W9-CUP-460

Blumberg

California
FAMILY CODE
Annotated

Grace Ganz Blumberg

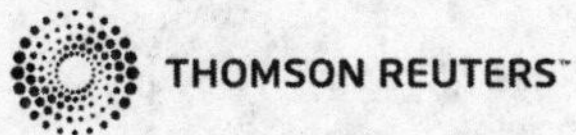

Mat# 42055008

© 2018 Thomson Reuters

ISBN: 978–0–314–69437–9

This publication was created to provide you with accurate and authoritative information concerning the subject matter covered; however, this publication was not necessarily prepared by persons licensed to practice law in a particular jurisdiction. The publisher is not engaged in rendering legal or other professional advice and this publication is not a substitute for the advice of an attorney. If you require legal or other expert advice, you should seek the services of a competent attorney or other professional.

West's and Westlaw are registered in the U.S. Patent and Trademark Office.
Thomson Reuters Westlaw is a trademark of Thomson Reuters and its affiliates.

PREFACE

Blumberg California Family Code Annotated features the complete text of the California Family Code, along with selected sections from other California codes, the California Constitution, and state court rules, to provide comprehensive coverage of California family law. Related federal statutes and regulations are also included, as well as materials on international child abduction. In order to aid in research and analysis, the author has provided commentary under particular statutory sections and court rules. Law Revision Commission Comments and research references are also provided.

WHAT'S NEW

Includes all laws through c. 859 of the 2017 portion of the 2017–2018 Regular Session, and Resolution chapters 30 (A.C.A.5), 105 (A.C.A.1), and 190 (A.C.A.17), subject to approval at the June 5, 2018 election.

Federal statutes are current through P.L. 115-82 approved 11-2-17.

Court rules reflect all amendments available through November 15, 2017.

ADDITIONAL INFORMATION

All California legislative enactments in 2017 are effective January 1, 2018, unless indicated otherwise. Additions or changes in statutes affected by 2017 legislation are indicated by underlining; deletions are indicated by asterisks. In court rules, additions or changes are indicated by underlining; deletions are indicated by strikethroughs.

Codified legislation which is subject to a governor's veto is followed by an italicized note indicating that fact. For the text of the message, please consult the Historical and Statutory Notes for the provision in *West's Annotated California Codes* or the material pertaining to the legislation affecting the provision in *West's California Legislative Service*.

To facilitate the inclusion of applicable provisions in one portable volume, repealed and reserved statutes and court rules are omitted.

CONTACT US

For additional information or research assistance call the Reference Attorneys at 1-800-REF-ATTY (1-800-733-2889). Contact our U.S. legal editorial department directly with your questions and suggestions by e-mail at editors.us-legal@tr.com.

Thank you for subscribing to this product. Should you have any questions regarding this product, please contact Customer Service at 1-800-328-4880 or by fax at 1-800-340-9378. If you would like to inquire about related publications, or to place an order, please contact us at 1-888-728-7677 or visit us at legalsolutions.thomsonreuters.com.

THE PUBLISHER

January 2018

ABOUT THE AUTHOR

Grace Ganz Blumberg is Distinguished Professor of Law Emerita at the UCLA School of Law, where she continues to teach a course in Community Property every fall. Since retiring from full-time teaching, Professor Blumberg has been consulting and writing appellate briefs in her areas of expertise, which include community property and family law.

Professor Blumberg is the author of COMMUNITY PROPERTY IN CALIFORNIA (6th ed. 2016) and she writes bi-monthly commentary for California Family Law Monthly (Matthew Bender). She was named R. Ammi Cutter Reporter for her work on the American Law Institute's PRINCIPLES OF THE LAW OF FAMILY DISSOLUTION (2002).

TABLE OF SECTIONS AFFECTED

This table indicates sections affected by 2017 legislation

Family Code

Sec.	Effect	Chap.	Sec.
400	Amended	42	1
3170	Amended	330	1
	Added	330	2
4055	Amended	730	1
			2
6301.5	Added	384	2
prec. § 6450 Div. 10 Pt. 6	Added	98	1
6450	Added	98	1
6451	Added	98	1
6452	Added	98	1
6453	Added	98	1
6454	Added	98	1
6455	Added	98	1
6456	Added	98	1
6457	Added	98	1
6458	Added	98	1
6459	Added	98	1
6460	Added	98	1
7962	Amended	326	1
8704.5	Amended	732	2
8708	Amended	732	3
8712	Amended	733	1
17202	Amended	19	7
17706	Amended	24	4

TABLE OF CONTENTS

FAMILY CODE

TABLE OF CONTENTS

TABLE OF CONTENTS

EVIDENCE CODE

GOVERNMENT CODE

INSURANCE CODE

PENAL CODE

TABLE OF CONTENTS

CODE OF FEDERAL REGULATIONS

UNITED STATES CODE

CONVENTION ON THE CIVIL ASPECTS OF INTERNATIONAL CHILD ABDUCTION [HAGUE CONVENTION]

CALIFORNIA RULES OF COURT

TABLE OF CONTENTS

STANDARDS OF JUDICIAL ADMINISTRATION

JUDICIAL COUNCIL FORMS; JURY INSTRUCTIONS

TABLE OF CASES

INDEX

FAMILY CODE

The Family Code was enacted by Stats.1992, c. 162 (A.B.2650), § 10, operative Jan. 1, 1994.

Division 1

PRELIMINARY PROVISIONS AND DEFINITIONS

Part 1

PRELIMINARY PROVISIONS

§ 1. Title of code

This code shall be known as the Family Code. *(Stats.1992, c. 162 (A.B.2650), § 10, operative Jan. 1, 1994.)*

Law Revision Commission Comments

Enactment [Revised Comment]

Section 1 is a standard type of provision found in many other codes. See, e.g., Bus. & Prof. Code § 1; Evid. Code § 1; Prob. Code § 1; Veh. Code § 1; see also Civ. Code §§ 1, 21. The operative date of this code is January 1, 1994. See 1992 Cal. Stat. ch. 162, § 13. [23 Cal.L.Rev.Comm. Reports 1 (1993)].

Research References

Treatises and Practice Aids

Witkin, California Summary 10th Husband and Wife § 3, Statutory Framework.

§ 2. Continuation of existing statutes; construction

A provision of this code, insofar as it is substantially the same as a previously existing provision relating to the same subject matter, shall be considered as a restatement and continuation thereof and not as a new enactment, and a reference in a statute to the provision of this code shall be deemed to include a reference to the previously existing provision unless a contrary intent appears. *(Stats.1992, c. 162 (A.B.2650), § 10, operative Jan. 1, 1994. Amended by Stats. 1993, c. 219 (A.B.1500), § 78.)*

Law Revision Commission Comments

Enactment [Revised Comment]

The first part of Section 2 is comparable to Civil Code Section 5 and is a standard provision found in many other codes. See, e.g., Bus. & Prof. Code § 2; Corp. Code § 2; Prob. Code § 2(a); Veh. Code § 2. See also Gov't Code §§ 9604 (construction of restatements and continuations), 9605 (construction of amended statutory provision). The last clause makes clear that a statutory reference to a new Family Code provision includes a reference to the former law from which it is drawn. *Cf.* Gov't Code § 9604 (reference to previously existing provision deemed reference to restatement or continuation).

A number of terms and phrases are used in the Comments to the sections of the Family Code to indicate the sources of the sections and to describe how they compare with prior law. The following discussion is intended to provide guidance in interpreting the terminology most commonly used in the Comments.

(1) *Continues without change.* A new provision "continues" a former provision "without change" if the two provisions are identical or nearly so. In some cases, there may be insignificant technical differences, such as where punctuation is changed without a change in meaning. Some Comments may describe the relationship by simply stating that the Family Code provision "continues" or is "the same as" a former provision, or is "the same as" a provision of a uniform act.

(2) *Continues without substantive change.* A new provision "continues" a former provision "without substantive change" if the substantive law remains the same, but the language differs to an insignificant degree.

(3) *Restates without substantive change.* A new provision "restates" a former provision "without substantive change" if the substantive law remains the same but the language differs to a significant degree. Some Comments may describe the new provision as being the "same in substance."

(4) *Exceptions, additions, omissions.* If part of a former provision is "continued" or "restated," the Comment may say that the former provision is continued or restated, but also note the specific differences as "exceptions to," "additions to," or "omissions from" the former provision.

(5) *Generalizes, broadens, restates in general terms.* A new provision may be described as "generalizing," "broadening," or "restating in general terms" a provision of prior law. This description means that a limited rule has been expanded to cover a broader class of cases.

(6) *Supersedes, replaces.* A provision "supersedes" or "replaces" a former provision if the new provision deals with the same subject as the former provision, but treats it in a significantly different manner.

(7) *New.* A provision is described as "new" where it has no direct source in prior statutes.

(8) *Drawn from, similar to, consistent with.* A variety of terms are used to indicate a source for a new provision, typically a source other than California statutes. For example, a provision may be "drawn from" a uniform act, model code, or the statutes of another state. In these cases, it may be useful to consult any available commentary or interpretation of the source from which the new provision is drawn for background information.

(9) *Codifies.* A Comment may state that a new provision "codifies" a case-law rule that has not previously been enacted into statutory law.

(10) *Makes clear, clarifies.* A new provision may be described as "making clear" a particular rule or "clarifying" a rule as a way of emphasizing the rule, particularly if the situation under prior law was doubtful or contradictory.

(11) *Statement in Comment that section is "comparable" to another section.* A Comment may state that a provision is "comparable" to another provision. If the Comment to a section notes that another section is "comparable," that does not mean that the other section is the same or substantially the same. The statement is included in the Comment so that the statute user is alerted to the other section and can review the cases under that section for possible use in interpreting the section containing the statement in the Comment. [23 Cal.L.Rev.Comm. Reports 1 (1993)].

Research References

Treatises and Practice Aids

Witkin, California Summary 10th Husband and Wife § 2, in General.

§ 3. Construction as provision of uniform act

A provision of this code, insofar as it is the same in substance as a provision of a uniform act, shall be construed to effectuate the general purpose to make uniform the law in those states which enact that provision. *(Stats.1992, c. 162 (A.B.2650), § 10, operative Jan. 1, 1994.)*

Law Revision Commission Comments

Enactment [Revised Comment]

Section 3 generalizes former Civil Code Sections 5003, 5150(1)(i), and 5301, Code of Civil Procedure Section 1651, and Evidence Code Section 891. This section expands the uniform construction rule to the Uniform Parentage Act, which formerly lacked a uniform construction provision. Provisions of the Family Code drawn from uniform acts include:

Uniform Premarital Agreement Act (§§ 1600–1617)
Uniform Divorce Recognition Act (§§ 2090–2093)
Uniform Child Custody Jurisdiction Act (§§ 3400–3425)
Uniform Reciprocal Enforcement of Support Act (§§ 4800–4854)
Uniform Act on Blood Tests to Determine Paternity (§§ 7550–7557)
Uniform Parentage Act (§§ 7600–7730)

See also Sections 7900–7910 (Interstate Compact on Placement of Children).

The former Uniform Civil Liability for Support Act has not been continued as a uniform act. For the disposition of the former sections, see the Comments to Sections 3550–3551, 3554, 3651, 3900, 3910(a), 4000, 4002, 4300, 4303, 4320, 4400, 4402–4405. [23 Cal. L.Rev.Comm. Reports 1 (1993)].

Research References

Forms

California Transactions Forms--Family Law § 1:71, Binding Agreement With Specific Family Code Waivers.

Treatises and Practice Aids

Witkin, California Summary 10th Community Property § 24, in General.

Witkin, California Summary 10th Husband and Wife § 2, in General.

§ 4. Change in code; operative date; application of new law; filings; orders; liability for action taken before operative date

(a) As used in this section:

(1) "New law" means either of the following, as the case may be:

(A) The act that enacted this code.

(B) The act that makes a change in this code, whether effectuated by amendment, addition, or repeal of a provision of this code.

(2) "Old law" means the applicable law in effect before the operative date of the new law.

(3) "Operative date" means the operative date of the new law.

(b) This section governs the application of the new law except to the extent otherwise expressly provided in the new law.

(c) Subject to the limitations provided in this section, the new law applies on the operative date to all matters governed by the new law, regardless of whether an event occurred or circumstance existed before, on, or after the operative date, including, but not limited to, commencement of a proceeding, making of an order, or taking of an action.

(d) If a document or paper is filed before the operative date, the contents, execution, and notice thereof are governed by the old law and not by the new law; but subsequent proceedings taken after the operative date concerning the document or paper, including an objection or response, a hearing, an order, or other matter relating thereto is governed by the new law and not by the old law.

(e) If an order is made before the operative date, or an action on an order is taken before the operative date, the validity of the order or action is governed by the old law and not by the new law. Nothing in this subdivision precludes proceedings after the operative date to modify an order made, or alter a course of action commenced, before the operative date to the extent proceedings for modification of an order or alteration of a course of action of that type are otherwise provided in the new law.

(f) No person is liable for an action taken before the operative date that was proper at the time the action was taken, even though the action would be improper if taken on or after the operative date, and the person has no duty, as a result of the enactment of the new law, to take any step to alter the course of action or its consequences.

(g) If the new law does not apply to a matter that occurred before the operative date, the old law continues to govern the matter notwithstanding its repeal or amendment by the new law.

(h) If a party shows, and the court determines, that application of a particular provision of the new law or of the old law in the manner required by this section or by the new law would substantially interfere with the effective conduct of the proceedings or the rights of the parties or other interested persons in connection with an event that occurred or circumstance that existed before the operative date, the court may, notwithstanding this section or the new law, apply either the new law or the old law to the extent reasonably necessary to mitigate the substantial interference. *(Stats.1992, c. 162 (A.B.2650), § 10, operative Jan. 1, 1994.)*

Law Revision Commission Comments

Enactment [Revised Comment]

Section 4 is comparable to Probate Code Section 3. This section provides general transitional rules applicable to the Family Code. This section applies both to the act that enacted the Family Code and to any later act that changes the code, whether the change is effectuated by amendment, addition, or repeal of a provision of the code.

The rules stated in this section are general provisions that apply absent a special rule stated in a new law. Special rules may defer or accelerate application of a new law despite the general rules stated in this section. See subdivision (b).

The general rule prescribed in subdivision (c) is that a new law applies immediately on its operative date to all matters, including pending proceedings. The general rule is qualified by the exceptions listed in subdivision (d) (contents, execution, and notice of papers and documents are governed by the law applicable when the paper or document was filed), subdivision (e) (orders are governed by the law applicable when the order was made, subject to any applicable modification procedures), and subdivision (f) (acts are governed by the law applicable when the act was done).

Where a new law fails to address a matter that occurred before its operative date, subdivision (g) makes clear that old law continues to govern the matter.

Because it is impractical to attempt to deal with all the possible transitional problems that may arise in the application of a new law to various circumstances, subdivision (h) provides a safety valve that permits the court to vary the application of the new law where there would otherwise be a substantial impairment of procedure or justice. This provision is intended to apply only in the extreme and unusual case, and is not intended to excuse compliance with the basic transitional provisions simply because of minor inconveniences or minor impacts on expectations or other interests.

In addition to governing other substantive provisions, Section 4 also governs itself. It therefore becomes operative on the date the Family Code becomes operative and applies to provisions enacted and operative before, on, or after that date. [23 Cal.L.Rev.Comm. Reports 1 (1993)].

Commentary

In its treatment of *In re Marriage of Rosendale*, the California Supreme Court gave full effect to this section. On October 13, 2004, the Supreme Court granted review to *Rosendale*, in which the depublished opinion of the court of appeal, *15 Cal.Rptr.3d 137 (2004)*, purported to hold that Section 1612(c), which is silent on the issue of retroactivity, applied to all premarital spousal support waivers whether executed before or after the 2001 addition of Section 1612(c), on the ground that its date of enactment was immaterial because Section 1612(c) merely codified existing common law. However, on July 13, 2005, the Supreme Court, under California Rules of Court rule 29.3b, dismissed review of *Rosendale*, citing Section 4(c), which provides that amendments to the Family Code apply to all matters governed by those amendments without regard to when the operative events occurred. Thus, the Supreme Court would seem to be taking the view that, by virtue of Section 4(c), Section 1612(c) applies retroactively to all premarital spousal support waivers, subject only to the limitations of this section and due process requirements.

Similarly, Section 4502 (c) was amended in 2002 to provide that the defense of laches is available only with respect to any portion of a child, family or spousal support judgment owed to the *state*. *In re Marriage of Fellows, 39 Cal.4th 179, 46 Cal.Rptr.3d 49, 138 P.3d 200 (2006)*, held that the amendment applies retroactively to support due before the amendment's effective date. The California Supreme Court relied on this section, which provides that the Code and future amendments to the Code apply on their operative dates to all matters governed by them. Thus every amendment to the Code applies retroactively unless the amendment or this section specifically provides otherwise, or retroactive application would violate the due process clause by impairing a vested right without a serving an important state interest.

In re Marriage of Howell, 195 Cal.App.4th 1062, 126 Cal.Rptr.3d 539 (2011), declined to retroactively apply Family Code section 1612(c), a 2002 amendment, insofar as it would invalidate a 1999 spousal support waiver because the party resisting enforcement was not represented by counsel. *Howell* concluded that retroactive application of the attorney-representation requirement would violate subsection (f) of this section by making the party seeking enforcement "liable for an action taken before the operative date that was proper at the time…even if the action would be improper if taken on or after the operative date," reasoning that the party seeking enforcement became "liable" for failing to make sure that the other party was represented by counsel.

In re Marriage of Hill and Dittmer, 202 Cal.App.4th 1046, 136 Cal.Rptr.3d 700 (2011), held that a pre-2002 premarital agreement was enforceable when the wife was a successful business woman, was represented by counsel, and voluntarily waived disclosure. *Hill and Dittmer* declined to retroactively apply the 2002 amendment to section 1615 (subsection c) on the ground it materially changed the law and therefore could not be retroactively applied.

For further discussion of retroactive application of amendments to the Family Code, see the Commentary to Family Code sections 1612, 1615, and 4325.

Research References

Treatises and Practice Aids

Witkin, California Summary 10th Husband and Wife § 2A, (New) Retroactivity Of Provisions.

Witkin, California Summary 10th Husband and Wife § 220, Laches Defense Limited.

Witkin, California Summary 10th Husband and Wife § 371, Civil Remedies.

§ 5. Construction of headings

Division, part, chapter, article, and section headings do not in any manner affect the scope, meaning, or intent of this code. *(Stats.1992, c. 162 (A.B.2650), § 10, operative Jan. 1, 1994.)*

Law Revision Commission Comments

Enactment [Revised Comment]

Section 5 is comparable to Probate Code Section 4. This section is a standard provision found in many other codes. See, e.g., Bus. & Prof. Code § 9; Corp. Code § 6; Evid. Code § 5; Gov't Code § 6; Veh. Code § 7. [23 Cal.L.Rev.Comm. Reports 1 (1993)].

Research References

Treatises and Practice Aids

Witkin, California Summary 10th Husband and Wife § 2, in General.

§ 6. Construction of code

Unless the provision or context otherwise requires, the general provisions and rules of construction in this part govern the construction of this code. *(Stats.1992, c. 162 (A.B.2650), § 10, operative Jan. 1, 1994.)*

Law Revision Commission Comments

Enactment [Revised Comment]

Section 6 is comparable to Probate Code Section 6. This section is a standard provision found in many other codes. See, e.g., Bus. & Prof. Code § 8; Corp. Code § 5; Evid. Code § 4; Lab. Code § 5; Veh. Code § 6. See also Section 2 Comment. [23 Cal.L.Rev. Comm. Reports 1 (1993)].

Research References

Treatises and Practice Aids

Witkin, California Summary 10th Husband and Wife § 2, in General.

§ 7. References to statutes; application

Whenever a reference is made to a portion of this code or to another law, the reference applies to all amendments and additions regardless of when made. *(Stats.1992, c. 162 (A.B.2650), § 10, operative Jan. 1, 1994.)*

Law Revision Commission Comments

Enactment [Revised Comment]

Section 7 is comparable to Probate Code Section 7. This section is a standard provision found in many other codes. See, e.g., Bus. & Prof. Code § 12; Corp. Code § 9; Evid. Code § 6; Gov't Code § 9; Veh. Code § 10. See also Gov't Code §§ 9604 (construction of restatements and continuations), 9605 (construction of amended statutory provision). [23 Cal.L.Rev.Comm. Reports 1 (1993)].

Research References

Treatises and Practice Aids

Witkin, California Summary 10th Husband and Wife § 2, in General.

§ 8. Definitions

Unless otherwise expressly stated:

(a) "Division" means a division of this code.

(b) "Part" means a part of the division in which that term occurs.

(c) "Chapter" means a chapter of the division or part, as the case may be, in which that term occurs.

(d) "Article" means an article of the chapter in which that term occurs.

(e) "Section" means a section of this code.

(f) "Subdivision" means a subdivision of the section in which that term occurs.

(g) "Paragraph" means a paragraph of the subdivision in which that term occurs.

(h) "Subparagraph" means a subparagraph of the paragraph in which that term occurs. *(Stats.1992, c. 162 (A.B. 2650), § 10, operative Jan. 1, 1994.)*

Law Revision Commission Comments

Enactment [Revised Comment]

Section 8 is comparable to Civil Code Section 14(6). This section is a standard provision found in many other codes. See, e.g., Bus. & Prof. Code § 15; Corp. Code § 10; Veh. Code § 11. More recent codes have expanded the section to include additional definitions found in Section 8. See, e.g., Evid. Code § 7; Prob. Code § 8. [23 Cal.L.Rev.Comm. Reports 1 (1993)].

§ 9. Present, past, and future tenses

The present tense includes the past and future tenses, and the future, the present. *(Stats.1992, c. 162 (A.B.2650), § 10, operative Jan. 1, 1994.)*

Law Revision Commission Comments

Enactment [Revised Comment]

Section 9 is comparable to part of Civil Code Section 14. This section is a standard provision found in many other codes. See, e.g., Bus. & Prof. Code § 14; Food & Agric. Code § 19; Lab. Code § 11; Prob. Code § 9; Veh. Code § 12. [23 Cal.L.Rev.Comm. Reports 1 (1993)].

Research References

Treatises and Practice Aids

Witkin, California Summary 10th Husband and Wife § 2, in General.

§ 10. Numbers; singular and plural

The singular number includes the plural, and the plural, the singular. *(Stats.1992, c. 162 (A.B.2650), § 10, operative Jan. 1, 1994.)*

Law Revision Commission Comments

Enactment [Revised Comment]

Section 10 is comparable to part of Civil Code Section 14. This section is a standard provision found in many other codes. See, e.g., Corp. Code § 13; Food & Agric. Code § 21; Lab. Code § 13; Prob. Code § 10; Veh. Code § 14. [23 Cal.L.Rev.Comm. Reports 1 (1993)].

Research References

Treatises and Practice Aids

Witkin, California Summary 10th Husband and Wife § 2, in General.

§ 11. Husband, wife, spouses, and married persons

A reference to "husband" and "wife," "spouses," or "married persons," or a comparable term, includes persons who are lawfully married to each other and persons who were previously lawfully married to each other, as is appropriate under the circumstances of the particular case. *(Stats.1992, c. 162 (A.B.2650), § 10, operative Jan. 1, 1994.)*

Law Revision Commission Comments

Enactment [Revised Comment]

Section 11 restates without substantive change and generalizes former Civil Code Section 4350.5. The terms "spouses" and "married persons," and the reference to a "comparable term," have been added. The former provision applied only to the former Family Law Act (former Part 5 (commencing with former Section 4000) of Division 4 of the Civil Code), whereas Section 11 applies to the entire Family Code. The rule stated in Section 11 applies unless the provision or context otherwise requires. See Section 6. [23 Cal.L.Rev.Comm. Reports 1 (1993)].

Research References

Treatises and Practice Aids

Witkin, California Summary 10th Husband and Wife § 2, in General.

§ 12. Meaning of "shall" and "may"

"Shall" is mandatory and "may" is permissive. "Shall not" and "may not" are prohibitory. *(Stats.1992, c. 162 (A.B. 2650), § 10, operative Jan. 1, 1994.)*

Law Revision Commission Comments

Enactment [Revised Comment]

The first sentence of Section 12 is a standard provision found in many other codes. See, e.g., Bus. & Prof. Code § 19; Corp. Code § 15; Lab. Code § 15; Prob. Code § 12; Veh. Code § 15. The first sentence also generalizes former Code of Civil Procedure Section 1732, which applied only to conciliation proceedings (former Title 11.5 (commencing with former Section 1730) of the Code of Civil Procedure, now Division 5 (commencing with Section 1800) of the Family Code).

The second sentence is a new provision making clear that "shall not" and "may not" are equivalent prohibitory expressions. This is not a substantive change. [23 Cal.L.Rev.Comm. Reports 1 (1993)].

Research References

Treatises and Practice Aids

Witkin, California Summary 10th Husband and Wife § 2, in General.

§ 13. Severability

If a provision or clause of this code or its application to any person or circumstances is held invalid, the invalidity does not affect other provisions or applications of the code which can be given effect without the invalid provision or application, and to this end the provisions of this code are severable. *(Stats.1992, c. 162 (A.B.2650), § 10, operative Jan. 1, 1994.)*

Law Revision Commission Comments

Enactment [Revised Comment]

Section 13 generalizes former Civil Code Section 7018 and former Code of Civil Procedure Section 1656. The scope of the former provisions has been expanded to apply to the entire Family Code. The former provisions applied only to the uniform acts of which they were a part, i.e., the Uniform Parentage Act (former Part 7 (commencing with former Section 7000) of Division 4 of the Civil Code, now Part 3 (commencing with Section 7600) of Division 12 of the Family Code), and the Revised Uniform Reciprocal Enforcement of Support Act of 1968 (former Title 10a (commencing with former Section 1650) of Part 3 of the Code of Civil Procedure, now Chapter 6 (commencing with 4800) of Part 5 of Division 9 of the Family Code). This section is a standard provision found in many other codes. See, e.g., Bus. & Prof. Code § 24; Corp. Code § 19; Food & Agric. Code § 17; Lab. Code § 24; Prob. Code § 11. [23 Cal. L.Rev.Comm. Reports 1 (1993)].

Research References

Treatises and Practice Aids

Witkin, California Summary 10th Husband and Wife § 2, in General.

Part 2

DEFINITIONS

Section

§ 50. Applicability of part

Unless the provision or context otherwise requires, the definitions and rules of construction in this part govern the construction of this code. *(Stats.1992, c. 162 (A.B.2650), § 10, operative Jan. 1, 1994.)*

Law Revision Commission Comments

Enactment [Revised Comment]

Section 50 is comparable to Probate Code Section 20. This section is a standard provision found in many other codes. See, e.g., Corp. Code § 5; Evid. Code § 100; Food & Agric. Code § 25; Veh. Code § 100. See also Sections 11 (reference to married person includes formerly married person), 12 (meaning of "shall," "may," "shall not," and "may not"). For comparable provisions, see Sections 6, 900, 2500, 3000, 3500, 3760, 4802, 5200, 6900, 8500. [23 Cal.L.Rev.Comm. Reports 1 (1993)].

Research References

Treatises and Practice Aids

Witkin, California Summary 10th Community Property § 176, Nature and Scope Of Revision.

Witkin, California Summary 10th Husband and Wife § 4, Definitions.

Witkin, California Summary 10th Husband and Wife § 174, in General.

§ 58. Child for whom support may be ordered

"Child for whom support may be ordered" means a minor child and a child for whom support is authorized under Section 3587, 3901, or 3910. *(Added by Stats.1993, c. 219 (A.B.1500), § 79.)*

Law Revision Commission Comments

Enactment [Revised Comment]

Section 58 is added for convenience in drafting. For provisions concerning situations in which a child may be supported, see Sections 3587 (court order to effectuate agreement for support of adult child), 3901 (duration of duty to support child), 3910 (duty to maintain incapacitated child), 4000 (civil action to enforce parent's duty to support), 4001 (order for child support). [23 Cal.L.Rev.Comm. Reports 1 (1993)].

Commentary

See generally *In re Marriage of Lambe & Meehan, 37 Cal.App.4th 388, 44 Cal.Rptr.2d 641 (1995)* (parents' court-ratified agreement to divest family court of jurisdiction to order support for their adult indigent child is unenforceable). Cf. *Marriage of Goodarzirad, 185 Cal.App.3d 1020, 1026, 230 Cal.Rptr. 203 (1986)* (husband's stipulation to surrender rights of custody and visitation of his minor child is unenforceable as is the portion of the judgment incorporating the stipulation).

Research References

Treatises and Practice Aids

Witkin, California Summary 10th Husband and Wife § 4, Definitions.

Witkin, California Summary 10th Parent and Child § 379, Children to Whom Duty is Owed.

§ 63. Community estate

"Community estate" includes both community property and quasi-community property. *(Added by Stats.1993, c. 219 (A.B.1500), § 79.3.)*

Law Revision Commission Comments

Enactment [Revised Comment]

Section 63 generalizes definitions in former Civil Code Sections 4800(a) (property division) and 5120.020 (liability for debts). Former Civil Code Section 5120.020 provided a special definition of community *property,* whereas this section defines community *estate*. This is not a substantive change. Generalization of the definition of community estate to apply to the entire code is not intended to make any substantive changes. Thus, while generalization of this definition makes it newly applicable to Section 1101 (remedies for breach of fiduciary duty between spouses), no substantive change results, because the fiduciary duties between spouses to which the remedies apply are provided in Sections 1100 and 1102.

The language in former Civil Code Section 4800(a) concerning assets and liabilities is omitted as surplus. This is not a substantive change. See, e.g., Sections 2551 (characterization of liabilities), 2552 (valuation date), 2556 (continuing jurisdiction).

This section omits the language found in former Civil Code Section 5120.020(a) stating that community property includes real property situated in another state that would be community property if situated in this state. This language is no longer necessary, since Section 760 provides that community property includes real and personal property, wherever situated, acquired by a married person during marriage while domiciled in this state. See Section 760 Comment. When enacted in 1984 (as former Civil Code Section 5120.020), the inclusion of quasi-community property within the formerly-used term "community property" was intended to help implement the policy of Section 912 that quasi-community property is treated as community property rather than separate property for purposes of liability. For background on former Civ. Code § 5120.020, see *Recommendation Relating to Liability of Marital Property for Debts,* 17 Cal. L. Revision Comm'n Reports 1 (1984).

See also Sections 65 ("community property" defined in Section 760 *et seq.*), 125 ("quasi-community property" defined), 700 (real property includes leasehold interests in real property), 912 (liability of quasi-community property). [23 Cal.L.Rev.Comm. Reports 1 (1993)].

Research References

Forms

California Transactions Forms--Estate Planning § 1:26, Quasi-Community Property; Separate Property.

California Transactions Forms--Estate Planning § 10:5, Quasi-Community Property.

Am. Jur. Pl. & Pr. Forms Community Property § 1, Introductory Comments.

Am. Jur. Pl. & Pr. Forms Community Property § 36, Complaint, Petition, or Declaration--For Divorce or Other Legal Separation--Allegation Of Quasi-Community Property.

Treatises and Practice Aids

Witkin, California Summary 10th Community Property § 176, Nature and Scope Of Revision.

Witkin, California Summary 10th Community Property § 247, Post-judgment Motion.

Witkin, California Summary 10th Husband and Wife § 4, Definitions.

§ 65. Community property

"Community property" is property that is community property under Part 2 (commencing with Section 760) of Division 4. *(Stats.1992, c. 162 (A.B.2650), § 10, operative Jan. 1, 1994.)*

Law Revision Commission Comments

Enactment [Revised Comment]

Section 65 is a new provision included for drafting convenience. See also Section 751 (respective interests of spouses in community property during marriage). [23 Cal.L.Rev.Comm. Reports 1 (1993)].

Research References

Forms

Am. Jur. Pl. & Pr. Forms Community Property § 1, Introductory Comments.

Treatises and Practice Aids

Witkin, California Summary 10th Husband and Wife § 4, Definitions.

§ 67. County

"County" includes city and county. *(Stats.1992, c. 162 (A.B.2650), § 10, operative Jan. 1, 1994.)*

Law Revision Commission Comments

Enactment [Revised Comment]

Section 67 is a new provision drawn from part of Civil Code Section 14. [23 Cal.L.Rev.Comm. Reports 1 (1993)].

Research References

Treatises and Practice Aids

Witkin, California Summary 10th Husband and Wife § 4, Definitions.

§ 70. "Date of separation" defined

(a) "Date of separation" means the date that a complete and final break in the marital relationship has occurred, as evidenced by both of the following:

(1) The spouse has expressed to the other spouse his or her intent to end the marriage.

(2) The conduct of the spouse is consistent with his or her intent to end the marriage.

(b) In determining the date of separation, the court shall take into consideration all relevant evidence.

(c) It is the intent of the Legislature in enacting this section to abrogate the decisions in In re Marriage of Davis (2015) 61 Cal.4th 846 and In re Marriage of Norviel (2002) 102 Cal.App.4th 1152. *(Added by Stats.2016, c. 114 (S.B. 1255), § 1, eff. Jan. 1, 2017.)*

Commentary

This section was added in 2016 to abrogate two decisions holding that spouses were not living "separate and apart" within the meaning of former section 771 unless they were living in separate residences (*In re Marriage of Davis, 61 Cal.4th 846, 352 P.3d 401, 189 Cal.Rptr.3d 835 (2015)* and *In re Marriage of Norviel, 102 Cal.App.4th 1152, 126 Cal.Rptr.2d 148 (2002)*). In addition to allowing spouses to separate for purposes of section 771 while continuing to occupy a single residence, the first line of this section would seem to indicate that a temporary reconciliation negates any prior separation that would otherwise satisfy this section. The question was posed by *In re Marriage of Jaschke, 50 Cal.Rptr.2d 658 (1996)*, which was denied review and depublished by the California Supreme Court. This section also specifies that a spouse's intent to end the marriage must be communicated to the other spouse.

§ 80. Employee benefit plan

"Employee benefit plan" includes public and private retirement, pension, annuity, savings, profit sharing, stock bonus, stock option, thrift, vacation pay, and similar plans of deferred or fringe benefit compensation, whether of the defined contribution or defined benefit type whether or not such plan is qualified under the Employee Retirement Income Security Act of 1974 (P.L. 93-406) (ERISA), as amended. The term also includes "employee benefit plan" as defined in Section 3 of ERISA (29 U.S.C.A. Sec. 1002(3)). *(Stats.1992, c. 162 (A.B.2650), § 10, operative Jan. 1, 1994. Amended by Stats.1994, c. 1269 (A.B.2208), § 9.)*

Law Revision Commission Comments

Enactment [Revised Comment]

Section 80 continues without change and generalizes former Civil Code Section 4363.3. The former provision applied only to the former Family Law Act (former Part 5 (commencing with former Section 4000) of Division 4 of the Civil Code), whereas Section 80 applies to the entire Family Code. For a special definition of "employee benefit plan," see Section 755. [23 Cal.L.Rev.Comm. Reports 1 (1993)].

Research References

Forms

California Practice Guide: Rutter Family Law Forms Form 1:32, Glossary Of Common Family Law Terms, Phrases and Concepts (Enclosure to Form 1:31).

West's California Code Forms, Family § 2060, Comment Overview--Application and Order for Joinder.

West's California Judicial Council Forms FL-374, Notice Of Appearance and Response Of Employee Benefit Plan.

West's California Judicial Council Forms FL-460, Qualified Domestic Relations Order for Support.

Treatises and Practice Aids

Witkin, California Summary 10th Husband and Wife § 4, Definitions.

Witkin, California Summary 10th Husband and Wife § 79, in General.

§ 92. Family support

"Family support" means an agreement between the parents, or an order or judgment, that combines child support and spousal support without designating the amount to be paid for child support and the amount to be paid for spousal support. *(Stats.1992, c. 162 (A.B.2650), § 10, operative Jan. 1, 1994.)*

Law Revision Commission Comments

Enactment [Revised Comment]

Section 92 continues parts of the first and second sentences of former Civil Code Section 4811(d) without substantive change and adds language that expands the definition to include family support orders and judgments. [23 Cal.L.Rev.Comm. Reports 1 (1993)].

Research References

Forms

California Practice Guide: Rutter Family Law Forms Form 1:32, Glossary Of Common Family Law Terms, Phrases and Concepts (Enclosure to Form 1:31).

California Transactions Forms--Family Law § 2:66, Overview.

Treatises and Practice Aids

Witkin, California Summary 10th Husband and Wife § 4, Definitions.

Witkin, California Summary 10th Husband and Wife § 248, in General.

§ 95. Income and expense declaration

"Income and expense declaration" means the form for an income and expense declaration in family law matters adopted by the Judicial Council. *(Stats.1992, c. 162 (A.B. 2650), § 10, operative Jan. 1, 1994.)*

Law Revision Commission Comments

Enactment [Revised Comment]

Section 95 continues without change and generalizes the last paragraph of former Civil Code Section 4357.5(a). Former Section 4357.5 applied only to expedited support orders, whereas Section 95 applies to the entire Family Code. See Cal. R. Ct. 1243 (rev. July 1, 1985) (financial declarations), 1285.50 (income and expense declaration form); Sections 115 (property declaration), 211 (Judicial Council rules of practice and procedure). [23 Cal.L.Rev.Comm. Reports 1 (1993)].

Research References

Treatises and Practice Aids

Witkin, California Summary 10th Husband and Wife § 4, Definitions.

§ 100. Judgment; order

"Judgment" and "order" include a decree, as appropriate under the circumstances. *(Stats.1992, c. 162 (A.B.2650), § 10, operative Jan. 1, 1994.)*

Law Revision Commission Comments

Enactment [Revised Comment]

Section 100 is a new provision. Throughout this code references to "decree" have been eliminated as surplus. See, e.g., Sections 155, 215, 233, 290–291, 310, 772, 781, 2310, 2313, 2330.5, 2336, 2340, 2346, 3120, 3131, 4338, 4414, 4500, 4506, 5100–5103, 7611–7612, 7642, 8503, 8604, 9100–9102. This section recognizes that the term "decree" will still be used in certain instances. See, e.g., Sections 3400–3425 (Uniform Child Custody Jurisdiction Act), 4800–4854 (Uniform Reciprocal Enforcement of Support Act). [23 Cal.L.Rev. Comm. Reports 1 (1993)].

Research References

Treatises and Practice Aids

Witkin, California Summary 10th Husband and Wife § 4, Definitions.

§ 105. Person

"Person" includes a natural person, firm, association, organization, partnership, business trust, corporation, limited liability company, or public entity. *(Added by Stats.1993, c. 219 (A.B.1500), § 80. Amended by Stats.1994, c. 1010 (S.B.2053), § 107.)*

Law Revision Commission Comments

Enactment [Revised Comment]

Section 105 is new and is drawn from Evidence Code Section 175 and Government Code Section 17. [23 Cal.L.Rev.Comm. Reports 1 (1993)].

Research References

Treatises and Practice Aids

Witkin, California Summary 10th Husband and Wife § 4, Definitions.

§ 110. Proceeding

"Proceeding" includes an action. *(Added by Stats.1993, c. 219 (A.B.1500), § 81.)*

Law Revision Commission Comments

Enactment [Revised Comment]

Section 110 is a new provision added for drafting convenience. One purpose of this section is to make clear that where "proceeding" is used in this code, there is no intention to exclude an "action." This section rejects hypertechnical arguments that the application of a particular rule depends on the fortuity of whether a particular matter is termed an action or a proceeding. Thus, for example, Section 200 concerning the jurisdiction of the superior court in "proceedings" under this code, applies with equal force to any matter referred to as an "action." [23 Cal.L.Rev.Comm. Reports 1 (1993)].

Research References

Treatises and Practice Aids

Witkin, California Summary 10th Husband and Wife § 4, Definitions.

§ 113. Property

"Property" includes real and personal property and any interest therein. *(Added by Stats.2000, c. 808 (A.B.1358), § 21, eff. Sept. 28, 2000.)*

Law Revision Commission Comments

2000 Addition

Section 113 is a new provision added for drafting convenience. It is the same as Code of Civil Procedure Section 680.310. The context of a particular section may require that a word or phrase in that section be given a meaning different from the definition in this section. See Section 50. Special definitions used for a particular portion of this code would override the general definition in this section. *Id.* [30 Cal.L.Rev.Comm.Reports 717 (2000)].

Research References

Treatises and Practice Aids

Witkin, California Summary 10th Husband and Wife § 4, Definitions.

§ 115. Property declaration

"Property declaration" means the form for a property declaration in family law matters adopted by the Judicial Council. *(Stats.1992, c. 162 (A.B.2650), § 10, operative Jan. 1, 1994.)*

Law Revision Commission Comments

Enactment [Revised Comment]

Section 115 is a new provision designed to permit easy reference to the property declaration form adopted by the Judicial Council. See Cal. R. Ct. 1243 (rev. July 1, 1985) (financial declarations), 1285.55 (property declaration form); Sections 95 (income and expense declaration), 211 (Judicial Council rules of practice and procedure). [23 Cal.L.Rev.Comm. Reports 1 (1993)].

Research References

Forms

West's California Judicial Council Forms FL-160, Property Declaration.

West's California Judicial Council Forms FL-161, Continuation Of Property Declaration.

Treatises and Practice Aids

Witkin, California Summary 10th Husband and Wife § 4, Definitions.

§ 125. Quasi-community property

"Quasi-community property" means all real or personal property, wherever situated, acquired before or after the operative date of this code in any of the following ways:

(a) By either spouse while domiciled elsewhere which would have been community property if the spouse who acquired the property had been domiciled in this state at the time of its acquisition.

(b) In exchange for real or personal property, wherever situated, which would have been community property if the spouse who acquired the property so exchanged had been domiciled in this state at the time of its acquisition. *(Stats. 1992, c. 162 (A.B.2650), § 10, operative Jan. 1, 1994.)*

Law Revision Commission Comments

Enactment [Revised Comment]

Section 125 continues without substantive change and generalizes former Civil Code Section 4803. The former provision applied only to the former Family Law Act (former Part 5 (commencing with former Section 4000) of Division 4 of the Civil Code), whereas Section 125 applies to the entire Family Code.

By defining "quasi-community property" to include all property, wherever situated, that would have been treated as community property had the acquiring spouse been domiciled in California at the time of acquisition, Section 125 ensures that the division of marital property on dissolution of marriage, nullity of marriage, or legal separation of the parties will not be controlled by the fortuity of when or where the property was initially acquired. Section 125 makes clear that property of the type described in Sections 771, 772, and 781 is not quasi-community property. For background on former Civ. Code § 4803, see *Recommendation Relating to Quasi–Community Property,* 9 Cal. L. Revision Comm'n Reports 113 (1969). [23 Cal.L.Rev.Comm. Reports 1 (1993)].

Commentary

Family Code § 125 is essentially a choice-of-law rule. Choice-of-law rules tell the forum court whether it should apply the law of the forum or the law of some other jurisdiction to each particular legal issue in the case. That a court has subject matter and personal jurisdiction over the parties does not necessarily mean that it will decide each issue in the case according to the law of the forum.

Absent any statute to the contrary, traditional American common-law rules determine ownership of personal property according to the law of the jurisdiction in which the party was domiciled when the property was acquired, and ownership of real property (realty) according to the law of the jurisdiction in which the realty is located. However, common-law rules are subject to legislative alteration. Family Code § 125 is such a legislative alteration. California would have preferred simply to treat property described in § 125 as community property, and California initially legislated accordingly in the early part of the 20th century. However, the California Supreme Court held that this early legislation was unconstitutional. A law changing the ownership of property merely upon a person's move from another state to California violated the due process and privileges and immunities clauses of the U.S. Constitution. *Estate of Thornton, 1 Cal.2d 1, 33 P.2d 1 (1934)*. Current quasi-community-property (QCP) legislation avoids that constitutional objection by altering the ownership of property acquired by a person before he moves to California only at divorce or death, two junctures at which the state has long been understood to have the power to alter or redetermine property ownership and rights. Thus during the on-going marriage, QCP largely retains the character it had before a person moved to California. The QCP characterization only becomes operative at death or divorce. (But see Family Code § 914.)

Addison v. Addison, 62 Cal.2d 558, 43 Cal.Rptr. 97, 399 P.2d 897 (1965), held this section constitutional insofar as it operates to alter property ownership at divorce. In *Addison*, a couple moved from Illinois to California, where the wife subsequently sued the husband for divorce, claiming a quasi-community-property interest in California property traceable to property acquired in Illinois by her husband during marriage. Rejecting the husband's claim that, by changing ownership rights, application of the statute infringed the due process and privileges and immunities clauses of the Unites States Constitution, *Addison* constitutionally justified this section in terms of the state's power to alter property ownership at divorce and death.

If an out-of-state couple separates and only one spouse moves to California and later petitions for divorce, may the out-of-state respondent voluntarily appear in the California action and assert a quasi-community-property claim to property acquired during the marriage by the California spouse? As a matter of statutory interpretation, this section appears to allow such a claim. However, *In re Marriage of Roesch, 83 Cal.App.3d 96, 147 Cal.Rptr. 586 (1978)*, suggests that application of this section would be unconstitutional. In *Roesch,* the husband left his wife in Pennsylvania and moved to California, where he sought a divorce. The Pennsylvania wife appeared in the California divorce proceeding and requested a QCP distribution of property acquired by the husband. The trial court granted the husband a California no-fault divorce, awarded the wife alimony and child support, and made the QCP distribution requested by the wife. When the wife appealed some of the particulars of the QCP distribution, the intermediate court of appeal declined to consider her appeal on the ground that she was not entitled to the benefit of the California QCP statute because she was not a California domiciliary. *Roesch* understood the facts of *Addison* (that couple moved to California together and resided there before one of them filed for divorce) as constitutional prerequisites for the application of this section. However, *Roesch* would seem to misread of *Addison. Addison* merely describes the facts of the particular case before the court. It neither holds that those facts are constitutionally required, nor does it purport to set the constitutional limits of application of this section. *Addison* relies instead, for its constitutional holding, on the general power of courts to reallocate property rights at divorce.

Although *Roesch* has never been directly rejected or overruled in California, subsequent California cases either ignore or narrowly distinguish *Roesch* and apply this section according to its express terms. Ignoring *Roesch* entirely, *In re Marriage of Ben–Yehosua, 91 Cal.App.3d 259, 154 Cal.Rptr. 80 (1979)*, involved a wife who left her husband in Israel when she came to visit her mother in California, bringing the children with her. During the visit she decided not to return to Israel, and she petitioned for divorce. The husband appeared in the California action. The trial court applied quasi-community-property law to all of the parties' property, including real property in Israel. The court of appeal read the language of this section literally and approved its application. Cases distinguishing *Roesch* and applying this section include *In re Marriage of Jacobson, 161 Cal.App.3d 465, 207 Cal.Rptr.512 (1984)* (applying this section to divide husband's military pension notwithstanding that husband was a domiciliary of Iowa because husband voluntarily consented to the court's jurisdiction, distinguishing *Roesch* on the ground that it did not address one spouse's consent to jurisdiction as an alternative to domicile); and *In re Marriage of Fransen, 142 Cal.App.3d 419, 190 Cal.Rptr.885, as modified 143 Cal.App.3d 357H* (distinguishing *Roesch* and applying this section to husband's pension).

Arizona and Texas have the same quasi-community-property statute as California. Their appellate courts have strongly rejected the result and reasoning of *Roesch*. Both states apply their quasi-community property statute even though only one spouse is a state domiciliary so long as the other spouse is participating in the proceeding. The most persuasive rejection of *Roesch* is *In re Marriage of Martin, 156 Ariz. 440, 752 P.2d 1026 (Ariz. Ct. App. 1986)*. *Martin* applies the Arizona quasi-community-property law to property acquired by a non-resident husband who voluntarily appeared in the jurisdiction to respond to his Arizona wife's divorce petition. See additionally *Ismail v. Ismail, 702 S.W.2d 216 (Tex. Ct. App. 1985)* (rejecting *Roesch* and applying Texas quasi-community-property statute when one spouse is a domiciliary and the other consents to the court's jurisdiction) and Grace Ganz Blumberg, Community Property in California 586–592 (4th ed. 2003) (criticizing *Roesch*).

Roesch reveals its own fatal flaw. All elements of a jurisdiction's divorce law—its grounds for divorce and its support and property distribution rules, are interdependent. Judicial economy, as *Martin* notes, and more importantly, justice require that those elements be administered in their entirety when the forum has subject-matter jurisdiction and personal jurisdiction over the parties. When Mr. Roesch availed himself of California's liberal no-fault divorce ground, Pennsylvania had only fault grounds for divorce and had no marital property system at all. In Pennsylvania, fault grounds served as contractual bargaining chips for negotiated property distributions. By contrast, California had no need of fault grounds to work economic justice because it had already legislated an invariable rule of 50–50 distribution of the parties' community and quasi-community property. The result, under *Roesch*, was that Mrs. Roesch was divorced by her husband under California's liberal no-fault law and informed that she would have to look to Pennsylvania law for (nonexistent) property distribution. If a spouse chooses to avail himself of the very liberal divorce-on-demand law of California, he should also be bound by the property distribution rules that go with that unusually liberal law, under which economic justice is achieved through rules of property distribution, rather than reliance on party bargaining about the grounds for divorce.

Arguably, *Roesch* is factually distinguishable from all other reported cases because in *Roesch* the person asserting a quasi-community-property interest in the other spouse's property was the out-of-state domiciliary, while in all other cases the claimant was a California domiciliary and the spouse objecting to the application of this section was domiciled in another state. Thus, California's interest in the claimant was greater in the cases applying this section than in *Roesch*. However, reliance on this distinction entails an unduly narrow view of California's interests. California should be unwilling to allow a divorce petitioner to use its liberal divorce law to undermine the negotiating posture an out-of-state spouse would enjoy in his or home state. California's interest in assuring justice for all persons who are summoned and voluntarily appear before its courts requires that this section be equally applied whether the quasi-community-property claimant is a domiciliary or a nondomiciliary, so long as the California court has subject-matter jurisdiction and personal jurisdiction over both parties.

Research References

Forms

California Practice Guide: Rutter Family Law Forms Form 1:32, Glossary Of Common Family Law Terms, Phrases and Concepts (Enclosure to Form 1:31).

California Transactions Forms--Estate Planning § 1:26, Quasi-Community Property; Separate Property.

California Transactions Forms--Estate Planning § 10:5, Quasi-Community Property.

California Transactions Forms--Estate Planning § 19:19, Quasi-Community Property.

California Transactions Forms--Family Law § 1:27, Complete Agreement.

Nichols Cyclopedia of Legal Forms Annotated § 100:40, Premarital Agreement--Community Property--California.

Am. Jur. Pl. & Pr. Forms Community Property § 36, Complaint, Petition, or Declaration--For Divorce or Other Legal Separation--Allegation Of Quasi-Community Property.

West's California Code Forms, Family § 1611 Form 1, Premarital Agreement.

Treatises and Practice Aids

Witkin, California Summary 10th Community Property § 176, Nature and Scope Of Revision.

Witkin, California Summary 10th Community Property § 256, Nature and Purpose Of Legislation.

Witkin, California Summary 10th Community Property § 257, Clarifications and Distinctions.

Witkin, California Summary 10th Community Property § 258, Statutory Rule.

Witkin, California Summary 10th Husband and Wife § 4, Definitions.

§ 126. Petitioner

"Petitioner" includes plaintiff, where appropriate. *(Added by Stats.1999, c. 980 (A.B.1671), § 1.)*

Research References

Treatises and Practice Aids

Witkin, California Summary 10th Husband and Wife § 4, Definitions.

§ 127. Respondent

"Respondent" includes defendant, where appropriate. *(Stats.1992, c. 162 (A.B.2650), § 10, operative Jan. 1, 1994.)*

Law Revision Commission Comments

Enactment [Revised Comment]

Section 127 is a new provision included for drafting convenience. [23 Cal.L.Rev.Comm. Reports 1 (1993)].

Research References

Treatises and Practice Aids

Witkin, California Summary 10th Husband and Wife § 4, Definitions.

§ 130. Separate property

"Separate property" is property that is separate property under Part 2 (commencing with Section 760) of Division 4. *(Stats.1992, c. 162 (A.B.2650), § 10, operative Jan. 1, 1994.)*

Law Revision Commission Comments

Enactment [Revised Comment]

Section 130 is a new provision included for drafting convenience. See also Sections 2502 (defining "separate property" for purposes of division of community estate), 3515 (defining "separate property" for purposes of support). [23 Cal.L.Rev.Comm. Reports 1 (1993)].

Research References

Treatises and Practice Aids

Witkin, California Summary 10th Husband and Wife § 4, Definitions.

§ 142. Spousal support

"Spousal support" means support of the spouse of the obligor. *(Stats.1992, c. 162 (A.B.2650), § 10, operative Jan. 1, 1994.)*

Law Revision Commission Comments

Enactment [Revised Comment]

Section 142 is a new provision included for drafting convenience. As used in this section, "spouse" refers to persons who are lawfully married to each other and to persons who were previously lawfully married to each other. See Section 11. As used in a particular provision, this definition does not apply if the provision or context otherwise requires. See Section 50. [23 Cal.L.Rev.Comm. Reports 1 (1993)].

Research References

Treatises and Practice Aids

Witkin, California Summary 10th Husband and Wife § 4, Definitions.

§ 143. Spouse

"Spouse" includes "registered domestic partner," as required by Section 297.5. *(Added by Stats.2016, c. 50 (S.B. 1005), § 35, eff. Jan. 1, 2017.)*

§ 145. State

"State" means a state of the United States, the District of Columbia, or a commonwealth, territory, or insular possession subject to the jurisdiction of the United States. *(Stats. 1992, c. 162 (A.B.2650), § 10, operative Jan. 1, 1994. Amended by Stats.1999, c. 661 (A.B.825), § 3.)*

Law Revision Commission Comments

Enactment [Revised Comment]

Section 145 is a new provision drawn from Code of Civil Procedure Section 676.1(12). For special definitions of "state" applicable to specific acts, see Sections 3402(j) (Uniform Child Custody Jurisdiction Act), 4802(j) (Uniform Reciprocal Enforcement of Support Act). [23 Cal.L.Rev.Comm. Reports 1 (1993)].

Research References

Treatises and Practice Aids

Witkin, California Summary 10th Husband and Wife § 4, Definitions.

§ 150. Support

"Support" refers to a support obligation owing on behalf of a child, spouse, or family, or an amount owing pursuant to Section 17402. It also includes past due support or arrearage when it exists. "Support," when used with reference to a minor child or a child described in Section 3901, includes maintenance and education. *(Stats.1992, c. 162 (A.B.2650), § 10, operative Jan. 1, 1994. Amended by Stats.1993, c. 219 (A.B.1500), § 82; Stats.2000, c. 808 (A.B.1358), § 22, eff. Sept. 28, 2000.)*

Law Revision Commission Comments

Enactment [Revised Comment]

The first and second sentences of Section 150 continue without change and generalize former Civil Code Section 4390(h). The third sentence of Section 150 is a new provision that makes clear that "support" includes maintenance and education of a minor child or an unmarried child described in Section 3901. As used in a particular provision, this all-inclusive definition does not apply if the provision or context otherwise requires. See Section 50. [23 Cal.L.Rev. Comm. Reports 1 (1993)].

Commentary

Monterey County v. Banuelos, 82 Cal.App.4th 1299, 98 Cal.Rptr.2d 710 (2000), holds that post–1993 amendments to this section enlarged the definition of "child support" to include amounts owed to individuals or the county for current support or arrearages, and thus allow a court to use the contempt remedy and issue a seek-work order under § 290 when a county attempts to recover child support arrearages or reimbursement for public assistance. See commentary to § 290.

Research References

Forms

West's California Code Forms, Family § 3900, Comment Overview--Duty Of Parent to Support Child.

West's California Judicial Council Forms FL-343, Spousal, Partner, or Family Support Order Attachment.

Treatises and Practice Aids

Witkin, California Summary 10th Husband and Wife § 4, Definitions.

Witkin, California Summary 10th Husband and Wife § 343, CalWORKs Aid.

Witkin, California Summary 10th Parent and Child § 422, Support Of High School Student.

§ 155. Support order

"Support order" means a judgment or order of support in favor of an obligee, whether temporary or final, or subject to modification, termination, or remission, regardless of the kind of action or proceeding in which it is entered. For the purposes of Section 685.020 of the Code of Civil Procedure, only the initial support order, whether temporary or final, whether or not the order is contained in a judgment, shall be considered an installment judgment. No support order or other order or notice issued, which sets forth the amount of support owed for prior periods of time or establishes a periodic payment to liquidate the support owed for prior periods, shall be considered a money judgment for purposes of subdivision (b) of Section 685.020 of the Code of Civil Procedure. *(Stats.1992, c. 162 (A.B.2650), § 10, operative Jan. 1, 1994. Amended by Stats.2002, c. 539 (S.B.97), § 2.)*

Law Revision Commission Comments

Enactment [Revised Comment]

Section 155 provides a general definition of "support order" that is drawn from the definition of "support order" in the Uniform Reciprocal Enforcement of Support Act, continued in Section 4802(k), except that the definition provided by Section 155 does not include the word "decree." See Section 100 ("judgment" and "order" include decree, as appropriate). The word "termination" is used in place of "revocation." This is not a substantive change. As used in a particular provision, this all-inclusive definition does not apply if the provision or context otherwise requires. See Section 50. [23 Cal.L.Rev.Comm. Reports 1 (1993)].

Commentary

The 2002 amendment of this section, which refers to Code of Civil Procedure Section 685.020, was intended to abrogate the installment-payment holding of *Dupont v. Dupont, 88 Cal.App.4th 192, 105 Cal.Rptr.2d 607 (2001)*. For further discussion, see Commentary to Code of Civil Procedure § 685.020.

In re Marriage of McClellan, 130 Cal.App.4th 247, 30 Cal.Rptr.3d 5 (2005), holds that the 2000 amendment to this section applies retroactively because it clarified, rather than altered, existing law. Accordingly, it applies in calculating the interest due on child support arrearages that were the subject of arrearage orders entered before the amendment took effect.

Research References

Treatises and Practice Aids

Witkin, California Summary 10th Community Property § 29, Lack Of Independent Counsel.

Witkin, California Summary 10th Husband and Wife § 4, Definitions.

Part 3

INDIAN CHILDREN

§ 170. Definitions; eligible membership in more than one tribe

(a) As used in this code, unless the context otherwise requires, the terms "Indian," "Indian child," "Indian child's tribe," "Indian custodian," "Indian organization," "Indian tribe," "reservation," and "tribal court" shall be defined as provided in Section 1903 of the Indian Child Welfare Act (25 U.S.C. Sec. 1901 et seq.).

(b) When used in connection with an Indian child custody proceeding, the terms "extended family member" and "parent" shall be defined as provided in Section 1903 of the Indian Child Welfare Act.

(c) "Indian child custody proceeding" means a "child custody proceeding" within the meaning of Section 1903 of the Indian Child Welfare Act, including a voluntary or involuntary proceeding that may result in an Indian child's temporary or long-term foster care or guardianship placement if the parent or Indian custodian cannot have the child returned upon demand, termination of parental rights, or adoptive placement. An "Indian child custody proceeding" does not include a proceeding under this code commenced by the parent of an Indian child to determine the custodial rights of the child's parents, unless the proceeding involves a petition to declare an Indian child free from the custody or control of a parent or involves a grant of custody to a person or persons other than a parent, over the objection of a parent.

(d) If an Indian child is a member of more than one tribe or is eligible for membership in more than one tribe, the court shall make a determination, in writing together with the reasons for it, as to which tribe is the Indian child's tribe for purposes of the Indian child custody proceeding. The court shall make that determination as follows:

(1) If the Indian child is or becomes a member of only one tribe, that tribe shall be designated as the Indian child's tribe, even though the child is eligible for membership in another tribe.

(2) If an Indian child is or becomes a member of more than one tribe, or is not a member of any tribe but is eligible for membership in more than one tribe, the tribe with which the child has the more significant contacts shall be designated as the Indian child's tribe. In determining which tribe the child has the more significant contacts with, the court shall consider, among other things, the following factors:

(A) The length of residence on or near the reservation of each tribe and frequency of contact with each tribe.

(B) The child's participation in activities of each tribe.

(C) The child's fluency in the language of each tribe.

(D) Whether there has been a previous adjudication with respect to the child by a court of one of the tribes.

(E) Residence on or near one of the tribes' reservations by the child's parents, Indian custodian or extended family members.

(F) Tribal membership of custodial parent or Indian custodian.

(G) Interest asserted by each tribe in response to the notice specified in Section 180.

(H) The child's self identification.

(3) If an Indian child becomes a member of a tribe other than the one designated by the court as the Indian child's tribe under paragraph (2), actions taken based on the court's determination prior to the child's becoming a tribal member shall continue to be valid. *(Added by Stats.2006, c. 838 (S.B.678), § 1.)*

Commentary

California provides a higher standard of protection for the rights of an Indian child's parents than does the federal Indian Child Welfare Act. Compare this section, Welfare and Institutions Code section 224, and California Rules of Court, Rule 5.481 with 25 U.S.C. § 1903. Thus a trial court, a court-connected investigator, and a petitioner have an affirmative duty to inquire whether a child is or may be an Indian child in proceedings for foster care placement, guardianship, conservatorship, custody placement with a non-parent pursuant to Family Code section 3041, a declaration freeing a child from parental custody and control, termination of parental rights, or adoption. *In re Noreen G., 181 Cal.App.4th 1359, 105 Cal.Rptr.3d 521 (2010), review denied.*

Research References

Forms

California Transactions Forms--Family Law § 3:7, Custody Issues Outside the Scope Of the Family Code.

California Transactions Forms--Family Law § 6:143, Overview Of Indian Child Welfare Act (ICWA).

California Transactions Forms--Family Law § 6:144, Scope and Implementation Of ICWA.

California Transactions Forms--Family Law § 6:145, Definitions.

West's California Judicial Council Forms ADOPT-200, Adoption Request.

Treatises and Practice Aids

Witkin, California Summary 10th Parent and Child § 288A, (New) Definitions.

Witkin, California Summary 10th Parent and Child § 288D, (New) Determination Of Tribal Membership.

Witkin, California Summary 10th Parent and Child § 288E, (New) Notice Of Proceedings.

Witkin, California Summary 10th Parent and Child § 288F, (New) Participation by Unrecognized Tribe.

Witkin, California Summary 10th Parent and Child § 527A, (New) Participation Of Unrecognized Tribe.

§ 175. Legislative findings and declarations

(a) The Legislature finds and declares the following:

(1) There is no resource that is more vital to the continued existence and integrity of recognized Indian tribes than their children, and the State of California has an interest in protecting Indian children who are members of, or are eligible for membership in, an Indian tribe. The state is committed to protecting the essential tribal relations and best interest of an Indian child by promoting practices, in accordance with the Indian Child Welfare Act (25 U.S.C. Sec. 1901 et seq.) and other applicable law, designed to prevent the child's involuntary out-of-home placement and, whenever the placement is necessary or ordered, by placing the child, whenever possible, in a placement that reflects the unique values of the child's tribal culture and is best able to assist the child in establishing, developing, and maintaining a political, cultural, and social relationship with the child's tribe and tribal community.

(2) It is in the interest of an Indian child that the child's membership in the child's Indian tribe and connection to the tribal community be encouraged and protected, regardless of any of the following:

(A) Whether the child is in the physical custody of an Indian parent or Indian custodian at the commencement of a child custody proceeding.

(B) Whether the parental rights of the child's parents have been terminated.

(C) Where the child has resided or been domiciled.

(b) In all Indian child custody proceedings the court shall consider all of the findings contained in subdivision (a), strive to promote the stability and security of Indian tribes and families, comply with the federal Indian Child Welfare Act, and seek to protect the best interest of the child. Whenever an Indian child is removed from a foster care home or institution, guardianship, or adoptive placement for the purpose of further foster care, guardianship, or adoptive placement, placement of the child shall be in accordance with the Indian Child Welfare Act.

(c) A determination by an Indian tribe that an unmarried person, who is under the age of 18 years, is either (1) a member of an Indian tribe or (2) eligible for membership in an Indian tribe and a biological child of a member of an Indian tribe shall constitute a significant political affiliation with the tribe and shall require the application of the federal Indian Child Welfare Act to the proceedings.

(d) In any case in which this code or other applicable state or federal law provides a higher standard of protection to the rights of the parent or Indian custodian of an Indian child, or the Indian child's tribe, than the rights provided under the Indian Child Welfare Act, the court shall apply the higher standard.

(e) Any Indian child, the Indian child's tribe, or the parent or Indian custodian from whose custody the child has been removed, may petition the court to invalidate an action in an Indian child custody proceeding for foster care, guardianship placement, or termination of parental rights if the action violated Sections 1911, 1912, and 1913 of the Indian Child Welfare Act (25 U.S.C. Sec. 1901 et seq.). Nothing in this section is intended to prohibit, restrict, or otherwise limit any rights under Section 1914 of the Indian Child Welfare Act (25 U.S.C. Sec. 1901 et seq.). *(Added by Stats.2006, c. 838 (S.B.678), § 1.)*

Commentary

Compliance with the notice provision of the Indian Child Welfare Act (ICWA), 25 U.S.C.A. § 1912, is required in a parental rights termination proceeding under this part even though the "existing Indian family doctrine" may ultimately render the ICWA inapplicable. *In re Suzanna L., 104 Cal.App.4th 223, 127 Cal.Rptr.2d 860 (2002)*. For discussion of the "existing Indian family doctrine," see Commentary to 25 U.S.C.A. § 1913.

Research References

Forms

California Transactions Forms--Family Law § 3:8, No Statutory Custody Preferences.

California Transactions Forms--Family Law § 6:143, Overview Of Indian Child Welfare Act (ICWA).

Treatises and Practice Aids

Witkin, California Summary 10th Parent and Child § 288B, (New) Legislative Findings and Policies.

Witkin, California Summary 10th Parent and Child § 288D, (New) Determination Of Tribal Membership.

§ 177. Governing law in Indian child custody proceedings

(a) In an Indian child custody proceeding, the court shall apply Sections 224.2 to 224.6, inclusive, and Sections 305.5, 361.31, and 361.7 of the Welfare and Institutions Code, and the following rules from the California Rules of Court, as they read on January 1, 2007:

(1) Paragraph (7) of subdivision (b) of Rule 5.530.

(2) Subdivision (i) of Rule 5.534.

(b) In the provisions cited in subdivision (a), references to social workers, probation officers, county welfare department, or probation department shall be construed as meaning the party seeking a foster care placement, guardianship, or adoption under this code.

(c) This section shall only apply to proceedings involving an Indian child. *(Added by Stats.2006, c. 838 (S.B.678), § 1. Amended by Stats.2007, c. 130 (A.B.299), § 85.)*

Research References

Forms

California Transactions Forms--Family Law § 3:4, Subject Matter Jurisdiction for Custody Determinations.

California Transactions Forms--Family Law § 6:143, Overview Of Indian Child Welfare Act (ICWA).

California Transactions Forms--Family Law § 6:149, Rights Of Indian Child's Tribe.

West's California Judicial Council Forms ICWA-020, Parental Notification Of Indian Status.

West's California Judicial Council Forms ICWA-040, Notice Of Designation Of Tribal Representative and Notice Of Intervention in a Court Proceeding Involving an Indian Child.

West's California Judicial Council Forms ICWA-050, Notice Of Petition and Petition to Transfer Case Involving an Indian Child to Tribal Jurisdiction.

West's California Judicial Council Forms ICWA-060, Order on Petition to Transfer Case Involving an Indian Child to Tribal Jurisdiction.

Treatises and Practice Aids

Witkin, California Summary 10th Parent and Child § 524, Jurisdiction.

Witkin, California Summary 10th Parent and Child § 535, Placement Standards and Preferences.

Witkin, California Summary 10th Parent and Child § 288C, (New) Applicable Law.

§ 180. Notice of proceedings; parties; requirements; time to send

(a) In an Indian child custody proceeding notice shall comply with subdivision (b) of this section.

(b) Any notice sent under this section shall be sent to the minor's parent or legal guardian, Indian custodian, if any, and the Indian child's tribe and shall comply with all of the following requirements:

(1) Notice shall be sent by registered or certified mail with return receipt requested. Additional notice by first-class mail is recommended, but not required.

(2) Notice to the tribe shall be to the tribal chairperson, unless the tribe has designated another agent for service.

(3) Notice shall be sent to all tribes of which the child may be a member or eligible for membership until the court makes a determination as to which tribe is the Indian child's tribe in accordance with subdivision (d) of Section 170, after which notice need only be sent to the tribe determined to be the Indian child's tribe.

(4) Notice, to the extent required by federal law, shall be sent to the Secretary of the Interior's designated agent, the Sacramento Area Director, Bureau of Indian Affairs. If the identity or location of the Indian child's tribe is known, a copy of the notice shall also be sent directly to the Secretary of the Interior unless the Secretary of the Interior has waived that notice in writing and the person responsible for giving notice under this section has filed proof of the waiver with the court.

(5) In addition to the information specified in other sections of this article, notice shall include all of the following information:

(A) The name, birthdate, and birthplace of the Indian child, if known.

(B) The name of any Indian tribe in which the child is a member or may be eligible for membership, if known.

(C) All names known of the Indian child's biological parents, grandparents, and great-grandparents, or Indian custodians, including maiden, married, and former names or aliases, as well as their current and former addresses, birthdates, places of birth and death, tribal enrollment numbers, and any other identifying information, if known.

(D) A copy of the petition by which the proceeding was initiated.

(E) A copy of the child's birth certificate, if available.

(F) The location, mailing address, and telephone number of the court and all parties notified pursuant to this section.

(G) A statement of the following:

(i) The absolute right of the child's parents, Indian custodians, and tribe to intervene in the proceeding.

(ii) The right of the child's parents, Indian custodians, and tribe to petition the court to transfer the proceeding to the tribal court of the Indian child's tribe, absent objection by either parent and subject to declination by the tribal court.

(iii) The right of the child's parents, Indian custodians, and tribe to, upon request, be granted up to an additional 20 days from the receipt of the notice to prepare for the proceeding.

(iv) The potential legal consequences of the proceedings on the future custodial rights of the child's parents or Indian custodians.

(v) That if the parents or Indian custodians are unable to afford counsel, counsel will be appointed to represent the parents or Indian custodians pursuant to Section 1912 of the Indian Child Welfare Act (25 U.S.C. Sec. 1901 et seq.).

(vi) That the information contained in the notice, petition, pleading, and other court documents is confidential, so any person or entity notified shall maintain the confidentiality of the information contained in the notice concerning the particular proceeding and not reveal it to anyone who does not need the information in order to exercise the tribe's rights under the Indian Child Welfare Act (25 U.S.C. Sec. 1901 et seq.).

(c) Notice shall be sent whenever it is known or there is reason to know that an Indian child is involved, and for every hearing thereafter, including, but not limited to, the hearing at which a final adoption order is to be granted. After a tribe acknowledges that the child is a member or eligible for membership in that tribe, or after the Indian child's tribe intervenes in a proceeding, the information set out in subparagraphs (C), (D), (E), and (G) of paragraph (5) of subdivision (b) need not be included with the notice.

(d) Proof of the notice, including copies of notices sent and all return receipts and responses received, shall be filed with the court in advance of the hearing except as permitted under subdivision (e).

(e) No proceeding shall be held until at least 10 days after receipt of notice by the parent, Indian custodian, the tribe, or the Bureau of Indian Affairs. The parent, Indian custodian, or the tribe shall, upon request, be granted up to 20 additional days to prepare for the proceeding. Nothing herein shall be construed as limiting the rights of the parent, Indian custodian, or tribe to 10 days' notice if a lengthier notice period is required under this code.

(f) With respect to giving notice to Indian tribes, a party shall be subject to court sanctions if that person knowingly and willfully falsifies or conceals a material fact concerning whether the child is an Indian child, or counsels a party to do so.

(g) The inclusion of contact information of any adult or child that would otherwise be required to be included in the notification pursuant to this section, shall not be required if that person is at risk of harm as a result of domestic violence, child abuse, sexual abuse, or stalking. *(Added by Stats.2006, c. 838 (S.B.678), § 1.)*

Research References

Forms

California Transactions Forms--Family Law § 6:143, Overview Of Indian Child Welfare Act (ICWA).

West's California Judicial Council Forms ADOPT-200, Adoption Request.

West's California Judicial Council Forms ICWA-030(A), Attachment to Notice Of Child Custody Proceeding for Indian Child (Indian Child Welfare Act).

Treatises and Practice Aids

Witkin, California Summary 10th Parent and Child § 78, Child Of Indian Ancestry.

Witkin, California Summary 10th Parent and Child § 529, Formal Requisites.

Witkin, California Summary 10th Parent and Child § 288E, (New) Notice Of Proceedings.

Witkin, California Summary 10th Parent and Child § 288F, (New) Participation by Unrecognized Tribe.

§ 185. Indian child of tribe not recognized to have tribal status under federal law; tribal participation at hearings

(a) In a custody proceeding involving a child who would otherwise be an Indian child based on the definition contained in paragraph (4) of Section 1903 of the federal Indian Child Welfare Act (25 U.S.C. Sec. 1901 et seq.), but is not an Indian child based on status of the child's tribe, as defined in paragraph (8) of Section 1903 of the federal Indian Child Welfare Act (25 U.S.C. Sec. 1901 et seq.), the court may permit the tribe from which the child is descended to participate in the proceeding upon request of the tribe.

(b) If the court permits a tribe to participate in a proceeding, the tribe may do all of the following, upon consent of the court:

(1) Be present at the hearing.

(2) Address the court.

(3) Request and receive notice of hearings.

(4) Request to examine court documents relating to the proceeding.

(5) Present information to the court that is relevant to the proceeding.

(6) Submit written reports and recommendations to the court.

(7) Perform other duties and responsibilities as requested or approved by the court.

(c) If more than one tribe requests to participate in a proceeding under subdivision (a), the court may limit participation to the tribe with which the child has the most significant contacts, as determined in accordance with paragraph (2) of subdivision (d) of Section 170.

(d) This section is intended to assist the court in making decisions that are in the best interest of the child by permitting a tribe in the circumstances set out in subdivision (a) to inform the court and parties to the proceeding about placement options for the child within the child's extended family or the tribal community, services and programs available to the child and the child's parents as Indians, and other unique interests the child or the child's parents may have as Indians. This section shall not be construed to make the Indian Child Welfare Act (25 U.S.C. Sec. 1901 et seq.), or any state law implementing the Indian Child Welfare Act, applicable to the proceedings, or to limit the court's discretion to permit other interested persons to participate in these or any other proceedings.

(e) This section shall only apply to proceedings involving an Indian child. *(Added by Stats.2006, c. 838 (S.B.678), § 1.)*

Research References

Treatises and Practice Aids

Witkin, California Summary 10th Parent and Child § 288F, (New) Participation by Unrecognized Tribe.

Division 2

GENERAL PROVISIONS

Part 1

JURISDICTION

§ 200. Jurisdiction in superior court

The superior court has jurisdiction in proceedings under this code. *(Stats.1992, c. 162 (A.B.2650), § 10, operative Jan. 1, 1994.)*

Law Revision Commission Comments

Enactment [Revised Comment]

Section 200 generalizes provisions found throughout former law. See, e.g., former Civ. Code §§ 36.1, 36.2, 65, 197.5, 206.5, 221.60, 221.72, 222.20, 222.70, 222.72, 224.30, 222.90, 224.45, 224.47, 224.64, 224.66, 224.80, 224.93, 226.64, 227.10, 227.40, 227.46, 228.10, 229.30, 230.20, 233, 233.5, 233.6, 245, 4101, 4102, 4212, 4213, 4306, 4351, 4351.5, 4357, 4359, 4365, 4450, 4503, 4551, 4703, 7007, 7017, 7020; former Code Civ. Proc. §§ 1672.5, 1771; former Prob. Code § 3301. Each of the former sections is continued in the Family Code, but the reference to the "superior" court has been omitted as surplus. [23 Cal.L.Rev.Comm. Reports 1 (1993)].

Commentary

Under this section, section 2010(c), and section 4908, in a proceeding to dissolve a marriage a California Superior Court has jurisdiction to award child support even though a child's home state is Japan, when no support action has ever been initiated in the child's home state. *In re Marriage of Richardson, 179 Cal.App.4th 1240, 102 Cal.Rptr.3d 391 (2009)*.

See Section 290, Commentary.

Research References

Forms

California Transactions Forms--Family Law § 4:104, Paternity Acknowledgment.

West's California Code Forms, Family § 4400, Comment Overview--Duty Of Adult Children to Support Parents.

West's California Code Forms, Family § 303 Form 1, Order Consenting to Marriage Of Minor.

West's California Code Forms, Family § 4303 Form 1, Complaint by Spouse to Enforce Duty Of Spousal Support.

Treatises and Practice Aids

Witkin, California Summary 10th Husband and Wife § 3, Statutory Framework.

Witkin, California Summary 10th Husband and Wife § 5, Generally Applicable Procedures.

Witkin, California Summary 10th Husband and Wife § 69, Superior Court and Departments.

Part 2

GENERAL PROCEDURAL PROVISIONS

§ 210. Rules for practice and procedure

Except to the extent that any other statute or rules adopted by the Judicial Council provide applicable rules, the rules of practice and procedure applicable to civil actions generally, including the provisions of Title 3a (commencing with Section 391) of Part 2 of the Code of Civil Procedure, apply to, and constitute the rules of practice and procedure in, proceedings under this code. *(Stats.1992, c. 162 (A.B.2650), § 10, operative Jan. 1, 1994. Amended by Stats.2002, c. 1118 (A.B.1938), § 2.)*

Law Revision Commission Comments

Enactment [Revised Comment]

Section 210 is a new provision drawn from Probate Code Section 1000. Section 210 is consistent with prior practice. See Cal. R. Ct. 1206, 1207 (1970).

Section 210 provides a default rule that applies in circumstances where there is not a special statutory or court rule applicable to proceedings under this code. The general rule stated in this section is subject to many special provisions in this code and other statutes governing practice and procedure, and also is subject to the rulemaking power of the Judicial Council. See Section 211 (Judicial Council rules of practice and procedure).

This code does not include a general rule regarding appeals. Therefore, the rule applicable to civil actions generally applies except to the extent that another statute or a rule adopted by the Judicial Council provides otherwise. See Code of Civ. Proc. §§ 904.1 [sic] (when appeal may be taken from superior court judgment or order). For provisions of this code dealing with rights of appeal, see Sections 2025 (appeal of bifurcated issue), 2400, 2404 (waiver of appeal in summary dissolution proceeding), 2554 (court valuation of property for purposes of arbitration not appealable), 2555 (disposition of property subject to revision on appeal), 3554 (support order or judgment appealable as in other civil actions), 4847 (appeal by Attorney General from support order under URESA), 7669 (appeal from order as to father's consent for adoption), 7894 (appeal from order or judgment freeing child from parental custody and control), 7895 (appeal by indigent appellant from judgment freeing child from parental custody and control), 8815 (appeal from order as to withdrawal of consent in independent adoption), 8820 (appeal from department or agency disapproval of independent adoption), 9005 (appeal from order as to consent to adoption in stepparent adoption).

For other provisions of this code dealing with appeals, see Section 2341 (effect of appeal from judgment of dissolution), 2346 (entry of judgment nunc pro tunc where no appeal taken), 4853 (stay of enforcement of registered foreign support order under URESA where appeal pending), 7805 (persons entitled to inspect court papers in appeal from proceeding to declare freedom from parental custody and control). See also Code Civ. Proc. § 917.7 (special rules regarding stay on appeal of provisions regarding child custody and exclusion from dwelling.) [23 Cal.L.Rev.Comm. Reports 1 (1993)].

Commentary

Invoking this section, *Elkins v. Superior Court, 41 Cal.4th 1337, 163 P.3d 160, 63 Cal.Rptr.3d 483 (2007)*, held that a local superior court rule, which required divorcing parties to present their case by means of written declarations was unenforceable because it was inconsistent with state law limiting introduction of hearsay evidence.

In re Marriage of Woolsey, 220 Cal.App.4th 881, 163 Cal.Rptr.3d 551 (2013), review denied, held that a county rule requiring notarization of unrepresented parties' signatures on a marital settlement agreement was invalid because it was in conflict with statewide rules of court and did not reasonably advance any statutory purpose.

Loeffler v. Medina, 174 Cal.App.4th 1495, 95 Cal.Rptr.3d 343 (2009), holds that Code of Civil Procedure section 533 sets forth the applicable standard for a trial court considering whether to terminate a domestic violence restraining order issued under the Domestic Violence Prevention Act (Family Code sections 6200–6409.)

Research References

Treatises and Practice Aids

Witkin, California Summary 10th Husband and Wife § 5, Generally Applicable Procedures.

Witkin, California Summary 10th Husband and Wife § 67, in General.

Witkin, California Summary 10th Husband and Wife § 82, in General.

Witkin, California Summary 10th Husband and Wife § 86, in General.

Witkin, California Summary 10th Husband and Wife § 99, in General.

Witkin, California Summary 10th Husband and Wife § 119, Entry After Death Of Party.

§ 211. Provision by rule for practice and procedure

Notwithstanding any other provision of law, the Judicial Council may provide by rule for the practice and procedure in proceedings under this code. *(Stats.1992, c. 162 (A.B.2650), § 10, operative Jan. 1, 1994.)*

Law Revision Commission Comments

Enactment [Revised Comment]

Section 211 continues without change and generalizes former Civil Code Section 4001. The former provision applied only to former Part 5 (commencing with Section 4000) of Division 4 of the Civil Code (the former Family Law Act), whereas Section 211 applies to the entire Family Code.

For other provisions relating to Judicial Council rules, see, e.g., Sections 2021 (joinder of interested person), 2025 (appeal of bifurcated issue), 2070 (joinder), 2321 (notice of amendment), 3830 (standards for software to determine support).

For provisions relating to Judicial Council forms, see, e.g., Sections 95 ("income and expense declaration"), 115 ("property declaration"), 2062 (notice of appearance), 2104 (preliminary declaration of disclosure), 2105 (final declaration of disclosure), 2250 (petition for judgment of nullity), 2331 (petition and summons), 2401 (joint petition), 2402 (revocation of joint petition), 3417 (affidavit), 3634 (expedited child support order), 3668 (discovery before modification or termination of support order), 3694 (simplified modification of support order), 3772 (health insurance coverage assignment), 4068 (child support worksheets and forms), 4506 (abstract of judgment), 4732 (civil penalty for child support delinquency), 5295 (earnings assignment order for support), 6222 (in forma pauperis), 6226 (orders intended to prevent domestic violence), 7110 (court declaration of emancipation of minor).

For provisions relating to other Judicial Council matters, see, e.g., Sections 1816 (development of training program), 1850–1852 (duties in connection with statewide coordination of family mediation and conciliation services), 2400 (adjustment of dollar amounts to reflect California Consumer Price Index), 2406 (summary dissolution brochure), 3153 (guidelines for determining eligibility for county payment of counsel), 3162 (uniform standards of practice for mediation), 3686 (age increase factor), 4054 (periodic review of statewide uniform guideline), 4067 (continuing review of statewide uniform guideline), 4071 (maximum hardship deduction table), 4552 (duties regarding procedure for deposit of money to secure future child support payments, including development of rules and forms). [23 Cal.L.Rev.Comm. Reports 1 (1993)].

Commentary

Relying on this section and California Rules of Court, Rules 5.21, 5.106, and 5.118, *In re Marriage of Guasch, 201 Cal.App.4th 942, 134 Cal.Rptr.3d 358 (2011)*, affirmed a judgment in favor of a wife, who was not the debtor spouse, which quashed a judgment creditor's writ of execution and enjoined further enforcement against community property, without requiring the wife to post an undertaking under Code of Civil Procedure section 529. *Guasch* declined to read the requirement of that statute into Family Code section 2010 (e), upon which the trial court relied in granting the wife relief.

Research References

Treatises and Practice Aids

Witkin, California Summary 10th Husband and Wife § 11, Family Law Rules.

§ 212. Verification of pleadings

A petition, response, application, opposition, or other pleading filed with the court under this code shall be verified. *(Stats.1992, c. 162 (A.B.2650), § 10, operative Jan. 1, 1994.)*

Law Revision Commission Comments

Enactment [Revised Comment]

Section 212 generalizes provisions found throughout former law. See, e.g., former Civ. Code §§ 64, 206.5, 230.20, 232.9, 4102, 4710. Each of the former sections is continued in the Family Code, but the reference to a "verified" pleading has been omitted as surplus, since Section 212 applies to the entire Family Code. Section 212 codifies existing family law practice. See, e.g., Cal. R. Ct. 1281 (rev. Jan. 1, 1993) (petition), 1282 (response), 1285.20 (application for order and supporting declaration). See also Code Civ. Proc. § 446 (verification of pleadings). [23 Cal.L.Rev.Comm. Reports 1 (1993)].

Research References

Forms

California Transactions Forms--Family Law § 6:41, Initiating the Adoption.

California Transactions Forms--Family Law § 6:47, Matters to Consider in Drafting Petition for Independent Adoption Of Unmarried Minor.

California Transactions Forms--Family Law § 6:98, Form Drafting Considerations.

California Transactions Forms--Family Law § 6:112, Form Drafting Considerations.

California Transactions Forms--Family Law § 6:162, Termination Of Adoption.

Treatises and Practice Aids

Witkin, California Summary 10th Husband and Wife § 5, Generally Applicable Procedures.

§ 213. Responsive declaration to seek affirmative relief alternative to moving party's requested relief; proceedings

(a) In a hearing on an order to show cause, or on a modification thereof, or in a hearing on a motion, other than for contempt, the responding party may seek affirmative relief alternative to that requested by the moving party, on the same issues raised by the moving party, by filing a responsive declaration within the time set by statute or rules of court.

(b) This section applies in any of the following proceedings:

(1) A proceeding for dissolution of marriage, for nullity of marriage, or for legal separation of the parties.

(2) A proceeding relating to a protective order described in Section 6218.

(3) Any other proceeding in which there is at issue the visitation, custody, or support of a child. *(Stats.1992, c. 162 (A.B.2650), § 10, operative Jan. 1, 1994. Amended by Stats. 1993, c. 219 (A.B.1500), § 83.)*

Law Revision Commission Comments

Enactment [Revised Comment]

Subdivision (a) of Section 213 continues former Civil Code Section 4355.6 without substantive change.

Subdivision (b) is new and has been added to state the application of this section. The application of former Civil Code Section 4355.6 was unclear, because the section did not include any language specifying the proceedings to which it applied.

For provisions concerning situations in which a child may be supported, see Sections 3587 (court order to effectuate agreement for support of adult child), 3901 (duration of duty to support child), 3910 (duty to maintain incapacitated child), 4000 (civil action to enforce parent's duty to support), 4001 (order for child support). [23 Cal.L.Rev.Comm. Reports 1 (1993)].

Research References

Forms

West's California Judicial Council Forms FL-685, Response to Governmental Notice Of Motion or Order to Show Cause.

Treatises and Practice Aids

Witkin, California Summary 10th Husband and Wife § 5, Generally Applicable Procedures.

Witkin, California Summary 10th Husband and Wife § 87, Methods Of Obtaining Orders.

§ 214. Joinder of issues of fact; private trial

Except as otherwise provided in this code or by court rule, the court may, when it considers it necessary in the interests of justice and the persons involved, direct the trial of any issue of fact joined in a proceeding under this code to be private, and may exclude all persons except the officers of the court, the parties, their witnesses, and counsel. *(Stats.1992, c. 162 (A.B.2650), § 10, operative Jan. 1, 1994.)*

Law Revision Commission Comments

Enactment [Revised Comment]

Section 214 continues without change and generalizes former Civil Code Section 4360. The former provision applied only to former Part 5 (commencing with Section 4000) of Division 4 of the Civil Code (the former Family Law Act), whereas Section 214 applies to the entire Family Code. Section 214 is also made subject to exceptions provided in this code or by court rule. Section 214 provides an exception to the general rule stated by Code of Civil Procedure Section 124 (court proceedings to be public).

Special provisions of the Family Code may provide more restrictive rules that prevail over the rule stated in Section 214. See, e.g., Sections 1818 (mandatory exclusion from conciliation proceedings), 7884 (mandatory exclusion from proceeding to declare child free from parental custody and control), 8611 (mandatory exclusion from adoption proceeding). Particular statutes may provide special rules concerning exclusion of the public from hearings that also prevail over the general rule of Section 214. See, e.g., Sections 591(e) (confidentiality of proceeding for waiver of premarital examinations prior to issuance of marriage license), 7643 (confidentiality of Uniform Parentage Act hearings and records). [23 Cal.L.Rev. Comm. Reports 1 (1993)].

Commentary

See generally *Green v. Uccelli, 207 Cal.App.3d 1112, 1119, 255 Cal.Rptr. 315 (1989)*; *Whitney v. Whitney, 164 Cal.App.2d 577, 330 P.2d 947 (1958)*.

In re Marriage of Lechowick, 65 Cal.App.4th 1406, 77 Cal.Rptr.2d 395 (1998), review denied November 18, 1998, holds that this Section merely authorizes the closing, under some circumstances, of court hearings and proceedings; it is not generally applicable to the issue of sealing court files, except that exhibits and transcripts from a closed hearing should likewise be confidential, unless the court orders to the contrary. An order under this Section must relate to the trial of one or more issues of fact and must be justified by a showing of particular need by the moving party. A journalist who seeks unsealing of court records in a dissolution proceeding must rebut the presumption that records on the trial of an issue of fact from which the court has excluded the public, should be kept confidential. *Id.*

Research References

Treatises and Practice Aids

Witkin, California Summary 10th Constitutional Law § 423, Civil Trial.

Witkin, California Summary 10th Husband and Wife § 5, Generally Applicable Procedures.

Witkin, California Summary 10th Parent and Child § 284, Trial.

§ 215. Modification of judgment or order; service of notice

(a) Except as provided in subdivision (b) or (c), after entry of a judgment of dissolution of marriage, nullity of marriage, legal separation of the parties, or paternity, or after a permanent order in any other proceeding in which there was at issue the visitation, custody, or support of a child, no modification of the judgment or order, and no subsequent order in the proceedings, is valid unless any prior notice otherwise required to be given to a party to the proceeding is served, in the same manner as the notice is otherwise permitted by law to be served, upon the party. For the purposes of this section, service upon the attorney of record is not sufficient.

(b) A postjudgment motion to modify a custody, visitation, or child support order may be served on the other party or parties by first-class mail or airmail, postage prepaid, to the persons to be served. For any party served by mail, the proof of service shall include an address verification.

(c) This section does not apply if the court has ordered an issue or issues bifurcated for separate trial in advance of the disposition of the entire case. In those cases, service of a motion on any outstanding matter shall be served either upon the attorney of record, if the parties are represented, or upon the parties, if unrepresented. However, if there has been no pleading filed in the action for a period of six months after the entry of the bifurcated judgment, service shall be upon both the party, at the party's last known address, and the attorney of record. *(Stats.1992, c. 162 (A.B.2650), § 10, operative Jan. 1, 1994. Amended by Stats.1993, c. 219 (A.B.1500), § 84; Stats.1999, c. 980 (A.B.1671), § 2; Stats. 2010, c. 352 (A.B.939), § 2; Stats.2016, c. 67 (A.B.1735), § 1, eff. Jan. 1, 2017.)*

Law Revision Commission Comments

Enactment [Revised Comment]

Section 215 continues former Civil Code Section 4809 without substantive change and adds "visitation" to the introductory clause. The reference to a "minor" child has been omitted to recognize that the proceeding may have been for support of an adult child. See Sections 3587 (court order to effectuate agreement for support of adult child), 3901 (duration of duty to support child), 3910 (duty to maintain incapacitated child), 4000 (civil action to enforce parent's duty to support), 4001 (order for child support). The word "support" has been substituted for "support, maintenance, or education," since "support" includes maintenance and education when used in reference to a minor child or a child described by Section 3901. See Section 150. References to "decree" have been omitted as surplus. See Section 100 ("judgment" and "order" include decree, as appropriate). [23 Cal.L.Rev.Comm. Reports 1 (1993)].

Commentary

For discussion of the purpose of the Section 215 requirement that the party be served and the insufficiency of service solely upon the party's attorney of record, see *In re Marriage of Kreiss, 224 Cal.App.3d 1033, 1036–1037, 274 Cal.Rptr. 226 (1990)* (divorced husband's failure to serve former wife with notice of motion to terminate spousal support required that the order to terminate spousal support be set aside; service on wife's attorney alone did not satisfy the letter or the spirit of Section 215).

For treatment of the claim that a party has waived, by her behavior, her Section 215 right to notice, compare *Kreiss, supra,* (no waiver) with *Ruszovan v. Ruszovan, 268 Cal.App.2d 902, 906, 74 Cal.Rptr. 507 (1969)* (waiver).

Research References

Forms

West's California Judicial Council Forms FL-334, Declaration Regarding Address Verification--Postjudgment Request to Modify a Child Custody, Visitation, or Child Support Order.
West's California Judicial Council Forms FL-683, Order to Show Cause.
West's California Judicial Council Forms FL-684, Request for Order and Supporting Declaration (Governmental).
West's California Judicial Council Forms FL-686, Proof Of Service by Mail.

Treatises and Practice Aids

Witkin, California Summary 10th Husband and Wife § 5, Generally Applicable Procedures.
Witkin, California Summary 10th Husband and Wife § 260, Improper Service on Attorney.
Witkin, California Summary 10th Husband and Wife § 290, Service on Party.
Witkin, California Summary 10th Parent and Child § 249, Power to Modify.
Witkin, California Summary 10th Parent and Child § 253, Move-Away Cases.

§ 216. Mediators or evaluators appointed by or connected to the court; limitations upon communication with said persons; exceptions

(a) In the absence of a stipulation by the parties to the contrary, there shall be no ex parte communication between the attorneys for any party to an action and any court-appointed or court-connected evaluator or mediator, or between a court-appointed or court-connected evaluator or mediator and the court, in any proceedings under this code, except with regard to the scheduling of appointments.

(b) There shall be no ex parte communications between counsel appointed by the court pursuant to Section 3150 and any court-appointed or court-connected evaluator or mediator, except where it is expressly authorized by the court or undertaken pursuant to paragraph (5) of subdivision (c) of Section 3151.

(c) Subdivisions (a) and (b) shall not apply in the following situations:

(1) To allow a mediator or evaluator to address a case involving allegations of domestic violence as set forth in Sections 3113, 3181, and 3192.

(2) To allow a mediator or evaluator to address a case involving allegations of domestic violence as set forth in Rule 5.215 of the California Rules of Court.

(3) If the mediator or evaluator determines that ex parte communication is needed to inform the court of his or her belief that a restraining order is necessary to prevent an imminent risk to the physical safety of the child or the party.

(d) Nothing in this section shall be construed to limit the responsibilities a mediator or evaluator may have as a mandated reporter pursuant to Section 11165.9 of the Penal Code or the responsibilities a mediator or evaluator may have to warn under Tarasoff v. Regents of the University of California (1976) 17 Cal.3d 425, Hedlund v. Superior Court (1983) 34 Cal.3d 695, and Section 43.92 of the Civil Code.

(e) The Judicial Council shall, by July 1, 2006, adopt a rule of court to implement this section. *(Added by Stats.2005, c.*

489 (S.B.1088), § 1. Amended by Stats.2007, c. 130 (A.B. 299), § 86.)

Implementation

For implementation of this section, see its terms.

Research References

Treatises and Practice Aids

Witkin, California Summary 10th Husband and Wife § 91, Family Conciliation Courts.

Witkin, California Summary 10th Husband and Wife § 10A, (New) Ex Parte Communications With Mediator or Evaluator.

Witkin, California Summary 10th Parent and Child § 253, Move-Away Cases.

§ 217. Hearing on motion; live, competent testimony to be received; refusal to hear testimony for good cause with written reasons; service of witness list

(a) At a hearing on any order to show cause or notice of motion brought pursuant to this code, absent a stipulation of the parties or a finding of good cause pursuant to subdivision (b), the court shall receive any live, competent testimony that is relevant and within the scope of the hearing and the court may ask questions of the parties.

(b) In appropriate cases, a court may make a finding of good cause to refuse to receive live testimony and shall state its reasons for the finding on the record or in writing. The Judicial Council shall, by January 1, 2012, adopt a statewide rule of court regarding the factors a court shall consider in making a finding of good cause.

(c) A party seeking to present live testimony from witnesses other than the parties shall, prior to the hearing, file and serve a witness list with a brief description of the anticipated testimony. If the witness list is not served prior to the hearing, the court may, on request, grant a brief continuance and may make appropriate temporary orders pending the continued hearing. *(Added by Stats.2010, c. 352 (A.B.939), § 3.)*

Commentary

Interpreting this section's requirement of live testimony absent a stipulation of the parties or a finding of good cause, *In re Marriage of Shimkus, 244 Cal.App.4th 1262, 198 Cal.Rptr.3d 799 (2016)*, held that declarations in support of a request for order (RFO) are not automatically admitted into evidence. Although California Rule of Court 5.111 requires that declarations be filed in support of an RFO, the declarations are not automatically evidence that may be considered by the court in making its findings or order.

Research References

Forms

West's California Judicial Council Forms FL-321, Witness List.

Treatises and Practice Aids

Witkin, California Summary 10th Husband and Wife § 5, Generally Applicable Procedures.

§ 218. Postjudgment pleadings; automatic reopening of discovery

With respect to the ability to conduct formal discovery in family law proceedings, when a request for order or other motion is filed and served after entry of judgment, discovery shall automatically reopen as to the issues raised in the postjudgment pleadings currently before the court. The date initially set for trial of the action specified in subdivision (a) of Section 2024.020 of the Code of Civil Procedure shall mean the date the postjudgment proceeding is set for hearing on the motion or any continuance thereof, or evidentiary trial, whichever is later. *(Added by Stats.2014, c. 169 (A.B.2586), § 1, eff. Jan. 1, 2015.)*

Commentary

This section was added to overrule *In re Marriage of Boblitt, 223 Cal.App.4th 1004, 167 Cal.Rptr.3d 777 (2014)*, which held that a motion to reopen discovery is required in postjudgment family law proceedings.

Research References

Treatises and Practice Aids

Witkin, California Summary 10th Husband and Wife § 5, Generally Applicable Procedures.

Witkin, California Summary 10th Husband and Wife § 291, Discovery.

Part 3

TEMPORARY RESTRAINING ORDER IN SUMMONS

§ 231. Application of part

This part applies to a temporary restraining order in a summons issued under any of the following provisions:

(a) Section 2040 (proceeding for dissolution of marriage, for nullity of marriage, or for legal separation of the parties).

(b) Section 7700 (proceeding under Uniform Parentage Act). *(Stats.1992, c. 162 (A.B.2650), § 10, operative Jan. 1, 1994. Amended by Stats.1993, c. 219 (A.B.1500), § 84.5.)*

Law Revision Commission Comments

Enactment [Revised Comment]

Section 231 is new. This part collects general provisions applicable to any restraining order contained in a summons in the proceedings referred to in this section. [23 Cal.L.Rev.Comm. Reports 1 (1993)].

Research References

Treatises and Practice Aids

Witkin, California Summary 10th Husband and Wife § 6, Order in Summons.

Witkin, California Summary 10th Husband and Wife § 83, Petition.

§ 232. Statement in summons as to enforceability of order

The summons shall state on its face that the order is enforceable in any place in this state by any law enforcement agency that has received mailed notice of the order or has otherwise received a copy of the order and any officer who has been shown a copy of the order. *(Stats.1992, c. 162 (A.B.2650), § 10, operative Jan. 1, 1994.)*

Law Revision Commission Comments

Enactment [Revised Comment]

Section 232 continues without substantive change the first sentence of the sixth paragraph of subdivision (a) and the first sentence of the third paragraph of subdivision (b) of former Code of Civil Procedure Section 412.21. [23 Cal.L.Rev.Comm. Reports 1 (1993)].

Research References

Forms

West's California Judicial Council Forms FL-110, Summons (Family Law).

West's California Judicial Council Forms FL-210, Summons (Percentage - Custody and Support).

Treatises and Practice Aids

Witkin, California Summary 10th Husband and Wife § 6, Order in Summons.

§ 233. Duration of order; enforceability; violation; punishment

(a) Upon filing the petition and issuance of the summons and upon personal service of the petition and summons on the respondent or upon waiver and acceptance of service by the respondent, the temporary restraining order under this part shall be in effect against the parties until the final judgment is entered or the petition is dismissed, or until further order of the court.

(b) The temporary restraining order is enforceable in any place in this state, but is not enforceable by a law enforcement agency of a political subdivision unless that law enforcement agency has received mailed notice of the order or has otherwise received a copy of the order or the officer enforcing the order has been shown a copy of the order.

(c) A willful and knowing violation of the order included in the summons by removing a child from the state without the written consent of the other party or an order of the court is punishable as provided in Section 278.5 of the Penal Code. A willful and knowing violation of any of the other orders included in the summons is punishable as provided in Section 273.6 of the Penal Code. *(Stats.1992, c. 162 (A.B.2650), § 10, operative Jan. 1, 1994.)*

Law Revision Commission Comments

Enactment [Revised Comment]

Subdivision (a) of Section 233 continues without substantive change the first part of the second sentences of subdivisions (a) and (b) former Code of Civil Procedure Section 412.21. The word "judgment" has been substituted for "decree." This is not a substantive change. See Section 100 ("judgment" includes decree, as appropriate).

Subdivision (b) continues without substantive change the fifth paragraph of subdivision (a) and the second paragraph of subdivision (b) of former Code of Civil Procedure Section 412.21.

Subdivision (c) continues without substantive change the second and third sentences of the sixth paragraph of subdivision (a) and the second and third sentences of the third paragraph of subdivision (b) of former Code of Civil Procedure Section 412.21. [23 Cal.L.Rev. Comm. Reports 1 (1993)].

Commentary

When a spouse violated a Section 2040 (a)(2) automatic restraining order by selling community securities without a court order or the other spouse's consent, the trial court, under subsections (a) and (g) of Section 1101, properly awarded the wronged spouse one-half of the lost profits, that is, the appreciation of the securities between the date of sale and the subsequent divorce. *In re Marriage of McTiernan & Dubrow, 133 Cal.App.4th 1090, 35 Cal.Rptr.3d 287 (2005), review denied.*

Research References

Forms

California Practice Guide: Rutter Family Law Forms Form 1:32, Glossary Of Common Family Law Terms, Phrases and Concepts (Enclosure to Form 1:31).

West's California Judicial Council Forms FL-110, Summons (Family Law).

West's California Judicial Council Forms FL-210, Summons (Percentage - Custody and Support).

Treatises and Practice Aids

Witkin, California Summary 10th Husband and Wife § 6, Order in Summons.

Witkin, California Summary 10th Husband and Wife § 7, Other Ex Parte Orders.

§ 234. Ex parte orders; admissibility as evidence

The automatic granting of the ex parte temporary restraining order under this part is not a court determination or competent evidence in any proceeding of any prior history of the conduct so proscribed occurring between the parties. *(Stats.1992, c. 162 (A.B.2650), § 10, operative Jan. 1, 1994.)*

Law Revision Commission Comments

Enactment [Revised Comment]

Section 234 continues without substantive change the last paragraphs of subdivisions (a) and (b) of former Code of Civil Procedure Section 412.21. The phrase "ex parte temporary restraining order under this part" has been substituted for the former references to "these ex parte orders." This is not a substantive change, since "these ex parte orders" referred to temporary restraining orders in summons and these orders are the subject of this part. [23 Cal.L.Rev.Comm. Reports 1 (1993)].

Research References

Treatises and Practice Aids

Witkin, California Summary 10th Husband and Wife § 6, Order in Summons.

§ 235. Modification or revocation of orders

Nothing in this part precludes either party from applying to the court for modification or revocation of the temporary restraining order provided for in this part or for further temporary orders or an expanded temporary ex parte order. *(Stats.1992, c. 162 (A.B.2650), § 10, operative Jan. 1, 1994.)*

Law Revision Commission Comments

Enactment [Revised Comment]

Section 235 continues without substantive change the next to last paragraphs of subdivisions (a) and (b) of former Code of Civil Procedure Section 412.21. The phrase "this part" has been substituted for the former reference to "this subdivision" and "temporary restraining order provided for in this part" has been substituted for the former reference to "the order." These are not substantive changes, since the former phrases referred to temporary restraining orders in summons and these orders are the subject of this part. [23 Cal.L.Rev.Comm. Reports 1 (1993)].

Research References

Treatises and Practice Aids

Witkin, California Summary 10th Husband and Wife § 6, Order in Summons.

Part 4

EX PARTE TEMPORARY RESTRAINING ORDERS

§ 240. Application of part

This part applies where a temporary restraining order, including a protective order as defined in Section 6218, is issued under any of the following provisions:

(a) Article 2 (commencing with Section 2045) of Chapter 4 of Part 1 of Division 6 (dissolution of marriage, nullity of marriage, or legal separation of the parties).

(b) Article 3 (commencing with Section 4620) of Chapter 3 of Part 5 of Division 9 (deposit of assets to secure future child support payments).

(c) Article 1 (commencing with Section 6320) of Chapter 2 of Part 4 of Division 10 (Domestic Violence Prevention Act), other than an order under Section 6322.5.

(d) Article 2 (commencing with Section 7710) of Chapter 6 of Part 3 of Division 12 (Uniform Parentage Act). *(Added by Stats.1993, c. 219 (A.B.1500), § 85.1. Amended by Stats.1998, c. 511 (A.B.1900), § 1.)*

Law Revision Commission Comments

Enactment [Revised Comment]

Section 240 continues without substantive change the fourth sentence of former Code of Civil Procedure Section 545 and parts of former Civil Code Sections 4359(a), 4701.1(d), and 7020. The former sections required that ex parte restraining orders be obtained in the manner provided in Code of Civil Procedure Section 527. The provisions of Part 4 (commencing with Section 240) of Division 2 of the Family Code are drawn from and supersede the provisions of Code of Civil Procedure Section 527, insofar as that section formerly applied to these ex parte restraining orders. See also Section 210 (general rules of practice and procedure); Code Civ. Proc. §§ 527(b) (section not applicable to this part), 529 (exemption from undertaking requirement). [23 Cal.L.Rev.Comm. Reports 1 (1993)].

Research References

Forms

California Practice Guide: Rutter Family Law Forms Form 1:32, Glossary Of Common Family Law Terms, Phrases and Concepts (Enclosure to Form 1:31).

West's California Code Forms, Family § 2045, Comment Overview-- Ex Parte Protective Orders.

Treatises and Practice Aids

Witkin, California Summary 10th Husband and Wife § 7, Other Ex Parte Orders.

Witkin, California Summary 10th Husband and Wife § 89, Other Orders.

Witkin, California Summary 10th Husband and Wife § 382, in General.

Witkin, California Summary 10th Parent and Child § 51, Protective Orders.

Witkin, California Summary 10th Parent and Child § 434, Ex Parte Restraining Order.

§ 241. Notice requirement; exception

Except as provided in Section 6300, an order described in Section 240 may not be granted without notice to the respondent unless it appears from facts shown by the declaration in support of the petition for the order, or in the petition for the order, that great or irreparable injury would result to the petitioner before the matter can be heard on notice. *(Stats.1992, c. 162 (A.B.2650), § 10, operative Jan. 1, 1994. Amended by Stats.1993, c. 219 (A.B.1500), § 85.2; Stats.2010, c. 572 (A.B.1596), § 6, operative Jan. 1, 2012.)*

Law Revision Commission Comments

Enactment [Revised Comment]

Section 241 is a new provision drawn from a part of the first sentence of the last paragraph of Code of Civil Procedure Section 527(a). The introductory clause has been added to Section 241 to recognize that Section 6300 provides for the issuance of an order under Division 10 (prevention of domestic violence) on an affidavit showing reasonable proof of a past act of abuse. The reference to a "verified" application has been omitted as surplus. See Section 212 (pleadings to be verified). [23 Cal.L.Rev.Comm. Reports 1 (1993)].

Research References

Treatises and Practice Aids

Witkin, California Summary 10th Husband and Wife § 7, Other Ex Parte Orders.

§ 242. Deadline for hearing on the petition

(a) Within 21 days, or, if good cause appears to the court, 25 days from the date that a temporary restraining order is granted or denied, a hearing shall be held on the petition. If no request for a temporary restraining order is made, the hearing shall be held within 21 days, or, if good cause appears to the court, 25 days from the date that the petition is filed.

(b) If a hearing is not held within the time provided in subdivision (a), the court may nonetheless hear the matter, but the temporary restraining order shall no longer be enforceable unless it is extended under Section 245. *(Added by Stats.1993, c. 219 (A.B.1500), § 85.4. Amended by Stats. 2010, c. 572 (A.B.1596), § 7, operative Jan. 1, 2012; Stats. 2015, c. 411 (A.B.1081), § 4, eff. Jan. 1, 2016.)*

Law Revision Commission Comments

Enactment [Revised Comment]

Subdivision (a) of Section 242 continues without substantive change the third sentence of the last paragraph of former Code of Civil Procedure Section 527(a), the second sentence of former Code of Civil Procedure Section 546(a), and the second sentence of former Civil Code Section 7020(a).

Subdivision (b) is new. Under subdivision (b), if a hearing is not held within the time provided in subdivision (a), the court may hear the order to show cause as though it were a notice of motion, and may hear the application for a long term order. This changes the result in McDonald v. Superior Court, 18 Cal.App.2d 652, 64 P.2d 738 (1937). A temporary restraining order issued without notice that is not heard within the time prescribed by subdivision (a) and not reissued is unenforceable. This is consistent with Agricultural Prorate Commission v. Superior Court, 30 Cal.App.2d 154, 85 P.2d 898 (1938). [23 Cal.L.Rev.Comm. Reports 1 (1993)].

Research References

Forms

West's California Judicial Council Forms DV-109, Notice Of Court Hearing.

Treatises and Practice Aids

Witkin, California Summary 10th Husband and Wife § 7, Other Ex Parte Orders.

§ 243. Service and response

(a) If a petition under this part has been filed, the respondent shall be personally served with a copy of the petition, the temporary restraining order, if any, and the notice of hearing on the petition. Service shall be made at least five days before the hearing.

(b) On motion of the petitioner or on its own motion, the court may shorten the time for service on the respondent.

(c) If service on the respondent is made, the respondent may file a response that explains or denies the allegations in the petition. *(Stats.1992, c. 162 (A.B.2650), § 10, operative Jan. 1, 1994. Amended by Stats.1993, c. 219 (A.B.1500), § 85.5; Stats.1999, c. 980 (A.B.1671), § 3; Stats.2000, c. 135 (A.B.2539), § 56; Stats.2000, c. 90 (A.B.2914), § 1, eff. July 5, 2000; Stats.2010, c. 572 (A.B.1596), § 8, operative Jan. 1, 2012; Stats.2015, c. 411 (A.B.1081), § 5, eff. Jan. 1, 2016.)*

Law Revision Commission Comments

Enactment [Revised Comment]

Section 243 is a new provision. Subdivisions (a)-(d) and (f) are drawn from the fourth, fifth, and sixth sentences of the last paragraph of Code of Civil Procedure Section 527(a). Section 243 is amended to require that the order to show cause be served within two days of the hearing, and to further broaden the service requirements to include "any other supporting papers filed with the court." This would include an income and expense declaration, if filed.

Subdivision (e) continues without substantive change and generalizes the third sentences of former Code of Civil Procedure Section 546(a) and former Civil Code Section 7020(a). The reference to "applicant" has been substituted for the former reference to "plaintiff." This is not a substantive change.

If an order to show cause is issued without an accompanying ex parte temporary restraining order, the provisions of this part are not applicable. See Section 240 (application of provisions of this part). The order to show cause is subject to the time requirements of a noticed motion. See Section 210 (general rules of practice and procedure); Code Civ. Proc. §§ 1003, 1005(b). [23 Cal.L.Rev. Comm. Reports 1 (1993)].

Research References

Forms

West's California Judicial Council Forms DV-115, Request to Continue Court Hearing and Reissue Temporary Restraining Order.

West's California Judicial Council Forms DV-200, Proof Of Personal Service.

Treatises and Practice Aids

Witkin, California Summary 10th Husband and Wife § 7, Other Ex Parte Orders.

§ 244. Precedence of hearing and trial

(a) On the day of the hearing, the hearing on the petition shall take precedence over all other matters on the calendar that day, except older matters of the same character, and matters to which special precedence may be given by law.

(b) The hearing on the petition shall be set for trial at the earliest possible date and shall take precedence over all other matters, except older matters of the same character, and matters to which special precedence may be given by law. *(Stats.1992, c. 162 (A.B.2650), § 10, operative Jan. 1, 1994. Amended by Stats.2010, c. 572 (A.B.1596), § 9, operative Jan. 1, 2012.)*

Law Revision Commission Comments

Enactment [Revised Comment]

Section 244 is a new provision drawn from the last two sentences of the last paragraph of Code of Civil Procedure Section 527(a). See also Section 240 (application of provisions of this part). [23 Cal.L.Rev.Comm. Reports 1 (1993)].

Research References

Treatises and Practice Aids

Witkin, California Summary 10th Husband and Wife § 7, Other Ex Parte Orders.

§ 245. Continuance

(a) The respondent shall be entitled, as a matter of course, to one continuance for a reasonable period, to respond to the petition.

(b) Either party may request a continuance of the hearing, which the court shall grant on a showing of good cause. The request may be made in writing before or at the hearing or orally at the hearing. The court may also grant a continuance on its own motion.

(c) If the court grants a continuance, any temporary restraining order that has been issued shall remain in effect until the end of the continued hearing, unless otherwise ordered by the court. In granting a continuance, the court may modify or terminate a temporary restraining order.

(d) If the court grants a continuance, the extended temporary restraining order shall state on its face the new date of expiration of the order.

(e) A fee shall not be charged for the extension of the temporary restraining order. *(Stats.1992, c. 162 (A.B.2650), § 10, operative Jan. 1, 1994. Amended by Stats.2010, c. 572 (A.B.1596), § 10, operative Jan. 1, 2012; Stats.2015, c. 411 (A.B.1081), § 6, eff. Jan. 1, 2016.)*

Law Revision Commission Comments

Enactment [Revised Comment]

Section 245 continues former Code of Civil Procedure Section 527(b) without substantive change and expands the scope of the former provision to apply to all orders listed in Section 240. Former Code of Civil Procedure Section 527(b) applied only to a temporary restraining order issued pursuant to former Code of Civil Procedure Section 546, now Article 1 (commencing with Section 6320) of Part 4 of Division 10 (ex parte protective and restraining orders issued under Domestic Violence Prevention Act). [23 Cal.L.Rev.Comm. Reports 1 (1993)].

Research References

Forms

West's California Judicial Council Forms DV-116, Notice Of New Hearing and Order on Reissuance.
West's California Judicial Council Forms DV-200, Proof Of Personal Service.

Treatises and Practice Aids

Witkin, California Summary 10th Husband and Wife § 7, Other Ex Parte Orders.

§ 246. Grant or denial on date petition submitted

A request for a temporary restraining order described in Section 240, issued without notice, shall be granted or denied on the same day that the petition is submitted to the court, unless the petition is filed too late in the day to permit effective review, in which case the order shall be granted or denied on the next day of judicial business in sufficient time for the order to be filed that day with the clerk of the court. *(Added by Stats.1993, c. 148 (A.B.1331), § 1. Amended by Stats.2010, c. 572 (A.B.1596), § 11, operative Jan. 1, 2012.)*

Research References

Treatises and Practice Aids

Witkin, California Summary 10th Husband and Wife § 7, Other Ex Parte Orders.

Part 5

ATTORNEY'S FEES AND COSTS

Section

§ 270. Order for attorney's fees and costs; ability to pay

If a court orders a party to pay attorney's fees or costs under this code, the court shall first determine that the party has or is reasonably likely to have the ability to pay. *(Added by Stats.1993, c. 219 (A.B.1500), § 87.)*

Law Revision Commission Comments

Enactment [Revised Comment]

Section 270 is new and generalizes provisions in former Civil Code Sections 224.10(d), 4370(a), and 4700(b). See also former Civ. Code §§ 237.5(c) (party "unable to afford counsel"), 237.7 (appellant "unable to afford counsel"), 4606(g) (party "financially unable to pay"), 4763(a) ("extreme hardship"). Section 270 is consistent with existing practice. See 1 S. Adams & N. Sevitch, California Family Law Practice § A.18 *et seq.* (8th ed. rev. Feb. 1991); 2 C. Markey, California Family Law Practice and Procedure § 25.12[1]. See also Rosenthal v. Rosenthal, 197 Cal.App.2d 289, 297–98, 17 Cal.Rptr. 186 (1961) (order to pay attorney's fees not precluded even though party's expenses exceed income); Section 271 (sanction may not put "unreasonable financial burden" on sanctioned party). [23 Cal. L.Rev.Comm. Reports 1 (1993)].

Research References

Forms

West's California Code Forms, Family § 270, Comment Overview--Attorney's Fees.
West's California Judicial Council Forms FL-157, Spousal or Partner Support Declaration Attachment.
West's California Judicial Council Forms FL-158, Supporting Declaration for Attorney's Fees and Costs Attachment.
West's California Judicial Council Forms FL-319, Request for Attorney's Fees and Costs Attachment.
West's California Judicial Council Forms FL-346, Attorney's Fees and Costs Order Attachment.

Treatises and Practice Aids

Witkin, California Summary 10th Husband and Wife § 8, in General.

§ 271. Alternative basis for award; encouragement of cooperation; award as sanction; notice; property or income of sanctioned party

(a) Notwithstanding any other provision of this code, the court may base an award of attorney's fees and costs on the extent to which the conduct of each party or attorney furthers or frustrates the policy of the law to promote settlement of litigation and, where possible, to reduce the cost of litigation by encouraging cooperation between the parties and attorneys. An award of attorney's fees and costs pursuant to this section is in the nature of a sanction. In making an award pursuant to this section, the court shall take into consideration all evidence concerning the parties' incomes, assets, and liabilities. The court shall not impose a sanction pursuant to this section that imposes an unreasonable financial burden on the party against whom the sanction is imposed. In order to obtain an award under this section, the party requesting an award of attorney's fees and costs is not required to demonstrate any financial need for the award.

(b) An award of attorney's fees and costs as a sanction pursuant to this section shall be imposed only after notice to the party against whom the sanction is proposed to be imposed and opportunity for that party to be heard.

(c) An award of attorney's fees and costs as a sanction pursuant to this section is payable only from the property or income of the party against whom the sanction is imposed, except that the award may be against the sanctioned party's share of the community property. *(Added by Stats.1993, c. 219 (A.B.1500), § 87.)*

Law Revision Commission Comments

Enactment [Revised Comment]

Section 271 continues former Civil Code Section 4370.6 without substantive change, except that Section 271 is broadened to apply to all proceedings under the Family Code. See also Section 65 ("community property" defined in Section 760 *et seq.*). [23 Cal. L.Rev.Comm. Reports 1 (1993)].

Commentary

Webb v. Webb, 12 Cal.App.5th 876, 219 Cal.Rptr.3d 785 (2017), held that this section does not authorize an award of sanctions to a nonparty, reasoning that the purpose of the section is to promote settlement by means of fee shifting between the parties.

In re Marriage of Duris and Urbany, 193 Cal.App.4th 510, 123 Cal.Rptr.3d 150 (2011), held that a trial court erred in awarding sanctions under this section without giving the party advance notice that sanctions were at issue and failing to hold a hearing to allow the party to contest the imposition and amount of sanctions.

In re Marriage of Tharp, 188 Cal.App.4th 1295, 116 Cal.Rptr.3d 375 (2010), review denied, held that a family court abused its discretion, under this section and section 2107(c), in denying a divorcing wife's request for sanctions when her husband frustrated and blocked discovery and falsely asserted the existence of a premarital agreement.

In re Marriage of Greenberg, 194 Cal.App.4th 1095, 125 Cal.Rptr.3d 238 (2011), held that an attorney husband's appeal that was premised on facts expressly not credited by the trial court, was a frivolous sanctionable appeal. However, *Greenberg* did not issue an order to show cause for sanctions payable to the court of appeal because the wife did not request sanctions on appeal.

Parker v. Harbert, 212 Cal.App.4th 1172, 151 Cal.Rptr.3d 642 (2013), affirmed a trial court order requiring a father to pay attorney's fees and costs as sanctions under this section, because he brought contempt proceedings against the mother for trivial violations of custody orders. Even though the trial court denied the mother's pretrial motion for acquittal, the contempt proceedings delayed resolution of the custody issues and frustrated the public policy of promoting settlement. *Parker* reasons that conduct need not be frivolous to be sanctioned under this section.

A court ordering attorney's fees under section 6344(a) is not ordering attorney's fees in the nature of a sanction under this section, but is simply awarding attorney's fees and costs to the prevailing party. *Loeffler v. Medina, 174 Cal.App.4th 1495, 95 Cal.Rptr.3d 343 (2009)*.

See *In re Marriage of Schnabel, 30 Cal.App.4th 747, 36 Cal.Rptr.2d 682, review denied 2/23/95* (*Schnabel IV*) (sanctions for frivolous appeal imposed against husband and his attorney); *In re Marriage of Daniels, 19 Cal.App.4th 1102, 23 Cal.Rptr.2d 865 (1993)* (wife ordered to pay attorney's fees incurred by husband because of her attorney's misconduct); *In re Marriage of Quay, 18 Cal.App.4th 961, 22 Cal.Rptr.2d 537 (1993), review denied 12/2/93* (husband properly required to pay a portion of his ex-wife's attorney fees where his uncooperative conduct increased the cost of litigation and necessitated the appointment of an expert and a trustee to manage community funds) and *In re Marriage of Falcone & Fyke, 164 Cal.App.4th 814, 79 Cal.Rptr.3d 588 (2008)* (holding that a trial court, under this section and Family Code section 271, properly imposed $64,500 in sanctions against a self-represented ex-spouse, because she prosecuted a motion for contempt without any factual or legal basis and pursued a meritless motion for a new trial). *Burkle v. Burkle, 144 Cal.App.4th 387, 50 Cal.Rptr.3d 436 (2006), review denied Feb. 21, 2007*, affirmed a trial court dismissal of a wife's civil action for intentional infliction of emotional distress arising from her husband's failure to comply with an interim support order in a pending dissolution proceeding, on the ground that bringing a separate action pertaining to a pending dissolution proceeding violates well-established California precedent prohibiting such separate actions, and concluded that the wife's contentions about the proper forum for her civil action were frivolous; therefore the trial court properly ordered, as sanctions, that the wife make substantial payments to her husband under this section and that the wife and her attorneys make substantial payments to the husband under Code of Civil Procedure section 128.7. Compare *In re Marriage of Benjamins, 26 Cal.App.4th 423, 31 Cal. Rptr.2d 313, 319 (1994)* (disapproving imposition of sanctions on former husband when his motion was neither frivolous nor without merit). See also *Bidna v. Rosen, 19 Cal.App.4th 27, 23 Cal.Rptr.2d 251 (1993), review denied 12/30/93* (barring malicious prosecution claims based on family law motions, finding Section 271 an effective substitute); *Green v. Uccelli, 207 Cal.App.3d 1112, 1116, 255 Cal.Rptr. 315 (1989)* (relief from bad faith or harassing litigation appropriately sought in Section 271 award, not through independent tort action). With *Green v. Uccelli*, contrast *Dale v. Dale, 66 Cal.App.4th 1172, 78 Cal.Rptr.2d 513 (1998), review denied January 13, 1999* (absent a pending dissolution proceeding, a divorced spouse may bring a common law tort action against a former spouse for injury resulting from the latter's concealment of community assets at dissolution) and *In the Matter of Varakin, 3 Cal. State Bar Ct. Rptr. 179 (1994)* (disbarment recommended for attorney who repeatedly filed frivolous motions and appeals in proceedings related to his own dissolution). *Bidna* and *Green, supra,* are not followed in *Nicholson v. Fazeli, 113 Cal.App.4th 1091, 6 Cal.Rptr.3d 881 (2003), review denied*, which holds that a cross-complaint originating in a dissolution action may form the basis for an independent malicious prosecution action and a former spouse's malicious prosecution action is not precluded by an award to that spouse of attorney fees, costs, and sanctions in the dissolution action.

In re Marriage of Feldman, 153 Cal.App.4th 1470, 64 Cal.Rptr.3d 29 (2007), held that a trial did not abuse its discretion in ordering a husband, under subsection (a) of this section and section 2107(c), to pay his wife $250,000 in sanctions and $140,000 in attorney's fees, because the husband failed to disclose the existence of privately held companies and failed to disclose financial information about many assets, in violation of Family Code sections 1100(e), 2100(c), 2102(a), 2103, and 2104(c). *Feldman* additionally held that imposition of sanctions did not require a showing of harm to the wife and she was not required to seek statutory procedural remedies before imposition of sanctions.

In re Marriage of Falcone & Fyke, 203 Cal.App.4th 964, 138 Cal.Rptr.3d 44 (2012), review denied, affirmed, under this section, a trial court order awarding attorney fees, costs, and sanctions against a wife for taking a meritless appeal from a sanctions order and for misconduct in trying to obtain a trial continuance. *Falcone & Fyke* also found that the wife, who had previously filed at least 11 nonmeritorious appeals, was a vexatious litigant within the meaning of Code of Civil Procedure § 391.7.

See also *In re Marriage of Christy, 26 Cal.App.4th 256 (1994), rehearing granted 7/11/94* (imposing Code of Civil Procedure Section 907 sanctions on the sister of the children's mother because the sister brought frivolous support and custody actions against the father on behalf of herself and the children's mother); and *Simonian v. Patterson, 27 Cal.App.4th 773, 32 Cal.Rptr.2d 722 (1994)* (attorney-plaintiff and plaintiff's attorney sanctioned $50,000 for frivolous appeal from dismissal of plaintiff's action against father of plaintiff's former fiancee).

Application for post-judgment attorney's fees under this section must be filed within the 40–day time limit set out by Cal. Rules of Court 870.2(c) and 26(d). *In re Marriage of Freeman, 132 Cal.App.4th 1, 33 Cal.Rptr.3d 237 (2005), review denied.*

Research References

Forms

California Practice Guide: Rutter Family Law Forms Form 14:4, Request for Order Re Attorney Fees and Costs as Sanctions (Family Code S271).

West's California Code Forms, Family § 270, Comment Overview--Attorney's Fees.

Treatises and Practice Aids

Witkin, California Summary 10th Husband and Wife § 8, in General.
Witkin, California Summary 10th Husband and Wife § 10, Imposition Of Award as Sanction.
Witkin, California Summary 10th Husband and Wife § 175, Development Of Law.
Witkin, California Summary 10th Husband and Wife § 180, in General.
Witkin, California Summary 10th Parent and Child § 283, Sexual Abuse Allegation.
Witkin, California Summary 10th Torts § 496, Family Law Proceedings.

§ 272. Method of payment; enforcement of order for costs and fees

(a) Where the court orders one of the parties to pay attorney's fees and costs for the benefit of the other party, the fees and costs may, in the discretion of the court, be made payable in whole or in part to the attorney entitled thereto.

(b) Subject to subdivision (c), the order providing for payment of the attorney's fees and costs may be enforced directly by the attorney in the attorney's own name or by the party in whose behalf the order was made.

(c) If the attorney has ceased to be the attorney for the party in whose behalf the order was made, the attorney may enforce the order only if it appears of record that the attorney has given to the former client or successor counsel 10 days' written notice of the application for enforcement of the order. During the 10-day period, the client may file in the proceeding a motion directed to the former attorney for partial or total reallocation of fees and costs to cover the services and cost of successor counsel. On the filing of the motion, the enforcement of the order by the former attorney shall be stayed until the court has resolved the motion. *(Added by Stats.1993, c. 219 (A.B.1500), § 87.)*

Law Revision Commission Comments

Enactment [Revised Comment]

Section 272 restates former Civil Code Section 4371 without substantive change. [23 Cal.L.Rev.Comm. Reports 1 (1993)].

Commentary

For discussion of the court's jurisdiction to order a spouse to pay attorney's fees to a discharged attorney of the other spouse, see Commentary to Section 2030.

Entry of a judgment ordering, under this section, a deceased spouse's trustee to pay attorney fees to the other spouse's former attorneys gave the attorneys an independent right to enforce the judgment under this section, and the former attorneys were entitled to postjudgment interest after the wife barred payment, which she had no right to do under this section, and the trustee consequently failed to satisfy the judgment for seven months. *In re Marriage of Green, 143 Cal.App.4th 1312, 49 Cal.Rptr.3d 908 (2006).*

Research References

Forms

West's California Code Forms, Family § 270, Comment Overview--Attorney's Fees.
West's California Code Forms, Family § 272 Form 1, Notice Of Enforcement Of Attorney's Fees Award.
West's California Code Forms, Family § 272 Form 2, Declaration in Support Of Motion for Reallocation Of Attorney's Fees.

Treatises and Practice Aids

Witkin, California Summary 10th Husband and Wife § 9, Payment Directly to Attorney.
Witkin, California Summary 10th Husband and Wife § 193, in General.
Witkin, California Summary 10th Husband and Wife § 204, in General.

§ 273. Attorney's fees awarded against governmental agencies

Notwithstanding any other provision of this code, the court shall not award attorney's fees against any governmental agency involved in a family law matter or child support proceeding except when sanctions are appropriate pursuant to Section 128.5 of the Code of Civil Procedure or Section 271 of this code. *(Added by Stats.1994, c. 1269 (A.B.2208), § 10.)*

Research References

Treatises and Practice Aids

Witkin, California Summary 10th Husband and Wife § 8, in General.

§ 274. Attempted murder of a spouse; attorney's fees and costs; notice and hearing; source of funds

(a) Notwithstanding any other provision of law, if the injured spouse is entitled to a remedy authorized pursuant to Section 4324, the injured spouse shall be entitled to an award of reasonable attorney's fees and costs as a sanction pursuant to this section.

(b) An award of attorney's fees and costs as a sanction pursuant to this section shall be imposed only after notice to the party against whom the sanction is proposed to be imposed and opportunity for that party to be heard.

(c) An award of attorney's fees and costs as a sanction pursuant to this section is payable only from the property or income of the party against whom the sanction is imposed, except that the award may be against the sanctioned party's share of the community property. In order to obtain an award under this section, the party requesting an award of attorney's fees and costs is not required to demonstrate any financial need for the award. *(Added by Stats.1995, c. 364 (A.B.16), § 1. Amended by Stats.2006, c. 538 (S.B.1852), § 156.)*

Research References

Treatises and Practice Aids

Witkin, California Summary 10th Community Property § 187, Attempted Murder Of Spouse.
Witkin, California Summary 10th Husband and Wife § 10, Imposition Of Award as Sanction.
Witkin, California Summary 10th Husband and Wife § 174, in General.

Part 6

ENFORCEMENT OF JUDGMENTS AND ORDERS

§ 290. Methods of enforcement

A judgment or order made or entered pursuant to this code may be enforced by the court by execution, the appointment of a receiver, or contempt, or by any other order as the court in its discretion determines from time to time to be necessary. *(Stats.1992, c. 162 (A.B.2650), § 10, operative Jan. 1, 1994. Amended by Stats.2000, c. 808 (A.B.1358), § 23, eff. Sept. 28, 2000; Stats.2006, c. 86 (A.B.2126), § 2.)*

Law Revision Commission Comments

Enactment [Revised Comment]

Section 290 continues former Civil Code Section 4380 without substantive change and expands the scope of the former provision to apply to the entire Family Code. The former provision applied only to a judgment or order made or entered "pursuant to this part," meaning the former Family Law Act (former Part 5 (commencing with former Section 4000) of Division 4 of the Civil Code). The phrase "or decree of the court" has been omitted as surplus. See Section 100 ("judgment" and "order" include decree, as appropriate). "Order" has been substituted for "order or orders." See Section 10 (singular includes plural).

The authority granted by Section 290 is subject to the general provisions governing enforcement of judgments and orders and to any special provisions applicable to enforcement of a judgment or order made or entered pursuant to this code. For provisions governing enforcement of support orders, see Part 5 (commencing with former Section 4500) of Division 9. For provisions permitting enforcement by writ of execution without prior court approval, see Sections 5100–5101. See also Code Civ. Proc. §§ 683.130 (renewal of judgment), 1209–1222 (contempt of court).

For background on former Civ. Code § 4380, see *Recommendation Relating to Prejudgment Attachment,* 11 Cal. L. Revision Comm'n Reports 701, 747 (1973). [23 Cal.L.Rev.Comm. Reports 1 (1993)].

2000 Amendment

Section 290 provides the general rule on enforcement of judgments under the Family Code. The introductory clause is added to recognize the exception in Section 291, which makes the general rules concerning the period of enforceability and renewal of judgments in the Enforcement of Judgments Law applicable to judgments for the possession or sale of property under the Family Code. Thus, for example, a judgment for sale would be unenforceable if it is not renewed within the 10–year period of Code of Civil Procedure Section 683.020. However, an action on the judgment may still be possible subject to the statute of limitations in Code of Civil Procedure Section 337.5. See Code Civ. Proc. §683.020 & Comment. This amendment does not affect the rules concerning enforcement of child, family, or spousal support. See, e.g., Sections 4502, 5100 *et seq.* [30 Cal.L.Rev.Comm.Reports 717 (2000)].

2006 Amendment

Section 290 is amended to reflect the fact that new Section 291 does not limit the enforcement of a judgment or order made or entered pursuant to this code. [35 Cal.L.Rev.Comm. Reports 176 (2005)].

Commentary

In re Marriage of Fithian, 74 Cal.App.3d 397, 403–406, 141 Cal.Rptr. 506 (1977), holds that failure to deliver a specific item of property pursuant to a court-ordered property division may be punished by contempt. *Fithian* provides excellent discussion of the use of the contempt remedy to enforce *property division obligations* and the limits of the constitutional prohibition of imprisonment for debt. *Fithian* draws a distinction between an obligation to deliver a specific item of property, which may be enforced by contempt, and an obligation to pay, as property division, a designated sum from private resources, which may not.

Cases approving the appointment of a receiver to enforce a child support judgment include *Alderson v. Alderson, 180 Cal.App.3d 450, 225 Cal.Rptr. 610 (1986), review denied 7/16/86*, and *Quaglino v. Quaglino, 88 Cal.App.3d 542, 152 Cal.Rptr. 47 (1979)*.

Crider v. Superior Court, 15 Cal.App.4th 227, 231, 18 Cal.Rptr.2d 757 (1993), review denied 8/26/93, holds that an order to reimburse the county for AFDC benefits provided to the parent-obligor's children is not a Family Law Act (Family Code) proceeding and thus may not be enforced by contempt. However, *Monterey County v. Banuelos, 82 Cal.App.4th 1299, 98 Cal.Rptr.2d 710 (2000)*, holds that post–1993 amendments to the child and family support statutes superseded the holding of *Crider* by enlarging the definition of "child support" to include amounts owed to individuals or a county for current support or arrearages. Thus, a court may use the contempt remedy and issue a seek-work order when a county attempts to recover child support arrearages or reimbursement for public assistance. *People v. Lindemann, 8 Cal.App.4th Supp. 7, 11 Cal.Rptr.2d 886 (1992)*, holds that a *criminal* complaint alleging contempt of a family law court order is not a Family Law Act (Family Code) proceeding giving the superior court jurisdiction under Sections 200 and 2010; instead the municipal court has exclusive jurisdiction. *In re Marriage of Lackey, 143 Cal.App.3d 698, 191 Cal.Rptr. 309 (1983)*, holds that small claims court has no subject matter jurisdiction to determine and liquidate child support arrearages.

Research References

Forms

West's California Code Forms, Family § 270, Comment Overview--Attorney's Fees.

West's California Code Forms, Family § 290, Comment Overview--Enforcement Of Judgments and Orders.

Treatises and Practice Aids

Witkin, California Summary 10th Community Property § 232, in General.

Witkin, California Summary 10th Husband and Wife § 5, Generally Applicable Procedures.

Witkin, California Summary 10th Husband and Wife § 78, Joinder Of Third Persons.

Witkin, California Summary 10th Husband and Wife § 204, in General.

Witkin, California Summary 10th Husband and Wife § 205, Contempt.

Witkin, California Summary 10th Husband and Wife § 206, Other Remedies.

Witkin, California Summary 10th Husband and Wife § 248, in General.

Witkin, California Summary 10th Husband and Wife § 258, Nature Of Remedy.

Witkin, California Summary 10th Husband and Wife § 260, Improper Service on Attorney.

Witkin, California Summary 10th Husband and Wife § 262, in General.

Witkin, California Summary 10th Husband and Wife § 266, Appointment Of Receiver.

Witkin, California Summary 10th Husband and Wife § 268, Charging Order Against Interest in Partnership or Limited Liability Company.

Witkin, California Summary 10th Husband and Wife § 360, Execution and Receivership.

Witkin, California Summary 10th Husband and Wife § 362, Integrated Agreement.
Witkin, California Summary 10th Parent and Child § 285, in General.
Witkin, California Summary 10th Parent and Child § 410, Uninsured Health Care Costs.

§ 291. Judgment for possession or sale of property; enforceability; renewal; laches; enforcement after death; self-help materials; definition

(a) A money judgment or judgment for possession or sale of property that is made or entered under this code, including a judgment for child, family, or spousal support, is enforceable until paid in full or otherwise satisfied.

(b) A judgment described in this section is exempt from any requirement that a judgment be renewed. Failure to renew a judgment described in this section has no effect on the enforceability of the judgment.

(c) A judgment described in this section may be renewed pursuant to Article 2 (commencing with Section 683.110) of Chapter 3 of Division 1 of Title 9 of Part 2 of the Code of Civil Procedure. An application for renewal of a judgment described in this section, whether or not payable in installments, may be filed:

(1) If the judgment has not previously been renewed as to past due amounts, at any time.

(2) If the judgment has previously been renewed, the amount of the judgment as previously renewed and any past due amount that became due and payable after the previous renewal may be renewed at any time after a period of at least five years has elapsed from the time the judgment was previously renewed.

(d) In an action to enforce a judgment for child, family, or spousal support, the defendant may raise, and the court may consider, the defense of laches only with respect to any portion of the judgment that is owed to the state.

(e) Nothing in this section supersedes the law governing enforcement of a judgment after the death of the judgment creditor or judgment debtor.

(f) On or before January 1, 2008, the Judicial Council shall develop self-help materials that include: (1) a description of the remedies available for enforcement of a judgment under this code, and (2) practical advice on how to avoid disputes relating to the enforcement of a support obligation. The self-help materials shall be made available to the public through the Judicial Council self-help Internet Web site.

(g) As used in this section, "judgment" includes an order. *(Added by Stats.2006, c. 86 (A.B.2126), § 4. Amended by Stats.2007, c. 130 (A.B.299), § 87.)*

Law Revision Commission Comments

2006 Repeal and Addition

Section 291 is repealed. New Section 291 provides a general rule for enforcement of a judgment under this code. [35 Cal.L.Rev. Comm. Reports 176 (2005)].

Subdivisions (a)-(c) of Section 291 continue the substance of former subdivisions (a)-(b) of Section 4502 and generalize the substance of those provisions so that it applies to any judgment or order for the payment of money or the possession or sale of property that is made or entered under this code.

The reference in former Section 4502(a) to an order for reimbursement under Section 17402 is not continued. This is not a substantive change. Section 291 applies to any judgment or order for payment of money made or entered under this code. This includes an order to pay money under Section 17402.

Subdivision (d) continues former Section 4502(c) without substantive change.

Subdivision (e) is new. It is consistent with a recent appellate decision that stated, in dictum, that Family Code Section 4502 "does not address the procedural requirements for reaching the assets of a judgment debtor after that debtor's death." Embree v. Embree, 125 Cal.App.4th 487, 495, 22 Cal.Rptr.3d 782 (2004).

Subdivision (g) makes clear that the section applies to both judgments and orders. [35 Cal.L.Rev.Comm. Reports 178 (2005)].

Commentary

As amended by Stats.2006, c. 86 (A.B.2126), effective January 1, 2007, this section provides that all money *and property* judgments entered under the Family Code are enforceable until paid in full and need not be renewed. It also incorporates, in subsection (d), the rule, formerly articulated in Section 4502(c), that the defense of laches may only be asserted against the state.

Schelb v. Stein, 190 Cal.App.4th 1440, 119 Cal.Rptr.3d 267 (2010), harmonizes this section with the Marketable Record Title Act (MRTA, Civil Code § 880.020 et seq.), which provides that a deed of trust or other instrument that creates a security interest of record in real property to secure a debt expires 10 years from the final maturity date of the note creating the debt. Although a security interest expires after 10 years under the MRTA, the underlying family law debt remains enforceable.

Subsection (d), enacted as Section 4502(c) by 2002 Cal.Stat., ch. 304, settled a previously unsettled area of caselaw. Compare prior law. *In re Marriage of Plescia, 59 Cal.App.4th 252, 69 Cal.Rptr.2d 120 (1997),* held that even though spousal support is generally enforceable until paid in full, the defense of laches is available in an action for spousal support arrears. In *Plescia*, the court found the obligee's nine-year delay unreasonable and injurious to the obligor, who entertained a reasonable good faith belief that he owed no support obligation and who had retired and was now unable to pay the support judgment. *In re Marriage of Fogarty & Rasbeary, 78 Cal.App.4th 1353, 93 Cal.Rptr.2d 653 (2000)*, applied the reasoning of *Plescia* to past due child support. *In re Marriage of Cutler, 79 Cal.App.4th 460, 94 Cal.Rptr.2d 156 (2000), review denied June 21, 2000*, concluded that enactment of this section eliminated the Family Code § 291 "lack of diligence" defense to enforcement and further observed that the defense of laches requires undue delay by the party seeking enforcement and, for the party asserting laches, clean hands and undue prejudice. *In re Marriage of Copeman, 90 Cal.App.4th 324, 108 Cal.Rptr.2d 801 (2001), review denied September 26, 2001*, held that laches is available as a defense to the payment of child support arrearages even when a child is still a minor.*Copeman* reasoned that the pre-2002 language of this section does not explicitly bar the pre-existing defense of laches and the legislative history of this section indicates that the legislature intended to continue the defense of laches. *Copeman* concluded that the legislative amendment removing the defense of "lack of diligence" in enforcement proceedings should not be understand to eliminate the defense of laches because laches additionally requires undue prejudice to the support obligor. *In re Marriage of Dancy, 82 Cal.App.4th 1142, 98 Cal.Rptr.2d 775 (2000), review denied November 15, 2000*, agreed, in dictum, with *Fogarty* that laches is available as a defense in an action to recover past due child support, spousal support, and family support, but nevertheless sustained the trial court's failure to apply laches because the party resisting enforcement failed to make the necessary showing of unreasonable delay by the claimant and consequential prejudice to the support obligor.

Subsection (d) provides that the defense of laches is available only with respect to any portion of a child, family or spousal support judgment owed to the state. *In re Marriage of Fellows, 39 Cal.4th 179, 46 Cal.Rptr.3d 49, 138 P.3d 200 (2006)*, held that subsection (d) applies retroactively to support due before the subsection's effective date. The California Supreme Court relied on Section 4 of the Family Code, which provides that the Code and future amendments to the Code apply on their operative dates to all matters governed by them. Thus every amendment to the Code applies retroactively unless the amendment or Section 4 specifically provides otherwise, or retroactive application would violate the due process clause by impairing a vested right without a serving an important state interest. Cf. *Marriage of Buol, 39 Cal.3d 751, 705 P.2d 354, 218 Cal.Rptr.31 (1985)*, in which the California Supreme Court disapproved retroactive application of section 2581 when the law changed between the trial court judgment and appeal.

Fellows disapproved *In re Marriage of Garcia, 67 Cal.App.4th 693, 79 Cal.Rptr.2d 242 (1998),* which held that subsection (a), which makes child, family and spousal support orders infinitely enforceable, may not be applied retroactively to an order made before its effective date. *Garcia* held that pre–1993 orders were controlled by former Civil Code Section 4383, which provided that arrears could be collected for 10 years as of right and thereafter at the discretion of the court.

In re Marriage of Sweeney,76 Cal.App.4th 343, 90 Cal.Rptr.2d 298 (1999), held that a claim under this section was barred by the doctrine of res judicata after an unappealed 1979 ruling, decided under prior law, denied the payee's motion for execution of a 1963 support judgment.

Research References

Forms

West's California Code Forms, Family § 5104, Comment Overview--Enforcement by Writ Of Execution.

Treatises and Practice Aids

Witkin, California Summary 10th Husband and Wife § 5, Generally Applicable Procedures.

Witkin, California Summary 10th Husband and Wife § 219, Waiver After Judgment.

Witkin, California Summary 10th Husband and Wife § 220, Laches Defense Limited.

Witkin, California Summary 10th Husband and Wife § 248, in General.

Witkin, California Summary 10th Husband and Wife § 263, Period Of Enforcement.

Witkin, California Summary 10th Husband and Wife § 267, Judgment Lien.

Witkin, California Summary 10th Wills and Probate § 517, Action Against Decedent.

§ 292. Judicial Council; modification and creation of contempt forms; content

(a) The Judicial Council shall modify the title of its existing form, "Order to Show Cause and Declaration for Contempt (Family Law)," to "Order to Show Cause and Affidavit for Contempt (Family Law)."

(b) The Judicial Council shall prescribe a form entitled "Affidavit of Facts Constituting Contempt" that a party seeking to enforce a judgment or order made or entered pursuant to this code by contempt may use as an attachment to the Judicial Council form entitled "Order to Show Cause and Affidavit for Contempt (Family Law)." The form shall provide in the simplest language possible:

(1) The basic information needed to sustain a cause of action for contempt, including, but not limited to, the elements of a cause of action for contempt.

(2) Instructions on how to prepare and submit the Order to Show Cause and Affidavit for Contempt (Family Law) and the Affidavit of Facts Constituting Contempt.

(3) Lines for the date and a signature made under penalty of perjury.

(c) Section 1211.5 of the Code of Civil Procedure shall apply to the Order to Show Cause and Affidavit for Contempt (Family Law) and the Affidavit of Facts Constituting Contempt. *(Added by Stats.1995, c. 904 (A.B.965), § 2.)*

Research References

Forms

West's California Judicial Council Forms FL-410, Order to Show Cause and Affidavit for Contempt.

West's California Judicial Council Forms FL-411, Affidavit Of Facts Constituting Contempt.

West's California Judicial Council Forms FL-412, Affidavit Of Facts Constituting Contempt.

Treatises and Practice Aids

Witkin, California Summary 10th Husband and Wife § 205, Contempt.

Witkin, California Summary 10th Husband and Wife § 259, Procedure.

Part 7

TRIBAL MARRIAGES AND DIVORCES

Section

§ 295. Validity of marriages and divorces

(a) For the purpose of application of the laws of succession set forth in the Probate Code to a decedent, and for the purpose of determining the validity of a marriage under the laws of this state, an alliance entered into before 1958, which, by custom of the Indian tribe, band, or group of which the parties to the alliance, or either of them, are members, is commonly recognized in the tribe, band, or group as marriage, is deemed a valid marriage under the laws of this state.

(b) In the case of these marriages and for the purposes described in subdivision (a), a separation, which, by custom of the Indian tribe, band, or group of which the separating parties, or either of them, are members, is commonly recognized in the tribe, band, or group as a dissolution of marriage, is deemed a valid divorce under the laws of this state. *(Stats.1992, c. 162 (A.B.2650), § 10, operative Jan. 1, 1994.)*

Law Revision Commission Comments

Enactment [Revised Comment]

Section 295 continues former Civil Code Section 5138 without substantive change. [23 Cal.L.Rev.Comm. Reports 1 (1993)].

Research References

Treatises and Practice Aids

Witkin, California Summary 10th Husband and Wife § 50, Illustrations.

Division 2.5

DOMESTIC PARTNER REGISTRATION

Part 1

DEFINITIONS

§ 297. Domestic partners and partnership; establishment

(a) Domestic partners are two adults who have chosen to share one another's lives in an intimate and committed relationship of mutual caring.

(b) A domestic partnership shall be established in California when both persons file a Declaration of Domestic Partnership with the Secretary of State pursuant to this division, and, at the time of filing, all of the following requirements are met:

(1) Neither person is married to someone else or is a member of another domestic partnership with someone else that has not been terminated, dissolved, or adjudged a nullity.

(2) The two persons are not related by blood in a way that would prevent them from being married to each other in this state.

(3) Both persons are at least 18 years of age, except as provided in Section 297.1.

(4) Either of the following:

(A) Both persons are members of the same sex.

(B) One or both of the persons meet the eligibility criteria under Title II of the Social Security Act as defined in Section 402(a) of Title 42 of the United States Code for old-age insurance benefits or Title XVI of the Social Security Act as defined in Section 1381 of Title 42 of the United States Code for aged individuals. Notwithstanding any other provision of this section, persons of opposite sexes may not constitute a domestic partnership unless one or both of the persons are over 62 years of age.

(5) Both persons are capable of consenting to the domestic partnership. *(Added by Stats.1999, c. 588 (A.B.26), § 2. Amended by Stats.2001, c. 893 (A.B.25), § 3; Stats.2003, c. 421 (A.B.205), § 3, operative Jan. 1, 2005; Stats.2011, c. 721 (S.B.651), § 1.)*

Commentary

Holguin v. Flores, 122 Cal.App.4th 428, 18 Cal.Rptr.3d 749 (2004), holds that the state does not violate the equal protection clause when it denies opposite-sex unmarried partners, both of whom are under the age of 62, the wrongful death rights accorded to married persons and, under Section 297.5, to same-sex registered domestic partners who are under the age of 62. *Holguin* reasons that there is a rational basis for extending the status of domestic partnership only to couples who are legally or practically prevented from marrying and, further, that the factor distinguishing claimant from persons eligible for wrongful death benefits is that the latter have publicly registered their relationship and assumed mutual legal obligations as well as legal rights.

Strong v. State Board of Equalization, 155 Cal.App.4th 1182, 66 Cal.Rptr.3d 657 (2007), review denied, sustained legislation exempting real property transfers between registered domestic partners from the increase in property tax assessment that normally accompanies a change of ownership.

Velez v. Smith, 142 Cal.App.4th 1154, 48 Cal.Rptr.3d 642 (2006), review denied Nov. 29, 2006, held that filing a declaration of domestic partnership with the City and County of San Francisco in 1994 did not establish a domestic partnership within the meaning of this section.

A person's objectively reasonable, good faith belief that his California domestic partnership was validly registered entitles him to all the rights and benefits of domestic partnership as a putative domestic partner, even though registration never occurred. *In re Domestic Partnership of Ellis and Arriaga, 162 Cal.App.4th 1000, 76 Cal.Rptr.3d 401 (2008)*. Thus when two men signed and notarized a California declaration of domestic partnership and one of them failed to keep his promise to send the declaration to the California Secretary of State, his partner could claim the status of putative domestic partner.

Research References

Forms

California Practice Guide: Rutter Family Law Forms Form 1:32, Glossary Of Common Family Law Terms, Phrases and Concepts (Enclosure to Form 1:31).

California Transactions Forms--Family Law § 4:4, Application Of Agreements to Same Sex Couples.

West's California Code Forms, Civil Procedure § 377.60 Form 2, Parties--Complaint--Wrongful Death Of Domestic Partner.

West's California Code Forms, Family § 297.5, Comment Overview--Domestic Partnerships.

West's California Code Forms, Probate § 21351 Form 1, Certificate Of Independent Review.

West's California Code Forms, Revenue and Taxation § 7651 Form 1, Supplier Of Motor Vehicle Fuel Tax Return (BOE-501-PS).

West's California Code Forms, Revenue and Taxation § 30182 Form 1, Cigarette Distributor's Tax Return (BOE-501-CD).

West's California Code Forms, Revenue and Taxation § 32251 Form 1, Beer Manufacturer Tax Return (BOE-501-BM).

West's California Code Forms, Revenue and Taxation § 38402 Form 2, Timber Tax Return (BOE-401-1PT).

West's California Code Forms, Revenue and Taxation § 40063 Form 1, Consumer's Electrical Energy Surcharge Return (BOE-501-EC).

West's California Code Forms, Revenue and Taxation § 41052 Form 1, Emergency Telephone Users Surcharge Return (BOE-501-TE).

West's California Code Forms, Revenue and Taxation § 45051 Form 1, Integrated Waste Management Fee Return (BOE-501-SQ).
West's California Code Forms, Revenue and Taxation § 60115 Form 1, Interstate User Diesel Fuel Tax Return (BOE-501-DI).
West's California Code Forms, Revenue and Taxation § 43152.16 Form 1, Hazardous Waste Facility Fee Return--Annual (BOE-501-HF).
West's California Judicial Council Forms FL-100, Petition - Marriage/Domestic Partnership.
West's California Judicial Council Forms FL-910, Request Of Minor to Marry or Establish a Domestic Partnership.
West's California Judicial Council Forms FL-915, Order on Request Of Minor to Marry or Establish a Domestic Partnership.

Treatises and Practice Aids

Witkin, California Summary 10th Agency and Employment § 404, Duties Of Employers.
Witkin, California Summary 10th Agency and Employment § 502, Leaving to Join Spouse or Domestic Partner.
Witkin, California Summary 10th Community Property § 281, in General.
Witkin, California Summary 10th Community Property § 282, Legal Effect Of Status.
Witkin, California Summary 10th Constitutional Law § 908A, (New) Marital Status Discrimination.
Witkin, California Summary 10th Husband and Wife § 3, Statutory Framework.
Witkin, California Summary 10th Husband and Wife § 25, in General.
Witkin, California Summary 10th Husband and Wife § 27, Establishment Of Domestic Partnership.
Witkin, California Summary 10th Husband and Wife § 28, Registration Procedure.
Witkin, California Summary 10th Husband and Wife § 29, Preemption Of Local Laws.
Witkin, California Summary 10th Husband and Wife § 31, Patient Visitation.
Witkin, California Summary 10th Husband and Wife § 32, Health Care Benefits.
Witkin, California Summary 10th Parent and Child § 141, in General.
Witkin, California Summary 10th Parent and Child § 60A, (New) Lesbian Partner Who is Not Biological Mother Of Child.
Witkin, California Summary 10th Taxation § 151, in General.
Witkin, California Summary 10th Torts § 1020, Unmarried Cohabitant.
Witkin, California Summary 10th Torts § 1391, Domestic Partner.
Witkin, California Summary 10th Wills and Probate § 49, Persons and Entities.
Witkin, California Summary 10th Wills and Probate § 303, in General.
Witkin, California Summary 10th Wills and Probate § 521, Wrongful Death.
Witkin, California Summary 10th Wills and Probate § 891, Health Care Surrogates.
Witkin, California Summary 10th Wills and Probate § 969, Statewide Registry.
Witkin, California Summary 10th Wills and Probate § 304A, (New) in General.

§ 297.1. Domestic partnership with underage person; court order and written consent of parents

(a) A person under 18 years of age who, together with the person with whom he or she proposes to establish a domestic partnership, otherwise meets the requirements for a domestic partnership other than the requirement of being at least 18 years of age, is capable of consenting to and establishing a domestic partnership upon obtaining a court order granting permission to the underage person or persons to establish a domestic partnership.

(b)(1) The court order and written consent of the parents of each person under 18 years of age or of one of the parents or the guardian of each person under 18 years of age, except as provided in paragraph (2), shall be filed with the clerk of the court, and a certified copy of the order shall be filed with the Secretary of State with the Declaration of Domestic Partnership.

(2) If it appears to the satisfaction of the court by application of a person under 18 years of age that the person requires a written consent to establish a domestic partnership and that the minor has no parent or guardian, or has no parent or guardian capable of consenting, the court may make an order consenting to establishing the domestic partnership. The order shall be filed with the clerk of the court and a certified copy of the order shall be filed with the Secretary of State with the Declaration of Domestic Partnership. *(Added by Stats.2011, c. 721 (S.B.651), § 2.)*

Research References

Forms

California Transactions Forms--Family Law § 4:4, Application Of Agreements to Same Sex Couples.
West's California Judicial Council Forms FL-910, Request Of Minor to Marry or Establish a Domestic Partnership.
West's California Judicial Council Forms FL-915, Order on Request Of Minor to Marry or Establish a Domestic Partnership.

Treatises and Practice Aids

Witkin, California Summary 10th Husband and Wife § 27, Establishment Of Domestic Partnership.

§ 297.5. Rights, protections and benefits; responsibilities; obligations and duties under law; date of registration as equivalent of date of marriage

(a) Registered domestic partners shall have the same rights, protections, and benefits, and shall be subject to the same responsibilities, obligations, and duties under law, whether they derive from statutes, administrative regulations, court rules, government policies, common law, or any other provisions or sources of law, as are granted to and imposed upon spouses.

(b) Former registered domestic partners shall have the same rights, protections, and benefits, and shall be subject to the same responsibilities, obligations, and duties under law, whether they derive from statutes, administrative regulations, court rules, government policies, common law, or any other provisions or sources of law, as are granted to and imposed upon former spouses.

(c) A surviving registered domestic partner, following the death of the other partner, shall have the same rights, protections, and benefits, and shall be subject to the same responsibilities, obligations, and duties under law, whether they derive from statutes, administrative regulations, court rules, government policies, common law, or any other provisions or sources of law, as are granted to and imposed upon a widow or a widower.

(d) The rights and obligations of registered domestic partners with respect to a child of either of them shall be the same as those of spouses. The rights and obligations of former or surviving registered domestic partners with respect to a child of either of them shall be the same as those of former or surviving spouses.

(e) To the extent that provisions of California law adopt, refer to, or rely upon, provisions of federal law in a way that otherwise would cause registered domestic partners to be treated differently than spouses, registered domestic partners shall be treated by California law as if federal law recognized a domestic partnership in the same manner as California law.

(f) Registered domestic partners shall have the same rights regarding nondiscrimination as those provided to spouses.

(g) No public agency in this state may discriminate against any person or couple on the ground that the person is a registered domestic partner rather than a spouse or that the couple are registered domestic partners rather than spouses, except that nothing in this section applies to modify eligibility for long-term care plans pursuant to Chapter 15 (commencing with Section 21660) of Part 3 of Division 5 of Title 2 of the Government Code.

(h) This act does not preclude any state or local agency from exercising its regulatory authority to implement statutes providing rights to, or imposing responsibilities upon, domestic partners.

(i) This section does not amend or modify any provision of the California Constitution or any provision of any statute that was adopted by initiative.

(j) Where necessary to implement the rights of registered domestic partners under this act, gender-specific terms referring to spouses shall be construed to include domestic partners.

(k)(1) For purposes of the statutes, administrative regulations, court rules, government policies, common law, and any other provision or source of law governing the rights, protections, and benefits, and the responsibilities, obligations, and duties of registered domestic partners in this state, as effectuated by this section, with respect to community property, mutual responsibility for debts to third parties, the right in particular circumstances of either partner to seek financial support from the other following the dissolution of the partnership, and other rights and duties as between the partners concerning ownership of property, any reference to the date of a marriage shall be deemed to refer to the date of registration of a domestic partnership with the state.

(2) Notwithstanding paragraph (1), for domestic partnerships registered with the state before January 1, 2005, an agreement between the domestic partners that the partners intend to be governed by the requirements set forth in Sections 1600 to 1620, inclusive, and which complies with those sections, except for the agreement's effective date, shall be enforceable as provided by Sections 1600 to 1620, inclusive, if that agreement was fully executed and in force as of June 30, 2005. *(Added by Stats.2003, c. 421 (A.B.205), § 4, operative Jan. 1, 2005. Amended by Stats.2004, c. 947 (A.B.2580), § 2; Stats.2006, c. 802 (S.B.1827), § 2.)*

Commentary

Holguin v. Flores, 122 Cal.App.4th 428, 18 Cal.Rptr.3d 749 (2004), holds that the state does not violate the equal protection clause when it denies opposite-sex unmarried partners, both of whom are under the age of 62, the wrongful death rights accorded to married persons and, under Section 297 and this section, to same-sex registered domestic partners under the age of 62. *Holguin* reasons that there is a rational basis for extending the status of domestic partnership only to couples who are legally or practically prevented from marrying and, further, that the factor distinguishing claimant from persons eligible for wrongful death benefits is that the latter have publicly registered their relationship and assumed mutual legal obligations as well as legal rights.

Strong v. State Board of Equalization, 155 Cal.App.4th 1182, 66 Cal.Rptr.3d 657 (2007), review denied, sustained legislation exempting real property transfers between registered domestic partners from the increase in property tax assessment that normally accompanies a change of ownership.

Velez v. Smith, 142 Cal.App.4th 1154, 48 Cal.Rptr.3d 642 (2006), review denied Nov. 29, 2006, held that filing a declaration of domestic partnership with the City and County of San Francisco in 1994 did not establish a domestic partnership within the meaning of section 297. Thus a former San Francisco-registered domestic partner was not a registered domestic partner for purposes of subsection (d).

A person's objectively reasonable, good faith belief that his California domestic partnership was validly registered entitles him to all the rights and benefits of domestic partnership as a putative domestic partner, even though registration never occurred. *In re Domestic Partnership of Ellis and Arriaga, 162 Cal.App.4th 1000, 76 Cal.Rptr.3d 401 (2008)*. Thus when two men signed and notarized a California declaration of domestic partnership and one of them failed to keep his promise to send the declaration to the California Secretary of State, his partner could claim the status of putative domestic partner.

In re Rabin, 359 B.R. 242 (9th Cir. Bankr. App. Pan., 2007), interpreting and applying California law, held that California registered domestic partners, who are treated under this section as if they were spouses, are required, like spouses under California Code of Civil Procedure section 703.110, to share a single bankruptcy exemption in bankruptcy proceedings. Each may not claim the full homestead exemption granted to individuals under California Code of Civil Procedure section 704.730(a)(2).

Note that subsection (d) gives domestic partners the same rights and obligations as spouses with respect to a child. A registered domestic partner who consents to insemination of the other partner or a third party for the purpose of conceiving a child for the partners should be able to avail himself or herself of the section 7613 rights and obligations of the husband of a wife artificially inseminated with his consent. Thus, recourse to section 7611(d) presumed parenthood may be unnecessary.

Estate of Wilson, 211 Cal.App.4th 1284, 150 Cal.Rptr.3d 699 (2012), review denied, held that domestic partnership agreements that satisfy the requirements of Family Code sections 1600-1617 and were made after the enactment of statutes providing domestic partners with the same property rights as spouses, are not automatically invalidated by the partners' subsequent same-sex marriage. Thus, a pre-registration California domestic partnership agreement in which the parties waived any interest in each other's estate and that required a signed writing to terminate the agreement, was not revoked by the parties' subsequent same-sex marriage. Although the surviving spouse was an omitted spouse for purposes of Probate Code section 21610, under Probate Code section 21611(c) he waived his right to any interest in the decedent spouse's estate in the domestic partnership agreement.

Research References

Forms

California Transactions Forms--Family Law § 4:4, Application Of Agreements to Same Sex Couples.

16 West's Legal Forms PT I INTRO, Introduction.

West's California Code Forms, Family § 297.5, Comment Overview--Domestic Partnerships.

West's California Judicial Council Forms DE-221, Spousal or Domestic Partner Property Petition.

West's California Judicial Council Forms DE-226, Spousal or Domestic Partner Property Order.

Treatises and Practice Aids

Witkin, California Summary 10th Community Property § 282, Legal Effect Of Status.

Witkin, California Summary 10th Husband and Wife § 30, in General.

Witkin, California Summary 10th Parent and Child § 18, Parent and Child Relationship.

Witkin, California Summary 10th Parent and Child § 203, Homosexuality.

Witkin, California Summary 10th Parent and Child § 220, Illustrations: Guardianship Cases.

Witkin, California Summary 10th Parent and Child § 236, Former Lesbian Partner Opposed by Other Partner.

Witkin, California Summary 10th Parent and Child § 363, Applicability Of Family Code Custody Provisions.

Witkin, California Summary 10th Wills and Probate § 78, Surviving Spouse or Domestic Partner.

Part 2

REGISTRATION

§ 298. Declaration of Domestic Partnership and Notice of Termination of Domestic Partnership forms

(a)(1) The Secretary of State shall prepare forms entitled "Declaration of Domestic Partnership" and "Notice of Termination of Domestic Partnership" to meet the requirements of this division. These forms shall require the signature and seal of an acknowledgment by a notary public to be binding and valid.

(2) When funding allows, the Secretary of State shall include on the form notice that a lesbian, gay, bisexual, and transgender specific domestic abuse brochure is available upon request.

(b)(1) The Secretary of State shall distribute these forms to each county clerk. These forms shall be available to the public at the office of the Secretary of State and each county clerk.

(2) The Secretary of State shall, by regulation, establish fees for the actual costs of processing each of these forms, and the cost for preparing and sending the mailings and notices required pursuant to Section 299.3, and shall charge these fees to persons filing the forms.

(3) There is hereby established a fee of twenty-three dollars ($23) to be charged in addition to the existing fees established by regulation to persons filing domestic partner registrations pursuant to Section 297 for development and support of a lesbian, gay, bisexual, and transgender curriculum for training workshops on domestic violence, conducted pursuant to Section 13823.15 of the Penal Code, and for the support of a grant program to promote healthy nonviolent relationships in the lesbian, gay, bisexual, and transgender community. This paragraph shall not apply to persons of opposite sexes filing a domestic partnership registration and who meet the qualifications described in subparagraph (B) of paragraph (5) of subdivision (b) of Section 297.

(4) The fee established by paragraph (3) shall be deposited in the Equality in Prevention and Services for Domestic Abuse Fund, which is hereby established. The fund shall be administered by the Office of Emergency Services, and expenditures from the fund shall be used to support the purposes of paragraph (3).

(c) The Declaration of Domestic Partnership shall require each person who wants to become a domestic partner to (1) state that he or she meets the requirements of Section 297 at the time the form is signed, (2) provide a mailing address, (3) state that he or she consents to the jurisdiction of the Superior Courts of California for the purpose of a proceeding to obtain a judgment of dissolution or nullity of the domestic partnership or for legal separation of partners in the domestic partnership, or for any other proceeding related to the partners' rights and obligations, even if one or both partners ceases to be a resident of, or to maintain a domicile in, this state, (4) sign the form with a declaration that representations made therein are true, correct, and contain no material omissions of fact to the best knowledge and belief of the applicant, and (5) have a notary public acknowledge his or her signature. Both partners' signatures shall be affixed to one Declaration of Domestic Partnership form, which form shall then be transmitted to the Secretary of State according to the instructions provided on the form. Filing an intentionally and materially false Declaration of Domestic Partnership shall be punishable as a misdemeanor.

(d) The Declaration of Domestic Partnership form shall contain an optional section for either party or both parties to indicate a change in name pursuant to Section 298.6. The optional section shall require a party indicating a change in name to provide his or her date of birth. *(Added by Stats.1999, c. 588 (A.B.26), § 2. Amended by Stats.2003, c. 421 (A.B.205), § 5, operative Jan. 1, 2005; Stats.2006, c. 856 (A.B.2051), § 2; Stats.2007, c. 179 (S.B.86), § 7, eff. Aug. 24, 2007; Stats.2007, c. 567 (A.B.102), § 4; Stats.2010, c. 618 (A.B.2791), § 14; Stats.2013, c. 352 (A.B.1317), § 78, eff. Sept. 26, 2013, operative July 1, 2013.)*

Research References

Forms

California Practice Guide: Rutter Family Law Forms Form 1:32, Glossary Of Common Family Law Terms, Phrases and Concepts (Enclosure to Form 1:31).

California Transactions Forms--Family Law § 4:4.50, Declaration Of Domestic Partnership.

Nichols Cyclopedia of Legal Forms Annotated § 100:1, Definitions and Status Of Persons as Spouses or Domestic or Civil Partners, Generally.

Nichols Cyclopedia of Legal Forms Annotated § 100:4, Dissolution or Termination Of Marital Relationship, Generally.

Treatises and Practice Aids

Witkin, California Summary 10th Husband and Wife § 25, in General.

Witkin, California Summary 10th Husband and Wife § 28, Registration Procedure.

§ 298.5. Filing of Declaration of Domestic Partnership forms; registration

(a) Two persons desiring to become domestic partners may complete and file a Declaration of Domestic Partnership with the Secretary of State.

(b) The Secretary of State shall register the Declaration of Domestic Partnership in a registry for those partnerships, and shall return a copy of the registered form and a Certificate of Registered Domestic Partnership and, except for those opposite sex domestic partners who meet the qualifications described in subparagraph (B) of paragraph (5) of subdivision (b) of Section 297, a copy of the brochure that is made available to county clerks and the Secretary of State by the State Department of Public Health pursuant to Section 358 and distributed to individuals receiving a confidential marriage license pursuant to Section 503, to the domestic partners at the mailing address provided by the domestic partners.

(c) No person who has filed a Declaration of Domestic Partnership may file a new Declaration of Domestic Partnership or enter a civil marriage with someone other than their registered domestic partner unless the most recent domestic partnership has been terminated or a final judgment of dissolution or nullity of the most recent domestic partnership has been entered. This prohibition does not apply if the previous domestic partnership ended because one of the partners died.

(d) When funding allows, the Secretary of State shall print and make available upon request, pursuant to Section 358, a lesbian, gay, bisexual, and transgender specific domestic abuse brochure developed by the State Department of Public Health and made available to the Secretary of State to domestic partners who qualify pursuant to Section 297.

(e) The Certificate of Registered Domestic Partnership shall include the name used by each party before registration of the domestic partnership and the new name, if any, selected by each party upon registration of the domestic partnership. *(Added by Stats.1999, c. 588 (A.B.26), § 2. Amended by Stats.2003, c. 421 (A.B.205), § 6, operative Jan. 1, 2005; Stats.2006, c. 856 (A.B.2051), § 3; Stats.2007, c. 483 (S.B.1039), § 8; Stats.2007, c. 567 (A.B.102), § 5.)*

Commentary

Velez v. Smith, 142 Cal.App.4th 1154, 48 Cal.Rptr.3d 642 (2006), review denied Nov. 29, 2006, held that filing a declaration of domestic partnership with the City and County of San Francisco in 1994 did not establish a domestic partnership within the meaning of section 297.

A person's objectively reasonable, good faith belief that his California domestic partnership was validly registered entitles him to all the rights and benefits of domestic partnership as a putative domestic partner, even though registration never occurred. *In re Domestic Partnership of Ellis and Arriaga, 162 Cal.App.4th 1000, 76 Cal.Rptr.3d 401 (2008).* Thus when two men signed and notarized a California declaration of domestic partnership and one of them failed to keep his promise to send the declaration to the California Secretary of State, his partner could claim the status of putative domestic partner.

Research References

Forms

California Practice Guide: Rutter Family Law Forms Form 1:32, Glossary Of Common Family Law Terms, Phrases and Concepts (Enclosure to Form 1:31).

Nichols Cyclopedia of Legal Forms Annotated § 100:1, Definitions and Status Of Persons as Spouses or Domestic or Civil Partners, Generally.

West's California Code Forms, Family § 298, Comment Overview--Declaration Of Domestic Partnership.

Treatises and Practice Aids

Witkin, California Summary 10th Husband and Wife § 28, Registration Procedure.

Witkin, California Summary 10th Husband and Wife § 29, Preemption Of Local Laws.

§ 298.6. Parties to registered domestic partnership; names; procedure for change of name

(a) Parties to a registered domestic partnership shall not be required to have the same name. Neither party shall be required to change his or her name. A person's name shall not change upon registration as a domestic partner unless that person elects to change his or her name pursuant to subdivision (b).

(b)(1) One party or both parties to a registered domestic partnership may elect to change the middle or last names by which that party wishes to be known after registration of the domestic partnership by entering the new name in the space provided on the Declaration of Domestic Partnership form without intent to defraud.

(2) A person may adopt any of the following middle or last names pursuant to paragraph (1):

(A) The current last name of the other domestic partner.

(B) The last name of either domestic partner given at birth.

(C) A name combining into a single last name all or a segment of the current last name or the last name of either domestic partner given at birth.

(D) A hyphenated combination of last names.

(3)(A) An election by a person to change his or her name pursuant to paragraph (1) shall serve as a record of the name change. A certified copy of the Certificate of Registered Domestic Partnership containing the new name, or retaining the former name, shall constitute proof that the use of the new name or retention of the former name is lawful.

(B) A certified copy of a Certificate of Registered Domestic Partnership shall be accepted as identification establishing a true, full name for purposes of Section 12800.7 of the Vehicle Code.

(C) Nothing in this section shall be construed to prohibit the Department of Motor Vehicles from accepting as identification other documents establishing a true, full name for purposes of Section 12800.7 of the Vehicle Code. Those documents may include, without limitation, a certified copy of a document that is substantially equivalent to a Certificate of Registered Domestic Partnership that records either of the following:

(i) A legal union of two persons that was validly formed in another jurisdiction and is recognized as a valid domestic partnership in this state pursuant to Section 299.2.

(ii) A legal union of domestic partners as defined by a local jurisdiction pursuant to Section 299.6.

(D) This section shall be applied in a manner consistent with the requirements of Sections 1653.5 and 12801 of the Vehicle Code.

(4) The adoption of a new name, or the choice not to adopt a new name, by means of a Declaration of Domestic Partnership pursuant to paragraph (1) shall not abrogate the right of either party to adopt a different name through usage at a future date, or to petition the superior court for a change of name pursuant to Title 8 (commencing with Section 1275) of Part 3 of the Code of Civil Procedure.

(c) Nothing in this section shall be construed to abrogate the common law right of any person to change his or her name, or the right of any person to petition the superior court for a change of name pursuant to Title 8 (commencing with Section 1275) of Part 3 of the Code of Civil Procedure. *(Added by Stats.2007, c. 567 (A.B.102), § 6.)*

Research References

Forms

California Transactions Forms--Family Law § 4:4.50, Declaration Of Domestic Partnership.

Treatises and Practice Aids

Witkin, California Summary 10th Husband and Wife § 25, in General.

Witkin, California Summary 10th Husband and Wife § 33, Other Rights.

Witkin, California Summary 10th Personal Property § 25A, (New) Right to Maintain or Change Name Following Marriage or Domestic Partnership Registration.

§ 298.7. Confidential domestic partnership

The Secretary of State shall establish a process by which two persons, who have been living together as domestic partners and who meet the requirements of paragraphs (1) to (5), inclusive, of subdivision (b) of Section 297, may enter into a confidential domestic partnership. This process shall do all of the following:

(a) Maintain each confidential Declaration of Domestic Partnership as a permanent record that is not open to public inspection except upon order of the court issued upon a showing of good cause.

(b) Authorize the Secretary of State to charge a reasonable fee to offset costs directly connected with maintaining confidentiality of a Declaration of Domestic Partnership. *(Added by Stats.2011, c. 721 (S.B.651), § 3.)*

Research References

Treatises and Practice Aids

Witkin, California Summary 10th Husband and Wife § 28, Registration Procedure.

Part 3

TERMINATION

§ 299. Termination of registered domestic partnership; filing of Notice of Termination of Domestic Partnership; conditions; effective date; setting aside termination; jurisdiction; dissolution of marriage

(a) A registered domestic partnership may be terminated without filing a proceeding for dissolution of domestic partnership by the filing of a Notice of Termination of Domestic Partnership with the Secretary of State pursuant to this section, provided that all of the following conditions exist at the time of the filing:

(1) The Notice of Termination of Domestic Partnership is signed by both registered domestic partners.

(2) There are no children of the relationship of the parties born before or after registration of the domestic partnership or adopted by the parties after registration of the domestic partnership, and neither of the registered domestic partners, to their knowledge, is pregnant.

(3) The registered domestic partnership is not more than five years in duration.

(4) Neither party has any interest in real property wherever situated, with the exception of the lease of a residence occupied by either party which satisfies the following requirements:

(A) The lease does not include an option to purchase.

(B) The lease terminates within one year from the date of filing of the Notice of Termination of Domestic Partnership.

(5) There are no unpaid obligations in excess of the amount described in paragraph (6) of subdivision (a) of Section 2400, as adjusted by subdivision (b) of Section 2400, incurred by either or both of the parties after registration of the domestic partnership, excluding the amount of any unpaid obligation with respect to an automobile.

(6) The total fair market value of community property assets, excluding all encumbrances and automobiles, including any deferred compensation or retirement plan, is less than the amount described in paragraph (7) of subdivision (a) of Section 2400, as adjusted by subdivision (b) of Section 2400, and neither party has separate property assets, excluding all encumbrances and automobiles, in excess of that amount.

(7) The parties have executed an agreement setting forth the division of assets and the assumption of liabilities of the community property, and have executed any documents, title certificates, bills of sale, or other evidence of transfer necessary to effectuate the agreement.

(8) The parties waive any rights to support by the other domestic partner.

(9) The parties have read and understand a brochure prepared by the Secretary of State describing the requirements, nature, and effect of terminating a domestic partnership.

(10) Both parties desire that the domestic partnership be terminated.

(b) The registered domestic partnership shall be terminated effective six months after the date of filing of the Notice of

Termination of Domestic Partnership with the Secretary of State pursuant to this section, provided that neither party has, before that date, filed with the Secretary of State a notice of revocation of the termination of domestic partnership, in the form and content as shall be prescribed by the Secretary of State, and sent to the other party a copy of the notice of revocation by first-class mail, postage prepaid, at the other party's last known address. The effect of termination of a domestic partnership pursuant to this section shall be the same as, and shall be treated for all purposes as, the entry of a judgment of dissolution of a domestic partnership.

(c) The termination of a domestic partnership pursuant to subdivision (b) does not prejudice nor bar the rights of either of the parties to institute an action in the superior court to set aside the termination for fraud, duress, mistake, or any other ground recognized at law or in equity. A court may set aside the termination of domestic partnership and declare the termination of the domestic partnership null and void upon proof that the parties did not meet the requirements of subdivision (a) at the time of the filing of the Notice of Termination of Domestic Partnership with the Secretary of State.

(d) The superior courts shall have jurisdiction over all proceedings relating to the dissolution of domestic partnerships, nullity of domestic partnerships, and legal separation of partners in a domestic partnership. The dissolution of a domestic partnership, nullity of a domestic partnership, and legal separation of partners in a domestic partnership shall follow the same procedures, and the partners shall possess the same rights, protections, and benefits, and be subject to the same responsibilities, obligations, and duties, as apply to the dissolution of marriage, nullity of marriage, and legal separation of spouses in a marriage, respectively, except as provided in subdivision (a), and except that, in accordance with the consent acknowledged by domestic partners in the Declaration of Domestic Partnership form, proceedings for dissolution, nullity, or legal separation of a domestic partnership registered in this state may be filed in the superior courts of this state even if neither domestic partner is a resident of, or maintains a domicile in, the state at the time the proceedings are filed.

(e) Parties to a registered domestic partnership who are also married to one another may petition the court to dissolve both their domestic partnership and their marriage in a single proceeding, in a form that shall be prescribed by the Judicial Council. *(Added by Stats.2003, c. 421 (A.B.205), § 8, operative Jan. 1, 2005. Amended by Stats.2004, c. 947 (A.B.2580), § 3; Stats.2010, c. 397 (A.B.2700), § 1.)*

Commentary

Note that 2013 amendments to Code of Civil Procedure section 583.161 expanded the definition of petitions and orders that are not subject to mandatory dismissal, including petitions and orders under this section.

Velez v. Smith, 142 Cal.App.4th 1154, 48 Cal.Rptr.3d 642 (2006), review denied Nov. 29.2006, held that filing a declaration of domestic partnership with the City and County of San Francisco in 1994 did not establish a domestic partnership within the meaning of section 297. Thus a former San Francisco-registered domestic partner could not bring a dissolution action under subsection (d).

A person's objectively reasonable, good faith belief that his California domestic partnership was validly registered entitles him to all the rights and benefits of domestic partnership as a putative domestic partner, even though registration never occurred. *In re Domestic Partnership of Ellis and Arriaga, 162 Cal.App.4th 1000, 76 Cal.Rptr.3d 401 (2008).* Thus when two men signed and notarized a California declaration of domestic partnership and one of them failed to keep his promise to send the declaration to the California Secretary of State, his partner could claim the status of putative domestic partner.

Research References

Forms

California Transactions Forms--Family Law § 1:2, Nature and Advantages Of Agreement.
California Transactions Forms--Family Law § 4:4.60, Termination Of Registered Domestic Partnership.
West's California Code Forms, Family § 299, Comment Overview--Termination Of Registered Domestic Partnership.
West's California Judicial Council Forms FL-100, Petition - Marriage/Domestic Partnership.
West's California Judicial Council Forms FL-343, Spousal, Partner, or Family Support Order Attachment.
West's California Judicial Council Forms FL-345, Property Order Attachment to Judgment.
West's California Judicial Council Forms FL-435, Earnings Assignment Order for Spousal or Partner Support.
West's California Judicial Council Forms FL-800, Joint Petition for Summary Dissolution.

Treatises and Practice Aids

Witkin, California Summary 10th Community Property § 282, Legal Effect Of Status.
Witkin, California Summary 10th Husband and Wife § 34, Termination Of Status.
Witkin, California Summary 10th Parent and Child § 363, Applicability Of Family Code Custody Provisions.
Witkin, California Summary 10th Torts § 1391, Domestic Partner.
Witkin, California Summary 10th Wills and Probate § 49, Persons and Entities.
Witkin, California Summary 10th Wills and Probate § 935, Limitation on Appointment Of Spouse or Domestic Partner.

Part 4

LEGAL EFFECT

§ 299.2. Recognizing same sex unions from another jurisdiction as a valid domestic partnership

A legal union of two persons of the same sex, other than a marriage, that was validly formed in another jurisdiction, and that is substantially equivalent to a domestic partnership as defined in this part, shall be recognized as a valid domestic partnership in this state regardless of whether it bears the name domestic partnership. *(Added by Stats.2003, c. 421 (A.B.205), § 9, operative Jan. 1, 2005.)*

Research References

Forms

Nichols Cyclopedia of Legal Forms Annotated § 100:4, Dissolution or Termination Of Marital Relationship, Generally.

Treatises and Practice Aids

Witkin, California Summary 10th Community Property § 282, Legal Effect Of Status.

Witkin, California Summary 10th Husband and Wife § 30, in General.

Witkin, California Summary 10th Husband and Wife § 32, Health Care Benefits.

§ 299.3. Letter to be sent to each registered domestic partner from Secretary of State; notice to potential domestic partner registrants

(a) On or before June 30, 2004, and again on or before December 1, 2004, and again on or before January 31, 2005, the Secretary of State shall send the following letter to the mailing address on file of each registered domestic partner who registered more than one month prior to each of those dates:

"Dear Registered Domestic Partner:

This letter is being sent to all persons who have registered with the Secretary of State as a domestic partner.

Effective January 1, 2005, California's law related to the rights and responsibilities of registered domestic partners will change (or, if you are receiving this letter after that date, the law has changed, as of January 1, 2005). With this new legislation, for purposes of California law, domestic partners will have a great many new rights and responsibilities, including laws governing community property, those governing property transfer, those regarding duties of mutual financial support and mutual responsibilities for certain debts to third parties, and many others. The way domestic partnerships are terminated is also changing. After January 1, 2005, under certain circumstances, it will be necessary to participate in a dissolution proceeding in court to end a domestic partnership.

Domestic partners who do not wish to be subject to these new rights and responsibilities MUST terminate their domestic partnership before January 1, 2005. Under the law in effect until January 1, 2005, your domestic partnership is automatically terminated if you or your partner marry or die while you are registered as domestic partners. It is also terminated if you send to your partner or your partner sends to you, by certified mail, a notice terminating the domestic partnership, or if you and your partner no longer share a common residence. In all cases, you are required to file a Notice of Termination of Domestic Partnership.

If you do not terminate your domestic partnership before January 1, 2005, as provided above, you will be subject to these new rights and responsibilities and, under certain circumstances, you will only be able to terminate your domestic partnership, other than as a result of your domestic partner's death, by the filing of a court action.

Further, if you registered your domestic partnership with the state prior to January 1, 2005, you have until June 30, 2005, to enter into a written agreement with your domestic partner that will be enforceable in the same manner as a premarital agreement under California law, if you intend to be so governed.

If you have any questions about any of these changes, please consult an attorney. If you cannot find an attorney in your locale, please contact your county bar association for a referral.

Sincerely,

The Secretary of State"

(b) From January 1, 2004, to December 31, 2004, inclusive, the Secretary of State shall provide the following notice with all requests for the Declaration of Domestic Partnership form. The Secretary of State also shall attach the Notice to the Declaration of Domestic Partnership form that is provided to the general public on the Secretary of State's Web site:

"NOTICE TO POTENTIAL DOMESTIC PARTNER REGISTRANTS

As of January 1, 2005, California's law of domestic partnership will change.

Beginning at that time, for purposes of California law, domestic partners will have a great many new rights and responsibilities, including laws governing community property, those governing property transfer, those regarding duties of mutual financial support and mutual responsibilities for certain debts to third parties, and many others. The way domestic partnerships are terminated will also change. Unlike current law, which allows partners to end their partnership simply by filing a "Termination of Domestic Partnership" form with the Secretary of State, after January 1, 2005, it will be necessary under certain circumstances to participate in a dissolution proceeding in court to end a domestic partnership.

If you have questions about these changes, please consult an attorney. If you cannot find an attorney in your area, please contact your county bar association for a referral." *(Added by Stats.2003, c. 421 (A.B.205), § 10. Amended by Stats.2004, c. 947 (A.B.2580), § 4; Stats.2005, c. 22 (S.B. 1108), § 59.)*

Research References

Forms

California Transactions Forms--Family Law § 1:2, Nature and Advantages Of Agreement.

Treatises and Practice Aids

Witkin, California Summary 10th Husband and Wife § 25, in General.

Witkin, California Summary 10th Husband and Wife § 26, California Domestic Partner Rights and Responsibilities Act.

Witkin, California Summary 10th Husband and Wife § 34, Termination Of Status.

Part 5

PREEMPTION

Section

§ 299.6. Preemption of local ordinances or laws

(a) Any local ordinance or law that provides for the creation of a "domestic partnership" shall be preempted on and after July 1, 2000, except as provided in subdivision (c).

(b) Domestic partnerships created under any local domestic partnership ordinance or law before July 1, 2000, shall remain valid. On and after July 1, 2000, domestic partnerships previously established under a local ordinance or law shall be governed by this division and the rights and duties of the partners shall be those set out in this division, except as provided in subdivision (c), provided a Declaration of Domestic Partnership is filed by the domestic partners under Section 298.5.

(c) Any local jurisdiction may retain or adopt ordinances, policies, or laws that offer rights within that jurisdiction to domestic partners as defined by Section 297 or as more broadly defined by the local jurisdiction's ordinances, policies, or laws, or that impose duties upon third parties regarding domestic partners as defined by Section 297 or as more broadly defined by the local jurisdiction's ordinances, policies, or laws, that are in addition to the rights and duties set out in this division, and the local rights may be conditioned upon the agreement of the domestic partners to assume the additional obligations set forth in this division. *(Added by Stats.1999, c. 588 (A.B.26), § 2.)*

Research References

Treatises and Practice Aids

Witkin, California Summary 10th Husband and Wife § 29, Preemption Of Local Laws.

Division 3

MARRIAGE

Part 1

VALIDITY OF MARRIAGE

§ 300. Consent; issuance of license and solemnization; marriage license and marriage certificate

(a) Marriage is a personal relation arising out of a civil contract between two persons, to which the consent of the parties capable of making that contract is necessary. Consent alone does not constitute marriage. Consent must be followed by the issuance of a license and solemnization as authorized by this division, except as provided by Section 425 and Part 4 (commencing with Section 500).

(b) For purposes of this part, the document issued by the county clerk is a marriage license until it is registered with the county recorder, at which time the license becomes a marriage certificate. *(Stats.1992, c. 162 (A.B.2650), § 10, operative Jan. 1, 1994. Amended by Stats.1993, c. 219 (A.B.1500), § 88; Stats.2006, c. 816 (A.B.1102), § 1, operative Jan. 1, 2008; Stats.2014, c. 82 (S.B.1306), § 2, eff. Jan. 1, 2015.)*

Validity

Language in a prior version of this section ("between a man and a woman") was held unconstitutional as a violation of the equal protection clause in the decision of In re Marriage Cases (2008) 76 Cal. Rptr.3d 683, 43 Cal.4th 757, 183 P.3d 384, rehearing denied, on subsequent appeal 2009 WL 2515727, unpublished. See, also, Const. Art. 1, § 7.5.

Law Revision Commission Comments

Enactment [Revised Comment]

Section 300 continues former Civil Code Section 4100 without substantive change. In the last sentence of Section 300, "this division" has been substituted for the broader reference to "this code," formerly meaning the Civil Code. This is not a substantive change, since all sections dealing with issuance of a license and solemnization formerly in the Civil Code are continued in this division of the Family Code. [23 Cal.L.Rev.Comm. Reports 1 (1993)].

Commentary

In re Marriage Cases, 43 Cal.4th 757, 183 P.3d 384, 76 Cal.Rptr.3d 683 (2008), held that, under the California constitution, a fundamental right to marry extends equally to all individuals, and discrimination on the basis of sexual orientation is subject to strict judicial scrutiny, with the consequence that this section and Family Code section 308.5 are unconstitutional insofar as they purport to limit marriage to opposite-sex couples. California domestic partners may marry each other without terminating their domestic partnership. Their accumulation of community property dates from the initial registration of their domestic partnership. In the November 2008 election, California voters approved Proposition 8, an initiative amending the California constitution to define marriage as "a union between a man and a woman." In *Strauss v. Horton, 46 Cal.4th 364, 93 Cal.Rptr.3d 591, 207 P.3d 48 (2009)*, the California Supreme Court concluded that Proposition 8 was a permissible constitutional amendment. However, Proposition 8 could not be applied retroactively to invalidate lawful marriages of same-sex couples contracted prior to its effective date, November 5, 2008. Thus, those same-sex marriages remain lawful under California law. Proposition 8 was subsequently challenged in federal court. In *Perry v. Schwarzenegger, 704 F.Supp. 921 (2010)*, Chief District Judge Vaughn R. Walker held that Proposition 8 violates the Due Process and Equal Protection clauses of the Fourteenth Amendment of the United States Constitution, because it both unconstitutionally burdens the exercise of the fundamental right to marry and creates an irrational classification on the basis of sexual orientation. Judge Vaughn concluded that Proposition 8 did not withstand rational basis review, the lowest level of constitutional scrutiny. Although the State of California declined to appeal Judge Vaughn's decision to the Ninth Circuit Court of Appeals, the official proponents of Proposition 8 appealed the decision. The Ninth Circuit Court of Appeals referred the case to the California Supreme Court to determine whether the official proponents had standing to appeal the district court's decision. In *Perry v. Brown, 52 Cal.4th 1116, 134 Cal.Rptr.3d 499, 265 P.3d 1002 (2011)*, the California Supreme Court held that the proponents had standing when the state declined to appeal. Subsequently, a three-judge panel of the Court of Appeals, one judge dissenting, affirmed the district court's decision. *Perry v. Brown, 671 F.3d 1052 (9th Cir. 2012), petition for cert. filed*. The panel affirmed on a relatively narrow ground. Relying on *Romer v. Evans, 517 U.S. 620, 623 (1996)*, the panel held that Proposition 8 served no purpose other than to take away from gays and lesbians an existing civil right to use the term marriage to designate their relationship and to thereby lessen the status and dignity of gays and lesbians in California. However, the Ninth Circuit stayed judgment pending appeal to the United States Supreme Court, which granted certiorari and ultimately held that the proponents did not have federal standing to appeal the district court's order. Thus, the court vacated the judgment of the Ninth Circuit and remanded the case to the Ninth Circuit with instructions to dismiss the appeal for lack of jurisdiction. *Hollingsworth v. Perry, 133 S.Ct. 2652 (2013)*. Accordingly, the Ninth Circuit lifted its stay and vacated its judgment, enabling state officials to again marry same-sex couples. *Perry v. Brown, 725 F.3d 968, 725 F.3d 1140 (2013)*.

United States v. Windsor, 133 S.Ct. 2675 (2013), requires the federal government to recognize same-sex marriages lawfully contracted in a state authorizing such marriages, holding that the first section of the Defense of Marriage Act (1 USC 7), which declined to do so, violates the Fifth and Fourteenth Amendments. *Obergefell v. Hodges, 135 S.Ct. 2584 (2015)*, constitutionally established a national right to same-sex marriage and requires that states recognize such marriages lawfully contracted elsewhere.

In order to contract a lawful marriage, the parties must satisfy certain substantive and formal requirements. Each party must have legal capacity to marry. Neither may, for example, have a prior undissolved marriage. See Sections 2200–2255.

Additionally, in order to contract a valid California marriage, the parties must observe certain formal requirements, which are set out in Sections 300–536. California does not recognize informal, or common-law, marriages purportedly contracted within its borders. In 1895, California abolished common-law marriage; the statutory abolition is codified in the last two sentences of Section 300.

Although California does not recognize common-law marriages contracted within its borders, it does recognize common-law marriages validly contracted in the fourteen American jurisdictions where common-law marriages may validly be contracted. See Section 308. Thus, a common-law marriage may have been contracted by current California domiciliaries when they previously resided in a common-law marriage state. *In re Marriage of Smyklo, 180 Cal.App.3d 1095, 226 Cal.Rptr. 174 (1986)* (recognizing Alabama common-law marriage); *People v. Badgett, 10 Cal.4th 330, 895 P.2d 877, 41 Cal.Rptr.2d 635 (1995)* (evidence supported trial court determination that defendant and witness had not contracted a valid Texas common law marriage and thus the defendant could not assert the Evidence Code Section 980 privilege for confidential marriage communications in order to bar the testimony of witness). Under some circumstances, a common-law marriage may even be contracted by California domiciliaries who are merely traveling through a common-law marriage state. Moreover, a good faith common-law marriage invalidly contracted in a common-law marriage state may be treated as a putative marriage in California. See *Sancha v. Arnold, 114 Cal.App.2d 772, 251 P.2d 67 (1952), rehearing denied 114 Cal.App.2d 781, 252 P.2d 55 (1953)* (recognizing as a putative marriage an apparently invalid Nevada common-law marriage contracted when Nevada still recognized common-law marriage). For further discussion of putative marriage, see Section 2251, Commentary.

An informal relationship, or cohabitation, that does not qualify as a lawful or putative *marriage* or as a registered domestic partnership is not regulated by the Family Code but is instead subject to the law of contract. See generally *Marvin v. Marvin, 18 Cal.3d 660, 557 P.2d 106, 134 Cal.Rptr. 815 (1976)* (applying contractual remedies at the dissolution of a six-year cohabitation); *Byrne v. Laura, 52 Cal.App.4th 1054, 60 Cal.Rptr.2d 908 (1997), review denied May 28, 1997* (primer for cohabitation claims after the death of a nonmarital partner); and *Della Zoppa v. Della Zoppa, 86 Cal.App.4th 1144, 103 Cal.Rptr.2d 901 (2001)* (holding that trial court erred in concluding that agreement to cohabit was meretricious and hence unenforceable because the parties planned to have sexual relations and to have children together). *Cochran v. Cochran, 89 Cal.App.4th 283, 106 Cal.Rptr.2d 899 (2001)*, holds that, for *Marvin* purposes, the parties may cohabit ("live together as husband and wife") even though they do not live together on a full-time basis. See also *Elden v. Sheldon, 46 Cal.3d 267, 250 Cal.Rptr. 254 (1988)* (no loss of consortium recovery when cohabitant is tortiously killed because marriage is a prerequisite for a loss of consortium claim; cohabitant not sufficiently "closely related" to victim to maintain an action for negligent infliction of emotional distress). *Cf. Kahn v. INS, 20 F.3d 960 (9th Cir. 1994)*, which holds that state law characterization of a family relationship, in this case California non-recognition of "common law" cohabitation, does not conclusively determine whether claimant has "family ties" in the United States for purposes of federal law waiver of deportation. For further discussion of cohabitation, see Section 2251, Commentary.

Holguin v. Flores, 122 Cal.App.4th 428, 18 Cal.Rptr.3d 749 (2004), holds that the state does not violate the equal protection clause when it denies opposite-sex unmarried partners, both of whom are under the age of 62, the wrongful death rights accorded to married persons and, under Sections 297 and 297.5, to same-sex registered domestic partners under the age of 62. *Holguin* reasons that there is a rational basis for extending the status of domestic partnership only to couples who are legally or practically prevented from marrying and, further, that the factor distinguishing claimant from persons eligible for wrongful death benefits is that the latter have publicly registered their relationship and assumed mutual legal obligations as well as legal rights.

Research References

Forms

California Practice Guide: Rutter Family Law Forms Form 1:32, Glossary Of Common Family Law Terms, Phrases and Concepts (Enclosure to Form 1:31).

California Transactions Forms--Family Law § 4:4, Application Of Agreements to Same Sex Couples.

West's California Code Forms, Family § 400, Comment Overview--Solemnize Marriage.

Treatises and Practice Aids

Witkin, California Summary 10th Community Property § 259B, (New) California Law.

Witkin, California Summary 10th Constitutional Law § 910, Classification Based on Marital Status.

Witkin, California Summary 10th Constitutional Law § 226A, (New) Historical Development.

Witkin, California Summary 10th Constitutional Law § 226B, (New) Constitutional and Statutory Amendments.

Witkin, California Summary 10th Contracts § 31, Statutory Right and Methods.

Witkin, California Summary 10th Husband and Wife § 3, Statutory Framework.

Witkin, California Summary 10th Husband and Wife § 42, in General.

Witkin, California Summary 10th Husband and Wife § 44, Same-Sex Marriage.

Witkin, California Summary 10th Husband and Wife § 45, License.

Witkin, California Summary 10th Husband and Wife § 46, Certificate Of Registry.

Witkin, California Summary 10th Husband and Wife § 47, Solemnization.

Witkin, California Summary 10th Husband and Wife § 53, in General.

Witkin, California Summary 10th Husband and Wife § 154, in General.

§ 301. Adults; capability to consent to and consummate marriage

Two unmarried persons 18 years of age or older, who are not otherwise disqualified, are capable of consenting to and consummating marriage. *(Stats.1992, c. 162 (A.B.2650), § 10, operative Jan. 1, 1994. Amended by Stats.2014, c. 82 (S.B.1306), § 3, eff. Jan. 1, 2015.)*

Law Revision Commission Comments

Enactment [Revised Comment]

Section 301 continues former Civil Code Section 4101(a) without substantive change. [23 Cal.L.Rev.Comm. Reports 1 (1993)].

Research References

Forms

Am. Jur. Pl. & Pr. Forms Marriage § 1, Introductory Comments.
Am. Jur. Pl. & Pr. Forms Marriage § 2, Introductory Comments.

Treatises and Practice Aids

Witkin, California Summary 10th Community Property § 259B, (New) California Law.
Witkin, California Summary 10th Husband and Wife § 43, Capacity Of Parties.
Witkin, California Summary 10th Husband and Wife § 44, Same-Sex Marriage.
Witkin, California Summary 10th Husband and Wife § 160, Minority.

§ 302. Minors; capability of consenting to and consummating marriage; court order and parental consent; filing

(a) An unmarried person under 18 years of age is capable of consenting to and consummating marriage upon obtaining a court order granting permission to the underage person or persons to marry.

(b) The court order and written consent of at least one of the parents or the guardian of each underage person shall be filed with the clerk of the court, and a certified copy of the order shall be presented to the county clerk at the time the marriage license is issued. *(Stats.1992, c. 162 (A.B.2650), § 10, operative Jan. 1, 1994. Amended by Stats.2006, c. 816 (A.B.1102), § 2, operative Jan. 1, 2008; Stats.2014, c. 82 (S.B.1306), § 4, eff. Jan. 1, 2015; Stats.2016, c. 474 (A.B. 2882), § 1, eff. Jan. 1, 2017.)*

Law Revision Commission Comments

Enactment [Revised Comment]

Section 302 continues former Civil Code Section 4101(b) without substantive change. In the introductory clause, the cross reference to former Civil Code Section 4201 has been omitted and the word "county" has been added. This is not a substantive change, since former Civil Code Section 4201 required filing with the "county" clerk. The reference to the "superior" court has been omitted as surplus. See Section 200 (jurisdiction in superior court). See also Sections 303 (consent of court where minor has no parent), 353 (requirements for underage applicant for marriage license). [23 Cal.L.Rev.Comm. Reports 1 (1993)].

Commentary

Note that a minor is "capable of consenting" when Section 302 requirements are met and thus the minor would appear ineligible for a Section 2210(a) annulment even though he or she has not yet reached the age of majority when the annulment is sought.

Research References

Forms

West's California Code Forms, Family § 302, Comment Overview--Marriage Of Minor.
West's California Judicial Council Forms FL-910, Request Of Minor to Marry or Establish a Domestic Partnership.
West's California Judicial Council Forms FL-915, Order on Request Of Minor to Marry or Establish a Domestic Partnership.

Treatises and Practice Aids

Witkin, California Summary 10th Husband and Wife § 43, Capacity Of Parties.
Witkin, California Summary 10th Husband and Wife § 45, License.
Witkin, California Summary 10th Husband and Wife § 160, Minority.

§ 303. Consent of court to marriage of minor

If it appears to the satisfaction of the court by application of a minor that the minor requires a written consent to marry and that the minor has no parent or has no parent capable of consenting, the court may make an order consenting to the issuance of a marriage license and granting permission to the minor to marry. The order shall be filed with the clerk of the court and a certified copy of the order shall be presented to the county clerk at the time the marriage license is issued. *(Stats.1992, c. 162 (A.B.2650), § 10, operative Jan. 1, 1994. Amended by Stats.2006, c. 816 (A.B.1102), § 3, operative Jan. 1, 2008.)*

Law Revision Commission Comments

Enactment [Revised Comment]

Section 303 continues former Civil Code Section 4102 without substantive change. The references to the "superior" court and to a "verified" application have been omitted as surplus. See Sections 200 (jurisdiction in superior court), 212 (pleadings to be verified). [23 Cal.L.Rev.Comm. Reports 1 (1993)].

Research References

Forms

West's California Code Forms, Family § 302, Comment Overview--Marriage Of Minor.
West's California Code Forms, Family § 303 Form 1, Order Consenting to Marriage Of Minor.

Treatises and Practice Aids

Witkin, California Summary 10th Husband and Wife § 43, Capacity Of Parties.
Witkin, California Summary 10th Husband and Wife § 45, License.

§ 304. Premarital counseling; fees

As part of the court order granting permission to marry under Section 302 or 303, the court shall, if it considers it necessary, require the parties to the prospective marriage of a minor to participate in premarital counseling concerning social, economic, and personal responsibilities incident to marriage. The parties shall not be required, without their consent, to confer with counselors provided by religious organizations of any denomination. In determining whether to order the parties to participate in the premarital counseling, the court shall consider, among other factors, the ability of the parties to pay for the counseling. The court may impose a reasonable fee to cover the cost of any premarital counseling provided by the county or the court. The fees shall be used exclusively to cover the cost of the counseling services authorized by this section. *(Stats.1992, c. 162 (A.B.2650), § 10, operative Jan. 1, 1994. Amended by Stats. 2007, c. 738 (A.B.1248), § 12; Stats.2016, c. 474 (A.B.2882), § 2, eff. Jan. 1, 2017.)*

Law Revision Commission Comments

Enactment [Revised Comment]

Section 304 continues former Civil Code Section 4101(c) without substantive change. The word "minor" has been substituted for "person under the age of 18 years." See Section 6500 (minor). [23 Cal.L.Rev.Comm. Reports 1 (1993)].

Research References

Forms

West's California Code Forms, Family § 303 Form 1, Order Consenting to Marriage Of Minor.
West's California Judicial Council Forms FL-910, Request Of Minor to Marry or Establish a Domestic Partnership.
West's California Judicial Council Forms FL-915, Order on Request Of Minor to Marry or Establish a Domestic Partnership.

Treatises and Practice Aids

Witkin, California Summary 10th Husband and Wife § 43, Capacity Of Parties.

§ 305. Proof of consent and solemnization

Consent to and solemnization of marriage may be proved under the same general rules of evidence as facts are proved in other cases. *(Stats.1992, c. 162 (A.B.2650), § 10, operative Jan. 1, 1994.)*

Law Revision Commission Comments

Enactment [Revised Comment]

Section 305 continues former Civil Code Section 4103 without substantive change. [23 Cal.L.Rev.Comm. Reports 1 (1993)].

Research References

Treatises and Practice Aids

Witkin, California Summary 10th Husband and Wife § 53, in General.

§ 306. Procedural requirements; effect of noncompliance

Except as provided in Section 307, a marriage shall be licensed, solemnized, and authenticated, and the authenticated marriage license shall be returned to the county recorder of the county where the marriage license was issued, as provided in this part. Noncompliance with this part by a nonparty to the marriage does not invalidate the marriage. *(Stats.1992, c. 162 (A.B.2650), § 10, operative Jan. 1, 1994. Amended by Stats.1993, c. 219 (A.B.1500), § 89; Stats.2006, c. 816 (A.B.1102), § 4, operative Jan. 1, 2008.)*

Law Revision Commission Comments

Enactment [Revised Comment]

Section 306 continues former Civil Code Section 4200 without substantive change. The introductory clause has been added to recognize the exception provided in Section 307. The word "nonparty" has been substituted for "others than a party." [23 Cal.L.Rev. Comm. Reports 1 (1993)].

Commentary

When a formal, or ceremonial, marriage fails to satisfy statutory licensing or recording requirements, California case law tends to give it effect by treating it as a putative marriage. See, for example, *Estate of Leslie, 37 Cal.3d 186, 207 Cal.Rptr. 561 (1984)*. For further discussion of putative marriage, see Section 2251, Commentary. Nevertheless, in some circumstances it may be desirable to have a lawful, as opposed to merely a putative, marriage. See, for example, *Estate of Hafner, 184 Cal.App.3d 1371, 229 Cal.Rptr. 676 (1986), review denied 11/20/86* (putative, as opposed to lawful, spouse ineligible for Probate Code Section 6540 family allowance) and *Allen v. Western Conference of Teamsters Pension Trust Fund, 788 F.2d 648 (9th Cir. 1986)* (pension benefit for "surviving spouse" available only to lawfully wedded spouses). See, for example, N.Y. Dom. Rel. Law § 25 (McKinney 1988).

Because California uses putative spouse doctrine liberally, California law was not required to define the minimum requirements for a valid formal marriage until *Estate of DePasse, 97 Cal.App.4th 92, 118 Cal.Rptr.2d 143 (2002), review denied June 26, 2002,* which held that issuance of a marriage license is a mandatory requirement for a valid marriage in California. The claimed marriage found invalid in *DePasse* was a deathbed marriage conducted by a hospital chaplain without a license, because there was insufficient time to obtain one. Compare N.Y. Domestic Relations Law § 25, which provides that a marriage is valid when it has been evidenced by a witnessed ceremony, even though licensing and recordation requirements have not been met. *DePasse* further held that the surviving spouse was not a putative spouse because he knew of the license requirement and thus had no objectively reasonable belief that he had contracted a valid marriage. For further discussion of putative marriage, see Commentary to Section 2551.

By contrast, *In re Marriage of Cantarella, 191 Cal.App.4th 916, 119 Cal.Rptr.3d 829 (2011)*, interpreting the Family Law Act (FLA — former Civil Code § 4000 et seq.), held that a couple's 1991 duly licensed and ceremonialized marriage was valid even though the couple never registered the certificate of marriage.

Research References

Treatises and Practice Aids

Witkin, California Summary 10th Husband and Wife § 42, in General.
Witkin, California Summary 10th Husband and Wife § 45, License.
Witkin, California Summary 10th Husband and Wife § 47, Solemnization.
Witkin, California Summary 10th Husband and Wife § 53, in General.
Witkin, California Summary 10th Husband and Wife § 154, in General.

§ 306.5. Parties to marriage; names; procedure for change of name

(a) Parties to a marriage shall not be required to have the same name. Neither party shall be required to change his or her name. A person's name shall not change upon marriage unless that person elects to change his or her name pursuant to subdivision (b).

(b)(1) One party or both parties to a marriage may elect to change the middle or last names, or both, by which that party wishes to be known after solemnization of the marriage by entering the new name in the spaces provided on the marriage license application without intent to defraud.

(2) A person may adopt any of the following last names pursuant to paragraph (1):

(A) The current last name of the other spouse.

(B) The last name of either spouse given at birth.

(C) A name combining into a single last name all or a segment of the current last name or the last name of either spouse given at birth.

(D) A combination of last names.

(3) A person may adopt any of the following middle names pursuant to paragraph (1):

(A) The current last name of either spouse.

(B) The last name of either spouse given at birth.

(C) A combination of the current middle name and the current last name of the person or spouse.

(D) A combination of the current middle name and the last name given at birth of the person or spouse.

(4)(A) An election by a person to change his or her name pursuant to paragraph (1) shall serve as a record of the name change. A certified copy of a marriage certificate containing the new name, or retaining the former name, shall constitute proof that the use of the new name or retention of the former name is lawful.

(B) A certified copy of a marriage certificate shall be accepted as identification establishing a true, full name for purposes of Section 12800.7 of the Vehicle Code.

(C) Nothing in this section shall be construed to prohibit the Department of Motor Vehicles from accepting as identification other documents establishing a true, full name for purposes of Section 12800.7 of the Vehicle Code. Those documents may include, without limitation, a certified copy of a marriage certificate recording a marriage outside of this state.

(D) This section shall be applied in a manner consistent with the requirements of Sections 1653.5 and 12801 of the Vehicle Code.

(5) The adoption of a new name, or the choice not to adopt a new name, by means of a marriage license application pursuant to paragraph (1) shall only be made at the time the marriage license is issued. After a marriage certificate is registered by the local registrar, the certificate shall not be amended to add a new name or change the name adopted pursuant to paragraph (1). An amendment may be issued to correct a clerical error in the new name fields on the marriage license. In this instance, the amendment shall be signed by one of the parties to the marriage and the county clerk or his or her deputy, and the reason for the amendment shall be stated as correcting a clerical error. A clerical error as used in this part is an error made by the county clerk, his or her deputy, or a notary authorized to issue confidential marriage licenses, whereby the information shown in the new name field does not match the information shown on the marriage license application. This requirement shall not abrogate the right of either party to adopt a different name through usage at a future date, or to petition the superior court for a change of name pursuant to Title 8 (commencing with Section 1275) of Part 3 of the Code of Civil Procedure.

(c) Nothing in this section shall be construed to abrogate the common law right of any person to change his or her name, or the right of any person to petition the superior court for a change of name pursuant to Title 8 (commencing with Section 1275) of Part 3 of the Code of Civil Procedure. *(Added by Stats.2007, c. 567 (A.B.102), § 7, operative Jan. 1, 2009. Amended by Stats.2009, c. 512 (A.B.1143), § 1; Stats. 2016, c. 474 (A.B.2882), § 3, eff. Jan. 1, 2017.)*

Research References

Forms

West's California Code Forms, Family § 350, Comment Overview--Marriage License and Certificate Of Registry.

West's California Code Forms, Family § 351 Form 1, Marriage License Application.

Treatises and Practice Aids

Witkin, California Summary 10th Husband and Wife § 42, in General.

Witkin, California Summary 10th Husband and Wife § 45, License.

Witkin, California Summary 10th Personal Property § 25A, (New) Right to Maintain or Change Name Following Marriage or Domestic Partnership Registration.

§ 307. Marriage of members of religious society or denomination; requirements

This division, so far as it relates to the solemnizing of marriage, is not applicable to members of a particular religious society or denomination not having clergy for the purpose of solemnizing marriage or entering the marriage relation, if all of the following requirements are met:

(a) The parties to the marriage sign and endorse on the form prescribed by the State Department of Public Health, showing all of the following:

(1) The fact, time, and place of entering into the marriage.

(2) The printed names, signatures, and mailing addresses of two witnesses to the ceremony.

(3) The religious society or denomination of the parties to the marriage, and that the marriage was entered into in accordance with the rules and customs of that religious society or denomination. The statement of the parties to the marriage that the marriage was entered into in accordance with the rules and customs of the religious society or denomination is conclusively presumed to be true.

(b) The License and Certificate of Non–Clergy Marriage, endorsed pursuant to subdivision (a), is returned to the county recorder of the county in which the license was issued within 10 days after the ceremony. *(Stats.1992, c. 162 (A.B.2650), § 10, operative Jan. 1, 1994. Amended by Stats. 1993, c. 219 (A.B.1500), § 90; Stats.2006, c. 816 (A.B.1102), § 5, operative Jan. 1, 2008; Stats.2007, c. 483 (S.B.1039), § 9.)*

Law Revision Commission Comments

Enactment [Revised Comment]

Section 307 continues former Civil Code Section 4216 without substantive change. In the introductory part of this section, a reference to this division has been substituted for the narrower reference to "this article" in former law. This is not a substantive change, since the former article contained the sections relating to solemnization that are continued in this division. [23 Cal.L.Rev. Comm. Reports 1 (1993)].

Research References

Forms

West's California Code Forms, Family § 400, Comment Overview--Solemnize Marriage.

Treatises and Practice Aids

Witkin, California Summary 10th Husband and Wife § 42, in General.

Witkin, California Summary 10th Husband and Wife § 47, Solemnization.

§ 308. Validity of foreign marriages

A marriage contracted outside this state that would be valid by laws of the jurisdiction in which the marriage was contracted is valid in California. *(Added by Stats.2014, c. 82 (S.B.1306), § 6, eff. Jan. 1, 2015. Amended by Stats.2016, c. 474 (A.B.2882), § 4, eff. Jan. 1, 2017.)*

Research References

Forms

California Transactions Forms--Family Law § 4:65, Effect Of Valid Marriage.

Treatises and Practice Aids

Witkin, California Summary 10th Constitutional Law § 226A, (New) Historical Development.
Witkin, California Summary 10th Constitutional Law § 226B, (New) Constitutional and Statutory Amendments.
Witkin, California Summary 10th Husband and Wife § 51, Valid Marriage Evading Law Of Domicile.
Witkin, California Summary 10th Husband and Wife § 68, in General.

§ 309. Action to test validity of marriage

If either party to a marriage denies the marriage, or refuses to join in a declaration of the marriage, the other party may proceed, by action pursuant to Section 103450 of the Health and Safety Code, to have the validity of the marriage determined and declared. *(Stats.1992, c. 162 (A.B.2650), § 10, operative Jan. 1, 1994. Amended by Stats.2006, c. 816 (A.B.1102), § 6, operative Jan. 1, 2008.)*

Law Revision Commission Comments

Enactment [Revised Comment]

Section 309 continues former Civil Code Section 4212 without substantive change. The reference to the "superior" court has been omitted as surplus. See Section 200 (jurisdiction in superior court). See also Prob. Code § 1901 (determination of conservatee's capacity to marry). [23 Cal.L.Rev.Comm. Reports 1 (1993)].

Commentary

See, for example, *In re Marriage of Smyklo, 180 Cal.App.3d 1095, 226 Cal.Rptr. 174 (1986)* (Section 309 action brought by California resident to establish the validity of an Alabama common law marriage entered many years earlier). A Section 309 action may be brought by one of the spouses at any time during their joint lives. *Stierlen v. Stierlen, 6 Cal.App. 420, 424, 92 P. 329 (1907)*. Laches is not a defense. *Smyklo*, supra, 180 Cal.App.3d at 1100.

Research References

Forms

West's California Code Forms, Family § 309, Comment Overview-- Action to Test Validity Of Marriage.
West's California Code Forms, Family § 309 Form 2, Judgment Establishing Validity Of Marriage.

Treatises and Practice Aids

Witkin, California Summary 10th Husband and Wife § 42, in General.
Witkin, California Summary 10th Wills and Probate § 958, Capacity to Marry.

§ 310. Methods of dissolution

Marriage is dissolved only by one of the following:

(a) The death of one of the parties.

(b) A judgment of dissolution of marriage.

(c) A judgment of nullity of marriage. *(Stats.1992, c. 162 (A.B.2650), § 10, operative Jan. 1, 1994.)*

Law Revision Commission Comments

Enactment [Revised Comment]

Section 310 continues former Civil Code Section 4350 without substantive change. In subdivision (b), the phrase "of a court of competent jurisdiction" has been omitted as surplus. The reference to "decree" has been omitted as surplus. See Section 100 ("judgment" includes decree, as appropriate). See also Section 2344 (effect of death of either party after entry of judgment of dissolution). [23 Cal.L.Rev.Comm. Reports 1 (1993)].

Research References

Treatises and Practice Aids

Witkin, California Summary 10th Husband and Wife § 42, in General.

Part 2

MARRIAGE LICENSE

§ 350. Necessity of license; armed forces members serving overseas in conflict or war; appearance of attorney-in-fact

(a) Before entering a marriage, or declaring a marriage pursuant to Section 425, the parties shall first obtain a marriage license from a county clerk.

(b) If a marriage is to be entered into pursuant to subdivision (b) of Section 420, the attorney-in-fact shall appear before the county clerk on behalf of the party who is overseas, as prescribed in subdivision (a). *(Stats.1992, c. 162 (A.B.2650), § 10, operative Jan. 1, 1994. Amended by Stats. 2004, c. 476 (S.B.7), § 1, eff. Sept. 10, 2004.)*

Law Revision Commission Comments

Enactment [Revised Comment]

Section 350 continues the first part of former Civil Code Section 4201(a) without substantive change. [23 Cal.L.Rev.Comm. Reports (1993)].

Research References

Forms

West's California Code Forms, Family § 350, Comment Overview--Marriage License and Certificate Of Registry.

Treatises and Practice Aids

Witkin, California Summary 10th Husband and Wife § 45, License.

§ 351. Contents of license

The marriage license shall show all of the following:

(a) The identity of the parties to the marriage.

(b) The parties' full given names at birth or by court order, and mailing addresses.

(c) The parties' dates of birth. *(Stats.1992, c. 162 (A.B. 2650), § 10, operative Jan. 1, 1994. Amended by Stats.2006, c. 816 (A.B.1102), § 8, operative Jan. 1, 2008.)*

Law Revision Commission Comments

Enactment [Revised Comment]

Section 351 continues the last part of former Civil Code Section 4201(a) without substantive change. [23 Cal.L.Rev.Comm. Reports 1 (1993)].

Research References

Forms

West's California Code Forms, Family § 350, Comment Overview--Marriage License and Certificate Of Registry.

Treatises and Practice Aids

Witkin, California Summary 10th Husband and Wife § 45, License.

§ 351.5. Certificate of registry and marriage license; address information

Notwithstanding subdivision (b) of Section 351 or 359 of this code, or Section 103175 of the Health and Safety Code, if either of the applicants for, or any witness to, a certificate of registry of marriage and a marriage license requests, the certificate of registry and the marriage license shall show the business address or United States Postal Service post office box for that applicant or witness instead of the residential address of that person. *(Added by Stats.2006, c. 60 (S.B. 1364), § 1.)*

Research References

Treatises and Practice Aids

Witkin, California Summary 10th Husband and Wife § 42, in General.

§ 351.6. Mailing address

Notwithstanding Section 307, 351, 351.5, 359, or 422 of this code, or Section 103175 or 103180 of the Health and Safety Code, a mailing address used by an applicant, witness, or person solemnizing or performing the marriage ceremony shall be a residential address, a business address, or a United States Postal Service post office box. *(Added by Stats.2006, c. 816 (A.B.1102), § 8.5, operative Jan. 1, 2007.)*

Operative Effect

For operative effect of Stats.2006, c. 816 (A.B.1102), see § 55 of that act.

Research References

Treatises and Practice Aids

Witkin, California Summary 10th Husband and Wife § 42, in General.

§ 352. Grounds for denial of license

No marriage license shall be granted if either of the applicants lacks the capacity to enter into a valid marriage or is, at the time of making the application for the license, under the influence of an intoxicating liquor or narcotic drug. *(Stats.1992, c. 162 (A.B.2650), § 10, operative Jan. 1, 1994.)*

Law Revision Commission Comments

Enactment [Revised Comment]

Section 352 continues the first sentence of former Civil Code Section 4201(b) without substantive change. The phrase "lacks the capacity to enter into a valid marriage" has been substituted for "is an imbecile, is insane." This revision is consistent with Probate Code Section 1901 (determination of conservatee's capacity to marry). [23 Cal.L.Rev.Comm. Reports 1 (1993)].

Research References

Treatises and Practice Aids

Witkin, California Summary 10th Husband and Wife § 45, License.

§ 354. Identification; examination of applicants; additional documentary proof; armed forces members serving overseas in war or conflict; compliance by attorney-in-fact

(a) Each applicant for a marriage license shall be required to present authentic photo identification acceptable to the county clerk as to name and date of birth. A credible witness affidavit or affidavits may be used in lieu of authentic photo identification.

(b) For the purpose of ascertaining the facts mentioned or required in this part, if the clerk deems it necessary, the clerk may examine the applicants for a marriage license on oath at the time of the application. The clerk shall reduce the examination to writing and the applicants shall sign it.

(c) If necessary, the clerk may request additional documentary proof as to the accuracy of the facts stated.

(d) Applicants for a marriage license shall not be required to state, for any purpose, their race or color.

(e) If a marriage is to be entered into pursuant to subdivision (b) of Section 420, the attorney in fact shall comply with the requirements of this section on behalf of the applicant who is overseas, if necessary. *(Stats.1992, c. 162 (A.B.2650), § 10, operative Jan. 1, 1994. Amended by Stats. 2004, c. 476 (S.B.7), § 2, eff. Sept. 10, 2004; Stats.2006, c. 816 (A.B.1102), § 10, operative Jan. 1, 2008.)*

Law Revision Commission Comments

Enactment [Revised Comment]

Section 354 restates without substantive change the third, fourth, and fifth sentences of former Civil Code Section 4201(b). In subdivision (b), the phrase "the applicants shall sign it" has been substituted for "subscribed by them." [23 Cal.L.Rev.Comm. Reports 1 (1993)].

Research References

Treatises and Practice Aids

Witkin, California Summary 10th Constitutional Law § 747, Anti-Miscegenation Law.

Witkin, California Summary 10th Husband and Wife § 45, License.

§ 355. Forms

(a) The forms for the marriage license shall be prescribed by the State Department of Public Health, and shall be adapted to set forth the facts required in this part.

(b) The marriage license shall include an affidavit, which the applicants shall sign, affirming that they have received the brochure provided for in Section 358. If the marriage is to be entered into pursuant to subdivision (b) of Section 420, the attorney in fact shall sign the affidavit on behalf of the applicant who is overseas.

(c) The forms for the marriage license shall contain spaces for either party or both parties to indicate a change in name pursuant to Section 306.5. *(Stats.1992, c. 162 (A.B.2650), § 10, operative Jan. 1, 1994. Amended by Stats.2004, c. 476 (S.B.7), § 3, eff. Sept. 10, 2004; Stats.2006, c. 816 (A.B.1102), § 11, operative Jan. 1, 2008; Stats.2007, c. 483 (S.B.1039), § 10; Stats.2007, c. 567 (A.B.102), § 8, operative Jan. 1, 2009.)*

Law Revision Commission Comments

Enactment [Revised Comment]

Section 355 continues former Civil Code Section 4201(c)-(d) without substantive change. In subdivision (b), "applicants" has been substituted for "bride and groom" for consistency with other sections in this part. See, e.g., Sections 352, 354. [23 Cal.L.Rev. Comm. Reports 1 (1993)].

Research References

Forms

West's California Code Forms, Family § 350, Comment Overview--Marriage License and Certificate Of Registry.

Treatises and Practice Aids

Witkin, California Summary 10th Husband and Wife § 45, License.

§ 356. Expiration of license

A marriage license issued pursuant to this part expires 90 days after its issuance. The calendar date of expiration shall be clearly noted on the face of the license. *(Stats.1992, c. 162 (A.B.2650), § 10, operative Jan. 1, 1994.)*

Law Revision Commission Comments

Enactment [Revised Comment]

Section 356 continues the first sentence of former Civil Code Section 4204 without substantive change. [23 Cal.L.Rev.Comm. Reports 1 (1993)].

Research References

Forms

West's California Code Forms, Family § 350, Comment Overview--Marriage License and Certificate Of Registry.

Treatises and Practice Aids

Witkin, California Summary 10th Husband and Wife § 45, License.

§ 357. Numbering of licenses; transmittal of list of issued licenses; notice of expiration of license

(a) The county clerk shall number each marriage license issued and shall transmit at periodic intervals to the county recorder a list or copies of the licenses issued.

(b) Not later than 60 days after the date of issuance, the county recorder shall notify licenseholders whose marriage license has not been returned of that fact and that the marriage license will automatically expire on the date shown on its face.

(c) The county recorder shall notify the licenseholders of the obligation of the person solemnizing their marriage to return the marriage license to the recorder's office within 10 days after the ceremony. *(Stats.1992, c. 162 (A.B.2650), § 10, operative Jan. 1, 1994. Amended by Stats.1993, c. 219 (A.B.1500), § 91; Stats.2001, c. 39 (A.B.1323), § 1; Stats. 2006, c. 816 (A.B.1102), § 12, operative Jan. 1, 2008.)*

Law Revision Commission Comments

Enactment [Revised Comment]

Section 357 restates without substantive change the second paragraph of former Civil Code Section 4204. In subdivision (c), the phrase "person solemnizing their marriage" has been substituted for "person marrying them" to conform with other sections in this division. See, e.g., Section 420. [23 Cal.L.Rev.Comm. Reports 1 (1993)].

Research References

Treatises and Practice Aids

Witkin, California Summary 10th Husband and Wife § 45, License.

Witkin, California Summary 10th Husband and Wife § 46, Certificate Of Registry.

§ 358. Informational brochure; preparation and publication; contents

(a) The State Department of Public Health shall prepare and publish a brochure that shall contain the following:

(1) Information concerning the possibilities of genetic defects and diseases and a listing of centers available for the testing and treatment of genetic defects and diseases.

(2) Information concerning acquired immunodeficiency syndrome (AIDS) and the availability of testing for antibodies to the probable causative agent of AIDS.

(3) Information concerning domestic violence, including resources available to victims and a statement that physical, emotional, psychological, and sexual abuse, and assault and battery, are against the law.

(4) Information concerning options for changing a name upon solemnization of marriage pursuant to Section 306.5, or upon registration of a domestic partnership pursuant to Section 298.6. That information shall include a notice that the recording of a change in name or the absence of a change in name on a marriage license application and certificate pursuant to Section 306.5 may not be amended once the marriage license is issued, but that options to adopt a change in name in the future through usage, common law, or petitioning the superior court are preserved, as set forth in Section 306.5.

(b) The State Department of Public Health shall make the brochures available to county clerks who shall distribute a copy of the brochure to each applicant for a marriage license, including applicants for a confidential marriage license and notaries public receiving a confidential marriage license pursuant to Section 503. The department shall also make the brochure available to the Secretary of State, who shall distribute a copy of the brochure to persons who qualify as domestic partners pursuant to Section 297 and shall make the brochure available electronically on the Internet Web site of the Secretary of State.

(c) The department shall prepare a lesbian, gay, bisexual, and transgender specific domestic abuse brochure and make the brochure available to the Secretary of State who shall print and make available the brochure, as funding allows, pursuant to Section 298.5.

(d) Each notary public issuing a confidential marriage license under Section 503 shall distribute a copy of the brochure to the applicants for a confidential marriage license.

(e) To the extent possible, the State Department of Public Health shall seek to combine in a single brochure all statutorily required information for marriage license applicants. *(Stats.1992, c. 162 (A.B.2650), § 10, operative Jan. 1, 1994. Amended by Stats.1996, c. 1075 (S.B.1444), § 8; Stats.2006, c. 816 (A.B.1102), § 13; Stats.2006, c. 856 (A.B. 2051), § 4.5; Stats.2007, c. 483 (S.B.1039), § 11; Stats.2007, c. 567 (A.B.102), § 9.)*

Law Revision Commission Comments

Enactment [Revised Comment]

Section 358 continues former Civil Code Section 4201.5 without substantive change. In subdivision (c), a reference to Section 503 has been substituted for the broader reference to former Civil Code Section 4213. This is not a substantive change, since the relevant part of the former section is continued in Section 503. [23 Cal.L.Rev.Comm. 1 (1993)].

Research References

Forms

West's California Code Forms, Family § 350, Comment Overview--Marriage License and Certificate Of Registry.

Treatises and Practice Aids

Witkin, California Summary 10th Husband and Wife § 28, Registration Procedure.

Witkin, California Summary 10th Husband and Wife § 45, License.

§ 359. Marriage license; completion and return to county recorder

(a) Except as provided in Sections 420 and 426, applicants to be married shall first appear together in person before the county clerk to obtain a marriage license.

(b) The contents of the marriage license are provided in Part 1 (commencing with Section 102100) of Division 102 of the Health and Safety Code.

(c) The issued marriage license shall be presented to the person solemnizing the marriage by the parties to be married.

(d) The person solemnizing the marriage shall complete the solemnization sections on the marriage license, and shall cause to be entered on the marriage license the printed name, signature, and mailing address of at least one, and no more than two, witnesses to the marriage ceremony.

(e) The marriage license shall be returned by the person solemnizing the marriage to the county recorder of the county in which the license was issued within 10 days after the ceremony.

(f) As used in this division, "returned" means presented to the appropriate person in person, or postmarked, before the expiration of the specified time period. *(Stats.1992, c. 162 (A.B.2650), § 10, operative Jan. 1, 1994. Amended by Stats. 1993, c. 219 (A.B.1500), § 92; Stats.1996, c. 1023 (S.B.1497), § 44, eff. Sept. 29, 1996; Stats.2001, c. 39 (A.B.1323), § 2; Stats.2006, c. 816 (A.B.1102), § 14, operative Jan. 1, 2008.)*

Law Revision Commission Comments

Enactment [Revised Comment]

Section 359 restates former Civil Code Section 4202 without substantive change. The phrase "person solemnizing the marriage" has been substituted for "person performing the ceremony" throughout this section for consistency with other sections in this division. See, e.g., Section 420. [23 Cal.L.Rev.Comm. Reports 1 (1993)].

Research References

Forms

West's California Code Forms, Family § 350, Comment Overview--Marriage License and Certificate Of Registry.

Treatises and Practice Aids

Witkin, California Summary 10th Husband and Wife § 45, License.

Witkin, California Summary 10th Husband and Wife § 46, Certificate Of Registry.

Witkin, California Summary 10th Husband and Wife § 47, Solemnization.

§ 360. Duplicate marriage license; affidavit; issuance; fee; licenses lost, damaged, or destroyed before marriage ceremony

(a) If a marriage license is lost, damaged, or destroyed after the marriage ceremony, but before it is returned to the county recorder, or deemed unacceptable for registration by the county recorder, the person solemnizing the marriage, in order to comply with Section 359, shall obtain a duplicate marriage license by filing an affidavit setting forth the facts with the county clerk of the county in which the license was issued.

(b) The duplicate marriage license shall not be issued later than one year after the date of marriage and shall be returned by the person solemnizing the marriage to the county recorder within one year of the date of marriage.

(c) The county clerk may charge a fee to cover the actual costs of issuing a duplicate marriage license.

(d) If a marriage license is lost, damaged, or destroyed before a marriage ceremony takes place, the applicants shall purchase a new marriage license and the old license shall be voided. *(Stats.1992, c. 162 (A.B.2650), § 10, operative Jan. 1, 1994. Amended by Stats.1993, c. 219 (A.B.1500), § 93; Stats.2001, c. 39 (A.B.1323), § 3; Stats.2006, c. 816 (A.B. 1102), § 15, operative Jan. 1, 2008; Stats.2016, c. 474 (A.B. 2882), § 5, eff. Jan. 1, 2017.)*

Law Revision Commission Comments

Enactment [Revised Comment]

Section 360 restates former Civil Code Section 4203 without substantive change. [23 Cal.L.Rev.Comm. Reports 1 (1993)].

Research References

Treatises and Practice Aids

Witkin, California Summary 10th Husband and Wife § 45, License.
Witkin, California Summary 10th Husband and Wife § 46, Certificate Of Registry.

Part 3

SOLEMNIZATION OF MARRIAGE

CHAPTER 1. PERSONS AUTHORIZED TO SOLEMNIZE MARRIAGE

§ 400. Authorized persons; refusal to solemnize marriage; tax-exempt status

(a) Although marriage is a personal relation arising out of a civil, and not a religious, contract, a marriage may be solemnized by a priest, minister, rabbi, or authorized person of any religious denomination who is 18 years of age or older. A person authorized by this subdivision shall not be required to solemnize a marriage that is contrary to the tenets of his or her faith. Any refusal to solemnize a marriage under this subdivision, either by an individual or by a religious denomination, shall not affect the tax-exempt status of any entity.

(b) Consistent with Section 94.5 of the Penal Code and provided that any compensation received is reasonable, including payment of actual expenses, a marriage may also be solemnized by any of the following persons:

(1) A judge or retired judge, commissioner of civil marriages or retired commissioner of civil marriages, commissioner or retired commissioner, or assistant commissioner of a court of record in this state.

(2) A judge or magistrate who has resigned from office.

(3) Any of the following judges or magistrates of the United States:

(A) A justice or retired justice of the United States Supreme Court.

(B) A judge or retired judge of a court of appeals, a district court, or a court created by an act of the United States Congress the judges of which are entitled to hold office during good behavior.

(C) A judge or retired judge of a bankruptcy court or a tax court.

(D) A United States magistrate or retired magistrate.

(c) Except as provided in subdivision (d), a marriage may also be solemnized by any of the following persons who are 18 years of age or older:

(1) A Member of the Legislature or constitutional officer of this state or a Member of Congress of the United States who represents a district within this state, or a former Member of the Legislature or constitutional officer of this state or a former Member of Congress of the United States who represented a district within this state.

(2) A person that holds or formerly held an elected office of a city, county, or city and county.

(3) A city clerk of a charter city or serving in accordance with subdivision (b) of Section 36501 of the Government Code, while that person holds office.

(d)(1) A person listed in subdivision (c) shall not accept compensation for solemnizing a marriage while holding office.

(2) A person listed in subdivision (c) shall not solemnize a marriage pursuant to this section if they have been removed from office due to committing an offense or have been convicted of an offense that involves moral turpitude, dishonesty, or fraud. *(Stats.1992, c. 162 (A.B.2650), § 10, operative Jan. 1, 1994. Amended by Stats.1998, c. 931 (S.B.2139), § 142, eff. Sept. 28, 1998; Stats.1998, c. 932 (A.B.1094), § 31.5, operative Jan. 1, 1999; Stats.2006, c. 816 (A.B.1102), § 16, operative Jan. 1, 2008; Stats.2012, c. 834 (S.B.1140), § 1; Stats.2016, c. 211 (S.B.875), § 1, eff. Jan. 1, 2017; Stats.2016, c. 528 (A.B.2761), § 1, eff. Jan. 1, 2017; Stats.2017, c. 42 (A.B.430), § 1, eff. July 10, 2017.)*

Law Revision Commission Comments

Enactment [Revised Comment]

Section 400 restates former Civil Code Section 4205 without substantive change. See also Section 402 (official of nonprofit religious institution licensed by county to solemnize marriages). [23 Cal.L.Rev.Comm. Reports 1 (1993)].

1998 Amendment

Section 400 is amended to reflect elimination of the justice court. Cal. Const. art. VI, §§ 1, 5(b). [28 Cal.L.Rev.Comm. Reports 51 (1998)].

Research References

Forms

West's California Code Forms, Family § 400, Comment Overview--Solemnize Marriage.

Treatises and Practice Aids

Witkin, California Summary 10th Husband and Wife § 47, Solemnization.
Witkin, California Summary 10th Husband and Wife § 48, Confidential Marriage.

§ 401. Commissioner of civil marriages; designation of county clerk; deputies

(a) For each county, the county clerk is designated as a commissioner of civil marriages.

(b) The commissioner of civil marriages may appoint deputy commissioners of civil marriages who may solemnize marriages under the direction of the commissioner of civil marriages and shall perform other duties directed by the commissioner. *(Stats.1992, c. 162 (A.B.2650), § 10, operative Jan. 1, 1994.)*

Law Revision Commission Comments

Enactment [Revised Comment]

Section 401 continues former Civil Code Section 4205.1 without substantive change. [23 Cal.L.Rev.Comm. Reports 1 (1993)].

Research References

Treatises and Practice Aids

Witkin, California Summary 10th Husband and Wife § 47, Solemnization.

§ 402. Officials of nonprofit religious institutions

In addition to the persons permitted to solemnize marriages under Section 400, a county may license officials of a nonprofit religious institution, whose articles of incorporation are registered with the Secretary of State, to solemnize the marriages of persons who are affiliated with or are members of the religious institution. The licensee shall possess the degree of doctor of philosophy and must perform religious services or rites for the institution on a regular basis. The marriages shall be performed without fee to the parties. *(Stats.1992, c. 162 (A.B.2650), § 10, operative Jan. 1, 1994.)*

Law Revision Commission Comments

Enactment [Revised Comment]

Section 402 continues former Civil Code Section 4205.5 without substantive change. [23 Cal.L.Rev.Comm. Reports 1 (1993)].

Research References

Treatises and Practice Aids

Witkin, California Summary 10th Husband and Wife § 47, Solemnization.

CHAPTER 2. SOLEMNIZATION OF MARRIAGE

§ 420. Requirements for solemnization; appearance by attorney-in-fact on behalf of armed forces member serving overseas in conflict or war

(a) No particular form for the ceremony of marriage is required for solemnization of the marriage, but the parties shall declare, in the physical presence of the person solemnizing the marriage and necessary witnesses, that they take each other as spouses.

(b) Notwithstanding subdivision (a), a member of the Armed Forces of the United States who is stationed overseas and serving in a conflict or a war and is unable to appear for the licensure and solemnization of the marriage may enter into that marriage by the appearance of an attorney in fact, commissioned and empowered in writing for that purpose through a power of attorney. The attorney in fact shall personally appear at the county clerk's office with the party who is not stationed overseas and present the original power of attorney duly signed by the party stationed overseas and acknowledged before a notary or witnessed by two officers of the United States Armed Forces. Copies in any form, including by facsimile, are not acceptable. The power of attorney shall state the full given names at birth, or by court order, of the parties to be married, and that the power of attorney is solely for the purpose of authorizing the attorney in fact to obtain a marriage license on the person's behalf and participate in the solemnization of the marriage. The original power of attorney shall be a part of the marriage certificate upon registration. The completion of a power of attorney shall be the sole determinant as to whether the county clerk's office and the State Registrar will accept the power of attorney.

(c) A contract of marriage, if otherwise duly made, shall not be invalidated for want of conformity to the requirements of any religious sect. *(Stats.1992, c. 162 (A.B.2650), § 10, operative Jan. 1, 1994. Amended by Stats.1993, c. 219 (A.B.1500), § 94; Stats.2004, c. 476 (S.B.7), § 4, eff. Sept. 10, 2004; Stats.2005, c. 22 (S.B.1108), § 60; Stats.2006, c. 816 (A.B.1102), § 17, operative Jan. 1, 2008; Stats.2014, c. 82 (S.B.1306), § 8, eff. Jan. 1, 2015; Stats.2016, c. 130 (A.B. 2128), § 1, eff. Jan. 1, 2017.)*

Law Revision Commission Comments

Enactment [Revised Comment]

Subdivision (a) of Section 420 continues former Civil Code Section 4206 without substantive change. Subdivision (b) continues former Civil Code Section 4206.5 without substantive change. [23 Cal. L.Rev.Comm. Reports 1 (1993)].

Commentary

See Section 306, Commentary.

Research References

Treatises and Practice Aids

Witkin, California Summary 10th Husband and Wife § 17, Vital Statistics.

Witkin, California Summary 10th Husband and Wife § 42, in General.

Witkin, California Summary 10th Husband and Wife § 45, License.

Witkin, California Summary 10th Husband and Wife § 47, Solemnization.

§ 421. Duties of persons solemnizing marriage

Before solemnizing a marriage, the person solemnizing the marriage shall require the presentation of the marriage license. If the person solemnizing the marriage has reason to doubt the correctness of the statement of facts in the marriage license, the person must be satisfied as to the correctness of the statement of facts before solemnizing the marriage. For this purpose, the person may administer oaths and examine the parties and witnesses in the same manner as the county clerk does before issuing the license. *(Stats.1992, c. 162 (A.B.2650), § 10, operative Jan. 1, 1994.)*

Law Revision Commission Comments

Enactment [Revised Comment]

Section 421 restates former Civil Code Section 4207 without substantive change. [23 Cal.L.Rev.Comm. Reports 1 (1993)].

Research References

Treatises and Practice Aids

Witkin, California Summary 10th Husband and Wife § 47, Solemnization.

§ 422. License; statement of person solemnizing marriage

The person solemnizing a marriage shall, sign and print or type upon the marriage license a statement, in the form prescribed by the State Department of Public Health, showing all of the following:

(a) The fact, date (month, day, year), and place (city and county) of solemnization.

(b) The printed names, signatures, and mailing addresses of at least one, and no more than two, witnesses to the ceremony.

(c) The official position of the person solemnizing the marriage, or of the denomination of which that person is a priest, minister, rabbi, or other authorized person of any religious denomination.

(d) The person solemnizing the marriage shall also type or print his or her name and mailing address. *(Stats.1992, c. 162 (A.B.2650), § 10, operative Jan. 1, 1994. Amended by Stats. 1993, c. 219 (A.B.1500), § 95; Stats.2006, c. 816 (A.B.1102), § 18, operative Jan. 1, 2008; Stats.2007, c. 483 (S.B.1039), § 12.)*

Law Revision Commission Comments

Enactment [Revised Comment]

Section 422 continues former Civil Code Section 4208(a) without substantive change. The reference to "rabbi" has been added to subdivision (c) for consistency with Section 400 (persons authorized to solemnize). [23 Cal.L.Rev.Comm. Reports 1 (1993)].

Research References

Forms

West's California Code Forms, Family § 350, Comment Overview--Marriage License and Certificate Of Registry.

West's California Code Forms, Family § 400, Comment Overview--Solemnize Marriage.

Treatises and Practice Aids

Witkin, California Summary 10th Husband and Wife § 47, Solemnization.

§ 423. Return of license

The person solemnizing the marriage shall return the marriage license, endorsed as required in Section 422, to the county recorder of the county in which the license was issued within 10 days after the ceremony. *(Stats.1992, c. 162 (A.B.2650), § 10, operative Jan. 1, 1994. Amended by Stats. 1993, c. 219 (A.B.1500), § 96; Stats.2001, c. 39 (A.B.1323), § 4.)*

Law Revision Commission Comments

Enactment [Revised Comment]

Section 423 continues former Civil Code Section 4208(b) without substantive change. [23 Cal.L.Rev.Comm. Reports 1 (1993)].

Research References

Treatises and Practice Aids

Witkin, California Summary 10th Husband and Wife § 47, Solemnization.

§ 425. Unrecorded marriage; license and certificate of declaration of marriage; filing

If no record of the solemnization of a California marriage previously contracted under this division for that marriage is known to exist, the parties may purchase a License and Certificate of Declaration of Marriage from the county clerk in the parties' county of residence one year or more from the date of the marriage. The license and certificate shall be returned to the county recorder of the county in which the license was issued. *(Stats.1992, c. 162 (A.B.2650), § 10, operative Jan. 1, 1994. Amended by Stats.1993, c. 219 (A.B.1500), § 97; Stats.2006, c. 816 (A.B.1102), § 20, operative Jan. 1, 2008.)*

Law Revision Commission Comments

Enactment [Revised Comment]

Section 425 continues former Civil Code Section 4210 without substantive change. In the last sentence of this section, the phrase "returned to the county recorder of the county in which the license was issued" has been substituted for "returned in the manner specified in subdivision (b) of Section 4216." Section 307(b) (continuing former Civil Code Section 4216(b)) requires the filing within thirty days after the ceremony. This requirement is not relevant to a "previously contracted" marriage under Section 425. [23 Cal.L.Rev.Comm. Reports 1 (1993)].

Commentary

Estate of DePasse, 97 Cal.App.4th 92, 118 Cal.Rptr.2d 143 (2002), review denied June 26, 2002, held that issuance of a marriage license is a mandatory requirement for a valid marriage in California. The claimed marriage found invalid in *DePasse* was a deathbed marriage conducted by a hospital chaplain without a license, because there was insufficient time to obtain one. *DePasse* further held that this section may not be used the cure the absence of a marriage license when one spouse is already deceased, and that the surviving spouse was not a putative spouse because he knew of the license requirement and thus had no objectively reasonable belief that the had contracted a valid marriage. For further discussion of putative marriage, see Commentary to Section 2551.

By contrast, *In re Marriage of Cantarella, 191 Cal.App.4th 916, 119 Cal.Rptr.3d 829 (2011)*, interpreting the Family Law Act (FLA — former Civil Code § 4000 et seq.), held that a couple's 1991 duly licensed and ceremonialized marriage was valid even though the couple never registered the certificate of marriage.

Research References

Forms

West's California Code Forms, Family § 309, Comment Overview--Action to Test Validity Of Marriage.

West's California Code Forms, Family § 400, Comment Overview--Solemnize Marriage.

West's California Code Forms, Family § 309 Form 1, Complaint to Establish Validity Of Marriage.

Treatises and Practice Aids

Witkin, California Summary 10th Husband and Wife § 42, in General.

Witkin, California Summary 10th Husband and Wife § 47, Solemnization.

§ 426. Physical inability of party to appear before clerk; issuance of license; requirements

If for sufficient reason, as described in subdivision (d), either or both of the parties to be married are physically unable to appear in person before the county clerk, a marriage license may be issued by the county clerk to the person solemnizing the marriage if the following requirements are met:

(a) The person solemnizing the marriage physically presents an affidavit to the county clerk explaining the reason for the inability to appear.

(b) The affidavit is signed under penalty of perjury by the person solemnizing the marriage and by both parties.

(c) The signature of any party to be married who is unable to appear in person before the county clerk is authenticated by a notary public or a court prior to the county clerk issuing the marriage license.

(d) Sufficient reason includes proof of hospitalization, incarceration, or any other reason proved to the satisfaction of the county clerk. *(Added by Stats.2006, c. 816 (A.B.1102), § 21, operative Jan. 1, 2008.)*

Research References

Treatises and Practice Aids

Witkin, California Summary 10th Husband and Wife § 45, License.
Witkin, California Summary 10th Husband and Wife § 47, Solemnization.

Part 4

CONFIDENTIAL MARRIAGE

CHAPTER 1. GENERAL PROVISIONS

§ 500. Unmarried persons who have been living together as spouses

When two unmarried people, not minors, have been living together as spouses, they may be married pursuant to this chapter by a person authorized to solemnize a marriage under Chapter 1 (commencing with Section 400) of Part 3. *(Stats.1992, c. 162 (A.B.2650), § 10, operative Jan. 1, 1994. Amended by Stats.2014, c. 82 (S.B.1306), § 9, eff. Jan. 1, 2015; Stats.2016, c. 474 (A.B.2882), § 6, eff. Jan. 1, 2017.)*

Law Revision Commission Comments

Enactment [Revised Comment]

Section 500 continues the first sentence of former Civil Code Section 4213(a) without substantive change. [23 Cal.L.Rev.Comm. Reports 1 (1993)].

Research References

Forms

West's California Code Forms, Family § 500, Comment Overview--Requirements for Confidential Marriages.

Treatises and Practice Aids

Witkin, California Summary 10th Husband and Wife § 42, in General.
Witkin, California Summary 10th Husband and Wife § 48, Confidential Marriage.

§ 500.5. Marriage license and marriage certificate

For purposes of this part, the document issued by the county clerk is a marriage license until it is registered with the county clerk, at which time the license becomes a marriage certificate. *(Added by Stats.2006, c. 816 (A.B.1102), § 22, operative Jan. 1, 2008.)*

Research References

Forms

West's California Code Forms, Family § 500, Comment Overview--Requirements for Confidential Marriages.

Treatises and Practice Aids

Witkin, California Summary 10th Husband and Wife § 48, Confidential Marriage.

§ 501. Issuance of license

Except as provided in Section 502, a confidential marriage license shall be issued by the county clerk upon the personal appearance together of the parties to be married and their payment of the fees required by Sections 26840.1 and 26840.8 of the Government Code and any fee imposed pursuant to the authorization of Section 26840.3 of the Government Code. *(Stats.1992, c. 162 (A.B.2650), § 10, operative Jan. 1, 1994. Amended by Stats.2006, c. 816 (A.B.1102), § 23, operative Jan. 1, 2008.)*

Law Revision Commission Comments

Enactment [Revised Comment]

Section 501 continues the second sentence of former Civil Code Section 4213(a) without substantive change. [23 Cal.L.Rev.Comm. Reports 1 (1993)].

Research References

Forms

West's California Code Forms, Family § 500, Comment Overview--Requirements for Confidential Marriages.

Treatises and Practice Aids

Witkin, California Summary 10th Husband and Wife § 48, Confidential Marriage.

§ 502. Inability to personally appear; issuance of license

If for sufficient reason, as described in subdivision (d), either or both of the parties to be married are physically unable to appear in person before the county clerk, a confidential marriage license may be issued by the county clerk to the person solemnizing the marriage if the following requirements are met:

(a) The person solemnizing the marriage physically presents an affidavit to the county clerk explaining the reason for the inability to appear.

(b) The affidavit is signed under penalty of perjury by the person solemnizing the marriage and by both parties.

(c) The signature of any party to be married who is unable to appear in person before the county clerk is authenticated by a notary public or a court prior to the county clerk issuing the confidential marriage license.

(d) Sufficient reason includes proof of hospitalization, incarceration, or any other reason proved to the satisfaction of the county clerk. *(Stats.1992, c. 162 (A.B.2650), § 10, operative Jan. 1, 1994. Amended by Stats.2006, c. 816 (A.B.1102), § 24, operative Jan. 1, 2008.)*

Law Revision Commission Comments

Enactment [Revised Comment]

Section 502 continues former Civil Code Section 4213.1 without substantive change. The phrase "person solemnizing the marriage" has been substituted for "person performing the ceremony" for consistency with other sections in this division. See, e.g., Section 420. [23 Cal.L.Rev.Comm. Reports 1 (1993)].

Research References

Forms

West's California Code Forms, Family § 500, Comment Overview--Requirements for Confidential Marriages.

Treatises and Practice Aids

Witkin, California Summary 10th Husband and Wife § 48, Confidential Marriage.

§ 503. Issuance of confidential marriage license upon request of notary public; fees

The county clerk shall issue a confidential marriage license upon the request of a notary public approved by the county clerk to issue confidential marriage licenses pursuant to Chapter 2 (commencing with Section 530) and upon payment by the notary public of the fees specified in Sections 26840.1 and 26840.8 of the Government Code. The parties shall reimburse a notary public who issues a confidential marriage license for the amount of the fees. *(Stats.1992, c. 162 (A.B.2650), § 10, operative Jan. 1, 1994. Amended by Stats. 2006, c. 816 (A.B.1102), § 25, operative Jan. 1, 2008.)*

Law Revision Commission Comments

Enactment [Revised Comment]

Section 503 continues the first two sentences of former Civil Code Section 4213(b) without substantive change. [23 Cal.L.Rev.Comm. Reports 1 (1993)].

Research References

Forms

West's California Code Forms, Family § 500, Comment Overview--Requirements for Confidential Marriages.

Treatises and Practice Aids

Witkin, California Summary 10th Husband and Wife § 48, Confidential Marriage.

§ 504. Duration of license

A confidential marriage license is valid only for a period of 90 days after its issuance by the county clerk. *(Stats.1992, c. 162 (A.B.2650), § 10, operative Jan. 1, 1994. Amended by Stats.2014, c. 913 (A.B.2747), § 16, eff. Jan. 1, 2015.)*

Law Revision Commission Comments

Enactment [Revised Comment]

Section 504 continues without substantive change the third sentence of subdivision (a) and the last sentence of former Civil Code Section 4213(b). [23 Cal.L.Rev.Comm. Reports 1 (1993)].

Research References

Forms

West's California Code Forms, Family § 500, Comment Overview--Requirements for Confidential Marriages.

Treatises and Practice Aids

Witkin, California Summary 10th Husband and Wife § 48, Confidential Marriage.

§ 505. Form of license; contents

(a) The form of the confidential marriage license shall be prescribed by the State Registrar of Vital Statistics.

(b) The form shall be designed to require that the parties to be married declare or affirm that they meet all of the requirements of this chapter.

(c) The form shall include an affidavit, which the bride and groom shall sign, affirming that they have received the brochure provided for in Section 358. *(Stats.1992, c. 162 (A.B.2650), § 10, operative Jan. 1, 1994. Amended by Stats. 2006, c. 816 (A.B.1102), § 26, operative Jan. 1, 2008.)*

Law Revision Commission Comments

Enactment [Revised Comment]

Section 505 continues without substantive change the last paragraph of subdivision (a) and all of subdivision (i) of former Civil Code Section 4213. In subdivision (c), the phrase "person solemnizing the marriage" has been substituted for "person performing the ceremony" for consistency with other sections in this division. See, e.g., Section 420. [23 Cal.L.Rev.Comm. Reports 1 (1993)].

Research References

Treatises and Practice Aids

Witkin, California Summary 10th Husband and Wife § 48, Confidential Marriage.

§ 506. Completion of license; filing

(a) The confidential marriage license shall be presented to the person solemnizing the marriage.

(b) Upon performance of the ceremony, the solemnization section on the confidential marriage license shall be completed by the person solemnizing the marriage.

(c) The confidential marriage license shall be returned by the person solemnizing the marriage to the office of the county clerk in the county in which the license was issued within 10 days after the ceremony. *(Stats.1992, c. 162 (A.B.2650), § 10, operative Jan. 1, 1994. Amended by Stats. 1993, c. 219 (A.B.1500), § 98; Stats.2001, c. 39 (A.B.1323), § 5; Stats.2006, c. 816 (A.B.1102), § 27, operative Jan. 1, 2008.)*

Law Revision Commission Comments

Enactment [Revised Comment]

Section 506 continues the fourth, fifth, and sixth sentences of former Civil Code Section 4213(a) without substantive change. The phrase "person solemnizing the marriage" has been substituted for "person performing the ceremony" throughout this section for consistency with other sections in this division. See, e.g., Section 420. The reference to "performance" of the ceremony has been omitted from subdivision (c) for consistency with Section 423 (return of license and statement to local registrar). [23 Cal.L.Rev.Comm. Reports 1 (1993)].

Research References

Forms

West's California Code Forms, Family § 500, Comment Overview--Requirements for Confidential Marriages.

Treatises and Practice Aids

Witkin, California Summary 10th Husband and Wife § 48, Confidential Marriage.

§ 508. Application to obtain certified copy of confidential marriage license

Upon issuance of a confidential marriage license, parties shall be provided with an application to obtain a certified copy of the confidential marriage certificate from the county clerk. *(Stats.1992, c. 162 (A.B.2650), § 10, operative Jan. 1, 1994. Amended by Stats.2001, c. 39 (A.B.1323), § 7; Stats. 2006, c. 816 (A.B.1102), § 28, operative Jan. 1, 2008.)*

Law Revision Commission Comments

Enactment [Revised Comment]

Section 508 continues without substantive change the last sentence of the second paragraph of former Civil Code Section 4213(a). The phrase "person solemnizing the marriage" has been substituted for "person performing the ceremony" for consistency with other sections in this division. See, e.g., Section 420. [23 Cal.L.Rev. Comm. Reports 1 (1993)].

Research References

Treatises and Practice Aids

Witkin, California Summary 10th Husband and Wife § 48, Confidential Marriage.

§ 509. Application to obtain certified copy of certificate; fee

(a) A party to a confidential marriage may obtain a certified copy of the confidential marriage certificate from the county clerk of the county in which the certificate is filed by submitting an application that satisfies the requirements of Chapter 14 (commencing with Section 103525) of Part 1 of Division 102 of the Health and Safety Code.

(b) Copies of a confidential marriage certificate may be issued to the parties to the marriage upon payment of the fee equivalent to that charged for copies of a marriage certificate. *(Stats.1992, c. 162 (A.B.2650), § 10, operative Jan. 1, 1994. Amended by Stats.2001, c. 39 (A.B.1323), § 8; Stats.2006, c. 816 (A.B.1102), § 29, operative Jan. 1, 2008; Stats.2009, c. 412 (A.B.130), § 2.)*

Law Revision Commission Comments

Enactment [Revised Comment]

Section 509 continues former Civil Code Section 4213(g) without substantive change. [23 Cal.L.Rev.Comm. Reports 1 (1993)].

Research References

Treatises and Practice Aids

Witkin, California Summary 10th Husband and Wife § 48, Confidential Marriage.

§ 510. Replacement of marriage certificate; issuance of duplicate license

(a) If a confidential marriage license is lost, damaged, or destroyed after the performance of the marriage, but before it is returned to the county clerk, or deemed unacceptable for registration by the county clerk, the person solemnizing the marriage, in order to comply with Section 506, shall obtain a duplicate marriage license by filing an affidavit setting forth the facts with the county clerk of the county in which the license was issued.

(b) The duplicate license may not be issued later than one year after issuance of the original license and shall be returned by the person solemnizing the marriage to the county clerk within one year of the issuance date shown on the original marriage license.

(c) The county clerk may charge a fee to cover the actual costs of issuing a duplicate marriage license.

(d) If a marriage license is lost, damaged, or destroyed before a marriage ceremony takes place, the applicants shall purchase a new marriage license and the old license shall be voided. *(Stats.1992, c. 162 (A.B.2650), § 10, operative Jan. 1, 1994. Amended by Stats.1993, c. 219 (A.B.1500), § 99; Stats.2001, c. 39 (A.B.1323), § 9; Stats.2006, c. 816 (A.B. 1102), § 30, operative Jan. 1, 2008.)*

Law Revision Commission Comments

Enactment [Revised Comment]

Section 510 continues former Civil Code Section 4213(h) without substantive change. The phrase "confidential marriage certificate" has been substituted for "certificate furnished pursuant to this section." This is not a substantive change, since the certificates furnished pursuant to former Civil Code Section 4213 are confidential marriage certificates. [23 Cal.L.Rev.Comm. Reports 1 (1993)].

Research References

Treatises and Practice Aids

Witkin, California Summary 10th Husband and Wife § 48, Confidential Marriage.

§ 511. Maintenance of marriage certificates; inspections; preservation of record; reproductions; disclosure of information

(a) Except as provided in subdivision (b), the county clerk shall maintain confidential marriage certificates filed pursuant to Section 506 as permanent records which shall not be open to public inspection except upon order of the court issued upon a showing of good cause. The confidential marriage license is a confidential record and not open to public inspection without an order from the court.

(b) The county clerk shall keep all original certificates of confidential marriages for one year from the date of filing. After one year, the clerk may reproduce the certificates pursuant to Section 26205 of the Government Code, and dispose of the original certificates. The county clerk shall promptly seal and store at least one original negative of each microphotographic film made in a manner and place as reasonable to ensure its preservation indefinitely against loss, theft, defacement, or destruction. The microphotograph shall be made in a manner that complies with the minimum standards or guidelines, or both, recommended by the American National Standards Institute or the Association for Information and Image Management. Every reproduction shall be deemed and considered an original. A certified copy of any reproduction shall be deemed and considered a certified copy of the original.

(c) The county clerk may conduct a search for a confidential marriage certificate for the purpose of confirming the existence of a marriage, but the date of the marriage and any other information contained in the certificate shall not be disclosed except upon order of the court.

(d) The county clerk shall, not less than quarterly, transmit copies of all original confidential marriage certificates retained, or originals of reproduced confidential marriage certificates filed after January 1, 1982, to the State Registrar of Vital Statistics. The registrar may destroy the copies so transmitted after they have been indexed. The registrar may respond to an inquiry as to the existence of a marriage performed pursuant to this chapter, but shall not disclose the date of the marriage. *(Stats.1992, c. 162 (A.B.2650), § 10, operative Jan. 1, 1994. Amended by Stats.1994, c. 1269 (A.B.2208), § 11; Stats.2006, c. 816 (A.B.1102), § 31, operative Jan. 1, 2008.)*

Law Revision Commission Comments

Enactment [Revised Comment]

Subdivision (a) of Section 511 continues without substantive change the last sentence of the first paragraph of former Civil Code Section 4213(a). The reference to the "superior" court has been omitted as surplus. See Section 200 (jurisdiction in superior court).

Subdivision (b) continues former Civil Code Section 4213.2 without substantive change.

Subdivision (c) continues former Civil Code Section 4213(f) without substantive change. The reference to the "superior" court has been omitted as surplus. See Section 200 (jurisdiction in superior court).

Subdivision (d) continues former Civil Code Section 4213(e) without substantive change. The reference to filings after January 1, 1982, has been omitted as obsolete. [23 Cal.L.Rev.Comm. Reports 1 (1993)].

Research References

Forms

West's California Code Forms, Family § 500, Comment Overview--Requirements for Confidential Marriages.

Treatises and Practice Aids

Witkin, California Summary 10th Husband and Wife § 48, Confidential Marriage.

CHAPTER 2. APPROVAL OF NOTARIES TO AUTHORIZE CONFIDENTIAL MARRIAGES

§ 530. Compliance with chapter; violation; penalty

(a) No notary public shall issue a confidential marriage license pursuant to this part unless the notary public is approved by the county clerk to issue confidential marriage licenses pursuant to this chapter.

(b) A violation of subdivision (a) is a misdemeanor punishable by a fine not to exceed one thousand dollars ($1,000) or six months in jail. *(Stats.1992, c. 162 (A.B.2650), § 10, operative Jan. 1, 1994. Amended by Stats.2006, c. 816 (A.B.1102), § 32, operative Jan. 1, 2008.)*

Law Revision Commission Comments

Enactment [Revised Comment]

Section 530 continues former Civil Code Section 4213(c)(1) and (d) without substantive change. [23 Cal.L.Rev.Comm. Reports 1 (1993)].

Research References

Treatises and Practice Aids

Witkin, California Summary 10th Husband and Wife § 48, Confidential Marriage.

§ 531. Application by notary for approval to authorize marriage; contents; fees

(a) An application for approval to authorize confidential marriages pursuant to this part shall be submitted to the county clerk in the county in which the notary public who is applying for the approval resides. The county clerk shall exercise reasonable discretion as to whether to approve applications.

(b) The application shall include all of the following:

(1) The full name of the applicant.

(2) The date of birth of the applicant.

(3) The applicant's current residential address and telephone number.

(4) The address and telephone number of the place where the applicant will issue confidential marriage licenses.

(5) The full name of the applicant's employer if the applicant is employed by another person.

(6) Whether or not the applicant has engaged in any of the acts specified in Section 8214.1 of the Government Code.

(c) The application shall be accompanied by the fee provided for in Section 536. *(Stats.1992, c. 162 (A.B.2650), § 10, operative Jan. 1, 1994. Amended by Stats.2001, c. 39 (A.B.1323), § 10; Stats.2006, c. 816 (A.B.1102), § 33, operative Jan. 1, 2008.)*

Law Revision Commission Comments

Enactment [Revised Comment]

Subdivisions (a) and (b) of Section 531 continue former Civil Code Section 4213(c)(2) without substantive change. Subdivision (c) continues part of the first sentence of former Civil Code Section 4213(c)(3). [23 Cal.L.Rev.Comm. Reports 1 (1993)].

§ 532. Proof of completion of course of instruction

No approval, or renewal of the approval, shall be granted pursuant to this chapter unless the notary public shows evidence of successful completion of a course of instruction concerning the issuance of confidential marriage licenses that was conducted by the county clerk in the county of registration. The course of instruction shall not exceed six hours in duration. *(Stats.1992, c. 162 (A.B.2650), § 10, operative Jan. 1, 1994. Amended by Stats.2006, c. 816 (A.B.1102), § 34, operative Jan. 1, 2008.)*

Law Revision Commission Comments

Enactment [Revised Comment]

Section 532 continues former Civil Code Section 4213(c)(5) without substantive change. [23 Cal.L.Rev.Comm. Reports 1 (1993)].

§ 533. Validity of approval; renewal of approval; conditions

An approval to issue confidential marriage licenses pursuant to this chapter is valid for one year. The approval may be renewed for additional one-year periods provided the following conditions are met:

(a) The applicant has not violated any of the provisions provided for in Section 531.

(b) The applicant has successfully completed the course prescribed in Section 532.

(c) The applicant has paid the renewal fee provided for in Section 536. *(Stats.1992, c. 162 (A.B.2650), § 10, operative Jan. 1, 1994. Amended by Stats.2006, c. 816 (A.B.1102), § 35, operative Jan. 1, 2008.)*

Law Revision Commission Comments

Enactment [Revised Comment]

The first sentence of Section 533 continues the second sentence of former Civil Code Section 4213(c)(3) without substantive change. The second sentence is new and is drawn from the third sentence of former Civil Code Section 4213(c)(3). [23 Cal.L.Rev.Comm. Reports 1 (1993)].

§ 534. List of notaries public approved to issue confidential marriage licenses; public inspection; currentness of information

(a) The county clerk shall maintain a list of the notaries public who are approved to issue confidential marriage licenses. The list shall be available for inspection by the public.

(b) It is the responsibility of a notary public approved to issue confidential marriage licenses pursuant to this chapter to keep current the information required in paragraphs (1), (3), (4), and (5) of subdivision (b) of Section 531. This information shall be used by the county clerk to update the list required to be maintained by this section. *(Stats.1992, c. 162 (A.B.2650), § 10, operative Jan. 1, 1994. Amended by Stats.2006, c. 816 (A.B.1102), § 36, operative Jan. 1, 2008.)*

Law Revision Commission Comments

Enactment [Revised Comment]

Section 534 continues former Civil Code Section 4213(c)(6) without substantive change. [23 Cal.L.Rev.Comm. Reports 1 (1993)].

§ 535. Suspension or revocation of approval; hearing

(a) If, after an approval to issue confidential marriage licenses is granted pursuant to this chapter, it is discovered that the notary public has engaged in any of the actions specified in Section 8214.1 of the Government Code, the approval shall be revoked, and the county clerk shall notify the Secretary of State for whatever action the Secretary of State deems appropriate. Any fees paid by the notary public shall be retained by the county clerk.

(b) If a notary public who is approved to authorize confidential marriages pursuant to this chapter is alleged to have violated a provision of this division, the county clerk shall conduct a hearing to determine if the approval of the notary public should be suspended or revoked. The notary public may present any evidence as is necessary in the notary public's defense. If the county clerk determines that the notary public has violated a provision of this division, the county clerk may place the notary public on probation or suspend or revoke the notary public's registration, and any fees paid by the notary public shall be retained by the county clerk. The county clerk shall report the findings of the hearing to the Secretary of State for whatever action the Secretary of State deems appropriate. *(Stats.1992, c. 162 (A.B.2650), § 10, operative Jan. 1, 1994. Amended by Stats. 2006, c. 816 (A.B.1102), § 37, operative Jan. 1, 2008.)*

Law Revision Commission Comments

Enactment [Revised Comment]

Section 535 continues former Civil Code Section 4213(c)(4) and (c)(7) without substantive change. In subdivision (b), a reference to this division has been substituted for the narrower reference to "this article." This is not a substantive change, since the sections in the former article are continued in this division and the other sections in this division do not impose any new obligations on notaries. In the third sentence of subdivision (b), the provision for retaining fees is new and is drawn from the last sentence of former Civil Code Section 4213(c)(3), now Family Code Section 536(c). [23 Cal.L.Rev.Comm. Reports 1 (1993)].

§ 536. Application fees; renewal fees; deposit of fees

(a) The fee for an application for approval to authorize confidential marriages pursuant to this chapter is three hundred dollars ($300).

(b) The fee for renewal of an approval is three hundred dollars ($300).

(c) Fees received pursuant to this chapter shall be deposited in a trust fund established by the county clerk. The money in the trust fund shall be used exclusively for the administration of the programs described in this chapter. *(Stats.1992, c. 162 (A.B.2650), § 10, operative Jan. 1, 1994. Amended by Stats.2006, c. 816 (A.B.1102), § 38, operative Jan. 1, 2008.)*

Law Revision Commission Comments

Enactment [Revised Comment]

Section 536 continues without substantive change part of the first sentence and the last two sentences of former Civil Code Section 4213(c)(3). [23 Cal.L.Rev.Comm. Reports 1 (1993)].

Division 4

RIGHTS AND OBLIGATIONS DURING MARRIAGE

Part 1

GENERAL PROVISIONS

CHAPTER 1. DEFINITIONS

§ 700. Leasehold interest in real property

For the purposes of this division, a leasehold interest in real property is real property, not personal property. *(Stats. 1992, c. 162 (A.B.2650), § 10, operative Jan. 1, 1994.)*

Law Revision Commission Comments

Enactment [Revised Comment]

Section 700 restates the last sentence of former Civil Code Section 5110 without substantive change, and expands the coverage of the definition to apply to the entire division. The former provision applied only to former Civil Code Section 5110. [23 Cal.L.Rev. Comm. Reports 1 (1993)].

Research References

Treatises and Practice Aids

Witkin, California Summary 10th Community Property § 3, Property Rights During Marriage.

Witkin, California Summary 10th Husband and Wife § 3, Statutory Framework.

CHAPTER 2. RELATION OF SPOUSES

§ 720. Mutual obligations

Spouses contract toward each other obligations of mutual respect, fidelity, and support. *(Stats.1992, c. 162 (A.B.2650), § 10, operative Jan. 1, 1994. Amended by Stats.2014, c. 82 (S.B.1306), § 11, eff. Jan. 1, 2015.)*

Law Revision Commission Comments

Enactment [Revised Comment]

Section 720 continues former Civil Code Section 5100 without change. [23 Cal.L.Rev.Comm. Reports 1 (1993)].

Commentary

For discussion of the duty of support, see *Borelli v. Brusseau, 12 Cal.App.4th 647, 654, 16 Cal.Rptr.2d 16 (1993), review denied 4/1/93*, holding that the section 4300 duty of support includes the obligation to care personally for a spouse who is ill. See additionally Section 1620, Commentary. See also *In re Marriage of Mathiasen, 268 Cal.Rptr. 895, 897 (1990), review denied and depublished 7/25/90* (holding the spouses' household expense reimbursement agreement unenforceable because it altered the statutory obligation of mutual support).

Kilroy v. Kilroy, 35 Cal.App.4th 1141, 41 Cal.Rptr.2d 812 (1995), review denied 8/24/95, holds that a trial court may award temporary support and attorney's fees in a civil action brought by one spouse to enforce the other spouse's Section 4300 duty of support during marriage. Although neither spouse had brought any action for dissolution, it appears that the spouses were not living together when the wife brought her Section 4303 action. Thus *Kilroy* does not directly challenge the venerable American rule that when the spouses are still living together as husband and wife, the courts will not intervene in an ongoing marriage to order spousal support absent jeopardy to the health or basic welfare of the petitioning spouse. See, for example, *McGuire v. McGuire, 59 N.W.2d 336 (Neb. 1953)*. In any event, a California spouse may enlist the court's assistance indirectly during an ongoing marriage by bringing a Section 1101(c) action to add his or her name to the title of the parties' community property assets.

Despite the requirement of 28 USC § 1360(c) that state courts give full force and effect to American Indian tribal law and custom in civil matters, *In re Marriage of Jacobsen, 121 Cal.App.4th 1187, 18 Cal.Rptr.3d 162 (2004)*, holds that, in a divorce proceeding initiated by a tribal member, a California family court is not required to give effect to the Chumash Indian custom that funds distributed by the tribe to its members should not be used to pay spousal support to non-members, because once a tribal member invokes the court's jurisdiction in a domestic relations matter, the court has jurisdiction to grant any appropriate relief. *Jacobsen* additionally observes that the Chumash custom is not binding in family court because it is inconsistent with California law and policy, which is expressed in this section and Sections 3600 and 4300.

Research References

Forms

California Transactions Forms--Estate Planning § 11:45, Introduction.

Treatises and Practice Aids

Witkin, California Summary 10th Community Property § 133, Statutory Requirement.

Witkin, California Summary 10th Husband and Wife § 36, Mutual Obligations.

§ 721. Contracts with each other and third parties; fiduciary relationship

(a) Subject to subdivision (b), either spouse may enter into any transaction with the other, or with any other person, respecting property, which either might if unmarried.

(b) Except as provided in Sections 143, 144, 146, 16040, and 16047 of the Probate Code, in transactions between themselves, spouses are subject to the general rules governing fiduciary relationships that control the actions of persons occupying confidential relations with each other. This confidential relationship imposes a duty of the highest good faith and fair dealing on each spouse, and neither shall take any unfair advantage of the other. This confidential relationship is a fiduciary relationship subject to the same rights and duties of nonmarital business partners, as provided in Sections 16403, 16404, and 16503 of the Corporations Code, including, but not limited to, the following:

(1) Providing each spouse access at all times to any books kept regarding a transaction for the purposes of inspection and copying.

(2) Rendering upon request, true and full information of all things affecting any transaction that concerns the community property. Nothing in this section is intended to impose a duty for either spouse to keep detailed books and records of community property transactions.

(3) Accounting to the spouse, and holding as a trustee, any benefit or profit derived from any transaction by one spouse without the consent of the other spouse that concerns the community property. *(Stats.1992, c. 162 (A.B.2650), § 10, operative Jan. 1, 1994. Amended by Stats.2002, c. 310 (S.B.1936), § 1; Stats.2014, c. 82 (S.B.1306), § 12, eff. Jan. 1, 2015.)*

Law Revision Commission Comments

Enactment [Revised Comment]

Section 721 continues former Civil Code Section 5103 without change, except that "one spouse" has been substituted for "him or her" in subdivision (b)(3) for clarity. See also Section 1101 (claims and remedies for breach of fiduciary duty); Code Civ. Proc. §§ 370 (right of married person to sue without spouse being joined as a party), 371 (right of married person to defend suit for spouse's right). [23 Cal.L.Rev.Comm. Reports 1 (1993)].

Commentary

Although married couples may freely contract to alter the separate or community character of their property, unless the marriage has entirely broken down, any agreement that promotes divorce violates public policy. See generally *Glickman v. Collins, 13 Cal.3d 852, 857, 120 Cal.Rptr. 76 (1975)*. For discussion of contract provisions that are deemed to promote divorce, see Section 1612, Commentary.

Mejia v. Reed, 31 Cal.4th 657, 74 P.3d 166, 3 Cal.Rptr.3d 390 (2003), holds that the Uniform Fraudulent Transfer Act (Civil Code §§ 3439–3439.12) applies to marital settlement agreements. *Filip v. Bucurenciu, 129 Cal.App.4th 825, 28 Cal.Rptr.3d 884 (2005)*, approves a trial court's finding that the spouses' marital settlement agreement violates the Uniform Fraudulent Transfer Act.

Reversing the Bankruptcy Court, *In re Beverly, 374 B.R. 221 (U.S. Bankr. App. Pan., 9th Cir. 2007)*, held that a divorcing attorney's marital settlement agreement, which transferred nonexempt community property to his wife in exchange for an equivalent amount of his exempt community property retirement fund, was a fraudulent transfer under California Civil Code § 3439.04(a)(1) and therefore under 11 U.S.C. § 544(b). Thus, in the attorney's involuntary bankruptcy proceeding, the Bankruptcy Trustee could avoid the transfer and reach the attorney's community property interest in the nonexempt property.

A rebuttable presumption of undue influence arises when one spouse gains an advantage over the other in an interspousal transaction. The spouse who obtained the advantage bears the burden of rebutting the presumption. *In re Marriage of Haines, 33 Cal.App.4th 277, 39 Cal.Rptr.2d 673 (1995)*. *In re Marriage of Lange, 102 Cal.App.4th 360, 125 Cal.Rptr.2d 379 (2002)*, held that a husband's promissory note for a wife's separate property contribution to the acquisition of the family home and the deed of trust on the home securing the note were unenforceable under this section because they gave the wife an advantage and thus gave rise to a presumption of undue influence, which the wife failed to rebut. However, the wife remained entitled to § 2640 reimbursement of her separate property contributions to the acquisition of community property because the unenforceable instruments did not constitute a written waiver of that right. *In re Marriage of Delaney, 111 Cal.App.4th 991, 4 Cal.Rptr.3d 378 (2003)*, applies the holding of *Haines, supra,* to a spouse's routine transfer of his separate property home into joint tenancy in connection with the couple's application for a home improvement loan. *Delaney* requires that the spouse who benefited from the transfer by gaining a property interest show that the transfer "was freely and voluntarily made, with full knowledge of all the facts, and with a complete understanding of the effect of a transfer from his unencumbered separate interest to a joint interest."

In re Marriage of Balcof, 141 Cal.App.4th 1509, 47 Cal.Rptr.3d 183 (2006), review denied Feb. 18, 2004, approved a trial court finding that a formally adequate transmutation was ineffective because the spouse advantaged by the agreement exercised duress and undue influence when she secured her spouse's consent to the transmutation document. *Balcof* concluded that a preponderance of the evidence, as contrasted to the higher standard of clear and convincing evidence, is all that is required to rebut the presumption of undue influence that arises when one spouse is advantaged by a formally adequate transmutation. In view of the clear evidence of duress and undue influence in *Balcof*, the court's discussion of the applicable evidentiary standard is arguably dictum. Under either standard, the presumption of undue influence could not have been rebutted.

In re Marriage of Mathews, 133 Cal.App.4th 624, 35 Cal.Rptr.3d 1 (2005), concluded that a husband rebutted the presumption of undue influence with evidence that a wife with a poor credit rating "freely and voluntarily" quitclaimed her interest in what otherwise would have been a community property home, even though she did so solely for the purpose of obtaining a lower interest rate and both husband and wife continued to believe during marriage that the home was community property.

Matthews was narrowly distinguished by *Starr v. Starr, 189 Cal. App.4th 277, 116 Cal.Rptr.3d 813 (2010)*, and *In re Marriage of Fossum, 192 Cal.App.4th 336, 121 Cal.Rptr.3d 195 (2011), review denied*. In each case, a realtor recommended title in one spouse's name alone and further recommended that the other spouse sign a quit-claim deed relinquishing all interest in the home. The spouses complied with the realtors' suggestions in order to obtain a beneficial interest rate. However, in each case, the quit-claim deed was set aside and the home was held to be community property on the ground that the titled spouse exercised undue influence (breached his fiduciary duty). Because the titled spouse promised to re-convey the property into joint title after financing was obtained and did not do so, the non-titled spouse's consent to title in the other spouse's name alone and the supplementary quit-claim deed was not "voluntary." In *Matthews*, by contrast, the titled spouse did not promise to re-convey.

In re Marriage of Burkle, 139 Cal.App.4th 712, 43 Cal.Rptr.3d 181 (2006), review denied, states in dictum that the presumption of undue influence does not arise unless a spouse obtains an "unfair advantage." This would effectively shift the burden of proof to the spouse who is disadvantaged to show that the disadvantage was unfair.

In re Marriage of Kieturakis, 138 Cal.App.4th 56, 41 Cal.Rptr.3d 119 (2006), review denied, held that the presumption of undue influence is not applicable to mediated settlement agreements. To the same effect, see *In re Marriage of Woolsey, 220 Cal.App.4th 881, 163 Cal.Rptr.3d 551 (2013), review denied*.

The content of subsection (b) is relatively recent. It was initially introduced by 1991 Cal. Stat., Ch. 1026 (S.B.716). See additionally Section 1100(e), also added by Ch. 1026 (Section 721 fiduciary duties continue until the property has been divided by the parties or by a court), and Commentary on Section 1100(e). For discussion of the current fiduciary standard, see *In re Marriage of Reuling, 23 Cal. App.4th 1428, 28 Cal.Rptr.2d 726 (1994)*. See also *In re Marriage of Haines, 33 Cal.App.4th 277, 39 Cal.Rptr.2d 673 (1995)*, which holds that Evidence Code Section 662, which provides that "[t]he owner of the legal title to property is presumed to be the owner of the full beneficial title," does not apply in family law proceedings insofar as its application would be inconsistent with the presumption of undue influence that arises from the Family Code Section 721 principle that the spouses have a confidential relationship in their transactions with each other. For further discussion of this issue, see the Commentary to Family Code Section 852.

In re Marriage of Margulis, 198 Cal.App.4th 1252, 130 Cal.Rptr.3d 327 (2011), relying in part on subsection (b), held that in a marriage dissolution proceeding a managing spouse has the burden of proof to account for missing assets when the nonmanaging spouse has made a prima facie showing of the existence and value of community assets that have disappeared after separation while controlled by the managing spouse. The managing spouse must either rebut the showing or prove the proper disposition or lesser value of the assets. If the managing spouse fails to do so, the court should charge the managing spouse with the prima facie value of the assets. *Margulis* interprets this section, along with Family Code sections 1100, 1101, 2100, and 2107, to impose upon a managing spouse a duty to disclose and account for the existence, valuation and distribution of all community assets from the date of separation to the final property distribution.

D'Elia v. D'Elia, 58 Cal.App.4th 415, 68 Cal.Rptr.2d 324 (1997), holds that California security laws (Corp. Code § 25401 et seq.) do not apply to an ostensible breach of the subsection (b) fiduciary duty. Compare *Dale v. Dale, 66 Cal.App.4th 1172, 78 Cal.Rptr.2d 513 (1998), review denied January 13, 1999* (absent a pending dissolution proceeding, a divorced spouse may bring a common law tort action against a former spouse for injury resulting from the latter's concealment of community assets at dissolution). Dissolution of the Dales' marriage occurred before enactment of Sections 2120–2129, and the court thus did not address whether such an action might be brought with respect to judgments entered on or after January 1, 1993, the effective date of Sections 2120–2129.

In re Marriage of Duffy, 91 Cal.App.4th 923, 111 Cal.Rptr.2d 160 (2001), held that so long as a managing spouse acts in good faith, he has not breached the fiduciary duty even though he makes unwise or improvident investments. However, Duffy was decided under a prior version of this section, which incorporated by reference former Corporations Code §§ 15019–15022, sections that were superseded in 1996 by Corporations Code §§ 16401–16503. This section was not amended to incorporate the new Corporations Code sections until 2002. 2002 Cal.Stat., ch. 310 (S.B.1936).[1] Although the 2002 amendment expresses legislative intent merely to clarify existing law, thus paving the way for retroactive application of the amendment, to the extent that the amendment imposes duties that did not exist under prior law, it may not be applied retroactively to events that occurred before its effective date. *In re Marriage of Walker, 138 Cal.App.4th 1408, 42 Cal.Rptr.3d 325 (2006)* (duty to disclose without demand applies prospectively only because pre-amendment duty was duty to disclose "on demand").

Subsection (c) of Corporations Code § 16404 adds an element to the fiduciary duties prescribed by the superseded sections; it provides that "[a] partner's duty of care to the partnership . . . is limited to refraining from engaging in grossly negligent or reckless conduct. . . ." Section (2) of chapter 310 expresses legislative intent "to abrogate the ruling in In re Marriage of Duffy . . . to the extent that it is in conflict with this clarification." Thus, highly improvident investments may now violate a spouse's fiduciary duty under this section.

In re Marriage of Leni, 144 Cal.App.4th 1087, 50 Cal.Rptr.3d 886 (2006), held that the fiduciary duty that spouses bear to one another does not compel a spouse to give the other spouse a right of first refusal in the sale of a community property asset.

[1] Former §§ 15019–15022 provided:

§ 15019. Partnership books; right to inspect

The partnership books shall be kept, subject to any agreement between the partners, at the principal place of business of the partnership, and every partner shall at all times have access to and may inspect and copy any of them.

§ 15020. Disclosure of information on demand

Partners shall render on demand true and full information of all things affecting the partnership to any partner or the legal representative of any deceased partner or partner under legal disability.

§ 15021. Accounting of partner to partnership; personal representatives of deceased last surviving partner

(1) Every partner must account to the partnership for any benefit, and hold as trustee for it any profits derived by him without the consent of the other partners from any transaction connected with the formation, conduct, or liquidation of the partnership or from any use by him of its property.

(2) This section applies also to the representatives of a deceased partner engaged in the liquidation of the affairs of the partnership as the personal representatives of the last surviving partner.

§ 15022. Partner's right to formal accounting

Any partner shall have the right to a formal account as to partnership affairs:

(a) If he is wrongfully excluded from the partnership business or possession of its property by his copartners,

(b) If the right exists under the terms of any agreement,

(c) As provided by Section 15021,

(d) Whenever other circumstances render it just and reasonable.

Research References

Forms

California Practice Guide: Rutter Family Law Forms Form 8:1, Request for Order Re Separate Trial Re Validity Of Interspousal Deed.

California Practice Guide: Rutter Family Law Forms Form 9:2, Marital Agreement.

California Practice Guide: Rutter Family Law Forms Form 9:3, Marital Settlement Agreement.

California Transactions Forms--Business Entities § 19:82, Consent Of Spouse.

California Transactions Forms--Estate Planning § 10:4, Community Property.

California Transactions Forms--Estate Planning § 11:34, Agreement Entered Into Before January 1, 1985.

California Transactions Forms--Estate Planning § 11:36, Family Code S852 Transmutations and Rules Governing Fiduciary Relationships.

California Transactions Forms--Estate Planning § 11:40, Premarital Agreements Entered Into Before January 1, 1986.

California Transactions Forms--Estate Planning § 11:45, Introduction.

California Transactions Forms--Estate Planning § 11:47, Formalities.

California Transactions Forms--Estate Planning § 11:48, Governing Contractual Provisions [CC §§ 1550 et seq., Fam C S721(B)].

California Transactions Forms--Estate Planning § 11:52, Enforceability Under Probate Code § 143.

California Transactions Forms--Estate Planning § 11:53, Enforceability Under Probate Code § 144.

California Transactions Forms--Estate Planning § 11:54, Revocation and Amendment Of Waiver by Agreement.

California Transactions Forms--Estate Planning § 19:15, Waiver Of Family Protection.
California Transactions Forms--Family Law § 2:3, Comprehensive Drafting.
California Transactions Forms--Family Law § 2:4, Fiduciary Duty.
California Transactions Forms--Family Law § 1:18, Capacity and Consent; Undue Influence.
California Transactions Forms--Family Law § 1:99, Waiver Of Management and Control Of Property.
West's California Code Forms, Family § 850, Comment Overview--Transmutation by Agreement or Transfer.
West's California Code Forms, Family § 1500 Form 1, Marital Agreement.
West's California Code Forms, Family § 2338 Form 9, Marital Agreement--Both Spouses Employed.
West's California Code Forms, Family § 2550 Form 3, Marital Agreement.
West's California Code Forms, Probate § 3080 Form 1, Petition for Support; for Injunctive Orders; for Determination Of the Character Of Property; for an Accounting; for Employment Of Counsel; and for Attorney Fees and Costs.

Treatises and Practice Aids

Witkin, California Summary 10th Community Property § 24, in General.
Witkin, California Summary 10th Community Property § 133, Statutory Requirement.
Witkin, California Summary 10th Community Property § 134, Action for Breach Of Duty.
Witkin, California Summary 10th Community Property § 155, Writing Requirement.
Witkin, California Summary 10th Community Property § 159, Management, Control, and Disposition.
Witkin, California Summary 10th Community Property § 200, Division by Agreement.
Witkin, California Summary 10th Community Property § 235, Fiduciary Duties.
Witkin, California Summary 10th Husband and Wife § 18, in General.
Witkin, California Summary 10th Husband and Wife § 39, in General.
Witkin, California Summary 10th Husband and Wife § 349, Approval Of Court.
Witkin, California Summary 10th Real Property § 206, Capacity to Acquire and Transfer Land.
Witkin, California Summary 10th Wills and Probate § 324, Enforcement.
Witkin, California Summary 10th Wills and Probate § 325, Alteration or Revocation.

CHAPTER 3. PROPERTY RIGHTS DURING MARRIAGE

§ 750. Methods of holding property

Spouses may hold property as joint tenants or tenants in common, or as community property, or as community property with a right of survivorship. *(Stats.1992, c. 162 (A.B.2650), § 10, operative Jan. 1, 1994. Amended by Stats.2001, c. 754 (A.B.1697), § 2; Stats.2014, c. 82 (S.B.1306), § 13, eff. Jan. 1, 2015.)*

Law Revision Commission Comments

Enactment [Revised Comment]

Section 750 continues former Civil Code Section 5104 without substantive change. See also Section 65 ("community property" defined in Section 760 *et seq.*); Code Civ. Proc. §§ 370 (right of married person to sue without spouse being joined as a party), 371 (right of married person to defend suit for spouse's right). [23 Cal.L.Rev.Comm. Reports 1 (1993)].

Commentary

To create a joint tenancy, the governing instrument must expressly declare that the spouses hold in joint tenancy. Civil Code Section 683. Concurrent ownership that is not held in joint tenancy is held either as community property or as tenancy in common. Civil Code Section 686. To explicitly create community property title, the governing instrument may either specify that the property is held as community property or that the co-owners are husband and wife. When a husband and wife took pre–1975 unqualified title that was insufficient to create either joint tenancy or community property title, they took as tenants in common, often with odd results. See Section 803(b) and Commentary. With the 1975 prospective repeal of the married woman's presumption (Section 803), there is no longer precise statutory instruction on the effect of concurrent title held by a husband and wife who are not identified as husband and wife and who do not hold as joint tenants. The Section 760 principle that property acquired during marriage is community property may be understood to suggest that post–1974 title held in the names of both spouses be treated as community property title. Cf. Probate Code Section 5305: "[I]f parties to . . . [a bank] account are married to each other, whether or not they are so described in the deposit agreement, their net contribution to the account is presumed to be and remain their community property."

Research References

Forms

Am. Jur. Pl. & Pr. Forms Community Property § 1, Introductory Comments.
Am. Jur. Pl. & Pr. Forms Husband and Wife § 2, Introductory Comments.
West's California Code Forms, Family § 754, Comment Overview--Property Rights During Marriage.

Treatises and Practice Aids

Witkin, California Summary 10th Community Property § 3, Property Rights During Marriage.
Witkin, California Summary 10th Husband and Wife § 18, in General.

§ 751. Community property; interests of parties

The respective interests of each spouse in community property during continuance of the marriage relation are present, existing, and equal interests. *(Stats.1992, c. 162 (A.B.2650), § 10, operative Jan. 1, 1994. Amended by Stats. 2014, c. 82 (S.B.1306), § 14, eff. Jan. 1, 2015.)*

Law Revision Commission Comments

Enactment [Revised Comment]

Section 751 continues the first sentence of former Civil Code Section 5105 without change. The last sentence of former Civil Code Section 5105 has been omitted as surplus. See also Section 65 ("community property" defined in Section 760 *et seq.*); Code Civ.

Proc. §§ 370 (right of married person to sue without spouse being joined as a party), 371 (right of married person to defend suit for spouse's right). [23 Cal.L.Rev.Comm. Reports 1 (1993)].

Commentary

Patrick v. Alacer Corp., 167 Cal.App.4th 995, 84 Cal.Rptr.3d 642 (2008), review denied, held that a surviving spouse had standing to assert shareholder derivative claims against her deceased husband's corporation even though she was not a shareholder of record, when she alleged that during marriage the community had acquired an interest in the corporation because its increase in value was attributable to community labor.

People v. Kahanic, 196 Cal.App.3d 461, 241 Cal.Rptr. 722 (1987), sustained the conviction of a divorcing wife for vandalizing property "not his [her] own" by tossing a beer bottle through the rear window of an automobile that she owned as community property with her husband because, under Civil Code Section 5105 (now Family Code Section 751), she did not have exclusive ownership of the automobile but instead shared ownership with her husband.

For treatment of California community property ownership and debt liability rules in the context of federal law, compare *United States v. Lester, 85 F.3d 1409 (9th Cir. 1996)* with *U.S. v. Hooper, 229 F.3d 818 (9th Cir. 2000)*, and *In re Soderling, 998 F.2d 730, 733 (9th Cir. 1993)*. *Lester* holds that the federal Comprehensive Drug Abuse Prevention and Control Act substitute property forfeiture section ("substitute property" is property not used in the commission of a crime but taken instead because property used in commission of the crime is unavailable) looks to state law only for the purpose of determining property ownership (Family Code Section 751), and not for the purpose of determining debt liability (Family Code Section 910(a)). Thus an innocent wife's one-half interest in the community property cannot be reached on account of her husband's criminal behavior. Distinguishing *Lester*, which applied to "substitute property," *Hooper* held that the federal criminal statute governing forfeiture of property derived from illicit drug sale (21 USC § 853) allows forfeiture of an innocent spouse's community property interest in the illicit sale proceeds or property purchased with those proceeds. *Soderling* determined that, for purposes of dischargeability in bankruptcy, a criminal restitution order is a "debt" under California law and federal bankruptcy law, and hence may be satisfied, according to state law, from community property assets.

Research References

Forms

California Transactions Forms--Estate Planning § 10:4, Community Property.
California Transactions Forms--Estate Planning § 3:75, Community Property.
California Transactions Forms--Estate Planning § 19:18, Community Property.

Treatises and Practice Aids

Witkin, California Summary 10th Community Property § 3, Property Rights During Marriage.
Witkin, California Summary 10th Community Property § 130, Present, Existing, and Equal Interest.
Witkin, California Summary 10th Community Property § 153, Authority to Transmute.
Witkin, California Summary 10th Real Property § 32, in General.

§ 752. Separate property; interest of parties

Except as otherwise provided by statute, neither spouse has any interest in the separate property of the other. *(Stats. 1992, c. 162 (A.B.2650), § 10, operative Jan. 1, 1994. Amended by Stats.2014, c. 82 (S.B.1306), § 15, eff. Jan. 1, 2015.)*

Law Revision Commission Comments

Enactment [Revised Comment]

Section 752 continues the first part of former Civil Code Section 5102(a) without substantive change. "Except as otherwise provided by statute" has been substituted for "[e]xcept as provided in this section." See also Sections 130 ("separate property" defined in Section 760 *et seq.*), 754 (limitation on disposition of separate property residence if notice of pendency of proceeding recorded); Code Civ. Proc. §§ 370 (right of married person to sue without spouse being joined as a party), 371 (right of married person to defend suit for spouse's right). [23 Cal.L.Rev.Comm. Reports 1 (1993)].

Research References

Forms

West's California Code Forms, Family § 754, Comment Overview--Property Rights During Marriage.

Treatises and Practice Aids

Witkin, California Summary 10th Community Property § 3, Property Rights During Marriage.
Witkin, California Summary 10th Husband and Wife § 18, in General.

§ 753. Exclusion of spouse from other's dwelling

Notwithstanding Section 752 and except as provided in Article 2 (commencing with Section 2045), Article 3 (commencing with Section 2047), or Article 4 (commencing with Section 2049) of Chapter 4 of Part 1 of Division 6, neither spouse may be excluded from the other's dwelling. *(Stats. 1992, c. 162 (A.B.2650), § 10, operative Jan. 1, 1994. Amended by Stats.1993, c. 219 (A.B.1500), § 99.5.)*

Law Revision Commission Comments

Enactment [Revised Comment]

Section 753 restates the second part of former Civil Code Section 5102(a) without substantive change. [23 Cal.L.Rev.Comm. Reports 1 (1993)].

Commentary

For discussion of the use of Section 753 as a defense to the criminal charge of burglary, see *People v. Davenport, 219 Cal.App.3d 885, 268 Cal.Rptr. 501 (1990), review denied 7/18/90* (Section 753 does not confer right to burglarize the dwelling of an estranged spouse), and cases cited therein.

Research References

Forms

West's California Code Forms, Family § 754, Comment Overview--Property Rights During Marriage.

§ 754. Disposition of separate property residence during pendency of proceedings

If notice of the pendency of a proceeding for dissolution of the marriage, for nullity of the marriage, or for legal separation of the parties is recorded in any county in which either spouse resides on real property that is the separate property of the other, the real property shall not for a period of three months thereafter be transferred, encumbered, or otherwise disposed of voluntarily or involuntarily without the joinder of both spouses, unless the court otherwise orders. *(Stats.1992, c. 162 (A.B.2650), § 10, operative Jan. 1, 1994.*

Amended by Stats.2014, c. 82 (S.B.1306), § 16, eff. Jan. 1, 2015.)

Law Revision Commission Comments

Enactment [Revised Comment]

Section 754 continues former Civil Code Section 5102(b) without substantive change. See also Section 700 (real property includes leasehold interests in real property).

Section 754 provides a means of restraining transfer or encumbrance of a separate property dwelling for a three-month period during the pendency of separation, annulment, or dissolution proceedings. The restraint applies to voluntary dispositions of the dwelling, as well as involuntary dispositions, such as pursuant to a writ of execution. As to the authority of the court to restrain transfer during pendency of these proceedings, see Section 2045. See also Section 2030 (temporary restraining order in summons). A community property dwelling may not be transferred or encumbered without joinder or consent of both spouses. See Sections 1100(c) (disposition or encumbrance of personal property family dwelling), 1102 (lease, transfer, or encumbrance of real property).

For background on former Civ. Code § 5102, see *Tentative Recommendation Proposing the Enforcement of Judgments Law,* 15 Cal. L. Revision Comm'n Reports 2001, 2630 (1980). [23 Cal.L.Rev. Comm. Reports 1 (1993)].

Research References

Forms

West's California Code Forms, Family § 754, Comment Overview--Property Rights During Marriage.

Treatises and Practice Aids

Witkin, California Summary 10th Community Property § 3, Property Rights During Marriage.

§ 755. Employee benefit plan; payment or refund; discharge from adverse claims; notice of claims

(a) The terms "participant," "beneficiary," "employer," "employee organization," "named fiduciary," "fiduciary," and "administrator," as used in subdivision (b), have the same meaning as provided in Section 3 of the Employee Retirement Income Security Act of 1974 (P.L. 93-406) (ERISA), as amended (29 U.S.C.A. Sec. 1002). The term "employee benefit plan" has the same meaning as provided in Section 80 of this code. The term "trustee" shall include a "named fiduciary" as that term is employed in ERISA. The term "plan sponsor" shall include an "employer" or "employee organization," as those terms are used in ERISA (29 U.S.C.A. Sec. 1002).

(b) Notwithstanding Sections 751 and 1100, if payment or refund is made to a participant or the participant's, employee's, or former employee's beneficiary or estate pursuant to an employee benefit plan including a plan governed by the Employee Retirement Income Security Act of 1974 (P.L. 93-406), as amended, the payment or refund fully discharges the plan sponsor and the administrator, trustee, or insurance company making the payment or refund from all adverse claims thereto unless, before the payment or refund is made, the plan sponsor or the administrator of the plan has received written notice by or on behalf of some other person that the other person claims to be entitled to the payment or refund or some part thereof. Nothing in this section affects or releases the participant from claims which may exist against the participant by a person other than the plan sponsor, trustee, administrator, or other person making the benefit payment. *(Stats.1992, c. 162 (A.B.2650), § 10, operative Jan. 1, 1994. Amended by Stats.1994, c. 1269 (A.B.2208), § 12.)*

Law Revision Commission Comments

Enactment [Revised Comment]

Section 755 continues former Civil Code Section 5106 without substantive change. In the last sentences of subdivisions (a) and (b), the phrase "all persons" has been shortened to "persons," since the word "all" was surplus. [23 Cal.L.Rev.Comm. Reports 1 (1993)].

Research References

Forms

California Practice Guide: Rutter Family Law Forms Form 8:5, Notice Of Adverse Interest in Employee Benefit Plan(S).

West's California Code Forms, Family § 754, Comment Overview--Property Rights During Marriage.

West's California Code Forms, Family § 2060, Comment Overview--Application and Order for Joinder.

West's California Code Forms, Family § 755 Form 1, Notice Of Claim to Retirement Benefits.

Treatises and Practice Aids

Witkin, California Summary 10th Community Property § 71, Payment as Discharge.

Part 2

CHARACTERIZATION OF MARITAL PROPERTY

CHAPTER 1. COMMUNITY PROPERTY

§ 760. "Community property" defined

Except as otherwise provided by statute, all property, real or personal, wherever situated, acquired by a married person during the marriage while domiciled in this state is community property. *(Stats.1992, c. 162 (A.B.2650), § 10, operative Jan. 1, 1994.)*

Law Revision Commission Comments

Enactment [Revised Comment]

Section 760 restates the first part of former Civil Code Section 5110, and extends the definition of community property to include real property situated outside California. The phrase "[e]xcept as otherwise provided by statute" has been substituted for the narrower reference to specific statutory provisions in the former section. The former reference to property held in trust has been eliminated as surplus. See Section 761 (property in certain revocable trusts as community property).

The effect of defining community property to include out-of-state real property is that California courts will treat it as community property for all purposes, including management and control.

Under former law, such property was treated as community property for the purpose of liability for debts and for purposes of division at dissolution of marriage or legal separation. See former Civ. Code § 5120.020 (liability for debts). See also Section 63 ("community estate" defined) & Comment. As to division at dissolution, see, e.g., Rozan v. Rozan, 49 Cal.2d 322, 317 P.2d 11 (1957); Ford v. Ford, 276 Cal.App.2d 9, 80 Cal.Rptr. 435 (1969). The treatment given such property by the courts of the state in which the property is located may depend on the applicable choice of law rules of the state. See also Section 2660 & Comment (division where community estate includes real property located in another state).

Section 760 states the basic rule that all property acquired during marriage is community property unless it comes within a specified exception. The major exceptions to the basic community property rule are those relating to separate property. See, e.g., Sections 130 ("separate property" defined in Section 760 *et seq.*), 770 (separate property of married person), 771 (earnings and accumulations while living separate and apart), 772 (earnings and accumulations after judgment of legal separation), 781 (cases where damages for personal injury are separate property).

Section 760 is not an exclusive statement of property classified as community. See, e.g., Sections 761 (property in certain revocable trusts as community property), 780 (damages for personal injury to married person as community property).

See also Sections 65 ("community property" defined in Section 760 *et seq.*), 802–803 (presumptions concerning nature of property), 850–853 (transmutation of property), 1500–1620 (marital property agreements). [23 Cal.L.Rev.Comm. Reports 1 (1993)].

Commentary

Although Sections 760 and 770 define community property and separate property, they do not establish the vital evidentiary presumptions in favor of community property. See *In re Marriage of Lusk, 86 Cal.App.3d 228, 234, 150 Cal.Rptr. 63 (1978)*. But see Section 802. In California, these presumptions have been formulated by case law, and the case law is not consistent. At the very least, there is a presumption, arising from proof of acquisition during marriage, that property acquired during marriage is community property. Once acquisition during marriage has been established, the separate property proponent has the burden of proving that the property is nevertheless Section 770 separate property. *In re Duncan's Estate, 9 Cal.2d 207, 217, 70 P.2d 174 (1937)*; *Fidelity & Casualty Company v. Mahoney, 71 Cal.App.2d 65, 161 P.2d 944 (1945)*.

Yet who has the burden of proving acquisition during marriage? *Mahoney* allocates the burden to the community property proponent. In contrast, other cases hold that possession during marriage gives rise to a presumption of acquisition during marriage, effectively imposing on the separate property proponent the burden of demonstrating that the property was not acquired during marriage. See, for example, *Lynam v. Vorwerk, 13 Cal.App. 507, 110 P. 355 (1910)*. Allocation of the burden of proof may also turn on whether the classification issue arises in an interspousal dispute or involves parties who do not claim on behalf of either spouse. See, for example, *Meyer v. Kinzer, 12 Cal. 247, 252–253 (1859)* (using the "possession during marriage" formulation to protect a creditor's access to the debtor's property). For further discussion of the burden of proof issues, see Blumberg, *Community Property in California* 165–182 (2d ed. 1993).

What amount of proof is required to overcome the community property presumption? *Meyer* states, in dictum, that "clear and certain proof" is required to overcome the community property presumption. See additionally *In re Duncan's Estate, supra,* at 217. This dictum has been repeated in relatively recent appellate decisions. See, for example, *In re Marriage of Saslow, 40 Cal.3d 848, 863, 221 Cal.Rptr. 546 (1985)*; *In re Marriage of Ashodian, 96 Cal.App.3d 43, 47, 157 Cal.Rptr. 555 (1979), hearing denied 11/8/79*; and *Bank of California v. Connolly, 36 Cal.App.3d 350, 375, 11 Cal.Rptr 468 (1973)*. But see *In re Marriage of Ettefagh, 150 Cal.App.4th 1578, 59 Cal.Rptr.3d 419 (2007), review denied Aug. 8, 2007*, which held that only a preponderance of the evidence is required to overcome the presumption that property acquired during marriage is community property. Yet the supreme court repudiated the *Meyer* dictum in *Freese v. Hibernia Savings and Loan Society, 139 Cal. 392, 394–395, 73 P. 172 (1903)* (holding that a mere preponderance of the evidence is sufficient to overcome the community property presumption). Although the two competing evidentiary standards are prescribed by appellate courts for use by trial courts, they are not the standards applied in appellate review, where the issue is whether the trial court's determination of the character of property is supported by substantial evidence. See, for example, *In re Marriage of Knickerbocker, 43 Cal.App.3d 1039, 1042, 118 Cal.Rptr. 232 (1974)*: "Only where the evidence to rebut the presumption is so weak and improbable that the finding is without substantial support may the appellate court set aside the decision of the trier of fact." See additionally *Saslow, supra,* at 863.

A Ninth Circuit Bankruptcy Appellate Panel, purporting to apply California community property law, held that a married couple's property held in joint tenancy title is community property for purposes of inclusion, in its entirety, in the husband's bankruptcy estate. Characterizing joint tenancy held by spouses in an intact marriage, *In re Brace, 566 B.R. 13 (B.A.P. 9th Cir. 2017)*, relied on this section, the case law presumption that property acquired during marriage is community property, the section 2581 presumption that, at dissolution, property acquired in joint tenancy title is community property, the transmutation provisions, including sections 850 through 852, and *In re Marriage of Valli, 58 Cal. 4th 1396 (2014)*. The reasoning of *Brace* is ahistorical and unpersuasive. Its holding should be treated with circumspection.

Research References

Forms

California Practice Guide: Rutter Family Law Forms Form 1:32, Glossary Of Common Family Law Terms, Phrases and Concepts (Enclosure to Form 1:31).

Cal. Transaction Forms - Bus. Transactions § 18:14, Spouses.

California Transactions Forms--Estate Planning § 1:22, Community Property.

California Transactions Forms--Estate Planning § 10:4, Community Property.

California Transactions Forms--Estate Planning § 19:18, Community Property.

California Transactions Forms--Family Law § 1:27, Complete Agreement.

California Transactions Forms--Family Law § 2:34, Mixed-Character Asset Described.

Nichols Cyclopedia of Legal Forms Annotated § 100:40, Premarital Agreement--Community Property--California.

West's California Code Forms, Family § 803, Comment Overview--Presumptions Concerning Nature Of Property.

West's California Code Forms, Family § 2550, Comment Overview--Manner Of Division Of Community Estate.

West's California Code Forms, Family § 1611 Form 1, Premarital Agreement.

Treatises and Practice Aids

Witkin, California Summary 10th Community Property § 4, Community Property.

Witkin, California Summary 10th Community Property § 15, Nature and Effect.

Witkin, California Summary 10th Community Property § 20, Abolition Of Presumption.

Witkin, California Summary 10th Community Property § 21, to Wife and Stranger.

Witkin, California Summary 10th Community Property § 22, Community Property.

Witkin, California Summary 10th Community Property § 35, Real Property Purchased Elsewhere.

Witkin, California Summary 10th Community Property § 61, Enhanced Early Retirement Benefits.
Witkin, California Summary 10th Community Property § 176, Nature and Scope Of Revision.
Witkin, California Summary 10th Husband and Wife § 4, Definitions.

§ 761. Property of certain revocable trusts as community property

(a) Unless the trust instrument or the instrument of transfer expressly provides otherwise, community property that is transferred in trust remains community property during the marriage, regardless of the identity of the trustee, if the trust, originally or as amended before or after the transfer, provides that the trust is revocable as to that property during the marriage and the power, if any, to modify the trust as to the rights and interests in that property during the marriage may be exercised only with the joinder or consent of both spouses.

(b) Unless the trust instrument expressly provides otherwise, a power to revoke as to community property may be exercised by either spouse acting alone. Community property, including any income or appreciation, that is distributed or withdrawn from a trust by revocation, power of withdrawal, or otherwise, remains community property unless there is a valid transmutation of the property at the time of distribution or withdrawal.

(c) The trustee may convey and otherwise manage and control the trust property in accordance with the provisions of the trust without the joinder or consent of either spouse unless the trust expressly requires the joinder or consent of one or both spouses.

(d) This section applies to a transfer made before, on, or after July 1, 1987.

(e) Nothing in this section affects the community character of property that is transferred before, on, or after July 1, 1987, in any manner or to a trust other than described in this section. *(Stats.1992, c. 162 (A.B.2650), § 10, operative Jan. 1, 1994. Amended by Stats.2014, c. 82 (S.B.1306), § 17, eff. Jan. 1, 2015.)*

Law Revision Commission Comments

Enactment [Revised Comment]

Section 761 continues former Civil Code Section 5110.150 without change. It should be noted that a transfer in trust by a married person is not exempt from the general limitations on transfers and transmutations by married persons acting alone. See Sections 850–853 (limitations on transmutations), 1100, 1102 (limitations on transfers).

Subdivision (a) is intended to be consistent with Revenue Ruling 66–283 in order to obtain community property income tax treatment for the trust property under Internal Revenue Code Section 1014(b)(6), but whether the terms of a particular trust are sufficient to obtain such treatment is ultimately a matter of federal law.

One consequence of retention of its community character is that the trust property is subject to claims of creditors and to division at dissolution to the same extent as any other community property. See Sections 910–916 (general rules of liability); Prob. Code § 18200 (creditors' rights against revocable trust during settlor's lifetime). Likewise, the interest of the decedent in the community property is subject to testamentary disposition at death, unless a contrary method of disposition is provided in the trust instrument, as is typically the case. Prob. Code § 104. In this situation, the spouses' traditional community property right of testamentary disposition is substantially preserved by the unilateral power of revocation. See subdivision (b). Where the trust requires joint action for revocation, the trust could preserve the power of testamentary disposition by granting the first spouse to die a testamentary power of modification, appointment, or disposition as to the spouse's share of the community property.

Subdivision (b) establishes the presumption that either spouse acting alone may revoke the trust as to the community property. The statute makes clear, however, that a unilateral revocation does not change the community property character of property received by the revoking spouse.

Subdivision (c) makes clear that the trustee may manage the trust community property in the same manner as other trust assets, free from the general limitations on disposition of community property imposed on spouses, unless the trust expressly provides such limitations.

Section 761 is not restrictive and does not provide the exclusive means by which community property may be held in trust without loss of its community character. See subdivision (e). [23 Cal.L.Rev. Comm. Reports 1 (1993)].

Commentary

For general discussion of Section 761, see *Estate of Wernicke, 16 Cal.App.4th 1069, 1076 n.7, 20 Cal.Rptr.2d 481 (1993)*.

Research References

Forms

California Transactions Forms--Estate Planning § 10:4, Community Property.
California Transactions Forms--Estate Planning § 13:10, Revocation Of Trust Created by More Than One Settlor.
California Transactions Forms--Estate Planning § 13:17, Joinder and Consent.
California Transactions Forms--Estate Planning § 13:18, Revocable Trust Property Retains Community Property Status.
California Transactions Forms--Estate Planning § 13:19, Legal Effect Of Retention Of Community Character.
California Transactions Forms--Estate Planning § 13:20, Tax Effect Of Retention Of Community Character.
California Transactions Forms--Estate Planning § 13:21, Transmutation.
California Transactions Forms--Estate Planning § 13:22, Agent May Amend or Revoke.
California Transactions Forms--Family Law § 2:45, Trust Terms Obsolete.
California Transactions Forms--Family Law § 2:46, No Transmutation.

Treatises and Practice Aids

Witkin, California Summary 10th Community Property § 4, Community Property.
Witkin, California Summary 10th Community Property § 147, Requirement Of Spouse's Consent.
Witkin, California Summary 10th Community Property § 250, Probate Code Revision.
Witkin, California Summary 10th Trusts § 23, Other Provisions Governing Trusts.
Witkin, California Summary 10th Trusts § 196, Methods Of Revocation.
Witkin, California Summary 10th Trusts § 198, Trust Of Community Property.
Witkin, California Summary 10th Wills and Probate § 265, Disposition.

Witkin, California Summary 10th Wills and Probate § 818, Property Passing Without Administration.

CHAPTER 2. SEPARATE PROPERTY

§ 770. Separate property of married person

(a) Separate property of a married person includes all of the following:

(1) All property owned by the person before marriage.

(2) All property acquired by the person after marriage by gift, bequest, devise, or descent.

(3) The rents, issues, and profits of the property described in this section.

(b) A married person may, without the consent of the person's spouse, convey the person's separate property. *(Stats.1992, c. 162 (A.B.2650), § 10, operative Jan. 1, 1994.)*

Law Revision Commission Comments

Enactment [Revised Comment]

Section 770 restates former Civil Code Sections 5107 and 5108 without substantive change. The two former sections (which separately stated the same rule, one in relation to a wife and the other to a husband) have been combined and made gender-neutral. For special definitions of separate property in other contexts, see Sections 2502 (division of property), 3515 (support). See also Cal. Const. Art. I, § 21 (separate property). [23 Cal.L.Rev.Comm. Reports 1 (1993)].

Commentary

Once the community property presumption arises, the burden shifts to the separate property proponent to show that the asset in question is nevertheless section 770 property, or that it is traceable to Section 770 property. *Meyer v. Kinzer, 12 Cal. 247 (1859)*; *Estate of Clark, 94 Cal.App. 453, 271 P. 542 (1928)*. See Section 760, Commentary. When separate and community funds have been commingled in a single bank account, the separate property proponent has the burden of tracing the separate funds. See *In re Marriage of Mix, 14 Cal.3d 604, 122 Cal.Rptr. 79 (1975)* ("direct tracing"); *See v. See, 64 Cal.2d 778, 51 Cal.Rptr. 888 (1966)* ("exhaustion" method of tracing); *In re Marriage of Braud, 45 Cal.App.4th 797, 822–826, 53 Cal.Rptr.2d 179 (1996)* (explaining and applying tracing rules); and *In re Marriage of Frick, 181 Cal.App.3d 997, 226 Cal.Rptr. 766 (1986), review denied 8/28/86* (both tracing methods and implicit criticism of *Mix, supra*). See also Probate Code Section 5305(b)(1) (funds deposited by married persons in jointly titled bank accounts may be traced to separate property unless there is a written agreement to the contrary). Compare Family Code Section 2640 (separate contributions to the purchase price or improvement of community property are merely reimbursed without interest).

Subsection (2), which includes all property acquired by a person during marriage by gift, bequest, devise, or descent, includes only those acquisitions that have not been earned by the labor of a spouse. Thus, an acquisition that might be termed a "gift" to one spouse for other legal purposes may nevertheless be community property. See, for example, *Downer v. Bramet, 152 Cal.App.3d 837, 199 Cal.Rptr. 830 (1984)* (holding that although a retirement "gift" from husband's employer was legally in the form of a gift in that it was made voluntarily without legal obligation, nevertheless it was community property to the extent that it was made in recognition of the husband's employment services.) See also *Andrews v. Andrews, 116 Wash. 513, 199 P. 981 (1921)* (Washington court holds that recovery under a contract to make a bequest in exchange for care and support of aged parents would be community property). Moreover, the definition of "gift" for purposes of Section 770 may be more restrictive than the definition of "gift" for purposes of the Section 1100(b) requirement that neither spouse may make a gift of community property without the written consent of the other spouse. Compare *Bramet, supra*, with *Estate of Bray, 230 Cal.App.2d 136, 40 Cal.Rptr. 750 (1964)* (husband's transfers to employee-son "gifts" for purpose of requiring wife's written consent).

Property that would otherwise be community property under Section 760 may be made separate property by the parties' agreement before or during marriage. See generally Sections 850–853 (transmutation during marriage), 1500–1502, 1620 (premarital and marital agreements) and 1503–1617 (premarital agreements). Such agreements are effective with respect to third-party creditor claims. See, for example, *Leasefirst v. Borrelli, 13 Cal.App.4th Supp. 28, 30, 17 Cal.Rptr.2d 114 (1993)* and cases cited therein.

Research References

Forms

California Practice Guide: Rutter Family Law Forms Form 1:32, Glossary Of Common Family Law Terms, Phrases and Concepts (Enclosure to Form 1:31).

California Transactions Forms--Estate Planning § 10:3, Separate Property.

California Transactions Forms--Estate Planning § 19:17, Separate Property.

California Transactions Forms--Family Law § 2:28, Dividing Defined Contribution Plan.

California Transactions Forms--Family Law § 2:34, Mixed-Character Asset Described.

Am. Jur. Pl. & Pr. Forms Community Property § 3, Complaint, Petition, or Declaration--By Spouse--To Determine Defendant Spouse's Adverse Claims to Community Interest in Plaintiff's Real Property Acquired After Marriage.

West's California Code Forms, Family § 2550, Comment Overview--Manner Of Division Of Community Estate.

Treatises and Practice Aids

Witkin, California Summary 10th Community Property § 5, Separate Property.

Witkin, California Summary 10th Community Property § 14, Separate Property Acquired During Marriage.

Witkin, California Summary 10th Husband and Wife § 18, in General.

§ 771. Earnings and accumulations after date of separation

(a) The earnings and accumulations of a spouse and the minor children living with, or in the custody of, the spouse, after the date of separation of the spouses, are the separate property of the spouse.

(b) Notwithstanding subdivision (a), the earnings and accumulations of an unemancipated minor child related to a contract of a type described in Section 6750 shall remain the sole legal property of the minor child. *(Stats.1992, c. 162 (A.B.2650), § 10, operative Jan. 1, 1994. Amended by Stats. 1999, c. 940 (S.B.1162), § 1; Stats.2016, c. 114 (S.B.1255), § 2, eff. Jan. 1, 2017.)*

Law Revision Commission Comments

Enactment [Revised Comment]

Section 771 continues former Civil Code Section 5118 without change. [23 Cal.L.Rev.Comm. Reports 1 (1993)].

Commentary

This section was amended in 2016 to replace "living separate and apart" with "the date of separation of the spouses." The latter term is defined by section 70 of the Family Code. The purpose of the 2016 amendments was to abrogate two cases holding that spouses could not satisfy the requirements of this section unless they lived in separate residences (*In re Marriage of Davis, 61 Cal.4th 846, 352 P.3d 401, 189 Cal.Rptr.3d 835 (2015)* and *In re Marriage of Norviel, 102 Cal.App.4th 1152, 126 Cal.Rptr.2d 148 (2002)*).

Separation, defined by section 70, requires that the marriage have come to an end both objectively and subjectively. Objectively, the parties must no longer be living and working together as a marital economic community. Subjectively, at least one spouse must have no present intention of ever resuming the marital relationship. *In re Marriage of Baragry, 73 Cal.App.3d 444, 140 Cal.Rptr. 779 (1977)*. See additionally *In re Marriage of Von der Nuell, 23 Cal.App.4th 730, 28 Cal.Rptr.2d 447 (1994)* (trial court erred in ruling that the date the husband moved out of the family home was the couple's date of separation when the parties' subsequent conduct did not evidence a complete and final break in the marital relationship); and *In re Marriage of Hardin, 38 Cal.App.4th 448, 45 Cal.Rptr.2d 308 (1995)* (trial court erred in finding Section 771 separation of the parties when neither party subjectively believed that the marital rift was permanent). See also *In re Marriage of Marsden, 130 Cal.App.3d 426, 434, 181 Cal.Rptr. 910 (1982)*; *Makeig v. U.S. Security Bank & Trust Co., 112 Cal.App. 138, 143–144, 296 P. 673 (1931)*.

In re Marriage of Manfer, 144 Cal.App.4th 925, 50 Cal.Rptr.3d 785 (2006) held, for purposes of this section, a couple lived "separate and apart" when they agreed that their marriage was over and one of them moved out of the family residence, even though they kept their separation secret for some time to spare the feelings of their daughters and friends. *Manfer* rejects the notion, suggested by *Baragry* dictum, that public perception, or the "outsider's viewpoint," is determinative. So long as there is adequate evidence of physical separation and the intentions of the parties, public perception is immaterial.

Determination of the date of separation merely requires proof by a preponderance of the evidence, rather than by clear and convincing evidence. *In re Marriage of Peters, 52 Cal.App.4th 1487, 61 Cal.Rptr.2d 493 (1997), review denied May 21, 1997.*

As property acquired during marriage may be traced to separate property (see Section 770, Commentary), so earnings and accumulations received after separation may be traced to marital labor or capital and hence characterized as community property. See, for example, *In re Marriage of Imperato, 45 Cal.App.3d 432, 119 Cal.Rptr. 590 (1975)*.

Research References

Forms

California Transactions Forms--Estate Planning § 10:3, Separate Property.

California Transactions Forms--Estate Planning § 19:17, Separate Property.

Treatises and Practice Aids

Witkin, California Summary 10th Community Property § 10, Current Law.

Witkin, California Summary 10th Community Property § 11, Valuation Based on Date Of Separation.

Witkin, California Summary 10th Community Property § 12, Permanent Separation.

Witkin, California Summary 10th Community Property § 14, Separate Property Acquired During Marriage.

Witkin, California Summary 10th Community Property § 46, Profits from Community Property Business.

Witkin, California Summary 10th Community Property § 61, Enhanced Early Retirement Benefits.

Witkin, California Summary 10th Community Property § 106, Date Of Valuation Of Law Practice.

Witkin, California Summary 10th Community Property § 192, Consideration Of Covenant Not to Compete.

Witkin, California Summary 10th Community Property § 257, Clarifications and Distinctions.

Witkin, California Summary 10th Community Property § 266, Where Legal Spouse Also Claims.

Witkin, California Summary 10th Parent and Child § 296, in General.

§ 772. Earnings or accumulations after entry of judgment of legal separation

After entry of a judgment of legal separation of the parties, the earnings or accumulations of each party are the separate property of the party acquiring the earnings or accumulations. *(Stats.1992, c. 162 (A.B.2650), § 10, operative Jan. 1, 1994.)*

Law Revision Commission Comments

Enactment [Revised Comment]

Section 772 continues former Civil Code Section 5119 without substantive change. The phrase "entry of a judgment of legal separation" has been substituted for "the rendition of a judgment decreeing legal separation." This is not a substantive change. See Section 100 ("judgment" includes decree, as appropriate). [23 Cal.L.Rev.Comm. Reports 1 (1993)].

Research References

Forms

California Transactions Forms--Estate Planning § 10:3, Separate Property.

California Transactions Forms--Estate Planning § 19:17, Separate Property.

Treatises and Practice Aids

Witkin, California Summary 10th Community Property § 10, Current Law.

Witkin, California Summary 10th Community Property § 257, Clarifications and Distinctions.

CHAPTER 3. DAMAGES FOR INJURIES TO MARRIED PERSON

§ 780. Community property

Except as provided in Section 781 and subject to the rules of allocation set forth in Section 2603, money and other property received or to be received by a married person in satisfaction of a judgment for damages for personal injuries, or pursuant to an agreement for the settlement or compromise of a claim for such damages, is community property if the cause of action for the damages arose during the marriage. *(Stats.1992, c. 162 (A.B.2650), § 10, operative Jan. 1, 1994.)*

Law Revision Commission Comments

Enactment [Revised Comment]

Section 780 is new and is drawn from the last sentence of former Civil Code Section 4800(b)(4). This section continues existing law. See, e.g., *In re* Marriage of Devlin, 138 Cal.App.3d 804, 807, 189 Cal.Rptr. 1 (1982). See also Code Civ. Proc. § 370 (right of married person to sue without spouse being joined as a party). [23 Cal.L.Rev.Comm. Reports 1 (1993)].

Commentary

Section 780 is new in the sense that it is the first general codification of the old case-law rule that personal injury damages and settlements may be characterized as community property. *McFadden v. Santa Ana, Orange, and Tustin Street Railway Co., 87 Cal. 464, 467–468, 25 P. 681 (1891)*. In contrast, Civil Code Section 4800(b)(4) provided only for the treatment of personal injury recoveries at divorce. Nevertheless, Section 780 makes no substantive change in the law.

Research References

Forms

Cal. Transaction Forms - Bus. Transactions § 18:14, Spouses.
California Transactions Forms--Estate Planning § 19:17, Separate Property.
California Transactions Forms--Estate Planning § 19:18, Community Property.

Treatises and Practice Aids

Witkin, California Summary 10th Community Property § 40, Community Property Rule Restored.

§ 781. Separate property

(a) Money or other property received or to be received by a married person in satisfaction of a judgment for damages for personal injuries, or pursuant to an agreement for the settlement or compromise of a claim for those damages, is the separate property of the injured person if the cause of action for the damages arose as follows:

(1) After the entry of a judgment of dissolution of a marriage or legal separation of the parties.

(2) While either spouse, if he or she is the injured person, is living separate from the other spouse.

(b) Notwithstanding subdivision (a), if the spouse of the injured person has paid expenses by reason of the personal injuries from separate property or from the community property, the spouse is entitled to reimbursement of the separate property or the community property for those expenses from the separate property received by the injured person under subdivision (a).

(c) Notwithstanding subdivision (a), if one spouse has a cause of action against the other spouse which arose during the marriage of the parties, money or property paid or to be paid by or on behalf of a party to the party's spouse of that marriage in satisfaction of a judgment for damages for personal injuries to that spouse, or pursuant to an agreement for the settlement or compromise of a claim for the damages, is the separate property of the injured spouse. *(Stats.1992, c. 162 (A.B.2650), § 10, operative Jan. 1, 1994.)*

Law Revision Commission Comments

Enactment [Revised Comment]

Section 781 continues former Civil Code Section 5126 without substantive change. In subdivision (a)(1), the phrase "entry of a judgment of legal separation" has been substituted for "rendition of a decree of legal separation." This is not a substantive change. See Section 100 ("judgment" includes decree, as appropriate). The last paragraph of former Civil Code Section 5126(a), which dealt with retroactive application of the former section, has been omitted as temporary and obsolete. [23 Cal.L.Rev.Comm. Reports 1 (1993)].

Commentary

For discussion of the meaning of subsection (a)(2) "living separate from the other spouse," see Section 771, Commentary.

In re Marriage of Fisk, 2 Cal.App.4th 1698, 4 Cal.Rptr.2d 95 (1992), declined to allow subsection (b) reimbursement from a worker's compensation, as opposed to a personal injury, award.

Research References

Forms

California Transactions Forms--Estate Planning § 10:3, Separate Property.
California Transactions Forms--Estate Planning § 19:17, Separate Property.
West's California Code Forms, Family § 781, Comment Overview--Damages for Injuries to Married Person.
West's California Code Forms, Family § 2550, Comment Overview--Manner Of Division Of Community Estate.

Treatises and Practice Aids

Witkin, California Summary 10th Community Property § 40, Community Property Rule Restored.
Witkin, California Summary 10th Community Property § 41, Exceptions: Separate Property.
Witkin, California Summary 10th Community Property § 42, Reimbursement for Expenses.
Witkin, California Summary 10th Community Property § 202, Personal Injury Damages.
Witkin, California Summary 10th Community Property § 257, Clarifications and Distinctions.
Witkin, California Summary 10th Community Property § 266, Where Legal Spouse Also Claims.

§ 782. Injuries to married person by spouse; primary resort to separate property; consent of injured spouse to use of community property; indemnity

(a) Where an injury to a married person is caused in whole or in part by the negligent or wrongful act or omission of the person's spouse, the community property may not be used to discharge the liability of the tortfeasor spouse to the injured spouse or the liability to make contribution to a joint tortfeasor until the separate property of the tortfeasor spouse, not exempt from enforcement of a money judgment, is exhausted.

(b) This section does not prevent the use of community property to discharge a liability referred to in subdivision (a) if the injured spouse gives written consent thereto after the occurrence of the injury.

(c) This section does not affect the right to indemnity provided by an insurance or other contract to discharge the tortfeasor spouse's liability, whether or not the consideration given for the contract consisted of community property. *(Stats.1992, c. 162 (A.B.2650), § 10, operative Jan. 1, 1994.)*

Law Revision Commission Comments

Enactment [Revised Comment]

Section 782 continues former Civil Code Section 5113 without substantive change. The phrase "not exempt from enforcement of a money judgment" has been substituted for "not exempt from execution," in order to conform to the terminology of the Enforcement of Judgments Law. See, e.g., Code Civ. Proc. § 703.010. [23 Cal.L.Rev.Comm. Reports 1 (1993)].

Research References

Forms

West's California Code Forms, Family § 781, Comment Overview--Damages for Injuries to Married Person.

Treatises and Practice Aids

Witkin, California Summary 10th Community Property § 186, Interspousal Injuries.

§ 782.5. Attempted murder or soliciting the murder of a spouse; remedies; community property interests

In addition to any other remedy authorized by law, when a spouse is convicted of attempting to murder the other spouse, as punishable pursuant to subdivision (a) of Section 664 of the Penal Code, or of soliciting the murder of the other spouse, as punishable pursuant to subdivision (b) of Section 653f of the Penal Code, the injured spouse shall be entitled to an award to the injured spouse of 100 percent of the community property interest in the retirement and pension benefits of the injured spouse.

As used in this section, "injured spouse" has the same meaning as defined in Section 4324. *(Added by Stats.1995, c. 364 (A.B.16), § 2. Amended by Stats.2010, c. 65 (A.B.2674), § 1.)*

Research References

Treatises and Practice Aids

Witkin, California Summary 10th Community Property § 187, Attempted Murder Of Spouse.

§ 783. Injuries to married person by third party; extent concurring negligence of spouse allowable as defense

If a married person is injured by the negligent or wrongful act or omission of a person other than the married person's spouse, the fact that the negligent or wrongful act or omission of the spouse of the injured person was a concurring cause of the injury is not a defense in an action brought by the injured person to recover damages for the injury except in cases where the concurring negligent or wrongful act or omission would be a defense if the marriage did not exist. *(Stats.1992, c. 162 (A.B.2650), § 10, operative Jan. 1, 1994.)*

Law Revision Commission Comments

Enactment [Revised Comment]

Section 783 continues former Civil Code Section 5112 without substantive change. See also Code Civ. Proc. § 370 (right of married person to sue without spouse being joined as a party). [23 Cal.L.Rev.Comm. Reports 1 (1993)].

Research References

Treatises and Practice Aids

Witkin, California Summary 10th Community Property § 43, Spouse's Negligence as Concurring Cause.

Witkin, California Summary 10th Community Property § 186, Interspousal Injuries.

CHAPTER 4. PRESUMPTIONS CONCERNING NATURE OF PROPERTY

§ 802. Property acquired during marriage terminated by dissolution more than four years prior to death

The presumption that property acquired during marriage is community property does not apply to any property to which legal or equitable title is held by a person at the time of the person's death if the marriage during which the property was acquired was terminated by dissolution of marriage more than four years before the death. *(Stats.1992, c. 162 (A.B. 2650), § 10, operative Jan. 1, 1994.)*

Law Revision Commission Comments

Enactment [Revised Comment]

Section 802 continues former Civil Code Section 5111 without substantive change. [23 Cal.L.Rev.Comm. Reports 1 (1993)].

Research References

Forms

California Transactions Forms--Estate Planning § 19:18, Community Property.

Treatises and Practice Aids

Witkin, California Summary 10th Community Property § 15, Nature and Effect.

Witkin, California Summary 10th Community Property § 221, Effect Of Party's Death After Dissolution But Before Division.

§ 803. Property acquired by married woman before January 1, 1975; conclusiveness of presumptions

Notwithstanding any other provision of this part, whenever any real or personal property, or any interest therein or encumbrance thereon, was acquired before January 1, 1975, by a married woman by an instrument in writing, the following presumptions apply, and are conclusive in favor of any person dealing in good faith and for a valuable consideration with the married woman or her legal representatives or successors in interest, regardless of any change in her marital status after acquisition of the property:

(a) If acquired by the married woman, the presumption is that the property is the married woman's separate property.

(b) If acquired by the married woman and any other person, the presumption is that the married woman takes the part acquired by her as tenant in common, unless a different intention is expressed in the instrument.

(c) If acquired by husband and wife by an instrument in which they are described as husband and wife, the presumption is that the property is the community property of the husband and wife, unless a different intention is expressed in the instrument. *(Stats.1992, c. 162 (A.B.2650), § 10, operative Jan. 1, 1994.)*

Law Revision Commission Comments

Enactment [Revised Comment]

Section 803 restates without substantive change the last part of the first paragraph of former Civil Code Section 5110. The second paragraph of former Civil Code Section 5110 has been omitted as obsolete. [23 Cal.l.Rev.Comm. Reports 1 (1993)].

Commentary

Although the married woman's presumption is conclusive when asserted in favor of a good faith purchaser from a married woman or from her successors in interest, the presumption is otherwise rebuttable. Because the statute effectively presumes a gift to a married woman when title was placed in her name during the era of male management, that is, before 1975, it is not enough merely to trace the purchase money to community property. Instead, the husband or his successor in interest must rebut the presumption of gift by showing that the husband did not intend to make a gift to his wife. *Holmes v. Holmes, 27 Cal.App. 546, 150 P. 793 (1915)*. See also *Louknitsky v. Louknitsky, 123 Cal.App.2d 406, 266 P.2d 910 (1954)*.

Under subsection (b), an unqualified pre–1975 tenancy in common held by a husband and wife is owned 75 percent by the wife and 25 percent by the husband. See *Dunn v. Mullan, 211 Cal. 583, 296 P. 604 (1931)*. The spouses hold as tenants in common when their unqualified pre–1975 co-ownership title is inadequate to create a joint tenancy or community property title. *Cardew v. Cardew, 192 Cal. App.2d 502, 514, 13 Cal.Rptr. 620 (1961)*. If their title is sufficient to create a joint tenancy (see Civil Code Section 683), they hold equal interests as joint tenants because their title expresses a "different intention" within the meaning of subsection (b). *Siberell v. Siberell, 214 Cal. 767, 7 P.2d 1003 (1932)*. Similarly, explicit community property title expresses "a different intention" within the meaning of subsection (b).

Research References

Forms

West's California Code Forms, Family § 803, Comment Overview--Presumptions Concerning Nature Of Property.

Treatises and Practice Aids

Witkin, California Summary 10th Community Property § 20, Abolition Of Presumption.

Witkin, California Summary 10th Community Property § 21, to Wife and Stranger.

Witkin, California Summary 10th Community Property § 22, Community Property.

Witkin, California Summary 10th Community Property § 23, Exception: Driving With Permission Law.

CHAPTER 5. TRANSMUTATION OF PROPERTY

§ 850. Transmutation by agreem

Subject to Sections 851 to 853, may by agreement or transfer, with do any of the following:

(a) Transmute community prop of either spouse.

(b) Transmute separate proper community property.

(c) Transmute separate property property of the other spouse. *(Stats.1992, c. 162 (A.B.2650), § 10, operative Jan. 1, 1994.)*

Law Revision Commission Comments

Enactment [Revised Comment]

Section 850 continues former Civil Code Section 5110.710 without substantive change. When enacted in 1984 (as former Civil Code Section 5110.710), this provision codified the basic rule that spouses may transmute the character of community or separate property. See, e.g., Reppy, *Debt Collection from Married Californians: Problems Caused by Transmutations, Single–Spouse Management, and Invalid Marriage,* 18 San Diego L. Rev. 143 (1981).

In addition to the limitations on transmutation provided in Sections 851–853, the spouses are subject to the general rules governing the validity of agreements and transfers, as well as the special rules that control the actions of persons occupying confidential relations with each other. See Section 721. The characterization of community and separate property may be affected by a general marital property agreement, prenuptial or otherwise, as well as by a transmutation of specific property.

For background on former Civ. Code § 5110.710, see *Recommendation Relating to Marital Property Presumptions and Transmutations,* 17 Cal. L. Revision Comm'n Reports 205 (1984); 18 Cal. L. Revision Comm'n Reports 67 (1986). [23 Cal.L.Rev.Comm. Reports 1 (1993)].

Commentary

Note that Section 850 includes only interspousal transfers within the definition of "transmutation". It does not include spousal transfers to third parties. Spousal gifts to third parties are instead regulated by Section 1100(b).

In re Marriage of Valli, 58 Cal.4th 1396, 324 P.2d 274, 171 Cal.Rptr.3d 454 (2014), held that spousal purchases from a third party where the character of the purchase funds and the character of the asset are claimed to differ *are* transmutations subject to this Chapter. In order to relinquish a property interest that a spouse would otherwise have based on the character of the purchase funds, he must, under section 852, expressly declare in writing that he is giving up any interest he may have in the purchased asset. Thus, when Frankie Valli used community property funds to purchase a life insurance policy on his life and named his spouse as the owner of the policy, the policy remained community property because Frankie did not expressly declare in writing that he was giving up any interest he had in the policy. *Valli* overrules *In re Summers, 332 F.3d 1240 (9th Cir. 2003)* and *In re Marriage of Brooks & Robinson, 169 Cal.App.4th 176, 86 Cal.Rptr.3d 624 (2008)*, to the extent they hold that spousal purchases from third parties are not subject to the requirements of this Chapter. *Valli* also holds that the Evidence Code section 662 presumption arising from the form of title, a common law presumption, is inapplicable when it conflicts with the transmutation statutes. Justice Chin's concurrence in *Valli* further considers the relationship between the Evidence Code section 622 common law title presumption and California community property law.

Invoking *Valli*, *In re Marriage of Lafkas, 237 Cal.App.4th 921, 188 Cal.Rptr.3d 484 (2015), review denied*, held that the husband's separate property interest in a partnership agreement was not community property despite a modification of the ...igned by the husband, that named husband and wife as ... the partnership interest, because the modification did not ... an express declaration that the character of ownership was ...g changed.

Also invoking *Valli*, a Ninth Circuit Bankruptcy Appellate Panel, purporting to apply California community property law, held that a married couple's property held in joint tenancy title was community property for purposes of inclusion, in its entirety, in the husband's bankruptcy estate. Characterizing joint tenancy held by spouses in an intact marriage, *In re Brace, 566 B.R. 13 (B.A.P. 9th Cir. 2017)*, relied on section 760, the case law presumption that property acquired during marriage is community property, the section 2581 presumption that, at dissolution, property acquired in joint tenancy title is community property, and the transmutation provisions, including sections 850 through 852. The reasoning of *Brace* is ahistorical and unpersuasive. Its holding should be treated with circumspection.

Reversing the Bankruptcy Court, *In re Beverly, 374 B.R. 221 (U.S. Bankr. App. Pan., 9th Cir. 2007)*, held that a divorcing attorney's marital settlement agreement, which transferred nonexempt community property to his wife in exchange for an equivalent amount of his exempt community property retirement fund, was a fraudulent transfer under California Civil Code § 3439.04(a)(1) and therefore under 11 U.S.C. § 544(b). Thus, in the attorney's involuntary bankruptcy proceeding, the Bankruptcy Trustee could avoid the transfer and reach the attorney's community property interest in the nonexempt property.

Mejia v. Reed, 31 Cal.4th 657, 74 P.3d 166, 3 Cal.Rptr.3d 390 (2003), holds that the Uniform Fraudulent Transfer Act (Civil Code §§ 3439–3439.12) applies to marital settlement agreements. *Filip v. Bucurenciu, 129 Cal.App.4th 825, 28 Cal.Rptr.3d 884 (2005)*, approves a trial court's finding that the spouses' marital settlement agreement violates the Uniform Fraudulent Transfer Act.

Research References

Forms

California Transactions Forms--Estate Planning § 10:3, Separate Property.

California Transactions Forms--Estate Planning § 9:77, Beneficiary Designations Of Community Property Interests in Plan or IRA [Prob C §§ 5000 et seq.].

California Transactions Forms--Estate Planning § 11:35, Agreement Entered Into on or After January 1, 1985.

California Transactions Forms--Estate Planning § 11:47, Formalities.

California Transactions Forms--Estate Planning § 11:48, Governing Contractual Provisions [CC §§ 1550 et seq., Fam C S721(B)].

California Transactions Forms--Estate Planning § 11:59, Matters to Include in Transmutation Agreement.

California Transactions Forms--Estate Planning § 11:68, General Transmutation Agreement.

California Transactions Forms--Estate Planning § 13:21, Transmutation.

West's California Code Forms, Family § 850, Comment Overview--Transmutation by Agreement or Transfer.

West's California Code Forms, Family § 850 Form 2, Agreement Transmuting Separate Property to Community Property.

West's California Code Forms, Family § 850 Form 3, Agreement Transmuting Separate Property Of Spouse to Separate Property Of Other Spouse.

Treatises and Practice Aids

Witkin, California Summary 10th Community Property § 14, Separate Property Acquired During Marriage.

Witkin, California Summary 10th Community Property § 152, Law Revision Commission Report.

Witkin, California Summary 10th Community Property § 153, Authority to Transmute.

Witkin, California Summary 10th Community Property § 155, Writing Requirement.

Witkin, California Summary 10th Community Property § 222, Statutory Rule.

§ 851. Transmutation subject to fraudulent transfer laws

A transmutation is subject to the laws governing fraudulent transfers. *(Stats.1992, c. 162 (A.B.2650), § 10, operative Jan. 1, 1994.)*

Law Revision Commission Comments

Enactment [Revised Comment]

Section 851 continues former Civil Code Section 5110.720 without change. When enacted in 1984 (as former Civil Code Section 5110.720), this provision codified case law. *Cf.* Bailey v. Leeper, 142 Cal.App.2d 460, 298 P.2d 684 (1956) (transfer of property from husband to wife); Frankel v. Boyd, 106 Cal. 608, 614, 39 P. 939, 941 (1895) (dictum); Wikes v. Smith, 465 F.2d 1142 (1972) (bankruptcy). See also Civ. Code § 3439 *et seq.* (general law regarding fraudulent transfers).

For background on former Civ. Code § 5110.720, see *Recommendation Relating to Marital Property Presumptions and Transmutations,* 17 Cal. L. Revision Comm'n Reports 205 (1984); 18 Cal. L. Revision Comm'n Reports 68 (1986). [23 Cal.L.Rev.Comm. Reports 1 (1993)].

Commentary

State Board of Equalization v. Woo, 82 Cal.App.4th 481, 98 Cal.Rptr.2d 206 (2000), holds that a marital agreement transmuting the wife's future earnings into her separate property, which was entered by the spouses after the wife was notified that the Board would seek to reach her future earnings to satisfy her husband's tax debt, was a fraudulent transfer.

Mejia v. Reed, 31 Cal.4th 657, 74 P.3d 166, 3 Cal.Rptr.3d 390 (2003), holds that the Uniform Fraudulent Transfer Act (Civil Code §§ 3439–3439.12) applies to marital settlement agreements. *Filip v. Bucurenciu, 129 Cal.App.4th 825, 28 Cal.Rptr.3d 884 (2005)*, approves a trial court's finding that the spouses' marital settlement agreement violates the Uniform Fraudulent Transfer Act.

Reversing the Bankruptcy Court, *In re Beverly, 374 B.R. 221 (U.S. Bankr. App. Pan., 9th Cir. 2007)*, held that a divorcing attorney's marital settlement agreement, which transferred nonexempt community property to his wife in exchange for an equivalent amount of his exempt community property retirement fund, was a fraudulent transfer under California Civil Code § 3439.04(a)(1) and therefore under 11 U.S.C. § 544(b). Thus, in the attorney's involuntary bankruptcy proceeding, the Bankruptcy Trustee could avoid the transfer and reach the attorney's community property interest in the nonexempt property.

A Ninth Circuit Bankruptcy Appellate Panel, purporting to apply California community property law, held that a married couple's property held in joint tenancy title is community property for purposes of inclusion, in its entirety, in the husband's bankruptcy estate. Characterizing joint tenancy held by spouses in an intact marriage, *In re Brace, 566 B.R. 13 (B.A.P. 9th Cir. 2017)*, relied on this section, the case law presumption that property acquired during marriage is community property, the section 2581 presumption that, at dissolution, property acquired in joint tenancy title is community property, the transmutation provisions, including sections 850 through 852, and *In re Marriage of Valli, 58 Cal. 4th 1396 (2014)*. The reasoning of *Brace* is ahistorical and unpersuasive. Its holding should be treated with circumspection.

Research References

Forms

California Transactions Forms--Estate Planning § 11:35, Agreement Entered Into on or After January 1, 1985.

West's California Code Forms, Family § 850, Comment Overview--Transmutation by Agreement or Transfer.

Treatises and Practice Aids

Witkin, California Summary 10th Community Property § 153, Authority to Transmute.

§ 852. Requirements

(a) A transmutation of real or personal property is not valid unless made in writing by an express declaration that is made, joined in, consented to, or accepted by the spouse whose interest in the property is adversely affected.

(b) A transmutation of real property is not effective as to third parties without notice thereof unless recorded.

(c) This section does not apply to a gift between the spouses of clothing, wearing apparel, jewelry, or other tangible articles of a personal nature that is used solely or principally by the spouse to whom the gift is made and that is not substantial in value taking into account the circumstances of the marriage.

(d) Nothing in this section affects the law governing characterization of property in which separate property and community property are commingled or otherwise combined.

(e) This section does not apply to or affect a transmutation of property made before January 1, 1985, and the law that would otherwise be applicable to that transmutation shall continue to apply. *(Stats.1992, c. 162 (A.B.2650), § 10, operative Jan. 1, 1994.)*

Law Revision Commission Comments

Enactment [Revised Comment]

Section 852 continues former Civil Code Section 5110.730 without change. See also Section 700 (real property includes leasehold interests in real property).

Section 852 imposes formalities on interspousal transmutations for the purpose of increasing certainty in the determination whether a transmutation has in fact occurred. Section 852 makes clear that the ordinary rules and formalities applicable to real property transfers apply also to transmutations of real property between the spouses. See Civ. Code §§ 1091, 1624 (statute of frauds), 1213–1217 (effect of recording). When enacted in 1984 (as former Civil Code Section 5110.730), this provision overruled case law. See, e.g., Woods v. Security First Nat'l Bank, 46 Cal.2d 697, 701, 299 P.2d 657, 659 (1956). It also overruled prior law that permitted oral transmutation of personal property; however, transmutation by gift of certain personal property was recognized.

For background on former Civ. Code § 5110.730, see *Recommendation Relating to Marital Property Presumptions and Transmutations,* 17 Cal. L. Revision Comm'n Reports 205 (1984); 18 Cal. L. Revision Comm'n Reports 68 (1986). [23 Cal.L.Rev.Comm. Reports 1 (1993)].

Commentary

Estate of MacDonald, 51 Cal.3d 262, 264, 272 Cal.Rptr. 153 (1990), holds that "a writing is not an 'express declaration' for the purposes of section [852(a)] unless it contains language which expressly states that a change in the characterization or ownership of the property is being made." A purported transfer that does not satisfy the rigorous *MacDonald* "express declaration" requirement and hence fails to work a present transmutation, may nevertheless be effective as spousal consent to a nonprobate beneficiary designation. Such consent remains revocable while both spouses are living. At the death of either spouse after January 1, 1993, the consent becomes irrevocable. Stats 1992 Ch 51, codified at Family Code Section 853 and Probate Code Sections 5002–5032.

Applying *MacDonald, In re Marriage of Barneson, 69 Cal.App.4th 583, 81 Cal.Rptr.2d 726 (1999),* holds that a husband's written order to "transfer" stocks to his wife's name did not satisfy the subsection (a) express declaration requirement because the word "transfer" does not necessarily imply a change in ownership. *Estate of Bibb, 87 Cal.App.4th 461, 104 Cal.Rptr.2d 415 (2001), review denied May 16, 2001,* holds that a grant deed transferring a husband's separate property to himself and his wife satisfied subsection (a), but that a Department of Motor Vehicles registration form indicating a change in registration from the husband alone to the husband or wife did not satisfy subsection (a).

In re Marriage of Starkman, 129 Cal.App.4th 659, 28 Cal.Rptr.3d 639 (2005), review denied, holds that, as between husband and wife, a revocable living trust provision stating that all property that is not identified as the separate property of the husband or wife is the community property of the parties, was not sufficient to work a transmutation under this section because there was no unambiguous indication that the husband intended thereby to change the character of the separate property he placed in the trust into the community property of the parties. Compare *In re Marriage of Holtemann, 166 Cal.App.4th 1166, 83 Cal.Rptr.3d 385 (2008), review denied,* which found a transmutation when a "transmutation agreement" contained explicit and unambiguous language of present transmutation, even though the agreement was incident to an estate planning trust. Accord, *In re Marriage of Lund, 174 Cal.App.4th 40, 94 Cal.Rptr.3d 84 (2009).*

In re Marriage of Leni, 144 Cal.App.4th 1087, 50 Cal.Rptr.3d 886 (2006), held that a separated couple's escrow instruction that proceeds from the sale of a community property home be split 50–50 between them did not transmute each spouse's share of the sale proceeds into that spouse's separate property.

Also interpreting *MacDonald, In re Marriage of Campbell, 74 Cal.App.4th 1058, 88 Cal.Rptr.2d 580 (1999), review denied November 17, 1999,* held that the § 852(a) requirement of an express written declaration of transmutation bars the use of extrinsic oral evidence to estop the promisor from asserting the § 852(a) statute of frauds in order to enable the promisee to enforce an oral transmutation agreement. Compare § 1611, the statute of frauds requirement for premarital agreements. Section 1611 has been interpreted to incorporate the usual exceptions to the statute of frauds, including equitable estoppel. When, under § 1611, a promisee has relied to her detriment on an oral premarital promise, the promisor is estopped to assert the statute of frauds, and thus the promisee may avoid the statute of frauds and enforce the oral promise. *In re Marriage of Benson, 36 Cal.4th 1096, 116 P.3d 1152, 32 Cal.Rptr.3d 471(2005),* holds that the usual exceptions to the statute of frauds (see Commentary to Section 1611) may not be used to avoid the subsection (a) writing requirement.

In re Marriage of Valli, 58 Cal.4th 1396, 324 P.2d 274, 171 Cal.Rptr.3d 454 (2014), held that spousal purchases from a third party where the character of the purchase funds and the character of the asset are claimed to differ *are* transmutations subject to this Chapter. In order to relinquish a property interest that a spouse would otherwise have based on the character of the purchase funds, he must, under section 852, expressly declare in writing that he is giving up any interest he may have in the purchased asset. Thus, when Frankie Valli used community property funds to purchase a life insurance policy on his life and named his spouse as the owner of the policy, the policy remained community property because Frankie did not expressly declare in writing that he was giving up any interest he had in the policy. *Valli* overrules *In re Summers, 332 F.3d 1240 (9th Cir. 2003)* and *In re Marriage of Brooks & Robinson, 169 Cal.App.4th*

176, 86 Cal.Rptr.3d 624 (2008), to the extent they hold that spousal purchases from third parties are not subject to the requirements of this Chapter. *Valli* also holds that the Evidence Code section 662 presumption arising from the form of title, a common law presumption, is inapplicable when it conflicts with the transmutation statutes. Justice Chin's concurrence in *Valli* further considers the relationship between the Evidence Code section 622 common law title presumption and California community property law.

Invoking *Valli*, *In re Marriage of Lafkas, 237 Cal.App.4th 921, 188 Cal.Rptr.3d 484 (2015), review denied*, held that the husband's separate property interest in a partnership agreement was not transmuted to community property despite a modification of the agreement, signed by husband, that named husband and wife as owners of the partnership interest, because the modification did not contain an express declaration that the character of ownership was being changed.

Also invoking *Valli*, a Ninth Circuit Bankruptcy Appellate Panel, purporting to apply California community property law, held that a married couple's property held in joint tenancy title was community property for purposes of inclusion, in its entirety, in the husband's bankruptcy estate. Characterizing joint tenancy held by spouses in an intact marriage, *In re Brace, 566 B.R. 13 (B.A.P. 9th Cir. 2017), relied on section 760,* the case law presumption that property acquired during marriage is community property, the section 2581 presumption that, at dissolution, property acquired in joint tenancy title is community property, and the transmutation provisions, including sections 850 through 852. The reasoning of *Brace* is ahistorical and unpersuasive. Its holding should be treated with circumspection.

For further discussion of Section 852, see *Estate of Petersen 28 Cal.App.4th 1742, 34 Cal.Rptr.2d 449 (1994)* (ruling on various transmutation issues); *In re Marriage of Steinberger, 91 Cal.App.4th 1449, 111 Cal.Rptr.2d 521 (2001), review denied November 14, 2001* (affirming trial court's holding that diamond ring worth between $13,000 and $14,000 and purchased by spouses with community funds as a gift for high-earning wife was, for purposes of subsection (c), "substantial in value taking into account the circumstances of the marriage"). Also interpreting subsection (c), *In re Marriage of Neighbors, 179 Cal.App.4th 1170, 102 Cal.Rptr.3d 387 (2009)*, held that an automobile is not "a tangible article of a personal nature" within the meaning of that subsection.

Note that the writing requirement of Section 852 applies only to transmutations made on or after January 1, 1985. Transmutations before that date are regulated by more generous case law, which recognizes oral and even implied-in-fact transmutation on the theory that married persons are likely to engage in informal transactions. See, for example, *Estate of Nelson, 224 Cal.App.2d 138, 36 Cal.Rptr. 352 (1964)* and *Estate of Raphael, 91 Cal.App.2d 931, 206 P.2d 391 (1949)*. Compare *In re Marriage of Jafeman, 29 Cal.App.3d 244, 105 Cal.Rptr. 483 (1972)*. Although prior case law applied the usual "preponderance of the evidence" standard to pre–1985 oral transmutation, *In re Marriage of Weaver, 224 Cal.App.3d 478, 273 Cal.Rptr. 696 (1990)*, holds that Evidence Code Section 662 applies to pre–1985 oral transmutation. Evidence Code Section 662 provides: "The owner of the legal title to property is presumed to be the owner of the full beneficial title. This presumption may be rebutted only by clear and convincing proof." See also *Tannehill v. Finch, 188 Cal.App.3d 224, 232 Cal.Rptr. 749 (1986), review denied 3/11/87* (applying Section 662 in a *Marvin* cohabitation action). But see *In re Marriage of Haines, 33 Cal.App.4th 277, 39 Cal.Rptr.2d 673 (1995)*, which holds that Evidence Code Section 662 does not apply in family law proceedings insofar as its application would be inconsistent with the presumption of undue influence that arises from the Family Code Section 721 principle that the spouses have a confidential relationship in their transactions with each other.

Mejia v. Reed, 31 Cal.4th 657, 74 P.3d 166, 3 Cal.Rptr.3d 390 (2003), holds that the Uniform Fraudulent Transfer Act (Civil Code §§ 3439–3439.12) applies to marital settlement agreements. *Filip v. Bucurenciu, 129 Cal.App.4th 825, 28 Cal.Rptr.3d 884 (2005)*, approves a trial court's finding that the spouses' marital settlement agreement violates the Uniform Fraudulent Transfer Act.

Reversing the Bankruptcy Court, *In re Beverly, 374 B.R. 221 (U.S. Bankr. App. Pan., 9th Cir. 2007)*, held that a divorcing attorney's marital settlement agreement, which transferred nonexempt community property to his wife in exchange for an equivalent amount of his exempt community property retirement fund, was a fraudulent transfer under California Civil Code § 3439.04(a)(1) and therefore under 11 U.S.C. § 544(b). Thus, in the attorney's involuntary bankruptcy proceeding, the Bankruptcy Trustee could avoid the transfer and reach the attorney's community property interest in the nonexempt property.

Although an interspousal transaction satisfies the formal requirements of this section, it may nevertheless be ineffective because it violates the fiduciary duty that spouses owe to one another. A rebuttable presumption of undue influence arises when one spouse gains an advantage over the other in an interspousal transaction. For discussion of the presumption, see commentary to Section 721.

Research References

Forms

California Transactions Forms--Estate Planning § 1:21, Severing Joint Tenancies in Real Property.

California Transactions Forms--Estate Planning § 1:24, Community Property Versus Joint Tenancy.

California Transactions Forms--Estate Planning § 1:25, Joint Tenancy or Community Property Treatment Of Property in Revocable Trust.

California Transactions Forms--Estate Planning § 10:4, Community Property.

California Transactions Forms--Estate Planning § 10:7, Joint Tenancy.

California Transactions Forms--Estate Planning § 10:14, Formalities Required.

California Transactions Forms--Estate Planning § 10:19, Joint Tenancy Property.

California Transactions Forms--Estate Planning § 11:34, Agreement Entered Into Before January 1, 1985.

California Transactions Forms--Estate Planning § 11:35, Agreement Entered Into on or After January 1, 1985.

California Transactions Forms--Estate Planning § 11:36, Family Code S852 Transmutations and Rules Governing Fiduciary Relationships.

California Transactions Forms--Estate Planning § 11:59, Matters to Include in Transmutation Agreement.

California Transactions Forms--Estate Planning § 13:21, Transmutation.

California Transactions Forms--Estate Planning § 19:17, Separate Property.

California Transactions Forms--Estate Planning § 19:70, Characterization Of Property.

California Transactions Forms--Family Law § 2:18, Reimbursement Of Separate Property Contribution [Fam C § 2640].

California Transactions Forms--Family Law § 2:42, Excess Tax Payments.

West's California Code Forms, Family § 850, Comment Overview--Transmutation by Agreement or Transfer.

Treatises and Practice Aids

Witkin, California Summary 10th Community Property § 154, in General.

Witkin, California Summary 10th Community Property § 155, Writing Requirement.

Witkin, California Summary 10th Community Property § 156, Estate Planning Transactions.

Witkin, California Summary 10th Wills and Probate § 310, Consent.

§ 853. Characterization of property in will; admissibility in proceedings commenced before death of testator; waiver of right to joint and survivor annuity or survivor's benefits; written joinders or consents to nonprobate transfers of community property

(a) A statement in a will of the character of property is not admissible as evidence of a transmutation of the property in a proceeding commenced before the death of the person who made the will.

(b) A waiver of a right to a joint and survivor annuity or survivor's benefits under the federal Retirement Equity Act of 1984 (Public Law 98-397) [1] is not a transmutation of the community property rights of the person executing the waiver.

(c) A written joinder or written consent to a nonprobate transfer of community property on death that satisfies Section 852 is a transmutation and is governed by the law applicable to transmutations and not by Chapter 2 (commencing with Section 5010) of Part 1 of Division 5 of the Probate Code. *(Stats.1992, c. 162 (A.B.2650), § 10, operative Jan. 1, 1994. Amended by Stats.1993, c. 219 (A.B.1500), § 100.)*

[1] See Short Title of 1984 Amendment note under 29 U.S.C.A. § 1001 for classifications of the Act.

Law Revision Commission Comments

Enactment [Revised Comment]

Section 853 continues former Civil Code Section 5110.740 without substantive change. When enacted in 1984 (as former Civil Code Section 5110.740), subdivision (a) of this provision reversed the case-law rule that a declaration made in a will as to the character of property may be an effective transmutation of the property before the death of the declarant. See, e.g., *In re* Marriage of Lotz, 120 Cal.App.3d 379, 174 Cal.Rptr. 618 (1981); Estate of Wilson, 64 Cal.App.3d 786, 134 Cal.Rptr. 749 (1976). Section 853 is consistent with the general concepts that a will is ambulatory and subject to subsequent revocation or modification and does not speak until the testator's death.

For background on former Civ. Code § 5110.740, see *Recommendation Relating to Marital Property Presumptions and Transmutations,* 17 Cal. L. Revision Comm'n Reports 205 (1984); *Nonprobate Transfers of Community Property,* 21 Cal. L. Revision Comm'n Reports 163 (1991). [23 Cal.L.Rev.Comm. Reports 1 (1993)].

Commentary

In re Marriage of Weaver, 224 Cal.App.3d 478, 489, 273 Cal.Rptr. 696 (1990), holds that subsection (a) applies in any action brought after the statute's effective date (January 1, 1985), without regard to the date of the purported transmutation or the date of the will. Compare Section 852, which applies only to post–1984 transmutation.

Relying in part on Family Code Section 853, *Estate of Gallio, 33 Cal.App.4th 592, 39 Cal.Rptr.2d 470 (1995)*, holds that a stepmother's will is not discoverable by decedent's children for the purpose of proving an agreement between decedent and stepmother to transmute joint tenancy property to community property.

This section does not by its terms apply to inter vivos trusts. However, *In re Marriage of Starkman, 129 Cal.App.4th 659, 28 Cal.Rptr.3d 639 (2005), review denied*, holds that, as between a living husband and wife, a revocable living trust provision stating that all property that is not identified as the separate property of the husband or wife is the community property of the parties, was not sufficient to work a transmutation under Section 852 because there was no unambiguous indication that the husband intended thereby to change the character of the separate property he placed into the trust into the community property of the parties. Compare *In re Marriage of Holtemann, 166 Cal.App.4th 1166, 83 Cal.Rptr.3d 385 (2008)*, review denied, which found a transmutation when a "transmutation agreement" contained explicit and unambiguous language of present transmutation, even though the agreement was incident to an estate planning trust. Accord, *In re Marriage of Lund, 174 Cal.App.4th 40, 94 Cal.Rptr.3d 84 (2009)*.

Research References

Forms

California Transactions Forms--Estate Planning § 11:35, Agreement Entered Into on or After January 1, 1985.

California Transactions Forms--Estate Planning § 19:57, Maintaining Confidentiality.

California Transactions Forms--Estate Planning § 19:70, Characterization Of Property.

California Transactions Forms--Family Law § 2:46, No Transmutation.

Treatises and Practice Aids

Witkin, California Summary 10th Community Property § 153, Authority to Transmute.

Witkin, California Summary 10th Community Property § 156, Estate Planning Transactions.

Part 3

LIABILITY OF MARITAL PROPERTY

CHAPTER 1. DEFINITIONS

§ 900. Construction of part

Unless the provision or context otherwise requires, the definitions in this chapter govern the construction of this part. *(Stats.1992, c. 162 (A.B.2650), § 10, operative Jan. 1, 1994.)*

Law Revision Commission Comments

Enactment [Revised Comment]

Section 900 continues former Civil Code Section 5120.010 without substantive change. For background on former Civ. Code § 5120.010, see *Recommendation Relating to Liability of Marital Property for Debts,* 17 Cal. L. Revision Comm'n Reports 1 (1984). [23 Cal.L.Rev.Comm. Reports 1 (1993)].

Research References

Forms

West's California Code Forms, Family § 781, Comment Overview--Damages for Injuries to Married Person.

Treatises and Practice Aids

Witkin, California Summary 10th Community Property § 176, Nature and Scope Of Revision.

Witkin, California Summary 10th Community Property § 183, Reimbursement.

§ 902. Debt

"Debt" means an obligation incurred by a married person before or during marriage, whether based on contract, tort, or otherwise. *(Stats.1992, c. 162 (A.B.2650), § 10, operative Jan. 1, 1994.)*

Law Revision Commission Comments

Enactment [Revised Comment]

Section 902 continues former Civil Code Section 5120.030 without change. For background on former Civ. Code § 5120.030, see *Recommendation Relating to Liability of Marital Property for Debts,* 17 Cal. L. Revision Comm'n Reports 1 (1984). [23 Cal.L.Rev.Comm. Reports 1 (1993)].

Research References

Treatises and Practice Aids

Witkin, California Summary 10th Community Property § 176, Nature and Scope Of Revision.

§ 903. Time debt is incurred

A debt is "incurred" at the following time:

(a) In the case of a contract, at the time the contract is made.

(b) In the case of a tort, at the time the tort occurs.

(c) In other cases, at the time the obligation arises. *(Stats.1992, c. 162 (A.B.2650), § 10, operative Jan. 1, 1994.)*

Law Revision Commission Comments

Enactment [Revised Comment]

Section 903 continues former Civil Code Section 5120.040 without change. For background on former Civ. Code § 5120.040, see *Recommendation Relating to Liability of Marital Property for Debts,* 17 Cal. L. Revision Comm'n Reports 1 (1984). [23 Cal.L.Rev.Comm. Reports 1 (1993)].

Commentary

Applying the literal language of subsection (a), *In re Marriage of Feldner, 40 Cal.App.4th 617, 47 Cal.Rptr.2d 312 (1995)*, holds that damages caused the husband's breach of a contract, which breach occurred after the parties' final separation, gave rise to a community debt because the underlying contract was made by the husband before the parties separated.

Research References

Treatises and Practice Aids

Witkin, California Summary 10th Community Property § 176, Nature and Scope Of Revision.

CHAPTER 2. GENERAL RULES OF LIABILITY

§ 910. Community estate; liability for debts

(a) Except as otherwise expressly provided by statute, the community estate is liable for a debt incurred by either spouse before or during marriage, regardless of which spouse has the management and control of the property and regardless of whether one or both spouses are parties to the debt or to a judgment for the debt.

(b) "During marriage" for purposes of this section does not include the period after the date of separation, as defined in Section 70, and before a judgment of dissolution of marriage or legal separation of the parties. *(Stats.1992, c. 162 (A.B.2650), § 10, operative Jan. 1, 1994. Amended by Stats.2016, c. 114 (S.B.1255), § 3, eff. Jan. 1, 2017.)*

Law Revision Commission Comments

Enactment [Revised Comment]

Section 910 continues former Civil Code Section 5120.110(a) and (c) without substantive change. The term "community estate" has been substituted for "community property." This is not a substantive change. See Section 63 ("community estate" defined) & Comment. In subdivision (b), the definition of "during marriage" has been limited in application to this section. This is not a substantive change. See Section 911 Comment.

Section 910 makes clear that the community estate is liable for the prenuptial contracts of the spouses. But see Section 911 (liability of earnings of the nondebtor spouse). The nondebtor spouse need not be made a party for the purpose of enforcing a judgment out of the community estate. However, special procedural provisions may apply. See, e.g., Code Civ. Proc. § 706.109 (issuance of earnings withholding order against spouse of judgment debtor). For rules governing liability after division of the community estate, see Section 916. See also Code Civ. Proc. § 371 (right of married person to defend suit for spouse's right).

The introductory and concluding clauses of subdivision (a) make clear that the community estate is liable for all debts of either spouse absent an express statutory exception. Thus, community property under the management and control of one spouse pursuant to Section 1100(d) (spouse operating or managing business), Financial Code Section 851 (one-spouse bank account), or Probate Code Section 3051 (conservatorship) remains liable for the debts of the other spouse. For an express statutory exception from liability of a community estate, see Section 911 (liability of earnings of nondebtor spouse). See also Welf. & Inst. Code §§ 14006.1–14006.6 (eligibility for Medi–Cal).

Section 915 provides that a child or spousal support obligation that does not arise out of the marriage is to be treated as a debt incurred before marriage. Hence, such an obligation is governed by the provisions of Sections 910 and 911. If property sought to be applied to the satisfaction of a judgment for child support is liable for the payment of the judgment but is shown to be exempt, in determining under Code of Civil Procedure Section 703.070 the extent to which the exempt property nevertheless shall be applied to the satisfaction of the support judgment, the court shall take into account, among other relevant circumstances, all of the other property of the spouses, including the separate property of each and the earnings that are not liable for child support under Sections 910 and 911. Although Code of Civil Procedure Section 703.070 requires the court to take into account property that is not liable under Section 911, Section 703.070 does not make the property described in Section 911 liable for payment of the support judgment. Nothing in Section 911 limits or affects the payment under Article 8 (commencing with Section 708.710) of Chapter 6 of Division 2 of the Code of Civil Procedure of a claim based on a judgment for child support, whether the money to be applied to the claim is owed to the judgment debtor alone or to the judgment debtor and the spouse of the judgment debtor. This is clear because the protection for earnings after payment extends only to earnings deposited in a deposit account that meets the requirements of Section 911.

For background on former Civ. Code § 5120.110, see *Recommendation Relating to Liability of Marital Property for Debts,* 17 Cal. L. Revision Comm'n Reports 1 (1984); 18 Cal. L. Revision Comm'n Reports 56–57 (1986). [23 Cal.L.Rev.Comm. Reports 1 (1993)].

Commentary

For treatment of California community property ownership and debt liability rules in the context of federal law, compare *United States v. Lester, 85 F.3d 1409 (9th Cir. 1996)* with *U.S. v. Hooper, 229 F.3d 818 (9th Cir. 2000)*, and *In re Soderling, 998 F.2d 730, 733 (9th Cir. 1993)*. *Lester* holds that the federal Comprehensive Drug Abuse Prevention and Control Act substitute property forfeiture section ("substitute property" is that property not used in the commission of a crime but taken instead because property used in commission of the crime is unavailable) looks to state law only for the purpose of determining property ownership (Family Code Section 751), and not for the purpose of determining debt liability (Family Code Section 910(a)). Thus an innocent wife's one-half interest in the community property cannot be reached on account of her husband's criminal behavior. Distinguishing *Lester*, which applied to "substitute property," *Hooper* held that the federal criminal statute governing forfeiture of property derived from illicit drug sale (21 USC § 853) allows forfeiture of an innocent spouse's community property interest in the illicit sale proceeds or property purchased with those proceeds. *Soderling* determined that, for purposes of dischargeability in bankruptcy, a criminal restitution order is a "debt" under California law and federal bankruptcy law, and hence may be satisfied, according to state law, from community property assets. See also *McIntyre v. United States, 222 F.3d 655 (9th Cir. 2000)*. Reading 29 USC §§ 1056 (d) and 1144 (d) together with California Family Code § 910 (a), *McIntyre* holds that the Internal Revenue Service may levy, under 26 USC § 6331 (a), on the entire contents of a spouse's ERISA-regulated pension plan, including the other spouse's California community property interest, in order to satisfy the spouse's tax debt. To similar effect, see *Babb v. Schmidt, 496 F.2d 957, 959 (9th Cir.1974)* (relying on § 910(a) to conclude that a tax debtor has a "right to property" sufficient to allow the Internal Revenue Service to levy, under 26 USC § 6331(a), on all the community property to satisfy that spouse's delinquent tax obligations). Relying on subsection (a) of this section, *United States v. Berger, 574 F.3d 1202 (9th Cir. 2009)*, holds that the portion of community property that would potentially be awarded upon dissolution of marriage to a spouse who was not involved in criminal activity is available to satisfy a restitution judgment obtained against a criminally liable spouse under the Mandatory Victim Restitution Act (18 U.S.C. § 3663(a)).

When a landlord brings an action against a husband who has personally guaranteed obligations under a lease, the landlord has no cause of action against the defendant's wife based solely on the liability of community property under this section. *11601 Wilshire Associates v. Grebow, 64 Cal.App.4th 453, 74 Cal.Rptr.2d 912 (1998), review denied August 19, 1998.*

When a debt for which community property is liable under this section, was not assigned, under section 916(a)(2), to the non-debtor spouse in the judgment of dissolution, *Litke O'Farrell, LLC v. Tipton, 204 Cal.App.4th 1178, 139 Cal.Rptr.3d 548 (2012)*, held that a marital settlement agreement (MSA) dividing the community property, assigning the debt solely to husband, providing that the court would be requested to incorporate the MSA in the judgment of dissolution, but that the MSA was enforceable whether or not it was incorporated into a final judgment, became effective on the date it was signed by the parties. Thus, a motion to charge interests served by the husband's creditors after the MSA was executed but before the judgment of dissolution was entered did not attach to the property received by the wife in the MSA.

Research References

Forms

California Transactions Forms--Estate Planning § 10:14, Formalities Required.

California Transactions Forms--Estate Planning § 13:19, Legal Effect Of Retention Of Community Character.

Treatises and Practice Aids

Witkin, California Summary 10th Community Property § 153, Authority to Transmute.

Witkin, California Summary 10th Community Property § 177, General Rule.

Witkin, California Summary 10th Trusts § 198, Trust Of Community Property.

§ 911. Earnings of married persons; liability for premarital debts; earnings held in deposit accounts

(a) The earnings of a married person during marriage are not liable for a debt incurred by the person's spouse before marriage. After the earnings of the married person are paid, they remain not liable so long as they are held in a deposit account in which the person's spouse has no right of withdrawal and are uncommingled with other property in the community estate, except property insignificant in amount.

(b) As used in this section:

(1) "Deposit account" has the meaning prescribed in paragraph (29) of subdivision (a) of Section 9102 of the Commercial Code.

(2) "Earnings" means compensation for personal services performed, whether as an employee or otherwise. *(Stats. 1992, c. 162 (A.B.2650), § 10, operative Jan. 1, 1994. Amended by Stats.1999, c. 991 (S.B.45), § 42.5, operative July 1, 2001.)*

Law Revision Commission Comments

Enactment [Revised Comment]

Section 911 continues former Civil Code Section 5120.110(b) without substantive change. The term "community estate" has been substituted for "community property." This is not a substantive change. See Section 63 ("community estate" defined) & Comment. The definition of "during marriage" in former Civil Code Section 5120.110(c) is not continued in this section because it was not intended to apply to the rule in this section. See also Section 910 Comment.

When enacted in 1984 (as former Civil Code Section 5120.110), the second sentence of subdivision (a) codified the rule that, for purposes of liability, earnings may not be traced through changes in form. See, e.g., Pfunder v. Goodwin, 83 Cal.App. 551, 257 P. 119 (1927).

The second sentence of subdivision (a) also makes clear the extent to which paid earnings remain not liable. The effect of the sentence is to protect a deposit account only where the nonobligor spouse has an account into which only his or her earnings and separate property or property of a third person are deposited (unless the amount of other community estate property deposited in the account is insignificant). In such a situation, it is clear that the nonobligor spouse has carefully set aside his or her earnings and separate property and it is appropriate to continue the protection given the earnings. Where the account is commingled with any significant amount of other property in the community estate (such as the earnings of the other spouse or income from other property in the community estate), the intent to segregate the earnings and separate property is not clear, and hence the protection is not continued. The same reasoning justifies not protecting the account where the obligor spouse has a right to withdraw funds from the account.

For background on former Civ. Code § 5120.110, see *Recommendation Relating to Liability of Marital Property for Debts,* 17 Cal. L. Revision Comm'n Reports 1 (1984); 18 Cal. L. Revision Comm'n Reports 56–57 (1986). [23 Cal.L.Rev.Comm. Reports 1 (1993)].

Research References

Treatises and Practice Aids

Witkin, California Summary 10th Community Property § 178, Exception for Earnings.

Witkin, California Summary 10th Parent and Child § 390, Liability Of Stepparent.

§ 912. Quasi-community property; treatment

For the purposes of this part, quasi-community property is liable to the same extent, and shall be treated the same in all other respects, as community property. *(Stats.1992, c. 162 (A.B.2650), § 10, operative Jan. 1, 1994.)*

Law Revision Commission Comments

Enactment [Revised Comment]

Section 912 continues former Civil Code Section 5120.120 without substantive change.

When enacted in 1984 (as former Civil Code Section 5120.120), this provision reversed existing law which treated quasi-community property as separate property rather than community property for purposes of liability for debts. This change in the law was necessary to effectuate the public policy of the state to achieve sharing of marital assets and liabilities, to promote equal access to credit for both spouses, to treat all residents of the state equally, and to protect the interests of California creditors.

For background on former Civ. Code § 5120.120, see *Recommendation Relating to Liability of Marital Property for Debts,* 17 Cal. L. Revision Comm'n Reports 1 (1984). [23 Cal.L.Rev.Comm. Reports 1 (1993)].

Commentary

This provision is of questionable constitutionality. See *Addison v. Addison, 62 Cal.2d 558, 43 Cal.Rptr. 97 (1965)*, which holds constitutional, at death and divorce, the application of California quasi-community property law to property acquired in common-law states by persons who later become domiciled in California. *Addison* constitutionally justifies such treatment in terms of the state's power to alter property ownership at death and divorce. The state has no similar power or interest in altering property ownership to enlarge creditor access to a spouse's property. The Law Revision Commission's effort to justify the statute, *supra,* is not persuasive. The promotion of equal spousal access to credit is hardly served by a statutory scheme that gives the nonowner spouse no rights in the quasi-community property during marriage and hence does not allow the nonowner spouse to manage or pledge the quasi-community property in order to establish credit.

Research References

Treatises and Practice Aids

Witkin, California Summary 10th Community Property § 176, Nature and Scope Of Revision.

§ 913. Separate property of married person; liability for debt

(a) The separate property of a married person is liable for a debt incurred by the person before or during marriage.

(b) Except as otherwise provided by statute:

(1) The separate property of a married person is not liable for a debt incurred by the person's spouse before or during marriage.

(2) The joinder or consent of a married person to an encumbrance of community estate property to secure payment of a debt incurred by the person's spouse does not subject the person's separate property to liability for the debt unless the person also incurred the debt. *(Stats.1992, c. 162 (A.B.2650), § 10, operative Jan. 1, 1994.)*

Law Revision Commission Comments

Enactment [Revised Comment]

Section 913 continues former Civil Code Section 5120.130 without substantive change. The term "community estate" has been substituted for "community property." This is not a substantive change. See Section 63 ("community estate" defined) & Comment. For an exception to the rule of subdivision (b), see Section 914 (liability for necessaries).

For background on former Civ. Code § 5120.130, see *Recommendation Relating to Liability of Marital Property for Debts,* 17 Cal. L. Revision Comm'n Reports 1 (1984); 18 Cal. L. Revision Comm'n Reports 57 (1986). [23 Cal.L.Rev.Comm. Reports 1 (1993)].

Research References

Treatises and Practice Aids

Witkin, California Summary 10th Community Property § 179, Debt Incurred Before or During Marriage.

Witkin, California Summary 10th Community Property § 180, Personal Liability for Debts for Spouse's Necessaries.

§ 914. Personal liability for debts incurred by spouse; separate property applied to satisfaction of debt; statute of limitations

(a) Notwithstanding Section 913, a married person is personally liable for the following debts incurred by the person's spouse during marriage:

(1) A debt incurred for necessaries of life of the person's spouse before the date of separation of the spouses.

(2) Except as provided in Section 4302, a debt incurred for common necessaries of life of the person's spouse after the date of separation of the spouses.

(b) The separate property of a married person may be applied to the satisfaction of a debt for which the person is personally liable pursuant to this section. If separate property is so applied at a time when nonexempt property in the community estate or separate property of the person's spouse is available but is not applied to the satisfaction of the debt, the married person is entitled to reimbursement to the extent such property was available.

(c)(1) Except as provided in paragraph (2), the statute of limitations set forth in Section 366.2 of the Code of Civil Procedure shall apply if the spouse for whom the married person is personally liable dies.

(2) If the surviving spouse had actual knowledge of the debt prior to expiration of the period set forth in Section 366.2 of the Code of Civil Procedure and the personal representative of the deceased spouse's estate failed to provide the creditor asserting the claim under this section with a timely written notice of the probate administration of

the estate in the manner provided for pursuant to Section 9050 of the Probate Code, the statute of limitations set forth in Section 337 or 339 of the Code of Civil Procedure, as applicable, shall apply.

(d) For purposes of this section, "date of separation" has the same meaning as set forth in Section 70. *(Stats.1992, c. 162 (A.B.2650), § 10, operative Jan. 1, 1994. Amended by Stats.1993, c. 219 (A.B.1500), § 100.4; Stats.2001, c. 702 (A.B.539), § 1; Stats.2014, c. 71 (S.B.1304), § 53, eff. Jan. 1, 2015; Stats.2016, c. 114 (S.B.1255), § 4, eff. Jan. 1, 2017.)*

Law Revision Commission Comments

Enactment [Revised Comment]

Section 914 continues former Civil Code Section 5120.140 without substantive change. The term "community estate" has been substituted for "community property." This is not a substantive change. See Section 63 ("community estate" defined) & Comment.

Section 914 is an exception to the rule of Section 913 that the separate property of a spouse is not liable for a debt of the other spouse incurred during marriage. The separate property of a spouse may not be subjected to process by necessaries creditors of the other spouse unless the spouse is made a party for the purpose of enforcing the liability. See, e.g., Evans v. Noonan, 20 Cal.App. 288, 128 P. 794 (1912); Credit Bureau of Santa Monica Bay Dist. v. Terranova, 15 Cal.App.3d 854, 93 Cal.Rptr. 538 (1971).

Subdivision (a)(1) is consistent with Section 4301 (use of separate property for support while living together), but does not require exhaustion of community estate property before separate property of a nondebtor spouse can be reached. But see subdivision (b) (reimbursement). For general provisions governing reimbursement, see Section 920.

Subdivision (a)(2) applies where the spouses are living separate not by agreement, as where one spouse leaves without an agreement between the spouses to live separate and apart. Compare Section 4302, which abrogates the obligation of support between spouses living separate by agreement, unless support is stipulated in the agreement. Nothing in subdivision (a)(2) should be deemed to limit the obligation of a spouse for support pursuant to a court order pendente lite or in a judgment of legal separation of the spouses. A spouse who desires to limit the liability pursuant to subdivision (a)(2), or a spouse who desires a greater support obligation than provided in subdivision (a)(2), may seek a support order, which supersedes liability under subdivision (a)(2).

When enacted in 1984 (as former Civil Code Section 5120.140), subdivision (a)(2) abolished the "station in life" test in determining what is a necessary of life. See, e.g., Wisnom v. McCarthy, 48 Cal.App. 697, 192 P. 337 (1920) (maid necessary because of economic and social position of spouses). The separate property of the nondebtor spouse is liable only for debts for the "common" necessaries of life of the other spouse while living separate and apart. *Cf.* Ratzlaff v. Portillo, 14 Cal.App.3d 1013, 92 Cal.Rptr. 722 (1971) ("common" necessary is that required to sustain life).

For background on former Civ. Code § 5120.140, see *Recommendation Relating to Liability of Marital Property for Debts,* 17 Cal. L. Revision Comm'n Reports 1 (1984); 18 Cal. L. Revision Comm'n Reports 58–59 (1986). [23 Cal.L.Rev.Comm. Reports 1 (1993)].

Commentary

The next to the last paragraph of the Law Revision Commission Comment, *supra,* is confusing and inconsistent with the plain language of the statute. Subsection (a)(2) does not abolish "the station in life test in determining what is a necessary of life." Instead, it merely prescribes the lesser standard of "common necessaries of life" when the parties are living separately. Subsection (a)(1) provides that a married person is personally liable for a debt incurred for the necessaries of life of the person's spouse when the spouses are living together. *Necessaries* are living costs consistent with the parties' station in life. See *Wisnom v. McCarthy, 48 Cal.App. 697, 701, 192 P. 337 (1920)*. When the parties are living separately, subsection (a)(2) provides instead that a spouse is personally liable only for debts incurred for the *common necessaries* of the person's spouse. *Common necessaries* are "such things as are ordinarily required for the sustenance of all men." *Ratzlaff v. Portillo, 14 Cal.App.3d 1013, 1015, 92 Cal.Rptr. 722 (1971)*.

Although under this section a person is personally liable for a spouse's necessaries, under section 916 a non-debtor spouse is liable for debts incurred by a former spouse during their marriage only if the debt was assigned to the non-debtor spouse by the judgment of dissolution. *CMRE Financial Services, Inc. v. Parton, 184 Cal.App.4th 263, 109 Cal.Rptr.3d 139 (2010), review denied,* held that a former wife was not liable for fees for common necessaries incurred by her husband after separation but before dissolution, because liability for the debt was not assigned to her in the judgment of dissolution. The court relied on the "notwithstanding any other provision of this chapter" language of section 916. Effectively, the judgment of dissolution relieved the wife of liability under this section.

Research References

Treatises and Practice Aids

Witkin, California Summary 10th Community Property § 179, Debt Incurred Before or During Marriage.

Witkin, California Summary 10th Community Property § 180, Personal Liability for Debts for Spouse's Necessaries.

Witkin, California Summary 10th Husband and Wife § 36, Mutual Obligations.

Witkin, California Summary 10th Wills and Probate § 517, Action Against Decedent.

Witkin, California Summary 10th Wills and Probate § 823, Debts Of Deceased Spouse.

§ 915. Child or spousal support obligation not arising out of marriage; reimbursement of community

(a) For the purpose of this part, a child or spousal support obligation of a married person that does not arise out of the marriage shall be treated as a debt incurred before marriage, regardless of whether a court order for support is made or modified before or during marriage and regardless of whether any installment payment on the obligation accrues before or during marriage.

(b) If property in the community estate is applied to the satisfaction of a child or spousal support obligation of a married person that does not arise out of the marriage, at a time when nonexempt separate income of the person is available but is not applied to the satisfaction of the obligation, the community estate is entitled to reimbursement from the person in the amount of the separate income, not exceeding the property in the community estate so applied.

(c) Nothing in this section limits the matters a court may take into consideration in determining or modifying the amount of a support order, including, but not limited to, the earnings of the spouses of the parties. *(Stats.1992, c. 162 (A.B.2650), § 10, operative Jan. 1, 1994. Amended by Stats. 1993, c. 219 (A.B.1500), § 100.5.)*

Law Revision Commission Comments

Enactment [Revised Comment]

Section 915 continues former Civil Code Section 5120.150 without substantive change. The term "community estate" has been substituted for "community property." This is not a substantive change. See Section 63 ("community estate" defined) & Comment.

Subdivision (a) makes clear that a support obligation that arises before the marriage is a prenuptial debt for purposes of liability of marital property. As a result, the general rule is that the separate property of the obligor spouse and the community estate of the marriage is liable for the support obligation, other than the earnings of the non-obligor spouse. See Sections 910 (liability of community estate), 911 (liability of married person's earnings for premarital debt of spouse), 913 (liability of separate property). Subdivision (a) also applies to an extramarital support obligation of a spouse that arises during the marriage.

When enacted in 1984 (as former Civil Code Section 5120.150), subdivision (b) codified the rule of Weinberg v. Weinberg, 67 Cal.2d 557, 432 P.2d 709, 63 Cal.Rptr. 13 (1967), that the community is entitled to reimbursement, but prescribed a fixed measure for the community reimbursement based on the separate income of the obligor spouse. See also Bare v. Bare, 256 Cal.App.2d 684, 64 Cal.Rptr. 335 (1967); *In re* Marriage of Smaltz, 82 Cal.App.3d 568, 147 Cal.Rptr. 154 (1978).

Subdivision (c) makes clear that, despite the general rule that earnings of the non-obligor spouse are not liable for the support obligation, the earnings of the spouses of both parties may be taken into account by the court in setting the amount of the support obligation. When enacted in 1984 (as former Civil Code Section 5120.150), subdivision (c) codified prior case law. See, e.g., *In re* Marriage of Havens, 125 Cal.App.3d 1012, 178 Cal.Rptr. 477 (1981).

For background on former Civ. Code § 5120.150, see *Recommendation Relating to Liability of Marital Property for Debts,* 17 Cal. L. Revision Comm'n Reports 1 (1984); 18 Cal. L. Revision Comm'n Reports 59 (1986). [23 Cal.L.Rev.Comm. Reports 1 (1993)].

Commentary

In *re Marriage of Leni, 144 Cal.App.4th 1087, 50 Cal.Rptr.3d 886 (2006),* held that a spouse's use of community funds to care for his ailing mother was not a gift for purposes of section 1100(b) because section 4400 imposes upon an adult child a legal duty to support a parent who is in need and is unable to maintain herself by work. Moreover, the community has no right of reimbursement under this section because it creates a right of reimbursement only for "a child or spousal support obligation that does not arise out of the marriage."

Research References

Treatises and Practice Aids

Witkin, California Summary 10th Community Property § 181, Child or Spousal Support Obligations.

Witkin, California Summary 10th Parent and Child § 390, Liability Of Stepparent.

§ 916. Division of property; subsequent liability; right of reimbursement, interest and attorney's fees

(a) Notwithstanding any other provision of this chapter, after division of community and quasi-community property pursuant to Division 7 (commencing with Section 2500):

(1) The separate property owned by a married person at the time of the division and the property received by the person in the division is liable for a debt incurred by the person before or during marriage and the person is personally liable for the debt, whether or not the debt was assigned for payment by the person's spouse in the division.

(2) The separate property owned by a married person at the time of the division and the property received by the person in the division is not liable for a debt incurred by the person's spouse before or during marriage, and the person is not personally liable for the debt, unless the debt was assigned for payment by the person in the division of the property. Nothing in this paragraph affects the liability of property for the satisfaction of a lien on the property.

(3) The separate property owned by a married person at the time of the division and the property received by the person in the division is liable for a debt incurred by the person's spouse before or during marriage, and the person is personally liable for the debt, if the debt was assigned for payment by the person in the division of the property. If a money judgment for the debt is entered after the division, the property is not subject to enforcement of the judgment and the judgment may not be enforced against the married person, unless the person is made a party to the judgment for the purpose of this paragraph.

(b) If property of a married person is applied to the satisfaction of a money judgment pursuant to subdivision (a) for a debt incurred by the person that is assigned for payment by the person's spouse, the person has a right of reimbursement from the person's spouse to the extent of the property applied, with interest at the legal rate, and may recover reasonable attorney's fees incurred in enforcing the right of reimbursement. *(Stats.1992, c. 162 (A.B.2650), § 10, operative Jan. 1, 1994.)*

Law Revision Commission Comments

Enactment [Revised Comment]

Section 916 continues former Civil Code Section 5120.160 without substantive change. In subdivision (a), a reference to Division 7 has been substituted for the narrower reference to former Civil Code Section 4800. This is not a substantive change, since all of the former section is included in Division 7. See also Sections 2620–2627 (division of debts and liabilities).

Section 916 prescribes rules of liability of former community, quasi-community, or community estate property and former separate property following a division of the property pursuant to a court judgment of separation, dissolution, or later division.

Subdivision (a)(1) states the rule that the rights of a creditor against the property of a debtor are not affected by assignment of the debt to the other spouse for payment pursuant to a property division. A creditor who is not paid may seek to satisfy the debt out of property of the debtor. The debtor in such a case will have a right of reimbursement against the former spouse pursuant to subdivision (b).

When enacted in 1984 (as former Civil Code Section 5120.160), subdivisions (a)(2)–(3) reversed the former case law rule that a creditor may seek enforcement of a money judgment against the former community property in the hands of a nondebtor spouse after dissolution of the marriage. See, e.g., Bank of America N.T. & S.A. v. Mantz, 4 Cal.2d 322, 49 P.2d 279 (1935).

Subdivision (a)(2) makes clear that former community estate property received by the nondebtor spouse at division is liable only if the nondebtor spouse is assigned the debt in division. In the case of a judgment entered after the division of property, the nondebtor spouse must be made a party for due process reasons. If the property division calls for the one spouse to pay the debt and the creditor satisfies the judgment out of property of the other spouse, the other spouse will have a right of reimbursement pursuant to subdivision (b). Subdivision (a)(2) does not affect enforceability of liens on the property. See, e.g., Kinney v. Vallentyne, 15 Cal.3d 475, 541 P.2d 537, 124 Cal.Rptr. 897 (1975).

Subdivision (b) states the rule as to reimbursement where a debt is satisfied out of the property of a spouse other than the spouse to whom the debt was assigned pursuant to a property division. For general provisions governing reimbursement, see Section 920. This subdivision is not intended to authorize reimbursement if reimbursement is precluded under Title 11 of the United States Code (Bankruptcy) by discharge of the debt in a case concerning the married person's spouse. *Cf. In re* Marriage of Clements, 134 Cal.App.3d 737, 184 Cal.Rptr. 756 (1982).

For background on former Civ. Code § 5120.160, see *Recommendation Relating to Liability of Marital Property for Debts,* 17 Cal. L. Revision Comm'n Reports 1 (1984); 18 Cal. L. Revision Comm'n Reports 59–60 (1986). [23 Cal.L.Rev.Comm. Reports 1 (1993)].

Commentary

Mejia v. Reed, 31 Cal.4th 657, 74 P.3d 166, 3 Cal.Rptr.3d 390 (2003), holds that the Uniform Fraudulent Transfer Act (Civil Code §§ 3439–3439.12) applies to marital settlement agreements. *Filip v. Bucurenciu, 129 Cal.App.4th 825, 28 Cal.Rptr.3d 884 (2005)*, approves a trial court's finding that the spouses' marital settlement agreement violates the Uniform Fraudulent Transfer Act.

Reversing the Bankruptcy Court, *In re Beverly, 374 B.R. 221 (U.S. Bankr. App. Pan., 9th Cir. 2007)*, held that a divorcing attorney's marital settlement agreement, which transferred nonexempt community property to his wife in exchange for an equivalent amount of his exempt community property retirement fund, was a fraudulent transfer under California Civil Code § 3439.04(a)(1) and therefore under 11 U.S.C. § 544(b). Thus, in the attorney's involuntary bankruptcy proceeding, the Bankruptcy Trustee could avoid the transfer and reach the attorney's community property interest in the nonexempt property.

Although under section 914 a person is personally liable for a spouse's necessaries, under this section a non-debtor spouse is liable for debts incurred by a former spouse during their marriage only if the debt was assigned to the non-debtor spouse by the judgment of dissolution. *CMRE Financial Services, Inc. v. Parton, 184 Cal.App.4th 263, 109 Cal.Rptr.3d 139 (2010), review denied*, held that a former wife was not liable for fees for common necessaries incurred by her husband after separation but before dissolution, because liability for the debt was not assigned to her in the judgment of dissolution. The court relied on the "notwithstanding any other provision of this chapter" language of this section. Effectively, the judgment of dissolution relieved the wife of liability under section 914.

When a debt for which community property is liable under section 910 was not assigned to the non-debtor spouse in the judgment of dissolution, *Litke O'Farrell, LLC v. Tipton, 204 Cal.App.4th 1178, 139 Cal.Rptr.3d 548 (2012)*, held that a marital settlement agreement (MSA) dividing the community property, assigning the debt solely to husband, providing that the court would be requested to incorporate the MSA in the judgment of dissolution, but that the MSA was enforceable whether or not it was incorporated into a final judgment, became effective on the date it was signed by the parties. Thus, a motion to charge interests served by the husband's creditors after the MSA was executed but before the judgment of dissolution was entered did not attach to the property received by the wife in the MSA.

Research References

Forms

California Transactions Forms--Estate Planning § 13:19, Legal Effect Of Retention Of Community Character.

Treatises and Practice Aids

Witkin, California Summary 10th Community Property § 182, Property Owned or Received at Division.

CHAPTER 3. REIMBURSEMENT

§ 920. Conditions governing right of reimbursement

A right of reimbursement provided by this part is subject to the following provisions:

(a) The right arises regardless of which spouse applies the property to the satisfaction of the debt, regardless of whether the property is applied to the satisfaction of the debt voluntarily or involuntarily, and regardless of whether the debt to which the property is applied is satisfied in whole or in part. The right is subject to an express written waiver of the right by the spouse in whose favor the right arises.

(b) The measure of reimbursement is the value of the property or interest in property at the time the right arises.

(c) The right shall be exercised not later than the earlier of the following times:

(1) Within three years after the spouse in whose favor the right arises has actual knowledge of the application of the property to the satisfaction of the debt.

(2) In proceedings for division of community and quasi-community property pursuant to Division 7 (commencing with Section 2500) or in proceedings upon the death of a spouse. *(Stats.1992, c. 162 (A.B.2650), § 10, operative Jan. 1, 1994.)*

Law Revision Commission Comments

Enactment [Revised Comment]

Section 920 continues former Civil Code Section 5120.210 without substantive change. In subdivision (a), a reference to Division 7 has been substituted for the narrower reference to former Civil Code Section 4800. This is not a substantive change, since all of the former section is included in Division 7.

Section 920 limits reimbursement rights to a three-year enforceability period after discovery of the application of the property to the satisfaction of the debt, or less if a dissolution occurs before the end of the three-year period. Contrast Weinberg v. Weinberg, 67 Cal.2d 557, 432 P.2d 709, 63 Cal.Rptr. 13 (1967) (community property applied to support payments entitled to reimbursement at dissolution); *In re* Marriage of Walter, 57 Cal.App.3d 802, 129 Cal.Rptr. 351 (1976) (community property applied to separate tax and mortgage debts entitled to reimbursement at dissolution). Under Section 920, the reimbursement right applies even though the spouse seeking reimbursement may have satisfied or consented to satisfaction of the debt out of a particular type of property, unless the spouse expressly waived in writing the reimbursement right. Contrast *In re* Marriage of Smaltz, 82 Cal.App.3d 568, 147 Cal.Rptr. 154 (1978) (no reimbursement where community property applied to support payments and no separate property available to make payments).

For background on former Civ. Code § 5120.210, see *Recommendation Relating to Liability of Marital Property for Debts,* 17 Cal. L. Revision Comm'n Reports 1 (1984); 18 Cal. L. Revision Comm'n Reports 60–61 (1986). [23 Cal.L.Rev.Comm. Reports 1 (1993)].

Research References

Treatises and Practice Aids

Witkin, California Summary 10th Community Property § 183, Reimbursement.

Witkin, California Summary 10th Community Property § 184, in General.

CHAPTER 4. TRANSITIONAL PROVISIONS

§ 930. Liability for debts enforced on or after Jan. 1, 1985

Except as otherwise provided by statute, this part governs the liability of separate property and property in the community estate and the personal liability of a married person for a debt enforced on or after January 1, 1985, regardless of whether the debt was incurred before, on, or after that date. *(Stats.1992, c. 162 (A.B.2650), § 10, operative Jan. 1, 1994. Amended by Stats.1993, c. 219 (A.B.1500), § 100.6.)*

Law Revision Commission Comments

Enactment [Revised Comment]

Section 930 continues without substantive change former Civil Code Section 5120.320 and former Civil Code Section 5120.310 (operative date). The term "community estate" has been substituted for "community property." This is not a substantive change. See Section 63 ("community estate" defined) & Comment.

Section 930 states the general rule that this part applies to all debts enforced on or after January 1, 1985, regardless of the time they were incurred. For an exception to the general rule, see Section 931 (reimbursement rights).

For background on former Civ. Code §§ 5120.310 and 5120.320, see *Recommendation Relating to Liability of Marital Property for Debts,* 17 Cal. L. Revision Comm'n Reports 1 (1984). [23 Cal.L.Rev. Comm. Reports 1 (1993)].

Research References

Treatises and Practice Aids

Witkin, California Summary 10th Community Property § 176, Nature and Scope Of Revision.

§ 931. Application of provisions governing reimbursement

The provisions of this part that govern reimbursement apply to all debts, regardless of whether satisfied before, on, or after January 1, 1985. *(Stats.1992, c. 162 (A.B.2650), § 10, operative Jan. 1, 1994.)*

Law Revision Commission Comments

Enactment [Revised Comment]

Section 931 continues without substantive change former Civil Code Section 5120.330(a) and former Civil Code Section 5120.310 (operative date). Section 931 makes clear that reimbursement rights provided in this part apply to debts satisfied before as well as after January 1, 1985.

Former Civil Code Section 5120.330(b), which dealt with retroactive application of the former section, has been omitted as obsolete. For background on former Civ. Code § 5120.330, see *Recommendation Relating to Liability of Marital Property for Debts,* 17 Cal. L. Revision Comm'n Reports 1 (1984). [23 Cal.L.Rev.Comm. Reports 1 (1993)].

Research References

Treatises and Practice Aids

Witkin, California Summary 10th Community Property § 176, Nature and Scope Of Revision.

CHAPTER 5. LIABILITY FOR DEATH OR INJURY

§ 1000. Liability for injury or damage caused by spouse; property subject to satisfaction of liability; satisfaction out of insurance proceeds; limitation on exercise of reimbursement right

(a) A married person is not liable for any injury or damage caused by the other spouse except in cases where the married person would be liable therefor if the marriage did not exist.

(b) The liability of a married person for death or injury to person or property shall be satisfied as follows:

(1) If the liability of the married person is based upon an act or omission which occurred while the married person was performing an activity for the benefit of the community, the liability shall first be satisfied from the community estate and second from the separate property of the married person.

(2) If the liability of the married person is not based upon an act or omission which occurred while the married person was performing an activity for the benefit of the community, the liability shall first be satisfied from the separate property of the married person and second from the community estate.

(c) This section does not apply to the extent the liability is satisfied out of proceeds of insurance for the liability, whether the proceeds are from property in the community estate or from separate property. Notwithstanding Section 920, no right of reimbursement under this section shall be exercised more than seven years after the spouse in whose favor the right arises has actual knowledge of the application of the property to the satisfaction of the debt. *(Stats.1992, c. 162 (A.B.2650), § 10, operative Jan. 1, 1994. Amended by Stats. 1993, c. 219 (A.B.1500), § 100.7.)*

Law Revision Commission Comments

Enactment [Revised Comment]

Section 1000 continues former Civil Code Section 5122 without substantive change. The term "community estate" has been substituted for "community property." This is not a substantive change, since former Civil Code Section 5120.020 (which formerly applied to this section) defined community property to include quasi-community property. See Section 63 ("community estate" defined) & Comment.

Subdivision (c) limits the order of satisfaction requirement to liabilities not covered by insurance. Subdivision (c) also imposes a seven-year limitation period on any reimbursement right implied by the order of satisfaction requirement. *Cf. In re* Marriage of Stitt, 147 Cal.App.3d 579, 195 Cal.Rptr. 172 (1983).

See also Section 2627 (assignment of tort liability upon division of property).

For background on former Civ. Code § 5122, see *Recommendation Relating to Liability of Marital Property for Debts,* 17 Cal. L. Revision Comm'n Reports 1 (1984); 18 Cal. L. Revision Comm'n Reports 61 (1986). [23 Cal.L.Rev.Comm. Reports 1 (1993)].

Commentary

Note that Section 1000 creates only an order of satisfaction. Ultimately, it insulates neither the community property nor a married person's separate property from liability for that person's torts. The basic liability rules are laid out in Sections 902–913. Nor does Section 1000 define the spouses' rights against each other arising from either spouse's tort liabilities to third parties. The limited scope of Section 1000 is addressed by *In re Marriage of Hirsch, 211 Cal.App.3d 104, 110–111, 259 Cal.Rptr. 39 (1989), review denied 8/17/89*. But compare *In re Marriage of Stitt, 147 Cal.App.3d 579, 195 Cal.Rptr. 172 (1983)*. For further discussion of *Hirsch* and *Stitt*, see *In re Marriage of*

Seaman, 1 Cal.App.4th 1489, 1500, 2 Cal.Rptr.2d 690 (1991), review denied 3/26/92, and Section 2602, Commentary.

See also *Oyakawa v. Gillett, 8 Cal.App.4th 628, 10 Cal.Rptr.2d 469 (1992)*, which holds that even though the community property is liable for a tort obligation incurred by either spouse during marriage, a wife may not subsequently be added as an additional judgment debtor to a tort judgment previously obtained against the husband when she was not named as a party, no claim was made against her personally, and she had no opportunity to defend.

Research References

Forms

West's California Code Forms, Family § 781, Comment Overview--Damages for Injuries to Married Person.

Treatises and Practice Aids

Witkin, California Summary 10th Community Property § 184, in General.
Witkin, California Summary 10th Community Property § 185, Illustrations.
Witkin, California Summary 10th Community Property § 203, Other Exceptions.
Witkin, California Summary 10th Husband and Wife § 18, in General.
Witkin, California Summary 10th Torts § 24, in General.
Witkin, California Summary 10th Torts § 1220, Circumstances Justifying Vicarious Liability.

Part 4

MANAGEMENT AND CONTROL OF MARITAL PROPERTY

§ 1100. Community personal property; management and control; restrictions on disposition

(a) Except as provided in subdivisions (b), (c), and (d) and Sections 761 and 1103, either spouse has the management and control of the community personal property, whether acquired prior to or on or after January 1, 1975, with like absolute power of disposition, other than testamentary, as the spouse has of the separate estate of the spouse.

(b) A spouse may not make a gift of community personal property, or dispose of community personal property for less than fair and reasonable value, without the written consent of the other spouse. This subdivision does not apply to gifts mutually given by both spouses to third parties and to gifts given by one spouse to the other spouse.

(c) A spouse may not sell, convey, or encumber community personal property used as the family dwelling, or the furniture, furnishings, or fittings of the home, or the clothing or wearing apparel of the other spouse or minor children which is community personal property, without the written consent of the other spouse.

(d) Except as provided in subdivisions (b) and (c), and in Section 1102, a spouse who is operating or managing a business or an interest in a business that is all or substantially all community personal property has the primary management and control of the business or interest. Primary management and control means that the managing spouse may act alone in all transactions but shall give prior written notice to the other spouse of any sale, lease, exchange, encumbrance, or other disposition of all or substantially all of the personal property used in the operation of the business (including personal property used for agricultural purposes), whether or not title to that property is held in the name of only one spouse. Written notice is not, however, required when prohibited by the law otherwise applicable to the transaction.

Remedies for the failure by a managing spouse to give prior written notice as required by this subdivision are only as specified in Section 1101. A failure to give prior written notice shall not adversely affect the validity of a transaction nor of any interest transferred.

(e) Each spouse shall act with respect to the other spouse in the management and control of the community assets and liabilities in accordance with the general rules governing fiduciary relationships which control the actions of persons having relationships of personal confidence as specified in Section 721, until such time as the assets and liabilities have been divided by the parties or by a court. This duty includes the obligation to make full disclosure to the other spouse of all material facts and information regarding the existence, characterization, and valuation of all assets in which the community has or may have an interest and debts for which the community is or may be liable, and to provide equal access to all information, records, and books that pertain to the value and character of those assets and debts, upon request. *(Stats.1992, c. 162 (A.B.2650), § 10, operative Jan. 1, 1994. Amended by Stats.1993, c. 219 (A.B.1500), § 100.8.)*

Law Revision Commission Comments

Enactment [Revised Comment]

Section 1100 continues former Civil Code Section 5125 without change, except that section references have been adjusted. In subdivision (e), references to community "property" have been replaced by more specific references to community "assets and liabilities." These changes are technical and nonsubstantive. See also Section 700 (personal property does not include a leasehold interest in real property); Prob. Code §§ 3057 (protection of rights of spouse who lacks legal capacity), 5100–5407 (multiple-party account held by financial institution).

For background on former Civ. Code § 5125, see *Tentative Recommendation Proposing the Enforcement of Judgments Law*, 15 Cal. L. Revision Comm'n Reports 2001 (1980); 16 Cal. L. Revision Comm'n Reports 1784–85 (1982); *Recommendation Relating to Technical Revisions in the Trust Law*, 18 Cal. L. Revision Comm'n Reports 1823 (1986). [23 Cal.L.Rev.Comm. Reports 1 (1993)].

Commentary

Subsection (a) states the general rule that either spouse, acting alone, may manage, with absolute power of disposition, all the community personal property. Nevertheless, absent a judicial proceeding (see Section 1101(c)), the nonearner's right to manage the community property may be more abstract than real. See, for example, Financial Code Section 851, which provides that a "bank account . . . in the name of a married person shall be held for the exclusive right and benefit of the person [and] shall be free from the control or lien of any other person except a creditor."

In re Marriage of Leni, 144 Cal.App.4th 1087, 50 Cal.Rptr.3d 886 (2006), held that a spouse's use of community funds to care for his ailing mother was not a gift for purposes of subsection (b) because section 4400 imposes upon an adult child a legal duty to support a parent who is in need and is unable to maintain herself by work. Moreover, the community has no right of reimbursement under section 915, because it creates a right of reimbursement only for "a child or spousal support obligation that does not arise out of the marriage."

Even though a spouse did not initially consent to a subsection (b) gift, she may ratify the gift in a later writing. *Spreckels v. Spreckels, 172 Cal. 775, 158 P. 537 (1916)*. During the marriage, an unauthorized subsection (b) gift may be revoked in its entirety by the nonconsenting spouse, but after one spouse's death, it may be revoked only to the extent of the nonconsenting spouse's one-half interest. After the donor's death, the unauthorized gift is effectively treated as a testamentary transfer of the deceased donor's one-half interest. *Dargie v. Patterson, 176 Cal. 714, 169 P. 360 (1917)*. An unauthorized gift may be recovered from the donee. *Dargie, supra*. Or, after the donor spouse's death, one-half its value may be recovered from the donor spouse's estate. *Fields v. Michael, 91 Cal.App.2d 443, 205 P.2d 402 (1949)*. Even though the nondonor spouse has not acted during her lifetime, her estate may avoid the gift to the extent of her one-half interest. *Harris v. Harris, 57 Cal.2d 367, 19 Cal.Rptr. 793 (1962)*. In a dissolution proceeding, when one spouse claims that the other spouse has made a subsection (b) unauthorized gift of community funds, the putative donee may be joined in the dissolution action. *Babcock v. Superior Court, 29 Cal.App.4th 721, 35 Cal.Rptr.2d 462 (1994)*.

Subsection (c) has been broadly interpreted to protect the community's interest in household furnishings and family clothing. During marriage, a spouse may revoke any transfer to which he or she did not consent. *Matthews v. Hamburger, 36 Cal.App.2d 182, 97 P.2d 465 (1939)*. Even after the death of the transferor spouse, the nonconsenting survivor may set aside the entire transfer. *Dynan v. Gallinatti, 87 Cal.App.2d 553, 557, 197 P.2d 391 (1948)*. Compare postdeath gift revocation under subsection (b), supra.

Subsection (e) has been much rewritten in recent years. See also Family Code Sections 721 and 1101 which, together with subsection (e), were amended by Stats 1991, Ch 1026, in order to strengthen the position of the nonmanaging spouse, particularly at divorce. Although the full meaning of the amended provisions has not yet been illuminated by case law, they were intended to reverse a good deal of pre–1991 case law, which did not hold the managing spouse to a high standard in divorce negotiations. See, for example, *In re Marriage of Connolly, 23 Cal.3d 590, 153 Cal.Rptr. 423 (1979)*; *Boeseke v. Boeseke, 10 Cal.3d 844, 112 Cal.Rptr. 401 (1974)*; *In re Marriage of Alexander, 212 Cal.App.3d 677, 261 Cal.Rptr. 9 (1989)*. Thus pre–1991 case law must be evaluated in light of the 1991 amendments. See additionally Sections 2100–2129, added in 1992. Sections 2100–2113 apply to proceedings commenced on or after January 1, 1993, and Sections 2120–2129 apply to judgments entered on or after January 1, 1993. For discussion of the current Section 1100(e) fiduciary standard and the Section 2100–2133 disclosure provisions, see *In re Marriage of Reuling, 23 Cal.App.4th 1428, 28 Cal.Rptr.2d 726 (1994)*. The Section 1100(e) fiduciary duty does not require a spouse to disclose "insider" information about community property stock shares and options when such disclosure is prohibited by federal law. *Reuling, supra*. *Reuling* also states, in dictum, that the recently amended heightened fiduciary standard of Section 1100(e) should not be applied to conduct that occurred before the statute was amended. 23 Cal. App.4th at 1439.

In re Marriage of Duffy, 91 Cal.App.4th 923, 111 Cal.Rptr.2d 160 (2001), holds that the fiduciary duty imposed by § 721 and subsection (e) of this section does not encompass the "prudent investor" rule. A managing spouse is not held to the standard of a trustee. So long as a managing spouse acts in good faith, he has not breached the fiduciary duty even though he makes unwise or improvident investments. However, see Commentary to Family Code section 721.

Interpreting subsection 11 U.S.C. § 523 (a)(4), the Ninth Circuit Bankruptcy Appellate Panel held that a former husband's debt to his wife for pension benefits, which were received by him prior to the decree dividing the parties' community property, was nondischargeable in bankruptcy because, under subsection (e) of this section, California imposes a fiduciary duty on each spouse with respect to the other in the management of community property. *In re Stanifer, 236 B.R. 709 (1999)*. *Stanifer* distinguished on two grounds *In re Teichman, 774 F.2d 1395 (9th Cir. 1985)*, in which the Court of Appeals held that the § 523 (a)(4) exception to bankruptcy discharge does not apply to obligations created by a dissolution decree with respect to post-decretal pension benefits. First, the property in *Stanifer* was still community property when it was received; the property in *Teichman* was no longer community property for the marriage had already been dissolved and the community property distributed. Second, since *Teichman*, the California legislature has upgraded the "good faith" duty between spouses to a "fiduciary duty." (In addition to this section, see Family Code §§ 721, 1101, and 2102.)

Schnabel v. Superior Court, 5 Cal.4th 704, 21 Cal.Rptr.2d 200 (1993), holds that the wife's right of access to records that pertain to the value of community assets extends to records of a close corporation of which the husband is a 30% stockholder so long as such records are reasonably related to the dissolution proceeding. *Schnabel* further holds that tax information about third-party employees is not absolutely privileged from discovery, but that the request for inspection must be adequately justified, thus disapproving *Rifkind v. Superior Court, 123 Cal.App.3d 1045, 177 Cal.Rptr. 82 (1981)*, which held that all such tax returns were absolutely privileged.

Subsection (e) incorporates by reference the § 721 fiduciary duty. Under § 721, a rebuttable presumption of undue influence arises when one spouses gains an advantage over another in a community property transaction. The spouse who obtained the advantage bears the burden of rebutting the presumption. *In re Marriage of Haines, 33 Cal.App.4th 277, 39 Cal.Rptr.2d 673 (1995)*. *In re Marriage of Lange, 102 Cal.App.4th 360, 125 Cal.Rptr.2d 379 (2002)*, held that a husband's promissory note for a wife's separate property contributions to the acquisition of the family home and the deed of trust on the home securing the note were unenforceable under § 721 because they gave the wife an advantage and thus gave rise to a presumption of undue influence, which the wife failed to rebut. However, the wife remained entitled to § 2640 reimbursement of her separate property contributions to the acquisition of community property because the unenforceable instruments did not constitute a written waiver of that right.

In re Marriage of Mathews, 133 Cal.App.4th 624, 35 Cal.Rptr.3d 1 (2005), concluded that a husband rebutted the presumption of undue influence with evidence that a wife with a poor credit rating "freely and voluntarily" quitclaimed her interest in what otherwise would have been a community property home, even though she did so solely for the purpose of obtaining a lower interest rate and both husband and wife continued to believe during marriage that the home was community property.

Similarly, *In re Marriage of Brooks & Robinson, 169 Cal.App.4th 176, 86 Cal.Rptr.3d 624 (2008)*, held that a husband who agreed that his wife would take title to the family home acquired during marriage in her name alone solely for the purpose of obtaining a lower interest rate, thereby gave up all ownership interest in the home. *Brooks & Robinson* reached this conclusion by applying Evidence Code section 662, which creates a presumption that the owner of legal title is also the owner of beneficial title, and then requiring a contrary agreement of the parties to overcome the presumption. The husband's claim to an ownership interest failed because although it was undisputed that the husband agreed to take title in the wife's name solely to obtain a lower interest rate, the wife never agreed that he would have an ownership interest in the home.

Matthews and *Brooks & Robinson* were narrowly distinguished by *Starr v. Starr, 189 Cal.App.4th 277, 116 Cal.Rptr.3d 813 (2010)*, and *In re Marriage of Fossum, 192 Cal.App.4th 336, 121 Cal.Rptr.3d 195 (2011), review denied*. In each case, a realtor recommended title in one spouse's name alone and further recommended that the other spouse sign a quit-claim deed relinquishing all interest in the home. The spouses complied with the realtors' suggestions in order to obtain a beneficial interest rate. Each case followed *Brooks & Robinson* in applying the Evidence Code section 662 presumption. However, in each case, the quit-claim deed was set aside and the home was held to be community property on the ground that the titled spouse exercised undue influence (breached his fiduciary duty). Because the titled spouse promised to re-convey the property into joint title after financing was obtained and did not do so, the non-titled spouse's consent to title in the other spouse's name alone and the supplementary quit-claim deed was not "voluntary." In *Brooks & Robinson* and *Matthews*, by contrast, the titled spouse did not promise to re-convey.

In re Marriage of Burkle, 139 Cal.App.4th 712, 43 Cal.Rptr.3d 181 (2006), review denied, states in dictum that the presumption of undue influence does not arise unless a spouse obtains an "unfair advantage." This would effectively shift the burden of proof to the spouse who is disadvantaged to show that the disadvantage was unfair.

In re Marriage of Kieturakis, 138 Cal.App.4th 56, 41 Cal.Rptr.3d 119 (2006), review denied, held that the presumption of undue influence is not applicable to mediated settlement agreements. To the same effect, see *In re Marriage of Woolsey, 220 Cal.App.4th 881, 163 Cal.Rptr.3d 551 (2013), review denied*.

In re Marriage of Margulis, 198 Cal.App.4th 1252, 130 Cal.Rptr.3d 327 (2011), relying in part on subsection (e), held that in a marriage dissolution proceeding a managing spouse has the burden of proof to account for missing assets when the nonmanaging spouse has made a prima facie showing of the existence and value of community assets that have disappeared after separation while controlled by the managing spouse. The managing spouse must either rebut the showing or prove the proper disposition or lesser value of the assets. If the managing spouse fails to do so, the court should charge the managing spouse with the prima facie value of the assets. *Margulis* interprets this section, along with Family Code sections 721, 1101, 2100, and 2107, to impose upon a managing spouse a duty to disclose and account for the existence, valuation, and distribution of all community assets from the date of separation to the final property distribution.

Research References

Forms

California Practice Guide: Rutter Family Law Forms Form 9:2, Marital Agreement.
California Practice Guide: Rutter Family Law Forms Form 9:3, Marital Settlement Agreement.
California Transactions Forms--Business Entities § 19:82, Consent Of Spouse.
Cal. Transaction Forms - Bus. Transactions § 18:14, Spouses.
California Transactions Forms--Estate Planning § 7:2, Types Of Gifts.
California Transactions Forms--Estate Planning § 10:4, Community Property.
California Transactions Forms--Estate Planning § 7:14, Grant Deed Making Gift Of Real Property.
California Transactions Forms--Estate Planning § 7:20, Declaration Of Gift in View Of Impending Death.
California Transactions Forms--Estate Planning § 7:26, Consent Of Spouse to Gift.
California Transactions Forms--Estate Planning § 7:33, Restricted Endowment to Charitable Organization.
California Transactions Forms--Estate Planning § 10:21, Life Insurance Generally.
California Transactions Forms--Estate Planning § 11:49, Introduction and Definition [Prob C § 140].
California Transactions Forms--Family Law § 2:3, Comprehensive Drafting.
California Transactions Forms--Family Law § 2:4, Fiduciary Duty.
California Transactions Forms--Family Law § 2:5, Disclosure Requirements.
California Transactions Forms--Family Law § 1:99, Waiver Of Management and Control Of Property.
California Transactions Forms--Family Law § 2:30, Overview.
California Transactions Forms--Family Law § 2:88, Marital Settlement Agreement.
Am. Jur. Pl. & Pr. Forms Community Property § 64, Introductory Comments.
West's California Code Forms, Family § 781, Comment Overview--Damages for Injuries to Married Person.
West's California Code Forms, Family § 1100, Comment Overview--Community Personal Property.
West's California Code Forms, Family § 1100 Form 1, Consent Of Spouse to Gift by Other Spouse Of Community Personal Property.
West's California Code Forms, Family § 1500 Form 1, Marital Agreement.
West's California Code Forms, Family § 2338 Form 8, Marital Agreement.
West's California Code Forms, Family § 2338 Form 9, Marital Agreement--Both Spouses Employed.
West's California Code Forms, Family § 2550 Form 3, Marital Agreement.
West's California Code Forms, Family § 2550 Form 4, Division Of Property Clauses in Dissolution Settlement Agreement.
West's California Code Forms, Probate § 3080 Form 1, Petition for Support; for Injunctive Orders; for Determination Of the Character Of Property; for an Accounting; for Employment Of Counsel; and for Attorney Fees and Costs.

Treatises and Practice Aids

Witkin, California Summary 10th Community Property § 3, Property Rights During Marriage.
Witkin, California Summary 10th Community Property § 129, Former Law.
Witkin, California Summary 10th Community Property § 132, Current Law: Control by Either Spouse.
Witkin, California Summary 10th Community Property § 133, Statutory Requirement.
Witkin, California Summary 10th Community Property § 134, Action for Breach Of Duty.
Witkin, California Summary 10th Community Property § 135, Spouse Operating Business.
Witkin, California Summary 10th Community Property § 136, in General.
Witkin, California Summary 10th Community Property § 137, Statutory Limitation.
Witkin, California Summary 10th Community Property § 138, Permissible Transactions.
Witkin, California Summary 10th Community Property § 146, Personal Property.
Witkin, California Summary 10th Community Property § 158, in General.
Witkin, California Summary 10th Community Property § 159, Management, Control, and Disposition.

Witkin, California Summary 10th Community Property § 160, Substitute for Joinder or Consent.
Witkin, California Summary 10th Community Property § 200, Division by Agreement.
Witkin, California Summary 10th Community Property § 209, Family Business.
Witkin, California Summary 10th Husband and Wife § 349, Approval Of Court.
Witkin, California Summary 10th Personal Property § 146, Effect Of Transfer.

§ 1101. Claim for breach of fiduciary duty; court ordered accounting; addition of name of spouse to community property; limitation of action; consent of spouse not required; remedies

(a) A spouse has a claim against the other spouse for any breach of the fiduciary duty that results in impairment to the claimant spouse's present undivided one-half interest in the community estate, including, but not limited to, a single transaction or a pattern or series of transactions, which transaction or transactions have caused or will cause a detrimental impact to the claimant spouse's undivided one-half interest in the community estate.

(b) A court may order an accounting of the property and obligations of the parties to a marriage and may determine the rights of ownership in, the beneficial enjoyment of, or access to, community property, and the classification of all property of the parties to a marriage.

(c) A court may order that the name of a spouse shall be added to community property held in the name of the other spouse alone or that the title of community property held in some other title form shall be reformed to reflect its community character, except with respect to any of the following:

(1) A partnership interest held by the other spouse as a general partner.

(2) An interest in a professional corporation or professional association.

(3) An asset of an unincorporated business if the other spouse is the only spouse involved in operating and managing the business.

(4) Any other property, if the revision would adversely affect the rights of a third person.

(d)(1) Except as provided in paragraph (2), any action under subdivision (a) shall be commenced within three years of the date a petitioning spouse had actual knowledge that the transaction or event for which the remedy is being sought occurred.

(2) An action may be commenced under this section upon the death of a spouse or in conjunction with an action for legal separation, dissolution of marriage, or nullity without regard to the time limitations set forth in paragraph (1).

(3) The defense of laches may be raised in any action brought under this section.

(4) Except as to actions authorized by paragraph (2), remedies under subdivision (a) apply only to transactions or events occurring on or after July 1, 1987.

(e) In any transaction affecting community property in which the consent of both spouses is required, the court may, upon the motion of a spouse, dispense with the requirement of the other spouse's consent if both of the following requirements are met:

(1) The proposed transaction is in the best interest of the community.

(2) Consent has been arbitrarily refused or cannot be obtained due to the physical incapacity, mental incapacity, or prolonged absence of the nonconsenting spouse.

(f) Any action may be brought under this section without filing an action for dissolution of marriage, legal separation, or nullity, or may be brought in conjunction with the action or upon the death of a spouse.

(g) Remedies for breach of the fiduciary duty by one spouse, including those set out in Sections 721 and 1100, shall include, but not be limited to, an award to the other spouse of 50 percent, or an amount equal to 50 percent, of any asset undisclosed or transferred in breach of the fiduciary duty plus attorney's fees and court costs. The value of the asset shall be determined to be its highest value at the date of the breach of the fiduciary duty, the date of the sale or disposition of the asset, or the date of the award by the court.

(h) Remedies for the breach of the fiduciary duty by one spouse, as set forth in Sections 721 and 1100, when the breach falls within the ambit of Section 3294 of the Civil Code shall include, but not be limited to, an award to the other spouse of 100 percent, or an amount equal to 100 percent, of any asset undisclosed or transferred in breach of the fiduciary duty. *(Stats.1992, c. 162 (A.B.2650), § 10, operative Jan. 1, 1994. Amended by Stats.2001, c. 703 (A.B.583), § 1.)*

Application

For application of Stats.2001, c. 703 (A.B.583), see § 8 of that act.

Law Revision Commission Comments

Enactment [Revised Comment]

Section 1101 continues former Civil Code Section 5125.1 without change, except that (1) section references have been adjusted and (2) "community estate" has been substituted for "community interest" in subdivision (a) for internal consistency. These are technical, nonsubstantive changes. See Section 63 ("community estate" defined) & Comment. See also Prob. Code §§ 3057 (protection of rights of spouse who lacks legal capacity), 3101 (proceeding for court order to authorize particular transaction). [23 Cal.L.Rev.Comm. Reports 1 (1993)].

Commentary

In re Marriage of Margulis, 198 Cal.App.4th 1252, 130 Cal.Rptr.3d 327 (2011), relying in part on this section, held that in a marriage dissolution proceeding a managing spouse has the burden of proof to account for missing assets when the nonmanaging spouse has made a prima facie showing of the existence and value of community assets that have disappeared after separation while controlled by the managing spouse. The managing spouse must either rebut the showing or prove the proper disposition or lesser value of the assets. If the managing spouse fails to do so, the court should charge the managing spouse with the prima facie value of the assets. *Margulis* interprets this section, along with Family Code sections 721, 1100, 2100, and 2107, to impose upon a managing spouse a duty to disclose and account for the existence, valuation, and distribution of all community assets from the date of separation to the final property distribution.

In re Marriage of Georgiou and Leslie, 218 Cal.App.4th 561, 160 Cal.Rptr.3d 254 (2013) review denied, holds that this section does not permit a postjudgment action for breach of the fiduciary duty of disclosure when the asset was adjudicated and divided in the dissolution proceeding. In such case, the former spouse's remedy is an action to set aside the judgment under Family Code section 2122.

Some rights provided by this section are available in the absence of any breach of fiduciary duty. The legislative history of Section 1101 indicates that the first three subsections provide independent claims and remedies. A subsection (b) accounting and a subsection (c) add-a-name remedy are available without any showing of a subsection (a) breach of fiduciary duty. Assembly Judiciary Committee Analysis, Senate Bill 1071, July 1, 1986; Letter from Senator Bill Lockyer to Assembly Member Elihu Harris, July 8, 1986.

When a spouse violated a Section 2040 (a)(2) automatic restraining order by selling community securities without a court order or the other spouse's consent, the trial court, under subsections (a) and (g) of this section, properly awarded the wronged spouse one-half of the lost profits, that is, the appreciation of the securities between the date of sale and the subsequent divorce. *In re Marriage of McTiernan & Dubrow, 133 Cal.App.4th 1090, 35 Cal.Rptr.3d 287 (2005), review denied.*

In re Marriage of Hokanson, 68 Cal.App.4th 987, 80 Cal.Rptr.2d 699 (1998), holds that once a court finds a breach of fiduciary duty, subsection (g) requires that the court award attorney's fees to the injured party. Going even further than *Hokanson*, *In re Marriage of Fossum, 192 Cal.App.4th 336, 121 Cal.Rptr.3d 195 (2011), review denied*, holds that the court must award attorney's fees to the injured party even if that party did not request them.

Subsection (h) incorporates Civil Code Section 3294, which provides for exemplary, or punitive, damages when "it is proven by clear and convincing evidence that the defendant has been guilty of oppression, fraud, or malice." Applying subsection (h), *In re Marriage of Rossi, 90 Cal.App.4th 34, 108 Cal.Rptr.2d 270 (2001)*, holds that a spouse's intentional concealment of community property lottery winnings constituted fraud under Civil Code § 3294 (c)(3) and justified a trial court award of 100 percent of the winnings to the other spouse. *Rossi* also holds that subsection (h), unlike subsection (g), does not require the imposition of attorney's fees and court costs on the breaching party.

In re Marriage of Simmons, 215 Cal.App.4th 584, 155 Cal.Rptr.3d 685 (2013), holds that the subsection (h) value-of-the-asset remedy does not apply to a spouse's nondisclosure of his separate property.

Marriage of Schleich, 8 Cal.App.5th 267, 213 Cal.Rptr.3d 665 (2017), review denied, held that the subsection (g) and (h) remedies for a spouse's breach of fiduciary duty do not apply to (1) a spouse's failure to disclose separate property in dissolution proceedings or (2) a spouse's failure to disclose community property received preseparation when that property was spent for community purposes prior to separation. *Schleich* additionally held that a spouse who receives 50 percent or 100 percent of the value of an asset under subsections (g) or (h) is not additionally entitled to receive 50 percent of the value of the asset in the division of community property; instead the aggrieved spouse's remedy for nondisclosure during dissolution lies in section 2107(c) money sanctions for failure to comply with disclosure rules.

A spouse may be criminally liable for intentionally causing harm to property in which the other spouse has a community or separate interest, even though that harm occurs in the marital home and the parties are cohabiting as husband and wife. In *People v. Wallace, 123 Cal.App.4th 144, 19 Cal.Rptr.3d 790 (2004), review denied*, a husband was convicted of felony vandalism for causing more than $15,000 of damages to his wife's house and belongings. Although burglary and trespass cannot be committed against one's own home, vandalism can be.

Michaely v. Michaely, 150 Cal.App.4th 802, 59 Cal.Rptr.3d 56 (2007), review denied July 25, 2007, held that the remedies provided in this section for breach of fiduciary duty are applicable to a spouse whose intentional and obstreperous behavior during a deposition effectively deprived his wife of meaningful discovery. In *Michaely*, the trial court awarded the wife all the community property, pursuant to subsection (h).

Research References

Forms

California Transactions Forms--Estate Planning § 10:4, Community Property.

California Transactions Forms--Estate Planning § 10:21, Life Insurance Generally.

California Transactions Forms--Family Law § 2:9, Remedies for False Disclosure.

California Transactions Forms--Family Law § 1:99, Waiver Of Management and Control Of Property.

California Transactions Forms--Family Law § 2:81, Potential Community Assets and Obligations.

West's California Code Forms, Family § 1100, Comment Overview--Community Personal Property.

Treatises and Practice Aids

Witkin, California Summary 10th Community Property § 134, Action for Breach Of Duty.

Witkin, California Summary 10th Community Property § 135, Spouse Operating Business.

Witkin, California Summary 10th Equity § 16, Nature Of Defense.

§ 1102. Community real property; spouse's joinder in conveyances; application of section; limitation of actions

(a) Except as provided in Sections 761 and 1103, either spouse has the management and control of the community real property, whether acquired prior to or on or after January 1, 1975, but both spouses, either personally or by a duly authorized agent, must join in executing any instrument by which that community real property or any interest therein is leased for a longer period than one year, or is sold, conveyed, or encumbered.

(b) Nothing in this section shall be construed to apply to a lease, mortgage, conveyance, or transfer of real property or of any interest in real property between spouses.

(c) Notwithstanding subdivision (b):

(1) The sole lease, contract, mortgage, or deed of the husband, holding the record title to community real property, to a lessee, purchaser, or encumbrancer, in good faith without knowledge of the marriage relation, shall be presumed to be valid if executed prior to January 1, 1975.

(2) The sole lease, contract, mortgage, or deed of either spouse, holding the record title to community real property to a lessee, purchaser, or encumbrancer, in good faith without knowledge of the marriage relation, shall be presumed to be valid if executed on or after January 1, 1975.

(d) No action to avoid any instrument mentioned in this section, affecting any property standing of record in the name of either spouse alone, executed by the spouse alone, shall be commenced after the expiration of one year from the filing for record of that instrument in the recorder's office in the county in which the land is situated.

(e) Nothing in this section precludes either spouse from encumbering his or her interest in community real property, as provided in Section 2033, to pay reasonable attorney's fees in order to retain or maintain legal counsel in a proceeding for dissolution of marriage, for nullity of marriage, or for legal separation of the parties. *(Stats.1992, c. 162 (A.B.2650), § 10, operative Jan. 1, 1994. Amended by Stats.1993, c. 219 (A.B.1500), § 101; Stats.2014, c. 82 (S.B.1306), § 18, eff. Jan. 1, 2015.)*

Law Revision Commission Comments

Enactment [Revised Comment]

Section 1102 continues former Civil Code Section 5127 without substantive change. The section has been divided into subdivisions and some minor, nonsubstantive wording changes have been made, such as changing "situate" to "situated" in subdivision (d). In subdivision (e), the phrase "proceeding for dissolution of marriage, nullity of marriage, or legal separation of the parties" has been substituted for "action under this part," which referred to the former Family Law Act (former Part 5 (commencing with former Section 4000) of Division 4 of the Civil Code). [23 Cal.L.Rev.Comm. Reports 1 (1993)].

Commentary

Subsection (c) gives presumptive validity to real property purchases, leases, and encumbrances from one spouse alone when the property is titled in that spouse's name alone and the third-party purchaser, lessee, or encumbrancer takes in good faith without notice of the marriage relationship. The presumption may be rebutted by evidence that the nonconsenting spouse did not know of or participate in the transfer she seeks to avoid. *Bush v. Rogers, 42 Cal.App.2d 477, 109 P.2d 379 (1941)*. Even when the nonconsenting spouse rebuts the presumption, she may also have to tender back the purchase price. *Mark v. Title Guarantee & Trust Company, 122 Cal.App. 301, 9 P.2d 839 (1932)*.

The subsection (d) one-year statute of limitations "only protects bona fide transferees with no knowledge of the marital relation who have no reason to suspect another signature is necessary." *Byrd v. Blanton, 149 Cal.App.3d 987, 993, 197 Cal.Rptr. 190 (1983)*.

Subsection (e) was added in 1992 to limit the holding of *Droeger v. Friedman, Sloan & Ross, 54 Cal.3d 26, 812 P.2d 931, 283 Cal.Rptr. 584 (1991)*. Stats 1992, Ch 356 (AB 3399). See also Family Code Section 2033, providing for a "family law attorney's real property lien." *Droeger* held that a subsection (a) encumbrance made without the consent of a spouse may be avoided in its entirety by the nonconsenting spouse *during the parties' marriage*. Compare *Hyatt v. Mabie, 24 Cal.App.4th 541, 29 Cal.Rptr.2d 447 (1994)* (when community realty has been encumbered during marriage without one spouse's consent, after the spouses are divorced the nonconsenting spouse may invalidate the encumbrance only to the extent of her one-half interest).

With *Droeger*, supra, compare *Lezine v. Security Pacific Financial Services, 14 Cal.4th 56, 925 P.2d 1002, 58 Cal.Rptr.2d 756 (1996)*. In *Lezine*, the husband forged the wife's signature on a quit claim deed to the family home and then, as security for a loan, executed two trust deeds on the home. At the wife's request, the trial court voided the trust deeds on the ground that encumbrances of community realty require the consent of both spouses. The trial court also awarded the lender money judgments against the debtor, which the lender then recorded. Later, at divorce, the family home was awarded to the wife and the debts to the husband. The California Supreme Court held that the judgment lien attached to all of the couple's community property, and that the wife took the home subject to the lien.

Research References

Forms

California Practice Guide: Rutter Family Law Forms Form 1:20, Ex Parte Application and Request for Order Re Objection to Family Law Attorney's Real Property Lien and Request to Stay Recordation.
Cal. Transaction Forms - Bus. Transactions § 18:14, Spouses.
California Transactions Forms--Estate Planning § 10:4, Community Property.
Am. Jur. Pl. & Pr. Forms Community Property § 17, Introductory Comments.
West's California Code Forms, Family § 1100, Comment Overview--Community Personal Property.
West's California Code Forms, Family § 2033 Form 2, Trust Deed Creating Attorney's Lien.

Treatises and Practice Aids

Witkin, California Summary 10th Community Property § 3, Property Rights During Marriage.
Witkin, California Summary 10th Community Property § 132, Current Law: Control by Either Spouse.
Witkin, California Summary 10th Community Property § 135, Spouse Operating Business.
Witkin, California Summary 10th Community Property § 136, in General.
Witkin, California Summary 10th Community Property § 137, Statutory Limitation.
Witkin, California Summary 10th Community Property § 147, Requirement Of Spouse's Consent.
Witkin, California Summary 10th Community Property § 148, Entire Lien is Voidable.
Witkin, California Summary 10th Community Property § 149, Distinction: Family Law Attorney's Lien.
Witkin, California Summary 10th Community Property § 150, Bona Fide Purchasers.
Witkin, California Summary 10th Community Property § 158, in General.
Witkin, California Summary 10th Community Property § 160, Substitute for Joinder or Consent.

§ 1103. Management and control of community property; one or both spouses having conservator of estate or lacking legal capacity

(a) Where one or both of the spouses either has a conservator of the estate or lacks legal capacity to manage and control community property, the procedure for management and control (which includes disposition) of the community property is that prescribed in Part 6 (commencing with Section 3000) of Division 4 of the Probate Code.

(b) Where one or both spouses either has a conservator of the estate or lacks legal capacity to give consent to a gift of community personal property or a disposition of community personal property without a valuable consideration as required by Section 1100 or to a sale, conveyance, or encumbrance of community personal property for which a consent is required by Section 1100, the procedure for that gift, disposition, sale, conveyance, or encumbrance is that prescribed in Part 6 (commencing with Section 3000) of Division 4 of the Probate Code.

(c) Where one or both spouses either has a conservator of the estate or lacks legal capacity to join in executing a lease, sale, conveyance, or encumbrance of community real property or any interest therein as required by Section 1102, the procedure for that lease, sale, conveyance, or encumbrance is that prescribed in Part 6 (commencing with Section 3000) of Division 4 of the Probate Code. *(Stats.1992, c. 162 (A.B. 2650), § 10, operative Jan. 1, 1994.)*

Law Revision Commission Comments

Enactment [Revised Comment]

Section 1103 continues former Civil Code Section 5128 without change, except that section references have been adjusted and "that" has been substituted for "such" in subdivisions (b) and (c).

This section makes provisions of the Probate Code applicable in two situations:

(1) Where one or both spouses have a conservator of the estate or lack legal capacity to manage and control community property (which includes the disposition of community property). See, e.g., Prob. Code § 3051.

(2) Where one or both spouses have a conservator of the estate or lack legal capacity for a transaction requiring joinder or consent under Section 1100(b)–(c) or 1102. See, e.g., Prob. Code §§ 3012 (legal capacity), 3071 (substitute for joinder or consent). [23 Cal.L.Rev.Comm. Reports 1 (1993)].

Research References

Forms

Am. Jur. Pl. & Pr. Forms Community Property § 64, Introductory Comments.
West's California Code Forms, Family § 781, Comment Overview--Damages for Injuries to Married Person.

Treatises and Practice Aids

Witkin, California Summary 10th Community Property § 136, in General.
Witkin, California Summary 10th Community Property § 147, Requirement Of Spouse's Consent.
Witkin, California Summary 10th Community Property § 158, in General.

Part 5

MARITAL AGREEMENTS

CHAPTER 1. GENERAL PROVISIONS

§ 1500. Effect of premarital agreements and other marital property agreements

The property rights of spouses prescribed by statute may be altered by a premarital agreement or other marital property agreement. *(Stats.1992, c. 162 (A.B.2650), § 10, operative Jan. 1, 1994. Amended by Stats.2014, c. 82 (S.B.1306), § 19, eff. Jan. 1, 2015.)*

Law Revision Commission Comments

Enactment [Revised Comment]

Section 1500 continues former Civil Code Section 5200 without change. See also Sections 1600–1617 (premarital agreements); Prob. Code §§ 140–147 (surviving spouse's waiver of rights). [23 Cal.L.Rev.Comm. Reports 1 (1993)].

Research References

Forms

California Transactions Forms--Estate Planning § 11:39, General Considerations.
California Transactions Forms--Estate Planning § 11:45, Introduction.
California Transactions Forms--Family Law § 1:71, Binding Agreement With Specific Family Code Waivers.
West's California Code Forms, Family § 1500, Comment Overview--Marital Agreements and Premarital Agreements.

Treatises and Practice Aids

Witkin, California Summary 10th Community Property § 24, in General.
Witkin, California Summary 10th Community Property § 153, Authority to Transmute.
Witkin, California Summary 10th Husband and Wife § 39, in General.

§ 1501. Agreements by minors

A minor may make a valid premarital agreement or other marital property agreement if the minor is emancipated or is otherwise capable of contracting marriage. *(Stats.1992, c. 162 (A.B.2650), § 10, operative Jan. 1, 1994.)*

Law Revision Commission Comments

Enactment [Revised Comment]

Section 1501 continues former Civil Code Section 5201 without change. [23 Cal.L.Rev.Comm. Reports 1 (1993)].

Research References

Forms

California Transactions Forms--Estate Planning § 11:39, General Considerations.
West's California Code Forms, Family § 1500, Comment Overview--Marital Agreements and Premarital Agreements.

Treatises and Practice Aids

Witkin, California Summary 10th Community Property § 25, Requisites Of Premarital Agreements.

§ 1502. Recording of agreements

(a) A premarital agreement or other marital property agreement that is executed and acknowledged or proved in the manner that a grant of real property is required to be executed and acknowledged or proved may be recorded in the office of the recorder of each county in which real property affected by the agreement is situated.

(b) Recording or nonrecording of a premarital agreement or other marital property agreement has the same effect as recording or nonrecording of a grant of real property. *(Stats.1992, c. 162 (A.B.2650), § 10, operative Jan. 1, 1994.)*

Law Revision Commission Comments

Enactment [Revised Comment]

Section 1502 continues former Civil Code Section 5202 without change. See also Section 700 (real property includes leasehold interests in real property). [23 Cal.L.Rev.Comm. Reports 1 (1993)].

Research References

Forms

California Transactions Forms--Estate Planning § 11:39, General Considerations.

California Transactions Forms--Estate Planning § 11:45, Introduction.
California Transactions Forms--Family Law § 1:8, Acknowledgment and Recordation.
West's California Code Forms, Family § 1500, Comment Overview--Marital Agreements and Premarital Agreements.

Treatises and Practice Aids

Witkin, California Summary 10th Community Property § 25, Requisites Of Premarital Agreements.

§ 1503. Law applicable to preexisting premarital agreements

Nothing in this chapter affects the validity or effect of premarital agreements made before January 1, 1986, and the validity and effect of those agreements shall continue to be determined by the law applicable to the agreements before January 1, 1986. *(Stats.1992, c. 162 (A.B.2650), § 10, operative Jan. 1, 1994.)*

Law Revision Commission Comments

Enactment [Revised Comment]

Section 1503 continues former Civil Code Section 5203 without substantive change. [23 Cal.L.Rev.Comm. Reports 1 (1993)].

Research References

Forms

California Transactions Forms--Family Law § 1:5, Governing Law, Form, and Execution.

Treatises and Practice Aids

Witkin, California Summary 10th Community Property § 24, in General.

CHAPTER 2. UNIFORM PREMARITAL AGREEMENT ACT

ARTICLE 1. PRELIMINARY PROVISIONS

§ 1600. Short title

This chapter may be cited as the Uniform Premarital Agreement Act. *(Stats.1992, c.162 (A.B.2650), § 10, operative Jan. 1, 1994.)*

Law Revision Commission Comments

Enactment [Revised Comment]

Section 1600 continues former Civil Code Section 5300 without substantive change. Section 1600 is the same as Section 10 of the Uniform Premarital Agreement Act (1983). See also Sections 3 (construction of provision drawn from uniform act), 14 (severability of provisions). [23 Cal.L.Rev.Comm. Reports 1 (1993)].

Research References

Forms

California Transactions Forms--Estate Planning § 6:28, Exceptions to Omitted Spouse Statute.
California Transactions Forms--Estate Planning § 6:99, Omitted Spouse Made Valid Agreement Waiving Right to Share in Decedent's Estate.
California Transactions Forms--Estate Planning § 11:37, Introduction.
California Transactions Forms--Family Law § 1:2, Nature and Advantages Of Agreement.
California Transactions Forms--Family Law § 1:5, Governing Law, Form, and Execution.
California Transactions Forms--Family Law § 4:7, Effect Of Subsequent Marriage Between Cohabitants.
West's California Code Forms, Family § 1500, Comment Overview--Marital Agreements and Premarital Agreements.

Treatises and Practice Aids

Witkin, California Summary 10th Community Property § 24, in General.
Witkin, California Summary 10th Contracts § 255, Premarital Agreements.
Witkin, California Summary 10th Contracts § 399, Marital and Premarital Agreements.
Witkin, California Summary 10th Contracts § 629, Other Agreements.
Witkin, California Summary 10th Wills and Probate § 324, Enforcement.

§ 1601. Effective date of chapter

This chapter is effective on and after January 1, 1986, and applies to any premarital agreement executed on or after that date. *(Stats.1992, c. 162 (A.B.2650), § 10, operative Jan. 1, 1994.)*

Law Revision Commission Comments

Enactment [Revised Comment]

Section 1601 continues former Civil Code Section 5302 without change. Section 1601 is the same as Section 12 of the Uniform Premarital Agreement Act (1983). See also Section 1503 (law applicable to premarital agreements made before January 1, 1986). [23 Cal.L.Rev.Comm. Reports 1 (1993)].

Research References

Forms

California Transactions Forms--Estate Planning § 11:41, Formalities.
California Transactions Forms--Family Law § 1:5, Governing Law, Form, and Execution.

Treatises and Practice Aids

Witkin, California Summary 10th Community Property § 24, in General.

ARTICLE 2. PREMARITAL AGREEMENTS

§ 1610. Definitions

As used in this chapter:

(a) "Premarital agreement" means an agreement between prospective spouses made in contemplation of marriage and to be effective upon marriage.

(b) "Property" means an interest, present or future, legal or equitable, vested or contingent, in real or personal property, including income and earnings. *(Stats.1992, c. 162 (A.B.2650), § 10, operative Jan. 1, 1994.)*

Law Revision Commission Comments

Enactment [Revised Comment]

Section 1610 continues former Civil Code Section 5310 without change. Section 1610 is the same as Section 1 of the Uniform Premarital Agreement Act (1983). [23 Cal.L.Rev.Comm. Reports 1 (1993)].

Commentary

Estate of Wilson, 211 Cal.App.4th 1284, 150 Cal.Rptr.3d 699 (2012), review denied, held that domestic partnership agreements that satisfy the requirements of sections 1600-1617 and were made after the enactment of statutes that provided domestic partners with essentially the same property rights as spouses are not automatically invalidated by the partners' subsequent same-sex marriage. Thus, a pre-registration California domestic partnership agreement in which the parties waived any interest in each other's estate and that required a signed writing to terminate the agreement, was not revoked by the parties' subsequent same-sex marriage. Although the surviving spouse was an omitted spouse for purposes of Probate Code section 21610, under section 21611(c) he waived his right to any interest in the decedent spouse's estate in the domestic partnership agreement.

Research References

Forms

California Practice Guide: Rutter Family Law Forms Form 9:1, Premarital Agreement.
California Transactions Forms--Estate Planning § 6:28, Exceptions to Omitted Spouse Statute.
California Transactions Forms--Estate Planning § 11:37, Introduction.
California Transactions Forms--Estate Planning § 11:39, General Considerations.
California Transactions Forms--Estate Planning § 11:41, Formalities.
California Transactions Forms--Family Law § 1:2, Nature and Advantages Of Agreement.
California Transactions Forms--Family Law § 1:6, Subject Matter; Altering Rights.
California Transactions Forms--Family Law § 4:7, Effect Of Subsequent Marriage Between Cohabitants.
California Transactions Forms--Family Law § 4:9, Rights to Income.
California Transactions Forms--Family Law § 1:27, Complete Agreement.
California Transactions Forms--Family Law § 1:37, Agreement in Contemplation and Consideration Of Marriage; Complex Provision.
Nichols Cyclopedia of Legal Forms Annotated § 100:40, Premarital Agreement--Community Property--California.
West's California Code Forms, Family § 1611, Comment Overview--Premarital Agreements.

Treatises and Practice Aids

Witkin, California Summary 10th Community Property § 24, in General.
Witkin, California Summary 10th Contracts § 399, Marital and Premarital Agreements.
Witkin, California Summary 10th Contracts § 629, Other Agreements.

§ 1611. Form and execution of agreement; consideration

A premarital agreement shall be in writing and signed by both parties. It is enforceable without consideration. *(Stats. 1992, c. 162 (A.B.2650), § 10, operative Jan. 1, 1994.)*

Law Revision Commission Comments

Enactment [Revised Comment]

Section 1611 continues former Civil Code Section 5311 without change. Section 1611 is the same as Section 2 of the Uniform Premarital Agreement Act (1983). See also Sections 1501 (agreements by minors), 1502 (recording of agreements). [23 Cal.L.Rev. Comm. Reports 1 (1993)].

Commentary

A waiver of death rights contained in an antenuptial agreement that satisfies the requirements of Family Code Sections 1600 et seq. (the Uniform Premarital Agreement Act) is enforceable even though the agreement does not satisfy the requirements of Probate Code Sections 140 et seq. *Estate of Gagnier, 21 Cal.App.4th 124, 26 Cal.Rptr.2d 128 (1993)* (upholding wife's waiver of death rights in antenuptial agreement despite lack of Probate Code Section 143 representation by independent counsel).

This section of the Uniform Premarital Agreement Act recodifies the long-standing California requirement that premarital agreements satisfy the statute of frauds. The current recodification has been interpreted to preserve pre-existing case law exceptions to the statute of frauds. *Hall v. Hall, 222 Cal.App.3d 578, 587, 271 Cal.Rptr. 773 (1990), review denied*. The California courts have long recognized two exceptions to the statute of frauds: execution and detrimental reliance. An oral premarital agreement is enforceable when the promisor has executed his promise. *In re Marriage of Garrity & Bishton, 181 Cal.App.3d 675, 685, 226 Cal.Rptr. 485 (1986)*; *Freitas v. Freitas, 31 Cal.App. 16, 159 P. 611 (1916)*. When one spouse has relied to her detriment upon the other's oral promise, the promisor may be estopped to assert the statute of frauds. Detrimental reliance may consist of affirmative action or mere forbearance to act. *Estate of Sheldon, 75 Cal.App.3d 364, 142 Cal.Rptr. 119 (1977)*. Yet marriage alone does not work an estoppel. *Hall, supra at 586*. For further discussion of equitable estoppel to assert the statute of frauds, see *Juran v. Epstein, 23 Cal.App.4th 882, 28 Cal.Rptr.2d 588 (1994)* (Probate Code Section 150(a)(3), which requires a writing in order to enforce a contract not to revoke a will, does not abolish use of the doctrine of equitable estoppel to enforce an oral agreement not to revoke a will). See also equitable estoppel cases cited in Civil Code Section 683, Commentary.

But compare judicial interpretation of Family Code § 852(a), which governs transmutation of property *during marriage*. *In re Marriage of Benson, 36 Cal.4th 1096, 116 P.3d 1152, 32 Cal.Rptr.3d 471 (2005)*, holds that the usual exceptions to the statute of frauds (see Commentary to Section 1611) may not be used to avoid the subsection (a) writing requirement.

In re Marriage of Shaban, 88 Cal.App.4th 398, 105 Cal.Rptr.2d 863 (2001), review denied July 11, 2001, holds that parol evidence is inadmissible to establish the terms of an Islamic marriage contract when the writing fails to state with reasonable certainty the terms and conditions of the contract. *Shaban* reasons that, in the context of the statute of frauds, the limited purpose of the parol evidence rule is to illuminate the meaning of specific words of the contract, but not to create missing terms of the contract.

Research References

Forms

California Transactions Forms--Estate Planning § 6:28, Exceptions to Omitted Spouse Statute.
California Transactions Forms--Estate Planning § 11:41, Formalities.
California Transactions Forms--Family Law § 1:5, Governing Law, Form, and Execution.
California Transactions Forms--Family Law § 1:8, Acknowledgment and Recordation.
California Transactions Forms--Family Law § 1:19, Consideration.
West's California Code Forms, Family § 1611, Comment Overview--Premarital Agreements.

Treatises and Practice Aids

Witkin, California Summary 10th Community Property § 25, Requisites Of Premarital Agreements.
Witkin, California Summary 10th Contracts § 255, Premarital Agreements.
Witkin, California Summary 10th Contracts § 399, Marital and Premarital Agreements.

§ 1612. Subject matter of premarital agreements

(a) Parties to a premarital agreement may contract with respect to all of the following:

(1) The rights and obligations of each of the parties in any of the property of either or both of them whenever and wherever acquired or located.

(2) The right to buy, sell, use, transfer, exchange, abandon, lease, consume, expend, assign, create a security interest in, mortgage, encumber, dispose of, or otherwise manage and control property.

(3) The disposition of property upon separation, marital dissolution, death, or the occurrence or nonoccurrence of any other event.

(4) The making of a will, trust, or other arrangement to carry out the provisions of the agreement.

(5) The ownership rights in and disposition of the death benefit from a life insurance policy.

(6) The choice of law governing the construction of the agreement.

(7) Any other matter, including their personal rights and obligations, not in violation of public policy or a statute imposing a criminal penalty.

(b) The right of a child to support may not be adversely affected by a premarital agreement.

(c) Any provision in a premarital agreement regarding spousal support, including, but not limited to, a waiver of it, is not enforceable if the party against whom enforcement of the spousal support provision is sought was not represented by independent counsel at the time the agreement containing the provision was signed, or if the provision regarding spousal support is unconscionable at the time of enforcement. An otherwise unenforceable provision in a premarital agreement regarding spousal support may not become enforceable solely because the party against whom enforcement is sought was represented by independent counsel. *(Stats.1992, c. 162 (A.B.2650), § 10, operative Jan. 1, 1994. Amended by Stats. 2001, c. 286 (S.B.78), § 1.)*

Law Revision Commission Comments

Enactment [Revised Comment]

Section 1612 continues former Civil Code Section 5312 without change. Section 1612 is the same as Section 3 of the Uniform Premarital Agreement Act (1983), except that Section 1612 omits the provision of the uniform act providing that the parties to a premarital agreement may contract with respect to "the modification or elimination of spousal support." See also Prob. Code §§ 140–147 (surviving spouse's waiver of rights), 150 (contracts concerning will or succession). [23 Cal.L.Rev.Comm. Reports 1 (1993)].

Commentary

For contracts made before January 1, 1986 (see Sections 1503 and 1601), the public policy against promoting divorce is also violated by premarital contract clauses providing for property transfer at divorce. Hence such clauses are also unenforceable. See *In re Marriage of Noghrey, 169 Cal.App.3d 326, 215 Cal.Rptr. 153 (1985)* and *In re Marriage of Dajani, 204 Cal.App.3d 1387, 251 Cal.Rptr. 871 (1988)*. It is uncertain whether, with respect to post–1985 contracts, this caselaw rule survives enactment of the Uniform Act. Compare subsections (a)(3) and (a)(7).

In re Marriage of Bellio, 105 Cal.App.4th 630, 129 Cal.Rptr.2d 556 (2003), purports to apply the public policy restriction of *Noghrey* and *Dajani* to a premarital contract entered after the effective date of the Uniform Act, but nevertheless concludes that the contract term providing for payment of $100,000 to the wife in the event of divorce did not violate public policy because the term, in light of the reason for the payment, would not promote dissolution of a viable marriage.

In re Marriage of Weiss, 42 Cal.App.4th 106, 49 Cal.Rptr.2d 339 (1996), review denied May 1, 1996, declined to enforce the parties' formal antenuptial agreement that any children of the marriage would be reared in the Jewish faith on the ground that enforcement would infringe the free exercise rights of the breaching parent.

On October 13, 2004, the California Supreme Court granted review to *In re Marriage of Rosendale, 15 Cal.Rptr.3d 137 (2004)*, in which the depublished opinion of the court of appeal purported to hold that whether a spousal support waiver in a premarital agreement was executed before or after the effective date of the 2001 enactment of subsection (c), a support waiver is unenforceable if at the time enforcement is sought, enforcement would be unconscionable. The court reasoned that the effective date of the amendment was immaterial because the statutory amendment codified existing common law, citing *In re Marriage of Pendleton & Fireman, 24 Cal.4th 39, 99 Cal.Rptr.2d 278, 5 P.3d 839 (2000)*, which held that premarital spousal support waivers were not per se unenforceable, but declined to expressly decide "whether circumstances existing at the time enforcement of a waiver of spousal support is sought might make enforcement unjust." 24 Cal.4th at 53. On July 13, 2005, the Supreme Court, under California Rules of Court, Rule 29.3b, dismissed review of *Rosendale*, citing subsection (c) of this section and Section 4(c), which provides that amendments to the Family Code apply to all matters governed by those amendments without regard to when the operative events occurred. Thus, the Supreme Court would seem to be taking the view that subsection (c) of this section applies retroactively to all premarital spousal support waivers, subject only to Section 4(h) and due process requirements. *Rosendale* remains depublished because the Supreme Court did not specifically order otherwise when it dismissed review. California Rules of Court, Rule 8.528 (renumbered from 29.3b in 2007).

However, *In re Marriage of Howell, 195 Cal.App.4th 1062, 126 Cal.Rptr.3d 539 (2011)*, declined to retroactively apply Family Code section 1612(c), which is a 2002 amendment, insofar as it would invalidate a 1999 spousal support waiver because the party resisting enforcement was not represented by counsel. *Howell* concluded that retroactive application of the attorney-representation requirement would violate Family Code section 4(f) by making the party seeking enforcement "liable for an action taken before the operative date that was proper at the time…even if the action would be improper if taken on or after the operative date," reasoning that the party seeking enforcement became "liable" for failing to make sure that the other party was represented by counsel.

In re Marriage of Melissa, 212 Cal.App.4th 598, 151 Cal.Rptr.3d 608 (2013), review denied, holds that a spousal support waiver in a premarital agreement executed before 1986, that is, before the Uniform Premarital Agreement Act became effective, is unenforceable, because when the agreement was executed spousal support waivers were entirely unenforceable under California case law.

By contrast, *In re Marriage of Facter, 212 Cal.App.4th 967, 152 Cal.Rptr.3d 79 (2013), review denied*, states that a premarital spousal support waiver executed in 1994 was not per se unenforceable under *Pendleton*, decided in 2000 and interpreting an earlier version of this section of the Uniform Premarital Agreement Act. Subsection (c) of this section, added in 2002, did not apply because its application would be impermissibly retroactive, citing *Howell*. However, *Facter* concluded that, under *Pendleton*, enforcement would be unconscionable at the time of divorce in light of the great disparity in the parties' income and the inability of the wife to achieve the marital standard of living. Effectively, *Facter* applied dictum of *Pendleton*, which promised a result that could not be achieved under the UPAA at the time *Pendleton* was decided (*enforcement* of support waiver would be unconscionable), in order to apply the substance of subsection (c), enacted in 2002. *Facter* may also be read to find that the support waiver also was unconscionable at the time of *execution*. While the agreement's support waiver was unenforceable, its property provisions were severable and enforceable.

For further discussion of retroactive application of amendments to the Family Code, see the Commentary to Family Code sections 4 and 1615.

Research References

Forms

California Practice Guide: Rutter Family Law Forms Form 9:1, Premarital Agreement.
California Transactions Forms--Estate Planning § 11:37, Introduction.
California Transactions Forms--Estate Planning § 11:42, Scope Of Statutory Framework.
California Transactions Forms--Estate Planning § 11:48, Governing Contractual Provisions [CC §§ 1550 et seq., Fam C S721(B)].
California Transactions Forms--Estate Planning § 11:60, Matters to be Included in Premarital Agreement.
California Transactions Forms--Estate Planning § 11:69, Premarital Agreement.
California Transactions Forms--Family Law § 1:2, Nature and Advantages Of Agreement.
California Transactions Forms--Family Law § 1:6, Subject Matter; Altering Rights.
California Transactions Forms--Family Law § 4:67, Agreement Becoming Prenuptial Agreement.
California Transactions Forms--Family Law § 1:105, Spousal Support.

Treatises and Practice Aids

Witkin, California Summary 10th Community Property § 26, Subjects Of Premarital Agreements.
Witkin, California Summary 10th Community Property § 29, Lack Of Independent Counsel.
Witkin, California Summary 10th Community Property § 32, Agreements Violating Public Policy.
Witkin, California Summary 10th Contracts § 629, Other Agreements.

§ 1613. Effective date of agreements

A premarital agreement becomes effective upon marriage. *(Stats.1992, c. 162 (A.B.2650), § 10, operative Jan. 1, 1994.)*

Law Revision Commission Comments

Enactment [Revised Comment]

Section 1613 continues former Civil Code Section 5313 without change. Section 1613 is the same as Section 4 of the Uniform Premarital Agreement Act (1983). [23 Cal.L.Rev.Comm. Reports 1 (1993)].

Research References

Forms

California Transactions Forms--Family Law § 1:5, Governing Law, Form, and Execution.
West's California Code Forms, Family § 1611, Comment Overview--Premarital Agreements.

Treatises and Practice Aids

Witkin, California Summary 10th Community Property § 25, Requisites Of Premarital Agreements.

§ 1614. Amendment or revocation of agreements

After marriage, a premarital agreement may be amended or revoked only by a written agreement signed by the parties. The amended agreement or the revocation is enforceable without consideration. *(Stats.1992, c. 162 (A.B.2650), § 10, operative Jan. 1, 1994.)*

Law Revision Commission Comments

Enactment [Revised Comment]

Section 1614 continues former Civil Code Section 5314 without change. Section 1614 is the same as Section 5 of the Uniform Premarital Agreement Act (1983). [23 Cal.L.Rev.Comm. Reports 1 (1993)].

Commentary

Estate of Wilson, 211 Cal.App.4th 1284, 150 Cal.Rptr.3d 699 (2012), review denied, held that a pre-registration California domestic partnership agreement in which the parties waived any interest in each other's estate and required a signed writing to terminate the agreement, remained valid after the parties subsequently married. Thus, the surviving spouse was not entitled to claim an omitted spouse's share of decedent spouse's estate.

Research References

Forms

California Transactions Forms--Estate Planning § 11:43, Amendment or Revocation After Marriage.
California Transactions Forms--Estate Planning § 11:47, Formalities.
California Transactions Forms--Estate Planning § 11:48, Governing Contractual Provisions [CC §§ 1550 et seq., Fam C S721(B)].
California Transactions Forms--Family Law § 1:5, Governing Law, Form, and Execution.
West's California Code Forms, Family § 1611, Comment Overview--Premarital Agreements.

Treatises and Practice Aids

Witkin, California Summary 10th Community Property § 25, Requisites Of Premarital Agreements.

Witkin, California Summary 10th Contracts § 255, Premarital Agreements.

Witkin, California Summary 10th Contracts § 399, Marital and Premarital Agreements.

§ 1615. Unenforceable agreements; unconscionability; voluntariness

(a) A premarital agreement is not enforceable if the party against whom enforcement is sought proves either of the following:

(1) That party did not execute the agreement voluntarily.

(2) The agreement was unconscionable when it was executed and, before execution of the agreement, all of the following applied to that party:

(A) That party was not provided a fair, reasonable, and full disclosure of the property or financial obligations of the other party.

(B) That party did not voluntarily and expressly waive, in writing, any right to disclosure of the property or financial obligations of the other party beyond the disclosure provided.

(C) That party did not have, or reasonably could not have had, an adequate knowledge of the property or financial obligations of the other party.

(b) An issue of unconscionability of a premarital agreement shall be decided by the court as a matter of law.

(c) For the purposes of subdivision (a), it shall be deemed that a premarital agreement was not executed voluntarily unless the court finds in writing or on the record all of the following:

(1) The party against whom enforcement is sought was represented by independent legal counsel at the time of signing the agreement or, after being advised to seek independent legal counsel, expressly waived, in a separate writing, representation by independent legal counsel.

(2) The party against whom enforcement is sought had not less than seven calendar days between the time that party was first presented with the agreement and advised to seek independent legal counsel and the time the agreement was signed.

(3) The party against whom enforcement is sought, if unrepresented by legal counsel, was fully informed of the terms and basic effect of the agreement as well as the rights and obligations he or she was giving up by signing the agreement, and was proficient in the language in which the explanation of the party's rights was conducted and in which the agreement was written. The explanation of the rights and obligations relinquished shall be memorialized in writing and delivered to the party prior to signing the agreement. The unrepresented party shall, on or before the signing of the premarital agreement, execute a document declaring that he or she received the information required by this paragraph and indicating who provided that information.

(4) The agreement and the writings executed pursuant to paragraphs (1) and (3) were not executed under duress, fraud, or undue influence, and the parties did not lack capacity to enter into the agreement.

(5) Any other factors the court deems relevant. *(Stats. 1992, c. 162 (A.B.2650), § 10, operative Jan. 1, 1994. Amended by Stats.2001, c. 286 (S.B.78), § 2.)*

Law Revision Commission Comments

Enactment [Revised Comment]

Section 1615 continues former Civil Code Section 5315 without substantive change. Section 1615 is the same as Section 6(a) and (c) of the Uniform Premarital Agreement Act (1983). Section 6(b) of the uniform act was omitted since it applies to a premarital agreement that modifies or eliminates spousal support. The uniform provision allowing for modification or elimination of spousal support by premarital agreement was also omitted. See Section 912 Comment. See also Prob. Code §§ 140–147 (surviving spouse's waiver of rights). [23 Cal.L.Rev.Comm. Reports 1 (1993)].

Commentary

Subsection (a) codifies prior law with respect to the burden of proof: The party attacking the validity of the premarital agreement has the burden of proof on the issue of the validity of the contract. *In re Marriage of Iverson, 11 Cal.App.4th 1495, 15 Cal.Rptr.2d 70 (1992)*. The California Supreme Court declined to reverse the burden of proof when one party was not represented by counsel in the negotiation of the agreement. *In re Marriage of Bonds, 5 P.3d 815, 99 Cal.Rptr.2d 252 (2000)* (rejecting "strict scrutiny" standard of review formulated by court of appeal for cases in which a party represented by counsel seeks to enforce the agreement against a party who was not represented by counsel; and finding that the consent of the party resisting enforcement was "voluntary"). However, subsection (c), added in 2001 in response to the holding of *Bonds*, effectively imposes upon the party seeking enforcement of the agreement the burden of showing that the other party's execution of the agreement was "voluntary" within the meaning of subsection (c).

In re Marriage of Cadwell-Faso & Faso, 191 Cal.App.4th 945, 119 Cal.Rptr.3d 818 (2011), review denied, holds that the subsection (c) requirement of a seven-day waiting period is inapplicable when the party against whom enforcement is sought was represented by counsel from the beginning of the protracted negotiation that resulted in the agreement.

In re Marriage of Hill and Dittmer, 202 Cal.App.4th 1046, 136 Cal.Rptr.3d 700 (2011), held that a pre-2002 premarital agreement was enforceable when the wife was a successful business woman, was represented by counsel and voluntarily waived disclosure. *Hill and Dittmer* declined to retroactively apply the 2002 amendment to this section, which added subsection (c), on the ground it materially changed the law and therefore could not be retroactively applied.

For further discussion of retroactive application of amendments to the Family Code, see the Commentary to Family Code sections 4 and 1612.

A waiver of death rights contained in an antenuptial agreement that satisfies the requirements of Family Code sections 1600 et seq. (the Uniform Premarital Agreement Act) is enforceable even though it does not satisfy the requirements of Probate Code Sections 140 et seq. *Estate of Gagnier, 21 Cal.App.4th 124, 26 Cal.Rptr.2d 128 (1993)* (upholding wife's waiver of death rights in antenuptial agreement despite lack of Probate Code Section 143 representation by independent counsel).

In re Estate of Will, 170 Cal.App.4th 902, 88 Cal.Rptr.3d 502 (2009), review denied, held that although a premarital agreement did not satisfy current subsection (c), it was independently enforceable as a waiver of inheritance rights when it satisfied Probate Code sections 140–147, which set out the Probate Code requirements for an enforceable surviving spouse's waiver of death rights. Thus a surviving wife who married decedent-husband after he had written his final will, was barred from claiming that she was an "omitted spouse" under Probate Code § 21611(c).

Research References

Forms

California Transactions Forms--Estate Planning § 6:28, Exceptions to Omitted Spouse Statute.
California Transactions Forms--Estate Planning § 6:99, Omitted Spouse Made Valid Agreement Waiving Right to Share in Decedent's Estate.
California Transactions Forms--Estate Planning § 11:44, Enforceability.
California Transactions Forms--Family Law § 1:7, Unenforceable Agreements; Severability.
California Transactions Forms--Family Law § 1:71, Binding Agreement With Specific Family Code Waivers.
West's California Code Forms, Family § 1611, Comment Overview--Premarital Agreements.

Treatises and Practice Aids

Witkin, California Summary 10th Community Property § 26, Subjects Of Premarital Agreements.
Witkin, California Summary 10th Community Property § 28, in General.
Witkin, California Summary 10th Community Property § 29, Lack Of Independent Counsel.
Witkin, California Summary 10th Wills and Probate § 324, Enforcement.

§ 1616. Void marriage, effect on agreement

If a marriage is determined to be void, an agreement that would otherwise have been a premarital agreement is enforceable only to the extent necessary to avoid an inequitable result. *(Stats.1992, c. 162 (A.B.2650), § 10, operative Jan. 1, 1994.)*

Law Revision Commission Comments

Enactment [Revised Comment]

Section 1616 continues former Civil Code Section 5316 without change. Section 1616 is the same as Section 7 of the Uniform Premarital Agreement Act (1983). [23 Cal.L.Rev.Comm. Reports 1 (1993)].

Research References

Forms

California Transactions Forms--Estate Planning § 11:44, Enforceability.
California Transactions Forms--Family Law § 1:9, Effect Of Void Marriage; Limitations Of Actions and Equitable Defenses.
California Transactions Forms--Family Law § 1:34, Waiver Of Family Code S1616 Provisions.

Treatises and Practice Aids

Witkin, California Summary 10th Community Property § 30, Void Marriage.

§ 1617. Limitation of actions; equitable defenses including laches and estoppel

Any statute of limitations applicable to an action asserting a claim for relief under a premarital agreement is tolled during the marriage of the parties to the agreement. However, equitable defenses limiting the time for enforcement, including laches and estoppel, are available to either party. *(Stats.1992, c. 162 (A.B.2650), § 10, operative Jan. 1, 1994.)*

Law Revision Commission Comments

Enactment [Revised Comment]

Section 1617 continues former Civil Code Section 5317 without change. Section 1617 is the same as Section 8 of the Uniform Premarital Agreement Act (1983). [23 Cal.L.Rev.Comm. Reports 1 (1993)].

Research References

Forms

California Transactions Forms--Estate Planning § 6:28, Exceptions to Omitted Spouse Statute.
California Transactions Forms--Estate Planning § 6:99, Omitted Spouse Made Valid Agreement Waiving Right to Share in Decedent's Estate.
California Transactions Forms--Estate Planning § 11:44, Enforceability.
California Transactions Forms--Family Law § 1:9, Effect Of Void Marriage; Limitations Of Actions and Equitable Defenses.
California Transactions Forms--Family Law § 4:7, Effect Of Subsequent Marriage Between Cohabitants.
California Transactions Forms--Family Law § 1:71, Binding Agreement With Specific Family Code Waivers.

Treatises and Practice Aids

Witkin, California Summary 10th Community Property § 31, Statute Of Limitations and Equitable Defenses.

CHAPTER 3. AGREEMENTS BETWEEN SPOUSES

Section

§ 1620. Contracts altering legal relations of spouses; restrictions

Except as otherwise provided by law, spouses cannot, by a contract with each other, alter their legal relations, except as to property. *(Stats.1992, c. 162 (A.B.2650), § 10, operative Jan. 1, 1994. Amended by Stats.2014, c. 82 (S.B.1306), § 21, eff. Jan. 1, 2015.)*

Law Revision Commission Comments

Enactment [Revised Comment]

Section 1620 continues the first part of former Civil Code Section 4802 without substantive change. The phrase "[e]xcept as otherwise provided by law" has been substituted for specific references to former Civil Code Sections 4801(b) and 4811, since the former specific references were no longer a complete listing of exceptions to this rule. Section 1620 does not purport to limit the statutory and case-law exceptions to the rule stated in this section. A more extensive list of exceptions to this rule includes, for example, Sections 2550 (agreement concerning division of community estate), 2641 (agreement concerning community contributions and loans for education or training of spouse), 3580–3592 (support agreements), 3651 (modification or termination of support order if agreement between parties on support), 4302 (spouse living separate by agreement), 4323 (agreement regarding effect of cohabitation on spousal support), 4337 (unless otherwise agreed by parties in writing, support obligation terminates upon death of either party or remarriage of supported party).

See also Prob. Code §§ 140–147 (requirements for waiver, agreement, or property settlement affecting certain rights of surviving spouse on death of other spouse). See also Section 11 (reference to married person includes formerly married person). [23 Cal.L.Rev. Comm. Reports 1 (1993)].

Commentary

For a recent application of this venerable principle, see *Borelli v. Brusseau, 12 Cal.App.4th 647, 654, 16 Cal.Rptr.2d 16 (1993), review denied 4/1/93. Borelli* holds that a wife's personal nursing care of her invalid husband is a personal nondelegable duty required of the wife by the marriage contract and thus does not provide consideration for the husband's marital promise to leave property to his wife in exchange for the nursing care. See also *In re Marriage of Mathiasen, 268 Cal.Rptr. 895, 897 (1990), review denied and depublished 7/25/90* (holding the spouses' household expense reimbursement agreement unenforceable because it altered the statutory obligation of mutual support).

Cf. *In re Marriage of Dargan, 118 Cal.App.4th 1167, 13 Cal.Rptr.3d 522 (2004), review denied*, holding that an agreement made pursuant to a married couple's reconciliation, which provided that the wife would receive all of husband's interest in certain community property if he resumed the use of illicit drugs, was unenforceable because it violated the public policy favoring no-fault divorce. To similar effect, see *Diosdado v. Diosdado, 97 Cal.App.4th 470, 118 Cal.Rptr.2d 494 (2002)*, which, on the same ground, declined to enforce an agreement providing for $50,000 liquidated damages to be paid at divorce if either spouse were unfaithful to the other.

Research References

Forms

California Transactions Forms--Estate Planning § 11:39, General Considerations.

California Transactions Forms--Estate Planning § 11:45, Introduction.

California Transactions Forms--Estate Planning § 11:48, Governing Contractual Provisions [CC §§ 1550 et seq., Fam C S721(B)].

Treatises and Practice Aids

Witkin, California Summary 10th Community Property § 24, in General.

Witkin, California Summary 10th Community Property § 33, Restrictions on Alteration Of Spouses' Legal Relations.

Witkin, California Summary 10th Contracts § 626, Separation and Property Agreements.

Witkin, California Summary 10th Husband and Wife § 40, Agreements Altering Spouses' Legal Relations.

Witkin, California Summary 10th Husband and Wife § 152, Survival Of Cause Of Action.

Division 5

CONCILIATION PROCEEDINGS

Part 1

FAMILY CONCILIATION COURT LAW

CHAPTER 1. GENERAL PROVISIONS

§ 1800. Short title

This part may be cited as the Family Conciliation Court Law. *(Stats.1992, c. 162 (A.B.2650), § 10, operative Jan. 1, 1994.)*

Law Revision Commission Comments

Enactment [Revised Comment]

Section 1800 continues former Code of Civil Procedure Section 1731 without change. [23 Cal.L.Rev.Comm. Reports 1 (1993)].

Research References

Forms

Cal. Transaction Forms - Bus. Transactions § 14:50, Confidentiality Of Mediation Process.

West's California Code Forms, Family § 1830, Comment Overview-- Jurisdiction.

Treatises and Practice Aids

Witkin, California Summary 10th Husband and Wife § 3, Statutory Framework.

Witkin, California Summary 10th Husband and Wife § 69, Superior Court and Departments.

Witkin, California Summary 10th Husband and Wife § 90, in General.

Witkin, California Summary 10th Husband and Wife § 371, Civil Remedies.

§ 1801. Purposes of part

The purposes of this part are to protect the rights of children and to promote the public welfare by preserving, promoting, and protecting family life and the institution of matrimony, and to provide means for the reconciliation of spouses and the amicable settlement of domestic and family controversies. *(Stats.1992, c. 162 (A.B.2650), § 10, operative Jan. 1, 1994.)*

Law Revision Commission Comments

Enactment [Revised Comment]

Section 1801 continues former Code of Civil Procedure Section 1730 without substantive change. [23 Cal.L.Rev.Comm. Reports 1 (1993)].

Research References

Forms

West's California Code Forms, Family § 1830, Comment Overview-- Jurisdiction.

Treatises and Practice Aids

Witkin, California Summary 10th Husband and Wife § 90, in General.

Witkin, California Summary 10th Husband and Wife § 371, Civil Remedies.

§ 1802. Application of part

(a) This part applies only in counties in which the superior court determines that the social conditions in the county and the number of domestic relations cases in the courts render the procedures provided in this part necessary to the full and proper consideration of those cases and the effectuation of the purposes of this part.

(b) The determination under subdivision (a) shall be made annually in the month of January by:

(1) The judge of the superior court in counties having only one superior court judge.

(2) A majority of the judges of the superior court in counties having more than one superior court judge. *(Stats. 1992, c. 162 (A.B.2650), § 10, operative Jan. 1, 1994.)*

Law Revision Commission Comments

Enactment [Revised Comment]

Section 1802 continues former Code of Civil Procedure Section 1733 without substantive change. [23 Cal.L.Rev.Comm. Reports 1 (1993)].

Research References

Treatises and Practice Aids

Witkin, California Summary 10th Husband and Wife § 90, in General.

CHAPTER 2. FAMILY CONCILIATION COURTS

§ 1810. Jurisdiction; designation of court

Each superior court shall exercise the jurisdiction conferred by this part. While sitting in the exercise of this jurisdiction, the court shall be known and referred to as the "family conciliation court." *(Stats.1992, c. 162 (A.B.2650), § 10, operative Jan. 1, 1994.)*

Law Revision Commission Comments

Enactment [Revised Comment]

Section 1810 continues former Code of Civil Procedure Section 1740 without substantive change. [23 Cal.L.Rev.Comm. Reports 1 (1993)].

§ 1811. Assignment of judges; number of sessions

The presiding judge of the superior court shall annually, in the month of January, designate at least one judge to hear all cases under this part. *(Stats.1992, c. 162 (A.B.2650), § 10, operative Jan. 1, 1994. Amended by Stats.2003, c. 149 (S.B.79), § 11.)*

Law Revision Commission Comments

Enactment [Revised Comment]

Section 1811 continues former Code of Civil Procedure Section 1741 without substantive change. [23 Cal.L.Rev.Comm. Reports 1 (1993)].

2003 Amendment

Section 1811 is amended to reflect enactment of Government Code Section 69740(a) (number and location of trial court sessions).

The section is also amended to reflect the fact that every superior court has at least two judgeships as a result of trial court unification. See Gov't Code § 69580 *et seq.* (number of judges). [33 Cal.L.Rev. Comm. Reports 193 (2003)].

Research References

Treatises and Practice Aids

Witkin, California Summary 10th Husband and Wife § 91, Family Conciliation Courts.

§ 1812. Transfer of cases; reasons; duties of transferee judge

(a) The judge of the family conciliation court may transfer any case before the family conciliation court pursuant to this part to the department of the presiding judge of the superior court for assignment for trial or other proceedings by another judge of the court, whenever in the opinion of the judge of the family conciliation court the transfer is necessary to expedite the business of the family conciliation court or to ensure the prompt consideration of the case.

(b) When a case is transferred pursuant to subdivision (a), the judge to whom it is transferred shall act as the judge of the family conciliation court in the matter. *(Stats.1992, c. 162 (A.B.2650), § 10, operative Jan. 1, 1994.)*

Law Revision Commission Comments

Enactment [Revised Comment]

Section 1812 continues former Code of Civil Procedure Section 1742 without substantive change. [23 Cal.L.Rev.Comm. Reports 1 (1993)].

Research References

Treatises and Practice Aids

Witkin, California Summary 10th Husband and Wife § 86, in General.

Witkin, California Summary 10th Husband and Wife § 91, Family Conciliation Courts.

§ 1813. Substitute judge; appointment; powers and authority

(a) The presiding judge of the superior court may appoint a judge of the superior court other than the judge of the family conciliation court to act as judge of the family conciliation court during any period when the judge of the family conciliation court is on vacation, absent, or for any reason unable to perform the duties as judge of the family conciliation court.

(b) The judge appointed under subdivision (a) has all of the powers and authority of a judge of the family conciliation court in cases under this part. *(Stats.1992, c. 162 (A.B.2650), § 10, operative Jan. 1, 1994.)*

Law Revision Commission Comments

Enactment [Revised Comment]

Section 1813 continues former Code of Civil Procedure Section 1743 without substantive change. [23 Cal.L.Rev.Comm. Reports 1 (1993)].

Research References

Treatises and Practice Aids

Witkin, California Summary 10th Husband and Wife § 91, Family Conciliation Courts.

§ 1814. Supervising counselor; secretary; powers and duties; other assistants; classification; compensation

(a) In each county in which a family conciliation court is established, the superior court may appoint one supervising counselor of conciliation and one secretary to assist the family conciliation court in disposing of its business and carrying out its functions. When superior courts by contract have established joint family conciliation court services, the contracting courts jointly may make the appointments under this subdivision.

(b) The supervising counselor of conciliation has the power to do all of the following:

(1) Hold conciliation conferences with parties to, and hearings in, proceedings under this part, and make recommendations concerning the proceedings to the judge of the family conciliation court.

(2) Provide supervision in connection with the exercise of the counselor's jurisdiction as the judge of the family conciliation court may direct.

(3) Cause reports to be made, statistics to be compiled, and records to be kept as the judge of the family conciliation court may direct.

(4) Hold hearings in all family conciliation court cases as may be required by the judge of the family conciliation court, and make investigations as may be required by the court to carry out the intent of this part.

(5) Make recommendations relating to marriages where one or both parties are underage.

(6) Make investigations, reports, and recommendations as provided in Section 281 of the Welfare and Institutions Code under the authority provided the probation officer in that code.

(7) Act as domestic relations cases investigator.

(8) Conduct mediation of child custody and visitation disputes.

(c) The superior court, or contracting superior courts, may also appoint associate counselors of conciliation and other office assistants as may be necessary to assist the family conciliation court in disposing of its business. The associate counselors shall carry out their duties under the supervision of the supervising counselor of conciliation and have the powers of the supervising counselor of conciliation. Office assistants shall work under the supervision and direction of the supervising counselor of conciliation.

(d) The classification and salaries of persons appointed under this section shall be determined by:

(1) The superior court of the county in which a noncontracting family conciliation court operates.

(2) The superior court of the county which by contract has the responsibility to administer funds of the joint family conciliation court service. *(Stats.1992, c. 162 (A.B.2650), § 10, operative Jan. 1, 1994. Amended by Stats.2012, c. 470 (A.B.1529), § 12.)*

Law Revision Commission Comments

Enactment [Revised Comment]

Section 1814 restates former Code of Civil Procedure Section 1744 without substantive change. In subdivision (b)(5), the phrase "relating to marriages where one or both parties are underage" has been substituted for "relating to preage marriages," to conform to language used in other sections of this code. See, e.g., Sections 302, 353 (underage applicants for marriage license). [23 Cal.L.Rev. Comm. Reports 1 (1993)].

2012 Amendment

Subdivision (a) of Section 1814 is amended to reflect enactment of the Lockyer–Isenberg Trial Court Funding Act, 1997 Cal. Stat. ch. 850 (see generally Gov't Code §§ 77000–77655). See, e.g., Gov't Code §§ 77001 (local trial court management), 77003 ("court operations" defined), 77200 (state funding of "court operations"); see also Cal. R. Ct. 10.810.

Subdivisions (c) and (d) are amended to reflect enactment of the Trial Court Employment Protection and Governance Act, 2000 Cal. Stat. ch. 1010 (codified as Gov't Code §§ 71600–71675). See, e.g., Gov't Code §§ 71620(a) (job classifications and appointments), 71623(a) ("Each trial court may establish a salary range for each of its employee classifications."). [39 Cal.L.Rev.Comm. Reports 157 (2009)].

Research References

Treatises and Practice Aids

Witkin, California Summary 10th Husband and Wife § 92, Qualifications and Appointment.

Witkin, California Summary 10th Husband and Wife § 93, Powers Of Supervising Counselor.

§ 1815. Supervising and associate counselors; qualifications

(a) A person employed as a supervising counselor of conciliation or as an associate counselor of conciliation shall have all of the following minimum qualifications:

(1) A master's degree in psychology, social work, marriage, family and child counseling, or other behavioral science substantially related to marriage and family interpersonal relationships.

(2) At least two years of experience in counseling or psychotherapy, or both, preferably in a setting related to the areas of responsibility of the family conciliation court and with the ethnic population to be served.

(3) Knowledge of the court system of California and the procedures used in family law cases.

(4) Knowledge of other resources in the community that clients can be referred to for assistance.

(5) Knowledge of adult psychopathology and the psychology of families.

(6) Knowledge of child development, child abuse, clinical issues relating to children, the effects of divorce on children, the effects of domestic violence on children, and child custody research sufficient to enable a counselor to assess the mental health needs of children.

(7) Training in domestic violence issues as described in Section 1816.

(b) The family conciliation court may substitute additional experience for a portion of the education, or additional education for a portion of the experience, required under subdivision (a).

(c) This section does not apply to any supervising counselor of conciliation who was in office on March 27, 1980. *(Stats.1992, c. 162 (A.B.2650), § 10, operative Jan. 1, 1994. Amended by Stats.2006, c. 130 (A.B.2853), § 1.)*

Law Revision Commission Comments

Enactment [Revised Comment]

Section 1815 continues former Code of Civil Procedure Section 1745 without substantive change. In subdivision (c), the specific effective date of the former section has been substituted for the former general reference. See 1980 Cal. Stat. ch. 48, § 9. The first sentence of former Code of Civil Procedure Section 1745(c), which required counselors of conciliation to meet provisions of the section by January 1, 1984, has been omitted as obsolete. [23 Cal.L.Rev. Comm. Reports 1 (1993)].

Research References

Treatises and Practice Aids

Witkin, California Summary 10th Husband and Wife § 92, Qualifications and Appointment.

Witkin, California Summary 10th Parent and Child § 278, in General.

§ 1816. Domestic violence training for evaluators; areas of basic, advanced, and updated training; eligible providers

(a) For purposes of this section, the following definitions apply:

(1) "Eligible provider" means the Administrative Office of the Courts or an educational institution, professional association, professional continuing education group, a group connected to the courts, or a public or private group that has been authorized by the Administrative Office of the Courts to provide domestic violence training.

(2) "Evaluator" means a supervising or associate counselor described in Section 1815, a mediator described in Section 3164, a court-connected or private child custody evaluator described in Section 3110.5, or a court-appointed investigator or evaluator as described in Section 3110 or Section 730 of the Evidence Code.

(b) An evaluator shall participate in a program of continuing instruction in domestic violence, including child abuse, as may be arranged and provided to that evaluator. This training may utilize domestic violence training programs conducted by nonprofit community organizations with an expertise in domestic violence issues.

(c) Areas of basic instruction shall include, but are not limited to, the following:

(1) The effects of domestic violence on children.

(2) The nature and extent of domestic violence.

(3) The social and family dynamics of domestic violence.

(4) Techniques for identifying and assisting families affected by domestic violence.

(5) Interviewing, documentation of, and appropriate recommendations for families affected by domestic violence.

(6) The legal rights of, and remedies available to, victims.

(7) Availability of community and legal domestic violence resources.

(d) An evaluator shall also complete 16 hours of advanced training within a 12–month period. Four hours of that advanced training shall include community resource networking intended to acquaint the evaluator with domestic violence resources in the geographical communities where the family being evaluated may reside. Twelve hours of instruction, as approved by the Administrative Office of the Courts, shall include all of the following:

(1) The appropriate structuring of the child custody evaluation process, including, but not limited to, all of the following:

(A) Maximizing safety for clients, evaluators, and court personnel.

(B) Maintaining objectivity.

(C) Providing and gathering balanced information from the parties and controlling for bias.

(D) Providing separate sessions at separate times as described in Section 3113.

(E) Considering the impact of the evaluation report and recommendations with particular attention to the dynamics of domestic violence.

(2) The relevant sections of local, state, and federal laws, rules, or regulations.

(3) The range, availability, and applicability of domestic violence resources available to victims, including, but not limited to, all of the following:

(A) Shelters for battered women.

(B) Counseling, including drug and alcohol counseling.

(C) Legal assistance.

(D) Job training.

(E) Parenting classes.

(F) Resources for a victim who is an immigrant.

(4) The range, availability, and applicability of domestic violence intervention available to perpetrators, including, but not limited to, all of the following:

(A) Certified treatment programs described in Section 1203.097 of the Penal Code.

(B) Drug and alcohol counseling.

(C) Legal assistance.

(D) Job training.

(E) Parenting classes.

(5) The unique issues in a family and psychological assessment in a domestic violence case, including all of the following:

(A) The effects of exposure to domestic violence and psychological trauma on children, the relationship between child physical abuse, child sexual abuse, and domestic violence, the differential family dynamics related to parent-child attachments in families with domestic violence, intergenerational transmission of familial violence, and manifestations of post-traumatic stress disorders in children.

(B) The nature and extent of domestic violence, and the relationship of gender, class, race, culture, and sexual orientation to domestic violence.

(C) Current legal, psychosocial, public policy, and mental health research related to the dynamics of family violence, the impact of victimization, the psychology of perpetration, and the dynamics of power and control in battering relationships.

(D) The assessment of family history based on the type, severity, and frequency of violence.

(E) The impact on parenting abilities of being a victim or perpetrator of domestic violence.

(F) The uses and limitations of psychological testing and psychiatric diagnosis in assessing parenting abilities in domestic violence cases.

(G) The influence of alcohol and drug use and abuse on the incidence of domestic violence.

(H) Understanding the dynamics of high conflict relationships and relationships between an abuser and victim.

(I) The importance of and procedures for obtaining collateral information from a probation department, children's protective services, police incident report, a pleading regarding a restraining order, medical records, a school, and other relevant sources.

(J) Accepted methods for structuring safe and enforceable child custody and parenting plans that ensure the health, safety, welfare, and best interest of the child, and safeguards for the parties.

(K) The importance of discouraging participants in child custody matters from blaming victims of domestic violence for the violence and from minimizing allegations of domestic violence, child abuse, or abuse against a family member.

(e) After an evaluator has completed the advanced training described in subdivision (d), that evaluator shall complete four hours of updated training annually that shall include, but is not limited to, all of the following:

(1) Changes in local court practices, case law, and state and federal legislation related to domestic violence.

(2) An update of current social science research and theory, including the impact of exposure to domestic violence on children.

(f) Training described in this section shall be acquired from an eligible provider and that eligible provider shall comply with all of the following:

(1) Ensure that a training instructor or consultant delivering the education and training programs either meets the training requirements of this section or is an expert in the subject matter.

(2) Monitor and evaluate the quality of courses, curricula, training, instructors, and consultants.

(3) Emphasize the importance of focusing child custody evaluations on the health, safety, welfare, and best interest of the child.

(4) Develop a procedure to verify that an evaluator completes the education and training program.

(5) Distribute a certificate of completion to each evaluator who has completed the training. That certificate shall document the number of hours of training offered, the number of hours the evaluator completed, the dates of the training, and the name of the training provider.

(g)(1) If there is a local court rule regarding the procedure to notify the court that an evaluator has completed training as described in this section, the evaluator shall comply with that local court rule.

(2) Except as provided in paragraph (1), an evaluator shall attach copies of his or her certificates of completion of the training described in subdivision (d) and the most recent updated training described in subdivision (e).

(h) An evaluator may satisfy the requirement for 12 hours of instruction described in subdivision (d) by training from an eligible provider that was obtained on or after January 1, 1996. The advanced training of that evaluator shall not be complete until that evaluator completes the four hours of community resource networking described in subdivision (d).

(i) The Judicial Council shall develop standards for the training programs. The Judicial Council shall solicit the assistance of community organizations concerned with domestic violence and child abuse and shall seek to develop training programs that will maximize coordination between conciliation courts and local agencies concerned with domestic violence. *(Stats.1992, c. 162 (A.B.2650), § 10, operative Jan. 1, 1994. Amended by Stats.1993, c. 219 (A.B.1500), § 101.5; Stats.2000, c. 926 (S.B.1716), § 1; Stats.2006, c. 130 (A.B.2853), § 2; Stats.2007, c. 130 (A.B.299), § 88.)*

Law Revision Commission Comments

Enactment [Revised Comment]

Section 1816 continues former Code of Civil Procedure Section 1745.5 without substantive change. See also Sections 6201 (application of definitions), 6203 ("abuse" defined), 6211 ("domestic violence" defined). [23 Cal.L.Rev.Comm. Reports 1 (1993)].

Research References

Forms

California Transactions Forms--Family Law § 2:70, Deciding Custody.

West's California Judicial Council Forms FL-325, Declaration Of Court-Connected Child Custody Evaluator Regarding Qualifications.

West's California Judicial Council Forms FL-326, Declaration Of Private Child Custody Evaluator Regarding Qualifications.

Treatises and Practice Aids

Witkin, California Summary 10th Husband and Wife § 92, Qualifications and Appointment.

Witkin, California Summary 10th Husband and Wife § 94, Participation in Domestic Violence Programs.

§ 1817. Probation officers; duties

The probation officer in every county shall do all of the following:

(a) Give assistance to the family conciliation court that the court may request to carry out the purposes of this part, and to that end shall, upon request, make investigations and reports as requested.

(b) In cases pursuant to this part, exercise all the powers and perform all the duties granted or imposed by the laws of this state relating to probation or to probation officers. *(Stats.1992, c. 162 (A.B.2650), § 10, operative Jan. 1, 1994.)*

Law Revision Commission Comments

Enactment [Revised Comment]

Section 1817 continues former Code of Civil Procedure Section 1746 without substantive change. [23 Cal.L.Rev.Comm. Reports 1 (1993)].

Research References

Treatises and Practice Aids

Witkin, California Summary 10th Husband and Wife § 93, Powers Of Supervising Counselor.

§ 1818. Privacy of hearings; conferences; confidential nature of communications; closed files; inspection of papers

(a) All superior court hearings or conferences in proceedings under this part shall be held in private and the court shall exclude all persons except the officers of the court, the parties, their counsel, and witnesses. The court shall not allow ex parte communications, except as authorized by Section 216. All communications, verbal or written, from parties to the judge, commissioner, or counselor in a proceeding under this part shall be deemed to be official information within the meaning of Section 1040 of the Evidence Code.

(b) The files of the family conciliation court shall be closed. The petition, supporting affidavit, conciliation agreement, and any court order made in the matter may be opened to inspection by a party or the party's counsel upon the written authority of the judge of the family conciliation court. *(Stats.1992, c. 162 (A.B.2650), § 10, operative Jan. 1, 1994. Amended by Stats.2005, c. 489 (S.B.1088), § 2.)*

Law Revision Commission Comments

Enactment [Revised Comment]

Section 1818 continues former Code of Civil Procedure Section 1747 without substantive change. The introductory phrase "[n]otwithstanding the provisions of Section 124" in former Code of Civil Procedure Section 1747 has been omitted as unnecessary. See Section 214 Comment; Code of Civ. Proc. § 124 (court proceedings to be public). [23 Cal.L.Rev.Comm. Reports 1 (1993)].

Research References

Treatises and Practice Aids

Witkin, California Summary 10th Husband and Wife § 91, Family Conciliation Courts.

§ 1819. Destruction of records, papers or documents in office of counselor; exception; microfilming

(a) Except as provided in subdivision (b), upon order of the judge of the family conciliation court, the supervising counselor of conciliation may destroy any record, paper, or document filed or kept in the office of the supervising counselor of conciliation which is more than two years old.

(b) Records described in subdivision (a) of child custody or visitation mediation may be destroyed when the minor or minors involved are 18 years of age.

(c) In the judge's discretion, the judge of the family conciliation court may order the microfilming of any record, paper, or document described in subdivision (a) or (b). *(Stats.1992, c. 162 (A.B.2650), § 10, operative Jan. 1, 1994.)*

Law Revision Commission Comments

Enactment [Revised Comment]

Section 1819 restates former Code of Civil Procedure Section 1748 without substantive change. [23 Cal.L.Rev.Comm. Reports 1 (1993)].

Research References

Treatises and Practice Aids

Witkin, California Summary 10th Husband and Wife § 91, Family Conciliation Courts.

§ 1820. Joint family conciliation court services; agreement between courts

(a) A court may contract with any other court or courts to provide joint family conciliation court services.

(b) An agreement between two or more courts for the operation of a joint family conciliation court service may provide that one participating court shall be the custodian of moneys made available for the purposes of the joint services, and that the custodian court may make payments from the moneys upon audit of the appropriate auditing officer or body of the court.

(c) An agreement between two or more courts for the operation of a joint family conciliation court service may also provide:

(1) For the joint provision or operation of services and facilities or for the provision or operation of services and facilities by one participating court under contract for the other participating courts.

(2) For appointments of members of the staff of the family conciliation court including the supervising counselor.

(3) That, for specified purposes, the members of the staff of the family conciliation court including the supervising counselor, but excluding the judges of the family conciliation court, shall be considered to be employees of one participating court.

(4) For other matters that are necessary or proper to effectuate the purposes of the Family Conciliation Court Law.

(d) The provisions of this part relating to family conciliation court services provided by a single court shall be equally applicable to courts which contract, pursuant to this section, to provide joint family conciliation court services. *(Stats. 1992, c. 162 (A.B.2650), § 10, operative Jan. 1, 1994. Amended by Stats.2012, c. 470 (A.B.1529), § 13.)*

Law Revision Commission Comments

Enactment [Revised Comment]

Section 1820 continues former Code of Civil Procedure Section 1749 without substantive change. [23 Cal.L.Rev.Comm. Reports 1 (1993)].

2012 Amendment

Section 1820 is amended to reflect enactment of the Lockyer–Isenberg Trial Court Funding Act, 1997 Cal. Stat. ch. 850 (see generally Gov't Code §§ 77000–77655). See, e.g., Gov't Code §§ 77001 (local trial court management), 77003 ("court operations" defined), 77200 (state funding of "court operations"); see also Cal. R. Ct. 10.810.

The section is also amended to reflect enactment of the Trial Court Employment Protection and Governance Act, 2000 Cal. Stat. ch. 1010 (codified as Gov't Code §§ 71600–71675). See, e.g., Gov't Code § 71620(a) (job classifications and appointments). [39 Cal. L.Rev.Comm. Reports 157 (2009)].

Research References

Treatises and Practice Aids

Witkin, California Summary 10th Husband and Wife § 90, in General.

CHAPTER 3. PROCEEDINGS FOR CONCILIATION

Section

§ 1830. Jurisdiction

(a) When a controversy exists between spouses, or when a controversy relating to child custody or visitation exists between parents regardless of their marital status, and the controversy may, unless a reconciliation is achieved, result in dissolution of the marriage, nullity of the marriage, or legal separation of the parties, or in the disruption of the household, and there is a minor child of the spouses or parents or of either of them whose welfare might be affected thereby, the family conciliation court has jurisdiction as provided in this part over the controversy and over the parties to the controversy and over all persons having any relation to the controversy.

(b) The family conciliation court also has jurisdiction over the controversy, whether or not there is a minor child of the parties or either of them, where the controversy involves domestic violence. *(Stats.1992, c. 162 (A.B.2650), § 10, operative Jan. 1, 1994.)*

Law Revision Commission Comments

Enactment [Revised Comment]

Section 1830 restates former Code of Civil Procedure Section 1760 without substantive change. The reference to legal separation has been added to conform with other sections. See, e.g., Sections 1831, 1840, 1841. See also Sections 1842 (conciliation court may accept other cases where no minor children involved), 3160–3186 (mediation of custody and visitation issues), 3190–3192 (counseling of parents and child), 6201 (application of definitions), 6211 ("domestic violence" defined). [23 Cal.L.Rev.Comm. Reports 1 (1993)].

Research References

Forms

West's California Code Forms, Family § 1830, Comment Overview--Jurisdiction.

Treatises and Practice Aids

Witkin, California Summary 10th Husband and Wife § 95, Jurisdiction.

§ 1831. Petition; right to file; purpose

Before the filing of a proceeding for determination of custody or visitation rights, for dissolution of marriage, for nullity of a voidable marriage, or for legal separation of the parties, either spouse or parent, or both, may file in the family conciliation court a petition invoking the jurisdiction of the court for the purpose of preserving the marriage by effecting a reconciliation between the parties, or for amicable settlement of the controversy between the spouses or parents, so as to avoid further litigation over the issue involved. *(Stats.1992, c. 162 (A.B.2650), § 10, operative Jan. 1, 1994.)*

Law Revision Commission Comments

Enactment [Revised Comment]

Section 1831 continues former Code of Civil Procedure Section 1761 without substantive change. See also Sections 3160–3186 (mediation of custody and visitation issues), 3190–3192 (counseling of parents and child). [23 Cal.L.Rev.Comm. Reports 1 (1993)].

Research References

Forms

West's California Code Forms, Family § 1830, Comment Overview--Jurisdiction.

Treatises and Practice Aids

Witkin, California Summary 10th Husband and Wife § 96, Petition.

§ 1832. Petition; caption

The petition shall be captioned substantially as follows:

In the Superior Court of the State of California
in and for the County of ________

Upon the petition of	)	
________________	)	Petition for
(Petitioner)	)	Conciliation
And concerning	)	(Under the Family
________________ and	)	Conciliation
________________	)	Court Law)
________________, Respondents	)	

To the Family Conciliation Court:

(Stats.1992, c. 162 (A.B.2650), § 10, operative Jan. 1, 1994.)

Law Revision Commission Comments

Enactment [Revised Comment]

Section 1832 continues former Code of Civil Procedure Section 1762 without change. [23 Cal.L.Rev.Comm. Reports 1 (1993)].

Research References

Treatises and Practice Aids

Witkin, California Summary 10th Husband and Wife § 96, Petition.

§ 1833. Petition; contents

The petition shall:

(a) Allege that a controversy exists between the spouses or parents and request the aid of the court to effect a reconciliation or an amicable settlement of the controversy.

(b) State the name and age of each minor child whose welfare may be affected by the controversy.

(c) State the name and address of the petitioner or the names and addresses of the petitioners.

(d) If the petition is presented by one spouse or parent only, the name of the other spouse or parent as a respondent, and state the address of that spouse or parent.

(e) Name as a respondent any other person who has any relation to the controversy, and state the address of the person if known to the petitioner.

(f) If the petition arises out of an instance of domestic violence, so state generally and without specific allegations as to the incident.

(g) State any other information the court by rule requires. *(Stats.1992, c. 162 (A.B.2650), § 10, operative Jan. 1, 1994.)*

Law Revision Commission Comments

Enactment [Revised Comment]

Section 1833 continues former Code of Civil Procedure Section 1763 without substantive change. See also Sections 6201 (application of definitions), 6211 ("domestic violence" defined). [23 Cal. L.Rev.Comm. Reports 1 (1993)].

Research References

Treatises and Practice Aids

Witkin, California Summary 10th Husband and Wife § 96, Petition.

§ 1834. Blank forms; assistance in preparing and presenting petition; references; coextensive jurisdiction

(a) The clerk of the court shall provide, at the expense of the court, blank forms for petitions for filing pursuant to this part.

(b) The probation officers of the county and the attachés and employees of the family conciliation court shall assist a person in the preparation and presentation of a petition under this part if the person requests assistance.

(c) All public officers in each county shall refer to the family conciliation court all petitions and complaints made to them in respect to controversies within the jurisdiction of the family conciliation court.

(d) The jurisdiction of the family conciliation court in respect to controversies arising out of an instance of domestic violence is not exclusive but is coextensive with any other remedies either civil or criminal in nature that may be available. *(Stats.1992, c. 162 (A.B.2650), § 10, operative Jan. 1, 1994. Amended by Stats.2012, c. 470 (A.B.1529), § 14.)*

Law Revision Commission Comments

Enactment [Revised Comment]

Section 1834 continues former Code of Civil Procedure Section 1764 without substantive change. See also Sections 6201 (application of definitions), 6211 ("domestic violence" defined). [23 Cal. L.Rev.Comm. Reports 1 (1993)].

2012 Amendment

Subdivision (a) of Section 1834 is amended to reflect enactment of the Lockyer–Isenberg Trial Court Funding Act, 1997 Cal. Stat. ch. 850 (see generally Gov't Code §§ 77000–77655). See, e.g., Gov't Code §§ 77001 (local trial court management), 77003 ("court operations" defined), 77200 (state funding of "court operations"); see also Cal. R. Ct. 10.810(d), Function 10 ("court operations" include "publications and legal notices, by the court"); *cf.* Cal. R. Ct. 10.810(d), Function 6 (listing "court operations" relating to dispute resolution programs, including conciliators, but signaling that "[a]ny other related services, supplies, and equipment" are allowable under Function 10"). [42 Cal.L.Rev.Comm. Reports 413 (2012)].

Research References

Treatises and Practice Aids

Witkin, California Summary 10th Husband and Wife § 95, Jurisdiction.

Witkin, California Summary 10th Husband and Wife § 96, Petition.

§ 1835. Fees

No fee shall be charged by any officer for filing the petition. *(Stats.1992, c. 162 (A.B.2650), § 10, operative Jan. 1, 1994.)*

Law Revision Commission Comments

Enactment [Revised Comment]

Section 1835 continues former Code of Civil Procedure Section 1765 without change. [23 Cal.L.Rev.Comm. Reports 1 (1993)].

Research References

Treatises and Practice Aids

Witkin, California Summary 10th Husband and Wife § 96, Petition.

§ 1836. Hearing; time; place; notice; citation; witnesses

(a) The court shall fix a reasonable time and place for hearing on the petition. The court shall cause notice to be given to the respondents of the filing of the petition and of the time and place of the hearing that the court deems necessary.

(b) The court may, when it deems it necessary, issue a citation to a respondent requiring the respondent to appear at the time and place stated in the citation. The court may require the attendance of witnesses as in other civil cases. *(Stats.1992, c. 162 (A.B.2650), § 10, operative Jan. 1, 1994.)*

Law Revision Commission Comments

Enactment [Revised Comment]

Section 1836 continues former Code of Civil Procedure Section 1766 without substantive change. [23 Cal.L.Rev.Comm. Reports 1 (1993)].

Research References

Treatises and Practice Aids

Witkin, California Summary 10th Husband and Wife § 97, Hearing.

§ 1837. Time and place of holding court; hearings in chambers or otherwise

(a) Except as provided in subdivision (b), for the purpose of conducting hearings pursuant to this part, the family conciliation court may be convened at any time and place within the county, and the hearing may be had in chambers or otherwise.

(b) The time and place for hearing shall not be different from the time and place provided by law for the trial of civil actions if any party, before the hearing, objects to any different time or place. *(Stats.1992, c. 162 (A.B.2650), § 10, operative Jan. 1, 1994.)*

Law Revision Commission Comments

Enactment [Revised Comment]

Section 1837 continues former Code of Civil Procedure Section 1767 without substantive change. [23 Cal.L.Rev.Comm. Reports 1 (1993)].

Research References

Treatises and Practice Aids

Witkin, California Summary 10th Husband and Wife § 97, Hearing.

§ 1838. Informal hearings; conferences; purpose; aid of specialists or experts

(a) The hearing shall be conducted informally as a conference or a series of conferences to effect a reconciliation of the spouses or an amicable adjustment or settlement of the issues in controversy.

(b) To facilitate and promote the purposes of this part, the court may, with the consent of both parties to the proceeding, recommend or invoke the aid of medical or other specialists or scientific experts, or of the pastor or director of any religious denomination to which the parties may belong. Aid under this subdivision shall not be at the expense of the court unless the presiding judge specifically authorizes the aid, nor at the expense of the county unless the board of supervisors of the county specifically provides and authorizes the aid. *(Stats.1992, c. 162 (A.B.2650), § 10, operative Jan. 1, 1994. Amended by Stats.2012, c. 470 (A.B.1529), § 15.)*

Law Revision Commission Comments

Enactment [Revised Comment]

Section 1838 continues former Code of Civil Procedure Section 1768 without substantive change. [23 Cal.L.Rev.Comm. Reports 1 (1993)].

2012 Amendment

Section 1838 is amended to reflect enactment of the Lockyer–Isenberg Trial Court Funding Act, 1997 Cal. Stat. ch. 850 (see generally Gov't Code §§ 77000–77655). See, e.g., Gov't Code §§ 77001 (local trial court management), 77003 ("court operations" defined), 77200 (state funding of "court operations"); see also Cal. R. Ct. 10.603(a) (responsibilities of presiding judge of superior court). [39 Cal.L.Rev.Comm. Reports 157 (2009)].

Research References

Treatises and Practice Aids

Witkin, California Summary 10th Husband and Wife § 97, Hearing.

§ 1839. Orders, duration; reconciliation agreement; temporary support

(a) At or after the hearing, the court may make orders in respect to the conduct of the spouses or parents and the subject matter of the controversy that the court deems necessary to preserve the marriage or to implement the reconciliation of the spouses. No such order shall be effective for more than 30 days from the hearing of the petition unless the parties mutually consent to a continuation of the time the order remains effective.

(b) A reconciliation agreement between the parties may be reduced to writing and, with the consent of the parties, a court order may be made requiring the parties to comply fully with the agreement.

(c) During the pendency of a proceeding under this part, the superior court may order a spouse or parent, as the case may be, to pay an amount necessary for the support and maintenance of the other spouse and for the support, maintenance, and education of the minor children, as the case may be. In determining the amount, the superior court may take into consideration the recommendations of a financial referee if one is available to the court. An order made pursuant to this subdivision shall not prejudice the rights of the parties or children with respect to any subsequent order that may be made. An order made pursuant to this subdivision may be modified or terminated at any time except as to an amount that accrued before the date of filing of the notice of motion or order to show cause to modify or terminate. *(Stats.1992, c. 162 (A.B.2650), § 10, operative Jan. 1, 1994. Amended by Stats.1993, c. 219 (A.B.1500), § 102; Stats.2014, c. 82 (S.B.1306), § 22, eff. Jan. 1, 2015.)*

Law Revision Commission Comments

Enactment [Revised Comment]

Section 1839 continues former Code of Civil Procedure Section 1769 without substantive change. References to "termination" have been substituted for the former references to "revocation." [23 Cal.L.Rev.Comm. Reports 1 (1993)].

Research References

Treatises and Practice Aids

Witkin, California Summary 10th Husband and Wife § 98, Orders.
Witkin, California Summary 10th Husband and Wife § 371, Civil Remedies.

§ 1840. Dissolution, legal separation or judgment of nullity; stay of right to file; effect of pendency of action upon conciliation proceedings

(a) During a period beginning upon the filing of the petition for conciliation and continuing until 30 days after the hearing of the petition for conciliation, neither spouse shall file a petition for dissolution of marriage, for nullity of a voidable marriage, or for legal separation of the parties.

(b) After the expiration of the period under subdivision (a), if the controversy between the spouses, or the parents, has not been terminated, either spouse may institute a proceeding for dissolution of marriage, for nullity of a voidable marriage, or for legal separation of the parties, or a proceeding to determine custody or visitation of the minor child or children.

(c) The pendency of a proceeding for dissolution of marriage, for nullity of marriage, or for legal separation of the parties, or a proceeding to determine custody or visitation of the minor child or children, does not operate as a bar to the instituting of proceedings for conciliation under this part. *(Stats.1992, c. 162 (A.B.2650), § 10, operative Jan. 1, 1994.)*

Law Revision Commission Comments

Enactment [Revised Comment]

Section 1840 continues former Code of Civil Procedure Section 1770 without substantive change. See also Sections 3160–3186 (mediation of custody and visitation issues), 3190–3192 (counseling of parents and child). [23 Cal.L.Rev.Comm. Reports 1 (1993)].

Research References

Treatises and Practice Aids

Witkin, California Summary 10th Husband and Wife § 95, Jurisdiction.

§ 1841. Dissolution, legal separation or judgment of nullity; minor child involved; transfer

If a petition for dissolution of marriage, for nullity of marriage, or for legal separation of the parties is filed, the case may be transferred at any time during the pendency of the proceeding to the family conciliation court for proceedings for reconciliation of the spouses or amicable settlement of issues in controversy in accordance with this part if both of the following appear to the court:

(a) There is a minor child of the spouses, or of either of them, whose welfare may be adversely affected by the dissolution of the marriage or the disruption of the household or a controversy involving child custody.

(b) There is some reasonable possibility of a reconciliation being effected. *(Stats.1992, c. 162 (A.B.2650), § 10, operative Jan. 1, 1994.)*

Law Revision Commission Comments

Enactment [Revised Comment]

Section 1841 restates former Code of Civil Procedure Section 1771 without substantive change. In the introductory paragraph of this section, the phrase "nullity of marriage" has been substituted for "declaration of nullity of a voidable marriage." The reference to the "superior" court has been omitted as surplus. See Section 200 (jurisdiction in superior court). [23 Cal.L.Rev.Comm. Reports 1 (1993)].

Research References

Forms

West's California Code Forms, Family § 1830, Comment Overview--Jurisdiction.

West's California Code Forms, Family § 1841 Form 1, Order Transferring Action to Family Conciliation Court.

Treatises and Practice Aids

Witkin, California Summary 10th Husband and Wife § 95, Jurisdiction.

§ 1842. Dissolution, legal separation or judgment of nullity; no minor children; application for and acceptance of transfer; jurisdiction

(a) If an application is made to the family conciliation court for conciliation proceedings in respect to a controversy between spouses, or a contested proceeding for dissolution of marriage, for nullity of a voidable marriage, or for legal separation of the parties, but there is no minor child whose welfare may be affected by the results of the controversy, and it appears to the court that reconciliation of the spouses or amicable adjustment of the controversy can probably be achieved, and that the work of the court in cases involving children will not be seriously impeded by acceptance of the case, the court may accept and dispose of the case in the same manner as similar cases involving the welfare of children are disposed of.

(b) If the court accepts the case under subdivision (a), the court has the same jurisdiction over the controversy and the parties to the controversy and those having a relation to the controversy that it has under this part in similar cases involving the welfare of children. *(Stats.1992, c. 162 (A.B. 2650), § 10, operative Jan. 1, 1994.)*

Law Revision Commission Comments

Enactment [Revised Comment]

Section 1842 continues former Code of Civil Procedure Section 1772 without substantive change. [23 Cal.L.Rev.Comm. Reports 1 (1993)].

Research References

Treatises and Practice Aids

Witkin, California Summary 10th Husband and Wife § 95, Jurisdiction.

Part 2

STATEWIDE COORDINATION OF FAMILY MEDIATION AND CONCILIATION SERVICES

§ 1850. Duties of Judicial Council

The Judicial Council shall do all of the following:

(a) Assist courts in implementing mediation and conciliation proceedings under this code.

(b) Establish and implement a uniform statistical reporting system relating to proceedings brought for dissolution of marriage, for nullity of marriage, or for legal separation of the parties, including, but not limited to, a custody disposition survey.

(c) Administer a program of grants to public and private agencies submitting proposals for research, study, and demonstration projects in the area of family law, including, but not limited to, all of the following:

(1) The development of conciliation and mediation and other newer dispute resolution techniques, particularly as they relate to child custody and to avoidance of litigation.

(2) The establishment of criteria to ensure that a child support order is adequate.

(3) The development of methods to ensure that a child support order is paid.

(4) The study of the feasibility and desirability of guidelines to assist judges in making custody decisions.

(d) Administer a program for the training of court personnel involved in family law proceedings, which shall be available to the court personnel and which shall be totally funded from funds specified in Section 1852. The training shall include, but not be limited to, the order of preference for custody of minor children and the meaning of the custody arrangements under Part 2 (commencing with Section 3020) of Division 8.

(e) Conduct research on the effectiveness of current family law for the purpose of shaping future public policy. *(Stats. 1992, c. 162 (A.B.2650), § 10, operative Jan. 1, 1994. Amended by Stats.1993, c. 219 (A.B.1500), § 102.5; Stats.2012, c. 470 (A.B.1529), § 16.)*

Law Revision Commission Comments

Enactment [Revised Comment]

Subdivisions (a)–(d) of Section 1850 continue former Civil Code Section 5181 without substantive change. The application of subdivision (a) has been expanded to cover all mediation and conciliation proceedings under this code. The former section applied only to implementation of former Civil Code Sections 4351.5 and 4607. See Sections 3160–3186 (mediation of custody and visitation issues).

In subdivision (b), the phrase "relating to proceedings brought for dissolution of marriage, for nullity of marriage, or for legal separation of the parties" has been substituted for "relating to actions brought pursuant to this part." The former reference to "this part" referred to the former Family Law Act (former Part 5 (commencing with former Section 4000) of Division 4 of the Civil Code).

In subdivision (d), a reference to Part 2 (commencing with Section 3020) of Division 8 has been substituted for a narrower reference to specific sections continued in Part 2. This is not a substantive change.

Subdivision (e) is new to this section, but continues authority implied under the last part of former Civil Code Section 5180.

Addition of this subdivision is not intended to mandate any new duties or require the Judicial Council to undertake any research that was not ongoing under former law. [23 Cal.L.Rev.Comm. Reports 1 (1993)].

2012 Amendment

Subdivision (a) of Section 1850 is amended to reflect enactment of the Lockyer–Isenberg Trial Court Funding Act, 1997 Cal. Stat. ch. 850 (see generally Gov't Code §§ 77000–77655). See, e.g., Gov't Code §§ 77001 (local trial court management), 77003 ("court operations" defined), 77200 (state funding of "court operations"); see also Cal. R. Ct. 10.810. [39 Cal.L.Rev.Comm. Reports 157 (2009)].

Research References

Treatises and Practice Aids

Witkin, California Summary 10th Husband and Wife § 91, Family Conciliation Courts.

Witkin, California Summary 10th Parent and Child § 278, in General.

§ 1851. Advisory committee

The Judicial Council shall establish an advisory committee of persons representing a broad spectrum of interest in and knowledge about family law. The committee shall recommend criteria for determining grant recipients pursuant to subdivision (c) of Section 1850, which shall include proposal evaluation guidelines and procedures for submission of the results to the Legislature, the Governor, and family law courts. In accordance with established criteria, the committee shall receive grant proposals and shall recommend the priority of submitted proposals. *(Stats.1992, c. 162 (A.B. 2650), § 10, operative Jan. 1, 1994.)*

Law Revision Commission Comments

Enactment [Revised Comment]

Section 1851 continues former Civil Code Section 5182 without substantive change. [23 Cal.L.Rev.Comm. Reports 1 (1993)].

§ 1852. Family Law Trust Fund; deposits; disbursements

(a) There is in the State Treasury the Family Law Trust Fund.

(b) Moneys collected by the state pursuant to subdivision (c) of Section 103625 of the Health and Safety Code, Section 70674 of the Government Code, and grants, gifts, or devises made to the state from private sources to be used for the purposes of this part shall be deposited into the Family Law Trust Fund.

(c) Moneys deposited in the Family Law Trust Fund shall be placed in an interest bearing account. Any interest earned shall accrue to the fund and shall be disbursed pursuant to subdivision (d).

(d) Money deposited in the Family Law Trust Fund shall be disbursed for purposes specified in this part and for other family law related activities.

(e) Moneys deposited in the Family Law Trust Fund shall be administered by the Judicial Council. The Judicial Council may, with appropriate guidelines, delegate the administration of the fund to the Administrative Office of the Courts.

(f) Any moneys in the Family Law Trust Fund that are unencumbered at the end of the fiscal year are automatically appropriated to the Family Law Trust Fund of the following year.

(g) In order to defray the costs of collection of these funds, pursuant to this section, the local registrar, county clerk, or county recorder may retain a percentage of the funds collected, not to exceed 10 percent of the fee payable to the state pursuant to subdivision (c) of Section 103625 of the Health and Safety Code. *(Stats.1992, c. 162 (A.B.2650), § 10, operative Jan. 1, 1994. Amended by Stats.1996, c. 1023 (S.B.1497), § 45, eff. Sept. 29, 1996; Stats.1997, c. 850 (A.B.233), § 5; Stats.2005, c. 75 (A.B.145), § 45, eff. July 19, 2005, operative Jan. 1, 2006.)*

Law Revision Commission Comments

Enactment [Revised Comment]

Section 1852 continues former Civil Code Section 5183 without substantive change. The word "devises" has been substituted for "bequests" to conform with the Probate Code. See Prob. Code § 32 ("devise" defined). [23 Cal.L.Rev.Comm. Reports 1 (1993)].

Division 6

NULLITY, DISSOLUTION, AND LEGAL SEPARATION

Part 1

GENERAL PROVISIONS

CHAPTER 1. APPLICATION OF PART

§ 2000. Application of part

This part applies to a proceeding for dissolution of marriage, for nullity of marriage, or for legal separation of the parties. *(Stats.1992, c. 162 (A.B.2650), § 10, operative Jan. 1, 1994.)*

Law Revision Commission Comments

Enactment [Revised Comment]

Section 2000 is new and is drawn from Rule 1201(c) ("proceeding" defined) of the California Rules of Court (Family Law Rules). A proceeding for dissolution of marriage, for nullity of marriage, or for legal separation of the parties includes not only a determination of marital status, but also determinations of property rights, support, and custody matters. See Section 2010 (authority of court). See also Cal. R. Ct. 1206 (1970) (general law applicable), 1207 (1970) (other proceedings); Division 1 (commencing with Section 1) (preliminary provisions and definitions), Division 2 (commencing with Section 200) (general provisions). [23 Cal.L.Rev.Comm. Reports 1 (1993)].

Research References

Treatises and Practice Aids

Witkin, California Summary 10th Husband and Wife § 3, Statutory Framework.
Witkin, California Summary 10th Husband and Wife § 5, Generally Applicable Procedures.
Witkin, California Summary 10th Husband and Wife § 57, Methods Of Altering Marital Status.
Witkin, California Summary 10th Husband and Wife § 67, in General.
Witkin, California Summary 10th Husband and Wife § 165, in General.
Witkin, California Summary 10th Husband and Wife § 128A, (New) Collaborative Law Process.

CHAPTER 2. JURISDICTION

§ 2010. Scope of jurisdiction

In a proceeding for dissolution of marriage, for nullity of marriage, or for legal separation of the parties, the court has jurisdiction to inquire into and render any judgment and make orders that are appropriate concerning the following:

(a) The status of the marriage, including any marriage under subdivision (c) of Section 308.

(b) The custody of minor children of the marriage.

(c) The support of children for whom support may be ordered, including children born after the filing of the initial petition or the final decree of dissolution.

(d) The support of either party.

(e) The settlement of the property rights of the parties.

(f) The award of attorney's fees and costs. *(Stats.1992, c. 162 (A.B.2650), § 10, operative Jan. 1, 1994. Amended by Stats.1993, c. 219 (A.B.1500), § 103; Stats.1994, c. 1269 (A.B.2208), § 12.5; Stats.2010, c. 397 (A.B.2700), § 2.)*

Law Revision Commission Comments

Enactment [Revised Comment]

Section 2010 continues the first part of former Civil Code Section 4351 without substantive change. The reference to the "superior" court has been omitted as surplus. See Section 200 (jurisdiction in superior court). The phrase "proceeding for dissolution of marriage, nullity of marriage, or legal separation of the parties" has been substituted for "proceedings under this part," which referred to the former Family Law Act (former Part 5 (commencing with former Section 4000) of Division 4 of the Civil Code). In subdivision (c), a reference to "children for whom support may be ordered" has been substituted for the former reference to "minor" children and children for whom support could be ordered pursuant to former Civil Code Section 206. This is not a substantive change. See Section 58 ("children for whom support may be ordered" defined). See also Section 2556 (continuing jurisdiction to award community estate property or adjudicate debts). [23 Cal.L.Rev.Comm. Reports 1 (1993)].

Commentary

Relying on subsection (b) of this section and § 3022, *In re Marriage of Jensen, 114 Cal.App.4th 587, 7 Cal.Rptr.3d 701 (2003), review denied*, held that a court lacks jurisdiction to enforce the terms of a marital settlement agreement, incorporated into a judgment of dissolution, that required an adult disabled child living in Thailand to visit his father in California and required the child's mother to encourage and implement visitation and give the father written updates on the child's activities.

Read together, subsection (b) and Section 3101 generally limit stepparent claims to visitation, as opposed to custody. *In re Marriage of Goetz and Lewis, 203 Cal.App.3d 514, 250 Cal.Rptr. 30 (1988)* (in divorce action stepparent may not be awarded joint custody of wife's minor child). See also Section 290, Commentary.

Although a tort claim may be consolidated with a *pending* dissolution action in appropriate circumstances, *Sosnick v. Sosnick, 71 Cal.App.4th 1335, 84 Cal.Rptr.2d 700 (1999),* holds that the divorce court lacks jurisdiction to consolidate a former wife's tort claim against her former husband with a closed dissolution action.

Gale v. Superior Court, 122 Cal.App.4th 1388, 19 Cal.Rptr.3d 554 (2004), holds that a party to a dissolution proceeding may file a lis pendens on property only if the pleadings have alleged a community interest in that property and the reference is sufficient to enable third parties to ascertain from the pleadings the nature of any claim to that property. A general reference to, for example, "such assets as may be discovered at a later date" is insufficient to support the filing of a lis pendens. See Code of Civil Procedure § 405.4.

Under subsection (c) of this section, section 200, and section 4908, in a proceeding to dissolve a marriage a California Superior Court has jurisdiction to award child support even though a child's home state is Japan, when no support action has ever been initiated in the child's home state. *In re Marriage of Richardson, 179 Cal.App.4th 1240, 102 Cal.Rptr.3d 391 (2009)*.

When a wife was not the debtor spouse, *In re Marriage of Guasch, 201 Cal.App.4th 942, 134 Cal.Rptr.3d 358 (2011)*, affirmed a judgment granting a wife's motion to quash a judgment creditor's writ of execution and enjoining further enforcement against community property, without requiring the wife to post an undertaking under Code of Civil Procedure section 529. *Guasch* declined to read the requirement of that statute into subsection (e) of this section, upon which the trial court relied in granting the wife relief.

Research References

Forms

California Practice Guide: Rutter Family Law Forms Form 1:32, Glossary Of Common Family Law Terms, Phrases and Concepts (Enclosure to Form 1:31).

California Practice Guide: Rutter Family Law Forms Form 4:12, Request for Order to Strike Petition.

California Transactions Forms--Family Law § 3:4, Subject Matter Jurisdiction for Custody Determinations.

California Transactions Forms--Family Law § 2:55, Continuing Jurisdiction.

West's California Judicial Council Forms FL-372, Request for Joinder Of Employee Benefit Plan and Order.

West's California Judicial Council Forms FL-374, Notice Of Appearance and Response Of Employee Benefit Plan.

Treatises and Practice Aids

Witkin, California Summary 10th Community Property § 149, Distinction: Family Law Attorney's Lien.

Witkin, California Summary 10th Husband and Wife § 68, in General.

Witkin, California Summary 10th Husband and Wife § 78, Joinder Of Third Persons.

Witkin, California Summary 10th Husband and Wife § 144, in General.

Witkin, California Summary 10th Husband and Wife § 166, Subject Matter Jurisdiction.

Witkin, California Summary 10th Parent and Child § 267, Jurisdiction and Venue.

Witkin, California Summary 10th Parent and Child § 423, Support Of Disabled Indigent Adult Child.

§ 2011. Service by publication; scope of jurisdiction

When service of summons on a spouse is made pursuant to Section 415.50 of the Code of Civil Procedure, the court, without the aid of attachment or the appointment of a receiver, shall have and may exercise the same jurisdiction over:

(a) The community real property of the spouse so served situated in this state as it has or may exercise over the community real property of a spouse who is personally served with process within this state.

(b) The quasi-community real property of the spouse so served situated in this state as it has or may exercise over the quasi-community real property of a spouse who is personally served with process within this state. *(Stats.1992, c. 162 (A.B.2650), § 10, operative Jan. 1, 1994.)*

Law Revision Commission Comments

Enactment [Revised Comment]

Section 2011 continues former Civil Code Section 4813 without substantive change. The references to proceedings under "this part," meaning proceedings under the former Family Law Act (former Part 5 (commencing with former Section 4000) of Division 4 of the Civil Code), have been omitted as surplus. See Section 2000 (application to dissolution, nullity, or legal separation proceedings). See also Sections 65 ("community property" defined in Section 760 *et seq.*), 125 ("quasi-community property" defined). [23 Cal.L.Rev. Comm. Reports 1 (1993)].

Research References

Treatises and Practice Aids

Witkin, California Summary 10th Contracts § 42, Minors Exposed to Communicable Disease.

Witkin, California Summary 10th Husband and Wife § 68, in General.

§ 2012. Pendency of motion to quash service of summons or to stay or dismiss action; appearance of respondent

(a) During the time a motion pursuant to Section 418.10 of the Code of Civil Procedure is pending, the respondent may appear in opposition to an order made during the pendency of the proceeding and the appearance shall not be deemed a general appearance by the respondent.

(b) As used in this section, a motion pursuant to Section 418.10 of the Code of Civil Procedure is pending from the time notice of motion is served and filed until the time within which to petition for a writ of mandate has expired or, if a petition is made, until the time final judgment in the mandate proceeding is entered. *(Stats.1992, c. 162 (A.B.2650), § 10, operative Jan. 1, 1994.)*

Law Revision Commission Comments

Enactment [Revised Comment]

Section 2012 continues former Civil Code Section 4356 without substantive change. The reference to proceedings under "this part," meaning the former Family Law Act (former Part 5 (commencing with former Section 4000) of Division 4 of the Civil Code), has been omitted as surplus. See Section 2000 (application to dissolution, nullity, or legal separation proceedings).

Section 2012 enables the respondent to contest preliminary orders in family law proceedings without prejudicing the respondent's right to litigate the personal jurisdiction of the court by special appearance pursuant to Code of Civil Procedure Section 418.10. For background on former Civ. Code § 4356, see *Recommendation Relating to Special Appearance in Family Law Proceedings,* 17 Cal. L. Revision Comm'n Reports 243 (1984). [23 Cal.L.Rev.Comm. Reports 1 (1993)].

Research References

Treatises and Practice Aids

Witkin, California Summary 10th Husband and Wife § 70, Special Appearance by Respondent.
Witkin, California Summary 10th Parent and Child § 144, Procedure.

§ 2013. Collaborative law process

(a) If a written agreement is entered into by the parties, the parties may utilize a collaborative law process to resolve any matter governed by this code over which the court is granted jurisdiction pursuant to Section 2000.

(b) "Collaborative law process" means the process in which the parties and any professionals engaged by the parties to assist them agree in writing to use their best efforts and to make a good faith attempt to resolve disputes related to the family law matters as referenced in subdivision (a) on an agreed basis without resorting to adversary judicial intervention. *(Added by Stats.2006, c. 496 (A.B.402), § 2.)*

Research References

Forms

West's California Code Forms, Family § 2013, Comment Overview--Collaborative Law.

Treatises and Practice Aids

Witkin, California Summary 10th Contracts § 1024, Payment Of Support Due to Mistaken Belief Of Biological Fatherhood.
Witkin, California Summary 10th Husband and Wife § 384, Orders After Notice and Hearing.
Witkin, California Summary 10th Husband and Wife § 128A, (New) Collaborative Law Process.
Witkin, California Summary 10th Parent and Child § 19, General Provisions.
Witkin, California Summary 10th Parent and Child § 33, Effect Of Declaration.
Witkin, California Summary 10th Parent and Child § 35, in General.
Witkin, California Summary 10th Parent and Child § 36, Nonbiological Father as Presumed Father.
Witkin, California Summary 10th Parent and Child § 235, Biologically Unrelated Persons Opposed by Parent.
Witkin, California Summary 10th Parent and Child § 603, Identification Of Presumed or Alleged Fathers.

CHAPTER 3. PROCEDURAL PROVISIONS

§ 2020. Responsive pleadings

A responsive pleading, if any, shall be filed and a copy served on the petitioner within 30 days of the date of the service on the respondent of a copy of the petition and summons. *(Stats.1992, c. 162 (A.B.2650), § 10, operative Jan. 1, 1994. Amended by Stats.1998, c. 581 (A.B.2801), § 4.)*

Law Revision Commission Comments

Enactment [Revised Comment]

Section 2020 continues former Civil Code Section 4355 without substantive change. The reference to proceedings under "this part," meaning the former Family Law Act (former Part 5 (commencing with former Section 4000) of Division 4 of the Civil Code), has been omitted as surplus. See Section 2000 (application to dissolution, nullity, or legal separation proceedings). [23 Cal.L.Rev.Comm. Reports 1 (1993)].

Commentary

Gale v. Superior Court, 122 Cal.App.4th 1388, 19 Cal.Rptr.3d 554 (2004), holds that a party to a dissolution proceeding may file a lis pendens on property only if the pleadings have alleged a community interest in that property and the reference is sufficient to enable third parties to ascertain from the pleadings the nature of any claim to that property. A general reference to, for example, such assets as may be discovered at a later date is insufficient to support the filing of a lis pendens. See Code of Civil Procedure § 405.4.

Research References

Forms

West's California Code Forms, Family § 2020, Comment Overview--Nullity, Dissolution, and Legal Separation.
West's California Judicial Council Forms FL-120, Response--Marriage/Domestic Partnership.

Treatises and Practice Aids

Witkin, California Summary 10th Husband and Wife § 75, Process.
Witkin, California Summary 10th Husband and Wife § 84, Response.

§ 2021. Joinder; interested parties; employee benefit plans

(a) Subject to subdivision (b), the court may order that a person who claims an interest in the proceeding be joined as a party to the proceeding in accordance with rules adopted by the Judicial Council pursuant to Section 211.

(b) An employee benefit plan may be joined as a party only in accordance with Chapter 6 (commencing with Section 2060). *(Stats.1992, c. 162 (A.B.2650), § 10, operative Jan. 1, 1994. Amended by Stats.1996, c. 1061 (S.B.1033), § 3.)*

Law Revision Commission Comments

Enactment [Revised Comment]

Section 2021 continues former Civil Code Section 4363 without substantive change. The references to proceedings under "this part," meaning the former Family Law Act (former Part 5 (commencing with former Section 4000) of Division 4 of the Civil Code), have been omitted as surplus. See Section 2000 (application to dissolution, nullity, or legal separation proceedings). See also Sections 80 ("employee pension benefit plan" defined), 755 (discharge of employee benefit plan from adverse claims). [23 Cal. L.Rev.Comm. Reports 1 (1993)].

Commentary

See generally *Schnabel v. Superior Court, 21 Cal.App.4th 548, 26 Cal.Rptr.2d 169 (1993)* (*Schnabel III*).

Research References

Forms

West's California Code Forms, Family § 2020, Comment Overview--Nullity, Dissolution, and Legal Separation.

West's California Judicial Council Forms FL-371, Notice Of Motion and Declaration for Joinder.

West's California Judicial Council Forms FL-372, Request for Joinder Of Employee Benefit Plan and Order.

West's California Judicial Council Forms FL-374, Notice Of Appearance and Response Of Employee Benefit Plan.

Treatises and Practice Aids

Witkin, California Summary 10th Community Property § 239, Claims Of Third Parties.

Witkin, California Summary 10th Husband and Wife § 78, Joinder Of Third Persons.

§ 2022. Evidence collected by eavesdropping; admissibility

(a) Evidence collected by eavesdropping in violation of Chapter 1.5 (commencing with Section 630) of Title 15 of Part 1 of the Penal Code is inadmissible.

(b) If it appears that a violation described in subdivision (a) exists, the court may refer the matter to the proper authority for investigation and prosecution. *(Stats.1992, c. 162 (A.B.2650), § 10, operative Jan. 1, 1994.)*

Law Revision Commission Comments

Enactment [Revised Comment]

Section 2022 continues former Civil Code Section 4361 without substantive change. Language in the former section limiting its application to proceedings for dissolution, nullity, or legal separation has been omitted as surplus. See Section 2000 (application of part). [23 Cal.L.Rev.Comm. Reports 1 (1993)].

Research References

Forms

California Transactions Forms--Family Law § 3:16, Identifying Areas Of Parental Decision Making and Participation.

Treatises and Practice Aids

Witkin, California Summary 10th Husband and Wife § 62, Evidence Of Misconduct is Ordinarily Inadmissible.

§ 2023. Payment of obligation directly to creditor

(a) On a determination that payment of an obligation of a party would benefit either party or a child for whom support may be ordered, the court may order one of the parties to pay the obligation, or a portion thereof, directly to the creditor.

(b) The creditor has no right to enforce the order made under this section, nor are the creditor's rights affected by the determination made under this section. *(Stats.1992, c. 162 (A.B.2650), § 10, operative Jan. 1, 1994. Amended by Stats. 1993, c. 219 (A.B.1500), § 104.)*

Law Revision Commission Comments

Enactment [Revised Comment]

Section 2023 continues former Civil Code Section 4358 without substantive change. The reference to any proceeding under "this part," meaning the former Family Law Act (former Part 5 (commencing with former Section 4000) of Division 4 of the Civil Code), has been omitted as surplus. See Section 2000 (application to dissolution, nullity, or legal separation proceedings). A reference to a "child for whom support may be ordered" has been substituted for the former reference to a "minor" child. This is not a substantive change, but rather recognizes that support may be ordered for children who are not minors. See Section 58 ("child for whom support may be ordered" defined). [23 Cal.L.Rev.Comm. Reports 1 (1993)].

Commentary

Pinson v. Cole, 106 Cal.App.4th 494, 131 Cal.Rptr.2d 113 (2003), holds that this section means exactly what it says: A creditor has no right to enforce an order made under this section, nor are creditors' rights enlarged by a determination made under this section.

Research References

Treatises and Practice Aids

Witkin, California Summary 10th Husband and Wife § 215, Provision for Creditors.

§ 2024. Petitions or judgments for dissolution of marriage, nullity of marriage, or for legal separation of the parties; notice

(a) A petition for dissolution of marriage, nullity of marriage, or legal separation of the parties, or a joint petition for summary dissolution of marriage, shall contain the following notice:

"Dissolution or annulment of your marriage may automatically cancel your spouse's rights under your will, trust, retirement benefit plan, power of attorney, pay on death bank account, transfer on death vehicle registration, survivorship rights to any property owned in joint tenancy, and any other similar thing. It does not automatically cancel your spouse's rights as beneficiary of your life insurance policy. If these are not the results that you want, you must change your will, trust, account agreement, or other similar document to reflect your actual wishes.

Dissolution or annulment of your marriage may also automatically cancel your rights under your spouse's will, trust, retirement benefit plan, power of attorney, pay on death bank account, transfer on death vehicle registration, and survivorship rights to any property owned in joint tenancy, and any other similar thing. It does not automatically cancel your rights as beneficiary of your spouse's life insurance policy.

You should review these matters, as well as any credit cards, other credit accounts, insurance policies, retirement benefit plans, and credit reports to determine whether they should be changed or whether you should take any other actions in view of the dissolution or annulment of your marriage, or your legal separation. However, some changes may require the agreement of your spouse or a court order (see Part 3 (commencing with Section 231) of Division 2 of the Family Code)."

(b) A judgment for dissolution of marriage, for nullity of marriage, or for legal separation of the parties shall contain the following notice:

"Dissolution or annulment of your marriage may automatically cancel your spouse's rights under your will, trust, retirement benefit plan, power of attorney, pay on death bank account, transfer on death vehicle registration, survivorship rights to any property owned in joint tenancy, and any other similar thing. It does not automatically cancel your spouse's rights as beneficiary of your life insurance policy. If these are not the results that you want, you must change your will, trust, account agreement, or other similar document to reflect your actual wishes.

Dissolution or annulment of your marriage may also automatically cancel your rights under your spouse's will, trust, retirement benefit plan, power of attorney, pay on death bank account, transfer on death vehicle registration, survivorship rights to any property owned in joint tenancy, and any other similar thing. It does not automatically cancel your rights as beneficiary of your spouse's life insurance policy.

You should review these matters, as well as any credit cards, other credit accounts, insurance policies, retirement benefit plans, and credit reports to determine whether they should be changed or whether you should take any other actions in view of the dissolution or annulment of your marriage, or your legal separation." *(Stats.1992, c. 162 (A.B.2650), § 10, operative Jan. 1, 1994. Amended by Stats. 1993, c. 219 (A.B.1500), § 105; Stats.2001, c. 417 (A.B.873), § 1.)*

Law Revision Commission Comments

Enactment [Revised Comment]

Section 2024 continues without substantive change former Civil Code Sections 4352 and 4800.6. A reference to the possible effect of dissolution or annulment on a will has been added to subdivision (a) for consistency with subdivision (b). See also Prob. Code § 6122 & Comment (provisions in will revoked by dissolution or annulment of testator's marriage). For background on former Civ. Code § 4352, see *Tentative Recommendation Relating to Wills and Intestate Succession,* 16 Cal. L. Revision Comm'n Reports 2301, 2485 (1982). [23 Cal.L.Rev.Comm. Reports 1 (1993)].

2001 Amendment

Section 2024 is amended to refer to the effect of dissolution or annulment of marriage on the designation of a former spouse as attorney-in-fact, nonprobate transfers to a former spouse, and joint tenancy survivorship as between former spouses. See Prob. Code 3722, 4154, 4727(e) (power of attorney), 5600 (nonprobate transfer), 5601 (joint tenancy). [28 Cal.L.Rev.Comm. Reports 599 (1998)].

Research References

Forms

West's California Code Forms, Family § 2020, Comment Overview--Nullity, Dissolution, and Legal Separation.

West's California Judicial Council Forms FL-180, Judgment (Family Law).

Treatises and Practice Aids

Witkin, California Summary 10th Husband and Wife § 83, Petition.

Witkin, California Summary 10th Husband and Wife § 112, Contents Of Judgment.

Witkin, California Summary 10th Wills and Probate § 177, Dissolution or Annulment Of Marriage.

§ 2024.5. Redacting social security numbers from pleadings, attachments, documents or other written material filed pursuant to petitions for dissolution of marriage, nullity of marriage or legal separation; exceptions

(a) Except as provided in subdivision (b), the petitioner or respondent may redact any social security number from any pleading, attachment, document, or other written material filed with the court pursuant to a petition for dissolution of marriage, nullity of marriage, or legal separation. The Judicial Council form used to file such a petition, or a response to such a petition, shall contain a notice that the parties may redact any social security numbers from those pleadings, attachments, documents, or other material filed with the court.

(b) An abstract of support judgment, the form required pursuant to subdivision (b) of Section 4014, or any similar form created for the purpose of collecting child or spousal support payments may not be redacted pursuant to subdivision (a). *(Added by Stats.2004, c. 45 (A.B.782), § 2, eff. June 7, 2004.)*

Research References

Treatises and Practice Aids

Witkin, California Summary 10th Husband and Wife § 82, in General.

§ 2024.6. Sealing of pleadings listing parties' financial assets and liabilities and their location and identifying information; forms; service of copy of pleading

(a) Upon request by a party to a petition for dissolution of marriage, nullity of marriage, or legal separation, the court shall order a pleading that lists the parties' financial assets and liabilities and provides the location or identifying information about those assets and liabilities sealed. The request may be made by ex parte application. Nothing sealed pursuant to this section may be unsealed except upon petition to the court and good cause shown.

(b) Commencing not later than July 1, 2005, the Judicial Council form used to declare assets and liabilities of the parties in a proceeding for dissolution of marriage, nullity of marriage, or legal separation of the parties shall require the party filing the form to state whether the declaration contains identifying information on the assets and liabilities listed therein. If the party making the request uses a pleading other than the Judicial Council form, the pleading shall exhibit a notice on the front page, in bold capital letters, that the pleading lists and identifies financial information and is therefore subject to this section.

(c) For purposes of this section, "pleading" means a document that sets forth or declares the parties' assets and liabilities, income and expenses, a marital settlement agreement that lists and identifies the parties' assets and liabilities, or any document filed with the court incidental to the declaration or agreement that lists and identifies financial information.

(d) The party making the request to seal a pleading pursuant to subdivision (a) shall serve a copy of the pleading on the other party to the proceeding and file a proof of service with the request to seal the pleading.

(e) Nothing in this section precludes a party to a proceeding described in this section from using any document or information contained in a sealed pleading in any manner that is not otherwise prohibited by law. *(Added by Stats.2004, c. 45 (A.B.782), § 3, eff. June 7, 2004. Amended by Stats.2005, c. 22 (S.B.1108), § 61.)*

Validity

This section was held unconstitutional on its face as an undue burden on the right of public access to court records, in the case of Burkle v. Burkle (App. 2 Dist. 2006) 37 Cal.Rptr.3d 805, 135 Cal.App.4th 1045, as modified, review denied.

Commentary

Burkle v. Burkle, 135 Cal.App.4th 1045, 37 Cal.Rptr.3d 805 (2006), review denied, holds that this section is unconstitutional on its face, because the statute is not narrowly tailored enough to strike a balance between the parties' privacy rights and the public's First Amendment right of access to court records in divorce proceedings.

Research References

Forms

West's California Code Forms, Family § 2020, Comment Overview--Nullity, Dissolution, and Legal Separation.

West's California Code Forms, Family § 2104 Form 4, Schedule Of Assets and Debts.

Treatises and Practice Aids

Witkin, California Summary 10th Husband and Wife § 82, in General.

§ 2024.7. Notice of eligibility for reduced-cost or no-cost health coverage

On and after January 1, 2014, upon the filing of a petition for dissolution of marriage, nullity of marriage, or legal separation, the court shall provide to the petitioner and the respondent a notice informing him or her that he or she may be eligible for reduced-cost coverage through the California Health Benefit Exchange established under Title 22 (commencing with Section 100500) of the Government Code or no-cost coverage through Medi-Cal. The notice shall include information on obtaining coverage pursuant to those programs, and shall be developed by the California Health Benefit Exchange. *(Added by Stats.2012, c. 851 (A.B.792), § 1.)*

Research References

Forms

West's California Judicial Council Forms FL-110, Summons (Family Law).

Treatises and Practice Aids

Witkin, California Summary 10th Husband and Wife § 83, Petition.

§ 2025. Appeals of bifurcated issues; certification by superior court

Notwithstanding any other provision of law, if the court has ordered an issue or issues bifurcated for separate trial or hearing in advance of the disposition of the entire case, a court of appeal may order an issue or issues transferred to it for hearing and decision when the court that heard the issue or issues certifies that the appeal is appropriate. Certification by the court shall be in accordance with rules promulgated by the Judicial Council. *(Stats.1992, c. 162 (A.B.2650), § 10, operative Jan. 1, 1994.)*

Law Revision Commission Comments

Enactment [Revised Comment]

Section 2025 continues former Civil Code Section 4365(a) without substantive change. References to the "superior" court have been omitted as surplus. See Section 200 (jurisdiction in superior court). The reference to any proceeding under "this part," meaning the former Family Law Act (former Part 5 (commencing with former Section 4000) of Division 4 of the Civil Code), has been omitted as surplus. See Section 2000 (application to dissolution, nullity, or legal separation proceedings).

Former Civil Code Section 4365(b), which required the Judicial Council to establish rules for certification of appeals of bifurcated issues by July 1, 1989, has been omitted as obsolete. See Cal. R. Ct. 1269.5 (July 1, 1989) (certification of appeals of bifurcated issues other than marital status). See also Section 211 (Judicial Council rules of practice and procedure). [23 Cal.L.Rev.Comm. Reports 1 (1993)].

Research References

Treatises and Practice Aids

Witkin, California Summary 10th Husband and Wife § 122, Appeals Where Issues Are Bifurcated.

Witkin, California Summary 10th Husband and Wife § 123, Certification Procedure for Bifurcated Issues.

§ 2026. Reconciliation of parties; amelioration of contempt

The reconciliation of the parties, whether conditional or unconditional, is an ameliorating factor to be considered by the court in considering a contempt of an existing court order. *(Stats.1992, c. 162 (A.B.2650), § 10, operative Jan. 1, 1994.)*

Law Revision Commission Comments

Enactment [Revised Comment]

Section 2026 continues former Civil Code Section 4381 without substantive change. The reference to a court order under "this part," meaning the former Family Law Act (former Part 5 (commencing with former Section 4000) of Division 4 of the Civil Code), has been omitted as surplus. See Section 2000 (application to dissolution, nullity, or legal separation proceedings). [23 Cal.L.Rev. Comm. Reports 1 (1993)].

Research References

Treatises and Practice Aids

Witkin, California Summary 10th Husband and Wife § 113, in General.

Witkin, California Summary 10th Husband and Wife § 258, Nature Of Remedy.

CHAPTER 3.5. ATTORNEY'S FEES AND COSTS

§ 2030. Award; findings; timing; modification; limitation; statewide rule of court

(a)(1) In a proceeding for dissolution of marriage, nullity of marriage, or legal separation of the parties, and in any proceeding subsequent to entry of a related judgment, the court shall ensure that each party has access to legal representation, including access early in the proceedings, to preserve each party's rights by ordering, if necessary based on the income and needs assessments, one party, except a governmental entity, to pay to the other party, or to the other party's attorney, whatever amount is reasonably necessary for attorney's fees and for the cost of maintaining or defending the proceeding during the pendency of the proceeding.

(2) When a request for attorney's fees and costs is made, the court shall make findings on whether an award of attorney's fees and costs under this section is appropriate, whether there is a disparity in access to funds to retain counsel, and whether one party is able to pay for legal representation of both parties. If the findings demonstrate disparity in access and ability to pay, the court shall make an order awarding attorney's fees and costs. A party who lacks the financial ability to hire an attorney may request, as an in pro per litigant, that the court order the other party, if that other party has the financial ability, to pay a reasonable amount to allow the unrepresented party to retain an attorney in a timely manner before proceedings in the matter go forward.

(b) Attorney's fees and costs within this section may be awarded for legal services rendered or costs incurred before or after the commencement of the proceeding.

(c) The court shall augment or modify the original award for attorney's fees and costs as may be reasonably necessary for the prosecution or defense of the proceeding, or any proceeding related thereto, including after any appeal has been concluded.

(d) Any order requiring a party who is not the spouse of another party to the proceeding to pay attorney's fees or costs shall be limited to an amount reasonably necessary to maintain or defend the action on the issues relating to that party.

(e) The Judicial Council shall, by January 1, 2012, adopt a statewide rule of court to implement this section and develop a form for the information that shall be submitted to the court to obtain an award of attorney's fees under this section.
(Added by Stats.1993, c. 219 (A.B.1500), § 106.1. Amended by Stats.2004, c. 472 (A.B.2148), § 1; Stats.2010, c. 352 (A.B.939), § 4.)

Law Revision Commission Comments

Enactment [Revised Comment]

Section 2030 continues former Civil Code Section 4370(a) without substantive change. The phrase "proceeding for dissolution of marriage, for nullity of marriage, or for legal separation of the parties" replaces the former reference to "proceeding under this part." The phrase "proceeding under this part" as used in former Civil Code Section 4370(a) referred to the former Family Law Act (former Part 5 (commencing with former Section 4000) of Division 4 of the Civil Code).

Section 2032 requires that the award of attorney's fees and costs under Section 2030 be just and reasonable under relevant circumstances of the parties. See, e.g., *In re* Marriage of Hublou, 231 Cal.App.3d 956, 282 Cal.Rptr. 695 (1991).

Special provisions may govern attorney's fees and costs in particular circumstances. See, e.g., Sections 916 (attorney's fees in enforcing right to reimbursement after division of community property), 1101(g) (breach of fiduciary duty), 2255 (attorney's fees and costs in proceeding for judgment of nullity of marriage), 2334 (order for attorney's fees during period of continuance for reconciliation), 3027 (attorney's fees in proceeding to recover monetary sanction for false accusation of child abuse or neglect), 3028 (attorney's fees in proceeding to recover compensation for failure to assume caretaker responsibility or for thwarting other parent's visitation or custody rights), 3114, 3150–3153, 3184 (appointment of counsel to represent child in custody or visitation proceeding), 3407 (attorney's fees where custody or visitation proceeding commenced in clearly inappropriate forum), 3408 (attorney's fees where jurisdiction declined by reason of conduct), 3416 (attorney's fees for enforcement of sister state custody order), 3557 (attorney's fees for enforcing support order or civil penalty), 3652 (attorney's fees in proceeding to modify or terminate child support order), 4002 (attorney's fees for county enforcement of child support), 4303 (attorney's fees for county enforcement of spousal support), 4403 (attorney's fees for county enforcement of parent's right to support), 4803 (limitation on recovery of attorney's fees in proceeding under Uniform Reciprocal Enforcement of Support Act), 5283(d) (earnings assignment order), 6344, 6386 (attorney's fees in proceeding under Domestic Violence Prevention Act), 6602 (contract for attorney's fees for services in litigation for minor), 7640 (counsel fees and costs under Uniform Parentage Act), 7827, 7860–7864, 7895 (appointment of counsel in proceeding to declare child free from parental custody and control), 8800 (independent adoption). [23 Cal.L.Rev.Comm. Reports 1 (1993)].

Commentary

The Judicial Council form for requesting attorney fees and costs pendente lite in a dissolution proceeding is not mandatory when comparable declarations are submitted. To the extent that a local court rule makes the Judicial Council form mandatory, it is unenforceable because it conflicts with California Rule of Court 5.427(b)(1)(B), which makes the form optional. *In re Marriage of Sharples, 223 Cal.App.4th 160, 166 Cal.Rptr.3d 818 (2014).*

In re Marriage of Tharp, 188 Cal.App.4th 1295, 116 Cal.Rptr.3d 375 (2010), review denied, held that a family court abused its discretion, under this section and section 2032, by denying a wife's request for an award of previously incurred attorney's fees when it failed to examine the records submitted by the attorney and failed to make a needs analysis and consider the relative ability of the parties to pay the attorney's fees.

A request for need-based attorney's fees that is filed after an earlier denial of such fees is not required to satisfy the Code of Civil Procedure § 1008 requirements for a motion for reconsideration. Moreover, the "augment or modify" language of subsection (c) does not preclude reconsideration of a trial court order that initially denied attorney's fees. *In re Marriage of Hobdy, 123 Cal.App.4th 360, 20 Cal.Rptr.3d 104 (2004).*

Subsection (a) provides for attorney's fees in a dissolution proceeding and "any proceeding related thereto." In *Askew v. Askew, 22 Cal.App.4th 942, 28 Cal.Rptr.2d 284 (1994)*, the court held that it was error for the trial court to deny wife's request for attorney's fees to defend against husband's civil action, explaining that although the trial court might exercise its discretion not to consolidate a divorce action and a civil action, the two actions may nevertheless be "related" for purposes of Section 2030 attorney's fees.

In re Marriage of Read, 97 Cal.App.4th 476, 1269F, 118 Cal.Rptr.2d 497 (2002), held that a trial court lacked jurisdiction to award attorney's fees to a spouse's former attorneys when the spouse discharged the attorneys and withdrew her motion for the fee award before the court signed the order awarding fees. *Read* distinguished *In re Marriage of Borson, 37 Cal.App.3d 632, 112 Cal.Rptr. 432 (1974)*, where an award of fees was allowed, on the ground that in *Borson* the wife requested fees in her dissolution petition, so that her attorneys reasonably believed that, despite their discharge, they had implied authority from her to file a motion for additional fees and costs. *In re Marriage of Erickson and Simpson, 141 Cal.App.4th 707, 46 Cal. Rptr.3d 253 (2006)*, explains that a court has jurisdiction, under Section 272(a), to order a spouse to pay attorney fees to the other spouse's discharged attorney when the client expressly or impliedly authorized the attorney to make the fee request on behalf of the former client and the attorney made such fee request while he was still the attorney of record. Otherwise, the discharged attorney's only remedy is to seek fees from the former client in an independent action.

In re Marriage of O'Connor, 59 Cal.App.4th 877, 69 Cal.Rptr.2d 480 (1998), review denied February 18, 1998, sustained a trial court award to a rich husband of $450,000 in pendente lite attorney's fees and costs payable by his even richer wife. *In re Marriage of Keech, 75 Cal.App.4th 860, 89 Cal.Rptr.2d 525 (1999)*, held that the trial court abused its discretion when it ordered the husband to pay a "contributive share" of the wife's attorney's fees without consideration of the husband's ability to pay and whether the fees were reasonably necessary in light of the parties' litigation needs.

When a family attorney has been awarded attorney's fees in a dissolution proceeding and the parties to the action appeal the award, may the family attorney additionally recover section 2030 fees from his client and her former spouse for the expense of defending the appeal? *Selvin & Weiner v. Diller, 25 Cal.App.4th 728, 30 Cal.Rptr.2d 742 (1994)*, answered this question affirmatively, but the California Supreme Court ordered that the opinion not be officially published when it denied review on 8/25/94.

AT & T Management Plan v. Tucker, 902 F.Supp. 1168 (1995), holds that the ERISA anti-alienation clause (29 U.S.C. § 1056(d)(1)), which provides that benefits may not be alienated or assigned, preempts a California state order for attorney's fees against an ERISA-regulated pension plan. An order for attorney's fees does not constitute a Qualified Domestic Relations Order (QDRO) because the order is a prohibited assignment of funds held by the plan.

For treatment of a Section 2030(d) order requiring a nonspouse to pay attorney's fees, see *In re Marriage of Jovel, 49 Cal.App.4th 575, 56 Cal.Rptr.2d 740 (1996)* (defining and applying the term "issues relating to that party"). *In re Marriage of Bendetti, 214 Cal.App.4th 863, 154 Cal.Rptr.3d 329 (2013)*, holds that under subsection (d), a court has discretion to award attorney fees to a spouse against a third party joined in a dissolution proceeding without a showing that the spouse is likely to prevail on the merits. Also interpreting subsection (d), *In re Marriage of Perry, 61 Cal.App.4th 295, 71 Cal.Rptr.2d 499 (1998),* holds that a grandparent who is a party to a custody or visitation proceeding may be ordered to pay for a child's court-appointed counsel and for another party's attorney's fees to defend on issues involving the grandparent. For further discussion of *Perry*, see Commentary to Section 3103.

In re Marriage of Guilardi, 200 Cal.App.4th 770, 132 Cal.Rptr.3d 798 (2011), review denied, holds that a trial court has discretion to find that a relinquishment of all claims in a voluntarily executed marital settlement agreement constitutes a waiver of need-based attorney fees for a party who unsuccessfully challenges the agreement. There appears, however, to be a conflict of authority on the issue. *Guilardi* collects and discusses conflicting California appellate cases.

Applying the disentitlement doctrine, *In re Marriage of Hofer, 208 Cal.App.4th 454, 145 Cal.Rptr.3d 697 (2012), review denied*, held that a husband who refused to comply with orders to produce financial documents showing his income and the extent of the community property, was not entitled to appeal an award of attorney's fees to his wife. The disentitlement doctrine is an equitable doctrine that allows an appellate court to dismiss or stay the appeal of a party who has not complied with legal orders.

In re Marriage of Smith, 242 Cal.App.4th 529, 195 Cal.Rptr.3d 162 (2015), held that a trial court properly considered large sums that a wife's father paid to her attorney on her behalf in determining the parties' relative circumstances for the purpose of awarding attorney's fees under this section.

Research References

Forms

California Practice Guide: Rutter Family Law Forms Form 5:2, Request for Order Re Child Custody, Child Support, Spousal Support, Attorney Fees, etc.
California Practice Guide: Rutter Family Law Forms Form 14:1, Request for Order Re Need-Based Attorney Fees and Costs.
California Practice Guide: Rutter Family Law Forms Form 14:2, Request for Order Re Need-Based Attorney Fees and Costs (Pro Per Litigant).
California Practice Guide: Rutter Family Law Forms Form 14:3, Request for Order Re Need-Based Attorney Fees and Costs ("Borson Motion").
California Transactions Forms--Family Law § 3:2, Child Custody.
California Transactions Forms--Family Law § 2:48, Nondischargeable Debts.
West's California Code Forms, Family § 2030, Comment Overview--Attorney's Fees.
West's California Judicial Council Forms FL-150, Income and Expense Declaration.
West's California Judicial Council Forms FL-157, Spousal or Partner Support Declaration Attachment.
West's California Judicial Council Forms FL-158, Supporting Declaration for Attorney's Fees and Costs Attachment.
West's California Judicial Council Forms FL-319, Request for Attorney's Fees and Costs Attachment.
West's California Judicial Council Forms FL-346, Attorney's Fees and Costs Order Attachment.

Treatises and Practice Aids

Witkin, California Summary 10th Husband and Wife § 10, Imposition Of Award as Sanction.
Witkin, California Summary 10th Husband and Wife § 86, in General.
Witkin, California Summary 10th Husband and Wife § 112, Contents Of Judgment.
Witkin, California Summary 10th Husband and Wife § 173, Attorneys' Fees and Costs Pending Proceeding.
Witkin, California Summary 10th Husband and Wife § 175, Development Of Law.
Witkin, California Summary 10th Husband and Wife § 176, Purpose and Public Policy.
Witkin, California Summary 10th Husband and Wife § 177, Types Of Actions.
Witkin, California Summary 10th Husband and Wife § 178, Main Proceeding in Trial Court.
Witkin, California Summary 10th Husband and Wife § 179, Main Proceeding on Appeal.
Witkin, California Summary 10th Husband and Wife § 180, in General.

Witkin, California Summary 10th Husband and Wife § 184, Payee's Needs.

Witkin, California Summary 10th Husband and Wife § 185, Payor's Ability.

Witkin, California Summary 10th Husband and Wife § 188, Legal Services Already Rendered.

Witkin, California Summary 10th Husband and Wife § 190, Award Of Attorneys' Fees and Costs Against Third Party.

Witkin, California Summary 10th Husband and Wife § 193, in General.

Witkin, California Summary 10th Husband and Wife § 197, in General.

Witkin, California Summary 10th Husband and Wife § 207, Modification.

Witkin, California Summary 10th Parent and Child § 19, General Provisions.

§ 2031. Applications for temporary orders

(a)(1) Except as provided in subdivision (b), during the pendency of a proceeding for dissolution of marriage, for nullity of marriage, for legal separation of the parties, or any proceeding subsequent to entry of a related judgment, an application for a temporary order making, augmenting, or modifying an award of attorney's fees, including a reasonable retainer to hire an attorney, or costs or both shall be made by motion on notice or by an order to show cause.

(2) The court shall rule on an application within 15 days of the hearing on the motion or order to show cause.

(b) An order described in subdivision (a) may be made without notice by an oral motion in open court at either of the following times:

(1) At the time of the hearing of the cause on the merits.

(2) At any time before entry of judgment against a party whose default has been entered pursuant to Section 585 or 586 of the Code of Civil Procedure. The court shall rule on any motion made pursuant to this subdivision within 15 days and prior to the entry of any judgment. *(Added by Stats.1993, c. 219 (A.B.1500), § 106.1. Amended by Stats.2004, c. 472 (A.B.2148), § 2.)*

Law Revision Commission Comments

Enactment [Revised Comment]

Section 2031 continues former Civil Code Section 4370(b) without substantive change. The phrase "proceeding for dissolution of marriage, for nullity of marriage, or for legal separation of the parties" replaces the former reference to "proceeding under this part." The phrase "proceeding under this part" as used in former Civil Code Section 4370(b) referred to the former Family Law Act (former Part 5 (commencing with former Section 4000) of Division 4 of the Civil Code). [23 Cal.L.Rev.Comm. Reports 1 (1993)].

Research References

Forms

West's California Code Forms, Family § 2030, Comment Overview--Attorney's Fees.

Treatises and Practice Aids

Witkin, California Summary 10th Husband and Wife § 87, Methods Of Obtaining Orders.

Witkin, California Summary 10th Husband and Wife § 198, Order to Show Cause or Motion.

Witkin, California Summary 10th Husband and Wife § 207, Modification.

Witkin, California Summary 10th Husband and Wife § 203A, (New) Attorneys' Fees and Costs.

§ 2032. Reasonableness of award; findings; property from which fees can be awarded; allocation of fees and costs in light of complex issues

(a) The court may make an award of attorney's fees and costs under Section 2030 or 2031 where the making of the award, and the amount of the award, are just and reasonable under the relative circumstances of the respective parties.

(b) In determining what is just and reasonable under the relative circumstances, the court shall take into consideration the need for the award to enable each party, to the extent practical, to have sufficient financial resources to present the party's case adequately, taking into consideration, to the extent relevant, the circumstances of the respective parties described in Section 4320. The fact that the party requesting an award of attorney's fees and costs has resources from which the party could pay the party's own attorney's fees and costs is not itself a bar to an order that the other party pay part or all of the fees and costs requested. Financial resources are only one factor for the court to consider in determining how to apportion the overall cost of the litigation equitably between the parties under their relative circumstances.

(c) The court may order payment of an award of attorney's fees and costs from any type of property, whether community or separate, principal or income.

(d) Either party may, at any time before the hearing of the cause on the merits, on noticed motion, request the court to make a finding that the case involves complex or substantial issues of fact or law related to property rights, visitation, custody, or support. Upon that finding, the court may in its discretion determine the appropriate, equitable allocation of attorney's fees, court costs, expert fees, and consultant fees between the parties. The court order may provide for the allocation of separate or community assets, security against these assets, and for payments from income or anticipated income of either party for the purpose described in this subdivision and for the benefit of one or both parties. Payments shall be authorized only on agreement of the parties or, in the absence thereof, by court order. The court may order that a referee be appointed pursuant to Section 639 of the Code of Civil Procedure to oversee the allocation of fees and costs. *(Added by Stats.1993, c. 219 (A.B.1500), § 106.1. Amended by Stats.2010, c. 352 (A.B.939), § 5.)*

Law Revision Commission Comments

Enactment [Revised Comment]

Section 2032 continues former Civil Code Section 4370.5 without substantive change. In subdivision (b), a reference to Section 4320 has been substituted for the broader reference to former Civil Code Section 4801(a). Section 4320 continues the relevant part of former Civil Code Section 4801(a). See also Sections 65 ("community property" defined in Section 760 *et seq.*), 125 ("quasi-community property" defined), 130 ("separate property" defined in Section 760 *et seq.*).

Subdivision (a) of Section 2032 states the general standard for an award of costs and attorney's fees in family law proceedings. Subdivision (b) lists two important factors the court should consider in making such an award. The factors listed in subdivision (b) are not exclusive, and the court may consider any other proper factors, including the likelihood of collection, tax considerations, and other factors announced in the cases. See, e.g., *In re* Marriage of Lopez, 38 Cal.App.3d 93, 113 Cal.Rptr. 58 (1974). Subdivision (c) expressly authorizes the court to order payment from any source that appears proper, including the community and separate estates of the parties. When enacted in 1985 (as former Civil Code Section 4370.5), this provision overruled language in the cases holding, for example, that the court could not require a wife to impair the capital of her separate estate in order to defray her litigation expenses. See, e.g., *In re* Marriage of Jafeman, 29 Cal.App.3d 244, 105 Cal.Rptr. 483 (1972); *In re* Marriage of Hopkins, 74 Cal.App.3d 591, 141 Cal.Rptr. 597 (1977).

For background on former Civ. Code § 4370.5, see *Recommendation Relating to Litigation Expenses in Family Law Proceedings,* 18 Cal. L. Revision Comm'n Reports 351 (1986). [23 Cal.L.Rev.Comm. Reports 1 (1993)].

Commentary

The Judicial Council form for requesting attorney fees and costs pendent lite in a dissolution proceeding is not mandatory when comparable declarations are submitted. To the extent that a local court rule makes the Judicial Council form mandatory, it is unenforceable because it conflicts with California Rule of Court 5.427(b)(1)(B), which makes the form optional. *In re Marriage of Sharples, 223 Cal.App.4th 160, 166 Cal.Rptr.3d 818 (2014).*

In re Marriage of Tharp, 188 Cal.App.4th 1295, 116 Cal.Rptr.3d 375 (2010), review denied, held that a family court abused its discretion, under this section and section 2030, by denying a wife's request for an award of previously incurred attorney's fees when it failed to examine the records submitted by the attorney and failed to make a needs analysis and consider the relative ability of the parties to pay the attorney's fees.

See generally *In re Marriage of Drake, 53 Cal.App.4th 1139, 62 Cal.Rptr.2d 466 (1997), review denied June 11, 1997.*

Applying subsection (b), *In re Marriage of O'Connor, 59 Cal. App.4th 877, 69 Cal.Rptr.2d 480 (1998), review denied February 18, 1998,* sustained a trial court award to a rich husband of $450,000 in pendente lite attorney's fees and costs payable by his even richer wife. *In re Marriage of Keech, 75 Cal.App.4th 860, 89 Cal.Rptr.2d 525 (1999)*, held that the trial court abused its discretion when it ordered the husband to pay a "contributive share" of the wife's attorney's fees without consideration of the husband's ability to pay and whether the fees were reasonably necessary in light of the parties' litigation needs.

In applying sections 7605 and 7640 to a request for attorney's fees in a paternity proceeding, *Kevin Q. v. Lauren W., 195 Cal.App.4th 633, 124 Cal.Rptr.3d 676 (2011)*, holds that a trial court properly relied this section to establish the standards for an award.

Applying the disentitlement doctrine, *In re Marriage of Hofer, 208 Cal.App.4th 454, 145 Cal.Rptr.3d 697 (2012), review denied*, held that a husband who refused to comply with orders to produce financial documents showing his income and the extent of the community property, was not entitled to appeal an award of attorney's fees to his wife. The disentitlement doctrine is an equitable doctrine that allows an appellate court to dismiss or stay the appeal of a party who has not complied with legal orders.

Mooney v. Superior Court of Santa Cruz County, 245 Cal.App.4th 523, 199 Cal.Rptr.3d 647 (2016), held that a trial court abused its discretion in awarding attorney's fees under this section when the requirements of this section were not satisfied in that no request for attorney's fees was made, the court did not make the necessary findings, and there was no adequate basis for awarding attorney's fees.

Research References

Forms

California Practice Guide: Rutter Family Law Forms Form 14:1, Request for Order Re Need-Based Attorney Fees and Costs.

California Practice Guide: Rutter Family Law Forms Form 14:2, Request for Order Re Need-Based Attorney Fees and Costs (Pro Per Litigant).

California Practice Guide: Rutter Family Law Forms Form 14:3, Request for Order Re Need-Based Attorney Fees and Costs ("Borson Motion").

California Transactions Forms--Family Law § 3:2, Child Custody.

California Transactions Forms--Family Law § 3:6, Unenforceability Of Limitation Of Jurisdiction.

West's California Code Forms, Family § 2030, Comment Overview--Attorney's Fees.

West's California Judicial Council Forms FL-150, Income and Expense Declaration.

West's California Judicial Council Forms FL-157, Spousal or Partner Support Declaration Attachment.

West's California Judicial Council Forms FL-158, Supporting Declaration for Attorney's Fees and Costs Attachment.

West's California Judicial Council Forms FL-319, Request for Attorney's Fees and Costs Attachment.

Treatises and Practice Aids

Witkin, California Summary 10th Community Property § 149, Distinction: Family Law Attorney's Lien.

Witkin, California Summary 10th Husband and Wife § 71, Case Management.

Witkin, California Summary 10th Husband and Wife § 186, Effect Of Payee's Property, Income, and Earning Capacity.

Witkin, California Summary 10th Husband and Wife § 193, in General.

Witkin, California Summary 10th Husband and Wife § 194, Factors to be Considered.

Witkin, California Summary 10th Husband and Wife § 201, Case Management Plan.

Witkin, California Summary 10th Husband and Wife § 368, California Statute.

Witkin, California Summary 10th Parent and Child § 19, General Provisions.

§ 2033. Family law attorney's real property lien; notice; objections

(a) Either party may encumber his or her interest in community real property to pay reasonable attorney's fees in order to retain or maintain legal counsel in a proceeding for dissolution of marriage, for nullity of marriage, or for legal separation of the parties. This encumbrance shall be known as a "family law attorney's real property lien" and attaches only to the encumbering party's interest in the community real property.

(b) Notice of a family law attorney's real property lien shall be served either personally or on the other party's attorney of record at least 15 days before the encumbrance is recorded. This notice shall contain a declaration signed under penalty of perjury containing all of the following:

(1) A full description of the real property.

(2) The party's belief as to the fair market value of the property and documentation supporting that belief.

(3) Encumbrances on the property as of the date of the declaration.

(4) A list of community assets and liabilities and their estimated values as of the date of the declaration.

(5) The amount of the family law attorney's real property lien.

(c) The nonencumbering party may file an ex parte objection to the family law attorney's real property lien. The objection shall include a request to stay the recordation until further notice of the court and shall contain a copy of the notice received. The objection shall also include a declaration signed under penalty of perjury as to all of the following:

(1) Specific objections to the family law attorney's real property lien and to the specific items in the notice.

(2) The objector's belief as to the appropriate items or value and any documentation supporting that belief.

(3) A declaration specifically stating why recordation of the encumbrance at this time would likely result in an unequal division of property or would otherwise be unjust under the circumstances of the case.

(d) Except as otherwise provided by this section, general procedural rules regarding ex parte motions apply.

(e) An attorney for whom a family law attorney's real property lien is obtained shall comply with Rule 3-300 of the Rules of Professional Conduct of the State Bar of California. *(Added by Stats.1993, c. 219 (A.B.1500), § 106.1.)*

Law Revision Commission Comments

Enactment [Revised Comment]

Section 2033 continues without substantive change former Civil Code Section 4372 relating to the Family Law Attorney's Real Property Lien (FLARPL). In subdivision (a), the reference to a "proceeding for dissolution of marriage, for nullity of marriage, or for legal separation of the parties" replaces the reference in former Section 4372 to an "action under this part," meaning the former Family Law Act (former Part 5 (commencing with former Section 4000) of Division 4 of the Civil Code). [23 Cal.L.Rev.Comm. Reports 1 (1993)].

Commentary

Section 2033 was enacted to carve out a narrow exception to the rule of *Droeger v. Friedman, Sloan & Ross, 54 Cal.3d 26, 812 P.2d 931, 283 Cal.Rptr. 584 (1991)* (a security interest in community realty given by only one spouse may be voided in its entirety by the other spouse during marriage). *Droeger* construed former Civil Code Section 5127, now Family Code Section 1102, which generally requires that both spouses join together to execute any instrument encumbering community realty. After *Droeger*, former Civil Code Section 5127 was amended to exempt liens created in favor of family law attorneys from the general requirement of joinder. For further discussion, see Family Code Section 1102, Commentary.

In re Scott, 400 B.R. 257 (U.S. Bankr. Ct. C.D. California 2009), holds that a debtor may not use 11 U.S.C. § 522(f)(1) to avoid a family law attorney's real property lien recorded on his spouse's interest in community real property.

In re Marriage of Ramirez, 198 Cal.App.4th 336, 132 Cal.Rptr.3d 41 (2011), holds that an attorney holding a lien under this section is an indispensable party to a proceeding to extinguish the lien.

Even though the requirements of this section have been satisfied, *In re Marriage of Turkanis, 213 Cal.App.4th 332, 152 Cal.Rptr.3d 498 (2013), review denied*, held that section 2034 permits a non-encumbering spouse to challenge the propriety of a family law attorney's real property lien that was recorded and to which the spouse consented.

Research References

Forms

California Practice Guide: Rutter Family Law Forms Form 1:17, Family Law Attorney's Real Property Lien.

California Practice Guide: Rutter Family Law Forms Form 1:19, Notice Of Family Law Attorney's Real Property Lien.

California Practice Guide: Rutter Family Law Forms Form 1:20, Ex Parte Application and Request for Order Re Objection to Family Law Attorney's Real Property Lien and Request to Stay Recordation.

West's California Code Forms, Family § 2030, Comment Overview--Attorney's Fees.

West's California Code Forms, Family § 2033 Form 2, Trust Deed Creating Attorney's Lien.

West's California Code Forms, Family § 2033 Form 3, Notice Of Attorney's Real Property Lien.

Treatises and Practice Aids

Witkin, California Summary 10th Community Property § 149, Distinction: Family Law Attorney's Lien.

Witkin, California Summary 10th Husband and Wife § 193, in General.

§ 2034. Denial of lien on real property; limitation of lien amount; determination of appropriate, equitable allocation

(a) On application of either party, the court may deny the family law attorney's real property lien described in Section 2033 based on a finding that the encumbrance would likely result in an unequal division of property because it would impair the encumbering party's ability to meet his or her fair share of the community obligations or would otherwise be unjust under the circumstances of the case. The court may also for good cause limit the amount of the family law attorney's real property lien. A limitation by the court is not to be construed as a determination of reasonable attorney's fees.

(b) On receiving an objection to the establishment of a family law attorney's real property lien, the court may on its own motion determine whether the case involves complex or substantial issues of fact or law related to property rights, visitation, custody, or support. If the court finds that the case involves one or more of these complex or substantial issues, the court may determine the appropriate, equitable allocation of fees and costs as provided in subdivision (d) of Section 2032.

(c) The court has jurisdiction to resolve any dispute arising from the existence of a family law attorney's real property lien. *(Added by Stats.1993, c. 219 (A.B.1500), § 106.1. Amended by Stats.2010, c. 352 (A.B.939), § 6.)*

Law Revision Commission Comments

Enactment [Revised Comment]

Section 2034 continues former Civil Code Section 4373 without substantive change. [23 Cal.L.Rev.Comm. Reports 1 (1993)].

Commentary

In re Marriage of Turkanis, 213 Cal.App.4th 332, 152 Cal.Rptr.3d 498 (2013), review denied, held that this section permits a non-encumbering spouse to challenge the propriety of a family law attorney's real property lien that was recorded and to which the spouse consented.

Research References

Forms

California Practice Guide: Rutter Family Law Forms Form 1:20, Ex Parte Application and Request for Order Re Objection to Family Law Attorney's Real Property Lien and Request to Stay Recordation.

West's California Code Forms, Family § 2030, Comment Overview--Attorney's Fees.

West's California Code Forms, Family § 2033 Form 2, Trust Deed Creating Attorney's Lien.

Treatises and Practice Aids

Witkin, California Summary 10th Community Property § 149, Distinction: Family Law Attorney's Lien.

Witkin, California Summary 10th Husband and Wife § 71, Case Management.

Witkin, California Summary 10th Husband and Wife § 193, in General.

CHAPTER 4. PROTECTIVE AND RESTRAINING ORDERS

ARTICLE 1. ORDERS IN SUMMONS

§ 2040. Temporary restraining order; contents; notice; definitions

(a) In addition to the contents required by Section 412.20 of the Code of Civil Procedure, the summons shall contain a temporary restraining order:

(1) Restraining both parties from removing the minor child or children of the parties, if any, from the state, or from applying for a new or replacement passport for the minor child or children, without the prior written consent of the other party or an order of the court.

(2) Restraining both parties from transferring, encumbering, hypothecating, concealing, or in any way disposing of any property, real or personal, whether community, quasi-community, or separate, without the written consent of the other party or an order of the court, except in the usual course of business or for the necessities of life, and requiring each party to notify the other party of any proposed extraordinary expenditures at least five business days before incurring those expenditures and to account to the court for all extraordinary expenditures made after service of the summons on that party.

Notwithstanding the foregoing, nothing in the restraining order shall preclude a party from using community property, quasi-community property, or the party's own separate property to pay reasonable attorney's fees and costs in order to retain legal counsel in the proceeding. A party who uses community property or quasi-community property to pay his or her attorney's retainer for fees and costs under this provision shall account to the community for the use of the property. A party who uses other property that is subsequently determined to be the separate property of the other party to pay his or her attorney's retainer for fees and costs under this provision shall account to the other party for the use of the property.

(3) Restraining both parties from cashing, borrowing against, canceling, transferring, disposing of, or changing the beneficiaries of any insurance or other coverage, including life, health, automobile, and disability, held for the benefit of the parties and their child or children for whom support may be ordered.

(4) Restraining both parties from creating a nonprobate transfer or modifying a nonprobate transfer in a manner that affects the disposition of property subject to the transfer, without the written consent of the other party or an order of the court.

(b) Nothing in this section restrains any of the following:

(1) Creation, modification, or revocation of a will.

(2) Revocation of a nonprobate transfer, including a revocable trust, pursuant to the instrument, provided that notice of the change is filed and served on the other party before the change takes effect.

(3) Elimination of a right of survivorship to property, provided that notice of the change is filed and served on the other party before the change takes effect.

(4) Creation of an unfunded revocable or irrevocable trust.

(5) Execution and filing of a disclaimer pursuant to Part 8 (commencing with Section 260) of Division 2 of the Probate Code.

(c) In all actions filed on and after January 1, 1995, the summons shall contain the following notice:

"WARNING: California law provides that, for purposes of division of property upon dissolution of marriage or legal separation, property acquired by the parties during marriage in joint form is presumed to be community property. If either party to this action should die before the jointly held community property is divided, the language of how title is held in the deed (i.e., joint tenancy, tenants in common, or community property) will be controlling and not the community property presumption. You should consult your attorney if you want the community property presumption to be written into the recorded title to the property."

(d) For the purposes of this section:

(1) "Nonprobate transfer" means an instrument, other than a will, that makes a transfer of property on death, including a revocable trust, pay on death account in a financial institution, Totten trust, transfer on death registration of personal property, revocable transfer on death deed, or other instrument of a type described in Section 5000 of the Probate Code.

(2) "Nonprobate transfer" does not include a provision for the transfer of property on death in an insurance policy or other coverage held for the benefit of the parties and their child or children for whom support may be ordered, to the extent that the provision is subject to paragraph (3) of subdivision (a).

(e) The restraining order included in the summons shall include descriptions of the notices required by paragraphs (2) and (3) of subdivision (b). *(Added by Stats.1993, c. 219 (A.B.1500), § 106.7. Amended by Stats.1994, c. 1269 (A.B. 2208), § 13; Stats.1999, c. 118 (S.B.357), § 1; Stats.2000, c. 135 (A.B.2539), § 57; Stats.2001, c. 417 (A.B.873), § 2; Stats.2012, c. 276 (S.B.1206), § 2; Stats.2015, c. 293 (A.B. 139), § 2, eff. Jan. 1, 2016.)*

Law Revision Commission Comments

Enactment [Revised Comment]

The introductory part of Section 2040 restates the first sentence of former Code of Civil Procedure Section 412.21(a) without substantive change. Subdivisions (a), (b), and (c) continue former Code of Civil Procedure Section 412.21(a)(1)–(3) without substantive change. The former limitation to proceedings commenced on or after July 1, 1990, has been omitted as obsolete. The former language limiting application of the former section to dissolution, nullity, or legal separation proceedings has been omitted as surplus. See Section 2000 (application of part). In subdivision (c), a reference to a "child for whom support may be ordered" has been substituted for the former reference to a "minor" child. This is not a substantive change, but rather recognizes that support may be ordered for children who are not minors. See Section 58 ("child for whom support may be ordered" defined).

For general provisions on temporary restraining orders in summons, see Part 3 (commencing with Section 231) of Division 2. [23 Cal.L.Rev.Comm. Reports 1 (1993)].

2001 Amendment

Section 2040 is amended to clarify the scope of the automatic temporary restraining order with respect to estate planning changes.

Subdivision (a)(4) restrains modification of a nonprobate transfer "in a manner that affects the disposition of property subject to the transfer." Modifications that are restrained as affecting the disposition of property include a change of beneficiary and a donor's modification of the terms of a power of appointment (this would not include exercise of a power of appointment by a donee). Modifications that are not restrained include naming a new trustee or successor trustee (so long as the change does not affect the trustee's powers or duties with respect to disposition of trust property).

Subdivision (b)(2) provides that the restraining order does not restrain revocation of a nonprobate transfer, provided that notice of the change has been filed and served on the other party. This does not mean that a nonprobate transfer is necessarily subject to revocation by one party without the consent of the other party. The question of whether a nonprobate transfer is subject to unilateral revocation is governed by the terms of the nonprobate transfer and applicable substantive law. See, e.g., Prob. Code 5506 (action by all surviving joint owners required to cancel beneficiary registration of jointly-owned security); 31 C.F.R. 353.51 (2000) (restricting changes in ownership of jointly-owned Series EE savings bond).

Subdivision (b)(3) provides that the restraining order does not restrain elimination of a right of survivorship, provided that notice of the change has been filed and served on the other party. This is consistent with *Estate of Mitchell*, 76 Cal.App.4th 1378, 91 Cal. Rptr.2d 192 (1999) (restraining order does not restrain severance of joint tenancy).

Subdivision (b)(4) provides that the restraining order does not restrain creation of one or more revocable or irrevocable unfunded trusts. However, the transfer of property to fund a trust would be restrained under subdivision (a)(2). An unfunded trust created during a dissolution proceeding could serve as a receptacle for property subject to a pour-over provision in a will. Such a trust could also be funded by property that has been released from restraint by the restraining order.

Subdivision (d) defines "nonprobate transfer" for the purposes of this section. The definition expressly incorporates instruments described in Probate Code Section 5000, including a "marital property agreement." Thus, an agreement between spouses as to how to divide community property between them on either of their deaths is a nonprobate transfer for the purposes of this section. See Prob. Code 100(b) (agreement as to division of community property on death of spouse). [31 Cal.L.Rev.Comm. Reports 75 (2001)].

2015 Amendment

Section 2040 is amended to make explicit its application to a revocable TOD deed. See Part 4 (commencing with Section 5600) of Division 5 of the Probate Code (revocable transfer on death deed). [36 Cal.L.Rev.Comm. Reports 103 (2006)].

Commentary

Goold v. Superior Court, 145 Cal.App.4th 1, 51 Cal.Rptr.3d 455 (2006), sustained a trial court's award to a wife of attorney's fees under subsection (a) and the imposition on her husband of 360 hours in custody under subsection (c) of section 1218 of the Code of Civil Procedure, after finding the husband in contempt for repeatedly violating this section's restraining orders prohibiting either spouse from encumbering or transferring property during dissolution proceedings.

Estate of Mitchell, 76 Cal.App.4th 1378, 91 Cal.Rptr.2d 192 (1999), holds that severance of a joint tenancy by recordation of a declaration of severance is not a "transfer" or "disposition" within the meaning of subsection (a)(2) and therefore does not violate the temporary restraining order issued under this section.

Applying subsection (a)(2), *Gale v. Superior Court, 122 Cal.App.4th 1388, 19 Cal.Rptr.3d 554 (2004)*, notes that prima facie evidence that property is being sold in the ordinary course of business exempts the sale from the automatic operation of the restraining order, but points out that the party resisting sale may nevertheless seek a restraining order.

In *Minnesota Mutual Life Insurance Company v. Ensley, 174 F.3d 977 (9th Cir. 1999)*, the Ninth Circuit Court of Appeals held that a divorcing husband's change of beneficiary designation of his life insurance from his wife to his brother did not violate an Arizona divorce court's preliminary injunction restraining either party from "transferring . . . or otherwise disposing of . . . any community property" because, under Arizona law, the wife would still realize her one-half community property interest in the proceeds. However, the husband's change of beneficiary designation would violate a California restraining order. See subsection (a)(3).

When a spouse violated the subsection (a)(2) automatic restraining order by selling community securities without a court order or the other spouse's consent, the trial court, under subsections (a) and (g) of Section 1101, properly awarded the wronged spouse one-half of the lost profits, that is, the appreciation of the securities between the date of sale and the subsequent divorce. *In re Marriage of McTiernan & Dubrow, 133 Cal.App.4th 1090, 35 Cal.Rptr.3d 287 (2005), review denied.*

The warning required by subsection (c) is somewhat misleading. The warning accurately states California law when the death of a spouse abates the divorce action before any decree has been entered. *Estate of Blair, 199 Cal.App.3d 161, 244 Cal.Rptr. 627 (1988).* However, if the divorce proceeding has been bifurcated and the decree of divorce has already been entered before the death of either party, Probate Code section 5601 severs a decedent's interest in a joint tenancy.

Research References

Forms

California Practice Guide: Rutter Family Law Forms Form 1:32, Glossary Of Common Family Law Terms, Phrases and Concepts (Enclosure to Form 1:31).

West's California Judicial Council Forms FL-110, Summons (Family Law).

West's California Judicial Council Forms FL-210, Summons (Percentage - Custody and Support).

Treatises and Practice Aids

Witkin, California Summary 10th Husband and Wife § 6, Order in Summons.

Witkin, California Summary 10th Husband and Wife § 75, Process.

Witkin, California Summary 10th Husband and Wife § 87, Methods Of Obtaining Orders.

Witkin, California Summary 10th Husband and Wife § 88, Order in Summons.

Witkin, California Summary 10th Real Property § 63, Severance Under Statute is Not Transfer Of Property.

§ 2041. Application of temporary restraining order provisions to rights, title and interest of purchaser for value

Nothing in Section 2040 adversely affects the rights, title, and interest of a purchaser for value, encumbrancer for value, or lessee for value who is without actual knowledge of the restraining order. *(Added by Stats.1993, c. 219 (A.B.1500), § 106.7.)*

Law Revision Commission Comments

Enactment [Revised Comment]

Section 2041 is new. [23 Cal.L.Rev.Comm. Reports 1 (1993)].

Research References

Treatises and Practice Aids

Witkin, California Summary 10th Husband and Wife § 88, Order in Summons.

ARTICLE 2. EX PARTE ORDERS

§ 2045. Ex parte protective orders

During the pendency of the proceeding, on application of a party in the manner provided by Part 4 (commencing with Section 240) of Division 2, the court may issue ex parte any of the following orders:

(a) An order restraining any person from transferring, encumbering, hypothecating, concealing, or in any way disposing of any property, real or personal, whether community, quasi-community, or separate, except in the usual course of business or for the necessities of life, and if the order is directed against a party, requiring that party to notify the other party of any proposed extraordinary expenditures and to account to the court for all extraordinary expenditures.

(b) A protective order, as defined in Section 6218, and any other order as provided in Article 1 (commencing with Section 6320) of Chapter 2 of Part 4 of Division 10. *(Added by Stats.1993, c. 219 (A.B.1500), § 106.7.)*

Law Revision Commission Comments

Enactment [Revised Comment]

The introductory clause of Section 2045 restates without substantive change the introductory clause of former Civil Code Section 4359(a). A reference to the "superior" court has been omitted as surplus. See Section 200 (jurisdiction in superior court). The former reference to Code of Civil Procedure Section 527 has been omitted. This is not a substantive change. See Section 240 & Comment.

Subdivision (a) continues without substantive change former Civil Code Section 4359(a)(1).

Subdivision (b) is new and has been added to provide a reference to the provisions in Division 10 (Domestic Violence Prevention Act) for the issuance of ex parte restraining orders intended to prevent domestic violence. See also Section 6221 (application of division) & Comment.

For general provisions relating to ex parte restraining orders, see Part 4 (commencing with Section 240) of Division 2. See also Sections 2000 (application of part), 6303 (support person for victim of domestic violence). [23 Cal.L.Rev.Comm. Reports 1 (1993)].

Commentary

See generally *Schnabel v. Superior Court, 21 Cal.App.4th 548, 26 Cal.Rptr.2d 169 (1993)* (*Schnabel III*).

Research References

Forms

California Practice Guide: Rutter Family Law Forms Form 5:5, Ex Parte Application and Request for Order Re Child Custody, Visitation and Property Control.

West's California Code Forms, Family § 2045, Comment Overview--Ex Parte Protective Orders.

West's California Judicial Council Forms FL-300, Request for Order.

West's California Judicial Council Forms FL-303, Declaration Regarding Notice and Service Of Request for Temporary Emergency (Ex Parte) Orders.

West's California Judicial Council Forms FL-305, Temporary Emergency Court Orders.

West's California Judicial Council Forms FL-344, Property Order Attachment to Findings and Order After Hearing.

Treatises and Practice Aids

Witkin, California Summary 10th Husband and Wife § 86, in General.

Witkin, California Summary 10th Husband and Wife § 89, Other Orders.

Witkin, California Summary 10th Husband and Wife § 12B, (New) Amount Of Filing Fees.

Witkin, California Summary 10th Husband and Wife § 382, in General.

Witkin, California Summary 10th Parent and Child § 271, Temporary Custody During Pendency Of Proceeding.

Witkin, California Summary 10th Parent and Child § 653, Ex Parte Orders Pending Nullity or Dissolution Proceedings.

ARTICLE 3. ORDERS AFTER NOTICE AND HEARING

§ 2047. Protective orders; restraining orders

(a) After notice and a hearing, the court may issue a protective order, as defined in Section 6218, and any other restraining order as provided in Article 2 (commencing with Section 6340) of Chapter 2 of Part 4 of Division 10.

(b) The court may not issue a mutual protective order pursuant to subdivision (a) unless it meets the requirements of Section 6305. *(Added by Stats.1993, c. 219 (A.B.1500), § 106.7. Amended by Stats.1995, c. 246 (S.B.591), § 1.)*

Law Revision Commission Comments

Enactment [Revised Comment]

Section 2047 is new. The former Family Law Act, applicable to dissolution, nullity, and legal separation proceedings, did not contain a general provision for the issuance, after notice and hearing, of restraining orders intended to prevent domestic violence, despite a provision for issuance of an order excluding a party from a dwelling after notice and hearing. The addition of this general provision is not a substantive change. See Cal. R. Ct. 1296.29 (July 1, 1991) (restraining order after hearing).

This section is added to provide a reference to the provisions in Division 10 (Domestic Violence Prevention Act) for the issuance, after notice and hearing, of restraining orders intended to prevent domestic violence. See also Sections 2000 (application of part), 6221 (application of division), 6303 (support person for victim of domestic violence). [23 Cal.L.Rev.Comm. Reports 1 (1993)].

Research References

Forms

West's California Code Forms, Family § 2047, Comment Overview--Orders After Notice and Hearing.

Treatises and Practice Aids

Witkin, California Summary 10th Husband and Wife § 89, Other Orders.

Witkin, California Summary 10th Husband and Wife § 12B, (New) Amount Of Filing Fees.

ARTICLE 4. ORDERS INCLUDED IN JUDGMENT

§ 2049. Protective orders included in judgments; restraining orders

A judgment may include a protective order, as defined in Section 6218, and any other restraining order as provided in Article 3 (commencing with Section 6360) of Chapter 2 of Part 4 of Division 10. *(Added by Stats.1993, c. 219 (A.B. 1500), § 106.7.)*

Law Revision Commission Comments

Enactment [Revised Comment]

Section 2049 is new and is added to provide a reference to the provisions in Division 10 (Domestic Violence Prevention Act) that authorizing restraining orders intended to prevent domestic violence to be included in a judgment. See Section 6200 Comment (consolidation of substantive provisions regarding issuance of restraining orders intended to prevent domestic violence). See also Sections 2000 (application of part), 6221 (application of division), 6303 (support person for victim of domestic violence). [23 Cal.L.Rev. Comm. Reports 1 (1993)].

Research References

Forms

West's California Code Forms, Family § 2049, Comment Overview--Orders Included in Judgment.

Treatises and Practice Aids

Witkin, California Summary 10th Husband and Wife § 112, Contents Of Judgment.

Witkin, California Summary 10th Husband and Wife § 12B, (New) Amount Of Filing Fees.

CHAPTER 5. NOTICE TO INSURANCE CARRIERS

§ 2050. Notice to health, life, or disability insurance carrier; form

Upon filing of the petition, or at any time during the proceeding, a party may transmit to, or the court may order transmittal to, a health, life, or disability insurance carrier or plan the following notice in substantially the following form:

"YOU ARE HEREBY NOTIFIED, PURSUANT TO A PENDING PROCEEDING, IN RE MARRIAGE OF ________, CASE NUMBER ________, FILED IN THE SUPERIOR COURT OF THE STATE OF CALIFORNIA, COUNTY OF ________, THAT OWNERSHIP OF, OR BENEFITS PAYABLE UNDER, A POLICY OF HEALTH, LIFE, OR DISABILITY INSURANCE WHICH YOU HAVE ISSUED TO ONE OF THE PARTIES TO THIS PROCEEDING, POLICY NO. ________, IS AT ISSUE OR MAY BE AT ISSUE IN THE PROCEEDING.

YOU ARE HEREBY INSTRUCTED TO MAINTAIN THE NAMED BENEFICIARIES OR COVERED DEPENDENTS UNDER THE POLICY, UNLESS THE TERMS OF THE POLICY OR OTHER PROVISIONS OF LAW REQUIRE OTHERWISE, OR UNTIL RECEIPT OF A COURT ORDER, JUDGMENT, OR STIPULATION BETWEEN THE PARTIES PROVIDING OTHER INSTRUCTIONS.

YOU ARE FURTHER INSTRUCTED TO SEND NOTICE TO THE NAMED BENEFICIARIES, COVERED DEPENDENTS, OR OTHER SPECIFIED PERSONS UPON CANCELLATION, LAPSE, OR CHANGE OF THE COVERAGE, OR CHANGE OF DESIGNATED BENEFICIARIES UNDER THE POLICY." *(Stats.1992, c. 162 (A.B.2650), § 10, operative Jan. 1, 1994.)*

Law Revision Commission Comments

Enactment [Revised Comment]

Section 2050 continues former Civil Code Section 4366(a) without substantive change. The language limiting the application of the former section to dissolution, nullity, or legal separation proceedings has been omitted as surplus. See Section 2000 (application of part). [23 Cal.L.Rev.Comm. Reports 1 (1993)].

Research References

Forms

California Practice Guide: Rutter Family Law Forms Form 3:7, Notice Of Pending Proceeding to Health/Life/Disability Insurance Carrier (Family Code § 2050).

California Practice Guide: Rutter Family Law Forms Form 6:13, Notice to Health/Life/Disability Carrier Of Order to Maintain Insurance Coverage (Family Code § 2051).

West's California Code Forms, Family § 2050, Comment Overview--Notice to Insurance Carrier.

Treatises and Practice Aids

Witkin, California Summary 10th Husband and Wife § 85, Notices Concerning Insurance.

§ 2051. Transmittal of order or judgment and notice

Upon the entry of an order or judgment in the proceeding requiring a party to maintain existing health, life, or disability insurance coverage for a spouse or children or after an order or judgment in the proceeding requiring a party to purchase life or disability insurance and name the spouse or children as beneficiaries and upon receipt of the name, title, and address of the insurer, or the name of the plan's trustee, administrator, or agent for service of process, a party may transmit to, or the court may order transmittal to, the insurer or plan a copy of the order or judgment endorsed by the court, together with the following notice in substantially the following form:

"PURSUANT TO A PROCEEDING, IN RE MARRIAGE OF ________, CASE NUMBER ________, IN THE SUPERIOR COURT OF THE STATE OF CALIFORNIA, COUNTY OF ________, YOUR INSURED, ________, HAS BEEN ORDERED TO MAINTAIN THE EXISTING (HEALTH) (LIFE) (DISABILITY) INSURANCE COVERAGE, POLICY NO. ________, IN FORCE FOR THE NAMED BENEFICIARIES OR COVERED DEPENDENTS AS SPECIFIED IN THE ATTACHED ORDER OR JUDGMENT.

THE ATTACHED ORDER OR JUDGMENT REQUIRES YOU TO MAINTAIN THE NAMED BENEFICIARIES UNDER THE POLICY AS IRREVOCABLE BENEFICIARIES OR COVERED DEPENDENTS OF THE POLICY AND YOU MUST ADMINISTER THE COVERAGE ACCORDINGLY, UNTIL THE DATE SPECIFIED, IF ANY, IN THE ORDER OR JUDGMENT, OR UNTIL THE RECEIPT OF A COURT ORDER, JUDGMENT, OR STIPULATION PROVIDING OTHER INSTRUCTIONS.

YOU ARE FURTHER INSTRUCTED TO SEND NOTICE TO THE NAMED BENEFICIARIES, COVERED DEPENDENTS, OR OTHER SPECIFIED PERSONS UPON ANY CANCELLATION, LAPSE, OR CHANGE OF COVERAGE, OR CHANGE OF DESIGNATED BENEFICIARIES UNDER THIS POLICY." *(Stats.1992, c. 162 (A.B.2650), § 10, operative Jan. 1, 1994.)*

Law Revision Commission Comments

Enactment [Revised Comment]

Section 2051 continues former Civil Code Section 4366(b) without substantive change. The language limiting the application of the former section to dissolution, nullity, or legal separation proceedings has been omitted as surplus. See Section 2000 (application of part). [23 Cal.L.Rev.Comm. Reports 1 (1993)].

Research References

Forms

California Practice Guide: Rutter Family Law Forms Form 6:13, Notice to Health/Life/Disability Carrier Of Order to Maintain Insurance Coverage (Family Code S2051).

West's California Code Forms, Family § 2050, Comment Overview--Notice to Insurance Carrier.

Treatises and Practice Aids

Witkin, California Summary 10th Husband and Wife § 85, Notices Concerning Insurance.

§ 2052. Method of notice

Notice pursuant to this chapter may be sent by first-class mail, postage prepaid, to the last known address of the covered dependents, named beneficiaries, or other specified persons who have requested receipt of notification. *(Stats. 1992, c. 162 (A.B.2650), § 10, operative Jan. 1, 1994.)*

Law Revision Commission Comments

Enactment [Revised Comment]

Section 2052 continues former Civil Code Section 4366(c) without substantive change. A reference to "first class" mail has been substituted for the former reference to "regular" mail to conform to similar sections that allow service of similar notices by mail. See, e.g., Section 5252 (service of notice of intent to seek earnings assignment order for support). [23 Cal.L.Rev.Comm. Reports 1 (1993)].

Research References

Forms

West's California Code Forms, Family § 2050, Comment Overview--Notice to Insurance Carrier.

Treatises and Practice Aids

Witkin, California Summary 10th Husband and Wife § 85, Notices Concerning Insurance.

§ 2053. Insured or policyholder to furnish information to other party

The insured or policyholder who is a party to the proceeding shall furnish to the other party the name, title, and address of the insurer or the insurer's agent for service of process. *(Stats.1992, c. 162 (A.B.2650), § 10, operative Jan. 1, 1994.)*

Law Revision Commission Comments

Enactment [Revised Comment]

Section 2053 continues former Civil Code Section 4366(d) without change. [23 Cal.L.Rev.Comm. Reports 1 (1993)].

Research References

Forms

West's California Code Forms, Family § 2050, Comment Overview--Notice to Insurance Carrier.

Treatises and Practice Aids

Witkin, California Summary 10th Husband and Wife § 85, Notices Concerning Insurance.

CHAPTER 6. EMPLOYEE PENSION BENEFIT PLAN AS PARTY

ARTICLE 1. JOINDER OF PLAN

§ 2060. Application and order for joinder

(a) Upon written application by a party, the clerk shall enter an order joining as a party to the proceeding any employee benefit plan in which either party to the proceeding claims an interest that is or may be subject to disposition by the court.

(b) An order or judgment in the proceeding is not enforceable against an employee benefit plan unless the plan has been joined as a party to the proceeding. *(Stats.1992, c. 162 (A.B.2650), § 10, operative Jan. 1, 1994. Amended by Stats.1996, c. 1061 (S.B.1033), § 4.)*

Law Revision Commission Comments

Enactment [Revised Comment]

Subdivision (a) of Section 2060 continues the first sentence of former Civil Code Section 4363.1(a) without substantive change. The reference to a proceeding under "this part," meaning the former Family Law Act (former Part 5 (commencing with former Section 4000) of Division 4 of the Civil Code), has been omitted as surplus. See Section 2000 (application to dissolution, nullity, or legal separation proceedings).

Subdivision (b) continues the last part of former Civil Code Section 4351 without substantive change. For an exception to this general rule, see Section 5103 (support order enforceable against employee pension benefit plan regardless of whether joined as party). See also Sections 80 ("employee pension benefit plan" defined), 755 (discharge of employee benefit plan from adverse claims). [23 Cal.L.Rev.Comm. Reports 1 (1993)].

Research References

Forms

West's California Code Forms, Family § 2060, Comment Overview--Application and Order for Joinder.
West's California Code Forms, Family § 2061 Form 1, Pleading on Joinder.
West's California Judicial Council Forms FL-370, Pleading on Joinder--Employee Benefit Plan.
West's California Judicial Council Forms FL-372, Request for Joinder Of Employee Benefit Plan and Order.
West's California Judicial Council Forms FL-374, Notice Of Appearance and Response Of Employee Benefit Plan.

Treatises and Practice Aids

Witkin, California Summary 10th Husband and Wife § 78, Joinder Of Third Persons.
Witkin, California Summary 10th Husband and Wife § 79, in General.
Witkin, California Summary 10th Husband and Wife § 80, Joinder Of Plan.
Witkin, California Summary 10th Husband and Wife § 264, Enforcement Against Employee Benefit Plan.

§ 2061. Pleading of party requesting joinder

Upon entry of the order under Section 2060, the party requesting joinder shall file an appropriate pleading setting forth the party's claim against the plan and the nature of the relief sought. *(Stats.1992, c. 162 (A.B.2650), § 10, operative Jan. 1, 1994.)*

Law Revision Commission Comments

Enactment [Revised Comment]

Section 2061 continues the second sentence of former Civil Code Section 4363.1(a) without substantive change. See also Sections 80 ("employee pension benefit plan" defined), 755 (discharge of employee benefit plan from adverse claims), 2000 (application to dissolution, nullity, or legal separation proceedings). [23 Cal.L.Rev. Comm. Reports 1 (1993)].

Research References

Forms

West's California Code Forms, Family § 2060, Comment Overview--Application and Order for Joinder.

Treatises and Practice Aids

Witkin, California Summary 10th Husband and Wife § 80, Joinder Of Plan.

§ 2062. Service of documents by party requesting joinder

(a) The party requesting joinder shall serve all of the following upon the employee benefit plan:

(1) A copy of the pleading on joinder.

(2) A copy of the request for joinder and order of joinder.

(3) A copy of the summons (joinder).

(4) A blank copy of a notice of appearance in form and content approved by the Judicial Council.

(b) Service shall be made in the same manner as service of papers generally. Service of the summons upon a trustee or administrator of the plan in its capacity as trustee or administrator, or upon an agent designated by the plan for service of process in its capacity as agent, constitutes service upon the plan.

(c) To facilitate identification and service, the employee spouse shall furnish to the nonemployee spouse within 30 days after written request, as to each employee benefit plan covering the employee, the name of the plan, the name, title, address, and telephone number of the plan's trustee, administrator, or agent for service of process. If necessary, the employee shall obtain the information from the plan or plan sponsor. *(Stats.1992, c. 162 (A.B.2650), § 10, operative Jan. 1, 1994. Amended by Stats.1994, c. 1269 (A.B.2208), § 15.)*

Law Revision Commission Comments

Enactment [Revised Comment]

Section 2062 restates the last four sentences of former Civil Code Section 4363.1(a) without substantive change. See also Sections 80 ("employee pension benefit plan" defined), 755 (discharge of employee benefit plan from adverse claims), 2000 (application to dissolution, nullity, or legal separation proceedings). [23 Cal.L.Rev. Comm. Reports 1 (1993)].

Research References

Forms

West's California Code Forms, Family § 2060, Comment Overview--Application and Order for Joinder.

Treatises and Practice Aids

Witkin, California Summary 10th Husband and Wife § 80, Joinder Of Plan.

§ 2063. Employee pension benefit plan; notice of appearance; responsive pleadings

(a) The employee benefit plan shall file and serve a copy of a notice of appearance upon the party requesting joinder within 30 days of the date of the service upon the plan of a copy of the joinder request and summons.

(b) The employee benefit plan may, but need not, file an appropriate responsive pleading with its notice of appearance. If the plan does not file a responsive pleading, all statements of fact and requests for relief contained in any pleading served on the plan are deemed to be controverted by the plan's notice of appearance. *(Stats.1992, c. 162 (A.B. 2650), § 10, operative Jan. 1, 1994. Amended by Stats.1994, c. 1269 (A.B.2208), § 16.)*

Law Revision Commission Comments

Enactment [Revised Comment]

Subdivision (a) of Section 2063 continues the first sentence of former Civil Code Section 4363.1(b) without substantive change. Subdivision (b) continues former Civil Code Section 4363.2(b) without substantive change. See also Sections 80 ("employee pension benefit plan" defined), 755 (discharge of employee benefit plan from adverse claims), 2000 (application to dissolution, nullity, or legal separation proceedings). [23 Cal.L.Rev.Comm. Reports 1 (1993)].

Research References

Forms

West's California Code Forms, Family § 2060, Comment Overview--Application and Order for Joinder.

West's California Code Forms, Family § 2063 Form 1, Notice Of Appearance and Response Of Employee Pension Benefit Plan.

Treatises and Practice Aids

Witkin, California Summary 10th Husband and Wife § 80, Joinder Of Plan.

§ 2064. Filing fees

Notwithstanding any contrary provision of law, the employee benefit plan is not required to pay any fee to the clerk of the court as a condition to filing the notice of appearance or any subsequent paper in the proceeding. *(Stats.1992, c. 162 (A.B.2650), § 10, operative Jan. 1, 1994. Amended by Stats. 1994, c. 1269 (A.B.2208), § 17.)*

Law Revision Commission Comments

Enactment [Revised Comment]

Section 2064 continues the last sentence of former Civil Code Section 4363.1(b) without substantive change. See also Sections 80 ("employee pension benefit plan" defined), 755 (discharge of employee benefit plan from adverse claims), 2000 (application to dissolution, nullity, or legal separation proceedings). [23 Cal.L.Rev. Comm. Reports 1 (1993)].

Research References

Treatises and Practice Aids

Witkin, California Summary 10th Husband and Wife § 80, Joinder Of Plan.

§ 2065. Default of plan

If the employee benefit plan has been served and no notice of appearance, notice of motion to quash service of summons pursuant to Section 418.10 of the Code of Civil Procedure, or notice of the filing of a petition for writ of mandate as provided in that section, has been filed with the clerk of the court within the time specified in the summons or such further time as may be allowed, the clerk, upon written application of the party requesting joinder, shall enter the default of the employee benefit plan in accordance with Chapter 2 (commencing with Section 585) of Title 8 of Part 2 of the Code of Civil Procedure. *(Stats.1992, c. 162 (A.B. 2650), § 10, operative Jan. 1, 1994. Amended by Stats.1994, c. 1269 (A.B.2208), § 18.)*

Law Revision Commission Comments

Enactment [Revised Comment]

Section 2065 continues former Civil Code Section 4363.1(c) without substantive change. See also Sections 80 ("employee pension benefit plan" defined), 755 (discharge of employee benefit plan from adverse claims), 2000 (application to dissolution, nullity, or legal separation proceedings). [23 Cal.L.Rev.Comm. Reports 1 (1993)].

Research References

Forms

West's California Code Forms, Family § 2060, Comment Overview--Application and Order for Joinder.

West's California Judicial Council Forms FL-370, Pleading on Joinder--Employee Benefit Plan.

West's California Judicial Council Forms FL-372, Request for Joinder Of Employee Benefit Plan and Order.

West's California Judicial Council Forms FL-374, Notice Of Appearance and Response Of Employee Benefit Plan.

Treatises and Practice Aids

Witkin, California Summary 10th Husband and Wife § 80, Joinder Of Plan.

ARTICLE 2. PROCEEDINGS AFTER JOINDER

§ 2070. Application of article; application of law applicable to civil actions

(a) This article governs a proceeding in which an employee benefit plan has been joined as a party.

(b) To the extent not in conflict with this article and except as otherwise provided by rules adopted by the Judicial Council pursuant to Section 211, all provisions of law applicable to civil actions generally apply, regardless of nomenclature, to the portion of the proceeding as to which an employee benefit plan has been joined as a party if those provisions would otherwise apply to the proceeding without reference to this article. *(Stats.1992, c. 162 (A.B.2650), § 10, operative Jan. 1, 1994. Amended by Stats.1994, c. 1269 (A.B.2208), § 19.)*

Law Revision Commission Comments

Enactment [Revised Comment]

Section 2070 continues former Civil Code Section 4363.2(a) without substantive change. See also Sections 80 ("employee pension benefit plan" defined), 755 (discharge of employee benefit plan from adverse claims), 2000 (application to dissolution, nullity, or legal separation proceedings). [23 Cal.L.Rev.Comm. Reports 1 (1993)].

Research References

Forms

West's California Code Forms, Family § 2060, Comment Overview--Application and Order for Joinder.

West's California Judicial Council Forms FL-372, Request for Joinder Of Employee Benefit Plan and Order.

West's California Judicial Council Forms FL-374, Notice Of Appearance and Response Of Employee Benefit Plan.

Treatises and Practice Aids

Witkin, California Summary 10th Husband and Wife § 81, Proceedings After Joinder.

§ 2071. Notice and reply to proposed property settlement

Either party or their representatives may notify the employee benefit plan of any proposed property settlement as it concerns the plan before any hearing at which the proposed property settlement will be a matter before the court. If so notified, the plan may stipulate to the proposed settlement or advise the representative that it will contest the proposed settlement. *(Stats.1992, c. 162 (A.B.2650), § 10, operative Jan. 1, 1994. Amended by Stats.1994, c. 1269 (A.B.2208), § 20.)*

Law Revision Commission Comments

Enactment [Revised Comment]

Section 2071 continues former Civil Code Section 4363.2(c) without substantive change. The phrase "before any hearing at which the proposed property settlement will be a matter before the court" has been substituted for "prior to the interlocutory hearing." This is a technical, nonsubstantive change. See also Sections 80 ("employee pension benefit plan" defined), 755 (discharge of employee benefit plan from adverse claims), 2000 (application to dissolution, nullity, or legal separation proceedings). [23 Cal.L.Rev. Comm. Reports 1 (1993)].

Research References

Treatises and Practice Aids

Witkin, California Summary 10th Husband and Wife § 81, Proceedings After Joinder.

§ 2072. Hearings; appearances

The employee benefit plan is not required to, but may, appear at any hearing in the proceeding. For purposes of the Code of Civil Procedure, the plan shall be considered a party appearing at the trial with respect to any hearing at which the interest of the parties in the plan is an issue before the court. *(Stats.1992, c. 162 (A.B.2650), § 10, operative Jan. 1, 1994. Amended by Stats.1994, c. 1269 (A.B.2208), § 21.)*

Law Revision Commission Comments

Enactment [Revised Comment]

Section 2072 continues without substantive change the first two sentences of the first paragraph of former Civil Code Section 4363.2(d). See also Sections 80 ("employee pension benefit plan" defined), 755 (discharge of employee benefit plan from adverse claims), 2000 (application to dissolution, nullity, or legal separation proceedings). [23 Cal.L.Rev.Comm. Reports 1 (1993)].

Research References

Treatises and Practice Aids

Witkin, California Summary 10th Husband and Wife § 81, Proceedings After Joinder.

§ 2073. Order affecting plan; stay

(a) Subject to subdivisions (b) and (c), the provisions of an order entered by stipulation of the parties or entered at or as a result of a hearing not attended by the employee benefit plan (whether or not the plan received notice of the hearing) which affect the plan or which affect any interest either the petitioner or respondent may have or claim under the plan, shall be stayed until 30 days after the order has been served upon the plan.

(b) The plan may waive all or any portion of the 30-day period under subdivision (a).

(c) If within the 30-day period, the plan files in the proceeding a motion to set aside or modify those provisions of the order affecting it, those provisions shall be stayed until the court has resolved the motion.

(d) The duration of the stay described in subdivision (a), and the time period for filing the motion to set aside or modify provisions of the order, shall be extended to 60 days if the plan files with the court and serves on all affected parties a request for extension within the 30-day period.

(e) Either spousal party may seek an order staying any other provisions of the order and associated orders or judgments related to or affected by the provisions to which the plan has objected, until the court has resolved the motion, in order to protect the right of the party to seek relief under subdivision (c) of Section 2074. *(Stats.1992, c. 162 (A.B. 2650), § 10, operative Jan. 1, 1994. Amended by Stats.1994, c. 1269 (A.B.2208), § 22.)*

Law Revision Commission Comments

Enactment [Revised Comment]

Section 2073 continues without substantive change the last two sentences of the first paragraph of former Civil Code Section 4363.2(d). See also Sections 80 ("employee pension benefit plan" defined), 755 (discharge of employee benefit plan from adverse claims), 2000 (application to dissolution, nullity, or legal separation proceedings). [23 Cal.L.Rev.Comm. Reports 1 (1993)].

Research References

Treatises and Practice Aids

Witkin, California Summary 10th Husband and Wife § 81, Proceedings After Joinder.

§ 2074. Motion to set aside or modify; hearing

(a) At any hearing on a motion to set aside or modify an order pursuant to Section 2073, any party may present further evidence on any issue relating to the rights of the parties under the employee benefit plan or the extent of the parties' community or quasi-community property interest in the plan, except where the parties have agreed in writing to the contrary.

(b) Any statement of decision issued by the court with respect to the order which is the subject of the motion shall take account of the evidence referred to in subdivision (a).

(c) If the provisions of the order affecting the employee benefit plan are modified or set aside, the court, on motion by either party, may set aside or modify other provisions of the order and associated orders or judgments related to or affected by the provisions affecting the plan. *(Stats.1992, c. 162 (A.B.2650), § 10, operative Jan. 1, 1994. Amended by Stats.1994, c. 1269 (A.B.2208), § 23.)*

Law Revision Commission Comments

Enactment [Revised Comment]

Subdivisions (a) and (b) of Section 2074 continue former Civil Code Section 4363.2(e) without substantive change. Subdivision (c) continues the last paragraph of former Civil Code Section 4363.2(d) without substantive change. In subdivision (a), a reference to Section 2073 has been substituted for the broader reference to former Civil Code Section 4363.2(d). This is not a substantive change, since the relevant part of the former subdivision is continued in Section 2073.

See also Sections 65 ("community property" defined in Section 760 *et seq.*), 80 ("employee pension benefit plan" defined), 125 ("quasi-community property" defined), 755 (discharge of employee benefit plan from adverse claims), 2000 (application to dissolution, nullity, or legal separation proceedings). [23 Cal.L.Rev.Comm. Reports 1 (1993)].

Research References

Forms

West's California Code Forms, Family § 2060, Comment Overview--Application and Order for Joinder.

West's California Judicial Council Forms FL-372, Request for Joinder Of Employee Benefit Plan and Order.

West's California Judicial Council Forms FL-374, Notice Of Appearance and Response Of Employee Benefit Plan.

Treatises and Practice Aids

Witkin, California Summary 10th Husband and Wife § 81, Proceedings After Joinder.

CHAPTER 7. RESTORATION OF WIFE'S FORMER NAME

§ 2080. Request for restoration

In a proceeding for dissolution of marriage or for nullity of marriage, but not in a proceeding for legal separation of the parties, the court, upon the request of a party, shall restore the birth name or former name of that party, regardless of whether or not a request for restoration of the name was included in the petition. *(Stats.1992, c. 162 (A.B.2650), § 10, operative Jan. 1, 1994. Amended by Stats.1996, c. 1061 (S.B.1033), § 5.)*

Law Revision Commission Comments

Enactment [Revised Comment]

Section 2080 continues former Civil Code Sections 4362(a) and 4457(a) without substantive change. This section retains the application of the former sections to proceedings for dissolution and nullity, but not to proceedings for legal separation.

Former Civil Code Sections 4362(d) and 4457(d), which prohibited certain actions by businesses based on a woman's use of her birth name or former name, are continued in Code of Civil Procedure Section 1279.6 without substantive change. [23 Cal.L.Rev.Comm. Reports 1 (1993)].

Commentary

For the legislative history of prior versions of this statute, see *In re Marriage of Banks, 42 Cal.App.3d 631, 634–638, 117 Cal.Rptr. 37 (1974)*. The current provision makes restoration of a party's former name mandatory, rather than discretionary, upon request.

Research References

Forms

West's California Code Forms, Family § 2080, Comment Overview--Request for Restoration.

West's California Judicial Council Forms FL-395, Ex Parte Application for Restoration Of Former Name After Entry Of Judgment and Order.

Treatises and Practice Aids

Witkin, California Summary 10th Husband and Wife § 20, After Judgment Of Dissolution or Nullity.

Witkin, California Summary 10th Husband and Wife § 112, Contents Of Judgment.

Witkin, California Summary 10th Personal Property § 23, in General.

§ 2081. Grounds for denial

The restoration of a former name or birth name requested under Section 2080 shall not be denied (a) on the basis that the party has custody of a minor child who bears a different name or (b) for any other reason other than fraud. *(Stats. 1992, c. 162 (A.B.2650), § 10, operative Jan. 1, 1994. Amended by Stats.1996, c. 1061 (S.B.1033), § 6.)*

Law Revision Commission Comments

Enactment [Revised Comment]

Section 2081 continues former Civil Code Sections 4362(c) and 4457(c) without substantive change. [23 Cal.L.Rev.Comm. Reports 1 (1993)].

Research References

Forms

West's California Code Forms, Family § 2080, Comment Overview--Request for Restoration.

Treatises and Practice Aids

Witkin, California Summary 10th Husband and Wife § 20, After Judgment Of Dissolution or Nullity.

§ 2082. Common law rights

Nothing in this code shall be construed to abrogate the common law right of any person to change one's name. *(Stats.1992, c. 162 (A.B.2650), § 10, operative Jan. 1, 1994.)*

Law Revision Commission Comments

Enactment [Revised Comment]

Section 2082 continues without change and generalizes former Civil Code Sections 4362(b) and 4457(b). This section applies to the entire Family Code; the broader of the two former sections, former Civil Code Section 4362(b), applied only to the former Family Law Act (former Part 5 (commencing with former Section 4000) of Division 4 of the Civil Code). [23 Cal.L.Rev.Comm. Reports 1 (1993)].

Research References

Treatises and Practice Aids

Witkin, California Summary 10th Husband and Wife § 20, After Judgment Of Dissolution or Nullity.

CHAPTER 8. UNIFORM DIVORCE RECOGNITION ACT

§ 2090. Short title

This chapter may be cited as the Uniform Divorce Recognition Act. *(Stats.1992, c. 162 (A.B.2650), § 10, operative Jan. 1, 1994.)*

Law Revision Commission Comments

Enactment [Revised Comment]

Section 2090 continues former Civil Code Section 5000 without substantive change. See also Sections 3 (construction of provisions drawn from uniform act), 13 (severability of provisions). [23 Cal.L.Rev.Comm. Reports 1 (1993)].

Research References

Treatises and Practice Aids

Witkin, California Summary 10th Husband and Wife § 139, Uniform Divorce Recognition Act.

§ 2091. Foreign divorce of parties domiciled in state; effect

A divorce obtained in another jurisdiction shall be of no force or effect in this state if both parties to the marriage were domiciled in this state at the time the proceeding for the divorce was commenced. *(Stats.1992, c. 162 (A.B.2650), § 10, operative Jan. 1, 1994.)*

Law Revision Commission Comments

Enactment [Revised Comment]

Section 2091 continues former Civil Code Section 5001 without change. [23 Cal.L.Rev.Comm. Reports 1 (1993)].

Commentary

For application of Section 2091 to a foreign-country divorce, see *Estate of Atherly, 44 Cal.App.3d 758, 763, 119 Cal.Rptr. 41 (1975)*. Application of Section 2091 to sister-state divorces is constrained by full faith and credit requirements. See Section 2093, Commentary.

Research References

Treatises and Practice Aids

Witkin, California Summary 10th Husband and Wife § 129, Background.

Witkin, California Summary 10th Husband and Wife § 139, Uniform Divorce Recognition Act.

Witkin, California Summary 10th Husband and Wife § 140, in General.

§ 2092. Domicile; prima facie evidence

Proof that a person hereafter obtaining a divorce from the bonds of matrimony in another jurisdiction was (a) domiciled in this state within 12 months before the commencement of the proceeding therefor, and resumed residence in this state within 18 months after the date of the person's departure therefrom, or (b) at all times after the person's departure from this state and until the person's return maintained a place of residence within this state, shall be prima facie evidence that the person was domiciled in this state when the divorce proceeding was commenced. *(Stats.1992, c. 162 (A.B.2650), § 10, operative Jan. 1, 1994.)*

Law Revision Commission Comments

Enactment [Revised Comment]

Section 2092 continues former Civil Code Section 5002 without substantive change. The word "hereafter" used in Section 2092 is to be construed as of the time former Civil Code Section 5002 was enacted. See 1969 Cal. Stat. ch. 1608 (former Civ. Code § 5002, enacted Sept. 6, 1969); Section 2 (provision to be construed as restatement and continuation and not as new enactment). [23 Cal.L.Rev.Comm. Reports 1 (1993)].

Commentary

But see Section 2093, Commentary.

Research References

Treatises and Practice Aids

Witkin, California Summary 10th Husband and Wife § 139, Uniform Divorce Recognition Act.

§ 2093. Application of title; full faith and credit

The application of this chapter is limited by the requirement of the Constitution of the United States that full faith and credit shall be given in each state to the public acts, records, and judicial proceedings of every other state. *(Stats. 1992, c. 162 (A.B.2650), § 10, operative Jan. 1, 1994.)*

Law Revision Commission Comments

Enactment [Revised Comment]

Section 2093 continues former Civil Code Section 5004 without substantive change. See also Section 13 (severability of provisions). [23 Cal.L.Rev.Comm. Reports 1 (1993)].

Commentary

Constitutional full faith and credit requirements severely limit the application of Sections 2091 and 2092 to sister state divorce decrees. *Williams v. North Carolina (I), 317 U.S. 287 (1942)*, requires that every state accord presumptive good faith to the ex parte divorce decree of a sister state. *Williams v. North Carolina (II), 325 U.S. 226 (1945)*, nevertheless allows collateral attack on the ground that the divorcing state was without jurisdiction to render the decree because neither party was domiciled in the state at the time of divorce. The burden of proof is on the party who would upset the decree.

In contrast, a *bilateral* decree is generally immune from such collateral jurisdictional attack. A decree is bilateral when both parties have participated in the proceeding, or have consented or are subject to the general jurisdiction of the court. In such case, the parties are deemed to have had their day in court, and thus jurisdictional issues may not subsequently be raised by them or by their privies. See *Sherrer v. Sherrer, 334 U.S. 343 (1948)*, and *Johnson v. Muelberger, 340 U.S. 581 (1951)*.

Even though a California party has secured an ex parte divorce in a sister state, the stay-at-home spouse who did not participate in that divorce may bring a California action for property division and support. California follows the doctrine of "divisible divorce." *Hudson v. Hudson, 52 Cal.2d 735, 344 P.2d 295 (1959)*. See, for example, *In re Marriage of Fransen, 142 Cal.App.3d 419, 190 Cal.Rptr. 885 (1983)*. The United States Supreme Court has constitutionally approved the doctrine of divisible divorce. *Vanderbilt v. Vanderbilt, 354 U.S. 416 (1957)*. See also Section 2011 (court's in rem jurisdiction over community and quasi-community property).

Research References

Treatises and Practice Aids

Witkin, California Summary 10th Husband and Wife § 139, Uniform Divorce Recognition Act.

CHAPTER 9. DISCLOSURE OF ASSETS AND LIABILITIES

Section

§ 2100. Legislative findings and declarations; disclosure of assets and liabilities

The Legislature finds and declares the following:

(a) It is the policy of the State of California (1) to marshal, preserve, and protect community and quasi-community assets and liabilities that exist at the date of separation so as to avoid dissipation of the community estate before distribution, (2) to ensure fair and sufficient child and spousal support awards, and (3) to achieve a division of community and quasi-community assets and liabilities on the dissolution or nullity of marriage or legal separation of the parties as provided under California law.

(b) Sound public policy further favors the reduction of the adversarial nature of marital dissolution and the attendant costs by fostering full disclosure and cooperative discovery.

(c) In order to promote this public policy, a full and accurate disclosure of all assets and liabilities in which one or both parties have or may have an interest must be made in the early stages of a proceeding for dissolution of marriage or legal separation of the parties, regardless of the characterization as community or separate, together with a disclosure of all income and expenses of the parties. Moreover, each party has a continuing duty to immediately, fully, and accurately update and augment that disclosure to the extent there have been any material changes so that at the time the parties enter into an agreement for the resolution of any of these issues, or at the time of trial on these issues, each party will have a full and complete knowledge of the relevant underlying facts. *(Added by Stats.1993, c. 219 (A.B.1500), § 107. Amended by Stats.1993, c. 1101 (A.B.1469), § 3, eff. Oct. 11, 1993, operative Jan. 1, 1994; Stats.2001, c. 703 (A.B.583), § 2.)*

Application

For application of Stats.2001, c. 703 (A.B.583), see § 8 of that act.

Law Revision Commission Comments

Enactment [Revised Comment]

Section 2100 continues former Civil Code Section 4800.10(a) without substantive change. References to legal separation have been added in subdivisions (a) and (b) for consistency with the rules governing division of property. See, e.g., Section 2550 (equal division of community estate). See also Section 63 ("community estate" defined). [23 Cal.L.Rev.Comm. Reports 1 (1993)].

Commentary

Elden v. Superior Court, 53 Cal.App.4th 1497, 62 Cal.Rptr.2d 322 (1997), held that when parties agree to private arbitration of property issues, compliance with the technical requirements of sections 2104 and 2105 is not required. The parties may adopt less formal methods of financial disclosure. *In re Marriage of Woolsey, 220 Cal.App.4th 881, 163 Cal.Rptr.3d 551 (2013), review denied*, extended the holding of Elden to parties who agree to private mediation of property issues.

On a motion to set aside a judgment incorporating a mediation settlement, *Lappe v. Superior Court, 232 Cal.App.4th 774, 181 Cal.Rptr.3d 510 (2014), review denied*, holds that the contractual provisions of the parties' stipulation regarding the confidentiality of the declarations of disclosure were an impermissible attempt to preclude the court from receiving the declarations into evidence.

In re Marriage of Margulis, 198 Cal.App.4th 1252, 130 Cal.Rptr.3d 327 (2011), invoking, inter alia, this section, held that in a marriage dissolution proceeding a managing spouse has the burden of proof to account for missing assets when the nonmanaging spouse has made a prima facie showing of the existence and value of community assets that have disappeared after separation while controlled by the managing spouse. The managing spouse must either rebut the showing or prove the proper disposition or lesser value of the assets. If the managing spouse fails to do so, the court should charge the managing spouse with the prima facie value of the assets. *Margulis* interprets this section, along with Family Code sections 721, 1100, 1101, and 2107, to impose upon a managing spouse a duty to disclose and account for the existence, valuation, and distribution of all community assets from the date of separation to the final property distribution.

For discussion of the Section 2100–2133 disclosure provisions, see *In re Marriage of Varner, 55 Cal.App.4th 128, 63 Cal.Rptr.2d 894 (1997)* (setting aside a stipulated judgment on the ground of mistake under Section 2122(e)); *Elden v. Superior Court, 53 Cal.App.4th 1497, 62 Cal.Rptr.2d 322 (1997)* (application of disclosure provisions when parties agree to arbitration); and *In re Marriage of Reuling, 23 Cal.App.4th 1428, 28 Cal.Rptr.2d 726 (1994)*.

D'Elia v. D'Elia, 58 Cal.App.4th 415, 68 Cal.Rptr.2d 324 (1997), holds that California security laws (Corp. Code § 25401 et seq.) do not apply to an ostensible breach of the Section 721 fiduciary duty.

Research References

Forms

California Practice Guide: Rutter Family Law Forms Form 1:6, Letter to Opposing Counsel to Exchange Information.
California Practice Guide: Rutter Family Law Forms Form 9:3, Marital Settlement Agreement.
California Transactions Forms--Family Law § 2:4, Fiduciary Duty.
California Transactions Forms--Family Law § 2:5, Disclosure Requirements.
West's California Code Forms, Family § 2104, Comment Overview--Disclosure Of Assets.
West's California Judicial Council Forms FL-150, Income and Expense Declaration.

Treatises and Practice Aids

Witkin, California Summary 10th Community Property § 232, in General.
Witkin, California Summary 10th Community Property § 233, in General.
Witkin, California Summary 10th Community Property § 234, Scope Of Disclosure Requirements.
Witkin, California Summary 10th Community Property § 243, Grounds and Time Limits.
Witkin, California Summary 10th Husband and Wife § 11A, (New) Generally Applicable Procedures.
Witkin, California Summary 10th Husband and Wife § 126, Joint Petition.
Witkin, California Summary 10th Husband and Wife § 346, Nature and Validity.

§ 2101. Definitions

Unless the provision or context otherwise requires, the following definitions apply to this chapter:

(a) "Asset" includes, but is not limited to, any real or personal property of any nature, whether tangible or intangible, and whether currently existing or contingent.

(b) "Default judgment" does not include a stipulated judgment or any judgment pursuant to a marital settlement agreement.

(c) "Earnings and accumulations" includes income from whatever source derived, as provided in Section 4058.

(d) "Expenses" includes, but is not limited to, all personal living expenses, but does not include business related expenses.

(e) "Income and expense declaration" includes the Income and Expense Declaration forms approved for use by the Judicial Council, and any other financial statement that is approved for use by the Judicial Council in lieu of the Income and Expense Declaration, if the financial statement form satisfies all other applicable criteria.

(f) "Liability" includes, but is not limited to, any debt or obligation, whether currently existing or contingent. *(Added by Stats.1993, c. 219 (A.B.1500), § 107. Amended by Stats. 1993, c. 1101 (A.B.1469), § 4, eff. Oct. 11, 1993, operative Jan. 1, 1994; Stats.1998, c. 581 (A.B.2801), § 5.)*

Law Revision Commission Comments

Enactment [Revised Comment]

Section 2101 continues former Civil Code Section 4800.10(*l*) without substantive change. [23 Cal.L.Rev.Comm. Reports 1 (1993)].

Commentary

For discussion of the fiduciary standard and the Section 2100–2133 disclosure provisions, see *In re Marriage of Reuling, 23 Cal.App.4th 1428, 28 Cal.Rptr.2d 726 (1994)*.

Research References

Treatises and Practice Aids

Witkin, California Summary 10th Community Property § 233, in General.

§ 2102. Fiduciary relationship; length and scope of duty; termination

(a) From the date of separation to the date of the distribution of the community or quasi-community asset or liability in question, each party is subject to the standards provided in Section 721, as to all activities that affect the assets and liabilities of the other party, including, but not limited to, the following activities:

(1) The accurate and complete disclosure of all assets and liabilities in which the party has or may have an interest or obligation and all current earnings, accumulations, and expenses, including an immediate, full, and accurate update or augmentation to the extent there have been any material changes.

(2) The accurate and complete written disclosure of any investment opportunity, business opportunity, or other income-producing opportunity that presents itself after the date of separation, but that results from any investment, significant business activity outside the ordinary course of business, or other income-producing opportunity of either spouse from the date of marriage to the date of separation, inclusive. The written disclosure shall be made in sufficient time for the other spouse to make an informed decision as to whether he or she desires to participate in the investment opportunity, business, or other potential income-producing opportunity, and for the court to resolve any dispute regarding the right of the other spouse to participate in the opportunity. In the event of nondisclosure of an investment opportunity, the division of any gain resulting from that opportunity is governed by the standard provided in Section 2556.

(3) The operation or management of a business or an interest in a business in which the community may have an interest.

(b) From the date that a valid, enforceable, and binding resolution of the disposition of the asset or liability in question is reached, until the asset or liability has actually been distributed, each party is subject to the standards provided in Section 721 as to all activities that affect the assets or liabilities of the other party. Once a particular asset or liability has been distributed, the duties and standards set forth in Section 721 shall end as to that asset or liability.

(c) From the date of separation to the date of a valid, enforceable, and binding resolution of all issues relating to child or spousal support and professional fees, each party is subject to the standards provided in Section 721 as to all issues relating to the support and fees, including immediate, full, and accurate disclosure of all material facts and information regarding the income or expenses of the party. *(Added by Stats.1993, c. 219 (A.B.1500), § 107. Amended by Stats. 1993, c. 1101 (A.B.1469), § 5, eff. Oct. 11, 1993, operative Jan. 1, 1994; Stats.2001, c. 703 (A.B.583), § 3.)*

Application

For application of Stats.2001, c. 703 (A.B.583), see § 8 of that act.

Law Revision Commission Comments

Enactment [Revised Comment]

Section 2102 continues former Civil Code Section 4800.10(b) without substantive change. [23 Cal.L.Rev.Comm. Reports 1 (1993)].

Commentary

For discussion of the fiduciary standard and the Section 2100–2133 disclosure provisions, see *In re Marriage of Brewer, 93 Cal.App.4th 1334, 113 Cal.Rptr.2d 849 (2001)* (trial court properly set aside stipulated judgment and marital settlement agreement on the basis of mistake under § 2122(e), when wife did not give the husband accurate and complete valuation of the her pension plans); *In re Marriage of Varner, 55 Cal.App.4th 128, 63 Cal.Rptr.2d 894 (1997)* (setting aside a stipulated judgment on the ground of mistake under Section 2122(e)); and *In re Marriage of Reuling, 23 Cal.App.4th 1428, 28 Cal.Rptr.2d 726 (1994)*.

D'Elia v. D'Elia, 58 Cal.App.4th 415, 68 Cal.Rptr.2d 324 (1997), holds that California security laws (Corp. Code § 25401 et seq.) do not apply to an ostensible breach of the Section 2105 (b)(2) requirement to disclose all material facts relating to the valuation of community property assets.

In re Marriage of Sorge, 202 Cal.App.4th 626, 134 Cal.Rptr.3d 751 (2012), review denied, holds that the fiduciary duty of disclosure established by this section terminates when a final judgment resolves all divorce-related issues. It does not continue during the minority of children to whom child support may be owed. Thus a former husband did not violate his fiduciary duty under this section by failing voluntarily to disclose his current financial circumstances when his former wife filed a motion to modify child support. Instead, the support obligee must serve the support obligor with a section 3664 request for a current income and expense declaration.

Research References

Forms

California Practice Guide: Rutter Family Law Forms Form 8:1, Request for Order Re Separate Trial Re Validity Of Interspousal Deed.

California Practice Guide: Rutter Family Law Forms Form 9:3, Marital Settlement Agreement.

California Practice Guide: Rutter Family Law Forms Form 11:6, Final Declaration Of Disclosure Separate Statement (Attorney-Drafted Sample).

West's California Code Forms, Family § 2338 Form 9, Marital Agreement--Both Spouses Employed.

West's California Judicial Council Forms FL-140, Declaration Of Disclosure.

West's California Judicial Council Forms FL-141, Declaration Regarding Service Of Declaration Of Disclosure and Income and Expense Declaration.

West's California Judicial Council Forms FL-144, Stipulation and Waiver Of Final Declaration Of Disclosure.

Treatises and Practice Aids

Witkin, California Summary 10th Community Property § 234, Scope Of Disclosure Requirements.

Witkin, California Summary 10th Community Property § 235, Fiduciary Duties.

Witkin, California Summary 10th Community Property § 237, Final Declaration.

Witkin, California Summary 10th Community Property § 238, Effect Of Failure to Disclose.

§ 2103. Declarations of disclosure; requirements

In order to provide full and accurate disclosure of all assets and liabilities in which one or both parties may have an interest, each party to a proceeding for dissolution of the marriage or legal separation of the parties shall serve on the other party a preliminary declaration of disclosure under Section 2104, unless service of the preliminary declaration of disclosure is waived as provided in Section 2107 or is not required pursuant to Section 2110, and a final declaration of disclosure under Section 2105, unless service of the final declaration of disclosure is waived pursuant to Section 2105, 2107, or 2110, and shall file proof of service of each with the court. *(Added by Stats.1993, c. 219 (A.B.1500), § 107. Amended by Stats.1998, c. 581 (A.B.2801), § 6; Stats.2015, c. 46 (S.B.340), § 1, eff. Jan. 1, 2016; Stats.2016, c. 474 (A.B.2882), § 7, eff. Jan. 1, 2017.)*

Law Revision Commission Comments

Enactment [Revised Comment]

Section 2103 continues the first paragraph of former Civil Code Section 4800.10(c) without substantive change. A reference to legal separation has been added for consistency with the rules governing division of property. See, e.g., Section 2550 (equal division of community estate). Cross-references have been added for clarity. These are not substantive changes. [23 Cal.L.Rev.Comm. Reports 1 (1993)].

Research References

Treatises and Practice Aids

Witkin, California Summary 10th Community Property § 234, Scope Of Disclosure Requirements.

§ 2104. Preliminary declaration of disclosure

(a) Except by court order for good cause, as provided in Section 2107, or when service of the preliminary declaration of disclosure is not required pursuant to Section 2110, in the time period set forth in subdivision (f), each party shall serve on the other party a preliminary declaration of disclosure, executed under penalty of perjury on a form prescribed by the Judicial Council. The commission of perjury on the preliminary declaration of disclosure may be grounds for setting aside the judgment, or any part or parts thereof, pursuant to Chapter 10 (commencing with Section 2120), in addition to any and all other remedies, civil or criminal, that otherwise are available under law for the commission of perjury. The preliminary declaration of disclosure shall include all tax returns filed by the declarant within the two years prior to the date that the party served the declaration.

(b) The preliminary declaration of disclosure shall not be filed with the court, except on court order. However, the parties shall file proof of service of the preliminary declaration of disclosure with the court.

(c) The preliminary declaration of disclosure shall set forth with sufficient particularity, that a person of reasonable and ordinary intelligence can ascertain, all of the following:

(1) The identity of all assets in which the declarant has or may have an interest and all liabilities for which the declarant is or may be liable, regardless of the characterization of the asset or liability as community, quasi-community, or separate.

(2) The declarant's percentage of ownership in each asset and percentage of obligation for each liability when property is not solely owned by one or both of the parties. The preliminary declaration may also set forth the declarant's characterization of each asset or liability.

(d) A declarant may amend his or her preliminary declaration of disclosure without leave of the court. Proof of service of any amendment shall be filed with the court.

(e) Along with the preliminary declaration of disclosure, each party shall provide the other party with a completed income and expense declaration unless an income and expense declaration has already been provided and is current and valid.

(f) The petitioner shall serve the other party with the preliminary declaration of disclosure either concurrently with the petition for dissolution or legal separation, or within 60 days of filing the petition. When a petitioner serves the summons and petition by publication or posting pursuant to court order and the respondent files a response prior to a default judgment being entered, the petitioner shall serve the other party with the preliminary declaration of disclosure within 30 days of the response being filed. The respondent shall serve the other party with the preliminary declaration of disclosure either concurrently with the response to the petition, or within 60 days of filing the response. The time periods specified in this subdivision may be extended by written agreement of the parties or by court order. *(Added by Stats.1993, c. 219 (A.B.1500), § 107. Amended by Stats. 1993, c. 1101 (A.B.1469), § 6, eff. Oct. 11, 1993, operative Jan. 1, 1994; Stats.1998, c. 581 (A.B.2801), § 7; Stats.2009, c. 110 (A.B.459), § 1; Stats.2012, c. 107 (A.B.1406), § 1; Stats.2015, c. 46 (S.B.340), § 2, eff. Jan. 1, 2016; Stats.2015, c. 416 (A.B.1519), § 1.5, eff. Jan. 1, 2016.)*

Law Revision Commission Comments

Enactment [Revised Comment]

Section 2104 continues former Civil Code Section 4800.10(c)(1) without substantive change. A reference to legal separation has been added in subdivision (a) for consistency with the rules governing division of property. See, e.g., Section 2550 (equal division of community estate). In subdivision (a), the reference to penalties for perjury has been revised to eliminate the reference to "existing" law. This is not a substantive change. [23 Cal.L.Rev.Comm. Reports 1 (1993)].

Commentary

Elden v. Superior Court, 53 Cal.App.4th 1497, 62 Cal.Rptr.2d 322 (1997), held that when parties agree to private arbitration of property issues, compliance with the technical requirements of sections 2104 and 2105 is not required. The parties may adopt less formal methods of financial disclosure. *In re Marriage of Woolsey, 220 Cal.App.4th 881, 163 Cal.Rptr.3d 551 (2013), review denied*, extended the holding of Elden to parties who agree to private mediation of property issues.

On a motion to set aside a judgment incorporating a mediation settlement, *Lappe v. Superior Court, 232 Cal.App.4th 774, 181 Cal.Rptr.3d 510 (2014), review denied*, holds that the contractual provisions of the parties' stipulation regarding the confidentiality of the declarations of disclosure were an impermissible attempt to preclude the court from receiving the declarations into evidence.

Interpreting this section and section 2105, *In re Marriage of Evans, 229 Cal.App.4th 374, 177 Cal.Rptr.3d 256 (2014)*, held that a property settlement agreement executed by the parties before the filing of a petition for dissolution is enforceable even though the parties have not exchanged declarations of disclosure, which are required only after a petition as been filed.

Section 2107 (d) overruled *In re Marriage of McLaughlin, 82 Cal.App.4th 327, 98 Cal.Rptr.2d 136 (2000)*, which held that a husband's failure to file preliminary and final declarations was harmless error absent showing of prejudice.

Research References

Forms

California Practice Guide: Rutter Family Law Forms Form 1:32, Glossary Of Common Family Law Terms, Phrases and Concepts (Enclosure to Form 1:31).

California Transactions Forms--Family Law § 2:6, Preliminary Declaration Of Disclosure.

California Transactions Forms--Family Law § 2:7, Final Declaration Of Disclosure.

California Transactions Forms--Family Law § 2:8, Waiver Of Final Declaration Of Disclosure.

California Transactions Forms--Family Law § 2:9, Remedies for False Disclosure.

California Transactions Forms--Family Law § 2:88, Marital Settlement Agreement.

West's California Code Forms, Family § 2104, Comment Overview--Disclosure Of Assets.

West's California Code Forms, Family § 2338 Form 8, Marital Agreement.

West's California Code Forms, Family § 2550 Form 4, Division Of Property Clauses in Dissolution Settlement Agreement.

West's California Judicial Council Forms FL-140, Declaration Of Disclosure.

West's California Judicial Council Forms FL-141, Declaration Regarding Service Of Declaration Of Disclosure and Income and Expense Declaration.

West's California Judicial Council Forms FL-144, Stipulation and Waiver Of Final Declaration Of Disclosure.

West's California Judicial Council Forms FL-160, Property Declaration.

West's California Judicial Council Forms FL-161, Continuation Of Property Declaration.

Treatises and Practice Aids

Witkin, California Summary 10th Community Property § 233, in General.

Witkin, California Summary 10th Community Property § 236, Preliminary Declaration.

Witkin, California Summary 10th Community Property § 237, Final Declaration.

Witkin, California Summary 10th Community Property § 238, Effect Of Failure to Disclose.

Witkin, California Summary 10th Community Property § 243, Grounds and Time Limits.

§ 2105. Final declaration of disclosure of current income and expenses; execution and service; contents; waiver; perjury or noncompliance with chapter

(a) Except by court order for good cause, before or at the time the parties enter into an agreement for the resolution of property or support issues other than pendente lite support, or, if the case goes to trial, no later than 45 days before the first assigned trial date, each party, or the attorney for the party in this matter, shall serve on the other party a final declaration of disclosure and a current income and expense declaration, executed under penalty of perjury on a form prescribed by the Judicial Council, unless the parties mutually waive the final declaration of disclosure. The commission of perjury on the final declaration of disclosure by a party may be grounds for setting aside the judgment, or any part or parts thereof, pursuant to Chapter 10 (commencing with Section 2120), in addition to any and all other remedies, civil or criminal, that otherwise are available under law for the commission of perjury.

(b) The final declaration of disclosure shall include all of the following information:

(1) All material facts and information regarding the characterization of all assets and liabilities.

(2) All material facts and information regarding the valuation of all assets that are contended to be community property or in which it is contended the community has an interest.

(3) All material facts and information regarding the amounts of all obligations that are contended to be community obligations or for which it is contended the community has liability.

(4) All material facts and information regarding the earnings, accumulations, and expenses of each party that have been set forth in the income and expense declaration.

(c) In making an order setting aside a judgment for failure to comply with this section, the court may limit the set aside to those portions of the judgment materially affected by the nondisclosure.

(d) The parties may stipulate to a mutual waiver of the requirements of subdivision (a) concerning the final declaration of disclosure, by execution of a waiver under penalty of perjury entered into in open court or by separate stipulation. The waiver shall include all of the following representations:

(1) Both parties have complied with Section 2104 and the preliminary declarations of disclosure have been completed and exchanged.

(2) Both parties have completed and exchanged a current income and expense declaration, that includes all material facts and information regarding that party's earnings, accumulations, and expenses.

(3) Both parties have fully complied with Section 2102 and have fully augmented the preliminary declarations of disclosure, including disclosure of all material facts and information regarding the characterization of all assets and liabilities, the valuation of all assets that are contended to be community property or in which it is contended the community has an interest, and the amounts of all obligations that are contended to be community obligations or for which it is contended the community has liability.

(4) The waiver is knowingly, intelligently, and voluntarily entered into by each of the parties.

(5) Each party understands that this waiver does not limit the legal disclosure obligations of the parties, but rather is a statement under penalty of perjury that those obligations have been fulfilled. Each party further understands that noncompliance with those obligations will result in the court setting aside the judgment. *(Added by Stats.1993, c. 219 (A.B.1500), § 107. Amended by Stats.1993, c. 1101 (A.B. 1469), § 7, eff. Oct. 11, 1993, operative Jan. 1, 1994; Stats. 1995, c. 233 (A.B.806), § 1; Stats.1996, c. 1061 (S.B.1033), § 7; Stats.1998, c. 581 (A.B.2801), § 8; Stats.2001, c. 703 (A.B.583), § 4.)*

Application

For application of Stats.2001, c. 703 (A.B.583), see § 8 of that act.

Law Revision Commission Comments

Enactment [Revised Comment]

Section 2105 continues former Civil Code Section 4800.10(c)(2) without substantive change. In subdivision (a), the reference to penalties for perjury has been revised to eliminate the reference to "existing" law. This is not a substantive change. The provision concerning the filing of an income and expense declaration in subdivision (c) has been revised for consistency with the income and expense declaration provided with the preliminary declaration of disclosure. [23 Cal.L.Rev.Comm. Reports 1 (1993)].

Commentary

Elden v. Superior Court, 53 Cal.App.4th 1497, 62 Cal.Rptr.2d 322 (1997), held that when parties agree to private arbitration of property issues, compliance with the technical requirements of sections 2104 and 2105 is not required. The parties may adopt less formal methods of financial disclosure. *In re Marriage of Woolsey, 220 Cal.App.4th 881, 163 Cal.Rptr.3d 551 (2013), review denied*, extended the holding of Elden to parties who agree to private mediation of property issues.

On a motion to set aside a judgment incorporating a mediation settlement, *Lappe v. Superior Court, 232 Cal.App.4th 774, 181 Cal.Rptr.3d 510 (2014), review denied*, holds that the contractual provisions of the parties' stipulation regarding the confidentiality of the declarations of disclosure were an impermissible attempt to preclude the court from receiving the declarations into evidence.

Interpreting section 2104 and this section, *In re Marriage of Evans, 229 Cal.App.4th 374, 177 Cal.Rptr.3d 256 (2014)*, held that a property settlement agreement executed by the parties before the filing of a petition for dissolution is enforceable even though the parties have not exchanged declarations of disclosure, which are required only after a petition as been filed.

For discussion of waiver of the statutory disclosure provisions, see *In re Marriage of Fell, 55 Cal.App.4th 1058, 64 Cal.Rptr.2d 522 (1997), review denied September 3, 1997* (affirming trial court setting aside dissolution judgment when parties by agreement waived the disclosure requirements before Section 2105 was amended in 1995 to permit limited waiver, and analyzing the 1995 amendments). Section 2107 (d) overruled *In re Marriage of Jones, 60 Cal.App.4th 685, 70 Cal.Rptr.2d 542 (1998)* (sustaining trial court entry of dissolution judgment despite husband's failure to execute final declaration of disclosure on the ground that wife did not show that she was prejudiced thereby); and *In re Marriage of McLaughlin, 82 Cal. App.4th 327, 98 Cal.Rptr.2d 136 (2000)* (failure to file preliminary and final declarations was harmless error absent showing of prejudice). However, *In re Marriage of Steiner, 117 Cal.App.4th 519, 11 Cal. Rptr.3d 671 (2004), review denied*, holds that when *both* divorcing spouses fail to exchange final declarations of disclosure, neither spouse has a right to reversal of judgment or a new trial unless the moving spouse shows a miscarriage of justice. *Steiner* reasons that insofar as § 2107(d) would effectively require that a judgment be set aside for harmless error, it is inconsistent with California Constitution, art. VI, § 13, which provides that "[n]o judgment shall be set aside...for any error as to any manner of procedure, unless...the court shall be of the opinion that the error...has resulted in a miscarriage of justice." Moreover, *Steiner* notes the tension between subsection (c) of this section and § 2107(d). Reconciling both Family Code provisions and the California Constitution, *Steiner* concludes that a *noncomplying* party must identify some portion of the judgment that is materially affected by the parties' failure to exchange final disclosure declarations.

D'Elia v. D'Elia, 58 Cal.App.4th 415, 68 Cal.Rptr.2d 324 (1997), holds that California security laws (Corp. Code § 25401 et seq.) do not apply to an ostensible breach of the subsection (b)(2) requirement to disclose all material facts relating to the valuation of community property assets.

See generally In re Marriage of Varner, 55 Cal.App.4th 128, 63 Cal.Rptr.2d 894 (1997) (setting aside a stipulated judgment on the ground of mistake under Section 2122(e)).

Research References

Forms

California Practice Guide: Rutter Family Law Forms Form 1:32, Glossary Of Common Family Law Terms, Phrases and Concepts (Enclosure to Form 1:31).
California Practice Guide: Rutter Family Law Forms Form 11:6, Final Declaration Of Disclosure Separate Statement (Attorney-Drafted Sample).
California Transactions Forms--Family Law § 2:6, Preliminary Declaration Of Disclosure.
California Transactions Forms--Family Law § 2:7, Final Declaration Of Disclosure.
California Transactions Forms--Family Law § 2:8, Waiver Of Final Declaration Of Disclosure.
California Transactions Forms--Family Law § 2:9, Remedies for False Disclosure.
California Transactions Forms--Family Law § 2:88, Marital Settlement Agreement.
West's California Code Forms, Family § 2104, Comment Overview--Disclosure Of Assets.
West's California Code Forms, Family § 2338 Form 8, Marital Agreement.
West's California Code Forms, Family § 2550 Form 4, Division Of Property Clauses in Dissolution Settlement Agreement.
West's California Judicial Council Forms FL-140, Declaration Of Disclosure.
West's California Judicial Council Forms FL-141, Declaration Regarding Service Of Declaration Of Disclosure and Income and Expense Declaration.
West's California Judicial Council Forms FL-144, Stipulation and Waiver Of Final Declaration Of Disclosure.

Treatises and Practice Aids

Witkin, California Summary 10th Community Property § 233, in General.
Witkin, California Summary 10th Community Property § 237, Final Declaration.
Witkin, California Summary 10th Community Property § 238, Effect Of Failure to Disclose.
Witkin, California Summary 10th Community Property § 243, Grounds and Time Limits.

§ 2106. Entry of judgment; requirement of execution and service of declarations; exceptions; execution and filing of declaration of execution and service or of waiver

Except as provided in subdivision (d) of Section 2105, Section 2110, or absent good cause as provided in Section 2107, no judgment shall be entered with respect to the parties' property rights without each party, or the attorney for that party in this matter, having executed and served a copy of the final declaration of disclosure and current income and expense declaration. Each party, or his or her attorney, shall execute and file with the court a declaration signed under penalty of perjury stating that service of the final declaration of disclosure and current income and expense declaration was made on the other party or that service of the final declaration of disclosure has been waived pursuant to subdivision (d) of Section 2105 or in Section 2110. *(Added by Stats.1993, c. 219 (A.B.1500), § 107. Amended by Stats.1993, c. 1101 (A.B.1469), § 8, eff. Oct. 11, 1993, operative Jan. 1, 1994; Stats.1995, c. 233 (A.B.806), § 2; Stats.1996, c. 1061 (S.B.1033), § 8; Stats.1998, c. 581 (A.B.2801), § 9; Stats. 2001, c. 703 (A.B.583), § 5; Stats.2002, c. 1008 (A.B.3028), § 15; Stats.2009, c. 110 (A.B.459), § 2.)*

Law Revision Commission Comments

Enactment [Revised Comment]

Section 2106 continues former Civil Code Section 4800.10(d) without substantive change. [23 Cal.L.Rev.Comm. Reports 1 (1993)].

Commentary

Despite this section, *In re Marriage of Jones, 60 Cal.App.4th 685, 70 Cal.Rptr.2d 542 (1998),* sustained trial court entry of a dissolution judgment even though the husband failed to execute final declaration of disclosure on the ground that wife did not show that she was prejudiced thereby.

Research References

Forms

California Transactions Forms--Family Law § 2:7, Final Declaration Of Disclosure.
California Transactions Forms--Family Law § 2:8, Waiver Of Final Declaration Of Disclosure.
West's California Code Forms, Family § 2104, Comment Overview--Disclosure Of Assets.
West's California Judicial Council Forms FL-140, Declaration Of Disclosure.
West's California Judicial Council Forms FL-141, Declaration Regarding Service Of Declaration Of Disclosure and Income and Expense Declaration.

Treatises and Practice Aids

Witkin, California Summary 10th Community Property § 234, Scope Of Disclosure Requirements.
Witkin, California Summary 10th Community Property § 237, Final Declaration.
Witkin, California Summary 10th Community Property § 238, Effect Of Failure to Disclose.
Witkin, California Summary 10th Husband and Wife § 359, Action on Agreement.

§ 2107. Noncomplying declarations; requests to comply; remedies

(a) If one party fails to serve on the other party a preliminary declaration of disclosure under Section 2104, unless that party is not required to serve a preliminary declaration of disclosure pursuant to Section 2110, or a final declaration of disclosure under Section 2105, or fails to provide the information required in the respective declarations with sufficient particularity, and if the other party has served the respective declaration of disclosure on the noncomplying party, the complying party may, within a reasonable time, request preparation of the appropriate declaration of disclosure or further particularity.

(b) If the noncomplying party fails to comply with a request under subdivision (a), the complying party may do one or more of the following:

(1) File a motion to compel a further response.

(2) File a motion for an order preventing the noncomplying party from presenting evidence on issues that should have been covered in the declaration of disclosure.

(3) File a motion showing good cause for the court to grant the complying party's voluntary waiver of receipt of the noncomplying party's preliminary declaration of disclosure pursuant to Section 2104 or final declaration of disclosure pursuant to Section 2105. The voluntary waiver does not affect the rights enumerated in subdivision (d).

(c) If a party fails to comply with any provision of this chapter, the court shall, in addition to any other remedy provided by law, impose money sanctions against the noncomplying party. Sanctions shall be in an amount sufficient to deter repetition of the conduct or comparable conduct, and shall include reasonable attorney's fees, costs incurred, or both, unless the court finds that the noncomplying party acted with substantial justification or that other circumstances make the imposition of the sanction unjust.

(d) Except as otherwise provided in this subdivision, if a court enters a judgment when the parties have failed to comply with all disclosure requirements of this chapter, the court shall set aside the judgment. The failure to comply with the disclosure requirements does not constitute harmless error. If the court granted the complying party's voluntary waiver of receipt of the noncomplying party's preliminary declaration of disclosure pursuant to paragraph (3) of subdivision (b), the court shall set aside the judgment only at the request of the complying party, unless the motion to set aside the judgment is based on one of the following:

(1) Actual fraud if the defrauded party was kept in ignorance or in some other manner was fraudulently prevented from fully participating in the proceeding.

(2) Perjury, as defined in Section 118 of the Penal Code, in the preliminary or final declaration of disclosure, in the waiver of the final declaration of disclosure, or in the current income and expense statement.

(e) Upon the motion to set aside judgment, the court may order the parties to provide the preliminary and final declarations of disclosure that were exchanged between them. Absent a court order to the contrary, the disclosure declarations shall not be filed with the court and shall be returned to the parties. *(Added by Stats.1993, c. 219 (A.B.1500), § 107. Amended by Stats.1993, c. 1101 (A.B.1469), § 9, eff. Oct. 11, 1993, operative Jan. 1, 1994; Stats.2001, c. 703 (A.B.583), § 6; Stats.2009, c. 110 (A.B.459), § 3; Stats.2015, c. 46 (S.B.340), § 3, eff. Jan. 1, 2016.)*

Law Revision Commission Comments

Enactment [Revised Comment]

Section 2107 continues former Civil Code Section 4800.10(e)-(f) without substantive change. In subdivision (a), the word "exchange" has been omitted as surplus and the cross-references added for clarity. These are not substantive changes. Subdivision (a) has also been revised to make clear that the complying party "may" (rather than "shall") request the declaration or particularity, since the complying party is not compelled to seek compliance by the other party. However, as subdivision (b) makes clear, the request is a prerequisite to seeking a court order compelling a response from the noncomplying party. [23 Cal.L.Rev.Comm. Reports 1 (1993)].

Commentary

In re Marriage of Margulis, 198 Cal.App.4th 1252, 130 Cal.Rptr.3d 327 (2011), relying in part on subsection (c), held that in a marriage dissolution proceeding a managing spouse has the burden of proof to account for missing assets when the nonmanaging spouse has made a prima facie showing of the existence and value of community assets that have disappeared after separation while controlled by the managing spouse. The managing spouse must either rebut the showing or prove the proper disposition or lesser value of the assets. If the managing spouse fails to do so, the court should charge the managing spouse with the prima facie value of the assets. *Margulis* interprets this section, along with Family Code sections 271, 1100, 1101, and 2100, to impose upon a managing spouse a duty to disclose and account for the existence, valuation, and distribution of all community assets from the date of separation to the final property distribution.

In re Marriage of Tharp, 188 Cal.App.4th 1295, 116 Cal.Rptr.3d 375 (2010), review denied, held that a family court abused its discretion, under subsection (c) of this section and section 2071, in denying a divorcing wife's request for sanctions when her husband frustrated and blocked discovery and falsely asserted the existence of a premarital agreement.

Marriage of Schleich, 8 Cal.App.5th 267, 213 Cal.Rptr.3d 665 (2017), review denied, held that a spouse who receives 50 percent or 100 percent of the value of an asset under subsections (g) or (h) of section 1101 is not additionally entitled to receive 50 percent of the value of the asset in the division of community property; instead the aggrieved spouse's remedy for nondisclosure during dissolution lies in subsection (c) of this section, that is, in money sanctions for failure to comply with disclosure rules.

Note that subsection (c), unlike subsections (a) and (b), does not restrict relief to a "complying party." Nevertheless, *In re Marriage of Fong, 193 Cal.App.4th 278, 123 Cal.Rptr.3d 260 (2011)*, held that a trial court erred in imposing subsection (c) money sanctions on a grossly noncomplying husband for failure to comply with disclosure requirements when his wife failed to serve her final declaration of disclosure before bringing her motion for sanctions.

In re Marriage of Steiner, 117 Cal.App.4th 519, 11 Cal.Rptr.3d 671 (2004), review denied, holds that when *both* divorcing spouses fail to exchange final declarations of disclosure neither spouse has a right to reversal of judgment or a new trial unless the moving spouse shows a miscarriage of justice. *Steiner* reasons that insofar as subsection (d) would effectively require that a judgment be set aside for harmless error, it is inconsistent with California Constitution, art. VI, § 13, which provides that "[n]o judgment shall be set aside . . . for any error as to any manner of procedure, unless . . . the court shall be of the opinion that the error . . . has resulted in a miscarriage of justice." Moreover, *Steiner* notes the tension between subsection (d) of this section and § 2105(c). Reconciling both Family Code provisions and the California Constitution, *Steiner* concludes that a *noncomplying* party must identify some portion of the judgment that is materially affected by the parties' failure to exchange final disclosure declarations.

When, in the course of a child support proceeding, a father failed to comply with a court order to provide income and expense declarations, income tax returns, and other relevant financial documents, the trial court properly imposed an "issue sanction" (see Code of Civil Procedure § 2023(b)(2) as well as subsection (b)(2) of this section) declaring the support obligor's income to be $40,000 monthly, based on a home loan application he had made, and barring him from offering evidence to the contrary. *In re Marriage of Chakko, 115 Cal.App.4th 104, 8 Cal.Rptr.3d 699 (2004).*

In re Marriage of Feldman, 153 Cal.App.4th 1470, 64 Cal.Rptr.3d 29 (2007), held that a trial did not abuse its discretion in ordering a husband, under subsection (c) of this section and section 271(a), to pay his wife $250,000 in sanctions and $140,000 in attorney's fees, because the husband failed to disclose the existence of privately held companies and failed to disclose financial information about many assets, in violation of Family Code sections 1100(e), 2100(c), 1202(a), 2103, and 2104(c). *Feldman* additionally held that imposition of sanctions did not require a showing of harm to the wife and she was not required to seek statutory procedural remedies before imposition of sanctions.

In re Marriage of Sorge, 202 Cal.App.4th 626, 134 Cal.Rptr.3d 751 (2012), holds that the fiduciary duty of disclosure established by section 2102 terminates when a final judgment resolves all divorce-related issues. It does not continue during the minority of children to whom child support may be owed. Thus a former husband did not violate his fiduciary duty under section 2102 and could not be sanctioned under this section by failing voluntarily to disclose his current financial circumstances when his former wife filed a motion to modify child support. (Instead, the support obligee must serve a section 3664 request upon the support obligor for a current income and expense declaration.) However, the husband could be sanctioned for other misbehavior under section 271.

Research References

Forms

California Practice Guide: Rutter Family Law Forms Form 11:4, Request for Order Re Service Of Declaration Of Disclosure.
West's California Judicial Council Forms FL-300, Request for Order.
West's California Judicial Council Forms FL-316, Request for Orders Regarding Noncompliance With Disclosure Requirements.

Treatises and Practice Aids

Witkin, California Summary 10th Community Property § 236, Preliminary Declaration.
Witkin, California Summary 10th Community Property § 237, Final Declaration.
Witkin, California Summary 10th Community Property § 238, Effect Of Failure to Disclose.
Witkin, California Summary 10th Husband and Wife § 10, Imposition Of Award as Sanction.
Witkin, California Summary 10th Husband and Wife § 86, in General.

§ 2108. Liquidation of community or quasi-community assets to avoid market or investment risks; authority of court

At any time during the proceeding, the court has the authority, on application of a party and for good cause, to order the liquidation of community or quasi-community assets so as to avoid unreasonable market or investment risks, given the relative nature, scope, and extent of the community estate. However, in no event shall the court grant the application unless, as provided in this chapter, the appropriate declaration of disclosure has been served by the moving party. *(Added by Stats.1993, c. 219 (A.B.1500), § 107.)*

Law Revision Commission Comments

Enactment [Revised Comment]

Section 2108 continues former Civil Code Section 4800.10(g) without substantive change. See also Section 63 ("community estate" defined). [23 Cal.L.Rev.Comm. Reports 1 (1993)].

Research References

Forms

California Practice Guide: Rutter Family Law Forms Form 5:9, Request for Order to Liquidate Family Residence (Family Code S2108).
California Practice Guide: Rutter Family Law Forms Form 5:10, Responsive Declaration to Request for Order to Liquidate Family Residence (Family Code S2108).

Treatises and Practice Aids

Witkin, California Summary 10th Community Property § 232, in General.

§ 2109. Summary dissolution of marriage; required disclosures

The provisions of this chapter requiring a final declaration of disclosure do not apply to a summary dissolution of marriage, but a preliminary declaration of disclosure is required. *(Added by Stats.1993, c. 1101 (A.B.1469), § 11, eff. Oct. 11, 1993, operative Jan. 1, 1994.)*

Law Revision Commission Comments

Enactment [Revised Comment]

Section 2109 continues former Civil Code Section 4800.10(h) without substantive change. [23 Cal.L.Rev.Comm. Reports 1 (1993)].

Research References

Forms

West's California Judicial Council Forms FL-800, Joint Petition for Summary Dissolution.

Treatises and Practice Aids

Witkin, California Summary 10th Community Property § 234, Scope Of Disclosure Requirements.
Witkin, California Summary 10th Community Property § 237, Final Declaration.

§ 2110. Default judgments; declarations of disclosure

In the case of a default judgment, the petitioner may waive the final declaration of disclosure requirements provided in this chapter, and shall not be required to serve a final declaration of disclosure on the respondent nor receive a final declaration of disclosure from the respondent. However, a preliminary declaration of disclosure by the petitioner is required unless the petitioner served the summons and petition by publication or posting pursuant to court order and the respondent has defaulted. *(Added by Stats.1993, c. 1101 (A.B.1469), § 12, eff. Oct. 11, 1993, operative Jan. 1, 1994. Amended by Stats.1994, c. 146 (A.B.3601), § 41; Stats.1998, c. 581 (A.B.2801), § 10; Stats.2015, c. 46 (S.B.340), § 4, eff. Jan. 1, 2016.)*

Law Revision Commission Comments

Enactment [Revised Comment]

Section 2110 continues former Civil Code Section 4800.10(i) without substantive change. [23 Cal.L.Rev.Comm. Reports 1 (1993)].

Research References

Treatises and Practice Aids

Witkin, California Summary 10th Community Property § 234, Scope Of Disclosure Requirements.
Witkin, California Summary 10th Community Property § 236, Preliminary Declaration.
Witkin, California Summary 10th Community Property § 237, Final Declaration.
Witkin, California Summary 10th Community Property § 238, Effect Of Failure to Disclose.

§ 2111. Attorney work product privilege; protective orders

A disclosure required by this chapter does not abrogate the attorney work product privilege or impede the power of the court to issue protective orders. *(Added by Stats.1993, c. 1101 (A.B.1469), § 13, eff. Oct. 11, 1993, operative Jan. 1, 1994.)*

Law Revision Commission Comments

Enactment [Revised Comment]

Section 2111 continues former Civil Code Section 4800.10(j) without substantive change. [23 Cal.L.Rev.Comm. Reports 1 (1993)].

Research References

Forms

West's California Code Forms, Family § 2104, Comment Overview--Disclosure Of Assets.

Treatises and Practice Aids

Witkin, California Summary 10th Community Property § 233, in General.

§ 2112. Forms

The Judicial Council shall adopt appropriate forms and modify existing forms to effectuate the purposes of this chapter. *(Added by Stats.1993, c. 1101 (A.B.1469), § 14, eff. Oct. 11, 1993, operative Jan. 1, 1994.)*

Law Revision Commission Comments

Enactment [Revised Comment]

Section 2112 continues former Civil Code Section 4800.10(k) without substantive change. [23 Cal.L.Rev.Comm. Reports 1 (1993)].

Research References

Forms

California Practice Guide: Rutter Family Law Forms Form 1:32, Glossary Of Common Family Law Terms, Phrases and Concepts (Enclosure to Form 1:31).
West's California Code Forms, Family § 2112 Form 1, Form Interrogatories.
West's California Judicial Council Forms FL-140, Declaration Of Disclosure.
West's California Judicial Council Forms FL-141, Declaration Regarding Service Of Declaration Of Disclosure and Income and Expense Declaration.

Treatises and Practice Aids

Witkin, California Summary 10th Community Property § 233, in General.

§ 2113. Application of chapter

This chapter applies to any proceeding commenced on or after January 1, 1993. *(Formerly § 2109, added by Stats.1993, c. 219, (A.B.1500), § 107. Renumbered § 2113 and amended by Stats.1993, c. 1101 (A.B.1469), § 10, eff. Oct. 11, 1993, operative Jan. 1, 1994.)*

Law Revision Commission Comments

Enactment [Revised Comment]

Section 2113 continues former Civil Code Section 4800.10(m) without substantive change. [23 Cal.L.Rev.Comm. Reports 1 (1993)].

Research References

Forms

West's California Code Forms, Family § 2104, Comment Overview--Disclosure Of Assets.
West's California Judicial Council Forms FL-150, Income and Expense Declaration.

CHAPTER 10. RELIEF FROM JUDGMENT

§ 2120. Legislative findings and declarations; public policy

The Legislature finds and declares the following:

(a) The State of California has a strong policy of ensuring the division of community and quasi-community property in the dissolution of a marriage as set forth in Division 7 (commencing with Section 2500), and of providing for fair and sufficient child and spousal support awards. These policy goals can only be implemented with full disclosure of community, quasi-community, and separate assets, liabilities, income, and expenses, as provided in Chapter 9 (commencing with Section 2100), and decisions freely and knowingly made.

(b) It occasionally happens that the division of property or the award of support, whether made as a result of agreement or trial, is inequitable when made due to the nondisclosure or other misconduct of one of the parties.

(c) The public policy of assuring finality of judgments must be balanced against the public interest in ensuring proper division of marital property, in ensuring sufficient support awards, and in deterring misconduct.

(d) The law governing the circumstances under which a judgment can be set aside, after the time for relief under Section 473 of the Code of Civil Procedure has passed, has been the subject of considerable confusion which has led to increased litigation and unpredictable and inconsistent decisions at the trial and appellate levels. *(Added by Stats.1993, c. 219 (A.B.1500), § 108.)*

Law Revision Commission Comments

Enactment [Revised Comment]

Section 2120 continues former Civil Code Section 4800.11(a) without substantive change. In subdivision (a), a reference to Division 7 (commencing with Section 2500) has been substituted for the narrower reference to former Civil Code Section 4800. This is not a substantive change. [23 Cal.L.Rev.Comm. Reports 1 (1993)].

Commentary

Sections 2120–29 do not extend the statutory time limit for filing a notice of *appeal* from a dissolution judgment. Sections 2120–29 extend the time in which a party may seek relief from judgment in the trial court, not the time in which a party may file a notice of appeal from a judgment of the trial court. *In re Marriage of Eben–King & King, 80 Cal.App.4th 92, 95 Cal.Rptr.2d 113 (2000)*.

To the extent that Sections 2120–29 allow the setting aside of a judgment, the doctrine of res judicata is inoperative. *Rubenstein v. Rubenstein, 81 Cal.App.4th 1131, 97 Cal.Rptr.2d 707 (2000)*.

See generally *In re Marriage of Brewer, 93 Cal.App.4th 1334, 113 Cal.Rptr.2d 849 (2001)* (trial court properly set aside stipulated judgment and marital settlement agreement on the basis of mistake under § 2122(e), when wife did not give the husband accurate and complete valuation of the her pension plans); *In re Marriage of Varner, 55 Cal.App.4th 128, 63 Cal.Rptr.2d 894 (1997)* (setting aside a stipulated judgment on the ground of mistake under Section 2122(e)).

Research References

Forms

California Practice Guide: Rutter Family Law Forms Form 16:1, Request for Order to Set Aside Judgment (Family Code S2120 et seq.).

West's California Code Forms, Family § 2104, Comment Overview--Disclosure Of Assets.

Treatises and Practice Aids

Witkin, California Summary 10th Community Property § 190, General Rule Of Equal Division.

Witkin, California Summary 10th Community Property § 217, Nonjudicial Division.

Witkin, California Summary 10th Community Property § 242, in General.

Witkin, California Summary 10th Community Property § 243, Grounds and Time Limits.

Witkin, California Summary 10th Community Property § 248, Tort Action for Concealment.

Witkin, California Summary 10th Husband and Wife § 115, Setting Aside Judgment.

Witkin, California Summary 10th Husband and Wife § 306, in General.

Witkin, California Summary 10th Husband and Wife § 352, in General.

§ 2121. Authority of court to provide relief

(a) In proceedings for dissolution of marriage, for nullity of marriage, or for legal separation of the parties, the court may, on any terms that may be just, relieve a spouse from a judgment, or any part or parts thereof, adjudicating support or division of property, after the six-month time limit of Section 473 of the Code of Civil Procedure has run, based on the grounds, and within the time limits, provided in this chapter.

(b) In all proceedings under this chapter, before granting relief, the court shall find that the facts alleged as the grounds for relief materially affected the original outcome and that the moving party would materially benefit from the granting of the relief. *(Added by Stats.1993, c. 219 (A.B.1500), § 108.)*

Law Revision Commission Comments

Enactment [Revised Comment]

Section 2121 continues former Civil Code Section 4800.11(b)-(c) without substantive change. In subdivision (a), the phrase "proceeding for dissolution of marriage, nullity of marriage, or legal separation of the parties" has been substituted for the reference to the former Family Law Act (former Part 5 (commencing with former Section 4000) of Division 4 of the Civil Code). This is not a substantive change. [23 Cal.L.Rev.Comm. Reports 1 (1993)].

Commentary

See generally *In re Marriage of Brewer, 93 Cal.App.4th 1334, 113 Cal.Rptr.2d 849 (2001)* (trial court properly set aside stipulated judgment and marital settlement agreement on the basis of mistake under § 2122(e), when wife did not give the husband accurate and complete valuation of the her pension plans); and *In re Marriage of Varner, 55 Cal.App.4th 128, 63 Cal.Rptr.2d 894 (1997)* (setting aside a stipulated judgment on the ground of mistake under Section 2122(e)).

Interpreting subsection (b), *In re Marriage of Rosevear, 65 Cal.App.4th 673, 76 Cal.Rptr.2d 691 (1998),* holds that the moving party must show that he or she would materially benefit from the granting of relief.

Invoking § 2123, *In re Marriage of Heggie, 99 Cal.App.4th 28, 120 Cal.Rptr.2d 707 (2002)*, holds that a stipulated dissolution judgment may not be set aside under this section or Code of Civil Procedure § 473 solely because of inequality in the distribution of community property attributable to a postjudgment increase in the value of community property stock.

Research References

Forms

California Practice Guide: Rutter Family Law Forms Form 16:1, Request for Order to Set Aside Judgment (Family Code S2120 et seq.).

Treatises and Practice Aids

Witkin, California Summary 10th Community Property § 243, Grounds and Time Limits.

Witkin, California Summary 10th Husband and Wife § 115, Setting Aside Judgment.

§ 2122. Grounds for relief; limitation of actions

The grounds and time limits for a motion to set aside a judgment, or any part or parts thereof, are governed by this section and shall be one of the following:

(a) Actual fraud where the defrauded party was kept in ignorance or in some other manner was fraudulently prevented from fully participating in the proceeding. An action or motion based on fraud shall be brought within one year after the date on which the complaining party either did discover, or should have discovered, the fraud.

(b) Perjury. An action or motion based on perjury in the preliminary or final declaration of disclosure, the waiver of the final declaration of disclosure, or in the current income and expense statement shall be brought within one year after the date on which the complaining party either did discover, or should have discovered, the perjury.

(c) Duress. An action or motion based upon duress shall be brought within two years after the date of entry of judgment.

(d) Mental incapacity. An action or motion based on mental incapacity shall be brought within two years after the date of entry of judgment.

(e) As to stipulated or uncontested judgments or that part of a judgment stipulated to by the parties, mistake, either mutual or unilateral, whether mistake of law or mistake of fact. An action or motion based on mistake shall be brought within one year after the date of entry of judgment.

(f) Failure to comply with the disclosure requirements of Chapter 9 (commencing with Section 2100). An action or motion based on failure to comply with the disclosure requirements shall be brought within one year after the date on which the complaining party either discovered, or should have discovered, the failure to comply. *(Added by Stats.1993, c. 219 (A.B.1500), § 108. Amended by Stats.1993, c. 1101 (A.B.1469), § 15, eff. Oct. 11, 1993, operative Jan. 1, 1994; Stats.2001, c. 703 (A.B.583), § 7.)*

Application

For application of Stats.2001, c. 703 (A.B.583), see § 8 of that act.

Law Revision Commission Comments

Enactment [Revised Comment]

Section 2122 continues former Civil Code Section 4800.11(d) without substantive change. [23 Cal.L.Rev.Comm. Reports 1 (1993)].

Commentary

Compare this section with section 3691. Section 3691, with its six-month limitation, applies to support orders, while this section applies to motions to set aside a judgment. *In re Marriage of Zimmerman, 183 Cal.App.4th 900, 109 Cal.Rptr.3d 96 (2010), review denied* (holding that motion to set aside a child support order for fraud and perjury was barred by the six-month limitation of section 3691).

Sections 2120–29 do not extend the statutory time limit for filing a notice of *appeal* from a dissolution judgment. Sections 2120–29 extend the time in which a party may seek relief from judgment in the trial court, not the time in which a party may file a notice of appeal from a judgment of the trial court. *In re Marriage of Eben-King & King, 80 Cal.App.4th 92, 95 Cal.Rptr.2d 113 (2000)*.

Interpreting subsection (a), *Rubenstein v. Rubenstein, 81 Cal. App.4th 1131, 97 Cal.Rptr.2d 707 (2000)*, holds that the one-year limitation begins to run when the defrauded party discovers, or should have discovered, the *facts* constituting the alleged fraud, rather than the prior date on which that party merely suspects or asserts, without knowledge of the necessary facts, that she was defrauded. Cf. Code of Civil Procedure § 338(d). Compare Family Code § 1101 (action for breach of fiduciary duty may be commenced within three years of the date on which petitioner had notice of the transaction or event for which the remedy is sought; and remedy for breach of fiduciary duty involving fraud is 100 percent of the asset undisclosed or transferred in breach of the fiduciary duty) and § 2556 (no statute of limitations for division of an omitted or unadjudicated community estate asset or liability).

In denying review, the California Supreme Court depublished *In re Marriage of Deffner*, in which the depublished opinion of the court of appeal, *49 Cal.Rptr.3d 424 (2006)*, had held that the subsection (a) statute of limitations, which applies only to fraud upon a party, has no application when there has been fraud *upon the court*. The court of appeal reasoned that setting aside a judgment involving fraud upon the court, as contrasted to fraud against a party, is necessary to protect the integrity of the judicial process. In *Deffner*, the claimed fraud upon the court was the representation of the husband's attorney that he was instead the wife's attorney, resulting in the court's approval of the parties' settlement agreement despite its patent unfairness to the wife. Even though the attorney persuaded the unsophisticated wife to participate in his misrepresentation and even though she would be an incidental beneficiary of an order setting aside the settlement agreement, the gravamen of her complaint was fraud upon the court.

In re Marriage of Varner, 55 Cal.App.4th 128, 63 Cal.Rptr.2d 894 (1997), holds that a spouse's uncontested but patently incorrect valuation of community property assets is a ground for setting aside a judgment under subsection (e), which allows relief for mistake of fact in an uncontested judgment. To the same effect, see *In re Marriage of Brewer, 93 Cal.App.4th 1334, 113 Cal.Rptr.2d 849 (2001)* (trial court properly set aside stipulated judgment and marital settlement agreement on the basis of mistake under subsection (e), when wife did not give the husband accurate and complete valuation of the her pension plans).

In re Marriage of Thorne & Raccina, 203 Cal.App.4th 492, 136 Cal.Rptr.3d 887 (2012), held that the parties' reliance on incorrect information provided by the military justice advocate general, which resulted in gross understatement of the wife's interest in the husband's pension, although a ground for avoiding the parties' stipulated final judgment under Family Code section 2122(e), was unavailable to the wife because the one-year time limitation of that section had expired by the time the husband retired and the wife sought to realize her interest in the pension. Relief for fraud was unavailable under section 2122(a) because both parties intended to enter an agreement that complied with California law. Moreover, the difference between the larger correctly calculated value of her interest and smaller incorrectly calculated value of her interest was not an omitted asset for purposes of section 2556.

See generally *In re Marriage of Rosevear, 65 Cal.App.4th 673, 76 Cal.Rptr.2d 691 (1998)* (holding that movant failed to demonstrate any ground for relief).

Dale v. Dale, 66 Cal.App.4th 1172, 78 Cal.Rptr.2d 513 (1998), review denied January 13, 1999, holds that absent a pending dissolution proceeding, a divorced spouse may bring a common law tort action against a former spouse for injury resulting from the latter's concealment of community assets at dissolution. Dissolution of the Dales' marriage occurred before enactment of Sections 2120–2129, and the court thus did not address whether such an action might be brought with respect to judgments entered on or after January 1, 1993, the effective date of Sections 2120–2129.

In re Marriage of Georgiou and Leslie, 218 Cal.App.4th 561, 160 Cal.Rptr.3d 254 (2013) review denied, holds that section 1101 does not permit a postjudgment action for breach of the fiduciary duty of disclosure when the asset was adjudicated and divided in the dissolution proceeding. In such case, the former spouse's remedy is an action to set aside the judgment under this section.

With respect to subsection (f), strict compliance with Chapter 9 disclosure requirements is not required in private mediation or arbitration of property issues. *Elden v. Superior Court, 53 Cal.App.4th 1497, 62 Cal.Rptr.2d 322 (1997)*, held that when parties agree to private arbitration of property issues, compliance with the technical requirements of sections 2104 and 2105 is not required. The parties may adopt less formal methods of financial disclosure. *In re Marriage of Woolsey, 220 Cal.App.4th 881, 163 Cal.Rptr.3d 551 (2013), review denied*, extended the holding of *Elden* to parties who agree to private mediation of property issues.

Research References

Forms

California Practice Guide: Rutter Family Law Forms Form 16:1, Request for Order to Set Aside Judgment (Family Code S2120 et seq.).

Treatises and Practice Aids

Witkin, California Summary 10th Community Property § 133, Statutory Requirement.
Witkin, California Summary 10th Community Property § 182, Property Owned or Received at Division.
Witkin, California Summary 10th Community Property § 200, Division by Agreement.
Witkin, California Summary 10th Community Property § 237, Final Declaration.
Witkin, California Summary 10th Community Property § 242, in General.
Witkin, California Summary 10th Community Property § 243, Grounds and Time Limits.
Witkin, California Summary 10th Husband and Wife § 307, Grounds and Time Limits.

§ 2123. Restrictions on grounds for relief; inequitable judgments

Notwithstanding any other provision of this chapter, or any other law, a judgment may not be set aside simply because the court finds that it was inequitable when made, nor simply because subsequent circumstances caused the division of assets or liabilities to become inequitable, or the support to become inadequate. *(Added by Stats.1993, c. 219 (A.B.1500), § 108.)*

Law Revision Commission Comments

Enactment [Revised Comment]

Section 2123 continues former Civil Code Section 4800.11(e) without substantive change. [23 Cal.L.Rev.Comm. Reports 1 (1993)].

Commentary

Invoking this section, *In re Marriage of Heggie, 99 Cal.App.4th 28, 120 Cal.Rptr.2d 707 (2002)*, holds that a stipulated dissolution judgment may not be set aside under Family Code § 2121 or Code of Civil Procedure § 473 solely because of inequality in the distribution of community property attributable to a postjudgment increase in the value of community property stock.

Research References

Treatises and Practice Aids

Witkin, California Summary 10th Community Property § 243, Grounds and Time Limits.

§ 2124. Attorney negligence

The negligence of an attorney shall not be imputed to a client to bar an order setting aside a judgment, unless the court finds that the client knew, or should have known, of the attorney's negligence and unreasonably failed to protect himself or herself. *(Added by Stats.1993, c. 219 (A.B.1500), § 108.)*

Law Revision Commission Comments

Enactment [Revised Comment]

Section 2124 continues former Civil Code Section 4800.11(f) without substantive change. [23 Cal.L.Rev.Comm. Reports 1 (1993)].

Research References

Treatises and Practice Aids

Witkin, California Summary 10th Community Property § 243, Grounds and Time Limits.

§ 2125. Actions or motions to set aside judgment

When ruling on an action or motion to set aside a judgment, the court shall set aside only those provisions materially affected by the circumstances leading to the court's decision to grant relief. However, the court has discretion to set aside the entire judgment, if necessary, for equitable considerations. *(Added by Stats.1993, c. 219 (A.B.1500), § 108. Amended by Stats.1993, c. 1101 (A.B.1469), § 16, eff. Oct. 11, 1993, operative Jan. 1, 1994.)*

Law Revision Commission Comments

Enactment [Revised Comment]

Section 2125 continues former Civil Code Section 4800.11(g) without substantive change. [23 Cal.L.Rev.Comm. Reports 1 (1993)].

Commentary

See generally *In re Marriage of Brewer, 93 Cal.App.4th 1334, 113 Cal.Rptr.2d 849 (2001)* (trial court properly set aside stipulated judgment and marital settlement agreement on the basis of mistake under § 2122(e), when wife did not give the husband accurate and complete valuation of the her pension plans); and *In re Marriage of Varner, 55 Cal.App.4th 128, 63 Cal.Rptr.2d 894 (1997)* (setting aside a stipulated judgment on the ground of mistake under Section 2122(e)).

Research References

Treatises and Practice Aids

Witkin, California Summary 10th Community Property § 193, in General.
Witkin, California Summary 10th Community Property § 201, Misappropriation by Spouse.
Witkin, California Summary 10th Community Property § 243, Grounds and Time Limits.

§ 2126. Valuation date of assets or liabilities for which judgment was set aside; equal division

As to assets or liabilities for which a judgment or part of a judgment is set aside, the date of valuation shall be subject to equitable considerations. The court shall equally divide the asset or liability, unless the court finds upon good cause shown that the interests of justice require an unequal division. *(Added by Stats.1993, c. 219 (A.B.1500), § 108.)*

Law Revision Commission Comments

Enactment [Revised Comment]

Section 2126 continues former Civil Code Section 4800.11(h) without substantive change. [23 Cal.L.Rev.Comm. Reports 1 (1993)].

Research References

Treatises and Practice Aids

Witkin, California Summary 10th Community Property § 243, Grounds and Time Limits.

§ 2127. Actions or motions; statement of decision

As to actions or motions filed under this chapter, if a timely request is made, the court shall render a statement of decision where the court has resolved controverted factual evidence. *(Added by Stats.1993, c. 219 (A.B.1500), § 108. Amended by Stats.1993, c. 1101 (A.B.1469), § 17, eff. Oct. 11, 1993, operative Jan. 1, 1994.)*

Law Revision Commission Comments

Enactment [Revised Comment]

Section 2127 continues former Civil Code Section 4800.11(i) without substantive change. [23 Cal.L.Rev.Comm. Reports 1 (1993)].

Research References

Treatises and Practice Aids

Witkin, California Summary 10th Community Property § 243, Grounds and Time Limits.

§ 2128. Construction of chapter with other provisions

(a) Nothing in this chapter prohibits a party from seeking relief under Section 2556.

(b) Nothing in this chapter changes existing law with respect to contract remedies where the contract has not been merged or incorporated into a judgment.

(c) Nothing in this chapter is intended to restrict a family law court from acting as a court of equity.

(d) Nothing in this chapter is intended to limit existing law with respect to the modification or enforcement of support orders.

(e) Nothing in this chapter affects the rights of a bona fide lessee, purchaser, or encumbrancer for value of real property. *(Added by Stats.1993, c. 219 (A.B.1500), § 108.)*

Law Revision Commission Comments

Enactment [Revised Comment]

Section 2128 continues former Civil Code Section 4800.11(j)-(n) without substantive change. [23 Cal.L.Rev.Comm. Reports 1 (1993)].

Research References

Treatises and Practice Aids

Witkin, California Summary 10th Community Property § 243, Grounds and Time Limits.

Witkin, California Summary 10th Community Property § 248, Tort Action for Concealment.

§ 2129. Application of chapter

This chapter applies to judgments entered on or after January 1, 1993. *(Added by Stats.1993, c. 219 (A.B.1500), § 108.)*

Law Revision Commission Comments

Enactment [Revised Comment]

Section 2129 continues former Civil Code Section 4800.11(*o*) without substantive change. [23 Cal.L.Rev.Comm. Reports 1 (1993)].

Research References

Treatises and Practice Aids

Witkin, California Summary 10th Community Property § 242, in General.

Witkin, California Summary 10th Husband and Wife § 115, Setting Aside Judgment.

Part 2

JUDICIAL DETERMINATION OF VOID OR VOIDABLE MARRIAGE

CHAPTER 1. VOID MARRIAGE

§ 2200. Incestuous marriages

Marriages between parents and children, ancestors and descendants of every degree, and between siblings of the half as well as the whole blood, and between uncles or aunts and nieces or nephews, are incestuous, and void from the beginning, whether the relationship is legitimate or illegitimate. *(Stats.1992, c. 162 (A.B.2650), § 10, operative Jan. 1, 1994. Amended by Stats.2014, c. 82 (S.B.1306), § 23, eff. Jan. 1, 2015.)*

Law Revision Commission Comments

Enactment [Revised Comment]

Section 2200 continues former Civil Code Section 4400 without change. [23 Cal.L.Rev.Comm. Reports 1 (1993)].

Commentary

Even though a marriage is void because it is incestuous, one or both parties may enjoy the status of putative spouse if either or both believed that the marriage was valid. See Section 2251, including Commentary.

Research References

Forms

California Practice Guide: Rutter Family Law Forms Form 1:32, Glossary Of Common Family Law Terms, Phrases and Concepts (Enclosure to Form 1:31).

West's California Code Forms, Family § 2250, Comment Overview--Judgment Of Nullity.

Treatises and Practice Aids

Witkin, California Summary 10th Husband and Wife § 57, Methods Of Altering Marital Status.

Witkin, California Summary 10th Husband and Wife § 154, in General.

Witkin, California Summary 10th Husband and Wife § 155, Incest.

Witkin, California Summary 10th Husband and Wife § 165, in General.

Witkin, California Summary 10th Parent and Child § 60, Action to Determine Mother and Child Relationship.

Witkin, California Summary 10th Wills and Probate § 958, Capacity to Marry.

§ 2201. Bigamous and polygamous marriages; exceptions; absentees

(a) A subsequent marriage contracted by a person during the life of his or her former spouse, with a person other than the former spouse, is illegal and void, unless:

(1) The former marriage has been dissolved or adjudged a nullity before the date of the subsequent marriage.

(2) The former spouse (A) is absent, and not known to the person to be living for the period of five successive years immediately preceding the subsequent marriage, or (B) is generally reputed or believed by the person to be dead at the time the subsequent marriage was contracted.

(b) In either of the cases described in paragraph (2) of subdivision (a), the subsequent marriage is valid until its nullity is adjudged pursuant to subdivision (b) of Section 2210. *(Stats.1992, c. 162 (A.B.2650), § 10, operative Jan. 1, 1994. Amended by Stats.2014, c. 82 (S.B.1306), § 24, eff. Jan. 1, 2015.)*

Law Revision Commission Comments

Enactment [Revised Comment]

Section 2201 continues former Civil Code Section 4401 without substantive change. [23 Cal.L.Rev.Comm. Reports 1 (1993)].

Commentary

Because a bigamous marriage was, under applicable state law, illegal and void from the beginning, a wife's subsequent marriage was valid despite her failure to annul the prior bigamous marriage. *In re Marriage of Seaton, 200 Cal.App.4th 800, 133 Cal.Rptr.3d 50 (2011).*

Even though a marriage is void because it is bigamous, one or both parties may enjoy the status of putative spouse if either or both believed that the marriage was valid. See Section 2251, including Commentary.

The operation of the "Enoch Arden" provisions, subsections (a)(2) and (b), is illustrated in *Estate of LeMont, 7 Cal.App.3d 437, 86 Cal.Rptr. 810 (1970).*

Research References

Forms

California Practice Guide: Rutter Family Law Forms Form 1:32, Glossary Of Common Family Law Terms, Phrases and Concepts (Enclosure to Form 1:31).

West's California Code Forms, Family § 2250, Comment Overview--Judgment Of Nullity.

Treatises and Practice Aids

Witkin, California Summary 10th Husband and Wife § 154, in General.

Witkin, California Summary 10th Husband and Wife § 156, Bigamy.

CHAPTER 2. VOIDABLE MARRIAGE

§ 2210. Annulment, causes for

A marriage is voidable and may be adjudged a nullity if any of the following conditions existed at the time of the marriage:

(a) The party who commences the proceeding or on whose behalf the proceeding is commenced was without the capability of consenting to the marriage as provided in Section 301 or 302, unless, after attaining the age of consent, the party for any time freely cohabited with the other as his or her spouse.

(b) The spouse of either party was living and the marriage with that spouse was then in force and that spouse (1) was absent and not known to the party commencing the proceeding to be living for a period of five successive years immediately preceding the subsequent marriage for which the judgment of nullity is sought or (2) was generally reputed or believed by the party commencing the proceeding to be dead at the time the subsequent marriage was contracted.

(c) Either party was of unsound mind, unless the party of unsound mind, after coming to reason, freely cohabited with the other as his or her spouse.

(d) The consent of either party was obtained by fraud, unless the party whose consent was obtained by fraud afterwards, with full knowledge of the facts constituting the fraud, freely cohabited with the other as his or her spouse.

(e) The consent of either party was obtained by force, unless the party whose consent was obtained by force afterwards freely cohabited with the other as his or her spouse.

(f) Either party was, at the time of marriage, physically incapable of entering into the marriage state, and that incapacity continues, and appears to be incurable. *(Stats. 1992, c. 162 (A.B.2650), § 10, operative Jan. 1, 1994. Amended by Stats.2014, c. 82 (S.B.1306), § 25, eff. Jan. 1, 2015.)*

Law Revision Commission Comments

Enactment [Revised Comment]

Section 2210 continues former Civil Code Section 4425 without substantive change. [23 Cal.L.Rev.Comm. Reports 1 (1993)].

Commentary

Note that a minor is "capable of consenting" when Section 302 requirements are met, and thus the minor would appear ineligible for a subsection (a) annulment even though he or she has not yet reached the age of majority when the annulment is sought.

In re Marriage of Meagher & Maleki, 131 Cal.App.4th 1, 31 Cal.Rptr.3d 663 (2005), holds that the subsection (d) ground of fraud may not be satisfied by misrepresentation of a purely financial nature. Instead, actionable fraud must go to the "very essence of the marriage relationship," generally understood as misrepresentation of a sexual or procreative character.

For comprehensive discussion of subsection (d) *fraud*, see *In re Marriage of Johnston, 18 Cal.App.4th 499, 22 Cal.Rptr.2d 253 (1993).* See also *In re Marriage of Buckley, 133 Cal.App.3d 927, 933, 184 Cal.Rptr. 290 (1982)* (fraud action alleging fraudulent inducement into a void marriage is barred by Civil Code Section 43.4, the anti-heart-balm statute). *In re Marriage of Ramirez, 165 Cal.App.4th 751, 81 Cal.Rptr.3d 180 (2008)*, affirmed a trial court decision that a wife was entitled to an annulment under subsection (d), because her husband married her without intending to fulfill his section 720 duty of fidelity. Instead he intended to continue his preexisting affair with the bride's sister. No other California case has concluded that adultery alone constitutes *fraud* for purposes of subsection (d).

For discussion of subsection (e) *force*, see *In re Marriage of Weintraub, 167 Cal.App.3d 420, 213 Cal.Rptr. 159 (1985).*

Even though a marriage is voidable and is ultimately adjudged a nullity, one or both parties may enjoy the status of putative spouse if either or both believed that the marriage was valid. See Section 2251, Commentary.

Research References

Forms

California Practice Guide: Rutter Family Law Forms Form 1:32, Glossary Of Common Family Law Terms, Phrases and Concepts (Enclosure to Form 1:31).

West's California Code Forms, Family § 2250, Comment Overview--Judgment Of Nullity.

Treatises and Practice Aids

Witkin, California Summary 10th Husband and Wife § 154, in General.

Witkin, California Summary 10th Husband and Wife § 156, Bigamy.

Witkin, California Summary 10th Husband and Wife § 157, in General.

Witkin, California Summary 10th Husband and Wife § 160, Minority.

Witkin, California Summary 10th Husband and Wife § 161, Insanity.

Witkin, California Summary 10th Husband and Wife § 162, Physical Incapacity.

Witkin, California Summary 10th Husband and Wife § 163, Force.

§ 2211. Limitation of actions

A proceeding to obtain a judgment of nullity of marriage, for causes set forth in Section 2210, must be commenced within the periods and by the parties, as follows:

(a) For causes mentioned in subdivision (a) of Section 2210, by any of the following:

(1) The party to the marriage who was married under the age of legal consent, within four years after arriving at the age of consent.

(2) A parent, guardian, conservator, or other person having charge of the minor, at any time before the married minor has arrived at the age of legal consent.

(b) For causes mentioned in subdivision (b) of Section 2210, by either of the following:

(1) Either party during the life of the other.

(2) The former spouse.

(c) For causes mentioned in subdivision (c) of Section 2210, by the party injured, or by a relative or conservator of the party of unsound mind, at any time before the death of either party.

(d) For causes mentioned in subdivision (d) of Section 2210, by the party whose consent was obtained by fraud, within four years after the discovery of the facts constituting the fraud.

(e) For causes mentioned in subdivision (e) of Section 2210, by the party whose consent was obtained by force, within four years after the marriage.

(f) For causes mentioned in subdivision (f) of Section 2210, by the injured party, within four years after the marriage. *(Stats.1992, c. 162 (A.B.2650), § 10, operative Jan. 1, 1994. Amended by Stats.2014, c. 82 (S.B.1306), § 26, eff. Jan. 1, 2015.)*

Law Revision Commission Comments

Enactment [Revised Comment]

Section 2211 continues former Civil Code Section 4426 without substantive change. In subdivision (a)(2), "underage" has been substituted for "nonaged" to conform to language used in other sections of this code. See, e.g., Sections 302, 353 (underage applicants for marriage license), 1814(b)(5) (conciliation counselor recommendations on marriage where party underage). In subdivisions (d) and (e), specific descriptions of the party have been substituted for the general reference to the injured party. For background on former Civ. Code § 4426, see *Recommendation Relating to Guardianship–Conservatorship Law,* 14 Cal. L. Revision Comm'n Reports 501 (1978). [23 Cal.L.Rev.Comm. Reports 1 (1993)].

Commentary

Applying subsection (d), *Pryor v. Pryor, 177 Cal.App.4th 1448, 99 Cal.Rptr.3d 853 (2009)*, held that a decedent's daughter lacked standing to seek annulment of decedent's allegedly fraudulent confidential marriage. However, *Pryor*'s invocation of the subsection (d) limitations may have been inapt insofar as the daughter's contention was not that her father's consent to marriage was fraudulently obtained, but that her father's signature on the confidential marriage license was forged, in which case there may have been no confidential marriage at all.

In re Marriage of Higgason, 10 Cal.3d 476, 483, 110 Cal.Rptr. 897 (1973), holds that subsection (d) and (f) actions may be brought by a spouse's guardian ad litem.

Does an annulment action survive the death of a spouse? The law is unsettled. *In re Marriage of Goldberg, 22 Cal.App.4th 265, 27 Cal.Rptr.2d 298 (1994), review denied 5/19/94*, held that a husband's action for an annulment based on fraud initiated before the husband's death did not abate at the husband's death but instead survived it. In contrast, *Greene v. Williams, 9 Cal.App.3d 559, 88 Cal.Rptr. 261 (1970)*, held that a parent could not bring an annulment action based on her deceased son's nonage after the son's death. Although *Goldberg* narrowly distinguishes *Greene* on its facts, the reasoning of the two cases is not reconcilable.

Research References

Treatises and Practice Aids

Witkin, California Summary 10th Husband and Wife § 148, in General.

Witkin, California Summary 10th Husband and Wife § 152, Survival Of Cause Of Action.

Witkin, California Summary 10th Husband and Wife § 153, Dissolution Distinguished.

Witkin, California Summary 10th Husband and Wife § 160, Minority.

Witkin, California Summary 10th Husband and Wife § 161, Insanity.

Witkin, California Summary 10th Husband and Wife § 170, Venue, Limitations, Parties, and Pleadings.

Witkin, California Summary 10th Wills and Probate § 958, Capacity to Marry.

§ 2212. Effect of judgment of nullity; conclusiveness

(a) The effect of a judgment of nullity of marriage is to restore the parties to the status of unmarried persons.

(b) A judgment of nullity of marriage is conclusive only as to the parties to the proceeding and those claiming under them. *(Stats.1992, c. 162 (A.B.2650), § 10, operative Jan. 1, 1994.)*

Law Revision Commission Comments

Enactment [Revised Comment]

Subdivision (a) of Section 2212 continues former Civil Code Section 4429 without substantive change. Subdivision (b) continues former Civil Code Section 4451 without substantive change. [23 Cal.L.Rev.Comm. Reports 1 (1993)].

Research References

Forms

West's California Code Forms, Family § 2250, Comment Overview--Judgment Of Nullity.

Treatises and Practice Aids

Witkin, California Summary 10th Husband and Wife § 169, Effect Of Foreign Decree.

Witkin, California Summary 10th Husband and Wife § 171, Hearing, Incidental Orders, and Judgment.

CHAPTER 3. PROCEDURAL PROVISIONS

§ 2250. Petition for judgment of nullity; filing; service

(a) A proceeding based on void or voidable marriage is commenced by filing a petition entitled "In re the marriage of ________ and ________" which shall state that it is a petition for a judgment of nullity of the marriage.

(b) A copy of the petition together with a copy of a summons in form and content approved by the Judicial Council shall be served upon the other party to the marriage in the same manner as service of papers in civil actions generally. *(Stats.1992, c. 162 (A.B.2650), § 10, operative Jan. 1, 1994.)*

Law Revision Commission Comments

Enactment [Revised Comment]

Section 2250 continues former Civil Code Section 4450 without substantive change. The reference to the "superior" court has been omitted as surplus. See Section 200 (jurisdiction in superior court). See also Sections 2080–2082 (restoration of wife's former name). [23 Cal.L.Rev.Comm. Reports 1 (1993)].

Commentary

Note that 2013 amendments to Code of Civil Procedure section 583.161 expanded the definition of petitions and orders that are not subject to mandatory dismissal, including petitions and orders under this section.

In re Marriage of Garcia, 13 Cal.App.5th 1334, 221 Cal.Rptr.3d 319 (2017), held that a court's determination that the parties had never been legally married did not bar a subsequent action for nullity of marriage, because actions for dissolution and nullity involve different claims and rights.

Research References

Forms

California Practice Guide: Rutter Family Law Forms Form 1:32, Glossary Of Common Family Law Terms, Phrases and Concepts (Enclosure to Form 1:31).

West's California Code Forms, Family § 2250, Comment Overview--Judgment Of Nullity.

Treatises and Practice Aids

Witkin, California Summary 10th Husband and Wife § 148, in General.

Witkin, California Summary 10th Husband and Wife § 170, Venue, Limitations, Parties, and Pleadings.

§ 2251. Status of putative spouse; division of community or quasi-community property

(a) If a determination is made that a marriage is void or voidable and the court finds that either party or both parties believed in good faith that the marriage was valid, the court shall:

(1) Declare the party or parties, who believed in good faith that the marriage was valid, to have the status of a putative spouse.

(2) If the division of property is in issue, divide, in accordance with Division 7 (commencing with Section 2500), that property acquired during the union that would have been community property or quasi-community property if the union had not been void or voidable, only upon request of a party who is declared a putative spouse under paragraph (1). This property is known as "quasi-marital property."

(b) If the court expressly reserves jurisdiction, it may make the property division at a time after the judgment. *(Stats. 1992, c. 162 (A.B.2650), § 10, operative Jan. 1, 1994. Amended by Stats.2015, c. 196 (A.B.380), § 1, eff. Jan. 1, 2016.)*

Law Revision Commission Comments

Enactment [Revised Comment]

Section 2251 continues the first three sentences of former Civil Code Section 4452 without substantive change. A reference to the division governing property division has been substituted for the narrower reference to former Civil Code Section 4800. This is not a substantive change. [23 Cal.L.Rev.Comm. Reports 1 (1993)].

Commentary

In re Marriage of Garcia, 13 Cal.App.5th 1334, 221 Cal.Rptr.3d 319 (2017), held that a court's determination that the parties had never been legally married did not bar a subsequent action for nullity of marriage, because actions for dissolution and nullity involve different claims and rights.

This section codifies the putative spouse doctrine, which may apply when parties attempt to contract a lawful marriage and one or both maintain a good faith belief that the marriage is valid. Putative spouse status continues only as long as the good faith belief. Once a putative spouse learns that the marriage is not valid, he or she loses her putative spouse status with respect to subsequently acquired property. *Lazzarevich v. Lazzarevich, 88 Cal.App.2d 708, 718, 200 P.2d 49 (1948)*.

A person's objectively reasonable, good faith belief that his California domestic partnership was validly registered entitles him to all the rights and benefits of domestic partnership as a putative domestic partner, even though registration never occurred. *In re Domestic Partnership of Ellis and Arriaga, 162 Cal.App.4th 1000, 76 Cal.Rptr.3d 401 (2008)*. Thus when two men signed and notarized a

California declaration of domestic partnership and one of them failed to keep his promise to send the declaration to the California Secretary of State, his partner could claim the status of putative domestic partner.

But compare *Velez v. Smith, 142 Cal.App.4th 1154, 1173-1174, 48 Cal.Rptr.3d 642 (2006)*, refusing to recognize as state putative domestic partners parties who registered only for the more limited legal status of municipal domestic partners. Also compare *Burnham v. California Public Employees' Retirement System, 208 Cal.App.4th 1576, 146 Cal.Rptr.3d 607 (2012)*, declining to recognize as a putative spouse the survivor of a couple when the parties notarized a declaration of partnership, but one party died before it was registered with the Secretary of State.

The putative spouse doctrine is generally understood to remedy a defect in legal capacity, as opposed to failure to satisfy the formal legal requirements for contracting a marriage. (For discussion of the distinction between legal capacity and the formal requirements for contracting a marriage, see Sections 300 and 2200, Commentary.) See, for example, *Estate of Vargas, 36 Cal.App.3d 714, 716–717, 111 Cal.Rptr. 779 (1974)*, defining a putative spouse as "an innocent participant who has duly solemnized a matrimonial union which is void because of some legal infirmity." The usual legal infirmity is a prior undissolved marriage.

Nevertheless, some California cases have found a putative marriage when the parties have failed to comply with some or all of the formal marriage requirements. See, for example, *Santos v. Santos, 32 Cal.App.2d 62, 89 P.2d 164 (1939)*, finding a putative marriage when a non-English-speaking couple secured a California marriage license and, believing they were thereby married, began living together as husband and wife. Before the California Supreme Court's decision in *Ceja infra*, the courts of appeal split on whether the doctrine extends to informal California unions, that is, to relationships that might have been common-law marriages if they had been contracted before California abolished the doctrine of common-law marriage in 1895. Compare *Wagner v. Imperial County, 145 Cal.App.3d 980, 193 Cal.Rptr. 820 (1983)* (finding a putative marriage when parties had a good faith, albeit erroneous, belief that they had contracted a common-law marriage in California) with *Centinela Hospital Medical Center v. Superior Court, 215 Cal.App.3d 971, 263 Cal.Rptr. 672 (1989), review denied* (declining to find a putative marriage on similar facts). (For discussion of California recognition of common-law marriages contracted in other states, see Commentary to section 300.)

Subjective or objective good faith belief? In *Ceja v. Rudolph & Sletten, 56 Cal.4th 1113, 302 P.3d 211, 158 Cal.Rptr.3d 211 (2013)*, the California Supreme Court held that the sole issue is whether the person claiming the status of putative spouse had a subjective belief that she was lawfully married. *Ceja* prescribes an "all the factors" test, in which the claimant's effort to comply with legal formalities is merely one fact. Presumably, the objective reasonableness of a claimant's belief that she had satisfied the legal formalities would go to the question of her subjective belief that she was lawfully married. *Ceja* purports to disapprove the line of cases discussed below, which required, when the parties did not satisfy the legal formalities, an objectively reasonable belief that the parties contracted any marriage at all, be it lawful, void, or voidable. However, it is not clear whether the *Ceja* formulation would require different results on the facts of those cases.

Arguably, *Ceja* conflates two distinct issues. First, was there *any marriage at all*, albeit one that was void or voidable? If so, did the claimant maintain a subjective good faith belief in the validity of that marriage? If the marriage was a duly licensed ceremonial marriage, the only issue is the claimant's subjective good faith belief in its validity. *Estate of Vargas, supra*. Yet when there was no duly licensed formal marriage, the claimant must also prove that there was a marriage. In such circumstance, some recent cases have required that the claimant's belief *that there was a lawful marriage* be objectively reasonable. See, for example, *Estate of DePasse, 97 Cal.App.4th 92, 118 Cal.Rptr.2d 143 (2002), review denied June 26, 2002* (holding that issuance of a marriage license is a mandatory requirement for a valid marriage in California and that surviving spouse was not a putative spouse because he knew of the license requirement and thus had no objectively reasonable belief that he had contracted a valid marriage); *In re Marriage of Vryonis, 202 Cal.App.3d 712, 720–723, 248 Cal.Rptr. 807 (1988)* (holding objectively unreasonable a foreign claimant's belief that she had entered a California marriage when she neglected to inquire about or follow California marriage law); *Centinela Hospital, supra* at 975 (requiring an objectively reasonable belief in the existence of a marriage and holding that California's 1895 abolition of common-law marriage renders unreasonable, as a matter of law, a putative spouse claim predicated upon a subjective good faith belief in the lawfulness of a California attempt to enter a common-law marriage); and *Welch v. State of California, 83 Cal.App.4th 1374, 100 Cal.Rptr.2d 430 (2000)* (accord). Compare *Wagner, supra*, where the court required only a subjective good faith belief, albeit erroneous, that the parties had successfully contracted a California common law marriage.

What about the bad faith spouse? When there is a putative marriage because one spouse qualifies as a putative spouse, the California Supreme Court has pointedly left open the question of how the other spouse, who knew about the legal defect, should be treated. See *Marvin v. Marvin, 18 Cal.3d 660, 680 n. 18, 557 P.2d 106, 134 Cal.Rptr. 815 (1976)*. Section 2251, subsection (a)(2), may be read to indicate that both spouses should effectively be treated as putative spouses. Apparently unaware that the question was reserved by the Supreme Court in *Marvin*, *In re Marriage of Ramirez, 165 Cal.App.4th 751, 81 Cal.Rptr.3d 180 (2008)*, summarily concluded that a good faith putative spouse was a putative spouse, but that person's spouse, who could not claim good faith, was not a putative spouse. However, after careful analysis of the statutory language, *In re Marriage of Tejeda, 179 Cal.App.4th 973, 102 Cal.Rptr.3d 361 (2009)*, concluded that once a court finds one party to be a putative spouse, it must treat all property earned by the labor of either party during the relationship as quasi-marital property and divide that property equally between the parties. *In re Marriage of Guo & Sun, 186 Cal.App.4th 1491, 112 Cal.Rptr.3d 906 (2010)*, rejected the holding of *Tejeda*. Relying instead on the case law history of the putative spouse doctrine, *Guo & Sun* held that a claim for quasi-marital property dissolution may only be asserted by a good-faith putative spouse.

Although the cases often do not clearly distinguish between the two distinct questions identified in this Commentary (Did the claimant have an objectively reasonable basis for believing that the parties had contracted a marriage, albeit voidable or void? If so, did the claimant have a subjective good faith belief in the lawfulness of that marriage?), case decisions are generally consistent with the rubric laid out in the Commentary. The California Supreme Court has granted review to *Ceja v. Rudolph & Sletten*, in which the superseded court of appeal opinion, *125 Cal.Rptr.3d 98 (2011)*, conflated the two issues and purported to hold that only a subjective belief is required for both issues.

When a putative spouse claim fails because the claimant knew that her duly regularized marriage was invalid, the doctrine of estoppel may provide an effective substitute. When the spouse asserting the invalidity of a marriage knew that it was invalid but nevertheless continued to cohabit, he may be estopped to assert the invalidity of the marriage. See, for example, *In re Marriage of Recknor, 138 Cal.App.3d 539, 546, 187 Cal.Rptr. 887 (1982)*. But see *In re Marriage of Vryonis, 202 Cal.App.3d 712, 248 Cal.Rptr. 807 (1988)* (criticizing the estoppel analysis of *Recknor*). See generally *Spellens v. Spellens, 49 Cal.2d 210, 317 P.2d 613 (1957)*.

Putative spouse status suffices for most, but not all, entitlements due the lawful spouse. See generally *Estate of Leslie, 37 Cal.3d 186, 207 Cal.Rptr. 561 (1984)*. But see *Estate of Hafner, 184 Cal.App.3d 1371, 1396, 229 Cal.Rptr. 676 (1986), review denied 11/20/86* (statutory allowance for "surviving spouse" not available to a putative spouse). Compare *Estate of Sax, 214 Cal.App.3d 1300, 263 Cal.Rptr. 190 (1989)* (putative spouse is surviving spouse within meaning of "omitted spouse" provision). See additionally Section 306, Commentary.

An informal relationship, or cohabitation, that does not qualify as a lawful or putative *marriage* under any California doctrine is not regulated by the Family Code but is instead subject only to the law of contract. See generally *Marvin v. Marvin, 18 Cal.3d 660, 134 Cal.Rptr. 815 (1976)* (applying contractual remedies at the dissolution of a six-year cohabitation) and *Byrne v. Laura, 52 Cal.App.4th 1054, 60 Cal.Rptr.2d 908 (1997), review denied May 28, 1997* (primer for cohabitation claims after the death of a nonmarital partner). *Cochran v. Cochran, 89 Cal.App.4th 283, 106 Cal.Rptr.2d 899 (2001)*, holds that, for *Marvin* purposes, the parties may cohabit ("live together as husband and wife") even though they do not live together on a full-time basis. See also *Elden v. Sheldon, 46 Cal.3d 267, 250 Cal.Rptr. 254 (1988)* (no loss of consortium recovery when cohabitant is tortiously killed because marriage is a prerequisite for a loss of consortium claim; cohabitant is not sufficiently "closely related" to victim to maintain an action for negligent infliction of emotional distress); and *Friedman v. Friedman, 20 Cal.App.4th 876, 24 Cal. Rptr.2d 892 (1993)* (trial court lacks authority to award temporary "spousal support" to disabled cohabitant pending trial of *Marvin* contract action). Case law is divided on whether actual cohabitation, that is, living in a common household, is required in order to enforce a contract arising from a companionate sexual relationship. Compare *Bergen v. Wood, 14 Cal.App.4th 854, 18 Cal.Rptr.2d 75 (1993), review denied 7/15/93* (support contract not enforced) with *Milian v. De Leon, 181 Cal.App.3d 1185, 226 Cal.Rptr. 831 (1986)* (property contract enforced). *Bergen v. Wood* concludes, despite facts suggesting the contrary, that without the performance of domestic services in cohabitation, a contract is necessarily solely for sexual services and hence is unenforceable. *Bergen* is criticized at 1993 Cal. Family Law Monthly 144. Compare *Della Zoppa v. Della Zoppa, 86 Cal. App.4th 1144, 103 Cal.Rptr.2d 901 (2001)* (holding that trial court erred in concluding that agreement was meretricious and hence unenforceable because the parties planned to have sexual relations and to have children together). For discussion of quantum meruit recovery in cohabitation cases, see *Maglica v. Maglica, 66 Cal.App.4th 442, 78 Cal.Rptr.2d 101 (1998), review denied December 16, 1998* (measure of quantum meruit recovery is reasonable market value of services provided, not the greater amount by which defendant's solely owned business was benefited by the services; quantum meruit claim did not accrue until parties ended their cohabitation).

A cause of action for breach of a ("Marvin") cohabitation agreement accrues, and the statute of limitations begins to run, when a cohabitant fails to perform the agreement, not when the cohabitants separate. *Cochran v. Cochran, 56 Cal.App.4th 1115, 66 Cal. Rptr.2d 337 (1997).*

Research References

Forms

West's California Code Forms, Family § 2250, Comment Overview--Judgment Of Nullity.

Treatises and Practice Aids

Witkin, California Summary 10th Community Property § 190, General Rule Of Equal Division.

Witkin, California Summary 10th Community Property § 263, Modern View.

Witkin, California Summary 10th Community Property § 265, Codification.

Witkin, California Summary 10th Community Property § 266, Where Legal Spouse Also Claims.

Witkin, California Summary 10th Husband and Wife § 149, Void Marriage.

Witkin, California Summary 10th Husband and Wife § 150, in General.

Witkin, California Summary 10th Husband and Wife § 171, Hearing, Incidental Orders, and Judgment.

§ 2252. Liability of quasi-marital property for debts of parties

The property divided pursuant to Section 2251 is liable for debts of the parties to the same extent as if the property had been community property or quasi-community property. *(Stats.1992, c. 162 (A.B.2650), § 10, operative Jan. 1, 1994.)*

Law Revision Commission Comments

Enactment [Revised Comment]

Section 2252 continues the last sentence of former Civil Code Section 4452 without substantive change. Under Section 2252, quasi-marital property is treated the same as community and quasi-community property for purposes of creditors' remedies. See Section 916 (liability of property after division). For background on former Civ. Code § 4452, see *Recommendation Relating to Liability of Marital Property for Debts,* 17 Cal. L. Revision Comm'n Reports 1 (1984). [23 Cal.L.Rev.Comm. Reports 1 (1993)].

Research References

Treatises and Practice Aids

Witkin, California Summary 10th Community Property § 190, General Rule Of Equal Division.

Witkin, California Summary 10th Community Property § 263, Modern View.

Witkin, California Summary 10th Community Property § 265, Codification.

Witkin, California Summary 10th Community Property § 266, Where Legal Spouse Also Claims.

Witkin, California Summary 10th Husband and Wife § 171, Hearing, Incidental Orders, and Judgment.

§ 2253. Children of annulled marriage; determination of custody

In a proceeding under this part, custody of the children shall be determined according to Division 8 (commencing with Section 3000). *(Stats.1992, c. 162 (A.B.2650), § 10, operative Jan. 1, 1994.)*

Law Revision Commission Comments

Enactment [Revised Comment]

Section 2253 continues former Civil Code Section 4454 without substantive change. A reference to the division governing custody has been substituted for the narrower reference to former Civil Code Section 4600. This is not a substantive change. [23 Cal.L.Rev. Comm. Reports 1 (1993)].

Research References

Forms

California Transactions Forms--Family Law § 3:4, Subject Matter Jurisdiction for Custody Determinations.

Treatises and Practice Aids

Witkin, California Summary 10th Husband and Wife § 171, Hearing, Incidental Orders, and Judgment.

Witkin, California Summary 10th Parent and Child § 267, Jurisdiction and Venue.

§ 2254. Order for support; putative spouse

The court may, during the pendency of a proceeding for nullity of marriage or upon judgment of nullity of marriage, order a party to pay for the support of the other party in the same manner as if the marriage had not been void or voidable if the party for whose benefit the order is made is found to be a putative spouse. *(Stats.1992, c. 162 (A.B.2650), § 10, operative Jan. 1, 1994.)*

Law Revision Commission Comments

Enactment [Revised Comment]

Section 2254 continues former Civil Code Section 4455 without substantive change. [23 Cal.L.Rev.Comm. Reports 1 (1993)].

Commentary

See generally Section 2251, Commentary. Even though a party to a void marriage may be ineligible to claim as a putative spouse, the other party may be estopped to deny the marriage, in which case the first party is eligible for ordinary Section 4330 support. *In re Marriage of Recknor, 138 Cal.App.3d 539, 542, 187 Cal.Rptr. 887 (1982)*. But see *In re Marriage of Vryonis, 202 Cal.App.3d 712, 248 Cal.Rptr. 807 (1988)* (criticizing the estoppel analysis of *Recknor*).

Research References

Treatises and Practice Aids

Witkin, California Summary 10th Community Property § 265, Codification.
Witkin, California Summary 10th Community Property § 268, Codification.
Witkin, California Summary 10th Husband and Wife § 149, Void Marriage.
Witkin, California Summary 10th Husband and Wife § 151, Relation Back Theory.
Witkin, California Summary 10th Husband and Wife § 171, Hearing, Incidental Orders, and Judgment.
Witkin, California Summary 10th Husband and Wife § 172, Temporary Support.
Witkin, California Summary 10th Husband and Wife § 177, Types Of Actions.
Witkin, California Summary 10th Husband and Wife § 183, Marital Relationship.
Witkin, California Summary 10th Husband and Wife § 208, Basis Of Award.

§ 2255. Grant of attorney's fees and costs

The court may grant attorney's fees and costs in accordance with Chapter 3.5 (commencing with Section 2030) of Part 1 in proceedings to have the marriage adjudged void and in those proceedings based upon voidable marriage in which the party applying for attorney's fees and costs is found to be innocent of fraud or wrongdoing in inducing or entering into the marriage, and free from knowledge of the then existence of any prior marriage or other impediment to the contracting of the marriage for which a judgment of nullity is sought. *(Stats.1992, c. 162 (A.B.2650), § 10, operative Jan. 1, 1994. Amended by Stats.1993, c. 219 (A.B.1500), § 108.5.)*

Law Revision Commission Comments

Enactment [Revised Comment]

Section 2255 continues former Civil Code Section 4456 without substantive change. A reference to Chapter 3.5 (commencing with Section 2030) of Part 1 has been substituted for the narrower reference to former Civil Code Section 4370. This is not a substantive change. See also Sections 270–272 (attorney's fees and costs generally). [23 Cal.L.Rev.Comm. Reports 1 (1993)].

Research References

Forms

West's California Code Forms, Family § 2250, Comment Overview--Judgment Of Nullity.

Treatises and Practice Aids

Witkin, California Summary 10th Husband and Wife § 149, Void Marriage.
Witkin, California Summary 10th Husband and Wife § 151, Relation Back Theory.
Witkin, California Summary 10th Husband and Wife § 173, Attorneys' Fees and Costs Pending Proceeding.
Witkin, California Summary 10th Husband and Wife § 177, Types Of Actions.
Witkin, California Summary 10th Husband and Wife § 183, Marital Relationship.

Part 3

DISSOLUTION OF MARRIAGE AND LEGAL SEPARATION

CHAPTER 1. EFFECT OF DISSOLUTION

§ 2300. Effect of dissolution

The effect of a judgment of dissolution of marriage when it becomes final is to restore the parties to the state of unmarried persons. *(Stats.1992, c. 162 (A.B.2650), § 10, operative Jan. 1, 1994.)*

Law Revision Commission Comments

Enactment [Revised Comment]

Section 2300 continues former Civil Code Section 4501 without substantive change. The words "when it becomes final" have been added to recognize that there is a waiting period before the judgment of dissolution becomes final. See Section 2339 (waiting period before dissolution judgment becomes final). See also Sections 2340–2344 (date of termination). [23 Cal.L.Rev.Comm. Reports 1 (1993)].

Research References

Forms

California Practice Guide: Rutter Family Law Forms Form 1:32, Glossary Of Common Family Law Terms, Phrases and Concepts (Enclosure to Form 1:31).
California Transactions Forms--Family Law § 2:51, Preparation Of Future Returns.

Treatises and Practice Aids

Witkin, California Summary 10th Husband and Wife § 57, Methods Of Altering Marital Status.

Witkin, California Summary 10th Husband and Wife § 59, Fault Theory Eliminated for Dissolution.

CHAPTER 2. GROUNDS FOR DISSOLUTION OR LEGAL SEPARATION

§ 2310. Grounds for dissolution or legal separation

Dissolution of the marriage or legal separation of the parties may be based on either of the following grounds, which shall be pleaded generally:

(a) Irreconcilable differences, which have caused the irremediable breakdown of the marriage.

(b) Permanent legal incapacity to make decisions. *(Stats. 1992, c. 162 (A.B.2650), § 10, operative Jan. 1, 1994. Amended by Stats.2014, c. 144 (A.B.1847), § 9, eff. Jan. 1, 2015.)*

Law Revision Commission Comments

Enactment [Revised Comment]

Section 2310 continues former Civil Code Section 4506 without substantive change. The reference to the court decree has been omitted as surplus. See Section 100 ("judgment" and "order" include decree, as appropriate). [23 Cal.L.Rev.Comm. Reports 1 (1993)].

Commentary

Diosdado v. Diosdado, 97 Cal.App.4th 470, 118 Cal.Rptr.2d 494 (2002), holds that a contract between husband and wife providing for liquidated damages if either is sexually unfaithful to the other, is unenforceable because it violates the public policy underlying California's no-fault divorce laws. Similarly, Cf. *In re Marriage of Dargan, 118 Cal.App.4th 1167, 13 Cal.Rptr.3d 522 (2004), review denied*, holding that an agreement made pursuant to a married couple's reconciliation, which provided that the wife would receive all of husband's interest in certain community property if he resumed the use of illicit drugs, was unenforceable because it violated the public policy favoring no-fault divorce.

Research References

Forms

California Practice Guide: Rutter Family Law Forms Form 1:32, Glossary Of Common Family Law Terms, Phrases and Concepts (Enclosure to Form 1:31).

Treatises and Practice Aids

Witkin, California Summary 10th Community Property § 32, Agreements Violating Public Policy.
Witkin, California Summary 10th Husband and Wife § 60, Nature Of Ground.
Witkin, California Summary 10th Husband and Wife § 61, Substantial Reasons for Dissolution.
Witkin, California Summary 10th Husband and Wife § 62, Evidence Of Misconduct is Ordinarily Inadmissible.
Witkin, California Summary 10th Husband and Wife § 63, Nature Of Ground.
Witkin, California Summary 10th Husband and Wife § 83, Petition.
Witkin, California Summary 10th Husband and Wife § 144, in General.
Witkin, California Summary 10th Husband and Wife § 145, Grounds and Defenses.

§ 2311. "Irreconcilable differences" defined

Irreconcilable differences are those grounds which are determined by the court to be substantial reasons for not continuing the marriage and which make it appear that the marriage should be dissolved. *(Stats.1992, c. 162 (A.B.2650), § 10, operative Jan. 1, 1994.)*

Law Revision Commission Comments

Enactment [Revised Comment]

Section 2311 continues former Civil Code Section 4507 without change. [23 Cal.L.Rev.Comm. Reports 1 (1993)].

Research References

Treatises and Practice Aids

Witkin, California Summary 10th Husband and Wife § 60, Nature Of Ground.
Witkin, California Summary 10th Husband and Wife § 61, Substantial Reasons for Dissolution.

§ 2312. Permanent legal incapacity to make decisions

A marriage may be dissolved on the grounds of permanent legal incapacity to make decisions only upon proof, including competent medical or psychiatric testimony, that the spouse was at the time the petition was filed, and remains, permanently lacking the legal capacity to make decisions. *(Stats. 1992, c. 162 (A.B.2650), § 10, operative Jan. 1, 1994. Amended by Stats.2014, c. 144 (A.B.1847), § 10, eff. Jan. 1, 2015.)*

Law Revision Commission Comments

Enactment [Revised Comment]

Section 2312 continues former Civil Code Section 4510(a) without change. For background on former Civ. Code § 4510, see *Recommendation Relating to Guardianship–Conservatorship Law,* 14 Cal. L. Revision Comm'n Reports 501, 930 (1978). [23 Cal.L.Rev.Comm. Reports 1 (1993)].

Research References

Forms

West's California Code Forms, Family § 2330, Comment Overview--Procedures.

Treatises and Practice Aids

Witkin, California Summary 10th Husband and Wife § 64, Proof.

§ 2313. Support of spouse lacking legal capacity to make decisions

No dissolution of marriage granted on the ground of permanent legal incapacity to make decisions relieves a spouse from any obligation imposed by law as a result of the marriage for the support of the spouse who lacks legal capacity to make decisions, and the court may make an order for support, or require a bond therefor, as the circumstances require. *(Stats.1992, c. 162 (A.B.2650), § 10, operative Jan. 1, 1994. Amended by Stats.2014, c. 144 (A.B.1847), § 11, eff. Jan. 1, 2015.)*

Law Revision Commission Comments

Enactment [Revised Comment]

Section 2313 continues former Civil Code Section 4510(b) without substantive change. The former reference to "decree" has been omitted as surplus. See Section 100 ("judgment" and "order" include decree, as appropriate). For background on former Civ. Code § 4510, see *Recommendation Relating to Guardianship–Conservatorship Law,* 14 Cal. L. Revision Comm'n Reports 501, 930 (1978). [23 Cal.L.Rev.Comm. Reports 1 (1993)].

Research References

Forms

West's California Code Forms, Family § 2330, Comment Overview-- Procedures.

Treatises and Practice Aids

Witkin, California Summary 10th Husband and Wife § 65, Support Of Insane Spouse.

CHAPTER 3. RESIDENCE REQUIREMENTS

§ 2320. Entry of judgment of dissolution; entry of judgment for dissolution, nullity, or legal separation of a marriage between persons of the same sex

(a) Except as provided in subdivision (b), a judgment of dissolution of marriage may not be entered unless one of the parties to the marriage has been a resident of this state for six months and of the county in which the proceeding is filed for three months next preceding the filing of the petition.

(b)(1) A judgment for dissolution, nullity, or legal separation of a marriage between persons of the same sex may be entered, even if neither spouse is a resident of, or maintains a domicile in, this state at the time the proceedings are filed, if the following apply:

(A) The marriage was entered in California.

(B) Neither party to the marriage resides in a jurisdiction that will dissolve the marriage. If the jurisdiction does not recognize the marriage, there shall be a rebuttable presumption that the jurisdiction will not dissolve the marriage.

(2) For the purposes of this subdivision, the superior court in the county where the marriage was entered shall be the proper court for the proceeding. The dissolution, nullity, or legal separation shall be adjudicated in accordance with California law. *(Stats.1992, c. 162 (A.B.2650), § 10, operative Jan. 1, 1994. Amended by Stats.2011, c. 721 (S.B.651), § 4.)*

Law Revision Commission Comments

Enactment [Revised Comment]

Section 2320 continues former Civil Code Section 4530(a) without substantive change. See also Code Civ. Proc. § 395 (venue for marriage dissolution proceeding). [23 Cal.L.Rev.Comm. Reports 1 (1993)].

Commentary

"Resident" is synonymous with "domiciliary." *Whealton v. Whealton, 67 Cal.2d 656, 660, 63 Cal.Rptr. 291 (1967)*. Domicile requires both the act of residence and the intention to make that place one's home. *In re Marriage of Thornton, 135 Cal.App.3d 500, 507, 185 Cal.Rptr. 388 (1982)* (distinguishing domicile from residence). A nonimmigrant alien may establish residence for purposes of obtaining a California dissolution. *In re Marriage of Dick, 15 Cal.App.4th 144, 18 Cal.Rptr.2d 743 (1993), review denied 8/26/93* (allowing a Canadian tourist to establish California divorce residence).

To the same effect see, *In re Marriage of Amezquita & Archuleta, 101 Cal.App.4th 1415, 124 Cal.Rptr.2d 887 (2002)*, which holds that, for purposes of § 4962 modification of out-of-state child support orders, a person does not "reside" in California if the person is domiciled in another state. As in this section, "residence" means "domicile."

Research References

Forms

California Practice Guide: Rutter Family Law Forms Form 4:19, Request for Order to Quash Proceeding.

West's California Code Forms, Family § 2330, Comment Overview-- Procedures.

West's California Judicial Council Forms FL-100, Petition - Marriage/Domestic Partnership.

West's California Judicial Council Forms FL-800, Joint Petition for Summary Dissolution.

Treatises and Practice Aids

Witkin, California Summary 10th Husband and Wife § 73, Residence and Venue.

Witkin, California Summary 10th Husband and Wife § 125, Conditions.

Witkin, California Summary 10th Husband and Wife § 129, Background.

Witkin, California Summary 10th Husband and Wife § 138, Exception for "Unique Circumstances.".

Witkin, California Summary 10th Husband and Wife § 153, Dissolution Distinguished.

§ 2321. Conversion of separation proceeding to dissolution proceeding; notice

(a) In a proceeding for legal separation of the parties in which neither party, at the time the proceeding was commenced, has complied with the residence requirements of Section 2320, either party may, upon complying with the residence requirements, amend the party's petition or responsive pleading in the proceeding to request that a judgment of dissolution of the marriage be entered. The date of the filing of the amended petition or pleading shall be deemed to be the date of commencement of the proceeding for the dissolution of the marriage for the purposes only of the residence requirements of Section 2320.

(b) If the other party has appeared in the proceeding, notice of the amendment shall be given to the other party in the manner provided by rules adopted by the Judicial Council. If no appearance has been made by the other party in the proceeding, notice of the amendment may be given to the other party by mail to the last known address of the other party, or by personal service, if the intent of the party to so amend upon satisfaction of the residence requirements of Section 2320 is set forth in the initial petition or pleading in the manner provided by rules adopted by the Judicial

Council. *(Stats.1992, c. 162 (A.B.2650), § 10, operative Jan. 1, 1994.)*

Law Revision Commission Comments

Enactment [Revised Comment]

Section 2321 continues former Civil Code Section 4530(b) without substantive change. [23 Cal.L.Rev.Comm. Reports 1 (1993)].

Research References

Treatises and Practice Aids

Witkin, California Summary 10th Husband and Wife § 146, Proceedings.

§ 2322. Separate domicile or residence

For the purpose of a proceeding for dissolution of marriage, each spouse may have a separate domicile or residence depending upon proof of the fact and not upon legal presumptions. *(Stats.1992, c. 162 (A.B.2650), § 10, operative Jan. 1, 1994. Amended by Stats.2014, c. 82 (S.B.1306), § 27, eff. Jan. 1, 2015.)*

Law Revision Commission Comments

Enactment [Revised Comment]

Section 2322 continues former Civil Code Section 4531 without substantive change. [23 Cal.L.Rev.Comm. Reports 1 (1993)].

Research References

Treatises and Practice Aids

Witkin, California Summary 10th Husband and Wife § 73, Residence and Venue.

CHAPTER 4. GENERAL PROCEDURAL PROVISIONS

§ 2330. Petition

(a) A proceeding for dissolution of marriage or for legal separation of the parties is commenced by filing a petition entitled "In re the marriage of ______ and ______" which shall state whether it is a petition for dissolution of the marriage or for legal separation of the parties.

(b) In a proceeding for dissolution of marriage or for legal separation of the parties, the petition shall set forth among other matters, as nearly as can be ascertained, the following facts:

(1) The date of marriage.

(2) The date of separation.

(3) The number of years from marriage to separation.

(4) The number of children of the marriage, if any, and if none a statement of that fact.

(5) The age and birth date of each minor child of the marriage. *(Stats.1992, c. 162 (A.B.2650), § 10, operative Jan. 1, 1994. Amended by Stats.1998, c. 581 (A.B.2801), § 11.)*

Law Revision Commission Comments

Enactment [Revised Comment]

Subdivision (a) of Section 2330 continues the first sentence of former Civil Code Section 4503 without substantive change. The reference to the "superior" court has been omitted as surplus. See Section 200 (jurisdiction in superior court).

Subdivision (b) continues former Code of Civil Procedure Section 429.10 without substantive change. The reference to legal separation has been added. This is not a substantive change, since the mandatory Judicial Council form for a petition for legal separation includes this information. See Cal. R. Ct. 1281 (rev. Jan. 1, 1993). [23 Cal.L.Rev.Comm. Reports 1 (1993)].

Research References

Forms

West's California Code Forms, Family § 2330, Comment Overview--Procedures.

West's California Judicial Council Forms FL-100, Petition - Marriage/Domestic Partnership.

Treatises and Practice Aids

Witkin, California Summary 10th Husband and Wife § 83, Petition.

Witkin, California Summary 10th Husband and Wife § 111, When Judgment Becomes Final.

Witkin, California Summary 10th Husband and Wife § 127, Revocation Of Petition.

Witkin, California Summary 10th Husband and Wife § 144, in General.

§ 2330.1. Supplemental complaint; paternity or child support

In any proceeding for dissolution of marriage, for legal separation of the parties, or for the support of children, the petition or complaint may list children born before the marriage to the same parties and, pursuant to the terms of the Uniform Parentage Act, a determination of paternity may be made in the action. In addition, a supplemental complaint may be filed, in any of those proceedings, pursuant to Section 464 of the Code of Civil Procedure, seeking a judgment or order of paternity or support for a child of the mother and father of the child whose paternity and support are already in issue before the court. A supplemental complaint for paternity or support of children may be filed without leave of court either before or after final judgment in the underlying action. Service of the supplemental summons and complaint shall be made in the manner provided for the initial service of a summons by this code. *(Added by Stats.1994, c. 1269 (A.B.2208), § 23.5. Amended by Stats. 1998, c. 581 (A.B.2801), § 12.)*

Research References

Forms

West's California Code Forms, Family § 2330, Comment Overview--Procedures.
West's California Code Forms, Family § 3650, Comment Overview--Modification, Termination, or Set Aside Of Support Orders.
West's California Judicial Council Forms FL-600, Summons and Complaint or Supplemental Complaint Regarding Parental Obligations.
West's California Judicial Council Forms FL-610, Answer to Complaint or Supplemental Complaint Regarding Parental Obligations.
West's California Judicial Council Forms FL-640, Notice and Motion to Cancel (Set Aside) Support Order Based on Presumed Income.
West's California Judicial Council Forms FL-643, Declaration Of Obligor's Income During Judgment Period--Presumed Income Set--Aside Request.
West's California Judicial Council Forms FL-640-INFO, Information Sheet for Notice and Motion to Cancel (Set Aside) Support Order Based on Presumed Income.

Treatises and Practice Aids

Witkin, California Summary 10th Husband and Wife § 83, Petition.
Witkin, California Summary 10th Husband and Wife § 324, Pleadings.
Witkin, California Summary 10th Parent and Child § 439, Modification or Termination Of Support Order.

§ 2330.3. Assignment to same court and judicial officer; minimum length of judicial officer assignment

(a) All dissolution actions, to the greatest extent possible, shall be assigned to the same superior court department for all purposes, in order that all decisions in a case through final judgment shall be made by the same judicial officer. However, if the assignment will result in a significant delay of any family law matter, the dissolution action need not be assigned to the same superior court department for all purposes, unless the parties stipulate otherwise.

(b) The Judicial Council shall adopt a standard of judicial administration prescribing a minimum length of assignment of a judicial officer to a family law assignment.

(c) This section shall be operative on July 1, 1997. *(Added by Stats.1996, c. 56 (S.B.389), § 2, operative July 1, 1997. Amended by Stats.2010, c. 352 (A.B.939), § 7.)*

Commentary

Blumenthal v. Superior Court, 137 Cal.App.4th 672, 40 Cal.Rptr.3d 509 (2006), understands this provision to authorize a family law judge to take along an in-progress dissolution proceeding to a new assignment and consequently holds that a family law judge abused her discretion by declaring a mistrial against the wishes of both parties when they failed to complete a long-cause dissolution trial before the start of the judge's new assignment.

Research References

Treatises and Practice Aids

Witkin, California Summary 10th Husband and Wife § 69, Superior Court and Departments.

§ 2330.5. Financial declarations; filing; exception

Notwithstanding any other provision of law, if no demand for money, property, costs, or attorney's fees is contained in the petition and the judgment of dissolution of marriage is entered by default, the filing of income and expense declarations and property declarations in connection therewith shall not be required. *(Stats.1992, c. 162 (A.B.2650), § 10, operative Jan. 1, 1994.)*

Law Revision Commission Comments

Enactment [Revised Comment]

Section 2330.5 continues former Civil Code Section 4364 without substantive change. The word "judgment" has been substituted for "decree." This is not a substantive change. See Section 100 ("judgment" includes decree, as appropriate). The phrase "income and expense declarations and property declarations" has been substituted for "a financial declaration" to conform with the language of California Rule of Court 1243. See also Sections 95 ("income and expense declaration" defined), 115 ("property declaration" defined). [23 Cal.L.Rev.Comm. Reports 1 (1993)].

Research References

Forms

West's California Judicial Council Forms FL-165, Request to Enter Default (Family Law--Uniform Parentage).

Treatises and Practice Aids

Witkin, California Summary 10th Community Property § 234, Scope Of Disclosure Requirements.
Witkin, California Summary 10th Community Property § 237, Final Declaration.
Witkin, California Summary 10th Husband and Wife § 87, Methods Of Obtaining Orders.

§ 2331. Service of petitions and summons

A copy of the petition, together with a copy of a summons, in form and content approved by the Judicial Council shall be served upon the other party to the marriage in the same manner as service of papers in civil actions generally. *(Stats.1992, c. 162 (A.B.2650), § 10, operative Jan. 1, 1994.)*

Law Revision Commission Comments

Enactment [Revised Comment]

Section 2331 continues the last sentence of former Civil Code Section 4503 without substantive change. See also Section 2332 (service on guardian or conservator of insane spouse where dissolution based on incurable insanity). [23 Cal.L.Rev.Comm. Reports 1 (1993)].

Research References

Treatises and Practice Aids

Witkin, California Summary 10th Husband and Wife § 75, Process.

§ 2332. Service of petition for dissolution on grounds of permanent legal incapacity to make decisions; appointment of guardian ad litem

(a) If the petition for dissolution of the marriage is based on the ground of permanent legal incapacity to make decisions and the spouse who lacks legal capacity to make decisions has a guardian or conservator, other than the spouse filing the petition, the petition and summons shall be served upon the spouse and the guardian or conservator. The guardian or conservator shall defend and protect the interests of the spouse who lacks legal capacity to make decisions.

(b) If the spouse who lacks legal capacity to make decisions has no guardian or conservator, or if the spouse filing the petition is the guardian or conservator, the court shall appoint a guardian ad litem, who may be the district attorney or the county counsel, if any, to defend and protect the interests of the spouse who lacks legal capacity to make decisions. If a district attorney or county counsel is appointed guardian ad litem pursuant to this subdivision, the successor in the office of district attorney or county counsel, as the case may be, succeeds as guardian ad litem, without further action by the court or parties.

(c) "Guardian or conservator" as used in this section means:

(1) With respect to the issue of the dissolution of the marriage relationship, the guardian or conservator of the person.

(2) With respect to support and property division issues, the guardian or conservator of the estate. *(Stats.1992, c. 162 (A.B.2650), § 10, operative Jan. 1, 1994. Amended by Stats. 2014, c. 144 (A.B.1847), § 12, eff. Jan. 1, 2015.)*

Law Revision Commission Comments

Enactment [Revised Comment]

Section 2332 continues former Civil Code Section 4510(c)-(d) without substantive change. In subdivisions (a) and (b), "filing the petition" has been substituted for "bringing the action." For background on former Civ. Code § 4510, see *Recommendation Relating to Guardianship–Conservatorship Law,* 14 Cal. L. Revision Comm'n Reports 501, 930 (1978). [23 Cal.L.Rev.Comm. Reports 1 (1993)].

Research References

Forms

West's California Code Forms, Family § 2330, Comment Overview--Procedures.

Treatises and Practice Aids

Witkin, California Summary 10th Husband and Wife § 66, Procedure.

§ 2333. Irreconcilable differences; order for dissolution

Subject to Section 2334, if from the evidence at the hearing the court finds that there are irreconcilable differences which have caused the irremediable breakdown of the marriage, the court shall order the dissolution of the marriage or a legal separation of the parties. *(Stats.1992, c. 162 (A.B.2650), § 10, operative Jan. 1, 1994.)*

Law Revision Commission Comments

Enactment [Revised Comment]

Section 2333 continues the first sentence of former Civil Code Section 4508(a) without substantive change. [23 Cal.L.Rev.Comm. Reports 1 (1993)].

Research References

Treatises and Practice Aids

Witkin, California Summary 10th Husband and Wife § 60, Nature Of Ground.

§ 2334. Grounds for continuance; authority of court

(a) If it appears that there is a reasonable possibility of reconciliation, the court shall continue the proceeding for the dissolution of the marriage or for a legal separation of the parties for a period not to exceed 30 days.

(b) During the period of the continuance, the court may make orders for the support and maintenance of the parties, the custody of the minor children of the marriage, the support of children for whom support may be ordered, attorney's fees, and for the preservation of the property of the parties.

(c) At any time after the termination of the period of the continuance, either party may move for the dissolution of the marriage or a legal separation of the parties, and the court may enter a judgment of dissolution of the marriage or legal separation of the parties. *(Stats.1992, c. 162 (A.B.2650), § 10, operative Jan. 1, 1994. Amended by Stats.1993, c. 219 (A.B.1500), § 109.)*

Law Revision Commission Comments

Enactment [Revised Comment]

Section 2334 continues the last three sentences of former Civil Code Section 4508(a) without substantive change. In subdivision (b), the former reference to "maintenance and education" of children has been omitted as surplus. See Section 150 ("support" when used as to minor child or child described in Section 3901 includes maintenance and education). A reference to "the support of children for whom support may be ordered" has been substituted for the former reference to support of "minor" children, since in some cases support may be ordered for adult children. See Section 58 ("child for whom support may be ordered" defined). In subdivision (c), "termination of the period of the continuance" has been substituted for "termination of such 30-day period" to conform with other language in this section. [23 Cal.L.Rev.Comm. Reports 1 (1993)].

Research References

Treatises and Practice Aids

Witkin, California Summary 10th Husband and Wife § 60, Nature Of Ground.

§ 2335. Misconduct; admissibility of specific acts of misconduct

Except as otherwise provided by statute, in a pleading or proceeding for dissolution of marriage or legal separation of the parties, including depositions and discovery proceedings, evidence of specific acts of misconduct is improper and inadmissible. *(Stats.1992, c. 162 (A.B.2650), § 10, operative*

Jan. 1, 1994. Amended by Stats.1993, c. 219 (A.B.1500), § 110.)

Law Revision Commission Comments

Enactment [Revised Comment]

Section 2335 restates the central rule of former Civil Code Section 4509 without substantive change. The phrase "under this part," meaning the former Family Law Act (former Part 5 (commencing with former Section 4000) of Division 4 of the Civil Code), has been omitted as surplus. The former exception for child custody matters is superseded by the introductory clause, which recognizes all statutory exceptions. See, e.g. Sections 3011 (history of abuse of child or other parent must be considered in determining best interest of child for purposes of custody), 6305 (presentation of evidence of abuse or domestic violence required for mutual restraining order). [23 Cal.L.Rev.Comm. Reports 1 (1993)].

Commentary

Notwithstanding the Law Revision Comments, reproduced directly above, it does not appear that "Section 2335 restates the central rule of former Civil Code Section 4509 without substantive change." Former Civil Code Section 4509 provides: "In any pleadings or proceedings for legal separation or dissolution of marriage ..., evidence of specific acts of misconduct shall be improper and inadmissible, except where child custody is in issue and such evidence is relevant to that issue." All the statutory provisions cited in the Law Revision Comments refer to spousal or child abuse and hence are more narrowly drawn than the omnibus former Section 4509 reference to "specific acts of misconduct" that are relevant to child custody. Acts of misconduct may, for example, involve moral turpitude unrelated to spousal or child abuse but nevertheless affecting parenting capacity. The Law Revision Commission erred in interpreting the former Section 4509 "specific acts of misconduct" to include only other statutory references to particular forms of misconduct. The error is both illogical and ahistorical. Section 4509 was enacted before the more recent statutes dealing specifically with spousal and child abuse.

Research References

Treatises and Practice Aids

Witkin, California Summary 10th Husband and Wife § 62, Evidence Of Misconduct is Ordinarily Inadmissible.

§ 2335.5. Requests to enter default judgment; dissolution or legal separation; notice to defaulting spouse

In a proceeding for dissolution of marriage or legal separation of the parties, where the judgment is to be entered by default, the petitioner shall provide the court clerk with a stamped envelope bearing sufficient postage addressed to the spouse who has defaulted, with the address of the court clerk as the return address, and the court clerk shall mail a copy of the request to enter default to that spouse in the envelope provided. A judgment of dissolution or legal separation, including relief requested in the petition, shall not be denied solely on the basis that the request to enter default was returned unopened to the court. The court clerk shall maintain any such document returned by the post office as part of the court file in the case. *(Added by Stats.1996, c. 810 (A.B.2149), § 1.)*

Research References

Forms

West's California Code Forms, Family § 2330, Comment Overview--Procedures.

West's California Judicial Council Forms FL-165, Request to Enter Default (Family Law--Uniform Parentage).

Treatises and Practice Aids

Witkin, California Summary 10th Husband and Wife § 101, Entry Of Default and Application for Relief.

§ 2336. Default; proof required

(a) No judgment of dissolution or of legal separation of the parties may be granted upon the default of one of the parties or upon a statement or finding of fact made by a referee; but the court shall, in addition to the statement or finding of the referee, require proof of the grounds alleged, and the proof, if not taken before the court, shall be by affidavit. In all cases where there are minor children of the parties, each affidavit or offer of proof shall include an estimate by the declarant or affiant of the monthly gross income of each party. If the declarant or affiant has no knowledge of the estimated monthly income of a party, the declarant or affiant shall state why he or she has no knowledge. In all cases where there is a community estate, each affidavit or offer of proof shall include an estimate of the value of the assets and the debts the declarant or affiant proposes to be distributed to each party, unless the declarant or affiant has filed, or concurrently files, a complete and accurate property declaration with the court.

(b) If the proof is by affidavit, the personal appearance of the affiant is required only when it appears to the court that any of the following circumstances exist:

(1) Reconciliation of the parties is reasonably possible.

(2) A proposed child custody order is not in the best interest of the child.

(3) A proposed child support order is less than a noncustodial parent is capable of paying.

(4) A personal appearance of a party or interested person would be in the best interests of justice.

(c) An affidavit submitted pursuant to this section shall contain a stipulation by the affiant that the affiant understands that proof will be by affidavit and that the affiant will not appear before the court unless so ordered by the court. *(Stats.1992, c. 162 (A.B.2650), § 10, operative Jan. 1, 1994. Amended by Stats.1996, c. 810 (A.B.2149), § 2; Stats.1998, c. 581 (A.B.2801), § 13.)*

Law Revision Commission Comments

Enactment [Revised Comment]

Section 2336 continues former Civil Code Section 4511 without substantive change. In subdivision (a), "judgment" has been substituted for "decree." This is not a substantive change. See Section 100 ("judgment" includes decree, as appropriate). See also Section 3011 (factors in determining best interest of child). [23 Cal.L.Rev. Comm. Reports 1 (1993)].

Commentary

See generally *McKim v. McKim, 6 Cal.3d 673, 679, 100 Cal.Rptr. 140 (1972); Lakkees v. Superior Court, 222 Cal.App.3d 531, 537, 271 Cal.Rptr. 845 (1990).*

Research References

Forms

West's California Code Forms, Family § 2330, Comment Overview--Procedures.

West's California Judicial Council Forms FL-170, Declaration for Default or Uncontested Dissolution or Legal Separation.

Treatises and Practice Aids

Witkin, California Summary 10th Husband and Wife § 100, No Requirement Of Corroboration.

Witkin, California Summary 10th Husband and Wife § 102, Requirement Of Proof.

Witkin, California Summary 10th Husband and Wife § 117, Power to Enter Judgment.

Witkin, California Summary 10th Husband and Wife § 171, Hearing, Incidental Orders, and Judgment.

§ 2337. Early and separate trial on dissolution; preliminary declaration; conditions; effect on retirement plan; service on plan administrator; reservation of jurisdiction; effect of party's death

(a) In a proceeding for dissolution of marriage, the court, upon noticed motion, may sever and grant an early and separate trial on the issue of the dissolution of the status of the marriage apart from other issues.

(b) A preliminary declaration of disclosure with a completed schedule of assets and debts shall be served on the nonmoving party with the noticed motion unless it has been served previously, or unless the parties stipulate in writing to defer service of the preliminary declaration of disclosure until a later time.

(c) The court may impose upon a party any of the following conditions on granting a severance of the issue of the dissolution of the status of the marriage, and in case of that party's death, an order of any of the following conditions continues to be binding upon that party's estate:

(1) The party shall indemnify and hold the other party harmless from any taxes, reassessments, interest, and penalties payable by the other party in connection with the division of the community estate that would not have been payable if the parties were still married at the time the division was made.

(2) Until judgment has been entered on all remaining issues and has become final, the party shall maintain all existing health and medical insurance coverage for the other party and any minor children as named dependents, so long as the party is eligible to do so. If at any time during this period the party is not eligible to maintain that coverage, the party shall, at the party's sole expense, provide and maintain health and medical insurance coverage that is comparable to the existing health and medical insurance coverage to the extent it is available. To the extent that coverage is not available, the party shall be responsible to pay, and shall demonstrate to the court's satisfaction the ability to pay, for the health and medical care for the other party and the minor children, to the extent that care would have been covered by the existing insurance coverage but for the dissolution of marital status, and shall otherwise indemnify and hold the other party harmless from any adverse consequences resulting from the loss or reduction of the existing coverage. For purposes of this subdivision, "health and medical insurance coverage" includes any coverage for which the parties are eligible under any group or individual health or other medical plan, fund, policy, or program.

(3) Until judgment has been entered on all remaining issues and has become final, the party shall indemnify and hold the other party harmless from any adverse consequences to the other party if the bifurcation results in a termination of the other party's right to a probate homestead in the residence in which the other party resides at the time the severance is granted.

(4) Until judgment has been entered on all remaining issues and has become final, the party shall indemnify and hold the other party harmless from any adverse consequences to the other party if the bifurcation results in the loss of the rights of the other party to a probate family allowance as the surviving spouse of the party.

(5) Until judgment has been entered on all remaining issues and has become final, the party shall indemnify and hold the other party harmless from any adverse consequences to the other party if the bifurcation results in the loss of the other party's rights with respect to any retirement, survivor, or deferred compensation benefits under any plan, fund, or arrangement, or to any elections or options associated therewith, to the extent that the other party would have been entitled to those benefits or elections as the spouse or surviving spouse of the party.

(6) The party shall indemnify and hold the other party harmless from any adverse consequences if the bifurcation results in the loss of rights to social security benefits or elections to the extent the other party would have been entitled to those benefits or elections as the surviving spouse of the party.

(7)(A) The court may make an order pursuant to paragraph (3) of subdivision (b) of Section 5040 of the Probate Code, if appropriate, that a party maintain a beneficiary designation for a nonprobate transfer, as described in Section 5000 of the Probate Code, for a spouse or domestic partner for up to one-half of or, upon a showing of good cause, for all of a nonprobate transfer asset until judgment has been entered with respect to the community ownership of that asset, and until the other party's interest therein has been distributed to him or her.

(B) Except upon a showing of good cause, this paragraph does not apply to any of the following:

(i) A nonprobate transfer described in Section 5000 of the Probate Code that was not created by either party or that was acquired by either party by gift, descent, or devise.

(ii) An irrevocable trust.

(iii) A trust of which neither party is the grantor.

(iv) Powers of appointment under a trust instrument that was not created by either party or of which neither party is a grantor.

(v) The execution and filing of a disclaimer pursuant to Part 8 (commencing with Section 260) of Division 2 of the Probate Code.

(vi) The appointment of a party as a trustee.

(8) In order to preserve the ability of the party to defer the distribution of the Individual Retirement Account or annuity

(IRA) established under Section 408 or 408A of the Internal Revenue Code [1] of 1986, as amended, (IRC) upon the death of the other party, the court may require that one-half, or all upon a showing of good cause, of the community interest in any IRA, by or for the benefit of the party, be assigned and transferred to the other party pursuant to Section 408(d)(6) of the Internal Revenue Code. This paragraph does not limit the power granted pursuant to subdivision (g).

(9) Upon a showing that circumstances exist that would place a substantial burden of enforcement upon either party's community property rights or would eliminate the ability of the surviving party to enforce his or her community property rights if the other party died before the division and distribution or compliance with any court-ordered payment of any community property interest therein, including, but not limited to, a situation in which preemption under federal law applies to an asset of a party, or purchase by a bona fide purchaser has occurred, the court may order a specific security interest designed to reduce or eliminate the likelihood that a postmortem enforcement proceeding would be ineffective or unduly burdensome to the surviving party. For this purpose, those orders may include, but are not limited to, any of the following:

(A) An order that the party provide an undertaking.

(B) An order to provide a security interest by Qualified Domestic Relations Order from that party's share of a retirement plan or plans.

(C) An order for the creation of a trust as defined in paragraph (2) of subdivision (a) of Section 82 of the Probate Code.

(D) An order for other arrangements as may be reasonably necessary and feasible to provide appropriate security in the event of the party's death before judgment has been entered with respect to the community ownership of that asset, and until the other party's interest therein has been distributed to him or her.

(E) If a retirement plan is not subject to an enforceable court order for the payment of spousal survivor benefits to the other party, an interim order requiring the party to pay or cause to be paid, and to post adequate security for the payment of, any survivor benefit that would have been payable to the other party on the death of the party but for the judgment granting a dissolution of the status of the marriage, pending entry of judgment on all remaining issues.

(10) Any other condition the court determines is just and equitable.

(d) Prior to, or simultaneously with, entry of judgment granting dissolution of the status of the marriage, all of the following shall occur:

(1) The party's retirement or pension plan shall be joined as a party to the proceeding for dissolution, unless joinder is precluded or made unnecessary by Title 1 of the federal Employee Retirement Income Security Act of 1974 (29 U.S.C. Sec. 1001 et seq.), as amended (ERISA), or any other applicable law.

(2) To preserve the claims of each spouse in all retirement plan benefits upon entry of judgment granting a dissolution of the status of the marriage, the court shall enter one of the following in connection with the judgment for each retirement plan in which either party is a participant:

(A) An order pursuant to Section 2610 disposing of each party's interest in retirement plan benefits, including survivor and death benefits.

(B) An interim order preserving the nonemployee party's right to retirement plan benefits, including survivor and death benefits, pending entry of judgment on all remaining issues.

(C) An attachment to the judgment granting a dissolution of the status of the marriage, as follows:

EACH PARTY (insert names and addresses) IS PROVISIONALLY AWARDED WITHOUT PREJUDICE AND SUBJECT TO ADJUSTMENT BY A SUBSEQUENT DOMESTIC RELATIONS ORDER, A SEPARATE INTEREST EQUAL TO ONE–HALF OF ALL BENEFITS ACCRUED OR TO BE ACCRUED UNDER THE PLAN (name each plan individually) AS A RESULT OF EMPLOYMENT OF THE OTHER PARTY DURING THE MARRIAGE OR DOMESTIC PARTNERSHIP AND PRIOR TO THE DATE OF SEPARATION. IN ADDITION, PENDING FURTHER NOTICE, THE PLAN SHALL, AS ALLOWED BY LAW, OR IN THE CASE OF A GOVERNMENTAL PLAN, AS ALLOWED BY THE TERMS OF THE PLAN, CONTINUE TO TREAT THE PARTIES AS MARRIED OR DOMESTIC PARTNERS FOR PURPOSES OF ANY SURVIVOR RIGHTS OR BENEFITS AVAILABLE UNDER THE PLAN TO THE EXTENT NECESSARY TO PROVIDE FOR PAYMENT OF AN AMOUNT EQUAL TO THAT SEPARATE INTEREST OR FOR ALL OF THE SURVIVOR BENEFIT IF AT THE TIME OF THE DEATH OF THE PARTICIPANT, THERE IS NO OTHER ELIGIBLE RECIPIENT OF THE SURVIVOR BENEFIT.

(e) The moving party shall promptly serve a copy of any order, interim order, or attachment entered pursuant to paragraph (2) of subdivision (d), and a copy of the judgment granting a dissolution of the status of the marriage, on the retirement or pension plan administrator.

(f) A judgment granting a dissolution of the status of the marriage shall expressly reserve jurisdiction for later determination of all other pending issues.

(g) If the party dies after the entry of judgment granting a dissolution of marriage, any obligation imposed by this section shall be enforceable against any asset, including the proceeds thereof, against which these obligations would have been enforceable prior to the person's death. *(Stats.1992, c. 162 (A.B.2650), § 10, operative Jan. 1, 1994. Amended by Stats.1994, c. 1269 (A.B.2208), § 24; Stats.1997, c. 56 (A.B. 1098), § 1; Stats.1998, c. 581 (A.B.2801), § 14; Stats.2007, c. 141 (A.B.861), § 1; Stats.2015, c. 293 (A.B.139), § 1, eff. Jan. 1, 2016.)*

[1] Internal Revenue Code sections are in Title 26 of the U.S.C.A.

Law Revision Commission Comments

Enactment [Revised Comment]

Section 2337 continues former Civil Code Section 4515 without substantive change. The phrase "under this part," meaning the former Family Law Act (former Part 5 (commencing with former Section 4000) of Division 4 of the Civil Code), has been omitted as surplus. In subdivision (a), "proceeding" has been substituted for "action." In subdivision (b)(1), "community estate" has been substituted for "community property" to conform to the language of Division 7 (commencing with Section 2500). See, e.g., Section 2550 (equal division of community estate). See also Section 63 ("community estate" defined). Throughout this section, "any" has been substituted for "any and all," since "all" is surplus. [23 Cal.L.Rev. Comm. Reports 1 (1993)].

Commentary

Note that 2013 amendments to Code of Civil Procedure section 583.161 expanded the definition of petitions and orders that are not subject to mandatory dismissal, including petitions and orders under this section.

In re Marriage of Dunmore, 45 Cal.App.4th 1372, 53 Cal.Rptr.2d 450 (1996), review denied August 28, 1996, holds that Code of Civil Procedure Section 583.161(c) protection against dismissal extends as well to a bifurcated uncontested proceeding in which a trial court dissolved the parties' marital status and reserved judgment over unresolved economic issues. For further discussion of bifurcation, see Section 2550, Commentary.

Research References

Forms

California Practice Guide: Rutter Family Law Forms Form 1:32, Glossary Of Common Family Law Terms, Phrases and Concepts (Enclosure to Form 1:31).
California Practice Guide: Rutter Family Law Forms Form 11:13, Request for Order to Sever (Bifurcate) and Grant an Early and Separate Trial on the Issue Of Dissolution Of Marital Status.
California Transactions Forms--Family Law § 2:27, Joinder Of Pension Plan.
California Transactions Forms--Family Law § 2:108.50, Statement Attached to Judgment Granting Dissolution Of Marriage.
West's California Code Forms, Family § 2330, Comment Overview--Procedures.
West's California Judicial Council Forms FL-315, Request or Response to Request for Separate Trial (Family Law).
West's California Judicial Council Forms FL-347, Bifurcation Of Status Of Marriage or Domestic Partnership--Attachment.
West's California Judicial Council Forms FL-348, Pension Benefits--Attachment to Judgment.
West's California Judicial Council Forms FL-318-INFO, Retirement Plan Joinder--Information Sheet (Family Law).

Treatises and Practice Aids

Witkin, California Summary 10th Husband and Wife § 105, Statutory Rule.

§ 2338. Decisions; judgments

(a) In a proceeding for dissolution of the marriage or legal separation of the parties, the court shall file its decision and any statement of decision as in other cases.

(b) If the court determines that no dissolution should be granted, a judgment to that effect only shall be entered.

(c) If the court determines that a dissolution should be granted, a judgment of dissolution of marriage shall be entered. After the entry of the judgment and before it becomes final, neither party has the right to dismiss the proceeding without the consent of the other. *(Stats.1992, c. 162 (A.B.2650), § 10, operative Jan. 1, 1994.)*

Law Revision Commission Comments

Enactment [Revised Comment]

Section 2338 continues former Civil Code Section 4512 without substantive change. In subdivision (a), "proceeding" has been substituted for "action" and the reference to legal separation has been added. This is not a substantive change. See Section 210 (general rules of practice and procedure); Cal. R. Ct. 1206 (1970) (general law applicable). The effect of subdivision (a) is that the rule regarding filing of decisions and statements applicable to civil actions generally is the rule in proceedings for dissolution or legal separation. See also Code Civ. Proc. § 632 (statement of decision not required unless requested).

In subdivision (b), the phrase "judgment of dissolution shall be entered" has been substituted for "a judgment shall be entered declaring that the parties are entitled to have their marriage dissolved." This conforms with the language of Section 2340 and with the mandatory Judicial Council judgment form. See Cal. R. Ct. 1287 (rev. Jan. 1, 1993). [23 Cal.L.Rev.Comm. Reports 1 (1993)].

Research References

Forms

West's California Judicial Council Forms FL-190, Notice Of Entry Of Judgment (Family Law--Uniform Parentage--Custody and Support).

Treatises and Practice Aids

Witkin, California Summary 10th Community Property § 241, Statutory Requirement Of Division.
Witkin, California Summary 10th Husband and Wife § 107, Statement Of Decision.
Witkin, California Summary 10th Husband and Wife § 109, Elimination Of Interlocutory Judgment.
Witkin, California Summary 10th Husband and Wife § 110, Entry Of Judgment.
Witkin, California Summary 10th Husband and Wife § 112, Contents Of Judgment.
Witkin, California Summary 10th Husband and Wife § 113, in General.

§ 2338.5. Default judgments; dissolution or nullity of marriage, or legal separation

Where a judgment of dissolution or nullity of marriage or legal separation of the parties is to be granted upon the default of one of the parties:

(a) The signature of the spouse who has defaulted on any marital settlement agreement or on any stipulated judgment shall be notarized.

(b) The court clerk shall give notice of entry of judgment of dissolution of marriage, nullity of marriage, or legal separation to the attorney for each party or to the party, if unrepresented.

(c) For the purpose of mailing the notice of entry of judgment, the party submitting the judgment shall provide the court clerk with a stamped envelope bearing sufficient postage addressed to the attorney for the other party or to the party, if unrepresented, with the address of the court clerk as the return address. The court clerk shall maintain any such document returned by the post office as part of the court file in the case. *(Added by Stats.1996, c. 810 (A.B. 2149), § 3.)*

Research References

Treatises and Practice Aids

Witkin, California Summary 10th Husband and Wife § 103, Notice Of Entry Of Judgment.

Witkin, California Summary 10th Husband and Wife § 346, Nature and Validity.

§ 2339. Finality of judgment; waiting period

(a) Subject to subdivision (b) and to Sections 2340 to 2344, inclusive, no judgment of dissolution is final for the purpose of terminating the marriage relationship of the parties until six months have expired from the date of service of a copy of summons and petition or the date of appearance of the respondent, whichever occurs first.

(b) The court may extend the six-month period described in subdivision (a) for good cause shown. *(Stats.1992, c. 162 (A.B.2650), § 10, operative Jan. 1, 1994.)*

Law Revision Commission Comments

Enactment [Revised Comment]

Section 2339 restates the first sentence of former Civil Code Section 4514(a) without substantive change. In subdivision (a), "judgment of dissolution" has been substituted for "judgment entered pursuant to Section 4512." This is not a substantive change, since former Civil Code Section 4512 provided for a judgment of dissolution. Subdivision (a) includes new language concerning the effect of the expiration of the waiting period. This is not a substantive change. See Sections 2300 (effect of judgment of dissolution when it becomes final), 2340 (date judgment becomes final for purpose of terminating marriage relationship). [23 Cal. L.Rev.Comm. Reports 1 (1993)].

Commentary

In re Marriage of Sanabia, 95 Cal.App.3d 483, 157 Cal.Rptr. 56 (1979), holds that the court may not condition entry of final judgment on reimbursement to the county for AFDC benefits and filing fees previously waived because of the party's indigence.

Research References

Forms

West's California Judicial Council Forms FL-970, Request and Declaration for Final Judgment Of Dissolution Of Marriage.

Treatises and Practice Aids

Witkin, California Summary 10th Husband and Wife § 51, Valid Marriage Evading Law Of Domicile.

Witkin, California Summary 10th Husband and Wife § 111, When Judgment Becomes Final.

Witkin, California Summary 10th Husband and Wife § 127, Revocation Of Petition.

§ 2340. Statement of effective date of judgment

A judgment of dissolution of marriage shall specify the date on which the judgment becomes finally effective for the purpose of terminating the marriage relationship of the parties. *(Stats.1992, c. 162 (A.B.2650), § 10, operative Jan. 1, 1994.)*

Law Revision Commission Comments

Enactment [Revised Comment]

Section 2340 continues second sentence of former Civil Code Section 4514(a) without substantive change. The word "judgment" has been substituted for "decree." This is not a substantive change. See Section 100 ("judgment" includes decree, as appropriate). [23 Cal.L.Rev.Comm. Reports 1 (1993)].

Research References

Forms

West's California Judicial Council Forms FL-180, Judgment (Family Law).

Treatises and Practice Aids

Witkin, California Summary 10th Husband and Wife § 111, When Judgment Becomes Final.

§ 2341. Appeal or motion for new trial; finality of judgment

(a) Notwithstanding Section 2340, if an appeal is taken from the judgment or a motion for a new trial is made, the dissolution of marriage does not become final until the motion or appeal has been finally disposed of, nor then, if the motion has been granted or judgment reversed.

(b) Notwithstanding any other provision of law, the filing of an appeal or of a motion for a new trial does not stay the effect of a judgment insofar as it relates to the dissolution of the marriage status and restoring the parties to the status of unmarried persons, unless the appealing or moving party specifies in the notice of appeal or motion for new trial an objection to the termination of the marriage status. No party may make such an objection to the termination of the marriage status unless such an objection was also made at the time of trial. *(Stats.1992, c. 162 (A.B.2650), § 10, operative Jan. 1, 1994.)*

Law Revision Commission Comments

Enactment [Revised Comment]

Subdivision (a) of Section 2341 continues the last sentence of former Civil Code Section 4514(a) without substantive change. Subdivision (b) continues former Civil Code Section 4514(b) without substantive change. [23 Cal.L.Rev.Comm. Reports 1 (1993)].

Research References

Treatises and Practice Aids

Witkin, California Summary 10th Husband and Wife § 111, When Judgment Becomes Final.

§ 2342. Joint petitions for summary dissolutions; revocation; final judgment

Where a joint petition under Chapter 5 (commencing with Section 2400) is thereafter revoked and either party commences a proceeding pursuant to Section 2330 within 90 days from the date of the filing of the revocation, the date the judgment becomes a final judgment under Section 2339 shall be calculated by deducting the period of time which has elapsed from the date of filing the joint petition to the date of filing the revocation. *(Stats.1992, c. 162 (A.B.2650), § 10, operative Jan. 1, 1994.)*

Law Revision Commission Comments

Enactment [Revised Comment]

Section 2342 continues former Civil Code Section 4514(c) without substantive change. The phrase "the date the judgment becomes a final judgment under Section 2339" replaces "the permissible date of entry of judgment pursuant to this section." This is not a substantive change, since the relevant part of the former section is continued in Section 2339. [23 Cal.L.Rev.Comm. Reports 1 (1993)].

Research References

Treatises and Practice Aids

Witkin, California Summary 10th Husband and Wife § 111, When Judgment Becomes Final.

Witkin, California Summary 10th Husband and Wife § 127, Revocation Of Petition.

§ 2343. Retention of jurisdiction; purposes; effect of date of termination of marital status

The court may, upon notice and for good cause shown, or on stipulation of the parties, retain jurisdiction over the date of termination of the marital status, or may order that the marital status be terminated at a future specified date. On the date of termination of the marital status, the parties are restored to the status of unmarried persons. *(Stats.1992, c. 162 (A.B.2650), § 10, operative Jan. 1, 1994.)*

Law Revision Commission Comments

Enactment [Revised Comment]

Section 2343 continues former Civil Code Section 4514(e) without change. [23 Cal.L.Rev.Comm. Reports 1 (1993)].

Research References

Forms

West's California Judicial Council Forms FL-180, Judgment (Family Law).

Treatises and Practice Aids

Witkin, California Summary 10th Husband and Wife § 111, When Judgment Becomes Final.

§ 2344. Death of party after entry of judgment

(a) The death of either party after entry of the judgment does not prevent the judgment from becoming a final judgment under Sections 2339 to 2343, inclusive.

(b) Subdivision (a) does not validate a marriage by either party before the judgment becomes final, nor does it constitute a defense in a criminal prosecution against either party. *(Stats.1992, c. 162 (A.B.2650), § 10, operative Jan. 1, 1994.)*

Law Revision Commission Comments

Enactment [Revised Comment]

Section 2344 restates former Civil Code Section 4514(d) without substantive change. The language of the former provision has been revised to recognize that the judgment is entered and becomes final when the time runs, without further action by the court. Subdivision (b) has been revised to omit the reference to a marriage having been "contracted," since this language is surplus. This is not a substantive change and a marriage entered into before the judgment becomes final is not validated by subdivision (a). See also Section 310(a) (death of party dissolves marriage). [23 Cal.L.Rev.Comm. Reports 1 (1993)].

Research References

Forms

West's California Judicial Council Forms FL-970, Request and Declaration for Final Judgment Of Dissolution Of Marriage.

Treatises and Practice Aids

Witkin, California Summary 10th Husband and Wife § 111, When Judgment Becomes Final.

§ 2345. Consent to legal separation

The court may not render a judgment of the legal separation of the parties without the consent of both parties unless one party has not made a general appearance and the petition is one for legal separation. *(Stats.1992, c. 162 (A.B.2650), § 10, operative Jan. 1, 1994.)*

Law Revision Commission Comments

Enactment [Revised Comment]

Section 2345 continues the first sentence of former Civil Code Section 4508(b) without substantive change. [23 Cal.L.Rev.Comm. Reports 1 (1993)].

Research References

Treatises and Practice Aids

Witkin, California Summary 10th Husband and Wife § 144, in General.

§ 2346. Judgments; nunc pro tunc entry; rights to judgment

(a) If the court determines that a judgment of dissolution of the marriage should be granted, but by mistake, negligence, or inadvertence, the judgment has not been signed, filed, and entered, the court may cause the judgment to be signed, dated, filed, and entered in the proceeding as of the date when the judgment could have been signed, dated, filed, and entered originally, if it appears to the satisfaction of the court that no appeal is to be taken in the proceeding or motion made for a new trial, to annul or set aside the judgment, or for relief under Chapter 8 (commencing with Section 469) of Title 6 of Part 2 of the Code of Civil Procedure.

(b) The court may act under subdivision (a) on its own motion or upon the motion of either party to the proceeding. In contested cases, the motion of a party shall be with notice to the other party.

(c) The court may cause the judgment to be entered nunc pro tunc as provided in this section, even though the judgment may have been previously entered, where through mistake, negligence, or inadvertence the judgment was not entered as soon as it could have been entered under the law if applied for.

(d) The court shall not cause a judgment to be entered nunc pro tunc as provided in this section as of a date before trial in the matter, before the date of an uncontested judgment hearing in the matter, or before the date of submission to the court of an application for judgment on affidavit pursuant to Section 2336. Upon the entry of the judgment, the parties have the same rights with regard to the dissolution of marriage becoming final on the date that it would have become final had the judgment been entered upon the date when it could have been originally entered. *(Stats.1992, c. 162 (A.B.2650), § 10, operative Jan. 1, 1994.)*

Law Revision Commission Comments

Enactment [Revised Comment]

Section 2346 continues former Civil Code Section 4513 without substantive change. In subdivision (a), "judgment of dissolution of the marriage" has been substituted for "decree of dissolution." This is not a substantive change. See Section 100 ("judgment" includes decree, as appropriate). Throughout this section "proceeding" has been substituted for "action." [23 Cal.L.Rev.Comm. Reports 1 (1993)].

Commentary

Compare *In re Marriage of Coefield, 92 Cal.App.3d 959, 155 Cal.Rptr. 335 (1979)* (nunc pro tunc decree of divorce in first marriage entered to benefit second spouse by validating subsequent out-of-state common-law marriage) with *In re Marriage of Frapwell, 53 Cal.App.3d 479, 125 Cal.Rptr. 878 (1975)* (abuse of discretion to order nunc pro tunc entry of divorce decree when no interests of second spouse involved and effect of entry would be to cut off homestead rights that surviving spouse would otherwise have). But see *Estate of Casimir, 19 Cal.App.3d 773, 97 Cal.Rptr. 623 (1971)*.

In re Marriage of Tamraz, 24 Cal.App.4th 1740, 30 Cal.Rptr.2d 233 (1994), review denied 7/27/94, affirmed the trial court's 1989 award of a nunc pro tunc judgment in a 1976 dissolution action where the absence of any judgment in the 1976 action arose from the failure of the attorney husband to prepare a stipulation for default and interlocutory judgment, which he had promised to do in the parties' separation agreement. See also *In re Marriage of Shayman, 35 Cal.App.3d 648, 111 Cal.Rptr. 11 (1973)* (although death normally abates a dissolution proceeding, nunc pro tunc judgment appropriate when party dies after court filed facts and conclusions of law but before court issued formal judgment) and *In re Marriage of Mallory, 55 Cal.App.4th 1165, 64 Cal.Rptr.2d 667 (1997)* (when a party to a dissolution action dies after trial and after the case is submitted for decision, the court may subsequently enter a judgment *nunc pro tunc* to a date prior to the party's death). Cf. *Kinsler v. Superior Court, 121 Cal.App.3d 808, 175 Cal.Rptr. 564 (1981)* (where trial court entered judgment dissolving marriage and reserved jurisdiction to determine property issues, party's subsequent death did not abate remainder of dissolution action nor deprive court of jurisdiction to decide those issues); *Frederick v. Superior Court, 223 Cal.App.4th 988, 167 Cal. Rptr.3d 773 (2014)* (where a party dies after a court orally delivers a judgment of dissolution but before written judgment is entered, the court has jurisdiction to enter a written judgment nunc pro tunc).

Research References

Forms

California Practice Guide: Rutter Family Law Forms Form 15:8, Request for Order Re Entry Of Judgment Of Dissolution Nunc Pro Tunc.

West's California Code Forms, Family § 2330, Comment Overview--Procedures.

West's California Judicial Council Forms FL-180, Judgment (Family Law).

Treatises and Practice Aids

Witkin, California Summary 10th Husband and Wife § 116, Development Of Law.

Witkin, California Summary 10th Husband and Wife § 117, Power to Enter Judgment.

Witkin, California Summary 10th Husband and Wife § 118, Who May Seek Entry.

Witkin, California Summary 10th Husband and Wife § 119, Entry After Death Of Party.

§ 2347. Judgment of legal separation; effect on subsequent judgment of dissolution

A judgment of legal separation of the parties does not bar a subsequent judgment of dissolution of the marriage granted pursuant to a petition for dissolution filed by either party. *(Stats.1992, c. 162 (A.B.2650), § 10, operative Jan. 1, 1994.)*

Law Revision Commission Comments

Enactment [Revised Comment]

Section 2347 continues the last sentence of former Civil Code Section 4508(b) without substantive change. [23 Cal.L.Rev.Comm. Reports 1 (1993)].

Research References

Treatises and Practice Aids

Witkin, California Summary 10th Husband and Wife § 147, Effect Of Judgment.

§ 2348. Annual report to Judicial Council; superior court clerks

(a) In addition to the requirements of Section 103200 of the Health and Safety Code, the clerk of the superior court of each county shall report annually to the Judicial Council the number of judgments entered in the county during the preceding calendar year or other 12–month period as required by the Judicial Council for each of the following:

(1) Dissolution of marriage.

(2) Legal separation of the parties.

(3) Nullity of marriage.

(b) After the Judicial Branch Statistical Information System (JBSIS) is operational statewide, the clerk of the superior court of each county shall also report annually to the Judicial Council the number of each of those judgments specified in paragraphs (1), (2), and (3) of subdivision (a), entered in the county during the preceding calendar year or other 12–month period as required by the Judicial Council, that include orders relating to child custody, visitation, or support.

(c) The Judicial Council shall include in its annual report to the Legislature on court statistics the number of each of the types of judgments entered in the state reported pursuant to subdivisions (a) and (b).

(d) The Judicial Council shall establish the applicable 12–month reporting period, the due date, and forms to be used, for submission of data pursuant to subdivisions (a) and (b). Until the Judicial Branch Statistical Information System (JBSIS) is operational statewide, the clerk of the superior court may report the data described in subdivision (a) using existing data collection systems, according to current Judicial Council statistical reporting regulations. *(Added by Stats. 1998, c. 225 (A.B.913), § 1.)*

CHAPTER 5. SUMMARY DISSOLUTION

§ 2400. Conditions necessary at commencement of proceedings

(a) A marriage may be dissolved by the summary dissolution procedure provided in this chapter if all of the following conditions exist at the time the proceeding is commenced:

(1) Either party has met the jurisdictional requirements of Chapter 3 (commencing with Section 2320) with regard to dissolution of marriage.

(2) Irreconcilable differences have caused the irremediable breakdown of the marriage and the marriage should be dissolved.

(3) There are no children of the relationship of the parties born before or during the marriage or adopted by the parties during the marriage, and neither party, to that party's knowledge, is pregnant.

(4) The marriage is not more than five years in duration as of the date of separation of the parties.

(5) Neither party has any interest in real property wherever situated, with the exception of the lease of a residence occupied by either party which satisfies the following requirements:

(A) The lease does not include an option to purchase.

(B) The lease terminates within one year from the date of the filing of the petition.

(6) There are no unpaid obligations in excess of four thousand dollars ($4,000) incurred by either or both of the parties after the date of their marriage, excluding the amount of any unpaid obligation with respect to an automobile.

(7) The total fair market value of community property assets, excluding all encumbrances and automobiles, including any deferred compensation or retirement plan, is less than twenty-five thousand dollars ($25,000), and neither party has separate property assets, excluding all encumbrances and automobiles, in excess of twenty-five thousand dollars ($25,000).

(8) The parties have executed an agreement setting forth the division of assets and the assumption of liabilities of the community, and have executed any documents, title certificates, bills of sale, or other evidence of transfer necessary to effectuate the agreement.

(9) The parties waive any rights to spousal support.

(10) The parties, upon entry of the judgment of dissolution of marriage pursuant to Section 2403, irrevocably waive their respective rights to appeal and their rights to move for a new trial.

(11) The parties have read and understand the summary dissolution brochure provided for in Section 2406.

(12) The parties desire that the court dissolve the marriage.

(b) On January 1, 1985, and on January 1 of each odd-numbered year thereafter, the amounts in paragraph (6) of subdivision (a) shall be adjusted to reflect any change in the value of the dollar. On January 1, 1993, and on January 1 of each odd-numbered year thereafter, the amounts in paragraph (7) of subdivision (a) shall be adjusted to reflect any change in the value of the dollar. The adjustments shall be made by multiplying the base amounts by the percentage change in the California Consumer Price Index as compiled by the Department of Industrial Relations, with the result rounded to the nearest thousand dollars. The Judicial Council shall compute and publish the amounts. *(Stats.1992, c. 162 (A.B.2650), § 10, operative Jan. 1, 1994. Amended by Stats.1993, c. 219 (A.B.1500), § 110.2; Stats.2010, c. 352 (A.B.939), § 8; Stats.2014, c. 82 (S.B.1306), § 28, eff. Jan. 1, 2015.)*

Law Revision Commission Comments

Enactment [Revised Comment]

Section 2400 continues former Civil Code Section 4550 without substantive change. In subdivision (a)(8), "executed" has been substituted for "duly executed," since the word "duly" is surplus. In subdivision (a)(10), "judgment of dissolution of marriage pursuant to Section 2403" has been substituted for "final judgment" to recognize that the judgment can be set aside pursuant to Section 2405. This substitution has been made throughout this chapter. [23 Cal.L.Rev. Comm. Reports 1 (1993)].

Research References

Forms

California Transactions Forms--Family Law § 4:4.60, Termination Of Registered Domestic Partnership.

West's California Code Forms, Family § 2401, Comment Overview--Summary Dissolution.

West's California Judicial Council Forms FL-800, Joint Petition for Summary Dissolution.

West's California Judicial Council Forms FL-810, Summary Dissolution Information.

Treatises and Practice Aids

Witkin, California Summary 10th Husband and Wife § 34, Termination Of Status.

Witkin, California Summary 10th Husband and Wife § 124, in General.

Witkin, California Summary 10th Husband and Wife § 125, Conditions.

Witkin, California Summary 10th Husband and Wife § 126, Joint Petition.

Witkin, California Summary 10th Husband and Wife § 128, Judgment.

§ 2401. Joint petition; filing; form; contents

(a) A proceeding for summary dissolution of the marriage shall be commenced by filing a joint petition in the form prescribed by the Judicial Council.

(b) The petition shall be signed under oath by both spouses, and shall include all of the following:

(1) A statement that as of the date of the filing of the joint petition all of the conditions set forth in Section 2400 have been met.

(2) The mailing address of each spouse.

(3) A statement whether a spouse elects to have his or her former name restored, and, if so, the name to be restored. *(Stats.1992, c. 162 (A.B.2650), § 10, operative Jan. 1, 1994. Amended by Stats.2014, c. 82 (S.B.1306), § 29, eff. Jan. 1, 2015.)*

Law Revision Commission Comments

Enactment [Revised Comment]

Section 2401 continues former Civil Code Section 4551 without substantive change. The reference to the "superior" court has been omitted as surplus. See Section 200 (jurisdiction in superior court). [23 Cal.L.Rev.Comm. Reports 1 (1993)].

Research References

Forms

West's California Code Forms, Family § 2401, Comment Overview--Summary Dissolution.

Treatises and Practice Aids

Witkin, California Summary 10th Husband and Wife § 126, Joint Petition.

§ 2402. Revocation of joint petition; termination of proceedings; notice; filing; copy to other party

(a) At any time before the filing of application for judgment pursuant to Section 2403, either party to the marriage may revoke the joint petition and thereby terminate the summary dissolution proceeding filed pursuant to this chapter.

(b) The revocation shall be effected by filing with the clerk of the court where the proceeding was commenced a notice of revocation in such form and content as shall be prescribed by the Judicial Council.

(c) The revoking party shall send a copy of the notice of revocation to the other party by first-class mail, postage prepaid, at the other party's last known address. *(Stats.1992, c. 162 (A.B.2650), § 10, operative Jan. 1, 1994.)*

Law Revision Commission Comments

Enactment [Revised Comment]

Section 2402 continues former Civil Code Section 4552 without substantive change. [23 Cal.L.Rev.Comm. Reports 1 (1993)].

Research References

Forms

California Practice Guide: Rutter Family Law Forms Form 2:5, Notice Of Revocation Of Joint Petition for Summary Dissolution.

West's California Code Forms, Family § 2401, Comment Overview--Summary Dissolution.

West's California Judicial Council Forms FL-830, Notice Of Revocation Of Petition for Summary Dissolution.

Treatises and Practice Aids

Witkin, California Summary 10th Husband and Wife § 127, Revocation Of Petition.

Witkin, California Summary 10th Husband and Wife § 128, Judgment.

§ 2403. Entry of judgment of dissolution; notice

When six months have expired from the date of the filing of the joint petition for summary dissolution, the court shall, unless a revocation has been filed pursuant to Section 2402, enter the judgment dissolving the marriage. The judgment restores to the parties the status of single persons, and either party may marry after the entry of the judgment. The clerk shall send a notice of entry of judgment to each of the parties at the party's last known address. *(Stats.1992, c. 162 (A.B.2650), § 10, operative Jan. 1, 1994. Amended by Stats. 2010, c. 352 (A.B.939), § 9.)*

Law Revision Commission Comments

Enactment [Revised Comment]

Section 2403 continues former Civil Code Section 4553 without substantive change. [23 Cal.L.Rev.Comm. Reports 1 (1993)].

Research References

Forms

West's California Code Forms, Family § 2401, Comment Overview--Summary Dissolution.

West's California Judicial Council Forms FL-820, Request for Judgment, Judgment Of Dissolution Of Marriage, and Notice Of Entry Of Judgment.

West's California Judicial Council Forms FL-825, Judgment Of Dissolution and Notice Of Entry Of Judgment.

Treatises and Practice Aids

Witkin, California Summary 10th Husband and Wife § 125, Conditions.

Witkin, California Summary 10th Husband and Wife § 128, Judgment.

§ 2404. Final judgment as final adjudication of rights and obligations

Entry of the judgment pursuant to Section 2403 constitutes:

(a) A final adjudication of the rights and obligations of the parties with respect to the status of the marriage and property rights.

(b) A waiver of their respective rights to spousal support, rights to appeal, and rights to move for a new trial. *(Stats.1992, c. 162 (A.B.2650), § 10, operative Jan. 1, 1994.)*

Law Revision Commission Comments

Enactment [Revised Comment]

Section 2404 continues former Civil Code Section 4554 without substantive change. [23 Cal.L.Rev.Comm. Reports 1 (1993)].

Research References

Forms

West's California Code Forms, Family § 2401, Comment Overview--Summary Dissolution.

Treatises and Practice Aids

Witkin, California Summary 10th Husband and Wife § 128, Judgment.

§ 2405. Actions to set aside final judgment

(a) Entry of the judgment pursuant to Section 2403 does not prejudice nor bar the rights of either of the parties to institute an action to set aside the judgment for fraud, duress, accident, mistake, or other grounds recognized at law or in equity or to make a motion pursuant to Section 473 of the Code of Civil Procedure.

(b) The court shall set aside a judgment entered pursuant to Section 2403 regarding all matters except the status of the marriage, upon proof that the parties did not meet the requirements of Section 2400 at the time the petition was filed. *(Stats.1992, c. 162 (A.B.2650), § 10, operative Jan. 1, 1994.)*

Law Revision Commission Comments

Enactment [Revised Comment]

Section 2405 continues former Civil Code Section 4555 without substantive change. [23 Cal.L.Rev.Comm. Reports 1 (1993)].

Research References

Forms

West's California Code Forms, Family § 2401, Comment Overview--Summary Dissolution.

Treatises and Practice Aids

Witkin, California Summary 10th Husband and Wife § 128, Judgment.

§ 2406. Brochure to describe proceedings; availability; distribution; contents and form

(a) Each superior court shall make available a brochure, the contents and form of which shall be prescribed by the Judicial Council, describing the requirements, nature, and effect of proceedings under this chapter. The brochure shall be printed and distributed by the Judicial Council in both English and Spanish.

(b) The brochure shall state, in nontechnical language, all the following:

(1) It is in the best interests of the parties to consult an attorney regarding the dissolution of their marriage. The services of an attorney may be obtained through lawyer referral services, group or prepaid legal services, or legal aid organizations.

(2) The parties should not rely exclusively on this brochure which is not intended as a guide for self-representation in proceedings under this chapter.

(3) A concise summary of the provisions and procedures of this chapter and Sections 2320 and 2322 and Sections 2339 to 2344, inclusive.

(4) The nature of services of the conciliation court, where available.

(5) Neither party to the marriage can in the future obtain spousal support from the other.

(6) A statement in boldface type to the effect that upon entry of the judgment, the rights and obligations of the parties to the marriage with respect to the marriage, including property and spousal support rights, will be permanently adjudicated without right of appeal, except that neither party will be barred from instituting an action to set aside the judgment for fraud, duress, accident, mistake, or other grounds at law or in equity, or to make a motion pursuant to Section 473 of the Code of Civil Procedure.

(7) The parties to the marriage retain the status of married persons and cannot remarry until the judgment dissolving the marriage is entered.

(8) Other matters as the Judicial Council considers appropriate. *(Stats.1992, c. 162 (A.B.2650), § 10, operative Jan. 1, 1994.)*

Law Revision Commission Comments

Enactment [Revised Comment]

Section 2406 continues former Civil Code Section 4556 without substantive change. [23 Cal.L.Rev.Comm. Reports 1 (1993)].

Research References

Forms

West's California Code Forms, Family § 2406 Form 1, Summary Dissolution Information.

West's California Judicial Council Forms FL-800, Joint Petition for Summary Dissolution.

West's California Judicial Council Forms FL-810, Summary Dissolution Information.

Treatises and Practice Aids

Witkin, California Summary 10th Husband and Wife § 124, in General.

Witkin, California Summary 10th Husband and Wife § 125, Conditions.

CHAPTER 6. CASE MANAGEMENT

§ 2450. Family centered case resolution; purpose; order

(a) The purpose of family centered case resolution is to benefit the parties by providing judicial assistance and management to the parties in actions for dissolution of marriage for the purpose of expediting the processing of the case, reducing the expense of litigation, and focusing on early resolution by settlement. Family centered case resolution is a tool to allow the courts to better assist families. It does not increase the authority of the court to appoint any third parties to the case.

(b) The court may order a family centered case resolution plan as provided in Section 2451. If the court orders family centered case resolution, it shall state the family centered case resolution plan in writing or on the record. *(Added by Stats.1996, c. 56 (S.B.389), § 3. Amended by Stats.2010, c. 352 (A.B.939), § 10.)*

Research References

Forms

California Practice Guide: Rutter Family Law Forms Form 1:32, Glossary Of Common Family Law Terms, Phrases and Concepts (Enclosure to Form 1:31).

West's California Judicial Council Forms FL-174, Family Centered Case Resolution Order.

Treatises and Practice Aids

Witkin, California Summary 10th Community Property § 232, in General.

Witkin, California Summary 10th Husband and Wife § 71, Case Management.

§ 2451. Family centered case resolution plan; contents; appointment of experts; statewide rule of court

(a) A court-ordered family centered case resolution plan must be in conformance with due process requirements and may include, but is not limited to, all of the following:

(1) Early neutral case evaluation.

(2) Alternative dispute resolution consistent with the requirements of subdivision (a) of Section 3181.

(3) Limitations on discovery, including temporary suspension pending exploration of settlement. There is a rebuttable presumption that an attorney who carries out discovery as provided in a family centered case resolution plan has

fulfilled his or her duty of care to the client as to the existence of community property.

(4) Use of telephone conference calls to ascertain the status of the case, encourage cooperation, and assist counsel in reaching agreement. However, if the court is required to issue an order other than by stipulation, a hearing shall be held.

(5) If stipulated by the parties, modification or waiver of the requirements of procedural statutes.

(6) A requirement that any expert witness be selected by the parties jointly or be appointed by the court. However, if at any time the court determines that the issues for which experts are required cannot be settled under these conditions, the court shall permit each party to employ his or her own expert.

(7) Bifurcation of issues for trial.

(b) This section does not provide any additional authority to the court to appoint experts beyond that permitted under other provisions of law.

(c) The Judicial Council shall, by January 1, 2012, adopt a statewide rule of court to implement this section.

(d) The changes made to this section by the act adding this subdivision [1] shall become operative on January 1, 2012. *(Added by Stats.1996, c. 56 (S.B.389), § 3. Amended by Stats.2010, c. 352 (A.B.939), § 11, operative Jan. 1, 2012.)*

[1] Stats.2010, c. 352 (A.B.939).

Research References

Forms

California Practice Guide: Rutter Family Law Forms Form 1:32, Glossary Of Common Family Law Terms, Phrases and Concepts (Enclosure to Form 1:31).

West's California Judicial Council Forms FL-174, Family Centered Case Resolution Order.

Treatises and Practice Aids

Witkin, California Summary 10th Husband and Wife § 71, Case Management.

§ 2452. Increase of procedures

The Judicial Council may, by rule, increase the procedures set forth in this chapter. *(Added by Stats.1996, c. 56 (S.B.389), § 3. Amended by Stats.2014, c. 311 (A.B.2745), § 1, eff. Jan. 1, 2015.)*

Research References

Treatises and Practice Aids

Witkin, California Summary 10th Husband and Wife § 71, Case Management.

Division 7

DIVISION OF PROPERTY

Part 1

DEFINITIONS

§ 2500. Construction of division

Unless the provision or context otherwise requires, the definitions in this part govern the construction of this division. *(Stats.1992, c. 162 (A.B.2650), § 10, operative Jan. 1, 1994.)*

Law Revision Commission Comments

Enactment [Revised Comment]

Section 2500 is new and is comparable to Section 50. [23 Cal.L.Rev.Comm. Reports 1 (1993)].

Research References

Forms

West's California Code Forms, Family § 2550, Comment Overview--Manner Of Division Of Community Estate.

West's California Judicial Council Forms FL-160, Property Declaration.

West's California Judicial Council Forms FL-161, Continuation Of Property Declaration.

West's California Judicial Council Forms FL-345, Property Order Attachment to Judgment.

Treatises and Practice Aids

Witkin, California Summary 10th Community Property § 182, Property Owned or Received at Division.

Witkin, California Summary 10th Community Property § 183, Reimbursement.

Witkin, California Summary 10th Community Property § 189, Current Law Eliminating Fault.

Witkin, California Summary 10th Community Property § 190, General Rule Of Equal Division.

Witkin, California Summary 10th Community Property § 215, Sale Of Property and Division Of Proceeds.

Witkin, California Summary 10th Community Property § 232, in General.

Witkin, California Summary 10th Community Property § 241, Statutory Requirement Of Division.

Witkin, California Summary 10th Community Property § 258, Statutory Rule.

Witkin, California Summary 10th Husband and Wife § 3, Statutory Framework.

§ 2502. Separate property

"Separate property" does not include quasi-community property. *(Stats.1992, c. 162 (A.B.2650), § 10, operative Jan. 1, 1994.)*

Law Revision Commission Comments

Enactment [Revised Comment]

Section 2502 continues former Civil Code Section 4804 without substantive change, insofar as it applied to division of property. See also Sections 125 ("quasi-community property" defined), 130 ("separate property" defined in Section 760 *et seq.*). For a comparable definition applicable to support, see Section 3515. [23 Cal.L.Rev. Comm. Reports 1 (1993)].

Research References

Forms

California Transactions Forms--Estate Planning § 1:26, Quasi-Community Property; Separate Property.

Treatises and Practice Aids

Witkin, California Summary 10th Community Property § 257, Clarifications and Distinctions.

Part 2

GENERAL PROVISIONS

§ 2550. Manner of division of community estate

Except upon the written agreement of the parties, or on oral stipulation of the parties in open court, or as otherwise provided in this division, in a proceeding for dissolution of marriage or for legal separation of the parties, the court shall, either in its judgment of dissolution of the marriage, in its judgment of legal separation of the parties, or at a later time if it expressly reserves jurisdiction to make such a property division, divide the community estate of the parties equally. *(Stats.1992, c. 162 (A.B.2650), § 10, operative Jan. 1, 1994.)*

Law Revision Commission Comments

Enactment [Revised Comment]

Section 2550 continues without substantive change the first sentence of the first paragraph of former Civil Code Section 4800(a). The phrase "or as otherwise provided in this division" has been substituted for "or as otherwise provided in this section," which referred to former Civil Code Section 4800. For the special rules for division of the community estate, see Sections 2600–2604.

For applicability of this division to a proceeding for nullity of marriage, see Sections 2251 (where court finds putative spouse, "quasi-marital property" divided in accordance with Division 7), 2252 (liability of "quasi-marital property" same as community or quasi-community property). See also Sections 63 ("community estate" defined), 1620 (contract between married persons concerning their property), 2554 (use of arbitration where parties do not voluntarily agree to division), 2650 (division of jointly held separate property), 2660 (real property located in another state), 3592 (obligations of property settlement discharged in bankruptcy). [23 Cal.L.Rev. Comm. Reports 1 (1993)].

Commentary

Relying on this section, *In re Marriage of Dellaria, 172 Cal.App.4th 196, 90 Cal.Rptr.3d 802 (2009), review denied*, held unenforceable a post-separation oral property division agreement that was neither reduced to writing nor stipulated in open court, even though the trial court found that the agreement, which did not divide the property equally, had been fully executed.

To similar effect, see *In re Marriage of Huntley, 10 Cal.App.5th 1053, 216 Cal.Rptr.3d 904 (2017)*, applying the holding of *Dellaria* to allow a former wife to bring a section 2556 proceeding to divide unadjudicated assets although the parties may have already executed an informal agreement to divide those assets.

In re Marriage of Walker, 240 Cal.App.4th 986, 193 Cal.Rptr.3d 134 (2015), held that a wife's discharge of her debts in bankruptcy did not entitle her to more than one-half the proceeds from the sale of the community property home. Although bankruptcy discharged the wife's personal liability on a purchase-money loan from the bank, it did not affect the bank's lien on the home, which had to be satisfied before net sale proceeds could be divided.

Except as otherwise provided, the divorce court has jurisdiction to divide only the community property. *Robinson v. Robinson, 65 Cal.App.2d 118, 150 P.2d 7 (1944)* (trial court may not award divorcing wife a life estate in husband's separate property home). This jurisdictional limitation is qualified by Section 2650, which additionally allows the divorce court to divide the spouses' jointly held separate property. Moreover, when both parties so request, the divorce court may resolve other separate property ownership issues. See, for example, *Crook v. Crook, 184 Cal.App.2d 745, 748, 7 Cal.Rptr. 892 (1960)*. For further recent case-law discussion of the divorce court's jurisdiction with respect to property claims, see *In re Marriage of Hebbring, 207 Cal.App.3d 1260, 255 Cal.Rptr. 488 (1989)* (divorce court has jurisdiction to order reimbursement for the value of a spouse's separate property willfully destroyed by the other spouse from the community property share of the latter) and cases cited therein. For discussion of the consolidation of independent claims with a divorce action, see *In re Marriage of McNeill, 160 Cal.App.3d 548, 206 Cal.Rptr. 641 (1984)* (consolidation of divorce and fraud action) and *In re Marriage of Buford, 155 Cal.App.3d 74, 202 Cal.Rptr. 20 (1984)*. Although a tort claim may be consolidated with a *pending* dissolution action in appropriate circumstances, *Sosnick v. Sosnick, 71 Cal.App.4th 1335, 84 Cal.Rptr.2d 700 (1999)*, holds that the divorce court lacks jurisdiction to consolidate a former wife's tort claim against her former husband with a closed dissolution action. For discussion of the exclusive and preemptive nature of the divorce court's jurisdiction, see *Askew v. Askew, 22 Cal.App.4th 942, 28 Cal.Rptr.2d 284 (1994)*; and *Neal v. Superior Court, 90 Cal.App.4th 22, 108 Cal.Rptr.2d 262 (2001)* (trial court should have granted former wife's demurrer to former husband's civil action that was clearly duplicative of parties' family law action). See additionally *Burkle v. Burkle, 144 Cal.App.4th 387, 50 Cal.Rptr.3d 436 (2006), review denied Feb. 21, 2007*, affirming a trial court dismissal of a wife's civil action for intentional infliction of emotional distress arising from her husband's failure to comply with an interim support order in a pending dissolution proceeding, on the ground that bringing a separate action pertaining to a pending dissolution proceeding violates well-established California precedent prohibiting such separate actions, and concluded that the wife's contentions about the proper forum for her civil action were frivolous; and therefore concluding that the trial court properly ordered the wife to make, as sanctions, substantial payments to her husband under Family Code section 271, and the wife and her attorneys to make substantial payments to the husband under Code of Civil Procedure section 128.7.

Sections 3800 et seq., which provide that a court may delay the sale of the family home to award temporary use and possession to the children and their custodial parent, has been interpreted as an exception to the general rule limiting the divorce court's jurisdiction to the community property. *In re Marriage of Braud, 45 Cal.App.4th 797, 811, 53 Cal.Rptr.2d 179 (1996)*. *Braud* involved a community property home to which the noncustodial parent had made significant Section 2640 separate property contributions.

The requirement that the community estate be divided equally is elaborated and qualified by Sections 2600–2627.

The tax consequences of division are not codified, but are controlled instead by case law, which provides that adjustment for tax consequences shall be made only when such consequences are relatively immediate and occur as a direct consequence of the community property division. Compare *In re Marriage of Fonstein, 17 Cal.3d 738, 131 Cal.Rptr. 873 (1976)* (in valuing husband's community property law partnership by his contractual right to withdraw from the firm, court may not take into account the taxes he would incur if he did later withdraw) with *In re Marriage of Epstein, 24 Cal.3d. 76, 154 Cal.Rptr. 413 (1979)* (tax consequences must be taken into account, at least through Internal Revenue Code rollover period, when court ordered the family residence sold and the proceeds divided between the parties). See also *In re Marriage of Marx, 97 Cal.App.3d 552, 159 Cal.Rptr. 215 (1979)* (future income taxation of pension benefits must be ignored in valuing a pension interest); accord, *In re Marriage of Bergman, 168 Cal.App.3d 742, 754, 214 Cal.Rptr. 661, 669 (1985)*.

The principle that tax consequences may be taken into account only when they are relatively certain and immediate and occur as a direct consequence of community property division has been extended to other speculative factors. *In re Marriage of Duncan, 90 Cal.App.4th 617, 108 Cal.Rptr.2d 833 (2001), review denied October 10, 2001*, holds that in valuing a business retained by a manager-spouse, the trial court should not reduce the value of the business by the value of any long-term contract for key employees that would ordinarily be included in a sale if the business were sold to a third party. *In re Marriage of Czapar, 232 Cal.App.3d 1308, 1315, 285 Cal.Rptr. 479 (1991)*, similarly holds that the value of a covenant not to compete, which might be required if the business were sold, should not serve to reduce the value of a business that is not being sold at divorce. (Note that *Duncan* and *Czapar* assume that the value of such a long-term contract or covenant not to compete should reduce the value of a community property business when sale is incident to dissolution. This assumption is undercut by *Duncan*'s recognition that such provisions negotiated incident to the sale of a business at divorce are simply means of protecting the value of the community property goodwill.)

Section 2550 implicitly allows the court to bifurcate dissolution and property division. See *In re Marriage of Lusk, 86 Cal.App.3d 228, 232, 150 Cal.Rptr. 63 (1978)* and *In re Marriage of Fink, 54 Cal.App.3d 357, 364, 126 Cal.Rptr. 626 (1976)*. See also Section 2337, explicitly authorizing and regulating bifurcation.

In a bifurcated proceeding, absent a waiver or stipulation to the contrary, a party is entitled to have the same judge try all portions of the proceeding that involve weighing of the evidence and issues of credibility. If the same judge is not available, a mistrial must be declared. *European Beverage, Inc. v. Superior Court, 43 Cal.App.4th 1211, 51 Cal.Rptr.2d 147 (1996)*. See also *In re Marriage of Colombo, 197 Cal.App.3d 572, 242 Cal.Rptr. 100 (1987)* (when interlocutory judgment is ordered by judge and certain issues remain to be decided, successor judge must hear the evidence and make decisions on all issues, unless parties stipulate otherwise).

When a debt for which community property is liable under section 910 was not assigned to the non-debtor spouse in the judgment of dissolution, *Litke O'Farrell, LLC v. Tipton, 204 Cal.App.4th 1178, 139 Cal.Rptr.3d 548 (2012)*, held that a marital settlement agreement (MSA) dividing the community property, assigning the debt solely to husband, providing that the court would be requested to incorporate the MSA in the judgment of dissolution but that the MSA was enforceable whether or not it was incorporated into a final judgment, became effective on the date it was signed by the parties. Thus, a motion to charge interests served by the husband's creditors after the MSA was executed but before the judgment of dissolution was entered did not attach to the property received by the wife in the MSA.

Research References

Forms

California Practice Guide: Rutter Family Law Forms Form 1:32, Glossary Of Common Family Law Terms, Phrases and Concepts (Enclosure to Form 1:31).
California Transactions Forms--Estate Planning § 1:23, Aggregate or Asset-By-Asset Division Of Community Property.
California Transactions Forms--Estate Planning § 1:26, Quasi-Community Property; Separate Property.
California Transactions Forms--Estate Planning § 1:36, Conflicts Between Clients.
California Transactions Forms--Estate Planning § 10:4, Community Property.
California Transactions Forms--Estate Planning § 10:5, Quasi-Community Property.
California Transactions Forms--Family Law § 2:12, Overview.
California Transactions Forms--Family Law § 2:13, Equalizing Payments.
Am. Jur. Pl. & Pr. Forms Community Property § 36, Complaint, Petition, or Declaration--For Divorce or Other Legal Separation--Allegation Of Quasi-Community Property.
West's California Code Forms, Family § 2550, Comment Overview--Manner Of Division Of Community Estate.
West's California Code Forms, Family § 2338 Form 6, Provision in Judgment--Awarding Community Estate.

Treatises and Practice Aids

Witkin, California Summary 10th Community Property § 33, Restrictions on Alteration Of Spouses' Legal Relations.
Witkin, California Summary 10th Community Property § 68, Statutory Abrogation Of Rule.
Witkin, California Summary 10th Community Property § 76, Award to Employee Spouse With Offset.
Witkin, California Summary 10th Community Property § 185, Illustrations.
Witkin, California Summary 10th Community Property § 190, General Rule Of Equal Division.
Witkin, California Summary 10th Community Property § 200, Division by Agreement.
Witkin, California Summary 10th Community Property § 203, Other Exceptions.
Witkin, California Summary 10th Community Property § 212, Characterization and Confirmation Of Debts.
Witkin, California Summary 10th Community Property § 213, in General.
Witkin, California Summary 10th Community Property § 216, Reservation Of Jurisdiction to Divide.
Witkin, California Summary 10th Community Property § 217, Nonjudicial Division.
Witkin, California Summary 10th Community Property § 241, Statutory Requirement Of Division.
Witkin, California Summary 10th Community Property § 258, Statutory Rule.
Witkin, California Summary 10th Husband and Wife § 112, Contents Of Judgment.
Witkin, California Summary 10th Insurance § 181, Personal Injury Coverage: Uninsured Motorists.

§ 2551. Characterization of liabilities; confirmation or assignment

For the purposes of division and in confirming or assigning the liabilities of the parties for which the community estate is liable, the court shall characterize liabilities as separate or community and confirm or assign them to the parties in accordance with Part 6 (commencing with Section 2620). *(Stats.1992, c. 162 (A.B.2650), § 10, operative Jan. 1, 1994.)*

Law Revision Commission Comments

Enactment [Revised Comment]

Section 2551 continues the second paragraph of former Civil Code Section 4800(a) without substantive change. A reference to Part 6 has been substituted for the narrower reference to former Civil Code Section 4800(c). This is not a substantive change. See also Sections 63 ("community estate" defined), 2251 (where court finds putative spouse, "quasi-marital property" divided in accordance with Division 7), 2252 (liability of "quasi-marital property" same as community or quasi-community property). [23 Cal.L.Rev.Comm. Reports 1 (1993)].

Research References

Treatises and Practice Aids

Witkin, California Summary 10th Community Property § 212, Characterization and Confirmation Of Debts.

§ 2552. Valuation of assets and liabilities

(a) For the purpose of division of the community estate upon dissolution of marriage or legal separation of the parties, except as provided in subdivision (b), the court shall value the assets and liabilities as near as practicable to the time of trial.

(b) Upon 30 days' notice by the moving party to the other party, the court for good cause shown may value all or any portion of the assets and liabilities at a date after separation and before trial to accomplish an equal division of the community estate of the parties in an equitable manner. *(Stats.1992, c. 162 (A.B.2650), § 10, operative Jan. 1, 1994.)*

Law Revision Commission Comments

Enactment [Revised Comment]

Section 2552 continues without substantive change the last sentence of the first paragraph of former Civil Code Section 4800(a). The reference to the "community estate" in the introductory clause of subdivision (a) replaces the former reference to "community property." This revision is consistent with the language of subdivision (b). See Section 63 ("community estate" defined). In subdivision (a), the reference to dissolution and legal separation has been added and is drawn from the first sentence of former Civil Code

Section 4800(a). See also Sections 2251 (where court finds putative spouse, "quasi-marital property" divided in accordance with Division 7), 2252 (liability of "quasi-marital property" same as community or quasi-community property). [23 Cal.L.Rev.Comm. Reports 1 (1993)].

Commentary

For discussion of the general rule that assets and liabilities be valued as near as practicable to the time of trial, see *In re Marriage of Reuling, 23 Cal.App.4th 1428, 1435, 28 Cal.Rptr.2d 726 (1994).*

In re Marriage of Campi, 212 Cal.App.4th 1565, 152 Cal.Rptr.3d 179 (2013), holds that a trial court properly valued a family residence according to a stipulated order filed three years before the trial, when neither party objected to the stipulated value at trial.

Although Section 2552 provides that assets shall generally be valued as near as practicable to the time of trial, assets that reflect or incorporate a spouse's personal activity or labor should be valued at the date of Section 771 separation. *In re Marriage of Duncan, 90 Cal.App.4th 617, 108 Cal.Rptr.2d 833 (2001), review denied October 10, 2001* (company that managed pension funds should be valued at the time of separation because its value and success depended almost exclusively on husband's skill, industry, guidance and reputation); *In re Marriage of Stevenson, 20 Cal.App.4th 250, 24 Cal.Rptr.2d 411 (1993)* (small contracting business dependent on husband's skill and reputation should be valued at the time of separation); *In re Marriage of Green, 213 Cal.App.3d 14, 20–21, 261 Cal.Rptr. 294 (1989)*. See also *In re Marriage of Stallcup, 97 Cal.App.3d 294, 301, 158 Cal.Rptr. 679 (1979)*, and *In re Marriage of Barnert, 85 Cal.App.3d 413, 422–424, 149 Cal.Rptr. 616 (1978)*.

Compare *In re Marriage of Sherman, 133 Cal.App.4th 795, 35 Cal.Rptr.3d 137 (2005)*, which held that in making a *Moore-Marsden* apportionment, the trial court erred in valuing an appreciated family home at the time of separation rather than the time of trial, because the increase in value was due to market forces rather than to either spouse's personal efforts. *Sherman* criticizes the analysis of *Bono v. Clark, 103 Cal.App.4th 1409, 128 Cal.Rptr.2d 31 (2002), review denied*, which used the time of separation in a death proceeding.

In re Marriage of Nelson, 139 Cal.App.4th 1546, 44 Cal.Rptr.3d 52 (2006), holds that the trial court properly valued the wife's business at the time of separation when her poor recordkeeping made it difficult to value at any later date.

Although it may sometimes be appropriate to value a business at the time of the separation, when the business has increased in value between the date of separation and the date of divorce, it may also be appropriate to apportion that increase in value between the community and separate estates. *In re Marriage of Imperato, 45 Cal.App.3d 432, 119 Cal.Rptr.590 (1975)* (*Van Camp* or *Pereira* accounting should be used to apportion the post separation increase in value). For discussion of *Van Camp* and *Pereira* accounting, see Section 2640, Commentary. Compare *In re Marriage of Honer, 236 Cal. App. 4th 687, 186 Cal.Rptr.3d 607 (2015), review denied*, which held that the trial court did not err in considering, inter alia, an appraisal of the parties' community business that was a year old. Moreover, the court of appeals, after an extensive discussion of valuation methods, found no abuse of discretion in the trial court's denial of wife's motion to reopen judgment to admit evidence that the business's retained profits had increased since the appraisal was prepared.

See also *In re Marriage of Cream, 13 Cal.App.4th 81, 16 Cal.Rptr.2d 575 (1993), review denied* (trial court may not value property by means of interspousal auction when one spouse disapproves).

Research References

Forms

California Practice Guide: Rutter Family Law Forms Form 8:8, Request for Order Re Separate Trial Re Alternate Valuation Date (Community Bank Accounts).

California Transactions Forms--Family Law § 2:32, Date Of Valuation.

West's California Code Forms, Family § 2550, Comment Overview--Manner Of Division Of Community Estate.

Treatises and Practice Aids

Witkin, California Summary 10th Community Property § 106, Date Of Valuation Of Law Practice.

Witkin, California Summary 10th Community Property § 193, in General.

§ 2553. Powers of court

The court may make any orders the court considers necessary to carry out the purposes of this division. *(Stats. 1992, c. 162 (A.B.2650), § 10, operative Jan. 1, 1994.)*

Law Revision Commission Comments

Enactment [Revised Comment]

Section 2553 continues former Civil Code Section 4800(f) without substantive change. The phrase "the purposes of this division" has been substituted for "the purposes of this section," which referred to former Civil Code Section 4800. See also Section 3592 (obligations of property settlement discharged in bankruptcy). [23 Cal.L.Rev. Comm. Reports 1 (1993)].

Commentary

In re Marriage of Cream, 13 Cal.App.4th 81, 16 Cal.Rptr.2d 575 (1993), review denied, holds that the trial court may not order an interspousal auction of property when one spouse disapproves.

Research References

Forms

Am. Jur. Pl. & Pr. Forms Community Property § 32, Introductory Comments.

Treatises and Practice Aids

Witkin, California Summary 10th Community Property § 215, Sale Of Property and Division Of Proceeds.

Witkin, California Summary 10th Community Property § 232, in General.

§ 2554. Failure to agree to voluntary division of property; submission to arbitration

(a) Notwithstanding any other provision of this division, in any case in which the parties do not agree in writing to a voluntary division of the community estate of the parties, the issue of the character, the value, and the division of the community estate may be submitted by the court to arbitration for resolution pursuant to Chapter 2.5 (commencing with Section 1141.10) of Title 3 of Part 3 of the Code of Civil Procedure, if the total value of the community and quasi-community property in controversy in the opinion of the court does not exceed fifty thousand dollars ($50,000). The decision of the court regarding the value of the community and quasi-community property for purposes of this section is not appealable.

(b) The court may submit the matter to arbitration at any time it believes the parties are unable to agree upon a division of the property. *(Stats.1992, c. 162 (A.B.2650), § 10, operative Jan. 1, 1994.)*

Law Revision Commission Comments

Enactment [Revised Comment]

Section 2554 continues former Civil Code Section 4800.9 without substantive change. In the introductory clause of subdivision (a), "this division" has been substituted for the reference to former Civil Code Section 4800. In the part of subdivision (a) that refers to division of property, references to "community estate" have been substituted for references to "community property and quasi-community property." These are not substantive changes. See Section 63 ("community estate" defined). In the parts of subdivision (a) that refer to valuation of property, references to quasi-community property have been added. This conforms the valuation rule to the division rule. [23 Cal.L.Rev.Comm. Reports 1 (1993)].

Research References

Forms

26 West's Legal Forms § 1:3, Statutes Mandating or Encouraging Alternative Dispute Resolution.

Treatises and Practice Aids

Witkin, California Summary 10th Community Property § 213, in General.
Witkin, California Summary 10th Community Property § 232, in General.

§ 2555. Disposition of community estate; revision on appeal

The disposition of the community estate, as provided in this division, is subject to revision on appeal in all particulars, including those which are stated to be in the discretion of the court. *(Stats.1992, c. 162 (A.B.2650), § 10, operative Jan. 1, 1994.)*

Law Revision Commission Comments

Enactment [Revised Comment]

Section 2555 continues former Civil Code Section 4810 without substantive change. The term "community estate" replaces the former reference to "community and quasi-community property" for consistency with other sections in this part. See, e.g., Section 2550 (equal division of community estate). This is not a substantive change. See Section 63 ("community estate" defined). The phrase "as provided in this division" has been substituted for "as above provided." This is not a substantive change, since the "above provided" provisions having to do with disposition of property are continued in this division. [23 Cal.L.Rev.Comm. Reports 1 (1993)].

Research References

Treatises and Practice Aids

Witkin, California Summary 10th Community Property § 232, in General.

§ 2556. Community property or debts; continuing jurisdiction

In a proceeding for dissolution of marriage, for nullity of marriage, or for legal separation of the parties, the court has continuing jurisdiction to award community estate assets or community estate liabilities to the parties that have not been previously adjudicated by a judgment in the proceeding. A party may file a postjudgment motion or order to show cause in the proceeding in order to obtain adjudication of any community estate asset or liability omitted or not adjudicated by the judgment. In these cases, the court shall equally divide the omitted or unadjudicated community estate asset or liability, unless the court finds upon good cause shown that the interests of justice require an unequal division of the asset or liability. *(Stats.1992, c. 162 (A.B.2650), § 10, operative Jan. 1, 1994. Amended by Stats.1993, c. 219 (A.B.1500), § 111.)*

Law Revision Commission Comments

Enactment [Revised Comment]

Section 2556 continues former Civil Code Section 4353 without substantive change. In the introductory clause, "proceeding" has been substituted for "action." The term "community estate" has been substituted for "community" to conform with the language of Section 2550 regarding property subject to division. See Section 63 ("community estate" defined). See also *In re* Marriage of Craig, 219 Cal.App.3d 683, 686, 268 Cal.Rptr. 396 (1990) ("California's marital property laws are designed to provide for uniform treatment of quasi-community and community property when the parties have changed their domicile to this state and seek to legally alter their marital status in a California court. This intent is apparent from statutes such as [former Civil Code Section] 4800 (equal division of 'community estate' consisting of community and quasi-community property) and [former Civil Code Section] 4800.5 (power to order conveyance of out-of-state property)."). The terms "asset" and "liability" are used in place of "property" and "debt" for consistency with other sections. See, e.g., Sections 1100 (fiduciary duty in management and control of community personal property), 2033 (family law attorney's real property lien), 2100 *et seq.* (disclosure of assets and liabilities), 2120 *et seq.* (relief from judgment). [23 Cal.L.Rev.Comm. Reports 1 (1993)].

Commentary

Section 2556 codifies the substantive rule articulated in *Henn v. Henn, 26 Cal.3d 323, 161 Cal.Rptr. 502 (1980)* (community assets not distributed in the dissolution decree patiently await later division as tenancy in common property). See also *Brunson v. Brunson, 168 Cal.App.3d 786, 214 Cal.Rptr. 378 (1985)* (*Henn* action to divide a pension may be brought even though prior divorce decree mentioned pension in connection with spousal support payments so long as divorce court did not adjudicate the parties' property rights in the pension). Yet Section 2556 modifies the procedural rules set out in *Henn*. The claimant need no longer bring an independent partition action; instead the claimant shall file a postjudgment motion or order to show cause in the dissolution action.

In re Marriage of Nassimi, 3 Cal.App.5th 667, 207 Cal.Rptr.3d 764 (2016), review denied, held that the liability arising from a third party's claim after dissolution to rescind a contract to purchase a community property business was an obligation omitted from the parties' marital dissolution judgment, subject to division under this section, and each spouse was obliged to pay half the cost of settling the litigation.

In re Marriage of Huntley, 10 Cal.App.5th 1053, 216 Cal.Rptr.3d 904 (2017), reversed a trial court order denying a former wife's post-judgment motion to divide an unadjudicated asset, holding that the former wife was not required to set aside a default judgment of dissolution that did not address division of the parties' community property. *Huntley* held that it did not matter than the wife may have been aware of the unadjudicated assets at the time of dissolution and emphasized that there is no time limit for a motion under this section. For further discussion of *Huntley*, see Commentary to section 2550.

Does a "final settlement of all property claims" clause bar a subsequent Section 2556 claim? Compare *Huddleson v. Huddleson, 187 Cal.App.3d 1564, 1572–1573, 232 Cal.Rptr. 722 (1986)* (general release does not bar subsequent *Henn* [Section 2556] action) with *Espy v. Espy, 238 Cal.Rptr. 182 (1987), review denied and depublished by the supreme court on 9/3/87* (general release does bar subsequent *Henn* action).

See also *In re Marriage of Moore and Ferrie, 14 Cal.App.4th 1472, 1478, 18 Cal.Rptr.2d 543 (1993), review denied 7/29/93* (wife may bring action in California to divide California community property portion of pension where Ohio court entered earlier judgment but omitted pension from the parties' property division); *Lakkees v. Superior Court, 222 Cal.App.3d 531, 271 Cal.Rptr. 845 (1990)*.

In re Marriage of Simundza, 121 Cal.App.4th 1513, 18 Cal.Rptr.3d 377 (2004), concluded that a stipulated dissolution judgment that awarded the wife a monthly sum from her husband's pension check for 12 years did not result in a partially omitted asset within the meaning of this section, because there was no indication in the judgment that the parties intended to divide the community property interest in the pension equally. *Simundza* distinguished *In re Marriage of Melton, 28 Cal.App.4th 931, 33 Cal.Rptr.2d 761 (1994)*, which found that there was an omitted asset when the parties' judgment specified that the wife was entitled to a one-half interest in her husband's pension but understated the monthly value of that interest.

With *Melton*, compare *In re Marriage of Thorne & Raccina, 203 Cal.App.4th 492, 136 Cal.Rptr.3d 887 (2012)*, which held that a stipulated final judgment awarding a wife a percentage of retirement pay based on the husband's rank and pay at the time the settlement agreement was executed rather than at the time he ultimately retired did not justify trial court recalculation of the wife's interest in the pension as of the time of retirement, because the difference between the greater and lesser amount was not an omitted asset for purposes of this section. Moreover, the wife's reliance on incorrect information provided by the military justice advocate general, although a ground for avoiding a judgment under Family Code section 2122(e), was unavailable to the wife because the one-year time limitation of that section had expired by the time the husband retired and the wife sought to realize her interest in the pension. Relief for fraud was unavailable under section 2122(a) because both parties intended to enter an agreement that complied with California law.

With respect to federal military pensions, the operation of Section 2556 may be preempted by federal law. In 1990, Congress amended the Uniformed Services Former Spouses Protection Act (USFSPA) to provide, effective November 8, 1990, that a court may not treat retired pay as property in any proceeding to divide or partition retired pay if a final decree of dissolution or legal separation was issued before June 21, 1981 (the date of *McCarty v. McCarty, 453 U.S. 210*) and the decree did not reserve jurisdiction to treat the retired pay as property. 10 U.S.C. § 1408(c)(1). Otherwise, undistributed community property interests in military retired pay are subject to section 2556 distribution. See also *In re Marriage of Olsen, 24 Cal.App.4th 1702, 30 Cal.Rptr.2d 306 (1994), review denied 9/7/94* (even though trial court had terminated spousal support in 1989 without reserving continuing jurisdiction, pursuant to wife's waiver of further support on condition of receiving a share of husband's military retirement benefits, nevertheless the trial court had jurisdiction and grounds to order spousal support in 1993 because the 1990 amendment to USFSPA had retroactively deprived wife of her share of those military retirement benefits).

Cf. In re Marriage of Mason, 46 Cal.App.4th 1025, 54 Cal.Rptr.2d 263 (1996), which raises but does not decide the question whether the goodwill of a business may be treated as a Section 2556 "omitted asset" when the other assets of the business were divided in the original divorce action.

In Marriage of Hixson, 111 Cal.App.4th 1116, 4 Cal.Rptr.3d 483 (2003), review denied, held that the trial court did not abuse its discretion in quashing discovery and denying relief on an order to show cause brought under this section when a former wife failed to present any evidence or argument as to the existence of community estate unadjudicated assets or investment opportunities.

The doctrine of judicial estoppel gives a court discretionary power to bar a party from taking a factual or legal position that is inconsistent with a position the party successfully asserted in prior litigation. In *Levin v. Ligon, 140 Cal.App.4th 1456, 45 Cal.Rptr.3d 560 (2006), review denied*, the court of appeal affirmed a trial court's application of the doctrine to a former husband in an action under this section. The husband and wife were divorced in England. Due to attorney negligence, under English law the husband lost all interest in pension rights his wife earned during their marriage. Taking the position that the attorney's negligence caused him to lose all interest in his former wife's pension rights, the husband successfully recovered malpractice damages from the attorney. The successful assertion of that position warranted a California trial court's application of the doctrine of judicial estoppel to bar the husband from subsequently asserting a community property interest in pension rights earned by his wife during marriage.

Research References

Treatises and Practice Aids

Witkin, California Summary 10th Community Property § 238, Effect Of Failure to Disclose.

Witkin, California Summary 10th Community Property § 243, Grounds and Time Limits.

Witkin, California Summary 10th Community Property § 244, in General.

Witkin, California Summary 10th Community Property § 247, Post-judgment Motion.

Part 3

PRESUMPTION CONCERNING PROPERTY HELD IN JOINT FORM

§ 2580. Legislative findings and declarations; public policy

The Legislature hereby finds and declares as follows:

(a) It is the public policy of this state to provide uniformly and consistently for the standard of proof in establishing the character of property acquired by spouses during marriage in joint title form, and for the allocation of community and separate interests in that property between the spouses.

(b) The methods provided by case and statutory law have not resulted in consistency in the treatment of spouses' interests in property they hold in joint title, but rather, have created confusion as to which law applies to property at a particular point in time, depending on the form of title, and, as a result, spouses cannot have reliable expectations as to the characterization of their property and the allocation of the interests therein, and attorneys cannot reliably advise their clients regarding applicable law.

(c) Therefore, a compelling state interest exists to provide for uniform treatment of property. Thus, former Sections 4800.1 and 4800.2 of the Civil Code, as operative on January 1, 1987, and as continued in Sections 2581 and 2640 of this code, apply to all property held in joint title regardless of the date of acquisition of the property or the date of any agreement affecting the character of the property, and those sections apply in all proceedings commenced on or after January 1, 1984. However, those sections do not apply to property settlement agreements executed before January 1, 1987, or proceedings in which judgments were rendered before January 1, 1987, regardless of whether those judgments have become final. *(Added by Stats.1993, c. 219*

(A.B.1500), § 111.6. Amended by Stats.1993, c. 876 (S.B. 1068), § 15.2, eff. Oct. 6, 1993, operative Jan. 1, 1994.)

Law Revision Commission Comments

Enactment [Revised Comment]

Section 2580 continues former Civil Code Section 4800.1(a) without substantive change. *Cf.* Marriage of Hilke, 4 Cal.4th 215, 841 P.2d 891, 14 Cal.Rptr.2d 371 (1992). The references to the former Civil Code provisions (Sections 4800.1 and 4800.2, repealed by 1992 Cal. Stat. ch. 162, § 3, operative Jan. 1, 1994) and their Family Code successors is consistent with Section 2 ("A provision of this code, insofar as it is substantially the same as a previously existing provision relating to the same subject matter, shall be considered as a restatement and continuation thereof and not as a new enactment.").

Under Section 2581, all property held in joint form by the spouses is presumed to be community property, absent a written agreement otherwise. Under Section 2640, all community property is divided subject to a right of reimbursement for separate property contributions, absent an express agreement otherwise. When enacted in 1983 (as former Civil Code Sections 4800.1 and 4800.2), these provisions were intended to remedy the injustice in former law resulting from the following factors:

(1) The Supreme Court's interpretation of former law in the *Lucas* case of the community property presumption for a joint tenancy single-family residence to find a gift of separate funds used to acquire a community asset absent an express agreement otherwise. See *In re* Marriage of Lucas, 27 Cal.3d 808, 614 P.2d 285, 166 Cal.Rptr. 853 (1980). The *Lucas* decision was widely considered to cause injustice to persons who contributed their separate funds for use by the community and then lost the funds entirely to the community at dissolution of marriage. Often the parties were unaware that taking title in joint tenancy had the effect of making a gift of the separate property to the community.

(2) The rule that a spouse could disprove the community property presumption for a joint tenancy single-family residence under former law by evidence of an oral agreement that the residence is separate property. This rule promoted actions characterized by conflicting and inconsistent testimony, with each side offering different explanations for the effect of a joint tenancy deed. Often the intent of the parties who long before filed a joint tenancy deed could be confused by faded memories or altered to self-serving testimony. The requirement of a writing provides a reliable test by which to determine the understanding of the parties. It seeks to prevent the abuses and unpredictability that have resulted from the oral agreement standard. See discussion in *In re* Marriage of Martinez, 156 Cal.App.3d 20, 29, 202 Cal.Rptr. 646 (1984), disapproved in *In re* Marriage of Buol, 39 Cal.3d 751, 705 P.2d 354, 218 Cal.Rptr. 31 (1985). [23 Cal.L.Rev.Comm. Reports 1 (1993)].

Research References

Forms

California Transactions Forms--Family Law § 1:90, Real and Personal Property.

Treatises and Practice Aids

Witkin, California Summary 10th Community Property § 231, Attempted Statutory Solution.

§ 2581. Division of property; presumptions

For the purpose of division of property on dissolution of marriage or legal separation of the parties, property acquired by the parties during marriage in joint form, including property held in tenancy in common, joint tenancy, or tenancy by the entirety, or as community property, is presumed to be community property. This presumption is a presumption affecting the burden of proof and may be rebutted by either of the following:

(a) A clear statement in the deed or other documentary evidence of title by which the property is acquired that the property is separate property and not community property.

(b) Proof that the parties have made a written agreement that the property is separate property. *(Added by Stats.1993, c. 219 (A.B.1500), § 111.7.)*

Law Revision Commission Comments

Enactment [Revised Comment]

Section 2581 continues former Civil Code Section 4800.1(b) without substantive change. Section 2581 applies to all property acquired during marriage in joint form regardless of the date of acquisition. Section 2580 (legislative finding and declaration); Marriage of Hilke, 4 Cal.4th 215, 841 P.2d 891, 14 Cal.Rptr.2d 371 (1992). See also Section 2251 (division of property in nullity proceeding).

The community property presumptions created by Section 2581 are applicable only in dissolution and legal separation proceedings. The presumptions govern both real and personal property, whether situated in California or another jurisdiction, and include property acquired during marriage while domiciled in another jurisdiction. The presumptions also govern property initially acquired before marriage, the title to which is taken in joint form or as community property by the spouses during marriage. The measure of the separate property contribution under Section 2640 in such a case is the value of the property at the time of its conversion to joint or community property form.

Section 2581 requires a writing to rebut the community property presumption. Permitting oral statements to defeat the community property presumption for purposes of dissolution of marriage would frustrate the strong public policy favoring community ownership of property acquired during marriage. The requirement of a writing is important to help ensure that a party waives community property rights only on mature consideration.

Section 2581 does not affect the validity of an oral agreement for any purpose other than division of property at dissolution of marriage. For purposes of division, Section 2581, together with Section 2640, recognizes and reimburses separate property contributions. This treatment of an oral agreement for purposes of division is fair because an oral agreement, whatever other purpose it might have (management and control, disposition at death, etc.), is not ordinarily intended to affect rights at dissolution or to make a present gift for that purpose. Casual statements made during marriage generally are not made with full knowledge of their consequences or with the intention that they change the rights of the parties if the marriage is dissolved.

For background on former Civ. Code § 4800.1, see *Recommendation Relating to Division of Joint Tenancy and Tenancy in Common Property at Dissolution of Marriage,* 16 Cal. L. Revision Comm'n Reports 2165 (1982); 17 Cal. L. Revision Comm'n Reports 863 (1984); *Recommendation Relating to Civil Code Sections 4800.1 and 4800.2,* 18 Cal. L. Revision Comm'n Reports 383 (1986); 18 Cal. L. Revision Comm'n Reports 1741 (1986). [23 Cal.L.Rev.Comm. Reports 1 (1993)].

Commentary

In its first version (reproduced below), the California Law Revision Commission finally conceded the constitutional point and incorporated the constitutional rules announced by the supreme court and refined by the courts of appeal. The first version applied only to property *acquired after the statute's effective date*. See Commission comment reproduced below under Author's Note for informational purposes only. Then the California Supreme Court decided *In re Marriage of Hilke, 4 Cal.4th 215, 14 Cal.Rptr.2d 371 (1992). Hilke* emboldened the Commission to return to its original retroactive formulation of Civil Code Sections 4800.1 and 4800.2, the so-called "anti-Lucas legislation," which it did in the second, current version of Family Code Sections 2580, 2581 and 2640. Yet *Hilke* seemed to provide inadequate support for full retroactive application of those sections. In 1969, Robert and Joyce Hilke purchased a home with community property funds and took title in joint tenancy. Joyce died after their divorce but shortly before the bifurcated divorce-related property distribution, where Robert resisted the application of Civil Code Section 4800.1 (current Family Code Sections 2580 and 2581) on the ground that any retroactive application is constitutionally impermissible. Rejecting his argument, the Supreme Court held that retroactive application is impermissible only when *vested* rights would thereby be impaired. When the only consequence of treating a joint tenancy as community property is the destruction of each spouse's right of survivorship, no vested right is destroyed because, as between living co-owners, a right of survivorship is a mere expectancy. (Robert's survivorship right vested only at Joyce's death, which occurred long after the statute was enacted.) Thus, in the ordinary case of jointly-titled property purchased by married persons with community property funds, Sections 2580 and 2581 may be retroactively applied. Although the holding of *Hilke* rests on the distinction between vested and unvested rights, the court observed in a footnote that "[a]n additional difference between this case, on the one hand, and *Fabian* and *Buol*, on the other, is that [Civil Code] Section 4800.1 was enacted well before Mrs. Hilke filed for dissolution." *4 Cal.4th 223 n.4*. The Law Revision Commission apparently relied on this footnote to conclude that any retroactive application of the anti-*Lucas* statutes is constitutional so long as the divorce proceeding was commenced after their effective date. This seemed an excessively broad reading in view of the reasoning of *Hilke* and the court of appeal decisions cited in the Law Revision Commission Comment to its first version of Sections 2580 and 2640. Nevertheless, one court of appeal summarily extended the holding of *Hilke* to vested interests and to Section 2640 reimbursement, concluding that both Sections 2581 and 2640 could be applied retroactively in any case brought after their effective dates even though the transaction in question occurred before the effective dates of the statutes. *In re Marriage of Heikes, 31 Cal.Rptr.2d 721 (1994)*. The Supreme Court granted review and reversed the decision of the court of appeal. *In re Marriage of Heikes, 10 Cal.4th 1211, 899 P.2d 1349, 44 Cal.Rptr.2d 155 (1995)*. The Supreme Court reaffirmed the ostensible holdings of *In re Marriage of Buol, 39 Cal.3d 751, 705 P.2d 354, 218 Cal.Rptr. 31 (1985)*, *In re Marriage of Fabian, 41 Cal.3d 440, 715 P.2d 253, 224 Cal.Rptr. 333 (1986)*, and *In re Marriage of Hilke,* supra. Family Code Sections 2581 and 2640 may not be applied retroactively to transactions occurring before their effective dates when the effect of such retroactive application would be the destruction of vested property rights. Effectively, Section 2581 may be applied retroactively to property acquired before its effective date when the only result of its application would be to destroy an unvested right of survivorship by treating a joint tenancy as community property or to treat one form of equal ownership, for example, tenancy in common, as community property, an equivalent form of equal ownership. Section 2581 may not be applied retroactively when the effect would be material alteration of a vested property interest. Thus Section 2581 may not be applied to a claim that property acquired before the statute's effective date is not jointly owned at all, despite its joint title. This was Mrs. Buol's claim (*In re Marriage of Buol*, supra), and she was constitutionally entitled to prove her sole ownership of the disputed property according to the law in effect at the time that she and her husband took title to the property. For purposes of this rule of nonretroactivity, there are two effective dates. When Section 2581 was initially enacted, effective January 1, 1984, it applied to joint tenancies only. Section 2581 was subsequently amended, effective January 1, 1987, to additionally apply to all other forms of joint ownership. When Section 2581 may not constitutionally be applied, prior case law controls. Prior case law allows oral as well as written evidence of a spousal agreement or understanding to hold property differently than as indicated in the joint and equal title. See generally *In re Marriage of Lucas, 27 Cal.3d 808, 614 P.2d 285, 166 Cal.Rptr. 853 (1980)*.

Similarly, Section 2640 may be applied retroactively only when such application would not alter any property right that vested before its effective date. Thus a spouse who made a separate property contribution to the acquisition of community property before 1984 may not seek reimbursement of the separate property contribution because there was no right of reimbursement before 1984 unless the parties had a reimbursement agreement; otherwise, a gift was presumed. *Lucas*, supra.

The substance, including the effective dates, of these constitutional rules is captured in the Law Revision Commission's first abandoned version of Family Code Sections 2580, reproduced below, and 2640. This first version need only be glossed by *Hilke* (retroactive application permissible when only unvested rights are affected thereby) to accurately describe the current state of this complex area of law.

The central issue presented by *Hilke* is the treatment of joint tenancy property when a spouse dies after the entry of the divorce decree but before the bifurcated property proceeding. The supreme court held that Sections 2580 and 2581 are generally applicable. Hence the survivor's right of survivorship is inoperative and each spouse owns a one-half interest in the property. On the other hand, if a spouse dies before there has been any judgment respecting the parties' marital status, the divorce action abates entirely and Section 2581 has no application. In such case, property held by the spouses in joint tenancy is subject to the surviving spouse's right of survivorship. *Estate of Blair, 199 Cal.App.3d 161, 244 Cal.Rptr. 627 (1988)*. See also *Dorn v. Solomon, 57 Cal.App.4th 650, 67 Cal.Rptr.2d 311 (1997)* (quit claim deed of separated spouse, which failed to meet Civil Code § 683.2 requirements for severance of joint tenancy, was ineffective to transfer dying spouse's one-half interest to third party; interest passed instead to surviving spouse by joint tenancy right of survivorship); *Estate of Layton, 44 Cal.App.4th 1337, 52 Cal.Rptr.2d 251 (1996)* (a status-only dissolution does not automatically sever a joint tenancy).

Inter vivos severance will avoid joint tenancy treatment in the event that the subsequent death of one of the parties abates the divorce proceeding. *Estate of Mitchell, 76 Cal.App.4th 1378, 91 Cal.Rptr.2d 192 (1999)*, holds that severance of a joint tenancy by recordation of a declaration of severance is not a "transfer" or "disposition" within the meaning of § 2040(a)(2) and therefore does not violate the temporary restraining order issued under § 2040.

Although a family residence titled in joint tenancy is deemed community property for purposes of Section 2581, it may nevertheless remain a joint tenancy for purposes of a third party's execution of a judgment against the husband. *Abbett Electric Corp. v. Storek, 22 Cal.App.4th 1460, 27 Cal.Rptr.2d 845 (1994), review denied 6/23/94.*

A Ninth Circuit Bankruptcy Appellate Panel, purporting to apply California community property law, held that a married couple's property held in joint tenancy title is community property for purposes of inclusion, in its entirety, in the husband's bankruptcy estate. Characterizing joint tenancy held by spouses in an intact marriage, *In re Brace, 566 B.R. 13 (B.A.P. 9th Cir. 2017)*, relied on the case law presumption that property acquired during marriage is community property, this section's presumption that, at dissolution, property acquired in joint tenancy title is community property, the transmutation provisions, including sections 850 through 852, and *In re Marriage of Valli, 58 Cal. 4th 1396 (2014)*. The reasoning of *Brace* is ahistorical and unpersuasive. Its holding should be treated with circumspection.

Former Section 2580

The former version of Section 2580, enacted by Stats 1992 Ch 162 § 10, effective January 1, 1993, operative January 1, 1994, was repealed by Stats 1993 Ch 219 § 111.5. It provides:

(a) For the purpose of division of property upon dissolution of marriage or legal separation of the parties:

(1) Property acquired by the parties during marriage on or after January 1, 1984, and before January 1, 1987, in joint tenancy form is presumed to be community property.

(2) Property acquired by the parties during marriage on or after January 1, 1987, in joint form, including property held in tenancy in common, joint tenancy, tenancy by the entirety, or as community property is presumed to be community property.

(b) The presumptions under subdivision (a) are presumptions affecting the burden of proof and may be rebutted by either of the following:

(1) A clear statement in the deed or other documentary evidence of title by which the property is acquired that the property is separate property and not community property.

(2) Proof that the parties have made a written agreement that the property is separate property.

(c) Nothing in this section affects the character of property acquired by married persons that is not described in subdivision (a).

The Law Revision Commission's Comments regarding this former Section 2580, which are provided for informational purposes only, read as follows:

Subdivision (a)(1) of Section 2580 restates the first sentence of former Civil Code Section 4800.1(b) (as enacted by 1983 Cal. Stat. ch. 342, § 1), with the addition of language that codifies the constitutional limitations on the application of Section 2580. Subdivision (a)(2) restates the first sentence of former Civil Code Section 4800.1(b) (as amended by 1986 Cal. Stat. ch. 539, § 1), with the addition of language that codifies the constitutional limitations on the application of Section 2580.

Subdivision (b) of Section 2580 continues the last part of former Civil Code Section 4800.1(b) without substantive change.

Subdivision (c) of Section 2580 is new and makes clear that the law concerning property not described in subdivision (a) is not affected by Section 2580. Accordingly, the character of the interest in property acquired in joint tenancy form by the parties before January 1, 1984, is not determined under or affected by Section 2580. Likewise, the character of the interest in property acquired by the parties before January 1, 1987, and held in tenancy in common, tenancy by the entirety, or as community property is not determined under or affected by Section 2580. See also Section 2650 (division of jointly held separate property).

Former Civil Code Section 4800.1(a), which sought to justify the application of former Civil Code Sections 4800.1 and 4800.2 without regard to the date the property was acquired, has not been continued. Instead, subdivision (a) codifies case law holding that the section cannot constitutionally be applied to the property described in subdivision (a) prior to the date of acquisition specified in paragraph (1) or (2) of subdivision (a), whichever is applicable. See, e.g., *In re Marriage of Cairo, 204 Cal.App.3d 1255, 251 Cal.Rptr. 731 (1988)*; *In re Marriage of Lockman, 204 Cal.App.3d 782, 251 Cal.Rptr. 434 (1988)*; *In re Marriage of Bankovich, 203 Cal.App.3d 49, 249 Cal.Rptr. 713 (1988)*; *In re Marriage of Hopkins and Axene, 199 Cal.App.3d 288, 245 Cal.Rptr. 433 (1987)*; *In re Marriage of Griffis, 187 Cal.App.3d 156, 231 Cal.Rptr. 510 (1986)*; see also *In re Marriage of Fabian, 41 Cal.3d 440, 715 P.2d 253, 224 Cal.Rptr. 333 (1986)*; *In re Marriage of Buol, 39 Cal.3d 751, 705 P.2d 354, 218 Cal.Rptr. 31 (1985)*.

Under Section 2580, all property held in joint form by the spouses is presumed to be community property, absent a written agreement otherwise. Under Section 2640, all community property is divided subject to a right of reimbursement for separate property contributions, absent an express agreement otherwise. When enacted in 1983 (as former Civil Code Sections 4800.1 and 4800.2), these provisions were intended to remedy the rank injustice in former law that resulted from the following two factors:

(1) The Supreme Court's interpretation of former law in the Lucas case of the community property presumption for a joint tenancy single-family residence to find a gift of separate funds used to acquire a community asset absent an express agreement otherwise. See *In re Marriage of Lucas, 27 Cal.3d 808, 614 P.2d 285, 166 Cal.Rptr. 853 (1980)*. The Lucas decision was widely considered to cause injustice to persons who contributed their separate funds for use by the community and then lost the funds entirely to the community at dissolution of marriage. Often the parties were unaware that taking title in joint tenancy had the effect of making a gift of the separate property to the community.

(2) The rule that a spouse could disprove the community property presumption for a joint tenancy single-family residence under former law by evidence of an oral agreement that the residence is separate property. This rule promoted actions characterized by conflicting and inconsistent testimony, with each side offering different explanations for the effect of a joint tenancy deed. Often the intent of the parties who long before filed a joint tenancy deed could be confused by faded memories or altered to self-serving testimony. The requirement of a writing provides a reliable test by which to determine the understanding of the parties. It seeks to prevent the abuses and unpredictability that have resulted from the oral agreement standard. See discussion in *In re Marriage of Martinez, 156 Cal.App.3d 20, 29, 202 Cal.Rptr. 646 (1984), disapproved in In re Marriage of Buol, 39 Cal.3d 751, 705 P.2d 354, 218 Cal.Rptr. 31 (1985)*.

The community property presumptions created by subdivision (a) of Section 2580 are applicable only in dissolution and legal separation proceedings. The presumptions govern both real and personal property, whether situated in California or another jurisdiction, and include property acquired during marriage while domiciled in another jurisdiction. The presumptions also govern property initially acquired before marriage, the title to which is taken in joint form or as community property by the spouses during marriage. The measure of the separate property contribution under Section 2640 in such a case is the value of the property at the time of its conversion to joint or community property form.

Subdivision (b) of Section 2580 requires a writing to rebut the community property presumption. To permit or al statements to defeat the community property presumption for purposes of dissolution of marriage would frustrate the strong public policy favoring community ownership of property acquired during marriage. The requirement of a writing is important to help ensure that a party waives his or her community property rights only upon mature consideration.

Section 2580 does not affect the validity of an oral agreement for any purpose other than division of property at dissolution of marriage. For purposes of division, Section 2580, together with Section 2640, recognizes and reimburses separate property contributions. This treatment of an oral agreement for purposes of division is fair because an oral agreement, whatever other purpose it might have (management and control, disposition at death, etc.), is not ordinarily intended to affect rights at dissolution or to make a present gift for that purpose. Casual statements made during marriage generally are not made with full knowledge of their consequences or with the intention that they change the rights of the parties if the marriage is dissolved.

For background on former Civil Code Section 4800.1, see *Recommendation Relating to Division of Joint Tenancy and Tenancy in Common Property at Dissolution of Marriage,* 16 Cal. L. Revision Comm'n Reports 2165 (1982); 17 Cal. L. Revision Comm'n Reports 863 (1984); *Recommendation Relating to Civil Code Sections 4800.1 and 4800.2,* 18 Cal. L. Revision Comm'n Reports 383 (1986); 18 Cal. L. Revision Comm'n Reports 1741 (1986).

Research References

Forms

California Transactions Forms--Estate Planning § 10:6, Tenancy in Common.

California Transactions Forms--Estate Planning § 10:7, Joint Tenancy.

California Transactions Forms--Estate Planning § 10:19, Joint Tenancy Property.
California Transactions Forms--Family Law § 1:90, Real and Personal Property.

Treatises and Practice Aids

Witkin, California Summary 10th Community Property § 45, Proceeds Of Personal Injury Damages.
Witkin, California Summary 10th Community Property § 220, in General.
Witkin, California Summary 10th Community Property § 221, Effect Of Party's Death After Dissolution But Before Division.
Witkin, California Summary 10th Community Property § 223, Conversion Of Separate Property Into Joint Tenancy.
Witkin, California Summary 10th Community Property § 229, Community Property Presumption.
Witkin, California Summary 10th Community Property § 230, Right to Reimbursement.
Witkin, California Summary 10th Community Property § 231, Attempted Statutory Solution.

Part 4

SPECIAL RULES FOR DIVISION OF COMMUNITY ESTATE

§ 2600. Powers of court

Notwithstanding Sections 2550 to 2552, inclusive, the court may divide the community estate as provided in this part. *(Stats.1992, c. 162 (A.B.2650), § 10, operative Jan. 1, 1994.)*

Law Revision Commission Comments

Enactment [Revised Comment]

Section 2600 continues the introductory part of former Civil Code Section 4800(b) without substantive change. See also Section 63 ("community estate" defined). [23 Cal.L.Rev.Comm. Reports 1 (1993)].

Research References

Forms

Am. Jur. Pl. & Pr. Forms Community Property § 1, Introductory Comments.
West's California Code Forms, Family § 2338 Form 6, Provision in Judgment--Awarding Community Estate.

Treatises and Practice Aids

Witkin, California Summary 10th Community Property § 76, Award to Employee Spouse With Offset.
Witkin, California Summary 10th Community Property § 204, Statutory Rule.

§ 2601. Conditional award of an asset of the community estate to one party

Where economic circumstances warrant, the court may award an asset of the community estate to one party on such conditions as the court deems proper to effect a substantially equal division of the community estate. *(Stats.1992, c. 162 (A.B.2650), § 10, operative Jan. 1, 1994.)*

Law Revision Commission Comments

Enactment [Revised Comment]

Section 2601 continues former Civil Code Section 4800(b)(1) without substantive change. References to "community estate" have been added here to conform with language in the remainder of this division. See, e.g. Section 2550 (equal division of community estate). See also Section 63 ("community estate" defined). [23 Cal.L.Rev. Comm. Reports 1 (1993)].

Commentary

Section 2601 contemplates equal *in-kind* division of the community estate at divorce, but allows the court to award an asset entirely to one spouse "when economic circumstances warrant" so long as the aggregate community estate is substantially equally divided. In contrast, when a marriage survives until the death of one of the spouses, a party may insist absolutely on in-kind division of each community asset. *Dargie v. Patterson, 176 Cal. 714, 169 P. 360 (1917)*.

When do "economic circumstances warrant" deviation from in-kind division? The case law is not entirely consistent. Compare *In re Marriage of Brigden, 80 Cal.App.3d 380, 145 Cal.Rptr. 716 (1978)* (requiring in-kind division of publicly traded community property stock in corporation where husband was a director, because economic circumstances did not warrant awarding stock entirely to husband) with *In re Marriage of Connolly, 23 Cal.3d 590, 153 Cal.Rptr. 423 (1979)* (distinguishing *Brigden* on "its unique facts" and suggesting, in dictum, that the trial court has "a maximum degree of allowable flexibility" to avoid in-kind division when it would disserve the interests of either spouse). To the same effect, see *In re Marriage of Fink, 25 Cal.3d 877, 885–886, 160 Cal.Rptr. 516 (1979)*.

The legislative history of this provision clearly contemplates that in-kind division may be inappropriate for the family business and the family home. See discussion in *Brigden, supra*. Distribution of the family home is now also regulated by Sections 3800–3810.

Research References

Forms

California Transactions Forms--Estate Planning § 1:23, Aggregate or Asset-By-Asset Division Of Community Property.
California Transactions Forms--Family Law § 2:13, Equalizing Payments.

Treatises and Practice Aids

Witkin, California Summary 10th Community Property § 202, Personal Injury Damages.
Witkin, California Summary 10th Community Property § 204, Statutory Rule.
Witkin, California Summary 10th Community Property § 210, Publicly Traded Stock.
Witkin, California Summary 10th Community Property § 212, Characterization and Confirmation Of Debts.

§ 2602. Additional award or offset against existing property; award of amount determined to have been misappropriated

As an additional award or offset against existing property, the court may award, from a party's share, the amount the court determines to have been deliberately misappropriated by the party to the exclusion of the interest of the other party in the community estate. *(Stats.1992, c. 162 (A.B.2650), § 10, operative Jan. 1, 1994.)*

Law Revision Commission Comments

Enactment [Revised Comment]

Section 2602 continues former Civil Code Section 4800(b)(2) without substantive change. See also Section 63 ("community estate" defined). [23 Cal.L.Rev.Comm. Reports 1 (1993)].

Commentary

The term "deliberately misappropriated" contemplates more than mere "mishandling of assets." *In re Marriage of Schultz, 105 Cal. App.3d 846, 164 Cal.Rptr. 653 (1980)*. See also *In re Marriage of Economou, 224 Cal.App.3d 1466, 1483, 274 Cal.Rptr. 473 (1990)* (deliberate misappropriation of community property). See additionally *In re Marriage of Hirsch, 211 Cal.App.3d 104, 259 Cal.Rptr. 39 (1989), review denied 8/17/89* (negligent conduct of a spouse engaged in an activity benefiting the community is not a sufficient reason to characterize the resultant debt as a separate obligation at divorce). But compare *In re Marriage of Beltran, 183 Cal.App.3d 292, 227 Cal.Rptr. 924 (1986)*, and *In re Marriage of Stitt, 147 Cal.App.3d 579, 195 Cal.Rptr. 172 (1983)* (criminal activity of spouse causing pecuniary loss to community estate requires reimbursement to community estate at divorce).

Even a spouse who acts criminally for the benefit of the community is liable to the community only to the extent that the costs exceed the benefits. *In re Marriage of Bell, 49 Cal.App.4th 300, 56 Cal.Rptr.2d 623 (1996), review denied December 11, 1996,* holds that the amount of the legal settlement to the wife's employer required by the wife's embezzlement should not be assigned to the wife at dissolution as her share of the community property when the marital community benefited in an equal amount from the wife's embezzlement.

A spouse may be criminally liable for intentionally causing harm to property in which the other spouse has a community or separate interest, even though that harm occurs in the marital home and the parties are cohabiting as husband and wife. In *People v. Wallace, 123 Cal.App.4th 144, 19 Cal.Rptr.3d 790 (2004), review denied*, a husband was convicted of felony vandalism for causing more than $15,000 of damages to his wife's house and belongings. Although burglary and trespass cannot be committed against one's own home, vandalism can.

Research References

Treatises and Practice Aids

Witkin, California Summary 10th Community Property § 201, Misappropriation by Spouse.

§ 2603. Community estate personal injury damages; assignment

(a) "Community estate personal injury damages" as used in this section means all money or other property received or to be received by a person in satisfaction of a judgment for damages for the person's personal injuries or pursuant to an agreement for the settlement or compromise of a claim for the damages, if the cause of action for the damages arose during the marriage but is not separate property as described in Section 781, unless the money or other property has been commingled with other assets of the community estate.

(b) Community estate personal injury damages shall be assigned to the party who suffered the injuries unless the court, after taking into account the economic condition and needs of each party, the time that has elapsed since the recovery of the damages or the accrual of the cause of action, and all other facts of the case, determines that the interests of justice require another disposition. In such a case, the community estate personal injury damages shall be assigned to the respective parties in such proportions as the court determines to be just, except that at least one-half of the damages shall be assigned to the party who suffered the injuries. *(Stats.1992, c. 162 (A.B.2650), § 10, operative Jan. 1, 1994.)*

Law Revision Commission Comments

Enactment [Revised Comment]

Section 2603 continues former Civil Code Section 4800(b)(4) without substantive change. In the second sentence of subdivision (b), the former reference to community "property" personal injury damages has been changed to community "estate" personal injury damages for internal consistency. See Section 63 ("community estate" defined). See also Sections 780–783 (damages for injuries to married person). [23 Cal.L.Rev.Comm. Reports 1 (1993)].

Commentary

The meaning of the final clause of subsection (a), the commingling clause, is uncertain. The Law Revision Commission, which drafted the original legislation, contemplated the application of ordinary tracing rules. See Damages for Personal Injuries to a Married Person as Separate or Community Property, 8 Cal. L. Revision Comm'n Reports 1389, 1398 (1967). Yet the Law Revision proposal did not include the commingling clause, which was added later in the legislative process and which would seem to prohibit ordinary tracing when community estate personal injury damages have been commingled with other community property.

For divorce-related treatment of personal injury recoveries that have been used to purchase property taken in joint tenancy or community property title, see *In re Marriage of Devlin, 138 Cal.App.3d 804, 809–810, 189 Cal.Rptr. 1 (1982)*, and *In re Marriage of Mason, 93 Cal.App.3d 215, 222–223, 155 Cal.Rptr. 350 (1979)*.

Although Section 2603 makes no specific provision for reimbursement when community property or the separate property of the other spouse has been applied to pay injury-related expenses, it should be one of the "other facts of the case" for purposes of subsection (b). See Section 781(b), which specifically requires reimbursement for such expenses when the cause of action arose after separation and thus is the injured spouse's separate property.

Research References

Forms

West's California Code Forms, Family § 2550, Comment Overview--Manner Of Division Of Community Estate.

West's California Code Forms, Family § 2338 Form 7, Provision in Judgment--Awarding Community Estate Personal Injury Damages.

Treatises and Practice Aids

Witkin, California Summary 10th Community Property § 40, Community Property Rule Restored.

Witkin, California Summary 10th Community Property § 45, Proceeds Of Personal Injury Damages.

Witkin, California Summary 10th Community Property § 202, Personal Injury Damages.

Witkin, California Summary 10th Insurance § 181, Personal Injury Coverage: Uninsured Motorists.

§ 2603.5. Civil damages in a domestic violence action; enforcement of judgment

The court may, if there is a judgment for civil damages for an act of domestic violence perpetrated by one spouse against the other spouse, enforce that judgment against the abusive spouse's share of community property, if a proceeding for dissolution of marriage or legal separation of the parties is pending prior to the entry of final judgment. *(Added by Stats.2004, c. 299 (A.B.2018), § 1.)*

Research References

Treatises and Practice Aids

Witkin, California Summary 10th Community Property § 202, Personal Injury Damages.

Witkin, California Summary 10th Torts § 467, Domestic Violence.

§ 2604. Community estates of less than $5,000; award of entire estate

If the net value of the community estate is less than five thousand dollars ($5,000) and one party cannot be located through the exercise of reasonable diligence, the court may award all the community estate to the other party on conditions the court deems proper in its judgment of dissolution of marriage or legal separation of the parties. *(Stats.1992, c. 162 (A.B.2650), § 10, operative Jan. 1, 1994.)*

Law Revision Commission Comments

Enactment [Revised Comment]

Section 2604 continues former Civil Code Section 4800(b)(3) without substantive change. A reference to the "community estate" has been added to conform with language in the remainder of this division. See, e.g., Section 2550 (equal division of community estate). See also Section 63 ("community estate" defined). [23 Cal.L.Rev.Comm. Reports 1 (1993)].

Research References

Forms

West's California Code Forms, Family § 2338 Form 6, Provision in Judgment--Awarding Community Estate.

Treatises and Practice Aids

Witkin, California Summary 10th Community Property § 203, Other Exceptions.

Part 5

RETIREMENT PLAN BENEFITS

§ 2610. Retirement plans; orders to ensure benefits

(a) Except as provided in subdivision (b), the court shall make whatever orders are necessary or appropriate to ensure that each party receives the party's full community property share in any retirement plan, whether public or private, including all survivor and death benefits, including, but not limited to, any of the following:

(1) Order the disposition of any retirement benefits payable upon or after the death of either party in a manner consistent with Section 2550.

(2) Order a party to elect a survivor benefit annuity or other similar election for the benefit of the other party, as specified by the court, in any case in which a retirement plan provides for such an election, provided that no court shall order a retirement plan to provide increased benefits determined on the basis of actuarial value.

(3) Upon the agreement of the nonemployee spouse, order the division of accumulated community property contributions and service credit as provided in the following or similar enactments:

(A) Article 2 (commencing with Section 21290) of Chapter 9 of Part 3 of Division 5 of Title 2 of the Government Code.

(B) Chapter 12 (commencing with Section 22650) of Part 13 of the Education Code.

(C) Article 8.4 (commencing with Section 31685) of Chapter 3 of Part 3 of Division 4 of Title 3 of the Government Code.

(D) Article 2.5 (commencing with Section 75050) of Chapter 11 of Title 8 of the Government Code.

(E) Chapter 15 (commencing with Section 27400) of Part 14 of the Education Code.

(4) Order a retirement plan to make payments directly to a nonmember party of his or her community property interest in retirement benefits.

(b) A court shall not make any order that requires a retirement plan to do either of the following:

(1) Make payments in any manner that will result in an increase in the amount of benefits provided by the plan.

(2) Make the payment of benefits to any party at any time before the member retires, except as provided in paragraph (3) of subdivision (a), unless the plan so provides.

(c) This section shall not be applied retroactively to payments made by a retirement plan to any person who retired or died prior to January 1, 1987, or to payments made to any person who retired or died prior to June 1, 1988, for plans subject to paragraph (3) of subdivision (a). *(Stats.1992, c. 162 (A.B.2650), § 10, operative Jan. 1, 1994. Amended by Stats.1993, c. 219 (A.B.1500), § 112; Stats.1994, c. 670 (S.B.1500), § 1; Stats.1994, c. 1269 (A.B.2208), § 25.5; Stats. 1998, c. 965 (A.B.2765), § 322; Stats.2009, c. 130 (A.B.966), § 1.)*

Validity

This section was held preempted by ERISA in the decision of Branco v. UFCW-Northern California Employers Joint Pension Plan, C.A.9 (Cal.)2002, 279 F.3d 1154.

Law Revision Commission Comments

Enactment [Revised Comment]

Section 2610 continues former Civil Code Section 4800.8 without change. In subdivision (a), a reference to "this division" has been substituted for the narrower reference to former Civil Code Section 4800. This is not a substantive change. In subdivision (a)(3), the reference to Article 2.5 (commencing with Government Code Section 75050) restores an amendment made by Section 1 of Chapter 176 of the Statutes of 1992 that was inadvertently chaptered out by Section 1 of Chapter 431 of the Statutes of 1992. [23 Cal.L.Rev.Comm. Reports 1 (1993)].

1994 Amendment

Subdivision (a) of Section 2610 is amended to reflect the reorganization of the State Teachers' Retirement System statutes. See 1993

Cal. Stat. ch. 893, § 2 (AB 1796). This is a technical, nonsubstantive change. [24 Cal.L.Rev.Comm. Reports 621 (1994)].

Commentary

Former Civil Code Section 4800.8 was enacted in 1986 to repeal the California terminable interest rule, a case-law doctrine holding that a nonemployee divorced spouse's interest in an employee spouse's pension survived neither the death of the employee nor the death of the nonemployee. For exposition of the terminable interest rule, see *Benson v. City of Los Angeles, 60 Cal.2d 355, 33 Cal.Rptr. 257 (1963)* (death of employee spouse), and *Waite v. Waite, 6 Cal.3d 461, 99 Cal.Rptr. 325 (1972)* (death of nonemployee spouse). The statement of legislative intent to repeal the terminable interest rule was included in an uncodified portion of the 1986 law, Stats 1986, Ch 686, § 2. Former Civil Code Section 4800.8, now Family Code Section 2610, has been generously interpreted by the courts of appeal. *Estate of Austin, 206 Cal.App.3d 1249, 254 Cal.Rptr. 372 (1988)*, holds that the section applies equally to marriages that last until the death of one of the spouses. With *Austin*, compare *Regents of the University of California v. Benford, 128 Cal.App.4th 867, 27 Cal.Rptr.3d 441 (2005)*, which held that this section applies only when trial courts are dividing property in divorce proceedings and has no application when a marriage continues until the death of one of the spouses. Thus, in *Benford*, the University of California pension plan's anti-alienation provision prohibiting the transfer of a community property interest in the plan by a nonemployee spouse who predeceases an employee spouse, was controlling. *In re Marriage of Powers, 218 Cal.App.3d 626, 267 Cal.Rptr. 350 (1990), review denied 5/31/90*, holds that it applies to all cases, whenever decided, in which the court has retained continuing jurisdiction over a pension. See also *In re Marriage of Carnall, 216 Cal.App.3d 1010, 265 Cal.Rptr. 271 (1989)*.

Nevertheless, a portion of the terminable interest rule has effectively been revived by the United States Ninth Circuit Court of Appeals. With respect to a marriage that lasted until the death of the wife, *Ablamis v. Roper, 937 F.2d 1450, 1452 (9th Cir. 1991)*, held that the federal Employee Retirement Income Security Act (ERISA) preempts California law insofar as it purports to give a predeceasing nonmember spouse testamentary capacity over her share of the surviving member-spouse's pension. Moreover, in broad dictum, *Ablamis* interprets ERISA to prohibit any community property pension distribution, even under a divorce-related qualified domestic relations order (QDRO), to a person other than a *living* spouse or former spouse. In other words, *Ablamis* construes ERISA "alternate payees" to include only *living* spouses or former spouses. Effectively, the dictum of *Ablamis* would revive the *Waite* arm of the terminable interest rule. Similarly, in *Boggs v. Boggs, 117 S.Ct. 1754, 138 L.Ed.2d 45 (1997)*, the United States Supreme Court held that ERISA preempts Louisiana community property law insofar as it purports to allow a predeceased first wife to will to third parties her interest in her husband's pension, specifically, her interest in the survivor's annuity payable to the deceased husband's surviving second wife. Under ERISA, a surviving spouse's annuity may not be diverted to third parties. *Boggs* also held that ERISA equally preempts the predeceased wife's testamentary transfer of her Louisiana community property interest in her surviving husband's other ERISA–regulated benefits, including shares of stock from an employee stock ownership plan (ESOP). Interpreting *Boggs*, *Branco v. UFCW–Northern California Employers Joint Pension Plan, 279 F.3d 1154 (9th Cir.2002)*, applies the dictum of *Ablamis* and holds that ERISA preempts a California divorce court distribution of a community property pension insofar as it purports to enable a wife to leave her share of a community property pension earned by her former husband to her heirs at her death. Under *Branco*, the interest of a former spouse who is an Alternate Payee under an ERISA QDRO expires at his or her death and reverts to the surviving employee spouse. *Branco* thus revives the *Waite* arm of the terminable interest rule. See also *Kimble v. Metropolitan Life Ins. Co., 969 F. Supp. 599 (E.D. Cal. 1997)* (holding that beneficiary designation under employee group life insurance policy regulated by ERISA controls disposition of proceeds at employee's death, preempting California community property rights of employee's surviving spouse) and *In re Marriage of Shelstead, 66 Cal.App.4th 893, 78 Cal.Rptr.2d 365 (1998)* (holding unenforceable a qualified domestic relations order (QDRO) requiring ERISA-regulated pension plan to pay a portion of the pension benefits to the wife of the participant and, at the wife's death, to a successor in interest named by the wife; QDRO may designate as "alternate payee" only a participant or a person included within the ERISA category of alternate payee, i.e., "a spouse, former spouse, child or other dependent"). *Kimble*, supra, was not mentioned by the Ninth Circuit Court of Appeals panel that subsequently decided *Emard v. Hughes Aircraft Co., 153 F.3d 949 (9th Cir. 1998)*. Although every other circuit addressing the issue has agreed with *Kimble, Emard* states, arguably in dictum, that a spouse's community property interest in the proceeds of an ERISA-regulated life insurance policy is not preempted by the participant's beneficiary designation. *Cf. Egelhoff v. Egelhoff, 121 S.Ct. 1322, 149 L.Ed.2d 264 (2001)*, in which the United States Supreme Court held that, with respect to ERISA-regulated plans, ERISA preempts a Washington statute that, upon divorce, revokes any nonprobate designation of the divorced spouse as beneficiary. *Egelhoff* involved both life insurance and pension benefits. Although ERISA preempts inconsistent state law, it does not preempt inconsistent federal common law, which gives effect to divorce settlement waivers of interests in ERISA-regulated benefits. Nevertheless, in *Kennedy v. Plan Administrator, 129 S.Ct. 865, 172 L.Ed.2d 662 (2009)*, the United States Supreme Court concluded that a plan administrator has a duty under ERISA to follow the participant's beneficiary designation of his ex-spouse, which the participant had neglected to revoke, despite his former wife's federal common law waiver. The court reasoned that although federal common law is not preempted by ERISA's anti-alienation clause, federal common law does not include the power to rewrite federal statutes. Specifically, federal common law generally applicable to contractual waivers may not override an express ERISA provision. The court noted, however, that the ex-spouse's waiver was not necessarily a nullity, and suggested the possibility that the participant's estate might bring an action in federal or state court to enforce the waiver and thereby obtain the benefits after the ERISA plan administrator distributed them to the ex-spouse, as per her former husband's ERISA beneficiary designation.

Following the suggestion of *Kennedy*, in *Estate of Kensinger v. URL Pharma, Inc., 674 F.3d 131 (2012)*, the federal Third Circuit Court of Appeals held that a decedent's estate could bring an action against decedent's former wife to recover the proceeds of an ERISA plan after they were distributed to her, when she had waived all rights to the plan in the parties' settlement agreement although she remained the designated beneficiary on plan documents. To the same effect, see *Andochick v. Byrd, 709 F.3d 296 (4th Cir. 2013)*.

But see *Hillman v. Maretta, 133 S.Ct. 194 (2013)*, holding that the express preemption provision of the Federal Employees Group Life Insurance Act (FEGLIA), 5 U.S.C. § 8709(d)(1), pre-empts a Virginia statute that makes the recipient of a former spouse's life insurance proceeds liable to whoever would have received the proceeds had the recipient not been the policy's designated beneficiary. *Hillman* concluded that Congress intended not only that the employee's designated beneficiary would receive the life insurance proceeds, but also that the proceeds would belong to the designated beneficiary. FEGLIA's sole exception to an employee's right of designation provides that benefits shall be paid to another person if required by a divorce decree that is received by the employing agency before the employee's death. 5 U.S.C. §§ 8705(e)(1)-(2).

Relying on 29 U.S.C. §§ 1055 (a)(2) and 1056 (d)(3)(F), *Hamilton v. Washington State Plumbing and Pipefitting Industry Pension Plan, 433 F.3d 1091 (9th Cir. 2006)*, concludes that a surviving spouse's Qualified Preretirement Survivor Annuity can be diverted *only* to a former surviving spouse. Thus, a dissolution decree requiring decedent ex-husband to name the parties' two children as the beneficiaries of his pension in lieu of life insurance that he was unable to obtain, was insufficient to divest decedent's surviving second wife of her Preretirement Survivor Annuity benefits.

Resolving a conflict between the final two wives of a deceased participant, *Carmona v. Carmona, 544 F.3d 988 (9th Cir. 2008)*, held that a participant in an ERISA-regulated Qualified Joint and Survivor Annuity (QJSA) may not change his surviving spouse beneficiary after he has retired and the annuity has started to pay out. The QJSA surviving spouse's benefit irrevocably vests in the participant's spouse at the time of the annuity start date and may not be reassigned to a subsequent spouse. Accord, *Hopkins v. AT & T Global Solutions Co., 105 F.3d 153 (4th Cir. 1997)*.

When a beneficiary designation form for ERISA-regulated life insurance failed to unambiguously designate a beneficiary through a relationship code or reference to the insured's will, the proper beneficiary was the default beneficiary under the plan in effect at the time of the insured's death. *Metropolitan Life Insurance Co. v. Parker, 436 F.3d 1109 (9th Cir. 2005)*.

Citing *Kennedy, Becker v. Williams, 777 F.3d 1035 (9th Cir. 2015)*, held that decedent effectively changed his beneficiary by phone and was not required to sign and return a beneficiary designation form to confirm the change, because a beneficiary designation form that was neither a governing plan document nor incorporated into the governing plan documents is not a plan document under 29 U.S.C. sections 1024(b)(4) and 1104(a)(1)(D).

In re Marriage of Gillmore, 29 Cal.3d 418, 629 P.2d 1, 174 Cal.Rptr. 493 (1981), holds that when an employee is eligible to retire but has not chosen to do so, his former spouse may nevertheless require the immediate payment of her interest in the employee's retirement benefit. Effectively, the employee is required to pay his former spouse her share of the benefit he would receive had he retired. *In re Marriage of Cornejo, 13 Cal.4th 381, 916 P.2d 476, 53 Cal.Rptr.2d 81 (1996)*, holds that the former spouse who wishes to claim *Gillmore* payments before the employee actually retires must file a motion to obtain her share of the employee's retirement benefits, and the date of filing is controlling for purposes of entitlement to benefits. *Gillmore* payments may not be awarded retroactively to the date, if earlier, on which the employee was first eligible to retire.

Despite *Gillmore, In re Marriage of Moore, 226 Cal.App.4th 92, 171 Cal.Rptr.3d 762 (2014)*, held that, because of valuation uncertainties, a trial court properly reserved jurisdiction to divide a husband's accrued sick leave and medical reimbursement plan until the husband retired even though he was eligible to retire at the time of trial.

With respect to ERISA-regulated pensions, the need for a *Gillmore* order is avoided by 29 U.S.C. § 1056(d)(3)(E), which provides that a qualified domestic relations order may require the *plan* to make payments to an alternate payee on the date on which an employee is eligible to retire, but does not do so. This type of order is called a "separate interest QDRO." See Commentary to 29 U.S.C. § 1056.

Section 2610 was amended by Stats 1992, Ch 431, which was apparently intended to codify the case law rule that, unless otherwise provided by state legislation or by the plan itself, a court may not order a *public* pension plan to make payments to any party before the member retires. This is because the only general authority for requiring that pension plans make such preretirement payments comes from ERISA, and ERISA applies only to ERISA-regulated *private* pension plans. 29 U.S.C. § 1001 et seq. (1985 and 1992 Supp). See particularly § 1056(d)(3)(E). Thus, unless otherwise authorized by the public pension plan or by a specific California statute, a payout order requiring that public pension payments be made before a member has retired may be directed only against the member himself. *In re Marriage of Jensen, 235 Cal.App.3d 1137, 286 Cal.Rptr. 911 (1991)*; *In re Marriage of Nice, 230 Cal.App.3d 444, 281 Cal.Rptr. 415 (1991), review denied 9/19/91*.

In *Commissioner v. Dunkin, 500 F.3d 1065 (9th Cir. 2007)*, a Los Angeles policeman who remained on the job although his pension rights were fully vested and matured, was required to make such payments to his former wife. The Ninth Circuit Court of Appeals held that the earnings Dunkin used to satisfy his wife's entitlement were taxable to him, not to her. (Compare payments made directly to a former spouse under an ERISA bifurcated pension; they are taxable to the recipient, not to the other spouse.)

The 1992 amendments to this section were inadvertently drafted more broadly than necessary to codify the case-law rule. The language of Section 2610(b)(2) is not restricted to *public* pension plans, but instead prohibits a court from ordering any pension plan to make payments to a party before the member retires. Nevertheless, according to the sponsor's legislative staff, the amendments were intended to reach only public pensions, and a statement of legislative intent was to be prepared to clarify this point. 9 Cal. Fam. Law Monthly 150 (1992). Alternatively, it is likely that ERISA preempts state legislation that would prohibit courts from ordering ERISA-regulated plans to make payments before a member has retired. See 29 U.S.C. § 1056(d)(3)(E).

Like community property law generally, Section 2610 only recognizes community property interests in existing pension rights. It does not create new or independent pension rights. Thus, Section 2610 does not empower a divorce court to require that a pension plan pay a "surviving spouse's" benefit to a surviving former spouse. Under Section 2610, a surviving divorced spouse may have a community property ownership interest in otherwise existing benefits, but California community property law does not engender new benefits. *In re Marriage of Cramer, 20 Cal.App.4th 73, 24 Cal.Rptr.2d 372 (1993)*. Compare ERISA, 29 U.S.C. § 1056(d)(3)(F) (enabling divorce court to provide in a qualified domestic relations order that ERISA-regulated pension plan shall treat a surviving divorced spouse as a "surviving spouse"). Cf. *Willis v. State of California, 22 Cal.App.4th 287, 27 Cal.Rptr.2d 413 (1994)* (although California Government Code Section 12479 requires the State of California to release a deceased employee's outstanding payroll warrants to the employee's designated recipient even after being notified of a surviving spouse's community property interest in the warrants, neither the statute nor the payment alters the community property nature of the warrants); and *Fatemi v. Los Angeles County Employees, 21 Cal.App.4th 1797, 27 Cal.Rptr.2d 105 (1994)* (interpreting Government Code Sections 31781.1 and 31781.3).

In re Marriage of LaMoure, 221 Cal.App.4th 1463, 165 Cal.Rptr.3d 417 (2013), relying on California Code of Civil Procedure section 704.115(b), affirmed a trial court order determining that husband's pension plan, which had originally qualified for ERISA protection, no longer qualified because the husband used the plan to secrete and shield community property assets.

Retirement benefits must be distinguished from disability benefits. While retirement benefits are community property to the extent that they were earned during marriage, the character of disability benefits turns on the character of the wages they are intended to replace. See generally *In re Marriage of Saslow, 40 Cal.3d 848, 221 Cal.Rptr. 546 (1985)* (although community funds alone were used to purchase husband's disability insurance, disability payments received by husband after separation are his separate property; nevertheless, when disability benefits continue past the age of retirement and effectively become retirement benefits, they must be characterized as community property). The wage-replacement analysis applied to disability benefits would seem to suggest that when a disability policy is purchased before marriage and pays wage-replacement benefits during marriage, the benefits received during marriage are community property because they replace lost community property wages. Nevertheless, *In re Marriage of Rossin, 172 Cal.App.4th 725, 91 Cal.Rptr.3d 427 (2009)*, holds that disability benefits paid to a spouse during marriage are the spouse's separate property when the spouse acquired the disability insurance policy before marriage without any contribution from the community. See also *In re Marriage of Elfmont, 9 Cal.4th 1026, 891 P.2d 136, 39 Cal.Rptr.2d 590 (1995)* (where only the bare right to renew a disability policy is traceable to community premiums paid for terms that expired before former husband became disabled and where former husband renewed policy with separate funds after separation and became disabled after separation, there is no cognizable community property interest in resultant disability benefits even though they may be characterized as retirement benefits because they will continue after the intended or normative age of retirement). Although severance benefits have generally been analogized to disability pay and classified according to the character of the wages they replace, early retirement benefits may instead be characterized as ordinary retirements benefits and hence classified according to when they were earned. See generally *In re Marriage of Gram, 25 Cal.App.4th 859, 30 Cal.Rptr.2d 792 (1994)* (reviewing the case law and characterizing a spouse's postseparation enhanced early retirement benefits as partially community property because they were intended primarily to enhance expected retirement benefits, not to compensate for loss of earnings). Compare *In re Marriage of Frahm, 45 Cal.App.4th 536, 53 Cal.Rptr.3d 31 (1996), review denied August 21, 1996* (additional retirement benefits offered to induce former husband to take early retirement were husband's separate property because the right to them did not accrue during marriage from the husband's employment; instead the benefits "resulted solely from [the employer's] beneficence"). *In re Marriage of Lehman, 18 Cal.4th 169, 955 P.2d 451, 74 Cal.Rptr.2d 825 (1998),* holds that a nonemployee spouse's community property ownership interest in retirement benefits earned by the other spouse extends to all subsequent "enhancements" to those benefits. *Lehman* reconciles the holdings of *Gram* and *Frahm* on the ground that *Gram* involved an early retirement package expressed entirely in terms of retirement benefits (community property to the extent earned during marriage) and *Frahm* involved a retirement package combining enhanced retirement benefits (community property to the extent earned during marriage) and severance pay (the earner's separate property). See also *In re Marriage of Oddino, 16 Cal.4th 67, 939 P.2d 1266, 65 Cal.Rptr.2d 566 (1997)* (holding that "Rule of 75" early retirement benefits are an "employer subsidy for early retirement" within the meaning of ERISA, 29 U.S.C. § 1056(d)(3)(E)(i)(II), and hence a QDRO may not require a pension plan to pay such benefits to an alternate payee *before* the participant's actual retirement.) *In re Marriage of Babauta, 66 Cal.App.4th 784, 78 Cal.Rptr.2d 281 (1998),* relied on *Lehman* to conclude that Marine Corps voluntary separation pay is a "retirement benefit" and therefore distributable by a California court at divorce. For additional discussion of *Babauta,* see Commentary to 10 U.S.C.A. § 1408. Also relying on *Lehman*, *In re Marriage of Drapeau, 93 Cal.App.4th 1086, 114 Cal.Rptr.2d 6 (2001), review denied February 13, 2002,* held that an "early retirement benefit" that was earned with marital employment and arose from the term of a contract entered during marriage, was community property. Following *Lehman*, *In re Marriage of Davis, 120 Cal. App.4th 1007, 16 Cal.Rptr.3d 220 (2004)*, characterizes as community property the enhanced retirement benefits from a Los Angeles policeman's "Deferred Retirement Option," which was offered to and elected by the husband after permanent separation.

In re Marriage of Walker, 203 Cal.App.4th 137, 137 Cal.Rptr.3d 611 (2012), held that a husband's post-separation, pre-retirement disability allowance was his separate property when the disability allowance would terminate as soon as the husband reached the age of eligibility for a retirement pension, which itself would be partially community property because it was earned during marriage.

Raphael v. Bloomfield, 113 Cal.App.4th 617, 6 Cal.Rptr.3d 583 (2003), treats a lump sum workers' compensation award in the same manner as disability pay. In *Raphael*, the lump-sum award, received before the parties separated, was intended to provide lifetime support for the permanently disabled wife. *Raphael* holds that the award must be apportioned between wage replacement for the preseparation period and medical expenses paid with community funds, which are community property, and post-separation wage replacement, which is the wife's separate property.

In the absence of any evidence as to how a lump-sum worker's compensation award was calculated and allocated, *In re Marriage of Ruiz, 194 Cal.App.4th 348, 122 Cal.Rptr.3d 914 (2011)*, held that a trial court did not abuse its discretion in dividing the award by the number of years from the date of disability to the date of likely retirement and apportioning the award pro rata from the date of the wife's injury to the date of separation as community property and the balance as her separate property.

When a divorced spouse is entitled to either disability pay, which is characterized as separate property after divorce (see supra), or community property retirement benefits and elects or is required to take disability pay in lieu of community property retirement benefits, the other spouse is entitled to half the value of the community property retirement benefits that would otherwise have been received. *In re Marriage of Stenquist, 21 Cal.3d 779, 582 P.2d 96, 148 Cal.Rptr. 9 (1978)*. However, when the spouse's entitlement arises from federal military service, *Mansell v. Mansell, 490 U.S. 581 (1999)*, holds that federal law preempts any direct or indirect community property distribution of military disability pay. Thus *Stenquist* treatment is barred for such benefits.

Moreover, *Howell v. Howell, 137 S.Ct. 1400, 197 L.Ed.2d 781 (2017)*, held that when a former spouse has been awarded a portion of a service member's retirement pay at divorce and, after divorce the service member elects to receive disability pay instead of retirement pay, a state court may not compensate the former spouse for the loss of her share of the service member's retirement pay. *Howell* suggests that harm to the former spouse may be mitigated by means of spousal support.

Although *In re Marriage of Smith, 148 Cal.App.4th 1115, 56 Cal.Rptr.3d 341 (2007)*, is factually distinguishable from *Howell*, where there was no indemnity clause in the parties' stipulation, it is uncertain whether *Smith* survives *Howell*. *Smith* approved a trial court judgment stipulated by the parties, which divided the community property portion of a husband's future retirement pay, required that the husband name the wife the beneficiary of a survivor's benefit so that she would not lose her interest in the retirement pay if he were to predecease her, and provided that if the husband elected in the future to receive disability in lieu of retirement pay, he would indemnify his former wife for his unilateral reduction of the value of the retirement benefits. The final provision was intended to insure that the wife received the value of the bargain she made at dissolution.

In re Marriage of Lucero, 118 Cal.App.3d 836, 173 Cal.Rptr. 680 (1981), holds that the right to reinstate a pension earned during marriage is a community asset even though that right may have been exercised with a divorced spouse's separate property funds. *Lucero* analyzes and finds wanting *In re Marriage of Forrest, 97 Cal.App.3d 850, 159 Cal.Rptr. 229 (1979)*, an earlier decision of a different panel of the Fourth District, which held to the contrary. The California Supreme Court approved the reasoning of *Lucero* in *In re Marriage of Sonne, 48 Cal.4th 118, 105 Cal.Rptr.3d 414, 225 P.3d 546 (2010)*.

In re Marriage of Green, 56 Cal.4th 1130, 302 P.3d 562, 158 Cal.Rptr.3d 247 (2013), reversing a decision of the court of appeal, the California Supreme Court held that when CalPERS military service credits were purchased with community funds during the marriage, but the military service was performed by the husband before marriage and he was employed by a CalPERS participant before marriage, the military service credits were the husband's separate property subject to his reimbursement to the community for the cost of their purchase.

In re Marriage of Havins, 43 Cal.App.4th, 50 Cal.Rptr.2d 763 (1996), holds that an employer's subsidy of a divorced spouse's post-retirement medical insurance premiums, which is part of the husband's retirement package earned during marriage, is not community property. *In re Marriage of Ellis, 101 Cal.App.4th 400, 124 Cal.Rptr.2d 719 (2002), review denied October 16, 2002*, follows *Havins*. *Ellis* and *Havins* may be incorrectly decided. See commentary at California Family Law Monthly 267–269 (October 2002).

When, pursuant to an ERISA qualified domestic relations order (QDRO), a pension plan distributes benefits to a former spouse, those benefits are taxable to the former spouse and not to the pension-earner spouse. Internal Revenue Code § 402 (a)(9). However, absent a QDRO, a pension distribution is entirely taxable to the participant even though one-half is distributed to the participant's ex-spouse according to state community property law. *Robert L. Karem v. Commissioner, 100 T.C. No. 34 (1993)*.

When a retirement pension is earned partly during marriage and partly before marriage or after permanent separation, the pension must be apportioned between the community estate and the earner's separate estate. For comprehensive discussion of the "time rule" generally used to make such apportionment, see *In re Marriage of Gowan, 54 Cal.App.4th 80, 62 Cal.Rptr.2d 453 (1997)* (pension based on employee's years of service from two separate periods of employment properly apportioned according to the "time rule").

Research References

Forms

California Practice Guide: Rutter Family Law Forms Form 8:6, Qualified Domestic Relations Order (Qdro).
California Transactions Forms--Estate Planning § 10:4, Community Property.
California Transactions Forms--Estate Planning § 9:76, Community Property Interest in Retirement Benefits.
California Transactions Forms--Estate Planning § 19:16, Overview.
California Transactions Forms--Family Law § 2:23, Overview.
West's California Code Forms, Family § 2060, Comment Overview--Application and Order for Joinder.
West's California Code Forms, Family § 2550, Comment Overview--Manner Of Division Of Community Estate.
West's California Judicial Council Forms FL-347, Bifurcation Of Status Of Marriage or Domestic Partnership--Attachment.
West's California Judicial Council Forms FL-348, Pension Benefits--Attachment to Judgment.

Treatises and Practice Aids

Witkin, California Summary 10th Community Property § 68, Statutory Abrogation Of Rule.
Witkin, California Summary 10th Community Property § 69, Election Not to Retire.
Witkin, California Summary 10th Community Property § 75, Waiver Of Immediate Payment Rights.
Witkin, California Summary 10th Community Property § 77, Survivor and Death Benefits.
Witkin, California Summary 10th Community Property § 96, Application Of Time Rule.
Witkin, California Summary 10th Husband and Wife § 105, Statutory Rule.

Part 6

DEBTS AND LIABILITIES

Section

Section

§ 2620. Community estate debts; confirmation or division

The debts for which the community estate is liable which are unpaid at the time of trial, or for which the community estate becomes liable after trial, shall be confirmed or divided as provided in this part. *(Stats.1992, c. 162 (A.B.2650), § 10, operative Jan. 1, 1994.)*

Law Revision Commission Comments

Enactment [Revised Comment]

Section 2620 continues the introductory part of former Civil Code Section 4800(c) without substantive change. See also Sections 63 ("community estate" defined), 916 (liability after property division), 2551 (court characterization of liabilities as separate or community and confirmation or assignment to parties), 2552 (valuation date for liabilities). [23 Cal.L.Rev.Comm. Reports 1 (1993)].

Research References

Forms

West's California Code Forms, Family § 2550, Comment Overview--Manner Of Division Of Community Estate.

Treatises and Practice Aids

Witkin, California Summary 10th Community Property § 203, Other Exceptions.
Witkin, California Summary 10th Community Property § 212, Characterization and Confirmation Of Debts.

§ 2621. Premarital debts; confirmation

Debts incurred by either spouse before the date of marriage shall be confirmed without offset to the spouse who incurred the debt. *(Stats.1992, c. 162 (A.B.2650), § 10, operative Jan. 1, 1994.)*

Law Revision Commission Comments

Enactment [Revised Comment]

Section 2621 continues former Civil Code Section 4800(c)(1) without change. [23 Cal.L.Rev.Comm. Reports 1 (1993)].

Research References

Treatises and Practice Aids

Witkin, California Summary 10th Community Property § 212, Characterization and Confirmation Of Debts.

§ 2622. Marital debts incurred before the date of separation; division

(a) Except as provided in subdivision (b), debts incurred by either spouse after the date of marriage but before the date of separation shall be divided as set forth in Sections 2550 to 2552, inclusive, and Sections 2601 to 2604, inclusive.

(b) To the extent that community debts exceed total community and quasi-community assets, the excess of debt shall be assigned as the court deems just and equitable, taking into account factors such as the parties' relative ability to pay. *(Stats.1992, c. 162 (A.B.2650), § 10, operative Jan. 1, 1994.)*

Law Revision Commission Comments

Enactment [Revised Comment]

Section 2622 continues former Civil Code Section 4800(c)(2) without substantive change. [23 Cal.L.Rev.Comm. Reports 1 (1993)].

Research References

Treatises and Practice Aids

Witkin, California Summary 10th Community Property § 212, Characterization and Confirmation Of Debts.

§ 2623. Marital debts incurred after the date of separation; confirmation

Debts incurred by either spouse after the date of separation but before entry of a judgment of dissolution of marriage or legal separation of the parties shall be confirmed as follows:

(a) Debts incurred by either spouse for the common necessaries of life of either spouse or the necessaries of life of the children of the marriage for whom support may be ordered, in the absence of a court order or written agreement for support or for the payment of these debts, shall be confirmed to either spouse according to the parties' respective needs and abilities to pay at the time the debt was incurred.

(b) Debts incurred by either spouse for nonnecessaries of that spouse or children of the marriage for whom support may be ordered shall be confirmed without offset to the spouse who incurred the debt. *(Stats.1992, c. 162 (A.B.2650), § 10, operative Jan. 1, 1994. Amended by Stats.1993, c. 219 (A.B.1500), § 113.)*

Law Revision Commission Comments

Enactment [Revised Comment]

Section 2623 continues former Civil Code Section 4800(c)(3) without substantive change. References to children "for whom support may be ordered" have been substituted for former references to "minor" children, since in some cases support may be ordered for adult children. See Section 58 ("child for whom support may be ordered" defined). [23 Cal.L.Rev.Comm. Reports 1 (1993)].

Research References

Treatises and Practice Aids

Witkin, California Summary 10th Community Property § 212, Characterization and Confirmation Of Debts.

§ 2624. Marital debts incurred after entry of judgment of dissolution or after entry of judgment of legal separation; confirmation

Debts incurred by either spouse after entry of a judgment of dissolution of marriage but before termination of the parties' marital status or after entry of a judgment of legal separation of the parties shall be confirmed without offset to the spouse who incurred the debt. *(Stats.1992, c. 162 (A.B.2650), § 10, operative Jan. 1, 1994.)*

Law Revision Commission Comments

Enactment [Revised Comment]

Section 2624 continues former Civil Code Section 4800(c)(4) without substantive change. [23 Cal.L.Rev.Comm. Reports 1 (1993)].

Research References

Treatises and Practice Aids

Witkin, California Summary 10th Community Property § 212, Characterization and Confirmation Of Debts.

§ 2625. Separate debts incurred before date of separation; confirmation

Notwithstanding Sections 2620 to 2624, inclusive, all separate debts, including those debts incurred by a spouse during marriage and before the date of separation that were not incurred for the benefit of the community, shall be confirmed without offset to the spouse who incurred the debt. *(Stats. 1992, c. 162 (A.B.2650), § 10, operative Jan. 1, 1994.)*

Law Revision Commission Comments

Enactment [Revised Comment]

Section 2625 continues former Civil Code Section 4800(d) without substantive change. [23 Cal.L.Rev.Comm. Reports 1 (1993)].

Commentary

Section 2625 is anomalous in a community property system that does not have, for purposes of debtor-creditor liability, a "community debt" doctrine. (Compare prior Washington law discussed in *Grolemund v. Cafferata, 17 Cal.2d 679, 111 P.2d 641 (1941), cert. denied 314 U.S. 612 (1941).*) Before the 1986 enactment of Civil Code Section 4800(d), now Section 2625, several cases had treated certain debts incurred during marriage as the separate obligation of one spouse for purposes of debt apportionment at divorce. See, for example, *In re Marriage of Lister, 152 Cal.App.3d 411, 416, 199 Cal.Rptr. 321 (1984)* (use of community property to discharge premarital debts), and *In re Marriage of Stitt, 147 Cal.App.3d 579, 195 Cal.Rptr 172 (1983)* (wife's debt incurred during marriage to defend against embezzlement charges assigned to her as her separate obligation at divorce). Although those cases were unexceptionable, the statute seems conceptually overbroad. Characterization of debts "incurred by a spouse during marriage . . . that were not incurred for the benefit of the community" as "separate debts" could conceivably capture any personal expenditure by a spouse during marriage. See, for example, *In re Marriage of Cairo, 204 Cal.App.3d 1255, 251 Cal.Rptr. 731 (1988)*, approving the assignment of a $1,100 credit card debt to the husband as his "separate debt" because he had used some of the money for gambling and had not given his wife any household money from the borrowed funds. Yet "community benefit" arguably should be understood to include each spouse's individual welfare and hence to include each spouse's lawful personal consumption expenditure.

Research References

Treatises and Practice Aids

Witkin, California Summary 10th Community Property § 185, Illustrations.

Witkin, California Summary 10th Community Property § 212, Characterization and Confirmation Of Debts.

Witkin, California Summary 10th Parent and Child § 12, Parental or Marital Rights Of Prisoners.

§ 2626. Reimbursements

The court has jurisdiction to order reimbursement in cases it deems appropriate for debts paid after separation but before trial. *(Stats.1992, c. 162 (A.B.2650), § 10, operative Jan. 1, 1994.)*

Law Revision Commission Comments

Enactment [Revised Comment]

Section 2626 continues former Civil Code Section 4800(e) without substantive change. [23 Cal.L.Rev.Comm. Reports 1 (1993)].

Commentary

The court may order reimbursement under this section even though there is no authority for reimbursement other than this section. *In re Marriage of Williams, 213 Cal.App.3d 1239, 262 Cal.Rptr. 317 (1989)*. In *Williams*, after the parties separated, the district attorney levied on community property to satisfy the husband's child support obligation arising from a prior marriage. Although there had been no separate property available to pay the debt when the district attorney levied on the property (see Section 915(b)), the court held that reimbursement to the community was appropriate. *Williams* indicates that Section 2626 may be used to require reimbursement when community property has been applied after separation to satisfy any "separate" debt enumerated in Sections 2621–2625. (In contrast, the use of community property to satisfy such debts *before separation* does not ordinarily give rise to any claim for reimbursement.)

When one party uses his or her separate property for community purposes after separation, that party is normally entitled to reimbursement. See generally *In re Marriage of Epstein, 24 Cal.3d 76, 82–86, 154 Cal.Rptr. 413 (1979)*, and *In re Marriage of Hebbring, 207 Cal.App.3d 1260, 1269–1272, 255 Cal.Rptr. 488 (1989)*. (Compare treatment of the use of separate property funds for community purposes before separation. See Section 2640, Commentary.)

For discussion of the meaning of the term "separation," see Section 771, Commentary.

Research References

Forms

California Practice Guide: Rutter Family Law Forms Form 1:32, Glossary Of Common Family Law Terms, Phrases and Concepts (Enclosure to Form 1:31).

Treatises and Practice Aids

Witkin, California Summary 10th Community Property § 212, Characterization and Confirmation Of Debts.

Witkin, California Summary 10th Community Property § 225, Postseparation Payments.

§ 2627. Educational loans; liabilities for death or injuries; assignment

Notwithstanding Sections 2550 to 2552, inclusive, and Sections 2620 to 2624, inclusive, educational loans shall be assigned pursuant to Section 2641 and liabilities subject to paragraph (2) of subdivision (b) of Section 1000 shall be assigned to the spouse whose act or omission provided the basis for the liability, without offset. *(Stats.1992, c. 162 (A.B.2650), § 10, operative Jan. 1, 1994.)*

Law Revision Commission Comments

Enactment [Revised Comment]

Section 2627 continues former Civil Code Section 4800(b)(5) without substantive change. [23 Cal.L.Rev.Comm. Reports 1 (1993)].

Commentary

See Section 2641, Commentary, and Section 1000, Commentary.

Research References

Treatises and Practice Aids

Witkin, California Summary 10th Community Property § 203, Other Exceptions.

§ 2628. Joint California income tax liabilities; revision by court in marriage dissolution proceeding

Notwithstanding Sections 2550 to 2552, inclusive, and Sections 2620 to 2624, inclusive, joint California income tax liabilities may be revised by a court in a proceeding for dissolution of marriage, provided the requirements of Section 19006 of the Revenue and Taxation Code are satisfied. *(Added by Stats.2002, c. 374 (A.B.2979), § 1.)*

Research References

Treatises and Practice Aids

Witkin, California Summary 10th Community Property § 203, Other Exceptions.

Part 7

REIMBURSEMENTS

§ 2640. Contribution to the acquisition of property of the community property estate; waivers; amount of reimbursement

(a) "Contributions to the acquisition of property," as used in this section, include downpayments, payments for improvements, and payments that reduce the principal of a loan used to finance the purchase or improvement of the property but do not include payments of interest on the loan or payments made for maintenance, insurance, or taxation of the property.

(b) In the division of the community estate under this division, unless a party has made a written waiver of the right to reimbursement or has signed a writing that has the effect of a waiver, the party shall be reimbursed for the party's contributions to the acquisition of property of the community property estate to the extent the party traces the contributions to a separate property source. The amount reimbursed shall be without interest or adjustment for change in monetary values and may not exceed the net value of the property at the time of the division.

(c) A party shall be reimbursed for the party's separate property contributions to the acquisition of property of the other spouse's separate property estate during the marriage, unless there has been a transmutation in writing pursuant to Chapter 5 (commencing with Section 850) of Part 2 of Division 4, or a written waiver of the right to reimbursement. The amount reimbursed shall be without interest or adjustment for change in monetary values and may not exceed the net value of the property at the time of the division. *(Stats.1992, c. 162 (A.B.2650), § 10, operative Jan. 1, 1994. Amended by Stats.1993, c. 219 (A.B.1500), § 114.5; Stats. 2004, c. 119 (S.B.1407), § 1.)*

Law Revision Commission Comments

Enactment [Revised Comment]

Section 2640 continues former Civil Code Section 4800.2 without substantive change. Section 2640 is intended to apply to all community estate property regardless of the date of acquisition. See Section 2580 (legislative findings and declarations).

In subdivision (b), "community estate" has been substituted for "community property" to codify case law holding that this provision applies to quasi-community property as well as to community property. See *In re* Marriage of Craig, 219 Cal.App.3d 683, 268 Cal.Rptr. 396 (1990). See also Sections 63 ("community estate" defined), 2502 ("separate property" defined). A reference to division of property "under this division" has been substituted for the former reference to division "under this part," meaning the former Family Law Act (former Part 5 (commencing with former Section 4000) of Division 4 of the Civil Code). See also Section 2251 (division of property in nullity proceeding).

When enacted in 1983 (as former Civil Code Section 4800.2), Section 2640 reversed the rule of *In re* Marriage of Lucas, 27 Cal.3d 808, 614 P.2d 285, 166 Cal.Rptr. 853 (1980), and cases following it, which precluded recognition of the separate property contribution of one of the parties to the acquisition of community property, unless the party could show an agreement between the spouses to the effect that the contribution was not intended to be a gift. Under Section 2640, in case of dissolution of the marriage, a party making a separate property contribution to the acquisition of the property is not presumed to have made a gift, unless it is shown that the parties agreed in writing that it was a gift, but is entitled to reimbursement for the separate property contribution at dissolution of marriage. The separate property contribution is measured by the value of the contribution at the time the contribution is made. Under this rule, if the property has since appreciated in value, the community is entitled to the appreciation. If the property has since depreciated in value, reimbursement may not exceed the value of the property; if both parties are entitled to reimbursement and the property has insufficient value to permit full reimbursement of both, reimbursement should be on a proportionate basis.

For background on former Civ. Code § 4800.2, see *Recommendation Relating to Division of Joint Tenancy and Tenancy in Common Property at Dissolution of Marriage,* 16 Cal. L. Revision Comm'n Reports 2165 (1982); 17 Cal. L. Revision Comm'n Reports 863 (1984); *Recommendation Relating to Civil Code Sections 4800.1 and 4800.2,* 18 Cal. L. Revision Comm'n Reports 383 (1986); 18 Cal. L. Revision Comm'n Reports 1741 (1986). [23 Cal.L.Rev.Comm. Reports 1 (1993)].

Commentary

For discussion of the constitutionality of retroactive application of Section 2640 to transactions occurring before its effective date, January 1, 1984, see Section 2581 Commentary and the Law Revision Comment to an earlier constitutionalized draft of Section 2640, reproduced below for informational purposes only. See particularly *In re Marriage of Heikes, 10 Cal.4th 1211, 899 P.2d 1349, 44 Cal.Rptr.2d 155 (1995)* (Family Code Sections 2581 and 2640 may be applied retroactively to transactions that occurred before their effective dates only when such retroactive application would not affect vested property rights created before the statutes' effective dates). See also *In re Marriage of Rico, 10 Cal.App.4th 706, 12 Cal.Rptr.2d 659 (1992)* (treatment of tenancy in common acquired in 1979 and redeeded as joint tenancy in 1986).

In light of the constitutional rule articulated in *Heikes, supra,* subsection (c), should be understood to apply only to those separate property contributions of one spouse to the acquisition of the separate property estate of the other spouse that were made *on or after* January 1, 2005, the effective date of subsection (c).

In one respect, this section treats separate property contributions to the acquisition of the other spouse's separate property differently from separate contributions to the acquisition of community property. Subsection (c) bars reimbursement of one spouse's separate property contributions to the separate estate of the other spouse when there has been a section 852 written transmutation. For example, if a husband were to take a separate property asset titled in his name alone and convey it in writing to his wife as her separate property, there would be no reimbursement to the husband of the value of the asset at the time of its conveyance to the wife. However, case law interpreting subsection (b), which does not mention transmutation, allows reimbursement to a spouse's separate estate when the spouse conveyed his separate property home to the parties together as community property or joint tenancy, even though section 852 transmutations requirements have been met. See, for example, *In re Marriage of Heikes, 10 Cal.4th 1211 (1995)* (separate property contribution is the value at the time of conveyance). This treatment has been criticized by Mary Charles McRae in *Contribution or Transmutation?,* 49 UCLA L.Rev.1187 (2002) (arguing that when separate property has been transmuted into community property under section 852, there should be no section 2640 reimbursement to the separate estate).

For discussion of tracing when separate and community funds are commingled, see Section 770 Commentary.

For purposes of Section 2640, the term "community estate" includes only property that cannot otherwise be demonstrated to be the separate property of one or both spouses. It does not include all property covered by the general presumption arising merely from acquisition during marriage (see Section 760, Commentary), but rather includes only property for which the presumption may not be overcome. Thus, an untitled asset purchased by one spouse with separate and community funds is an asset of mixed character allocated to the separate and community estates according to the percentage of funds that each estate contributed to the purchase price. Similarly, when a husband took title to real property in *his name alone* and contributed separate and community property to the purchase price, it was error to apply this section to grant the husband mere reimbursement of his separate property contributions. Instead, separate and community interests in the property should have been apportioned according to each estate's relative contribution, because the husband never transmuted his separate property interest in the purchase funds. *In re Marriage of Bonvino, 241 Cal.App.4th 1411, 194 Cal.Rptr.3d 754 (2015)*. With respect to untitled property and property titled in a form that is consistent with the assertion of a separate property interest, such as title in one spouse's name alone, this section has no application. For discussion of apportionment, see *In re Marriage of Moore, 28 Cal.3d 366, 618 P.2d 208, 168 Cal.Rptr 662 (1980)*. In contrast, Section 2640 applies when written title has been taken by the spouses in joint form, and neither can rebut the presumption that arises from the form of title. See Sections 2580 and 2581, and *In re Marriage of Buol, 39 Cal.3d 751, 762, 705 P.2d 354, 218 Cal.Rptr. 31, 38 (1985)*. When Section 2640 is properly applicable, the separate estate is reimbursed for the amount of the separate property contribution to the debt reduction, not for the value of the debt extinguished. *In re Marriage of Tallman, 22 Cal.App.4th 1697, 28 Cal.Rptr.2d 323 (1994)*.

In re Marriage of Walrath, 17 Cal.4th 907, 952 P.2d 1124, 72 Cal.Rptr.2d 856 (1998), holds that a spouse may seek reimbursement for separate property contribution to the acquisition of community property both from the asset initially purchased with the separate property contribution and also from any other community property subsequently acquired from funds derived from the initial asset. When funds used to make a subsequent purchase have been secured by hypothecation of the first acquisition, the separate property interest in those purchase funds is determined by the relationship of the separate property contribution to the total equity in the initial asset at the time of hypothecation. For example, if the separate contribution represented 40% of the value of the equity at the time of hypothecation (refinancing), the separate property interest in the funds derived from refinancing would also be 40%. See also *In re*

Marriage of Stoll, 63 Cal.App.4th 837, 74 Cal.Rptr.2d 506 (1998) (applying relaxed proof requirements to *Walrath* valuation of the separate property asset when it was transmuted into community property).

In re Marriage of Cochran, 89 Cal.App.4th 1144, 103 Cal.Rptr.2d 901 (2001), holds that a spouse is entitled to reimbursement under this section for his (i) separate property payment of school fees, which were required to obtain a permit to build the family home, and (ii) separate property payment of home construction loan earnest money to the extent that the earnest money was used for home improvements. Compare *In re Marriage of Nicholson and Sparks, 104 Cal.App.4th 289, 127 Cal.Rptr.2d 882 (2003)*, which rejects a reimbursement claim for separate property funds used to pay off credit-card debt in order to qualify for a loan to purchase a community property family residence, on the ground that such payment of credit-card debt does not qualify, under this section, as a contribution to the acquisition or improvement of the community property residence.

As currently drafted and constitutionally glossed, this reimbursement provision allows reimbursement for separate contributions to the acquisition or improvement of community property made on or after January 1, 1984 and for one spouse's separate contributions to the acquisition or improvement of the other spouse's separate property made on or after January 1, 2005. This section does not address community contributions to the acquisition or improvement of a spouse's separate property. That topic and all prestatutory separate property contributions are controlled by case law, which generally provides that when one spouse applies his separate property or community property to improve the other spouse's separate property, in the absence of any reimbursement agreement between the spouses, a gift is presumed. In contrast, when a spouse uses community property to improve his own separate property, absent a reimbursement agreement or the consent of the other spouse, the acting spouse must reimburse the community estate for the amount so used or the value added, whichever is greater. See *In re Marriage of Frick, 181 Cal.App.3d 997, 1019–1020, 226 Cal.Rptr. 766 (1986), review denied 8/28/86* (dictum), and *In re Marriage of Warren, 28 Cal.App.3d 777, 104 Cal.Rptr. 860 (1972)*. However, some courts have expressed dissatisfaction with the incoherence of California rules of reimbursement when one estate contributes to another, and two cases have entirely rejected the case law presumption of gift. *In re Marriage of Wolfe, 91 Cal.App.4th 962, 110 Cal.Rptr.2d 921 (2001), review denied December 12, 2001*, holds that the divorce court properly ordered the husband to reimburse the community for the amount of community funds used to improve his separate property. Rejecting the traditional case law rubric, *Wolfe* does not specify which spouse applied the funds or whether the wife consented to their application to husband's separate property. *Wolfe* was not followed in *In re Marriage of Cross, 94 Cal.App.4th 1143, 114 Cal.Rptr.2d 839 (2001)*, which holds that the divorce court properly refused to reimburse the husband or the community estate for improvements made to the wife's separate property residence, to which the husband contributed his separate funds property and community services. *Wolfe* was followed in *In re Marriage of Allen, 96 Cal.App.4th 497, 116 Cal.Rptr.2d 887 (2002)*, which holds that a wife's consent to the use of community property funds to improve the separate property of her husband does not raise a presumption that the wife intended to make a gift of her interest in the funds to her husband; instead the community is entitled either to reimbursement of the funds spent or a pro rata interest in the property. *Wolfe* was also followed in *Bono v. Clark, 103 Cal.App.4th 1409, 128 Cal.Rptr.2d 31 (2002), review denied March 5, 2003*, which allowed the surviving widow recovery for expenditure of community funds used to improve the decedent husband's separate property. The measure of community property recovery was, to the extent that value was added, a pro tanto interest in the property, or if no value was added, the community funds so spent.

When community *funds* are applied to reduce an encumbrance on a spouse's separate property, the community estate becomes an owner in the proportion that community property encumbrance reduction bears to the total purchase price. *In re Marriage of Moore, 28 Cal.3d 366, 168 Cal.Rptr. 662 (1980)*. Although *Moore* did not present any claim that the acting spouse had made a gift to the other spouse's separate property, the issue was raised in *In re Marriage of Gowdy, 178 Cal.App.3d 1228, 224 Cal.Rptr. 400 (1986)*, which held that the application of community property funds to reduce the "encumbrance on the husband's separate property, even though done with knowledge and apparent consent of the wife, gave the community a pro tanto interest in that separate property." *Id. at 1234*. There is obvious tension between *Gowdy* and the improvement cases supra. Compare also *In re Marriage of Branco, 47 Cal.App.4th 1621, 55 Cal.Rptr.2d 493 (1996)* (community property loan proceeds used by spouses to pay off debt on wife's separate property home gave rise to *Moore* community property interest in home even though husband executed quitclaim deed to wife after the couple obtained the loan proceeds) with *In re Marriage of Stoner, 147 Cal.App.3d 858, 195 Cal.Rptr. 351 (1983)* (finding no *Moore* community property interest on similar facts). See also *In re Marriage of Frick, 181 Cal.App.3d 997, 1007–1009, 226 Cal.Rptr. 766 (1986)*; *In re Marriage of Marsden, 130 Cal.App.3d 426, 436–439, 181 Cal.Rptr. 910 (1982)* (treatment of mixed-character asset when there has been premarital appreciation); and *In re Marriage of Rico, 10 Cal.App.4th 706, 12 Cal.Rptr.2d 659 (1992)* (*Moore-Marsden* accounting used when both parties contributed separate funds to purchase real property before marriage and then made payments after marriage with community property).See also *In re Marriage of Sherman, 133 Cal.App.4th 795, 35 Cal.Rptr.3d 137 (2005)*, which held that in making a *Moore-Marsden* apportionment, the trial court erred in valuing an appreciated family home at the time of separation rather than the time of trial, because the increase in value was due to market forces rather than to either spouse's personal efforts. Sherman criticizes the analysis of *Bono v. Clark, 103 Cal.App.4th 1409, 128 Cal.Rptr.2d 31 (2002), review denied*, which used the time of separation in a death proceeding.

In re Marriage of Nelson, 139 Cal.App.4th 1546, 44 Cal.Rptr.3d 52 (2006), holds that the trial court erred in offsetting the community property Moore–Marsden interest in a home that the husband brought into marriage with the fair rental value of the community's occupancy of the home.

When the community property *labor* of either spouse has been applied to a business initially owned as separate property by one spouse, business profits and appreciation must be apportioned between community labor and separate capital. *In re Marriage of Dekker, 17 Cal.App.4th 842, 21 Cal.Rptr.2d 642 (1993), review denied* (husband's community labor applied to business held in wife's name). California courts have used at least two apportionment methods. The *Pereira* approach imputes an ordinary rate of return to the separate capital and assigns the remainder to the community. *Pereira v. Pereira, 156 Cal. 1, 103 P. 488 (1909)*. *Van Camp*, in contrast, imputes to the community ordinary wages for the spouse's community labor (reduced by any funds withdrawn from the business for family expenses) and then assigns the remainder as the separate property of the spouse who initially owned the business. *Van Camp v. Van Camp, 53 Cal.App. 17, 27–28, 199 P. 885 (1921)*. See generally *Beam v. Bank of America, 6 Cal.3d 12, 98 Cal.Rptr. 137 (1971)*. When the labor of a spouse has been the primary factor in business success, *Pereira* accounting should be used. When the separate capital has been the primary factor in business success, *Van Camp* accounting may be used. *In re Marriage of Dekker, supra, 21 Cal.Rptr.2d at 648–50*. See additionally *Gilmore v. Gilmore, 45 Cal.2d 142, 287 P.2d 769 (1955); Tassi v. Tassi, 160 Cal.App.2d 680, 325 P.2d 872 (1958)*. Such apportionment must also be made when a spouse's postseparation separate property labor is applied to an otherwise community property business. See *In re Marriage of Imperato, 45 Cal.App.3d 432, 119 Cal.Rptr. 590 (1975)*. The incorporation of a separate property sole proprietorship during marriage does not subject it to Section 2640 reimbursement. A change in form does not change the character of the business; it still must be apportioned according too

Pereira/Van Camp principles. *In re Marriage of Koester, 73 Cal. App.4th 1032, 87 Cal.Rptr.2d 76 (1999).*

In re Marriage of Brandes, 239 Cal.App.4th 1461, 192 Cal.Rptr.3d 1 (2015), review denied, held that a court may use a hybrid *Pereira/Van Camp* approach to determine the community property interest in a separate property business that grew enormously during marriage when the managing spouse's personal labor was the primary cause of early business growth (*Pereira*), but the spouse later delegated management of the business to others and market conditions were unusually favorable (*Van Camp*). The effect of *Brandes* was to minimize the community property interest in a separate property business that initially grew because of the quality of a spouse's personal labor, when the managing spouse later delegated management responsibilities to others and no longer personally participated in the management of the business.

Patrick v. Alacer Corp., 167 Cal.App.4th 995, 84 Cal.Rptr.3d 642 (2008), review denied, held that a surviving spouse had standing to assert shareholder derivative claims against her deceased husband's corporation even though she was not a shareholder of record, when she alleged that during marriage the community had acquired an interest in the corporation because its increase in value was attributable to community labor.

When a spouse has applied community property to preserve his own separate property, the community is entitled to reimbursement. *In re Marriage of Avril, 57 Cal.App.3d 802, 129 Cal.Rptr. 351 (1976)* (payment of taxes); *Somps v. Somps, 25 Cal.App.2d 328, 58 Cal.Rptr. 304 (1967)* (taxes and incidental expenses); *Estate of Turner, 35 Cal.App.2d 576, 96 P.2d 363 (1939)* (taxes and special assessments).

Although the statute is not entirely clear (compare Section 2581), the Section 2640 right of reimbursement would appear to apply only at dissolution and not when a marriage ends in death. When marriage ends because of the death of one of the parties, *In re Marriage of Lucas, 27 Cal.3d 808 (1980),* should be controlling. Absent an agreement to the contrary, when the parties have taken title in joint form, *Lucas* does not allow tracing to separate funds. However, Section 2640 has been applied when a marriage ended in death because one joint tenant spouse killed the other. See Probate Code Section 251 and *Estate of Castiglioni, 40 Cal.App.4th 367, 47 Cal.Rptr.2d 288 (1995), review denied February 15, 1996* (when real property is held in joint tenancy and one joint tenant feloniously and intentionally kills the other, the joint tenancy is severed and the portion of property that passes as decedent's property must be calculated according to the principles of tracing and reimbursement of contributions ordinarily used in marital dissolution cases).

For discussion of the treatment of Section 2640 contributions to the acquisition of a family home subject to a Section 3800 deferred sale of home order, see *In re Marriage of Braud, 45 Cal.App.4th 797, 53 Cal.Rptr.3d 179 (1996). Braud* holds that when the trial court makes a deferral order, it should treat a spouse's separate property contribution, which would otherwise be immediately reimbursable under Section 2640, as a court-ordered reinvestment in the family home. The court may then "reconfigure . . . the title to the family home recognizing the parties as tenants in common with unequal ownership interests and, concomitantly, order that they be paid in proportion to those ownership interests at the time of sale of the family home." 45 Cal.App.4th at 822.

Even though a petition of dissolution has been filed, when one spouse files a bankruptcy petition *before* the community property has been distributed to the parties in the dissolution action, subsection (a)(2) includes in the bankruptcy estate the entire equity in the couple's community property home despite the other spouse's Family Code Section 2640 right of reimbursement for separate funds contributed to the purchase price of the home. *In re Mantle, 153 F.3d 1082 (9th Cir. 1998), cert. denied 119 S.Ct. 1461, 143 L.Ed.2d 547 (1999).*

In re Marriage of Lange, 102 Cal.App.4th 360, 125 Cal.Rptr.2d 379 (2003), held that a husband's promissory note for a wife's separate property contributions to the acquisition of the family home and the deed of trust on the home securing the note were unenforceable under § 721 because they gave the wife an advantage and thus gave rise to a presumption of undue influence, which the wife failed to rebut. However, the wife remained entitled to § 2640 reimbursement of her separate property contributions to the acquisition of community property because the unenforceable instruments did not constitute a subsection (b) written waiver of that right.

Former Section 2640

The version of Section 2640, enacted by Stats 1992 Ch 162 § 10, effective January 1, 1993, operative January 1, 1994, prior to its amendment by Stats 1993 Ch 219 § 114.5, provides:

(a) "Contributions to the acquisition of the property," as used in this section, include downpayments, payments for improvements, and payments that reduce the principal of a loan used to finance the purchase or improvement of the property but do not include payments of interest on the loan or payments made for maintenance, insurance, or taxation of the property.

(b) In the division of community estate property acquired on or after January 1, 1984, by the parties during marriage unless a party has made a written waiver of the right to reimbursement or signed a writing that has the effect of a waiver, the party shall be reimbursed for the party's contributions to the acquisition of the property to the extent the party traces the contributions to a separate property source. The amount reimbursed shall be without interest or adjustment for change in monetary values and shall not exceed the net value of the property at the time of the division.

The Law Revision Commission's Comments regarding this prior version of Section 2640, which are provided for informational purposes only, read as follows:

Section 2640 continues former Civil Code Section 4800.2 without substantive change. In subdivision (b), "community estate property" has been substituted for "community property" to codify case law holding that the section applies to quasi-community property as well as to community property. See *In re Marriage of Craig, 219 Cal.App.3d 683, 268 Cal. Rptr 396 (1990).* See also Section 2501 ("community estate" defined). See also Section 2502 ("separate property" defined).

In subdivision (b), the phrase "acquired on or after January 1, 1984, by the parties during marriage" has been added to codify a case-law rule, based on impairment of vested rights without due process, that the section cannot constitutionally be applied to a case where the property was acquired before the effective date of the section. See, e.g., *In re Marriage of Craig, 219 Cal.App.3d 683, 268 Cal.Rptr. 396 (1990)*; *In re Marriage of Cairo, 204 Cal.App.3d 1255, 251 Cal.Rptr. 731 (1988)*; *In re Marriage of Lockman, 204 Cal.App.3d 782, 251 Cal.Rptr. 434 (1988)*; *In re Marriage of Bankovich, 203 Cal.App.3d 49, 249 Cal.Rptr. 713 (1988)*; *In re Marriage of Hopkins and Axene, 199 Cal.App.3d 288, 245 Cal.Rptr. 433 (1987)*; *In re Marriage of Griffis, 187 Cal.App.3d 156, 231 Cal.Rptr. 510 (1986)*; see also *In re Marriage of Fabian, 41 Cal.3d 440, 715 P.2d 253, 224 Cal.Rptr. 333 (1986)*; *In re Marriage of Buol, 39 Cal.3d 751, 705 P.2d 354, 218 Cal.Rptr. 31 (1985)*; Section 2580 & Comment (community property presumption for property held in joint form).

When enacted in 1983 (as former Civil Code Section 4800.2), Section 2640 reversed the rule of *In re Marriage of Lucas, 27 Cal.3d 8 08, 614 P.2d 285, 166 Cal.Rptr. 853 (1980)*, and cases following it, which precluded recognition of the separate property contribution of one of the parties to the acquisition of community property, unless the party could show an agreement between the spouses to the effect that the contribution was not intended to be a gift. Under Section 2640, in case of dissolution of the marriage, a party making a separate property contribution to the acquisition of the property is not presumed to have made a gift, unless it is shown that the parties agreed in writing that it was a gift, but is entitled to reimbursement for the separate property contribution at dissolution of marriage. The separate property contribution is measured by the value of the contribution at the time the contribution is made. Under this rule, if the property has since appreciated in value, the community is entitled to the appreciation. If the property has since depreciated in value, reimbursement may not exceed the value of the property; if both parties are entitled to reimbursement and the property has insufficient value to permit full reimbursement of both, reimbursement should be on a proportionate basis.

For background on former Civil Code Section 4800.2, see *Recommendation Relating to Division of Joint Tenancy and Tenancy in Common Property at Dissolution of Marriage,* 16 Cal. L. Revision Comm'n Reports 2165 (1982); 17 Cal. L. Revision Comm'n Reports 863 (1984); *Recommendation Relating to Civil Code Sections 4800.1 and 4800.2,* 18 Cal. L. Revision Comm'n Reports 383 (1986); 18 Cal. L. Revision Comm'n Reports 1741 (1986).

Research References

Forms

California Transactions Forms--Estate Planning § 1:25, Joint Tenancy or Community Property Treatment Of Property in Revocable Trust.
California Transactions Forms--Estate Planning § 2:13, Separate Versus Community Property Issues.
California Transactions Forms--Estate Planning § 10:45, Property Characterization Agreement.
California Transactions Forms--Estate Planning § 11:49, Introduction and Definition [Prob C § 140].
California Transactions Forms--Family Law § 1:90, Real and Personal Property.
California Transactions Forms--Family Law § 2:17, Drafting Principles Regarding Disposition Of Residence.
California Transactions Forms--Family Law § 2:18, Reimbursement Of Separate Property Contribution [Fam C § 2640].
California Transactions Forms--Family Law § 2:81, Potential Community Assets and Obligations.
California Transactions Forms--Family Law § 2:88, Marital Settlement Agreement.
California Transactions Forms--Family Law § 2:97, Confirmation Of Capital Gains Tax and Division Of Proceeds After Separate Property Reimbursement [Fam C § 2640].
West's California Code Forms, Family § 2338 Form 8, Marital Agreement.

Treatises and Practice Aids

Witkin, California Summary 10th Community Property § 14, Separate Property Acquired During Marriage.
Witkin, California Summary 10th Community Property § 18, Payments Made After Separation.
Witkin, California Summary 10th Community Property § 111, Other Assets.
Witkin, California Summary 10th Community Property § 114, Recordkeeping Requirements.
Witkin, California Summary 10th Community Property § 116, Current Rule: Reimbursement to Community.
Witkin, California Summary 10th Community Property § 117, Taxes or Encumbrances.
Witkin, California Summary 10th Community Property § 118, Community Interest in Enhanced Value.
Witkin, California Summary 10th Community Property § 222, Statutory Rule.
Witkin, California Summary 10th Community Property § 223, Conversion Of Separate Property Into Joint Tenancy.
Witkin, California Summary 10th Community Property § 224, Later Acquired Assets.
Witkin, California Summary 10th Community Property § 225, Postseparation Payments.
Witkin, California Summary 10th Community Property § 227, Statutory Revision.
Witkin, California Summary 10th Community Property § 230, Right to Reimbursement.
Witkin, California Summary 10th Community Property § 231, Attempted Statutory Solution.
Witkin, California Summary 10th Contracts § 400, Miscellaneous Provisions.

§ 2641. Community contributions to education or training

(a) "Community contributions to education or training" as used in this section means payments made with community or quasi-community property for education or training or for the repayment of a loan incurred for education or training, whether the payments were made while the parties were resident in this state or resident outside this state.

(b) Subject to the limitations provided in this section, upon dissolution of marriage or legal separation of the parties:

(1) The community shall be reimbursed for community contributions to education or training of a party that substantially enhances the earning capacity of the party. The amount reimbursed shall be with interest at the legal rate, accruing from the end of the calendar year in which the contributions were made.

(2) A loan incurred during marriage for the education or training of a party shall not be included among the liabilities of the community for the purpose of division pursuant to this division but shall be assigned for payment by the party.

(c) The reimbursement and assignment required by this section shall be reduced or modified to the extent circumstances render such a disposition unjust, including, but not limited to, any of the following:

(1) The community has substantially benefited from the education, training, or loan incurred for the education or training of the party. There is a rebuttable presumption, affecting the burden of proof, that the community has not substantially benefited from community contributions to the education or training made less than 10 years before the commencement of the proceeding, and that the community has substantially benefited from community contributions to the education or training made more than 10 years before the commencement of the proceeding.

(2) The education or training received by the party is offset by the education or training received by the other party for which community contributions have been made.

(3) The education or training enables the party receiving the education or training to engage in gainful employment that substantially reduces the need of the party for support that would otherwise be required.

(d) Reimbursement for community contributions and assignment of loans pursuant to this section is the exclusive remedy of the community or a party for the education or training and any resulting enhancement of the earning capacity of a party. However, nothing in this subdivision limits consideration of the effect of the education, training, or enhancement, or the amount reimbursed pursuant to this section, on the circumstances of the parties for the purpose of an order for support pursuant to Section 4320.

(e) This section is subject to an express written agreement of the parties to the contrary. *(Stats.1992, c. 162 (A.B.2650), § 10, operative Jan. 1, 1994.)*

Law Revision Commission Comments

Enactment [Revised Comment]

Section 2641 continues former Civil Code Section 4800.3 without substantive change. Section 2641 provides authority for reimbursement of educational expenses that have benefited primarily one party to the marriage. Although the education, degree, or license or the resulting enhanced earning capacity is not "property" subject to division, community expenditures for them are properly subject to reimbursement. See subdivision (d).

In subdivision (a), the reference to quasi-community property has been added. Former Civil Code Section 4800.3 referred only to community property. See *In re* Marriage of Craig, 219 Cal.App.3d 683, 686, 268 Cal.Rptr. 396 (1990) ("California's marital property laws are designed to provide for uniform treatment of quasi-community and community property when the parties have changed their domicile to this state and seek to legally alter their marital status in a California court. This intent is apparent from statutes such as [former Civil Code Section] 4800 (equal division of 'community estate' consisting of community and quasi-community property) and [former Civil Code Section] 4800.5 (power to order conveyance of out-of-state property)."). Subdivision (a) does not detail the expenditures that might be included within the concept of "community contributions." These expenditures would at least include the cost of tuition, fees, books and supplies, and transportation.

Subdivision (b)(1) states the basic rule that community contributions must be reimbursed. The reimbursement right is limited to cases where the earning capacity of a party is substantially enhanced. This limitation is intended to restrict litigation by requiring that the education or training must demonstrably enhance earning capacity and to implement the policy of the section to redress economic inequity. However, it is not required that the party actually work in an occupation to which the enhancement applies; community contributions were made to the enhancement for the benefit of one party, who retains the potential to realize the enhancement in the future. Unless the rebuttable presumption of subdivision (c)(1) is overcome, reimbursement is limited to contributions made during the preceding ten years to minimize proof problems as well as potential inequity. Interest at the legal rate (Code Civ. Proc. § 685.010) accrues only from the end of each year in which expenditures were made, in order to simplify accounting for numerous small expenditures made over the course of the education or training. In subdivision (b)(2), the reference to this division has been substituted for the narrower reference to former Civil Code Section 4800. This is not a substantive change.

Subdivision (c) is intended to permit the court to avoid the provisions of this section in an appropriate case. For example, if one party receives a medical education, degree, and license at community expense, but the marriage endures for some time with a high standard of living and substantial accumulation of community assets attributable to the medical training, it may be inappropriate to require reimbursement. Subdivision (c)(1). If both parties receive education or training at community expense, it may be inappropriate to require reimbursement even though the exact amounts expended for each are not equal. Subdivision (c)(2). This limitation is especially important where one party received education or training more than 10 years before the commencement of the dissolution or legal separation proceeding. See subdivision (c)(1). If toward the end of a lengthy marriage one party, who had been a homemaker during the marriage and had never completed an education or developed job skills, receives education or training to enable him or her to be gainfully employed, reimbursement may be improper. Subdivision (c)(3). Absent the education or training, support may be necessary to maintain the party or to permit the party to obtain education or training.

In subdivision (d), a reference to Section 4320 has been substituted for the broader reference to former Civil Code Section 4801. This is not a substantive change, since the relevant part of the former section is continued in Section 4320.

Subdivision (e) recognizes that at the time community contributions are made to the education or training of a spouse, the parties may have an agreement as to the conditions of the contributions. Since such agreements may be subject to litigation, subdivision (e) requires a writing.

For background on former Civ. Code § 4800.3, see *Recommendation Relating to Reimbursement of Educational Expenses,* 17 Cal. L. Revision Comm'n Reports 229 (1984). See also *In re* Marriage of Sullivan, 37 Cal.3d 762, 691 P.2d 1020, 209 Cal.Rptr. 354 (1984). [23 Cal.L.Rev.Comm. Reports 1 (1993)].

Commentary

In re Marriage of Watt, 214 Cal.App.3d 340, 262 Cal.Rptr. 783 (1989), holds that subsection (b)(1) reimbursable community expenditures for the student spouse's education generally do not include ordinary living expenses, which would be incurred in any event, but instead include only expenses related to the education itself. Compare the trial court's treatment of subsection (b)(2) student loans, which were assigned solely to the student spouse without any allocation between their use for living and educational expenses. Also compare *Watt's* more expansive treatment of professional education for purposes of Section 4320 spousal support. See Section 4320, Commentary.

Weiner v. Weiner, 105 Cal.App.4th 235, 129 Cal.Rptr.2d 288 (2003), holds that reimbursement under this section is available when a spouse's education was acquired before marriage and community funds were used to repay the spouse's premarital educational loans.

In re Marriage of Graham, 109 Cal.App.4th 1321, 135 Cal.Rptr.2d 685 (2003), sustained a trial court's denial of reimbursement to the community for community funds spent on the legal education of a husband who was a police officer and had no plans to take the bar examination or practice law after graduation. *Graham* reasoned that it was speculative whether his eventual graduation from law school would substantially increase his earning capacity and the evidence did not support the conclusion that it would. *Graham* declined to rule, as a matter of law, that a law degree substantially enhances earning capacity.

In re Marriage of Slivka, 183 Cal.App.3d 159, 228 Cal.Rptr. 76 (1986), holds that Section 2641 may constitutionally be applied to education obtained before the statute's effective date, January 1, 1985. For general discussion of Section 2641, see *In re Marriage of Sullivan, 37 Cal.3d 762, 691 P.2d 1020, 209 Cal.Rptr. 354 (1984)*.

Research References

Forms

California Transactions Forms--Estate Planning § 11:49, Introduction and Definition [Prob C § 140].

California Transactions Forms--Family Law § 2:88, Marital Settlement Agreement.

West's California Code Forms, Family § 2550, Comment Overview--Manner Of Division Of Community Estate.

West's California Code Forms, Family § 2338 Form 8, Marital Agreement.

Treatises and Practice Aids

Witkin, California Summary 10th Community Property § 33, Restrictions on Alteration Of Spouses' Legal Relations.

Witkin, California Summary 10th Community Property § 109, Nature and Scope Of Reimbursement Statute.

Witkin, California Summary 10th Community Property § 110, Reimbursement Requirements.

Witkin, California Summary 10th Community Property § 203, Other Exceptions.

Part 8

JOINTLY HELD SEPARATE PROPERTY

§ 2650. Jurisdiction; division of real and personal property

In a proceeding for division of the community estate, the court has jurisdiction, at the request of either party, to divide the separate property interests of the parties in real and personal property, wherever situated and whenever acquired, held by the parties as joint tenants or tenants in common. The property shall be divided together with, and in accordance with the same procedure for and limitations on, division of community estate. *(Stats.1992, c. 162 (A.B.2650), § 10, operative Jan. 1, 1994.)*

Law Revision Commission Comments

Enactment [Revised Comment]

Section 2650 continues former Civil Code Section 4800.4(a) without substantive change. The term "community estate" has been substituted for "community property and quasi-community property." This is not a substantive change. See Sections 63 ("community estate" defined), 2502 ("separate property" defined).

Section 2650 applies regardless of when the separate property was acquired. Former Civil Code Section 4800.4(b), which provided that the "section applies to proceedings commenced on or after January 1, 1986, regardless of whether the property was acquired before, on, or after January 1, 1986" has been omitted as unnecessary in view of Section 4(c).

When enacted in 1985 (as former Civil Code Section 4800.4), Section 2650 reversed the former rule that the court in a dissolution or legal separation proceeding had no jurisdiction over property of the parties other than community or quasi-community property. Section 2650 supplements provisions governing community property held in joint tenancy form by extending the jurisdiction of the court to separate property held in joint tenancy form as well. The section is consistent with the general rule that the court has jurisdiction to settle the property rights of the parties and with the principle that the court has jurisdiction to settle matters submitted to it by the parties. See Section 2010 (authority of court). The section is also consistent with the rule that the court may reserve jurisdiction to divide community property that has become tenancy in common by operation of law upon dissolution or separation. See, e.g., Marriage of Borges, 83 Cal.App.3d 771, 148 Cal.Rptr. 118 (1978); Comment, *Post–Dissolution Suits to Divide Community Property: A Proposal for Legislative Action,* 10 Pac. L.J. 825 (1979).

Section 2650 supplements the other provisions of this division by giving the court express jurisdiction over joint tenancy or tenancy in common separate property submitted by a party in a proceeding for division of the community estate. Property subject to division includes property acquired by the parties either before or during marriage. It also includes property acquired or situated either in this state or elsewhere. For a special rule governing treatment of real property situated in another state, see Section 2660 (community and quasi-community property). See also Section 2011 (jurisdiction over property of spouse served by publication). The court's jurisdiction extends only to the interests of the spouses, whether equal or unequal, and the court may not affect interests of third parties in the property. The interests of third parties may be subject to partition pursuant to Title 10.5 (commencing with Section 872.010) of Part 2 of the Code of Civil Procedure.

It should be noted that division of property pursuant to this section is subject to the same limitations applicable to division of the community estate. Therefore, an express agreement of the parties precluding partition or other division of the property and providing a mechanism for dispute resolution or otherwise governing their rights in the property prevails over this section. See Section 2550 (equal division of community estate "[e]xcept upon the written agreement of the parties").

For background on former Civ. Code § 4800.4, see *Recommendation Relating to Dividing Jointly Owned Property Upon Marriage Dissolution,* 18 Cal. L. Revision Comm'n Reports 147 (1986); 18 Cal. L. Revision Comm'n Reports 365 (1986). [23 Cal.L.Rev.Comm. Reports 1 (1993)].

Commentary

For discussion of Section 2650, see *In re Marriage of Gagne, 225 Cal.App.3d 277, 281–282, 274 Cal.Rptr. 750 (1990), review denied 2/14/91,* and *Askew v. Askew, 22 Cal.App.4th 942, 962, 28 Cal.Rptr.2d 284, 296 (1994)*. For further discussion of the divorce court's jurisdiction, see Section 2550, Commentary.

See also *In re Marriage of Rico, 10 Cal.App.4th 706, 12 Cal.Rptr.2d 659 (1992)* (treatment of tenancy in common acquired in 1979 and redeeded as joint tenancy in 1986). Compare *In re Marriage of Romant, 21 Cal.App.4th 542 (1993), rehearing granted 1/18/94, opinion filed June 14, 1994, not for publication*, (possibly unconstitutional retroactive application of sections 2581 and 2640), criticized at 1994 Cal. Fam. L. Monthly 35.

Research References

Forms

West's California Code Forms, Family § 2550, Comment Overview--Manner Of Division Of Community Estate.

Treatises and Practice Aids

Witkin, California Summary 10th Community Property § 227, Statutory Revision.

Witkin, California Summary 10th Community Property § 228, Enforcement Of Premarital Loan.

Part 9

REAL PROPERTY LOCATED IN ANOTHER STATE

§ 2660. Division of real property situated in another state

(a) Except as provided in subdivision (b), if the property subject to division includes real property situated in another state, the court shall, if possible, divide the community property and quasi-community property as provided for in this division in such a manner that it is not necessary to change the nature of the interests held in the real property situated in the other state.

(b) If it is not possible to divide the property in the manner provided for in subdivision (a), the court may do any of the following in order to effect a division of the property as provided for in this division:

(1) Require the parties to execute conveyances or take other actions with respect to the real property situated in the other state as are necessary.

(2) Award to the party who would have been benefited by the conveyances or other actions the money value of the interest in the property that the party would have received if the conveyances had been executed or other actions taken. *(Stats.1992, c. 162 (A.B.2650), § 10, operative Jan. 1, 1994.)*

Law Revision Commission Comments

Enactment [Revised Comment]

Section 2660 continues former Civil Code Section 4800.5 without substantive change. References to this division have been substituted for narrower references to former Civil Code Section 4800. Section 2660 specifies the procedure to be followed when the property subject to division includes real property situated in another state.

When real property is acquired in another state with community funds, the property is treated as community property for the purpose of division on dissolution of the marriage or on legal separation. See Rozan v. Rozan, 49 Cal.2d 322, 317 P.2d 11 (1957); Tomaier v. Tomaier, 23 Cal.2d 754, 146 P.2d 905 (1944); *Recommendation Relating to Quasi–Community Property,* 9 Cal. L. Revision Comm'n Reports 113, 119 n. 12 (1969). Quasi-community property likewise may include real property situated in another state. See Section 125 ("quasi-community property" defined). See also *Recommendation Relating to Quasi–Community Property,* 9 Cal. L. Revision Comm'n Reports 113 (1969).

Section 2660 recognizes that the judgment of the court dividing the property cannot directly affect real property in another state, even though the court has personal jurisdiction over both spouses, unless the judgment is allowed that effect by the laws of the state in which the property is situated. Fall v. Eastin, 215 U.S. 1 (1909); Rozan v. Rozan, 49 Cal.2d 322, 317 P.2d 11 (1957); Taylor v. Taylor, 192 Cal. 71, 218 P. 756 (1923). On the other hand, where the court has personal jurisdiction over both parties, it may order one of the parties to execute a deed by acting in personam; if the person so ordered does execute the deed, it effectively conveys the interest transferred, even though executed under threat of contempt proceedings. Fall v. Fall, 75 Neb. 104, 113 N.W. 175 (1907), *aff'd,* Fall v. Eastin, 215 U.S. 1 (1909).

Section 2660 requires that the court first attempt to effect the equal division of the community property and quasi-community property required by this division without making any change in the nature of the interests held in the real property situated in the other state. This will be the result where the value of the other community and quasi-community property is equal to or exceeds the value of the real property situated in the other state that is subject to division. Where the court determines that the real property situated in another state or an interest in such property must be transferred from one party to the other to effect the equal division of community and quasi-community property required by this division, the court may order the parties to execute the necessary conveyances or to take other actions—such as selling the property and including the proceeds in the property division—that may be necessary to effect an equal division of the community and quasi-community property, and may enforce its order by contempt proceedings. If a party refuses to execute the instrument necessary to effect the transfer or sale of the property or to take some other necessary action, the problem may be dealt with by awarding the money value of the property or interest therein to the other party, which award must be given full faith and credit. Fall v. Fall, 75 Neb. 104, 113 N.W. 175 (1907), *aff'd,* Fall v. Eastin, 215 U.S. 1 (1909).

For background on former Civ. Code § 4800.5, see *Recommendation Relating to Quasi–Community Property,* 9 Cal. L. Revision Comm'n Reports 113 (1969); *Report of Assembly Committee on Judiciary on Assembly Bill 124,* 10 Cal. L. Revision Comm'n Reports 1042–43 (1971). [23 Cal.L.Rev.Comm. Reports 1 (1993)].

Commentary

For discussion of Section 2660, see *In re Marriage of Fink, 25 Cal.3d 877, 883, 160 Cal.Rptr. 516 (1979),* and *In re Marriage of Economou, 224 Cal.App.3d 1466, 1479, 274 Cal.Rptr. 473 (1990).*

Research References

Forms

California Transactions Forms--Estate Planning § 19:19, Quasi-Community Property.

West's California Code Forms, Family § 2550, Comment Overview--Manner Of Division Of Community Estate.

West's California Judicial Council Forms FL-160, Property Declaration.

West's California Judicial Council Forms FL-161, Continuation Of Property Declaration.

West's California Judicial Council Forms FL-345, Property Order Attachment to Judgment.

Treatises and Practice Aids

Witkin, California Summary 10th Community Property § 258, Statutory Rule.

Witkin, California Summary 10th Community Property § 259, Illustrations.

Division 8

CUSTODY OF CHILDREN

Part 1

DEFINITIONS AND GENERAL PROVISIONS

CHAPTER 1. DEFINITIONS

§ 3000. Construction of division

Unless the provision or context otherwise requires, the definitions in this chapter govern the construction of this division. *(Stats.1992, c. 162 (A.B.2650), § 10, operative Jan. 1, 1994.)*

Law Revision Commission Comments

Enactment [Revised Comment]

Section 3000 is new and is comparable to Section 50. [23 Cal.L.Rev.Comm. Reports 1 (1993)].

Research References

Forms

California Transactions Forms--Family Law § 3:2, Child Custody.
California Transactions Forms--Family Law § 3:4, Subject Matter Jurisdiction for Custody Determinations.
California Transactions Forms--Family Law § 2:70, Deciding Custody.

Treatises and Practice Aids

Witkin, California Summary 10th Community Property § 272, Nature Of Theory.
Witkin, California Summary 10th Husband and Wife § 3, Statutory Framework.
Witkin, California Summary 10th Husband and Wife § 171, Hearing, Incidental Orders, and Judgment.
Witkin, California Summary 10th Parent and Child § 63, in General.
Witkin, California Summary 10th Parent and Child § 195, Statutory Framework.
Witkin, California Summary 10th Parent and Child § 222, Statutory Authorization.
Witkin, California Summary 10th Parent and Child § 235, Biologically Unrelated Persons Opposed by Parent.
Witkin, California Summary 10th Parent and Child § 277, Investigation Of Child Sexual Abuse Allegations.
Witkin, California Summary 10th Parent and Child § 311, Other Proceedings Stayed.
Witkin, California Summary 10th Parent and Child § 363, Applicability Of Family Code Custody Provisions.
Witkin, California Summary 10th Parent and Child § 385, Support During Action.

§ 3002. Joint custody

"Joint custody" means joint physical custody and joint legal custody. *(Stats.1992, c. 162 (A.B.2650), § 10, operative Jan. 1, 1994.)*

Law Revision Commission Comments

Enactment [Revised Comment]

Section 3002 continues former Civil Code Section 4600.5(d)(1) without change. [23 Cal.L.Rev.Comm. Reports 1 (1993)].

Research References

Forms

California Transactions Forms--Family Law § 5:2, Overview.
California Transactions Forms--Family Law § 2:69, Terminology Of Custody.

Treatises and Practice Aids

Witkin, California Summary 10th Parent and Child § 222, Statutory Authorization.

§ 3003. Joint legal custody

"Joint legal custody" means that both parents shall share the right and the responsibility to make the decisions relating to the health, education, and welfare of a child. *(Stats.1992, c. 162 (A.B.2650), § 10, operative Jan. 1, 1994.)*

Law Revision Commission Comments

Enactment [Revised Comment]

Section 3003 continues former Civil Code Section 4600.5(d)(5) without change. [23 Cal.L.Rev.Comm. Reports 1 (1993)].

Research References

Forms

California Transactions Forms--Family Law § 3:9, Statutory Custody Definitions.
California Transactions Forms--Family Law § 2:69, Terminology Of Custody.
California Transactions Forms--Family Law § 3:15, Overview; Scope Of Agreement.
California Transactions Forms--Family Law § 3:53, Sample Basic Custody Provisions.
California Transactions Forms--Family Law § 5:16, School and Extracurricular Activities; Religious Upbringing; Medical Care.
West's California Judicial Council Forms FL-341(C), Children's Holiday Schedule Attachment.
West's California Judicial Council Forms FL-341(D), Additional Provisions--Physical Custody Attachment.

West's California Judicial Council Forms FL-341(E), Joint Legal Custody Attachment.

Treatises and Practice Aids

Witkin, California Summary 10th Parent and Child § 222, Statutory Authorization.

§ 3004. Joint physical custody

"Joint physical custody" means that each of the parents shall have significant periods of physical custody. Joint physical custody shall be shared by the parents in such a way so as to assure a child of frequent and continuing contact with both parents, subject to Sections 3011 and 3020. *(Stats.1992, c. 162 (A.B.2650), § 10, operative Jan. 1, 1994. Amended by Stats.1997, c. 849 (A.B.200), § 1.)*

Law Revision Commission Comments

Enactment [Revised Comment]

Section 3004 continues former Civil Code Section 4600.5(d)(3) without change. [23 Cal.L.Rev.Comm. Reports 1 (1993)].

Research References

Forms

California Transactions Forms--Family Law § 2:69, Terminology Of Custody.
California Transactions Forms--Family Law § 3:18, Overview.
California Transactions Forms--Family Law § 3:53, Sample Basic Custody Provisions.

Treatises and Practice Aids

Witkin, California Summary 10th Parent and Child § 222, Statutory Authorization.

§ 3006. Sole legal custody

"Sole legal custody" means that one parent shall have the right and the responsibility to make the decisions relating to the health, education, and welfare of a child. *(Stats.1992, c. 162 (A.B.2650), § 10, operative Jan. 1, 1994.)*

Law Revision Commission Comments

Enactment [Revised Comment]

Section 3006 continues former Civil Code Section 4600.5(d)(4) without change. [23 Cal.L.Rev.Comm. Reports 1 (1993)].

Research References

Forms

California Transactions Forms--Family Law § 2:69, Terminology Of Custody.

Treatises and Practice Aids

Witkin, California Summary 10th Parent and Child § 222, Statutory Authorization.
Witkin, California Summary 10th Parent and Child § 253, Move-Away Cases.

§ 3007. Sole physical custody

"Sole physical custody" means that a child shall reside with and be under the supervision of one parent, subject to the power of the court to order visitation. *(Stats.1992, c. 162 (A.B.2650), § 10, operative Jan. 1, 1994.)*

Law Revision Commission Comments

Enactment [Revised Comment]

Section 3007 continues former Civil Code Section 4600.5(d)(2) without change. [23 Cal.L.Rev.Comm. Reports 1 (1993)].

Research References

Forms

California Transactions Forms--Family Law § 3:9, Statutory Custody Definitions.
California Transactions Forms--Family Law § 5:2, Overview.
California Transactions Forms--Family Law § 2:69, Terminology Of Custody.

Treatises and Practice Aids

Witkin, California Summary 10th Parent and Child § 222, Statutory Authorization.
Witkin, California Summary 10th Parent and Child § 253, Move-Away Cases.

CHAPTER 2. GENERAL PROVISIONS

§ 3010. Custody of unemancipated minor children

(a) The mother of an unemancipated minor child and the father, if presumed to be the father under Section 7611, are equally entitled to the custody of the child.

(b) If one parent is dead, is unable or refuses to take custody, or has abandoned the child, the other parent is entitled to custody of the child. *(Added by Stats.1993, c. 219 (A.B.1500), § 115.5.)*

Law Revision Commission Comments

Enactment [Revised Comment]

Section 3010 restates the general right to custody in former Civil Code Section 197 without substantive change. The word "unemancipated" has been substituted for "unmarried." This is not a substantive change, but resolves a conflict with the rules governing emancipation of minors. See Section 7002 (conditions of emancipation).

The abandonment standard in former Civil Code Section 197, which referred to abandonment of the family, has been revised in subdivision (b) to refer to abandonment of the child. This is not a substantive change, but recognizes that where child custody is the issue, abandonment of the child is the relevant consideration. This change is also made for general consistency with judicial standards stated elsewhere concerning parental rights and child custody. See Sections 3011 (factors considered in determining best interest of child), 3040 (preference in ordering custody), 7822 (proceeding to declare child free from parental custody and control on ground of abandonment); see also *In re* Guardianship of Schwartz, 171 Cal. 633, 635, 154 P. 304 (1915); Guardianship of Case, 57 Cal.App.2d 844, 848, 135 P.2d 681 (1943).

For additional rights dependent on the right to custody, see Part 1 (commencing with Section 7500) of Division 12. [23 Cal.L.Rev. Comm. Reports 1 (1993)].

Commentary

See *In re Phoenix B., 218 Cal.App.3d 787, 267 Cal.Rptr. 269 (1990)* (dependency proceeding initiated on mother's involuntary hospitalization dismissed when presumed natural father ready and able to take custody of child).

Absent a court order affecting custody, this section provides that a mother and a man presumed to be the father under Section 7611 have an equal right to custody of an unemancipated minor child. On March 9, 1999, the Supreme Court denied review and depublished the Court of Appeal opinion in *People v. Zeghtchanian, 79 Cal.Rptr.2d 866 (1998),* in which the Court of Appeal ruled that when a parent is prosecuted for child-stealing under Penal Code Section 278, the prosecution bears the burden of showing that the parent does not have a right to custody of the child and that the parent took the child from a person or agency that had "lawful custody" of the child; the Court of Appeal also ruled that the invalidity of a custody order may be asserted as a defense to a Section 278 prosecution.

See also *People v. Johnson, 151 Cal.App.3d 1021, 1024, 199 Cal.Rptr. 231 (1984)* (dismissing charges of child abduction and false imprisonment against child's natural presumed father who had not been served with court order awarding custody of children to mother). Compare *People v. Carrillo, 162 Cal.App.3d 585, 208 Cal.Rptr. 684 (1984)* (nonpresumed natural father has no Section 3010 right to custody and hence may be prosecuted for child stealing when taking child from unwed mother). But cf. *Adoption of Kelsey S., 1 Cal.4th 816, 4 Cal.Rptr.2d 615 (1992)*, discussed in Section 7611, Commentary. See also *In re Guardianship of Donaldson, 178 Cal. App.3d 477, 486, 223 Cal.Rptr. 707 (1986)* (at father's death, mother entitled to sole custody of children whose custody had been granted to father in marital dissolution order).

Research References

Forms

California Transactions Forms--Family Law § 5:2, Overview.

Treatises and Practice Aids

Witkin, California Summary 10th Parent and Child § 87, Private Adoptions.

Witkin, California Summary 10th Parent and Child § 195, Statutory Framework.

Witkin, California Summary 10th Parent and Child § 215, Current Statute: No Preference.

§ 3011. Best interest of child; considerations

In making a determination of the best interest of the child in a proceeding described in Section 3021, the court shall, among any other factors it finds relevant, consider all of the following:

(a) The health, safety, and welfare of the child.

(b) Any history of abuse by one parent or any other person seeking custody against any of the following:

(1) Any child to whom he or she is related by blood or affinity or with whom he or she has had a caretaking relationship, no matter how temporary.

(2) The other parent.

(3) A parent, current spouse, or cohabitant, of the parent or person seeking custody, or a person with whom the parent or person seeking custody has a dating or engagement relationship.

As a prerequisite to considering allegations of abuse, the court may require substantial independent corroboration, including, but not limited to, written reports by law enforcement agencies, child protective services or other social welfare agencies, courts, medical facilities, or other public agencies or private nonprofit organizations providing services to victims of sexual assault or domestic violence. As used in this subdivision, "abuse against a child" means "child abuse" as defined in Section 11165.6 of the Penal Code and abuse against any of the other persons described in paragraph (2) or (3) means "abuse" as defined in Section 6203 of this code.

(c) The nature and amount of contact with both parents, except as provided in Section 3046.

(d) The habitual or continual illegal use of controlled substances, the habitual or continual abuse of alcohol, or the habitual or continual abuse of prescribed controlled substances by either parent. Before considering these allegations, the court may first require independent corroboration, including, but not limited to, written reports from law enforcement agencies, courts, probation departments, social welfare agencies, medical facilities, rehabilitation facilities, or other public agencies or nonprofit organizations providing drug and alcohol abuse services. As used in this subdivision, "controlled substances" has the same meaning as defined in the California Uniform Controlled Substances Act, Division 10 (commencing with Section 11000) of the Health and Safety Code.

(e)(1) Where allegations about a parent pursuant to subdivision (b) or (d) have been brought to the attention of the court in the current proceeding, and the court makes an order for sole or joint custody to that parent, the court shall state its reasons in writing or on the record. In these circumstances, the court shall ensure that any order regarding custody or visitation is specific as to time, day, place, and manner of transfer of the child as set forth in subdivision (b) of Section 6323.

(2) The provisions of this subdivision shall not apply if the parties stipulate in writing or on the record regarding custody or visitation. *(Added by Stats.1993, c. 219 (A.B.1500), § 115.5. Amended by Stats.1996, c. 835 (A.B.2474), § 1; Stats.1996, c. 836 (S.B.384), § 1.5; Stats.1997, c. 849 (A.B. 200), § 2; Stats.1999, c. 980 (A.B.1671), § 4; Stats.2012, c. 258 (A.B.2365), § 1.)*

Law Revision Commission Comments

Enactment [Revised Comment]

Section 3011 continues former Civil Code Section 4608 without substantive change. The reference to "a proceeding described in Section 3021" has been substituted for the former reference to a "proceeding under this title," which referred to the custody title of the former Family Law Act (former Title 4 (commencing with former Civil Code Section 4600) of Part 5 of Division 4 of the Civil Code). See Section 3021 (application of custody provisions) & Comment.

For provisions adopting this section by reference, see Sections 3020 (legislative findings and declarations), 3040 (order of preference in ordering custody), 3080 (presumption for joint custody where parents agree to joint custody), 3081 (joint custody order absent agreement of parents).

For provisions in this division referring to the best interest of the child, see Sections 3031 (custody order not to be inconsistent with civil or criminal protective orders), 3041 (additional requirements of custody award to nonparent), 3082 (statement by court of reasons for grant or denial of joint custody request), 3087 (modification or termination of joint custody order), 3100 (visitation rights of a parent), 3101 (visitation rights of stepparent), 3102 (visitation rights of grandparent and other relatives where parent of unmarried minor child is deceased), 3103 (visitation rights of grandparent in proceeding described in Section 3021), 3114 (recommendation for appointment of counsel for minor child), 3120 (independent action for exclusive custody), 3133 (temporary custody order upon request of district attorney), 3150 (appointment of private counsel to represent child in custody or visitation proceeding), 3161 (purpose of mediation), 3162 (uniform standards of practice for mediation), 3184 (recommendations that counsel be appointed for minor child), 3190 (order requiring counseling), 3191 (purpose of counseling), 3403 (jurisdictional requirements). [23 Cal.L.Rev.Comm. Reports 1 (1993)].

Commentary

In granting a father's motion to modify a final child custody order, *Christina L. v. Chauncey B., 229 Cal.App.4th 731, 177 Cal.Rptr.3d 178 (2014)*, held that the trial court erred in not considering an existing domestic violence restraining order against the father in determining the child's best interest under this section; in not applying the section 3044 rebuttable presumption that the father should not have custody because of his history of domestic violence within the past five years; and in not requiring that the father show changed circumstances justifying modification of the final custody order.

Wainwright v. Superior Court, 84 Cal.App.4th 262, 100 Cal.Rptr.2d 749 (2000), holds that subsection (d) does not authorize the family court to order drug testing of parents in custody proceedings. *Wainwright* reasons that the independent corroboration requirement is intended to protect parents from drug abuse allegations, not to enable the court to subject them to drug testing.

For discussion of custody modification and "move-away" requests, see Section 3022, Commentary.

In re Marriage of Williams, 88 Cal.App.4th 808, 105 Cal.Rptr.2d 923 (2001), holds that family court may enter an order that separates siblings only when compelling circumstances require separation in order to serve the children's best interests. With *Williams*, compare *J.M. v. G.H., 228 Cal.App.4th 925, 175 Cal.Rptr.3d 371 (2014)*, which declined to apply the compelling circumstances requirement to the separation of stepsiblings.

Research References

Forms

California Practice Guide: Rutter Family Law Forms Form 5:5, Ex Parte Application and Request for Order Re Child Custody, Visitation and Property Control.
California Practice Guide: Rutter Family Law Forms Form 1:32, Glossary Of Common Family Law Terms, Phrases and Concepts (Enclosure to Form 1:31).
California Practice Guide: Rutter Family Law Forms Form 7:19.2, Request for Order Re Move-Away Request.
California Transactions Forms--Family Law § 3:2, Child Custody.
California Transactions Forms--Family Law § 3:8, No Statutory Custody Preferences.
California Transactions Forms--Family Law § 5:2, Overview.
California Transactions Forms--Family Law § 2:70, Deciding Custody.
California Transactions Forms--Family Law § 2:76, Drug and Alcohol Use.
California Transactions Forms--Family Law § 3:11, Permanent Custody.
California Transactions Forms--Family Law § 3:16, Identifying Areas Of Parental Decision Making and Participation.
West's California Code Forms, Family § 3120, Comment Overview--Action for Exclusive Custody.
West's California Judicial Council Forms GC-212, Confidential Guardian Screening Form.

Treatises and Practice Aids

Witkin, California Summary 10th Husband and Wife § 62, Evidence Of Misconduct is Ordinarily Inadmissible.
Witkin, California Summary 10th Parent and Child § 196, Best Interest Of Child.
Witkin, California Summary 10th Parent and Child § 197, Discretion Of Court.
Witkin, California Summary 10th Parent and Child § 198, Domestic Violence.
Witkin, California Summary 10th Parent and Child § 199, Substance Abuse.
Witkin, California Summary 10th Parent and Child § 210, Other Factors.
Witkin, California Summary 10th Parent and Child § 217, Statutory Order Of Preference.
Witkin, California Summary 10th Parent and Child § 222, Statutory Authorization.
Witkin, California Summary 10th Parent and Child § 255, Stipulation for Temporary Custody.
Witkin, California Summary 10th Parent and Child § 277, Investigation Of Child Sexual Abuse Allegations.
Witkin, California Summary 10th Parent and Child § 278, in General.

§ 3012. Use of telepresence in child custody proceedings

(a) If a party's deportation or detention by the United States Immigration and Customs Enforcement of the Department of Homeland Security will have a material effect on his or her ability, or anticipated ability, to appear in person at a child custody proceeding, the court shall, upon motion of the party, allow the party to present testimony and evidence and participate in mandatory child custody mediation by electronic means, including, but not limited to, telephone, video teleconferencing, or other electronic means that provide remote access to the hearing, to the extent that this technology is reasonably available to the court and protects the due process rights of all parties.

(b) This section does not authorize the use of electronic recording for the purpose of taking the official record of these proceedings. *(Added by Stats.2015, c. 69 (A.B.365), § 1, eff. Jan. 1, 2016.)*

Research References

Treatises and Practice Aids

Witkin, California Summary 10th Parent and Child § 183, Notice and Hearing.

Part 2

RIGHT TO CUSTODY OF MINOR CHILD

CHAPTER 1. GENERAL PROVISIONS

§ 3020. Legislative findings and declarations; health, safety, and welfare of children; continuing contact with parents

(a) The Legislature finds and declares that it is the public policy of this state to assure that the health, safety, and welfare of children shall be the court's primary concern in determining the best interest of children when making any orders regarding the physical or legal custody or visitation of children. The Legislature further finds and declares that the perpetration of child abuse or domestic violence in a household where a child resides is detrimental to the child.

(b) The Legislature finds and declares that it is the public policy of this state to assure that children have frequent and continuing contact with both parents after the parents have separated or dissolved their marriage, or ended their relationship, and to encourage parents to share the rights and responsibilities of child rearing in order to effect this policy, except where the contact would not be in the best interest of the child, as provided in Section 3011.

(c) Where the policies set forth in subdivisions (a) and (b) of this section are in conflict, any court's order regarding physical or legal custody or visitation shall be made in a manner that ensures the health, safety, and welfare of the child and the safety of all family members. *(Stats.1992, c. 162 (A.B.2650), § 10, operative Jan. 1, 1994. Amended by Stats. 1993, c. 219 (A.B.1500), § 116; Stats.1997, c. 849 (A.B.200), § 3; Stats.1999, c. 980 (A.B.1671), § 5.)*

Law Revision Commission Comments

Enactment [Revised Comment]

Section 3020 continues the first paragraph of former Civil Code Section 4600(a) without substantive change. See also Sections 2253 (determining custody in nullity proceeding), 3021 (application of part). [23 Cal.L.Rev.Comm. Reports 1 (1993)].

Commentary

For discussion of custody modification and "move-away" requests, see Section 3022, Commentary.

In a relocation case (see Family Code § 7501 and commentary to that section), *Wilson v. Shea, 87 Cal.App.4th 887, 104 Cal.Rptr.2d 880 (2001)*, invokes the subsection (b) legislative purpose of assuring a child's frequent and continuing contact with both parents to justify § 4057 (b)(5) reduction of the guideline child support amount by an amount intended to cover the noncustodial parent's transportation expenses in visiting the child.

Holding that the trial court abused its discretion in separating two siblings without a careful analysis of (1) the actual impact of one child's disability on the other child and (2) the impact of separation on both children, *In re Marriage of Heath, 122 Cal.App.4th 444, 18 Cal.Rptr.3d 760 (2004)*, discerns, in Welfare and Institutions Code §§ 366.26(c)(1)(E) and 16002.5, which treat the placement of children in foster homes, a state policy that the sibling bond should be preserved whenever possible. However, *J.M. v. G.H., 228 Cal. App.4th 925, 175 Cal.Rptr.3d 371 (2014)*, declined to apply the same standard to the separation of stepsiblings.

Research References

Forms

California Practice Guide: Rutter Family Law Forms Form 5:2, Request for Order Re Child Custody, Child Support, Spousal Support, Attorney Fees, etc.
California Practice Guide: Rutter Family Law Forms Form 5:5, Ex Parte Application and Request for Order Re Child Custody, Visitation and Property Control.
California Practice Guide: Rutter Family Law Forms Form 1:32, Glossary Of Common Family Law Terms, Phrases and Concepts (Enclosure to Form 1:31).
California Transactions Forms--Family Law § 3:2, Child Custody.
California Transactions Forms--Family Law § 3:4, Subject Matter Jurisdiction for Custody Determinations.
California Transactions Forms--Family Law § 3:8, No Statutory Custody Preferences.
California Transactions Forms--Family Law § 5:2, Overview.
California Transactions Forms--Family Law § 5:3, Rights Of Nonparents Generally.
California Transactions Forms--Family Law § 5:9, Use Of Parenting Agreement to Define Rights and Responsibilities Relating to Child on Termination Of Partners' Relationship Where Both Partners Are Biological Parents.
California Transactions Forms--Family Law § 2:70, Deciding Custody.
California Transactions Forms--Family Law § 3:11, Permanent Custody.
California Transactions Forms--Family Law § 4:104, Paternity Acknowledgment.
West's California Code Forms, Family § 3022, Comment Overview--Order for Custody.

West's California Code Forms, Family § 7841 Form 1, Petition for Freedom from Parental Control--Abandonment.
West's California Code Forms, Probate § 1514 Form 1, Order Appointing Guardian Of Minor--Judicial Council Form GC-240.
West's California Judicial Council Forms DV-140, Child Custody and Visitation Order.
West's California Judicial Council Forms FL-341, Child Custody and Visitation (Parenting Time) Order Attachment.
West's California Judicial Council Forms FL-356, Request for Special Immigrant Juvenile Findings--Family Law.
West's California Judicial Council Forms JV-200, Custody Order - Juvenile - Final Judgment.
West's California Judicial Council Forms JV-205, Visitation Order--Juvenile.

Treatises and Practice Aids

Witkin, California Summary 10th Husband and Wife § 373, in General.
Witkin, California Summary 10th Husband and Wife § 383, Temporary Custody and Visitation.
Witkin, California Summary 10th Parent and Child § 59, Visitation Privileges.
Witkin, California Summary 10th Parent and Child § 194, in General.
Witkin, California Summary 10th Parent and Child § 195, Statutory Framework.
Witkin, California Summary 10th Parent and Child § 198, Domestic Violence.
Witkin, California Summary 10th Parent and Child § 211, in General.
Witkin, California Summary 10th Parent and Child § 217, Statutory Order Of Preference.
Witkin, California Summary 10th Parent and Child § 218, Statutory Rule.
Witkin, California Summary 10th Parent and Child § 222, Statutory Authorization.
Witkin, California Summary 10th Parent and Child § 224, Nature Of Right.
Witkin, California Summary 10th Parent and Child § 255, Stipulation for Temporary Custody.
Witkin, California Summary 10th Parent and Child § 278, in General.
Witkin, California Summary 10th Parent and Child § 282, Agreement.
Witkin, California Summary 10th Parent and Child § 320, Statutory Ground.
Witkin, California Summary 10th Parent and Child § 322, Insufficient Showing.
Witkin, California Summary 10th Parent and Child § 363, Applicability Of Family Code Custody Provisions.
Witkin, California Summary 10th Parent and Child § 680, Statutory Procedure is Exclusive.
Witkin, California Summary 10th Wills and Probate § 924, Factors Considered in Appointment.
Witkin, California Summary 10th Wills and Probate § 928, Illustrations.

§ 3021. Application of part

This part applies in any of the following:

(a) A proceeding for dissolution of marriage.

(b) A proceeding for nullity of marriage.

(c) A proceeding for legal separation of the parties.

(d) An action for exclusive custody pursuant to Section 3120.

(e) A proceeding to determine physical or legal custody or for visitation in a proceeding pursuant to the Domestic Violence Prevention Act (Division 10 (commencing with Section 6200)).

In an action under Section 6323, nothing in this subdivision shall be construed to authorize physical or legal custody, or visitation rights, to be granted to any party to a Domestic Violence Prevention Act proceeding who has not established a parent and child relationship pursuant to paragraph (2) of subdivision (a) of Section 6323.

(f) A proceeding to determine physical or legal custody or visitation in an action pursuant to the Uniform Parentage Act (Part 3 (commencing with Section 7600) of Division 12).

(g) A proceeding to determine physical or legal custody or visitation in an action brought by the district attorney pursuant to Section 17404. *(Added by Stats.1993, c. 219 (A.B.1500), § 116.11. Amended by Stats.1996, c. 1075 (S.B. 1444), § 9; Stats.1997, c. 396 (S.B.564), § 1; Stats.1999, c. 980 (A.B.1671), § 6; Stats.2000, c. 135 (A.B.2539), § 58.)*

Law Revision Commission Comments

Enactment [Revised Comment]

Section 3021 is a new provision that generalizes the parts of former Civil Code Sections 4351.5, 4600.1, 4600.5, 4602, 4606, 4608.1, 4609, and 4611 stating the scope of application of the former sections. The former provisions applied to proceedings under the former Family Law Act (former Part 5 (commencing with former Section 4000) of Division 4 of the Civil Code), which included proceedings for dissolution of marriage, nullity of marriage, and legal separation of the parties, and actions for exclusive custody.

This section expands the application of this part to proceedings in which custody or visitation is determined in an action pursuant to the Domestic Violence Prevention Act or the Uniform Parentage Act. Application of this part to these acts provides a complete set of rules where custody or visitation is determined in proceedings pursuant to these acts, as well as providing for related matters such as investigations, appointment of counsel to represent the child, mediation, and counseling.

See also Prob. Code § 1514 (Fam. Code §§ 3040–3043 applicable in proceeding to establish guardianship of person). For provisions excluding application of this part, see Section 7807 (specific provisions not applicable in proceeding to terminate parental rights pursuant to Uniform Parentage Act); Welf. & Inst. Code § 366.26 (specific provisions not applicable to dependency proceedings). [23 Cal.L.Rev.Comm. Reports 1 (1993)].

Commentary

Even though a dissolution judgment has been entered, a stipulation of the parties signed during dissolution proceedings allowing mutual discovery of psychological evidence "through the pendency of this action" is enforceable throughout a child's minority because family court has continuing jurisdiction over child custody matters. *In re Marriage of Kreiss, 122 Cal.App.4th 1082, 19 Cal.Rptr.3d 260 (2004).*

Research References

Forms

California Practice Guide: Rutter Family Law Forms Form 5:5, Ex Parte Application and Request for Order Re Child Custody, Visitation and Property Control.
California Practice Guide: Rutter Family Law Forms Form 7:17, Notice Of Motion and Declaration for Joinder (Grandparent Visitation Claim).
California Practice Guide: Rutter Family Law Forms Form 7:18, Complaint for Joinder (Grandparent Visitation Claim).

California Practice Guide: Rutter Family Law Forms Form 7:19, Memorandum in Support Of Motion and Declaration for Joinder (Grandparent Visitation Claim).
California Transactions Forms--Family Law § 3:4, Subject Matter Jurisdiction for Custody Determinations.
California Transactions Forms--Family Law § 5:2, Overview.

Treatises and Practice Aids

Witkin, California Summary 10th Husband and Wife § 380, Support Person for Victim.
Witkin, California Summary 10th Parent and Child § 196, Best Interest Of Child.
Witkin, California Summary 10th Parent and Child § 363, Applicability Of Family Code Custody Provisions.
Witkin, California Summary 10th Parent and Child § 371, Modification Of Order.

§ 3022. Order for custody

The court may, during the pendency of a proceeding or at any time thereafter, make an order for the custody of a child during minority that seems necessary or proper. *(Formerly § 3021, enacted by Stats.1992, c. 162 (A.B.2650), § 10, operative Jan. 1, 1994. Renumbered § 3022 and amended by Stats.1993, c. 219 (A.B.1500), § 116.12.)*

Law Revision Commission Comments

Enactment [Revised Comment]

Section 3022 continues without substantive change the first sentence of the second paragraph of former Civil Code Section 4600(a). The former reference to "any proceeding where there is at issue the custody of a minor child" has been omitted. See Section 3021 (application of part). As to the court's jurisdiction, see Sections 3400–3425 (Uniform Child Custody Jurisdiction Act). See also Code Civ. Proc. § 917.7 (order not automatically stayed by appeal). [23 Cal.L.Rev.Comm. Reports 1 (1993)].

Commentary

Note that 2013 amendments to Code of Civil Procedure section 583.161 expanded the definition of petitions and orders that are not subject to mandatory dismissal, including petitions and orders under this section.

In re Marriage of Olson, 238 Cal.App.4th 1458, 190 Cal.Rptr.3d 715 (2015), holds that a parent who defaulted in a dissolution proceeding has standing to seek modification of child custody without seeking relief from the default.

Relying on this section and § 2010(b), *In re Marriage of Jensen, 114 Cal.App.4th 587, 7 Cal.Rptr.3d 701 (2003), review denied*, held that a court lacks jurisdiction to enforce the terms of a marital settlement agreement, incorporated into a judgment of dissolution, that required an *adult* disabled child living in Thailand to visit his father in California and required the child's mother to encourage and implement visitation and give the father written updates on the child's activities.

Even though a dissolution judgment has been entered, a stipulation of the parties signed during dissolution proceedings allowing mutual discovery of psychological evidence "through the pendency of this action" is enforceable throughout a child's minority because family court has continuing jurisdiction over child custody matters. *In re Marriage of Kreiss, 122 Cal.App.4th 1082, 19 Cal.Rptr.3d 260 (2004)*.

For custody modification, see generally *In re Marriage of Carney, 24 Cal.3d 725, 157 Cal.Rptr. 383 (1979)* (court may modify custody only upon a showing of "changed circumstances"); *Montenegro v. Diaz, 26 Cal.4th 249, 27 P.3d 289, 109 Cal.Rptr.2d 575 (2001)* (a custody order stipulated by the parties is a final judicial determination of custody for purposes of the "changed circumstances" rule only if there is clear affirmative indication that the parties intended such result; otherwise the "best interests" test applies in a modification proceeding); *In re Marriage of Lewin, 186 Cal.App.3d 1482, 1488, 231 Cal.Rptr. 433 (1986)* (where mother's custody of child was based solely on pendente lite stipulation, no need to show "changed circumstances" at custody hearing); *In re Marriage of Rose and Richardson, 102 Cal.App.4th 941, 126 Cal.Rptr.2d 45 (2002)* (initial custody order awarding mother custody pursuant to parents' stipulation did not constitute final judicial custody determination within the meaning of *Montenegro v. Diaz*; thus trial court should not have applied the "changed circumstances" test in a "move away" case, but should instead have made a de novo "best interests" child custody determination). *Ragghanti v. Reyes, 123 Cal.App.4th 989, 20 Cal. Rptr.3d 522 (2004)*, approved, in a move-away case involving a 5–year-old temporary custody order, the trial court's application of the "best interests," rather than the "changed circumstances" standard.

Keith R. v. Superior Court, 174 Cal.App.4th 1047, 96 Cal.Rptr.3d 298 (2009), holds that a domestic violence order issued in a dissolution proceeding, which granted the abused parent sole legal and physical custody of a child, does not constitute a final custody determination for purposes of *Montenegro*. Thus the trial court erred in applying the "changed circumstances" rather than the "best interest" standard to a move-away request in a child custody case.

In granting a father's motion to modify a final child custody order, *Christina L. v. Chauncey B., 229 Cal.App.4th 731, 177 Cal.Rptr.3d 178 (2014)*, held that the trial court erred in not requiring that the father show *changed circumstances* justifying modification of a final custody order; in not considering an existing domestic violence restraining order against the father in determining the child's best interests under section 3011; and in not applying the section 3044 rebuttable presumption that the father should not have custody because of his history of domestic violence within the past five years.

In re Marriage of Loyd, 106 Cal.App.4th 754, 131 Cal.Rptr.2d 80 (2003), held that a trial court abused its discretion in modifying a child custody order to change custody to the noncustodial mother on the ground that she would care for the children at home. *Loyd* reasons that custody may not be based on the assumption that a nonworking parent provides better care, relying on *Burchard v. Garay, 42 Cal.3d 531, 229 Cal.Rptr. 800, 724 P.2d 486 (1986)*, where the California Supreme Court reversed a trial court's grant of custody to one parent on the ground that he was wealthier, that is, better able to provide for the child, and had remarried so that the child could be cared for in his home by his new wife, while the mother in contrast was gainfully employed. In *Loyd,* the trial court arguably also erred in finding "changed circumstances" within the meaning of the rule requiring changed circumstances for custody modification. To warrant a change in custody, the change in circumstances must materially undermine the efficacy of the existing custodial arrangement. The mother's recovery from drug and alcohol abuse, identified by the trial court as the required "changed circumstance," was not a factor affecting the well-being of the children with respect to their existing custodial placement in their father's home.

Anne H. v. Michael B., 1 Cal.App.5th 488, 204 Cal.Rptr.3d 495 (2016), held that a judge's statement, in a final custody order, that a mother's subsequent move would constitute a change of circumstances sufficient to allow reconsideration of the order, was dictum that was not binding on subsequent judges, because the identification of future events that might constitute a change of circumstances was not an issue before the court nor was it necessary to the court's ruling when it entered its final custody order.

In re Marriage of Birnbaum, 211 Cal.App.3rd 1508, 260 Cal.Rptr.2d 210 (1989), purported to hold that the party who moves for modification of a joint custody award need not show a change of circumstances justifying the requested modification, as would the movant in an ordinary motion to change custody, reasoning that alteration of the details of a joint custody arrangement is not a change of custody. However, the ostensible holding was dictum because *Birnbaum* did involve a substantial change of circumstances: the mother changed her residence, necessitating a change of schools for the children or alteration of the parenting plan. However, *Niko v. Forman, 144 Cal.App.4th 344, 50 Cal.Rptr.3d 398 (2006), review denied Feb. 7, 2007*, applied the dictum of *Birnbaum* to a case in which there were no changed circumstances, other than the decision of a California mother to relocate to Colorado. *Niko* held that changed circumstances were not required because the trial court continued joint custody with a modified parenting plan and thus did not "change" custody. The California Supreme Court initially granted review to *In re Marriage of Congdon, 977 P.2d 693, 85 Cal.Rptr.2d 696 (1999),* thereby depublishing the opinion of the Court of Appeal, 82 Cal.Rptr.2d 686 (1999), which rejected the dictum of *Birnbaum* and held that a parent who seeks to modify a joint physical custody order must show a change of circumstances justifying the requested modification. *Congdon* reasoned that the change of circumstances threshold is necessary to avoid unwarranted and harassing relitigation and to provide stability in the lives of the children and the nonmovant parent. Ultimately, the Supreme Court dismissed the petition for review in *Congdon* after the parties' voluntary settlement, and remanded the case to the court of appeal.

Following the dictum of *Birnbaum*, *Enrique M. v. Angelina V., 121 Cal.App.4th 1371, 18 Cal.Rptr.3d 306 (2004)*, holds that the standard of proof required of a joint physical custodian who wishes to change joint custodial parenting time is the best interests of the child, not changed circumstances.

When a noncustodial parent merely seeks to alter or increase visitation, his request is decided according to the "best interest of the child" standard. *In re Marriage of Lucio, 161 Cal.App.4th 1068, 74 Cal.Rptr.3d 803 (2008)*.

For discussion of the custodial parent's right to change the child's residence, see Section 7501, Commentary.

When a noncustodial parent dies after the entry of a divorce decree, the court has limited power to modify, impose conditions, or order third-party visitation. *In re Marriage of Jenkens, 116 Cal.App.3d 767, 172 Cal.Rptr. 331 (1981), hearing denied 5/6/81* (the surviving custodial parent should be no more subject to restriction than she would if the marriage had ended in the other parent's death). See also *In re Marriage of Williams, 101 Cal.App.3d 507, 161 Cal.Rptr. 808 (1980)* (abatement of dissolution proceeding because of death of wife deprived divorce court of jurisdiction to award custody and visitation to wife's mother and brother although they may still seek visitation in an independent Section 3102 proceeding).

Research References

Forms

California Practice Guide: Rutter Family Law Forms Form 5:2, Request for Order Re Child Custody, Child Support, Spousal Support, Attorney Fees, etc.
California Practice Guide: Rutter Family Law Forms Form 5:5, Ex Parte Application and Request for Order Re Child Custody, Visitation and Property Control.
California Practice Guide: Rutter Family Law Forms Form 17:5, Request for Order Re Modification Of Child Custody, Visitation and Child Support.
California Transactions Forms--Family Law § 3:2, Child Custody.
California Transactions Forms--Family Law § 2:70, Deciding Custody.
California Transactions Forms--Family Law § 3:11, Permanent Custody.
West's California Code Forms, Family § 3022, Comment Overview--Order for Custody.
West's California Code Forms, Family § 7841 Form 1, Petition for Freedom from Parental Control--Abandonment.
West's California Judicial Council Forms DV-140, Child Custody and Visitation Order.
West's California Judicial Council Forms FL-341, Child Custody and Visitation (Parenting Time) Order Attachment.

Treatises and Practice Aids

Witkin, California Summary 10th Husband and Wife § 112, Contents Of Judgment.
Witkin, California Summary 10th Parent and Child § 232, Statutory Authorization.
Witkin, California Summary 10th Parent and Child § 233, in General.
Witkin, California Summary 10th Parent and Child § 249, Power to Modify.
Witkin, California Summary 10th Parent and Child § 285, in General.
Witkin, California Summary 10th Parent and Child § 359, Dissolution Proceedings.
Witkin, California Summary 10th Parent and Child § 363, Applicability Of Family Code Custody Provisions.
Witkin, California Summary 10th Parent and Child § 259A, (New) Military Deployment.

§ 3022.3. Statement of decision

Upon the trial of a question of fact in a proceeding to determine the custody of a minor child, the court shall, upon the request of either party, issue a statement of the decision explaining the factual and legal basis for its decision pursuant to Section 632 of the Code of Civil Procedure. *(Added by Stats.2006, c. 496 (A.B.402), § 3.)*

Research References

Treatises and Practice Aids

Witkin, California Summary 10th Parent and Child § 285, in General.

§ 3022.5. Motion by parent for reconsideration of child custody order after conviction of spouse for false accusation of child abuse against parent

A motion by a parent for reconsideration of an existing child custody order shall be granted if the motion is based on the fact that the other parent was convicted of a crime in connection with falsely accusing the moving parent of child abuse. *(Added by Stats.1995, c. 406 (S.B.558), § 1.)*

Research References

Forms

West's California Code Forms, Family § 3022, Comment Overview--Order for Custody.

Treatises and Practice Aids

Witkin, California Summary 10th Parent and Child § 285, in General.

§ 3023. Sole contested issue or order for separate trial on issue; preference for trial date

(a) If custody of a minor child is the sole contested issue, the case shall be given preference over other civil cases, except matters to which special precedence may be given by law, for assigning a trial date and shall be given an early hearing.

(b) If there is more than one contested issue and one of the issues is the custody of a minor child, the court, as to the issue of custody, shall order a separate trial. The separate trial shall be given preference over other civil cases, except matters to which special precedence may be given by law, for assigning a trial date. *(Stats.1992, c. 162 (A.B.2650), § 10, operative Jan. 1, 1994. Amended by Stats.1993, c. 219 (A.B.1500), § 116.14.)*

Law Revision Commission Comments

Enactment [Revised Comment]

Section 3023 continues former Civil Code Section 4600.6 without substantive change. The former reference to a "contested issue" of custody has been omitted as surplus. See Section 3021 (application of part).

See also Sections 3041 (excluding public from hearing on award of custody to nonparent), 4003 (separate trial on issue of child support). [23 Cal.L.Rev.Comm. Reports 1 (1993)].

Commentary

See generally *Miller v. Superior Court, 221 Cal.App.3d 1200, 270 Cal.Rptr. 766 (1990)* (statutory trial preferences). For discussion of bifurcated proceedings, see Commentary to Sections 2337 and 2550.

Research References

Treatises and Practice Aids

Witkin, California Summary 10th Husband and Wife § 105, Statutory Rule.

Witkin, California Summary 10th Parent and Child § 284, Trial.

Witkin, California Summary 10th Parent and Child § 383, in General.

§ 3024. Notice to other parent of change of residence of child

In making an order for custody, if the court does not consider it inappropriate, the court may specify that a parent shall notify the other parent if the parent plans to change the residence of the child for more than 30 days, unless there is prior written agreement to the removal. The notice shall be given before the contemplated move, by mail, return receipt requested, postage prepaid, to the last known address of the parent to be notified. A copy of the notice shall also be sent to that parent's counsel of record. To the extent feasible, the notice shall be provided within a minimum of 45 days before the proposed change of residence so as to allow time for mediation of a new agreement concerning custody. This section does not affect orders made before January 1, 1989. *(Stats.1992, c. 162 (A.B.2650), § 10, operative Jan. 1, 1994.)*

Law Revision Commission Comments

Enactment [Revised Comment]

Section 3024 continues former Civil Code Section 4600.5(m) without substantive change. Although former Civil Code Section 4600.5 related to joint custody, subdivision (m) of that section was not by its terms limited to a joint custody order. Accordingly, Section 3024 applies to any custody order, not only a joint custody order. See also Section 3131 (action by district attorney where child taken or detained in violation of custody order). [23 Cal.L.Rev. Comm. Reports 1 (1993)].

Commentary

For discussion of custody modification and "move-away" requests, see Section 3022, Commentary.

In re Maribel T., 96 Cal.App.4th 82, 116 Cal.Rptr.2d 631 (2002), holds that a juvenile court order requiring a father with sole custody of a child to notify the child's mother before removing the child from the state is a proper method of protecting the mother's interest in continued monitored visitation. However, *Maribel T.* disapproved the juvenile court order to the extent that it prohibited the father from removing the daughter from the state without the written consent of the mother or order of the court.

Research References

Forms

California Transactions Forms--Family Law § 2:74, Move-Away Cases.

California Transactions Forms--Family Law § 2:88, Marital Settlement Agreement.

California Transactions Forms--Family Law § 3:16, Identifying Areas Of Parental Decision Making and Participation.

West's California Judicial Council Forms FL-341(D), Additional Provisions--Physical Custody Attachment.

Treatises and Practice Aids

Witkin, California Summary 10th Parent and Child § 223, Procedure.

§ 3025. Parental access to records

Notwithstanding any other provision of law, access to records and information pertaining to a minor child, including, but not limited to, medical, dental, and school records, shall not be denied to a parent because that parent is not the child's custodial parent. *(Stats.1992, c. 162 (A.B.2650), § 10, operative Jan. 1, 1994.)*

Law Revision Commission Comments

Enactment [Revised Comment]

Section 3025 continues former Civil Code Section 4600.5(*l*) without substantive change. Although former Civil Code Section 4600.5 related to joint custody, subdivision (*l*) of that section was not by its terms limited to a joint custody order. Accordingly, Section 3025 applies whether or not custody is pursuant to a joint custody order. [23 Cal.L.Rev.Comm. Reports 1 (1993)].

Commentary

This section merely grants the noncustodial parent rights that he or she would have as a custodial parent. It does not create any further rights of access and hence does not override denial of access to medical records based on the psychotherapist-patient relationship. *In re Daniel C. H., 220 Cal.App.3d 814, 827, 269 Cal.Rptr. 624 (1990), review denied 8/1/90.*

Research References

Forms

California Transactions Forms--Family Law § 2:75, Access to Records.

California Transactions Forms--Family Law § 2:88, Marital Settlement Agreement.

California Transactions Forms--Family Law § 3:16, Identifying Areas Of Parental Decision Making and Participation.

California Transactions Forms--Family Law § 5:21, Access to Information.

California Transactions Forms--Family Law § 5:31, Parenting Agreement Providing for Joint Legal and Sole Physical Custody Where Both Partners Are Biological Parents Of Child.

California Transactions Forms--Family Law § 5:33, Parenting Agreement Providing for Joint Legal and Sole Physical Custody Where Neither or Only One Partner is Biological Parent Of Child.

West's California Code Forms, Family § 2338 Form 8, Marital Agreement.

West's California Code Forms, Family § 3081 Form 2, Clauses Regarding Custody and Visitation.

West's California Judicial Council Forms FL-341, Child Custody and Visitation (Parenting Time) Order Attachment.

West's California Judicial Council Forms FL-341(E), Joint Legal Custody Attachment.

Treatises and Practice Aids

Witkin, California Summary 10th Parent and Child § 194, in General.

§ 3025.5. Psychological evaluations of children; confidentiality; exceptions; confidential information contained in child custody evaluation reports

(a) In a proceeding involving child custody or visitation rights, if a report containing psychological evaluations of a child or recommendations regarding custody of, or visitation with, a child is submitted to the court, including, but not limited to, a report created pursuant to Chapter 6 (commencing with Section 3110) of this part and a recommendation made to the court pursuant to Section 3183, that information shall be contained in a document that shall be placed in the confidential portion of the court file of the proceeding, and may not be disclosed, except to the following persons:

(1) A party to the proceeding and his or her attorney.

(2) A federal or state law enforcement officer, the licensing entity of a child custody evaluator, a judicial officer, court employee, or family court facilitator of the superior court of the county in which the action was filed, or an employee or agent of that facilitator, acting within the scope of his or her duties.

(3) Counsel appointed for the child pursuant to Section 3150.

(4) Any other person upon order of the court for good cause.

(b) Confidential information contained in a report prepared pursuant to Section 3111 that is disclosed to the licensing entity of a child custody evaluator pursuant to subdivision (a) shall remain confidential and shall only be used for purposes of investigating allegations of unprofessional conduct by the child custody evaluator, or in a criminal, civil, or administrative proceeding involving the child custody evaluator. All confidential information, including, but not limited to, the identity of any minors, shall retain their confidential nature in any criminal, civil, or administrative proceeding resulting from the investigation of unprofessional conduct and shall be sealed at the conclusion of the proceeding and shall not subsequently be released. Names that are confidential shall be listed in attachments separate from the general pleadings. If the confidential information does not result in a criminal, civil, or administrative proceeding, it shall be sealed after the licensing entity decides that no further action will be taken in the matter of suspected licensing violations. *(Added by Stats.2004, c. 102 (S.B.1284), § 1. Amended by Stats.2012, c. 470 (A.B.1529), § 17; Stats. 2014, c. 283 (A.B.1843), § 2, eff. Jan. 1, 2015.)*

Law Revision Commission Comments

2012 Amendment

Subdivision (b) of Section 3025.5 is amended to reflect enactment of the Lockyer–Isenberg Trial Court Funding Act, 1997 Cal. Stat. ch. 850 (see generally Gov't Code §§ 77000–77655). [39 Cal.L.Rev. Comm. Reports 157 (2009)].

Research References

Forms

West's California Judicial Council Forms FL-329-INFO, Child Custody Evaluation Information Sheet.

Treatises and Practice Aids

Witkin, California Summary 10th Parent and Child § 276, Report.

Witkin, California Summary 10th Parent and Child § 284, Trial.

§ 3026. Family reunification services

Family reunification services shall not be ordered as a part of a child custody or visitation rights proceeding. Nothing in this section affects the applicability of Section 16507 of the Welfare and Institutions Code. *(Stats.1992, c. 162 (A.B. 2650), § 10, operative Jan. 1, 1994. Amended by Stats.1993, c. 219 (A.B.1500), § 116.16.)*

Law Revision Commission Comments

Enactment [Revised Comment]

Section 3026 restates former Civil Code Section 4609 without substantive change. The reference to a custody or visitation rights proceeding "brought under this part," meaning the former Family Law Act (former Part 5 (commencing with former Section 4000) of Division 4 of the Civil Code), has been omitted as unnecessary. See Section 3021 (application of part). [23 Cal.L.Rev.Comm. Reports 1 (1993)].

Research References

Treatises and Practice Aids

Witkin, California Summary 10th Parent and Child § 194, in General.

§ 3027. Allegations of child abuse or child sexual abuse

(a) If allegations of child abuse, including child sexual abuse, are made during a child custody proceeding and the court has concerns regarding the child's safety, the court may take any reasonable, temporary steps as the court, in its discretion, deems appropriate under the circumstances to protect the child's safety until an investigation can be completed. Nothing in this section shall affect the applicability of Section 16504 or 16506 of the Welfare and Institutions Code.

(b) If allegations of child abuse, including child sexual abuse, are made during a child custody proceeding, the court may request that the local child welfare services agency conduct an investigation of the allegations pursuant to Section 328 of the Welfare and Institutions Code. Upon completion of the investigation, the agency shall report its findings to the court. *(Added by Stats.2000, c. 926 (S.B.1716), § 3. Amended by Stats.2010, c. 352 (A.B.939), § 12.)*

Research References

Treatises and Practice Aids

Witkin, California Summary 10th Parent and Child § 283, Sexual Abuse Allegation.

Witkin, California Summary 10th Parent and Child § 561, Investigation by Social Worker.

§ 3027.1. False accusations of child abuse or neglect during child custody proceedings; knowledge; penalties

(a) If a court determines, based on the investigation described in Section 3027 or other evidence presented to it, that an accusation of child abuse or neglect made during a child custody proceeding is false and the person making the accusation knew it to be false at the time the accusation was made, the court may impose reasonable money sanctions, not to exceed all costs incurred by the party accused as a direct result of defending the accusation, and reasonable attorney's fees incurred in recovering the sanctions, against the person making the accusation. For the purposes of this section, "person" includes a witness, a party, or a party's attorney.

(b) On motion by any person requesting sanctions under this section, the court shall issue its order to show cause why the requested sanctions should not be imposed. The order to show cause shall be served on the person against whom the sanctions are sought and a hearing thereon shall be scheduled by the court to be conducted at least 15 days after the order is served.

(c) The remedy provided by this section is in addition to any other remedy provided by law. *(Formerly § 3027, enacted by Stats.1992, c. 162 (A.B.2650), § 10, operative Jan. 1, 1994. Amended by Stats.1993, c. 219 (A.B.1500), § 116.17; Stats.1994, c. 688 (A.B.2845), § 1. Renumbered § 3027.1 and amended by Stats.2000, c. 926 (S.B.1716), § 2.)*

Law Revision Commission Comments

Enactment [Revised Comment]

Section 3027 [Renumbered as § 3027.1] continues former Civil Code Section 4611 without substantive change. The former reference to a "proceeding under this title," meaning the custody title of the former Family Law Act (former Title 4 (commencing with former Civil Code Section 4600) of Part 5 of Division 4 of the Civil Code), has been omitted as unnecessary. See Section 3021 (application of part). [23 Cal.L.Rev.Comm. Reports 1 (1993)].

Commentary

In re Marriage of Dupre, 127 Cal.App.4th 1517, 26 Cal.Rptr.3d 328 (2005), review denied, holds that the issue of whether allegations of child abuse made during a child custody proceeding were false need not be determined in the custody proceeding itself; instead the issue of falsity can be determined in an independent action.

A party filing a motion for sanctions under this section must file the motion 60 days after service of a judgment or order exonerating the party from the false allegations, or 180 days from the entry of such judgment or order, whichever is earliest. *Robert J. v. Catherine D., 171 Cal.App.4th 1500, 91 Cal.Rptr.3d 6 (2009).*

Research References

Forms

California Practice Guide: Rutter Family Law Forms Form 7:10, Request for Order Re Sanctions for False Child Abuse Allegations.

West's California Code Forms, Civil § 47 Form 2, Affirmative Defense to Defamation--Official Proceeding Privilege.

Treatises and Practice Aids

Witkin, California Summary 10th Parent and Child § 283, Sexual Abuse Allegation.

§ 3027.5. Sexual abuse of child; report or treatment; limitations on custody or visitation

(a) No parent shall be placed on supervised visitation, or be denied custody of or visitation with his or her child, and no custody or visitation rights shall be limited, solely because the parent (1) lawfully reported suspected sexual abuse of the child, (2) otherwise acted lawfully, based on a reasonable belief, to determine if his or her child was the victim of sexual abuse, or (3) sought treatment for the child from a licensed mental health professional for suspected sexual abuse.

(b) The court may order supervised visitation or limit a parent's custody or visitation if the court finds substantial evidence that the parent, with the intent to interfere with the other parent's lawful contact with the child, made a report of child sexual abuse, during a child custody proceeding or at any other time, that he or she knew was false at the time it was made. Any limitation of custody or visitation, including an order for supervised visitation, pursuant to this subdivision, or any statute regarding the making of a false child abuse report, shall be imposed only after the court has determined that the limitation is necessary to protect the health, safety, and welfare of the child, and the court has considered the state's policy of assuring that children have frequent and continuing contact with both parents as declared in subdivision (b) of Section 3020. *(Added by Stats. 1999, c. 985 (S.B.792), § 1.)*

Research References

Treatises and Practice Aids

Witkin, California Summary 10th Parent and Child § 283, Sexual Abuse Allegation.

§ 3028. Compensation; failure to assume caretaker responsibility; thwarting of other parent's visitation or custody rights; attorney's fees

(a) The court may order financial compensation for periods when a parent fails to assume the caretaker responsibility or when a parent has been thwarted by the other parent when attempting to exercise custody or visitation rights contemplated by a custody or visitation order, including, but not limited to, an order for joint physical custody, or by a written or oral agreement between the parents.

(b) The compensation shall be limited to (1) the reasonable expenses incurred for or on behalf of a child, resulting from the other parent's failure to assume caretaker responsibility or (2) the reasonable expenses incurred by a parent for or on behalf of a child, resulting from the other parent's thwarting of the parent's efforts to exercise custody or visitation rights. The expenses may include the value of caretaker services but are not limited to the cost of services provided by a third party during the relevant period.

(c) The compensation may be requested by noticed motion or an order to show cause, which shall allege, under penalty of perjury, (1) a minimum of one hundred dollars ($100) of expenses incurred or (2) at least three occurrences of failure to exercise custody or visitation rights or (3) at least three occurrences of the thwarting of efforts to exercise custody or visitation rights within the six months before filing of the motion or order.

(d) Attorney's fees shall be awarded to the prevailing party upon a showing of the nonprevailing party's ability to pay as required by Section 270. *(Stats.1992, c. 162 (A.B.2650), § 10, operative Jan. 1, 1994. Amended by Stats.1993, c. 219 (A.B.1500), § 116.18.)*

Law Revision Commission Comments

Enactment [Revised Comment]

Section 3028 continues former Civil Code Section 4700(b) without substantive change. In subdivision (a), the former reference to an order "entered pursuant to this part," meaning the former Family Law Act (former Part 5 (commencing with former Section 4000) of Division 4 of the Civil Code), has been omitted as unnecessary. See Section 3021 (application of part).

See also Sections 3003 ("joint legal custody" defined), 3004 ("joint physical custody" defined), 3556 (custodial parent's failure to implement noncustodial parent's custody or visitation rights does not affect noncustodial parent's duty of support). [23 Cal.L.Rev.Comm. Reports 1 (1993)].

Research References

Treatises and Practice Aids

Witkin, California Summary 10th Parent and Child § 245, in General.

Witkin, California Summary 10th Parent and Child § 382, Compensation for Custodial Parent's Breach.

§ 3029. Noncustodial parent's liability for support if custodial parent is receiving AFDC assistance; order

An order granting custody to a parent who is receiving, or in the opinion of the court is likely to receive, assistance pursuant to the Family Economic Security Act of 1982 (Chapter 2 (commencing with Section 11200) of Part 3 of Division 9 of the Welfare and Institutions Code) for the maintenance of the child shall include an order pursuant to Chapter 2 (commencing with Section 4000) of Part 2 of Division 9 of this code, directing the noncustodial parent to pay any amount necessary for the support of the child, to the extent of the noncustodial parent's ability to pay. *(Added by Stats.1993, c. 219 (A.B.1500), § 116.19.)*

Law Revision Commission Comments

Enactment [Revised Comment]

Section 3029 continues former Civil Code Section 4600.2 without substantive change. A reference to sections in the Family Code has been substituted for the narrower references in former Civil Code Section 4600.2. This is not a substantive change. This is not a substantive change. [sic] See also Sections 4200–4203 (payment of child support to court-designated county officer). [23 Cal.L.Rev. Comm. Reports 1 (1993)].

Research References

Treatises and Practice Aids

Witkin, California Summary 10th Parent and Child § 285, in General.

§ 3030. Sex offenders; murderers; custody and visitation; child support; disclosure of information relating to custodial parent

(a)(1) No person shall be granted physical or legal custody of, or unsupervised visitation with, a child if the person is required to be registered as a sex offender under Section 290 of the Penal Code where the victim was a minor, or if the person has been convicted under Section 273a, 273d, or 647.6 of the Penal Code, unless the court finds that there is no significant risk to the child and states its reasons in writing or on the record. The child may not be placed in a home in which that person resides, nor permitted to have unsupervised visitation with that person, unless the court states the reasons for its findings in writing or on the record.

(2) No person shall be granted physical or legal custody of, or unsupervised visitation with, a child if anyone residing in the person's household is required, as a result of a felony conviction in which the victim was a minor, to register as a sex offender under Section 290 of the Penal Code, unless the court finds there is no significant risk to the child and states its reasons in writing or on the record. The child may not be placed in a home in which that person resides, nor permitted to have unsupervised visitation with that person, unless the court states the reasons for its findings in writing or on the record.

(3) The fact that a child is permitted unsupervised contact with a person who is required, as a result of a felony conviction in which the victim was a minor, to be registered as a sex offender under Section 290 of the Penal Code, shall be prima facie evidence that the child is at significant risk. When making a determination regarding significant risk to the child, the prima facie evidence shall constitute a presumption affecting the burden of producing evidence. However, this presumption shall not apply if there are factors mitigating against its application, including whether the party seeking custody or visitation is also required, as the result of a felony conviction in which the victim was a minor, to register as a sex offender under Section 290 of the Penal Code.

(b) No person shall be granted custody of, or visitation with, a child if the person has been convicted under Section 261 of the Penal Code and the child was conceived as a result of that violation.

(c) No person shall be granted custody of, or unsupervised visitation with, a child if the person has been convicted of murder in the first degree, as defined in Section 189 of the Penal Code, and the victim of the murder was the other parent of the child who is the subject of the order, unless the court finds that there is no risk to the child's health, safety, and welfare, and states the reasons for its finding in writing or on the record. In making its finding, the court may consider, among other things, the following:

(1) The wishes of the child, if the child is of sufficient age and capacity to reason so as to form an intelligent preference.

(2) Credible evidence that the convicted parent was a victim of abuse, as defined in Section 6203, committed by the deceased parent. That evidence may include, but is not limited to, written reports by law enforcement agencies, child protective services or other social welfare agencies, courts, medical facilities, or other public agencies or private nonprofit organizations providing services to victims of domestic abuse.

(3) Testimony of an expert witness, qualified under Section 1107 of the Evidence Code, that the convicted parent experiences intimate partner battering.

Unless and until a custody or visitation order is issued pursuant to this subdivision, no person shall permit or cause the child to visit or remain in the custody of the convicted parent without the consent of the child's custodian or legal guardian.

(d) The court may order child support that is to be paid by a person subject to subdivision (a), (b), or (c) to be paid through the local child support agency, as authorized by Section 4573 of the Family Code and Division 17 (commencing with Section 17000) of this code.

(e) The court shall not disclose, or cause to be disclosed, the custodial parent's place of residence, place of employment, or the child's school, unless the court finds that the disclosure would be in the best interest of the child. *(Added by Stats.1993, c. 219 (A.B.1500), § 116.20. Amended by Stats.1993–94, 1st Ex.Sess., c. 5 (S.B.25), § 1, eff. Nov. 30, 1994; Stats.1997, c. 594 (A.B.1222), § 1; Stats.1998, c. 131 (A.B.1645), § 1; Stats.1998, c. 485 (A.B.2803), § 64; Stats. 1998, c. 704 (A.B.2745), § 1.5; Stats.1998, c. 705 (A.B.2386), § 1.5; Stats.2000, c. 808 (A.B.1358), § 26, eff. Sept. 28, 2000; Stats.2005, c. 215 (A.B.220), § 2; Stats.2005, c. 483 (S.B.594), § 2.5; Stats.2006, c. 207 (A.B.2893), § 1.)*

Law Revision Commission Comments

Enactment [Revised Comment]

Section 3030 continues former Civil Code Section 4610 without substantive change. See also Sections 3100(b) (visitation limited to situations where third party present in case involving domestic violence), 3101(b), 3103(b) (limitation on stepparent or grandparent visitation in case involving domestic violence). [23 Cal.L.Rev. Comm. Report 1 (1993)].

Research References

Forms

West's California Code Forms, Family § 3022, Comment Overview--Order for Custody.

Treatises and Practice Aids

Witkin, California Summary 10th Parent and Child § 200, Commission Of Crime.

Witkin, California Summary 10th Parent and Child § 641, Visitation Rights.

§ 3030.5. Modification or termination of order for physical or legal custody or unsupervised visitation order; sex offenders required to be registered

(a) Upon the motion of one or both parents, or the legal guardian or custodian, or upon the court's own motion, an order granting physical or legal custody of, or unsupervised visitation with, a child may be modified or terminated if either of the following circumstances has occurred since the order was entered, unless the court finds that there is no significant risk to the child and states its reasons in writing or on the record:

(1) The person who has been granted physical or legal custody of, or unsupervised visitation with the child is required, as a result of a felony conviction in which the victim was a minor, to be registered as a sex offender under Section 290 of the Penal Code.

(2) The person who has been granted physical or legal custody of, or unsupervised visitation with, the child resides with another person who is required, as a result of a felony conviction in which the victim was a minor, to be registered as a sex offender under Section 290 of the Penal Code.

(b) The fact that a child is permitted unsupervised contact with a person who is required, as a result of a felony conviction in which the victim was a minor, to be registered as a sex offender under Section 290 of the Penal Code, shall be prima facie evidence that the child is at significant risk. When making a determination regarding significant risk to the child, the prima facie evidence shall constitute a presumption affecting the burden of producing evidence. However, this presumption shall not apply if there are factors mitigating against its application, including whether the party seeking custody or visitation is also required, as the result of a felony conviction in which the victim was a minor, to register as a sex offender under Section 290 of the Penal Code.

(c) The court shall not modify an existing custody or visitation order upon the ex parte petition of one party pursuant to this section without providing notice to the other party and an opportunity to be heard. This notice provision applies only when the motion for custody or visitation change is based solely on the fact that the child is allowed unsupervised contact with a person required, as a result of a felony conviction in which the victim was a minor, to register as a sex offender under Section 290 of the Penal Code and does not affect the court's ability to remove a child upon an ex parte motion when there is a showing of immediate harm to the child. *(Added by Stats.2005, c. 483 (S.B.594), § 3.)*

Research References

Treatises and Practice Aids

Witkin, California Summary 10th Parent and Child § 253A, (New) Registration as Sex Offender.

§ 3031. Protective or restraining orders; findings; transfer of children; detail specific custody or visitation orders; required presence of third party

(a) Where the court considers the issue of custody or visitation the court is encouraged to make a reasonable effort to ascertain whether or not any emergency protective order, protective order, or other restraining order is in effect that concerns the parties or the minor. The court is encouraged not to make a custody or visitation order that is inconsistent with the emergency protective order, protective order, or other restraining order, unless the court makes both of the following findings:

(1) The custody or visitation order cannot be made consistent with the emergency protective order, protective order, or other restraining order.

(2) The custody or visitation order is in the best interest of the minor.

(b) Whenever custody or visitation is granted to a parent in a case in which domestic violence is alleged and an emergency protective order, protective order, or other restraining order has been issued, the custody or visitation order shall specify the time, day, place, and manner of transfer of the child for custody or visitation to limit the child's exposure to potential domestic conflict or violence and to ensure the safety of all family members. Where the court finds a party is staying in a place designated as a shelter for victims of domestic violence or other confidential location, the court's order for time, day, place, and manner of transfer of the child for custody or visitation shall be designed to prevent disclosure of the location of the shelter or other confidential location.

(c) When making an order for custody or visitation in a case in which domestic violence is alleged and an emergency protective order, protective order, or other restraining order has been issued, the court shall consider whether the best interest of the child, based upon the circumstances of the case, requires that any custody or visitation arrangement shall be limited to situations in which a third person, specified by the court, is present, or whether custody or visitation shall be suspended or denied. *(Added by Stats.1993, c. 219 (A.B. 1500), § 116.30. Amended by Stats.1994, c. 320 (A.B.356), § 1.)*

Law Revision Commission Comments

Enactment [Revised Comment]

Section 3031 continues without substantive change former Civil Code Sections 4612 and 7009 and former Code of Civil Procedure Section 547.7. The former reference to "a proceeding concerning the custody of, or visitation with, a minor" has been omitted. This section applies to a determination of custody or visitation in a proceeding for dissolution, nullity, or legal separation, and in proceedings pursuant to the Domestic Violence Prevention Act and the Uniform Parentage Act. See Section 3021 (application of part). See also Section 3011 (factors in determining best interest of child). [23 Cal.L.Rev.Comm. Report 1 (1993)].

Research References

Forms

California Transactions Forms--Family Law § 3:2, Child Custody.
West's California Judicial Council Forms DV-150, Supervised Visitation and Exchange Order.
West's California Judicial Council Forms FL-356, Request for Special Immigrant Juvenile Findings--Family Law.
West's California Judicial Council Forms FL-341(A), Supervised Visitation Order.

Treatises and Practice Aids

Witkin, California Summary 10th Parent and Child § 286, Where Domestic Violence is Alleged and Protective Order is Issued.

§ 3032. Pilot program to provide interpreter in child custody or protective order cases; lack of English proficiency and financial ability of party; report to Legislature

(a) The Judicial Council shall establish a state-funded one-year pilot project beginning July 1, 1999, in at least two counties, including Los Angeles County, pursuant to which, in any child custody proceeding, including mediation proceedings pursuant to Section 3170, any action or proceeding under Division 10 (commencing with Section 6200), any action or proceeding under the Uniform Parentage Act (Part 3 (commencing with Section 7600) of Division 12), and any proceeding for dissolution or nullity of marriage or legal separation of the parties in which a protective order as been granted or is being sought pursuant to Section 6221, the court shall, notwithstanding Section 68092 of the Government Code, appoint an interpreter to interpret the proceedings at court expense, if both of the following conditions are met:

(1) One or both of the parties is unable to participate fully in the proceeding due to a lack of proficiency in the English language.

(2) The party who needs an interpreter appears in forma pauperis, pursuant to Section 68511.3 of the Government Code, or the court otherwise determines that the parties are financially unable to pay the cost of an interpreter. In all other cases where an interpreter is required pursuant to this section, interpreter fees shall be paid as provided in Section 68092 of the Government Code.

(3) This section shall not prohibit the court doing any of the following when an interpreter is not present:

(A) Issuing an order when the necessity for the order outweighs the necessity for an interpreter.

(B) Extending the duration of a previously issued temporary order if an interpreter is not readily available.

(C) Issuing a permanent order where a party who requires an interpreter fails to make appropriate arrangements for an interpreter after receiving proper notice of the hearing, including notice of the requirement to have an interpreter present, along with information about obtaining an interpreter.

(b) The Judicial Council shall submit its findings and recommendations with respect to the pilot project to the Legislature by January 31, 2001. Measurable objectives of the program may include increased utilization of the court by parties not fluent in English, increased efficiency in proceedings, increased compliance with orders, enhanced coordination between courts and culturally relevant services in the community, increased client satisfaction, and increased public satisfaction. *(Added by Stats.1998, c. 981 (A.B.1884), § 2.)*

CHAPTER 2. MATTERS TO BE CONSIDERED IN GRANTING CUSTODY

§ 3040. Order of preference; child with more than two parents

(a) Custody should be granted in the following order of preference according to the best interest of the child as provided in Sections 3011 and 3020:

(1) To both parents jointly pursuant to Chapter 4 (commencing with Section 3080) or to either parent. In making an order granting custody to either parent, the court shall consider, among other factors, which parent is more likely to allow the child frequent and continuing contact with the noncustodial parent, consistent with Sections 3011 and 3020, and shall not prefer a parent as custodian because of that parent's sex. The court, in its discretion, may require the parents to submit to the court a plan for the implementation of the custody order.

(2) If to neither parent, to the person or persons in whose home the child has been living in a wholesome and stable environment.

(3) To any other person or persons deemed by the court to be suitable and able to provide adequate and proper care and guidance for the child.

(b) The immigration status of a parent, legal guardian, or relative shall not disqualify the parent, legal guardian, or relative from receiving custody under subdivision (a).

(c) This section establishes neither a preference nor a presumption for or against joint legal custody, joint physical custody, or sole custody, but allows the court and the family the widest discretion to choose a parenting plan that is in the best interest of the child.

(d) In cases where a child has more than two parents, the court shall allocate custody and visitation among the parents based on the best interest of the child, including, but not limited to, addressing the child's need for continuity and stability by preserving established patterns of care and emotional bonds. The court may order that not all parents share legal or physical custody of the child if the court finds that it would not be in the best interest of the child as provided in Sections 3011 and 3020. *(Added by Stats.1993, c. 219 (A.B.1500), § 116.50. Amended by Stats.1997, c. 849 (A.B.200), § 4; Stats.2012, c. 845 (S.B.1064), § 1; Stats.2013, c. 564 (S.B.274), § 2.)*

Law Revision Commission Comments

Enactment [Revised Comment]

Section 3040 continues former Civil Code Section 4600(b) and (d) without substantive change. The reference to "children" has been omitted as surplus. See Section 10 (singular includes plural). See also Sections 2253 (determination of custody in nullity proceeding), 3003 ("joint legal custody" defined), 3004 ("joint physical custody" defined), 3021 (application of part), 3131 (action by district attorney where child taken or detained in violation of custody order). [23 Cal.L.Rev.Comm. Reports 1 (1993)].

Commentary

Although Section 3040 sets out substantive rules for custody determinations, it does not itself create subject matter jurisdiction. There must be an independent statutory basis for the court's exercise of jurisdiction to determine custody, such as a dissolution or dependency proceeding. See *In re Marriage of Goetz and Lewis, 203 Cal.App.3d 514, 250 Cal.Rptr. 30 (1988)* for general discussion and extensive citation. For recent application of this principle, see *Polin v. Cosio, 16 Cal.App.4th 1451, 20 Cal.Rptr.2d 714 (1993)*. See also Section 3100, Commentary.

Unless otherwise indicated by case law or statute, the substantive rules of Section 3040 apply in any proceeding in which custody is at issue. *In re B.G., 11 Cal.3d 679, 695–696, 114 Cal.Rptr. 444 (1974)* (juvenile dependency proceeding); *Guardianship of Diana B., 30 Cal.App.4th 1766, 36 Cal.Rptr.2d 447 (1994)* (applying Sections 3040 and 3041 in a Probate Code Section 1514 guardianship proceeding and requiring only a preponderance of the evidence, as opposed to clear and convincing evidence, that returning the child to parental custody would create a substantial risk of detriment to the child). For extensive citation, see *In re Guardianship of Martha M., 204 Cal. App.3d 909, 912, 251 Cal.Rptr. 567 (1988)*.

Research References

Forms

California Transactions Forms--Estate Planning § 19:94, Appointment Of Guardian Of Person.
California Transactions Forms--Family Law § 3:7, Custody Issues Outside the Scope Of the Family Code.
California Transactions Forms--Family Law § 3:8, No Statutory Custody Preferences.
California Transactions Forms--Family Law § 5:2, Overview.
California Transactions Forms--Family Law § 2:70, Deciding Custody.
California Transactions Forms--Family Law § 3:11, Permanent Custody.
West's California Code Forms, Family § 3022, Comment Overview--Order for Custody.
West's California Code Forms, Family § 7841 Form 1, Petition for Freedom from Parental Control--Abandonment.
West's California Code Forms, Probate § 1514 Form 1, Order Appointing Guardian Of Minor--Judicial Council Form GC-240.
West's California Judicial Council Forms DV-140, Child Custody and Visitation Order.
West's California Judicial Council Forms FL-341, Child Custody and Visitation (Parenting Time) Order Attachment.

Treatises and Practice Aids

Witkin, California Summary 10th Parent and Child § 195, Statutory Framework.
Witkin, California Summary 10th Parent and Child § 198, Domestic Violence.
Witkin, California Summary 10th Parent and Child § 211, in General.
Witkin, California Summary 10th Parent and Child § 215, Current Statute: No Preference.
Witkin, California Summary 10th Parent and Child § 217, Statutory Order Of Preference.
Witkin, California Summary 10th Parent and Child § 218, Statutory Rule.
Witkin, California Summary 10th Parent and Child § 222, Statutory Authorization.
Witkin, California Summary 10th Parent and Child § 223, Procedure.
Witkin, California Summary 10th Parent and Child § 255, Stipulation for Temporary Custody.
Witkin, California Summary 10th Parent and Child § 282, Agreement.
Witkin, California Summary 10th Parent and Child § 285, in General.
Witkin, California Summary 10th Parent and Child § 363, Applicability Of Family Code Custody Provisions.
Witkin, California Summary 10th Wills and Probate § 924, Factors Considered in Appointment.

§ 3041. Custody award to nonparent; findings of court; hearing

(a) Before making an order granting custody to a person or persons other than a parent, over the objection of a parent, the court shall make a finding that granting custody to a parent would be detrimental to the child and that granting custody to the nonparent is required to serve the best interest of the child. Allegations that parental custody would be detrimental to the child, other than a statement of that ultimate fact, shall not appear in the pleadings. The court may, in its discretion, exclude the public from the hearing on this issue.

(b) Subject to subdivision (d), a finding that parental custody would be detrimental to the child shall be supported by clear and convincing evidence.

(c) As used in this section, "detriment to the child" includes the harm of removal from a stable placement of a child with a person who has assumed, on a day-to-day basis, the role of his or her parent, fulfilling both the child's physical needs and the child's psychological needs for care and affection, and who has assumed that role for a substantial period of time. A finding of detriment does not require any finding of unfitness of the parents.

(d) Notwithstanding subdivision (b), if the court finds by a preponderance of the evidence that the person to whom custody may be given is a person described in subdivision (c), this finding shall constitute a finding that the custody is in the best interest of the child and that parental custody would be detrimental to the child absent a showing by a preponderance of the evidence to the contrary.

(e) Notwithstanding subdivisions (a) to (d), inclusive, if the child is an Indian child, when an allegation is made that parental custody would be detrimental to the child, before making an order granting custody to a person or persons other than a parent, over the objection of a parent, the court shall apply the evidentiary standards described in subdivisions (d), (e), and (f) of Section 1912 of the Indian Child Welfare Act (25 U.S.C. Sec. 1901 et seq.) and Sections 224.6 and 361.7 of the Welfare and Institutions Code and the placement preferences and standards set out in Section 361.31 of the Welfare and Institutions Code and Section 1922 of the Indian Child Welfare Act (25 U.S.C. Sec. 1901 et seq.). *(Added by Stats.1993, c. 219 (A.B.1500), § 116.50. Amended by Stats. 2002, c. 1118 (A.B.1938), § 3; Stats.2006, c. 838 (S.B.678), § 2.)*

Law Revision Commission Comments

Enactment [Revised Comment]

Section 3041 continues former Civil Code Section 4600(c) without substantive change. See also Section 3011 (factors to be considered in determining best interest of child). [23 Cal.L.Rev.Comm. Reports 1 (1993)].

Commentary

In re E.S., 173 Cal.App.4th 1131, 93 Cal.Rptr.3d 470 (2009), review denied, held that a parent's due process rights are not violated when, pursuant to subsections (c) and (d), custody of a child is awarded to a nonparent on a showing of detriment, which is established by a rebuttable presumption in favor of a nonparent who has acted as a child's de facto parent for a substantial period of time.

See generally *In re B.G., 11 Cal.3d 679, 695–696, 114 Cal.Rptr. 444 (1974)* (granting children to third party in dependency proceeding on ground that granting custody to parent would be detrimental to children). *B.G.* also holds that a de facto parent has party standing in a dependency proceeding. For the definition of a *de facto* parent, see California Rules of Court, Rule 5.502(10) and accompanying Commentary. Compare *Guardianship of Diana B., 30 Cal.App.4th 1766, 36 Cal.Rptr.2d 447 (1994)* (applying Sections 3040 and 3041 in a Probate Code Section 1514 guardianship proceeding and requiring only a preponderance of the evidence, as opposed to clear and convincing evidence, that returning the child to parental custody would create a substantial risk of detriment to the child) with *Guardianship of Stephen G., 40 Cal.App.4th 1418, 47 Cal.Rptr.2d 409 (1995)* (holding that, in a guardianship proceeding, Section 3041 requires "clear and convincing" proof that "granting custody to a parent would be detrimental to the child and that granting custody to the nonparent is required to serve the best interest of the child"). *Stephen G.* is followed by *Guardianship of Jenna G., 63 Cal.App.4th 387, 74 Cal.Rptr.2d 47 (1998)* (requiring "clear and convincing" evidence to grant guardianship over objection of natural parent; and criticizing *Diana B.* as based on inapposite authority, that is, on dependency cases in which natural parent had already been found unfit). *Guardianship of Zachary H., 73 Cal.App.4th 51, 86 Cal.Rptr.2d 7 (1999),* holds that the trial court properly appointed prospective adoptive parents, with whom the child had been placed from birth, as the guardians of the child after their adoption of the child failed because of the father's opposition, when changing custody to the father, who was not otherwise shown to be unfit, would cause detriment to the child, and the best interest of the child required that custody be continued with the guardians. Although the federal due process clause requires a showing of "unfitness" before parental rights are terminated, the appointment of a guardian does not terminate parental rights. Similarly, see *Adoption of Daniele G., 87 Cal.App.4th 1392, 105 Cal.Rptr.2d 341 (2001),* which holds that the trial court improperly denied the guardianship petition of prospective adoptive parents currently caring for the child when the court found that removal from the current home would cause detriment to the child and remaining in the current home was required to serve the child's best interests. Although adoption might not proceed without the father's consent, granting guardianship to the prospective adoptive parents was warranted by the court's findings.

See also *Guardianship of Z.C.W. & K.G.W., 71 Cal.App.4th 524, 84 Cal.Rptr.2d 48 (1999), review denied July 21, 1999* (woman claiming to be a "de facto" parent of the children of her former lesbian partner is not entitled to a limited guardianship that would provide for visitation, absent a showing of detriment to the children from continued parental custody). But compare *Guardianship of Olivia J., 84 Cal.App.4th 1146, 101 Cal.Rptr.2d 364 (2000),* which held that the trial court should not have dismissed, without a hearing on the merits, a guardianship proceeding brought by a former same-sex domestic partner who alleged that parental custody would be detrimental to the child because the child's parent would cause the child psychological harm by terminating the child's relationship with the former same-sex partner, and thus an award of custody to the same-sex partner would be necessary to serve the best interests of the child.

Guardianship of Vaughan, 207 Cal.App.4th 1055, 144 Cal.Rptr.3d 216 (2012), held that when grandchildren have been residing with their grandparents for over a year, subsection (c) does not require a showing that the children were abandoned by their parent in order for a trial court to grant the grandparents' petition for a probate guardianship (Probate Code sections 1510(a) and 1514 (a) and (b)).

Research References

Forms

California Practice Guide: Rutter Family Law Forms Form 7:16, Memorandum in Support Of Motion and Declaration for Joinder (Nonparent Custody Claim).

California Transactions Forms--Family Law § 5:3, Rights Of Nonparents Generally.

California Transactions Forms--Family Law § 5:4, Rights Of De Facto Parents.

California Transactions Forms--Family Law § 5:26, Inheritance and Custody on Death.

California Transactions Forms--Family Law § 6:11, Initiating Proceeding Under Uniform Parentage Act [Fam C §§ 7600 to 7730].

West's California Code Forms, Family § 3022, Comment Overview--Order for Custody.

West's California Code Forms, Probate § 1510 Form 1, Petition for Appointment Of Guardian Of Estate Of Minor--Judicial Council Form GC-210.

West's California Code Forms, Probate § 1514 Form 1, Order Appointing Guardian Of Minor--Judicial Council Form GC-240.

Treatises and Practice Aids

Witkin, California Summary 10th Parent and Child § 66, Statutory Requirements.

Witkin, California Summary 10th Parent and Child § 68, Constitutional Rights Of Natural Father.

Witkin, California Summary 10th Parent and Child § 102, Failure to Support and Communicate.

Witkin, California Summary 10th Parent and Child § 136, Withdrawal, Denial, or Dismissal Of Petition.

Witkin, California Summary 10th Parent and Child § 218, Statutory Rule.

Witkin, California Summary 10th Parent and Child § 220, Illustrations: Guardianship Cases.

Witkin, California Summary 10th Parent and Child § 284, Trial.

Witkin, California Summary 10th Parent and Child § 320, Statutory Ground.

Witkin, California Summary 10th Parent and Child § 346, Detriment.

Witkin, California Summary 10th Parent and Child § 363, Applicability Of Family Code Custody Provisions.

Witkin, California Summary 10th Parent and Child § 522, Nature and Scope Of Indian Child Welfare Act.

Witkin, California Summary 10th Parent and Child § 526, Determination Of Indian Status.

Witkin, California Summary 10th Parent and Child § 632, Standard Of Proof.

Witkin, California Summary 10th Wills and Probate § 924, Factors Considered in Appointment.

Witkin, California Summary 10th Wills and Probate § 930, Termination Of Guardianship.

Witkin, California Summary 10th Wills and Probate § 963, Joint Guardians or Conservators.

§ 3041.5. Controlled substances or alcohol abuse testing of persons seeking custody or visitation; grounds for testing; confidentiality of results; penalties for unauthorized disclosure

In any custody or visitation proceeding brought under this part, as described in Section 3021, or any guardianship proceeding brought under the Probate Code, the court may order any person who is seeking custody of, or visitation with, a child who is the subject of the proceeding to undergo testing for the illegal use of controlled substances and the use of alcohol if there is a judicial determination based upon a preponderance of evidence that there is the habitual, frequent, or continual illegal use of controlled substances or the habitual or continual abuse of alcohol by the parent, legal custodian, person seeking guardianship, or person seeking visitation in a guardianship. This evidence may include, but may not be limited to, a conviction within the last five years for the illegal use or possession of a controlled substance. The court shall order the least intrusive method of testing for the illegal use of controlled substances or the habitual or continual abuse of alcohol by either or both parents, the legal custodian, person seeking guardianship, or person seeking visitation in a guardianship. If substance abuse testing is ordered by the court, the testing shall be performed in conformance with procedures and standards established by the United States Department of Health and Human Services for drug testing of federal employees. The parent, legal custodian, person seeking guardianship, or person seeking visitation in a guardianship who has undergone drug testing shall have the right to a hearing, if requested, to challenge a positive test result. A positive test result, even if challenged and upheld, shall not, by itself, constitute grounds for an adverse custody or guardianship decision. Determining the best interests of the child requires weighing all relevant factors. The court shall also consider any reports provided to the court pursuant to the Probate Code. The results of this testing shall be confidential, shall be maintained as a sealed record in the court file, and may not be released to any person except the court, the parties, their attorneys, the Judicial Council, until completion of its authorized study of the testing process, and any person to whom the court expressly grants access by written order made with prior notice to all parties. Any person who has access to the test results may not disseminate copies or disclose information about the test results to any person other than a person who is authorized to receive the test results pursuant to this section. Any breach of the confidentiality of the test results shall be punishable by civil sanctions not to exceed two thousand five hundred dollars ($2,500). The results of the testing may not be used for any purpose, including any criminal, civil, or administrative proceeding, except to assist the court in determining, for purposes of the proceeding, the best interest of the child pursuant to Section 3011 and the content of the order or judgment determining custody or visitation. The court may order either party, or both parties, to pay the costs of the drug or alcohol testing ordered pursuant to this section. As used in this section, "controlled substances" has the same meaning as defined in the California Uniform Controlled Substances Act (Division 10 (commencing with Section 11000) of the Health and Safety Code). *(Added by Stats.2004, c. 19 (A.B.1108), § 1, eff. Feb. 23, 2004. Amended by Stats.2005, c. 302 (A.B.541), § 1; Stats.2007, c. 152 (S.B.403), § 1; Stats.2008, c. 57 (S.B.1255), § 1; Stats. 2009, c. 140 (A.B.1164), § 66; Stats.2012, c. 258 (A.B.2365), § 2.)*

Commentary

Heidi S. v. David H., 1 Cal App.5th 1150, 205 Cal.Rptr.3d 335 (2016), held that a trial court order could provide that a positive drug test would trigger a reduction in visitation, because this section contains no restrictions on the court's power to alter visitation, as opposed to custody or guardianship, based on a positive test result.

Deborah M. v. Superior Court, 128 Cal.App.4th 1181, 27 Cal.Rptr.3d 757 (2005), holds that section does not allow hair follicle testing because, as of 2005, the United States Department of Health and Human Services (DHHS) only allows urine testing for federal employees. Even if DHHS were eventually to allow hair follicle testing, it might not be "the least intrusive method of testing" within the meaning of this section.

Research References

Treatises and Practice Aids

Witkin, California Summary 10th Parent and Child § 199, Substance Abuse.

Witkin, California Summary 10th Wills and Probate § 922, Investigation and Report.

§ 3042. Preference of child; custody or visitation; examination of child witnesses; addressing the court; means other than direct testimony; determination of wish to express preference; rule of court

(a) If a child is of sufficient age and capacity to reason so as to form an intelligent preference as to custody or visitation, the court shall consider, and give due weight to, the wishes of the child in making an order granting or modifying custody or visitation.

(b) In addition to the requirements of subdivision (b) of Section 765 of the Evidence Code, the court shall control the examination of a child witness so as to protect the best interests of the child.

(c) If the child is 14 years of age or older and wishes to address the court regarding custody or visitation, the child shall be permitted to do so, unless the court determines that doing so is not in the child's best interests. In that case, the court shall state its reasons for that finding on the record.

(d) Nothing in this section shall be interpreted to prevent a child who is less than 14 years of age from addressing the court regarding custody or visitation, if the court determines that is appropriate pursuant to the child's best interests.

(e) If the court precludes the calling of any child as a witness, the court shall provide alternative means of obtaining input from the child and other information regarding the child's preferences.

(f) To assist the court in determining whether the child wishes to express his or her preference or to provide other input regarding custody or visitation to the court, a minor's counsel, an evaluator, an investigator, or a mediator who provides recommendations to the judge pursuant to Section 3183 shall indicate to the judge that the child wishes to address the court, or the judge may make that inquiry in the absence of that request. A party or a party's attorney may also indicate to the judge that the child wishes to address the court or judge.

(g) Nothing in this section shall be construed to require the child to express to the court his or her preference or to provide other input regarding custody or visitation.

(h) The Judicial Council shall, no later than January 1, 2012, promulgate a rule of court establishing procedures for the examination of a child witness, and include guidelines on methods other than direct testimony for obtaining information or other input from the child regarding custody or visitation.

(i) The changes made to subdivisions (a) to (g), inclusive, by the act [1] adding this subdivision shall become operative on January 1, 2012. *(Added by Stats.1993, c. 219 (A.B.1500), § 116.50. Amended by Stats.1994, c. 596 (S.B.1700), § 1; Stats.1995, c. 91 (S.B.975), § 38; Stats.2010, c. 187 (A.B. 1050), § 1.)*

[1] Stats.2010, c. 187 (A.B.1050).

Operative Effect

For operative effect of the amendment by Stats.2010, c. 187 (A.B.1050), see the terms of this section.

Law Revision Commission Comments

Enactment [Revised Comment]

Section 3042 continues without substantive change the second sentence of the second paragraph of former Civil Code Section 4600(a). [23 Cal.L.Rev.Comm. Reports 1 (1993)].

Commentary

Compare *In re Marriage of Rosson, 178 Cal.App.3d 1094, 224 Cal.Rptr. 250 (1986)* (giving great weight to custodial preference of children ages 10 and 13) with *In re Marriage of Melmauer, 60 Cal.App.3d 104, 131 Cal.Rptr. 325 (1976)* (finding preference of 14–year-old "unpersuasive").

Research References

Forms

California Transactions Forms--Estate Planning § 19:94, Appointment Of Guardian Of Person.

California Transactions Forms--Family Law § 3:12, Preferences Of the Child.

Treatises and Practice Aids

Witkin, California Summary 10th Husband and Wife § 5, Generally Applicable Procedures.

Witkin, California Summary 10th Parent and Child § 165, Home State.

Witkin, California Summary 10th Parent and Child § 208, Child's Preference.

Witkin, California Summary 10th Parent and Child § 260, Child's Preference.

Witkin, California Summary 10th Parent and Child § 273, Rights and Duties.

Witkin, California Summary 10th Parent and Child § 284, Trial.

Witkin, California Summary 10th Parent and Child § 344, Testimony.

Witkin, California Summary 10th Parent and Child § 363, Applicability Of Family Code Custody Provisions.

Witkin, California Summary 10th Parent and Child § 225A, (New) Right Of Child to Express Preference.

Witkin, California Summary 10th Wills and Probate § 916, in General.

§ 3043. Nomination of guardian by parent

In determining the person or persons to whom custody should be granted under paragraph (2) or (3) of subdivision (a) of Section 3040, the court shall consider and give due weight to the nomination of a guardian of the person of the child by a parent under Article 1 (commencing with Section 1500) of Chapter 1 of Part 2 of Division 4 of the Probate Code. *(Added by Stats.1993, c. 219 (A.B.1500), § 116.50.)*

Law Revision Commission Comments

Enactment [Revised Comment]

Section 3043 continues without substantive change the last sentence of the second paragraph of former Civil Code Section 4600(a). Section 3043 makes clear that a nomination under the Probate Code provisions is to be considered and given due weight, regardless of the nature of the custody proceeding. For background on former Civ. Code § 4600, see *Recommendation Relating to Guardianship–Conservatorship Law,* 14 Cal. L. Revision Comm'n Reports 501 (1978). [23 Cal.L.Rev.Comm. Reports 1 (1993)].

Commentary

A person nominated as guardian of the child by a deceased parent is entitled to de facto parent status at the child's dependency proceeding. *In re Vanessa P., 38 Cal.App.4th 1763, 45 Cal.Rptr.2d 760 (1995), review denied January 31, 1996.*

Research References

Forms

California Transactions Forms--Estate Planning § 19:94, Appointment Of Guardian Of Person.

West's California Code Forms, Family § 7841 Form 1, Petition for Freedom from Parental Control--Abandonment.

West's California Judicial Council Forms DV-140, Child Custody and Visitation Order.

West's California Judicial Council Forms FL-341, Child Custody and Visitation (Parenting Time) Order Attachment.

Treatises and Practice Aids

Witkin, California Summary 10th Parent and Child § 209, Nomination Of Guardian by Parent.

Witkin, California Summary 10th Parent and Child § 363, Applicability Of Family Code Custody Provisions.

§ 3044. Presumption against persons perpetrating domestic violence

(a) Upon a finding by the court that a party seeking custody of a child has perpetrated domestic violence against the other party seeking custody of the child or against the child or the child's siblings within the previous five years, there is a rebuttable presumption that an award of sole or joint physical or legal custody of a child to a person who has perpetrated domestic violence is detrimental to the best interest of the child, pursuant to Section 3011. This presumption may only be rebutted by a preponderance of the evidence.

(b) In determining whether the presumption set forth in subdivision (a) has been overcome, the court shall consider all of the following factors:

(1) Whether the perpetrator of domestic violence has demonstrated that giving sole or joint physical or legal custody of a child to the perpetrator is in the best interest of the child. In determining the best interest of the child, the preference for frequent and continuing contact with both parents, as set forth in subdivision (b) of Section 3020, or with the noncustodial parent, as set forth in paragraph (1) of subdivision (a) of Section 3040, may not be used to rebut the presumption, in whole or in part.

(2) Whether the perpetrator has successfully completed a batterer's treatment program that meets the criteria outlined in subdivision (c) of Section 1203.097 of the Penal Code.

(3) Whether the perpetrator has successfully completed a program of alcohol or drug abuse counseling if the court determines that counseling is appropriate.

(4) Whether the perpetrator has successfully completed a parenting class if the court determines the class to be appropriate.

(5) Whether the perpetrator is on probation or parole, and whether he or she has complied with the terms and conditions of probation or parole.

(6) Whether the perpetrator is restrained by a protective order or restraining order, and whether he or she has complied with its terms and conditions.

(7) Whether the perpetrator of domestic violence has committed any further acts of domestic violence.

(c) For purposes of this section, a person has "perpetrated domestic violence" when he or she is found by the court to have intentionally or recklessly caused or attempted to cause bodily injury, or sexual assault, or to have placed a person in reasonable apprehension of imminent serious bodily injury to that person or to another, or to have engaged in any behavior involving, but not limited to, threatening, striking, harassing, destroying personal property or disturbing the peace of another, for which a court may issue an ex parte order pursuant to Section 6320 to protect the other party seeking custody of the child or to protect the child and the child's siblings.

(d)(1) For purposes of this section, the requirement of a finding by the court shall be satisfied by, among other things, and not limited to, evidence that a party seeking custody has been convicted within the previous five years, after a trial or a plea of guilty or no contest, of any crime against the other party that comes within the definition of domestic violence contained in Section 6211 and of abuse contained in Section 6203, including, but not limited to, a crime described in subdivision (e) of Section 243 of, or Section 261, 262, 273.5, 422, or 646.9 of, the Penal Code.

(2) The requirement of a finding by the court shall also be satisfied if any court, whether that court hears or has heard the child custody proceedings or not, has made a finding pursuant to subdivision (a) based on conduct occurring within the previous five years.

(e) When a court makes a finding that a party has perpetrated domestic violence, the court may not base its findings solely on conclusions reached by a child custody evaluator or on the recommendation of the Family Court Services staff, but shall consider any relevant, admissible evidence submitted by the parties.

(f) In any custody or restraining order proceeding in which a party has alleged that the other party has perpetrated domestic violence in accordance with the terms of this section, the court shall inform the parties of the existence of this section and shall give them a copy of this section prior to any custody mediation in the case. *(Added by Stats.1999, c. 445 (A.B.840), § 1. Amended by Stats.2003, c. 243 (S.B.265), § 1.)*

Commentary

Celia S. v. Hugo H., 3 Cal.App.5th 655, 207 Cal.Rptr.3d 756 (2016), held that a court erred when, in a domestic violence proceeding, it awarded sole custody to the abused parent but nevertheless maintained the 50 percent time share of the abusing parent, who failed to rebut this section's presumption against awarding sole or joint custody to a parent who committed domestic violence. *Celia S.* reasoned that a 50 percent time share is equivalent to joint physical custody.

Jason P. v. Danielle S., 9 Cal.App.5th 1000, 215 Cal.Rptr.3d 542 (2017), review denied, held that a trial court erred in (1) concluding that the presumption of this section carried less force because a domestic violence restraining order against a father was not based on any physical violence and (2) ordering joint custody upon the completion of court-ordered joint counseling before determining that the father had completed the counseling required to rebut the presumption.

In granting a father's motion to modify a final child custody order, *Christina L. v. Chauncey B., 229 Cal.App.4th 731, 177 Cal.Rptr.3d 178 (2014)*, held that the trial court erred in failing to apply this section's rebuttable presumption that the father should not have custody because of his history of domestic violence evidenced by a domestic violence restraining order within the past five years. The trial court additionally erred in not considering the existing restraining order in determining the child's best interests under section 3011, and in not requiring the father to show that *changed circumstances* warranted modification of the final custody order.

This section's presumption must be applied whenever a parent has been found to have perpetrated domestic violence against the other parent within the last five years, without regard to whether a court has issued a permanent restraining order. *In re Marriage of Fajota, 230 Cal.App.4th 1487, 179 Cal.Rptr.3d 569 (2014).*

Ellis v. Lyons, 2 Cal.App.5th 404, 206 Cal.Rptr.3d 687 (2016), held that a California trial court erred when it denied a Massachusetts mother's request for modification of joint custody without considering this section's rebuttable presumption against awarding joint custody of a child to a California father after the mother had obtained a Massachusetts domestic violence restraining order against the father on the ground that the father caused the child to fear imminent serious physical injury. The proper procedure would have been to apply this section and require the father to rebut the presumption.

Keith R. v. Superior Court, 174 Cal.App.4th 1047, 96 Cal.Rptr.3d 298 (2009), holds that a subsection (a) order granting an abused parent sole legal and physical custody of a child, incident to a domestic violence order issued in a dissolution proceeding, does not constitute a final custody determination for purposes of *Montenegro*. (See commentary to section 3022.) Thus the trial court erred in applying the "changed circumstances" rather than the "best interest" standard to a move-away request in a child custody case.

Sabbah v. Sabbah, 151 Cal.App.4th 818, 60 Cal.Rptr.3d 175 (2007), held that subsection (f) applies only when a party is about to enter custody mediation. It imposes no duty on a court issuing a restraining order after finding that one party has perpetrated domestic violence on the other.

S.M. v. E.P., 184 Cal.App.4th 1249, 109 Cal.Rptr.3d 792 (2010), holds that a trial court abused its discretion by issuing, after hearing, a domestic violence restraining order against a parent without making a finding that the parent had engaged in domestic abuse within the meaning of section 6203. *S.M. v. E.P.* points out that, under this section, a domestic violence restraining order creates a presumption that an award of custody to a parent subject to the restraining order would be detrimental to the best interest of a child.

Research References

Treatises and Practice Aids

Witkin, California Summary 10th Parent and Child § 198, Domestic Violence.

Witkin, California Summary 10th Parent and Child § 211, in General.

§ 3046. Party absence or relocation from residence; consideration; interference with contact; application

(a) If a party is absent or relocates from the family residence, the court shall not consider the absence or relocation as a factor in determining custody or visitation in either of the following circumstances:

(1) The absence or relocation is of short duration and the court finds that, during the period of absence or relocation, the party has demonstrated an interest in maintaining custody or visitation, the party maintains, or makes reasonable efforts to maintain, regular contact with the child, and the party's behavior demonstrates no intent to abandon the child.

(2) The party is absent or relocates because of an act or acts of actual or threatened domestic or family violence by the other party.

(b) The court may consider attempts by one party to interfere with the other party's regular contact with the child in determining if the party has satisfied the requirements of subdivision (a).

(c) This section does not apply to either of the following:

(1) A party against whom a protective or restraining order has been issued excluding the party from the dwelling of the other party or the child, or otherwise enjoining the party from assault or harassment against the other party or the child, including, but not limited to, orders issued under Part 4 (commencing with Section 6300) of Division 10, orders preventing civil harassment or workplace violence issued pursuant to Section 527.6 or 527.8 of the Code of Civil Procedure, and criminal protective orders issued pursuant to Section 136.2 of the Penal Code.

(2) A party who abandons a child as provided in Section 7822. *(Added by Stats.1999, c. 980 (A.B.1671), § 7. Amended by Stats.2006, c. 538 (S.B.1852), § 157.)*

Research References

Forms

California Transactions Forms--Family Law § 2:70, Deciding Custody.

California Transactions Forms--Family Law § 3:16, Identifying Areas Of Parental Decision Making and Participation.

Treatises and Practice Aids

Witkin, California Summary 10th Parent and Child § 196, Best Interest Of Child.

Witkin, California Summary 10th Parent and Child § 205, Absence from Family Residence.

§ 3047. Military duty, temporary duty, mobilization, or deployment as justification; modification of custody or visitation orders; ability to appear at hearing; relocation of nondeploying parent; deployment as basis for inconvenience; legislative intent

(a) A party's absence, relocation, or failure to comply with custody and visitation orders shall not, by itself, be sufficient to justify a modification of a custody or visitation order if the reason for the absence, relocation, or failure to comply is the party's activation to military duty or temporary duty, mobilization in support of combat or other military operation, or military deployment out of state.

(b)(1) If a party with sole or joint physical custody or visitation receives temporary duty, deployment, or mobilization orders from the military that require the party to move a substantial distance from his or her residence or otherwise has a material effect on the ability of the party to exercise custody or visitation rights, any necessary modification of the existing custody order shall be deemed a temporary custody order made without prejudice, which shall be subject to review and reconsideration upon the return of the party from military deployment, mobilization, or temporary duty.

(2) If the temporary order is reviewed upon return of the party from military deployment, mobilization, or temporary duty, there shall be a presumption that the custody order shall revert to the order that was in place before the

modification, unless the court determines that it is not in the best interest of the child. The court shall not, as part of its review of the temporary order upon the return of the deploying party, order a child custody evaluation under Section 3111 of this code or Section 730 of the Evidence Code, unless the party opposing reversion of the order makes a prima facie showing that reversion is not in the best interest of the child.

(3)(A) If the court makes a temporary custody order, it shall consider any appropriate orders to ensure that the relocating party can maintain frequent and continuing contact with the child by means that are reasonably available.

(B) Upon a motion by the relocating party, the court may grant reasonable visitation rights to a stepparent, grandparent, or other family member if the court does all of the following:

(i) Finds that there is a preexisting relationship between the family member and the child that has engendered a bond such that visitation is in the best interest of the child.

(ii) Finds that the visitation will facilitate the child's contact with the relocating party.

(iii) Balances the interest of the child in having visitation with the family member against the right of the parents to exercise parental authority.

(C) Nothing in this paragraph shall increase the authority of the persons described in subparagraph (B) to seek visitation orders independently.

(D) The granting of visitation rights to a nonparent pursuant to subparagraph (B) shall not impact the calculation of child support.

(c) If a party's deployment, mobilization, or temporary duty will have a material effect on his or her ability, or anticipated ability, to appear in person at a regularly scheduled hearing, the court shall do either of the following:

(1) Upon motion of the party, hold an expedited hearing to determine custody and visitation issues prior to the departure of the party.

(2) Upon motion of the party, allow the party to present testimony and evidence and participate in court-ordered child custody mediation by electronic means, including, but not limited to, telephone, video teleconferencing, or the Internet, to the extent that this technology is reasonably available to the court and protects the due process rights of all parties.

(d) A relocation by a nondeploying parent during a period of a deployed parent's absence while a temporary modification order for a parenting plan is in effect shall not, by itself, terminate the exclusive and continuing jurisdiction of the court for purposes of later determining custody or parenting time under this chapter.

(e) When a court of this state has issued a custody or visitation order, the absence of a child from this state during the deployment of a parent shall be considered a "temporary absence" for purposes of the Uniform Child Custody Jurisdiction and Enforcement Act (Part 3 (commencing with Section 3400)), and the court shall retain exclusive continuing jurisdiction under Section 3422.

(f) The deployment of a parent shall not be used as a basis to assert inconvenience of the forum under Section 3427.

(g) For purposes of this section, the following terms have the following meanings:

(1) "Deployment" means the temporary transfer of a member of the Armed Forces in active-duty status in support of combat or some other military operation.

(2) "Mobilization" means the transfer of a member of the National Guard or Military Reserve to extended active-duty status, but does not include National Guard or Military Reserve annual training.

(3) "Temporary duty" means the transfer of a service member from one military base to a different location, usually another base, for a limited period of time to accomplish training or to assist in the performance of a noncombat mission.

(h) It is the intent of the Legislature that this section provide a fair, efficient, and expeditious process to resolve child custody and visitation issues when a party receives temporary duty, deployment, or mobilization orders from the military, as well as at the time that the party returns from service and files a motion to revert back to the custody order in place before the deployment. The Legislature intends that family courts shall, to the extent feasible within existing resources and court practices, prioritize the calendaring of these cases, avoid unnecessary delay or continuances, and ensure that parties who serve in the military are not penalized for their service by a delay in appropriate access to their children. *(Added by Stats.2005, c. 154 (S.B.1082), § 1, eff. Aug. 30, 2005. Amended by Stats.2010, c. 466 (A.B.2416), § 1; Stats.2012, c. 116 (A.B.1807), § 1; Stats.2013, c. 76 (A.B.383), § 59.)*

Commentary

In re Marriage of E.U. & J.E., *212 Cal.App.4th 1377, 152 Cal.Rptr.3d 58 (2013), review denied*, applying an earlier version of this section, held that a trial court erred when it failed to enforce a court order providing that father's custody be reinstated upon his return from military service and, absent any serious concerns, instead required a custody evaluation and a hearing on the best interests of the child.

Research References

Treatises and Practice Aids

Witkin, California Summary 10th Parent and Child § 259A, (New) Military Deployment.

§ 3048. Required contents for custody or visitation orders; risk of child abduction; risk factors and preventative measures; notation of preventative conditions on minute order of court proceedings; Child Abduction Unit; child custody order forms

(a) Notwithstanding any other provision of law, in any proceeding to determine child custody or visitation with a child, every custody or visitation order shall contain all of the following:

(1) The basis for the court's exercise of jurisdiction.

(2) The manner in which notice and opportunity to be heard were given.

(3) A clear description of the custody and visitation rights of each party.

(4) A provision stating that a violation of the order may subject the party in violation to civil or criminal penalties, or both.

(5) Identification of the country of habitual residence of the child or children.

(b)(1) In cases in which the court becomes aware of facts which may indicate that there is a risk of abduction of a child, the court shall, either on its own motion or at the request of a party, determine whether measures are needed to prevent the abduction of the child by one parent. To make that determination, the court shall consider the risk of abduction of the child, obstacles to location, recovery, and return if the child is abducted, and potential harm to the child if he or she is abducted. To determine whether there is a risk of abduction, the court shall consider the following factors:

(A) Whether a party has previously taken, enticed away, kept, withheld, or concealed a child in violation of the right of custody or of visitation of a person.

(B) Whether a party has previously threatened to take, entice away, keep, withhold, or conceal a child in violation of the right of custody or of visitation of a person.

(C) Whether a party lacks strong ties to this state.

(D) Whether a party has strong familial, emotional, or cultural ties to another state or country, including foreign citizenship. This factor shall be considered only if evidence exists in support of another factor specified in this section.

(E) Whether a party has no financial reason to stay in this state, including whether the party is unemployed, is able to work anywhere, or is financially independent.

(F) Whether a party has engaged in planning activities that would facilitate the removal of a child from the state, including quitting a job, selling his or her primary residence, terminating a lease, closing a bank account, liquidating other assets, hiding or destroying documents, applying for a passport, applying to obtain a birth certificate or school or medical records, or purchasing airplane or other travel tickets, with consideration given to whether a party is carrying out a safety plan to flee from domestic violence.

(G) Whether a party has a history of a lack of parental cooperation or child abuse, or there is substantiated evidence that a party has perpetrated domestic violence.

(H) Whether a party has a criminal record.

(2) If the court makes a finding that there is a need for preventative measures after considering the factors listed in paragraph (1), the court shall consider taking one or more of the following measures to prevent the abduction of the child:

(A) Ordering supervised visitation.

(B) Requiring a parent to post a bond in an amount sufficient to serve as a financial deterrent to abduction, the proceeds of which may be used to offset the cost of recovery of the child in the event there is an abduction.

(C) Restricting the right of the custodial or noncustodial parent to remove the child from the county, the state, or the country.

(D) Restricting the right of the custodial parent to relocate with the child, unless the custodial parent provides advance notice to, and obtains the written agreement of, the noncustodial parent, or obtains the approval of the court, before relocating with the child.

(E) Requiring the surrender of passports and other travel documents.

(F) Prohibiting a parent from applying for a new or replacement passport for the child.

(G) Requiring a parent to notify a relevant foreign consulate or embassy of passport restrictions and to provide the court with proof of that notification.

(H) Requiring a party to register a California order in another state as a prerequisite to allowing a child to travel to that state for visits, or to obtain an order from another country containing terms identical to the custody and visitation order issued in the United States (recognizing that these orders may be modified or enforced pursuant to the laws of the other country), as a prerequisite to allowing a child to travel to that county for visits.

(I) Obtaining assurances that a party will return from foreign visits by requiring the traveling parent to provide the court or the other parent or guardian with any of the following:

(i) The travel itinerary of the child.

(ii) Copies of round trip airline tickets.

(iii) A list of addresses and telephone numbers where the child can be reached at all times.

(iv) An open airline ticket for the left-behind parent in case the child is not returned.

(J) Including provisions in the custody order to facilitate use of the Uniform Child Custody Jurisdiction and Enforcement Act (Part 3 (commencing with Section 3400)) and the Hague Convention on the Civil Aspects of International Child Abduction (implemented pursuant to 42 U.S.C. Sec. 11601 et seq.), such as identifying California as the home state of the child or otherwise defining the basis for the California court's exercise of jurisdiction under Part 3 (commencing with Section 3400), identifying the United States as the country of habitual residence of the child pursuant to the Hague Convention, defining custody rights pursuant to the Hague Convention, obtaining the express agreement of the parents that the United States is the country of habitual residence of the child, or that California or the United States is the most appropriate forum for addressing custody and visitation orders.

(K) Authorizing the assistance of law enforcement.

(3) If the court imposes any or all of the conditions listed in paragraph (2), those conditions shall be specifically noted on the minute order of the court proceedings.

(4) If the court determines there is a risk of abduction that is sufficient to warrant the application of one or more of the prevention measures authorized by this section, the court shall inform the parties of the telephone number and address of the Child Abduction Unit in the office of the district attorney in the county where the custody or visitation order is being entered.

(c) The Judicial Council shall make the changes to its child custody order forms that are necessary for the implementation of subdivision (b). This subdivision shall become operative on July 1, 2003.

(d) Nothing in this section affects the applicability of Section 278.7 of the Penal Code. *(Added by Stats.2002, c. 856 (A.B.2441), § 2. Amended by Stats.2003, c. 62 (S.B.600), § 86; Stats.2003, c. 52 (A.B.1516) § 1, eff. July 14, 2003.)*

Research References

Forms

California Practice Guide: Rutter Family Law Forms Form 9:3, Marital Settlement Agreement.
West's California Code Forms, Family § 2338 Form 9, Marital Agreement--Both Spouses Employed.
West's California Code Forms, Family § 3081 Form 3, Clauses Regarding Custody and Visitation--Additional Clauses.
West's California Judicial Council Forms DV-108, Request for Order: No Travel With Children.
West's California Judicial Council Forms DV-145, Order: No Travel With Children.
West's California Judicial Council Forms FL-312, Request for Child Abduction Prevention Orders.
West's California Judicial Council Forms FL-341, Child Custody and Visitation (Parenting Time) Order Attachment.
West's California Judicial Council Forms FL-341(B), Child Abduction Prevention Order Attachment.

Treatises and Practice Aids

Witkin, California Summary 10th Parent and Child § 270, Risk Of Abduction and Missing Person Check.
Witkin, California Summary 10th Parent and Child § 285, in General.

§ 3049. Disabled parents; legislative intent

It is the intent of the Legislature in enacting this section to codify the decision of the California Supreme Court in In re Marriage of Carney (1979) 24 Cal.3d 725, with respect to custody and visitation determinations by the court involving a disabled parent. *(Added by Stats.2010, c. 179 (S.B.1188), § 1.)*

Commentary

This section codifies *In re Marriage of Carney, 24 Cal.3d 725, 598 P.2d 36, 157 Cal.Rptr. 383 (1979)*, which held that a parent's disability per se is not a proper basis for determining child custody or visitation. Before taking into account a parent's disability, a court must determine whether the parent's condition will have a substantial and lasting adverse effect on the best interest of the child. A newly disabled custodial parent's inability to participate with his children in purely physical activities is not a changed circumstance of sufficient relevance and materiality to make it either essential or expedient to warrant a change in custody to the other parent.

Research References

Forms

California Transactions Forms--Family Law § 3:11, Permanent Custody.

Treatises and Practice Aids

Witkin, California Summary 10th Parent and Child § 210, Other Factors.
Witkin, California Summary 10th Parent and Child § 257, Physical Handicap Of Custodial Parent.

CHAPTER 3. TEMPORARY CUSTODY ORDER DURING PENDENCY OF PROCEEDING

§ 3060. Petition for temporary custody order

A petition for a temporary custody order, containing the statement required by Section 3409, may be included with the initial filing of the petition or action or may be filed at any time after the initial filing. *(Stats.1992, c. 162 (A.B.2650), § 10, operative Jan. 1, 1994. Amended by Stats.1993, c. 219 (A.B.1500), § 116.60.)*

Law Revision Commission Comments

Enactment [Revised Comment]

Section 3060 continues former Civil Code Section 4600.1(a) without substantive change. The language making this section applicable to proceedings for dissolution, nullity, legal separation, and exclusive custody has been omitted as unnecessary. See Section 3021 (application of part) & Comment. See also Sections 3131 (action by district attorney where child taken or detained in violation of custody order), 3133 (temporary custody order at request of district attorney). As to the court's jurisdiction, see Sections 3400–3425 (Uniform Child Custody Jurisdiction Act). [23 Cal.L.Rev. Comm. Reports 1 (1993)].

Commentary

For discussion and history of Sections 3060–3064, see *People v. Beach, 194 Cal.App.3d 955, 968, 240 Cal.Rptr. 50 (1987), review denied 12/2/87.*

Lester v. Lennane, 84 Cal.App.4th 536, 101 Cal.Rptr.2d 86 (2000), holds that temporary child custody orders are unappealable and are reviewable only by extraordinary writ.

Research References

Forms

California Transactions Forms--Family Law § 3:10, Temporary Custody.

Treatises and Practice Aids

Witkin, California Summary 10th Husband and Wife § 86, in General.
Witkin, California Summary 10th Parent and Child § 195, Statutory Framework.
Witkin, California Summary 10th Parent and Child § 271, Temporary Custody During Pendency Of Proceeding.

§ 3061. Agreement or understanding on custody; temporary custody order

If the parties have agreed to or reached an understanding on the custody or temporary custody of their children, a copy of the agreement or an affidavit as to their understanding shall be attached to the petition or action. As promptly as possible after this filing, the court shall, except in exceptional circumstances, enter an order granting temporary custody in accordance with the agreement or understanding or in accordance with any stipulation of the parties. *(Stats.1992, c. 162 (A.B.2650), § 10, operative Jan. 1, 1994. Amended by Stats.1993, c. 219 (A.B.1500), § 116.61.)*

Law Revision Commission Comments

Enactment [Revised Comment]

Section 3061 continues former Civil Code Section 4600.1(b) without substantive change. [23 Cal.L.Rev.Comm. Reports 1 (1993)].

Commentary

For discussion and history of Sections 3060–3064, see *People v. Beach, 194 Cal.App.3d 955, 968, 240 Cal.Rptr. 50 (1987), review denied 12/2/87.*

Research References

Forms

California Transactions Forms--Family Law § 2:70, Deciding Custody.

California Transactions Forms--Family Law § 3:10, Temporary Custody.

Treatises and Practice Aids

Witkin, California Summary 10th Parent and Child § 271, Temporary Custody During Pendency Of Proceeding.

§ 3062. Ex parte temporary custody orders; hearing; extension of order if responding party avoiding jurisdiction

(a) In the absence of an agreement, understanding, or stipulation, the court may, if jurisdiction is appropriate, enter an ex parte temporary custody order, set a hearing date within 20 days, and issue an order to show cause on the responding party. If the responding party does not appear or respond within the time set, the temporary custody order may be extended as necessary, pending the termination of the proceedings.

(b) If, despite good faith efforts, service of the ex parte order and order to show cause has not been effected in a timely fashion and there is reason to believe, based on an affidavit, or other manner of proof made under penalty of perjury, by the petitioner, that the responding party has possession of the minor child and seeks to avoid the jurisdiction of the court or is concealing the whereabouts of the child, then the hearing date may be reset and the ex parte order extended up to an additional 90 days. After service has been effected, either party may request ex parte that the hearing date be advanced or the ex parte order be dissolved or modified. *(Stats.1992, c. 162 (A.B.2650), § 10, operative Jan. 1, 1994.)*

Law Revision Commission Comments

Enactment [Revised Comment]

Section 3062 continues former Civil Code Section 4600.1(c)-(d) without substantive change. The reference to "children" has been omitted as surplus. See Section 10 (singular includes plural). See also Section 3130 (action by district attorney to locate missing party and child and to procure compliance with order to appear). [23 Cal.L.Rev.Comm. Reports 1 (1993)].

Commentary

For discussion and history of Sections 3060–3064, see *People v. Beach, 194 Cal.App.3d 955, 968, 240 Cal.Rptr. 50 (1987), review denied 12/2/87.*

Research References

Forms

California Practice Guide: Rutter Family Law Forms Form 5:5, Ex Parte Application and Request for Order Re Child Custody, Visitation and Property Control.

West's California Judicial Council Forms FL-303, Declaration Regarding Notice and Service Of Request for Temporary Emergency (Ex Parte) Orders.

West's California Judicial Council Forms FL-305, Temporary Emergency Court Orders.

Treatises and Practice Aids

Witkin, California Summary 10th Parent and Child § 249, Power to Modify.

Witkin, California Summary 10th Parent and Child § 271, Temporary Custody During Pendency Of Proceeding.

§ 3063. Order restraining removal of child from state

In conjunction with any ex parte order seeking or modifying an order of custody, the court shall enter an order restraining the person receiving custody from removing the child from the state pending notice and a hearing on the order seeking or modifying custody. *(Stats.1992, c. 162 (A.B.2650), § 10, operative Jan. 1, 1994.)*

Law Revision Commission Comments

Enactment [Revised Comment]

Section 3063 continues the first sentence of former Civil Code Section 4600.1(e) without change. See also Section 3131 (action by district attorney where child taken or detained in violation of custody order). [23 Cal.L.Rev.Comm. Reports 1 (1993)].

Commentary

For discussion and history of Sections 3060–3064, see *People v. Beach, 194 Cal.App.3d 955, 968, 240 Cal.Rptr. 50 (1987), review denied 12/2/87.*

Research References

Forms

West's California Judicial Council Forms DV-105, Request for Child Custody and Visitation Orders.

Treatises and Practice Aids

Witkin, California Summary 10th Parent and Child § 271, Temporary Custody During Pendency Of Proceeding.

§ 3064. Restrictions on ex parte orders granting or modifying custody order

(a) The court shall refrain from making an order granting or modifying a custody order on an ex parte basis unless there has been a showing of immediate harm to the child or immediate risk that the child will be removed from the State of California.

(b) "Immediate harm to the child" includes, but is not limited to, the following:

(1) Having a parent who has committed acts of domestic violence, where the court determines that the acts of domestic violence are of recent origin or are a part of a demonstrated and continuing pattern of acts of domestic violence.

(2) Sexual abuse of the child, where the court determines that the acts of sexual abuse are of recent origin or are a part of a demonstrated and continuing pattern of acts of sexual

abuse. *(Stats.1992, c. 162 (A.B.2650), § 10, operative Jan. 1, 1994. Amended by Stats.2008, c. 54 (A.B.2960), § 1.)*

Law Revision Commission Comments

Enactment [Revised Comment]

Section 3064 continues the last two sentences of former Civil Code Section 4600.1(e) without substantive change. Unlike the former section, this section does not contain a reference to the section defining "domestic violence." This is not a substantive change. See Sections 6201 (application of definitions), 6211 ("domestic violence" defined). [23 Cal.L.Rev.Comm. Reports 1 (1993)].

Commentary

For discussion and history of Sections 3060–3064, see *People v. Beach, 194 Cal.App.3d 955, 968, 240 Cal.Rptr. 50 (1987), review denied 12/2/87.*

In re Marriage of Biggums–Slayton, 86 Cal.App.4th 653, 103 Cal.Rptr.2d 545 (2001), review denied May 16, 2001, held that the trial court properly issued an ex parte order changing child custody to the father after a custodial mother left her four-year-old son alone at home, because the mother's failure to supervise the child satisfied the statutory requisite of "immediate harm" to the child.

Research References

Forms

California Transactions Forms--Family Law § 3:10, Temporary Custody.

West's California Judicial Council Forms FL-303, Declaration Regarding Notice and Service Of Request for Temporary Emergency (Ex Parte) Orders.

West's California Judicial Council Forms FL-305, Temporary Emergency Court Orders.

Treatises and Practice Aids

Witkin, California Summary 10th Husband and Wife § 383, Temporary Custody and Visitation.

Witkin, California Summary 10th Parent and Child § 271, Temporary Custody During Pendency Of Proceeding.

CHAPTER 4. JOINT CUSTODY

§ 3080. Presumption of joint custody

There is a presumption, affecting the burden of proof, that joint custody is in the best interest of a minor child, subject to Section 3011, where the parents have agreed to joint custody or so agree in open court at a hearing for the purpose of determining the custody of the minor child. *(Stats.1992, c. 162 (A.B.2650), § 10, operative Jan. 1, 1994. Amended by Stats.1993, c. 219 (A.B.1500), § 116.70.)*

Law Revision Commission Comments

Enactment [Revised Comment]

Section 3080 continues former Civil Code Section 4600.5(a) without substantive change. The former reference to a child "of the marriage" has been omitted as unnecessary. See Section 3021 (application of part). The reference to "an award of" joint custody is omitted as surplus.

See also Sections 3002 ("joint custody" defined), 3131 (action by district attorney where child taken or detained in violation of custody order). [23 Cal.L.Rev.Comm. Reports 1 (1993)].

Research References

Forms

California Transactions Forms--Family Law § 3:8, No Statutory Custody Preferences.

West's California Code Forms, Family § 3080, Comment Overview--Joint Custody.

Treatises and Practice Aids

Witkin, California Summary 10th Parent and Child § 195, Statutory Framework.

Witkin, California Summary 10th Parent and Child § 222, Statutory Authorization.

Witkin, California Summary 10th Parent and Child § 224, Nature Of Right.

Witkin, California Summary 10th Parent and Child § 282, Agreement.

§ 3081. Application by parents; custody investigation

On application of either parent, joint custody may be ordered in the discretion of the court in cases other than those described in Section 3080, subject to Section 3011. For the purpose of assisting the court in making a determination whether joint custody is appropriate under this section, the court may direct that an investigation be conducted pursuant to Chapter 6 (commencing with Section 3110). *(Stats.1992, c. 162 (A.B.2650), § 10, operative Jan. 1, 1994. Amended by Stats.1993, c. 219 (A.B.1500), § 116.71.)*

Law Revision Commission Comments

Enactment [Revised Comment]

Section 3081 continues former Civil Code Section 4600.5(b) without substantive change. The reference to "an award" of joint custody is omitted as surplus. See Section 3002 ("joint custody" defined); see also Section 3131 (action by district attorney where child taken or detained in violation of custody order); Code Civ. Proc. § 917.7 (order not automatically stayed by appeal). [23 Cal.L.Rev.Comm. Reports 1 (1993)].

Research References

Forms

West's California Code Forms, Family § 3080, Comment Overview--Joint Custody.

Treatises and Practice Aids

Witkin, California Summary 10th Parent and Child § 223, Procedure.

§ 3082. Statement of reasons for grant or denial

When a request for joint custody is granted or denied, the court, upon the request of any party, shall state in its decision the reasons for granting or denying the request. A statement that joint physical custody is, or is not, in the best interest of the child is not sufficient to satisfy the requirements of this section. *(Stats.1992, c. 162 (A.B.2650), § 10, operative Jan. 1, 1994.)*

Law Revision Commission Comments

Enactment [Revised Comment]

Section 3082 continues former Civil Code Section 4600.5(c) without substantive change. See also Sections 3002 ("joint custody" defined), 3004 ("joint physical custody" defined), 3011 (factors to be considered in determining best interest of child). [23 Cal.L.Rev. Comm. Reports 1 (1993)].

Commentary

See generally *In re Marriage of Buser, 190 Cal.App.3d 639, 642, 235 Cal.Rptr. 785 (1987), review denied 7/2/87.*

Research References

Forms

West's California Code Forms, Family § 3080, Comment Overview--Joint Custody.

Treatises and Practice Aids

Witkin, California Summary 10th Parent and Child § 223, Procedure.

§ 3083. Contents and construction of joint legal custody order

In making an order of joint legal custody, the court shall specify the circumstances under which the consent of both parents is required to be obtained in order to exercise legal control of the child and the consequences of the failure to obtain mutual consent. In all other circumstances, either parent acting alone may exercise legal control of the child. An order of joint legal custody shall not be construed to permit an action that is inconsistent with the physical custody order unless the action is expressly authorized by the court. *(Stats.1992, c. 162 (A.B.2650), § 10, operative Jan. 1, 1994.)*

Law Revision Commission Comments

Enactment [Revised Comment]

Section 3083 continues former Civil Code Section 4600.5(e) without change. See also Section 3003 ("joint legal custody" defined); Code Civ. Proc. § 917.7 (order not automatically stayed by appeal). [23 Cal.L.Rev.Comm. Reports 1 (1993)].

Research References

Forms

California Transactions Forms--Family Law § 3:9, Statutory Custody Definitions.

California Transactions Forms--Family Law § 3:15, Overview; Scope Of Agreement.

California Transactions Forms--Family Law § 3:17, Deciding How to Implement and Enforce the Agreement.

California Transactions Forms--Family Law § 5:16, School and Extracurricular Activities; Religious Upbringing; Medical Care.

California Transactions Forms--Family Law § 5:26, Inheritance and Custody on Death.

West's California Code Forms, Family § 3080, Comment Overview--Joint Custody.

West's California Judicial Council Forms FL-341(C), Children's Holiday Schedule Attachment.

West's California Judicial Council Forms FL-341(D), Additional Provisions--Physical Custody Attachment.

West's California Judicial Council Forms FL-341(E), Joint Legal Custody Attachment.

Treatises and Practice Aids

Witkin, California Summary 10th Parent and Child § 223, Procedure.

§ 3084. Rights of parents to physical control of child

In making an order of joint physical custody, the court shall specify the rights of each parent to physical control of the child in sufficient detail to enable a parent deprived of that control to implement laws for relief of child snatching and kidnapping. *(Stats.1992, c. 162 (A.B.2650), § 10, operative Jan. 1, 1994.)*

Law Revision Commission Comments

Enactment [Revised Comment]

Section 3084 continues former Civil Code Section 4600.5(f) without change. See also Section 3004 ("joint physical custody" defined). [23 Cal.L.Rev.Comm. Reports 1 (1993)].

Research References

Forms

California Transactions Forms--Family Law § 3:9, Statutory Custody Definitions.

California Transactions Forms--Family Law § 3:18, Overview.

Treatises and Practice Aids

Witkin, California Summary 10th Parent and Child § 223, Procedure.

§ 3085. Grant of joint legal custody without joint physical custody

In making an order for custody with respect to both parents, the court may grant joint legal custody without granting joint physical custody. *(Stats.1992, c. 162 (A.B. 2650), § 10, operative Jan. 1, 1994. Amended by Stats.1993, c. 219 (A.B.1500), § 116.72.)*

Law Revision Commission Comments

Enactment [Revised Comment]

Section 3085 continues former Civil Code Section 4600.5(g) without substantive change. See also Sections 3003 ("joint legal custody" defined), 3004 ("joint physical custody" defined). [23 Cal.L.Rev.Comm. Reports 1 (1993)].

Research References

Forms

California Transactions Forms--Family Law § 3:9, Statutory Custody Definitions.

Treatises and Practice Aids

Witkin, California Summary 10th Parent and Child § 223, Procedure.

§ 3086. Orders of joint physical custody or joint legal custody; designation of primary caretaker and primary home of child

In making an order of joint physical custody or joint legal custody, the court may specify one parent as the primary caretaker of the child and one home as the primary home of the child, for the purposes of determining eligibility for public assistance. *(Stats.1992, c. 162 (A.B.2650), § 10, operative Jan. 1, 1994.)*

Law Revision Commission Comments

Enactment [Revised Comment]

Section 3086 continues former Civil Code Section 4600.5(h) without change. See also Sections 3003 ("joint legal custody" defined), 3004 ("joint physical custody" defined), 3028 (compensation for failure to assume caretaker responsibility). [23 Cal.L.Rev. Comm. Reports 1 (1993)].

Research References

Forms

California Transactions Forms--Family Law § 3:9, Statutory Custody Definitions.

California Transactions Forms--Family Law § 3:18, Overview.

Treatises and Practice Aids

Witkin, California Summary 10th Parent and Child § 223, Procedure.

§ 3087. Modification or termination of joint custody order; statement of reasons

An order for joint custody may be modified or terminated upon the petition of one or both parents or on the court's own motion if it is shown that the best interest of the child requires modification or termination of the order. If either parent opposes the modification or termination order, the court shall state in its decision the reasons for modification or termination of the joint custody order. *(Stats.1992, c. 162 (A.B.2650), § 10, operative Jan. 1, 1994.)*

Law Revision Commission Comments

Enactment [Revised Comment]

Section 3087 continues former Civil Code Section 4600.5(i) without substantive change. See also Sections 3002 ("joint custody" defined), 3011 (factors to be considered in determining best interest of child); Code Civ. Proc. § 917.7 (order not automatically stayed by appeal). [23 Cal.L.Rev.Comm. Reports 1 (1993)].

Commentary

In re Marriage of Olson, 238 Cal.App.4th 1458, 190 Cal.Rptr.3d 715 (2015), holds that a parent who defaulted in a dissolution proceeding has standing to seek modification of child custody without seeking relief from the default.

In re Marriage of Birnbaum, 211 Cal.App.3rd 1508, 260 Cal.Rptr.2d 210 (1989), purported to hold that the party who moves for modification of a joint custody award need not show a change of circumstances justifying the requested modification, as would the movant in an ordinary motion to change custody, reasoning that alteration of the details of a joint custody arrangement is not a change of custody. However, the ostensible holding was dictum because *Birnbaum* did involve a substantial change of circumstances: the mother changed her residence, necessitating a change of schools for the children or alteration of the parenting plan. However, *Niko v. Forman, 144 Cal.App.4th 344, 50 Cal.Rptr.3d 398 (2006), review denied Feb. 7, 2007*, applied the dictum of *Birnbaum* to a case in which there were no changed circumstances, other than the decision of a California mother to relocate to Colorado. *Niko* held that changed circumstances were not required because the trial court continued joint custody with a modified parenting plan and thus did not "change" custody. The California Supreme Court granted review to *In re Marriage of Congdon, 977 P.2d 693, 85 Cal.Rptr.2d 696 (1999)*, thereby depublishing the opinion of the Court of Appeal, 82 Cal.Rptr.2d 686 (1999), which rejected the dictum of *Birnbaum* and held that a parent who seeks to modify a joint physical custody order must show a change of circumstances justifying the requested modification. *Congdon* reasoned that the change of circumstances threshold is necessary to avoid unwarranted and harassing relitigation and to provide stability in the lives of the children and the nonmovant parent. For further discussion of the requirement that the movant show changed circumstances, see Section 3022, Commentary.

Following the dictum of *Birnbaum*, *Enrique M. v. Angelina V., 121 Cal.App.4th 1371, 18 Cal.Rptr.3d 306 (2004)*, holds that the standard of proof required of a joint physical custodian who wishes to change joint custodial parenting time is the best interests of the child, not changed circumstances.

For discussion of modification when parents in fact exercise joint physical custody and one parent proposes to relocate, see Section 7501, Commentary.

Research References

Forms

California Transactions Forms--Family Law § 3:18, Overview.

Treatises and Practice Aids

Witkin, California Summary 10th Parent and Child § 223, Procedure.

Witkin, California Summary 10th Parent and Child § 249, Power to Modify.

Witkin, California Summary 10th Parent and Child § 253, Move-Away Cases.

Witkin, California Summary 10th Parent and Child § 255, Stipulation for Temporary Custody.

Witkin, California Summary 10th Parent and Child § 265, Application and Decision.

Witkin, California Summary 10th Parent and Child § 259A, (New) Military Deployment.

§ 3088. Modification of custody order to joint custody order

An order for the custody of a minor child entered by a court in this state or any other state may, subject to the jurisdictional requirements in Sections 3403 and 3414, be modified at any time to an order for joint custody in accordance with this chapter. *(Stats.1992, c. 162 (A.B.2650), § 10, operative Jan. 1, 1994. Amended by Stats.1993, c. 219 (A.B.1500), § 116.73.)*

Law Revision Commission Comments

Enactment [Revised Comment]

Section 3088 continues former Civil Code Section 4600.5(j) without substantive change. The former reference to a child "of the marriage" has been omitted as unnecessary. See Section 3021 (application of part). See also Section 3002 ("joint custody" defined). [23 Cal.L.Rev.Comm. Reports 1 (1993)].

Research References

Treatises and Practice Aids

Witkin, California Summary 10th Parent and Child § 223, Procedure.

§ 3089. Conciliation court; consultation by court or parties

In counties having a conciliation court, the court or the parties may, at any time, pursuant to local rules of court, consult with the conciliation court for the purpose of assisting the parties to formulate a plan for implementation of the custody order or to resolve a controversy which has arisen in the implementation of a plan for custody. *(Stats.1992, c. 162 (A.B.2650), § 10, operative Jan. 1, 1994.)*

Law Revision Commission Comments

Enactment [Revised Comment]

Section 3089 continues former Civil Code Section 4600.5(k) without change. [23 Cal.L.Rev.Comm. Reports 1 (1993)].

Research References

Forms

California Transactions Forms--Family Law § 3:17, Deciding How to Implement and Enforce the Agreement.

Treatises and Practice Aids

Witkin, California Summary 10th Parent and Child § 223, Procedure.

CHAPTER 5. VISITATION RIGHTS

§ 3100. Joint custody orders; visitation rights; domestic violence prevention orders; transfer of children; detail specific orders; confidentiality of shelter locations

(a) In making an order pursuant to Chapter 4 (commencing with Section 3080), the court shall grant reasonable visitation rights to a parent unless it is shown that the visitation would be detrimental to the best interest of the child. In the discretion of the court, reasonable visitation rights may be granted to any other person having an interest in the welfare of the child.

(b) If a protective order, as defined in Section 6218, has been directed to a parent, the court shall consider whether the best interest of the child requires that any visitation by that parent be limited to situations in which a third person, specified by the court, is present, or whether visitation shall be suspended or denied. The court shall include in its deliberations a consideration of the nature of the acts from which the parent was enjoined and the period of time that has elapsed since that order. A parent may submit to the court the name of a person that the parent deems suitable to be present during visitation.

(c) If visitation is ordered in a case in which domestic violence is alleged and an emergency protective order, protective order, or other restraining order has been issued, the visitation order shall specify the time, day, place, and manner of transfer of the child, so as to limit the child's exposure to potential domestic conflict or violence and to ensure the safety of all family members. If a criminal protective order has been issued pursuant to Section 136.2 of the Penal Code, the visitation order shall make reference to, and, unless there is an emergency protective order that has precedence in enforcement pursuant to paragraph (1) of subdivision (c) of Section 136.2 of the Penal Code or a no-contact order, as described in Section 6320, acknowledge the precedence of enforcement of, an appropriate criminal protective order.

(d) If the court finds a party is staying in a place designated as a shelter for victims of domestic violence or other confidential location, the court's order for time, day, place, and manner of transfer of the child for visitation shall be designed to prevent disclosure of the location of the shelter or other confidential location. *(Stats.1992, c. 162 (A.B.2650), § 10, operative Jan. 1, 1994. Amended by Stats. 1993, c. 219 (A.B.1500), § 116.74; Stats.1994, c. 320 (A.B. 356), § 2; Stats.2005, c. 465 (A.B.118), § 1; Stats.2013, c. 263 (A.B.176), § 1, operative July 1, 2014.)*

Law Revision Commission Comments

Enactment [Revised Comment]

Subdivision (a) of Section 3100 continues former Civil Code Section 4601 without substantive change.

Subdivision (b) continues former Civil Code Section 4601.5 without substantive change. The introductory clause has been omitted as surplus. The term "protective order" has been substituted for the references to orders under specific sections formerly in the Civil Code and the Code of Civil Procedure. This is not a substantive change, since Section 6218 defines "protective order" to include these orders.

See also Sections 3011 (factors to be considered in determining best interest of child), 3030 (parent convicted under certain Penal Code provisions not allowed unsupervised visitation with child), 3131 (action by district attorney where child taken or detained in violation of visitation order); Code Civ. Proc. § 917.7 (order not automatically stayed by appeal). [23 Cal.L.Rev.Comm. Reports 1 (1993)].

Commentary

When a noncustodial parent merely seeks to alter or increase visitation, his request is decided according to the "best interest of the child" standard. *In re Marriage of Lucio, 161 Cal.App.4th 1068, 74 Cal.Rptr.3d 803 (2008)*. Compare the standard applied in a request to change custody, discussed in Commentary to section 3022.

Hoversten v. Superior Court, 74 Cal.App.4th 636, 88 Cal.Rptr.2d 197 (1999), holds that subsection (a) requires that a prisoner, no matter how egregious the nature of his crime, be granted a hearing to determine whether he should have legal custody and visitation of his minor child. It was error for the trial court to determine that the prisoner was not entitled to a hearing to determine whether it would be in the child's best interests to have visitation despite the crime and incarceration of the prisoner. Although prisoners do not ordinarily appear personally in civil proceedings, trial courts should devise alternative means to insure participation in the proceeding. *Hoversten* additionally suggests, under § 3170(a), the use of a mediator in contested cases.

A court generally may not entertain an independent action for nonparent visitation. *White v. Jacobs, 198 Cal.App.3d 122, 243 Cal.Rptr. 597 (1988)*. A request for nonparent visitation must usually be made in the course of a proceeding in which custody otherwise is or may be at issue. *Perry v. Superior Court, 108 Cal.App.3d 480, 482, 166 Cal.Rptr. 583 (1980)*. Section 3100 visitation may, for example, be granted to an interested but unrelated person in the course of an existing guardianship proceeding. *Guardianship of Martha M., 204 Cal.App.3d 909, 251 Cal.Rptr. 567 (1988)*. See also Section 3021. But see Section 3102, which allows specified persons to bring an independent action for visitation when the parent of the child is deceased. *White, supra.* See also Section 3104, added by Stats 1993 Ch 832, § 1 (SB 306), which, under special circumstances, grants grandparents the right to file an independent petition for visitation.

In re Marriage of Gayden, 229 Cal.App.3d 1510, 280 Cal.Rptr. 862 (1991), holds that visitation may not be granted to a nonparent over the opposition of both parents merely upon a finding that visitation would promote the best interests of the child. Instead, such an award may be made only when there is clear and convincing evidence that denial of nonparent visitation would be detrimental to the child. Cf. *In re Hirenia C., 18 Cal.App.4th 504, 22 Cal.Rptr.2d 443 (1993)* and *In re Robin N., 7 Cal.App.4th 1140, 1146, 9 Cal.Rptr.2d 512 (1992), review denied 9/23/92.* But see Section 3104.

Research References

Forms

California Practice Guide: Rutter Family Law Forms Form 5:5, Ex Parte Application and Request for Order Re Child Custody, Visitation and Property Control.

California Practice Guide: Rutter Family Law Forms Form 7:19, Memorandum in Support Of Motion and Declaration for Joinder (Grandparent Visitation Claim).

California Transactions Forms--Family Law § 5:2, Overview.

California Transactions Forms--Family Law § 3:13, Rights Of Third Parties.

California Transactions Forms--Family Law § 4:104, Paternity Acknowledgment.

West's California Code Forms, Family § 3103, Comment Overview--Visitation Rights.

West's California Judicial Council Forms DV-140, Child Custody and Visitation Order.

West's California Judicial Council Forms DV-150, Supervised Visitation and Exchange Order.

West's California Judicial Council Forms FL-341, Child Custody and Visitation (Parenting Time) Order Attachment.

West's California Judicial Council Forms FL-341(A), Supervised Visitation Order.

Treatises and Practice Aids

Witkin, California Summary 10th Husband and Wife § 383, Temporary Custody and Visitation.

Witkin, California Summary 10th Parent and Child § 195, Statutory Framework.

Witkin, California Summary 10th Parent and Child § 224, Nature Of Right.

Witkin, California Summary 10th Parent and Child § 225, Circumstances Warranting Denial.

Witkin, California Summary 10th Parent and Child § 233, in General.

Witkin, California Summary 10th Parent and Child § 234, Biologically Unrelated Persons Not Opposed by Parent.

Witkin, California Summary 10th Parent and Child § 235, Biologically Unrelated Persons Opposed by Parent.

Witkin, California Summary 10th Parent and Child § 238, Valid Conditions.

Witkin, California Summary 10th Parent and Child § 279, Availability Of Mediation.

Witkin, California Summary 10th Parent and Child § 282, Agreement.

§ 3101. Stepparent's visitation rights

(a) Notwithstanding any other provision of law, the court may grant reasonable visitation to a stepparent, if visitation by the stepparent is determined to be in the best interest of the minor child.

(b) If a protective order, as defined in Section 6218, has been directed to a stepparent to whom visitation may be granted pursuant to this section, the court shall consider whether the best interest of the child requires that any visitation by the stepparent be denied.

(c) Visitation rights may not be ordered under this section that would conflict with a right of custody or visitation of a birth parent who is not a party to the proceeding.

(d) As used in this section:

(1) "Birth parent" means "birth parent" as defined in Section 8512.

(2) "Stepparent" means a person who is a party to the marriage that is the subject of the proceeding, with respect to a minor child of the other party to the marriage. *(Added by Stats.1993, c. 219 (A.B.1500), § 116.76.)*

Law Revision Commission Comments

Enactment [Revised Comment]

Subdivision (a) of Section 3101 restates former Civil Code Section 4351.5(a) without substantive change. The section is revised to use the term "stepparent." This is not a substantive change, since subdivision (d)(1), defining "stepparent," is drawn from the language of former Civil Code Section 4351.5(a). References to the "superior" court have been omitted as surplus. See Section 200 (jurisdiction in superior court). The language making this section applicable to proceedings for dissolution, nullity, or legal separation has been omitted as unnecessary. See Section 3021 (application of part) & Comment.

Subdivision (b) continues former Civil Code Section 4351.5(*l*) without substantive change insofar as it applied to stepparents. The term "protective order" has been substituted for the references to orders under specific sections formerly in the Civil Code and the Code of Civil Procedure. This is not a substantive change, since Section 6218 defines "protective order" to include these orders.

Subdivision (c) continues former Civil Code Section 4351.5(j) without substantive change insofar as it applied to stepparents. The reference to "birth parent" has been substituted for the former reference to "a natural or adoptive parent." This is not a substantive change, since under subdivision (d)(1),"birth parent" include a biological and adoptive parent. This amendment is intended to improve clarity by using a defined term.

Subdivision (d) is new. Paragraph (1) is drawn from former Civil Code Section 4351.5(a).

See also Sections 3011 (factors to be considered in determining best interest of child), 3131 (action by district attorney where child taken or detained in violation of custody order), 3133 (temporary custody order at request of district attorney); Code Civ. Proc. § 917.7 (order not automatically stayed by appeal). As to the court's jurisdiction, see Sections 3400–3425 (Uniform Child Custody Jurisdiction Act). [23 Cal.L.Rev.Comm. Reports 1 (1993)].

Commentary

For discussion of this provision, see generally *Michelle W. v. Ronald W., 39 Cal.3d 354, 368, 216 Cal.Rptr. 748 (1985), appeal dismissed, 474 U.S. 1043 (1986)*; *In re Marriage of Goetz and Lewis, 203 Cal.App.3d 514, 517, 250 Cal.Rptr. 30 (1988)*; *In re Robert D. v. Carol F., 151 Cal.App.3d 391, 404, 198 Cal.Rptr. 801 (1984)*. See also *In re Marriage of Hinman, 6 Cal.App.4th 711, 716, 8 Cal.Rptr.2d 245 (1992)* (wife's characterization of her children as Section 2010 "children of the marriage" in dissolution provision and her later stipulation that husband have primary physical custody estopped her from later challenging stepparent custody order on jurisdictional grounds).

Visitation is not available to a natural parent who has relinquished the child for adoption. *Marckwardt v. Superior Court, 150 Cal.App.3d 471, 479, 198 Cal.Rptr. 41 (1984)* (natural parent who has given consent that wife's new husband adopt the children is neither a

Section 2010 parent nor a Section 3101 stepparent). But see Section 3100(a), which gives the divorce court discretion to award reasonable visitation rights to "any other person having an interest in the welfare of the child."

But cf. *Troxel v. Granville, 120 S.Ct. 2054, 147 L.Ed.2d 49 (2000)*, which involved a Washington statute permitting "any person" to petition for visitation rights at any time and allowing the court to grant visitation "whenever visitation may serve the best interests of the child." Despite the objections of the legal parents, the Washington trial court, applying the statute, granted the paternal grandparents extensive visitation of their deceased son's natural children, who resided with their mother and her husband, who had adopted the children. The U.S. Supreme Court held that, in the context of grandparent visitation, the Washington statute violated the due process rights of a fit parent and her family to make decisions concerning the "care, custody, and control" of their children. In *In re Marriage of Harris, 34 Cal.4th 210, 96 P.3d 141, 17 Cal. Rptr.3d 842 (2004)*, the California Supreme Court sustained the constitutionality of Section 3104 and held that it, rather than Section 3103, applies when grandparents request visitation outside of any action in which custody is otherwise at issue, that is, outside of any proceeding described in Section 3021.

Relying on *Troxel*, *In re Marriage of James W., 114 Cal.App.4th 68, 7 Cal.Rptr.3d 461 (2003)*, held that when a child has a father, mother and stepfather, respect for the parents' due process right to the care, custody, and control of their child requires that the trial court apply a presumption that the parents' decision to terminate stepfather visitation is in the child's best interests. The presumption may be overcome only by a showing that visitation with a stepparent is in the best interest of the child and denial of visitation would be detrimental to the child. Of course, *Troxel* does not limit the court's power to order or enforce nonparent visitation when the child's parents do not object. *In re Marriage of Ross & Kelley, 114 Cal.App.4th 130, 7 Cal.Rptr.3d 287 (2003)* (trial court erred in declining to order stipulated grandparent visitation on mistaken belief that it had no power to order grandparent visitation under *Troxel*).

For further discussion of the implications of *Troxel v. Granville*, supra, see Commentary to Section 3102.

Chalmers v. Hirschkop, 213 Cal.App.4th 289, 152 Cal.Rptr.3d 361 (2013), held that a stepparent cannot request a modification of a prior court order that denied subsection (a) visitation.

Research References

Forms

California Transactions Forms--Family Law § 3:7, Custody Issues Outside the Scope Of the Family Code.

California Transactions Forms--Family Law § 5:3, Rights Of Non-parents Generally.

California Transactions Forms--Family Law § 3:13, Rights Of Third Parties.

California Transactions Forms--Family Law § 5:10, Use Of Parenting Agreement to Define Rights and Responsibilities Relating to Child on Termination Of Partners' Relationship Where Neither or Only One Partner is Biological Parent.

Treatises and Practice Aids

Witkin, California Summary 10th Parent and Child § 232, Statutory Authorization.

Witkin, California Summary 10th Parent and Child § 237, Constitutional Limitations.

§ 3102. Deceased parent; visitation rights of close relatives; adoption of child

(a) If either parent of an unemancipated minor child is deceased, the children, siblings, parents, and grandparents of the deceased parent may be granted reasonable visitation with the child during the child's minority upon a finding that the visitation would be in the best interest of the minor child.

(b) In granting visitation pursuant to this section to a person other than a grandparent of the child, the court shall consider the amount of personal contact between the person and the child before the application for the visitation order.

(c) This section does not apply if the child has been adopted by a person other than a stepparent or grandparent of the child. Any visitation rights granted pursuant to this section before the adoption of the child automatically terminate if the child is adopted by a person other than a stepparent or grandparent of the child. *(Stats.1992, c. 162 (A.B.2650), § 10, operative Jan. 1, 1994. Amended by Stats. 1993, c. 219 (A.B.1500), § 116.77; Stats.1994, c. 164 (A.B. 3042), § 1.)*

Law Revision Commission Comments

Enactment [Revised Comment]

Section 3102 continues former Civil Code Section 197.5 without substantive change. The reference to the "superior" court has been omitted as surplus. See Section 200 (jurisdiction in superior court). In subdivision (a), the word "unemancipated" has been substituted for "unmarried." This is not a substantive change. See Section 7002 (conditions of emancipation). See also Section 3011 (factors to be considered in determining best interest of child); Code Civ. Proc. § 917.7 (order not automatically stayed by appeal). [23 Cal.L.Rev. Comm. Reports 1 (1993)].

Commentary

Section 3102 visitation may be requested at any time by the children, siblings, parents, and grandparents of a deceased parent of a child with whom visitation is sought. No other jurisdictional basis is required for a Section 3102 proceeding. Compare sections 3021, 3100 and 3103. *Guardianship of Martha M., 204 Cal.App.3d 909, 913, 251 Cal.Rptr. 567 (1988)*; *White v. Jacobs, 198 Cal.App.3d 122, 124, 243 Cal.Rptr. 597 (1988)*.

See also *Huffman v. Grob, 172 Cal.App.3d 1153, 218 Cal.Rptr. 659 (1985), review denied 12/30/85* (mother, brother, and sister of child's deceased adoptive mother were not entitled to visitation after child was adopted by new mother). But compare Section 3100 (a), which gives the court discretion to award reasonable visitation rights to "any other person having an interest in the welfare of the child." Section 3102 is not an exclusive listing of persons who may seek visitation when a parent dies. *Guardianship of Martha M., supra*.

But see *Troxel v. Granville, 120 S.Ct. 2054, 147 L.Ed.2d 49 (2000)*, which involved a Washington statute, permitting "any person" to petition for visitation rights at any time and allowing the court to grant visitation "whenever visitation may serve the best interests of the child." Despite the objections of the legal parents, the Washington trial court, applying the statute, granted the paternal grandparents extensive visitation of their deceased son's natural children, who resided with their mother and her husband, who had adopted the children. The U.S. Supreme Court held that, in the context of grandparent visitation, the Washington statute violated the due process rights of a fit parent and her family to make decisions concerning the "care, custody, and control" of their children.

Relying on *Troxel*, *In re Marriage of James W., 114 Cal.App.4th 68, 7 Cal.Rptr.3d 461(2003)*, held that when a child has a father, mother and stepfather, respect for the parents' due process right to the care, custody, and control of their child requires that the trial court apply a presumption that the parents' decision to terminate stepfather visitation is in the child's best interests. The presumption may be overcome only by a showing that visitation with a stepparent is in the best interest of the child and denial of visitation would be detrimental to the child. Of course, *Troxel* does not limit the court's power to order or enforce nonparent visitation when the child's parents do not object. *In re Marriage of Ross & Kelley, 114 Cal.App.4th 130, 7 Cal.Rptr.3d 287 (2003)* (trial court erred in declining to order stipulated grandparent visitation on mistaken belief that it had no power to order grandparent visitation under *Troxel*).

Kyle O. v. Donald R., 85 Cal.App.4th 848, 102 Cal.Rptr.2d 476 (2000), constitutionally glosses this section to conform to *Troxel*. *Kyle O.* effectively holds that a grandparent may not petition for "reasonable visitation" under this section when the child's fit parent has been willing to grant ordinary grandparent visitation. Similarly, *Punsly v. Ho, 87 Cal.App.4th 1099, 105 Cal.Rptr.2d 139 (2001)*, holds that the trial court infringed the constitutional rights of a fit parent who was willing to schedule grandparent visitation when it substituted its judgment for the parent's judgment by granting the visitation schedule requested by the grandparents. In *In re Marriage of Harris, 34 Cal.4th 210, 96 P.3d 141, 17 Cal.Rptr.3d 842 (2004)*, the California Supreme Court sustained the constitutionality of Section 3104 and held that it, rather than Section 3103, applies when grandparents request visitation outside of any action in which custody is otherwise at issue, that is, outside of any proceeding described in Section 3021.

Hoag v. Diedjomahor, 200 Cal.App.4th 1008, 132 Cal.Rptr.3d 256 (2011), review denied, holds that the Troxel presumption that a parent's denial or severe limitation of visitation is in a child's best interests is overcome when the parent's objections to visitation by the parent of a child's deceased parent are unreasonable and lack credibility.

Ian J. v. Peter M., 213 Cal.App.4th 189, 152 Cal.Rptr.3d 323 (2013), held that the trial court erred in ordering unsupervised visitation for deceased mother's relatives when the children's fit father had a reasonable basis for believing that the mother's father might sexually abuse the children.

Rich v. Thatcher, 200 Cal.App.4th 1176, 132 Cal.Rptr.3d 897 (2011), holds that the *Troxel* presumption that a fit parent is acting in the best interests of the child imposes upon a grandparent the burden of proving by clear and convincing evidence that denial of grandparent visitation would be detrimental to the child and is therefore not in the child's best interests.

Herbst v. Swan, 102 Cal.App.4th 813, 125 Cal.Rptr.2d 836 (2002), sustained a trial court order dismissing the visitation petition of an adult half-sibling on the ground that granting it would unconstitutionally infringe the surviving parent's liberty interest in controlling her child. In *Herbst*, the surviving parent declined to allow the half-sibling any visitation. Compare *Kyle O.* and *Punsley*, supra. Similarly, in *Zasueta v. Zasueta, 102 Cal.App.4th 1242, 126 Cal.Rptr.2d 245 (2002)*, the court of appeal reversed a trial court order granting grandparent visitation over the objection of the surviving parent, on the ground that the order unconstitutionally infringed the surviving parent's liberty interest in making decisions about the care and custody of her child. The trial court effectively presumed that the parent was unfit insofar as she opposed grandparent visitation, thus shifting to the parent the burden of proving that grandparent visitation was not in the child's best interests. Instead, the parent's decision should have been granted deference, placing on the grandparents the burden of showing that visitation was in the child's best interests. Similarly, interpreting *Troxel*, supra, *Fenn v. Sherriff, 109 Cal.App.4th 1466, 1 Cal.Rptr.3d 185 (2003)*, held that a court may, under this section, constitutionally order grandparent visitation over the objection of fit parents so long as the court grants "special weight" to the decision of the parents regarding grandparent visitation.

Research References

Forms

California Transactions Forms--Family Law § 5:3, Rights Of Nonparents Generally.

California Transactions Forms--Family Law § 5:10, Use Of Parenting Agreement to Define Rights and Responsibilities Relating to Child on Termination Of Partners' Relationship Where Neither or Only One Partner is Biological Parent.

Treatises and Practice Aids

Witkin, California Summary 10th Parent and Child § 226, in General.

Witkin, California Summary 10th Parent and Child § 228, Statutory Right.

Witkin, California Summary 10th Parent and Child § 229, Constitutionality.

Witkin, California Summary 10th Parent and Child § 230, Effect Of Adoption.

Witkin, California Summary 10th Parent and Child § 233, in General.

Witkin, California Summary 10th Parent and Child § 237, Constitutional Limitations.

§ 3103. Grandparent's rights; custody proceeding

(a) Notwithstanding any other provision of law, in a proceeding described in Section 3021, the court may grant reasonable visitation to a grandparent of a minor child of a party to the proceeding if the court determines that visitation by the grandparent is in the best interest of the child.

(b) If a protective order as defined in Section 6218 has been directed to the grandparent during the pendency of the proceeding, the court shall consider whether the best interest of the child requires that visitation by the grandparent be denied.

(c) The petitioner shall give notice of the petition to each of the parents of the child, any stepparent, and any person who has physical custody of the child, by certified mail, return receipt requested, postage prepaid, to the person's last known address, or to the attorneys of record of the parties to the proceeding.

(d) There is a rebuttable presumption affecting the burden of proof that the visitation of a grandparent is not in the best interest of a minor child if the child's parents agree that the grandparent should not be granted visitation rights.

(e) Visitation rights may not be ordered under this section if that would conflict with a right of custody or visitation of a birth parent who is not a party to the proceeding.

(f) Visitation ordered pursuant to this section shall not create a basis for or against a change of residence of the child, but shall be one of the factors for the court to consider in ordering a change of residence.

(g) When a court orders grandparental visitation pursuant to this section, the court in its discretion may, based upon the relevant circumstances of the case:

(1) Allocate the percentage of grandparental visitation between the parents for purposes of the calculation of child support pursuant to the statewide uniform guideline (Article 2 (commencing with Section 4050) of Chapter 2 of Part 2 of Division 9).

(2) Notwithstanding Sections 3930 and 3951, order a parent or grandparent to pay to the other, an amount for the support of the child or grandchild. For purposes of this paragraph, "support" means costs related to visitation such as any of the following:

(A) Transportation.

(B) Provision of basic expenses for the child or grandchild, such as medical expenses, day care costs, and other necessities.

(h) As used in this section, "birth parent" means "birth parent" as defined in Section 8512. *(Added by Stats.1993, c. 219 (A.B.1500), § 116.78. Amended by Stats.1993, c. 832 (S.B.306), § 1.)*

Law Revision Commission Comments

Enactment [Revised Comment]

Subdivision (a) of Section 3103 restates former Civil Code Section 4351.5(b) without substantive change. The reference to former Civil Code Section 4601 has been omitted as surplus. References to the "superior" court have been omitted as surplus. See Section 200 (jurisdiction in superior court). The reference to proceedings "described in Section 3021" has been substituted for the former language making this section applicable to proceedings for dissolution, nullity, or legal separation. Other language has been revised to make clear that this section is applicable to situations in which the parents of the child are not married, such as where visitation is determined in a proceeding pursuant to the Domestic Violence Prevention Act or the Uniform Parentage Act. See Section 3021 (application of part) & Comment.

Subdivision (b) continues former Civil Code Section 4351.5(*l*) without substantive change, insofar as it applied to grandparents. The term "protective order" has been substituted for the references to orders under specific sections formerly in the Civil Code and the Code of Civil Procedure. This is not a substantive change, since Section 6218 defines "protective order" to include these orders.

Subdivision (d) continues former Civil Code Section 4351.5(k) without substantive change. The subdivision has been revised to make it clear that it is applicable to situations in which the parents of the child are not married, such as where visitation is determined in a proceeding pursuant to the Domestic Violence Prevention Act or the Uniform Parentage Act.

Subdivision (e) continues former Civil Code Section 4351.5(j) without substantive change, insofar as it applied to grandparents. A reference to "birth parent" has been substituted for the former reference to "a natural or adoptive parent." This is not a substantive change, since subdivision (h) defines "birth parent" to include a biological or adoptive parent. This amendment is intended to improve clarity by using a defined term.

Subdivision (h) is new.

See also Sections 3011 (factors to be considered in determining best interest of child), 3131 (action by district attorney where child taken or detained in violation of custody order), 3133 (temporary custody order at request of district attorney); Code Civ. Proc. § 917.7 (order not automatically stayed by appeal). As to the court's jurisdiction, see Sections 3400–3425 (Uniform Child Custody Jurisdiction Act).

The provisions in subdivisions (c), (f), and (g) were added by 1993 Cal. Stat. ch. 832, § 1. [23 Cal.L.Rev.Comm. Reports 1 (1993)].

Commentary

Subsection (a) makes explicit the case law requirement that Section 3103 grandparent visitation may only be sought when child custody and visitation are otherwise before the court. *White v. Jacobs, 198 Cal.App.3d 122, 124, 243 Cal.Rptr. 597 (1988)*. Accordingly, *In re Marriage of Harris, 34 Cal.4th 210, 96 P.3d 141, 17 Cal.Rptr.3d 842 (2004)*, held that this section does not apply to a grandparent's request for visitation when the issue of custody is not otherwise before the court under Section 3021. Instead Section 3104 controls. Compare Section 3102, Commentary. See also Section 3104 which, under special circumstances, grants grandparents the right to file an independent petition for visitation.

Interpreting subsection (g)(2), *In re Marriage of Perry, 61 Cal. App.4th 295, 71 Cal.Rptr.2d 499 (1998),* holds that a grandparent who is a party to a custody or visitation proceeding may be ordered to pay for a child's court-appointed counsel, for another party's attorney's fees to defend on issues involving the grandparent, and for costs related to visitation, but not for counseling costs for a grandchild.

But cf. *Troxel v. Granville, 120 S.Ct. 2054, 147 L.Ed.2d 49 (2000)*, which involved a Washington statute permitting "any person" to petition for visitation rights at any time and allowing the court to grant visitation "whenever visitation may serve the best interests of the child." Despite the objections of the legal parents, the Washington trial court, applying the statute, granted the paternal grandparents extensive visitation of their deceased son's natural children, who resided with their mother and her husband, who had adopted the children. The U.S. Supreme Court held that, in the context of grandparent visitation, the Washington statute violated the due process rights of a fit parent and her family to make decisions concerning the "care, custody, and control" of their children. In *In re Marriage of Harris*, supra, the California Supreme Court sustained the constitutionality of Section 3104.

Relying on *Troxel*, *In re Marriage of James W., 114 Cal.App.4th 68, 7 Cal.Rptr.3d 461 (2003)*, held that when a child has a father, mother and stepfather, respect for the parents' due process right to the care, custody, and control of their child requires that the trial court apply a presumption that the parents' decision to terminate stepfather visitation is in the child's best interests. The presumption may be over come only by a showing that visitation with a stepparent is in the best interest of the child and denial of visitation would be detrimental to the child. Of course, *Troxel* does not limit the court's power to order or enforce nonparent visitation when the child's parents do not object. *In re Marriage of Ross & Kelley, 114 Cal.App.4th 130, 7 Cal.Rptr.3d 287 (2003)* (trial court erred in declining to order stipulated grandparent visitation on mistaken belief that it had no power to order grandparent visitation under *Troxel*).

For further discussion of the implications of *Troxel v. Granville,* supra, see Commentary to Section 3102.

Research References

Forms

California Practice Guide: Rutter Family Law Forms Form 7:17, Notice Of Motion and Declaration for Joinder (Grandparent Visitation Claim).

California Practice Guide: Rutter Family Law Forms Form 7:18, Complaint for Joinder (Grandparent Visitation Claim).

California Practice Guide: Rutter Family Law Forms Form 7:19, Memorandum in Support Of Motion and Declaration for Joinder (Grandparent Visitation Claim).

California Transactions Forms--Family Law § 3:7, Custody Issues Outside the Scope Of the Family Code.

California Transactions Forms--Family Law § 5:3, Rights Of Non-parents Generally.

California Transactions Forms--Family Law § 5:5, Rights Of Grand-parents and Close Relatives.

California Transactions Forms--Family Law § 5:10, Use Of Parenting Agreement to Define Rights and Responsibilities Relating to Child on Termination Of Partners' Relationship Where Neither or Only One Partner is Biological Parent.

West's California Code Forms, Family § 3103, Comment Overview--Visitation Rights.

Treatises and Practice Aids

Witkin, California Summary 10th Parent and Child § 226, in General.

Witkin, California Summary 10th Parent and Child § 227, Visitation Order Made After Judgment Of Dissolution.

Witkin, California Summary 10th Parent and Child § 235, Biologically Unrelated Persons Opposed by Parent.

§ 3104. Grandparent's rights; petition by grandparent; notice; protective order directed to grandparent; rebuttable presumptions; conflict with rights of non-party birth parent; change of residence of child; discretion of court

(a) On petition to the court by a grandparent of a minor child, the court may grant reasonable visitation rights to the grandparent if the court does both of the following:

(1) Finds that there is a preexisting relationship between the grandparent and the grandchild that has engendered a bond such that visitation is in the best interest of the child.

(2) Balances the interest of the child in having visitation with the grandparent against the right of the parents to exercise their parental authority.

(b) A petition for visitation under this section shall not be filed while the natural or adoptive parents are married, unless one or more of the following circumstances exist:

(1) The parents are currently living separately and apart on a permanent or indefinite basis.

(2) One of the parents has been absent for more than one month without the other spouse knowing the whereabouts of the absent spouse.

(3) One of the parents joins in the petition with the grandparents.

(4) The child is not residing with either parent.

(5) The child has been adopted by a stepparent.

(6) One of the parents is incarcerated or involuntarily institutionalized.

At any time that a change of circumstances occurs such that none of these circumstances exist, the parent or parents may move the court to terminate grandparental visitation and the court shall grant the termination.

(c) The petitioner shall give notice of the petition to each of the parents of the child, any stepparent, and any person who has physical custody of the child, by personal service pursuant to Section 415.10 of the Code of Civil Procedure.

(d) If a protective order as defined in Section 6218 has been directed to the grandparent during the pendency of the proceeding, the court shall consider whether the best interest of the child requires that any visitation by that grandparent should be denied.

(e) There is a rebuttable presumption that the visitation of a grandparent is not in the best interest of a minor child if the natural or adoptive parents agree that the grandparent should not be granted visitation rights.

(f) There is a rebuttable presumption affecting the burden of proof that the visitation of a grandparent is not in the best interest of a minor child if the parent who has been awarded sole legal and physical custody of the child in another proceeding, or the parent with whom the child resides if there is currently no operative custody order objects to visitation by the grandparent.

(g) Visitation rights may not be ordered under this section if that would conflict with a right of custody or visitation of a birth parent who is not a party to the proceeding.

(h) Visitation ordered pursuant to this section shall not create a basis for or against a change of residence of the child, but shall be one of the factors for the court to consider in ordering a change of residence.

(i) When a court orders grandparental visitation pursuant to this section, the court in its discretion may, based upon the relevant circumstances of the case:

(1) Allocate the percentage of grandparental visitation between the parents for purposes of the calculation of child support pursuant to the statewide uniform guideline (Article 2 (commencing with Section 4050) of Chapter 2 of Part 2 of Division 9).

(2) Notwithstanding Sections 3930 and 3951, order a parent or grandparent to pay to the other, an amount for the support of the child or grandchild. For purposes of this paragraph, "support" means costs related to visitation such as any of the following:

(A) Transportation.

(B) Provision of basic expenses for the child or grandchild, such as medical expenses, day care costs, and other necessities.

(j) As used in this section, "birth parent" means "birth parent" as defined in Section 8512. *(Added by Stats.1993, c. 832 (S.B.306), § 2. Amended by Stats.2006, c. 138 (A.B. 2517), § 1; Stats.2014, c. 328 (A.B.1628), § 1, eff. Jan. 1, 2015.)*

Commentary

In *In re Marriage of Harris, 34 Cal.4th 210, 96 P.3d 141, 17 Cal.Rptr.3d 842 (2004)*, the California Supreme Court held that this section, rather than Section 3103, applies to a grandparent's petition for visitation when the issue of custody is not otherwise before the court under Section 3021.

But cf. *Troxel v. Granville, 120 S.Ct. 2054, 147 L.Ed.2d 49 (2000)*, which involved a Washington statute permitting "any person" to petition for visitation rights at any time and allowing the court to grant visitation "whenever visitation may serve the best interests of the child." Despite the objections of the legal parents, the Washington trial court, applying the statute, granted the paternal grandparents extensive visitation of their deceased son's natural children, who resided with their mother and her husband, who had adopted the children. The U.S. Supreme Court held that, in the context of grandparent visitation, the Washington statute violated the due process rights of a fit parent and her family to make decisions concerning the "care, custody, and control" of their children. However, *In re Marriage of Harris* sustained the constitutionality of Section 3104. The California Supreme Court reasoned that by imposing a rebuttable presumption that grandparent visitation is not in the child's best interest when the parents so agree or when a parent granted sole legal and physical custody objects to grandparent visitation, this section satisfies the *Troxel* requirement that "special weight" be granted to the parental decision to deny grandparent visitation.

Relying on *Troxel*, *In re Marriage of James W., 114 Cal.App.4th 68, 7 Cal.Rptr.3d 461 (2003)*, held that when a child has a father, mother and stepfather, respect for the parents' due process right to the care, custody, and control of their child requires that the trial court apply a presumption that the parents' decision to terminate stepfather visitation is in the child's best interests. The presumption may be overcome only by a showing that visitation with a stepparent is in the best interest of the child and denial of visitation would be detrimental to the child. Of course, *Troxel* does not limit the court's power to order or enforce nonparent visitation when the child's parents do not object. *In re Marriage of Ross & Kelley, 114 Cal.App.4th 130, 7 Cal.Rptr.3d 287 (2003)* (trial court erred in declining to order stipulated grandparent visitation on mistaken belief that it had no power to order grandparent visitation under *Troxel*).

Hoag v. Diedjomahor, 200 Cal.App.4th 1008, 132 Cal.Rptr.3d 256 (2011), review denied, holds that the *Troxel* presumption that a parent's denial or severe limitation of visitation is in a child's best interests is overcome when the parent's objections to visitation by a parent of the child's deceased parent are unreasonable and lack credibility.

Rich v. Thatcher, 200 Cal.App.4th 1176, 132 Cal.Rptr.3d 897 (2011), holds that the *Troxel* presumption that a fit parent is acting in the best interests of the child imposes upon a grandparent the burden of proving by clear and convincing evidence that denial of grandparent visitation would be detrimental to the child and is therefore not in the child's best interests.

Stuard v. Stuard, 244 Cal.App.4th 768, 199 Cal.Rptr.3d 821 (2016), sustained a trial court's award of visitation to two grandparents against the objection of both divorced parents even though they were fit parents, on the ground that the parents themselves had fostered the child's subsection (a)(1) relationship with her grandparents. The court of appeal declined to consider the father's inadequately developed equal protection claim that there was no constitutionally adequate basis for this section's distinction between cohabiting parents and parents who do not live together.

Subsection (b)(5) was added to overturn *Lopez v. Martinez, 85 Cal.App.4th 279, 102 Cal.Rptr.2d 71 (2000)*, which held that a stepparent adoption is a change of circumstances requiring termination of grandparent visitation upon request of the child's parents. Subsection (b) was added to remove the possibility of a stepparent preventing grandparent visitation under this section by adopting a stepchild.

Finberg v. Mansett, 223 Cal.App.4th 529, 167 Cal.Rptr.3d 109 (2014), review denied, rejected an equal protection claim that, under (b)(5), adopting stepparents must be treated equally with natural parents and adoptive parents who are stepparents.

For further discussion of the implications of *Troxel v. Granville*, supra, see Commentary to Section 3102.

In re J.T., 228 Cal.App.4th 953, 175 Cal.Rptr.3d 744 (2014), held that the juvenile court acted within its authority in granting visitation to a grandparent, over the objection of the child's mother, in a proceeding terminating jurisdiction over the child. Although termination of jurisdiction may have reinstated the mother's presumption of parental fitness, the subsection (e) and (f) presumption that visitation with a grandparent over the objection of the custodial parent is not in the child's best interest does not apply in dependency proceedings, where the court has special responsibility to children on the termination of dependency jurisdiction.

Research References

Forms

California Practice Guide: Rutter Family Law Forms Form 7:17, Notice Of Motion and Declaration for Joinder (Grandparent Visitation Claim).

California Practice Guide: Rutter Family Law Forms Form 7:18, Complaint for Joinder (Grandparent Visitation Claim).

California Practice Guide: Rutter Family Law Forms Form 7:19, Memorandum in Support Of Motion and Declaration for Joinder (Grandparent Visitation Claim).

California Transactions Forms--Family Law § 3:7, Custody Issues Outside the Scope Of the Family Code.

California Transactions Forms--Family Law § 5:3, Rights Of Non-parents Generally.

California Transactions Forms--Family Law § 5:5, Rights Of Grand-parents and Close Relatives.

California Transactions Forms--Family Law § 5:10, Use Of Parenting Agreement to Define Rights and Responsibilities Relating to Child on Termination Of Partners' Relationship Where Neither or Only One Partner is Biological Parent.

Treatises and Practice Aids

Witkin, California Summary 10th Parent and Child § 226, in General.

Witkin, California Summary 10th Parent and Child § 227, Visitation Order Made After Judgment Of Dissolution.

Witkin, California Summary 10th Parent and Child § 229, Constitutionality.

Witkin, California Summary 10th Parent and Child § 237, Constitutional Limitations.

§ 3105. Former legal guardians; visitation rights

(a) The Legislature finds and declares that a parent's fundamental right to provide for the care, custody, companionship, and management of his or her children, while compelling, is not absolute. Children have a fundamental right to maintain healthy, stable relationships with a person who has served in a significant, judicially approved parental role.

(b) The court may grant reasonable visitation rights to a person who previously served as the legal guardian of a child, if visitation is determined to be in the best interest of the minor child.

(c) In the absence of a court order granting or denying visitation between a former legal guardian and his or her former minor ward, and if a dependency proceeding is not pending, a former legal guardian may maintain an independent action for visitation with his or her former minor ward. If the child does not have at least one living parent, visitation shall not be determined in a proceeding under the Family Code, but shall instead be determined in a guardianship proceeding which may be initiated for that purpose. *(Added by Stats.2004, c. 301 (A.B.2292), § 1.)*

Research References

Treatises and Practice Aids

Witkin, California Summary 10th Parent and Child § 233, in General.

CHAPTER 6. CUSTODY INVESTIGATION AND REPORT

Section

§ 3110. Court-appointed investigator

As used in this chapter, "court-appointed investigator" means a probation officer, domestic relations investigator, or court-appointed evaluator directed by the court to conduct an investigation pursuant to this chapter. *(Added by Stats.1993, c. 219 (A.B.1500), § 116.81.)*

Law Revision Commission Comments

Enactment [Revised Comment]

Section 3110 is a new section added to facilitate drafting by avoiding repetition of the list of persons referred to throughout this chapter. [23 Cal.L.Rev.Comm. Reports 1 (1993)].

Research References

Forms

California Practice Guide: Rutter Family Law Forms Form 1:32, Glossary Of Common Family Law Terms, Phrases and Concepts (Enclosure to Form 1:31).

California Transactions Forms--Family Law § 2:70, Deciding Custody.

Treatises and Practice Aids

Witkin, California Summary 10th Husband and Wife § 94, Participation in Domestic Violence Programs.

Witkin, California Summary 10th Parent and Child § 195, Statutory Framework.

Witkin, California Summary 10th Parent and Child § 223, Procedure.

Witkin, California Summary 10th Parent and Child § 275, in General.

Witkin, California Summary 10th Parent and Child § 281, Recommendations.

§ 3110.5. Child custody evaluator

(a) No person may be a court-connected or private child custody evaluator under this chapter unless the person has completed the domestic violence and child abuse training program described in Section 1816 and has complied with Rules 5.220 and 5.230 of the California Rules of Court.

(b)(1) On or before January 1, 2002, the Judicial Council shall formulate a statewide rule of court that establishes education, experience, and training requirements for all child custody evaluators appointed pursuant to this chapter, Section 730 of the Evidence Code, or Chapter 15 (commencing with Section 2032.010) of Title 4 of Part 4 of the Code of Civil Procedure.

(A) The rule shall require a child custody evaluator to declare under penalty of perjury that he or she meets all of the education, experience, and training requirements specified in the rule and, if applicable, possesses a license in good standing. The Judicial Council shall establish forms to implement this section. The rule shall permit court-connected evaluators to conduct evaluations if they meet all of the qualifications established by the Judicial Council. The education, experience, and training requirements to be specified for court-connected evaluators shall include, but not be limited to, knowledge of the psychological and developmental needs of children and parent-child relationships.

(B) The rule shall require all evaluators to utilize comparable interview, assessment, and testing procedures for all parties that are consistent with generally accepted clinical, forensic, scientific, diagnostic, or medical standards. The rule shall also require evaluators to inform each adult party of the purpose, nature, and method of the evaluation.

(C) The rule may allow courts to permit the parties to stipulate to an evaluator of their choosing with the approval of the court under the circumstances set forth in subdivision (d). The rule may require courts to provide general information about how parties can contact qualified child custody evaluators in their county.

(2) On or before January 1, 2004, the Judicial Council shall include in the statewide rule of court created pursuant to this section a requirement that all court-connected and private child custody evaluators receive training in the nature of child sexual abuse. The Judicial Council shall develop standards for this training that shall include, but not be limited to, the following:

(A) Children's patterns of hiding and disclosing sexual abuse occurring in a family setting.

(B) The effects of sexual abuse on children.

(C) The nature and extent of child sexual abuse.

(D) The social and family dynamics of child sexual abuse.

(E) Techniques for identifying and assisting families affected by child sexual abuse.

(F) Legal rights, protections, and remedies available to victims of child sexual abuse.

(c) In addition to the education, experience, and training requirements established by the Judicial Council pursuant to subdivision (b), on or after January 1, 2005, no person may be a child custody evaluator under this chapter, Section 730 of the Evidence Code, or Chapter 15 (commencing with Section 2032.010) of Title 4 of Part 4 of the Code of Civil Procedure unless the person meets one of the following criteria:

(1) He or she is licensed as a physician under Chapter 5 (commencing with Section 2000) of Division 2 of the Business and Professions Code and either is a board certified psychiatrist or has completed a residency in psychiatry.

(2) He or she is licensed as a psychologist under Chapte 6.6 (commencing with Section 2900) of Division 2 of th Business and Professions Code.

(3) He or she is licensed as a marriage and family therap under Chapter 13 (commencing with Section 4980) of Di sion 2 of the Business and Professions Code.

(4) He or she is licensed as a clinical social worker un Article 4 (commencing with Section 4996) of Chapter 1 Division 2 of the Business and Professions Code.

(5) He or she is a court-connected evaluator who has certified by the court as meeting all of the qualificatio court-connected evaluators as specified by the Judicial cil pursuant to subdivision (b).

(d) Subdivision (c) does not apply in any case whe court determines that there are no evaluators who m criteria of subdivision (c) who are willing and available a reasonable period of time, to perform child custody evaluations. In those cases, the parties may stipulate to an individual who does not meet the criteria of subdivision (c), subject to approval by the court.

(e) A child custody evaluator who is licensed by the Medical Board of California, the Board of Psychology, or the Board of Behavioral Sciences shall be subject to disciplinary action by that board for unprofessional conduct, as defined in the licensing law applicable to that licensee.

(f) On or after January 1, 2005, a court-connected or private child custody evaluator may not evaluate, investigate, or mediate an issue of child custody in a proceeding pursuant to this division unless that person has completed child sexual abuse training as required by this section. *(Added by Stats.1999, c. 932 (S.B.433), § 1. Amended by Stats.2000, c. 926 (S.B.1716), § 4; Stats.2004, c. 811 (A.B.3079), § 1; Stats.2004, c. 182 (A.B.3081), § 33, operative July 1, 2005; Stats.2004, c. 811 (A.B.3079), § 1.5, operative July 1, 2005.)*

Law Revision Commission Comments

2004 Amendment

Subdivisions (b) and (c) of Section 3110.5 are amended to reflect nonsubstantive reorganization of the rules governing civil discovery. [33 Cal.L.Rev.Comm. Reports 1020 (2003)].

Research References

Forms

California Transactions Forms--Family Law § 2:70, Deciding Custody.

West's California Code Forms, Family § 3110, Comment Overview--Custody Investigation and Report.

West's California Judicial Council Forms FL-325, Declaration Of Court-Connected Child Custody Evaluator Regarding Qualifications.

West's California Judicial Council Forms FL-326, Declaration Of Private Child Custody Evaluator Regarding Qualifications.

West's California Judicial Council Forms FL-327, Order Appointing Child Custody Evaluator.

Treatises and Practice Aids

Witkin, California Summary 10th Husband and Wife § 94, Participation in Domestic Violence Programs.

Witkin, California Summary 10th Parent and Child § 275, in General.

§ 3111. Child custody evaluations; confidentiality and use of report; monetary sanction for unwarranted disclosure; adoption of form regarding confidentiality

(a) In any contested proceeding involving child custody or visitation rights, the court may appoint a child custody evaluator to conduct a child custody evaluation in cases where the court determines it is in the best interests of the child. The child custody evaluation shall be conducted in accordance with the standards adopted by the Judicial Council pursuant to Section 3117, and all other standards adopted by the Judicial Council regarding child custody evaluations. If directed by the court, the court-appointed child custody evaluator shall file a written confidential report on his or her evaluation. At least 10 days before any hearing regarding custody of the child, the report shall be filed with the clerk of the court in which the custody hearing will be conducted and served on the parties or their attorneys, and any other counsel appointed for the child pursuant to Section 3150. A child custody evaluation, investigation, or assessment, and any resulting report, may be considered by the court only if it is conducted in accordance with the requirements set forth in the standards adopted by the Judicial Council pursuant to Section 3117; however, this does not preclude the consideration of a child custody evaluation report that contains nonsubstantive or inconsequential errors or both.

(b) The report shall not be made available other than as provided in subdivision (a) or Section 3025.5, or as described in Section 204 of the Welfare and Institutions Code or Section 1514.5 of the Probate Code. Any information obtained from access to a juvenile court case file, as defined in subdivision (e) of Section 827 of the Welfare and Institutions Code, is confidential and shall only be disseminated as provided by paragraph (4) of subdivision (a) of Section 827 of the Welfare and Institutions Code.

(c) The report may be received in evidence on stipulation of all interested parties and is competent evidence as to all matters contained in the report.

(d) If the court determines that an unwarranted disclosure of a written confidential report has been made, the court may impose a monetary sanction against the disclosing party. The sanction shall be in an amount sufficient to deter repetition of the conduct, and may include reasonable attorney's fees, costs incurred, or both, unless the court finds that the disclosing party acted with substantial justification or that other circumstances make the imposition of the sanction unjust. The court shall not impose a sanction pursuant to this subdivision that imposes an unreasonable financial burden on the party against whom the sanction is imposed. This subdivision shall become operative on January 1, 2010.

(e) The Judicial Council shall, by January 1, 2010, do the following:

(1) Adopt a form to be served with every child custody evaluation report that informs the report recipient of the confidentiality of the report and the potential consequences for the unwarranted disclosure of the report.

(2) Adopt a rule of court to require that, when a court-ordered child custody evaluation report is served on the parties, the form specified in paragraph (1) shall be included with the report.

(f) For purposes of this section, a disclosure is unwarranted if it is done either recklessly or maliciously, and is not in the best interests of the child. *(Added by Stats.1993, c. 219 (A.B.1500), § 116.81. Amended by Stats.1996, c. 761 (S.B. 1995), § 1; Stats.1999, c. 932 (S.B.433), § 2; Stats.2002, c. 1008 (A.B.3028), § 16; Stats.2004, c. 574 (A.B.2228), § 1; Stats.2005, c. 22 (S.B.1108), § 62; Stats.2008, c. 215 (A.B. 1877), § 1; Stats.2014, c. 283 (A.B.1843), § 3, eff. Jan. 1, 2015; Stats.2015, c. 130 (S.B.594), § 1, eff. Jan. 1, 2016.)*

Law Revision Commission Comments

Enactment [Revised Comment]

Section 3111 restates without substantive change the first paragraph of former Civil Code Section 4602 and the first three paragraphs of former Code of Civil Procedure Section 263. The former reference to a proceeding "brought under this part," meaning the former Family Law Act (former Part 5 (commencing with former

Section 4000) of Division 4 of the Civil Code), has been omitted as unnecessary. See Section 3021 (application of part). The reference to "court-appointed investigator" has been substituted for the former list of officers. This is not a substantive change. See Section 3110 ("court-appointed investigator" defined).

See also Section 3081 (investigation concerning whether joint custody appropriate). [23 Cal.L.Rev.Comm. Reports 1 (1993)].

Commentary

The 2015 amendments to this section (SB 594) are intended to overrule *In re Marriage of Winternitz, 235 Cal.App.4th 644, 185 Cal.Rptr.3d 458 (2015), review denied* (affirming a trial court order denying a mother's request to strike a defective child custody evaluation report).

Research References

Forms

California Practice Guide: Rutter Family Law Forms Form 7:5, Stipulation Appointing Child Custody Evaluator (Attorney-Drafted).

California Practice Guide: Rutter Family Law Forms Form 1:32, Glossary Of Common Family Law Terms, Phrases and Concepts (Enclosure to Form 1:31).

California Transactions Forms--Family Law § 2:70, Deciding Custody.

West's California Code Forms, Family § 3110, Comment Overview--Custody Investigation and Report.

West's California Judicial Council Forms FL-327, Order Appointing Child Custody Evaluator.

West's California Judicial Council Forms FL-328, Notice Regarding Confidentiality Of Child Custody Evaluation Report.

West's California Judicial Council Forms FL-329-INFO, Child Custody Evaluation Information Sheet.

Treatises and Practice Aids

Witkin, California Summary 10th Husband and Wife § 381, Criminal Background Search.

Witkin, California Summary 10th Parent and Child § 275, in General.

Witkin, California Summary 10th Parent and Child § 276, Report.

Witkin, California Summary 10th Parent and Child § 277, Investigation Of Child Sexual Abuse Allegations.

Witkin, California Summary 10th Parent and Child § 493, Persons Entitled to Inspect Records.

Witkin, California Summary 10th Parent and Child § 259A, (New) Military Deployment.

§ 3112. Repayment of expenses

(a) Where a court-appointed investigator is directed by the court to conduct a custody investigation or evaluation pursuant to this chapter or to undertake visitation work, including necessary evaluation, supervision, and reporting, the court shall inquire into the financial condition of the parent, guardian, or other person charged with the support of the minor. If the court finds the parent, guardian, or other person able to pay all or part of the expense of the investigation, report, and recommendation, the court may make an order requiring the parent, guardian, or other person to repay the court the amount the court determines proper.

(b) The repayment shall be made to the court. The court shall keep suitable accounts of the expenses and repayments and shall deposit the collections as directed by the Judicial Council. *(Added by Stats.1993, c. 219 (A.B.1500), § 116.81. Amended by Stats.2000, c. 926 (S.B.1716), § 5.)*

Law Revision Commission Comments

Enactment [Revised Comment]

Section 3112 continues the third paragraph of former Civil Code Section 4602 without substantive change. The reference to "court-appointed investigator" has been substituted for the former list of officers. This is not a substantive change. See Section 3110 ("court-appointed investigator" defined). The reference to "maintenance" of a minor child has been omitted as surplus. See Section 150 ("support" when used with reference to minor child includes maintenance and education). [23 Cal.L.Rev.Comm. Reports 1 (1993)].

Research References

Treatises and Practice Aids

Witkin, California Summary 10th Parent and Child § 275, in General.

§ 3113. Domestic violence history between parties; custody investigation procedures

Where there has been a history of domestic violence between the parties, or where a protective order as defined in Section 6218 is in effect, at the request of the party alleging domestic violence in a written declaration under penalty of perjury or at the request of a party who is protected by the order, the parties shall meet with the court-appointed investigator separately and at separate times. *(Added by Stats.1993, c. 219 (A.B.1500), § 116.81.)*

Law Revision Commission Comments

Enactment [Revised Comment]

Section 3113 continues the second paragraph of former Civil Code Section 4602 without substantive change. The reference to "court-appointed investigator" has been substituted for the former list of officers. This is not a substantive change. See Section 3110 ("court-appointed investigator" defined). Unlike the former section, this section does not contain a reference to the section defining "domestic violence." This is not a substantive change. See Section 6211 ("domestic violence" defined). The term "protective order" has been substituted for the references to orders under specific former sections in the Civil Code and the Code of Civil Procedure. This is not a substantive change, since Section 6218 defines "protective order" to include these orders. [23 Cal.L.Rev.Comm. Reports 1 (1993)].

Research References

Treatises and Practice Aids

Witkin, California Summary 10th Husband and Wife § 10A, (New) Ex Parte Communications With Mediator or Evaluator.

Witkin, California Summary 10th Parent and Child § 275, in General.

§ 3114. Appointment of counsel for minor children; recommendations

Nothing in this chapter prohibits a court-appointed investigator from recommending to the court that counsel be appointed pursuant to Chapter 10 (commencing with Section 3150) to represent the minor child. In making that recommendation, the court-appointed investigator shall inform the court of the reasons why it would be in the best interest of the child to have counsel appointed. *(Added by Stats.1993, c. 219 (A.B.1500), § 116.81.)*

Law Revision Commission Comments

Enactment [Revised Comment]

Section 3114 continues the last paragraph of former Civil Code Section 4602 without substantive change. The reference to "court-appointed investigator" has been substituted for the former list of officers. This is not a substantive change. See Section 3110 ("court-appointed investigator" defined). The reference to "children" has been omitted as surplus. See Section 10 (singular includes plural). See also Section 3011 (factors to be considered in determining best interest of child). [23 Cal.L.Rev.Comm. Reports 1 (1993)].

Research References

Treatises and Practice Aids

Witkin, California Summary 10th Parent and Child § 275, in General.

§ 3115. Cross–examination of court–appointed investigator; waiver of right

No statement, whether written or oral, or conduct shall be held to constitute a waiver by a party of the right to cross-examine the court-appointed investigator, unless the statement is made, or the conduct occurs, after the report has been received by a party or his or her attorney. *(Added by Stats.1993, c. 219 (A.B.1500), § 116.81. Amended by Stats. 1996, c. 761 (S.B.1995), § 2.)*

Law Revision Commission Comments

Enactment [Revised Comment]

Section 3115 continues without substantive change and generalizes the fourth paragraph of former Code of Civil Procedure Section 263. The reference to "court-appointed investigator" has been added to conform to other sections in this chapter. See Section 3110 ("court-appointed investigator" defined). The former reference to a "divorce" action has been omitted as unnecessary. See Section 3021 (application of part). [23 Cal.L.Rev.Comm. Reports 1 (1993)].

Research References

Treatises and Practice Aids

Witkin, California Summary 10th Parent and Child § 276, Report.

§ 3116. Investigator's duty to assist court; scope of duty

Nothing in this chapter limits the duty of a court-appointed investigator to assist the appointing court in the transaction of the business of the court. *(Added by Stats.1993, c. 219 (A.B.1500), § 116.81.)*

Law Revision Commission Comments

Enactment [Revised Comment]

Section 3116 continues without substantive change and generalizes the last paragraph of former Code of Civil Procedure Section 263. The reference to "court-appointed investigator" has been added to conform to other sections in this chapter. See Section 3110 ("court-appointed investigator" defined) & Comment. The former reference to a "divorce" action has been omitted as unnecessary. See Section 3021 (application of part). The reference to the "superior" court has been omitted as surplus. See Section 200 (jurisdiction in superior court). [23 Cal.L.Rev.Comm. Reports 1 (1993)].

Research References

Treatises and Practice Aids

Witkin, California Summary 10th Parent and Child § 275, in General.

§ 3117. Standards for court–connected child custody actions; guidelines for cross–examination of court–appointed investigators; deadline

The Judicial Council shall, by January 1, 1999, do both of the following:

(a) Adopt standards for full and partial court-connected evaluations, investigations, and assessments related to child custody.

(b) Adopt procedural guidelines for the expeditious and cost-effective cross-examination of court-appointed investigators, including, but not limited to, the use of electronic technology whereby the court-appointed investigator may not need to be present in the courtroom. These guidelines shall in no way limit the requirement that the court-appointed investigator be available for the purposes of cross-examination. These guidelines shall also provide for written notification to the parties of the right to cross-examine these investigators after the parties have had a reasonable time to review the investigator's report. *(Added by Stats.1996, c. 761 (S.B.1995), § 3.)*

Research References

Treatises and Practice Aids

Witkin, California Summary 10th Parent and Child § 275, in General.

Witkin, California Summary 10th Parent and Child § 276, Report.

§ 3118. Child sex abuse allegations; child custody evaluation, investigation or assessment

(a) In any contested proceeding involving child custody or visitation rights, where the court has appointed a child custody evaluator or has referred a case for a full or partial court-connected evaluation, investigation, or assessment, and the court determines that there is a serious allegation of child sexual abuse, the court shall require an evaluation, investigation, or assessment pursuant to this section. When the court has determined that there is a serious allegation of child sexual abuse, any child custody evaluation, investigation, or assessment conducted subsequent to that determination shall be considered by the court only if the evaluation, investigation, or assessment is conducted in accordance with the minimum requirements set forth in this section in determining custody or visitation rights, except as specified in paragraph (1). For purposes of this section, a serious allegation of child sexual abuse means an allegation of child sexual abuse, as defined in Section 11165.1 of the Penal Code, that is based in whole or in part on statements made by the child to law enforcement, a child welfare services agency investigator, any person required by statute to report suspected child abuse, or any other court-appointed personnel, or that is supported by substantial independent corroboration as provided for in subdivision (b) of Section 3011. When an allegation of child abuse arises in any other circumstances in any proceeding involving child custody or visitation rights, the court may require an evaluator or investigator to conduct an evaluation, investigation, or assessment pursuant to this section. The order appointing a child custody evaluator or investigator pursuant to this section shall provide that the evaluator or investigator have access to all juvenile court records pertaining to the child who is the subject of the evaluation, investigation, or assessment. The order shall also provide that any juvenile court records or information gained from those records remain confidential and shall only be released as specified in Section 3111.

(1) This section does not apply to any emergency court-ordered partial investigation that is conducted for the purpose of assisting the court in determining what immediate temporary orders may be necessary to protect and meet the immediate needs of a child. This section does apply when the emergency is resolved and the court is considering permanent child custody or visitation orders.

(2) This section does not prohibit a court from considering evidence relevant to determining the safety and protection needs of the child.

(3) Any evaluation, investigation, or assessment conducted pursuant to this section shall be conducted by an evaluator or investigator who meets the qualifications set forth in Section 3110.5.

(b) The evaluator or investigator shall, at a minimum, do all of the following:

(1) Consult with the agency providing child welfare services and law enforcement regarding the allegations of child sexual abuse, and obtain recommendations from these professionals regarding the child's safety and the child's need for protection.

(2) Review and summarize the child welfare services agency file. No document contained in the child welfare services agency file may be photocopied, but a summary of the information in the file, including statements made by the children and the parents, and the recommendations made or anticipated to be made by the child welfare services agency to the juvenile court, may be recorded by the evaluator or investigator, except for the identity of the reporting party. The evaluator's or investigator's notes summarizing the child welfare services agency information shall be stored in a file separate from the evaluator's or investigator's file and may only be released to either party under order of the court.

(3) Obtain from a law enforcement investigator all available information obtained from criminal background checks of the parents and any suspected perpetrator that is not a parent, including information regarding child abuse, domestic violence, or substance abuse.

(4) Review the results of a multidisciplinary child interview team (hereafter MDIT) interview if available, or if not, or if the evaluator or investigator believes the MDIT interview is inadequate for purposes of the evaluation, investigation, or assessment, interview the child or request an MDIT interview, and shall wherever possible avoid repeated interviews of the child.

(5) Request a forensic medical examination of the child from the appropriate agency, or include in the report required by paragraph (6) a written statement explaining why the examination is not needed.

(6) File a confidential written report with the clerk of the court in which the custody hearing will be conducted and which shall be served on the parties or their attorneys at least 10 days prior to the hearing. This report may not be made available other than as provided in this subdivision. This report shall include, but is not limited to, the following:

(A) Documentation of material interviews, including any MDIT interview of the child or the evaluator or investigator, written documentation of interviews with both parents by the evaluator or investigator, and interviews with other witnesses who provided relevant information.

(B) A summary of any law enforcement investigator's investigation, including information obtained from the criminal background check of the parents and any suspected perpetrator that is not a parent, including information regarding child abuse, domestic violence, or substance abuse.

(C) Relevant background material, including, but not limited to, a summary of a written report from any therapist treating the child for suspected child sexual abuse, excluding any communication subject to Section 1014 of the Evidence Code, reports from other professionals, and the results of any forensic medical examination and any other medical examination or treatment that could help establish or disprove whether the child has been the victim of sexual abuse.

(D) The written recommendations of the evaluator or investigator regarding the therapeutic needs of the child and how to ensure the safety of the child.

(E) A summary of the following information: whether the child and his or her parents are or have been the subject of a child abuse investigation and the disposition of that investigation; the name, location, and telephone number of the children's services worker; the status of the investigation and the recommendations made or anticipated to be made regarding the child's safety; and any dependency court orders or findings that might have a bearing on the custody dispute.

(F) Any information regarding the presence of domestic violence or substance abuse in the family that has been obtained from a child protective agency in accordance with paragraphs (1) and (2), a law enforcement agency, medical personnel or records, prior or currently treating therapists, excluding any communication subject to Section 1014 of the Evidence Code, or from interviews conducted or reviewed for this evaluation, investigation, or assessment.

(G) Which, if any, family members are known to have been deemed eligible for assistance from the Victims of Crime Program due to child abuse or domestic violence.

(H) Any other information the evaluator or investigator believes would be helpful to the court in determining what is in the best interests of the child.

(c) If the evaluator or investigator obtains information as part of a family court mediation, that information shall be maintained in the family court file, which is not subject to subpoena by either party. If, however, the members of the family are the subject of an ongoing child welfare services investigation, or the evaluator or investigator has made a child welfare services referral, the evaluator or investigator shall so inform the family law judicial officer in writing and this information shall become part of the family law file. This subdivision may not be construed to authorize or require a mediator to disclose any information not otherwise authorized or required by law to be disclosed.

(d) In accordance with subdivision (d) of Section 11167 of the Penal Code, the evaluator or investigator may not disclose any information regarding the identity of any person making a report of suspected child abuse. Nothing in this section is intended to limit any disclosure of information by any agency that is otherwise required by law or court order.

(e) The evaluation, investigation, or assessment standards set forth in this section represent minimum requirements of evaluation and the court shall order further evaluation beyond these minimum requirements when necessary to determine the safety needs of the child.

(f) If the court orders an evaluation, investigation, or assessment pursuant to this section, the court shall consider whether the best interests of the child require that a temporary order be issued that limits visitation with the parent against whom the allegations have been made to situations in which a third person specified by the court is present or whether visitation will be suspended or denied in accordance with Section 3011.

(g) An evaluation, investigation, or assessment pursuant to this section shall be suspended if a petition is filed to declare the child a dependent child of the juvenile court pursuant to Section 300 of the Welfare and Institutions Code, and all information gathered by the evaluator or investigator shall be made available to the juvenile court.

(h) This section may not be construed to authorize a court to issue any orders in a proceeding pursuant to this division regarding custody or visitation with respect to a minor child who is the subject of a dependency hearing in juvenile court or to otherwise supersede Section 302 of the Welfare and Institutions Code. *(Added by Stats.2000, c. 926 (S.B.1716), § 6. Amended by Stats.2002, c. 305 (S.B.1704), § 1; Stats. 2003, c. 62 (S.B.600), § 87.)*

Research References

Forms

California Practice Guide: Rutter Family Law Forms Form 7:5, Stipulation Appointing Child Custody Evaluator (Attorney-Drafted).

California Practice Guide: Rutter Family Law Forms Form 1:32, Glossary Of Common Family Law Terms, Phrases and Concepts (Enclosure to Form 1:31).

West's California Judicial Council Forms FL-329-INFO, Child Custody Evaluation Information Sheet.

Treatises and Practice Aids

Witkin, California Summary 10th Parent and Child § 277, Investigation Of Child Sexual Abuse Allegations.

Witkin, California Summary 10th Parent and Child § 493, Persons Entitled to Inspect Records.

CHAPTER 7. ACTION FOR EXCLUSIVE CUSTODY

§ 3120. Action for exclusive custody; order

Without filing a petition for dissolution of marriage or legal separation of the parties, a spouse may bring an action for the exclusive custody of the children of the marriage. The court may, during the pendency of the action, or at the final hearing thereof, or afterwards, make such order regarding the support, care, custody, education, and control of the children of the marriage as may be just and in accordance with the natural rights of the parents and the best interest of the children. The order may be modified or terminated at any time thereafter as the natural rights of the parties and the best interest of the children may require. *(Stats.1992, c. 162 (A.B.2650), § 10, operative Jan. 1, 1994. Amended by Stats. 2014, c. 82 (S.B.1306), § 30, eff. Jan. 1, 2015.)*

Law Revision Commission Comments

Enactment [Revised Comment]

Section 3120 continues former Civil Code Section 4603 without substantive change. The reference to "decree" has been omitted as surplus. See Section 100 ("order" includes decree, as appropriate). The reference to "terminated" has been substituted for the former reference to "revoked." This is not a substantive change. See also Section 3011 (factors to be considered in determining best interest of child); Code Civ. Proc. § 917.7 (order not automatically stayed by appeal). [23 Cal.L.Rev.Comm. Reports 1 (1993)].

Research References

Forms

California Transactions Forms--Family Law § 3:4, Subject Matter Jurisdiction for Custody Determinations.

West's California Code Forms, Family § 3120, Comment Overview--Action for Exclusive Custody.

West's California Judicial Council Forms FL-230, Declaration for Default or Uncontested Judgment.

West's California Judicial Council Forms FL-250, Judgment.

West's California Judicial Council Forms FL-260, Petition for Custody and Support Of Minor Children.

West's California Judicial Council Forms FL-270, Response to Petition for Custody and Support Of Minor Children.

Treatises and Practice Aids

Witkin, California Summary 10th Husband and Wife § 177, Types Of Actions.

Witkin, California Summary 10th Parent and Child § 195, Statutory Framework.

Witkin, California Summary 10th Parent and Child § 249, Power to Modify.

Witkin, California Summary 10th Parent and Child § 267, Jurisdiction and Venue.

Witkin, California Summary 10th Parent and Child § 359, Dissolution Proceedings.

Witkin, California Summary 10th Parent and Child § 363, Applicability Of Family Code Custody Provisions.

Witkin, California Summary 10th Parent and Child § 385, Support During Action.

§ 3121. Attorney's fees and costs; findings; temporary order; default; statewide rule of court

(a) In any proceeding pursuant to Section 3120, and in any proceeding subsequent to entry of a related judgment, the court shall ensure that each party has access to legal representation, including access early in the proceedings, to preserve each party's rights by ordering, if necessary based on the income and needs assessments, one party, except a government entity, to pay to the other party, or to the other party's attorney, whatever amount is reasonably necessary for attorney's fees and for the cost of maintaining or defending the proceeding during the pendency of the proceeding.

(b) When a request for attorney's fees and costs is made, the court shall make findings on whether an award of attorney's fees and costs under this section is appropriate, whether there is a disparity in access to funds to retain counsel, and whether one party is able to pay for legal representation of both parties. If the findings demonstrate disparity in access and ability to pay, the court shall make an order awarding attorney's fees and costs. A party who lacks the financial ability to hire an attorney may request, as an in pro per litigant, that the court order the other party, if that other party has the financial ability, to pay a reasonable amount to allow the unrepresented party to retain an attorney in a timely manner before proceedings in the matter go forward.

(c) Attorney's fees and costs within this section may be awarded for legal services rendered or costs incurred before or after the commencement of the proceeding.

(d) The court shall augment or modify the original award for attorney's fees and costs as may be reasonably necessary for the prosecution or defense of a proceeding described in Section 3120, or any proceeding related thereto, including after any appeal has been concluded.

(e) Except as provided in subdivision (f), an application for a temporary order making, augmenting, or modifying an award of attorney's fees, including a reasonable retainer to hire an attorney, or costs, or both, shall be made by motion on notice or by an order to show cause during the pendency of any proceeding described in Section 3120.

(f) The court shall rule on an application for fees under this section within 15 days of the hearing on the motion or order to show cause. An order described in subdivision (a) may be made without notice by an oral motion in open court at either of the following times:

(1) At the time of the hearing of the cause on the merits.

(2) At any time before entry of judgment against a party whose default has been entered pursuant to Section 585 or 586 of the Code of Civil Procedure. The court shall rule on any motion made pursuant to this subdivision within 15 days and prior to the entry of any judgment.

(g) The Judicial Council shall, by January 1, 2012, adopt a statewide rule of court to implement this section and develop a form for the information that shall be submitted to the court to obtain an award of attorney's fees under this section. *(Added by Stats.2004, c. 472 (A.B.2148), § 3. Amended by Stats.2006, c. 538 (S.B.1852), § 158; Stats.2010, c. 352 (A.B.939), § 13.)*

Research References

Forms

West's California Code Forms, Family § 3120, Comment Overview--Action for Exclusive Custody.

West's California Judicial Council Forms FL-158, Supporting Declaration for Attorney's Fees and Costs Attachment.

West's California Judicial Council Forms FL-319, Request for Attorney's Fees and Costs Attachment.

West's California Judicial Council Forms FL-346, Attorney's Fees and Costs Order Attachment.

Treatises and Practice Aids

Witkin, California Summary 10th Husband and Wife § 177, Types Of Actions.

Witkin, California Summary 10th Parent and Child § 363, Applicability Of Family Code Custody Provisions.

CHAPTER 8. LOCATION OF MISSING PARTY OR CHILD

§ 3130. Custody petitions or temporary custody orders; duties of district attorney

If a petition to determine custody of a child has been filed in a court of competent jurisdiction, or if a temporary order pending determination of custody has been entered in accordance with Chapter 3 (commencing with Section 3060), and the whereabouts of a party in possession of the child are not known, or there is reason to believe that the party may not appear in the proceedings although ordered to appear personally with the child pursuant to Section 3430, the district attorney shall take all actions necessary to locate the party and the child and to procure compliance with the order to appear with the child for purposes of adjudication of custody. The petition to determine custody may be filed by the district attorney. *(Stats.1992, c. 162 (A.B.2650), § 10, operative Jan. 1, 1994. Amended by Stats.2008, c. 699 (S.B.1241), § 2.)*

Law Revision Commission Comments

Enactment [Revised Comment]

Section 3130 continues former Civil Code Section 4604(a) without substantive change. [23 Cal.L.Rev.Comm. Reports 1 (1993)].

Research References

Treatises and Practice Aids

Witkin, California Summary 10th Husband and Wife § 86, in General.

Witkin, California Summary 10th Parent and Child § 162, Locating Missing Child or Party.

Witkin, California Summary 10th Parent and Child § 195, Statutory Framework.

Witkin, California Summary 10th Parent and Child § 269, Locating Missing Party or Child.

Witkin, California Summary 10th Parent and Child § 271, Temporary Custody During Pendency Of Proceeding.

§ 3131. Custody or visitation orders; duties of district attorney

If a custody or visitation order has been entered by a court of competent jurisdiction and the child is taken or detained by another person in violation of the order, the distric[illegible] attorney shall take all actions necessary to locate and retu[illegible] the child and the person who violated the order and to as[illegible] in the enforcement of the custody or visitation order or [illegible] order of the court by use of an appropriate civil or criminal proceeding. *(Stats.1992, c. 162 (A.B.2650), § 10, operative Jan. 1, 1994.)*

Law Revision Commission Comments

Enactment [Revised Comment]

Section 3131 continues former Civil Code Section 4604(b) without substantive change. The word "order" has been substituted for "decree." This is not a substantive change. See Section 100 ("order" includes decree, as appropriate). The phrase "and the child" has been omitted as surplus. [23 Cal.L.Rev.Comm. Reports 1 (1993)].

Commentary

See generally *In re Marriage of Damico, 7 Cal.4th 673, 691, 29 Cal.Rptr.2d 787 (1984)* (dissent).

Research References

Treatises and Practice Aids

Witkin, California Summary 10th Parent and Child § 246, Custodial Parent Entitled to Obtain Child Support Despite Violation.
Witkin, California Summary 10th Parent and Child § 269, Locating Missing Party or Child.

§ 3132. District attorney to act on behalf of court

In performing the functions described in Sections 3130 and 3131, the district attorney shall act on behalf of the court and shall not represent any party to the custody proceedings. *(Stats.1992, c. 162 (A.B.2650), § 10, operative Jan. 1, 1994.)*

Law Revision Commission Comments

Enactment [Revised Comment]

Section 3132 continues first sentence of former Civil Code Section 4604(c) without substantive change. [23 Cal.L.Rev.Comm. Reports 1 (1993)].

Research References

Treatises and Practice Aids

Witkin, California Summary 10th Parent and Child § 269, Locating Missing Party or Child.

§ 3133. Temporary custody orders; temporary sole physical custody

If the district attorney represents to the court, by a written declaration under penalty of perjury, that a temporary custody order is needed to recover a child who is being detained or concealed in violation of a court order or a parent's right to custody, the court may issue an order, placing temporary sole physical custody in the parent or person recommended by the district attorney to facilitate the return of the child to the jurisdiction of the court, pending further hearings. If the court determines that it is not in the best interest of the child to place temporary sole physical custody in the parent or person recommended by the district attorney, the court shall appoint a person to take charge of the child and return the child to the jurisdiction of the court. *(Stats.1992, c. 162 (A.B.2650), § 10, operative Jan. 1, 1994.)*

Law Revision Commission Comments

Enactment [Revised Comment]

Section 3133 continues the last two sentences of former Civil Code Section 4604(c) without substantive change. See also Sections 3007 ("sole physical custody" defined), 3011 (factors to be considered in determining best interest of child). [23 Cal.L.Rev.Comm. Reports 1 (1993)].

Research References

Treatises and Practice Aids

Witkin, California Summary 10th Parent and Child § 269, Locating Missing Party or Child.

§ 3134. Payment of district attorney's expenses

(a) When the district attorney incurs expenses pursuant to this chapter, including expenses incurred in a sister state, payment of the expenses may be advanced by the county subject to reimbursement by the state, and shall be audited by the Controller and paid by the State Treasury according to law.

(b) The court in which the custody proceeding is pending or which has continuing jurisdiction shall, if appropriate, allocate liability for the reimbursement of actual expenses incurred by the district attorney to either or both parties to the proceedings, and that allocation shall constitute a judgment for the state for the funds advanced pursuant to this section. The county shall take reasonable action to enforce that liability and shall transmit all recovered funds to the state. *(Stats.1992, c. 162 (A.B.2650), § 10, operative Jan. 1, 1994.)*

Law Revision Commission Comments

Enactment [Revised Comment]

Section 3134 continues former Civil Code Section 4605 without substantive change. [23 Cal.L.Rev.Comm. Reports 1 (1993)].

Research References

Treatises and Practice Aids

Witkin, California Summary 10th Parent and Child § 162, Locating Missing Child or Party.
Witkin, California Summary 10th Parent and Child § 193, California Criminal Statutes.
Witkin, California Summary 10th Parent and Child § 269, Locating Missing Party or Child.

§ 3134.5. Protective custody warrant; order to freeze assets; service; dismissal of warrant; order terminated, modified, or vacated; service of notice of dismissal

(a) Upon request of the district attorney, the court may issue a protective custody warrant to secure the recovery of an unlawfully detained or concealed child. The request by the district attorney shall include a written declaration under penalty of perjury that a warrant for the child is necessary in order for the district attorney to perform the duties described in Sections 3130 and 3131. The protective custody warrant for the child shall contain an order that the arresting agency shall place the child in protective custody, or return the child as directed by the court. The protective custody warrant for the child may also contain an order to freeze the California assets of the party alleged to be in possession of the child. The protective custody warrant may be served in any county in the same manner as a warrant of arrest and may be served at any time of the day or night. For purposes of this subdivision, "assets" means funds held in a depository institution, as defined in subdivision (a) of Section 1420 of the Financial Code, in California.

(b) Upon a declaration of the district attorney that the child has been recovered or that the warrant is otherwise no longer required, the court may dismiss the warrant without further court proceedings.

(c) Upon noticed motion, any order to freeze assets pursuant to subdivision (a) may be terminated, modified, or vacated by the court upon a finding that the release of the assets will not jeopardize the safety or best interest of the child.

(d) If an asset freeze order is entered pursuant to subdivision (a), and the court subsequently dismisses the warrant pursuant to subdivision (b), notice of the dismissal shall be immediately served on the depository institutions holding any assets pursuant to the freeze order. *(Added by Stats.1996, c. 988 (A.B.2936), § 1.5. Amended by Stats.2012, c. 276 (S.B. 1206), § 3.)*

Research References

Treatises and Practice Aids

Witkin, California Summary 10th Parent and Child § 269, Locating Missing Party or Child.

§ 3135. Effect of Part 3 on authority of district attorney or arresting agency

Part 3 (commencing with Section 3400) does not limit the authority of a district attorney or arresting agency to act pursuant to this chapter, Section 279.6 of the Penal Code, or any other applicable law. *(Added by Stats.1999, c. 867 (S.B.668), § 1.)*

Research References

Treatises and Practice Aids

Witkin, California Summary 10th Parent and Child § 269, Locating Missing Party or Child.

CHAPTER 9. CHECK TO DETERMINE WHETHER CHILD IS MISSING PERSON

§ 3140. Parent not appearing in court or by counsel; submission of child's birth certificate; missing children

(a) Subject to subdivisions (b) and (c), before granting or modifying a custody order in a case in which one or both parents of the child have not appeared either personally or by counsel, the court shall require the parent, petitioner, or other party appearing in the case to submit a certified copy of the child's birth certificate to the court. The court or its designee shall forward the certified copy of the birth certificate to the local police or sheriff's department which shall check with the National Crime Information Center Missing Person System to ascertain whether the child has been reported missing or is the victim of an abduction and shall report the results of the check to the court.

(b) If the custody matter before the court also involves a petition for the dissolution of marriage or the adjudication of paternity rights or duties, this section applies only to a case in which there is no proof of personal service of the petition on the absent parent.

(c) For good cause shown, the court may waive the requirements of this section. *(Stats.1992, c. 162 (A.B.2650), § 10, operative Jan. 1, 1994.)*

Law Revision Commission Comments

Enactment [Revised Comment]

Section 3140 continues former Civil Code Section 4604.5 without substantive change. See also Sections 3415 (Section 3140 applies to proceedings pursuant to Uniform Child Custody Jurisdiction Act), 7603 (Section 3140 applies to proceedings pursuant to Uniform Parentage Act); Welf. & Inst. Code § 11478.5 (California Parent Locator Service and Central Registry). [23 Cal.L.Rev.Comm. Reports 1 (1993)].

Research References

Treatises and Practice Aids

Witkin, California Summary 10th Parent and Child § 19, General Provisions.

Witkin, California Summary 10th Parent and Child § 195, Statutory Framework.

Witkin, California Summary 10th Parent and Child § 270, Risk Of Abduction and Missing Person Check.

CHAPTER 10. APPOINTMENT OF COUNSEL TO REPRESENT CHILD

§ 3150. Appointment of private counsel

(a) If the court determines that it would be in the best interest of the minor child, the court may appoint private counsel to represent the interests of the child in a custody or visitation proceeding, provided that the court and counsel comply with the requirements set forth in Rules 5.240, 5.241, and 5.242 of the California Rules of Court.

(b) Upon entering an appearance on behalf of a child pursuant to this chapter, counsel shall continue to represent that child unless relieved by the court upon the substitution of other counsel by the court or for cause. *(Stats.1992, c. 162 (A.B.2650), § 10, operative Jan. 1, 1994. Amended by Stats. 1993, c. 219 (A.B.1500), § 116.85; Stats.2010, c. 352 (A.B. 939), § 14.)*

Law Revision Commission Comments

Enactment [Revised Comment]

Section 3150 continues former Civil Code Section 4606(a)-(b) without substantive change. The former reference to a proceeding "brought under this part," meaning the former Family Law Act (former Part 5 (commencing with former Section 4000) of Division 4 of the Civil Code), has been omitted as unnecessary. See Section 3021 (application of part). See also Section 3011 (factors to be considered in determining best interest of child). [23 Cal.L.Rev. Comm. Reports 1 (1993)].

Commentary

In re Marriage of Metzger, 224 Cal.App.4th 1441, 169 Cal.Rptr.3d 382 (2014), review denied, held that judicial appointment of counsel to represent the parties' minor child in a custody dispute did not violate the father's constitutional rights and was not an abuse of discretion.

In re Marriage of Lloyd, 55 Cal.App.4th 216, 64 Cal.Rptr.2d 37 (1997), holds that the trial court may not appoint guardians ad litem to represent children in family law cases because there is no statutory authority for such appointment. Nevertheless, the trial court may appoint counsel to represent the children under this section.

Research References

Forms

California Transactions Forms--Family Law § 2:72, Counsel for the Children.
West's California Judicial Council Forms FL-322, Declaration Of Counsel for a Child Regarding Qualifications.
West's California Judicial Council Forms FL-323, Order Appointing Counsel for a Child.
West's California Judicial Council Forms FL-321-INFO, Attorney for Child in a Family Law Case--Information Sheet.

Treatises and Practice Aids

Witkin, California Summary 10th Husband and Wife § 10A, (New) Ex Parte Communications With Mediator or Evaluator.
Witkin, California Summary 10th Parent and Child § 46, in General.
Witkin, California Summary 10th Parent and Child § 49, Joinder and Alignment Of Parties.
Witkin, California Summary 10th Parent and Child § 195, Statutory Framework.
Witkin, California Summary 10th Parent and Child § 272, in General.
Witkin, California Summary 10th Parent and Child § 275, in General.
Witkin, California Summary 10th Parent and Child § 276, Report.
Witkin, California Summary 10th Parent and Child § 281, Recommendations.
Witkin, California Summary 10th Parent and Child § 493, Persons Entitled to Inspect Records.

§ 3151. Duties and rights of private counsel

(a) The child's counsel appointed under this chapter is charged with the representation of the child's best interests. The role of the child's counsel is to gather evidence that bears on the best interests of the child, and present that admissible evidence to the court in any manner appropriate for the counsel of a party. If the child so desires, the child's counsel shall present the child's wishes to the court. The counsel's duties, unless under the circumstances it is inappropriate to exercise the duty, include interviewing the child, reviewing the court files and all accessible relevant records available to both parties, and making any further investigations as the counsel considers necessary to ascertain evidence relevant to the custody or visitation hearings.

(b) Counsel shall serve notices and pleadings on all parties, consistent with requirements for parties. Counsel shall not be called as a witness in the proceeding. Counsel may introduce and examine counsel's own witnesses, present arguments to the court concerning the child's welfare, and participate further in the proceeding to the degree necessary to represent the child adequately.

(c) The child's counsel shall have the following rights:

(1) Reasonable access to the child.

(2) Standing to seek affirmative relief on behalf of the child.

(3) Notice of any proceeding, and all phases of that proceeding, including a request for examination affecting the child.

(4) The right to take any action that is available to a party to the proceeding, including, but not limited to, the following: filing pleadings, making evidentiary objections, and presenting evidence and being heard in the proceeding, which may include, but shall not be limited to, presenting motions and orders to show cause, and participating in settlement conferences, trials, seeking writs, appeals, and arbitrations.

(5) Access to the child's medical, dental, mental health, and other health care records, school and educational records, and the right to interview school personnel, caretakers, health care providers, mental health professionals, and others who have assessed the child or provided care to the child. The release of this information to counsel shall not constitute a waiver of the confidentiality of the reports, files, and any disclosed communications. Counsel may interview mediators; however, the provisions of Sections 3177 and 3182 shall apply.

(6) The right to reasonable advance notice of and the right to refuse any physical or psychological examination or evaluation, for purposes of the proceeding, which has not been ordered by the court.

(7) The right to assert or waive any privilege on behalf of the child.

(8) The right to seek independent psychological or physical examination or evaluation of the child for purposes of the pending proceeding, upon approval by the court. *(Stats.1992, c. 162 (A.B.2650), § 10, operative Jan. 1, 1994. Amended by Stats.1997, c. 449 (A.B.1526), § 1; Stats.2010, c. 352 (A.B. 939), § 15.)*

Law Revision Commission Comments

Enactment [Revised Comment]

Section 3151 continues former Civil Code Section 4606(c)-(d) without substantive change. The word "any" has been substituted for "any and all," since "all" is surplus. [23 Cal.L.Rev.Comm. Reports 1 (1993)].

Research References

Forms

California Transactions Forms--Family Law § 2:72, Counsel for the Children.
West's California Judicial Council Forms FL-323, Order Appointing Counsel for a Child.

Treatises and Practice Aids

Witkin, California Summary 10th Husband and Wife § 10A, (New) Ex Parte Communications With Mediator or Evaluator.
Witkin, California Summary 10th Parent and Child § 272, in General.
Witkin, California Summary 10th Parent and Child § 273, Rights and Duties.
Witkin, California Summary 10th Parent and Child § 278, in General.

§ 3152. Reports or files of local child protective services agencies; release; review

(a) The child's counsel may, upon noticed motion to all parties and the local child protective services agency, request the court to authorize release of relevant reports or files, concerning the child represented by the counsel, of the relevant local child protective services agency.

(b) The court shall review the reports or files in camera in order to determine whether they are relevant to the pending action and whether and to what extent they should be released to the child's counsel.

(c) Neither the review by the court nor the release to counsel shall constitute a waiver of the confidentiality of the reports and files. Counsel shall not disclose the contents or existence of the reports or files to anyone unless otherwise permitted by law. *(Stats.1992, c. 162 (A.B.2650), § 10, operative Jan. 1, 1994.)*

Law Revision Commission Comments

Enactment [Revised Comment]

Section 3152 continues former Civil Code Section 4606(e) without substantive change. The word "reports" has been substituted for "records" in subdivision (c) to conform to subdivisions (a) and (b). [23 Cal.L.Rev.Comm. Reports 1 (1993)].

Research References

Forms

West's California Judicial Council Forms FL-323, Order Appointing Counsel for a Child.

West's California Judicial Council Forms FL-321-INFO, Attorney for Child in a Family Law Case--Information Sheet.

Treatises and Practice Aids

Witkin, California Summary 10th Parent and Child § 272, in General.

§ 3153. Compensation and expenses of private counsel

(a) If the court appoints counsel under this chapter to represent the child, counsel shall receive a reasonable sum for compensation and expenses, the amount of which shall be determined by the court. Except as provided in subdivision (b), this amount shall be paid by the parties in the proportions the court deems just.

(b) Upon its own motion or that of a party, the court shall determine whether both parties together are financially unable to pay all or a portion of the cost of counsel appointed pursuant to this chapter, and the portion of the cost of that counsel which the court finds the parties are unable to pay shall be paid by the county. The Judicial Council shall adopt guidelines to assist in determining financial eligibility for county payment of counsel appointed by the court pursuant to this chapter. *(Stats.1992, c. 162 (A.B.2650), § 10, operative Jan. 1, 1994.)*

Law Revision Commission Comments

Enactment [Revised Comment]

Section 3153 continues former Civil Code Section 4606(f)-(g) without substantive change. [23 Cal.L.Rev.Comm. Reports 1 (1993)].

Commentary

See *In re Marriage of Lisi, 39 Cal.App.4th. 1573, 46 Cal.Rptr.2d 623 (1995)* (although death of a party normally abates a dissolution action, counsel appointed by court to represent the children may nevertheless be awarded attorney's fee against estate of deceased party when, during lifetime of party, the court appointed the attorney and ordered "reasonable compensation," to be later determined).

Research References

Forms

California Transactions Forms--Family Law § 2:72, Counsel for the Children.

Treatises and Practice Aids

Witkin, California Summary 10th Parent and Child § 49, Joinder and Alignment Of Parties.

Witkin, California Summary 10th Parent and Child § 272, in General.

CHAPTER 11. MEDIATION OF CUSTODY AND VISITATION ISSUES

ARTICLE 1. GENERAL PROVISIONS

§ 3160. Mediators; availability; duties of court

Each superior court shall make a mediator available. The court is not required to institute a family conciliation court in order to provide mediation services. *(Added by Stats.1993, c. 219 (A.B.1500), § 116.87.)*

Law Revision Commission Comments

Enactment [Revised Comment]

Section 3160 continues without substantive change and generalizes the first and third sentences of former Civil Code Section 4607(b). Generalizing this provision means that it is also applicable to mediation involving a stepparent or grandparent.

This chapter continues the rules in former Civil Code Section 4351.5 (mediation of stepparent or grandparent visitation) and former Civil Code Sections 4607–4607.2 (mediation of contested custody or visitation). Where one of the former sections provided a rule, but the other did not, the chapter generalizes the rule to apply to both types of mediation. See Sections 3160 (superior courts to provide mediation services), 3162 (uniform standards of practice for mediation), 3163 (local court rules), 3164 (qualifications of mediator), 3172 (mediation available where paternity is at issue), 3173 (mediation of dispute concerning existing order), 3175 (mediation to be set before or concurrent with hearing), 3176 (notice of mediation or hearing), 3180(b) (requirement that mediator effect settlement in best interest of child), 3181 (separate mediation where domestic violence), 3183 (recommendations to court), 3184 (recommendations that counsel be appointed for minor child), 3185 (hearing on issues not settled by mediation). [23 Cal.L.Rev.Comm. Reports 1 (1993)].

Research References

Forms

Alternative Dispute Resolution with Forms § 1:9, Statutes Mandating or Encouraging Alternative Dispute Resolution.
California Practice Guide: Rutter Family Law Forms Form 1:32, Glossary Of Common Family Law Terms, Phrases and Concepts (Enclosure to Form 1:31).
Cal. Transaction Forms - Bus. Transactions § 14:50, Confidentiality Of Mediation Process.
California Transactions Forms--Family Law § 2:70, Deciding Custody.
California Transactions Forms--Family Law § 3:16, Identifying Areas Of Parental Decision Making and Participation.
California Transactions Forms--Family Law § 3:59, Basis for Modification Of Physical Custody.
California Transactions Forms--Family Law § 3:87, Appointment Of a Special Master.
26 West's Legal Forms § 1:3, Statutes Mandating or Encouraging Alternative Dispute Resolution.
West's California Code Forms, Family § 3160, Comment Overview--Mediation Of Custody and Visitation Issues.

Treatises and Practice Aids

Witkin, California Summary 10th Husband and Wife § 12A, (New) in General.
Witkin, California Summary 10th Parent and Child § 195, Statutory Framework.
Witkin, California Summary 10th Parent and Child § 278, in General.
Witkin, California Summary 10th Parent and Child § 280, Mediation Proceeding.
Witkin, California Summary 10th Parent and Child § 281, Recommendations.
Witkin, California Summary 10th Parent and Child § 493, Persons Entitled to Inspect Records.

§ 3161. Purpose of mediation proceedings

The purposes of a mediation proceeding are as follows:

(a) To reduce acrimony that may exist between the parties.

(b) To develop an agreement assuring the child close and continuing contact with both parents that is in the best interest of the child, consistent with Sections 3011 and 3020.

(c) To effect a settlement of the issue of visitation rights of all parties that is in the best interest of the child. *(Added by Stats.1993, c. 219 (A.B.1500), § 116.87. Amended by Stats. 1997, c. 849 (A.B.200), § 5.)*

Law Revision Commission Comments

Enactment [Revised Comment]

Section 3161 continues without substantive change the third sentence of former Civil Code Section 4607(a) and the second sentence of former Civil Code Section 4351.5(c). The reference to "children" has been omitted as surplus. See Section 10 (singular includes plural). See also Section 3011 (factors to be considered in determining best interest of child). [23 Cal.L.Rev.Comm. Reports 1 (1993)].

Research References

Forms

Alternative Dispute Resolution with Forms § 23:7, Child Custody Disputes.
West's California Code Forms, Family § 3160, Comment Overview--Mediation Of Custody and Visitation Issues.

Treatises and Practice Aids

Witkin, California Summary 10th Parent and Child § 278, in General.

§ 3162. Uniform standards of practice; contents; adoption by Judicial Council

(a) Mediation of cases involving custody and visitation concerning children shall be governed by uniform standards of practice adopted by the Judicial Council.

(b) The standards of practice shall include, but not be limited to, all of the following:

(1) Provision for the best interest of the child and the safeguarding of the rights of the child to frequent and continuing contact with both parents, consistent with Sections 3011 and 3020.

(2) Facilitation of the transition of the family by detailing factors to be considered in decisions concerning the child's future.

(3) The conducting of negotiations in such a way as to equalize power relationships between the parties.

(c) In adopting the standards of practice, the Judicial Council shall consider standards developed by recognized associations of mediators and attorneys and other relevant standards governing mediation of proceedings for the dissolution of marriage.

(d) The Judicial Council shall offer training with respect to the standards to mediators. *(Added by Stats.1993, c. 219 (A.B.1500), § 116.87. Amended by Stats.1997, c. 849 (A.B. 200), § 6.)*

Law Revision Commission Comments

Enactment [Revised Comment]

Section 3162 continues without substantive change and generalizes former Civil Code Section 4607.1. The part of the former section that directed the Judicial Council to adopt uniform standards of practice by Jan. 1, 1991, has been omitted as surplus. See Cal. R. Ct. App. Div. I § 26 (1992) (Judicial Council Uniform Standards of Practice for Court–Connected Mediation of Child Custody and Visitation Disputes). See Section 3160 Comment (generalization of provisions to apply both to mediation of stepparent or grandparent visitation and to mediation of contested issues).

See also Sections 1819 (destruction of records of child custody or visitation mediation), 1850 (statewide coordination of family mediation and conciliation services), 3011 (factors to be considered in determining best interest of child). [23 Cal.L.Rev.Comm. Reports 1 (1993)].

Research References

Treatises and Practice Aids

Witkin, California Summary 10th Parent and Child § 278, in General.

§ 3163. Local rules; development

Courts shall develop local rules to respond to requests for a change of mediators or to general problems relating to mediation. *(Added by Stats.1993, c. 219 (A.B.1500), § 116.87.)*

Law Revision Commission Comments

Enactment [Revised Comment]

Section 3163 continues without substantive change and generalizes former Civil Code Section 4607(g). See Section 3160 Comment (generalization of provisions to apply both to mediation of stepparent or grandparent visitation and to mediation of contested issues). [23 Cal.L.Rev.Comm. Reports 1 (1993)].

Research References

Treatises and Practice Aids

Witkin, California Summary 10th Parent and Child § 278, in General.

§ 3164. Qualifications of mediators

(a) The mediator may be a member of the professional staff of a family conciliation court, probation department, or mental health services agency, or may be any other person or agency designated by the court.

(b) The mediator shall meet the minimum qualifications required of a counselor of conciliation as provided in Section 1815. *(Added by Stats.1993, c. 219 (A.B.1500), § 116.87.)*

Law Revision Commission Comments

Enactment [Revised Comment]

Subdivision (a) of Section 3164 continues without substantive change and generalizes the second sentence of former Civil Code Section 4607(b). Subdivision (b) continues without substantive change the last sentence of former Civil Code Section 4607(b) and the last sentence of former Civil Code Section 4351.5(c). See Section 3160 Comment (generalization of provisions to apply both to mediation of stepparent or grandparent visitation and to mediation of contested issues). See also Section 1816 (continuing instruction programs in domestic violence). [23 Cal.L.Rev.Comm. Reports 1 (1993)].

Research References

Treatises and Practice Aids

Witkin, California Summary 10th Husband and Wife § 94, Participation in Domestic Violence Programs.

Witkin, California Summary 10th Parent and Child § 278, in General.

§ 3165. Continuing education; clinical supervisors of evaluators, investigators, and mediators

Any person, regardless of administrative title, hired on or after January 1, 1998, who is responsible for clinical supervision of evaluators, investigators, or mediators or who directly supervises or administers the Family Court Services evaluation or mediation programs shall meet the same continuing education requirements specified in Section 1816 for supervising and associate counselors of conciliation. *(Added by Stats.1996, c. 761 (S.B.1995), § 4.)*

Research References

Treatises and Practice Aids

Witkin, California Summary 10th Parent and Child § 278, in General.

ARTICLE 2. AVAILABILITY OF MEDIATION

Section

3170. Setting matters for mediation; guidelines for handling domestic violence cases.

§ 3170. Setting matters for mediation; guidelines for handling domestic violence cases

Section operative until Jan. 1, 2020. See, also, § 3170 operative Jan. 1, 2020.

(a)(1) If it appears on the face of a petition, application, or other pleading to obtain or modify a temporary or permanent custody or visitation order that custody, visitation, or both are contested, the court shall set the contested issues for mediation.

(2) Prior to filing the petition, application, or other pleading to obtain or modify a temporary or permanent custody or visitation order, a party to an existing case may request that the court set a custody or visitation issue for mediation, and the court may set that issue for mediation.

(b) Domestic violence cases shall be handled by Family Court Services in accordance with a separate written protocol approved by the Judicial Council. The Judicial Council shall adopt guidelines for services, other than services provided under this chapter, that courts or counties may offer to parents who have been unable to resolve their disputes. These services may include, but are not limited to, parent education programs, booklets, video recordings, or referrals to additional community resources.

(c) This section shall remain in effect only until January 1, 2020, and as of that date is repealed. *(Added by Stats.1993, c. 219 (A.B.1500), § 116.87. Amended by Stats.1996, c. 761 (S.B.1995), § 5; Stats.2009, c. 88 (A.B.176), § 37; Stats.2012, c. 470 (A.B.1529), § 18; Stats.2017, c. 330 (A.B.1692), § 1, eff. Jan. 1, 2018.)*

Repeal

For repeal of this section, see its terms.

Law Revision Commission Comments

Enactment [Revised Comment]

Section 3170 restates the first part of the first sentence of former Civil Code Section 4607(a) without substantive change. The reference to "to obtain or modify a temporary or permanent custody or visitation order" has been substituted for "as provided in Section 4600, 4600.1, or 4601." This is not a substantive change. The reference to "children" has been omitted as surplus. See Section 10 (singular includes plural). See also Section 3175 (mediation to be set before or concurrent with hearing). [23 Cal.L.Rev.Comm. Reports 1 (1993)].

2009 Amendment

Section 3170 is amended to reflect advances in recording technology and for consistency of terminology. For a similar reform, see 2002 Cal. Stat. ch. 1068 (replacing numerous references to "audiotape" in Civil Discovery Act with either "audio technology," "audio recording," or "audio record," as context required). [37 Cal. L. Revision Comm'n Reports 211 (2007)].

2012 Amendment

Subdivision (b) of Section 3170 is amended to reflect the Lockyer–Isenberg Trial Court Funding Act, 1997 Cal. Stat. ch. 850 (see generally Gov't Code §§ 77000–77655). [39 Cal.L.Rev.Comm. Reports 157 (2009)].

Commentary

Hoversten v. Superior Court, 74 Cal.App.4th 636, 88 Cal.Rptr.2d 197 (1999), holds that subsection (a) requires that a prisoner, no matter how egregious the nature of his crime, be granted a hearing to determine whether he should have legal custody and visitation of his minor child. It was error for the trial court to determine that the prisoner was not entitled to a hearing to determine whether it would be in the child's best interests to have visitation despite the crime and incarceration of the prisoner. Although prisoners do not ordinarily appear personally in civil proceedings, trial courts should devise alternative means to insure participation in the proceeding. *Hoversten* additionally suggests, under subsection (a), the use of a mediator in contested cases.

Research References

Forms

Alternative Dispute Resolution with Forms § 1:9, Statutes Mandating or Encouraging Alternative Dispute Resolution.
Alternative Dispute Resolution with Forms § 4:4, Mandated Mediation.
Alternative Dispute Resolution with Forms § 23:7, Child Custody Disputes.
California Transactions Forms--Family Law § 2:70, Deciding Custody.

Treatises and Practice Aids

Witkin, California Summary 10th Husband and Wife § 327, Hearing.
Witkin, California Summary 10th Parent and Child § 253, Move-Away Cases.
Witkin, California Summary 10th Parent and Child § 279, Availability Of Mediation.

§ 3170. Setting matters for mediation; guidelines for handling domestic violence cases

Section operative Jan. 1, 2020. See, also, § 3170 operative until Jan. 1, 2020.

(a) If it appears on the face of a petition, application, or other pleading to obtain or modify a temporary or permanent custody or visitation order that custody, visitation, or both are contested, the court shall set the contested issues for mediation.

(b) Domestic violence cases shall be handled by Family Court Services in accordance with a separate written protocol approved by the Judicial Council. The Judicial Council shall adopt guidelines for services, other than services provided under this chapter, that courts or counties may offer to parents who have been unable to resolve their disputes. These services may include, but are not limited to, parent education programs, booklets, video recordings, or referrals to additional community resources.

(c) This section shall become operative on January 1, 2020. *(Added by Stats.2017, c. 330 (A.B.1692), § 2, eff. Jan. 1, 2018, operative Jan. 1, 2020.)*

§ 3171. Stepparent or grandparent visitation; setting matter for mediation; waiver of parental right to object or require a hearing

(a) If a stepparent or grandparent has petitioned, or otherwise applied, for a visitation order pursuant to Chapter 5 (commencing with Section 3100), the court shall set the matter for mediation.

(b) A natural or adoptive parent who is not a party to the proceeding is not required to participate in the mediation proceeding, but failure to participate is a waiver of that parent's right to object to a settlement reached by the other parties during mediation or to require a hearing on the matter. *(Added by Stats.1993, c. 219 (A.B.1500), § 116.87.)*

Law Revision Commission Comments

Enactment [Revised Comment]

Subdivision (a) of Section 3171 continues the first sentence of former Civil Code Section 4351.5(c) without substantive change. Subdivision (b) continues former Civil Code Section 4351.5(g) without substantive change.

In subdivision (a), a reference to Chapter 5 (commencing with Section 3100) has been substituted for the narrower reference to stepparent and grandparent visitation pursuant to former Civil Code Section 4351.5. This makes mediation available in the situations described in Family Code Section 3102 (former Civil Code Section 197.5)—cases where grandparents and other relatives seek visitation of a minor child whose parent or parents are deceased. The former reference to a request for an order of "reasonable" visitation rights has been omitted. This is not a substantive change, since the sections in Chapter 5 (commencing with Section 3100) control the type of visitation order that may be issued and these sections require that visitation rights must be in the best interest of the child.

See also Section 3011 (factors to be considered in determining best interest of child). [23 Cal.L.Rev.Comm. Reports 1 (1993)].

Research References

Treatises and Practice Aids

Witkin, California Summary 10th Parent and Child § 279, Availability Of Mediation.

§ 3172. Paternity disputes; availability of mediation proceedings

Mediation shall not be denied to the parties on the basis that paternity is at issue in a proceeding before the court. *(Added by Stats.1993, c. 219 (A.B.1500), § 116.87.)*

Law Revision Commission Comments

Enactment [Revised Comment]

Section 3172 continues without substantive change and generalizes the last sentence of former Civil Code Section 4607(a). See Section 3160 Comment (generalization of provisions to apply both to mediation of stepparent or grandparent visitation and to mediation of contested issues). [23 Cal.L.Rev.Comm. Reports 1 (1993)].

Research References

Treatises and Practice Aids

Witkin, California Summary 10th Parent and Child § 279, Availability Of Mediation.

§ 3173. Mediation of disputes relating to existing custody or visitation orders; filing of petition

(a) Upon an order of the presiding judge of a superior court authorizing the procedure in that court, a petition may be filed pursuant to this chapter for mediation of a dispute relating to an existing order for custody, visitation, or both.

(b) The mediation of a dispute concerning an existing order shall be set not later than 60 days after the filing of the petition. *(Added by Stats.1993, c. 219 (A.B.1500), § 116.87. Amended by Stats.2012, c. 470 (A.B.1529), § 19.)*

Law Revision Commission Comments

Enactment [Revised Comment]

Section 3173 continues without substantive change and generalizes the second sentence of former Civil Code Section 4607(a). See Section 3160 Comment (generalization of provisions to apply both to mediation of stepparent or grandparent visitation and to mediation of contested issues). In subdivision (a), the reference to "or both" has been added. This is not a substantive change. [23 Cal.L.Rev. Comm. Reports 1 (1993)].

2012 Amendment

Subdivision (a) of Section 3173 is amended to reflect enactment of the Lockyer–Isenberg Trial Court Funding Act, 1997 Cal. Stat. ch. 850 (see generally Gov't Code §§ 77000–77655). See, e.g., Gov't Code §§ 77001 (local trial court management), 77003 ("court operations" defined), 77200 (state funding of "court operations"); see also Cal. R. Ct. 10.603(a) (responsibilities of presiding judge of superior court). [39 Cal.L.Rev.Comm. Reports 157 (2009)].

Research References

Treatises and Practice Aids

Witkin, California Summary 10th Parent and Child § 279, Availability Of Mediation.

ARTICLE 3. MEDIATION PROCEEDINGS

§ 3175. Setting matter before or concurrent with hearing

If a matter is set for mediation pursuant to this chapter, the mediation shall be set before or concurrent with the setting of the matter for hearing. *(Added by Stats.1993, c. 219 (A.B. 1500), § 116.87.)*

Law Revision Commission Comments

Enactment [Revised Comment]

Section 3175 restates without substantive change and generalizes the last part of the first sentence of former Civil Code Section 4607(a). See Section 3160 Comment (generalization of provisions to apply both to mediation of stepparent or grandparent visitation and to mediation of contested issues). [23 Cal.L.Rev.Comm. Reports 1 (1993)].

Research References

Forms

Alternative Dispute Resolution with Forms § 23:7, Child Custody Disputes.

Treatises and Practice Aids

Witkin, California Summary 10th Parent and Child § 280, Mediation Proceeding.

§ 3176. Notice of mediation and hearing

(a) Notice of mediation and of any hearing to be held pursuant to this chapter shall be given to the following persons:

(1) Where mediation is required to settle a contested issue of custody or visitation, to each party and to each party's counsel of record.

(2) Where a stepparent or grandparent seeks visitation rights, to the stepparent or grandparent seeking visitation rights, to each parent of the child, and to each parent's counsel of record.

(b) Notice shall be given by certified mail, return receipt requested, postage prepaid, to the last known address.

(c) Notice of mediation pursuant to Section 3188 shall state that all communications involving the mediator shall be kept confidential between the mediator and the disputing parties. *(Added by Stats.1993, c. 219 (A.B.1500), § 116.87. Amended by Stats.2002, c. 1077 (S.B.174), § 1.)*

Law Revision Commission Comments

Enactment [Revised Comment]

Section 3176 restates without substantive change and generalizes former Civil Code Section 4351.5(i). The former reference to proceedings for dissolution of marriage, for nullity of marriage, or for legal separation of the parties has been omitted as unnecessary. See Section 3021 (application of part) & Comment. See also Section 3160 Comment (generalization of provisions to apply both to mediation of stepparent or grandparent visitation and to mediation of contested issues). [23 Cal.L.Rev.Comm. Reports 1 (1993)].

Research References

Treatises and Practice Aids

Witkin, California Summary 10th Parent and Child § 280, Mediation Proceeding.

§ 3177. Confidentiality of proceedings

Mediation proceedings pursuant to this chapter shall be held in private and shall be confidential. All communications, verbal or written, from the parties to the mediator made in the proceeding are official information within the meaning of Section 1040 of the Evidence Code. *(Added by Stats.1993, c. 219 (A.B.1500), § 116.87.)*

Law Revision Commission Comments

Enactment [Revised Comment]

Section 3177 continues former Civil Code Sections 4351.5(d) and 4607(c) without substantive change. See also Section 1819 (destruction of records of child custody or visitation mediation). [23 Cal.L.Rev.Comm. Reports 1 (1993)].

Research References

Treatises and Practice Aids

Witkin, California Summary 10th Parent and Child § 273, Rights and Duties.

Witkin, California Summary 10th Parent and Child § 280, Mediation Proceeding.

§ 3178. Restrictions on mediation agreements

An agreement reached by the parties as a result of mediation shall be limited as follows:

(a) Where mediation is required to settle a contested issue of custody or visitation, the agreement shall be limited to the resolution of issues relating to parenting plans, custody, visitation, or a combination of these issues.

(b) Where a stepparent or grandparent seeks visitation rights, the agreement shall be limited to the resolution of issues relating to visitation. *(Added by Stats.1993, c. 219 (A.B.1500), § 116.87.)*

Law Revision Commission Comments

Enactment [Revised Comment]

Section 3178 restates without substantive change the fifth sentence of former Civil Code Section 4351.5(f) and the fifth sentence of former Civil Code Section 4607(e). See also Section 3185 (hearing on issues not settled by mediation). [23 Cal.L.Rev.Comm. Reports 1 (1993)].

Research References

Treatises and Practice Aids

Witkin, California Summary 10th Parent and Child § 280, Mediation Proceeding.

Witkin, California Summary 10th Parent and Child § 282, Agreement.

§ 3179. Modification of agreements

A custody or visitation agreement reached as a result of mediation may be modified at any time at the discretion of the court, subject to Chapter 1 (commencing with Section 3020), Chapter 2 (commencing with Section 3040), Chapter 4 (commencing with Section 3080), and Chapter 5 (commencing with Section 3100). *(Added by Stats.1993, c. 219 (A.B. 1500), § 116.87.)*

Law Revision Commission Comments

Enactment [Revised Comment]

Section 3179 restates the last sentences of former Civil Code Sections 4351.5(f) and 4607(e) without substantive change. Broader references to Family Code sections have been substituted for the references to former Civil Code Sections 4600, 4600.5, and 4601. These are not substantive changes. [23 Cal.L.Rev.Comm. Reports 1 (1993)].

Research References

Treatises and Practice Aids

Witkin, California Summary 10th Parent and Child § 282, Agreement.

§ 3180. Duties of mediators

(a) In mediation proceedings pursuant to this chapter, the mediator has the duty to assess the needs and interests of the child involved in the controversy, and is entitled to interview the child where the mediator considers the interview appropriate or necessary.

(b) The mediator shall use his or her best efforts to effect a settlement of the custody or visitation dispute that is in the best interest of the child, as provided in Section 3011. *(Added by Stats.1993, c. 219 (A.B.1500), § 116.87.)*

Law Revision Commission Comments

Enactment [Revised Comment]

Subdivision (a) of Section 3180 continues without substantive change the second sentence of former Civil Code Section 4351.5(e) and the second sentence of former Civil Code Section 4607(d). The reference to "children" has been omitted as surplus. See Section 10 (singular includes plural).

Subdivision (b) continues without substantive change and generalizes the fourth sentence of former Civil Code Section 4607(a). See Section 3160 Comment (generalization of provisions to apply both to mediation of stepparent or grandparent visitation and to mediation of contested issues). The phrase "as provided in" has been substituted for "consistent with the considerations required by" for consistency with other sections. See, e.g., Sections 3020 (legislative findings and declarations), 3040 (order of preference in ordering custody). This is not a substantive change. [23 Cal.L.Rev.Comm. Reports 1 (1993)].

Research References

Treatises and Practice Aids

Witkin, California Summary 10th Parent and Child § 280, Mediation Proceeding.

§ 3181. Domestic violence history between the parties; separate meetings; intake forms

(a) In a proceeding in which mediation is required pursuant to this chapter, where there has been a history of domestic violence between the parties or where a protective order as defined in Section 6218 is in effect, at the request of the party alleging domestic violence in a written declaration under penalty of perjury or protected by the order, the mediator appointed pursuant to this chapter shall meet with the parties separately and at separate times.

(b) Any intake form that an agency charged with providing family court services requires the parties to complete before the commencement of mediation shall state that, if a party alleging domestic violence in a written declaration under penalty of perjury or a party protected by a protective order so requests, the mediator will meet with the parties separately and at separate times. *(Added by Stats.1993, c. 219 (A.B. 1500), § 116.87.)*

Law Revision Commission Comments

Enactment [Revised Comment]

Section 3181 restates without substantive change and generalizes former Civil Code Section 4607.2. See Section 3160 Comment (generalization of provisions to apply both to mediation of stepparent or grandparent visitation and to mediation of contested issues). In subdivision (a), the requirement that the allegation of domestic violence be made in a written declaration under penalty of perjury has been added for consistency with subdivision (b). The "notwithstanding" clause in the former section has been omitted as surplus.

Unlike the former section, this section does not contain a reference to the section defining "domestic violence." This is not a substantive change. See Sections 6201 (application of definitions), 6211 ("domestic violence" defined). The term "protective order" has been substituted for the former references to orders under specific sections formerly in the Civil Code and the Code of Civil Procedure. This is not a substantive change, since Section 6218 defines "protective order" to include these orders.

This section supersedes the last sentence of former Civil Code Section 4607(d) which provided that mediators have the authority to meet with parties separately under the circumstances described in this section. The authority to hold the meetings is inherent in the requirement that the mediator do so. [23 Cal.L.Rev.Comm. Reports 1 (1993)].

Research References

Treatises and Practice Aids

Witkin, California Summary 10th Husband and Wife § 71, Case Management.

Witkin, California Summary 10th Husband and Wife § 10A, (New) Ex Parte Communications With Mediator or Evaluator.

Witkin, California Summary 10th Husband and Wife § 371, Civil Remedies.

Witkin, California Summary 10th Parent and Child § 280, Mediation Proceeding.

§ 3182. Authority of mediators; exclusion of counsel; exclusion of domestic violence support person

(a) The mediator has authority to exclude counsel from participation in the mediation proceedings pursuant to this chapter if, in the mediator's discretion, exclusion of counsel is appropriate or necessary.

(b) The mediator has authority to exclude a domestic violence support person from a mediation proceeding as provided in Section 6303. *(Added by Stats.1993, c. 219 (A.B.1500), § 116.87.)*

Law Revision Commission Comments

Enactment [Revised Comment]

Subdivision (a) of Section 3182 restates without substantive change the first sentence of former Civil Code Section 4351.5(e) and the first sentence of former Civil Code Section 4607(d).

Subdivision (b) is new and is added to provide a reference to the rule regarding exclusion of a domestic violence support person. This is not a substantive change. [23 Cal.L.Rev.Comm. Reports 1 (1993)].

Research References

Forms

26 West's Legal Forms APP. 2B, Uniform Mediation Act.

Treatises and Practice Aids

Witkin, California Summary 10th Parent and Child § 273, Rights and Duties.

Witkin, California Summary 10th Parent and Child § 280, Mediation Proceeding.

§ 3183. Child custody recommending counseling; written report provided to parties and counsel; investigation when agreement not reached; restraining order to protect child well-being

(a) Except as provided in Section 3188, the mediator may, consistent with local court rules, submit a recommendation to the court as to the custody of or visitation with the child, if the mediator has first provided the parties and their attorneys, including counsel for any minor children, with the recommendations in writing in advance of the hearing. The court shall make an inquiry at the hearing as to whether the parties and their attorneys have received the recommendations in writing. If the mediator is authorized to submit a recommendation to the court pursuant to this subdivision, the mediation and recommendation process shall be referred to as "child custody recommending counseling" and the mediator shall be referred to as a "child custody recommending counselor." Mediators who make those recommendations are considered mediators for purposes of Chapter 11 (commencing with Section 3160), and shall be subject to all requirements for mediators for all purposes under this code and the California Rules of Court. On and after January 1, 2012, all court communications and information regarding the child custody recommending counseling process shall reflect the change in the name of the process and the name of the providers.

(b) If the parties have not reached agreement as a result of the mediation proceedings, the mediator may recommend to the court that an investigation be conducted pursuant to Chapter 6 (commencing with Section 3110) or that other services be offered to assist the parties to effect a resolution of the controversy before a hearing on the issues.

(c) In appropriate cases, the mediator may recommend that restraining orders be issued, pending determination of the controversy, to protect the well-being of the child involved in the controversy. *(Added by Stats.1993, c. 219 (A.B.1500), § 116.87. Amended by Stats.1996, c. 761 (S.B. 1995), § 6; Stats.2002, c. 1077 (S.B.174), § 2; Stats.2010, c. 352 (A.B.939), § 16.)*

Law Revision Commission Comments

Enactment [Revised Comment]

Section 3183 continues without substantive change the first three sentences of former Civil Code Section 4351.5(f) and the first three sentences of former Civil Code Section 4607(e). The word "child" has been substituted for "children." This is not a substantive change. See Section 10 (singular includes plural).

The provisions in subdivision (b) that the mediator may recommend to the court that the investigation be conducted "pursuant to Chapter 6 (commencing with Section 3110)" and that "other action be taken" to assist the parties to effect a resolution of the controversy have been generalized. The provision in subdivision (c) that restraining orders (rather than "mutual" restraining orders) may be issued has been generalized. Each of these provisions formerly applied only to mediation in contested custody or visitation proceedings pursuant to former Civil Code Section 4607. See Section 3160 Comment (generalization of provisions to apply both to mediation of stepparent or grandparent visitation and to mediation of contested issues). [23 Cal.L.Rev.Comm. Reports 1 (1993)].

Research References

Treatises and Practice Aids

Witkin, California Summary 10th Parent and Child § 208, Child's Preference.

Witkin, California Summary 10th Parent and Child § 281, Recommendations.

Witkin, California Summary 10th Parent and Child § 225A, (New) Right Of Child to Express Preference.

§ 3184. Appointment of counsel to represent minor child; recommendations

Except as provided in Section 3188, nothing in this chapter prohibits the mediator from recommending to the court that counsel be appointed, pursuant to Chapter 10 (commencing with Section 3150), to represent the minor child. In making this recommendation, the mediator shall inform the court of the reasons why it would be in the best interest of the minor child to have counsel appointed. *(Added by Stats.1993, c. 219 (A.B.1500), § 116.87. Amended by Stats.2002, c. 1077 (S.B. 174), § 3.)*

Law Revision Commission Comments

Enactment [Revised Comment]

Section 3184 continues without substantive change and generalizes former Civil Code Section 4607(f). The reference to "children" has been omitted as surplus. See Section 10 (singular includes plural). See Section 3160 Comment (generalization of provisions to apply both to mediation of stepparent or grandparent visitation and to mediation of contested issues). See also Section 3011 (factors to be considered in determining best interest of child). [23 Cal.L.Rev. Comm. Reports 1 (1993)].

Research References

Treatises and Practice Aids

Witkin, California Summary 10th Parent and Child § 281, Recommendations.

§ 3185. Failure to reach mediation agreement; visitation rights hearing

(a) If issues that may be resolved by agreement pursuant to Section 3178 are not resolved by an agreement of all the parties who participate in mediation, the mediator shall inform the court in writing and the court shall set the matter for hearing on the unresolved issues.

(b) Where a stepparent or grandparent requests visitation, each natural or adoptive parent and the stepparent or grandparent shall be given an opportunity to appear and be heard on the issue of visitation. *(Added by Stats.1993, c. 219 (A.B.1500), § 116.87.)*

Law Revision Commission Comments

Enactment [Revised Comment]

Subdivision (a) of Section 3185 restates without substantive change and generalizes the first sentence of former Civil Code Section 4351.5(h). Subdivision (b) restates the last sentence of former Civil Code Section 4351.5 (h) without substantive change. See Section 3160 Comment (generalization of provisions to apply both to mediation of stepparent or grandparent visitation and to mediation of contested issues). [23 Cal.L.Rev.Comm. Reports 1 (1993)].

Commentary

Invoking this section, *In re Marriage of Dunn, 103 Cal.App.4th 345, 126 Cal.Rptr.2d 636 (2002)*, holds that the trial court erred in issuing a child custody modification order that limited former husband's new wife's participation in the children's school and social activities without first conducting a formal hearing in open court on the former wife's motion to so modify the custody order.

Research References

Treatises and Practice Aids

Witkin, California Summary 10th Parent and Child § 253, Move-Away Cases.

Witkin, California Summary 10th Parent and Child § 280, Mediation Proceeding.

§ 3186. Report of agreement; confirmation or incorporation of agreement in order

(a) An agreement reached by the parties as a result of mediation shall be reported to counsel for the parties by the mediator on the day set for mediation or as soon thereafter as practical, but before the agreement is reported to the court.

(b) An agreement may not be confirmed or otherwise incorporated in an order unless each party, in person or by counsel of record, has affirmed and assented to the agreement in open court or by written stipulation.

(c) An agreement may be confirmed or otherwise incorporated in an order if a party fails to appear at a noticed hearing on the issue involved in the agreement. *(Added by Stats.1993, c. 219 (A.B.1500), § 116.87.)*

Law Revision Commission Comments

Enactment [Revised Comment]

Section 3186 continues without substantive change the fourth, sixth, and seventh sentences of former Civil Code Section 4351.5(f) and the fourth, sixth, and seventh sentences of former Civil Code Section 4607(e). In subdivision (b), a reference to "may not" has been substituted for the former reference to "[n]o agreement shall." This is not a substantive change. See Section 12 (shall not and may not are prohibitory). See also Section 1819 (destruction of records of child custody or visitation mediation). [23 Cal.L.Rev.Comm. Reports 1 (1993)].

Research References

Treatises and Practice Aids

Witkin, California Summary 10th Parent and Child § 282, Agreement.

§ 3188. Confidential mediation program

(a) Any court selected by the Judicial Council under subdivision (c) may voluntarily adopt a confidential mediation program that provides for all of the following:

(1) The mediator may not make a recommendation as to custody or visitation to anyone other than the disputing parties, except as otherwise provided in this section.

(2) If total or partial agreement is reached in mediation, the mediator may report this fact to the court. If both parties consent in writing, where there is a partial agreement, the mediator may report to the court a description of the issues still in dispute, without specific reference to either party.

(3) In making the recommendation described in Section 3184, the mediator may not inform the court of the reasons why it would be in the best interest of the minor child to have counsel appointed.

(4) If the parties have not reached agreement as a result of the initial mediation, this section does not prohibit the court from requiring subsequent mediation that may result in a recommendation as to custody or visitation with the child if the subsequent mediation is conducted by a different mediator with no prior involvement with the case or knowledge of any communications, as defined in Section 1040 of the Evidence Code, with respect to the initial mediation. The court, however, shall inform the parties that the mediator will make a recommendation to the court regarding custody or visitation in the event that the parties cannot reach agreement on these issues.

(5) If an initial screening or intake process indicates that the case involves serious safety risks to the child, such as domestic violence, sexual abuse, or serious substance abuse, the mediator may provide an initial emergency assessment service that includes a recommendation to the court concerning temporary custody or visitation orders in order to expeditiously address those safety issues.

(b) This section shall become operative upon the appropriation of funds in the annual Budget Act sufficient to implement this section.

(c) This section shall apply only in four or more superior courts selected by the Judicial Council that currently allow a mediator to make custody recommendations to the court and have more than 1,000 family law case filings per year. The Judicial Council may also make this section applicable to additional superior courts that have fewer than 1,000 family law case filings per year. *(Added by Stats.2002, c. 1077 (S.B.174), § 4. Amended by Stats.2012, c. 470 (A.B.1529), § 20.)*

Law Revision Commission Comments

2012 Amendment

Paragraph (5) of subdivision (a) of Section 3188 is amended to make a technical correction. An erroneous reference to "the court" is replaced with a reference to "the mediator."

Subdivision (c) of Section 3188 is amended to reflect enactment of the Lockyer–Isenberg Trial Court Funding Act, 1997 Cal. Stat. ch. 850 (see generally Gov't Code §§ 77000–77655). See, e.g., Gov't Code § 77001 (local trial court management); see also Fam. Code § 3183(a) (authorizing mediator to make recommendations, except as provided in Section 3188, to court consistent with local rules). [39 Cal.L.Rev.Comm. Reports 157 (2009)].

Research References

Treatises and Practice Aids

Witkin, California Summary 10th Parent and Child § 280, Mediation Proceeding.
Witkin, California Summary 10th Parent and Child § 281, Recommendations.

CHAPTER 12. COUNSELING OF PARENTS AND CHILD

§ 3190. Court order to participate in counseling; costs

(a) The court may require parents or any other party involved in a custody or visitation dispute, and the minor child, to participate in outpatient counseling with a licensed mental health professional, or through other community programs and services that provide appropriate counseling, including, but not limited to, mental health or substance abuse services, for not more than one year, provided that the program selected has counseling available for the designated period of time, if the court finds both of the following:

(1) The dispute between the parents, between the parent or parents and the child, between the parent or parents and another party seeking custody or visitation rights with the child, or between a party seeking custody or visitation rights and the child, poses a substantial danger to the best interest of the child.

(2) The counseling is in the best interest of the child.

(b) In determining whether a dispute, as described in paragraph (1) of subdivision (a), poses a substantial danger to the best interest of the child, the court shall consider, in addition to any other factors the court determines relevant, any history of domestic violence, as defined in Section 6211, within the past five years between the parents, between the parent or parents and the child, between the parent or parents and another party seeking custody or visitation rights with the child, or between a party seeking custody or visitation rights and the child.

(c) Subject to Section 3192, if the court finds that the financial burden created by the order for counseling does not otherwise jeopardize a party's other financial obligations, the court shall fix the cost and shall order the entire cost of the services to be borne by the parties in the proportions the court deems reasonable.

(d) The court, in its finding, shall set forth reasons why it has found both of the following:

(1) The dispute poses a substantial danger to the best interest of the child and the counseling is in the best interest of the child.

(2) The financial burden created by the court order for counseling does not otherwise jeopardize a party's other financial obligations.

(e) The court shall not order the parties to return to court upon the completion of counseling. Any party may file a new order to show cause or motion after counseling has been completed, and the court may again order counseling consistent with this chapter. *(Stats.1992, c. 162 (A.B.2650), § 10, operative Jan. 1, 1994. Amended by Stats.1993, c. 219 (A.B.1500), § 116.90; Stats.1993, c. 301, (A.B.197), § 1; Stats.1993, c. 876 (S.B.1068), § 15.4, eff. Oct. 6, 1993, operative Jan. 1, 1994; Stats.1994, c. 1269 (A.B.2208), § 30; Stats.1998, c. 229 (A.B.1837), § 1.)*

Law Revision Commission Comments

Enactment [Revised Comment]

Section 3190 supersedes the first paragraph of former Civil Code Section 4608.1(a). In subdivision (a), the reference to proceedings "under this part," meaning the former Family Law Act (former Part 5 (commencing with former Section 4000) of Division 4 of the Civil Code), has been omitted as unnecessary. See Section 3021 (application of part) & Comment. See also Section 3011 (factors to be considered in determining best interest of child). [23 Cal.L.Rev. Comm. Reports 1 (1993)].

1994 Amendment

Subdivision (b) of Section 3190 is amended for consistency with Section 3192 as amended. See Section 3192 Comment. [24 Cal.L.Rev.Comm. Reports 621 (1994)].

Commentary

Section 3190 has no application to dependency proceedings. *In re Chantal, 13 Cal.4th 196, 913 P.2d 1075, 51 Cal.Rptr.2d 866 (1996),* holds that a juvenile court, when terminating its dependency jurisdiction, may order as a condition of visitation that a parent receive psychotherapy; a juvenile court is not limited by Family Code Section 3190, which applies only to counseling ordered by a family court. Compare *In re Donnovan J., 58 Cal.App.4th 1474, 68 Cal.Rptr.2d 714 (1997),* holding that the juvenile court unlawfully delegated judicial authority to therapists when it provided that a parent was to have "no visitation rights without permission of minors' therapists," because the court set no criteria to instruct the therapists when to allow visitation.

Research References

Forms

California Transactions Forms--Family Law § 2:76, Drug and Alcohol Use.

Treatises and Practice Aids

Witkin, California Summary 10th Parent and Child § 195, Statutory Framework.

Witkin, California Summary 10th Parent and Child § 242, Other Restrictions.

Witkin, California Summary 10th Parent and Child § 287, Order to Participate in Counseling.

Witkin, California Summary 10th Parent and Child § 373, Order Requiring Therapy.

§ 3191. Goals of outpatient counseling

The counseling pursuant to this chapter shall be specifically designed to facilitate communication between the parties regarding their minor child's best interest, to reduce conflict regarding custody or visitation, and to improve the quality of parenting skills of each parent. *(Stats.1992, c. 162 (A.B. 2650), § 10, operative Jan. 1, 1994. Amended by Stats.1993, c. 219 (A.B.1500), § 116.91.)*

Law Revision Commission Comments

Enactment [Revised Comment]

Section 3191 continues the last paragraph of former Civil Code Section 4608.1(a) without substantive change. See also Section 3011 (factors to be considered in determining best interest of child). [23 Cal.L.Rev.Comm. Reports 1 (1993)].

Research References

Treatises and Practice Aids

Witkin, California Summary 10th Parent and Child § 287, Order to Participate in Counseling.

§ 3192. Separate counseling sessions; history of abuse in family relationship

In a proceeding in which counseling is ordered pursuant to this chapter, where there has been a history of abuse by either parent against the child or by one parent against the other parent and a protective order as defined in Section 6218 is in effect, the court may order the parties to participate in counseling separately and at separate times. Each party shall bear the cost of his or her own counseling separately, unless good cause is shown for a different apportionment. The costs associated with a minor child participating in counseling shall be apportioned in accordance with Section 4062. *(Stats.1992, c. 162 (A.B.2650), § 10, operative Jan. 1, 1994. Amended by Stats.1993, c. 219 (A.B.1500), § 116.92; Stats. 1994, c. 1269 (A.B.2208), § 31.)*

Law Revision Commission Comments

Enactment [Revised Comment]

Section 3192 continues former Civil Code Section 4608.1(b) without substantive change. Unlike the former section, this section does not contain a reference to the section defining "domestic violence." This is not a substantive change. See Sections 6201 (application of definitions), 6211 ("domestic violence" defined). The phrase "protective order" has been substituted for the references to orders under specific former sections in the Civil Code and the Code of Civil Procedure. This is not a substantive change, since Section 6218 defines "protective order" to include these orders. [23 Cal.L.Rev.Comm. Reports 1 (1993)].

1994 Amendment

Section 3192 is amended to conform to the substance of 1993 Cal. Stat. ch. 301, § 1 (AB 197), which was unintentionally chaptered out by 1993 Cal. Stat. ch. 876, § 15.4 (SB 1068). [24 Cal.L.Rev.Comm. Reports 621 (1994)].

Research References

Treatises and Practice Aids

Witkin, California Summary 10th Husband and Wife § 10A, (New) Ex Parte Communications With Mediator or Evaluator.

Witkin, California Summary 10th Parent and Child § 287, Order to Participate in Counseling.

CHAPTER 13. SUPERVISED VISITATION AND EXCHANGE SERVICES, EDUCATION, AND COUNSELING

§ 3200. Supervised visitation provider standards; guidelines

The Judicial Council shall develop standards for supervised visitation providers in accordance with the guidelines set forth in this section. For the purposes of the development of these standards, the term "provider" shall include any individual who functions as a visitation monitor, as well as supervised visitation centers. Provisions shall be made within the standards to allow for the diversity of supervised visitation providers.

(a) When developing standards, the Judicial Council shall consider all of the following issues:

(1) The provider's qualifications, experience, and education.

(2) Safety and security procedures, including ratios of children per supervisor.

(3) Any conflict of interest.

(4) Maintenance and disclosure of records, including confidentiality policies.

(5) Procedures for screening, delineation of terms and conditions, and termination of supervised visitation services.

(6) Procedures for emergency or extenuating situations.

(7) Orientation to and guidelines for cases in which there are allegations of domestic violence, child abuse, substance abuse, or special circumstances.

(8) The legal obligations and responsibilities of supervisors.

(b) The Judicial Council shall consult with visitation centers, mothers' groups, fathers' groups, judges, the State Bar of California, children's advocacy groups, domestic violence prevention groups, Family Court Services, and other groups it regards as necessary in connection with these standards.

(c) It is the intent of the Legislature that the safety of children, adults, and visitation supervisors be a precondition to providing visitation services. Once safety is assured, the best interest of the child is the paramount consideration at all stages and particularly in deciding the manner in which supervision is provided. *(Added by Stats.1996, c. 387 (S.B. 1643), § 1. Amended by Stats.2004, c. 193 (S.B.111), § 17.)*

Law Revision Commission Comments

2004 Amendment

Section 3200 is amended to delete reference to an obsolete reporting requirement. The required report was to be completed by April 1, 1997. [33 Cal.L.Rev.Comm. Reports 302 (2003)].

Commentary

The uniform standards required by this section are found in Standard 5.20 (renumbered from Section 26.2 in 2007) of the Standards of Judicial Administration. They are recommended, not mandatory.

Research References

Forms

California Transactions Forms--Family Law § 5:2, Overview.

California Transactions Forms--Family Law § 5:9, Use Of Parenting Agreement to Define Rights and Responsibilities Relating to Child on Termination Of Partners' Relationship Where Both Partners Are Biological Parents.

West's California Code Forms, Family § 3022, Comment Overview--Order for Custody.

Treatises and Practice Aids

Witkin, California Summary 10th Parent and Child § 195, Statutory Framework.

Witkin, California Summary 10th Parent and Child § 243, Standards for Supervised Visitation.

§ 3200.5. Standards for professional or nonprofessional supervised visitation providers; cases of domestic violence or child abuse or neglect; court to determine provider based on best interest of child; definitions; training; child to provider ratio; duties of professional providers

(a) Any standards for supervised visitation providers adopted by the Judicial Council pursuant to Section 3200 shall conform to this section. A provider, as described in Section 3200, shall be a professional provider or nonprofessional provider.

(b) In any case in which the court has determined that there is domestic violence or child abuse or neglect, as defined in Section 11165.6 of the Penal Code, and the court determines supervision is necessary, the court shall consider whether to use a professional or nonprofessional provider based upon the child's best interest.

(c) For the purposes of this section, the following definitions apply:

(1) "Nonprofessional provider" means any person who is not paid for providing supervised visitation services. Unless otherwise ordered by the court or stipulated by the parties, the nonprofessional provider shall:

(A) Have no record of a conviction for child molestation, child abuse, or other crimes against a person.

(B) Have proof of automobile insurance if transporting the child.

(C) Have no current or past court order in which the provider is the person being supervised.

(D) Agree to adhere to and enforce the court order regarding supervised visitation.

(2) "Professional provider" means any person paid for providing supervised visitation services, or an independent contractor, employee, intern, or volunteer operating independently or through a supervised visitation center or agency. The professional provider shall:

(A) Be at least 21 years of age.

(B) Have no record of a conviction for driving under the influence (DUI) within the last five years.

(C) Not have been on probation or parole for the last 10 years.

(D) Have no record of a conviction for child molestation, child abuse, or other crimes against a person.

(E) Have proof of automobile insurance if transporting the child.

(F) Have no civil, criminal, or juvenile restraining orders within the last 10 years.

(G) Have no current or past court order in which the provider is the person being supervised.

(H) Be able to speak the language of the party being supervised and of the child, or the provider must provide a neutral interpreter over 18 years of age who is able to do so.

(I) Agree to adhere to and enforce the court order regarding supervised visitation.

(J) Meet the training requirements set forth in subdivision (d).

(d)(1) Professional providers shall have received 24 hours of training that includes training in the following subjects:

(A) The role of a professional provider.

(B) Child abuse reporting laws.

(C) Recordkeeping procedures.

(D) Screening, monitoring, and termination of visitation.

(E) Developmental needs of children.

(F) Legal responsibilities and obligations of a provider.

(G) Cultural sensitivity.

(H) Conflicts of interest.

(I) Confidentiality.

(J) Issues relating to substance abuse, child abuse, sexual abuse, and domestic violence.

(K) Basic knowledge of family and juvenile law.

(2) Professional providers shall sign a declaration or any Judicial Council form that they meet the training and qualifications of a provider.

(e) The ratio of children to a professional provider shall be contingent on:

(1) The degree of risk factors present in each case.

(2) The nature of supervision required in each case.

(3) The number and ages of the children to be supervised during a visit.

(4) The number of people visiting the child during the visit.

(5) The duration and location of the visit.

(6) The experience of the provider.

(f) Professional providers of supervised visitation shall:

(1) Advise the parties before commencement of supervised visitation that no confidential privilege exists.

(2) Report suspected child abuse to the appropriate agency, as provided by law, and inform the parties of the provider's obligation to make those reports.

(3) Suspend or terminate visitation under subdivision (h).

(g) Professional providers shall:

(1) Prepare a written contract to be signed by the parties before commencement of the supervised visitation. The contract should inform each party of the terms and conditions of supervised visitation.

(2) Review custody and visitation orders relevant to the supervised visitation.

(3) Keep a record for each case, including, at least, all of the following:

(A) A written record of each contact and visit.

(B) Who attended the visit.

(C) Any failure to comply with the terms and conditions of the visitation.

(D) Any incidence of abuse, as required by law.

(h)(1) Each provider shall make every reasonable effort to provide a safe visit for the child and the noncustodial party.

(2) If a provider determines that the rules of the visit have been violated, the child has become acutely distressed, or the safety of the child or the provider is at risk, the visit may be temporarily interrupted, rescheduled at a later date, or terminated.

(3) All interruptions or terminations of visits shall be recorded in the case file.

(4) All providers shall advise both parties of the reasons for the interruption or termination of a visit.

(i) A professional provider shall state the reasons for temporary suspension or termination of supervised visitation in writing and shall provide the written statement to both parties, their attorneys, the attorney for the child, and the court. *(Added by Stats.2012, c. 692 (A.B.1674), § 1. Amended by Stats.2013, c. 76 (A.B.383), § 60.)*

Research References

Forms

West's California Judicial Council Forms FL-324, Declaration Of Supervised Visitation Provider.

Treatises and Practice Aids

Witkin, California Summary 10th Parent and Child § 243, Standards for Supervised Visitation.

§ 3201. Administration of supervised visitation

Any supervised visitation maintained or imposed by the court shall be administered in accordance with Section 26.2 of the California Standards of Judicial Administration recommended by the Judicial Council. *(Added by Stats.1999, c. 985 (S.B.792), § 2.)*

Research References

Treatises and Practice Aids

Witkin, California Summary 10th Parent and Child § 243, Standards for Supervised Visitation.

§ 3201.5. Administration of programs; education about protecting children during family disruption

(a) The programs described in this chapter shall be administered by the family law division of the superior court in the county.

(b) For purposes of this chapter, "education about protecting children during family disruption" includes education on parenting skills and the impact of parental conflict on children, how to put a parenting agreement into effect, and the responsibility of both parents to comply with custody and visitation orders. *(Formerly § 3201, added by Stats.1999, c. 1004 (A.B.673), § 2. Renumbered § 3201.5 and amended by Stats.2015, c. 303 (A.B.731), § 145, eff. Jan. 1, 2016.)*

§ 3202. Uniform Standards of Practice for Providers of Supervised Visitation; eligible providers

(a) All supervised visitation and exchange programs funded pursuant to this chapter shall comply with all requirements of the Uniform Standards of Practice for Providers of Supervised Visitation set forth in Standard 5.20 of the Standards of Judicial Administration as amended. The family law division of the superior court may contract with eligible providers of supervised visitation and exchange services, education, and group counseling to provide services under this chapter.

(b) As used in this section, "eligible provider" means:

(1) For providers of supervised visitation and exchange services, a local public agency or nonprofit entity that satisfies the Uniform Standards of Practice for Providers of Supervised Visitation.

(2) For providers of group counseling, a professional licensed to practice psychotherapy in this state, including, but not limited to, a licensed psychiatrist, licensed psychologist, licensed clinical social worker, licensed marriage and family therapist, or licensed professional clinical counselor; or a mental health intern working under the direct supervision of a professional licensed to practice psychotherapy.

(3) For providers of education, a professional with a bachelor's or master's degree in human behavior, child development, psychology, counseling, family-life education, or a related field, having specific training in issues relating to child and family development, substance abuse, child abuse, domestic violence, effective parenting, and the impact of divorce and interparental conflict on children; or an intern working under the supervision of that professional. *(Added by Stats.1999, c. 1004 (A.B.673), § 3. Amended by Stats.2011, c. 381 (S.B.146), § 24; Stats.2013, c. 61 (S.B.826), § 1.)*

§ 3203. Establishment and administration of programs by family law division of county superior courts

Subject to the availability of federal funding for the purposes of this chapter, the family law division of the superior court in each county may establish and administer a supervised visitation and exchange program, programs for education about protecting children during family disruption, and group counseling programs for parents and children under this chapter. The programs shall allow parties and children to participate in supervised visitation between a custodial party and a noncustodial party or joint custodians, and to participate in the education and group counseling programs, irrespective of whether the parties are or are not married to each other or are currently living separately and apart on a permanent or temporary basis. *(Added by Stats.1999, c. 1004 (A.B.673), § 4.)*

§ 3204. Judicial Council; application for grants from the federal Administration for Children and Families; legislative intent; reports

(a) The Judicial Council shall annually submit an application to the federal Administration for Children and Families, pursuant to Section 669B of the "1996 Federal Personal Responsibility and Work Opportunity Recovery Act" (PRWORA), for a grant to fund child custody and visitation programs pursuant to this chapter.

The Judicial Council shall be charged with the administration of the grant funds.

(b)(1) It is the intention of the Legislature that, effective October 1, 2000, the grant funds described in subdivision (a) shall be used to fund the following three types of programs: supervised visitation and exchange services, education about protecting children during family disruption, and group counseling for parents and children, as set forth in this chapter. Contracts shall follow a standard request for proposal procedure, that may include multiple year funding. Requests for proposals shall meet all state and federal requirements for receiving access and visitation grant funds.

(2) The grant funds shall be awarded with the intent of approving as many requests for proposals as possible while assuring that each approved proposal would provide beneficial services and satisfy the overall goals of the program under this chapter. The Judicial Council shall determine the final number and amount of grants. Requests for proposals shall be evaluated based on the following criteria:

(A) Availability of services to a broad population of parties.

(B) The ability to expand existing services.

(C) Coordination with other community services.

(D) The hours of service delivery.

(E) The number of counties or regions participating.

(F) Overall cost-effectiveness.

(G) The purpose of the program to promote and encourage healthy parent and child relationships between noncustodial parents and their children, while ensuring the health, safety, and welfare of the children.

(3) Special consideration for grant funds shall be given to proposals that coordinate supervised visitation and exchange services, education, and group counseling with existing court-based programs and services.

(c) The family law division of the superior court in each county shall approve sliding scale fees that are based on the ability to pay for all parties, including low-income families, participating in a supervised visitation and exchange, education, and group counseling programs under this chapter.

(d) The Judicial Council shall, on March 1, 2002, and on the first day of March of each subsequent even-numbered year, report to the Legislature on the programs funded pursuant to this chapter and whether and to what extent those programs are achieving the goal of promoting and encouraging healthy parent and child relationships between noncustodial or joint custodial parents and their children while ensuring the health, safety, and welfare of children, and the other goals described in this chapter. *(Added by Stats. 1999, c. 1004 (A.B.673), § 5. Amended by Stats.2007, c. 738 (A.B.1248), § 13.)*

Part 3

UNIFORM CHILD CUSTODY JURISDICTION AND ENFORCEMENT ACT

CHAPTER 1. GENERAL PROVISIONS

§ 3400. Short title

This part may be cited as the Uniform Child Custody Jurisdiction and Enforcement Act. *(Added by Stats.1999, c. 867 (S.B.668), § 3.)*

Commentary

The Uniform Child Custody Jurisdiction and Enforcement Act (UCCJEA) supersedes the Uniform Child Custody Jurisdiction Act (UCCJA).

For general discussion of the purposes and content of the superseded Uniform Child Custody Jurisdiction Act, see *In re Marriage of Newsome, 68 Cal.App.4th 949, 80 Cal.Rptr.2d 555 (1998)* (UCCJA gives preference to child's "home state" even when there is no custody proceeding pending in child's home state); and *Zenide v. Superior Court, 22 Cal.App.4th 1287, 27 Cal.Rptr.2d 703 (1994)* (French court's child custody order, rather than Texas court's subsequent modification, properly enforced in California because Texas court lacked modification jurisdiction in view of French court's continuing jurisdiction over custody). See also *Kumar v. Superior Court, 32 Cal.3d 689, 186 Cal.Rptr. 772 (1982)*; In *re Marriage of Hopson, 110 Cal.App.3d 884, 891, 168 Cal.Rptr. 345 (1980)* ("The exclusive method of determining subject matter jurisdiction in custody cases in California is the [UCCJA] . . .").

As to appeals and stay of proceedings as to judgment or order affecting custody generally, see Code of Civil Procedure § 917.7.

Research References

Forms

California Transactions Forms--Family Law § 3:4, Subject Matter Jurisdiction for Custody Determinations.
California Transactions Forms--Family Law § 7:33, Parentage Testing.
California Transactions Forms--Family Law § 6:119, Continuing Jurisdiction.
West's California Code Forms, Family § 3400, Comment Overview--Uniform Child Custody Jurisdiction and Enforcement Act.
West's California Judicial Council Forms FL-260, Petition for Custody and Support Of Minor Children.
West's California Judicial Council Forms FL-270, Response to Petition for Custody and Support Of Minor Children.
West's California Judicial Council Forms GC-120, Declaration Under Uniform Child Custody Jurisdiction and Enforcement Act (UCCJEA).
West's California Judicial Council Forms GC-120(A), Attachment to Declaration Under Uniform Child Custody Jurisdiction and Enforcement Act (UCCJEA).
West's California Judicial Council Forms FL-105/GC-120, Declaration Under Uniform Child Custody Jurisdiction and Enforcement Act (UCCJEA).
West's California Judicial Council Forms FL-105(A)/GC-120(A), Attachment to Declaration Under Uniform Child Custody Jurisdiction and Enforcement Act (UCCJEA).

Treatises and Practice Aids

Witkin, California Summary 10th Parent and Child § 158, Enactment and Principal Changes.
Witkin, California Summary 10th Parent and Child § 159, in General.
Witkin, California Summary 10th Parent and Child § 195, Statutory Framework.
Witkin, California Summary 10th Parent and Child § 269, Locating Missing Party or Child.
Witkin, California Summary 10th Parent and Child § 374, Appellate Court Proceeding.
Witkin, California Summary 10th Parent and Child § 520, Jurisdiction.
Witkin, California Summary 10th Parent and Child § 259A, (New) Military Deployment.
Witkin, California Summary 10th Wills and Probate § 959B, (New) Nature and Scope Of Act.

§ 3402. Definitions

As used in this part:

(a) "Abandoned" means left without provision for reasonable and necessary care or supervision.

(b) "Child" means an individual who has not attained 18 years of age.

(c) "Child custody determination" means a judgment, decree, or other order of a court providing for the legal custody, physical custody, or visitation with respect to a child. The term includes a permanent, temporary, initial, and modification order. The term does not include an order relating to child support or other monetary obligation of an individual.

(d) "Child custody proceeding" means a proceeding in which legal custody, physical custody, or visitation with respect to a child is an issue. The term includes a proceeding for dissolution of marriage, legal separation of the parties, neglect, abuse, dependency, guardianship, paternity, termination of parental rights, and protection from domestic violence, in which the issue may appear. The term does not include a proceeding involving juvenile delinquency, contractual emancipation, or enforcement under Chapter 3 (commencing with Section 3441).

(e) "Commencement" means the filing of the first pleading in a proceeding.

(f) "Court" means an entity authorized under the law of a state to establish, enforce, or modify a child custody determination.

(g) "Home state" means the state in which a child lived with a parent or a person acting as a parent for at least six consecutive months immediately before the commencement of a child custody proceeding. In the case of a child less than six months of age, the term means the state in which the child lived from birth with any of the persons mentioned. A period of temporary absence of any of the mentioned persons is part of the period.

(h) "Initial determination" means the first child custody determination concerning a particular child.

(i) "Issuing court" means the court that makes a child custody determination for which enforcement is sought under this part.

(j) "Issuing state" means the state in which a child custody determination is made.

(k) "Modification" means a child custody determination that changes, replaces, supersedes, or is otherwise made after a previous determination concerning the same child, whether or not it is made by the court that made the previous determination.

(*l*) "Person" means an individual, corporation, business trust, estate, trust, partnership, limited liability company, association, joint venture, or government; governmental subdivision, agency, or instrumentality; public corporation; or any other legal or commercial entity.

(m) "Person acting as a parent" means a person, other than a parent, who: (1) has physical custody of the child or has had physical custody for a period of six consecutive months, including any temporary absence, within one year immediately before the commencement of a child custody proceeding; and (2) has been awarded legal custody by a court or claims a right to legal custody under the law of this state.

(n) "Physical custody" means the physical care and supervision of a child.

(*o*) "State" means a state of the United States, the District of Columbia, Puerto Rico, the United States Virgin Islands, or any territory or insular possession subject to the jurisdiction of the United States.

(p) "Tribe" means an Indian tribe or band, or Alaskan Native village, that is recognized by federal law or formally acknowledged by a state.

(q) "Warrant" means an order issued by a court authorizing law enforcement officers to take physical custody of a child. *(Added by Stats.1999, c. 867 (S.B.668), § 3.)*

Commentary

For general discussion of the purposes and content of the superseded Uniform Child Custody Jurisdiction Act, see *In re Marriage of Newsome, 68 Cal.App4th 949, 80 Cal.Rptr.2d 555 (1998)* (UCCJA gives preference to child's "home state" even when there is no custody proceeding pending in child's home state); and *Zenide v. Superior Court, 22 Cal.App.4th 1287, 27 Cal.Rptr.2d 703 (1994)* (French court's child custody order, rather than Texas court's subsequent modification, properly enforced in California because Texas court lacked modification jurisdiction in view of French court's continuing jurisdiction over custody). See also *Kumar v. Superior Court, 32 Cal.3d 689, 186 Cal.Rptr. 772 (1982)*; In *re Marriage of Hopson, 110 Cal.App.3d 884, 891, 168 Cal.Rptr. 345 (1980)* ("The exclusive method of determining subject matter jurisdiction in custody cases in California is the [UCCJA] ....").

Under the UCCJA, an out-of-state parent could participate in a "custody determination" without submitting to the personal jurisdiction of the forum state. *In re Marriage of Fitzgerald and King, 39 Cal.App.4th 1419, 46 Cal.Rptr.2d 558 (1995)*.

Interpreting subsection (g), *In re Marriage of Sareen, 153 Cal. App.4th 371, 62 Cal.Rptr.3d 687 (2007)*, held that the time spent by a child *after* the filing of a child custody petition may not be counted toward the six months necessary for "home state" jurisdiction. *Ocegueda v. Perreira, 232 Cal.App.4th 1079, 181 Cal.Rptr.3d 845 (2015), review denied*, applied subsection (g) of this section and section 3421 to conclude that when a child is less than six months old at the commencement of custody proceedings, the location of his or her birth is essential in determining the child's home state. Additionally, deciding an issue of first impression, *Ocegueda* held that, for the purposes of determining home state jurisdiction under the UCCJEA, the state where a child "lived" is that in which he or she was physically present, regardless of parental domiciliary intent.

Applying subsection (g), *In re Gloria A., 213 Cal.App.4th 476, 152 Cal.Rptr.3d 550 (2013)*, held that the juvenile court did not have home state jurisdiction because the child did not reside with his mother in California for six consecutive months immediately before the commencement of the dependency proceeding.

Interpreting subsection (g) of this section and § 3421(a)(1), *Guardianship of Ariana K., 120 Cal.App.4th 690, 15 Cal.Rptr.3d 817 (2004)*, holds that the UCCJEA does not deprive a California trial court of continuing subject matter jurisdiction to adjudicate a guardianship dispute when the court properly acquired subject matter jurisdiction in an earlier guardianship proceeding. Under the doctrine of continuing jurisdiction, once custody jurisdiction in California is initially established, it continues so long as the child or a parent or guardian of the child continues to reside in California. *Ariana K.* also concludes that nothing in the Hague Convention deprives a California court of continuing subject matter jurisdiction because federal law implementing that convention provides that "[t]he remedies established by the Convention and this chapter shall be in addition to remedies available under other law or international agreements." 42 U.S.C. § 11603(h).

In re Jaheim B., 169 Cal.App.4th 1343, 87 Cal.Rptr.3d 504 (2008), holds that when a neglected child has no "home state," as defined by subsection (g) and section 3421 (a), under section 3421 (b) the court has jurisdiction to declare the child a dependent of the juvenile court, remove the child from parental custody, and place him in out-of-home care.

In re S.W., 148 Cal.App.4th 1501, 56 Cal.Rptr.3d 665 (2007), review denied June 13, 2007, held that a juvenile court has subject matter jurisdiction, under subsection (g) of this section and subsection (a) of section 3421, to terminate the parental rights of a mother from Nebraska who was living in a van in California, when neither state qualified as a "home state."

In re A. C., 130 Cal.App.4th 854, 30 Cal.Rptr.3d 431 (2005), observes that subsection (d) subjects a California juvenile court's exercise of dependency jurisdiction to the provisions of the UCCJEA. Accordingly, *A.C.* held that the juvenile court lacked subject matter jurisdiction under the UCCJEA to invoke California dependency law in order to shift responsibility for the care of a severely injured child from the child's subsection (g) "home state" of Mexico to San Diego County. *A.C.* additionally held that Section 3403 was inapplicable because it is limited by the Section 3424(a) requirement of "mistreatment or abuse."

Research References

Forms

West's California Code Forms, Probate § 1510 Form 3, Declaration Under Uniform Child Custody Jurisdiction and Enforcement Act (UCCJEA)-Judicial Council Form FL-105/GC-120.

Treatises and Practice Aids

Witkin, California Summary 10th Parent and Child § 160, Scope Of Child Custody Proceedings.

Witkin, California Summary 10th Parent and Child § 165, Home State.

Witkin, California Summary 10th Parent and Child § 520, Jurisdiction.

§ 3403. Adoption proceedings; emergency medical care

This part does not govern an adoption proceeding or a proceeding pertaining to the authorization of emergency medical care for a child. *(Added by Stats.1999, c. 867 (S.B.668), § 3.)*

Commentary

Applying this section, *Adoption of K.C., 247 Cal.App.4th 1412, 203 Cal.Rptr.3d 110 (2016), review denied,* held that the UCCJEA does not apply to adoption proceedings in which a New York father's parental rights under a New York divorce decree were terminated under sections 7782 and 8604.

In re A. C., 130 Cal.App.4th 854, 30 Cal.Rptr.3d 431 (2005), observes that Section 3402(d) subjects a California juvenile court's exercise of dependency jurisdiction to the provisions of the UCCJEA. Accordingly, *A.C.* held that the juvenile court lacked subject matter jurisdiction under the UCCJEA to invoke California dependency law in order to shift responsibility for the care of a severely injured child from the child's Section 3402(g) "home state" of Mexico to San Diego County. *A.C.* additionally held that this section was inapplicable because is limited by the Section 3424(a) requirement of "mistreatment or abuse."

Research References

Forms

California Transactions Forms--Family Law § 6:119, Continuing Jurisdiction.

Treatises and Practice Aids

Witkin, California Summary 10th Parent and Child § 160, Scope Of Child Custody Proceedings.

Witkin, California Summary 10th Parent and Child § 170, in General.

§ 3404. Native American children

(a) A child custody proceeding that pertains to an Indian child as defined in the Indian Child Welfare Act (25 U.S.C. Sec. 1901 et seq.) is not subject to this part to the extent that it is governed by the Indian Child Welfare Act.

(b) A court of this state shall treat a tribe as if it were a state of the United States for the purpose of applying this chapter and Chapter 2 (commencing with Section 3421).

(c) A child custody determination made by a tribe under factual circumstances in substantial conformity with the jurisdictional standards of this part must be recognized and enforced under Chapter 3 (commencing with Section 3441). *(Added by Stats.1999, c. 867 (S.B.668), § 3.)*

Research References

Forms

California Transactions Forms--Family Law § 3:4, Subject Matter Jurisdiction for Custody Determinations.

Treatises and Practice Aids

Witkin, California Summary 10th Parent and Child § 159, in General.

Witkin, California Summary 10th Parent and Child § 160, Scope Of Child Custody Proceedings.

Witkin, California Summary 10th Parent and Child § 185, Enforceable Orders and Determinations.

§ 3405. Foreign countries; application of this Part; recognition of foreign custody determinations; exception

(a) A court of this state shall treat a foreign country as if it were a state of the United States for the purpose of applying this chapter and Chapter 2 (commencing with Section 3421).

(b) Except as otherwise provided in subdivision (c), a child custody determination made in a foreign country under factual circumstances in substantial conformity with the jurisdictional standards of this part must be recognized and enforced under Chapter 3 (commencing with Section 3441).

(c) A court of this state need not apply this part if the child custody law of a foreign country violates fundamental principles of human rights. *(Added by Stats.1999, c. 867 (S.B.668), § 3.)*

Commentary

For application of this section to a request for California recognition of a Pakistani custody decree, see *In re Marriage of Nurie, 176 Cal.App.4th 478, 98 Cal.Rptr.3d 200 (2009), review denied.*

Research References

Treatises and Practice Aids

Witkin, California Summary 10th Parent and Child § 159, in General.

Witkin, California Summary 10th Parent and Child § 173, Exclusive Continuing Jurisdiction.

Witkin, California Summary 10th Parent and Child § 185, Enforceable Orders and Determinations.

§ 3406. Binding effect of custody determinations

A child custody determination made by a court of this state that had jurisdiction under this part binds all persons who have been served in accordance with the laws of this state or notified in accordance with Section 3408 or who have submitted to the jurisdiction of the court, and who have been given an opportunity to be heard. As to those persons, the determination is conclusive as to all decided issues of law and fact except to the extent the determination is modified. *(Added by Stats.1999, c. 867 (S.B.668), § 3.)*

Research References

Treatises and Practice Aids

Witkin, California Summary 10th Parent and Child § 159, in General.

§ 3407. Questions regarding jurisdiction; priority handling

If a question of existence or exercise of jurisdiction under this part is raised in a child custody proceeding, the question, upon request of a party, must be given priority on the calendar and handled expeditiously. *(Added by Stats.1999, c. 867 (S.B.668), § 3.)*

Research References

Treatises and Practice Aids

Witkin, California Summary 10th Parent and Child § 163, in General.

Witkin, California Summary 10th Parent and Child § 284, Trial.

Witkin, California Summary 10th Parent and Child § 288, Appeal.

§ 3408. Notice to persons outside California

(a) Notice required for the exercise of jurisdiction when a person is outside this state may be given in a manner prescribed by the law of this state for service of process or by the law of the state in which the service is made. Notice must be given in a manner reasonably calculated to give actual notice but may be by publication if other means are not effective.

(b) Proof of service may be made in the manner prescribed by the law of this state or by the law of the state in which the service is made.

(c) Notice is not required for the exercise of jurisdiction with respect to a person who submits to the jurisdiction of the court. *(Added by Stats.1999, c. 867 (S.B.668), § 3.)*

Commentary

This Section is substantially similar to Section 3405 of the superseded UCCJA. Under the superseded UCCJA, an out-of-state parent could participate in custody and visitation proceedings without submitting to the personal jurisdiction of the forum state. *In re Marriage of Fitzgerald and King, 39 Cal.App.4th 1419, 46 Cal.Rptr.2d 558 (1995)*.

Nevertheless, under the superseded Act, an out-of-state parent was deemed to submit to the personal jurisdiction of the court by appending a claim for additional relief. See, for example, *In re Marriage of Torres, 62 Cal.App.4th 1357, 73 Cal.Rptr.2d 344 (1998)* (parent's request for child support in UCCJA proceeding constituted a general appearance, curing, under subsection (d), arguably inadequate notice). *Torres* also stated, in dictum, that United Postal Service Next Day Air Letter Delivery was adequate notice under superseded Act even though no receipt was requested.

Research References

Treatises and Practice Aids

Witkin, California Summary 10th Parent and Child § 159, in General.

Witkin, California Summary 10th Parent and Child § 161, Registration Of Foreign Child Custody Determination.

Witkin, California Summary 10th Parent and Child § 182, Order to Appear.

Witkin, California Summary 10th Parent and Child § 183, Notice and Hearing.

Witkin, California Summary 10th Parent and Child § 187, Petition and Order to Appear.

Witkin, California Summary 10th Parent and Child § 188, Order.

§ 3409. Child custody proceedings; parties; immunity from personal jurisdiction in other proceedings

(a) A party to a child custody proceeding, including a modification proceeding, or a petitioner or respondent in a proceeding to enforce or register a child custody determination, is not subject to personal jurisdiction in this state for another proceeding or purpose solely by reason of having participated, or of having been physically present for the purpose of participating, in the proceeding.

(b) A person who is subject to personal jurisdiction in this state on a basis other than physical presence is not immune from service of process in this state. A party present in this state who is subject to the jurisdiction of another state is not immune from service of process allowable under the laws of that state.

(c) The immunity granted by subdivision (a) does not extend to civil litigation based on acts unrelated to the participation in a proceeding under this part committed by an individual while present in this state. *(Added by Stats.1999, c. 867 (S.B.668), § 3.)*

Research References

Forms

West's California Code Forms, Family § 3400, Comment Overview--Uniform Child Custody Jurisdiction and Enforcement Act.

West's California Code Forms, Family § 7841 Form 1, Petition for Freedom from Parental Control--Abandonment.

West's California Judicial Council Forms FL-100, Petition - Marriage/Domestic Partnership.

Treatises and Practice Aids

Witkin, California Summary 10th Parent and Child § 163, in General.

Witkin, California Summary 10th Parent and Child § 271, Temporary Custody During Pendency Of Proceeding.

Witkin, California Summary 10th Parent and Child § 363, Applicability Of Family Code Custody Provisions.

§ 3410. Communication between courts

(a) A court of this state may communicate with a court in another state concerning a proceeding arising under this part.

(b) The court may allow the parties to participate in the communication. If the parties are not able to participate in the communication, they must be given the opportunity to present facts and legal arguments before a decision on jurisdiction is made.

(c) Communication between courts on schedules, calendars, court records, and similar matters may occur without informing the parties. A record need not be made of the communication.

(d) Except as otherwise provided in subdivision (c), a record must be made of a communication under this section. The parties must be informed promptly of the communication and granted access to the record.

(e) For the purposes of this section, "record" means information that is inscribed on a tangible medium or that is stored in an electronic or other medium and is retrievable in perceivable form. *(Added by Stats.1999, c. 867 (S.B.668), § 3.)*

Research References

Treatises and Practice Aids

Witkin, California Summary 10th Parent and Child § 175, in General.

Witkin, California Summary 10th Parent and Child § 180, Intercourt Communications and Requests.

§ 3411. Witnesses in another state; testimony by deposition; documentary evidence transmitted by technological means

(a) In addition to other procedures available to a party, a party to a child custody proceeding may offer testimony of witnesses who are located in another state, including testimony of the parties and the child, by deposition or other means allowable in this state for testimony taken in another state. The court, on its own motion, may order that the testimony of a person be taken in another state and may prescribe the manner in which and the terms upon which the testimony is taken.

(b) A court of this state may permit an individual residing in another state to be deposed or to testify by telephone, audiovisual means, or other electronic means before a designated court or at another location in that state. A court of this state shall cooperate with courts of other states in designating an appropriate location for the deposition or testimony.

(c) Documentary evidence transmitted from another state to a court of this state by technological means that do not produce an original writing may not be excluded from evidence on an objection based on the means of transmission. *(Added by Stats.1999, c. 867 (S.B.668), § 3.)*

Research References

Treatises and Practice Aids

Witkin, California Summary 10th Parent and Child § 176, Relevant Factors.

Witkin, California Summary 10th Parent and Child § 182, Order to Appear.

Witkin, California Summary 10th Parent and Child § 183, Notice and Hearing.

§ 3412. Request of another court to hold hearing or enter an order; preservation of pleadings and records

(a) A court of this state may request the appropriate court of another state to do all of the following:

(1) Hold an evidentiary hearing.

(2) Order a person to produce or give evidence pursuant to procedures of that state.

(3) Order that an evaluation be made with respect to the custody of a child involved in a pending proceeding.

(4) Forward to the court of this state a certified copy of the transcript of the record of the hearing, the evidence otherwise presented, and any evaluation prepared in compliance with the request.

(5) Order a party to a child custody proceeding or any person having physical custody of the child to appear in the proceeding with or without the child.

(b) Upon request of a court of another state, a court of this state may hold a hearing or enter an order described in subdivision (a).

(c) Travel and other necessary and reasonable expenses incurred under subdivisions (a) and (b) may be assessed against the parties according to the law of this state.

(d) A court of this state shall preserve the pleadings, orders, decrees, records of hearings, evaluations, and other pertinent records with respect to a child custody proceeding until the child attains 18 years of age. Upon appropriate request by a court or law enforcement official of another state, the court shall forward a certified copy of those records. *(Added by Stats.1999, c. 867 (S.B.668), § 3.)*

Research References

Treatises and Practice Aids

Witkin, California Summary 10th Parent and Child § 159, in General.

Witkin, California Summary 10th Parent and Child § 176, Relevant Factors.

Witkin, California Summary 10th Parent and Child § 180, Intercourt Communications and Requests.

CHAPTER 2. JURISDICTION

Section

§ 3421. Jurisdiction to make initial child custody determination

(a) Except as otherwise provided in Section 3424, a court of this state has jurisdiction to make an initial child custody determination only if any of the following are true:

(1) This state is the home state of the child on the date of the commencement of the proceeding, or was the home state of the child within six months before the commencement of the proceeding and the child is absent from this state but a parent or person acting as a parent continues to live in this state.

(2) A court of another state does not have jurisdiction under paragraph (1), or a court of the home state of the child has declined to exercise jurisdiction on the grounds that this state is the more appropriate forum under Section 3427 or 3428, and both of the following are true:

(A) The child and the child's parents, or the child and at least one parent or a person acting as a parent, have a significant connection with this state other than mere physical presence.

(B) Substantial evidence is available in this state concerning the child's care, protection, training, and personal relationships.

(3) All courts having jurisdiction under paragraph (1) or (2) have declined to exercise jurisdiction on the ground that a court of this state is the more appropriate forum to determine the custody of the child under Section 3427 or 3428.

(4) No court of any other state would have jurisdiction under the criteria specified in paragraph (1), (2), or (3).

(b) Subdivision (a) is the exclusive jurisdictional basis for making a child custody determination by a court of this state.

(c) Physical presence of, or personal jurisdiction over, a party or a child is not necessary or sufficient to make a child custody determination. *(Added by Stats.1999, c. 867 (S.B. 668), § 3.)*

Commentary

When a woman residing in Tijuana crossed the border to give birth in a California hospital, the child's birth in California was insufficient to give California home state jurisdiction under this section. However, California had emergency jurisdiction under section 3424 because the child was present in California and jurisdiction was necessary to protect the child from mistreatment or abuse. *In re R.L., 4 Cal.App.5th 125, 208 Cal.Rptr.3d 523 (2016)*.

For interpretation of the substantially identical Section 3403 (a) of the UCCJA, see *Brossoit v. Brossoit, 31 Cal.App.4th 361, 36 Cal. Rptr.2d 919 (1995)* (California trial court improperly declined to exercise its continuing custody jurisdiction in favor of Tennessee court when California jurisdiction was exclusive and, although children resided with grandmother in Tennessee, both parents continued to reside in California); and *In re Marriage of Torres, 62 Cal.App.4th 1357, 73 Cal.Rptr.2d 344 (1998)* (six months provision satisfied, making California the "home state," when children lived in California from birth until removal from state by mother, and California father filed divorce proceedings within six months of removal). See also 28 U.S.C. § 1738A (c)(2)(A) (Federal Parental Kidnapping Prevention Act).

Although a Texas court had already assumed jurisdiction over custody, *Keisha W. v. Marvin M., 229 Cal.App.4th 581, 177 Cal.Rptr.3d 161 (2014), review denied*, affirmed a restraining order issued by a California trial court, which awarded custody of the child to the mother, because neither parent nor the child was residing in Texas when the restraining order was issued and no other state had jurisdiction at the time. Under section 3423, a California court may modify a child custody determination made by another state if the California court has jurisdiction to make an initial custody determination under subdivision (a)(1) or (2) of this section and neither parent nor the child currently resides in the other state.

In re Jaheim B., 169 Cal.App.4th 1343, 87 Cal.Rptr.3d 504 (2008), holds that when a neglected child has no "home state," as defined by section 3402(g) and subsection (a) of this section, under subsection (b) the court has jurisdiction to declare the child a dependent of the juvenile court, remove the child from parental custody, and place him in out-of-home care.

Interpreting subsection (a)(1) of this section as well as § 3402(g), *Guardianship of Ariana K., 120 Cal.App.4th 690, 15 Cal.Rptr.3d 817 (2004)*, holds that the UCCJEA does not deprive a California trial court of continuing subject matter jurisdiction to adjudicate a guardianship dispute when the court properly acquired subject matter jurisdiction in an earlier guardianship proceeding. Under the doctrine of continuing jurisdiction, once custody jurisdiction in California is initially established, it continues so long as the child or a parent or guardian of the child continues to reside in California. *Ariana K.* also concludes that nothing in the Hague Convention deprives the California court of jurisdiction because federal law implementing that convention provides that "[t]he remedies established by the Convention and this chapter shall be in addition to remedies available under other law or international agreements." 42 U.S.C. § 11603(h).

In re S.W., 148 Cal.App.4th 1501, 56 Cal.Rptr.3d 665 (2007), review denied June 13, 2007, held that a juvenile court has jurisdiction, under subsection (a) of this section and subsection (g) of section 3402, to terminate the parental rights of a mother from Nebraska who was living in a van in California when neither state qualified as a "home state."

Applying subsection (a)(2), *In re M.M., 240 Cal.App.4th 703, 192 Cal.Rptr.3d 849 (2015)*, held that a juvenile court, having initially exercised emergency jurisdiction, properly assumed permanent jurisdiction when, although Japan had home state jurisdiction, Japan implicitly declined to exercise jurisdiction by repeatedly failing to assume jurisdiction and refusing to discuss jurisdiction.

Also interpreting subsection (a)(2), *In re A.C., 13 Cal.App.5th 661, 220 Cal.Rptr.3d 725 (2017)*, held a juvenile court properly assumed subject matter jurisdiction with respect to two children whose home state was Mexico, after making several unsuccessful attempts to contact the appropriate Mexican judicial officials by telephone and email. The court of appeal reasoned that in failing to timely respond, the Mexican authorities were declining to exercise jurisdiction.

Interpreting subsection (g) of section 3402, *In re Marriage of Sareen, 153 Cal.App.4th 371, 62 Cal.Rptr.3d 687 (2007)*, held that the time spent by a child *after* the filing of a child custody petition may not be counted toward the six months necessary for "home state" jurisdiction.

For interpretation and application of Section 3403 (a)(3) of the UCCJA, see *In re Stephanie M., 7 Cal.4th 295, 7 Cal.4th 724a, 27 Cal.Rptr.2d 595 (1994)* (juvenile court properly exercised its emergency jurisdiction over Mexican child). See additionally *In re Joseph D., 19 Cal.App.4th 678, 23 Cal.Rptr.2d 574 (1993), review denied 1/20/94* (although a California court may assume emergency jurisdiction under subsection (a)(3)(B), the exercise of such jurisdiction is temporary, and the California court should ultimately relinquish jurisdiction to the home state).

In re Baby Boy M., 141 Cal.App.4th 588, 46 Cal.Rptr.3d 196 (2006), held that a juvenile court lacked jurisdiction under the UCCJEA to make nonemergency custody determinations with respect to a missing child when there was insufficient evidence to determine that California was the child's home state within the meaning of subsection (a) of this section and subsection (g) of Section 3402. See also *Ocegueda v. Perreira, 232 Cal.App.4th 1079, 181 Cal.Rptr.3d 845 (2015), review denied*, in which the court relied on *In re Baby Boy M.*, and applied this section and section 3402 to conclude that when a child is less than six months old at the commencement of custody proceedings, the location of his or her birth is essential in determining the child's home state. Moreover, deciding an issue of first impression, *Ocegueda* holds that, for the purposes of determining home state jurisdiction under the UCCJEA, the state where a child "lived" is that in which he or she was physically present, regardless of parental domiciliary intent.

In re A. C., 130 Cal.App.4th 854, 30 Cal.Rptr.3d 431 (2005), observes that Section 3402(d) subjects a California juvenile court's exercise of dependency jurisdiction to the provisions of the UCCJEA. Accordingly, *A.C.* held that the juvenile court lacked subject matter jurisdiction under the UCCJEA to invoke California dependency law in order to shift responsibility for the care of a severely injured child from the child's Section 3402(g) "home state" of Mexico to San Diego County. *A.C.* additionally held that Section 3403 was inapplicable because it is limited by the Section 3424(a) requirement of "mistreatment or abuse."

For discussion of the jurisdictional relationship between the Federal Parental Kidnapping Prevention Act of 1980, 28 U.S.C. § 1738A (reprinted infra), and the superseded Uniform Child Custody Jurisdiction Act (California Family Code Sections 3400 et seq.), see *Wallace v. Superior Court, 15 Cal.App.4th 1182, 19 Cal.Rptr.2d 157, review denied 9/02/93* (when California is the "home state" and Kentucky merely meets the subsection (a)(2) significant connection test, California is not required to give full faith and credit to Kentucky modification of a Kentucky divorce decree nor to stay a California proceeding because a Kentucky proceeding is already pending).

Research References

Forms

California Transactions Forms--Family Law § 3:4, Subject Matter Jurisdiction for Custody Determinations.

Am. Jur. Pl. & Pr. Forms Parent and Child § 6, Introductory Comments.

West's California Code Forms, Probate § 1510 Form 3, Declaration Under Uniform Child Custody Jurisdiction and Enforcement Act (UCCJEA)-Judicial Council Form FL-105/GC-120.

Treatises and Practice Aids

Witkin, California Summary 10th Parent and Child § 159, in General.

Witkin, California Summary 10th Parent and Child § 161, Registration Of Foreign Child Custody Determination.
Witkin, California Summary 10th Parent and Child § 164, in General.
Witkin, California Summary 10th Parent and Child § 165, Home State.
Witkin, California Summary 10th Parent and Child § 166, Statutory Requirements.
Witkin, California Summary 10th Parent and Child § 168, More Appropriate Forum.
Witkin, California Summary 10th Parent and Child § 169, No Other Available Forum.
Witkin, California Summary 10th Parent and Child § 170, in General.
Witkin, California Summary 10th Parent and Child § 172, Modification Jurisdiction.
Witkin, California Summary 10th Parent and Child § 173, Exclusive Continuing Jurisdiction.
Witkin, California Summary 10th Parent and Child § 174, Simultaneous Proceeding in Another State.
Witkin, California Summary 10th Parent and Child § 177, in General.
Witkin, California Summary 10th Parent and Child § 178, After Jurisdiction is Declined.
Witkin, California Summary 10th Parent and Child § 184, in General.
Witkin, California Summary 10th Parent and Child § 185, Enforceable Orders and Determinations.
Witkin, California Summary 10th Parent and Child § 186, Modification Proceeding Pending in Another State.
Witkin, California Summary 10th Parent and Child § 187, Petition and Order to Appear.
Witkin, California Summary 10th Parent and Child § 188, Order.
Witkin, California Summary 10th Parent and Child § 195, Statutory Framework.

§ 3422. Continuing jurisdiction

(a) Except as otherwise provided in Section 3424, a court of this state that has made a child custody determination consistent with Section 3421 or 3423 has exclusive, continuing jurisdiction over the determination until either of the following occurs:

(1) A court of this state determines that neither the child, nor the child and one parent, nor the child and a person acting as a parent have a significant connection with this state and that substantial evidence is no longer available in this state concerning the child's care, protection, training, and personal relationships.

(2) A court of this state or a court of another state determines that the child, the child's parents, and any person acting as a parent do not presently reside in this state.

(b) A court of this state that has made a child custody determination and does not have exclusive, continuing jurisdiction under this section may modify that determination only if it has jurisdiction to make an initial determination under Section 3421. *(Added by Stats.1999, c. 867 (S.B.668), § 3.)*

Commentary

When a custodial parent and child move from California to another state, *Grahm v. Superior Court, 132 Cal.App.4th 1193, 34 Cal.Rptr.3d 270 (2005),* interprets subsection (a)(1) to grant California continuing exclusive jurisdiction so long as (1) the parent exercising visitation rights still lives in California and (2) the relationship between the California parent and the child has not deteriorated to the point at which California's exercise of jurisdiction would be unreasonable.

Research References

Forms

California Transactions Forms--Family Law § 3:4, Subject Matter Jurisdiction for Custody Determinations.
California Transactions Forms--Family Law § 3:16, Identifying Areas Of Parental Decision Making and Participation.

Treatises and Practice Aids

Witkin, California Summary 10th Parent and Child § 172, Modification Jurisdiction.
Witkin, California Summary 10th Parent and Child § 173, Exclusive Continuing Jurisdiction.
Witkin, California Summary 10th Parent and Child § 177, in General.
Witkin, California Summary 10th Parent and Child § 186, Modification Proceeding Pending in Another State.
Witkin, California Summary 10th Parent and Child § 259A, (New) Military Deployment.

§ 3423. Modification of custody determination made by court of another state

Except as otherwise provided in Section 3424, a court of this state may not modify a child custody determination made by a court of another state unless a court of this state has jurisdiction to make an initial determination under paragraph (1) or (2) of subdivision (a) of Section 3421 and either of the following determinations is made:

(a) The court of the other state determines it no longer has exclusive, continuing jurisdiction under Section 3422 or that a court of this state would be a more convenient forum under Section 3427.

(b) A court of this state or a court of the other state determines that the child, the child's parents, and any person acting as a parent do not presently reside in the other state. *(Added by Stats.1999, c. 867 (S.B.668), § 3.)*

Commentary

Although a Texas court had already assumed jurisdiction over custody, *Keisha W. v. Marvin M., 229 Cal.App.4th 581, 177 Cal.Rptr.3d 161 (2014), review denied,* affirmed a restraining order issued by a California trial court, which awarded custody of the child to the mother, because neither parent nor the child was residing in Texas when the restraining order was issued and no other state had jurisdiction at the time. Under this section, a California court may modify a child custody determination made by another state if the California court has jurisdiction to make an initial custody determination under subdivision (a)(1) or (2) of section 3421 and neither parents nor the child currently resides in the other state.

Research References

Forms

California Transactions Forms--Family Law § 3:16, Identifying Areas Of Parental Decision Making and Participation.

Treatises and Practice Aids

Witkin, California Summary 10th Parent and Child § 172, Modification Jurisdiction.
Witkin, California Summary 10th Parent and Child § 173, Exclusive Continuing Jurisdiction.
Witkin, California Summary 10th Parent and Child § 177, in General.

Witkin, California Summary 10th Parent and Child § 186, Modification Proceeding Pending in Another State.

§ 3424. Temporary emergency jurisdiction

(a) A court of this state has temporary emergency jurisdiction if the child is present in this state and the child has been abandoned or it is necessary in an emergency to protect the child because the child, or a sibling or parent of the child, is subjected to, or threatened with, mistreatment or abuse.

(b) If there is no previous child custody determination that is entitled to be enforced under this part and a child custody proceeding has not been commenced in a court of a state having jurisdiction under Sections 3421 to 3423, inclusive, a child custody determination made under this section remains in effect until an order is obtained from a court of a state having jurisdiction under Sections 3421 to 3423, inclusive. If a child custody proceeding has not been or is not commenced in a court of a state having jurisdiction under Sections 3421 to 3423, inclusive, a child custody determination made under this section becomes a final determination, if it so provides and this state becomes the home state of the child.

(c) If there is a previous child custody determination that is entitled to be enforced under this part, or a child custody proceeding has been commenced in a court of a state having jurisdiction under Sections 3421 to 3423, inclusive, any order issued by a court of this state under this section must specify in the order a period that the court considers adequate to allow the person seeking an order to obtain an order from the state having jurisdiction under Sections 3421 to 3423, inclusive. The order issued in this state remains in effect until an order is obtained from the other state within the period specified or the period expires.

(d) A court of this state that has been asked to make a child custody determination under this section, upon being informed that a child custody proceeding has been commenced in, or a child custody determination has been made by, a court of a state having jurisdiction under Sections 3421 to 3423, inclusive, shall immediately communicate with the other court. A court of this state which is exercising jurisdiction pursuant to Sections 3421 to 3423, inclusive, upon being informed that a child custody proceeding has been commenced in, or a child custody determination has been made by, a court of another state under a statute similar to this section shall immediately communicate with the court of that state to resolve the emergency, protect the safety of the parties and the child, and determine a period for the duration of the temporary order.

(e) It is the intent of the Legislature in enacting subdivision (a) that the grounds on which a court may exercise temporary emergency jurisdiction be expanded. It is further the intent of the Legislature that these grounds include those that existed under Section 3403 of the Family Code as that section read on December 31, 1999, particularly including cases involving domestic violence. *(Added by Stats.1999, c. 867 (S.B.668), § 3.)*

Commentary

When a woman residing in Tijuana crossed the border to give birth in a California hospital, the child's birth in California was insufficient to give California home state jurisdiction under section 3421. However, California had emergency jurisdiction under this section because the child was present in California and the exercise of jurisdiction was necessary to protect the child from mistreatment or abuse. *In re R. L., 4 Cal.App.5th 125, 208 Cal.Rptr.3d 523 (2016).*

In re Marriage of Fernandez-Abin & Sanchez, 191 Cal.App.4th 1015, 120 Cal.Rptr.3d 227 (2011), holds that a California trial court lacked jurisdiction to issue a permanent domestic violence restraining order (Family Code §§ 6200 et seq.) that included children when a Mexican court already had exclusive jurisdiction over the children under the Uniform Child Custody Jurisdiction and Enforcement Act (UCCJEA). Nevertheless, a California court may exercise temporary emergency jurisdiction under this section of the UCCJEA if a child is present in California and the exercise of jurisdiction is necessary to protect the child because the child, a sibling, or a parent has been threatened with abuse.

In re A. C., 130 Cal.App.4th 854, 30 Cal.Rptr.3d 431 (2005), observes that Section 3402(d) subjects a California juvenile court's exercise of dependency jurisdiction to the provisions of the UCCJEA. Accordingly, *A.C.* held that the juvenile court lacked subject matter jurisdiction under the UCCJEA to invoke California dependency law in order to shift responsibility for the care of a severely injured child from the child's Section 3402(g) "home state" of Mexico to San Diego County. *A.C.* additionally held that Section 3403 was inapplicable because it is limited by this section's subsection (a) requirement of "mistreatment or abuse."

Although a juvenile court had temporary emergency subject matter jurisdiction over a Mexican teenager who entered the United States illegally after being abandoned by his parents, the juvenile court lacked authority to make jurisdictional and dispositional orders until personal jurisdiction over his Mexican parents could be established in compliance with the notice provisions of the Hague Service Convention (20 U.S.T. 361 (1965)). *In re Jorge G., 164 Cal.App.4th 125, 78 Cal.Rptr.3d 552 (2008).*

In re A.M., 224 Cal.App.4th 593, 168 Cal.Rptr.3d 494 (2014), held that a juvenile court properly exercised emergency jurisdiction over two children from Mexico when their mother used the children to avoid detection while smuggling drugs from Mexico to California.

In re Cristian I., 224 Cal.App.4th 1088, 169 Cal.Rptr.3d 265 (2014), held that a juvenile court properly exercised jurisdiction over a physically abused child whose removal was necessary for his protection and placed him with his presumed father in Arizona. Procedural errors in communication with the Arizona court were harmless because each court was fully aware of proceedings in the other court.

In re Jaheim B., 169 Cal.App.4th 1343, 87 Cal.Rptr.3d 504 (2008), held that a court had emergency jurisdiction under subsection (a) of a neglected child present in California. Moreover, as the neglected child had no "home state," as defined by sections 3402(g) and 3421(a), under section 3421(b) the court had jurisdiction to declare the child a dependent of the juvenile court, remove the child from parental custody, and place him in out-of-home care.

Research References

Treatises and Practice Aids

Witkin, California Summary 10th Parent and Child § 170, in General.

Witkin, California Summary 10th Parent and Child § 171, Illustrations.

Witkin, California Summary 10th Parent and Child § 172, Modification Jurisdiction.

Witkin, California Summary 10th Parent and Child § 173, Exclusive Continuing Jurisdiction.

Witkin, California Summary 10th Parent and Child § 174, Simultaneous Proceeding in Another State.

Witkin, California Summary 10th Parent and Child § 177, in General.

Witkin, California Summary 10th Parent and Child § 188, Order.

Witkin, California Summary 10th Parent and Child § 190, Appeal.

§ 3425. Notice and opportunity to be heard

(a) Before a child custody determination is made under this part, notice and an opportunity to be heard in accordance with the standards of Section 3408 must be given to all persons entitled to notice under the law of this state as in child custody proceedings between residents of this state, any parent whose parental rights have not been previously terminated, and any person having physical custody of the child.

(b) This part does not govern the enforceability of a child custody determination made without notice or an opportunity to be heard.

(c) The obligation to join a party and the right to intervene as a party in a child custody proceeding under this part are governed by the law of this state as in child custody proceedings between residents of this state. *(Added by Stats.1999, c. 867 (S.B.668), § 3. Amended by Stats.2008, c. 699 (S.B.1241), § 3.)*

Commentary

Although a juvenile court had temporary emergency subject matter jurisdiction over a Mexican teenager who entered the United States illegally after being abandoned by his parents, the juvenile court lacked authority to make jurisdictional and dispositional orders until personal jurisdiction over his Mexican parents could be established in compliance with the notice provisions of the Hague Service Convention (20 U.S.T. 361 (1965)). *In re Jorge G., 164 Cal.App.4th 125, 78 Cal.Rptr.3d 552 (2008)*.

Research References

Treatises and Practice Aids

Witkin, California Summary 10th Parent and Child § 170, in General.

Witkin, California Summary 10th Parent and Child § 179, Joinder and Intervention.

Witkin, California Summary 10th Parent and Child § 183, Notice and Hearing.

§ 3426. Simultaneous proceedings in another state

(a) Except as otherwise provided in Section 3424, a court of this state may not exercise its jurisdiction under this chapter if, at the time of the commencement of the proceeding, a proceeding concerning the custody of the child has been commenced in a court of another state having jurisdiction substantially in conformity with this part, unless the proceeding has been terminated or is stayed by the court of the other state because a court of this state is a more convenient forum under Section 3427.

(b) Except as otherwise provided in Section 3424, a court of this state, before hearing a child custody proceeding, shall examine the court documents and other information supplied by the parties pursuant to Section 3429. If the court determines that a child custody proceeding has been commenced in a court in another state having jurisdiction substantially in accordance with this part, the court of this state shall stay its proceeding and communicate with the court of the other state. If the court of the state having jurisdiction substantially in accordance with this part does not determine that the court of this state is a more appropriate forum, the court of this state shall dismiss the proceeding.

(c) In a proceeding to modify a child custody determination, a court of this state shall determine whether a proceeding to enforce the determination has been commenced in another state. If a proceeding to enforce a child custody determination has been commenced in another state, the court may do any of the following:

(1) Stay the proceeding for modification pending the entry of an order of a court of the other state enforcing, staying, denying, or dismissing the proceeding for enforcement.

(2) Enjoin the parties from continuing with the proceeding for enforcement.

(3) Proceed with the modification under conditions it considers appropriate. *(Added by Stats.1999, c. 867 (S.B. 668), § 3.)*

Commentary

For interpretation of the similar jurisdictional and inconvenient forum provisions of the superseded UCCJA, see *Zenide v. Superior Court, 22 Cal.App.4th 1287, 27 Cal.Rptr.2d 703 (1994)* (French court's child custody order, rather than Texas court's subsequent modification, properly enforced in California because Texas court lacked modification jurisdiction in view of French court's continuing jurisdiction over custody).

Research References

Treatises and Practice Aids

Witkin, California Summary 10th Parent and Child § 166, Statutory Requirements.

Witkin, California Summary 10th Parent and Child § 174, Simultaneous Proceeding in Another State.

§ 3427. Inconvenient forum; declining to exercise jurisdiction

(a) A court of this state that has jurisdiction under this part to make a child custody determination may decline to exercise its jurisdiction at any time if it determines that it is an inconvenient forum under the circumstances and that a court of another state is a more appropriate forum. The issue of inconvenient forum may be raised upon motion of a party, the court's own motion, or request of another court.

(b) Before determining whether it is an inconvenient forum, a court of this state shall consider whether it is appropriate for a court of another state to exercise jurisdiction. For this purpose, the court shall allow the parties to submit information and shall consider all relevant factors, including:

(1) Whether domestic violence has occurred and is likely to continue in the future and which state could best protect the parties and the child.

(2) The length of time the child has resided outside this state.

(3) The distance between the court in this state and the court in the state that would assume jurisdiction.

(4) The degree of financial hardship to the parties in litigating in one forum over the other.

(5) Any agreement of the parties as to which state should assume jurisdiction.

(6) The nature and location of the evidence required to resolve the pending litigation, including testimony of the child.

(7) The ability of the court of each state to decide the issue expeditiously and the procedures necessary to present the evidence.

(8) The familiarity of the court of each state with the facts and issues in the pending litigation.

(c) If a court of this state determines that it is an inconvenient forum and that a court of another state is a more appropriate forum, it shall stay the proceedings upon condition that a child custody proceeding be promptly commenced in another designated state and may impose any other condition the court considers just and proper.

(d) A court of this state may decline to exercise its jurisdiction under this part if a child custody determination is incidental to an action for dissolution of marriage or another proceeding while still retaining jurisdiction over the dissolution of marriage or other proceeding.

(e) If it appears to the court that it is clearly an inappropriate forum, the court may require the party who commenced the proceeding to pay, in addition to the costs of the proceeding in this state, necessary travel and other expenses, including attorney's fees, incurred by the other parties or their witnesses. Payment is to be made to the clerk of the court for remittance to the proper party. *(Added by Stats. 1999, c. 867 (S.B.668), § 3.)*

Commentary

For interpretation of the similar jurisdictional and inconvenient forum provisions of the superseded UCCJA, see *Zenide v. Superior Court, 22 Cal.App.4th 1287, 27 Cal.Rptr.2d 703 (1994)* (French court's child custody order, rather than Texas court's subsequent modification, properly enforced in California because Texas court lacked modification jurisdiction in view of French court's continuing jurisdiction over custody).

Brewer v. Carter, 218 Cal.App.4th 1312, 160 Cal.Rptr.3d 853 (2013), holds that before a court determines that California is an inconvenient forum to decide custody issues, it must give the parties an opportunity to present evidence on the issue and must make the findings required by this section.

Research References

Forms

California Transactions Forms--Family Law § 3:4, Subject Matter Jurisdiction for Custody Determinations.

Treatises and Practice Aids

Witkin, California Summary 10th Parent and Child § 166, Statutory Requirements.

Witkin, California Summary 10th Parent and Child § 168, More Appropriate Forum.

Witkin, California Summary 10th Parent and Child § 172, Modification Jurisdiction.

Witkin, California Summary 10th Parent and Child § 174, Simultaneous Proceeding in Another State.

Witkin, California Summary 10th Parent and Child § 175, in General.

Witkin, California Summary 10th Parent and Child § 176, Relevant Factors.

Witkin, California Summary 10th Parent and Child § 177, in General.

Witkin, California Summary 10th Parent and Child § 259A, (New) Military Deployment.

§ 3428. Declining to exercise jurisdiction due to unjustifiable conduct of person

(a) Except as otherwise provided in Section 3424 or by any other law of this state, if a court of this state has jurisdiction under this part because a person seeking to invoke its jurisdiction has engaged in unjustifiable conduct, the court shall decline to exercise its jurisdiction unless one of the following are true:

(1) The parents and all persons acting as parents have acquiesced in the exercise of jurisdiction.

(2) A court of the state otherwise having jurisdiction under Sections 3421 to 3423, inclusive, determines that this state is a more appropriate forum under Section 3427.

(3) No court of any other state would have jurisdiction under the criteria specified in Sections 3421 to 3423, inclusive.

(b) If a court of this state declines to exercise its jurisdiction pursuant to subdivision (a), it may fashion an appropriate remedy to ensure the safety of the child and prevent a repetition of the unjustifiable conduct, including staying the proceeding until a child custody proceeding is commenced in a court having jurisdiction under Sections 3421 to 3423, inclusive.

(c) If a court dismisses a petition or stays a proceeding because it declines to exercise its jurisdiction pursuant to subdivision (a), it shall assess against the party seeking to invoke its jurisdiction necessary and reasonable expenses including costs, communication expenses, attorney's fees, investigative fees, expenses for witnesses, travel expenses, and child care during the course of the proceedings, unless the party from whom fees are sought establishes that the assessment would be clearly inappropriate. The court may not assess fees, costs, or expenses against this state unless authorized by law other than this part.

(d) In making a determination under this section, a court shall not consider as a factor weighing against the petitioner any taking of the child, or retention of the child after a visit or other temporary relinquishment of physical custody, from the person who has legal custody, if there is evidence that the taking or retention of the child was a result of domestic violence against the petitioner, as defined in Section 6211. *(Added by Stats.1999, c. 867 (S.B.668), § 3.)*

Research References

Treatises and Practice Aids

Witkin, California Summary 10th Parent and Child § 166, Statutory Requirements.

Witkin, California Summary 10th Parent and Child § 168, More Appropriate Forum.

Witkin, California Summary 10th Parent and Child § 173, Exclusive Continuing Jurisdiction.

Witkin, California Summary 10th Parent and Child § 177, in General.

Witkin, California Summary 10th Parent and Child § 178, After Jurisdiction is Declined.

Witkin, California Summary 10th Wills and Probate § 959-I, (New) Jurisdiction Based on Unjustifiable Conduct.

§ 3429. Required information in first pleading

(a) In a child custody proceeding, each party, in its first pleading or in an attached affidavit, shall give information, if reasonably ascertainable, under oath as to the child's present address or whereabouts, the places where the child has lived during the last five years, and the names and present addresses of the persons with whom the child has lived during that period. However, where there are allegations of domestic violence or child abuse, any addresses of the party alleging violence or abuse and of the child which are unknown to the other party are confidential and may not be disclosed in the pleading or affidavit. The pleading or affidavit must state whether the party:

(1) Has participated, as a party or witness or in any other capacity, in any other proceeding concerning the custody of, or visitation with, the child and, if so, identify the court, the case number, and the date of the child custody determination, if any.

(2) Knows of any proceeding that could affect the current proceeding, including proceedings for enforcement and proceedings relating to domestic violence, protective orders, termination of parental rights, and adoptions and, if so, identify the court, the case number, and the nature of the proceeding.

(3) Knows the names and addresses of any person not a party to the proceeding who has physical custody of the child or claims rights of legal custody or physical custody of, or visitation with, the child and, if so, the names and addresses of those persons.

(b) If the information required by subdivision (a) is not furnished, the court, upon motion of a party or its own motion, may stay the proceeding until the information is furnished.

(c) If the declaration as to any of the items described in paragraphs (1) to (3), inclusive, of subdivision (a) is in the affirmative, the declarant shall give additional information under oath as required by the court. The court may examine the parties under oath as to details of the information furnished and other matters pertinent to the court's jurisdiction and the disposition of the case.

(d) Each party has a continuing duty to inform the court of any proceeding in this or any other state that could affect the current proceeding. *(Added by Stats.1999, c. 867 (S.B.668), § 3.)*

Research References

Forms

West's California Judicial Council Forms FL-580, Registration Of Out-Of-State Custody Decree.

Treatises and Practice Aids

Witkin, California Summary 10th Parent and Child § 161, Registration Of Foreign Child Custody Determination.

Witkin, California Summary 10th Parent and Child § 174, Simultaneous Proceeding in Another State.

Witkin, California Summary 10th Parent and Child § 181, Information in First Pleading.

Witkin, California Summary 10th Parent and Child § 271, Temporary Custody During Pendency Of Proceeding.

Witkin, California Summary 10th Parent and Child § 331, Venue, Petition, and Investigation.

§ 3430. Appearance by party and child

(a) In a child custody proceeding in this state, the court may order a party to the proceeding who is in this state to appear before the court in person with or without the child. The court may order any person who is in this state and who has physical custody or control of the child to appear in person with the child.

(b) If a party to a child custody proceeding whose presence is desired by the court is outside this state, the court may order that a notice given pursuant to Section 3408 include a statement directing the party to appear in person with or without the child and informing the party that failure to appear may result in a decision adverse to the party.

(c) The court may enter any orders necessary to ensure the safety of the child and of any person ordered to appear under this section.

(d) If a party to a child custody proceeding who is outside this state is directed to appear under subdivision (b) or desires to appear personally before the court with or without the child, the court may require another party to pay reasonable and necessary travel and other expenses of the party so appearing and of the child. *(Added by Stats.1999, c. 867 (S.B.668), § 3.)*

Research References

Treatises and Practice Aids

Witkin, California Summary 10th Parent and Child § 182, Order to Appear.

CHAPTER 3. ENFORCEMENT

Section

§ 3441. "Petitioner"; "respondent"

In this chapter:

(a) "Petitioner" means a person who seeks enforcement of an order for return of a child under the Hague Convention on the Civil Aspects of International Child Abduction or enforcement of a child custody determination.

(b) "Respondent" means a person against whom a proceeding has been commenced for enforcement of an order for return of a child under the Hague Convention on the Civil Aspects of International Child Abduction or enforcement of a child custody determination. *(Added by Stats.1999, c. 867 (S.B.668), § 3.)*

Research References

Treatises and Practice Aids

Witkin, California Summary 10th Parent and Child § 160, Scope Of Child Custody Proceedings.
Witkin, California Summary 10th Parent and Child § 184, in General.
Witkin, California Summary 10th Parent and Child § 185, Enforceable Orders and Determinations.
Witkin, California Summary 10th Parent and Child § 186, Modification Proceeding Pending in Another State.
Witkin, California Summary 10th Parent and Child § 187, Petition and Order to Appear.
Witkin, California Summary 10th Parent and Child § 188, Order.
Witkin, California Summary 10th Parent and Child § 190, Appeal.
Witkin, California Summary 10th Parent and Child § 195, Statutory Framework.

§ 3442. Orders made under the Hague Convention on the Civil Aspects of International Child Abduction

Under this chapter, a court of this state may enforce an order for the return of a child made under the Hague Convention on the Civil Aspects of International Child Abduction as if it were a child custody determination. *(Added by Stats.1999, c. 867 (S.B.668), § 3.)*

Research References

Treatises and Practice Aids

Witkin, California Summary 10th Parent and Child § 185, Enforceable Orders and Determinations.

§ 3443. Recognition and enforcement of out-of-state custody decrees

(a) A court of this state shall recognize and enforce a child custody determination of a court of another state if the latter court exercised jurisdiction in substantial conformity with this part or the determination was made under factual circumstances meeting the jurisdictional standards of this part and the determination has not been modified in accordance with this part.

(b) A court of this state may utilize any remedy available under other laws of this state to enforce a child custody determination made by a court of another state. The remedies provided in this chapter are cumulative and do not affect the availability of other remedies to enforce a child custody determination. *(Added by Stats.1999, c. 867 (S.B. 668), § 3.)*

Research References

Treatises and Practice Aids

Witkin, California Summary 10th Parent and Child § 184, in General.
Witkin, California Summary 10th Parent and Child § 185, Enforceable Orders and Determinations.

§ 3444. Temporary order enforcing out-of-state visitation order

(a) A court of this state which does not have jurisdiction to modify a child custody determination may issue a temporary order enforcing either:

(1) A visitation schedule made by a court of another state.

(2) The visitation provisions of a child custody determination of another state that does not provide for a specific visitation schedule.

(b) If a court of this state makes an order under paragraph (2) of subdivision (a), it shall specify in the order a period that it considers adequate to allow the petitioner to obtain an order from a court having jurisdiction under the criteria specified in Chapter 2 (commencing with Section 3421). The order remains in effect until an order is obtained from the other court or the period expires. *(Added by Stats.1999, c. 867 (S.B.668), § 3.)*

Research References

Treatises and Practice Aids

Witkin, California Summary 10th Parent and Child § 185, Enforceable Orders and Determinations.

§ 3445. Registration of out-of-state custody determination; method; duties of court; notice; contesting validity of registration; confirmation of registered order

(a) A child custody determination issued by a court of another state may be registered in this state, with or without a simultaneous request for enforcement, by sending all of the following to the appropriate court in this state:

(1) A letter or other document requesting registration.

(2) Two copies, including one certified copy, of the determination sought to be registered, and a statement under penalty of perjury that to the best of the knowledge and belief of the person seeking registration the order has not been modified.

(3) Except as otherwise provided in Section 3429, the name and address of the person seeking registration and any parent or person acting as a parent who has been awarded custody or visitation in the child custody determination sought to be registered.

(b) On receipt of the documents required by subdivision (a), the registering court shall do both of the following:

(1) Cause the determination to be filed as a foreign judgment, together with one copy of any accompanying documents and information, regardless of their form.

(2) Serve notice upon the persons named pursuant to paragraph (3) of subdivision (a) and provide them with an opportunity to contest the registration in accordance with this section.

(c) The notice required by paragraph (2) of subdivision (b) shall state all of the following:

(1) That a registered determination is enforceable as of the date of the registration in the same manner as a determination issued by a court of this state.

(2) That a hearing to contest the validity of the registered determination must be requested within 20 days after service of the notice.

(3) That failure to contest the registration will result in confirmation of the child custody determination and preclude further contest of that determination with respect to any matter that could have been asserted.

(d) A person seeking to contest the validity of a registered order must request a hearing within 20 days after service of the notice. At that hearing, the court shall confirm the registered order unless the person contesting registration establishes any of the following:

(1) That the issuing court did not have jurisdiction under Chapter 2 (commencing with Section 3421).

(2) That the child custody determination sought to be registered has been vacated, stayed, or modified by a court having jurisdiction to do so under Chapter 2 (commencing with Section 3421).

(3) That the person contesting registration was entitled to notice, but notice was not given in accordance with the standards of Section 3408, in the proceedings before the court that issued the order for which registration is sought.

(e) If a timely request for a hearing to contest the validity of the registration is not made, the registration is confirmed as a matter of law and the person requesting registration and all persons served shall be notified of the confirmation.

(f) Confirmation of a registered order, whether by operation of law or after notice and hearing, precludes further contest of the order with respect to any matter that could have been asserted at the time of registration. *(Added by Stats.1999, c. 867 (S.B.668), § 3.)*

Research References

Forms

West's California Judicial Council Forms FL-580, Registration Of Out-Of-State Custody Decree.

West's California Judicial Council Forms FL-585, Request for Hearing Regarding Registration Of Out-Of-State Custody Decree.

Treatises and Practice Aids

Witkin, California Summary 10th Parent and Child § 161, Registration Of Foreign Child Custody Determination.

Witkin, California Summary 10th Parent and Child § 187, Petition and Order to Appear.

Witkin, California Summary 10th Parent and Child § 188, Order.

§ 3446. Enforcement of registered child custody determination

(a) A court of this state may grant any relief normally available under the law of this state to enforce a registered child custody determination made by a court of another state.

(b) A court of this state shall recognize and enforce, but may not modify, except in accordance with Chapter 2 (commencing with Section 3421), a registered child custody determination of a court of another state. *(Added by Stats.1999, c. 867 (S.B.668), § 3.)*

Research References

Treatises and Practice Aids

Witkin, California Summary 10th Parent and Child § 185, Enforceable Orders and Determinations.

§ 3447. Pending proceeding in another state to modify order

If a proceeding for enforcement under this chapter is commenced in a court of this state and the court determines that a proceeding to modify the determination is pending in a court of another state having jurisdiction to modify the determination under Chapter 2 (commencing with Section 3421), the enforcing court shall immediately communicate with the modifying court. The proceeding for enforcement continues unless the enforcing court, after consultation with the modifying court, stays or dismisses the proceeding. *(Added by Stats.1999, c. 867 (S.B.668), § 3.)*

Research References

Treatises and Practice Aids

Witkin, California Summary 10th Parent and Child § 174, Simultaneous Proceeding in Another State.

Witkin, California Summary 10th Parent and Child § 186, Modification Proceeding Pending in Another State.

§ 3448. Petition; verification; contents; order directing respondent to appear

(a) A petition under this chapter must be verified. Certified copies of all orders sought to be enforced and of any order confirming registration must be attached to the petition. A copy of a certified copy of an order may be attached instead of the original.

(b) A petition for enforcement of a child custody determination must state all of the following:

(1) Whether the court that issued the determination identified the jurisdictional basis it relied upon in exercising jurisdiction and, if so, what the basis was.

(2) Whether the determination for which enforcement is sought has been vacated, stayed, or modified by a court whose decision must be enforced under this part and, if so, identify the court, the case number, and the nature of the proceeding.

(3) Whether any proceeding has been commenced that could affect the current proceeding, including proceedings relating to domestic violence, protective orders, termination of parental rights, and adoptions and, if so, identify the court, the case number, and the nature of the proceeding.

(4) The present physical address of the child and the respondent, if known.

(5) Whether relief in addition to the immediate physical custody of the child and attorney's fees is sought, including a request for assistance from law enforcement officials and, if so, the relief sought.

(6) If the child custody determination has been registered and confirmed under Section 3445, the date and place of registration.

(c) Upon the filing of a petition, the court shall issue an order directing the respondent to appear in person with or without the child at a hearing and may enter any order necessary to ensure the safety of the parties and the child. The hearing must be held on the next judicial day after service of the order unless that date is impossible. In that event, the court shall hold the hearing on the first judicial day possible. The court may extend the date of hearing at the request of the petitioner.

(d) An order issued under subdivision (c) must state the time and place of the hearing and advise the respondent that, at the hearing, the court will order that the petitioner may take immediate physical custody of the child and the payment of fees, costs, and expenses under Section 3452, and may schedule a hearing to determine whether further relief is appropriate, unless the respondent appears and establishes either of the following:

(1) That the child custody determination has not been registered and confirmed under Section 3445 and all of the following are true:

(A) The issuing court did not have jurisdiction under Chapter 2 (commencing with Section 3421).

(B) The child custody determination for which enforcement is sought has been vacated, stayed, or modified by a court having jurisdiction to do so under Chapter 2 (commencing with Section 3421).

(C) The respondent was entitled to notice, but notice was not given in accordance with the standards of Section 3408, in the proceedings before the court that issued the order for which enforcement is sought.

(2) That the child custody determination for which enforcement is sought was registered and confirmed under Section 3445, but has been vacated, stayed, or modified by a court of a state having jurisdiction to do so under Chapter 2 (commencing with Section 3421). *(Added by Stats.1999, c. 867 (S.B.668), § 3. Amended by Stats.2008, c. 699 (S.B.1241), § 4.)*

Research References

Treatises and Practice Aids

Witkin, California Summary 10th Parent and Child § 187, Petition and Order to Appear.

Witkin, California Summary 10th Parent and Child § 189, Warrant to Take Physical Custody.

§ 3449. Service of petition and order

Except as otherwise provided in Section 3451, the petition and order shall be served, by any method authorized by the law of this state, upon the respondent and any person who has physical custody of the child. *(Added by Stats.1999, c. 867 (S.B.668), § 3.)*

Research References

Treatises and Practice Aids

Witkin, California Summary 10th Parent and Child § 187, Petition and Order to Appear.

§ 3450. Order for immediate physical custody; fees and costs; inferences; spousal privilege

(a) Unless the court issues a temporary emergency order pursuant to Section 3424, upon a finding that a petitioner is entitled to immediate physical custody of the child, the court shall order that the petitioner may take immediate physical custody of the child unless the respondent establishes either of the following:

(1) That the child custody determination has not been registered and confirmed under Section 3445 and one of the following is true:

(A) The issuing court did not have jurisdiction under Chapter 2 (commencing with Section 3421).

(B) The child custody determination for which enforcement is sought has been vacated, stayed, or modified by a court of a state having jurisdiction to do so under Chapter 2 (commencing with Section 3421).

(C) The respondent was entitled to notice, but notice was not given in accordance with the standards of Section 3408, in the proceedings before the court that issued the order for which enforcement is sought.

(2) That the child custody determination for which enforcement is sought was registered and confirmed under Section 3445 but has been vacated, stayed, or modified by a court of a state having jurisdiction to do so under Chapter 2 (commencing with Section 3421).

(b) The court shall award the fees, costs, and expenses authorized under Section 3452 and may grant additional relief, including a request for the assistance of law enforcement officials, and set a further hearing to determine whether additional relief is appropriate.

(c) If a party called to testify refuses to answer on the ground that the testimony may be self-incriminating, the court may draw an adverse inference from the refusal.

(d) A privilege against disclosure of communications between spouses and a defense of immunity based on the relationship of spouses or parent and child may not be invoked in a proceeding under this chapter. *(Added by Stats.1999, c. 867 (S.B.668), § 3. Amended by Stats.2014, c. 82 (S.B.1306), § 31, eff. Jan. 1, 2015.)*

Research References

Treatises and Practice Aids

Witkin, California Summary 10th Parent and Child § 188, Order.

§ 3451. Warrant to take physical custody

(a) Upon the filing of a petition seeking enforcement of a child custody determination, the petitioner may file a verified application for the issuance of a warrant to take physical custody of the child if the child is imminently likely to suffer serious physical harm or be removed from this state.

(b) If the court, upon the testimony of the petitioner or other witness, finds that the child is imminently likely to suffer serious physical harm or be removed from this state, it may issue a warrant to take physical custody of the child. The petition must be heard on the next judicial day after the warrant is executed unless that date is impossible. In that event, the court shall hold the hearing on the first judicial day possible. The application for the warrant must include the statements required by subdivision (b) of Section 3448.

(c) A warrant to take physical custody of a child must do all of the following:

(1) Recite the facts upon which a conclusion of imminent serious physical harm or removal from the jurisdiction is based.

(2) Direct law enforcement officers to take physical custody of the child immediately.

(3) Provide for the placement of the child pending final relief.

(d) The respondent must be served with the petition, warrant, and order immediately after the child is taken into physical custody.

(e) A warrant to take physical custody of a child is enforceable throughout this state. If the court finds on the basis of the testimony of the petitioner or other witness that a less intrusive remedy is not effective, it may authorize law enforcement officers to enter private property to take physical custody of the child. If required by exigent circumstances of the case, the court may authorize law enforcement officers to make a forcible entry at any hour.

(f) The court may impose conditions upon placement of a child to ensure the appearance of the child and the child's custodian. *(Added by Stats.1999, c. 867 (S.B.668), § 3.)*

Research References

Treatises and Practice Aids

Witkin, California Summary 10th Parent and Child § 187, Petition and Order to Appear.

Witkin, California Summary 10th Parent and Child § 189, Warrant to Take Physical Custody.

§ 3452. Prevailing party; award of necessary and reasonable expenses

(a) The court shall award the prevailing party, including a state, necessary and reasonable expenses incurred by or on behalf of the party, including costs, communication expenses, attorney's fees, investigative fees, expenses for witnesses, travel expenses, and child care during the course of the proceedings, unless the party from whom fees or expenses are sought establishes that the award would be clearly inappropriate.

(b) The court may not assess fees, costs, or expenses against a state unless authorized by law other than this part. *(Added by Stats.1999, c. 867 (S.B.668), § 3.)*

Research References

Treatises and Practice Aids

Witkin, California Summary 10th Parent and Child § 187, Petition and Order to Appear.

Witkin, California Summary 10th Parent and Child § 188, Order.

§ 3453. Full faith and credit to order issued by another state

A court of this state shall accord full faith and credit to an order issued by another state, and consistent with this part, enforce a child custody determination by a court of another state unless the order has been vacated, stayed, or modified by a court having jurisdiction to do so under Chapter 2 (commencing with Section 3421). *(Added by Stats.1999, c. 867 (S.B.668), § 3.)*

Research References

Treatises and Practice Aids

Witkin, California Summary 10th Parent and Child § 184, in General.

§ 3454. Appeals

An appeal may be taken from a final order in a proceeding under this chapter in accordance with expedited appellate procedures in other civil cases. Unless the court enters a temporary emergency order under Section 3424, the enforcing court may not stay an order enforcing a child custody determination pending appeal. *(Added by Stats.1999, c. 867 (S.B.668), § 3.)*

Research References

Treatises and Practice Aids

Witkin, California Summary 10th Parent and Child § 190, Appeal.

§ 3455. Locating missing child or party; district attorney authorized to proceed pursuant to § 3130 et seq.

(a) In a case arising under this part or involving the Hague Convention on the Civil Aspects of International Child Abduction, a district attorney is authorized to proceed pursuant to Chapter 8 (commencing with Section 3130) of Part 2.

(b) A district attorney acting under this section acts on behalf of the court and may not represent any party. *(Added by Stats.1999, c. 867 (S.B.668), § 3.)*

Research References

Treatises and Practice Aids

Witkin, California Summary 10th Parent and Child § 162, Locating Missing Child or Party.

§ 3456. Law enforcement officers; locating child or party

At the request of a district attorney acting under Section 3455, a law enforcement officer may take any lawful action reasonably necessary to locate a child or a party and assist the district attorney with responsibilities under Section 3455. *(Added by Stats.1999, c. 867 (S.B.668), § 3.)*

Research References

Treatises and Practice Aids

Witkin, California Summary 10th Parent and Child § 162, Locating Missing Child or Party.

§ 3457. Expenses incurred under § 3455 or 3456

The court may assess all direct expenses and costs incurred by a district attorney under Section 3455 or 3456 pursuant to the provisions of Section 3134. *(Added by Stats.1999, c. 867 (S.B.668), § 3.)*

Research References

Treatises and Practice Aids

Witkin, California Summary 10th Parent and Child § 162, Locating Missing Child or Party.

CHAPTER 4. MISCELLANEOUS PROVISIONS

Section

§ 3461. Construction of act; promoting uniformity

In applying and construing this Uniform Child Custody Jurisdiction and Enforcement Act, consideration shall be given to the need to promote uniformity of the law with respect to its subject matter among states that enact it. *(Added by Stats.1999, c. 867 (S.B.668), § 3.)*

Research References

Treatises and Practice Aids

Witkin, California Summary 10th Parent and Child § 159, in General.
Witkin, California Summary 10th Parent and Child § 195, Statutory Framework.

§ 3462. Severability

If any provision of this part or its application to any person or circumstance is held invalid, the invalidity does not affect other provisions or applications of this part that can be given effect without the invalid provision or application, and to this end the provisions of this part are severable. *(Added by Stats.1999, c. 867 (S.B.668), § 3.)*

Research References

Treatises and Practice Aids

Witkin, California Summary 10th Parent and Child § 159, in General.

§ 3465. Proceedings begun before effective date of this act

A motion or other request for relief made in a child custody proceeding or to enforce a child custody determination that was commenced before the effective date of this part is governed by the law in effect at the time the motion or other request was made. *(Added by Stats.1999, c. 867 (S.B.668), § 3.)*

Research References

Forms

California Transactions Forms--Family Law § 3:2, Child Custody.
California Transactions Forms--Family Law § 2:70, Deciding Custody.
California Transactions Forms--Family Law § 6:119, Continuing Jurisdiction.

Division 9

SUPPORT

Part 1

DEFINITIONS AND GENERAL PROVISIONS

CHAPTER 1. DEFINITIONS

§ 3500. Construction of division

Unless the provision or context otherwise requires, the definitions in this chapter govern the construction of this division. *(Stats.1992, c. 162 (A.B.2650), § 10, operative Jan. 1, 1994.)*

Law Revision Commission Comments

Enactment [Revised Comment]

Section 3500 is new and is comparable to Section 50. This chapter supplements the general definitions in Part 2 (commencing with Section 50) of Division 1 with special definitions that apply only to this division. For general definitions frequently used in this division, see Sections 92 ("family support"), 142 ("spousal support"), 150 ("support"), and 155 ("support order"). See also Section 11 (reference to married person includes formerly married person). [23 Cal.L.Rev.Comm. Reports 1 (1993)].

Research References

Forms

West's California Code Forms, Family § 4300, Comment Overview--Duty to Support Spouse.

West's California Code Forms, Family § 6340, Comment Overview--Issuance Of Orders After Notice and Hearing.

Treatises and Practice Aids

Witkin, California Summary 10th Community Property § 272, Nature Of Theory.

Witkin, California Summary 10th Husband and Wife § 3, Statutory Framework.

Witkin, California Summary 10th Husband and Wife § 36, Mutual Obligations.

Witkin, California Summary 10th Husband and Wife § 174, in General.

Witkin, California Summary 10th Husband and Wife § 259, Procedure.

Witkin, California Summary 10th Husband and Wife § 384, Orders After Notice and Hearing.

Witkin, California Summary 10th Parent and Child § 63, in General.

Witkin, California Summary 10th Parent and Child § 311, Other Proceedings Stayed.

Witkin, California Summary 10th Parent and Child § 415, in General.

§ 3515. Separate property; quasi-community property

"Separate property" does not include quasi-community property. *(Stats.1992, c. 162 (A.B.2650), § 10, operative Jan. 1, 1994.)*

Law Revision Commission Comments

Enactment [Revised Comment]

Section 3515 continues former Civil Code Section 4804 without substantive change, insofar as it applied to support. For a comparable provision applicable to property division, see Section 2502. See also Section 125 ("quasi-community property" defined). Compare Section 130 ("separate property" defined in Section 760 *et seq.*). [23 Cal.L.Rev.Comm. Reports 1 (1993)].

Research References

Treatises and Practice Aids

Witkin, California Summary 10th Community Property § 257, Clarifications and Distinctions.

Witkin, California Summary 10th Husband and Wife § 174, in General.

CHAPTER 2. GENERAL PROVISIONS

§ 3550. Obligee; obligor; duties of support of obligors

(a) As used in this section:

(1) "Obligee" means a person to whom a duty of support is owed.

(2) "Obligor" means a person who owes a duty of support.

(b) An obligor present or resident in this state has the duty of support as defined in Sections 3900, 3901, 3910, 4300, and 4400, regardless of the presence or residence of the obligee. *(Stats.1992, c. 162 (A.B.2650), § 10, operative Jan. 1, 1994.)*

Law Revision Commission Comments

Enactment [Revised Comment]

Subdivision (a) of Section 3550 continues former Civil Code Section 241(b)-(c) without substantive change. Subdivision (b) continues former Civil Code Section 244 without substantive change. [23 Cal.L.Rev.Comm. Reports 1 (1993)].

Research References

Forms

West's California Code Forms, Family § 4300, Comment Overview--Duty to Support Spouse.

Treatises and Practice Aids

Witkin, California Summary 10th Husband and Wife § 174, in General.

§ 3551. Inapplicability of privilege; competency of husband and wife to testify

Laws attaching a privilege against the disclosure of communications between spouses are inapplicable under this division. Spouses are competent witnesses to testify to any relevant matter, including marriage and parentage. *(Stats. 1992, c. 162 (A.B.2650), § 10, operative Jan. 1, 1994. Amended by Stats.2014, c. 82 (S.B.1306), § 32, eff. Jan. 1, 2015.)*

Law Revision Commission Comments

Enactment [Revised Comment]

Section 3551 continues former Civil Code Section 250 without substantive change and expands its application to this division. This is not a substantive change. See Evid. Code § 972(g) (when spousal privilege not applicable in support proceedings). For a similar provision, see Section 4839 (Uniform Reciprocal Enforcement of Support Act). [23 Cal.L.Rev.Comm. Reports 1 (1993)].

Research References

Treatises and Practice Aids

Witkin, California Summary 10th Husband and Wife § 174, in General.

§ 3552. State and federal income tax returns; submission to court; examination and discovery

(a) In a proceeding involving child, family, or spousal support, no party to the proceeding may refuse to submit copies of the party's state and federal income tax returns to the court, whether individual or joint.

(b) The tax returns may be examined by the other party and are discoverable by the other party. A party also may be examined by the other party as to the contents of a tax return submitted pursuant to this section.

(c) If the court finds that it is relevant to the case to retain the tax return, the tax return shall be sealed and maintained as a confidential record of the court. If the court finds that the tax return is not relevant to disposition of the case, all copies of the tax return shall be returned to the party who submitted it. *(Stats.1992, c. 162 (A.B.2650), § 10, operative Jan. 1, 1994.)*

Law Revision Commission Comments

Enactment [Revised Comment]

Section 3552 continues former Civil Code Section 4700.7 without substantive change and expands the rule to apply to family support. See also Sections 3629 (tax returns in proceeding for expedited support order), 3665 (tax returns in discovery proceedings for modification or termination of support order), 3689 (tax returns in simplified procedure for modification of support order). [23 Cal. L.Rev.Comm. Reports 1 (1993)].

Commentary

In re Marriage of Sachs, 95 Cal.App.4th 1144, 116 Cal.Rptr.2d 273 (2002), review denied May 15, 2002, holds that a parent who has failed to pay court-ordered child support may not invoke the 5th Amendment privilege against self-incrimination in order to avoid providing financial information sought for the purpose of collecting child support arrearages. The court reasoned, inter alia, that the privilege against self-incrimination has no application in support-based contempt proceedings, because the support obligor bears the burden of showing inability to pay court-ordered support. Thus, withholding financial information would not protect him from liability; instead it would cause him to be found guilty of contempt.

Despite the language of Sections 3552, 4055(b)(2), 4058, and 4059, *Estevez v. Superior Court, 22 Cal.App.4th 423, 27 Cal.Rptr.2d 470 (1994), review denied 4/21/94,* holds that a parent may not be required to disclose financial information when he has a very high income and he stipulates that he can pay any reasonable amount of child support ordered by the trial court. In *Estevez*, the parent stipulated that he had annual income of not less that $1.4 million and that he could pay any reasonable amount of support ordered by the trial court. *Estevez* relied upon Section 4057(b)(3), which provides that the presumed guideline amount may be rebutted by evidence that the "parent being ordered to pay child support has an extraordinarily high income and the amount determined under the formula would exceed the needs of the children." *Estevez* is discussed approvingly by *In re Marriage of Fini, 26 Cal.App.4th 1033, 31 Cal.Rptr.2d 749, 756 (1994)*. See also *White v. Marciano, 190 Cal.App.3d 1026, 1032, 235 Cal.Rptr. 779 (1987)* (reaching a similar conclusion under prior law).

Johnson v. Superior Court, 66 Cal.App.4th 68, 77 Cal.Rptr.2d 624 (1998), holds that a parent with extraordinarily high income who offers to pay any reasonable amount of court-ordered support is not required to provide full financial discovery to the child's other parent in a support proceeding if the trial court makes financial assumptions that are "least beneficial to the ... high earner." The other parent is, however, entitled to discovery of information sufficient to enable the trial court to make such assumptions.

In re Marriage of Hubner, 94 Cal.App.4th 175, 114 Cal.Rptr.2d 646 (2001), review denied March 13, 2002, holds that a child support obligor with extraordinarily high income must inform the court of the actual amount of his income when that amount is disputed and the parties have not agreed on the appropriate amount of child support. Effectively, *Hubner* restricts the holding of *Estevez* to cases in which the parties have agreed on the appropriate amount of child support.

Research References

Forms

West's California Judicial Council Forms FL-150, Income and Expense Declaration.

Treatises and Practice Aids

Witkin, California Summary 10th Husband and Wife § 174, in General.

Witkin, California Summary 10th Husband and Wife § 273, Continuing Jurisdiction.

Witkin, California Summary 10th Husband and Wife § 291, Discovery.

§ 3554. Appeals

An appeal may be taken from an order or judgment under this division as in other civil actions. *(Stats.1992, c. 162 (A.B.2650), § 10, operative Jan. 1, 1994.)*

Law Revision Commission Comments

Enactment [Revised Comment]

Section 3554 continues former Civil Code Section 249 without substantive change and expands the rule to apply to this division. This is not a substantive change. See Section 210 (except as provided by statute or rule, procedural rules applicable to civil actions generally applicable to this code). See also Code Civ. Proc. § 904.1 (when appeal may be taken from superior court judgment or order). [23 Cal.L.Rev.Comm. Reports 1 (1993)].

Research References

Treatises and Practice Aids

Witkin, California Summary 10th Husband and Wife § 174, in General.

§ 3555. Support paid through county officer; forwarding of payments

Where support is ordered to be paid through the county officer designated by the court on behalf of a child or other party not receiving public assistance pursuant to the Family Economic Security Act of 1982 (Chapter 2 (commencing with Section 11200) of Part 3 of Division 9 of the Welfare and Institutions Code), the designated county officer shall forward the support received to the designated payee within the time standards prescribed by federal law and the Department of Child Support Services. *(Stats.1992, c. 162 (A.B.2650), § 10, operative Jan. 1, 1994. Amended by Stats.1993, c. 219 (A.B.1500), § 120; Stats.2000, c. 808 (A.B.1358), § 27, eff. Sept. 28, 2000.)*

Law Revision Commission Comments

Enactment [Revised Comment]

Section 3555 continues former Civil Code Section 4390.18 without substantive change. The reference to support of a "minor" child has been omitted. This is not a substantive change, but recognizes that in some cases support may be ordered for an adult child. See Sections 58 ("child for whom support may be ordered" defined), 3587 (court order to effectuate agreement for support of adult child), 3901 (duration of duty to support child), 3910 (duty to maintain incapacitated adult child), 4000 (civil action to enforce parent's duty to support child), 4001 (order for child support).

The application of the former section was ambiguous, since it was written in broad terms, but located in an earnings assignment order chapter. This section makes clear that it applies to any support paid to a designated county officer, whether or not paid pursuant to an earnings assignment order. See also Sections 3752 (providing district attorney designated as assigned payee with information concerning health insurance coverage for child), 4200–4203 (designation of county officer to be paid child support payments), 4350–4352 (designation of county officer to be paid spousal support payments), 4573 (payment where support paid through district attorney for child not receiving public assistance), 5237(b) (providing designated county officer notice of change of address under earnings assignment order for support). [23 Cal.L.Rev.Comm. Reports 1 (1993)].

Research References

Treatises and Practice Aids

Witkin, California Summary 10th Husband and Wife § 313, Payment to County by Court and Referral.

§ 3556. Child support; failure or refusal to implement custody or visitation rights

The existence or enforcement of a duty of support owed by a noncustodial parent for the support of a minor child is not affected by a failure or refusal by the custodial parent to implement any rights as to custody or visitation granted by a court to the noncustodial parent. *(Stats.1992, c. 162 (A.B. 2650), § 10, operative Jan. 1, 1994.)*

Law Revision Commission Comments

Enactment [Revised Comment]

Section 3556 continues former Civil Code Section 4382 without change. [23 Cal.L.Rev.Comm. Reports 1 (1993)].

Commentary

See generally *Moffat v. Moffat, 27 Cal.3d 645, 165 Cal.Rptr. 877, 612 P.2d 967 (1980)* (a parent under a court order to pay support for a minor child must pay that support even if the custodial parent interferes with the support obligor's right to visitation).

Despite the language of the statute, which might seem to sever any link between the duty to support and the right to custody or visitation, the courts of appeal were long divided on whether one parent's concealment of a child, as opposed to mere interference with visitation, was a defense to the other parent's obligation to pay child support. *In re Marriage of Damico, 7 Cal.4th 673, 29 Cal.Rptr.2d 787 (1994)*, partially resolved this conflict among the courts of appeal. At issue in *Damico* were arrearages payable to a parent for the support of a child who had long since reached the age of majority. In such case, the Supreme Court held that the parent may be equitably estopped to recover arrearages that accumulated while she concealed the child from the obligor parent. *Damico* specifically reserved two issues: whether estoppel is available when recovery is sought while the child is still a minor; and whether the state may be estopped to recover arrearages assigned to it by a custodial parent as a condition of receipt of public assistance. Both questions were presented by *In re Marriage of Comer, Cal.4th 504, 927 P.2d 265, 59 Cal.Rptr.2d 155 (1996)*, which held that estoppel based on child concealment is not available as a defense to arrearages when the child is still a minor and would thus benefit from the payment of arrearages, and that the custodial parent's concealment of the child may not estop the state to recover arrearages from the other parent as reimbursement for public assistance benefits paid to the custodial household. *In re Marriage of Vroenen, 94 Cal.App.4th 1176, 114 Cal.Rptr.2d 860 (2001)*, held that a custodial parent who actively concealed her children from the noncustodial parent was not estopped from collecting, after the children reached majority, child support arrearages that accrued during the concealment, because the concealment ended when the children were still minors. See also *In re Marriage of Padilla,* 932 P.2d 756, 61 Cal.Rptr.2d 809 (1997), remanded by the California Supreme Court to the court of appeal with directions to vacate in light of *Comer, supra.* The superseded court of appeal opinion, originally published at 34 Cal.Rptr.2d 165 (1994), held that the county assignee of the custodial parent's child support rights was estopped to collect arrearages accumulated before the assignment because the child's whereabouts were concealed from the support obligor parent by the obligee parent. To similar effect, see *In re Marriage of Walters, 59 Cal.App.4th 998, 70 Cal.Rptr.2d 354 (1998)*, holding that a custodial parent's active concealment of the child until the age of majority does not estop the County from collecting child support arrearages as reimbursement for public assistance payments and does not estop the custodial parent from collecting child support arrearages when the noncustodial parent has been ordered to pay child support to a court trustee. Compare *County of Orange v. Carl D., 76 Cal.App.4th 429, 90 Cal.Rptr.2d 440 (1999)*, where the court of appeal held that the county was estopped to obtain reimbursement from the father for public assistance expenditures unnecessarily incurred to provide his children with foster care when the county had misrepresented that the father, who was willing and able to assume custody, could not be located.

Focusing on the age of majority instead of *Comer*'s underlying concern about the child's eligibility and continuing need for support, *Stanislaus County Department of Child Services v. Jensen, 112 Cal. App.4th 453, 5 Cal.Rptr.3d 178 (2003)*, held that concealment ending after the child reaches the age of majority estops collection of child support arrearages even though the child is still in high school and eligible for support under § 3901.

Even when concealment is a defense to arrearages, the principle of res judicata prohibits the obligor from later raising this defense with respect to arrearages already included in a stipulated judgment when he failed to timely raise the defense in the earlier enforcement proceeding. *Warga v. Cooper, 44 Cal.App.4th 371, 51 Cal.Rptr.2d 684 (1996)*.

With the concealment cases, compare *Cooper v. O'Rourke, 32 Cal.App.4th 243, 38 Cal.Rptr.2d 444 (1995)* (mother's mere interference with visitation, absent child concealment, does not warrant termination of father's child support obligation).

Research References

Treatises and Practice Aids

Witkin, California Summary 10th Parent and Child § 245, in General.

Witkin, California Summary 10th Parent and Child § 380, Duty to Support Minor Child.

§ 3557. Award of attorney's fees

(a) Notwithstanding any other provision of law, absent good cause to the contrary, the court, in order to ensure that each party has access to legal representation to preserve each party's rights, upon determining (1) an award of attorney's fees and cost under this section is appropriate, (2) there is a disparity in access to funds to retain counsel, and (3) one party is able to pay for legal representation for both parties, shall award reasonable attorney's fees to any of the following persons:

(1) A custodial parent or other person to whom payments should be made in any action to enforce any of the following:

(A) An existing order for child support.

(B) A penalty incurred pursuant to Chapter 5 (commencing with Section 4720) of Part 5 of Division 9.

(2) A supported spouse in an action to enforce an existing order for spousal support.

(b) This section shall not be construed to allow an award of attorney's fees to or against a governmental entity. *(Added by Stats.1993, c. 219 (A.B.1500), § 120.3. Amended by Stats.1994, c. 1269 (A.B.2208), § 31.2; Stats.2010, c. 352 (A.B.939), § 17.)*

Law Revision Commission Comments

Enactment [Revised Comment]

Section 3557 continues former Civil Code Section 4370(c)-(d) without substantive change. Subdivision (a)(2) continues language that was added in 1991, but chaptered out by a later-enacted bill. See 1991 Cal. Stat. ch. 110, § 4, chaptered out by 1991 Cal. Stat. ch. 500, § 1. See also Section 3652 (attorney's fees in order modifying or terminating child support order). [23 Cal.L.Rev.Comm. Reports 1 (1993)].

Research References

Forms

West's California Judicial Council Forms FL-158, Supporting Declaration for Attorney's Fees and Costs Attachment.

West's California Judicial Council Forms FL-319, Request for Attorney's Fees and Costs Attachment.

West's California Judicial Council Forms FL-346, Attorney's Fees and Costs Order Attachment.

Treatises and Practice Aids

Witkin, California Summary 10th Husband and Wife § 174, in General.

Witkin, California Summary 10th Parent and Child § 426, Action by Child or Parent.

§ 3558. Child or family support proceedings; court-ordered job training, placement, or vocation rehabilitation; documentation

In a proceeding involving child or family support, a court may require either parent to attend job training, job placement and vocational rehabilitation, and work programs, as designated by the court, at regular intervals and times and for durations specified by the court, and provide documentation of participation in the programs, in a format that is acceptable to the court, in order to enable the court to make a finding that good faith attempts at job training and placement have been undertaken by the parent. *(Added by Stats.1996, c. 490 (A.B.932), § 1.)*

Commentary

Under former California law, a criminal contempt sentence of incarceration could not constitutionally be imposed on a parent who chose not to seek employment or earn money, although required to do so by a child support order. The California Supreme Court disapproved this long standing rule in *Moss v. Superior Court, 17 Cal.4th 396, 950 P.2d 59, 71 Cal.Rptr.2d 215 (1998),* which held that a parent who willfully fails to seek and accept employment may be held in criminal contempt. Additionally, inability to comply with a child support order is an affirmative defense, and thus the petitioner need not prove the nonsupporting parent's ability to pay.

Research References

Treatises and Practice Aids

Witkin, California Summary 10th Husband and Wife § 174, in General.

Witkin, California Summary 10th Parent and Child § 425, in General.

Witkin, California Summary 10th Parent and Child § 437, Contempt Proceedings.

CHAPTER 3. SUPPORT AGREEMENTS

ARTICLE 1. GENERAL PROVISIONS

§ 3580. Immediate separation agreements; consent to support agreements

Subject to this chapter and to Section 3651, spouses may agree, in writing, to an immediate separation, and may provide in the agreement for the support of either of them and of their children during the separation or upon the dissolution of their marriage. The mutual consent of the parties is sufficient consideration for the agreement. *(Stats. 1992, c. 162 (A.B.2650), § 10, operative Jan. 1, 1994. Amended by Stats.2014, c. 82 (S.B.1306), § 33, eff. Jan. 1, 2015.)*

Law Revision Commission Comments

Enactment [Revised Comment]

Section 3580 continues the last part of former Civil Code Section 4802 without substantive change. See also Sections 1620 (restrictions on contract altering spouses' legal relations), 3592 (agreement discharged in bankruptcy), 4302 (no support for spouse living separate by agreement unless stipulated), 4323 (agreement concerning effect of cohabitation on spousal support). [23 Cal.L.Rev. Comm. Reports 1 (1993)].

Research References

Forms

California Transactions Forms--Estate Planning § 11:48, Governing Contractual Provisions [CC §§ 1550 et seq., Fam C S721(B)].
California Transactions Forms--Family Law § 2:52, Overview.
California Transactions Forms--Family Law § 2:53, Temporary Support.
California Transactions Forms--Family Law § 2:63, Authority for Child Support.
West's California Code Forms, Family § 3580, Comment Overview--Support Agreements.

Treatises and Practice Aids

Witkin, California Summary 10th Community Property § 33, Restrictions on Alteration Of Spouses' Legal Relations.
Witkin, California Summary 10th Contracts § 626, Separation and Property Agreements.
Witkin, California Summary 10th Husband and Wife § 40, Agreements Altering Spouses' Legal Relations.
Witkin, California Summary 10th Husband and Wife § 41, Separation Agreements.
Witkin, California Summary 10th Husband and Wife § 174, in General.
Witkin, California Summary 10th Parent and Child § 389, Agreement Between Spouses.

ARTICLE 2. CHILD SUPPORT

§ 3585. Severability of child support provisions; orders based on agreements

The provisions of an agreement between the parents for child support shall be deemed to be separate and severable from all other provisions of the agreement relating to property and support of either spouse. An order for child support based on the agreement shall be imposed by law and shall be made under the power of the court to order child support. *(Stats.1992, c. 162 (A.B.2650), § 10, operative Jan. 1, 1994. Amended by Stats.2014, c. 82 (S.B.1306), § 34, eff. Jan. 1, 2015.)*

Law Revision Commission Comments

Enactment [Revised Comment]

Section 3585 continues the first two sentences of former Civil Code Section 4811(a) without substantive change. A reference to "parents" has been substituted for the former reference to "parties." The phrase "based on the agreement" has been added to the second sentence. Neither change is intended to be substantive. The rule in former Civil Code Section 4811(c), limiting application of this section to property settlement agreements entered into on or after January 1, 1970, has been omitted as obsolete. See also Sections 3029 (support order required where parent receiving public assistance), 3557 (attorney's fees for enforcement of support order), 3651 (modification or termination of support order based on agreement), 4013 (child support obligation discharged in bankruptcy). For a comparable provision relating to spousal support, see Section 3590. [23 Cal.L.Rev.Comm. Reports 1 (1993)].

Commentary

Relying on this section as well as subsections (a) and (e) of section 3651, *In re Marriage of Alter, 171 Cal.App.4th 718, 89 Cal.Rptr.3d 849 (2009)*, holds that a trial court always has power to modify an existing child support order upward *or downward*, regardless of the parties' contrary marital settlement agreement. *Alter* establishes that child support may be modified downward despite the parties' agreement to the contrary.

Research References

Forms

California Transactions Forms--Family Law § 2:63, Authority for Child Support.
West's California Code Forms, Family § 3580, Comment Overview--Support Agreements.
West's California Code Forms, Family § 3585, Comment Overview--Child Support.

Treatises and Practice Aids

Witkin, California Summary 10th Parent and Child § 389, Agreement Between Spouses.

§ 3586. Child support and spousal support agreements; failure to designate amount of payments

If an agreement between the parents combines child support and spousal support without designating the amount to be paid for child support and the amount to be paid for spousal support, the court is not required to make a separate order for child support. *(Stats.1992, c. 162 (A.B.2650), § 10, operative Jan. 1, 1994.)*

Law Revision Commission Comments

Enactment [Revised Comment]

Section 3586 continues the first paragraph of former Civil Code Section 4811(d) without substantive change. A reference to "parents" has been substituted for the former reference to "parties." This is not a substantive change. The rule in former Civil Code Section 4811(c), limiting application of this section to property settlement agreements entered into on or after January 1, 1970, has been omitted as obsolete. See also Sections 92 ("family support" defined), 3029 (support order required where parent receiving public assistance), 4500 (enforcement of support order). [23 Cal.L.Rev. Comm. Reports 1 (1993)].

Research References

Forms

West's California Code Forms, Family § 3585, Comment Overview--Child Support.

Treatises and Practice Aids

Witkin, California Summary 10th Parent and Child § 389, Agreement Between Spouses.

§ 3587. Approval of stipulated agreements to pay support for adult children

Notwithstanding any other provision of law, the court has the authority to approve a stipulated agreement by the parents to pay for the support of an adult child or for the continuation of child support after a child attains the age of 18 years and to make a support order to effectuate the agreement. *(Stats.1992, c. 162 (A.B.2650), § 10, operative Jan. 1, 1994.)*

Law Revision Commission Comments

Enactment [Revised Comment]

Section 3587 continues the first sentence of former Civil Code Section 4700.9 without substantive change. A reference to "parents" has been substituted for the former reference to "parties." This is not a substantive change. The language "and to make a support order to effectuate the agreement" is new, but was implied by the last sentence of former Civil Code Section 4700.9, which is superseded by Family Code Section 4500. See also Sections 3557 (attorney's fees for enforcement of support order), 3901 (duty to support high school student), 3910 (duty to support incapacitated adult child), 4000 (civil action to enforce parent's duty to support), 4500 (support orders enforceable under this code). [23 Cal.L.Rev.Comm. Reports 1 (1993)].

Commentary

See generally *In re Marriage of Lambe & Meehan, 37 Cal.App.4th 388, 44 Cal.Rptr.2d 641 (1995)* (parents' court-ratified agreement to divest family court of jurisdiction to order support for their adult indigent child is unenforceable). Cf. *Marriage of Goodarzirad, 185 Cal.App.3d 1020, 1026, 230 Cal.Rptr. 203 (1986)* (husband's stipulation to surrender rights of custody and visitation of his minor child is unenforceable as is the portion of the judgment incorporating the stipulation).

In re Marriage of Rosenfeld & Gross, 225 Cal.App.4th 478, 169 Cal.Rptr.3d 918 (2014), holds that an order for adult child support based solely on the parties' agreement is judicially modifiable unless the agreement expressly and specifically provides that it is not modifiable. The holding of *Rosenfeld & Gross* parallels section 3591(c) modification of spousal support: It is modifiable unless the parties specifically agree that it is not modifiable.

Research References

Forms

California Transactions Forms--Family Law § 3:26, Voluntary Support After Age Of Majority.

West's California Code Forms, Family § 3585, Comment Overview--Child Support.

Treatises and Practice Aids

Witkin, California Summary 10th Husband and Wife § 4, Definitions.

Witkin, California Summary 10th Husband and Wife § 273, Continuing Jurisdiction.

Witkin, California Summary 10th Parent and Child § 421, Agreement to Support Adult Child.

ARTICLE 3. SPOUSAL SUPPORT

§ 3590. Severability of support provisions; orders based on agreements

The provisions of an agreement for support of either party shall be deemed to be separate and severable from the provisions of the agreement relating to property. An order for support of either party based on the agreement shall be law-imposed and shall be made under the power of the court to order spousal support. *(Stats.1992, c. 162 (A.B.2650), § 10, operative Jan. 1, 1994.)*

Law Revision Commission Comments

Enactment [Revised Comment]

Section 3590 continues the first two sentences of former Civil Code Section 4811(b) without substantive change. For a provision limiting applicability of this section, see Section 3593. For a comparable provision relating to child support, see Section 3585.

Absent a written agreement otherwise, spousal support terminates at the death of either party or on remarriage of the supported party. See Section 4337. See also Sections 3557 (attorney's fees for enforcement of support order), 3592 (agreement discharged in bankruptcy), 4302 (no support for spouse living separate by agreement unless stipulated), 4323 (agreement concerning effect of cohabitation on spousal support), 4336 (agreement terminating spousal support jurisdiction), 4360(b) (agreement that annuity, life insurance, or trust for spousal support may not be modified or terminated). [23 Cal.L.Rev.Comm. Reports 1 (1993)].

Commentary

See Section 3593, providing that Sections 3590 and 3591 apply only to property settlement agreements made on or after January 1, 1970. Agreements made earlier are controlled by prior law.

Research References

Forms

West's California Code Forms, Family § 3590, Comment Overview--Spousal Support.

Treatises and Practice Aids

Witkin, California Summary 10th Husband and Wife § 112, Contents Of Judgment.

Witkin, California Summary 10th Husband and Wife § 356, General Rule: Support Provisions Are Modifiable.

Witkin, California Summary 10th Husband and Wife § 362, Integrated Agreement.

§ 3591. Modification or termination of agreements

(a) Except as provided in subdivisions (b) and (c), the provisions of an agreement for the support of either party are subject to subsequent modification or termination by court order.

(b) An agreement may not be modified or terminated as to an amount that accrued before the date of the filing of the notice of motion or order to show cause to modify or terminate.

(c) An agreement for spousal support may not be modified or revoked to the extent that a written agreement, or, if there is no written agreement, an oral agreement entered into in open court between the parties, specifically provides that the spousal support is not subject to modification or termination. *(Stats.1992, c. 162 (A.B.2650), § 10, operative Jan. 1, 1994.)*

Law Revision Commission Comments

Enactment [Revised Comment]

Section 3591 continues the last sentence of former Civil Code Section 4811(b) without substantive change, insofar as that sentence applied to spousal support agreements. References to "terminate" and "termination" have been substituted for "revoke" and "revocation." These are not substantive changes. For a provision limiting applicability of this section, see Section 3593. See also Section 3592 (agreement discharged in bankruptcy). For a comparable provision relating to orders for support, see Section 3651. [23 Cal.L.Rev. Comm. Reports 1 (1993)].

Commentary

See Section 3593, providing that Sections 3590 and 3591 apply only to property settlement agreements made on or after January 1, 1970. Agreements made earlier are controlled by prior law.

Section 3591 applies to all support agreements, even those that have not been incorporated in a divorce decree. *In re Marriage of Maytag, 26 Cal.App.4th 1711, 32 Cal.Rptr.2d 334 (1994)* (although the parties' separation agreement was never approved by the court or incorporated in the parties' judgment of dissolution, the agreement was subject to subsequent modification by court order).

In re Marriage of Cauley, 138 Cal.App.4th 1100, 41 Cal.Rptr.3d 902 (2006), review denied, holds that a trial court properly terminated a former wife's spousal support under Section 4325 when she was convicted of domestic violence against her former husband, even though the parties' marital settlement agreement provided that spousal support could not be modified or terminated.

In re Marriage of Dietz, 176 Cal.App.4th 387, 97 Cal.Rptr.3d 616 (2009), held that a former wife's attainment of the age at which retirement accounts awarded to her in the division of community property could be accessed without penalty was not a change of circumstances sufficient to warrant a downward modification of her spousal support. *Dietz* does not purport to set a per se rule, but rather looks to the parties' marital settlement agreement to see whether the parties anticipated this event and intended it to have any bearing on the amount of support payable to the former wife under their agreement.

In re Marriage of Shaughnessy, 139 Cal.App.4th 1225, 43 Cal.Rptr.3d 642 (2006), holds that the trial court did not abuse its discretion in ordering a reduction and termination of spousal support due to changed circumstances when the supported spouse, after adequate judicial notice, failed to make diligent effort to be self-supporting.

In re Marriage of West, 152 Cal.App.4th 240, 60 Cal.Rptr.3d 858 (2007), held that a former wife's change of career sufficed as a material change of circumstances justifying reconsideration of spousal support. *West* also held that a wife's receipt of cash from the sale of her share of a community property asset did not justify a reduction in spousal support.

Under subsection (c), the parties may preclude any modification of the spousal support agreement, effectively ousting the court from all aspects of its jurisdiction to modify spousal support. See, for example, *In re Marriage of Sasson, 129 Cal.App.3d 140, 146–147, 180 Cal.Rptr. 815 (1982)* (agreement that spousal support not modifiable unless wife remarried precluded termination on account of her marriage-like cohabitation); *In re Marriage of Hibbard, 212 Cal.App.4th 1007, 151 Cal.Rptr.3d 553 (2013), review denied* (trial court properly interpreted the parties' marital settlement agreement as setting a spousal support minimum that could not be modified by the court despite the support obligor's total disability). Because support is generally modifiable, provisions to the contrary should be unambiguous. *In re Marriage of Hufford, 152 Cal.App.3d 825, 199 Cal.Rptr. 726 (1984)*; *In re Marriage of Forcum, 145 Cal.App.3d 599, 604–605, 193 Cal.Rptr. 596 (1983)*. For drafting guidance, see *In re Marriage of Vomacka, 36 Cal.3d 459, 683 P.2d 248, 204 Cal.Rptr. 568 (1984)* (jurisdiction to modify or award support implies jurisdiction to extend it); *In re Marriage of Brown, 35 Cal.App.4th 785, 41 Cal.Rptr.2d 506 (1995)* (construing parties' agreement, which provided a 60–month spousal support limit, to allow judicial modification and extension of the time limit so long as the judicial modification and extension occurred *before* expiration of the 60–month period). Compare the similar but sufficiently different agreement language of *In re Marriage of Zlatnik, 197 Cal.App.3d 1284, 243 Cal.Rptr. 454 (1988), review denied* (judicial modification precluded by parties' agreement) with *In re Marriage of Jones, 222 Cal.App.3d 505, 271 Cal.Rptr. 761 (1990), review denied* (agreement language insufficient to bar judicial modification). Although the cases are not entirely consistent, the operative distinction would seem to be between agreement language that merely deprives the court of jurisdiction to modify after a certain date, which language has been judicially construed to allow extension of support beyond that date so long as the court acts before or by the stated date, and language which provides absolutely and unconditionally that spousal support shall terminate by a date certain. See also *In re Marriage of Iberti, 55 Cal.App.4th 1435, 64 Cal.Rptr.2d 766 (1997)* (spousal support terminated by unambiguous language of agreement when wife dropped out of college) and *In re Marriage of Ousterman, 46 Cal.App.4th 1090, 54 Cal.Rptr.2d 403 (1996)* (holding that parties' agreement that spousal support of a certain amount be payable until a specified date and not be modifiable before that date did not preclude trial court from continuing and modifying spousal support after that date).

For modification of "step-down" provisions, see *In re Marriage of Beust, 23 Cal.App.4th 24, 28 Cal.Rptr.2d 201 (1994), review denied 6/23/94*. In *Beust*, the court of appeal held that, in light of the parties' 32–year marriage and the wife's efforts to be self-supporting, the trial court abused its discretion in denying the wife's motion to modify an agreement containing a step-down provision reducing her support to $1 a year after six years of support payments. Although the wife was required to demonstrate a change of circumstances in order to modify the provision, she did so by showing that despite her best efforts she had been unable to satisfy the parties' contractual expectation that she would become self-supporting in six years. Compare *In re Marriage of Aninger, 220 Cal.App.3d 230, 269 Cal.Rptr. 388 (1990)* (wife's increased need was not based on failure of parties' expectations about her self-sufficiency but rather on her improvident expenditure).

In re Marriage of Khera and Sameer, 206 Cal.App.4th 1464, 143 Cal.Rptr.3d 81 (2012), held that a wife's post-divorce decision to pursue a doctoral degree instead of completing her MSW degree and entering the job market, as contemplated by the parties' marital settlement agreement, was not a change of circumstances justifying the modification of a *Richmond* step-down spousal support order.

In a motion to modify spousal support, the trial court properly considered a recent increase in the obligor's child support obligation to the children of the marriage; the increase in child support constitutes the "material change of circumstances" necessary to maintain an action to modify spousal support. *In re Marriage of McCann, 41 Cal.App.4th 978, 48 Cal.Rptr.2d 864 (1996), review denied April 11, 1996.*

Family Code section 4326 was added to overturn *In re Marriage of Lautsbaugh, 72 Cal.App.4th 1131, 85 Cal.Rptr.2d 688 (1999)*, which held that termination of child support when a child reached the age of majority was not a sufficient change of circumstances to justify a spousal support modification. Interpreting the section 4326 requirement that "a companion child support order is in effect," *In re Marriage of Kacik, 179 Cal.App.4th 410, 101 Cal.Rptr.3d 745 (2009)*, concluded that a request for modification of spousal support must be reasonably contemporaneous with the termination of child support, although it need not precede termination of child support. *Kacik* held that a modification request made 17 months after termination of child support could not rely on section 4326 to claim that the termination was the necessary change of circumstances, because it would be unreasonable to believe that the termination of child support 17 months earlier prompted the request for modification of spousal support.

Research References

Forms

California Transactions Forms--Family Law § 2:61, Modifiability.

Treatises and Practice Aids

Witkin, California Summary 10th Contracts § 79, Public Policy Exception.
Witkin, California Summary 10th Husband and Wife § 300, Jurisdiction Reserved.
Witkin, California Summary 10th Husband and Wife § 356, General Rule: Support Provisions Are Modifiable.
Witkin, California Summary 10th Husband and Wife § 357, Agreement Made Expressly Nonmodifiable.
Witkin, California Summary 10th Husband and Wife § 358, Purely Private Agreement.
Witkin, California Summary 10th Husband and Wife § 371, Civil Remedies.

§ 3592. Discharge in bankruptcy; power of court to make new orders

If an obligation under an agreement for settlement of property to a spouse or for support of a spouse is discharged in bankruptcy, the court may make all proper orders for the support of the spouse, as the court determines are just, having regard for the circumstances of the parties and the amount of the obligations under the agreement that are discharged. *(Stats.1992, c. 162 (A.B.2650), § 10, operative Jan. 1, 1994.)*

Law Revision Commission Comments

Enactment [Revised Comment]

Section 3592 continues the substance of former Civil Code Section 4812. See also Section 4013 (child support obligation discharged in bankruptcy). [23 Cal.L.Rev.Comm. Reports 1 (1993)].

Commentary

In re Marriage of Lynn, 101 Cal.App.4th 120, 123 Cal.Rptr.2d 611 (2002), holds that this section applies only to a bankruptcy discharge of a spouse's obligation under a *property settlement agreement*. If the obligation was instead established by court adjudication, this section is inapplicable and any modification of spousal support must be made according to § 4320, in which case the discharge in bankruptcy of a spouse's obligation is merely one of many factors.

Research References

Treatises and Practice Aids

Witkin, California Summary 10th Husband and Wife § 285, Supported Spouse's Discharge in Bankruptcy.
Witkin, California Summary 10th Husband and Wife § 368, California Statute.

§ 3593. Application of §§ 3590 and 3591

Sections 3590 and 3591 are effective only with respect to a property settlement agreement entered into on or after January 1, 1970, and do not affect an agreement entered into before January 1, 1970, as to which Chapter 1308 of the Statutes of 1967 shall apply. *(Stats.1992, c. 162 (A.B.2650), § 10, operative Jan. 1, 1994.)*

Law Revision Commission Comments

Enactment [Revised Comment]

Section 3593 continues former Civil Code Section 4811(c) without substantive change, insofar as it applied to spousal support agreements. [23 Cal.L.Rev.Comm. Reports 1 (1993)].

Research References

Treatises and Practice Aids

Witkin, California Summary 10th Husband and Wife § 356, General Rule: Support Provisions Are Modifiable.

CHAPTER 4. SPOUSAL AND CHILD SUPPORT DURING PENDENCY OF PROCEEDING

§ 3600. Support orders

During the pendency of any proceeding for dissolution of marriage or for legal separation of the parties or under Division 8 (commencing with Section 3000) (custody of children) or in any proceeding where there is at issue the support of a minor child or a child for whom support is authorized under Section 3901 or 3910, the court may order (a) either spouse to pay any amount that is necessary for the support of the other spouse, consistent with the requirements of subdivisions (i) and (m) of Section 4320 and Section 4325, or (b) either or both parents to pay any amount necessary for the support of the child, as the case may be. *(Stats.1992, c. 162 (A.B.2650), § 10, operative Jan. 1, 1994. Amended by Stats.2001, c. 293 (S.B.1221), § 1; Stats.2002, c. 759 (A.B. 3033), § 1; Stats.2014, c. 82 (S.B.1306), § 35, eff. Jan. 1, 2015.)*

Law Revision Commission Comments

Enactment [Revised Comment]

Section 3600 continues the first sentence of former Civil Code Section 4357(a) without substantive change. The language describing the support proceedings to which this section applies is drawn from the first sentence of former Civil Code Section 4700(a), with the addition of language to make clear that this section applies to a child for whom support is authorized under Section 3901. This is not a substantive change. The word "support" has been substituted for "support and maintenance" with reference to support of a husband or wife, since "maintenance" is surplus. The word "support" has been substituted for "support and education" with reference to support of a child. This is not a substantive change. See Section 150 (when used with reference to minor child, "support" includes education). A reference to "child" has been substituted for "children." This is not a substantive change. See Section 10 (singular includes plural). A reference to the "superior" court has been omitted as surplus. See Section 200 (jurisdiction in superior court).

See also Sections 2254 (order for support of putative spouse), 3029 (support order required where parent receiving public assistance), 3557 (attorney's fees for enforcement of support order). [23 Cal.L.Rev.Comm. Reports 1 (1993)].

Commentary

In re Marriage of Williamson, 226 Cal.App.4th 1303, 172 Cal.Rptr.3d 699 (2014), holds that a trial court impermissibly modified a husband's temporary support obligation retroactively by ordering that support payments already made were to come from the general community property funds in a blocked account, rather than from the husband's share of those funds, when the court had not specifically reserved jurisdiction to modify with respect to any date earlier than the day on which the petition for modification was filed.

In re Marriage of Freitas, 209 Cal.App.4th 1059, 147 Cal.Rptr.3d 453 (2012), review denied, held that a trial court did not abuse its discretion when it terminated temporary spousal support because of the obligee's conviction for domestic abuse, despite the absence of any showing of changed circumstances. In *Freitas*, spousal support should not have been initially ordered because the support obligee had earlier been convicted of domestic violence and had not rebutted the section 4325 presumption that spousal support should not be awarded to a perpetrator of domestic violence. Additionally, *Freitas* states in dictum that temporary support is retroactively modifiable when a court reserves jurisdiction to retroactively modify based on further evidentiary developments.

Despite the requirement of 28 USC § 1360(c) that state courts give full force and effect to American Indian tribal law and custom in civil matters, *In re Marriage of Jacobsen, 121 Cal.App.4th 1187, 18 Cal.Rptr.3d 162 (2004)*, holds that, in a divorce proceeding initiated by a tribal member, a California family court is not required to give effect to a Chumash Indian custom that funds distributed by the tribe to its members should not be used to pay spousal support to nonmembers, because once a tribal member invokes the court's jurisdiction in a domestic relations matter, the court has jurisdiction to grant any appropriate relief. *Jacobsen* additionally observes that the Chumash custom is not binding in family court because it is inconsistent with California law and policy, which is expressed in this section and Sections 720 and 4300.

For general discussion of spousal support pendente lite, see *In re Marriage of Dick, 15 Cal.App.4th 144, 159–166, 18 Cal.Rptr.2d 743 (1993), review denied 8/26/93* (trial court may make temporary spousal support retroactive to date wife filed petition for legal separation). See also *In re Marriage of Economou, 224 Cal.App.3d 1466, 1477, 274 Cal.Rptr. 473 (1990)*.

This section gives the trial court jurisdiction to award pendente lite spousal support and attorney's fees during the pendency of an appeal in a dissolution action seeking relief from a default judgment. *In re Marriage of Askmo, 85 Cal.App.4th 1032, 102 Cal.Rptr.2d 662 (2000)*.

Pendente lite spousal support is not available to unmarried cohabitants. *Friedman v. Friedman, 20 Cal.App.4th 876, 24 Cal. Rptr.2d 892 (1993)* (trial court lacks authority to award temporary "spousal support" to disabled cohabitant pending trial of *Marvin* contract action). For discussion of the rights of cohabitants, see generally Section 2251, Commentary.

County of Orange v. Quinn, 97 Cal.App.4th 956, 118 Cal.Rptr.2d 833 (2002), holds that, despite the apparent restriction of Code of Civil Procedure § 583.161 to marital dissolution cases, by virtue of this section, the exception to the five-year dismissal rule expressed in § 3601 applies to any case in which continuing pendente lite child support has been ordered. Compare *County of Orange v. Rosales, 99 Cal.App.4th 1214, 121 Cal.Rptr.2d 788 (2002)* (once father's parental rights were terminated, there was no "continuing child support order" and county's child support action was subject to dismissal five years after filing of claim).

Jaycee B. v. Superior Court, 42 Cal.App.4th 718, 49 Cal.Rptr.2d 694 (1996), review denied May 1, 1996, holds that family court has jurisdiction to order payment of Section 3600 pendente lite child support by the child's "intended father" to the child's "intended mother" when the child was conceived pursuant to a surrogacy contract signed by the divorcing contractual parties even though the child is not genetically related to either party or to the surrogate mother and even though the child's legal parents are not yet established. *Jaycee B.* found that the husband's (intended father's) signature on the surrogacy contract was a sufficient basis for a temporary support order.

Cf. *In re Marriage of Schulze, 60 Cal.App.4th 519, 70 Cal.Rptr.2d 488 (1997)*, holding that it is reversible error for the trial court to use a computer program designed for temporary support to calculate permanent support. The trial court used the Dissomaster program which, according to *Schulze*, bases the spousal support award on the Santa Clara guideline for temporary support. In dictum, *Schulze* suggests that no computer program would satisfy the court's duty to consider the enumerated factors of this section in setting permanent spousal support. See also *In re Marriage of Olson, 14 Cal.App.4th 1, 17 Cal.Rptr.2d 480 (1993)* (distinguishing temporary, or pendente lite, spousal support from permanent support).

Although a husband's attorney was negligent in calculating the husband's permanent support obligation based on the DissoMaster program for temporary spousal support and not obtaining a forensic standard of living analysis, the husband's malpractice action against his attorney was unsuccessful because he failed to prove that his attorney would have obtained a better outcome either through settlement or trial. *Namikas v. Miller, 225 Cal.App.4th 1574, 171 Cal.Rptr.3d 23 (2014)*.

Research References

Forms

California Practice Guide: Rutter Family Law Forms Form 5:2, Request for Order Re Child Custody, Child Support, Spousal Support, Attorney Fees, etc.

California Practice Guide: Rutter Family Law Forms Form 1:32, Glossary Of Common Family Law Terms, Phrases and Concepts (Enclosure to Form 1:31).

California Practice Guide: Rutter Family Law Forms Form 6:11, Request for Order Re Guideline Child Support, Temporary "Guideline" Spousal Support and Family Code S4062 "Add-On" Child Support.

California Practice Guide: Rutter Family Law Forms Form 6:23, Request for Order Re Temporary "Guideline" Spousal Support and Family Code S4360 Provision for Support After Death Of Supporting Party.

California Transactions Forms--Family Law § 2:52, Overview.

California Transactions Forms--Family Law § 2:53, Temporary Support.

California Transactions Forms--Family Law § 2:63, Authority for Child Support.

California Transactions Forms--Family Law § 3:21, Jurisdiction for Orders to Pay Child Support.

West's California Code Forms, Family § 3600, Comment Overview--Spousal and Child Support During Pendency Of Proceeding.

Treatises and Practice Aids

Witkin, California Summary 10th Husband and Wife § 86, in General.

Witkin, California Summary 10th Husband and Wife § 87, Methods Of Obtaining Orders.

Witkin, California Summary 10th Husband and Wife § 171, Hearing, Incidental Orders, and Judgment.

Witkin, California Summary 10th Husband and Wife § 174, in General.

Witkin, California Summary 10th Husband and Wife § 175, Development Of Law.

Witkin, California Summary 10th Husband and Wife § 177, Types Of Actions.

Witkin, California Summary 10th Husband and Wife § 178, Main Proceeding in Trial Court.

Witkin, California Summary 10th Husband and Wife § 179, Main Proceeding on Appeal.

Witkin, California Summary 10th Husband and Wife § 184, Payee's Needs.

Witkin, California Summary 10th Husband and Wife § 191, in General.

Witkin, California Summary 10th Husband and Wife § 197, in General.

Witkin, California Summary 10th Parent and Child § 385, Support During Action.

§ 3601. Duration of child support orders

(a) An order for child support entered pursuant to this chapter continues in effect until the order (1) is terminated by the court or (2) terminates by operation of law pursuant to Sections 3900, 3901, 4007, and 4013.

(b) Subject to Section 3602, subdivision (a) applies notwithstanding any other provision of law and notwithstanding that the proceeding has not been brought to trial within the time limits specified in Chapter 1.5 (commencing with Section 583.110) of Title 8 of Part 2 of the Code of Civil Procedure. *(Stats.1992, c. 162 (A.B.2650), § 10, operative Jan. 1, 1994. Amended by Stats.1993, c. 219 (A.B.1500), § 121.)*

Law Revision Commission Comments

Enactment [Revised Comment]

Section 3601 continues the first sentence of former Civil Code Section 4357(b) without substantive change. In subdivision (a), the references to specific Family Code sections are narrower than the former references to former Civil Code sections. These are not substantive changes, since the relevant parts of the former sections are continued in the Family Code sections. In subdivision (a)(1), a reference to "terminated" has been substituted for "revoked." This is not a substantive change. [23 Cal.L.Rev.Comm. Reports 1 (1993)].

Commentary

County of Orange v. Quinn, 97 Cal.App.4th 956, 118 Cal.Rptr.2d 833 (2002), holds that, despite the apparent restriction of Code of Civil Procedure § 583.310 to marital dissolution cases, by virtue of Family Code § 3600, the exception to the five-year dismissal rule expressed in this section applies to any case in which continuing pendente lite child support has been ordered. Compare *County of Orange v. Rosales, 99 Cal.App.4th 1214, 121 Cal.Rptr.2d 788 (2002)* (once father's parental rights were terminated, there was no "continuing child support order" and county's child support action was subject to dismissal five years after filing of claim).

Research References

Treatises and Practice Aids

Witkin, California Summary 10th Husband and Wife § 113, in General.

Witkin, California Summary 10th Parent and Child § 385, Support During Action.

§ 3602. Reconciliation

Unless the order specifies otherwise, an order made pursuant to this chapter is not enforceable during any period in which the parties have reconciled and are living together. *(Stats.1992, c. 162 (A.B.2650), § 10, operative Jan. 1, 1994.)*

Law Revision Commission Comments

Enactment [Revised Comment]

Section 3602 continues the last sentence of former Civil Code Section 4357(b) without substantive change. [23 Cal.L.Rev.Comm. Reports 1 (1993)].

Research References

Treatises and Practice Aids

Witkin, California Summary 10th Husband and Wife § 113, in General.

Witkin, California Summary 10th Husband and Wife § 204, in General.

Witkin, California Summary 10th Parent and Child § 385, Support During Action.

§ 3603. Time for modification or termination of orders; exceptions

An order made pursuant to this chapter may be modified or terminated at any time except as to an amount that accrued before the date of the filing of the notice of motion or order to show cause to modify or terminate. *(Stats.1992, c. 162 (A.B.2650), § 10, operative Jan. 1, 1994.)*

Law Revision Commission Comments

Enactment [Revised Comment]

Section 3603 continues the last sentence of former Civil Code Section 4357(a) without substantive change. A reference to "terminated" has been substituted for "revoked." This is not a substantive change. For provisions relating to modification or termination of support orders, see Chapter 6 (commencing with Section 3650). [23 Cal.L.Rev.Comm. Reports 1 (1993)].

Commentary

Relying on this section, *In re Marriage of Goodman & Gruen, 191 Cal.App.4th 627, 120 Cal.Rptr.3d 184 (2011)*, held that a family court exceeded its jurisdiction by modifying a temporary child and spousal support order retroactively and by modifying the temporary order absent a pending order to show cause or motion for modification.

Research References

Treatises and Practice Aids

Witkin, California Summary 10th Husband and Wife § 198, Order to Show Cause or Motion.

Witkin, California Summary 10th Husband and Wife § 207, Modification.

§ 3604. Rights of the parties or children with respect to subsequent orders

An order made pursuant to this chapter does not prejudice the rights of the parties or the child with respect to any subsequent order which may be made. *(Stats.1992, c. 162 (A.B.2650), § 10, operative Jan. 1, 1994.)*

Law Revision Commission Comments

Enactment [Revised Comment]

Section 3604 continues the second sentence of former Civil Code Section 4357(a) without substantive change. A reference to "child" has been substituted for "children." This is not a substantive change. See Section 10 (singular includes plural). [23 Cal.L.Rev.Comm. Reports 1 (1993)].

Research References

Forms

West's California Code Forms, Family § 3600, Comment Overview-- Spousal and Child Support During Pendency Of Proceeding.

Treatises and Practice Aids

Witkin, California Summary 10th Husband and Wife § 204, in General.

CHAPTER 5. EXPEDITED CHILD SUPPORT ORDER

§ 3620. Expedited support order

An order under this chapter shall be known as an expedited support order. *(Stats.1992, c. 162 (A.B.2650), § 10, operative Jan. 1, 1994.)*

Law Revision Commission Comments

Enactment [Revised Comment]

Section 3620 continues the second sentence of former Civil Code Section 4357.5(a) without substantive change. [23 Cal.L.Rev.Comm. Reports 1 (1993)].

Research References

Forms

West's California Judicial Council Forms FL-150, Income and Expense Declaration.
West's California Judicial Council Forms FL-380, Application for Expedited Child Support Order.
West's California Judicial Council Forms FL-381, Response to Application for Expedited Child Support Order and Notice Of Hearing (Family Code, §§ 3620-3634).
West's California Judicial Council Forms FL-382, Expedited Child Support Order (Family Code, §§ 3620-3634).

Treatises and Practice Aids

Witkin, California Summary 10th Husband and Wife § 174, in General.
Witkin, California Summary 10th Parent and Child § 386, in General.

§ 3621. Amount of support orders

In an action for child support that has been filed and served, the court may, without a hearing, make an order requiring a parent or parents to pay for the support of their minor child or children during the pendency of that action, pursuant to this chapter, the amount required by Section 4055 or, if the income of the obligated parent or parents is unknown to the applicant, then the minimum amount of support as provided in Section 11452 of the Welfare and Institutions Code. *(Stats.1992, c. 162 (A.B.2650), § 10, operative Jan. 1, 1994. Amended by Stats.1993, c. 219 (A.B.1500), § 122.)*

Law Revision Commission Comments

Enactment [Revised Comment]

Section 3621 continues the first sentence of former Civil Code Section 4357.5(a) without substantive change. A reference to Section 4055 has been substituted for the broader reference to former Civil Code Section 4721 (as added by 1990 Cal. Stat. ch. 1493, § 14, and repealed by 1992 Cal. Stat. ch. 46, § 8). This is not a substantive change, since the relevant part of the former section is continued in Section 4055. A reference to maintenance and education of the child has been omitted as surplus. See Section 150 (when used in reference to a child, "support" includes maintenance and education). [23 Cal.L.Rev.Comm. Reports 1 (1993)].

Research References

Forms

West's California Code Forms, Family § 3620, Comment Overview-- Expedited Child Support Order.

Treatises and Practice Aids

Witkin, California Summary 10th Parent and Child § 386, in General.

§ 3622. Application for order; forms and required information

The court shall make an expedited support order upon the filing of all of the following:

(a) An application for an expedited child support order, setting forth the minimum amount the obligated parent or parents are required to pay pursuant to Section 4055 of this code or the minimum basic standards of adequate care for Region 1 as specified in Sections 11452 and 11452.018 of the Welfare and Institutions Code.

(b) An income and expense declaration for both parents, completed by the applicant.

(c) A worksheet setting forth the basis of the amount of support requested.

(d) A proposed expedited child support order. *(Stats. 1992, c. 162 (A.B.2650), § 10, operative Jan. 1, 1994. Amended by Stats.1993, c. 219 (A.B.1500), § 123; Stats.1997, c. 14 (A.B.239), § 2, eff. May 30, 1997.)*

Law Revision Commission Comments

Enactment [Revised Comment]

Section 3622 continues the first sentence of former Civil Code Section 4357.5(b) without substantive change. A reference to Section 4055 has been substituted for the broader reference to former Civil Code Section 4721 (as added by 1990 Cal. Stat. ch. 1493, § 14, and repealed by 1992 Cal. Stat. ch. 46, § 8). This is not a substantive change, since the relevant part of the former section is continued in Section 4055. The reference to the "superior" court has been omitted as surplus. See Section 200 (jurisdiction in superior court). See also Section 95 ("income and expense declaration" defined). [23 Cal.L.Rev.Comm. Reports 1 (1993)].

Research References

Forms

West's California Code Forms, Family § 3620, Comment Overview-- Expedited Child Support Order.

Treatises and Practice Aids

Witkin, California Summary 10th Parent and Child § 387, Application and Order or Response.

§ 3623. Jurisdiction of court

(a) An application for the expedited support order confers jurisdiction on the court to hear only the issue of support of the child or children for whom support may be ordered.

(b) Nothing in this chapter prevents either party from bringing before the court at the hearing other separately noticed issues otherwise relevant and proper to the action in which the application for the expedited support order has been filed. *(Stats.1992, c. 162 (A.B.2650), § 10, operative Jan. 1, 1994. Amended by Stats.1993, c. 219 (A.B.1500), § 124.)*

Law Revision Commission Comments

Enactment [Revised Comment]

Section 3623 continues former Civil Code Section 4357.5(f) without substantive change. The reference to support of a "minor" child has been omitted. This is not a substantive change, but recognizes that in some cases support may be ordered for an adult child. See Sections 58 ("child for whom support may be ordered" defined), 3587 (court order to effectuate agreement for support of adult child), 3901 (duration of duty to support child), 3910 (duty to maintain incapacitated adult child), 4000 (civil action to enforce parent's duty to support child), 4001 (order for child support). [23 Cal.L.Rev.Comm. Reports 1 (1993)].

Research References

Treatises and Practice Aids

Witkin, California Summary 10th Parent and Child § 387, Application and Order or Response.

§ 3624. Effective date of expedited support order; service of application; effect of failure to respond

(a) Subject to Section 3625, an expedited support order becomes effective 30 days after service on the obligated parent of all of the following:

(1) The application for an expedited child support order.

(2) The proposed expedited child support order, which shall include a notice of consequences of failure to file a response.

(3) The completed income and expense declaration for both parents.

(4) A worksheet setting forth the basis of the amount of support requested.

(5) Three blank copies of the income and expense declaration form.

(6) Three blank copies of the response to an application for expedited child support order and notice of hearing form.

(b) Service on the obligated parent of the application and other required documents as set forth in subdivision (a) shall be by personal service or by any method available under Sections 415.10 to 415.40, inclusive, of the Code of Civil Procedure.

(c) Unless there is a response to the application for an expedited support order as provided in Section 3625, the expedited support order shall be effective on the obligated parent without further action by the court. *(Stats.1992, c. 162 (A.B.2650), § 10, operative Jan. 1, 1994.)*

Law Revision Commission Comments

Enactment [Revised Comment]

Subdivision (a) of Section 3624 continues the last sentence of the second paragraph of former Civil Code Section 4357.5(b) without substantive change. This subdivision has been rephrased to adopt language used in the Judicial Council form. See Cal. R. Ct. 1297 (Jan. 1, 1986) (application for expedited child support order). See also Section 95 ("income and expense declaration" defined).

Subdivision (b) continues former Civil Code Section 4357.5(c) without substantive change. Subdivision (c) continues the last paragraph of former Civil Code Section 4357.5(b) without substantive change. [23 Cal.L.Rev.Comm. Reports 1 (1993)].

Research References

Forms

West's California Code Forms, Family § 3620, Comment Overview-- Expedited Child Support Order.

Treatises and Practice Aids

Witkin, California Summary 10th Parent and Child § 387, Application and Order or Response.

Witkin, California Summary 10th Parent and Child § 388, Hearing and Order After Hearing.

§ 3625. Response to application; service; effect of filing

(a) A response to the application for the proposed expedited support order and the obligated parent's income and expense declaration may be filed with the court at any time before the effective date of the expedited support order and, on filing, shall be served upon the applicant by any method by which a response to a notice of motion may be served.

(b) The response to the application for an expedited support order shall state the objections of the obligated parent to the proposed expedited support order.

(c) The simultaneous filing of the response to the application for an expedited support order and the obligated parent's income and expense declaration shall stay the effective date of the expedited support order.

(d) No fee shall be charged for, or in connection with, the filing of the response. *(Stats.1992, c. 162 (A.B.2650), § 10, operative Jan. 1, 1994.)*

Law Revision Commission Comments

Enactment [Revised Comment]

Section 3625 continues former Civil Code Section 4357.5(d) without substantive change. See also Section 95 ("income and expense declaration" defined). [23 Cal.L.Rev.Comm. Reports 1 (1993)].

Research References

Forms

West's California Code Forms, Family § 3620, Comment Overview--Expedited Child Support Order.

Treatises and Practice Aids

Witkin, California Summary 10th Parent and Child § 387, Application and Order or Response.

§ 3626. Time set for hearing

The obligated parent shall cause the court clerk to, and the court clerk shall, set a hearing on the application for the expedited support order not less than 20 nor more than 30 days after the filing of the response to the application for the expedited support order and income and expense declaration. *(Stats.1992, c. 162 (A.B.2650), § 10, operative Jan. 1, 1994.)*

Law Revision Commission Comments

Enactment [Revised Comment]

Section 3626 continues the first sentence of former Civil Code Section 4357.5(e) without substantive change. [23 Cal.L.Rev.Comm. Reports 1 (1993)].

Research References

Forms

West's California Code Forms, Family § 3620, Comment Overview--Expedited Child Support Order.

Treatises and Practice Aids

Witkin, California Summary 10th Parent and Child § 388, Hearing and Order After Hearing.

§ 3627. Notice of hearing

The obligated parent shall give notice of the hearing to the other parties or their counsel by first-class mail not less than 15 days before the hearing. *(Stats.1992, c. 162 (A.B.2650), § 10, operative Jan. 1, 1994.)*

Law Revision Commission Comments

Enactment [Revised Comment]

Section 3627 continues the second sentence of former Civil Code Section 4357.5(e) without substantive change. [23 Cal.L.Rev.Comm. Reports 1 (1993)].

Research References

Treatises and Practice Aids

Witkin, California Summary 10th Parent and Child § 388, Hearing and Order After Hearing.

§ 3628. Failure to give notice of hearing

If notice of the hearing is not given as provided in Section 3627, the expedited support order becomes effective as provided in Section 3624, subject to the relief available to the responding party as provided by Section 473 of the Code of Civil Procedure or any other available relief whether in law or in equity. *(Stats.1992, c. 162 (A.B.2650), § 10, operative Jan. 1, 1994.)*

Law Revision Commission Comments

Enactment [Revised Comment]

Section 3628 continues the last sentence of former Civil Code Section 4357.5(e) without substantive change. The reference to Section 3624 has been substituted for the broader reference to former Civil Code Section 4357.5(b). This is not a substantive change, since the relevant part of the former section is continued in Family Code Section 3624. [23 Cal.L.Rev.Comm. Reports 1 (1993)].

Research References

Treatises and Practice Aids

Witkin, California Summary 10th Parent and Child § 388, Hearing and Order After Hearing.

§ 3629. Submission of state and federal income tax returns; review and examination; enforcement

(a) At the hearing on the application for the expedited support order, all parties who are parents of the child or children who are the subject of the action shall produce copies of their most recently filed federal and state income tax returns.

(b) A tax return so submitted may be reviewed by the other parties, and a party also may be examined by the other parties as to the contents of the return.

(c) Except as provided in subdivision (d), a party who fails to submit documents to the court as required by this chapter shall not be granted the relief that the party has requested.

(d) The court may grant the requested relief if the party submits a declaration under penalty of perjury that (1) no such document exists, or (2) in the case of a tax return, it cannot be produced, but a copy has been requested from the Internal Revenue Service or Franchise Tax Board. *(Stats. 1992, c. 162 (A.B.2650), § 10, operative Jan. 1, 1994.)*

Law Revision Commission Comments

Enactment [Revised Comment]

Section 3629 continues former Civil Code Section 4357.5(g) without substantive change. [23 Cal.L.Rev.Comm. Reports 1 (1993)].

Research References

Treatises and Practice Aids

Witkin, California Summary 10th Parent and Child § 388, Hearing and Order After Hearing.

§ 3630. Amount of expedited support order

(a) Except as provided in subdivision (b), the amount of the expedited support order shall be the minimum amount the obligated parent is required to pay as set forth in the application.

(b) If a hearing is held on the application, the court shall order an amount of support in accordance with Article 2 (commencing with Section 4050) of Chapter 2 of Part 2. *(Stats.1992, c. 162 (A.B.2650), § 10, operative Jan. 1, 1994.)*

Law Revision Commission Comments

Enactment [Revised Comment]

Subdivision (a) of Section 3630 continues without substantive change the first sentence of the second paragraph of former Civil Code Section 4357.5(b). Subdivision (b) continues former Civil Code Section 4357.5(h) without substantive change. [23 Cal.L.Rev. Comm. Reports 1 (1993)].

Research References

Treatises and Practice Aids

Witkin, California Summary 10th Parent and Child § 387, Application and Order or Response.

Witkin, California Summary 10th Parent and Child § 388, Hearing and Order After Hearing.

§ 3631. Order after hearing

When there is a hearing, the resulting order shall be called an order after hearing. *(Stats.1992, c. 162 (A.B.2650), § 10, operative Jan. 1, 1994.)*

Law Revision Commission Comments

Enactment [Revised Comment]

Section 3631 continues the first sentence of former Civil Code Section 4357.5(i) without substantive change. [23 Cal.L.Rev.Comm. Reports 1 (1993)].

Research References

Treatises and Practice Aids

Witkin, California Summary 10th Parent and Child § 388, Hearing and Order After Hearing.

§ 3632. Effective date of order after hearing; retroactive effect

An order after hearing shall become effective not more than 30 days after the filing of the response to the application for the expedited support order and may be given retroactive effect to the date of the filing of the application. *(Stats.1992, c. 162 (A.B.2650), § 10, operative Jan. 1, 1994.)*

Law Revision Commission Comments

Enactment [Revised Comment]

Section 3632 continues the last sentence of former Civil Code Section 4357.5(i) without substantive change. [23 Cal.L.Rev.Comm. Reports 1 (1993)].

Research References

Treatises and Practice Aids

Witkin, California Summary 10th Parent and Child § 388, Hearing and Order After Hearing.

§ 3633. Time for modification or termination of order

An order entered under this chapter may be modified or terminated at any time on the same basis as any other order for child support. *(Stats.1992, c. 162 (A.B.2650), § 10, operative Jan. 1, 1994.)*

Law Revision Commission Comments

Enactment [Revised Comment]

Section 3633 continues former Civil Code Section 4357.5(j) without substantive change. The words "or terminated" have been added. For provisions relating to modification or termination of a support order, see Chapter 6 (commencing with Section 3650). [23 Cal.L.Rev.Comm. Reports 1 (1993)].

Research References

Treatises and Practice Aids

Witkin, California Summary 10th Parent and Child § 386, in General.

§ 3634. Forms; preparation by Judicial Council

The Judicial Council shall prepare all forms necessary to give effect to this chapter. *(Stats.1992, c. 162 (A.B.2650), § 10, operative Jan. 1, 1994.)*

Law Revision Commission Comments

Enactment [Revised Comment]

Section 3634 continues former Civil Code Section 4357.5(k) without substantive change. See also Sections 95 ("income and expense declaration" defined), 115 ("property declaration" defined). [23 Cal.L.Rev.Comm. Reports 1 (1993)].

Research References

Forms

West's California Judicial Council Forms FL-150, Income and Expense Declaration.

West's California Judicial Council Forms FL-380, Application for Expedited Child Support Order.

West's California Judicial Council Forms FL-381, Response to Application for Expedited Child Support Order and Notice Of Hearing (Family Code, §§ 3620-3634).

West's California Judicial Council Forms FL-382, Expedited Child Support Order (Family Code, §§ 3620-3634).

CHAPTER 6. MODIFICATION, TERMINATION, OR SET ASIDE OF SUPPORT ORDERS

ARTICLE 1. GENERAL PROVISIONS

§ 3650. Support order

Unless the provision or context otherwise requires, as used in this chapter, "support order" means a child, family, or spousal support order. *(Stats.1992, c. 162 (A.B.2650), § 10, operative Jan. 1, 1994. Amended by Stats.1993, c. 219 (A.B.1500), § 124.5.)*

Law Revision Commission Comments

Enactment [Revised Comment]

Section 3650 is a new provision designed to facilitate drafting. Throughout this chapter this definition of "support order" applies, in addition to the general definition of this term. See Section 155 ("support order" defined). [23 Cal.L.Rev.Comm. Reports 1 (1993)].

Research References

Forms

West's California Code Forms, Family § 4405 Form 1, Notice Of Motion and Motion to Modify Order for Support.

Treatises and Practice Aids

Witkin, California Summary 10th Husband and Wife § 174, in General.

Witkin, California Summary 10th Husband and Wife § 273, Continuing Jurisdiction.

§ 3651. Powers of court; application of section

(a) Except as provided in subdivisions (c) and (d) and subject to Article 3 (commencing with Section 3680) and Sections 3552, 3587, and 4004, a support order may be modified or terminated at any time as the court determines to be necessary.

(b) Upon the filing of a supplemental complaint pursuant to Section 2330.1, a child support order in the original proceeding may be modified in conformity with the statewide uniform guideline for child support to provide for the support of all of the children of the same parents who were named in the initial and supplemental pleadings, to consolidate arrearages and wage assignments for children of the parties, and to consolidate orders for support.

(c)(1) Except as provided in paragraph (2) and subdivision (b), a support order may not be modified or terminated as to an amount that accrued before the date of the filing of the notice of motion or order to show cause to modify or terminate.

(2) If a party to a support order is activated to United States military duty or National Guard service and deployed out of state, the service member may file and serve a notice of activation of military service and request to modify a support order, in lieu of a notice of motion or order to show cause, by informing the court and the other party of the request to modify the support order based on the change in circumstance. The service member shall indicate the date of deployment, and if possible, the court shall schedule the hearing prior to that date. If the court cannot hear the matter prior to the date of deployment out of state, and the service member complies with the conditions set forth in the Servicemembers Civil Relief Act, Section 522 of the Appendix of Title 50 of the United States Code, the court shall grant a stay of proceedings consistent with the timelines for stays set forth in that section. If, after granting the mandatory stay required by Section 522 of the Appendix of Title 50 of the United States Code, the court fails to grant the discretionary stay described under the law, it shall comply with the federal mandate to appoint counsel to represent the interests of the deployed service member. The court may not proceed with the matter if it does not appoint counsel, unless the service member is represented by other counsel. If the court stays the proceeding until after the return of the service member, the service member shall request the court to set the matter for hearing within 90 days of return from deployment or the matter shall be taken off calendar and the existing order may not be made retroactive pursuant to subdivision (c) of Section 3653.

(3) A service member who does not file a notice of activation of military service and request to modify a support order or order to show cause or notice of motion prior to deployment out of state nonetheless shall not be subject to penalties otherwise authorized by Chapter 5 (commencing with Section 4720) of Part 5 on the amount of child support that would not have accrued if the order had been modified pursuant to paragraph (2), absent a finding by the court of good cause. Any such finding shall be stated on the record.

(4) Notwithstanding any other provision of law, no interest shall accrue on that amount of a child support obligation that would not have become due and owing if the activated service member modified his or her support order upon activation to reflect the change in income due to the activation. Upon a finding by the court that good cause did not exist for the service member's failure to seek, or delay in seeking, the modification, interest shall accrue as otherwise allowed by law.

(d) An order for spousal support may not be modified or terminated to the extent that a written agreement, or, if there is no written agreement, an oral agreement entered into in open court between the parties, specifically provides that the spousal support is not subject to modification or termination.

(e) This section applies whether or not the support order is based upon an agreement between the parties.

(f) This section is effective only with respect to a property settlement agreement entered into on or after January 1, 1970, and does not affect an agreement entered into before January 1, 1970, as to which Chapter 1308 of the Statutes of 1967 shall apply.

(g)(1) The Judicial Council, no later than 90 days after the effective date of the act adding this section, shall develop any forms and procedures necessary to implement paragraph (2) of subdivision (c). The Judicial Council shall ensure that all forms adopted pursuant to this section are in plain language.

(2) The form developed by the Judicial Council, in addition to other items the Judicial Council determines to be necessary or appropriate, shall include the following:

(A) The date of deployment and all information relevant to the determination of the amount of child support, including whether the service member's employer will supplement the service member's income during the deployment.

(B) A notice informing the opposing party that, absent a finding of good cause, the order will be made retroactive to the date of service of the form or the date of deployment, whichever is later.

(C) Notice that the requesting party must notify the court and the other party upon return from military duty and seek to bring any unresolved request for modification to hearing within 90 days of return, or else lose the right to modify the order pursuant to this section. *(Stats.1992, c. 162 (A.B.2650), § 10, operative Jan. 1, 1994. Amended by Stats.1994, c. 1269 (A.B.2208), § 31.4; Stats.1997, c. 599 (A.B.573), § 6; Stats. 2005, c. 154 (S.B.1082), § 2, eff. Aug. 30, 2005.)*

Law Revision Commission Comments

Enactment [Revised Comment]

Section 3651 continues without substantive change the fifth sentence of former Civil Code Section 4700(a), the third sentence of the last paragraph of former Civil Code Section 4801(a), the last sentences of subdivisions (a) and (b) of former Civil Code Section 4811, and, to the extent it applied to support orders, former Civil Code Section 4811(c). In subdivision (a), the "subject to" clause, which applied only to orders for child support, is extended to cover spousal support orders. This section has been revised to use "terminate" in place of "revoke." This is not a substantive change.

This section supersedes former Civil Code Section 247, insofar as that section applied to child, family, or spousal support orders. See also Sections 215 (service of notice prerequisite to validity of modification or subsequent order), 3580–3592 (support agreements), 3591 (authority to modify or terminate spousal support agreement), 3603 (modification or termination of order for child or spousal support during pendency of proceeding), 3653 (retroactivity of modification or termination), 3660–3668 (discovery before modification or termination), 3680–3694 (simplified procedure for modification of support order). [23 Cal.L.Rev.Comm. Reports 1 (1993)].

Commentary

Interpreting subsection (a) with respect to section 3587 adult child support, *In re Marriage of Rosenfeld & Gross, 225 Cal.App.4th 478, 169 Cal.Rptr.3d 918 (2014)*, holds that an order for adult child support based solely on the parties' agreement is judicially modifiable unless the agreement expressly and specifically provides that it is not modifiable. The holding of *Rosenfeld & Gross* parallels section 3591(c) modification of spousal support: It is modifiable unless the parties specifically agree that it is not modifiable.

In re Marriage of Alter, 171 Cal.App.4th 718, 89 Cal.Rptr.3d 849 (2009), holds that a trial court always has power, under subsections (a) and (e) and section 3585, to modify an existing child support order for a minor child upward *or downward*, regardless of the parties' contrary marital settlement agreement. *Alter* establishes that child support may be modified downward despite the parties' agreement to the contrary.

See Section 3591, Commentary.

In re Marriage of Shaughnessy, 139 Cal.App.4th 1225, 43 Cal.Rptr.3d 642 (2006), holds that the trial court did not abuse its discretion in ordering a reduction and termination of spousal support due to changed circumstances when the supported spouse, after adequate judicial notice, failed to make diligent effort to be self-supporting.

In re Marriage of West, 152 Cal.App.4th 240, 60 Cal.Rptr.3d 858 (2007), held that a former wife's change of career sufficed as a material change of circumstances justifying reconsideration of spousal support. *West* also held that a wife's receipt of cash from the sale of her share of a community property asset did not justify a reduction in spousal support.

In re Marriage of Khera and Sameer, 206 Cal.App.4th 1464, 143 Cal.Rptr.3d 81 (2012), held that a wife's post-divorce decision to pursue a doctoral degree instead of completing her MSW degree and entering the job market, as contemplated by the parties' marital settlement agreement, was not a change of circumstances justifying the modification of a *Richmond* step-down spousal support order. For further discussion of step-down orders, see Commentary to section 3591.

In re Marriage of Mosley, 165 Cal.App.4th 1375, 82 Cal.Rptr.3d 479 (2008), held that a trial court erred in denying an ex-spouse's request to modify his child and spousal support obligation based on changed circumstances when his income remained relatively constant, but changed from regular predictable periodic earnings to reduced periodic earnings and the uncertain possibility of a large year-end bonus. Although a bonus is income for purposes of child support, in view of the uncertainty of its receipt, his monthly child support should have been reduced to reflect his reduced monthly earnings, and the bonus should have been subject to child support if and when it was received.

For discussion and application of subsection (c), which prohibits judicial reduction of arrearages, see *County of Santa Clara v. Wilson, 111 Cal.App.4th 1324, 4 Cal.Rptr.3d 653 (2003)* (trial court lacks equitable power to forgive child support arrearages that accrued when the petitioner was incarcerated); *In re Marriage of Perez, 35 Cal.App.4th 77, 41 Cal.Rptr.2d 377 (1995)* (trial court's reduction of child support arrearages and forgiveness of interest due on arrearages were impermissible retroactive modifications within the meaning of Section 3651 (c), and they also ran afoul of the principles articulated in Code of Civil Procedure Sections 695.211 and 695.221); and *In re Marriage of Hamer, 81 Cal.App.4th 712, 97 Cal.Rptr.2d 195 (2000)* (trial court improperly held that by accepting former husband's payment of lesser amounts, former wife waived her right to collect the full amount of spousal and child support due under the judgment of dissolution). See also *In re Marriage of Brinkman, 111 Cal.App.4th 1281, 4 Cal.Rptr.3d 722 (2003)* (mother not estopped to present evidence of child support arrearages by accepting reduced payments recommended by family court settlement officer when she objected to the reduction and the settlement officer's recommendation was never implemented by court order).

Helgestad v. Vargas, 231 Cal.App.4th 719, 180 Cal.Rptr.3d 318 (2014), held that a nonmarital father who was ordered to pay child support in a paternity action could receive credit for any actual in-the-home child support he provided for the children in a period of reconciliation when he lived with the children and their mother in the home of the mother. *Helgestad* reasoned that such credit was not an impermissible subsection (c)(1) modification of arrearage, but rather an aspect of the court's calculation of the amount of arrearage. Credits for actual support when a child is living with a support obligor parent are known as *Jackson* credits, after *Jackson v. Jackson, 51 Cal.App.3d 363, 124 Cal.Rptr. 101 (1975)*, which applied such credits with respect to a period in which a divorced couple reconciled.

Although subsection (c) prohibits retroactive modification of support obligations and subsection (d) of Family Code section 291 permits a court to consider the defense of laches *only* with respect to obligations owed to the state, a court may stay enforcement of an arrears judgment on equitable grounds under certain circumstances. *Jackson*, supra, justified its use of credits as an exercise of this equitable power. Following *Jackson*, *In re Marriage of Wilson, 4 Cal.App.5th 1011, 208 Cal.Rptr.3d 779 (2016)*, held that a trial court had discretion to set aside or stay child support arrears incurred when the child lived with his paternal grandparents, the support obligor paid support to the grandparents, and the mother did not contribute to the support or care of the child.

In re Marriage of Tavares, 151 Cal.App.4th 620, 60 Cal.Rptr.3d 39 (2007), review denied Aug. 8, 2007, held that a noncustodial parent who failed to seek a modification of a child support order may not seek modification of accrued child support arrearages based on that order on the ground that certain expenses were never incurred by the custodial parent.

Relying on subsection (c), *In re Marriage of Sabine and Toshio M., 153 Cal.App.4th 1203, 63 Cal.Rptr.3d 757 (2007)*, held that an agreement between parties to forgive a portion of support arrearages is unenforceable when it does not resolve any bona fide dispute between the parties.

On January 13, 1999, the California Supreme Court depublished *County of Fresno v. Ruiz, 79 Cal.Rptr.2d 684 (1998),* in which the Court of Appeal ruled that subsection (c) bars retroactive modification of a support order even when there has been a subsequent determination of nonpaternity.

Research References

Forms

California Transactions Forms--Family Law § 2:61, Modifiability.

West's California Code Forms, Family § 3650, Comment Overview--Modification, Termination, or Set Aside Of Support Orders.

West's California Code Forms, Family § 4405 Form 1, Notice Of Motion and Motion to Modify Order for Support.

West's California Judicial Council Forms FL-343, Spousal, Partner, or Family Support Order Attachment.

Treatises and Practice Aids

Witkin, California Summary 10th Community Property § 33, Restrictions on Alteration Of Spouses' Legal Relations.

Witkin, California Summary 10th Contracts § 79, Public Policy Exception.

Witkin, California Summary 10th Husband and Wife § 41, Separation Agreements.

Witkin, California Summary 10th Husband and Wife § 219, Waiver After Judgment.

Witkin, California Summary 10th Husband and Wife § 273, Continuing Jurisdiction.
Witkin, California Summary 10th Husband and Wife § 276, Retroactive Modification.
Witkin, California Summary 10th Husband and Wife § 293, Change in Circumstances.
Witkin, California Summary 10th Husband and Wife § 356, General Rule: Support Provisions Are Modifiable.
Witkin, California Summary 10th Husband and Wife § 288A, (New) Activation and Out-Of-State Deployment Of Military Service Member.
Witkin, California Summary 10th Parent and Child § 383, in General.
Witkin, California Summary 10th Parent and Child § 421, Agreement to Support Adult Child.
Witkin, California Summary 10th Parent and Child § 439, Modification or Termination Of Support Order.
Witkin, California Summary 10th Parent and Child § 424A, (New) Suspension on Incarceration.

§ 3652. Attorney's fees and court costs

Except as against a governmental agency, an order modifying, terminating, or setting aside a support order may include an award of attorney's fees and court costs to the prevailing party. *(Stats.1992, c. 162 (A.B.2650), § 10, operative Jan. 1, 1994. Amended by Stats.1994, c. 1269 (A.B.2208), § 31.6; Stats.1999, c. 653 (A.B.380), § 3.)*

Law Revision Commission Comments

Enactment [Revised Comment]

Section 3652 continues the seventh sentence of former Civil Code Section 4700(a) without substantive change. A reference to "terminating" has been substituted for "revoking." This is not a substantive change. See also Section 3557 (attorney's fees for enforcement of support order). [23 Cal.L.Rev.Comm. Reports 1 (1993)].

Research References

Forms

West's California Code Forms, Family § 3650, Comment Overview--Modification, Termination, or Set Aside Of Support Orders.

Treatises and Practice Aids

Witkin, California Summary 10th Husband and Wife § 289, in General.
Witkin, California Summary 10th Husband and Wife § 306, in General.

§ 3653. Retroactive application of modification or termination of support orders

(a) An order modifying or terminating a support order may be made retroactive to the date of the filing of the notice of motion or order to show cause to modify or terminate, or to any subsequent date, except as provided in subdivision (b) or by federal law (42 U.S.C. Sec. 666(a)(9)).

(b) If an order modifying or terminating a support order is entered due to the unemployment of either the support obligor or the support obligee, the order shall be made retroactive to the later of the date of the service on the opposing party of the notice of motion or order to show cause to modify or terminate or the date of unemployment, subject to the notice requirements of federal law (42 U.S.C. Sec. 666(a)(9)), unless the court finds good cause not to make the order retroactive and states its reasons on the record.

(c) If an order modifying or terminating a support order is entered due to a change in income resulting from the activation to United States military service or National Guard duty and deployment out of state for either the support obligor or the support obligee, the order shall be made retroactive to the later of the date of the service on the opposing party of the notice of activation, notice of motion, order to show cause to modify or terminate, or the date of activation, subject to the notice requirements of federal law (42 U.S.C. Sec. 666(a)(9)), unless the court finds good cause not to make the order retroactive and states its reasons on the record. Good cause shall include, but not be limited to, a finding by the court that the delay in seeking the modification was not reasonable under the circumstances faced by the service member.

(d) If an order decreasing or terminating a support order is entered retroactively pursuant to this section, the support obligor may be entitled to, and the support obligee may be ordered to repay, according to the terms specified in the order, any amounts previously paid by the support obligor pursuant to the prior order that are in excess of the amounts due pursuant to the retroactive order. The court may order that the repayment by the support obligee shall be made over any period of time and in any manner, including, but not limited to, by an offset against future support payments or wage assignment, as the court deems just and reasonable. In determining whether to order a repayment, and in establishing the terms of repayment, the court shall consider all of the following factors:

(1) The amount to be repaid.

(2) The duration of the support order prior to modification or termination.

(3) The financial impact on the support obligee of any particular method of repayment such as an offset against future support payments or wage assignment.

(4) Any other facts or circumstances that the court deems relevant. *(Stats.1992, c. 162 (A.B.2650), § 10, operative Jan. 1, 1994. Amended by Stats.1998, c. 854 (A.B.960), § 1; Stats.1999, c. 653 (A.B.380), § 4; Stats.2005, c. 154 (S.B. 1082), § 3, eff. Aug. 30, 2005.)*

Law Revision Commission Comments

Enactment [Revised Comment]

Section 3653 continues without substantive change the sixth sentence of former Civil Code Section 4700(a), insofar as it related to modification or termination of a support order, and the last part of the last sentence of the last paragraph of former Civil Code Section 4801(a). References to "terminate" and its variants have been substituted for "revoke." These are not substantive changes. See also Section 4009 (retroactivity of child support order), 4333 (retroactivity of spousal support order). [23 Cal.L.Rev.Comm. Reports 1 (1993)].

Commentary

In 1998, the legislature amended this section to prohibit support obligors from recouping overpayments resulting from any retroactive reduction or termination of spousal support. In 1999, the legislature rewrote this section to reverse the effect of the 1998 amendment. *In re Marriage of Dandona & Araluce, 91 Cal.App.4th 1120, 111 Cal.Rptr.2d 390 (2001)*, and *In re Marriage of Petropoulos, 91 Cal.App.4th 161, 110 Cal.Rptr.2d 111 (2001)*, permit retroactive application of the statute to allow recovery of payments made during

1999, the year in which the 1998 amendment would otherwise control. They reasoned that the 1998 amendment was erroneously enacted, that the legislature corrected it the following year, that it was always the intention of the legislature to allow retroactive recovery, and that retroactive application would not violate due process because retroactive application is necessary to avoid a patent unfairness.

Applying subsection (b), *In re Marriage of Leonard, 119 Cal.App.4th 546, 14 Cal.Rptr.3d 482 (2004)*, held that a trial court did not abuse its discretion in denying a request to make retroactive a child support modification based on the parent's unemployment when the trial court provided specific reasons that were supported by evidence and sufficient to constitute "good cause" within the meaning of subsection (b).

Despite a child support order permitting future modification of child support retroactive to the date the children were no longer enrolled in child care, a trial court erred by modifying child support retroactive to that date, which was prior to the date the child support obligor filed his motion to modify support. *Stover v. Bruntz, 12 Cal.App.5th 19, 218 Cal.Rptr.3d 551 (2017)*, reasoned that this section's limitation on retroactivity could not be altered by court order.

Research References

Forms

West's California Code Forms, Family § 3650, Comment Overview--Modification, Termination, or Set Aside Of Support Orders.
West's California Judicial Council Forms FL-343, Spousal, Partner, or Family Support Order Attachment.

Treatises and Practice Aids

Witkin, California Summary 10th Husband and Wife § 276, Retroactive Modification.
Witkin, California Summary 10th Husband and Wife § 289, in General.
Witkin, California Summary 10th Husband and Wife § 288A, (New) Activation and Out-Of-State Deployment Of Military Service Member.
Witkin, California Summary 10th Parent and Child § 439, Modification or Termination Of Support Order.

§ 3654. Statement of decision

At the request of either party, an order modifying, terminating, or setting aside a support order shall include a statement of decision. *(Stats.1992, c. 162 (A.B.2650), § 10, operative Jan. 1, 1994. Amended by Stats.1999, c. 653 (A.B.380), § 5.)*

Law Revision Commission Comments

Enactment [Revised Comment]

Section 3654 continues without substantive change the first part of the last sentence of the last paragraph of former Civil Code Section 4801(a). The word "terminating" has been substituted for "revoking." This is not a substantive change. [23 Cal.L.Rev.Comm. Reports 1 (1993)].

Commentary

In re Marriage of Sellers, 110 Cal.App.4th 1007, 2 Cal.Rptr.3d 293 (2003), held that the trial court erred in failing to issue a statement of decision under this section when the party who initially requested the statement later waived the request, but the nonrequesting party sought compliance with the request.

Research References

Forms

West's California Judicial Council Forms FL-343, Spousal, Partner, or Family Support Order Attachment.

Treatises and Practice Aids

Witkin, California Summary 10th Husband and Wife § 289, in General.
Witkin, California Summary 10th Husband and Wife § 306, in General.

ARTICLE 2. DISCOVERY BEFORE COMMENCING MODIFICATION OR TERMINATION PROCEEDING

§ 3660. Purpose of article

The purpose of this article is to permit inexpensive discovery of facts before the commencement of a proceeding for modification or termination of an order for child, family, or spousal support. *(Stats.1992, c. 162 (A.B.2650), § 10, operative Jan. 1, 1994.)*

Law Revision Commission Comments

Enactment [Revised Comment]

Section 3660 continues former Civil Code Sections 4700.2(a) and 4801.1(a) without substantive change. The phrase "or termination" has been added to make clear that this article applies to a proceeding for termination of a support order. The same phrase has also been added to Sections 3662, 3663, and 3667 for consistency. [23 Cal.L.Rev.Comm. Reports 1 (1993)].

Research References

Forms

California Transactions Forms--Family Law § 3:52, Simplified Method Of Discovery for Purposes Of Modification Of Child Support or Family Support.
West's California Code Forms, Family § 3660, Comment Overview--Discovery Before Commencing Modification or Termination Proceeding.

Treatises and Practice Aids

Witkin, California Summary 10th Husband and Wife § 291, Discovery.

§ 3662. Methods of discovery; restrictions

Methods of discovery other than that described in this article may only be used if a motion for modification or termination of the support order is pending. *(Stats.1992, c. 162 (A.B.2650), § 10, operative Jan. 1, 1994.)*

Law Revision Commission Comments

Enactment [Revised Comment]

Section 3662 continues without substantive change the first sentence of the last paragraph of former Civil Code Section 4700.2(b) and the first sentence of the last paragraph of former Civil Code Section 4801.1(b). [23 Cal.L.Rev.Comm. Reports 1 (1993)].

Research References

Forms

West's California Code Forms, Family § 3620, Comment Overview--Expedited Child Support Order.

West's California Code Forms, Family § 3660, Comment Overview--Discovery Before Commencing Modification or Termination Proceeding.

Treatises and Practice Aids

Witkin, California Summary 10th Husband and Wife § 291, Discovery.

§ 3663. Discovery requests; restrictions

In the absence of a pending motion for modification or termination of a support order, a request for discovery pursuant to this article may be undertaken not more frequently than once every 12 months. *(Stats.1992, c. 162 (A.B.2650), § 10, operative Jan. 1, 1994.)*

Law Revision Commission Comments

Enactment [Revised Comment]

Section 3663 continues without substantive change the second sentence of the last paragraph of former Civil Code Section 4700.2(b) and the second sentence of the last paragraph of former Civil Code Section 4801.1(b). [23 Cal.L.Rev.Comm. Reports 1 (1993)].

Research References

Forms

West's California Code Forms, Family § 3620, Comment Overview--Expedited Child Support Order.

West's California Code Forms, Family § 3660, Comment Overview--Discovery Before Commencing Modification or Termination Proceeding.

Treatises and Practice Aids

Witkin, California Summary 10th Husband and Wife § 291, Discovery.

§ 3664. Requests for current income and expense declaration; authorized forms; requests to employer for income and benefit information; service

(a) At any time following a judgment of dissolution of marriage or legal separation of the parties, or a determination of paternity, that provides for payment of support, either the party ordered to pay support or the party to whom support was ordered to be paid or that party's assignee, without leave of court, may serve a request on the other party for the production of a completed current income and expense declaration in the form adopted by the Judicial Council.

(b) If there is no response within 35 days of service of the request or if the responsive income and expense declaration is incomplete as to any wage information, including the attachment of pay stubs and income tax returns, the requesting party may serve a request on the employer of the other party for information limited to the income and benefits provided to the party in the form adopted by the Judicial Council. The employer may require the requesting party to pay the reasonable costs of copying this information for the requesting party. The date specified in the request served on the employer for the production of income and benefit information shall not be less than 15 days from the date this request is issued.

(c) The requesting party shall serve or cause to be served on the employee described in this section or on his or her attorney a copy of the request served on the employer prior to the date specified in the request served on the employer for the production of income and benefit information. This copy shall be accompanied by a notice that, in a typeface that is intended to call attention to its terms, indicates all of the following:

(1) That information limited to the income and benefits provided to the employee by his or her employer is being sought from the employer named in the request for production.

(2) That the information may be protected by right of privacy.

(3) That, if the employee objects to the production of this information by the employer to the requesting party, the employee shall notify the court, in writing, of this objection prior to the date specified in the request served on the employer for the production of income and benefit information.

(4) That, if the requesting party does not agree, in writing, to cancel or narrow the scope of the request for the production of this information by the employer, the employee should consult an attorney regarding the employee's right to privacy and how to protect this right.

(d) The employee described in this section may, prior to the date specified in the request served on the employer for the production of income and benefit information, bring a motion pursuant to Section 1987.1 of the Code of Civil Procedure to quash or modify this request in the same manner as a subpoena duces tecum. Notice of this motion shall be given to the employer prior to the date specified in the request served on the employer for the production of income and benefit information. No employer shall be required to produce information limited to the income and benefits of the employee, except upon order of the court or upon agreement of the parties, employers, and employee affected.

(e) Service of a request for production of an income and expense declaration or for income and benefit information pursuant to this section or a copy thereof shall be by certified mail, postage prepaid, return receipt requested, to the last known address of the party to be served, or by personal service.

(f) The form adopted by the Judicial Council for purposes of the request on an employer described in subdivision (b) shall state that compliance with the request is voluntary, except upon order of the court or upon agreement of the parties, employers, and employee affected. *(Stats.1992, c. 162 (A.B.2650), § 10, operative Jan. 1, 1994. Amended by Stats.1995, c. 506 (A.B.413), § 2.)*

Law Revision Commission Comments

Enactment [Revised Comment]

Subdivision (a) of Section 3664 continues without substantive change the first paragraph of former Civil Code Section 4700.2(b) and the first paragraph of former Civil Code Section 4801.1(b). Subdivision (b) continues former Civil Code Sections 4700.2(d) and 4801.1(d) without substantive change. See also Section 95 ("income and expense declaration" defined). [23 Cal.L.Rev.Comm. Reports 1 (1993)].

Commentary

In re Marriage of Sorge, 202 Cal.App.4th 626, 134 Cal.Rptr.3d 751 (2012), holds that the section 2102 fiduciary duty terminates when a final judgment resolves all divorce-related issues. It does not continue during the minority of children to whom child support may be owed. Thus a former husband did not violate his fiduciary duty under this section by failing voluntarily to disclose his current financial circumstances when his former wife filed a motion to modify child support. Instead, the support obligee must serve a request upon the support obligor for a current income and expense declaration under this section.

Research References

Forms

California Transactions Forms--Family Law § 3:52, Simplified Method Of Discovery for Purposes Of Modification Of Child Support or Family Support.
West's California Code Forms, Family § 3620, Comment Overview--Expedited Child Support Order.
West's California Code Forms, Family § 3660, Comment Overview--Discovery Before Commencing Modification or Termination Proceeding.
West's California Judicial Council Forms FL-396, Request for Production Of an Income and Expense Declaration After Judgment.
West's California Judicial Council Forms FL-397, Request for Income and Benefit Information from Employer.

Treatises and Practice Aids

Witkin, California Summary 10th Husband and Wife § 291, Discovery.

§ 3665. Attachments to income and expense declaration; tax returns; disclosure

(a) A copy of the prior year's federal and state personal income tax returns shall be attached to the income and expense declaration of each party.

(b) A party shall not disclose the contents or provide copies of the other party's tax returns to anyone except the court, the party's attorney, the party's accountant, or other financial consultant assisting with matters relating to the proceeding, or any other person permitted by the court.

(c) The tax returns shall be controlled by the court as provided in Section 3552. *(Stats.1992, c. 162 (A.B.2650), § 10, operative Jan. 1, 1994.)*

Law Revision Commission Comments

Enactment [Revised Comment]

Section 3665 continues former Civil Code Sections 4700.2(c) and 4801.1(c) without substantive change. See also Section 95 ("income and expense declaration" defined). [23 Cal.L.Rev.Comm. Reports 1 (1993)].

Research References

Forms

California Transactions Forms--Family Law § 3:52, Simplified Method Of Discovery for Purposes Of Modification Of Child Support or Family Support.
West's California Code Forms, Family § 3660, Comment Overview--Discovery Before Commencing Modification or Termination Proceeding.
West's California Judicial Council Forms FL-396, Request for Production Of an Income and Expense Declaration After Judgment.

Treatises and Practice Aids

Witkin, California Summary 10th Husband and Wife § 174, in General.
Witkin, California Summary 10th Husband and Wife § 291, Discovery.

§ 3666. Enforcement of article

This article may be enforced in the manner specified in Sections 1991, 1991.1, 1991.2, 1992, and 1993 of the Code of Civil Procedure and in the Civil Discovery Act (Title 4 (commencing with Section 2016.010) of Part 4 of the Code of Civil Procedure), and any other statutes applicable to the enforcement of procedures for discovery. *(Stats.1992, c. 162 (A.B.2650), § 10, operative Jan. 1, 1994. Amended by Stats. 2004, c. 182 (A.B.3081), § 34, operative July 1, 2005.)*

Law Revision Commission Comments

2004 Amendment

Section 3666 is amended to reflect nonsubstantive reorganization of the rules governing civil discovery. [33 Cal.L.Rev.Comm. Reports 1023 (2003)].

Enactment [Revised Comment]

Section 3666 continues without substantive change the third sentence of the last paragraph of former Civil Code Section 4700.2(b) and the third sentence of the last paragraph of former Civil Code Section 4801.1(b). See also Section 3557 (attorney's fees for enforcement of support order). [23 Cal.L.Rev.Comm. Reports 1 (1993)].

Research References

Treatises and Practice Aids

Witkin, California Summary 10th Husband and Wife § 291, Discovery.

§ 3667. Incomplete or inaccurate income and expense declaration; penalties

Upon the subsequent filing of a motion for modification or termination of the support order by the requesting party, if the court finds that the income and expense declaration submitted by the responding party pursuant to this article was incomplete, inaccurate, or missing the prior year's federal and state personal income tax returns, or that the declaration was not submitted in good faith, the court may order sanctions against the responding party in the form of payment of all costs of the motion, including the filing fee and the costs of the depositions and subpoenas necessary to be utilized in order to obtain complete and accurate information. This section is applicable regardless of whether a party has utilized subdivision (b) of Section 3664. *(Stats.1992, c. 162 (A.B.*

2650), § 10, operative Jan. 1, 1994. Amended by Stats.1995, c. 506 (A.B.413), § 3.)

Law Revision Commission Comments

Enactment [Revised Comment]

Section 3667 continues former Civil Code Sections 4700.2(e) and 4801.1(e) without substantive change. See also Section 95 ("income and expense declaration" defined). [23 Cal.L.Rev.Comm. Reports 1 (1993)].

Research References

Treatises and Practice Aids

Witkin, California Summary 10th Husband and Wife § 291, Discovery.

§ 3668. Forms; adoption by Judicial Council

The Judicial Council shall adopt forms which shall be used in the procedure provided by this article. *(Stats.1992, c. 162 (A.B.2650), § 10, operative Jan. 1, 1994.)*

Law Revision Commission Comments

Enactment [Revised Comment]

Section 3668 continues without substantive change the last sentence of the last paragraph of former Civil Code Section 4700.2(b) and the last sentence of the last paragraph of former Civil Code Section 4801.1(b). [23 Cal.L.Rev.Comm. Reports 1 (1993)].

Research References

Forms

West's California Judicial Council Forms FL-396, Request for Production Of an Income and Expense Declaration After Judgment.

ARTICLE 3. SIMPLIFIED PROCEDURE FOR MODIFICATION OF SUPPORT ORDER

§ 3680. Legislative findings and declaration

(a) The Legislature finds and declares the following:

(1) There is currently no simple method available to parents to quickly modify their support orders when circumstances warrant a change in the amount of support.

(2) The lack of a simple method for parents to use to modify support orders has led to orders in which the amount of support ordered is inappropriate based on the parents' financial circumstances.

(3) Parents should not have to incur significant costs or experience significant delays in obtaining an appropriate support order.

(b) Therefore, it is the intent of the Legislature that the Judicial Council adopt rules of court and forms for a simplified method to modify support orders. This simplified method should be designed to be used by parents who are not represented by counsel. *(Added by Stats.1996, c. 957 (A.B. 1058), § 5.)*

Research References

Forms

West's California Code Forms, Family § 3680, Comment Overview--Simplified Procedure for Modification Of Support Order.

West's California Code Forms, Family § 3680 Form 1, Notice Of Motion and Motion for Simplified Modification Of Order for Child, Spousal, or Family Support.

West's California Code Forms, Family § 3680 Form 6, Responsive Declaration to Motion for Simplified Modification Of Order for Child, Spousal, or Family Support.

West's California Judicial Council Forms FL-390, Notice Of Motion and Motion for Simplified Modification Of Order for Child, Spousal, or Family Support.

West's California Judicial Council Forms FL-391, Information Sheet--Simplified Way to Change Child, Spousal, or Family Support.

West's California Judicial Council Forms FL-392, Responsive Declaration to Motion for Simplified Modification Of Order for Child, Spousal, or Family Support.

West's California Judicial Council Forms FL-393, Information Sheet--How to Oppose a Request to Change Child, Spousal, or Family Support.

Treatises and Practice Aids

Witkin, California Summary 10th Husband and Wife § 273, Continuing Jurisdiction.

Witkin, California Summary 10th Husband and Wife § 292, Simplified Procedure.

§ 3680.5. Local child support agency; monitoring; modifications

(a) The local child support agency shall monitor child support cases and seek modifications, when needed.

(b) At least once every three years, the local child support agency shall review, and, if appropriate, seek modification of, each child support case for which assistance is being provided under the CalWORKs program, pursuant to Chapter 2 (commencing with Section 11200) of Part 3 of Division 9 of the Welfare and Institutions Code. *(Added by Stats.1999, c. 652 (S.B.240), § 3. Amended by Stats.2007, c. 488 (A.B.176), § 1.)*

Research References

Treatises and Practice Aids

Witkin, California Summary 10th Husband and Wife § 273, Continuing Jurisdiction.

Witkin, California Summary 10th Parent and Child § 439, Modification or Termination Of Support Order.

ARTICLE 4. RELIEF FROM ORDERS

§ 3690. Authority to grant relief; findings; limitations operation

(a) The court may, on any terms that may be just, relieve a party from a support order, or any part or parts thereof, after the six-month time limit of Section 473 of the Code of Civil

Procedure has run, based on the grounds, and within the time limits, provided in this article.

(b) In all proceedings under this division, before granting relief, the court shall find that the facts alleged as the grounds for relief materially affected the original order and that the moving party would materially benefit from the granting of the relief.

(c) Nothing in this article shall limit or modify the provisions of Section 17432 or 17433.

(d) This section shall only be operative if Assembly Bill 196 [1], of the 1999–2000 Regular Session, is enacted and becomes operative. *(Added by Stats.1999, c. 653 (A.B.380), § 6.)*

[1] Stats.1999, c. 478 (A.B.196).

Research References

Forms

West's California Code Forms, Family § 3690, Comment Overview--Relief from Order.

West's California Judicial Council Forms FL-360, Request for Hearing and Application to Set Aside Support Order Under Family Code Section 3691.

West's California Judicial Council Forms FL-365, Responsive Declaration to Application to Set Aside Support Order.

West's California Judicial Council Forms FL-367, Order After Hearing on Motion to Set Aside Support Order.

Treatises and Practice Aids

Witkin, California Summary 10th Husband and Wife § 274, Default Award.

Witkin, California Summary 10th Husband and Wife § 289, in General.

Witkin, California Summary 10th Husband and Wife § 306, in General.

Witkin, California Summary 10th Husband and Wife § 307, Grounds and Time Limits.

Witkin, California Summary 10th Husband and Wife § 352, in General.

§ 3691. Grounds and time limits

The grounds and time limits for an action or motion to set aside a support order, or any part or parts thereof, are governed by this section and shall be one of the following:

(a) Actual fraud. Where the defrauded party was kept in ignorance or in some other manner, other than his or her own lack of care or attention, was fraudulently prevented from fully participating in the proceeding. An action or motion based on fraud shall be brought within six months after the date on which the complaining party discovered or reasonably should have discovered the fraud.

(b) Perjury. An action or motion based on perjury shall be brought within six months after the date on which the complaining party discovered or reasonably should have discovered the perjury.

(c) Lack of Notice.

(1) When service of a summons has not resulted in notice to a party in time to defend the action for support and a default or default judgment has been entered against him or her in the action, he or she may serve and file a notice of motion to set aside the default and for leave to defend the action. The notice of motion shall be served and filed within a reasonable time, but in no event later than six months after the party obtains or reasonably should have obtained notice (A) of the support order, or (B) that the party's income and assets are subject to attachment pursuant to the order.

(2) A notice of motion to set aside a support order pursuant to this subdivision shall be accompanied by an affidavit showing, under oath, that the party's lack of notice in time to defend the action was not caused by his or her avoidance of service or inexcusable neglect. The party shall serve and file with the notice a copy of the answer, motion, or other pleading proposed to be filed in the action.

(3) The court may not set aside or otherwise relieve a party from a support order pursuant to this subdivision if service of the summons was accomplished in accordance with existing requirements of law regarding service of process. *(Added by Stats.1999, c. 653 (A.B.380), § 6.)*

Commentary

Compare this section with section 2122. This section, with its six-month limitation, applies to support orders, while section 2122 applies to motions to set aside a judgment. *In re Marriage of Zimmerman, 183 Cal.App.4th 900, 109 Cal.Rptr.3d 96 (2010), review denied* (holding that motion to set aside a child support order for fraud and perjury was barred by the six-month limitation of this section).

Of course, a default child support judgment is absolutely void for lack of personal jurisdiction over the defendant when service of the summons and complaint was fraudulent. In such case, dismissal of a motion to enforce is mandatory. *County of San Diego v. Gorham, 186 Cal.App.4th 1215, 113 Cal.Rptr.3d 147 (2010)* (defendant was incarcerated on the date summons was purportedly served personally at his home address).

Research References

Forms

California Practice Guide: Rutter Family Law Forms Form 16:2, Request for Hearing and Application to Set Aside Support Order Under Family Code Section 3691.

West's California Code Forms, Family § 3690, Comment Overview--Relief from Order.

Treatises and Practice Aids

Witkin, California Summary 10th Husband and Wife § 307, Grounds and Time Limits.

§ 3692. Limits on set aside; inequity or changed circumstances

Notwithstanding any other provision of this article, or any other law, a support order may not be set aside simply because the court finds that it was inequitable when made, nor simply because subsequent circumstances caused the support ordered to become excessive or inadequate. *(Added by Stats.1999, c. 653 (A.B.380), § 6.)*

Research References

Treatises and Practice Aids

Witkin, California Summary 10th Husband and Wife § 306, in General.

§ 3693. Set aside of materially affected provisions

When ruling on an action or motion to set aside a support order, the court shall set aside only those provisions materially affected by the circumstances leading to the court's decision to grant relief. However, the court has discretion to set aside the entire order, if necessary, for equitable considerations. *(Added by Stats.1999, c. 653 (A.B.380), § 6.)*

Research References

Forms

West's California Judicial Council Forms FL-360, Request for Hearing and Application to Set Aside Support Order Under Family Code Section 3691.
West's California Judicial Council Forms FL-365, Responsive Declaration to Application to Set Aside Support Order.
West's California Judicial Council Forms FL-367, Order After Hearing on Motion to Set Aside Support Order.

Treatises and Practice Aids

Witkin, California Summary 10th Husband and Wife § 306, in General.

CHAPTER 7. HEALTH INSURANCE

ARTICLE 1. HEALTH INSURANCE COVERAGE FOR SUPPORTED CHILD

§ 3750. Health insurance coverage

"Health insurance coverage" as used in this article includes all of the following:

(a) Vision care and dental care coverage whether the vision care or dental care coverage is part of existing health insurance coverage or is issued as a separate policy or plan.

(b) Provision for the delivery of health care services by a fee for service, health maintenance organization, preferred provider organization, or any other type of health care delivery system under which medical services could be provided to a dependent child of an absent parent. *(Stats. 1992, c. 162 (A.B.2650), § 10, operative Jan. 1, 1994. Amended by Stats.1994, c. 147 (A.B.2377), § 1, eff. July 11, 1994; Stats.1996, c. 1062 (A.B.1832), § 1.)*

Law Revision Commission Comments

Enactment [Revised Comment]

Section 3750 continues former Civil Code Section 4726(a)(3) without substantive change. The reference to "children" has been omitted as surplus. See Section 10 (singular includes plural). [23 Cal.L.Rev.Comm. Reports 1 (1993)].

Research References

Treatises and Practice Aids

Witkin, California Summary 10th Husband and Wife § 174, in General.
Witkin, California Summary 10th Parent and Child § 415, in General.
Witkin, California Summary 10th Parent and Child § 416, Application and Order.
Witkin, California Summary 10th Parent and Child § 417, Provision and Termination Of Coverage.

§ 3751. Maintenance of health insurance coverage; cost of insurance; application by parents for coverage; continuation of coverage for supported child upon attainment of limiting age for dependent child

(a)(1) Support orders issued or modified pursuant to this chapter shall include a provision requiring the child support obligor to keep the agency designated under Title IV–D of the Social Security Act (42 U.S.C. Sec. 651 et seq.) informed of whether the obligor has health insurance coverage at a reasonable cost and, if so, the health insurance policy information.

(2) In any case in which an amount is set for current support, the court shall require that health insurance coverage for a supported child shall be maintained by either or both parents if that insurance is available at no cost or at a reasonable cost to the parent. Health insurance coverage shall be rebuttably presumed to be reasonable in cost if the cost to the responsible parent providing medical support does not exceed 5 percent of his or her gross income. In applying the 5 percent for the cost of health insurance, the cost is the difference between self-only and family coverage. If the obligor is entitled to a low-income adjustment as provided in paragraph (7) of subdivision (b) of Section 4055, medical support shall be deemed not reasonable, unless the court determines that not requiring medical support would be unjust and inappropriate in the particular case. If the court determines that the cost of health insurance coverage is not reasonable, the court shall state its reasons on the record. If the court determines that, although the obligor is entitled to a low-income adjustment, not requiring medical support would be unjust and inappropriate, the court shall state its reasons on the record.

(b) If the court determines that health insurance coverage is not available at no cost or at a reasonable cost, the court's order for support shall contain a provision that specifies that health insurance coverage shall be obtained if it becomes available at no cost or at a reasonable cost. Upon health insurance coverage at no cost or at a reasonable cost becoming available to a parent, the parent shall apply for that coverage.

(c) The court's order for support shall require the parent who, at the time of the order or subsequently, provides health insurance coverage for a supported child to seek continuation of coverage for the child upon attainment of the limiting age for a dependent child under the health insurance coverage if the child meets the criteria specified under Section 1373 of the Health and Safety Code or Section 10277 or 10278 of the Insurance Code and that health insurance coverage is available at no cost or at a reasonable cost to the parent or parents, as applicable. *(Stats.1992, c. 162 (A.B.2650), § 10, operative Jan. 1, 1994. Amended by Stats.1993, c. 876 (S.B.1068), § 16, eff. Oct. 6, 1993, operative Jan. 1, 1994; Stats.1994, c. 1269 (A.B.2208), § 33; Stats.2007, c. 617 (A.B.910), § 1; Stats.2010, c. 103 (S.B.580), § 1.)*

Law Revision Commission Comments

Enactment [Revised Comment]

Subdivisions (a)(2) and (b) of Section 3751 continues former Civil Code Section 4726(a)(1)-(2) without substantive change. References to "parents" have been omitted as surplus. See Section 10 (singular includes plural). See also Sections 2050–2053 (notice to insurance carriers in dissolution, nullity, or legal separation proceeding), 4006 (health insurance coverage as factor in determining child support).

Subdivision (a)(1) was added by 1993 Cal. Stat. ch. 876, § 16. [23 Cal.L.Rev.Comm. Reports 1 (1993)].

Commentary

For guidance on which parent's health insurance is primarily responsible for a child's health care expenses, see *Inter Valley Health Plan v. Blue Cross, 16 Cal.App.4th 60, 19 Cal.Rptr.2d 782 (1993), review denied 8/19/93, cert. denied sub nom Blue Cross/Blue Shield of Connecticut v. Inter Valley Health Plan, 114 S.Ct. 881 (1994)* (noncustodial father's insurance plan, rather than custodial mother's plan, primarily responsible under ERISA for child's hospital expenses by reference to California law; father's plan was made primary by California divorce decree that required father to maintain his children as beneficiaries on any health insurance available through his employment).

Research References

Forms

California Practice Guide: Rutter Family Law Forms Form 5:1, Stipulation to Orders Pending Trial (Attorney-Drafted).
California Practice Guide: Rutter Family Law Forms Form 5:2, Request for Order Re Child Custody, Child Support, Spousal Support, Attorney Fees, etc.
California Practice Guide: Rutter Family Law Forms Form 6:2, Stipulation Re Child Support and Order Thereon (Attorney-Drafted).
California Practice Guide: Rutter Family Law Forms Form 11:20, Sample Trial Brief.
West's California Judicial Council Forms FL-684, Request for Order and Supporting Declaration (Governmental).

Treatises and Practice Aids

Witkin, California Summary 10th Husband and Wife § 310, Local Child Support Agency.
Witkin, California Summary 10th Parent and Child § 415, in General.

§ 3751.5. Denial of enrollment; prohibited grounds; court or administrative order requiring parent to provide coverage; duties of employers or insurers

(a) Notwithstanding any other provision of law, an employer or insurer shall not deny enrollment of a child under the health insurance coverage of a child's parent on any of the following grounds:

(1) The child was born out of wedlock.

(2) The child is not claimed as a dependent on the parent's federal income tax return.

(3) The child does not reside with the parent or within the insurer's service area.

(b) Notwithstanding any other provision of law, in any case in which a parent is required by a court or administrative order to provide health insurance coverage for a child and the parent is eligible for family health coverage through an employer or an insurer, the employer or insurer shall do all of the following, as applicable:

(1) Permit the parent to enroll under health insurance coverage any child who is otherwise eligible to enroll for that coverage, without regard to any enrollment period restrictions.

(2) If the parent is enrolled in health insurance coverage but fails to apply to obtain coverage of the child, enroll that child under the health coverage upon presentation of the court order or request by the local child support agency, the other parent or person having custody of the child, or the Medi–Cal program.

(3) The employer or insurer shall not disenroll or eliminate coverage of a child unless either of the following applies:

(A) The employer has eliminated family health insurance coverage for all of the employer's employees.

(B) The employer or insurer is provided with satisfactory written evidence that either of the following apply:

(i) The court order or administrative order is no longer in effect or is terminated pursuant to Section 3770.

(ii) The child is or will be enrolled in comparable health insurance coverage through another insurer that will take effect not later than the effective date of the child's disenrollment.

(c) In any case in which health insurance coverage is provided for a child pursuant to a court or administrative order, the insurer shall do all of the following:

(1) Provide any information, including, but not limited to, the health insurance membership or identification card regarding the child, the evidence of coverage and disclosure form, and any other information provided to the covered parent about the child's health care coverage to the noncovered parent having custody of the child or any other person having custody of the child and to the local child support agency when requested by the local child support agency.

(2) Permit the noncovered parent or person having custody of the child, or a provider with the approval of the noncovered parent or person having custody, to submit claims for covered services without the approval of the covered parent.

(3) Make payment on claims submitted in accordance with subparagraph (2) directly to the noncovered parent or person having custody, the provider, or to the Medi–Cal program. Payment on claims for services provided to the child shall be made to the covered parent for claims submitted or paid by the covered parent.

(d) For purposes of this section, "insurer" includes every health care service plan, self-insured welfare benefit plan, including those regulated pursuant to the Employee Retirement Income Security Act of 1974 (29 U.S.C. Sec. 1001, et seq.), self-funded employer plan, disability insurer, nonprofit hospital service plan, labor union trust fund, employer, and any other similar plan, insurer, or entity offering a health coverage plan.

(e) For purposes of this section, "person having custody of the child" is defined as a legal guardian, a caregiver who is authorized to enroll the child in school or to authorize medical care for the child pursuant to Section 6550, or a person with whom the child resides.

(f) For purposes of this section, "employer" has the meaning provided in Section 5210.

(g) For purposes of this section, the insurer shall notify the covered parent and noncovered parent having custody of the child or any other person having custody of the child in writing at any time that health insurance for the child is terminated.

(h) The requirements of subdivision (g) shall not apply unless the court, employer, or person having custody of the child provides the insurer with one of the following:

(1) A qualified medical child support order that meets the requirements of subdivision (a) of Section 1169 of Title 29 of the United States Code.

(2) A health insurance coverage assignment or assignment order made pursuant to Section 3761.

(3) A national medical support notice made pursuant to Section 3773.

(i) The noncovered parent or person having custody of the child may contact the insurer, by telephone or in writing, and request information about the health insurance coverage for the child. Upon request of the noncovered parent or person having custody of the child, the insurer shall provide the requested information that is specific to the health insurance coverage for the child. *(Added by Stats.1996, c. 1062 (A.B.1832), § 2. Amended by Stats.1997, c. 599 (A.B.573), § 7; Stats.2000, c. 808 (A.B.1358), § 28, eff. Sept. 28, 2000; Stats.2000, c. 809 (A.B.2130), § 1; Stats.2001, c. 755 (S.B. 943), § 2, eff. Oct. 12, 2001.)*

Research References

Treatises and Practice Aids

Witkin, California Summary 10th Parent and Child § 415, in General.

§ 3752. Notice to the local child support agency designated as assigned payee for child support; policy information to be provided to custodial parent

(a) If the local child support agency has been designated as the assigned payee for child support, the court shall order the parent to notify the local child support agency upon applying for and obtaining health insurance coverage for the child within a reasonable period of time.

(b) The local child support agency shall obtain a completed medical form from the parent in accordance with Section 17422 and shall forward the completed form to the State Department of Health Services.

(c) In those cases where the local child support agency is providing medical support enforcement services, the local child support agency shall provide the parent or person having custody of the child with information pertaining to the health insurance policy that has been secured for the child. *(Stats.1992, c. 162 (A.B.2650), § 10, operative Jan. 1, 1994. Amended by Stats.2000, c. 808 (A.B.1358), § 30, eff. Sept. 28, 2000.)*

Law Revision Commission Comments

Enactment [Revised Comment]

Section 3752 continues former Civil Code Section 4726(b)-(c) without substantive change. References to "parents" and to "children" have been omitted as surplus. See Section 10 (singular includes plural). [23 Cal.L.Rev.Comm. Reports 1 (1993)].

Research References

Treatises and Practice Aids

Witkin, California Summary 10th Parent and Child § 415, in General.

§ 3752.5. Notice of availability of coverage; continuation of health insurance coverage upon child or adult attaining limiting age; modification of form of order by Judicial Council

(a) A child support order issued or modified pursuant to this division shall include a provision requiring the child support obligor to keep the obligee informed of whether the obligor has health insurance made available through the obligor's employer or has other group health insurance and, if so, the health insurance policy information. The support obligee under a child support order shall inform the support obligor of whether the obligee has health insurance made available through the employer or other group health insurance and, if so, the health insurance policy information.

(b) A child support order issued or modified pursuant to this division shall include a provision requiring the child support obligor and obligee to provide the information described in subdivision (a) for a child or an adult who meets the criteria for continuation of health insurance coverage upon attaining the limiting age pursuant to Section 1373 of the Health and Safety Code or Section 10277 or 10278 of the Insurance Code.

(c) The Judicial Council shall modify the form of the order for health insurance coverage (family law) to notify child support obligors of the requirements of this section and of Section 3752. Notwithstanding any other provision of law, the Judicial Council shall not be required to modify the form of the order for health insurance coverage (family law) to include the provisions described in subdivision (b) until January 1, 2010. *(Added by Stats.1993, c. 876 (S.B.1068), § 17, eff. Oct. 6, 1993, operative Jan. 1, 1994. Amended by Stats.2007, c. 617 (A.B.910), § 2.)*

Research References

Forms

California Practice Guide: Rutter Family Law Forms Form 5:1, Stipulation to Orders Pending Trial (Attorney-Drafted).

California Practice Guide: Rutter Family Law Forms Form 6:2, Stipulation Re Child Support and Order Thereon (Attorney-Drafted).

California Practice Guide: Rutter Family Law Forms Form 11:20, Sample Trial Brief.

Treatises and Practice Aids

Witkin, California Summary 10th Parent and Child § 415, in General.

§ 3753. Health insurance cost; separation from child support

The cost of the health insurance shall be in addition to the child support amount ordered under Article 2 (commencing with Section 4050), with allowance for the costs of health insurance actually obtained given due consideration under subdivision (d) of Section 4059. *(Added by Stats.1994, c. 1269 (A.B.2208), § 36.)*

Research References

Treatises and Practice Aids

Witkin, California Summary 10th Parent and Child § 415, in General.

ARTICLE 2. HEALTH INSURANCE COVERAGE ASSIGNMENT

Section

§ 3760. Definitions

As used in this article, unless the provision or context otherwise requires:

(a) "Employer" includes the United States government and any public entity as defined in Section 811.2 of the Government Code.

(b) "Health insurance," "health insurance plan," "health insurance coverage," "health care services," or "health insurance coverage assignment" includes vision care and dental care coverage whether the vision care or dental care coverage is part of existing health insurance coverage or is issued as a separate policy or plan.

(c) "Health insurance coverage assignment" or "assignment order" means an order made under Section 3761.

(d) "National medical support notice" means the notice required by Section 666(a)(19) of Title 42 of the United States Code with respect to an order made pursuant to Section 3773. *(Stats.1992, c. 162 (A.B.2650), § 10, operative Jan. 1, 1994. Amended by Stats.2000, c. 119 (S.B.2045), § 1.)*

Law Revision Commission Comments

Enactment [Revised Comment]

Subdivision (a) of Section 3760 continues former Civil Code Section 4726.1(m) without substantive change. Subdivision (b) continues former Civil Code Section 4726.1(p) without substantive change. Subdivision (c) continues the last sentence of former Civil Code Section 4726.1(a)(1) without substantive change. [23 Cal. L.Rev.Comm. Reports 1 (1993)].

Research References

Forms

West's California Judicial Council Forms FL-470, Application and Order for Health Insurance Coverage.

Treatises and Practice Aids

Witkin, California Summary 10th Parent and Child § 416, Application and Order.

§ 3761. Application for health insurance coverage assignment; assignment order

(a) Upon application by a party or local child support agency in any proceeding where the court has ordered either or both parents to maintain health insurance coverage under Article 1 (commencing with Section 3750), the court shall order the employer of the obligor parent or other person providing health insurance to the obligor to enroll the supported child in the health insurance plan available to the obligor through the employer or other person and to deduct the appropriate premium or costs, if any, from the earnings of the obligor unless the court makes a finding of good cause for not making the order.

(b)(1) The application shall state that the party or local child support agency seeking the assignment order has given the obligor a written notice of the intent to seek a health insurance coverage assignment order in the event of a default in instituting coverage required by court order on behalf of the parties' child and that the notice was transmitted by first-class mail, postage prepaid, or personally served at least 15 days before the date of the filing of the application for the order. The written notice of the intent to seek an assignment order required by this subdivision may be given at the time of filing a petition or complaint for support or at any later time, but shall be given at least 15 days before the date of filing the application under this section. The obligor may at any time waive the written notice required by this subdivision.

(2) The party or local child support agency seeking the assignment order shall file a certificate of service showing the method and date of service of the order and the statements required under Section 3772 upon the employer or provider of health insurance.

(c) The total amount that may be withheld from earnings for all obligations, including health insurance assignments, is limited by subdivision (a) of Section 706.052 of the Code of Civil Procedure or Section 1673 of Title 15 of the United States Code, whichever is less. *(Stats.1992, c. 162 (A.B.2650), § 10, operative Jan. 1, 1994. Amended by Stats.1993, c. 219 (A.B.1500), § 127; Stats.1994, c. 1269 (A.B.2208), § 37; Stats.2000, c. 808 (A.B.1358), § 31, eff. Sept. 28, 2000.)*

Law Revision Commission Comments

Enactment [Revised Comment]

Subdivision (a) of Section 3761 continues the first sentence of former Civil Code Section 4726.1(a)(1) without substantive change. Subdivision (b) continues former Civil Code Section 4726.1(c) without substantive change. A reference to "wages" has been omitted as surplus. This is not a substantive change. See also Sections 2050–2053 (notice to insurance carriers in dissolution, nullity, or legal separation proceeding), 5206 ("earnings" defined). [23 Cal.L.Rev.Comm. Reports 1 (1993)].

Research References

Forms

West's California Code Forms, Family § 3760, Comment Overview-- Health Insurance Coverage Assignment.
West's California Judicial Council Forms FL-478, Request and Notice Of Hearing Regarding Health Insurance Assignment.
West's California Judicial Council Forms FL-650, Statement for Registration Of California Support Order.
West's California Judicial Council Forms FL-684, Request for Order and Supporting Declaration (Governmental).
West's California Judicial Council Forms FL-478-INFO, Information Sheet and Instructions for Request and Notice Of Hearing Regarding Health Insurance Assignment.

Treatises and Practice Aids

Witkin, California Summary 10th Parent and Child § 416, Application and Order.

§ 3762. Denial of health insurance coverage assignment order; findings of court

Good cause for not making a health insurance coverage assignment order shall be limited to either of the following:

(a) The court finds that one of the conditions listed in subdivision (a) of Section 3765 or in Section 3770 exists.

(b) The court finds that the health insurance coverage assignment order would cause extraordinary hardship to the obligor. The court shall specify the nature of the extraordinary hardship and, whenever possible, a date by which the obligor shall obtain health insurance coverage or be subject to a health insurance coverage assignment. *(Stats.1992, c. 162 (A.B.2650), § 10, operative Jan. 1, 1994. Amended by Stats. 1994, c. 1269 (A.B.2208), § 38.)*

Law Revision Commission Comments

Enactment [Revised Comment]

Section 3762 continues former Civil Code Section 4726.1(a)(2) without substantive change. [23 Cal.L.Rev.Comm. Reports 1 (1993)].

Research References

Forms

West's California Code Forms, Family § 3760, Comment Overview-- Health Insurance Coverage Assignment.

Treatises and Practice Aids

Witkin, California Summary 10th Parent and Child § 416, Application and Order.

Witkin, California Summary 10th Parent and Child § 417, Provision and Termination Of Coverage.

§ 3763. Time for order of health insurance coverage assignment order; modification

(a) The health insurance coverage assignment order may be ordered at the time of trial or entry of a judgment ordering health insurance coverage. The order operates as an assignment and is binding on any existing or future employer of the obligor parent, or other person providing health insurance to the obligor, upon whom a copy of the order has been served.

(b) The order of assignment may be modified at any time by the court. *(Stats.1992, c. 162 (A.B.2650), § 10, operative Jan. 1, 1994. Amended by Stats.1994, c. 1269 (A.B.2208), § 39.)*

Law Revision Commission Comments

Enactment [Revised Comment]

Section 3763 continues former Civil Code Section 4726.1(b) without substantive change. In subdivision (a), the phrase "or other person providing health insurance to the obligor" has been added. This conforms with other sections in this article. See, e.g., Sections 3761, 3764–3765, 3767–3768, 3770. See also Sections 2050–2053 (notice to insurance carriers in dissolution, nullity, or legal separation proceeding). [23 Cal.L.Rev.Comm. Reports 1 (1993)].

Research References

Treatises and Practice Aids

Witkin, California Summary 10th Parent and Child § 416, Application and Order.

§ 3764. Effective date of assignment; copy of order and information to obligor; service of assignment order

(a) A health insurance coverage assignment order does not become effective until 20 days after service by the applicant of the assignment order on the employer.

(b) Within 10 days after service of the order, the employer or other person providing health insurance to the obligor shall deliver a copy of the order to the obligor, together with a written statement of the obligor's rights and the relevant procedures under the law to move to quash the order.

(c) Service of a health insurance coverage assignment order on any employer or other person providing health insurance may be made by first class mail in the manner prescribed in Section 1013 of the Code of Civil Procedure. *(Stats.1992, c. 162 (A.B.2650), § 10, operative Jan. 1, 1994. Amended by Stats.1994, c. 1269 (A.B.2208), § 40.)*

Law Revision Commission Comments

Enactment [Revised Comment]

Section 3764 continues former Civil Code Section 4726.1(d) without substantive change. See also Sections 2050–2053 (notice to insurance carriers in dissolution, nullity, or legal separation proceeding). [23 Cal.L.Rev.Comm. Reports 1 (1993)].

Research References

Treatises and Practice Aids

Witkin, California Summary 10th Parent and Child § 416, Application and Order.

§ 3765. Motion to quash assignment; grounds

(a) The obligor may move to quash a health insurance coverage assignment order as provided in this section if the obligor declares under penalty of perjury that there is error on any of the following grounds:

(1) No order to maintain health insurance has been issued under Article 1 (commencing with Section 3750).

(2) The amount to be withheld for premiums is greater than that permissible under Article 1 (commencing with Section 3750) or greater than the amount otherwise ordered by the court.

(3) The amount of the increased premium is unreasonable.

(4) The alleged obligor is not the obligor from whom health insurance coverage is due.

(5) The child is or will be otherwise provided health care coverage.

(6) The employer's choice of coverage is inappropriate.

(b) The motion and notice of motion to quash the assignment order, including the declaration required by subdivision (a), shall be filed with the court issuing the assignment order within 15 days after delivery of a copy of the order to the obligor pursuant to subdivision (b) of Section 3764. The court clerk shall set the motion for hearing not less than 15 days, nor more than 30 days, after receipt of the notice of motion. The clerk shall, within five days after receipt of the notice of motion, deliver a copy of the notice of motion to (1) the district attorney personally or by first-class mail, and (2) the applicant and the employer or other person providing health insurance, at the appropriate addresses contained in the application, by first-class mail.

(c) Upon a finding of error described in subdivision (a), the court shall quash the assignment. *(Stats.1992, c. 162 (A.B.2650), § 10, operative Jan. 1, 1994. Amended by Stats. 1994, c. 1269 (A.B.2208), § 41.)*

Law Revision Commission Comments

Enactment [Revised Comment]

Section 3765 restates former Civil Code Section 4726.1(e) without substantive change. A reference to "children" has been omitted as surplus. See Section 10 (singular includes plural). [23 Cal.L.Rev. Comm. Reports 1 (1993)].

Research References

Forms

West's California Judicial Council Forms FL-478, Request and Notice Of Hearing Regarding Health Insurance Assignment.
West's California Judicial Council Forms FL-478-INFO, Information Sheet and Instructions for Request and Notice Of Hearing Regarding Health Insurance Assignment.

Treatises and Practice Aids

Witkin, California Summary 10th Parent and Child § 416, Application and Order.

§ 3766. Commencement of coverage; selection of plan

(a) The employer, or other person providing health insurance, shall take steps to commence coverage, consistent with the order for the health insurance coverage assignment, within 30 days after service of the assignment order upon the obligor under Section 3764 unless the employer or other person providing health insurance coverage receives an order issued pursuant to Section 3765 to quash the health insurance coverage assignment. The employer, or the person providing health insurance, shall commence coverage at the earliest possible time and, if applicable, consistent with the group plan enrollment rules.

(b) If the obligor has made a selection of health coverage prior to the issuance of the court order, the selection shall not be superseded unless the child to be enrolled in the plan will not be provided benefits or coverage where the child resides or the court order specifically directs other health coverage.

(c) If the obligor has not enrolled in an available health plan, there is a choice of coverage, and the court has not ordered coverage by a specific plan, the employer or other person providing health insurance shall enroll the child in the plan that will provide reasonable benefits or coverage where the child resides. If that coverage is not available, the employer or other person providing health insurance shall, within 20 days, return the assignment order to the attorney or person initiating the assignment.

(d) If an assignment order is served on an employer or other person providing health insurance and no coverage is available for the supported child, the employer or other person shall, within 20 days, return the assignment to the attorney or person initiating the assignment. *(Stats.1992, c. 162 (A.B.2650), § 10, operative Jan. 1, 1994. Amended by Stats.1994, c. 1269 (A.B.2208), § 42; Stats.2002, c. 927 (A.B.3032), § 2.)*

Law Revision Commission Comments

Enactment [Revised Comment]

Section 3766 continues former Civil Code Section 4726.1(f) and (j) without substantive change. References to "children" have been omitted as surplus. See Section 10 (singular includes plural). In the last part of the second sentence of subdivision (a) and in the first sentence of subdivision (c), references to the "other person providing health insurance to the obligor" have been added. This conforms with the remainder of this section and with other sections in this article. See, e.g., Sections 3761, 3764–3765, 3767–3768, 3770. See also Sections 2050–2053 (notice to insurance carriers in dissolution, nullity, or legal separation proceeding). [23 Cal.L.Rev.Comm. Reports 1 (1993)].

Research References

Treatises and Practice Aids

Witkin, California Summary 10th Parent and Child § 417, Provision and Termination Of Coverage.

§ 3767. Duties of employer or health insurance provider

The employer or other person providing health insurance shall do all of the following:

(a) Notify the applicant for the assignment order or notice of assignment of the commencement date of the coverage of the child.

(b) Provide evidence of coverage and any information necessary for the child to obtain benefits through the coverage to both parents or the person having custody of the child and to the local child support agency when requested by the local child support agency.

(c) Upon request by the parents or person having custody of the child, provide all forms and other documentation necessary for the purpose of submitting claims to the insurance carrier which the employer or other person providing health insurance usually provides to insureds. *(Stats.*

1992, c. 162 (A.B.2650), § 10, operative Jan. 1, 1994. Amended by Stats.1996, c. 1062 (A.B.1832), § 3; Stats.1997, c. 599 (A.B.573), § 8; Stats.2001, c. 755 (S.B.943), § 3, eff. Oct. 12, 2001.)

Law Revision Commission Comments

Enactment [Revised Comment]

Section 3767 continues former Civil Code Section 4726.1(h)-(i) without substantive change. [23 Cal.L.Rev.Comm. Reports 1 (1993)].

Research References

Treatises and Practice Aids

Witkin, California Summary 10th Parent and Child § 417, Provision and Termination Of Coverage.

§ 3768. Failure to comply with a valid assignment order; liability

(a) An employer or other person providing health insurance who willfully fails to comply with a valid health insurance coverage assignment order entered and served on the employer or other person pursuant to this article is liable to the applicant for the amount incurred in health care services that would otherwise have been covered under the insurance policy but for the conduct of the employer or other person that was contrary to the assignment order.

(b) Willful failure of an employer or other person providing health insurance to comply with a health insurance coverage assignment order is punishable as contempt of court under Section 1218 of the Code of Civil Procedure. *(Stats. 1992, c. 162 (A.B.2650), § 10, operative Jan. 1, 1994. Amended by Stats.1994, c. 1269 (A.B.2208), § 43.)*

Law Revision Commission Comments

Enactment [Revised Comment]

Section 3768 continues former Civil Code Section 4726.1(g) without substantive change. See also Sections 2050–2053 (notice to insurance carriers in dissolution, nullity, or legal separation proceeding), 3557 (attorney's fees for enforcement of support order). [23 Cal.L.Rev.Comm. Reports 1 (1993)].

Research References

Treatises and Practice Aids

Witkin, California Summary 10th Parent and Child § 417, Provision and Termination Of Coverage.

§ 3769. Discrimination prohibited; violation; penalty

No employer shall use a health insurance coverage assignment order as grounds for refusing to hire a person or for discharging or taking disciplinary action against an employee. An employer who violates this section may be assessed a civil penalty of a maximum of five hundred dollars ($500). *(Stats.1992, c. 162 (A.B.2650), § 10, operative Jan. 1, 1994. Amended by Stats.1994, c. 1269 (A.B.2208), § 44.)*

Law Revision Commission Comments

Enactment [Revised Comment]

Section 3769 continues former Civil Code Section 4726.1(*l*) without substantive change. [23 Cal.L.Rev.Comm. Reports 1 (1993)].

Research References

Treatises and Practice Aids

Witkin, California Summary 10th Parent and Child § 416, Application and Order.

§ 3770. Termination of assignment order; grounds

Upon notice of motion by the obligor, the court shall terminate a health insurance coverage assignment order if any of the following conditions exist:

(a) A new order has been issued under Article 1 (commencing with Section 3750) that is inconsistent with the existing assignment.

(b) The employer or other person providing health insurance has discontinued that coverage to the obligor.

(c) The court determines that there is good cause, consistent with Section 3762, to terminate the assignment.

(d) The death or emancipation of the child for whom the health insurance has been obtained. *(Stats.1992, c. 162 (A.B.2650), § 10, operative Jan. 1, 1994. Amended by Stats. 1994, c. 1269 (A.B.2208), § 45.)*

Law Revision Commission Comments

Enactment [Revised Comment]

Section 3770 continues former Civil Code Section 4726.1(k) without substantive change. [23 Cal.L.Rev.Comm. Reports 1 (1993)].

Research References

Treatises and Practice Aids

Witkin, California Summary 10th Parent and Child § 416, Application and Order.

Witkin, California Summary 10th Parent and Child § 417, Provision and Termination Of Coverage.

§ 3771. Information provided to the local child support agency

Upon request of the local child support agency the employer shall provide the following information to the local child support agency within 30 days:

(a) The social security number of the absent parent.

(b) The home address of the absent parent.

(c) Whether the absent parent has a health insurance policy and, if so, the policy names and numbers, and the names of the persons covered.

(d) Whether the health insurance policy provides coverage for dependent children of the absent parent who do not reside in the absent parent's home.

(e) If there is a subsequent lapse in health insurance coverage, the employer shall notify the local child support agency, giving the date the coverage ended, the reason for the lapse in coverage and, if the lapse is temporary, the date upon which coverage is expected to resume. *(Stats.1992, c. 162 (A.B.2650), § 10, operative Jan. 1, 1994. Amended by Stats. 2000, c. 808 (A.B.1358), § 32, eff. Sept. 28, 2000.)*

Law Revision Commission Comments

Enactment [Revised Comment]

Section 3771 continues former Civil Code Section 4726.1(*o*) without substantive change. [23 Cal.L.Rev.Comm. Reports 1 (1993)].

Research References

Forms

West's California Code Forms, Family § 3760, Comment Overview--Health Insurance Coverage Assignment.

West's California Judicial Council Forms FL-475, Employer's Health Insurance Return.

Treatises and Practice Aids

Witkin, California Summary 10th Parent and Child § 417, Provision and Termination Of Coverage.

§ 3772. Forms; adoption by Judicial Council

The Judicial Council shall adopt forms for the health insurance coverage assignment required or authorized by this article, including, but not limited to, the application, the order, the statement of the obligor's rights, and an employer's return form which shall include information on the limitations on the total amount that may be withheld from earnings for obligations, including health insurance assignments, under subdivision (a) of Section 706.052 of the Code of Civil Procedure and Section 1673 of Title 15 of the United States Code, and the information required by Section 3771. The parties and child shall be sufficiently identified on the forms by the inclusion of birth dates, social security numbers, and any other information the Judicial Council determines is necessary. *(Stats.1992, c. 162 (A.B.2650), § 10, operative Jan. 1, 1994. Amended by Stats.1994, c. 1269 (A.B.2208), § 46.)*

Law Revision Commission Comments

Enactment [Revised Comment]

Section 3772 continues former Civil Code Section 4726.1(n) without substantive change. [23 Cal.L.Rev.Comm. Reports 1 (1993)].

Research References

Forms

West's California Judicial Council Forms FL-470, Application and Order for Health Insurance Coverage.

West's California Judicial Council Forms FL-475, Employer's Health Insurance Return.

Treatises and Practice Aids

Witkin, California Summary 10th Parent and Child § 416, Application and Order.

§ 3773. Title IV–D cases where support enforcement services are provided by local child support agency

(a) This section applies only to Title IV–D cases where support enforcement services are being provided by the local child support agency pursuant to Section 17400.

(b) After the court has ordered that a parent provide health insurance coverage, the local child support agency shall serve on the employer a national medical support notice in lieu of the health insurance coverage assignment order. The national medical support notice may be combined with the order/notice to withhold income for child support that is authorized by Section 5246.

(c) A national medical support notice shall have the same force and effect as a health insurance coverage assignment order.

(d) The obligor shall have the same right to move to quash or terminate a national medical support notice as provided in this article for a health insurance coverage assignment order. *(Added by Stats.1997, c. 599 (A.B.573), § 9. Amended by Stats.1998, c. 858 (A.B.2169), § 1; Stats.2000, c. 119 (S.B. 2045), § 2.)*

Research References

Forms

West's California Judicial Council Forms FL-478, Request and Notice Of Hearing Regarding Health Insurance Assignment.

West's California Judicial Council Forms FL-478-INFO, Information Sheet and Instructions for Request and Notice Of Hearing Regarding Health Insurance Assignment.

Treatises and Practice Aids

Witkin, California Summary 10th Parent and Child § 416, Application and Order.

CHAPTER 8. DEFERRED SALE OF HOME ORDER

§ 3800. Definitions

As used in this chapter:

(a) "Custodial parent" means a party awarded physical custody of a child.

(b) "Deferred sale of home order" means an order that temporarily delays the sale and awards the temporary exclusive use and possession of the family home to a custodial parent of a minor child or child for whom support is authorized under Sections 3900 and 3901 or under Section 3910, whether or not the custodial parent has sole or joint custody, in order to minimize the adverse impact of dissolution of marriage or legal separation of the parties on the welfare of the child.

(c) "Resident parent" means a party who has requested or who has already been awarded a deferred sale of home order. *(Stats.1992, c. 162 (A.B.2650), § 10, operative Jan. 1, 1994.)*

Law Revision Commission Comments

Enactment [Revised Comment]

Section 3800 continues former Civil Code Section 4700.10(a) without substantive change. [23 Cal.L.Rev.Comm. Reports 1 (1993)].

Commentary

In re Marriage of Braud, 45 Cal.App.4th 797, 53 Cal.Rptr.2d 179 (1996), interprets Section 3800 to allow a deferred sale of home order even when the noncustodial parent, that is, the parent who will not enjoy use and possession of the family home, has a separate property interest in the home. *Braud* involved a community property family home to which the noncustodial spouse had made significant Section 2640 separate property contributions. For further discussion, see Section 2550, Commentary and Section 2640, Commentary.

Research References

Forms

California Transactions Forms--Family Law § 3:38, Deferred Sale Of Residence.

Treatises and Practice Aids

Witkin, California Summary 10th Community Property § 207, Statutory Procedure and Factors.
Witkin, California Summary 10th Husband and Wife § 174, in General.
Witkin, California Summary 10th Parent and Child § 284, Trial.
Witkin, California Summary 10th Parent and Child § 411, Factors Rebutting Presumption.

§ 3801. Determination of economic feasibility of deferred sale

(a) If one of the parties has requested a deferred sale of home order pursuant to this chapter, the court shall first determine whether it is economically feasible to maintain the payments of any note secured by a deed of trust, property taxes, insurance for the home during the period the sale of the home is deferred, and the condition of the home comparable to that at the time of trial.

(b) In making this determination, the court shall consider all of the following:

(1) The resident parent's income.

(2) The availability of spousal support, child support, or both spousal and child support.

(3) Any other sources of funds available to make those payments.

(c) It is the intent of the Legislature, by requiring the determination under this section, to do all of the following:

(1) Avoid the likelihood of possible defaults on the payments of notes and resulting foreclosures.

(2) Avoid inadequate insurance coverage.

(3) Prevent deterioration of the condition of the family home.

(4) Prevent any other circumstance which would jeopardize both parents' equity in the home. *(Stats.1992, c. 162 (A.B.2650), § 10, operative Jan. 1, 1994.)*

Law Revision Commission Comments

Enactment [Revised Comment]

Section 3801 continues the first three sentences of former Civil Code Section 4700.10(b) without substantive change. [23 Cal.L.Rev. Comm. Reports 1 (1993)].

Research References

Forms

California Transactions Forms--Family Law § 3:38, Deferred Sale Of Residence.

Treatises and Practice Aids

Witkin, California Summary 10th Community Property § 207, Statutory Procedure and Factors.
Witkin, California Summary 10th Community Property § 208, Orders.

§ 3802. Grant or denial of order; discretion of court

(a) If the court determines pursuant to Section 3801 that it is economically feasible to consider ordering a deferred sale of the family home, the court may grant a deferred sale of home order to a custodial parent if the court determines that the order is necessary in order to minimize the adverse impact of dissolution of marriage or legal separation of the parties on the child.

(b) In exercising its discretion to grant or deny a deferred sale of home order, the court shall consider all of the following:

(1) The length of time the child has resided in the home.

(2) The child's placement or grade in school.

(3) The accessibility and convenience of the home to the child's school and other services or facilities used by and available to the child, including child care.

(4) Whether the home has been adapted or modified to accommodate any physical disabilities of a child or a resident parent in a manner that a change in residence may adversely affect the ability of the resident parent to meet the needs of the child.

(5) The emotional detriment to the child associated with a change in residence.

(6) The extent to which the location of the home permits the resident parent to continue employment.

(7) The financial ability of each parent to obtain suitable housing.

(8) The tax consequences to the parents.

(9) The economic detriment to the nonresident parent in the event of a deferred sale of home order.

(10) Any other factors the court deems just and equitable. *(Stats.1992, c. 162 (A.B.2650), § 10, operative Jan. 1, 1994.)*

Law Revision Commission Comments

Enactment [Revised Comment]

Subdivision (a) of Section 3802 continues without substantive change the introductory clause of the fourth sentence of subdivision (b) and the first sentence of subdivision (c) of former Civil Code Section 4700.10. Subdivision (b) continues the remainder of the fourth sentence of former Civil Code Section 4700.10(b) without substantive change. [23 Cal.L.Rev.Comm. Reports 1 (1993)].

Commentary

For legislative history and analysis of this section, see *In re Marriage of Braud, 45 Cal.App.4th 797, 814–19, 53 Cal.Rptr.2d 179 (1996)*.

Research References

Forms

California Transactions Forms--Family Law § 3:38, Deferred Sale Of Residence.

Treatises and Practice Aids

Witkin, California Summary 10th Community Property § 207, Statutory Procedure and Factors.

Witkin, California Summary 10th Community Property § 208, Orders.

§ 3803. Contents of order

A deferred sale of home order shall state the duration of the order and may include the legal description and assessor's parcel number of the real property which is subject to the order. *(Stats.1992, c. 162 (A.B.2650), § 10, operative Jan. 1, 1994.)*

Law Revision Commission Comments

Enactment [Revised Comment]

Section 3803 continues without substantive change the first part of the second sentence of former Civil Code Section 4700.10(c). [23 Cal.L.Rev.Comm. Reports 1 (1993)].

Research References

Treatises and Practice Aids

Witkin, California Summary 10th Community Property § 208, Orders.

§ 3804. Recordation of order

A deferred sale of home order may be recorded in the office of the county recorder of the county in which the real property is located. *(Stats.1992, c. 162 (A.B.2650), § 10, operative Jan. 1, 1994.)*

Law Revision Commission Comments

Enactment [Revised Comment]

Section 3804 continues without substantive change the last part of the second sentence of former Civil Code Section 4700.10(c). [23 Cal.L.Rev.Comm. Reports 1 (1993)].

Research References

Treatises and Practice Aids

Witkin, California Summary 10th Community Property § 208, Orders.

§ 3806. Payment of maintenance and capital improvement costs; order

The court may make an order specifying the parties' respective responsibilities for the payment of the costs of routine maintenance and capital improvements. *(Stats.1992, c. 162 (A.B.2650), § 10, operative Jan. 1, 1994.)*

Law Revision Commission Comments

Enactment [Revised Comment]

Section 3806 continues former Civil Code Section 4700.10(d) without change. [23 Cal.L.Rev.Comm. Reports 1 (1993)].

Research References

Treatises and Practice Aids

Witkin, California Summary 10th Community Property § 208, Orders.

§ 3807. Time for modification or termination of orders; exceptions

Except as otherwise agreed to by the parties in writing, a deferred sale of home order may be modified or terminated at any time at the discretion of the court. *(Stats.1992, c. 162 (A.B.2650), § 10, operative Jan. 1, 1994.)*

Law Revision Commission Comments

Enactment [Revised Comment]

Section 3807 continues former Civil Code Section 4700.10(e)(1) without substantive change. [23 Cal.L.Rev.Comm. Reports 1 (1993)].

Research References

Treatises and Practice Aids

Witkin, California Summary 10th Community Property § 208, Orders.

§ 3808. Remarriage or other change in circumstances; rebuttable presumption

Except as otherwise agreed to by the parties in writing, if the party awarded the deferred sale of home order remarries, or if there is otherwise a change in circumstances affecting the determinations made pursuant to Section 3801 or 3802 or affecting the economic status of the parties or the children on which the award is based, a rebuttable presumption, affecting the burden of proof, is created that further deferral of the sale is no longer an equitable method of minimizing the adverse impact of the dissolution of marriage or legal separation of the parties on the children. *(Stats.1992, c. 162 (A.B.2650), § 10, operative Jan. 1, 1994.)*

Law Revision Commission Comments

Enactment [Revised Comment]

Section 3808 continues former Civil Code Section 4700.10(e)(2) without substantive change. [23 Cal.L.Rev.Comm. Reports 1 (1993)].

Commentary

For legislative history and analysis of this section, see *In re Marriage of Braud, 45 Cal.App.4th 797, 814–19, 53 Cal.Rptr.2d 179 (1996)*.

Research References

Forms

California Transactions Forms--Family Law § 3:38, Deferred Sale Of Residence.

Treatises and Practice Aids

Witkin, California Summary 10th Community Property § 208, Orders.

§ 3809. Reservation of jurisdiction

In making an order pursuant to this chapter, the court shall reserve jurisdiction to determine any issues that arise with respect to the deferred sale of home order including, but not limited to, the maintenance of the home and the tax consequences to each party. *(Stats.1992, c. 162 (A.B.2650), § 10, operative Jan. 1, 1994.)*

Law Revision Commission Comments

Enactment [Revised Comment]

Section 3809 continues former Civil Code Section 4700.10(f) without substantive change. The word "any" has been substituted for "any and all," since "all" is surplus. [23 Cal.L.Rev.Comm. Reports 1 (1993)].

Research References

Treatises and Practice Aids

Witkin, California Summary 10th Community Property § 208, Orders.

§ 3810. Application of chapter

This chapter is applicable regardless of whether the deferred sale of home order is made before or after January 1, 1989. *(Stats.1992, c. 162 (A.B.2650), § 10, operative Jan. 1, 1994.)*

Law Revision Commission Comments

Enactment [Revised Comment]

Section 3810 continues former Civil Code Section 4700.10(g) without substantive change. [23 Cal.L.Rev.Comm. Reports 1 (1993)].

Research References

Forms

California Transactions Forms--Family Law § 3:38, Deferred Sale Of Residence.

CHAPTER 9. SOFTWARE USED TO DETERMINE SUPPORT

§ 3830. Conformation of software to rules of court; analysis; costs

(a) On and after January 1, 1994, no court shall use any computer software to assist in determining the appropriate amount of child support or spousal support obligations, unless the software conforms to rules of court adopted by the Judicial Council prescribing standards for the software, which shall ensure that it performs in a manner consistent with the applicable statutes and rules of court for determination of child support or spousal support.

(b) The Judicial Council may contract with an outside agency or organization to analyze software to ensure that it conforms to the standards established by the Judicial Council. The cost of this analysis shall be paid by the applicant software producers and fees therefor shall be established by the Judicial Council in an amount that in the aggregate will defray its costs of administering this section. *(Added by Stats.1993, c. 219 (A.B.1500), § 129.)*

Law Revision Commission Comments

Enactment [Revised Comment]

Section 3830 continues former Civil Code Section 4395 without substantive change. [23 Cal.L.Rev.Comm. Reports 1 (1993)].

Commentary

See Rule 5.275, California Rules of Court (Family Law Rules). For discussion, see 1993 Cal. Fam. L. Monthly 322, and George Norton, *Calculating Spousal Support: "Fixed" and "Floating Shares" Explained,* 1994 Cal. Fam. L. Monthly 24.

Research References

Forms

California Practice Guide: Rutter Family Law Forms Form 5:2, Request for Order Re Child Custody, Child Support, Spousal Support, Attorney Fees, etc.

California Practice Guide: Rutter Family Law Forms Form 6:11, Request for Order Re Guideline Child Support, Temporary "Guideline" Spousal Support and Family Code S4062 "Add-On" Child Support.

California Transactions Forms--Family Law § 3:22, Mandatory Compliance With Statewide Guidelines.

Treatises and Practice Aids

Witkin, California Summary 10th Husband and Wife § 192, Use Of Guidelines.

Witkin, California Summary 10th Parent and Child § 394, in General.

Part 2

CHILD SUPPORT

CHAPTER 1. DUTY OF PARENT TO SUPPORT CHILD

ARTICLE 1. SUPPORT OF MINOR CHILD

§ 3900. Equal duty of parents to support child

Subject to this division, the father and mother of a minor child have an equal responsibility to support their child in the manner suitable to the child's circumstances. *(Stats.1992, c. 162 (A.B.2650), § 10, operative Jan. 1, 1994.)*

Law Revision Commission Comments

Enactment [Revised Comment]

Section 3900 continues without substantive change former Civil Code Section 196(a), the first sentence of former Civil Code Section 196a, and former Civil Code Section 242 to the extent that section applied to the duty to support a child. The introductory clause has been substituted for the sections referred to in the second sentence of former Civil Code Section 242. This is not a substantive change. References to the duty to provide for education have been omitted as surplus. See Section 150 ("support" defined to include education when used in reference to child). The provision of former Civil Code Section 196(a) requiring consideration of "the respective earnings or earning capacities of the parents" has been omitted. The factors to be considered in determining child support are provided in Article 2 (commencing with Section 4050) of Chapter 3.

The duty provided in Section 3900 is subject to the other provisions in this division, including but not limited to, Article 2 (commencing with Section 4050) of Chapter 3 (child support guideline). See also Sections 3028 (compensation for failure to assume caretaker responsibility or thwarting other parent attempting to exercise custody or visitation rights), 3556 (effect of failure to implement custody or visitation rights), 3901 (duration of duty); Code Civ. Proc. § 395 (venue for action to enforce support obligation). [23 Cal.L.Rev. Comm. Reports 1 (1993)].

Commentary

Even though the child's minor father was the victim of statutory rape (unlawful intercourse with a minor under 16 years of age), the father is legally responsible for the child's support. *County of San Luis Obispo v. Nathaniel J., 50 Cal.App.4th 842, 57 Cal.Rptr.2d 843 (1996).*

Even though a man is not a child's biological parent, he may be required to support the child under the doctrine of parentage by estoppel, which requires (1) that the child have accepted a putative father's express or implied representation that he is the child's father and (2) that the representation continue for a sufficient time to establish a parent-child relationship and frustrate the opportunity of discovering the child's biological father. *Clevenger v. Clevenger, 189 Cal.App.2d 658, 11 Cal.Rptr. 707 (1961)*. For a review of the parentage-by-estoppel cases, see *In re Marriage of Pedregon, 107 Cal.App.4th 1284, 132 Cal.Rptr.2d 861 (2003)* (requiring husband to pay child support for his divorced wife's child even though he was not the biological father). Although all the parentage-by-estoppel cases have involved men, the doctrine would seem equally applicable to women.

Relying on this section as well as Sections 4053 and 7632, *Kristine M. v. David P., 135 Cal.App.4th 783, 37 Cal.Rptr.3d 748 (2006),* holds that a trial court's termination of a father's parental rights pursuant to the parents' stipulation is void as a matter of public policy and is an act that exceeds the court's jurisdiction. To similar effect, see *In re Marriage of Jackson, 136 Cal.App.4th 980, 39 Cal.Rptr.3d 365 (2006), review denied*, holding that a trial court's order granting a mother's motion, based on an agreement of the parents, to terminate her own parental rights was void because the order exceeded the court's jurisdiction.

Research References

Forms

California Practice Guide: Rutter Family Law Forms Form 1:32, Glossary Of Common Family Law Terms, Phrases and Concepts (Enclosure to Form 1:31).
California Transactions Forms--Family Law § 3:3, Child Support.
California Transactions Forms--Family Law § 7:43, Characterization Of Payments as Child Support.
California Transactions Forms--Family Law § 4:104, Paternity Acknowledgment.
Am. Jur. Pl. & Pr. Forms Parent and Child § 56, Introductory Comments.
West's California Code Forms, Family § 3900, Comment Overview--Duty Of Parent to Support Child.
West's California Judicial Council Forms FL-230, Declaration for Default or Uncontested Judgment.
West's California Judicial Council Forms FL-250, Judgment.
West's California Judicial Council Forms FL-260, Petition for Custody and Support Of Minor Children.
West's California Judicial Council Forms FL-270, Response to Petition for Custody and Support Of Minor Children.
West's California Judicial Council Forms FL-684, Request for Order and Supporting Declaration (Governmental).

Treatises and Practice Aids

Witkin, California Summary 10th Community Property § 207, Statutory Procedure and Factors.
Witkin, California Summary 10th Husband and Wife § 174, in General.
Witkin, California Summary 10th Parent and Child § 378, Former Law.
Witkin, California Summary 10th Parent and Child § 380, Duty to Support Minor Child.
Witkin, California Summary 10th Parent and Child § 385, Support During Action.
Witkin, California Summary 10th Parent and Child § 397, Annual Gross Income.
Witkin, California Summary 10th Parent and Child § 423, Support Of Disabled Indigent Adult Child.

§ 3901. Duration of duty of support

(a) The duty of support imposed by Section 3900 continues as to an unmarried child who has attained the age of 18 years, is a full-time high school student, and who is not self-supporting, until the time the child completes the 12th grade or attains the age of 19 years, whichever occurs first.

(b) Nothing in this section limits a parent's ability to agree to provide additional support or the court's power to inquire whether an agreement to provide additional support has been made. *(Stats.1992, c. 162 (A.B.2650), § 10, operative Jan. 1, 1994. Amended by Stats.1993, c. 219 (A.B.1500), § 130.)*

Law Revision Commission Comments

Enactment [Revised Comment]

Section 3901 continues without substantive change the first and last sentences of former Civil Code Section 196.5 and the first and last sentences of former Civil Code Section 4704.5. The transitional provisions found in the former sections—that the section does not apply to support agreements made or judgments entered before March 4, 1972—have been omitted as obsolete.

This duty may be enforced in the manner described in Section 4000 (civil action against parent to enforce duty of support). For provisions relating to enforcement of support orders, see Part 5 (commencing with Section 4500). See also Sections 3580–3587 (child support agreements), 3600–3604 (child support during pendency of proceeding), 3620–3634 (expedited child support order). [23 Cal.L.Rev.Comm. Reports 1 (1993)].

Commentary

Interpreting this section, *In re Marriage of Hubner, 94 Cal.App.4th 175, 114 Cal.Rptr.2d 646 (2001), review denied March 13, 2002*, holds that the trial court erred in suspending a parent's support obligation to an 18–year-old who was attending an American Field Service educational program in Japan, for which he would receive credit in his local American high school. *Hubner* observes that a child is not required to graduate high school as soon as possible or required to take only those courses necessary to graduate from high school in order to maintain eligibility for child support. In subsequent litigation between the same parties, *In re Marriage of Hubner, 124 Cal.App.4th 1082, 22 Cal.Rptr.3d 549 (2004)*, held that statutory interest on unpaid child support accrues from the period each payment originally came due during a period in which the trial court erroneously suspended the parent's child support obligation, and that the obligation to pay support ordered for a child who has reached the age of 18 but is still in high school is not contingent upon a monthly showing that all the conditions specified in subsection (a) remain satisfied.

Interpreting subsection (b) together with section 3587, *In re Marriage of Rosenfeld & Gross, 225 Cal.App.4th 478, 169 Cal.Rptr.3d 918 (2014)*, holds that an order for adult child support based solely on the parties' agreement is judicially modifiable unless the agreement expressly and specifically provides that it is not modifiable. The holding of *Rosenfeld & Gross* parallels section 3591(c) modification of spousal support: It is modifiable unless the parties specifically agree that it is not modifiable.

Research References

Forms

California Practice Guide: Rutter Family Law Forms Form 1:32, Glossary Of Common Family Law Terms, Phrases and Concepts (Enclosure to Form 1:31).

California Transactions Forms--Family Law § 3:25, Duration Of Child Support Obligation.

California Transactions Forms--Family Law § 3:26, Voluntary Support After Age Of Majority.

West's California Code Forms, Family § 3900, Comment Overview--Duty Of Parent to Support Child.

West's California Code Forms, Family § 4000, Comment Overview--Court-Ordered Child Support.

West's California Judicial Council Forms FL-430, Ex Parte Application to Issue, Modify, or Terminate an Earnings Assignment Order.

West's California Judicial Council Forms FL-684, Request for Order and Supporting Declaration (Governmental).

Treatises and Practice Aids

Witkin, California Summary 10th Community Property § 207, Statutory Procedure and Factors.

Witkin, California Summary 10th Husband and Wife § 4, Definitions.

Witkin, California Summary 10th Husband and Wife § 287, Change in Cost Of Child Support.

Witkin, California Summary 10th Parent and Child § 247, Custodial Parent Estopped by Violation from Obtaining Child Support.

Witkin, California Summary 10th Parent and Child § 385, Support During Action.

Witkin, California Summary 10th Parent and Child § 422, Support Of High School Student.

Witkin, California Summary 10th Parent and Child § 423, Support Of Disabled Indigent Adult Child.

§ 3902. Property of child; allowance to parent

The court may direct that an allowance be made to the parent of a child for whom support may be ordered out of the child's property for the child's past or future support, on conditions that are proper, if the direction is for the child's benefit. *(Stats.1992, c. 162 (A.B.2650), § 10, operative Jan. 1, 1994. Amended by Stats.1993, c. 219 (A.B.1500), § 131.)*

Law Revision Commission Comments

Enactment [Revised Comment]

Section 3902 continues former Civil Code Section 201 without substantive change. The reference to support of a "minor" child has been omitted. This is not a substantive change, but recognizes that in some cases support may be ordered for an adult child. See Sections 58 ("child for whom support may be ordered" defined), 3587 (court order to effectuate agreement for support of adult child), 3901 (duration of duty to support child), 3910 (duty to maintain incapacitated adult child), 4000 (civil action to enforce parent's duty to support child), 4001 (order for child support). A reference to the duty to provide for education has been omitted as surplus. See Section 150 ("support" includes maintenance and education when used in reference to child). [23 Cal.L.Rev.Comm. Reports 1 (1993)].

Research References

Forms

California Transactions Forms--Family Law § 3:43, Use Of Child's Property or Income.

West's California Code Forms, Family § 3900, Comment Overview--Duty Of Parent to Support Child.

Treatises and Practice Aids

Witkin, California Summary 10th Parent and Child § 380, Duty to Support Minor Child.

ARTICLE 2. SUPPORT OF ADULT CHILD

Section

§ 3910. Duty to support incapacitated adult child

(a) The father and mother have an equal responsibility to maintain, to the extent of their ability, a child of whatever age who is incapacitated from earning a living and without sufficient means.

(b) Nothing in this section limits the duty of support under Sections 3900 and 3901. *(Stats.1992, c. 162 (A.B.2650), § 10, operative Jan. 1, 1994.)*

Law Revision Commission Comments

Enactment [Revised Comment]

Subdivision (a) of Section 3910 restates without substantive change the first sentence of former Civil Code Section 206 and former Civil Code Sections 241(d) and 242 to the extent those sections applied to the duty to maintain an incapacitated adult child. The "equal responsibility" language is new and is drawn from Section 3900.

Subdivision (b) is new. It makes clear that the duty stated in this section does not supersede or limit the duty of support under Sections 3900 and 3901.

See also Sections 3587 (court order to effectuate agreement for support of adult child); Welf. & Inst. Code § 12350 (no liability for support or reimbursement of support to applicant for aid under Burton–Moscone–Bagley Citizens' Security Act for Aged, Blind and Disabled Californians). [23 Cal.L.Rev.Comm. Reports 1 (1993)].

Commentary

A court may not order adult child support unless it finds that a child is unable to become self-supporting because of a physical or mental disability and the child is likely to become a public charge absent parental support. *In re Marriage of Cecilia and David W., 241 Cal.App.4th 1277, 194 Cal.Rptr.3d 559 (2015)*.

In re Marriage of Drake, 241 Cal.App.4th 934, 194 Cal.Rptr.3d 252 (2015), held that a court erred in ordering a father to pay adult child support for his disabled son to the child's mother, when the child did not live with the mother and the mother was not his conservator, guardian or legal representative.

See generally *In re Marriage of Lambe & Meehan, 37 Cal.App.4th 388, 44 Cal.Rptr.2d 641 (1995)* (parents' court-ratified agreement to divest family court of jurisdiction to order support for their adult indigent child is unenforceable). Cf. *Marriage of Goodarzirad, 185 Cal.App.3d 1020, 1026, 230 Cal.Rptr. 203 (1986)* (husband's stipulation to surrender rights of custody and visitation of his minor child is unenforceable as is the portion of the judgment incorporating the stipulation).

In re Marriage of Drake, 53 Cal.App.4th 1139, 62 Cal.Rptr.2d 466 (1997), review denied June 11, 1997, holds that the statewide uniform child support guideline (Sections 4050–4076) applies to disabled adult children.

Research References

Forms

California Practice Guide: Rutter Family Law Forms Form 6:7, Request for Order Re Child Support (Needy, Incapacitated Adult Child).
California Transactions Forms--Family Law § 3:27, Support for Incapacitated Adult Child.
West's California Code Forms, Family § 3900, Comment Overview--Duty Of Parent to Support Child.
West's California Code Forms, Family § 3910, Comment Overview--Support Of Adult Child.
West's California Code Forms, Family § 4000, Comment Overview--Court-Ordered Child Support.
West's California Code Forms, Family § 4400, Comment Overview--Duty Of Adult Children to Support Parents.

Treatises and Practice Aids

Witkin, California Summary 10th Community Property § 207, Statutory Procedure and Factors.
Witkin, California Summary 10th Husband and Wife § 4, Definitions.
Witkin, California Summary 10th Husband and Wife § 287, Change in Cost Of Child Support.
Witkin, California Summary 10th Husband and Wife § 340, Aid to Aged, Blind, and Disabled.
Witkin, California Summary 10th Husband and Wife § 342, Aid to Mentally Ill.
Witkin, California Summary 10th Parent and Child § 385, Support During Action.
Witkin, California Summary 10th Parent and Child § 420, Emancipation.
Witkin, California Summary 10th Parent and Child § 423, Support Of Disabled Indigent Adult Child.

ARTICLE 3. SUPPORT OF GRANDCHILD

§ 3930. Duty to support grandchild

A parent does not have the duty to support a child of the parent's child. *(Stats.1992, c. 162 (A.B.2650), § 10, operative Jan. 1, 1994. Amended by Stats.1993, c. 219 (A.B.1500), § 132.)*

Law Revision Commission Comments

Enactment [Revised Comment]

Section 3930 continues former Civil Code Section 208.5 without substantive change. References to support of a "minor" child have been omitted. This is not a substantive change, but recognizes that in some cases support may be ordered for an adult child. See Sections 58 ("child for whom support may be ordered" defined), 3587 (court order to effectuate agreement for support of adult child), 3901 (duration of duty to support child), 3910 (duty to maintain incapacitated adult child), 4000 (civil action to enforce parent's duty to support child), 4001 (order for child support). [23 Cal.L.Rev. Comm. Reports 1 (1993)].

Commentary

Although a grandparent normally has no duty to support a grandchild, *In re Marriage of Perry, 61 Cal.App.4th 295, 71 Cal.Rptr.2d 499 (1998),* interpreting Sections 2030 (d) and 3103 (g)(2), holds that a grandparent who is a party to a custody or visitation proceeding may be ordered to pay for a child's court-appointed counsel, for another party's attorney's fees to defend on issues involving the grandparent, and for costs related to visitation, but not for counseling costs for a grandchild.

Research References

Forms

California Transactions Forms--Family Law § 5:5, Rights Of Grandparents and Close Relatives.
West's California Code Forms, Family § 3930, Comment Overview--Support Of Grandchild.
West's California Code Forms, Family § 3950, Comment Overview--Liability to Others Who Provide Support for Child.

Treatises and Practice Aids

Witkin, California Summary 10th Parent and Child § 226, in General.
Witkin, California Summary 10th Parent and Child § 379, Children to Whom Duty is Owed.

ARTICLE 4. LIABILITY TO OTHERS WHO PROVIDE SUPPORT FOR CHILD

§ 3950. Necessaries furnished to child

If a parent neglects to provide articles necessary for the parent's child who is under the charge of the parent, according to the circumstances of the parent, a third person may in good faith supply the necessaries and recover their reasonable value from the parent. *(Stats.1992, c. 162 (A.B. 2650), § 10, operative Jan. 1, 1994.)*

Law Revision Commission Comments

Enactment [Revised Comment]

Section 3950 continues former Civil Code Section 207 without substantive change. [23 Cal.L.Rev.Comm. Reports 1 (1993)].

Research References

Forms

West's California Code Forms, Family § 3950, Comment Overview--Liability to Others Who Provide Support for Child.
West's California Code Forms, Family § 4400, Comment Overview--Duty Of Adult Children to Support Parents.

Treatises and Practice Aids

Witkin, California Summary 10th Contracts § 1021, Exception: Performing Defendant's Duty.
Witkin, California Summary 10th Parent and Child § 381, Liability to Others Who Support Child.

§ 3951. Circumstances where liability is not incurred

(a) A parent is not bound to compensate the other parent, or a relative, for the voluntary support of the parent's child, without an agreement for compensation.

(b) A parent is not bound to compensate a stranger for the support of a child who has abandoned the parent without just cause.

(c) Nothing in this section relieves a parent of the obligation to support a child during any period in which the state, county, or other governmental entity provides support for the child. *(Stats.1992, c. 162 (A.B.2650), § 10, operative Jan. 1, 1994.)*

Law Revision Commission Comments

Enactment [Revised Comment]

Section 3951 continues former Civil Code Section 208 without substantive change. [23 Cal.L.Rev.Comm. Reports 1 (1993)].

Commentary

Plumas County Child Support Services v. Rodriquez, 161 Cal.App.4th 1021, 76 Cal.Rptr.3d 1 (2008), relied in part on subsection (a) of this section when it concluded that a county has no authority to seek child support on behalf of non-parent relatives who are supporting a child and sharing their home with him, unless there is a contractual agreement between the parents and the relatives. Correspondingly, see section 17404, which does not authorize a county action that would require a parent to compensate a relative for voluntary support of a child.

County of San Bernardino v. Martinez, 51 Cal.App.4th 600, 59 Cal.Rptr.3d 142 (1996), review denied March 12, 1997, invoking subsection (c), holds that a parent is liable to the county for reimbursement of public welfare benefits paid to his minor daughter for the support of herself and her two infant children even though the minor daughter may have abandoned her father without just cause.

Research References

Forms

California Transactions Forms--Family Law § 5:5, Rights Of Grandparents and Close Relatives.
West's California Code Forms, Family § 3950, Comment Overview--Liability to Others Who Provide Support for Child.

Treatises and Practice Aids

Witkin, California Summary 10th Parent and Child § 226, in General.
Witkin, California Summary 10th Parent and Child § 381, Liability to Others Who Support Child.

§ 3952. Estate of deceased parent; action for support of child

If a parent chargeable with the support of a child dies leaving the child chargeable to the county or leaving the child confined in a state institution to be cared for in whole or in part at the expense of the state, and the parent leaves an estate sufficient for the child's support, the supervisors of the county or the director of the state department having jurisdiction over the institution may claim provision for the child's support from the parent's estate, and for this purpose has the same remedies as a creditor against the estate of the parent and may obtain reimbursement from the successor of the deceased parent to the extent provided in Division 8 (commencing with Section 13000) of the Probate Code. *(Stats.1992, c. 162 (A.B.2650), § 10, operative Jan. 1, 1994.)*

Law Revision Commission Comments

Enactment [Revised Comment]

Section 3952 continues former Civil Code Section 205 without substantive change. A reference to Division 8 (commencing with Section 13000) of the Probate Code (disposition of estate without administration) has been substituted for the reference in the former section to a civil action against the heirs, devisees, and next of kin of the parent. See, e.g., Prob. Code § 13112 (limitation on liability of successor). If there is an administration of the deceased parent's estate, a claim may be submitted to the personal representative administering the estate in the manner provided for the submission of claims. See Part 4 (commencing with Section 9000) of Division 7 of the Probate Code. [23 Cal.L.Rev.Comm. Reports 1 (1993)].

Commentary

A child support obligation fixed by a divorce decree or property settlement agreement survives a supporting parent's death and is a charge against the parent's estate. *Taylor v. George, 34 Cal.2d 552, 556, 212 P.2d 505 (1949)* and authorities cited therein. For purposes of a decedent's support obligation to a child, *In re Marriage of Perry, 58 Cal.App.4th 1104, 68 Cal.Rptr.2d 445 (1997),* holds that a living trust is indistinguishable from a probate estate, and that the family court has jurisdiction to make an order against the trustee of a living trust because Probate Code Section 17000(b)(2) provides for concurrent jurisdiction.

Research References

Forms

California Transactions Forms--Estate Planning § 19:11, Child Support.
West's California Code Forms, Family § 3950, Comment Overview--Liability to Others Who Provide Support for Child.

Treatises and Practice Aids

Witkin, California Summary 10th Parent and Child § 381, Liability to Others Who Support Child.
Witkin, California Summary 10th Parent and Child § 418, Liability Of Parent's Estate or Trust.

CHAPTER 2. COURT–ORDERED CHILD SUPPORT

ARTICLE 1. GENERAL PROVISIONS

§ 4000. Actions to enforce parent's duty to support

If a parent has the duty to provide for the support of the parent's child and willfully fails to so provide, the other parent, or the child by a guardian ad litem, may bring an action against the parent to enforce the duty. *(Stats.1992, c. 162 (A.B.2650), § 10, operative Jan. 1, 1994.)*

Law Revision Commission Comments

Enactment [Revised Comment]

Section 4000 continues former Civil Code Section 4703 without substantive change. The reference to the "superior" court has been omitted as surplus. See Section 200 (jurisdiction in superior court). The reference to the duty to provide maintenance and education to a child has been omitted as surplus. See Section 150 ("support" includes maintenance and education when used in reference to child).

Section 4000 supersedes the second sentence of former Civil Code Section 196a, the second sentence of the first paragraph of former Civil Code Section 196.5, the first sentence of former Civil Code Section 248, insofar as it gave a child the right to enforce the duty of support, and the second sentence of the first paragraph of former Civil Code Section 4704.5.

For a provision allowing a county to proceed on behalf of the child to enforce the parent's duty of support, see Section 4002. For general provisions relating to support, see Part 1 (commencing with Section 3500). For provisions relating to enforcement of support orders, see Part 5 (commencing with Section 4500). See also Sections 3028 (compensation for failure to assume caretaker responsibility or for thwarting other parent's visitation or custody rights), 3029 (support order required where parent receiving public assistance), 3556 (effect of failure to implement custody or visitation rights), 3557 (attorney's fees for enforcement of support order). [23 Cal.L.Rev.Comm. Reports 1 (1993)].

Commentary

County of San Diego v. Lamb, 63 Cal.App.4th 845, 73 Cal.Rptr.2d 912 (1998), review denied August 12, 1998, holds that Welfare and Institutions Code Section 11350(a) does not authorize a county to seek reimbursement from the "noncustodial parent" of a minor child who receives benefits on behalf of the minor's own child. But see *County of San Bernadino v. Martinez, 51 Cal.App.4th 600, 59 Cal.Rptr.2d 142 (1996), review denied March 12, 1997* (contra). *Lamb* also says, in dictum, that this section would not be applicable when a minor child has left home and refused to accept parental control, because failure to support the minor child would not be "willful."

Research References

Forms

California Transactions Forms--Family Law § 2:88, Marital Settlement Agreement.
California Transactions Forms--Family Law § 2:91, Add-On Expenses in Conjunction With Family Support.
West's California Code Forms, Family § 3900, Comment Overview--Duty Of Parent to Support Child.
West's California Code Forms, Family § 4000, Comment Overview--Court-Ordered Child Support.
West's California Code Forms, Family § 2338 Form 8, Marital Agreement.
West's California Code Forms, Family § 3585 Form 2, Child Support Provisions.
West's California Code Forms, Family § 4001 Form 1, Order for Support Of Child.

Treatises and Practice Aids

Witkin, California Summary 10th Husband and Wife § 174, in General.
Witkin, California Summary 10th Parent and Child § 304, Notice Of Hearing.
Witkin, California Summary 10th Parent and Child § 422, Support Of High School Student.
Witkin, California Summary 10th Parent and Child § 423, Support Of Disabled Indigent Adult Child.
Witkin, California Summary 10th Parent and Child § 426, Action by Child or Parent.

§ 4001. Order for support

In any proceeding where there is at issue the support of a minor child or a child for whom support is authorized under Section 3901 or 3910, the court may order either or both parents to pay an amount necessary for the support of the child. *(Stats.1992, c. 162 (A.B.2650), § 10, operative Jan. 1, 1994.)*

Law Revision Commission Comments

Enactment [Revised Comment]

Section 4001 continues the first sentence of former Civil Code Section 4700(a) without substantive change. The reference to the duty to provide maintenance and education to a child has been omitted as surplus. See Section 150 ("support" includes maintenance and education when used in reference to child). A reference to Section 3901 has been added to make clear that this section applies to a child for whom support is authorized under that section.

For general provisions relating to support, see Part 1 (commencing with Section 3500). For provisions relating to enforcement of support orders, see Part 5 (commencing with Section 4500). See also Sections 3028 (compensation for failure to assume caretaker responsibility or thwarting other parent attempting to exercise custody or visitation rights), 3029 (support order required where parent receiving public assistance), 3556 (effect of failure to implement custody or visitation rights), 3557 (attorney's fees for enforcement of support order). [23 Cal.L.Rev.Comm. Reports 1 (1993)].

Commentary

Although Section 4001 gives the trial court power to make a child support order, adequate notice of the request for child support must nevertheless be given to the support obligor. *In re Marriage of Lippel, 51 Cal.3d 1160, 1171, 801 P.2d 1041, 1047, 276 Cal.Rptr. 290, 295 (1990)* (vacating default child support order entered at dissolution proceeding where petitioner did not request child support and no notice of such request was ever subsequently served on obligor father).

Research References

Forms

California Transactions Forms--Family Law § 2:63, Authority for Child Support.

California Transactions Forms--Family Law § 3:21, Jurisdiction for Orders to Pay Child Support.
West's California Code Forms, Family § 4000, Comment Overview--Court-Ordered Child Support.
West's California Judicial Council Forms FL-683, Order to Show Cause.
West's California Judicial Council Forms FL-684, Request for Order and Supporting Declaration (Governmental).

Treatises and Practice Aids

Witkin, California Summary 10th Husband and Wife § 112, Contents Of Judgment.
Witkin, California Summary 10th Parent and Child § 383, in General.

§ 4002. Enforcement of right of support; reimbursement of county

(a) The county may proceed on behalf of a child to enforce the child's right of support against a parent.

(b) If the county furnishes support to a child, the county has the same right as the child to secure reimbursement and obtain continuing support. The right of the county to reimbursement is subject to any limitation otherwise imposed by the law of this state.

(c) The court may order the parent to pay the county reasonable attorney's fees and court costs in a proceeding brought by the county pursuant to this section. *(Stats.1992, c. 162 (A.B.2650), § 10, operative Jan. 1, 1994.)*

Law Revision Commission Comments

Enactment [Revised Comment]

Section 4002 continues former Civil Code Section 248 without substantive change to the extent that the former section related to enforcement of child support by the county.

For general provisions relating to support, see Part 1 (commencing with Section 3500). For provisions relating to enforcement of support orders, see Part 5 (commencing with Section 4500). See also Sections 3029 (support order required where parent receiving public assistance), 3556 (effect of failure to implement custody or visitation rights), 3557 (attorney's fees for enforcement of support order). For comparable provisions, see Section 4303 (county enforcement of duty to provide spousal support), 4403 (county enforcement of duty to support parent). [23 Cal.L.Rev.Comm. Reports 1 (1993)].

Commentary

County of San Diego v. Lamb, 63 Cal.App.4th 845, 73 Cal.Rptr.2d 912 (1998), review denied August 12, 1998, holds that Welfare and Institutions Code Section 11350(a) does not authorize a county to seek reimbursement from the "noncustodial parent" of a minor child who receives benefits on behalf of the minor's own child. But see *County of San Bernadino v. Martinez, 51 Cal.App.4th 600, 59 Cal.Rptr.2d 142 (1996)* (contra). *Lamb* also says, in dictum, that this section would not be applicable when a minor child has left home and refused to accept parental control, because a parent's failure to support the minor child would not be "willful" within the meaning of Section 4000(a).

Research References

Forms

West's California Code Forms, Family § 3900, Comment Overview--Duty Of Parent to Support Child.
West's California Code Forms, Family § 4000, Comment Overview--Court-Ordered Child Support.
West's California Judicial Council Forms FL-683, Order to Show Cause.
West's California Judicial Council Forms FL-684, Request for Order and Supporting Declaration (Governmental).

Treatises and Practice Aids

Witkin, California Summary 10th Husband and Wife § 310, Local Child Support Agency.
Witkin, California Summary 10th Husband and Wife § 311, Duties Of Public Assistance Recipient.
Witkin, California Summary 10th Husband and Wife § 339, in General.

§ 4003. Separate trial; calendar preference; joinder with custody

In any case in which the support of a child is at issue, the court may, upon a showing of good cause, order a separate trial on that issue. The separate trial shall be given preference over other civil cases, except matters to which special precedence may be given by law, for assigning a trial date. If the court has also ordered a separate trial on the issue of custody pursuant to Section 3023, the two issues shall be tried together. *(Stats.1992, c. 162 (A.B.2650), § 10, operative Jan. 1, 1994. Amended by Stats.1993, c. 219 (A.B.1500), § 133.)*

Law Revision Commission Comments

Enactment [Revised Comment]

Section 4003 continues former Civil Code Section 4707 without substantive change. The reference to support of a "minor" child has been omitted. This is not a substantive change, but recognizes that in some cases support may be ordered for an adult child. See Sections 58 ("child for whom support may be ordered" defined), 3587 (court order to effectuate agreement for support of adult child), 3901 (duration of duty to support child), 3910 (duty to maintain incapacitated adult child), 4000 (civil action to enforce parent's duty to support child), 4001 (order for child support).

For general provisions relating to support, see Part 1 (commencing with Section 3500). For provisions relating to enforcement of support orders, see Part 5 (commencing with Section 4500). [23 Cal.L.Rev.Comm. Reports 1 (1993)].

Commentary

See generally *Miller v. Superior Court, 221 Cal.App.3d 1200, 270 Cal.Rptr. 766 (1990)* (statutory trial preferences). For discussion of bifurcated proceedings, see Commentary to Sections 2337 and 2550.

Research References

Treatises and Practice Aids

Witkin, California Summary 10th Husband and Wife § 105, Statutory Rule.
Witkin, California Summary 10th Parent and Child § 383, in General.

§ 4004. Disclosure of party receiving or intending to receive public assistance for maintenance of child

In a proceeding where there is at issue the support of a child, the court shall require the parties to reveal whether a party is currently receiving, or intends to apply for, public assistance under the Family Economic Security Act of 1982 (Chapter 2 (commencing with Section 11200) of Part 3 of Division 9 of the Welfare and Institutions Code) for the maintenance of the child. *(Stats.1992, c. 162 (A.B.2650), § 10, operative Jan. 1, 1994. Amended by Stats.1993, c. 219 (A.B.1500), § 134.)*

Law Revision Commission Comments

Enactment [Revised Comment]

Section 4004 continues former Civil Code Section 4700.5 without substantive change. See also Section 3029 (support order required where parent receiving public assistance). The reference to support of a "minor" child has been omitted. This is not a substantive change, but recognizes that in some cases support may be ordered for an adult child. See Sections 58 ("child for whom support may be ordered" defined), 3587 (court order to effectuate agreement for support of adult child), 3901 (duration of duty to support child), 3910 (duty to maintain incapacitated adult child), 4000 (civil action to enforce parent's duty to support child), 4001 (order for child support). [23 Cal.L.Rev.Comm. Reports 1 (1993)].

Research References

Treatises and Practice Aids

Witkin, California Summary 10th Husband and Wife § 273, Continuing Jurisdiction.

Witkin, California Summary 10th Parent and Child § 383, in General.

§ 4005. Circumstances forming basis for child support order; findings

At the request of either party, the court shall make appropriate findings with respect to the circumstances on which the order for support of a child is based. *(Added by Stats.1994, c. 1269 (A.B.2208), § 47.)*

Law Revision Commission Comments

1994 Addition

Section 4005 is added to restore a provision in the second sentence of former Civil Code Section 4700(a) which had been carried forward in Family Code Section 4005(b) as enacted in 1992 and erroneously repealed. [24 Cal.L.Rev.Comm. Reports 621 (1994)].

Research References

Treatises and Practice Aids

Witkin, California Summary 10th Parent and Child § 383, in General.

§ 4006. Health insurance coverage; consideration by court

In a proceeding for child support under this code, including, but not limited to, Division 17 (commencing with Section 17000), the court shall consider the health insurance coverage, if any, of the parties to the proceeding. *(Stats.1992, c. 162 (A.B.2650), § 10, operative Jan. 1, 1994. Amended by Stats.2000, c. 808 (A.B.1358), § 33, eff. Sept. 28, 2000.)*

Law Revision Commission Comments

Enactment [Revised Comment]

Section 4006 continues former Civil Code Section 4706 without substantive change and expands the section to apply to any child support proceeding under this code. The former section applied in an "action for support" brought under former Chapter 1 (commencing with Section 4700) of Title 5 of the former Family Law Act. The substitution of "proceeding" for "action" is not a substantive change. The reference to "health insurance coverage" has been substituted for the former reference to "medical insurance coverage." This conforms with the terminology of the related sections dealing with health insurance coverage assignments. For provisions relating to health insurance coverage assignments, see Chapter 7 (commencing with Section 3750). [23 Cal.L.Rev.Comm. Reports 1 (1993)].

Research References

Treatises and Practice Aids

Witkin, California Summary 10th Parent and Child § 383, in General.

§ 4007. Termination of duty to pay support on happening of contingency; notice of contingency

(a) If a court orders a person to make specified payments for support of a child during the child's minority, or until the child is married or otherwise emancipated, or until the death of, or the occurrence of a specified event as to, a child for whom support is authorized under Section 3901 or 3910, the obligation of the person ordered to pay support terminates on the happening of the contingency. The court may, in the original order for support, order the custodial parent or other person to whom payments are to be made to notify the person ordered to make the payments, or the person's attorney of record, of the happening of the contingency.

(b) If the custodial parent or other person having physical custody of the child, to whom payments are to be made, fails to notify the person ordered to make the payments, or the attorney of record of the person ordered to make the payments, of the happening of the contingency and continues to accept support payments, the person shall refund all moneys received that accrued after the happening of the contingency, except that the overpayments shall first be applied to any support payments that are then in default. *(Stats.1992, c. 162 (A.B.2650), § 10, operative Jan. 1, 1994.)*

Law Revision Commission Comments

Enactment [Revised Comment]

Section 4007 continues former Civil Code Section 4700(c) without substantive change. The reference to Section 3901 has been added. In subdivision (b), references to "all" and to "any" have been substituted for the former references to "any and all," since the phrase "any and all" is redundant. For a comparable provision relating to spousal support, see Section 4334 (spousal support for contingent period of time). [23 Cal.L.Rev.Comm. Reports 1 (1993)].

Research References

Forms

West's California Judicial Council Forms FL-684, Request for Order and Supporting Declaration (Governmental).

Treatises and Practice Aids

Witkin, California Summary 10th Husband and Wife § 265, Security for Payment.

Witkin, California Summary 10th Parent and Child § 385, Support During Action.

Witkin, California Summary 10th Parent and Child § 424, Termination on Contingency or Other Event.

§ 4007.5. Suspension of money judgment or order for support of a child; exceptions; resumption of obligation; administrative adjustment

(a) Every money judgment or order for support of a child shall be suspended, by operation of law, for any period exceeding 90 consecutive days in which the person ordered to pay support is incarcerated or involuntarily institutionalized, unless either of the following conditions exist:

(1) The person owing support has the means to pay support while incarcerated or involuntarily institutionalized.

(2) The person owing support was incarcerated or involuntarily institutionalized for an offense constituting domestic violence, as defined in Section 6211, against the supported party or supported child, or for an offense that could be enjoined by a protective order pursuant to Section 6320, or as a result of his or her failure to comply with a court order to pay child support.

(b) The child support obligation shall resume on the first day of the first full month after the release of the person owing support in the amount previously ordered, and that amount is presumed to be appropriate under federal and state law. This section does not preclude a person owing support from seeking a modification of the child support order pursuant to Section 3651, based on a change in circumstances or other appropriate reason.

(c)(1) A local child support agency enforcing a child support order under Title IV–D of the Social Security Act (42 U.S.C. Sec. 651 et seq.) may, upon written notice of the proposed adjustment to the support obligor and obligee along with a blank form provided for the support obligor or obligee to object to the administrative adjustment to the local child support agency, administratively adjust account balances for a money judgment or order for support of a child suspended pursuant to subdivision (a) if all of the following occurs:

(A) The agency verifies that arrears and interest were accrued in violation of this section.

(B) The agency verifies that neither of the conditions set forth in paragraph (1) or (2) of subdivision (a) exist.

(C) Neither the support obligor nor obligee objects, within 30 days of receipt of the notice of proposed adjustment, whether in writing or by telephone, to the administrative adjustment by the local child support agency.

(2) If either the support obligor or obligee objects to the administrative adjustment set forth in this subdivision, the agency shall not adjust the order, but shall file a motion with the court to seek to adjust the arrears and shall serve copies of the motion on the parties, who may file an objection to the agency's motion with the court. The obligor's arrears shall not be adjusted unless the court approves the adjustment.

(3) The agency may perform this adjustment without regard to whether it was enforcing the child support order at the time the parent owing support qualified for relief under this section.

(d) This section does not prohibit the local child support agency or a party from petitioning a court for a determination of child support or arrears amounts.

(e) For purposes of this section, the following definitions shall apply:

(1) "Incarcerated or involuntarily institutionalized" includes, but is not limited to, involuntary confinement to the state prison, a county jail, a juvenile facility operated by the Division of Juvenile Facilities in the Department of Corrections and Rehabilitation, or a mental health facility.

(2) "Suspend" means that the payment due on the current child support order, an arrears payment on a preexisting arrears balance, or interest on arrears created during a qualifying period of incarceration pursuant to this section is, by operation of law, set to zero dollars ($0) for the period in which the person owing support is incarcerated or involuntarily institutionalized.

(f) This section applies to every money judgment or child support order issued or modified on or after the enactment of this section.

(g) The Department of Child Support Services shall, by January 1, 2016, and in consultation with the Judicial Council, develop forms to implement this section.

(h) On or before January 1, 2019, the Department of Child Support Services and the Judicial Council shall conduct an evaluation of the effectiveness of the administrative adjustment process authorized by this section and shall report the results of the review, as well as any recommended changes, to the Assembly Judiciary Committee and the Senate Judiciary Committee. The evaluation shall include a review of the ease of the process to both the obligor and obligee, as well as an analysis of the number of cases administratively adjusted, the number of cases adjusted in court, and the number of cases not adjusted.

(i) This section shall remain in effect only until January 1, 2020, and as of that date is repealed, unless a later enacted statute, that is enacted before January 1, 2020, deletes or extends that date. *(Added by Stats.2015, c. 629 (A.B.610), § 2, eff. Oct. 8, 2015.)*

Repeal

For repeal of this section, see its terms.

Research References

Forms

West's California Judicial Council Forms FL-676, Request for Judicial Determination Of Support Arrearages or Adjustment Of Arrearages Due to Incarceration or Involuntary Institutionalization.

Treatises and Practice Aids

Witkin, California Summary 10th Parent and Child § 424A, (New) Suspension on Incarceration.

§ 4008. Property which may be subjected to support of children

The community property, the quasi-community property, and the separate property may be subjected to the support of the children in the proportions the court determines are just. *(Stats.1992, c. 162 (A.B.2650), § 10, operative Jan. 1, 1994.)*

Law Revision Commission Comments

Enactment [Revised Comment]

Section 4008 continues former Civil Code Section 4807 without substantive change. For a provision relating to spousal support, see Section 4338 (order of resort to property for payment of spousal support). [23 Cal.L.Rev.Comm. Reports 1 (1993)].

Research References

Treatises and Practice Aids

Witkin, California Summary 10th Parent and Child § 383, in General.

§ 4009. Retroactive application of order for support

An original order for child support may be made retroactive to the date of filing the petition, complaint, or other initial pleading. If the parent ordered to pay support was not served with the petition, complaint, or other initial pleading within 90 days after filing and the court finds that the parent was not intentionally evading service, the child support order shall be effective no earlier than the date of service. *(Stats.1992, c. 162 (A.B.2650), § 10, operative Jan. 1, 1994. Amended by Stats.1999, c. 653 (A.B.380), § 8; Stats.2000, c. 808 (A.B.1358), § 34, eff. Sept. 28, 2000; Stats.2004, c. 305 (A.B.2669), § 3.)*

Law Revision Commission Comments

Enactment [Revised Comment]

Section 4009 continues the sixth sentence of former Civil Code Section 4700(a) without substantive change, to the extent that sentence related to the making of the order for child support. See also Section 3653 (retroactivity of order modifying or terminating child support order). For a provision relating to spousal support, see Section 4333 (retroactivity of spousal support order). [23 Cal.L.Rev. Comm. Reports 1 (1993)].

Commentary

Invoking this section, *In re Marriage of Barth, 210 Cal.App.4th 363, 147 Cal.Rptr.3d 910 (2012), review denied*, holds that a California trial court did not abuse its discretion when it ordered child support retroactive to the date when the support obligor originally filed a California petition for divorce six years earlier, even though the California proceeding was stayed because the obligee had earlier filed an Ohio petition for divorce, which was ultimately dismissed for lack of jurisdiction.

Section 4009 means what it says: A child support order may only be made retroactive to the date of filing the notice of motion or order to show cause for establishment or modification of a child support obligation. *In re Marriage of Goosmann, 26 Cal.App.4th 838, 31 Cal.Rptr.2d 613 (1994)*. *County of Santa Clara v. Perry, 18 Cal.4th 435, 956 P.2d 1191, 75 Cal.Rptr.2d 738 (1998)*, holds that this section applies to original support orders as well as to orders modifying support, and it equally applies to support orders in paternity actions brought by the district attorney. Thus, for many children born out of wedlock, the support obligation of the noncustodial parent may be made retroactive only to the establishment of paternity.

Nevertheless, *County of Riverside v. Burt, 78 Cal.App.4th 28, 92 Cal.Rptr.2d 619 (2000)*, holds that *Perry, supra*, does not apply to cases in which reimbursement is sought for public assistance payments on behalf of a child. In such case, reimbursement is subject only to the three-year statute of limitations (Civil Code § 338) and the parent's reasonable ability to pay. Effectively, *Burt* holds that Welfare and Institutions Code § 11350 (amended and reenacted as Family Code § 17402, effective January 1, 2000) provides an alternative path for reimbursement in public assistance cases. Family Code § 17402 adds a one-year statute of limitations: the period may not exceed one year from the filing of the petition or complaint.

Research References

Forms

West's California Judicial Council Forms FL-684, Request for Order and Supporting Declaration (Governmental).

Treatises and Practice Aids

Witkin, California Summary 10th Parent and Child § 383, in General.

§ 4010. Information on procedures to modify support order

In a proceeding in which the court orders a payment for the support of a child, the court shall, at the time of providing written notice of the order, provide the parties with a document describing the procedures by which the order may be modified. *(Stats.1992, c. 162 (A.B.2650), § 10, operative Jan. 1, 1994. Amended by Stats.1993, c. 219 (A.B.1500), § 136.)*

Law Revision Commission Comments

Enactment [Revised Comment]

Section 4010 continues former Civil Code Section 4700.1(f) without substantive change. For provisions relating to modification or termination of support orders, see Chapter 6 (commencing with Section 3650). The reference to support of a "minor" child has been omitted. This is not a substantive change, but recognizes that in some cases support may be ordered for an adult child. See Sections 58 ("child for whom support may be ordered" defined), 3587 (court order to effectuate agreement for support of adult child), 3901 (duration of duty to support child), 3910 (duty to maintain incapacitated adult child), 4000 (civil action to enforce parent's duty to support child), 4001 (order for child support). [23 Cal.L.Rev.Comm. Reports 1 (1993)].

Research References

Treatises and Practice Aids

Witkin, California Summary 10th Parent and Child § 439, Modification or Termination Of Support Order.

§ 4011. Priority of payments; creditors

Payment of child support ordered by the court shall be made by the person owing the support payment before payment of any debts owed to creditors. *(Stats.1992, c. 162 (A.B.2650), § 10, operative Jan. 1, 1994.)*

Law Revision Commission Comments

Enactment [Revised Comment]

Section 4011 continues the fourth sentence of former Civil Code Section 4700(a) without substantive change. [23 Cal.L.Rev.Comm. Reports 1 (1993)].

Commentary

Despite the language of Section 4011, a custodial parent's lien for past and present child support against the proceeds of a noncustodial parent's personal injury award does not take priority over prior liens of legal and medical providers. *Wujcik v. Wujcik, 21 Cal.App.4th 1790, 27 Cal.Rptr.2d 102 (1994), review denied 4/21/94*. See California Civil Code Section 2897 (priority of liens on same property determined according to time of creation). See also Family Code Section 2033 ("family law attorney's real property lien"). But compare Family Code Section 5243.

The claims of crime victims in "Freeze and Seize" proceedings under Penal Code section 186.11 have priority over child support claims, unless the child support obligee establishes a legitimately acquired interest in defendant's frozen assets. *People v. Mozes, 192 Cal.App.4th 1124, 121 Cal.Rptr.3d 808 (2011), review denied.*

Research References

Forms

California Transactions Forms--Family Law § 3:3, Child Support.

Treatises and Practice Aids

Witkin, California Summary 10th Parent and Child § 383, in General.

§ 4012. Security for payment of child support

Upon a showing of good cause, the court may order a parent required to make a payment of child support to give reasonable security for the payment. *(Stats.1992, c. 162 (A.B.2650), § 10, operative Jan. 1, 1994.)*

Law Revision Commission Comments

Enactment [Revised Comment]

Section 4012 continues the third sentence of former Civil Code Section 4700(a) without substantive change. The former reference to parents has been omitted as surplus. See Section 10 (singular includes plural). See also Sections 3557 (attorney's fees for enforcement of support order), 4550–4573 (deposit of money to secure future child support payments), 4600–4641 (deposit of assets to secure future child support payments). For a provision relating to spousal support, see Section 4339 (security for payment of spousal support). [23 Cal.L.Rev.Comm. Reports 1 (1993)].

Commentary

See generally *Taylor v. Superior Court, 218 Cal.App.3d 1185, 267 Cal.Rptr. 519 (1990)* (custodial parent has standing to compel noncustodial parent to post security for future child support even though custodial parent, in order to receive welfare benefits, has assigned to County all her rights to support "which have accrued at the time such assignment was made"). *See also In re Marriage of Drake, 53 Cal.App.4th 1139, 62 Cal.Rptr.2d 466 (1997), review denied June 11, 1997* (requiring parent to pledge $300,000 as security for support of adult disabled child).

Research References

Forms

California Transactions Forms--Family Law § 2:43, Life Insurance.

Treatises and Practice Aids

Witkin, California Summary 10th Husband and Wife § 265, Security for Payment.

§ 4013. Duty for child support discharged in bankruptcy; order for child support

If obligations for support of a child are discharged in bankruptcy, the court may make all proper orders for the support of the child that the court determines are just. *(Stats.1992, c. 162 (A.B.2650), § 10, operative Jan. 1, 1994.)*

Law Revision Commission Comments

Enactment [Revised Comment]

Section 4013 continues former Civil Code Section 4700(d) without substantive change. The reference to the duty to provide maintenance and education to a child has been omitted as surplus. See Section 150 ("support" includes maintenance and education when used in reference to child). For a provision relating to spousal support, see Section 3592 (agreement for property settlement or support of spouse discharged in bankruptcy). [23 Cal.L.Rev.Comm. Reports 1 (1993)].

Research References

Treatises and Practice Aids

Witkin, California Summary 10th Parent and Child § 383, in General.

Witkin, California Summary 10th Parent and Child § 385, Support During Action.

§ 4014. Notice of obligation to provide name and address of employer; notice of information to be filed with the court

(a) Any order for child support issued or modified pursuant to this chapter shall include a provision requiring the obligor and child support obligee to notify the other parent or, if the order requires payment through an agency designated under Title IV–D of the Social Security Act (42 U.S.C. Sec. 651 et seq.), the agency named in the order, of the name and address of his or her current employer.

(b) The requirements set forth in this subdivision apply only in cases in which the local child support agency is not providing child support services pursuant to Section 17400. To the extent required by federal law, and subject to applicable confidentiality provisions of state or federal law, any judgment for paternity and any order for child support entered or modified pursuant to any provision of law shall include a provision requiring the child support obligor and obligee to file with the court all of the following information:

(1) Residential and mailing address.

(2) Social security number.

(3) Telephone number.

(4) Driver's license number.

(5) Name, address, and telephone number of the employer.

(6) Any other information prescribed by the Judicial Council.

The judgment or order shall specify that each parent is responsible for providing his or her own information, that the information must be filed with the court within 10 days of the court order, and that new or different information must be filed with the court within 10 days after any event causing a change in the previously provided information.

(c) The requirements set forth in this subdivision shall only apply in cases in which the local child support agency is not providing child support services pursuant to Section 17400. Once the child support registry, as described in Section 17391 is operational, any judgment for paternity and any order for child support entered or modified pursuant to any provision of law shall include a provision requiring the child support obligor and obligee to file and keep updated the information specified in subdivision (b) with the child support registry.

(d) The Judicial Council shall develop forms to implement this section. The forms shall be developed so as not to delay the implementation of the Statewide Child Support Registry described in Section 17391 and shall be available no later than 30 days prior to the implementation of the Statewide Child Support Registry. *(Added by Stats.1993, c. 876 (S.B. 1068), § 18, eff. Oct. 6, 1993, operative Jan. 1, 1994. Amended by Stats.1997, c. 599 (A.B.573), § 13; Stats.1998, c. 858 (A.B.2169), § 2; Stats.2004, c. 339 (A.B.1704), § 2; Stats. 2016, c. 474 (A.B.2882), § 8, eff. Jan. 1, 2017.)*

Research References

Forms

West's California Code Forms, Family § 4000, Comment Overview--Court-Ordered Child Support.

West's California Judicial Council Forms FL-191, Child Support Case Registry Form.

West's California Judicial Council Forms FL-684, Request for Order and Supporting Declaration (Governmental).

Treatises and Practice Aids

Witkin, California Summary 10th Parent and Child § 384, Information Required.

ARTICLE 2. STATEWIDE UNIFORM GUIDELINE

§ 4050. Legislative intent; compliance with federal law

In adopting the statewide uniform guideline provided in this article, it is the intention of the Legislature to ensure that this state remains in compliance with federal regulations for child support guidelines. *(Added by Stats.1993, c. 219 (A.B.1500), § 138.)*

Law Revision Commission Comments

Enactment [Revised Comment]

Section 4050 continues without substantive change the first sentence and the first part of the second sentence of former Civil Code Section 4720(a)(1). A reference to this article has been substituted for the narrower reference to former Civil Code Section 4721. This is not a substantive change, since the former section is continued in this article. [23 Cal.L.Rev.Comm. Reports 1 (1993)].

Research References

Forms

California Practice Guide: Rutter Family Law Forms Form 5:1, Stipulation to Orders Pending Trial (Attorney-Drafted).
California Practice Guide: Rutter Family Law Forms Form 6:2, Stipulation Re Child Support and Order Thereon (Attorney-Drafted).
California Practice Guide: Rutter Family Law Forms Form 1:32, Glossary Of Common Family Law Terms, Phrases and Concepts (Enclosure to Form 1:31).
California Practice Guide: Rutter Family Law Forms Form 17:1, Stipulation and Order for Modification Of Spousal Support, Child Support, Custody and Visitation.
California Practice Guide: Rutter Family Law Forms Form 11:20, Sample Trial Brief.
California Transactions Forms--Family Law § 3:3, Child Support.
California Transactions Forms--Family Law § 3:22, Mandatory Compliance With Statewide Guidelines.
West's California Code Forms, Family § 3900, Comment Overview--Duty Of Parent to Support Child.
West's California Code Forms, Family § 4050, Comment Overview--Statewide Uniform Guideline.
West's California Code Forms, Family § 4068 Form 2, Financial Statement--Simplified.
West's California Judicial Council Forms FL-150, Income and Expense Declaration.
West's California Judicial Council Forms FL-684, Request for Order and Supporting Declaration (Governmental).

Treatises and Practice Aids

Witkin, California Summary 10th Husband and Wife § 287, Change in Cost Of Child Support.
Witkin, California Summary 10th Parent and Child § 380, Duty to Support Minor Child.
Witkin, California Summary 10th Parent and Child § 383, in General.
Witkin, California Summary 10th Parent and Child § 388, Hearing and Order After Hearing.
Witkin, California Summary 10th Parent and Child § 394, in General.
Witkin, California Summary 10th Parent and Child § 402, Family Support.
Witkin, California Summary 10th Parent and Child § 404, Hardship Deduction.
Witkin, California Summary 10th Parent and Child § 413, Special Circumstances.
Witkin, California Summary 10th Parent and Child § 415, in General.
Witkin, California Summary 10th Parent and Child § 439, Modification or Termination Of Support Order.

§ 4052. Adherence of courts to uniform guidelines

The court shall adhere to the statewide uniform guideline and may depart from the guideline only in the special circumstances set forth in this article. *(Added by Stats.1993, c. 219 (A.B.1500), § 138.)*

Law Revision Commission Comments

Enactment [Revised Comment]

Section 4052 restates former Civil Code Section 4720(a)(2) without substantive change, but states a positive rule rather than a legislative intent. A reference to this article has been substituted for the narrower reference to former Civil Code Section 4721. This is not a substantive change, since the former section is continued in this article. [23 Cal.L.Rev.Comm. Reports 1 (1993)].

Research References

Forms

California Practice Guide: Rutter Family Law Forms Form 5:2, Request for Order Re Child Custody, Child Support, Spousal Support, Attorney Fees, etc.

California Practice Guide: Rutter Family Law Forms Form 6:11, Request for Order Re Guideline Child Support, Temporary "Guideline" Spousal Support and Family Code S4062 "Add-On" Child Support.

West's California Code Forms, Family § 4050, Comment Overview--Statewide Uniform Guideline.

Treatises and Practice Aids

Witkin, California Summary 10th Parent and Child § 392, Discretion Of Lower Court.

Witkin, California Summary 10th Parent and Child § 395, Guiding Principles.

Witkin, California Summary 10th Parent and Child § 439, Modification or Termination Of Support Order.

§ 4052.5. Child with more than two parents; application of uniform guideline; amount of support adjusted if presumption rebutted; effect on existing guidelines, regulations, etc.

(a) The statewide uniform guideline, as required by federal regulations, shall apply in any case in which a child has more than two parents. The court shall apply the guideline by dividing child support obligations among the parents based on income and amount of time spent with the child by each parent, pursuant to Section 4053.

(b) Consistent with federal regulations, after calculating the amount of support owed by each parent under the guideline, the presumption that the guideline amount of support is correct may be rebutted if the court finds that the application of the guideline in that case would be unjust or inappropriate due to special circumstances, pursuant to Section 4057. If the court makes that finding, the court shall divide child support obligations among the parents in a manner that is just and appropriate based on income and amount of time spent with the child by each parent, applying the principles set forth in Section 4053 and this article.

(c) Nothing in this section shall be construed to require reprogramming of the California Child Support Enforcement System, a change to the statewide uniform guideline for determining child support set forth in Section 4055, or a revision by the Department of Child Support Services of its regulations, policies, procedures, forms, or training materials. *(Added by Stats.2013, c. 564 (S.B.274), § 3. Amended by Stats.2016, c. 474 (A.B.2882), § 9, eff. Jan. 1, 2017.)*

Research References

Treatises and Practice Aids

Witkin, California Summary 10th Parent and Child § 413, Special Circumstances.

Witkin, California Summary 10th Parent and Child § 401A, (New) Where Child Has More Than Two Parents.

§ 4053. Implementation of statewide uniform guideline; principles to be followed by court

In implementing the statewide uniform guideline, the courts shall adhere to the following principles:

(a) A parent's first and principal obligation is to support his or her minor children according to the parent's circumstances and station in life.

(b) Both parents are mutually responsible for the support of their children.

(c) The guideline takes into account each parent's actual income and level of responsibility for the children.

(d) Each parent should pay for the support of the children according to his or her ability.

(e) The guideline seeks to place the interests of children as the state's top priority.

(f) Children should share in the standard of living of both parents. Child support may therefore appropriately improve the standard of living of the custodial household to improve the lives of the children.

(g) Child support orders in cases in which both parents have high levels of responsibility for the children should reflect the increased costs of raising the children in two homes and should minimize significant disparities in the children's living standards in the two homes.

(h) The financial needs of the children should be met through private financial resources as much as possible.

(i) It is presumed that a parent having primary physical responsibility for the children contributes a significant portion of available resources for the support of the children.

(j) The guideline seeks to encourage fair and efficient settlements of conflicts between parents and seeks to minimize the need for litigation.

(k) The guideline is intended to be presumptively correct in all cases, and only under special circumstances should child support orders fall below the child support mandated by the guideline formula.

(*l*) Child support orders must ensure that children actually receive fair, timely, and sufficient support reflecting the state's high standard of living and high costs of raising children compared to other states. *(Added by Stats.1993, c. 219 (A.B.1500), § 138.)*

Law Revision Commission Comments

Enactment [Revised Comment]

Section 4053 continues former Civil Code Section 4720(a)(3) without substantive change. [23 Cal.L.Rev.Comm. Reports 1 (1993)].

Commentary

Wilson v. Shea, 87 Cal.App.4th 887, 104 Cal.Rptr.2d 880 (2001), invokes subsection (*l*) to suggest in dictum that a custodial parent's relocation to a "less expensive" state might be a special circumstance justifying a reduction in the guideline amount of child support under § 4057 (b)(5).

Relying on this section as well as Sections 3900 and 7632, *Kristine M. v. David P., 135 Cal.App.4th 783, 37 Cal.Rptr.3d 748 (2006),* holds that a trial court's termination of a father's parental rights pursuant to the parents' stipulation is void as a matter of public policy and is an act that exceeds the court's jurisdiction. To similar effect, see *In re Marriage of Jackson, 136 Cal.App.4th 980, 39 Cal.Rptr.3d 365 (2006), review denied,* holding that a trial court's order granting a mother's motion, based on an agreement of the parents, to terminate her own parental rights was void because the order exceeded the court's jurisdiction.

Research References

Forms

California Practice Guide: Rutter Family Law Forms Form 6:8, Request for Order Re Child Support (Guideline Based on Earning Capacity in Lieu Of Actual Income).
California Transactions Forms--Family Law § 2:64, Amount Of Support.
California Transactions Forms--Family Law § 2:65, Add-Ons.
California Transactions Forms--Family Law § 3:23, Legislative Principles.
California Transactions Forms--Family Law § 3:36, Permitted Adjustments.
California Transactions Forms--Family Law § 3:39, Extraordinarily High Income.
West's California Code Forms, Family § 4000, Comment Overview--Court-Ordered Child Support.
West's California Code Forms, Family § 4050, Comment Overview--Statewide Uniform Guideline.

Treatises and Practice Aids

Witkin, California Summary 10th Parent and Child § 392, Discretion Of Lower Court.
Witkin, California Summary 10th Parent and Child § 395, Guiding Principles.
Witkin, California Summary 10th Parent and Child § 397, Annual Gross Income.
Witkin, California Summary 10th Parent and Child § 399, Earning Capacity Of Assets.
Witkin, California Summary 10th Parent and Child § 406, Other Adjustments.
Witkin, California Summary 10th Parent and Child § 411, Factors Rebutting Presumption.
Witkin, California Summary 10th Parent and Child § 413, Special Circumstances.
Witkin, California Summary 10th Parent and Child § 401A, (New) Where Child Has More Than Two Parents.

§ 4054. Review of statewide uniform guideline by Judicial Council; recommendations to Legislature

(a) The Judicial Council shall periodically review the statewide uniform guideline to recommend to the Legislature appropriate revisions.

(b) The review shall include economic data on the cost of raising children and analysis of case data, gathered through sampling or other methods, on the actual application of the guideline after the guideline's operative date. The review shall also include an analysis of guidelines and studies from other states, and other research and studies available to or undertaken by the Judicial Council.

(c) Any recommendations for revisions to the guideline shall be made to ensure that the guideline results in appropriate child support orders, to limit deviations from the guideline, or otherwise to help ensure that the guideline is in compliance with federal law.

(d) The Judicial Council may also review and report on other matters, including, but not limited to, the following:

(1) The treatment of the income of a subsequent spouse or nonmarital partner.

(2) The treatment of children from prior or subsequent relationships.

(3) The application of the guideline in a case where a payer parent has extraordinarily low or extraordinarily high income, or where each parent has primary physical custody of one or more of the children of the marriage.

(4) The benefits and limitations of a uniform statewide spousal support guideline and the interrelationship of that guideline with the state child support guideline.

(5) Whether the use of gross or net income in the guideline is preferable.

(6) Whether the guideline affects child custody litigation or the efficiency of the judicial process.

(7) Whether the various assumptions used in computer software used by some courts to calculate child support comport with state law and should be made available to parties and counsel.

(e) The initial review by the Judicial Council shall be submitted to the Legislature and to the Department of Child Support Services on or before December 31, 1993, and subsequent reviews shall occur at least every four years thereafter unless federal law requires a different interval.

(f) In developing its recommendations, the Judicial Council shall consult with a broad cross-section of groups involved in child support issues, including, but not limited to, the following:

(1) Custodial and noncustodial parents.

(2) Representatives of established women's rights and fathers' rights groups.

(3) Representatives of established organizations that advocate for the economic well-being of children.

(4) Members of the judiciary, district attorney's offices, the Attorney General's office, and the Department of Child Support Services.

(5) Certified family law specialists.

(6) Academicians specializing in family law.

(7) Persons representing low-income parents.

(8) Persons representing recipients of assistance under the CalWORKs program seeking child support services.

(g) In developing its recommendations, the Judicial Council shall seek public comment and shall be guided by the legislative intent that children share in the standard of living of both of their parents. *(Added by Stats.1993, c. 219 (A.B.1500), § 138. Amended by Stats.2002, c. 927 (A.B.3032), § 2.5.)*

Law Revision Commission Comments

Enactment [Revised Comment]

Section 4054 continues former Civil Code Section 4720(b)-(d) without substantive change. In subdivisions (a) and (c), the references to "the statewide uniform guideline" and "the" guideline have been substituted for the former references to the "guideline established in [former Civil Code] Section 4721." These are not substantive changes. [23 Cal.L.Rev.Comm. Reports 1 (1993)].

Research References

Treatises and Practice Aids

Witkin, California Summary 10th Parent and Child § 394, in General.

§ 4055. Statewide uniform guideline for determining child support

Section operative until Jan. 1, 2021. See, also, § 4055 operative Jan. 1, 2021.

(a) The statewide uniform guideline for determining child support orders is as follows: CS = K[HN − (H%)(TN)].

(b)(1) The components of the formula are as follows:

(A) CS = child support amount.

(B) K = amount of both parents' income to be allocated for child support as set forth in paragraph (3).

(C) HN = high earner's net monthly disposable income.

(D) H% = approximate percentage of time that the high earner has or will have primary physical responsibility for the children compared to the other parent. In cases in which parents have different time-sharing arrangements for different children, H% equals the average of the approximate percentages of time the high earner parent spends with each child.

(E) TN = total net monthly disposable income of both parties.

(2) To compute net disposable income, see Section 4059.

(3) K (amount of both parents' income allocated for child support) equals one plus H% (if H% is less than or equal to 50 percent) or two minus H% (if H% is greater than 50 percent) times the following fraction:

Total Net Disposable Income Per Month	K
$0–800	0.20 + TN/16,000
$801–6,666	0.25
$6,667–10,000	0.10 + 1,000/TN
Over $10,000	0.12 + 800/TN

For example, if H% equals 20 percent and the total monthly net disposable income of the parents is $1,000, K = (1 + 0.20) × 0.25, or 0.30. If H% equals 80 percent and the total monthly net disposable income of the parents is $1,000, K = (2 − 0.80) × 0.25, or 0.30.

(4) For more than one child, multiply CS by:

2 children	1.6
3 children	2
4 children	2.3
5 children	2.5
6 children	2.625
7 children	2.75
8 children	2.813
9 children	2.844
10 children	2.86

(5) If the amount calculated under the formula results in a positive number, the higher earner shall pay that amount to the lower earner. If the amount calculated under the formula results in a negative number, the lower earner shall pay the absolute value of that amount to the higher earner.

(6) In any default proceeding where proof is by affidavit pursuant to Section 2336, or in any proceeding for child support in which a party fails to appear after being duly noticed, H% shall be set at zero in the formula if the noncustodial parent is the higher earner or at 100 if the custodial parent is the higher earner, where there is no evidence presented demonstrating the percentage of time that the noncustodial parent has primary physical responsibility for the children. H% shall not be set as described * * * in paragraph (3) if the moving party in a default proceeding is the noncustodial parent or if the party who fails to appear after being duly noticed is the custodial parent. A statement by the party who is not in default as to the percentage of time that the noncustodial parent has primary physical responsibility for the children shall be deemed sufficient evidence.

(7) In all cases in which the net disposable income per month of the obligor is less than one thousand five hundred dollars ($1,500), adjusted annually for cost-of-living increases, there * * * is a rebuttable presumption that the obligor is entitled to a low-income adjustment. * * * The Judicial Council shall annually determine the amount of the net disposable income adjustment based on the change in the annual California Consumer Price Index for All Urban Consumers, published by the California Department of Industrial Relations, Division of Labor Statistics and Research. The presumption may be rebutted by evidence showing that the application of the low-income adjustment would be unjust and inappropriate in the particular case. In determining whether the presumption is rebutted, the court shall consider the principles provided in Section 4053, and the impact of the contemplated adjustment on the respective net incomes of the obligor and the obligee. The low-income adjustment shall reduce the child support amount otherwise determined under this section by an amount that is no greater than the amount calculated by multiplying the child support amount otherwise determined under this section by a fraction, the numerator of which is 1,500, adjusted annually for cost-of-living increases, minus the obligor's net disposable income per month, and the denominator of which is 1,500, adjusted annually for cost-of-living increases.

(8) Unless the court orders otherwise, the order for child support shall allocate the support amount so that the amount of support for the youngest child is the amount of support for one child, and the amount for the next youngest child is the difference between that amount and the amount for two children, with similar allocations for additional children. However, this paragraph does not apply to cases in which there are different time-sharing arrangements for different children or where the court determines that the allocation would be inappropriate in the particular case.

(c) If a court uses a computer to calculate the child support order, the computer program shall not automatically default affirmatively or negatively on whether a low-income adjustment is to be applied. If the low-income adjustment is applied, the computer program shall not provide the amount of the low-income adjustment. Instead, the computer program shall ask the user whether or not to apply the low-income adjustment, and if answered affirmatively, the computer program shall provide the range of the adjustment permitted by paragraph (7) of subdivision (b).

(d) This section shall remain in effect only until January 1, 2021, and as of that date is repealed, unless a later enacted statute, that is enacted before January 1, 2021, deletes or extends that date. *(Added by Stats.1993, c. 219 (A.B.1500), § 138. Amended by Stats.1993, c. 1156 (S.B.541), § 1; Stats.1994, c. 906 (A.B.923), § 1.5; Stats.1998, c. 581 (A.B. 2801), § 15; Stats.2003, c. 225 (A.B.1752), § 1, eff. Aug. 11, 2003; Stats.2012, c. 646 (A.B.2393), § 1; Stats.2013, c. 76 (A.B.383), § 61; Stats.2017, c. 730 (S.B.469), § 1, eff. Jan. 1, 2018.)*

Repeal

For repeal of this section, see its terms.

Law Revision Commission Comments

Enactment [Revised Comment]

Section 4055 supersedes former Civil Code Section 4721(a)-(b). [23 Cal.L.Rev.Comm. Reports 1 (1993)].

Commentary

In re Marriage of Katzberg, 88 Cal.App.4th 974, 106 Cal.Rptr.2d 157 (2001), holds that, for the purpose of determining the time share of each parent, the trial court properly imputed the time the child spent at boarding school to the parent who had primary custodial responsibility for the child and was paying the child's schooling expenses.

DaSilva v. DaSilva, 119 Cal.App.4th 1030, 15 Cal.Rptr.3d 59 (2004), explains that subsection (b)(1)(D) defines the H% factor as the "approximate percentage of time that the high earner has or will have *primary physical responsibility* for the children compared to the other parent" (emphasis added). It does not refer to "physical custody." Thus, time may be imputed to a parent when a child is not in the physical custody of either parent so long as the child is under the physical supervision of a parent. *DaSilva* lists criteria for determining which parent should be treated as bearing primary physical responsibility for a child during periods in which the child is in the physical custody of neither parent.

Note that Stats 1993 Ch 1156, § 1 (SB 541) eliminated former subsection (b)(6), which denied time reduction to parents whose children receive AFDC benefits. This disparate treatment had been held constitutional in *County of Los Angeles v. Patrick, 11 Cal.App.4th 1246, 14 Cal.Rptr.2d 665 (1992)*. See also *County of Yolo v. Worrell, 208 Cal.App.3d 471, 256 Cal.Rptr. 259 (1989)*. See, additionally, *State of Washington v. Cobb, 194 Cal.App.3d 773, 239 Cal.Rptr. 726 (1987)* (holding constitutional a more onerous support requirement for parents of children receiving AFDC benefits).

In re Marriage of Drake, 53 Cal.App.4th 1139, 62 Cal.Rptr.2d 466 (1997), review denied June 11, 1997, holds that the statewide uniform child support guideline (Sections 4050–4076) applies to disabled adult children.

Research References

Forms

California Practice Guide: Rutter Family Law Forms Form 5:19, Non-Guideline Child Support Findings Attachment.

California Transactions Forms--Family Law § 2:64, Amount Of Support.

California Transactions Forms--Family Law § 3:22, Mandatory Compliance With Statewide Guidelines.

California Transactions Forms--Family Law § 3:36, Permitted Adjustments.

California Transactions Forms--Family Law § 3:112, Alternating the Dependency Exemption.

West's California Code Forms, Family § 4050, Comment Overview--Statewide Uniform Guideline.

West's California Code Forms, Family § 4068 Form 2, Financial Statement--Simplified.

West's California Judicial Council Forms FL-342, Child Support Information and Order Attachment.

Treatises and Practice Aids

Witkin, California Summary 10th Husband and Wife § 310, Local Child Support Agency.

Witkin, California Summary 10th Parent and Child § 387, Application and Order or Response.

Witkin, California Summary 10th Parent and Child § 396, Basic Formula.

Witkin, California Summary 10th Parent and Child § 405, Adjustment for More Than One Child.

Witkin, California Summary 10th Parent and Child § 406, Other Adjustments.

Witkin, California Summary 10th Parent and Child § 409, Allocation Of Additional Support.

Witkin, California Summary 10th Parent and Child § 411, Factors Rebutting Presumption.

Witkin, California Summary 10th Parent and Child § 415, in General.

Witkin, California Summary 10th Parent and Child § 512, Illustrations.

§ 4055. Statewide uniform guideline for determining child support

Section operative Jan. 1, 2021. See, also, § 4055 operative until Jan. 1, 2021.

(a) The statewide uniform guideline for determining child support orders is as follows: CS = K[HN − (H%)(TN)].

(b)(1) The components of the formula are as follows:

(A) CS = child support amount.

(B) K = amount of both parents' income to be allocated for child support as set forth in paragraph (3).

(C) HN = high earner's net monthly disposable income.

(D) H% = approximate percentage of time that the high earner has or will have primary physical responsibility for the children compared to the other parent. In cases in which parents have different time-sharing arrangements for different children, H% equals the average of the approximate percentages of time the high earner parent spends with each child.

(E) TN = total net monthly disposable income of both parties.

(2) To compute net disposable income, see Section 4059.

(3) K (amount of both parents' income allocated for child support) equals one plus H% (if H% is less than or equal to 50 percent) or two minus H% (if H% is greater than 50 percent) times the following fraction:

Total Net Disposable Income Per Month	K
$0–800	0.20 + TN/16,000

$801–6,666	0.25
$6,667–10,000	0.10 + 1,000/TN
Over $10,000	0.12 + 800/TN

For example, if H% equals 20 percent and the total monthly net disposable income of the parents is $1,000, K = (1 + 0.20) × 0.25, or 0.30. If H% equals 80 percent and the total monthly net disposable income of the parents is $1,000, K = (2 − 0.80) × 0.25, or 0.30.

(4) For more than one child, multiply CS by:

2 children	1.6
3 children	2
4 children	2.3
5 children	2.5
6 children	2.625
7 children	2.75
8 children	2.813
9 children	2.844
10 children	2.86

(5) If the amount calculated under the formula results in a positive number, the higher earner shall pay that amount to the lower earner. If the amount calculated under the formula results in a negative number, the lower earner shall pay the absolute value of that amount to the higher earner.

(6) In any default proceeding where proof is by affidavit pursuant to Section 2336, or in any proceeding for child support in which a party fails to appear after being duly noticed, H% shall be set at zero in the formula if the noncustodial parent is the higher earner or at 100 if the custodial parent is the higher earner, where there is no evidence presented demonstrating the percentage of time that the noncustodial parent has primary physical responsibility for the children. H% shall not be set as described above if the moving party in a default proceeding is the noncustodial parent or if the party who fails to appear after being duly noticed is the custodial parent. A statement by the party who is not in default as to the percentage of time that the noncustodial parent has primary physical responsibility for the children shall be deemed sufficient evidence.

(7) In all cases in which the net disposable income per month of the obligor is less than one thousand dollars ($1,000), there shall be a rebuttable presumption that the obligor is entitled to a low-income adjustment. The presumption may be rebutted by evidence showing that the application of the low-income adjustment would be unjust and inappropriate in the particular case. In determining whether the presumption is rebutted, the court shall consider the principles provided in Section 4053, and the impact of the contemplated adjustment on the respective net incomes of the obligor and the obligee. The low-income adjustment shall reduce the child support amount otherwise determined under this section by an amount that is no greater than the amount calculated by multiplying the child support amount otherwise determined under this section by a fraction, the numerator of which is 1,000 minus the obligor's net disposable income per month, and the denominator of which is 1,000.

(8) Unless the court orders otherwise, the order for child support shall allocate the support amount so that the amount of support for the youngest child is the amount of support for one child, and the amount for the next youngest child is the difference between that amount and the amount for two children, with similar allocations for additional children. However, this paragraph does not apply to cases in which there are different time-sharing arrangements for different children or where the court determines that the allocation would be inappropriate in the particular case.

(c) If a court uses a computer to calculate the child support order, the computer program shall not automatically default affirmatively or negatively on whether a low-income adjustment is to be applied. If the low-income adjustment is applied, the computer program shall not provide the amount of the low-income adjustment. Instead, the computer program shall ask the user whether or not to apply the low-income adjustment, and if answered affirmatively, the computer program shall provide the range of the adjustment permitted by paragraph (7) of subdivision (b).

(d) This section shall become operative on January 1, 2021. *(Added by Stats.2012, c. 646 (A.B.2393), § 2, operative Jan. 1, 2018. Amended by Stats.2013, c. 76 (A.B.383), § 62, operative Jan. 1, 2018; Stats.2017, c. 730 (S.B.469), § 2, eff. Jan. 1, 2018, operative Jan. 1, 2021.)*

Research References

Forms

California Practice Guide: Rutter Family Law Forms Form 5:19, Non-Guideline Child Support Findings Attachment.

California Transactions Forms--Family Law § 2:64, Amount Of Support.

California Transactions Forms--Family Law § 3:22, Mandatory Compliance With Statewide Guidelines.

California Transactions Forms--Family Law § 3:36, Permitted Adjustments.

California Transactions Forms--Family Law § 3:112, Alternating the Dependency Exemption.

West's California Code Forms, Family § 4050, Comment Overview--Statewide Uniform Guideline.

West's California Code Forms, Family § 4068 Form 2, Financial Statement--Simplified.

West's California Judicial Council Forms FL-342, Child Support Information and Order Attachment.

Treatises and Practice Aids

Witkin, California Summary 10th Husband and Wife § 310, Local Child Support Agency.

Witkin, California Summary 10th Parent and Child § 387, Application and Order or Response.

Witkin, California Summary 10th Parent and Child § 396, Basic Formula.

Witkin, California Summary 10th Parent and Child § 405, Adjustment for More Than One Child.

Witkin, California Summary 10th Parent and Child § 406, Other Adjustments.

Witkin, California Summary 10th Parent and Child § 409, Allocation Of Additional Support.

Witkin, California Summary 10th Parent and Child § 411, Factors Rebutting Presumption.

Witkin, California Summary 10th Parent and Child § 415, in General.

Witkin, California Summary 10th Parent and Child § 512, Illustrations.

§ 4056. Amount differing from guideline formula; information used in determining statewide uniform guideline amount

(a) To comply with federal law, the court shall state, in writing or on the record, the following information whenever the court is ordering an amount for support that differs from the statewide uniform guideline formula amount under this article:

(1) The amount of support that would have been ordered under the guideline formula.

(2) The reasons the amount of support ordered differs from the guideline formula amount.

(3) The reasons the amount of support ordered is consistent with the best interests of the children.

(b) At the request of any party, the court shall state in writing or on the record the following information used in determining the guideline amount under this article:

(1) The net monthly disposable income of each parent.

(2) The actual federal income tax filing status of each parent (for example, single, married, married filing separately, or head of household and number of exemptions).

(3) Deductions from gross income for each parent.

(4) The approximate percentage of time pursuant to paragraph (1) of subdivision (b) of Section 4055 that each parent has primary physical responsibility for the children compared to the other parent. *(Added by Stats.1993, c. 219 (A.B.1500), § 138. Amended by Stats.1993, c. 1156 (S.B.541), § 2.)*

Law Revision Commission Comments

Enactment [Revised Comment]

Section 4056 supersedes former Civil Code Section 4721(c). See also Section 3011 (factors in determining best interest of child). [23 Cal.L.Rev.Comm. Reports 1 (1993)].

Commentary

For discussion and strict application of the subsection (a) requirement that any deviation from the guideline amount be fully justified in writing with appropriate findings, see *In re Marriage of Gigliotti, 33 Cal.App.4th 518, 39 Cal.Rptr.2d 367, 372 (1995). See also Rojas v. Mitchell, 50 Cal.App.4th 1445, 58 Cal.Rptr.2d 354 (1996)* (when court deviates from guideline amount, it must *sua sponte* provide the information required by Section 4056).

Y.R. v. A.F., 9 Cal.App.5th 974, 215 Cal.Rptr.3d 577 (2017), reversed a trial court order requiring a father who was an extraordinarily high earner to pay child support of $8,500 a month when the guideline amount was over $25,000 a month because, inter alia, the court failed to satisfy the subsection (a) requirement of stating its reasons for deviating from the guideline amount and explaining why the deviation was in the best interest of the child.

When a party points out a factual error in the trial court's application of the child support formula, the court must reapply the formula to the corrected facts; it may not merely "estimate" the corrected child support obligation. *In re Marriage of Whealon, 53 Cal.App.4th 132, 61 Cal.Rptr.2d 559 (1997).*

Absent compliance with this section, a court may not make an order requiring a percentage of appellant's income above a certain dollar amount without regard to changes in the custodial parent's income, because the resultant payments would differ from those required by the formula, which takes into account the income of both parents. *In re Marriage of Hall, 81 Cal.App.4th 313, 96 Cal.Rptr.2d 772 (2000).*

Research References

Forms

California Practice Guide: Rutter Family Law Forms Form 1:32, Glossary Of Common Family Law Terms, Phrases and Concepts (Enclosure to Form 1:31).

California Transactions Forms--Family Law § 2:64, Amount Of Support.

California Transactions Forms--Family Law § 2:65, Add-Ons.

California Transactions Forms--Family Law § 2:88, Marital Settlement Agreement.

California Transactions Forms--Family Law § 3:28, Statutory Findings as Basis for Support.

California Transactions Forms--Family Law § 3:32, Determination Of Net Monthly Disposable Income.

West's California Code Forms, Family § 4050, Comment Overview--Statewide Uniform Guideline.

West's California Code Forms, Family § 2338 Form 8, Marital Agreement.

West's California Code Forms, Family § 3585 Form 2, Child Support Provisions.

West's California Judicial Council Forms FL-693, Guideline Findings Attachment.

West's California Judicial Council Forms FL-342(A), Non-Guideline Child Support Findings Attachment.

Treatises and Practice Aids

Witkin, California Summary 10th Parent and Child § 407, Statement Supporting Deviation from Guideline.

Witkin, California Summary 10th Parent and Child § 411, Factors Rebutting Presumption.

Witkin, California Summary 10th Parent and Child § 412, Extraordinarily High Earner.

Witkin, California Summary 10th Parent and Child § 414, Stipulated Support Agreements.

Witkin, California Summary 10th Parent and Child § 428, Recovery Of Arrearages.

§ 4057. Amount of child support established by formula; rebuttable presumption

(a) The amount of child support established by the formula provided in subdivision (a) of Section 4055 is presumed to be the correct amount of child support to be ordered.

(b) The presumption of subdivision (a) is a rebuttable presumption affecting the burden of proof and may be rebutted by admissible evidence showing that application of the formula would be unjust or inappropriate in the particular case, consistent with the principles set forth in Section 4053, because one or more of the following factors is found to be applicable by a preponderance of the evidence, and the court states in writing or on the record the information required in subdivision (a) of Section 4056:

(1) The parties have stipulated to a different amount of child support under subdivision (a) of Section 4065.

(2) The sale of the family residence is deferred pursuant to Chapter 8 (commencing with Section 3800) of Part 1 and the rental value of the family residence where the children reside exceeds the mortgage payments, homeowner's insurance, and property taxes. The amount of any adjustment pursuant to this paragraph shall not be greater than the excess amount.

(3) The parent being ordered to pay child support has an extraordinarily high income and the amount determined under the formula would exceed the needs of the children.

(4) A party is not contributing to the needs of the children at a level commensurate with that party's custodial time.

(5) Application of the formula would be unjust or inappropriate due to special circumstances in the particular case. These special circumstances include, but are not limited to, the following:

(A) Cases in which the parents have different time-sharing arrangements for different children.

(B) Cases in which both parents have substantially equal time-sharing of the children and one parent has a much lower or higher percentage of income used for housing than the other parent.

(C) Cases in which the children have special medical or other needs that could require child support that would be greater than the formula amount.

(D) Cases in which a child is found to have more than two parents. *(Added by Stats.1993, c. 219 (A.B.1500), § 138. Amended by Stats.1993, c. 935 (S.B.145), § 1; Stats.1993, c. 1156 (S.B.541), § 3.5; Stats.2013, c. 564 (S.B.274), § 4.)*

Law Revision Commission Comments

Enactment [Revised Comment]

Section 4057 supersedes former Civil Code Section 4721(d)-(e). The language in subdivisions (a) and (b) has been revised to conform with the language of the Evidence Code sections dealing with presumptions. See, e.g., Evid. Code §§ 660–669.5 (presumptions affecting the burden of proof). This is not a substantive change. In subdivision (b), the reference to Section 4053 has been substituted for the broader reference to former Civil Code Section 4720. This is not a substantive change, since Section 4053 continues the relevant part of former Civil Code Section 4720 without substantive change. See also Section 3011 (factors in determining best interest of child). [23 Cal.L.Rev.Comm. Reports 1 (1993)].

Commentary

Subsection (b)(3) allows downward deviation from the formula when the parent ordered to pay child support has an extraordinarily high income and the amount determined under the formula would exceed the needs of the children. There is some tension between this provision and the section 4053 statement of legislative intent that "...the children should share in the standard of living of both parents. Child support may therefore appropriately improve the standard of living in the custodial household to improve the lives of the children." *S.P. v. F.G., 4 Cal.App.5th 921, 208 Cal.Rptr.3d 903 (2016)*, review denied, affirmed a child support award that was far below the guideline amount when the obligor had an extraordinarily high income and the amount of support ordered would provide the obligor's daughter with the standard of living of a "financially privileged child." Compare *Y.R. v. A.F., 9 Cal.App.5th 974, 215 Cal.Rptr.3d 577 (2017)*, which reversed a trial court order requiring a father who was an extraordinarily high earner to pay child support of $8,500 a month when the guideline amount was over $25,000 a month, because the court (1) failed to satisfy the section 4056(a) requirement of stating its reasons for deviating from the guideline amount and explaining why the deviation was in the best interest of the child; (2) erred in determining the child's needs based solely on the mother's historic expenses and not the father's station in life; (3) erred in determining that the father should not be required to pay expenses that also benefitted the mother's other children; and (4) erred in placing the burden of establishing the child's needs on the mother, rather than the father who was seeking a deviation from the guideline amount.

County of Lake v. Antoni, 18 Cal.App.4th 1102, 22 Cal.Rptr.2d 804 (1993), broadly interprets Subsection (b)(5) "special circumstances," giving the trial court considerable discretion to deviate from the child support figure established by the Section 4055 guideline. *Antoni* approves a trial court's substantial reduction of the guideline figure on the ground that the child support obligor had an "extraordinarily high amount of debt seemingly incurred for living needs," was probably entitled to a hardship deduction for a child of his new marriage, and provided support for a stepchild of his new marriage. Rejecting the County's argument that neither Section 4057 nor Sections 4070–4071 provide hardship relief for consumer debt or stepchild support, the court of appeal rested its affirmance on the language of Section 4057 (b)(5), which provides that the special circumstances enumerated by the statute are not exclusive or exhaustive: "These special circumstances include, but are not limited to, the following . . . . ." But see Justice King's dictum to the contrary in *In re Marriage of Carter, 26 Cal.App.4th 1024, 33 Cal.Rptr.2d 1 (1994)* (trial court lacks discretion to vary from the presumptively correct amount "unless one or more of the statutorily enumerated rebuttal factors is found to exist"); *In re Marriage of C., 57 Cal.App.4th 1100, 67 Cal.Rptr.2d 508 (1997)* (obligor's discretionary spending is not a "special circumstance" justifying deviation from child support prescribed by formula; child support is determined by parents' income, not parents' discretionary consumption expenditure); and *Haggard v. Haggard, 38 Cal.App.4th 1566, 45 Cal.Rptr.2d 638 (1995)* (noncustodial support obligor parent's voluntary support of nonadopted children of new mate does not entitle support obligor either to a Section 4057(b)(5) finding of "special circumstances" or to a Section 4059(g) hardship deduction). For additional discussion of subsection (b), see *In re Marriage of Gigliotti, 33 Cal.App.4th 518, 39 Cal.Rptr.2d 367, 372 (1995)* (noncustodial parent's increased visitation costs due to custodial parent's court-approved move away not a subsection (b)(5) "special circumstance" absent a court finding that application of the formula would be unjust or inappropriate). *Gigliotti* is further discussed in Section 4062 Commentary. With *Gigliotti*, compare *Wilson v. Shea, 87 Cal.App.4th 887, 104 Cal.Rptr.2d 880 (2001)*, where the court held, after the custodial parent's relocation, that the need to assure a child's frequent and continuing contact with both parents justified reducing, under subsection (b)(5), the guideline child support amount by an amount intended to cover the noncustodial parent's transportation expenses in visiting the child. *Wilson* also invokes § 4053 *(l)* to suggest in dictum that a custodial parent's relocation to a "less expensive" state might be a special circumstance justifying a reduction in the guideline amount of child support under subsection (b)(5).

Applying subsection (b)(5), *Brothers v. Kern, 154 Cal.App.4th 126, 64 Cal.Rptr.3d 239 (2007)*, justified a substantial increase in the obligation otherwise due under the formula on the ground that the obligor's standard of living would not be affected because he was incarcerated and the child's standard of living could not be sustained if the guideline figure were used. For further discussion of *Brothers*, see commentary to section 4058.

County of Stanislaus v. Gibbs, 59 Cal.App.4th 1417, 69 Cal.Rptr.2d 819 (1998), held that a trial court abused its discretion by finding "special circumstances" and reducing the presumptively correct amount of child support because the obligor had high consumer debt and other children to support, when the child who was the subject of the child support order was receiving public assistance. (Family Code Section 4071.5, which provided that no hardship deduction could be granted to a parent when the child who was the subject of the child support order was receiving public assistance, was repealed in 1999.) Additionally, in order to reduce a presumptively correct child support obligation on the ground of consumer debt, *Gibbs* says that the trial court must take into account all the income of the obligor's household, not just the income of the obligor alone.

Relying on subsection (b)(5)(B) and Section 4058(a)(1), *County of Orange v. Smith, 132 Cal.App.4th 1434, 34 Cal.Rptr.3d 383 (2005), review denied,* treated as "income" $600 that a father received monthly from a roommate, which the father passed on immediately to his landlord to satisfy his $1,600 monthly rent obligation to the landlord.

Invoking subsection (b)(5)(C) of this section and § 4058, *In re Marriage of de Guigne, 97 Cal.App.4th 1353, 119 Cal.Rptr.2d 430 (2002)*, held that the trial court did not abuse its discretion in ordering a support obligor to pay child support and spousal support in an amount greater than the obligor's total monthly income when the obligor had extensive property holdings that were not yielding income (see Commentary to § 4058) and the support was necessary to reduce the disparity between the support obligees' marital and postdivorce standards of living even though the marital standard of living was based on overspending.

Distinguishing *de Guigne, In re Marriage of Williams, 150 Cal. App.4th 1221, 58 Cal.Rptr.3d 877 (2007)*, held that a trial court erred in imputing, under section 4058, a reasonable rate of return to a portion of a support obligor's equity in a 11,000 square foot Pebble Beach home absent a showing, under this section, of special circumstances that would render guideline support unjust or inappropriate.

In re Marriage of Schlafly, 149 Cal.App.4th 747, 57 Cal.Rptr.3d 274 (2007), held that a trial court erred in determining child support by imputing, under section 4058, $3,000 a month of nontaxable income to a support obligor based on his mortgage-free housing. The court reasoned that mortgage-free housing might be considered a special circumstance justifying deviation from the guideline under this section, but it is not imputed income for purposes of section 4058.

Similarly, *M.S. v. O.S, 176 Cal.App.4th 548, 97 Cal.Rptr.3d 812 (2009)*, held that a trial court abused its discretion when it included the value of tribal payment of a support obligor's attorney fees in the annual gross income of the obligor, because the tribal benefit did not create any disposable income for the obligor. Nevertheless, the court opined that a trial court might consider the value of the benefit as a special circumstance within the meaning of section 4057.

Although declining to impute to a support obligor the higher income previously earned by the obligor, *In re Marriage of Berger, 170 Cal.App.4th 1070, 88 Cal.Rptr.3d 766 (2009)*, holds that the obligor's practice of "deferring" his salary in order to protect his investment in his business was a subsection (b)(5) "special circumstance" that would justify treating his deferred income as current income for purposes of child support. Alternatively, deferral would warrant including the deferred salary as current income for purposes of section 4058(a).

Interpreting Section 4058 (a)(1), *In re Marriage of Corman, 59 Cal.App.4th 1492, 69 Cal.Rptr.2d 880 (1997)*, holds that spousal support received by the noncustodial parent from the custodial parent is not "gross income" for purposes of application of the Section 4055 child support guideline. (Compare Section 4061, which takes spousal support payable by a party into account for purposes of calculating Section 4062 "add-on" expenses.) Nor is such spousal support a "special circumstance" for purposes of Section 4057 deviation from the presumptively correct guideline amount.

When the payment of child support would leave the support obligor with insufficient funds for basic subsistence, the trial court, under subsection (b)(5), may reduce the presumptive child support obligation to zero. *City and County of San Francisco v. Miller, 49 Cal.App.4th 866, 56 Cal.Rptr.2d 887 (1996), review denied December 23, 1996.*

A court may not make a subsection (b)(5) finding that "application of the formula would be unjust or inappropriate due to special circumstances in the particular case" when the basis of such finding is the new mate of the custodial parent, because the consideration of such income is generally prohibited, absent specified circumstances, by Section 4057.5. *In re Marriage of Wood, 37 Cal.App.4th 1059, 44 Cal.Rptr.2d 236 (1995), review denied December 14, 1995.* For further discussion of *Wood*, see Section 4057.5, Commentary.

Interpreting prior but similar law (Cal. Rules of Court, former Rule 1274(e)(8): "Application of the guideline would be unjust or inappropriate due to the special circumstances of the case"; compare Family Code Section 4057(b)(5)), *County of San Diego v. Guy C., 30 Cal.App.4th 1325, 36 Cal.Rptr.2d 222 (1994)*, holds that "special circumstances" are limited to the parties' economic circumstances and do not authorize consideration of non-economic factors, in this case the severe behavioral problems of an adopted child, which required AFDC expenditure for out-of-home dependency placement.

The subsection (b)(5) cases are analyzed and reconciled in *In re Marriage of Butler & Gill, 53 Cal.App.4th 462, 61 Cal.Rptr.2d 781 (1997)* (holding that the (b)(5) "special circumstances" exception permits a trial court to deviate from the guideline amount only when the obligor parent would otherwise experience unusual hardship).

When a child was removed from a custodial support obligee in a dependency proceeding and, in the early stages of the proceeding, was placed with the support obligor, *In re Marriage of Cryer, 198 Cal.App.4th 1039, 131 Cal.Rptr.3d 424 (2011)*, held that a trial court acted within its discretion in continuing the high-income support obligor's above-guideline support despite the other parent's reduced time share. *Cryer* invoked subsection (b)(5) in concluding that reduction to the guideline amount would be unjust to the support obligee and the child.

When a child will, in any event, be supported by public funds, the child's interests are not adversely affected by reduction of child support. A court may, therefore, be more liberal in its application of this section. See, for example, *City and County of San Francisco v. Funches, 75 Cal.App.4th 243, 89 Cal.Rptr.2d 49 (1999)* (holding that trial court's reduction of the guideline amount to reflect weekends spent with obligor, whose paternity of 16–year-old in foster care had just been adjudicated, and reduction of reimbursement to City for past support of child was not an abuse of discretion).

For discussion of the reduction of guideline child support in light of a subsection (b)(2) deferred sale of family residence order, see *In re Marriage of Braud, 45 Cal.App.4th 797, 818–819, 53 Cal.Rptr.2d 179 (1996)*. For treatment of subsection (b)(3) high income support obligors, see *McGinley v. Herman, 50 Cal.App.4th 936, 57 Cal.Rptr.2d 921 (1997)* (requiring specified findings when uniform formula is not applied because the obligor has extraordinarily high income and the amount of support determined under the formula would exceed the child's needs) and *Estevez v. Superior Court, 22 Cal.App.4th 423, 27 Cal.Rptr.2d 470 (1994), review denied 4/21/94*. *Estevez* is discussed in Section 3552 Commentary. See also *In re Marriage of Chandler, 60 Cal.App.4th 124, 70 Cal.Rptr.2d 109 (1997)*, disapproving trial court treatment of child support payable by a support obligor with unusually high income. In *Chandler*, the guideline obligation was more than $9,000 monthly. The trial court awarded $3,000 ordinary support and $4,000 in trust, the trust funds to be distributed for the child's reasonable Section 4062 "add-on" costs, and the balance to be distributed to the child when she reached the age of majority. The court of appeal rejected the trust for several reasons: (1) a trust should be used only when there is a compelling need to limit the custodial parent's access to child support funds; (2) the $3,000 monthly child support, standing alone, would have constituted an abuse of discretion; and (3) the trust device improperly limited the custodial parent's access to Section 4062 child support payable to the trust.

Interpreting § 4059(a), *In re Marriage of Carlton & D'Allessandro, 91 Cal.App.4th 1213, 111 Cal.Rptr.2d 329 (2001)*, holds that the trial court erred in assigning a child support obligor the tax filing status of "married filing jointly" when his actual status was "married filing separately" and in allocating to the obligor a tax deduction arising from his new spouse's separate property ("separate property" because the couple had a premarital agreement providing for the segregation and separate ownership of all funds and assets) mortgage payments on the home in which the couple resided. The latter error also runs afoul of § 4057.5(a), which provides that the income of a parent's subsequent spouse or marital partner shall not be considered in determining or modifying child support. (But query whether the obligor's cost-free housing is "income...from whatever source derived" within the meaning of § 4058(a), or a "special circumstance" within the meaning of subsection (b)(5) of this section.)

Research References

Forms

California Practice Guide: Rutter Family Law Forms Form 6:10, Responsive Declaration to Request for Order Re Child Support Based on Guideline Formula (Extraordinarily High Income Earner Rebuttal).
California Transactions Forms--Family Law § 2:64, Amount Of Support.
California Transactions Forms--Family Law § 2:88, Marital Settlement Agreement.
California Transactions Forms--Family Law § 3:36, Permitted Adjustments.
California Transactions Forms--Family Law § 3:39, Extraordinarily High Income.
West's California Code Forms, Family § 4050, Comment Overview--Statewide Uniform Guideline.
West's California Code Forms, Family § 2338 Form 8, Marital Agreement.
West's California Code Forms, Family § 3585 Form 2, Child Support Provisions.
West's California Judicial Council Forms FL-693, Guideline Findings Attachment.

Treatises and Practice Aids

Witkin, California Summary 10th Community Property § 207, Statutory Procedure and Factors.
Witkin, California Summary 10th Parent and Child § 392, Discretion Of Lower Court.
Witkin, California Summary 10th Parent and Child § 395, Guiding Principles.
Witkin, California Summary 10th Parent and Child § 397, Annual Gross Income.
Witkin, California Summary 10th Parent and Child § 409, Allocation Of Additional Support.
Witkin, California Summary 10th Parent and Child § 411, Factors Rebutting Presumption.
Witkin, California Summary 10th Parent and Child § 412, Extraordinarily High Earner.
Witkin, California Summary 10th Parent and Child § 413, Special Circumstances.
Witkin, California Summary 10th Parent and Child § 423, Support Of Disabled Indigent Adult Child.

§ 4057.5. Income of obligor parent's subsequent spouse or nonmarital partner; consideration

(a)(1) The income of the obligor parent's subsequent spouse or nonmarital partner shall not be considered when determining or modifying child support, except in an extraordinary case where excluding that income would lead to extreme and severe hardship to any child subject to the child support award, in which case the court shall also consider whether including that income would lead to extreme and severe hardship to any child supported by the obligor or by the obligor's subsequent spouse or nonmarital partner.

(2) The income of the obligee parent's subsequent spouse or nonmarital partner shall not be considered when determining or modifying child support, except in an extraordinary case where excluding that income would lead to extreme and severe hardship to any child subject to the child support award, in which case the court shall also consider whether including that income would lead to extreme and severe hardship to any child supported by the obligee or by the obligee's subsequent spouse or nonmarital partner.

(b) For purposes of this section, an extraordinary case may include a parent who voluntarily or intentionally quits work or reduces income, or who intentionally remains unemployed or underemployed and relies on a subsequent spouse's income.

(c) If any portion of the income of either parent's subsequent spouse or nonmarital partner is allowed to be considered pursuant to this section, discovery for the purposes of determining income shall be based on W2 and 1099 income tax forms, except where the court determines that application would be unjust or inappropriate.

(d) If any portion of the income of either parent's subsequent spouse or nonmarital partner is allowed to be considered pursuant to this section, the court shall allow a hardship deduction based on the minimum living expenses for one or more stepchildren of the party subject to the order.

(e) The enactment of this section constitutes cause to bring an action for modification of a child support order entered prior to the operative date of this section. *(Added by Stats.1993, c. 935 (S.B.145), § 2. Amended by Stats.1994, c. 1140 (S.B.279), § 1; Stats.1994, c. 1269 (A.B.2208), § 47.5.)*

Commentary

In re Marriage of Wood, 37 Cal.App.4th 1059, 44 Cal.Rptr.2d 236 (1995), review denied December 14, 1995, holds that a trial court modification of child support based upon an increase in the custodial mother's standard of living due to her remarriage is an impermissible modification because it is effectively predicated upon her new mate's income, in violation of Section 4057.5. Under this section, new mate income may be taken into account only when a child will suffer if the court does not consider such income. Effectively, the statute cannot be invoked when the new mate in question is the spouse or nonmarital partner of the custodial parent. Despite an apparent statutory effort at evenhandedness, the statutory formulation has no possible application when the new mate is the obligee's, as opposed to the obligor's, new mate. Compare subsections (a)(2) and (a)(1).

Wood also emphasizes that each subsection of Section 4057.5 is limited by the requirement that new mate income may be taken into account only to prevent hardship to a supported child. Thus, under this section, the intentional unemployment of a custodial parent is normally immaterial. Such unemployment may only be taken into account under Section 4058(b), where it may, or may not, affect the obligor's guideline obligation.

In re Marriage of Carlsen, 50 Cal.App.4th 212, 57 Cal.Rptr.2d 630 (1996), holds that for purposes of determining the support obligee's Section 4059(a) tax rate in order to calculate the obligee's net disposable income, the court may properly take into account the income of the obligee's new spouse. *Carlsen* concludes that such treatment violates neither the letter nor the spirit of Section 4057.5. *Accord, County of Tulare v. Campbell, 50 Cal.App.4th 847, 57 Cal.Rptr.2d 902 (1996)* (same holding with respect to income of support obligor's new spouse). Although *Carlsen* and *Campbell* allow inclusion of new spouse income, neither case considers how such new spouse should be taken into account. For excellent discussion of this question, see George Norton, Using New Spouse Income for Tax Allocation of Child Support—An Equitable Method for Allocation of Joint Taxes, 1997 California Family Law Monthly 1–6 (January).

Interpreting § 4059(a), *In re Marriage of Carlton & D'Allessandro, 91 Cal.App.4th 1213, 111 Cal.Rptr.2d 329 (2001)*, held that the trial court erred in assigning a child support obligor the tax filing status of "married filing jointly" when his actual status was "married filing separately" and in allocating to the obligor a tax deduction arising from his new spouse's separate property ("separate property" because the couple had a premarital agreement providing for the segregation and separate ownership of all funds and assets) mortgage payments on the home in which the couple resided. The latter error also runs afoul of subsection (a) of this section, which provides that the income of a parent's subsequent spouse or marital partner shall not be considered in determining or modifying child support. (But query whether the obligor's "free housing" is "income...from whatever source derived" within the meaning of § 4058(a) or a "special circumstance" within the meaning of § 4057(b)(5).)

Also interpreting § 4059, *In re Marriage of Loh, 93 Cal.App.4th 325, 112 Cal.Rptr.2d 893 (2001)*, held that the trial court erred when, in a child support modification proceeding, it disregarded a support obligor's income tax returns and instead used evidence of his current life style, which was subsidized by a nonmarital partner, to establish his income. *Loh* concluded that the evidence was insufficient to establish obligor's income, and its use also violated § 4057.5, which does not allow trial courts to look at the income of a new spouse or nonmarital partner in determining or modifying child support.

Research References

Forms

California Transactions Forms--Family Law § 3:35, Consideration Of New Spouse's Income for Tax Purposes.

Treatises and Practice Aids

Witkin, California Summary 10th Parent and Child § 400, Annual Net Disposable Income.

Witkin, California Summary 10th Parent and Child § 401, Income Of Subsequent Spouse or Nonmarital Partner.

§ 4058. Annual gross income of parents

(a) The annual gross income of each parent means income from whatever source derived, except as specified in subdivision (c) and includes, but is not limited to, the following:

(1) Income such as commissions, salaries, royalties, wages, bonuses, rents, dividends, pensions, interest, trust income, annuities, workers' compensation benefits, unemployment insurance benefits, disability insurance benefits, social security benefits, and spousal support actually received from a person not a party to the proceeding to establish a child support order under this article.

(2) Income from the proprietorship of a business, such as gross receipts from the business reduced by expenditures required for the operation of the business.

(3) In the discretion of the court, employee benefits or self-employment benefits, taking into consideration the benefit to the employee, any corresponding reduction in living expenses, and other relevant facts.

(b) The court may, in its discretion, consider the earning capacity of a parent in lieu of the parent's income, consistent with the best interests of the children.

(c) Annual gross income does not include any income derived from child support payments actually received, and income derived from any public assistance program, eligibility for which is based on a determination of need. Child support received by a party for children from another relationship shall not be included as part of that party's gross or net income. *(Added by Stats.1993, c. 219 (A.B.1500), § 138.)*

Law Revision Commission Comments

Enactment [Revised Comment]

Section 4058 continues former Civil Code Section 4721(f) without substantive change. In subdivision (a)(1), "the proceeding to establish a child support order under this article" has been substituted for "this order." This is not a substantive change. In subdivision (c), "does not" has been substituted for "shall not." This is not a substantive change. See also Section 3011 (factors in determining best interest of child). [23 Cal.L.Rev.Comm. Reports 1 (1993)].

Commentary

Ventura County Department of Child Support Services v. Brown, 117 Cal.App.4th 144, 11 Cal.Rptr.3d 489 (2004), relying on Probate Code § 15305(c), holds that when there is an enforceable child support judgment against a trust beneficiary, which the trustee refuses to satisfy, a trial court may overcome the trustee's discretion and order the trustee to satisfy the past due and ongoing child support obligations of the beneficiary directly from the trust. The analysis and rationale of *Brown* would seem to apply equally to spousal support judgments.

For divergent treatment of the income of high income support obligors, see *Estevez v. Superior Court, 22 Cal.App.4th 423, 27 Cal.Rptr.2d 470 (1994), review denied 4/21/94*; *Johnson v. Superior Court, 66 Cal.App.4th 68, 77 Cal.Rptr.2d 624 (1998)*; and *In re Marriage of Hubner, 94 Cal.App.4th 175, 114 Cal.Rptr.2d 646 (2001), review denied March 13, 2002*. *Estevez, Johnson and Hubner* are discussed in the Commentary to Section 3552.

Relying on subsection (a), *Brothers v. Kern, 154 Cal.App.4th 126, 64 Cal.Rptr.3d 239 (2007)*, held that unspent client funds held in an attorney trust account are reachable to satisfy a father's child support obligation. The court rejected the father's claim that his Sixth Amendment right to counsel in a criminal proceeding was violated because satisfaction of his child support obligation lessened his ability to retain counsel of his choice.

In re Marriage of Stanton, 190 Cal.App.4th 547, 118 Cal.Rptr.3d 249 (2010), review denied, petition for certiorari filed March 10, 2011, held that military cash allowances for housing and food, which under federal law are neither taxable nor subject to wage garnishment, are includible in a support obligor's gross income for purposes of California child or spousal support. *Stanton* rejected the claim that state law inclusion is pre-empted by the federal provisions.

Relying on subsection (a)(1) and Section 4057(b)(5)(B), *County of Orange v. Smith, 132 Cal.App.4th 1434, 34 Cal.Rptr.3d 383 (2005), review denied,* approved a trial court's conclusion that the $600 rent that a father received monthly from a roommate, which amount the father passed on immediately to his landlord to satisfy a portion of his $1,600 monthly rent obligation to the landlord, was "rental income" to the father. Presumably, if the roommate were the primary lessee who paid $1,600 monthly to the landlord, and the father paid the lessee $1,000 a month, the court would not have found that the father had rental income.

County of Placer v. Andrade, 55 Cal.App.4th 1393, 64 Cal.Rptr.2d 739 (1997), holds that a parent's past bonus and overtime pay must be included in "annual gross income" unless the court concludes that the parent is not likely to receive bonus and overtime pay in the future. *M.S. v. O.S, 176 Cal.App.4th 548, 97 Cal.Rptr.3d 812 (2009)*, held that regular bonuses in the past should be included in annual gross income unless the support obligor persuades the court that he is unlikely to receive them in the future, in which case they should only be considered when actually received. Similarly, *In re Marriage of Scheppers, 86 Cal.App.4th 646, 103 Cal.Rptr.2d 529 (2001)*, holds that although a support obligor may not be required to work more than 40 hours a week, if he does in fact do so, all his income is available for child support.

In re Marriage of Williamson, 226 Cal.App.4th 1303, 172 Cal.Rptr.3d 699 (2014), held that former cash advances from a husband's wealthy parents could not be used to impute income to the husband for purposes of child support or spousal support, when the advances had ceased before trial and there was no evidence that they would resume.

In re Marriage of Henry, 126 Cal.App.4th 111, 23 Cal.Rptr.3d 707 (2005), holds that a noncustodial parent's share of the unrealized increased equity in the family home owned by that parent and her new spouse is not "income" within the meaning of subsection (a).

Although declining to impute to a support obligor the higher income previously earned by the obligor, *In re Marriage of Berger, 170 Cal.App.4th 1070, 88 Cal.Rptr.3d 766 (2009)*, holds that the obligor's practice of "deferring" his salary in order to protect his investment in his business would warrant including that salary as current income for purposes of subsection (a). Alternatively, deferral was a section 4057 (b)(5) "special circumstance" that would justify treating the deferred salary as current income for purposes of child support.

Interpreting subsection (a)(1), *In re Marriage of Corman, 59 Cal.App.4th 1492, 69 Cal.Rptr.2d 880 (1997)*, holds that spousal support received by the noncustodial parent from the custodial parent is not "gross income" for purposes of application of the Section 4055 child support guideline. (Compare Section 4061, which takes spousal support payable by a party into account for purposes of calculating Section 4062 "add-on" expenses.) Nor is such spousal support a "special circumstance" for purposes of Section 4057 deviation from the presumptively correct guideline amount.

In re Marriage of Daugherty, 232 Cal.App.4th 463, 181 Cal.Rptr.3d 427 (2014), holds that a child's derivative social security benefits paid to a custodial parent, which are based on an obligor parent's disability, are not included as income to the support obligor for determining child support under subsection (a).

Also interpreting subsection (a)(1), *In re Marriage of Scheppers, 86 Cal.App.4th 646, 103 Cal.Rptr.2d 529 (2001)*, holds that life insurance proceeds are not included within the definition of income.

In re Marriage of Daugherty, 232 Cal.App.4th 463, 181 Cal.Rptr.3d 427 (2014), holds that social security disability payments made to the custodial parent on behalf of the children of a disabled obligor are not includible in the obligor's income for the purpose of determining his child support obligation. Those payments are, however, to be credited against the disabled parent's child support obligation under subsection (b) of section 4504.

In re Marriage of Rocha, 68 Cal.App.4th 514, 80 Cal.Rptr.2d 376 (1998), holds that the proceeds of an educational loan are not income for purposes of child support even though the proceeds exceed the cost of the support obligor's books and tuition.

County of Kern v. Castle, 75 Cal.App.4th 1442, 89 Cal.Rptr.2d 874 (1999), held that a parent's $1,000,000 inheritance, including a lump-sum distribution and two rental properties, was not "income" for purposes of this section. (But compare *County of Contra Costa v. Lemon, 205 Cal.App.3d 683, 688, 252 Cal.Rptr. 455 (1988)* (treating lottery winnings as income in the context of public assistance to a dependent child). Nevertheless, *Castle* states that the inheritance could be considered in child support calculations under § 4058(a)(3), by considering the extent to which it reduced the obligor's living expenses. Of course, actual net profit on the rental properties was properly treated as "income" and, under subsection (b), the court may impute income on the inheritance corpus based on the amount the corpus could have earned if invested or rented. *In re Marriage of Destein, 91 Cal.App.4th 1385, 111 Cal.Rptr.2d 487 (2001)*, held that the trial court properly calculated a husband's income for purposes of child support by imputing, under subsection (b), a reasonable rate of return to husband's non-income-producing separate property assets. See also *In re Marriage of Dacumos, 76 Cal.App.4th 150, 90 Cal.Rptr.2d 159 (1999)* (in determining a parent's income for purposes of child support, subsection (b) earning capacity includes income derived from capital, as well as labor; when obligor "underutilizes" capital, court may impute a fair return on that capital). Invoking § 4057 (b)(5)(C) and this section, *In re Marriage of de Guigne, 97 Cal.App.4th 1353, 119 Cal.Rptr.2d 430 (2002)*, held that the trial court did not abuse its discretion in ordering a support obligor to pay child support and spousal support in an amount greater than the obligor's total monthly income when the obligor had extensive property holdings that were not yielding income and the support was necessary to reduce the disparity between the support obligees' marital and postdivorce standards of living, even though the marital standard of living was based on overspending.

Distinguishing County of Kern v. Castle, *In re Marriage of Alter, 171 Cal.App.4th 718, 89 Cal.Rptr.3d 849 (2009)*, holds that a court may consider recurring gifts to a support obligor as income in determining child support. Compare *Anna M. v. Jeffrey E., 7 Cal.App.5th 439, 212 Cal.Rptr.3d 652 (2017)*, which held that a trial court did not abuse its discretion when it declined to consider a friend's recurring payment of mother's substantial living expenses as income to the mother.

Distinguishing *de Guigne, In re Marriage of Williams, 150 Cal. App.4th 1221, 58 Cal.Rptr.3d 877 (2007)*, held that a trial court erred in imputing a reasonable rate of return to a portion of a support obligor's equity in a 11,000 square foot Pebble Beach home absent a showing, under section 4057, of special circumstances that would render guideline support unjust or inappropriate.

In re Marriage of Schlafly, 149 Cal.App.4th 747, 57 Cal.Rptr.3d 274 (2007), held that a trial court erred in determining child support by imputing $3,000 a month of nontaxable income to a support obligor based on his mortgage-free housing. The court reasoned that mortgage-free housing might be considered a special circumstance justifying deviation from the guideline under section 4057, but it is not imputed income for purposes of this section.

Similarly, *M.S. v. O.S, 176 Cal.App.4th 548, 97 Cal.Rptr.3d 812 (2009)*, held that a trial court abused its discretion when it included the value of tribal payment of a support obligor's attorney fees in the annual gross income of the obligor, because the tribal benefit did not create any disposable income for the obligor. Nevertheless, the court opined that a trial court might consider the value of the benefit as a special circumstance within the meaning of section 4057.

In re Marriage of Heiner, 136 Cal.App.4th 1514, 39 Cal.Rptr.3d 730 (2006), holds that the entire amount of an undifferentiated lump-sum personal injury award is not income for purposes of this section, but that the trial court has discretion to determine whether some portion of the award should be treated as income because it replaces lost earnings. *In re Marriage of Rothrock, 159 Cal.App.4th 223, 70 Cal.Rptr.3d 881 (2008)*, held that a parent's undifferentiated personal injury settlement annuity payments were properly excluded from his income in determining his child support obligation. *Rothrock* held that the parent seeking to include a portion of the payments as income bears the burden of proving that some component of the payments was compensation for lost wages.

In re Marriage of Pearlstein, 137 Cal.App.4th 1361, 40 Cal.Rptr.3d 910 (2006), holds that the market value of unsold stock received from the sale of a business is not income for purposes of child support. Of course, when a supporting party maintains non-income-producing assets, the court has discretion, under subsection (b) to impute income to those assets by estimating a reasonable rate of return.

Interpreting § 4059 (a), *In re Marriage of Carlton & D'Allesandro, 91 Cal.App.4th 1213, 111 Cal.Rptr.2d 329 (2001)*, holds that the trial court erred in assigning a child support obligor the tax filing status of "married filing jointly" when his actual status was "married filing separately" and in allocating to the obligor a tax deduction arising from his new spouse's separate property ("separate property" because the couple had a premarital agreement providing for the segregation and separate ownership of all funds and assets) mortgage payments on the home in which the couple resided. The latter error also runs afoul of § 4057.5(a), which provides that the income of a parent's subsequent spouse or marital partner shall not be considered in determining or modifying child support. (But query whether the obligor's cost-free housing is "income. . . from whatever source derived" within the meaning of subsection (a) of this section, or a "special circumstance" within the meaning of § 4057 (b)(5).)

In re Marriage of Loh, 93 Cal.App.4th 325, 112 Cal.Rptr.2d 893 (2001), held that the trial court erred when, in a child support modification proceeding, it disregarded a support obligor's income tax returns and instead used evidence of his current life style, which was subsidized by a nonmarital partner, to establish his income. *Loh* concluded that the evidence was insufficient to establish obligor's income, and its use also ran afoul of § 4057.5, which does not allow trial courts to look at the income of a new spouse or nonmarital partner in determining or modifying child support.

Interpreting subsections (a)(1) and (2) of this section together with section 4059, *Asfaw v. Woldberhan, 147 Cal.App.4th 1407, 55 Cal. Rptr.3d 323 (2007)*, held that tax depreciation of rental realty, which it characterized as "illusory" and "fictional," was not deductible from income under either section. *Asfaw* should not be understood to bar depreciation deduction in all circumstances, as when depreciated business personalty does require periodic replacement.

In re Marriage of Barth, 210 Cal.App.4th 363, 147 Cal.Rptr.3d 910 (2012), review denied, interprets subsection (b) to require only the ability of the paying spouse to work and the availability of suitable jobs. It does not require a showing that the parent would actually be hired for an available position.

In re Marriage of Lim and Carrasco, 214 Cal.App.4th 768, 154 Cal.Rptr.3d 179 (2013), holds that the trial court acted within its discretion, under subsection (b), in awarding ex-husband spousal child support based on the ex-wife's earnings while working an 80% schedule as an attorney. The trial court declined to impute full-time earnings to the attorney, because a full-time schedule as a partner at a big law firm would not be in the children's best interest.

In re Marriage of Ficke, 217 Cal.App.4th 10, 157 Cal.Rptr.3d 870 (2013), reversed an order imputing income to the custodial mother and ordering her to pay spousal support to the father as well as reducing his child support obligation to her, without making an express finding supported by substantial evidence that income imputation would benefit the children.

Interpreting subsection (b), *In re Marriage of Padilla, 38 Cal. App.4th 1212, 45 Cal.Rptr.2d 555 (1995)*, holds that a trial court may consider a parent's earning capacity instead of his actual earnings even though the court has not found that the parent acted in bad faith in leaving his well salaried job in order to start a new business on his own. *In re Marriage of Cohn, 65 Cal.App.4th 923, 76 Cal.Rptr.2d 866 (1998)*, held that the trial court properly undertook the task of imputing income to the support obligor, but determined that the court's calculations were not supported by substantial evidence. *In re Marriage of Bardzik, 165 Cal.App.4th 1291, 83 Cal.Rptr.3d 72 (2008)*, held that a trial court properly declined to impute income to a parent who took early retirement when the other parent failed to discharge his burden of showing ability and opportunity to earn imputed income. See also *In re Marriage of Hinman, 55 Cal.App.4th 988, 64 Cal.Rptr.2d 383 (1997), review denied August 27, 1997*, holding that court may impute income to noncustodial mother who is not earning income because she is caring for three preschool children born in a subsequent nonmarital relationship. Compare *State of Oregon v. Vargas, 70 Cal.App.4th 1123, 83 Cal.Rptr.2d 229 (1999)*, holding that income from earnings cannot be imputed to an incarcerated support obligor unless the obligor actually has the opportunity to work. For discussion of imputed earnings in the context of spousal support, see Family Code Section 4320, Commentary. Similarly, *In re Marriage of Smith, 90 Cal.App.4th 74, 108 Cal.Rptr.2d 537 (2001)*, holds that a court may not impute income to an incarcerated parent absent evidence that the parent has the opportunity to work and may not deny child support modification on the ground that the incarcerated parent committed a crime against a family member. *In re Marriage of Eggers, 131 Cal.App.4th 695, 32 Cal.Rptr.3d 292 (2005)*, holds that the trial court abused its discretion when it imputed income to an unemployed support obligor, who had lost his job due to misconduct, without determining whether he had the ability or opportunity to work.

In re Marriage of McHugh, 231 Cal.App.4th 1238, 180 Cal.Rptr.3d 448 (2014), affirmed a trial court order imputing a support obligor's former earnings to him because he lost or left his high-paying job in an effort to avoid his support obligation, even though there was no evidence that the obligor currently had the opportunity to earn at the same level. Unlike *Eggers, supra*, where the obligor was discharged for misconduct unrelated to his support obligation, the *McHugh* misconduct was for the purpose of avoiding the support obligation, and thus the job loss was effectively voluntary.

Interpreting subsection (b), *Mendoza v. Ramos, 182 Cal.App.4th 680, 105 Cal.Rptr.3d 853 (2010)*, held that a trial court properly declined to impute income to a custodial parent who was a recipient of CalWORKS and in compliance with the terms of the program.

Also interpreting subsection (b), *Stewart v. Gomez, 47 Cal.App.4th 1748, 55 Cal.Rptr.2d 531 (1996)*, holds that a father's earning capacity and disability benefits may be properly combined in determining his gross income so long as he would continue to collect disability benefits even if he were employed. Additionally, under subsection (a)(3), the value of his rent-free housing and of his meal allowance while he attended a vocational training program may be included as gross income. 55 Cal.Rptr.2d at 535–536. *In re Marriage of Schulze, 60 Cal.App.4th 519, 70 Cal.Rptr.2d 488 (1997)*, holds that employee fringe benefits should be treated as taxable income to the extent that the value of the benefits is taxable income under federal law (reversing trial court treatment of taxable employee benefits as nontaxable income when employee had not in fact paid tax on their value). (For further discussion of *Schulze*, see commentary to Section 4059.) *In re Marriage of Cheriton, 92 Cal.App.4th 269, 111 Cal.Rptr.2d 755 (2001), review denied December 19, 2001*, holds that stock options should be treated as income available for child support at the time of exercise or, at the very latest, when the stock is sold for gain.

All subsection (b) cases cited above involve imputation of income to a noncustodial parent in order to increase his or her child support payment. In contrast, *In re Marriage of LaBass & Munsee, 56 Cal.App.4th 1331, 66 Cal.Rptr.2d 393 (1997)*, approves imputation of full-time earnings as a school teacher to a custodial parent of young children employed part-time as a community college instructor, in order to decrease the child support payment of the noncustodial parent. *In re Marriage of Cheriton, 92 Cal.App.4th 269, 111 Cal. Rptr.2d 755 (2001), review denied December 19, 2001*, holds that the trial court erred in imputing income to the custodial parent without considering whether imputation would be in the children's best interests.

See also *Moss v. Superior Court, 17 Cal.4th 396, 950 P.2d 59, 71 Cal.Rptr.2d 215 (1998)*. Under former California law, a criminal contempt sentence of incarceration could not constitutionally be imposed on a parent who chose not to seek employment or earn money, although required to do so by a child support order. In *Moss*, the California Supreme Court disapproved this long standing rule and held that a parent who willfully fails to seek and accept employment is subject to criminal contempt. Additionally, inability to comply with a child support order is an affirmative defense, and thus the petitioner need not prove the nonsupporting parent's ability to pay.

Interpreting subsection (c), *Elsenheimer v. Elsenheimer, 124 Cal. App.4th 1532, 22 Cal.Rptr.3d 447 (2004)*, holds that Supplemental Security Income (SSI) benefits must be excluded from a parent's gross annual income for purposes of the California child support formula. Although *Elsenheimer* perceives a conflict between subsections (a) and (c) because subsection (a)(1) includes social security benefits as income and SSI is administered under the Social Security Act, *Elsenheimer* reasons that SSI is nevertheless a "public assistance program, eligibility for which is based on need" within the meaning of subsection (c).

Research References

Forms

California Practice Guide: Rutter Family Law Forms Form 6:8, Request for Order Re Child Support (Guideline Based on Earning Capacity in Lieu Of Actual Income).

California Transactions Forms--Family Law § 3:29, Determination Of Gross Income.
West's California Code Forms, Family § 4050, Comment Overview--Statewide Uniform Guideline.

Treatises and Practice Aids

Witkin, California Summary 10th Community Property § 233, in General.
Witkin, California Summary 10th Husband and Wife § 236, in General.
Witkin, California Summary 10th Parent and Child § 397, Annual Gross Income.
Witkin, California Summary 10th Parent and Child § 398, Earning Capacity from Employment.
Witkin, California Summary 10th Parent and Child § 399, Earning Capacity Of Assets.

§ 4059. Annual net disposable income of parents

The annual net disposable income of each parent shall be computed by deducting from his or her annual gross income the actual amounts attributable to the following items or other items permitted under this article:

(a) The state and federal income tax liability resulting from the parties' taxable income. Federal and state income tax deductions shall bear an accurate relationship to the tax status of the parties (that is, single, married, married filing separately, or head of household) and number of dependents. State and federal income taxes shall be those actually payable (not necessarily current withholding) after considering appropriate filing status, all available exclusions, deductions, and credits. Unless the parties stipulate otherwise, the tax effects of spousal support shall not be considered in determining the net disposable income of the parties for determining child support, but shall be considered in determining spousal support consistent with Chapter 3 (commencing with Section 4330) of Part 3.

(b) Deductions attributed to the employee's contribution or the self-employed worker's contribution pursuant to the Federal Insurance Contributions Act (FICA), or an amount not to exceed that allowed under FICA for persons not subject to FICA, provided that the deducted amount is used to secure retirement or disability benefits for the parent.

(c) Deductions for mandatory union dues and retirement benefits, provided that they are required as a condition of employment.

(d) Deductions for health insurance or health plan premiums for the parent and for any children the parent has an obligation to support and deductions for state disability insurance premiums.

(e) Any child or spousal support actually being paid by the parent pursuant to a court order, to or for the benefit of any person who is not a subject of the order to be established by the court. In the absence of a court order, any child support actually being paid, not to exceed the amount established by the guideline, for natural or adopted children of the parent not residing in that parent's home, who are not the subject of the order to be established by the court, and of whom the parent has a duty of support. Unless the parent proves payment of the support, no deduction shall be allowed under this subdivision.

(f) Job-related expenses, if allowed by the court after consideration of whether the expenses are necessary, the benefit to the employee, and any other relevant facts.

(g) A deduction for hardship, as defined by Sections 4070 to 4073, inclusive, and applicable published appellate court decisions. The amount of the hardship shall not be deducted from the amount of child support, but shall be deducted from the income of the party to whom it applies. In applying any hardship under paragraph (2) of subdivision (a) of Section 4071, the court shall seek to provide equity between competing child support orders. The Judicial Council shall develop a formula for calculating the maximum hardship deduction and shall submit it to the Legislature for its consideration on or before July 1, 1995. *(Added by Stats.1993, c. 219 (A.B.1500), § 138. Amended by Stats.1994, c. 1056 (A.B. 3258), § 1.)*

Law Revision Commission Comments

Enactment [Revised Comment]

Section 4059 continues former Civil Code Section 4721(g) without substantive change. In subdivision (g), the reference to Section 4070 has been substituted for the broader reference to former Civil Code Section 4722. This is not a substantive change, since Section 4070 continues the relevant part of the former section without substantive change. [23 Cal.L.Rev.Comm. Reports 1 (1993)].

Commentary

In re Marriage of McQuoid, 9 Cal.App.4th 1353, 12 Cal.Rprt.2d 737 (1991), held that, for purposes of subsection (a), "income tax liability" should be understood to include only taxes actually paid, because the purpose of the section is to determine a parent's net disposable income. When a self-employed parent does not pay taxes on his income, that income should not be reduced by the amount of tax that might be due, but has not been paid. If and when the parent pays that tax, he may move for a modification of child support. Compare *In re Marriage of Schulze, 60 Cal.App.4th 519, 70 Cal.Rptr.2d 488 (1997)*, in which the court of appeal held when, under section 4058(a)(3), a court treats the value of employee benefits received by a parent as gross income, the court should deduct the parent's tax liability on those benefits, even though the parent has not reported the benefits as taxable employee benefits and has therefore paid no tax on them. *Schulze* is also discussed in the commentary to Section 4058.

Interpreting subsection (a), *In re Marriage of Carlton & D'Allessandro, 91 Cal.App.4th 1213, 111 Cal.Rptr.2d 329 (2001)*, holds that the trial court erred in assigning a child support obligor the tax filing status of "married filing jointly" when his actual status was "married filing separately" and in allocating to the obligor a tax deduction arising from his new spouse's separate property ("separate property" because the couple had a premarital agreement providing for the segregation and separate ownership of all funds and assets) mortgage payments on the home in which the couple resided. The latter error also runs afoul of § 4057.5(a)(1), which provides that the income of a parent's subsequent spouse or marital partner shall not be considered in determining or modifying child support. (But query whether the obligor's "free housing" is "income...from whatever source derived" within the meaning of § 4058(a) or a "special circumstance" within the meaning of § 4057(b)(5).)

For divergent treatment of the income of high income support obligors, see *Estevez v. Superior Court, 22 Cal.App.4th 423, 27 Cal.Rptr.2d 470 (1994), review denied 4/21/94*; *Johnson v. Superior Court, 66 Cal.App.4th. 68, 77 Cal.Rptr.2d 624 (1998); and* In re Marriage of Hubner, 94 Cal.App.4th 175, 114 Cal.Rptr.2d 646 (2001), review denied March 13, 2002. *Estevez, Johnson and Hubner* are discussed in the Commentary to Section 3552.

Although subsection (e) allows, as a deduction from income, child support actually paid by the obligor for a child who does not reside with the obligor, a subsection (g) hardship deduction for children residing with the obligor is discretionary with the court. (See Sections 4070, 4071, and 4072.) Former Section 4071.5 additionally provided that a subsection (g) hardship deduction could not be granted to a parent when the child for whom support was being determined was receiving public assistance payments. Section 4071.5 was repealed in 1999. *County of Orange v. Ivansco, 67 Cal.App.4th 328, 78 Cal.Rptr.2d 886 (1998),* held former Section 4071.5 unconstitutional insofar as it denied the court discretion to grant a hardship deduction for children living with the obligor when children who are the subject of the instant order are receiving public assistance. The holding of *Ivansco* was rejected by *City and County of San Francisco v. Garnett, 70 Cal.App.4th 845, 82 Cal.Rptr.2d 924 (1999)* (former Section 4071.5, providing that a parent's income may not be reduced by discretionary hardship deductions when welfare payments are being made for a child of the obligor, constitutional); *City and County of San Francisco v. Freeman, 71 Cal.App.4th 869, 84 Cal.Rptr.2d 132 (1999)* (accord); and *Moreno v. Draper, 70 Cal.App.4th 886, 83 Cal.Rptr.2d 82 (1999)* (nor, in light of former Section 4071.5, could Section 4057(b)(5) "special circumstances" deduction be made when child of obligor was receiving public assistance).

Haggard v. Haggard, 38 Cal.App.4th 1566, 45 Cal.Rptr.2d 638 (1995), holds that a support obligor parent's voluntary support of the nonadopted children of his new mate does not entitle the support obligor to a Section 4057(b)(5) finding of "special circumstances" nor to a Section 4059(g) hardship deduction. Compare *In re Marriage of Paulin, 46 Cal.App.4th 1378, 54 Cal.Rptr.2d 314 (1996)* (sustaining trial court finding that middle-income child support obligor was entitled to hardship deduction on account of expenses resulting from birth of twins in obligor's new marriage).

For discussion of subsection (f) job-related expenses, see *Stewart v. Gomez, 47 Cal.App.4th 1748, 55 Cal.Rptr.2d 531, 535–536 (1996)* (reimbursed meal expenses are not deductible under subsection (f) but are instead a Section 4058(a)(3) employee benefit, the value of which is includible in gross income).

Interpreting this section and section 4058 (a)(1) and (2), *Asfaw v. Woldberhan, 147 Cal.App.4th 1407, 55 Cal.Rptr.3d 323 (2007)*, held that tax depreciation of rental realty, which it characterized as "illusory" and "fictional," was not deductible from income under either section. *Asfaw* should not be understood to bar depreciation deduction in all circumstances, as when depreciated business personalty does require periodic replacement.

In re Marriage of Carlsen, 50 Cal.App.4th 212, 57 Cal.Rptr.2d 630 (1996), holds that for purposes of determining the support obligee's Section 4059(a) tax rate in order to calculate the obligee's net disposable income, the court may properly take into account the income of the obligee's new spouse. *Carlsen* concludes that such treatment violates neither the letter nor the spirit of Section 4057.5. *Accord, County of Tulare v. Campbell, 50 Cal.App.4th 847, 57 Cal.Rptr.2d 902 (1996)* (same holding with respect to income of support obligor's new spouse). Although *Carlsen* and *Campbell* allow inclusion of new spouse income, neither case considers how such new spouse should be taken into account. For excellent discussion of this question, see George Norton, Using New Spouse Income for Tax Allocation of Child Support—An Equitable Method for Allocation of Joint Taxes, 1997 California Family Law Monthly 1–6 (January).

In re Marriage of Riddle, 125 Cal.App.4th 1075, 23 Cal.Rptr.3d 273 (2005), holds that the trial court erred in basing pendente lite support orders on an unrepresentative two-month sample of the obligor's earnings. *Riddle* proposes standards for determining a representative sample.

Research References

Forms

California Transactions Forms--Family Law § 3:29, Determination Of Gross Income.

California Transactions Forms--Family Law § 3:32, Determination Of Net Monthly Disposable Income.

California Transactions Forms--Family Law § 3:33, Adjustments for Tax Filing Status, Itemized Deductions, and Credits.

Treatises and Practice Aids

Witkin, California Summary 10th Parent and Child § 396, Basic Formula.

Witkin, California Summary 10th Parent and Child § 397, Annual Gross Income.

Witkin, California Summary 10th Parent and Child § 400, Annual Net Disposable Income.

Witkin, California Summary 10th Parent and Child § 404, Hardship Deduction.

Witkin, California Summary 10th Parent and Child § 415, in General.

§ 4060. Computation of monthly net disposable income

The monthly net disposable income shall be computed by dividing the annual net disposable income by 12. If the monthly net disposable income figure does not accurately reflect the actual or prospective earnings of the parties at the time the determination of support is made, the court may adjust the amount appropriately. *(Added by Stats.1993, c. 219 (A.B.1500), § 138.)*

Law Revision Commission Comments

Enactment [Revised Comment]

Section 4060 continues former Civil Code Section 4721(h) without substantive change. The first sentence has been revised to conform with the first sentence [of] Section 4059. [23 Cal.L.Rev.Comm. Reports 1 (1993)].

Commentary

In re Marriage of Riddle, 125 Cal.App.4th 1075, 23 Cal.Rptr.3d 273 (2005), holds that the trial court erred in basing pendente lite support orders on an unrepresentative two-month sample of the obligor's earnings. *Riddle* proposes standards for determining a representative sample.

Research References

Forms

California Transactions Forms--Family Law § 3:32, Determination Of Net Monthly Disposable Income.

California Transactions Forms--Family Law § 3:40, Bonuses and Other Nonrecurring Income.

Treatises and Practice Aids

Witkin, California Summary 10th Parent and Child § 400, Annual Net Disposable Income.

§ 4061. Additional support for children; computation

The amounts in Section 4062 shall be considered additional support for the children and shall be computed in accordance with the following:

(a) If there needs to be an apportionment of expenses pursuant to Section 4062, the expenses shall be divided one-half to each parent, unless either parent requests a different apportionment pursuant to subdivision (b) and presents documentation which demonstrates that a different apportionment would be more appropriate.

(b) If requested by either parent, and the court determines it is appropriate to apportion expenses under Section 4062 other than one-half to each parent, the apportionment shall be as follows:

(1) The basic child support obligation shall first be computed using the formula set forth in subdivision (a) of Section 4055, as adjusted for any appropriate rebuttal factors in subdivision (b) of Section 4057.

(2) Any additional child support required for expenses pursuant to Section 4062 shall thereafter be ordered to be paid by the parents in proportion to their net disposable incomes as adjusted pursuant to subdivisions (c) and (d).

(c) In cases where spousal support is or has been ordered to be paid by one parent to the other, for purposes of allocating additional expenses pursuant to Section 4062, the gross income of the parent paying spousal support shall be decreased by the amount of the spousal support paid and the gross income of the parent receiving the spousal support shall be increased by the amount of the spousal support received for as long as the spousal support order is in effect and is paid.

(d) For purposes of computing the adjusted net disposable income of the parent paying child support for allocating any additional expenses pursuant to Section 4062, the net disposable income of the parent paying child support shall be reduced by the amount of any basic child support ordered to be paid under subdivision (a) of Section 4055. However, the net disposable income of the parent receiving child support shall not be increased by any amount of child support received. *(Added by Stats.1993, c. 219 (A.B.1500), § 138. Amended by Stats.2010, c. 103 (S.B.580), § 2.)*

Law Revision Commission Comments

Enactment [Revised Comment]

Section 4061 continues former Civil Code Section 4721(i) without substantive change. [23 Cal.L.Rev.Comm. Reports 1 (1993)].

Commentary

For general discussion of Section 4061, see *In re Marriage of Fini, 26 Cal.App.4th 1033, 31 Cal.Rptr.2d 749 (1994)*.

In re Marriage of Lusby, 64 Cal.App.4th 459, 75 Cal.Rptr.2d 263 (1998), holds that the trial court has jurisdiction to make a postjudgment retroactive award of section 4062 expenses, and that the trial court has discretion to allocate the expenses according to the parents' incomes when the expenses were incurred.

Research References

Forms

California Practice Guide: Rutter Family Law Forms Form 5:2, Request for Order Re Child Custody, Child Support, Spousal Support, Attorney Fees, etc.

California Transactions Forms--Family Law § 2:65, Add-Ons.

California Transactions Forms--Family Law § 3:44, Mandatory Additional Child Support.

Treatises and Practice Aids

Witkin, California Summary 10th Parent and Child § 409, Allocation Of Additional Support.

§ 4062. Additional child support

(a) The court shall order the following as additional child support:

(1) Child care costs related to employment or to reasonably necessary education or training for employment skills.

(2) The reasonable uninsured health care costs for the children as provided in Section 4063.

(b) The court may order the following as additional child support:

(1) Costs related to the educational or other special needs of the children.

(2) Travel expenses for visitation. *(Added by Stats.1993, c. 219 (A.B.1500), § 138. Amended by Stats.1994, c. 466 (S.B.1807), § 1.)*

Law Revision Commission Comments

Enactment [Revised Comment]

Section 4062 continues former Civil Code Section 4721(j) without substantive change. [23 Cal.L.Rev.Comm. Reports 1 (1993)].

Commentary

In re Marriage of de Guigne, 97 Cal.App.4th 1353, 119 Cal.Rptr.2d 430 (2002), holds that this section is exclusive, and the trial court has no authority to create new add-on categories.

In re Marriage of Lusby, 64 Cal.App.4th 459, 75 Cal.Rptr.2d 263 (1998), holds that the trial court has jurisdiction to make a postjudgment retroactive award of section 4062 expenses, and that the trial court has discretion to allocate the expenses according to the parents' incomes when the expenses were incurred.

See generally *In re Marriage of Gigliotti, 33 Cal.App.4th 518, 39 Cal.Rptr.2d 367 (1995)*. *Gigliotti* holds that it was error for the trial court to reduce the noncustodial parent's child support obligation by that parent's projected travel expenses for visitation. Instead, a support obligor's travel expenses may only be taken into account under this section. If, as in *Gigliotti*, both parents incur travel expenses to enable the noncustodial parent's visitation, both parents' expenditure should be taken into account under this section. With *Gigliotti*, compare *Wilson v. Shea, 87 Cal.App.4th 887, 104 Cal.Rptr.2d 880 (2001)*, where the court held, after a custodial parent's relocation, that the need to assure a child's frequent and continuing contact with both parents justified reducing, under § 4057 (b)(5), the guideline child support amount by an amount intended to cover that parent's transportation expenses in visiting the child.

In *Gigliotti*, the trial court also reduced the actual cost of the child's subsection (a)(1) Montessori day care, $980 monthly, to the "reasonable" figure of $750. The propriety of this reduction was not appealed by the custodial parent. Nevertheless, the court of appeal observed: "Although we question the trial court's interpretation of subdivision (a)(1) of Family Code section 4062 as authorizing the court to fashion a "reasonable" expense which does not correlate to the actual expense borne by the parent, we have no occasion to resolve this issue here." *39 Cal.Rptr.2d 367, 370*. Compare the language of subsection (a)(2), which provides for the "*reasonable* uninsured health care costs for the children." Compare also subsection (b), which gives the court discretion whether to order *educational* costs as additional child support. In contrast, the court must order subsection (a) child care costs as additional child support.

Boutte v. Nears, 50 Cal.App.4th 162, 57 Cal.Rptr.2d 655 (1996), holds that a child support obligor may not be ordered to pay attorney's fees, which were incurred by the other parent to modify the child support order, as Section 4062 "additional child support." Instead, the other parent must seek attorney's fees under Section 3652, which allows a trial court to award attorney's fees to the prevailing party in a support modification proceeding. Nevertheless, some courts have awarded attorney's fees under Section 4062 in order to ensure that, as "child support," the obligation is not dischargeable by the debtor in bankruptcy. In any event, federal bankruptcy court is receptive to the claim that attorney's fees awarded under either section are "in the nature of child support" because they are incurred to obtain support for the child, and hence the award of attorney's fees is not dischargeable in bankruptcy. See discussion at 1996 California Family Law Monthly 345–346 (December).

See also *Hoover-Reynolds v. Superior Court, 50 Cal.App.4th 1273, 58 Cal.Rptr.2d 173 (1996),* which holds that an attorney's contractual lien for attorney's fees, which is otherwise enforceable against recovery in a lawsuit, does not attach to payment of court-ordered child support, including payment of arrearages.

In re Marriage of Chandler, 60 Cal.App.4th 124, 70 Cal.Rptr.2d 109 (1997), disapproves trial court treatment of Section 4062 child support payable by a support obligor with unusually high income. In *Chandler*, the guideline obligation was more than $9,000 monthly. The trial court awarded $3,000 ordinary support and $4,000 in trust, the trust funds to be distributed for the child's reasonable Section 4062 "add-on" costs, and the balance to be distributed to the child when she reached the age of majority. The court of appeal rejected the trust for several reasons: (1) a trust should be used only when there is a compelling need to limit the custodial parent's access to child support funds; (2) the $3,000 monthly child support, standing alone, would have constituted an abuse of discretion; and (3) the trust device improperly limited the custodial parent's access to Section 4062 child support payable to the trust.

Research References

Forms

California Practice Guide: Rutter Family Law Forms Form 5:2, Request for Order Re Child Custody, Child Support, Spousal Support, Attorney Fees, etc.

California Practice Guide: Rutter Family Law Forms Form 6:11, Request for Order Re Guideline Child Support, Temporary "Guideline" Spousal Support and Family Code S4062 "Add-On" Child Support.

California Transactions Forms--Family Law § 2:65, Add-Ons.

California Transactions Forms--Family Law § 3:44, Mandatory Additional Child Support.

California Transactions Forms--Family Law § 3:45, Discretionary Additional Child Support.

West's California Judicial Council Forms FL-192, Notice Of Rights and Responsibilities (Health-Care Costs and Reimbursement Procedures).

Treatises and Practice Aids

Witkin, California Summary 10th Parent and Child § 287, Order to Participate in Counseling.

Witkin, California Summary 10th Parent and Child § 408, in General.

Witkin, California Summary 10th Parent and Child § 409, Allocation Of Additional Support.

Witkin, California Summary 10th Parent and Child § 410, Uninsured Health Care Costs.

§ 4063. Uninsured health care costs; payment procedures

(a) When making an order pursuant to paragraph (2) of subdivision (a) of Section 4062, the court shall:

(1) Advise each parent, in writing or on the record, of his or her rights and liabilities, including financial responsibilities.

(2) Include in its order the time period for a parent to reimburse the other parent for the reimbursing parent's share of the reasonable additional child support costs subject to the requirements of this section.

(b) Unless there has been an assignment of rights pursuant to Section 11477 of the Welfare and Institutions Code, when either parent accrues or pays costs pursuant to an order under this section, that parent shall provide the other parent with an itemized statement of the costs within a reasonable time, but not more than 30 days after accruing the costs. These costs shall then be paid as follows:

(1) If a parent has already paid all of these costs, that parent shall provide proof of payment and a request for reimbursement of his or her court-ordered share to the other parent.

(2) If a parent has paid his or her court-ordered share of the costs only, that parent shall provide proof of payment to the other parent, request the other parent to pay the remainder of the costs directly to the provider, and provide the reimbursing parent with any necessary information about how to make the payment to the provider.

(3) The other parent shall make the reimbursement or pay the remaining costs within the time period specified by the court, or, if no period is specified, within a reasonable time not to exceed 30 days from notification of the amount due, or according to any payment schedule set by the health care provider for either parent unless the parties agree in writing to another payment schedule or the court finds good cause for setting another payment schedule.

(4) If the reimbursing parent disputes a request for payment, that parent shall pay the requested amount and thereafter may seek judicial relief under this section and Section 290. If the reimbursing parent fails to pay the other parent as required by this subdivision, the other parent may seek judicial relief under this section and Section 290.

(c) Either parent may file a noticed motion to enforce an order issued pursuant to this section. In addition to the court's powers under Section 290, the court may award filing costs and reasonable attorney's fees if it finds that either party acted without reasonable cause regarding his or her obligations pursuant to this section.

(d) There is a rebuttable presumption that the costs actually paid for the uninsured health care needs of the children are reasonable, except as provided in subdivision (e).

(e) Except as provided in subdivision (g):

(1) The health care insurance coverage, including, but not limited to, coverage for emergency treatment, provided by a parent pursuant to a court order, shall be the coverage to be utilized at all times, consistent with the requirements of that coverage, unless the other parent can show that the health care insurance coverage is inadequate to meet the child's needs.

(2) If either parent obtains health care insurance coverage in addition to that provided pursuant to the court order, that parent shall bear sole financial responsibility for the costs of that additional coverage and the costs of any care or treatment obtained pursuant thereto in excess of the costs that would have been incurred under the health care insurance coverage provided for in the court order.

(f) Except as provided in subdivision (g):

(1) If the health care insurance coverage provided by a parent pursuant to a court order designates a preferred health care provider, that preferred provider shall be used at

all times, consistent with the terms and requirements of that coverage.

(2) If either parent uses a health care provider other than the preferred provider inconsistent with the terms and requirements of the court-ordered health care insurance coverage, the parent obtaining that care shall bear the sole responsibility for any nonreimbursable health care costs in excess of the costs that would have been incurred under the court-ordered health care insurance coverage had the preferred provider been used.

(g) When ruling on a motion made pursuant to this section, in order to ensure that the health care needs of the child under this section are met, the court shall consider all relevant facts, including, but not limited to, the following:

(1) The geographic access and reasonable availability of necessary health care for the child which complies with the terms of the health care insurance coverage paid for by either parent pursuant to a court order. Health insurance shall be rebuttably presumed to be accessible if services to be provided are within 50 miles of the residence of the child subject to the support order. If the court determines that health insurance is not accessible, the court shall state the reason on the record.

(2) The necessity of emergency medical treatment that may have precluded the use of the health care insurance, or the preferred health care provider required under the insurance, provided by either parent pursuant to a court order.

(3) The special medical needs of the child.

(4) The reasonable inability of a parent to pay the full amount of reimbursement within a 30–day period and the resulting necessity for a court-ordered payment schedule. *(Added by Stats.1994, c. 466 (S.B.1807), § 3. Amended by Stats.2010, c. 103 (S.B.580), § 3.)*

Law Revision Commission Comments

Enactment [Revised Comment]

Section 4063 continues former Civil Code Section 4721(k) without substantive change. [23 Cal.L.Rev.Comm. Reports 1 (1993)].

Research References

Forms

California Practice Guide: Rutter Family Law Forms Form 5:2, Request for Order Re Child Custody, Child Support, Spousal Support, Attorney Fees, etc.

California Practice Guide: Rutter Family Law Forms Form 11:20, Sample Trial Brief.

California Transactions Forms--Family Law § 3:44, Mandatory Additional Child Support.

West's California Judicial Council Forms FL-192, Notice Of Rights and Responsibilities (Health-Care Costs and Reimbursement Procedures).

Treatises and Practice Aids

Witkin, California Summary 10th Parent and Child § 408, in General.

Witkin, California Summary 10th Parent and Child § 410, Uninsured Health Care Costs.

§ 4064. Adjustment of award to accommodate parent's seasonal or fluctuating income

The court may adjust the child support order as appropriate to accommodate seasonal or fluctuating income of either parent. *(Added by Stats.1993, c. 219 (A.B.1500), § 138.)*

Law Revision Commission Comments

Enactment [Revised Comment]

Section 4064 continues former Civil Code Section 4721(*l*) without change. [23 Cal.L.Rev.Comm. Reports 1 (1993)].

Commentary

In re Marriage of Riddle, 125 Cal.App.4th 1075, 23 Cal.Rptr.3d 273 (2005), holds that the trial court erred in basing pendente lite support orders on an unrepresentative two-month sample of the obligor's earnings. *Riddle* proposes standards for determining a representative sample.

In re Marriage of Mosley, 165 Cal.App.4th 1375, 82 Cal.Rptr.3d 479 (2008), held that a trial court erred when it denied a ex-spouse's request to modify his child and support obligation based on changed circumstances when his income remained relatively constant, but changed from regular predictable periodic earnings to reduced periodic earnings and the uncertain possibility of a large year-end bonus. Although a bonus is income for purposes of child support, in view of the uncertainty of its receipt his monthly child support should have been reduced to reflect his reduced monthly earnings, and the bonus should have been subject to child support when and if it was received.

Research References

Forms

California Transactions Forms--Family Law § 3:41, Seasonal or Fluctuating Income.

Treatises and Practice Aids

Witkin, California Summary 10th Parent and Child § 406, Other Adjustments.

§ 4065. Stipulated agreements for child support awards; conditions; modification

(a) Unless prohibited by applicable federal law, the parties may stipulate to a child support amount subject to approval of the court. However, the court shall not approve a stipulated agreement for child support below the guideline formula amount unless the parties declare all of the following:

(1) They are fully informed of their rights concerning child support.

(2) The order is being agreed to without coercion or duress.

(3) The agreement is in the best interests of the children involved.

(4) The needs of the children will be adequately met by the stipulated amount.

(5) The right to support has not been assigned to the county pursuant to Section 11477 of the Welfare and Institutions Code and no public assistance application is pending.

(b) The parties may, by stipulation, require the child support obligor to designate an account for the purpose of paying the child support obligation by electronic funds transfer pursuant to Section 4508.

(c) A stipulated agreement of child support is not valid unless the local child support agency has joined in the stipulation by signing it in any case in which the local child support agency is providing services pursuant to Section 17400. The local child support agency shall not stipulate to a child support order below the guideline amount if the children are receiving assistance under the CalWORKs program, if an application for public assistance is pending, or if the parent receiving support has not consented to the order.

(d) If the parties to a stipulated agreement stipulate to a child support order below the amount established by the statewide uniform guideline, no change of circumstances need be demonstrated to obtain a modification of the child support order to the applicable guideline level or above. *(Added by Stats.1993, c. 219 (A.B.1500), § 138. Amended by Stats.1993, c. 1156 (S.B.541), § 4; Stats.1999, c. 980 (A.B. 1671), § 8; Stats.2000, c. 135 (A.B.2539), § 59; Stats.2000, c. 808 (A.B.1358), § 35, eff. Sept. 28, 2000.)*

Law Revision Commission Comments

Enactment [Revised Comment]

Section 4065 supersedes former Civil Code Section 4721(m)-(*o*). In subdivision (c), the reference to the amount established "by the statewide uniform guideline" has been substituted for the former reference to the amount established by "this section," meaning former Civil Code Section 4721. This is not a substantive change. See also Section 3011 (factors in determining best interest of child). [23 Cal.L.Rev.Comm. Reports 1 (1993)].

Commentary

Relying on section 3585 as well as subsections (a) and (e) of section 3651, *In re Marriage of Alter, 171 Cal.App.4th 718, 89 Cal.Rptr.3d 849 (2009)*, holds that a trial court always has power to modify an existing child support order upward *or downward*, regardless of the parties' contrary marital settlement agreement. *Alter* establishes that child support may be modified downward despite the parties' agreement to the contrary.

Although no change of circumstances is required to raise a stipulated amount of child support to the guideline level (subsection (d)), when parents have agreed to an amount above the guideline level, the support obligor must demonstrate a change of circumstances to obtain a downward modification of the child support obligation. *In re Marriage of Laudeman, 92 Cal.App.4th 1009, 112 Cal.Rptr.2d 378 (2001)*. *Laudeman* reasons that because the statute is silent on downward modification of a stipulated amount, the prestatutory requirement that the movant must show material changed circumstances to justify downward modification remains the rule. Accord, *In re Marriage of Bodo, 198 Cal.App.4th 373, 129 Cal.Rptr.3d 298 (2011)* (there is no difference between "material change in circumstances" and "substantial change in circumstances" for purposes of modifying child support).

When parties agreed to a stipulated amount below the guideline amount and the support obligor later sought a reduction of the stipulated amount because his earned income declined, that decline was not a *material* change of circumstances because, taking into account all the obligor's assets, he could still afford to pay the stipulated amount. *In re Marriage of Usher, 6 Cal.App.5th 347, 210 Cal.Rptr.3d 875 (2016)*.

The parties' agreement to waive the "materially changed circumstances" requirement when one party seeks a downward modification of a stipulated amount, is unenforceable. The parties cannot, by agreement, require a court to consider or recalculate support de novo, because the changed circumstances requirement is an aspect of res judicata. *In re Marriage of Cohen, 6 Cal.App.5th 1014, 207 Cal.Rptr.3d 846 (2016), review denied.*

In re Marriage of Bereznak & Heminger, 110 Cal.App.4th 1062, 2 Cal.Rptr.3d 351 (2003), held that a stipulation of the parents to submit child support issues to binding arbitration is void to the extent that it would deprive a court of jurisdiction to modify child support.

Research References

Forms

California Practice Guide: Rutter Family Law Forms Form 5:1, Stipulation to Orders Pending Trial (Attorney-Drafted).

California Practice Guide: Rutter Family Law Forms Form 17:1, Stipulation and Order for Modification Of Spousal Support, Child Support, Custody and Visitation.

California Transactions Forms--Family Law § 2:63, Authority for Child Support.

California Transactions Forms--Family Law § 2:64, Amount Of Support.

California Transactions Forms--Family Law § 2:65, Add-Ons.

California Transactions Forms--Family Law § 2:88, Marital Settlement Agreement.

California Transactions Forms--Family Law § 2:91, Add-On Expenses in Conjunction With Family Support.

California Transactions Forms--Family Law § 3:37, Stipulation Of the Parties.

California Transactions Forms--Family Law § 3:112, Alternating the Dependency Exemption.

California Transactions Forms--Family Law § 2:93.5, Child Support Provision Regarding Electronic Transfer Of Funds.

California Transactions Forms--Family Law § 3:112.5, Designation Of Electronic Fund Transfer Account Number.

West's California Code Forms, Family § 4050, Comment Overview--Statewide Uniform Guideline.

West's California Code Forms, Family § 2338 Form 8, Marital Agreement.

West's California Code Forms, Family § 3585 Form 2, Child Support Provisions.

West's California Judicial Council Forms FL-350, Stipulation to Establish or Modify Child Support and Order.

West's California Judicial Council Forms FL-693, Guideline Findings Attachment.

Treatises and Practice Aids

Witkin, California Summary 10th Parent and Child § 411, Factors Rebutting Presumption.

Witkin, California Summary 10th Parent and Child § 414, Stipulated Support Agreements.

§ 4066. "Family support" designation; maximization of tax benefits

Orders and stipulations otherwise in compliance with the statewide uniform guideline may designate as "family support" an unallocated total sum for support of the spouse and any children without specifically labeling all or any portion as "child support" as long as the amount is adjusted to reflect the effect of additional deductibility. The amount of the order shall be adjusted to maximize the tax benefits for both parents. *(Added by Stats.1993, c. 219 (A.B.1500), § 138.)*

Law Revision Commission Comments

Enactment [Revised Comment]

Section 4066 continues former Civil Code Section 4721(p) without substantive change. The reference to the "statewide uniform guideline" has been substituted for the former reference to "this guideline." This is not a substantive change. [23 Cal.L.Rev.Comm. Reports 1 (1993)].

Research References

Forms

California Practice Guide: Rutter Family Law Forms Form 1:32, Glossary Of Common Family Law Terms, Phrases and Concepts (Enclosure to Form 1:31).

California Transactions Forms--Family Law § 3:24, Family Support.
California Transactions Forms--Family Law § 3:25, Duration Of Child Support Obligation.

Treatises and Practice Aids

Witkin, California Summary 10th Parent and Child § 402, Family Support.

§ 4067. Legislative review of statewide uniform guideline

It is the intent of the Legislature that the statewide uniform guideline shall be reviewed by the Legislature at least every four years and shall be revised by the Legislature as appropriate to ensure that its application results in the determination of appropriate child support amounts. The review shall include consideration of changes required by applicable federal laws and regulations or recommended from time to time by the Judicial Council pursuant to Section 4054. *(Added by Stats.1993, c. 219 (A.B.1500), § 138.)*

Law Revision Commission Comments

Enactment [Revised Comment]

Section 4067 continues former Civil Code Section 4721(q) without substantive change. The reference to Section 4054 has been substituted for the narrower reference to former Civil Code Section 4720(b). This is not a substantive change. The reference to the "statewide uniform guideline" has been substituted for the former reference to the "uniform guideline provided by this chapter." This is not a substantive change. [23 Cal.L.Rev.Comm. Reports 1 (1993)].

Research References

Treatises and Practice Aids

Witkin, California Summary 10th Parent and Child § 394, in General.

§ 4068. Model worksheets for determination of amount of support due; form to assist courts in making findings and orders; development of simplified income and expense form

(a) The Judicial Council may develop the following:

(1) Model worksheets to assist parties in determining the approximate amount of child support due under the formula provided in subdivision (a) of Section 4055 and the approximate percentage of time each parent has primary physical responsibility for the children.

(2) A form to assist the courts in making the findings and orders required by this article.

(b) The Judicial Council, in consultation with representatives of the State Department of Social Services, the California Family Support Council, the Senate Judiciary Committee, the Assembly Judiciary Committee, the Family Law Section of the State Bar of California, a legal services organization providing representation on child support matters, a custodial parent group, and a noncustodial parent group, shall develop a simplified income and expense form for determining child support under the formula provided in subdivision (a) of Section 4055, by June 1, 1995. The Judicial Council, also in consultation with these groups, shall develop factors to use to determine when the simplified income and expense form may be used and when the standard income and expense form must be used. *(Added by Stats.1993, c. 219 (A.B.1500), § 138. Amended by Stats.1994, c. 415 (S.B.1715), § 2; Stats.1994, c. 953 (A.B.2142), § 1.)*

Law Revision Commission Comments

Enactment [Revised Comment]

Section 4068 continues former Civil Code Section 4721(r) without substantive change. The phrase "the following" has been added and the section subdivided. The addition of "the following" makes this section consistent with other sections. See, e.g., Section 4058. These are not substantive changes. [23 Cal.L.Rev.Comm. Reports 1 (1993)].

Research References

Forms

West's California Code Forms, Family § 4050, Comment Overview--Statewide Uniform Guideline.

West's California Code Forms, Family § 4068 Form 2, Financial Statement--Simplified.

West's California Judicial Council Forms FL-155, Financial Statement (Simplified).

Treatises and Practice Aids

Witkin, California Summary 10th Parent and Child § 403, Judicial Council Worksheets and Forms.

§ 4069. Establishment of statewide uniform guideline as change of circumstances

The establishment of the statewide uniform guideline constitutes a change of circumstances. *(Added by Stats.1993, c. 219 (A.B.1500), § 138. Amended by Stats.1993, c. 1156 (S.B.541), § 5.)*

Law Revision Commission Comments

Enactment [Revised Comment]

Section 4069 supersedes former Civil Code Section 4721(s). The reference to the "statewide uniform guideline" has been substituted for the former reference to "this guideline." This is not a substantive change. [23 Cal.L.Rev.Comm. Reports 1 (1993)].

Commentary

For discussion and application of this section, see *In re Marriage of Gigliotti, 33 Cal.App.4th 518, 39 Cal.Rptr.2d 367 (1995)*. Identifying additional changed circumstances that would also independently warrant modification of a child support judgment, *Gigliotti* observes: "[N]umerous changed circumstances existed in this case, including an increase in respondent's [obligor's] income, a decrease in appellant's [obligee's] anticipated income, and increased ... child care expenses incurred by appellant [obligee]." Although the Statewide Uniform Guideline provisions (Sections 4050–4076) do not explicitly identify each of these changed circumstances as sufficient to warrant child support modification, the income-sharing principles articulated in Section 4053 (see particularly subsections (b), (c), (d), and (f)) and executed in Sections 4055 (guideline formula) and 4062 (child care costs as mandatory add-on) support the dictum of *Gigliotti*.

Research References

Forms

West's California Judicial Council Forms FL-342, Child Support Information and Order Attachment.

Treatises and Practice Aids

Witkin, California Summary 10th Parent and Child § 439, Modification or Termination Of Support Order.

§ 4070. Financial hardship; income deductions

If a parent is experiencing extreme financial hardship due to justifiable expenses resulting from the circumstances enumerated in Section 4071, on the request of a party, the court may allow the income deductions under Section 4059 that may be necessary to accommodate those circumstances. *(Added by Stats.1993, c. 219 (A.B.1500), § 138.)*

Law Revision Commission Comments

Enactment [Revised Comment]

Section 4070 continues the introductory sentence of former Civil Code Section 4722 without substantive change. [23 Cal.L.Rev. Comm. Reports 1 (1993)].

Research References

Forms

California Transactions Forms--Family Law § 2:65, Add-Ons.
California Transactions Forms--Family Law § 3:32, Determination Of Net Monthly Disposable Income.
California Transactions Forms--Family Law § 3:34, Hardship Deductions.

Treatises and Practice Aids

Witkin, California Summary 10th Parent and Child § 400, Annual Net Disposable Income.
Witkin, California Summary 10th Parent and Child § 404, Hardship Deduction.

§ 4071. Financial hardship; evidence

(a) Circumstances evidencing hardship include the following:

(1) Extraordinary health expenses for which the parent is financially responsible, and uninsured catastrophic losses.

(2) The minimum basic living expenses of either parent's natural or adopted children for whom the parent has the obligation to support from other marriages or relationships who reside with the parent. The court, on its own motion or on the request of a party, may allow these income deductions as necessary to accommodate these expenses after making the deductions allowable under paragraph (1).

(b) The maximum hardship deduction under paragraph (2) of subdivision (a) for each child who resides with the parent may be equal to, but shall not exceed, the support allocated each child subject to the order. For purposes of calculating this deduction, the amount of support per child established by the statewide uniform guideline shall be the total amount ordered divided by the number of children and not the amount established under paragraph (8) of subdivision (b) of Section 4055.

(c) The Judicial Council may develop tables in accordance with this section to reflect the maximum hardship deduction, taking into consideration the parent's net disposable income before the hardship deduction, the number of children for whom the deduction is being given, and the number of children for whom the support award is being made. *(Added by Stats.1993, c. 219 (A.B.1500), § 138. Amended by Stats. 1993, c. 1156 (S.B.541), § 6.)*

Law Revision Commission Comments

Enactment [Revised Comment]

Section 4071 supersedes former Civil Code Section 4722(a)-(b). [23 Cal.L.Rev.Comm. Reports 1 (1993)].

Commentary

See *Haggard v. Haggard, 38 Cal.App.4th 1566, 45 Cal.Rptr.2d 638 (1995)* (noncustodial support obligor parent's voluntary support of nonadopted children of new mate does not entitle support obligor either to a Section 4057(b)(5) finding of "special circumstances" or to a Section 4059(g) hardship deduction. See also Section 4057, Commentary. Compare *In re Marriage of Paulin, 46 Cal.App.4th 1378, 54 Cal.Rptr.2d 314 (1996)* (sustaining trial court finding that middle-income child support obligor was entitled to hardship deduction on account of expenses resulting from birth of twins in obligor's new marriage).

Research References

Forms

California Transactions Forms--Family Law § 2:88, Marital Settlement Agreement.
California Transactions Forms--Family Law § 3:34, Hardship Deductions.
West's California Code Forms, Family § 2338 Form 8, Marital Agreement.
West's California Code Forms, Family § 3585 Form 2, Child Support Provisions.

Treatises and Practice Aids

Witkin, California Summary 10th Parent and Child § 400, Annual Net Disposable Income.
Witkin, California Summary 10th Parent and Child § 404, Hardship Deduction.

§ 4072. Deduction for hardship expenses; statement by court of reasons for supporting deductions; statement of amount and underlying facts; duration

(a) If a deduction for hardship expenses is allowed, the court shall do both of the following:

(1) State the reasons supporting the deduction in writing or on the record.

(2) Document the amount of the deduction and the underlying facts and circumstances.

(b) Whenever possible, the court shall specify the duration of the deduction. *(Added by Stats.1993, c. 219 (A.B.1500), § 138.)*

Law Revision Commission Comments

Enactment [Revised Comment]

Section 4072 continues former Civil Code Section 4722(c) without substantive change. The language of the former section has been revised for clarity. See also Section 10 (singular includes plural). [23 Cal.L.Rev.Comm. Reports 1 (1993)].

Commentary

In re Marriage of Carlsen, 50 Cal.App.4th 212, 57 Cal.Rptr.2d 630 (1996), holds that a trial court may not grant a hardship deduction without making the express evidentiary findings required by this section and stating its reasons in writing or on the record.

Research References

Treatises and Practice Aids

Witkin, California Summary 10th Parent and Child § 404, Hardship Deduction.

§ 4073. Considerations of court in deciding whether or not to allow hardship deduction

The court shall be guided by the goals set forth in this article when considering whether or not to allow a financial hardship deduction, and, if allowed, when determining the amount of the deduction. *(Added by Stats.1993, c. 219 (A.B.1500), § 138.)*

Law Revision Commission Comments

Enactment [Revised Comment]

Section 4073 continues former Civil Code Section 4722(d) without substantive change. The language of the former section has been revised for clarity. The reference to this article has been substituted for the narrower reference to former Civil Code Section 4720. This is not a substantive change, since the former section is continued in this article. [23 Cal.L.Rev.Comm. Reports 1 (1993)].

Research References

Forms

California Transactions Forms--Family Law § 3:32, Determination Of Net Monthly Disposable Income.

Treatises and Practice Aids

Witkin, California Summary 10th Parent and Child § 404, Hardship Deduction.

§ 4074. Application of article to all awards for support of children

This article applies to an award for the support of children, including those awards designated as "family support," that contain provisions for the support of children as well as for the support of the spouse. *(Added by Stats.1993, c. 219 (A.B.1500), § 138.)*

Law Revision Commission Comments

Enactment [Revised Comment]

Section 4074 continues former Civil Code Section 4731 without substantive change. [23 Cal.L.Rev.Comm. Reports 1 (1993)].

Research References

Treatises and Practice Aids

Witkin, California Summary 10th Parent and Child § 402, Family Support.

§ 4075. Tax treatment of spousal support and separate maintenance; application of article

This article shall not be construed to affect the treatment of spousal support and separate maintenance payments pursuant to Section 71 of the Internal Revenue Code of 1954 (26 U.S.C. Sec. 71). *(Added by Stats.1993, c. 219 (A.B.1500), § 138.)*

Law Revision Commission Comments

Enactment [Revised Comment]

Section 4075 continues former Civil Code Section 4732 without substantive change. [23 Cal.L.Rev.Comm. Reports 1 (1993)].

Research References

Treatises and Practice Aids

Witkin, California Summary 10th Parent and Child § 402, Family Support.

§ 4076. Modification of child support orders; two-step phasein of formula amount of support; conditions

(a) Whenever the court is requested to modify a child support order issued prior to July 1, 1992, for the purpose of conforming to the statewide child support guideline, and it is not using its discretionary authority to depart from the guideline pursuant to paragraph (3), (4), or (5) of subdivision (b) of Section 4057, and the amount of child support to be ordered is the amount provided under the guideline formula in subdivision (a) of Section 4055, the court may, in its discretion, order a two-step phasein of the formula amount of support to provide the obligor with time for transition to the full formula amount if all of the following are true:

(1) The period of the phasein is carefully limited to the time necessary for the obligor to rearrange his or her financial obligations in order to meet the full formula amount of support.

(2) The obligor is immediately being ordered to pay not less than 30 percent of the amount of the child support increase, in addition to the amount of child support required under the prior order.

(3) The obligor has not unreasonably increased his or her financial obligations following notice of the motion for modification of support, has no arrearages owing, and has a history of good faith compliance with prior support orders.

(b) Whenever the court grants a request for a phasein pursuant to this section, the court shall state the following in writing:

(1) The specific reasons why (A) the immediate imposition of the full formula amount of support would place an extraordinary hardship on the obligor, and (B) this extraordinary hardship on the obligor would outweigh the hardship caused the supported children by the temporary phasein of the full formula amount of support.

(2) The full guideline amount of support, the date and amount of each phasein, and the date that the obligor must commence paying the full formula amount of support, which in no event shall be later than one year after the filing of the motion for modification of support.

(c) In the event the court orders a phasein pursuant to this section, and the court thereafter determines that the obligor has violated the phasein schedule or has intentionally lowered the income available for the payment of child support during the phasein period, the court may order the immediate payment of the full formula amount of child support and the difference in the amount of support that would have been due without the phasein and the amount of support due with the phasein, in addition to any other penalties provided for by law. *(Added by Stats.1993, c. 1156 (S.B.541), § 7.5.)*

Research References

Forms

California Transactions Forms--Family Law § 3:21, Jurisdiction for Orders to Pay Child Support.

West's California Code Forms, Family § 4068 Form 2, Financial Statement--Simplified.

West's California Judicial Council Forms FL-150, Income and Expense Declaration.

West's California Judicial Council Forms FL-684, Request for Order and Supporting Declaration (Governmental).

Treatises and Practice Aids

Witkin, California Summary 10th Parent and Child § 439, Modification or Termination Of Support Order.

ARTICLE 3. PAYMENT TO COURT DESIGNATED COUNTY OFFICER; ENFORCEMENT BY DISTRICT ATTORNEY

§ 4200. Child support orders to parents receiving welfare; duties of court

In any proceeding where a court makes or has made an order requiring the payment of child support to a parent receiving welfare moneys for the maintenance of children for whom support may be ordered, the court shall do both of the following:

(a) Direct that the payments of support shall be made to the county officer designated by the court for that purpose. Once the State Disbursement Unit is implemented pursuant to Section 17309, all payments shall be directed to the State Disbursement Unit instead of the county officer designated by the court.

(b) Direct the local child support agency to appear on behalf of the welfare recipient in any proceeding to enforce the order. *(Stats.1992, c. 162 (A.B.2650), § 10, operative Jan. 1, 1994. Amended by Stats.1993, c. 219 (A.B.1500), § 140; Stats.1997, c. 599 (A.B.573), § 14; Stats.2000, c. 808 (A.B. 1358) § 36, eff. Sept. 28, 2000; Stats.2003, c. 387 (A.B.739), § 2.)*

Law Revision Commission Comments

Enactment [Revised Comment]

Section 4200 continues former Civil Code Section 4702(a) without substantive change. The reference to support of a "minor" child has been omitted. This is not a substantive change, but recognizes that in some cases support may be ordered for an adult child. See Sections 58 ("child for whom support may be ordered" defined), 3587 (court order to effectuate agreement for support of adult child), 3901 (duration of duty to support child), 3910 (duty to maintain incapacitated adult child), 4000 (civil action to enforce parent's duty to support child), 4001 (order for child support). The reference in former law to Civil Code Section 4701 has been omitted as obsolete, since Section 4701 was repealed by its own terms on January 1, 1991. See 1989 Cal. Stat. ch. 1359, § 3.5.

See also Sections 3029 (order for support required when custodial parent receiving public assistance), 3555 (forwarding of support payments paid through county officer), 4550–4573 (deposit of money to secure future child support payments), 4600–4641 (deposit of assets to secure future child support payments). For a comparable procedure for spousal support payments, see Section 4350 *et seq.* [23 Cal.L.Rev.Comm. Reports 1 (1993)].

Research References

Forms

West's California Code Forms, Family § 4200, Comment Overview--Child Support Orders to Parents.

West's California Judicial Council Forms FL-632, Notice Regarding Payment Of Support.

West's California Judicial Council Forms FL-684, Request for Order and Supporting Declaration (Governmental).

Treatises and Practice Aids

Witkin, California Summary 10th Husband and Wife § 313, Payment to County by Court and Referral.

§ 4201. Child support orders; payment to county officer; appearance by local child support agency in enforcement proceeding

In any proceeding where a court makes or has made an order requiring the payment of child support to the person having custody of a child for whom support may be ordered, the court may do either or both of the following:

(a) Direct that the payments shall be made to the county officer designated by the court for that purpose. Once the State Disbursement Unit is implemented pursuant to Section 17309, all payments shall be directed to the State Disbursement Unit instead of the county officer designated by the court.

(b) Direct the local child support agency to appear on behalf of the minor children in any proceeding to enforce the order. *(Stats.1992, c. 162 (A.B.2650), § 10, operative Jan. 1, 1994. Amended by Stats.1993, c. 219 (A.B.1500), § 141; Stats.1997, c. 599 (A.B.573), § 15; Stats.2000, c. 808 (A.B. 1358), § 37, eff. Sept. 28, 2000; Stats.2003, c. 387 (A.B.739), § 3.)*

Law Revision Commission Comments

Enactment [Revised Comment]

Section 4201 continues former Civil Code Section 4702(b) without substantive change. The reference to support of a "minor" child has been omitted. This is not a substantive change, but recognizes that in some cases support may be ordered for an adult child. See Sections 58 ("child for whom support may be ordered" defined), 3587 (court order to effectuate agreement for support of adult child), 3901 (duration of duty to support child), 3910 (duty to maintain incapacitated adult child), 4000 (civil action to enforce parent's duty to support child), 4001 (order for child support). The limitation to children "of the marriage" has been omitted, since this section applies to proceedings for support involving unmarried parents. See, e.g., Section 7637 (court authorized to order child support in Uniform Parentage Act proceeding). In subdivision (b), the reference to "proceeding" has been substituted for "action." This is a nonsubstantive change that conforms with Section 4200(b).

See also Sections 3555 (forwarding of support payments paid through county officer), 4550–4573 (deposit of money to secure future child support payments), 4600–4641 (deposit of assets to secure future child support payments). [23 Cal.L.Rev.Comm. Reports 1 (1993)].

Research References

Forms

West's California Code Forms, Family § 4200, Comment Overview--Child Support Orders to Parents.

West's California Judicial Council Forms FL-632, Notice Regarding Payment Of Support.

Treatises and Practice Aids

Witkin, California Summary 10th Husband and Wife § 313, Payment to County by Court and Referral.

§ 4202. Parents residing in different counties

(a) Notwithstanding any other provision of law, in a proceeding where the custodial parent resides in one county and the parent ordered to pay support resides in another county, the court may direct payment to be made to the county officer designated by the court for those purposes in the county of residence of the custodial parent, and may direct the local child support agency of either county to enforce the order.

(b) If the court directs the local child support agency of the county of residence of the noncustodial parent to enforce the order, the expenses of the local child support agency with respect to the enforcement is a charge upon the county of residence of the noncustodial parent. *(Stats.1992, c. 162 (A.B.2650), § 10, operative Jan. 1, 1994. Amended by Stats. 2000, c. 808 (A.B.1358), § 38, eff. Sept. 28, 2000; Stats.2004, c. 339 (A.B.1704), § 3.)*

Law Revision Commission Comments

Enactment [Revised Comment]

Section 4202 continues former Civil Code Section 4702(c) without substantive change. See also Section 3555 (forwarding of support payments paid through county officer). [23 Cal.L.Rev.Comm. Reports 1 (1993)].

Research References

Treatises and Practice Aids

Witkin, California Summary 10th Husband and Wife § 313, Payment to County by Court and Referral.

§ 4203. Charges and expenses

(a) Except as provided in Section 4202, expenses of the county officer designated by the court, and expenses of the local child support agency incurred in the enforcement of an order of the type described in Section 4200 or 4201, are a charge upon the county where the proceedings are pending.

(b) Fees for service of process in the enforcement of an order of the type described in Section 4200 or 4201 are a charge upon the county where the process is served. *(Stats. 1992, c. 162 (A.B.2650), § 10, operative Jan. 1, 1994. Amended by Stats.2000, c. 808 (A.B.1358), § 39, eff. Sept. 28, 2000.)*

Law Revision Commission Comments

Enactment [Revised Comment]

Section 4203 continues former Civil Code Section 4702(d) without substantive change. [23 Cal.L.Rev.Comm. Reports 1 (1993)].

§ 4204. Child support assigned to county; local child support agency providing child support enforcement services; notice regarding where payments should be directed

Notwithstanding any other provision of law, in any proceeding where the court has made an order requiring the payment of child support to a person having custody of a child and the child support is subsequently assigned to the county pursuant to Section 11477 of the Welfare and Institutions Code or the person having custody has requested the local child support agency to provide child support enforcement services pursuant to Section 17400, the local child support agency may issue a notice directing that the payments shall be made to the local child support agency, another county office, or the State Disbursement Unit pursuant to Section 17309. The notice shall be served on both the support obligor and obligee in compliance with Section 1013 of the Code of Civil Procedure. The local child support agency shall file the notice in the action in which the support order was issued. *(Added by Stats.1997, c. 599 (A.B.573), § 16. Amended by Stats.2000, c. 808 (A.B.1358), § 40, eff. Sept. 28, 2000; Stats.2003, c. 387 (A.B.739), § 4.)*

Research References

Forms

West's California Judicial Council Forms FL-632, Notice Regarding Payment Of Support.

West's California Judicial Council Forms FL-684, Request for Order and Supporting Declaration (Governmental).

Treatises and Practice Aids

Witkin, California Summary 10th Husband and Wife § 313, Payment to County by Court and Referral.

§ 4205. Notice requesting meeting with support obligor; contents

Any notice from the local child support agency requesting a meeting with the support obligor for any purpose authorized under this part shall contain a statement advising the support obligor of his or her right to have an attorney present at the meeting. *(Added by Stats.1998, c. 854 (A.B.960), § 2. Amended by Stats.2000, c. 808 (A.B.1358), § 41, eff. Sept. 28, 2000.)*

Research References

Forms

West's California Code Forms, Family § 4200, Comment Overview--Child Support Orders to Parents.

Treatises and Practice Aids

Witkin, California Summary 10th Husband and Wife § 314, Acquisition and Confidentiality Of Information.

ARTICLE 4. CHILD SUPPORT COMMISSIONERS

§ 4250. Legislative findings and declarations

(a) The Legislature finds and declares the following:

(1) Child and spousal support are serious legal obligations.

(2) The current system for obtaining, modifying, and enforcing child and spousal support orders is inadequate to meet the future needs of California's children due to burgeoning caseloads within local child support agencies and the growing number of parents who are representing themselves in family law actions.

(3) The success of California's child support enforcement program depends upon its ability to establish and enforce child support orders quickly and efficiently.

(4) There is a compelling state interest in creating an expedited process in the courts that is cost-effective and

accessible to families, for establishing and enforcing child support orders in cases being enforced by the local child support agency.

(5) There is a compelling state interest in having a simple, speedy, conflict-reducing system, that is both cost-effective and accessible to families, for resolving all issues concerning children, including support, health insurance, custody, and visitation in family law cases that do not involve enforcement by the local child support agency.

(b) Therefore, it is the intent of the Legislature to: (1) provide for commissioners to hear child support cases being enforced by the local child support agency; (2) adopt uniform and simplified procedures for all child support cases; and (3) create an Office of the Family Law Facilitator in the courts to provide education, information, and assistance to parents with child support issues. *(Added by Stats.1996, c. 957 (A.B.1058), § 6. Amended by Stats.2000, c. 808 (A.B.1358), § 42, eff. Sept. 28, 2000.)*

Research References

Forms

West's California Code Forms, Family § 4250, Comment Overview--Child Support Commissioners.

Treatises and Practice Aids

Witkin, California Summary 10th Husband and Wife § 327, Hearing.
Witkin, California Summary 10th Parent and Child § 383, in General.

§ 4251. Provision of commissioners; referral of actions or proceedings; authority of commissioners

(a) Commencing July 1, 1997, each superior court shall provide sufficient commissioners to hear Title IV–D child support cases filed by the local child support agency. The number of child support commissioners required in each county shall be determined by the Judicial Council as prescribed by paragraph (3) of subdivision (b) of Section 4252. All actions or proceedings filed by the local child support agency in a support action or proceeding in which enforcement services are being provided pursuant to Section 17400, for an order to establish, modify, or enforce child or spousal support, including actions to establish paternity, shall be referred for hearing to a child support commissioner unless a child support commissioner is not available due to exceptional circumstances, as prescribed by the Judicial Council pursuant to paragraph (7) of subdivision (b) of Section 4252. All actions or proceedings filed by a party other than the local child support agency to modify or enforce a support order established by the local child support agency or for which enforcement services are being provided pursuant to Section 17400 shall be referred for hearing to a child support commissioner unless a child support commissioner is not available due to exceptional circumstances, as prescribed by the Judicial Council pursuant to paragraph (7) of subdivision (b) of Section 4252.

(b) The commissioner shall act as a temporary judge unless an objection is made by the local child support agency or any other party. The Judicial Council shall develop a notice which shall be included on all forms and pleadings used to initiate a child support action or proceeding that advises the parties of their right to review by a superior court judge and how to exercise that right. The parties shall also be advised by the court prior to the commencement of the hearing that the matter is being heard by a commissioner who shall act as a temporary judge unless any party objects to the commissioner acting as a temporary judge. While acting as a temporary judge, the commissioner shall receive no compensation other than compensation as a commissioner.

(c) If any party objects to the commissioner acting as a temporary judge, the commissioner may hear the matter and make findings of fact and a recommended order. Within 10 court days, a judge shall ratify the recommended order unless either party objects to the recommended order, or where a recommended order is in error. In both cases, the judge shall issue a temporary order and schedule a hearing de novo within 10 court days. Any party may waive his or her right to the review hearing at any time.

(d) The commissioner shall, where appropriate, do any of the following:

(1) Review and determine ex parte applications for orders and writs.

(2) Take testimony.

(3) Establish a record, evaluate evidence, and make recommendations or decisions.

(4) Enter judgments or orders based upon voluntary acknowledgments of support liability and parentage and stipulated agreements respecting the amount of child support to be paid.

(5) Enter default orders and judgments pursuant to Section 4253.

(6) In actions in which paternity is at issue, order the mother, child, and alleged father to submit to genetic tests.

(e) The commissioner shall, upon application of any party, join issues concerning custody, visitation, and protective orders in the action filed by the local child support agency, subject to Section 17404. After joinder, the commissioner shall:

(1) Refer the parents for mediation of disputed custody or visitation issues pursuant to Section 3170 of the Family Code.

(2) Accept stipulated agreements concerning custody, visitation, and protective orders and enter orders pursuant to the agreements.

(3) Refer contested issues of custody, visitation, and protective orders to a judge or to another commissioner for hearing. A child support commissioner may hear contested custody, visitation, and restraining order issues only if the court has adopted procedures to segregate the costs of hearing Title IV–D child support issues from the costs of hearing other issues pursuant to applicable federal requirements.

(f) The local child support agency shall be served notice by the moving party of any proceeding under this section in which support is at issue. Any order for support that is entered without the local child support agency having received proper notice shall be voidable upon the motion of the local child support agency. *(Added by Stats.1996, c. 957 (A.B.1058), § 6. Amended by Stats.1998, c. 932 (A.B.1094), § 32; Stats.2000, c. 808 (A.B.1358), § 43, eff. Sept. 28, 2000.)*

Commentary

Kern County Department of Child Support Services v. Camacho, 209 Cal.App.4th 1028, 147 Cal.Rptr.3d 354 (2012), holds that failure to comply with the notification procedure of subsection (c) did not require set-aside of commissioner's order when the support obligor had prior notice of his right to object.

In re Marriage of M.A., 234 Cal.App.4th 894, 184 Cal.Rptr.3d 315 (2015), review denied, held that orders made by a commissioner who declined to "entertain" a father's statement of disqualification were invalid, because under Code of Civil Procedure section 170.3(4), a commissioner who fails to act on a statement of disqualification is deemed to have consented to disqualification.

Research References

Forms

West's California Judicial Council Forms FL-665, Findings and Recommendation Of Commissioner.

West's California Judicial Council Forms FL-666, Notice Of Objection.

West's California Judicial Council Forms FL-667, Review Of Commissioner's Findings Of Fact and Recommendation.

West's California Judicial Council Forms FL-679, Request for Telephone Appearance.

West's California Judicial Council Forms FL-683, Order to Show Cause.

Treatises and Practice Aids

Witkin, California Summary 10th Husband and Wife § 327, Hearing.

§ 4252. Appointment of subordinate judicial officers as child support commissioners; priority of cases; number of commissioner positions allotted to each court; responsibility of Judicial Council

(a) The superior court shall appoint one or more subordinate judicial officers as child support commissioners to perform the duties specified in Section 4251. The child support commissioners' first priority always shall be to hear Title IV–D child support cases. The child support commissioners shall specialize in hearing child support cases, and their primary responsibility shall be to hear Title IV–D child support cases. Notwithstanding Section 71622 of the Government Code, the number of child support commissioner positions allotted to each court shall be determined by the Judicial Council in accordance with caseload standards developed pursuant to paragraph (3) of subdivision (b), subject to appropriations in the annual Budget Act.

(b) The Judicial Council shall do all of the following:

(1) Establish minimum qualifications for child support commissioners.

(2) Establish minimum educational and training requirements for child support commissioners and other court personnel that are assigned to Title IV–D child support cases. Training programs shall include both federal and state laws concerning child support and related issues.

(3) Establish caseload, case processing, and staffing standards for child support commissioners on or before April 1, 1997, which shall set forth the maximum number of cases that each child support commissioner can process. These standards shall be reviewed and, if appropriate, revised by the Judicial Council every two years.

(4) Adopt uniform rules of court and forms for use in Title IV–D child support cases.

(5) Offer technical assistance to courts regarding issues relating to implementation and operation of the child support commissioner system, including assistance related to funding, staffing, and the sharing of resources between courts.

(6) Establish procedures for the distribution of funding to the courts for child support commissioners, family law facilitators pursuant to Division 14 (commencing with Section 10000), and related allowable costs.

(7) Adopt rules that define the exceptional circumstances in which judges may hear Title IV–D child support matters as provided in subdivision (a) of Section 4251.

(8) Undertake other actions as appropriate to ensure the successful implementation and operation of child support commissioners in the counties.

(c) As used in this article, "Title IV–D" means Title IV–D of the federal Social Security Act (42 U.S.C. Sec. 651 et seq.). *(Added by Stats.1996, c. 957 (A.B.1058), § 6. Amended by Stats.1998, c. 249 (A.B.2498), § 1; Stats.1999, c. 83 (S.B.966), § 49; Stats.2002, c. 784 (S.B.1316), § 105.)*

Law Revision Commission Comments

2002 Amendment

Section 4252 is amended to reflect enactment of the Trial Court Employment Protection and Governance Act. See Gov't Code § 71622 (subordinate judicial officers).

The section is also amended to reflect enactment of the Trial Court Funding Act. See Gov't Code §§ 77001 (local trial court management), 77003 ("court operations" defined), 77200 (state funding of trial court operations).

The section is also amended to delete the reference in subdivision (a) to former Article 13 (commencing with Section 70140) of Chapter 5 of Title 8 of the Government Code.

The section is also amended to delete former subdivision (b)(8) as obsolete.

Subdivision (c) is added for purposes of clarity. [32 Cal.L.Rev. Comm. Reports 162 (2002)].

Research References

Treatises and Practice Aids

Witkin, California Summary 10th Husband and Wife § 327, Hearing.

§ 4253. Default orders

Notwithstanding any other provision of law, when hearing child support matters, a commissioner or referee may enter default orders if the defendant does not respond to notice or other process within the time prescribed to respond to that notice. *(Added by Stats.1996, c. 957 (A.B.1058), § 6.)*

Research References

Treatises and Practice Aids

Witkin, California Summary 10th Husband and Wife § 327, Hearing.

Part 3

SPOUSAL SUPPORT

CHAPTER 1. DUTY TO SUPPORT SPOUSE

§ 4300. Individual's duty of support

Subject to this division, a person shall support the person's spouse. *(Stats.1992, c. 162 (A.B.2650), § 10, operative Jan. 1, 1994.)*

Law Revision Commission Comments

Enactment [Revised Comment]

Section 4300 restates former Civil Code Section 242 without substantive change, to the extent the former section applied to support of a spouse. The introductory clause has been substituted for the specific sections referred to in the second sentence of former Civil Code Section 242. This is not a substantive change. The former reference to the requirement that the spouse be supported "when in need" has been omitted as surplus. See Sections 4320–4323 (factors to be considered in ordering spousal support).

See also Sections 720 (husband and wife contract toward each other obligations of mutual respect, fidelity, and support), 2254 (duty to support putative spouse), 4302 (no liability for support of spouse living separate by agreement unless stipulated). [23 Cal.L.Rev. Comm. Reports 1 (1993)].

Commentary

For recent discussion of the duty of support, see *Borelli v. Brusseau, 12 Cal.App.4th 647, 654, 16 Cal.Rptr.2d 16 (1993), review denied 4/1/93*, holding that the Section 4300 duty of support includes the obligation to care personally for a spouse who is ill. See additionally Section 1620, Commentary.

For the principle that the duty of support may not be altered or waived other than by a separation agreement, see *In re Marriage of Higgason, 10 Cal.3d 476, 487, 110 Cal.Rptr. 897 (1973)*. See also *In re Marriage of Mathiasen, 268 Cal.Rptr. 895, 897 (1990), review denied and depublished 7/25/90* (holding the spouses' household expense reimbursement agreement unenforceable because it altered the statutory obligation of mutual support).

Kilroy v. Kilroy, 35 Cal.App.4th 1141, 41 Cal.Rptr.2d 812 (1995), review denied 8/24/95, holds that a trial court may award temporary support and attorney's fees in a civil action brought by one spouse to enforce the other spouse's Section 4300 duty of support during marriage. Although neither spouse had brought any action for dissolution, it appears that the spouses were not living together when the wife brought her Section 4303 action. Thus *Kilroy* does not directly challenge the venerable American rule that when the spouses are still living together as husband and wife, the courts will not intervene in an ongoing marriage to order spousal support absent jeopardy to the health or basic welfare of the petitioning spouse. See, for example, *McGuire v. McGuire, 59 N.W.2d 336 (Neb. 1953)*. In any event, a California spouse may enlist the court's assistance indirectly during an ongoing marriage by bringing a Section 1101(c) action to add his or her name to the title of the parties' community property assets.

Despite the requirement of 28 USC § 1360(c) that state courts give full force and effect to American Indian tribal law and custom in civil matters, *In re Marriage of Jacobsen, 121 Cal.App.4th 1187, 18 Cal.Rptr.3d 162 (2004)*, holds that, in a divorce proceeding initiated by a tribal member, a California family court is not required to give effect to a Chumash Indian custom that funds distributed by the tribe to its members should not be used to pay spousal support to non-members, because once a tribal member invokes the court's jurisdiction in a domestic relations matter, the court has jurisdiction to grant any appropriate relief. *Jacobsen* additionally observes that the Chumash custom is not binding in family court because it is inconsistent with California law and policy, which is expressed in this section and Sections 720 and 3600.

Research References

Forms

Alternative Dispute Resolution with Forms § 22:5, Parties.
California Transactions Forms--Family Law § 2:52, Overview.
Am. Jur. Pl. & Pr. Forms Husband and Wife § 64, Introductory Comments.
West's California Code Forms, Family § 4300, Comment Overview--Duty to Support Spouse.
West's California Code Forms, Probate § 3080 Form 1, Petition for Support; for Injunctive Orders; for Determination Of the Character Of Property; for an Accounting; for Employment Of Counsel; and for Attorney Fees and Costs.
West's California Judicial Council Forms FL-150, Income and Expense Declaration.

Treatises and Practice Aids

Witkin, California Summary 10th Husband and Wife § 36, Mutual Obligations.
Witkin, California Summary 10th Husband and Wife § 174, in General.
Witkin, California Summary 10th Husband and Wife § 384, Orders After Notice and Hearing.

§ 4301. Support of spouse from separate property

Subject to Section 914, a person shall support the person's spouse while they are living together out of the separate property of the person when there is no community property or quasi-community property. *(Stats.1992, c. 162 (A.B.2650), § 10, operative Jan. 1, 1994.)*

Law Revision Commission Comments

Enactment [Revised Comment]

Section 4301 continues former Civil Code Section 5132 without substantive change. The second sentence of the former section, which made the definitions set out in former Civil Code Sections 4803 and 4804 applicable to this section, has been omitted as surplus. This is not a substantive change, since the former definitions are continued in Sections 125 ("quasi-community property" defined) and 3515 ("separate property" defined). See also Sections 65 ("community property" defined in Section 760 *et seq.*), 130 ("separate property" defined in Section 760 *et seq.*).

This section is consistent with Section 914(a)(1) and (b), but Section 914(a)(1) and (b) do not require exhaustion of community and quasi-community property before separate property of a non-debtor spouse can be reached by a third-party creditor.

For background on former Civ. Code § 5132, see *Recommendation Relating to Liability of Marital Property for Debts,* 17 Cal. L. Revision Comm'n Reports 1 (1984). [23 Cal.L.Rev.Comm. Reports 1 (1993)].

Commentary

Section 4301 provides support for the case-law tracing rule that a spouse who uses his separate property to pay for family expenses when the community property has been exhausted, may not later claim reimbursement from the community estate. *See v. See, 64 Cal.2d 778, 51 Cal.Rptr. 888 (1966)*. See also Sections 1620 and 4300, Commentary.

Research References

Treatises and Practice Aids

Witkin, California Summary 10th Community Property § 180, Personal Liability for Debts for Spouse's Necessaries.

Witkin, California Summary 10th Husband and Wife § 36, Mutual Obligations.

§ 4302. Support of spouse living separate by agreement

A person is not liable for support of the person's spouse when the person is living separate from the spouse by agreement unless support is stipulated in the agreement. *(Stats.1992, c. 162 (A.B.2650), § 10, operative Jan. 1, 1994.)*

Law Revision Commission Comments

Enactment [Revised Comment]

Section 4302 continues former Civil Code Section 5131 without substantive change. See also Section 3580 (spousal support in separation agreement). [23 Cal.L.Rev.Comm. Reports 1 (1993)].

Commentary

Section 4302 applies only when the parties entered a separation agreement and the agreement contains no provision for support. *In re Marriage of Epstein, 24 Cal.3d 76, 85, 154 Cal.Rptr. 413 (1979)*; *In re Marriage of Stallworth, 192 Cal.App.3d 742, 752, 237 Cal.Rptr. 829 (1987)*.

Research References

Treatises and Practice Aids

Witkin, California Summary 10th Community Property § 9, Former Law.

Witkin, California Summary 10th Community Property § 33, Restrictions on Alteration Of Spouses' Legal Relations.

Witkin, California Summary 10th Community Property § 180, Personal Liability for Debts for Spouse's Necessaries.

Witkin, California Summary 10th Husband and Wife § 37, Spouse Living Apart.

Witkin, California Summary 10th Husband and Wife § 40, Agreements Altering Spouses' Legal Relations.

§ 4303. Enforcement of duty of support; reimbursement of county

(a) The obligee spouse, or the county on behalf of the obligee spouse, may bring an action against the obligor spouse to enforce the duty of support.

(b) If the county furnishes support to a spouse, the county has the same right as the spouse to whom the support was furnished to secure reimbursement and obtain continuing support. The right of the county to reimbursement is subject to any limitation otherwise imposed by the law of this state.

(c) The court may order the obligor to pay the county reasonable attorney's fees and court costs in a proceeding brought by the county under this section. *(Stats.1992, c. 162 (A.B.2650), § 10, operative Jan. 1, 1994.)*

Law Revision Commission Comments

Enactment [Revised Comment]

Section 4303 continues without substantive change former Civil Code Section 248, insofar as that section applied to enforcement of spousal support. For comparable provisions, see Sections 4002 (county enforcement of duty to support child), 4403 (county enforcement of duty to support parent). [23 Cal.L.Rev.Comm. Reports 1 (1993)].

Commentary

Kilroy v. Kilroy, 35 Cal.App.4th 1141, 41 Cal.Rptr.2d 812 (1995), review denied 8/24/95, holds that a trial court may award temporary support and attorney's fees in a civil action brought by one spouse to enforce the other spouse's Section 4300 duty of support during marriage. Although neither spouse had brought any action for dissolution, it appears that the spouses were not living together when the wife brought her Section 4303 action. Thus *Kilroy* does not directly challenge the venerable American rule that when the spouses are still living together as husband and wife, the courts will not intervene in an ongoing marriage to order spousal support absent jeopardy to the health or basic welfare of the petitioning spouse. See, for example, *McGuire v. McGuire, 59 N.W.2d 336 (Neb. 1953)*. In any event, a California spouse may enlist the court's assistance indirectly during an ongoing marriage by bringing a Section 1101 (c) action to add his or her name to the title of the parties' community property assets.

Research References

Forms

California Transactions Forms--Family Law § 2:52, Overview.

West's California Code Forms, Family § 4300, Comment Overview--Duty to Support Spouse.

Treatises and Practice Aids

Witkin, California Summary 10th Husband and Wife § 36, Mutual Obligations.

Witkin, California Summary 10th Husband and Wife § 310, Local Child Support Agency.

Witkin, California Summary 10th Husband and Wife § 339, in General.

CHAPTER 2. FACTORS TO BE CONSIDERED IN ORDERING SUPPORT

§ 4320. Determination of amount due for support; considerations

In ordering spousal support under this part, the court shall consider all of the following circumstances:

(a) The extent to which the earning capacity of each party is sufficient to maintain the standard of living established during the marriage, taking into account all of the following:

(1) The marketable skills of the supported party; the job market for those skills; the time and expenses required for the supported party to acquire the appropriate education or training to develop those skills; and the possible need for retraining or education to acquire other, more marketable skills or employment.

(2) The extent to which the supported party's present or future earning capacity is impaired by periods of unemployment that were incurred during the marriage to permit the supported party to devote time to domestic duties.

(b) The extent to which the supported party contributed to the attainment of an education, training, a career position, or a license by the supporting party.

(c) The ability of the supporting party to pay spousal support, taking into account the supporting party's earning capacity, earned and unearned income, assets, and standard of living.

(d) The needs of each party based on the standard of living established during the marriage.

(e) The obligations and assets, including the separate property, of each party.

(f) The duration of the marriage.

(g) The ability of the supported party to engage in gainful employment without unduly interfering with the interests of dependent children in the custody of the party.

(h) The age and health of the parties.

(i) Documented evidence, including a plea of nolo contendere, of any history of domestic violence, as defined in Section 6211, between the parties or perpetrated by either party against either party's child, including, but not limited to, consideration of emotional distress resulting from domestic violence perpetrated against the supported party by the supporting party, and consideration of any history of violence against the supporting party by the supported party.

(j) The immediate and specific tax consequences to each party.

(k) The balance of the hardships to each party.

(*l*) The goal that the supported party shall be self-supporting within a reasonable period of time. Except in the case of a marriage of long duration as described in Section 4336, a "reasonable period of time" for purposes of this section generally shall be one-half the length of the marriage. However, nothing in this section is intended to limit the court's discretion to order support for a greater or lesser length of time, based on any of the other factors listed in this section, Section 4336, and the circumstances of the parties.

(m) The criminal conviction of an abusive spouse shall be considered in making a reduction or elimination of a spousal support award in accordance with Section 4324.5 or 4325.

(n) Any other factors the court determines are just and equitable. *(Stats.1992, c. 162 (A.B.2650), § 10, operative Jan. 1, 1994. Amended by Stats.1996, c. 1163 (S.B.509), § 1; Stats.1999, c. 284 (A.B.808), § 1; Stats.1999, c. 846 (A.B.391), § 1.5; Stats.2001, c. 293 (S.B.1221), § 2; Stats.2012, c. 718 (A.B.1522), § 1; Stats.2013, c. 455 (A.B.681), § 1; Stats.2015, c. 137 (S.B.28), § 1, eff. Jan. 1, 2016.)*

Law Revision Commission Comments

Enactment [Revised Comment]

Section 4320 continues former Civil Code Section 4801(a)(1)-(10) without substantive change. In the introductory clause, the reference to "under this part" has been added to make clear that the court is only required to consider these factors when making an order for permanent spousal support.

For provisions dealing with temporary support orders, see Chapter 4 (commencing with Section 3600) of Part 1. In subdivisions (a)-(c), the references to parties have been substituted for the former references to spouses. These are not substantive changes, but conform to the terminology of the remainder of this section.

See Section 4360 (in determining supported spouse's needs under Section 4320, court may include amount sufficient for annuity, insurance, or trust to provide support in event of supporting spouse's death). See also Sections 2641 (reimbursement for community contributions to education or training), 3557 (attorney's fees for enforcement of support order), 3592 (support order where agreement for support of spouse discharged in bankruptcy). [23 Cal. L.Rev.Comm. Reports 1 (1993)].

Commentary

In 1988, the legislature amended the predecessors to subsections (a) and (d) to revive the principle that the marital standard of living, as opposed to some lesser standard, shall be the touchstone for spousal support awards. See also Section 4332 (requiring that the court make specific factual findings with respect to the standard of living during the marriage.) For discussion of the 1988 amendments, see *In re Marriage of Smith, 225 Cal.App.3d 469, 484–485, 274 Cal.Rptr. 911 (1990)*. Recent cases treating the marital standard of living include *In re Marriage of Winter, 7 Cal.App.4th 1926, 10 Cal.Rptr.2d 225 (1992)* (spouses lived below their means), and *In re Marriage of Weinstein, 4 Cal.App.4th 555, 5 Cal.Rptr.2d 558 (1991)* (spouses lived above their means). *Winter, supra,* considering temporary (*pendente lite*) support, and *In re Marriage of Kerr, 77 Cal.App.4th 87, 91 Cal.Rptr.2d 374 (1999)*, considering postdivorce support, hold that the marital standard of living may include savings and investment, as well as current consumption. *In re Marriage of Drapeau, 93 Cal.App.4th 1086, 114 Cal.Rptr.2d 6 (2001), review denied February 13, 2002,* applies the reasoning of *Winter* to permanent support and concludes that, at least where ability to pay is not a limiting factor, savings should be treated as an aspect of the marital standard of living for the purpose of determining permanent support. *Kerr* also holds that the trial court erred in awarding spousal support (and child support) based on a fixed percentage of stock option income without setting an upper limit on the amount of income paid as spousal or child support. *Kerr* reasoned that the stock option income might exceed the marital standard of living, in the case of spousal support, or the child's needs (see Family Code § 4057(b)(3)), in the case of child support.

With respect to whether the court may take into account the support obligee's expenditure for postmajority educational support of the parties' children in determining spousal support, compare *In re Marriage of Paul, 173 Cal.App.3d 913, 219 Cal.Rptr. 318 (1985)* and *In re Marriage of Siegel, 26 Cal.App.3d 88, 102 Cal.Rptr. 613 (1972)* (court may do so) with *In re Marriage of Serna, 85 Cal.App.4th 482, 102 Cal.Rptr.2d 188 (2000)* (court may not do so).

Subsection (b) contributions to the supporting spouse's education are not limited to direct education expenses but instead include "*all* of the working spouse's efforts to assist the student spouse in acquiring an education and enhanced earning capacity . . ., including contributions for ordinary living expenses." *In re Marriage of Watt, 214 Cal.App.3d 340, 262 Cal.Rptr. 783 (1989)*. Compare *Watt's* much narrower definition of education expenses reimbursable under Section 2641 (ordinary living expenses not reimbursable). See Section 2641, Commentary.

With respect to both subsections (a)(2) and (b), see *In re Marriage of Ostler and Smith, 223 Cal.App.3d 33, 46–49, 272 Cal.Rptr. 560 (1990)* (homemaker cared for children while spouse developed career).

In re Marriage of Ostler and Smith, supra, held that, in the case of fluctuating or uncertain income, a support order might include a percentage of income in excess of a certain dollar amount. When, contemplating fluctuating monthly sales commissions, a temporary support order specified a percentage of monthly income and the support obligor was unexpectedly terminated with lump-sum severance pay, the entire amount of the severance pay should not have been attributed entirely to the month in which it was received. Instead, the trial court should have allocated the severance pay according to its terms. *In re Marriage of Tong & Samson, 197 Cal.App.4th 23, 127 Cal.Rptr.3d 857 (2011)*.

The supporting spouse's subsection (c) earning capacity includes actual earnings or, when the supporting spouse is not earning all that he could in normal full-time employment, the amount that he could earn. See *In re Marriage of Regnery, 214 Cal.App.3d 1367, 263 Cal.Rptr. 243 (1989)*. But see *In re Marriage of Meegan, 11 Cal.App.4th 156, 13 Cal.Rptr.2d 799 (1992), review denied 2/18/93* (trial court did not abuse discretion by eliminating husband's spousal support obligation when, in good faith, he resigned his job to enter a monastery). Compare *In re Marriage of Ilas, 12 Cal.App.4th 1630, 16 Cal.Rptr.2d 345 (1993)* and *In re Marriage of Sinks, 204 Cal.App.3d 586, 251 Cal.Rptr. 379 (1988)*. For discussion of income imputation to child support obligors, see Section 4058, Commentary. *In re Marriage of Eggers, 131 Cal.App.4th 695, 32 Cal.Rptr.3d 292 (2005)*, holds that the trial court abused its discretion when it imputed income to an unemployed support obligor, who had lost his job due to misconduct, without determining whether he had the ability or opportunity to work. See also *In re Marriage of Simpson, 4 Cal.4th 225, 14 Cal.Rptr.2d 411 (1992)* (supporting spouse's earning capacity should not be based on greater than normal hours of work even when spouse worked unusually long hours during marriage); and *In re Marriage of Reynolds, 63 Cal.App.4th 1373, 74 Cal.Rptr.2d 636 (1998)* (supporting spouse cannot be required to work after the normal age of retirement in order to maintain spousal support at pre-retirement level). *In re Marriage of Shimkus, 244 Cal.App.4th 1262, 198 Cal. Rptr.3d 799 (2016)*, held that the normative age of retirement in the support obligor's profession must be considered. Thus Shimkus did not impute employment income to a fireman who retired at the age of 61 when, due to the physical requirements of the job, the normative age of retirement was 55. Nor may additional income be imputed to a long-term employee on the ground that he would increase his income by exercising his right to retire, collect his pension, and return to work with the same employer in a different position. *In re Marriage of Kochan, 193 Cal.App.4th 420, 122 Cal.Rptr.3d 61 (2011)*. Yet a spouse's actual income includes income from all sources, including overtime and bonus pay. *County of Placer v. Andrade, 55 Cal.App.4th 1393, 64 Cal.Rptr.2d 739 (1997)* (definition of Section 4320 annual gross income for purposes of child support determination). When a supporting spouse was forced to take early retirement, the trial court properly treated severance pay as normal salary for purposes of maintaining the existing support obligation; at expiration of the severance pay period, the trial court should reconsider spousal support in light of changed circumstances. *In re Marriage of Stephenson, 39 Cal.App.4th 71, 46 Cal.Rptr.2d 8 (1995)*. Subsection (c) includes the supporting spouse's separate property as well as the assets distributed to the supporting spouse in the community property division. California case law rejects the argument that this treatment entails "double counting." *In re Marriage of Epstein, 24 Cal.3d 76, 91 n. 14, 154 Cal.Rptr. 413 (1979)*; *In re Marriage of White, 192 Cal.App.3d 1022, 1027–1029, 237 Cal.Rptr. 764 (1987)*. See also *In re Marriage of de Guigne, 97 Cal.App.4th 1353, 119 Cal.Rptr.2d 430 (2002)*, which held that the trial court did not abuse its discretion in ordering a support obligor to pay child support and spousal support in an amount greater than the obligor's total monthly income when the obligor had extensive separate property holdings that were not yielding income and the support was necessary to reduce the disparity between the support obligees' marital and postdivorce standards of living, even though the marital standard of living was based on overspending.

Unlike the child support provisions (see particularly section 4058), the spousal support provisions do not define "income." *In re Marriage of Blazer, 176 Cal.App.4th 1438, 99 Cal.Rptr.3d 42 (2009)*, held that a trial court did not abuse its discretion when it excluded from consideration business income that a support obligor used to capitalize and vertically integrate his business, on the ground that the income so expended was a reasonable business expense.

In re Marriage of Williamson, 226 Cal.App.4th 1303, 172 Cal.Rptr.3d 699 (2014), held that former cash advances from a husband's wealthy parents could not be used to impute income to the husband for purposes of child support or spousal support, when the advances had ceased before trial and there was no evidence that they would resume. With respect to spousal support, *Williamson* noted that the definition of income and whether familial gifts may be treated as income are issues that have not been definitively resolved.

The duration of the marriage (subsection (f)) is a significant factor in determining the amount and duration of support. For recent case-law discussion, see *In re Marriage of Baker, 3 Cal.App.4th 491, 4 Cal.Rptr.2d 553 (1992)*; *In re Marriage of Wilson, 201 Cal.App.3d 913, 247 Cal.Rptr. 522 (1988), review denied 8/17/88*; and *In re Marriage of Prietsch & Calhoun, 190 Cal.App.3d 645, 662–667, 235 Cal.Rptr. 587 (1987)*. For cases stating that, after a long marriage, one spouse should not have a substantially higher standard of living than the other, see *In re Marriage of Beust, 23 Cal.App.4th 24, 28, 28 Cal.Rptr.2d 201 (1994), review denied 6/23/94*, and *In re Marriage of Andreen, 76 Cal.App.3d 667, 671, 143 Cal.Rptr.94 (1978)*.

Subsection (f) *duration of the marriage* does not include premarital and postmarital periods of nonmarital cohabitation. *In re Marriage of Bukaty, 180 Cal.App.3d 143, 225 Cal.Rptr.2d 492 (1986)*. However, the duration of successive marriages is added together to determine the duration of the final marriage. *In re Marriage of Chapman, 191 Cal.App.3d 1308, 237 Cal.Rptr. 84 (1987)*.

Compare subsection (g) with section 4058 (b). For purposes of spousal support, as one factor among many, subsection (g) would effectively impute income to a custodial parent so long as it would not "unduly" interfere "with the interests of the dependent children" in his or her custody. By contrast, for purposes of child support, section 4058 (b) provides that a court may consider the earning capacity of a parent in lieu of the parent's income, consistent with the best interests of the children. *In re Marriage of Mosley, 165 Cal. App.4th 1375, 82 Cal.Rptr.3d 497 (2008)*, discerns a distinction between the two standards. It opines that although a trial court may not impute earning capacity to a parent unless doing so is in the child's best interest, a spousal support award does not require the court to consider the child's best interests. However, when a custodial parent is eligible for child support and may also be eligible for spousal support, the application of different imputation standards could result in anomalous results. Imputation of income to a custodial parent might be impermissible for child support purposes, but allowable for spousal support purposes. In such case, if the custodial parent seeks to earn the income imputed to her for purposes of spousal support, she is not acting in her child's best interest. If she declines to earn that imputed income, she and her child jointly suffer a reduced standard of living because child support must now be applied to support the child and custodial parent.

The subsection (*l*) goal of self-support is implemented by subsection (b) of section 4330, which allows the court discretion whether to give a supported party notice that he or she is expected to become self-supporting. A section 4330 warning is commonly called a "*Gavron* warning." *In re Marriage of Gavron, 203 Cal.App.3d 705, 712, 250 Cal.Rptr. 148 (1988)* (court notice to supported party regarding employment expectations and whether party is required to become self-supporting). For further discussion of such a warning, see *In re Schmir, 134 Cal.App.4th 43, 55, 35 Cal.Rptr.3d 716 (2005)*, review denied (fair notice of expectation of self-sufficiency and a reasonable opportunity to achieve such goal).

When a supported spouse had surpassed the normative age of retirement and was in fact retired at the time of divorce, *In re Marriage of McLain, 7 Cal.App.5th 262, 212 Cal.Rptr.3d 537 (2017)*, held that a trial court did not abuse its discretion when it declined to impute income to the supported spouse or to issue a *Gavron* warning. Relying on *Reynolds* and *Shimkus*, supra, *McLain* applied their reasoning equally to retired support obligees. In addition, McLain characterized retirement as an element of the support obligee's standard of living.

In re Marriage of Schu, 6 Cal.App.5th 470, 211 Cal.Rptr.3d 413 (2016), affirming a trial court denial of spousal support to a mother who committed acts of domestic violence against her two children, acknowledged that, in the case of domestic violence, fault is a consideration in awarding spousal support.

A judgment of dissolution does not necessarily preclude an abused spouse's domestic violence tort action. A court's consideration, with respect to spousal support, of subsection (i) evidence of domestic violence does not bar a tort action on the ground of res judicata because the dissolution action and the tort action do not involve the same primary right. Collateral estoppel, or issue preclusion, does not apply unless the particular issues were litigated and decided in a prior final judgment. *Boblitt v. Boblitt, 190 Cal.App.4th 603, 118 Cal.Rptr.3d 788 (2010)*. For additional cases considering whether a dissolution proceeding precludes a tort action arising from common factual allegations, see Commentary to section 271.

In re Marriage of Lynn, 101 Cal.App.4th 120, 123 Cal.Rptr.2d 611 (2002), holds that § 3592 applies only to a bankruptcy discharge of a spouse's obligation under a *property settlement agreement*. If the obligation was instead established by court adjudication, § 3592 is inapplicable and any modification of spousal support must be made according to § 4320, in which case the discharge in bankruptcy of a spouse's obligation is merely one of many factors.

In re Marriage of West, 152 Cal.App.4th 240, 60 Cal.Rptr.3d 858 (2007), held that a former wife's change of career sufficed as a material change of circumstances justifying reconsideration of spousal support. *West* also held that a wife's receipt of cash from the sale of her share of a community property asset did not justify a reduction in spousal support.

When a support obligor retired, *In re Marriage of Shimkus, 244 Cal.App.4th 1262, 198 Cal.Rptr.3d 799 (2016)*, held that his former wife's receipt of her community property share of his retirement benefits was a change of circumstance that allowed modification of spousal support.

In re Marriage of Schaffer, 69 Cal.App.4th 801, 81 Cal.Rptr.2d 797 (1999), holds that a trial court considering a spousal support modification need not confine its inquiry to whether there has been a change of circumstances since the last modification, but may instead consider the obligee's conduct since the judgment of divorce. In *Shaffer*, the trial court properly took into account the wife's conduct during the fifteen years following the dissolution of her twenty-four year marriage and did not abuse its discretion when it refused to extend spousal support, even though there was no material change of circumstances since support was last modified. *Shaffer* explains that a full review of the past may be required to serve the subsection (k) "goal that the supported party shall be self-supporting within a reasonable period of time."

In re Marriage of Schulze, 60 Cal.App.4th 519, 70 Cal.Rptr.2d 488 (1997), holds that it is reversible error for the trial court to use a computer program designed for temporary support to calculate permanent support. The trial court used the Dissomaster program which, according to *Schulze*, bases the spousal support award on the Santa Clara guideline for temporary support. In dictum, *Schulze* suggests that no computer program would satisfy the court's duty to consider the enumerated factors of this section in setting permanent spousal support. To the same effect, see *In re Marriage of Zywiciel, 83 Cal.App.4th 1078, 100 Cal.Rptr.2d 242 (2000)*. See also *In re Marriage of Olson, 14 Cal.App.4th 1, 17 Cal.Rptr.2d 480 (1993)* and *In re Marriage of Burlini, 143 Cal.App.3d 65, 191 Cal.Rptr. 541 (1993)* (distinguishing temporary, or pendente lite, spousal support from permanent support).

Although a husband's attorney was negligent in calculating the husband's permanent support obligation based on the DissoMaster program for temporary spousal support, and not obtaining a forensic standard of living analysis, the husband's malpractice action against his attorney was unsuccessful because he failed to prove that his attorney would have obtained a better outcome either through settlement or trial. *Namikas v. Miller, 225 Cal.App.4th 1574, 171 Cal.Rptr.3d 23 (2014)*.

Although failure to seek work may affect a former wife's state law entitlement to spousal support, it does not excuse the former husband's support obligation under a federal immigration I-864 affidavit in which he agreed to support her as a prerequisite to her entry into the United States as his spouse. *Liu v. Mund, 686 F.3d 418 (7th Cir. 2012)*.

In re Marriage of Kumar, 13 Cal.App.5th 1072, 220 Cal.Rptr.3d 863 (2017), held that an immigrant spouse may seek enforcement of an I-864 agreement in a marital dissolution proceeding and, agreeing with *Liu v. Mund*, supra, additionally held that a person seeking I-864 enforcement has no duty to mitigate damages by seeking employment.

Research References

Forms

California Practice Guide: Rutter Family Law Forms Form 9:3, Marital Settlement Agreement.
California Practice Guide: Rutter Family Law Forms Form 11:20, Sample Trial Brief.
California Transactions Forms--Family Law § 2:54, Permanent Support.
California Transactions Forms--Family Law § 2:62, Grounds for Modification Post-Judgment.
California Transactions Forms--Family Law § 2:88, Marital Settlement Agreement.
California Transactions Forms--Family Law § 2:92, Family Support.
West's California Code Forms, Family § 3600, Comment Overview--Spousal and Child Support During Pendency Of Proceeding.
West's California Code Forms, Family § 4300, Comment Overview--Duty to Support Spouse.
West's California Code Forms, Family § 4330, Comment Overview--Spousal Support Upon Dissolution or Legal Separation.
West's California Code Forms, Family § 2338 Form 8, Marital Agreement.
West's California Code Forms, Family § 2338 Form 9, Marital Agreement--Both Spouses Employed.
West's California Code Forms, Family § 3590 Form 3, Spousal Support Provisions.
West's California Code Forms, Family § 3590 Form 4, Spousal Support Provisions--Good Faith Efforts.
West's California Code Forms, Family § 4303 Form 1, Complaint by Spouse to Enforce Duty Of Spousal Support.
West's California Judicial Council Forms FL-157, Spousal or Partner Support Declaration Attachment.
West's California Judicial Council Forms FL-158, Supporting Declaration for Attorney's Fees and Costs Attachment.
West's California Judicial Council Forms FL-343, Spousal, Partner, or Family Support Order Attachment.

Treatises and Practice Aids

Witkin, California Summary 10th Community Property § 187A, (New) Violent Felony Against Spouse.

Witkin, California Summary 10th Husband and Wife § 174, in General.
Witkin, California Summary 10th Husband and Wife § 175, Development Of Law.
Witkin, California Summary 10th Husband and Wife § 191, in General.
Witkin, California Summary 10th Husband and Wife § 194, Factors to be Considered.
Witkin, California Summary 10th Husband and Wife § 214, Payments for Insurance, Annuity, or Trust.
Witkin, California Summary 10th Husband and Wife § 221, Tax Aspects Of Award.
Witkin, California Summary 10th Husband and Wife § 225, Statutory Factors.
Witkin, California Summary 10th Husband and Wife § 229, Advice to Supported Spouse.
Witkin, California Summary 10th Husband and Wife § 230, in General.
Witkin, California Summary 10th Husband and Wife § 233, Separate Property.
Witkin, California Summary 10th Husband and Wife § 234, Marital Savings History.
Witkin, California Summary 10th Husband and Wife § 235, Postseparation Lifestyles.
Witkin, California Summary 10th Husband and Wife § 236, in General.
Witkin, California Summary 10th Husband and Wife § 278, Necessity Of Showing.
Witkin, California Summary 10th Husband and Wife § 279, Considerations Generally.
Witkin, California Summary 10th Husband and Wife § 281, Career Change or Retirement.
Witkin, California Summary 10th Husband and Wife § 293, Change in Circumstances.
Witkin, California Summary 10th Husband and Wife § 368, California Statute.
Witkin, California Summary 10th Husband and Wife § 371, Civil Remedies.
Witkin, California Summary 10th Husband and Wife § 235A, (New) Gifts from Third Parties.
Witkin, California Summary 10th Parent and Child § 19, General Provisions.

§ 4321. Denial of support from separate property of other party; grounds

In a judgment of dissolution of marriage or legal separation of the parties, the court may deny support to a party out of the separate property of the other party in any of the following circumstances:

(a) The party has separate property, or is earning the party's own livelihood, or there is community property or quasi-community property sufficient to give the party proper support.

(b) The custody of the children has been awarded to the other party, who is supporting them. *(Stats.1992, c. 162 (A.B.2650), § 10, operative Jan. 1, 1994. Amended by Stats. 1993, c. 219 (A.B.1500), § 141.5.)*

Law Revision Commission Comments

Enactment [Revised Comment]

Section 4321 restates the first sentence of former Civil Code Section 4806 without substantive change. In the introductory clause, the reference to a "judgment of dissolution of marriage or legal separation of the parties" has been substituted for the former reference to a "proceeding under this part," meaning the former Family Law Act (former Part 5 (commencing with former Section 4000) of Division 4 of the Civil Code). The reference to the court's authority to "deny support" has been substituted for the former reference to withholding an allowance. This is not a substantive change. A reference to the defined term "separate property" has been substituted for the former reference to the undefined term "separate estate." This is not a substantive change.

See also Sections 65 ("community property" defined in Section 760 *et seq.*), 125 ("quasi-community property" defined), 130 ("separate property" defined in Section 760 *et seq.*), 2254 (support of putative spouse), 3515 ("separate property" defined). [23 Cal.L.Rev.Comm. Reports 1 (1993)].

Research References

Treatises and Practice Aids

Witkin, California Summary 10th Husband and Wife § 233, Separate Property.

§ 4322. Childless party has or acquires a separate estate sufficient for support; prohibition on order or continuation of support

In an original or modification proceeding, where there are no children, and a party has or acquires a separate estate, including income from employment, sufficient for the party's proper support, no support shall be ordered or continued against the other party. *(Stats.1992, c. 162 (A.B.2650), § 10, operative Jan. 1, 1994.)*

Law Revision Commission Comments

Enactment [Revised Comment]

Section 4322 continues the second sentence of former Civil Code Section 4806 without substantive change. [23 Cal.L.Rev.Comm. Reports 1 (1993)].

Commentary

In re Marriage of Terry, 80 Cal.App.4th 921, 95 Cal.Rptr.2d 760 (2000), review denied July 26, 2000, holds that the court erred in failing to terminate spousal support under this section when the supported spouse's estate was sufficient, if properly invested, to yield income that would satisfy her support needs.

Research References

Treatises and Practice Aids

Witkin, California Summary 10th Husband and Wife § 233, Separate Property.

§ 4323. Cohabitation with nonmarital partner; rebuttable presumption of decreased need for support; modification or termination of support

(a)(1) Except as otherwise agreed to by the parties in writing, there is a rebuttable presumption, affecting the burden of proof, of decreased need for spousal support if the supported party is cohabiting with a nonmarital partner. Upon a determination that circumstances have changed, the court may modify or terminate the spousal support as provided for in Chapter 6 (commencing with Section 3650) of Part 1.

(2) Holding oneself out to be the spouse of the person with whom one is cohabiting is not necessary to constitute cohabitation as the term is used in this subdivision.

(b) The income of a supporting spouse's subsequent spouse or nonmarital partner shall not be considered when determining or modifying spousal support.

(c) Nothing in this section precludes later modification or termination of spousal support on proof of change of circumstances. *(Stats.1992, c. 162 (A.B.2650), § 10, operative Jan. 1, 1994. Amended by Stats.1993, c. 935 (S.B.145), § 3; Stats.2014, c. 82 (S.B.1306), § 36, eff. Jan. 1, 2015.)*

Law Revision Commission Comments

Enactment [Revised Comment]

Subdivisions (a) and (c) of Section 4323 continue former Civil Code Section 4801.5 without substantive change. In subdivision (a)(1), the reference to Chapter 6 (commencing with Section 3650) of Part 1 has been substituted for the broader reference to former Civil Code Section 4801(a). This is not a substantive change, since the relevant parts of the former section are continued in the Family Code sections. The references to termination have been added. These are nonsubstantive changes that conform with the court's authority pursuant to Chapter 6 (commencing with Section 3650) of Part 1.

Subdivision (b) was added by 1993 Cal. Stat. ch. 935, § 3. [23 Cal.L.Rev.Comm. Reports 1 (1993)].

Commentary

"Cohabitation" entails more than expense-sharing in a common household. It requires a sexual, romantic, or companionate relationship. *In re Marriage of Thweatt, 96 Cal.App.3d 530, 534, 157 Cal.Rptr. 826 (1979)* (former wife not "cohabiting" with male boarders). See also *In re Marriage of Regnery, 214 Cal.App.3d 1367, 1378, 263 Cal.Rptr. 243 (1989)*, and *In re Marriage of Lieb, 80 Cal.App.3d 629, 145 Cal.Rptr. 763 (1978)*.

For application of the rebuttable presumption of this section, see *In re Marriage of Bower, 96 Cal.App.4th 893, 117 Cal.Rptr.2d 520 (2002)* (holding that trial court properly applied presumption to reduce and then terminate former wife's spousal support).

In re Marriage of Romero, 99 Cal.App.4th 1436, 122 Cal.Rptr.2d 220 (2002), invoked subsection (b) in concluding that a trial court abused its discretion in denying a former husband's motion for spousal support modification when it indirectly considered the income of the husband's new wife as it related to the husband's standard of living and his ability to pay spousal support. On its face, *Romero*'s reliance on subsection (b) seems misplaced because the former wife was not cohabiting with a person of the other sex and hence the entire section would seem inapplicable. However, the legislative history of subsection (b) suggests that its sponsors intended it as a universal rule applicable in all spousal support proceedings.

Research References

Forms

California Transactions Forms--Family Law § 2:56, Effect Of Death, Remarriage, or Cohabitation.

Treatises and Practice Aids

Witkin, California Summary 10th Community Property § 33, Restrictions on Alteration Of Spouses' Legal Relations.

Witkin, California Summary 10th Husband and Wife § 40, Agreements Altering Spouses' Legal Relations.

Witkin, California Summary 10th Husband and Wife § 225, Statutory Factors.

Witkin, California Summary 10th Husband and Wife § 283, Income Of Supporting Spouse's New Spouse or Nonmarital Partner.

Witkin, California Summary 10th Husband and Wife § 286, Supported Spouse's Nonmarital Cohabitation.

Witkin, California Summary 10th Husband and Wife § 365, in General.

§ 4324. Attempted murder or soliciting the murder of spouse; prohibited awards

In addition to any other remedy authorized by law, when a spouse is convicted of attempting to murder the other spouse, as punishable pursuant to subdivision (a) of Section 664 of the Penal Code, or of soliciting the murder of the other spouse, as punishable pursuant to subdivision (b) of Section 653f of the Penal Code, the injured spouse shall be entitled to a prohibition of any temporary or permanent award for spousal support or medical, life, or other insurance benefits or payments from the injured spouse to the other spouse.

As used in this section, "injured spouse" means the spouse who has been the subject of the attempted murder or the solicitation of murder for which the other spouse was convicted, whether or not actual physical injury occurred. *(Added by Stats.1995, c. 364 (A.B.16), § 3. Amended by Stats.2010, c. 65 (A.B.2674), § 2.)*

Research References

Forms

West's California Code Forms, Family § 4330, Comment Overview--Spousal Support Upon Dissolution or Legal Separation.

Treatises and Practice Aids

Witkin, California Summary 10th Community Property § 187, Attempted Murder Of Spouse.

Witkin, California Summary 10th Husband and Wife § 10, Imposition Of Award as Sanction.

Witkin, California Summary 10th Husband and Wife § 174, in General.

§ 4324.5. Violent sexual felony; prohibited awards

(a) In any proceeding for dissolution of marriage where there is a criminal conviction for a violent sexual felony perpetrated by one spouse against the other spouse and the petition for dissolution is filed before five years following the conviction and any time served in custody, on probation, or on parole, the following shall apply:

(1) An award of spousal support to the convicted spouse from the injured spouse is prohibited.

(2) Where economic circumstances warrant, the court shall order the attorney's fees and costs incurred by the parties to be paid from the community assets. The injured spouse shall not be required to pay any attorney's fees of the convicted spouse out of the injured spouse's separate property.

(3) At the request of the injured spouse, the date of legal separation shall be the date of the incident giving rise to the conviction, or earlier, if the court finds circumstances that justify an earlier date.

(4) The injured spouse shall be entitled to 100 percent of the community property interest in the retirement and pension benefits of the injured spouse.

(b) As used in this section, "violent sexual felony" means those offenses described in paragraphs (3), (4), (5), (11), and (18) of subdivision (c) of Section 667.5 of the Penal Code.

(c) As used in this section, "injured spouse" means the spouse who has been the subject of the violent sexual felony for which the other spouse was convicted. *(Added by Stats.2012, c. 718 (A.B.1522), § 2.)*

Research References

Treatises and Practice Aids

Witkin, California Summary 10th Community Property § 187A, (New) Violent Felony Against Spouse.

Witkin, California Summary 10th Husband and Wife § 225, Statutory Factors.

Witkin, California Summary 10th Husband and Wife § 371, Civil Remedies.

§ 4325. Temporary or permanent support to abusive spouse; rebuttable presumption disfavoring award; evidence

(a) In any proceeding for dissolution of marriage where there is a criminal conviction for an act of domestic violence perpetrated by one spouse against the other spouse entered by the court within five years prior to the filing of the dissolution proceeding, or at any time thereafter, there shall be a rebuttable presumption affecting the burden of proof that any award of temporary or permanent spousal support to the abusive spouse otherwise awardable pursuant to the standards of this part should not be made.

(b) The court may consider documented evidence of a convicted spouse's history as a victim of domestic violence, as defined in Section 6211, perpetrated by the other spouse, or any other factors the court deems just and equitable, as conditions for rebutting this presumption.

(c) The rebuttable presumption created in this section may be rebutted by a preponderance of the evidence. *(Added by Stats.2001, c. 293 (S.B.1221), § 3.)*

Commentary

This section was amended in 2015 (SB 28) to codify the holdings of *Priem* and *Kelkar*, discussed below.

In re Marriage of Freitas, 209 Cal.App.4th 1059, 147 Cal.Rptr.3d 453 (2012), review denied, held that a trial court did not abuse its discretion when it terminated section 3600 temporary spousal support because of the obligee's conviction for domestic abuse, despite the absence of any showing of changed circumstances. In *Freitas*, spousal support should not have initially been ordered because the support obligee had earlier been convicted of domestic violence and had not rebutted this section's presumption that spousal support should not be awarded to a perpetrator of domestic violence. Additionally, *Freitas* states in dictum that temporary support is retroactively modifiable when a court reserves jurisdiction to retroactively modify based on further evidentiary developments.

In re Marriage of Priem, 214 Cal.App.4th 505, 153 Cal.Rptr.3d 842 (2013), held that a plea of nolo contendere to a charge of misdemeanor domestic violence made within five years prior to the filing of a dissolution proceeding may be used, under this section, as the basis for presumptive denial of temporary spousal support and denial of a portion of the spouse's request for professional fees.

In re Marriage of Cauley, 138 Cal.App.4th 1100, 41 Cal.Rptr.3d 902 (2006), review denied, holds that a trial court properly terminated a former wife's spousal support under this section when she was convicted of domestic violence against her former husband, even though the parties' marital settlement agreement provided that spousal support could not be modified or terminated.

Relying on the strong public policy against domestic abuse, *In re Marriage of Kelkar, 229 Cal.App.4th 833, 176 Cal.Rptr.3d 905 (2014), review denied*, approved retroactive application of this section to terminate support to a spouse who, prior to the enactment of this section, pleaded no contest to an act of domestic violence.

Research References

Forms

California Transactions Forms--Family Law § 2:54, Permanent Support.

West's California Code Forms, Family § 3600, Comment Overview--Spousal and Child Support During Pendency Of Proceeding.

Treatises and Practice Aids

Witkin, California Summary 10th Husband and Wife § 2A, (New) Retroactivity Of Provisions.

Witkin, California Summary 10th Husband and Wife § 175, Development Of Law.

Witkin, California Summary 10th Husband and Wife § 191, in General.

Witkin, California Summary 10th Husband and Wife § 225, Statutory Factors.

Witkin, California Summary 10th Husband and Wife § 273, Continuing Jurisdiction.

Witkin, California Summary 10th Husband and Wife § 371, Civil Remedies.

§ 4326. Termination of child support as change of circumstances; time for filing motion to modify spousal support; appointment of vocational training counselor; exceptions

(a) Except as provided in subdivision (d), in a proceeding in which a spousal support order exists or in which the court has retained jurisdiction over a spousal support order, if a companion child support order is in effect, the termination of child support pursuant to subdivision (a) of Section 3901 constitutes a change of circumstances that may be the basis for a request by either party for modification of spousal support.

(b) A motion to modify spousal support based on the change of circumstances described in subdivision (a) shall be filed by either party no later than six months from the date the child support order terminates.

(c) If a motion to modify a spousal support order pursuant to subdivision (a) is filed, either party may request the appointment of a vocational training counselor pursuant to Section 4331.

(d) Notwithstanding subdivision (a), termination of the child support order does not constitute a change of circumstances under subdivision (a) in any of the following circumstances:

(1) The child and spousal support orders are the result of a marital settlement agreement or judgment and the marital settlement agreement or judgment contains a provision regarding what is to occur when the child support order terminates.

(2) The child and spousal support orders are the result of a marital settlement agreement or judgment, which provides that the spousal support order is nonmodifiable or that spousal support is waived and the court's jurisdiction over spousal support has been terminated.

(3) The court's jurisdiction over spousal support was previously terminated.

(e) Notwithstanding subdivision (b), a party whose six-month deadline to file expired between January 1, 2014, and September 30, 2014, may file a motion pursuant to this section until December 31, 2014. *(Added by Stats.2014, c. 202 (A.B.414), § 1, eff. Aug. 15, 2014.)*

CHAPTER 3. SPOUSAL SUPPORT UPON DISSOLUTION OR LEGAL SEPARATION

§ 4330. Order of support; advice to support recipient

(a) In a judgment of dissolution of marriage or legal separation of the parties, the court may order a party to pay for the support of the other party an amount, for a period of time, that the court determines is just and reasonable, based on the standard of living established during the marriage, taking into consideration the circumstances as provided in Chapter 2 (commencing with Section 4320).

(b) When making an order for spousal support, the court may advise the recipient of support that he or she should make reasonable efforts to assist in providing for his or her support needs, taking into account the particular circumstances considered by the court pursuant to Section 4320, unless, in the case of a marriage of long duration as provided for in Section 4336, the court decides this warning is inadvisable. *(Stats.1992, c. 162 (A.B.2650), § 10, operative Jan. 1, 1994. Amended by Stats.1996, c. 1163 (S.B.509), § 2; Stats.1999, c. 846 (A.B.391), § 2.)*

Law Revision Commission Comments

Enactment [Revised Comment]

Section 4330 continues the first sentence of former Civil Code Section 4801(a) without substantive change. The reference to Chapter 2 (commencing with Section 4320) has been added. This is not a substantive change. See also Sections 2254 (putative spouse to be supported as if marriage not nullified), 3557 (attorney's fees for enforcement of support order). [23 Cal.L.Rev.Comm. Reports 1 (1993)].

Commentary

Although originally mandatory, the warning described in subsection (b) is now discretionary. A subsection (b) warning is commonly called a "*Gavron* warning." *In re Marriage of Gavron, 203 Cal.App.3d 705, 712, 250 Cal.Rptr. 148 (1988)* (court notice to supported party regarding employment expectations and whether party is required to become self-supporting). For further discussion of such a warning, see *In re Schmir, 134 Cal.App.4th 43, 55, 35 Cal.Rptr.3d 716 (2005)* (fair notice of expectation of self-sufficiency and a reasonable opportunity to achieve such goal).

When a supported spouse had surpassed the normative age of retirement and was in fact retired at the time of divorce, *In re Marriage of McLain, 7 Cal.App.5th 262, 212 Cal.Rptr.3d 537 (2017)*, held that a trial court did not abuse its discretion when it declined to impute income to the supported spouse or to issue a *Gavron* warning.

See generally *In re Marriage of Morrison, 20 Cal.3d 437, 143 Cal.Rptr. 139 (1978)*; *In re Marriage of Baker, 3 Cal.App.4th 491, 4 Cal.Rptr.2d 553 (1992)*; *In re Marriage of Smith, 225 Cal.App.3d 469, 274 Cal.Rptr. 911 (1990)*, and cases cited therein.

In re Marriage of Schaffer, 69 Cal.App.4th 801, 81 Cal.Rptr.2d 797 (1999), holds that a trial court considering a spousal support modification need not confine its inquiry to whether there has been a change of circumstances since the last modification, but may instead consider the obligee's conduct since the judgment of divorce. In *Shaffer*, the trial court properly took into account the wife's conduct during the fifteen years following the dissolution of her twenty-four year marriage and did not abuse its discretion when it refused to extend spousal support, even though there was no material change of circumstances since support was last modified. *Shaffer* explains that a full review of the past may be required to serve the subsection (b) goal of self-support.

Although the spousal support statute does not specifically provide that one spouse may be required to maintain health insurance for the other, a court may so order. (Compare Section 3751, specifically providing for health insurance as child support, and Section 4360 providing for life insurance as spousal support.) See generally *In re Marriage of Benjamins, 26 Cal.App.4th 423, 31 Cal.Rptr.2d 313 (1994)* (former husband's contractual obligation to pay for wife's health insurance premiums terminated at her death because obligation was in the nature of spousal support).

Research References

Forms

California Practice Guide: Rutter Family Law Forms Form 9:3, Marital Settlement Agreement.
California Practice Guide: Rutter Family Law Forms Form 1:32, Glossary Of Common Family Law Terms, Phrases and Concepts (Enclosure to Form 1:31).
California Transactions Forms--Family Law § 2:52, Overview.
California Transactions Forms--Family Law § 2:54, Permanent Support.
California Transactions Forms--Family Law § 2:62, Grounds for Modification Post-Judgment.
California Transactions Forms--Family Law § 2:88, Marital Settlement Agreement.
California Transactions Forms--Family Law § 2:92, Family Support.
West's California Code Forms, Family § 4330, Comment Overview--Spousal Support Upon Dissolution or Legal Separation.
West's California Code Forms, Family § 2338 Form 8, Marital Agreement.
West's California Code Forms, Family § 2338 Form 9, Marital Agreement--Both Spouses Employed.
West's California Code Forms, Family § 3590 Form 3, Spousal Support Provisions.
West's California Code Forms, Family § 3590 Form 4, Spousal Support Provisions--Good Faith Efforts.
West's California Judicial Council Forms FL-343, Spousal, Partner, or Family Support Order Attachment.

Treatises and Practice Aids

Witkin, California Summary 10th Husband and Wife § 112, Contents Of Judgment.
Witkin, California Summary 10th Husband and Wife § 174, in General.
Witkin, California Summary 10th Husband and Wife § 208, Basis Of Award.

Witkin, California Summary 10th Husband and Wife § 209, Money Judgment Distinguished.
Witkin, California Summary 10th Husband and Wife § 210, in General.
Witkin, California Summary 10th Husband and Wife § 223, Statutory Standard.
Witkin, California Summary 10th Husband and Wife § 224, Marital Standard Of Living as Point Of Reference.
Witkin, California Summary 10th Husband and Wife § 229, Advice to Supported Spouse.
Witkin, California Summary 10th Husband and Wife § 287, Change in Cost Of Child Support.

§ 4331. Examination by vocational training counselor; order; payment of expenses and costs

(a) In a proceeding for dissolution of marriage or for legal separation of the parties, the court may order a party to submit to an examination by a vocational training counselor. The examination shall include an assessment of the party's ability to obtain employment based upon the party's age, health, education, marketable skills, employment history, and the current availability of employment opportunities. The focus of the examination shall be on an assessment of the party's ability to obtain employment that would allow the party to maintain herself or himself at the marital standard of living.

(b) The order may be made only on motion, for good cause, and on notice to the party to be examined and to all parties. The order shall specify the time, place, manner, conditions, scope of the examination, and the person or persons by whom it is to be made.

(c) A party who does not comply with an order under this section is subject to the same consequences provided for failure to comply with an examination ordered pursuant to Chapter 15 (commencing with Section 2032.010) of Title 4 of Part 4 of the Code of Civil Procedure.

(d) "Vocational training counselor" for the purpose of this section means an individual with sufficient knowledge, skill, experience, training, or education in interviewing, administering, and interpreting tests for analysis of marketable skills, formulating career goals, planning courses of training and study, and assessing the job market, to qualify as an expert in vocational training under Section 720 of the Evidence Code.

(e) A vocational training counselor shall have at least the following qualifications:

(1) A master's degree in the behavioral sciences.

(2) Be qualified to administer and interpret inventories for assessing career potential.

(3) Demonstrated ability in interviewing clients and assessing marketable skills with understanding of age constraints, physical and mental health, previous education and experience, and time and geographic mobility constraints.

(4) Knowledge of current employment conditions, job market, and wages in the indicated geographic area.

(5) Knowledge of education and training programs in the area with costs and time plans for these programs.

(f) The court may order the supporting spouse to pay, in addition to spousal support, the necessary expenses and costs of the counseling, retraining, or education. *(Stats.1992, c. 162 (A.B.2650), § 10, operative Jan. 1, 1994. Amended by Stats.2004, c. 182 (A.B.3081), § 35, operative July 1, 2005.)*

Law Revision Commission Comments

2004 Amendment

Subdivision (c) of Section 4331 is amended to reflect nonsubstantive reorganization of the rules governing civil discovery. [33 Cal.L.Rev.Comm. Reports 1024 (2003)].

Enactment [Revised Comment]

Section 4331 continues former Civil Code Section 4801(e)-(g) without substantive change. The reference to a proceeding for dissolution or legal separation has been substituted for the reference to former Civil Code Section 4801. This is not a substantive change. See also Section 2254 (putative spouse to be supported as if marriage not nullified). [23 Cal.L.Rev.Comm. Reports 1 (1993)].

Commentary

In re Marriage of Stupp & Schilders, 11 Cal.App.5th 907, 217 Cal.Rptr.3d 825 (2017), held that a trial court abused its discretion by ordering a former wife to obtain a postjudgment vocational examination under this section when there was no pending support-related motion.

Research References

Forms

California Practice Guide: Rutter Family Law Forms Form 6:14, Request for Order Re Vocational Examination.

Treatises and Practice Aids

Witkin, California Summary 10th Husband and Wife § 245, Examination by Vocational Training Counselor.

§ 4332. Findings of court; standard of living during marriage; other circumstances

In a proceeding for dissolution of marriage or for legal separation of the parties, the court shall make specific factual findings with respect to the standard of living during the marriage, and, at the request of either party, the court shall make appropriate factual determinations with respect to other circumstances. *(Stats.1992, c. 162 (A.B.2650), § 10, operative Jan. 1, 1994.)*

Law Revision Commission Comments

Enactment [Revised Comment]

Section 4332 continues the first sentence of the last paragraph of former Civil Code Section 4801(a) without substantive change. The reference to a proceeding for dissolution or legal separation has been added. This is not a substantive change. See also Sections 2254 (putative spouse to be supported as if marriage not nullified), 4320–4323 (factors to be considered in ordering spousal support). [23 Cal.L.Rev.Comm. Reports 1 (1993)].

Commentary

For discussion of the 1988 "standard of living" amendments, see Section 4320, Commentary.

Research References

Forms

California Transactions Forms--Family Law § 2:54, Permanent Support.

Treatises and Practice Aids

Witkin, California Summary 10th Husband and Wife § 107, Statement Of Decision.

Witkin, California Summary 10th Husband and Wife § 224, Marital Standard Of Living as Point Of Reference.

Witkin, California Summary 10th Husband and Wife § 225, Statutory Factors.

§ 4333. Retroactive application of order

An order for spousal support in a proceeding for dissolution of marriage or for legal separation of the parties may be made retroactive to the date of filing the notice of motion or order to show cause, or to any subsequent date. *(Stats.1992, c. 162 (A.B.2650), § 10, operative Jan. 1, 1994.)*

Law Revision Commission Comments

Enactment [Revised Comment]

Section 4333 continues the fourth sentence of the last paragraph of former Civil Code Section 4801(a) without substantive change. The reference to a proceeding for dissolution or legal separation has been added. This is not a substantive change. [23 Cal.L.Rev.Comm. Reports 1 (1993)].

Research References

Forms

California Transactions Forms--Family Law § 2:53, Temporary Support.

Treatises and Practice Aids

Witkin, California Summary 10th Husband and Wife § 210, in General.

§ 4334. Orders for contingent periods of time; termination; notification

(a) If a court orders spousal support for a contingent period of time, the obligation of the supporting party terminates on the happening of the contingency. The court may, in the order, order the supported party to notify the supporting party, or the supporting party's attorney of record, of the happening of the contingency.

(b) If the supported party fails to notify the supporting party, or the attorney of record of the supporting party, of the happening of the contingency and continues to accept spousal support payments, the supported party shall refund payments received that accrued after the happening of the contingency, except that the overpayments shall first be applied to spousal support payments that are then in default. *(Stats.1992, c. 162 (A.B.2650), § 10, operative Jan. 1, 1994.)*

Law Revision Commission Comments

Enactment [Revised Comment]

Section 4334 restates former Civil Code Section 4801(c) without substantive change. The reference in the former section to the court making the order requiring notification of the happening of the contingency in the "original" order has been omitted. This is not a substantive change. For a provision relating to child support, see Section 4007 (child support for contingent period of time). [23 Cal.L.Rev.Comm. Reports 1 (1993)].

Research References

Treatises and Practice Aids

Witkin, California Summary 10th Husband and Wife § 298, Order for Contingent Period.

§ 4335. Termination of spousal support order; extension of order

An order for spousal support terminates at the end of the period provided in the order and shall not be extended unless the court retains jurisdiction in the order or under Section 4336. *(Stats.1992, c. 162 (A.B.2650), § 10, operative Jan. 1, 1994.)*

Law Revision Commission Comments

Enactment [Revised Comment]

Section 4335 continues without substantive change the first sentence of the first paragraph of former Civil Code Section 4801(d). The reference to an order for "spousal support" has been substituted for the former reference to an "allowance" for support. This is not a substantive change. The reference in the former section to the court's retaining jurisdiction in the "original" order has been omitted. This is not a substantive change. The reference to Section 4336 has been added. [23 Cal.L.Rev.Comm. Reports 1 (1993)].

Commentary

See generally *In re Marriage of Liss, 10 Cal.App.4th 1426, 13 Cal.Rptr.2d 397 (1992)*, and cases cited therein. Reservation of jurisdiction to extend spousal support beyond its specified termination date need not be explicit. *In re Marriage of Vomacka, 36 Cal.3d 459, 467, 683 P.2d 248, 204 Cal.Rptr. 568 (1984)*; *In re Marriage of Benson, 171 Cal.App.3d 907, 217 Cal.Rptr. 589 (1985)*, and cases cited therein.

Research References

Treatises and Practice Aids

Witkin, California Summary 10th Husband and Wife § 297, in General.

Witkin, California Summary 10th Husband and Wife § 299, in General.

Witkin, California Summary 10th Husband and Wife § 300, Jurisdiction Reserved.

Witkin, California Summary 10th Husband and Wife § 302, in General.

§ 4336. Retention of jurisdiction; application of section

(a) Except on written agreement of the parties to the contrary or a court order terminating spousal support, the court retains jurisdiction indefinitely in a proceeding for dissolution of marriage or for legal separation of the parties where the marriage is of long duration.

(b) For the purpose of retaining jurisdiction, there is a presumption affecting the burden of producing evidence that a marriage of 10 years or more, from the date of marriage to the date of separation, is a marriage of long duration. However, the court may consider periods of separation during the marriage in determining whether the marriage is in fact of long duration. Nothing in this subdivision precludes a court from determining that a marriage of less than 10 years is a marriage of long duration.

(c) Nothing in this section limits the court's discretion to terminate spousal support in later proceedings on a showing of changed circumstances.

(d) This section applies to the following:

(1) A proceeding filed on or after January 1, 1988.

(2) A proceeding pending on January 1, 1988, in which the court has not entered a permanent spousal support order or in which the court order is subject to modification. *(Stats. 1992, c. 162 (A.B.2650), § 10, operative Jan. 1, 1994.)*

Law Revision Commission Comments

Enactment [Revised Comment]

Section 4336 continues without substantive change former Civil Code Section 4801(d) from the last sentence of the first paragraph to the end of that subdivision. In subdivision (a), the reference to a proceeding for dissolution or legal separation has been added. This is not a substantive change. See also Section 2254 (putative spouse to be supported as if marriage not nullified). [23 Cal.L.Rev.Comm. Reports 1 (1993)].

Commentary

The length of a marriage does not include premarital and postmarital periods of nonmarital cohabitation. *In re Marriage of Bukaty, 180 Cal.App.3d 143, 225 Cal.Rptr.2d 492 (1986)*. However, the length of successive marriages is cumulated in determining whether a marriage is of long duration. *In re Marriage of Chapman, 191 Cal.App.3d 1308, 237 Cal.Rptr. 84 (1987)*.

See generally *In re Marriage of Liss, 10 Cal.App.4th 1426, 1430, 13 Cal.Rptr. 397 (1992)* (not abuse of discretion to retain jurisdiction to award spousal support to either party after lengthy marriage even though one spouse did not initially request spousal support) and cases cited therein. See additionally Section 3591, Commentary and Section 4335, Commentary.

In re Marriage of Ostrander, 53 Cal.App.4th 63, 61 Cal.Rptr.2d 348 (1997), review denied April 23, 1997, holds that subsection (a) means what it says: In a marriage of long duration, the divorce court has continuing jurisdiction to award spousal support; the judgment of dissolution need not specifically reserve jurisdiction. Compare Section 4335.

See also *In re Marriage of Beck, 57 Cal.App.4th 341, 67 Cal.Rptr.2d 79 (1997)* (even though marriage was of "long duration," trial court lacked jurisdiction to modify a 1972 dissolution judgment to reinstate spousal support that had ended 16 years earlier and ten years before 1988 enactment authorizing retention of jurisdiction in marriages of long duration).

In re Marriage of Schaffer, 69 Cal.App.4th 801, 81 Cal.Rptr.2d 797 (1999), holds that a trial court considering a spousal support modification need not confine its inquiry to whether there has been a change of circumstances since the last modification, but may instead consider the obligee's conduct since the judgment of divorce. In *Shaffer*, the trial court properly took into account the wife's conduct during the fifteen years following the dissolution of her twenty-four year marriage and did not abuse its discretion when it refused to extend spousal support, even though there was no subsection (c) change of circumstances since support was last modified. *Shaffer* explains that a full review of the past may be required to serve the Section 4320 (k) "goal that the supported party shall be self-supporting within a reasonable period of time."

Although a trial court may alter spousal support during the pendency of an appeal of a judgment affecting spousal support or property division, it may not terminate jurisdiction over spousal support until the appeal is concluded. *In re Marriage of Varner, 68 Cal.App.4th 932, 80 Cal.Rptr.2d 628 (1998). Varner* reasons that the trial court may not make any order that might lessen the effectiveness of the decision of the appellate court.

Research References

Forms

California Practice Guide: Rutter Family Law Forms Form 6:24, Request for Order Re Modification Contingent Termination Of Spousal Support Jurisdiction ("Richmond Order").

California Transactions Forms--Family Law § 2:55, Continuing Jurisdiction.

Treatises and Practice Aids

Witkin, California Summary 10th Husband and Wife § 225, Statutory Factors.

Witkin, California Summary 10th Husband and Wife § 229, Advice to Supported Spouse.

Witkin, California Summary 10th Husband and Wife § 297, in General.

Witkin, California Summary 10th Husband and Wife § 300, Jurisdiction Reserved.

Witkin, California Summary 10th Husband and Wife § 301, Jurisdiction Not Reserved.

Witkin, California Summary 10th Husband and Wife § 302, in General.

Witkin, California Summary 10th Husband and Wife § 305, Statutory Jurisdiction After Lengthy Marriage.

§ 4337. Termination of support order; death; remarriage

Except as otherwise agreed by the parties in writing, the obligation of a party under an order for the support of the other party terminates upon the death of either party or the remarriage of the other party. *(Stats.1992, c. 162 (A.B.2650), § 10, operative Jan. 1, 1994.)*

Law Revision Commission Comments

Enactment [Revised Comment]

Section 4337 continues former Civil Code Section 4801(b) without substantive change. The reference to a "judgment" for support has been omitted as surplus. See Section 155 ("support order" means a judgment or order of support). The reference to the duty to provide for "maintenance" of a spouse has been omitted as surplus. Neither of these revisions is a substantive change. See also Sections 4334 (support for contingent period of time), 4335 (support for fixed period to time), 4360 (provision for support after death of supporting party). [23 Cal.L.Rev.Comm. Reports 1 (1993)].

Commentary

In re Marriage of Left, 208 Cal.App.4th 1137, 146 Cal.Rptr.3d 181 (2012), review denied, holds that this section does not apply when former wife went through a marriage ceremony with her fiancé because neither intended to marry and they never obtained a marriage license, facts of which the support obligor was aware. Nevertheless, under section 4323, the trial court could and did reduce spousal support because of the wife's cohabitation with her fiancé.

When a marital settlement agreement waived the general rule expressed in this section and provided for continuing spousal support payments to a former wife after a decedent's death, the decedent's surviving spouse was personally liable, under Probate Code section 13551, for the continuing support payments to the extent of the fair market value (less encumbrances) at the time of decedent's death of the real property held in joint tenancy by the decedent and surviving spouse. *Kircher v. Kircher, 189 Cal.App.4th 1105, 117 Cal.Rptr.3d 254 (2010), review denied*.

In re Marriage of Campbell, 136 Cal.App.4th 502, 38 Cal.Rptr.3d 908 (2006), review denied, holds that this section does not terminate a temporary spousal support order when the supported spouse "remarries" prior to entry of a judgment of dissolution of the existing marriage.

Although, absent agreement of the parties, court-ordered spousal support terminates at the death of either party, nevertheless a court may order an effective substitute by requiring that the supporting spouse maintain life insurance naming the supported spouse as beneficiary. See Section 4360, including Commentary.

In re Marriage of Benjamins, 26 Cal.App.4th 423, 31 Cal.Rptr.2d 313 (1994), holds that a husband's obligation to pay his former wife's medical insurance premiums is "spousal support" within the meaning of Section 4337. Under Section 4337, the duty to pay terminated at her death because the spouses' separation agreement did not provide that the husband's payment of premiums would continue after his former wife's death. The court found it immaterial that the separation agreement prohibited modification except by a writing, reasoning that "modification" is different from Section 4337 "termination." In other words, a general provision limiting modification does not constitute a Section 4337 agreement "otherwise" by the parties. Compare Family Code Section 3591. Similarly, *In re Marriage of Thornton, 95 Cal.App.4th 251, 115 Cal.Rptr.2d 380 (2002)*, holds that this section terminated a husband's spousal support obligation on the remarriage of his former wife, even though the parties' stipulated judgment provided that spousal support was non-modifiable and omitted remarriage as a factor terminating spousal support. *Thornton* reasoned that "non-modifiable," as contrasted with "non-terminable," is insufficient to avoid the operation of this section. Compare *In re Marriage of Cesnalis, 106 Cal.App.4th 1267, 131 Cal.Rptr.2d 436 (2003), review denied June 18, 2003*, which affirmed the trial court's conclusion that the husband waived his right to terminate spousal support on the wife's remarriage because the stipulated judgment, drafted by the husband's attorney, characterized a specified "termination date" as "absolute." *Cesnalis* also relies on the doctrine of estoppel and extrinsic evidence admitted under the parol evidence rule.

John R. Okerson v. Commissioner, 123 T.C. Memo 258 (U.S. Tax Ct. 2004), holds that payments to be made in 113 installments to a Tennessee ex-wife did not qualify as alimony where they would continue to be paid to the couple's children should the ex-wife die before full satisfaction of the obligation. Compare *Michael K. Berry v. Commissioner, T.C. Memo 2005–91, 89 T.C.M. (CCH) 1090 (U.S. Tax Ct. 2005)*, holding that despite the absence of an explicit provision in the divorce instrument for termination at the death of the payee spouse, unallocated family support payments qualified as alimony because, under this section, support payments to a spouse terminate at her death and the possibility, upon her death, that the children would not be in obligor's custody and the obligor would continue to be required to pay child support is insufficient to prevent treatment of the family support payments as alimony. *Okerson* and *Berry* are reconcilable in terms of state law. In *Okerson*, the law of Tennessee conducts an open-ended inquiry into the intent of the parties to determine whether spousal support ends at the payee's death, while this section provides: "Except as otherwise agreed by the parties in writing, the obligation of a party under an order for the support of the other party terminates upon the death of either party."

Research References

Forms

California Transactions Forms--Estate Planning § 19:11, Child Support.

California Transactions Forms--Family Law § 2:56, Effect Of Death, Remarriage, or Cohabitation.

West's California Judicial Council Forms FL-343, Spousal, Partner, or Family Support Order Attachment.

Treatises and Practice Aids

Witkin, California Summary 10th Community Property § 33, Restrictions on Alteration Of Spouses' Legal Relations.

Witkin, California Summary 10th Husband and Wife § 40, Agreements Altering Spouses' Legal Relations.

Witkin, California Summary 10th Husband and Wife § 294, Death Of Spouse.

Witkin, California Summary 10th Husband and Wife § 295, in General.

Witkin, California Summary 10th Husband and Wife § 296, Agreement to Continue Support.

Witkin, California Summary 10th Husband and Wife § 363, in General.

Witkin, California Summary 10th Husband and Wife § 364, Agreement that Obligations Survive.

Witkin, California Summary 10th Husband and Wife § 365, in General.

§ 4338. Enforcement of order for support; property to be utilized by court

In the enforcement of an order for spousal support, the court shall resort to the property described below in the order indicated:

(a) The earnings, income, or accumulations of either spouse after the date of separation, as defined in Section 70, which would have been community property if the spouse had not been separated from the other spouse.

(b) The community property.

(c) The quasi-community property.

(d) The other separate property of the party required to make the support payments. *(Stats.1992, c. 162 (A.B.2650), § 10, operative Jan. 1, 1994. Amended by Stats.2016, c. 114 (S.B.1255), § 5, eff. Jan. 1, 2017.)*

Law Revision Commission Comments

Enactment [Revised Comment]

Section 4338 continues former Civil Code Section 4805 without substantive change. References to both "decree" and "judgment" have been omitted as surplus. See Sections 100 ("order" includes decree, as appropriate), 155 ("support order" means a judgment or order of support). The reference to an order rendered pursuant to "this part," meaning the former Family Law Act (former Part 5 (commencing with former Section 4000) of Division 4 of the Civil Code), has been omitted. These revisions are not substantive changes. Language has been added to make clear that application of this section is limited to spousal support.

See also Sections 65 ("community property" defined in Section 760 *et seq.*), 125 ("quasi-community property" defined), 130 ("separate property" defined in Section 760 *et seq.*), 3515 ("separate property" defined). For a provision relating to child support, see Section 4008 (property available for child support). [23 Cal.L.Rev.Comm. Reports 1 (1993)].

Commentary

For discussion of Section 4338, see *Burkhart v. Burkhart, 180 Cal.App.3d 198, 204, 225 Cal.Rptr. 390 (1986)*.

Research References

Treatises and Practice Aids

Witkin, California Summary 10th Husband and Wife § 222, Source Of Payments.

§ 4339. Security for payment

The court may order the supporting party to give reasonable security for payment of spousal support. *(Stats.1992, c. 162 (A.B.2650), § 10, operative Jan. 1, 1994.)*

Law Revision Commission Comments

Enactment [Revised Comment]

Section 4339 continues without substantive change the second sentence of the last paragraph of former Civil Code Section 4801(a). For provisions relating to child support, see Sections 4012 (security for payment of child support), 4550–4573 (deposit of money to secure future child support payments), 4600–4641 (deposit of assets to secure future child support payments). [23 Cal.L.Rev.Comm. Reports 1 (1993)].

Research References

Forms

California Transactions Forms--Family Law § 2:43, Life Insurance.

West's California Judicial Council Forms FL-150, Income and Expense Declaration.

Treatises and Practice Aids

Witkin, California Summary 10th Husband and Wife § 206, Other Remedies.

Witkin, California Summary 10th Husband and Wife § 265, Security for Payment.

CHAPTER 4. PAYMENT TO COURT-DESIGNATED OFFICER; ENFORCEMENT BY DISTRICT ATTORNEY

§ 4350. Payments to county officer

In any proceeding where a court makes or has made an order requiring the payment of spousal support, the court may direct that payment shall be made to the county officer designated by the court for that purpose. The court may include in its order made pursuant to this section any service charge imposed under the authority of Section 279 of the Welfare and Institutions Code. *(Stats.1992, c. 162 (A.B. 2650), § 10, operative Jan. 1, 1994.)*

Law Revision Commission Comments

Enactment [Revised Comment]

Section 4350 continues former Civil Code Section 4801.7(a) without substantive change. See also Section 3555 (forwarding of support payments paid through county officer). For similar provisions relating to child support, see Sections 4200–4203. [23 Cal. L.Rev.Comm. Reports 1 (1993)].

Research References

Forms

West's California Code Forms, Family § 4350, Comment Overview--Payment to Court-Designated Officer.

West's California Judicial Council Forms FL-632, Notice Regarding Payment Of Support.

Treatises and Practice Aids

Witkin, California Summary 10th Husband and Wife § 174, in General.

Witkin, California Summary 10th Husband and Wife § 210, in General.

Witkin, California Summary 10th Husband and Wife § 313, Payment to County by Court and Referral.

§ 4351. Referral of enforcement to local child support agency; enforcement proceedings; notice requesting meeting with support obligor; contents

(a) In any proceeding where the court has entered an order pursuant to Section 4350, the court may also refer the matter of enforcement of the spousal support order to the local child support agency. The local child support agency may bring those enforcement proceedings it determines to be appropriate.

(b) Notwithstanding subdivision (a), in any case in which the local child support agency is required to appear on behalf of a welfare recipient in a proceeding to enforce an order requiring payment of child support, the local child support agency shall also enforce any order requiring payment to the welfare recipient of spousal support that is in arrears.

(c) Nothing in this section shall be construed to prohibit the district attorney or the local child support agency from bringing an action or initiating process to enforce or punish the failure to obey an order for spousal support under any provision of law that empowers the district attorney or the local child support agency to bring an action or initiate a process, whether or not there has been a referral by the court pursuant to this chapter.

(d) Any notice from the district attorney or the local child support agency requesting a meeting with the support obligor for any purpose authorized under this part shall contain a statement advising the support obligor of his or her right to have an attorney present at the meeting. *(Stats.1992, c. 162 (A.B.2650), § 10, operative Jan. 1, 1994. Amended by Stats. 1998, c. 854 (A.B.960), § 3; Stats.1999, c. 83 (S.B.966), § 50; Stats.2000, c. 808 (A.B.1358), § 44, eff. Sept. 28, 2000.)*

Law Revision Commission Comments

Enactment [Revised Comment]

Section 4351 continues former Civil Code Section 4801.7(b)-(c) without substantive change. [23 Cal.L.Rev.Comm. Reports 1 (1993)].

Research References

Forms

West's California Code Forms, Family § 4350, Comment Overview--Payment to Court-Designated Officer.

West's California Judicial Council Forms FL-632, Notice Regarding Payment Of Support.

Treatises and Practice Aids

Witkin, California Summary 10th Husband and Wife § 313, Payment to County by Court and Referral.

Witkin, California Summary 10th Husband and Wife § 314, Acquisition and Confidentiality Of Information.

§ 4352. Expenses and charges

(a) Insofar as expenses of the county officer designated by the court and expenses of the local child support agency incurred in the enforcement of an order referred by the court under this chapter exceed any service charge imposed under Section 279 of the Welfare and Institutions Code, the expenses are a charge upon the county where the proceedings are pending.

(b) Fees for service of process in the enforcement of an order referred by the court under this chapter are a charge upon the county where the process is served. *(Stats.1992, c. 162 (A.B.2650), § 10, operative Jan. 1, 1994. Amended by Stats.2000, c. 808 (A.B.1358), § 45, eff. Sept. 28, 2000.)*

Law Revision Commission Comments

Enactment [Revised Comment]

Section 4352 continues former Civil Code Section 4801.7(d) without substantive change. [23 Cal.L.Rev.Comm. Reports 1 (1993)].

CHAPTER 5. PROVISION FOR SUPPORT AFTER DEATH OF SUPPORTING PARTY

§ 4360. Needs of supported spouse; annuity, life insurance, or trust; modification or termination of order

(a) For the purpose of Section 4320, where it is just and reasonable in view of the circumstances of the parties, the court, in determining the needs of a supported spouse, may include an amount sufficient to purchase an annuity for the supported spouse or to maintain insurance for the benefit of the supported spouse on the life of the spouse required to make the payment of support, or may require the spouse required to make the payment of support to establish a trust to provide for the support of the supported spouse, so that the supported spouse will not be left without means of support in the event that the spousal support is terminated by the death of the party required to make the payment of support.

(b) Except as otherwise agreed to by the parties in writing, an order made under this section may be modified or terminated at the discretion of the court at any time before the death of the party required to make the payment of support. *(Stats.1992, c. 162 (A.B.2650), § 10, operative Jan. 1, 1994.)*

Law Revision Commission Comments

Enactment [Revised Comment]

Section 4360 continues former Civil Code Section 4801.4 without substantive change. This section gives the court authority to order the purchase of an annuity for the supported spouse or to order that the support obligor establish a trust to provide for the support of the supported spouse. This authority is given in recognition that in some circumstances the amount of insurance in force, if any, on the life of the support obligor may be insufficient and the support obligor may no longer be insurable or insurance can be obtained only at a prohibitive cost.

If insurance is already in force on the life of the support obligor, this section authorizes the court to order that the support obligor maintain some or all of the insurance in force and name the supported spouse as the beneficiary of the insurance. And, if the support obligor is insurable, this section authorizes the court to order that the support obligor obtain and maintain insurance and name the supported spouse as beneficiary. The support obligor can change the beneficiary on the insurance if the supported spouse dies before the support obligor. Instead of ordering the support obligor to maintain insurance and name the supported spouse as beneficiary, the court may order the support obligor to purchase an annuity for the supported spouse to provide support in the event that the support obligor dies before the supported spouse. In some cases, this may be less expensive than insurance. In other cases, the establishment of a trust to provide for the support of the supported spouse during that spouse's lifetime may be the best solution. If a trust is used, after the death of the supported spouse, the income or assets of the trust, or both, could be paid to the person designated by the support obligor.

This section does not change the rule that the support order terminates when the support obligor dies. See Section 4337 (effect of death or remarriage). This section permits the court, where it is just and reasonable, to do so in view of the circumstances of the particular case to order (as a part of the support) insurance, an annuity, or establishment of a trust, where necessary so that the supported spouse will not be left without means for support if the support obligor dies. This section supplements Section 4320, which requires the court to consider a number of factors in determining the amount and duration of support.

For background on former Civ. Code § 4801.4, see *Recommendation Relating to Provision for Support if Support Obligor Dies,* 18 Cal. L. Revision Comm'n Reports 119 (1986). [23 Cal.L.Rev.Comm. Reports 1 (1993)].

Commentary

Although Section 4337 nominally provides that court-required spousal support does not survive the death of the support obligor, Section 4360 effectively allows the court to anticipate and provide for the supported spouse after the death of the supporting spouse. See *In re Marriage of O'Connell, 8 Cal.App.4th 565, 10 Cal.Rptr.2d 334 (1992); In re Marriage of Ziegler, 207 Cal.App.3d 788, 255 Cal.Rptr 100 (1989), review denied 4/19/89* (former husband ordered to make monthly payments to maintain military survivor plan for benefit of former wife); *In re Marriage of Gonzalez, 168 Cal.App.3d 1021, 214 Cal.Rptr. 634 (1985)*.

"Maintaining life insurance" means more than merely purchasing life insurance and paying the premiums; it also includes an obligation to refrain from doing anything that would interfere with receipt of the insurance benefits. Thus in *Tintocalis v. Tintocalis, 20 Cal.App.4th 1590, 25 Cal.Rptr.2d 655 (1993)*, the husband failed "to maintain insurance," as required by a Section 4360 order, when he committed suicide within two years of the date of policy issue. His estate was required to pay his surviving ex-wife an amount equal to the policy benefits.

In re Marriage of Stimel, 49 Cal.App.4th 991, 57 Cal.Rptr.2d 18 (1996), holds that a spousal support obligee's request for an order directing the support obligor to purchase life insurance naming the obligee as the beneficiary, premiums to be paid by the obligee, is not a request for a spousal support modification and therefore does not require a showing of changed circumstances.

Research References

Forms

California Practice Guide: Rutter Family Law Forms Form 6:23, Request for Order Re Temporary "Guideline" Spousal Support and Family Code S4360 Provision for Support After Death Of Supporting Party.

California Transactions Forms--Family Law § 2:43, Life Insurance.

Treatises and Practice Aids

Witkin, California Summary 10th Community Property § 48, Term Life Insurance.

Witkin, California Summary 10th Husband and Wife § 174, in General.

Witkin, California Summary 10th Husband and Wife § 214, Payments for Insurance, Annuity, or Trust.

Witkin, California Summary 10th Husband and Wife § 294, Death Of Spouse.

Part 4

SUPPORT OF PARENTS

CHAPTER 1. GENERAL PROVISIONS

§ 4400. Duty of adult children to support parents

Except as otherwise provided by law, an adult child shall, to the extent of his or her ability, support a parent who is in need and unable to maintain himself or herself by work. *(Stats.1992, c. 162 (A.B.2650), § 10, operative Jan. 1, 1994.)*

Law Revision Commission Comments

Enactment [Revised Comment]

Section 4400 restates without substantive change the first sentence of former Civil Code Section 206 and former Civil Code Section 242, insofar as those sections applied to the duty of an adult child to support a parent. The introductory clause recognizes exceptions such as that found in Welfare and Institutions Code Section 12350 (no liability for support or reimbursement to applicant for aid under Burton–Moscone–Bagley Citizens' Security Act for Aged, Blind and Disabled Californians). The last sentence of former Civil Code Section 206 (which defined a parent who receives aid to the aged as one in need) has been omitted as obsolete. See Welf. & Inst. Code § 12350.

The duty of support stated in Section 4400 is subject to Chapter 2 (commencing with Section 4410) (relief from duty to support parent on ground of abandonment). [23 Cal.L.Rev.Comm. Reports 1 (1993)].

Commentary

In re Marriage of Leni, 144 Cal.App.4th 1087, 50 Cal.Rptr.3d 886 (2006), held that a spouse's use of community funds to care for his ailing mother was not a gift for purposes of section 1100 (b) because this section imposes upon an adult child a legal duty to support a parent who is in need and is unable to maintain herself by work. Moreover, the community has no right of reimbursement under section 915, because it creates a right of reimbursement only for "a child or spousal support obligation that does not arise out of the marriage."

Research References

Forms

West's California Code Forms, Family § 4400, Comment Overview-- Duty Of Adult Children to Support Parents.
West's California Code Forms, Family § 4405 Form 2, Order Modifying Order for Support.

Treatises and Practice Aids

Witkin, California Summary 10th Husband and Wife § 174, in General.
Witkin, California Summary 10th Husband and Wife § 340, Aid to Aged, Blind, and Disabled.
Witkin, California Summary 10th Parent and Child § 376, Civil and Criminal Liability.

§ 4401. Promise of adult child to pay for necessaries

The promise of an adult child to pay for necessaries previously furnished to a parent described in Section 4400 is binding. *(Stats.1992, c. 162 (A.B.2650), § 10, operative Jan. 1, 1994.)*

Law Revision Commission Comments

Enactment [Revised Comment]

Section 4401 continues the second sentence of former Civil Code Section 206 without substantive change. [23 Cal.L.Rev.Comm. Reports 1 (1993)].

Research References

Forms

West's California Code Forms, Family § 4400, Comment Overview-- Duty Of Adult Children to Support Parents.

Treatises and Practice Aids

Witkin, California Summary 10th Husband and Wife § 340, Aid to Aged, Blind, and Disabled.
Witkin, California Summary 10th Parent and Child § 376, Civil and Criminal Liability.

§ 4402. Cumulative nature of duties

The duty of support under this part is cumulative and not in substitution for any other duty. *(Stats.1992, c. 162 (A.B.2650), § 10, operative Jan. 1, 1994.)*

Law Revision Commission Comments

Enactment [Revised Comment]

Section 4402 continues former Civil Code Section 251 without substantive change, insofar as that section applied to the duty of an adult child to support a parent. [23 Cal.L.Rev.Comm. Reports 1 (1993)].

Research References

Forms

West's California Code Forms, Family § 4400, Comment Overview-- Duty Of Adult Children to Support Parents.

Treatises and Practice Aids

Witkin, California Summary 10th Parent and Child § 376, Civil and Criminal Liability.

§ 4403. Enforcement of right of support; reimbursement of county

(a) Subject to subdivision (b):

(1) A parent, or the county on behalf of the parent, may bring an action against the child to enforce the duty of support under this part.

(2) If the county furnishes support to a parent, the county has the same right as the parent to whom the support was furnished to secure reimbursement and obtain continuing support.

(b) The right of the county to proceed on behalf of the parent or to obtain reimbursement is subject to any limitation otherwise imposed by the law of this state.

(c) The court may order the child to pay the county reasonable attorney's fees and court costs in a proceeding by the county under this section. *(Stats.1992, c. 162 (A.B.2650), § 10, operative Jan. 1, 1994.)*

Law Revision Commission Comments

Enactment [Revised Comment]

Section 4403 continues former Civil Code Section 248 without substantive change, insofar as that section applied to enforcement of the duty of an adult child to support a parent. For a provision limiting the right of the county to bring an action or to obtain reimbursement, see, e.g., Welf. & Inst. Code § 12350 (no relative liable under Burton–Moscone–Bagley Citizens' Security Act for Aged, Blind and Disabled Californians).

For comparable provisions, see Sections 4002 (county enforcement of duty to support child), 4303 (county enforcement of duty to support spouse). [23 Cal.L.Rev.Comm. Reports 1 (1993)].

Research References

Forms

West's California Code Forms, Family § 4400, Comment Overview--Duty Of Adult Children to Support Parents.

Treatises and Practice Aids

Witkin, California Summary 10th Parent and Child § 376, Civil and Criminal Liability.

§ 4404. Determination of amount due for support; circumstances

In determining the amount to be ordered for support, the court shall consider the following circumstances of each party:

(a) Earning capacity and needs.

(b) Obligations and assets.

(c) Age and health.

(d) Standard of living.

(e) Other factors the court deems just and equitable. *(Stats.1992, c. 162 (A.B.2650), § 10, operative Jan. 1, 1994.)*

Law Revision Commission Comments

Enactment [Revised Comment]

Section 4404 continues without substantive change former Civil Code Section 246 (repealed by 1993 [sic] Cal. Stat. ch. 46, § 1), insofar as that section applied to an order for support of a parent. [23 Cal.L.Rev.Comm. Reports 1 (1993)].

Research References

Forms

West's California Code Forms, Family § 4400, Comment Overview--Duty Of Adult Children to Support Parents.

West's California Code Forms, Family § 4400 Form 1, Complaint to Enforce Reciprocal Duty Of Support Of Needy Parent.

West's California Code Forms, Family § 4405 Form 1, Notice Of Motion and Motion to Modify Order for Support.

Treatises and Practice Aids

Witkin, California Summary 10th Parent and Child § 376, Civil and Criminal Liability.

§ 4405. Jurisdiction to modify or terminate order of support

The court retains jurisdiction to modify or terminate an order for support where justice requires. *(Stats.1992, c. 162 (A.B.2650), § 10, operative Jan. 1, 1994.)*

Law Revision Commission Comments

Enactment [Revised Comment]

Section 4405 continues the substance of former Civil Code Section 247, insofar as that section applied to an order for support of a parent. A reference to "terminate" has been substituted for "vacate." This is not a substantive change. [23 Cal.L.Rev.Comm. Reports 1 (1993)].

Research References

Forms

West's California Code Forms, Family § 4405 Form 1, Notice Of Motion and Motion to Modify Order for Support.

Treatises and Practice Aids

Witkin, California Summary 10th Parent and Child § 376, Civil and Criminal Liability.

CHAPTER 2. RELIEF FROM DUTY TO SUPPORT PARENT WHO ABANDONED CHILD

§ 4410. Petition for relief from duty; filing

An adult child may file a petition in the county where a parent of the child resides requesting that the court make an order freeing the petitioner from the obligation otherwise imposed by law to support the parent. If the parent does not reside in this state, the petition shall be filed in the county where the adult child resides. *(Stats.1992, c. 162 (A.B.2650), § 10, operative Jan. 1, 1994.)*

Law Revision Commission Comments

Enactment [Revised Comment]

The first sentence of Section 4410 continues without substantive change the first and last parts of the first sentence of former Civil Code Section 206.5. The second sentence of this section is new and has been added to make clear the correct venue where the parent is not a California resident. References to the "superior" court and to a "verified" petition have been omitted as surplus. See Sections 200 (jurisdiction in superior court), 212 (pleadings to be verified).

The provision of former Civil Code Section 206.7, requiring an adult child to request relief from the county board of supervisors before filing a court petition for relief from the duty to support a parent, has been omitted as obsolete. The request was required to be directed to the board of supervisors in the county responsible for granting public aid to the parent. Since public aid programs, such as the Burton–Moscone–Bagley Citizens' Security Act for Aged, Blind and Disabled Californians, no longer require reimbursement for such aid, the former section is obsolete. See Welf. & Inst. Code § 12350. [23 Cal.L.Rev.Comm. Reports 1 (1993)].

Research References

Forms

West's California Code Forms, Family § 4410, Comment Overview--Petition for Relief from Duty to Support Parent Who Abandoned Child.

West's California Code Forms, Family § 4410 Form 3, Notice Of Pendency Of Proceedings to Obtain Relief from Obligation to Support Parent Who Abandoned Child.

Treatises and Practice Aids

Witkin, California Summary 10th Husband and Wife § 174, in General.

Witkin, California Summary 10th Parent and Child § 377, Limitations on Parent's Right.

§ 4411. Grounds for order

The court shall make the order requested pursuant to Section 4410 only if the petition alleges and the court finds all of the following:

(a) The child was abandoned by the parent when the child was a minor.

(b) The abandonment continued for a period of two or more years before the time the child attained the age of 18 years.

(c) During the period of abandonment the parent was physically and mentally able to provide support for the child. *(Stats.1992, c. 162 (A.B.2650), § 10, operative Jan. 1, 1994.)*

Law Revision Commission Comments

Enactment [Revised Comment]

Section 4411 restates without substantive change the middle part of the first sentence of former Civil Code Section 206.5. [23 Cal.L.Rev.Comm. Reports 1 (1993)].

Research References

Forms

West's California Code Forms, Family § 4410, Comment Overview--Petition for Relief from Duty to Support Parent Who Abandoned Child.

Treatises and Practice Aids

Witkin, California Summary 10th Parent and Child § 377, Limitations on Parent's Right.

§ 4412. Time for hearing; service of citation and petition

On the filing of a petition under this chapter, the clerk shall set the matter for hearing by the court and shall issue a citation, stating the time and place of the hearing, directed to the parent and to the parent's conservator, if any, or, if the parent is deceased, the personal representative of the parent's estate. At least five days before the date of the hearing, the citation and a copy of the petition shall be personally served on each person to whom it is directed, in the same manner as provided by law for the service of summons. *(Stats.1992, c. 162 (A.B.2650), § 10, operative Jan. 1, 1994.)*

Law Revision Commission Comments

Enactment [Revised Comment]

Section 4412 restates without substantive change the second and third sentences of the first paragraph of former Civil Code Section 206.5. [23 Cal.L.Rev.Comm. Reports 1 (1993)].

Research References

Forms

West's California Code Forms, Family § 4410, Comment Overview--Petition for Relief from Duty to Support Parent Who Abandoned Child.

West's California Code Forms, Family § 4410 Form 2, Citation--Petition to Obtain Relief from Obligation to Support Parent.

West's California Code Forms, Family § 4410 Form 4, Order Granting Relief from Obligation to Support Parent.

Treatises and Practice Aids

Witkin, California Summary 10th Parent and Child § 377, Limitations on Parent's Right.

§ 4413. Jurisdiction; notice to district attorney or county counsel

If the parent is a resident of this state, the court does not have jurisdiction to make an order under this chapter until 30 days after the county counsel, or the district attorney in a county not having a county counsel, of the county in which the parent resides has been served with notice of the pendency of the proceeding. *(Stats.1992, c. 162 (A.B.2650), § 10, operative Jan. 1, 1994.)*

Law Revision Commission Comments

Enactment [Revised Comment]

Section 4413 restates former Civil Code Section 206.6 without substantive change. The reference to making an "order" has been substituted for the former reference to rendering a "judgment." This is not a substantive change. See also Section 155 ("support order" means a judgment or order of support). [23 Cal.L.Rev. Comm. Reports 1 (1993)].

Research References

Forms

West's California Code Forms, Family § 4410, Comment Overview--Petition for Relief from Duty to Support Parent Who Abandoned Child.

West's California Code Forms, Family § 4410 Form 3, Notice Of Pendency Of Proceedings to Obtain Relief from Obligation to Support Parent Who Abandoned Child.

West's California Code Forms, Family § 4410 Form 4, Order Granting Relief from Obligation to Support Parent.

§ 4414. Order for relief; effect of order

(a) If, upon hearing, the court determines that the requirements of Section 4411 are satisfied, the court shall make an order that the petitioner is relieved from the obligation otherwise imposed by law to support the parent.

(b) An order under this section also releases the petitioner with respect to any state law under which a child is required to do any of the following:

(1) Pay for the support, care, maintenance, and the like of a parent.

(2) Reimburse the state or a local public agency for furnishing the support, care, maintenance, or the like of a parent. *(Stats.1992, c. 162 (A.B.2650), § 10, operative Jan. 1, 1994.)*

Law Revision Commission Comments

Enactment [Revised Comment]

Section 4414 restates without substantive change the last sentence of the first paragraph and the last paragraph of former Section 206.5. In subdivision (a), the reference to the court "making an order" has been substituted for the former reference to "issuing a decree." This is not a substantive change. See Section 100 ("order" includes decree, as appropriate). [23 Cal.L.Rev.Comm. Reports 1 (1993)].

Research References

Forms

West's California Code Forms, Family § 4410, Comment Overview-- Petition for Relief from Duty to Support Parent Who Abandoned Child.

Treatises and Practice Aids

Witkin, California Summary 10th Parent and Child § 377, Limitations on Parent's Right.

Part 5

ENFORCEMENT OF SUPPORT ORDERS

CHAPTER 1. GENERAL PROVISIONS

§ 4500. Orders enforceable under this code

An order for child, family, or spousal support that is made, entered, or enforceable in this state is enforceable under this code, whether or not the order was made or entered pursuant to this code. *(Stats.1992, c. 162 (A.B.2650), § 10, operative Jan. 1, 1994.)*

Law Revision Commission Comments

Enactment [Revised Comment]

Section 4500 continues former Civil Code Section 4385 without substantive change. References to "this code" have been substituted for the former references to "this chapter" and "this part," which formerly referred to the provisions for enforcement found in the former Family Law Act. The former references to both "judgment" and "decree" have been omitted as surplus. See Sections 100 ("order" includes decree, as appropriate), 155 ("support order" means judgment or order of support). The reference to "family" support is new and is consistent with Section 4501. See also Sections 290–291 (enforcement of judgments and orders), 3557 (attorney's fees and costs for enforcement of support order).

This section supersedes the last sentence of former Civil Code Section 4700.9 (child support orders based on agreement of parties to pay for support of adult child enforceable in same manner as other child support award).

For background on former Civ. Code § 4385, see 16 Cal. L. Revision Comm'n Reports 2143 (1982). [23 Cal.L.Rev.Comm. Reports 1 (1993)].

Research References

Forms

West's California Code Forms, Family § 4500, Comment Overview-- Enforcement Of Support Orders.

Treatises and Practice Aids

Witkin, California Summary 10th Husband and Wife § 174, in General.

Witkin, California Summary 10th Husband and Wife § 248, in General.

Witkin, California Summary 10th Parent and Child § 425, in General.

§ 4501. Family support orders

A family support order is enforceable in the same manner and to the same extent as a child support order. *(Stats.1992, c. 162 (A.B.2650), § 10, operative Jan. 1, 1994.)*

Law Revision Commission Comments

Enactment [Revised Comment]

Section 4501 continues without substantive change the last part of the first sentence of the second paragraph of former Civil Code Section 4811(d). The rule in former Civil Code Section 4811(c) limiting application of this section to property settlement agreements entered into on or after January 1, 1970, has been omitted as obsolete. The last sentence of former Civil Code Section 4811(d) also has been omitted. See also Section 92 ("family support" defined). [23 Cal.L.Rev.Comm. Reports 1 (1993)].

Research References

Forms

West's California Code Forms, Family § 4500, Comment Overview-- Enforcement Of Support Orders.

Treatises and Practice Aids

Witkin, California Summary 10th Husband and Wife § 248, in General.

Witkin, California Summary 10th Parent and Child § 425, in General.

§ 4502. Judgments or orders for support; enforcement and renewal; governing provisions

The period for enforcement and procedure for renewal of a judgment or order for child, family, or spousal support is governed by Section 291. *(Added by Stats.2006, c. 86 (A.B.2126), § 6.)*

Law Revision Commission Comments

2006 Repeal and Addition

Section 4502 is repealed. Its substance is continued in Section 291. New Section 4502 provides a cross-reference to Section 291. [35 Cal.L.Rev.Comm. Reports 179 (2005)].

Section 4502 provides a cross-reference to the general rule on enforcement of a judgment under the Family Code. Section 291 continues the substance of former Section 4502. [35 Cal.L.Rev. Comm. Reports 179 (2005)].

Research References

Forms

West's California Code Forms, Family § 4500, Comment Overview--Enforcement Of Support Orders.

Treatises and Practice Aids

Witkin, California Summary 10th Husband and Wife § 2A, (New) Retroactivity Of Provisions.

Witkin, California Summary 10th Husband and Wife § 219, Waiver After Judgment.

Witkin, California Summary 10th Husband and Wife § 220, Laches Defense Limited.

Witkin, California Summary 10th Husband and Wife § 248, in General.

Witkin, California Summary 10th Husband and Wife § 263, Period Of Enforcement.

Witkin, California Summary 10th Husband and Wife § 267, Judgment Lien.

Witkin, California Summary 10th Wills and Probate § 517, Action Against Decedent.

§ 4503. Actions to recover arrearages; limitation of actions

If a parent has been ordered to make payments for the support of a minor child, an action to recover an arrearage in those payments may be maintained at any time within the period otherwise specified for the enforcement of such a judgment, notwithstanding the fact that the child has attained the age of 18 years. *(Stats.1992, c. 162 (A.B.2650), § 10, operative Jan. 1, 1994.)*

Law Revision Commission Comments

Enactment [Revised Comment]

Section 4503 continues former Civil Code Section 4708 without substantive change. The reference to paying for maintenance and education of a child has been omitted as surplus. See Section 150 ("support" includes maintenance and education when used with reference to a minor child). See also Section 4011 (priority of child support payments). [23 Cal.L.Rev.Comm. Reports 1 (1993)].

Commentary

Although Section 4054 provides that social security "child's insurance benefits" payable on account of the disability or retirement of the noncustodial parent shall be credited against the amount of child support otherwise payable by the noncustodial parent, current benefits may not be applied against child support arrearages. *In re Marriage of Robinson, 65 Cal.App.4th 93, 76 Cal.Rptr.2d 134 (1998).*

Research References

Forms

West's California Code Forms, Family § 4500, Comment Overview--Enforcement Of Support Orders.

West's California Judicial Council Forms FL-626, Stipulation and Order Waiving Unassigned Arrears (Governmental).

Treatises and Practice Aids

Witkin, California Summary 10th Husband and Wife § 248, in General.

Witkin, California Summary 10th Husband and Wife § 263, Period Of Enforcement.

Witkin, California Summary 10th Parent and Child § 428, Recovery Of Arrearages.

§ 4504. Payments received from the federal government under specified federal acts or from specified agencies due to retirement or disability of noncustodial parent; application for benefits on behalf of each eligible child; cooperation requirements; credit toward amount ordered to be paid by court

(a) If the noncustodial parent is receiving payments from the federal government pursuant to the Social Security Act or Railroad Retirement Act, or from the Department of Veterans Affairs because of the retirement or disability of the noncustodial parent and the noncustodial parent notifies the custodial person, or notifies the local child support agency in a case being enforced by the local child support agency pursuant to Title IV–D of the Social Security Act, then the custodial parent or other child support obligee shall contact the appropriate federal agency within 30 days of receiving notification that the noncustodial parent is receiving those payments to verify eligibility for each child to receive payments from the federal government because of the disability of the noncustodial parent. If the child is potentially eligible for those payments, the custodial parent or other child support obligee shall apply for and cooperate with the appropriate federal agency for the receipt of those benefits on behalf of each child. The noncustodial parent shall cooperate with the custodial parent or other child support obligee in making that application and shall provide any information necessary to complete the application.

(b) If the court has ordered a noncustodial parent to pay for the support of a child, payments for the support of the child made by the federal government pursuant to the Social Security Act or Railroad Retirement Act, or by the Department of Veterans Affairs because of the retirement or disability of the noncustodial parent and received by the custodial parent or other child support obligee shall be credited toward the amount ordered by the court to be paid by the noncustodial parent for support of the child unless the payments made by the federal government were taken into consideration by the court in determining the amount of support to be paid. Any payments shall be credited in the order set forth in Section 695.221 of the Code of Civil Procedure.

(c) If the custodial parent or other child support obligee refuses to apply for those benefits or fails to cooperate with the appropriate federal agency in completing the application but the child or children otherwise are eligible to receive those benefits, the noncustodial parent shall be credited toward the amount ordered by the court to be paid for that month by the noncustodial parent for support of the child or children in the amount of payment that the child or children would have received that month had the custodial parent or other child support obligee completed an application for the benefits if the noncustodial parent provides evidence to the local child support agency indicating the amount the child or children would have received. The credit for those payments shall continue until the child or children would no longer be eligible for those benefits or the order for child support for the child or children is no longer in effect, whichever occurs first. *(Stats.1992, c. 162 (A.B.2650), § 10, operative Jan. 1, 1994. Amended by Stats.1996, c. 912 (A.B.1751), § 2; Stats. 2001, c. 651 (A.B.891), § 1; Stats.2004, c. 305 (A.B.2669), § 4.)*

Law Revision Commission Comments

Enactment [Revised Comment]

Section 4504 continues former Civil Code Section 4705 without substantive change. The reference to paying for maintenance and education of a child has been omitted as surplus. See Section 150 ("support" includes maintenance and education when used with reference to a minor child). [23 Cal.L.Rev.Comm. Reports 1 (1993)].

Commentary

Applying this section, *In re Marriage of Hall and Frencher, 247 Cal.App.4th 23, 201 Cal.Rptr.3d 769 (2016)*, held that the trial court erred when it failed to apply a child's derivative social security benefits to his father's child support arrears and interest to the extent that the derivative benefits exceeded the father's current monthly support obligation. Note that subsection (b) of this section was amended in 2004 to repeal the contrary holding of *In re Marriage of Robinson, 65 Cal.App.4th 93, 76 Cal.Rptr.2d 134 (1998)*, decided under prior law, which provided that excess derivative benefits could not be applied to support arrearage.

In re Marriage of Daugherty, 232 Cal.App.4th 463, 181 Cal.Rptr.3d 427 (2014), holds that social security disability payments made to the custodial parent on behalf of the children of a disabled obligor are not includible, under section 4058, in the obligor's income for the purpose of determining his child support obligation. Those payments are, however, to be credited against the disabled parent's child support obligation under subsection (b) of this section.

In re Marriage of Bertrand, 33 Cal.App.4th 437, 39 Cal.Rptr.2d 151 (1995), holds that social security payments received by a child on account of decedent's death may not be credited against decedent's support obligation because Section 4504 allows credit against a support obligation only for social security retirement or disability benefits, but trial court may consider such death benefits in ruling on executor's motion to modify decedent father's support obligation.

Research References

Forms

California Practice Guide: Rutter Family Law Forms Form 6:9, Responsive Declaration to Request for Order Re Child Support Based on Earning Capacity.

Treatises and Practice Aids

Witkin, California Summary 10th Parent and Child § 393, Crediting Federal Retirement or Disability Payments.

Witkin, California Summary 10th Parent and Child § 397, Annual Gross Income.

§ 4505. Default due to unemployment; allegation by parent; list of places applied for employment

(a) A court may require a parent who alleges that the parent's default in a child or family support order is due to the parent's unemployment to submit to the appropriate child support enforcement agency or any other entity designated by the court, including, but not limited to, the court itself, each two weeks, or at a frequency deemed appropriate by the court, a list of at least five different places the parent has applied for employment.

(b) This section shall become operative on January 1, 2011. *(Added by Stats.2007, c. 249 (S.B.523), § 2, operative Jan. 1, 2011.)*

Research References

Treatises and Practice Aids

Witkin, California Summary 10th Parent and Child § 425, in General.

Witkin, California Summary 10th Parent and Child § 437, Contempt Proceedings.

§ 4506. Certification of abstract of judgment; contents; form; notice of support judgment

(a) An abstract of a judgment ordering a party to pay spousal, child, or family support to the other party shall be certified by the clerk of the court where the judgment was entered and shall contain all of the following:

(1) The title of the court where the judgment is entered and the cause and number of the proceeding.

(2) The date of entry of the judgment and of any renewal of the judgment.

(3) Where the judgment and any renewals are entered in the records of the court.

(4) The name and last known address of the party ordered to pay support.

(5) The name and address of the party to whom support payments are ordered to be paid.

(6) Only the last four digits of the social security number, birth date, and driver's license number of the party who is ordered to pay support. If any of those numbers are not known to the party to whom support payments are to be paid, that fact shall be indicated on the abstract of the court judgment. This paragraph shall not apply to documents created prior to January 1, 2010.

(7) Whether a stay of enforcement has been ordered by the court and, if so, the date the stay ends.

(8) The date of issuance of the abstract.

(9) Any other information deemed reasonable and appropriate by the Judicial Council.

(b) The Judicial Council may develop a form for an abstract of a judgment ordering a party to pay child, family, or spousal support to another party which contains the information required by subdivision (a).

(c) Notwithstanding any other provision of law, when a support obligation is being enforced pursuant to Title IV–D of the Social Security Act, the agency enforcing the obligation may record a notice of support judgment. The notice of support judgment shall contain the same information as the form adopted by the Judicial Council pursuant to subdivision (b) and Section 4506.1. The notice of support judgment shall have the same force and effect as an abstract of judgment certified by the clerk of the court where the judgment was entered. The local child support agency or other Title IV–D agency shall not be subject to any civil liability as a consequence of causing a notice of support judgment to be recorded.

(d) As used in this section, "judgment" includes an order for child, family, or spousal support. *(Stats.1992, c. 162 (A.B.2650), § 10, operative Jan. 1, 1994. Amended by Stats. 2002, c. 927 (A.B.3032), § 3; Stats.2009, c. 552 (S.B.40), § 3.)*

Law Revision Commission Comments

Enactment [Revised Comment]

Subdivisions (a) and (b) of Section 4506 continue without substantive change former Code of Civil Procedure Section 674(b)-(c) (as amended by 1988 Cal. Stat. ch. 1411, § 1). Subdivision (c) is new.

In subdivision (a)(1), the reference to "proceeding" has been substituted for the former reference to "action." This is not a substantive change. In subdivision (a)(6), the reference to an abstract of "judgment" has been substituted for the former reference to an abstract of a "court order." This is not a substantive change and is consistent with the remainder of the section. References to "decree" have been omitted as surplus. See Section 100 ("judgment" includes decree, as appropriate). See also Code Civ. Proc. § 674(b) (amendment to abstract of judgment). [23 Cal.L.Rev. Comm. Reports 1 (1993)].

Research References

Forms

West's California Code Forms, Family § 4500, Comment Overview--Enforcement Of Support Orders.

Treatises and Practice Aids

Witkin, California Summary 10th Husband and Wife § 267, Judgment Lien.

§ 4506.1. Obligations enforced pursuant to Title IV–D of the Social Security Act; filing and recording abstract of support judgment

Notwithstanding any other provision of law, when a support obligation is being enforced pursuant to Title IV–D of the Social Security Act, the agency enforcing the obligation may file and record an abstract of support judgment as authorized by Section 4506 and substitute the office address of the agency designated to receive support payments for the address of the party to whom support was ordered to be paid. *(Added by Stats.1994, c. 1269 (A.B.2208), § 48.)*

Research References

Treatises and Practice Aids

Witkin, California Summary 10th Husband and Wife § 267, Judgment Lien.

§ 4506.2. Enforcement of obligation pursuant to Title IV–D of the Social Security Act; filing and recording record of substitution of payee

(a) Notwithstanding any other provision of law, when a support obligation is being enforced pursuant to Title IV–D of the Social Security Act, the agency enforcing the obligation may file and record a substitution of payee, if a judgment or abstract of judgment has previously been recorded pursuant to Section 697.320 of the Code of Civil Procedure by the support obligee or by a different governmental agency.

(b) Notwithstanding any other provision of law, when the Title IV–D agency ceases enforcement of a support obligation at the request of the support obligee, the agency may file and record a substitution of payee, if a judgment or abstract of judgment has been previously recorded pursuant to Section 697.320 of the Code of Civil Procedure.

(c) The substitution of payee shall contain all of the following:

(1) The name and address of the governmental agency or substituted payee filing the substitution and a notice that the substituted payee is to be contacted when notice to a lienholder may or must be given.

(2) The title of the court, the cause, and number of the proceeding where the substituted payee has registered the judgment.

(3) The name and last known address of the party ordered to pay support.

(4) The recorder identification number or book and page of the recorded document to which the substitution of payee applies.

(5) Any other information deemed reasonable and appropriate by the Judicial Council.

(d) The recorded substitution of payee shall not affect the priorities created by earlier recordations of support judgments or abstracts of support judgments.

(e) An agency enforcing the support obligation pursuant to Title IV–D of the Social Security Act is not required to obtain prior court approval or a clerk's certification when filing and recording a substitution of payee under this section. *(Added by Stats.1994, c. 1269 (A.B.2208), § 48.2. Amended by Stats.1997, c. 599 (A.B.573), § 17.)*

Research References

Treatises and Practice Aids

Witkin, California Summary 10th Husband and Wife § 267, Judgment Lien.

§ 4506.3. Notice directing payment of support to local child support agency and notice that support has been assigned; single form

The Judicial Council, in consultation with the California Family Support Council, the Department of Child Support Services, and title insurance industry representatives, shall develop a single form, which conforms with the requirements of Section 27361.6 of the Government Code, for the substitution of payee, for notice directing payment of support to the local child support agency pursuant to Section 4204, and for notice that support has been assigned pursuant to Section 11477 of the Welfare and Institutions Code. The form shall be available no later than July 1, 1998. *(Added by Stats.1994, c. 1269 (A.B.2208), § 48.4. Amended by Stats.1996, c. 957 (A.B.1058), § 7; Stats.1997, c. 599 (A.B.573), § 18; Stats. 2000, c. 808 (A.B.1358), § 46, eff. Sept. 28, 2000.)*

Research References

Forms

West's California Judicial Council Forms FL-632, Notice Regarding Payment Of Support.

Treatises and Practice Aids

Witkin, California Summary 10th Husband and Wife § 267, Judgment Lien.

§ 4507. Payment of court order for support in accordance with Government Code § 1151.5

When a court orders a person to make payment for child support or family support, the court may order that individual to make that payment as provided in Section 1151.5 of the Government Code. *(Added by Stats.1993, c. 176 (A.B.877), § 1.)*

Research References

Treatises and Practice Aids

Witkin, California Summary 10th Parent and Child § 425, in General.

§ 4508. Electronic funds transfer; designation of account; application of section

(a) This section does not apply to any child support obligor who is subject to an earnings assignment order pursuant to Chapter 8 (commencing with Section 5200).

(b) Except as provided in subdivision (a), every order or judgment to pay child support may require a child support obligor to designate an account for the purpose of paying the child support obligation by electronic funds transfer, as defined in subdivision (a) of Section 6479.5 of the Revenue and Taxation Code. The order or judgment may require the obligor to deposit funds in an interest-bearing account with a state or federally chartered commercial bank, a savings and loan association, or in shares of a federally insured credit union doing business in this state, and shall require the obligor to maintain funds in the account sufficient to pay the monthly child support obligation. The court may order that each payment be electronically transferred to either the obligee's account or the local child support agency account. The obligor shall be required to notify the obligee if the depository institution or the account number is changed. No interest shall accrue on any amount subject to electronic funds transfer as long as funds are maintained in the account that are sufficient to pay the monthly child support obligation. *(Added by Stats.1994, c. 906 (A.B.923), § 2. Amended by Stats.1999, c. 980 (A.B.1671), § 9; Stats.2001, c. 755 (S.B.943), § 4, eff. Oct. 12, 2001.)*

Research References

Forms

California Transactions Forms--Family Law § 2:63, Authority for Child Support.

California Transactions Forms--Family Law § 3:37, Stipulation Of the Parties.

California Transactions Forms--Family Law § 2:93.5, Child Support Provision Regarding Electronic Transfer Of Funds.

California Transactions Forms--Family Law § 3:112.5, Designation Of Electronic Fund Transfer Account Number.

Treatises and Practice Aids

Witkin, California Summary 10th Parent and Child § 414, Stipulated Support Agreements.

Witkin, California Summary 10th Parent and Child § 425, in General.

CHAPTER 2. DEPOSIT OF MONEY TO SECURE FUTURE CHILD SUPPORT PAYMENTS

ARTICLE 1. GENERAL PROVISIONS

§ 4550. "Child support obligee" defined

"Child support obligee" as used in this chapter means either the parent, guardian, or other person to whom child support has been ordered to be paid or the local child support agency designated by the court to receive the payment. The local child support agency is the "child support obligee" for the purposes of this chapter for all cases in which an application for services has been filed under Part D of Title IV of the Social Security Act (42 U.S.C. Sec. 651 et seq.). *(Stats.1992, c. 162 (A.B.2650), § 10, operative Jan. 1, 1994; Stats.2001, c. 755 (S.B.943), § 5, eff. Oct. 12, 2001.)*

Law Revision Commission Comments

Enactment [Revised Comment]

Section 4550 continues the first two sentences of former Civil Code Section 4710(f) without substantive change. The reference to "other person" has been substituted for "conservatee." This is not a substantive change. See also Section 4573 (payment to custodial parent or other person where support paid through district attorney for child not receiving public assistance). [23 Cal.L.Rev.Comm. Reports 1 (1993)].

Research References

Treatises and Practice Aids

Witkin, California Summary 10th Husband and Wife § 174, in General.

Witkin, California Summary 10th Husband and Wife § 265, Security for Payment.

Witkin, California Summary 10th Parent and Child § 429, Child Support Security Deposit.

§ 4551. Application of chapter

Except as provided in this section, this chapter:

(a) Does not apply to a temporary child support order.

(b) Applies to an application for modification of child support filed on or after January 1, 1992, but this chapter does not constitute the basis for the modification.

(c) Applies to an application for modification of child support in a case where the child support obligee has previously waived the establishment of a child support trust account pursuant to subdivision (b) of Section 4560 and now seeks the establishment of the child support trust account.

(d) Applies to an order or judgment entered by the court on or after January 1, 1993, ordering a child support obligor to pay a then existing child support arrearage that the child support obligor has unlawfully failed to pay as of the date of that order or judgment, including the arrearages which were incurred before January 1, 1992. *(Stats.1992, c. 162 (A.B. 2650), § 10, operative Jan. 1, 1994.)*

Law Revision Commission Comments

Enactment [Revised Comment]

Section 4551 continues former Civil Code Section 4710(g) without substantive change. In subdivision (b), the word "filed" has been substituted for "entered into." This is not a substantive change. [23 Cal.L.Rev.Comm. Reports 1 (1993)].

Research References

Treatises and Practice Aids

Witkin, California Summary 10th Parent and Child § 429, Child Support Security Deposit.

§ 4552. Rules of court; promulgation and publication of forms by Judicial Council

The Judicial Council shall promulgate such rules of court and publish such related judicial forms as the Judicial Council determines are necessary and appropriate to implement this chapter. In taking these steps, the Judicial Council shall ensure the uniform statewide application of this chapter and compliance with Part D of Title IV of the Social Security Act (42 U.S.C. Sec. 651 et seq.) and any regulations promulgated thereunder. *(Stats.1992, c. 162 (A.B.2650), § 10, operative Jan. 1, 1994.)*

Law Revision Commission Comments

Enactment [Revised Comment]

Section 4552 continues without substantive change Section 4 of Chapter 1141 of the Statutes of 1991. [23 Cal.L.Rev.Comm. Reports 1 (1993)].

§ 4553. Construction of chapter; compliance with federal law

Nothing in this chapter shall be construed to permit any action or omission by the state or any of its political subdivisions that would place the state in noncompliance with any requirement of federal law, including, but not limited to, the state reimbursement requirements of Part D of Title IV of the Social Security Act (42 U.S.C. Sec. 651 et seq.) and any regulations promulgated thereunder. *(Stats.1992, c. 162 (A.B.2650), § 10, operative Jan. 1, 1994.)*

Law Revision Commission Comments

Enactment [Revised Comment]

Section 4552 [sic] continues without substantive change Section 5 of Chapter 1141 of the Statutes of 1991. [23 Cal.L.Rev.Comm. Reports 1 (1993)].

§ 4554. Application of chapter

This chapter applies notwithstanding any other law. *(Stats. 1992, c. 162 (A.B.2650), § 10, operative Jan. 1, 1994.)*

Law Revision Commission Comments

Enactment [Revised Comment]

Section 4554 continues the introductory clause of former Civil Code Section 4710 without substantive change. See also Section 4553 (compliance with requirements of federal law). [23 Cal.L.Rev. Comm. Reports 1 (1993)].

ARTICLE 2. ORDER FOR DEPOSIT OF MONEY

Section

§ 4560. Child support security deposit; trust account

(a) Except as provided in subdivision (b) or in Article 3 (commencing with Section 4565), every order or judgment to pay child support may also require the payment by the child support obligor of up to one year's child support or such lesser amount as is equal to the child support amount due to be paid by the child support obligor between the time of the date of the order and the date when the support obligation will be terminated by operation of law. This amount shall be known as the "child support security deposit."

(b) Unless expressly waived by the child support obligee, the court may order the establishment of a child support trust account pursuant to this chapter in every proceeding in which a child support obligation is imposed by order of the court. Among other reasons, the court may decline to establish a child support trust account upon its finding that an adequately funded child support trust account already exists pursuant to this chapter for the benefit of the child or children involved in the proceeding or that the child support obligor has provided adequate alternative security which is equivalent to the child support security deposit otherwise required by this chapter. *(Stats.1992, c. 162 (A.B.2650), § 10, operative Jan. 1, 1994.)*

Law Revision Commission Comments

Enactment [Revised Comment]

Subdivision (a) of Section 4560 continues the first two sentences of former Civil Code Section 4710(a) without substantive change. Subdivision (b) continues former Civil Code Section 4710(d) without substantive change. In subdivision (b), a reference to "every proceeding in which a child support obligation is imposed by order of the court" has been substituted for "every proceeding to establish paternity or for dissolution of a marriage" for consistency with subdivision (a).

See also Sections 4551 (application of chapter), 4565 (grounds for application to reduce or eliminate deposit), 4600–4641 (deposit of assets to secure future child support payments). [23 Cal.L.Rev. Comm. Reports 1 (1993)].

Research References

Forms

California Transactions Forms--Family Law § 3:48, Deposit Into Trust Account.

West's California Code Forms, Family § 4560, Comment Overview--Deposit Of Money to Secure Future Child Support Payments.

West's California Judicial Council Forms FL-400, Order for Child Support Security Deposit and Evidence Of Deposit.

Treatises and Practice Aids

Witkin, California Summary 10th Parent and Child § 429, Child Support Security Deposit.

§ 4561. Deposit of funds

If a child support security deposit is ordered, the court shall order that the moneys be deposited by the child support obligor in an interest-bearing account with a state or federally chartered commercial bank, a trust company authorized to transact trust business in this state, or a savings and loan association, or in shares of a federally insured credit union doing business in this state and having a trust department, subject to withdrawal only upon authorization of the court. The moneys so deposited shall be used exclusively to guarantee the monthly payment of child support. *(Stats. 1992, c. 162 (A.B.2650), § 10, operative Jan. 1, 1994.)*

Law Revision Commission Comments

Enactment [Revised Comment]

Section 4561 continues the third and last sentences of former Civil Code Section 4710(a) without substantive change. See also Section 4560(a) (amount of "child support security deposit"). [23 Cal.L.Rev. Comm. Reports 1 (1993)].

Research References

Treatises and Practice Aids

Witkin, California Summary 10th Parent and Child § 429, Child Support Security Deposit.

§ 4562. Evidence of deposit

The court shall also order that evidence of the deposit shall be provided by the child support obligor in the form specified by the court, which shall be served upon the child support obligee and filed with the court within a reasonable time specified by the court, not to exceed 30 days. *(Stats.1992, c. 162 (A.B.2650), § 10, operative Jan. 1, 1994.)*

Law Revision Commission Comments

Enactment [Revised Comment]

Section 4562 continues the next to last sentence of former Civil Code Section 4710(a) without substantive change. [23 Cal.L.Rev. Comm. Reports 1 (1993)].

Research References

Forms

West's California Judicial Council Forms FL-400, Order for Child Support Security Deposit and Evidence Of Deposit.

Treatises and Practice Aids

Witkin, California Summary 10th Parent and Child § 429, Child Support Security Deposit.

§ 4563. Dissolution of account; return of funds

An account established pursuant to this chapter shall be dissolved and any remaining funds in the account shall be returned to the support obligor, with any interest earned thereon, upon the full payment and cessation of the child support obligation as provided by court order or operation of law. *(Stats.1992, c. 162 (A.B.2650), § 10, operative Jan. 1, 1994.)*

Law Revision Commission Comments

Enactment [Revised Comment]

Section 4563 continues former Civil Code Section 4710(c) without substantive change. [23 Cal.L.Rev.Comm. Reports 1 (1993)].

Research References

Forms

California Transactions Forms--Family Law § 3:48, Deposit Into Trust Account.

Treatises and Practice Aids

Witkin, California Summary 10th Parent and Child § 429, Child Support Security Deposit.

ARTICLE 3. APPLICATION TO REDUCE OR ELIMINATE DEPOSIT

Section

§ 4565. Filing of application; grounds for relief

(a) Before entry of a child support order pursuant to Section 4560, the court shall give the child support obligor reasonable notice and opportunity to file an application to reduce or eliminate the child support security deposit on either of the following grounds:

(1) The obligor has provided adequate alternative equivalent security to assure timely payment of the amount required by Section 4560.

(2) The obligor is unable, without undue financial hardship, to pay the support deposit required by Section 4560.

(b) The application shall be supported by all reasonable and necessary financial and other information required by the court to establish the existence of either ground for relief.

(c) After the filing of an application, the child support obligor shall also serve the application and supporting financial and other information submitted pursuant to subdivision (b) upon the child support obligee and any other party to the proceeding. *(Stats.1992, c. 162 (A.B.2650), § 10, operative Jan. 1, 1994. Amended by Stats.2007, c. 441 (S.B.892), § 1.)*

Law Revision Commission Comments

Enactment [Revised Comment]

Section 4565 continues the first two sentences of former Civil Code Section 4710(e) without substantive change. See also Sections 4600–4641 (deposit of assets to secure future child support payments). [23 Cal.L.Rev.Comm. Reports 1 (1993)].

Research References

Forms

West's California Code Forms, Family § 4560, Comment Overview--Deposit Of Money to Secure Future Child Support Payments.

Treatises and Practice Aids

Witkin, California Summary 10th Parent and Child § 429, Child Support Security Deposit.

§ 4566. Notice of application; response

Upon the filing of an application under Section 4565 with the court and the service of the application upon the child support obligee and any other party to the proceedings, the court shall provide notice and opportunity for any party opposing the application to file responsive financial and other information setting forth the factual and legal bases for the party's opposition. *(Stats.1992, c. 162 (A.B.2650), § 10, operative Jan. 1, 1994.)*

Law Revision Commission Comments

Enactment [Revised Comment]

Section 4566 continues the third sentence of former Civil Code Section 4710(e) without substantive change. [23 Cal.L.Rev.Comm. Reports 1 (1993)].

§ 4567. Hearing; entry of orders; reduction of amount of deposit

The court shall then provide an opportunity for hearing, and shall thereafter enter its order exercising its discretion under all the facts and circumstances as disclosed in the admissible evidence before it so as to maximize the payment and deposit of the amount required by Section 4560, or an equivalent adequate security for the payment thereof, without imposition of undue financial hardship on the support obligor. If the court finds that the deposit of the amount required by Section 4560 would impose an undue financial hardship upon the child support obligor, the court shall reduce this amount to an amount that the child support obligor can pay as the child support security deposit without undue financial hardship. *(Stats.1992, c. 162 (A.B.2650), § 10, operative Jan. 1, 1994.)*

Law Revision Commission Comments

Enactment [Revised Comment]

Section 4567 continues the last two sentences of former Civil Code Section 4710(e) without substantive change. See also Sections 4600–4641 (deposit of assets to secure future child support payments). [23 Cal.L.Rev.Comm. Reports 1 (1993)].

Research References

Treatises and Practice Aids

Witkin, California Summary 10th Parent and Child § 429, Child Support Security Deposit.

ARTICLE 4. USE OF DEPOSIT TO MAKE DELINQUENT SUPPORT PAYMENT

§ 4570. Disbursement of funds; use of funds; replenishment of account

(a) Upon the application of the child support obligee stating that the support payment is 10 or more days late, the court shall immediately order disbursement of funds from the account established pursuant to this chapter solely for the purpose of providing the amount of child support then in arrears.

(b) Funds so disbursed shall be used exclusively for the support, maintenance, and education of the child or children subject to the child support order.

(c) The court shall also order the account to be replenished by the child support obligor in the same amounts as are expended from the account to pay the amount of child support which the child support obligor has failed to pay the child support obligee in a timely manner. *(Stats.1992, c. 162 (A.B.2650), § 10, operative Jan. 1, 1994.)*

Law Revision Commission Comments

Enactment [Revised Comment]

Section 4570 continues the first three sentences of former Civil Code Section 4710(b) without substantive change. The reference to a "verified" application has been omitted as surplus. See Section 212 (pleadings to be verified). [23 Cal.L.Rev.Comm. Reports 1 (1993)].

Research References

Forms

California Transactions Forms--Family Law § 3:48, Deposit Into Trust Account.

West's California Code Forms, Family § 4570, Comment Overview--Use Of Deposit to Make Delinquent Support Payment.

Treatises and Practice Aids

Witkin, California Summary 10th Parent and Child § 429, Child Support Security Deposit.

§ 4571. Service upon support obligor

The court shall cause a copy of the application, as well as its order to disburse and replenish funds, to be served upon the child support obligor, who shall be subject to contempt of court for failure to comply with the order. *(Stats.1992, c. 162 (A.B.2650), § 10, operative Jan. 1, 1994.)*

Law Revision Commission Comments

Enactment [Revised Comment]

Section 4571 continues the next to last sentence of former Civil Code Section 4710(b) without substantive change. The reference to a "verified" application has been omitted as surplus. See Section 212 (pleadings to be verified). [23 Cal.L.Rev.Comm. Reports 1 (1993)].

Research References

Forms

West's California Code Forms, Family § 4570, Comment Overview--Use Of Deposit to Make Delinquent Support Payment.

Treatises and Practice Aids

Witkin, California Summary 10th Parent and Child § 429, Child Support Security Deposit.

§ 4572. Service upon depository institution and local child support agency

The court shall cause a copy of its order to disburse and replenish funds to be served upon the depository institution where the child support security deposit is maintained, and upon the child support agency with jurisdiction over the case. *(Stats.1992, c. 162 (A.B.2650), § 10, operative Jan. 1, 1994. Amended by Stats.2001, c. 755 (S.B.943), § 6, eff. Oct. 12, 2001.)*

Law Revision Commission Comments

Enactment [Revised Comment]

Section 4572 continues the last sentence of former Civil Code Section 4710(b) without substantive change. [23 Cal.L.Rev.Comm. Reports 1 (1993)].

Research References

Treatises and Practice Aids

Witkin, California Summary 10th Parent and Child § 429, Child Support Security Deposit.

§ 4573. Support payments ordered paid through local child support agency; duties

If support is ordered to be paid through the local child support agency on behalf of a child not receiving public assistance pursuant to the Family Economic Security Act of 1982 (Chapter 2 (commencing with Section 11200) of Part 3 of Division 9 of the Welfare and Institutions Code), the local child support agency shall forward the support received pursuant to this chapter to the custodial parent or other person having care or control of the child or children involved. *(Stats.1992, c. 162 (A.B.2650), § 10, operative Jan. 1, 1994. Amended by Stats.1993, c. 219 (A.B.1500), § 144; Stats.2000, c. 808 (A.B.1358), § 47, eff. Sept. 28, 2000.)*

Law Revision Commission Comments

Enactment [Revised Comment]

Section 4573 continues the third sentence of former Civil Code Section 4710(f) without substantive change. References to support of a "minor" child have been omitted. These are not substantive changes, but recognize that in some cases support may be ordered for an adult child. See Sections 58 ("child for whom support may be ordered" defined), 3587 (court order to effectuate agreement for support of adult child), 3901 (duration of duty to support child), 3910 (duty to maintain incapacitated adult child), 4000 (civil action to enforce parent's duty to support child), 4001 (order for child support). See also Section 3555 (forwarding support paid through designated county officer). [23 Cal.L.Rev.Comm. Reports 1 (1993)].

Research References

Forms

California Transactions Forms--Family Law § 3:48, Deposit Into Trust Account.

Treatises and Practice Aids

Witkin, California Summary 10th Parent and Child § 200, Commission Of Crime.

Witkin, California Summary 10th Parent and Child § 429, Child Support Security Deposit.

CHAPTER 3. DEPOSIT OF ASSETS TO SECURE FUTURE CHILD SUPPORT PAYMENTS

ARTICLE 1. GENERAL PROVISIONS

§ 4600. Purpose of chapter

The purpose of this chapter is to provide an extraordinary remedy for cases of bad faith failure to pay child support obligations. *(Stats.1992, c. 162 (A.B.2650), § 10, operative Jan. 1, 1994.)*

Law Revision Commission Comments

Enactment [Revised Comment]

Section 4600 continues former Civil Code Section 4701.1(i) without substantive change. See also Section 4011 (priority of child support payments). [23 Cal.L.Rev.Comm. Reports 1 (1993)].

Research References

Forms

California Transactions Forms--Family Law § 3:49, Deposit Of Assets.

Treatises and Practice Aids

Witkin, California Summary 10th Husband and Wife § 174, in General.

Witkin, California Summary 10th Parent and Child § 430, in General.

§ 4601. "Deposit holder" defined

"Deposit holder" as used in this chapter means the district attorney, county officer, or trustee designated by the court to receive assets deposited pursuant to this chapter to secure future support payments. *(Stats.1992, c. 162 (A.B.2650), § 10, operative Jan. 1, 1994.)*

Law Revision Commission Comments

Enactment [Revised Comment]

Section 4601 is new and is drawn from former Civil Code Section 4701.1. This provision is included for drafting convenience. Throughout this chapter the new term has been substituted, without substantive change, for the former specific references to those persons now referred to as the "deposit holder." See, e.g., Sections 4602–4604, 4610, 4616, 4630, 4640–4641. [23 Cal.L.Rev.Comm. Reports 1 (1993)].

Research References

Treatises and Practice Aids

Witkin, California Summary 10th Parent and Child § 430, in General.

§ 4602. Statement of disbursements and receipts by deposit holder

If requested by an obligor-parent, the deposit holder shall prepare a statement setting forth disbursements and receipts made under this chapter. *(Stats.1992, c. 162 (A.B.2650), § 10, operative Jan. 1, 1994.)*

Law Revision Commission Comments

Enactment [Revised Comment]

Section 4602 continues former Civil Code Section 4701.1(g) without substantive change. [23 Cal.L.Rev.Comm. Reports 1 (1993)].

Research References

Treatises and Practice Aids

Witkin, California Summary 10th Parent and Child § 430, in General.

§ 4603. Liability of deposit holder

The deposit holder who is responsible for any money or property and for any disbursements under this chapter is not liable for any action undertaken in good faith and in conformance with this chapter. *(Stats.1992, c. 162 (A.B. 2650), § 10, operative Jan. 1, 1994.)*

Law Revision Commission Comments

Enactment [Revised Comment]

Section 4603 continues former Civil Code Section 4701.1(e) without substantive change. [23 Cal.L.Rev.Comm. Reports 1 (1993)].

Research References

Treatises and Practice Aids

Witkin, California Summary 10th Parent and Child § 430, in General.

§ 4604. Payment of fees and costs of deposit holders; hearing

(a) If the deposit holder incurs fees or costs under this chapter which are not compensated by the deduction under subdivision (c) of Section 4630 (including, but not limited to, fees or costs incurred in a sale of assets pursuant to this chapter and in the preparation of a statement pursuant to Section 4602), the court shall, after a hearing, order the obligor-parent to pay the reasonable fees and costs incurred by the deposit holder. The hearing shall be held not less than 20 days after the deposit holder serves notice of motion or order to show cause upon the obligor-parent.

(b) Fees and costs ordered to be paid under this section shall be in addition to any deposit made under this chapter but shall not exceed whichever of the following is less:

(1) Five percent of one year's child support obligation.

(2) The total amount ordered deposited under Section 4614. *(Stats.1992, c. 162 (A.B.2650), § 10, operative Jan. 1, 1994.)*

Law Revision Commission Comments

Enactment [Revised Comment]

Section 4604 continues former Civil Code Section 4701.1(h) without substantive change. The reference to Section 4614 has been substituted for the former reference to former Civil Code Section 4701.1(a)(1). This is not a substantive change. [23 Cal.L.Rev. Comm. Reports 1 (1993)].

Research References

Treatises and Practice Aids

Witkin, California Summary 10th Parent and Child § 430, in General.

ARTICLE 2. ORDER FOR DEPOSIT OF ASSETS

§ 4610. Notice and hearing; order to deposit assets

(a) Subject to Sections 4613, 4614, and 4615, in any proceeding where the court has ordered either or both parents to pay any amount for the support of a child for whom support may be ordered, upon an order to show cause or notice of motion, application, and declaration signed under penalty of perjury by the person or county officer to whom support has been ordered to have been paid stating that the parent or parents so ordered is in arrears in payment in a sum equal to the amount of 60 days of payments, the court shall issue to the parent or parents ordered to pay support, following notice and opportunity for a hearing, an order requiring that the parent or parents deposit assets to secure future support payments with the deposit holder designated by the court.

(b) In a proceeding under this article, upon request of any party, the court may also issue an ex parte restraining order as specified in Section 4620. *(Stats.1992, c. 162 (A.B.2650), § 10, operative Jan. 1, 1994. Amended by Stats.1993, c. 219 (A.B.1500), § 145.)*

Law Revision Commission Comments

Enactment [Revised Comment]

Section 4610 continues the first two sentences of former Civil Code Section 4701.1(a)(1) without substantive change. The reference to support of a "minor" child has been omitted. This is not a substantive change, but recognizes that in some cases support may be ordered for an adult child. See Sections 58 ("child for whom support may be ordered" defined), 3587 (court order to effectuate agreement for support of adult child), 3901 (duration of duty to support child), 3910 (duty to maintain incapacitated adult child), 4000 (civil action to enforce parent's duty to support child), 4001 (order for child support). [23 Cal.L.Rev.Comm. Reports 1 (1993)].

Research References

Forms

California Transactions Forms--Family Law § 3:49, Deposit Of Assets.

Treatises and Practice Aids

Witkin, California Summary 10th Parent and Child § 430, in General.

Witkin, California Summary 10th Parent and Child § 431, Order for Deposit.

Witkin, California Summary 10th Parent and Child § 434, Ex Parte Restraining Order.

§ 4611. Presumptions; rebuttal

In a proceeding under this chapter, an obligor-parent shall rebut both of the following presumptions:

(a) The nonpayment of child support was willful, without good faith.

(b) The obligor had the ability to pay the support. *(Stats.1992, c. 162 (A.B.2650), § 10, operative Jan. 1, 1994.)*

Law Revision Commission Comments

Enactment [Revised Comment]

Section 4611 continues the next to last paragraph of former Civil Code Section 4701.1(a)(4) without substantive change. [23 Cal. L.Rev.Comm. Reports 1 (1993)].

Research References

Forms

California Transactions Forms--Family Law § 3:49, Deposit Of Assets.

Treatises and Practice Aids

Witkin, California Summary 10th Parent and Child § 430, in General.

§ 4612. Grounds for defense of obligor-parent alleged to be in arrears

An obligor-parent alleged to be in arrears may use any of the following grounds as a defense to the motion filed pursuant to this article or as a basis for filing a motion to stop a sale or use of assets under Section 4631:

(a) Child support payments are not in arrears.

(b) Laches.

(c) There has been a change in the custody of the children.

(d) There is a pending motion for reduction in support due to a reduction in income.

(e) Illness or disability.

(f) Unemployment.

(g) Serious adverse impact on the immediate family of the obligor-parent residing with the obligor-parent that outweighs the impact of denial of the motion or stopping the sale on obligee.

(h) Serious impairment of the ability of the obligor-parent to generate income.

(i) Other emergency conditions. *(Stats.1992, c. 162 (A.B. 2650), § 10, operative Jan. 1, 1994.)*

Law Revision Commission Comments

Enactment [Revised Comment]

Section 4612 restates without substantive change former Civil Code Section 4701.1(a)(4)(A)-(I), including the introductory clause. See also Sections 4011 (priority of child support payments), 4505 (submitting list of places applied for employment where default in support due to unemployment), 4632 (grounds for motion to stop sale or use of asset listed in Section 4612). [23 Cal.L.Rev.Comm. Reports 1 (1993)].

Research References

Forms

California Transactions Forms--Family Law § 3:49, Deposit Of Assets.

Treatises and Practice Aids

Witkin, California Summary 10th Parent and Child § 433, Defenses.

Witkin, California Summary 10th Parent and Child § 435, Use or Sale Of Assets.

§ 4613. Issuance of orders; conditions

The court shall not issue an order pursuant to this article unless the court determines that one or more of the following conditions exist:

(a) The obligor-parent is not receiving salary or wages subject to an assignment pursuant to Chapter 8 (commencing with Section 5200) and there is reason to believe that the obligor-parent has earned income from some source of employment.

(b) An assignment of a portion of salary or wages pursuant to Chapter 8 (commencing with Section 5200) would not be sufficient to meet the amount of the support obligation, for reasons other than a change of circumstances which would qualify for a reduction in the amount of child support ordered.

(c) The job history of the obligor-parent shows that an assignment of a portion of salary or wages pursuant to Chapter 8 (commencing with Section 5200), would be difficult to enforce or would not be a practical means for securing the payment of the support obligation, due to circumstances including, but not limited to, multiple concurrent or consecutive employers. *(Stats.1992, c. 162 (A.B.2650), § 10, operative Jan. 1, 1994.)*

Law Revision Commission Comments

Enactment [Revised Comment]

Section 4613 continues former Civil Code Section 4701.1(b) without substantive change. In the introductory clause, the language has been revised to state that the court may not make the order unless one or more of the conditions are met. This is not a substantive change. [23 Cal.L.Rev.Comm. Reports 1 (1993)].

Research References

Treatises and Practice Aids

Witkin, California Summary 10th Parent and Child § 431, Order for Deposit.

§ 4614. Designation of assets subject to order

The designation of assets subject to an order pursuant to this article shall be based upon concern for maximizing the liquidity and ready conversion into cash of the deposited asset. In all instances, the assets shall include a sum of money up to or equal in value to one year of support payments or six thousand dollars ($6,000) whichever is less, or any other assets, personal or real, designated by the court which equal in value up to one year of payments for support of the child, or six thousand dollars ($6,000), whichever is less, subject to Section 703.070 of the Code of Civil Procedure. *(Stats.1992, c. 162 (A.B.2650), § 10, operative Jan. 1, 1994. Amended by Stats.1993, c. 219 (A.B.1500), § 146.)*

Law Revision Commission Comments

Enactment [Revised Comment]

Section 4614 continues the first two sentences of former Civil Code Section 4701.1(c) without substantive change. The reference to support of a "minor" child has been omitted. This is not a substantive change, but recognizes that in some cases support may be ordered for an adult child. See Sections 58 ("child for whom support may be ordered" defined), 3587 (court order to effectuate agreement for support of adult child), 3901 (duration of duty to support child), 3910 (duty to maintain incapacitated adult child), 4000 (civil action to enforce parent's duty to support child), 4001 (order for child support). [23 Cal.L.Rev.Comm. Reports 1 (1993)].

Research References

Treatises and Practice Aids

Witkin, California Summary 10th Parent and Child § 432, Assets Subject to Order.

§ 4615. Performance bonds

In lieu of depositing cash or other assets as provided in Section 4614, the obligor-parent may, if approved by the court, provide a performance bond secured by real property or other assets of the obligor-parent and equal in value to one year of payments. *(Stats.1992, c. 162 (A.B.2650), § 10, operative Jan. 1, 1994.)*

Law Revision Commission Comments

Enactment [Revised Comment]

Section 4615 continues the last sentence of former Civil Code Section 4701.1(c) without substantive change. [23 Cal.L.Rev.Comm. Reports 1 (1993)].

Research References

Forms

California Transactions Forms--Family Law § 3:49, Deposit Of Assets.

Treatises and Practice Aids

Witkin, California Summary 10th Parent and Child § 430, in General.

§ 4616. Sale of assets; hearing; notice

Upon deposit of an asset which is not readily convertible into money, the court may, after a hearing, order the sale of that asset and the deposit of the proceeds with the deposit holder. Not less than 20 days written notice of the hearing shall be served on the obligor-parent. *(Stats.1992, c. 162 (A.B.2650), § 10, operative Jan. 1, 1994.)*

Law Revision Commission Comments

Enactment [Revised Comment]

Section 4616 restates the third sentence of former Civil Code Section 4701.1(a)(1) without substantive change. The references to "parents" and to "assets" have been omitted as surplus. See Section 10 (singular includes plural). [23 Cal.L.Rev.Comm. Reports 1 (1993)].

Research References

Forms

California Transactions Forms--Family Law § 3:49, Deposit Of Assets.

Treatises and Practice Aids

Witkin, California Summary 10th Parent and Child § 432, Assets Subject to Order.

§ 4617. Deposit of real property; certification of order as abstract of judgment; recordation

(a) If the asset ordered to be deposited is real property, the order shall be certified as an abstract of judgment in accordance with Section 674 of the Code of Civil Procedure.

(b) A deposit of real property is made effective by recordation of the certified abstract with the county recorder.

(c) The deposited real property and the rights, benefits, and liabilities attached to that property shall continue in the possession of the legal owner.

(d) For purposes of Section 701.545 of the Code of Civil Procedure, the date of the issuance of the order to deposit assets shall be construed as the date notice of levy on an interest in real property was served on the judgment debtor. *(Stats.1992, c. 162 (A.B.2650), § 10, operative Jan. 1, 1994.)*

Law Revision Commission Comments

Enactment [Revised Comment]

Section 4617 continues the last four sentences of former Civil Code Section 4701.1(a)(1) without substantive change. [23 Cal.L.Rev. Comm. Reports 1 (1993)].

Research References

Forms

California Transactions Forms--Family Law § 3:49, Deposit Of Assets.

Treatises and Practice Aids

Witkin, California Summary 10th Parent and Child § 432, Assets Subject to Order.

ARTICLE 3. EX PARTE RESTRAINING ORDERS

§ 4620. Issuance of orders; notification and account of extraordinary expenditures; expiration of order

(a) During the pendency of a proceeding under this chapter, upon the application of either party in the manner provided by Part 4 (commencing with Section 240) of Division 2, the court may, without a hearing, issue ex parte orders restraining any person from transferring, encumbering, hypothecating, concealing, or in any way disposing of any property, real or personal, whether community, quasi-community, or separate, except in the usual course of business or for the necessities of life, and if the order is directed against a party, requiring the party to notify the other party of any proposed extraordinary expenditures and to account to the court for all such extraordinary expenditures.

(b) The matter shall be made returnable not later than 20 days, or if good cause appears to the court, 25 days from the date of the order at which time the ex parte order shall expire.

(c) The court, at the hearing, shall determine for which property the obligor-parent shall be required to report extraordinary expenditures and shall specify what is deemed an extraordinary expenditure for purposes of this subdivision.

(d) An order issued pursuant to this section after the hearing shall state on its face the date of expiration of the order, which shall expire in one year or upon deposit of assets or money pursuant to Article 2 (commencing with Section 4610), whichever first occurs. *(Stats.1992, c. 162 (A.B.2650), § 10, operative Jan. 1, 1994.)*

Law Revision Commission Comments

Enactment [Revised Comment]

Section 4620 continues former Civil Code Section 4701.1(d) without substantive change. In subdivision (a), the reference to Part 4 (commencing with Section 240) of Division 2 has been substituted for the former reference to Code of Civil Procedure Section 527. This is not a substantive change, since Part 4 (commencing with Section 240) of Division 2 is drawn from and duplicates the applicable parts of Code of Civil Procedure Section 527.

In subdivision (d), the reference to this section has been substituted for the broader reference to all of former Civil Code Section 4701.1. This revision makes it clear that subdivision (d) only applies to an ex parte order issued under this section. The duration of the order that assets be deposited is specified in Section 4640. [23 Cal.L.Rev.Comm. Reports 1 (1993)].

Research References

Forms

West's California Judicial Council Forms FL-303, Declaration Regarding Notice and Service Of Request for Temporary Emergency (Ex Parte) Orders.

Treatises and Practice Aids

Witkin, California Summary 10th Parent and Child § 431, Order for Deposit.

Witkin, California Summary 10th Parent and Child § 434, Ex Parte Restraining Order.

ARTICLE 4. USE OR SALE OF ASSETS TO MAKE SUPPORT PAYMENTS

§ 4630. Authority to use or sell assets; conduct of sale

(a) Upon an obligor-parent's failure, within the time specified by the court, to make reasonable efforts to cure the default in child support payments or to comply with a court-approved payment plan, if payments continue in arrears, the deposit holder shall, not less than 25 days after providing the obligor-parent or parents with a written notice served personally or with return receipt requested, unless a motion or order to show cause has been filed to stop the use or sale, use the money or sell or otherwise process the deposited assets for an amount sufficient to pay the arrearage and the amount ordered by the court for the support currently due for the child for whom support may be ordered.

(b) Assets deposited pursuant to an order issued under Article 2 (commencing with Section 4610) shall be construed as being assets subject to levy pursuant to Article 6 (commencing with Section 701.510) of Chapter 3 of Division 2 of Title 9 of Part 2 of the Code of Civil Procedure. The sale of assets shall be conducted in accordance with Article 6 (commencing with Section 701.510) and Article 7 (commencing with Section 701.810) of Chapter 3 of Division 2 of Title 9 of Part 2 of the Code of Civil Procedure.

(c) The deposit holder may deduct from the deposited money the sum of one dollar ($1) for each payment made pursuant to this section. *(Stats.1992, c. 162 (A.B.2650), § 10, operative Jan. 1, 1994. Amended by Stats.1993, c. 219 (A.B.1500), § 147.)*

Law Revision Commission Comments

Enactment [Revised Comment]

Section 4630 continues former Civil Code Section 4701.1(a)(2)-(3) without substantive change. In subdivision (a), the reference to the maintenance and education of the minor child has been omitted as surplus. See Section 150 ("support" includes maintenance and education when used in reference to minor child). See also Section 4011 (priority of child support payments). The reference to support of a "minor" child has been omitted. This is not a substantive change, but recognizes that in some cases support may be ordered for an adult child. See Sections 58 ("child for whom support may be ordered" defined), 3587 (court order to effectuate agreement for support of adult child), 3901 (duration of duty to support child), 3910 (duty to maintain incapacitated adult child), 4000 (civil action to enforce parent's duty to support child), 4001 (order for child support). [23 Cal.L.Rev.Comm. Reports 1 (1993)].

Research References

Treatises and Practice Aids

Witkin, California Summary 10th Parent and Child § 430, in General.

Witkin, California Summary 10th Parent and Child § 435, Use or Sale Of Assets.

§ 4631. Motion to stop use or sale of assets; time of hearing

(a) An obligor-parent may file a motion to stop the use of the money or the sale of the asset under this article within 15 days after service of notice on the obligor-parent pursuant to Section 4630.

(b) The clerk of the court shall set the motion for hearing not less than 20 days after service of the notice of motion and the motion on the person or county officer to whom support has been ordered to have been paid. *(Stats.1992, c. 162 (A.B.2650), § 10, operative Jan. 1, 1994.)*

Law Revision Commission Comments

Enactment [Revised Comment]

Section 4631 continues the last paragraph of former Civil Code Section 4701.1(a)(4) without substantive change. [23 Cal.L.Rev. Comm. Reports 1 (1993)].

Research References

Treatises and Practice Aids

Witkin, California Summary 10th Parent and Child § 433, Defenses.
Witkin, California Summary 10th Parent and Child § 435, Use or Sale Of Assets.

§ 4632. Grounds for filing motion to stop sale or use of assets

An obligor-parent alleged to be in arrears under this article may use any ground set forth in Section 4612 as a basis for filing a motion under Section 4631 to stop a sale or use of assets under this article. *(Stats.1992, c. 162 (A.B.2650), § 10, operative Jan. 1, 1994.)*

Law Revision Commission Comments

Enactment [Revised Comment]

Section 4632 is new and is drawn from the part of former Civil Code Section 4701.1(a) that is continued in Section 4612. See also Section 4011 (priority of child support payments). [23 Cal.L.Rev. Comm. Reports 1 (1993)].

Research References

Treatises and Practice Aids

Witkin, California Summary 10th Parent and Child § 435, Use or Sale Of Assets.

ARTICLE 5. RETURN OF ASSETS OF OBLIGOR

§ 4640. Conditions for return of assets

The deposit holder shall return all assets subject to court order under Article 2 (commencing with Section 4610) to the obligor-parent when both of the following occur:

(a) One year has elapsed since the court issued the order described under Article 2 (commencing with Section 4610).

(b) The obligor-parent has made all support payments on time during that one-year period. *(Stats.1992, c. 162 (A.B. 2650), § 10, operative Jan. 1, 1994.)*

Law Revision Commission Comments

Enactment [Revised Comment]

Section 4640 continues without substantive change former Civil Code Section 4701.1(f)(1)-(2), including the introductory clause. References to "parents" have been omitted as surplus. See Section 10 (singular includes plural). [23 Cal.L.Rev.Comm. Reports 1 (1993)].

Research References

Treatises and Practice Aids

Witkin, California Summary 10th Parent and Child § 431, Order for Deposit.

§ 4641. Release of real property; duties of deposit holder

If the deposited asset is real property and the requirements of Section 4640 have been satisfied, the deposit holder shall do all of the following:

(a) Prepare a release in accordance with Section 697.370 of the Code of Civil Procedure.

(b) Request the clerk of the court where the order to deposit assets was made to certify the release.

(c) Record the certified release in the office of the county recorder where the certified abstract was recorded under Section 4617. *(Stats.1992, c. 162 (A.B.2650), § 10, operative Jan. 1, 1994.)*

Law Revision Commission Comments

Enactment [Revised Comment]

Section 4641 continues the last paragraph of former Civil Code Section 4701.1(f) without substantive change. Revisions to the former section make clear that the deposit holder, and not the court clerk, has the duty to record the certified release. In subdivision (c), language has been added to make clear where the certified release must be recorded. [23 Cal.L.Rev.Comm. Reports 1 (1993)].

Research References

Forms

California Transactions Forms--Family Law § 3:49, Deposit Of Assets.

Treatises and Practice Aids

Witkin, California Summary 10th Parent and Child § 431, Order for Deposit.

CHAPTER 4. CHILD SUPPORT DELINQUENCY REPORTING

§ 4700. Short title

This chapter may be cited as the Child Support Delinquency Reporting Law. *(Stats.1992, c. 162 (A.B.2650), § 10, operative Jan. 1, 1994.)*

Law Revision Commission Comments

Enactment [Revised Comment]

Section 4700 replaces former Civil Code Section 4750. The title of the former statute was "Child Support Delinquency Reporting Act of 1984." [23 Cal.L.Rev.Comm. Reports 1 (1993)].

Research References

Treatises and Practice Aids

Witkin, California Summary 10th Husband and Wife § 174, in General.

Witkin, California Summary 10th Parent and Child § 427, Collection Of Information About Support Obligations.

§ 4701. Statewide automated system for reporting

(a) The Department of Child Support Services shall administer a statewide automated system for the reporting of court-ordered child support obligations to credit reporting agencies.

(b) The department shall design and develop standards for the system in conjunction with representatives of the California Family Support Council and the credit reporting industry.

(c) The standards for the system shall be consistent with credit reporting industry standards and reporting format and with the department's statewide central automated system for support enforcement.

(d) The standards shall include, but not be limited to, all of the following:

(1) Court–ordered child support obligations and delinquent payments, including amounts owed and by whom. The California local child support agencies, on a monthly basis, shall update this information, and then submit it to the department which, in turn, shall consolidate and transmit it to the credit reporting agencies.

(2) Before the initial reporting of a court-ordered child support obligation or a delinquent payment, the local child support agency shall attempt to notify the obligor parent of the proposed action and give 30 days to contest in writing the accuracy of the information, or to pay the arrearage, if any, in compliance with the due process requirements of the laws of this state.

(e) The department and the local child support agencies are responsible for the accuracy of information provided pursuant to this section, and the information shall be based upon the data available at the time the information is provided. Each of these organizations and the credit reporting agencies shall follow reasonable procedures to ensure maximum possible accuracy of the information provided. Neither the department, nor the local child support agencies are liable for any consequences of the failure of a parent to contest the accuracy of the information within the time allowed under paragraph (2) of subdivision (d). *(Stats.1992, c. 162 (A.B.2650), § 10, operative Jan. 1, 1994. Amended by Stats.2000, c. 808 (A.B.1358), § 48, eff. Sept. 28, 2000.)*

Law Revision Commission Comments

Enactment [Revised Comment]

Section 4701 restates former Civil Code Section 4752 without substantive change. The parts of the former section that were temporary or transitional in nature have been omitted. Federal law contains provisions for the program provided in this section. See Pub. L. No. 98–378, Aug. 16, 1984. See also Section 4011 (priority of child support payments). [23 Cal.L.Rev.Comm. Reports 1 (1993)].

Research References

Treatises and Practice Aids

Witkin, California Summary 10th Husband and Wife § 174, in General.

Witkin, California Summary 10th Parent and Child § 427, Collection Of Information About Support Obligations.

CHAPTER 5. CIVIL PENALTY FOR CHILD SUPPORT DELINQUENCY

§ 4720. "Support" defined

"Support" for the purposes of this chapter means support as defined in Section 150. *(Stats.1992, c. 162 (A.B.2650), § 10, operative Jan. 1, 1994.)*

Law Revision Commission Comments

Enactment [Revised Comment]

Section 4720 continues former Civil Code Section 4700.11(m) without substantive change. [23 Cal.L.Rev.Comm. Reports 1 (1993)].

Research References

Forms

California Practice Guide: Rutter Family Law Forms Form 6:19, Request for Order to Determine Arrearages and to Show Cause Why Family Code S4720 et seq. Penalties Should Not be Imposed.

West's California Judicial Council Forms FL-485, Notice Of Delinquency.

West's California Judicial Council Forms FL-490, Application to Determine Arrearages.

Treatises and Practice Aids

Witkin, California Summary 10th Husband and Wife § 174, in General.

Witkin, California Summary 10th Husband and Wife § 288A, (New) Activation and Out-Of-State Deployment Of Military Service Member.

Witkin, California Summary 10th Parent and Child § 426, Action by Child or Parent.

Witkin, California Summary 10th Parent and Child § 436, Civil Penalty for Child Support Delinquency.

§ 4721. Application of chapter; legislative intent; timely payments

(a) This chapter applies only to installments of child support that are due on or after January 1, 1992.

(b) It is the intent of the Legislature that the penalties provided under this chapter shall be applied in egregious instances of noncompliance with child support orders.

(c) It is the intent of the Legislature that for the purposes of this chapter, payments made through wage assignments are considered timely regardless of the date of receipt by the local child support agency or obligee. *(Stats.1992, c. 162 (A.B.2650), § 10, operative Jan. 1, 1994. Amended by Stats. 1994, c. 959 (A.B.3072), § 2, eff. Sept. 28, 1994; Stats.2000, c. 808 (A.B.1358), § 49, eff. Sept. 28, 2000.)*

Law Revision Commission Comments

Enactment [Revised Comment]

Section 4721 continues former Civil Code Section 4700.11(k) without substantive change. [23 Cal.L.Rev.Comm. Reports 1 (1993)].

Research References

Treatises and Practice Aids

Witkin, California Summary 10th Parent and Child § 436, Civil Penalty for Child Support Delinquency.

§ 4722. Notice of delinquency; penalties

(a) Any person with a court order for child support, the payments on which are more than 30 days in arrears, may file and then serve a notice of delinquency, as described in this chapter.

(b) Except as provided in Section 4726, and subject to Section 4727, any amount of child support specified in a notice of delinquency that remains unpaid for more than 30 days after the notice of delinquency has been filed and served shall incur a penalty of 6 percent of the delinquent payment for each month that it remains unpaid, up to a maximum of 72 percent of the unpaid balance due. *(Stats.1992, c. 162 (A.B.2650), § 10, operative Jan. 1, 1994.)*

Law Revision Commission Comments

Enactment [Revised Comment]

Section 4722 continues former Civil Code Section 4700.11(a) without substantive change. The reference to Section 4727 has been added. This is not a substantive change. [23 Cal.L.Rev.Comm. Reports 1 (1993)].

Commentary

In re Marriage of De Prieto, 104 Cal.App.4th 748, 128 Cal.Rptr.2d 380 (2002), holds that when child support remains unpaid for more than 30 days after service of a notice of delinquency, the trial court, in ruling on a § 4726 motion, may exercise its discretion to reduce the penalty in the interests of justice. Under § 4726, the trial court is not required to apply either the entire penalty or no penalty at all.

Research References

Forms

West's California Code Forms, Family § 4720, Comment Overview--Civil Penalty for Child Support Delinquency.

Treatises and Practice Aids

Witkin, California Summary 10th Parent and Child § 436, Civil Penalty for Child Support Delinquency.

§ 4723. Execution and contents of notice

(a) The notice of delinquency shall be signed under penalty of perjury by the support obligee.

(b) The notice of delinquency shall state all of the following:

(1) The amount that the child support obligor is in arrears.

(2) The installments of support due, the amounts, if any, that have been paid, and the balance due.

(3) That any unpaid installment of child support will incur a penalty of 6 percent of the unpaid support per month until paid, to a maximum of 72 percent of the original amount of the unpaid support, unless the support arrearage is paid within 30 days of the date of service of the notice of delinquency.

(c) In the absence of a protective order prohibiting the support obligor from knowing the whereabouts of the child or children for whom support is payable, or otherwise excusing the requirements of this subdivision, the notice of delinquency shall also include a current address and telephone number of all of the children for whom support is due and, if different from that of the support obligee, the address at which court papers may be served upon the support obligee. *(Stats.1992, c. 162 (A.B.2650), § 10, operative Jan. 1, 1994.)*

Law Revision Commission Comments

Enactment [Revised Comment]

Subdivisions (a) and (b) of Section 4723 continue former Civil Code Section 4700.11(b) without substantive change. Subdivision (c) continues former Civil Code Section 4700.11(g) without substantive change. [23 Cal.L.Rev.Comm. Reports 1 (1993)].

Research References

Treatises and Practice Aids

Witkin, California Summary 10th Parent and Child § 436, Civil Penalty for Child Support Delinquency.

§ 4724. Service of notice

The notice of delinquency may be served personally or by certified mail or in any manner provided for service of summons. *(Stats.1992, c. 162 (A.B.2650), § 10, operative Jan. 1, 1994.)*

Law Revision Commission Comments

Enactment [Revised Comment]

Section 4724 continues former Civil Code Section 4700.11(c) without substantive change. [23 Cal.L.Rev.Comm. Reports 1 (1993)].

Research References

Treatises and Practice Aids

Witkin, California Summary 10th Parent and Child § 436, Civil Penalty for Child Support Delinquency.

§ 4725. Motion for judgment; enforcement

If the child support owed, or any arrearages, interest, or penalty, remains unpaid more than 30 days after serving the notice of delinquency, the support obligee may file a motion to obtain a judgment for the amount owed, which shall be enforceable in any manner provided by law for the enforcement of judgments. *(Stats.1992, c. 162 (A.B.2650), § 10, operative Jan. 1, 1994.)*

Law Revision Commission Comments

Enactment [Revised Comment]

Section 4725 continues former Civil Code Section 4700.11(e) without substantive change. [23 Cal.L.Rev.Comm. Reports 1 (1993)].

Research References

Treatises and Practice Aids

Witkin, California Summary 10th Parent and Child § 436, Civil Penalty for Child Support Delinquency.

§ 4726. Penalties; exceptions

No penalties may be imposed pursuant to this chapter if, in the discretion of the court, all of the following conditions are met:

(a) Within a timely fashion after service of the notice of delinquency, the support obligor files and serves a motion to determine arrearages and to show cause why the penalties provided in this chapter should not be imposed.

(b) At the hearing on the motion filed by the support obligor, the court finds that the support obligor has proved any of the following:

(1) The child support payments were not 30 days in arrears as of the date of service of the notice of delinquency and are not in arrears as of the date of the hearing.

(2) The support obligor suffered serious illness, disability, or unemployment which substantially impaired the ability of the support obligor to comply fully with the support order and the support obligor has made every possible effort to comply with the support order.

(3) The support obligor is a public employee and for reasons relating to fiscal difficulties of the employing entity the obligor has not received a paycheck for 30 or more days.

(4) It would not be in the interests of justice to impose a penalty. *(Stats.1992, c. 162 (A.B.2650), § 10, operative Jan. 1, 1994.)*

Law Revision Commission Comments

Enactment [Revised Comment]

Section 4726 continues former Civil Code Section 4700.11(d) without substantive change. [23 Cal.L.Rev.Comm. Reports 1 (1993)].

Commentary

In re Marriage of De Prieto, 104 Cal.App.4th 748, 128 Cal.Rptr.2d 380 (2002), holds that when, under § 4722, child support remains unpaid for more than 30 days after service of a notice of delinquency, the trial court, in ruling on a motion brought under this section, may exercise its discretion to reduce the penalty in the interests of justice. The trial court is not required to apply either the entire penalty or no penalty at all.

Research References

Forms

California Practice Guide: Rutter Family Law Forms Form 6:19, Request for Order to Determine Arrearages and to Show Cause Why Family Code S4720 et seq. Penalties Should Not be Imposed.

West's California Code Forms, Family § 4720, Comment Overview--Civil Penalty for Child Support Delinquency.

Treatises and Practice Aids

Witkin, California Summary 10th Parent and Child § 436, Civil Penalty for Child Support Delinquency.

§ 4727. Amount of penalties

Any penalty due under this chapter shall not be greater than 6 percent per month of the original amount of support arrearages or support installment, nor may the penalties on any arrearage amount or support installment exceed 72 percent of the original amount due, regardless of whether or not the installments have been listed on more than one notice of delinquency. *(Stats.1992, c. 162 (A.B.2650), § 10, operative Jan. 1, 1994.)*

Law Revision Commission Comments

Enactment [Revised Comment]

Section 4727 continues the last sentence of former Civil Code Section 4700.11(h) without substantive change. [23 Cal.L.Rev. Comm. Reports 1 (1993)].

Research References

Forms

West's California Code Forms, Family § 4720, Comment Overview--Civil Penalty for Child Support Delinquency.

Treatises and Practice Aids

Witkin, California Summary 10th Parent and Child § 436, Civil Penalty for Child Support Delinquency.

§ 4728. Enforcement of penalties; priorities

Penalties due pursuant to this chapter may be enforced by the issuance of a writ of execution in the same manner as a writ of execution may be issued for unpaid installments of child support, as described in Chapter 7 (commencing with Section 5100), except that payment of penalties under this chapter may not take priority over payment of arrearages or current support. *(Stats.1992, c. 162 (A.B.2650), § 10, operative Jan. 1, 1994.)*

Law Revision Commission Comments

Enactment [Revised Comment]

Section 4728 continues former Civil Code Section 4700.11(i) without substantive change. See also Section 3557 (attorney's fees in action to enforce penalty). [23 Cal.L.Rev.Comm. Reports 1 (1993)].

Research References

Treatises and Practice Aids

Witkin, California Summary 10th Parent and Child § 436, Civil Penalty for Child Support Delinquency.

§ 4729. Enforcement of child support obligations by local child support agency or other agency

The local child support agency or any other agency providing support enforcement services pursuant to Title IV–D of the federal Social Security Act may not enforce child support obligations utilizing the penalties provided for by this chapter. *(Stats.1992, c. 162 (A.B.2650), § 10, operative Jan. 1, 1994. Amended by Stats.1993, c. 219 (A.B.1500), § 148;*

Stats.1994, c. 959 (A.B.3072), § 3, eff. Sept. 28, 1994; Stats. 2000, c. 808 (A.B.1358), § 50, eff. Sept. 28, 2000.)

Law Revision Commission Comments

Enactment [Revised Comment]

Section 4729 continues former Civil Code Section 4700.11(*l*) without substantive change. [23 Cal.L.Rev.Comm. Reports 1 (1993)].

Research References

Treatises and Practice Aids

Witkin, California Summary 10th Parent and Child § 436, Civil Penalty for Child Support Delinquency.

§ 4730. Hearings to set or modify amount of child support; consideration of penalties

At any hearing to set or modify the amount payable for the support of a child, the court shall not consider any penalties imposed under this chapter in determining the amount of current support to be paid. *(Stats.1992, c. 162 (A.B.2650), § 10, operative Jan. 1, 1994. Amended by Stats.1993, c. 219 (A.B.1500), § 149.)*

Law Revision Commission Comments

Enactment [Revised Comment]

Section 4730 continues former Civil Code Section 4700.11(f) without substantive change. The reference to support of a "minor" child has been omitted. This is not a substantive change, but recognizes that in some cases support may be ordered for an adult child. See Sections 58 ("child for whom support may be ordered" defined), 3587 (court order to effectuate agreement for support of adult child), 3901 (duration of duty to support child), 3910 (duty to maintain incapacitated adult child), 4000 (civil action to enforce parent's duty to support child), 4001 (order for child support). [23 Cal.L.Rev.Comm. Reports 1 (1993)].

Research References

Treatises and Practice Aids

Witkin, California Summary 10th Parent and Child § 436, Civil Penalty for Child Support Delinquency.

§ 4731. Subsequent notices of delinquency

A subsequent notice of delinquency may be served and filed at any time. The subsequent notice shall indicate those child support arrearages and ongoing installments that have been listed on a previous notice. *(Stats.1992, c. 162 (A.B. 2650), § 10, operative Jan. 1, 1994.)*

Law Revision Commission Comments

Enactment [Revised Comment]

Section 4731 continues the first two sentences of former Civil Code Section 4700.11(h) without substantive change. [23 Cal.L.Rev. Comm. Reports 1 (1993)].

Research References

Treatises and Practice Aids

Witkin, California Summary 10th Parent and Child § 436, Civil Penalty for Child Support Delinquency.

§ 4732. Adoption of forms or notices by Judicial Counsel

The Judicial Council shall adopt forms or notices for the use of the procedures provided by this chapter. *(Stats.1992, c. 162 (A.B.2650), § 10, operative Jan. 1, 1994.)*

Law Revision Commission Comments

Enactment [Revised Comment]

Section 4732 continues former Civil Code Section 4700.11(j) without substantive change. [23 Cal.L.Rev.Comm. Reports 1 (1993)].

Research References

Forms

West's California Judicial Council Forms FL-490, Application to Determine Arrearages.

§ 4733. Penalties; payment to custodian of child

Penalties collected pursuant to this chapter shall be paid to the custodian of the child who is the subject of the child support judgment or order, whether or not the child is a recipient of public assistance. *(Added by Stats.1993, c. 219 (A.B.1500), § 150.)*

Law Revision Commission Comments

Enactment [Revised Comment]

Section 4733 continues former Civil Code Section 4700.11(n) without substantive change. The former reference to "children" is omitted as surplus. See Section 10 (singular includes plural). The former reference to a decree is omitted as surplus. See Section 100 ("judgment" includes decree, as appropriate). [23 Cal.L.Rev.Comm. Reports 1 (1993)].

Research References

Forms

West's California Judicial Council Forms FL-485, Notice Of Delinquency.

Treatises and Practice Aids

Witkin, California Summary 10th Parent and Child § 436, Civil Penalty for Child Support Delinquency.

CHAPTER 7. ENFORCEMENT BY WRIT OF EXECUTION

§ 5100. Enforcement of support orders without prior court approval

Notwithstanding Section 290, a child, family, or spousal support order may be enforced by a writ of execution or a notice of levy pursuant to Section 706.030 of the Code of Civil Procedure or Section 17522 of this code without prior court approval. *(Stats.1992, c. 162 (A.B.2650), § 10, operative Jan. 1, 1994. Amended by Stats.1993, c. 876 (S.B.1068), § 21, eff. Oct. 6, 1993, operative Jan. 1, 1994; Stats.1994, c. 1269 (A.B.2208), § 49.2; Stats.1997, c. 599 (A.B.573), § 19; Stats.2000, c. 808 (A.B.1358), § 54, eff. Sept. 28, 2000.)*

Law Revision Commission Comments

Enactment [Revised Comment]

Section 5100 supersedes the first sentence of former Civil Code Section 4383(a). The former references to both "judgment" and "decree" have been omitted as surplus. See Sections 100 ("order" includes decree, as appropriate), 155 ("support order" means judgment or order of support).

See also Sections 150 ("support" includes maintenance and education when used in reference to minor child), 3557 (attorney's fees and costs for enforcement of support order), 4011 (priority of child support payments), 4500 (support orders enforceable under this code), 4502 (exception to renewal requirement); Code Civ. Proc. § 683.130 (renewal of judgment). For a similar rule relating to spousal support, see Section 5101 (enforcement of spousal support without prior court approval).

For background on former Civ. Code § 4383, see *Tentative Recommendation Proposing the Enforcement of Judgments Law,* 15 Cal. L. Revision Comm'n Reports 2001, 2616 (1980). [23 Cal.L.Rev. Comm. Reports 1 (1993)].

2000 Amendment

Section 5100 is amended to change the introductory "notwithstanding" clause to refer to Section 290 instead of Section 291. Section 290 provides the general rule concerning judicial discretion in enforcing judgments under the Family Code to which this section is an exception. Additionally, former Section 291 has been repealed and replaced by a new Section 291 that is not relevant to this section.

The scope of this section has been expanded to cover enforcement of spousal support, formerly governed by Section 5101. This is not a substantive change. Separate treatment of spousal support became unnecessary when the rules governing support enforcement were unified. See Sections 290, 290, 4502.

The erroneous reference to former Welfare and Institutions Code Section 11350.7 (repealed by 1999 Cal. Stat. ch. 478, §15) has been corrected. [30 Cal.L.Rev.Comm.Reports 717 (2000)].

Research References

Forms

California Practice Guide: Rutter Family Law Forms Form 18:7, Application for Issuance Of Writ Of Execution (Family Code S5100 et seq.).

West's California Code Forms, Family § 5104, Comment Overview--Enforcement by Writ Of Execution.

Treatises and Practice Aids

Witkin, California Summary 10th Husband and Wife § 174, in General.

Witkin, California Summary 10th Husband and Wife § 206, Other Remedies.

Witkin, California Summary 10th Husband and Wife § 262, in General.

Witkin, California Summary 10th Husband and Wife § 276, Retroactive Modification.

Witkin, California Summary 10th Parent and Child § 436, Civil Penalty for Child Support Delinquency.

§ 5103. Enforcement of support against employee pension benefit plan

(a) Notwithstanding Section 2060, an order for the payment of child, family, or spousal support may be enforced against an employee benefit plan regardless of whether the plan has been joined as a party to the proceeding in which the support order was obtained.

(b) Notwithstanding Section 697.710 of the Code of Civil Procedure, an execution lien created by a levy on the judgment debtor's right to payment of benefits from an employee benefit plan to enforce an order for the payment of child, family, or spousal support continues until the date the plan has withheld and paid over to the levying officer, as provided in Section 701.010 of the Code of Civil Procedure, the full amount specified in the notice of levy, unless the plan is directed to stop withholding and paying over before that time by court order or by the levying officer.

(c) A writ of execution pursuant to which a levy is made on the judgment debtor's right to payment of benefits from an employee benefit plan under an order for the payment of child, family, or spousal support shall be returned not later than one year after the date the execution lien expires under subdivision (b). *(Stats.1992, c. 162 (A.B.2650), § 10, operative Jan. 1, 1994. Amended by Stats.1994, c. 1269 (A.B.2208), § 50.)*

Law Revision Commission Comments

Enactment [Revised Comment]

Subdivisions (a) and (b) of Section 5103 continue the last two sentences of former Civil Code Section 4383(a) without substantive change. The former references to both "judgment" and "decree" have been omitted as surplus. See Sections 100 ("order" includes decree, as appropriate), 155 ("support order" means judgment or order of support). In subdivision (a), "the proceeding in which the support order was obtained" has been substituted for "a proceeding under this part," meaning the former Family Law Act, former Part 5 (commencing with former Section 4000) of Division 4 of the Civil Code. In subdivisions (a) and (b), references to "family" support are new and are consistent with the rule stated in Section 4501. See Section 4501 (family support order enforceable in same manner and to same extent as child support order).

Subdivision (c) continues former Civil Code Section 4383(c) without substantive change. See also Sections 80 ("employee pension benefit plan" defined), 3557 (attorney's fees and costs for enforcement of support order), 4011 (priority of child support payments).

For background on former Civ. Code § 4383, see *Tentative Recommendation Proposing the Enforcement of Judgments Law,* 15 Cal. L. Revision Comm'n Reports 2001, 2616 (1980). [23 Cal.L.Rev. Comm. Reports 1 (1993)].

Research References

Forms

West's California Code Forms, Family § 2060, Comment Overview--Application and Order for Joinder.

Treatises and Practice Aids

Witkin, California Summary 10th Husband and Wife § 79, in General.

Witkin, California Summary 10th Husband and Wife § 262, in General.

Witkin, California Summary 10th Husband and Wife § 264, Enforcement Against Employee Benefit Plan.

§ 5104. Application for writ

(a) The application for a writ of execution shall be accompanied by an affidavit stating the total amount due and unpaid that is authorized to be enforced pursuant to Sections 5100 to 5103, inclusive, on the date of the application.

(b) If interest on the overdue installments is sought, the affidavit shall state the total amount of the interest and the amount of each due and unpaid installment and the date it became due.

(c) The affidavit shall be filed in the action and a copy shall be attached to the writ of execution delivered to the levying officer. The levying officer shall serve the copy of the affidavit on the judgment debtor when the writ of execution is first served on the judgment debtor pursuant to a levy under the writ. *(Stats.1992, c. 162 (A.B.2650), § 10, operative Jan. 1, 1994.)*

Law Revision Commission Comments

Enactment [Revised Comment]

Section 5104 continues subdivision (b) of former Civil Code Section 4383 without substantive change. This section provides technical requirements that must be complied with in addition to the general provisions governing execution. The affidavit provides the court clerk with the information needed to issue the writ and informs the judgment debtor concerning the nature of the debt sought to be collected. If no interest is sought on the amount due and unpaid, the affidavit need state only the total amount. If interest is sought, the affidavit need state only the total amount of interest and also state the amount of each unpaid installment and the date it became due so that the judgment debtor can verify that the interest was accurately computed. See also Sections 3557 (attorney's fees and costs for enforcement of support order), 4502 (exception to renewal requirement); Code Civ. Proc. § 683.130 (renewal of judgment).

For background on former Civ. Code § 4383, see *Tentative Recommendation Proposing the Enforcement of Judgments Law,* 15 Cal. L. Revision Comm'n Reports 2001, 2616 (1980). [23 Cal.L.Rev. Comm. Reports 1 (1993)].

Research References

Forms

California Practice Guide: Rutter Family Law Forms Form 18:7, Application for Issuance Of Writ Of Execution (Family Code S5100 et seq.).

West's California Code Forms, Family § 5104, Comment Overview--Enforcement by Writ Of Execution.

Treatises and Practice Aids

Witkin, California Summary 10th Husband and Wife § 262, in General.

CHAPTER 8. EARNINGS ASSIGNMENT ORDER

ARTICLE 1. DEFINITIONS

§ 5200. Construction of chapter

Unless the provision or context otherwise requires, the definitions in this article govern the construction of this chapter. *(Stats.1992, c. 162 (A.B.2650), § 10, operative Jan. 1, 1994.)*

Law Revision Commission Comments

Enactment [Revised Comment]

Section 5200 continues the introductory clause of former Civil Code Section 4390 without substantive change. For additional definitions of terms used in this chapter, see, e.g., Section 150 ("support" defined). [23 Cal.L.Rev.Comm. Reports 1 (1993)].

Research References

Forms

Cal. Transaction Forms - Bus. Transactions § 16:83, Exclusions.

Treatises and Practice Aids

Witkin, California Summary 10th Husband and Wife § 174, in General.

Witkin, California Summary 10th Husband and Wife § 206, Other Remedies.

Witkin, California Summary 10th Husband and Wife § 249, in General.

Witkin, California Summary 10th Husband and Wife § 250, Definitions.

Witkin, California Summary 10th Husband and Wife § 253, Rights and Obligations Of Employer.

Witkin, California Summary 10th Husband and Wife § 270, Registration by Local Child Support Agency.

Witkin, California Summary 10th Husband and Wife § 271, Registration by Obligee.

Witkin, California Summary 10th Husband and Wife § 310, Local Child Support Agency.

§ 5201. "Arrearage" or "arrearages" defined

"Arrearage" or "arrearages" is the amount necessary to satisfy a support judgment or order pursuant to Section 695.210 of the Code of Civil Procedure. *(Added by Stats. 1997, c. 599 (A.B.573), § 21.)*

Research References

Treatises and Practice Aids

Witkin, California Summary 10th Husband and Wife § 250, Definitions.

§ 5202. Assignment order; earnings assignment order for support

"Assignment order" has the same meaning as "earnings assignment order for support." *(Stats.1992, c. 162 (A.B. 2650), § 10, operative Jan. 1, 1994.)*

Law Revision Commission Comments

Enactment [Revised Comment]

Section 5202 restates former Civil Code Section 4390(a) without substantive change. See also Section 5208 ("earnings assignment order for support" defined). [23 Cal.L.Rev.Comm. Reports 1 (1993)].

Research References

Treatises and Practice Aids

Witkin, California Summary 10th Husband and Wife § 250, Definitions.

§ 5204. "Due date of support payments" defined

"Due date of support payments" is the date specifically stated in the order of support or, if no date is stated in the support order, the last day of the month in which the support payment is to be paid. *(Stats.1992, c. 162 (A.B.2650), § 10, operative Jan. 1, 1994.)*

Law Revision Commission Comments

Enactment [Revised Comment]

Section 5204 continues former Civil Code Section 4390(b) without substantive change. [23 Cal.L.Rev.Comm. Reports 1 (1993)].

Research References

Treatises and Practice Aids

Witkin, California Summary 10th Husband and Wife § 250, Definitions.

§ 5206. "Earnings" defined

"Earnings," to the extent that they are subject to an earnings assignment order for support under Chapter 4 (commencing with Section 703.010) of Division 2 of Title 9 of Part 2 of the Code of Civil Procedure, include:

(a) Wages, salary, bonus, money, and benefits described in Sections 704.110, 704.113, and 704.115 of the Code of Civil Procedure.

(b) Payments due for services of independent contractors, interest, dividends, rents, royalties, residuals, patent rights, or mineral or other natural resource rights.

(c) Payments or credits due or becoming due as a result of written or oral contracts for services or sales whether denominated as wages, salary, commission, bonus, or otherwise.

(d) Payments due for workers' compensation temporary disability benefits.

(e) Payments due as a result of disability from benefits described in Section 704.130 of the Code of Civil Procedure.

(f) Any other payments or credits due or becoming due, regardless of source. *(Stats.1992, c. 162 (A.B.2650), § 10, operative Jan. 1, 1994. Amended by Stats.1993, c. 219 (A.B.1500), § 152.5; Stats.1997, c. 599 (A.B.573), § 22.)*

Law Revision Commission Comments

Enactment [Revised Comment]

Section 5206 continues former Civil Code Section 4390(c) without substantive change. In subdivision (c), the reference to payments "or" credits was substituted for consistency with subdivision (e). In subdivision (d), the reference to "[a]ny" payments is omitted as surplus. This is not a substantive change. [23 Cal.L.Rev.Comm. Reports 1 (1993)].

Commentary

Although subsection (d) includes "workers' compensation temporary disability benefits," *In re Marriage of Johnson–Wilkes & Wilkes, 48 Cal.App.4th 1569, 56 Cal.Rptr.2d 323 (1996), review denied November 20, 1996*, holds that benefits from a disability insurance policy are exempt from an earnings assignment order to enforce support because Code of Civil Procedure Sections 703.070(b) and 704.130(a) provide that "benefits from a disability ... insurance policy" are exempt from an assignment order.

Research References

Treatises and Practice Aids

Witkin, California Summary 10th Husband and Wife § 250, Definitions.

§ 5208. "Earnings assignment order for support" defined

(a) "Earnings assignment order for support" means an order that assigns to an obligee a portion of the earnings of a support obligor due or to become due in the future.

(b) Commencing January 1, 2000, all earnings assignment orders for support in any action in which child support or family support is ordered shall be issued on an "order/notice to withhold income for child support" mandated by Section 666 of Title 42 of the United States Code. *(Stats.1992, c. 162 (A.B.2650), § 10, operative Jan. 1, 1994. Amended by Stats. 1999, c. 480 (S.B.542), § 1.)*

Law Revision Commission Comments

Enactment [Revised Comment]

Section 5208 is new and is drawn from the first sentence of former Civil Code Section 4390.3(a). This section is based on the concept that the assignment order operates without the need for the obligor to make an assignment to the obligee. This section supersedes the last sentence of former Civil Code Section 4390.5(c). See also Section 5202 ("assignment order" has same meaning as "earnings assignment order for support").

Throughout this chapter references to "earnings assignment order for support" or to "assignment order" have been substituted, without substantive change, for former references to wage assignments and earnings assignments. See, e.g., Sections 5202, 5206, 5230–5231, 5235–5236, 5240, 5242, 5250–5252, 5260, 5270–5271, 5281–5282, 5295. [23 Cal.L.Rev.Comm. Reports 1 (1993)].

Research References

Forms

California Practice Guide: Rutter Family Law Forms Form 1:32, Glossary Of Common Family Law Terms, Phrases and Concepts (Enclosure to Form 1:31).

West's California Judicial Council Forms FL-435, Earnings Assignment Order for Spousal or Partner Support.

West's California Judicial Council Forms FL-460, Qualified Domestic Relations Order for Support.

West's California Judicial Council Forms FL-461, Attachment to Qualified Domestic Relations Order for Support.

Treatises and Practice Aids

Witkin, California Summary 10th Husband and Wife § 249, in General.

Witkin, California Summary 10th Husband and Wife § 250, Definitions.

§ 5210. "Employer" defined

"Employer" includes all of the following:

(a) A person for whom an individual performs services as an employee, as defined in Section 706.011 of the Code of Civil Procedure.

(b) The United States government and any public entity as defined in Section 811.2 of the Government Code.

(c) Any person or entity paying earnings as defined under Section 5206. *(Stats.1992, c. 162 (A.B.2650), § 10, operative Jan. 1, 1994.)*

Law Revision Commission Comments

Enactment [Revised Comment]

Section 5210 continues former Civil Code Section 4390(d) without substantive change. [23 Cal.L.Rev.Comm. Reports 1 (1993)].

Research References

Treatises and Practice Aids

Witkin, California Summary 10th Husband and Wife § 250, Definitions.

Witkin, California Summary 10th Husband and Wife § 314, Acquisition and Confidentiality Of Information.

§ 5212. "IV–D Case" defined

"IV–D Case" means any case being established, modified, or enforced by the local child support agency pursuant to Section 654 of Title 42 of the United States Code (Section 454 of the Social Security Act). *(Stats.1992, c. 162 (A.B. 2650), § 10, operative Jan. 1, 1994. Amended by Stats.1999, c. 480 (S.B.542), § 2.)*

Law Revision Commission Comments

Enactment [Revised Comment]

Section 5212 continues former Civil Code Section 4390(e) without change. [23 Cal.L.Rev.Comm. Reports 1 (1993)].

Research References

Treatises and Practice Aids

Witkin, California Summary 10th Husband and Wife § 250, Definitions.

§ 5214. "Obligee" or "assigned obligee" defined

"Obligee" or "assigned obligee" means either the person to whom support has been ordered to be paid, the local child support agency, or other person designated by the court to receive the payment. The local child support agency is the obligee for all Title IV–D cases as defined under Section 5212 or in which an application for services has been filed under Part D (commencing with Section 651) and Part E (commencing with Section 670) of Subchapter IV of Chapter 7 of Title 42 of the United States Code (Title IV–D or IV–E of the Social Security Act). *(Stats.1992, c. 162 (A.B.2650), § 10, operative Jan. 1, 1994. Amended by Stats.2000, c. 808 (A.B.1358), § 57, eff. Sept. 28, 2000; Stats.2001, c. 755 (S.B.943), § 7, eff. Oct. 12, 2001.)*

Law Revision Commission Comments

Enactment [Revised Comment]

Section 5214 continues former Civil Code Section 4390(f) without substantive change. [23 Cal.L.Rev.Comm. Reports 1 (1993)].

Research References

Treatises and Practice Aids

Witkin, California Summary 10th Husband and Wife § 250, Definitions.

§ 5216. "Obligor" defined

"Obligor" means a person owing a duty of support. *(Stats.1992, c. 162 (A.B.2650), § 10, operative Jan. 1, 1994.)*

Law Revision Commission Comments

Enactment [Revised Comment]

Section 5216 continues former Civil Code Section 4390(g) without substantive change. [23 Cal.L.Rev.Comm. Reports 1 (1993)].

Research References

Treatises and Practice Aids

Witkin, California Summary 10th Husband and Wife § 250, Definitions.

§ 5220. "Timely payment" defined

"Timely payment" means receipt of support payments by the obligee or assigned obligee within five days of the due date. *(Stats.1992, c. 162 (A.B.2650), § 10, operative Jan. 1, 1994.)*

Law Revision Commission Comments

Enactment [Revised Comment]

Section 5220 continues former Civil Code Section 4390(i) without change. [23 Cal.L.Rev.Comm. Reports 1 (1993)].

Research References

Treatises and Practice Aids

Witkin, California Summary 10th Husband and Wife § 250, Definitions.

ARTICLE 2. GENERAL PROVISIONS

Section

§ 5230. Support orders; inclusion of earnings assignment order

(a) When the court orders a party to pay an amount for support or orders a modification of the amount of support to be paid, the court shall include in its order an earnings assignment order for support that orders the employer of the obligor to pay to the obligee that portion of the obligor's earnings due or to become due in the future as will be sufficient to pay an amount to cover both of the following:

(1) The amount ordered by the court for support.

(2) An amount which shall be ordered by the court to be paid toward the liquidation of any arrearage.

(b) An earnings assignment order for support shall be issued, and shall be effective and enforceable pursuant to Section 5231, notwithstanding the absence of the name, address, or other identifying information regarding the obligor's employer. *(Stats.1992, c. 162 (A.B.2650), § 10, operative Jan. 1, 1994. Amended by Stats.1993, c. 876 (S.B.1068), § 22.5, eff. Oct. 6, 1993, operative Jan. 1, 1994; Stats.1997, c. 599 (A.B.573), § 23; Stats.2000, c. 808 (A.B.1358), § 57.3, eff. Sept. 28, 2000.)*

Law Revision Commission Comments

Enactment [Revised Comment]

Section 5230 restates former Civil Code Section 4390.3(a) without substantive change. In subdivision (a), the reference to the requirement that the earnings assignment order for support include an order that the employer make the specified payments has been substituted for the former reference to an order that the obligor make the assignment. This is not a substantive change. See Section 5208 & Comment ("earnings assignment order for support" defined as order that assigns to obligee part of earnings of obligor). The former reference to a "judgment" of support has been omitted as surplus. See Section 155 ("support order" means a judgment or order of support). The introductory clause of the first sentence of former Civil Code Section 4390.3, which made the provision now found in subdivision (a) applicable on and after July 1, 1990, has been omitted as unnecessary. In subdivision (b), reference to a support order made or modified before July 1, 1990, has been substituted for the former reference to an "existing" support order. This is not a substantive change. See also Section 5251 (procedure for obtaining assignment order where support order issued or modified before July 1, 1990). [23 Cal.L.Rev.Comm. Reports 1 (1993)].

Research References

Forms

California Practice Guide: Rutter Family Law Forms Form 9:3, Marital Settlement Agreement.

California Practice Guide: Rutter Family Law Forms Form 1:32, Glossary Of Common Family Law Terms, Phrases and Concepts (Enclosure to Form 1:31).

Cal. Transaction Forms - Bus. Transactions § 16:83, Exclusions.

California Transactions Forms--Family Law § 3:46, Earnings Assignment.

West's California Code Forms, Family § 5230, Comment Overview--Earnings Assignment Order.

West's California Code Forms, Family § 2338 Form 9, Marital Agreement--Both Spouses Employed.

West's California Code Forms, Government § 37103 Form 5, Standard Provisions for City Personal Services Contracts.

West's California Judicial Council Forms FL-430, Ex Parte Application to Issue, Modify, or Terminate an Earnings Assignment Order.

Treatises and Practice Aids

Witkin, California Summary 10th Husband and Wife § 249, in General.

Witkin, California Summary 10th Husband and Wife § 251, Issuance Of Order.

§ 5230.1. Earning assignment or income withholding order of another state; enforceability; applicable law

(a) An earnings assignment or income withholding order for support issued by a court or administrative agency of another state is binding upon an employer of the obligor to the same extent as an earnings assignment order made by a court of this state.

(b) When an employer receives an earnings assignment order or an income withholding order for support from a court or administrative agency in another state, all of the provisions of this chapter shall apply. *(Added by Stats.1997, c. 599 (A.B.573), § 24.)*

Research References

Forms

West's California Code Forms, Family § 5230, Comment Overview--Earnings Assignment Order.

Treatises and Practice Aids

Witkin, California Summary 10th Husband and Wife § 249, in General.

§ 5230.5. Allegation of child support arrearage amount; perjury

Any obligee alleging arrearages in child support shall specify the amount thereof under penalty of perjury. *(Added by Stats.1994, c. 1140 (S.B.279), § 2.)*

Research References

Forms

West's California Judicial Council Forms FL-420, Declaration Of Support Arrearage.

West's California Judicial Council Forms FL-421, Attachment to Declaration Of Support Arrearage (Family Law--Domestic Violence Prevention--Uniform Parentage Act).

Treatises and Practice Aids

Witkin, California Summary 10th Husband and Wife § 251, Issuance Of Order.

§ 5231. Binding effect of assignment order upon employers

Unless stayed pursuant to Article 4 (commencing with Section 5260), an assignment order is effective and binding upon any existing or future employer of the obligor upon whom a copy of the order is served in compliance with Sections 5232 and 5233, notwithstanding the absence of the name, address, or other identifying information regarding the obligor's employer, or the inclusion of incorrect information regarding the support obligor's employer. *(Stats.1992, c. 162 (A.B.2650), § 10, operative Jan. 1, 1994. Amended by Stats. 2000, c. 808 (A.B.1358), § 57.5, eff. Sept. 28, 2000.)*

Law Revision Commission Comments

Enactment [Revised Comment]

Section 5231 restates former Civil Code Sections 4390.3(b) and 4390.7(c) without substantive change. [23 Cal.L.Rev.Comm. Reports 1 (1993)].

Research References

Forms

West's California Code Forms, Family § 5230, Comment Overview--Earnings Assignment Order.

Treatises and Practice Aids

Witkin, California Summary 10th Husband and Wife § 249, in General.

Witkin, California Summary 10th Husband and Wife § 251, Issuance Of Order.

§ 5232. Service of order on employer

Service on an employer of an assignment order may be made by first-class mail in the manner prescribed in Section 1013 of the Code of Civil Procedure. The obligee shall serve the documents specified in Section 5234. *(Stats.1992, c. 162 (A.B.2650), § 10, operative Jan. 1, 1994. Amended by Stats. 1997, c. 599 (A.B.573), § 25.)*

Law Revision Commission Comments

Enactment [Revised Comment]

Section 5232 continues the last sentence of former Civil Code Section 4390.8(a) without substantive change. [23 Cal.L.Rev.Comm. Reports 1 (1993)].

Research References

Forms

California Transactions Forms--Family Law § 3:46, Earnings Assignment.

Treatises and Practice Aids

Witkin, California Summary 10th Husband and Wife § 251, Issuance Of Order.

Witkin, California Summary 10th Husband and Wife § 257, Alternative Procedure in Title IV-D Cases.

§ 5233. Commencement of withholding

Unless the order states a later date, beginning as soon as possible after service of the order on the employer but not later than 10 days after service of the order on the employer, the employer shall commence withholding pursuant to the assignment order from all earnings payable to the employee. *(Stats.1992, c. 162 (A.B.2650), § 10, operative Jan. 1, 1994.)*

Law Revision Commission Comments

Enactment [Revised Comment]

Section 5233 restates the first two sentences of former Civil Code Section 4390.8(a) without substantive change. The former provision for withholding from all earnings of the employee payable for a pay period ending after the assignment becomes effective has been revised. This section only requires withholding from earnings payable to the employee after the order becomes effective. This is not a substantive change. The introductory clause is new and recognizes that the order itself may provide for a later effective date. [23 Cal.L.Rev.Comm. Reports 1 (1993)].

Research References

Forms

California Transactions Forms--Family Law § 3:46, Earnings Assignment.

Treatises and Practice Aids

Witkin, California Summary 10th Husband and Wife § 253, Rights and Obligations Of Employer.

§ 5234. Delivery to obligor by employer; copy of order; statement of rights

Within 10 days of service of an assignment order or an order/notice to withhold income for child support on an employer, the employer shall deliver both of the following to the obligor:

(a) A copy of the assignment order or the order/notice to withhold income for child support.

(b) A written statement of the obligor's rights under the law to seek to quash, modify, or stay service of the earnings assignment order, together with a blank form that the obligor can file with the court to request a hearing to quash, modify, or stay service of the earnings assignment order with instructions on how to file the form and obtain a hearing date. *(Stats.1992, c. 162 (A.B.2650), § 10, operative Jan. 1, 1994. Amended by Stats.1997, c. 599 (A.B.573), § 26; Stats.1999, c. 480 (S.B.542), § 3.)*

Law Revision Commission Comments

Enactment [Revised Comment]

Section 5234 continues former Civil Code Section 4390.8(b) without substantive change. See also Section 5295 (Judicial Council to prepare form for written statement of obligor's rights). [23 Cal.L.Rev.Comm. Reports 1 (1993)].

Research References

Treatises and Practice Aids

Witkin, California Summary 10th Husband and Wife § 251, Issuance Of Order.

§ 5235. Duties of employer; withholding and forwarding of support; liability

(a) The employer shall continue to withhold and forward support as required by the assignment order until served with notice terminating the assignment order. If an employer withholds support as required by the assignment order, the obligor shall not be held in contempt or subject to criminal prosecution for nonpayment of the support that was withheld by the employer but not received by the obligee. If the employer withheld the support but failed to forward the payments to the obligee, the employer shall be liable for the payments, including interest, as provided in Section 5241.

(b) Within 10 days of service of a substitution of payee on the employer, the employer shall forward all subsequent support to the governmental entity or other payee that sent the substitution.

(c) The employer shall send the amounts withheld to the obligee within the timeframe specified in federal law and shall report to the obligee the date on which the amount was withheld from the obligor's wages.

(d) The employer may deduct from the earnings of the employee the sum of one dollar and fifty cents ($1.50) for each payment made pursuant to the order.

(e) Once the State Disbursement Unit as required by Section 17309 is operational, the employer shall send all earnings withheld pursuant to this chapter to the State Disbursement Unit instead of the obligee. *(Stats.1992, c. 162 (A.B.2650), § 10, operative Jan. 1, 1994. Amended by Stats. 1993, c. 876 (S.B.1068), § 23, eff. Oct. 6, 1993, operative Jan. 1, 1994; Stats.1994, c. 1269 (A.B.2208), § 50.2; Stats.1997, c. 599 (A.B.573), § 27; Stats.1998, c. 854 (A.B.960), § 4; Stats.2000, c. 808 (A.B.1358), § 58, eff. Sept. 28, 2000; Stats.2003, c. 387 (A.B.739), § 5; Stats.2004, c. 520 (A.B. 2530), § 3.)*

Law Revision Commission Comments

Enactment [Revised Comment]

Section 5235 continues former Civil Code Section 4390.10(a) without substantive change. [23 Cal.L.Rev.Comm. Reports 1 (1993)].

Research References

Forms

California Transactions Forms--Family Law § 3:46, Earnings Assignment.

Treatises and Practice Aids

Witkin, California Summary 10th Husband and Wife § 253, Rights and Obligations Of Employer.

§ 5236. Simplification of wage withholding

The state agency or the local agency, designated to enforce support obligations as required by federal law, shall allow employers to simplify the process of assignment order withholding by forwarding, as ordered by the court, the amounts of support withheld under more than one order in a consolidated check, accompanied by an itemized accounting providing names, social security number or other identifying number, and the amount attributable to each obligor. *(Stats. 1992, c. 162 (A.B.2650), § 10, operative Jan. 1, 1994.)*

Law Revision Commission Comments

Enactment [Revised Comment]

Section 5236 continues former Civil Code Section 4390.16(b) without substantive change. [23 Cal.L.Rev.Comm. Reports 1 (1993)].

Research References

Treatises and Practice Aids

Witkin, California Summary 10th Husband and Wife § 253, Rights and Obligations Of Employer.

§ 5237. Notice of obligee of change of address; effect of failure to notify

(a) Except as provided in subdivisions (b) and (c), the obligee shall notify the employer of the obligor, by first-class mail, postage prepaid, of any change of address within a reasonable period of time after the change.

(b) Where payments have been ordered to be made to a county officer designated by the court, the obligee who is the parent, guardian, or other person entitled to receive payment through the designated county officer shall notify the designated county officer by first-class mail, postage prepaid, of any address change within a reasonable period of time after the change.

(c) If the obligee is receiving support payments from the State Disbursement Unit as required by Section 17309, the obligee shall notify the State Disbursement Unit instead of the employer of the obligor as provided in subdivision (a).

(d)(1) Except as set forth in paragraph (2), if the employer, designated county officer, or the State Disbursement Unit is unable to deliver payments under the assignment order for a period of six months due to the failure of the obligee to notify the employer, designated county officer, or State Disbursement Unit, of a change of address, the employer, designated county officer, or State Disbursement Unit shall not make any further payments under the assignment order and shall return all undeliverable payments to the obligor.

(2) If payments are being directed to the State Disbursement Unit pursuant to subdivision (e) of Section 5235, but the case is not otherwise receiving services from the Title IV–D agency, and the State Disbursement Unit is unable to deliver payments under the assignment order for a period of 45 days due to the failure of the obligee to notify the employer, designated county officer, or State Disbursement Unit of a change of address, the Title IV–D agency shall take the following actions:

(A) Immediately return the undeliverable payments to the obligor if the obligee cannot be located.

(B) Notify the employer to suspend withholding pursuant to the wage assignment until the employer or Title IV–D agency is notified of the obligee's whereabouts. *(Stats.1992, c. 162 (A.B.2650), § 10, operative Jan. 1, 1994. Amended by Stats.1997, c. 599 (A.B.573), § 28; Stats.2000, c. 808 (A.B. 1358), § 59, eff. Sept. 28, 2000; Stats.2003, c. 387 (A.B.739), § 6; Stats.2004, c. 806 (A.B.2358), § 1.)*

Law Revision Commission Comments

Enactment [Revised Comment]

Section 5237 continues former Civil Code Section 4390.13 without substantive change. See also Section 3555 (forwarding support payments paid through designated county officer). [23 Cal.L.Rev. Comm. Reports 1 (1993)].

Research References

Treatises and Practice Aids

Witkin, California Summary 10th Husband and Wife § 249, in General.

Witkin, California Summary 10th Husband and Wife § 253, Rights and Obligations Of Employer.

§ 5238. Assignments including both current support and arrearages; priority; multiple assignment orders for the same employee; proration of withheld payments

(a) Where an assignment order or assignment orders include both current support and payments towards the liquidation of arrearages, priority shall be given first to the current child support obligation, then the current spousal support obligation, and thereafter to the liquidation of child and then spousal support arrearages.

(b) Where there are multiple assignment orders for the same employee, the employer shall prorate the withheld payments as follows:

(1) If the obligor has more than one assignment for support, the employer shall add together the amount of support due for each assignment.

(2) If 50 percent of the obligor's net disposable earnings will not pay in full all of the assignments for support, the employer shall prorate it first among all of the current support assignments in the same proportion that each assignment bears to the total current support owed.

(3) The employer shall apply any remainder to the assignments for arrearage support in the same proportion that each assignment bears to the total arrearage owed. *(Stats.1992, c. 162 (A.B.2650), § 10, operative Jan. 1, 1994. Amended by Stats.1997, c. 599 (A.B.573), § 29.)*

Law Revision Commission Comments

Enactment [Revised Comment]

Section 5238 continues former Civil Code Section 4390.12(a) without substantive change. [23 Cal.L.Rev.Comm. Reports 1 (1993)].

Research References

Treatises and Practice Aids

Witkin, California Summary 10th Husband and Wife § 254, Priorities.

§ 5239. Arrearages of support payments; computation

Arrearages of support payments shall be computed on the basis of the payments owed and unpaid on the date that the obligor has been given notice of the assignment order as required by Section 5234. *(Stats.1992, c. 162 (A.B.2650), § 10, operative Jan. 1, 1994.)*

Law Revision Commission Comments

Enactment [Revised Comment]

Section 5239 continues former Civil Code Section 4390.2 without substantive change. The reference to Section 5234 is new and is not a substantive change. [23 Cal.L.Rev.Comm. Reports 1 (1993)].

Research References

Treatises and Practice Aids

Witkin, California Summary 10th Husband and Wife § 250, Definitions.

§ 5240. Payment of past due support; termination of service of order of assignment; grounds; ex parte relief

(a) Upon the filing and service of a motion and a notice of motion by the obligor, the court shall terminate the service of an assignment order if past due support has been paid in full, including any interest due, and if any of the following conditions exist:

(1) With regard to orders for spousal support, the death or remarriage of the spouse to whom support is owed.

(2) With regard to orders for child support, the death or emancipation of the child for whom support is owed.

(3) The court determines that there is good cause, as defined in Section 5260, to terminate the assignment order. This subdivision does not apply if there has been more than one application for an assignment order.

(4) The obligor meets the conditions of an alternative arrangement specified in paragraph (2) of subdivision (b) of Section 5260, and a wage assignment has not been previously terminated and subsequently initiated.

(5) There is no longer a current order for support.

(6) The termination of the stay of an assignment order under Section 5261 was improper, but only if that termination was based upon the obligor's failure to make timely support payments as described in subdivision (b) of Section 5261.

(7) The employer or agency designated to provide services under Title IV–D of the Social Security Act or the State Disbursement Unit is unable to deliver payment for a period of six months due to the failure of the obligee to notify that employer or agency or the State Disbursement Unit of a change in the obligee's address.

(b) In lieu of filing and serving a motion and a notice of motion pursuant to subdivision (a), an obligor may request ex parte relief, except ex parte relief shall not be available in the circumstances described in paragraphs (3) and (4) of subdivision (a). *(Stats.1992, c. 162 (A.B.2650), § 10, operative Jan. 1, 1994. Amended by Stats.1993, c. 876 (S.B.1068), § 24, eff. Oct. 6, 1993, operative Jan. 1, 1994; Stats.1997, c. 599 (A.B.573), § 30; Stats.2003, c. 387 (A.B.739), § 7; Stats.2012, c. 77 (A.B.1727), § 1.)*

Law Revision Commission Comments

Enactment [Revised Comment]

Section 5240 continues former Civil Code Section 4390.14 without substantive change. [23 Cal.L.Rev.Comm. Reports 1 (1993)].

Research References

Forms

West's California Judicial Council Forms FL-430, Ex Parte Application to Issue, Modify, or Terminate an Earnings Assignment Order.

Treatises and Practice Aids

Witkin, California Summary 10th Husband and Wife § 256, Termination Of Order.

§ 5241. Wilful failure to withhold or forward support; penalties; actions to collect withheld sums not forwarded; electronic transfer and employer awareness

(a) An employer who willfully fails to withhold and forward support pursuant to a currently valid assignment order entered and served upon the employer pursuant to this chapter is liable to the obligee for the amount of support not withheld, forwarded, or otherwise paid to the obligee, including any interest thereon.

(b) If an employer withholds support as required by the assignment order, the obligor shall not be held in contempt or subject to criminal prosecution for nonpayment of the support that was withheld by the employer but not received by the obligee. In addition, the employer is liable to the obligee for any interest incurred as a result of the employer's failure to timely forward the withheld support pursuant to an assignment earnings order.

(c) In addition to any other penalty or liability provided by law, willful failure by an employer to comply with an assignment order is punishable as a contempt pursuant to Section 1218 of the Code of Civil Procedure.

(d) If an employer withholds support, as required by the assignment order, but fails to forward the support to the obligee, the local child support agency shall take appropriate action to collect the withheld sums from the employer. The child support obligee or the local child support agency upon application may obtain an order requiring payment of support by electronic transfer from the employer's bank account if the employer has willfully failed to comply with the assignment order or if the employer has failed to comply with the assignment order on three separate occasions within a 12–month period. Where a court finds that an employer has willfully failed to comply with the assignment order or has otherwise failed to comply with the assignment order on three separate occasions within a 12–month period, the court may impose a civil penalty, in addition to any other penalty required by law, of up to 50 percent of the support amount that has not been received by the obligee.

(e) To facilitate employer awareness, the local child support agency shall make reasonable efforts to notify any employer subject to an assignment order pursuant to this chapter of the electronic fund transfer provision and enhanced penalties provided by this act.

(f) Notwithstanding any other provision of law, any penalty payable pursuant to this subdivision shall be payable directly to the obligee. The local child support agency shall not be required to establish or collect this penalty on behalf of the obligee. The penalty shall not be included when determining the income of the obligee for the purpose of determining the eligibility of the obligee for benefits payable pursuant to state supplemental income programs. A court may issue the order requiring payment of support by electronic transfer from the employer's bank account and impose the penalty described in this subdivision, after notice and hearing. This provision shall not be construed to expand or limit the duties and obligations of the Labor Commissioner, as set forth in Section 200 and following of the Labor Code. *(Stats.1992, c. 162 (A.B.2650), § 10, operative Jan. 1, 1994. Amended by Stats.1993, c. 745 (S.B.788), § 2; Stats.1993, c. 876 (S.B.1068), § 25, eff. Oct. 6, 1993, operative Jan. 1, 1994; Stats.1998, c. 854 (A.B.960), § 5; Stats.2000, c. 808 (A.B.1358), § 60, eff. Sept. 28, 2000; Stats.2001, c. 371 (A.B.1426), § 1; Stats.2003, c. 308 (A.B.738), § 2.)*

Law Revision Commission Comments

Enactment [Revised Comment]

Section 5241 continues former Civil Code Section 4390.10(b) without substantive change. See also Sections 3557 (attorney's fees and costs for enforcement of support order), 5290 (civil penalty for using assignment order as grounds for refusing to hire or for discharging or taking disciplinary action against employee). [23 Cal.L.Rev.Comm. Reports 1 (1993)].

Commentary

Although a support obligee may proceed against the obligor's employer under this section, the support obligor is not entitled to a credit on his child support obligation for wage withholding wrongfully taken by now bankrupt employer. The support obligee may proceed against either defendant, the support obligor or his employer, to satisfy the support obligation. *County of Shasta v. Smith, 38 Cal. App.4th 329, 45 Cal.Rptr.2d 52 (1995)*. After *Smith* was decided, subsections (b) and (d) were added to protect the obligor whose employer has withheld child support from the obligor's wages, but failed to pay it to the obligee.

Research References

Treatises and Practice Aids

Witkin, California Summary 10th Husband and Wife § 253, Rights and Obligations Of Employer.

§ 5242. Lien on earnings; service of order

Service of the assignment order creates a lien on the earnings of the employee and the property of the employer to the same extent as the service of an earnings withholding order as provided in Section 706.029 of the Code of Civil Procedure. *(Stats.1992, c. 162 (A.B.2650), § 10, operative Jan. 1, 1994.)*

Law Revision Commission Comments

Enactment [Revised Comment]

Section 5242 continues former Civil Code Section 4390.10(c) without substantive change. [23 Cal.L.Rev.Comm. Reports 1 (1993)].

Research References

Treatises and Practice Aids

Witkin, California Summary 10th Husband and Wife § 249, in General.

§ 5243. Priority of order

An assignment order for support has priority as against any attachment, execution, or other assignment as specified in Section 706.031 of the Code of Civil Procedure. *(Stats.1992, c. 162 (A.B.2650), § 10, operative Jan. 1, 1994. Amended by Stats.1993, c. 876 (S.B.1068), § 26, eff. Oct. 6, 1993, operative Jan. 1, 1994.)*

Law Revision Commission Comments

Enactment [Revised Comment]

Section 5243 continues former Civil Code Section 4390.12(b) without substantive change. [23 Cal.L.Rev.Comm. Reports 1 (1993)].

Commentary

See Family Code Section 4011, Commentary.

Research References

Treatises and Practice Aids

Witkin, California Summary 10th Husband and Wife § 254, Priorities.

§ 5244. Local child support agency; enforcement or collection duties

A reference to the local child support agency in this chapter applies only when the local child support agency is otherwise ordered or required to act pursuant to law. Nothing in this chapter shall be deemed to mandate additional enforcement or collection duties upon the local child support agency beyond those otherwise imposed by law. *(Stats.1992, c. 162 (A.B.2650), § 10, operative Jan. 1, 1994.*

Amended by Stats.2000, c. 808 (A.B.1358), § 61, eff. Sept. 28, 2000.)

Law Revision Commission Comments

Enactment [Revised Comment]

Section 5244 continues former Civil Code Section 4390.1 without substantive change. This section has been revised to omit references to "existing" law. These are not substantive changes. [23 Cal. L.Rev.Comm. Reports 1 (1993)].

Research References

Treatises and Practice Aids

Witkin, California Summary 10th Husband and Wife § 250, Definitions.

§ 5245. Enforcement of support obligations; authority of local child support agency to use civil and criminal remedies

Nothing in this chapter limits the authority of the local child support agency to use any other civil and criminal remedies to enforce support obligations, regardless of whether or not the child or the obligee who is the parent, guardian, or other person entitled to receive payment is the recipient of welfare moneys. *(Stats.1992, c. 162 (A.B.2650), § 10, operative Jan. 1, 1994. Amended by Stats.1993, c. 219 (A.B.1500), § 153; Stats.2000, c. 808 (A.B.1358), § 62, eff. Sept. 28, 2000.)*

Law Revision Commission Comments

Enactment [Revised Comment]

Section 5245 continues former Civil Code Section 4390.19 without substantive change. The former reference to any "and all" enforcement remedies has been omitted. This is not a substantive change, since "all" is surplus. The reference to support of a "minor" child has been omitted. This is not a substantive change, but recognizes that in some cases support may be ordered for an adult child. See Sections 58 ("child for whom support may be ordered" defined), 3587 (court order to effectuate agreement for support of adult child), 3901 (duration of duty to support child), 3910 (duty to maintain incapacitated adult child), 4000 (civil action to enforce parent's duty to support child), 4001 (order for child support). [23 Cal.L.Rev. Comm. Reports 1 (1993)].

Research References

Treatises and Practice Aids

Witkin, California Summary 10th Husband and Wife § 249, in General.

§ 5246. Assignment of earnings; notice to employer; employer's duties; application of section

(a) This section applies only to Title IV–D cases where support enforcement services are being provided by the local child support agency pursuant to Section 17400.

(b) In lieu of an earnings assignment order signed by a judicial officer, the local child support agency may serve on the employer a notice of assignment in the manner specified in Section 5232. An order/notice to withhold income for child support shall have the same force and effect as an earnings assignment order signed by a judicial officer. An order/notice to withhold income for child support, when used under this section, shall be considered a notice and shall not require the signature of a judicial officer.

(c) Pursuant to Section 666 of Title 42 of the United States Code, the federally mandated order/notice to withhold income for child support shall be used for the purposes described in this section.

(d)(1) An order/notice to withhold income may not reduce the current amount withheld for court-ordered child support.

(2) If the underlying court order for support does not provide for an arrearage payment, or if an additional arrearage accrues after the date of the court order for support, the local child support agency may send an order/notice to withhold income for child support that shall be used for the purposes described in this section directly to the employer which specifies the updated arrearage amount and directs the employer to withhold an additional amount to be applied towards liquidation of the arrearages not to exceed the maximum amount permitted by Section 1673(b) of Title 15 of the United States Code.

(3) Notwithstanding paragraph (2), if an obligor is disabled, meets the SSI resource test, and is receiving Supplemental Security Income/State Supplementary Payments (SSI/SSP) or, but for excess income as described in Section 416.1100 et seq. of Part 416 of Title 20 of the Code of Federal Regulations, would be eligible to receive SSI/SSP, pursuant to Section 12200 of the Welfare and Institutions Code, and the obligor has supplied the local child support agency with proof of his or her eligibility for and, if applicable, receipt of, SSI/SSP or Social Security Disability Insurance benefits, then the order/notice to withhold income issued by the local child support agency for the liquidation of the arrearage shall not exceed 5 percent of the obligor's total monthly Social Security Disability payments under Title II of the Social Security Act.

(e) If the obligor requests a hearing, a hearing date shall be scheduled within 20 days of the filing of the request with the court. The clerk of the court shall provide notice of the hearing to the local child support agency and the obligor no later than 10 days prior to the hearing.

(1) If at the hearing the obligor establishes that he or she is not the obligor or good cause or an alternative arrangement as provided in Section 5260, the court may order that service of the order/notice to withhold income for child support be quashed. If the court quashes service of the order/notice to withhold income for child support, the local child support agency shall notify the employer within 10 days.

(2) If the obligor contends at the hearing that the payment of arrearages at the rate specified in the order/notice to withhold income for child support is excessive or that the total arrearages owing is incorrect, and if it is determined that payment of the arrearages at the rate specified in this section creates an undue hardship upon the obligor or that the withholding would exceed the maximum amount permitted by Section 1673(b) of Title 15 of the United States Code Annotated, the rate at which the arrearages must be paid shall be reduced to a rate that is fair and reasonable considering the circumstances of the parties and the best interest of the child. If it is determined at a hearing that the total amount of arrearages calculated is erroneous, the court shall modify the amount calculated to the correct amount. If the court modifies the total amount of arrearages owed or reduces the monthly payment due on the arrearages, the local child support agency shall serve the employer with an

amended order/notice to withhold income for child support within 10 days.

(f) If an obligor's current support obligation has terminated by operation of law, the local child support agency may serve an order/notice to withhold income for child support on the employer which directs the employer to continue withholding from the obligor's earnings an amount to be applied towards liquidation of the arrearages, not to exceed the maximum amount permitted by Section 1673(b) of Title 15 of the United States Code, until such time that the employer is notified by the local child support agency that the arrearages have been paid in full. The employer shall provide the obligor with a copy of the order/notice to withhold income for child support and a blank form that the obligor may file with the court to request a hearing to modify or quash the assignment with instructions on how to file the form and obtain a hearing date. The obligor shall be entitled to the same rights to a hearing as specified in subdivision (e).

(g) The local child support agency shall retain a copy of the order/notice to withhold income for child support and shall file a copy with the court whenever a hearing concerning the order/notice to withhold income for child support is requested.

(h) The local child support agency may transmit an order/notice to withhold income for child support and other forms required by this section to the employer through electronic means. *(Added by Stats.1996, c. 957 (A.B.1058), § 8. Amended by Stats.1997, c. 599 (A.B.573), § 31; Stats. 1999, c. 480 (S.B.542), § 4; Stats.2000, c. 808 (A.B.1358), § 62.3, eff. Sept. 28, 2000; Stats.2001, c. 111 (A.B.429), § 1, eff. July 30, 2001; Stats.2001, c. 651 (A.B.891), § 2.)*

Research References

Forms

West's California Code Forms, Family § 5246 Form 1, Request for Hearing Regarding Wage and Earnings Assignment.

West's California Judicial Council Forms FL-450, Request for Hearing Regarding Earnings Assignment.

Treatises and Practice Aids

Witkin, California Summary 10th Husband and Wife § 257, Alternative Procedure in Title IV-D Cases.

Witkin, California Summary 10th Parent and Child § 416, Application and Order.

§ 5247. Civil liability of local child support agency or employer

Neither the local child support agency nor an employer shall be subject to any civil liability for any amount withheld and paid to the obligee, the local child support agency, or the State Disbursement Unit pursuant to an earnings assignment order or notice of assignment. *(Added by Stats.1997, c. 599 (A.B.573), § 32. Amended by Stats.2000, c. 808 (A.B.1358), § 63, eff. Sept. 28, 2000; Stats.2003, c. 387 (A.B.739), § 8.)*

Research References

Treatises and Practice Aids

Witkin, California Summary 10th Husband and Wife § 253, Rights and Obligations Of Employer.

ARTICLE 3. SUPPORT ORDERS ISSUED OR MODIFIED BEFORE JULY 1, 1990

§ 5250. Application of article

For a support order first issued or modified before July 1, 1990, this article provides a procedure for obtaining an earnings assignment order for support when the court in ordering support or modification of support did not issue an assignment order. *(Stats.1992, c. 162 (A.B.2650), § 10, operative Jan. 1, 1994.)*

Law Revision Commission Comments

Enactment [Revised Comment]

Section 5250 continues without substantive change the first sentence of the first paragraph of former Civil Code Section 4390.5(a). [23 Cal.L.Rev.Comm. Reports 1 (1993)].

Research References

Treatises and Practice Aids

Witkin, California Summary 10th Husband and Wife § 251, Issuance Of Order.

§ 5251. Procedure for obtaining assignment

The obligee seeking issuance of an assignment order to enforce a support order described in Section 5250 may use the procedure set forth in this article by filing an application under Section 5252, or by notice of motion or order to show cause, or pursuant to subdivision (b) of Section 5230. *(Stats.1992, c. 162 (A.B.2650), § 10, operative Jan. 1, 1994.)*

Law Revision Commission Comments

Enactment [Revised Comment]

Section 5251 continues without substantive change the last sentence of the first paragraph of former Civil Code Section 4390.5(a). [23 Cal.L.Rev.Comm. Reports 1 (1993)].

§ 5252. Application for assignment order; false declarations or notices; punishment

(a) An assignment order under this article may be issued only upon an application signed under penalty of perjury by the obligee that the obligor is in default in support payments in a sum equal to the amount of support payable for one month, for any other occurrence specified by the court in the support order, or earlier by court order if requested by the local child support agency or the obligor.

(b) If the order for support does not contain a provision for an earnings assignment order for support, the application shall state that the obligee has given the obligor a written notice of the obligee's intent to seek an assignment order if there is a default in support payments and that the notice was transmitted by first-class mail, postage prepaid, or personally served at least 15 days before the date of the filing of the application. The written notice of the intent to seek an assignment order may be given at any time, including at the time of filing a petition or complaint in which support is requested or at any time subsequent thereto. The obligor may at any time waive the written notice required by this subdivision.

(c) In addition to any other penalty provided by law, the filing of the application with knowledge of the falsity of the declaration or notice is punishable as a contempt pursuant to Section 1209 of the Code of Civil Procedure. *(Stats.1992, c. 162 (A.B.2650), § 10, operative Jan. 1, 1994. Amended by Stats.2000, c. 808 (A.B.1358), § 64, eff. Sept. 28, 2000.)*

Law Revision Commission Comments

Enactment [Revised Comment]

Subdivision (a) of Section 5252 continues without substantive change the last paragraph of former Civil Code Section 4390.5(a). Subdivision (b) continues former Civil Code Section 4390.5(d)-(e) without substantive change. Subdivision (c) continues former Civil Code Section 4390.5(b) without substantive change. [23 Cal.L.Rev. Comm. Reports 1 (1993)].

Research References

Forms

West's California Judicial Council Forms FL-430, Ex Parte Application to Issue, Modify, or Terminate an Earnings Assignment Order.

§ 5253. Issuance of assignment order

Upon receipt of the application, the court shall issue, without notice to the obligor, an assignment order requiring the employer of the obligor to pay to the obligee or the State Disbursement Unit that portion of the earnings of the obligor due or to become due in the future as will be sufficient to pay an amount to cover both of the following:

(a) The amount ordered by the court for support.

(b) An amount which shall be ordered by the court to be paid toward the liquidation of any arrearage or past due support amount. *(Stats.1992, c. 162 (A.B.2650), § 10, operative Jan. 1, 1994. Amended by Stats.1997, c. 599 (A.B.573), § 33; Stats.2003, c. 387 (A.B.739), § 9.)*

Law Revision Commission Comments

Enactment [Revised Comment]

Section 5253 restates the first sentence of former Civil Code Section 4390.5(c) without substantive change. The reference to the requirement that the earnings assignment order for support include an order that the employer make the specified payments has been substituted for the former reference to an order that the obligor make the assignment. This is not a substantive change. See Section 5208 & Comment ("earnings assignment order for support" defined as order that assigns to obligee part of earnings of obligor). [23 Cal.L.Rev.Comm. Reports 1 (1993)].

ARTICLE 4. STAY OF SERVICE OF ASSIGNMENT ORDER

§ 5260. Finding of good cause necessary to stay order; restrictions

(a) The court may order that service of the assignment order be stayed only if the court makes a finding of good cause or if an alternative arrangement exists for payment in accordance with paragraph (2) of subdivision (b). Notwithstanding any other provision of law, service of wage assignments issued for foreign orders for support, and service of foreign orders for the assignment of wages registered pursuant to Chapter 6 (commencing with Section 5700.601) of Part 6 shall not be stayed pursuant to this subdivision.

(b) For purposes of this section, good cause or an alternative arrangement for staying an assignment order is as follows:

(1) Good cause for staying a wage assignment exists only when all of the following conditions exist:

(A) The court provides a written explanation of why the stay of the wage assignment would be in the best interests of the child.

(B) The obligor has a history of uninterrupted, full, and timely payment, other than through a wage assignment or other mandatory process of previously ordered support, during the previous 12 months.

(C) The obligor does not owe an arrearage for prior support.

(D) The obligor proves, and the court finds, by clear and convincing evidence that service of the wage assignment would cause extraordinary hardship upon the obligor. Whenever possible, the court shall specify a date that any stay ordered under this section will automatically terminate.

(2) An alternative arrangement for staying a wage assignment order shall require a written agreement between the parties that provides for payment of the support obligation as ordered other than through the immediate service of a wage assignment. Any agreement between the parties which includes the staying of a service of a wage assignment shall include the concurrence of the local child support agency in any case in which support is ordered to be paid through a county officer designated for that purpose. The execution of an agreement pursuant to this paragraph shall not preclude a party from thereafter seeking a wage assignment in accordance with the procedures specified in Section 5261 upon violation of the agreement. *(Stats.1992, c. 162 (A.B.2650), § 10, operative Jan. 1, 1994. Amended by Stats.1993, c. 219 (A.B.1500), § 153.2; Stats.1993, c. 876 (S.B.1068), § 27, eff. Oct. 6, 1993, operative Jan. 1, 1994; Stats.1994, c. 1269 (A.B.2208), § 50.4; Stats.2000, c. 808 (A.B.1358), § 65, eff. Sept. 28, 2000; Stats.2001, c. 755 (S.B.943), § 8, eff. Oct. 12, 2001; Stats.2015, c. 493 (S.B.646), § 3, eff. Jan. 1, 2016.)*

Law Revision Commission Comments

Enactment [Revised Comment]

Section 5260 continues former Civil Code Section 4390.3(c) without substantive change. [23 Cal.L.Rev.Comm. Reports 1 (1993)].

1994 Amendment

Subdivision (b)(2) of Section 5260 is amended to correct an erroneous cross-reference made in 1993 Cal. Stat. ch. 876, § 27 (SB 1068). This is a technical, nonsubstantive change. [24 Cal.L.Rev. Comm. Reports 621 (1994)].

Research References

Forms

California Transactions Forms--Family Law § 3:46, Earnings Assignment.

California Transactions Forms--Family Law § 3:104, Basic Child Support Agreement.

West's California Code Forms, Family § 5260, Comment Overview--Stay Of Service Of Assignment Order.

West's California Judicial Council Forms FL-455, Stay Of Service Of Wage Assignment Order and Order.

Treatises and Practice Aids

Witkin, California Summary 10th Husband and Wife § 252, Stay Of Service.

Witkin, California Summary 10th Husband and Wife § 256, Termination Of Order.

Witkin, California Summary 10th Husband and Wife § 257, Alternative Procedure in Title IV-D Cases.

§ 5261. Termination of stay; declaration; falsification of declaration; penalty

(a) If service of the assignment order has been ordered stayed, the stay shall terminate pursuant to subdivision (b) upon the obligor's failure to make timely support payments or earlier by court order if requested by the local child support agency or by the obligor. The stay shall terminate earlier by court order if requested by any other obligee who can establish that good cause, as defined in Section 5260, no longer exists.

(b) To terminate a stay of the service of the assignment order, the obligee shall file a declaration signed under penalty of perjury by the obligee that the obligor is in arrears in payment of any portion of the support. At the time of filing the declaration, the stay shall terminate by operation of law without notice to the obligor.

(c) In addition to any other penalty provided by law, the filing of a declaration under subdivision (b) with knowledge of the falsity of its contents is punishable as a contempt pursuant to Section 1209 of the Code of Civil Procedure. *(Stats.1992, c. 162 (A.B.2650), § 10, operative Jan. 1, 1994. Amended by Stats.2000, c. 808 (A.B.1358), § 66, eff. Sept. 28, 2000.)*

Law Revision Commission Comments

Enactment [Revised Comment]

Section 5261 continues former Civil Code Section 4390.4 without substantive change. [23 Cal.L.Rev.Comm. Reports 1 (1993)].

Research References

Forms

California Transactions Forms--Family Law § 3:46, Earnings Assignment.

West's California Code Forms, Family § 5260, Comment Overview--Stay Of Service Of Assignment Order.

West's California Judicial Council Forms FL-455, Stay Of Service Of Wage Assignment Order and Order.

Treatises and Practice Aids

Witkin, California Summary 10th Husband and Wife § 252, Stay Of Service.

Witkin, California Summary 10th Husband and Wife § 256, Termination Of Order.

ARTICLE 5. MOTION TO QUASH ASSIGNMENT ORDER

§ 5270. Grounds for motion

(a) An obligor may move to quash an assignment order on any of the following grounds:

(1) The assignment order does not correctly state the amount of current or overdue support ordered by the courts.

(2) The alleged obligor is not the obligor from whom support is due.

(3) The amount to be withheld exceeds that allowable under federal law in subsection (b) of Section 1673 of Title 15 of the United States Code.

(b) If an assignment order is sought under Article 3 (commencing with Section 5250), the party ordered to pay support may also move to quash the service of the order based upon Section 5260.

(c) The obligor shall state under oath the ground on which the motion to quash is made.

(d) If an assignment order which has been issued and served on a prior employer is served on the obligor's new employer, the obligor does not have the right to move to quash the assignment order on any grounds which the obligor previously raised when the assignment order was served on the prior employer or on any grounds which the obligor could have raised when the assignment order was served on the prior employer but failed to raise. *(Stats.1992, c. 162 (A.B.2650), § 10, operative Jan. 1, 1994.)*

Law Revision Commission Comments

Enactment [Revised Comment]

Section 5270 continues former Civil Code Section 4390.9(a)-(c) without substantive change. The reference to the time for making the motion in former Civil Code Section 4390.9(a) has been omitted as unnecessary, because this duplicated a provision of former Civil Code Section 4390.11, now Family Code Section 5271(a). [23 Cal.L.Rev.Comm. Reports 1 (1993)].

Research References

Treatises and Practice Aids

Witkin, California Summary 10th Husband and Wife § 255, Motion to Quash.

§ 5271. Motion and notice of motion to quash; filing; hearing; service on obligee

(a) The motion and notice of motion to quash the assignment order shall be filed with the court issuing the order within 10 days after delivery of the copy of the assignment order to the obligor by the employer.

(b) The clerk of the court shall set the motion to quash for hearing within not less than 15 days, nor more than 20 days, after receipt of the notice of motion.

(c) The obligor shall serve personally or by first-class mail, postage prepaid, a copy of the motion and notice of motion on the obligee named in the assignment order no less than 10 days before the date of the hearing. *(Stats.1992, c. 162 (A.B.2650), § 10, operative Jan. 1, 1994.)*

Law Revision Commission Comments

Enactment [Revised Comment]

Section 5271 continues former Civil Code Section 4390.11 without substantive change. In subdivision (a), the phrase "delivery of the copy of the assignment order to the obligor" has been substituted for "service on the obligor of notice of the order," which was used in the former provision. This revision makes subdivision (a) consistent with Section 5234 and is not a substantive change. See Section 5234 (delivery of copy of assignment order to obligor). [23 Cal.L.Rev. Comm. Reports 1 (1993)].

Research References

Treatises and Practice Aids

Witkin, California Summary 10th Husband and Wife § 255, Motion to Quash.

§ 5272. Error or excess in amount of current support or arrearage; modification of order

A finding of error in the amount of the current support or arrearage or that the amount exceeds federal or state limits is not grounds to vacate the assignment order. The court shall modify the order to reflect the correct or allowable amount of support or arrearages. The fact that the obligor may have subsequently paid the arrearages does not relieve the court of its duty to enter the assignment order. *(Stats.1992, c. 162 (A.B.2650), § 10, operative Jan. 1, 1994.)*

Law Revision Commission Comments

Enactment [Revised Comment]

Section 5272 continues former Civil Code Section 4390.9(d) without substantive change. [23 Cal.L.Rev.Comm. Reports 1 (1993)].

Research References

Treatises and Practice Aids

Witkin, California Summary 10th Husband and Wife § 255, Motion to Quash.

ARTICLE 6. INFORMATION CONCERNING ADDRESS AND EMPLOYMENT OF OBLIGOR

§ 5280. Obligor's whereabouts or identity of employer unknown; duties of local child support agency

If the obligee making the application under this chapter also states that the whereabouts of the obligor or the identity of the obligor's employer is unknown to the party to whom support has been ordered to be paid, the local child support agency shall do both of the following:

(a) Contact the California parent locator service maintained by the Department of Justice in the manner prescribed in Section 17506.

(b) Upon receiving the requested information, notify the court of the last known address of the obligor and the name and address of the obligor's last known employer. *(Stats. 1992, c. 162 (A.B.2650), § 10, operative Jan. 1, 1994. Amended by Stats.2000, c. 808 (A.B.1358), § 67, eff. Sept. 28, 2000.)*

Law Revision Commission Comments

Enactment [Revised Comment]

Section 5280 continues former Civil Code Section 4390.6 without substantive change. [23 Cal.L.Rev.Comm. Reports 1 (1993)].

Research References

Treatises and Practice Aids

Witkin, California Summary 10th Husband and Wife § 251, Issuance Of Order.

§ 5281. Duty of obligor to inform obligee of change of employment

An assignment order required or authorized by this chapter shall include a requirement that the obligor notify the obligee of any change of employment and of the name and address of the obligor's new employer within 10 days of obtaining new employment. *(Stats.1992, c. 162 (A.B.2650), § 10, operative Jan. 1, 1994.)*

Law Revision Commission Comments

Enactment [Revised Comment]

Section 5281 continues former Civil Code Section 4390.7(a) without substantive change. [23 Cal.L.Rev.Comm. Reports 1 (1993)].

Research References

Treatises and Practice Aids

Witkin, California Summary 10th Husband and Wife § 251, Issuance Of Order.

§ 5282. Duty of employer to inform obligee of obligor's change of employment

After the obligor has left employment with the employer, the employer, at the time the next payment is due on the assignment order, shall notify the obligee designated in the assignment order by first-class mail, postage prepaid, to the last known address of the obligee that the obligor has left employment. *(Stats.1992, c. 162 (A.B.2650), § 10, operative Jan. 1, 1994.)*

Law Revision Commission Comments

Enactment [Revised Comment]

Section 5282 continues former Civil Code Section 4390.7(b) without substantive change. The phrase "designated in the assignment order" has been added to make clear that the notice is to be given to the district attorney or other person designated in the order to receive the payment. See also Section 5214 ("obligee" defined). [23 Cal.L.Rev.Comm. Reports 1 (1993)].

Research References

Treatises and Practice Aids

Witkin, California Summary 10th Husband and Wife § 253, Rights and Obligations Of Employer.

ARTICLE 7. PROHIBITED PRACTICES

§ 5290. Use of assignment order under chapter as basis of adverse employment action; violations; civil penalty

No employer shall use an assignment order authorized by this chapter as grounds for refusing to hire a person, or for discharging, taking disciplinary action against, denying a promotion to, or for taking any other action adversely affecting the terms and conditions of employment of, an employee. An employer who engages in the conduct prohibited by this section may be assessed a civil penalty of a maximum of five hundred dollars ($500). *(Stats.1992, c. 162 (A.B.2650), § 10, operative Jan. 1, 1994. Amended by Stats. 2004, c. 369 (A.B.1706), § 1.)*

Law Revision Commission Comments

Enactment [Revised Comment]

Section 5290 continues former Civil Code Section 4390.17 without substantive change. See also Section 5241 (penalty for employer failing to comply with order). [23 Cal.L.Rev.Comm. Reports 1 (1993)].

Research References

Treatises and Practice Aids

Witkin, California Summary 10th Husband and Wife § 253, Rights and Obligations Of Employer.

ARTICLE 8. JUDICIAL COUNCIL FORMS

§ 5295. Forms

The Judicial Council shall prescribe forms necessary to carry out the requirements of this chapter, including the following:

(a) The written statement of the obligor's rights.

(b) The earnings assignment order for support.

(c) The instruction guide for obligees and obligors.

(d) The application forms required under Sections 5230, 5252, and 5261.

(e) The notice form required under Section 5252.

(f) Revised judgment and assignment order forms as necessary. *(Stats.1992, c. 162 (A.B.2650), § 10, operative Jan. 1, 1994.)*

Law Revision Commission Comments

Enactment [Revised Comment]

Section 5295 continues former Civil Code Section 4390.15 without substantive change. [23 Cal.L.Rev.Comm. Reports 1 (1993)].

Research References

Forms

Cal. Transaction Forms - Bus. Transactions § 16:83, Exclusions.
Cal. Transaction Forms - Bus. Transactions § 16:84, Form Drafting Principles.
Cal. Transaction Forms - Bus. Transactions § 16:88, Assignment Of Wages or Salary (General).

Treatises and Practice Aids

Witkin, California Summary 10th Husband and Wife § 249, in General.

ARTICLE 9. INTERCOUNTY SUPPORT OBLIGATIONS

§ 5600. Registration of order for support or earnings withholding obtained in another county

(a) A local child support agency or obligee may register an order for support or earnings withholding, or both, obtained in another county of the state.

(b) An obligee may register a support order in the court of another county of this state in the manner, with the effect, and for the purposes provided in this part. The orders may be registered in any county in which the obligor, the obligee, or the child who is the subject of the order resides, or in any county in which the obligor has income, assets, or any other property. *(Added by Stats.1997, c. 599 (A.B.573), § 35. Amended by Stats.2000, c. 808 (A.B.1358), § 68, eff. Sept. 28, 2000.)*

Research References

Forms

West's California Code Forms, Family § 5600, Comment Overview--Intercounty Support Obligations.

Treatises and Practice Aids

Witkin, California Summary 10th Husband and Wife § 269, in General.

§ 5601. Registration by local child support agency of support order made in another county; procedures; motion to vacate; notice of registration

(a) When the local child support agency is responsible for the enforcement of a support order pursuant to Section 17400, the local child support agency may register a support order made in another county by utilizing the procedures set forth in Section 5602 or by filing all of the following in the superior court of his or her county:

(1) An endorsed file copy of the most recent support order or a copy thereof.

(2) A statement of arrearages, including an accounting of amounts ordered and paid each month, together with any added costs, fees, and interest.

(3) A statement prepared by the local child support agency showing the post office address of the local child support agency, the last known place of residence or post office

address of the obligor; the most recent address of the obligor set forth in the licensing records of the Department of Motor Vehicles, if known; and a list of other states and counties in California that are known to the local child support agency in which the original order of support and any modifications are registered.

(b) The filing of the documents described in subdivision (a) constitutes registration under this chapter.

(c) Promptly upon registration, the local child support agency shall, in compliance with the requirements of Section 1013 of the Code of Civil Procedure, or in any other manner as provided by law, serve the obligor with copies of the documents described in subdivision (a).

(d) If a motion to vacate registration is filed under Section 5603, any party may introduce into evidence copies of any pleadings, documents, or orders that have been filed in the original court or other courts where the support order has been registered or modified. Certified copies of the documents shall not be required unless a party objects to the authenticity or accuracy of the document in which case it shall be the responsibility of the party who is asserting the authenticity of the document to obtain a certified copy of the questioned document.

(e) Upon registration, the clerk of the court shall forward a notice of registration to the courts in other counties and states in which the original order for support and any modifications were issued or registered. No further proceedings regarding the obligor's support obligations shall be filed in other counties.

(f) The procedure prescribed by this section may also be used to register support or wage and earnings assignment orders of other California jurisdictions that previously have been registered for purposes of enforcement only pursuant to the Uniform Interstate Family Support Act (Part 6 (commencing with Section 5700.101)) in another California county. The local child support agency may register such an order by filing an endorsed file copy of the registered California order plus any subsequent orders, including procedural amendments.

(g) The Judicial Council shall develop the forms necessary to effectuate this section. These forms shall be available no later than July 1, 1998. *(Added by Stats.1997, c. 599 (A.B.573), § 35. Amended by Stats.2000, c. 808 (A.B.1358), § 69, eff. Sept. 28, 2000; Stats.2015, c. 493 (S.B.646), § 4, eff. Jan. 1, 2016.)*

Research References

Forms

West's California Code Forms, Family § 5230, Comment Overview--Earnings Assignment Order.
West's California Code Forms, Family § 5600, Comment Overview--Intercounty Support Obligations.
West's California Judicial Council Forms FL-650, Statement for Registration Of California Support Order.
West's California Judicial Council Forms FL-651, Notice Of Registration Of California Support Order.

Treatises and Practice Aids

Witkin, California Summary 10th Husband and Wife § 270, Registration by Local Child Support Agency.
Witkin, California Summary 10th Husband and Wife § 271, Registration by Obligee.
Witkin, California Summary 10th Husband and Wife § 272, Vacation Of Registration.

§ 5602. Registration of order by obligee; procedure; notice

(a) An obligee other than the local child support agency may register an order issued in this state using the same procedures specified in subdivision (a) of Section 5601, except that the obligee shall prepare and file the statement of registration. The statement shall be verified and signed by the obligee showing the mailing address of the obligee, the last known place of residence or mailing address of the obligor, and a list of other states and counties in California in which, to the obligee's knowledge, the original order of support and any modifications are registered.

(b) Upon receipt of the documents described in subdivision (a) of Section 5601, the clerk of the court shall file them without payment of a filing fee or other cost to the obligee. The filing constitutes registration under this chapter.

(c) Promptly upon registration, the clerk of the court shall send, by any form of mail requiring a return receipt from the addressee only, to the obligor at the address given a notice of the registration with a copy of the registered support order and the post office address of the obligee. Proof shall be made to the satisfaction of the court that the obligor personally received the notice of registration by mail or other method of service. A return receipt signed by the obligor shall be satisfactory evidence of personal receipt. *(Added by Stats.1997, c. 599 (A.B.573), § 35. Amended by Stats.2000, c. 808 (A.B.1358), § 70, eff. Sept. 28, 2000.)*

Research References

Forms

West's California Code Forms, Family § 5230, Comment Overview--Earnings Assignment Order.
West's California Code Forms, Family § 5600, Comment Overview--Intercounty Support Obligations.
West's California Judicial Council Forms FL-440, Statement for Registration Of California Support Order.

Treatises and Practice Aids

Witkin, California Summary 10th Husband and Wife § 270, Registration by Local Child Support Agency.
Witkin, California Summary 10th Husband and Wife § 271, Registration by Obligee.
Witkin, California Summary 10th Husband and Wife § 272, Vacation Of Registration.

§ 5603. Motion to vacate registration; procedure; hearing

(a) An obligor shall have 20 days after the service of notice of the registration of a California order of support in which to file a noticed motion requesting the court to vacate the registration or for other relief. In an action under this section, there shall be no joinder of actions, coordination of actions, or cross-complaints, and the claims or defenses shall be limited strictly to the identity of the obligor, the validity of the underlying California support order, or the accuracy of the obligee's statement of the amount of support remaining unpaid unless the amount has been previously established by a judgment or order. The obligor shall serve a copy of the motion, personally or by first-class mail, on the local child support agency, private attorney representing the obligee, or obligee representing himself or herself who filed the request for registration of the order, not less than 15 days prior to the date on which the motion is to be heard. If service is by mail, Section 1013 of the Code of Civil Procedure applies. If the obligor does not file the motion within 20 days, the registered California support order and all other documents filed pursuant to subdivision (a) of Section 5601 or Section 5602 are confirmed.

(b) At the hearing on the motion to vacate the registration of the order, the obligor may present only matters that would be available to the obligor as defenses in an action to enforce a support judgment. If the obligor shows, and the court finds, that an appeal from the order is pending or that a stay of execution has been granted, the court shall stay enforcement of the order until the appeal is concluded, the time for appeal has expired, or the order is vacated, upon satisfactory proof that the obligor has furnished security for payment of the support ordered. If the obligor shows, and the court finds, any ground upon which enforcement of a California support order may be stayed, the court shall stay enforcement of the order for an appropriate period if the obligor furnishes security for payment of support. *(Added by Stats.1997, c. 599 (A.B.573), § 35. Amended by Stats.2000, c. 808 (A.B.1358), § 71, eff. Sept. 28, 2000.)*

Research References

Forms

West's California Code Forms, Family § 5230, Comment Overview-- Earnings Assignment Order.

West's California Judicial Council Forms FL-440, Statement for Registration Of California Support Order.

West's California Judicial Council Forms FL-575, Request for Hearing Regarding Registration Of Support Order.

West's California Judicial Council Forms FL-650, Statement for Registration Of California Support Order.

Treatises and Practice Aids

Witkin, California Summary 10th Husband and Wife § 272, Vacation Of Registration.

§ 5604. Effect of previous determination of paternity made by another state

A previous determination of paternity made by another state, whether established through voluntary acknowledgment procedures in effect in that state or through an administrative or judicial process shall be given full faith and credit by the courts in this state, and shall have the same effect as a paternity determination made in this state and may be enforced and satisfied in a like manner. *(Added by Stats. 1997, c. 599 (A.B.573), § 35.)*

Commentary

Adoption of A.S., 212 Cal.App.4th 188, 151 Cal.Rptr.3d 15 (2012), review denied, held that a New York order of filiation did not confer presumed father status and the right to veto a California adoption, because a California judgment of paternity would not make a man a presumed father under California law.

CHAPTER 9. PRIVATE CHILD SUPPORT COLLECTORS

§ 5610. "Private child support collector" defined

For the purposes of this chapter, "private child support collector" means any individual, corporation, attorney, nonprofit organization, or other nongovernmental entity who is engaged by an obligee to collect child support ordered by a court or other tribunal for a fee or other consideration. The term does not include any attorney who addresses issues of ongoing child support or child support arrearages in the course of an action to establish parentage or a child support obligation, a proceeding under Division 10 (commencing with Section 6200), a proceeding for dissolution of marriage, legal separation, or nullity of marriage, or in postjudgment or modification proceedings related to any of those actions. A "private child support collector" includes any private, nongovernmental attorney whose business is substantially comprised of the collection or enforcement of child support. As used in this section, substantially means that at least 50 percent of the attorney's business, either in terms of remuneration or time spent, is comprised of the activity of seeking to collect or enforce child support obligations for other individuals. *(Added by Stats.2006, c. 797 (A.B.2781), § 1.)*

Research References

Treatises and Practice Aids

Witkin, California Summary 10th Parent and Child § 438A, (New) Private Child Support Collectors.

§ 5611. Contract for child support collection between private child support collector and obligee; contents; notice of cancellation

(a) Any contract for the collection of child support between a private child support collector and an obligee shall be in writing and written in simple language, in at least 10-point type, signed by the private child support collector and the obligee. The contract shall be delivered to the obligee in a paper form that the obligee may retain for his or her records. The contract shall include all of the following:

(1) An explanation of the fees imposed by contract and otherwise permitted by law and an example of how they are calculated and deducted.

(2) A statement that the amount of fees to be charged is set by the agency and is not set by state law.

(3) A statement that the private child support collector cannot charge fees on current support if the obligee received

any current child support during the 6 months preceding execution of the contract with the private collector.

(4) An explanation of the nature of the services to be provided.

(5) The expected duration of the contract, stated as a length of time or as an amount to be collected by the collection agency.

(6) An explanation of the opportunities available to the obligee or private child support collector to cancel the contract or other conditions under which the contract terminates.

(7) The mailing address, street address, telephone numbers, facsimile numbers, and Internet address or location of the private child support collector.

(8) A statement that the private child support collector is not a governmental entity and that governmental entities in California provide child support collection and enforcement services free of charge.

(9) A statement that the private child support collector collects only money owed to the obligee and not support assigned to the state or county due to the receipt of CalWORKs or Temporary Assistance to Needy Families.

(10) A statement that the private child support collector will not retain fees from collections that are primarily attributable to the actions of a governmental entity or any other person or entity and is required by law to refund any fees improperly retained.

(11) A statement that the obligee may continue to receive, or may pursue, services through a governmental entity to collect support, and the private child support collection agency will not require or request that the obligee cease or refrain from engaging those services.

(12) A notice that the private child support collector is required to keep and maintain case records for a period of four years and four months, after the expiration of the contract and may thereafter destroy or otherwise dispose of the records. The obligee may, prior to destruction or disposal, retrieve those portions of the records that are not confidential.

(13) A "Notice of Cancellation," which shall be included with the contract and which shall contain, in the same size font as the contract, the following statement, written in the same language as the contract:

"Notice of Cancellation

You may cancel this contract, without any penalty or obligation, within 15 business days from the date the contract is signed or you receive this notice, whichever is later, or at any time if the private child support collector commits a material breach of any provision of the contract or a material violation of any provision of this chapter with respect to the obligee or the obligor, or __________ (all other reasons for cancellation permitted).
To cancel this contract, mail or deliver a signed copy of this cancellation notice or any other written notice to __________ (name of private child support collector) at __________ (address for mail or delivery) no later than midnight on ______(date).
I am canceling this contract.______(date)
__________(signature)"

(14) The following statement by the obligee on the first page of the contract:

"I understand that this contract calls for (name of private child support collector) to collect money owed to me, and not money owed to the state or county. If child support is owed to the state or county because I am receiving or have received program benefits from CalWORKs or Temporary Assistance to Needy Families, then (name of private child support collector) cannot collect that money for me. If I start to receive program benefits from CalWORKs or Temporary Assistance to Needy Families during this contract, I must notify (name of private child support collector) in writing."

"I declare by my signature below that the child support to be collected for me pursuant to this contract is not assigned to the state or county as of the time I sign this contract. I agree that I will give written notice to the private child support collector if I apply for program benefits under CalWORKs or Temporary Assistance to Needy Families during the term of this contract."

(15)(A) The following statement by the obligee immediately above the signature line of the contract:

"I understand that (name of private child support collector) will charge a fee for all the current child support and arrears it collects for me until the entire contract amount is collected or the contract terminates for another reason. I also understand that depending on the frequency and size of payments, it could take years for the amount specified in my contract to be collected. This means that if (name of private child support collector) is collecting my current support by wage withholding or other means, I will not receive the full amount of my periodic court-ordered current support until the contract terminates since (name of private child support collector) will be deducting its fee from the periodic court-ordered current support it collects for me."

(B) The statement required by subparagraph (A) shall:

(i) Be in a type size that is at least equal to one-quarter of the largest type size used in the contract. In no event shall the disclosure be printed in less than 8–point type.

(ii) Be in a contrasting style, and contrasting color or bold type, which is equally or more visible than the type used in the contract.

(b) The disclosures required by paragraph (1) of subdivision (a) of Section 5612 shall be printed in the contract, as follows:

(1) In a type size that is at least equal to one-quarter of the largest type size used in the contract. In no event shall the disclosure be printed in less than 8–point type.

(2) In a contrasting style, and contrasting color or bold type that is equally or more visible than the type used in the contract.

(3) Immediately above, below, or beside the stated fee without any intervening words, pictures, marks, or symbols.

(4) In the same language as the contract. *(Added by Stats.2006, c. 797 (A.B.2781), § 1.)*

Research References

Treatises and Practice Aids

Witkin, California Summary 10th Parent and Child § 438A, (New) Private Child Support Collectors.

§ 5612. Advertising disclosures

(a) Each private child support collector:

(1) That charges any initial fee, processing fee, application fee, filing fee, or other fee or assessment that must be paid by an obligee regardless of whether any child support collection is made on behalf of the obligee shall make the following disclosure in every radio, television, or print advertisement intended for a target audience consisting primarily of California residents:

"(Name of private child support collector) is not a governmental entity and charges an upfront fee for its services even if it does not collect anything."

(2) That does not charge any fee or assessment specified in paragraph (1) shall make the following disclosure in every radio, television, or print advertisement aired for a target audience consisting primarily of California residents:

"(Name of private child support collector) is not a governmental entity and charges a fee for its services."

(b) The disclosures required in subdivision (a) shall also be stated during the first 30 seconds of any initial telephone conversation with an obligee and in the private child support collector's contract. *(Added by Stats.2006, c. 797 (A.B.2781), § 1.)*

Research References

Treatises and Practice Aids

Witkin, California Summary 10th Parent and Child § 438A, (New) Private Child Support Collectors.

§ 5613. Cancellation or termination of contract with private child support collector

(a) An obligee shall have the right to cancel a contract with a private support collector under either of the following circumstances:

(1) Within 15 business days of the later of signing the contract, or receiving a blank notice of cancellation form, or at any time if the private child support collector commits a material breach of any provision of the contract or a material violation of any provision of this chapter with respect to the obligee or the obligor.

(2) At the end of any 12–month period in which the total amount collected by the private child support collector is less than 50 percent of the amount scheduled to be paid under a payment plan.

(b) A contract shall automatically terminate when the contract term has expired or the contract amount has been collected, whichever occurs first. *(Added by Stats.2006, c. 797 (A.B.2781), § 1.)*

Research References

Treatises and Practice Aids

Witkin, California Summary 10th Parent and Child § 438A, (New) Private Child Support Collectors.

§ 5614. Duties of private child support collector; prohibited acts

(a) A private child support collector shall do all of the following:

(1)(A) Provide to an obligee all of the following information:

(i) The name of, and any other identifying information relating to, any obligor who made child support payments collected by the private child support collector.

(ii) The amount of support collected by the private child support collector.

(iii) The date on which each amount was received by the private child support collector.

(iv) The date on which each amount received by the private child support collector was sent to the obligee.

(v) The amount of the payment sent to the obligee.

(vi) The source of payment of support collected and the actions affirmatively taken by the private child support collector that resulted in the payment.

(vii) The amount and percentage of each payment kept by the private child support collector as its fee.

(B) The information required by paragraph (A) shall be made available, at the option of the obligee, by mail, telephone, or via secure Internet access. If provided by mail, the notice shall be sent at least quarterly and, if provided by any other method, the information shall be updated and made available at least monthly. Information accessed by telephone and the Internet shall be up to date.

(2) Establish a direct deposit account with the state disbursement unit and shall within two business days from the date the funds are disbursed from the state disbursement unit to the private child support collector, if a portion of the funds constitute an obligor's fee, notify the Department of Child Support Services of the portion of each collection that constitutes a fee. The notification shall be sent by the private child support collector to the department in an electronic format to be determined by the department.

(3) Maintain records of all child support collections made on behalf of a client who is an obligee. The records required under this section shall be maintained by the private child support collector for the duration of the contract plus a period of four years and four months from the date of the last child support payment collected by the private child support collector on behalf of an obligee. In addition to information required by paragraph (1), the private child support collector shall maintain the following:

(A) A copy of the order establishing the child support obligation under which a collection was made by the private child support collector.

(B) Records of all correspondence between the private child support collector and the obligee or obligor in a case.

(C) Any other pertinent information relating to the child support obligation, including any case, cause, or docket number of the court having jurisdiction over the matter and official government payment records obtained by the private child support collector on behalf of, and at the request of, the obligee.

(4) Safeguard case records in a manner reasonably expected to prevent intentional or accidental disclosure of confidential information pertaining to the obligee or obligor, including providing necessary protections for records maintained in an automated system.

(5) Ensure that every person who contracts with a private child support collector has the right to review all files and documents, both paper and electronic, in the possession of the private child support collector for the information specified in this paragraph regarding that obligee's case that are not required by law to be kept confidential. The obligee, during regular business hours, shall be provided reasonable access to and copies of the files and records of the private child support collector regarding all moneys received, collection attempts made, fees retained or paid to the private child support collector, and moneys disbursed to the obligee. The private child support collector may not charge a fee for access to the files and records, but may require the obligee to pay up to three cents ($0.03) per page for the copies prior to their release.

(6) Provide, prior to commencing collection activities, written notice of any contract with an obligee to the local child support agency that is enforcing the obligee's support order, if known, or the local child support agency for the county in which the obligee resides as of the time the contract is signed by the obligee. The notice shall identify the obligee, the obligor, and the amount of the arrearage claimed by the obligee.

(b) A private child support collector shall not do any of the following:

(1) Charge fees on current support if the obligee received any current child support during the six months preceding execution of the contract with the private child support collector. A private child support collector shall inquire of the obligee and record the month and year of the last current support payment and may rely on information provided by the obligee in determining whether a fee may be charged on current support.

(2) Improperly retain fees from collections that are primarily attributable to the actions of a governmental entity. The private child support collector shall refund all of those fees to the obligee immediately upon discovery or notice of the improper retention of fees.

(3) Collect or attempt to collect child support by means of any conduct that is prohibited of a debt collector collecting a consumer debt under Sections 1788.10 to 1788.16, inclusive, of the Civil Code. This chapter does not modify, alter, or amend the definition of a debt or a debt collector under the Rosenthal Fair Debt Collection Practices Act (Title 1.6C (commencing with Section 1788) of Part 4 of Division 3 of the Civil Code).

(4) Misstate the amount of the fee that may be lawfully paid to the private child support collector for the performance of the contract or the identity of the person who is obligated to pay that fee.

(5) Make a false representation of the amount of child support to be collected. A private child support collector is not in violation of this paragraph if it reasonably relied on sufficient documentation provided by the government entity collecting child support, a court with jurisdiction over the support obligation, or from the obligee, or upon sufficient documentation provided by the obligor.

(6) Ask any party other than the obligor to pay the child support obligation, unless that party is legally responsible for the obligation or is the legal representative of the obligor.

(7) Require, on or after January 1, 2007, as a condition of providing services to the obligee, that the obligee waive any right or procedure provided for in any state law regarding the right to file and pursue a civil action, or that the obligee agree to resolve disputes in a jurisdiction outside of California or to the application of laws other than those of California, as provided by law. Any waiver by the obligee of the right to file and pursue a civil action, the right to file and pursue a civil action in California, or the right to rely upon California law as provided by law must be knowing, voluntary, and not made a condition of doing business with the private child support collector. Any waiver, including, but not limited to, an agreement to arbitrate or regarding choice of forum or choice of law, that is required as a condition of doing business with the private child support collector, shall be presumed involuntary, unconscionable, against public policy, and unenforceable. The private child support collector has the burden of proving that any waiver of rights, including any agreement to arbitrate a claim or regarding choice of forum or choice of law, was knowing, voluntary, and not made a condition of the contract with the obligee. *(Added by Stats.2006, c. 797 (A.B.2781), § 1. Amended by Stats.2007, c. 130 (A.B.299), § 89.)*

Research References

Treatises and Practice Aids

Witkin, California Summary 10th Parent and Child § 438A, (New) Private Child Support Collectors.

§ 5615. Remedies for violations of chapter; attorney acting as private child support collector subject to statutes, rules, and cases governing attorney conduct

(a)(1) A person may bring an action for actual damages incurred as a result of a violation of this chapter.

(2) In addition to actual damages, a private child support collector who willfully and knowingly violates the provisions of this chapter shall be liable for a civil penalty in an amount determined by the court, which may not be less than one hundred dollars ($100) nor more than one thousand dollars ($1,000).

(3)(A) The prevailing party in any action pursuant to this chapter shall be entitled to recover the costs of the action. Reasonable attorney's fees, which shall be based on the time necessarily expended to enforce the liability, shall be awarded to a prevailing party, other than the private child support collector, asserting rights under this chapter. Reasonable attorney's fees may be awarded to a prevailing private child support collector if the court finds that the party bringing the action did not prosecute the action in good faith.

(B) In an action by an obligor under this chapter, the private child support collector shall have no civil liability under this chapter to the obligor under any circumstance in which a debt collector would not have civil liability under Section 1788.30 of the Civil Code.

(4) A private child support collector is not in violation of this chapter if the private child support collector shows, by a preponderance of the evidence, that the action complained of was not intentional and resulted from a bona fide error that occurred notwithstanding the use of reasonable procedures to avoid the error.

(5) The remedies provided in this section are cumulative and are in addition to any other procedures, rights, or remedies available under any other law.

(b) Any waiver of the rights, requirements, and remedies provided by this chapter violates public policy and is void.

(c) Notwithstanding any other provision of this chapter, including provisions establishing a right of cancellation and requiring notice thereof, any contract for the collection of child support between an attorney who is a "private child support collector" pursuant to Section 5610 shall conform to the statutes, rules, and case law governing attorney conduct, including the provisions of law providing that a contract with an attorney is cancelable by the attorney's client at any time. Upon cancellation of that contract, the attorney may seek compensation as provided by law, including, if applicable, a claim for the reasonable value of any services rendered to the attorney's client pursuant to the doctrine of quantum meruit, provided those services lead to the collection of support and the compensation is limited to what would have been collected had the contract been in effect. To the extent that the provisions of this chapter are in conflict with the provisions of state law governing the conduct of attorneys, this chapter shall control. If there is no conflict, an attorney who is a "private child support collector" pursuant to Section 5610 shall conform to the provisions of this chapter. *(Added by Stats.2006, c. 797 (A.B.2781), § 1.)*

Research References

Treatises and Practice Aids

Witkin, California Summary 10th Parent and Child § 438A, (New) Private Child Support Collectors.

§ 5616. Court orders for child support and child support agreements; inclusion of provision for separate money judgment to pay fee of private child support collector; enforcement; assignment

(a) Every court order for child support issued on or after January 1, 2010, and every child support agreement providing for the payment of child support approved by a court on or after January 1, 2010, shall include a separate money judgment owed by the child support obligor to pay a fee not to exceed 33 and ⅓ percent of the total amount in arrears, and not to exceed 50 percent of the fee as charged by a private child support collector pursuant to a contract complying with this chapter and any other child support collections costs expressly permitted by the child support order for the collection efforts undertaken by the private child support collector. The money judgment shall be in favor of the private child support collector and the child support obligee, jointly, but shall not constitute a private child support collector lien on real property unless an abstract of judgment is recorded pursuant to subdivision (d). Except as provided in subdivision (c), the money judgment may be enforced by the private child support collector by any means available to the obligee for the enforcement of the child support order without any additional action or order by the court. Nothing in this chapter shall be construed to grant the private child support collector any enforcement remedies beyond those authorized by federal or state law. Any fee collected from the obligor pursuant to a contract complying with this chapter, shall not constitute child support.

(b) If the child support order makes the obligor responsible for payment of collection fees and costs, fees that are deducted by a private child support collector may not be credited against child support arrearages or interest owing on arrearages or any other money owed by the obligor to the obligee.

(c) If the order for child support requires payment of collection fees and costs by the obligor, then not later than five days after the date that the private child support collector makes its first collection, written notice shall be provided to the obligor of (1) the amount of arrearages subject to collection, (2) the amount of the collection that shall be applied to the arrearage, and (3) the amount of the collection that shall be applied to the fees and costs of collection. The notice shall provide that, in addition to any other procedures available, the obligor has 30 days to file a motion to contest the amount of collection fees and costs assessed against the obligor.

(d) Any fees or monetary obligations resulting from the contract between an obligee parent and a private child support collector, or moneys owed to a private child support collector by the obligor parent or obligee parent as a result of the private child support collector's efforts, does not create a lien on real property, unless an abstract of judgment is obtained from the court and recorded by the private child support collector against the real property in the county in which it is located, nor shall that amount be added to any existing lien created by a recorded abstract of support or be added to an obligation on any abstract of judgment. A private child support collector lien shall have the force, effect, and priority of a judgment lien.

(e) An assignment to a private child support collector is a voluntary assignment for the purpose of collecting the domestic support obligation as defined in Section 101 of Title 11 of the United States Bankruptcy Code (11 U.S.C. Sec. 101 (14 A)). *(Added by Stats.2006, c. 797 (A.B.2781), § 1. Amended by Stats.2011, c. 296 (A.B.1023), § 92.)*

Research References

Forms

California Practice Guide: Rutter Family Law Forms Form 5:1, Stipulation to Orders Pending Trial (Attorney-Drafted).
California Practice Guide: Rutter Family Law Forms Form 6:2, Stipulation Re Child Support and Order Thereon (Attorney-Drafted).

California Practice Guide: Rutter Family Law Forms Form 17:1, Stipulation and Order for Modification Of Spousal Support, Child Support, Custody and Visitation.

California Practice Guide: Rutter Family Law Forms Form 11:20, Sample Trial Brief.

Treatises and Practice Aids

Witkin, California Summary 10th Parent and Child § 438A, (New) Private Child Support Collectors.

Part 6

UNIFORM INTERSTATE FAMILY SUPPORT ACT

CHAPTER 1. GENERAL PROVISIONS

§ 5700.101. Short title; federal mandate

(a) This part may be cited as the Uniform Interstate Family Support Act.

(b) There is a federal mandate set forth in Section 666(f) of Title 42 of the United States Code requiring California to adopt and have in effect the Uniform Interstate Family Support Act, including any amendments officially adopted by the National Council of Commissioners on Uniform State Laws as of September 30, 2008. *(Added by Stats.2015, c. 493 (S.B.646), § 5, eff. Jan. 1, 2016.)*

Research References

Treatises and Practice Aids

Witkin, California Summary 10th Husband and Wife § 174, in General.

Witkin, California Summary 10th Husband and Wife § 252, Stay Of Service.

Witkin, California Summary 10th Husband and Wife § 270, Registration by Local Child Support Agency.

Witkin, California Summary 10th Husband and Wife § 345, Proceedings Under UIFSA.

§ 5700.102. Definitions

In this part:

(1) "Child" means an individual, whether over or under the age of majority, who is or is alleged to be owed a duty of support by the individual's parent or who is or is alleged to be the beneficiary of a support order directed to the parent.

(2) "Child–support order" means a support order for a child, including a child who has attained the age of majority under the law of the issuing state or foreign country.

(3) "Convention" means the Convention on the International Recovery of Child Support and Other Forms of Family Maintenance, concluded at The Hague on November 23, 2007.

(4) "Duty of support" means an obligation imposed or imposable by law to provide support for a child, spouse, or former spouse, including an unsatisfied obligation to provide support.

(5) "Foreign country" means a country, including a political subdivision thereof, other than the United States, that authorizes the issuance of support orders and:

(A) Which has been declared under the law of the United States to be a foreign reciprocating country;

(B) Which has established a reciprocal arrangement for child support with this state as provided in Section 5700.308;

(C) Which has enacted a law or established procedures for the issuance and enforcement of support orders which are substantially similar to the procedures under this part; or

(D) In which the Convention is in force with respect to the United States.

(6) "Foreign support order" means a support order of a foreign tribunal.

(7) "Foreign tribunal" means a court, administrative agency, or quasi-judicial entity of a foreign country which is authorized to establish, enforce, or modify support orders or to determine parentage of a child. The term includes a competent authority under the Convention.

(8) "Home state" means the state or foreign country in which a child lived with a parent or a person acting as parent for at least six consecutive months immediately preceding the time of filing of a petition or comparable pleading for support and, if a child is less than six months old, the state or foreign country in which the child lived from birth with any of them. A period of temporary absence of any of them is counted as part of the six-month or other period.

(9) "Income" includes earnings or other periodic entitlements to money from any source and any other property subject to withholding for support under the law of this state.

(10) "Income–withholding order" means an order or other legal process directed to an obligor's employer, or other debtor, as defined by Section 5208, to withhold support from the income of the obligor.

(11) "Initiating tribunal" means the tribunal of a state or foreign country from which a petition or comparable pleading is forwarded or in which a petition or comparable pleading is filed for forwarding to another state or foreign country.

(12) "Issuing foreign country" means the foreign country in which a tribunal issues a support order or a judgment determining parentage of a child.

(13) "Issuing state" means the state in which a tribunal issues a support order or a judgment determining parentage of a child.

(14) "Issuing tribunal" means the tribunal of a state or foreign country that issues a support order or a judgment determining parentage of a child.

(15) "Law" includes decisional and statutory law and rules and regulations having the force of law.

(16) "Obligee" means:

(A) an individual to whom a duty of support is or is alleged to be owed or in whose favor a support order or a judgment determining parentage of a child has been issued;

(B) a foreign country, state, or political subdivision of a state to which the rights under a duty of support or support order have been assigned or which has independent claims based on financial assistance provided to an individual obligee in place of child support;

(C) an individual seeking a judgment determining parentage of the individual's child; or

(D) a person that is a creditor in a proceeding under Chapter 7.

(17) "Obligor" means an individual, or the estate of a decedent that:

(A) owes or is alleged to owe a duty of support;

(B) is alleged but has not been adjudicated to be a parent of a child;

(C) is liable under a support order; or

(D) is a debtor in a proceeding under Chapter 7.

(18) "Outside this state" means a location in another state or a country other than the United States, whether or not the country is a foreign country.

(19) "Person" means an individual, corporation, business trust, estate, trust, partnership, limited liability company, association, joint venture, public corporation, government or governmental subdivision, agency, or instrumentality, or any other legal or commercial entity.

(20) "Record" means information that is inscribed on a tangible medium or that is stored in an electronic or other medium and is retrievable in perceivable form.

(21) "Register" means to file in a tribunal of this state a support order or judgment determining parentage of a child issued in another state or a foreign country.

(22) "Registering tribunal" means a tribunal in which a support order or judgment determining parentage of a child is registered.

(23) "Responding state" means a state in which a petition or comparable pleading for support or to determine parentage of a child is filed or to which a petition or comparable pleading is forwarded for filing from another state or a foreign country.

(24) "Responding tribunal" means the authorized tribunal in a responding state or foreign country.

(25) "Spousal–support order" means a support order for a spouse or former spouse of the obligor.

(26) "State" means a state of the United States, the District of Columbia, Puerto Rico, the United States Virgin Islands, or any territory or insular possession under the jurisdiction of the United States. The term includes an Indian nation or tribe.

(27) "Support enforcement agency" means a public official, governmental entity, or private agency authorized to:

(A) seek enforcement of support orders or laws relating to the duty of support;

(B) seek establishment or modification of child support;

(C) request determination of parentage of a child;

(D) attempt to locate obligors or their assets; or

(E) request determination of the controlling child-support order.

(28) "Support order" means a judgment, decree, order, decision, or directive, whether temporary, final, or subject to modification, issued in a state or foreign country for the benefit of a child, a spouse, or a former spouse, which provides for monetary support, health care, arrearages, retroactive support, or reimbursement for financial assistance provided to an individual obligee in place of child support. The term may include related costs and fees, interest, income withholding, automatic adjustment, reasonable attorney's fees, and other relief.

(29) "Tribunal" means a court, administrative agency, or quasi-judicial entity authorized to establish, enforce, or modify support orders or to determine parentage of a child. *(Added by Stats.2015, c. 493 (S.B.646), § 5, eff. Jan. 1, 2016.)*

§ 5700.103. State tribunal and state enforcement agency

(a) The superior court is the tribunal of this state.

(b) The Department of Child Support Services is the support enforcement agency of this state. *(Added by Stats. 2015, c. 493 (S.B.646), § 5, eff. Jan. 1, 2016.)*

§ 5700.104. Cumulative remedies

(a) Remedies provided by this part are cumulative and do not affect the availability of remedies under other law or the recognition of a foreign support order on the basis of comity.

(b) This part does not:

(1) provide the exclusive method of establishing or enforcing a support order under the law of this state; or

(2) grant a tribunal of this state jurisdiction to render judgment or issue an order relating to child custody or visitation in a proceeding under this part. *(Added by Stats.2015, c. 493 (S.B.646), § 5, eff. Jan. 1, 2016.)*

Research References

Treatises and Practice Aids

Witkin, California Summary 10th Husband and Wife § 345, Proceedings Under UIFSA.

§ 5700.105. Application of part to resident of foreign country and foreign support proceeding

(a) A tribunal of this state shall apply Chapters 1 through 6 and, as applicable, Chapter 7, to a support proceeding involving:

(1) a foreign support order;

(2) a foreign tribunal; or

(3) an obligee, obligor, or child residing in a foreign country.

(b) A tribunal of this state that is requested to recognize and enforce a support order on the basis of comity may apply the procedural and substantive provisions of Chapters 1 through 6.

(c) Chapter 7 applies only to a support proceeding under the Convention. In such a proceeding, if a provision of Chapter 7 is inconsistent with Chapters 1 through 6, Chapter 7 controls. *(Added by Stats.2015, c. 493 (S.B.646), § 5, eff. Jan. 1, 2016.)*

CHAPTER 2. JURISDICTION

§ 5700.201. Bases for jurisdiction over nonresident

(a) In a proceeding to establish or enforce a support order or to determine parentage of a child, a tribunal of this state may exercise personal jurisdiction over a nonresident individual or the individual's guardian or conservator if:

(1) the individual is personally served with notice within this state;

(2) the individual submits to the jurisdiction of this state by consent in a record, by entering a general appearance, or by filing a responsive document having the effect of waiving any contest to personal jurisdiction;

(3) the individual resided with the child in this state;

(4) the individual resided in this state and provided prenatal expenses or support for the child;

(5) the child resides in this state as a result of the acts or directives of the individual;

(6) the individual engaged in sexual intercourse in this state and the child may have been conceived by that act of intercourse;

(7) the individual has filed a declaration of paternity pursuant to Chapter 3 (commencing with Section 7570) of Part 2 of Division 12, maintained in this state by the Department of Child Support Services; or

(8) there is any other basis consistent with the constitutions of this state and the United States for the exercise of personal jurisdiction.

(b) The bases of personal jurisdiction set forth in subsection (a) or in any other law of this state may not be used to acquire personal jurisdiction for a tribunal of this state to modify a child-support order of another state unless the requirements of Section 5700.611 are met, or, in the case of a foreign support order, unless the requirements of Section 5700.615 are met. *(Added by Stats.2015, c. 493 (S.B.646), § 5, eff. Jan. 1, 2016.)*

Research References

Treatises and Practice Aids

Witkin, California Summary 10th Husband and Wife § 345, Proceedings Under UIFSA.

§ 5700.202. Duration of personal jurisdiction

Personal jurisdiction acquired by a tribunal of this state in a proceeding under this part or other law of this state relating to a support order continues as long as a tribunal of this state has continuing, exclusive jurisdiction to modify its order or continuing jurisdiction to enforce its order as provided by Sections 5700.205, 5700.206, and 5700.211. *(Added by Stats. 2015, c. 493 (S.B.646), § 5, eff. Jan. 1, 2016.)*

§ 5700.203. Initiating and responding tribunal of state

Under this part, a tribunal of this state may serve as an initiating tribunal to forward proceedings to a tribunal of another state, and as a responding tribunal for proceedings initiated in another state or a foreign country. *(Added by Stats.2015, c. 493 (S.B.646), § 5, eff. Jan. 1, 2016.)*

§ 5700.204. Simultaneous proceedings

(a) A tribunal of this state may exercise jurisdiction to establish a support order if the petition or comparable pleading is filed after a pleading is filed in another state or a foreign country only if:

(1) the petition or comparable pleading in this state is filed before the expiration of the time allowed in the other state or the foreign country for filing a responsive pleading challenging the exercise of jurisdiction by the other state or the foreign country;

(2) the contesting party timely challenges the exercise of jurisdiction in the other state or the foreign country; and

(3) if relevant, this state is the home state of the child.

(b) A tribunal of this state may not exercise jurisdiction to establish a support order if the petition or comparable pleading is filed before a petition or comparable pleading is filed in another state or a foreign country if:

(1) the petition or comparable pleading in the other state or foreign country is filed before the expiration of the time allowed in this state for filing a responsive pleading challenging the exercise of jurisdiction by this state;

(2) the contesting party timely challenges the exercise of jurisdiction in this state; and

(3) if relevant, the other state or foreign country is the home state of the child. *(Added by Stats.2015, c. 493 (S.B.646), § 5, eff. Jan. 1, 2016.)*

Commentary

This section repeats the substance of former Family Code section 4908. Decided under that section, section 200 and section 2010(c), in a proceeding to dissolve a marriage a California Superior Court has jurisdiction to award child support even though a child's home state is Japan, when no support action has ever been initiated in the child's home state. *In re Marriage of Richardson, 179 Cal.App.4th 1240, 102 Cal.Rptr.3d 391 (2009).*

So long as the issue of support has not been raised in a divorce action pending in another jurisdiction, a California court is not divested of jurisdiction to order support. Under former Family code section 4908, *In re Marriage of Newman, 80 Cal.App.4th 846, 95 Cal.Rptr.3d 691 (2000)*, interpreted a subsection (a) "petition or comparable pleading" to refer only to a support proceeding or a proceeding that raises a support issue, rather than any proceeding in which support could be sought.

§ 5700.205. Continuing, exclusive jurisdiction to modify child-support order

(a) A tribunal of this state that has issued a child-support order consistent with the law of this state has and shall exercise continuing, exclusive jurisdiction to modify its child-support order if the order is the controlling order and:

(1) at the time of the filing of a request for modification this state is the residence of the obligor, the individual obligee, or the child for whose benefit the support order is issued; or

(2) even if this state is not the residence of the obligor, the individual obligee, or the child for whose benefit the support order is issued, the parties consent in a record or in open court that the tribunal of this state may continue to exercise jurisdiction to modify its order.

(b) A tribunal of this state that has issued a child-support order consistent with the law of this state may not exercise continuing, exclusive jurisdiction to modify the order if:

(1) all of the parties who are individuals file consent in a record with the tribunal of this state that a tribunal of another state that has jurisdiction over at least one of the parties who is an individual or that is located in the state of residence of the child may modify the order and assume continuing, exclusive jurisdiction; or

(2) its order is not the controlling order.

(c) If a tribunal of another state has issued a child-support order pursuant to the Uniform Interstate Family Support Act or a law substantially similar to that Act which modifies a child-support order of a tribunal of this state, tribunals of this state shall recognize the continuing, exclusive jurisdiction of the tribunal of the other state.

(d) A tribunal of this state that lacks continuing, exclusive jurisdiction to modify a child-support order may serve as an initiating tribunal to request a tribunal of another state to modify a support order issued in that state.

(e) A temporary support order issued ex parte or pending resolution of a jurisdictional conflict does not create continuing, exclusive jurisdiction in the issuing tribunal. *(Added by Stats.2015, c. 493 (S.B.646), § 5, eff. Jan. 1, 2016.)*

Commentary

This section repeats a portion of the content of former Family Code section 4909. Interpreting subsection (a) of the prior section, *Stone v. Davis, 148 Cal.App.4th 596, 55 Cal.Rptr.3d 833 (2007)*, held that a trial court improperly transferred continuing exclusive jurisdiction of a child support order to another state when one party continued to reside in California and the other parties had not filed consent in writing to jurisdiction in another state.

Research References

Treatises and Practice Aids

Witkin, California Summary 10th Husband and Wife § 273, Continuing Jurisdiction.

§ 5700.206. Initiating tribunal to request tribunal of another state to enforce; continuing jurisdiction to enforce child-support order

(a) A tribunal of this state that has issued a child-support order consistent with the law of this state may serve as an initiating tribunal to request a tribunal of another state to enforce:

(1) the order if the order is the controlling order and has not been modified by a tribunal of another state that assumed jurisdiction pursuant to the Uniform Interstate Family Support Act; or

(2) a money judgment for arrears of support and interest on the order accrued before a determination that an order of a tribunal of another state is the controlling order.

(b) A tribunal of this state having continuing jurisdiction over a support order may act as a responding tribunal to enforce the order. *(Added by Stats.2015, c. 493 (S.B.646), § 5, eff. Jan. 1, 2016.)*

§ 5700.207. Determination of controlling child-support order

(a) If a proceeding is brought under this part and only one tribunal has issued a child-support order, the order of that tribunal controls and must be recognized.

(b) If a proceeding is brought under this part, and two or more child-support orders have been issued by tribunals of this state, another state, or a foreign country with regard to the same obligor and same child, a tribunal of this state having personal jurisdiction over both the obligor and individual obligee shall apply the following rules and by order shall determine which order controls and must be recognized:

(1) If only one of the tribunals would have continuing, exclusive jurisdiction under this part, the order of that tribunal controls.

(2) If more than one of the tribunals would have continuing, exclusive jurisdiction under this part:

(A) an order issued by a tribunal in the current home state of the child controls; or

(B) if an order has not been issued in the current home state of the child, the order most recently issued controls.

(3) If none of the tribunals would have continuing, exclusive jurisdiction under this part, the tribunal of this state shall issue a child-support order, which controls.

(c) If two or more child-support orders have been issued for the same obligor and same child, upon request of a party who is an individual or that is a support enforcement agency, a tribunal of this state having personal jurisdiction over both the obligor and the obligee who is an individual shall determine which order controls under subsection (b). The request may be filed with a registration for enforcement or registration for modification pursuant to Chapter 6, or may be filed as a separate proceeding.

(d) A request to determine which is the controlling order must be accompanied by a copy of every child-support order in effect and the applicable record of payments. The requesting party shall give notice of the request to each party whose rights may be affected by the determination.

(e) The tribunal that issued the controlling order under subsection (a), (b), or (c) has continuing jurisdiction to the extent provided in Section 5700.205 or 5700.206.

(f) A tribunal of this state that determines by order which is the controlling order under subsection (b)(1) or (2) or (c), or that issues a new controlling order under subsection(b)(3), shall state in that order:

(1) the basis upon which the tribunal made its determination;

(2) the amount of prospective support, if any; and

(3) the total amount of consolidated arrears and accrued interest, if any, under all of the orders after all payments made are credited as provided by Section 5700.209.

(g) Within 30 days after issuance of an order determining which is the controlling order, the party obtaining the order shall file a certified copy of it in each tribunal that issued or registered an earlier order of child support. A party or support enforcement agency obtaining the order that fails to file a certified copy is subject to appropriate sanctions by a tribunal in which the issue of failure to file arises. The failure to file does not affect the validity or enforceability of the controlling order.

(h) An order that has been determined to be the controlling order, or a judgment for consolidated arrears of support and interest, if any, made pursuant to this section must be recognized in proceedings under this part. *(Added by Stats.2015, c. 493 (S.B.646), § 5, eff. Jan. 1, 2016.)*

§ 5700.208. Child-support order for two or more obligees

In responding to registrations or petitions for enforcement of two or more child-support orders in effect at the same time with regard to the same obligor and different individual obligees, at least one of which was issued by a tribunal of another state or a foreign country, a tribunal of this state shall enforce those orders in the same manner as if the orders had been issued by a tribunal of this state. *(Added by Stats.2015, c. 493 (S.B.646), § 5, eff. Jan. 1, 2016.)*

§ 5700.209. Credit for payments

A tribunal of this state shall credit amounts collected for a particular period pursuant to any child-support order against the amounts owed for the same period under any other child-support order for support of the same child issued by a tribunal of this state, another state, or a foreign country. *(Added by Stats.2015, c. 493 (S.B.646), § 5, eff. Jan. 1, 2016.)*

§ 5700.210. Application of part to nonresident subject to personal jurisdiction

A tribunal of this state exercising personal jurisdiction over a nonresident in a proceeding under this part, under other law of this state relating to a support order, or recognizing a foreign support order may receive evidence from outside this state pursuant to Section 5700.316, communicate with a tribunal outside this state pursuant to Section 5700.317, and obtain discovery through a tribunal outside this state pursuant to Section 5700.318. In all other respects, Chapters 3 through 6 do not apply, and the tribunal shall apply the procedural and substantive law of this state. *(Added by Stats.2015, c. 493 (S.B.646), § 5, eff. Jan. 1, 2016.)*

§ 5700.211. Continuing, exclusive jurisdiction to modify spousal-support order

(a) A tribunal of this state issuing a spousal-support order consistent with the law of this state has continuing, exclusive jurisdiction to modify the spousal-support order throughout the existence of the support obligation.

(b) A tribunal of this state may not modify a spousal-support order issued by a tribunal of another state or a foreign country having continuing, exclusive jurisdiction over that order under the law of that state or foreign country.

(c) A tribunal of this state that has continuing, exclusive jurisdiction over a spousal-support order may serve as:

(1) an initiating tribunal to request a tribunal of another state to enforce the spousal-support order issued in this state; or

(2) a responding tribunal to enforce or modify its own spousal-support order. *(Added by Stats.2015, c. 493 (S.B. 646), § 5, eff. Jan. 1, 2016.)*

Commentary

This section repeats the content of former Family Code section 4914. Although the Uniform Interstate Family Support Act (UIFSA) provides for a controlling child support order (§§ 5700.206, 5700.207, 5700.211), there is no comparable provision for spousal support orders. Instead, UIFSA contemplates the possibility of multiple support orders properly issued under the earlier interstate acts (URESA and RURESA) and provides, in subsection (a), that the state initially issuing the spousal support order has continuing exclusive jurisdiction to modify it and, in subsection (b), that it may not be modified by a tribunal in any other state. For extensive discussion of this aspect of UIFSA, see *Lundahl v. Telford, 116 Cal.App.4th 305, 9 Cal.Rptr.3d 902 (2004).*

CHAPTER 3. CIVIL PROVISIONS OF GENERAL APPLICATION

Section

§ 5700.301. Proceedings under part

(a) Except as otherwise provided in this part, this chapter applies to all proceedings under this part.

(b) An individual petitioner or a support enforcement agency may initiate a proceeding authorized under this part by filing a petition in an initiating tribunal for forwarding to a responding tribunal or by filing a petition or a comparable pleading directly in a tribunal of another state or a foreign country which has or can obtain personal jurisdiction over the respondent. *(Added by Stats.2015, c. 493 (S.B.646), § 5, eff. Jan. 1, 2016.)*

§ 5700.302. Proceeding by minor parent

A minor parent, or a guardian or other legal representative of a minor parent, may maintain a proceeding on behalf of or for the benefit of the minor's child. *(Added by Stats.2015, c. 493 (S.B.646), § 5, eff. Jan. 1, 2016.)*

§ 5700.303. Application of law of state

Except as otherwise provided in this part, a responding tribunal of this state shall:

(1) apply the procedural and substantive law generally applicable to similar proceedings originating in this state and may exercise all powers and provide all remedies available in those proceedings; and

(2) determine the duty of support and the amount payable in accordance with the law and support guidelines of this state. *(Added by Stats.2015, c. 493 (S.B.646), § 5, eff. Jan. 1, 2016.)*

§ 5700.304. Duties of initiating tribunal

(a) Upon the filing of a petition authorized by this part, an initiating tribunal of this state shall forward the petition and its accompanying documents:

(1) to the responding tribunal or appropriate support enforcement agency in the responding state; or

(2) if the identity of the responding tribunal is unknown, to the state information agency of the responding state with a request that they be forwarded to the appropriate tribunal and that receipt be acknowledged.

(b) If requested by the responding tribunal, a tribunal of this state shall issue a certificate or other document and make findings required by the law of the responding state. If the responding tribunal is in a foreign country, upon request the tribunal of this state shall specify the amount of support sought, convert that amount into the equivalent amount in the foreign currency under applicable official or market exchange rate as publicly reported, and provide any other documents necessary to satisfy the requirements of the responding foreign tribunal. *(Added by Stats.2015, c. 493 (S.B.646), § 5, eff. Jan. 1, 2016.)*

§ 5700.305. Duties and powers of responding tribunal

(a) When a responding tribunal of this state receives a petition or comparable pleading from an initiating tribunal or directly pursuant to Section 5700.301(b), it shall cause the petition or pleading to be filed and notify the petitioner where and when it was filed.

(b) A responding tribunal of this state, to the extent not prohibited by other law, may do one or more of the following:

(1) establish or enforce a support order, modify a child-support order, determine the controlling child-support order, or determine parentage of a child;

(2) order an obligor to comply with a support order, specifying the amount and the manner of compliance;

(3) order income withholding;

(4) determine the amount of any arrearages, and specify a method of payment;

(5) enforce orders by civil or criminal contempt, or both;

(6) set aside property for satisfaction of the support order;

(7) place liens and order execution on the obligor's property;

(8) order an obligor to keep the tribunal informed of the obligor's current residential address, electronic-mail address, telephone number, employer, address of employment, and telephone number at the place of employment;

(9) issue a bench warrant for an obligor who has failed after proper notice to appear at a hearing ordered by the tribunal and enter the bench warrant in any local and state computer systems for criminal warrants;

(10) order the obligor to seek appropriate employment by specified methods;

(11) award reasonable attorney's fees and other fees and costs; and

(12) grant any other available remedy.

(c) A responding tribunal of this state shall include in a support order issued under this part, or in the documents accompanying the order, the calculations on which the support order is based.

(d) A responding tribunal of this state may not condition the payment of a support order issued under this part upon compliance by a party with provisions for visitation.

(e) If a responding tribunal of this state issues an order under this part, the tribunal shall send a copy of the order to the petitioner and the respondent and to the initiating tribunal, if any.

(f) If requested to enforce a support order, arrears, or judgment or modify a support order stated in a foreign currency, a responding tribunal of this state shall convert the amount stated in the foreign currency to the equivalent amount in dollars under the applicable official or market exchange rate as publicly reported. *(Added by Stats.2015, c. 493 (S.B.646), § 5, eff. Jan. 1, 2016.)*

§ 5700.306. Inappropriate tribunal

If a petition or comparable pleading is received by an inappropriate tribunal of this state, the tribunal shall forward the pleading and accompanying documents to an appropriate tribunal of this state or another state and notify the petitioner where and when the pleading was sent. *(Added by Stats.2015, c. 493 (S.B.646), § 5, eff. Jan. 1, 2016.)*

§ 5700.307. Duties of support enforcement agency

(a) A support enforcement agency of this state, upon request, shall provide services to a petitioner in a proceeding under this part.

(b) A support enforcement agency of this state that is providing services to the petitioner shall:

(1) take all steps necessary to enable an appropriate tribunal of this state, another state, or a foreign country to obtain jurisdiction over the respondent;

(2) request an appropriate tribunal to set a date, time, and place for a hearing;

(3) make a reasonable effort to obtain all relevant information, including information as to income and property of the parties;

(4) within 14 days, exclusive of Saturdays, Sundays, and legal holidays, after receipt of notice in a record from an initiating, responding, or registering tribunal, send a copy of the notice to the petitioner;

(5) within 14 days, exclusive of Saturdays, Sundays, and legal holidays, after receipt of communication in a record from the respondent or the respondent's attorney, send a copy of the communication to the petitioner; and

(6) notify the petitioner if jurisdiction over the respondent cannot be obtained.

(c) A support enforcement agency of this state that requests registration of a child-support order in this state for enforcement or for modification shall make reasonable efforts:

(1) to ensure that the order to be registered is the controlling order; or

(2) if two or more child-support orders exist and the identity of the controlling order has not been determined, to ensure that a request for such a determination is made in a tribunal having jurisdiction to do so.

(d) A support enforcement agency of this state that requests registration and enforcement of a support order, arrears, or judgment stated in a foreign currency shall convert the amounts stated in the foreign currency into the equivalent amounts in dollars under the applicable official or market exchange rate as publicly reported.

(e) A support enforcement agency of this state shall issue or request a tribunal of this state to issue a child-support order and an income-withholding order that redirect payment of current support, arrears, and interest if requested to do so by a support enforcement agency of another state pursuant to Section 5700.319.

(f) This part does not create or negate a relationship of attorney and client or other fiduciary relationship between a support enforcement agency or the attorney for the agency and the individual being assisted by the agency. *(Added by Stats.2015, c. 493 (S.B.646), § 5, eff. Jan. 1, 2016.)*

§ 5700.308. Duty of Attorney General or Department of Child Support Services

(a) If the Attorney General or the Department of Child Support Services determines that the support enforcement agency is neglecting or refusing to provide services to an individual, the Attorney General or the department may order the agency to perform its duties under this part or may provide those services directly to the individual.

(b) The Department of Child Support Services, in consultation with the Attorney General, may determine that a foreign country has established a reciprocal arrangement for child support with this state and take appropriate action for notification of the determination. *(Added by Stats.2015, c. 493 (S.B.646), § 5, eff. Jan. 1, 2016.)*

§ 5700.309. Private counsel

An individual may employ private counsel to represent the individual in proceedings authorized by this part. *(Added by Stats.2015, c. 493 (S.B.646), § 5, eff. Jan. 1, 2016.)*

§ 5700.310. Duties of state information agency

(a) The Department of Child Support Services is the state information agency under this part.

(b) The state information agency shall:

(1) compile and maintain a current list, including addresses, of the tribunals in this state which have jurisdiction under this part and any support enforcement agencies in this state and transmit a copy to the state information agency of every other state;

(2) maintain a register of names and addresses of tribunals and support enforcement agencies received from other states;

(3) forward to the appropriate tribunal in the county in this state in which the obligee who is an individual or the obligor resides, or in which the obligor's property is believed to be located, all documents concerning a proceeding under this part received from another state or a foreign country; and

(4) obtain information concerning the location of the obligor and the obligor's property within this state not exempt from execution, by such means as postal verification and federal or state locator services, examination of telephone directories, requests for the obligor's address from employers, and examination of governmental records, including, to the extent not prohibited by other law, those relating to real property, vital statistics, law enforcement, taxation, motor vehicles, driver's licenses, and social security. *(Added by Stats.2015, c. 493 (S.B.646), § 5, eff. Jan. 1, 2016.)*

§ 5700.311. Pleadings and accompanying documents

(a) In a proceeding under this part, a petitioner seeking to establish a support order, to determine parentage of a child, or to register and modify a support order of a tribunal of another state or a foreign country must file a petition. Unless otherwise ordered under Section 5700.312, the petition or accompanying documents must provide, so far as known, the name, residential address, and social security numbers of the obligor and the obligee or the parent and alleged parent, and the name, sex, residential address, social security number, and date of birth of each child for whose benefit support is sought or whose parentage is to be determined. Unless filed at the time of registration, the petition must be accompanied by a copy of any support order known to have been issued by another tribunal. The petition may include any other information that may assist in locating or identifying the respondent.

(b) The petition must specify the relief sought. The petition and accompanying documents must conform substantially with the requirements imposed by the forms mandated by federal law for use in cases filed by a support enforcement agency. *(Added by Stats.2015, c. 493 (S.B.646), § 5, eff. Jan. 1, 2016.)*

§ 5700.312. Nondisclosure of information in exceptional circumstances

If a party alleges in an affidavit or a pleading under oath that the health, safety, or liberty of a party or child would be jeopardized by disclosure of specific identifying information, that information must be sealed and may not be disclosed to the other party or the public. After a hearing in which a tribunal takes into consideration the health, safety, or liberty of the party or child, the tribunal may order disclosure of information that the tribunal determines to be in the interest of justice. *(Added by Stats.2015, c. 493 (S.B.646), § 5, eff. Jan. 1, 2016.)*

§ 5700.313. Costs and fees

(a) The petitioner may not be required to pay a filing fee or other costs.

(b) If an obligee prevails, a responding tribunal of this state may assess against an obligor filing fees, reasonable attorney's fees, other costs, and necessary travel and other reasonable expenses incurred by the obligee and the obligee's witnesses. The tribunal may not assess fees, costs, or expenses against the obligee or the support enforcement agency of either the initiating or responding state or foreign country, except as provided by other law. Attorney's fees may be taxed as costs, and may be ordered paid directly to the attorney, who may enforce the order in the attorney's own name. Payment of support owed to the obligee has priority over fees, costs, and expenses.

(c) The tribunal shall order the payment of costs and reasonable attorney's fees if it determines that a hearing was requested primarily for delay. In a proceeding under Chapter 6, a hearing is presumed to have been requested primarily for delay if a registered support order is confirmed or enforced without change. *(Added by Stats.2015, c. 493 (S.B.646), § 5, eff. Jan. 1, 2016.)*

§ 5700.314. Limited immunity of petitioner

(a) Participation by a petitioner in a proceeding under this part before a responding tribunal, whether in person, by private attorney, or through services provided by the support enforcement agency, does not confer personal jurisdiction over the petitioner in another proceeding.

(b) A petitioner is not amenable to service of civil process while physically present in this state to participate in a proceeding under this part.

(c) The immunity granted by this section does not extend to civil litigation based on acts unrelated to a proceeding under this part committed by a party while physically present in this state to participate in the proceeding. *(Added by Stats.2015, c. 493 (S.B.646), § 5, eff. Jan. 1, 2016.)*

§ 5700.315. Nonparentage as defense

A party whose parentage of a child has been previously determined by or pursuant to law may not plead nonparentage as a defense to a proceeding under this part. *(Added by Stats.2015, c. 493 (S.B.646), § 5, eff. Jan. 1, 2016.)*

§ 5700.316. Special rules of evidence and procedure

(a) The physical presence of a nonresident party who is an individual in a tribunal of this state is not required for the establishment, enforcement, or modification of a support order or the rendition of a judgment determining parentage of a child.

(b) An affidavit, a document substantially complying with federally mandated forms, or a document incorporated by reference in any of them, which would not be excluded under the hearsay rule if given in person, is admissible in evidence if given under penalty of perjury by a party or witness residing outside this state.

(c) A copy of the record of child-support payments certified as a true copy of the original by the custodian of the record may be forwarded to a responding tribunal. The copy is evidence of facts asserted in it, and is admissible to show whether payments were made.

(d) Copies of bills for testing for parentage of a child, and for prenatal and postnatal health care of the mother and child, furnished to the adverse party at least 10 days before trial, are admissible in evidence to prove the amount of the charges billed and that the charges were reasonable, necessary, and customary.

(e) Documentary evidence transmitted from outside this state to a tribunal of this state by telephone, telecopier, or other electronic means that do not provide an original record may not be excluded from evidence on an objection based on the means of transmission.

(f) In a proceeding under this part, a tribunal of this state shall permit a party or witness residing outside this state to be deposed or to testify under penalty of perjury by telephone, audiovisual means, or other electronic means at a designated tribunal or other location. A tribunal of this state shall cooperate with other tribunals in designating an appropriate location for the deposition or testimony.

(g) If a party called to testify at a civil hearing refuses to answer on the ground that the testimony may be self-incriminating, the trier of fact may draw an adverse inference from the refusal.

(h) A privilege against disclosure of communications between spouses does not apply in a proceeding under this part.

(i) The defense of immunity based on the relationship of husband and wife or parent and child does not apply in a proceeding under this part.

(j) A voluntary acknowledgment of paternity, certified as a true copy, is admissible to establish parentage of the child. *(Added by Stats.2015, c. 493 (S.B.646), § 5, eff. Jan. 1, 2016.)*

Research References

Treatises and Practice Aids

Witkin, California Summary 10th Husband and Wife § 327, Hearing.

§ 5700.317. Communications between tribunals

A tribunal of this state may communicate with a tribunal outside this state in a record or by telephone, electronic mail, or other means, to obtain information concerning the laws, the legal effect of a judgment, decree, or order of that tribunal, and the status of a proceeding. A tribunal of this state may furnish similar information by similar means to a tribunal outside this state. *(Added by Stats.2015, c. 493 (S.B.646), § 5, eff. Jan. 1, 2016.)*

§ 5700.318. Assistance with discovery

A tribunal of this state may:

(1) request a tribunal outside this state to assist in obtaining discovery; and

(2) upon request, compel a person over which it has jurisdiction to respond to a discovery order issued by a tribunal outside this state. *(Added by Stats.2015, c. 493 (S.B.646), § 5, eff. Jan. 1, 2016.)*

§ 5700.319. Receipt and disbursement of payments

(a) A support enforcement agency or tribunal of this state shall disburse promptly any amounts received pursuant to a support order, as directed by the order. The agency or tribunal shall furnish to a requesting party or tribunal of another state or a foreign country a certified statement by the custodian of the record of the amounts and dates of all payments received.

(b) If neither the obligor, nor the obligee who is an individual, nor the child resides in this state, upon request from the support enforcement agency of this state or another state, the Department of Child Support Services or a tribunal of this state shall:

(1) direct that the support payment be made to the support enforcement agency in the state in which the obligee is receiving services; and

(2) issue and send to the obligor's employer a conforming income-withholding order or an administrative notice of change of payee, reflecting the redirected payments.

(c) The support enforcement agency of this state receiving redirected payments from another state pursuant to a law similar to subsection (b) shall furnish to a requesting party or tribunal of the other state a certified statement by the custodian of the record of the amount and dates of all payments received. *(Added by Stats.2015, c. 493 (S.B.646), § 5, eff. Jan. 1, 2016.)*

CHAPTER 4. ESTABLISHMENT OF SUPPORT ORDER OR DETERMINATION OF PARENTAGE

§ 5700.401. Issuance of support orders; temporary child-support orders

(a) If a support order entitled to recognition under this part has not been issued, a responding tribunal of this state with personal jurisdiction over the parties may issue a support order if:

(1) the individual seeking the order resides outside this state; or

(2) the support enforcement agency seeking the order is located outside this state.

(b) The tribunal may issue a temporary child-support order if the tribunal determines that such an order is appropriate and the individual ordered to pay is:

(1) a presumed father of the child;

(2) petitioning to have his paternity adjudicated;

(3) identified as the father of the child through genetic testing;

(4) an alleged father who has declined to submit to genetic testing;

(5) shown by clear and convincing evidence to be the father of the child;

(6) an acknowledged father as provided by applicable state law;

(7) the mother of the child; or

(8) an individual who has been ordered to pay child support in a previous proceeding and the order has not been reversed or vacated.

(c) Upon finding, after notice and opportunity to be heard, that an obligor owes a duty of support, the tribunal shall issue a support order directed to the obligor and may issue other orders pursuant to Section 5700.305. *(Added by Stats.2015, c. 493 (S.B.646), § 5, eff. Jan. 1, 2016.)*

§ 5700.402. Proceeding to determine parentage

A tribunal of this state authorized to determine parentage of a child may serve as a responding tribunal in a proceeding to determine parentage of a child brought under this part or a law or procedure substantially similar to this part. *(Added by Stats.2015, c. 493 (S.B.646), § 5, eff. Jan. 1, 2016.)*

CHAPTER 5. ENFORCEMENT OF SUPPORT ORDER WITHOUT REGISTRATION

§ 5700.501. Employer's receipt of income-withholding order of another state

An income-withholding order issued in another state may be sent by or on behalf of the obligee, or by the support enforcement agency, to the person defined as the obligor's employer under Section 5210 without first filing a petition or comparable pleading or registering the order with a tribunal of this state. *(Added by Stats.2015, c. 493 (S.B.646), § 5, eff. Jan. 1, 2016.)*

Research References

Treatises and Practice Aids

Witkin, California Summary 10th Husband and Wife § 345, Proceedings Under UIFSA.

§ 5700.502. Employer's compliance with income-withholding order of another state

(a) Upon receipt of an income-withholding order, the obligor's employer shall immediately provide a copy of the order to the obligor.

(b) The employer shall treat an income-withholding order issued in another state which appears regular on its face as if it had been issued by a tribunal of this state.

(c) Except as otherwise provided in subsection (d) and Section 5700.503, the employer shall withhold and distribute the funds as directed in the withholding order by complying with terms of the order which specify:

(1) the duration and amount of periodic payments of current child support, stated as a sum certain;

(2) the person designated to receive payments and the address to which the payments are to be forwarded;

(3) medical support, whether in the form of periodic cash payment, stated as a sum certain, or ordering the obligor to provide health insurance coverage for the child under a policy available through the obligor's employment;

(4) the amount of periodic payments of fees and costs for a support enforcement agency, the issuing tribunal, and the obligee's attorney, stated as sums certain; and

(5) the amount of periodic payments of arrearages and interest on arrearages, stated as sums certain.

(d) An employer shall comply with the law of the state of the obligor's principal place of employment for withholding from income with respect to:

(1) the employer's fee for processing an income-withholding order;

(2) the maximum amount permitted to be withheld from the obligor's income; and

(3) the times within which the employer must implement the withholding order and forward the child-support payment. *(Added by Stats.2015, c. 493 (S.B.646), § 5, eff. Jan. 1, 2016.)*

§ 5700.503. Employer's compliance with two or more income-withholding orders

If an obligor's employer receives two or more income-withholding orders with respect to the earnings of the same obligor, the employer satisfies the terms of the orders if the employer complies with the law of the state of the obligor's principal place of employment to establish the priorities for withholding and allocating income withheld for two or more child-support obligees. *(Added by Stats.2015, c. 493 (S.B. 646), § 5, eff. Jan. 1, 2016.)*

§ 5700.504. Immunity from civil liability

An employer that complies with an income-withholding order issued in another state in accordance with this chapter is not subject to civil liability to an individual or agency with regard to the employer's withholding of child support from the obligor's income. *(Added by Stats.2015, c. 493 (S.B.646), § 5, eff. Jan. 1, 2016.)*

§ 5700.505. Penalties for noncompliance

An employer that willfully fails to comply with an income-withholding order issued in another state and received for enforcement is subject to the same penalties that may be imposed for noncompliance with an order issued by a tribunal of this state. *(Added by Stats.2015, c. 493 (S.B.646), § 5, eff. Jan. 1, 2016.)*

§ 5700.506. Contest by obligor

(a) An obligor may contest the validity or enforcement of an income-withholding order issued in another state and received directly by an employer in this state by registering the order in a tribunal of this state and filing a contest to that order as provided in Chapter 6, or otherwise contesting the order in the same manner as if the order had been issued by a tribunal of this state.

(b) The obligor shall give notice of the contest to:

(1) a support enforcement agency providing services to the obligee;

(2) each employer that has directly received an income-withholding order relating to the obligor; and

(3) the person designated to receive payments in the income-withholding order or, if no person is designated, to the obligee. *(Added by Stats.2015, c. 493 (S.B.646), § 5, eff. Jan. 1, 2016.)*

§ 5700.507. Administrative enforcement of orders

(a) A party or support enforcement agency seeking to enforce a support order or an income-withholding order, or both, issued in another state or a foreign support order may send the documents required for registering the order to a support enforcement agency of this state.

(b) Upon receipt of the documents, the support enforcement agency, without initially seeking to register the order, shall consider and, if appropriate, use any administrative procedure authorized by the law of this state to enforce a support order or an income-withholding order, or both. If the obligor does not contest administrative enforcement, the order need not be registered. If the obligor contests the validity or administrative enforcement of the order, the support enforcement agency shall register the order pursuant to this part. *(Added by Stats.2015, c. 493 (S.B.646), § 5, eff. Jan. 1, 2016.)*

CHAPTER 6. REGISTRATION, ENFORCEMENT, AND MODIFICATION OF SUPPORT ORDER

ARTICLE 1. REGISTRATION FOR ENFORCEMENT OF SUPPORT ORDER

§ 5700.601. Registration of order for enforcement

A support order or income-withholding order issued in another state or a foreign support order may be registered in this state for enforcement. *(Added by Stats.2015, c. 493 (S.B.646), § 5, eff. Jan. 1, 2016.)*

Commentary

This section repeats the content of former Family Code section 4950.

The registration of a foreign divorce decree does not give the county standing to initiate a section 17400(a) child support enforcement proceeding unless the registration includes a proper request for enforcement services. If a family is receiving public assistance, the welfare department providing public assistance may request enforcement services; if not, the support obligee must request those services. *Codoni v. Codoni, 103 Cal.App.4th 18, 126 Cal.Rptr.2d 423 (2002).*

Research References

Treatises and Practice Aids

Witkin, California Summary 10th Husband and Wife § 252, Stay Of Service.

Witkin, California Summary 10th Husband and Wife § 345, Proceedings Under UIFSA.

§ 5700.602. Procedure to register order for enforcement

(a) Except as otherwise provided in Section 5700.706, a support order or income-withholding order of another state or a foreign support order may be registered in this state by sending the following records to the appropriate tribunal in this state:

(1) a letter of transmittal to the tribunal requesting registration and enforcement;

(2) two copies, including one certified copy, of the order to be registered, including any modification of the order;

(3) a sworn statement by the person requesting registration or a certified statement by the custodian of the records showing the amount of any arrearage;

(4) the name of the obligor and, if known:

(A) the obligor's address and social security number;

(B) the name and address of the obligor's employer and any other source of income of the obligor; and

(C) a description and the location of property of the obligor in this state not exempt from execution; and

(5) except as otherwise provided in Section 5700.312, the name and address of the obligee and, if applicable, the person to whom support payments are to be remitted.

(b) On receipt of a request for registration, the registering tribunal shall cause the order to be filed as an order of a tribunal of another state or a foreign support order, together with one copy of the documents and information, regardless of their form.

(c) A petition or comparable pleading seeking a remedy that must be affirmatively sought under other law of this state may be filed at the same time as the request for registration or later. The pleading must specify the grounds for the remedy sought.

(d) If two or more orders are in effect, the person requesting registration shall:

(1) furnish to the tribunal a copy of every support order asserted to be in effect in addition to the documents specified in this section;

(2) specify the order alleged to be the controlling order, if any; and

(3) specify the amount of consolidated arrears, if any.

(e) A request for a determination of which is the controlling order may be filed separately or with a request for registration and enforcement or for registration and modification. The person requesting registration shall give notice of the request to each party whose rights may be affected by the determination. *(Added by Stats.2015, c. 493 (S.B.646), § 5, eff. Jan. 1, 2016.)*

Commentary

This section repeats the content of former Family Code section 4951.

The registration of a foreign divorce decree does not give the county standing to initiate a section 17400(a) child support enforcement proceeding unless the registration includes a proper request for enforcement services. If a family is receiving public assistance, the welfare department providing public assistance may request enforcement services; if not, the support obligee must request those services. *Codoni v. Codoni, 103 Cal.App.4th 18, 126 Cal.Rptr.2d 423 (2002).*

Research References

Treatises and Practice Aids

Witkin, California Summary 10th Husband and Wife § 12B, (New) Amount Of Filing Fees.

§ 5700.603. Effect of registration for enforcement

(a) A support order or income-withholding order issued in another state or a foreign support order is registered when the order is filed in the registering tribunal of this state.

(b) A registered support order issued in another state or a foreign country is enforceable in the same manner and is subject to the same procedures as an order issued by a tribunal of this state.

(c) Except as otherwise provided in this part, a tribunal of this state shall recognize and enforce, but may not modify, a registered support order if the issuing tribunal had jurisdiction. *(Added by Stats.2015, c. 493 (S.B.646), § 5, eff. Jan. 1, 2016.)*

Commentary

This section repeats the content of former Family Code section 4952.

The registration of a foreign divorce decree does not give the county standing to initiate a section 17400(a) child support enforcement proceeding unless the registration includes a proper request for enforcement services. If a family is receiving public assistance, the welfare department providing public assistance may request enforcement services; if not, the support obligee must request those services. *Codoni v. Codoni, 103 Cal.App.4th 18, 126 Cal.Rptr.2d 423 (2002).*

§ 5700.604. Choice of law

(a) Except as otherwise provided in subsection (d), the law of the issuing state or foreign country governs:

(1) the nature, extent, amount, and duration of current payments under a registered support order;

(2) the computation and payment of arrearages and accrual of interest on the arrearages under the support order; and

(3) the existence and satisfaction of other obligations under the support order.

(b) In a proceeding for arrears under a registered support order, the statute of limitation of this state, or of the issuing state or foreign country, whichever is longer, applies.

(c) A responding tribunal of this state shall apply the procedures and remedies of this state to enforce current support and collect arrears and interest due on a support order of another state or a foreign country registered in this state.

(d) After a tribunal of this state or another state determines which is the controlling order and issues an order consolidating arrears, if any, a tribunal of this state shall prospectively apply the law of the state or foreign country issuing the controlling order, including its law on interest on arrears, on current and future support, and on consolidated arrears. *(Added by Stats.2015, c. 493 (S.B.646), § 5, eff. Jan. 1, 2016.)*

Commentary

This section repeats the content of former Family Code section 4953.

Despite the clear language of subsection (b), *Scheuerman v. Hauk, 116 Cal.App.4th 1140, 11 Cal.Rptr.3d 125 (2004)*, held that a trial court properly refused to register an Arizona child support order after an Arizona court had judicially determined that it was no longer enforceable because the Arizona statute of limitations had expired, although the California statute of limitations had not. Scheuerman reasoned that enforcement of the Arizona support order would violate the full faith and credit clause of the United States Constitution.

ARTICLE 2. CONTEST OF VALIDITY OR ENFORCEMENT

§ 5700.605. Notice of registration of order

(a) When a support order or income-withholding order issued in another state or a foreign support order is registered, the registering tribunal of this state shall notify the nonregistering party. The notice must be accompanied by a copy of the registered order and the documents and relevant information accompanying the order.

(b) A notice must inform the nonregistering party:

(1) that a registered support order is enforceable as of the date of registration in the same manner as an order issued by a tribunal of this state;

(2) that a hearing to contest the validity or enforcement of the registered order must be requested within 20 days after notice unless the registered order is under Section 5700.707;

(3) that failure to contest the validity or enforcement of the registered order in a timely manner will result in confirmation of the order and enforcement of the order and the alleged arrearages; and

(4) of the amount of any alleged arrearages.

(c) If the registering party asserts that two or more orders are in effect, a notice must also:

(1) identify the two or more orders and the order alleged by the registering party to be the controlling order and the consolidated arrears, if any;

(2) notify the nonregistering party of the right to a determination of which is the controlling order;

(3) state that the procedures provided in subsection (b) apply to the determination of which is the controlling order; and

(4) state that failure to contest the validity or enforcement of the order alleged to be the controlling order in a timely manner may result in confirmation that the order is the controlling order.

(d) Upon registration of an income-withholding order for enforcement, the support enforcement agency or the registering tribunal shall notify the obligor's employer pursuant to Chapter 8 (commencing with Section 5200) of Part 5. *(Added by Stats.2015, c. 493 (S.B.646), § 5, eff. Jan. 1, 2016.)*

§ 5700.606. Procedure to contest validity or enforcement of registered support order

(a) A nonregistering party seeking to contest the validity or enforcement of a registered support order in this state shall request a hearing within the time required by Section 5700.605. The nonregistering party may seek to vacate the registration, to assert any defense to an allegation of noncompliance with the registered order, or to contest the remedies being sought or the amount of any alleged arrearages pursuant to Section 5700.607.

(b) If the nonregistering party fails to contest the validity or enforcement of the registered support order in a timely manner, the order is confirmed by operation of law.

(c) If a nonregistering party requests a hearing to contest the validity or enforcement of the registered support order, the registering tribunal shall schedule the matter for hearing and give notice to the parties of the date, time, and place of the hearing. *(Added by Stats.2015, c. 493 (S.B.646), § 5, eff. Jan. 1, 2016.)*

§ 5700.607. Contest of registration or enforcement

(a) A party contesting the validity or enforcement of a registered support order or seeking to vacate the registration has the burden of proving one or more of the following defenses:

(1) the issuing tribunal lacked personal jurisdiction over the contesting party;

(2) the order was obtained by fraud;

(3) the order has been vacated, suspended, or modified by a later order;

(4) the issuing tribunal has stayed the order pending appeal;

(5) there is a defense under the law of this state to the remedy sought;

(6) full or partial payment has been made;

(7) the statute of limitation under Section 5700.604 precludes enforcement of some or all of the alleged arrearages; or

(8) the alleged controlling order is not the controlling order.

(b) If a party presents evidence establishing a full or partial defense under subsection (a), a tribunal may stay enforcement of a registered support order, continue the proceeding to permit production of additional relevant evidence, and issue other appropriate orders. An uncontested portion of the registered support order may be enforced by all remedies available under the law of this state.

(c) If the contesting party does not establish a defense under subsection (a) to the validity or enforcement of a registered support order, the registering tribunal shall issue an order confirming the order. *(Added by Stats.2015, c. 493 (S.B.646), § 5, eff. Jan. 1, 2016.)*

Commentary

This section repeats the content of former Family Code section 4956.

Interpreting subsection (a)(1) "personal jurisdiction," *Willmer v. Willmer, 144 Cal.App.4th 951, 51 Cal.Rptr.3d 10 (2006)*, held that a German child or spousal support judgment is enforceable in California even though Germany based its child and spousal support jurisdiction on grounds that California does not have, so long as those grounds did not violate fundamental American principles of due process.

County of Los Angeles Child Support Services Department v. Youngblood, 243 Cal.App.4th 230, ___ Cal.Rptr.3d ___ (2015), held that a trial court erred in ordering genetic testing to challenge a Swiss child support order registered in this state under UIFSA, because nonparentage is not a defense in a UIFSA enforcement proceeding.

§ 5700.608. Confirmed order

Confirmation of a registered support order, whether by operation of law or after notice and hearing, precludes further contest of the order with respect to any matter that could have been asserted at the time of registration. *(Added by Stats.2015, c. 493 (S.B.646), § 5, eff. Jan. 1, 2016.)*

ARTICLE 3. REGISTRATION AND MODIFICATION OF CHILD–SUPPORT ORDER OF ANOTHER STATE

§ 5700.609. Procedure to register child-support order of another state for modification

A party or support enforcement agency seeking to modify, or to modify and enforce, a child-support order issued in another state shall register that order in this state in the same manner provided in Sections 5700.601 through 5700.608 if the order has not been registered. A petition for modification may be filed at the same time as a request for registration, or later. The pleading must specify the grounds for modification. *(Added by Stats.2015, c. 493 (S.B.646), § 5, eff. Jan. 1, 2016.)*

§ 5700.610. Effect of registration for modification

A tribunal of this state may enforce a child-support order of another state registered for purposes of modification, in the same manner as if the order had been issued by a tribunal of this state, but the registered support order may be modified only if the requirements of Section 5700.611 or 5700.613 have been met. *(Added by Stats.2015, c. 493 (S.B.646), § 5, eff. Jan. 1, 2016.)*

§ 5700.611. Modification of child-support order of another state

(a) If Section 5700.613 does not apply, upon petition a tribunal of this state may modify a child-support order issued in another state which is registered in this state if, after notice and hearing, the tribunal finds that:

(1) the following requirements are met:

(A) neither the child, nor the obligee who is an individual, nor the obligor resides in the issuing state;

(B) a petitioner who is a nonresident of this state seeks modification; and

(C) the respondent is subject to the personal jurisdiction of the tribunal of this state; or

(2) this state is the residence of the child, or a party who is an individual is subject to the personal jurisdiction of the tribunal of this state, and all of the parties who are individuals have filed consents in a record in the issuing tribunal for a tribunal of this state to modify the support order and assume continuing, exclusive jurisdiction.

(b) Modification of a registered child-support order is subject to the same requirements, procedures, and defenses that apply to the modification of an order issued by a tribunal of this state and the order may be enforced and satisfied in the same manner.

(c) A tribunal of this state may not modify any aspect of a child-support order that may not be modified under the law of the issuing state, including the duration of the obligation of support. If two or more tribunals have issued child-support orders for the same obligor and same child, the order that controls and must be so recognized under Section 5700.207 establishes the aspects of the support order which are nonmodifiable.

(d) In a proceeding to modify a child-support order, the law of the state that is determined to have issued the initial controlling order governs the duration of the obligation of support. The obligor's fulfillment of the duty of support established by that order precludes imposition of a further obligation of support by a tribunal of this state.

(e) On the issuance of an order by a tribunal of this state modifying a child-support order issued in another state, the tribunal of this state becomes the tribunal having continuing, exclusive jurisdiction.

(f) Notwithstanding subsections (a) through (e) and Section 5700.201(b), a tribunal of this state retains jurisdiction to modify an order issued by a tribunal of this state if:

(1) one party resides in another state; and

(2) the other party resides outside the United States. *(Added by Stats.2015, c. 493 (S.B.646), § 5, eff. Jan. 1, 2016.)*

Commentary

This section replaces portions of former Family Code section 4960.

Interpreting subsection (a)(1)(a), *Harding v. Harding, 99 Cal. App.4th 626, 121 Cal.Rptr.2d 450 (2002)*, held that a trial court properly concluded that it lacked subject matter jurisdiction to modify a child support order of another state when the support obligor remained a resident of that state. *Harding* upheld the constitutionality of former Family Code sections 4900-5005 (California Uniform Interstate Family Support Act and 28 USC section 1738B (Full Faith and Credit for Child Support Orders Act).

In re Marriage of Crosby and Grooms, 116 Cal.App.4th 201, 10 Cal.Rptr.3d 146 (2004), held that when the requirements of subsection (a) have been met, a California court will apply the child support guidelines of California even though the parties' marital settlement agreement provided that "all matters affecting the interpretation of this Agreement and the rights of parties hereto shall be governed by the State of Idaho." Observing that Idaho has also enacted the Uniform Interstate Family Support Act (UIFSA), *Crosby* reasons that, as the laws of Idaho include its choice of law provisions as well as its child support guidelines, application of California guidelines is consistent with the law of Idaho. Moreover, even if Idaho had not enacted UIFSA, parents may not contract away their children's right to support.

Knabe v. Brister, 154 Cal.App.4th 1316, 65 Cal.Rptr.3d 493 (2007), review denied, holds that, pursuant to this section, a written stipulation to transfer child support jurisdiction to California is enforceable when signed by the parties' attorneys but not the parties themselves.

In re Marriage of Amezquita & Archuleta, 101 Cal.App.4th 1415, 124 Cal.Rptr.2d 887 (2002), holds that, for purposes of this section, a person does not "reside" in California if the person is domiciled in another state. As in Family Code section 2320, "residence" means "domicile." *Amezquita* concluded that an ex-husband stationed in California did not "reside" in California within the meaning of this section.

§ 5700.612. Recognition of order modified in another state

If a child-support order issued by a tribunal of this state is modified by a tribunal of another state which assumed jurisdiction pursuant to the Uniform Interstate Family Support Act, a tribunal of this state:

(1) may enforce its order that was modified only as to arrears and interest accruing before the modification;

(2) may provide appropriate relief for violations of its order which occurred before the effective date of the modification; and

(3) shall recognize the modifying order of the other state, upon registration, for the purpose of enforcement. *(Added by Stats.2015, c. 493 (S.B.646), § 5, eff. Jan. 1, 2016.)*

§ 5700.613. Jurisdiction to modify child-support order of another state when individual parties reside in this state

(a) If all of the parties who are individuals reside in this state and the child does not reside in the issuing state, a tribunal of this state has jurisdiction to enforce and to modify the issuing state's child-support order in a proceeding to register that order.

(b) A tribunal of this state exercising jurisdiction under this section shall apply the provisions of Chapters 1 and 2, and this chapter, and the procedural and substantive law of this state to the proceeding for enforcement or modification. Chapters 3, 4, 5, 7, and 8 do not apply. *(Added by Stats.2015, c. 493 (S.B.646), § 5, eff. Jan. 1, 2016.)*

§ 5700.614. Notice to issuing tribunal of modification

Within 30 days after issuance of a modified child-support order, the party obtaining the modification shall file a certified copy of the order with the issuing tribunal that had continuing, exclusive jurisdiction over the earlier order, and in each tribunal in which the party knows the earlier order has been registered. A party who obtains the order and fails to file a certified copy is subject to appropriate sanctions by a tribunal in which the issue of failure to file arises. The failure to file does not affect the validity or enforceability of the modified order of the new tribunal having continuing, exclusive jurisdiction. *(Added by Stats.2015, c. 493 (S.B.646), § 5, eff. Jan. 1, 2016.)*

ARTICLE 4. REGISTRATION AND MODIFICATION OF FOREIGN CHILD–SUPPORT ORDER

Section

§ 5700.615. Jurisdiction to modify child-support order of foreign country

(a) Except as otherwise provided in Section 5700.711, if a foreign country lacks or refuses to exercise jurisdiction to modify its child-support order pursuant to its laws, a tribunal of this state may assume jurisdiction to modify the child-support order and bind all individuals subject to the personal jurisdiction of the tribunal whether the consent to modification of a child-support order otherwise required of the individual pursuant to Section 5700.611 has been given or whether the individual seeking modification is a resident of this state or of the foreign country.

(b) An order issued by a tribunal of this state modifying a foreign child-support order pursuant to this section is the controlling order. *(Added by Stats.2015, c. 493 (S.B.646), § 5, eff. Jan. 1, 2016.)*

§ 5700.616. Procedure to register child-support order of foreign country for modification

A party or support enforcement agency seeking to modify, or to modify and enforce, a foreign child-support order not under the Convention may register that order in this state under Sections 5700.601 through 5700.608 if the order has not been registered. A petition for modification may be filed at the same time as a request for registration, or at another time. The petition must specify the grounds for modification. *(Added by Stats.2015, c. 493 (S.B.646), § 5, eff. Jan. 1, 2016.)*

CHAPTER 7. SUPPORT PROCEEDING UNDER CONVENTION

§ 5700.701. Definitions

In this chapter:

(1) "Application" means a request under the Convention by an obligee or obligor, or on behalf of a child, made through a central authority for assistance from another central authority.

(2) "Central authority" means the entity designated by the United States or a foreign country described in Section 5700.102(5)(D) to perform the functions specified in the Convention.

(3) "Convention support order" means a support order of a tribunal of a foreign country described in Section 5700.102(5)(D).

(4) "Direct request" means a petition filed by an individual in a tribunal of this state in a proceeding involving an obligee, obligor, or child residing outside the United States.

(5) "Foreign central authority" means the entity designated by a foreign country described in Section 5700.102(5)(D) to perform the functions specified in the Convention.

(6) "Foreign support agreement":

(A) means an agreement for support in a record that:

(i) is enforceable as a support order in the country of origin;

(ii) has been:

(I) formally drawn up or registered as an authentic instrument by a foreign tribunal; or

(II) authenticated by, or concluded, registered, or filed with a foreign tribunal; and

(iii) may be reviewed and modified by a foreign tribunal; and

(B) includes a maintenance arrangement or authentic instrument under the Convention.

(7) "United States central authority" means the Secretary of the United States Department of Health and Human Services. *(Added by Stats.2015, c. 493 (S.B.646), § 5, eff. Jan. 1, 2016.)*

§ 5700.702. Applicability

This chapter applies only to a support proceeding under the Convention. In such a proceeding, if a provision of this chapter is inconsistent with Chapters 1 through 6, this chapter controls. *(Added by Stats.2015, c. 493 (S.B.646), § 5, eff. Jan. 1, 2016.)*

§ 5700.703. Relationship of Department of Child Support Services to United States central authority

The Department of Child Support Services is recognized as the agency designated by the United States central authority to perform specific functions under the Convention. *(Added by Stats.2015, c. 493 (S.B.646), § 5, eff. Jan. 1, 2016.)*

§ 5700.704. Initiation by Department of Child Support Services of support proceeding under Convention

(a) In a support proceeding under this chapter, the Department of Child Support Services shall:

(1) transmit and receive applications; and

(2) initiate or facilitate the institution of a proceeding regarding an application in a tribunal of this state.

(b) The following support proceedings are available to an obligee under the Convention:

(1) recognition or recognition and enforcement of a foreign support order;

(2) enforcement of a support order issued or recognized in this state;

(3) establishment of a support order if there is no existing order, including, if necessary, determination of parentage of a child;

(4) establishment of a support order if recognition of a foreign support order is refused under Section 5700.708(b)(2), (4), or (9);

(5) modification of a support order of a tribunal of this state; and

(6) modification of a support order of a tribunal of another state or a foreign country.

(c) The following support proceedings are available under the Convention to an obligor against which there is an existing support order:

(1) recognition of an order suspending or limiting enforcement of an existing support order of a tribunal of this state;

(2) modification of a support order of a tribunal of this state; and

(3) modification of a support order of a tribunal of another state or a foreign country.

(d) A tribunal of this state may not require security, bond, or deposit, however described, to guarantee the payment of costs and expenses in proceedings under the Convention. *(Added by Stats.2015, c. 493 (S.B.646), § 5, eff. Jan. 1, 2016.)*

§ 5700.705. Direct request

(a) A petitioner may file a direct request seeking establishment or modification of a support order or determination of parentage of a child. In the proceeding, the law of this state applies.

(b) A petitioner may file a direct request seeking recognition and enforcement of a support order or support agreement. In the proceeding, Sections 5700.706 through 5700.713 apply.

(c) In a direct request for recognition and enforcement of a Convention support order or foreign support agreement:

(1) a security, bond, or deposit is not required to guarantee the payment of costs and expenses; and

(2) an obligee or obligor that in the issuing country has benefited from free legal assistance is entitled to benefit, at least to the same extent, from any free legal assistance provided for by the law of this state under the same circumstances.

(d) A petitioner filing a direct request is not entitled to assistance from the Department of Child Support Services.

(e) This chapter does not prevent the application of laws of this state that provide simplified, more expeditious rules regarding a direct request for recognition and enforcement of a foreign support order or foreign support agreement. *(Added by Stats.2015, c. 493 (S.B.646), § 5, eff. Jan. 1, 2016.)*

§ 5700.706. Registration of Convention support order

(a) Except as otherwise provided in this chapter, a party who is an individual or a support enforcement agency seeking recognition of a Convention support order shall register the order in this state as provided in Chapter 6.

(b) Notwithstanding Sections 5700.311 and 5700.602(a), a request for registration of a Convention support order must be accompanied by:

(1) a complete text of the support order or an abstract or extract of the support order drawn up by the issuing foreign tribunal, which may be in the form recommended by the Hague Conference on Private International Law;

(2) a record stating that the support order is enforceable in the issuing country;

(3) if the respondent did not appear and was not represented in the proceedings in the issuing country, a record attesting, as appropriate, either that the respondent had proper notice of the proceedings and an opportunity to be heard or that the respondent had proper notice of the support order and an opportunity to be heard in a challenge or appeal on fact or law before a tribunal;

(4) a record showing the amount of arrears, if any, and the date the amount was calculated;

(5) a record showing a requirement for automatic adjustment of the amount of support, if any, and the information necessary to make the appropriate calculations; and

(6) if necessary, a record showing the extent to which the applicant received free legal assistance in the issuing country.

(c) A request for registration of a Convention support order may seek recognition and partial enforcement of the order.

(d) A tribunal of this state may vacate the registration of a Convention support order without the filing of a contest under Section 5700.707 only if, acting on its own motion, the tribunal finds that recognition and enforcement of the order would be manifestly incompatible with public policy.

(e) The tribunal shall promptly notify the parties of the registration or the order vacating the registration of a Convention support order. *(Added by Stats.2015, c. 493 (S.B.646), § 5, eff. Jan. 1, 2016.)*

§ 5700.707. Contest of registered Convention support order

(a) Except as otherwise provided in this chapter, Sections 5700.605 through 5700.608 apply to a contest of a registered Convention support order.

(b) A party contesting a registered Convention support order shall file a contest not later than 30 days after notice of the registration, but if the contesting party does not reside in the United States, the contest must be filed not later than 60 days after notice of the registration.

(c) If the nonregistering party fails to contest the registered Convention support order by the time specified in subsection (b), the order is enforceable.

(d) A contest of a registered Convention support order may be based only on grounds set forth in Section 5700.708. The contesting party bears the burden of proof.

(e) In a contest of a registered Convention support order, a tribunal of this state:

(1) is bound by the findings of fact on which the foreign tribunal based its jurisdiction; and

(2) may not review the merits of the order.

(f) A tribunal of this state deciding a contest of a registered Convention support order shall promptly notify the parties of its decision.

(g) A challenge or appeal, if any, does not stay the enforcement of a Convention support order unless there are exceptional circumstances. *(Added by Stats.2015, c. 493 (S.B.646), § 5, eff. Jan. 1, 2016.)*

§ 5700.708. Recognition and enforcement of registered Convention support order

(a) Except as otherwise provided in subsection (b), a tribunal of this state shall recognize and enforce a registered Convention support order.

(b) The following grounds are the only grounds on which a tribunal of this state may refuse recognition and enforcement of a registered Convention support order:

(1) recognition and enforcement of the order is manifestly incompatible with public policy, including the failure of the issuing tribunal to observe minimum standards of due process, which include notice and an opportunity to be heard;

(2) the issuing tribunal lacked personal jurisdiction consistent with Section 5700.201;

(3) the order is not enforceable in the issuing country;

(4) the order was obtained by fraud in connection with a matter of procedure;

(5) a record transmitted in accordance with Section 5700.706 lacks authenticity or integrity;

(6) a proceeding between the same parties and having the same purpose is pending before a tribunal of this state and that proceeding was the first to be filed;

(7) the order is incompatible with a more recent support order involving the same parties and having the same purpose if the more recent support order is entitled to recognition and enforcement under this part in this state;

(8) payment, to the extent alleged arrears have been paid in whole or in part;

(9) in a case in which the respondent neither appeared nor was represented in the proceeding in the issuing foreign country:

(A) if the law of that country provides for prior notice of proceedings, the respondent did not have proper notice of the proceedings and an opportunity to be heard; or

(B) if the law of that country does not provide for prior notice of the proceedings, the respondent did not have proper notice of the order and an opportunity to be heard in a challenge or appeal on fact or law before a tribunal; or

(10) the order was made in violation of Section 5700.711.

(c) If a tribunal of this state does not recognize a Convention support order under subsection (b)(2), (4), or (9):

(1) the tribunal may not dismiss the proceeding without allowing a reasonable time for a party to request the establishment of a new Convention support order; and

(2) the Department of Child Support Services shall take all appropriate measures to request a child-support order for the obligee if the application for recognition and enforcement was received under Section 5700.704. *(Added by Stats.2015, c. 493 (S.B.646), § 5, eff. Jan. 1, 2016.)*

§ 5700.709. Partial enforcement

If a tribunal of this state does not recognize and enforce a Convention support order in its entirety, it shall enforce any severable part of the order. An application or direct request may seek recognition and partial enforcement of a Convention support order. *(Added by Stats.2015, c. 493 (S.B.646), § 5, eff. Jan. 1, 2016.)*

§ 5700.710. Foreign support agreement

(a) Except as otherwise provided in subsections (c) and (d), a tribunal of this state shall recognize and enforce a foreign support agreement registered in this state.

(b) An application or direct request for recognition and enforcement of a foreign support agreement must be accompanied by:

(1) a complete text of the foreign support agreement; and

(2) a record stating that the foreign support agreement is enforceable as an order of support in the issuing country.

(c) A tribunal of this state may vacate the registration of a foreign support agreement only if, acting on its own motion, the tribunal finds that recognition and enforcement would be manifestly incompatible with public policy.

(d) In a contest of a foreign support agreement, a tribunal of this state may refuse recognition and enforcement of the agreement if it finds:

(1) recognition and enforcement of the agreement is manifestly incompatible with public policy;

(2) the agreement was obtained by fraud or falsification;

(3) the agreement is incompatible with a support order involving the same parties and having the same purpose in this state, another state, or a foreign country if the support order is entitled to recognition and enforcement under this act in this state; or

(4) the record submitted under subsection (b) lacks authenticity or integrity.

(e) A proceeding for recognition and enforcement of a foreign support agreement must be suspended during the pendency of a challenge to or appeal of the agreement before a tribunal of another state or a foreign country. *(Added by Stats.2015, c. 493 (S.B.646), § 5, eff. Jan. 1, 2016.)*

§ 5700.711. Modification of Convention child-support order

(a) A tribunal of this state may not modify a Convention child-support order if the obligee remains a resident of the foreign country where the support order was issued unless:

(1) the obligee submits to the jurisdiction of a tribunal of this state, either expressly or by defending on the merits of the case without objecting to the jurisdiction at the first available opportunity; or

(2) the foreign tribunal lacks or refuses to exercise jurisdiction to modify its support order or issue a new support order.

(b) If a tribunal of this state does not modify a Convention child-support order because the order is not recognized in this state, Section 5700.708(c) applies. *(Added by Stats.2015, c. 493 (S.B.646), § 5, eff. Jan. 1, 2016.)*

§ 5700.712. Personal information; limit on use

Personal information gathered or transmitted under this chapter may be used only for the purposes for which it was gathered or transmitted. *(Added by Stats.2015, c. 493 (S.B. 646), § 5, eff. Jan. 1, 2016.)*

§ 5700.713. Record in original language; English translation

A record filed with a tribunal of this state under this chapter must be in the original language and, if not in English, must be accompanied by an English translation. *(Added by Stats.2015, c. 493 (S.B.646), § 5, eff. Jan. 1, 2016.)*

CHAPTER 8. INTERSTATE RENDITION

§ 5700.801. Grounds for rendition

(a) For purposes of this chapter, "governor" includes an individual performing the functions of governor or the executive authority of a state covered by this part.

(b) The Governor may:

(1) demand that the governor of another state surrender an individual found in the other state who is charged

criminally in this state with having failed to provide for the support of an obligee; or

(2) on the demand of the governor of another state, surrender an individual found in this state who is charged criminally in the other state with having failed to provide for the support of an obligee.

(c) A provision for extradition of individuals not inconsistent with this act applies to the demand even if the individual whose surrender is demanded was not in the demanding state when the crime was allegedly committed and has not fled therefrom. *(Added by Stats.2015, c. 493 (S.B.646), § 5, eff. Jan. 1, 2016.)*

§ 5700.802. Conditions of rendition

(a) Before making a demand that the governor of another state surrender an individual charged criminally in this state with having failed to provide for the support of an obligee, the Governor may require a prosecutor of this state to demonstrate that at least 60 days previously the obligee had initiated proceedings for support pursuant to this act or that the proceeding would be of no avail.

(b) If, under this act or a law substantially similar to this act, the Governor of another state makes a demand that the Governor of this state surrender an individual charged criminally in that state with having failed to provide for the support of a child or other individual to whom a duty of support is owed, the Governor may require a prosecutor to investigate the demand and report whether a proceeding for support has been initiated or would be effective. If it appears that a proceeding would be effective but has not been initiated, the Governor may delay honoring the demand for a reasonable time to permit the initiation of a proceeding.

(c) If a proceeding for support has been initiated and the individual whose rendition is demanded prevails, the Governor may decline to honor the demand. If the petitioner prevails and the individual whose rendition is demanded is subject to a support order, the Governor may decline to honor the demand if the individual is complying with the support order. *(Added by Stats.2015, c. 493 (S.B.646), § 5, eff. Jan. 1, 2016.)*

CHAPTER 9. MISCELLANEOUS PROVISIONS

§ 5700.901. Uniformity of application and construction

In applying and construing this uniform act, consideration must be given to the need to promote uniformity of the law with respect to its subject matter among states that enact it. *(Added by Stats.2015, c. 493 (S.B.646), § 5, eff. Jan. 1, 2016.)*

§ 5700.902. Transitional provision

This part applies to proceedings begun on or after January 1, 2016, to establish a support order or determine parentage of a child or to register, recognize, enforce, or modify a prior support order, determination, or agreement, whenever issued or entered. *(Added by Stats.2015, c. 493 (S.B.646), § 5, eff. Jan. 1, 2016.)*

§ 5700.903. Severability

If any provision of this part or its application to any person or circumstance is held invalid, the invalidity does not affect other provisions or applications of this part which can be given effect without the invalid provision or application, and to this end the provisions of this part are severable. *(Added by Stats.2015, c. 493 (S.B.646), § 5, eff. Jan. 1, 2016.)*

§ 5700.905. Emergency regulations

The Department of Child Support Services may adopt emergency regulations as appropriate to implement this part. *(Added by Stats.2015, c. 493 (S.B.646), § 5, eff. Jan. 1, 2016.)*

Division 10

PREVENTION OF DOMESTIC VIOLENCE

Part 1

SHORT TITLE AND DEFINITIONS

§ 6200. Short title

This division may be cited as the Domestic Violence Prevention Act. *(Added by Stats.1993, c. 219 (A.B.1500), § 154.)*

Law Revision Commission Comments

Enactment [Revised Comment]

Section 6200 continues former Code of Civil Procedure Section 541 without substantive change.

This division collects the substantive provisions for issuance of restraining orders intended to prevent domestic violence. Formerly these substantive provisions were duplicated in substantial part in the former Family Law Act, the Domestic Violence Prevention Act, and the Uniform Parentage Act. Now that these bodies of law have been consolidated in the Family Code, these duplicative provisions have been consolidated and continued in this division.

The orders that may be issued under this division may be issued in a proceeding brought pursuant to this division. These orders may also be issued in a proceeding for dissolution, nullity, or legal separation, and in an action brought pursuant to the Uniform Parentage Act. See Section 6221 (application of this division). See also Sections 2045, 2047, 2049 (restraining orders in dissolution, nullity, or legal separation proceeding), 7710, 7720, 7730 (restraining orders in Uniform Parentage Act proceeding).

See also Welf. & Inst. Code § 213.5 (protective orders during pendency of proceeding to declare minor dependent). [23 Cal. L.Rev.Comm. Reports 1 (1993)].

Commentary

Note that 2013 amendments to Code of Civil Procedure section 583.161 expanded the definition of petitions and orders that are not subject to mandatory dismissal, including petitions and orders under this division.

In re Marriage of Fernandez-Abin & Sanchez, 191 Cal.App.4th 1015, 120 Cal.Rptr.3d 227 (2011), holds that a California trial court lacked jurisdiction to issue a permanent domestic violence restraining order that included children when a Mexican court already had exclusive jurisdiction over the children under the Uniform Child Custody Jurisdiction and Enforcement Act (UCCJEA Family Code §§ 3400 et seq.). Nevertheless, a California court may exercise temporary emergency jurisdiction under the UCCJEA (Family Code § 3424) if a child is present in California and the exercise of jurisdiction is necessary to protect the child because the child, a sibling, or a parent has been threatened with abuse.

Research References

Forms

California Transactions Forms--Family Law § 3:4, Subject Matter Jurisdiction for Custody Determinations.

California Transactions Forms--Family Law § 4:14, Domestic Violence and Restraining Orders.

West's California Code Forms, Civil Procedure § 372 Form 8, Parties--Notice Of Motion for Order Appointing Guardian Ad Litem for Minor 12 Years or Older to Assist Minor in Obtaining Protective Order.

West's California Code Forms, Civil Procedure § 372 Form 9, Parties--Order Appointing Guardian Ad Litem for Minor 12 Years or Older to Assist Minor in Obtaining Protective Order.

West's California Code Forms, Family § 2045, Comment Overview--Ex Parte Protective Orders.

West's California Code Forms, Family § 6200, Comment Overview--Prevention Of Domestic Violence.

West's California Judicial Council Forms DV-100, Request for Domestic Violence Restraining Order.

West's California Judicial Council Forms DV-101, Description Of Abuse.

West's California Judicial Council Forms DV-110, Temporary Restraining Order.

West's California Judicial Council Forms DV-120, Response to Request for Domestic Violence Restraining Order.

West's California Judicial Council Forms DV-130, Restraining Order After Hearing (Order Of Protection).

West's California Judicial Council Forms FL-303, Declaration Regarding Notice and Service Of Request for Temporary Emergency (Ex Parte) Orders.

West's California Judicial Council Forms FL-311, Child Custody and Visitation Application Attachment.

Treatises and Practice Aids

Witkin, California Summary 10th Husband and Wife § 3, Statutory Framework.

Witkin, California Summary 10th Husband and Wife § 89, Other Orders.

Witkin, California Summary 10th Husband and Wife § 12B, (New) Amount Of Filing Fees.

Witkin, California Summary 10th Husband and Wife § 373, in General.

Witkin, California Summary 10th Parent and Child § 63, in General.

Witkin, California Summary 10th Parent and Child § 160, Scope Of Child Custody Proceedings.
Witkin, California Summary 10th Parent and Child § 171, Illustrations.
Witkin, California Summary 10th Parent and Child § 211, in General.
Witkin, California Summary 10th Parent and Child § 235, Biologically Unrelated Persons Opposed by Parent.
Witkin, California Summary 10th Parent and Child § 238, Valid Conditions.
Witkin, California Summary 10th Parent and Child § 311, Other Proceedings Stayed.
Witkin, California Summary 10th Parent and Child § 363, Applicability Of Family Code Custody Provisions.
Witkin, California Summary 10th Torts § 467, Domestic Violence.

§ 6201. Construction of code; application of definitions

Unless the provision or context otherwise requires, the definitions in this part govern the construction of this code. *(Added by Stats.1993, c. 219 (A.B.1500), § 154.)*

Law Revision Commission Comments

Enactment [Revised Comment]

Section 6201 continues without substantive change and generalizes the introductory clause of former Code of Civil Procedure Section 542. The introductory clause of this section has been added for conformity with other sections in this code. See Section 50 & Comment.

For provisions outside this division that use the definitions in this division, see Sections 213 (responding party's request for affirmative relief alternative to moving party's requested relief), 3064 (limitation on ex parte order granting or modifying custody order), 3100 (visitation rights of a parent), 3101 (visitation rights of stepparent), 3103 (visitation rights of grandparent), 3113 (separate meetings with court appointed investigator), 3181 (separate meetings with mediator), 3192 (separate meetings with counselor appointed in custody proceeding). [23 Cal.L.Rev.Comm. Reports 1 (1993)].

Research References

Treatises and Practice Aids

Witkin, California Summary 10th Husband and Wife § 374, Definitions.
Witkin, California Summary 10th Parent and Child § 271, Temporary Custody During Pendency Of Proceeding.

§ 6203. "Abuse" defined

(a) For purposes of this act, "abuse" means any of the following:

(1) To intentionally or recklessly cause or attempt to cause bodily injury.

(2) Sexual assault.

(3) To place a person in reasonable apprehension of imminent serious bodily injury to that person or to another.

(4) To engage in any behavior that has been or could be enjoined pursuant to Section 6320.

(b) Abuse is not limited to the actual infliction of physical injury or assault. *(Added by Stats.1993, c. 219 (A.B.1500), § 154. Amended by Stats.1998, c. 581 (A.B.2801), § 16; Stats.2014, c. 635 (A.B.2089), § 2, eff. Jan. 1, 2015; Stats.2015, c. 303 (A.B.731), § 149, eff. Jan. 1, 2016.)*

Law Revision Commission Comments

Enactment [Revised Comment]

Section 6203 continues former Code of Civil Procedure Section 542(a) without substantive change. For provisions adopting this definition by reference, see Section 3011 (determining best interest of child in custody proceeding); Evid. Code § 1107 (admissibility of expert witness testimony regarding battered women's syndrome). [23 Cal.L.Rev.Comm. Reports 1 (1993)].

Commentary

Applying subsection (c), *Guo v. Xiao, 228 Cal.App.4th 812, 175 Cal.Rptr.3d 635 (2014)*, held that a wife could be a victim of violence based on her husband's physical abuse of the parties' son and, under section 6320(a), the consequential disturbance of her peace.

People v. Kovacich, 201 Cal.App.4th 863, 133 Cal.Rptr.3d 924 (2011), review denied, held that a criminal defendant's violent assault on a family dog in front of his wife and children constituted abuse under this section.

In re Marriage of Nadkarni, 173 Cal.App.4th 1483, 93 Cal.Rptr.3d 723 (2009), holds that allegations that a former husband accessed, used, and publicly disclosed his former wife's confidential email were facially sufficient to satisfy subsection (d).

S.M. v. E.P., 184 Cal.App.4th 1249, 109 Cal.Rptr.3d 792 (2010), holds that a trial court abused its discretion by issuing, after hearing, a restraining order against a parent without making a finding that the parent had engaged in domestic abuse within the meaning of this section. *S.M. v. E.P.* points out that, under section 3044, a restraining order issued under this division creates a presumption that an award of custody to a parent subject to a domestic violence restraining order would be detrimental to the best interest of a child.

In re Marriage of Fregoso and Hernandez, 5 Cal.App.5th 698, 209 Cal.Rptr.3d 884 (2016), held that a trial court did not abuse its discretion in issuing a domestic violence restraining order against a husband, even though after the issuance of the restraining order the wife had consensual sex with him, because the wife explained that consensual sex was part of husband's pattern of violence followed by attempted reconciliation.

In re Marriage of G., 11 Cal.App.5th 773, 218 Cal.Rptr.3d 200 (2017), held that a trial court did not abuse its discretion in denying a wife's request for a domestic violence restraining order against her husband when her injuries were sustained in physical altercations that she initiated and the evidence was sufficient to support the trial court's finding that the husband used reasonable force to protect himself and his possessions from the wife's aggression. Therefore, the husband's actions did not constitute abuse within the meaning of this section. Although this section does not mention self-defense, section 6305 provides that a court cannot issue a mutual restraining order if it finds that one spouse acted primarily in self-defense.

Research References

Treatises and Practice Aids

Witkin, California Summary 10th Husband and Wife § 374, Definitions.
Witkin, California Summary 10th Parent and Child § 198, Domestic Violence.

§ 6205. "Affinity" defined

"Affinity," when applied to the marriage relation, signifies the connection existing in consequence of marriage between each of the married persons and the blood relatives of the other. *(Added by Stats.1993, c. 219 (A.B.1500), § 154.)*

Law Revision Commission Comments

Enactment [Revised Comment]

Section 6205 is a new provision drawn from Code of Civil Procedure Section 17(9). [23 Cal.L.Rev.Comm. Reports 1 (1993)].

Research References

Treatises and Practice Aids

Witkin, California Summary 10th Husband and Wife § 374, Definitions.

§ 6209. "Cohabitant" defined

"Cohabitant" means a person who regularly resides in the household. "Former cohabitant" means a person who formerly regularly resided in the household. *(Added by Stats. 1993, c. 219 (A.B.1500), § 154.)*

Law Revision Commission Comments

Enactment [Revised Comment]

Section 6209 continues former Code of Civil Procedure Section 542(c) without change. [23 Cal.L.Rev.Comm. Reports 1 (1993)].

Commentary

For purposes of Section 6209, a "household" includes persons who live together as a permanent or domestic group and share a common goal; it does not include two unacquainted, unrelated persons who sublet portions of a house, including common areas, from a third party. *O'Kane v. Irvine, 47 Cal.App.4th 207, 54 Cal.Rptr.2d 549 (1996).*

Research References

Forms

California Transactions Forms--Family Law § 4:3, Validity and Scope Of Agreement.

California Transactions Forms--Family Law § 4:14, Domestic Violence and Restraining Orders.

Treatises and Practice Aids

Witkin, California Summary 10th Husband and Wife § 374, Definitions.

§ 6210. "Dating relationship" defined

"Dating relationship" means frequent, intimate associations primarily characterized by the expectation of affection or sexual involvement independent of financial considerations. *(Added by Stats.2001, c. 110 (A.B.362), § 1.)*

Commentary

This section was added to disapprove *Oriola v. Thaler, 84 Cal. App.4th 397, 100 Cal.Rptr.2d 822 (2000)*. Interpreting § 6211 (c), *Oriola* held that the parties did not have a "dating relationship" even though they went on four social outings and had telephone conversations, e-mail correspondence, and frequent contacts at a gym, because appellant told respondent immediately after their first date that she was not interested in a romantic relationship and their relationship was never exclusive.

Research References

Treatises and Practice Aids

Witkin, California Summary 10th Husband and Wife § 374, Definitions.

§ 6211. "Domestic violence" defined

"Domestic violence" is abuse perpetrated against any of the following persons:

(a) A spouse or former spouse.

(b) A cohabitant or former cohabitant, as defined in Section 6209.

(c) A person with whom the respondent is having or has had a dating or engagement relationship.

(d) A person with whom the respondent has had a child, where the presumption applies that the male parent is the father of the child of the female parent under the Uniform Parentage Act (Part 3 (commencing with Section 7600) of Division 12).

(e) A child of a party or a child who is the subject of an action under the Uniform Parentage Act, where the presumption applies that the male parent is the father of the child to be protected.

(f) Any other person related by consanguinity or affinity within the second degree. *(Added by Stats.1993, c. 219 (A.B.1500), § 154.)*

Law Revision Commission Comments

Enactment [Revised Comment]

Subdivisions (a)-(d) and (f) of Section 6211 continue without substantive change and broaden former Code of Civil Procedure Section 542(b). In subdivision (c), the reference to an ongoing dating or engagement relationship has been added. This is drawn from the definition of domestic violence in Penal Code Section 13700. In subdivision (f), the reference to any "adult" person related by consanguinity or affinity has been omitted. This is consistent with the addition of children in subdivision (e).

Subdivision (e) is drawn from former Civil Code Section 7020 and eliminates any implication that children are not covered by this statute. Former Civil Code Section 7020 authorized restraining orders to protect children who are the subject of a proceeding pursuant to the Uniform Parentage Act. The former Domestic Violence Protection Act protected "cohabitants" but did not specifically mention children. See former Code Civ. Proc. § 542(b)-(c). Subdivision (e) continues the protection explicit in the former Uniform Parentage Act and extends it explicitly to include a child of a party to the proceeding in which the orders are sought. See Section 6221 (application of division).

Where a child has been declared a dependent of the juvenile court, that court may issue orders to protect the child from violence pursuant to the Welfare and Institutions Code. See, e.g., Welf. & Inst. Code §§ 213.5 (ex parte orders during pendency of proceeding to declare child a dependent), 304 (juvenile court authority to issue protective orders sua sponte). See also Section 6221(b) (nothing in this division affects the jurisdiction of the juvenile court).

See Sections 6320 (ex parte order enjoining harassment, threats, and violence), 6321 (ex parte order excluding party from dwelling), 6340 (orders that may be issued after notice and hearing); see also Sections 6203 ("abuse" defined), 6205 ("affinity" defined), 6209 ("cohabitant" and "former cohabitant" defined); Welf. & Inst. Code § 213.5 (issuance of restraining order during pendency of proceeding to determine minor dependent).

For provisions adopting this definition by reference, see Sections 3064 (limitation on ex parte order granting or modifying custody order), 3113 (separate meetings with court appointed investigator), 3181 (separate meetings with mediator), 3192 (separate meetings with counselor appointed in custody proceeding); Code Civ. Proc. §§ 128 (contempt powers of court), 1219 (punishment for contempt); Evid. Code §§ 1037.7 (victim-counselor privilege), 1107 (admissibility of expert witness testimony regarding battered women's syndrome); Penal Code §§ 273.6 (penalty for violation of protective order), 977 (appearance in misdemeanors), 1377 (compromise of misdemeanors).

For other domestic violence provisions, see, e.g., Penal Code §§ 136.2 (penalty for intimidation of witness), 273.83 (individuals subject to prosecution by district attorney's "spousal abuser" unit), 277 (penalty for child abduction), 653m (penalty for annoying telephone calls), 853.6 (citation and release not automatically available for misdemeanor violation of order to prevent domestic violence), 1000.6 (diversion of misdemeanant to counseling), 12028.5 (confiscating weapons at scene of domestic violence), 13700 (law enforcement response to domestic violence); Welf. & Inst. Code § 18291 ("domestic violence" defined for purposes of the Domestic Violence Centers Act). [23 Cal.L.Rev.Comm. Reports 1 (1993)].

Commentary

People v. Kovacich, 201 Cal.App.4th 863, 133 Cal.Rptr.3d 924 (2011), review denied, held that a criminal defendant's violent assault on a family dog in front of his wife and children constituted domestic violence under this section.

Hauck v. Riehl, 224 Cal.App.4th 695, 168 Cal.Rptr.3d 795 (2014), held that, under this division, a trial court lacked jurisdiction to grant a father's request for a permanent injunction against his child's stepfather when the father did not bring an action on behalf of the child.

Research References

Forms

California Practice Guide: Rutter Family Law Forms Form 1:32, Glossary Of Common Family Law Terms, Phrases and Concepts (Enclosure to Form 1:31).
California Transactions Forms--Family Law § 2:54, Permanent Support.
California Transactions Forms--Family Law § 4:14, Domestic Violence and Restraining Orders.
West's California Code Forms, Family § 6300, Comment Overview--Protective Orders.

Treatises and Practice Aids

Witkin, California Summary 10th Agency and Employment § 424, Jurors, Witnesses, and Victims.
Witkin, California Summary 10th Husband and Wife § 225, Statutory Factors.
Witkin, California Summary 10th Husband and Wife § 374, Definitions.
Witkin, California Summary 10th Husband and Wife § 379, in General.
Witkin, California Summary 10th Parent and Child § 177, in General.
Witkin, California Summary 10th Parent and Child § 271, Temporary Custody During Pendency Of Proceeding.
Witkin, California Summary 10th Parent and Child § 424A, (New) Suspension on Incarceration.

§ 6215. "Emergency protective order" defined

"Emergency protective order" means an order issued under Part 3 (commencing with Section 6240). *(Added by Stats.1993, c. 219 (A.B.1500), § 154.)*

Law Revision Commission Comments

Enactment [Revised Comment]

Section 6215 is a new provision included for drafting convenience. [23 Cal.L.Rev.Comm. Reports 1 (1993)].

Research References

Treatises and Practice Aids

Witkin, California Summary 10th Husband and Wife § 374, Definitions.

§ 6218. "Protective order" defined

"Protective order" means an order that includes any of the following restraining orders, whether issued ex parte, after notice and hearing, or in a judgment:

(a) An order described in Section 6320 enjoining specific acts of abuse.

(b) An order described in Section 6321 excluding a person from a dwelling.

(c) An order described in Section 6322 enjoining other specified behavior. *(Added by Stats.1993, c. 219 (A.B.1500), § 154.)*

Law Revision Commission Comments

Enactment [Revised Comment]

Section 6218 restates former Code of Civil Procedure Section 542(d) and expands the definition to include orders described in Sections 6321 and 6322. As revised, this term describes the three orders that most directly protect a victim of domestic violence from abuse. These are the orders to prevent specific acts of abuse, such as contacting, molesting, and striking, to exclude a party from a dwelling, and to enjoin other specified behaviors necessary to effectuate the first two orders. See Sections 6320 (enjoining harassment, threats, and violence), 6321 (exclusion from dwelling), 6322 (enjoining additional specified behaviors).

In this division, the term "protective order" is used in Sections 6252 (orders included in emergency protective order), 6303 (support person for victim of domestic violence), 6304 (court to provide information to parties concerning terms and effect of order), 6343 (participation in counseling), 6360 (orders included in judgment), 6385 (notice to Department of Justice), 6386 (appointment of counsel and payment if fees and costs to enforce order), 6388 (criminal penalty for violation of order).

For provisions adopting this definition by reference, see Sections 213 (responding party's request for affirmative relief alternative to moving party's requested relief), 2045, 2047, 2049 (restraining orders in proceeding for dissolution, nullity, and legal separation), 3100 (visitation rights of a parent), 3101 (visitation rights of stepparent), 3113 (separate meetings with court appointed investigator), 3103 (visitation rights of grandparent), 3181 (separate meetings with mediator), 3192 (separate meetings with counselor appointed in custody proceeding), 7710, 7720, 7730 (restraining orders in action pursuant to the Uniform Parentage Act); Gov't Code § 26841 (fees for protective order); Penal Code §§ 273.6 (willful violation of court order), 12021 (firearms), 14152 (referrals by district attorney to community conflict resolution program); Welf. & Inst. Code §§ 304 (custody of dependent children of the court), 362.4 (juvenile court order concerning custody or visitation). [23 Cal.L.Rev.Comm. Reports 1 (1993)].

Research References

Forms

West's California Code Forms, Family § 6200, Comment Overview--Prevention Of Domestic Violence.
West's California Code Forms, Family § 6250, Comment Overview--Issuance and Effect Of Emergency Protective Order.
West's California Judicial Council Forms JV-245, Request for Restraining Order--Juvenile.
West's California Judicial Council Forms JV-250, Notice Of Hearing and Temporary Restraining Order--Juvenile.
West's California Judicial Council Forms JV-255, Restraining Order - Juvenile Order After Hearing.

Treatises and Practice Aids

Witkin, California Summary 10th Husband and Wife § 71, Case Management.
Witkin, California Summary 10th Husband and Wife § 86, in General.
Witkin, California Summary 10th Husband and Wife § 89, Other Orders.

Witkin, California Summary 10th Husband and Wife § 112, Contents Of Judgment.
Witkin, California Summary 10th Husband and Wife § 371, Civil Remedies.
Witkin, California Summary 10th Husband and Wife § 374, Definitions.
Witkin, California Summary 10th Husband and Wife § 376, Issuance and Effect.
Witkin, California Summary 10th Husband and Wife § 380, Support Person for Victim.
Witkin, California Summary 10th Husband and Wife § 384, Orders After Notice and Hearing.
Witkin, California Summary 10th Husband and Wife § 385, Orders Included in Judgment.
Witkin, California Summary 10th Husband and Wife § 386, in General.
Witkin, California Summary 10th Parent and Child § 51, Protective Orders.
Witkin, California Summary 10th Parent and Child § 370, in General.
Witkin, California Summary 10th Parent and Child § 451, in General.
Witkin, California Summary 10th Parent and Child § 453, Jurisdiction Over Adults.
Witkin, California Summary 10th Parent and Child § 637, Priority Right Of Noncustodial Parent.
Witkin, California Summary 10th Parent and Child § 653, Ex Parte Orders Pending Nullity or Dissolution Proceedings.
Witkin, California Summary 10th Parent and Child § 892, in General.

§ 6219. Demonstration project to identify best practices in domestic violence court cases; participation in project; findings and recommendations

Subject to adequate, discretionary funding from a city or a county, the superior courts in San Diego County and in Santa Clara County may develop a demonstration project to identify the best practices in civil, juvenile, and criminal court cases involving domestic violence. The superior courts in any other county that is able and willing may also participate in the demonstration project. The superior courts participating in this demonstration project shall report their findings and recommendations to the Judicial Council and the Legislature on or before May 1, 2004. The Judicial Council may make those recommendations available to any court or county. *(Added by Stats.2002, c. 192 (A.B.1909), § 1.)*

Part 2

GENERAL PROVISIONS

Section

§ 6220. Purpose

The purpose of this division is to prevent acts of domestic violence, abuse, and sexual abuse and to provide for a separation of the persons involved in the domestic violence for a period sufficient to enable these persons to seek a resolution of the causes of the violence. *(Added by Stats. 1993, c. 219 (A.B.1500), § 154. Amended by Stats.2014, c. 635 (A.B.2089), § 3, eff. Jan. 1, 2015.)*

Law Revision Commission Comments

Enactment [Revised Comment]

Section 6220 continues former Code of Civil Procedure Section 540 without substantive change. The list of persons in the former section has been omitted. This is not a substantive change, since the list is duplicated in the definition of domestic violence that applies to this section. See Section 6211 ("domestic violence" defined). [23 Cal.L.Rev.Comm. Reports 1 (1993)].

Commentary

Quintana v. Guijosa, 107 Cal.App.4th 1077, 132 Cal.Rptr.2d 538 (2003), held that the trial court abused its discretion by denying a domestic relations restraining order to a woman whose husband had repeatedly physically and emotionally abused her, because the court disapproved the woman's leaving her children in Mexico.

Research References

Treatises and Practice Aids

Witkin, California Summary 10th Husband and Wife § 373, in General.
Witkin, California Summary 10th Husband and Wife § 379, in General.

§ 6221. Application of division; forms for issuance of orders

(a) Unless the provision or context otherwise requires, this division applies to any order described in this division, whether the order is issued in a proceeding brought pursuant to this division, in an action brought pursuant to the Uniform Parentage Act (Part 3 (commencing with Section 7600) of Division 12), or in a proceeding for dissolution of marriage, for nullity of marriage, or for legal separation of the parties.

(b) Nothing in this division affects the jurisdiction of the juvenile court.

(c) Any order issued by a court to which this division applies shall be issued on forms adopted by the Judicial Council of California and that have been approved by the Department of Justice pursuant to subdivision (i) of Section 6380. However, the fact that an order issued by a court pursuant to this section was not issued on forms adopted by the Judicial Council and approved by the Department of Justice shall not, in and of itself, make the order unenforceable. *(Added by Stats.1993, c. 219 (A.B.1500), § 154. Amended by Stats.1999, c. 661 (A.B.825), § 4.)*

Law Revision Commission Comments

Enactment [Revised Comment]

Subdivision (a) of Section 6221 is new and is added to make clear that the provisions of this division are applicable not only to proceedings brought pursuant to this division, but also in proceedings for dissolution, nullity, and legal separation and in actions brought pursuant to the Uniform Parentage Act.

Subdivision (b) is new [and] is added to help to ensure that conflicts of jurisdiction between the family court and the juvenile court do not arise. [23 Cal.L.Rev.Comm. Reports 1 (1993)].

Commentary

Relying in part on subsection (c) of this section, *Faton v. Ahmedo, 236 Cal.App.4th 1160, 187 Cal.Rptr.3d 201 (2015)*, holds that a prevailing party's failure to request attorney's fees on Judicial Council Form DV-100 did not deprive the trial court of jurisdiction to award attorney's fees, under section 6344, after notice and hearing in a domestic violence restraining order proceeding.

Research References

Forms

West's California Code Forms, Family § 6200, Comment Overview--Prevention Of Domestic Violence.

West's California Code Forms, Family § 6220, Comment Overview--General Provisions.

West's California Code Forms, Family § 6380, Comment Overview--Registration and Enforcement Of Orders.

Treatises and Practice Aids

Witkin, California Summary 10th Husband and Wife § 373, in General.

Witkin, California Summary 10th Husband and Wife § 387, Electronic Transmission and Recording Of Data.

§ 6222. Application, responsive pleading, or show cause order seeking to acquire, modify, or enforce a protective order; subpoena filed in connection; fees

There is no filing fee for an application, a responsive pleading, or an order to show cause that seeks to obtain, modify, or enforce a protective order or other order authorized by this division when the request for the other order is necessary to obtain or give effect to a protective order. There is no fee for a subpoena filed in connection with that application, responsive pleading, or order to show cause. *(Added by Stats.2002, c. 1009 (A.B.2030), § 4, operative Jan. 1, 2007. Amended by Stats.2006, c. 476 (A.B.2695), § 3.)*

Research References

Forms

West's California Code Forms, Family § 6220, Comment Overview--General Provisions.

Treatises and Practice Aids

Witkin, California Summary 10th Husband and Wife § 373, in General.

§ 6223. Custody or visitation order; application of Part 2 of Division 8

A custody or visitation order issued in a proceeding brought pursuant to this division is subject to Part 2 (commencing with Section 3020) of Division 8 (custody of children). *(Added by Stats.1993, c. 219 (A.B.1500), § 154.)*

Law Revision Commission Comments

Enactment [Revised Comment]

Section 6223 is a new provision that provides a cross-reference to the main custody statute in Division 8. This section makes clear that, where a custody or visitation order is issued in a proceeding brought pursuant to the Domestic Violence Prevention Act, the court is to apply the same substantive and procedural rules as would be applied in any other proceeding in which these issues may be determined.

For sections of particular importance in situations involving domestic violence, see Sections 3030 (custody and unsupervised visitation prohibited where parent convicted under certain Penal Code provisions), 3031 (custody or visitation should not be inconsistent with restraining orders), 3100(b) (limiting visitation to situation where third party present), 3131 (action by district attorney where child taken or detained in violation of visitation order). [23 Cal.L.Rev.Comm. Reports 1 (1993)].

Commentary

Keith R. v. Superior Court, 174 Cal.App.4th 1047, 96 Cal.Rptr.3d 298 (2009), holds that a section 3044(a) order granting an abused parent sole legal and physical custody of a child, incident to a domestic violence order issued in a dissolution proceeding, does not constitute a final custody determination for purposes of *Montenegro*. (See commentary to section 3022.) Thus the trial court erred in applying the "changed circumstances" rather than the "best interest" standard to a move-away request in a child custody case.

Barkaloff v. Woodward, 47 Cal.App.4th 393, 55 Cal.Rptr.2d 167 (1996), holds that a trial court lacks jurisdiction under the Domestic Violence Prevention Act (DVPA) (Section 6200 et seq.) and the Uniform Parentage Act (UPA) (Section 7600 et seq.) to award visitation rights to a man who is not the father of the child and who was never married to the child's mother when both the child's mother and the child's biological father object to visitation, even though such visitation may be in the child's best interests. *Barkaloff* holds that jurisdiction to order visitation of minor children under the DVPA is limited, pursuant to Section 6323, to cases where there is a marital relationship between the parties. 47 Cal.App.4th at 398.

Research References

Forms

California Transactions Forms--Family Law § 3:4, Subject Matter Jurisdiction for Custody Determinations.

Treatises and Practice Aids

Witkin, California Summary 10th Husband and Wife § 373, in General.

Witkin, California Summary 10th Parent and Child § 238, Valid Conditions.

§ 6224. Statement on face of order; expiration date and notice

An order described in this division shall state on its face the date of expiration of the order and the following statements in substantially the following form:

"This order is effective when made. The law enforcement agency shall enforce it immediately on receipt. It is enforceable anywhere in California by any law enforcement agency that has received the order or is shown a copy of the order. If proof of service on the restrained person has not been received, the law enforcement agency shall advise the restrained person of the terms of the order and then shall enforce it." *(Added by Stats.1993, c. 219 (A.B.1500), § 154.)*

Law Revision Commission Comments

Enactment [Revised Comment]

Section 6224 continues without substantive change former Code of Civil Procedure Section 552, the third paragraph of former Civil Code Section 4359(a), the first sentence of former Civil Code Section 4359(c), and former Civil Code Section 7020(c). This section generalizes the requirements of the former sections to apply to all orders issued pursuant to this division. This is not a substantive change. See Cal. R. Ct. 1285.05 (rev. July 1, 1987) (temporary restraining order in dissolution, nullity, or legal separation proceeding), 1296.10 (rev. Jan. 1, 1991) (order to show cause and temporary restraining order in proceeding pursuant to Domestic Violence Prevention Act or Uniform Parentage Act), 1296.29 (new July 1, 1991) (restraining order after hearing in dissolution, nullity, or legal separation or in proceedings under Domestic Violence Prevention Act or Uniform Parentage Act). [23 Cal.L.Rev.Comm. Reports 1 (1993)].

Research References

Forms

West's California Judicial Council Forms FL-300, Request for Order.

Treatises and Practice Aids

Witkin, California Summary 10th Husband and Wife § 373, in General.

§ 6225. Explicit statement of address not required

A petition for an order described in this division is valid and the order is enforceable without explicitly stating the address of the petitioner or the petitioner's place of residence, school, employment, the place where the petitioner's child is provided child care services, or the child's school. *(Added by Stats.1993, c. 219 (A.B.1500), § 154.)*

Law Revision Commission Comments

Enactment [Revised Comment]

Section 6225 generalizes and continues the last sentence of former Code of Civil Procedure Section 545 without substantive change. This section has been expanded to apply to orders contained in a judgment. The references to "petitioner" have been substituted for the former references to "applicant." These are not substantive changes. [23 Cal.L.Rev.Comm. Reports 1 (1993)].

Research References

Treatises and Practice Aids

Witkin, California Summary 10th Husband and Wife § 373, in General.

§ 6226. Forms and instructions; promulgation by Judicial Council

The Judicial Council shall prescribe the form of the orders and any other documents required by this division and shall promulgate forms and instructions for applying for orders described in this division. *(Added by Stats.1993, c. 219 (A.B.1500), § 154.)*

Law Revision Commission Comments

Enactment [Revised Comment]

Section 6226 continues without substantive change former Code of Civil Procedure Section 543, the first sentence of the third paragraph of subdivision (b) and the first sentence of the fourth paragraph of subdivision (c) of former Code of Civil Procedure Section 546, and the last paragraph of former Civil Code Section 4359(a). [23 Cal.L.Rev.Comm. Reports 1 (1993)].

Commentary

Although this section requires the Judicial Council to promulgate forms for applying for orders prescribed by this division, *Faton v. Ahmedo, 236 Cal.App.4th 1160, 187 Cal.Rptr.3d 201 (2015)*, holds that a prevailing party's failure to request attorney's fees on Judicial Council Form DV-100 did not deprive the trial court of jurisdiction to award section 6344 attorney's fees after notice and hearing in a domestic violence restraining order proceeding.

Research References

Forms

West's California Judicial Council Forms FL-300, Request for Order.

Treatises and Practice Aids

Witkin, California Summary 10th Husband and Wife § 373, in General.

§ 6227. Remedies in this chapter additional to other remedies

The remedies provided in this division are in addition to any other civil or criminal remedies that may be available to the petitioner. *(Added by Stats.1993, c. 219 (A.B.1500), § 154.)*

Law Revision Commission Comments

Enactment [Revised Comment]

Section 6227 continues former Code of Civil Procedure Section 549 without substantive change. The word "petitioner" has been substituted for "plaintiff" to conform to revisions made in former law. See 1990 Cal. Stat. ch. 752. [23 Cal.L.Rev.Comm. Reports 1 (1993)].

Research References

Treatises and Practice Aids

Witkin, California Summary 10th Husband and Wife § 373, in General.

§ 6228. Access to Domestic Violence Reports Act of 1999

(a) State and local law enforcement agencies shall provide, upon request and without charging a fee, one copy of all incident report face sheets, one copy of all incident reports, or both, to a victim, or his or her representative as defined in subdivision (g), of a crime that constitutes an act of any of the following:

(1) Domestic violence, as defined in Section 6211.

(2) Sexual assault, as defined in Sections 261, 261.5, 262, 265, 266, 266a, 266b, 266c, 266g, 266j, 267, 269, 273.4, 285, 286, 288, 288a, 288.5, 289, or 311.4 of the Penal Code.

(3) Stalking, as defined in Section 1708.7 of the Civil Code or Section 646.9 of the Penal Code.

(4) Human trafficking, as defined in Section 236.1 of the Penal Code.

(5) Abuse of an elder or a dependent adult, as defined in Section 15610.07 of the Welfare and Institutions Code.

(b)(1) A copy of an incident report face sheet shall be made available during regular business hours to a victim or his or her representative no later than 48 hours after being requested by the victim or his or her representative, unless the state or local law enforcement agency informs the victim or his or her representative of the reasons why, for good cause, the incident report face sheet is not available, in which case the incident report face sheet shall be made available to the victim or his or her representative no later than five working days after the request is made.

(2) A copy of the incident report shall be made available during regular business hours to a victim or his or her representative no later than five working days after being requested by a victim or his or her representative, unless the state or local law enforcement agency informs the victim or

his or her representative of the reasons why, for good cause, the incident report is not available, in which case the incident report shall be made available to the victim or his or her representative no later than 10 working days after the request is made.

(c) Any person requesting copies under this section shall present state or local law enforcement with his or her identification, including a current, valid driver's license, a state-issued identification card, or a passport. If the person is a representative of the victim and the victim is deceased, the representative shall also present a certified copy of the death certificate or other satisfactory evidence of the death of the victim at the time a request is made. If the person is a representative of the victim and the victim is alive and not the subject of a conservatorship, the representative shall also present a written authorization, signed by the victim, making him or her the victim's personal representative.

(d)(1) This section shall apply to requests for domestic violence face sheets or incident reports made within five years from the date of completion of the incident report.

(2) This section shall apply to requests for sexual assault, stalking, human trafficking, or abuse of an elder or a dependent adult face sheets or incident reports made within two years from the date of completion of the incident report.

(e) This section shall be known and may be cited as the Access to Domestic Violence Reports Act of 1999.

(f) For purposes of this section, "victim" includes a minor who is 12 years of age or older.

(g)(1) For purposes of this section, if the victim is deceased, a "representative of the victim" means any of the following:

(A) The surviving spouse.

(B) A surviving child of the decedent who has attained 18 years of age.

(C) A domestic partner, as defined in subdivision (a) of Section 297.

(D) A surviving parent of the decedent.

(E) A surviving adult relative.

(F) The personal representative of the victim, as defined in Section 58 of the Probate Code, if one is appointed.

(G) The public administrator if one has been appointed.

(2) For purposes of this section, if the victim is not deceased, a "representative of the victim" means any of the following:

(A) A parent, guardian, or adult child of the victim, or an adult sibling of a victim 12 years of age or older, who shall present to law enforcement identification pursuant to subdivision (c). A guardian shall also present to law enforcement a copy of his or her letters of guardianship demonstrating that he or she is the appointed guardian of the victim.

(B) An attorney for the victim, who shall present to law enforcement identification pursuant to subdivision (c) and written proof that he or she is the attorney for the victim.

(C) A conservator of the victim who shall present to law enforcement identification pursuant to subdivision (c) and a copy of his or her letters of conservatorship demonstrating that he or she is the appointed conservator of the victim.

(3) A representative of the victim does not include any person who has been convicted of murder in the first degree, as defined in Section 189 of the Penal Code, of the victim, or any person identified in the incident report face sheet as a suspect. *(Added by Stats.1999, c. 1022 (A.B.403), § 1. Amended by Stats.2002, c. 377 (S.B.1265), § 1; Stats.2010, c. 363 (A.B.1738), § 1; Stats.2011, c. 296 (A.B.1023), § 93; Stats.2016, c. 875 (A.B.1678), § 1, eff. Jan. 1, 2017.)*

Research References

Treatises and Practice Aids

Witkin, California Summary 10th Husband and Wife § 373, in General.

§ 6229. Minor under 12 years of age appearing without counsel

A minor, under 12 years of age, accompanied by a duly appointed and acting guardian ad litem, shall be permitted to appear in court without counsel for the limited purpose of requesting or opposing a request for a temporary restraining order or injunction, or both, under this division as provided in Section 374 of the Code of Civil Procedure. *(Added by Stats.2010, c. 572 (A.B.1596), § 12, operative Jan. 1, 2012.)*

Research References

Treatises and Practice Aids

Witkin, California Summary 10th Husband and Wife § 373, in General.

Part 3

EMERGENCY PROTECTIVE ORDERS

CHAPTER 1. GENERAL PROVISIONS

§ 6240. Definitions

As used in this part:

(a) "Judicial officer" means a judge, commissioner, or referee designated under Section 6241.

(b) "Law enforcement officer" means one of the following officers who requests or enforces an emergency protective order under this part:

(1) A police officer.

(2) A sheriff's officer.

(3) A peace officer of the Department of the California Highway Patrol.

(4) A peace officer of the University of California Police Department.

(5) A peace officer of the California State University and College Police Departments.

(6) A peace officer of the Department of Parks and Recreation, as defined in subdivision (f) of Section 830.2 of the Penal Code.

(7) A peace officer of the Department of General Services of the City of Los Angeles, as defined in subdivision (c) of Section 830.31 of the Penal Code.

(8) A housing authority patrol officer, as defined in subdivision (d) of Section 830.31 of the Penal Code.

(9) A peace officer for a district attorney, as defined in Section 830.1 or 830.35 of the Penal Code.

(10) A parole officer, probation officer, or deputy probation officer, as defined in Section 830.5 of the Penal Code.

(11) A peace officer of a California Community College police department, as defined in subdivision (a) of Section 830.32.

(12) A peace officer employed by a police department of a school district, as defined in subdivision (b) of Section 830.32.

(c) "Abduct" means take, entice away, keep, withhold, or conceal. *(Added by Stats.1993, c. 219 (A.B.1500), § 154. Amended by Stats.1993, c. 1229 (A.B.224), § 1; Gov.Reorg. Plan No. 1 of 1995, § 4, eff. July 12, 1995; Stats.1996, c. 305 (A.B.3103), § 5; Stats.1996, c. 988 (A.B.2936), § 3; Stats. 1999, c. 659 (S.B.355), § 1; Stats.2004, c. 250 (S.B.1391), § 1.)*

Law Revision Commission Comments

Enactment [Revised Comment]

Section 6240 is a new section that defines terms for the purposes of this part relating exclusively to emergency protective orders. The terms "judicial officer" and "law enforcement officer" are consistent with the Judicial Council form for the emergency protective order. See Cal. R. Ct. 1295.90 (rev. Jan. 1, 1992). See also Section 6215 ("emergency protective order" defined).

In this part, provisions concerning emergency protective orders relating to domestic violence from former Code of Civil Procedure Section 546(b) and provisions concerning emergency protective orders relating to child abuse from former Code of Civil Procedure Section 546(c) have been unified to the extent practicable. This approach is consistent with the unified Judicial Council form for the emergency protective order. [23 Cal.L.Rev.Comm. Reports 1 (1993)].

Research References

Treatises and Practice Aids

Witkin, California Summary 10th Husband and Wife § 87, Methods Of Obtaining Orders.

Witkin, California Summary 10th Husband and Wife § 374, Definitions.

Witkin, California Summary 10th Husband and Wife § 375, in General.

Witkin, California Summary 10th Parent and Child § 311, Other Proceedings Stayed.

§ 6241. Designation of judge, commissioner, or referee to orally issue emergency protective orders

The presiding judge of the superior court in each county shall designate at least one judge, commissioner, or referee to be reasonably available to issue orally, by telephone or otherwise, emergency protective orders at all times whether or not the court is in session. *(Added by Stats.1993, c. 219 (A.B.1500), § 154.)*

Law Revision Commission Comments

Enactment [Revised Comment]

Section 6241 continues without substantive change the first sentence of the first paragraph of former Code of Civil Procedure Section 546(b). See Section 6240(a) ("judicial officer" defined by reference to this section). See also Section 6215 ("emergency protective order" defined). [23 Cal.L.Rev.Comm. Reports 1 (1993)].

Research References

Forms

West's California Code Forms, Family § 6240, Comment Overview--Emergency Protective Orders.

Treatises and Practice Aids

Witkin, California Summary 10th Husband and Wife § 375, in General.

CHAPTER 2. ISSUANCE AND EFFECT OF EMERGENCY PROTECTIVE ORDER

Section

§ 6250. Grounds for issuance

A judicial officer may issue an ex parte emergency protective order where a law enforcement officer asserts reasonable grounds to believe any of the following:

(a) That a person is in immediate and present danger of domestic violence, based on the person's allegation of a recent incident of abuse or threat of abuse by the person against whom the order is sought.

(b) That a child is in immediate and present danger of abuse by a family or household member, based on an allegation of a recent incident of abuse or threat of abuse by the family or household member.

(c) That a child is in immediate and present danger of being abducted by a parent or relative, based on a reasonable belief that a person has an intent to abduct the child or flee with the child from the jurisdiction or based on an allegation of a recent threat to abduct the child or flee with the child from the jurisdiction.

(d) That an elder or dependent adult is in immediate and present danger of abuse as defined in Section 15610.07 of the Welfare and Institutions Code, based on an allegation of a recent incident of abuse or threat of abuse by the person against whom the order is sought, except that no emergency protective order shall be issued based solely on an allegation of financial abuse. *(Added by Stats.1993, c. 219 (A.B.1500), § 154. Amended by Stats.1996, c. 988 (A.B.2936), § 4; Stats.1999, c. 561 (A.B.59), § 1; Stats.2003, c. 468 (S.B.851), § 3.)*

Law Revision Commission Comments

Enactment [Revised Comment]

Section 6250 continues without substantive change the second sentence of the first paragraph of subdivision (b) and the first sentence of the first paragraph of subdivision (c) of former Code of Civil Procedure Section 546. In subdivision (a), the phrase "by the person against whom the order is sought" has been added. This is not a substantive change. See Sections 6203 ("abuse" defined), 6211 ("domestic violence" defined).

See also Sections 6215 ("emergency protective order" defined), 6240(a) ("judicial officer" defined). [23 Cal.L.Rev.Comm. Reports 1 (1993)].

Research References

Forms

California Practice Guide: Rutter Family Law Forms Form 1:32, Glossary Of Common Family Law Terms, Phrases and Concepts (Enclosure to Form 1:31).

West's California Code Forms, Family § 6250, Comment Overview--Issuance and Effect Of Emergency Protective Order.

Treatises and Practice Aids

Witkin, California Summary 10th Husband and Wife § 376, Issuance and Effect.

§ 6250.3. Valid orders

An emergency protective order is valid only if it is issued by a judicial officer after making the findings required by Section 6251 and pursuant to a specific request by a law enforcement officer. *(Added by Stats.2006, c. 82 (A.B.1787), § 1.)*

Research References

Treatises and Practice Aids

Witkin, California Summary 10th Husband and Wife § 376, Issuance and Effect.

§ 6250.5. Issuance of ex parte emergency protective orders to peace officers

A judicial officer may issue an ex parte emergency protective order to a peace officer defined in subdivisions (a) and (b) of Section 830.32 if the issuance of that order is consistent with an existing memorandum of understanding between the college or school police department where the peace officer is employed and the sheriff or police chief of the city in whose jurisdiction the peace officer's college or school is located and the peace officer asserts reasonable grounds to believe that there is a demonstrated threat to campus safety. *(Added by Stats.1999, c. 659 (S.B.355), § 1.5.)*

Research References

Forms

West's California Code Forms, Family § 6250, Comment Overview--Issuance and Effect Of Emergency Protective Order.

Treatises and Practice Aids

Witkin, California Summary 10th Husband and Wife § 376, Issuance and Effect.

§ 6251. Findings of court

An emergency protective order may be issued only if the judicial officer finds both of the following:

(a) That reasonable grounds have been asserted to believe that an immediate and present danger of domestic violence exists, that a child is in immediate and present danger of abuse or abduction, or that an elder or dependent adult is in immediate and present danger of abuse as defined in Section 15610.07 of the Welfare and Institutions Code.

(b) That an emergency protective order is necessary to prevent the occurrence or recurrence of domestic violence, child abuse, child abduction, or abuse of an elder or dependent adult. *(Added by Stats.1993, c. 219 (A.B.1500), § 154. Amended by Stats.1996, c. 988 (A.B.2936), § 5; Stats.1999, c. 561 (A.B.59), § 2.)*

Law Revision Commission Comments

Enactment [Revised Comment]

Section 6251 continues without substantive change the first sentence of the second paragraph of subdivision (b) and the first sentence of the second paragraph of subdivision (c) of former Code of Civil Procedure Section 546. See also Sections 6203 ("abuse" defined), 6211 ("domestic violence" defined), 6215 ("emergency protective order" defined), 6240(a) ("judicial officer" defined). [23 Cal.L.Rev.Comm. Reports 1 (1993)].

Research References

Forms

West's California Code Forms, Family § 6250, Comment Overview--Issuance and Effect Of Emergency Protective Order.

Treatises and Practice Aids

Witkin, California Summary 10th Husband and Wife § 376, Issuance and Effect.

§ 6252. Inclusion of other orders

An emergency protective order may include any of the following specific orders, as appropriate:

(a) A protective order, as defined in Section 6218.

(b) An order determining the temporary care and control of any minor child of the endangered person and the person against whom the order is sought.

(c) An order authorized in Section 213.5 of the Welfare and Institutions Code, including provisions placing the temporary care and control of the endangered child and any other minor children in the family or household with the parent or guardian of the endangered child who is not a restrained party.

(d) An order determining the temporary care and control of any minor child who is in danger of being abducted.

(e) An order authorized by Section 15657.03 of the Welfare and Institutions Code. *(Added by Stats.1993, c. 219 (A.B.1500), § 154. Amended by Stats.1996, c. 988 (A.B.2936), § 6; Stats.1999, c. 561 (A.B.59), § 3.)*

Law Revision Commission Comments

Enactment [Revised Comment]

The introductory clause and subdivisions (a) and (b) of Section 6252 continue without substantive change the third sentence of the first paragraph of former Code of Civil Procedure Section 546(b). A reference to "child" has been substituted for "children." This is not a substantive change. See Section 10 (singular includes plural).

The introductory clause and subdivision (c) continue without substantive change the second sentence of the first paragraph of former Code of Civil Procedure Section 546(c). The reference to the "legal" guardian has been omitted as surplus. This conforms with terminology in the Probate Code. See Prob. Code §§ 2350(b), 2400(b) ("guardian" defined).

See also Sections 6203 ("abuse" defined), 6211 ("domestic violence" defined), 6215 ("emergency protective order" defined). [23 Cal.L.Rev.Comm. Reports 1 (1993)].

Research References

Forms

West's California Code Forms, Family § 6250, Comment Overview--Issuance and Effect Of Emergency Protective Order.

Treatises and Practice Aids

Witkin, California Summary 10th Husband and Wife § 376, Issuance and Effect.

Witkin, California Summary 10th Parent and Child § 271, Temporary Custody During Pendency Of Proceeding.

§ 6252.5. Addresses or locations of persons protected under court order; prohibition upon certain enjoined parties from acting to obtain such information

(a) The court shall order that any party enjoined pursuant to an order issued under this part be prohibited from taking any action to obtain the address or location of a protected party or a protected party's family members, caretakers, or guardian, unless there is good cause not to make that order.

(b) The Judicial Council shall promulgate forms necessary to effectuate this section. *(Added by Stats.2005, c. 472 (A.B.978), § 2.)*

Research References

Forms

West's California Code Forms, Family § 6250, Comment Overview--Issuance and Effect Of Emergency Protective Order.

Treatises and Practice Aids

Witkin, California Summary 10th Husband and Wife § 371, Civil Remedies.

§ 6253. Contents of orders

An emergency protective order shall include all of the following:

(a) A statement of the grounds asserted for the order.

(b) The date and time the order expires.

(c) The address of the superior court for the district or county in which the endangered person or child in danger of being abducted resides.

(d) The following statements, which shall be printed in English and Spanish:

(1) "To the Protected Person: This order will last only until the date and time noted above. If you wish to seek continuing protection, you will have to apply for an order from the court, at the address noted above. You may seek the advice of an attorney as to any matter connected with your application for any future court orders. The attorney should be consulted promptly so that the attorney may assist you in making your application."

(2) "To the Restrained Person: This order will last until the date and time noted above. The protected party may, however, obtain a more permanent restraining order from the court. You may seek the advice of an attorney as to any matter connected with the application. The attorney should be consulted promptly so that the attorney may assist you in responding to the application."

(e) In the case of an endangered child, the following statement, which shall be printed in English and Spanish: "This order will last only until the date and time noted above. You may apply for a more permanent restraining order under Section 213.5 of the Welfare and Institutions Code from the court at the address noted above. You may seek the advice of an attorney in connection with the application for a more permanent restraining order."

(f) In the case of a child in danger of being abducted, the following statement, which shall be printed in English and Spanish: "This order will last only until the date and time noted above. You may apply for a child custody order from the court, at the address noted above. You may seek the advice of an attorney as to any matter connected with the application. The attorney should be consulted promptly so that the attorney may assist you in responding to the application." *(Added by Stats.1993, c. 219 (A.B.1500), § 154. Amended by Stats.1996, c. 988 (A.B.2936), § 7.)*

Law Revision Commission Comments

Enactment [Revised Comment]

Section 6253 continues without substantive change the parts of the second paragraphs of subdivisions (b) and (c) of former Code of Civil Procedure Section 546 that enumerated the contents of an emergency protective order, and the last sentence of the third paragraph of subdivision (b) and the last sentence of the fourth paragraph of subdivision (c) of former Code of Civil Procedure Section 546. The language concerning attorney advice in subdivision (e) has been conformed to the language of subdivision (d)(1). See also Section 6215 ("emergency protective order" defined). [23 Cal.L.Rev.Comm. Reports 1 (1993)].

Research References

Forms

West's California Code Forms, Family § 6250, Comment Overview--Issuance and Effect Of Emergency Protective Order.

Treatises and Practice Aids

Witkin, California Summary 10th Husband and Wife § 376, Issuance and Effect.

§ 6254. Availability of orders; effect of vacation of household

The fact that the endangered person has left the household to avoid abuse does not affect the availability of an emergency protective order. *(Added by Stats.1993, c. 219 (A.B.1500), § 154.)*

Law Revision Commission Comments

Enactment [Revised Comment]

Section 6254 continues without substantive change the seventh paragraph of subdivision (b) and the seventh paragraph of subdivision (c) of former Code of Civil Procedure Section 546. The endangered person may be an adult or a child. See also Section 6203 ("abuse" defined), 6215 ("emergency protective order" defined). [23 Cal.L.Rev.Comm. Reports 1 (1993)].

Research References

Forms

West's California Code Forms, Family § 6250, Comment Overview--Issuance and Effect Of Emergency Protective Order.

Treatises and Practice Aids

Witkin, California Summary 10th Husband and Wife § 376, Issuance and Effect.

§ 6255. Issuance of orders without prejudice

An emergency protective order shall be issued without prejudice to any person. *(Added by Stats.1993, c. 219 (A.B.1500), § 154.)*

Law Revision Commission Comments

Enactment [Revised Comment]

Section 6255 continues without substantive change the last sentence of the first paragraph of subdivision (b) and the last sentence of the first paragraph of subdivision (c) of former Code of Civil Procedure Section 546. See also Section 6215 ("emergency protective order" defined). [23 Cal.L.Rev.Comm. Reports 1 (1993)].

Research References

Treatises and Practice Aids

Witkin, California Summary 10th Husband and Wife § 376, Issuance and Effect.

§ 6256. Expiration of orders

An emergency protective order expires at the earlier of the following times:

(a) The close of judicial business on the fifth court day following the day of its issuance.

(b) The seventh calendar day following the day of its issuance. *(Added by Stats.1993, c. 219 (A.B.1500), § 154. Amended by Stats.1993, c. 1229 (A.B.224), § 2.)*

Law Revision Commission Comments

Enactment [Revised Comment]

Section 6256 supersedes the sixth paragraph of subdivision (b) and the third sentence of the first paragraph of subdivision (c) of former Code of Civil Procedure Section 546. See also Section 6215 ("emergency protective order" defined). [23 Cal.L.Rev.Comm. Reports 1 (1993)].

Research References

Forms

West's California Code Forms, Family § 6250, Comment Overview--Issuance and Effect Of Emergency Protective Order.

Treatises and Practice Aids

Witkin, California Summary 10th Husband and Wife § 376, Issuance and Effect.

§ 6257. Application for restraining orders under Welfare and Institutions Code § 213.5

If an emergency protective order concerns an endangered child, the child's parent or guardian who is not a restrained person, or a person having temporary custody of the endangered child, may apply to the court for a restraining order under Section 213.5 of the Welfare and Institutions Code. *(Added by Stats.1993, c. 219 (A.B.1500), § 154.)*

Law Revision Commission Comments

Enactment [Revised Comment]

Section 6257 continues the third paragraph of former Code of Civil Procedure Section 546(c) without substantive change. For provisions relating to orders concerning endangered children, see Section 6250(b), 6251(a), 6252(b)-(c). See also Section 6215 ("emergency protective order" defined). The reference to the "legal" guardian has been omitted as surplus. This conforms with terminology in the Probate Code. See Prob. Code §§ 2350(b), 2400(b) ("guardian" defined). [23 Cal.L.Rev.Comm. Reports 1 (1993)].

Research References

Forms

West's California Code Forms, Family § 6250, Comment Overview--Issuance and Effect Of Emergency Protective Order.

Treatises and Practice Aids

Witkin, California Summary 10th Husband and Wife § 376, Issuance and Effect.

Witkin, California Summary 10th Parent and Child § 271, Temporary Custody During Pendency Of Proceeding.

CHAPTER 3. DUTIES OF LAW ENFORCEMENT OFFICER

Section

§ 6270. Reduction of orders to writing

A law enforcement officer who requests an emergency protective order shall reduce the order to writing and sign it. *(Added by Stats.1993, c. 219 (A.B.1500), § 154.)*

Law Revision Commission Comments

Enactment [Revised Comment]

Section 6270 continues without substantive change the second sentence of the second paragraph of subdivision (b) and the second sentence of the second paragraph of subdivision (c) of former Code of Civil Procedure Section 546. The requirement of this section is satisfied by use of the Judicial Council form. See Cal. R. Ct. 1295.90 (rev. Jan. 1, 1992). See also Sections 6215 ("emergency protective order" defined), 6240(b) ("law enforcement officer" defined). [23 Cal.L.Rev.Comm. Reports 1 (1993)].

Research References

Treatises and Practice Aids

Witkin, California Summary 10th Husband and Wife § 377, Duties Of Law Enforcement Officer.

§ 6271. Duties of officer who requested order

A law enforcement officer who requests an emergency protective order shall do all of the following:

(a) Serve the order on the restrained person, if the restrained person can reasonably be located.

(b) Give a copy of the order to the protected person or, if the protected person is a minor child, to a parent or guardian of the endangered child who is not a restrained person, if the parent or guardian can reasonably be located, or to a person having temporary custody of the endangered child.

(c) File a copy of the order with the court as soon as practicable after issuance.

(d) Have the order entered into the computer database system for protective and restraining orders maintained by the Department of Justice. *(Added by Stats.1993, c. 219 (A.B.1500), § 154. Amended by Stats.2013, c. 145 (A.B.238), § 1.)*

Law Revision Commission Comments

Enactment [Revised Comment]

Section 6271 continues without substantive change the fifth paragraph of subdivision (b) and the sixth paragraph of subdivision (c) of former Code of Civil Procedure Section 546. References to the "legal" guardian have been omitted as surplus. This conforms with terminology in the Probate Code. See Prob. Code §§ 2350(b), 2400(b) ("guardian" defined).

See Section 6252 (b)–(c) (orders concerning endangered child); see also Sections 6215 ("emergency protective order" defined), 6240(b) ("law enforcement officer" defined). [23 Cal.L.Rev.Comm. Reports 1 (1993)].

Research References

Treatises and Practice Aids

Witkin, California Summary 10th Husband and Wife § 377, Duties Of Law Enforcement Officer.

§ 6272. Enforcement of orders; liability of officers enforcing orders

(a) A law enforcement officer shall use every reasonable means to enforce an emergency protective order.

(b) A law enforcement officer who acts in good faith to enforce an emergency protective order is not civilly or criminally liable. *(Added by Stats.1993, c. 219 (A.B.1500), § 154.)*

Law Revision Commission Comments

Enactment [Revised Comment]

Section 6272 restates without substantive change the last paragraph of subdivision (b) and the last paragraph of subdivision (c) of former Code of Civil Procedure Section 546. See also Sections 6215 ("emergency protective order" defined), 6240(b) ("law enforcement officer" defined). [23 Cal.L.Rev.Comm. Reports 1 (1993)].

Research References

Treatises and Practice Aids

Witkin, California Summary 10th Husband and Wife § 377, Duties Of Law Enforcement Officer.

§ 6274. Stalking; emergency protective order

A peace officer, as defined in Section 830.1 or 830.2 of the Penal Code, may seek an emergency protective order relating to stalking under Section 646.91 of the Penal Code if the requirements of that section are complied with. *(Added by Stats.1997, c. 169 (A.B.350), § 1.)*

Research References

Forms

West's California Code Forms, Family § 6274, Comment Overview--Stalking.

Treatises and Practice Aids

Witkin, California Summary 10th Husband and Wife § 372, Criminal Proceedings.

Witkin, California Summary 10th Husband and Wife § 378, Antistalking Order.

§ 6275. Conditions under which an officer is to inform a person for whom emergency protective order may be sought

(a) A law enforcement officer who responds to a situation in which the officer believes that there may be grounds for the issuance of an emergency protective order pursuant to Section 6250 of this code or Section 646.91 of the Penal Code, shall inform the person for whom an emergency protective order may be sought, or, if that person is a minor, his or her parent or guardian, provided that the parent or guardian is not the person against whom the emergency protective order may be obtained, that he or she may request the officer to request an emergency protective order pursuant to this part.

(b) Notwithstanding Section 6250, and pursuant to this part, an officer shall request an emergency protective order if the officer believes that the person requesting an emergency protective order is in immediate and present danger. *(Added by Stats.2006, c. 479 (A.B.2139), § 1.)*

Research References

Forms

West's California Code Forms, Family § 6250, Comment Overview--Issuance and Effect Of Emergency Protective Order.

West's California Code Forms, Family § 6274, Comment Overview--Stalking.

Treatises and Practice Aids

Witkin, California Summary 10th Husband and Wife § 377, Duties Of Law Enforcement Officer.

Part 4

PROTECTIVE ORDERS AND OTHER DOMESTIC VIOLENCE PREVENTION ORDERS

CHAPTER 1. GENERAL PROVISIONS

§ 6300. Issuance of order upon affidavit or testimony

An order may be issued under this part, with or without notice, to restrain any person for the purpose specified in Section 6220, if an affidavit or testimony and any additional information provided to the court pursuant to Section 6306, shows, to the satisfaction of the court, reasonable proof of a past act or acts of abuse. The court may issue an order under this part based solely on the affidavit or testimony of the person requesting the restraining order. *(Added by Stats. 1993, c. 219 (A.B.1500), § 154. Amended by Stats.2001, c. 572 (S.B.66), § 2; Stats.2014, c. 635 (A.B.2089), § 4, eff. Jan. 1, 2015.)*

Implementation

Implementation of Stats.2001, c. 572 (S.B.66), see § 7 of that act.

Law Revision Commission Comments

Enactment [Revised Comment]

Section 6300 continues without substantive change and generalizes the first sentence of former Code of Civil Procedure Section 545 and supersedes the fourth sentence of Section 545. A reference to an order issued under "this part" has been substituted for the former reference to a "temporary" restraining order. This is not a substantive change. See also Sections 6203 ("abuse" defined), 6211 ("domestic violence" defined).

For general provisions relating to ex parte restraining orders, see Part 4 (commencing with Section 240) of Division 2. [23 Cal.L.Rev. Comm. Reports 1 (1993)].

Commentary

When two parties separately apply for and receive, under this section, restraining orders against each other on different dates, the second application is not a request for a mutual restraining order and therefore need not meet the requirements of Section 6305. *Conness v. Satram, 122 Cal.App.4th 197, 18 Cal.Rptr.3d 577 (2004).*

Research References

Forms

West's California Code Forms, Family § 6300, Comment Overview-- Protective Orders.

West's California Judicial Council Forms FL-303, Declaration Regarding Notice and Service Of Request for Temporary Emergency (Ex Parte) Orders.

Treatises and Practice Aids

Witkin, California Summary 10th Husband and Wife § 7, Other Ex Parte Orders.

Witkin, California Summary 10th Husband and Wife § 379, in General.

Witkin, California Summary 10th Husband and Wife § 381, Criminal Background Search.

Witkin, California Summary 10th Husband and Wife § 386, in General.

Witkin, California Summary 10th Husband and Wife § 388, Service Of Order.

Witkin, California Summary 10th Parent and Child § 63, in General.

Witkin, California Summary 10th Parent and Child § 271, Temporary Custody During Pendency Of Proceeding.

Witkin, California Summary 10th Parent and Child § 311, Other Proceedings Stayed.

Witkin, California Summary 10th Parent and Child § 453, Jurisdiction Over Adults.

§ 6301. Persons who may be granted order

(a) An order under this part may be granted to any person described in Section 6211, including a minor pursuant to subdivision (b) of Section 372 of the Code of Civil Procedure.

(b) The right to petition for relief shall not be denied because the petitioner has vacated the household to avoid abuse, and in the case of a marital relationship, notwithstanding that a petition for dissolution of marriage, for nullity of marriage, or for legal separation of the parties has not been filed.

(c) The length of time since the most recent act of abuse is not, by itself, determinative. The court shall consider the totality of the circumstances in determining whether to grant or deny a petition for relief. *(Added by Stats.1993, c. 219 (A.B.1500), § 154. Amended by Stats.1996, c. 727 (A.B.2155), § 3; Stats.2014, c. 635 (A.B.2089), § 5, eff. Jan. 1, 2015; Stats.2015, c. 303 (A.B.731), § 150, eff. Jan. 1, 2016.)*

Law Revision Commission Comments

Enactment [Revised Comment]

Section 6301 continues the second and third sentences of former Code of Civil Procedure Section 545 without substantive change. A reference to Section 6211 has been substituted for the reference to former Code of Civil Procedure Section 542. This is not a substantive change, since the relevant part of the former section is continued in Section 6211. The former reference to a "temporary" restraining order has been omitted, for consistency with other sections in this part. This is not a substantive change. See also Section 6203 ("abuse" defined). [23 Cal.L.Rev.Comm. Reports 1 (1993)].

Research References

Forms

West's California Code Forms, Family § 6300, Comment Overview-- Protective Orders.

Treatises and Practice Aids

Witkin, California Summary 10th Husband and Wife § 379, in General.

§ 6301.5. Confidentiality of information relating to minors

(a) A minor or the minor's legal guardian may petition the court to have information regarding a minor obtained when issuing a protective order pursuant to this division, including, but not limited to, the minor's name, address, and the circumstances surrounding the protective order with respect to that minor, be kept confidential.

(b) The court may order the information specified in subdivision (a) be kept confidential if the court expressly finds all of the following:

(1) The minor's right to privacy overcomes the right of public access to the information.

(2) There is a substantial probability that the minor's interest will be prejudiced if the information is not kept confidential.

(3) The order to keep the information confidential is narrowly tailored.

(4) No less restrictive means exist to protect the minor's privacy.

(c) If the request is granted, except as provided in subdivision (d), information regarding the minor shall be maintained in a confidential case file and shall not become part of the public file in the proceeding or any other civil proceeding. Disclosure or misuse of that information is punishable as civil contempt of court with a fine of up to one thousand dollars ($1,000). An order of civil contempt under this subdivision shall not include imprisonment.

(d)(1) Information about a minor who is protected by an order issued pursuant to this division shall be made available to law enforcement pursuant to Section 6380, to the extent necessary and only for the purpose of enforcing the order.

(2) To the extent necessary for the enforcement of the order and to allow the respondent to comply with and respond to the order, confidential information shall be included in the notice sent to the respondent pursuant to this part. The notice shall identify the specific information that has been made confidential and shall include a statement that disclosure or misuse of that information is punishable as a contempt of court. *(Added by Stats.2017, c. 384 (A.B.953), § 2, eff. Jan. 1, 2018.)*

§ 6302. Notice of hearing

A notice of hearing under this part shall notify the respondent that if he or she does not attend the hearing, the court may make orders against him or her that could last up to five years. *(Added by Stats.2010, c. 572 (A.B.1596), § 14, operative Jan. 1, 2012.)*

Commentary

Relying on this section, *Isidora M. v. Silvino M., 239 Cal.App.4th, 190 Cal.Rptr.3d 502 (2015)*, holds that a court may not issue a mutual restraining order without prior notice to the person who would thereby be restrained.

Research References

Treatises and Practice Aids

Witkin, California Summary 10th Husband and Wife § 379, in General.

§ 6303. Support persons for victims of domestic violence; powers and duties; discretion of court

(a) It is the function of a support person to provide moral and emotional support for a person who alleges he or she is a victim of domestic violence. The person who alleges that he or she is a victim of domestic violence may select any individual to act as a support person. No certification, training, or other special qualification is required for an individual to act as a support person. The support person shall assist the person in feeling more confident that he or she will not be injured or threatened by the other party during the proceedings where the person and the other party must be present in close proximity. The support person is not present as a legal adviser and shall not give legal advice.

(b) A support person shall be permitted to accompany either party to any proceeding to obtain a protective order, as defined in Section 6218. Where the party is not represented by an attorney, the support person may sit with the party at the table that is generally reserved for the party and the party's attorney.

(c) Notwithstanding any other provision of law to the contrary, if a court has issued a protective order, a support person shall be permitted to accompany a party protected by the order during any mediation orientation or mediation session, including separate mediation sessions, held pursuant to a proceeding described in Section 3021. Family Court Services, and any agency charged with providing family court services, shall advise the party protected by the order of the right to have a support person during mediation. A mediator may exclude a support person from a mediation session if the support person participates in the mediation session, or acts as an advocate, or the presence of a particular support person is disruptive or disrupts the process of mediation. The presence of the support person does not waive the confidentiality of the mediation, and the support person is bound by the confidentiality of the mediation.

(d) In a proceeding subject to this section, a support person shall be permitted to accompany a party in court where there are allegations or threats of domestic violence and, where the party is not represented by an attorney, may sit with the party at the table that is generally reserved for the party and the party's attorney.

(e) Nothing in this section precludes a court from exercising its discretion to remove a person from the courtroom when it would be in the interest of justice to do so, or when the court believes the person is prompting, swaying, or influencing the party protected by the order. *(Added by Stats.1993, c. 219 (A.B.1500), § 154. Amended by Stats.1996, c. 761 (S.B.1995), § 7; Stats.2012, c. 470 (A.B.1529), § 21.)*

Law Revision Commission Comments

Enactment [Revised Comment]

Section 6303 continues without substantive change and generalizes former Civil Code Section 4351.6. Subdivision (a) has been revised to refer to the function of a support person, rather than the legislative intent regarding that function. This is not a substantive change. Duplicative references to "the person who alleges he or she is a victim of domestic violence" have been omitted and references to "the person" substituted. In subdivisions (b) and (c), the term "protective order" has been substituted for the references to orders under specific sections formerly in the Civil Code and the Code of Civil Procedure. Section 6218 defines "protective order" to include the orders formerly listed, except as to orders under Code of Civil Procedure 527.6, which provides for similar orders in situations not covered by this division. This is not a substantive change, since, insofar as former Civil Code Section 4351.6 applied to Code of Civil Procedure Section 527.6, the former section is continued in new subdivision (f) of Code of Civil Procedure Section 527.6. See Code Civ. Proc. § 527.6 (civil harassment orders) & Comment. See also Section 6211 ("domestic violence" defined).

In subdivision (c), a reference to a "proceeding described in Section 3021" has been substituted for the narrower reference to an "action or proceeding under this part," meaning the former Family Law Act (former Part 5 (commencing with former Section 4000) of Division 4 of the Civil Code). See Section 3021 Comment.

Former Civil Code Section 4351.6(e) has been omitted. This is not a substantive change, since the former subdivision duplicated a provision that is continued in Section 6303(a). [23 Cal.L.Rev.Comm. Reports 1 (1993)].

2012 Amendment

Subdivision (c) of Section 6303 is amended to reflect enactment of the Lockyer–Isenberg Trial Court Funding Act, 1997 Cal. Stat. ch. 850 (see generally Gov't Code §§ 77000–77655). See, e.g., Gov't Code §§ 77001 (local trial court management), 77003 ("court operations" defined), 77200 (state funding of "court operations"); see also Fam. Code § 3170(b) (requiring domestic violence cases to be handled by Family Court Services according to approved protocol by Judicial Council); Cal. R. Ct. 5.215(b) ("This rule sets forth protocol for Family Court Services‘ handling of domestic violence cases consistent with requirement of Family Code section 3170(b)."), Cal. R. Ct. 5.215(h)(1) ("Family Court Services staff must advise the party protected by a protective order of the right to have a support person attend any mediation orientation or mediation sessions, including separate mediation sessions, under Family Code section 6303."). [39 Cal.L.Rev.Comm. Reports 157 (2009)].

Research References

Treatises and Practice Aids

Witkin, California Summary 10th Husband and Wife § 380, Support Person for Victim.

Witkin, California Summary 10th Parent and Child § 280, Mediation Proceeding.

§ 6304. Protective orders; court to inform parties of terms of orders

When making a protective order, as defined in Section 6218, where both parties are present in court, the court shall inform both the petitioner and the respondent of the terms of the order, including notice that the respondent is prohibited from owning, possessing, purchasing or receiving or attempting to own, possess, purchase or receive a firearm or ammunition, and including notice of the penalty for violation. *(Added by Stats.1993, c. 219 (A.B.1500), § 154. Amended by Stats.1999, c. 662 (S.B.218), § 2; Stats.2010, c. 572 (A.B. 1596), § 15, operative Jan. 1, 2012.)*

Law Revision Commission Comments

Enactment [Revised Comment]

Section 6304 continues former Code of Civil Procedure Section 550(f) without substantive change. The reference to "protective order" has been substituted for the reference to an order "predicated on" what are now Sections 6320–6322. This is not a substantive change, since "protective order" has been defined to include the same orders. See Section 6218 ("protective order" defined). See also Penal Code § 12021 (penalty for violation of firearm prohibition in restraining order). [23 Cal.L.Rev.Comm. Reports 1 (1993)].

Research References

Treatises and Practice Aids

Witkin, California Summary 10th Husband and Wife § 379, in General.

§ 6305. Mutual orders; personal appearance of parties; application for relief

(a) The court shall not issue a mutual order enjoining the parties from specific acts of abuse described in Section 6320 unless both of the following apply:

(1) Both parties personally appear and each party presents written evidence of abuse or domestic violence in an application for relief using a mandatory Judicial Council restraining order application form. For purposes of this paragraph, written evidence of abuse or domestic violence in a responsive pleading does not satisfy the party's obligation to present written evidence of abuse or domestic violence. By July 1, 2016, the Judicial Council shall modify forms as necessary to provide notice of this information.

(2) The court makes detailed findings of fact indicating that both parties acted as a primary aggressor and that neither party acted primarily in self-defense.

(b) For purposes of subdivision (a), in determining if both parties acted primarily as aggressors, the court shall consider the provisions concerning dominant aggressors set forth in paragraph (3) of subdivision (c) of Section 836 of the Penal Code. *(Added by Stats.1993, c. 219 (A.B.1500), § 154. Amended by Stats.1995, c. 246 (S.B.591), § 2; Stats.2014, c. 635 (A.B.2089), § 6, eff. Jan. 1, 2015; Stats.2015, c. 73 (A.B.536), § 1, eff. Jan. 1, 2016.)*

Law Revision Commission Comments

Enactment [Revised Comment]

Section 6305 continues without substantive change former Code of Civil Procedure Section 545.5, the second paragraph of former Civil Code Section 4359(a), and former Civil Code Section 7020(f). The references in the former sections to the definition of domestic violence have been omitted. These are not substantive changes, since the definition applicable to this section is the same. See Section 6211 ("domestic violence" defined); see also Section 6302 ("abuse" defined). A reference to Section 6320 has been substituted for a specific list of acts. This is not a substantive change, since Section 6320 duplicates the omitted list. [23 Cal.L.Rev.Comm. Reports 1 (1993)].

Commentary

In re Marriage of G., 11 Cal.App.5th 773, 218 Cal.Rptr.3d 200 (2017), held that a trial court did not abuse its discretion in denying a wife's request for a domestic violence restraining order against her husband when her injuries were sustained in physical altercations that she initiated and the evidence was sufficient to support the trial court's finding that the husband used reasonable force to protect himself and his possessions from the wife's aggression. Therefore, the husband's actions did not constitute abuse within the meaning of section 6203. Although section 6203 does not mention self-defense, this section provides that a court cannot issue a mutual restraining order if it finds that one spouse acted primarily in self-defense.

When two parties separately apply for and receive Section 6300 restraining orders against each other on different dates, the second application is not a request for a mutual restraining order and therefore need not meet the requirements of this section. *Conness v. Satram, 122 Cal.App.4th 197, 18 Cal.Rptr.3d 577 (2004).*

Monterroso v. Moran, 135 Cal.App.4th 732, 37 Cal.Rptr.3d 694 (2006), holds that a trial court may not enter a mutual restraining order without making detailed findings that both parties acted primarily as aggressors and neither acted primarily in self-defense. To the same effect, see *J.J. v. M.F., 223 Cal.App.4th 968, 167 Cal.Rptr.3d 670 (2014).*

Relying on section 6302, *Isidora M. v. Silvino M., 239 Cal.App.4th, 190 Cal.Rptr.3d 502 (2015)*, holds that a court may not issue a mutual restraining order without prior notice to the person who would be restrained thereby.

Research References

Forms

West's California Code Forms, Family § 2047, Comment Overview-- Orders After Notice and Hearing.

Treatises and Practice Aids

Witkin, California Summary 10th Husband and Wife § 62, Evidence Of Misconduct is Ordinarily Inadmissible.

Witkin, California Summary 10th Husband and Wife § 89, Other Orders.
Witkin, California Summary 10th Husband and Wife § 379, in General.
Witkin, California Summary 10th Parent and Child § 51, Protective Orders.

§ 6306. Criminal history search; prior restraining orders

(a) Prior to a hearing on the issuance or denial of an order under this part, the court shall ensure that a search is or has been conducted to determine if the subject of the proposed order has any prior criminal conviction for a violent felony specified in Section 667.5 of the Penal Code or a serious felony specified in Section 1192.7 of the Penal Code; has any misdemeanor conviction involving domestic violence, weapons, or other violence; has any outstanding warrant; is currently on parole or probation; has a registered firearm; or has any prior restraining order or any violation of a prior restraining order. The search shall be conducted of all records and databases readily available and reasonably accessible to the court, including, but not limited to, the following:

(1) The California Sex and Arson Registry (CSAR).

(2) The Supervised Release File.

(3) State summary criminal history information maintained by the Department of Justice pursuant to Section 11105 of the Penal Code.

(4) The Federal Bureau of Investigation's nationwide database.

(5) Locally maintained criminal history records or databases.

However, a record or database need not be searched if the information available in that record or database can be obtained as a result of a search conducted in another record or database.

(b)(1) Prior to deciding whether to issue an order under this part or when determining appropriate temporary custody and visitation orders, the court shall consider the following information obtained pursuant to a search conducted under subdivision (a): any conviction for a violent felony specified in Section 667.5 of the Penal Code or a serious felony specified in Section 1192.7 of the Penal Code; any misdemeanor conviction involving domestic violence, weapons, or other violence; any outstanding warrant; parole or probation status; any prior restraining order; and any violation of a prior restraining order.

(2) Information obtained as a result of the search that does not involve a conviction described in this subdivision shall not be considered by the court in making a determination regarding the issuance of an order pursuant to this part. That information shall be destroyed and shall not become part of the public file in this or any other civil proceeding.

(c)(1) After issuing its ruling, the court shall advise the parties that they may request the information described in subdivision (b) upon which the court relied. The court shall admonish the party seeking the proposed order that it is unlawful, pursuant to Sections 11142 and 13303 of the Penal Code, to willfully release the information, except as authorized by law.

(2) Upon the request of either party to obtain the information described in subdivision (b) upon which the court relied, the court shall release the information to the parties or, upon either party's request, to his or her attorney in that proceeding.

(3) The party seeking the proposed order may release the information to his or her counsel, court personnel, and court-appointed mediators for the purpose of seeking judicial review of the court's order or for purposes of court proceedings under Section 213.5 of the Welfare and Institutions Code.

(d) Any information obtained as a result of the search conducted pursuant to subdivision (a) and relied upon by the court shall be maintained in a confidential case file and shall not become part of the public file in the proceeding or any other civil proceeding. However, the contents of the confidential case file shall be disclosed to the court-appointed mediator assigned to the case or to a child custody evaluator appointed by the court pursuant to Section 3111 of the Family Code or Section 730 of the Evidence Code. All court-appointed mediators and child custody evaluators appointed or contracted by the court pursuant to Section 3111 of the Family Code or Section 730 of the Evidence Code who may receive information from the search conducted pursuant to subdivision (a) shall be subject to, and shall comply with, the California Law Enforcement Telecommunications System policies, practices, and procedures adopted pursuant to Section 15160 of the Government Code.

(e) If the results of the search conducted pursuant to subdivision (a) indicate that an outstanding warrant exists against the subject of the order, the court shall order the clerk of the court to immediately notify, by the most effective means available, appropriate law enforcement officials of the issuance and contents of any protective order and of any other information obtained through the search that the court determines is appropriate. The law enforcement officials so notified shall take all actions necessary to execute any outstanding warrants or any other actions, with respect to the restrained person, as appropriate and as soon as practicable.

(f) If the results of the search conducted pursuant to subdivision (a) indicate that the subject of the order is currently on parole or probation, the court shall order the clerk of the court to immediately notify, by the most effective means available, the appropriate parole or probation officer of the issuance and contents of any protective order issued by the court and of any other information obtained through the search that the court determines is appropriate. That officer shall take all actions necessary to revoke any parole or probation, or any other actions, with respect to the restrained person, as appropriate and as soon as practicable.

(g) Nothing in this section shall delay the granting of an application for an order that may otherwise be granted without the information resulting from the database search. If the court finds that a protective order under this part should be granted on the basis of the affidavit presented with the petition, the court shall issue the protective order and shall then ensure that a search is conducted pursuant to subdivision (a) prior to the hearing. *(Added by Stats.2001, c. 572 (S.B.66), § 3. Amended by Stats.2012, c. 765 (S.B.1433), § 1; Stats.2014, c. 54 (S.B.1461), § 2, eff. Jan. 1, 2015.)*

Research References

Treatises and Practice Aids

Witkin, California Summary 10th Husband and Wife § 379, in General.

Witkin, California Summary 10th Husband and Wife § 381, Criminal Background Search.

CHAPTER 2. ISSUANCE OF ORDERS

ARTICLE 1. EX PARTE ORDERS

§ 6320. Ex parte order enjoining contact, credibly or falsely impersonating, or destroying personal property; protection for companion animals

(a) The court may issue an ex parte order enjoining a party from molesting, attacking, striking, stalking, threatening, sexually assaulting, battering, credibly impersonating as described in Section 528.5 of the Penal Code, falsely personating as described in Section 529 of the Penal Code, harassing, telephoning, including, but not limited to, making annoying telephone calls as described in Section 653m of the Penal Code, destroying personal property, contacting, either directly or indirectly, by mail or otherwise, coming within a specified distance of, or disturbing the peace of the other party, and, in the discretion of the court, on a showing of good cause, of other named family or household members.

(b) On a showing of good cause, the court may include in a protective order a grant to the petitioner of the exclusive care, possession, or control of any animal owned, possessed, leased, kept, or held by either the petitioner or the respondent or a minor child residing in the residence or household of either the petitioner or the respondent. The court may order the respondent to stay away from the animal and forbid the respondent from taking, transferring, encumbering, concealing, molesting, attacking, striking, threatening, harming, or otherwise disposing of the animal.

(c) This section shall become operative on July 1, 2014. *(Added by Stats.2013, c. 260 (A.B.157), § 2, operative July 1, 2014.)*

Commentary

Applying section 6203(c), *Guo v. Xiao, 228 Cal.App.4th 812, 175 Cal.Rptr.3d 635 (2014)*, held that a wife could be a victim of violence based on her husband's physical abuse of the parties' son and, under subsection (a) of this section, the consequential disturbance of her peace.

In re Marriage of Nadkarni, 173 Cal.App.4th 483, 93 Cal.Rptr.3d 723 (2009), holds that allegations that a former husband accessed, used, and publicly disclosed his former wife's confidential email were facially sufficient to satisfy subsection (a).

Altafulla v. Ervin, 238 Cal.App.4th 571, 189 Cal.Rptr.3d 316 (2015), holds that a protective order may be issued even if the statements disseminated to harass a victim are true, reasoning that abusive conduct may involve the use of accurate information in a manner that causes the victim severe emotional distress.

Defining subsection (a) "disturbing the peace of the other party," *Burquet v. Brumbaugh, 223 Cal.App.4th 1140, 167 Cal.Rptr.3d 664 (2014), review denied*, holds that the term includes defendant's persistent unwanted contact and advances, due to his inability to accept that his relationship with plaintiff was over.

Nakamura v. Parker, 156 Cal.App.4th 327, 67 Cal.Rptr.3d 286 (2007), held that a trial court abused its discretion by denying summarily without a hearing a wife's ex parte application for a temporary restraining order against her husband under this section, when the facts alleged by the wife would, if proven, show abuse.

S.M. v. E.P., 184 Cal.App.4th 1249, 109 Cal.Rptr.3d 792 (2010), holds that a trial court abused its discretion by issuing, after hearing, a restraining order against a parent without making a finding that the parent had engaged in domestic abuse within the meaning of this section. *S.M. v. E.P.* points out that, under section 3044, a restraining order issued under this division creates a presumption that an award of custody to a parent subject to a domestic violence restraining order would be detrimental to the best interest of a child.

Research References

Forms

California Practice Guide: Rutter Family Law Forms Form 1:32, Glossary Of Common Family Law Terms, Phrases and Concepts (Enclosure to Form 1:31).

West's California Code Forms, Family § 6320, Comment Overview--Ex Parte Orders.

West's California Code Forms, Family § 6340, Comment Overview--Issuance Of Orders After Notice and Hearing.

West's California Judicial Council Forms FL-300, Request for Order.

West's California Judicial Council Forms JV-245, Request for Restraining Order--Juvenile.

Treatises and Practice Aids

Witkin, California Summary 10th Husband and Wife § 89, Other Orders.

Witkin, California Summary 10th Husband and Wife § 374, Definitions.

Witkin, California Summary 10th Husband and Wife § 376, Issuance and Effect.

Witkin, California Summary 10th Husband and Wife § 379, in General.

Witkin, California Summary 10th Husband and Wife § 382, in General.

Witkin, California Summary 10th Husband and Wife § 384, Orders After Notice and Hearing.

Witkin, California Summary 10th Husband and Wife § 386, in General.

Witkin, California Summary 10th Husband and Wife § 389, Foreign Orders.

Witkin, California Summary 10th Parent and Child § 51, Protective Orders.

Witkin, California Summary 10th Parent and Child § 238, Valid Conditions.

Witkin, California Summary 10th Parent and Child § 424A, (New) Suspension on Incarceration.

§ 6320.5. Order denying petition for ex parte order; reasons; right to noticed hearing; right to waive hearing

(a) An order denying a petition for an ex parte order pursuant to Section 6320 shall include the reasons for denying the petition.

(b) An order denying a jurisdictionally adequate petition for an ex parte order, pursuant to Section 6320, shall provide the petitioner the right to a noticed hearing on the earliest date that the business of the court will permit, but not later than 21 days or, if good cause appears to the court, 25 days from the date of the order. The petitioner shall serve on the respondent, at least 5 days before the hearing, copies of all supporting papers filed with the court, including the application and affidavits.

(c) Notwithstanding subdivision (b), upon the denial of the ex parte order pursuant to Section 6320, the petitioner shall have the option of waiving his or her right to a noticed hearing. However, nothing in this section shall preclude a petitioner who waives his or her right to a noticed hearing from refiling a new petition, without prejudice, at a later time. *(Added by Stats.2008, c. 263 (A.B.2553), § 1. Amended by Stats.2010, c. 572 (A.B.1596), § 17, operative Jan. 1, 2012.)*

Research References

Forms

West's California Judicial Council Forms DV-112, Waiver Of Hearing on Denied Request for Temporary Restraining Order.

Treatises and Practice Aids

Witkin, California Summary 10th Husband and Wife § 382, in General.

§ 6321. Ex parte order excluding party from dwelling

(a) The court may issue an ex parte order excluding a party from the family dwelling, the dwelling of the other party, the common dwelling of both parties, or the dwelling of the person who has care, custody, and control of a child to be protected from domestic violence for the period of time and on the conditions the court determines, regardless of which party holds legal or equitable title or is the lessee of the dwelling.

(b) The court may issue an order under subdivision (a) only on a showing of all of the following:

(1) Facts sufficient for the court to ascertain that the party who will stay in the dwelling has a right under color of law to possession of the premises.

(2) That the party to be excluded has assaulted or threatens to assault the other party or any other person under the care, custody, and control of the other party, or any minor child of the parties or of the other party.

(3) That physical or emotional harm would otherwise result to the other party, to any person under the care, custody, and control of the other party, or to any minor child of the parties or of the other party. *(Added by Stats.1993, c. 219 (A.B.1500), § 154.)*

Law Revision Commission Comments

Enactment [Revised Comment]

Section 6321 restates without substantive change part of the first sentence of Code of Civil Procedure Section 546(a), and continues without substantive change the last paragraph of former Code of Civil Procedure Section 546(a) and former Civil Code Sections 4359(a)(3) and 7020(a)(2). This section supersedes the third part of former Civil Code Section 5102(a). The reference to "the common dwelling of both parties" is drawn from former Civil Code Section 7020(b). This is not a substantive change, but rather is added to clarify application of the section to unmarried persons. A reference to the "superior" court has been omitted as surplus. See Section 200 (jurisdiction in superior court). The former reference to Code of Civil Procedure Section 527 has been omitted. This is not a substantive change. See Section 240 & Comment.

For general provisions relating to ex parte restraining orders, see Part 4 (commencing with Section 240) of Division 2. [23 Cal.L.Rev. Comm. Reports 1 (1993)].

Research References

Forms

California Practice Guide: Rutter Family Law Forms Form 1:32, Glossary Of Common Family Law Terms, Phrases and Concepts (Enclosure to Form 1:31).

West's California Code Forms, Family § 6320, Comment Overview--Ex Parte Orders.

West's California Code Forms, Family § 6340, Comment Overview--Issuance Of Orders After Notice and Hearing.

West's California Judicial Council Forms JV-245, Request for Restraining Order--Juvenile.

Treatises and Practice Aids

Witkin, California Summary 10th Husband and Wife § 374, Definitions.

Witkin, California Summary 10th Husband and Wife § 382, in General.

Witkin, California Summary 10th Husband and Wife § 384, Orders After Notice and Hearing.

§ 6322. Ex parte order enjoining specified behavior

The court may issue an ex parte order enjoining a party from specified behavior that the court determines is necessary to effectuate orders under Section 6320 or 6321. *(Added by Stats.1993, c. 219 (A.B.1500), § 154.)*

Law Revision Commission Comments

Enactment [Revised Comment]

Section 6322 restates without substantive change part of the first sentence of former Code of Civil Procedure Section 546(a), and continues without substantive change former Civil Code Sections 4359(a)(6) and 7020(a)(3). A reference to the "superior" court has been omitted as surplus. See Section 200 (jurisdiction in superior court). The former reference to Code of Civil Procedure Section 527 has been omitted. This is not a substantive change. See Section 240 & Comment.

For general provisions relating to ex parte restraining orders, see Part 4 (commencing with Section 240) of Division 2. [23 Cal.L.Rev. Comm. Reports 1 (1993)].

Research References

Forms

California Practice Guide: Rutter Family Law Forms Form 1:32, Glossary Of Common Family Law Terms, Phrases and Concepts (Enclosure to Form 1:31).

West's California Judicial Council Forms JV-245, Request for Restraining Order--Juvenile.

Treatises and Practice Aids

Witkin, California Summary 10th Husband and Wife § 374, Definitions.

Witkin, California Summary 10th Husband and Wife § 382, in General.

§ 6322.7. Addresses or locations of persons protected under court order; prohibition upon certain enjoined parties from acting to obtain such information

(a) The court shall order that any party enjoined pursuant to an order issued under this part be prohibited from taking any action to obtain the address or location of any protected person, unless there is good cause not to make that order.

(b) The Judicial Council shall develop forms necessary to effectuate this section. *(Added by Stats.2005, c. 472 (A.B. 978), § 3. Amended by Stats.2010, c. 572 (A.B.1596), § 18, operative Jan. 1, 2012.)*

Research References

Forms

West's California Code Forms, Family § 6320, Comment Overview--Ex Parte Orders.

Treatises and Practice Aids

Witkin, California Summary 10th Husband and Wife § 371, Civil Remedies.

§ 6323. Ex parte orders regarding temporary custody and visitation of minor children; stipulation of paternity; considerations

(a) Subject to Section 3064:

(1) The court may issue an ex parte order determining the temporary custody and visitation of a minor child on the conditions the court determines to a party who has established a parent and child relationship pursuant to paragraph (2). The parties shall inform the court if any custody or visitation orders have already been issued in any other proceeding.

(2)(A) In making a determination of the best interests of the child and in order to limit the child's exposure to potential domestic violence and to ensure the safety of all family members, if the party who has obtained the restraining order has established a parent and child relationship and the other party has not established that relationship, the court may award temporary sole legal and physical custody to the party to whom the restraining order was issued and may make an order of no visitation to the other party pending the establishment of a parent and child relationship between the child and the other party.

(B) A party may establish a parent and child relationship for purposes of subparagraph (A) only by offering proof of any of the following:

(i) The party gave birth to the child.

(ii) The child is conclusively presumed to be a child of the marriage between the parties, pursuant to Section 7540, or the party has been determined by a court to be a parent of the child, pursuant to Section 7541.

(iii) Legal adoption or pending legal adoption of the child by the party.

(iv) The party has signed a valid voluntary declaration of paternity, which has been in effect more than 60 days prior to the issuance of the restraining order, and that declaration has not been rescinded or set aside.

(v) A determination made by the juvenile court that there is a parent and child relationship between the party offering the proof and the child.

(vi) A determination of paternity made in a proceeding to determine custody or visitation in a case brought by the district attorney pursuant to Section 11350.1 of the Welfare and Institutions Code.

(vii) The party has been determined to be the parent of the child through a proceeding under the Uniform Parentage Act (Part 3 (commencing with Section 7600) of Division 12).

(viii) Both parties stipulate, in writing or on the record, for purposes of this proceeding, that they are the parents of the child.

(b)(1) Except as provided in paragraph (2), the court shall not make a finding of paternity in this proceeding, and any order issued pursuant to this section shall be without prejudice in any other action brought to establish a parent and child relationship.

(2) The court may accept a stipulation of paternity by the parties and, if paternity is uncontested, enter a judgment establishing paternity, subject to the set-aside provisions in Section 7646.

(c) When making any order for custody or visitation pursuant to this section, the court's order shall specify the time, day, place, and manner of transfer of the child for custody or visitation to limit the child's exposure to potential domestic conflict or violence and to ensure the safety of all family members. Where the court finds a party is staying in a place designated as a shelter for victims of domestic violence or other confidential location, the court's order for time, day, place, and manner of transfer of the child for custody or visitation shall be designed to prevent disclosure of the location of the shelter or other confidential location.

(d) When making an order for custody or visitation pursuant to this section, the court shall consider whether the best interest of the child, based upon the circumstances of the case, requires that any visitation or custody arrangement shall be limited to situations in which a third person, specified by the court, is present, or whether visitation or custody shall be suspended or denied. *(Added by Stats.1993, c. 219 (A.B. 1500), § 154. Amended by Stats.1994, c. 320 (A.B.356), § 3; Stats.1997, c. 396 (S.B.564), § 2; Stats.2010, c. 352 (A.B.939), § 18.)*

Law Revision Commission Comments

Enactment [Revised Comment]

Section 6323 restates without substantive change part of the first sentence of Code of Civil Procedure Section 546(a), and continues without substantive change former Civil Code Sections 4359(a)(4) and 7020(a)(4). The intention of this section is to continue the prior law and practice. The reference to Section 3064 has been added. To the extent that the court's authority to issue custody orders ex parte is limited by Section 3064, this limitation also applies to visitation. A reference to the "superior" court has been omitted as surplus. See Section 200 (jurisdiction in superior court). The former reference to Code of Civil Procedure Section 527 has been omitted. This is not a substantive change. See Section 240 & Comment.

Section 6223 requires that procedural and substantive rules contained in Part 2 (commencing with Section 3020) of Division 8 of this code be applied where a court determines custody or visitation in a proceeding brought pursuant to the Domestic Violence Prevention Act. For sections of particular importance in situations involving domestic violence, see Sections 3030 (custody and unsupervised visitation prohibited where parent convicted under certain Penal Code provisions), 3031 (custody or visitation should not be inconsistent with restraining orders), 3100(b) (limiting visitation to situation where third party present), 3131 (action by district attorney where child taken or detained in violation of visitation order). See also Cal. R. Ct. 1285.05 (rev. July 1, 1991) (temporary restraining order), 1296.10 (rev. Jan. 1, 1991) (order to show cause and temporary restraining order).

For general provisions relating to ex parte restraining orders, see Part 4 (commencing with Section 240) of Division 2. See also Section 3021 (Part 2 of Division 8 applicable to proceeding for dissolution, nullity, and legal separation and to action pursuant to the Uniform Parentage Act). [23 Cal.L.Rev.Comm. Reports 1 (1993)].

Commentary

Invoking subsection (a)(2)(A) and section 6340(a), *Gonzalez v. Munoz, 156 Cal.App.4th 413, 67 Cal.Rptr.3d 317 (2007)*, held that a trial court erred by failing to grant a mother's request for permanent custody of her daughter when the mother, who obtained a restraining order against the child's alleged father under the DVPA, had established a parent-child relationship with her daughter and there was no evidence that the child's alleged father, who denied paternity, had established a parental relationship with the child. *Gonzalez* emphasizes that when the parties are unrepresented in a DVPA proceeding, the court must inquire into the statutory facts because the parties cannot be assumed to know controlling law. Thus the trial court ought to have inquired whether the alleged father had a parental relationship with the child.

Barkaloff v. Woodward, 47 Cal.App.4th 393, 55 Cal.Rptr.2d 167 (1996), holds that a trial court lacks jurisdiction under the Domestic Violence Prevention Act (DVPA) (Section 6200 et seq.) and the Uniform Parentage Act (UPA) (Section 7600 et seq.) to award visitation rights to a man who is not the father of the child and who was never married to the child's mother when both the child's mother and the child's biological father object to visitation, even though such visitation may be in the child's best interests. *Barkaloff* holds that jurisdiction to order visitation of minor children under the DVPA is limited, pursuant to Section 6323, to cases where there is a marital relationship between the parties. 47 Cal.App.4th at 398.

Research References

Forms

California Transactions Forms--Family Law § 3:4, Subject Matter Jurisdiction for Custody Determinations.

West's California Judicial Council Forms DV-180, Agreement and Judgment Of Parentage.

Treatises and Practice Aids

Witkin, California Summary 10th Husband and Wife § 86, in General.

Witkin, California Summary 10th Husband and Wife § 383, Temporary Custody and Visitation.

Witkin, California Summary 10th Husband and Wife § 384, Orders After Notice and Hearing.

Witkin, California Summary 10th Parent and Child § 198, Domestic Violence.

Witkin, California Summary 10th Parent and Child § 199, Substance Abuse.

Witkin, California Summary 10th Parent and Child § 235, Biologically Unrelated Persons Opposed by Parent.

Witkin, California Summary 10th Parent and Child § 363, Applicability Of Family Code Custody Provisions.

§ 6324. Ex parte order regarding real or personal property

The court may issue an ex parte order determining the temporary use, possession, and control of real or personal property of the parties and the payment of any liens or encumbrances coming due during the period the order is in effect. *(Added by Stats.1993, c. 219 (A.B.1500), § 154.)*

Law Revision Commission Comments

Enactment [Revised Comment]

Section 6324 restates part of the first sentence of Code of Civil Procedure Section 546(a) without substantive change, and continues part of former Civil Code Section 4359(a)(5) without substantive change. Former Code of Civil Procedure Section 546(a) did not provide for issuance of an ex parte order determining temporary the use of property and the payment of debts for unmarried parties. This section has been generalized to allow issuance of the order in cases where the parties are not married, both in a proceeding brought pursuant to the Domestic Violence Prevention Act and in an action brought pursuant to the Uniform Parentage Act. Authorizing the court to issue an order determining the use of the property of unmarried parties is not a substantive change, since the Judicial Council form allows this order. See Cal. R. Ct. 1296.10 (rev. Jan. 1, 1991) (order to show cause and temporary restraining order). A reference to the "superior" court has been omitted as surplus. See Section 200 (jurisdiction in superior court). The former reference to Code of Civil Procedure Section 527 has been omitted. This is not a substantive change. See Section 240 & Comment.

For general provisions relating to ex parte restraining orders, see Part 4 (commencing with Section 240) of Division 2. [23 Cal.L.Rev. Comm. Reports 1 (1993)].

Research References

Forms

California Practice Guide: Rutter Family Law Forms Form 5:5, Ex Parte Application and Request for Order Re Child Custody, Visitation and Property Control.

California Practice Guide: Rutter Family Law Forms Form 1:32, Glossary Of Common Family Law Terms, Phrases and Concepts (Enclosure to Form 1:31).

West's California Judicial Council Forms DV-250, Proof Of Service by Mail.

West's California Judicial Council Forms FL-344, Property Order Attachment to Findings and Order After Hearing.

Treatises and Practice Aids

Witkin, California Summary 10th Husband and Wife § 86, in General.

Witkin, California Summary 10th Husband and Wife § 382, in General.

§ 6325. Ex parte order regarding community, quasi-community and separate property

The court may issue an ex parte order restraining a married person from specified acts in relation to community, quasi-community, and separate property as provided in Section 2045. *(Added by Stats.1993, c. 219 (A.B.1500), § 154.)*

Law Revision Commission Comments

Enactment [Revised Comment]

Section 6325 restates part of the first sentence of Code of Civil Procedure Section 546(a) without substantive change.

For general provisions relating to ex parte restraining orders, see Part 4 (commencing with Section 240) of Division 2. See also Section 11 (reference to married person includes formerly married person). [23 Cal.L.Rev.Comm. Reports 1 (1993)].

Research References

Forms

California Practice Guide: Rutter Family Law Forms Form 1:32, Glossary Of Common Family Law Terms, Phrases and Concepts (Enclosure to Form 1:31).

West's California Code Forms, Family § 6320, Comment Overview--Ex Parte Orders.

Treatises and Practice Aids

Witkin, California Summary 10th Husband and Wife § 382, in General.

§ 6325.5. Ex parte order regarding insurance coverage

(a) The court may issue an ex parte order restraining any party from cashing, borrowing against, canceling, transferring, disposing of, or changing the beneficiaries of any insurance or other coverage held for the benefit of the parties, or their child or children, if any, for whom support may be ordered, or both.

(b) This section shall become operative on July 1, 2014. *(Added by Stats.2013, c. 261 (A.B.161), § 1, operative July 1, 2014.)*

Research References

Treatises and Practice Aids

Witkin, California Summary 10th Husband and Wife § 382, in General.

§ 6326. Issuance or denial on date application submitted

An ex parte order under this article shall be issued or denied on the same day that the application is submitted to the court, unless the application is filed too late in the day to permit effective review, in which case the order shall be issued or denied on the next day of judicial business in sufficient time for the order to be filed that day with the clerk of the court. *(Added by Stats.1993, c. 148 (A.B.1331), § 2.)*

Research References

Forms

West's California Judicial Council Forms FL-300, Request for Order.

Treatises and Practice Aids

Witkin, California Summary 10th Husband and Wife § 382, in General.

§ 6327. Ex parte orders; application of Part 4 of Division 2

Part 4 (commencing with Section 240) of Division 2 applies to the issuance of any ex parte order under this article, other than an order under Section 6322.5. *(Formerly § 6326, added by Stats.1993, c. 219 (A.B.1500), § 154. Renumbered § 6327 and amended by Stats.1993, c. 876 (S.B.1068), § 27.2, eff. Oct. 6, 1993, operative Jan. 1, 1994. Amended by Stats.1998, c. 511 (A.B.1900), § 6.)*

Law Revision Commission Comments

Enactment [Revised Comment]

Section 6327 makes clear that the general rules concerning issuance of temporary restraining orders apply to this article. [23 Cal.L.Rev.Comm. Reports 1 (1993)].

Research References

Treatises and Practice Aids

Witkin, California Summary 10th Husband and Wife § 382, in General.

ARTICLE 2. ORDERS ISSUABLE AFTER NOTICE AND HEARING

§ 6340. Ex parte orders; survival of custody, visitation, or support order following expiration of protective order; court statement upon denial

(a) The court may issue any of the orders described in Article 1 (commencing with Section 6320) after notice and a hearing. When determining whether to make any orders under this subdivision, the court shall consider whether failure to make any of these orders may jeopardize the safety of the petitioner and the children for whom the custody or visitation orders are sought. If the court makes any order for custody, visitation, or support, that order shall survive the termination of any protective order. The Judicial Council shall provide notice of this provision on any Judicial Council forms related to this subdivision.

(b) The court shall, upon denying a petition under this part, provide a brief statement of the reasons for the decision in writing or on the record. A decision stating "denied" is insufficient.

(c) The court may issue an order described in Section 6321 excluding a person from a dwelling if the court finds that physical or emotional harm would otherwise result to the other party, to a person under the care, custody, and control of the other party, or to a minor child of the parties or of the other party. *(Added by Stats.1993, c. 219 (A.B.1500), § 154. Amended by Stats.2004, c. 472 (A.B.2148), § 4; Stats.2010, c.*

352 (A.B.939), § 19; Stats.2014, c. 635 (A.B.2089), § 7, eff. Jan. 1, 2015.)

Law Revision Commission Comments

Enactment [Revised Comment]

Section 6340 generalizes and continues without substantive change former Code of Civil Procedure Section 547(a), the last part of former Civil Code Section 5102(a), and the first two sentences of former Civil Code Section 7020(b). In subdivision (b), the phrase "if the court finds" has been substituted for inconsistent references in the former sections to a "showing" by the petitioner and a "finding" by the court.

This section generalizes the former sections as follows:

(1) The former Family Law Act, applicable to proceedings for dissolution, nullity, and legal separation, did not contain a provision for orders after hearing, except in the case of former Civil Code Section 5102 which provided for orders excluding a party from a dwelling. This section makes clear that any of the orders described in Section 6320 may be issued after notice and hearing in a proceeding for dissolution, nullity, or legal separation. This is not a substantive change. See Cal. R. Ct. 1296.29 (July 1, 1991) (restraining order after hearing).

(2) Former Civil Code Section 7020(b) did not provide for orders determining the temporary use of property or payment of debts in a proceeding under the Uniform Parentage Act. This section generalizes former Code of Civil Procedure Section 547(a) which provided for these orders as between unmarried parties in a proceeding under the Domestic Violence Prevention Act. This is not a substantive change. See Cal. R. Ct. 1296.31E (Jan. 1, 1992) (domestic violence miscellaneous orders attachment). [23 Cal.L.Rev.Comm. Reports 1 (1993)].

Commentary

Moore v. Bedard, 213 Cal.App.4th 1206, 152 Cal.Rptr.3d 809 (2013), holds that the parties' stipulation in which the mother agreed to drop her request for a restraining order did not deprive the court of jurisdiction to make subsequent child support orders, when the parties' stipulation also provided for child support.

Invoking subsection (a) and section 6323 (a)(2)(A), *Gonzalez v. Munoz, 156 Cal.App.4th 413, 67 Cal.Rptr.3d 317 (2007)*, held that a trial court erred by failing to grant a mother's request for sole legal and physical custody of her daughter when the mother, who obtained a restraining order against the child's alleged father under the DVPA, had established a parent-child relationship with her daughter and there was no evidence that the child's alleged father, who denied paternity, had established a parental relationship with the child. *Gonzalez* emphasizes that when the parties are unrepresented in a DVPA proceeding, the court must inquire into the statutory facts because the parties cannot be assumed to know controlling law. Thus the trial court ought to have inquired whether the alleged father had a parental relationship with the child.

Research References

Forms

West's California Code Forms, Family § 6340, Comment Overview--Issuance Of Orders After Notice and Hearing.
West's California Judicial Council Forms DV-140, Child Custody and Visitation Order.
West's California Judicial Council Forms DV-250, Proof Of Service by Mail.
West's California Judicial Council Forms FL-341, Child Custody and Visitation (Parenting Time) Order Attachment.

Treatises and Practice Aids

Witkin, California Summary 10th Husband and Wife § 89, Other Orders.
Witkin, California Summary 10th Husband and Wife § 384, Orders After Notice and Hearing.
Witkin, California Summary 10th Parent and Child § 51, Protective Orders.
Witkin, California Summary 10th Parent and Child § 271, Temporary Custody During Pendency Of Proceeding.
Witkin, California Summary 10th Parent and Child § 453, Jurisdiction Over Adults.

§ 6341. Married parties with no other child support order; presumptive father; considerations; order to pay child support; order to pay spousal support; considerations; effect of order in proceedings for dissolution, nullity of marriage or legal separation

(a) If the parties are married to each other and no other child support order exists or if there is a presumption under Section 7611 that the respondent is the natural father of a minor child and the child is in the custody of the petitioner, after notice and a hearing, the court may, if requested by the petitioner, order a party to pay an amount necessary for the support and maintenance of the child if the order would otherwise be authorized in an action brought pursuant to Division 9 (commencing with Section 3500) or the Uniform Parentage Act (Part 3 (commencing with Section 7600) of Division 12). When determining whether to make any orders under this subdivision, the court shall consider whether failure to make any of these orders may jeopardize the safety of the petitioner and the children for whom child support is requested, including safety concerns related to the financial needs of the petitioner and the children. The Judicial Council shall provide notice of this provision on any Judicial Council forms related to this subdivision.

(b) An order issued pursuant to subdivision (a) of this section shall be without prejudice in an action brought pursuant to the Uniform Parentage Act (Part 3 (commencing with Section 7600) of Division 12).

(c) If the parties are married to each other and no spousal support order exists, after notice and a hearing, the court may order the respondent to pay spousal support in an amount, if any, that would otherwise be authorized in an action pursuant to Part 1 (commencing with Section 3500) or Part 3 (commencing with Section 4300) of Division 9. When determining whether to make any orders under this subdivision, the court shall consider whether failure to make any of these orders may jeopardize the safety of the petitioner, including safety concerns related to the financial needs of the petitioner. The Judicial Council shall provide notice of this provision on any Judicial Council forms related to this subdivision.

(d) An order issued pursuant to subdivision (c) shall be without prejudice in a proceeding for dissolution of marriage, nullity of marriage, or legal separation of the parties. *(Added by Stats.1993, c. 219 (A.B.1500), § 154. Amended by Stats. 1999, c. 980 (A.B.1671), § 13; Stats.2004, c. 472 (A.B.2148), § 5; Stats.2005, c. 22 (S.B.1108), § 63.)*

Law Revision Commission Comments

Enactment [Revised Comment]

Section 6341 continues former Code of Civil Procedure Section 547(b) without substantive change. [23 Cal.L.Rev.Comm. Reports 1 (1993)].

Commentary

In re Marriage of J.Q. and T.B., 223 Cal.App.4th 687, 167 Cal.Rptr.3d 574 (2014), holds that spousal support can be ordered under this section to a plaintiff prior to a court's determination on the issue of domestic violence.

Research References

Forms

West's California Code Forms, Family § 6340, Comment Overview--Issuance Of Orders After Notice and Hearing.

Treatises and Practice Aids

Witkin, California Summary 10th Husband and Wife § 384, Orders After Notice and Hearing.

§ 6342. Orders for restitution

(a) After notice and a hearing, the court may issue any of the following orders:

(1) An order that restitution be paid to the petitioner for loss of earnings and out-of-pocket expenses, including, but not limited to, expenses for medical care and temporary housing, incurred as a direct result of the abuse inflicted by the respondent or any actual physical injuries sustained from the abuse.

(2) An order that restitution be paid by the petitioner for out-of-pocket expenses incurred by a party as a result of an ex parte order that is found by the court to have been issued on facts shown at a noticed hearing to be insufficient to support the order.

(3) An order that restitution be paid by the respondent to any public or private agency for the reasonable cost of providing services to the petitioner required as a direct result of the abuse inflicted by the respondent or any actual injuries sustained therefrom.

(b) An order for restitution under this section shall not include damages for pain and suffering. *(Added by Stats. 1993, c. 219 (A.B.1500), § 154.)*

Law Revision Commission Comments

Enactment [Revised Comment]

Section 6342 continues former Code of Civil Procedure Section 547(c) and the last two sentences of former Civil Code Section 7020(b) without substantive change. References to "petitioner" have been substituted for the former references to "family or household member" in the former Code of Civil Procedure section. References to "petitioner" have been substituted for references to "plaintiff" in the former Civil Code section. These are not substantive changes. See also Section 6203 ("abuse" defined). [23 Cal.L.Rev.Comm. Reports 1 (1993)].

Research References

Forms

West's California Code Forms, Family § 6340, Comment Overview--Issuance Of Orders After Notice and Hearing.

Treatises and Practice Aids

Witkin, California Summary 10th Husband and Wife § 384, Orders After Notice and Hearing.

§ 6343. Batterer's program; order to participate; enrollment; resource list

(a) After notice and a hearing, the court may issue an order requiring the restrained party to participate in a batterer's program approved by the probation department as provided in Section 1203.097 of the Penal Code.

(b)(1) Commencing July 1, 2016, if the court orders a restrained party to participate in a batterer's program pursuant to subdivision (a), the restrained party shall do all of the following:

(A) Register for the program by the deadline ordered by the court. If no deadline is ordered by the court, the restrained party shall register no later than 30 days from the date the order was issued.

(B) At the time of enrollment, sign all necessary program consent forms for the program to release proof of enrollment, attendance records, and completion or termination reports to the court and the protected party, or his or her attorney. The court and the protected party may provide to the program a fax number or mailing address for purposes of receiving proof of enrollment, attendance records, and completion or termination reports.

(C) Provide the court and the protected party with the name, address, and telephone number of the program.

(2) By July 1, 2016, the Judicial Council shall revise or promulgate forms as necessary to effectuate this subdivision.

(c) The courts shall, in consultation with local domestic violence shelters and programs, develop a resource list of referrals to appropriate community domestic violence programs and services to be provided to each applicant for an order under this section. *(Added by Stats.1993, c. 219 (A.B.1500), § 154. Amended by Stats.1993, c. 876 (S.B.1068), § 27.3, eff. Oct. 6, 1993, operative Jan. 1, 1994; Stats.1999, c. 662 (S.B.218), § 3; Stats.2015, c. 72 (A.B.439), § 1, eff. Jan. 1, 2016.)*

Law Revision Commission Comments

Enactment [Revised Comment]

Section 6343 continues former Code of Civil Procedure Section 547(d) without substantive change and includes 1993 amendments. See 1993 Cal. Stat. ch. 197, § 2 (amending repealed Fam. Code § 5754). The requirements for meeting separately with the counselor have been revised to provide that either a history of violence or the existence of a protective order is sufficient. This is consistent with other sections in the code. See Sections 3113 (separate meetings with court appointed investigator), 3181 (separate meetings with mediator), 3192 (separate meetings with counselor appointed in custody proceeding). See also Sections 6211 ("domestic violence" defined), 6218 ("protective order" defined). [23 Cal.L.Rev.Comm. Reports 1 (1993)].

Research References

Forms

West's California Code Forms, Family § 6340, Comment Overview--Issuance Of Orders After Notice and Hearing.

West's California Judicial Council Forms DV-805, Proof Of Enrollment for Batterer Intervention Program.

West's California Judicial Council Forms DV-815, Batterer Intervention Program Progress Report.

Treatises and Practice Aids

Witkin, California Summary 10th Husband and Wife § 384, Orders After Notice and Hearing.

§ 6344. Orders for payment of attorney's fees and costs; grounds for determination

(a) After notice and a hearing, the court may issue an order for the payment of attorney's fees and costs of the prevailing party.

(b) In any action in which the petitioner is the prevailing party and cannot afford to pay for the attorney's fees and costs, the court shall, if appropriate based on the parties' respective abilities to pay, order that the respondent pay petitioner's attorney's fees and costs for commencing and maintaining the proceeding. Whether the respondent shall be ordered to pay attorney's fees and costs for the prevailing petitioner, and what amount shall be paid, shall be determined based upon (1) the respective incomes and needs of the parties, and (2) any factors affecting the parties' respective abilities to pay. *(Added by Stats.1993, c. 219 (A.B.1500), § 154. Amended by Stats.2004, c. 472 (A.B.2148), § 6.)*

Law Revision Commission Comments

Enactment [Revised Comment]

Section 6344 continues former Code of Civil Procedure Section 547(e) without substantive change. See also Sections 270–272 (general provisions for attorney's fees and costs). [23 Cal.L.Rev. Comm. Reports 1 (1993)].

Commentary

A court ordering attorney's fees under subsection (a) is not ordering section 271 attorney's fees in the nature of a sanction, but is simply awarding attorney's fees and costs to the prevailing party. *Loeffler v. Medina, 174 Cal.App.4th 1495, 95 Cal.Rptr.3d 343 (2009).*

Although section 6226 requires the Judicial Council to promulgate forms for applying for orders prescribed by this division, *Faton v. Ahmedo, 236 Cal.App.4th 1160, 187 Cal.Rptr.3d 201 (2015)*, holds that a prevailing party's failure to request attorney's fees on Judicial Council Form DV-100 did not deprive the trial court of jurisdiction to award attorney's fees, under this section, after notice and hearing in a domestic violence restraining order proceeding.

Research References

Forms

West's California Code Forms, Family § 6340, Comment Overview--Issuance Of Orders After Notice and Hearing.

West's California Judicial Council Forms DV-250, Proof Of Service by Mail.

West's California Judicial Council Forms FL-157, Spousal or Partner Support Declaration Attachment.

Treatises and Practice Aids

Witkin, California Summary 10th Husband and Wife § 384, Orders After Notice and Hearing.

§ 6345. Duration of orders

(a) In the discretion of the court, the personal conduct, stay-away, and residence exclusion orders contained in a court order issued after notice and a hearing under this article may have a duration of not more than five years, subject to termination or modification by further order of the court either on written stipulation filed with the court or on the motion of a party. These orders may be renewed, upon the request of a party, either for five years or permanently, without a showing of any further abuse since the issuance of the original order, subject to termination or modification by further order of the court either on written stipulation filed with the court or on the motion of a party. The request for renewal may be brought at any time within the three months before the expiration of the orders.

(b) Notwithstanding subdivision (a), the duration of any orders, other than the protective orders described in subdivision (a), that are also contained in a court order issued after notice and a hearing under this article, including, but not limited to, orders for custody, visitation, support, and disposition of property, shall be governed by the law relating to those specific subjects.

(c) The failure to state the expiration date on the face of the form creates an order with a duration of three years from the date of issuance.

(d) If an action is filed for the purpose of terminating or modifying a protective order prior to the expiration date specified in the order by a party other than the protected party, the party who is protected by the order shall be given notice, pursuant to subdivision (b) of Section 1005 of the Code of Civil Procedure, of the proceeding by personal service or, if the protected party has satisfied the requirements of Chapter 3.1 (commencing with Section 6205) of Division 7 of Title 1 of the Government Code, by service on the Secretary of State. If the party who is protected by the order cannot be notified prior to the hearing for modification or termination of the protective order, the court shall deny the motion to modify or terminate the order without prejudice or continue the hearing until the party who is protected can be properly noticed and may, upon a showing of good cause, specify another method for service of process that is reasonably designed to afford actual notice to the protected party. The protected party may waive his or her right to notice if he or she is physically present in court and does not challenge the sufficiency of the notice. *(Added by Stats.1993, c. 219 (A.B.1500), § 154. Amended by Stats.1995, c. 907 (A.B.935), § 2; Stats.2005, c. 125 (A.B.99), § 1; Stats.2010, c. 572 (A.B.1596), § 19, operative Jan. 1, 2012; Stats.2011, c. 101 (A.B.454), § 4.)*

Law Revision Commission Comments

Enactment [Revised Comment]

Section 6345 continues without substantive change and generalizes former Code of Civil Procedure Section 548 and the third sentence of former Civil Code Section 7020(b). In subdivision (a), the requirement that the stipulation be written has been generalized. Former Civil Code Section 7020(b) did not contain a writing requirement, but rather allowed stipulation by "mutual consent." In subdivision (c), the reference to the former Family Law Act (former Part 5 (commencing with former Section 4000) of Division 4 of the Civil Code) has been omitted. This expands application of this subdivision to all orders that may be issued after notice and a hearing under this article, whether issued in a proceeding for dissolution, nullity, or legal separation, in an action brought pursuant to the Uniform Parentage Act, or in a proceeding brought pursuant to the Domestic Violence Prevention Act. [23 Cal.L.Rev.Comm. Reports 1 (1993)].

Commentary

Loeffler v. Medina, 174 Cal.App.4th 1495, 95 Cal.Rptr.3d 343 (2009), holds that Code of Civil Procedure section 533 sets forth the applicable standard for a trial court considering whether to terminate a domestic violence restraining order issued under the Domestic Violence Prevention Act (Family Code sections 6200–6409.)

The trial court should grant a requested extension of a domestic violence protection order if the request is not contested. If the request is contested, the court should renew the order only if it determines, by a preponderance of the evidence, that the protected party has a "reasonable apprehension" of future abusive conduct if the protective order is allowed to expire, that is, that the "evidence demonstrates it is more probable than not there is a sufficient risk of future abuse to find the protected party's apprehension is genuine and reasonable." *Ritchie v. Konrad, 115 Cal.App.4th 1275, 10 Cal.Rptr.3d 387 (2004), review denied.*

Eneaji v. Ubboe, 2014 WL 4756205, held that the trial court erred in denying the wife's request to renew a restraining order against her former husband on the ground that nothing had happened during the prior three-year order. Under subsection (a), renewal does not require a showing of further abuse since the issuance of the initial order, but only a reasonable apprehension of future abusive conduct if the initial order is allowed to expire.

Similarly, *Perez v. Torres-Hernandez, 1 Cal.App.5th 389, 206 Cal. Rptr.3d 873 (2016)*, held that lack of evidence of abuse during the period that the restraining order was in effect was not a ground for denial of appellant's request to renew the order when she had established a reasonable apprehension of future abuse. Additionally, evidence that defendant abused their children and continued to threaten their mother in harassing telephone calls while the restraining order was in effect, was relevant to the issue of renewal.

Cueto v. Dozier, 241 Cal.App.4th 550, 193 Cal.Rptr.3d 663 (2015), held that a trial court abused its discretion in declining to renew a restraining order under this section, because the facts supporting the original order and the defendant's failure to attend a court-ordered anger management program were sufficient evidence to require a finding of reasonable apprehension of future abuse.

Rodriguez v. Menjivar, 243 Cal.App.4th 816, 196 Cal.Rptr.3d 816 (2015), held that a trial court erred in declining to issue a permanent restraining order despite evidence of nonviolent emotional abuse and controlling behavior.

Lister v. Bowen, 215 Cal.App.4th 319, 155 Cal.Rptr.3d 50 (2013), affirmed a three-year renewal of a domestic restraining order because appellant's violation of the order sufficed to establish that the protected person had an objectively reasonable fear of future abuse.

Avalos v. Perez, 196 Cal.App.4th 663, 127 Cal.Rptr.3d 106 (2011), holds that a trial court erred in renewing a restraining order for only two years, instead of five years or permanently, as this section requires.

Research References

Forms

West's California Code Forms, Family § 6340, Comment Overview--Issuance Of Orders After Notice and Hearing.

West's California Judicial Council Forms DV-200, Proof Of Personal Service.

West's California Judicial Council Forms DV-400, Findings and Order to Terminate Restraining Order After Hearing.

West's California Judicial Council Forms DV-700, Request to Renew Restraining Order.

West's California Judicial Council Forms DV-710, Notice Of Hearing to Renew Restraining Order.

West's California Judicial Council Forms DV-720, Response to Request to Renew Restraining Order.

West's California Judicial Council Forms DV-730, Order to Renew Domestic Violence Restraining Order.

West's California Judicial Council Forms DV-400-INFO, How Do I Ask to Change or End a Domestic Violence Restraining Order After Hearing?

Treatises and Practice Aids

Witkin, California Summary 10th Husband and Wife § 384, Orders After Notice and Hearing.

§ 6346. Custody and visitation orders; notice and hearing

The court may make appropriate custody and visitation orders pursuant to the Uniform Parentage Act (Part 3 (commencing with Section 7600) of Division 12) after notice and a hearing under this section when the party who has requested custody or visitation has not established a parent and child relationship under subparagraph (B) of paragraph (2) of subdivision (a) of Section 6323, but has taken steps to establish that relationship by filing an action under the Uniform Parentage Act. *(Added by Stats.1997, c. 396 (S.B. 564), § 3.)*

Research References

Treatises and Practice Aids

Witkin, California Summary 10th Husband and Wife § 384, Orders After Notice and Hearing.

§ 6347. Order directing wireless telephone service provider to transfer billing responsibility and rights to requesting party

(a) Commencing July 1, 2016, in order to ensure that the requesting party can maintain an existing wireless telephone number, and the wireless numbers of any minor children in the care of the requesting party, the court may issue an order, after notice and a hearing, directing a wireless telephone service provider to transfer the billing responsibility for and rights to the wireless telephone number or numbers to the requesting party, if the requesting party is not the accountholder.

(b)(1) The order transferring billing responsibility for and rights to the wireless telephone number or numbers to a requesting party shall be a separate order that is directed to the wireless telephone service provider. The order shall list the name and billing telephone number of the accountholder, the name and contact information of the person to whom the telephone number or numbers will be transferred, and each telephone number to be transferred to that person. The court shall ensure that the contact information of the requesting party is not provided to the accountholder in proceedings held pursuant to Division 10 (commencing with Section 6200).

(2) The order shall be served on the wireless service provider's agent for service of process listed with the Secretary of State.

(3) Where the wireless service provider cannot operationally or technically effectuate the order due to certain circumstances, including, but not limited to, any of the following, the wireless service provider shall notify the requesting party within 72 hours of receipt of the order:

(A) When the accountholder has already terminated the account.

(B) When differences in network technology prevent the functionality of a device on the network.

(C) When there are geographic or other limitations on network or service availability.

(c)(1) Upon transfer of billing responsibility for and rights to a wireless telephone number or numbers to a requesting party pursuant to subdivision (b) by a wireless telephone service provider, the requesting party shall assume all financial responsibility for the transferred wireless telephone number or numbers, monthly service costs, and costs for any mobile device associated with the wireless telephone number or numbers.

(2) This section shall not preclude a wireless service provider from applying any routine and customary requirements for account establishment to the requesting party as part of this transfer of billing responsibility for a wireless telephone number or numbers and any devices attached to that number or numbers, including, but not limited to, identification, financial information, and customer preferences.

(d) This section shall not affect the ability of the court to apportion the assets and debts of the parties as provided for in law, or the ability to determine the temporary use, possession, and control of personal property pursuant to Sections 6324 and 6340.

(e) No cause of action shall lie against any wireless telephone service provider, its officers, employees, or agents, for actions taken in accordance with the terms of a court order issued pursuant to this section.

(f) The Judicial Council shall, on or before July 1, 2016, develop any forms or rules necessary to effectuate this section. *(Added by Stats.2015, c. 415 (A.B.1407), § 2, eff. Jan. 1, 2016.)*

Research References

Forms

West's California Judicial Council Forms DV-900, Order Transferring Wireless Phone Account.

West's California Judicial Council Forms DV-901, Attachment to Order Transferring Wireless Phone Account (Form Dv-900).

Treatises and Practice Aids

Witkin, California Summary 10th Husband and Wife § 384, Orders After Notice and Hearing.

ARTICLE 3. ORDERS INCLUDED IN JUDGMENT

§ 6360. Judgments which may include protective orders

A judgment entered in a proceeding for dissolution of marriage, for nullity of marriage, for legal separation of the parties, in a proceeding brought pursuant to this division, or in an action brought pursuant to the Uniform Parentage Act (Part 3 (commencing with Section 7600) of Division 12) may include a protective order as defined in Section 6218. *(Added by Stats.1993, c. 219 (A.B.1500), § 154.)*

Law Revision Commission Comments

Enactment [Revised Comment]

Section 6360 continues without substantive change and generalizes the first sentences of former Civil Code Sections 4458, 4516, and 7021. The former sections applied only to judgments pursuant to the former Family Law Act and the Uniform Parentage Act, whereas this section allows the inclusion of these orders in a judgment in a proceeding brought pursuant to the Domestic Violence Prevention Act. The reference to a "protective order" has been substituted for the former reference to orders that may be issued pursuant to what are now Sections 6320–6322. This is not a substantive change, since "protective order" has been defined to include the same orders. See Section 6218 ("protective order" defined). See also Sections 6380 (transmittal to local law enforcement agency), 6388 (criminal penalty for violation of order). [23 Cal.L.Rev.Comm. Reports 1 (1993)].

Research References

Treatises and Practice Aids

Witkin, California Summary 10th Husband and Wife § 112, Contents Of Judgment.

Witkin, California Summary 10th Husband and Wife § 385, Orders Included in Judgment.

Witkin, California Summary 10th Parent and Child § 51, Protective Orders.

§ 6361. Statements on face of order included in judgment

If an order is included in a judgment pursuant to this article, the judgment shall state on its face both of the following:

(a) Which provisions of the judgment are the orders.

(b) The date of expiration of the orders, which shall be not more than five years from the date the judgment is issued, unless extended by the court after notice and a hearing. *(Added by Stats.1993, c. 219 (A.B.1500), § 154. Amended by Stats.2005, c. 125 (A.B.99), § 2.)*

Law Revision Commission Comments

Enactment [Revised Comment]

Section 6361 continues without substantive change and generalizes the second sentences of former Civil Code Sections 4458, 4516, and 7021. The former sections applied only to judgments pursuant to the former Family Law Act and the Uniform Parentage Act, whereas this section allows the inclusion of these orders in any judgment under this code. See also Sections 6380 (transmittal to local law enforcement agency), 6388 (criminal penalty for violation of order). [23 Cal.L.Rev.Comm. Reports 1 (1993)].

Research References

Treatises and Practice Aids

Witkin, California Summary 10th Husband and Wife § 112, Contents Of Judgment.

Witkin, California Summary 10th Husband and Wife § 385, Orders Included in Judgment.

CHAPTER 3. REGISTRATION AND ENFORCEMENT OF ORDERS

§ 6380. California Law Enforcement Telecommunications System; information transmitted to Department of Justice; Domestic Violence Restraining Order System

(a) Each county, with the approval of the Department of Justice, shall, by July 1, 1996, develop a procedure, using existing systems, for the electronic transmission of data, as described in subdivision (b), to the Department of Justice. The data shall be electronically transmitted through the California Law Enforcement Telecommunications System (CLETS) of the Department of Justice by law enforcement personnel, or with the approval of the Department of Justice, court personnel, or another appropriate agency capable of maintaining and preserving the integrity of both the CLETS and the Domestic Violence Restraining Order System, as described in subdivision (e). Data entry is required to be entered only once under the requirements of this section, unless the order is served at a later time. A portion of all fees payable to the Department of Justice under subdivision (a) of Section 1203.097 of the Penal Code for the entry of the information required under this section, based upon the proportion of the costs incurred by the local agency and those incurred by the Department of Justice, shall be transferred to the local agency actually providing the data. All data with respect to criminal court protective orders issued, modified, extended, or terminated under subdivision (g) of Section 136.2 of the Penal Code, and all data filed with the court on the required Judicial Council forms with respect to protective orders, including their issuance, modification, extension, or termination, to which this division applies pursuant to Section 6221, shall be transmitted by the court or its designee within one business day to law enforcement personnel by either one of the following methods:

(1) Transmitting a physical copy of the order to a local law enforcement agency authorized by the Department of Justice to enter orders into CLETS.

(2) With the approval of the Department of Justice, entering the order into CLETS directly.

(b) Upon the issuance of a protective order to which this division applies pursuant to Section 6221, or the issuance of a temporary restraining order or injunction relating to harassment, unlawful violence, or the threat of violence pursuant to Section 527.6, 527.8, or 527.85 of the Code of Civil Procedure, or the issuance of a criminal court protective order under subdivision (g) of Section 136.2 of the Penal Code, or the issuance of a juvenile court restraining order related to domestic violence pursuant to Section 213.5, 304, or 362.4 of the Welfare and Institutions Code, or the issuance of a protective order pursuant to Section 15657.03 of the Welfare and Institutions Code, or upon registration with the court clerk of a domestic violence protective or restraining order issued by the tribunal of another state, as defined in Section 6401, and including any of the foregoing orders issued in connection with an order for modification of a custody or visitation order issued pursuant to a dissolution, legal separation, nullity, or paternity proceeding the Department of Justice shall be immediately notified of the contents of the order and the following information:

(1) The name, race, date of birth, and other personal descriptive information of the respondent as required by a form prescribed by the Department of Justice.

(2) The names of the protected persons.

(3) The date of issuance of the order.

(4) The duration or expiration date of the order.

(5) The terms and conditions of the protective order, including stay-away, no-contact, residency exclusion, custody, and visitation provisions of the order.

(6) The department or division number and the address of the court.

(7) Whether or not the order was served upon the respondent.

(8) The terms and conditions of any restrictions on the ownership or possession of firearms.

All available information shall be included; however, the inability to provide all categories of information shall not delay the entry of the information available.

(c) The information conveyed to the Department of Justice shall also indicate whether the respondent was present in court to be informed of the contents of the court order. The respondent's presence in court shall provide proof of service of notice of the terms of the protective order. The respondent's failure to appear shall also be included in the information provided to the Department of Justice.

(d)(1) Within one business day of service, any law enforcement officer who served a protective order shall submit the proof of service directly into the Department of Justice Domestic Violence Restraining Order System, including his or her name and law enforcement agency, and shall transmit the original proof of service form to the issuing court.

(2) Within one business day of receipt of proof of service by a person other than a law enforcement officer, the clerk of the court shall submit the proof of service of a protective order directly into the Department of Justice Domestic Violation Restraining Order System, including the name of the person who served the order. If the court is unable to provide this notification to the Department of Justice by electronic transmission, the court shall, within one business day of receipt, transmit a copy of the proof of service to a local law enforcement agency. The local law enforcement agency shall submit the proof of service directly into the Department of Justice Domestic Violence Restraining Order System within one business day of receipt from the court.

(e) The Department of Justice shall maintain a Domestic Violence Restraining Order System and shall make available to court clerks and law enforcement personnel, through computer access, all information regarding the protective and restraining orders and injunctions described in subdivision (b), whether or not served upon the respondent.

(f) If a court issues a modification, extension, or termination of a protective order, it shall be on forms adopted by the Judicial Council of California and that have been approved by the Department of Justice, and the transmitting agency for the county shall immediately notify the Department of Justice, by electronic transmission, of the terms of the modification, extension, or termination.

(g) The Judicial Council shall assist local courts charged with the responsibility for issuing protective orders by developing informational packets describing the general procedures for obtaining a domestic violence restraining order and indicating the appropriate Judicial Council forms. The informational packets shall include a design, that local courts shall complete, that describes local court procedures and maps to enable applicants to locate filing windows and appropriate courts, and shall also include information on how to return proofs of service, including mailing addresses and fax numbers. The court clerk shall provide a fee waiver form to all applicants for domestic violence protective orders. The court clerk shall provide all Judicial Council forms required by this chapter to applicants free of charge. The informational packet shall also contain a statement that the protective order is enforceable in any state, as defined in Section 6401, and general information about agencies in other jurisdictions that may be contacted regarding enforcement of an order issued by a court of this state.

(h) For the purposes of this part, "electronic transmission" shall include computer access through the California Law Enforcement Telecommunications System (CLETS).

(i) Only protective and restraining orders issued on forms adopted by the Judicial Council of California and that have been approved by the Department of Justice shall be transmitted to the Department of Justice. However, this provision shall not apply to a valid protective or restraining order related to domestic or family violence issued by a tribunal of another state, as defined in Section 6401. Those orders shall, upon request, be registered pursuant to Section 6404. *(Added by Stats.1994, c. 872 (A.B.3034), § 2. Amended by Stats.1995, c. 731 (A.B.233), § 1; Stats.1996, c. 1139 (A.B.2647), § 1; Stats.1996, c. 1140 (A.B.2231), § 1.5; Stats.1998, c. 187 (A.B.1531), § 1; Stats.1998, c. 581 (A.B.2801), § 17; Stats.1998, c. 702 (A.B.2177), § 1; Stats.1998, c. 707 (S.B.1682), § 2.7; Stats.1999, c. 83 (S.B.966), § 52; Stats.1999, c. 561 (A.B.59), § 4; Stats.1999, c. 661 (A.B.825), § 5.5; Stats.2001, c. 698 (A.B.160), § 2; Stats.2001, c. 816 (A.B.731), § 1.5; Stats.2002, c. 265 (S.B.1627), § 1; Stats.2005, c. 631 (S.B.720), § 2; Stats.2010, c. 572 (A.B.1596), § 20, operative Jan. 1, 2012.)*

Research References

Forms

West's California Code Forms, Family § 6300, Comment Overview--Protective Orders.

West's California Code Forms, Family § 6380, Comment Overview--Registration and Enforcement Of Orders.

West's California Code Forms, Family § 6400, Comment Overview--Uniform Interstate Enforcement Of Violence Protection Orders Act.

West's California Judicial Council Forms FL-300, Request for Order.

West's California Judicial Council Forms JV-250, Notice Of Hearing and Temporary Restraining Order--Juvenile.

West's California Judicial Council Forms JV-255, Restraining Order - Juvenile Order After Hearing.

Treatises and Practice Aids

Witkin, California Summary 10th Husband and Wife § 112, Contents Of Judgment.

Witkin, California Summary 10th Husband and Wife § 373, in General.

Witkin, California Summary 10th Husband and Wife § 386, in General.

Witkin, California Summary 10th Husband and Wife § 387, Electronic Transmission and Recording Of Data.

Witkin, California Summary 10th Husband and Wife § 389, Foreign Orders.

Witkin, California Summary 10th Torts § 162, Failure Of Court to Give Notice Of Protective Order.

§ 6381. Enforceability of orders; receipt of copy by law enforcement agency; domestic violence restraining order registry

(a) Notwithstanding Section 6380 and subject to subdivision (b), an order issued under this part is enforceable in any place in this state.

(b) An order issued under this part is not enforceable by a law enforcement agency of a political subdivision unless that law enforcement agency has received a copy of the order, or the officer enforcing the order has been shown a copy of the order or has obtained information, through the Domestic Violence Restraining Order System maintained by the Department of Justice, of the contents of the order, as described in subdivision (b).

(c) The data contained in the Domestic Violence Restraining Order System shall be deemed to be original, self-authenticating, documentary evidence of the court orders. Oral notification of the terms of the orders shall be sufficient notice for enforcement under subdivision (g) of Section 136.2 and Section 273.6 of the Penal Code. *(Added by Stats.1993, c. 219 (A.B.1500), § 154. Amended by Stats.1994, c. 872 (A.B.3034), § 3; Stats.1999, c. 661 (A.B.825), § 7.)*

Law Revision Commission Comments

Enactment [Revised Comment]

Section 6381 continues without substantive change and generalizes the last paragraph of former Civil Code Section 4359(b). The former section applied only to the former Family Law Act. [23 Cal.L.Rev.Comm. Reports 1 (1993)].

Research References

Forms

West's California Code Forms, Family § 6380, Comment Overview--Registration and Enforcement Of Orders.

Treatises and Practice Aids

Witkin, California Summary 10th Husband and Wife § 386, in General.

§ 6382. Availability of information concerning orders; law enforcement officers

Each appropriate law enforcement agency shall make available to any law enforcement officer responding to the scene of reported domestic violence, through an existing system for verification, information as to the existence, terms, and current status of an order issued under this part. *(Added by Stats.1993, c. 219 (A.B.1500), § 154.)*

Law Revision Commission Comments

Enactment [Revised Comment]

Section 6382 continues without substantive change the first sentence of the second paragraph of former Code of Civil Procedure Section 550(a), the last sentence of the first paragraph of former Civil Code Section 4359(b), and the last sentence of former Civil Code Section 7020(e). See also Section 6211 ("domestic violence" defined). [23 Cal.L.Rev.Comm. Reports 1 (1993)].

Research References

Forms

West's California Code Forms, Family § 6380, Comment Overview--Registration and Enforcement Of Orders.

Treatises and Practice Aids

Witkin, California Summary 10th Husband and Wife § 386, in General.

§ 6383. Service of order; verification; verbal notice; report; civil liability

(a) A temporary restraining order or emergency protective order issued under this part shall, on request of the petitioner, be served on the respondent, whether or not the respondent has been taken into custody, by a law enforcement officer who is present at the scene of reported domestic violence involving the parties to the proceeding.

(b) The petitioner shall provide the officer with an endorsed copy of the order and a proof of service that the officer shall complete and transmit to the issuing court.

(c) It is a rebuttable presumption that the proof of service was signed on the date of service.

(d) Upon receiving information at the scene of a domestic violence incident that a protective order has been issued under this part, or that a person who has been taken into custody is the respondent to that order, if the protected person cannot produce an endorsed copy of the order, a law enforcement officer shall immediately inquire of the Domestic Violence Restraining Order System to verify the existence of the order.

(e) If the law enforcement officer determines that a protective order has been issued, but not served, the officer shall immediately notify the respondent of the terms of the order and where a written copy of the order can be obtained and the officer shall, at that time, also enforce the order. The law enforcement officer's verbal notice of the terms of the order shall constitute service of the order and is sufficient notice for the purposes of this section and for the purposes of Sections 273.6 and 29825 of the Penal Code.

(f) If a report is required under Section 13730 of the Penal Code, or if no report is required, then in the daily incident log, the officer shall provide the name and assignment of the officer notifying the respondent pursuant to subdivision (e) and the case number of the order.

(g) Upon service of the order outside of the court, a law enforcement officer shall advise the respondent to go to the local court to obtain a copy of the order containing the full terms and conditions of the order.

(h)(1) There shall be no civil liability on the part of, and no cause of action for false arrest or false imprisonment against, a peace officer who makes an arrest pursuant to a protective or restraining order that is regular upon its face, if the peace officer, in making the arrest, acts in good faith and has reasonable cause to believe that the person against whom the order is issued has notice of the order and has committed an act in violation of the order.

(2) If there is more than one order issued and one of the orders is an emergency protective order that has precedence in enforcement pursuant to paragraph (1) of subdivision (c) of Section 136.2 of the Penal Code, the peace officer shall enforce the emergency protective order. If there is more than one order issued, none of the orders issued is an emergency protective order that has precedence in enforcement, and one of the orders issued is a no-contact order, as described in Section 6320, the peace officer shall enforce the no-contact order. If there is more than one civil order regarding the same parties and neither an emergency protective order that has precedence in enforcement nor a no-contact order has been issued, the peace officer shall enforce the order that was issued last. If there are both civil and criminal orders regarding the same parties and neither an emergency protective order that has precedence in enforcement nor a no-contact order has been issued, the peace officer shall enforce the criminal order issued last, subject to the provisions of subdivisions (h) and (i) of Section 136.2 of the Penal Code. Nothing in this section shall be deemed to exonerate a peace officer from liability for the unreasonable use of force in the enforcement of the order. The immunities afforded by this section shall not affect the availability of any other immunity that may apply, including, but not limited to, Sections 820.2 and 820.4 of the Government Code. *(Added by Stats.1993, c. 219 (A.B.1500), § 154. Amended by Stats.1994, c. 872 (A.B.3034), § 4; Stats.1997, c. 347 (A.B. 356), § 1; Stats.1999, c. 661 (A.B.825), § 8; Stats.2001, c. 698 (A.B.160), § 3; Stats.2005, c. 467 (A.B.429), § 2; Stats.2010, c. 178 (S.B.1115), § 24, operative Jan. 1, 2012; Stats.2013, c. 263 (A.B.176), § 2, operative July 1, 2014; Stats.2014, c. 71 (S.B.1304), § 54, eff. Jan. 1, 2015.)*

Law Revision Commission Comments

Enactment [Revised Comment]

Section 6383 continues without substantive change and generalizes the last two sentences of the second paragraph of former Code of Civil Procedure Section 550(a), former Code of Civil Procedure Section 550(h), former Civil Code Section 4359(e), and former Civil Code Section 7020(g). See also Section 6211 ("domestic violence" defined). [23 Cal.L.Rev.Comm. Reports 1 (1993)].

2010 Amendment

Subdivision (e) of Section 6383 is amended to reflect nonsubstantive reorganization of the statutes governing control of deadly weapons. [38 Cal.L.Rev.Comm. Reports 217 (2009)].

Research References

Forms

West's California Code Forms, Family § 6380, Comment Overview--Registration and Enforcement Of Orders.
West's California Judicial Council Forms FL-300, Request for Order.

Treatises and Practice Aids

Witkin, California Summary 10th Husband and Wife § 386, in General.

Witkin, California Summary 10th Husband and Wife § 387, Electronic Transmission and Recording Of Data.
Witkin, California Summary 10th Husband and Wife § 388, Service Of Order.

§ 6384. Personal service of order not required; forms for orders

(a) If a respondent named in an order issued under this part after a hearing has not been served personally with the order but has received actual notice of the existence and substance of the order through personal appearance in court to hear the terms of the order from the court, no additional proof of service is required for enforcement of the order.

If a respondent named in a temporary restraining order or emergency protective order is personally served with the order and notice of hearing with respect to a restraining order or protective order based on the temporary restraining order or emergency protective order, but the respondent does not appear at the hearing either in person or by counsel, and the terms and conditions of the restraining order or protective order issued at the hearing are identical to the temporary restraining or emergency protective order, except for the duration of the order, the restraining order or protective order issued at the hearing may be served on the respondent by first-class mail sent to the respondent at the most current address for the respondent that is available to the court.

(b) The Judicial Council forms for orders issued under this part shall contain a statement in substantially the following form:

"If you have been personally served with a temporary restraining order and notice of hearing, but you do not appear at the hearing either in person or by a lawyer, and a restraining order that is the same as this temporary restraining order except for the expiration date is issued at the hearing, a copy of the order will be served on you by mail at the following address: ____.

If that address is not correct or you wish to verify that the temporary restraining order was converted to a restraining order at the hearing without substantive change and to find out the duration of that order, contact the clerk of the court." *(Added by Stats.1993, c. 219 (A.B.1500), § 154. Amended by Stats.1997, c. 347 (A.B.356), § 2; Stats.2010, c. 572 (A.B. 1596), § 21, operative Jan. 1, 2012.)*

Law Revision Commission Comments

Enactment [Revised Comment]

Subdivision (a) of Section 6384 continues former Code of Civil Procedure Section 550(e) without substantive change. In subdivision (a), a reference to an order issued under "this part" has been substituted for the former reference to "this section." The former reference was unclear, since former Code of Civil Procedure Section 550 did not provide for the issuance of orders. The reference has been corrected to include any of the orders issued under Part 4 of this division.

Subdivision (b) of Section 6384 continues former Code of Civil Procedure Section 550(g) without substantive change. The former reference to "temporary restraining orders or restraining orders issued after a hearing" has been replaced by a reference to orders issued under "this part." This is not a substantive change. [23 Cal.L.Rev.Comm. Reports 1 (1993)].

Research References

Treatises and Practice Aids

Witkin, California Summary 10th Husband and Wife § 387, Electronic Transmission and Recording Of Data.
Witkin, California Summary 10th Husband and Wife § 388, Service Of Order.

§ 6385. Proof of service of protective orders; personal descriptive information; purchase or receipt of firearm

(a) Proof of service of the protective order is not required for the purposes of Section 6380 if the order indicates on its face that both parties were personally present at the hearing at which the order was issued and that, for the purpose of Section 6384, no proof of service is required, or if the order was served by a law enforcement officer pursuant to Section 6383.

(b) The failure of the petitioner to provide the Department of Justice with the personal descriptive information regarding the person restrained does not invalidate the protective order.

(c) There is no civil liability on the part of, and no cause of action arises against, an employee of a local law enforcement agency, a court, or the Department of Justice, acting within the scope of employment, if a person described in Section 29825 of the Penal Code unlawfully purchases or receives or attempts to purchase or receive a firearm and a person is injured by that firearm or a person who is otherwise entitled to receive a firearm is denied a firearm and either wrongful action is due to a failure of a court to provide the notification provided for in this chapter. *(Added by Stats.1993, c. 219 (A.B.1500), § 154. Amended by Stats.1994, c. 872 (A.B.3034), § 5; Stats.1995, c. 731 (A.B.233), § 2; Stats.2002, c. 265 (S.B.1627), § 2; Stats.2010, c. 178 (S.B.1115), § 25, operative Jan. 1, 2012.)*

Law Revision Commission Comments

Enactment [Revised Comment]

Section 6385 continues former Code of Civil Procedure Section 550(b)–(d) without substantive change. The word "petitioner" has been substituted for "plaintiff" to conform to revisions made to former law. See 1990 Cal. Stat. ch. 752. The reference to "protective order" has been substituted for the reference to an order based on what are now Sections 6320–6322. This is not a substantive change, since "protective order" has been defined to include the same orders. See Section 6218 ("protective order" defined). In subdivision (c), a reference to providing information to the "Department of Justice" has been substituted for the reference to "local law enforcement," since the purpose of this section is the provision of information to the Department of Justice. This is not a substantive change.

See also Section 6304 (court to provide information to parties concerning terms and effect of order); Penal Code § 12021 (criminal penalty for acquiring firearm while subject to restraining order against domestic violence). [23 Cal.L.Rev.Comm. Reports 1 (1993)].

2010 Amendment

Subdivision (c) of Section 6385 is amended to reflect nonsubstantive reorganization of the statutes governing control of deadly weapons. [38 Cal.L.Rev.Comm. Reports 217 (2009)].

Research References

Forms

West's California Code Forms, Family § 6380, Comment Overview--Registration and Enforcement Of Orders.

Treatises and Practice Aids

Witkin, California Summary 10th Husband and Wife § 386, in General.

Witkin, California Summary 10th Husband and Wife § 387, Electronic Transmission and Recording Of Data.

Witkin, California Summary 10th Torts § 162, Failure Of Court to Give Notice Of Protective Order.

§ 6386. Appointment of counsel; payment of attorney fees and costs

(a) The court may, in its discretion, appoint counsel to represent the petitioner in a proceeding to enforce the terms of a protective order, as defined in Section 6218.

(b) In a proceeding in which private counsel was appointed by the court pursuant to subdivision (a), the court may order the respondent to pay reasonable attorney's fees and costs incurred by the petitioner. *(Added by Stats.1993, c. 219 (A.B.1500), § 154.)*

Law Revision Commission Comments

Enactment [Revised Comment]

Section 6386 restates former Code of Civil Procedure Section 553 without substantive change. The words "petitioner" and "respondent" have been substituted for "plaintiff" and "defendant" to conform to revisions made to former law. See 1990 Cal. Stat. ch. 752. The reference to "protective order" has been substituted for the reference to an order based on what are now Sections 6320–6322. This is not a substantive change, since "protective order" has been defined to include the same orders. See Section 6218 ("protective order" defined). See also Sections 270–272 (general provisions for attorney's fees and costs). [23 Cal.L.Rev.Comm. Reports 1 (1993)].

Research References

Treatises and Practice Aids

Witkin, California Summary 10th Husband and Wife § 386, in General.

§ 6387. Copies of order to be provided to petitioner

The court shall order the clerk of the court to provide to a petitioner, without cost, up to three certified, stamped, and endorsed copies of any order issued under this part, and of an extension, modification, or termination of the order. *(Added by Stats.1993, c. 219 (A.B.1500), § 154. Amended by Stats. 2001, c. 176 (S.B.210), § 5; Stats.2010, c. 572 (A.B.1596), § 22, operative Jan. 1, 2012.)*

Law Revision Commission Comments

Enactment [Revised Comment]

Section 6387 continues without substantive change the last sentence of the first paragraph of former Code of Civil Procedure Section 550(a). [23 Cal.L.Rev.Comm. Reports 1 (1993)].

Research References

Treatises and Practice Aids

Witkin, California Summary 10th Husband and Wife § 386, in General.

§ 6388. Willful and knowing violation of order; penalty

A willful and knowing violation of a protective order, as defined in Section 6218, is a crime punishable as provided by Section 273.6 of the Penal Code. *(Added by Stats.1993, c. 219 (A.B.1500), § 154.)*

Law Revision Commission Comments

Enactment [Revised Comment]

Section 6388 continues without substantive change former Code of Civil Procedure Section 551, the last sentence of former Civil Code Section 4359(c), former Civil Code Section 7020(h), and the last sentences of former Civil Code Section 4458, 4516, and 7021. The reference to "protective order" has been substituted for the reference to an order based on what are now Sections 6320–6322. This is not a substantive change, since "protective order" has been defined to include the same orders. See Section 6218 ("protective order" defined). [23 Cal.L.Rev.Comm. Reports 1 (1993)].

Research References

Treatises and Practice Aids

Witkin, California Summary 10th Husband and Wife § 112, Contents Of Judgment.

Witkin, California Summary 10th Husband and Wife § 386, in General.

§ 6389. Firearm or ammunition ownership, possession, purchase, or receipt; relinquishment order; use immunity; storage fee; order content; exemption; sale; penalty

(a) A person subject to a protective order, as defined in Section 6218, shall not own, possess, purchase, or receive a firearm or ammunition while that protective order is in effect. Every person who owns, possesses, purchases or receives, or attempts to purchase or receive a firearm or ammunition while the protective order is in effect is punishable pursuant to Section 29825 of the Penal Code.

(b) On all forms providing notice that a protective order has been requested or granted, the Judicial Council shall include a notice that, upon service of the order, the respondent shall be ordered to relinquish possession or control of any firearms and not to purchase or receive or attempt to purchase or receive any firearms for a period not to exceed the duration of the restraining order.

(c)(1) Upon issuance of a protective order, as defined in Section 6218, the court shall order the respondent to relinquish any firearm in the respondent's immediate possession or control or subject to the respondent's immediate possession or control.

(2) The relinquishment ordered pursuant to paragraph (1) shall occur by immediately surrendering the firearm in a safe manner, upon request of any law enforcement officer, to the control of the officer, after being served with the protective order. A law enforcement officer serving a protective order that indicates that the respondent possesses weapons or ammunition shall request that the firearm be immediately surrendered. Alternatively, if no request is made by a law enforcement officer, the relinquishment shall occur within 24 hours of being served with the order, by either surrendering the firearm in a safe manner to the control of local law enforcement officials, or by selling the firearm to a licensed gun dealer, as specified in Article 1 (commencing with Section 26700) and Article 2 (commencing with Section 26800) of Chapter 2 of Division 6 of Title 4 of Part 6 of the Penal Code. The law enforcement officer or licensed gun dealer taking possession of the firearm pursuant to this

subdivision shall issue a receipt to the person relinquishing the firearm at the time of relinquishment. A person ordered to relinquish any firearm pursuant to this subdivision shall, within 48 hours after being served with the order, do both of the following:

(A) File, with the court that issued the protective order, the receipt showing the firearm was surrendered to a local law enforcement agency or sold to a licensed gun dealer. Failure to timely file a receipt shall constitute a violation of the protective order.

(B) File a copy of the receipt described in subparagraph (A) with the law enforcement agency that served the protective order. Failure to timely file a copy of the receipt shall constitute a violation of the protective order.

(3) The forms for protective orders adopted by the Judicial Council and approved by the Department of Justice shall require the petitioner to describe the number, types, and locations of any firearms presently known by the petitioner to be possessed or controlled by the respondent.

(4) It is recommended that every law enforcement agency in the state develop, adopt, and implement written policies and standards for law enforcement officers who request immediate relinquishment of firearms.

(d) If the respondent declines to relinquish possession of any firearm based on the assertion of the right against self-incrimination, as provided by the Fifth Amendment to the United States Constitution and Section 15 of Article I of the California Constitution, the court may grant use immunity for the act of relinquishing the firearm required under this section.

(e) A local law enforcement agency may charge the respondent a fee for the storage of any firearm pursuant to this section. This fee shall not exceed the actual cost incurred by the local law enforcement agency for the storage of the firearm. For purposes of this subdivision, "actual cost" means expenses directly related to taking possession of a firearm, storing the firearm, and surrendering possession of the firearm to a licensed dealer as defined in Section 26700 of the Penal Code or to the respondent.

(f) The restraining order requiring a person to relinquish a firearm pursuant to subdivision (c) shall state on its face that the respondent is prohibited from owning, possessing, purchasing, or receiving a firearm while the protective order is in effect and that the firearm shall be relinquished to the local law enforcement agency for that jurisdiction or sold to a licensed gun dealer, and that proof of surrender or sale shall be filed with the court within a specified period of receipt of the order. The order shall also state on its face the expiration date for relinquishment. Nothing in this section shall limit a respondent's right under existing law to petition the court at a later date for modification of the order.

(g) The restraining order requiring a person to relinquish a firearm pursuant to subdivision (c) shall prohibit the person from possessing or controlling any firearm for the duration of the order. At the expiration of the order, the local law enforcement agency shall return possession of any surrendered firearm to the respondent, within five days after the expiration of the relinquishment order, unless the local law enforcement agency determines that (1) the firearm has been stolen, (2) the respondent is prohibited from possessing a firearm because the respondent is in any prohibited class for the possession of firearms, as defined in Chapter 2 (commencing with Section 29800) and Chapter 3 (commencing with Section 29900) of Division 9 of Title 4 of Part 6 of the Penal Code and Sections 8100 and 8103 of the Welfare and Institutions Code, or (3) another successive restraining order is issued against the respondent under this section. If the local law enforcement agency determines that the respondent is the legal owner of any firearm deposited with the local law enforcement agency and is prohibited from possessing any firearm, the respondent shall be entitled to sell or transfer the firearm to a licensed dealer as defined in Section 26700 of the Penal Code. If the firearm has been stolen, the firearm shall be restored to the lawful owner upon his or her identification of the firearm and proof of ownership.

(h) The court may, as part of the relinquishment order, grant an exemption from the relinquishment requirements of this section for a particular firearm if the respondent can show that a particular firearm is necessary as a condition of continued employment and that the current employer is unable to reassign the respondent to another position where a firearm is unnecessary. If an exemption is granted pursuant to this subdivision, the order shall provide that the firearm shall be in the physical possession of the respondent only during scheduled work hours and during travel to and from his or her place of employment. In any case involving a peace officer who as a condition of employment and whose personal safety depends on the ability to carry a firearm, a court may allow the peace officer to continue to carry a firearm, either on duty or off duty, if the court finds by a preponderance of the evidence that the officer does not pose a threat of harm. Prior to making this finding, the court shall require a mandatory psychological evaluation of the peace officer and may require the peace officer to enter into counseling or other remedial treatment program to deal with any propensity for domestic violence.

(i) During the period of the relinquishment order, a respondent is entitled to make one sale of all firearms that are in the possession of a local law enforcement agency pursuant to this section. A licensed gun dealer, who presents a local law enforcement agency with a bill of sale indicating that all firearms owned by the respondent that are in the possession of the local law enforcement agency have been sold by the respondent to the licensed gun dealer, shall be given possession of those firearms, at the location where a respondent's firearms are stored, within five days of presenting the local law enforcement agency with a bill of sale.

(j) The disposition of any unclaimed property under this section shall be made pursuant to Section 1413 of the Penal Code.

(k) The return of a firearm to any person pursuant to subdivision (g) shall not be subject to the requirements of Section 27545 of the Penal Code.

(*l*) If the respondent notifies the court that he or she owns a firearm that is not in his or her immediate possession, the court may limit the order to exclude that firearm if the judge is satisfied the respondent is unable to gain access to that firearm while the protective order is in effect.

(m) Any respondent to a protective order who violates any order issued pursuant to this section shall be punished under the provisions of Section 29825 of the Penal Code. *(Added by Stats.1994, c. 871 (S.B.1278), § 2. Amended by Stats.1999, c. 662 (S.B.218), § 5; Stats.2003, c. 498 (S.B.226), § 5; Stats.2004, c. 250 (S.B.1391), § 2; Stats.2006, c. 467 (S.B.585), § 1; Stats.2010, c. 178 (S.B.1115), § 26, operative Jan. 1, 2012; Stats.2010, c. 572 (A.B.1596), § 23, operative Jan. 1, 2012; Stats.2011, c. 285 (A.B.1402), § 6; Stats.2012, c. 765 (S.B.1433), § 2.)*

Law Revision Commission Comments

2011 Amendment

Subdivisions (a), (c), (g), (k), and (m) of Section 6389 (as it reads in 2010 Cal. Stat. ch. 572, § 23) are amended to reflect nonsubstantive reorganization of the statutes governing control of deadly weapons. [41 Cal.L.Rev.Comm. Reports 135 (2011)].

Commentary

Invoking subsection (a), *Ritchie v. Konrad, 115 Cal.App.4th 1275, 10 Cal.Rptr.3d 387 (2004), review denied*, holds that a trial court has no power to delete the firearm proscription from a renewed protective order. For further discussion of *Ritchie*, see commentary to § 6345.

Altafulla v. Ervin, 238 Cal.App.4th 571, 189 Cal.Rptr.3d 316 (2015), holds that this section does not violate the Second Amendment of the United States Constitution, because it is analogous to constitutionally permissible prohibition of felon weapon possession and is narrowly tailored to accomplish the compelling state interest in reducing domestic violence.

Research References

Forms

California Practice Guide: Rutter Family Law Forms Form 1:32, Glossary Of Common Family Law Terms, Phrases and Concepts (Enclosure to Form 1:31).

West's California Judicial Council Forms JV-250, Notice Of Hearing and Temporary Restraining Order--Juvenile.

West's California Judicial Council Forms JV-255, Restraining Order - Juvenile Order After Hearing.

West's California Judicial Council Forms DV-800/JV-252, Proof Of Firearms Turned In, Sold, or Stored (Domestic Violence Prevention).

Treatises and Practice Aids

Witkin, California Summary 10th Husband and Wife § 386, in General.

Part 5

UNIFORM INTERSTATE ENFORCEMENT OF DOMESTIC VIOLENCE PROTECTION ORDERS ACT

§ 6400. Short title

This part may be cited as the Uniform Interstate Enforcement of Domestic Violence Protection Orders Act. *(Added by Stats.2001, c. 816 (A.B.731), § 3.)*

Research References

Treatises and Practice Aids

Witkin, California Summary 10th Husband and Wife § 389, Foreign Orders.

§ 6401. Definitions

In this part:

(1) "Foreign protection order" means a protection order issued by a tribunal of another state.

(2) "Issuing state" means the state whose tribunal issues a protection order.

(3) "Mutual foreign protection order" means a foreign protection order that includes provisions in favor of both the protected individual seeking enforcement of the order and the respondent.

(4) "Protected individual" means an individual protected by a protection order.

(5) "Protection order" means an injunction or other order, issued by a tribunal under the domestic violence, family violence, or antistalking laws of the issuing state, to prevent an individual from engaging in violent or threatening acts against, harassment of, contact or communication with, or physical proximity to, another individual.

(6) "Respondent" means the individual against whom enforcement of a protection order is sought.

(7) "State" means a state of the United States, the District of Columbia, Puerto Rico, the United States Virgin Islands, or any territory or insular possession subject to the jurisdiction of the United States. The term includes an Indian tribe or band, or any branch of the United States military, that has jurisdiction to issue protection orders.

(8) "Tribunal" means a court, agency, or other entity authorized by law to issue or modify a protection order. *(Added by Stats.2001, c. 816 (A.B.731), § 3. Amended by Stats.2003, c. 134 (S.B.399), § 1.)*

Research References

Treatises and Practice Aids

Witkin, California Summary 10th Husband and Wife § 387, Electronic Transmission and Recording Of Data.

Witkin, California Summary 10th Husband and Wife § 389, Foreign Orders.

§ 6402. Judicial enforcement of order

(a) A person authorized by the law of this state to seek enforcement of a protection order may seek enforcement of a valid foreign protection order in a tribunal of this state. The tribunal shall enforce the terms of the order, including terms that provide relief that a tribunal of this state would lack power to provide but for this section. The tribunal shall enforce the order, whether the order was obtained by independent action or in another proceeding, if it is an order issued in response to a complaint, petition, or motion filed by or on behalf of an individual seeking protection. In a proceeding to enforce a foreign protection order, the tribunal shall follow the procedures of this state for the enforcement of protection orders.

(b) A tribunal of this state may not enforce a foreign protection order issued by a tribunal of a state that does not recognize the standing of a protected individual to seek enforcement of the order.

(c) A tribunal of this state shall enforce the provisions of a valid foreign protection order which govern custody and visitation, if the order was issued in accordance with the jurisdictional requirements governing the issuance of custody and visitation orders in the issuing state.

(d) A foreign protection order is valid if it meets all of the following criteria:

(1) Identifies the protected individual and the respondent.

(2) Is currently in effect.

(3) Was issued by a tribunal that had jurisdiction over the parties and subject matter under the law of the issuing state.

(4) Was issued after the respondent was given reasonable notice and had an opportunity to be heard before the tribunal issued the order or, in the case of an order ex parte, the respondent was given notice and has had or will have an opportunity to be heard within a reasonable time after the order was issued, in a manner consistent with the rights of the respondent to due process.

(e) A foreign protection order valid on its face is prima facie evidence of its validity.

(f) Absence of any of the criteria for validity of a foreign protection order is an affirmative defense in an action seeking enforcement of the order.

(g) A tribunal of this state may enforce provisions of a mutual foreign protection order which favor a respondent only if both of the following are true:

(1) The respondent filed a written pleading seeking a protection order from the tribunal of the issuing state.

(2) The tribunal of the issuing state made specific findings in favor of the respondent. *(Added by Stats.2001, c. 816 (A.B.731), § 3.. Amended by Stats.2003, c. 134 (S.B.399), § 2.)*

Research References

Forms

West's California Code Forms, Family § 6400, Comment Overview--Uniform Interstate Enforcement Of Violence Protection Orders Act.

Treatises and Practice Aids

Witkin, California Summary 10th Husband and Wife § 389, Foreign Orders.

§ 6403. Nonjudicial enforcement of order

(a) A law enforcement officer of this state, upon determining that there is probable cause to believe that a valid foreign protection order exists and that the order has been violated, shall enforce the order as if it were the order of a tribunal of this state. Presentation of a protection order that identifies both the protected individual and the respondent and, on its face, is currently in effect constitutes, in and of itself, probable cause to believe that a valid foreign protection order exists. For the purposes of this section, the protection order may be inscribed on a tangible medium or may have been stored in an electronic or other medium if it is retrievable in perceivable form. Presentation of a certified copy of a protection order is not required for enforcement.

(b) If a foreign protection order is not presented, a law enforcement officer of this state may consider other information in determining whether there is probable cause to believe that a valid foreign protection order exists.

(c) If a law enforcement officer of this state determines that an otherwise valid foreign protection order cannot be enforced because the respondent has not been notified or served with the order, the officer shall inform the respondent of the order, make a reasonable effort to serve the order upon the respondent, and allow the respondent a reasonable opportunity to comply with the order before enforcing the order. Verbal notice of the terms of the order is sufficient notice for the purposes of this section.

(d) Registration or filing of an order in this state is not required for the enforcement of a valid foreign protection order pursuant to this part. *(Added by Stats.2001, c. 816 (A.B.731), § 3.)*

Research References

Forms

West's California Code Forms, Family § 6400, Comment Overview--Uniform Interstate Enforcement Of Violence Protection Orders Act.

Treatises and Practice Aids

Witkin, California Summary 10th Husband and Wife § 389, Foreign Orders.

§ 6404. Registration of order

(a) Any foreign protection order shall, upon request of the person in possession of the order, be registered with a court of this state in order to be entered in the Domestic Violence Restraining Order System established under Section 6380. The Judicial Council shall adopt rules of court to do the following:

(1) Set forth the process whereby a person in possession of a foreign protection order may voluntarily register the order with a court of this state for entry into the Domestic Violence Restraining Order System.

(2) Require the sealing of foreign protection orders and provide access only to law enforcement, the person who registered the order upon written request with proof of identification, the defense after arraignment on criminal charges involving an alleged violation of the order, or upon further order of the court.

(b) No fee may be charged for the registration of a foreign protection order. The court clerk shall provide all Judicial Council forms required by this part to a person in possession of a foreign protection order free of charge. *(Added by Stats.2001, c. 816 (A.B.731), § 3.)*

Research References

Forms

West's California Code Forms, Family § 6400, Comment Overview-- Uniform Interstate Enforcement Of Violence Protection Orders Act.

West's California Judicial Council Forms DV-600, Order to Register Out-Of-State or Tribal Court Protective/Restraining Order.

Treatises and Practice Aids

Witkin, California Summary 10th Husband and Wife § 389, Foreign Orders.

§ 6405. Immunity from civil liability; multiple orders; precedence in enforcement; unreasonable use of force

(a) There shall be no civil liability on the part of, and no cause of action for false arrest or false imprisonment against, a peace officer who makes an arrest pursuant to a foreign protection order that is regular upon its face, if the peace officer, in making the arrest, acts in good faith and has reasonable cause to believe that the person against whom the order is issued has notice of the order and has committed an act in violation of the order.

(b) If there is more than one order issued and one of the orders is an emergency protective order that has precedence in enforcement pursuant to paragraph (1) of subdivision (c) of Section 136.2 of the Penal Code, the peace officer shall enforce the emergency protective order. If there is more than one order issued, none of the orders issued is an emergency protective order that has precedence in enforcement, and one of the orders issued is a no-contact order, as described in Section 6320, the peace officer shall enforce the no-contact order. If there is more than one civil order regarding the same parties and neither an emergency protective order that has precedence in enforcement nor a no-contact order has been issued, the peace officer shall enforce the order that was issued last. If there are both civil and criminal orders regarding the same parties and neither an emergency protective order that has precedence in enforcement nor a no-contact order has been issued, the peace officer shall enforce the criminal order issued last.

(c) Nothing in this section shall be deemed to exonerate a peace officer from liability for the unreasonable use of force in the enforcement of the order. The immunities afforded by this section shall not affect the availability of any other immunity that may apply, including, but not limited to, Sections 820.2 and 820.4 of the Government Code. *(Added by Stats.2001, c. 816 (A.B.731), § 3. Amended by Stats.2013, c. 263 (A.B.176), § 3, operative July 1, 2014.)*

Research References

Treatises and Practice Aids

Witkin, California Summary 10th Husband and Wife § 389, Foreign Orders.

§ 6406. Other remedies

A protected individual who pursues remedies under this part is not precluded from pursuing other legal or equitable remedies against the respondent. *(Added by Stats.2001, c. 816 (A.B.731), § 3.)*

Research References

Treatises and Practice Aids

Witkin, California Summary 10th Husband and Wife § 389, Foreign Orders.

§ 6407. Uniformity of application and construction

In applying and construing this part, consideration shall be given to the need to promote uniformity of the law with respect to its subject matter among states that also have adopted the act cited in Section 6400. *(Added by Stats.2001, c. 816 (A.B.731), § 3.)*

Research References

Treatises and Practice Aids

Witkin, California Summary 10th Husband and Wife § 389, Foreign Orders.

§ 6408. Severability clause

If any provision of this part or its application to any person or circumstance is held invalid, the invalidity does not affect other provisions or applications of this part which can be given effect without the invalid provision or application, and to this end the provisions of this part are severable. *(Added by Stats.2001, c. 816 (A.B.731), § 3.)*

Research References

Treatises and Practice Aids

Witkin, California Summary 10th Husband and Wife § 389, Foreign Orders.

§ 6409. Application of Part

This part applies to protection orders issued before January 1, 2002, and to continuing actions for enforcement of foreign protection orders commenced before January 1, 2002. A request for enforcement of a foreign protection order made on or after January 1, 2002, for violations of a foreign protection order occurring before January 1, 2002, is governed by this part. *(Added by Stats.2001, c. 816 (A.B.731), § 3.)*

Research References

Treatises and Practice Aids

Witkin, California Summary 10th Husband and Wife § 389, Foreign Orders.

Part 6

UNIFORM RECOGNITION AND ENFORCEMENT OF CANADIAN DOMESTIC VIOLENCE PROTECTION ORDERS ACT

Section

§ 6450. Short title

This part may be cited as the Uniform Recognition and Enforcement of Canadian Domestic Violence Protection Orders Act. *(Added by Stats.2017, c. 98 (S.B.204), § 1, eff. Jan. 1, 2018.)*

§ 6451. Definitions

In this part:

(a) "Canadian domestic violence protection order" means a judgment or part of a judgment or order issued in English in a civil proceeding by a court of Canada under law of the issuing jurisdiction that relates to domestic violence and prohibits a respondent from doing any of the following:

(1) Being in physical proximity to a protected individual or following a protected individual.

(2) Directly or indirectly contacting or communicating with a protected individual or other individual described in the order.

(3) Being within a certain distance of a specified place or location associated with a protected individual.

(4) Molesting, annoying, harassing, or engaging in threatening conduct directed at a protected individual.

(b) "Domestic protection order" means an injunction or other order issued by a tribunal that relates to domestic or family violence laws to prevent an individual from engaging in violent or threatening acts against, harassment of, direct or indirect contact or communication with, or being in physical proximity to, another individual.

(c) "Issuing court" means the court that issues a Canadian domestic violence protection order.

(d) "Law enforcement officer" means an individual authorized by law of this state to enforce a domestic protection order.

(e) "Person" means an individual, estate, business or nonprofit entity, public corporation, government or governmental subdivision, agency, or instrumentality, or other legal entity.

(f) "Protected individual" means an individual protected by a Canadian domestic violence protection order.

(g) "Record" means information that is inscribed on a tangible medium or that is stored in an electronic or other medium and is retrievable in perceivable form.

(h) "Respondent" means an individual against whom a Canadian domestic violence protection order is issued.

(i) "State" means a state of the United States, the District of Columbia, Puerto Rico, the United States Virgin Islands, or any territory or insular possession subject to the jurisdiction of the United States. The term includes a federally recognized Indian tribe.

(j) "Tribunal" means a court, agency, or other entity authorized by law to establish, enforce, or modify a domestic protection order. *(Added by Stats.2017, c. 98 (S.B.204), § 1, eff. Jan. 1, 2018.)*

§ 6452. Enforcement of Canadian domestic violence protection order by law enforcement officer

(a) If a law enforcement officer determines under subdivision (b) or (c) that there is probable cause to believe a valid Canadian domestic violence protection order exists and the order has been violated, the officer shall enforce the terms of the Canadian domestic violence protection order as if the terms were in an order of a tribunal of this state. Presentation to a law enforcement officer of a certified copy of a Canadian domestic violence protection order is not required for enforcement.

(b) Presentation to a law enforcement officer of a record of a Canadian domestic violence protection order that identifies both a protected individual and a respondent and on its face is in effect constitutes probable cause to believe that a valid order exists.

(c) If a record of a Canadian domestic violence protection order is not presented as provided in subdivision (b), a law enforcement officer may consider other information in determining whether there is probable cause to believe that a valid Canadian domestic violence protection order exists.

(d) If a law enforcement officer determines that an otherwise valid Canadian domestic violence protection order cannot be enforced because the respondent has not been notified of or served with the order, the officer shall notify the protected individual that the officer will make reasonable efforts to contact the respondent, consistent with the safety of the protected individual. After notice to the protected individual and consistent with the safety of the individual, the officer shall make a reasonable effort to inform the respondent of the order, notify the respondent of the terms of the order, provide a record of the order, if available, to the respondent, and allow the respondent a reasonable opportunity to comply with the order before the officer enforces the order. Verbal notice of the terms of the order is sufficient for purposes of this subdivision.

(e) If a law enforcement officer determines that an individual is a protected individual, the officer shall inform the individual of available local victim services. *(Added by Stats.2017, c. 98 (S.B.204), § 1, eff. Jan. 1, 2018.)*

§ 6453. Enforcement of Canadian domestic violence protection order by tribunal

(a) A tribunal of this state may issue an order enforcing or refusing to enforce a Canadian domestic violence protection order on application of any of the following:

(1) A protected party or other person authorized by law of this state other than this part to seek enforcement of a domestic protection order.

(2) A respondent.

(b) In a proceeding under subdivision (a), the tribunal of this state shall follow the procedures of this state for enforcement of a domestic protection order. An order entered under this section is limited to the enforcement of the terms of the Canadian domestic violence protection order as described in subdivision (a) of Section 6451.

(c) A Canadian domestic violence protection order is enforceable under this section if all of the following apply:

(1) The order identifies a protected individual and a respondent.

(2) The order is valid and in effect.

(3) The issuing court had jurisdiction over the parties and the subject matter under law applicable in the issuing court.

(4) The order was issued after either of the following:

(A) The respondent was given reasonable notice and had an opportunity to be heard before the court issued the order.

(B) In the case of an ex parte order, the respondent was given reasonable notice and had or will have an opportunity to be heard within a reasonable time after the order was issued, in a manner consistent with the right of the respondent to due process.

(d) A Canadian domestic violence protection order valid on its face is prima facie evidence of its enforceability under this section.

(e) A claim that a Canadian domestic violence protection order does not comply with subdivision (c) is an affirmative defense in a proceeding seeking enforcement of the order. If the tribunal of this state determines that the order is not enforceable, the tribunal of this state shall issue an order that the Canadian domestic violence protection order is not enforceable under this section and Section 6452 and may not be registered under Section 6454.

(f) This section applies to enforcement of a provision of a Canadian domestic violence protection order against a party to the order in which each party is a protected individual and respondent only if both of the following apply:

(1) The party seeking enforcement of the order filed a pleading requesting the order from the issuing court.

(2) The court made detailed findings of fact indicating that both parties acted as a primary aggressor and that neither party acted primarily in self-defense. *(Added by Stats.2017, c. 98 (S.B.204), § 1, eff. Jan. 1, 2018.)*

§ 6454. Registration of Canadian domestic violence protection order

(a) An individual may register a Canadian domestic violence protection order in this state. To register the order, the individual must present a certified copy of the order to a court of this state to be entered into the Domestic Violence Restraining Order System established under Section 6380, pursuant to procedures set forth in Section 6404.

(b) A fee may not be charged for the registration of a Canadian domestic violence protection order under this section.

(c) Registration in this state or filing under law of this state other than this part of a Canadian domestic violence protection order is not required for its enforcement under this part. *(Added by Stats.2017, c. 98 (S.B.204), § 1, eff. Jan. 1, 2018.)*

§ 6455. Immunity

(a) There shall be no civil liability on the part of, and no cause of action for false arrest or false imprisonment against, a law enforcement officer who makes an arrest pursuant to a Canadian domestic violence protection order that is regular upon its face, if the law enforcement officer, in making the arrest, acts in good faith and has reasonable cause to believe that the person against whom the order is issued has notice of the order and has committed an act in violation of the order.

(b) Nothing in this section shall be deemed to exonerate a law enforcement officer from liability for the unreasonable use of force in the enforcement of the order. The immunities afforded by this section shall not affect the availability of any other immunity that may apply, including, but not limited to, Sections 820.2 and 820.4 of the Government Code. *(Added by Stats.2017, c. 98 (S.B.204), § 1, eff. Jan. 1, 2018.)*

§ 6456. Other remedies

An individual who seeks a remedy under this part may seek other legal or equitable remedies. *(Added by Stats.2017, c. 98 (S.B.204), § 1, eff. Jan. 1, 2018.)*

§ 6457. Multiple protective orders; priority of enforcement

If there is more than one order issued and one of the orders is an emergency protective order that has precedence in enforcement pursuant to paragraph (1) of subdivision (c) of Section 136.2 of the Penal Code, the law enforcement officer shall enforce the emergency protective order. If there is more than one order issued, none of the orders issued is an emergency protective order that has precedence in enforcement, and one of the orders issued is a no-contact order, as described in Section 6320, the law enforcement officer shall enforce the no-contact order. If there is more than one civil order regarding the same parties and neither an emergency protective order that has precedence in enforcement nor a no-contact order has been issued, the law enforcement officer shall enforce the order that was issued last. If there are both civil and criminal orders regarding the same parties and neither an emergency protective order that has precedence in enforcement nor a no-contact order has been issued, the law enforcement officer shall enforce the criminal order issued last. *(Added by Stats.2017, c. 98 (S.B.204), § 1, eff. Jan. 1, 2018.)*

§ 6458. Relation to Electronic Signatures in Global and National Commerce Act

This part modifies, limits, or supersedes the federal Electronic Signatures in Global and National Commerce Act (15 U.S.C. Sec. 7001 et seq.), but does not modify, limit, or supersede Section 101(c) of that act (15 U.S.C. Sec. 7001(c)), or authorize electronic delivery of any of the notices described in Section 103(b) of that act (15 U.S.C. Sec. 7003(b)). *(Added by Stats.2017, c. 98 (S.B.204), § 1, eff. Jan. 1, 2018.)*

§ 6459. Transition

This part applies to a Canadian domestic violence protection order issued before, on, or after January 1, 2018, and to a continuing action for enforcement of a Canadian domestic violence protection order commenced before, on, or after January 1, 2018. A request for enforcement of a Canadian domestic violence protection order made on or after January 1, 2018, for a violation of the order occurring before, on, or after January 1, 2018, is governed by this part. *(Added by Stats.2017, c. 98 (S.B.204), § 1, eff. Jan. 1, 2018.)*

§ 6460. Severability

If any provision of this part or its application to any person or circumstance is held invalid, the invalidity does not affect other provisions or applications of this part that can be given effect without the invalid provision or application, and to this end the provisions of this part are severable. *(Added by Stats.2017, c. 98 (S.B.204), § 1, eff. Jan. 1, 2018.)*

Division 11

MINORS

Part 1

AGE OF MAJORITY

§ 6500. "Minor" defined

A minor is an individual who is under 18 years of age. The period of minority is calculated from the first minute of the day on which the individual is born to the same minute of the corresponding day completing the period of minority. *(Stats. 1992, c. 162 (A.B.2650), § 10, operative Jan. 1, 1994.)*

Law Revision Commission Comments

Enactment [Revised Comment]

The first sentence of Section 6500 restates former Civil Code Section 25 without substantive change. The second sentence continues former Civil Code Section 26 without substantive change. The word "individual" has been substituted for "persons." This is not a substantive change. See also Sections 7002 (conditions for emancipation), 7050 (emancipated minor considered an adult). [23 Cal. L.Rev.Comm. Reports 1 (1993)].

Research References

Forms

California Practice Guide: Rutter Family Law Forms Form 1:32, Glossary Of Common Family Law Terms, Phrases and Concepts (Enclosure to Form 1:31).
California Transactions Forms--Business Entities § 5:103, Voting Rights--Administrator, Executor, Guardian, or Conservator.
Cal. Transaction Forms - Bus. Transactions § 6:9, Parties Who May Contract.
Cal. Transaction Forms - Bus. Transactions § 6:10, Minors.
Cal. Transaction Forms - Bus. Transactions § 8:53, Model Release for Images Included in Website.
Cal. Transaction Forms - Bus. Transactions § 17:25, Minors.
California Transactions Forms--Estate Planning § 2:5, Necessity Of Privity Between Estate Planner and Ultimate Beneficiary.
California Transactions Forms--Estate Planning § 1:29, Options Involving Gifts to Minors.
California Transactions Forms--Estate Planning § 6:15, Minors' Capacity to Take Devised Property.
California Transactions Forms--Estate Planning § 6:53, Matters to Consider in Drafting Gifts to Minors.
California Transactions Forms--Estate Planning § 11:39, General Considerations.
California Transactions Forms--Estate Planning § 11:48, Governing Contractual Provisions [CC §§ 1550 et seq., Fam C S721(B)].
California Transactions Forms--Estate Planning § 18:53, Irrevocable Asset Protection Discretionary Trust for Children With Spendthrift Provisions.
California Transactions Forms--Family Law § 1:2, Nature and Advantages Of Agreement.
California Transactions Forms--Family Law § 2:63, Authority for Child Support.
California Transactions Forms--Family Law § 3:53, Sample Basic Custody Provisions.
Am. Jur. Pl. & Pr. Forms Infants § 1, Introductory Comments.

Treatises and Practice Aids

Witkin, California Summary 10th Contracts § 26, Age Of Majority: 18 Years.
Witkin, California Summary 10th Husband and Wife § 3, Statutory Framework.
Witkin, California Summary 10th Parent and Child § 63, in General.
Witkin, California Summary 10th Parent and Child § 311, Other Proceedings Stayed.
Witkin, California Summary 10th Parent and Child § 419, in General.
Witkin, California Summary 10th Torts § 1256, Signer Of Driver's License.

§ 6501. "Adult" defined

An adult is an individual who is 18 years of age or older. *(Stats.1992, c. 162 (A.B.2650), § 10, operative Jan. 1, 1994.)*

Law Revision Commission Comments

Enactment [Revised Comment]

Section 6501 restates former Civil Code Section 27 without substantive change. The word "individual" has been substituted for "persons." This is not a substantive change. See also Sections 7002 (conditions for emancipation), 7050 (emancipated minor considered an adult). [23 Cal.L.Rev.Comm. Reports 1 (1993)].

Research References

Forms

Cal. Transaction Forms - Bus. Transactions § 6:10, Minors.
California Transactions Forms--Estate Planning § 6:17, Guardian Of Estate or Of Property.

§ 6502. Transitional provisions

(a) The use of or reference to the words "age of majority," "age of minority," "adult," "minor," or words of similar intent in any instrument, order, transfer, or governmental communication made in this state:

(1) Before March 4, 1972, makes reference to individuals 21 years of age and older, or younger than 21 years of age.

(2) On or after March 4, 1972, makes reference to individuals 18 years of age and older, or younger than 18 years of age.

(b) Nothing in subdivision (a) or in Chapter 1748 of the Statutes of 1971 prevents amendment of any court order, will, trust, contract, transfer, or instrument to refer to the 18-year-old age of majority if the court order, will, trust, contract, transfer, or instrument satisfies all of the following conditions:

(1) It was in existence on March 4, 1972.

(2) It is subject to amendment by law, and amendment is allowable or not prohibited by its terms.

(3) It is otherwise subject to the laws of this state. *(Stats.1992, c. 162 (A.B.2650), § 10, operative Jan. 1, 1994.)*

Law Revision Commission Comments

Enactment [Revised Comment]

Section 6502 continues former Civil Code Section 25.1 without substantive change. The word "individual" has been substituted for "persons." This is not a substantive change. [23 Cal.L.Rev.Comm. Reports 1 (1993)].

Research References

Forms

California Transactions Forms--Business Entities § 5:103, Voting Rights--Administrator, Executor, Guardian, or Conservator.
Cal. Transaction Forms - Bus. Transactions § 6:10, Minors.

Treatises and Practice Aids

Witkin, California Summary 10th Contracts § 26, Age Of Majority: 18 Years.
Witkin, California Summary 10th Parent and Child § 419, in General.

Part 1.5

CAREGIVERS

§ 6550. Authorization affidavits; scope of authority; reliance on affidavit

(a) A caregiver's authorization affidavit that meets the requirements of this part authorizes a caregiver 18 years of age or older who completes items 1 to 4, inclusive, of the affidavit provided in Section 6552 and signs the affidavit to enroll a minor in school and consent to school-related medical care on behalf of the minor. A caregiver who is a relative and who completes items 1 to 8, inclusive, of the affidavit provided in Section 6552 and signs the affidavit shall have the same rights to authorize medical care and dental care for the minor that are given to guardians under Section 2353 of the Probate Code. The medical care authorized by this caregiver who is a relative may include mental health treatment subject to the limitations of Section 2356 of the Probate Code.

(b) The decision of a caregiver to consent to or to refuse medical or dental care for a minor shall be superseded by any contravening decision of the parent or other person having legal custody of the minor, provided the decision of the parent or other person having legal custody of the minor does not jeopardize the life, health, or safety of the minor.

(c) A person who acts in good faith reliance on a caregiver's authorization affidavit to provide medical or dental care, without actual knowledge of facts contrary to those stated on the affidavit, is not subject to criminal liability or to civil liability to any person, and is not subject to professional disciplinary action, for that reliance if the applicable portions of the affidavit are completed. This subdivision applies even if medical or dental care is provided to a minor in contravention of the wishes of the parent or other person having legal custody of the minor as long as the person providing the medical or dental care has no actual knowledge of the wishes of the parent or other person having legal custody of the minor.

(d) A person who relies on the affidavit has no obligation to make any further inquiry or investigation.

(e) Nothing in this section relieves any individual from liability for violations of other provisions of law.

(f) If the minor stops living with the caregiver, the caregiver shall notify any school, health care provider, or health care service plan that has been given the affidavit. The affidavit is invalid after the school, health care provider, or health care service plan receives notice that the minor is no longer living with the caregiver.

(g) A caregiver's authorization affidavit shall be invalid, unless it substantially contains, in not less than 10–point boldface type or a reasonable equivalent thereof, the warning statement beginning with the word "warning" specified in Section 6552. The warning statement shall be enclosed in a box with 3–point rule lines.

(h) For purposes of this part, the following terms have the following meanings:

(1) "Person" includes an individual, corporation, partnership, association, the state, or any city, county, city and county, or other public entity or governmental subdivision or agency, or any other legal entity.

(2) "Relative" means a spouse, parent, stepparent, brother, sister, stepbrother, stepsister, half brother, half sister, uncle, aunt, niece, nephew, first cousin, or any person denoted by the prefix "grand" or "great," or the spouse of any of the persons specified in this definition, even after the marriage has been terminated by death or dissolution.

(3) "School-related medical care" means medical care that is required by state or local governmental authority as a condition for school enrollment, including immunizations, physical examinations, and medical examinations conducted in schools for pupils. *(Added by Stats.1994, c. 98 (S.B.592), § 4 eff. June 6, 1994. Amended by Stats.1996, c. 563 (S.B.392), § 1.5; Stats.2004, c. 895 (A.B.2855), § 12.)*

Research References

Forms

West's California Code Forms, Family § 6550, Comment Overview--Authorization Affidavits.
West's California Code Forms, Family § 6900, Comment Overview--Consent by Person Having Care Of Minor Of Consent by Court.
West's California Code Forms, Family § 6552 Form 1, Caregiver's Authorization Affidavit.

West's California Judicial Council Forms GC-205, Guardianship Pamphlet.

§ 6552. Form of authorization affidavit

The caregiver's authorization affidavit shall be in substantially the following form:

Caregiver's Authorization Affidavit

Use of this affidavit is authorized by Part 1.5 (commencing with Section 6550) of Division 11 of the California Family Code.

Instructions: Completion of items 1–4 and the signing of the affidavit is sufficient to authorize enrollment of a minor in school and authorize school-related medical care. Completion of items 5–8 is additionally required to authorize any other medical care. Print clearly.

The minor named below lives in my home and I am 18 years of age or older.

1. Name of minor: ________________

2. Minor's birth date: ________________

3. My name (adult giving authorization): ________________

4. My home address: ________________

____

____

5. ☐ I am a grandparent, aunt, uncle, or other qualified relative of the minor (see back of this form for a definition of "qualified relative").

6. Check one or both (for example, if one parent was advised and the other cannot be located):

☐ I have advised the parent(s) or other person(s) having legal custody of the minor of my intent to authorize medical care, and have received no objection.

☐ I am unable to contact the parent(s) or other person(s) having legal custody of the minor at this time, to notify them of my intended authorization.

7. My date of birth: ________________

8. My California driver's license or identification card number: ________________

Warning: Do not sign this form if any of the statements above are incorrect, or you will be committing a crime punishable by a fine, imprisonment, or both.

I declare under penalty of perjury under the laws of the State of California that the foregoing is true and correct.
Dated: ____________ Signed: ____________

Notices:

1. This declaration does not affect the rights of the minor's parents or legal guardian regarding the care, custody, and control of the minor, and does not mean that the caregiver has legal custody of the minor.

2. A person who relies on this affidavit has no obligation to make any further inquiry or investigation.

Additional Information:

TO CAREGIVERS:

1. "Qualified relative," for purposes of item 5, means a spouse, parent, stepparent, brother, sister, stepbrother, stepsister, half brother, half sister, uncle, aunt, niece, nephew, first cousin, or any person denoted by the prefix "grand" or "great," or the spouse of any of the persons specified in this definition, even after the marriage has been terminated by death or dissolution.

2. The law may require you, if you are not a relative or a currently licensed, certified, or approved foster parent, to obtain resource family approval pursuant to Section 1517 of the Health and Safety Code or Section 16519.5 of the Welfare and Institutions Code in order to care for a minor. If you have any questions, please contact your local department of social services.

3. If the minor stops living with you, you are required to notify any school, health care provider, or health care service plan to which you have given this affidavit. The affidavit is invalid after the school, health care provider, or health care service plan receives notice that the minor no longer lives with you.

4. If you do not have the information requested in item 8 (California driver's license or I.D.), provide another form of identification such as your social security number or Medi–Cal number.

TO SCHOOL OFFICIALS:

1. Section 48204 of the Education Code provides that this affidavit constitutes a sufficient basis for a determination of residency of the minor, without the requirement of a guardianship or other custody order, unless the school district determines from actual facts that the minor is not living with the caregiver.

2. The school district may require additional reasonable evidence that the caregiver lives at the address provided in item 4.

TO HEALTH CARE PROVIDERS AND HEALTH CARE SERVICE PLANS:

1. A person who acts in good faith reliance upon a caregiver's authorization affidavit to provide medical or dental care, without actual knowledge of facts contrary to those stated on the affidavit, is not subject to criminal liability

or to civil liability to any person, and is not subject to professional disciplinary action, for that reliance if the applicable portions of the form are completed.

2. This affidavit does not confer dependency for health care coverage purposes. *(Added by Stats.1994, c. 98 (S.B.592), § 4, eff. June 6, 1994. Amended by Stats.1994, c. 1269 (A.B.2208), § 50.6; Stats.2004, c. 895 (A.B.2855), § 13; Stats.2016, c. 612 (A.B.1997), § 6, eff. Jan. 1, 2017.)*

Research References

Forms

West's California Code Forms, Family § 6550, Comment Overview--Authorization Affidavits.
West's California Code Forms, Family § 6552 Form 1, Caregiver's Authorization Affidavit.
West's California Code Forms, Family § 6910 Form 2, Authorization by Parent to Allow Another Person to Consent to Minor's Medical Care.

Part 2

RIGHTS AND LIABILITIES; CIVIL ACTIONS AND PROCEEDINGS

§ 6600. Minors; civil liability

A minor is civilly liable for a wrong done by the minor, but is not liable in exemplary damages unless at the time of the act the minor was capable of knowing that the act was wrongful. *(Stats.1992, c. 162 (A.B.2650), § 10, operative Jan. 1, 1994.)*

Law Revision Commission Comments

Enactment [Revised Comment]

Section 6600 continues without substantive change the part of former Civil Code Section 41 that related to minors. The part of the former section that related to persons of unsound mind is continued in new Civil Code Section 41. [23 Cal.L.Rev.Comm. Reports 1 (1993)].

Research References

Forms

California Transactions Forms--Estate Planning § 1:29, Options Involving Gifts to Minors.

Treatises and Practice Aids

Witkin, California Summary 10th Torts § 25, Minors.
Witkin, California Summary 10th Torts § 1580, in General.

§ 6601. Enforcement of minor's rights

A minor may enforce the minor's rights by civil action or other legal proceedings in the same manner as an adult, except that a guardian must conduct the action or proceedings. *(Stats.1992, c. 162 (A.B.2650), § 10, operative Jan. 1, 1994.)*

Law Revision Commission Comments

Enactment [Revised Comment]

Section 6601 continues former Civil Code Section 42 without substantive change. See Code Civ. Proc. §§ 372 (minor must appear either by a guardian of the estate or by a guardian ad litem), 373 (appointment of guardian ad litem to represent interest of minor); Lab. Code §§ 5307.5, 5408 (appointment of trustee or guardian ad litem to represent minor in workers' compensation proceeding); Prob. Code §§ 1003 (appointment of guardian ad litem to represent interest of minor in proceeding under Probate Code), 2462 (representation by guardian of estate in actions and proceedings), 2500–2507 (compromise of claims, actions, and proceedings by guardian), 3500, 3600–3603 (compromise by parent of minor's disputed claim). For related provisions concerning emancipated minors, see Sections 7002 (conditions of emancipation), 7050(e)(4) (emancipated minor may sue in own name), 7050(e)(5) (emancipated minor may compromise claim). [23 Cal.L.Rev.Comm. Reports 1 (1993)].

Research References

Forms

West's California Code Forms, Family § 7500, Comment Overview--Rights Of Parents.

Treatises and Practice Aids

Witkin, California Summary 10th Contracts § 49, Parent's Agreement to Arbitrate.

§ 6602. Approval of contract for attorney's fees for minor; fees in absence of contract

A contract for attorney's fees for services in litigation, made by or on behalf of a minor, is void unless the contract is approved, on petition by an interested person, by the court in which the litigation is pending or by the court having jurisdiction of the guardianship estate of the minor. If the contract is not approved and a judgment is recovered by or on behalf of the minor, the attorney's fees chargeable against the minor shall be fixed by the court rendering the judgment. *(Stats.1992, c. 162 (A.B.2650), § 10, operative Jan. 1, 1994.)*

Law Revision Commission Comments

Enactment [Revised Comment]

Section 6602 continues former Probate Code Section 3302 without substantive change. For related provisions concerning emancipated minors, see Sections 7002 (conditions of emancipation), 7050(e)(2) (emancipated minor may enter binding contract), 7050(e)(4) (emancipated minor may sue in own name), 7050(e)(5) (emancipated minor may compromise claim). [23 Cal.L.Rev.Comm. Reports 1 (1993)].

Research References

Treatises and Practice Aids

Witkin, California Summary 10th Contracts § 35, Contract for Attorneys' Fees.

Part 3

CONTRACTS

CHAPTER 1. CAPACITY TO CONTRACT

§ 6700. Authority to contract

Except as provided in Section 6701, a minor may make a contract in the same manner as an adult, subject to the power of disaffirmance under Chapter 2 (commencing with Section 6710), and subject to Part 1 (commencing with Section 300) of Division 3 (validity of marriage). *(Stats.1992, c. 162 (A.B.2650), § 10, operative Jan. 1, 1994.)*

Law Revision Commission Comments

Enactment [Revised Comment]

Section 6700 restates former Civil Code Section 34 without substantive change. The former reference to the repealed title on master and servant has been omitted as obsolete. For related provisions concerning emancipated minors, see Sections 7002 (conditions of emancipation), 7050(e)(2) (emancipated minor may enter binding contract). [23 Cal.L.Rev.Comm. Reports 1 (1993)].

Research References

Forms

Cal. Transaction Forms - Bus. Transactions § 6:10, Minors.
Cal. Transaction Forms - Bus. Transactions § 17:25, Minors.

Treatises and Practice Aids

Witkin, California Summary 10th Contracts § 31, Statutory Right and Methods.

§ 6701. Restrictions on authority to contract

A minor cannot do any of the following:

(a) Give a delegation of power.

(b) Make a contract relating to real property or any interest therein.

(c) Make a contract relating to any personal property not in the immediate possession or control of the minor. *(Stats. 1992, c. 162 (A.B.2650), § 10, operative Jan. 1, 1994.)*

Law Revision Commission Comments

Enactment [Revised Comment]

Section 6701 continues former Civil Code Section 33 without substantive change. For related provisions concerning emancipated minors, see Sections 7002 (conditions of emancipation), 7050(e)(2) (emancipated minor may make binding contract or delegation), 7050(e)(3) (emancipated minor may convey real or personal property). [23 Cal.L.Rev.Comm. Reports 1 (1993)].

Research References

Forms

Cal. Transaction Forms - Bus. Transactions § 6:10, Minors.
Cal. Transaction Forms - Bus. Transactions § 6:11, Void Contracts Of Minors.
Cal. Transaction Forms - Bus. Transactions § 6:12, Voidable Contracts Of Minors.
Cal. Transaction Forms - Bus. Transactions § 15:5, Qualifications.
Cal. Transaction Forms - Bus. Transactions § 17:25, Minors.

Treatises and Practice Aids

Witkin, California Summary 10th Agency and Employment § 89, in General.
Witkin, California Summary 10th Contracts § 28, Delegation Of Power.
Witkin, California Summary 10th Contracts § 29, Contract Relating to Real Property.
Witkin, California Summary 10th Contracts § 30, Other Void Contracts.
Witkin, California Summary 10th Parent and Child § 301, Contracts, Ownership, and Litigation.
Witkin, California Summary 10th Sales § 233, Illustrations.

CHAPTER 2. DISAFFIRMANCE OF CONTRACTS

§ 6710. Right of disaffirmance

Except as otherwise provided by statute, a contract of a minor may be disaffirmed by the minor before majority or within a reasonable time afterwards or, in case of the minor's death within that period, by the minor's heirs or personal representative. *(Stats.1992, c. 162 (A.B.2650), § 10, operative Jan. 1, 1994.)*

Law Revision Commission Comments

Enactment [Revised Comment]

Section 6710 continues former Civil Code Section 35 without substantive change. "Except as otherwise provided by statute" has been substituted for the specific sections referred to in the introductory clause of the former section. For exceptions to the right of disaffirmance, see Sections 6711 (contract made under express statutory authority), 6712 (contracts for necessaries), 6713 (protection of good faith purchaser), 6751 (contract in arts, entertainment, or professional sports approved by court), 6921 (consent given by minor to medical or dental care). For related provisions concerning emancipated minors, sections 7002 (conditions for emancipation), 7050(e)(2) (emancipated minor may enter binding contract). [23 Cal.L.Rev.Comm. Reports 1 (1993)].

Commentary

Berg v. Traylor, 148 Cal.App.4th 809, 56 Cal.Rptr.3d 140 (2007), held that, under this section, a child actor could disaffirm a contract the child made with a personal manager, because a personal management contract with a minor for the purpose of advancing his career cannot be considered a contract for the provision of necessaries within the meaning of section 6712. However, the minor's adult mother remained liable for her obligations under the contract.

Research References

Forms

Cal. Transaction Forms - Bus. Transactions § 6:10, Minors.
Cal. Transaction Forms - Bus. Transactions § 6:12, Voidable Contracts Of Minors.
Cal. Transaction Forms - Bus. Transactions § 17:25, Minors.
West's California Code Forms, Family § 6710, Comment Overview--Right Of Disaffirmance.
West's California Code Forms, Family § 6710 Form 1, Notice Of Disaffirmance Of Contract Made by Minor.
West's California Code Forms, Family § 6710 Form 2, Complaint by Minor to Recover Consideration Paid Under Contract Subsequently Disaffirmed.

Treatises and Practice Aids

Witkin, California Summary 10th Contracts § 31, Statutory Right and Methods.
Witkin, California Summary 10th Contracts § 32, No Need to Restore Consideration.
Witkin, California Summary 10th Contracts § 49, Parent's Agreement to Arbitrate.
Witkin, California Summary 10th Sales § 233, Illustrations.

§ 6711. Obligations entered into under express statutory authority

A minor cannot disaffirm an obligation, otherwise valid, entered into by the minor under the express authority or direction of a statute. *(Stats.1992, c. 162 (A.B.2650), § 10, operative Jan. 1, 1994.)*

Law Revision Commission Comments

Enactment [Revised Comment]

Section 6711 continues former Civil Code Section 37 without substantive change. [23 Cal.L.Rev.Comm. Reports 1 (1993)].

Research References

Forms

Cal. Transaction Forms - Bus. Transactions § 6:13, Contracts Enforceable Against Minors.
Cal. Transaction Forms - Bus. Transactions § 6:10, Minors.
West's California Code Forms, Family § 6710, Comment Overview--Right Of Disaffirmance.

Treatises and Practice Aids

Witkin, California Summary 10th Contracts § 47, Miscellaneous Contracts.

§ 6712. Contracts minors cannot disaffirm; conditions

A contract, otherwise valid, entered into during minority, may not be disaffirmed on that ground either during the actual minority of the person entering into the contract, or at any time thereafter, if all of the following requirements are satisfied:

(a) The contract is to pay the reasonable value of things necessary for the support of the minor or the minor's family.

(b) These things have been actually furnished to the minor or to the minor's family.

(c) The contract is entered into by the minor when not under the care of a parent or guardian able to provide for the minor or the minor's family. *(Stats.1992, c. 162 (A.B.2650), § 10, operative Jan. 1, 1994.)*

Law Revision Commission Comments

Enactment [Revised Comment]

Section 6712 continues former Civil Code Section 36(a)(1) without substantive change. For related provisions concerning emancipated minors, see Sections 7002 (conditions for emancipation), 7050(e)(2) (emancipated minor may enter binding contract). [23 Cal.L.Rev. Comm. Reports 1 (1993)].

Commentary

Berg v. Traylor, 148 Cal.App.4th 809, 56 Cal.Rptr.3d 140 (2007), held that, under section 1610, a child actor could disaffirm a contract the child made with a personal manager, because a personal management contract with a minor for the purpose of advancing his career cannot be considered a contract for the provision of necessaries within the meaning of this section. However, the minor's adult mother remained liable for her obligations under the contract.

Research References

Forms

Cal. Transaction Forms - Bus. Transactions § 6:13, Contracts Enforceable Against Minors.
California Transactions Forms--Estate Planning § 1:29, Options Involving Gifts to Minors.
West's California Code Forms, Family § 6710, Comment Overview--Right Of Disaffirmance.

Treatises and Practice Aids

Witkin, California Summary 10th Contracts § 34, Contract for Necessaries.

§ 6713. Recovery from good faith purchaser

If, before the contract of a minor is disaffirmed, goods the minor has sold are transferred to another purchaser who bought them in good faith for value and without notice of the transferor's defect of title, the minor cannot recover the goods from an innocent purchaser. *(Stats.1992, c. 162 (A.B.2650), § 10, operative Jan. 1, 1994.)*

Law Revision Commission Comments

Enactment [Revised Comment]

Section 6713 continues former Civil Code Section 35a without substantive change. For related provisions concerning emancipated minors, see Sections 7002 (conditions for emancipation), 7050(e)(2) (emancipated minor may enter binding contract). [23 Cal.L.Rev. Comm. Reports 1 (1993)].

Research References

Forms

Cal. Transaction Forms - Bus. Transactions § 6:13, Contracts Enforceable Against Minors.
Cal. Transaction Forms - Bus. Transactions § 6:10, Minors.
California Transactions Forms--Family Law § 7:72, Parentage.
West's California Code Forms, Family § 6710, Comment Overview--Right Of Disaffirmance.
West's California Code Forms, Family § 6713 Form 1, Affirmative Defense--Goods Not Recoverable from Innocent Purchaser.

Treatises and Practice Aids

Witkin, California Summary 10th Contracts § 33, No Recovery from Bona Fide Purchaser.
Witkin, California Summary 10th Sales § 233, Illustrations.

CHAPTER 3. CONTRACTS IN ART, ENTERTAINMENT, AND PROFESSIONAL SPORTS

§ 6750. Application of chapter

(a) This chapter applies to the following contracts entered into between an unemancipated minor and any third party or parties on or after January 1, 2000:

(1) A contract pursuant to which a minor is employed or agrees to render artistic or creative services, either directly or through a third party, including, but not limited to, a personal services corporation (loan–out company), or through a casting agency. "Artistic or creative services" includes, but is not limited to, services as an actor, actress, dancer, musician, comedian, singer, stunt-person, voice-over artist, or other performer or entertainer, or as a songwriter, musical producer or arranger, writer, director, producer, production executive, choreographer, composer, conductor, or designer.

(2) A contract pursuant to which a minor agrees to purchase, or otherwise secure, sell, lease, license, or otherwise dispose of literary, musical, or dramatic properties, or use of a person's likeness, voice recording, performance, or story of or incidents in his or her life, either tangible or intangible, or any rights therein for use in motion pictures, television, the production of sound recordings in any format now known or hereafter devised, the legitimate or living stage, or otherwise in the entertainment field.

(3) A contract pursuant to which a minor is employed or agrees to render services as a participant or player in a sport.

(b)(1) If a minor is employed or agrees to render services directly for any person or entity, that person or entity shall be considered the minor's employer for purposes of this chapter.

(2) If a minor's services are being rendered through a third-party individual or personal services corporation (loan–out company), the person to whom or entity to which that third party is providing the minor's services shall be considered the minor's employer for purposes of this chapter.

(3) If a minor renders services as an extra, background performer, or in a similar capacity through an agency or service that provides one or more of those performers for a fee (casting agency), the agency or service shall be considered the minor's employer for the purposes of this chapter.

(c)(1) For purposes of this chapter, the minor's "gross earnings" shall mean the total compensation payable to the minor under the contract or, if the minor's services are being rendered through a third-party individual or personal services corporation (loan–out company), the total compensation payable to that third party for the services of the minor.

(2) Notwithstanding paragraph (1), with respect to contracts pursuant to which a minor is employed or agrees to render services as a musician, singer, songwriter, musical producer, or arranger only, for purposes of this chapter, the minor's "gross earnings" shall mean the total amount paid to the minor pursuant to the contract, including the payment of any advances to the minor pursuant to the contract, but excluding deductions to offset those advances or other expenses incurred by the employer pursuant to the contract, or, if the minor's services are being rendered through a third-party individual or personal services corporation (loan–out company), the total amount payable to that third party for the services of the minor. *(Stats.1992, c. 162 (A.B.2650), § 10, operative Jan. 1, 1994. Amended by Stats.1999, c. 940 (S.B.1162), § 2; Stats.2003, c. 667 (S.B.210), § 1.)*

Law Revision Commission Comments

Enactment [Revised Comment]

Section 6750 continues without substantive change the first part of subdivision (a)(2)(A), subdivision (a)(2)(B), and the first part of subdivision (a)(3) of former Civil Code Section 36. References to "agreement" have been omitted as surplus. See Civ. Code § 1549 ("contract" defined). See also Lab. Code § 1700.37 (limitation on minor's right to disaffirm contract with licensed talent agency). [23 Cal.L.Rev.Comm. Reports 1 (1993)].

Research References

Forms

Cal. Transaction Forms - Bus. Transactions § 10:8, Employment Of Minors.
Cal. Transaction Forms - Bus. Transactions § 8:53, Model Release for Images Included in Website.
West's California Code Forms, Family § 6710, Comment Overview--Right Of Disaffirmance.
West's California Code Forms, Family § 6751, Comment Overview--Minor's Employment Contract.

Treatises and Practice Aids

Witkin, California Summary 10th Community Property § 10, Current Law.
Witkin, California Summary 10th Contracts § 36, Scope Of Statute.
Witkin, California Summary 10th Contracts § 37, Court Approval.
Witkin, California Summary 10th Parent and Child § 296, in General.

§ 6751. Disaffirmance of contracts approved by court

(a) A contract, otherwise valid, of a type described in Section 6750, entered into during minority, cannot be disaffirmed on that ground either during the minority of the person entering into the contract, or at any time thereafter, if the contract has been approved by the superior court in any county in which the minor resides or is employed or in which any party to the contract has its principal office in this state for the transaction of business.

(b) Approval of the court may be given on petition of any party to the contract, after such reasonable notice to all other parties to the contract as is fixed by the court, with opportunity to such other parties to appear and be heard.

(c) Approval of the court given under this section extends to the whole of the contract and all of its terms and provisions, including, but not limited to, any optional or conditional provisions contained in the contract for extension, prolongation, or termination of the term of the contract.

(d) For the purposes of any proceeding under this chapter, a parent or legal guardian, as the case may be, entitled to the physical custody, care, and control of the minor at the time of the proceeding shall be considered the minor's guardian ad litem for the proceeding, unless the court shall determine that appointment of a different individual as guardian ad litem is required in the best interests of the minor. *(Stats.1992, c. 162 (A.B.2650), § 10, operative Jan. 1, 1994. Amended by Stats. 1999, c. 940 (S.B.1162), § 3.)*

Law Revision Commission Comments

Enactment [Revised Comment]

Section 6751 continues without substantive change the introductory part of subdivision (a), the last part of subdivision (a)(2)(A), the last part of subdivision (a)(3), and subdivision (b) of former Civil Code Section 36. References to "agreement" have been omitted as surplus. See Civ. Code § 1549 ("contract" defined). See also Lab. Code § 1700.37 (limitation on minor's right to disaffirm contract with licensed talent agency). For related provisions concerning emancipated minors, see Sections 7002 (conditions for emancipation), 7050(e)(2) (emancipated minor may enter binding contract). [23 Cal.L.Rev.Comm. Reports 1 (1993)].

Research References

Forms

Cal. Transaction Forms - Bus. Transactions § 6:13, Contracts Enforceable Against Minors.

Cal. Transaction Forms - Bus. Transactions § 10:8, Employment Of Minors.

Cal. Transaction Forms - Bus. Transactions § 6:10, Minors.

West's California Code Forms, Family § 6710, Comment Overview--Right Of Disaffirmance.

West's California Code Forms, Family § 6751, Comment Overview--Minor's Employment Contract.

West's California Code Forms, Family § 6751 Form 1, Petition by Employer for Approval Of Minor's Employment Contract.

Treatises and Practice Aids

Witkin, California Summary 10th Contracts § 36, Scope Of Statute.

Witkin, California Summary 10th Contracts § 37, Court Approval.

§ 6752. Providing copy of minor's birth certificate to other party; percentage of minor's gross earnings set aside in trust for minor's benefit; exceptions; trustee of funds; deposits or disbursements; The Actors' Fund of America as trustee of unclaimed set-aside funds; entitlement of beneficiary of such fund to imputed interest; forwarding of unclaimed funds to The Actors' Fund of America; application of Unclaimed Property Law

(a) A parent or guardian entitled to the physical custody, care, and control of a minor who enters into a contract of a type described in Section 6750 shall provide a certified copy of the minor's birth certificate indicating the minor's minority to the other party or parties to the contract and in addition, in the case of a guardian, a certified copy of the court document appointing the person as the minor's legal guardian.

(b)(1) Notwithstanding any other statute, in an order approving a minor's contract of a type described in Section 6750, the court shall require that 15 percent of the minor's gross earnings pursuant to the contract be set aside by the minor's employer, except an employer of a minor for services as an extra, background performer, or in a similar capacity, as described in paragraph (3) of subdivision (b) of Section 6750. These amounts shall be held in trust, in an account or other savings plan, and preserved for the benefit of the minor in accordance with Section 6753.

(2) The court shall require that at least one parent or legal guardian, as the case may be, entitled to the physical custody, care, and control of the minor at the time the order is issued be appointed as trustee of the funds ordered to be set aside in trust for the benefit of the minor, unless the court shall determine that appointment of a different individual, individuals, entity, or entities as trustee or trustees is required in the best interest of the minor.

(3) Within 10 business days after commencement of employment, the trustee or trustees of the funds ordered to be set aside in trust shall provide the minor's employer with a true and accurate photocopy of the trustee's statement pursuant to Section 6753. Upon presentation of the trustee's statement offered pursuant to this subdivision, the employer shall provide the parent or guardian with a written acknowledgment of receipt of the statement.

(4) The minor's employer shall deposit or disburse the 15 percent of the minor's gross earnings pursuant to the contract within 15 business days after receiving a true and accurate copy of the trustee's statement pursuant to subdivision (c) of Section 6753, a certified copy of the minor's birth certificate, and, in the case of a guardian, a certified copy of the court document appointing the person as the minor's guardian. Notwithstanding any other law, pending receipt of these documents, the minor's employer shall hold, for the benefit of the minor, the 15 percent of the minor's gross earnings pursuant to the contract. This paragraph does not apply to an employer of a minor for services as an extra, background performer, or in a similar capacity, as described in paragraph (3) of subdivision (b) of Section 6750.

(5) When making the initial deposit of funds, the minor's employer shall provide written notification to the financial institution or company that the funds are subject to Section 6753. Upon receipt of the court order, the minor's employer shall provide the financial institution with a copy of the order.

(6) Once the minor's employer deposits the set-aside funds pursuant to Section 6753, in trust, in an account or other savings plan, the minor's employer shall have no further obligation or duty to monitor or account for the funds. The trustee or trustees of the trust shall be the only individual, individuals, entity, or entities with the obligation or duty to monitor and account for those funds once they have been deposited by the minor's employer. The trustee or trustees shall do an annual accounting of the funds held in trust, in an account or other savings plan, in accordance with Sections 16062 and 16063 of the Probate Code.

(7) The court shall have continuing jurisdiction over the trust established pursuant to the order and may at any time, upon petition of the parent or legal guardian, the minor, through his or her guardian ad litem, or the trustee or trustees, on good cause shown, order that the trust be amended or terminated, notwithstanding the provisions of the declaration of trust. An order amending or terminating a trust may be made only after reasonable notice to the beneficiary and, if the beneficiary is then a minor, to the parent or guardian, if any, and to the trustee or trustees of the funds with opportunity for all parties to appear and be heard.

(8) A parent or guardian entitled to the physical custody, care, and control of the minor shall promptly notify the minor's employer in writing of any change in facts that affect the employer's obligation or ability to set aside the funds in accordance with the order, including, but not limited to, a change of financial institution or account number, or the existence of a new or amended order issued pursuant to paragraph (7) amending or terminating the employer's obli-

gations under this section. The written notification shall be accompanied by a true and accurate photocopy of the trustee's statement pursuant to Section 6753 and, if applicable, a true and accurate photocopy of the new or amended order.

(9)(A) If a parent, guardian, or trustee fails to provide the minor's employer with a true and accurate photocopy of the trustee's statement pursuant to Section 6753 within 180 days after the commencement of employment, the employer shall forward to The Actors' Fund of America 15 percent of the minor's gross earnings pursuant to the contract, together with the minor's name and, if known, the minor's social security number, birth date, last known address, telephone number, email address, dates of employment, and title of the project on which the minor was employed, and shall notify the parent, guardian, or trustee of that transfer by certified mail to the last known address. Upon receipt of those forwarded funds, The Actors' Fund of America shall become the trustee of those funds and the minor's employer shall have no further obligation or duty to monitor or account for the funds.

(B) The Actors' Fund of America shall make its best efforts to notify the parent, guardian, or trustee of their responsibilities to provide a true and accurate photocopy of the trustee's statement pursuant to Section 6753, and in the case of a guardian, a certified copy of the court document appointing the person as the minor's legal guardian. Within 15 business days after receiving those documents, The Actors' Fund of America shall deposit or disburse the funds as directed by the trustee's statement. When making that deposit or disbursal of the funds, The Actors' Fund of America shall provide to the financial institution notice that the funds are subject to Section 6753 and a copy of each applicable order, and shall thereafter have no further obligation or duty to monitor or account for the funds.

(C) The Actors' Fund of America shall notify each beneficiary of his or her entitlement to the funds that it holds for the beneficiary within 60 days after the date on which its records indicated that the beneficiary has attained 18 years of age or the date on which it received notice that the minor has been emancipated, by sending that notice to the last known address for the beneficiary or, if it has no specific separate address for the beneficiary, to the beneficiary's parent or guardian.

(c)(1) Notwithstanding any other statute, for any minor's contract of a type described in Section 6750 that is not being submitted for approval by the court pursuant to Section 6751, or for which the court has issued a final order denying approval, 15 percent of the minor's gross earnings pursuant to the contract shall be set aside by the minor's employer, except an employer of a minor for services as an extra, background performer, or in a similar capacity, as described in paragraph (3) of subdivision (b) of Section 6750. These amounts shall be held in trust, in an account or other savings plan, and preserved for the benefit of the minor in accordance with Section 6753. At least one parent or legal guardian, as the case may be, entitled to the physical custody, care, and control of the minor, shall be the trustee of the funds set aside for the benefit of the minor, unless the court, upon petition by the parent or legal guardian, the minor, through his or her guardian ad litem, or the trustee or trustees of the trust, shall determine that appointment of a different individual, individuals, entity, or entities as trustee or trustees is required in the best interest of the minor.

(2) Within 10 business days of commencement after employment, a parent or guardian, as the case may be, entitled to the physical custody, care, and control of the minor shall provide the minor's employer with a true and accurate photocopy of the trustee's statement pursuant to Section 6753 and in addition, in the case of a guardian, a certified copy of the court document appointing the person as the minor's legal guardian. Upon presentation of the trustee's statement offered pursuant to this subdivision, the employer shall provide the parent or guardian with a written acknowledgment of receipt of the statement.

(3) The minor's employer shall deposit 15 percent of the minor's gross earnings pursuant to the contract within 15 business days of receiving the trustee's statement pursuant to Section 6753, or if the court denies approval of the contract, within 15 business days of receiving a final order denying approval of the contract. Notwithstanding any other statute, pending receipt of the trustee's statement or the final court order, the minor's employer shall hold for the benefit of the minor the 15 percent of the minor's gross earnings pursuant to the contract. When making the initial deposit of funds, the minor's employer shall provide written notification to the financial institution or company that the funds are subject to Section 6753. This paragraph does not apply to an employer of a minor for services as an extra, background performer, or in a similar capacity, as described in paragraph (3) of subdivision (b) of Section 6750.

(4) Once the minor's employer deposits the set-aside funds in trust, in an account or other savings plan pursuant to Section 6753, the minor's employer shall have no further obligation or duty to monitor or account for the funds. The trustee or trustees of the trust shall be the only individual, individuals, entity, or entities with the obligation or duty to monitor and account for those funds once they have been deposited by the minor's employer. The trustee or trustees shall do an annual accounting of the funds held in trust, in an account or other savings plan, in accordance with Sections 16062 and 16063 of the Probate Code.

(5) Upon petition of the parent or legal guardian, the minor, through his or her guardian ad litem, or the trustee or trustees of the trust, to the superior court in any county in which the minor resides or in which the trust is established, the court may at any time, on good cause shown, order that the trust be amended or terminated, notwithstanding the provisions of the declaration of trust. An order amending or terminating a trust may be made only after reasonable notice to the beneficiary and, if the beneficiary is then a minor, to the parent or guardian, if any, and to the trustee or trustees of the funds with opportunity for all parties to appear and be heard.

(6) A parent or guardian entitled to the physical custody, care, and control of the minor shall promptly notify the minor's employer in writing of any change in facts that affect the employer's obligation or ability to set aside funds for the benefit of the minor in accordance with this section, including, but not limited to, a change of financial institution or account number, or the existence of a new or amended order issued pursuant to paragraph (5) amending or terminating

the employer's obligations under this section. The written notification shall be accompanied by a true and accurate photocopy of the trustee's statement and attachments pursuant to Section 6753 and, if applicable, a true and accurate photocopy of the new or amended order.

(7)(A) If a parent, guardian, or trustee fails to provide the minor's employer with a true and accurate photocopy of the trustee's statement pursuant to Section 6753, within 180 days after commencement of employment, the employer shall forward to The Actors' Fund of America the 15 percent of the minor's gross earnings pursuant to the contract, together with the minor's name and, if known, the minor's social security number, birth date, last known address, telephone number, email address, dates of employment, and the title of the project on which the minor was employed, and shall notify the parent, guardian, or trustee of that transfer by certified mail to the last known address. Upon receipt of those forwarded funds, The Actors' Fund of America shall become the trustee of those funds and the minor's employer shall have no further obligation or duty to monitor or account for the funds.

(B) The Actors' Fund of America shall make best efforts to notify the parent, guardian, or trustee of their responsibilities to provide a true and accurate photocopy of the trustee's statement pursuant to Section 6753 and in the case of a guardian, a certified copy of the court document appointing the person as the minor's legal guardian. After receiving those documents, The Actors' Fund of America shall deposit or disburse the funds as directed by the trustee's statement, and in accordance with Section 6753, within 15 business days. When making that deposit or disbursal of the funds, The Actors' Fund of America shall provide notice to the financial institution that the funds are subject to Section 6753, and shall thereafter have no further obligation or duty to monitor or account for the funds.

(C) The Actors' Fund of America shall notify each beneficiary of his or her entitlement to the funds that it holds for the beneficiary, within 60 days after the date on which its records indicate that the beneficiary has attained 18 years of age or the date on which it received notice that the minor has been emancipated, by sending that notice to the last known address that it has for the beneficiary, or to the beneficiary's parent or guardian, where it has no specific separate address for the beneficiary.

(d) Where a parent or guardian is entitled to the physical custody, care, and control of a minor who enters into a contract of a type described in Section 6750, the relationship between the parent or guardian and the minor is a fiduciary relationship that is governed by the law of trusts, whether or not a court has issued a formal order to that effect. The parent or guardian acting in his or her fiduciary relationship, shall, with the earnings and accumulations of the minor under the contract, pay all liabilities incurred by the minor under the contract, including, but not limited to, payments for taxes on all earnings, including taxes on the amounts set aside under subdivisions (b) and (c) of this section, and payments for personal or professional services rendered to the minor or the business related to the contract. Nothing in this subdivision shall be construed to alter any other existing responsibilities of a parent or legal guardian to provide for the support of a minor child.

(e)(1) Except as otherwise provided in this subdivision, The Actors' Fund of America, as trustee of unclaimed set-aside funds, shall manage and administer those funds in the same manner as a trustee under the Probate Code. Notwithstanding the foregoing, The Actors' Fund of America is not required to open separate, segregated individual trust accounts for each beneficiary but may hold the set-aside funds in a single, segregated master account for all beneficiaries, provided it maintains accounting records for each beneficiary's interest in the master account.

(2) The Actors' Fund of America shall have the right to transfer funds from the master account, or from a beneficiary's segregated account to its general account in an amount equal to the beneficiary's balance. The Actors' Fund of America shall have the right to use those funds transferred to its general account to provide programs and services for young performers. This use of the funds does not limit or alter The Actors' Fund of America's obligation to disburse the set-aside funds to the beneficiary, or the beneficiary's parent, guardian, trustee, or estate pursuant to this chapter.

(3)(A) Upon receiving a certified copy of the beneficiary's birth certificate, or United States passport, and a true and accurate photocopy of the trustee's statement pursuant to Section 6753, The Actors' Fund of America shall transfer the beneficiary's balance to the trust account established for the beneficiary.

(B) The Actors' Fund of America shall disburse the set-aside funds to a beneficiary who has attained 18 years of age, after receiving proof of the beneficiary's identity and a certified copy of the beneficiary's birth certificate or United States passport, or to a beneficiary who has been emancipated, after receiving proof of the beneficiary's identity and appropriate documentation evidencing the beneficiary's emancipation.

(C) The Actors' Fund of America shall disburse the set-aside funds to the estate of a deceased beneficiary after receiving appropriate documentation evidencing the death of the beneficiary and the claimant's authority to collect those funds on behalf of the beneficiary.

(f)(1) The beneficiary of an account held by The Actors' Fund of America pursuant to this section shall be entitled to receive imputed interest on the balance in his or her account for the entire period during which the account is held at a rate equal to the lesser of the federal reserve rate in effect on the last business day of the prior calendar quarter or the national average money market rate as published in the New York Times on the last Sunday of the prior calendar quarter, adjusted quarterly.

(2) The Actors' Fund of America may assess and deduct from the balance in the beneficiary's account reasonable management, administrative, and investment expenses, including beneficiary-specific fees for initial setup, account notifications and account disbursements, and a reasonably allocable share of management, administrative, and investment expenses of the master account. No fees may be charged to any beneficiary's account during the first year that the account is held by The Actors' Fund of America.

(3) Notwithstanding paragraph (2), the amount paid on any claim made by a beneficiary or the beneficiary's parent or guardian after The Actors' Fund of America receives and

holds funds pursuant to this section may not be less than the amount of the funds received plus the imputed interest.

(g) Notwithstanding any provision of this chapter to the contrary, any minor's employer holding set-aside funds under this chapter, which funds remain unclaimed 180 days after the effective date hereof, shall forward those unclaimed funds to The Actors' Fund of America, along with the minor's name and, if known, the minor's social security number, birth date, last known address, telephone number, email address, dates of employment, and the title of the project on which the minor was employed, and shall notify the parent, guardian, or trustee of that transfer by certified mail to the last known address. Upon receipt of those forwarded funds by The Actors' Fund of America, the minor's employer shall have no further obligation or duty to monitor or account for the funds.

(h) All funds received by The Actors' Fund of America pursuant to this section shall be exempt from the application of the Unclaimed Property Law (Title 10 (commencing with Section 1300) of Part 3 of the Code of Civil Procedure), including, but not limited to, Section 1510 of the Code of Civil Procedure. *(Added by Stats.1999, c. 940 (S.B.1162), § 5. Amended by Stats.2003, c. 667 (S.B.210), § 2; Stats.2013, c. 102 (A.B.533), § 1.)*

Research References

Forms

Cal. Transaction Forms - Bus. Transactions § 10:8, Employment Of Minors.
West's California Code Forms, Family § 6751, Comment Overview--Minor's Employment Contract.
West's California Code Forms, Family § 6751 Form 2, Order Approving Minor's Employment Contract.
West's California Code Forms, Family § 6752 Form 1, Parental Consent to Court Order With Savings Provision.
West's California Code Forms, Family § 6753 Form 1, Petition to Terminate Trust or Savings Plan Established by Court Order.
West's California Code Forms, Family § 6753 Form 2, Order Terminating Trust or Savings Plan Established by Court Order.

Treatises and Practice Aids

Witkin, California Summary 10th Contracts § 37, Court Approval.
Witkin, California Summary 10th Parent and Child § 296, in General.

§ 6753. Establishment of Coogan Trust Account; consent of court required for withdrawals; written statement; handling of funds

(a) The trustee or trustees shall establish a trust account, that shall be known as a Coogan Trust Account, pursuant to this section at a bank, savings and loan institution, credit union, brokerage firm, or company registered under the Investment Company Act of 1940, that is located in the State of California, unless a similar trust has been previously established, for the purpose of preserving for the benefit of the minor the portion of the minor's gross earnings pursuant to paragraph (1) of subdivision (b) of Section 6752 or pursuant to paragraph (1) of subdivision (c) of Section 6752. The trustee or trustees shall establish the trust pursuant to this section within seven business days after the minor's contract is signed by the minor, the third-party individual or personal services corporation (loan–out company), and the employer.

(b) Except as otherwise provided in this section, prior to the date on which the beneficiary of the trust attains the age of 18 years or the issuance of a declaration of emancipation of the minor under Section 7122, no withdrawal by the beneficiary or any other individual, individuals, entity, or entities may be made of funds on deposit in trust without written order of the superior court pursuant to paragraph (7) of subdivision (b) or paragraph (5) of subdivision (c) of Section 6752. Upon reaching the age of 18 years, the beneficiary may withdraw the funds on deposit in trust only after providing a certified copy of the beneficiary's birth certificate to the financial institution where the trust is located.

(c) The trustee or trustees shall, within 10 business days after the minor's contract is signed by the minor, the third-party individual or personal services corporation (loan–out company), and the employer, prepare a written statement under penalty of perjury that shall include the name, address, and telephone number of the financial institution, the name of the account, the number of the account, the name of the minor beneficiary, the name of the trustee or trustees of the account, and any additional information needed by the minor's employer to deposit into the account the portion of the minor's gross earnings prescribed by paragraph (1) of subdivision (b) or paragraph (1) of subdivision (c) of Section 6752. The trustee or trustees shall attach to the written statement a true and accurate photocopy of any information received from the financial institution confirming the creation of the account, such as an account agreement, account terms, passbook, or other similar writings.

(d) The trust shall be established in California either with a financial institution that is and remains insured at all times by the Federal Deposit Insurance Corporation (FDIC), the Securities Investor Protection Corporation (SIPC), or the National Credit Union Share Insurance Fund (NCUSIF) or their respective successors, or with a company that is and remains registered under the Investment Company Act of 1940. The trustee or trustees of the trust shall be the only individual, individuals, entity, or entities with the obligation or duty to ensure that the funds remain in trust, in an account or other savings plan insured in accordance with this section, or with a company that is and remains registered under the Investment Company Act of 1940 as authorized by this section.

(e) Upon application by the trustee or trustees to the financial institution or company in which the trust is held, the trust funds shall be handled by the financial institution or company in one or more of the following methods:

(1) The financial institution or company may transfer funds to another account or other savings plan at the same financial institution or company, provided that the funds transferred shall continue to be held in trust, and subject to this chapter.

(2) The financial institution or company may transfer funds to another financial institution or company, provided that the funds transferred shall continue to be held in trust, and subject to this chapter and that the transferring financial institution or company has provided written notification to

the financial institution or company to which the funds will be transferred that the funds are subject to this section and written notice of the requirements of this chapter.

(3) The financial institution or company may use all or a part of the funds to purchase, in the name of and for the benefit of the minor, (A) investment funds offered by a company registered under the Investment Company Act of 1940, provided that if the underlying investments are equity securities, the investment fund is a broad-based index fund or invests broadly across the domestic or a foreign regional economy, is not a sector fund, and has assets under management of at least two hundred fifty million dollars ($250,000,000); or (B) government securities and bonds, certificates of deposit, money market instruments, money market accounts, or mutual funds investing solely in those government securities and bonds, certificates, instruments, and accounts, that are available at the financial institution where the trust fund or other savings plan is held, provided that the funds shall continue to be held in trust and subject to this chapter, those purchases shall have a maturity date on or before the date upon which the minor will attain the age of 18 years, and any proceeds accruing from those purchases shall be redeposited into that account or accounts or used to further purchase any of those or similar securities, bonds, certificates, instruments, funds, or accounts. *(Added by Stats.1999, c. 940 (S.B.1162), § 7. Amended by Stats.2003, c. 667 (S.B.210), § 3.)*

Research References

Forms

Cal. Transaction Forms - Bus. Transactions § 10:8, Employment Of Minors.
Cal. Transaction Forms - Bus. Transactions § 8:53, Model Release for Images Included in Website.
West's California Code Forms, Family § 6751 Form 2, Order Approving Minor's Employment Contract.
West's California Code Forms, Family § 6753 Form 1, Petition to Terminate Trust or Savings Plan Established by Court Order.
West's California Code Forms, Family § 6753 Form 2, Order Terminating Trust or Savings Plan Established by Court Order.

Treatises and Practice Aids

Witkin, California Summary 10th Contracts § 37, Court Approval.
Witkin, California Summary 10th Parent and Child § 296, in General.

Part 4

MEDICAL TREATMENT

CHAPTER 1. DEFINITIONS

§ 6900. Construction of part

Unless the provision or context otherwise requires, the definitions in this chapter govern the construction of this part. *(Stats.1992, c. 162 (A.B.2650), § 10, operative Jan. 1, 1994.)*

Law Revision Commission Comments

Enactment [Revised Comment]

Section 6900 is new and is comparable to Section 50. [23 Cal.L.Rev.Comm. Reports 1 (1993)].

§ 6901. "Dental care" defined

"Dental care" means X-ray examination, anesthetic, dental or surgical diagnosis or treatment, and hospital care by a dentist licensed under the Dental Practice Act. [1] *(Stats.1992, c. 162 (A.B.2650), § 10, operative Jan. 1, 1994.)*

[1] See Business and Professions Code § 1600 et seq.

Law Revision Commission Comments

Enactment [Revised Comment]

Section 6901 continues without substantive change and generalizes the last part of former Civil Code Section 25.8 and the last part of the first sentence of the first paragraph of former Civil Code Section 34.6. [23 Cal.L.Rev.Comm. Reports 1 (1993)].

Research References

Forms

California Transactions Forms--Family Law § 6:65, Medical Authorization.

Treatises and Practice Aids

Witkin, California Summary 10th Contracts § 46, Living Apart.
Witkin, California Summary 10th Torts § 389, in General.

§ 6902. "Medical care" defined

"Medical care" means X-ray examination, anesthetic, medical or surgical diagnosis or treatment, and hospital care under the general or special supervision and upon the advice of or to be rendered by a physician and surgeon licensed under the Medical Practice Act. [1] *(Stats.1992, c. 162 (A.B. 2650), § 10, operative Jan. 1, 1994.)*

[1] See Business and Professions Code § 2000 et seq.

Law Revision Commission Comments

Enactment [Revised Comment]

Section 6902 continues without substantive change and generalizes the second part of former Civil Code Section 25.8 and part of the first sentence of the first paragraph of former Civil Code Section 34.6. [23 Cal.L.Rev.Comm. Reports 1 (1993)].

Research References

Forms

California Transactions Forms--Family Law § 6:65, Medical Authorization.

Treatises and Practice Aids

Witkin, California Summary 10th Contracts § 46, Living Apart.
Witkin, California Summary 10th Torts § 389, in General.

§ 6903. "Parent or guardian" defined

"Parent or guardian" means either parent if both parents have legal custody, or the parent or person having legal custody, or the guardian, of a minor. *(Stats.1992, c. 162 (A.B.2650), § 10, operative Jan. 1, 1994.)*

Law Revision Commission Comments

Enactment [Revised Comment]

Section 6903 continues without substantive change and generalizes the first part of former Civil Code Section 25.8. The reference to the "legal" guardian has been omitted as surplus. This conforms with terminology in the Probate Code. See Prob. Code §§ 2350(b), 2400(b) ("guardian" defined). [23 Cal.L.Rev.Comm. Reports 1 (1993)].

Research References

Forms

California Transactions Forms--Family Law § 6:65, Medical Authorization.

Treatises and Practice Aids

Witkin, California Summary 10th Torts § 389, in General.

CHAPTER 2. CONSENT BY PERSON HAVING CARE OF MINOR OR BY COURT

§ 6910. Medical treatment of minor; adult entrusted with consensual power

The parent, guardian, or caregiver of a minor who is a relative of the minor and who may authorize medical care and dental care under Section 6550, may authorize in writing an adult into whose care a minor has been entrusted to consent to medical care or dental care, or both, for the minor. *(Stats.1992, c. 162 (A.B.2650), § 10, operative Jan. 1, 1994. Amended by Stats.1996, c. 563 (S.B.392), § 2.)*

Law Revision Commission Comments

Enactment [Revised Comment]

Section 6910 restates former Civil Code Section 25.8 without substantive change. See Sections 6901 ("dental care" defined), 6902 ("medical care" defined), 6903 ("parent or guardian" defined). See also Prob. Code § 2353 (guardian's right to consent to medical treatment same as parent with legal custody); Health & Safety Code § 1530.6 (foster care licensees authorized to consent to ordinary medical and dental treatment for child). For related provisions concerning emancipated minors, see Sections 7002 (conditions for emancipation), 7050(e)(1) (emancipated minor may consent to medical, dental, or psychiatric care). [23 Cal.L.Rev.Comm. Reports 1 (1993)].

Research References

Forms

California Transactions Forms--Family Law § 6:65, Medical Authorization.
West's California Code Forms, Family § 6900, Comment Overview--Consent by Person Having Care Of Minor Of Consent by Court.
West's California Code Forms, Family § 6910 Form 1, Authorization by Parent to Allow Adopting Parents to Consent to Minor's Medical Care.

Treatises and Practice Aids

Witkin, California Summary 10th Parent and Child § 289, in General.
Witkin, California Summary 10th Torts § 389, in General.
Witkin, California Summary 10th Wills and Probate § 991, Consent to Treatment Of Ward.

§ 6911. Consent by court; conditions

(a) Upon application by a minor, the court may summarily grant consent for medical care or dental care or both for the minor if the court determines all of the following:

(1) The minor is 16 years of age or older and resides in this state.

(2) The consent of a parent or guardian is necessary to permit the medical care or dental care or both, and the minor has no parent or guardian available to give the consent.

(b) No fee may be charged for proceedings under this section. *(Stats.1992, c. 162 (A.B.2650), § 10, operative Jan. 1, 1994.)*

Law Revision Commission Comments

Enactment [Revised Comment]

Section 6911 restates without substantive change former Probate Code Section 3301, insofar as that section related to consent to medical care. The reference to "dental care" has been added. The reference to the "superior" court has been omitted as surplus. See Section 200 (jurisdiction in superior court). See also Sections 6901 ("dental care" defined), 6902 ("medical care" defined), 6903 ("parent or guardian" defined). Section 6911 does not apply if the minor is under the age of 16 years, but in such a case, a temporary guardian may be appointed to give consent to medical care or dental care. See Prob. Code §§ 2252(b)(1), 2353. For related provisions concerning emancipated minors, see Sections 7002 (conditions for emancipation), 7050(e)(1) (emancipated minor may consent to medical, dental, or psychiatric care). [23 Cal.L.Rev.Comm. Reports 1 (1993)].

Research References

Forms

West's California Code Forms, Family § 6900, Comment Overview--Consent by Person Having Care Of Minor Of Consent by Court.

Treatises and Practice Aids

Witkin, California Summary 10th Torts § 389, in General.

CHAPTER 3. CONSENT BY MINOR

§ 6920. Capacity of minor to consent

Subject to the limitations provided in this chapter, notwithstanding any other provision of law, a minor may consent to the matters provided in this chapter, and the consent of the minor's parent or guardian is not necessary. *(Stats.1992, c. 162 (A.B.2650), § 10, operative Jan. 1, 1994.)*

Law Revision Commission Comments

Enactment [Revised Comment]

Section 6920 generalizes provisions found in former Civil Code Sections 25.9, 34.5, 34.6, 34.7, 34.8, 34.9, and 34.10. References to "parents" have been omitted as surplus. See Section 10 (singular includes the plural). References to the "legal" guardian have been omitted as surplus. This conforms with terminology in the Probate Code. See Prob. Code §§ 2350(b), 2400(b) ("guardian" defined). See also Section 6903 ("parent or guardian" defined). For related provisions concerning emancipated minors, see Sections 7002 (conditions for emancipation), 7050(e)(1) (emancipated minor may consent to medical, dental, or psychiatric care).

Former Civil Code Section 25.5, which authorized a minor to consent to the donation of blood subject to certain limitations, has not been continued in this chapter, because it was surplus. See Health & Safety Code § 1607.5 (minor's right to consent to donation of blood). Where a minor consents to the donation of blood pursuant to Health and Safety Code Section 1607.5, this consent is not subject to disaffirmance. See Section 6711 (obligation entered into under express statutory authority not subject to disaffirmance). [23 Cal.L.Rev.Comm. Reports 1 (1993)].

Research References

Treatises and Practice Aids

Witkin, California Summary 10th Contracts § 38, Nature Of Statutes.
Witkin, California Summary 10th Parent and Child § 559, Medical Care.
Witkin, California Summary 10th Wills and Probate § 991, Consent to Treatment Of Ward.

§ 6921. Effect of minority upon consent

A consent given by a minor under this chapter is not subject to disaffirmance because of minority. *(Stats.1992, c. 162 (A.B.2650), § 10, operative Jan. 1, 1994.)*

Law Revision Commission Comments

Enactment [Revised Comment]

Section 6921 generalizes provisions found in former Civil Code Sections 25.9, 34.5, 34.6, 34.7, 34.8, 34.9, and 34.10. [23 Cal.L.Rev. Comm. Reports 1 (1993)].

Research References

Forms

West's California Code Forms, Family § 6920, Comment Overview--Consent by Minor.

Treatises and Practice Aids

Witkin, California Summary 10th Contracts § 38, Nature Of Statutes.

§ 6922. Conditions for consent of minor; liability of parents or guardians; notification of minor's parents or guardians

(a) A minor may consent to the minor's medical care or dental care if all of the following conditions are satisfied:

(1) The minor is 15 years of age or older.

(2) The minor is living separate and apart from the minor's parents or guardian, whether with or without the consent of a parent or guardian and regardless of the duration of the separate residence.

(3) The minor is managing the minor's own financial affairs, regardless of the source of the minor's income.

(b) The parents or guardian are not liable for medical care or dental care provided pursuant to this section.

(c) A physician and surgeon or dentist may, with or without the consent of the minor patient, advise the minor's parent or guardian of the treatment given or needed if the physician and surgeon or dentist has reason to know, on the basis of the information given by the minor, the whereabouts of the parent or guardian. *(Stats.1992, c. 162 (A.B.2650), § 10, operative Jan. 1, 1994.)*

Law Revision Commission Comments

Enactment [Revised Comment]

Section 6922 restates former Civil Code Section 34.6 without substantive change. See Sections 6901 ("dental care" defined), 6902 ("medical care" defined), 6920 (consent by parent or guardian not necessary), 6921 (consent not subject to disaffirmance). References to "parents" have been omitted as surplus. See Section 10 (singular includes plural). The reference to the "legal" guardian has been omitted as surplus. This conforms with terminology in the Probate Code. See Prob. Code §§ 2350(b), 2400(b) ("guardian" defined). See also Section 6903 ("parent or guardian" defined). For related provisions concerning emancipated minors, see Sections 7002 (conditions for emancipation), 7050(e)(1) (emancipated minor may consent to medical, dental, or psychiatric care). [23 Cal.L.Rev.Comm. Reports 1 (1993)].

Research References

Forms

West's California Code Forms, Family § 6920, Comment Overview--Consent by Minor.
West's California Code Forms, Family § 6922 Form 1, Consent by Minor Living Apart from Parents to Medical Care.

Treatises and Practice Aids

Witkin, California Summary 10th Contracts § 46, Living Apart.
Witkin, California Summary 10th Torts § 389, in General.

§ 6924. Mental health treatment or counseling services; involvement of parents or guardians; liability of parents or guardians

(a) As used in this section:

(1) "Mental health treatment or counseling services" means the provision of mental health treatment or counseling on an outpatient basis by any of the following:

(A) A governmental agency.

(B) A person or agency having a contract with a governmental agency to provide the services.

(C) An agency that receives funding from community united funds.

(D) A runaway house or crisis resolution center.

(E) A professional person, as defined in paragraph (2).

(2) "Professional person" means any of the following:

(A) A person designated as a mental health professional in Sections 622 to 626, inclusive, of Article 8 of Subchapter 3 of Chapter 1 of Title 9 of the California Code of Regulations.

(B) A marriage and family therapist as defined in Chapter 13 (commencing with Section 4980) of Division 2 of the Business and Professions Code.

(C) A licensed educational psychologist as defined in Article 5 (commencing with Section 4986) of Chapter 13 of Division 2 of the Business and Professions Code.

(D) A credentialed school psychologist as described in Section 49424 of the Education Code.

(E) A clinical psychologist as defined in Section 1316.5 of the Health and Safety Code.

(F) The chief administrator of an agency referred to in paragraph (1) or (3).

(G) A person registered as a marriage and family therapist intern, as defined in Chapter 13 (commencing with Section 4980) of Division 2 of the Business and Professions Code, while working under the supervision of a licensed professional specified in subdivision (g) of Section 4980.03 of the Business and Professions Code.

(H) A licensed professional clinical counselor, as defined in Chapter 16 (commencing with Section 4999.10) of Division 2 of the Business and Professions Code.

(I) A person registered as a clinical counselor intern, as defined in Chapter 16 (commencing with Section 4999.10) of Division 2 of the Business and Professions Code, while working under the supervision of a licensed professional specified in subdivision (h) of Section 4999.12 of the Business and Professions Code.

(3) "Residential shelter services" means any of the following:

(A) The provision of residential and other support services to minors on a temporary or emergency basis in a facility that services only minors by a governmental agency, a person or agency having a contract with a governmental agency to provide these services, an agency that receives funding from community funds, or a licensed community care facility or crisis resolution center.

(B) The provision of other support services on a temporary or emergency basis by any professional person as defined in paragraph (2).

(b) A minor who is 12 years of age or older may consent to mental health treatment or counseling on an outpatient basis, or to residential shelter services, if both of the following requirements are satisfied:

(1) The minor, in the opinion of the attending professional person, is mature enough to participate intelligently in the outpatient services or residential shelter services.

(2) The minor (A) would present a danger of serious physical or mental harm to self or to others without the mental health treatment or counseling or residential shelter services, or (B) is the alleged victim of incest or child abuse.

(c) A professional person offering residential shelter services, whether as an individual or as a representative of an entity specified in paragraph (3) of subdivision (a), shall make his or her best efforts to notify the parent or guardian of the provision of services.

(d) The mental health treatment or counseling of a minor authorized by this section shall include involvement of the minor's parent or guardian unless, in the opinion of the professional person who is treating or counseling the minor, the involvement would be inappropriate. The professional person who is treating or counseling the minor shall state in the client record whether and when the person attempted to contact the minor's parent or guardian, and whether the attempt to contact was successful or unsuccessful, or the reason why, in the professional person's opinion, it would be inappropriate to contact the minor's parent or guardian.

(e) The minor's parents or guardian are not liable for payment for mental health treatment or counseling services provided pursuant to this section unless the parent or guardian participates in the mental health treatment or counseling, and then only for services rendered with the participation of the parent or guardian. The minor's parents or guardian are not liable for payment for any residential shelter services provided pursuant to this section unless the parent or guardian consented to the provision of those services.

(f) This section does not authorize a minor to receive convulsive therapy or psychosurgery as defined in subdivisions (f) and (g) of Section 5325 of the Welfare and Institutions Code, or psychotropic drugs without the consent of the minor's parent or guardian. *(Stats.1992, c. 162 (A.B.2650), § 10, operative Jan. 1, 1994. Amended by Stats. 1993, c. 219 (A.B.1500), § 155; Stats.2000, c. 519 (A.B.2161), § 1; Stats.2009, c. 26 (S.B.33), § 22; Stats.2011, c. 381 (S.B.146), § 25.)*

Law Revision Commission Comments

Enactment [Revised Comment]

Section 6924 restates former Civil Code Section 25.9 without substantive change. See Sections 6920 (consent by parent or guardian not necessary), 6921 (consent not subject to disaffirmance). Most references to "parents" have been omitted as surplus. See Section 10 (singular includes plural). The reference to the "legal" guardian has been omitted as surplus. This conforms with terminology in the Probate Code. See Prob. Code §§ 2350(b), 2400(b) ("guardian" defined). See also Section 6903 ("parent or guardian" defined). For related provisions concerning emancipated minors, see Sections 7002 (conditions for emancipation), 7050(e)(1) (minor may consent to medical, dental, or psychiatric care). [23 Cal.L.Rev. Comm. Reports 1 (1993)].

Research References

Forms

West's California Code Forms, Family § 6920, Comment Overview--Consent by Minor.

Treatises and Practice Aids

Witkin, California Summary 10th Contracts § 45, Minor Needing Mental Health Treatment.

Witkin, California Summary 10th Parent and Child § 289, in General.

§ 6925. Prevention or treatment of pregnancy

(a) A minor may consent to medical care related to the prevention or treatment of pregnancy.

(b) This section does not authorize a minor:

(1) To be sterilized without the consent of the minor's parent or guardian.

(2) To receive an abortion without the consent of a parent or guardian other than as provided in Section 123450 of the Health and Safety Code. *(Stats.1992, c. 162 (A.B.2650), § 10, operative Jan. 1, 1994. Amended by Stats.1996, c. 1023 (S.B.1497), § 46, eff. Sept. 29, 1996.)*

Law Revision Commission Comments

Enactment [Revised Comment]

Section 6925 restates former Civil Code Section 34.5 without substantive change. See Sections 6920 (consent by parent or guardian not necessary), 6921 (consent not subject to disaffirmance). The reference to an "unemancipated minor" has been omitted. This is not a substantive change. The term "medical care" has been substituted for "the furnishing of hospital, medical and surgical care." This is not a substantive change. See Section 6902 ("medical care" defined). See also Section 6903 ("parent or guardian" defined). For related provisions concerning emancipated minors, see Sections 7002 (conditions of emancipation), 7050(e)(1) (emancipated minor may consent to medical, dental, or psychiatric care). [23 Cal.L.Rev.Comm. Reports 1 (1993)].

Research References

Forms

West's California Code Forms, Family § 6920, Comment Overview--Consent by Minor.

Treatises and Practice Aids

Witkin, California Summary 10th Contracts § 39, Unwed Pregnant Minors.

Witkin, California Summary 10th Parent and Child § 289, in General.

Witkin, California Summary 10th Torts § 389, in General.

Witkin, California Summary 10th Torts § 391, Abortion Without Parental Consent.

§ 6926. Diagnosis or treatment of infectious, contagious, or communicable diseases; consent by minor to certain medical care; liability of parents or guardians

(a) A minor who is 12 years of age or older and who may have come into contact with an infectious, contagious, or communicable disease may consent to medical care related to the diagnosis or treatment of the disease, if the disease or condition is one that is required by law or regulation adopted pursuant to law to be reported to the local health officer, or is a related sexually transmitted disease, as may be determined by the State Public Health Officer.

(b) A minor who is 12 years of age or older may consent to medical care related to the prevention of a sexually transmitted disease.

(c) The minor's parents or guardian are not liable for payment for medical care provided pursuant to this section. *(Stats.1992, c. 162 (A.B.2650), § 10, operative Jan. 1, 1994. Amended by Stats.2011, c. 652 (A.B.499), § 1.)*

Law Revision Commission Comments

Enactment [Revised Comment]

Section 6926 restates former Civil Code Section 34.7 without substantive change. See Sections 6920 (consent by parent or guardian not necessary), 6921 (consent not subject to disaffirmance). The term "medical care" has been substituted for "the furnishing of hospital, medical and surgical care." This is not a substantive change. See Sections 6902 ("medical care" defined). A reference to "parent" has been omitted as surplus. See Section 10 (plural includes the singular). The reference to the "legal" guardian has been omitted as surplus. This conforms with terminology in the Probate Code. See Prob. Code §§ 2350(b), 2400(b) ("guardian" defined). See also Section 6903 ("parent or guardian" defined). For related provisions concerning emancipated minors, see Sections 7002 (conditions for emancipation), 7050(e)(1) (emancipated minor may consent to medical, dental, or psychiatric care). [23 Cal.L.Rev. Comm. Reports 1 (1993)].

Research References

Forms

West's California Code Forms, Family § 6920, Comment Overview--Consent by Minor.

Treatises and Practice Aids

Witkin, California Summary 10th Contracts § 42, Minors Exposed to Communicable Disease.

Witkin, California Summary 10th Torts § 389, in General.

§ 6927. Diagnosis or treatment for rape

A minor who is 12 years of age or older and who is alleged to have been raped may consent to medical care related to the diagnosis or treatment of the condition and the collection of medical evidence with regard to the alleged rape. *(Stats. 1992, c. 162 (A.B.2650), § 10, operative Jan. 1, 1994.)*

Law Revision Commission Comments

Enactment [Revised Comment]

Section 6927 restates former Civil Code Section 34.8 without substantive change. See Sections 6920 (consent by parent or guardian not necessary), 6921 (consent not subject to disaffirmance). The term "medical care" has been substituted for "the furnishing of hospital, medical, and surgical care." This is not a substantive change. See Section 6902 ("medical care" defined). For related provisions concerning emancipated minors, see Sections 7002 (conditions for emancipation), 7050(e)(1) (emancipated minor may consent to medical, dental, or psychiatric care). [23 Cal.L.Rev.Comm. Reports 1 (1993)].

Research References

Forms

West's California Code Forms, Family § 6920, Comment Overview--Consent by Minor.

Treatises and Practice Aids

Witkin, California Summary 10th Contracts § 43, Minor Raped or Sexually Assaulted.

Witkin, California Summary 10th Torts § 389, in General.

§ 6928. Diagnosis or treatment for sexual assault

(a) "Sexually assaulted" as used in this section includes, but is not limited to, conduct coming within Section 261, 286, or 288a of the Penal Code.

(b) A minor who is alleged to have been sexually assaulted may consent to medical care related to the diagnosis and treatment of the condition, and the collection of medical evidence with regard to the alleged sexual assault.

(c) The professional person providing medical treatment shall attempt to contact the minor's parent or guardian and shall note in the minor's treatment record the date and time the professional person attempted to contact the parent or guardian and whether the attempt was successful or unsuccessful. This subdivision does not apply if the professional person reasonably believes that the minor's parent or guardian committed the sexual assault on the minor. *(Stats.1992, c. 162 (A.B.2650), § 10, operative Jan. 1, 1994.)*

Law Revision Commission Comments

Enactment [Revised Comment]

Section 6928 restates former Civil Code Section 34.9 without substantive change. See Sections 6920 (consent by parent or guardian not necessary), 6921 (consent not subject to disaffirmance). The term "medical care" has been substituted for "the furnishing of hospital, medical, and surgical care." This is not a substantive change. See Section 6902 ("medical care" defined). A reference to "parents" has been omitted as surplus. See Section 10 (plural includes the singular). The reference to the "legal" guardian has been omitted as surplus. This conforms with terminology in the Probate Code. See Prob. Code §§ 2350(b), 2400(b) ("guardian" defined). See also Section 6903 ("parent or guardian" defined). For related provisions concerning emancipated minors, see Sections 7002 (conditions for emancipation), 7050(e)(1) (emancipated minor may consent to medical, dental, or psychiatric care). [23 Cal.L.Rev. Comm. Reports 1 (1993)].

Research References

Forms

West's California Code Forms, Family § 6920, Comment Overview--Consent by Minor.

Treatises and Practice Aids

Witkin, California Summary 10th Contracts § 43, Minor Raped or Sexually Assaulted.
Witkin, California Summary 10th Torts § 389, in General.

§ 6929. Diagnosis or treatment of drug and alcohol abuse; liability for cost of services; disclosure of medical information

(a) As used in this section:

(1) "Counseling" means the provision of counseling services by a provider under a contract with the state or a county to provide alcohol or drug abuse counseling services pursuant to Part 2 (commencing with Section 5600) of Division 5 of the Welfare and Institutions Code or pursuant to Division 10.5 (commencing with Section 11750) of the Health and Safety Code.

(2) "Drug or alcohol" includes, but is not limited to, any substance listed in any of the following:

(A) Section 380 or 381 of the Penal Code.

(B) Division 10 (commencing with Section 11000) of the Health and Safety Code.

(C) Subdivision (f) of Section 647 of the Penal Code.

(3) "LAAM" means levoalphacetylmethadol as specified in paragraph (10) of subdivision (c) of Section 11055 of the Health and Safety Code.

(4) "Professional person" means a physician and surgeon, registered nurse, psychologist, clinical social worker, professional clinical counselor, marriage and family therapist, registered marriage and family therapist intern when appropriately employed and supervised pursuant to Section 4980.43 of the Business and Professions Code, psychological assistant when appropriately employed and supervised pursuant to Section 2913 of the Business and Professions Code, associate clinical social worker when appropriately employed and supervised pursuant to Section 4996.18 of the Business and Professions Code, or registered clinical counselor intern when appropriately employed and supervised pursuant to Section 4999.42 of the Business and Professions Code.

(b) A minor who is 12 years of age or older may consent to medical care and counseling relating to the diagnosis and treatment of a drug- or alcohol-related problem.

(c) The treatment plan of a minor authorized by this section shall include the involvement of the minor's parent or guardian, if appropriate, as determined by the professional person or treatment facility treating the minor. The professional person providing medical care or counseling to a minor shall state in the minor's treatment record whether and when the professional person attempted to contact the minor's parent or guardian, and whether the attempt to contact the parent or guardian was successful or unsuccessful, or the reason why, in the opinion of the professional person, it would not be appropriate to contact the minor's parent or guardian.

(d) The minor's parent or guardian is not liable for payment for any care provided to a minor pursuant to this section, except that if the minor's parent or guardian participates in a counseling program pursuant to this section, the parent or guardian is liable for the cost of the services provided to the minor and the parent or guardian.

(e) This section does not authorize a minor to receive replacement narcotic abuse treatment, in a program licensed pursuant to Article 3 (commencing with Section 11875) of Chapter 1 of Part 3 of Division 10.5 of the Health and Safety Code, without the consent of the minor's parent or guardian.

(f) It is the intent of the Legislature that the state shall respect the right of a parent or legal guardian to seek medical care and counseling for a drug- or alcohol-related problem of a minor child when the child does not consent to the medical care and counseling, and nothing in this section shall be construed to restrict or eliminate this right.

(g) Notwithstanding any other provision of law, in cases where a parent or legal guardian has sought the medical care and counseling for a drug- or alcohol-related problem of a minor child, the physician and surgeon shall disclose medical information concerning the care to the minor's parent or legal guardian upon his or her request, even if the minor child does not consent to disclosure, without liability for the disclosure. *(Stats.1992, c. 162 (A.B.2650), § 10, operative Jan. 1, 1994. Amended by Stats.1995, c. 455 (A.B.1113), § 1, eff. Sept. 5, 1995; Stats.1996, c. 656 (A.B.2883), § 1; Stats.2002, c. 1013 (S.B.2026), § 79; Stats.2004, c. 59 (A.B.2182), § 1; Stats.2009, c. 26 (S.B.33), § 23; Stats.2011, c. 381 (S.B.146), § 26.)*

Law Revision Commission Comments

Enactment [Revised Comment]

Section 6929 restates former Civil Code Section 34.10 without substantive change. This section has been revised to correct former references to repealed sections.

See Sections 6920 (consent by parent or guardian not necessary), 6921 (consent not subject to disaffirmance). See also Sections 6902 ("medical care" defined), 6903 ("parent or guardian" defined). For related provisions concerning emancipated minors, see Sections 7002 (conditions for emancipation), 7050(e)(1) (emancipated minor may consent to medical, dental, or psychiatric care). [23 Cal.L.Rev. Comm. Reports 1 (1993)].

Research References

Forms

West's California Code Forms, Family § 6920, Comment Overview--Consent by Minor.

Treatises and Practice Aids

Witkin, California Summary 10th Contracts § 44, Minor With Drug or Alcohol Problem.

Witkin, California Summary 10th Torts § 389, in General.

Part 5

ENLISTMENT IN ARMED FORCES

§ 6950. Consent of court; conditions

(a) Upon application by a minor, the court may summarily grant consent for enlistment by the minor in the armed forces of the United States if the court determines all of the following:

(1) The minor is 16 years of age or older and resides in this state.

(2) The consent of a parent or guardian is necessary to permit the enlistment, and the minor has no parent or guardian available to give the consent.

(b) No fee may be charged for proceedings under this section. *(Stats.1992, c. 162 (A.B.2650), § 10, operative Jan. 1, 1994.)*

Law Revision Commission Comments

Enactment [Revised Comment]

Section 6950 restates former Probate Code Section 3301 without substantive change, insofar as that section related to consent to enlist in the armed forces. The reference to the "superior" court has been omitted as surplus. See Section 200 (jurisdiction in superior court). The phrase "armed forces of the United States" has been substituted for "armed services" to conform to Section 7002(b). For related provisions concerning emancipated minors, see Sections 7002(b) (person on active duty in armed forces meets condition for emancipation), 7050 (effects of emancipation). [23 Cal.L.Rev.Comm. Reports 1 (1993)].

Part 6

EMANCIPATION OF MINORS LAW

CHAPTER 1. GENERAL PROVISIONS

§ 7000. Short title

This part may be cited as the Emancipation of Minors Law. *(Stats.1992, c. 162 (A.B.2650), § 10, operative Jan. 1, 1994.)*

Law Revision Commission Comments

Enactment [Revised Comment]

Section 7000 continues former Civil Code Section 60 without substantive change. [23 Cal.L.Rev.Comm. Reports 1 (1993)].

Research References

Forms

California Transactions Forms--Family Law § 1:2, Nature and Advantages Of Agreement.

West's California Code Forms, Family § 7110, Comment Overview--Emancipation Of Minor.

West's California Judicial Council Forms MC-300, Petition for Declaration Of Emancipation Of Minor, Order Prescribing Notice, Declaration Of Emancipation, and Order Denying Petition.

West's California Judicial Council Forms MC-305, Notice Of Hearing--Emancipation Of Minor.

West's California Judicial Council Forms MC-306, Emancipation Of Minor--Income and Expense Declaration.

West's California Judicial Council Forms MC-310, Declaration Of Emancipation Of Minor After Hearing.

West's California Judicial Council Forms MC-315, Emancipated Minor's Application to California Department Of Motor Vehicles.

Treatises and Practice Aids

Witkin, California Summary 10th Contracts § 48, Emancipated Minors.

Witkin, California Summary 10th Parent and Child § 299, Emancipation Of Minors Law.

§ 7001. Purpose of part

It is the purpose of this part to provide a clear statement defining emancipation and its consequences and to permit an emancipated minor to obtain a court declaration of the minor's status. This part is not intended to affect the status of minors who may become emancipated under the decisional case law that was in effect before the enactment of Chapter 1059 of the Statutes of 1978. *(Stats.1992, c. 162 (A.B.2650), § 10, operative Jan. 1, 1994.)*

Law Revision Commission Comments

Enactment [Revised Comment]

Section 7001 continues the last two sentences of former Civil Code Section 61 without substantive change. The part of the last sentence of former Civil Code Section 61 that referred to "minors who are now emancipated" under the 1978 case law has been omitted as obsolete.

Section 7001 omits the first sentence of former Civil Code Section 61. This sentence was an obsolete provision describing the need for the enactment of the former Emancipation of Minors Act. [23 Cal.L.Rev.Comm. Reports 1 (1993)].

Research References

Treatises and Practice Aids

Witkin, California Summary 10th Parent and Child § 299, Emancipation Of Minors Law.

§ 7002. Emancipated minor; description

A person under the age of 18 years is an emancipated minor if any of the following conditions is satisfied:

(a) The person has entered into a valid marriage, whether or not the marriage has been dissolved.

(b) The person is on active duty with the armed forces of the United States.

(c) The person has received a declaration of emancipation pursuant to Section 7122. *(Stats.1992, c. 162 (A.B.2650), § 10, operative Jan. 1, 1994.)*

Law Revision Commission Comments

Enactment [Revised Comment]

Section 7002 restates former Civil Code Section 62 without substantive change. In subdivision (c), a reference to Section 7122 has been substituted for the broader reference to former Civil Code Section 64. This is not a substantive change, since the relevant part of the former section is continued in Section 7122. See also Section 310 (methods of dissolution).

Sections 7002 and 7050(e)(1) supersede former Civil Code Sections 25.6 (furnishing hospital, medical, and surgical care to married minor) and 25.7 (furnishing hospital, medical, and surgical care to minor on active duty with armed services). [23 Cal.L.Rev.Comm. Reports 1 (1993)].

Commentary

Relying on subsection (a) and section 7050(c), *In re J.S., 199 Cal.App.4th 1291, 132 Cal.Rptr.3d 244 (2011)*, holds that a juvenile court erred in denying a human service agency's motion to dismiss a dependency proceeding when a minor child's marriage in Nevada, with her mother's consent, had emancipated the child.

Research References

Forms

California Practice Guide: Rutter Family Law Forms Form 9:3, Marital Settlement Agreement.
Cal. Transaction Forms - Bus. Transactions § 6:11, Void Contracts Of Minors.
California Transactions Forms--Estate Planning § 6:16, Guardian Of Person.
West's California Code Forms, Family § 7002, Comment Overview--Emancipated Minors.
West's California Code Forms, Family § 2338 Form 9, Marital Agreement--Both Spouses Employed.
West's California Code Forms, Probate § 1601 Form 1, Petition for Termination Of Guardianship--Judicial Council Form GC-255.

Treatises and Practice Aids

Witkin, California Summary 10th Contracts § 40, Married Minors.
Witkin, California Summary 10th Contracts § 41, Minors in Military Service.
Witkin, California Summary 10th Contracts § 48, Emancipated Minors.
Witkin, California Summary 10th Parent and Child § 298, Types Of Emancipation.
Witkin, California Summary 10th Parent and Child § 299, Emancipation Of Minors Law.
Witkin, California Summary 10th Parent and Child § 420, Emancipation.
Witkin, California Summary 10th Torts § 389, in General.
Witkin, California Summary 10th Wills and Probate § 930, Termination Of Guardianship.

CHAPTER 2. EFFECT OF EMANCIPATION

§ 7050. Purposes for which emancipated minors are considered an adult

An emancipated minor shall be considered as being an adult for the following purposes:

(a) The minor's right to support by the minor's parents.

(b) The right of the minor's parents to the minor's earnings and to control the minor.

(c) The application of Sections 300 and 601 of the Welfare and Institutions Code.

(d) Ending all vicarious or imputed liability of the minor's parents or guardian for the minor's torts. Nothing in this section affects any liability of a parent, guardian, spouse, or employer imposed by the Vehicle Code, or any vicarious liability that arises from an agency relationship.

(e) The minor's capacity to do any of the following:

(1) Consent to medical, dental, or psychiatric care, without parental consent, knowledge, or liability.

(2) Enter into a binding contract or give a delegation of power.

(3) Buy, sell, lease, encumber, exchange, or transfer an interest in real or personal property, including, but not limited to, shares of stock in a domestic or foreign corporation or a membership in a nonprofit corporation.

(4) Sue or be sued in the minor's own name.

(5) Compromise, settle, arbitrate, or otherwise adjust a claim, action, or proceeding by or against the minor.

(6) Make or revoke a will.

(7) Make a gift, outright or in trust.

(8) Convey or release contingent or expectant interests in property, including marital property rights and any right of survivorship incident to joint tenancy, and consent to a transfer, encumbrance, or gift of marital property.

(9) Exercise or release the minor's powers as donee of a power of appointment unless the creating instrument otherwise provides.

(10) Create for the minor's own benefit or for the benefit of others a revocable or irrevocable trust.

(11) Revoke a revocable trust.

(12) Elect to take under or against a will.

(13) Renounce or disclaim any interest acquired by testate or intestate succession or by inter vivos transfer, including exercise of the right to surrender the right to revoke a revocable trust.

(14) Make an election referred to in Section 13502 of, or an election and agreement referred to in Section 13503 of, the Probate Code.

(15) Establish the minor's own residence.

(16) Apply for a work permit pursuant to Section 49110 of the Education Code without the request of the minor's parents.

(17) Enroll in a school or college. *(Stats.1992, c. 162 (A.B.2650), § 10, operative Jan. 1, 1994.)*

Law Revision Commission Comments

Enactment [Revised Comment]

Section 7050 continues former Civil Code Section 63 without substantive change. A reference to "adult" has been substituted for "over the age of majority." This is not a substantive change. See Section 6501 ("adult" defined). In subdivisions (b) and (e)(16), the former references to "guardian" have been omitted. In subdivision (e)(2), the phrase "or give a delegation of power" is new. This makes clear that Section 6701(a) (limitation on authority of minor) does not limit the powers of an emancipated minor. In subdivision (d), the reference to "imputed" liability is new and is added, to conform with statutory provisions imposing "imputed" parental liability. See, e.g., Code Civ. Proc. §§ 1714.1 (liability of parents and guardian for willful misconduct or minor), 1714.3 (liability of parent or guardian for injury to person or property caused by discharge of firearm by minor).

Sections 7002 and 7050(e)(1) supersede former Civil Code Sections 25.6 (furnishing hospital, medical, and surgical care to married minor) and 25.7 (furnishing hospital, medical, and surgical care to minor on active duty with armed services). [23 Cal.L.Rev.Comm. Reports 1 (1993)].

Commentary

West Shield Investigations and Security Consultants v. Superior Court, 82 Cal.App.4th 935, 98 Cal.Rptr.2d 612 (2000), holds that Code of Civil Procedure § 352, which tolls the statute of limitations during a party's minority, has no application to an emancipated minor, because Family Code § 7050(e)(4) gives an emancipated minor the right "to sue and be sued."

Relying on subsection (c) and section 7002(a), *In re J.S., 199 Cal.App.4th 1291, 132 Cal.Rptr.3d 244 (2011)*, holds that a juvenile court erred in denying a human service agency's motion to dismiss a dependency proceeding when a minor child's marriage in Nevada, with her mother's consent, had emancipated the child.

Research References

Forms

Cal. Transaction Forms - Bus. Transactions § 6:11, Void Contracts Of Minors.

California Transactions Forms--Estate Planning § 19:32, Persons Who May Make Will.

California Transactions Forms--Estate Planning § 19:43, Who May Execute.

California Transactions Forms--Family Law § 1:2, Nature and Advantages Of Agreement.

West's California Code Forms, Family § 7002, Comment Overview--Emancipated Minors.

West's California Code Forms, Family § 7002 Form 2, Consent by Married Minor to Medical Care.

West's California Code Forms, Family § 7002 Form 3, Consent by Minor in Military to Medical Care.

West's California Judicial Council Forms MC-305, Notice Of Hearing--Emancipation Of Minor.

West's California Judicial Council Forms MC-310, Declaration Of Emancipation Of Minor After Hearing.

West's California Judicial Council Forms MC-315, Emancipated Minor's Application to California Department Of Motor Vehicles.

Treatises and Practice Aids

Witkin, California Summary 10th Contracts § 40, Married Minors.

Witkin, California Summary 10th Contracts § 41, Minors in Military Service.

Witkin, California Summary 10th Contracts § 48, Emancipated Minors.

Witkin, California Summary 10th Parent and Child § 289, in General.

Witkin, California Summary 10th Parent and Child § 300, Family Relationships.

Witkin, California Summary 10th Parent and Child § 301, Contracts, Ownership, and Litigation.

Witkin, California Summary 10th Parent and Child § 302, Estate Planning and Probate.

Witkin, California Summary 10th Parent and Child § 420, Emancipation.

§ 7051. Insurance contracts

An insurance contract entered into by an emancipated minor has the same effect as if it were entered into by an adult and, with respect to that contract, the minor has the same rights, duties, and liabilities as an adult. *(Stats.1992, c. 162 (A.B.2650), § 10, operative Jan. 1, 1994.)*

Law Revision Commission Comments

Enactment [Revised Comment]

Section 7051 continues former Civil Code Section 63.1 without substantive change. [23 Cal.L.Rev.Comm. Reports 1 (1993)].

Research References

Treatises and Practice Aids

Witkin, California Summary 10th Contracts § 48, Emancipated Minors.

Witkin, California Summary 10th Parent and Child § 301, Contracts, Ownership, and Litigation.

§ 7052. Powers of emancipated minor with respect to shares of stock and similar property

With respect to shares of stock in a domestic or foreign corporation held by an emancipated minor, a membership in a nonprofit corporation held by an emancipated minor, or other property held by an emancipated minor, the minor may do all of the following:

(a) Vote in person, and give proxies to exercise any voting rights, with respect to the shares, membership, or property.

(b) Waive notice of any meeting or give consent to the holding of any meeting.

(c) Authorize, ratify, approve, or confirm any action that could be taken by shareholders, members, or property owners. *(Stats.1992, c. 162 (A.B.2650), § 10, operative Jan. 1, 1994.)*

Law Revision Commission Comments

Enactment [Revised Comment]

Section 7052 continues former Civil Code Section 63.2 without substantive change. [23 Cal.L.Rev.Comm. Reports 1 (1993)].

Research References

Treatises and Practice Aids

Witkin, California Summary 10th Parent and Child § 301, Contracts, Ownership, and Litigation.

CHAPTER 3. COURT DECLARATION OF EMANCIPATION

ARTICLE 1. GENERAL PROVISIONS

§ 7110. Legislative intent; minimum expense; forms

It is the intent of the Legislature that proceedings under this part be as simple and inexpensive as possible. To that end, the Judicial Council is requested to prepare and distribute to the clerks of the superior courts appropriate forms for the proceedings that are suitable for use by minors acting as their own counsel. *(Stats.1992, c. 162 (A.B.2650), § 10, operative Jan. 1, 1994.)*

Law Revision Commission Comments

Enactment [Revised Comment]

Section 7110 continues former Civil Code Section 70 without substantive change. A reference to this part has been substituted for references to the former sections providing for proceedings to declare a minor emancipated and to rescind a declaration of emancipation. This expands the scope of this section to apply to a proceeding to void a declaration of emancipation obtained by fraud or withholding material information. [23 Cal.L.Rev.Comm. Reports 1 (1993)].

Research References

Forms

West's California Code Forms, Family § 7110 Form 1, Petition for Declaration Of Emancipation Of Minor.

Treatises and Practice Aids

Witkin, California Summary 10th Parent and Child § 303, in General.

Witkin, California Summary 10th Torts § 389, in General.

§ 7111. Issuance of declaration of emancipation; effect on public social service benefits

The issuance of a declaration of emancipation does not entitle the minor to any benefits under Division 9 (commencing with Section 10000) of the Welfare and Institutions Code which would not otherwise accrue to an emancipated minor. *(Stats.1992, c. 162 (A.B.2650), § 10, operative Jan. 1, 1994.)*

Law Revision Commission Comments

Enactment [Revised Comment]

Section 7111 continues former Civil Code Section 67 without substantive change. [23 Cal.L.Rev.Comm. Reports 1 (1993)].

Research References

Treatises and Practice Aids

Witkin, California Summary 10th Parent and Child § 299, Emancipation Of Minors Law.

ARTICLE 2. PROCEDURE FOR DECLARATION

§ 7120. Petitions for declaration of emancipation; contents

(a) A minor may petition the superior court of the county in which the minor resides or is temporarily domiciled for a declaration of emancipation.

(b) The petition shall set forth with specificity all of the following facts:

(1) The minor is at least 14 years of age.

(2) The minor willingly lives separate and apart from the minor's parents or guardian with the consent or acquiescence of the minor's parents or guardian.

(3) The minor is managing his or her own financial affairs. As evidence of this, the minor shall complete and attach a declaration of income and expenses as provided in Judicial Council form FL–150.

(4) The source of the minor's income is not derived from any activity declared to be a crime by the laws of this state or the laws of the United States. *(Stats.1992, c. 162 (A.B.2650), § 10, operative Jan. 1, 1994. Amended by Stats.1993, c. 219 (A.B.1500), § 156; Stats.2004, c. 811 (A.B.3079), § 3.)*

Law Revision Commission Comments

Enactment [Revised Comment]

Section 7120 continues former Civil Code Section 64(a) without substantive change. References to the "legal" guardian have been omitted as surplus. This conforms with terminology in the Probate Code. See Prob. Code §§ 2350(b), 2400(b) ("guardian" defined). The requirement that the petition be verified has been omitted as surplus. See Section 212 (pleadings to be verified). [23 Cal.L.Rev. Comm. Reports 1 (1993)].

Commentary

Interpreting and applying this section, *Bonnie P. v. Superior Court, 134 Cal.App.4th 1249, 37 Cal.Rptr.3d 77 (2005),* holds that the trial court erred in granting minor's petition for a declaration of emancipation when the minor was living apart from her parents without their consent and was not managing her own financial affairs, and witnesses were not sworn at the emancipation proceeding.

Research References

Forms

West's California Code Forms, Family § 7110, Comment Overview-- Emancipation Of Minor.

West's California Judicial Council Forms MC-310, Declaration Of Emancipation Of Minor After Hearing.

Treatises and Practice Aids

Witkin, California Summary 10th Contracts § 48, Emancipated Minors.
Witkin, California Summary 10th Parent and Child § 303, in General.
Witkin, California Summary 10th Parent and Child § 305, Action.

§ 7121. Notice of declaration proceedings

(a) Before the petition for a declaration of emancipation is heard, notice the court determines is reasonable shall be given to the minor's parents, guardian, or other person entitled to the custody of the minor, or proof shall be made to the court that their addresses are unknown or that for other reasons the notice cannot be given.

(b) The clerk of the court shall also notify the local child support agency of the county in which the matter is to be heard of the proceeding. If the minor is a ward of the court, notice shall be given to the probation department. If the child is a dependent child of the court, notice shall be given to the county welfare department.

(c) The notice shall include a form whereby the minor's parents, guardian, or other person entitled to the custody of the minor may give their written consent to the petitioner's emancipation. The notice shall include a warning that a court may void or rescind the declaration of emancipation and the parents may become liable for support and medical insurance coverage pursuant to Chapter 2 (commencing with Section 4000) of Part 2 of Division 9 and Sections 17400, 17402, 17404, and 17422. *(Stats.1992, c. 162 (A.B.2650), § 10, operative Jan. 1, 1994. Amended by Stats.1993, c. 219 (A.B.1500), § 157; Stats.2003, c. 365 (A.B.1710), § 1.)*

Law Revision Commission Comments

Enactment [Revised Comment]

Section 7121 continues without substantive change the first, second, and fourth sentences of subdivision (b)(1) and subdivision (b)(2) of former Civil Code Section 64. In subdivision (c), a reference to "medical insurance coverage" has been substituted for the former reference to "medical support." This is consistent with the language in Section 7133 and is not a substantive change. A reference to Chapter 2 (commencing with Section 4000) of Part 2 of Division 10 has been substituted for a narrower reference to former Civil Code Section 4700. This is not a substantive change. [23 Cal.L.Rev.Comm. Reports 1 (1993)].

Research References

Forms

West's California Code Forms, Family § 7110, Comment Overview--Emancipation Of Minor.

Treatises and Practice Aids

Witkin, California Summary 10th Parent and Child § 304, Notice Of Hearing.

§ 7122. Findings of court; issuance of declaration of emancipation

(a) The court shall sustain the petition if it finds that the minor is a person described by Section 7120 and that emancipation would not be contrary to the minor's best interest.

(b) If the petition is sustained, the court shall forthwith issue a declaration of emancipation, which shall be filed by the clerk of the court.

(c) A declaration is conclusive evidence that the minor is emancipated. *(Stats.1992, c. 162 (A.B.2650), § 10, operative Jan. 1, 1994. Amended by Stats.2002, c. 784 (S.B.1316), § 107.)*

Law Revision Commission Comments

Enactment [Revised Comment]

Section 7122 continues without substantive change the third sentence of subdivision (b)(1), the first sentence of subdivision (c), and subdivision (f) of former Civil Code Section 64. [23 Cal.L.Rev.Comm. Reports 1 (1993)].

2002 Amendment

Subdivision (b) of Section 7122 is amended to reflect elimination of the county clerk's role as ex officio clerk of the superior court. See former Gov't Code § 26800 (county clerk acting as clerk of superior court). The powers, duties, and responsibilities formerly exercised by the county clerk as ex officio clerk of the court are delegated to the court administrative or executive officer, and the county clerk is relieved of those powers, duties, and responsibilities. See Gov't Code §§ 69840 (powers, duties, and responsibilities of clerk of court and deputy clerk of court), 71620 (trial court personnel). [32 Cal.L.Rev.Comm. Reports 164 (2002)].

Research References

Forms

California Transactions Forms--Estate Planning § 6:16, Guardian Of Person.
West's California Code Forms, Family § 7110, Comment Overview--Emancipation Of Minor.

Treatises and Practice Aids

Witkin, California Summary 10th Parent and Child § 298, Types Of Emancipation.
Witkin, California Summary 10th Parent and Child § 299, Emancipation Of Minors Law.
Witkin, California Summary 10th Parent and Child § 305, Action.
Witkin, California Summary 10th Parent and Child § 420, Emancipation.

§ 7123. Grant or denial of petition; filing of petition for writ of mandate

(a) If the petition is denied, the minor has a right to file a petition for a writ of mandate.

(b) If the petition is sustained, the parents or guardian have a right to file a petition for a writ of mandate if they have appeared in the proceeding and opposed the granting of the petition. *(Stats.1992, c. 162 (A.B.2650), § 10, operative Jan. 1, 1994.)*

Law Revision Commission Comments

Enactment [Revised Comment]

Section 7123 continues former Civil Code Section 64(d)-(e) without substantive change. [23 Cal.L.Rev.Comm. Reports 1 (1993)].

Research References

Forms

West's California Code Forms, Family § 7110, Comment Overview--Emancipation Of Minor.

Treatises and Practice Aids

Witkin, California Summary 10th Parent and Child § 305, Action.

ARTICLE 3. VOIDING OR RESCINDING DECLARATION

§ 7130. Grounds for voiding or rescinding declaration

(a) A declaration of emancipation obtained by fraud or by the withholding of material information is voidable.

(b) A declaration of emancipation of a minor who is indigent and has no means of support is subject to rescission. *(Stats.1992, c. 162 (A.B.2650), § 10, operative Jan. 1, 1994.)*

Law Revision Commission Comments

Enactment [Revised Comment]

Section 7130 continues without substantive change the first sentence of the first paragraph of former Civil Code Section 69 and restates part of the first sentence of former Civil Code Section 65(c). [23 Cal.L.Rev.Comm. Reports 1 (1993)].

Research References

Treatises and Practice Aids

Witkin, California Summary 10th Parent and Child § 306, Voiding or Rescinding Declaration.

Witkin, California Summary 10th Parent and Child § 420, Emancipation.

§ 7131. Filing of petitions to void declarations

A petition to void a declaration of emancipation on the ground that the declaration was obtained by fraud or by the withholding of material information may be filed by any person or by any public or private agency. The petition shall be filed in the court that made the declaration. *(Stats.1992, c. 162 (A.B.2650), § 10, operative Jan. 1, 1994.)*

Law Revision Commission Comments

Enactment [Revised Comment]

The first sentence of Section 7131 restates without substantive change the first sentence of the second paragraph of former Civil Code Section 69. The second sentence is new. [23 Cal.L.Rev. Comm. Reports 1 (1993)].

Research References

Treatises and Practice Aids

Witkin, California Summary 10th Parent and Child § 306, Voiding or Rescinding Declaration.

§ 7132. Filing of petitions to rescind declarations

(a) A petition to rescind a declaration of emancipation on the ground that the minor is indigent and has no means of support may be filed by the minor declared emancipated, by the minor's conservator, or by the district attorney of the county in which the minor resides. The petition shall be filed in the county in which the minor or the conservator resides.

(b) The minor may be considered indigent if the minor's only source of income is from public assistance benefits. The court shall consider the impact of the rescission of the declaration of emancipation on the minor and shall find the rescission of the declaration of emancipation will not be contrary to the best interest of the minor before granting the order to rescind. *(Stats.1992, c. 162 (A.B.2650), § 10, operative Jan. 1, 1994. Amended by Stats.1993, c. 219 (A.B.1500), § 158.)*

Law Revision Commission Comments

Enactment [Revised Comment]

Subdivision (a) of Section 7132 restates former Civil Code Section 65(a) without substantive change, and adds the provision specifying the ground on which the petition is based, drawn from former Civil Code Section 65(c). The reference to the "superior" court has been omitted as surplus. See Section 200 (jurisdiction in superior court). The second sentence of Section 7132 also makes clear that a petition filed by the conservator may be filed either in the county where the minor resides or in the county where the conservator resides.

Subdivision (b) continues the second and third sentences of former Civil Code Section 65(c) without substantive change. The references to an "order of emancipation" have been changed to a "declaration of emancipation" for consistency with other sections. See, e.g., Section 7120 (petition for declaration of emancipation). [23 Cal. L.Rev.Comm. Reports 1 (1993)].

Research References

Treatises and Practice Aids

Witkin, California Summary 10th Parent and Child § 306, Voiding or Rescinding Declaration.

§ 7133. Notice of petition to void or rescind declaration

(a) Before a petition under this article is heard, notice the court determines is reasonable shall be given to the minor's parents or guardian, or proof shall be made to the court that their addresses are unknown or that for other reasons the notice cannot be given.

(b) The notice to parents shall state that if the declaration of emancipation is voided or rescinded, the parents may be liable to provide support and medical insurance coverage for the child pursuant to Chapter 2 (commencing with Section 4000) of Part 2 of Division 9 of this code and Sections 11350, 11350.1, 11475.1, and 11490 of the Welfare and Institutions Code.

(c) No liability accrues to a parent or guardian not given actual notice, as a result of voiding or rescinding the declaration of emancipation, until that parent or guardian is given actual notice. *(Stats.1992, c. 162 (A.B.2650), § 10, operative Jan. 1, 1994. Amended by Stats.1993, c. 219 (A.B.1500), § 159.)*

Law Revision Commission Comments

Enactment [Revised Comment]

Section 7133 continues without substantive change former Civil Code Section 65(b) and part of the last sentence of the last paragraph of former Civil Code Section 69. The reference to voiding the declaration of emancipation in subdivision (b) has been added for consistency with subdivision (c) and with Section 7130 (grounds for voiding or rescinding). In subdivision (b), a reference to Chapter 2 (commencing with Section 4000) of Part 2 of Division 10 has been substituted for a narrower reference to former Civil Code Section 4700. This is not a substantive change. [23 Cal.L.Rev.Comm. Reports 1 (1993)].

Research References

Treatises and Practice Aids

Witkin, California Summary 10th Parent and Child § 306, Voiding or Rescinding Declaration.

Witkin, California Summary 10th Parent and Child § 420, Emancipation.

§ 7134. Issuance of order

If the petition is sustained, the court shall forthwith issue an order voiding or rescinding the declaration of emancipation, which shall be filed by the clerk of the court. *(Stats. 1992, c. 162 (A.B.2650), § 10, operative Jan. 1, 1994. Amended by Stats.2002, c. 784 (S.B.1316), § 108.)*

Law Revision Commission Comments

Enactment [Revised Comment]

Section 7134 continues without substantive change the first sentence of former Civil Code Section 65(d) and part of the last sentence of the last paragraph of former Civil Code Section 69. [23 Cal.L.Rev.Comm. Reports 1 (1993)].

2002 Amendment

Section 7134 is amended to reflect elimination of the county clerk's role as ex officio clerk of the superior court. See former Gov't Code § 26800 (county clerk acting as clerk of superior court). The powers, duties, and responsibilities formerly exercised by the county clerk as ex officio clerk of the court are delegated to the court administrative or executive officer, and the county clerk is relieved of those powers, duties, and responsibilities. See Gov't Code §§ 69840 (powers, duties, and responsibilities of clerk of court and deputy clerk of court), 71620 (trial court personnel). [32 Cal.L.Rev.Comm. Reports 165 (2002)].

Research References

Treatises and Practice Aids

Witkin, California Summary 10th Parent and Child § 306, Voiding or Rescinding Declaration.

§ 7135. Effect upon contractual and property obligations

Voiding or rescission of the declaration of emancipation does not alter any contractual obligation or right or any property right or interest that arose during the period that the declaration was in effect. *(Stats.1992, c. 162 (A.B.2650), § 10, operative Jan. 1, 1994.)*

Law Revision Commission Comments

Enactment [Revised Comment]

Section 7135 continues without substantive change former Civil Code Section 65(e) and the last sentence of the first paragraph of former Civil Code Section 69. [23 Cal.L.Rev.Comm. Reports 1 (1993)].

Research References

Treatises and Practice Aids

Witkin, California Summary 10th Parent and Child § 306, Voiding or Rescinding Declaration.

ARTICLE 4. IDENTIFICATION CARDS AND INFORMATION

Section

§ 7140. Entry of identifying information into department of motor vehicles records systems; statement of emancipation upon identification card

On application of a minor declared emancipated under this chapter, the Department of Motor Vehicles shall enter identifying information in its law enforcement computer network, and the fact of emancipation shall be stated on the department's identification card issued to the emancipated minor. *(Stats.1992, c. 162 (A.B.2650), § 10, operative Jan. 1, 1994.)*

Law Revision Commission Comments

Enactment [Revised Comment]

Section 7140 continues the last sentence of former Civil Code Section 64(c) without substantive change. [23 Cal.L.Rev.Comm. Reports 1 (1993)].

Research References

Forms

West's California Code Forms, Family § 7110, Comment Overview--Emancipation Of Minor.

Treatises and Practice Aids

Witkin, California Summary 10th Parent and Child § 305, Action.

§ 7141. Reliance on representation of emancipation; effect

A person who, in good faith, has examined a minor's identification card and relies on a minor's representation that the minor is emancipated, has the same rights and obligations as if the minor were in fact emancipated at the time of the representation. *(Stats.1992, c. 162 (A.B.2650), § 10, operative Jan. 1, 1994.)*

Law Revision Commission Comments

Enactment [Revised Comment]

Section 7141 continues former Civil Code Section 66 without substantive change. [23 Cal.L.Rev.Comm. Reports 1 (1993)].

Research References

Treatises and Practice Aids

Witkin, California Summary 10th Parent and Child § 299, Emancipation Of Minors Law.

§ 7142. Liability of public entities or employees

No public entity or employee is liable for any loss or injury resulting directly or indirectly from false or inaccurate information contained in the Department of Motor Vehicles records system or identification cards as provided in this part. *(Stats.1992, c. 162 (A.B.2650), § 10, operative Jan. 1, 1994.)*

Law Revision Commission Comments

Enactment [Revised Comment]

Section 7142 continues former Civil Code Section 68 without substantive change. [23 Cal.L.Rev.Comm. Reports 1 (1993)].

Research References

Treatises and Practice Aids

Witkin, California Summary 10th Parent and Child § 299, Emancipation Of Minors Law.

§ 7143. Notification to Department of Motor Vehicles upon voiding or rescission of declaration of emancipation; invalidation of identification cards

If a declaration of emancipation is voided or rescinded, notice shall be sent immediately to the Department of Motor Vehicles which shall remove the information relating to emancipation in its law enforcement computer network. Any identification card issued stating emancipation shall be invalidated. *(Stats.1992, c. 162 (A.B.2650), § 10, operative Jan. 1, 1994.)*

Law Revision Commission Comments

Enactment [Revised Comment]

Section 7143 continues without substantive change the last two sentences of former Civil Code Section 65(d) and part of the last sentence of the last paragraph of former Civil Code Section 69. [23 Cal.L.Rev.Comm. Reports 1 (1993)].

Research References

Treatises and Practice Aids

Witkin, California Summary 10th Parent and Child § 299, Emancipation Of Minors Law.

Division 12

PARENT AND CHILD RELATIONSHIP

Part 1

RIGHTS OF PARENTS

Section

§ 7500. Services and earnings of child

(a) The mother of an unemancipated minor child, and the father, if presumed to be the father under Section 7611, are equally entitled to the services and earnings of the child.

(b) If one parent is dead, is unable or refuses to take custody, or has abandoned the child, the other parent is entitled to the services and earnings of the child.

(c) This section shall not apply to any services or earnings of an unemancipated minor child related to a contract of a type described in Section 6750. *(Added by Stats.1993, c. 219 (A.B.1500), § 162. Amended by Stats.1999, c. 940 (S.B.1162), § 8.)*

Law Revision Commission Comments

Enactment [Revised Comment]

Section 7500 restates without substantive change the part of former Civil Code Section 197 relating to services and earnings of a minor. The rule in this section is parallel to the general rule on the right to custody provided in Section 3010. The word "unemancipated" has been substituted for "unmarried." This is not a substantive change. See Section 7002 (conditions of emancipation). See also Sections 7503 (payment of earnings to minor), 7504 (parent may relinquish right of controlling child and receiving child's earnings). [23 Cal.L.Rev.Comm. Reports 1 (1993)].

Research References

Treatises and Practice Aids

Witkin, California Summary 10th Husband and Wife § 3, Statutory Framework.

Witkin, California Summary 10th Parent and Child § 63, in General.

Witkin, California Summary 10th Parent and Child § 296, in General.

Witkin, California Summary 10th Parent and Child § 311, Other Proceedings Stayed.

§ 7501. Residence of children; determination by parents; restrictions; public policy

(a) A parent entitled to the custody of a child has a right to change the residence of the child, subject to the power of the court to restrain a removal that would prejudice the rights or welfare of the child.

(b) It is the intent of the Legislature to affirm the decision in In re Marriage of Burgess (1996) 13 Cal.4th 25, and to declare that ruling to be the public policy and law of this state. *(Added by Stats.1993, c. 219 (A.B.1500), § 164. Amended by Stats.2003, c. 674 (S.B.156), § 1.)*

Law Revision Commission Comments

Enactment [Revised Comment]

Section 7501 continues former Civil Code Section 213 without substantive change. The reference to the "proper" court is omitted as surplus. See also Section 3063 (order restraining removal of child from state); Prob. Code § 2352 (guardian may fix residence of minor ward). [23 Cal.L.Rev.Comm. Reports 1 (1993)].

Commentary

In re Marriage of Burgess, 13 Cal.4th 25, 913 P.2d 473, 51 Cal.Rptr.2d 444 (1996), gave new life to Section 7501. Overruling a considerable body of doctrine developed by the courts of appeal, the California Supreme Court held that Section 7501 is controlling when the child's custodial parent wishes to change residence with the child. The custodial parent has the right to move, subject to the court's power to restrain the move if it would harm the welfare of the child. The reason for the move need only be "sound" and in "good faith," that is, not intended to frustrate the other parent's visitation. The custodian need not show that the move is "necessary," "essential," or "expedient." In rejecting the notion that the moving parent has any burden to justify the move (13 Cal.4th at 34), the Supreme Court disapproved language to the contrary in recent court of appeal cases, including *In re Marriage of Seltzer, 29 Cal.App.4th 637, 644–45, 34 Cal.Rptr.2d 824 (1994), review denied*; *In re Marriage of Roe, 18 Cal.App.4th 1483, 1489–90, 23 Cal.Rptr.2d 295 (1993)*; *In re Marriage of McGinnis, 7 Cal.App.4th 473, 479, 9 Cal.Rptr.2d 182 (1992)*; and *In re Marriage of Rosson, 178 Cal.App.3d 1094, 1102, 224 Cal.Rptr. 250 (1986)*. *Id.* at 38, note 10.

Nor is the custodial parent's decision to move ordinarily sufficient to warrant a change of custody. Instead, the proponent of a motion to change custody must bear the usual burden of showing changed circumstances that make "a change of custody . . . essential or expedient for the welfare of the child." *Id.* at 38. The court emphasized that the need for continuity in the child's relationship with the primary caretaker normally cautions against any change in custody. *Id.* at 37. Instead the court should refashion visitation so that the child may also maintain a relationship with the other parent. *Id.* at 40.

The intention of the California Supreme Court was to put an end to the de facto practice, enforced by court of appeal doctrine, of holding the custodial parent hostage to her children in the community in which she resided during her marriage. With surprising candor,

Mr. Burgess argued "that most custodial parents seeking to move are really 'bluffing'; they will not move if the move will result in loss of custody." In other words, Mr. Burgess argued, the true goal of the court of appeal doctrine disapproved by the Supreme Court was simply to prevent the custodial parent from moving away from the community in which the other parent resided. The Supreme Court rejected this goal as illegitimate; a custodial parent ought not be forced to such choices. *Id.* at 36, note 7. Stats.2003, ch. 674 amended this section to codify the holding of *Burgess.*

Nevertheless, the Supreme Court's subsequent decision in *In re Marriage of LaMusga, 32 Cal.4th 1072, 12 Cal.Rptr.3d 356, 88 P.3d 81 (2004)*, may be read to reintroduce that trial court practice. In *LaMusga*, the Supreme Court found that the trial court acted in accordance with *Burgess* and did not abuse its discretion when it (1) found the necessary detriment in the proposed move's disruption of the children's relationship with the noncustodial father, a relationship described by the trial court's expert as "tenuous at best," (2) applied the best interest standard without mentioning the importance of continuity in the children's relationship to their primary parent or the strength of their attachment to the custodial mother, and (3) ordered that custody remain with the mother if she did not move, but that custody change to the father if she did move. In disapproving the court of appeal's reversal of the trial court order, the Supreme Court restored to trial courts a large measure of the power and discretion that *Burgess* initially promised to curtail in move-away cases.

Although there was some confusion below, *Burgess* was ultimately treated as an initial custody and visitation order where one parent had de facto sole physical custody. The Supreme Court prescribed the same "change of circumstances" rubric when a parent who has sole physical custody under an existing order seeks to relocate. *Id.* at 37. The Court also noted that the "change of circumstances" rubric should not be applied in true (de facto as well as de jure) joint physical custody cases. "In such cases, the custody order 'may be modified or terminated upon the petition of one or both parents or on the court's own motion if it is shown that the best interest of the child requires modification or termination of the order.' (Fam. Code § 3087.) The trial court must determine de novo what arrangement for primary custody is in the best interest of the minor children." *Id.* at 40, note 12. But see *Brody v. Kroll, 53 Cal.Rptr.2d 280 (1996), review denied September 4, 1996* (court of appeal appears to invoke *Burgess* joint custody rubric on facts that arguably do not support its application). Compare *In re Marriage of Whealon, 53 Cal.App.4th 132, 61 Cal.Rptr.2d 559 (1997)* (parent with liberal visitation rights did not have "actual joint physical custody" for purposes of *Burgess* rubric); and *In re Marriage of Biallas, 65 Cal.App.4th 755, 76 Cal.Rptr.2d 717 (1998)* (parent with liberal visitation rights, i.e., one overnight a week plus every other weekend, did not have "actual joint physical custody" for purposes of *Burgess* rule). See also *In re Marriage of Edlund and Hales, 66 Cal.App.4th 1454, 78 Cal.Rptr.2d 671 (1998)* (holding that the trial court did not abuse its discretion in permitting custodial parent to relocate to Indiana with the parties' child and explaining the implications of *Burgess*). *In re Marriage of Bryant, 91 Cal.App.4th 789, 110 Cal.Rptr.2d 791 (2001)* (applying *Burgess*, trial court did not abuse its discretion in initial custody determination by awarding primary physical custody to mother who planned to move with the children from Santa Barbara to New Mexico when move was not motivated by bad faith, even though the best interests of the children would be served by remaining in Santa Barbara, where the father continued to reside); and *In re Marriage of Lasich, 99 Cal.App.4th 702, 121 Cal.Rptr.2d 356 (2002)* (granting mother permission to relocate with custodial children from California to Spain).

Jane J. v. Superior Court, 237 Cal.App.4th 894, 188 Cal.Rptr.3d 432 (2015), holds that when a noncustodial parent who resides out of state seeks primary custody, the noncustodial parent does not have the benefit of the presumption of this section and must show that the move away from the custodial parent would not be detrimental to the children and would serve the children's best interest. *Jane J.* stayed a court order awarding an out-of-state noncustodial parent physical custody of the children and granted a peremptory writ in the first instance because the custodial parent's entitlement to relief was so obvious that no purpose could be served by plenary consideration.

In re Marriage of Rose and Richardson, 102 Cal.App.4th 941, 126 Cal.Rptr.2d 45 (2002), holds that the *Burgess* "changed circumstances" rubric applies only when the initial order awarding one parent custody was a final judicial custody determination within the meaning of *Montenegro v. Diaz.* (see Family Code § 3022 Commentary.) When the initial order does not satisfy *Montenegro v. Diaz* standards, the trial count must instead make a de novo "best interests" custody determination.

Mark T. v. Jamie Z., 194 Cal.App.4th 1115, 124 Cal.Rptr.3d 200 (2011), review denied, held that a trial court erred in denying a move-away request of a parent who was sharing temporary joint physical custody of a child and failing to determine what custody arrangement would be in the child's best interest, assuming that the parent does relocate.

When one parent made a move-away motion in the course of an initial custody determination, *In re F.T. v. L.J., 194 Cal.App.4th 1, 123 Cal.Rptr.3d 120 (2011)*, held a trial court erred in denying the move-away motion without addressing the custody arrangement. A trial court should not deny a move-away motion. Instead the trial court should assume that the moving parent will move away and determine how, in that event, custody should be awarded consistent with the best interests of the child. To the same effect, see *Jacob A. v. C.H., 196 Cal.App.4th 1591, 127 Cal.Rptr.3d 611 (2011)*. However, *F.T. v. L.J.* allows the court to make its custody allocation conditional upon the parent's relocation.

Although *LaMusga* and its progeny require a court to make a best interest custody determination that assumes the relocation of one parent, when a trial court wishes to frustrate a parent's relocation, it is difficult to understand how making a custodial allocation conditional upon a parent's relocation materially differs from simple denial of a move-away motion. LaMusga, read with close attention to its facts, is illustrative.

In re Marriage of Abrams, 105 Cal.App.4th 979, 130 Cal.Rptr.2d 16 (2003), review denied May 14, 2003, held that a provision in a stipulated custody order barring the custodial parent from changing in the children's residence "without the written consent of both parties or until further order of the Court" was merely a means of insuring the noncustodial parent notice and opportunity to contest any impending move. Its inclusion did not alter application of the *Burgess* rubric.

In re Marriage of Campos, 108 Cal.App.4th 839, 134 Cal.Rptr.2d 300 (2003), holds that the trial court must give the noncustodial parent an opportunity to present evidence that a custodial parent's good faith move would be so detrimental to the children that a change in custody is essential for their welfare.

When a custodial parent seeks to relocate with the child, *Marriage of Brown and Yana, 37 Cal.4th 947, 38 Cal.Rptr.3d 610, 127 P.3d 28 (2006)*, holds that the noncustodial parent who seeks a change of custody must allege and offer proof of the detriment required for custody modification in order to obtain an evidentiary hearing. Thus *Brown and Yana* sustained the trial court's denial of an evidentiary hearing to a noncustodial parent after the trial court determined that the noncustodial parent's offer of proof did not tend to demonstrate that a move to Nevada would be detrimental to the child. The noncustodial parent's offer of proof related only to general living conditions and schools in Las Vegas, rather than to any fact specific to the welfare of the child. *Brown and Yana* also holds that the proposed relocation of a custodial parent awarded sole legal and physical custody is equally subject to the rubric applied when, more commonly, parents share legal custody and the relocating parent is the sole, or primary, custodian.

Jane J. v. Superior Court, 237 Cal.App.4th 894, 188 Cal.Rptr.3d 432 (2015), issued a peremptory writ directing a trial court to vacate a move-away order when the trial court had failed to hold a hearing on all California law issues pertaining to a move-away order. Read together, *Brown* and *Yana* and *Jane J.* support the proposition that a move-away order may not be granted unless all issues relevant to the move are heard and determined by the trial court.

For a post *Burgess* case denying a primary caretaker's request for permission to relocate with the child, see *Cassady v. Signorelli, 49 Cal.App.4th 55, 56 Cal.Rptr.2d 545 (1996), review denied November 20, 1996.* For a post-*Burgess*/ post-*LaMusga* decision approving a trial court's careful application of the Supreme Court's move-away rubric to the facts of the case and change of custody to the non-moving parent, see *In re Marriage of Melville, 122 Cal.App.4th 601, 18 Cal.Rptr.3d 685 (2004), review denied*. For a post-*Burgess*/post-*LaMusga* decision affirming a trial court's determination that a noncustodial father failed to show that the mother's relocation would cause detriment to the child, see *Osgood v. Landon, 127 Cal.App.4th 425, 25 Cal.Rptr.3d 379 (2005)*.

For treatment of the issues posed by a custodial parent's proposed relocation to a foreign country, including the problem of guaranteeing the continuing enforceability of the decree, see *In re Marriage of Abargil, 106 Cal.App.4th 1294, 131 Cal.Rptr.2d 429 (2003); In re Marriage of Condon, 62 Cal.App.4th 533, 73 Cal.Rptr.2d 33 (1998)*; and *J.M. v. G.H., 228 Cal.App.4th 925, 175 Cal.Rptr.3d 371 (2014)*.

J.M. v. G.H., 228 Cal.App.4th 925, 175 Cal.Rptr.3d 371 (2014), held that a trial court did not abuse its discretion in allowing a mother to relocate to Israel with the parties' child, based on the child's closer bond to his mother. Assuming that the mother would move to Israel, the trial court concluded that the son would suffer greater detriment if he were separated from the mother than from the father.

In re Marriage of Williams, 88 Cal.App.4th 808, 105 Cal.Rptr.2d 923 (2001), holds that family court may enter an order that separates siblings only when compelling circumstances require separation in order to serve the children's best interests. *Williams* was a move-away case in which the parents had been exercising joint physical custody of the parties' four children. The court of appeal disapproved the trial court's award of two children to one parent, and two children to the other.

With Williams, compare *J.M. v. G.H., 228 Cal.App.4th 925, 175 Cal.Rptr.3d 371 (2014)*, which declined to apply the compelling circumstances requirement to the separation of stepsiblings.

In a relocation case, *Wilson v. Shea, 87 Cal.App.4th 887, 104 Cal.Rptr.2d 880 (2001)*, invokes the subsection (b) legislative purpose to assure a child's frequent and continuing contact with both parents to justify § 4057 (b)(5) reduction of the guideline child support amount by an amount intended to cover that parent's transportation expenses in visiting the child.

For discussion of the standards applicable in a nonrelocation case in which one parent seeks to change an existing custody order, see Commentary to Sections 3022 and 3087.

Research References

Forms

California Transactions Forms--Family Law § 2:74, Move-Away Cases.

California Transactions Forms--Family Law § 3:16, Identifying Areas Of Parental Decision Making and Participation.

California Transactions Forms--Family Law § 3:18, Overview.

California Transactions Forms--Family Law § 3:76, Procedure in Event Of Moveaway.

West's California Code Forms, Family § 7500, Comment Overview--Rights Of Parents.

West's California Code Forms, Family § 7501 Form 1, Notice Of Motion and Supporting Declaration for Order Restraining Change Of Residence Of Child.

West's California Code Forms, Family § 7501 Form 2, Order Restraining Change Of Residence Of Child.

Treatises and Practice Aids

Witkin, California Summary 10th Parent and Child § 211, in General.

Witkin, California Summary 10th Parent and Child § 253, Move-Away Cases.

§ 7502. Property of child; control

The parent, as such, has no control over the property of the child. *(Added by Stats.1993, c. 219 (A.B.1500), § 165.)*

Law Revision Commission Comments

Enactment [Revised Comment]

Section 7502 continues former Civil Code Section 202 without change. See also Section 3902 (court allowance to parent for support of child from child's property). [23 Cal.L.Rev.Comm. Reports 1 (1993)].

Research References

Treatises and Practice Aids

Witkin, California Summary 10th Parent and Child § 296, in General.

§ 7503. Payment of earnings to minor

The employer of a minor shall pay the earnings of the minor to the minor until the parent or guardian entitled to the earnings gives the employer notice that the parent or guardian claims the earnings. *(Added by Stats.1993, c. 219 (A.B.1500), § 166.)*

Law Revision Commission Comments

Enactment [Revised Comment]

Section 7503 restates former Civil Code Section 212 without substantive change. The word "shall" has been substituted for "may." This is consistent with Probate Code Section 2601(a)(2) (earnings shall be paid to ward unless otherwise ordered by court). The word "earnings" has been substituted for "wages" to conform with terminology in other sections of this code and to provide consistent treatment of different forms of income. See, e.g., Section 5206 ("earnings" defined). The phrase "employed in service" has been omitted as obsolete. See also Section 7504 (relinquishment by parent of right to receive earnings of child). [23 Cal.L.Rev.Comm. Reports 1 (1993)].

Research References

Forms

West's California Code Forms, Family § 7503 Form 1, Notice by Parent or Guardian Claiming Wages Of Child.

Treatises and Practice Aids

Witkin, California Summary 10th Parent and Child § 296, in General.

§ 7504. Relinquishment of parental rights; abandonment

The parent, whether solvent or insolvent, may relinquish to the child the right of controlling the child and receiving the child's earnings. Abandonment by the parent is presumptive evidence of that relinquishment. *(Added by Stats.1993, c. 219 (A.B.1500), § 167.)*

Law Revision Commission Comments

Enactment [Revised Comment]

Section 7504 continues former Civil Code Section 211 without substantive change. [23 Cal.L.Rev.Comm. Reports 1 (1993)].

Research References

Forms

West's California Code Forms, Family § 7500, Comment Overview-- Rights Of Parents.

Treatises and Practice Aids

Witkin, California Summary 10th Constitutional Law § 237, Voters.
Witkin, California Summary 10th Parent and Child § 296, in General.
Witkin, California Summary 10th Parent and Child § 298, Types Of Emancipation.

§ 7505. Parental authority; termination

The authority of a parent ceases on any of the following:

(a) The appointment, by a court, of a guardian of the person of the child.

(b) The marriage of the child.

(c) The child attaining the age of majority. *(Added by Stats.1993, c. 219 (A.B.1500), § 168.)*

Law Revision Commission Comments

Enactment [Revised Comment]

Section 7505 continues former Civil Code Section 204 without substantive change. See also Sections 7050–7052 (effect of emancipation under Emancipation of Minors Law). [23 Cal.L.Rev.Comm. Reports 1 (1993)].

Commentary

Guardianship of Zachary H., 73 Cal.App.4th 51, 86 Cal.Rptr.2d 7 (1999), holds that the trial court properly appointed prospective adoptive parents, with whom the child had been placed from birth, as the guardians of the child after their adoption of the child failed because of the father's opposition, when changing custody to the father, who was not otherwise shown to be unfit, would cause detriment to the child, and the best interest of the child required that custody be continued with the guardians. Although the federal due process clause requires a showing of "unfitness" before parental rights are terminated, the appointment of a guardian does not terminate parental rights. Similarly, see *Adoption of Daniele G., 87 Cal.App.4th 1392, 105 Cal.Rptr.2d 341 (2001)*, which holds that the trial court improperly denied the guardianship petition of prospective adoptive parents currently caring for the child when the court found that removal from the current home would cause detriment to the child and remaining in the current home was in the child's best interests. Although adoption might not proceed without the father's consent, granting guardianship to the prospective adoptive parents was warranted by the court's findings.

Research References

Treatises and Practice Aids

Witkin, California Summary 10th Parent and Child § 298, Types Of Emancipation.

§ 7506. Support of adult child; compensation

Where a child, after attaining the age of majority, continues to serve and to be supported by the parent, neither party is entitled to compensation, in the absence of an agreement for the compensation. *(Added by Stats.1993, c. 219 (A.B. 1500), § 169.)*

Law Revision Commission Comments

Enactment [Revised Comment]

Section 7506 continues former Civil Code Section 210 without substantive change. [23 Cal.L.Rev.Comm. Reports 1 (1993)].

Research References

Forms

West's California Code Forms, Family § 7506, Comment Overview-- Support Of Adult Child.

Treatises and Practice Aids

Witkin, California Summary 10th Parent and Child § 296, in General.
Witkin, California Summary 10th Parent and Child § 421, Agreement to Support Adult Child.

§ 7507. Abuse of parental authority; remedy

The abuse of parental authority is the subject of judicial cognizance in a civil action brought by the child, or by the child's relative within the third degree, or by the supervisors of the county where the child resides; and when the abuse is established, the child may be freed from the dominion of the parent, and the duty of support and education enforced. *(Added by Stats.1993, c. 219 (A.B.1500), § 170.)*

Law Revision Commission Comments

Enactment [Revised Comment]

Section 7507 continues former Civil Code Section 203 without change. [23 Cal.L.Rev.Comm. Reports 1 (1993)].

Research References

Forms

West's California Code Forms, Family § 7500, Comment Overview-- Rights Of Parents.

Treatises and Practice Aids

Witkin, California Summary 10th Parent and Child § 289, in General.

Part 2

PRESUMPTION CONCERNING CHILD OF MARRIAGE AND BLOOD TESTS TO DETERMINE PATERNITY

CHAPTER 1. CHILD OF WIFE COHABITING WITH HUSBAND

§ 7540. Conclusive presumption as child of marriage; exceptions

Except as provided in Section 7541, the child of a wife cohabiting with her husband, who is not impotent or sterile, is conclusively presumed to be a child of the marriage. *(Formerly § 7500, enacted by Stats.1992, c. 162 (A.B.2650), § 10, operative Jan. 1, 1994. Renumbered § 7540 and amended by Stats.1993, c. 219 (A.B.1500), § 161.)*

Law Revision Commission Comments

Enactment [Revised Comment]

Section 7540 continues former Evidence Code Section 621(a) without substantive change. [23 Cal.L.Rev.Comm. Reports 1 (1993)].

Commentary

For purposes of this provision, "cohabiting" means living together in the same dwelling and making a home together, ostensibly as husband and wife. *Kusior v. Silver, 54 Cal.2d 603, 609–614, 7 Cal.Rptr. 129 (1960)*. The requirement of cohabitation is not satisfied merely by sexual relations or the opportunity for sexual relations. *Steven W. v. Matthew S., 33 Cal.App.4th 1108, 39 Cal.Rptr.2d 535 (1995)* (weekend sexual encounter of separated husband and wife away from their respective residences did not trigger conclusive presumption because couple was not "cohabiting" within meaning of statute). See generally *People v. Holifield, 205 Cal.App.3d 993, 252 Cal.Rptr. 729 (1988), review denied 2/16/89; People v. Ballard, 203 Cal.App.3d 311, 249 Cal.Rptr. 806 (1988). Steven W. v. Matthew S., 33 Cal.App.4th 1108, 1114, 39 Cal.Rptr.2d 535 (1995), review denied,* held that the conclusive presumption is not applicable to a husband who was not cohabiting with his wife at the time of the child's conception.

For purposes of this section, *In re Marriage of Freeman, 45 Cal.App.4th 1437, 53 Cal.Rptr.2d 439 (1996)*, holds that "sterile" means "incapable of producing live sperm" even though the husband's sperm count was only one-fourth the amount experts currently understand to be necessary for conception.

Alicia R. v. Timothy M., 29 Cal.App.4th 1232, 34 Cal.Rptr.2d 868 (1994), review denied 1/19/95, held that the trial court properly declined to apply, at the behest of a nonmarital putative father in a paternity action, the conclusive presumption of paternity to the child of a marriage previously determined void ab initio by a judgment of nullity, which judgment of nullity also declared that there were no children of the void marriage, even though the presumption of the husband's paternity had not been rebutted within two years of the child's birth.

Under California case law, the constitutionality of any particular application of the Section 7540 conclusive presumption must be determined by an ad hoc substantive due process balancing test. See generally *Michelle W. v. Ronald W., 39 Cal.3d 354, 216 Cal.Rptr. 748 (1985), appeal dismissed 474 U.S. 1043 (1986)*. This rubric was constitutionally approved by the United States Supreme Court in *Michael H. v. Gerald D., 491 U.S. 110 (1989)* (sustaining an application of a prior version of the Section 7540 conclusive presumption barring an extramarital natural father's paternity claim with respect to a child conceived in wedlock). See also *Susan H. v. Jack S., 30 Cal.App.4th 1435, 37 Cal.Rptr.2d 120 (1994)* (conclusive presumption of paternity properly applied to grant summary judgment to putative father in parentage action brought by mother despite blood tests ordered in related divorce action, which proved that the social father of the child, the "conclusively presumed father," was not the biological father of the child); and *Rodney F. v. Karen M., 61 Cal.App.4th 233, 71 Cal.Rptr.2d 399 (1998), review denied April 22, 1998* (applying conclusive presumption to sustain parentage of husband in ongoing marriage despite court-ordered blood tests indicating high probability that petitioner who had adulterous affair with mother was the child's biological father). *Rodney F.* also holds that a mother may not be estopped to deny a biological father's paternity because estoppel would injure the interests of the child, the husband and the state in preserving the integrity of the family. Compare *County of Orange v. Leslie B., 14 Cal.App.4th 976, 17 Cal.Rptr.2d 797 (1993)* (Section 7540 conclusive presumption of paternity inapplicable when its underlying policies are not served even though mother was married to another at time of conception). See also *Comino v. Kelley, 25 Cal.App.4th 678, 30 Cal.Rptr.2d 728 (1994), review denied 9/7/94* (trial court properly refused to apply the Section 7540 conclusive presumption even though husband and wife were cohabiting at the time of conception when their marriage was one of financial convenience only and the putative father subsequently received the child and mother into his home and held the child out as his own, giving rise to presumptive paternity under Section 7611(d)); and *Brian C. v. Ginger K., 77 Cal.App.4th 1198, 92 Cal.Rptr.2d 294 (2000)* (holding that trial court should not have applied the conclusive presumption of this section when (1) at the birth of the child, the mother and her husband were not living together—although they subsequently reconciled; (2) the biological father developed a substantial parent-child relationship with the child from the child's birth until a year and a half later; and (3) the biological father received the child into his home and acknowledged the child as his own (see Family Code § 7611(d)).

Cf. *Steve H. v. Wendy S., 57 Cal.App.4th 379, 67 Cal.Rptr.2d 90 (1997), review granted and opinion of the Court of Appeal superseded, 946 P.2d 817, 68 Cal.Rptr.2d 859 (1997), review dismissed on stipulation of the parties and cause remanded to the Court of Appeal, 960 P.2d 510, 77 Cal.Rptr.2d 706 (1998)* (Court of Appeal initially held that public policy concerns bar husband's action against wife for intentional infliction of emotional distress in the course of her unsuccessful attempt to terminate husband's relationship to a child born during marriage who was not his biological child).

Craig L. v. Sandy S., 125 Cal.App.4th 36, 22 Cal.Rptr.3d 606 (2004), holds that when a mother and her husband, who are cohabiting as husband and wife, permit an alleged biological father to receive her child into his home and hold the child out as his own within the meaning of Section 7611(d), and the two-year limitation of Section 7541(b) has not yet expired, the alleged biological father may assert the Section 7611(d) presumption; the husband may assert only the Section 7611(a) rebuttable presumption, as contrasted with the conclusive presumption of this section; and the court must apply the Section 7612(b) rubric to determine which presumption is the weightier. Only when the court determines that Section 7611(d) presumption is the weightier may the alleged biological father obtain blood tests under Section 7541(b).

Amy G. v. M.W., 142 Cal.App.4th 1, 47 Cal.Rptr.3d 297 (2006), review denied Nov. 29, 2006, held that a wife who has accepted into the marital household a child that her husband fathered in an extramarital relationship, may not assert that she is a presumed mother for purposes of this section or subsection (a) or (d) of section 7611 when the child's biological mother timely asserts her parental interest in the child, the identity of the child's father is undisputed, and he is a party in the proceeding and represents his wife's interests as well as his own.

Research References

Forms

California Transactions Forms--Family Law § 5:4, Rights Of De Facto Parents.

California Transactions Forms--Family Law § 5:9, Use Of Parenting Agreement to Define Rights and Responsibilities Relating to Child on Termination Of Partners' Relationship Where Both Partners Are Biological Parents.

California Transactions Forms--Family Law § 6:3, Definitions.
California Transactions Forms--Family Law § 6:8, Consent for Adoption Of Unmarried Minor.
California Transactions Forms--Family Law § 7:8, Traditional Surrogacy Agreements.
California Transactions Forms--Family Law § 6:11, Initiating Proceeding Under Uniform Parentage Act [Fam C §§ 7600 to 7730].
California Transactions Forms--Family Law § 6:40, Structuring the Adoption.
California Transactions Forms--Family Law § 6:47, Matters to Consider in Drafting Petition for Independent Adoption Of Unmarried Minor.
California Transactions Forms--Family Law § 6:72, Petition to Terminate Parental Rights Of Alleged Father.
California Transactions Forms--Family Law § 6:74, Petition to Terminate Parental Rights Of Alleged Father Served With Notice Of Alleged Paternity Without Timely Response.
California Transactions Forms--Family Law § 6:75, Order Terminating Parental Rights Of Alleged Father Served With Notice Of Alleged Paternity Without Timely Response.
California Transactions Forms--Family Law § 6:76, Ex Parte Application for Order to Terminate Parental Rights Of Alleged Father Who Waived Notice or Denied Paternity.
California Transactions Forms--Family Law § 7:45, Artificial Insemination Surrogacy Agreement Between Intended Father and Surrogate Couple.
California Transactions Forms--Family Law § 7:46, in Vitro Surrogacy Agreement Between Intended Parents and Surrogate Couple; Intended Parents Are Genetic Parents.
California Transactions Forms--Family Law § 7:47, in Vitro Fertilization Surrogacy Agreement Between Intended Mother and Surrogate Using Donated Genetic Material.
California Transactions Forms--Family Law § 7:60, Overview; Paternity Of Child [Fam C § 7613].
California Transactions Forms--Family Law § 3:126, Request for Hearing and Application to Set Aside Voluntary Declaration Of Paternity [Form FL-280].
California Transactions Forms--Family Law § 3:127, Responsive Declaration to Application to Set Aside Voluntary Declaration Of Paternity [Form FL-285].
California Transactions Forms--Family Law § 3:128, Order After Hearing on Motion to Set Aside Voluntary Declaration Of Paternity [Form FL-290].
California Transactions Forms--Family Law § 4:105, Declaration Of Paternity.
California Transactions Forms--Family Law § 3:126.50, Information Sheet for Completing Request for Hearing and Application to Set Aside Voluntary Declaration Of Paternity [Form FL-281].
West's California Code Forms, Family § 7540, Comment Overview--Conclusive Presumption as Child Of Marriage.
West's California Code Forms, Family § 7610, Comment Overview--Establishing Parent and Child Relationship.
West's California Code Forms, Family § 7645, Comment Overview--Setting Aside or Vacating Judgment Of Paternity.
West's California Judicial Council Forms JV-505, Statement Regarding Parentage (Juvenile).

Treatises and Practice Aids

Witkin, California Summary 10th Husband and Wife § 383, Temporary Custody and Visitation.
Witkin, California Summary 10th Parent and Child § 13, Nature and Effect Of Classification.
Witkin, California Summary 10th Parent and Child § 16, Estoppel to Assert Paternity.
Witkin, California Summary 10th Parent and Child § 17, Development Of Law.
Witkin, California Summary 10th Parent and Child § 23, Where Intended Mother is Not Genetic Mother.
Witkin, California Summary 10th Parent and Child § 25, Nature and Effect.
Witkin, California Summary 10th Parent and Child § 26, Constitutional Challenges.
Witkin, California Summary 10th Parent and Child § 27, Cohabitation Requirement.
Witkin, California Summary 10th Parent and Child § 29, Impotence or Sterility.
Witkin, California Summary 10th Parent and Child § 30, Blood Test Disproving Paternity.
Witkin, California Summary 10th Parent and Child § 31, in General.
Witkin, California Summary 10th Parent and Child § 33, Effect Of Declaration.
Witkin, California Summary 10th Parent and Child § 35, in General.
Witkin, California Summary 10th Parent and Child § 43, in General.
Witkin, California Summary 10th Parent and Child § 48, Where No Presumption Applies.
Witkin, California Summary 10th Parent and Child § 56, in General.
Witkin, California Summary 10th Parent and Child § 59, Visitation Privileges.
Witkin, California Summary 10th Parent and Child § 60, Action to Determine Mother and Child Relationship.
Witkin, California Summary 10th Parent and Child § 63, in General.
Witkin, California Summary 10th Parent and Child § 100, in General.
Witkin, California Summary 10th Parent and Child § 23A, (New) Assisted Reproduction Agreements for Gestational Carriers.
Witkin, California Summary 10th Parent and Child § 311, Other Proceedings Stayed.
Witkin, California Summary 10th Torts § 790, Representation Of Sterility.
Witkin, California Summary 10th Wills and Probate § 94, Parent and Child Relationship.

§ 7541. Resolution of question of paternity upon finding of court based upon blood test that husband is not father of child; notice of motion for blood tests

(a) Notwithstanding Section 7540, if the court finds that the conclusions of all the experts, as disclosed by the evidence based on blood tests performed pursuant to Chapter 2 (commencing with Section 7550), are that the husband is not the father of the child, the question of paternity of the husband shall be resolved accordingly.

(b) The notice of motion for blood tests under this section may be filed not later than two years from the child's date of birth by the husband, or for the purposes of establishing paternity by the presumed father or the child through or by the child's guardian ad litem. As used in this subdivision, "presumed father" has the meaning given in Sections 7611 and 7612.

(c) The notice of motion for blood tests under this section may be filed by the mother of the child not later than two years from the child's date of birth if the child's biological father has filed an affidavit with the court acknowledging paternity of the child.

(d) The notice of motion for blood tests pursuant to this section shall be supported by a declaration under oath submitted by the moving party stating the factual basis for placing the issue of paternity before the court.

(e) Subdivision (a) does not apply, and blood tests may not be used to challenge paternity, in any of the following cases:

(1) A case that reached final judgment of paternity on or before September 30, 1980.

(2) A case coming within Section 7613.

(3) A case in which the wife, with the consent of the husband, conceived by means of a surgical procedure. *(Formerly § 7501, enacted by Stats.1992, c. 162 (A.B.2650), § 10, operative Jan. 1, 1994. Renumbered § 7541 and amended by Stats.1993, c. 219 (A.B.1500), § 163. Amended by Stats.1998, c. 581 (A.B.2801), § 18.)*

Law Revision Commission Comments

Enactment [Revised Comment]

Section 7541 restates former Evidence Code Section 621(b)-(h) without substantive change. The last sentence of former Evidence Code Section 621(f), pertaining to cases pending on September 30, 1980, has been omitted as obsolete. [23 Cal.L.Rev.Comm. Reports 1 (1993)].

Commentary

See generally *Johnson v. Calvert, 5 Cal.4th 84, 19 Cal.Rptr.2d 494 (1993), cert. denied 510 U.S. 874, 114 S.Ct. 206, 126 L.Ed.2d 163 (1993); Susan H. v. Jack S., 30 Cal.App.4th 1435, 37 Cal.Rptr.2d 120 (1994)* (conclusive presumption of paternity properly applied to grant summary judgment to putative father in parentage action brought by mother despite blood tests ordered in related divorce action, which proved that the social father of the child, the "conclusively presumed father," was not the biological father of the child). See also *Miller v. Miller, 64 Cal.App.4th 111, 74 Cal.Rptr.2d 797 (1998), review denied August 19, 1998* (conclusive presumption of husband's paternity properly applied to disallow biological father's action to establish paternity of a child conceived and born to husband's wife during their marriage).

As a matter of statutory interpretation, *In re Marriage of Rebecca R., initially reported at 62 Cal.Rptr.2d 730 (1997),* held that the Section 7541 two-year statute of limitations does not apply when a court orders blood tests under Section 7551. In other words a court, unlike the parties, is unconstrained by Section 7541 time limitations. The holding of *Rebecca R.* is unpersuasive as a matter of statutory interpretation and social policy. On July 30, 1997, the Supreme Court ordered that *Rebecca R.* not be officially published. Compare *Rodney F. v. Karen M., 61 Cal.App.4th 233, 71 Cal.Rptr.2d 399 (1998), review denied April 22, 1998* (applying conclusive presumption to sustain parentage of husband in ongoing marriage despite blood tests erroneously ordered by court, which tests indicated high probability that petitioner who had adulterous affair with mother was the child's biological father).

Craig L. v. Sandy S., 125 Cal.App.4th 36, 22 Cal.Rptr.3d 606 (2004), holds that when a mother and her husband, who are cohabiting as husband and wife, permit an alleged biological father to receive her child into his home and hold the child out as his own within the meaning of Section 7611(d), and the two-year limitation of subsection (b) of this section has not yet expired, the alleged biological father may assert the Section 7611(d) presumption; the husband may assert only the Section 7611(a) rebuttable presumption, as contrasted with the Section 7640 conclusive presumption; and the court must apply the Section 7612(b) rubric to determine which presumption is the weightier. Only when the court determines that Section 7611(d) presumption is the weightier may the alleged biological father obtain blood tests under subsection (b) of this section.

Research References

Forms

California Transactions Forms--Family Law § 6:3, Definitions.
California Transactions Forms--Family Law § 6:11, Initiating Proceeding Under Uniform Parentage Act [Fam C §§ 7600 to 7730].
California Transactions Forms--Family Law § 7:45, Artificial Insemination Surrogacy Agreement Between Intended Father and Surrogate Couple.
California Transactions Forms--Family Law § 7:46, in Vitro Surrogacy Agreement Between Intended Parents and Surrogate Couple; Intended Parents Are Genetic Parents.
California Transactions Forms--Family Law § 7:47, in Vitro Fertilization Surrogacy Agreement Between Intended Mother and Surrogate Using Donated Genetic Material.
California Transactions Forms--Family Law § 7:60, Overview; Paternity Of Child [Fam C § 7613].
California Transactions Forms--Family Law § 7:64, Exception to Application Of Fam C § 7613 in Certain Surrogacy Cases.
California Transactions Forms--Family Law § 7:72, Parentage.
West's California Code Forms, Family § 7540, Comment Overview--Conclusive Presumption as Child Of Marriage.
West's California Judicial Council Forms JV-505, Statement Regarding Parentage (Juvenile).

Treatises and Practice Aids

Witkin, California Summary 10th Husband and Wife § 383, Temporary Custody and Visitation.
Witkin, California Summary 10th Parent and Child § 17, Development Of Law.
Witkin, California Summary 10th Parent and Child § 23, Where Intended Mother is Not Genetic Mother.
Witkin, California Summary 10th Parent and Child § 29, Impotence or Sterility.
Witkin, California Summary 10th Parent and Child § 30, Blood Test Disproving Paternity.
Witkin, California Summary 10th Parent and Child § 33, Effect Of Declaration.
Witkin, California Summary 10th Parent and Child § 35, in General.
Witkin, California Summary 10th Parent and Child § 43, in General.
Witkin, California Summary 10th Parent and Child § 48, Where No Presumption Applies.
Witkin, California Summary 10th Parent and Child § 59, Visitation Privileges.
Witkin, California Summary 10th Parent and Child § 60, Action to Determine Mother and Child Relationship.
Witkin, California Summary 10th Torts § 790, Representation Of Sterility.
Witkin, California Summary 10th Wills and Probate § 94, Parent and Child Relationship.

CHAPTER 2. BLOOD TESTS TO DETERMINE PATERNITY

Section

§ 7550. Short title

This chapter may be cited as the Uniform Act on Blood Tests to Determine Paternity. *(Stats.1992, c. 162 (A.B.2650), § 10, operative Jan. 1, 1994. Amended by Stats.1993, c. 219 (A.B.1500), § 174.)*

Law Revision Commission Comments

Enactment [Revised Comment]

Section 7550 continues former Evidence Code Section 890 without substantive change. This section is similar to Section 9 of the Uniform Act on Blood Tests to Determine Paternity (1952). See also Sections 3 (construction of provisions drawn from uniform acts), 13 (severability of provisions). [23 Cal.L.Rev.Comm. Reports 1 (1993)].

Research References

Forms

California Transactions Forms--Family Law § 6:2, Governing Law.

California Transactions Forms--Family Law § 6:11, Initiating Proceeding Under Uniform Parentage Act [Fam C §§ 7600 to 7730].

Treatises and Practice Aids

Witkin, California Summary 10th Parent and Child § 30, Blood Test Disproving Paternity.

Witkin, California Summary 10th Parent and Child § 33, Effect Of Declaration.

Witkin, California Summary 10th Parent and Child § 34, Rescinding or Setting Aside Declaration.

Witkin, California Summary 10th Parent and Child § 41, Blood Test Paternity Index Of 100 or More.

Witkin, California Summary 10th Parent and Child § 603, Identification Of Presumed or Alleged Fathers.

§ 7551. Order for genetic tests in civil actions involving paternity

In a civil action or proceeding in which paternity is a relevant fact, the court may upon its own initiative or upon suggestion made by or on behalf of any person who is involved, and shall upon motion of any party to the action or proceeding made at a time so as not to delay the proceedings unduly, order the mother, child, and alleged father to submit to genetic tests. If a party refuses to submit to the tests, the court may resolve the question of paternity against that party or enforce its order if the rights of others and the interests of justice so require. A party's refusal to submit to the tests is admissible in evidence in any proceeding to determine paternity. For the purposes of this chapter, "genetic tests" means any genetic test that is generally acknowledged as reliable by accreditation bodies designated by the United States Secretary of Health and Human Services. *(Stats.1992, c. 162 (A.B.2650), § 10, operative Jan. 1, 1994. Amended by Stats.1997, c. 599 (A.B.573), § 36.)*

Law Revision Commission Comments

Enactment [Revised Comment]

Section 7551 continues former Evidence Code Section 892 without substantive change. This section is similar to Section 1 of the Uniform Act on Blood Tests to Determine Paternity (1952). In the first sentence, the reference to "proceeding" has been added. This is not a substantive change. See Evid. Code § 120 ("civil action" defined to include civil proceeding). [23 Cal.L.Rev.Comm. Reports 1 (1993)].

Commentary

On the constitutionality of Section 7551, see generally *El Dorado County v. Schneider, 191 Cal.App.3d 1263, 237 Cal.Rptr. 51 (1987), review denied 7/29/87* (application of Section 7551 to resolve paternity against putative father because he refused blood tests does not violate first amendment freedom to practice religion when putative father does not indicate how blood tests would interfere with his religious beliefs; nor is there any state constitutional right to a jury trial).

In re Raphael P. III, 97 Cal.App.4th 716, 118 Cal.Rptr.2d 610 (2002), review denied June 19, 2002, holds that, in a dependency proceeding, Family Code §§ 7551 and 7554 do not authorize a court to order genetic testing of a man who meets the requirements of presumed fatherhood. *Raphael P.* also observes that this section allows a court to order paternity testing only when paternity is a relevant fact, which it arguably is not in a dependency proceeding when a man claims presumptive paternity and no other man asserts paternity.

Although grandparents may bring an action for paternity under Section 7630(c) when the putative father is deceased, either in their individual capacity or as representatives of the deceased putative father, they may not be made defendants in a paternity action nor required to submit to blood tests when their son, the putative father, is deceased. *William M. v. Superior Court, 225 Cal.App.3d 447, 452, 275 Cal.Rptr. 103 (1990), review denied 3/14/91.*

When an indigent putative father requests blood tests in the course of a civil paternity proceeding, he is entitled to have the county pay for the tests. *Michael B. v. Superior Court, 86 Cal.App.3d 1006, 150 Cal.Rptr. 586 (1978)*. See also *Tulare County v. Ybarra, 143 Cal.App.3d 580, 192 Cal.Rptr. 49 (1983)* (trial court abused discretion in dismissing paternity action brought by state because putative father was indigent and there were no public funds available to pay attorney; court should have appointed counsel to represent putative father). But compare *Cunningham v. Superior Court, 177 Cal.App.3d 336, 222 Cal.Rptr. 854 (1986), review denied 5/8/86* (compelling attorney to represent indigent putative father without compensation is denial of equal protection). Cf. *Santa Clara County v. Superior Court, 2 Cal.App.4th 1686, 5 Cal.Rptr.2d 7 (1992), review denied 4/16/92* (when indigent father may be jailed for civil contempt for failure to pay child support, county must provide attorney at public expense).

For discussion of the relationship between Section 7551 and Section 7541, see Section 7541, Commentary.

Research References

Forms

California Practice Guide: Rutter Family Law Forms Form 6:4, Request for Order Re Genetic Paternity Testing.

West's California Code Forms, Family § 7550, Comment Overview--Blood Tests to Determine Paternity.

West's California Judicial Council Forms FL-627, Order for Genetic (Parentage) Testing.

West's California Judicial Council Forms FL-684, Request for Order and Supporting Declaration (Governmental).

Treatises and Practice Aids

Witkin, California Summary 10th Parent and Child § 34, Rescinding or Setting Aside Declaration.

Witkin, California Summary 10th Parent and Child § 36, Nonbiological Father as Presumed Father.

Witkin, California Summary 10th Parent and Child § 47, Where Presumption Of Paternity Applies.

§ 7551.5. Genetic test facilitation for enforcement purposes

All hospitals, local child support agencies, welfare offices, and family courts shall facilitate genetic tests for purposes of enforcement of this chapter. This may include having a health care professional available for purposes of extracting samples to be used for genetic testing. *(Added by Stats.1999, c. 652 (S.B.240), § 6.)*

§ 7552. Party performing tests

The genetic tests shall be performed by a laboratory approved by any accreditation body that has been approved by the United States Secretary of Health and Human Services. Any party or person at whose suggestion the tests have been ordered may demand that other experts, qualified as examiners of blood types, perform independent tests under order of the court, the results of which may be offered in evidence. The number and qualifications of these experts shall be determined by the court. *(Stats.1992, c. 162 (A.B. 2650), § 10, operative Jan. 1, 1994. Amended by Stats.1994, c. 1266 (A.B.3804), § 3.5; Stats.1997, c. 599 (A.B.573), § 37; Stats.1998, c. 485 (A.B.2803), § 66.)*

Law Revision Commission Comments

Enactment [Revised Comment]

Section 7552 continues former Evidence Code Section 893 without substantive change. This section is the same as Section 2 of the Uniform Act on Blood Tests to Determine Paternity (1952). [23 Cal.L.Rev.Comm. Reports 1 (1993)].

Commentary

See Section 7551, Commentary.

Research References

Forms

California Practice Guide: Rutter Family Law Forms Form 6:4, Request for Order Re Genetic Paternity Testing.

Treatises and Practice Aids

Witkin, California Summary 10th Parent and Child § 56, in General.
Witkin, California Summary 10th Parent and Child § 58, Grant or Denial.

§ 7552.5. Genetic test results; copy to parties; declaration; admittance into evidence without foundation; written objections; expert witnesses

(a) A copy of the results of all genetic tests performed under Section 7552 or 7558 shall be served upon all parties, by any method of service authorized under Chapter 5 (commencing with Section 1010) of Title 14 of Part 2 of the Code of Civil Procedure except personal service, no later than 20 days prior to any hearing in which the genetic test results may be admitted into evidence. The genetic test results shall be accompanied by a declaration under penalty of perjury of the custodian of records or other qualified employee of the laboratory that conducted the genetic tests, stating in substance each of the following:

(1) The declarant is the duly authorized custodian of the records or other qualified employee of the laboratory, and has authority to certify the records.

(2) A statement which establishes in detail the chain of custody of all genetic samples collected, including the date on which the genetic sample was collected, the identity of each person from whom a genetic sample was collected, the identity of the person who performed or witnessed the collecting of the genetic samples and packaged them for transmission to the laboratory, the date on which the genetic samples were received by the laboratory, the identity of the person who unpacked the samples and forwarded them to the person who performed the laboratory analysis of the genetic sample, and the identification and qualifications of all persons who performed the laboratory analysis and published the results.

(3) A statement which establishes that the procedures used by the laboratory to conduct the tests for which the test results are attached are used in the laboratory's ordinary course of business to ensure accuracy and proper identification of genetic samples.

(4) The genetic test results were prepared at or near the time of completion of the genetic tests by personnel of the business qualified to perform genetic tests in the ordinary course of business.

(b) The genetic test results shall be admitted into evidence at the hearing or trial to establish paternity, without the need for foundation testimony of authenticity and accuracy, unless a written objection to the genetic test results is filed with the court and served on all other parties, by any party no later than five days prior to the hearing or trial where paternity is at issue.

(c) If a written objection is filed with the court and served on all parties within the time specified in subdivision (b), experts appointed by the court shall be called by the court as witnesses to testify to their findings and are subject to cross-examination by the parties.

(d) If a genetic test reflects a paternity index of 100 or greater, the copy of the results mailed under subdivision (a) shall be accompanied with a voluntary declaration of paternity form, information prepared according to Section 7572. *(Added by Stats.1994, c. 1266 (A.B.3804), § 3.7. Amended by Stats.1997, c. 599 (A.B.573), § 38; Stats.1999, c. 652 (S.B. 240), § 7.)*

Research References

Forms

California Practice Guide: Rutter Family Law Forms Form 6:4, Request for Order Re Genetic Paternity Testing.
West's California Judicial Council Forms FL-627, Order for Genetic (Parentage) Testing.

§ 7553. Compensation of experts

(a) The compensation of each expert witness appointed by the court shall be fixed at a reasonable amount. It shall be paid as the court shall order. Except as provided in subdivision (b), the court may order that it be paid by the parties in the proportions and at the times the court prescribes, or that the proportion of any party be paid by the county, and that, after payment by the parties or the county or both, all or part or none of it be taxed as costs in the action or proceeding.

(b) If the expert witness is appointed for the court's needs, the compensation shall be paid by the court. *(Stats.1992, c. 162 (A.B.2650), § 10, operative Jan. 1, 1994. Amended by Stats.2012, c. 470 (A.B.1529), § 22.)*

Law Revision Commission Comments

Enactment [Revised Comment]

Section 7553 continues former Evidence Code Section 894 without substantive change. This section is similar to the first three sentences of Section 3 of the Uniform Act on Blood Tests to Determine Paternity (1952). The reference to "proceeding" has been added. This is not a substantive change. See Evid. Code § 120 ("civil action" defined to include civil proceeding). [23 Cal.L.Rev.Comm. Reports 1 (1993)].

2012 Amendment

Section 7553 is amended to reflect enactment of the Lockyer–Isenberg Trial Court Funding Act, 1997 Cal. Stat. ch. 850 (see generally Gov't Code §§ 77000–77655). See, e.g., Gov't Code §§ 77001 (local trial court management), 77003 ("court operations" defined), 77200 (state funding of "court operations"); see also Cal. R. Ct. 10.810(d), Function 10 ("court operations" include "court-appointed expert witness fees (for the court's needs)").

The amendment reflects that an expert whose compensation is governed by Section 7553 may be appointed by the court for the court's needs. See Sections 7551 (providing that "court may upon its own initiative" order genetic test), 7552 (providing for genetic tests and appointment of other experts), 7556(a) (providing that order for tests may be made "on the court's initiative"). [39 Cal.L.Rev.Comm. Reports 157 (2009)].

Commentary

See Section 7551, Commentary.

§ 7554. Determination of paternity

(a) If the court finds that the conclusions of all the experts, as disclosed by the evidence based upon the tests, are that the alleged father is not the father of the child, the question of paternity shall be resolved accordingly.

(b) If the experts disagree in their findings or conclusions, or if the tests show the probability of the alleged father's paternity, the question, subject to Section 352 of the Evidence Code, shall be submitted upon all the evidence, including evidence based upon the tests. *(Stats.1992, c. 162 (A.B.2650), § 10, operative Jan. 1, 1994.)*

Law Revision Commission Comments

Enactment [Revised Comment]

Section 7554 continues former Evidence Code Section 895 without change. This section is similar to Section 4 of the Uniform Act on Blood Tests to Determine Paternity (1952). [23 Cal.L.Rev.Comm. Reports 1 (1993)].

Commentary

In re Raphael P. III, 97 Cal.App.4th 716, 118 Cal.Rptr.2d 610 (2002), review denied June 19, 2002, holds that, in a dependency proceeding, Family Code §§ 7551 and 7554 do not authorize a court to order genetic testing of a man who meets the requirements of presumed fatherhood. *Raphael P.* also observes that § 7511 allows a court to order paternity testing only when paternity is a relevant fact, which it arguably is not in a dependency proceeding when a man claims presumptive paternity and no other man asserts paternity.

Cramer v. Morrison, 88 Cal.App.3d 873, 880, 153 Cal.Rptr. 865 (1979), hearing denied 3/29/79, initially approved the use of Human Leucocyte Antigen (HLA) tests to affirmatively prove paternity. For discussion of the subsequent codification of this principle in subsection (b), and its application, see *Sonoma County v. Grant, 187 Cal.App.3d 1439, 1447, 232 Cal.Rptr. 471 (1986)*.

Research References

Treatises and Practice Aids

Witkin, California Summary 10th Parent and Child § 30, Blood Test Disproving Paternity.

§ 7555. Rebuttable presumption of paternity; paternity index of 100 or more

(a) There is a rebuttable presumption, affecting the burden of proof, of paternity, if the court finds that the paternity index, as calculated by the experts qualified as examiners of genetic markers, is 100 or greater. This presumption may be rebutted by a preponderance of the evidence.

(b) As used in this section:

(1) "Genetic markers" mean separate genes or complexes of genes identified as a result of genetic tests.

(2) "Paternity index" means the commonly accepted indicator used for denoting the existence of paternity. It expresses the relative strength of the test results for and against paternity. The paternity index, computed using results of various paternity tests following accepted statistical principles, shall be in accordance with the method of expression accepted at the International Conference on Parentage Testing at Airlie House, Virginia, May 1982, sponsored by the American Association of Blood Banks. *(Stats.1992, c. 162 (A.B.2650), § 10, operative Jan. 1, 1994. Amended by Stats.1993, c. 219 (A.B.1500), § 175; Stats.1997, c. 599 (A.B.573), § 39.)*

Law Revision Commission Comments

Enactment [Revised Comment]

Section 7555 continues former Evidence Code Section 895.5 without change. [23 Cal.L.Rev.Comm. Reports 1 (1993)].

Commentary

The Section 7555 presumption of paternity may not be rebutted by the mere existence of other untested men who may also be the child's father. *County of El Dorado v. Misura, 33 Cal.App.4th 73, 38 Cal.Rptr.2d 908 (1995)*.

Consider *City and County of San Francisco v. Givens, 85 Cal. App.4th 51, 101 Cal.Rptr.2d 859 (2000), review denied February 28, 2001*, where the defendant's index was 1290 and the likelihood of paternity was 99.92 percent. Nevertheless, the trial court found that there was no probability that defendant was the father, based on defendant's testimony, contested by plaintiff, that he did not have access to the plaintiff at the time of conception. The trial court's conclusion was sustained on appeal.

Research References

Treatises and Practice Aids

Witkin, California Summary 10th Parent and Child § 17, Development Of Law.
Witkin, California Summary 10th Parent and Child § 33, Effect Of Declaration.
Witkin, California Summary 10th Parent and Child § 35, in General.
Witkin, California Summary 10th Parent and Child § 41, Blood Test Paternity Index Of 100 or More.

§ 7556. Application of part to criminal actions

This part applies to criminal actions subject to the following limitations and provisions:

(a) An order for the tests shall be made only upon application of a party or on the court's initiative.

(b) The compensation of the experts, other than an expert witness appointed by the court for the court's needs, shall be paid by the county under order of court. The compensation of an expert witness appointed for the court's needs shall be paid by the court.

(c) The court may direct a verdict of acquittal upon the conclusions of all the experts under Section 7554; otherwise, the case shall be submitted for determination upon all the evidence. *(Stats.1992, c. 162 (A.B.2650), § 10, operative Jan. 1, 1994. Amended by Stats.2012, c. 470 (A.B.1529), § 23.)*

Law Revision Commission Comments

Enactment [Revised Comment]

Section 7556 continues former Evidence Code Section 896 without substantive change. This section is similar to Section 6 of the Uniform Act on Blood Tests to Determine Paternity (1952). [23 Cal.L.Rev.Comm. Reports 1 (1993)].

2012 Amendment

Section 7556 is amended to reflect enactment of the Lockyer–Isenberg Trial Court Funding Act, 1997 Cal. Stat. ch. 850 (see generally Gov't Code §§ 77000–77655). See, e.g., Gov't Code §§ 77001 (local trial court management), 77003 ("court operations" defined), 77200 (state funding of "court operations"); see also Cal. R. Ct. 10.810(d), Function 10 ("court operations" include "court-appointed expert witness fees (for the court's needs)"). [39 Cal. L.Rev.Comm. Reports 157 (2009)].

§ 7557. Right of parties to produce other expert evidence; payment of fees

Nothing in this part prevents a party to an action or proceeding from producing other expert evidence on the matter covered by this part; but, where other expert witnesses are called by a party to the action or proceeding, their fees shall be paid by the party calling them and only ordinary witness fees shall be taxed as costs in the action or proceeding. *(Stats.1992, c. 162 (A.B.2650), § 10, operative Jan. 1, 1994.)*

Law Revision Commission Comments

Enactment [Revised Comment]

Section 7557 continues former Evidence Code Section 897 without substantive change. The last part of this section is similar to the last sentence of Section 3 of the Uniform Act on Blood Tests to Determine Paternity (1952). The references to "proceeding" have been added. These are not substantive changes. See Evid. Code § 120 ("civil action" defined to include civil proceeding). [23 Cal.L.Rev.Comm. Reports 1 (1993)].

Research References

Forms

California Transactions Forms--Family Law § 6:2, Governing Law.
California Transactions Forms--Family Law § 6:11, Initiating Proceeding Under Uniform Parentage Act [Fam C §§ 7600 to 7730].

§ 7558. Administrative order for genetic testing

(a) This section applies only to cases where support enforcement services are being provided by the local child support agency pursuant to Section 17400.

(b) In any civil action or proceeding in which paternity is a relevant fact, and in which the issue of paternity is contested, the local child support agency may issue an administrative order requiring the mother, child, and the alleged father to submit to genetic testing if any of the following conditions exist:

(1) The person alleging paternity has signed a statement under penalty of perjury that sets forth facts that establish a reasonable possibility of the requisite sexual conduct between the mother and the alleged father.

(2) The person denying paternity has signed a statement under penalty of perjury that sets forth facts that establish a reasonable possibility of the nonexistence of the requisite sexual contact between the parties.

(3) The alleged father has filed an answer in the action or proceeding in which paternity is a relevant fact and has requested that genetic tests be performed.

(4) The mother and the alleged father agree in writing to submit to genetic tests.

(c) Notwithstanding subdivision (b), the local child support agency may not order an individual to submit to genetic tests if the individual has been found to have good cause for failure to cooperate in the determination of paternity pursuant to Section 11477 of the Welfare and Institutions Code.

(d) The local child support agency shall pay the costs of any genetic tests that are ordered under subdivision (b), subject to the county obtaining a court order for reimbursement from the alleged father if paternity is established under Section 7553.

(e) Nothing in this section prohibits any person who has been ordered by the local child support agency to submit to genetic tests pursuant to this section from filing a notice of motion with the court in the action or proceeding in which paternity is a relevant fact seeking relief from the local child support agency's order to submit to genetic tests. In that event, the court shall resolve the issue of whether genetic tests should be ordered as provided in Section 7551. If any person refuses to submit to the tests after receipt of the administrative order pursuant to this section and fails to seek relief from the court from the administrative order either prior to the scheduled tests or within 10 days after the tests are scheduled, the court may resolve the question of paternity against that person or enforce the administrative order if the rights of others or the interest of justice so require. Except as provided in subdivision (c), a person's refusal to submit to tests ordered by the local child support agency is admissible in evidence in any proceeding to determine paternity if a notice of motion is not filed within the timeframes specified in this subdivision.

(f) If the original test result creates a rebuttable presumption of paternity under Section 7555 and the result is contested, the local child support agency shall order an additional test only upon request and advance payment of the contestant. *(Added by Stats.1997, c. 599 (A.B.573), § 40. Amended by Stats.2000, c. 808 (A.B.1358), § 72, eff. Sept. 28, 2000.)*

CHAPTER 3. ESTABLISHMENT OF PATERNITY BY VOLUNTARY DECLARATION

Section

Commentary

Sections 7601 and 7612 have been amended to provide that a child may have more than two legal parents, where having only two legal parent would be detrimental to the child, overturning In re M.C., 195 Cal.App.4th 197, 123 Cal.Rptr.3d 856 (2011), which held that when a dependent child had more than two presumed parents, the court was required to resolve the conflicting presumptions of parentage by reducing the number of presumed parents to no more than two. To the extent that any cases discussed in the Commentary to this Chapter rely on the prior rule that a child may have only two parents and only one father, those cases no longer express controlling law. Nevertheless, prior case law may still be controlling on other issues and those cases might still yield the same results under revised section 7612(c).

§ 7570. Legislative findings and declarations

The Legislature hereby finds and declares as follows:

(a) There is a compelling state interest in establishing paternity for all children. Establishing paternity is the first step toward a child support award, which, in turn, provides children with equal rights and access to benefits, including, but not limited to, social security, health insurance, survivors' benefits, military benefits, and inheritance rights. Knowledge of family medical history is often necessary for correct medical diagnosis and treatment. Additionally, knowing one's father is important to a child's development.

(b) A simple system allowing for establishment of voluntary paternity will result in a significant increase in the ease of establishing paternity, a significant increase in paternity establishment, an increase in the number of children who have greater access to child support and other benefits, and a significant decrease in the time and money required to establish paternity due to the removal of the need for a lengthy and expensive court process to determine and establish paternity and is in the public interest. *(Added by Stats.1993, c. 1240 (A.B.1277), § 1.)*

Research References

Forms

California Transactions Forms--Family Law § 5:8, Effect Of Birth Certificate Paternity Designation; Declaration Of Paternity.
California Transactions Forms--Family Law § 5:9, Use Of Parenting Agreement to Define Rights and Responsibilities Relating to Child on Termination Of Partners' Relationship Where Both Partners Are Biological Parents.
California Transactions Forms--Family Law § 7:38, Parentage and Birth Certificate.
California Transactions Forms--Family Law § 7:52, Application to Amend Birth Record; Acknowledgment Of Paternity [Form vs 22].
California Transactions Forms--Family Law § 7:86, Overview.
Am. Jur. Pl. & Pr. Forms Bastards § 1, Introductory Comments.
West's California Code Forms, Family § 7610, Comment Overview--Establishing Parent and Child Relationship.

Treatises and Practice Aids

Witkin, California Summary 10th Parent and Child § 17, Development Of Law.
Witkin, California Summary 10th Parent and Child § 23, Where Intended Mother is Not Genetic Mother.
Witkin, California Summary 10th Parent and Child § 31, in General.
Witkin, California Summary 10th Parent and Child § 32, Declaration Of Paternity at Birth.
Witkin, California Summary 10th Parent and Child § 33, Effect Of Declaration.
Witkin, California Summary 10th Parent and Child § 34, Rescinding or Setting Aside Declaration.
Witkin, California Summary 10th Parent and Child § 35, in General.
Witkin, California Summary 10th Parent and Child § 46, in General.
Witkin, California Summary 10th Parent and Child § 100, in General.

§ 7571. Voluntary declaration of paternity; liability of health care provider; payment

(a) On and after January 1, 1995, upon the event of a live birth, prior to an unmarried mother leaving any hospital, the person responsible for registering live births under Section 102405 of the Health and Safety Code shall provide to the natural mother and shall attempt to provide, at the place of birth, to the man identified by the natural mother as the natural father, a voluntary declaration of paternity together with the written materials described in Section 7572. Staff in the hospital shall witness the signatures of parents signing a voluntary declaration of paternity and shall forward the signed declaration to the Department of Child Support Services within 20 days of the date the declaration was signed. A copy of the declaration shall be made available to each of the attesting parents.

(b) No health care provider shall be subject to any civil, criminal, or administrative liability for any negligent act or omission relative to the accuracy of the information provided, or for filing the declaration with the appropriate state or local agencies.

(c) The local child support agency shall pay the sum of ten dollars ($10) to birthing hospitals and other entities that provide prenatal services for each completed declaration of paternity that is filed with the Department of Child Support Services, provided that the local child support agency and the hospital or other entity providing prenatal services has entered into a written agreement that specifies the terms and conditions for the payment as required by federal law.

(d) If the declaration is not registered by the person responsible for registering live births at the hospital, it may be completed by the attesting parents, notarized, and mailed to the Department of Child Support Services at any time after the child's birth.

(e) Prenatal clinics shall offer prospective parents the opportunity to sign a voluntary declaration of paternity. In order to be paid for their services as provided in subdivision (c), prenatal clinics must ensure that the form is witnessed and forwarded to the Department of Child Support Services within 20 days of the date the declaration was signed.

(f) Declarations shall be made available without charge at all local child support agency offices, offices of local registrars of births and deaths, courts, and county welfare departments within this state. Staff in these offices shall witness the signatures of parents wishing to sign a voluntary declaration of paternity and shall be responsible for forwarding the signed declaration to the Department of Child Support Services within 20 days of the date the declaration was signed.

(g) The Department of Child Support Services, at its option, may pay the sum of ten dollars ($10) to local registrars of births and deaths, county welfare departments, or courts for each completed declaration of paternity that is witnessed by staff in these offices and filed with the Department of Child Support Services. In order to receive payment, the Department of Child Support Services and the entity shall enter into a written agreement that specifies the terms and conditions for payment as required by federal law. The Department of Child Support Services shall study the effect of the ten dollar ($10) payment on obtaining completed voluntary declaration of paternity forms.

(h) The Department of Child Support Services and local child support agencies shall publicize the availability of the declarations. The local child support agency shall make the declaration, together with the written materials described in subdivision (a) of Section 7572, available upon request to any parent and any agency or organization that is required to offer parents the opportunity to sign a voluntary declaration of paternity. The local child support agency shall also provide qualified staff to answer parents' questions regarding the declaration and the process of establishing paternity.

(i) Copies of the declaration and any rescissions filed with the Department of Child Support Services shall be made available only to the parents, the child, the local child support agency, the county welfare department, the county counsel, the State Department of Health Services, and the courts.

(j) Publicly funded or licensed health clinics, pediatric offices, Head Start programs, child care centers, social services providers, prisons, and schools may offer parents the opportunity to sign a voluntary declaration of paternity. In order to be paid for their services as provided in subdivision (c), publicly funded or licensed health clinics, pediatric offices, Head Start programs, child care centers, social services providers, prisons, and schools shall ensure that the form is witnessed and forwarded to the Department of Child Support Services.

(k) Any agency or organization required to offer parents the opportunity to sign a voluntary declaration of paternity shall also identify parents who are willing to sign, but were unavailable when the child was born. The organization shall then contact these parents within 10 days and again offer the parent the opportunity to sign a voluntary declaration of paternity. *(Added by Stats.1993, c. 1240 (A.B.1277), § 1. Amended by Stats.1994, c. 1269 (A.B.2208), § 51; Stats.1996, c. 1023 (S.B.1497), § 47, eff. Sept. 29, 1996; Stats.1996, c. 1062 (A.B.1832), § 4; Stats.1997, c. 599 (A.B.573), § 41; Stats.1998, c. 485 (A.B.2803), § 67; Stats.1998, c. 858 (A.B. 2169), § 3; Stats.1999, c. 652 (S.B.240), § 8; Stats.2001, c. 745 (S.B.1191), § 44, eff. Oct. 12, 2001; Stats.2001, c. 755 (S.B.943), § 9, eff. Oct. 12, 2001; Stats.2012, c. 728 (S.B.71), § 37.)*

Research References

Forms

California Transactions Forms--Family Law § 5:9, Use Of Parenting Agreement to Define Rights and Responsibilities Relating to Child on Termination Of Partners' Relationship Where Both Partners Are Biological Parents.

West's California Code Forms, Family § 7570, Comment Overview--Establishment Of Paternity by Voluntary Declaration.

Treatises and Practice Aids

Witkin, California Summary 10th Parent and Child § 32, Declaration Of Paternity at Birth.

Witkin, California Summary 10th Parent and Child § 34, Rescinding or Setting Aside Declaration.

Witkin, California Summary 10th Parent and Child § 603, Identification Of Presumed or Alleged Fathers.

§ 7572. Written informational materials; contents; regulations

(a) The Department of Child Support Services, in consultation with the State Department of Health Care Services, the California Association of Hospitals and Health Systems, and other affected health provider organizations, shall work cooperatively to develop written materials to assist providers and parents in complying with this chapter. This written material shall be updated periodically by the Department of Child Support Services to reflect changes in law, procedures, or public need.

(b) The written materials for parents which shall be attached to the form specified in Section 7574 and provided to unmarried parents shall contain the following information:

(1) A signed voluntary declaration of paternity that is filed with the Department of Child Support Services legally establishes paternity.

(2) The legal rights and obligations of both parents and the child that result from the establishment of paternity.

(3) An alleged father's constitutional rights to have the issue of paternity decided by a court; to notice of any hearing on the issue of paternity; to have an opportunity to present his case to the court, including his right to present and cross-examine witnesses; to have an attorney represent him; and to have an attorney appointed to represent him if he cannot afford one in a paternity action filed by a local child support agency.

(4) That by signing the voluntary declaration of paternity, the father is voluntarily waiving his constitutional rights.

(c) Parents shall also be given oral notice of the rights and responsibilities specified in subdivision (b). Oral notice may be accomplished through the use of audio or video recorded programs developed by the Department of Child Support Services to the extent permitted by federal law.

(d) The Department of Child Support Services shall, free of charge, make available to hospitals, clinics, and other places of birth any and all informational and training materials for the program under this chapter, as well as the paternity declaration form. The Department of Child Support Services shall make training available to every participating hospital, clinic, local registrar of births and deaths, and other place of birth no later than June 30, 1999.

(e) The Department of Child Support Services may adopt regulations, including emergency regulations, necessary to implement this chapter. *(Added by Stats.1993, c. 1240 (A.B.1277), § 1. Amended by Stats.1994, c. 1269 (A.B.2208), § 51.5; Stats.1996, c. 1062 (A.B.1832), § 5; Stats.1997, c. 599 (A.B.573), § 42; Stats.1998, c. 485 (A.B.2803), § 68; Stats. 1998, c. 858 (A.B.2169), § 4; Stats.1999, c. 83 (S.B.966), § 53; Stats.1999, c. 652 (S.B.240), § 10; Stats.2009, c. 88 (A.B.176), § 38; Stats.2010, c. 328 (S.B.1330), § 65.)*

Law Revision Commission Comments

2009 Amendment

Subdivision (c) of Section 7572 is amended to reflect advances in recording technology and for consistency of terminology. For a similar reform, see 2002 Cal. Stat. ch. 1068 (replacing numerous references to "audiotape" in Civil Discovery Act with either "audio technology," "audio recording," or "audio record," as context required). [37 Cal. L. Revision Comm'n Reports 211 (2007)].

Research References

Forms

California Transactions Forms--Family Law § 4:105, Declaration Of Paternity.

Treatises and Practice Aids

Witkin, California Summary 10th Parent and Child § 31, in General.

Witkin, California Summary 10th Parent and Child § 32, Declaration Of Paternity at Birth.

§ 7573. Voluntary declaration of paternity; establishment of paternity; force and effect

Except as provided in Sections 7575, 7576, 7577, and 7612, a completed voluntary declaration of paternity, as described in Section 7574, that has been filed with the Department of Child Support Services shall establish the paternity of a child and shall have the same force and effect as a judgment for paternity issued by a court of competent jurisdiction. The voluntary declaration of paternity shall be recognized as a basis for the establishment of an order for child custody, visitation, or child support. *(Added by Stats.1996, c. 1062 (A.B.1832), § 6. Amended by Stats.1998, c. 858 (A.B.2169), § 5; Stats.2000, c. 808 (A.B.1358), § 73, eff. Sept. 28, 2000; Stats.2011, c. 185 (A.B.1349), § 1.)*

Commentary

Kevin Q. v. Lauren W., 175 Cal.App.4th 1119, 95 Cal.Rptr.3d 477 (2009), review denied, held that a voluntary declaration of paternity signed when a child already had a section 7611(d) presumed father had the effect of rebutting the latter's presumption of paternity under section 7612(c), because this section gives a voluntary declaration of paternity the force and effect of a judgment of paternity. Mitigating *Kevin Q.*, section 7612(d), added in 2011, grants any section 7611 presumed father, including a subsection (d) presumed father, the right to file a petition to set aside a voluntary declaration within two years of its making. By contrast, under section 7612(e), also added by the 2011 legislation, when parenthood is presumed under section 7450 or subsections (a),(b), or (c) of section 7611 (but not subsection (d)), any subsequent voluntary declaration of paternity by another person is automatically invalid.

In re Levi H., 197 Cal.App.4th 1279, 128 Cal.Rptr.3d 814 (2011), holds that when a voluntary declaration of paternity qualifies for section 7612(c) treatment, the presumption of paternity arising under section 7611(d) is rebutted by another man's voluntary declaration of paternity, and there is no need to engage in a section 7612(b) weighing analysis.

However, when a child has both an alleged biological father, whose paternity is at issue in a dependency proceeding, and a presumed father, a court must hold an evidentiary hearing on the issue biological paternity. If the court concludes that one man is the biological father and the other man is a presumed father, the court must perform a section 7612(b) balancing analysis to determine which man should be considered the child's father. *In re P.A., 198 Cal.App.4th 974, 130 Cal.Rptr.3d 556 (2011)*. In re P.A. concludes that a finding that a man is a biological father is not a paternity judgment for purposes of section 7612(c). *In re P.A.* interprets subsection (c) to refer to a judgment that already exists when the instant action arises. *In re P.A.* relies on *In re A.A.*, discussed below in the Commentary to this section. By contrast, *In re Cheyenne B., 203 Cal.App.4th 1361, 138 Cal.Rptr.3d 267 (2012), review denied*, holds that a pre-existing judgment that a man is the father of a child for child support purposes is a paternity judgment within the meaning of section 7612(c) and therefore may preclude another man from establishing that the is a presumed father under section 7611(d). Nevertheless, the fact that the child support order satisfies section 7612(c) does not make the support obligor a presumed parent. The effect of *Cheyenne B.* was that the child, who initially had one adjudicated nonpresumptive biological father and one unadjudicated presumptive father, ultimately had no presumed father.

Note that a voluntary declaration of paternity not only has the force and effect of a judgment of paternity, but also entitles the declarer to presumed father status under section 7576.

In re Mary G., 151 Cal.App.4th 184, 59 Cal.Rptr.3d 703 (2007), held that this section violates the equal protection and full faith and credit clauses insofar as it would deny presumed father status to a man on the sole basis that his voluntary acknowledgement of paternity was executed in Michigan, rather than California.

Research References

Forms

California Transactions Forms--Family Law § 5:9, Use Of Parenting Agreement to Define Rights and Responsibilities Relating to Child on Termination Of Partners' Relationship Where Both Partners Are Biological Parents.

California Transactions Forms--Family Law § 6:3, Definitions.

West's California Judicial Council Forms JV-500, Paternity Inquiry.

Treatises and Practice Aids

Witkin, California Summary 10th Parent and Child § 33, Effect Of Declaration.

Witkin, California Summary 10th Parent and Child § 34, Rescinding or Setting Aside Declaration.

Witkin, California Summary 10th Parent and Child § 603, Identification Of Presumed or Alleged Fathers.

§ 7574. Voluntary declaration of paternity; form

(a) The voluntary declaration of paternity shall be executed on a form developed by the Department of Child Support Services in consultation with the State Department of Health Services, the California Family Support Council, and child support advocacy groups.

(b) The form described in subdivision (a) shall contain, at a minimum, the following:

(1) The name and the signature of the mother.

(2) The name and the signature of the father.

(3) The name of the child.

(4) The date of birth of the child.

(5) A statement by the mother that she has read and understands the written materials described in Section 7572, that the man who has signed the voluntary declaration of paternity is the only possible father, and that she consents to the establishment of paternity by signing the voluntary declaration of paternity.

(6) A statement by the father that he has read and understands the written materials described in Section 7572, that he understands that by signing the voluntary declaration of paternity he is waiving his rights as described in the written materials, that he is the biological father of the child, and that he consents to the establishment of paternity by signing the voluntary declaration of paternity.

(7) The name and the signature of the person who witnesses the signing of the declaration by the mother and the father. *(Added by Stats.1996, c. 1062 (A.B.1832), § 8. Amended by Stats.2000, c. 808 (A.B.1358), § 74, eff. Sept. 28, 2000.)*

Research References

Forms

California Transactions Forms--Family Law § 5:9, Use Of Parenting Agreement to Define Rights and Responsibilities Relating to Child on Termination Of Partners' Relationship Where Both Partners Are Biological Parents.

California Transactions Forms--Family Law § 4:105, Declaration Of Paternity.

West's California Code Forms, Family § 7570, Comment Overview--Establishment Of Paternity by Voluntary Declaration.

Treatises and Practice Aids

Witkin, California Summary 10th Parent and Child § 31, in General.

§ 7575. Rescission of voluntary declaration of paternity; factors; action to set aside

(a) Either parent may rescind the voluntary declaration of paternity by filing a rescission form with the Department of Child Support Services within 60 days of the date of execution of the declaration by the attesting father or attesting mother, whichever signature is later, unless a court order for custody, visitation, or child support has been entered in an action in which the signatory seeking to rescind was a party. The Department of Child Support Services shall develop a form to be used by parents to rescind the declaration of paternity and instruction on how to complete and file the rescission with the Department of Child Support Services. The form shall include a declaration under penalty of perjury completed by the person filing the rescission form that certifies that a copy of the rescission form was sent by any form of mail requiring a return receipt to the other person who signed the voluntary declaration of paternity. A copy of the return receipt shall be attached to the rescission form when filed with the Department of Child Support Services. The form and instructions shall be written in simple, easy to understand language and shall be made available at the local family support office and the office of local registrar of births and deaths. The department shall, upon written request, provide to a court or commissioner a copy of any rescission form filed with the department that is relevant to proceedings before the court or commissioner.

(b)(1) Notwithstanding Section 7573, if the court finds that the conclusions of all of the experts based upon the results of the genetic tests performed pursuant to Chapter 2 (commencing with Section 7550) are that the man who signed the voluntary declaration is not the father of the child, the court may set aside the voluntary declaration of paternity unless the court determines that denial of the action to set aside the voluntary declaration of paternity is in the best interest of the child, after consideration of all of the following factors:

(A) The age of the child.

(B) The length of time since the execution of the voluntary declaration of paternity by the man who signed the voluntary declaration.

(C) The nature, duration, and quality of any relationship between the man who signed the voluntary declaration and the child, including the duration and frequency of any time periods during which the child and the man who signed the voluntary declaration resided in the same household or enjoyed a parent-child relationship.

(D) The request of the man who signed the voluntary declaration that the parent-child relationship continue.

(E) Notice by the biological father of the child that he does not oppose preservation of the relationship between the man who signed the voluntary declaration and the child.

(F) The benefit or detriment to the child in establishing the biological parentage of the child.

(G) Whether the conduct of the man who signed the voluntary declaration has impaired the ability to ascertain the identity of, or get support from, the biological father.

(H) Additional factors deemed by the court to be relevant to its determination of the best interest of the child.

(2) If the court denies the action, the court shall state on the record the basis for the denial of the action and any supporting facts.

(3)(A) The notice of motion for genetic tests under this section may be filed not later than two years from the date of the child's birth by a local child support agency, the mother, the man who signed the voluntary declaration as the child's father, or in an action to determine the existence or nonexistence of the father and child relationship pursuant to Section 7630 or in any action to establish an order for child custody, visitation, or child support based upon the voluntary declaration of paternity.

(B) The local child support agency's authority under this subdivision is limited to those circumstances where there is a conflict between a voluntary acknowledgment of paternity and a judgment of paternity or a conflict between two or more voluntary acknowledgments of paternity.

(4) The notice of motion for genetic tests pursuant to this section shall be supported by a declaration under oath submitted by the moving party stating the factual basis for putting the issue of paternity before the court.

(c)(1) Nothing in this chapter shall be construed to prejudice or bar the rights of either parent to file an action or motion to set aside the voluntary declaration of paternity on any of the grounds described in, and within the time limits specified in, Section 473 of the Code of Civil Procedure. If the action or motion to set aside a judgment is required to be filed within a specified time period under Section 473 of the Code of Civil Procedure, the period within which the action or motion to set aside the voluntary declaration of paternity must be filed shall commence on the date that the court makes an initial order for custody, visitation, or child support based upon a voluntary declaration of paternity.

(2) The parent or local child support agency seeking to set aside the voluntary declaration of paternity shall have the burden of proof.

(3) Any order for custody, visitation, or child support shall remain in effect until the court determines that the voluntary declaration of paternity should be set aside, subject to the court's power to modify the orders as otherwise provided by law.

(4) Nothing in this section is intended to restrict a court from acting as a court of equity.

(5) If the voluntary declaration of paternity is set aside pursuant to paragraph (1), the court shall order that the mother, child, and alleged father submit to genetic tests pursuant to Chapter 2 (commencing with Section 7550). If the court finds that the conclusions of all the experts, as disclosed by the evidence based upon the genetic tests, are that the person who executed the voluntary declaration of paternity is not the father of the child, the question of paternity shall be resolved accordingly. If the person who executed the declaration as the father of the child is not excluded as a possible father, the question of paternity shall be resolved as otherwise provided by law. If the person who executed the declaration of paternity is ultimately determined to be the father of the child, any child support that accrued under an order based upon the voluntary declaration of paternity shall remain due and owing.

(6) The Judicial Council shall develop the forms and procedures necessary to effectuate this subdivision. *(Added by Stats.1996, c. 1062 (A.B.1832), § 10. Amended by Stats. 1997, c. 599 (A.B.573), § 43; Stats.1998, c. 485 (A.B.2803), § 69; Stats.1998, c. 858 (A.B.2169), § 6; Stats.1999, c. 83 (S.B.966), § 54; Stats.1999, c. 652 (S.B.240), § 11; Stats. 1999, c. 653 (A.B.380), § 10.5; Stats.2000, c. 808 (A.B.1358), § 75, eff. Sept. 28, 2000; Stats.2002, c. 927 (A.B.3032), § 3.3; Stats.2004, c. 849 (A.B.252), § 1.)*

Commentary

In re Jovanni B., 221 Cal.App.4th 1482, 165 Cal.Rptr.3d 430 (2013), held that the juvenile court erroneously dismissed a man who had signed a voluntary declaration of paternity from dependency proceedings, without determining whether the man was the child's presumed father under section 7611(d). However, the California Supreme Court *granted review, 317 P.3d 1182 (2014), superseding In re Brianna M., 163 Cal.Rptr.3d 665 (2013)*, where the juvenile court excused from a dependency proceeding a man who signed a voluntary declaration of paternity, on the basis of DNA tests showing that he was not the father, without considering whether he was a presumed father under section (d). The California Supreme Court later dismissed review for failure of petitioner to file an opening brief, *330 P.3d 327 (2014)*.

J.R. v. D.P., 212 Cal.App.4th 374, 150 Cal.Rptr.3d 882 (2012), review denied, affirmed a trial court decision resolving conflicting section 7611(d) presumptions of paternity in favor of a *Kelsey S.* father, rather than the mother's husband who had been her boyfriend at the time of the child's conception and birth, lived with the child and mother, and raised the child as his own. The court reasoned that resolving the conflict in favor of the *Kelsey S.* biological father would serve the child's best interests, because if the presumption were resolved in favor of the mother's husband, the mother would have prevented contact between the biological father and the child. In *J.R.*, the court also affirmed the trial court's rescission of the husband's voluntary declaration of paternity on the ground that the mother committed perjury in attesting that no other man could be the father of her child, when she already knew that the *Kelsey S.* father was the child's biological father.

After a trial court granted a married mother's motion, under this section, to set aside a declaration of paternity, the trial court erred in ordering genetic testing in an action brought by the putative nonmarital father of the child in order to establish the putative father's paternity of the child because, under section 7630, the putative father had no standing to bring a paternity action once his declaration of paternity had been set aside. *H.S. v. Superior Court, 183 Cal.App.4th 1502, 108 Cal.Rptr.3d 723 (2010)*.

In re J.L., 159 Cal.App.4th 1010, 72 Cal.Rptr.3d 27 (2008), review denied, held that a biological father had standing in a dependency proceeding to challenge another man's voluntary declaration of paternity under subsection (b)(1) and (b)(3)(A) by virtue of each of the following: (1) his standing to bring a section 7630(b) proceeding to declare his paternity of a child; (2) his participation in a proceeding to establish child custody based on the voluntary declaration; and (3) his status as a *Kelsey S.* constitutionally presumed father, that is, a father who accepted his parental obligations as soon as reasonably possible. But cf. *In re Christopher M, 113 Cal.App.4th 155, 6 Cal.Rptr.3d 197 (2003)* (limiting the parties who may make a (b)(3)(a) motion).

In re William K., 161 Cal.App.4th 1, 73 Cal.Rptr.3d 737 (2008), review denied, held that the juvenile court properly declined, in a dependency proceeding, to grant the motion of a sex offender, who was a biological father but not a presumed or *Kelsey S.* father, to set aside a declaration of paternity executed by another man who had a parent-child relationship with the child but was not the child's biological father. The court invoked the subsection (b)(1) ground that setting aside the declaration of paternity would not be in the best interest of the child.

Applying subsection (b)(3)(A) and section 7646(a)(2), *County of Orange v. Superior Court, 155 Cal.App.4th 1253, 66 Cal.Rptr.3d 689 (2007)*, concluded that a motion to set aside a paternity judgment based on a voluntary declaration of paternity is untimely when it is filed more than two years after the child's birth.

Gabriel P. v. Suedi D., 141 Cal.App.4th 850, 46 Cal.Rptr.3d 437 (2006), held that where there were two presumptive fathers, one a biological father and one a father by virtue of his voluntary declaration of paternity and subsequent marriage to the child's mother, the trial court erred in setting aside the latter's voluntary declaration of paternity without joining him as a necessary party in the biological father's paternity action, assessing his relationship to the child, and, under Section 7612, weighing the presumptions supporting the presumed father status of each of the two men. The court reasoned that this result is also required by subsection (b)(1) of this section, which provides that a court may set aside a voluntary declaration of paternity unless it determines that declining to do so would serve the best interests of the child.

Research References

Forms

California Transactions Forms--Family Law § 5:4, Rights Of De Facto Parents.
California Transactions Forms--Family Law § 5:9, Use Of Parenting Agreement to Define Rights and Responsibilities Relating to Child on Termination Of Partners' Relationship Where Both Partners Are Biological Parents.
California Transactions Forms--Family Law § 6:3, Definitions.
California Transactions Forms--Family Law § 6:8, Consent for Adoption Of Unmarried Minor.

California Transactions Forms--Family Law § 6:11, Initiating Proceeding Under Uniform Parentage Act [Fam C §§ 7600 to 7730].

California Transactions Forms--Family Law § 6:40, Structuring the Adoption.

California Transactions Forms--Family Law § 6:47, Matters to Consider in Drafting Petition for Independent Adoption Of Unmarried Minor.

California Transactions Forms--Family Law § 6:72, Petition to Terminate Parental Rights Of Alleged Father.

California Transactions Forms--Family Law § 6:74, Petition to Terminate Parental Rights Of Alleged Father Served With Notice Of Alleged Paternity Without Timely Response.

California Transactions Forms--Family Law § 6:75, Order Terminating Parental Rights Of Alleged Father Served With Notice Of Alleged Paternity Without Timely Response.

California Transactions Forms--Family Law § 6:76, Ex Parte Application for Order to Terminate Parental Rights Of Alleged Father Who Waived Notice or Denied Paternity.

California Transactions Forms--Family Law § 7:38, Parentage and Birth Certificate.

California Transactions Forms--Family Law § 7:86, Overview.

California Transactions Forms--Family Law § 3:126, Request for Hearing and Application to Set Aside Voluntary Declaration Of Paternity [Form FL-280].

California Transactions Forms--Family Law § 3:127, Responsive Declaration to Application to Set Aside Voluntary Declaration Of Paternity [Form FL-285].

California Transactions Forms--Family Law § 3:128, Order After Hearing on Motion to Set Aside Voluntary Declaration Of Paternity [Form FL-290].

California Transactions Forms--Family Law § 4:105, Declaration Of Paternity.

California Transactions Forms--Family Law § 3:126.50, Information Sheet for Completing Request for Hearing and Application to Set Aside Voluntary Declaration Of Paternity [Form FL-281].

West's California Code Forms, Family § 7570, Comment Overview--Establishment Of Paternity by Voluntary Declaration.

West's California Code Forms, Family § 7575 Form 2, Request for Hearing and Application to Set Aside Voluntary Declaration Of Paternity.

West's California Code Forms, Family § 7575 Form 3, Responsive Declaration to Application to Set Aside Voluntary Declaration Of Paternity.

West's California Judicial Council Forms FL-272, Notice Of Motion to Set Aside Judgment Of Paternity.

West's California Judicial Council Forms FL-274, Information Sheet for Completing Notice Of Motion to Set Aside Judgment Of Paternity.

West's California Judicial Council Forms FL-276, Response to Notice Of Motion to Set Aside Judgment Of Paternity.

West's California Judicial Council Forms FL-278, Order After Hearing on Motion to Set Aside Judgment Of Paternity.

West's California Judicial Council Forms FL-280, Request for Hearing and Application to Set Aside Voluntary Declaration Of Paternity.

West's California Judicial Council Forms FL-281, Information Sheet for Completing Request for Hearing and Application to Set Aside Voluntary Declaration Of Paternity.

West's California Judicial Council Forms FL-285, Responsive Declaration to Application to Set Aside Voluntary Declaration Of Paternity.

West's California Judicial Council Forms FL-290, Order After Hearing on Motion to Set Aside Voluntary Declaration Of Paternity.

Treatises and Practice Aids

Witkin, California Summary 10th Parent and Child § 33, Effect Of Declaration.

Witkin, California Summary 10th Parent and Child § 34, Rescinding or Setting Aside Declaration.

Witkin, California Summary 10th Parent and Child § 36, Nonbiological Father as Presumed Father.

Witkin, California Summary 10th Parent and Child § 47, Where Presumption Of Paternity Applies.

Witkin, California Summary 10th Parent and Child § 603, Identification Of Presumed or Alleged Fathers.

§ 7576. Voluntary declaration of paternity; presumption; admissibility of evidence; rebuttal; construction with other presumptions of paternity

The following provisions shall apply for voluntary declarations signed on or before December 31, 1996.

(a) Except as provided in subdivision (d), the child of a woman and a man executing a declaration of paternity under this chapter is conclusively presumed to be the man's child. The presumption under this section has the same force and effect as the presumption under Section 7540.

(b) A voluntary declaration of paternity shall be recognized as the basis for the establishment of an order for child custody or support.

(c) In any action to rebut the presumption created by this section, a voluntary declaration of paternity shall be admissible as evidence to determine paternity of the child named in the voluntary declaration of paternity.

(d) The presumption established by this chapter may be rebutted by any person by requesting blood or genetic tests pursuant to Chapter 2 (commencing with Section 7550). The notice of motion for blood or genetic tests pursuant to this section shall be supported by a declaration under oath submitted by the moving party stating the factual basis for placing the issue of paternity before the court. The notice of motion for blood tests shall be made within three years from the date of execution of the declaration by the attesting father, or by the attesting mother, whichever signature is later. The two-year statute of limitations specified in subdivision (b) of Section 7541 is inapplicable for purposes of this section.

(e) A presumption under this chapter shall override all statutory presumptions of paternity except a presumption arising under Section 7540 or 7555, or as provided in Section 7612. *(Added by Stats.1996, c. 1062 (A.B.1832), § 12. Amended by Stats.2011, c. 185 (A.B.1349), § 2.)*

Commentary

Note that a voluntary declaration of paternity not only entitles the declarer to presumed father status under section this section, but also has the force and effect of a judgment of paternity under section 7573. Additionally, see Commentary to sections 7573, 7611, and 7612.

Research References

Treatises and Practice Aids

Witkin, California Summary 10th Parent and Child § 33, Effect Of Declaration.

Witkin, California Summary 10th Parent and Child § 46, in General.

§ 7577. Voluntary declaration of paternity; minor parents; validity; rescission; presumption; admissibility

(a) Notwithstanding Section 7573, a voluntary declaration of paternity that is signed by a minor parent or minor parents shall not establish paternity until 60 days after both parents have reached the age of 18 years or are emancipated, whichever first occurs.

(b) A parent who signs a voluntary declaration of paternity when he or she is a minor may rescind the voluntary declaration of paternity at any time up to 60 days after the parent reaches the age of 18 or becomes emancipated whichever first occurs.

(c) A voluntary declaration of paternity signed by a minor creates a rebuttable presumption of paternity until the date that it establishes paternity as specified in subdivision (a).

(d) A voluntary declaration of paternity signed by a minor shall be admissible as evidence in any civil action to establish paternity of the minor named in the voluntary declaration.

(e) A voluntary declaration of paternity that is signed by a minor shall not be admissible as evidence in a criminal prosecution for violation of Section 261.5 of the Penal Code. *(Added by Stats.1996, c. 1062 (A.B.1832), § 13.)*

Research References

Forms

California Transactions Forms--Family Law § 4:105, Declaration Of Paternity.

Treatises and Practice Aids

Witkin, California Summary 10th Parent and Child § 33, Effect Of Declaration.

Part 3

UNIFORM PARENTAGE ACT

CHAPTER 1. GENERAL PROVISIONS

§ 7600. Short title

This part may be cited as the Uniform Parentage Act. *(Stats.1992, c. 162 (A.B.2650), § 10, operative Jan. 1, 1994.)*

Law Revision Commission Comments

Enactment [Revised Comment]

Section 7600 continues former Civil Code Section 7000 without substantive change. This section is similar to Section 27 of the Uniform Parentage Act (1973). See also Sections 3 (construction of provisions drawn from uniform acts), 13 (severability of provisions). [23 Cal.L.Rev.Comm. Reports 1 (1993)].

Commentary

Note that 2013 amendments to Code of Civil Procedure section 583.161 expanded the definition of petitions and orders that are not subject to mandatory dismissal, including petitions and orders under this section.

For general discussion of the Uniform Parentage Act, see *Johnson v. Calvert, 5 Cal.4th 84, 19 Cal.Rptr.2d 494 (1993), cert. denied 510 U.S. 874, 114 S.Ct. 206, 126 L.Ed.2d 163 (1993)*. See also Section 7610, Commentary.

Research References

Forms

California Transactions Forms--Estate Planning § 6:11, Existence Of Relationship.

California Transactions Forms--Estate Planning § 6:52, Matters to Consider in Drafting Class Gifts.

California Transactions Forms--Family Law § 3:4, Subject Matter Jurisdiction for Custody Determinations.

California Transactions Forms--Family Law § 5:1, Nature and Purpose Of Parenting Agreement.

California Transactions Forms--Family Law § 5:9, Use Of Parenting Agreement to Define Rights and Responsibilities Relating to Child on Termination Of Partners' Relationship Where Both Partners Are Biological Parents.

California Transactions Forms--Family Law § 6:2, Governing Law.

California Transactions Forms--Family Law § 6:3, Definitions.

California Transactions Forms--Family Law § 7:6, Overview; Gestational Surrogacy Agreements.

California Transactions Forms--Family Law § 7:7, Gestational Surrogacy Agreements Using Donated Egg and Sperm.

California Transactions Forms--Family Law § 5:30, Parenting Agreement Providing for Joint Legal and Joint Physical Custody Where Both Partners Are Biological Parents Of Child.

California Transactions Forms--Family Law § 5:31, Parenting Agreement Providing for Joint Legal and Sole Physical Custody Where Both Partners Are Biological Parents Of Child.

California Transactions Forms--Family Law § 6:10, Initiating Proceeding Under Fam. Code, §§ 7800 et seq.

California Transactions Forms--Family Law § 7:28, Overview.

California Transactions Forms--Family Law § 7:45, Artificial Insemination Surrogacy Agreement Between Intended Father and Surrogate Couple.

California Transactions Forms--Family Law § 7:46, in Vitro Surrogacy Agreement Between Intended Parents and Surrogate Couple; Intended Parents Are Genetic Parents.

California Transactions Forms--Family Law § 7:47, in Vitro Fertilization Surrogacy Agreement Between Intended Mother and Surrogate Using Donated Genetic Material.
West's California Code Forms, Family § 6200, Comment Overview--Prevention Of Domestic Violence.
West's California Code Forms, Family § 6340, Comment Overview--Issuance Of Orders After Notice and Hearing.
West's California Judicial Council Forms DV-180, Agreement and Judgment Of Parentage.
West's California Judicial Council Forms FL-220, Response to Petition to Establish Parental Relationship.
West's California Judicial Council Forms FL-230, Declaration for Default or Uncontested Judgment.
West's California Judicial Council Forms FL-235, Advisement and Waiver Of Rights Re: Establishment Of Parental Relationship.
West's California Judicial Council Forms FL-240, Stipulation for Entry Of Judgment Re: Establishment Of Parental Relationship.
West's California Judicial Council Forms FL-250, Judgment.

Treatises and Practice Aids

Witkin, California Summary 10th Constitutional Law § 780, Action for Wrongful Death Of Parent.
Witkin, California Summary 10th Husband and Wife § 373, in General.
Witkin, California Summary 10th Husband and Wife § 374, Definitions.
Witkin, California Summary 10th Husband and Wife § 383, Temporary Custody and Visitation.
Witkin, California Summary 10th Husband and Wife § 384, Orders After Notice and Hearing.
Witkin, California Summary 10th Husband and Wife § 385, Orders Included in Judgment.
Witkin, California Summary 10th Parent and Child § 17, Development Of Law.
Witkin, California Summary 10th Parent and Child § 24, in General.
Witkin, California Summary 10th Parent and Child § 46, in General.
Witkin, California Summary 10th Parent and Child § 47, Where Presumption Of Paternity Applies.
Witkin, California Summary 10th Parent and Child § 52, Confidentiality.
Witkin, California Summary 10th Parent and Child § 60, Action to Determine Mother and Child Relationship.
Witkin, California Summary 10th Parent and Child § 63, in General.
Witkin, California Summary 10th Parent and Child § 69, Hearing and Order.
Witkin, California Summary 10th Parent and Child § 206, Agreement Between Parents.
Witkin, California Summary 10th Parent and Child § 235, Biologically Unrelated Persons Opposed by Parent.
Witkin, California Summary 10th Parent and Child § 311, Other Proceedings Stayed.
Witkin, California Summary 10th Parent and Child § 363, Applicability Of Family Code Custody Provisions.
Witkin, California Summary 10th Parent and Child § 370, in General.
Witkin, California Summary 10th Parent and Child § 60A, (New) Lesbian Partner Who is Not Biological Mother Of Child.
Witkin, California Summary 10th Parent and Child § 603, Identification Of Presumed or Alleged Fathers.
Witkin, California Summary 10th Parent and Child § 622, Findings and Order.
Witkin, California Summary 10th Parent and Child § 882, Findings.
Witkin, California Summary 10th Wills and Probate § 90, Out Of Wedlock Children.
Witkin, California Summary 10th Wills and Probate § 94, Parent and Child Relationship.
Witkin, California Summary 10th Wills and Probate § 281, Nature and Scope Of Statute.

§ 7601. "Natural parent" defined; "parent and child relationship" defined; finding of parent and child relationship with more than two parents; interpretation of reference to two parents

(a) "Natural parent" as used in this code means a nonadoptive parent established under this part, whether biologically related to the child or not.

(b) "Parent and child relationship" as used in this part means the legal relationship existing between a child and the child's natural or adoptive parents incident to which the law confers or imposes rights, privileges, duties, and obligations. The term includes the mother and child relationship and the father and child relationship.

(c) This part does not preclude a finding that a child has a parent and child relationship with more than two parents.

(d) For purposes of state law, administrative regulations, court rules, government policies, common law, and any other provision or source of law governing the rights, protections, benefits, responsibilities, obligations, and duties of parents, any reference to two parents shall be interpreted to apply to every parent of a child where that child has been found to have more than two parents under this part. *(Stats.1992, c. 162 (A.B.2650), § 10, operative Jan. 1, 1994. Amended by Stats.2013, c. 510 (A.B.1403), § 1; Stats.2013, c. 564 (S.B. 274), § 5.5.)*

Law Revision Commission Comments

Enactment [Revised Comment]

Section 7601 continues former Civil Code Section 7001 without substantive change. This section is the same in substance as Section 1 of the Uniform Parentage Act (1973). [23 Cal.L.Rev.Comm. Reports 1 (1993)].

Commentary

This section and section 7612 have been amended to provide that a child may have more than two legal parents, where having only two legal parent would be detrimental to the child, *overturning In re M.C., 195 Cal.App.4th 197, 123 Cal.Rptr.3d 856 (2011)*, which held that when a dependent child had more than two presumed parents, the court was required to resolve the conflicting presumptions of parentage by reducing the number of presumed parents to no more than two. To the extent that any cases discussed in the Commentary to this Chapter rely on the prior rule that a child may have only two parents and only one father, those cases no longer express controlling law. Nevertheless, prior case law may still be controlling on other issues and those cases might still yield the same results under revised section 7612(c).

For general discussion of the Uniform Parentage Act, see *Johnson v. Calvert, 5 Cal.4th 84, 19 Cal.Rptr.2d 494 (1993), cert. denied 510 U.S. 874, 114 S.Ct. 206, 126 L.Ed.2d 163 (1993)*. See also Section 7610, Commentary.

Research References

Forms

California Transactions Forms--Family Law § 3:4, Subject Matter Jurisdiction for Custody Determinations.
California Transactions Forms--Family Law § 5:9, Use Of Parenting Agreement to Define Rights and Responsibilities Relating to Child on Termination Of Partners' Relationship Where Both Partners Are Biological Parents.

Treatises and Practice Aids

Witkin, California Summary 10th Parent and Child § 13, Nature and Effect Of Classification.

Witkin, California Summary 10th Parent and Child § 18, Parent and Child Relationship.

Witkin, California Summary 10th Parent and Child § 22, Where Intended Mother is Genetic Mother.

Witkin, California Summary 10th Parent and Child § 23, Where Intended Mother is Not Genetic Mother.

Witkin, California Summary 10th Parent and Child § 60, Action to Determine Mother and Child Relationship.

§ 7602. Application regardless of marital status of parents

The parent and child relationship extends equally to every child and to every parent, regardless of the marital status of the parents. *(Stats.1992, c. 162 (A.B.2650), § 10, operative Jan. 1, 1994.)*

Law Revision Commission Comments

Enactment [Revised Comment]

Section 7602 continues former Civil Code Section 7002 without change. This section is the same as Section 2 of the Uniform Parentage Act (1973). [23 Cal.L.Rev.Comm. Reports 1 (1993)].

Research References

Treatises and Practice Aids

Witkin, California Summary 10th Parent and Child § 13, Nature and Effect Of Classification.

Witkin, California Summary 10th Parent and Child § 18, Parent and Child Relationship.

Witkin, California Summary 10th Parent and Child § 206, Agreement Between Parents.

§ 7603. Application of § 3140

Section 3140 is applicable to proceedings pursuant to this part. *(Stats.1992, c. 162 (A.B.2650), § 10, operative Jan. 1, 1994.)*

Law Revision Commission Comments

Enactment [Revised Comment]

Section 7603 continues former Civil Code Section 7017.6 without substantive change. There is no comparable provision in the Uniform Parentage Act (1973). [23 Cal.L.Rev.Comm. Reports 1 (1993)].

Research References

Treatises and Practice Aids

Witkin, California Summary 10th Parent and Child § 19, General Provisions.

§ 7604. Pendente lite relief of custody or visitation order on finding of parent-child relationship

A court may order pendente lite relief consisting of a custody or visitation order pursuant to Part 2 (commencing with Section 3020) of Division 8, if the court finds both of the following:

(a) Based on the tests authorized by Section 7541, a parent and child relationship exists pursuant to Section 7540.

(b) The custody or visitation order would be in the best interest of the child. *(Stats.1992, c. 162 (A.B.2650), § 10, operative Jan. 1, 1994. Amended by Stats.1993, c. 219 (A.B.1500), § 175.5.)*

Law Revision Commission Comments

Enactment [Revised Comment]

Section 7604 continues without substantive change the first paragraph of former Civil Code Section 7004.5. The last two paragraphs of former Civil Code Section 7004.5 are superseded. There is no comparable provision in the Uniform Parentage Act (1973).

In the introductory clause, a reference to Part 2 (commencing with Section 3020) of Division 8 has been substituted for narrower references to former Civil Code Sections 4600 and 4601. This supersedes the last two paragraphs of former Civil Code Section 7004.5 and is not a substantive change. The substance of the superseded paragraphs is contained in Section 3100(b) of Part 2 of Division 8, made expressly applicable to a determination of custody or visitation under this section.

See also Sections 200 (jurisdiction in superior court), 3011 (factors in determining best interest of child), 3030 (parent convicted under certain Penal Code provisions not allowed unsupervised visitation), 3131 (action by district attorney where child taken or detained in violation of visitation order), 3160–3186 (mediation of custody or visitation issues); Code Civ. Proc. § 917.7 (order not automatically stayed by appeal). [23 Cal.L.Rev.Comm. Reports 1 (1993)].

Commentary

Barkaloff v. Woodward, 47 Cal.App.4th 393, 55 Cal.Rptr.2d 167 (1996), holds that a trial court lacks jurisdiction under the Domestic Violence Prevention Act (DVPA) (Section 6200 et seq.) and the Uniform Parentage Act (UPA) (Section 7600 et seq.) to award visitation rights to a man who is not the father of the child and who was never married to the child's mother when both the child's mother and the child's biological father object to visitation, even though such visitation may be in the child's best interests. *Barkaloff* holds that jurisdiction to order visitation of minor children under the DVPA is limited, pursuant to Section 6323, to cases where there is a marital relationship between the parties. 47 Cal.App.4th at 398. Jurisdiction to order visitation of a child under the UPA is limited to claims by persons who are, or are presumed to be, a child's natural parent. 47 Cal.App.4th at 399.

Research References

Forms

California Transactions Forms--Family Law § 3:4, Subject Matter Jurisdiction for Custody Determinations.

California Transactions Forms--Family Law § 5:9, Use Of Parenting Agreement to Define Rights and Responsibilities Relating to Child on Termination Of Partners' Relationship Where Both Partners Are Biological Parents.

West's California Judicial Council Forms DV-140, Child Custody and Visitation Order.

West's California Judicial Council Forms FL-341, Child Custody and Visitation (Parenting Time) Order Attachment.

Treatises and Practice Aids

Witkin, California Summary 10th Parent and Child § 59, Visitation Privileges.

§ 7604.5. Pregnancy, childbirth and genetic testing bills as evidence

Notwithstanding any other provision of law, bills for pregnancy, childbirth, and genetic testing shall be admissible as evidence without third-party foundation testimony and shall constitute prima facie evidence of costs incurred for those services. *(Added by Stats.1997, c. 599 (A.B.573), § 44.)*

Research References

Treatises and Practice Aids

Witkin, California Summary 10th Parent and Child § 19, General Provisions.

§ 7605. Attorney's fees and costs; court findings; standard for awarding fees and costs; augmentation or modification; temporary orders; time for determination of application

(a) In any proceeding to establish physical or legal custody of a child or a visitation order under this part, and in any proceeding subsequent to entry of a related judgment, the court shall ensure that each party has access to legal representation to preserve each party's rights by ordering, if necessary based on the income and needs assessments, one party, except a government entity, to pay to the other party, or to the other party's attorney, whatever amount is reasonably necessary for attorney's fees and for the cost of maintaining or defending the proceeding during the pendency of the proceeding.

(b) When a request for attorney's fees and costs is made under this section, the court shall make findings on whether an award of attorney's fees and costs is appropriate, whether there is a disparity in access to funds to retain counsel, and whether one party is able to pay for legal representation of both parties. If the findings demonstrate disparity in access and ability to pay, the court shall make an order awarding attorney's fees and costs. A party who lacks the financial ability to hire an attorney may request, as an in pro per litigant, that the court order the other party, if that other party has the financial ability, to pay a reasonable amount to allow the unrepresented party to retain an attorney in a timely manner before proceedings in the matter go forward.

(c) Attorney's fees and costs within this section may be awarded for legal services rendered or costs incurred before or after the commencement of the proceeding.

(d) The court shall augment or modify the original award for attorney's fees and costs as may be reasonably necessary for the prosecution or defense of a proceeding described in subdivision (a), or any proceeding related thereto, including after any appeal has been concluded.

(e) Except as provided in subdivision (f), an application for a temporary order making, augmenting, or modifying an award of attorney's fees, including a reasonable retainer to hire an attorney, or costs, or both, shall be made by motion on notice or by an order to show cause during the pendency of any proceeding described in subdivision (a).

(f) The court shall rule on an application for fees under this section within 15 days of the hearing on the motion or order to show cause. An order described in subdivision (a) may be made without notice by an oral motion in open court at either of the following times:

(1) At the time of the hearing of the cause on the merits.

(2) At any time before entry of judgment against a party whose default has been entered pursuant to Section 585 or 586 of the Code of Civil Procedure. The court shall rule on any motion made pursuant to this subdivision within 15 days and prior to the entry of any judgment. *(Added by Stats.2004, c. 472 (A.B.2148), § 7. Amended by Stats.2006, c. 538 (S.B.1852), § 160; Stats.2012, c. 107 (A.B.1406), § 3.)*

Commentary

For claims arising before the effective date of this section, *Robert J. v. Catherine D., 134 Cal.App.4th 1392, 37 Cal.Rptr.3d 104 (2005), review denied,* held that Section 7640 also grants the trial court discretion to award attorney's fees on matters relating to custody, visitation, and support that arise after paternity is adjudicated.

In applying this section and section 7640 to a request for attorney's fees in a paternity proceeding, *Kevin Q. v. Lauren W., 195 Cal.App.4th 633, 124 Cal.Rptr.3d 676 (2011),* holds that a trial court properly relied on section 2032, which establishes standards for awards of attorney's fees in marital dissolution cases.

Research References

Forms

West's California Judicial Council Forms FL-158, Supporting Declaration for Attorney's Fees and Costs Attachment.

West's California Judicial Council Forms FL-319, Request for Attorney's Fees and Costs Attachment.

West's California Judicial Council Forms FL-346, Attorney's Fees and Costs Order Attachment.

Treatises and Practice Aids

Witkin, California Summary 10th Husband and Wife § 177, Types Of Actions.

Witkin, California Summary 10th Parent and Child § 19, General Provisions.

Witkin, California Summary 10th Parent and Child § 53, Judgment.

§ 7606. "Assisted reproduction" and "assisted reproduction agreement" defined

As used in this part, the following definitions shall apply:

(a) "Assisted reproduction" means conception by any means other than sexual intercourse.

(b) "Assisted reproduction agreement" means a written contract that includes a person who intends to be the legal parent of a child or children born through assisted reproduction and that defines the terms of the relationship between the parties to the contract. *(Added by Stats.2006, c. 806 (S.B.1325), § 1.)*

Research References

Forms

California Transactions Forms--Family Law § 7:8.50, Surrogacy Facilitator.

Treatises and Practice Aids

Witkin, California Summary 10th Parent and Child § 19, General Provisions.

CHAPTER 2. ESTABLISHING PARENT AND CHILD RELATIONSHIP

Section

Section

aside voluntary declaration of paternity; invalid voluntary declarations of paternity.

7613. Conception through assisted reproduction with semen or ova donated by donor other than spouse; consent of another intended parent; treatment as natural parent; treatment of semen or ova donors.

7613.5. Intended parent; use of forms.

7614. Written promise to furnish support; enforcement; confidentiality.

§ 7610. Method of establishment

The parent and child relationship may be established as follows:

(a) Between a child and the natural parent, it may be established by proof of having given birth to the child, or under this part.

(b) Between a child and an adoptive parent, it may be established by proof of adoption. *(Stats.1992, c. 162 (A.B. 2650), § 10, operative Jan. 1, 1994. Amended by Stats.2013, c. 510 (A.B.1403), § 2.)*

Law Revision Commission Comments

Enactment [Revised Comment]

Section 7610 continues former Civil Code Section 7003 without change. This section is the same in substance as Section 3 of the Uniform Parentage Act (1973), except that Section 7610 omits the Uniform Parentage Act reference to the Revised Uniform Adoption Act. [23 Cal.L.Rev.Comm. Reports 1 (1993)].

Commentary

Johnson v. Calvert, 5 Cal.4th 84, 19 Cal.Rptr.2d 494 (1993), cert. denied 510 U.S. 874, 114 S.Ct.206, 126 L.Ed.2d 163 (1993), holds that California law recognizes only one "natural mother" and that when genetic endowment and fetal gestation are not provided by the same woman, the woman who intended to bring about the birth of the child and to raise the child is the "natural mother." *Johnson v. Calvert* also states, in dictum, that gestational surrogacy contracts do not violate public policy and that in "true egg donation," where a donor's fertilized ovum is implanted in an infertile woman's uterus, the latter is the "natural mother" because she is the intended social mother. Compare *In re Marriage of Moschetta, 25 Cal.App.4th 1218, 30 Cal.Rptr.2d 893 (1994)*. (In a traditional surrogacy arrangement, that is, where the surrogate mother provides both the ovum and the womb, the surrogate mother is a birth parent, and her consent is required under Section 8814 before the child may be adopted by another. Thus the terms of the traditional surrogacy contract are unenforceable insofar as they purport to create maternal rights in a different woman.)

Relying on *Johnson v. Calvert*, and reasoning by analogy from Section 7613, *In re Marriage of Buzzanca, 61 Cal.App.4th 1410, 72 Cal.Rptr.2d 280 (1998), review denied June 10, 1998,* holds that a husband who, with his wife, consented to the artificial insemination of a surrogate mother by an unknown donor for the purpose of bearing a child for the couple, is the legal father of the child. Similarly, the same principle applies, in conjunction with Section 7610 (a), to justify the conclusion that the wife is the child's legal mother.

K.M. v. E.G., 37 Cal.4th 130, 117 P.3d 673, 33 Cal.Rptr.3d 61 (2005), holds that Section 7613(b) has no application when a woman in a lesbian relationship provides ova to impregnate her partner in order to produce children who will be raised in their joint home. Consequently, the California Supreme Court recognized the ova donor's claim to parental status, holding that both the woman who provided the ova and the woman who bore the resulting twin children were the children's parents even though the ova donor did not hold the resultant children out as her own natural children within the meaning of Section 7611(d) and the trial court found that she formally relinquished any claim to offspring resulting from her ova donation. In other words, the intent of the parties on the question of maternity had no bearing on the result.

Although *K.M.*, narrowly distinguishes *Steven S. v. Deborah D., 127 Cal.App.4th 319, 25 Cal.Rptr.3d 482 (2005)*, *K.M.* may be understood to undermine the rationale of *Stephen S.*, in which the court of appeal held that when a child is conceived by the artificial insemination of an unmarried mother with sperm provided by a licensed physician, the biological father of the child may not assert parental rights even though he once had an intimate sexual relationship with the mother and had some social role in the child's life. *Stephen S.* reasoned that once the trial court determined that the child was conceived by artificial insemination, rather than natural conception, Section 7613(b) applied to bar the semen donor from asserting his parentage of the child.

In a companion case to *K.M.*, *Elisa B. v. Superior Court, 37 Cal.4th 108, 117 P.3d 660, 33 Cal.Rptr.3d 46 (2005)*, the California Supreme Court held that in a child support action filed by a county district attorney, a woman who agreed to raise children with her lesbian partner, supported her partner's artificial insemination by means of an anonymous donor, and received the resulting twins into her home and held them out as her own children was a Section 7611(d) presumed parent. Moreover, invoking Section 7612(a), the Supreme Court held that a child support action was not an "appropriate action" in which to rebut the Section 7611(d) presumption. Consequently the woman was subject to the parental child support obligation. *Charisma R. v. Kristina S., 140 Cal.App.4th 301, 44 Cal.Rptr.3d 332 (2006)*, extends *Elisa B.* by applying it when a child's biological mother opposed her former lesbian partner's petition to establish a parental relationship with a child conceived and born during their relationship. *Charisma R.* reasons that the preferences of a biological parent are immaterial in determining whether another person is a presumed parent under Section 7611(d) or whether, under Section 7612(a), rebuttal of presumed parent status is appropriate. On remand, *Charisma R. v. Kristina S., 175 Cal.App.4th 361, 96 Cal.Rptr.3d 26 (2009)*, held that section 7611(d) presumed parenthood requires only that a former domestic partner have received the child into her home and openly held the child out as her own; it does not require the former partner to co-parent for any particular length of time.

In another companion case, *Kristine H. v. Lisa R., 37 Cal.4th 156, 117 P.3d 690, 33 Cal.Rptr.3d 81 (2005)*, the California Supreme Court used the doctrine of estoppel to reach a similar result when a former lesbian partner of a child's mother sought custody of the child after the parties' separation. During the mother's pregnancy the partners sought and secured a judgment that they are the "only legally recognized parents [of the unborn child] and take full and complete legal, custodial and financial responsibility of said child." Without deciding whether the judgment was enforceable, the Supreme Court held that the mother was estopped to attack the validity of a judgment to which she had stipulated.

Elisa B. and *Kristine H.* overruled earlier court of appeal decisions declining to accord parental status to a parent's lesbian partner, such as *Nancy S. v. Michele G., 228 Cal.App.3d 831, 279 Cal.Rptr. 212 (1991)* and *Curiale v. Reagan, 222 Cal.App.3d 1597, 1600, 272 Cal.Rptr. 520 (1990)*.

S.Y. v. S.B., 201 Cal.App.4th 1023, 134 Cal.Rptr.3d 1 (2011), review denied, held that a woman who fully embraced the rights and obligations of being a parent to her same-sex partner's adopted children was properly found to be a section 7611(d) presumed parent when the woman spent three or four nights a week at the children's home and openly held the children out as her own children. Whether the adoptive mother intended her partner to have parental rights was immaterial. See also *R.M. v. T.A., 233 Cal.App.4th 760, 182 Cal. Rptr.3d 836 (2015)*, in which the court relied on *S.Y. v. S.B.* to reject a mother's argument that her intent, as opposed to her behavior, was determinative on whether her former partner was a presumed parent of her child.

Robert B. v. Susan B., 109 Cal.App.4th 1109, 135 Cal.Rptr.2d 785 (2003), review denied September 10, 2003, sorts out parentage that has been confused by clinical error. In *Robert B.*, a couple and a single woman sought the reproductive assistance of a fertility clinic. For the couple, the clinic was to fertilize the eggs of an anonymous donor with the husband's sperm. The single woman was to receive an embryo created from anonymous egg and sperm donors. Through clinical error, the single woman received one of the couple's embryos and she gave birth to a son. The wife gave birth to a daughter. Thus the two infants were siblings. The single woman and the couple disputed parentage of the son. The court held that the husband was the father under § 7630, the single woman who carried the child to term was the mother under this section, and the father's wife had no standing to bring an action to determine the existence or non-existence of a mother-child relationship under § 7650. In concluding that the husband was the father, the court reasoned that § 7613(b) was inapplicable because the husband provided semen for the purpose of inseminating only his wife.

Research References

Forms

California Practice Guide: Rutter Family Law Forms Form 1:32, Glossary Of Common Family Law Terms, Phrases and Concepts (Enclosure to Form 1:31).
California Transactions Forms--Family Law § 7:63, Application Of Fam C § 7613 to Egg Donors.
West's California Code Forms, Family § 7610, Comment Overview--Establishing Parent and Child Relationship.

Treatises and Practice Aids

Witkin, California Summary 10th Parent and Child § 17, Development Of Law.
Witkin, California Summary 10th Parent and Child § 18, Parent and Child Relationship.
Witkin, California Summary 10th Parent and Child § 20, in General.
Witkin, California Summary 10th Parent and Child § 22, Where Intended Mother is Genetic Mother.
Witkin, California Summary 10th Parent and Child § 23, Where Intended Mother is Not Genetic Mother.
Witkin, California Summary 10th Parent and Child § 24, in General.
Witkin, California Summary 10th Parent and Child § 35, in General.
Witkin, California Summary 10th Parent and Child § 36, Nonbiological Father as Presumed Father.
Witkin, California Summary 10th Parent and Child § 60, Action to Determine Mother and Child Relationship.
Witkin, California Summary 10th Parent and Child § 23A, (New) Assisted Reproduction Agreements for Gestational Carriers.

§ 7611. Status as natural parent; presumption; conditions

A person is presumed to be the natural parent of a child if the person meets the conditions provided in Chapter 1 (commencing with Section 7540) or Chapter 3 (commencing with Section 7570) of Part 2 or in any of the following subdivisions:

(a) The presumed parent and the child's natural mother are or have been married to each other and the child is born during the marriage, or within 300 days after the marriage is terminated by death, annulment, declaration of invalidity, or divorce, or after a judgment of separation is entered by a court.

(b) Before the child's birth, the presumed parent and the child's natural mother have attempted to marry each other by a marriage solemnized in apparent compliance with law, although the attempted marriage is or could be declared invalid, and either of the following is true:

(1) If the attempted marriage could be declared invalid only by a court, the child is born during the attempted marriage, or within 300 days after its termination by death, annulment, declaration of invalidity, or divorce.

(2) If the attempted marriage is invalid without a court order, the child is born within 300 days after the termination of cohabitation.

(c) After the child's birth, the presumed parent and the child's natural mother have married, or attempted to marry, each other by a marriage solemnized in apparent compliance with law, although the attempted marriage is or could be declared invalid, and either of the following is true:

(1) With his or her consent, the presumed parent is named as the child's parent on the child's birth certificate.

(2) The presumed parent is obligated to support the child under a written voluntary promise or by court order.

(d) The presumed parent receives the child into his or her home and openly holds out the child as his or her natural child.

(e) If the child was born and resides in a nation with which the United States engages in an Orderly Departure Program or successor program, he acknowledges that he is the child's father in a declaration under penalty of perjury, as specified in Section 2015.5 of the Code of Civil Procedure. This subdivision shall remain in effect only until January 1, 1997, and on that date shall become inoperative.

(f) The child is in utero after the death of the decedent and the conditions set forth in Section 249.5 of the Probate Code are satisfied. *(Stats.1992, c. 162 (A.B.2650), § 10, operative Jan. 1, 1994. Amended by Stats.1993, c. 219 (A.B.1500), § 176; Stats.1994, c. 1269 (A.B.2208), § 53; Stats.2004, c. 775 (A.B.1910), § 1; Stats.2013, c. 510 (A.B. 1403), § 3.)*

Law Revision Commission Comments

Enactment [Revised Comment]

Section 7611 continues former Civil Code Section 7004(a) without substantive change. This section is the same in substance as Section 4(a) of the Uniform Parentage Act (1973). In subdivision (a), "judgment" has been substituted for "decree." This is not a substantive change. See Section 100 ("judgment" includes decree, as appropriate). See also Section 7612 (nature of paternity presumptions). [23 Cal.L.Rev.Comm. Reports 1 (1993)].

Commentary

Sections 7601 and 7612 have been amended to provide that a child may have more than two legal parents, where having only two legal parent would be detrimental to the child, *overturning In re M.C., 195 Cal.App.4th 197, 123 Cal.Rptr.3d 856 (2011)*, which held that when a dependent child had more than two presumed parents, the court was required to resolve the conflicting presumptions of parentage by reducing the number of presumed parents to no more than two. To the extent that any cases discussed in the Commentary to this Chapter rely on the prior rule that a child may have only two parents and only one father, those cases no longer express controlling law. Nevertheless prior case law may still be controlling on other issues

and those cases might still yield the same results under revised section 7612(c).

In re Jovanni B., 221 Cal.App.4th 1482, 165 Cal.Rptr.3d 430 (2013), held that the juvenile court erroneously dismissed a man who had signed a voluntary declaration of paternity from dependency proceedings, without determining whether the man was the child's presumed father under section subsection (d). However, the California Supreme Court *granted review, 317 P.3d 1182 (2014), superseding In re Brianna M., 163 Cal.Rptr.3d 665 (2013)*, where the juvenile court excused from a dependency proceeding a man who signed a voluntary declaration of paternity, on the basis of DNA tests showing that he was not the father, without considering whether he was a presumed father under section (d). The California Supreme Court later dismissed review for failure of petitioner to file an opening brief, *330 P.3d 327 (2014)*.

Jason P. v. Danielle S., 226 Cal.App.4th 167, 171 Cal.Rptr.3d 789 (2014), review denied, held that even though section 7613(b) precluded a sperm donor from establishing paternity by virtue of his biological relationship to the child, a sperm donor could establish his paternity under subsection (d) of this section, based on his openly holding out the child as his natural child and receiving him into his home. On remand, *Jason P. v. Danielle S., 9 Cal.App.5th 1000, 215 Cal.Rptr.3d 542 (2017), review denied*, affirmed a trial court judgment that a sperm donor was a subsection (d) presumed father based on evidence that he received the child into his home and held him out as his own.

Although a child's biological father was a presumed parent for purposes of section subsection (d) because he held the child out as his own and received him into his home during the first years of the child's life, he was not eligible to be a third parent under section 7612, when he had no existing relationship with the child, who already had a mother and a presumed father. *In re L.L., 13 Cal.App.5th 1302, 220 Cal.Rptr.3d 904 (2017)*.

Kevin Q. v. Lauren W., 175 Cal.App.4th 1119, 95 Cal.Rptr.3d 477 (2009), review denied, held that a voluntary declaration of paternity signed when a child already had a subsection (d) presumed father had the effect of rebutting the latter's presumption of paternity under section 7612(c), because section 7573 gives a voluntary declaration of paternity the force and effect of a judgment of paternity. Mitigating *Kevin Q.*, subsection 7612(d), added in 2011, grants any man presumed a father under this section, including a subsection (d) presumed father, the right to file a petition to set aside the voluntary declaration of another man within two years of its making. By contrast, under section 7612(e), also added by the 2011 legislation, when parenthood is presumed under section 7450 or under subsections (a),(b), or (c) of this section (but not subsection (d)), any subsequent voluntary declaration of paternity by another person is automatically invalid.

In re Levi H., 197 Cal.App.4th 1279, 128 Cal.Rptr.3d 814 (2011), holds that when a voluntary declaration of paternity qualifies for section 7612(c) treatment, the presumption of paternity arising under subsection (d) of this section is rebutted by another man's voluntary declaration of paternity, and there is no need to engage in a section 7612(b) weighing analysis.

However, when a child has both an alleged biological father, whose paternity is at issue in a dependency proceeding, and a presumed father, a court must hold an evidentiary hearing on the issue biological paternity. If the court concludes that one man is the biological father and one man is a presumed father, the court must perform a section 7612(b) balancing to determine which man should be considered the child's father. *In re P.A., 198 Cal.App.4th 974, 130 Cal.Rptr.3d 556 (2011)*. *In re P.A.* concludes that a finding that a man is a biological father is not a paternity judgment for purposes of section 7612(c). *In re P.A.* interprets section 7612(c) to refer solely to a judgment that already exists when the instant action arises. *In re P.A.* relies on *In re A.A.*, discussed below in the Commentary to this section.

By contrast, *In re Cheyenne B., 203 Cal.App.4th 1361, 138 Cal.Rptr.3d 267 (2012), review denied*, holds that a pre-existing judgment that a man is the father of a child for child support purposes is a paternity judgment within the meaning of section 7612(c) and therefore may preclude another man from establishing that the is a presumed father under section 7611(d). Nevertheless, the fact that the child support order satisfies section 7612(c) does not make the support obligor a presumed parent. The effect of *Cheyenne B.* was that the child, who initially had one adjudicated nonpresumptive biological father and one unadjudicated presumptive father, ultimately had no presumed father.

In re Mary G., 151 Cal.App.4th 184, 59 Cal.Rptr.3d 703 (2007), held that this section violates the equal protection and full faith and credit clauses insofar as it would deny presumed father status to a man on the sole basis that his voluntary acknowledgement of paternity was executed in Michigan, rather than California. But see *Kevin Q.*, immediately above, which follows section 7573 in characterizing the voluntary declarant as a legal father, rather than merely a presumptive father.

See generally *In re Sarah C., 8 Cal.App.4th 964, 11 Cal.Rptr.2d 414 (1992)* (sufficiency of evidence to conclude that man was not a "presumed father"). Although Section 7612 requires that the plaintiff produce clear and convincing evidence to overcome a Section 7611 presumption of paternity, the plaintiff need only establish by a preponderance of the evidence that a putative natural father is the father of the child. *Walsh v. Palma, 154 Cal.App.3d 290, 293, 201 Cal.Rptr. 142 (1984)*. A man claiming the status of "presumed father" must prove the facts that give rise to the presumption of parenthood. Thus a man making a subsection (d) claim must show by a preponderance of the evidence that he received the child into his home and held the child out as his natural child. *In re Spencer W., 48 Cal.App.4th 1647, 56 Cal.Rptr.2d 524 (1996), review denied October 23, 1996*.

In re J.O., 178 Cal.App.4th 139, 100 Cal.Rptr.3d 276 (2009), holds that in a dependency proceeding a juvenile court erred in finding that a man's subsection (d) presumed father status was rebutted by his failure to contact or provide support for his children, when rebuttal of the man's presumed father status would leave the children without any father.

Although an unwed father is a section 7636 father because he has been judicially determined to be the children's father and has been ordered to pay child support, he is not a "presumed father" under this section because he never lived with the children or openly held them out to be his own. Therefore, in a dependency proceeding, a juvenile court could deny him reunification services because only presumed fathers are entitled to reunification services. *In re E.O., 182 Cal.App.4th 722, 107 Cal.Rptr.3d 1 (2010), review denied*. *E.O.* reasons that the category ""presumed father" functions in dependency cases to identify social fathers, even those who may not be biological fathers, while the issue in a paternity proceeding brought against an unwed father is biological paternity.

Compare *In re Bryan D., 199 Cal.App.4th 127, 130 Cal.Rptr.3d 821 (2011)*, which sustained a juvenile court's finding that a dependent child's grandmother was not a presumed mother within the meaning of subsection (d). Although the grandmother received the child into her home and performed all parental responsibilities with respect to the child, there was no evidence that she ever held the child out as her own child rather than as a grandchild. However, the juvenile court abused its discretion in denying the grandmother party de facto parent status when the grandmother's conduct was the cause of the dependency proceeding but was not fundamentally inconsistent with the role of a parent. For the definition of a de facto parent, see California Rules of Court, Rule 5.502(10) and accompanying Commentary.

Craig L. v. Sandy S., 125 Cal.App.4th 36, 22 Cal.Rptr.3d 606 (2004), holds that when a mother and her husband, who are cohabiting as husband and wife, permit an alleged biological father to receive her child in his home and hold the child out as his own and the two-year limitation of Section 7541(b) has not yet expired, the alleged biological father may assert the subsection (d) presumption; the husband may assert only the subsection (a) rebuttable presumption, as contrasted with the Section 7540 conclusive presumption; and the court must apply the Section 7612(b) rubric to determine which presumption is the weightier. Only when the court determines that the subsection (d) presumption is the weightier may the alleged biological father obtain blood tests under Section 7541(b).

The California Supreme Court held in *Elisa B. v. Superior Court, 37 Cal.4th 108, 117 P.3d 660, 33 Cal.Rptr.3d 46 (2005)*, a child support action filed by a county district attorney, that a woman who agreed to raise children with her lesbian partner, supported her partner's artificial insemination by means of an anonymous donor, and received the resulting twins into her home and held them out as her own children was a subsection (d) presumed parent. Moreover, invoking Section 7612 (a), the Supreme Court held that a child support action was not an "appropriate action" in which to rebut the subsection (d) presumption. Consequently the woman was subject to the parental child support obligation. *Charisma R. v. Kristina S., 140 Cal.App.4th 301, 44 Cal.Rptr.3d 332 (2006),* extends *Elisa B.* by applying it when a child's biological mother opposed her former lesbian partner's petition to establish a parental relationship with a child conceived and born during their relationship. *Charisma R.* reasons that the preferences of a biological parent are immaterial in determining whether another person is a presumed parent under subsection (d) or whether, under Section 7612(a), rebuttal of presumed parent status is appropriate. On remand, *Charisma R. v. Kristina S., 175 Cal.App.4th 361, 96 Cal.Rptr.3d 26 (2009)*, held that subsection (d) presumed parenthood requires only that a former domestic partner have received the child into her home and openly held the child out as her own; it does not require the former partner to co-parent for any particular length of time.

Note that section 297.5(d) gives California registered domestic partners the same rights and obligations as spouses with respect to a child. A registered domestic partner who consents to insemination of the other partner or a third party for the purpose of conceiving a child for the partners should be able to avail himself or herself of the section 7613 rights and obligations of the husband of a wife artificially inseminated with his consent. Thus, recourse to subsection (d) presumed parenthood may be unnecessary.

In the companion case of *Kristine H. v. Lisa R., 37 Cal.4th 156, 117 P.3d 690, 33 Cal.Rptr.3d 81 (2005)*, the California Supreme Court used the doctrine of estoppel to reach a similar result when a former lesbian partner of a child's mother sought custody of the child after the parties' separation. During the mother's pregnancy the partners sought and secured a judgment that they are the "only legally recognized parents [of the unborn child] and take full and complete legal, custodial and financial responsibility of said child." Without deciding whether the agreement was enforceable, the Supreme Court held that the mother was estopped to attack the validity of a judgment to which she had stipulated.

Elisa B. and *Kristine H.* overruled earlier court of appeal decisions declining to accord parental status to a parent's lesbian partner. Such decisions include *Nancy S. v. Michele G., 228 Cal.App.3d 831, 279 Cal.Rptr. 212 (1991)* and *Curiale v. Reagan, 222 Cal.App.3d 1597, 1600, 272 Cal.Rptr. 520 (1990)*.

S.Y. v. S.B., 201 Cal.App.4th 1023, 134 Cal.Rptr.3d 1 (2011), review denied, held that a woman who fully embraced the rights and obligations of being a parent to her same-sex partner's adopted children was properly found to be a subsection (d) presumed parent when the woman spent three or four nights a week at the children's home and openly held the children out as her own children. Whether the adoptive mother intended her partner to have parental rights was immaterial. To the same effect, see *E.C. v. J.V, 202 Cal.App.4th 1076, 136 Cal.Rptr.3d 339 (2012)*.

The presumption that a woman was a subsection (d) parent was not rebutted by her former same-sex partner's single parent adoption of the child. *L.M. v. M.G., 208 Cal.App.4th 133, 145 Cal.Rptr.3d 97 (2012)*.

Amy G. v. M.W., 142 Cal.App.4th 1, 47 Cal.Rptr.3d 297 (2006), review denied Nov. 29, 2006, held that a wife who has accepted into the marital household a child that her husband fathered in an extramarital relationship, may not assert that she is a presumed mother for purposes of section 7540 or subsection (a) or (d) of this section when the child's biological mother timely asserts her parental interest in the child, the identity of the child's father is undisputed, and he is a party in the proceeding and represents his wife's interests as well as his own.

Adoption of Kelsey S., 1 Cal.4th 816, 4 Cal.Rptr.2d 615 (1992) holds that Sections 7611 and 7664 are unconstitutional insofar as they allow a mother unilaterally to prevent a natural father from becoming a "presumed father" and then allow the state to terminate his parental rights merely upon a showing of "best interest of the child." *Kelsey S.* holds that the parental rights of an unwed father who demonstrates full commitment to his parental responsibilities may only be terminated by a showing of parental unfitness. To demonstrate full commitment, he must show willingness to assume full custody, not just to block adoption. *Id. at 849*. For clarification of *Kelsey S.*, see *Adoption of Michael H., 10 Cal.4th 1043, 898 P.2d 891, 43 Cal.Rptr.2d 445 (1995)* (unwed father who is not a "presumed father" has no federal constitutional right to withhold consent to adoption at his child's birth unless he proves that he demonstrated a full commitment to parental responsibilities as soon as he learned that the mother was pregnant with his child). See also *In re Zacharia D., 6 Cal.4th 435, 862 P.2d 751, 24 Cal.Rptr.2d 751 (1993)* (father who did not come forward to assume responsibilities); *In re Ariel H., 73 Cal.App.4th 70, 86 Cal.Rptr.2d 125 (1999)* (15-year-old father who did not come forward to assume his responsibilities); and *Adoption of Arthur M., 149 Cal.App.4th 704, 57 Cal.Rptr.3d 259 (2007), review denied June 20, 2007* (unwed father not entitled to withhold his consent to adoption because father, who allegedly feared criminal prosecution for date rape, failed to promptly assume responsibility for the child upon learning of the mother's pregnancy). Compare *In re Julia U., 64 Cal.App.4th 532, 74 Cal.Rptr.2d 920 (1998)* (juvenile court deprived unwed biological father who promptly came forward and demonstrated a full commitment to his parental responsibilities of his constitutional rights by refusing him reunification services and terminating his parental rights). See also *Adoption of Baby Boy W., 232 Cal.App.4th 438, 181 Cal.Rptr.3d 130 (2015), review denied.* *Adoption of Alexander M., 94 Cal.App.4th 430, 114 Cal.Rptr.2d 218 (2001)*, holds that a biological father may establish paternity under § 7631, but whether an adoption should proceed or the biological father should retain his parental rights shall be decided under the best interests of the child standard (§ 7664(b)), unless the father proves that he has demonstrated a full commitment to parental responsibilities in accordance with *Kelsey S.*, in which case the father shall be awarded custody unless such award would be detrimental to the child under § 3041.

In re D.A., 204 Cal.App.4th 811, 139 Cal.Rptr.3d 222 (2012), holds that a man who came forward to accept all the responsibilities of parenthood but was prevented from becoming a presumed father under subsection (d), was a *Kelsey S.* presumed father even though he did not accept those responsibilities until tests established his biological paternity, when another man might have been the child's biological father. Compare *In re William K., 161 Cal.App.4th 1, 73 Cal.Rptr.3d 737 (2008)*, where a man was denied *Kelsey S.* status because he did not immediately accept paternal responsibilities although he indicated willingness to take a paternity test, when the parents planned the pregnancy and there never was any doubt about the identity of the biological father.

Adoption of H.R., 205 Cal.App.4th 455, 140 Cal.Rptr.3d 327 (2012), held that a man who attempted to marry the mother during her pregnancy, attended prenatal appointments with her, petitioned the court to establish his paternity before the child was born, and was willing and able to take immediate custody of the child, but was prevented from establishing subsection (d) presumed father status by the mother, was a *Kelsey S.* father despite his failure to pay for pregnancy and birth-related expenses commensurate with his ability to do so. However, *Adoption of T.K., 240 Cal.App.4th 1392, 194 Cal.Rptr.3d 606 (2015), review denied*, affirming an order terminating an unwed father's parental rights after finding that he was not a *Kelsey S.* father, disagreed with Adoption of H.R., on the ground that a *Kelsey S.* full commitment to parental responsibilities requires, *at a minimum*, a demonstrated willingness to support the child financially and to support the mother emotionally during the pregnancy. Consequently, other factors may be considered only after both requirements have been satisfied.

In re D.S., 230 Cal.App.4th 1238, 179 Cal.Rptr.3d 348 (2014), held that once a juvenile court made a finding, supported by substantial evidence, that a child's biological father had not done all he could reasonably do under the circumstances to assume parental responsibilities, the court erred in treating him as a *Kelsey S.* father and concluding that the *Kelsey S.* presumption in favor of the biological father outweighed a stepfather's subsection (d) presumption of parenthood.

Purporting to rely on *Zacharia D., supra, In re Vincent M., 161 Cal.App.4th 943, 74 Cal.Rptr.3d 755 (2008), review denied*, holds that a biological father who is not a presumed father under this section and whose paternity was concealed from him by the mother, but who does not come forward in a dependency proceeding until after the reunification period has ended, cannot be treated as a *Kelsey S.* father entitled to reunification services without regard to the best interests of the child, who was placed with prospective adoptive parents when he was four days old and was thriving in their home for nine months before the biological father asserted his *Kelsey S.* claim. *Vincent M.* states, in dictum, that after the reunification period has expired, the biological father's only remedy is a Welfare and Institutions Code section 388 modification petition, which requires changed circumstances or new evidence showing that it is in the child's best interest to grant the biological father custody or reunification services.

The first paragraph of this section includes persons who have properly executed voluntary declarations of paternity. See *In re Liam L., 84 Cal.App.4th 739, 101 Cal.Rptr.2d 13 (2000)* (man may be presumed father solely on the basis of his voluntary declaration of paternity).

Scott v. Thompson, 184 Cal.App.4th 1506, 109 Cal.Rptr.3d 846 (2010), review denied, holds that, under section 7630, a decedent's sibling has no standing in a wrongful death action to challenge the paternity of a person presumed to be decedent's father under subsection (a) of this section.

For the meaning of subsection (b)(2) "cohabitation," see Section 7540, Commentary. For discussion of subsection (d) "constructive receipt," see *Kelsey S., supra, 1 Cal.4th at 827*. See also *Comino v. Kelley, 25 Cal.App.4th 678, 30 Cal.Rptr.2d 728 (1994), review denied 9/7/94* (trial court properly refused to apply the Section 7540 conclusive presumption even though husband and wife were cohabiting at the time of conception when their marriage was one of financial convenience only and the putative father subsequently received the child and mother into his home and held the child out as his own, giving rise to presumptive paternity under Section 7611 (d)); and *Brian C. v. Ginger K., 77 Cal.App.4th 1198, 92 Cal.Rptr.2d 294 (2000)* (holding that trial court should not have applied the conclusive presumption of § 7540 when (1) at the birth of the child, the mother and her husband were not living together—although they subsequently reconciled; (2) the biological father developed a substantial parent-child relationship with the child from the child's birth until a year and a half later; and (3) the biological father received the child into his home and acknowledged the child as his own (subsection (d) of this section). *In re Tanis H., 59 Cal.App.4th 1218, 69 Cal.Rptr.2d 380 (1997),* held that an unwed biological father's cohabitation with the mother when she was pregnant, but not after the child's birth, is insufficient to constitute subsection (d) receipt of the child into the father's home, with the result that the unwed father was not a presumed father. *Charisma R. v. Kristina S., 175 Cal.App.4th 361, 96 Cal.Rptr.3d 26 (2009)*, held that subsection (d) presumed parenthood requires only that a former domestic partner have received the child into her home and openly held the child out as her own; it does not require the former partner to co-parent for any particular length of time.

The Indian Child Welfare Act of 1974 [25 U.S.C. Sections 1901 et seq.] preempts inconsistent provisions of the California version of the Uniform Parentage Act. See *In re Adoption of Lindsay C., 229 Cal.App.3d 404, 408, 280 Cal.Rptr. 194 (1991), review denied 7/11/91* (Indian Child Welfare Act preempts California provisions when noncustodial father is Indian even though custodial mother is not Indian). But see *Matter of Adoption of Crews, 118 Wash.2d 561, 825 P.2d 305 (1992)*.

In *In re Nicholas H., 28 Cal.App.4th 56, 407A, 46 P.3d 932, 120 Cal.Rptr.2d 146 (2002)*, the California Supreme Court interpreted the "in an appropriate action" language of § 7612(a) to limit the rebuttal of presumed fatherhood to cases where rebuttal is appropriate rather than to allow it in all cases. In *Nicholas H.*, a dependency proceeding, a fit presumptive father seeking to assume parental obligations admitted that he was not the child's biological father. In reversing the court of appeal, which had held that his admission and the mother's testimony to the same effect rebutted the presumption that he was the child's father, the supreme court held that when no other man was asserting paternity and a presumed father sought to accept the responsibilities of paternity, an "appropriate action" was lacking. The supreme court opined that an "appropriate action" for rebuttal of a presumption of paternity might be one in which two men seek to establish paternity of a child or one in which a presumed father seeks to avoid the responsibilities of paternity. The court emphasized that it did not reach the question posed by *Steven W.* and *Kiana A.*, discussed in the Commentary to § 7612. Nor did it reach the question addressed by *In re Jerry P.*, to which the California Supreme Court granted review on May 1, 2002 (46 P.3d 331, 119 Cal.Rptr.2d 856), ordered published on June 6, 2002 (47 P.3d 988, 121 Cal. Rptr.2d 106), and dismissed review and remanded on August 28, 2002 (53 P.3d 133, 124 Cal.Rptr.2d 718). The published opinion of the court of appeal in *Jerry P.*, 95 Cal.App.4th 793, 116 Cal.Rptr.2d 123 (2002), held that the status of "presumed father" for purposes of a dependency proceeding (see Welfare and Institutions Code § 361.5(a)) suffices to qualify that person for child welfare services, including reunification services, without any inquiry whether the presumed father is also the biological father. *Jerry P.* reasoned that while the purpose of the paternity presumption (§ 7611) in the paternity provisions of the Family Code (§§ 7500–7952) is evidentiary, that same presumption is used in the Welfare and Institutions Code solely for the purpose of identifying fathers by reference to their familial bonds to a dependent child. *Jerry P.* was followed in *In re Raphael P. III, 97 Cal.App.4th 716, 118 Cal.Rptr.2d 610 (2002), review denied June 19, 2002*, which holds, in a dependency proceeding, that Family Code §§ 7551 and 7554 do not authorize the trial court to order genetic testing of a man who meets the requirements of presumed fatherhood. *Raphael P.* also observes that § 7551 allows a court to order paternity testing only when paternity is a relevant fact, which it arguably is not in a dependency proceeding when a man claims presumptive paternity and no other man asserts paternity. *In re T.R., 132 Cal.App.4th 1202, 34 Cal.Rptr.3d 215 (2005),* inverts the case law doctrine that, depending on the context, Section 7611 presumptions may not be rebuttable by evidence of non-paternity. Although a child's step-father received the child into his home and openly held the child as his own natural child, *T.R.* concludes that, for purposes of a dependency proceeding where biological paternity is immaterial, the Section 7611(d) presumption of paternity is rebutted under this section by the step-father's inappropriate conduct and prior convictions for sexually molesting children.

In re D.M., 210 Cal.App.4th 541, 148 Cal.Rptr.3d 349 (2012), review denied, held that an alleged father who was not the child's biological father, was not married to the mother, and did not meet the requirements for a statutory father could not, in a dependency proceeding, be a constitutionally presumed father under *Kelsey S.* and *Jerry P.* because he did not have an "existing familial bond with the child."

In re A.A., 114 Cal.App.4th 771, 7 Cal.Rptr.3d 755 (2003), review denied, held that in a dependency proceeding in which the child was declared a dependent, removed from his mother's care, and placed with a man who was a presumed father because he had long held the child out as his own, the juvenile court erred in finding that the child's biological father was a presumed father and that the man who held the child out as his own was merely a de facto parent. In other words, the court's determination of biological fatherhood in favor of one man does not necessarily defeat another man's presumed father status when the two issues arise in the same action. The court reasoned that § 7612(c) provides that a *judgment* establishing paternity by another man rebuts a presumption of paternity arising under this section. As no judgment had yet issued when the juvenile court made its finding of biological paternity, the requirement of a judgment was not satisfied in that proceeding. In *In re Jesusa V., 32 Cal.4th 588, 10 Cal.Rptr.3d 205, 85 P.3d 2 (2004)*, held that in a dependency proceeding concerning the placement of a child whose mother was hospitalized because she had been beaten and raped by the child's biological father, the trial court properly applied this section and § 7612 in finding that both the biological father and the mother's husband had the status of presumed father and in selecting the man who was not the child's biological father as the presumed father for purposes of the dependency proceeding. The Supreme Court emphasized that the designation of the mother's husband as "presumed father" for purposes of the dependency proceeding did not terminate the parental rights of the other presumed father, who was also the biological father. *Librers v. Black, 129 Cal.App.4th 114, 28 Cal.Rptr.3d 188 (2005)*, holds that the analysis of *Jesusa V.* applies equally to paternity actions that are not part of dependency cases and that the trial court erred in finding that a man who asserted subsection (d) presumed father status lacked standing to bring a paternity action to assert that status because he was not the child's biological father. *Librers* points out that Section 7630 (b) grants any "interested party" standing to bring an action to determine the existence of a father and child relationship presumed under subsection (d).

In re Karen C., 101 Cal.App.4th 932, 124 Cal.Rptr.2d 677 (2002), extends to women asserting the status of "presumed mother" the rule of *In re Nicholas H.*, supra. *Nicholas H.* holds that the subsection (d) presumption of paternity arising from a man's reception of a child into his home may, according to § 7612(a), be disputed only "in an appropriate action." *In re Salvador M., 111 Cal.App.4th 1353, 4 Cal.Rptr.3d 705 (2003)*, held that the juvenile court erred in not granting presumed mother status to a dependent child's adult half-sister who cared for the child since their mother's death, when the sister had established herself as the child's presumed mother long before she admitted to school authorities that she was not the child's biological mother. The court reasoned that this was not an appropriate case to allow rebuttal of the parental presumption because there was no competing maternal interest and the mother-child relationship was well established.

In re Cody B., 153 Cal.App.4th 1004, 63 Cal.Rptr.3d 652 (2007), held that a juvenile court lacked jurisdiction to entertain a mother's request to be designated a child's presumed mother under subsection (d) after the mother's parental rights had been terminated under Welfare and Institutions Code section 366.26, reasoning that the mother's request constituted an impermissible collateral attack on the judgment terminating her parental rights.

Even though a person has rebutted the subsection (d) presumption of paternity, he may still be required to support a child under the doctrine of parentage by estoppel, which requires that (1) the child have accepted a putative father's express or implied representation that he is the child's father and (2) the representation continue for a sufficient time to establish a parent-child relationship and frustrate the opportunity of discovering the child's biological father. *Clevenger v. Clevenger, 189 Cal.App.2d 658, 11 Cal.Rptr.707 (1961)*. For a review of the parentage-by-estoppel cases, see *In re Marriage of Pedregon, 107 Cal.App.4th 1284, 132 Cal.Rptr.2d 861 (2003)* (requiring husband to pay child support for his divorced wife's child even though he was not the biological father.) Although all the parentage-by-estoppel cases have involved men, the doctrine would seem equally applicable to women.

County of San Diego v. Arzaga, 152 Cal.App.4th 1336, 62 Cal.Rptr.3d 329 (2007), held that a trial court erred in applying the doctrine of parentage by estoppel to a man who did not know that he was not the child's biological father and who stopped acting as the child's father when he received negative paternity test results. *Arzaga* restricts application of the doctrine to a man who holds himself out as a child's father while knowing that he is not in fact the child's biological father.

Research References

Forms

California Transactions Forms--Family Law § 5:4, Rights Of De Facto Parents.
California Transactions Forms--Family Law § 5:9, Use Of Parenting Agreement to Define Rights and Responsibilities Relating to Child on Termination Of Partners' Relationship Where Both Partners Are Biological Parents.
California Transactions Forms--Family Law § 6:3, Definitions.
California Transactions Forms--Family Law § 6:8, Consent for Adoption Of Unmarried Minor.
California Transactions Forms--Family Law § 6:11, Initiating Proceeding Under Uniform Parentage Act [Fam C §§ 7600 to 7730].
California Transactions Forms--Family Law § 6:40, Structuring the Adoption.
California Transactions Forms--Family Law § 6:47, Matters to Consider in Drafting Petition for Independent Adoption Of Unmarried Minor.
California Transactions Forms--Family Law § 6:72, Petition to Terminate Parental Rights Of Alleged Father.
California Transactions Forms--Family Law § 6:74, Petition to Terminate Parental Rights Of Alleged Father Served With Notice Of Alleged Paternity Without Timely Response.
California Transactions Forms--Family Law § 6:75, Order Terminating Parental Rights Of Alleged Father Served With Notice Of Alleged Paternity Without Timely Response.
California Transactions Forms--Family Law § 6:76, Ex Parte Application for Order to Terminate Parental Rights Of Alleged Father Who Waived Notice or Denied Paternity.
California Transactions Forms--Family Law § 6:77, Order Terminating Parental Rights Of Alleged Father Who Waived Notice.
California Transactions Forms--Family Law § 7:38, Parentage and Birth Certificate.
California Transactions Forms--Family Law § 7:45, Artificial Insemination Surrogacy Agreement Between Intended Father and Surrogate Couple.
California Transactions Forms--Family Law § 7:46, in Vitro Surrogacy Agreement Between Intended Parents and Surrogate Couple; Intended Parents Are Genetic Parents.
California Transactions Forms--Family Law § 7:47, in Vitro Fertilization Surrogacy Agreement Between Intended Mother and Surrogate Using Donated Genetic Material.
California Transactions Forms--Family Law § 7:86, Overview.
California Transactions Forms--Family Law § 7:96, California Statutory Form for Assisted Reproduction--Intent to be Parents--Married Spouses or Registered Domestic Partners Using Assisted Reproduction to Conceive a Child (Form 1).

California Transactions Forms--Family Law § 7:97, California Statutory Form for Assisted Reproduction--Intent to be Parents--Unmarried, Intended Parents Using Intended Parent's Sperm to Conceive a Child (Form 2).
California Transactions Forms--Family Law § 7:98, California Statutory Form for Assisted Reproduction--Intent to be Parents--Intended Parents Conceiving a Child Using Eggs from One Parent and the Other Parent Will Give Birth (Form 3).
California Transactions Forms--Family Law § 3:126, Request for Hearing and Application to Set Aside Voluntary Declaration Of Paternity [Form FL-280].
California Transactions Forms--Family Law § 3:127, Responsive Declaration to Application to Set Aside Voluntary Declaration Of Paternity [Form FL-285].
California Transactions Forms--Family Law § 3:128, Order After Hearing on Motion to Set Aside Voluntary Declaration Of Paternity [Form FL-290].
California Transactions Forms--Family Law § 4:105, Declaration Of Paternity.
California Transactions Forms--Family Law § 3:126.50, Information Sheet for Completing Request for Hearing and Application to Set Aside Voluntary Declaration Of Paternity [Form FL-281].
West's California Code Forms, Family § 6340, Comment Overview--Issuance Of Orders After Notice and Hearing.
West's California Code Forms, Family § 7540, Comment Overview--Conclusive Presumption as Child Of Marriage.
West's California Code Forms, Family § 7610, Comment Overview--Establishing Parent and Child Relationship.
West's California Code Forms, Family § 7630, Comment Overview--Determining Parent and Child Relationship.
West's California Code Forms, Family § 7660, Comment Overview--Termination Of Parental Rights in Adoption Proceedings.
West's California Code Forms, Family § 8600, Comment Overview--Adoption Of Unmarried Minors.
West's California Code Forms, Family § 7630 Form 2, Complaint to Establish Nonexistence Of Parental Relationship.
West's California Judicial Council Forms JV-505, Statement Regarding Parentage (Juvenile).

Treatises and Practice Aids

Witkin, California Summary 10th Constitutional Law § 776, Right to Withhold Consent to Adoption.
Witkin, California Summary 10th Contracts § 1024, Payment Of Support Due to Mistaken Belief Of Biological Fatherhood.
Witkin, California Summary 10th Husband and Wife § 384, Orders After Notice and Hearing.
Witkin, California Summary 10th Parent and Child § 13, Nature and Effect Of Classification.
Witkin, California Summary 10th Parent and Child § 17, Development Of Law.
Witkin, California Summary 10th Parent and Child § 23, Where Intended Mother is Not Genetic Mother.
Witkin, California Summary 10th Parent and Child § 24, in General.
Witkin, California Summary 10th Parent and Child § 25, Nature and Effect.
Witkin, California Summary 10th Parent and Child § 26, Constitutional Challenges.
Witkin, California Summary 10th Parent and Child § 27, Cohabitation Requirement.
Witkin, California Summary 10th Parent and Child § 31, in General.
Witkin, California Summary 10th Parent and Child § 33, Effect Of Declaration.
Witkin, California Summary 10th Parent and Child § 34, Rescinding or Setting Aside Declaration.
Witkin, California Summary 10th Parent and Child § 35, in General.
Witkin, California Summary 10th Parent and Child § 36, Nonbiological Father as Presumed Father.
Witkin, California Summary 10th Parent and Child § 37, Birth During Marriage.
Witkin, California Summary 10th Parent and Child § 38, Subsequent Marriage.
Witkin, California Summary 10th Parent and Child § 39, Reception Into Home.
Witkin, California Summary 10th Parent and Child § 40, Child in Utero.
Witkin, California Summary 10th Parent and Child § 42, No Presumption in Cases Of Rape.
Witkin, California Summary 10th Parent and Child § 43, in General.
Witkin, California Summary 10th Parent and Child § 47, Where Presumption Of Paternity Applies.
Witkin, California Summary 10th Parent and Child § 48, Where No Presumption Applies.
Witkin, California Summary 10th Parent and Child § 49, Joinder and Alignment Of Parties.
Witkin, California Summary 10th Parent and Child § 59, Visitation Privileges.
Witkin, California Summary 10th Parent and Child § 60, Action to Determine Mother and Child Relationship.
Witkin, California Summary 10th Parent and Child § 61, Notice Of Adoption Proceeding.
Witkin, California Summary 10th Parent and Child § 66, Statutory Requirements.
Witkin, California Summary 10th Parent and Child § 68, Constitutional Rights Of Natural Father.
Witkin, California Summary 10th Parent and Child § 98, in General.
Witkin, California Summary 10th Parent and Child § 100, in General.
Witkin, California Summary 10th Parent and Child § 101, Unwed Father.
Witkin, California Summary 10th Parent and Child § 206, Agreement Between Parents.
Witkin, California Summary 10th Parent and Child § 215, Current Statute: No Preference.
Witkin, California Summary 10th Parent and Child § 23A, (New) Assisted Reproduction Agreements for Gestational Carriers.
Witkin, California Summary 10th Parent and Child § 235, Biologically Unrelated Persons Opposed by Parent.
Witkin, California Summary 10th Parent and Child § 236, Former Lesbian Partner Opposed by Other Partner.
Witkin, California Summary 10th Parent and Child § 36A, (New) Biological Father as Kelsey S. Father.
Witkin, California Summary 10th Parent and Child § 60A, (New) Lesbian Partner Who is Not Biological Mother Of Child.
Witkin, California Summary 10th Parent and Child § 60B, (New) Domestic Partner Who Donated Her Ova to Partner to Conceive Child.
Witkin, California Summary 10th Parent and Child § 60C, (New) Estoppel to Deny Motherhood Of Lesbian Partner.
Witkin, California Summary 10th Parent and Child § 60D, (New) Determination Of Rights Of Biological Mother, Presumed Mother, and Kelsey S. Father.
Witkin, California Summary 10th Parent and Child § 603, Identification Of Presumed or Alleged Fathers.
Witkin, California Summary 10th Parent and Child § 644, Persons Entitled to Services.
Witkin, California Summary 10th Torts § 1393, Child Of Presumed Parent.
Witkin, California Summary 10th Wills and Probate § 94, Parent and Child Relationship.

§ 7611.5. Presumption against natural father status; Section 7611 inapplicable

Where Section 7611 does not apply, a man shall not be presumed to be the natural father of a child if either of the following is true:

(a) The child was conceived as a result of an act in violation of Section 261 of the Penal Code and the father was convicted of that violation.

(b) The child was conceived as a result of an act in violation of Section 261.5 of the Penal Code, the father was convicted of that violation, and the mother was under the age of 15 years and the father was 21 years of age or older at the time of conception. *(Added by Stats.1993, c. 219 (A.B.1500), § 177.)*

Law Revision Commission Comments

Enactment [Revised Comment]

Section 7611.5 continues former Civil Code Section 7004(b) without substantive change. [23 Cal.L.Rev.Comm. Reports 1 (1993)].

Commentary

In re Kyle F., 112 Cal.App.4th 538, 5 Cal.Rptr.3d 190 (2003), review denied, holds that an unwed father who could have been charged with misdemeanor unlawful sexual intercourse under Penal Code § 261.5 was not barred from bringing an action to declare his paternity under Family Code § 7631, for the purpose of asserting his status as a presumed father under the constitutional holding of *Adoption of Kelsey S.* (see commentary to § 7611) and withholding his consent to the child's adoption. *Kyle F.* concluded that this section was inapplicable because the father was never charged and the child was conceived when the father was 18 and the mother was 16.

Research References

Forms

West's California Judicial Council Forms JV-505, Statement Regarding Parentage (Juvenile).

Treatises and Practice Aids

Witkin, California Summary 10th Constitutional Law § 776, Right to Withhold Consent to Adoption.

Witkin, California Summary 10th Parent and Child § 42, No Presumption in Cases Of Rape.

§ 7612. Presumption as natural parent; rebuttable presumption; conflicting presumptions; more than two persons with claim to parentage; petition to set aside voluntary declaration of paternity; invalid voluntary declarations of paternity

(a) Except as provided in Chapter 1 (commencing with Section 7540) and Chapter 3 (commencing with Section 7570) of Part 2, a presumption under Section 7611 is a rebuttable presumption affecting the burden of proof and may be rebutted in an appropriate action only by clear and convincing evidence.

(b) If two or more presumptions arise under Section 7610 or 7611 that conflict with each other, or if a presumption under Section 7611 conflicts with a claim pursuant to Section 7610, the presumption which on the facts is founded on the weightier considerations of policy and logic controls.

(c) In an appropriate action, a court may find that more than two persons with a claim to parentage under this division are parents if the court finds that recognizing only two parents would be detrimental to the child. In determining detriment to the child, the court shall consider all relevant factors, including, but not limited to, the harm of removing the child from a stable placement with a parent who has fulfilled the child's physical needs and the child's psychological needs for care and affection, and who has assumed that role for a substantial period of time. A finding of detriment to the child does not require a finding of unfitness of any of the parents or persons with a claim to parentage.

(d) Unless a court orders otherwise after making the determination specified in subdivision (c), a presumption under Section 7611 is rebutted by a judgment establishing parentage of the child by another person.

(e) Within two years of the execution of a voluntary declaration of paternity, a person who is presumed to be a parent under Section 7611 may file a petition pursuant to Section 7630 to set aside a voluntary declaration of paternity. The court's ruling on the petition to set aside the voluntary declaration of paternity shall be made taking into account the validity of the voluntary declaration of paternity, the best interests of the child based upon the court's consideration of the factors set forth in subdivision (b) of Section 7575, and the best interests of the child based upon the nature, duration, and quality of the petitioning party's relationship with the child and the benefit or detriment to the child of continuing that relationship. In the event of a conflict between the presumption under Section 7611 and the voluntary declaration of paternity, the weightier considerations of policy and logic shall control.

(f) A voluntary declaration of paternity is invalid if, at the time the declaration was signed, any of the following conditions exist:

(1) The child already had a presumed parent under Section 7540.

(2) The child already had a presumed parent under subdivision (a), (b), or (c) of Section 7611.

(3) The man signing the declaration is a sperm donor, consistent with subdivision (b) of Section 7613.

(g) A person's offer or refusal to sign a voluntary declaration of paternity may be considered as a factor, but shall not be determinative, as to the issue of legal parentage in any proceedings regarding the establishment or termination of parental rights. *(Stats.1992, c. 162 (A.B.2650), § 10, operative Jan. 1, 1994. Amended by Stats.1993, c. 219 (A.B.1500), § 178; Stats.1994, c. 1269 (A.B.2208), § 54; Stats.2008, c. 534 (S.B.1726), § 1; Stats.2011, c. 185 (A.B.1349), § 3; Stats. 2013, c. 510 (A.B.1403), § 4; Stats.2013, c. 564 (S.B.274), § 6.5; Stats.2015, c. 91 (A.B.1049), § 1, eff. Jan. 1, 2016; Stats.2016, c. 86 (S.B.1171), § 129, eff. Jan. 1, 2017.)*

Law Revision Commission Comments

Enactment [Revised Comment]

Section 7612 continues former Civil Code Section 7004(c) without substantive change. This section is similar to Section 4(b) of the Uniform Parentage Act (1973). In subdivision (c), "judgment" has been substituted for "decree." This is not a substantive change. See Section 100 ("judgment" includes decree, as appropriate). [23 Cal.L.Rev.Comm. Reports 1 (1993)].

Commentary

Section 7601 and this section have been amended to provide that a child may have more than two legal parents, where having only two legal parent would be detrimental to the child, *overturning In re M.C., 195 Cal.App.4th 197, 123 Cal.Rptr.3d 856 (2011)*, which held that

when a dependent child had more than two presumed parents, the court was required to resolve the conflicting presumptions of parentage by reducing the number of presumed parents to no more than two. To the extent that any cases discussed in the Commentary to this Chapter rely on the prior rule that a child may have only two parents and only one father, those cases no longer express controlling law. Nevertheless, prior case law may still be controlling on other issues and those cases might still yield the same results under revised section 7612(c).

Subsection (c) now provides that a child may have more than two legal parents, *overturning In re M.C., 195 Cal.App.4th 197, 123 Cal.Rptr.3d 856 (2011)*, which held that when a dependent child had more than two presumed parents, the court was required to resolve the conflicting presumptions of parentage by reducing the number of presumed parents to no more than two.

In re Donovan J., 244 Cal.App.4th 1075, 198 Cal.Rptr.3d 550 (2016), holds that, for purposes of subsection (c), "an appropriate action" requires that there already be an existing parent-child relationship between the child and the person who claims third-parent status, so that recognizing only two parents would be detrimental to the child.

Martinez v. Vaziri, 246 Cal.App.4th 373, 200 Cal.Rptr.3d 884 (2016), held that, in determining whether there is a subsection (c) "stable placement," the trial court erred in focusing solely on the living arrangements of the adult parties rather than the extent to which the third-parent claimant satisfied the child's physical and psychological needs. Martinez also considers whether each of the child's biological parents has an existing parental relationship to the child and, if not, whether denying parental status to the third-parent claimant would effectively leave the child with only one parent.

Although a child's biological father was a presumed parent for purposes of section 7611(d) because he held the child out as his own and received him into his home during the first years of the child's life, he was not eligible to be a third parent under this section when he had no existing relationship with the child, who already had a mother and a presumed father. *In re L.L., 13 Cal.App.5th 1302, 220 Cal.Rptr.3d 904 (2017)*.

In re M.R., 7 Cal.App.5th 886, 212 Cal.Rptr.3d 807 (2017), affirmed a juvenile court ruling that a child had two presumed fathers when ample evidence showed that recognizing only one presumed father would be detrimental to the child.

In re J.O., 178 Cal.App.4th 139, 100 Cal.Rptr.3d 276 (2009), holds that in a dependency proceeding a juvenile court erred in finding that a man's section 7611(d) presumed father status was rebutted by his failure to contact or provide support for his children, when rebuttal of the man's presumed father status would leave the children without any father.

Kevin Q. v. Lauren W., 175 Cal.App.4th 1119, 95 Cal.Rptr.3d 477 (2009), review denied, held that a voluntary declaration of paternity signed when a child already had a section 7611(d) presumed father had the effect of rebutting the latter's presumption of paternity under subsection (c), because section 7573 gives a voluntary declaration of paternity the force and effect of a judgment of paternity. Mitigating *Kevin Q.*, subsection (d), added in 2011, grants any section 7611 presumed father, including a subsection (d) presumed father, the right to file a petition to set aside a voluntary declaration within two years of its making. By contrast, under section (e), also added by the 2011 legislation, when parenthood is presumed under section 7450 or subsections (a),(b), or (c) of section 7611 (but not subsection (d)), any subsequent voluntary declaration of paternity by another person is automatically invalid

In re Levi H., 197 Cal.App.4th 1279, 128 Cal.Rptr.3d 814 (2011), holds that when a voluntary declaration of paternity qualifies for section (c) treatment, the presumption of paternity arising under section 7611(d) is rebutted by another man's voluntary declaration of paternity, and there is no need to engage in a subsection (b) weighing analysis.

However, when a child has both an alleged biological father, whose paternity is at issue in a dependency proceeding, and a presumed father, a court must hold an evidentiary hearing on the issue biological paternity. If the court concludes that one man is the biological father and the other man is a presumed father, the court must perform a subsection (b) balancing to determine which man should be considered the child's father. *In re P.A., 198 Cal.App.4th 974, 130 Cal.Rptr.3d 556 (2011)*. *In re P.A.* concludes that a finding that a man is a biological father is not a paternity judgment for purposes of subsection (c). *In re P.A.* interprets subsection (c) to refer to a judgment that already exists when the instant action arises. *In re P.A.* relies on *In re A.A.*, discussed below in the Commentary to this section.

By contrast, *In re Cheyenne B., 203 Cal.App.4th 1361, 138 Cal.Rptr.3d 267 (2012), review denied*, holds that a pre-existing judgment that a man is the father of a child for child support purposes is a paternity judgment within the meaning of subsection (c) and therefore may preclude another man from establishing that the is a presumed father under section 7611(d). Nevertheless, the fact that the child support order satisfies subsection (c) does not make the support obligor a presumed parent. The effect of *Cheyenne B.* was that the child, who initially had one adjudicated nonpresumptive biological father and one unadjudicated presumptive father, ultimately had no presumed father.

For discussion and application of subsection (b), see *Steven W. v. Matthew S., 33 Cal.App.4th 1108, 39 Cal.Rptr.2d 535 (1995)*, where the mother's separated husband invoked the Section 7611(a) presumption of paternity and the mother's cohabitant invoked the Section 7611(d) presumption. The court held that the social relationship between the cohabitant and the child weighed in favor of treating the presumption in the cohabitant's favor as the controlling presumption under subsection (b). The court did not seem to realize that, unlike the Section 7540 conclusive presumption, the Section 7611 presumptions are rebuttable, and that blood tests clearly excluded the cohabitant, while demonstrating a high degree of probability that the husband was the father. Compare *Barkaloff v. Woodward, 47 Cal. App.4th 393, 399, 55 Cal.Rptr.2d 167 (1996)* (although a man is presumed to be the father of a child under Section 7611(d) when he receives the child into his home and holds the child out as his natural child, this presumption is rebuttable and is overcome by a judgment establishing that another man is the biological father of the child). For discussion of the evidentiary standards for rebutting Section 7611 presumptions, see Section 7611, Commentary.

The methodology of *Steven W.* was applied, in dictum, in the context of a dependency proceeding in *In re Kiana A., 93 Cal.App.4th 1109, 113 Cal.Rptr.2d 669 (2001)*, where there were two § 7611 presumptive fathers and the juvenile court applied subsection (b) of this section to award the presumption to a man who may not have been the biological father. The court of appeal found that the other presumptive father, who may also have been the biological father, had waived his right to genetic testing in the juvenile court proceeding by failing to seek testing, although a request for genetic testing, which was denied by the juvenile court, had been made by the other presumptive father and the Department of Social Services. *Kiana A.* additionally states, by way of dictum, that even if the biological father could have raised the issue of paternity, his challenge would not necessarily have defeated the nonbiological father's § 7611(d) presumption of paternity, which arose from receiving a child into one's home and holding the child out as one's natural child. But see Family Code § 7630(b), which provides that "[a]ny interested party may bring an action at any time for the purpose of determining the existence or nonexistence of the father and child relationship presumed under subdivision (d) of Section 7611." *In re A.A., 114 Cal.App.4th 771, 7 Cal.Rptr.3d 755 (2003), review denied*, held that in a dependency proceeding in which the child was declared a dependent, removed from his mother's care, and placed with a man who was a presumed father because he had long held the child out as his own, the juvenile court erred in finding that the child's biological father was a presumed father and that the man who held the child out as his own was merely a de facto parent. In other words, the court's determination of biological fatherhood in favor of one man does not necessarily defeat another man's presumed father status when the two issues arise in the same action. The court reasoned that subsection (c) of this section provides that a *judgment* establishing paternity by another man rebuts a presumption of paternity arising under § 7611. As no judgment had yet issued when the juvenile court made its finding of biological paternity, the requirement of a judgment was not satisfied in that proceeding. *In re Jesusa V., 32 Cal.4th 588, 10 Cal.Rptr.3d 205, 85 P.3d 2 (2004)*, held that in a dependency proceeding concerning the placement of a child whose mother was hospitalized because she had been beaten and raped by the child's biological father, the trial court properly applied § 7611 and this section in finding that both the biological father and the mother's husband had the status of presumed father and in selecting the man who was not the child's biological father as the presumed father for purposes of the dependency proceeding. The Supreme Court emphasized that the designation of the mother's husband as presumed father for purposes of the dependency proceeding did not terminate the parental rights of the other presumed father, who was also the biological father. *Librers v. Black, 129 Cal.App.4th 114, 28 Cal.Rptr.3d 188 (2005)*, holds that the analysis of *Jesusa V.* applies equally to paternity actions that are not part of dependency cases and that the trial court erred in finding that a man who asserted Section 7611(d) presumed father status lacked standing to bring a paternity action to assert that status because he was not the child's biological father. *Librers* points out that Section 7630(b) grants any "interested party" standing to bring an action to determine the existence of a father and child relationship presumed under subsection (d).

Gabriel P. v. Suedi D., 141 Cal.App.4th 850, 46 Cal.Rptr.3d 437 (2006), held that where there were two presumptive fathers, one a biological father and the other a father by virtue of his voluntary declaration of paternity and subsequent marriage to the child's mother, the trial court erred in setting aside the latter's voluntary declaration of paternity without joining him as a necessary party in the biological father's paternity action, assessing his relationship to the child, and weighing the presumptions supporting the presumed father status of each of the two men. The court reasoned that this result is also required by Section 7675(b)(1), which provides that a court may set aside a voluntary declaration of paternity unless it determines that declining to do so would serve the best interests of the child.

On March 30, 2004, the California Supreme Court denied review and ordered depublication of the court of appeal opinion in *In re R.R.* The depublished opinion, *9 Cal.Rptr.3d 188 (2004)*, had ruled that where the mother's husband was a conclusively presumed father under §§ 7540 and 7541 because there was no challenge to his paternity during the two years following the child's birth, but a blood test later ruled out husband as the biological father and husband was released from his court-ordered reunification plan, the juvenile court erred in ordering adoptive placement before terminating the rights of the mother's husband because he remained the presumptive father even though he had been ruled out at the biological father.

Compare *In re Nicholas H., 28 Cal.4th 56, 407A, 46 P.3d 932, 120 Cal.Rptr.2d 146 (2002)*, in which the California Supreme Court interpreted the "in an appropriate action" language of § 7612(a) to limit the rebuttal of presumed fatherhood to cases where rebuttal is appropriate rather than to allow it in all cases. In *Nicholas H.*, a dependency proceeding, a fit presumptive father seeking to assume parental obligations admitted that he was not the child's biological father. In reversing the court of appeal, which had held that his admission and the mother's testimony to the same effect rebutted the presumption that he was the child's father, the supreme court held that when no other man was asserting paternity and a presumed father sought to accept the responsibilities of paternity, an "appropriate action" was lacking. The supreme court opined that an "appropriate action" for rebuttal of a presumption of paternity might be one in which two men seek to establish paternity of a child or one in which a presumed father seeks to avoid the responsibilities of paternity. The court emphasized that it did not reach the question posed by *Steven W.* and *Kiana A.*, discussed immediately above. Nor did it reach the question addressed by In re Jerry P., to which the California Supreme Court granted review on May 1, 2002 (46 P.3d 331, 119 Cal.Rptr.2d 856), ordered published on June 6, 2002 (47 P.3d 988, 121 Cal. Rptr.2d 106), and dismissed review and remanded on August 28, 2002 (53 P.3d 133, 124 Cal.Rptr.2d 718). The published opinion of the court of appeal in *Jerry P.*, 95 Cal.App.4th 793, 116 Cal.Rptr.2d 123 (2002), held that the status of "presumed father" for purposes of a dependency proceeding (see Welfare and Institutions Code § 361.5 (a)) suffices to qualify that person for child welfare services, including reunification services, without any inquiry whether the presumed father is also the biological father. *Jerry P.* reasoned that while the purpose of the paternity presumption (§ 7611) in the paternity provisions of the Family Code (§§ 7500–7952) is evidentiary, that same presumption is used in the Welfare and Institutions Code solely for the purpose of identifying fathers by reference to their familial bonds to a dependent child. *Jerry P.* was followed in *In re Raphael P. III, 97 Cal.App.4th 716, 118 Cal.Rptr.2d 610 (2002), review denied June 19, 2002*, which holds, in a dependency proceeding, that Family Code §§ 7551 and 7554 do not authorize the trial court to order genetic testing of a man who meets the requirements of presumed fatherhood. *Raphael P.* also observes that § 7551 allows a court to order paternity testing only when paternity is a relevant fact, which it arguably is not in a dependency proceeding when a man claims presumptive paternity and no other man asserts paternity.

In re D.M., 210 Cal.App.4th 541, 148 Cal.Rptr.3d 349 (2012), review denied, held that an alleged father who was not the child's biological father, was not married to the mother, and did not meet the requirements for a statutory father could not, in a dependency proceeding, be a constitutionally presumed father under *Kelsey S.* and *Jerry P.* because he did not have an "existing familial bond with the child."

J.R. v. D.P., 212 Cal.App.4th 374, 150 Cal.Rptr.3d 882 (2012), review denied, affirmed a trial court decision resolving conflicting section 7611(d) presumptions of paternity in favor of a *Kelsey S.* father, rather than the mother's husband, who had been her boyfriend at the time of the child's conception and birth, lived with the child and mother, and raised the child as his own. The court reasoned that resolving the conflict in favor of the *Kelsey S.* biological father would serve the child's best interests because if the presumption were resolved in favor of the mother's husband, the mother would have prevented contact between the biological father and the child.

In re Karen C., 101 Cal.App.4th 932, 124 Cal.Rptr.2d 677 (2002), extends to women asserting the status of "presumed mother" the rule of *In re Nicholas H.*, supra. *Nicholas H.* holds that the § 7611 (d) presumption of paternity arising from a man's reception of a child into his home may, according to subsection (a), be disputed only "in an appropriate action." *In re Salvador M., 111 Cal.App.4th 1353, 4 Cal.Rptr.3d 705 (2003)*, held that the juvenile court erred in not granting presumed mother status to a dependent child's adult half-sister who cared for the child since their mother's death, when the sister had established herself as the child's presumed mother long before she admitted to school authorities that she was not the child's biological mother. The court reasoned that this was not an appropriate case to allow rebuttal of the parental presumption because there was no competing maternal interest and the mother-child relationship was well established.

In re T.R., 132 Cal.App.4th 1202, 34 Cal.Rptr.3d 215 (2005), inverts the case law doctrine that, depending on the context, Section 7611 presumptions may not be rebuttable by evidence of non-paternity. Although a child's step-father received the child into his home and openly held the child as his own natural child, *T.R.* concludes that, for purposes of a dependency proceeding where biological paternity is immaterial, the Section 7611(d) presumption of paternity is rebutted under this section by the step-father's inappropriate conduct and prior convictions for sexually molesting children. For further discussion of the use of paternity presumptions in dependency proceedings, see commentary to Welfare and Institutions Code Section 361.5.

In re D.S., 207 Cal.App.4th 1088, 143 Cal.Rptr.3d 918 (2012), held that when a child has a natural mother, a child's stepmother may not challenge the natural mother's maternity under this section, even though the stepmother could be found to be a section 7611(d) presumed parent. *In re D.S.* reasoned that this is not an "appropriate action" within the meaning of subsection (a) of this section. If, as it appeared, the natural mother has abandoned the child, the appropriate action is a stepparent adoption proceeding.

Research References

Forms

California Transactions Forms--Family Law § 5:4, Rights Of De Facto Parents.
California Transactions Forms--Family Law § 5:9, Use Of Parenting Agreement to Define Rights and Responsibilities Relating to Child on Termination Of Partners' Relationship Where Both Partners Are Biological Parents.
California Transactions Forms--Family Law § 6:3, Definitions.
California Transactions Forms--Family Law § 6:8, Consent for Adoption Of Unmarried Minor.
California Transactions Forms--Family Law § 6:11, Initiating Proceeding Under Uniform Parentage Act [Fam C §§ 7600 to 7730].
California Transactions Forms--Family Law § 6:40, Structuring the Adoption.
California Transactions Forms--Family Law § 6:47, Matters to Consider in Drafting Petition for Independent Adoption Of Unmarried Minor.
California Transactions Forms--Family Law § 6:72, Petition to Terminate Parental Rights Of Alleged Father.
California Transactions Forms--Family Law § 6:74, Petition to Terminate Parental Rights Of Alleged Father Served With Notice Of Alleged Paternity Without Timely Response.
California Transactions Forms--Family Law § 6:75, Order Terminating Parental Rights Of Alleged Father Served With Notice Of Alleged Paternity Without Timely Response.
California Transactions Forms--Family Law § 6:76, Ex Parte Application for Order to Terminate Parental Rights Of Alleged Father Who Waived Notice or Denied Paternity.
California Transactions Forms--Family Law § 7:38, Parentage and Birth Certificate.
California Transactions Forms--Family Law § 7:45, Artificial Insemination Surrogacy Agreement Between Intended Father and Surrogate Couple.
California Transactions Forms--Family Law § 7:46, in Vitro Surrogacy Agreement Between Intended Parents and Surrogate Couple; Intended Parents Are Genetic Parents.
California Transactions Forms--Family Law § 7:47, in Vitro Fertilization Surrogacy Agreement Between Intended Mother and Surrogate Using Donated Genetic Material.
California Transactions Forms--Family Law § 7:86, Overview.
California Transactions Forms--Family Law § 3:126, Request for Hearing and Application to Set Aside Voluntary Declaration Of Paternity [Form FL-280].
California Transactions Forms--Family Law § 3:127, Responsive Declaration to Application to Set Aside Voluntary Declaration Of Paternity [Form FL-285].
California Transactions Forms--Family Law § 3:128, Order After Hearing on Motion to Set Aside Voluntary Declaration Of Paternity [Form FL-290].
California Transactions Forms--Family Law § 4:105, Declaration Of Paternity.
California Transactions Forms--Family Law § 3:126.50, Information Sheet for Completing Request for Hearing and Application to Set Aside Voluntary Declaration Of Paternity [Form FL-281].
West's California Judicial Council Forms JV-505, Statement Regarding Parentage (Juvenile).

Treatises and Practice Aids

Witkin, California Summary 10th Constitutional Law § 776, Right to Withhold Consent to Adoption.
Witkin, California Summary 10th Parent and Child § 18, Parent and Child Relationship.
Witkin, California Summary 10th Parent and Child § 25, Nature and Effect.
Witkin, California Summary 10th Parent and Child § 31, in General.
Witkin, California Summary 10th Parent and Child § 33, Effect Of Declaration.
Witkin, California Summary 10th Parent and Child § 34, Rescinding or Setting Aside Declaration.
Witkin, California Summary 10th Parent and Child § 35, in General.
Witkin, California Summary 10th Parent and Child § 36, Nonbiological Father as Presumed Father.
Witkin, California Summary 10th Parent and Child § 39, Reception Into Home.
Witkin, California Summary 10th Parent and Child § 47, Where Presumption Of Paternity Applies.
Witkin, California Summary 10th Parent and Child § 60, Action to Determine Mother and Child Relationship.
Witkin, California Summary 10th Parent and Child § 235, Biologically Unrelated Persons Opposed by Parent.
Witkin, California Summary 10th Parent and Child § 60A, (New) Lesbian Partner Who is Not Biological Mother Of Child.
Witkin, California Summary 10th Parent and Child § 60D, (New) Determination Of Rights Of Biological Mother, Presumed Mother, and Kelsey S. Father.
Witkin, California Summary 10th Parent and Child § 603, Identification Of Presumed or Alleged Fathers.

§ 7613. Conception through assisted reproduction with semen or ova donated by donor other than spouse; consent of another intended parent; treatment as natural parent; treatment of semen or ova donors

(a) If a woman conceives through assisted reproduction with semen or ova or both donated by a donor not her spouse, with the consent of another intended parent, that intended parent is treated in law as if he or she were the natural parent of a child thereby conceived. The other intended parent's consent shall be in writing and signed by the other intended parent and the woman conceiving through assisted reproduction.

(b)(1) The donor of semen provided to a licensed physician and surgeon or to a licensed sperm bank for use in assisted reproduction by a woman other than the donor's spouse is treated in law as if he were not the natural parent of a child thereby conceived, unless otherwise agreed to in a writing signed by the donor and the woman prior to the conception of the child.

(2) If the semen is not provided to a licensed physician and surgeon or a licensed sperm bank as specified in paragraph (1), the donor of semen for use in assisted reproduction by a woman other than the donor's spouse is treated in law as if he were not the natural parent of a child thereby conceived if either of the following are met:

(A) The donor and the woman agreed in a writing signed prior to conception that the donor would not be a parent.

(B) A court finds by clear and convincing evidence that the child was conceived through assisted reproduction and that, prior to the conception of the child, the woman and the donor had an oral agreement that the donor would not be a parent.

(3) Paragraphs (1) and (2) do not apply to a man who provided semen for use in assisted reproduction by a woman other than the man's spouse pursuant to a written agreement signed by the man and the woman prior to conception of the child stating that they intended for the man to be a parent.

(c) The donor of ova for use in assisted reproduction by a person other than the donor's spouse or nonmarital partner is treated in law as if the donor were not the natural parent of a child thereby conceived unless the court finds satisfactory evidence that the donor and the person intended for the donor to be a parent. *(Stats.1992, c. 162 (A.B.2650), § 10, operative Jan. 1, 1994. Amended by Stats.2008, c. 534 (S.B.1726), § 2; Stats.2011, c. 185 (A.B.1349), § 4; Stats. 2013, c. 510 (A.B.1403), § 5; Stats.2015, c. 566 (A.B.960), § 1, eff. Jan. 1, 2016; Stats.2016, c. 385 (A.B.2349), § 2, eff. Jan. 1, 2017.)*

Law Revision Commission Comments

Enactment [Revised Comment]

Section 7613 continues former Civil Code Section 7005 without substantive change. This section is similar to Section 5 of the Uniform Parentage Act (1973). The phrase "physician and surgeon" has been substituted for "physician." See Section 580 Comment. [23 Cal.L.Rev.Comm. Reports 1 (1993)].

Commentary

See generally *Jhordan C. v. Mary K., 179 Cal.App.3d 386, 389, 224 Cal.Rptr. 530 (1986)* (when requirements of the provision are not followed by the parties, the donor of semen may be determined to be the father in a paternity action). See also *Hecht v. Superior Court, 16 Cal.App.4th 836, 852, 20 Cal.Rptr.2d 275 (1993), review denied 9/2/93* (disposition of posthumous sperm); and *Sherwyn and Handel v. Department of Social Services, 173 Cal.App.3d 52, 218 Cal.Rptr. 778 (1985)* (surrogacy action dismissed for lack of standing and lack of a justiciable controversy).

Jason P. v. Danielle S., 226 Cal.App.4th 167, 171 Cal.Rptr.3d 789 (2014), review denied, held that even though subsection (b) precluded a sperm donor from establishing paternity by virtue of his biological relationship to the child, a sperm donor could establish his paternity under section 7611(d), based on his openly holding out the child as his natural child and receiving him into his home. On remand, *Jason P. v. Danielle S., 9 Cal.App.5th 1000, 215 Cal.Rptr.3d 542 (2017), review denied*, affirmed a trial court judgment that a sperm donor was a subsection (d) presumed father based on evidence that he received the child into his home and held him out as his own.

K.M. v. E.G., 37 Cal.4th 130, 117 P.3d 673, 33 Cal.Rptr.3d 61 (2005), holds that section (b) has no application when a woman in a lesbian relationship provides her ova to impregnate her partner in order to produce children who will be raised in their joint home. Accordingly, the California Supreme Court recognized the ova donor's claim to parental status, holding that both the woman who provided the ova and the woman who bore the resulting twin children were the children's parents even though the ova donor did not hold the resultant child out as her own natural child within the meaning of Section 7611(d) and the trial court found that she formally relinquished any claim to offspring resulting from her ova donation. In other words, the intent of the parties on the question of maternity had no bearing on the result.

Although *K.M.*, narrowly distinguishes *Steven S. v. Deborah D., 127 Cal.App.4th 319, 25 Cal.Rptr.3d 482 (2005)*, *K.M.* may be understood to undermine the rationale of *Stephen S.*, in which the court of appeal held that when a child is conceived by the artificial insemination of an unmarried mother with sperm provided by a licensed physician, the biological father of the child may not assert parental rights even though he once had an intimate sexual relationship with the mother and had some social role in the child's life. *Stephen S.* reasoned that once the trial court determined that the child was conceived by artificial insemination, rather than natural conception, subsection (b) applied to bar the semen donor from asserting his parentage of the child.

A child conceived through artificial insemination has no cause of action for malpractice against the fertility clinic for its failure to certify the husband's signature, as required by this section, because lack of certification does not invalidate the husband's written consent to be the child's legal father. *Alexandria S. v. Pacific Fertility Medical Center, 55 Cal.App.4th 110, 64 Cal.Rptr.2d 23 (1997), review denied July 30, 1997.*

This section does not impose a duty on a physician to secure a husband's consent to insemination of his wife. The husband may not seek tort damages against a physician for failure to seek his consent, for a physician owes no legal duty to the husband of a patient. *Shin v. Kong, 80 Cal.App.4th 498, 95 Cal.Rptr.2d 304 (2000), review denied July 19, 2000.*

In *Johnson v. Superior Court, 80 Cal.App.4th 1050, 95 Cal.Rptr.2d 864 (2000)*, the parents of a child conceived by anonymous sperm donation sought to compel the donor's deposition and production of documents in order to discover facts in their action against a sperm bank for providing sperm that may have transmitted a serious disease to the child. The court of appeal held that discovery is consistent with subsection (a) and should be granted, with due regard to preservation of the donor's anonymity insofar as possible.

Reasoning by analogy from this Section, *In re Marriage of Buzzanca, 61 Cal.App.4th 1410, 72 Cal.Rptr.2d 280 (1998), review denied June 10, 1998*, holds that a husband who, with his wife, consented to the artificial insemination of a surrogate mother by an unknown donor for the purpose of bearing a child for the couple is the legal father of the child. Similarly, the same principle applies, in conjunction with Section 7610(a), to support the conclusion that the wife is the child's legal mother.

Robert B. v. Susan B., 109 Cal.App.4th 1109, 135 Cal.Rptr.2d 785 (2003), review denied September 10, 2003, sorts out parentage that has been confused by clinical error. In *Robert B.*, a couple and a single woman sought the reproductive assistance of a fertility clinic. For the couple, the clinic was to fertilize the eggs of an anonymous donor with the husband's sperm. The single woman was to receive an embryo created from anonymous egg and sperm donors. Through clinical error, the single woman received one of the couple's embryos and she gave birth to a son. The wife gave birth to a daughter. Thus the two infants were siblings. The single woman and the couple disputed parentage of the son. The court held that the husband was the father under § 7630, the single woman who carried the child to term was the mother under § 7610, and the father's wife had no standing to bring an action to determine the existence or nonexistence of a mother-child relationship under § 7650. In concluding that the husband was the father, the court reasoned that subsection (b) was inapplicable because the husband had provided semen for the purpose of inseminating only his wife.

Cf. *Dunkin v. Boskey, 82 Cal.App.4th 171, 98 Cal.Rptr.2d 44 (2000)*, involving an unmarried woman's breach of an agreement to confer parental rights upon a man with respect to a child the woman conceived by artificial insemination from an anonymous sperm donor. *Dunkin* held that the agreement did not *per se* violate public policy and was enforceable for the limited purpose of supporting an unjust enrichment claim, for which the measure of damages was the amount the man spent in performance of the agreement. *Compare McBride v. Boughton, 123 Cal.App.4th 379, 20 Cal.Rptr.3d 115 (2004)*, holding that an unmarried man who supports a child because of the mother's representation that he is the father and later discovers that he is not the biological father, may not sue the mother for reimbursement on a theory of unjust enrichment.

In re Estate of Kievernagel, 166 Cal.App.4th 1024, 83 Cal.Rptr.3d 1024 (2008), held that a widow had no right to use her deceased husband's frozen sperm to conceive a child when the husband had signed an agreement with the frozen sperm storage company that directed the company to discard the sperm upon his death. The court reasoned that disposition of the decedent's frozen sperm, to which no other party had made any contribution, should be governed solely by the decedent's intention, because its disposition implicated the right to procreational autonomy of the decedent but not that of his widow.

Research References

Forms

California Transactions Forms--Family Law § 5:4, Rights Of De Facto Parents.
California Transactions Forms--Family Law § 5:9, Use Of Parenting Agreement to Define Rights and Responsibilities Relating to Child on Termination Of Partners' Relationship Where Both Partners Are Biological Parents.
California Transactions Forms--Family Law § 6:3, Definitions.
California Transactions Forms--Family Law § 6:8, Consent for Adoption Of Unmarried Minor.
California Transactions Forms--Family Law § 7:7, Gestational Surrogacy Agreements Using Donated Egg and Sperm.
California Transactions Forms--Family Law § 7:8, Traditional Surrogacy Agreements.
California Transactions Forms--Family Law § 5:11, Use Of Parenting Agreement to Define Rights and Responsibilities Relating to Child During Relationship Between Same-Sex Partners.
California Transactions Forms--Family Law § 5:34, Parenting Agreement Between Lesbian Partners Where One Partner is Egg Mother and One Partner is Gestational Mother.
California Transactions Forms--Family Law § 5:35, Parenting Agreement Between Lesbian Partners Where One Partner is Both Gestational and Egg Mother.
California Transactions Forms--Family Law § 6:11, Initiating Proceeding Under Uniform Parentage Act [Fam C §§ 7600 to 7730].
California Transactions Forms--Family Law § 6:40, Structuring the Adoption.
California Transactions Forms--Family Law § 6:47, Matters to Consider in Drafting Petition for Independent Adoption Of Unmarried Minor.
California Transactions Forms--Family Law § 6:72, Petition to Terminate Parental Rights Of Alleged Father.
California Transactions Forms--Family Law § 6:74, Petition to Terminate Parental Rights Of Alleged Father Served With Notice Of Alleged Paternity Without Timely Response.
California Transactions Forms--Family Law § 6:75, Order Terminating Parental Rights Of Alleged Father Served With Notice Of Alleged Paternity Without Timely Response.
California Transactions Forms--Family Law § 6:76, Ex Parte Application for Order to Terminate Parental Rights Of Alleged Father Who Waived Notice or Denied Paternity.
California Transactions Forms--Family Law § 7:33, Parentage Testing.
California Transactions Forms--Family Law § 7:45, Artificial Insemination Surrogacy Agreement Between Intended Father and Surrogate Couple.
California Transactions Forms--Family Law § 7:46, in Vitro Surrogacy Agreement Between Intended Parents and Surrogate Couple; Intended Parents Are Genetic Parents.
California Transactions Forms--Family Law § 7:47, in Vitro Fertilization Surrogacy Agreement Between Intended Mother and Surrogate Using Donated Genetic Material.
California Transactions Forms--Family Law § 7:49, Nonconsent Of Surrogate's Husband [Fam C § 7613].
California Transactions Forms--Family Law § 7:54, Introduction.
California Transactions Forms--Family Law § 7:60, Overview; Paternity Of Child [Fam C § 7613].
California Transactions Forms--Family Law § 7:61, Requirement Of Physician Involvement.
California Transactions Forms--Family Law § 7:62, Effect Of Failure to Certify Consent.
California Transactions Forms--Family Law § 7:63, Application Of Fam C § 7613 to Egg Donors.
California Transactions Forms--Family Law § 7:64, Exception to Application Of Fam C § 7613 in Certain Surrogacy Cases.
California Transactions Forms--Family Law § 7:67, Selecting Physician.
California Transactions Forms--Family Law § 7:68, Overview.
California Transactions Forms--Family Law § 7:79, Waiver Of Parental Rights by Donor, Acceptance Of Parental Rights by Recipient.
California Transactions Forms--Family Law § 7:90, Artificial Insemination Agreement Between Husband, Wife, and Licensed Physician.
California Transactions Forms--Family Law § 7:91, Implantation Agreement Between Husband, Wife, and Licensed Physician.
California Transactions Forms--Family Law § 7:92, Sperm Donation Agreement Between Sperm Donor and Agency.
California Transactions Forms--Family Law § 7:93, Sperm Donation Agreement Between Sperm Donor and Recipients for Insemination Of Recipients' Surrogate.
California Transactions Forms--Family Law § 7:94, Egg Donation Agreement Between Egg Donor and Agency.
California Transactions Forms--Family Law § 7:95, Agreement Between Agency and Recipients to Utilize Eggs from Anonymous Donor.
California Transactions Forms--Family Law § 7:96, California Statutory Form for Assisted Reproduction--Intent to be Parents--Married Spouses or Registered Domestic Partners Using Assisted Reproduction to Conceive a Child (Form 1).
California Transactions Forms--Family Law § 7:97, California Statutory Form for Assisted Reproduction--Intent to be Parents--Unmarried, Intended Parents Using Intended Parent's Sperm to Conceive a Child (Form 2).
California Transactions Forms--Family Law § 7:98, California Statutory Form for Assisted Reproduction--Intent to be Parents--Intended Parents Conceiving a Child Using Eggs from One Parent and the Other Parent Will Give Birth (Form 3).
California Transactions Forms--Family Law § 3:126, Request for Hearing and Application to Set Aside Voluntary Declaration Of Paternity [Form FL-280].
California Transactions Forms--Family Law § 3:127, Responsive Declaration to Application to Set Aside Voluntary Declaration Of Paternity [Form FL-285].
California Transactions Forms--Family Law § 3:128, Order After Hearing on Motion to Set Aside Voluntary Declaration Of Paternity [Form FL-290].
California Transactions Forms--Family Law § 4:105, Declaration Of Paternity.
California Transactions Forms--Family Law § 3:126.50, Information Sheet for Completing Request for Hearing and Application to Set Aside Voluntary Declaration Of Paternity [Form FL-281].
West's California Code Forms, Family § 7610, Comment Overview--Establishing Parent and Child Relationship.

Treatises and Practice Aids

Witkin, California Summary 10th Parent and Child § 14, Child Of Artificial Insemination is Legitimate.
Witkin, California Summary 10th Parent and Child § 23, Where Intended Mother is Not Genetic Mother.
Witkin, California Summary 10th Parent and Child § 30, Blood Test Disproving Paternity.
Witkin, California Summary 10th Parent and Child § 31, in General.

Witkin, California Summary 10th Parent and Child § 43, in General.
Witkin, California Summary 10th Parent and Child § 44, Semen Obtained Without Physician.
Witkin, California Summary 10th Parent and Child § 45, Semen Of Decedent.
Witkin, California Summary 10th Parent and Child § 56, in General.
Witkin, California Summary 10th Parent and Child § 206, Agreement Between Parents.
Witkin, California Summary 10th Parent and Child § 23A, (New) Assisted Reproduction Agreements for Gestational Carriers.
Witkin, California Summary 10th Parent and Child § 60B, (New) Domestic Partner Who Donated Her Ova to Partner to Conceive Child.
Witkin, California Summary 10th Torts § 985, Failure to Secure Consent Of Husband for Artificial Insemination.

§ 7613.5. Intended parent; use of forms

(a) An intended parent may, but is not required to, use the forms set forth in this section to demonstrate his or her intent to be a legal parent of a child conceived through assisted reproduction. These forms shall satisfy the writing requirement specified in Section 7613, and are designed to provide clarity regarding the intentions, at the time of conception, of intended parents using assisted reproduction. These forms do not affect any presumptions of parentage based on Section 7611, and do not preclude a court from considering any other claims to parentage under California statute or case law.

(b) These forms apply only in very limited circumstances. Please read the forms carefully to see if you qualify for use of the forms.

(c) These forms do not apply to assisted reproduction agreements for gestational carriers or surrogacy agreements.

(d) Nothing in this section shall be interpreted to require the use of one of these forms to satisfy the writing requirement of Section 7613.

(e) The following are the optional California Statutory Forms for Assisted Reproduction:

California Statutory Forms for Assisted Reproduction, Form 1:

Two Married or Unmarried People Using Assisted Reproduction to Conceive a Child

Use this form if: You and another intended parent, who may be your spouse or registered domestic partner, are conceiving a child through assisted reproduction using sperm and/or egg donation; and one of you will be giving birth.

WARNING: Signing this form does not terminate the parentage claim of a sperm donor. A sperm donor's claim to parentage is terminated if the sperm is provided to a licensed physician and surgeon or to a licensed sperm bank prior to insemination, or if you conceive without having sexual intercourse and you have a written agreement signed by you and the donor that you will conceive using assisted reproduction and do not intend for the donor to be a parent, as required by Section 7613(b) of the Family Code.

The laws about parentage of a child are complicated. **You are strongly encouraged to consult with an attorney about your rights.** Even if you do not fill out this form, a spouse or domestic partner of the parent giving birth is presumed to be a legal parent of any child born during the marriage or domestic partnership.

This form demonstrates your intent to be parents of the child you plan to conceive through assisted reproduction using sperm and/or egg donation.

I, ________ (print name of person not giving birth), intend to be a parent of a child that ________ (print name of person giving birth) will or has conceived through assisted reproduction using sperm and/or egg donation. I consent to the use of assisted reproduction by the person who will give birth. I INTEND to be a parent of the child conceived.

SIGNATURES

Intended parent who will give birth:
________(print name)
________(signature)
________(date)

Intended parent who will not give birth:
________(print name)
________(signature)
________(date)

NOTARY ACKNOWLEDGMENT

State of California
County of________)

On ________before me, ________
(insert name and title of the officer)
personally appeared ________,
who proved to me on the basis of satisfactory evidence to be the person(s) whose name(s) is/are subscribed to the within instrument and acknowledged to me that he/she/they executed the same in his/her/their authorized capacity, and that by his/her/their signature(s) on the instrument the person(s), or the entity upon behalf of which the person(s) acted, executed the instrument.

I certify under PENALTY OF PERJURY under the laws of the State of California that the fore going paragraph is true and correct.

WITNESS my hand and official seal.

Signature________
(Seal)

California Statutory Forms for Assisted Reproduction, Form 2:

Unmarried, Intended Parents Using Intended Parent's Sperm to Conceive a Child

Use this form if: (1) Neither you or the other person are married or in a registered domestic partnership (including a registered domestic partnership or civil union from another state); (2) one of you will give birth to a child conceived through assisted reproduction using the intended parent's sperm; and (3) you both intend to be parents of that child.

Do not use this form if you are conceiving using a surrogate.

WARNING: If you do not sign this form, or a similar agreement, you may be treated as a sperm donor if you conceive without having sexual intercourse according to Section 7613(b) of the Family Code.

The laws about parentage of a child are complicated. **You are strongly encouraged to consult with an attorney about your rights.**

This form demonstrates your intent to be parents of the child you plan to conceive through assisted reproduction using sperm donation.

I, ______________________________ (print name of parent giving birth), plan to use assisted reproduction with another intended parent who is providing sperm to conceive the child. I am not married and am not in a registered domestic partnership (including a registered domestic partnership or civil union from another jurisdiction), and I INTEND for the person providing sperm to be a parent of the child to be conceived.

I, ______________________________ (print name of parent providing sperm), plan to use assisted reproduction to conceive a child using my sperm with the parent giving birth. I am not married and am not in a registered domestic partnership (including a registered domestic partnership or civil union from another jurisdiction), and I INTEND to be a parent of the child to be conceived.

SIGNATURES

Intended parent giving birth:
______________________________(print name)
______________________________(signature)
_______________(date)

Intended parent providing sperm:
______________________________(print name)
______________________________(signature)
_______________(date)

NOTARY ACKNOWLEDGMENT

State of California
County of______________________________)

On ______________________________ before me, ______________________________
(insert name and title of the officer)
personally appeared______________________________,
who proved to me on the basis of satisfactory evidence to be the person(s) whose name(s) is/are subscribed to the within instrument and acknowledged to me that he/she/they executed the same in his/her/their authorized capacity, and that by his/her/their signature(s) on the instrument the person(s), or the entity upon behalf of which the person(s) acted, executed the instrument.

I certify under PENALTY OF PERJURY under the laws of the State of California that the fore going paragraph is true and correct.

WITNESS my hand and official seal.

Signature______________________________
(Seal)

California Statutory Forms for Assisted Reproduction, Form 3:

Intended Parents Conceiving a Child Using Eggs from One Parent and the Other Parent Will Give Birth
Use this form if: You are conceiving a child using the eggs from one of you and the other person will give birth to the child; (2) and you both intend to be parents to that child.

Do not use this form if you are conceiving using a surrogate.

WARNING: Signing this form does not terminate the parentage claim of a sperm donor. A sperm donor's claim to parentage is terminated if the sperm is provided to a licensed physician and surgeon or to a licensed sperm bank prior to insemination, or if you conceive without having sexual intercourse and you have a written agreement signed by you and the donor that you will conceive using assisted reproduction and do not intend for the donor to be a parent, as required by Section 7613(b) of the Family Code.

The laws about parentage of a child are complicated. **You are strongly encouraged to consult with an attorney about your rights.**

This form demonstrates your intent to be parents of the child you plan to conceive through assisted reproduction using eggs from one parent and the other parent will give birth to the child.

I, ______________________________ (print name of parent giving birth), plan to use assisted reproduction to conceive and give birth to a child with another person who will provide eggs to conceive the child. I INTEND for the person providing eggs to be a parent of the child to be conceived.

I, ______________________________ (print name of parent providing eggs), plan to use assisted reproduction to conceive a child with another person who will give birth to the child conceived using my eggs. I INTEND to be a parent of the child to be conceived.

SIGNATURES

Intended parent giving birth:
______________________________ (print name)
______________________________(signature)
_______________(date)

Intended parent providing eggs:
______________________________(print name)
______________________________(signature)
_______________(date)

____

NOTARY ACKNOWLEDGMENT

State of California
County of______________________________)

On ______________________________before me, ______________________________
(insert name and title of the officer)
personally appeared ______________________________, who proved to me on the basis of satisfactory evidence to be the person(s) whose name(s) is/are subscribed to the within instrument and acknowledged to me that he/she/they executed the same in his/her/their authorized capacity, and that by his/her/their signature(s) on the instrument the person(s), or the entity upon behalf of which the person(s) acted, executed the instrument.

I certify under PENALTY OF PERJURY under the laws of the State of California that the fore going paragraph is true and correct.

WITNESS my hand and official seal.

Signature______________________________
(Seal)

____

California Statutory Forms for Assisted Reproduction, Form 4:

Intended Parent(s) Using a Known Sperm and/or Egg Donor(s) to Conceive a Child

Use this form if: You are using a known sperm and/or egg donor(s), or embryo donation, to conceive a child and you do not intend for the donor(s) to be a parent.

Do not use this form if you are conceiving using a surrogate.

If you do not sign this form or a similar agreement, your sperm donor may be treated as a parent unless the sperm is provided to a licensed physician and surgeon or to a licensed sperm bank prior to insemination, or a court finds by clear and convincing evidence that you planned to conceive through assisted reproduction and did not intend for the donor to be a parent, as required by Section 7613(b) of the Family Code. If you do not sign this form or a similar agreement, your egg donor may be treated as a parent unless a court finds that there is satisfactory evidence that you planned to conceive through assisted reproduction and did not intend for the donor to be a parent, as required by Section 7613(c) of the Family Code.

The laws about parentage of a child are complicated. **You are strongly encouraged to consult with an attorney about your rights.**

____

This form demonstrates your intent that your sperm and/or egg or embryo donor(s) will not be a parent or parents of the child you plan to conceive through assisted reproduction.

I, ______________________________(print name of parent giving birth), plan to use assisted reproduction to conceive using a sperm and/or egg donor(s) or embryo donation, and I DO NOT INTEND for the sperm and/or egg or embryo donor(s) to be a parent of the child to be conceived.

(If applicable) I, ______________________________ (print name of sperm donor), plan to donate my sperm to ______________________________(print name of parent giving birth and second parent if applicable). I am not married to and am not in a registered domestic partnership (including a registered domestic partnership or a civil union from another jurisdiction) with ______________________________(print name of parent giving birth), and I DO NOT INTEND to be a parent of the child to be conceived.

(If applicable) I, ______________(print name of egg donor), plan to donate my ova to ______________________________(print name of parent giving birth and second parent if applicable). I am not married to and am not in a registered domestic partnership (including a registered domestic partnership or a civil union from another jurisdiction) with ______________ (print name of parent giving birth), or any intimate and nonmarital relationship with ______________________________(print name of parent giving birth) and I DO NOT INTEND to be a parent of the child to be conceived.

(If applicable) I, ______________________________ (print name of intended parent not giving birth), INTEND to be a parent of the child that______________________________(print name of parent giving birth) will conceive through assisted reproduction using sperm and/or egg donation and I DO NOT INTEND for the sperm and/or egg or embryo donor(s) to be a parent. I consent to the use of assisted reproduction by the person who will give birth.

SIGNATURES

Intended parent giving birth:
______________________________(print name)
______________________________(signature)
______________(date)

(If applicable) Sperm Donor:
______________________________(print name)
______________________________(signature)
______________(date)

(If applicable) Egg Donor:
______________________________(print name)
______________________________(signature)
______________(date)

(If applicable) Intended parent not giving birth:
______________________________(print name)
______________________________(signature)
______________(date)

____

NOTARY ACKNOWLEDGMENT

State of California

County of ______________________)

On ______________________ before me, ______________________
(insert name and title of the officer)
personally appeared ______________________,
who proved to me on the basis of satisfactory evidence to be the person(s) whose name(s) is/are subscribed to the within instrument and acknowledged to me that he/she/they executed the same in his/her/their authorized capacity, and that by his/her/their signature(s) on the instrument the person(s), or the entity upon behalf of which the person(s) acted, executed the instrument.

I certify under PENALTY OF PERJURY under the laws of the State of California that the fore
going paragraph is true and correct.

WITNESS my hand and official seal.

Signature______________________
(Seal)

(Added by Stats.2014, c. 636 (A.B.2344), § 1, eff. Jan. 1, 2015. Amended by Stats.2015, c. 566 (A.B.960), § 2, eff. Jan. 1, 2016; Stats.2016, c. 86 (S.B.1171), § 130, eff. Jan. 1, 2017.)

Research References

Forms

California Transactions Forms--Family Law § 7:96, California Statutory Form for Assisted Reproduction--Intent to be Parents--Married Spouses or Registered Domestic Partners Using Assisted Reproduction to Conceive a Child (Form 1).

California Transactions Forms--Family Law § 7:97, California Statutory Form for Assisted Reproduction--Intent to be Parents--Unmarried, Intended Parents Using Intended Parent's Sperm to Conceive a Child (Form 2).

California Transactions Forms--Family Law § 7:98, California Statutory Form for Assisted Reproduction--Intent to be Parents--Intended Parents Conceiving a Child Using Eggs from One Parent and the Other Parent Will Give Birth (Form 3).

Treatises and Practice Aids

Witkin, California Summary 10th Parent and Child § 43, in General.

§ 7614. Written promise to furnish support; enforcement; confidentiality

(a) A promise in writing to furnish support for a child, growing out of a presumed parent or alleged father and child relationship, does not require consideration and, subject to Section 7632, is enforceable according to its terms.

(b) In the best interest of the child or the other parent, the court may, and upon the promisor's request shall, order the promise to be kept in confidence and designate a person or agency to receive and disburse on behalf of the child all amounts paid in performance of the promise. *(Stats.1992, c. 162 (A.B.2650), § 10, operative Jan. 1, 1994. Amended by Stats.2013, c. 510 (A.B.1403), § 6.)*

Law Revision Commission Comments

Enactment [Revised Comment]

Section 7614 continues former Civil Code Section 7016 without substantive change. This section is the same in substance as Section 22 of the Uniform Parentage Act (1973). A reference to Section 7632 has been substituted for the reference to former Civil Code Section 7006(d). This corrects an error in former Civil Code Section 7016, which should have referred to former Civil Code Section 7006(e), now Family Code Section 7632. See also Section 3011 (factors in determining best interest of child). [23 Cal.L.Rev.Comm. Reports 1 (1993)].

Research References

Treatises and Practice Aids

Witkin, California Summary 10th Parent and Child § 19, General Provisions.

CHAPTER 3. JURISDICTION AND VENUE

§ 7620. Intent to become legal parent by assisted reproduction in state; consent to jurisdiction; jurisdiction to determine parentage; venue

(a) A person who has sexual intercourse or causes conception with the intent to become a legal parent by assisted reproduction in this state, or who enters into an assisted reproduction agreement for gestational carriers in this state, thereby submits to the jurisdiction of the courts of this state as to an action brought under this part with respect to a child who may have been conceived by that act of intercourse or assisted reproduction, or who may have been conceived as a result of that assisted reproduction agreement.

(b) If a child is conceived pursuant to an assisted reproduction agreement for gestational carriers, as defined in Section 7960 and as described in Section 7962, the courts of this state shall have jurisdiction over a proceeding to determine parentage of the child if any of the following conditions is satisfied:

(1) One or more of the parties to the assisted reproduction agreement for gestational carriers resides in this state, or resided in this state at the time the assisted reproduction agreement for gestational carriers was executed.

(2) The medical procedures leading to conception, including in vitro fertilization or embryo transfer, or both, were carried out in this state.

(3) The child is born in this state.

(c) An action under this part shall be brought in one of the following:

(1) The county in which the child resides or is found.

(2) If the child is the subject of a pending or proposed adoption, any county in which a licensed California adoption agency to which the child has been relinquished or is proposed to be relinquished maintains an office.

(3) If the child is the subject of a pending or proposed adoption, the county in which an office of the department or a public adoption agency investigating the petition is located.

(4) If the parent is deceased, the county in which proceedings for probate of the estate of the parent of the child have been or could be commenced.

(5) If the child was conceived pursuant to an assisted reproduction agreement for gestational carriers, any county

described in subdivision (e) of Section 7962. *(Stats.1992, c. 162 (A.B.2650), § 10, operative Jan. 1, 1994. Amended by Stats.2003, c. 251 (S.B.182), § 1; Stats.2005, c. 627 (S.B.302), § 1; Stats.2006, c. 806 (S.B.1325), § 2; Stats.2009, c. 492 (A.B.941), § 1; Stats.2013, c. 510 (A.B.1403), § 7; Stats.2016, c. 385 (A.B.2349), § 3, eff. Jan. 1, 2017.)*

Law Revision Commission Comments

Enactment [Revised Comment]

Section 7620 continues former Civil Code Section 7007(b)-(c) without substantive change. This section is the same in substance as parts of Section 8 of the Uniform Parentage Act (1973). Former Civil Code Section 7007(a), which stated that the superior court has jurisdiction of an action under the Uniform Parentage Act, has been generalized. See Section 200 (jurisdiction in superior court). [23 Cal.L.Rev.Comm. Reports 1 (1993)].

Commentary

Humboldt County v. Harris, 206 Cal.App.3d 857, 862, 254 Cal.Rptr. 49 (1988), holds that the statute may constitutionally be applied to achieve personal jurisdiction over a nonresident putative father when the conception, birth, and rearing of the child occurred in California.

Research References

Forms

California Transactions Forms--Family Law § 6:11, Initiating Proceeding Under Uniform Parentage Act [Fam C §§ 7600 to 7730].

California Transactions Forms--Family Law § 6:72, Petition to Terminate Parental Rights Of Alleged Father.

Treatises and Practice Aids

Witkin, California Summary 10th Parent and Child § 17, Development Of Law.

Witkin, California Summary 10th Parent and Child § 50, Jurisdiction and Venue.

Witkin, California Summary 10th Parent and Child § 267, Jurisdiction and Venue.

CHAPTER 4. DETERMINATION OF PARENT AND CHILD RELATIONSHIP

ARTICLE 1. DETERMINATION OF FATHER AND CHILD RELATIONSHIP

§ 7630. Action to determine existence or nonexistence of parent and child relationship; consolidated actions; notice of proceedings

(a) A child, the child's natural mother, a person presumed to be the child's parent under subdivision (a), (b), or (c) of Section 7611, an adoption agency to whom the child has been relinquished, or a prospective adoptive parent of the child may bring an action as follows:

(1) At any time for the purpose of declaring the existence of the parent and child relationship presumed under subdivision (a), (b), or (c) of Section 7611.

(2) For the purpose of declaring the nonexistence of the parent and child relationship presumed under subdivision (a), (b), or (c) of Section 7611 only if the action is brought within a reasonable time after obtaining knowledge of relevant facts. After the presumption has been rebutted, parentage of the child by another person may be determined in the same action, if that person has been made a party.

(b) Any interested party may bring an action at any time for the purpose of determining the existence or nonexistence of the parent and child relationship presumed under subdivision (d) or (f) of Section 7611.

(c) Except as to cases coming within Chapter 1 (commencing with Section 7540) of Part 2, an action to determine the existence of the parent and child relationship may be brought by the child, a personal representative of the child, the Department of Child Support Services, a presumed parent or the personal representative or a parent of that presumed parent if that parent has died or is a minor, or, in cases in which the natural mother is the only presumed parent or an action under Section 300 of the Welfare and Institutions Code or adoption is pending, a man alleged or alleging himself to be the father or the personal representative or a parent of the alleged father if the alleged father has died or is a minor.

(d)(1) If a proceeding has been filed under Chapter 2 (commencing with Section 7820) of Part 4, an action under subdivision (a) or (b) shall be consolidated with that proceeding. The parental rights of the presumed parent shall be determined as set forth in Sections 7820 to 7829, inclusive.

(2) If a proceeding pursuant to Section 7662 has been filed under Chapter 5 (commencing with Section 7660), an action under subdivision (c) shall be consolidated with that proceed-

ing. The parental rights of the alleged natural father shall be determined as set forth in Section 7664.

(3) The consolidated action under paragraph (1) or (2) shall be heard in the court in which the proceeding under Section 7662 or Chapter 2 (commencing with Section 7820) of Part 4 is filed, unless the court finds, by clear and convincing evidence, that transferring the action to the other court poses a substantial hardship to the petitioner. Mere inconvenience does not constitute a sufficient basis for a finding of substantial hardship. If the court determines there is a substantial hardship, the consolidated action shall be heard in the court in which the parentage action is filed.

(e)(1) If any prospective adoptive parent who has physical custody of the child, any licensed California adoption agency that has legal custody of the child or to which the mother proposes to relinquish the child for adoption, or any person whom the mother has designated as the prospective adoptive parent in a written statement executed before a hospital social worker, an adoption service provider, an adoption agency representative, or a notary public, has not been joined as a party to an action to determine the existence of a parent and child relationship under subdivision (a), (b), or (c), or an action for custody by the alleged natural father, the court shall join the prospective adoptive parent or licensed California adoption agency as a party upon application or on its own motion, without the necessity of a motion for joinder. A joined party shall not be required to pay a fee in connection with this action.

(2) If a person brings an action to determine parentage and custody of a child who he or she has reason to believe is in the physical or legal custody of an adoption agency, or of one or more persons other than the child's parent who are prospective adoptive parents, he or she shall serve his or her entire pleading on, and give notice of all proceedings to, the adoption agency or the prospective adoptive parents, or both.

(f) A party to an assisted reproduction agreement may bring an action at any time to establish a parent and child relationship consistent with the intent expressed in that assisted reproduction agreement.

(g)(1) In an action to determine the existence of the parent and child relationship brought pursuant to subdivision (b), if the child's other parent has died and there are no existing court orders or pending court actions involving custody or guardianship of the child, then the persons having physical custody of the child shall be served with notice of the proceeding at least 15 days prior to the hearing, either by mail or in any manner authorized by the court. If any person identified as having physical custody of the child cannot be located, the court shall prescribe the manner of giving notice.

(2) If known to the person bringing the parentage action, relatives within the second degree of the child shall be given notice of the proceeding at least 15 days prior to the hearing, either by mail or in any manner authorized by the court. If a person identified as a relative of the second degree of the child cannot be located, or his or her whereabouts are unknown or cannot be ascertained, the court shall prescribe the manner of giving notice, or shall dispense with giving notice to that person.

(3) Proof of notice pursuant to this subdivision shall be filed with the court before the proceeding to determine the existence of the parent and child relationship is heard. *(Stats.1992, c. 162 (A.B.2650), § 10, operative Jan. 1, 1994. Amended by Stats.2000, c. 808 (A.B.1358), § 76, eff. Sept. 28, 2000; Stats.2001, c. 353 (A.B.538), § 1; Stats.2003, c. 251 (S.B.182), § 2; Stats.2004, c. 775 (A.B.1910), § 2; Stats.2005, c. 627 (S.B.302), § 2; Stats.2006, c. 806 (S.B.1325), § 3; Stats.2007, c. 47 (S.B.313), § 1; Stats.2008, c. 534 (S.B.1726), § 3; Stats.2010, c. 588 (A.B.2020), § 1; Stats.2012, c. 155 (A.B.1337), § 1; Stats.2013, c. 510 (A.B.1403), § 8; Stats. 2014, c. 763 (A.B.1701), § 1, eff. Jan. 1, 2015.)*

Law Revision Commission Comments

Enactment [Revised Comment]

Section 7630 continues former Civil Code Section 7006(a)-(c) without substantive change. This section is similar to Section 6(a)-(c) of the Uniform Parentage Act (1973). In subdivision (c), a reference to the filing of a proceeding under Chapter 5 (commencing with Section 7660) has been substituted for a narrower reference to former Civil Code Section 7017 in former law. This is not a substantive change. [23 Cal.L.Rev.Comm. Reports 1 (1993)].

Commentary

A 2014 amendment to subsection (c), effective January 1, 2015, reinstated the substance of the second-to-the-last version of subsection (c), which allowed a man claiming to be a child's biological father to bring a parentage action *only* when the child's natural mother is the sole presumed parent. (The 2014 amendment also allows the action in dependency and adoption proceedings.) Effectively, the 2014 amendment revived *Dawn D. v. Superior Court, 17 Cal.4th 932, 952 P.2d 1139, 72 Cal.Rptr.2d 871 (1998)* (holding that the pre-2010 version of subsection (c) barred the action when a child already had two presumed parents, and that a biological father has no constitutionally protected interest in establishing his paternity of a child who already has two presumed parents) and its extensive case law progeny. The 2014 amendment *overruled V.S. v. M.L., 222 Cal.App.4th 730, 166 Cal.Rptr.3d 376 (2013)*, decided under a 2010 version of subsection (c) that appeared to allow a biological father to bring a parentage action even though a child already had two presumed parents. 2013 CA A.B. 1701, Senate Judiciary Comm. Bill Analysis, June 24, 2014.

When a mother extramaritally conceived a child while she was not cohabiting with her husband, she could bring an action to determine the father's paternity under subsection (c), and she was not limited by the subsection (a)(2) requirement that subsection (a) actions be brought within a reasonable time after obtaining knowledge of relevant facts. *Pangilinan v. Palisoc, 227 Cal.App.4th 765, 174 Cal.Rptr.3d 114 (2014)*.

J.R. v. D.P., 212 Cal.App.4th 374, 150 Cal.Rptr.3d 882 (2012), review denied, affirmed a trial court decision resolving conflicting section 7611(d) presumptions of paternity in favor of a *Kelsey S.* father, rather than the mother's husband who had been her boyfriend at the time of the child's conception and birth, lived with the child and mother, and raised the child as his own. The court reasoned that resolving the conflict in favor of the *Kelsey S.* biological father would serve the child's best interests, because if the presumption were resolved in favor of the mother's husband, the mother would have prevented contact between the biological father and the child. Invoking subsection (b), the court also affirmed the trial court's rescission of the husband's voluntary declaration of paternity on the ground that the mother committed perjury in attesting that no other man could be the father of her child, when she already knew that the *Kelsey S.* father was the child's biological father.

After a trial court granted a married mother's section 7575 motion to set aside a declaration of paternity, the trial court erred in ordering genetic testing in an action brought by the putative nonmarital father of the child in order to establish the putative father's paternity of the child because, under this section, the putative father had no standing to bring a paternity action once his declaration of paternity had been set aside. *H.S. v. Superior Court, 183 Cal.App.4th 1502, 108 Cal.Rptr.3d 723 (2010)*.

Scott v. Thompson, 184 Cal.App.4th 1506, 109 Cal.Rptr.3d 846 (2010), review denied, holds that, under this section, a decedent's sibling has no standing in a wrongful death action to challenge the section 7611(a) presumed paternity of decedent's father.

In re J.L., 159 Cal.App.4th 1010, 72 Cal.Rptr.3d 27 (2008), review denied, held that a biological father had standing in a dependency proceeding to challenge another man's voluntary declaration of paternity under section 7575 (b)(1) and (b)(3)(A) by virtue of each of the following: (1) his standing to bring a proceeding under this section to determine his paternity of a child; (2) his participation in a dependency proceeding to establish child custody based on the voluntary declaration; and (3) his status as a *Kelsey S.* constitutionally presumed father, that is, a father who accepted his parental obligations as soon as reasonably possible. But cf. *In re Christopher M, 113 Cal.App.4th 155, 6 Cal.Rptr.3d 197 (2003)* (limiting the parties who may make a section 7575 (b)(3)(a) motion).

In re William K., 161 Cal.App.4th 1, 73 Cal.Rptr.3d 737 (2008), review denied, held that the juvenile court properly declined, in a dependency proceeding, to grant the motion of a sex-offender, who was a biological father but not a presumed or *Kelsey S.* father, to set aside a declaration of paternity executed by another man who had a parent-child relationship with the child but was not the child's biological father. The court invoked the section 7575(b)(1) ground that setting aside the declaration of paternity would not be in the best interest of the child.

Librers v. Black, 129 Cal.App.4th 114, 28 Cal.Rptr.3d 188 (2005), holds that the trial court erred in finding that a man who asserted Section 7611(d) presumed father status lacked standing to bring a paternity action to assert that status because he was not the child's biological father. *Librers* points out that Section 7630(b) grants any "interested party" standing to bring an action to determine the existence of a father and child relationship presumed under subsection (d).

When, on a child's birth certificate, a former wife named a former husband as the father of a child born to her 17 months after their divorce, the father had standing under subsection (b) to bring an action to declare his nonpaternity of the child, because he was an alleged father and might also be a presumed father, depending on the facts determined in the action. *Said v. Jegan, 146 Cal.App.4th 1375, 53 Cal.Rptr.3d 661 (2007)*.

Although grandparents may bring an action for paternity under subsection (c) when the putative father is deceased, either in their individual capacity or as representatives of the deceased putative father, they may not be made defendants in a paternity action nor required to submit to blood tests when their son, the putative father, is deceased. *William M. v. Superior Court, 225 Cal.App.3d 447, 452, 275 Cal.Rptr. 103 (1990), review denied 3/14/91*.

Robert B. v. Susan B., 109 Cal.App.4th 1109, 135 Cal.Rptr.2d 785 (2003), review denied September 10, 2003, sorts out parentage that has been confused by clinical error. In *Robert B.*, a couple and a single woman sought the reproductive assistance of a fertility clinic. For the couple, the clinic was to fertilize the eggs of an anonymous donor with the husband's sperm. The single woman was to receive an embryo created from anonymous egg and sperm donors. Through clinical error, the single woman received one of the couple's embryos and she gave birth to a son. The wife gave birth to a daughter. Thus the two infants were siblings. The single woman and the couple disputed parentage of the son. The court held that the husband was the father under this section, the single woman who carried the child to term was the mother under § 7610, and the father's wife had no standing to bring an action to determine the existence or nonexistence of a mother-child relationship under § 7650. In concluding that the husband was the father, the court reasoned that § 7613(b) was inapplicable because the husband provided semen for the purpose of inseminating only his wife.

For the effect of collateral determinations of paternity, see *Ruddock v. Ohls, 91 Cal.App.3d 271, 284, 154 Cal.Rptr. 87 (1979)* (Oregon divorce decree containing judgment of nonpaternity binding on husband and wife, but not on child who was not a party to the divorce proceeding), and cases cited therein; cf. *D.P. v. Stewart, 189 Cal.App.3d 244, 234 Cal.Rptr. 420 (1987)* (Texas decision refusing to order child support because "paternity not established at this time" does not bar later California paternity proceeding). Compare *In re Marriage of Hotz, 168 Cal.App.3d 605, 214 Cal.Rptr. 658 (1985)* (husband divorced by Iowa decree adjudicating his paternity of marital child collaterally estopped from relitigating paternity in a later California support proceeding) with *County of Santa Barbara v. Patrick H., 179 Cal.App.3d 1206, 225 Cal.Rptr. 478 (1986), rehearing granted 5/14/86, later opinion not published* (no collateral estoppel in subsequent proceeding where dissolution decree "child of the marriage" was born before the marriage). See also *In re Guardianship of Claralyn S., 148 Cal.App.3d 81, 195 Cal.Rptr. 646 (1983), hearing denied 12/15/83* (public policy estops maternal grandparents from challenging paternity of their grandchild after purported father's stipulation to paternity in prior actions brought by county for AFDC reimbursement even though blood tests exclude purported father); and *In re Margarita D., 72 Cal.App.4th 1288, 85 Cal.Rptr.2d 713 (1999)* (trial court properly rejected petition by alleged biological father to set aside a paternity judgment finding another man to be the child's father when petitioner had adequate notice and opportunity to assert paternity, but failed to do so because mother identified another man as the father). On September 20, 2000, the Supreme Court denied review and depublished *City and County of San Francisco v. Tijerino, 98 Cal.Rptr.2d 30 (2000)*, in which the court of appeal purported to hold that the trial court improperly agreed to reconsider a motion to set aside a stipulated paternity judgment when the motion failed to present "new or different facts, circumstances, or law," as required by Code of Civil Procedure § 1008, which governs the reconsideration of court orders. But compare *County of Fresno v. Ruiz, 79 Cal.Rptr.2d 684 (1998), depublished and denied review by the California Supreme Court on January 13, 1999* (holding that trial court properly vacated a seven-year-old paternity default judgment when defendant putative father, who was not in fact the child's biological father, did not appear because mother assured him that he was the child's father). Similarly, on July 15, 1998, the California Supreme Court denied review and depublished *County of Los Angeles v. Warmoth, 72 Cal.Rptr.2d 902 (1998)*, in which the Court of Appeal vacated a trial court order denying a motion to set aside a default judgment of paternity against a man who was not in fact the child's biological father, and remanded for further equitable proceedings. See additionally Section 7632, Commentary.

See also *Garrett v. Superior Court, 100 Cal.App.3d 535, 161 Cal.Rptr. 117 (1980), hearing denied 3/16/80* (district attorney as guardian ad litem).

See also Probate Code Section 6453, which limits application of the Uniform Parentage Act to establish paternity when a putative father is deceased. Interpreting Probate Code Section 6453 (b)(3), *Cheyanna M. v. A.C. Nielsen Co., 66 Cal.App.4th 855, 78 Cal.Rptr.2d 335 (1998)*, holds that a posthumous child has standing to sue for the wrongful death of the child's biological father if the child can establish paternity through clear and convincing evidence. In other words, *Cheyanna M.* restricts the definition of "child" for purposes of Probate Code Section 6453 (b)(3) to children who are already born at the father's death; thus by definition it is impossible for a father to have held a posthumous child out as his own. *Cheyanna M.* invokes Civil Code Section 43.1, which seeks to advance the interests of unborn children who are ultimately born, as support for its holding.

An incarcerated indigent appealing from a default paternity judgment obtained by the district attorney is not entitled to a *Wende* review, that is, an independent review of the trial record to determine whether there are any arguable issues. *County of Kern v. Dillier, 69 Cal.App.4th 1412, 82 Cal.Rptr.2d 318 (1999).*

Research References

Forms

California Transactions Forms--Estate Planning § 6:11, Existence Of Relationship.
California Transactions Forms--Estate Planning § 6:52, Matters to Consider in Drafting Class Gifts.
California Transactions Forms--Family Law § 5:9, Use Of Parenting Agreement to Define Rights and Responsibilities Relating to Child on Termination Of Partners' Relationship Where Both Partners Are Biological Parents.
California Transactions Forms--Family Law § 6:8, Consent for Adoption Of Unmarried Minor.
California Transactions Forms--Family Law § 6:11, Initiating Proceeding Under Uniform Parentage Act [Fam C §§ 7600 to 7730].
California Transactions Forms--Family Law § 6:40, Structuring the Adoption.
California Transactions Forms--Family Law § 6:42, Rights Of Birth Father.
California Transactions Forms--Family Law § 6:71, Notice Of Alleged Paternity.
California Transactions Forms--Family Law § 6:72, Petition to Terminate Parental Rights Of Alleged Father.
California Transactions Forms--Family Law § 6:75, Order Terminating Parental Rights Of Alleged Father Served With Notice Of Alleged Paternity Without Timely Response.
California Transactions Forms--Family Law § 6:78, Petition to Terminate Parental Rights Of Alleged Father Who Cannot be Located.
California Transactions Forms--Family Law § 7:28, Overview.
California Transactions Forms--Family Law § 7:30, Parties to Proceeding.
California Transactions Forms--Family Law § 7:38, Parentage and Birth Certificate.
California Transactions Forms--Family Law § 7:86, Overview.
California Transactions Forms--Family Law § 3:126, Request for Hearing and Application to Set Aside Voluntary Declaration Of Paternity [Form FL-280].
California Transactions Forms--Family Law § 3:127, Responsive Declaration to Application to Set Aside Voluntary Declaration Of Paternity [Form FL-285].
California Transactions Forms--Family Law § 3:128, Order After Hearing on Motion to Set Aside Voluntary Declaration Of Paternity [Form FL-290].
California Transactions Forms--Family Law § 4:105, Declaration Of Paternity.
California Transactions Forms--Family Law § 3:126.50, Information Sheet for Completing Request for Hearing and Application to Set Aside Voluntary Declaration Of Paternity [Form FL-281].
West's California Code Forms, Family § 7630, Comment Overview--Determining Parent and Child Relationship.
West's California Judicial Council Forms FL-200, Petition to Establish Parental Relationship.

Treatises and Practice Aids

Witkin, California Summary 10th Parent and Child § 17, Development Of Law.
Witkin, California Summary 10th Parent and Child § 34, Rescinding or Setting Aside Declaration.
Witkin, California Summary 10th Parent and Child § 35, in General.
Witkin, California Summary 10th Parent and Child § 46, in General.
Witkin, California Summary 10th Parent and Child § 47, Where Presumption Of Paternity Applies.
Witkin, California Summary 10th Parent and Child § 48, Where No Presumption Applies.
Witkin, California Summary 10th Parent and Child § 49, Joinder and Alignment Of Parties.
Witkin, California Summary 10th Parent and Child § 59, Visitation Privileges.
Witkin, California Summary 10th Parent and Child § 62, Inquiry to Identify Natural Father.
Witkin, California Summary 10th Parent and Child § 63, in General.
Witkin, California Summary 10th Parent and Child § 64, Where Mother Does Not Consent to Adoption.
Witkin, California Summary 10th Parent and Child § 66, Statutory Requirements.
Witkin, California Summary 10th Parent and Child § 69, Hearing and Order.
Witkin, California Summary 10th Parent and Child § 23A, (New) Assisted Reproduction Agreements for Gestational Carriers.
Witkin, California Summary 10th Parent and Child § 48A, (New) Party to Assisted Reproduction Agreement.
Witkin, California Summary 10th Parent and Child § 520, Jurisdiction.
Witkin, California Summary 10th Parent and Child § 583, Alleged Father.
Witkin, California Summary 10th Parent and Child § 60C, (New) Estoppel to Deny Motherhood Of Lesbian Partner.
Witkin, California Summary 10th Parent and Child § 603, Identification Of Presumed or Alleged Fathers.
Witkin, California Summary 10th Parent and Child § 622, Findings and Order.
Witkin, California Summary 10th Parent and Child § 882, Findings.
Witkin, California Summary 10th Parent and Child § 886, Conduct Of Hearing.
Witkin, California Summary 10th Wills and Probate § 94, Parent and Child Relationship.

§ 7632. Agreement among parties does not bar action

Regardless of its terms, an agreement between an alleged father or a presumed parent and the other parent or child does not bar an action under this chapter. *(Stats.1992, c. 162 (A.B.2650), § 10, operative Jan. 1, 1994. Amended by Stats. 2013, c. 510 (A.B.1403), § 9.)*

Law Revision Commission Comments

Enactment [Revised Comment]

Section 7632 continues former Civil Code Section 7006(e) without substantive change. This section is similar to Section 6(d) of the Uniform Parentage Act (1973). [23 Cal.L.Rev.Comm. Reports 1 (1993)].

Commentary

For the history and effect of Section 7632, see *Roland v. Superior Court, 111 Cal.App.3d 234, 238, 168 Cal.Rptr. 438 (1980), hearing denied 1/21/81*. See also *County of Shasta v. Caruthers, 31 Cal.App.4th 1838, 38 Cal.Rptr.2d 18 (1995)* (putative father's $15,000 settlement of paternity suit in consideration for mother's dismissal of paternity suit with prejudice does not bar subsequent paternity suit by county attorney on behalf of child). See additionally Section 7630, Commentary.

Relying on this section as well as Sections 3900 and 4053, *Kristine M. v. David P., 135 Cal.App.4th 783, 37 Cal.Rptr.3d 748 (2006),* holds that a trial court's termination of a father's parental rights pursuant to the parents' stipulation is void as a matter of public policy and is an act that exceeds the court's jurisdiction. To similar effect, see *In re Marriage of Jackson, 136 Cal.App.4th 980, 39 Cal.Rptr.3d 365 (2006), review denied,* holding that a trial court's order granting a mother's motion, based on an agreement of the parents, to terminate her own parental rights was void because the order exceeded the court's jurisdiction.

Research References

Treatises and Practice Aids

Witkin, California Summary 10th Parent and Child § 19, General Provisions.

Witkin, California Summary 10th Parent and Child § 46, in General.

Witkin, California Summary 10th Parent and Child § 60B, (New) Domestic Partner Who Donated Her Ova to Partner to Conceive Child.

§ 7633. Time for action, order or judgment

An action under this chapter may be brought, an order or judgment may be entered before the birth of the child, and enforcement of that order or judgment shall be stayed until the birth of the child. *(Stats.1992, c. 162 (A.B.2650), § 10, operative Jan. 1, 1994. Amended by Stats.2006, c. 806 (S.B.1325), § 4.)*

Law Revision Commission Comments

Enactment [Revised Comment]

Section 7633 continues former Civil Code Section 7006(f) without substantive change. This section is a substitute for Section 6(e) of the Uniform Parentage Act (1973). [23 Cal.L.Rev.Comm. Reports 1 (1993)].

Research References

Forms

California Transactions Forms--Family Law § 7:28, Overview.

Treatises and Practice Aids

Witkin, California Summary 10th Parent and Child § 46, in General.

Witkin, California Summary 10th Parent and Child § 60, Action to Determine Mother and Child Relationship.

Witkin, California Summary 10th Parent and Child § 23A, (New) Assisted Reproduction Agreements for Gestational Carriers.

Witkin, California Summary 10th Parent and Child § 60C, (New) Estoppel to Deny Motherhood Of Lesbian Partner.

§ 7634. Action brought by local child support agency; review of current practices

(a) The local child support agency may, in the local child support agency's discretion, bring an action under this chapter in any case in which the local child support agency believes it to be appropriate.

(b) The Department of Child Support Services may review the current practices of service of process used by the local child support agencies pursuant to subdivision (a), and may develop methods to increase the number of persons served using personal delivery. *(Stats.1992, c. 162 (A.B.2650), § 10, operative Jan. 1, 1994. Amended by Stats.2000, c. 808 (A.B.1358), § 77, eff. Sept. 28, 2000; Stats.2004, c. 849 (A.B.252), § 2.)*

Law Revision Commission Comments

Enactment [Revised Comment]

Section 7634 continues former Civil Code Section 7006(g) without substantive change. There is no comparable provision in the Uniform Parentage Act (1973). [23 Cal.L.Rev.Comm. Reports 1 (1993)].

Commentary

See generally *Garrett v. Superior Court, 100 Cal.App.3d 535, 161 Cal.Rptr. 117 (1980), hearing denied 3/16/80* (district attorney as guardian ad litem).

Research References

Treatises and Practice Aids

Witkin, California Summary 10th Parent and Child § 46, in General.

§ 7635. Parties to action; representation of child by guardian ad litem or private counsel; notice; alignment

(a) The child may, if under the age of 12 years, and shall, if 12 years of age or older, be made a party to the action. If the child is a minor and a party to the action, the child shall be represented by a guardian ad litem appointed by the court. The guardian ad litem need not be represented by counsel if the guardian ad litem is a relative of the child.

(b) The natural parent, each person presumed to be a parent under Section 7611, and each man alleged to be the natural father, may be made parties and shall be given notice of the action in the manner prescribed in Section 7666 and an opportunity to be heard. Appointment of a guardian ad litem shall not be required for a minor who is a parent of the child who is the subject of the petition to establish parental relationship, unless the minor parent is unable to understand the nature of the proceedings or to assist counsel in preparing the case.

(c) The court may align the parties.

(d) In any initial or subsequent proceeding under this chapter where custody of, or visitation with, a minor child is in issue, the court may, if it determines it would be in the best interest of the minor child, appoint private counsel to represent the interests of the minor child pursuant to Chapter 10 (commencing with Section 3150) of Part 2 of Division 8. *(Stats.1992, c. 162 (A.B.2650), § 10, operative Jan. 1, 1994. Amended by Stats.1994, c. 1269 (A.B.2208), § 55; Stats.2008, c. 181 (S.B.1612), § 2; Stats.2013, c. 510 (A.B.1403), § 10.)*

Law Revision Commission Comments

Enactment [Revised Comment]

Section 7635 continues former Civil Code Section 7008 without substantive change. This section is similar to Section 9 of the Uniform Parentage Act (1973). [23 Cal.L.Rev.Comm. Reports 1 (1993)].

Commentary

Although subsection (a) requires that a child twelve years of age or older be made a party and represented by a guardian ad litem, *J.W. v. Superior Court, 17 Cal.App.4th 958, 22 Cal.Rptr.2d 527 (1993)*, holds that a non-attorney mother may not represent her minor child as guardian ad litem in a paternity action because such representation would constitute the unauthorized practice of law. See also Section 7634, Commentary.

Alex R. v. Superior Court of Los Angeles County, 248 Cal.App.4th 1, 203 Cal.Rptr.3d 251 (2016), held that a trial court erred in denying a 12-year-old-child's request for appointment of a guardian ad litem in a parentage proceeding because the child failed to provide notice of the request to his noncustodial father, when such notice was not required by statutory or case law.

Research References

Forms

West's California Judicial Council Forms FL-935, Application for and Appointment Of Guardian Ad Litem Of Minor--Family Law.

Treatises and Practice Aids

Witkin, California Summary 10th Parent and Child § 46, in General.
Witkin, California Summary 10th Parent and Child § 49, Joinder and Alignment Of Parties.
Witkin, California Summary 10th Parent and Child § 60, Action to Determine Mother and Child Relationship.

§ 7635.5. Right of alleged father to have genetic testing to determine parentage; right to make motion to set aside or vacate judgment

In any action brought pursuant to this article, if the alleged father is present in court for the action, the court shall inform the alleged father of his right to have genetic testing performed to determine if he is the biological father of the child. The court shall further inform the alleged father of his right to move to set aside or vacate a judgment of paternity pursuant to Section 7646 within two years of the date he received notice of the action to establish paternity, and that after that time has expired he may not move to set aside or vacate the judgment of paternity, regardless of whether genetic testing shows him not to be the biological father of the child. *(Added by Stats.2004, c. 849 (A.B.252), § 3.)*

Research References

Treatises and Practice Aids

Witkin, California Summary 10th Parent and Child § 49, Joinder and Alignment Of Parties.

§ 7636. Effect of judgment or order; exceptions

The judgment or order of the court determining the existence or nonexistence of the parent and child relationship is determinative for all purposes except for actions brought pursuant to Section 270 of the Penal Code. *(Stats.1992, c. 162 (A.B.2650), § 10, operative Jan. 1, 1994.)*

Law Revision Commission Comments

Enactment [Revised Comment]

Section 7636 continues former Civil Code Section 7010(a) without change. This section is similar to Section 15(a) of the Uniform Parentage Act (1973). [23 Cal.L.Rev.Comm. Reports 1 (1993)].

Commentary

See Section 7630, Commentary.

Weir v. Ferreira, 59 Cal.App.4th 1509, 70 Cal.Rptr.2d 33 (1997), review denied March 25, 1998, holds that principles of res judicata and collateral estoppel bar a decedent's son from challenging ward's right to inherit as decedent's issue after dissolution judgment expressly found that the ward was a child of decedent's marriage.

Although an unwed father is a father under this section because he has been judicially determined to be the children's father and has been ordered to pay child support, he is not a section 7611 "presumed father" because he never lived with the children or openly held them out to be his own. Therefore, in a dependency proceeding, a juvenile court could deny him reunification services because only presumed fathers are entitled to reunification services. *In re E.O., 182 Cal.App.4th 722, 107 Cal.Rptr.3d 1 (2010), review denied*. E.O. reasons that the category ""presumed father" functions in dependency cases to identify social fathers, even those who may not be biological fathers, while the issue in a paternity proceeding brought against an unwed father is biological paternity.

Research References

Forms

West's California Code Forms, Family § 7630, Comment Overview--Determining Parent and Child Relationship.
West's California Judicial Council Forms FL-190, Notice Of Entry Of Judgment (Family Law--Uniform Parentage--Custody and Support).

Treatises and Practice Aids

Witkin, California Summary 10th Parent and Child § 46, in General.
Witkin, California Summary 10th Parent and Child § 53, Judgment.
Witkin, California Summary 10th Parent and Child § 603, Identification Of Presumed or Alleged Fathers.

§ 7637. Contents of judgment or order

The judgment or order may contain any other provision directed against the appropriate party to the proceeding, concerning the duty of support, the custody and guardianship of the child, visitation privileges with the child, the furnishing of bond or other security for the payment of the judgment, or any other matter in the best interest of the child. The judgment or order may direct the parent to pay the reasonable expenses of the mother's pregnancy and confinement. *(Stats.1992, c. 162 (A.B.2650), § 10, operative Jan. 1, 1994. Amended by Stats.1993, c. 219 (A.B.1500), § 179; Stats.2013, c. 510 (A.B.1403), § 11.)*

Law Revision Commission Comments

Enactment [Revised Comment]

Section 7637 continues former Civil Code Section 7010(c) without change. This section is the same as Section 15(c) of the Uniform Parentage Act (1973). See also Section 3011 (factors in determining best interest of child). [23 Cal.L.Rev.Comm. Reports 1 (1993)].

Commentary

Barkaloff v. Woodward, 47 Cal.App.4th 393, 55 Cal.Rptr.2d 167 (1996), holds that a trial court lacks jurisdiction under the Domestic Violence Prevention Act (DVPA) (Section 6200 et seq.) and the Uniform Parentage Act (UPA) (Section 7600 et seq.) to award visitation rights to a man who is not the father of the child and who was never married to the child's mother when both the child's mother and the child's biological father object to visitation, even though such visitation may be in the child's best interests. *Barkaloff* holds that jurisdiction to order visitation of minor children under the DVPA is limited, pursuant to Section 6323, to cases where there is a marital relationship between the parties. 47 Cal.App.4th at 398. Jurisdiction to order visitation of a child under the UPA is limited to claims by persons who are, or are presumed to be, a child's natural parent. 47 Cal.App.4th at 399.

Research References

Forms

California Transactions Forms--Family Law § 3:4, Subject Matter Jurisdiction for Custody Determinations.
California Transactions Forms--Family Law § 5:9, Use Of Parenting Agreement to Define Rights and Responsibilities Relating to Child on Termination Of Partners' Relationship Where Both Partners Are Biological Parents.
California Transactions Forms--Family Law § 7:28, Overview.
West's California Code Forms, Family § 7630, Comment Overview--Determining Parent and Child Relationship.
West's California Judicial Council Forms FL-190, Notice Of Entry Of Judgment (Family Law--Uniform Parentage--Custody and Support).

Treatises and Practice Aids

Witkin, California Summary 10th Parent and Child § 46, in General.
Witkin, California Summary 10th Parent and Child § 53, Judgment.
Witkin, California Summary 10th Parent and Child § 59, Visitation Privileges.

§ 7638. Procedures to change name of child

The procedure in an action under this part to change the name of a minor or adult child for whom a parent and child relationship is established pursuant to Section 7636, upon application in accordance with Title 8 (commencing with Section 1275) of Part 3 of the Code of Civil Procedure shall conform to those provisions, except that the application for the change of name may be included with the petition filed under this part and except as provided in Sections 1277 and 1278 of the Code of Civil Procedure. *(Stats.1992, c. 162 (A.B.2650), § 10, operative Jan. 1, 1994.)*

Law Revision Commission Comments

Enactment [Revised Comment]

Section 7638 restates former Civil Code Section 7007(d) without substantive change. There is no comparable provision in the Uniform Parentage Act (1973). The reference to Section 7636 has been substituted for the broader reference to former Civil Code Section 7010. This is not a substantive change, since the relevant part of former Civil Code Section 7010 is continued in Section 7636. The reference to the "superior" court has been omitted as surplus. See Section 200 (jurisdiction in superior court). See also Section 7639 (issuance of new birth certificate). [23 Cal.L.Rev.Comm. Reports 1 (1993)].

Research References

Treatises and Practice Aids

Witkin, California Summary 10th Parent and Child § 46, in General.

§ 7639. Order for issuance of new birth certificate

If the judgment or order of the court is at variance with the child's birth certificate, the court shall order that a new birth certificate be issued as prescribed in Article 2 (commencing with Section 102725) of Chapter 5 of Part 1 of Division 102 of the Health and Safety Code. *(Stats.1992, c. 162 (A.B.2650), § 10, operative Jan. 1, 1994. Amended by Stats.1996, c. 1023 (S.B.1497), § 48, eff. Sept. 29, 1996.)*

Law Revision Commission Comments

Enactment [Revised Comment]

Section 7639 continues former Civil Code Section 7010(b) without change. This section is similar to Section 15(b) of the Uniform Parentage Act (1973). See also Section 7638 (change of name of child). [23 Cal.L.Rev.Comm. Reports 1 (1993)].

Research References

Forms

California Transactions Forms--Family Law § 5:8, Effect Of Birth Certificate Paternity Designation; Declaration Of Paternity.

Treatises and Practice Aids

Witkin, California Summary 10th Parent and Child § 53, Judgment.
Witkin, California Summary 10th Parent and Child § 60, Action to Determine Mother and Child Relationship.

§ 7640. Fees and costs

The court may order reasonable fees of counsel, experts, and the child's guardian ad litem, and other costs of the action and pretrial proceedings, including blood tests, to be paid by the parties, excluding any governmental entity, in proportions and at times determined by the court. *(Stats. 1992, c. 162 (A.B.2650), § 10, operative Jan. 1, 1994. Amended by Stats.1994, c. 1269 (A.B.2208), § 55.2.)*

Law Revision Commission Comments

Enactment [Revised Comment]

Section 7640 continues former Civil Code Section 7011 without change. This section is the same as the first sentence of Section 16 of the Uniform Parentage Act (1973). For general provisions relating to the award of attorney's fees and costs, see Sections 270–272. [23 Cal.L.Rev.Comm. Reports 1 (1993)].

Commentary

The constitutionality of this section was sustained by *Banning v. Newdow, 119 Cal.App.4th 438, 14 Cal.Rptr.3d 447 (2004)*, in which the court concluded that, even assuming arguendo that requiring one party to pay another's attorney fees implicates the burdened party's fundamental rights, the statute is constitutional because it serves the compelling state interest of promoting the best interests of the child by allowing both sides effective representation.

Robert J. v. Catherine D., 134 Cal.App.4th 1392, 37 Cal.Rptr.3d 104 (2005), review denied, holds that this section grants the trial court discretion to award attorney's fees on matters relating to custody, visitation, and support that arise after paternity is adjudicated. The court's authority to award attorney's fees is now more clearly granted by Section 7605, enacted in 2004.

In applying this section and section 7605 to a request for attorney's fees in a paternity proceeding, *Kevin Q. v. Lauren W., 195 Cal.App.4th 633, 124 Cal.Rptr.3d 676 (2011)*, holds that a trial court properly relied on section 2032, which establishes standards for awards of attorney's fees in marital dissolution cases.

Research References

Forms

West's California Code Forms, Family § 7630, Comment Overview--Determining Parent and Child Relationship.
West's California Judicial Council Forms FL-157, Spousal or Partner Support Declaration Attachment.

Treatises and Practice Aids

Witkin, California Summary 10th Parent and Child § 19, General Provisions.
Witkin, California Summary 10th Parent and Child § 53, Judgment.
Witkin, California Summary 10th Parent and Child § 63, in General.
Witkin, California Summary 10th Parent and Child § 188, Order.
Witkin, California Summary 10th Parent and Child § 311, Other Proceedings Stayed.

§ 7641. Obligation of parent; enforcement; parties; persons payable; willful failure to obey; civil contempt

(a) If there is a voluntary declaration of paternity in place, or parentage or a duty of support has been acknowledged or adjudicated under this part or under prior law, the obligation of the parent may be enforced in the same or other proceedings by any of the following:

(1) The other parent.

(2) The child.

(3) The public authority that has furnished or may furnish the reasonable expenses of pregnancy, confinement, education, support, or funeral.

(4) Any other person, including a private agency, to the extent the person has furnished or is furnishing these expenses.

(b) The court may order support payments to be made to any of the following:

(1) The other parent.

(2) The clerk of the court.

(3) A person, corporation, or agency designated to administer the payments for the benefit of the child under the supervision of the court.

(c) Willful failure to obey the judgment or order of the court is a civil contempt of the court. All remedies for the enforcement of judgments, including imprisonment for contempt, apply. *(Stats.1992, c. 162 (A.B.2650), § 10, operative Jan. 1, 1994. Amended by Stats.2013, c. 510 (A.B.1403), § 12.)*

Law Revision Commission Comments

Enactment [Revised Comment]

Section 7641 continues former Civil Code Section 7012 without substantive change. This section is the same in substance as Section 17 of the Uniform Parentage Act (1973). [23 Cal.L.Rev.Comm. Reports 1 (1993)].

Commentary

In re Marriage of Wilson and Bodine, 207 Cal.App.4th 768, 143 Cal.Rptr.3d 803 (2012), holds that a child support order entered in a paternity action is nullified by the parents' subsequent marriage.

Research References

Forms

California Transactions Forms--Family Law § 7:60, Overview; Paternity Of Child [Fam C § 7613].

West's California Code Forms, Family § 7630, Comment Overview--Determining Parent and Child Relationship.

Treatises and Practice Aids

Witkin, California Summary 10th Parent and Child § 54, Enforcement.

§ 7642. Modification or set aside of judgment or order; jurisdiction; manner

The court has continuing jurisdiction to modify or set aside a judgment or order made under this part. A judgment or order relating to an adoption may only be modified or set aside in the same manner and under the same conditions as an order of adoption may be modified or set aside under Section 9100 or 9102. *(Stats.1992, c. 162 (A.B.2650), § 10, operative Jan. 1, 1994. Amended by Stats.1999, c. 653 (A.B.380), § 11.)*

Law Revision Commission Comments

Enactment [Revised Comment]

Section 7642 continues former Civil Code Section 7013 without substantive change. This section is similar to Section 18 of the Uniform Parentage Act (1973). A reference to "order of adoption" has been substituted for the former reference to "decree of adoption." This is not a substantive change. See Section 100 ("order" includes decree, as appropriate). [23 Cal.L.Rev.Comm. Reports 1 (1993)].

Research References

Forms

California Transactions Forms--Family Law § 5:9, Use Of Parenting Agreement to Define Rights and Responsibilities Relating to Child on Termination Of Partners' Relationship Where Both Partners Are Biological Parents.

West's California Code Forms, Family § 7630, Comment Overview--Determining Parent and Child Relationship.

Treatises and Practice Aids

Witkin, California Summary 10th Parent and Child § 53, Judgment.

§ 7643. Hearing or trial in closed court; papers and records; inspection

(a) Notwithstanding any other law concerning public hearings and records, a hearing or trial held under this part may be held in closed court without admittance of any person other than those necessary to the action or proceeding. Except as provided in subdivision (b), all papers and records, other than the final judgment, pertaining to the action or proceeding, whether part of the permanent record of the court or of a file in a public agency or elsewhere, are subject to inspection and copying only in exceptional cases upon an order of the court for good cause shown.

(b) Papers and records pertaining to the action or proceeding that are part of the permanent record of the court are subject to inspection and copying by the parties to the action, their attorneys, and by agents acting pursuant to written authorization from the parties to the action or their attorneys. An attorney shall obtain the consent of the party to the action prior to authorizing an agent to inspect and copy the permanent record. An attorney shall also state on the written authorization that he or she has obtained the consent of the party to authorize an agent to inspect and copy the permanent record. *(Stats.1992, c. 162 (A.B.2650), § 10, operative Jan. 1, 1994. Amended by Stats.2008, c. 50 (A.B. 1679), § 1; Stats.2010, c. 212 (A.B.2767), § 5.)*

Law Revision Commission Comments

Enactment [Revised Comment]

Section 7643 continues former Civil Code Section 7014 without substantive change. This section is similar to Section 20 of the Uniform Parentage Act (1973). [23 Cal.L.Rev.Comm. Reports 1 (1993)].

Research References

Forms

California Transactions Forms--Family Law § 5:9, Use Of Parenting Agreement to Define Rights and Responsibilities Relating to Child on Termination Of Partners' Relationship Where Both Partners Are Biological Parents.

West's California Code Forms, Family § 7630, Comment Overview--Determining Parent and Child Relationship.

Treatises and Practice Aids

Witkin, California Summary 10th Parent and Child § 52, Confidentiality.

§ 7644. Voluntary declaration of paternity; child custody and support actions; force and effect

(a) Notwithstanding any other law, an action for child custody and support and for other relief as provided in

Section 7637 may be filed based upon a voluntary declaration of paternity as provided in Chapter 3 (commencing with Section 7570) of Part 2.

(b) Except as provided in Section 7576, the voluntary declaration of paternity shall be given the same force and effect as a judgment of parentage entered by a court of competent jurisdiction. The court shall make appropriate orders as specified in Section 7637 based upon the voluntary declaration of paternity unless evidence is presented that the voluntary declaration of paternity has been rescinded by the parties or set aside as provided in Section 7575 of the Family Code.

(c) The Judicial Council shall develop the forms and procedures necessary to implement this section. *(Added by Stats.1994, c. 1266 (A.B.3804), § 7. Amended by Stats.1996, c. 1062 (A.B.1832), § 14; Stats.2013, c. 510 (A.B.1403), § 13.)*

Research References

Treatises and Practice Aids

Witkin, California Summary 10th Parent and Child § 46, in General.

ARTICLE 1.5. SETTING ASIDE OR VACATING JUDGMENT OF PATERNITY

§ 7645. Definitions

For purposes of this article, the following definitions shall apply:

(a) "Child" means the child of a previously established father, as determined by the superior court in a judgment that is the subject of a motion brought pursuant to this article, or as a matter of law.

(b) "Judgment" means a judgment, order, or decree entered in a court of this state that establishes paternity, including a determination of paternity made pursuant to a petition filed under Section 300, 601, or 602 of the Welfare and Institutions Code, or a voluntary declaration of paternity. For purposes of this article, "judgment" does not include a judgment in any action for marital dissolution, legal separation, or nullity.

(c) "Previously established father" means a person identified as the father of a child in a judgment that is the subject of a motion brought pursuant to this article.

(d) "Previously established mother" means a person identified as the mother of a child in a judgment that is the subject of a motion brought pursuant to this article. *(Added by Stats.2004, c. 849 (A.B.252), § 4.)*

Research References

Treatises and Practice Aids

Witkin, California Summary 10th Husband and Wife § 307, Grounds and Time Limits.

Witkin, California Summary 10th Parent and Child § 56, in General.

Witkin, California Summary 10th Parent and Child § 58, Grant or Denial.

§ 7646. Setting aside or vacating judgments establishing paternity; time periods for bringing motion; application; reconsideration of motion

(a) Notwithstanding any other provision of law, a judgment establishing paternity may be set aside or vacated upon a motion by the previously established mother of a child, the previously established father of a child, the child, or the legal representative of any of these persons if genetic testing indicates that the previously established father of a child is not the biological father of the child. The motion shall be brought within one of the following time periods:

(1) Within a two-year period commencing with the date on which the previously established father knew or should have known of a judgment that established him as the father of the child or commencing with the date the previously established father knew or should have known of the existence of an action to adjudicate the issue of paternity, whichever is first, except as provided in paragraph (2) or (3) of this subdivision.

(2) Within a two-year period commencing with the date of the child's birth if paternity was established by a voluntary declaration of paternity. Nothing in this paragraph shall bar any rights under subdivision (c) of Section 7575.

(3) In the case of any previously established father who is the legal father as a result of a default judgment as of the effective date of this section, within a two-year period from January 1, 2005, to December 31, 2006, inclusive.

(b) Subdivision (a) does not apply if the child is presumed to be a child of a marriage pursuant to Section 7540.

(c) Reconsideration of a motion brought under paragraph (3) of subdivision (a) may be requested and granted if the following requirements are met:

(1) The motion was filed with the court between September 24, 2006, and December 31, 2006, inclusive.

(2) The motion was denied solely on the basis that it was untimely.

(3) The request for reconsideration of the motion is filed on or before December 31, 2009. *(Added by Stats.2004, c. 849 (A.B.252), § 4. Amended by Stats.2008, c. 58 (S.B.1333), § 1.)*

Commentary

An order setting aside or vacating a paternity judgment must be founded on genetic tests indicating that a previously established father of a child is not the biological father of the child. When a mother and child do not comply with court-ordered genetic testing, there are judicial and administrative means to compel their participation and testing. *San Mateo County Department of Child Support Services v. Clark, 168 Cal.App.4th 834, 85 Cal.Rptr.3d 763 (2008).*

County of Fresno v. Sanchez, 135 Cal.App.4th 15, 37 Cal.Rptr.3d 192 (2005), holds that a trial court properly denied an adjudicated father's motion to eliminate his child support obligation and accrued support arrearages based on a DNA parentage report indicating that he was not the child's father. Instead, the adjudicated father should have proceeded under this section to have the paternity judgment set aside.

Applying subsection (a)(2) and section 7575(b)(3)(A), *County of Orange v. Superior Court, 155 Cal.App.4th 1253, 66 Cal.Rptr.3d 689 (2007),* concluded that a motion to set aside a paternity judgment based on a voluntary declaration of paternity is untimely when it is filed more than two years after the child's birth.

Applying a former version of subsection (a)(3), *County of Sacramento v. Llanes, 168 Cal.App.4th 1165, 86 Cal.Rptr.3d 158 (2008),* sustained a trial court's finding that a legal father's motion to set aside a default paternity judgment issued on or before January 1, 2005 was untimely because it was filed on December 29, 2006. *Llanes* reasoned that although the motion was filed within two years of the effective date of the former version of subsection (a)(3), which was January 1, 2005, the former version required filing within two years of *enactment* of the statute, which occurred on September 28, 2004. The current version of the statute, effective January 1, 2009, avoids *Llanes* by extending the filing period from September 28, 2004 to December 31, 2006, and opens a one year window for reconsideration of motions which would have been timely under the current version but were denied solely because they were untimely under the prior version.

Research References

Forms

West's California Code Forms, Family § 7645, Comment Overview--Setting Aside or Vacating Judgment Of Paternity.
West's California Judicial Council Forms FL-272, Notice Of Motion to Set Aside Judgment Of Paternity.
West's California Judicial Council Forms FL-274, Information Sheet for Completing Notice Of Motion to Set Aside Judgment Of Paternity.
West's California Judicial Council Forms FL-276, Response to Notice Of Motion to Set Aside Judgment Of Paternity.
West's California Judicial Council Forms FL-278, Order After Hearing on Motion to Set Aside Judgment Of Paternity.

Treatises and Practice Aids

Witkin, California Summary 10th Husband and Wife § 383, Temporary Custody and Visitation.
Witkin, California Summary 10th Parent and Child § 34, Rescinding or Setting Aside Declaration.
Witkin, California Summary 10th Parent and Child § 49, Joinder and Alignment Of Parties.
Witkin, California Summary 10th Parent and Child § 56, in General.
Witkin, California Summary 10th Parent and Child § 58, Grant or Denial.

§ 7647. Requirements for granting motion to set aside or vacate paternity judgment; proof of service

(a) A court may grant a motion to set aside or vacate a judgment establishing paternity only if all of the following conditions are met:

(1) The motion is filed in a court of proper venue.

(2) The motion contains, at a minimum, all of the following information, if known:

(A) The legal name, age, county of residence, and residence address of the child.

(B) The names, mailing addresses, and counties of residence, or, if deceased, the date and place of death, of the following persons:

(i) The previously established father and the previously established mother, and the biological mother and father of the child.

(ii) The guardian of the child, if any.

(iii) Any person who has physical custody of the child.

(iv) The guardian ad litem of the child, if any, as appointed pursuant to Section 7647.5.

(C) A declaration that the person filing the motion believes that the previously established father is not the biological father of the child, the specific reasons for this belief, and a declaration that the person desires that the motion be granted. The moving party is not required to present evidence of a paternity test indicating that the previously established father is not the biological father of the child in order to bring this motion pursuant to Section 7646.

(D) A declaration that the marital presumption set forth in Section 7540 does not apply.

(3) The court finds that the conclusions of the expert, as described in Section 7552, and as supported by the evidence, are that the previously established father is not the biological father of the child.

(b) The motion shall include a proof of service upon the following persons, excluding the person bringing the motion:

(1) The previously established mother.

(2) The previously established father.

(3) The local child support agency, if services are being provided to the child pursuant to Title IV–D or IV–E of the Social Security Act (42 U.S.C. Sec. 651 et seq. and 42 U.S.C. Sec. 670 et seq.).

(4) The child's guardian ad litem, if any. *(Added by Stats.2004, c. 849 (A.B.252), § 4.)*

Commentary

An order setting aside or vacating a paternity judgment must be founded on genetic tests indicating that a previously established father of a child is not the biological father of the child. When a mother and child do not comply with court-ordered genetic testing, there are judicial and administrative means to compel their participation and testing. *San Mateo County Department of Child Support Services v. Clark, 168 Cal.App.4th 834, 85 Cal.Rptr.3d 763 (2008).*

Research References

Forms

West's California Code Forms, Family § 7645, Comment Overview--Setting Aside or Vacating Judgment Of Paternity.

Treatises and Practice Aids

Witkin, California Summary 10th Parent and Child § 56, in General.
Witkin, California Summary 10th Parent and Child § 57, Order for Genetic Testing.

Witkin, California Summary 10th Parent and Child § 58, Grant or Denial.

§ 7647.5. Appointment of guardian ad litem

A guardian ad litem may be appointed for the child to represent the best interests of the child in an action brought pursuant to this article. *(Added by Stats.2004, c. 849 (A.B. 252), § 4.)*

Research References

Treatises and Practice Aids

Witkin, California Summary 10th Parent and Child § 56, in General.

§ 7647.7. Genetic testing

Any genetic testing used to support the motion to set aside or vacate shall be conducted in accordance with Section 7552. The court shall, at the request of any person authorized to make a motion pursuant to this article, or may upon its own motion, order genetic testing to assist the court in making a determination whether the previously established father is the biological father of the child. *(Added by Stats.2004, c. 849 (A.B.252), § 4.)*

Research References

Treatises and Practice Aids

Witkin, California Summary 10th Parent and Child § 56, in General.
Witkin, California Summary 10th Parent and Child § 58, Grant or Denial.

§ 7648. Previously established father not biological father; denial of motion to set aside or vacation paternity judgment; factors

If the court finds that the conclusions of all of the experts, based upon the results of genetic tests performed pursuant to Chapter 2 (commencing with Section 7550) of Part 2, indicate that the previously established father is not the biological father of the child, the court may, nevertheless, deny the motion if it determines that denial of the motion is in the best interest of the child, after consideration of the following factors:

(a) The age of the child.

(b) The length of time since the entry of the judgment establishing paternity.

(c) The nature, duration, and quality of any relationship between the previously established father and the child, including the duration and frequency of any time periods during which the child and the previously established father resided in the same household or enjoyed a parent-child relationship.

(d) The request of the previously established father that the parent-child relationship continue.

(e) Notice by the biological father of the child that he does not oppose preservation of the relationship between the previously established father and the child.

(f) The benefit or detriment to the child in establishing the biological parentage of the child.

(g) Whether the conduct of the previously established father has impaired the ability to ascertain the identity of, or get support from, the biological father.

(h) Additional factors deemed by the court to be relevant to its determination of the best interest of the child. *(Added by Stats.2004, c. 849 (A.B.252), § 4.)*

Research References

Treatises and Practice Aids

Witkin, California Summary 10th Parent and Child § 58, Grant or Denial.

§ 7648.1. Statement of basis for denial of motion

If the court denies a motion pursuant to Section 7648, the court shall state on the record the basis for the denial of that motion and any supporting facts. *(Added by Stats.2004, c. 849 (A.B.252), § 4.)*

Research References

Treatises and Practice Aids

Witkin, California Summary 10th Parent and Child § 58, Grant or Denial.

§ 7648.2. Support enforcement services; administrative orders; payment of costs of genetic testing

(a) This section applies only to cases where support enforcement services are being provided by a local child support agency pursuant to Section 17400.

(b) Upon receipt of any motion brought pursuant to Section 7646, the local child support agency may issue an administrative order requiring the mother, child, and the previously established father to submit to genetic testing if all of the conditions of paragraphs (1) and (2) of subdivision (a) of Section 7647 are satisfied.

(c) The local child support agency shall pay the costs of any genetic tests that are ordered under subdivision (b) or are ordered by a court for cases in which the local child support agency is providing services under Title IV–D of the Social Security Act (42 U.S.C. Sec. 651 et seq.).

(d) Nothing in this section prohibits any person who has been ordered by a local child support agency to submit to genetic tests pursuant to this section from filing a notice of motion with the court seeking relief from the local child support agency's order to submit to genetic tests. In that event, the court shall resolve the issue of whether genetic tests should be ordered as provided in Section 7647.7. If any person refuses to submit to the tests after receipt of the administrative order pursuant to this section and fails to seek relief from the court from the administrative order either prior to the scheduled tests or within 10 days after the tests are scheduled, the court may resolve the question of paternity against that person or enforce the administrative order if the rights of others or the interest of justice so require. *(Added by Stats.2004, c. 849 (A.B.252), § 4.)*

Research References

Treatises and Practice Aids

Witkin, California Summary 10th Parent and Child § 57, Order for Genetic Testing.

§ 7648.3. Prohibition against setting aside or vacating paternity judgment; circumstances

A court may not issue an order setting aside or vacating a judgment establishing paternity pursuant to this article under any of the following circumstances:

(a) The judgment was made or entered by a tribunal of another state, even if the enforcement of that judgment is sought in this state.

(b) The judgment was made or entered in this state and genetic tests were conducted prior to the entry of the judgment which did not exclude the previously established father as the biological father of the child. *(Added by Stats.2004, c. 849 (A.B.252), § 4.)*

Research References

Treatises and Practice Aids

Witkin, California Summary 10th Parent and Child § 58, Grant or Denial.

§ 7648.4. Orders for child support and arrearages based on previous judgment of paternity; reimbursement

Notwithstanding any other provision of law, if the court grants a motion to set aside or vacate a paternity judgment pursuant to this article, the court shall vacate any order for child support and arrearages issued on the basis of that previous judgment of paternity. The previously established father has no right of reimbursement for any amount of support paid prior to the granting of the motion. *(Added by Stats.2004, c. 849 (A.B.252), § 4.)*

Commentary

County of Los Angeles v. James, 152 Cal.App.4th 253, 60 Cal.Rptr.3d 880 (2007), review denied Sept. 25, 2007, relied on this section in holding that an erroneously declared father (pursuant to a default judgment) may not be reimbursed for child support already paid.

Research References

Treatises and Practice Aids

Witkin, California Summary 10th Parent and Child § 58, Grant or Denial.

§ 7648.8. Termination of adoption; effect on obligations

This article does not establish a basis for termination of any adoption, and does not affect any obligation of an adoptive parent to an adoptive child. *(Added by Stats.2004, c. 849 (A.B.252), § 4.)*

Research References

Treatises and Practice Aids

Witkin, California Summary 10th Parent and Child § 56, in General.

§ 7648.9. Assisted reproduction and surrogacy agreements

This article does not establish a basis for setting aside or vacating a judgment establishing paternity with regard to a child conceived by assisted reproduction pursuant to Section 7613 or a child conceived pursuant to a surrogacy agreement. *(Added by Stats.2004, c. 849 (A.B.252), § 4. Amended by Stats.2013, c. 510 (A.B.1403), § 14.)*

Research References

Treatises and Practice Aids

Witkin, California Summary 10th Parent and Child § 56, in General.

§ 7649. Rights and remedies available under other provisions of law

Nothing in this article shall limit the rights and remedies available under any other provision of law with regard to setting aside or vacating a judgment of paternity or a voluntary declaration of paternity. *(Added by Stats.2004, c. 849 (A.B.252), § 4.)*

Research References

Treatises and Practice Aids

Witkin, California Summary 10th Parent and Child § 56, in General.

§ 7649.5. Distribution from estate of decedent made in good faith reliance on judgement establishing paternity; finality; appeal; liability of estate, trust, personal representative or trustee

Notwithstanding any other provision of this article, a distribution from the estate of a decedent or payment made by a trustee, insurance company, pension fund, or any other person or entity that was made in good faith reliance on a judgment establishing paternity that is final for purposes of direct appeal, may not be set aside or subject to direct or collateral attack because of the entry of an order setting aside or vacating a judgment under this article. An estate, trust, personal representative, trustee, or any other person or entity that made that distribution or payment may not incur any liability to any person because of the distribution or payment or because of the entry of an order under this article. *(Added by Stats.2004, c. 849 (A.B.252), § 4.)*

Research References

Treatises and Practice Aids

Witkin, California Summary 10th Parent and Child § 56, in General.

ARTICLE 2. DETERMINATION OF MOTHER AND CHILD RELATIONSHIP

§ 7650. Action to determine existence or nonexistence of mother and child relationship; parties; law governing

(a) Any interested person may bring an action to determine the existence or nonexistence of a mother and child relationship. Insofar as practicable, the provisions of this part applicable to the father and child relationship apply.

(b) A woman is presumed to be the natural mother of a child if the child is in utero after the death of the decedent and the conditions set forth in Section 249.5 of the Probate Code are satisfied. *(Stats.1992, c. 162 (A.B.2650), § 10, operative Jan. 1, 1994. Amended by Stats.2004, c. 775 (A.B.1910), § 2.3.)*

Law Revision Commission Comments

Enactment [Revised Comment]

Section 7650 continues former Civil Code Section 7015 without change. This section is the same in substance as Section 21 of the Uniform Parentage Act (1973). [23 Cal.L.Rev.Comm. Reports 1 (1993)].

Commentary

Amy G. v. M.W., 142 Cal.App.4th 1, 47 Cal.Rptr.3d 297 (2006), review denied Nov. 29, 2006, held that a wife who has accepted into the marital household a child that her husband fathered in an extramarital relationship, may not assert that she is a presumed mother for purposes of section 7540 or subsection (a) or (d) of section 7611 when the child's biological mother timely asserts her parental interest in the child, the identity of the child's father is undisputed, and he is a party in the proceeding and represents his wife's interests as well as his own. Thus, *Amy G.* reasoned, the wife is not an "interested party" authorized to bring a parentage action under this section.

See generally *Johnson v. Calvert, 5 Cal.4th 84, 89, 19 Cal.Rptr.2d 494 (1993), cert. denied 510 U.S. 874, 114 S. Ct. 206, 126 L.Ed.2d 163 (1993)* (determining "mother" when reproductive technology multiplies the claimants). Compare *Johnson v. Calvert* (when one woman is the genetic mother and another woman is the gestational mother, the "natural mother" is the woman who intended to bring about the birth of the child and to raise the child as her own) with *In re Marriage of Moschetta, 25 Cal.App.4th 1218, 30 Cal.Rptr.2d (1994)* (in a traditional surrogacy arrangement, that is, where the surrogate mother provides both the ovum and the womb, the surrogate mother is a birth parent, and her consent is required under section 8814 before the child may be adopted by another; thus the terms of the traditional surrogacy contract are unenforceable insofar as they purport to create maternal rights in a different woman).

K.M. v. E.G., 37 Cal.4th 130, 117 P.3d 673, 33 Cal.Rptr.3d 61 (2005), holds that Section 7613(b) has no application when a woman in a lesbian relationship provides ova to impregnate her partner in order to produce children who will be raised in their joint home. Consequently, the California Supreme Court recognized the ova donor's claim to parental status, holding that both the woman who provided the ova and the woman who bore the resulting twin children were the children's parents even though the ova donor did not hold the resultant children out as her own natural children within the meaning of Section 7611(d) and the trial court found that she formally relinquished any claim to offspring resulting from her ova donation. In other words, the intent of the parties on the question of maternity had no bearing on the result.

Although *K.M.*, narrowly distinguishes *Steven S. v. Deborah D., 127 Cal.App.4th 319, 25 Cal.Rptr.3d 482 (2005)*, *K.M.* may be understood to undermine the rationale of *Stephen S.*, in which the court of appeal held that when a child is conceived by the artificial insemination of an unmarried mother with sperm provided by a licensed physician, the biological father of the child may not assert parental rights even though he once had an intimate sexual relationship with the mother and had some social role in the child's life. *Stephen S.* reasoned that once the trial court determined that the child was conceived by artificial insemination, rather than natural conception, Section 7613(b) applied to bar the semen donor from asserting his parentage of the child.

In a companion case to *K.M.*, *Elisa B. v. Superior Court, 37 Cal.4th 108, 117 P.3d 660, 33 Cal.Rptr.3d 46 (2005)*, the California Supreme Court held that in a child support action filed by a county district attorney, a woman who agreed to raise children with her lesbian partner, supported her partner's artificial insemination by means of an anonymous donor, and received the resulting twins into her home and held them out as her own children was a Section 7611(d) presumed parent. Moreover, invoking Section 7612(a), the Supreme Court held that a child support action was not an "appropriate action" in which to rebut the Section 7611(d) presumption. Consequently the woman was subject to the parental child support obligation. *Charisma R. v. Kristina S., 140 Cal.App.4th 301, 44 Cal.Rptr.3d 332 (2006)*, extends *Elisa B.* by applying it when a child's biological mother opposed her former lesbian partner's petition to establish a parental relationship with a child conceived and born during their relationship. *Charisma R.* reasons that the preferences of a biological parent are immaterial in determining whether another person is a presumed parent under Section 7611(d) or whether, under Section 7612(a), rebuttal of presumed parent status is appropriate. On remand, *Charisma R. v. Kristina S., 175 Cal.App.4th 361, 96 Cal.Rptr.3d 26 (2009)*, held that section 7611(d) presumed parenthood requires only that a former domestic partner have received the child into her home and openly held the child out as her own; it does not require the former partner to co-parent for any particular length of time.

In another companion case, *Kristine H. v. Lisa R., 37 Cal.4th 156, 117 P.3d 690, 33 Cal.Rptr.3d 81 (2005)*, the California Supreme Court used the doctrine of estoppel to reach a similar result when a former lesbian partner of a child's mother sought custody of the child after the parties' separation. During the mother's pregnancy the partners sought and secured a judgment that they are the "only legally recognized parents [of the unborn child] and take full and complete legal, custodial and financial responsibility of said child." Without deciding whether the judgment was enforceable, the Supreme Court held that the mother was estopped to attack the validity of a judgment to which she stipulated.

Elisa B. and *Kristine H.* overruled earlier court of appeal decisions declining to accord parental status to a parent's lesbian partner, such as *Nancy S. v. Michele G., 228 Cal.App.3d 831, 279 Cal.Rptr. 212 (1991)* and *Curiale v. Reagan, 222 Cal.App.3d 1597, 1600, 272 Cal.Rptr. 520 (1990)*.

S.Y. v. S.B., 201 Cal.App.4th 1023, 134 Cal.Rptr.3d 1 (2011), review denied, held that a woman who fully embraced the rights and obligations of being a parent to her same-sex partner's adopted children was properly found to be a section 7611(d) presumed parent when the woman spent three or four nights a week at the children's home and openly held the children out as her own children. Whether the adoptive mother intended her partner to have parental rights was immaterial. See also *R.M. v. T.A., 233 Cal.App.4th 760, 182 Cal. Rptr.3d 836 (2015)*, in which the court relied on *S.Y. v. S.B.* to reject a mother's argument that her intent, as opposed to her behavior, was determinative in whether her former partner was a presumed parent of her child.

Robert B. v. Susan B., 109 Cal.App.4th 1109, 135 Cal.Rptr.2d 785 (2003), review denied September 10, 2003, sorts out parentage that has been confused by clinical error. In *Robert B.*, a couple and a single woman sought the reproductive assistance of a fertility clinic. For the couple, the clinic was to fertilize the eggs of an anonymous donor with the husband's sperm. The single woman was to receive an embryo created from anonymous egg and sperm donors. Through clinical error, the single woman received one of the couple's embryos and she gave birth to a son. The wife gave birth to a daughter. Thus the two infants were siblings. The single woman and the couple disputed parentage of the son. The court held that the husband was the father under § 7630, the single woman who carried the child to term was the mother under § 7610, and the father's wife had no standing under this section to bring an action to determine the existence of non-existence of a mother-child relationship. In concluding that the husband was the father, the court reasoned that § 7613(b) was inapplicable because the husband provided semen for the purpose of inseminating only his wife.

Research References

Treatises and Practice Aids

Witkin, California Summary 10th Parent and Child § 20, in General.

Witkin, California Summary 10th Parent and Child § 60, Action to Determine Mother and Child Relationship.

Witkin, California Summary 10th Parent and Child § 236, Former Lesbian Partner Opposed by Other Partner.

Witkin, California Summary 10th Parent and Child § 60A, (New) Lesbian Partner Who is Not Biological Mother Of Child.

CHAPTER 5. TERMINATION OF PARENTAL RIGHTS IN ADOPTION PROCEEDINGS

§ 7660. Relinquishment or consent by mother; notice to and rights of presumed parent

If a mother relinquishes for or consents to, or proposes to relinquish for or consent to, the adoption of a child who has a presumed parent under Section 7611, the presumed parent shall be given notice of the adoption proceeding and have the rights provided under Part 2 (commencing with Section 8600) of Division 13, unless that parent's relationship to the child has been previously terminated or determined by a court not to exist or the presumed parent has voluntarily relinquished for or consented to the adoption of the child. *(Stats.1992, c. 162 (A.B.2650), § 10, operative Jan. 1, 1994. Amended by Stats.2000, c. 937 (A.B.2433), § 1; Stats.2013, c. 510 (A.B. 1403), § 15.)*

Law Revision Commission Comments

Enactment [Revised Comment]

Section 7660 continues former Civil Code Section 7017(a)(1) without substantive change. This section is similar to Section 24 of the Uniform Parentage Act (1973). In clause (2), the reference to "prior" law has been omitted. [23 Cal.L.Rev.Comm. Reports 1 (1993)].

Commentary

For discussion of the father's rights, see Section 7611, Commentary.

Research References

Forms

California Transactions Forms--Family Law § 6:71, Notice Of Alleged Paternity.

West's California Code Forms, Family § 7660, Comment Overview--Termination Of Parental Rights in Adoption Proceedings.

Treatises and Practice Aids

Witkin, California Summary 10th Constitutional Law § 776, Right to Withhold Consent to Adoption.

Witkin, California Summary 10th Parent and Child § 17, Development Of Law.

Witkin, California Summary 10th Parent and Child § 46, in General.

Witkin, California Summary 10th Parent and Child § 48, Where No Presumption Applies.

Witkin, California Summary 10th Parent and Child § 61, Notice Of Adoption Proceeding.

Witkin, California Summary 10th Parent and Child § 63, in General.

Witkin, California Summary 10th Parent and Child § 79, Adoption Information.

Witkin, California Summary 10th Parent and Child § 308, Dependency Proceeding Distinguished.

Witkin, California Summary 10th Parent and Child § 680, Statutory Procedure is Exclusive.

§ 7660.5. Waiver of right to notice by presumed father; adoption proceedings under Indian Child Welfare Act

Notwithstanding any other provision of law, a presumed father may waive the right to notice of any adoption proceeding by executing a form developed by the department before an authorized representative of the department, an authorized representative of a licensed public or private adoption agency, or a notary public or other person authorized to perform notarial acts. The waiver of notice form may be validly executed before or after the birth of the child, and once signed no notice, relinquishment for, or consent to adoption of the child shall be required from the father for the adoption to proceed. This shall be a voluntary and informed waiver without undue influence. If the child is an Indian child as defined under the Indian Child Welfare Act (ICWA), [1] any waiver of consent by an Indian presumed father shall be executed in accordance with the requirements for voluntary adoptions set forth in Section 1913 of Title 25 of the United States Code. The waiver shall not affect the rights of any known federally recognized Indian tribe or tribes from which the child or the presumed father may be descended to notification of, or participation in, adoption proceedings as provided by the ICWA. Notice that the waiver has been executed shall be given to any known federally recognized Indian tribe or tribes from which the child or the presumed father may be descended, as required by the ICWA. *(Added by Stats.2004, c. 858 (S.B.1357), § 1. Amended by Stats.2008, c. 534 (S.B.1726), § 4.)*

[1] See 25 U.S.C.A. § 1901 et seq.

Research References

Treatises and Practice Aids

Witkin, California Summary 10th Parent and Child § 61, Notice Of Adoption Proceeding.

§ 7661. Relinquishment or consent by other parent; notice to and rights of mother

If the other parent relinquishes for or consents to, or proposes to relinquish for or consent to, the adoption of a child, the mother shall be given notice of the adoption proceeding and have the rights provided under Part 2 (commencing with Section 8600) of Division 13, unless the mother's relationship to the child has been previously terminated by a court or the mother has voluntarily relinquished for or consented to the adoption of the child. *(Stats.1992, c. 162 (A.B.2650), § 10, operative Jan. 1, 1994. Amended by Stats.2013, c. 510 (A.B.1403), § 16.)*

Law Revision Commission Comments

Enactment [Revised Comment]

Section 7661 continues former Civil Code Section 7017(a)(2) without substantive change. There is no comparable provision in the Uniform Parentage Act (1973). [23 Cal.L.Rev.Comm. Reports 1 (1993)].

Research References

Forms

West's California Code Forms, Family § 7660, Comment Overview--Termination Of Parental Rights in Adoption Proceedings.

Treatises and Practice Aids

Witkin, California Summary 10th Parent and Child § 61, Notice Of Adoption Proceeding.

§ 7662. Filing of petition to terminate parental rights of alleged father; conditions

(a) If a mother relinquishes for or consents to, or proposes to relinquish for or consent to, the adoption of a child, or if a child otherwise becomes the subject of an adoption proceeding, the agency or person to whom the child has been or is to be relinquished, or the mother or the person having physical or legal custody of the child, or the prospective adoptive parent, shall file a petition to terminate the parental rights of the alleged father, unless one of the following occurs:

(1) The alleged father's relationship to the child has been previously terminated or determined not to exist by a court.

(2) The alleged father has been served as prescribed in Section 7666 with a written notice alleging that he is or could be the biological father of the child to be adopted or placed for adoption and has failed to bring an action for the purpose of declaring the existence of the father and child relationship pursuant to subdivision (c) of Section 7630 within 30 days of service of the notice or the birth of the child, whichever is later.

(3) The alleged father has executed a written form developed by the department to waive notice, to deny his paternity, relinquish the child for adoption, or consent to the adoption of the child.

(b) The alleged father may validly execute a waiver or denial of paternity before or after the birth of the child, and, once signed, no notice of, relinquishment for, or consent to adoption of the child shall be required from the alleged father for the adoption to proceed.

(c) Except as provided in this subdivision and subdivision (d), all proceedings affecting a child, including proceedings under Divisions 8 (commencing with Section 3000) to 11 (commencing with Section 6500), inclusive, Part 1 (commencing with Section 7500) to Part 3 (commencing with Section 7600), inclusive, of this division, and Part 1 (commencing with Section 1400), Part 2 (commencing with Section 1500), and Part 4 (commencing with Section 2100) of Division 4 of the Probate Code, and any motion or petition for custody or visitation filed in a proceeding under this part, shall be stayed. The petition to terminate parental rights under this section is the only matter that may be heard during the stay until the court issues a final ruling on the petition.

(d) This section does not limit the jurisdiction of the court pursuant to Part 3 (commencing with Section 6240) and Part 4 (commencing with Section 6300) of Division 10 with respect to domestic violence orders, or pursuant to Article 6 (commencing with Section 300) of Chapter 2 of Part 1 of Division 2 of the Welfare and Institutions Code with respect to dependency proceedings. *(Stats.1992, c. 162 (A.B.2650), § 10, operative Jan. 1, 1994. Amended by Stats.2000, c. 937 (A.B.2433), § 2; Stats.2003, c. 251 (S.B.182), § 3; Stats.2008, c. 534 (S.B.1726), § 5; Stats.2010, c. 588 (A.B.2020), § 3; Stats.2013, c. 510 (A.B.1403), § 17; Stats.2014, c. 763 (A.B. 1701), § 2, eff. Jan. 1, 2015.)*

Law Revision Commission Comments

Enactment [Revised Comment]

Section 7662 continues former Civil Code Section 7017(b) without substantive change. This section replaces Section 25(a) of the Uniform Parentage Act (1973). The reference to the "superior" court has been omitted as surplus. See Section 200 (jurisdiction in superior court). In the introductory part of this section, the reference to "prior" law has been omitted. [23 Cal.L.Rev.Comm. Reports 1 (1993)].

Commentary

The 60-day period for filing a notice of appeal from a trial court order made under this section runs from the date the trial court's written ruling was served on the parties. *Adoption of Reed H., 3 Cal.App.5th 76, 206 Cal.Rptr.3d 905 (2016), review denied.*

Research References

Forms

California Transactions Forms--Family Law § 6:8, Consent for Adoption Of Unmarried Minor.
California Transactions Forms--Family Law § 6:11, Initiating Proceeding Under Uniform Parentage Act [Fam C §§ 7600 to 7730].
California Transactions Forms--Family Law § 6:40, Structuring the Adoption.
California Transactions Forms--Family Law § 6:69, Transmittal Letter to Department Of Social Services.
California Transactions Forms--Family Law § 6:70, Appearance, Waiver Of Notice, and Statement Regarding Paternity.
California Transactions Forms--Family Law § 6:71, Notice Of Alleged Paternity.
California Transactions Forms--Family Law § 6:72, Petition to Terminate Parental Rights Of Alleged Father.
California Transactions Forms--Family Law § 6:74, Petition to Terminate Parental Rights Of Alleged Father Served With Notice Of Alleged Paternity Without Timely Response.
California Transactions Forms--Family Law § 6:75, Order Terminating Parental Rights Of Alleged Father Served With Notice Of Alleged Paternity Without Timely Response.
California Transactions Forms--Family Law § 6:76, Ex Parte Application for Order to Terminate Parental Rights Of Alleged Father Who Waived Notice or Denied Paternity.
California Transactions Forms--Family Law § 6:77, Order Terminating Parental Rights Of Alleged Father Who Waived Notice.
West's California Code Forms, Family § 7660, Comment Overview--Termination Of Parental Rights in Adoption Proceedings.

Treatises and Practice Aids

Witkin, California Summary 10th Parent and Child § 48, Where No Presumption Applies.
Witkin, California Summary 10th Parent and Child § 63, in General.
Witkin, California Summary 10th Parent and Child § 64, Where Mother Does Not Consent to Adoption.
Witkin, California Summary 10th Parent and Child § 67, Thirty-Day Requirement.

Witkin, California Summary 10th Parent and Child § 68, Constitutional Rights Of Natural Father.

Witkin, California Summary 10th Parent and Child § 129, in General.

§ 7663. Inquiry to identify all alleged fathers and presumed parents; report

(a) In an effort to identify all alleged fathers and presumed parents, the court shall cause inquiry to be made of the mother and any other appropriate person by one of the following:

(1) The State Department of Social Services.

(2) A licensed county adoption agency.

(3) The licensed adoption agency to which the child is to be relinquished.

(4) In the case of a stepparent adoption, the licensed clinical social worker or licensed marriage and family therapist who is performing the investigation pursuant to Section 9001, if applicable. In the case of a stepparent adoption in which no licensed clinical social worker or licensed marriage and family therapist is performing the investigation pursuant to Section 9001, the board of supervisors may assign those inquiries to a licensed county adoption agency, the county department designated by the board of supervisors to administer the public social services program, or the county probation department.

(b) The inquiry shall include all of the following:

(1) Whether the mother was married at the time of conception of the child or at any time thereafter.

(2) Whether the mother was cohabiting with a man at the time of conception or birth of the child.

(3) Whether the mother has received support payments or promises of support with respect to the child or in connection with her pregnancy.

(4) Whether any person has formally or informally acknowledged or declared his or her possible parentage of the child.

(5) The names and whereabouts, if known, of every person presumed or man alleged to be the parent of the child, and the efforts made to give notice of the proposed adoption to each person identified.

(c) The agency that completes the inquiry shall file a written report of the findings with the court. *(Stats.1992, c. 162 (A.B.2650), § 10, operative Jan. 1, 1994. Amended by Stats.2011, c. 462 (A.B.687), § 1; Stats.2012, c. 638 (A.B. 1757), § 1; Stats.2013, c. 510 (A.B.1403), § 18.)*

Law Revision Commission Comments

Enactment [Revised Comment]

Section 7663 continues former Civil Code Section 7017(c) without substantive change. This section is similar to Section 25(b) of the Uniform Parentage Act (1973). [23 Cal.L.Rev.Comm. Reports 1 (1993)].

Research References

Forms

California Transactions Forms--Family Law § 6:78, Petition to Terminate Parental Rights Of Alleged Father Who Cannot be Located.

Treatises and Practice Aids

Witkin, California Summary 10th Parent and Child § 62, Inquiry to Identify Natural Father.

§ 7664. Identification of biological father or possible fathers; notice of proceedings; default; claim of parental rights; determination and order concerning parental rights

(a) If, after the inquiry, the biological father is identified to the satisfaction of the court, or if more than one man is identified as a possible biological father, notice of the proceeding shall be given in accordance with Section 7666. If any alleged biological father fails to appear or, if appearing, fails to claim parental rights, his parental rights with reference to the child shall be terminated.

(b) If the biological father or a man representing himself to be the biological father claims parental rights, the court shall determine if he is the biological father. The court shall then determine if it is in the best interest of the child that the biological father retain his parental rights, or that an adoption of the child be allowed to proceed. The court, in making that determination, may consider all relevant evidence, including the efforts made by the biological father to obtain custody, the age and prior placement of the child, and the effects of a change of placement on the child.

(c) If the court finds that it is in the best interest of the child that the biological father should be allowed to retain his parental rights, the court shall order that his consent is necessary for an adoption. If the court finds that the man claiming parental rights is not the biological father, or that if he is the biological father it is in the child's best interest that an adoption be allowed to proceed, the court shall order that the consent of that man is not required for an adoption. This finding terminates all parental rights and responsibilities with respect to the child. *(Stats.1992, c. 162 (A.B.2650), § 10, operative Jan. 1, 1994. Amended by Stats.2011, c. 462 (A.B.687), § 2; Stats.2013, c. 510 (A.B.1403), § 19.)*

Law Revision Commission Comments

Enactment [Revised Comment]

Section 7664 continues former Civil Code Section 7017(d) without substantive change. This section replaces Section 25(c) of the Uniform Parentage Act (1973). In subdivision (b), a reference to Section 3041 has been substituted for the broader reference to former Civil Code Section 4600. This is not a substantive change, since the relevant part of the former section is continued in Section 3041. See also Section 3011 (factors in determining best interest of child). [23 Cal.L.Rev.Comm. Reports 1 (1993)].

Commentary

Subsection (b) is unconstitutional insofar as it would terminate the parental rights of a natural father willing and able to assume custody merely upon a showing of the "best interest of the child." *Adoption of Kelsey S., 1 Cal.4th 816, 4 Cal.Rptr.2d 615 (1992)*. See Section 7611, Commentary.

Adoption of Alexander M., 94 Cal.App.4th 430, 114 Cal.Rptr.2d 218 (2001), holds that a biological father may establish paternity under § 7631, but whether an adoption should proceed or the biological father should retain his parental rights shall be decided under the best interests of the child standard (subsection (b)), unless the father proves that he has demonstrated a full commitment to parental responsibilities in accordance with *Kelsey S.,* in which case the father shall be awarded custody unless such award would be detrimental to the child under § 3041.

Adoption of Emilio G., 235 Cal.App.4th 1133, 185 Cal.Rptr.3d 605 (2015), affirmed a trial court order determining that a biological father who emotionally and physically abused the child's mother during her pregnancy, evidencing lack of concern for the health of his unborn child, did not qualify as a *Kelsey S.* father, and that it was in the child's best interest that the father's parental rights be terminated in order that the child might be adopted by his prospective adoptive parents.

Research References

Forms

California Transactions Forms--Family Law § 6:3, Definitions.
California Transactions Forms--Family Law § 6:8, Consent for Adoption Of Unmarried Minor.
California Transactions Forms--Family Law § 6:11, Initiating Proceeding Under Uniform Parentage Act [Fam C §§ 7600 to 7730].
California Transactions Forms--Family Law § 6:40, Structuring the Adoption.
California Transactions Forms--Family Law § 6:72, Petition to Terminate Parental Rights Of Alleged Father.
California Transactions Forms--Family Law § 6:74, Petition to Terminate Parental Rights Of Alleged Father Served With Notice Of Alleged Paternity Without Timely Response.
California Transactions Forms--Family Law § 6:76, Ex Parte Application for Order to Terminate Parental Rights Of Alleged Father Who Waived Notice or Denied Paternity.
California Transactions Forms--Family Law § 6:77, Order Terminating Parental Rights Of Alleged Father Who Waived Notice.

Treatises and Practice Aids

Witkin, California Summary 10th Parent and Child § 48, Where No Presumption Applies.
Witkin, California Summary 10th Parent and Child § 66, Statutory Requirements.
Witkin, California Summary 10th Parent and Child § 68, Constitutional Rights Of Natural Father.

§ 7665. Termination of unknown biological father's parental rights; entry of order

If, after the inquiry, the court is unable to identify the biological father or any possible biological father and no person has appeared claiming to be the biological father and claiming custodial rights, the court shall enter an order terminating the unknown biological father's parental rights with reference to the child. *(Stats.1992, c. 162 (A.B.2650), § 10, operative Jan. 1, 1994. Amended by Stats.2013, c. 510 (A.B.1403), § 20.)*

Law Revision Commission Comments

Enactment [Revised Comment]

Section 7665 continues former Civil Code Section 7017(e) without change. This section is the same as the first sentence of Section 25(d) of the Uniform Parentage Act (1973). [23 Cal.L.Rev.Comm. Reports 1 (1993)].

Research References

Forms

California Transactions Forms--Family Law § 6:78, Petition to Terminate Parental Rights Of Alleged Father Who Cannot be Located.

West's California Code Forms, Family § 7660, Comment Overview--Termination Of Parental Rights in Adoption Proceedings.

Treatises and Practice Aids

Witkin, California Summary 10th Parent and Child § 62, Inquiry to Identify Natural Father.

§ 7666. Notice of proceedings

(a) Except as provided in subdivision (b), notice of the proceeding shall be given to every person identified as the biological father or a possible biological father in accordance with the Code of Civil Procedure for the service of process in a civil action in this state at least 10 days before the date of the proceeding, except that publication or posting of the notice of the proceeding is not required, and service on the parent or guardian of a biological father or possible biological father who is a minor is not required unless the minor has previously provided written authorization to serve his or her parent or guardian. Proof of giving the notice shall be filed with the court before the petition is heard.

(b) Notice to a man identified as or alleged to be the biological father shall not be required, and the court shall issue an order dispensing with notice to him, under any of the following circumstances:

(1) The relationship to the child has been previously terminated or determined not to exist by a court.

(2) The alleged father has executed a written form to waive notice, deny his paternity, relinquish the child for adoption, or consent to the adoption of the child.

(3) The whereabouts or identity of the alleged father are unknown or cannot be ascertained.

(4) The alleged father has been served with written notice of his alleged paternity and the proposed adoption, and he has failed to bring an action pursuant to subdivision (c) of Section 7630 within 30 days of service of the notice or the birth of the child, whichever is later. *(Stats.1992, c. 162 (A.B.2650), § 10, operative Jan. 1, 1994. Amended by Stats. 2002, c. 260 (S.B.1512), § 1; Stats.2011, c. 462 (A.B.687), § 3; Stats.2013, c. 510 (A.B.1403), § 21; Stats.2014, c. 763 (A.B. 1701), § 3, eff. Jan. 1, 2015.)*

Law Revision Commission Comments

Enactment [Revised Comment]

Section 7666 continues former Civil Code Section 7017(f) without substantive change. This section is similar to Section 25(e) of the Uniform Parentage Act (1973). [23 Cal.L.Rev.Comm. Reports 1 (1993)].

Research References

Forms

California Transactions Forms--Family Law § 6:8, Consent for Adoption Of Unmarried Minor.
California Transactions Forms--Family Law § 6:40, Structuring the Adoption.
California Transactions Forms--Family Law § 6:42, Rights Of Birth Father.
California Transactions Forms--Family Law § 6:78, Petition to Terminate Parental Rights Of Alleged Father Who Cannot be Located.
California Transactions Forms--Family Law § 6:79, Order Terminating Parental Rights Of Alleged Father Who Cannot be Located.

West's California Code Forms, Family § 7630, Comment Overview--Determining Parent and Child Relationship.

West's California Code Forms, Family § 7660, Comment Overview--Termination Of Parental Rights in Adoption Proceedings.

Treatises and Practice Aids

Witkin, California Summary 10th Parent and Child § 48, Where No Presumption Applies.

Witkin, California Summary 10th Parent and Child § 49, Joinder and Alignment Of Parties.

Witkin, California Summary 10th Parent and Child § 62, Inquiry to Identify Natural Father.

Witkin, California Summary 10th Parent and Child § 63, in General.

Witkin, California Summary 10th Parent and Child § 66, Statutory Requirements.

§ 7667. Time of hearing; ex parte orders terminating parental rights

(a) Notwithstanding any other provision of law, an action to terminate the parental rights of an alleged father of a child as specified in this part shall be set for hearing not more than 45 days after filing of the petition, except as provided in subdivision (c).

(b) The matter so set shall have precedence over all other civil matters on the date set for trial, except an action to terminate parental rights pursuant to Part 4 (commencing with Section 7800).

(c) The court may dispense with a hearing and issue an ex parte order terminating parental rights if any of the following applies:

(1) The identity or whereabouts of the alleged father are unknown.

(2) The alleged father has validly executed a waiver of the right to notice or a denial of paternity.

(3) The alleged father has been served with written notice of his alleged paternity and the proposed adoption, and he has failed to bring an action pursuant to subdivision (c) of Section 7630 within 30 days of service of the notice or the birth of the child, whichever is later. *(Stats.1992, c. 162 (A.B.2650), § 10, operative Jan. 1, 1994. Amended by Stats. 2010, c. 588 (A.B.2020), § 4; Stats.2011, c. 462 (A.B.687), § 4; Stats.2013, c. 510 (A.B.1403), § 22.)*

Law Revision Commission Comments

Enactment [Revised Comment]

Section 7667 continues without substantive change subdivision (a) and the first sentence of subdivision (b) of former Civil Code Section 7017.2. There is no comparable provision in the Uniform Parentage Act (1973). In subdivision (a), a reference to this part has been substituted for the narrower reference to former Civil Code Section 7017. This is not a substantive change. In subdivision (b), a reference to Part 4 (commencing with Section 7800) has been substituted for the narrower reference to former Civil Code Section 232. This is not a substantive change. [23 Cal.L.Rev.Comm. Reports 1 (1993)].

Research References

Forms

California Transactions Forms--Family Law § 6:11, Initiating Proceeding Under Uniform Parentage Act [Fam C §§ 7600 to 7730].

California Transactions Forms--Family Law § 6:72, Petition to Terminate Parental Rights Of Alleged Father.

Treatises and Practice Aids

Witkin, California Summary 10th Parent and Child § 69, Hearing and Order.

§ 7668. Continuance of proceedings; purpose

(a) The court may continue the proceedings for not more than 30 days as necessary to appoint counsel and to enable counsel to prepare for the case adequately or for other good cause.

(b) In order to obtain an order for a continuance of the hearing, written notice shall be filed within two court days of the date set for the hearing, together with affidavits or declarations detailing specific facts showing that a continuance is necessary, unless the court for good cause entertains an oral motion for continuance.

(c) Continuances shall be granted only upon a showing of good cause. Neither a stipulation between counsel nor the convenience of the parties is in and of itself a good cause.

(d) A continuance shall be granted only for that period of time shown to be necessary by the evidence considered at the hearing on the motion. If a continuance is granted, the facts proven which require the continuance shall be entered upon the minutes of the court. *(Stats.1992, c. 162 (A.B.2650), § 10, operative Jan. 1, 1994.)*

Law Revision Commission Comments

Enactment [Revised Comment]

Section 7668 continues without substantive change the last sentence of subdivision (b) and subdivision (c) of former Civil Code Section 7017.2. There is no comparable provision in the Uniform Parentage Act (1973). [23 Cal.L.Rev.Comm. Reports 1 (1993)].

Research References

Treatises and Practice Aids

Witkin, California Summary 10th Parent and Child § 69, Hearing and Order.

§ 7669. Order requiring or dispensing with alleged father's consent for adoption; appeal from order and judgment

(a) An order requiring or dispensing with an alleged father's consent for the adoption of a child may be appealed from in the same manner as an order of the juvenile court declaring a person to be a ward of the juvenile court and is conclusive and binding upon the alleged father.

(b) After making the order, the court has no power to set aside, change, or modify that order.

(c) Nothing in this section limits the right to appeal from the order and judgment. *(Stats.1992, c. 162 (A.B.2650), § 10, operative Jan. 1, 1994. Amended by Stats.2002, c. 260 (S.B.1512), § 2; Stats.2003, c. 251 (S.B.182), § 4; Stats.2013, c. 510 (A.B.1403), § 23.)*

Law Revision Commission Comments

Enactment [Revised Comment]

Section 7669 continues former Civil Code Section 7017(g) without substantive change. This section replaces the second sentence of Section 25(d) of the Uniform Parentage Act (1973). [23 Cal.L.Rev. Comm. Reports 1 (1993)].

Research References

Forms

West's California Code Forms, Family § 7660, Comment Overview--Termination Of Parental Rights in Adoption Proceedings.

Treatises and Practice Aids

Witkin, California Summary 10th Parent and Child § 69, Hearing and Order.

§ 7670. Filing fee

There shall be no filing fee charged for a petition filed pursuant to Section 7662. *(Stats.1992, c. 162 (A.B.2650), § 10, operative Jan. 1, 1994.)*

Law Revision Commission Comments

Enactment [Revised Comment]

Section 7670 continues former Civil Code Section 7017.1 without substantive change. There is no comparable provision in the Uniform Parentage Act (1973). [23 Cal.L.Rev.Comm. Reports 1 (1993)].

Research References

Forms

California Transactions Forms--Family Law § 6:11, Initiating Proceeding Under Uniform Parentage Act [Fam C §§ 7600 to 7730].

California Transactions Forms--Family Law § 6:71, Notice Of Alleged Paternity.

California Transactions Forms--Family Law § 6:72, Petition to Terminate Parental Rights Of Alleged Father.

Treatises and Practice Aids

Witkin, California Summary 10th Parent and Child § 63, in General.

§ 7671. Multiple fathers or multiple children; single petition to terminate parental rights

A single petition may be filed pursuant to Section 7662 to terminate the parental rights of the alleged father or fathers of two or more biological siblings or to terminate the parental rights of two or more alleged fathers of the same child. A petition filed in accordance with this section may be granted in whole or in part in accordance with the procedures set forth in this chapter. The court shall retain discretion to bifurcate any case in which the petition was filed in accordance with this section, and shall do so whenever it is necessary to protect the interests of a party or a child who is the subject of the proceeding. *(Added by Stats.2014, c. 763 (A.B.1701), § 4, eff. Jan. 1, 2015.)*

Research References

Forms

California Transactions Forms--Family Law § 6:8, Consent for Adoption Of Unmarried Minor.

California Transactions Forms--Family Law § 6:11, Initiating Proceeding Under Uniform Parentage Act [Fam C §§ 7600 to 7730].

California Transactions Forms--Family Law § 6:40, Structuring the Adoption.

California Transactions Forms--Family Law § 6:72, Petition to Terminate Parental Rights Of Alleged Father.

Treatises and Practice Aids

Witkin, California Summary 10th Parent and Child § 63, in General.

CHAPTER 6. PROTECTIVE AND RESTRAINING ORDERS

ARTICLE 1. ORDERS IN SUMMONS

§ 7700. Temporary restraining orders contained in summons

In addition to the contents required by Section 412.20 of the Code of Civil Procedure, in a proceeding under this part the summons shall contain a temporary restraining order restraining all parties, without the prior written consent of the other party or an order of the court, from removing from the state any minor child for whom the proceeding seeks to establish a parent and child relationship. *(Added by Stats. 1993, c. 219 (A.B.1500), § 179.6.)*

Law Revision Commission Comments

Enactment [Revised Comment]

Section 7700 continues without substantive change the first sentence and the last part of the last sentence of the first paragraph of former Code of Civil Procedure Section 412.21(b). The reference to "children" has been omitted as surplus. See Section 10 (singular includes plural). For general provisions governing restraining orders in summons, see Sections 231–235. [23 Cal.L.Rev.Comm. Reports 1 (1993)].

Commentary

A mother who filed a California petition to determine a parental relationship after she had relocated with her child to another state did not violate this section's restraining order prohibiting a party from removing a child from the state without the other party's consent or a court order. *Sarah B. v. Floyd B., 159 Cal.App.4th 938, 71 Cal.Rptr.3d 923 (2008).*

Research References

Forms

West's California Judicial Council Forms FL-110, Summons (Family Law).

West's California Judicial Council Forms FL-210, Summons (Percentage - Custody and Support).

Treatises and Practice Aids

Witkin, California Summary 10th Husband and Wife § 6, Order in Summons.

Witkin, California Summary 10th Parent and Child § 17, Development Of Law.

Witkin, California Summary 10th Parent and Child § 51, Protective Orders.

ARTICLE 2. EX PARTE ORDERS

§ 7710. Issuance of orders

During the pendency of a proceeding under this part, on application of a party in the manner provided by Part 4 (commencing with Section 240) of Division 2, the court may issue ex parte a protective order as defined in Section 6218 and any other order as provided in Article 1 (commencing with Section 6320) of Chapter 2 of Part 4 of Division 10. *(Added by Stats.1993, c. 219 (A.B.1500), § 179.6.)*

Law Revision Commission Comments

Enactment [Revised Comment]

Section 7710 is new. This section provides a reference to the article in Division 10 (Domestic Violence Prevention Act) that contains the substantive provisions for the issuance of ex parte restraining orders. See Section 6200 Comment (consolidation of substantive provisions regarding issuance of restraining orders intended to prevent domestic violence). [23 Cal.L.Rev.Comm. Reports 1 (1993)].

Research References

Forms

West's California Judicial Council Forms FL-303, Declaration Regarding Notice and Service Of Request for Temporary Emergency (Ex Parte) Orders.

Treatises and Practice Aids

Witkin, California Summary 10th Husband and Wife § 12B, (New) Amount Of Filing Fees.

Witkin, California Summary 10th Parent and Child § 51, Protective Orders.

Witkin, California Summary 10th Parent and Child § 271, Temporary Custody During Pendency Of Proceeding.

ARTICLE 3. ORDERS AFTER NOTICE AND HEARING

§ 7720. Protective and restraining orders; issuance after notice and hearing

(a) After notice and a hearing, the court may issue a protective order as defined in Section 6218 and any other restraining order as provided in Article 2 (commencing with Section 6340) of Chapter 2 of Part 4 of Division 10.

(b) The court may not issue a mutual protective order pursuant to subdivision (a) unless it meets the requirements of Section 6305. *(Added by Stats.1993, c. 219 (A.B.1500), § 179.6. Amended by Stats.1995, c. 246 (S.B.591), § 3.)*

Law Revision Commission Comments

Enactment [Revised Comment]

Section 7720 is new. This section provides a reference to the article in Division 10 (Domestic Violence Prevention Act) that contains the substantive provisions for the issuance of restraining orders after notice and hearing. See Section 6200 Comment (consolidation of substantive provisions regarding issuance of restraining orders intended to prevent domestic violence).

The former provisions for issuance or orders after notice and hearing in a proceeding under the Uniform Parentage Act did not provide for issuance of the orders described in Sections 6343 (counseling) or 6344 (attorney's fees and costs). However, the Judicial Council form used for orders after hearing applies to proceedings under the Uniform Parentage Act and allows for attorney's fees and costs. See Cal. R. Ct. 1296.31 (rev. Jan. 1, 1992) (findings and order after hearing). Expanding the court's authority to issue a counseling order in an action pursuant to the Uniform Parentage Act resolves an inconsistency, since the counseling order could be obtained by unmarried parties under the Domestic Violence Prevention Act. [23 Cal.L.Rev.Comm. Reports 1 (1993)].

Research References

Treatises and Practice Aids

Witkin, California Summary 10th Husband and Wife § 12B, (New) Amount Of Filing Fees.

Witkin, California Summary 10th Parent and Child § 51, Protective Orders.

Witkin, California Summary 10th Parent and Child § 271, Temporary Custody During Pendency Of Proceeding.

ARTICLE 4. ORDERS INCLUDED IN JUDGMENT

§ 7730. Protective and restraining orders; inclusion in judgment

A judgment entered in a proceeding under this part may include a protective order as defined in Section 6218 and any other restraining order as provided in Article 3 (commencing with Section 6360) of Chapter 2 of Part 4 of Division 10. *(Added by Stats.1993, c. 219 (A.B.1500), § 179.6.)*

Law Revision Commission Comments

Enactment [Revised Comment]

Section 7730 is new. This section provides a reference to the chapter in Division 10 (Domestic Violence Prevention Act) that contains the substantive provisions for the inclusion of restraining orders in a judgment. See Section 6200 Comment (consolidation of substantive provisions regarding issuance of restraining orders to prevent domestic violence). [23 Cal.L.Rev.Comm. Reports 1 (1993)].

Research References

Forms

California Transactions Forms--Family Law § 6:2, Governing Law.

California Transactions Forms--Family Law § 6:3, Definitions.

California Transactions Forms--Family Law § 6:10, Initiating Proceeding Under Fam. Code, §§ 7800 et seq.

Treatises and Practice Aids

Witkin, California Summary 10th Husband and Wife § 12B, (New) Amount Of Filing Fees.

Witkin, California Summary 10th Parent and Child § 51, Protective Orders.

Part 4

FREEDOM FROM PARENTAL CUSTODY AND CONTROL

CHAPTER 1. GENERAL PROVISIONS

§ 7800. Purpose of part

The purpose of this part is to serve the welfare and best interest of a child by providing the stability and security of an adoptive home when those conditions are otherwise missing from the child's life. *(Stats.1992, c. 162 (A.B.2650), § 10, operative Jan. 1, 1994.)*

Law Revision Commission Comments

Enactment [Revised Comment]

Section 7800 continues the first sentence of former Civil Code Section 232.6 without substantive change. [23 Cal.L.Rev.Comm. Reports 1 (1993)].

Commentary

The "intent to abandon" a child, for purposes of section 7822, is intent to abandon for the periods specified in that section, not intent to abandon forever. *Adoption of Allison C., 164 Cal.App.4th 1004, 79 Cal.Rptr.3d 743 (2008). Allison C.* reasons that the purpose of this part is to protect a child's interests by providing the stability and security of an adoptive home. That purpose would be defeated if the statute were interpreted to require intent to abandon the child forever.

Compliance with the notice provision of the Indian Child Welfare Act (ICWA), 25 U.S.C.A. § 1912, is required in a parental rights termination proceeding under this part even though the "existing Indian family doctrine" may ultimately render the ICWA inapplicable. *In re Suzanna L., 104 Cal.App.4th 223, 127 Cal.Rptr.2d 860 (2002)*. For discussion of the "existing Indian family doctrine," see Commentary to 25 U.S.C.A. § 1913.

Research References

Forms

California Transactions Forms--Family Law § 6:10, Initiating Proceeding Under Fam. Code, §§ 7800 et seq.

California Transactions Forms--Family Law § 7:39, Adoption and Termination Of Parental Rights.

West's California Code Forms, Probate § 1510 Form 1, Petition for Appointment Of Guardian Of Estate Of Minor--Judicial Council Form GC-210.

Treatises and Practice Aids

Witkin, California Summary 10th Parent and Child § 12, Parental or Marital Rights Of Prisoners.

Witkin, California Summary 10th Parent and Child § 46, in General.

Witkin, California Summary 10th Parent and Child § 60, Action to Determine Mother and Child Relationship.

Witkin, California Summary 10th Parent and Child § 64, Where Mother Does Not Consent to Adoption.

Witkin, California Summary 10th Parent and Child § 69, Hearing and Order.

Witkin, California Summary 10th Parent and Child § 79, Adoption Information.

Witkin, California Summary 10th Parent and Child § 87, Private Adoptions.

Witkin, California Summary 10th Parent and Child § 307, Nature Of Action.

Witkin, California Summary 10th Parent and Child § 308, Dependency Proceeding Distinguished.

Witkin, California Summary 10th Parent and Child § 311, Other Proceedings Stayed.

Witkin, California Summary 10th Parent and Child § 320, Statutory Ground.

Witkin, California Summary 10th Parent and Child § 331, Venue, Petition, and Investigation.

Witkin, California Summary 10th Parent and Child § 346, Detriment.

Witkin, California Summary 10th Parent and Child § 355, Review on Appeal.

Witkin, California Summary 10th Parent and Child § 356, Change in Circumstances Pending Appeal.

Witkin, California Summary 10th Parent and Child § 424, Termination on Contingency or Other Event.

Witkin, California Summary 10th Parent and Child § 520, Jurisdiction.

Witkin, California Summary 10th Parent and Child § 580, Right to Competent Counsel.

Witkin, California Summary 10th Parent and Child § 667, Due Process Attack on Decree.

Witkin, California Summary 10th Parent and Child § 709, in General.

Witkin, California Summary 10th Parent and Child § 711, Expedited Appeal.

§ 7801. Liberal construction

This part shall be liberally construed to serve and protect the interests and welfare of the child. *(Stats.1992, c. 162 (A.B.2650), § 10, operative Jan. 1, 1994.)*

Law Revision Commission Comments

Enactment [Revised Comment]

Section 7801 continues the first sentence of former Civil Code Section 232.5 without substantive change. [23 Cal.L.Rev.Comm. Reports 1 (1993)].

Research References

Treatises and Practice Aids

Witkin, California Summary 10th Parent and Child § 307, Nature Of Action.

Witkin, California Summary 10th Parent and Child § 312, Statutory Ground.

§ 7802. Proceeding for declaration of freedom from parental custody and control

A proceeding may be brought under this part for the purpose of having a minor child declared free from the custody and control of either or both parents. *(Stats.1992, c. 162 (A.B.2650), § 10, operative Jan. 1, 1994.)*

Law Revision Commission Comments

Enactment [Revised Comment]

Section 7802 continues without substantive change the first part of the first sentence of former Civil Code Section 232(a). A reference to "proceeding" has been substituted for the former reference to "action." This is not a substantive change. A reference to "minor" child has been substituted for "child under the age of 18 years." This is not a substantive change. See Section 6500 (minor is individual under 18). See also Sections 7820–7829 (circumstances where proceeding may be brought).

As noted in the Comments to sections in this part, references to "child" have been substituted for the former references to a "minor" or "minor person." Formerly, the words "child" and "minor" were used interchangeably. Nevertheless, as provided in this section, only a minor child (one under 18 years of age) can be declared free from the custody and control of either or both of the child's parents. See also Section 7820 (proceeding to declare minor free from parental custody and control). [23 Cal.L.Rev.Comm. Reports 1 (1993)].

Commentary

Compliance with the notice provision of the Indian Child Welfare Act (ICWA), 25 U.S.C.A. § 1912, is required in a parental rights termination proceeding under this part even though the "existing Indian family doctrine" may ultimately render the ICWA inapplicable. *In re Suzanna L., 104 Cal.App.4th 223, 127 Cal.Rptr.2d 860 (2002)*. For discussion of the "existing Indian family doctrine," see Commentary to 25 U.S.C.A. § 1913.

Research References

Treatises and Practice Aids

Witkin, California Summary 10th Parent and Child § 64, Where Mother Does Not Consent to Adoption.

Witkin, California Summary 10th Parent and Child § 225, Circumstances Warranting Denial.

Witkin, California Summary 10th Parent and Child § 267, Jurisdiction and Venue.

Witkin, California Summary 10th Parent and Child § 274, Counsel for Parent.

Witkin, California Summary 10th Parent and Child § 307, Nature Of Action.

§ 7803. Effect of declaration of freedom

A declaration of freedom from parental custody and control pursuant to this part terminates all parental rights and responsibilities with regard to the child. *(Stats.1992, c. 162 (A.B.2650), § 10, operative Jan. 1, 1994.)*

Law Revision Commission Comments

Enactment [Revised Comment]

Section 7803 continues the second sentence of former Civil Code Section 232.6 without substantive change. [23 Cal.L.Rev.Comm. Reports 1 (1993)].

Commentary

Similarly, an order terminating parental rights under Welfare and Institutions Code § 366.26 fully severs the parent-child relationship. Therefore, the juvenile court has no authority to order child support from a parent whose rights have been terminated. *County of Ventura v. Gonzalez, 88 Cal.App.4th 1120, 106 Cal.Rptr.2d 461 (2001)*. See also Family Code § 7803.

Research References

Forms

West's California Code Forms, Family § 7890, Comment Overview--Hearing and Subsequent Proceedings.

Treatises and Practice Aids

Witkin, California Summary 10th Parent and Child § 349, in General.

Witkin, California Summary 10th Parent and Child § 424, Termination on Contingency or Other Event.

§ 7804. Appointment of party to act in minor's behalf

In a proceeding under this part, the court may appoint a suitable party to act in behalf of the child and may order such further notice of the proceedings to be given as the court deems proper. *(Stats.1992, c. 162 (A.B.2650), § 10, operative Jan. 1, 1994.)*

Law Revision Commission Comments

Enactment [Revised Comment]

Section 7804 restates former Civil Code Section 237 without substantive change. The reference to "child" has been substituted for the former reference to "minor." This is not a substantive change. See Section 7802 Comment. [23 Cal.L.Rev.Comm. Reports 1 (1993)].

Research References

Treatises and Practice Aids

Witkin, California Summary 10th Parent and Child § 336, Statutory Rights.

§ 7805. Inspection of petitions, reports, and court records and briefs

(a) A petition filed in a proceeding under this part, or a report of the probation officer or county department designated by the board of supervisors to administer the public social services program filed in a proceeding under this part, may be inspected only by the following persons:

(1) Court personnel.

(2) The child who is the subject of the proceeding.

(3) The parents or guardian of the child.

(4) The attorneys for the parties.

(5) Any other person designated by the judge.

(b) In a proceeding before the court of appeal or Supreme Court to review a judgment or order entered in a proceeding under this part, the court record and briefs filed by the parties may be inspected only by the following persons:

(1) Court personnel.

(2) A party to the proceeding.

(3) The attorneys for the parties.

(4) Any other person designated by the presiding judge of the court before which the matter is pending.

(c) Notwithstanding any other provision of law, if it is believed that the welfare of the child will be promoted thereby, the court and the probation officer may furnish information, pertaining to a petition under this part, to any of the following:

(1) The State Department of Social Services.

(2) A county welfare department.

(3) A public welfare agency.

(4) A private welfare agency licensed by the State Department of Social Services. *(Stats.1992, c. 162 (A.B.2650), § 10, operative Jan. 1, 1994.)*

Law Revision Commission Comments

Enactment [Revised Comment]

Subdivisions (a) and (b) of Section 7805 continue former Civil Code Section 233.5 without substantive change. In subdivision (a), a reference to "child" has been substituted for the former reference to "minor." This is not a substantive change. See Section 7802 Comment. Subdivision (c) continues former Civil Code Section 233.6 without substantive change. The references to the "superior" court have been omitted as surplus. See Section 200 (jurisdiction in superior court). [23 Cal.L.Rev.Comm. Reports 1 (1993)].

Research References

Treatises and Practice Aids

Witkin, California Summary 10th Parent and Child § 331, Venue, Petition, and Investigation.

§ 7806. Filing fees

There shall be no filing fee charged for a proceeding brought under this part. *(Stats.1992, c. 162 (A.B.2650), § 10, operative Jan. 1, 1994.)*

Law Revision Commission Comments

Enactment [Revised Comment]

Section 7806 continues without substantive change the second sentence of the first paragraph of former Civil Code Section 233(a). A reference to "proceeding" has been substituted for the former reference to "action." This is not a substantive change. [23 Cal.L.Rev.Comm. Reports 1 (1993)].

Research References

Forms

West's California Code Forms, Family § 7840, Comment Overview--Freedom from Parental Control.

Treatises and Practice Aids

Witkin, California Summary 10th Parent and Child § 331, Venue, Petition, and Investigation.

§ 7807. Applicability of proceedings; stay of proceedings under specified statutory provisions

(a) Sections 3020, 3022, 3040 to 3043, inclusive, and 3409 do not apply in a proceeding under this part.

(b) Except as provided in this subdivision and subdivision (c), all proceedings affecting a child, including proceedings under Divisions 8 (commencing with Section 3000) to 11 (commencing with Section 6500), inclusive, Part 1 (commencing with Section 7500) to Part 3 (commencing with Section 7600), inclusive, of this division, and Part 1 (commencing with Section 1400), Part 2 (commencing with Section 1500), and Part 4 (commencing with Section 2100) of Division 4 of the Probate Code, and any motion or petition for custody or visitation filed in a proceeding under this part, shall be stayed. The petition to free the minor from parental custody and control under this section is the only matter that may be heard during the stay until the court issues a final ruling on the petition.

(c) This section does not limit the jurisdiction of the court pursuant to Part 3 (commencing with Section 6240) and Part 4 (commencing with Section 6300) of Division 10 with respect to domestic violence orders, or pursuant to Article 6 (commencing with Section 300) of Chapter 2 of Part 1 of Division 2 of the Welfare and Institutions Code with respect to dependency proceedings. *(Stats.1992, c. 162 (A.B.2650), § 10, operative Jan. 1, 1994. Amended by Stats.1993, c. 219 (A.B.1500), § 179.9; Stats.2002, c. 260 (S.B.1512), § 3; Stats. 2014, c. 763 (A.B.1701), § 5, eff. Jan. 1, 2015.)*

Law Revision Commission Comments

Enactment [Revised Comment]

Section 7807 continues former Civil Code Section 232(d) without substantive change. [23 Cal.L.Rev.Comm. Reports 1 (1993)].

Commentary

In re E.M., 228 Cal.App.4th 828, 175 Cal.Rptr.3d 711 (2014), holds a court may order temporary visitation for a father despite this section when it concludes that the mother and her new husband filed a section 7822 petition to terminate the father's parental rights solely for the purpose of delaying a hearing on the father's petition to modify existing custody and visitation orders.

Research References

Forms

West's California Code Forms, Family § 7841 Form 1, Petition for Freedom from Parental Control--Abandonment.

Treatises and Practice Aids

Witkin, California Summary 10th Parent and Child § 311, Other Proceedings Stayed.

Witkin, California Summary 10th Parent and Child § 312, Statutory Ground.

Witkin, California Summary 10th Parent and Child § 331, Venue, Petition, and Investigation.

Witkin, California Summary 10th Parent and Child § 346, Detriment.

Witkin, California Summary 10th Parent and Child § 363, Applicability Of Family Code Custody Provisions.

§ 7808. Application of part

This part does not apply to a minor adjudged a dependent child of the juvenile court pursuant to subdivision (c) of Section 360 of the Welfare and Institutions Code on and after January 1, 1989, during the period in which the minor is a dependent child of the court. For those minors, the exclusive means for the termination of parental rights are provided in the following statutes:

(a) Section 366.26 of the Welfare and Institutions Code.

(b) Sections 8604 to 8606, inclusive, and 8700 of this code.

(c) Chapter 5 (commencing with Section 7660) of Part 3 of this division of this code. *(Stats.1992, c. 162 (A.B.2650), § 10, operative Jan. 1, 1994. Amended by Stats.1994, c. 1269 (A.B.2208), § 55.4.)*

Law Revision Commission Comments

Enactment [Revised Comment]

Section 7808 continues former Civil Code Section 232(e) without substantive change. A reference to Chapter 5 (commencing with Section 7660) of Part 3 has been substituted for a narrower reference to former Civil Code Section 7017. This is not a substantive change. [23 Cal.L.Rev.Comm. Reports 1 (1993)].

1994 Amendment

Subdivision (c) of Section 7808 is amended to correct an incomplete cross-reference. This is a technical, nonsubstantive change. [24 Cal.L.Rev.Comm. Reports 621 (1994)].

Research References

Treatises and Practice Aids

Witkin, California Summary 10th Parent and Child § 308, Dependency Proceeding Distinguished.

CHAPTER 2. CIRCUMSTANCES WHERE PROCEEDING MAY BE BROUGHT

§ 7820. Application of chapter

A proceeding may be brought under this part for the purpose of having a child under the age of 18 years declared free from the custody and control of either or both parents if the child comes within any of the descriptions set out in this chapter. *(Stats.1992, c. 162 (A.B.2650), § 10, operative Jan. 1, 1994.)*

Law Revision Commission Comments

Enactment [Revised Comment]

Section 7820 continues the introductory part of former Civil Code Section 232(a) without substantive change. A reference to "proceeding" has been substituted for the former reference to "action." This is not a substantive change. [23 Cal.L.Rev.Comm. Reports 1 (1993)].

Research References

Treatises and Practice Aids

Witkin, California Summary 10th Parent and Child § 47, Where Presumption Of Paternity Applies.

Witkin, California Summary 10th Parent and Child § 275, in General.

Witkin, California Summary 10th Parent and Child § 298, Types Of Emancipation.

Witkin, California Summary 10th Parent and Child § 307, Nature Of Action.

Witkin, California Summary 10th Parent and Child § 331, Venue, Petition, and Investigation.

Witkin, California Summary 10th Parent and Child § 648, Parent or Guardian Absent, Unwilling, or Incapable.

§ 7821. Findings; sufficiency of evidence

A finding pursuant to this chapter shall be supported by clear and convincing evidence, except as otherwise provided. *(Stats.1992, c. 162 (A.B.2650), § 10, operative Jan. 1, 1994. Amended by Stats.2006, c. 838 (S.B.678), § 4.)*

Law Revision Commission Comments

Enactment [Revised Comment]

Section 7821 continues former Civil Code Section 232(c) without substantive change. [23 Cal.L.Rev.Comm. Reports 1 (1993)].

Research References

Treatises and Practice Aids

Witkin, California Summary 10th Parent and Child § 345, Clear and Convincing Evidence is Required.

§ 7822. Abandoned children; right to action; declaration of abandonment; Indian children

(a) A proceeding under this part may be brought if any of the following occur:

(1) The child has been left without provision for the child's identification by the child's parent or parents.

(2) The child has been left by both parents or the sole parent in the care and custody of another person for a period of six months without any provision for the child's support, or without communication from the parent or parents, with the intent on the part of the parent or parents to abandon the child.

(3) One parent has left the child in the care and custody of the other parent for a period of one year without any provision for the child's support, or without communication from the parent, with the intent on the part of the parent to abandon the child.

(b) The failure to provide identification, failure to provide support, or failure to communicate is presumptive evidence of the intent to abandon. If the parent or parents have made only token efforts to support or communicate with the child, the court may declare the child abandoned by the parent or parents. In the event that a guardian has been appointed for the child, the court may still declare the child abandoned if the parent or parents have failed to communicate with or support the child within the meaning of this section.

(c) If the child has been left without provision for the child's identification and the whereabouts of the parents are unknown, a petition may be filed after the 120th day following the discovery of the child and citation by publication may be commenced. The petition may not be heard until after the 180th day following the discovery of the child.

(d) If the parent has agreed for the child to be in the physical custody of another person or persons for adoption and has not signed an adoption placement agreement pursuant to Section 8801.3, a consent to adoption pursuant to Section 8814, or a relinquishment to a licensed adoption agency pursuant to Section 8700, evidence of the adoptive placement shall not in itself preclude the court from finding an intent on the part of that parent to abandon the child. If the parent has placed the child for adoption pursuant to

Section 8801.3, consented to adoption pursuant to Section 8814, or relinquished the child to a licensed adoption agency pursuant to Section 8700, and has then either revoked the consent or rescinded the relinquishment, but has not taken reasonable action to obtain custody of the child, evidence of the adoptive placement shall not in itself preclude the court from finding an intent on the part of that parent to abandon the child.

(e) Notwithstanding subdivisions (a), (b), (c), and (d), if the parent of an Indian child has transferred physical care, custody and control of the child to an Indian custodian, that action shall not be deemed to constitute an abandonment of the child, unless the parent manifests the intent to abandon the child by either of the following:

(1) Failing to resume physical care, custody, and control of the child upon the request of the Indian custodian provided that if the Indian custodian is unable to make a request because the parent has failed to keep the Indian custodian apprised of his or her whereabouts and the Indian custodian has made reasonable efforts to determine the whereabouts of the parent without success, there may be evidence of intent to abandon.

(2) Failing to substantially comply with any obligations assumed by the parent in his or her agreement with the Indian custodian despite the Indian custodian's objection to the noncompliance. *(Stats.1992, c. 162 (A.B.2650), § 10, operative Jan. 1, 1994. Amended by Stats.2006, c. 838 (S.B.678), § 5; Stats.2007, c. 47 (S.B.313), § 2.)*

Law Revision Commission Comments

Enactment [Revised Comment]

Section 7822 continues former Civil Code Section 232(a)(1) without substantive change. [23 Cal.L.Rev.Comm. Reports 1 (1993)].

Commentary

Applying section 3403, *Adoption of K.C., 247 Cal.App.4th 1412, 203 Cal.Rptr.3d 110 (2016), review denied*, held that the UCCJEA does not apply to California adoption proceedings in which a New York father's parental rights under a New York divorce decree were terminated under this section and section 8604.

Applying section (a)(3), *Adoption of A.B., 2 Cal.App.5th 912, 206 Cal.Rptr.3d 531 (2016)*, held that the "one year" period of abandonment need not immediately precede the filing of a petition to terminate parental rights.

The "intent to abandon" a child, for purposes of this section, is intent to abandon for the periods specified in this section, not intent to abandon forever. *Adoption of Allison C., 164 Cal.App.4th 1004, 79 Cal.Rptr.3d 743 (2008). Allison C.* reasons that the purpose of this part is to protect a child's interests by providing the stability and security of an adoptive home. That purpose would be defeated if the statute were interpreted to require intent to abandon the child forever.

In re Amy A., 132 Cal.App.4th 63, 33 Cal.Rptr.3d 298 (2005), held that a trial court did not abuse its discretion in terminating the parental rights of a parent who failed to pay court-ordered child support or exercise court-ordered visitation rights for more than a year. *In re Jacklyn F., 144 Cal.App.4th 747, 7 Cal.Rptr.3d 768 (2003)*, holds that a child has not been "left" for purposes of subsection (a) when a child has been taken away from a parent by a court order resulting from the grandparents' guardianship proceeding, which the parent contested. However, a parent's voluntary inaction following a custody order may satisfy subsection (a)(3) and thus provide presumptive evidence of subsection (b) intent to abandon. *In re Marriage of Jill and Victor D., 185 Cal.App.4th 491, 110 Cal.Rptr.3d 369 (2010).*

In re Michael R., 137 Cal.App.4th 126, 39 Cal.Rptr.3d 773 (2006), review denied, holds that a family court properly dismissed a temporary guardian's petition seeking to (1) free a child from parental custody and control on the ground of abandonment and (2) independently adopt the child, because the guardian failed to make a prima facie case of parental abandonment under this section and did not have standing to adopt under Section 8802.

In re Bryce C., 12 Cal.4th 226, 906 P.2d 1275, 48 Cal.Rptr.2d 120 (1995), reads Section 7895 literally to require that an appellate court appoint counsel only when a parent is an appellant, as opposed to a respondent, in an appeal from a proceeding to terminate parental control and custody. *Bryce C.* further states that an appellate court nevertheless has discretionary power to appoint counsel for a parent in any appeal in which the parent's custody and control of a child is at stake and that the court should exercise that discretion whenever the presence of counsel may reasonably influence whether parental rights are terminated. *Bryce C.* specifically reserves the question whether a child must be a dependent child of the court to entitle the appellant parent to absolute, as opposed to discretionary, right to counsel. 12 Cal.4th 226, 233. Applying the discretionary rubric of *Bryce C.*, *In re Chanel S., 45 Cal.App.4th 1250, 53 Cal.Rptr.2d 253 (1996)*, determined that the court was required to appoint counsel for an indigent mother appealing from her termination of parental rights in a private step-parent adoption proceeding.

See also *Appellate Defenders, Inc. v. Cheri S., 35 Cal.App.4th 1819, 42 Cal.Rptr.2d 195 (1995)*, which holds that an indigent parent has a right to appointed counsel in any proceeding that terminates his or her parental rights (cf. Section 7895), including proceedings invoking Family Code Sections 7822, 8604, and 9000. Relying on *In re Jacqueline H., 21 Cal.3d 170, 577 P.2d 683, 145 Cal.Rptr. 548 (1978), Appellate Defenders* reasons that it is immaterial whether the proceeding is initiated by private parties or the state; the magnitude of the loss is identical. But see *In re Curtis S., 25 Cal.App.4th 687, 30 Cal.Rptr.2d 739 (1994), review denied 8/29/94*, (appointment of appellate counsel required only when parental rights of indigent parent have been terminated in a dependency proceeding).

In re Sade C., 13 Cal.4th 952, 920 P.2d 716, 55 Cal.Rptr.2d 771 (1996), holds that the court of appeal is not required to make an independent review of the entire record (a "Wende" review; see *People v. Wende, 25 Cal.3d 436, 600 P.2d 1071, 158 Cal.Rptr. 839 (1979)*) when a parent appeals from a judgment adversely affecting his custody of a child or his status as a parent if the appellate court does not find any arguably meritorious basis for the appeal. Interpreting *Sade C.*, *In re Sara H., 52 Cal.App.4th 198, 60 Cal.Rptr.2d 434 (1997)*, holds that the appellate court has no discretionary authority in dependency appeals to conduct an independent "Wende" review of the entire record to discover whether there exists some arguably meritorious basis for appeal from a judgment terminating parental rights.

In re Conservatorship of Ben C., 40 Cal.4th 529, 53 Cal.Rptr.3d 856, 150 P.3d 738 (2007), held that while *Wende* protections are inapplicable in conservatorship proceedings, the conservatee nevertheless has the right to file a supplemental brief in propria persona when his counsel finds no appealable issue.

A trial court finding under § 8604 that an adoption may proceed without a natural parent's consent does not terminate that parent's child support obligation. Thus, the natural parent's duty of support is not terminated until the child is adopted by another, as specified by § 8617. *In re Marriage of Dunmore, 83 Cal.App.4th 1, 98 Cal.Rptr.2d 885 (2000). Dunmore* reasons that the purpose of § 8604 is to facilitate adoption, not to terminate parental rights. *Dunmore* contrasts § 8604 with this section, which is designed to terminate parental rights. See also *County of Ventura v. Gonzalez, 88 Cal.App.4th 1120, 106 Cal.Rptr.2d 461 (2001)*, which holds that a Welfare and Institutions Code § 366.26 order terminating parental rights fully severs the parent-child relationship, including the duty of support.

Although section 7807 ordinarily stays custody proceedings during the pendency of a proceeding to terminate parental rights under this section, *In re E.M., 228 Cal.App.4th 828, 175 Cal.Rptr.3d 711 (2014)*, holds a court may nevertheless order temporary visitation for a father when it concludes that the mother and her new husband filed a petition to terminate the father's parental rights solely for the purpose of delaying a hearing on the father's petition to modify existing custody and visitation orders.

Research References

Forms

California Transactions Forms--Family Law § 6:10, Initiating Proceeding Under Fam. Code, §§ 7800 et seq.
California Transactions Forms--Family Law § 7:39, Adoption and Termination Of Parental Rights.
California Transactions Forms--Family Law § 6:107, Adoption Without Consent Of Noncustodial Parent.
West's California Code Forms, Family § 7840, Comment Overview--Freedom from Parental Control.
West's California Judicial Council Forms ADOPT-200, Adoption Request.

Treatises and Practice Aids

Witkin, California Summary 10th Constitutional Law § 633, General Rule.
Witkin, California Summary 10th Parent and Child § 102, Failure to Support and Communicate.
Witkin, California Summary 10th Parent and Child § 132, Petition.
Witkin, California Summary 10th Parent and Child § 312, Statutory Ground.
Witkin, California Summary 10th Parent and Child § 354, Statutory Right.
Witkin, California Summary 10th Parent and Child § 355, Review on Appeal.

§ 7823. Neglected or cruelly treated children; right to action

(a) A proceeding under this part may be brought where all of the following requirements are satisfied:

(1) The child has been neglected or cruelly treated by either or both parents.

(2) The child has been a dependent child of the juvenile court under any subdivision of Section 300 of the Welfare and Institutions Code and the parent or parents have been deprived of the child's custody for one year before the filing of a petition pursuant to this part.

(b) Physical custody by the parent or parents for insubstantial periods of time does not interrupt the running of the one-year period. *(Stats.1992, c. 162 (A.B.2650), § 10, operative Jan. 1, 1994.)*

Law Revision Commission Comments

Enactment [Revised Comment]

Section 7823 continues former Civil Code Section 232(a)(2) without substantive change. [23 Cal.L.Rev.Comm. Reports 1 (1993)].

Research References

Forms

West's California Code Forms, Family § 7840, Comment Overview--Freedom from Parental Control.

Treatises and Practice Aids

Witkin, California Summary 10th Parent and Child § 316, Statutory Ground.

§ 7824. Parents suffering from disability due to alcohol, or controlled substances, or moral depravity; right of action

(a) "Disability" as used in this section means any physical or mental incapacity which renders the parent or parents unable to care for and control the child adequately.

(b) A proceeding under this part may be brought where all of the following requirements are satisfied:

(1) The child is one whose parent or parents (A) suffer a disability because of the habitual use of alcohol, or any of the controlled substances specified in Schedules I to V, inclusive, of Division 10 (commencing with Section 11000) of the Health and Safety Code, except when these controlled substances are used as part of a medically prescribed plan, or (B) are morally depraved.

(2) The child has been a dependent child of the juvenile court, and the parent or parents have been deprived of the child's custody continuously for one year immediately before the filing of a petition pursuant to this part.

(c) Physical custody by the parent or parents for insubstantial periods of time does not interrupt the running of the one-year period. *(Stats.1992, c. 162 (A.B.2650), § 10, operative Jan. 1, 1994.)*

Law Revision Commission Comments

Enactment [Revised Comment]

Section 7824 continues former Civil Code Section 232(a)(3) without substantive change. [23 Cal.L.Rev.Comm. Reports 1 (1993)].

Research References

Forms

West's California Code Forms, Family § 7840, Comment Overview--Freedom from Parental Control.

Treatises and Practice Aids

Witkin, California Summary 10th Parent and Child § 319, Dependent Child Of Immoral or Substance-Abusing Parent.

§ 7825. Parent convicted of felony; consideration of criminal record prior to felony conviction; right of action

(a) A proceeding under this part may be brought where both of the following requirements are satisfied:

(1) The child is one whose parent or parents are convicted of a felony.

(2) The facts of the crime of which the parent or parents were convicted are of such a nature so as to prove the unfitness of the parent or parents to have the future custody and control of the child. In making a determination pursuant to this section, the court may consider the parent's criminal record prior to the felony conviction to the extent that the criminal record demonstrates a pattern of behavior substantially related to the welfare of the child or the parent's ability to exercise custody and control regarding his or her child.

(b) The mother of a child may bring a proceeding under this part against the father of the child, where the child was conceived as a result of an act in violation of Section 261 of the Penal Code, and where the father was convicted of that violation. For purposes of this subdivision, there is a conclusive presumption that the father is unfit to have custody or control of the child. *(Stats.1992, c. 162 (A.B. 2650), § 10, operative Jan. 1, 1994. Amended by Stats.1997, c. 594 (A.B.1222), § 2; Stats.2006, c. 806 (S.B.1325), § 5.)*

Law Revision Commission Comments

Enactment [Revised Comment]

Section 7825 continues former Civil Code Section 232(a)(4) without substantive change. [23 Cal.L.Rev.Comm. Reports 1 (1993)].

Commentary

This section applies only when the actual facts underlying the felony conviction show that a parent is unfit for future custody and control of a child. The conviction must show, for example, a propensity to violence or child abuse. Thus, *In re Baby Girl M., 135 Cal.App.4th 1528, 38 Cal.Rptr.3d 484 (2006), review denied,* held that the trial court erred in concluding that a father's felony convictions for burglary and possession of methamphetamine justified termination of his parental rights under this section.

Research References

Forms

California Transactions Forms--Family Law § 6:10, Initiating Proceeding Under Fam. Code, §§ 7800 et seq.

West's California Code Forms, Family § 7840, Comment Overview--Freedom from Parental Control.

Treatises and Practice Aids

Witkin, California Summary 10th Parent and Child § 320, Statutory Ground.

Witkin, California Summary 10th Parent and Child § 322, Insufficient Showing.

§ 7826. Parent declared developmentally disabled or mentally ill; right to action

A proceeding under this part may be brought where both of the following requirements are satisfied:

(a) The child is one whose parent or parents have been declared by a court of competent jurisdiction, wherever situated, to be developmentally disabled or mentally ill.

(b) In the state or country in which the parent or parents reside or are hospitalized, the Director of State Hospitals or the Director of Developmental Services, or their equivalent, if any, and the executive director of the hospital, if any, of which the parent or parents are inmates or patients, certify that the parent or parents so declared to be developmentally disabled or mentally ill will not be capable of supporting or controlling the child in a proper manner. *(Stats.1992, c. 162 (A.B.2650), § 10, operative Jan. 1, 1994. Amended by Stats. 2012, c. 440 (A.B.1488), § 6, eff. Sept. 22, 2012.)*

Law Revision Commission Comments

Enactment [Revised Comment]

Section 7826 continues former Civil Code Section 232(a)(5) without substantive change. [23 Cal.L.Rev.Comm. Reports 1 (1993)].

Commentary

Affirming the trial court's termination of a psychiatric patient's parental rights, *In re Anthony P., 84 Cal.App.4th 1112, 101 Cal.Rptr.2d 423 (2000), review denied January 24, 2001,* held that Title II of the Americans with Disabilities Act, 42 U.S.C.A. § 12131 et seq., does not preempt the state from terminating the rights of a severely disabled parent in a proceeding under this chapter.

Research References

Forms

West's California Code Forms, Family § 7840, Comment Overview--Freedom from Parental Control.

Treatises and Practice Aids

Witkin, California Summary 10th Constitutional Law § 787, Mentally Defective Parents.

Witkin, California Summary 10th Parent and Child § 323, Parents Previously Adjudged Disabled.

§ 7827. Mentally disabled parent; right to action

(a) "Mentally disabled" as used in this section means that a parent or parents suffer a mental incapacity or disorder that renders the parent or parents unable to care for and control the child adequately.

(b) A proceeding under this part may be brought where the child is one whose parent or parents are mentally disabled and are likely to remain so in the foreseeable future.

(c) Except as provided in subdivision (d), the evidence of any two experts, each of whom shall be a physician and surgeon, certified either by the American Board of Psychiatry and Neurology or under Section 6750 of the Welfare and Institutions Code, a licensed psychologist who has a doctoral degree in psychology and at least five years of postgraduate experience in the diagnosis and treatment of emotional and mental disorders, is required to support a finding under this section. In addition to this requirement, the court shall have the discretion to call a licensed marriage and family therapist, or a licensed clinical social worker, either of whom shall have at least five years of relevant postlicensure experience, in circumstances where the court determines that this testimony is in the best interest of the child and is warranted by the circumstances of the particular family or parenting issues involved. However, the court may not call a licensed marriage and family therapist or licensed clinical social worker pursuant to this section who is the adoption service provider, as defined in Section 8502, of the child who is the subject of the petition to terminate parental rights.

(d) If the parent or parents reside in another state or in a foreign country, the evidence required by this section may be supplied by the affidavits of two experts, each of whom shall be either of the following:

(1) A physician and surgeon who is a resident of that state or foreign country, and who has been certified by a medical organization or society of that state or foreign country to practice psychiatric or neurological medicine.

(2) A licensed psychologist who has a doctoral degree in psychology and at least five years of postgraduate experience in the diagnosis and treatment of emotional and mental disorders and who is licensed in that state or authorized to practice in that country.

(e) If the rights of a parent are sought to be terminated pursuant to this section, and the parent has no attorney, the court shall appoint an attorney for the parent pursuant to Article 4 (commencing with Section 7860) of Chapter 3, whether or not a request for the appointment is made by the parent. *(Stats.1992, c. 162 (A.B.2650), § 10, operative Jan. 1, 1994. Amended by Stats.1996, c. 288 (S.B.2027), § 1; Stats. 2002, c. 1013 (S.B.2026), § 80.)*

Law Revision Commission Comments

Enactment [Revised Comment]

Section 7827 continues former Civil Code Section 232(a)(6) without substantive change. [23 Cal.L.Rev.Comm. Reports 1 (1993)].

Commentary

Interpreting subsection (c), *Curtis F. v. Superior Court, 80 Cal. App.4th 470, 95 Cal.Rptr.2d 232 (2000), review denied June 21, 2000,* held that the two experts need not agree; instead the statute requires only evidence upon which the court can base findings.

Affirming the trial court's termination of a psychiatric patient's parental rights, *In re Anthony P., 84 Cal.App.4th 1112, 101 Cal.Rptr.2d 423 (2000), review denied January 24, 2001,* held that Title II of the Americans with Disabilities Act, 42 U.S.C.A. § 12131 et seq., does not preempt the state from terminating the rights of a severely disabled parent in a proceeding under this chapter.

In re Marriage of Stephen P., 213 Cal.App.4th 983, 153 Cal.Rptr.3d 154 (2013), review denied, affirmed a trial court order granting the petition of an adoptive mother to terminate the father's parental rights to the parties' minor child based on the father's mental disability.

Research References

Forms

California Transactions Forms--Family Law § 6:10, Initiating Proceeding Under Fam. Code, §§ 7800 et seq.

West's California Code Forms, Family § 7840, Comment Overview--Freedom from Parental Control.

Treatises and Practice Aids

Witkin, California Summary 10th Constitutional Law § 787, Mentally Defective Parents.

Witkin, California Summary 10th Parent and Child § 323, Parents Previously Adjudged Disabled.

Witkin, California Summary 10th Parent and Child § 324, Parents Found Disabled or Ill.

Witkin, California Summary 10th Parent and Child § 331, Venue, Petition, and Investigation.

Witkin, California Summary 10th Parent and Child § 355, Review on Appeal.

Witkin, California Summary 10th Parent and Child § 541, Mental Illness and Substance Abuse.

Witkin, California Summary 10th Parent and Child § 648, Parent or Guardian Absent, Unwilling, or Incapable.

CHAPTER 3. PROCEDURE

ARTICLE 1. AUTHORIZED PETITIONERS

§ 7840. Right of specified entities to file petition

(a) A petition may be filed under this part for an order or judgment declaring a child free from the custody and control of either or both parents by any of the following:

(1) The State Department of Social Services, a county welfare department, a licensed private or public adoption agency, a county adoption department, or a county probation department which is planning adoptive placement of the child with a licensed adoption agency.

(2) The State Department of Social Services acting as an adoption agency in counties which are not served by a county adoption agency.

(b) The fact that a child is in a foster care home subject to the requirements of Chapter 3 (commencing with Section 1500) of Division 2 of the Health and Safety Code does not prevent the filing of a petition under subdivision (a).

(c) The county counsel or, if there is no county counsel, the district attorney of the county specified in Section 7845 shall, in a proper case, institute the proceeding upon the request of any of the state or county agencies mentioned in subdivision (a). The proceeding shall be instituted pursuant to this part within 30 days of the request.

(d) If, at the time of the filing of a petition by a department or agency specified in subdivision (a), the child is in the custody of the petitioner, the petitioner may continue to have custody of the child pending the hearing on the petition unless the court, in its discretion, makes such other order regarding custody pending the hearing as it finds will best serve and protect the interest and welfare of the child. *(Stats.1992, c. 162 (A.B.2650), § 10, operative Jan. 1, 1994.)*

Law Revision Commission Comments

Enactment [Revised Comment]

Section 7840 restates former Civil Code Section 232.9 without substantive change. In subdivision (c), the reference to a "verified" petition has been omitted as surplus. See Section 212 (pleadings to be verified). In subdivision (d), references to "proceeding" have been substituted for the former references to "action." These are not substantive changes. See also Sections 7841 (any interested person may file petition), 7845 (venue). [23 Cal.L.Rev.Comm. Reports 1 (1993)].

Research References

Forms

West's California Code Forms, Family § 7840, Comment Overview--Freedom from Parental Control.

Treatises and Practice Aids

Witkin, California Summary 10th Parent and Child § 330, Who May Bring Action.

Witkin, California Summary 10th Parent and Child § 331, Venue, Petition, and Investigation.

§ 7841. Right of interested persons to file petition

(a) An interested person may file a petition under this part for an order or judgment declaring a child free from the custody and control of either or both parents.

(b) For purposes of this section, an "interested person" is one who has a direct interest in the action, and includes, but is not limited to, a person who has filed, or who intends to file within a period of 6 months, an adoption petition under

Section 8714, 8802, or 9000, or a licensed adoption agency to whom the child has been relinquished by the other parent. *(Stats.1992, c. 162 (A.B.2650), § 10, operative Jan. 1, 1994. Amended by Stats.2007, c. 47 (S.B.313), § 3.)*

Law Revision Commission Comments

Enactment [Revised Comment]

Section 7841 restates without substantive change the first and last parts of the first sentence of the first paragraph of former Civil Code Section 233(a). The reference to the "superior" court has been omitted as surplus. See Section 200 (jurisdiction in superior court). See also Section 7845 (venue). [23 Cal.L.Rev.Comm. Reports 1 (1993)].

Commentary

T.P. v. T.W, 191 Cal.App.4th 1428, 120 Cal.Rptr.3d 477 (2011), review denied, holds that a child's mother is an "interested person" for purposes of bringing an action to free a child from the custody and control of the child's other parent, even though no adoption petition has or will be filed.

Research References

Forms

West's California Code Forms, Family § 7840, Comment Overview--Freedom from Parental Control.

West's California Code Forms, Family § 7894 Form 1, Judgment Declaring Minor Free from Parental Control.

Treatises and Practice Aids

Witkin, California Summary 10th Parent and Child § 330, Who May Bring Action.

Witkin, California Summary 10th Parent and Child § 331, Venue, Petition, and Investigation.

§ 7842. Single petition to free child from custody and control of both parents

A single petition may be filed under this part to free a child, or more than one child if the children are biological siblings, from the custody and control of both parents. A petition filed in accordance with this section may be granted in whole or in part in accordance with the procedures set forth in this chapter. The court shall retain discretion to bifurcate any case in which the petition was filed in accordance with this section, and shall do so whenever it is necessary to protect the interests of a party or a child who is the subject of the proceeding. *(Added by Stats.2014, c. 763 (A.B.1701), § 6, eff. Jan. 1, 2015.)*

Research References

Treatises and Practice Aids

Witkin, California Summary 10th Parent and Child § 331, Venue, Petition, and Investigation.

ARTICLE 2. VENUE

§ 7845. Filing of petition

The petition shall be filed in any of the following:

(a) The county in which a minor described in Chapter 2 (commencing with Section 7820) resides or is found.

(b) The county in which any of the acts which are set forth in Chapter 2 (commencing with Section 7820) are alleged to have occurred.

(c) The county in which a petition for the adoption of the child has been filed or the adoption agency to which the child has been relinquished or proposed to be relinquished has an office. *(Stats.1992, c. 162 (A.B.2650), § 10, operative Jan. 1, 1994. Amended by Stats.2009, c. 492 (A.B.941), § 2.)*

Law Revision Commission Comments

Enactment [Revised Comment]

Section 7845 restates without substantive change the first half of the first sentence of the first paragraph of former Civil Code Section 233(a). See also Section 200 (jurisdiction in superior court). [23 Cal.L.Rev.Comm. Reports 1 (1993)].

Research References

Forms

West's California Code Forms, Family § 7840, Comment Overview--Freedom from Parental Control.

Treatises and Practice Aids

Witkin, California Summary 10th Parent and Child § 331, Venue, Petition, and Investigation.

ARTICLE 3. INVESTIGATION AND REPORT

§ 7850. Notification to investigate; scope of investigation

Upon the filing of a petition under Section 7841, the clerk of the court shall, in accordance with the direction of the court, immediately notify the juvenile probation officer, qualified court investigator, licensed clinical social worker, licensed marriage and family therapist, or the county department designated by the board of supervisors to administer the public social services program, who shall immediately investigate the circumstances of the child and the circumstances which are alleged to bring the child within any of the provisions of Chapter 2 (commencing with Section 7820). *(Stats.1992, c. 162 (A.B.2650), § 10, operative Jan. 1, 1994. Amended by Stats.1993, c. 219 (A.B.1500), § 180; Stats.2002, c. 260 (S.B.1512), § 4.)*

Law Revision Commission Comments

Enactment [Revised Comment]

Section 7850 continues the third sentence of former Civil Code Section 233(a) without substantive change. References to "child" have been substituted for the former references to "minor." These are not substantive changes. See Section 7802 Comment. Section 7850 does not require the notice and investigation if the petition is filed under Section 7840 (petition by licensed private or public adoption agency or state or county agency). [23 Cal.L.Rev.Comm. Reports 1 (1993)].

Research References

Treatises and Practice Aids

Witkin, California Summary 10th Parent and Child § 275, in General.
Witkin, California Summary 10th Parent and Child § 324, Parents Found Disabled or Ill.
Witkin, California Summary 10th Parent and Child § 331, Venue, Petition, and Investigation.
Witkin, California Summary 10th Parent and Child § 350, Vacating Order for Fraud.

§ 7851. Recommendations to court; contents of report

(a) The juvenile probation officer, qualified court investigator, licensed clinical social worker, licensed marriage and family therapist, or the county department shall render to the court a written report of the investigation with a recommendation of the proper disposition to be made in the proceeding in the best interest of the child.

(b) The report shall include all of the following:

(1) A statement that the person making the report explained to the child the nature of the proceeding to end parental custody and control.

(2) A statement of the child's feelings and thoughts concerning the pending proceeding.

(3) A statement of the child's attitude towards the child's parent or parents and particularly whether or not the child would prefer living with his or her parent or parents.

(4) A statement that the child was informed of the child's right to attend the hearing on the petition and the child's feelings concerning attending the hearing.

(c) If the age, or the physical, emotional, or other condition of the child precludes the child's meaningful response to the explanations, inquiries, and information required by subdivision (b), a description of the condition shall satisfy the requirement of that subdivision.

(d) The court shall receive the report in evidence and shall read and consider its contents in rendering the court's judgment. *(Stats.1992, c. 162 (A.B.2650), § 10, operative Jan. 1, 1994. Amended by Stats.1993, c. 219 (A.B.1500), § 181; Stats.2002, c. 260 (S.B.1512), § 5.)*

Law Revision Commission Comments

Enactment [Revised Comment]

Section 7851 continues without substantive change former Civil Code Section 233, from the last sentence of the first paragraph of subdivision (sic) (a) to the end of subdivision (a). In subdivisions (a) and (b)(1), references to "proceeding" have been substituted for the former references to "action." These are not substantive changes. Throughout this section, references to "child" have been substituted for the former references to "minor." These are not substantive changes. See Section 7802 Comment. [23 Cal.L.Rev.Comm. Reports 1 (1993)].

Commentary

In re Linda W., 209 Cal.App.3d 222, 257 Cal.Rptr. 52 (1989), holds that, in a termination of parental rights proceeding, failure to prepare the report required by Section 7851 requires that the judgment terminating parental rights be reversed.

In re Chanel S., 45 Cal.App.4th 1250, 53 Cal.Rptr.2d 253 (1996), holds that an investigator's failure to interview children is not reversible error when the investigator complies with the statutory requirement of providing reasons for failure to interview the children.

Research References

Treatises and Practice Aids

Witkin, California Summary 10th Parent and Child § 324, Parents Found Disabled or Ill.
Witkin, California Summary 10th Parent and Child § 331, Venue, Petition, and Investigation.
Witkin, California Summary 10th Parent and Child § 343, Conduct Of Hearing.

§ 7851.5. Costs in connection with termination of parental rights; liability of petitioner; investigation cost; monetary limit

The petitioner shall be liable for all reasonable costs incurred in connection with the termination of parental rights, including, but not limited to, costs incurred for the investigation required by this article. However, public agencies and nonprofit organizations are exempt from payment of the costs of the investigation. The liability of a petitioner for costs under this section shall not exceed nine hundred dollars ($900). The court may defer, waive, or reduce the costs when the payment would cause an economic hardship which would be detrimental to the welfare of the child. *(Added by Stats.1994, c. 1286 (A.B.2902), § 1.)*

Research References

Treatises and Practice Aids

Witkin, California Summary 10th Parent and Child § 331, Venue, Petition, and Investigation.

§ 7852. "Qualified court investigator" defined

"Qualified court investigator," as used in this article, has the meaning provided by Section 8543. *(Added by Stats.1993, c. 219 (A.B.1500), § 182.)*

Law Revision Commission Comments

Enactment [Revised Comment]

Section 7852 continues former Civil Code Section 233(b) without substantive change. [23 Cal.L.Rev.Comm. Reports 1 (1993)].

ARTICLE 4. APPOINTMENT OF COUNSEL

Section

§ 7860. Procedures for appointment

At the beginning of the proceeding on a petition filed pursuant to this part, counsel shall be appointed as provided in this article. The public defender or private counsel may be appointed as counsel pursuant to this article. The same counsel shall not be appointed to represent both the child and the child's parent. *(Stats.1992, c. 162 (A.B.2650), § 10, operative Jan. 1, 1994.)*

Law Revision Commission Comments

Enactment [Revised Comment]

Section 7860 continues without substantive change the introductory part, the last sentence of subdivision (b), and the first sentence of subdivision (c) of former Civil Code Section 237.5. The reference to "child" has been substituted for the former reference to "minor." This is not a substantive change. See Section 7802 Comment. See also Sections 7827(e) (mandatory appointment of counsel for mentally disabled parent), 7895 (appointment of counsel for indigent appellant). [23 Cal.L.Rev.Comm. Reports 1 (1993)].

Commentary

In re Bryce C., 12 Cal.4th 226, 906 P.2d 1275, 48 Cal.Rptr.2d 120 (1995), reads Section 7895 literally to require that an appellate court appoint counsel only when a parent is an appellant, as opposed to a respondent, in an appeal from a proceeding to terminate parental control and custody. *Bryce C.* further states that an appellate court nevertheless has discretionary power to appoint counsel for a parent in any appeal in which the parent's custody and control of a child is at stake and that the court should exercise that discretion whenever the presence of counsel may reasonably influence whether parental rights are terminated. *Bryce C.* specifically reserves the question whether a child must be a dependent child of the court to entitle the appellant parent to absolute, as opposed to discretionary, right to counsel. 12 Cal.4th 226, 233. Applying the discretionary rubric of *Bryce C., In re Chanel S., 45 Cal.App.4th 1250, 53 Cal.Rptr.2d 253 (1996)*, determined that the court was required to appoint counsel for an indigent mother appealing from her termination of parental rights in a private step-parent adoption proceeding.

See also *Appellate Defenders, Inc. v. Cheri S., 35 Cal.App.4th 1819, 42 Cal.Rptr.2d 195 (1995)*, which holds that an indigent parent has a right to appointed counsel in any proceeding that terminates his or her parental rights (cf. Section 7895), including proceedings invoking Family Code Sections 7822, 8604, and 9000. Relying on *In re Jacqueline H., 21 Cal.3d 170, 577 P.2d 683, 145 Cal.Rptr. 548 (1978), Appellate Defenders* reasons that it is immaterial whether the proceeding is initiated by private parties or the state; the magnitude of the loss is identical. But see *In re Curtis S., 25 Cal.App.4th 687, 30 Cal.Rptr.2d 739 (1994), review denied 8/29/94*, (appointment of appellate counsel required only when parental rights of indigent parent have been terminated in a dependency proceeding).

Research References

Forms

West's California Code Forms, Family § 7880, Comment Overview--Notice Of Proceeding and Attendance at Hearing.

Treatises and Practice Aids

Witkin, California Summary 10th Parent and Child § 324, Parents Found Disabled or Ill.

Witkin, California Summary 10th Parent and Child § 336, Statutory Rights.

§ 7861. Appointment of counsel for child; consideration of interests of child

The court shall consider whether the interests of the child require the appointment of counsel. If the court finds that the interests of the child require representation by counsel, the court shall appoint counsel to represent the child, whether or not the child is able to afford counsel. The child shall not be present in court unless the child so requests or the court so orders. *(Stats.1992, c. 162 (A.B.2650), § 10, operative Jan. 1, 1994.)*

Law Revision Commission Comments

Enactment [Revised Comment]

Section 7861 continues former Civil Code Section 237.5(a) without substantive change. References to "child" have been substituted for the former references to "minor." These are not substantive changes. See Section 7802 Comment. This section has been reworded to make it more concise. [23 Cal.L.Rev.Comm. Reports 1 (1993)].

Commentary

In re Mary C., 41 Cal.App.4th 71, 48 Cal.Rptr.2d 346 (1995), holds that, in an appeal from an order terminating parental rights, an appellate court is not required to provide separate counsel for the child unless there is a conflict of interest between the child and the local child protection agency, or protection of the child's best interest requires that the child be represented by separate counsel.

Research References

Treatises and Practice Aids

Witkin, California Summary 10th Parent and Child § 336, Statutory Rights.

Witkin, California Summary 10th Parent and Child § 343, Conduct Of Hearing.

§ 7862. Appointment of counsel for parent

If a parent appears without counsel and is unable to afford counsel, the court shall appoint counsel for the parent, unless that representation is knowingly and intelligently waived. *(Stats.1992, c. 162 (A.B.2650), § 10, operative Jan. 1, 1994.)*

Law Revision Commission Comments

Enactment [Revised Comment]

Section 7862 continues the first sentence of former Civil Code Section 237.5(b) without substantive change. [23 Cal.L.Rev.Comm. Reports 1 (1993)].

Commentary

Appellate Defenders, Inc. v. Cheri S., 35 Cal.App.4th 1819, 42 Cal.Rptr.2d 195 (1995), holds that an indigent parent has a right to appointed counsel in any proceeding that terminates his or her parental rights (cf. Section 7895), including proceedings invoking Family Code Sections 7822, 8604, and 9000. Relying on *In re Jacqueline H., 21 Cal.3d 170, 577 P.2d 683, 145 Cal.Rptr. 548 (1978), Appellate Defenders* reasons that it is immaterial whether the proceeding is initiated by private parties or the state; the magnitude of the loss is identical. But see *In re Curtis S., 25 Cal.App.4th 687, 30 Cal.Rptr.2d 739 (1994), review denied 8/29/94*, (appointment of appellate counsel required only when parental rights of indigent parent have been terminated in a dependency proceeding).

Research References

Forms

West's California Code Forms, Family § 7881 Form 1, Citation to Parent.

Treatises and Practice Aids

Witkin, California Summary 10th Parent and Child § 336, Statutory Rights.

§ 7863. Compensation and expenses

Private counsel appointed under this article shall receive a reasonable sum for compensation and expenses, the amount of which shall be determined by the court. The amount so determined shall be paid by the real parties in interest, other than the child, in proportions the court deems just. However, if the court finds that any of the real parties in interest are unable to afford counsel, the amount shall be paid out of the general fund of the county. *(Stats.1992, c. 162 (A.B.2650), § 10, operative Jan. 1, 1994.)*

Law Revision Commission Comments

Enactment [Revised Comment]

Section 7863 continues the last three sentences of former Civil Code Section 237.5(c) without substantive change. The reference to "child" has been substituted for the former reference to "minor." This is not a substantive change. See Section 7802 Comment. [23 Cal.L.Rev.Comm. Reports 1 (1993)].

Commentary

In re Bryce C., 12 Cal.4th 226, 906 P.2d 1275, 48 Cal.Rptr.2d 120 (1995), reads Section 7895 literally to require that an appellate court appoint counsel only when a parent is an appellant, as opposed to a respondent, in an appeal from a proceeding to terminate parental control and custody. *Bryce C.* further states that an appellate court nevertheless has discretionary power to appoint counsel for a parent in any appeal in which the parent's custody and control of a child is at stake and that the court should exercise that discretion whenever the presence of counsel may reasonably influence whether parental rights are terminated. *Bryce C.* specifically reserves the question whether a child must be a dependent child of the court to entitle the appellant parent to absolute, as opposed to discretionary, right to counsel. 12 Cal.4th 226, 233. Applying the discretionary rubric of *Bryce C., In re Chanel S., 45 Cal.App.4th 1250, 53 Cal.Rptr.2d 253 (1996)*, determined that the court was required to appoint counsel for an indigent mother appealing from her termination of parental rights in a private step-parent adoption proceeding.

See also *Appellate Defenders, Inc. v. Cheri S., 35 Cal.App.4th 1819, 42 Cal.Rptr.2d 195 (1995)*, which holds that an indigent parent has a right to appointed counsel in any proceeding that terminates his or her parental rights (cf. Section 7895), including proceedings invoking Family Code Sections 7822, 8604, and 9000. Relying on *In re Jacqueline H., 21 Cal.3d 170, 577 P.2d 683, 145 Cal.Rptr. 548 (1978)*, *Appellate Defenders* reasons that it is immaterial whether the proceeding is initiated by private parties or the state; the magnitude of the loss is identical. But see *In re Curtis S., 25 Cal.App.4th 687, 30 Cal.Rptr.2d 739 (1994), review denied 8/29/94*, (appointment of appellate counsel required only when parental rights of indigent parent have been terminated in a dependency proceeding).

Research References

Treatises and Practice Aids

Witkin, California Summary 10th Parent and Child § 336, Statutory Rights.

§ 7864. Continuance of proceedings; purpose

The court may continue the proceeding for not to exceed 30 days as necessary to appoint counsel and to enable counsel to become acquainted with the case. *(Stats.1992, c. 162 (A.B.2650), § 10, operative Jan. 1, 1994.)*

Law Revision Commission Comments

Enactment [Revised Comment]

Section 7864 continues former Civil Code Section 237.5(d) without substantive change. For a general provision on continuances, see Section 7871. [23 Cal.L.Rev.Comm. Reports 1 (1993)].

Research References

Forms

West's California Code Forms, Family § 7880, Comment Overview--Notice Of Proceeding and Attendance at Hearing.

Treatises and Practice Aids

Witkin, California Summary 10th Parent and Child § 336, Statutory Rights.

Witkin, California Summary 10th Parent and Child § 342, Speedy Trial.

ARTICLE 5. TIME FOR HEARING; CONTINUANCE

§ 7870. Setting for trial; precedence over other civil matters; continuances

(a) It is the public policy of this state that judicial proceedings to declare a child free from parental custody and control shall be fully determined as expeditiously as possible.

(b) Notwithstanding any other provision of law, a proceeding to declare a child free from parental custody and control pursuant to this part shall be set for hearing not more than 45 days after the filing of the petition. If, at the time set for hearing, or at any continuance thereof, service has been completed and no interested person appears to contest, the court may issue an order based on the verified pleadings and any other evidence as may be submitted. If any interested person appears to contest the matter, the court shall set the matter for trial. The matter so set has precedence over all other civil matters on the date set for trial.

(c) The court may continue the proceeding as provided in Section 7864 or Section 7871. *(Stats.1992, c. 162 (A.B.2650), § 10, operative Jan. 1, 1994. Amended by Stats.2012, c. 638 (A.B.1757), § 4.)*

Law Revision Commission Comments

Enactment [Revised Comment]

Section 7870 continues former Civil Code Section 232.3(a)-(b) without substantive change. In subdivision (c), a reference to Section 7871 has been added. [23 Cal.L.Rev.Comm. Reports 1 (1993)].

Research References

Forms

West's California Code Forms, Family § 7840, Comment Overview--Freedom from Parental Control.

Treatises and Practice Aids

Witkin, California Summary 10th Parent and Child § 342, Speedy Trial.

§ 7871. Grounds for continuance

(a) A continuance may be granted only upon a showing of good cause. Neither a stipulation between counsel nor the convenience of the parties is in and of itself a good cause.

(b) Unless the court for good cause entertains an oral motion for continuance, written notice of a motion for a continuance of the hearing shall be filed within two court days of the date set for the hearing, together with affidavits or declarations detailing specific facts showing that a continuance is necessary.

(c) A continuance shall be granted only for that period of time shown to be necessary by the evidence considered at the hearing on the motion. Whenever a continuance is granted, the facts proven which require the continuance shall be entered upon the minutes of the court. *(Stats.1992, c. 162 (A.B.2650), § 10, operative Jan. 1, 1994.)*

Law Revision Commission Comments

Enactment [Revised Comment]

Section 7871 restates former Civil Code Section 232.3(c) without substantive change. See also Section 7864 (continuance for up to 30 days as necessary to appoint counsel and to enable counsel to become acquainted with case). [23 Cal.L.Rev.Comm. Reports 1 (1993)].

Research References

Forms

West's California Code Forms, Family § 7840, Comment Overview--Freedom from Parental Control.

Treatises and Practice Aids

Witkin, California Summary 10th Parent and Child § 342, Speedy Trial.

ARTICLE 6. NOTICE OF PROCEEDING AND ATTENDANCE AT HEARING

Section

§ 7880. Citation requiring appearance of person having custody or control of child and child at hearing

(a) Upon the filing of the petition, a citation shall issue requiring any person having the custody or control of the child, or the person with whom the child is, to appear at a time and place stated in the citation.

(b) The citation shall also require the person to appear with the child except that, if the child is under the age of 10 years, appearance with the child is required only upon order of the court after necessity has been shown.

(c) Service of the citation shall be made in the manner prescribed by law for service of civil process at least 10 days before the time stated in the citation for the appearance. The party or attorney responsible for serving the citation shall do so in a timely manner in order to maximize the response time available to the party being served. *(Stats.1992, c. 162 (A.B.2650), § 10, operative Jan. 1, 1994. Amended by Stats. 2012, c. 638 (A.B.1757), § 5.)*

Law Revision Commission Comments

Enactment [Revised Comment]

Section 7880 continues the first paragraph of former Civil Code Section 234 without substantive change. The requirement that service "be made in the manner prescribed by law for service of civil process" is new and is drawn from the first paragraph of former Civil Code Section 232.3(b), now Family Code Section 7870(b). Throughout this section, references to "child" have been substituted for the former references to "minor." These are not substantive changes. See Section 7802 Comment. [23 Cal.L.Rev.Comm. Reports 1 (1993)].

Commentary

Compliance with the notice provision of the Indian Child Welfare Act (ICWA), 25 U.S.C.A. § 1912, is required in a parental rights termination proceeding under this part even though the "existing Indian family doctrine" may ultimately render the ICWA inapplicable. *In re Suzanna L., 104 Cal.App.4th 223, 127 Cal.Rptr.2d 860 (2002)*. For discussion of the "existing Indian family doctrine," see Commentary to 25 U.S.C.A. § 1913.

Research References

Forms

West's California Code Forms, Family § 7840, Comment Overview--Freedom from Parental Control.
West's California Code Forms, Family § 7880, Comment Overview--Notice Of Proceeding and Attendance at Hearing.

Treatises and Practice Aids

Witkin, California Summary 10th Parent and Child § 332, Citation.
Witkin, California Summary 10th Parent and Child § 343, Conduct Of Hearing.

§ 7881. Notice of proceeding by service of citation on parents or relatives; contents

(a) Notice of the proceeding shall be given by service of a citation on the father or mother of the child, if the place of residence of the father or mother is known to the petitioner. If the place of residence of the father or mother is not known to the petitioner, then the citation shall be served on the grandparents and adult brothers, sisters, uncles, aunts, and first cousins of the child, if there are any and if their residences and relationships to the child are known to the petitioner.

(b) The citation shall advise the person or persons that they may appear at the time and place stated in the citation. The citation shall also advise the person or persons of the rights and procedures set forth in Article 4 (commencing with Section 7860). If the petition is filed for the purpose of freeing the child for placement for adoption, the citation shall so state.

(c) The citation shall be served in the manner provided by law for the service of a summons in a civil action, other than by publication. If one parent has relinquished the child for the purpose of adoption, or has signed a consent for adoption as provided in Sections 8700, 8814, or 9003, notice as provided in this section need not be given to the parent who has signed the relinquishment or consent.

(d) Service of the citations required by this section shall be made at least 10 days before the time stated in the citation for the appearance. *(Stats.1992, c. 162 (A.B.2650), § 10, operative Jan. 1, 1994.)*

Law Revision Commission Comments

Enactment [Revised Comment]

Section 7881 continues former Civil Code Section 235(a) without substantive change. In subdivision (a), references to "child" have been substituted for the former references to "minor." These are not substantive changes. See Section 7802 Comment. [23 Cal. L.Rev.Comm. Reports 1 (1993)].

Research References

Forms

West's California Code Forms, Family § 7840, Comment Overview--Freedom from Parental Control.

West's California Code Forms, Family § 7880, Comment Overview--Notice Of Proceeding and Attendance at Hearing.

Treatises and Practice Aids

Witkin, California Summary 10th Parent and Child § 12, Parental or Marital Rights Of Prisoners.

Witkin, California Summary 10th Parent and Child § 332, Citation.

§ 7882. Filing of affidavit as to parent who cannot be served or whose residence is unknown; publication of citation

(a) If the father or mother of the child or a person alleged to be or claiming to be the father or mother cannot, with reasonable diligence, be served as provided for in Section 7881, or if his or her place of residence is not known to the petitioner, the petitioner or the petitioner's agent or attorney shall make and file an affidavit, which shall state the name of the father or mother or alleged father or mother and his or her place of residence, if known to the petitioner, and the name of the father or mother or alleged father or mother whose place of residence is unknown to the petitioner.

(b) Upon the filing of the affidavit, the court shall make an order that (1) the service shall be made by the publication of a citation requiring the father or mother or alleged father or mother to appear at the time and place stated in the citation and (2) the citation shall be published pursuant to Section 6064 of the Government Code in a newspaper to be named and designated in the order as most likely to give notice to the father or mother or alleged father or mother to be served.

(c) In case of publication where the residence of a parent or alleged parent is known, the court shall also direct a copy of the citation to be forthwith served upon that parent or alleged parent by mail by deposit in the post office properly addressed and with the postage thereon fully prepaid, directed to that parent or alleged parent at the place of residence. When publication is ordered, service of a copy of the citation in the manner provided for in Section 7881 is equivalent to publication and deposit in the post office.

(d) If one or both of the parents of the child are unknown or if the names of one or both of the child's parents are uncertain, that fact shall be set forth in the affidavit and the court shall order the citation to be directed to either or both of the child's parents, naming and otherwise describing the child, and to all persons claiming to be a parent of the child.

(e) Service is complete at the expiration of the time prescribed by the order for publication or when service is made as provided for in Section 7881, whichever event first occurs. *(Stats.1992, c. 162 (A.B.2650), § 10, operative Jan. 1, 1994.)*

Law Revision Commission Comments

Enactment [Revised Comment]

Section 7882 continues former Civil Code Section 235(b) without substantive change. In subdivisions (a) and (d), references to "child" have been substituted for the former references to "minor." These are not substantive changes. See Section 7802 Comment. In subdivision (b), a reference to Government Code Section 6064 has been substituted for the requirement that the notice be published once a week for four successive weeks. This is not a substantive change. [23 Cal.L.Rev.Comm. Reports 1 (1993)].

Research References

Forms

West's California Code Forms, Family § 7880, Comment Overview--Notice Of Proceeding and Attendance at Hearing.

Treatises and Practice Aids

Witkin, California Summary 10th Parent and Child § 12, Parental or Marital Rights Of Prisoners.

Witkin, California Summary 10th Parent and Child § 332, Citation.

§ 7883. Failure to appear; contempt

If a person personally served with a citation within this state as provided in Section 7880 fails without reasonable cause to appear and abide by the order of the court, or to bring the child before the court if so required in the citation, the failure constitutes a contempt of court. *(Stats.1992, c. 162 (A.B.2650), § 10, operative Jan. 1, 1994.)*

Law Revision Commission Comments

Enactment [Revised Comment]

Section 7883 continues former Civil Code Section 236 without substantive change. A reference to "child" has been substituted for the former reference to "minor." This is not a substantive change. See Section 7802 Comment. A reference to Section 7880 has been added to make clear that this section applies only when attendance by the person is required by the citation. A person served with a citation under Section 7881 may, but is not required to, attend the hearing. [23 Cal.L.Rev.Comm. Reports 1 (1993)].

Research References

Forms

West's California Code Forms, Family § 7880 Form 1, Citation to Person Having Custody.

West's California Code Forms, Family § 7881 Form 1, Citation to Parent.

Treatises and Practice Aids

Witkin, California Summary 10th Parent and Child § 332, Citation.

§ 7884. Admission to proceedings

(a) Unless requested by the child concerning whom the petition has been filed and any parent or guardian present, the public shall not be admitted to a proceeding under this part.

(b) Notwithstanding subdivision (a), the judge may admit those persons the judge determines have a direct and legitimate interest in the particular case or in the work of the court. *(Stats.1992, c. 162 (A.B.2650), § 10, operative Jan. 1, 1994.)*

Law Revision Commission Comments

Enactment [Revised Comment]

Section 7884 continues former Civil Code Section 235.5 without substantive change. In subdivision (a), a reference to "child" has been substituted for the former reference to "minor." This is not a substantive change. See Section 7802 Comment. [23 Cal.L.Rev. Comm. Reports 1 (1993)].

Research References

Treatises and Practice Aids

Witkin, California Summary 10th Parent and Child § 343, Conduct Of Hearing.

ARTICLE 7. HEARING AND SUBSEQUENT PROCEEDINGS

§ 7890. Consideration of wishes of child

In a proceeding under this part, the court shall consider the wishes of the child, bearing in mind the age of the child, and shall act in the best interest of the child. *(Stats.1992, c. 162 (A.B.2650), § 10, operative Jan. 1, 1994.)*

Law Revision Commission Comments

Enactment [Revised Comment]

Section 7890 restates without substantive change the last sentence of former Civil Code Section 232.5 and the first paragraph of former Civil Code Section 232(b). [23 Cal.L.Rev.Comm. Reports 1 (1993)].

Research References

Forms

West's California Code Forms, Family § 7840, Comment Overview--Freedom from Parental Control.

West's California Code Forms, Family § 7890, Comment Overview--Hearing and Subsequent Proceedings.

Treatises and Practice Aids

Witkin, California Summary 10th Parent and Child § 307, Nature Of Action.

Witkin, California Summary 10th Parent and Child § 312, Statutory Ground.

Witkin, California Summary 10th Parent and Child § 344, Testimony.

§ 7891. In chambers hearing; notice of right to attend; waiver

(a) Except as otherwise provided in this section, if the child who is the subject of the petition is 10 years of age or older, the child shall be heard by the court in chambers on at least the following matters:

(1) The feelings and thoughts of the child concerning the custody proceeding about to take place.

(2) The feelings and thoughts of the child about the child's parent or parents.

(3) The child's preference as to custody, according to Section 3042.

(b) The court shall inform the child of the child's right to attend the hearing. However, counsel for the child may waive the hearing in chambers by the court.

(c) This section does not apply if the child is confined because of illness or other incapacity to an institution or residence and is therefore unable to attend. *(Stats.1992, c. 162 (A.B.2650), § 10, operative Jan. 1, 1994. Amended by Stats.1993, c. 219 (A.B.1500), § 182.5.)*

Law Revision Commission Comments

Enactment [Revised Comment]

Section 7891 continues without substantive change the second paragraph and subdivisions (a)-(c) of former Civil Code Section 234. Throughout this section, references to "child" have been substituted for the former references to "minor." These are not substantive changes. See Section 7802 Comment. The reference to Section 3042 has been substituted for the broader reference to former Civil Code Section 4600. This is not a substantive change, since Section 3042 continues the relevant part of the former section. See also Section 7954 (minor's right to make statement in connection with priorities for foster care placement). [23 Cal.L.Rev.Comm. Reports 1 (1993)].

Research References

Forms

California Transactions Forms--Family Law § 3:12, Preferences Of the Child.

West's California Code Forms, Family § 7840, Comment Overview--Freedom from Parental Control.

Treatises and Practice Aids

Witkin, California Summary 10th Parent and Child § 343, Conduct Of Hearing.

Witkin, California Summary 10th Parent and Child § 344, Testimony.

§ 7892. Testimony of child in chambers and outside presence of child's parents; conditions

(a) The testimony of the child may be taken in chambers and outside the presence of the child's parent or parents if the child's parent or parents are represented by counsel, the counsel is present, and any of the following circumstances exist:

(1) The court determines that testimony in chambers is necessary to ensure truthful testimony.

(2) The child is likely to be intimidated by a formal courtroom setting.

(3) The child is afraid to testify in front of the child's parent or parents.

(b) The testimony of a child also may be taken in chambers and outside the presence of the guardian or guardians of a child under the circumstances specified in subdivision (a).

(c) A finding pursuant to this section shall be supported by clear and convincing evidence.

(d) After testimony in chambers, the parent or parents of the child may elect to have the court reporter read back the testimony or have the testimony summarized by counsel for the parent or parents. *(Stats.1992, c. 162 (A.B.2650), § 10, operative Jan. 1, 1994.)*

Law Revision Commission Comments

Enactment [Revised Comment]

Subdivisions (a), (b), and (d) of Section 7892 continue without substantive change former Civil Code Section 232(b) from the second paragraph to the end of the former subdivision. Subdivision (c) continues former Civil Code Section 232(c) without substantive change. Throughout this section, references to "child" have been substituted for the former references to "minor." These are not substantive changes. See Section 7802 Comment. [23 Cal.L.Rev. Comm. Reports 1 (1993)].

Research References

Forms

West's California Code Forms, Family § 7840, Comment Overview--Freedom from Parental Control.

Treatises and Practice Aids

Witkin, California Summary 10th Parent and Child § 344, Testimony.

Witkin, California Summary 10th Parent and Child § 345, Clear and Convincing Evidence is Required.

§ 7892.5. Declaration that Indian child is free from custody or control of parent

The court shall not declare an Indian child free from the custody or control of a parent, unless both of the following apply:

(a) The court finds, supported by clear and convincing evidence, that active efforts were made in accordance with Section 361.7 of the Welfare and Institutions Code.

(b) The court finds, supported by evidence beyond a reasonable doubt, including testimony of one or more "qualified expert witnesses" as described in Section 224.5 of the Welfare and Institutions Code, that the continued custody of the child by the parent is likely to result in serious emotional or physical damage to the child.

(c) This section shall only apply to proceedings involving an Indian child. *(Added by Stats.2006, c. 838 (S.B.678), § 6.)*

Research References

Forms

West's California Judicial Council Forms ADOPT-200, Adoption Request.

Treatises and Practice Aids

Witkin, California Summary 10th Parent and Child § 348A, (New) Additional Findings for Indian Child.

§ 7893. Guardianship or referral to adoption agency

(a) If the court, by order or judgment, declares a child free from the custody and control of both parents under this part, or one parent if the other no longer has custody and control, the court shall at the same time take one of the following actions:

(1) Appoint a guardian for the child.

(2) At the request of the State Department of Social Services or a licensed adoption agency, or where the court finds it is in the child's best interest, refer the child to a licensed adoption agency for adoptive placement by the agency.

(b) When the court refers the child to a licensed adoption agency for adoptive placement by the agency:

(1) The agency is responsible for the care of the child and is entitled to the exclusive custody and control of the child at all times until a petition for adoption has been granted.

(2) After the referral, no petition for guardianship may be filed without the consent of the agency.

(3) No petition for adoption may be heard until the appellate rights of the natural parents have been exhausted. *(Stats.1992, c. 162 (A.B.2650), § 10, operative Jan. 1, 1994.)*

Law Revision Commission Comments

Enactment [Revised Comment]

Section 7893 continues former Civil Code Section 239 without substantive change. Throughout this section, references to "child" have been substituted for the former references to "minor." These are not substantive changes. See Section 7802 Comment. [23 Cal.L.Rev.Comm. Reports 1 (1993)].

Research References

Forms

West's California Code Forms, Family § 7890, Comment Overview--Hearing and Subsequent Proceedings.

Treatises and Practice Aids

Witkin, California Summary 10th Parent and Child § 349, in General.

§ 7894. Effect of order

(a) An order and judgment of the court declaring a child free from the custody and control of a parent or parents under this part is conclusive and binding upon the child, upon the parent or parents, and upon all other persons who have been served with citations by publication or otherwise as provided in this part.

(b) After making the order and judgment, the court has no power to set aside, change, or modify it.

(c) Nothing in this section limits the right to appeal from the order and judgment. *(Stats.1992, c. 162 (A.B.2650), § 10, operative Jan. 1, 1994.)*

Law Revision Commission Comments

Enactment [Revised Comment]

Section 7894 continues former Civil Code Section 238 without substantive change. In subdivision (a), references to "child" have been substituted for the former references to "minor." These are not substantive changes. See Section 7802 Comment. See also Code Civ. Proc. § 45 (precedence for appeal from judgment freeing dependent child from parental custody and control). [23 Cal.L.Rev. Comm. Reports 1 (1993)].

Commentary

A judgment terminating parental rights under this section may not be set aside on appeal on the ground that the judgment was taken by default. *Adoption of Clarissa H., 105 Cal.App.4th 120, 129 Cal.Rptr.2d 223 (2003).*

Research References

Forms

West's California Code Forms, Family § 7890, Comment Overview--Hearing and Subsequent Proceedings.

Treatises and Practice Aids

Witkin, California Summary 10th Parent and Child § 349, in General.
Witkin, California Summary 10th Parent and Child § 350, Vacating Order for Fraud.
Witkin, California Summary 10th Parent and Child § 351, in General.
Witkin, California Summary 10th Parent and Child § 355, Review on Appeal.

§ 7895. Appointment of counsel for appellant; indigent appellant; free copy of transcripts

(a) Upon appeal from a judgment freeing a child who is a dependent child of the juvenile court from parental custody and control, the appellate court shall appoint counsel for the appellant as provided by this section.

(b) Upon motion by the appellant and a finding that the appellant is unable to afford counsel, the appellate court shall appoint counsel for the indigent appellant, and appellant's counsel shall be provided a free copy of the reporter's and clerk's transcript. All of those costs are a charge against the court.

(c) The reporter's and clerk's transcripts shall be prepared and transmitted immediately after filing of the notice of appeal, at court expense and without advance payment of fees. If the appellant is able to afford counsel, the court may seek reimbursement from the appellant for the cost of the transcripts under subdivision (c) of Section 68511.3 of the Government Code as though the appellant had been granted permission to proceed in forma pauperis. *(Stats.1992, c. 162 (A.B.2650), § 10, operative Jan. 1, 1994. Amended by Stats. 2000, c. 447 (S.B.1533), § 4; Stats.2001, c. 754 (A.B.1697), § 3.)*

Law Revision Commission Comments

Enactment [Revised Comment]

Section 7895 continues former Civil Code Section 237.7 without substantive change. In subdivision (a), a reference to "child" has been substituted for the former reference to "minor." This is not a substantive change. See Section 7802 Comment. See also Code Civ. Proc. § 45 (precedence for appeal from judgment freeing dependent child from parental custody and control). [23 Cal.L.Rev. Comm. Reports 1 (1993)].

Commentary

In re Bryce C., 12 Cal.4th 226, 906 P.2d 1275, 48 Cal.Rptr.2d 120 (1995), reads Section 7895 literally to require that an appellate court appoint counsel only when a parent is an appellant, as opposed to a respondent, in an appeal from a proceeding to terminate parental control and custody. *Bryce C.* further states that an appellate court nevertheless has discretionary power to appoint counsel for a parent in any appeal in which the parent's custody and control of a child is at stake and that the court should exercise that discretion whenever the presence of counsel may reasonably influence whether parental rights are terminated. *Bryce C.* specifically reserves the question whether a child must be a dependent child of the court to entitle the appellant parent to absolute, as opposed to discretionary, right to counsel. 12 Cal.4th 226, 233. Applying the discretionary rubric of *Bryce C., In re Chanel S., 45 Cal.App.4th 1250, 53 Cal.Rptr.2d 253 (1996)*, determined that the court was required to appoint counsel for an indigent mother appealing from her termination of parental rights in a private step-parent adoption proceeding.

See also *Appellate Defenders, Inc. v. Cheri S., 35 Cal.App.4th 1819, 42 Cal.Rptr.2d 195 (1995)*, which holds that an indigent parent has a right to appointed counsel in any proceeding that terminates his or her parental rights, including proceedings invoking Family Code Sections 7822, 8604, and 9000. Relying on *In re Jacqueline H., 21 Cal.3d 170, 577 P.2d 683, 145 Cal.Rptr. 548 (1978), Appellate Defenders* reasons that it is immaterial whether the proceeding is initiated by private parties or the state. But see *In re Curtis S., 25 Cal.App.4th 687, 30 Cal.Rptr.2d 739 (1994), review denied 8/29/94*, (appointment of appellate counsel required only when parental rights of indigent parent have been terminated in a dependency proceeding).

Research References

Treatises and Practice Aids

Witkin, California Summary 10th Parent and Child § 352, Free Transcript.
Witkin, California Summary 10th Parent and Child § 353, Case Law.
Witkin, California Summary 10th Parent and Child § 354, Statutory Right.

Part 5

INTERSTATE COMPACT ON PLACEMENT OF CHILDREN

Section

§ 7900. Adoption

The Interstate Compact on Placement of Children as set forth in Section 7901 is hereby adopted and entered into with all other jurisdictions joining therein. *(Stats.1992, c. 162 (A.B.2650), § 10, operative Jan. 1, 1994.)*

Law Revision Commission Comments

Enactment [Revised Comment]

Section 7900 continues former Civil Code Section 264 without substantive change. [23 Cal.L.Rev.Comm. Reports 1 (1993)].

Commentary

On November 17, 1994, the California Supreme court denied review and ordered depublished *In re Colonia L., 27 Cal.App.4th 588, 32 Cal.Rptr.2d 540 (1994)*, which purported to hold that the Interstate Compact on the Placement of Children does not apply to a request to permit a dependent child to move out of state with the current foster parents.

Research References

Forms

California Transactions Forms--Family Law § 6:2, Governing Law.

California Transactions Forms--Family Law § 6:116, Purpose and Background Of Interstate Compact.

West's California Code Forms, Family § 7900, Comment Overview--Interstate Compact on Placement Of Children.

West's California Judicial Council Forms JV-565, Request for Assistance With Expedited Placement Under the Interstate Compact on the Placement Of Children.

West's California Judicial Council Forms JV-567, Expedited Placement Under the Interstate Compact on the Placement Of Children: Findings and Orders.

Treatises and Practice Aids

Witkin, California Summary 10th Parent and Child § 80, Interstate Placement Of Children for Adoption.

Witkin, California Summary 10th Parent and Child § 637, Priority Right Of Noncustodial Parent.

§ 7901. Provisions

The provisions of the interstate compact referred to in Section 7900 are as follows:

INTERSTATE COMPACT ON THE PLACEMENT OF CHILDREN

Article 1. Purpose and Policy

It is the purpose and policy of the party states to cooperate with each other in the interstate placement of children to the end that:

(a) Each child requiring placement shall receive the maximum opportunity to be placed in a suitable environment and with persons or institutions having appropriate qualifications and facilities to provide a necessary and desirable degree and type of care.

(b) The appropriate authorities in a state where a child is to be placed may have full opportunity to ascertain the circumstances of the proposed placement, thereby promoting full compliance with applicable requirements for the protection of the child.

(c) The proper authorities of the state from which the placement is made may obtain the most complete information on the basis on which to evaluate a projected placement before it is made.

(d) Appropriate jurisdictional arrangements for the care of children will be promoted.

Article 2. Definitions

As used in this compact:

(a) "Child" means a person who, by reason of minority, is legally subject to parental, guardianship, or similar control.

(b) "Sending agency" means a party state, or officer or employee thereof; subdivision of a party state, or officer or employee thereof; a court of a party state; a person, corporation, association, charitable agency, or other entity which sends, brings, or causes to be sent or brought any child to another party state.

(c) "Receiving state" means the state to which a child is sent, brought, or caused to be sent or brought, whether by public authorities or private persons or agencies, and whether for placement with state or local public authorities or for placement with private agencies or persons.

(d) "Placement" means the arrangement for the care of a child in a family free or boarding home or in a child-caring agency or institution but does not include any institution caring for persons with developmental disabilities or mental health disorders or any institution primarily educational in character, and any hospital or other medical facility.

Article 3. Conditions for Placement

(a) No sending agency shall send, bring, or cause to be sent or brought into any other party state any child for placement in foster care or as a preliminary to a possible adoption unless the sending agency shall comply with each and every requirement set forth in this article and with the applicable laws of the receiving state governing the placement of children therein.

(b) Before sending, bringing, or causing any child to be sent or brought into a receiving state for placement in foster care or as a preliminary to a possible adoption, the sending agency shall furnish the appropriate public authorities in the receiving state written notice of the intention to send, bring, or place the child in the receiving state. The notice shall contain:

(1) The name, date, and place of birth of the child.

(2) The identity and address or addresses of the parents or legal guardian.

(3) The name and address of the person, agency, or institution to or with which the sending agency proposes to send, bring, or place the child.

(4) A full statement of the reasons for the proposed action and evidence of the authority pursuant to which the placement is proposed to be made.

(c) Any public officer or agency in a receiving state which is in receipt of a notice pursuant to paragraph (b) of this article may request of the sending agency, or any other appropriate officer or agency of or in the sending agency's state, and shall be entitled to receive therefrom, supporting or additional information as it may deem necessary under the circumstances to carry out the purpose and policy of this compact.

(d) The child shall not be sent, brought, or caused to be sent or brought into the receiving state until the appropriate public authorities in the receiving state shall notify the sending agency, in writing, to the effect that the proposed placement does not appear to be contrary to the interests of the child.

Article 4. Penalty for Illegal Placement

The sending, bringing, or causing to be sent or brought into any receiving state of a child in violation of the terms of this compact shall constitute a violation of the laws respecting the placement of children of both the state in which the sending agency is located or from which it sends or brings the child and of the receiving state. A violation may be punished or subjected to penalty in either jurisdiction in accordance with its laws. In addition to liability for any punishment or penalty, any violation shall constitute full and sufficient grounds for the suspension or revocation of any license, permit, or other legal authorization held by the sending agency which empowers or allows it to place, or care for children.

Article 5. Continuing Jurisdiction

(a) The sending agency shall retain jurisdiction over the child sufficient to determine all matters in relation to the custody, supervision, care, treatment, and disposition of the child which it would have had if the child had remained in the sending agency's state, until the child is adopted, reaches majority, becomes self-supporting, or is discharged with the concurrence of the appropriate authority in the receiving state. That jurisdiction shall also include the power to effect or cause the return of the child or its transfer to another location and custody pursuant to law. The sending agency shall continue to have financial responsibility for support and maintenance of the child during the period of the placement. Nothing contained herein shall defeat a claim of jurisdiction by a receiving state sufficient to deal with an act of delinquency or crime committed therein.

(b) When the sending agency is a public agency, it may enter into an agreement with an authorized public or private agency in the receiving state providing for the performance of one or more services in respect of that case by the latter as agent for the sending agency.

(c) Nothing in this compact shall be construed to prevent a private charitable agency authorized to place children in the receiving state from performing services or acting as agent in that state for a private charitable agency of the sending state; nor to prevent the agency in the receiving state from discharging financial responsibility for the support and maintenance of a child who has been placed on behalf of the sending agency without relieving the responsibility set forth in paragraph (a) of this article.

Article 6. Institutional Care of Delinquent Children

A child adjudicated delinquent may be placed in an institution in another party jurisdiction pursuant to this compact but no such placement shall be made unless the child is given a court hearing on notice to the parent or guardian with opportunity to be heard, before being sent to the other party jurisdiction for institutional care and the court finds that both of the following exist:

(a) Equivalent facilities for the child are not available in the sending agency's jurisdiction.

(b) Institutional care in the other jurisdiction is in the best interest of the child and will not produce undue hardship.

Article 7. Compact Administrator

The executive head of each jurisdiction party to this compact shall designate an officer who shall be general coordinator of activities under this compact in his or her jurisdiction and who, acting jointly with like officers of other party jurisdictions, shall have power to promulgate rules and regulations to carry out more effectively the terms and provisions of this compact.

Article 8. Limitations

This compact shall not apply to:

(a) The sending or bringing of a child into a receiving state by his or her parent, stepparent, grandparent, adult brother or sister, adult uncle or aunt, or his or her guardian and leaving the child with any such relative or nonagency guardian in the receiving state.

(b) Any placement, sending or bringing of a child into a receiving state pursuant to any other interstate compact to which both the state from which the child is sent or brought and the receiving state are party, or to any other agreement between said states which has the force of law.

Article 9. Enactment and Withdrawal

This compact shall be open to joinder by any state, territory, or possession of the United States, the District of Columbia, the Commonwealth of Puerto Rico, and, with the consent of Congress, the government of Canada or any province thereof. It shall become effective with respect to any of these jurisdictions when that jurisdiction has enacted the same into law. Withdrawal from this compact shall be by the enactment of a statute repealing the same, but shall not take effect until two years after the effective date of the statute and until written notice of the withdrawal has been given by the withdrawing state to the Governor of each other party jurisdiction. Withdrawal of a party state shall not affect the rights, duties, and obligations under this compact of any sending agency therein with respect to a placement made before the effective date of withdrawal.

Article 10. Construction and Severability

The provisions of this compact shall be liberally construed to effectuate the purposes thereof. The provisions of this compact shall be severable and if any phrase, clause, sentence, or provision of this compact is declared to be contrary to the constitution of any party state or of the United States or the applicability thereof to any government, agency, person, or circumstance is held invalid, the validity of the remainder of this compact and the applicability thereof to any government, agency, person, or circumstance shall not be affected thereby. If this compact shall be held contrary to the constitution of any state party thereto, the compact shall remain in full force and effect as to the remaining states and in full force and effect as to the state affected as to all severable matters. *(Stats.1992, c. 162 (A.B.2650), § 10, operative Jan. 1, 1994. Amended by Stats.2002, c. 260 (S.B.1512), § 6; Stats.2014, c. 144 (A.B.1847), § 13, eff. Jan. 1, 2015.)*

Law Revision Commission Comments

Enactment [Revised Comment]

Section 7901 continues former Civil Code Section 265 without substantive change. [23 Cal.L.Rev.Comm. Reports 1 (1993)].

Commentary

On November 17, 1994, the California Supreme court denied review and ordered depublished *In re Colonia L., 27 Cal.App.4th 588, 32 Cal.Rptr.2d 540 (1994)*, which purported to hold that the Interstate Compact on the Placement of Children does not apply to a request to permit a dependent child to move out of state with the current foster parents. On October 26, 1995, the Supreme Court similarly denied review and ordered depublished *In re Christina M., 36 Cal.App.4th 1249, 43 Cal.Rptr.2d 52 (1995)*, which purported to hold that the juvenile court may continue a foster home placement even if the foster family will move with the child to another state during the process of placing the child under the Interstate Compact.

In re Johnny S., 40 Cal.App.4th 969, 47 Cal.Rptr.2d 94 (1995), review denied February 15, 1996, holds that compliance with the Interstate Compact is not required when a California court places a child with a parent residing in another state. *In re C.B., 190 Cal.App.4th 102, 117 Cal.Rptr.3d 846 (2010)*, follows the rule expressed in *Johnny S.*, but notes that other states have reached the opposite conclusion.

In re Emmanuel R., 94 Cal.App.4th 452, 114 Cal.Rptr.2d 320 (2001), holds that the Interstate Compact on the Placement of Children [ICPC] does not apply to short-term visits with a natural parent. Thus, the juvenile court was not prevented from allowing a dependent child visitation with a Florida parent even though an ICPC evaluation had found the parent's home unsuitable for placement. The court additionally concluded that ICPC placement procedures are not required for placement of a dependent child with a natural parent.

Research References

Forms

California Transactions Forms--Family Law § 6:116, Purpose and Background Of Interstate Compact.
California Transactions Forms--Family Law § 6:117, Exclusions from Interstate Compact.
California Transactions Forms--Family Law § 6:118, Penalties for Noncompliance With ICPC.
California Transactions Forms--Family Law § 6:119, Continuing Jurisdiction.
California Transactions Forms--Family Law § 6:120, Compliance With Law Of Sending State.
California Transactions Forms--Family Law § 6:125, Interstate Travel by Birth Mother Prior to Child's Birth.
California Transactions Forms--Family Law § 6:137.50, Notice to Recipient State.
West's California Code Forms, Family § 7900, Comment Overview--Interstate Compact on Placement Of Children.

Treatises and Practice Aids

Witkin, California Summary 10th Parent and Child § 80, Interstate Placement Of Children for Adoption.
Witkin, California Summary 10th Parent and Child § 128, Adoption Placement Agreement.

§ 7901.1. Request outside state; home study to assess safety and suitability of child placement; requirements

(a) Within 60 days of receipt of a request from another state to conduct a study of a home environment for purposes of assessing the safety and suitability of placing a child in the home, a county child welfare agency shall, directly or by contract, do both of the following:

(1) Conduct and complete the study.

(2) Return a report to the requesting state on the results of the study. The report shall address the extent to which placement in the home would meet the needs of the child.

(b) Except as provided in subdivision (c), in the case of a home study commenced on or before September 30, 2008, if the agency fails to comply with subdivision (a) within the 60–day period as a result of circumstances beyond the control of the agency, the agency shall have 75 days to comply with subdivision (a). The agency shall document the circumstances involved and certify that completing the home study is in the best interests of the child. For purposes of this subdivision, "circumstances beyond the control of the agency" include, but are not limited to, the failure of a federal agency to provide the results of a background check or the failure of any entity to provide completed medical forms, if the background check or records were requested by the agency at least 45 days before the end of the 60–day period.

(c) Subdivision (b) shall not be construed to require the agency to have completed, within the applicable period, the parts of the home study involving the education and training of the prospective foster or adoptive parents.

(d) The agency shall treat any report described in subdivision (a) that is received from another state, an Indian tribe, or a private agency under contract with another state, as meeting any requirements imposed by the state for the completion of a home study before placing a child in the home, unless, within 14 days after receipt of the report, the agency determines, based on grounds that are specific to the content of the report, that making a decision in reliance on the report would be contrary to the welfare of the child.

(e) A county is not restricted from contracting with a private agency for the conduct of a home study described in subdivision (a).

(f) The department shall work with counties to identify barriers to meeting the timeframes specified in this section and to develop recommendations to reduce or eliminate those barriers. *(Added by Stats.2007, c. 583 (S.B.703), § 1.)*

Research References

Treatises and Practice Aids

Witkin, California Summary 10th Parent and Child § 80, Interstate Placement Of Children for Adoption.

§ 7902. Financial responsibility for child placed pursuant to compact

Financial responsibility for a child placed pursuant to the Interstate Compact on the Placement of Children shall be determined in accordance with Article 5 of the compact in the first instance. However, in the event of partial or complete default of performance thereunder, the provisions of other state laws also may be invoked. *(Stats.1992, c. 162 (A.B.2650), § 10, operative Jan. 1, 1994.)*

Law Revision Commission Comments

Enactment [Revised Comment]

Section 7902 continues former Civil Code Section 266 without change. [23 Cal.L.Rev.Comm. Reports 1 (1993)].

§ 7903. "Appropriate public authorities" defined

The phrase "appropriate public authorities" as used in Article 3 of the Interstate Compact on the Placement of Children means, with reference to this state, the State Department of Social Services, and that department shall receive and act with reference to notices required by Article 3 of the compact. *(Stats.1992, c. 162 (A.B.2650), § 10, operative Jan. 1, 1994.)*

Law Revision Commission Comments

Enactment [Revised Comment]

Section 7903 continues former Civil Code Section 267 without substantive change. [23 Cal.L.Rev.Comm. Reports 1 (1993)].

Research References

Forms

West's California Code Forms, Family § 7900, Comment Overview--Interstate Compact on Placement Of Children.

§ 7904. "Appropriate authority in receiving state" defined

The phrase "appropriate authority in receiving state" as used in paragraph (a) of Article 5 of the Interstate Compact on the Placement of Children, with reference to this state, means the State Department of Social Services. *(Stats.1992, c. 162 (A.B.2650), § 10, operative Jan. 1, 1994.)*

Law Revision Commission Comments

Enactment [Revised Comment]

Section 7904 continues former Civil Code Section 268 without substantive change. [23 Cal.L.Rev.Comm. Reports 1 (1993)].

Research References

Forms

West's California Code Forms, Family § 7900, Comment Overview--Interstate Compact on Placement Of Children.

§ 7905. Agreements with party states; approval of financial obligations

The officers and agencies of this state and its subdivisions having authority to place children are hereby empowered to enter into agreements with appropriate officers or agencies of or in other party states pursuant to paragraph (b) of Article 5 of the Interstate Compact on the Placement of Children. Any such agreement which contains a financial commitment or imposes a financial obligation on this state or subdivision or agency thereof is not binding unless it has the approval in writing of the Controller in the case of the state and of the chief local fiscal officer in the case of a subdivision of the state. *(Stats.1992, c. 162 (A.B.2650), § 10, operative Jan. 1, 1994.)*

Law Revision Commission Comments

Enactment [Revised Comment]

Section 7905 continues former Civil Code Section 269 without substantive change. [23 Cal.L.Rev.Comm. Reports 1 (1993)].

§ 7906. Requirements for visitation, inspection or supervision in another state

Any requirements for visitation, inspection, or supervision of children, homes, institutions, or other agencies in another party state which may apply under the law of this state shall be deemed to be met if performed pursuant to an agreement entered into by appropriate officers or agencies of this state or a subdivision thereof as contemplated by paragraph (b) of Article 5 of the Interstate Compact on the Placement of Children. *(Stats.1992, c. 162 (A.B.2650), § 10, operative Jan. 1, 1994.)*

Law Revision Commission Comments

Enactment [Revised Comment]

Section 7906 continues former Civil Code Section 270 without change. [23 Cal.L.Rev.Comm. Reports 1 (1993)].

§ 7906.5. Request inside state; home study to assess safety and suitability of child placement; requirements

(a) Within 60 days after an officer or agency of this state, or its political subdivision, receives a request from another state to conduct a study of a home environment for purposes of assessing the safety and suitability of placing a child, who is in the custody of the requesting state, in the home, the county child welfare agency shall, directly or indirectly, do both of the following:

(1) Conduct and complete the home study.

(2) Return to the requesting state a report on the results of the home study, which shall address the extent to which placement in the home would meet the needs of the child.

(b) A licensed private adoption agency may agree to provide the services listed in subdivision (a), and upon that agreement, shall comply with the requirements of paragraphs (1) and (2) of subdivision (a).

(c) Notwithstanding subdivision (a), in the case of a home study commenced on or before September 30, 2008, if the county fails to comply with subdivision (a) within the 60–day period as a result of circumstances beyond the control of the state, including, but not limited to, failure by a federal agency to provide the results of a background check or failure of any entity to provide completed medical forms requested by the state at least 45 days before the end of the 60–day period, the county shall have 75 days to comply with subdivision (a) if the county documents the circumstances involved and certifies that completing the home study is in the best interest of the child.

(d) Nothing in this section shall be construed to require the county to have completed, within the applicable period, those portions of the home study concerning the education and training of the prospective foster parent or adoptive parent.

(e) The county shall treat any report described in subdivision (a) that is received from another state, an Indian tribe, or a private agency under contract with another state, as meeting any requirements imposed by the state for the completion of a home study before placing a child in the home, unless, within 14 days after receipt of the report, the county determines, based on grounds that are specific to the content of the report, that making a decision in reliance on the report would be contrary to the welfare of the child.

(f) A county is not restricted from contracting with a private agency for the conduct of a home study described in subdivision (a). *(Added by Stats.2007, c. 583 (S.B.703), § 2.)*

Research References

Treatises and Practice Aids

Witkin, California Summary 10th Parent and Child § 80, Interstate Placement Of Children for Adoption.

§ 7907. Application of laws restricting out-of-state placements

No provision of law restricting out-of-state placement of children for adoption shall apply to placements made pursuant to the Interstate Compact on the Placement of Children. *(Stats.1992, c. 162 (A.B.2650), § 10, operative Jan. 1, 1994.)*

Law Revision Commission Comments

Enactment [Revised Comment]

Section 7907 continues former Civil Code Section 271 without change. [23 Cal.L.Rev.Comm. Reports 1 (1993)].

Commentary

On November 17, 1994, the California Supreme court denied review and ordered depublished *In re Colonia L., 27 Cal.App.4th 588, 32 Cal.Rptr.2d 540 (1994)*, which purported to hold that the Interstate Compact on the Placement of Children does not apply to a request to permit a dependent child to move out of state with the current foster parents. On October 26, 1995, the Supreme Court similarly denied review and ordered depublished *In re Christina M., 36 Cal.App.4th 1249, 43 Cal.Rptr.2d 52 (1995)*, which purported to hold that the juvenile court may continue a foster home placement even if the foster family will move with the child to another state during the process of placing the child under the Interstate Compact.

In re Johnny S., 40 Cal.App.4th 969, 47 Cal.Rptr.2d 94 (1995), review denied February 15, 1996, holds that compliance with the Interstate Compact is not required when a California court places a child with a parent residing in another state. *In re C.B., 190 Cal.App.4th 102, 117 Cal.Rptr.3d 846 (2010)*, follows the rule expressed in *Johnny S.*, but notes that other states have reached the opposite conclusion.

§ 7907.3. Bringing or sending of Indian child into another state

The Interstate Compact on the Placement of Children shall not apply to any placement, sending, or bringing of an Indian child into another state pursuant to a transfer of jurisdiction to a tribal court under Section 1911 of the Indian Child Welfare Act (25 U.S.C. Sec. 1901 et seq.). *(Added by Stats.2006, c. 838 (S.B.678), § 7.)*

Research References

Treatises and Practice Aids

Witkin, California Summary 10th Parent and Child § 80, Interstate Placement Of Children for Adoption.

§ 7907.5. Placement for adoption with state resident or nonresident; application of Interstate Compact on Placement of Children

(a) A child who is born in this state and placed for adoption in this state with a resident of this state is not subject to the provisions of the Interstate Compact on the Placement of Children.

(b) A child who is born in this state and placed for adoption with a person who is not a resident of this state is subject to the provisions of the Interstate Compact on the Placement of Children, regardless of whether the adoption petition is filed in this state. In interstate placements, this state shall be deemed the sending state for any child born in the state. *(Added by Stats.2004, c. 858 (S.B.1357), § 2.)*

Research References

Treatises and Practice Aids

Witkin, California Summary 10th Parent and Child § 80, Interstate Placement Of Children for Adoption.

§ 7908. Jurisdiction of courts to place delinquent children

A court having jurisdiction to place delinquent children may place a delinquent child in an institution in another state pursuant to Article 6 of the Interstate Compact on the Placement of Children and shall retain jurisdiction as provided in Article 5 of the compact. *(Stats.1992, c. 162 (A.B. 2650), § 10, operative Jan. 1, 1994.)*

Law Revision Commission Comments

Enactment [Revised Comment]

Section 7908 continues former Civil Code Section 272 without substantive change. [23 Cal.L.Rev.Comm. Reports 1 (1993)].

§ 7908.5. "Jurisdiction" defined; legislative intent

For the purposes of an interstate adoption placement, the term "jurisdiction" as used in Article 5 of the Interstate Compact on the Placement of Children means "jurisdiction over or legal responsibility for the child." It is the intent of the Legislature that this section make a technical clarification to the Interstate Compact on the Placement of Children and not a substantive change. *(Added by Stats.2002, c. 260 (S.B.1512), § 7.)*

§ 7909. "Executive head" defined; appointment of compact administrator

"Executive head" as used in Article 7 of the Interstate Compact on the Placement of Children means the Governor. The Governor shall appoint a compact administrator in accordance with the terms of Article 7 of the compact. *(Stats.1992, c. 162 (A.B.2650), § 10, operative Jan. 1, 1994.)*

Law Revision Commission Comments

Enactment [Revised Comment]

Section 7909 continues former Civil Code Section 273 without substantive change. [23 Cal.L.Rev.Comm. Reports 1 (1993)].

§ 7910. Refusal to grant approval of placement in violation of state law

Approval of an interstate placement of a child for adoption shall not be granted by the compact administrator if the placement is in violation of either Section 8801 of this code or Section 273 of the Penal Code. *(Stats.1992, c. 162 (A.B. 2650), § 10, operative Jan. 1, 1994.)*

Law Revision Commission Comments

Enactment [Revised Comment]

Section 7910 continues former Civil Code Section 274 without substantive change. [23 Cal.L.Rev.Comm. Reports 1 (1993)].

§ 7911. Authority of State Department of Social Services; out-of-state placements

The Legislature finds and declares all of the following:

(a) The health and safety of California children placed by a county social services agency or probation department out of state pursuant to the provisions of the Interstate Compact on the Placement of Children are a matter of statewide concern.

(b) The Legislature therefore affirms its intention that the State Department of Social Services has full authority to require an assessment and placement recommendation by a county multidisciplinary team prior to placement of a child in an out-of-state group home, to investigate allegations of child abuse or neglect of minors so placed, and to ensure that out-of-state group homes, accepting California children, meet all California group home licensing standards.

(c) The Legislature also affirms its intention that, on and after January 1, 2017, the licensing standards applicable to out-of-state group homes certified by the department shall be those required of short-term residential therapeutic programs operated in this state.

(d) This section is declaratory of existing law with respect to the Governor's designation of the State Department of Social Services to act as the compact administrator and of that department to act as the single state agency charged with supervision of public social services under Section 10600 of the Welfare and Institutions Code. *(Added by Stats.1998, c. 311 (S.B.933), § 9, eff. Aug. 19, 1998. Amended by Stats.1999, c. 881 (A.B.1659), § 1, eff. Oct. 10, 1999; Stats.2015, c. 773 (A.B.403), § 2, eff. Jan. 1, 2016; Stats.2016, c. 612 (A.B.1997), § 7, eff. Jan. 1, 2017.)*

§ 7911.1. Out-of-state placements; investigation authority; inspections; assessment and placement recommendations; denial, suspension or discontinuance of certification

(a) Notwithstanding any other law, the State Department of Social Services or its designee shall investigate any threat to the health and safety of children placed by a California county social services agency or probation department in an out-of-state group home pursuant to the provisions of the Interstate Compact on the Placement of Children. This authority shall include the authority to interview children or staff in private or review their file at the out-of-state facility or wherever the child or files may be at the time of the investigation. Notwithstanding any other law, the State Department of Social Services or its designee shall require certified out-of-state group homes to comply with the reporting requirements applicable to group homes licensed in California pursuant to Title 22 of the California Code of Regulations for each child in care regardless of whether he or she is a California placement, by submitting a copy of the required reports to the Compact Administrator within regulatory timeframes. The Compact Administrator within one business day of receiving a serious events report shall verbally notify the appropriate placement agencies and, within five working days of receiving a written report from the out-of-state group home, forward a copy of the written report to the appropriate placement agencies.

(b) Any contract, memorandum of understanding, or agreement entered into pursuant to paragraph (b) of Article 5 of the Interstate Compact on the Placement of Children regarding the placement of a child out of state by a California county social services agency or probation department shall include the language set forth in subdivision (a).

(c)(1) The State Department of Social Services or its designee shall perform initial and continuing inspection of out-of-state group homes in order to either certify that the out-of-state group home meets all licensure standards required of group homes operated in California or that the department has granted a waiver to a specific licensing standard upon a finding that there exists no adverse impact to health and safety.

(2)(A) On and after January 1, 2017, the licensing standards applicable to out-of-state group homes certified by the department, as described in paragraph (1), shall be those required of short-term residential therapeutic programs operated in this state, unless the out-of-state group home is granted an extension pursuant to subdivision (d) of Section 11462.04 of the Welfare and Institutions Code or has otherwise been granted a waiver pursuant to this subdivision.

(B) On and after January 1, 2017, the licensing standards applicable to out-of-state group homes certified by the department, as described in paragraph (1), shall include the licensing standards for mental health program approval in Section 1562.01 of the Health and Safety Code. These standards may be satisfied if the out-of-state group home has an equivalent mental health program approval in the state in which it is operating. If an out-of-state group home cannot satisfy the licensing standards for an equivalent mental health program approval, children shall not be placed in that facility.

(3) In order to receive certification, the out-of-state group home shall have a current license, or an equivalent approval, in good standing issued by the appropriate authority or authorities of the state in which it is operating.

(4) On and after January 1, 2017, an out-of-state group home program shall, in order to receive an AFDC–FC rate, meet the requirements of paragraph (2) of subdivision (c) of Section 11460 of the Welfare and Institutions Code.

(5) Any failure by an out-of-state group home facility to make children or staff available as required by subdivision (a) for a private interview or make files available for review shall be grounds to deny or discontinue the certification.

(6) Certifications made pursuant to this subdivision shall be reviewed annually.

(d) A county shall be required to obtain an assessment and placement recommendation by a county multidisciplinary team prior to placement of a child in an out-of-state group home facility.

(e) Any failure by an out-of-state group home to obtain or maintain its certification as required by subdivision (c) shall preclude the use of any public funds, whether county, state, or federal, in the payment for the placement of any child in that out-of-state group home, pursuant to the Interstate Compact on the Placement of Children.

(f)(1) A multidisciplinary team shall consist of participating members from county social services, county mental health, county probation, county superintendents of schools, and other members as determined by the county.

(2) Participants shall have knowledge or experience in the prevention, identification, and treatment of child abuse and neglect cases, and shall be qualified to recommend a broad range of services related to child abuse or neglect.

(g)(1) The department may deny, suspend, or discontinue the certification of the out-of-state group home if the department makes a finding that the group home is not operating in compliance with the requirements of subdivision (c).

(2) Any judicial proceeding to contest the department's determination as to the status of the out-of-state group home certificate shall be held in California pursuant to Section 1085 of the Code of Civil Procedure.

(h) The certification requirements of this section shall not impact placements of emotionally disturbed children made pursuant to an individualized education program developed pursuant to the federal Individuals with Disabilities Education Act (20 U.S.C. Sec. 1400 et seq.) if the placement is not funded with federal or state foster care funds.

(i) Only an out-of-state group home authorized by the Compact Administrator to receive state funds for the placement by a county social services agency or probation department of any child in that out-of-state group home from the effective date of this section shall be eligible for public funds pending the department's certification under this section. *(Added by Stats.1998, c. 311 (S.B.933), § 10, eff. Aug. 19, 1998. Amended by Stats.1999, c. 881 (A.B.1659), § 2, eff. Oct. 10, 1999; Stats.2011, c. 43 (A.B.114), § 31, eff. June 30, 2011; Stats.2015, c. 773 (A.B.403), § 3, eff. Jan. 1, 2016; Stats.2016, c. 612 (A.B.1997), § 8, eff. Jan. 1, 2017.)*

Research References

Forms

West's California Code Forms, Family § 7900, Comment Overview--Interstate Compact on Placement Of Children.

Treatises and Practice Aids

Witkin, California Summary 10th Parent and Child § 673, Child in Foster Care.
Witkin, California Summary 10th Parent and Child § 885, Case Plan.
Witkin, California Summary 10th Parent and Child § 941, Commitment Of Minor for Status Offense.

§ 7912. Out-of-state placements; rights of child; temporary suspension of placements

(a) The Legislature finds and declares that the health and safety of children in out-of-state group home care pursuant to the Interstate Compact on the Placement of Children is a matter of statewide concern. The Legislature therefore affirms its intention that children placed by a county social services agency or probation department in out-of-state group homes be accorded the same personal rights and safeguards of a child placed in a California group home. This section is in clarification of existing law.

(b)(1) The Compact Administrator may temporarily suspend any new placements in an out-of-state group home, for a period not to exceed 100 days, pending the completion of an investigation, pursuant to subdivision (a) of Section 7911.1, regarding a threat to the health and safety of children in care. During any suspension period the department or its designee shall have staff daily onsite at the out-of-state group home.

(2) On and after January 1, 2017, the licensing standards applicable to out-of-state group homes certified by the State Department of Social Services shall be those required of short-term residential therapeutic programs operated in this state. *(Added by Stats.1998, c. 311 (S.B.933), § 11, eff. Aug. 19, 1998. Amended by Stats.2015, c. 773 (A.B.403), § 4, eff. Jan. 1, 2016; Stats.2016, c. 612 (A.B.1997), § 9, eff. Jan. 1, 2017.)*

Research References

Forms

California Transactions Forms--Family Law § 6:2, Governing Law.
California Transactions Forms--Family Law § 6:116, Purpose and Background Of Interstate Compact.

§ 7913. Placement determinations by licensed private adoption agency; authority; limitations

(a) When a full service licensed private adoption agency has provided adoption-related services to a birth parent or prospective adoptive parent, that agency is delegated the authority to determine whether the placement shall or shall not be made pursuant to the Interstate Compact on the Placement of Children, and to sign the compact forms documenting that determination and date of placement.

(b) For children entering California in independent adoptions, prior to making a determination regarding placement and as soon as feasible, the private adoption agency shall notify the appropriate district office or delegated county adoption agency of the matter and verify that the preplacement interview of the prospective adoptive parent or parents has been completed.

(c) This section shall not apply to a child who is a dependent of the court or a child subject to a petition filed under Section 300 of the Welfare and Institutions Code. *(Added by Stats.2011, c. 462 (A.B.687), § 5.)*

Research References

Treatises and Practice Aids

Witkin, California Summary 10th Parent and Child § 80, Interstate Placement Of Children for Adoption.
Witkin, California Summary 10th Parent and Child § 116, in General.
Witkin, California Summary 10th Parent and Child § 127, Selection Of Prospective Adoptive Parents.

Part 6

FOSTER CARE PLACEMENT CONSIDERATIONS

Section

§ 7950. Relatives; race, color or national origin

(a) With full consideration for the proximity of the natural parents to the placement so as to facilitate visitation and family reunification, when a placement in foster care is being made, the following considerations shall be used:

(1) Placement shall, if possible, be made in the home of a relative, unless the placement would not be in the best interest of the child. Diligent efforts shall be made by an agency or entity to which this subdivision applies, to locate an appropriate relative, as defined in paragraph (2) of subdivision (f) of Section 319 of the Welfare and Institutions Code. At any permanency hearing in which the court terminates reunification services, or at any postpermanency hearing for a child not placed for adoption, the court shall find that the agency or entity to which this subdivision applies has made diligent efforts to locate an appropriate relative and that each relative whose name has been submitted to the agency or entity as a possible caretaker, either by himself or herself or by other persons, has been evaluated as an appropriate placement resource.

(2) No agency or entity that receives any state assistance and is involved in foster care placements may do either of the following:

(A) Deny to any person the opportunity to become a foster parent on the basis of the race, color, or national origin of the person or the child involved.

(B) Delay or deny the placement of a child into foster care on the basis of the race, color, or national origin of the foster parent or the child involved.

(b) Subdivision (a) shall not be construed to affect the application of the Indian Child Welfare Act of 1978 (25 U.S.C. Sec. 1901 et seq.).

(c) Nothing in this section precludes a search for an appropriate relative being conducted simultaneously with a search for a foster family. *(Added by Stats.1995, c. 884 (S.B.1743), § 2. Amended by Stats.2003, c. 323 (S.B.984), § 1; Stats.2003, c. 469 (S.B.947), § 3; Stats.2015, c. 425 (S.B.794), § 1, eff. Jan. 1, 2016.)*

Law Revision Commission Comments

Enactment [Revised Comment]

Section 7950 continues former Civil Code Section 275 without substantive change. [23 Cal.L.Rev.Comm. Reports 1 (1993)].

Research References

Treatises and Practice Aids

Witkin, California Summary 10th Parent and Child § 114, Ethnic, Cultural, and Jurisdictional Considerations.

Witkin, California Summary 10th Parent and Child § 635, in General.

Witkin, California Summary 10th Parent and Child § 638, Preferential Right Of Relatives.

Witkin, California Summary 10th Parent and Child § 639, Foster Care.

Witkin, California Summary 10th Parent and Child § 896, General Requirements.

§ 7951. Placement of less than 30 days

This part does not apply in determining the foster care setting in which the child may be placed for a period not intended to exceed 30 days. *(Added by Stats.1995, c. 884 (A.B.1743), § 2.)*

Research References

Treatises and Practice Aids

Witkin, California Summary 10th Parent and Child § 639, Foster Care.

§ 7952. Statement to court by minor

A minor 10 years of age or older being considered for placement in a foster home has the right to make a brief statement to the court making a decision on placement. The court may disregard any preferences expressed by the minor. The minor's right to make a statement is not limited to the initial placement, but continues for any proceedings concerning continued placement or a decision to return to parental custody. *(Added by Stats.1995, c. 884 (A.B.1743), § 2.)*

Research References

Treatises and Practice Aids

Witkin, California Summary 10th Parent and Child § 626, Conduct Of Hearing.

Part 7

SURROGACY AND DONOR FACILITATORS, ASSISTED REPRODUCTION AGREEMENTS FOR GESTATIONAL CARRIERS, AND OOCYTE DONATIONS

§ 7960. Definitions

For purposes of this part, the following terms have the following meanings:

(a) "Assisted reproduction agreement" has the same meaning as defined in subdivision (b) of Section 7606.

(b) "Fund management agreement" means the agreement between the intended parents and the surrogacy or donor facilitator relating to the fee or other valuable consideration for services rendered or that will be rendered by the surrogacy or donor facilitator.

(c) "Intended parent" means an individual, married or unmarried, who manifests the intent to be legally bound as the parent of a child resulting from assisted reproduction.

(d) "Nonattorney surrogacy or donor facilitator" means a surrogacy or donor practitioner who is not an attorney in good standing licensed to practice law in this state.

(e) "Surrogacy or donor facilitator" means a person or organization that engages in either of the following activities:

(1) Advertising for the purpose of soliciting parties to an assisted reproduction agreement or for the donation of

oocytes for use by a person other than the provider of the oocytes, or acting as an intermediary between the parties to an assisted reproduction agreement or oocyte donation.

(2) Charging a fee or other valuable consideration for services rendered relating to an assisted reproduction agreement or oocyte donation.

(f) "Surrogate" means a woman who bears and carries a child for another through medically assisted reproduction and pursuant to a written agreement, as set forth in Sections 7606 and 7962. Within the definition of surrogate are two different and distinct types:

(1) "Traditional surrogate" means a woman who agrees to gestate an embryo, in which the woman is the gamete donor and the embryo was created using the sperm of the intended father or a donor arranged by the intended parent or parents.

(2) "Gestational carrier" means a woman who is not an intended parent and who agrees to gestate an embryo that is genetically unrelated to her pursuant to an assisted reproduction agreement.

(g) "Donor" means a woman who provides her oocytes for use by another for the purpose of assisting the recipient of the oocytes in having a child or children of her own. *(Added by Stats.2010, c. 138 (A.B.2426), § 1. Amended by Stats.2012, c. 466 (A.B.1217), § 2; Stats.2015, c. 91 (A.B.1049), § 3, eff. Jan. 1, 2016.)*

Research References

Forms

California Transactions Forms--Family Law § 7:8.50, Surrogacy Facilitator.

Treatises and Practice Aids

Witkin, California Summary 10th Parent and Child § 21, in General.

§ 7961. Nonattorney surrogacy or donor facilitators; directing clients to deposit funds; financial interest or agency prohibited; disbursement; applicability

(a) A nonattorney surrogacy or donor facilitator shall direct the client to deposit all client funds into either of the following:

(1) An independent, bonded escrow depository maintained by a licensed, independent, bonded escrow company.

(2) A trust account maintained by an attorney.

(b) For purposes of this section, a nonattorney surrogacy or donor facilitator may not have a financial interest in any escrow company holding client funds. A nonattorney surrogacy or donor facilitator and any of its directors or employees shall not be an agent of any escrow company holding client funds.

(c) Client funds may only be disbursed by the attorney or escrow agent as set forth in the assisted reproduction agreement and fund management agreement.

(d) This section shall not apply to funds that are both of the following:

(1) Not provided for in the fund management agreement.

(2) Paid directly to a medical doctor for medical services or a psychologist for psychological services. *(Added by Stats.2010, c. 138 (A.B.2426), § 1. Amended by Stats.2015, c. 91 (A.B.1049), § 4, eff. Jan. 1, 2016.)*

Research References

Forms

California Transactions Forms--Family Law § 7:8.50, Surrogacy Facilitator.

Treatises and Practice Aids

Witkin, California Summary 10th Parent and Child § 21, in General.

§ 7962. Assisted reproduction agreements for gestational carriers; requirements; actions to establish parent-child relationship; rebuttal of presumptions; judgment or order; confidentiality; presumption of validity

(a) An assisted reproduction agreement for gestational carriers shall contain, but shall not be limited to, all of the following information:

(1) The date on which the assisted reproduction agreement for gestational carriers was executed.

(2) The persons from which the gametes originated, unless donated gametes were used, in which case the assisted reproduction agreement does not need to specify the name of the donor but shall specify whether the donated gamete or gametes were eggs, sperm, or embryos, or all.

(3) The identity of the intended parent or parents.

(4) Disclosure of how the intended parents will cover the medical expenses of the gestational carrier and of the newborn or newborns. If health care coverage is used to cover those medical expenses, the disclosure shall include a review of the health care policy provisions related to coverage for surrogate pregnancy, including any possible liability of the gestational carrier, third-party liability liens or other insurance coverage, and any notice requirements that could affect coverage or liability of the gestational carrier. The review and disclosure do not constitute legal advice. If coverage of liability is uncertain, a statement of that fact shall be sufficient to meet the requirements of this section.

(b) Prior to executing the written assisted reproduction agreement for gestational carriers, a surrogate and the intended parent or intended parents shall be represented by separate independent licensed attorneys of their choosing.

(c) The assisted reproduction agreement for gestational carriers shall be executed by the parties and the signatures on the assisted reproduction agreement for gestational carriers shall be notarized or witnessed by an equivalent method of affirmation as required in the jurisdiction where the assisted reproduction agreement for gestational carriers is executed.

(d) The parties to an assisted reproduction agreement for gestational carriers shall not undergo an embryo transfer procedure, or commence injectable medication in preparation for an embryo transfer for assisted reproduction purposes, until the assisted reproduction agreement for gestational carriers has been fully executed as required by subdivisions (b) and (c) of this section.

(e) An action to establish the parent-child relationship between the intended parent or parents and the child as to a child conceived pursuant to an assisted reproduction agreement for gestational carriers may be filed before the child's birth and may be filed in the county where the child is anticipated to be born, the county where the intended parent or intended parents reside, the county where the surrogate resides, the county where the assisted reproduction agreement for gestational carriers is executed, or the county where medical procedures pursuant to the agreement are to be performed. A copy of the assisted reproduction agreement for gestational carriers shall be lodged in the court action filed for the purpose of establishing the parent-child relationship. The parties to the assisted reproduction agreement for gestational carriers shall attest, under penalty of perjury, and to the best of their knowledge and belief, as to the parties' compliance with this section in entering into the assisted reproduction agreement for gestational carriers. Submitting those declarations shall not constitute a waiver, under Section 912 of the Evidence Code, of the lawyer-client privilege described in Article 3 (commencing with Section 950) of Chapter 4 of Division 8 of the Evidence Code.

(f)(1) A notarized assisted reproduction agreement for gestational carriers signed by all the parties, with the attached declarations of independent attorneys, and lodged with the superior court in accordance with this section, shall rebut any presumptions contained within Part 2 (commencing with Section 7540), subdivision (a) of Section 7610, and Sections 7611 and 7613, as to the gestational carrier surrogate, her spouse, or partner being a parent of the child or children.

(2) Upon petition of any party to a properly executed assisted reproduction agreement for gestational carriers, the court shall issue a judgment or order establishing a parent-child relationship, whether pursuant to Section 7630 or otherwise. The judgment or order may be issued before or after the child's or children's birth subject to the limitations of Section 7633. Subject to proof of compliance with this section, the judgment or order shall establish the parent-child relationship of the intended parent or intended parents identified in the surrogacy agreement and shall establish that the surrogate, her spouse, or partner is not a parent of, and has no parental rights or duties with respect to, the child or children. The judgment or order shall * * * be issued forthwith and * * * without further hearing or evidence, unless the court or a party to the assisted reproduction agreement for gestational carriers has a good faith, reasonable belief that the assisted reproduction agreement for gestational carriers or attorney declarations were not executed in accordance with this section. Upon motion by a party to the assisted reproduction agreement for gestational carriers, the matter shall be scheduled for hearing before a judgment or order is issued. Nothing in this section shall be construed to prevent a court from finding and declaring that the intended parent is or intended parents are the parent or parents of the child where compliance with this section has not been met; however, the court shall require sufficient proof entitling the parties to the relief sought.

(g) The petition, relinquishment or consent, agreement, order, report to the court from any investigating agency, and any power of attorney and deposition filed in the office of the clerk of the court pursuant to this part shall not be open to inspection by any person other than the parties to the proceeding and their attorneys and the State Department of Social Services, except upon the written authority of a judge of the superior court. A judge of the superior court shall not authorize anyone to inspect the petition, relinquishment or consent, agreement, order, report to the court from any investigating agency, or power of attorney or deposition, or any portion of those documents, except in exceptional circumstances and where necessary. The petitioner may be required to pay the expense of preparing the copies of the documents to be inspected.

(h) Upon the written request of any party to the proceeding and the order of any judge of the superior court, the clerk of the court shall not provide any documents referred to in subdivision (g) for inspection or copying to any other person, unless the name of the gestational carrier or any information tending to identify the gestational carrier is deleted from the documents or copies thereof.

(i) An assisted reproduction agreement for gestational carriers executed in accordance with this section is presumptively valid and shall not be rescinded or revoked without a court order. For purposes of this part, any failure to comply with the requirements of this section shall rebut the presumption of the validity of the assisted reproduction agreement for gestational carriers. *(Added by Stats.2012, c. 466 (A.B.1217), § 3. Amended by Stats.2014, c. 636 (A.B.2344), § 2, eff. Jan. 1, 2015; Stats.2016, c. 385 (A.B.2349), § 4, eff. Jan. 1, 2017; Stats.2017, c. 326 (A.B.1396), § 1, eff. Jan. 1, 2018.)*

Commentary

C.M. v. M.C., 7 Cal.App.5th 1188, 213 Cal.Rptr.3d 351 (2017), review denied, cert. denied, affirmed a trial court judgment, which found that when the requirements of this section were met, a man was the sole parent of triplets born as the result of a surrogacy agreement and terminated the parental rights of the surrogate mother. *C.M. v. M.C.* rejected the surrogate's constitutional claims on the ground that the California surrogacy scheme had already been constitutionally approved by *Johnson v. Calvert, 5 Cal.4th 84, 851 P.2d 776, 19 Cal.Rptr.2d 494 (1993)*. For discussion of *Johnson v. Calvert*, see Commentary to Family Code section 7650.

Research References

Forms

California Transactions Forms--Family Law § 7:8.50, Surrogacy Facilitator.

Treatises and Practice Aids

Witkin, California Summary 10th Parent and Child § 23A, (New) Assisted Reproduction Agreements for Gestational Carriers.

Division 13

ADOPTION

Part 1

DEFINITIONS

§ 8500. Construction of division

Unless the provision or context otherwise requires, the definitions in this part govern the construction of this division. *(Stats.1992, c. 162 (A.B.2650), § 10, operative Jan. 1, 1994.)*

Law Revision Commission Comments

Enactment [Revised Comment]

Section 8500 is new and is comparable to Section 50. Section 8500 supersedes the introductory clause of former Civil Code Section 220.20. The definitions in this part have been made applicable to both minor adoptions governed by Part 2 and adult adoptions governed by Part 3. [23 Cal.L.Rev.Comm. Reports 1 (1993)].

Research References

Forms

California Transactions Forms--Family Law § 6:2, Governing Law.
California Transactions Forms--Family Law § 6:83, Nature Of Agency Adoption--Governing Law.

Treatises and Practice Aids

Witkin, California Summary 10th Husband and Wife § 3, Statutory Framework.
Witkin, California Summary 10th Parent and Child § 72, Statutory Framework.

§ 8502. "Adoption service provider" defined

(a) "Adoption service provider" means any of the following:

(1) A licensed private adoption agency.

(2) An individual who has presented satisfactory evidence to the department that he or she is a licensed clinical social worker who also has a minimum of five years of experience providing professional social work services while employed by a licensed California adoption agency or the department.

(3) In a state other than California, or a country other than the United States, an adoption agency licensed or otherwise approved under the laws of that state or country, or an individual who is licensed or otherwise certified as a clinical social worker under the laws of that state or country.

(4) An individual who has presented satisfactory evidence to the department that he or she is a licensed marriage and family therapist who has a minimum of five years of experience providing professional adoption casework services while employed by a licensed California adoption agency or the department. The department shall review the qualifications of each individual to determine if he or she has performed professional adoption casework services for five years as required by this section while employed by a licensed California adoption agency or the department.

(b) If, in the case of a birth parent located in California, at least three adoption service providers are not reasonably available, or, in the case of a birth parent located outside of California or outside of the United States who has contacted at least three potential adoption service providers and been unsuccessful in obtaining the services of an adoption service provider who is reasonably available and willing to provide services, independent legal counsel for the birth parent may serve as an adoption service provider pursuant to subdivision (e) of Section 8801.5. "Reasonably available" means that an adoption service provider is all of the following:

(1) Available within five days for an advisement of rights pursuant to Section 8801.5, or within 24 hours for the signing of the placement agreement pursuant to paragraph (3) of subdivision (b) of Section 8801.3.

(2) Within 100 miles of the birth mother.

(3) Available for a cost not exceeding five hundred dollars ($500) to make an advisement of rights and to witness the signing of the placement agreement.

(c) Where an attorney acts as an adoption service provider, the fee to make an advisement of rights and to witness the signing of the placement agreement shall not exceed five hundred dollars ($500). *(Added by Stats.1993, c. 758 (S.B. 792), § 3, operative Jan. 1, 1995. Amended by Stats.1994, c. 585 (A.B.3336), § 1; Stats.1997, c. 559 (S.B.1121), § 1;*

Stats.2002, c. 1013 (S.B.2026), § 81; Stats.2004, c. 858 (S.B.1357), § 3.)

Research References

Forms

California Transactions Forms--Family Law § 6:34, Role Of Adoption Service Provider.

California Transactions Forms--Family Law § 6:40, Structuring the Adoption.

Treatises and Practice Aids

Witkin, California Summary 10th Parent and Child § 124, Adoption Service Providers.

§ 8503. "Adoptive parent" defined

"Adoptive parent" means a person who has obtained an order of adoption of a minor child or, in the case of an adult adoption, an adult. *(Stats.1992, c. 162 (A.B.2650), § 10, operative Jan. 1, 1994.)*

Law Revision Commission Comments

Enactment [Revised Comment]

Section 8503 supersedes former Civil Code Section 220.20(a). The definition has been broadened to apply to adoptions of minors and adults. The reference in the former law to petitioning for an adoption order has been omitted as surplus. The reference to final decrees of adoption has been omitted as surplus. See Section 100 ("order" includes decree, as appropriate). The reference to children is also omitted as surplus. See Section 10 (singular includes plural). [23 Cal.L.Rev.Comm. Reports 1 (1993)].

Research References

Forms

California Transactions Forms--Family Law § 6:3, Definitions.

Treatises and Practice Aids

Witkin, California Summary 10th Parent and Child § 77, Adoptive Parents.

Witkin, California Summary 10th Parent and Child § 154, in General.

§ 8506. "Agency adoption" defined

"Agency adoption" means the adoption of a minor, other than an intercountry adoption, in which the department, county adoption agency, or licensed adoption agency is a party to, or joins in, the adoption petition. *(Stats.1992, c. 162 (A.B.2650), § 10, operative Jan. 1, 1994. Amended by Stats. 2012, c. 35 (S.B.1013), § 2, eff. June 27, 2012.)*

Law Revision Commission Comments

Enactment [Revised Comment]

Section 8506 continues former Civil Code Section 220.20(b) without substantive change. The defined term "licensed adoption agency" is used instead of the former reference to "an agency licensed by the department." For provisions relating to agency adoptions, see Chapter 2 (commencing with Section 8700) of Part 2.

See also Sections 8518 ("department" defined), 8527 ("intercountry adoption" defined), 8530 ("licensed adoption agency" defined). [23 Cal.L.Rev.Comm. Reports 1 (1993)].

Research References

Forms

California Transactions Forms--Family Law § 6:4, Types Of Adoptions.

California Transactions Forms--Family Law § 6:83, Nature Of Agency Adoption--Governing Law.

Treatises and Practice Aids

Witkin, California Summary 10th Parent and Child § 70, Types Of Adoption.

Witkin, California Summary 10th Parent and Child § 106, Types Of Agencies.

§ 8509. "Applicant" defined

"Applicant" means a person who has submitted a written application to adopt a child from the department, county adoption agency, or licensed adoption agency and who is being considered by the adoption agency for the adoptive placement of a child. *(Stats.1992, c. 162 (A.B.2650), § 10, operative Jan. 1, 1994. Amended by Stats.2012, c. 35 (S.B. 1013), § 3, eff. June 27, 2012.)*

Law Revision Commission Comments

Enactment [Revised Comment]

Section 8509 continues former Civil Code Section 220.20(c) without change. See also Sections 8518 ("department" defined), 8530 ("licensed adoption agency" defined). [23 Cal.L.Rev.Comm. Reports 1 (1993)].

Research References

Treatises and Practice Aids

Witkin, California Summary 10th Parent and Child § 94, Investigation Of Prospective Adoptive Parents.

§ 8512. "Birth parent" defined

"Birth parent" means the biological parent or, in the case of a person previously adopted, the adoptive parent. *(Stats. 1992, c. 162 (A.B.2650), § 10, operative Jan. 1, 1994.)*

Law Revision Commission Comments

Enactment [Revised Comment]

Section 8512 continues former Civil Code Section 220.20(d) without substantive change. A reference to "person" has been substituted for "child," since this definition also applies to Part 3 (commencing with Section 9300) concerning adult adoptions. See also Section 8503 ("adoptive parent" defined). [23 Cal.L.Rev. Comm. Reports 1 (1993)].

Research References

Forms

California Transactions Forms--Family Law § 6:3, Definitions.

Treatises and Practice Aids

Witkin, California Summary 10th Parent and Child § 100, in General.

§ 8513. "County adoption agency" defined

"County adoption agency" means an adoption agency operated by a county or consortium of counties. *(Added by Stats.2012, c. 35 (S.B.1013), § 4, eff. June 27, 2012.)*

Research References

Treatises and Practice Aids

Witkin, California Summary 10th Parent and Child § 106, Types Of Agencies.

§ 8514. "Days" defined

"Days" means calendar days, unless otherwise specified. *(Added by Stats.1994, c. 585 (A.B.3336), § 2.)*

§ 8515. "Delegated county adoption agency" defined

"Delegated county adoption agency" means a county adoption agency that has agreed to provide the services described in Chapter 3 (commencing with Section 8800) of Part 2. *(Stats.1992, c. 162 (A.B.2650), § 10, operative Jan. 1, 1994. Amended by Stats.2012, c. 35 (S.B.1013), § 5, eff. June 27, 2012.)*

Law Revision Commission Comments

Enactment [Revised Comment]

Section 8515 continues former Civil Code Section 220.20(f) without substantive change. See also Section 8530 ("licensed adoption agency" defined). [23 Cal.L.Rev.Comm. Reports 1 (1993)].

Research References

Treatises and Practice Aids

Witkin, California Summary 10th Parent and Child § 128, Adoption Placement Agreement.

§ 8518. "Department" defined

"Department" means the State Department of Social Services. *(Stats.1992, c. 162 (A.B.2650), § 10, operative Jan. 1, 1994.)*

Law Revision Commission Comments

Enactment [Revised Comment]

Section 8518 continues former Civil Code Section 220.20(g) without change. [23 Cal.L.Rev.Comm. Reports 1 (1993)].

Research References

Treatises and Practice Aids

Witkin, California Summary 10th Parent and Child § 70, Types Of Adoption.

Witkin, California Summary 10th Parent and Child § 106, Types Of Agencies.

§ 8521. "Full-service adoption agency" defined

(a) "Full-service adoption agency" means a licensed or authorized entity engaged in the business of providing adoption services, that does all of the following:

(1) Assumes care, custody, and control of a child through relinquishment of the child to the agency or involuntary termination of parental rights to the child.

(2) Assesses the birth parents, prospective adoptive parents, or child.

(3) Places children for adoption.

(4) Supervises adoptive placements.

(b) Private full-service adoption agencies shall be organized and operated on a nonprofit basis. As a condition of licensure to provide intercountry adoption services, a private full-service adoption agency shall be accredited by the Council on Accreditation, or supervised by an accredited primary provider, or acting as an exempted provider, in compliance with Subpart F (commencing with Section 96.29) of Part 96 of Title 22 of the Code of Federal Regulations. *(Stats.1992, c. 162 (A.B.2650), § 10, operative Jan. 1, 1994. Amended by Stats.2007, c. 583 (S.B.703), § 3; Stats.2012, c. 35 (S.B.1013), § 6, eff. June 27, 2012.)*

Law Revision Commission Comments

Enactment [Revised Comment]

Section 8521 continues former Civil Code Section 220.20(h) without substantive change. Language in subdivision (b) that was subject to a January 1, 1994, sunset clause has been omitted. See also Sections 8512 ("birth parent" defined), 8542 ("prospective adoptive parent" defined). [23 Cal.L.Rev.Comm. Reports 1 (1993)].

Research References

Treatises and Practice Aids

Witkin, California Summary 10th Parent and Child § 106, Types Of Agencies.

Witkin, California Summary 10th Parent and Child § 137, in General.

§ 8524. "Independent adoption" defined

"Independent adoption" means the adoption of a child in which neither the department, county adoption agency, nor agency licensed by the department is a party to, or joins in, the adoption petition. *(Stats.1992, c. 162 (A.B.2650), § 10, operative Jan. 1, 1994. Amended by Stats.2012, c. 35 (S.B. 1013), § 7, eff. June 27, 2012.)*

Law Revision Commission Comments

Enactment [Revised Comment]

Section 8524 continues former Civil Code Section 220.20(i) without substantive change. For provisions relating to independent adoptions, see Chapter 3 (commencing with Section 8800) of Part 2.

See also Sections 8518 ("department" defined), 8530 ("licensed adoption agency" defined). [23 Cal.L.Rev.Comm. Reports 1 (1993)].

Research References

Forms

California Transactions Forms--Family Law § 6:4, Types Of Adoptions.

Treatises and Practice Aids

Witkin, California Summary 10th Parent and Child § 70, Types Of Adoption.

Witkin, California Summary 10th Parent and Child § 123, Nature Of Independent Adoption.

§ 8527. "Intercountry adoption" defined

"Intercountry adoption" means the adoption of a foreign-born child for whom federal law makes a special immigration visa available. Intercountry adoption includes completion of the adoption in the child's native country or completion of the adoption in this state. *(Stats.1992, c. 162 (A.B.2650), § 10, operative Jan. 1, 1994.)*

Law Revision Commission Comments

Enactment [Revised Comment]

Section 8527 continues former Civil Code Section 220.20(j) without substantive change. For provisions relating to intercountry adoptions, see Chapter 4 (commencing with Section 8900) of Part 2. [23 Cal.L.Rev.Comm. Reports 1 (1993)].

Research References

Forms

California Transactions Forms--Family Law § 6:139, Overview Of Intercountry Adoption.

Treatises and Practice Aids

Witkin, California Summary 10th Parent and Child § 70, Types Of Adoption.

Witkin, California Summary 10th Parent and Child § 137, in General.

§ 8530. "Licensed adoption agency" defined

"Licensed adoption agency" means an agency licensed by the department to provide adoption services. *(Stats.1992, c. 162 (A.B.2650), § 10, operative Jan. 1, 1994. Amended by Stats.2012, c. 35 (S.B.1013), § 8, eff. June 27, 2012.)*

Law Revision Commission Comments

Enactment [Revised Comment]

Section 8530 continues former Civil Code Section 220.20(k) without change. See also Section 8518 ("department" defined). [23 Cal.L.Rev.Comm. Reports 1 (1993)].

Research References

Treatises and Practice Aids

Witkin, California Summary 10th Parent and Child § 106, Types Of Agencies.

§ 8533. "Noncustodial adoption agency" defined

(a) "Noncustodial adoption agency" means any licensed entity engaged in the business of providing adoption services, which does all of the following:

(1) Assesses the prospective adoptive parents.

(2) Cooperatively matches children freed for adoption, who are under the care, custody, and control of a licensed adoption agency, for adoption, with assessed and approved prospective adoptive parents.

(3) Cooperatively supervises adoptive placements with a full-service adoption agency, but does not disrupt a placement or remove a child from a placement.

(b) Private noncustodial adoption agencies shall be organized and operated on a nonprofit basis. As a condition of licensure to provide intercountry adoption services, a noncustodial adoption agency shall be accredited by the Council on Accreditation, or supervised by an accredited primary provider, or acting as an exempted provider, in compliance with Subpart F (commencing with Section 96.29) of Part 96 of Title 22 of the Code of Federal Regulations. *(Stats.1992, c. 162 (A.B.2650), § 10, operative Jan. 1, 1994. Amended by Stats.2007, c. 583 (S.B.703), § 4.)*

Law Revision Commission Comments

Enactment [Revised Comment]

Section 8533 continues former Civil Code Section 220.20(*l*) without substantive change. In subdivision (a)(2), the reference to "prospective adoptive applicants" has been changed to "prospective adoptive parents." See Section 8542 ("prospective adoptive parent" defined). Language in subdivision (b) that was subject to a January 1, 1994, sunset clause has been omitted. See also Sections 8512 ("birth parent" defined), 8521 ("full-service adoption agency" defined), 8530 ("licensed adoption agency" defined). [23 Cal.L.Rev. Comm. Reports 1 (1993)].

Research References

Treatises and Practice Aids

Witkin, California Summary 10th Parent and Child § 106, Types Of Agencies.

Witkin, California Summary 10th Parent and Child § 137, in General.

§ 8539. "Place for adoption" defined

"Place for adoption" means, in the case of an independent adoption, the selection of a prospective adoptive parent or parents for a child by the birth parent or parents and the completion of an adoptive placement agreement on a form prescribed by the department by the birth parent or parents placing the child with prospective adoptive parents.

This section shall become operative on January 1, 1995. *(Added by Stats.1993, c. 758 (S.B.792), § 4, operative Jan. 1, 1995.)*

Research References

Forms

California Transactions Forms--Family Law § 6:3, Definitions.

Treatises and Practice Aids

Witkin, California Summary 10th Parent and Child § 123, Nature Of Independent Adoption.

§ 8542. "Prospective adoptive parent" defined

"Prospective adoptive parent" means a person who has filed or intends to file a petition under Part 2 (commencing with Section 8600) to adopt a child who has been or who is to be placed in the person's physical care or a petition under Part 3 (commencing with Section 9300) to adopt an adult. *(Stats.1992, c. 162 (A.B.2650), § 10, operative Jan. 1, 1994.)*

Law Revision Commission Comments

Enactment [Revised Comment]

Section 8542 restates former Civil Code Section 220.20(p) without substantive change and also applies the definition to adult adoptions. [23 Cal.L.Rev.Comm. Reports 1 (1993)].

Research References

Treatises and Practice Aids

Witkin, California Summary 10th Parent and Child § 77, Adoptive Parents.

Witkin, California Summary 10th Parent and Child § 154, in General.

§ 8543. "Qualified court investigator" defined

"Qualified court investigator" means a superior court investigator with the same minimum qualifications as a probation officer or county welfare worker designated to conduct stepparent adoption investigations in stepparent adoption proceedings and proceedings to declare a minor free from parental custody and control. *(Added by Stats. 1993, c. 219 (A.B.1500), § 185.)*

Law Revision Commission Comments

Enactment [Revised Comment]

Section 8543 continues without substantive change part of former Civil Code Section 220.20 added by Section 1 of Chapter 472 of the Statutes of 1992, but inadvertently chaptered out by amendments to the same section made by Section 2 of Chapter 1353 of the Statutes of 1992. [23 Cal.L.Rev.Comm. Reports 1 (1993)].

Research References

Treatises and Practice Aids

Witkin, California Summary 10th Parent and Child § 142, Consent Of Birth Parents.

§ 8545. "Special needs child" defined

"Special needs child" means a child for whom all of the following are true:

(a) It has been determined that the child cannot or should not be returned to the home of his or her parents, as evidenced by a petition for termination of parental rights, a court order terminating parental rights, or a signed relinquishment.

(b) The child has at least one of the following characteristics that is a barrier to his or her adoption:

(1) Adoptive placement without financial assistance is unlikely because of membership in a sibling group that should remain intact, or by virtue of race, ethnicity, color, language, age of three years or older, or parental background of a medical or behavioral nature that can be determined to adversely affect the development of the child.

(2) Adoptive placement without financial assistance is unlikely because the child has a mental, physical, emotional, or medical disability that has been certified by a licensed professional competent to make an assessment and operating within the scope of his or her profession. This paragraph shall also apply to children with a developmental disability as defined in subdivision (a) of Section 4512 of the Welfare and Institutions Code, including those determined to require out-of-home nonmedical care as described in Section 11464 of the Welfare and Institutions Code.

(c) The need for adoption subsidy is evidenced by an unsuccessful search for an adoptive home to take the child without financial assistance, as documented in the case file of the prospective adoptive child. The requirement for this search shall be waived when it would be against the best interest of the child because of the existence of significant emotional ties with prospective adoptive parents while in the care of these persons as a foster child. *(Stats.1992, c. 162 (A.B.2650), § 10, operative Jan. 1, 1994. Amended by Stats. 2009, c. 339 (S.B.597), § 1.)*

Law Revision Commission Comments

Enactment [Revised Comment]

Section 8545 continues former Civil Code Section 220.20(q) without substantive change. [23 Cal.L.Rev.Comm. Reports 1 (1993)].

Research References

Treatises and Practice Aids

Witkin, California Summary 10th Parent and Child § 86, Programs to Facilitate Adoption.

§ 8548. "Stepparent adoption" defined

"Stepparent adoption" means an adoption of a child by a stepparent where one birth parent retains custody and control of the child. *(Stats.1992, c. 162 (A.B.2650), § 10, operative Jan. 1, 1994.)*

Law Revision Commission Comments

Enactment [Revised Comment]

Section 8548 continues former Civil Code Section 220.20(r) without substantive change. For provisions relating to stepparent adoptions, see Chapter 5 (commencing with Section 9000) of Part 2. See also Section 8512 ("birth parent" defined). [23 Cal.L.Rev. Comm. Reports 1 (1993)].

Research References

Forms

California Transactions Forms--Family Law § 6:2, Governing Law.
California Transactions Forms--Family Law § 6:4, Types Of Adoptions.
California Transactions Forms--Family Law § 6:104, Nature and Purpose Of Stepparent Adoption.

Treatises and Practice Aids

Witkin, California Summary 10th Parent and Child § 70, Types Of Adoption.

Part 2

ADOPTION OF UNMARRIED MINORS

CHAPTER 1. GENERAL PROVISIONS

§ 8600. Children eligible for adoption

An unmarried minor may be adopted by an adult as provided in this part. *(Stats.1992, c. 162 (A.B.2650), § 10, operative Jan. 1, 1994.)*

Law Revision Commission Comments

Enactment [Revised Comment]

Section 8600 restates former Civil Code Section 221.10 without substantive change and supersedes former Civil Code Section 220.20(e) ("child" means minor child). The language of this section has been simplified. [23 Cal.L.Rev.Comm. Reports 1 (1993)].

Research References

Forms

California Transactions Forms--Family Law § 5:6, Obtaining Rights Through Adoption.
California Transactions Forms--Family Law § 6:2, Governing Law.
California Transactions Forms--Family Law § 6:6, Who May Adopt.
California Transactions Forms--Family Law § 6:47, Matters to Consider in Drafting Petition for Independent Adoption Of Unmarried Minor.
California Transactions Forms--Family Law § 6:112, Form Drafting Considerations.
West's California Code Forms, Family § 7660, Comment Overview--Termination Of Parental Rights in Adoption Proceedings.
West's California Code Forms, Family § 8600, Comment Overview--Adoption Of Unmarried Minors.
West's California Code Forms, Family § 9100, Comment Overview--Vacation Of Adoption.

Treatises and Practice Aids

Witkin, California Summary 10th Parent and Child § 46, in General.
Witkin, California Summary 10th Parent and Child § 61, Notice Of Adoption Proceeding.
Witkin, California Summary 10th Parent and Child § 70, Types Of Adoption.
Witkin, California Summary 10th Parent and Child § 72, Statutory Framework.
Witkin, California Summary 10th Parent and Child § 76, Nature and Effect Of Adoption.
Witkin, California Summary 10th Parent and Child § 77, Adoptive Parents.
Witkin, California Summary 10th Parent and Child § 91, Jurisdiction, Venue, and Conflict Of Laws.
Witkin, California Summary 10th Parent and Child § 93, Medical Report on Child and Birth Parents.
Witkin, California Summary 10th Parent and Child § 149, Confidentiality Of Records.
Witkin, California Summary 10th Parent and Child § 451, in General.

§ 8600.5. Tribal customary adoption not applicable to this part

Tribal customary adoption as defined in Section 366.24 of the Welfare and Institutions Code and as applied to Indian Children who are dependents of the court, does not apply to this part. *(Added by Stats.2009, c. 287 (A.B.1325), § 1, operative July 1, 2010. Amended by Stats.2012, c. 35 (S.B. 1013), § 9, eff. June 27, 2012.)*

Research References

Forms

California Transactions Forms--Family Law § 6:143, Overview Of Indian Child Welfare Act (ICWA).

Treatises and Practice Aids

Witkin, California Summary 10th Parent and Child § 70, Types Of Adoption.

§ 8601. Adoptive parent; age requirements; exception

(a) Except as otherwise provided in subdivision (b), a prospective adoptive parent or parents shall be at least 10 years older than the child.

(b) If the court is satisfied that the adoption of a child by a stepparent, or by a sister, brother, aunt, uncle, or first cousin and, if that person is married, by that person and that person's spouse, is in the best interest of the parties and is in the public interest, it may approve the adoption without regard to the ages of the child and the prospective adoptive parent or parents. *(Stats.1992, c. 162 (A.B.2650), § 10, operative Jan. 1, 1994.)*

Law Revision Commission Comments

Enactment [Revised Comment]

Section 8601 continues former Civil Code Section 221.12 without substantive change. In subdivision (a), "prospective adoptive parent or parents" has been substituted for "person adopting a child" for consistency with the language of subdivision (b) and Sections 8612, 8801, and 8815. As revised, subdivision (a) provides that both prospective adoptive parents are subject to the 10–year age difference rule. See Section 8542 ("prospective adoptive parent" defined). A reference to "child" has been substituted for "person adopted." This is not a substantive change.

In subdivision (b), a reference to "first cousin" has been substituted for "cousin-german." This is not a substantive change. [23 Cal.L.Rev.Comm. Reports 1 (1993)].

Research References

Forms

California Transactions Forms--Family Law § 5:6, Obtaining Rights Through Adoption.
California Transactions Forms--Family Law § 6:6, Who May Adopt.
California Transactions Forms--Family Law § 6:7, Who May be Adopted.
California Transactions Forms--Family Law § 6:47, Matters to Consider in Drafting Petition for Independent Adoption Of Unmarried Minor.
Nichols Cyclopedia of Legal Forms Annotated § 7:5, Statutory Provisions--Who May be Adopted.
West's California Code Forms, Family § 8600, Comment Overview--Adoption Of Unmarried Minors.

Treatises and Practice Aids

Witkin, California Summary 10th Parent and Child § 77, Adoptive Parents.

§ 8601.5. Nunc pro tunc entry of orders of adoption

(a) A court may issue an order of adoption and declare that it shall be entered nunc pro tunc when it will serve public policy and the best interests of the child, such as cases where adoption finalization has been delayed beyond the child's 18th birthday due to factors beyond the control of the prospective adoptive family and the proposed adoptee.

(b) The request for nunc pro tunc entry of the order shall be stated in the adoption request or an amendment thereto, and shall set forth specific facts in support thereof.

(c) To the extent that a child's eligibility for any publicly funded benefit program is or could be altered by the entry of an order of adoption, the change in eligibility shall not be determined as of the nunc pro tunc date, but shall be determined as of the date of the adoption finalization hearing.

(d) The nunc pro tunc date shall not precede the date upon which the parental rights of the birth parent or parents were initially terminated, whether voluntarily or involuntarily. *(Added by Stats.2011, c. 462 (A.B.687), § 6.)*

Research References

Forms

West's California Judicial Council Forms ADOPT-200, Adoption Request.
West's California Judicial Council Forms ADOPT-215, Adoption Order.

Treatises and Practice Aids

Witkin, California Summary 10th Parent and Child § 81A, (New) Nunc Pro Tunc Entry Of Adoption Order.

§ 8602. Consent of child

The consent of a child, if over the age of 12 years, is necessary to the child's adoption. *(Stats.1992, c. 162 (A.B. 2650), § 10, operative Jan. 1, 1994.)*

Law Revision Commission Comments

Enactment [Revised Comment]

Section 8602 continues former Civil Code Section 221.13 without substantive change. [23 Cal.L.Rev.Comm. Reports 1 (1993)].

Research References

Forms

California Transactions Forms--Family Law § 6:7, Who May be Adopted.
California Transactions Forms--Family Law § 6:8, Consent for Adoption Of Unmarried Minor.
California Transactions Forms--Family Law § 6:47, Matters to Consider in Drafting Petition for Independent Adoption Of Unmarried Minor.
Am. Jur. Pl. & Pr. Forms Adoption § 94, Person Other Than Natural Parent--Child.
West's California Code Forms, Family § 8600, Comment Overview--Adoption Of Unmarried Minors.
West's California Code Forms, Family § 8612 Form 2, Adoption Agreement.
West's California Judicial Council Forms ADOPT-210, Adoption Agreement.

Treatises and Practice Aids

Witkin, California Summary 10th Parent and Child § 98, in General.

§ 8603. Married adoptive parent; consent of spouse

(a) A married person, not lawfully separated from the person's spouse, shall not adopt a child without the consent of the spouse, provided that the spouse is capable of giving that consent.

(b) The consent of the spouse shall not establish any parental rights or responsibilities on the part of the consenting spouse unless he or she has consented to adopt the child in a writing filed with the court and is named in the final decree as an adoptive parent. The court shall not name the consenting spouse as an adoptive parent in the final decree unless the consenting spouse has filed a written consent to adopt the child with the court and has an approved adoption home study.

(c) The court may dispense with the consent of a spouse who cannot be located after diligent search, or a spouse determined by the court to lack the capacity to consent. A spouse for whom consent was dispensed shall not be named as an adoptive parent in the final decree. *(Stats.1992, c. 162 (A.B.2650), § 10, operative Jan. 1, 1994. Amended by Stats. 2014, c. 763 (A.B.1701), § 7, eff. Jan. 1, 2015.)*

Law Revision Commission Comments

Enactment [Revised Comment]

Section 8603 continues former Civil Code Section 221.14 without substantive change. The language of this section has been simplified by eliminating paired references to husband and wife. [23 Cal. L.Rev.Comm. Reports 1 (1993)].

Research References

Forms

California Transactions Forms--Family Law § 6:6, Who May Adopt.
California Transactions Forms--Family Law § 6:8, Consent for Adoption Of Unmarried Minor.
California Transactions Forms--Family Law § 6:105, Consent Of Custodial Parent.

California Transactions Forms--Family Law § 6:115, Consent to Stepparent Adoption by Custodial Parent.
Nichols Cyclopedia of Legal Forms Annotated § 7:5, Statutory Provisions--Who May be Adopted.
West's California Code Forms, Family § 8600, Comment Overview--Adoption Of Unmarried Minors.

Treatises and Practice Aids

Witkin, California Summary 10th Parent and Child § 98, in General.
Witkin, California Summary 10th Parent and Child § 99, Adoptive Parents.

§ 8604. Birth parents; presumed fathers; consent; temporary custody orders

(a) Except as provided in subdivision (b), a child having a presumed father under Section 7611 shall not be adopted without the consent of the child's birth parents, if living. The consent of a presumed father is not required for the child's adoption unless he became a presumed father as described in Chapter 1 (commencing with Section 7540) or Chapter 3 (commencing with Section 7570) of Part 2 of Division 12, or subdivision (a), (b), or (c) of Section 7611 before the mother's relinquishment or consent becomes irrevocable or before the mother's parental rights have been terminated.

(b) If one birth parent has been awarded custody by judicial order, or has custody by agreement of both parents, and the other birth parent for a period of one year willfully fails to communicate with, and to pay for, the care, support, and education of the child when able to do so, then the birth parent having sole custody may consent to the adoption, but only after the birth parent not having custody has been served with a copy of a citation in the manner provided by law for the service of a summons in a civil action that requires the birth parent not having custody to appear at the time and place set for the appearance in court under Section 8718, 8823, 8913, or 9007.

(c) Failure of a birth parent to pay for the care, support, and education of the child for the period of one year or failure of a birth parent to communicate with the child for the period of one year is prima facie evidence that the failure was willful and without lawful excuse. If the birth parent or parents have made only token efforts to support or communicate with the child, the court may disregard those token efforts.

(d)(1) If the birth mother of a child for whom there is not a presumed father leaves the child in the physical care of a licensed private adoption agency, in the physical care of a prospective adoptive parent who has an approved preplacement evaluation or private agency adoption home study, or in the hospital after designating a licensed private adoption agency or an approved prospective adoptive parent in a signed document, completed with a hospital social worker, adoption service provider, licensed private adoption agency worker, notary, or attorney, but fails to sign a placement agreement, consent, or relinquishment for adoption, the approved prospective adoptive parent or the licensed private adoption agency may apply for, and the court may issue, a temporary custody order placing the child in the care and custody of the applicant.

(2) A temporary custody order issued pursuant to this subdivision shall include all of the following:

(A) A requirement that the applicant keep the court informed of the child's residence at all times.

(B) A requirement that the child shall not be removed from the state or concealed within the state.

(C) The expiration date of the order, which shall not be more than six months after the order is issued.

(3) A temporary custody order issued pursuant to this subdivision may be voided upon the birth mother's request to have the child returned to her care and custody. *(Stats.1992, c. 162 (A.B.2650), § 10, operative Jan. 1, 1994. Amended by Stats.2005, c. 627 (S.B.302), § 3; Stats.2007, c. 47 (S.B.313), § 4; Stats.2014, c. 763 (A.B.1701), § 8, eff. Jan. 1, 2015.)*

Law Revision Commission Comments

Enactment [Revised Comment]

Section 8604 continues the first three sentences of former Civil Code Section 221.20 without substantive change. In subdivision (a), the word "birth" has been added preceding "parents" for consistency with the remainder of this section. See also Section 8512 ("birth parent" defined).

In subdivision (b), the reference to "parent having sole custody" has been substituted for "parent having custody alone" for consistency with the language of Sections 8700, 8814, and 9003. A reference to "order" has been substituted for "decree." This is not a substantive change. See Section 100 ("order" includes decree, as appropriate). A reference to agreement by "both parents" has been substituted for the former reference to "the birth parents." This is not a substantive change. [23 Cal.L.Rev.Comm. Reports 1 (1993)].

Commentary

Adoption of Kelsey S., 1 Cal.4th 816, 4 Cal.Rptr.2d 615 (1992), holds that Sections 7611 and 7664 are unconstitutional insofar as they allow a mother unilaterally to prevent a natural father from becoming a "presumed father" and then allow the state to terminate his parental rights merely upon a showing of "best interest of the child." *Kelsey S.* holds that the parental rights of an unwed father who demonstrates full commitment to his parental responsibilities may only be terminated by a showing of parental unfitness. To demonstrate full commitment, he must show willingness to assume custody, not just to block adoption. For clarification of *Kelsey S.*, see *Adoption of Michael H., 10 Cal.4th 1043, 898 P.2d 891, 43 Cal.Rptr.2d 445 (1995)* (unwed father who is not a "presumed father" has no federal constitutional right to withhold consent to adoption at his child's birth unless he proves that he demonstrated a full commitment to parental responsibilities as soon as he learned that the mother was pregnant with his child). See also *In re Zacharia D., 6 Cal.4th 435, 24 Cal.Rptr.2d 751 (1993)* (father who did not come forward to assume responsibilities); *In re Ariel H., 73 Cal.App.4th 70, 86 Cal.Rptr.2d 125 (1999)* (15-year-old father who did not come forward to assume his responsibilities); and *Adoption of Arthur M., 149 Cal.App.4th 704, 57 Cal.Rptr.3d 259 (2007), review denied June 20, 2007* (unwed father not entitled to withhold his consent to adoption because father, who allegedly feared criminal prosecution for date rape, failed to promptly assume responsibility for the child upon learning of the mother's pregnancy). Compare *In re Julia U., 64 Cal.App.4th 532, 74 Cal.Rptr.2d 920 (1998)* (juvenile court deprived unwed biological father who promptly came forward and demonstrated a full commitment to his parental responsibilities of his constitutional rights by refusing him reunification services and terminating his parental rights). See also *Adoption of Baby Boy W., 232 Cal.App.4th 438, 181 Cal.Rptr.3d 130 (2015), review denied*. *Adoption of Alexander M., 94 Cal.App.4th 430, 114 Cal.Rptr.2d 218 (2001)*, holds that a biological father may establish paternity under § 7631, but whether an adoption should proceed or the biological father should retain his parental rights shall be decided under the best interests of the child standard (§ 7664(b)), unless the father proves that he has demonstrated a full commitment to parental responsibilities in accordance with *Kelsey S.*, in which case the father shall be awarded custody unless such award would be detrimental to the child under § 3041.

In re D.A., 204 Cal.App.4th 811, 139 Cal.Rptr.3d 222 (2012), holds that a man who came forward to accept all the responsibilities of parenthood but was prevented from becoming a presumed father under section 7611(d), was a *Kelsey S.* presumed father even though he did not accept those responsibilities until tests established his biological paternity, when another man might have been the child's biological father. Compare *In re William K., 161 Cal.App.4th 1, 73 Cal.Rptr.3d 737 (2008)*, where a man was denied *Kelsey S.* status because he did not immediately accept paternal responsibilities although he indicated willingness to take a paternity test, when the parents planned the pregnancy and there never was any doubt about the identity of the biological father.

Adoption of H.R., 205 Cal.App.4th 455, 140 Cal.Rptr.3d 327 (2012), held that a man who attempted to marry the mother during her pregnancy, attended prenatal appointments with her, petitioned the court to establish his paternity before the child was born, and was able and willing to take immediate custody of the child, but was prevented from establishing section 7611(d) presumed father status by the mother, was a *Kelsey S.* father despite his failure to pay for pregnancy and birth-related expenses commensurate with his ability to do so. However, *Adoption of T.K., 240 Cal.App.4th 1392, 194 Cal.Rptr.3d 606 (2015), review denied*, affirming an order terminating an unwed father's parental rights after finding that he was not a *Kelsey S.* father, disagreed with Adoption of H.R., on the ground that a *Kelsey S.* full commitment to parental responsibilities requires, *at a minimum*, a demonstrated willingness to support the child financially and to support the mother emotionally during the pregnancy. Consequently, other factors may be considered only after both requirements have been satisfied.

Purporting to rely on *Zacharia D., supra, In re Vincent M., 161 Cal.App.4th 943, 74 Cal.Rptr.3d 755 (2008), review denied*, holds that a biological father who is not a presumed father under section 7611 and whose paternity was concealed from him by the mother, but who does not come forward in a dependency proceeding until after the reunification period has ended, cannot be treated as a *Kelsey S.* father entitled to reunification services without regard to the best interests of the child, who was placed with prospective adoptive parents when he was four days old and was thriving in their home for nine months before the biological father asserted his *Kelsey S.* claim. *Vincent M.* states, in dictum, that after the reunification period has expired, the biological father's only remedy is a Welfare and Institutions Code section 388 modification petition, which requires changed circumstances or new evidence showing that it is in the child's best interest to grant the biological father custody or reunification services. *Appellate Defenders, Inc. v. Cheri S., 35 Cal.App.4th 1819, 42 Cal.Rptr.2d 195 (1995)*, holds that an indigent parent has a right to appointed counsel in any proceeding that terminates his or her parental rights (cf. Section 7895), including proceedings invoking Family Code Sections 7822, 8604, and 9000. Relying on *In re Jacqueline H., 21 Cal.3d 170, 577 P.2d 683, 145 Cal.Rptr. 548 (1978)*, *Appellate Defenders* reasons that it is immaterial whether the proceeding is initiated by private parties or the state. But see *In re Curtis S., 25 Cal.App.4th 687, 30 Cal.Rptr.2d 739 (1994), review denied 8/29/94*, (appointment of appellate counsel required only when parental rights of indigent parent have been terminated in a dependency proceeding).

A trial court finding under this section that an adoption may proceed without a natural parent's consent does not terminate that parent's child support obligation. *In re Marriage of Dunmore, 83 Cal.App.4th 1, 98 Cal.Rptr.2d 885 (2000)*. *Dunmore* reasons that the purpose of this section is to facilitate adoption, not to terminate parental rights (compare § 7822) and that the natural parent's duty of support is not terminated until the child is adopted by another (see Family Code § 8617). Compare *County of Ventura v. Gonzalez, 88 Cal.App.4th 1120, 106 Cal.Rptr.2d 461 (2001)*, which holds that a Welfare and Institutions Code § 366.26 order terminating parental rights fully severs the parent-child relationship, including the duty of support.

Adoption of A.S., 212 Cal.App.4th 188, 151 Cal.Rptr.3d 15 (2012), review denied, held that a New York order of filiation did not confer presumed father status with its right to veto a California adoption, because a California judgment of paternity would not make a man a presumed father.

Applying section 3403, *Adoption of K.C., 247 Cal.App.4th 1412, 203 Cal.Rptr.3d 110 (2016), review denied*, held that the UCCJEA does not apply to California adoption proceedings in which a New York father's parental rights under a New York divorce decree were terminated under section 7822 and this section.

Research References

Forms

California Transactions Forms--Family Law § 6:3, Definitions.
California Transactions Forms--Family Law § 6:8, Consent for Adoption Of Unmarried Minor.
California Transactions Forms--Family Law § 6:47, Matters to Consider in Drafting Petition for Independent Adoption Of Unmarried Minor.
California Transactions Forms--Family Law § 6:72, Petition to Terminate Parental Rights Of Alleged Father.
California Transactions Forms--Family Law § 6:107, Adoption Without Consent Of Noncustodial Parent.
West's California Code Forms, Family § 8600, Comment Overview--Adoption Of Unmarried Minors.
West's California Judicial Council Forms ADOPT-200, Adoption Request.

Treatises and Practice Aids

Witkin, California Summary 10th Constitutional Law § 776, Right to Withhold Consent to Adoption.
Witkin, California Summary 10th Parent and Child § 12, Parental or Marital Rights Of Prisoners.
Witkin, California Summary 10th Parent and Child § 98, in General.
Witkin, California Summary 10th Parent and Child § 100, in General.
Witkin, California Summary 10th Parent and Child § 101, Unwed Father.
Witkin, California Summary 10th Parent and Child § 102, Failure to Support and Communicate.
Witkin, California Summary 10th Parent and Child § 308, Dependency Proceeding Distinguished.
Witkin, California Summary 10th Parent and Child § 354, Statutory Right.
Witkin, California Summary 10th Parent and Child § 680, Statutory Procedure is Exclusive.
Witkin, California Summary 10th Parent and Child § 100A, (New) Temporary Custody Order.

§ 8605. Children without presumed father; consent of mother required

A child not having a presumed father under Section 7611 may not be adopted without the consent of the child's mother, if living. *(Stats.1992, c. 162 (A.B.2650), § 10, operative Jan. 1, 1994.)*

Law Revision Commission Comments

Enactment [Revised Comment]

Section 8605 continues the fourth sentence of former Civil Code Section 221.20 without substantive change. [23 Cal.L.Rev.Comm. Reports 1 (1993)].

Research References

Forms

California Transactions Forms--Family Law § 6:3, Definitions.
California Transactions Forms--Family Law § 6:8, Consent for Adoption Of Unmarried Minor.
California Transactions Forms--Family Law § 6:40, Structuring the Adoption.
California Transactions Forms--Family Law § 6:47, Matters to Consider in Drafting Petition for Independent Adoption Of Unmarried Minor.
California Transactions Forms--Family Law § 6:72, Petition to Terminate Parental Rights Of Alleged Father.
Nichols Cyclopedia of Legal Forms Annotated § 7:6, Statutory Provisions--Consent to Adoption.

Treatises and Practice Aids

Witkin, California Summary 10th Parent and Child § 98, in General.
Witkin, California Summary 10th Parent and Child § 100, in General.

§ 8606. Consent of birth parents not required in specified cases

Notwithstanding Sections 8604 and 8605, the consent of a birth parent is not necessary in the following cases:

(a) Where the birth parent has been judicially deprived of the custody and control of the child (1) by a court order declaring the child to be free from the custody and control of either or both birth parents pursuant to Part 4 (commencing with Section 7800) of Division 12 of this code, or Section 366.25 or 366.26 of the Welfare and Institutions Code, or (2) by a similar order of a court of another jurisdiction, pursuant to a law of that jurisdiction authorizing the order.

(b) Where the birth parent has, in a judicial proceeding in another jurisdiction, voluntarily surrendered the right to the custody and control of the child pursuant to a law of that jurisdiction providing for the surrender.

(c) Where the birth parent has deserted the child without provision for identification of the child.

(d) Where the birth parent has relinquished the child for adoption as provided in Section 8700.

(e) Where the birth parent has relinquished the child for adoption to a licensed or authorized child-placing agency in another jurisdiction pursuant to the law of that jurisdiction. *(Stats.1992, c. 162 (A.B.2650), § 10, operative Jan. 1, 1994.)*

Law Revision Commission Comments

Enactment [Revised Comment]

Section 8606 continues without substantive change the last sentence of the first paragraph and subdivisions (a)-(c) of former Civil Code Section 221.20. Throughout this section, "birth parent" has been substituted for "birth father or mother." See Section 8512 ("birth parent" defined). See also Section 8530 ("licensed adoption agency" defined). [23 Cal.L.Rev.Comm. Reports 1 (1993)].

Commentary

See Section 8604 Commentary.

Research References

Forms

California Transactions Forms--Family Law § 6:8, Consent for Adoption Of Unmarried Minor.
West's California Judicial Council Forms ADOPT-200, Adoption Request.
West's California Judicial Council Forms ADOPT-210, Adoption Agreement.

Treatises and Practice Aids

Witkin, California Summary 10th Parent and Child § 103, Other Exceptions.

§ 8606.5. Consent to adoption of Indian children

(a) Notwithstanding any other section in this part, and in accordance with Section 1913 of the Indian Child Welfare Act (25 U.S.C. Sec. 1901 et seq.), consent to adoption given by an Indian child's parent is not valid unless both of the following occur:

(1) The consent is executed in writing at least 10 days after the child's birth and recorded before a judge.

(2) The judge certifies that the terms and consequences of the consent were fully explained in detail in English and were fully understood by the parent or that they were interpreted into a language that the parent understood.

(b) The parent of an Indian child may withdraw his or her consent to adoption for any reason at any time prior to the entry of a final decree of adoption and the child shall be returned to the parent.

(c) After the entry of a final decree of adoption of an Indian child, the Indian child's parent may withdraw consent to the adoption upon the grounds that consent was obtained through fraud or duress and may petition the court to vacate such decree. Upon a finding that such consent was obtained through fraud or duress, the court shall vacate such decree and return the child to the parent, provided that no adoption that has been effective for at least 2 years may be invalidated unless otherwise permitted under state law. *(Added by Stats.2006, c. 838 (S.B.678), § 8.)*

Research References

Forms

California Transactions Forms--Family Law § 6:143, Overview Of Indian Child Welfare Act (ICWA).
California Transactions Forms--Family Law § 6:148, Rights Of Indian Parents Of Indian Children.
California Transactions Forms--Family Law § 6:156, Consent to Termination Of Parental Rights and Certification--Adoption Of an Indian Child [Form Adopt-225].

Treatises and Practice Aids

Witkin, California Summary 10th Parent and Child § 78, Child Of Indian Ancestry.

§ 8607. Forms; contents

All forms adopted by the department authorizing the release of an infant from a health facility to the custody of persons other than the person entitled to custody of the child pursuant to Section 3010 and authorizing these other persons to obtain medical care for the infant shall contain a statement in boldface type delineating the various types of adoptions available, the birth parents' rights with regard thereto, including, but not limited to, rights with regard to revocation of consent to adoption, and a statement regarding the authority of the court under Part 4 (commencing with Section 7800) of Division 12 to declare the child abandoned by the birth parent or parents. *(Stats.1992, c. 162 (A.B.2650), § 10, operative Jan. 1, 1994.)*

Law Revision Commission Comments

Enactment [Revised Comment]

Section 8607 continues former Civil Code Section 221.30 without substantive change. The reference to Part 4 (commencing with Section 7800) of Division 12 has been substituted for the narrower reference to former Civil Code Section 232. This is not a substantive change. See also Sections 8512 ("birth parent" defined), 8518 ("department" defined). [23 Cal.L.Rev.Comm. Reports 1 (1993)].

Commentary

See generally *Tyler v. Children's Home Society of California, 29 Cal.App.4th 511, 35 Cal.Rptr.2d 291 (1994), review denied 1/5/95,* (private adoption agency's noncompliance with various requirements of state adoption law does not necessarily invalidate a parent's relinquishment of his or her child).

Research References

Treatises and Practice Aids

Witkin, California Summary 10th Parent and Child § 87, Private Adoptions.

§ 8608. Form and content of medical reports on child and biological parents; adoption of regulations

(a) The department shall adopt regulations specifying the form and content of the reports required by Sections 8706, 8817, and 8909. In addition to any other material that may be required by the department, the form shall include inquiries designed to elicit information on any illness, disease, or defect of a genetic or hereditary nature.

(b) All county adoption agencies and licensed adoption agencies shall cooperate with and assist the department in devising a plan that will effectuate the effective and discreet transmission to adoptees or prospective adoptive parents of pertinent medical information reported to the department, county adoption agency, or licensed adoption agency, upon the request of the person reporting the medical information. *(Stats.1992, c. 162 (A.B.2650), § 10, operative Jan. 1, 1994. Amended by Stats.2012, c. 35 (S.B.1013), § 10, eff. June 27, 2012.)*

Law Revision Commission Comments

Enactment [Revised Comment]

Section 8608 continues former Civil Code Sections 222.26(b), 224.70(b), and 226.35(b) without substantive change. See also Sections 8518 ("department" defined), 8530 ("licensed adoption agency" defined), 8542 ("prospective adoptive parent" defined).

For a related provision, see Section 9202 (regulations concerning availability of medical report). [23 Cal.L.Rev.Comm. Reports 1 (1993)].

Commentary

See generally *Tyler v. Children's Home Society of California, 29 Cal.App.4th 511, 35 Cal.Rptr.2d 291 (1994), review denied 1/5/95,* (private adoption agency's noncompliance with various requirements of state adoption law does not necessarily invalidate a parent's relinquishment of his or her child).

Research References

Treatises and Practice Aids

Witkin, California Summary 10th Parent and Child § 93, Medical Report on Child and Birth Parents.

§ 8609. Advertisement of placement or other adoptive services; unlicensed persons or organizations; misdemeanor

(a) Any person or organization that, without holding a valid and unrevoked license to place children for adoption issued by the department, advertises in any periodical or newspaper, by radio, or other public medium, that he, she, or it will place children for adoption, or accept, supply, provide, or obtain children for adoption, or that causes any advertisement to be published in or by any public medium soliciting, requesting, or asking for any child or children for adoption is guilty of a misdemeanor.

(b) Any person, other than a birth parent, or any organization, association, or corporation that, without holding a valid and unrevoked license to place children for adoption issued by the department, places any child for adoption is guilty of a misdemeanor. *(Stats.1992, c. 162 (A.B.2650), § 10, operative Jan. 1, 1994.)*

Law Revision Commission Comments

Enactment [Revised Comment]

Section 8609 continues former Civil Code Section 221.40 without change. See also Sections 8512 ("birth parent" defined), 8518 ("department" defined). [23 Cal.L.Rev.Comm. Reports 1 (1993)].

Research References

Forms

California Transactions Forms--Family Law § 6:2, Governing Law.

Treatises and Practice Aids

Witkin, California Summary 10th Parent and Child § 87, Private Adoptions.

§ 8609.5. Location of filing an adoption request for a nondependent minor

An adoption request for the adoption of a nondependent minor may be filed with the court in the county in which one of the following applies:

(a) The petitioner resides.

(b) The child was born or resides at the time of filing.

(c) An office of the agency that placed the child for adoption is located.

(d) An office of the department or a public adoption agency that is investigating the petition is located.

(e) The county in which a placing birth parent or parents resided when the adoptive placement agreement, consent, or relinquishment was signed.

(f) The county in which a placing birth parent or parents resided when the petition was filed.

(g) The county in which the child was freed for adoption. *(Added by Stats.2012, c. 638 (A.B.1757), § 6.)*

Research References

Treatises and Practice Aids

Witkin, California Summary 10th Parent and Child § 91, Jurisdiction, Venue, and Conflict Of Laws.
Witkin, California Summary 10th Parent and Child § 118, Petition.
Witkin, California Summary 10th Parent and Child § 132, Petition.
Witkin, California Summary 10th Parent and Child § 140, Petition, Hearing, and Order.
Witkin, California Summary 10th Parent and Child § 144, Procedure.

§ 8610. Accounting report; filing by petitioners; contents; application

(a) The petitioners in a proceeding for adoption of a child shall file with the court a full accounting report of all disbursements of anything of value made or agreed to be made by them or on their behalf in connection with the birth of the child, the placement of the child with the petitioners, any medical or hospital care received by the child's birth mother or by the child in connection with the child's birth, any other expenses of either birth parent, or the adoption. The accounting report shall be made under penalty of perjury and shall be submitted to the court on or before the date set for the hearing on the adoption petition, unless the court grants an extension of time.

(b) The accounting report shall be itemized in detail and shall show the services relating to the adoption or to the placement of the child for adoption that were received by the petitioners, by either birth parent, by the child, or by any other person for whom payment was made by or on behalf of the petitioners. The report shall also include the dates of each payment, the names and addresses of each attorney, physician and surgeon, hospital, licensed adoption agency, or other person or organization who received any funds of the petitioners in connection with the adoption or the placement of the child with them, or participated in any way in the handling of those funds, either directly or indirectly.

(c) This section does not apply to an adoption by a stepparent where one birth parent or adoptive parent retains custody and control of the child. *(Stats.1992, c. 162 (A.B. 2650), § 10, operative Jan. 1, 1994.)*

Law Revision Commission Comments

Enactment [Revised Comment]

Section 8610 continues former Civil Code Section 221.50 without substantive change. In subdivision (b), the phrase "physician and surgeon" has been substituted for "doctor." See Section 580 Comment. See also Sections 8503 ("adoptive parent" defined), 8512 ("birth parent" defined), 8530 ("licensed adoption agency" defined). [23 Cal.L.Rev.Comm. Reports 1 (1993)].

Research References

Forms

California Transactions Forms--Family Law § 6:14, Accounting Report.
California Transactions Forms--Family Law § 6:25, Matters to Consider in Preparing Accounting Report [Fam C S8610].
California Transactions Forms--Family Law § 6:44, Documentation and Final Hearing.
California Transactions Forms--Family Law § 6:54, Request by Birth Parent for Financial Assistance.
California Transactions Forms--Family Law § 6:83, Nature Of Agency Adoption--Governing Law.
California Transactions Forms--Family Law § 6:90, Adoptive Placement Agreement.
California Transactions Forms--Family Law § 6:112, Form Drafting Considerations.
West's California Code Forms, Family § 8600, Comment Overview--Adoption Of Unmarried Minors.
West's California Judicial Council Forms ADOPT-230, Adoption Expenses.

Treatises and Practice Aids

Witkin, California Summary 10th Parent and Child § 92, Accounting Report.

§ 8611. Hearings

All court hearings in an adoption proceeding shall be held in private, and the court shall exclude all persons except the officers of the court, the parties, their witnesses, counsel, and representatives of the agencies present to perform their official duties under the law governing adoptions. *(Stats. 1992, c. 162 (A.B.2650), § 10, operative Jan. 1, 1994.)*

Law Revision Commission Comments

Enactment [Revised Comment]

Section 8611 continues former Civil Code Section 221.60 without substantive change. The reference to the "superior" court has been omitted as surplus. See Section 200 (jurisdiction in superior court). [23 Cal.L.Rev.Comm. Reports 1 (1993)].

Research References

Forms

California Transactions Forms--Family Law § 6:12, Conduct Of Hearing.
California Transactions Forms--Family Law § 6:111, Hearing on Stepparent Adoption Petition.

Treatises and Practice Aids

Witkin, California Summary 10th Parent and Child § 95, Petition and Hearing.

§ 8612. Examination by court; agreement; execution; order of adoption

(a) The court shall examine all persons appearing before it pursuant to this part. The examination of each person shall be conducted separately but within the physical presence of every other person unless the court, in its discretion, orders otherwise.

(b) The prospective adoptive parent or parents shall execute and acknowledge an agreement in writing that the child will be treated in all respects as their lawful child.

(c) If satisfied that the interest of the child will be promoted by the adoption, the court may make and enter an order of adoption of the child by the prospective adoptive parent or parents. *(Stats.1992, c. 162 (A.B.2650), § 10, operative Jan. 1, 1994.)*

Law Revision Commission Comments

Enactment [Revised Comment]

Section 8612 continues former Civil Code Section 221.63 without substantive change, except for the last part of subdivision (c) of the former provision, which is continued in Section 8616. The reference to "persons" has been omitted as surplus. See Section 10 (singular includes plural).

In subdivision (b), the reference to "prospective adoptive parent or parents" has been substituted for "party or parties adopting." See Section 8542 ("prospective adoptive parent" defined). See also Section 8503 ("adoptive parent" defined). [23 Cal.L.Rev.Comm. Reports 1 (1993)].

Research References

Forms

California Transactions Forms--Family Law § 6:111, Hearing on Stepparent Adoption Petition.
West's California Code Forms, Family § 8612 Form 2, Adoption Agreement.
West's California Judicial Council Forms JV-505, Statement Regarding Parentage (Juvenile).
West's California Judicial Council Forms ADOPT-210, Adoption Agreement.
West's California Judicial Council Forms ADOPT-215, Adoption Order.

Treatises and Practice Aids

Witkin, California Summary 10th Parent and Child § 95, Petition and Hearing.
Witkin, California Summary 10th Parent and Child § 96, Agreement and Order.
Witkin, California Summary 10th Parent and Child § 120, Hearing and Order.
Witkin, California Summary 10th Parent and Child § 135, Hearing and Order.
Witkin, California Summary 10th Parent and Child § 140, Petition, Hearing, and Order.

§ 8613. Prospective adoptive parent in military, or in service for governmental entity, red cross, or charitable or religious organization; appearance by counsel; execution of agreement; deposition; adoption order

(a) If the prospective adoptive parent is commissioned or enlisted in the military service, or auxiliary thereof, of the United States, or of any of its allies, or is engaged in service on behalf of any governmental entity of the United States, or in the American Red Cross, or in any other recognized charitable or religious organization, so that it is impossible or impracticable, because of the prospective adoptive parent's absence from this state, or otherwise, to make an appearance in person, and the circumstances are established by satisfactory evidence, the appearance may be made for the prospective adoptive parent by counsel, commissioned and empowered in writing for that purpose. The power of attorney may be incorporated in the adoption petition.

(b) Where the prospective adoptive parent is permitted to appear by counsel, the agreement may be executed and acknowledged by the counsel, or may be executed by the absent party before a notary public, or any other person authorized to take acknowledgments including the persons authorized by Sections 1183 and 1183.5 of the Civil Code.

(c) Where the prospective adoptive parent is permitted to appear by counsel, or otherwise, the court may, in its discretion, cause an examination of the prospective adoptive parent, other interested person, or witness to be made upon deposition, as it deems necessary. The deposition shall be taken upon commission, as prescribed by the Code of Civil Procedure, and the expense thereof shall be borne by the petitioner.

(d) The petition, relinquishment or consent, agreement, order, report to the court from any investigating agency, and any power of attorney and deposition shall be filed in the office of the clerk of the court.

(e) The provisions of this section permitting an appearance through counsel are equally applicable to the spouse of a prospective adoptive parent who resides with the prospective adoptive parent outside this state.

(f) Where, pursuant to this section, neither prospective adoptive parent need appear before the court, the child proposed to be adopted need not appear. If the law otherwise requires that the child execute any document during the course of the hearing, the child may do so through counsel.

(g) Where none of the parties appears, the court may not make an order of adoption until after a report has been filed with the court pursuant to Section 8715, 8807, 8914, or 9001. *(Stats.1992, c. 162 (A.B.2650), § 10, operative Jan. 1, 1994. Amended by Stats.1993, c. 1158 (S.B.1152), § 1; Stats.2002, c. 784 (S.B.1316), § 109.)*

Law Revision Commission Comments

Enactment [Revised Comment]

Section 8613 supersedes former Civil Code Section 221.65. See also Section 8542 ("prospective adoptive parent" defined). [23 Cal.L.Rev.Comm. Reports 1 (1993)].

2002 Amendment

Subdivision (d) of Section 8613 is amended to reflect elimination of the county clerk's role as ex officio clerk of the superior court. See former Gov't Code § 26800 (county clerk acting as clerk of superior court). The powers, duties, and responsibilities formerly exercised by the county clerk as ex officio clerk of the court are delegated to the court administrative or executive officer, and the county clerk is relieved of those powers, duties, and responsibilities. See Gov't Code §§ 69840 (powers, duties, and responsibilities of clerk of court and deputy clerk of court), 71620 (trial court personnel). [32 Cal.L.Rev. Comm. Reports 165 (2002)].

Research References

Forms

California Transactions Forms--Family Law § 6:13, Appearance in Person or by Counsel.
California Transactions Forms--Family Law § 6:28, Power Of Attorney for Counsel to Appear at Final Hearing on Behalf Of Petitioners Who Are Absent from California.
California Transactions Forms--Family Law § 6:44, Documentation and Final Hearing.
California Transactions Forms--Family Law § 6:111, Hearing on Stepparent Adoption Petition.
West's California Code Forms, Family § 8600, Comment Overview--Adoption Of Unmarried Minors.

Treatises and Practice Aids

Witkin, California Summary 10th Parent and Child § 95, Petition and Hearing.
Witkin, California Summary 10th Parent and Child § 96, Agreement and Order.

Witkin, California Summary 10th Parent and Child § 135, Hearing and Order.

§ 8613.5. Waiver of personal appearance of prospective adoptive parent

(a)(1) If it is impossible or impracticable for either prospective adoptive parent to make an appearance in person, and the circumstances are established by clear and convincing documentary evidence, the court may, in its discretion, do either of the following:

(A) Waive the personal appearance of the prospective adoptive parent. The appearance may be made for the prospective adoptive parent by counsel, commissioned and empowered in writing for that purpose. The power of attorney may be incorporated in the adoption petition.

(B) Authorize the prospective adoptive parent to appear by telephone, videoconference, or other remote electronic means that the court deems reasonable, prudent, and reliable.

(2) For purposes of this section, if the circumstances that make an appearance in person by a prospective adoptive parent impossible or impracticable are temporary in nature or of a short duration, the court shall not waive the personal appearance of that prospective adoptive parent.

(b) If the prospective adoptive parent is permitted to appear by counsel, the agreement may be executed and acknowledged by the counsel, or may be executed by the absent party before a notary public, or any other person authorized to take acknowledgments including the persons authorized by Sections 1183 and 1183.5 of the Civil Code.

(c) If the prospective adoptive parent is permitted to appear by counsel, or otherwise, the court may, in its discretion, cause an examination of the prospective adoptive parent, other interested person, or witness to be made upon deposition, as it deems necessary. The deposition shall be taken upon commission, as prescribed by the Code of Civil Procedure, and the expense thereof shall be borne by the petitioner.

(d) The petition, relinquishment or consent, agreement, order, report to the court from any investigating agency, and any power of attorney and deposition shall be filed in the office of the clerk of the court.

(e) The provisions of this section permitting an appearance by counsel or electronically pursuant to subparagraph (B) of paragraph (1) of subdivision (a) are equally applicable to the spouse of a prospective adoptive parent who resides with the prospective adoptive parent outside this state.

(f) If, pursuant to this section, neither prospective adoptive parent need appear before the court, the child proposed to be adopted need not appear. If the law otherwise requires that the child execute any document during the course of the hearing, the child may do so through counsel.

(g) If none of the parties appear, the court may not make an order of adoption until after a report has been filed with the court pursuant to Section 8715, 8807, 8914, or 9001. *(Added by Stats.2006, c. 806 (S.B.1325), § 6. Amended by Stats.2014, c. 763 (A.B.1701), § 9, eff. Jan. 1, 2015.)*

Research References

Forms

West's California Code Forms, Family § 8600, Comment Overview--Adoption Of Unmarried Minors.

Treatises and Practice Aids

Witkin, California Summary 10th Parent and Child § 95, Petition and Hearing.

§ 8613.7. Notice of eligibility for reduced-cost or no-cost health coverage

On and after January 1, 2014, the court shall provide to any petitioner for adoption pursuant to this part a notice informing him or her that he or she may be eligible for reduced-cost coverage through the California Health Benefit Exchange established under Title 22 (commencing with Section 100500) of the Government Code or no-cost coverage through Medi–Cal. The notice shall include information on obtaining coverage pursuant to those programs, and shall be developed by the California Health Benefit Exchange. *(Added by Stats.2012, c. 851 (A.B.792), § 2.)*

Research References

Treatises and Practice Aids

Witkin, California Summary 10th Parent and Child § 86, Programs to Facilitate Adoption.

§ 8614. Certificate of adoption

Upon the request of the adoptive parents or the adopted child, a clerk of the superior court may issue a certificate of adoption that states the date and place of adoption, the birthday of the child, the names of the adoptive parents, and the name the child has taken. Unless the child has been adopted by a stepparent or by a relative, as defined in subdivision (c) of Section 8616.5, the certificate shall not state the name of the birth parents of the child. *(Stats.1992, c. 162 (A.B.2650), § 10, operative Jan. 1, 1994. Amended by Stats. 1997, c. 793 (A.B.1544), § 2; Stats.2002, c. 784 (S.B.1316), § 110; Stats.2003, c. 251 (S.B.182), § 5.)*

Law Revision Commission Comments

Enactment [Revised Comment]

Section 8614 continues former Civil Code Section 221.70 without substantive change. See also Sections 8503 ("adoptive parent" defined), 8512 ("birth parent" defined). [23 Cal.L.Rev.Comm. Reports 1 (1993)].

2002 Amendment

Section 8614 is amended to reflect elimination of the county clerk's role as ex officio clerk of the superior court. See former Gov't Code § 26800 (county clerk acting as clerk of superior court). The powers, duties, and responsibilities formerly exercised by the county clerk as ex officio clerk of the court are delegated to the court administrative or executive officer, and the county clerk is relieved of those powers, duties, and responsibilities. See Gov't Code §§ 69840 (powers, duties, and responsibilities of clerk of court and deputy clerk of court), 71620 (trial court personnel). [32 Cal.L.Rev.Comm. Reports 166 (2002)].

Research References

Forms

California Transactions Forms--Family Law § 6:15, Certificate Of Adoption--Birth Certificate.

West's California Code Forms, Family § 8600, Comment Overview--Adoption Of Unmarried Minors.
West's California Code Forms, Family § 8614 Form 1, Certificate Of Adoption.

Treatises and Practice Aids

Witkin, California Summary 10th Parent and Child § 97, Certificates Of Birth and Adoption.

§ 8615. New birth certificate

(a) Notwithstanding any other law, an action may be brought in the county in which the petitioner resides for the purpose of obtaining for a child adopted by the petitioner a new birth certificate specifying that a deceased spouse of the petitioner who was in the home at the time of the initial placement of the child is a parent of the child.

(b) In an adoption proceeding, the petitioner may request that the new birth certificate specify that a deceased spouse of the petitioner who was in the home at the time of the initial placement of the child is a parent of the child.

(c) The inclusion of the name of a deceased person in a birth certificate issued pursuant to a court order under this section does not affect any matter of testate or intestate succession, and is not competent evidence on the issue of the relationship between the adopted child and the deceased person in any action or proceeding. *(Stats.1992, c. 162 (A.B.2650), § 10, operative Jan. 1, 1994.)*

Law Revision Commission Comments

Enactment [Revised Comment]

Section 8615 continues former Civil Code Section 221.72 without substantive change. The reference to the "superior" court has been omitted as surplus. See Section 200 (jurisdiction in superior court).

In subdivision (b), the reference to "adoption proceeding" has been substituted for "action for adoption" for consistency with the language of this part. [23 Cal.L.Rev.Comm. Reports 1 (1993)].

Research References

Forms

California Transactions Forms--Family Law § 6:15, Certificate Of Adoption--Birth Certificate.
West's California Code Forms, Family § 8600, Comment Overview--Adoption Of Unmarried Minors.
West's California Code Forms, Family § 8615 Form 2, Order Requiring New Birth Certificate--Deceased Spouse as Parent.

Treatises and Practice Aids

Witkin, California Summary 10th Parent and Child § 97, Certificates Of Birth and Adoption.

§ 8616. Legal relationship of parent and child

After adoption, the adopted child and the adoptive parents shall sustain towards each other the legal relationship of parent and child and have all the rights and are subject to all the duties of that relationship. *(Stats.1992, c. 162 (A.B.2650), § 10, operative Jan. 1, 1994.)*

Law Revision Commission Comments

Enactment [Revised Comment]

Section 8616 continues without substantive change the last part of former Civil Code Section 221.63(c) and the last sentence of former Civil Code Section 221.74. See also Section 8503 ("adoptive parent" defined).

For a comparable provision, see Section 9305 (relationship in adoption of adults and married minors). [23 Cal.L.Rev.Comm. Reports 1 (1993)].

Commentary

Ehrenclou v. MacDonald, 117 Cal.App.4th 364, 12 Cal.Rptr.3d 411 (2004), review denied, held that two adults adopted by a trust beneficiary under Colorado adult adoption law were not the deceased trust beneficiary's "children then living" under a trust governed by California law, because the Colorado adult adoption statute gave the adoptees heir-at-law status, but did not create a parent-child relationship between the trust beneficiary and the adoptees.

Research References

Forms

California Transactions Forms--Family Law § 6:16, Legal Relationship Following Adoption Of Unmarried Minor.
California Transactions Forms--Family Law § 6:18, Intestate Succession Rights.

Treatises and Practice Aids

Witkin, California Summary 10th Parent and Child § 76, Nature and Effect Of Adoption.

§ 8616.5. Postadoption contact agreements

(a) The Legislature finds and declares that some adoptive children may benefit from either direct or indirect contact with birth relatives, including the birth parent or parents or any siblings, or an Indian tribe, after being adopted. Postadoption contact agreements are intended to ensure children of an achievable level of continuing contact when contact is beneficial to the children and the agreements are voluntarily executed by birth relatives, including the birth parent or parents or any siblings, or an Indian tribe, and adoptive parents. Nothing in this section requires all of the listed parties to participate in the development of a postadoption contact agreement in order for the agreement to be executed.

(b)(1) Nothing in the adoption laws of this state shall be construed to prevent the adopting parent or parents, the birth relatives, including the birth parent or parents or any siblings, or an Indian tribe, and the child from voluntarily executing a written agreement to permit continuing contact between the birth relatives, including the birth parent or parents or any siblings, or an Indian tribe, and the child if the agreement is found by the court to have been executed voluntarily and to be in the best interests of the child at the time the adoption petition is granted.

(2) The terms of any postadoption contact agreement executed under this section shall be limited to, but need not include, all of the following:

(A) Provisions for visitation between the child and a birth parent or parents and other birth relatives, including siblings, and the child's Indian tribe if the case is governed by the Indian Child Welfare Act (25 U.S.C. Sec. 1901 et seq.).

(B) Provisions for future contact between a birth parent or parents or other birth relatives, including siblings, or both, and the child or an adoptive parent, or both, and in cases governed by the Indian Child Welfare Act, the child's Indian tribe.

(C) Provisions for the sharing of information about the child in the future.

(3) The terms of any postadoption contact agreement with birth relatives, including siblings, other than the child's birth parent or parents shall be limited to the sharing of information about the child, unless the child has a preexisting relationship with the birth relative.

(c) At the time an adoption decree is entered pursuant to a petition filed pursuant to Section 8714, 8714.5, 8802, 8912, or 9000, the court entering the decree may grant postadoption privileges if an agreement for those privileges has been executed, including agreements executed pursuant to subdivision (f) of Section 8620. The hearing to grant the adoption petition and issue an order of adoption may be continued as necessary to permit parties who are in the process of negotiating a postadoption agreement to reach a final agreement.

(d) The child who is the subject of the adoption petition shall be considered a party to the postadoption contact agreement. The written consent to the terms and conditions of the postadoption contact agreement and any subsequent modifications of the agreement by a child who is 12 years of age or older is a necessary condition to the granting of privileges regarding visitation, contact, or sharing of information about the child, unless the court finds by a preponderance of the evidence that the agreement, as written, is in the best interests of the child. Any child who has been found to come within Section 300 of the Welfare and Institutions Code or who is the subject of a petition for jurisdiction of the juvenile court under Section 300 of the Welfare and Institutions Code shall be represented by an attorney for purposes of consent to the postadoption contact agreement.

(e) A postadoption contact agreement shall contain the following warnings in bold type:

(1) After the adoption petition has been granted by the court, the adoption cannot be set aside due to the failure of an adopting parent, a birth parent, a birth relative, including a sibling, an Indian tribe, or the child to follow the terms of this agreement or a later change to this agreement.

(2) A disagreement between the parties or litigation brought to enforce or modify the agreement shall not affect the validity of the adoption and shall not serve as a basis for orders affecting the custody of the child.

(3) A court will not act on a petition to change or enforce this agreement unless the petitioner has participated, or attempted to participate, in good faith in mediation or other appropriate dispute resolution proceedings to resolve the dispute.

(f) Upon the granting of the adoption petition and the issuing of the order of adoption of a child who is a dependent of the juvenile court, juvenile court dependency jurisdiction shall be terminated. Enforcement of the postadoption contact agreement shall be under the continuing jurisdiction of the court granting the petition of adoption. The court may not order compliance with the agreement absent a finding that the party seeking the enforcement participated, or attempted to participate, in good faith in mediation or other appropriate dispute resolution proceedings regarding the conflict, prior to the filing of the enforcement action, and that the enforcement is in the best interests of the child. Documentary evidence or offers of proof may serve as the basis for the court's decision regarding enforcement. No testimony or evidentiary hearing shall be required. The court shall not order further investigation or evaluation by any public or private agency or individual absent a finding by clear and convincing evidence that the best interests of the child may be protected or advanced only by that inquiry and that the inquiry will not disturb the stability of the child's home to the detriment of the child.

(g) The court may not award monetary damages as a result of the filing of the civil action pursuant to subdivision (e).

(h) A postadoption contact agreement may be modified or terminated only if either of the following occurs:

(1) All parties, including the child if the child is 12 years of age or older at the time of the requested termination or modification, have signed a modified postadoption contact agreement and the agreement is filed with the court that granted the petition of adoption.

(2) The court finds all of the following:

(A) The termination or modification is necessary to serve the best interests of the child.

(B) There has been a substantial change of circumstances since the original agreement was executed and approved by the court.

(C) The party seeking the termination or modification has participated, or attempted to participate, in good faith in mediation or other appropriate dispute resolution proceedings prior to seeking court approval of the proposed termination or modification.

Documentary evidence or offers of proof may serve as the basis for the court's decision. No testimony or evidentiary hearing shall be required. The court shall not order further investigation or evaluation by any public or private agency or individual absent a finding by clear and convincing evidence that the best interests of the child may be protected or advanced only by that inquiry and that the inquiry will not disturb the stability of the child's home to the detriment of the child.

(i) All costs and fees of mediation or other appropriate dispute resolution proceedings shall be borne by each party, excluding the child. All costs and fees of litigation shall be borne by the party filing the action to modify or enforce the agreement when no party has been found by the court as failing to comply with an existing postadoption contact agreement. Otherwise, a party, other than the child, found by the court as failing to comply without good cause with an existing agreement shall bear all the costs and fees of litigation.

(j) The Judicial Council shall adopt rules of court and forms for motions to enforce, terminate, or modify postadoption contact agreements.

(k) The court shall not set aside a decree of adoption, rescind a relinquishment, or modify an order to terminate parental rights or any other prior court order because of the failure of a birth parent, adoptive parent, birth relative, including a sibling, an Indian tribe, or the child to comply with any or all of the original terms of, or subsequent modifications to, the postadoption contact agreement, except as follows:

(1) Prior to issuing the order of adoption, in an adoption involving an Indian child, the court may, upon a petition of the birth parent, birth relative, including a sibling, or an Indian tribe, order the parties to engage in family mediation services for the purpose of reaching a postadoption contact agreement if the prospective adoptive parent fails to negotiate in good faith to execute a postadoption contact agreement, after having agreed to enter into negotiations, provided that the failure of the parties to reach an agreement is not in and of itself proof of bad faith.

(2) Prior to issuing the order of adoption, if the parties fail to negotiate in good faith to execute a postadoption contact agreement during the negotiations entered into pursuant to, and in accordance with, paragraph (1), the court may modify prior orders or issue new orders as necessary to ensure the best interest of the Indian child is met, including, but not limited to, requiring parties to engage in further family mediation services for the purpose of reaching a postadoption contact agreement, initiating guardianship proceeding in lieu of adoption, or authorizing a change of adoptive placement for the child.

(*l*) As used in this section, "sibling" means a person related to the identified child by blood, adoption, or affinity through a common legal or biological parent. *(Formerly § 8714.7, added by Stats.1997, c. 793 (A.B.1544), § 5. Amended by Stats.2000, c. 910 (A.B.2921), § 4; Stats.2000, c. 930 (S.B.2157), § 3. Renumbered § 8616.5 and amended by Stats.2003, c. 251 (S.B.182), § 8. Amended by Stats.2004, c. 858 (S.B.1357), § 4; Stats.2006, c. 838 (S.B.678), § 9; Stats. 2009, c. 492 (A.B.941), § 3; Stats.2016, c. 719 (S.B.1060), § 1, eff. Jan. 1, 2017.)*

Commentary

In re Zachary D., 70 Cal.App.4th 1392, 83 Cal.Rptr.2d 407 (1999), review denied June 23, 1999, holds that the juvenile court may properly terminate a mother's parental rights without providing her with notice of and opportunity to enter a kinship adoption agreement with the mother's parents, who were the child's prospective adoptive parents. *Zachary D.* is followed by *In re Kimberly S., 71 Cal.App.4th 405, 83 Cal.Rptr.2d 740 (1999), review denied July 14, 1999.*

In re Noreen G., 181 Cal.App.4th 1359, 105 Cal.Rptr.3d 521 (2010), review denied, held that a probate court erred when it terminated the parental rights of both parents, but granted them supervised visitation absent an agreement of the parties that complied with this section.

Research References

Forms

California Transactions Forms--Family Law § 6:15, Certificate Of Adoption--Birth Certificate.
California Transactions Forms--Family Law § 6:55, Agreement for Continuing Contact.
California Transactions Forms--Family Law § 6:97, Kinship Adoption.
California Transactions Forms--Family Law § 6:100, Postadoption Contact Agreement [Form Adopt-310].
West's California Code Forms, Family § 8700, Comment Overview--Relinquishment Of Child to Department Of Social Services or a Licensed Adoption Agency.
West's California Code Forms, Family § 8714.5 Form 1, Contact After Adoption Agreement.
West's California Code Forms, Family § 8714.5 Form 2, Request to End, Enforce, Change Contact After Adoption Agreement.
West's California Code Forms, Family § 8714.5 Form 3, Answer to Request for Enforcement, Modification, or End Contact After Adoption Agreement.
West's California Code Forms, Family § 8714.5 Form 4, Order on Request for Enforcement, Modification, or End Contact After Adoption Agreement.

Treatises and Practice Aids

Witkin, California Summary 10th Parent and Child § 95, Petition and Hearing.
Witkin, California Summary 10th Parent and Child § 104, in General.
Witkin, California Summary 10th Parent and Child § 119, Investigation, Report, and Recommendation.
Witkin, California Summary 10th Parent and Child § 680, Statutory Procedure is Exclusive.
Witkin, California Summary 10th Parent and Child § 692, in General.

§ 8617. Existing parents' responsibilities toward child; cessation; waiver prior to finalization of adoption

(a) Except as provided in subdivision (b), the existing parent or parents of an adopted child are, from the time of the adoption, relieved of all parental duties towards, and all responsibility for, the adopted child, and have no right over the child.

(b) The termination of the parental duties and responsibilities of the existing parent or parents under subdivision (a) may be waived if both the existing parent or parents and the prospective adoptive parent or parents sign a waiver at any time prior to the finalization of the adoption. The waiver shall be filed with the court. *(Stats.1992, c. 162 (A.B.2650), § 10, operative Jan. 1, 1994. Amended by Stats.2013, c. 564 (S.B.274), § 7.)*

Law Revision Commission Comments

Enactment [Revised Comment]

Section 8617 continues former Civil Code Section 221.76 without substantive change. See also Section 8512 ("birth parent" defined).

For a comparable provision, see Section 9306 (responsibility of birth parents of adults and unmarried minors). [23 Cal.L.Rev. Comm. Reports 1 (1993)].

Commentary

In *Sharon S. v. Superior Court, 31 Cal.4th 417, 73 P.3d 554, 2 Cal.Rptr.3d 699 (2003)*, the California Supreme Court held that termination of a birth parent's rights is not mandatory in every adoption and that second-parent adoptions are valid under California laws regulating independent adoption. The court reasoned that relief from parental duties under this section may be waived by the parties to an adoption.

Research References

Forms

California Transactions Forms--Family Law § 6:16, Legal Relationship Following Adoption Of Unmarried Minor.
California Transactions Forms--Family Law § 6:18, Intestate Succession Rights.
California Transactions Forms--Family Law § 6:106, Consent Of Noncustodial Parent.

California Transactions Forms--Family Law § 6:134, Financial Responsibility Agreement.

Treatises and Practice Aids

Witkin, California Summary 10th Parent and Child § 76, Nature and Effect Of Adoption.

§ 8618. Adopted child may take adoptive parent's family name

A child adopted pursuant to this part may take the family name of the adoptive parent. *(Stats.1992, c. 162 (A.B.2650), § 10, operative Jan. 1, 1994.)*

Law Revision Commission Comments

Enactment [Revised Comment]

Section 8618 continues the first sentence of former Civil Code Section 221.74 without substantive change. The reference to "adoptive parent" has been substituted for "person adopting." See also Section 8503 ("adoptive parent" defined).

For a comparable provision, see Section 9304 (name of adopted adult). [23 Cal.L.Rev.Comm. Reports 1 (1993)].

Research References

Treatises and Practice Aids

Witkin, California Summary 10th Parent and Child § 76, Nature and Effect Of Adoption.

§ 8619. Children of Indian ancestry; information; certificate of degree of Indian blood

The department shall adopt rules and regulations it determines are reasonably necessary to ensure that the birth parent or parents of Indian ancestry, seeking to relinquish a child for adoption, provide sufficient information to the department, county adoption agency, or licensed adoption agency so that a certificate of degree of Indian blood can be obtained from the Bureau of Indian Affairs. The department shall immediately request a certificate of degree of Indian blood from the Bureau of Indian Affairs upon obtaining the information. A copy of all documents pertaining to the degree of Indian blood and tribal enrollment, including a copy of the certificate of degree of Indian blood, shall become a permanent record in the adoption files and shall be housed in a central location and made available to authorized personnel from the Bureau of Indian Affairs when required to determine the adopted person's eligibility to receive services or benefits because of the adopted person's status as an Indian. This information shall be made available to the adopted person upon reaching the age of majority. *(Stats.1992, c. 162 (A.B.2650), § 10, operative Jan. 1, 1994. Amended by Stats.2012, c. 35 (S.B.1013), § 11, eff. June 27, 2012.)*

Law Revision Commission Comments

Enactment [Revised Comment]

Section 8619 continues former Civil Code Section 221.80 without substantive change. See also Sections 8512 ("birth parent" defined), 8518 ("department" defined), 8530 ("licensed adoption agency" defined). [23 Cal.L.Rev.Comm. Reports 1 (1993)].

Research References

Forms

California Transactions Forms--Family Law § 6:143, Overview Of Indian Child Welfare Act (ICWA).

West's California Code Forms, Family § 8600, Comment Overview--Adoption Of Unmarried Minors.

Treatises and Practice Aids

Witkin, California Summary 10th Parent and Child § 109, in General.

Witkin, California Summary 10th Parent and Child § 526, Determination Of Indian Status.

§ 8619.5. Children of Indian ancestry; vacated or set aside final decrees or voluntary return by adoptive parents; return of custody

Whenever a final decree of adoption of an Indian child has been vacated or set aside or the adoptive parent voluntary consents to termination of his or her parental rights to the child, a biological parent or prior Indian custodian may petition for return of custody and the court shall grant that petition unless there is a showing, in a proceeding subject to the provisions of Section 1912 of the Indian Child Welfare Act (25 U.S.C. Sec. 1901 et seq.), that the return of custody is not in the best interest of the child. *(Added by Stats.2006, c. 838 (S.B.678), § 10.)*

Research References

Forms

California Transactions Forms--Family Law § 6:143, Overview Of Indian Child Welfare Act (ICWA).

Treatises and Practice Aids

Witkin, California Summary 10th Parent and Child § 78, Child Of Indian Ancestry.

§ 8620. Determination of identity as Indian child for purposes of relinquishment or adoption placement; procedures; civil penalty for violations

(a)(1) If a parent is seeking to relinquish a child pursuant to Section 8700 or execute an adoption placement agreement pursuant to Section 8801.3, the department, county adoption agency, licensed adoption agency, or adoption service provider, as applicable, shall ask the child and the child's parent or custodian whether the child is, or may be, a member of, or eligible for membership in an Indian tribe or whether the child has been identified as a member of an Indian organization. The department, county adoption agency, licensed adoption agency, or adoption service provider, as applicable, shall complete the forms provided for this purpose by the department and shall make this completed form a part of the file.

(2) If there is any oral or written information that indicates that the child is, or may be, an Indian child, the department, county adoption agency, licensed adoption agency, or adoption service provider, as applicable, shall obtain the following information:

(A) The name of the child involved, and the actual date and place of birth of the child.

(B) The name, address, date of birth, and tribal affiliation of the birth parents, maternal and paternal grandparents, and maternal and paternal great-grandparents of the child.

(C) The name and address of extended family members of the child who have a tribal affiliation.

(D) The name and address of the Indian tribes or Indian organizations of which the child is, or may be, a member.

(E) A statement of the reasons why the child is, or may be, an Indian.

(3)(A) The department, county adoption agency, licensed adoption agency, attorney for the prospective adoptive parents, or adoption service provider shall send a notice, which shall include information obtained pursuant to paragraph (2) and a request for confirmation of the child's Indian status, to any parent and any custodian of the child, and to any Indian tribe of which the child is, or may be, a member or eligible for membership. If any of the information required under paragraph (2) cannot be obtained, the notice shall indicate that fact.

(B) The notice sent pursuant to subparagraph (A) shall describe the nature of the proceeding and advise the recipient of the Indian tribe's right to intervene in the proceeding on its own behalf or on behalf of a tribal member relative of the child.

(b) The department shall adopt regulations to ensure that if a child who is being voluntarily relinquished for adoption, pursuant to Section 8700, is an Indian child, the parent of the child shall be advised of his or her right to withdraw his or her consent and thereby rescind the relinquishment of an Indian child for any reason at any time prior to entry of a final decree of termination of parental rights or adoption, pursuant to Section 1913 of Title 25 of the United States Code.

(c) If a child who is the subject of an adoption proceeding after being relinquished for adoption pursuant to Section 8700, is an Indian child, the child's Indian tribe may intervene in that proceeding on behalf of a tribal member relative of the child.

(d) Any notice sent under this section shall comply with Section 180.

(e) If all prior notices required by this section have been provided to an Indian tribe, the Indian tribe receiving those prior notices is encouraged to provide notice to the department and to the licensed adoption agency, county adoption agency, or adoption service provider, not later than five calendar days prior to the date of the hearing to determine whether or not the final adoption order is to be granted, indicating whether or not it intends to intervene in the proceeding required by this section, either on its own behalf or on behalf of a tribal member who is a relative of the child.

(f) The Legislature finds and declares that some adoptive children may benefit from either direct or indirect contact with an Indian tribe. Nothing in the adoption laws of this state shall be construed to prevent the adopting parent or parents, the birth relatives, including the birth parent or parents, an Indian tribe, and the child, from voluntarily entering into a written agreement to permit continuing contact between the Indian tribe and the child, if the agreement is found by the court to have been entered into voluntarily and to be in the best interest of the child at the time the adoption petition is granted.

(g) With respect to giving notice to Indian tribes in the case of voluntary placements of Indian children pursuant to this section, a person, other than a birth parent of the child, shall be subject to a civil penalty if that person knowingly and willfully:

(1) Falsifies, conceals, or covers up by any trick, scheme, or device, a material fact concerning whether the child is an Indian child or the parent is an Indian.

(2) Makes any false, fictitious, or fraudulent statement, omission, or representation.

(3) Falsifies a written document knowing that the document contains a false, fictitious, or fraudulent statement or entry relating to a material fact.

(4) Assists any person in physically removing a child from the State of California in order to obstruct the application of notification.

(h) Civil penalties for a violation of subdivision (g) by a person other than a birth parent of the child are as follows:

(1) For the initial violation, a person shall be fined not more than ten thousand dollars ($10,000).

(2) For any subsequent violation, a person shall be fined not more than twenty thousand dollars ($20,000). *(Added by Stats.2003, c. 469 (S.B.947), § 4. Amended by Stats.2006, c. 838 (S.B.678), § 11; Stats.2010, c. 588 (A.B.2020), § 5; Stats.2012, c. 35 (S.B.1013), § 12, eff. June 27, 2012.)*

Research References

Forms

California Transactions Forms--Family Law § 6:83, Nature Of Agency Adoption--Governing Law.

California Transactions Forms--Family Law § 6:143, Overview Of Indian Child Welfare Act (ICWA).

West's California Code Forms, Family § 8600, Comment Overview--Adoption Of Unmarried Minors.

Treatises and Practice Aids

Witkin, California Summary 10th Parent and Child § 78, Child Of Indian Ancestry.

Witkin, California Summary 10th Parent and Child § 104, in General.

§ 8621. Regulations

The department shall adopt regulations regarding the provision of adoption services by the department, county adoption agencies, licensed adoption agencies, and other adoption service providers, and shall monitor the provision of those services by county adoption agencies, licensed adoption agencies, and other adoption providers. The department shall report violations of regulations to the appropriate licensing authority.

This section shall become operative on January 1, 1995. *(Added by Stats.1993, c. 758 (S.B.792), § 6, operative Jan. 1, 1995. Amended by Stats.2012, c. 35 (S.B.1013), § 13, eff. June 27, 2012.)*

§ 8622. Service limitations; notice

A licensed private adoption agency whose services are limited to a particular target population shall inform all birth parents and prospective adoptive parents of its service limitations before commencing any services, signing any documents or agreements, or accepting any fees.

This section shall become operative on January 1, 1995. *(Added by Stats.1993, c. 758 (S.B.792), § 6.2, operative Jan. 1, 1995.)*

Research References

Forms

California Transactions Forms--Family Law § 6:83, Nature Of Agency Adoption--Governing Law.

Treatises and Practice Aids

Witkin, California Summary 10th Parent and Child § 87, Private Adoptions.

CHAPTER 1.5. ADOPTION FACILITATORS

§ 8623. Description

A person or organization is an adoption facilitator if the person or organization is not licensed as an adoption agency by the State of California and engages in either of the following activities:

(a) Advertises for the purpose of soliciting parties to an adoption or locating children for an adoption or acting as an intermediary between the parties to an adoption.

(b) Charges a fee or other valuable consideration for services rendered relating to an adoption. *(Added by Stats. 1996, c. 1135 (S.B.2035), § 1. Amended by Stats.2007, c. 130 (A.B.299), § 90.)*

Research References

Forms

California Transactions Forms--Family Law § 6:3, Definitions.

Treatises and Practice Aids

Witkin, California Summary 10th Parent and Child § 72, Statutory Framework.

Witkin, California Summary 10th Parent and Child § 89, Adoption Facilitators.

§ 8624. Advertising

Any advertising by an adoption facilitator shall:

(a) Identify the name of the party placing the advertisement and shall state that the party is an adoption facilitator.

(b) Be subject to Section 17500 of the Business and Professions Code.

(c) Provide, in any written advertisement, the disclosure required by subdivision (a) in print that is the same size and typeface as the name required pursuant to subdivision (a) or any telephone number specified in the advertisement, whichever is the larger print size.

(d) Provide the disclosure required by subdivision (a) in the same color as the most prominent print in the advertisement where the advertisement contains more than one color.

(e) Present the disclosure required by subdivision (a) in a readily understandable manner and at the same speed and volume, if applicable, as the rest of the advertisement if the advertisement is a television advertisement. *(Added by Stats.1996, c. 1135 (S.B.2035), § 1.)*

Research References

Treatises and Practice Aids

Witkin, California Summary 10th Parent and Child § 89, Adoption Facilitators.

§ 8625. Prohibitions; misrepresentation; photolisting or advertising specific information about particular minor children

An adoption facilitator shall not:

(a) Mislead any person into believing, or imply by any document, including any form of advertising or by oral communications, that the adoption facilitator is a licensed adoption agency.

(b) Represent to any person that he or she is able to provide services for which the adoption facilitator is not properly licensed.

(c) Make use of photolisting to advertise minor children for placement in adoption.

(d) Post in any advertising specific information about particular minor children who are available for adoption placement. *(Added by Stats.1996, c. 1135 (S.B.2035), § 1. Amended by Stats.2006, c. 754 (S.B.1758), § 2.)*

Research References

Treatises and Practice Aids

Witkin, California Summary 10th Parent and Child § 89, Adoption Facilitators.

§ 8626. Description of services; disclosure of status

An adoption facilitator shall disclose in the first oral communication in which there is a description of services, that the facilitator is not a licensed adoption agency. *(Added by Stats.1996, c. 1135 (S.B.2035), § 1.)*

Research References

Treatises and Practice Aids

Witkin, California Summary 10th Parent and Child § 89, Adoption Facilitators.

§ 8627. Representation of multiple parties; written agreements

If the facilitator is acting on behalf of more than one party, all of the parties on whose behalf the facilitator is acting shall have signed a written agreement authorizing the facilitator to act on behalf of all of the parties. *(Added by Stats.1996, c. 1135 (S.B.2035), § 1.)*

Research References

Treatises and Practice Aids

Witkin, California Summary 10th Parent and Child § 89, Adoption Facilitators.

§ 8628. Information provided by birthparents; report to prospective adoptive parents

An adoption facilitator shall report in writing to the prospective adoptive parents all information that is provided to the facilitator by the birthparents concerning a particular child. *(Added by Stats.1996, c. 1135 (S.B.2035), § 1.)*

Research References

Treatises and Practice Aids

Witkin, California Summary 10th Parent and Child § 89, Adoption Facilitators.

§ 8629. Contracts; revocation without penalty

For a period of 72 hours after signing a contract or after the payment of any fee, the birthparents or the prospective adoptive parents may revoke the contract and request the return of any fees paid, without penalty, except for any reasonable fees actually earned by the facilitator and which are supported by written records or documentation. *(Added by Stats.1996, c. 1135 (S.B.2035), § 1.)*

Research References

Treatises and Practice Aids

Witkin, California Summary 10th Parent and Child § 89, Adoption Facilitators.

§ 8630. Fees and expenses; adoption accounting report

The amount of fees paid to an adoption facilitator and any fees or expenses an adoption facilitator pays to a third party shall be reported to the court in the adoption accounting report as an adoption-related expense. *(Added by Stats.1996, c. 1135 (S.B.2035), § 1.)*

Research References

Treatises and Practice Aids

Witkin, California Summary 10th Parent and Child § 89, Adoption Facilitators.

§ 8631. Contracts; requirements

All contracts entered into by an adoption facilitator shall be in writing and, at a minimum, shall include the following:

(a) A statement that the adoption facilitator is not licensed by the State of California as an adoption agency.

(b) A statement disclosing on whose behalf the facilitator is acting.

(c) A statement that the information provided by any party is not confidential but that this waiver of confidentiality shall only apply to the parties to the facilitation contract and any disclosures required by Chapter 7 (commencing with Section 9200) of Part 2 of Division 13.

(d) A statement that the adoption facilitator cannot provide any services for which the facilitator is not properly licensed, such as legal or therapeutic counseling.

(e) A list of all the services that the adoption facilitator is required to provide under the contract.

(f) Notice that for a period of 72 hours after signing the contract any party may revoke the contract, and if a fee has been paid by the prospective adoptive parents, they may, within that 72–hour period, request the return of the fees paid, except for any reasonable fee actually earned by the facilitator that is supported by written record or documentation. *(Added by Stats.1996, c. 1135 (S.B.2035), § 1.)*

Research References

Forms

California Transactions Forms--Family Law § 6:3, Definitions.

Treatises and Practice Aids

Witkin, California Summary 10th Parent and Child § 89, Adoption Facilitators.

§ 8632. Contracts; verbal explanation of terms

The adoption facilitator shall also explain the terms of the written contract verbally to the prospective adoptive parents and the birthparents. *(Added by Stats.1996, c. 1135 (S.B. 2035), § 1.)*

Research References

Treatises and Practice Aids

Witkin, California Summary 10th Parent and Child § 89, Adoption Facilitators.

§ 8632.5. Statewide registration and enforcement process for adoption facilitators

(a) The department shall establish and adopt regulations for a statewide registration and enforcement process for adoption facilitators. The department shall also establish and adopt regulations to require adoption facilitators to post a bond as required by this section.

(b) The department may adapt the process it uses to register adoption service providers in order to provide a similar registration process for adoption facilitators. The process used by the department shall include a procedure for determining the status of bond compliance by adoption facilitators, a means for accepting or denying organizations seeking inclusion in the adoption facilitator registry, a means for removing adoption facilitators from the adoption facilitator registry, and an appeals process for those entities denied inclusion in or removed from the adoption facilitator registry. The department may deny or revoke inclusion in the registry for adoption facilitators to an applicant who does not possess a criminal record clearance or exemption issued by the department pursuant to Section 1522 of the Health and

Safety Code and the criminal record clearance regulations applicable to personnel of private adoption agencies. Criminal record clearances and exemptions granted to adoption facilitators are not transferable.

(c) Upon the establishment by the department of a registration process, all adoption facilitators that operate independently from a licensed public or private adoption agency or an adoption attorney in this state shall be required to register with the department.

(d) An adoption facilitator, when posting a bond, shall also file with the department a disclosure form containing the adoption facilitator's name, date of birth, residence address, business address, residence telephone number, business telephone number, and the number of adoptions facilitated for the previous year. Along with the disclosure form, the adoption facilitator shall provide all of the following information to the department:

(1) Proof that the facilitator and any member of the staff who provides direct adoption services has completed two years of college courses, with at least half of the units and hours focusing on social work or a related field.

(2) Proof that the facilitator and any member of the staff who provides direct adoption services has a minimum of three years of experience employed by a public or private adoption agency licensed by the department, a registered adoption facilitator, or an adoption attorney who assists in bringing adopting persons and placing parents together for the purpose of adoption placement.

(A) An adoption facilitator and any member of the staff subject to this paragraph may waive the educational and experience requirements by satisfying all of the following requirements:

(i) He or she has over five years of work experience providing direct adoption services for a licensed adoption agency.

(ii) He or she has not been found liable of malfeasance in connection with providing adoption services.

(iii) He or she provides three separate letters of support attesting to his or her ethics and work providing direct adoption services from any of the following:

(I) A licensed public or private adoption agency.

(II) A member of the Academy of California Adoption Lawyers.

(III) The State Department of Social Services.

(B) An adoption facilitator who is registered with the department may also register staff members under the designation of "trainee." A trainee may provide direct adoption services without meeting the requirements of this paragraph. Any trainee registered with the department shall be directly supervised by an individual who meets all registration requirements.

(3) A valid business license.

(4) A valid, current, government-issued identification to determine the adoption facilitator's identity, such as a California driver's license, identification card, passport, or other form of identification that is acceptable to the department.

(5) Fingerprint images for a background check to be used by the department for the purposes described in this section.

(e) The State Department of Social Services may submit fingerprint images of adoption facilitators to the Department of Justice for the purpose of obtaining criminal offender record information regarding state- and federal-level convictions and arrests, including arrests for which the Department of Justice establishes that the person is free on bail or on his or her recognizance pending trial or appeal.

(1) The Department of Justice shall forward to the Federal Bureau of Investigation requests for federal summary criminal history information received pursuant to this section. The Department of Justice shall review the information returned from the Federal Bureau of Investigation and compile and disseminate a response to the department.

(2) The Department of Justice shall provide a response to the department pursuant to subdivision (m) of Section 11105 of the Penal Code.

(3) The department shall request from the Department of Justice subsequent arrest notification service, as provided pursuant to Section 11105.2 of the Penal Code.

(4) The Department of Justice shall charge a fee sufficient to cover the cost of processing the request described in this section.

(5) The department may only release an applicant's criminal record information search response as provided in subparagraph (G) of paragraph (4) of subdivision (a) of Section 1522 of the Health and Safety Code.

(f) The department may impose a fee upon applicants for each set of classifiable fingerprint cards that it processes pursuant to paragraph (5) of subdivision (d).

(g) The department shall post on its Internet Web site the registration and bond requirements required by this chapter and a list of adoption facilitators in compliance with the registration and bond requirements of this chapter. The department shall ensure that the information is current and shall update the information at least once every 30 days.

(h) The department shall develop the disclosure form required pursuant to subdivision (d) and shall make it available to any adoption facilitator posting a bond.

(i) The department may charge adoption facilitators an annual filing fee to recover all costs associated with the requirements of this section and that fee shall be set by regulation.

(j) The department may create an Adoption Facilitator Account for deposit of fees received from registrants.

(k) On or before January 1, 2008, the department shall make recommendations for the registry program to the Legislature, including a recommendation on how to implement a department program to accept and compile complaints against registered adoption facilitators and to provide public access to those complaints, by specific facilitator, through the department's Internet Web site.

(*l*) The adoption facilitator registry established pursuant to this section shall become operative on the first day of the first month following an appropriation from the Adoption Facilitator Account to the State Department of Social Services for the startup costs and the costs of administration of the adoption facilitator registry. *(Added by Stats.2006, c. 754 (S.B.1758), § 3. Amended by Stats.2007, c. 130 (A.B.299), § 91; Stats.2008, c. 534 (S.B.1726), § 6.)*

Research References

Treatises and Practice Aids

Witkin, California Summary 10th Parent and Child § 89, Adoption Facilitators.

Witkin, California Summary 10th Parent and Child § 137, in General.

§ 8633. Civil penalty

Any person or entity that violates this chapter is subject to a civil penalty of one thousand dollars ($1,000) or the amount of the contract fees, whichever is greater. *(Added by Stats.1996, c. 1135 (S.B.2035), § 1.)*

Research References

Treatises and Practice Aids

Witkin, California Summary 10th Parent and Child § 89, Adoption Facilitators.

§ 8634. Construction of contract; remedies

Any contract entered into pursuant to this chapter is subject to the rules and remedies relating to contracts generally. *(Added by Stats.1996, c. 1135 (S.B.2035), § 1.)*

Research References

Treatises and Practice Aids

Witkin, California Summary 10th Parent and Child § 89, Adoption Facilitators.

§ 8636. Licensure requirement; surety bond

(a) Prior to engaging in the business of, or acting in the capacity of, an adoption facilitator, any person shall (1) obtain a business license in the appropriate jurisdiction, and (2) post a bond in the amount of twenty-five thousand dollars ($25,000), executed by a corporate surety admitted to do business in this state, with the department in accordance with Section 8632.5.

(b) The surety bond required by subdivision (a) shall be in favor of, and payable to, the people of the State of California and shall be for the benefit of any person damaged by fraud, misstatement, misrepresentation, unlawful act or omission, or failure to provide the services of the adoption facilitator, or the agents, representatives, or employees of the adoption facilitator, while acting within the scope of that employment or agency.

(c) Whenever there is a recovery from a bond required by subdivision (a), the person shall replenish the bond or file a new bond if the former bond cannot be replenished in accordance with subdivision (a) before that person may conduct further business as an adoption facilitator.

(d) An adoption facilitator shall notify the department in writing within 30 days when a surety bond required by this section is renewed, and of any change of name, address, telephone number, or agent for service of process. *(Added by Stats.1996, c. 1135 (S.B.2035), § 1. Amended by Stats.2006, c. 754 (S.B.1758), § 5.)*

Research References

Forms

California Transactions Forms--Family Law § 6:3, Definitions.

Treatises and Practice Aids

Witkin, California Summary 10th Parent and Child § 89, Adoption Facilitators.

§ 8637. Attorneys; facilitating adoptions; application of law

Notwithstanding the provisions of this chapter, an attorney who provides services specified in Section 8623 related to facilitating an adoption shall be subject only to those provisions of law regulating the practice of law. *(Added by Stats.1996, c. 1135 (S.B.2035), § 1.)*

Research References

Forms

California Transactions Forms--Family Law § 6:3, Definitions.

Treatises and Practice Aids

Witkin, California Summary 10th Parent and Child § 89, Adoption Facilitators.

§ 8638. Remedies

(a) Any person aggrieved by any violation of this chapter may bring a civil action for damages, rescission, injunctive relief, or any other civil or equitable remedy.

(b) If the court finds that a person has violated this chapter, it shall award actual damages, plus an amount equal to treble the amount of the actual damages or one thousand dollars ($1,000) per violation, whichever is greater.

(c) In any civil action under this chapter, a prevailing party may recover reasonable attorney's fees and costs.

(d) The Attorney General, a district attorney, or a city attorney may bring a civil action for injunctive relief, restitution, or other equitable relief against the adoption facilitator in the name of the people of the State of California.

(e) Any other person who, based upon information or belief, claims a violation of this chapter has been committed may bring a civil action for injunctive relief on behalf of the general public. *(Added by Stats.1996, c. 1135 (S.B.2035), § 1. Amended by Stats.2006, c. 754 (S.B.1758), § 6.)*

Research References

Treatises and Practice Aids

Witkin, California Summary 10th Parent and Child § 89, Adoption Facilitators.

§ 8639. Civil penalty for failure to be in the registry; appeal; regulations

(a) Notwithstanding any other provision of this chapter, any adoption facilitator who operates without having met the requirements established in Section 8632.5 for inclusion into the adoption facilitator registry may be assessed by the department an immediate civil penalty in the amount of one hundred dollars ($100) per day of the violation.

(b) The civil penalty authorized in subdivision (a) shall be imposed if an adoption facilitator is involved in the facilitation of adoptions and the adoption facilitator refuses to seek inclusion in the adoption facilitator registry or if the adoption facilitator's application for inclusion into the adoption facilitator registry is denied and the adoption facilitator continues to facilitate adoptions, unless other available remedies, including criminal prosecution, are deemed more effective by the department.

(c) An adoption facilitator may appeal the assessment to the director.

(d) The department shall adopt regulations implementing this section, including the appeal process authorized in subdivision (c). *(Added by Stats.2008, c. 534 (S.B.1726), § 7.)*

Research References

Treatises and Practice Aids

Witkin, California Summary 10th Parent and Child § 89, Adoption Facilitators.

CHAPTER 2. AGENCY ADOPTIONS

§ 8700. Relinquishment of child to department, county adoption agency, or licensed adoption agency; minor parents; rescission; termination of parental rights

(a) Either birth parent may relinquish a child to the department, county adoption agency, or licensed adoption agency for adoption by a written statement signed before two subscribing witnesses and acknowledged before an authorized official of the department, county adoption agency, or licensed adoption agency. The relinquishment, when reciting that the person making it is entitled to the sole custody of the child and acknowledged before the officer, is prima facie evidence of the right of the person making it to the sole custody of the child and the person's sole right to relinquish.

(b) A relinquishing parent who is a minor has the right to relinquish his or her child for adoption to the department, county adoption agency, or licensed adoption agency, and the relinquishment is not subject to revocation by the relinquishing parent by reason of the minority, or because the parent or guardian of the relinquishing minor parent was not served with notice that the relinquishing minor parent relinquished his or her child for adoption, unless the relinquishing minor parent has previously provided written authorization to serve his or her parent or guardian with that notice.

(c) If a parent resides outside this state and the other parent has relinquished the child for adoption pursuant to subdivision (a) or (d), the parent residing out of state may relinquish the child by a written statement signed before a notary on a form prescribed by the department, and previously signed by an authorized official of the department, county adoption agency, or licensed adoption agency that signifies the willingness of the department, county adoption agency, or licensed adoption agency to accept the relinquishment.

(d) If a parent and child reside outside this state and the other parent has not relinquished the child for adoption to the department, county adoption agency, or licensed adoption agency, the parent residing out of state may relinquish the child to the department, county adoption agency, or licensed adoption agency by a written statement signed by the relinquishing parent, after the following requirements have been satisfied:

(1) Prior to signing the relinquishment, the relinquishing parent shall have received, from a representative of an agency

licensed or otherwise approved to provide adoption services under the laws of the relinquishing parent's state of residence, the same counseling and advisement services as if the relinquishing parent resided in this state.

(2) The relinquishment shall be signed before a representative of an agency licensed or otherwise approved to provide adoption services under the laws of the relinquishing parent's state of residence whenever possible or before a licensed social worker on a form prescribed by the department, and previously signed by an authorized official of the department, county adoption agency, or licensed adoption agency, that signifies the willingness of the department, county adoption agency, or licensed adoption agency to accept the relinquishment.

(e)(1) The relinquishment authorized by this section has no effect until a certified copy is sent to, and filed with, the department. The county adoption agency or licensed adoption agency shall send that copy by certified mail, return receipt requested, or by overnight courier or messenger, with proof of delivery, to the department no earlier than the end of the business day following the signing thereof. The agency shall inform the birth parent that during this time period he or she may request that the relinquishment be withdrawn and that, if he or she makes the request, the relinquishment shall be withdrawn. The relinquishment shall be final 10 business days after receipt of the filing by the department, unless any of the following applies:

(A) The department sends written acknowledgment of receipt of the relinquishment prior to the expiration of that 10–day period, at which time the relinquishment shall be final.

(B) A longer period of time is necessary due to a pending court action or some other cause beyond control of the department.

(C) The birth parent signs a waiver of right to revoke relinquishment pursuant to Section 8700.5, in which case the relinquishment shall become final as provided in that section.

(2) After the relinquishment is final, it may be rescinded only by the mutual consent of the department, county adoption agency, or licensed adoption agency to which the child was relinquished and the birth parent or parents relinquishing the child.

(f) The relinquishing parent may name in the relinquishment the person or persons with whom he or she intends that placement of the child for adoption be made by the department, county adoption agency, or licensed adoption agency.

(g) Notwithstanding subdivision (e), if the relinquishment names the person or persons with whom placement by the department, county adoption agency, or licensed adoption agency is intended and the child is not placed in the home of the named person or persons or the child is removed from the home prior to the granting of the adoption, the department, county adoption agency, or licensed adoption agency shall mail a notice by certified mail, return receipt requested, to the birth parent signing the relinquishment within 72 hours of the decision not to place the child for adoption or the decision to remove the child from the home.

(h) The relinquishing parent has 30 days from the date on which the notice described in subdivision (g) was mailed to rescind the relinquishment.

(1) If the relinquishing parent requests rescission during the 30–day period, the department, county adoption agency, or licensed adoption agency shall rescind the relinquishment.

(2) If the relinquishing parent does not request rescission during the 30–day period, the department, county adoption agency, or licensed adoption agency shall select adoptive parents for the child.

(3) If the relinquishing parent and the department, county adoption agency, or licensed adoption agency wish to identify a different person or persons during the 30–day period with whom the child is intended to be placed, the initial relinquishment shall be rescinded and a new relinquishment identifying the person or persons completed.

(i) Subject to the requirements of subdivision (b) of Section 361 of the Welfare and Institutions Code, a parent may sign a relinquishment of a child described in paragraph (1) of subdivision (b) of Section 361 of the Welfare and Institutions Code. If the relinquishment is to a licensed private adoption agency, the parent shall be advised, in writing, that the relinquishment shall have no effect and will be not be filed with, or acknowledged by, the department, unless the court approves the relinquishment pursuant to paragraph (3) of subdivision (b) of Section 361 of the Welfare and Institutions Code. If the court issues an order approving the relinquishment, the licensed private adoption agency shall file the relinquishment and the order with the department. If the court denies the relinquishment, the licensed private adoption agency shall void the relinquishment and inform the parent of that fact.

(j) The filing of the relinquishment with the department terminates all parental rights and responsibilities with regard to the child, except as provided in subdivisions (g) and (h).

(k) The department shall adopt regulations to administer the provisions of this section. *(Stats.1992, c. 162 (A.B.2650), § 10, operative Jan. 1, 1994. Amended by Stats.1993, c. 219 (A.B.1500), § 189; Stats.1994, c. 1269 (A.B.2208), § 56; Stats.1997, c. 793 (A.B.1544), § 3; Stats.1998, c. 1056 (A.B. 2773), § 1; Stats.2004, c. 306 (A.B.2674), § 1; Stats.2006, c. 806 (S.B.1325), § 7; Stats.2008, c. 534 (S.B.1726), § 8; Stats.2012, c. 35 (S.B.1013), § 14, eff. June 27, 2012; Stats. 2012, c. 638 (A.B.1757), § 7; Stats.2014, c. 763 (A.B.1701), § 10, eff. Jan. 1, 2015.)*

Law Revision Commission Comments

Enactment [Revised Comment]

Section 8700 continues former Civil Code Section 222.10 without substantive change. Throughout this section, "birth parent" has been substituted for "birth father or mother." See Section 8512 ("birth parent" defined). The word "duly," formerly preceding "acknowledged," has been omitted as surplus. See also Sections 8518 ("department" defined), 8530 ("licensed adoption agency" defined).

For related provisions, see Sections 8814 (consent to independent adoption), 9003 (consent to stepparent adoption). [23 Cal.L.Rev. Comm. Reports 1 (1993)].

Commentary

When a Welfare and Institutions Code Section 366.26 hearing has been set but has not yet commenced and the dependent child's birth parents voluntarily relinquish the child to a public adoption agency under this section, the relinquishment obviates any need for the hearing and the juvenile court may not make any order that interferes with the parents' unlimited right to voluntarily relinquish the child. *In re R.S., 179 Cal.App.4th 1137, 101 Cal.Rptr.3d 910 (2009).*

Adoption of Baby Boy D., 93 Cal.App.4th 1, 112 Cal.Rptr.2d 760 (2001), review denied January 16, 2002, holds that there was an effective relinquishment of a child by a birth mother in an agency adoption despite the mother's failure to initial one of the many boxes in a statement of understanding supplied by the California Department of Social Services and despite the Department's refusal to acknowledge her relinquishment because of that failure. The court reasoned that the relinquishment nevertheless was valid because it was knowingly and intelligently made and substantially complied with every reasonable objective of the Family Code provisions and the Department regulations.

Teresa J. v. Superior Court, 102 Cal.App.4th 366, 125 Cal.Rptr.2d 506 (2002), holds that even though a child has already been adjudicated a dependent of the juvenile court under Welfare and Institutions Code § 300, the child's birth mother may relinquish the child for adoption to a private adoption agency, subject to the juvenile court's power to limit the parent's control over the child.

Research References

Forms

California Transactions Forms--Family Law § 6:3, Definitions.
California Transactions Forms--Family Law § 6:5, Issues Common to All Types Of Adoptions.
California Transactions Forms--Family Law § 6:32, Nature Of Independent Adoption--Relinquishment Versus Consent.
California Transactions Forms--Family Law § 6:83, Nature Of Agency Adoption--Governing Law.
California Transactions Forms--Family Law § 6:84, Relinquishment as Distinguished from Consent.
California Transactions Forms--Family Law § 6:85, Identified or Designated Adoption.
California Transactions Forms--Family Law § 6:87, Required Formalities Of Relinquishment.
California Transactions Forms--Family Law § 6:88, Revocation Of Relinquishment Prior to Filing.
California Transactions Forms--Family Law § 7:39, Adoption and Termination Of Parental Rights.
California Transactions Forms--Family Law § 6:148, Rights Of Indian Parents Of Indian Children.
Nichols Cyclopedia of Legal Forms Annotated § 7:7, Statutory Provisions--Relinquishment Of Child to Another to Obtain Adoption.
West's California Code Forms, Family § 8600, Comment Overview--Adoption Of Unmarried Minors.
West's California Code Forms, Family § 8700, Comment Overview--Relinquishment Of Child to Department Of Social Services or a Licensed Adoption Agency.
West's California Code Forms, Family § 8700 Form 1, Relinquishment by Parent Residing in California.
West's California Code Forms, Family § 9102 Form 1, Petition to Vacate Adoption--Procedural Defect.
West's California Judicial Council Forms ADOPT-200, Adoption Request.

Treatises and Practice Aids

Witkin, California Summary 10th Contracts § 47, Miscellaneous Contracts.
Witkin, California Summary 10th Parent and Child § 70, Types Of Adoption.
Witkin, California Summary 10th Parent and Child § 72, Statutory Framework.
Witkin, California Summary 10th Parent and Child § 78, Child Of Indian Ancestry.
Witkin, California Summary 10th Parent and Child § 100, in General.
Witkin, California Summary 10th Parent and Child § 103, Other Exceptions.
Witkin, California Summary 10th Parent and Child § 109, in General.
Witkin, California Summary 10th Parent and Child § 110, Finality and Effect Of Relinquishment.
Witkin, California Summary 10th Parent and Child § 267, Jurisdiction and Venue.
Witkin, California Summary 10th Parent and Child § 308, Dependency Proceeding Distinguished.
Witkin, California Summary 10th Parent and Child § 629, Limitations on Parental Control.
Witkin, California Summary 10th Parent and Child § 638, Preferential Right Of Relatives.
Witkin, California Summary 10th Parent and Child § 680, Statutory Procedure is Exclusive.
Witkin, California Summary 10th Parent and Child § 681, Notice.
Witkin, California Summary 10th Parent and Child § 675A, (New) Setting Selection and Implementation Hearing.

§ 8700.5. Waiver of the right to revoke relinquishment; interview and witness; relinquishment final and irrevocable; conditions rendering waiver void

(a) A relinquishing birth parent may elect to sign a waiver of the right to revoke relinquishment in the presence of any of the following:

(1) A representative of the department or the delegated county adoption agency, or any public adoption agency of another state.

(2) A judicial officer of a court of record, within or outside of California, if the birth parent is represented by independent legal counsel.

(3) An authorized representative of a licensed private adoption agency within or outside of California, including a representative of the adoption agency that witnessed or accepted the relinquishment, if the birth parent is represented by independent legal counsel.

(b) The waiver of the right to revoke relinquishment may not be signed until the department, delegated county adoption agency, or public adoption agency of another state has completed an interview, unless the waiver is signed in the presence of a judicial officer of a court of record of any state or an authorized representative of a private adoption agency licensed within or outside of California. If the waiver is signed in the presence of a judicial officer, the interview and witnessing of the signing of the waiver shall be conducted by the judicial officer. If the waiver is signed in the presence of an authorized representative of a licensed adoption agency, the interview shall be conducted by the independent legal counsel for the birth parent or parents, who shall:

(1) Review the waiver with the birth parent or parents.

(2) Counsel the birth parent or parents about the nature of the intended waiver.

(3) Sign and deliver to the birth parent or parents and the licensed adoption agency a certificate in substantially the following form:

"I, (name of attorney), have counseled my client, (name of client), about the nature and legal effect of the waiver of the right to revoke the relinquishment for adoption. I am so disassociated from the interest of the prospective adoptive parent(s) and the licensed adoption agency as to be in a position to advise my client impartially and confidentially as to the consequences of the waiver. My client is aware that California law provides an indeterminate period, usually 2 to 10 business days, during which a birth parent may revoke a relinquishment for adoption. On the basis of this counsel, I conclude that it is the intent of my client to waive the right to revoke, and to make a permanent and irrevocable relinquishment for adoption. My client understands that upon signing this waiver, he or she will not be able to regain custody of the child unless the prospective adoptive parent or parents agree to withdraw the petition for adoption or the court denies the adoption petition."

(c) If the placing birth parent signs the waiver in front of a judicial officer or the department, the relinquishment shall become final and irrevocable at the time the waiver is signed. If the waiver is signed in the presence of an authorized representative of a private licensed adoption agency, the relinquishment shall become final and irrevocable at the close of the next business day after the relinquishment was signed, or at the close of the next business day after expiration of any holding period specified in writing, whichever is later.

(d) The licensed adoption agency shall submit the waiver and certificate to the department with the relinquishment, unless the relinquishment was submitted to the department before the waiver was signed, in which case the waiver and certificate shall be submitted to the department no later than two business days after signing.

(e) A waiver executed pursuant to this section shall be void if any of the following occur:

(1) The relinquishment is determined to be invalid.

(2) The relinquishment is revoked during any holding period specified in writing.

(3) The relinquishment is rescinded pursuant to Section 8700.

(f) This section does not limit the birth parent's right to rescind the relinquishment pursuant to Section 8700. *(Added by Stats.2012, c. 638 (A.B.1757), § 8. Amended by Stats.2013, c. 743 (A.B.848), § 1.)*

Research References

Treatises and Practice Aids

Witkin, California Summary 10th Parent and Child § 110, Finality and Effect Of Relinquishment.

§ 8701. Right of birth parents to request information on status of adoption

At or before the time a relinquishment is signed, the department, county adoption agency, or licensed adoption agency shall advise the birth parent signing the relinquishment, verbally and in writing, that the birth parent may, at any time in the future, request from the department, county adoption agency, or licensed adoption agency all known information about the status of the child's adoption, except for personal, identifying information about the adoptive family. The birth parent shall be advised that this information includes, but is not limited to, all of the following:

(a) Whether the child has been placed for adoption.

(b) The approximate date that an adoption was completed.

(c) If the adoption was not completed or was vacated, for any reason, whether adoptive placement of the child is again being considered. *(Stats.1992, c. 162 (A.B.2650), § 10, operative Jan. 1, 1994. Amended by Stats.2012, c. 35 (S.B. 1013), § 15, eff. June 27, 2012.)*

Law Revision Commission Comments

Enactment [Revised Comment]

Section 8701 continues former Civil Code Section 222.13 without substantive change. See also Sections 8512 ("birth parent" defined), 8518 ("department" defined), 8530 ("licensed adoption agency" defined).

For a comparable provision, see Section 8813 (request for information on status of independent adoption). [23 Cal.L.Rev.Comm. Reports 1 (1993)].

Research References

Treatises and Practice Aids

Witkin, California Summary 10th Parent and Child § 109, in General.

§ 8702. Statement presented to birth parents at time of relinquishment; content; form

(a) The department shall adopt a statement to be presented to the birth parents at the time a relinquishment is signed and to prospective adoptive parents at the time of the home study. The statement shall, in a clear and concise manner and in words calculated to ensure the confidence of the birth parents in the integrity of the adoption process, communicate to the birth parents of a child who is the subject of an adoption petition all of the following facts:

(1) It is in the child's best interest that the birth parent keep the department, county adoption agency, or licensed adoption agency to whom the child was relinquished for adoption informed of any health problems that the parent develops that could affect the child.

(2) It is extremely important that the birth parent keep an address current with the department, county adoption agency, or licensed adoption agency to whom the child was relinquished for adoption in order to permit a response to inquiries concerning medical or social history.

(3) Section 9203 of the Family Code authorizes a person who has been adopted and who attains the age of 21 years to request the department, county adoption agency, or the licensed adoption agency to disclose the name and address of the adoptee's birth parents. Consequently, it is of the utmost importance that the birth parent indicate whether to allow this disclosure by checking the appropriate box provided on the form.

(4) The birth parent may change the decision whether to permit disclosure of the birth parent's name and address, at any time, by sending a notarized letter to that effect, by certified mail, return receipt requested, to the department,

county adoption agency, or to the licensed adoption agency that joined in the adoption petition.

(5) The relinquishment will be filed in the office of the clerk of the court in which the adoption takes place. The file is not open to inspection by any persons other than the parties to the adoption proceeding, their attorneys, and the department, except upon order of a judge of the superior court.

(b) The department shall adopt a form to be signed by the birth parents at the time the relinquishment is signed, which shall provide as follows:

"Section 9203 of the Family Code authorizes a person who has been adopted and who attains the age of 21 years to make a request to the State Department of Social Services, county adoption agency, or licensed adoption agency that joined in the adoption petition, for the name and address of the adoptee's birth parents. Indicate by checking one of the boxes below whether or not you wish your name and address to be disclosed:

☐ YES

☐ NO

☐ UNCERTAIN AT THIS TIME; WILL NOTIFY AGENCY AT LATER DATE." *(Stats.1992, c. 162 (A.B. 2650), § 10, operative Jan. 1, 1994. Amended by Stats.2002, c. 784 (S.B.1316), § 111; Stats.2012, c. 35 (S.B.1013), § 16, eff. June 27, 2012.)*

Law Revision Commission Comments

Enactment [Revised Comment]

Section 8702 continues former Civil Code Section 222.15 without substantive change. The statement concerning the requirements of Section 9203 has been revised to conform to the language of that section. For example, "petition" has been changed to "request." See also Sections 8512 ("birth parent" defined), 8518 ("department" defined), 8530 ("licensed adoption agency" defined), 8542 ("prospective adoptive parent" defined).

For a comparable provision, see Section 8818 (statement to birth parents in independent adoption). [23 Cal.L.Rev.Comm. Reports 1 (1993)].

2002 Amendment

Subdivision (a)(5) of Section 8702 is amended to reflect elimination of the county clerk's role as ex officio clerk of the superior court. See former Gov't Code § 26800 (county clerk acting as clerk of superior court). The powers, duties, and responsibilities formerly exercised by the county clerk as ex officio clerk of the court are delegated to the court administrative or executive officer, and the county clerk is relieved of those powers, duties, and responsibilities. See Gov't Code §§ 69840 (powers, duties, and responsibilities of clerk of court and deputy clerk of court), 71620 (trial court personnel). [32 Cal.L.Rev.Comm. Reports 167 (2002)].

Research References

Forms

West's California Code Forms, Family § 8700, Comment Overview--Relinquishment Of Child to Department Of Social Services or a Licensed Adoption Agency.

Treatises and Practice Aids

Witkin, California Summary 10th Parent and Child § 79, Adoption Information.

Witkin, California Summary 10th Parent and Child § 151, Request for Disclosure.

§ 8703. Written notice to birth parent upon termination of parental rights; contents

When the parental rights of a birth parent are terminated pursuant to Chapter 5 (commencing with Section 7660) of Part 3 of Division 12 or Part 4 (commencing with Section 7800) of Division 12, or pursuant to Section 366.25 or 366.26 of the Welfare and Institutions Code, the department, county adoption agency, or licensed adoption agency responsible for the adoptive placement of the child shall send a written notice to the birth parent, if the birth parent's address is known, that contains the following statement:

(a) "You are encouraged to keep the department or this agency informed of your current address in order to permit a response to any inquiry concerning medical or social history made by or on behalf of the child who was the subject of the court action terminating parental rights.

(b) Section 9203 of the Family Code authorizes a person who has been adopted and who attains the age of 21 years to make a request to the State Department of Social Services, county adoption agency, or licensed adoption agency, that joined in the adoption petition, for the name and address of the adoptee's birth parents. Indicate by checking one of the boxes below whether or not you wish your name and address to be disclosed:

( ) YES

( ) NO

( ) UNCERTAIN AT THIS TIME; WILL NOTIFY AGENCY AT LATER DATE" *(Stats.1992, c. 162 (A.B. 2650), § 10, operative Jan. 1, 1994. Amended by Stats.2000, c. 910 (A.B.2921), § 1; Stats.2012, c. 35 (S.B.1013), § 17, eff. June 27, 2012.)*

Law Revision Commission Comments

Enactment [Revised Comment]

Section 8703 continues former Civil Code Section 222.18 without substantive change. The references to the Family Code sections are broader than the references in former law to former Civil Code Sections 232 and 7017. These are not substantive changes. The language of the required statement has been revised to refer to the department. This is consistent with other provisions of this section. See also Sections 8512 ("birth parent" defined), 8518 ("department" defined), 8530 ("licensed adoption agency" defined).

For a comparable provision, see Section 8819 (notice of termination of parental rights in independent adoption). [23 Cal.L.Rev. Comm. Reports 1 (1993)].

Research References

Forms

West's California Code Forms, Family § 7840, Comment Overview--Freedom from Parental Control.

Treatises and Practice Aids

Witkin, California Summary 10th Parent and Child § 79, Adoption Information.

§ 8704. Responsibilities of department, county adoption agency, or licensed adoption agency; termination of placement; adoption petition; removal of child; consent to adoption

(a) The department, county adoption agency, or licensed adoption agency to which a child has been freed for adoption by either relinquishment or termination of parental rights is responsible for the care of the child, and is entitled to the exclusive custody and control of the child until an order of adoption is granted. Any placement for temporary care, or for adoption, made by the department, county adoption agency, or licensed adoption agency may be terminated in its discretion at any time before the granting of an order of adoption. In the event of termination of any placement for temporary care or for adoption, the child shall be returned promptly to the physical custody of the department, county adoption agency, or licensed adoption agency.

(b) No petition may be filed to adopt a child relinquished to the department, county adoption agency, or licensed adoption agency or a child declared free from the custody and control of either or both birth parents and referred to the department, county adoption agency, or licensed adoption agency for adoptive placement, except by the prospective adoptive parents with whom the child has been placed for adoption by the department, county adoption agency, or licensed adoption agency. After the adoption petition has been filed, the department, county adoption agency, or licensed adoption agency may remove the child from the prospective adoptive parents only with the approval of the court, upon motion by the department, county adoption agency, or licensed adoption agency after notice to the prospective adoptive parents, supported by an affidavit or affidavits stating the grounds on which removal is sought. If the department, county adoption agency, or licensed adoption agency refuses to consent to the adoption of a child by the person or persons with whom the department, county adoption agency, or licensed adoption agency placed the child for adoption, the court may nevertheless order the adoption if it finds that the refusal to consent is not in the child's best interest. *(Stats.1992, c. 162 (A.B.2650), § 10, operative Jan. 1, 1994. Amended by Stats.1995, c. 884 (A.B.1743), § 3; Stats. 2012, c. 35 (S.B.1013), § 18, eff. June 27, 2012.)*

Law Revision Commission Comments

Enactment [Revised Comment]

Section 8704 continues former Civil Code Section 222.20 without substantive change. In subdivision (a), the provision for return of physical custody to the department is new and is added for consistency with the first sentence of the subdivision. The reference to the "superior" court has been omitted as surplus. See Section 200 (jurisdiction in superior court). In subdivision (c), the reference to "prospective adoptive families" has been changed to the defined term "prospective adoptive parents." In subdivision (e), the former provision that "[t]his subdivision does not apply" to a child adjudged a dependent of the juvenile court has been changed to "[s]ubdivisions (c) and (d) do not apply." This is consistent with former Civil Code Section 224n, the predecessor of former Civil Code Section 222.20.

See also Sections 8512 ("birth parent" defined), 8518 ("department" defined), 8530 ("licensed adoption agency" defined), 8542 ("prospective adoptive parent" defined). [23 Cal.L.Rev.Comm. Reports 1 (1993)].

Commentary

Department of Social Services v. Superior Court, 58 Cal.App.4th 721, 68 Cal.Rptr.2d 239 (1997), review denied January 21, 1998, holds that absent a showing that an interim adoptive placement made by the Department of Social Services is arbitrary and capricious in light of the child's best interest, the juvenile court may not interfere with or disapprove the placement, because this section grants the agency "exclusive" custody and control of the child until an order of adoption is granted. Accord, *Los Angeles County Department of Child and Family Services v. Superior Court, 62 Cal.App.4th 1, 72 Cal.Rptr.2d 369 (1998), review denied June 10, 1998.*

Interpreting this section together with Welfare and Institutions Code § 366.26 (j), *In re Jacob E., 121 Cal.App.4th 909, 18 Cal.Rptr.3d 15 (2004), review denied,* held that a grandmother was not entitled to a hearing before the Department of Family Services removed a dependent child from her custody for failure to provide adequate parenting, because the grandmother had not been identified as a prospective adoptive parent of the child after his mother's parental rights were terminated.

Research References

Forms

California Transactions Forms--Family Law § 6:86, Role Of Agency.
California Transactions Forms--Family Law § 6:99, Agency Consent.
West's California Code Forms, Family § 8704 Form 1, Notice Of Motion and Motion for Order Removing Child from Prospective Adoptive Parents.

Treatises and Practice Aids

Witkin, California Summary 10th Parent and Child § 109, in General.
Witkin, California Summary 10th Parent and Child § 116, in General.
Witkin, California Summary 10th Parent and Child § 117, Termination Of Placement.
Witkin, California Summary 10th Parent and Child § 118, Petition.
Witkin, California Summary 10th Parent and Child § 120, Hearing and Order.
Witkin, California Summary 10th Parent and Child § 693B, (New) Designation Of Prospective Adoptive Parent.

§ 8704.5. Foster care license or certification or resource family approval not required for placement of child by licensed private adoption agency; supervisory visits

(a) A foster care license or certification or resource family approval shall not be required for placement of a nondependent child who is relinquished for adoption to a licensed private adoption agency, if the child is placed in the care of prospective adoptive parents who have an approved adoption home study that meets the criteria established by the department for home studies conducted within the state.

* * *

(b) During a preadoptive placement made pursuant to subdivision (a), the licensed private adoption agency shall conduct in-home supervisory visits no less than once every 30 days, until the child has been legally freed and formally placed for adoption. *(Added by Stats.2011, c. 462 (A.B.687), § 7. Amended by Stats.2017, c. 732 (A.B.404), § 2, eff. Jan. 1, 2018.)*

Research References

Treatises and Practice Aids

Witkin, California Summary 10th Parent and Child § 116, in General.

§ 8705. Consent to adoption of child; deceased persons; court order granting agency custody; guardian appointed

(a) Where a child is in the custody of a public agency or licensed adoption agency, if it is established that the persons whose consent to the adoption is required by law are deceased, an action may be brought by the department, county adoption agency, or licensed adoption agency requesting the court to make an order establishing that the requesting agency has the right to custody and control of the child and the authority to place the child for adoption. The department, county adoption agency, or licensed adoption agency bringing the action shall give notice in the form prescribed by the court to all known relatives of the child up to and including the third degree of lineal or collateral consanguinity.

(b) This section does not apply where a guardian of the person of the child has been appointed pursuant to nomination by a will. *(Stats.1992, c. 162 (A.B.2650), § 10, operative Jan. 1, 1994. Amended by Stats.2012, c. 35 (S.B.1013), § 19, eff. June 27, 2012.)*

Law Revision Commission Comments

Enactment [Revised Comment]

Section 8705 continues former Civil Code Section 222.22 without substantive change. In the last sentence of subdivision (a), the reference to the "department" is new and has been added for consistency with the statement in the first sentence that an action may be brought by the department or an agency. See also Sections 8518 ("department" defined), 8530 ("licensed adoption agency" defined). [23 Cal.L.Rev.Comm. Reports 1 (1993)].

Research References

Treatises and Practice Aids

Witkin, California Summary 10th Parent and Child § 103, Other Exceptions.

Witkin, California Summary 10th Parent and Child § 111, Child Of Deceased Parents.

§ 8706. Medical report; background of child and biological parents; contents; blood sample

(a) An agency may not place a child for adoption unless a written report on the child's medical background and, if available, the medical background of the child's biological parents so far as ascertainable, has been submitted to the prospective adoptive parents and they have acknowledged in writing the receipt of the report.

(b) The report on the child's background shall contain all known diagnostic information, including current medical reports on the child, psychological evaluations, and scholastic information, as well as all known information regarding the child's developmental history and family life.

(c)(1) The biological parents may provide a blood sample at a clinic or hospital approved by the State Department of Health Services. The biological parents' failure to provide a blood sample shall not affect the adoption of the child.

(2) The blood sample shall be stored at a laboratory under contract with the State Department of Health Services for a period of 30 years following the adoption of the child.

(3) The purpose of the stored sample of blood is to provide a blood sample from which DNA testing can be done at a later date after entry of the order of adoption at the request of the adoptive parents or the adopted child. The cost of drawing and storing the blood samples shall be paid for by a separate fee in addition to the fee required under Section 8716. The amount of this additional fee shall be based on the cost of drawing and storing the blood samples but at no time shall the additional fee be more than one hundred dollars ($100).

(d)(1) The blood sample shall be stored and released in such a manner as to not identify any party to the adoption.

(2) Any results of the DNA testing shall be stored and released in such a manner as to not identify any party to the adoption. *(Stats.1992, c. 162 (A.B.2650), § 10, operative Jan. 1, 1994. Amended by Stats.1996, c. 1053 (A.B.3241), § 1.)*

Law Revision Commission Comments

Enactment [Revised Comment]

Section 8706 continues former Civil Code Section 222.26(a) without substantive change. See also Sections 8542 ("prospective adoptive parent" defined), 8608 (regulations concerning form and content of medical reports), 9202 (regulations concerning availability of medical reports).

For a comparable provision, see Section 8909 (medical report in intercountry adoption). For a related provision, see Section 8817 (medical report in independent adoption). [23 Cal.L.Rev.Comm. Reports 1 (1993)].

Commentary

See generally *Tyler v. Children's Home Society of California, 29 Cal.App.4th 511, 35 Cal.Rptr.2d 291 (1994), review denied 1/5/95*, (private adoption agency's noncompliance with various requirements of state adoption law does not necessarily invalidate a parent's relinquishment of his or her child).

Research References

Treatises and Practice Aids

Witkin, California Summary 10th Parent and Child § 93, Medical Report on Child and Birth Parents.

Witkin, California Summary 10th Parent and Child § 138, Powers and Duties Of Licensed Adoption Agencies.

Witkin, California Summary 10th Parent and Child § 149, Confidentiality Of Records.

§ 8707. Photo-listing service

(a) The department shall establish a statewide photo-listing service to serve all county adoption agencies and licensed adoption agencies in the state as a means of recruiting adoptive families. The department shall adopt regulations governing the operations of the photo-listing service and shall establish procedures for monitoring compliance with this section.

(b) The photo-listing service shall maintain child specific information that, except as provided in this section, contains a photograph and description of each child who has been legally freed for adoption and whose case plan goal is adoption. Registration of children with the photo-listing service and notification by the licensed adoption agency of changes in a child's photo-listing status shall be reflected in the photo-listing service within 30 working days of receipt of the registration or notification.

(c) The photo-listing service shall be provided to all county adoption agencies, licensed adoption agencies, adoption support groups, and state, regional, and national photo-listings and exchanges requesting copies of the photo-listing service.

(d) All children legally freed for adoption whose case plan goal is adoption shall be photo-listed, unless deferred as provided in subdivision (e) or (f). Adoption agencies shall send a recent photograph and description of each legally freed child to the photo-listing service within 15 working days of the time a child is legally freed for adoption. When adoption has become the case plan goal for a particular child, the adoption agency may photo-list that child before the child becomes legally freed for adoption.

(e) A child shall be deferred from the photo-listing service when the child's foster parents or other identified individuals who have applied to adopt the child are meeting the county adoption agency's or licensed adoption agency's requests for required documentation and are cooperating in the completion of a home study being conducted by the agency.

(f) A child who is 12 years old or older may be deferred from the photo-listing service if the child does not consent to being adopted.

(g) Within 15 working days following a one-year period in which a child is listed in the photo-listing service, the county adoption agency or licensed adoption agency shall submit a revised description and photograph of the child.

(h) County adoption agencies and licensed adoption agencies shall notify the photo-listing service, by telephone, of any adoptive placements or of significant changes in a child's photo-listing status within two working days of the change.

(i) The department shall establish procedures for semiannual review of the photo-listing status of all legally freed children whose case plan goal is adoption, including those who are registered with the photo-listing service and those whose registration has been deferred. *(Stats.1992, c. 162 (A.B.2650), § 10, operative Jan. 1, 1994. Amended by Stats. 1998, c. 1056 (A.B.2773), § 2; Stats.2012, c. 35 (S.B.1013), § 20, eff. June 27, 2012.)*

Law Revision Commission Comments

Enactment [Revised Comment]

Section 8707 restates former Civil Code Section 222.30 without substantive change. The order of some provisions in this section has been changed. See also Sections 8518 ("department" defined), 8530 ("licensed adoption agency" defined). [23 Cal.L.Rev.Comm. Reports 1 (1993)].

Research References

Treatises and Practice Aids

Witkin, California Summary 10th Parent and Child § 107, Photo-Listing Service.

§ 8707.1. Recruitment of potential adoptive parents; ethnic, racial, and cultural diversity

(a) The agency responsible for recruitment of potential adoptive parents shall make diligent efforts to recruit individuals who reflect the ethnic, racial, and cultural diversity of children for whom adoptive homes are needed.

(b) This section shall not be construed to affect the application of the federal Indian Child Welfare Act. *(Added by Stats.2014, c. 772 (S.B.1460), § 1, eff. Jan. 1, 2015.)*

Research References

Treatises and Practice Aids

Witkin, California Summary 10th Parent and Child § 114, Ethnic, Cultural, and Jurisdictional Considerations.

§ 8708. Race, color, or national origin of adoptive parent or child; nonresident status of adoptive parent

(a) The adoption agency to which a child has been freed for adoption by either relinquishment or termination of parental rights shall not do any of the following:

(1) Deny to any person the opportunity to become an adoptive parent on the basis of the race, color, or national origin of the person or the child involved.

(2) Delay or deny the placement of a child for adoption on the basis of the race, color, or national origin of the adoptive parent or the child involved.

(3) Delay or deny the placement of a child for adoption solely because the prospective, approved adoptive family resides outside the jurisdiction of the department, county adoption agency, or licensed adoption agency. For purposes of this paragraph, an approved adoptive family means a family approved pursuant to the California adoptive applicant assessment standards or approved as a resource family pursuant to Section 1517 of the Health and Safety Code or Section 16519.5 of the Welfare and Institutions Code. If the adoptive applicant assessment was conducted in another state according to that state's standards, the California placing agency shall determine whether the standards of the other state substantially meet the standards and criteria established in California adoption regulations.

(b) This section shall not be construed to affect the application of the federal Indian Child Welfare Act (25 U.S.C. Sec. 1901 and following). *(Added by Stats.1995, c. 884 (A.B.1743), § 4. Amended by Stats.1998, c. 1056 (A.B.2773), § 3; Stats.2003, c. 323 (S.B.984), § 2; Stats.2012, c. 35 (S.B.1013), § 21, eff. June 27, 2012; Stats.2017, c. 732 (A.B.404), § 3, eff. Jan. 1, 2018.)*

Commentary

See generally *Tyler v. Children's Home Society of California, 29 Cal.App.4th 511, 35 Cal.Rptr.2d 291 (1994), review denied 1/5/95,* (private adoption agency's noncompliance with various requirements of state adoption law does not necessarily invalidate a parent's relinquishment of his or her child).

Cf. *Mullins v. State of Oregon, 57 F.3d 789 (9th Cir. 1995)*, holding that the biological connection between a grandparent and a grandchild, standing alone, does not give the grandparent a constitutionally protected liberty interest in the adoption of a grandchild.

Research References

Forms

California Transactions Forms--Family Law § 6:94, Consideration Of Race, Color, National Origin, or Religion as Factor in Placement.

California Transactions Forms--Family Law § 6:95, Nonresident Status Of Adoptive Family.

Treatises and Practice Aids

Witkin, California Summary 10th Parent and Child § 108, Exchange System.

Witkin, California Summary 10th Parent and Child § 112, in General.

Witkin, California Summary 10th Parent and Child § 114, Ethnic, Cultural, and Jurisdictional Considerations.

Witkin, California Summary 10th Parent and Child § 688, Other Alternatives.

§ 8709. Consideration of religious background; best interest of child

(a) The department, county adoption agency, or licensed adoption agency to which a child has been freed for adoption by either relinquishment or termination of parental rights may consider the child's religious background in determining an appropriate placement.

(b) This section shall not be construed to affect the application of the federal Indian Child Welfare Act (25 U.S.C. Sec. 1901 and following). *(Added by Stats.1995, c. 884 (A.B.1743), § 6. Amended by Stats.2003, c. 323 (S.B.984), § 3; Stats.2012, c. 35 (S.B.1013), § 22, eff. June 27, 2012.)*

Research References

Forms

California Transactions Forms--Family Law § 6:94, Consideration Of Race, Color, National Origin, or Religion as Factor in Placement.

Treatises and Practice Aids

Witkin, California Summary 10th Parent and Child § 115, Religious Considerations.

Witkin, California Summary 10th Parent and Child § 688, Other Alternatives.

§ 8710. Adoptive placement with relatives; placement criteria

(a) If a child is being considered for adoption, the department, county adoption agency, or licensed adoption agency shall first consider adoptive placement in the home of a relative or, in the case of an Indian child, according to the placement preferences and standards set out in subdivisions (c), (d), (e), (f), (g), (h), and (i) of Section 361.31 of the Welfare and Institutions Code. However, if the birth parent refuses to consider a relative or sibling placement, if a relative is not available, if placement with an available relative is not in the child's best interest, or if placement would permanently separate the child from other siblings who are being considered for adoption or who are in foster care and an alternative placement would not require the permanent separation, the foster parent or parents of the child shall be considered with respect to the child along with all other prospective adoptive parents where all of the following conditions are present:

(1) The child has been in foster care with the foster parent or parents for a period of more than four months.

(2) The child has substantial emotional ties to the foster parent or parents.

(3) The child's removal from the foster home would be seriously detrimental to the child's well-being.

(4) The foster parent or parents have made a written request to be considered to adopt the child.

(b) In the case of an Indian child whose foster parent or parents or other prospective adoptive parents do not fall within the placement preferences established in subdivision (c) or (d) of Section 361.31 of the Welfare and Institutions Code, the foster parent or parents or other prospective adoptive parents shall only be considered if the court finds, supported by clear and convincing evidence, that good cause exists to deviate from these placement preferences.

(c) This section does not apply to a child who has been adjudged a dependent of the juvenile court pursuant to Section 300 of the Welfare and Institutions Code.

(d) Upon a request to move a child from a prospective adoptive home for the purpose of placement with siblings or other relatives, the court shall consider the best interests of the child. *(Added by Stats.1995, c. 884 (A.B.1743), § 8. Amended by Stats.2006, c. 838 (S.B.678), § 12; Stats.2010, c. 588 (A.B.2020), § 6; Stats.2012, c. 35 (S.B.1013), § 23, eff. June 27, 2012.)*

Research References

Forms

California Transactions Forms--Family Law § 6:96, Placement Preference for Foster Parents and Extended Family.

Treatises and Practice Aids

Witkin, California Summary 10th Parent and Child § 113, Consideration Of Relatives and Foster Parents.

Witkin, California Summary 10th Parent and Child § 114, Ethnic, Cultural, and Jurisdictional Considerations.

§ 8710.1. Exchange system; child without adoptive placement plan within department or agency jurisdiction

If there is not an adoptive placement plan for a child with an approved adoptive family, as defined in subdivision (c) of Section 8708, within the department's, county adoption agency's, or licensed adoption agency's jurisdiction, then the department, county adoption agency, or licensed adoption agency shall register the child with the exchange system described in Section 8710.2. *(Added by Stats.1998, c. 1056 (A.B.2773), § 4. Amended by Stats.2012, c. 35 (S.B.1013), § 24, eff. June 27, 2012.)*

Research References

Treatises and Practice Aids

Witkin, California Summary 10th Parent and Child § 108, Exchange System.

§ 8710.2. Exchange system; establishment

In order to preclude the delays or denials described in subdivision (c) of Section 8708, the department shall establish a statewide exchange system that interjurisdictionally matches waiting children and approved adoptive families. The department may create a new statewide exchange system, modify an existing statewide exchange system, such as the photo-listing service described in Section 8707, or designate an existing exchange system, such as the Adoption Exchange Enhancement Program, as the statewide exchange system for purposes of this section. *(Added by Stats.1998, c. 1056 (A.B.2773), § 5.)*

Research References

Forms

California Transactions Forms--Family Law § 6:95, Nonresident Status Of Adoptive Family.

Treatises and Practice Aids

Witkin, California Summary 10th Parent and Child § 108, Exchange System.

§ 8710.3. Exchange system; registration of families

If the department, county adoption agency, or licensed adoption agency has approved a family for adoption pursuant to subdivision (c) of Section 8708 and that family may be appropriate for placement of a child who has been adjudged a dependent child of the juvenile court, the department, county adoption agency, or licensed adoption agency shall register the family with the statewide exchange system established pursuant to Section 8710.2, except in either of the following circumstances:

(a) The family refuses to consent to the registration.

(b) A specific child or children have already been identified for adoptive placement with the family. *(Added by Stats.1998, c. 1056 (A.B.2773), § 6. Amended by Stats.2012, c. 35 (S.B.1013), § 25, eff. June 27, 2012.)*

Research References

Treatises and Practice Aids

Witkin, California Summary 10th Parent and Child § 108, Exchange System.

§ 8710.4. Exchange system; information access

(a) The department shall ensure that information regarding families and children registered with the statewide exchange system described in Section 8710.2 is accessible by licensed adoption agency personnel throughout the state. Provision shall be made for secure Internet, telephone, and facsimile access by authorized licensed adoption agency personnel.

(b) Information regarding children maintained by the statewide exchange system described in Section 8710.2 shall be confidential and shall not be disclosed to any parties other than authorized adoption agency personnel, except when consent to disclosure has been received in writing from the birth parents or the court that has jurisdiction. *(Added by Stats.1998, c. 1056 (A.B.2773), § 7.)*

Research References

Treatises and Practice Aids

Witkin, California Summary 10th Parent and Child § 108, Exchange System.

§ 8711. Application of §§ 8708 to 8710.4

Sections 8708 to 8710.4, inclusive, apply only in determining the placement of a child who has been relinquished for adoption or has been declared free from the custody and control of the birth parents. *(Stats.1992, c. 162 (A.B.2650), § 10, operative Jan. 1, 1994. Amended by Stats.1998, c. 1056 (A.B.2773), § 8.)*

Law Revision Commission Comments

Enactment [Revised Comment]

Section 8711 continues former Civil Code Section 222.38 without substantive change. In subdivision (c), the reference to "birth" parents has been added for clarity. See Section 8512 ("birth parent" defined). [23 Cal.L.Rev.Comm. Reports 1 (1993)].

Research References

Treatises and Practice Aids

Witkin, California Summary 10th Parent and Child § 112, in General.

§ 8711.5. Regulations

The department shall adopt regulations to administer the provisions of Sections 8708 to 8711, inclusive. *(Added by Stats.1995, c. 884 (A.B.1743), § 9.)*

Research References

Treatises and Practice Aids

Witkin, California Summary 10th Parent and Child § 112, in General.

§ 8712. Applicants; information required to be provided; fingerprints; criminal records; prohibited placements; fees

(a)(1) The department, county adoption agency, or licensed adoption agency shall require each person who files an application for adoption to be fingerprinted and shall secure from an appropriate law enforcement agency any criminal record of that person to determine whether the person has ever been convicted of a crime other than a minor traffic violation. The department, county adoption agency, or licensed adoption agency may also secure the person's full criminal record, if any, with the exception of any convictions for which relief has been granted pursuant to Section 1203.49 of the Penal Code. A federal-level criminal offender record request to the Department of Justice shall be submitted with fingerprint images and related information required by the Department of Justice for the purposes of obtaining information as to the existence and content of a record of an out-of-state or federal conviction or arrest of a person or information regarding any out-of-state or federal crimes or arrests for which the Department of Justice establishes that the person is free on bail, or on his or her own recognizance pending trial or appeal. The Department of Justice shall forward to the Federal Bureau of Investigation any requests for federal summary criminal history information received pursuant to this section. The Department of Justice shall review the information returned from the Federal Bureau of Investigation and shall compile and disseminate a response to the department, county adoption agency, or licensed adoption agency.

(2) The department, county adoption agency, or licensed adoption agency may obtain arrest or conviction records or reports from any law enforcement agency as necessary to the performance of its duties, as provided in this section.

(b) Notwithstanding subdivision (c), the criminal record, if any, shall be taken into consideration when evaluating the prospective adoptive parent, and an assessment of the effects of any criminal history on the ability of the prospective adoptive parent to provide adequate and proper care and guidance to the child shall be included in the report to the court.

(c) * * * The department, county adoption agency, or licensed adoption agency shall not give final approval for an adoptive placement in any home in which the prospective adoptive parent or any adult living in the prospective adoptive home has * * * been convicted of an offense for which an exemption cannot be granted pursuant to subparagraph (A) of paragraph (2) of subdivision (g) of Section 1522 of the Health and Safety Code.

* * *

(d) Any fee charged by a law enforcement agency for fingerprinting or for checking or obtaining the criminal record of the applicant shall be paid by the applicant. The department, county adoption agency, or licensed adoption agency may defer, waive, or reduce the fee when its payment would cause economic hardship to prospective adoptive parents detrimental to the welfare of the adopted child, when the child has been in the foster care of the prospective adoptive parents for at least one year, or if necessary for the placement of a special-needs child. *(Stats.1992, c. 162 (A.B.2650), § 10, operative Jan. 1, 1994. Amended by Stats. 2007, c. 464 (A.B.340), § 1; Stats.2008, c. 701 (A.B.2651), § 1, eff. Sept. 30, 2008; Stats.2012, c. 35 (S.B.1013), § 26, eff. June 27, 2012; Stats.2014, c. 708 (A.B.1585), § 1, eff. Jan. 1, 2015; Stats.2015, c. 303 (A.B.731), § 151, eff. Jan. 1, 2016; Stats.2016, c. 612 (A.B.1997), § 10, eff. Jan. 1, 2017; Stats. 2017, c. 733 (S.B.213), § 1, eff. Jan. 1, 2018.)*

Law Revision Commission Comments

Enactment [Revised Comment]

Section 8712 continues former Civil Code Section 222.40 without substantive change. See also Sections 8509 ("applicant" defined), 8518 ("department" defined), 8530 ("licensed adoption agency" defined), 8542 ("prospective adoptive parent" defined), 8545 ("special-needs child" defined).

For comparable provisions, see Sections 8811 (investigation in independent adoption), 8908 (investigation in intercountry adoption). For a related provision, see Section 9001(a) (investigation in stepparent adoption). [23 Cal.L.Rev.Comm. Reports 1 (1993)].

Research References

Treatises and Practice Aids

Witkin, California Summary 10th Parent and Child § 94, Investigation Of Prospective Adoptive Parents.

Witkin, California Summary 10th Parent and Child § 119, Investigation, Report, and Recommendation.

Witkin, California Summary 10th Parent and Child § 122, Adoption by Relative Caregiver or Foster Parent.

§ 8713. Removal of child from county in which placed; permission; proceedings; concealment of child; violation

(a) In no event may a child who has been freed for adoption be removed from the county in which the child was placed, by any person who has not petitioned to adopt the child, without first obtaining the written consent of the department, county adoption agency, or licensed adoption agency responsible for the child.

(b) During the pendency of an adoption proceeding:

(1) The child proposed to be adopted may not be concealed within the county in which the adoption proceeding is pending.

(2) The child may not be removed from the county in which the adoption proceeding is pending unless the petitioners or other interested persons first obtain permission for the removal from the court, after giving advance written notice of intent to obtain the court's permission to the department, county adoption agency, or licensed adoption agency responsible for the child. Upon proof of giving notice, permission may be granted by the court if, within a period of 15 days after the date of giving notice, no objections are filed with the court by the department, county adoption agency, or licensed adoption agency responsible for the child. If the department, county adoption agency, or licensed adoption agency files objections within the 15–day period, upon the request of the petitioners the court shall immediately set the matter for hearing and give to the objector, the petitioners, and the party or parties requesting permission for the removal reasonable notice of the hearing by certified mail, return receipt requested, to the address of each as shown in the records of the adoption proceeding. Upon a finding that the objections are without good cause, the court may grant the requested permission for removal of the child, subject to any limitations that appear to be in the child's best interest.

(c) This section does not apply in any of the following situations:

(1) Where the child is absent for a period of not more than 30 days from the county in which the adoption proceeding is pending, unless a notice of recommendation of denial of petition has been personally served on the petitioners or the court has issued an order prohibiting the child's removal from the county pending consideration of any of the following:

(A) The suitability of the petitioners.

(B) The care provided the child.

(C) The availability of the legally required agency consents to the adoption.

(2) Where the child has been returned to and remains in the custody and control of the child's birth parent or parents.

(3) Where written consent for the removal of the child is obtained from the department, county adoption agency, or licensed adoption agency responsible for the child.

(d) A violation of this section is a violation of Section 280 of the Penal Code.

(e) Neither this section nor Section 280 of the Penal Code may be construed to render lawful any act that is unlawful under any other applicable law. *(Stats.1992, c. 162 (A.B. 2650), § 10, operative Jan. 1, 1994. Amended by Stats.2012, c. 35 (S.B.1013), § 27, eff. June 27, 2012.)*

Law Revision Commission Comments

Enactment [Revised Comment]

Section 8713 continues former Civil Code Section 222.50 without substantive change. In subdivision (a), "freed for adoption" has been substituted for the narrower "relinquished for adoption" so that the scope of this section will not be artificially limited. The prohibition of removal "for any period of time" has been omitted as surplus. The two limitations on the exception provided in subdivision (c)(1) have been rephrased for clarity.

See also Sections 8512 ("birth parent" defined), 8518 ("department" defined), 8530 ("licensed adoption agency" defined).

For comparable provisions, see Sections 8803 (removal and concealment in independent adoption), 8910 (removal and concealment in intercountry adoption). [23 Cal.L.Rev.Comm. Reports 1 (1993)].

Research References

Forms

California Transactions Forms--Family Law § 6:2, Governing Law.

California Transactions Forms--Family Law § 6:90, Adoptive Placement Agreement.

Treatises and Practice Aids

Witkin, California Summary 10th Parent and Child § 81, Removal or Concealment Of Child Pending Adoption.

§ 8714. Petition for adoption; content; guardianship petition; order of adoption

(a) A person desiring to adopt a nondependent child may for that purpose file an adoption request in a county authorized by Section 8609.5. A person desiring to adopt a child who has been adjudged to be a dependent of the juvenile court pursuant to Section 300 of the Welfare and Institutions Code, freed for adoption by the juvenile court, and placed for adoption with the petitioner, may file the adoption request either in the county where the petitioner resides or in the county where the child was freed for adoption.

(b) The court clerk shall immediately notify the department at Sacramento in writing of the pendency of the proceeding and of any subsequent action taken.

(c) If the petitioner has entered into a postadoption contact agreement with the birth parent as set forth in Section 8616.5, the agreement, signed by the participating parties, shall be attached to and filed with the petition for adoption under subdivision (a).

(d) The caption of the adoption petition shall contain the names of the petitioners, but not the child's name. The petition shall state the child's sex and date of birth. The name the child had before adoption shall appear in the joinder signed by the licensed adoption agency.

(e) If the child is the subject of a guardianship petition, the adoption petition shall so state and shall include the caption and docket number or have attached a copy of the letters of the guardianship or temporary guardianship. The petitioners shall notify the court of any petition for guardianship or temporary guardianship filed after the adoption petition. The guardianship proceeding shall be consolidated with the adoption proceeding.

(f) The order of adoption shall contain the child's adopted name, but not the name the child had before adoption. *(Stats.1992, c. 162 (A.B.2650), § 10, operative Jan. 1, 1994. Amended by Stats.1993, c. 219 (A.B.1500), § 190; Stats.2000, c. 910 (A.B.2921), § 2; Stats.2000, c. 930 (S.B.2157), § 1; Stats.2002, c. 1112 (A.B.746), § 1; Stats.2003, c. 251 (S.B. 182), § 6; Stats.2012, c. 638 (A.B.1757), § 9; Stats.2016, c. 474 (A.B.2882), § 10, eff. Jan. 1, 2017.)*

Law Revision Commission Comments

Enactment [Revised Comment]

Section 8714 continues former Civil Code Sections 222.70 and 222.71 without substantive change. In subdivision (b), the reference to an "action" for adoption has been changed to "proceeding" for consistency with subdivision (d). The reference to the "superior" court has been omitted as surplus. See Section 200 (jurisdiction in superior court).

For comparable provisions, see Sections 8802 (petition for independent adoption), 8912 (petition for intercountry adoption), 9000 (petition for stepparent adoption). [23 Cal.l.Rev.Comm. Reports 1 (1993)].

Research References

Forms

California Transactions Forms--Family Law § 6:13, Appearance in Person or by Counsel.

California Transactions Forms--Family Law § 6:98, Form Drafting Considerations.

West's California Judicial Council Forms JV-505, Statement Regarding Parentage (Juvenile).

West's California Judicial Council Forms ADOPT-200, Adoption Request.

West's California Judicial Council Forms ADOPT-215, Adoption Order.

Treatises and Practice Aids

Witkin, California Summary 10th Parent and Child § 71, Special Statutory Proceeding.

Witkin, California Summary 10th Parent and Child § 90, Effect Of Guardianship Proceeding.

Witkin, California Summary 10th Parent and Child § 95, Petition and Hearing.

Witkin, California Summary 10th Parent and Child § 96, Agreement and Order.

Witkin, California Summary 10th Parent and Child § 104, in General.

Witkin, California Summary 10th Parent and Child § 118, Petition.

Witkin, California Summary 10th Parent and Child § 330, Who May Bring Action.

§ 8714.5. Legislative findings and declarations; adoptions by relatives; adoption petition; order of adoption; contents

(a) The Legislature finds and declares the following:

(1) It is the intent of the Legislature to expedite legal permanency for children who cannot return to their parents and to remove barriers to adoption by relatives of children who are already in the dependency system or who are at risk of entering the dependency system.

(2) This goal will be achieved by empowering families, including extended families, to care for their own children safely and permanently whenever possible, by preserving existing family relationships, thereby causing the least amount of disruption to the child and the family, and by recognizing the importance of sibling and half-sibling relationships.

(b) A relative desiring to adopt a child may for that purpose file a petition in the county in which the petitioner resides. Where a child has been adjudged to be a dependent of the juvenile court pursuant to Section 300 of the Welfare and Institutions Code, and thereafter has been freed for adoption by the juvenile court, the petition may be filed either in the county where the petitioner resides or in the county where the child was freed for adoption.

(c) Upon the filing of a petition for adoption by a relative, the clerk of the court shall immediately notify the State Department of Social Services in Sacramento in writing of the pendency of the proceeding and of any subsequent action taken.

(d) If the adopting relative has entered into a postadoption contact agreement with the birth parent as set forth in Section 8616.5 the agreement, signed by the participating parties, shall be attached to and filed with the petition for adoption under subdivision (b).

(e) The caption of the adoption petition shall contain the name of the relative petitioner. The petition shall state the child's name, sex, and date of birth.

(f) If the child is the subject of a guardianship petition, the adoption petition shall so state and shall include the caption and docket number or have attached a copy of the letters of the guardianship or temporary guardianship. The petitioner shall notify the court of any petition for adoption. The guardianship proceeding shall be consolidated with the adoption proceeding, and the consolidated case shall be heard and decided in the court in which the adoption is pending.

(g) The order of adoption shall contain the child's adopted name and, if requested by the adopting relative, or if requested by the child who is 12 years of age or older, the name the child had before adoption.

(h) For purposes of this section, "relative" means an adult who is related to the child or the child's half-sibling by blood or affinity, including all relatives whose status is preceded by the words "step," "great," "great-great," or "grand," or the spouse of any of these persons, even if the marriage was terminated by death or dissolution. *(Added by Stats.1997, c. 793 (A.B.1544), § 4. Amended by Stats.2000, c. 910 (A.B. 2921), § 3; Stats.2000, c. 930 (S.B.2157), § 2; Stats.2002, c. 784 (S.B.1316), § 112; Stats.2003, c. 251 (S.B.182), § 7; Stats.2008, c. 534 (S.B.1726), § 9.)*

Law Revision Commission Comments

2002 Amendment

Subdivision (c) of Section 8714.5 is amended to reflect elimination of the county clerk's role as ex officio clerk of the superior court. See former Gov't Code § 26800 (county clerk acting as clerk of superior court). The powers, duties, and responsibilities formerly exercised by the county clerk as ex officio clerk of the court are delegated to the court administrative or executive officer, and the county clerk is relieved of those powers, duties, and responsibilities. See Gov't Code §§ 69840 (powers, duties, and responsibilities of clerk of court and deputy clerk of court), 71620 (trial court personnel). [32 Cal.L.Rev. Comm. Reports 168 (2002)].

Commentary

In re Zachary D., 70 Cal.App.4th 1392, 83 Cal.Rptr.2d 407 (1999), review denied June 23, 1999, holds that the juvenile court may properly terminate a mother's parental rights without providing her with notice of and opportunity to enter a kinship adoption agreement with the mother's parents, who were the child's prospective adoptive parents. *Zachary D.* is followed by *In re Kimberly S., 71 Cal.App.4th 405, 83 Cal.Rptr.2d 740 (1999), review denied July 14, 1999.*

Research References

Forms

California Transactions Forms--Family Law § 6:55, Agreement for Continuing Contact.
California Transactions Forms--Family Law § 6:97, Kinship Adoption.
California Transactions Forms--Family Law § 6:100, Postadoption Contact Agreement [Form Adopt-310].
West's California Code Forms, Family § 8700, Comment Overview--Relinquishment Of Child to Department Of Social Services or a Licensed Adoption Agency.
West's California Judicial Council Forms JV-505, Statement Regarding Parentage (Juvenile).
West's California Judicial Council Forms ADOPT-200, Adoption Request.
West's California Judicial Council Forms ADOPT-215, Adoption Order.
West's California Judicial Council Forms ADOPT-310, Contact After Adoption Agreement.
West's California Judicial Council Forms ADOPT-315, Request To: Enforce, Change, End Contact After Adoption Agreement.
West's California Judicial Council Forms ADOPT-320, Answer to Request To: Enforce, Change, End Contact After Adoption Agreement.
West's California Judicial Council Forms ADOPT-325, Judge's Order To: Enforce, Change, End Contact After Adoption Agreement.

Treatises and Practice Aids

Witkin, California Summary 10th Parent and Child § 104, in General.
Witkin, California Summary 10th Parent and Child § 121, Adoption by Relative.

§ 8715. Report of department or agency; submission to court

(a) The department, county adoption agency, or licensed adoption agency, whichever is a party to, or joins in, the petition, shall submit a full report of the facts of the case to the court.

(b) If the child has been adjudged to be a dependent of the juvenile court pursuant to Section 300 of the Welfare and Institutions Code, and has thereafter been freed for adoption by the juvenile court, the report required by this section shall describe whether the requirements of subdivision (e) of Section 16002 of the Welfare and Institutions Code have been completed and what, if any, plan exists for facilitation of postadoptive contact between the child who is the subject of the adoption petition and his or her siblings and half siblings.

(c) If a petition for adoption has been filed with a postadoption contact agreement pursuant to Section 8616.5, the report shall address whether the postadoption contact agreement has been entered into voluntarily, and whether it is in the best interests of the child who is the subject of the petition.

(d) The department may also submit a report in those cases in which a county adoption agency, or licensed adoption agency is a party or joins in the adoption petition.

(e) If a petitioner is a resident of a state other than California, an updated and current homestudy report, conducted and approved by a licensed adoption agency or other authorized resource in the state in which the petitioner resides, shall be reviewed and endorsed by the department, county adoption agency, or licensed adoption agency, if the standards and criteria established for a homestudy report in the other state are substantially commensurate with the homestudy standards and criteria established in California adoption regulations. *(Stats.1992, c. 162 (A.B.2650), § 10, operative Jan. 1, 1994. Amended by Stats.1997, c. 793 (A.B.1544), § 6; Stats.1998, c. 1072 (A.B.2196), § 1; Stats. 2000, c. 910 (A.B.2921), § 4.5; Stats.2000, c. 930 (S.B.2157), § 4; Stats.2002, c. 1112 (A.B.746), § 2; Stats.2003, c. 251 (S.B.182), § 9; Stats.2012, c. 35 (S.B.1013), § 28, eff. June 27, 2012.)*

Law Revision Commission Comments

Enactment [Revised Comment]

Section 8715 continues former Civil Code Section 222.75 without substantive change. The language of this provision has been revised to use the mandatory "shall" in place of the former statement that "it shall be the duty" to submit the report. See Section 12 ("shall" is mandatory). See also Sections 8518 ("department" defined), 8530 ("licensed adoption agency" defined).

For related provisions, see Sections 8807 (report of department or agency in independent adoption), 8914 (report of department or agency in intercountry adoption), 9001 (report of county welfare department or probation officer in stepparent adoption). [23 Cal.L.Rev.Comm. Reports 1 (1993)].

Research References

Forms

California Transactions Forms--Family Law § 6:13, Appearance in Person or by Counsel.

Treatises and Practice Aids

Witkin, California Summary 10th Parent and Child § 95, Petition and Hearing.

Witkin, California Summary 10th Parent and Child § 119, Investigation, Report, and Recommendation.

Witkin, California Summary 10th Parent and Child § 694, Adoption Proceeding.

§ 8716. Fee paid by adoptive parents; exception

Where a petition is filed for the adoption of a child who has been placed for adoption by a county adoption agency, licensed county adoption agency, or the department, the county adoption agency, licensed adoption agency, or department may, at the time of filing a favorable report with the court, require the petitioners to pay to the agency, as agent of the state, or to the department, a fee of five hundred dollars ($500). The county adoption agency, licensed adoption agency, or department may defer, waive, or reduce the fee if its payment would cause economic hardship to the prospective adoptive parents detrimental to the welfare of the adopted child, if the child has been in the foster care of the prospective adoptive parents for at least one year, or if necessary for the placement of a special-needs child. *(Stats. 1992, c. 162 (A.B.2650), § 10, operative Jan. 1, 1994. Amended by Stats.2012, c. 35 (S.B.1013), § 29, eff. June 27, 2012.)*

Law Revision Commission Comments

Enactment [Revised Comment]

Section 8716 continues former Civil Code Section 222.72 without substantive change. The reference to the "superior" court has been omitted as surplus. See Section 200 (jurisdiction in superior court). See also Sections 8503 ("adoptive parent" defined), 8518 ("department" defined), 8542 ("prospective adoptive parent" defined), 8545 ("special-needs child" defined).

For related provisions, see Sections 8810 (fee for report in independent adoption), 9002 (fee for report in stepparent adoption). [23 Cal.L.Rev.Comm. Reports 1 (1993)].

Research References

Forms

California Transactions Forms--Family Law § 6:93, Agency Fees.

Treatises and Practice Aids

Witkin, California Summary 10th Parent and Child § 119, Investigation, Report, and Recommendation.

§ 8717. Report or findings submitted to court; copy to attorney for petitioner

When any report or findings are submitted to the court by the department, county adoption agency, or licensed adoption agency, a copy of the report or findings, whether favorable or unfavorable, shall be given to the petitioner's attorney in the proceeding, if the petitioner has an attorney of record, or to the petitioner. *(Stats.1992, c. 162 (A.B.2650), § 10, operative Jan. 1, 1994. Amended by Stats.2012, c. 35 (S.B.1013), § 30, eff. June 27, 2012.)*

Law Revision Commission Comments

Enactment [Revised Comment]

Section 8717 continues former Civil Code Section 222.77 without substantive change. See also Sections 8518 ("department" defined), 8530 ("licensed adoption agency" defined).

For comparable provisions, see Sections 8821 (copy of report in independent adoption), 8915 (copy of report in intercountry adoption). [23 Cal.L.Rev.Comm. Reports 1 (1993)].

Research References

Treatises and Practice Aids

Witkin, California Summary 10th Parent and Child § 119, Investigation, Report, and Recommendation.

§ 8718. Appearance before court; adoptive parents and child

The prospective adoptive parents and the child proposed to be adopted shall appear before the court pursuant to Sections 8612 and 8613. *(Stats.1992, c. 162 (A.B.2650), § 10, operative Jan. 1, 1994.)*

Law Revision Commission Comments

Enactment [Revised Comment]

Section 8718 continues former Civil Code Sections 221.62 and 222.78 without substantive change. The reference to "prospective adoptive parents" has been substituted for "person or persons desiring to adopt a child." This is not a substantive change. See Section 8542 ("prospective adoptive parent" defined).

For comparable provisions, see Sections 8823 (appearance in independent adoption), 8913 (appearance in intercountry adoption), 9007 (appearance in stepparent adoption). [23 Cal.L.Rev.Comm. Reports 1 (1993)].

Research References

Treatises and Practice Aids

Witkin, California Summary 10th Parent and Child § 95, Petition and Hearing.

Witkin, California Summary 10th Parent and Child § 120, Hearing and Order.

§ 8719. Withdrawal of petition; dismissal of proceedings; notification of department

If the petitioners move to withdraw the adoption petition or to dismiss the proceeding, the court clerk shall immediately notify the department at Sacramento of the action. *(Stats.1992, c. 162 (A.B.2650), § 10, operative Jan. 1, 1994.)*

Law Revision Commission Comments

Enactment [Revised Comment]

Section 8719 continues former Civil Code Section 222.80 without substantive change. The former reference to the "clerk of the court in which the proceeding is pending" has been shortened to the "court clerk" to eliminate surplus language. See also Section 8518 ("department" defined).

For related provisions, see Sections 8804 (notice of withdrawal or dismissal in independent adoption), 8916 (notice of withdrawal or dismissal in intercountry adoption), 9006 (notice of withdrawal or dismissal in stepparent adoption). [23 Cal.L.Rev.Comm. Reports 1 (1993)].

Research References

Treatises and Practice Aids

Witkin, California Summary 10th Parent and Child § 118, Petition.

§ 8720. Denial or withdrawal of petition; referral to superior court for review; hearing; notice

(a) If the department, county adoption agency, or licensed adoption agency finds that the home of the petitioners is not suitable for the child or that the required agency consents are not available and the department, county adoption agency, or licensed adoption agency recommends that the petition be denied, or if the petitioners desire to withdraw the petition and the department, county adoption agency, or licensed adoption agency recommends that the petition be denied, the clerk upon receipt of the report of the department, county adoption agency, or licensed adoption agency shall immediately refer it to the court for review.

(b) Upon receipt of the report, the court shall set a date for a hearing of the petition and shall give reasonable notice of the hearing to the department, county adoption agency, or licensed adoption agency, the petitioners, and, if necessary, the birth parents, by certified mail, return receipt requested, to the address of each as shown in the proceeding.

(c) The department, county adoption agency, or licensed adoption agency shall appear to represent the child. *(Stats. 1992, c. 162 (A.B.2650), § 10, operative Jan. 1, 1994. Amended by Stats.2012, c. 35 (S.B.1013), § 31, eff. June 27, 2012.)*

Law Revision Commission Comments

Enactment [Revised Comment]

Section 8720 continues former Civil Code Section 222.90 without substantive change. The reference to the "superior" court has been omitted as surplus. See Section 200 (jurisdiction in superior court). The reference to "county" clerk has been omitted. This is not a substantive change. See also Sections 8512 ("birth parent" defined), 8518 ("department" defined), 8530 ("licensed adoption agency" defined).

For comparable provisions, see Sections 8822 (unfavorable recommendation in independent adoption), 8917 (unfavorable recommendation in intercountry adoption). [23 Cal.L.Rev.Comm. Reports 1 (1993)].

Research References

Forms

California Transactions Forms--Family Law § 6:83, Nature Of Agency Adoption--Governing Law.

Treatises and Practice Aids

Witkin, California Summary 10th Parent and Child § 85, Recommendation Of Department or Agency.

Witkin, California Summary 10th Parent and Child § 119, Investigation, Report, and Recommendation.

CHAPTER 2.5. ADOPTIONS BY RELATIVE CAREGIVERS OR FOSTER PARENTS

§ 8730. Abbreviated home study assessments; requirements

(a) Subject to the requirements of subdivision (b), the department, county adoption agency, or licensed adoption agency may provide an abbreviated home study assessment for any of the following:

(1) A licensed or certified foster parent with whom the child has lived for a minimum of six months.

(2) An approved relative caregiver or nonrelated extended family member with whom the child has had an ongoing and significant relationship.

(3) A court-appointed relative guardian of the child who has been investigated and approved pursuant to the guardianship investigation process and has had physical custody of the child for at least one year.

(4) A prospective adoptive parent who has completed an agency-supervised adoption within the last two years.

(b) Unless otherwise ordered by a court with jurisdiction over the child, home study assessments completed pursuant to subdivision (a) shall include, at minimum, all of the following:

(1) A criminal records check, as required by all applicable state and federal statutes and regulations.

(2) A determination that the applicant has sufficient financial stability to support the child and ensure that an adoption assistance program payment or other government assistance to which the child is entitled is used exclusively to meet the child's needs. In making this determination, the experience of the applicant only while the child was in his or her care shall be considered. For purposes of this section, the applicant shall be required to provide verification of employment records or income or both.

(3) A determination that the applicant has not abused or neglected the child while the child has been in his or her care and has fostered the healthy growth and development of the child. This determination shall include a review of the disciplinary practices of the applicant to ensure that the practices are age appropriate and do not physically or emotionally endanger the child.

(4) A determination that the applicant is not likely to abuse or neglect the child in the future and that the applicant can protect the child, ensure necessary care and supervision, and foster the child's healthy growth and development.

(5) A determination that the applicant can address issues that may affect the child's well-being, including, but not limited to, the child's physical health, mental health, and educational needs.

(6) An interview with the applicant, an interview with each individual residing in the home, and an interview with the child to be adopted.

(7) A review by the department, county adoption agency, or licensed adoption agency of all previous guardianship investigation reports, home study assessments, and preplacement evaluations of each applicant. Notwithstanding any other law regarding the confidential nature of these reports, upon the written request of the department, county adoption agency, or licensed adoption agency that is accompanied by a signed release from the applicant, the department, county adoption agency, or licensed adoption agency may receive a copy of any of these reports from a court, investigating agency, or other person or entity in possession of the report. The department, county adoption agency, or licensed adoption agency shall document attempts to obtain the report and, if applicable, the reason the report is unavailable.

(c) The department may promulgate regulations as necessary or appropriate to implement this section.

(d) This section does not apply to independent adoptions filed pursuant to Chapter 3 (commencing with Section 8800). *(Added by Stats.1998, c. 983 (A.B.2286), § 3. Amended by Stats.2012, c. 35 (S.B.1013), § 32, eff. June 27, 2012; Stats. 2013, c. 743 (A.B.848), § 2; Stats.2014, c. 71 (S.B.1304), § 55, eff. Jan. 1, 2015.)*

Research References

Treatises and Practice Aids

Witkin, California Summary 10th Parent and Child § 70, Types Of Adoption.

Witkin, California Summary 10th Parent and Child § 72, Statutory Framework.

Witkin, California Summary 10th Parent and Child § 122, Adoption by Relative Caregiver or Foster Parent.

§ 8731. Adoption sought by foster parent; time for initiation; assessment or home study

If the prospective adoptive parent of a child is a foster parent, the assessment or home study described in Section 8730 shall not be initiated until the child to be adopted has resided in the home of the foster parent for at least six months. *(Added by Stats.1998, c. 983 (A.B.2286), § 3.)*

Research References

Treatises and Practice Aids

Witkin, California Summary 10th Parent and Child § 122, Adoption by Relative Caregiver or Foster Parent.

§ 8732. Adoption sought by foster parent of six months or relative caregiver; medical examination and report

A report of a medical examination of the foster parent with whom the child has lived for a minimum of six months or the relative caregiver who has had an ongoing and significant relationship with the child shall be included in the assessment of each applicant unless the department, county adoption agency, or licensed adoption agency determines that, based on other available information, this report is unnecessary. The assessment shall require certification that the applicant and each adult residing in the applicant's home has received a test for communicable tuberculosis. *(Added by Stats.1998, c. 983 (A.B.2286), § 3. Amended by Stats.2012, c. 35 (S.B. 1013), § 33, eff. June 27, 2012.)*

Research References

Treatises and Practice Aids

Witkin, California Summary 10th Parent and Child § 122, Adoption by Relative Caregiver or Foster Parent.

§ 8733. Report of special needs of child to be adopted; supply to adopting parents

The department, county adoption agency, or licensed adoption agency shall require the adoptive parent to be provided with information related to the specific needs of the child to be adopted, that, as determined by the licensed adoption agency, may include information regarding the following: issues surrounding birth parents, the effects of abuse and neglect on children, cultural and racial issues, sexuality, contingency planning for children in the event of the parents' death or disability, financial assistance for adopted children, common childhood disabilities, including, but not limited to, emotional disturbances, attention deficit disorder, learning disabilities, speech and hearing impairment, and dyslexia, the importance of sibling and half-sibling relationships, and other issues related to adoption and child development and the availability of counseling to deal with these issues. *(Added by Stats.1998, c. 983 (A.B.2286), § 3. Amended by Stats.2012, c. 35 (S.B.1013), § 34, eff. June 27, 2012.)*

Research References

Treatises and Practice Aids

Witkin, California Summary 10th Parent and Child § 122, Adoption by Relative Caregiver or Foster Parent.

§ 8734. Adoption training programs

The department shall encourage adoption agencies to make adoption training programs available to prospective adoptive families. *(Added by Stats.1998, c. 983 (A.B.2286), § 3.)*

Research References

Treatises and Practice Aids

Witkin, California Summary 10th Parent and Child § 70, Types Of Adoption.

§ 8735. Information to department when foster parent or relative caregiver denied right to adopt

The department shall adopt regulations requiring county adoption agencies and licensed adoption agencies to inform the agency responsible for the foster care placement when a relative caregiver or foster parent has been denied approval to adopt based on an inability of the relative caregiver or foster parent to provide for the mental and emotional health, safety, and security of the child and to recommend either that the relative caregiver or foster parent be provided with additional support and supervision or that the child be removed from the home of the relative caregiver or foster parent. *(Added by Stats.1998, c. 983 (A.B.2286), § 3. Amended by Stats.2012, c. 35 (S.B.1013), § 35, eff. June 27, 2012.)*

Research References

Treatises and Practice Aids

Witkin, California Summary 10th Parent and Child § 122, Adoption by Relative Caregiver or Foster Parent.

§ 8736. Chapter provisions as grounds for removal of child from placement

The requirements of this chapter shall not be used as basis for removing a child who has been placed with a relative caregiver or foster parent prior to January 1, 1999, unless the noncompliance with the standards described therein present a danger to the health, safety, or emotional well-being of the child. *(Added by Stats.1998, c. 983 (A.B.2286), § 3.)*

Research References

Treatises and Practice Aids

Witkin, California Summary 10th Parent and Child § 122, Adoption by Relative Caregiver or Foster Parent.

CHAPTER 3. INDEPENDENT ADOPTIONS

§ 8800. Attorney-client relationship; professional conduct; conflict of interest; birth parents right to revoke consent; dual representation

(a) The Legislature finds and declares that an attorney's ability to effectively represent his or her client may be seriously impaired when conflict of interest deprives the client of the attorney's undivided loyalty and effort. The Legislature further finds and declares that the relation between attorney and client is a fiduciary relation of the very highest character, and binds the attorney to the most conscientious fidelity.

(b) The Legislature finds that Rule 2-111(A)(2) of the State Bar Rules of Professional Conduct provides that an attorney shall not withdraw from employment until the attorney has taken reasonable steps to avoid foreseeable prejudice to the rights of the client, including giving due notice to the client, allowing time for employment of other counsel, delivering to the client all papers and property to which the client is entitled, and complying with applicable laws and rules.

(c) The Legislature declares that in an independent adoption proceeding, whether or not written consent is obtained, multiple representation by an attorney should be avoided whenever a birth parent displays the slightest reason for the attorney to believe any controversy might arise. The Legislature finds and declares that it is the duty of the attorney when a conflict of interest occurs to withdraw promptly from any case, advise the parties to retain independent counsel, refrain from taking positions in opposition to any of these former clients, and thereafter maintain an impartial, fair, and open attitude toward the new attorneys.

(d) Notwithstanding any other law, it is unethical for an attorney to undertake the representation of both the prospective adoptive parents and the birth parents of a child in any negotiations or proceedings in connection with an adoption unless a written consent is obtained from both parties. The written consent shall include all of the following:

(1) A notice to the birth parents, in the form specified in this section, of their right to have an independent attorney advise and represent them in the adoption proceeding and that the prospective adoptive parents may be required to pay the reasonable attorney's fees up to a maximum of five hundred dollars ($500) for that representation, unless a higher fee is agreed to by the parties.

(2) A notice to the birth parents that they may waive their right to an independent attorney and may be represented by the attorney representing the prospective adoptive parents.

(3) A waiver by the birth parents of representation by an independent attorney.

(4) An agreement that the attorney representing the prospective adoptive parents shall represent the birth parents.

(e) Upon the petition or motion of any party, or upon motion of the court, the court may appoint an attorney to represent a child's birth parent or parents in negotiations or proceedings in connection with the child's adoption.

(f) The birth parent or parents may have an attorney, other than the attorney representing the interests of the prospective adoptive parents, to advise them fully of the adoption procedures and of their legal rights. The birth parent or parents also may retain an attorney to represent them in negotiations or proceedings in connection with the child's adoption. The court may award attorney's fees and costs for just cause and based upon the ability of the parties to pay those fees and costs.

(g) In the initial communication between the attorney retained by or representing the prospective adoptive parents and the birth parents, or as soon thereafter as reasonable, but before any written consent for dual representation, the attorney shall advise the birth parents of their rights regarding an independent attorney and that it is possible to waive the independent attorney.

(h) The attorney retained by or representing the prospective adoptive parents shall inform the prospective adoptive parents in writing that the birth parent or parents can revoke consent to the adoption pursuant to Section 8814.5 and that any moneys expended in negotiations or proceedings in connection with the child's adoption are not reimbursable. The prospective adoptive parents shall sign a statement to indicate their understanding of this information.

(i) Any written consent to dual representation shall be filed with the court before the filing of the birth parent's consent to adoption. *(Stats.1992, c. 162 (A.B.2650), § 10, operative Jan. 1, 1994. Amended by Stats.1993, c. 450 (S.B.255), § 1; Stats.1993, c. 450 (S.B.255), § 2, operative Jan. 1, 1995.)*

Law Revision Commission Comments

Enactment [Revised Comment]

Section 8800 continues former Civil Code Section 224.10 without substantive change. In subdivisions (f) and (g), references to "attorney" have been substituted for "counsel" for internal consistency. See also Sections 8512 ("birth parent" defined), 8542 ("prospective adoptive parent" defined). [23 Cal.L.Rev.Comm. Reports 1 (1993)].

Research References

Forms

California Transactions Forms--Family Law § 6:21, Ethical Considerations.
California Transactions Forms--Family Law § 6:40, Structuring the Adoption.
California Transactions Forms--Family Law § 6:48, Consent to Representation Of Multiple Parties by Counsel.
California Transactions Forms--Family Law § 6:49, Statement Of Representation.
California Transactions Forms--Family Law § 6:50, Independent Adoption Retainer Agreement.
California Transactions Forms--Family Law § 6:52, Birth Mother Representation Agreement.
California Transactions Forms--Family Law § 6:54, Request by Birth Parent for Financial Assistance.
California Transactions Forms--Family Law § 6:84, Relinquishment as Distinguished from Consent.
California Transactions Forms--Family Law § 7:39, Adoption and Termination Of Parental Rights.
West's California Code Forms, Family § 8800, Comment Overview--Independent Adoptions.
West's California Code Forms, Family § 8800 Form 1, Consent to Representation Of Multiple Parties.

Treatises and Practice Aids

Witkin, California Summary 10th Parent and Child § 70, Types Of Adoption.
Witkin, California Summary 10th Parent and Child § 72, Statutory Framework.
Witkin, California Summary 10th Parent and Child § 122, Adoption by Relative Caregiver or Foster Parent.
Witkin, California Summary 10th Parent and Child § 125, Advising and Counseling Birth Parents.
Witkin, California Summary 10th Parent and Child § 126, Dual Representation Of Adoptive and Birth Parents.
Witkin, California Summary 10th Parent and Child § 131, Withdrawal After Signing Statutory Consent.

§ 8801. Selection of prospective adoptive parents

(a) The selection of a prospective adoptive parent or parents shall be personally made by the child's birth parent or parents and may not be delegated to an agent. The act of selection by the birth parent or parents shall be based upon his, her, or their personal knowledge of the prospective adoptive parent or parents.

(b) "Personal knowledge" as used in this section includes, but is not limited to, substantially correct knowledge of all of the following regarding the prospective adoptive parents: their full legal names, ages, religion, race or ethnicity, length of current marriage and number of previous marriages, employment, whether other children or adults reside in their home, whether there are other children who do not reside in their home and the child support obligation for these children and any failure to meet these obligations, any health conditions curtailing their normal daily activities or reducing their normal life expectancies, any convictions for crimes other than minor traffic violations, any removals of children from their care due to child abuse or neglect, and their general area of residence or, upon request, their address.

(c) This section shall become operative on January 1, 1995. *(Added by Stats.1993, c. 758 (S.B.792), § 6.4, operative Jan. 1, 1995.)*

Law Revision Commission Comments

Enactment [Revised Comment]

Subdivision (a) of Section 8801 continues former Civil Code Section 224.20 without substantive change. Subdivision (b) continues former Civil Code Section 220.20(m) without substantive change. See also Sections 8512 ("birth parent" defined), 8542 ("prospective adoptive parent" defined). [23 Cal.L.Rev.Comm. Reports 1 (1993)].

Research References

Forms

California Transactions Forms--Family Law § 6:3, Definitions.
California Transactions Forms--Family Law § 6:34, Role Of Adoption Service Provider.
California Transactions Forms--Family Law § 6:36, Independent Adoption Placement Agreement.

California Transactions Forms--Family Law § 6:39, Advising Prospective Adoptive Parents.

California Transactions Forms--Family Law § 6:40, Structuring the Adoption.

California Transactions Forms--Family Law § 6:45, Matters to Consider in Initial Interview and Representation Of Adoptive Parents.

California Transactions Forms--Family Law § 6:46, Matters to Consider in Structuring the Adoption.

California Transactions Forms--Family Law § 6:59, Statement Of Understanding: Independent Adoption Program [Department Of Social Services Form Ad 927].

California Transactions Forms--Family Law § 6:133, Statement Of Intent to Adopt and Statement Of Personal Knowledge.

Treatises and Practice Aids

Witkin, California Summary 10th Parent and Child § 123, Nature Of Independent Adoption.

Witkin, California Summary 10th Parent and Child § 127, Selection Of Prospective Adoptive Parents.

Witkin, California Summary 10th Parent and Child § 128, Adoption Placement Agreement.

§ 8801.3. Placement of child for adoption; requirements

A child shall not be considered to have been placed for adoption unless each of the following is true:

(a) Each birth parent placing the child for adoption has been advised of his or her rights, and if desired, has been counseled pursuant to Section 8801.5.

(b) The adoption service provider, each prospective adoptive parent, and each birth parent placing the child have signed an adoption placement agreement on a form prescribed by the department. The signing of the agreement shall satisfy all of the following requirements:

(1) Each birth parent shall have been advised of his or her rights pursuant to Section 8801.5 at least 10 days before signing the agreement, unless the adoption service provider finds exigent circumstances that shall be set forth in the adoption placement agreement.

(2) The agreement may not be signed by either the birth parents or the prospective adoptive parents until the time of discharge of the birth mother from the hospital. However, if the birth mother remains hospitalized for a period longer than the hospitalization of the child, the agreement may be signed by all parties at the time of or after the child's discharge from the hospital but prior to the birth mother's discharge from the hospital if her competency to sign is verified by her attending physician and surgeon before she signs the agreement.

(3) The birth parents and prospective adoptive parents shall sign the agreement in the presence of an adoption service provider.

(4) The adoption service provider who witnesses the signatures shall keep the original of the adoption placement agreement and immediately forward it and supporting documentation as required by the department to the department or delegated county adoption agency.

(5) The child is not deemed to be placed for adoption with the prospective adoptive parents until the adoption placement agreement has been signed and witnessed.

(6) If the birth parent is not located in this state or country, the adoption placement agreement shall be signed before an adoption service provider or, for purposes of identification of the birth parent only, before a notary or other person authorized to perform notarial acts in the state or country in which the birth parent is located. This paragraph is not applicable to intercountry adoptions, as defined in Section 8527, which shall be governed by Chapter 4 (commencing with Section 8900).

(c) The adoption placement agreement form shall include all of the following:

(1) A statement that the birth parent received the advisement of rights and the date upon which it was received.

(2) A statement that the birth parent understands that the placement is for the purpose of adoption and that if the birth parent takes no further action, on the 31st day after signing the adoption placement agreement, the agreement shall become a permanent and irrevocable consent to the adoption.

(3) A statement that the birth parent signs the agreement having personal knowledge of certain facts regarding the prospective adoptive parents as provided in Section 8801.

(4) A statement that the adoptive parents have been informed of the basic health and social history of the birth parents.

(5) A consent to the adoption that may be revoked as provided by Section 8814.5.

(d) The adoption placement agreement shall also meet the requirements of the Interstate Compact on the Placement of Children in Section 7901.

(e) This section shall become operative on January 1, 1995. *(Added by Stats.1993, c. 758 (S.B.792), § 7, operative Jan. 1, 1995. Amended by Stats.1994, c. 585 (A.B.3336), § 3; Stats.2000, c. 937 (A.B.2433), § 3; Stats.2001, c. 688 (S.B. 104), § 1.)*

Research References

Forms

California Transactions Forms--Family Law § 6:3, Definitions.

California Transactions Forms--Family Law § 7:8, Traditional Surrogacy Agreements.

California Transactions Forms--Family Law § 6:32, Nature Of Independent Adoption--Relinquishment Versus Consent.

California Transactions Forms--Family Law § 6:34, Role Of Adoption Service Provider.

California Transactions Forms--Family Law § 6:36, Independent Adoption Placement Agreement.

California Transactions Forms--Family Law § 6:40, Structuring the Adoption.

California Transactions Forms--Family Law § 6:123, Applicability Of ICPC.

Treatises and Practice Aids

Witkin, California Summary 10th Parent and Child § 78, Child Of Indian Ancestry.

Witkin, California Summary 10th Parent and Child § 123, Nature Of Independent Adoption.

Witkin, California Summary 10th Parent and Child § 128, Adoption Placement Agreement.

Witkin, California Summary 10th Parent and Child § 129, in General.

Witkin, California Summary 10th Parent and Child § 131, Withdrawal After Signing Statutory Consent.
Witkin, California Summary 10th Parent and Child § 136, Withdrawal, Denial, or Dismissal Of Petition.

§ 8801.5. Birth parents; advice of rights; role of counselor

(a) Each birth parent placing a child for adoption shall be advised of his or her rights by an adoption service provider.

(b) The birth parent shall be advised of his or her rights in a face-to-face meeting in which the birth parent may ask questions and have questions answered, as provided by Section 8801.3.

(c) The department shall prescribe the format and process for advising birth parents of their rights, the content of which shall include, but not be limited to, the following:

(1) The alternatives to adoption.

(2) The alternative types of adoption, including a description of the full procedures and timeframes involved in each type.

(3) The full rights and responsibilities of the birth parent with respect to adoption, including the need to keep the department informed of his or her current address in case of a medical emergency requiring contact and of providing a full health history.

(4) The right to separate legal counsel paid for by the prospective adoptive parents upon the request of the birth parent, as provided for by Section 8800.

(5) The right to a minimum of three separate counseling sessions, each to be held on different days, to be paid for by the prospective adoptive parents upon the request of the birth parents, as provided for by subdivision (d).

(d) Each person advised pursuant to this section shall be offered at least three separate counseling sessions, to be held on different days. Each counseling session shall be not less than 50 minutes in duration. The counseling may be provided by the adoption service provider who informs the birth parent of his or her rights, or by another adoption service provider, or by a licensed psychotherapist, as defined by Section 1010 of the Evidence Code, as elected by the person, and after having been informed of these choices.

(e) The counselor owes a duty of care to the birth parent being counseled, similar to the duty of care established by a psychotherapist-patient relationship, regardless of who pays the fees of the counselor. No counselor shall have a contractual relationship with the adoptive parents, an attorney for the adoptive parents, or any other individual or an organization performing any type of services for the adoptive parents and for which the adoptive parents are paying a fee, except as relates to payment of the birth parents' fee.

(f) The advisement and counseling fees shall be paid by the prospective adoptive parents at the request of the birth parent.

(g) Failure to fulfill the duties specified in this section shall not be construed as a basis for setting aside the consent or the adoption, but may give rise to a cause of action for malpractice or negligence against those professionals or agencies serving as adoption service providers that are responsible for fulfilling the duties. *(Added by Stats.1993, c. 758 (S.B.792), § 8, operative Jan. 1, 1995. Amended by Stats.1994, c. 585 (A.B.3336), § 4; Stats.1997, c. 559 (S.B. 1121), § 2.)*

Research References

Forms

California Transactions Forms--Family Law § 6:3, Definitions.
California Transactions Forms--Family Law § 6:34, Role Of Adoption Service Provider.
California Transactions Forms--Family Law § 6:39, Advising Prospective Adoptive Parents.
California Transactions Forms--Family Law § 6:40, Structuring the Adoption.
California Transactions Forms--Family Law § 6:46, Matters to Consider in Structuring the Adoption.

Treatises and Practice Aids

Witkin, California Summary 10th Parent and Child § 123, Nature Of Independent Adoption.
Witkin, California Summary 10th Parent and Child § 125, Advising and Counseling Birth Parents.
Witkin, California Summary 10th Parent and Child § 128, Adoption Placement Agreement.

§ 8801.7. Duties of adoption service provider; duty of care

(a) An adoption service provider shall also witness the signature of the adoption placement agreement and offer to interview the birth parent after the placement of the child with prospective adoptive parents. The interview shall occur within 10 working days after the placement of the child for adoption and shall include a consideration of any concerns or problems the birth parent has with the placement, a readvisement of the rights of the birth parent, and the taking of the health and social history of the birth parent, if not taken previously.

(b) The adoption service provider shall immediately notify the department or delegated county adoption agency if the birth parent is not interviewed as provided in subdivision (a) or if there are any concerns regarding the placement. If the birth parent wishes to revoke the consent, the adoption service provider shall assist the birth parent in obtaining the return of the child.

(c) The adoption service provider owes a very high duty of care to the birth parent being advised, regardless of who pays the provider's fees. The duty of care specifically does not include a duty to investigate information provided by the birth parents, prospective adoptive parents, or their attorneys or agents. No adoption service provider shall have a contractual relationship with prospective adoptive parents, an attorney or representative for prospective adoptive parents, or any individual or organization providing services of any type to prospective adoptive parents for which the adoptive parents are paying a fee, except as relates to the payment of the fees for the advising and counseling of the birth parents.

(d) This section shall become operative on January 1, 1995. *(Added by Stats.1993, c. 758 (S.B.792), § 9, operative Jan. 1, 1995.)*

Research References

Forms

California Transactions Forms--Family Law § 6:34, Role Of Adoption Service Provider.

California Transactions Forms--Family Law § 6:40, Structuring the Adoption.

California Transactions Forms--Family Law § 6:148, Rights Of Indian Parents Of Indian Children.

Treatises and Practice Aids

Witkin, California Summary 10th Parent and Child § 124, Adoption Service Providers.

Witkin, California Summary 10th Parent and Child § 131, Withdrawal After Signing Statutory Consent.

Witkin, California Summary 10th Parent and Child § 133, Notice and Interview.

§ 8802. Petition for adoption; contents; order of adoption

(a)(1) Any of the following persons who desire to adopt a child may, for that purpose, file an adoption request in a county authorized by Section 8609.5:

(A) An adult who is related to the child or the child's half sibling by blood or affinity, including all relatives whose status is preceded by the words "step," "great," "great-great," or "grand," or the spouse of any of these persons, even if the marriage was terminated by death or dissolution.

(B) A person named in the will of a deceased parent as an intended adoptive parent where the child has no other parent.

(C) A person with whom a child has been placed for adoption.

(D)(i) A legal guardian who has been the child's legal guardian for more than one year.

(ii) If the child is alleged to have been abandoned pursuant to Section 7822, a legal guardian who has been the child's legal guardian for more than six months. The legal guardian may file a petition pursuant to Section 7822 in the same court and concurrently with a petition under this section.

(iii) However, if the parent nominated the guardian for a purpose other than adoption for a specified time period, or if the guardianship was established pursuant to Section 360 of the Welfare and Institutions Code, the guardianship shall have been in existence for not less than three years.

(2) If the child has been placed for adoption, a copy of the adoptive placement agreement shall be attached to the petition. The court clerk shall immediately notify the department at Sacramento in writing of the pendency of the proceeding and of any subsequent action taken.

(3) If the petitioner has entered into a postadoption contact agreement with the birth parent as set forth in Section 8616.5, the agreement, signed by the participating parties, shall be attached to and filed with the petition for adoption.

(b) The petition shall contain an allegation that the petitioners will file promptly with the department or delegated county adoption agency information required by the department in the investigation of the proposed adoption. The omission of the allegation from a petition does not affect the jurisdiction of the court to proceed or the validity of an adoption order or other order based on the petition.

(c) The caption of the adoption petition shall contain the names of the petitioners, but not the child's name. The petition shall state the child's sex and date of birth and the name the child had before adoption.

(d) If the child is the subject of a guardianship petition, the adoption petition shall so state and shall include the caption and docket number or have attached a copy of the letters of the guardianship or temporary guardianship. The petitioners shall notify the court of any petition for guardianship or temporary guardianship filed after the adoption petition. The guardianship proceeding shall be consolidated with the adoption proceeding, and the consolidated case shall be heard and decided in the court in which the adoption is pending.

(e) The order of adoption shall contain the child's adopted name, but not the name the child had before adoption. *(Added by Stats.1993, c. 758 (S.B.792), § 9.2, operative Jan. 1, 1995. Amended by Stats.1996, c. 510 (A.B.2165), § 1; Stats. 2000, c. 937 (A.B.2433), § 4; Stats.2002, c. 1112 (A.B.746), § 3; Stats.2003, c. 62 (S.B.600), § 88; Stats.2003, c. 81 (A.B.416), § 1; Stats.2004, c. 858 (S.B.1357), § 5; Stats.2007, c. 47 (S.B.313), § 5; Stats.2008, c. 534 (S.B.1726), § 10; Stats.2012, c. 638 (A.B.1757), § 10.)*

Law Revision Commission Comments

Enactment [Revised Comment]

Subdivisions (a)–(e) of Section 8802 continue former Civil Code Section 224.30 without substantive change. The reference to the "superior" court has been omitted as surplus. See Section 200 (jurisdiction in superior court). In subdivision (a), the reference to an "action" for adoption has been changed to "proceeding" for consistency with other provisions in this chapter. Language in former Civil Code Section 224.30(a), which dealt with retroactive application of the allegation required by what is now subdivision (b), has been omitted as obsolete. See also Section 8518 ("department" defined).

For comparable provisions, see Sections 8714 (petition for agency adoption), 8912 (petition for intercountry adoption), 9000 (petition for stepparent adoption). [23 Cal.L.Rev.Comm. Reports 1 (1993)].

Commentary

In re Michael R., 137 Cal.App.4th 126, 39 Cal.Rptr.3d 773 (2006), review denied, holds that a family court properly dismissed a temporary guardian's petition seeking to (1) free a child from parental custody and control on the ground of abandonment and (2) independently adopt the child, because the guardian failed to make a prima facie case of parental abandonment under Section 7822 and did not have standing to adopt under this section.

Research References

Forms

California Transactions Forms--Family Law § 6:40, Structuring the Adoption.

California Transactions Forms--Family Law § 6:41, Initiating the Adoption.

California Transactions Forms--Family Law § 6:46, Matters to Consider in Structuring the Adoption.

California Transactions Forms--Family Law § 6:47, Matters to Consider in Drafting Petition for Independent Adoption Of Unmarried Minor.

California Transactions Forms--Family Law § 6:67, Petition for Adoption [Form Adopt-200].

West's California Judicial Council Forms ADOPT-200, Adoption Request.

Treatises and Practice Aids

Witkin, California Summary 10th Parent and Child § 71, Special Statutory Proceeding.
Witkin, California Summary 10th Parent and Child § 90, Effect Of Guardianship Proceeding.
Witkin, California Summary 10th Parent and Child § 95, Petition and Hearing.
Witkin, California Summary 10th Parent and Child § 96, Agreement and Order.
Witkin, California Summary 10th Parent and Child § 104, in General.
Witkin, California Summary 10th Parent and Child § 132, Petition.
Witkin, California Summary 10th Parent and Child § 133, Notice and Interview.
Witkin, California Summary 10th Parent and Child § 330, Who May Bring Action.

§ 8803. Concealment of child; removal of child from county; permission for removal; objections; hearing; application of section; violations

(a) During the pendency of an adoption proceeding:

(1) The child proposed to be adopted may not be concealed within the county in which the adoption proceeding is pending.

(2) The child may not be removed from the county in which the adoption proceeding is pending unless the petitioners or other interested persons first obtain permission for the removal from the court, after giving advance written notice of intent to obtain the court's permission to the department or delegated county adoption agency responsible for the investigation of the proposed adoption. Upon proof of giving notice, permission may be granted by the court if, within a period of 15 days after the date of giving notice, no objections are filed with the court by the department or delegated county adoption agency. If the department or delegated county adoption agency files objections within the 15-day period, upon the request of the petitioners the court shall immediately set the matter for hearing and give to the objector, the petitioners, and the party or parties requesting permission for the removal reasonable notice of the hearing by certified mail, return receipt requested, to the address of each as shown in the records of the adoption proceeding. Upon a finding that the objections are without good cause, the court may grant the requested permission for removal of the child, subject to any limitations that appear to be in the child's best interest.

(b) This section does not apply in any of the following situations:

(1) Where the child is absent for a period of not more than 30 days from the county in which the adoption proceeding is pending, unless a notice of recommendation of denial of petition has been personally served on the petitioners or the court has issued an order prohibiting the child's removal from the county pending consideration of any of the following:

(A) The suitability of the petitioners.

(B) The care provided the child.

(C) The availability of the legally required consents to the adoption.

(2) Where the child has been returned to and remains in the custody and control of the child's birth parent or parents.

(c) A violation of this section is a violation of Section 280 of the Penal Code.

(d) Neither this section nor Section 280 of the Penal Code may be construed to render lawful any act that is unlawful under any other applicable law. *(Stats.1992, c. 162 (A.B. 2650), § 10, operative Jan. 1, 1994.)*

Law Revision Commission Comments

Enactment [Revised Comment]

Section 8803 continues former Civil Code Section 224.33 without substantive change. The two limitations on the exception provided in subdivision (b)(1) have been rephrased for clarity. See also Sections 8512 ("birth parent" defined), 8515 ("delegated county adoption agency" defined), 8518 ("department" defined).

For comparable provisions, see Sections 8713 (removal and concealment in agency adoption), 8910 (removal and concealment in intercountry adoption). [23 Cal.L.Rev.Comm. Reports 1 (1993)].

Research References

Forms

California Transactions Forms--Family Law § 6:2, Governing Law.

Treatises and Practice Aids

Witkin, California Summary 10th Parent and Child § 81, Removal or Concealment Of Child Pending Adoption.

§ 8804. Withdrawal of petition

(a) Whenever the petitioners move to withdraw the petition for the adoption or to dismiss the proceeding, the clerk of the court in which the proceeding is pending shall immediately notify the department at Sacramento of the action. The department or the delegated county adoption agency shall file a full report with the court recommending a suitable plan for the child in every case where the petitioners move to withdraw the petition for the adoption or where the department or delegated county adoption agency recommends that the petition for adoption be denied and shall appear before the court for the purpose of representing the child.

(b) Notwithstanding the withdrawal or dismissal of the petition, the court may retain jurisdiction over the child for the purposes of making any order for the child's custody that the court deems to be in the child's best interest.

(c) If a birth parent who did not place a child for adoption as specified in Section 8801.3 has refused to give the required consent, or a birth parent revokes consent as specified in Section 8814.5, the child shall be restored to the care and custody of the birth parent or parents, unless the court orders otherwise, subject to Section 3041. *(Added by Stats.1993, c. 758 (S.B.792), § 10, operative Jan. 1, 1995. Amended by Stats.2002, c. 1118 (A.B.1938), § 4; Stats.2014, c. 763 (A.B. 1701), § 11, eff. Jan. 1, 2015.)*

Law Revision Commission Comments

Enactment [Revised Comment]

Subdivisions (a)–(c) of Section 8804 continue former Civil Code Section 224.36 without substantive change. The former reference to the "clerk of the court in which the proceeding is pending" has been shortened to the "court clerk" to eliminate surplus language. See also Sections 8512 ("birth parent" defined), 8515 ("delegated county adoption agency" defined), 8518 ("department" defined).

For related provisions, see Sections 8719 (notice of withdrawal or dismissal in agency adoption), 8916 (notice of withdrawal or dismissal in intercountry adoption), 9006 (notice of withdrawal or dismissal in stepparent adoption). [23 Cal.L.Rev.Comm. Reports 1 (1993)].

Commentary

The California Supreme Court granted review to *Adoption of Haley A. sub nom. Petition of Mark A., 930 P.2d 401, 60 Cal.Rptr.2d 608 (1997),* but granted the parties' joint request to dismiss review on May 12, 1999. The superseded Court of Appeal opinion, 57 Cal.Rptr.2d 361 (1996), held that a birth parent who refuses to consent to an adoption within the statutory period specified for revocation of consent to an adoptive placement is entitled to immediate return of the child without regard to the child's best interests.

Compare *Guardianship of Zachary H., 73 Cal.App.4th 51, 86 Cal.Rptr.2d 7 (1999),* which held that the trial court properly appointed prospective adoptive parents, with whom the child had been placed from birth, as the guardians of the child after their adoption of the child failed because of the father's opposition, when changing custody to the father, who was not otherwise shown to be unfit, would cause detriment to the child, and the best interest of the child required that custody be continued with the guardians. Although the federal due process clause requires a showing of "unfitness" before parental rights are terminated, the appointment of a guardian does not terminate parental rights. *Zachary H.* explains that subsection (c), which would otherwise control, is subject to the constitutional right of the child to a secure and stable home with the only family it has known since birth. Similarly, see *Adoption of Daniele G., 87 Cal.App.4th 1392, 105 Cal.Rptr.2d 341 (2001)*, which holds that the trial court improperly denied the guardianship petition of prospective adoptive parents currently caring for the child when the court found that removal from the current home would cause detriment to the child and remaining in the current home was in the child's best interests. Although adoption might not proceed without the father's consent, granting guardianship to the prospective adoptive parents was warranted by the court's findings.

Research References

Treatises and Practice Aids

Witkin, California Summary 10th Parent and Child § 130, Withdrawal Before Signing Statutory Consent.

Witkin, California Summary 10th Parent and Child § 136, Withdrawal, Denial, or Dismissal Of Petition.

Witkin, California Summary 10th Parent and Child § 267, Jurisdiction and Venue.

§ 8805. Removal of child from home of petitioners; transfer of care of child to department or agency

At the hearing, if the court sustains the recommendation of the department or delegated county adoption agency that the child be removed from the home of the petitioners because the department or agency recommends denial or if the petitioners move to withdraw the petition or if the court dismisses the petition and does not return the child to the birth parents, the court shall commit the child to the care of the department or delegated county adoption agency, whichever made the recommendation, for the department or agency to arrange adoptive placement or to make a suitable plan. In those counties not served by a delegated county adoption agency, the county welfare department shall act as the agent of the department and shall provide care for the child in accordance with rules and regulations established by the department. *(Stats.1992, c. 162 (A.B.2650), § 10, operative Jan. 1, 1994.)*

Law Revision Commission Comments

Enactment [Revised Comment]

Section 8805 continues former Civil Code Section 224.37 without substantive change. See also Sections 8515 ("delegated county adoption agency" defined), 8518 ("department" defined). [23 Cal.L.Rev.Comm. Reports 1 (1993)].

Research References

Treatises and Practice Aids

Witkin, California Summary 10th Parent and Child § 136, Withdrawal, Denial, or Dismissal Of Petition.

§ 8806. Acceptance of consent of birth parent; ascertainment of whether child is proper subject for adoption; determination of suitability of home

The department or delegated county adoption agency shall accept the consent of the birth parents to the adoption of the child by the petitioners and, before filing its report with the court, shall ascertain whether the child is a proper subject for adoption and whether the proposed home is suitable for the child. *(Stats.1992, c. 162 (A.B.2650), § 10, operative Jan. 1, 1994.)*

Law Revision Commission Comments

Enactment [Revised Comment]

Section 8806 continues former Civil Code Section 224.40 without substantive change. The language of this provision has been revised to use the mandatory "shall" in place of the former statement that "it shall be the duty" to accept the consent and to ascertain the stated matters. See Section 12 ("shall" is mandatory). See also Sections 8512 ("birth parent" defined), 8515 ("delegated county adoption agency" defined), 8518 ("department" defined). [23 Cal.L.Rev. Comm. Reports 1 (1993)].

Research References

Treatises and Practice Aids

Witkin, California Summary 10th Parent and Child § 93, Medical Report on Child and Birth Parents.

Witkin, California Summary 10th Parent and Child § 129, in General.

Witkin, California Summary 10th Parent and Child § 134, Investigation, Report, and Recommendation.

§ 8807. Investigation of proposed independent adoption; report; filing with court

(a) Except as provided in subdivisions (b) and (c), within 180 days after receiving 50 percent of the fee, the department or delegated county adoption agency shall investigate the proposed independent adoption and, after the remaining balance of the fee is paid, submit to the court a full report of the facts disclosed by its inquiry with a recommendation regarding the granting of the petition. If the petitioners have a valid preplacement evaluation or a valid private agency adoption home study, as described in paragraph (2) of subdivision (a) of Section 8810, and no new information has been discovered and no new event has occurred subsequent to the approval of the evaluation or home study that creates a reasonable belief that further investigation is necessary, the department or delegated county adoption agency may elect not to reinvestigate any matters covered in the evaluation or home study, except that the department shall complete all background clearances required by law.

(b) If the investigation establishes that there is a serious question concerning the suitability of the petitioners, the care provided to the child, or the availability of the consent to adoption, the report shall be filed immediately.

(c) In its discretion, the court may allow additional time for the filing of the report, after at least five days' notice to the petitioner or petitioners and an opportunity for the petitioner or petitioners to be heard with respect to the request for additional time.

(d) If a petitioner is a resident of a state other than California, an updated and current home study report, conducted and approved by a licensed adoption agency or other authorized resource in the state in which the petitioner resides, shall be reviewed and endorsed by the department or delegated county adoption agency, if the standards and criteria established for a home study report in the other state are substantially commensurate with the home study standards and criteria established in California adoption regulations. *(Added by Stats.2008, c. 759 (A.B.1279), § 8, eff. Sept. 30, 2008, operative Oct. 1, 2008. Amended by Stats.2014, c. 763 (A.B.1701), § 12, eff. Jan. 1, 2015.)*

Research References

Forms

California Transactions Forms--Family Law § 6:13, Appearance in Person or by Counsel.

California Transactions Forms--Family Law § 6:35, Home Study Preplacement Certification Versus Postplacement Study.

California Transactions Forms--Family Law § 6:67, Petition for Adoption [Form Adopt-200].

Treatises and Practice Aids

Witkin, California Summary 10th Parent and Child § 95, Petition and Hearing.

Witkin, California Summary 10th Parent and Child § 134, Investigation, Report, and Recommendation.

§ 8808. Interview of petitioners and persons from whom consent is required; filing of petition

(a) The department or delegated county adoption agency shall interview the petitioners within 45 working days, excluding legal holidays, after the department or delegated county adoption agency receives 50 percent of the investigation fee together with a stamped file copy of the adoption petition.

(b) The department or delegated county adoption agency shall interview all persons from whom consent is required and whose addresses are known. The interview with the placing parent or parents shall include, but not be limited to, discussion of any concerns or problems that the parent has with the placement and, if the placing parent was not interviewed as provided in Section 8801.7, the content required in that interview. At the interview, the agency shall give the parent an opportunity to sign either a statement revoking the consent, or a waiver of the right to revoke consent, as provided in Section 8814.5, unless the parent has already signed a waiver or the time period allowed to revoke consent has expired.

(c) In order to facilitate the interview described in this section, within five business days of filing the petition, the petitioners shall provide the department or delegated county adoption agency a stamped file copy of the petition together with 50 percent of the fee, a copy of any valid preplacement evaluation or any valid private agency adoption home study, as described in paragraph (2) of subdivision (a) of Section 8810, and the names, addresses, and telephone numbers of all parties to be interviewed, if known. *(Added by Stats.2008, c. 759 (A.B.1279), § 10, eff. Sept. 30, 2008, operative Oct. 1, 2008. Amended by Stats.2014, c. 763 (A.B.1701), § 13, eff. Jan. 1, 2015.)*

Research References

Forms

California Transactions Forms--Family Law § 6:3, Definitions.

West's California Code Forms, Family § 8800, Comment Overview--Independent Adoptions.

Treatises and Practice Aids

Witkin, California Summary 10th Parent and Child § 133, Notice and Interview.

§ 8810. Petition fees; use of revenues; reduction of fee

(a) Except as otherwise provided in this section, whenever a petition is filed under this chapter for the adoption of a child, the petitioner shall pay a nonrefundable fee to the department or to the delegated county adoption agency for the cost of investigating the adoption petition. Fifty percent of the payment shall be made to the department or delegated county adoption agency at the time the adoption petition is filed, and the remaining balance shall be paid no later than the date determined by the department or the delegated county adoption agency in an amount as follows:

(1) For petitions filed on and after October 1, 2008, four thousand five hundred dollars ($4,500).

(2) For petitioners who have a valid preplacement evaluation less than one year old pursuant to Section 8811.5, or a valid private agency adoption home study less than two years old at the time of filing a petition, one thousand five hundred fifty dollars ($1,550) for a postplacement evaluation pursuant to Sections 8806 and 8807.

(b) Revenues produced by fees collected by the department pursuant to subdivision (a) shall be used, when appropriated by the Legislature, to fund only the direct costs associated with the state program for independent adoptions. Revenues produced by fees collected by the delegated county adoption agency pursuant to subdivision (a) shall be used by the county to fund the county program for independent adoptions.

(c) The department or delegated county adoption agency may reduce the fee to no less than five hundred dollars ($500) when the prospective adoptive parents are lower income, according to the income limits published by the Department of Housing and Community Development, and when making the required payment would be detrimental to the welfare of an adopted child. The department shall develop additional guidelines regarding income and assets to determine the financial criteria for reduction of the fee under this subdivision. *(Added by Stats.2008, c. 759 (A.B.1279), § 12, eff. Sept. 30, 2008, operative Oct. 1, 2008. Amended by Stats.2012, c. 638 (A.B.1757), § 11; Stats.2013, c. 743 (A.B.848), § 3.)*

Research References

Forms

California Transactions Forms--Family Law § 6:31, Accounting Report--Adoptions [Judicial Council Form Adopt-230].
California Transactions Forms--Family Law § 6:35, Home Study Preplacement Certification Versus Postplacement Study.
California Transactions Forms--Family Law § 6:69, Transmittal Letter to Department Of Social Services.

Treatises and Practice Aids

Witkin, California Summary 10th Parent and Child § 132, Petition.
Witkin, California Summary 10th Parent and Child § 134, Investigation, Report, and Recommendation.

§ 8811. Adoptive parents; fingerprints; criminal record; prohibited placements; fee; waiver

(a) The department or delegated county adoption agency shall require each person who files an adoption petition to be fingerprinted and shall secure from an appropriate law enforcement agency any criminal record of that person to determine if the person has ever been convicted of a crime other than a minor traffic violation. The department or delegated county adoption agency may also secure the person's full criminal record, if any, with the exception of any convictions for which relief has been granted pursuant to Section 1203.49 of the Penal Code. Any federal-level criminal offender record requests to the Department of Justice shall be submitted with fingerprint images and related information required by the Department of Justice for the purposes of obtaining information as to the existence and content of a record of an out-of-state or federal conviction or arrest of a person or information regarding any out-of-state or federal crimes or arrests for which the Department of Justice establishes that the person is free on bail, or on his or her own recognizance pending trial or appeal. The Department of Justice shall forward to the Federal Bureau of Investigation any requests for federal summary criminal history information received pursuant to this section. The Department of Justice shall review the information returned from the Federal Bureau of Investigation and shall compile and disseminate a response to the department or delegated county adoption agency.

(b) Notwithstanding subdivision (c), the criminal record, if any, shall be taken into consideration when evaluating the prospective adoptive parent, and an assessment of the effects of any criminal history on the ability of the prospective adoptive parent to provide adequate and proper care and guidance to the child shall be included in the report to the court.

(c)(1) The department or a delegated county adoption agency shall not give final approval for an adoptive placement in any home in which the prospective adoptive parent or any adult living in the prospective adoptive home has either of the following:

(A) A felony conviction for child abuse or neglect, spousal abuse, crimes against a child, including child pornography, or for a crime involving violence, including rape, sexual assault, or homicide, but not including other physical assault and battery. For purposes of this subdivision, crimes involving violence means those violent crimes contained in clause (i) of subparagraph (A), and subparagraph (B), of paragraph (1) of subdivision (g) of Section 1522 of the Health and Safety Code.

(B) A felony conviction that occurred within the last five years for physical assault, battery, or a drug- or alcohol-related offense.

(2) This subdivision shall become operative on October 1, 2008, and shall remain operative only to the extent that compliance with its provisions is required by federal law as a condition of receiving funding under Title IV–E of the federal Social Security Act (42 U.S.C. Sec. 670 et seq.).

(d) Any fee charged by a law enforcement agency for fingerprinting or for checking or obtaining the criminal record of the petitioner shall be paid by the petitioner. The department or delegated county adoption agency may defer, waive, or reduce the fee if its payment would cause economic hardship to the prospective adoptive parents detrimental to the welfare of the adopted child, if the child has been in the foster care of the prospective adoptive parents for at least one year, or if necessary for the placement of a special-needs child. *(Stats.1992, c. 162 (A.B.2650), § 10, operative Jan. 1, 1994. Amended by Stats.2008, c. 701 (A.B.2651), § 2, eff. Sept. 30, 2008; Stats.2014, c. 708 (A.B.1585), § 2, eff. Jan. 1, 2015; Stats.2015, c. 303 (A.B.731), § 152, eff. Jan. 1, 2016; Stats.2016, c. 86 (S.B.1171), § 131, eff. Jan. 1, 2017.)*

Law Revision Commission Comments

Enactment [Revised Comment]

Section 8811 continues former Civil Code Section 224.49 without substantive change. See also Sections 8515 ("delegated county adoption agency" defined), 8518 ("department" defined), 8542 ("prospective adoptive parent" defined).

For comparable provisions, see Sections 8712 (investigation in agency adoption), 8908 (investigation in intercountry adoption). For a related provision, see Section 9001(a) (investigation in stepparent adoption). [23 Cal.L.Rev.Comm. Reports 1 (1993)].

Research References

Treatises and Practice Aids

Witkin, California Summary 10th Parent and Child § 94, Investigation Of Prospective Adoptive Parents.
Witkin, California Summary 10th Parent and Child § 134, Investigation, Report, and Recommendation.

§ 8811.5. Preplacement evaluations

(a) A licensed private or public adoption agency of the state of the petitioners' residency may certify prospective adoptive parents by a preplacement evaluation that contains a finding that an individual is suited to be an adoptive parent.

(b) The preplacement evaluation shall include an investigation pursuant to standards included in the regulations governing independent adoption investigations established by the department. Fees for the investigation shall be commensurate with those fees charged for a comparable investigation conducted by the department or by a delegated licensed county adoption agency.

(c) The preplacement evaluation, whether it is conducted for the purpose of initially certifying prospective adoptive parents or for renewing that certification, shall be completed no more than one year prior to the signing of an adoption placement agreement. The cost for renewal of that certification shall be in proportion to the extent of the work required to prepare the renewal that is attributable to changes in family circumstances. *(Added by Stats.1996, c. 510 (A.B. 2165), § 3. Amended by Stats.2004, c. 128 (A.B.2492), § 1.)*

Research References

Forms

California Transactions Forms--Family Law § 6:35, Home Study Preplacement Certification Versus Postplacement Study.

California Transactions Forms--Family Law § 6:69, Transmittal Letter to Department Of Social Services.

Treatises and Practice Aids

Witkin, California Summary 10th Parent and Child § 134, Investigation, Report, and Recommendation.

§ 8812. Attorney's fees, medical fees and expenses, counseling fees, or living expenses of birth mother; request for payment by adoptive parents

Any request by a birth parent or birth parents for payment by the prospective adoptive parents of attorney's fees, medical fees and expenses, counseling fees, or living expenses of the birth mother shall be in writing. The birth parent or parents shall, by first-class mail or other agreed upon means to ensure receipt, provide the prospective adoptive parents written receipts for any money provided to the birth parent or birth parents. The prospective adoptive parents shall provide the receipts to the court when the accounting report required pursuant to Section 8610 is filed. *(Added by Stats.1993, c. 450 (S.B.255), § 3.)*

Research References

Forms

California Transactions Forms--Family Law § 6:40, Structuring the Adoption.

California Transactions Forms--Family Law § 6:46, Matters to Consider in Structuring the Adoption.

California Transactions Forms--Family Law § 6:54, Request by Birth Parent for Financial Assistance.

Treatises and Practice Aids

Witkin, California Summary 10th Parent and Child § 123, Nature Of Independent Adoption.

§ 8813. Request for information about the status of the child's adoption; notification of birth parents of rights

At or before the time a consent to adoption is signed, the department or delegated county adoption agency shall advise the birth parent signing the consent, verbally and in writing, that the birth parent may, at any time in the future, request from the department or agency, all known information about the status of the child's adoption, except for personal, identifying information about the adoptive family. The birth parent shall be advised that this information includes, but is not limited to, all of the following:

(a) Whether the child has been placed for adoption.

(b) The approximate date that an adoption was completed.

(c) If the adoption was not completed or was vacated, for any reason, whether adoptive placement of the child is again being considered. *(Stats.1992, c. 162 (A.B.2650), § 10, operative Jan. 1, 1994.)*

Law Revision Commission Comments

Enactment [Revised Comment]

Section 8813 continues former Civil Code Section 224.61 without substantive change. See also Sections 8512 ("birth parent" defined), 8515 ("delegated county adoption agency" defined), 8518 ("department" defined).

For a comparable provision, see Section 8701 (information on status of agency adoption). [23 Cal.L.Rev.Comm. Reports 1 (1993)].

Research References

Treatises and Practice Aids

Witkin, California Summary 10th Parent and Child § 129, in General.

§ 8814. Consent of birth parent or parents; out-of-state birth parent; minor birth parent

(a) Except as provided in Section 7662, the consent of the birth parent or parents who did not place the child for adoption, as described in Section 8801.3, to the adoption shall be signed in the presence of an agent of the department or of a delegated county adoption agency on a form prescribed by the department. The consent shall be filed with the clerk of the appropriate superior court.

(b) The consent described in subdivision (a), when reciting that the person giving it is entitled to the sole custody of the child and when acknowledged before that agent, is prima facie evidence of the right of the person making it to the sole custody of the child and that person's sole right to consent.

(c) If the birth parent described in subdivision (a) is located outside this state for an extended period of time unrelated to the adoption at the time of signing the consent, the consent may be signed before a notary or other person authorized to perform notarial acts, and in that case the consent of the department or of the delegated county adoption agency is also necessary.

(d) A birth parent who is a minor has the right to sign a consent for the adoption of the birth parent's child and the consent is not subject to revocation by the birth parent by reason of minority, or because the parent or guardian of the consenting minor parent was not served with notice that the minor parent consented to the adoption, unless the minor parent has previously provided written authorization to serve his or her parent or guardian with that notice. *(Added by Stats.1993, c. 758 (S.B.792), § 12, operative Jan. 1, 1995. Amended by Stats.1994, c. 585 (A.B.3336), § 5, operative Jan. 1, 1995; Stats.1996, c. 510 (A.B.2165), § 4; Stats.2014, c. 763 (A.B.1701), § 14, eff. Jan. 1, 2015.)*

Law Revision Commission Comments

Enactment [Revised Comment]

Subdivisions (a)–(d) of Section 8814 continue former Civil Code Section 224.62 without substantive change. The word "duly" formerly preceding "acknowledged" has been omitted as surplus. See also Sections 8512 ("birth parent" defined), 8515 ("delegated county adoption agency" defined), 8518 ("department" defined).

For related provisions, see Sections 8700 (consent to agency adoption), 9003 (consent to stepparent adoption). [23 Cal.L.Rev. Comm. Reports 1 (1993)].

Commentary

In a traditional surrogacy arrangement, that is, where the surrogate mother provides both the ovum and the womb, the surrogate mother is a birth parent, and her consent is required under Section 8814 before the child may be adopted by another. Thus the terms of the traditional surrogacy contract are unenforceable insofar as they purport to create maternal rights in a different woman. *In re Marriage of Moschetta, 25 Cal.App.4th 1218, 30 Cal.Rptr.2d 893 (1994).* Compare ovum donation where there are two biological mothers, the ovum donor and the womb donor. In such case, the birth parent is the woman who intended to bring about the birth and to raise the child as her natural child. *Johnson v. Calvert, 5 Cal.4th 84, 19 Cal.Rptr.2d 494 (1993), cert. denied 510 U.S. 874, 114 S.Ct. 206, 126 L.Ed.2d 163 (1993).*

K.M. v. E.G., 37 Cal.4th 130, 117 P.3d 673, 33 Cal.Rptr.3d 61 (2005), holds that Section 7613(b) has no application when a woman in a lesbian relationship provides ova to impregnate her partner in order to produce children who will be raised in their joint home. Consequently, the California Supreme Court recognized the ova donor's claim to parental status, holding that both the woman who provided the ova and the woman who bore the resulting twin children were the children's parents even though the ova donor did not hold the resultant children out as her own natural children within the meaning of Section 7611(d) and the trial court found that she formally relinquished any claim to offspring resulting from her ova donation. In other words, the intent of the parties on the question of maternity had no bearing on the result.

Although *K.M.*, narrowly distinguishes *Steven S. v. Deborah D., 127 Cal.App.4th 319, 25 Cal.Rptr.3d 482 (2005)*, *K.M.* may be understood to undermine the rationale of *Stephen S.*, in which the court of appeal held that when a child is conceived by the artificial insemination of an unmarried mother with sperm provided by a licensed physician, the biological father of the child may not assert parental rights even though he once had an intimate sexual relationship with the mother and had some social role in the child's life. *Stephen S.* reasoned that once the trial court determined that the child was conceived by artificial insemination, rather than natural conception, Section 7613(b) applied to bar the semen donor from asserting his parentage of the child.

In a companion case to *K.M.*, *Elisa B. v. Superior Court, 37 Cal.4th 108, 117 P.3d 660, 33 Cal.Rptr.3d 46 (2005)*, the California Supreme Court held that in a child support action filed by a county district attorney, a woman who agreed to raise children with her lesbian partner, supported her partner's artificial insemination by means of an anonymous donor, and received the resulting twins into her home and held them out as her own children was a Section 7611(d) presumed parent. Moreover, invoking Section 7612(a), the Supreme Court held that a child support action was not an "appropriate action" in which to rebut the Section 7611(d) presumption. Consequently the woman was subject to the parental child support obligation. *Charisma R. v. Kristina S., 140 Cal.App.4th 301, 44 Cal.Rptr.3d 332 (2006)*, extends *Elisa B.* by applying it when a child's biological mother opposed her former lesbian partner's petition to establish a parental relationship with a child conceived and born during their relationship. *Charisma R.* reasons that the preferences of a biological parent are immaterial in determining whether another person is a presumed parent under Section 7611(d) or whether, under Section 7612(a), rebuttal of presumed parent status is appropriate. On remand, *Charisma R. v. Kristina S., 175 Cal.App.4th 361, 96 Cal.Rptr.3d 26 (2009)*, held that section 7611(d) presumed parenthood requires only that a former domestic partner have received the child into her home and openly held the child out as her own; it does not require the former partner to co-parent for any particular length of time.

In another companion case, *Kristine H. v. Lisa R., 37 Cal.4th 156, 117 P.3d 690, 33 Cal.Rptr.3d 81 (2005)*, the California Supreme Court used the doctrine of estoppel to reach a similar result when a former lesbian partner of a child's mother sought custody of the child after the parties' separation. During the mother's pregnancy the partners sought and secured a judgment that they are the "only legally recognized parents [of the unborn child] and take full and complete legal, custodial and financial responsibility of said child." Without deciding whether the judgment was enforceable, the Supreme Court held that the mother was estopped to attack the validity of a judgment to which she stipulated.

Elisa B. and *Kristine H.* overruled earlier court of appeal decisions declining to accord parental status to a parent's lesbian partner, such as *Nancy S. v. Michele G., 228 Cal.App.3d 831, 279 Cal.Rptr. 212 (1991)* and *Curiale v. Reagan, 222 Cal.App.3d 1597, 1600, 272 Cal.Rptr. 520 (1990).*

S.Y. v. S.B., 201 Cal.App.4th 1023, 134 Cal.Rptr.3d 1 (2011), review denied, held that a woman who fully embraced the rights and obligations of being a parent to her same-sex partner's adopted children was properly found to be a section 7611(d) presumed parent when the woman spent three or four nights a week at the children's home and openly held the children out as her own children. Whether the adoptive mother intended her partner to have parental rights was immaterial. See also *R.M. v. T.A., 233 Cal.App.4th 760, 182 Cal. Rptr.3d 836 (2015)*, in which the court relied on *S.Y. v. S.B.* to reject a mother's argument that her intent, as opposed to her behavior, was determinative in whether her former partner was a presumed parent of her child.

Research References

Forms

California Transactions Forms--Family Law § 6:5, Issues Common to All Types Of Adoptions.

Treatises and Practice Aids

Witkin, California Summary 10th Contracts § 47, Miscellaneous Contracts.

Witkin, California Summary 10th Contracts § 625, Traditional Surrogacy Contract.

Witkin, California Summary 10th Parent and Child § 23, Where Intended Mother is Not Genetic Mother.

Witkin, California Summary 10th Parent and Child § 100, in General.

Witkin, California Summary 10th Parent and Child § 129, in General.

Witkin, California Summary 10th Parent and Child § 131, Withdrawal After Signing Statutory Consent.

§ 8814.5. Revocation of consent; actions taken within 30 days of signing consent

(a) After a consent to the adoption is signed by the birth parent or parents pursuant to Section 8801.3 or 8814, the birth parent or parents signing the consent shall have 30 days to take one of the following actions:

(1) Sign and deliver to the department or delegated county adoption agency a written statement revoking the consent and requesting the child to be returned to the birth parent or parents. After revoking consent, in cases where the birth parent or parents have not regained custody, or the birth parent or parents have failed to make efforts to exercise their rights under subdivision (b) of Section 8815, a written notarized statement reinstating the original consent may be signed and delivered to the department or delegated county adoption agency, in which case the revocation of consent shall be void and the remainder of the original 30–day period shall commence. After revoking consent, in cases in which the birth parent or parents have regained custody or made efforts to exercise their rights under subdivision (b) of Section 8815 by requesting the return of the child, upon the delivery of a

written notarized statement reinstating the original consent to the department or delegated county adoption agency, the revocation of consent shall be void and a new 30–day period shall commence. The birth mother shall be informed of the operational timelines associated with this section at the time of signing of the statement reinstating the original consent.

(2)(A) Sign a waiver of the right to revoke consent on a form prescribed by the department in the presence of any of the following:

(i) A representative of the department or delegated county adoption agency.

(ii) A judicial officer of a court of record if the birth parent is represented by independent legal counsel.

(iii) An adoption service provider, including, but not limited to, the adoption service provider who advised the birth mother and witnessed the signing of the consent, if the birth parent or parents are represented by independent legal counsel. The adoption service provider shall ensure that the waiver is delivered to the department, the petitioners, or their counsel no earlier than the end of the business day following the signing of the waiver. The adoption service provider shall inform the birth parent that during this time period he or she may request that the waiver be withdrawn and that, if he or she makes that request, the waiver shall be withdrawn.

(B) An adoption service provider may assist the birth parent or parents in any activity where the primary purpose of that activity is to facilitate the signing of the waiver with the department, a delegated county agency, or a judicial officer. The adoption service provider or another person designated by the birth parent or parents may also be present at any interview conducted pursuant to this section to provide support to the birth parent or parents, except when the interview is conducted by independent legal counsel for the birth parent or parents.

(C) The waiver of the right to revoke consent may not be signed until an interview has been completed by the department or delegated county adoption agency unless the waiver of the right to revoke consent is signed in the presence of a judicial officer of a court of record or an adoption service provider as specified in this section. If the waiver is signed in the presence of a judicial officer, the interview and the witnessing of the signing of the waiver shall be conducted by the judicial officer. If the waiver is signed in the presence of an adoption service provider, the interview shall be conducted by the independent legal counsel for the birth parent or parents. If the waiver is to be signed in the presence of an adoption service provider, prior to the waiver being signed the waiver shall be reviewed by the independent legal counsel who (i) counsels the birth parent or parents about the nature of his or her intended waiver and (ii) signs and delivers to the birth parent or parents and the department a certificate in substantially the following form:

I, (name of attorney), have counseled my client, (name of client), on the nature and legal effect of the waiver of right to revoke consent to adoption. I am so disassociated from the interest of the petitioner(s)/prospective adoptive parent(s) as to be in a position to advise my client impartially and confidentially as to the consequences of the waiver. (Name of client) is aware that California law provides for a 30–day period during which a birth parent may revoke consent to adoption. On the basis of this counsel, I conclude that it is the intent of (name of client) to waive the right to revoke, and make a permanent and irrevocable consent to adoption. (Name of client) understands that he/she will not be able to regain custody of the child unless the petitioner(s)/prospective adoptive parent(s) agree(s) to withdraw their petition for adoption or the court denies the adoption petition.

(D) Within 10 working days of a request made after the department or the delegated county adoption agency has received a copy of the petition for the adoption and the names and addresses of the persons to be interviewed, the department or the delegated county adoption agency shall interview, at the department or agency office, any birth parent requesting to be interviewed.

(E) Notwithstanding subparagraphs (A) and (C), the interview, and the witnessing of the signing of a waiver of the right to revoke consent of a birth parent residing outside of California or located outside of California for an extended period of time unrelated to the adoption may be conducted in the state where the birth parent is located, by any of the following:

(i) A representative of a public adoption agency in that state.

(ii) A judicial officer in that state where the birth parent is represented by independent legal counsel.

(iii) An adoption service provider.

(3) Allow the consent to become a permanent consent on the 31st day after signing.

(b) The consent may not be revoked after a waiver of the right to revoke consent has been signed or after 30 days, beginning on the date the consent was signed or as provided in paragraph (1) of subdivision (a), whichever occurs first. *(Added by Stats.1993, c. 758 (S.B.792), § 13, operative Jan. 1, 1995. Amended by Stats.1994, c. 585 (A.B.3336), § 6, operative Jan. 1, 1995; Stats.1996, c. 510 (A.B.2165), § 5; Stats. 2000, c. 937 (A.B.2433), § 5; Stats.2001, c. 688 (S.B.104), § 2; Stats.2002, c. 664 (A.B.3034), § 79; Stats.2003, c. 251 (S.B. 182), § 10; Stats.2008, c. 534 (S.B.1726), § 11; Stats.2009, c. 492 (A.B.941), § 4; Stats.2010, c. 588 (A.B.2020), § 7.)*

Commentary

The California Supreme Court granted review to *Adoption of Haley A. sub. nom. Petition of Mark A., 930 P.2d 401, 60 Cal.Rptr.2d 608 (1997),* but granted the parties' joint request to dismiss review on May 12, 1999. The superseded court of appeal opinion, 57 Cal. Rptr.2d 361 (1996), held that a birth parent who refuses to consent to an adoption within the statutory period specified for revocation of consent to an adoptive placement is entitled to immediate return of the child without regard to the child's best interests.

Compare *Guardianship of Zachary H., 73 Cal.App.4th 51, 86 Cal.Rptr.2d 7 (1999),* which held that the trial court properly appointed prospective adoptive parents, with whom the child had been placed from birth, as the guardians of the child after their adoption of the child failed because of the father's opposition, when changing custody to the father, who was not otherwise shown to be unfit, would cause detriment to the child, and the best interest of the child required that custody be continued with the guardians. Although the federal due process clause requires a showing of "unfitness" before parental rights are terminated, the appointment of a guardian does not terminate parental rights. *Zachary H.* explains that Section 8804 (c), which would otherwise control, is subject to the constitutional right of the child to a secure and stable home with the only family it has known since birth. Similarly, see *Adoption of Daniele G., 87 Cal.App.4th 1392, 105 Cal.Rptr.2d 341 (2001)*, which holds that the trial court improperly denied the guardianship petition of prospective adoptive parents currently caring for the child when the court found that removal from the current home would cause detriment to the child and remaining in the current home was in the child's best interests. Although adoption might not proceed without the father's consent, granting guardianship to the prospective adoptive parents was warranted by the court's findings.

Research References

Forms

California Transactions Forms--Family Law § 6:3, Definitions.
California Transactions Forms--Family Law § 6:32, Nature Of Independent Adoption--Relinquishment Versus Consent.
California Transactions Forms--Family Law § 6:33, Reasons for Independent Adoption.
California Transactions Forms--Family Law § 6:37, Placing Parent's Right to Revoke Consent to Adoption.
California Transactions Forms--Family Law § 6:38, Waiver Of Placing Parent's Right to Revoke Consent to Adoption.
California Transactions Forms--Family Law § 6:50, Independent Adoption Retainer Agreement.
California Transactions Forms--Family Law § 6:60, Waiver Of Right to Revoke Consent to Adoption: Independent Adoption Program [Department Of Social Services Form Ad 929].
California Transactions Forms--Family Law § 6:68, Receipt for Child.
California Transactions Forms--Family Law § 6:84, Relinquishment as Distinguished from Consent.
California Transactions Forms--Family Law § 6:148, Rights Of Indian Parents Of Indian Children.

Treatises and Practice Aids

Witkin, California Summary 10th Parent and Child § 124, Adoption Service Providers.
Witkin, California Summary 10th Parent and Child § 128, Adoption Placement Agreement.
Witkin, California Summary 10th Parent and Child § 131, Withdrawal After Signing Statutory Consent.
Witkin, California Summary 10th Parent and Child § 133, Notice and Interview.
Witkin, California Summary 10th Parent and Child § 136, Withdrawal, Denial, or Dismissal Of Petition.

§ 8815. Withdrawal of consent

(a) Once the revocable consent to adoption has become permanent as provided in Section 8814.5, the consent to the adoption by the prospective adoptive parents may not be withdrawn.

(b) Before the time when the revocable consent becomes permanent as provided in Section 8814.5, the birth parent or parents may request return of the child. In that case the child shall immediately be returned to the requesting birth parent or parents, unless a court orders otherwise.

(c) If the person or persons with whom the child has been placed have concerns that the birth parent or parents requesting return of the child are unfit or present a danger of harm to the child, that person or those persons may report their concerns to the appropriate child welfare agency. These concerns shall not be a basis for failure to immediately return the child, unless a court orders otherwise. *(Added by Stats.1993, c. 758 (S.B.792), § 16, operative Jan. 1, 1995. Amended by Stats.2014, c. 763 (A.B.1701), § 15, eff. Jan. 1, 2015.)*

Research References

Forms

California Transactions Forms--Family Law § 6:37, Placing Parent's Right to Revoke Consent to Adoption.
California Transactions Forms--Family Law § 6:38, Waiver Of Placing Parent's Right to Revoke Consent to Adoption.
California Transactions Forms--Family Law § 6:60, Waiver Of Right to Revoke Consent to Adoption: Independent Adoption Program [Department Of Social Services Form Ad 929].

Treatises and Practice Aids

Witkin, California Summary 10th Parent and Child § 131, Withdrawal After Signing Statutory Consent.

§ 8816. Consent of agency or department when consent of birth parent not required; prerequisites

In an independent adoption where the consent of the birth parent or parents is not necessary, the department or delegated county adoption agency shall, before the hearing of the petition, file its consent to the adoption with the clerk of the court in which the petition is filed. The consent may not be given unless the child's welfare will be promoted by the adoption. *(Stats.1992, c. 162 (A.B.2650), § 10, operative Jan. 1, 1994.)*

Law Revision Commission Comments

Enactment [Revised Comment]

Section 8816 continues former Civil Code Section 224.66 without substantive change. The reference to the "superior" court has been omitted as surplus. See Section 200 (jurisdiction in superior court).

See also Sections 8512 ("birth parent" defined), 8515 ("delegated county adoption agency" defined), 8518 ("department" defined), 8524 ("independent adoption" defined). [23 Cal.L.Rev.Comm. Reports 1 (1993)].

Research References

Treatises and Practice Aids

Witkin, California Summary 10th Parent and Child § 129, in General.

§ 8817. Report on medical background of child and biological parents; contents; blood sample

(a) A written report on the child's medical background, and if available, the medical background of the child's biological parents so far as ascertainable, shall be made by the department or delegated county adoption agency as part of the study required by Section 8806.

(b) The report on the child's background shall contain all known diagnostic information, including current medical reports on the child, psychological evaluations, and scholastic information, as well as all known information regarding the child's developmental history and family life.

(c) The report shall be submitted to the prospective adoptive parents who shall acknowledge its receipt in writing.

(d)(1) The biological parents may provide a blood sample at a clinic or hospital approved by the State Department of Health Services. The biological parents' failure to provide a blood sample shall not affect the adoption of the child.

(2) The blood sample shall be stored at a laboratory under contract with the State Department of Health Services for a period of 30 years following the adoption of the child.

(3) The purpose of the stored sample of blood is to provide a blood sample from which DNA testing can be done at a later date after entry of the order of adoption at the request of the adoptive parents or the adopted child. The cost of drawing and storing the blood samples shall be paid for by a separate fee in addition to the fee required under Section 8810. The amount of this additional fee shall be based on the cost of drawing and storing the blood samples but at no time shall the additional fee be more than one hundred dollars ($100).

(e)(1) The blood sample shall be stored and released in such a manner as to not identify any party to the adoption.

(2) Any results of the DNA testing shall be stored and released in such a manner as to not identify any party to the adoption. *(Stats.1992, c. 162 (A.B.2650), § 10, operative Jan. 1, 1994. Amended by Stats.1996, c. 1053 (A.B.3241), § 2.)*

Law Revision Commission Comments

Enactment [Revised Comment]

Section 8817 continues former Civil Code Section 224.70(a) without substantive change. See also Sections 8515 ("delegated county adoption agency" defined), 8518 ("department" defined), 8542 ("prospective adoptive parent" defined), 8608 (regulations concerning form and content of medical reports), 9202 (regulations concerning availability of medical reports).

For related provisions, see Sections 8706 (medical report in agency adoption), 8909 (medical report in intercountry adoption). [23 Cal.L.Rev.Comm. Reports 1 (1993)].

Research References

Treatises and Practice Aids

Witkin, California Summary 10th Parent and Child § 93, Medical Report on Child and Birth Parents.

Witkin, California Summary 10th Parent and Child § 149, Confidentiality Of Records.

§ 8818. Statement to birth parents; contents; disclosure form; birth parent information

(a) The department shall adopt a statement to be presented to the birth parents at the time the consent to adoption is signed and to prospective adoptive parents at the time of the home study. The statement shall, in a clear and concise manner and in words calculated to ensure the confidence of the birth parents in the integrity of the adoption process, communicate to the birth parent of a child who is the subject of an adoption petition all of the following facts:

(1) It is in the child's best interest that the birth parents keep the department informed of any health problems that the parent develops that could affect the child.

(2) It is extremely important that the birth parent keep an address current with the department in order to permit a response to inquiries concerning medical or social history.

(3) Section 9203 of the Family Code authorizes a person who has been adopted and who attains the age of 21 years to request the department to disclose the name and address of the adoptee's birth parents. Consequently, it is of the utmost importance that the birth parent indicate whether to allow this disclosure by checking the appropriate box provided on the form.

(4) The birth parent may change the decision whether to permit disclosure of the birth parent's name and address, at any time, by sending a notarized letter to that effect, by certified mail, return receipt requested, to the department.

(5) The consent will be filed in the office of the clerk of the court in which the adoption takes place. The file is not open to inspection by any persons other than the parties to the adoption proceeding, their attorneys, and the department, except upon order of a judge of the superior court.

(b) The department shall adopt a form to be signed by the birth parents at the time the consent to adoption is signed, which shall provide as follows:

"Section 9203 of the Family Code authorizes a person who has been adopted and who attains the age of 21 years to make a request to the State Department of Social Services, or the licensed adoption agency that joined in the adoption petition, for the name and address of the adoptee's birth parents. Indicate by checking one of the boxes below whether or not you wish your name and address to be disclosed:

☐ YES
☐ NO
☐ UNCERTAIN AT THIS TIME; WILL NOTIFY AGENCY AT LATER DATE."

(Stats.1992, c. 162 (A.B.2650), § 10, operative Jan. 1, 1994. Amended by Stats.2002, c. 784 (S.B.1316), § 113.)

Law Revision Commission Comments

Enactment [Revised Comment]

Section 8818 continues former Civil Code Section 224.73 without substantive change. The statement concerning the requirements of Section 9203 has been revised to conform to the language of that section. For example, "petition" has been changed to "request." See also Sections 8512 ("birth parent" defined), 8518 ("department" defined), 8542 ("prospective adoptive parent" defined).

For a comparable provision, see Section 8702 (statement to birth parents in agency adoption). [23 Cal.L.Rev.Comm. Reports 1 (1993)].

2002 Amendment

Subdivision (a)(5) of Section 8818 is amended to reflect elimination of the county clerk's role as ex officio clerk of the superior court. See former Gov't Code § 26800 (county clerk acting as clerk of superior court). The powers, duties, and responsibilities formerly exercised by the county clerk as ex officio clerk of the court are delegated to the court administrative or executive officer, and the county clerk is relieved of those powers, duties, and responsibilities. See Gov't Code §§ 69840 (powers, duties, and responsibilities of clerk of court and deputy clerk of court), 71620 (trial court personnel). [32 Cal.L.Rev.Comm. Reports 170 (2002)].

Research References

Treatises and Practice Aids

Witkin, California Summary 10th Parent and Child § 79, Adoption Information.

Witkin, California Summary 10th Parent and Child § 151, Request for Disclosure.

§ 8819. Termination of parental rights of birth parent; notification

When the parental rights of a birth parent are terminated pursuant to Chapter 5 (commencing with Section 7660) of Part 3 of Division 12 or Part 4 (commencing with Section 7800) of Division 12, the department or delegated county adoption agency shall send a written notice to the birth parent, if the birth parent's address is known, that contains the following statement:

"You are encouraged to keep the department or this agency informed of your current address in order to permit a response to any inquiry concerning medical or social history made by or on behalf of the child who was the subject of the court action terminating parental rights." *(Stats.1992, c. 162 (A.B.2650), § 10, operative Jan. 1, 1994.)*

Law Revision Commission Comments

Enactment [Revised Comment]

Section 8819 continues former Civil Code Section 224.76 without substantive change. The references to the Family Code sections are broader than the references in former law to former Civil Code Sections 232 and 7017. These are not substantive changes. The language of the required statement has been revised to refer to the department. This is consistent with other provisions of this section. See also Sections 8512 ("birth parent" defined), 8515 ("delegated county adoption agency" defined), 8518 ("department" defined).

For a comparable provision, see Section 8703 (notice of termination of parental rights in agency adoption). [23 Cal.L.Rev.Comm. Reports 1 (1993)].

Research References

Treatises and Practice Aids

Witkin, California Summary 10th Parent and Child § 79, Adoption Information.

§ 8820. Failure of department or agency to accept consent of birth parent or give consent where appropriate; appeal; proceedings

(a) The birth parent or parents or the petitioner may appeal in either of the following cases:

(1) If for a period of 180 days from the date of paying 50 percent of the fee, or upon the expiration of any extension of the period granted by the court, the department or delegated county adoption agency fails or refuses to accept the consent of the birth parent or parents to the adoption.

(2) In a case where the consent of the department or delegated county adoption agency is required by this chapter, if the department or agency fails or refuses to file or give its consent to the adoption after full payment has been received.

(b) The appeal shall be filed in the court in which the adoption petition is filed. The court clerk shall immediately notify the department or delegated county adoption agency of the appeal and the department or agency shall, within 10 days, file a report of its findings and the reasons for its failure or refusal to consent to the adoption or to accept the consent of the birth parent or parents.

(c) After the filing of the report by the department or delegated county adoption agency, the court may, if it deems that the welfare of the child will be promoted by that adoption, allow the signing of the consent by the birth parent or parents in open court or, if the appeal is from the refusal of the department or delegated county adoption agency to consent thereto, grant the petition without the consent.

(d) This section shall become operative on October 1, 2008. *(Added by Stats.2008, c. 759 (A.B.1279), § 14, eff. Sept. 30, 2008, operative Oct. 1, 2008.)*

Research References

Forms

California Transactions Forms--Family Law § 6:5, Issues Common to All Types Of Adoptions.

West's California Code Forms, Family § 8800, Comment Overview--Independent Adoptions.

Treatises and Practice Aids

Witkin, California Summary 10th Parent and Child § 129, in General.

§ 8821. Report or findings of department or agency; submission of copy to attorney for petitioner

When any report or findings are submitted to the court by the department or a delegated county adoption agency, a copy of the report or findings, whether favorable or unfavorable, shall be given to the petitioner's attorney in the proceeding, if the petitioner has an attorney of record, or to the petitioner. *(Stats.1992, c. 162 (A.B.2650), § 10, operative Jan. 1, 1994.)*

Law Revision Commission Comments

Enactment [Revised Comment]

Section 8821 continues former Civil Code Section 224.91 without substantive change. See also Sections 8515 ("delegated county adoption agency" defined), 8518 ("department" defined).

For comparable provisions, see Sections 8717 (copy of report in agency adoption), 8915 (copy of report in intercountry adoption). [23 Cal.L.Rev.Comm. Reports 1 (1993)].

Research References

Treatises and Practice Aids

Witkin, California Summary 10th Parent and Child § 134, Investigation, Report, and Recommendation.

§ 8822. Denial or withdrawal of petition; referral to superior court for review; hearing; notice

(a) If the findings of the department or delegated county adoption agency are that the home of the petitioners is not suitable for the child or that the required consents are not available and the department or agency recommends that the petition be denied, or if the petitioners desire to withdraw the petition and the department or agency recommends that the petition be denied, the clerk upon receipt of the report of the department or agency shall immediately refer it to the court for review.

(b) Upon receipt of the report, the court shall set a date for a hearing of the petition and shall give reasonable notice of the hearing to the department or delegated county adoption agency, the petitioners, and the birth parents by certified mail, return receipt requested, to the address of each as shown in the proceeding.

(c) The department or delegated county adoption agency shall appear to represent the child. *(Stats.1992, c. 162 (A.B.2650), § 10, operative Jan. 1, 1994.)*

Law Revision Commission Comments

Enactment [Revised Comment]

Section 8822 continues former Civil Code Section 224.93 without substantive change. The reference to the "county" clerk has been omitted. This is not a substantive change. The reference to the "superior" court has been omitted as surplus. See Section 200 (jurisdiction in superior court). In subdivision (b), reference to the department has been added for consistency with subdivisions (a) and (c). See also Sections 8512 ("birth parent" defined), 8515 ("delegated county adoption agency" defined), 8518 ("department" defined).

For comparable provisions, see Sections 8720 (unfavorable recommendation in agency adoption), 8917 (unfavorable recommendation in intercountry adoption). [23 Cal.L.Rev.Comm. Reports 1 (1993)].

Commentary

A trial court may not refuse to hold an evidentiary hearing on an independent adoption petition after a social services agency has filed an adverse adoption report, because the prospective adoptive parents have a right to a hearing under this Section. *Adoption of Baby Girl B., 74 Cal.App.4th 43, 87 Cal.Rptr.2d 569 (1999).*

Research References

Forms

California Transactions Forms--Family Law § 6:5, Issues Common to All Types Of Adoptions.

Treatises and Practice Aids

Witkin, California Summary 10th Parent and Child § 85, Recommendation Of Department or Agency.

Witkin, California Summary 10th Parent and Child § 134, Investigation, Report, and Recommendation.

Witkin, California Summary 10th Parent and Child § 135, Hearing and Order.

§ 8823. Prospective adoptive parents; appearance before court

The prospective adoptive parents and the child proposed to be adopted shall appear before the court pursuant to Sections 8612 and 8613. *(Stats.1992, c. 162 (A.B.2650), § 10, operative Jan. 1, 1994.)*

Law Revision Commission Comments

Enactment [Revised Comment]

Section 8823 continues former Civil Code Sections 221.62 and 224.95 without substantive change. The reference to "prospective adoptive parents" has been substituted for "person or persons desiring to adopt a child." This is not a substantive change. See Section 8542 ("prospective adoptive parent" defined).

For comparable provisions, see Sections 8718 (appearance in agency adoption), 8913 (appearance in intercountry adoption), 9007 (appearance in stepparent adoption). [23 Cal.L.Rev.Comm. Reports 1 (1993)].

Research References

Treatises and Practice Aids

Witkin, California Summary 10th Parent and Child § 95, Petition and Hearing.

Witkin, California Summary 10th Parent and Child § 135, Hearing and Order.

CHAPTER 4. INTERCOUNTRY ADOPTIONS

§ 8900. Service providers; licensure conditions; primary provider; written agreement

(a) Intercountry adoption services described in this chapter shall be exclusively provided by private adoption agencies licensed by the department specifically to provide these services. As a condition of licensure to provide intercountry adoption services, any private full-service adoption agency and any noncustodial adoption agency shall be accredited by the Council on Accreditation, or supervised by an accredited primary provider, or acting as an exempted provider, in compliance with Subpart F (commencing with Section 96.29) of Part 96 of Title 22 of the Code of Federal Regulations.

(b) A private full-service adoption agency or a noncustodial adoption agency, when acting as the primary provider and using a supervised provider, shall ensure that each supervised provider operates under a written agreement with the primary provider pursuant to subdivision (b) of Section 96.45 of Title 22 of the Code of Federal Regulations.

(c) The primary provider shall provide to the department a copy of the written agreement with each supervised provider containing all provisions required pursuant to subdivision (b) of Section 96.45 of Title 22 of the Code of Federal Regulations. *(Stats.1992, c. 162 (A.B.2650), § 10, operative Jan. 1, 1994. Amended by Stats.2007, c. 583 (S.B.703), § 5.)*

Law Revision Commission Comments

Enactment [Revised Comment]

Section 8900 continues former Civil Code Section 226.10 without substantive change. See also Sections 8518 ("department" defined), 8527 ("intercountry adoption" defined). [23 Cal.L.Rev.Comm. Reports 1 (1993)].

Research References

Forms

California Transactions Forms--Family Law § 6:138, Prohibition Of Intercountry Independent Adoption.

California Transactions Forms--Family Law § 6:139, Overview Of Intercountry Adoption.

West's California Code Forms, Family § 8900, Comment Overview--Intercountry Adoptions.

West's California Judicial Council Forms ADOPT-200, Adoption Request.

West's California Judicial Council Forms ADOPT-215, Adoption Order.

West's California Judicial Council Forms ADOPT-216, Verification Of Compliance With Hague Adoption Convention Attachment.

Treatises and Practice Aids

Witkin, California Summary 10th Parent and Child § 70, Types Of Adoption.

Witkin, California Summary 10th Parent and Child § 72, Statutory Framework.

Witkin, California Summary 10th Parent and Child § 128, Adoption Placement Agreement.

Witkin, California Summary 10th Parent and Child § 137, in General.

Witkin, California Summary 10th Parent and Child § 138, Powers and Duties Of Licensed Adoption Agencies.

§ 8900.5. Definitions

As used in this chapter:

(a) "Accredited agency" means an agency that has been accredited by an accrediting entity, in accordance with the standards in Subpart F (commencing with Section 96.29) of Part 96 of Title 22 of the Code of Federal Regulations, to provide adoption services in the United States in cases subject to the convention. Accredited agency does not include a temporarily accredited agency.

(b) "Adoption service" means any of the following services:

(1) Identifying a child for adoption and arranging an adoption.

(2) Securing the necessary consent to termination of parental rights and to adoption.

(3) Performing a background study on a child or a home study on any prospective adoptive parent, and reporting on the study.

(4) Making nonjudicial determinations of the best interests of a child and the appropriateness of an adoptive placement for the child.

(5) Monitoring a case after a child has been placed with any prospective adoptive parent until final adoption.

(6) If necessary because of a disruption before final adoption, assuming custody and providing or facilitating child care or any other social service pending an alternative placement.

(c) "Central authority" means the entity designated under paragraph (1) of Article 6 of the convention by a convention country. The United States Department of State is designated as the United States Central Authority pursuant to the federal Intercountry Adoption Act of 2000 (42 U.S.C. Sec. 14911).

(d) "Convention" means the Hague Convention on Protection of Children and Co-operation in Respect of Intercountry Adoption, May 29, 1993.

(e) "Convention adoption" means the adoption of a child resident in a convention country by a United States citizen, or an adoption of a child resident in the United States by an individual or individuals residing in a convention country, if, in connection with the adoption, the child has moved or will move between the United States and the convention country.

(f) "Convention country" means a country that is party to the convention and with which the convention is in force for the United States.

(g) "Exempted provider" means a social work professional or organization that performs a home study on any prospective adoptive parent, or a child background study, or both, in the United States in connection with a convention adoption, and who is not currently providing and has not previously provided any other adoption service in the case.

(h) "Hague adoption certificate" means a certificate issued by the secretary in an outgoing case (where the child is emigrating from the United States to another convention country) certifying that a child has been adopted in the United States in accordance with the convention and, except as provided in subdivision (b) of Section 97.4 of Title 22 of the Code of Federal Regulations, the Intercountry Adoption Act of 2000 (42 U.S.C. Sec. 14901 et seq.; the IAA).

(i) "Hague custody declaration" means a declaration issued by the secretary in an outgoing case (where the child is emigrating from the United States to another convention country) declaring that custody of a child for purposes of adoption has been granted in the United States in accordance with the convention and, except as provided in subdivision (b) of Section 97.4 of Title 22 of the Code of Federal Regulations, the IAA.

(j) "Legal service" means any service, other than those defined in this section as an adoption service, that relates to the provision of legal advice and information or to the drafting of legal instruments. Legal service includes, but is not limited to, any of the following services:

(1) Drafting contracts, powers of attorney, and other legal instruments.

(2) Providing advice and counsel to an adoptive parent on completing forms for the State Department of Health Care Services or the United States Department of State.

(3) Providing advice and counsel to accredited agencies, temporarily accredited agencies, approved persons, or prospective adoptive parents on how to comply with the convention, the IAA, and any regulations implementing the IAA.

(k) "Primary provider" means the accredited agency that is identified pursuant to Section 96.14 of Title 22 of the Code of Federal Regulations as responsible for ensuring that all adoption services are provided and responsible for supervising any supervised providers when used.

(*l*) "Public domestic authority" means an authority operated by a state, local, or tribal government.

(m) "Secretary" means the United States Secretary of State, and includes any official of the United States Department of State exercising the authority of the Secretary of State under the convention, the IAA, or any regulations implementing the IAA, pursuant to a delegation of authority.

(n) "Supervised provider" means any agency, person, or other nongovernmental entity that is providing any adoption service in a convention adoption under the supervision and responsibility of an accredited agency that is acting as the primary provider in the case. *(Added by Stats.2007, c. 583 (S.B.703), § 6.)*

Research References

Forms

West's California Judicial Council Forms ADOPT-215, Adoption Order.

West's California Judicial Council Forms ADOPT-216, Verification Of Compliance With Hague Adoption Convention Attachment.

Treatises and Practice Aids

Witkin, California Summary 10th Parent and Child § 137, in General.

Witkin, California Summary 10th Parent and Child § 140, Petition, Hearing, and Order.

§ 8901. Administration of program

The department shall adopt regulations to administer the intercountry adoption program. *(Stats.1992, c. 162 (A.B. 2650), § 10, operative Jan. 1, 1994.)*

Law Revision Commission Comments

Enactment [Revised Comment]

Section 8901 continues former Civil Code Section 226.11 without change. See also Sections 8518 ("department" defined), 8527 ("intercountry adoption" defined). [23 Cal.L.Rev.Comm. Reports 1 (1993)].

Research References

Forms

West's California Code Forms, Family § 8900, Comment Overview--Intercountry Adoptions.

West's California Judicial Council Forms ADOPT-216, Verification Of Compliance With Hague Adoption Convention Attachment.

§ 8902. Agency services

For intercountry adoptions that will be finalized in this state, the licensed adoption agency shall provide all of the following services:

(a) Assessment of the suitability of the applicant's home.

(b) Placement of the foreign-born child in an approved home.

(c) Postplacement supervision.

(d) Submission to the court of a report on the intercountry adoptive placement with a recommendation regarding the granting of the petition.

(e) Services to applicants seeking to adopt related children living in foreign countries. The Legislature recognizes that these children have an impelling need for adoptive placement with their relatives. *(Stats.1992, c. 162 (A.B.2650), § 10, operative Jan. 1, 1994.)*

Law Revision Commission Comments

Enactment [Revised Comment]

Section 8902 continues former Civil Code Section 226.20 without substantive change. See also Sections 8509 ("applicant" defined), 8527 ("intercountry adoption" defined), 8530 ("licensed adoption agency" defined). [23 Cal.L.Rev.Comm. Reports 1 (1993)].

Research References

Forms

California Transactions Forms--Family Law § 6:139, Overview Of Intercountry Adoption.

West's California Judicial Council Forms JV-505, Statement Regarding Parentage (Juvenile).

West's California Judicial Council Forms ADOPT-215, Adoption Order.

West's California Judicial Council Forms ADOPT-216, Verification Of Compliance With Hague Adoption Convention Attachment.

Treatises and Practice Aids

Witkin, California Summary 10th Parent and Child § 138, Powers and Duties Of Licensed Adoption Agencies.

§ 8903. Intercountry adoptions finalized in state; care, custody and control of child; Medi–Cal eligibility

(a) For each intercountry adoption finalized in this state, the licensed adoption agency shall assume all responsibilities for the child including care, custody, and control as if the child had been relinquished for adoption in this state from the time the child left the child's native country.

(b) Notwithstanding subdivision (a), if the child's native country requires and has given full guardianship to the prospective adoptive parents, the prospective adoptive parents shall assume all responsibilities for the child including care, custody, control, and financial support.

(c) If the licensed adoption agency or prospective adoptive parents fail to meet the responsibilities under subdivision (a) or (b) and the child becomes a dependent of the court pursuant to Section 300 of the Welfare and Institutions Code, the state shall assume responsibility for the cost of care for the child. When the child becomes a dependent of the court and if, for any reason, is ineligible for AFDC under Section 14005.1 of the Welfare and Institutions Code and loses Medi–Cal eligibility, the child shall be deemed eligible for Medi–Cal under Section 14005.4 of the Welfare and Institutions Code and the State Director of Health Services has authority to provide payment for the medical services to the child that are necessary to meet the child's needs. *(Stats. 1992, c. 162 (A.B.2650), § 10, operative Jan. 1, 1994.)*

Law Revision Commission Comments

Enactment [Revised Comment]

Section 8903 continues former Civil Code Section 226.21 without substantive change. See also Sections 8527 ("intercountry adoption" defined), 8530 ("licensed adoption agency" defined), 8542 ("prospective adoptive parent" defined). [23 Cal.L.Rev.Comm. Reports 1 (1993)].

Research References

Forms

California Transactions Forms--Family Law § 6:139, Overview Of Intercountry Adoption.
West's California Judicial Council Forms ADOPT-216, Verification Of Compliance With Hague Adoption Convention Attachment.

Treatises and Practice Aids

Witkin, California Summary 10th Parent and Child § 137, in General.
Witkin, California Summary 10th Parent and Child § 138, Powers and Duties Of Licensed Adoption Agencies.

§ 8904. Intercountry adoptions finalized in foreign country; agency services

For an intercountry adoption that will be finalized in a foreign country, the licensed adoption agency shall provide all of the following services:

(a) Assessment of the suitability of the applicant's home.

(b) Certification to the Immigration and Naturalization Service that this state's intercountry adoption requirements have been met.

(c) Readoption services as required by the Immigration and Naturalization Service. *(Stats.1992, c. 162 (A.B.2650), § 10, operative Jan. 1, 1994. Amended by Stats.1993, c. 219 (A.B.1500), § 202.)*

Law Revision Commission Comments

Enactment [Revised Comment]

Section 8904 continues former Civil Code Section 226.23 without substantive change. See also Sections 8527 ("intercountry adoption" defined), 8530 ("licensed adoption agency" defined). [23 Cal.L.Rev. Comm. Reports 1 (1993)].

Research References

Forms

California Transactions Forms--Family Law § 6:139, Overview Of Intercountry Adoption.
West's California Judicial Council Forms ADOPT-216, Verification Of Compliance With Hague Adoption Convention Attachment.

Treatises and Practice Aids

Witkin, California Summary 10th Parent and Child § 138, Powers and Duties Of Licensed Adoption Agencies.

§ 8905. Domestic and foreign adoption agencies; work with state agencies; written agreement required

Licensed adoption agencies may work only with domestic and foreign adoption agencies with whom they have written agreements that specify the responsibilities of each. The agreements may not violate any statute or regulation of the United States or of this state. *(Stats.1992, c. 162 (A.B.2650), § 10, operative Jan. 1, 1994.)*

Law Revision Commission Comments

Enactment [Revised Comment]

Section 8905 continues former Civil Code Section 226.25 without substantive change. See also Section 8530 ("licensed adoption agency" defined). [23 Cal.L.Rev.Comm. Reports 1 (1993)].

Research References

Forms

California Transactions Forms--Family Law § 6:140, Specifying Nation Of Origin Of Child.
West's California Judicial Council Forms ADOPT-200, Adoption Request.
West's California Judicial Council Forms ADOPT-216, Verification Of Compliance With Hague Adoption Convention Attachment.

Treatises and Practice Aids

Witkin, California Summary 10th Parent and Child § 138, Powers and Duties Of Licensed Adoption Agencies.

§ 8906. Financial responsibility for child; transfer or sharing between agency and prospective adoptive parents

Nothing in this chapter may be construed to prohibit the licensed adoption agency from entering into an agreement with the prospective adoptive parents to share or transfer financial responsibility for the child. *(Stats.1992, c. 162 (A.B.2650), § 10, operative Jan. 1, 1994.)*

Law Revision Commission Comments

Enactment [Revised Comment]

Section 8906 continues former Civil Code Section 226.27 without substantive change. See also Sections 8530 ("licensed adoption agency" defined), 8542 ("prospective adoptive parent" defined). [23 Cal.L.Rev.Comm. Reports 1 (1993)].

Research References

Treatises and Practice Aids

Witkin, California Summary 10th Parent and Child § 138, Powers and Duties Of Licensed Adoption Agencies.

§ 8907. Fees; program funding

The costs incurred by a licensed adoption agency pursuant to programs established by this chapter shall be funded by fees charged by the agency for services required by this chapter. The agency's fee schedule is required to be approved by the department initially and whenever it is altered. *(Stats.1992, c. 162 (A.B.2650), § 10, operative Jan. 1, 1994.)*

Law Revision Commission Comments

Enactment [Revised Comment]

Section 8907 continues former Civil Code Section 226.28 without substantive change. See also Sections 8518 ("department" defined), 8530 ("licensed adoption agency" defined). [23 Cal.L.Rev.Comm. Reports 1 (1993)].

Research References

Treatises and Practice Aids

Witkin, California Summary 10th Parent and Child § 138, Powers and Duties Of Licensed Adoption Agencies.

§ 8908. Applicants; fingerprints; criminal record; prohibited placement; fee; waiver

(a) A licensed adoption agency shall require each person filing an application for adoption to be fingerprinted and shall secure from an appropriate law enforcement agency any criminal record of that person to determine if the person has ever been convicted of a crime other than a minor traffic violation. The licensed adoption agency may also secure the person's full criminal record, if any, with the exception of any convictions for which relief has been granted pursuant to Section 1203.49 of the Penal Code. Any federal-level criminal offender record requests to the Department of Justice shall be submitted with fingerprint images and related information required by the Department of Justice for the purposes of obtaining information as to the existence and content of a record of an out-of-state or federal conviction or arrest of a person or information regarding any out-of-state or federal crimes or arrests for which the Department of Justice establishes that the person is free on bail, or on his or her own recognizance pending trial or appeal. The Department of Justice shall forward to the Federal Bureau of Investigation any requests for federal summary criminal history information received pursuant to this section. The Department of Justice shall review the information returned from the Federal Bureau of Investigation and shall compile and disseminate a fitness determination to the licensed adoption agency.

(b) Notwithstanding subdivision (c), the criminal record, if any, shall be taken into consideration when evaluating the prospective adoptive parent, and an assessment of the effects of any criminal history on the ability of the prospective adoptive parent to provide adequate and proper care and guidance to the child shall be included in the report to the court.

(c)(1) A licensed adoption agency shall not give final approval for an adoptive placement in any home in which the prospective adoptive parent, or any adult living in the prospective adoptive home, has a felony conviction for either of the following:

(A) Any felony conviction for child abuse or neglect, spousal abuse, crimes against a child, including child pornography, or for a crime involving violence, including rape, sexual assault, or homicide, but not including other physical assault and battery. For purposes of this subdivision, crimes involving violence means those violent crimes contained in clause (i) of subparagraph (A), and subparagraph (B), of paragraph (1) of subdivision (g) of Section 1522 of the Health and Safety Code.

(B) A felony conviction that occurred within the last five years for physical assault, battery, or a drug- or alcohol-related offense.

(2) This subdivision shall become operative on October 1, 2008, and shall remain operative only to the extent that compliance with its provisions is required by federal law as a condition of receiving funding under Title IV–E of the federal Social Security Act (42 U.S.C. Sec. 670 et seq.).

(d) Any fee charged by a law enforcement agency for fingerprinting or for checking or obtaining the criminal record of the applicant shall be paid by the applicant. The licensed adoption agency may defer, waive, or reduce the fee if its payment would cause economic hardship to the prospective adoptive parents detrimental to the welfare of the adopted child. *(Stats.1992, c. 162 (A.B.2650), § 10, operative Jan. 1, 1994. Amended by Stats.2008, c. 701 (A.B.2651), § 3, eff. Sept. 30, 2008; Stats.2014, c. 708 (A.B.1585), § 3, eff. Jan. 1, 2015; Stats.2015, c. 303 (A.B.731), § 153, eff. Jan. 1, 2016; Stats.2016, c. 86 (S.B.1171), § 132, eff. Jan. 1, 2017.)*

Law Revision Commission Comments

Enactment [Revised Comment]

Section 8908 continues former Civil Code Section 226.30 without substantive change. See also Section 8530 ("licensed adoption agency" defined).

For comparable provisions, see Sections 8712 (investigation in agency adoption, 8811 (investigation in independent adoption). For a related provision, see Section 9001(a) (investigation in stepparent adoption). [23 Cal.L.Rev.Comm. Reports 1 (1993)].

Research References

Forms

California Transactions Forms--Family Law § 6:139, Overview Of Intercountry Adoption.

West's California Judicial Council Forms ADOPT-200, Adoption Request.

West's California Judicial Council Forms ADOPT-216, Verification Of Compliance With Hague Adoption Convention Attachment.

Treatises and Practice Aids

Witkin, California Summary 10th Parent and Child § 94, Investigation Of Prospective Adoptive Parents.

Witkin, California Summary 10th Parent and Child § 139, Investigation and Report.

§ 8909. Medical report on child and biological parents; contents; blood sample

(a) An agency may not place a child for adoption unless a written report on the child's medical background and, if available, the medical background of the child's biological parents so far as ascertainable, has been submitted to the prospective adoptive parents and they have acknowledged in writing the receipt of the report.

(b) The report on the child's background shall contain all known diagnostic information, including current medical reports on the child, psychological evaluations, and scholastic information, as well as all known information regarding the child's developmental history and family life.

(c)(1) The biological parents may provide a blood sample at a clinic or hospital approved by the State Department of Health Services. The biological parents' failure to provide a blood sample shall not affect the adoption of the child.

(2) The blood sample shall be stored at a laboratory under contract with the State Department of Health Services for a period of 30 years following the adoption of the child.

(3) The purpose of the stored sample of blood is to provide a blood sample from which DNA testing can be done at a later date after entry of the order of adoption at the request of the adoptive parents or the adopted child. The cost of drawing and storing the blood samples shall be paid for by a separate fee in addition to any fee required under Section 8907. The amount of this additional fee shall be based on the cost of drawing and storing the blood samples but at no time shall the additional fee be more than one hundred dollars ($100).

(d)(1) The blood sample shall be stored and released in such a manner as to not identify any party to the adoption.

(2) Any results of the DNA testing shall be stored and released in such a manner as to not identify any party to the adoption. *(Stats.1992, c. 162 (A.B.2650), § 10, operative Jan. 1, 1994. Amended by Stats.1996, c. 1053 (A.B.3241), § 3.)*

Law Revision Commission Comments

Enactment [Revised Comment]

Section 8909 continues former Civil Code Section 226.35(a) without substantive change. See also Sections 8518 ("department" defined), 8542 ("prospective adoptive parent" defined), 8608 (regulations concerning form and content of medical reports), 9202 (regulations concerning availability of medical reports).

For a comparable provision, see Section 8706 (medical report in agency adoption). For a related provision, see Section 8817 (medical report in independent adoption). [23 Cal.L.Rev.Comm. Reports 1 (1993)].

Research References

Forms

California Transactions Forms--Family Law § 6:141, Required Medical Report on Child and Birth Parents.

Treatises and Practice Aids

Witkin, California Summary 10th Parent and Child § 93, Medical Report on Child and Birth Parents.

Witkin, California Summary 10th Parent and Child § 149, Confidentiality Of Records.

§ 8910. Removal of child from county; concealment of child; permission for removal; objections; hearing; notice; application of section

(a) In no event may a child who has been placed for adoption be removed from the county in which the child was placed, by any person who has not petitioned to adopt the child, without first obtaining the written consent of the licensed adoption agency responsible for the child.

(b) During the pendency of an adoption proceeding:

(1) The child proposed to be adopted may not be concealed within the county in which the adoption proceeding is pending.

(2) The child may not be removed from the county in which the adoption proceeding is pending unless the petitioners or other interested persons first obtain permission for the removal from the court, after giving advance written notice of intent to obtain the court's permission to the licensed adoption agency responsible for the child. Upon proof of giving notice, permission may be granted by the court if, within a period of 15 days after the date of giving notice, no objections are filed with the court by the licensed adoption agency responsible for the child. If the licensed adoption agency files objections within the 15-day period, upon the request of the petitioners the court shall immediately set the matter for hearing and give to the objector, the petitioners, and the party or parties requesting permission for the removal reasonable notice of the hearing by certified mail, return receipt requested, to the address of each as shown in the records of the adoption proceeding. Upon a finding that the objections are without good cause, the court may grant the requested permission for removal of the child, subject to any limitations that appear to be in the child's best interest.

(c) This section does not apply in any of the following situations:

(1) Where the child is absent for a period of not more than 30 days from the county in which the adoption proceeding is pending, unless a notice of recommendation of denial of petition has been personally served on the petitioners or the court has issued an order prohibiting the removal of the child from the county pending consideration of any of the following:

(A) The suitability of the petitioners.

(B) The care provided the child.

(C) The availability of the legally required agency consents to the adoption.

(2) Where the child has been returned to and remains in the custody and control of the child's birth parent or parents.

(3) Where written consent for the removal of the child is obtained from the licensed adoption agency responsible for the child.

(d) A violation of this section is a violation of Section 280 of the Penal Code.

(e) Neither this section nor Section 280 of the Penal Code may be construed to render lawful any act that is unlawful under any other applicable law. *(Stats.1992, c. 162 (A.B. 2650), § 10, operative Jan. 1, 1994.)*

Law Revision Commission Comments

Enactment [Revised Comment]

Section 8910 continues former Civil Code Section 226.40 without substantive change. The prohibition of removal "for any period of time" has been omitted as surplus. The two limitations on the exception provided in subdivision (c)(1) have been rephrased for clarity. See also Sections 8512 ("birth parent" defined), 8530 ("licensed adoption agency" defined).

For comparable provisions, see Sections 8713 (removal and concealment in agency adoption, 8803 (removal and concealment in independent adoption). [23 Cal.L.Rev.Comm. Reports 1 (1993)].

Research References

Forms

California Transactions Forms--Family Law § 6:2, Governing Law.

West's California Code Forms, Family § 8900, Comment Overview--Intercountry Adoptions.

West's California Code Forms, Family § 8910 Form 2, Notice Of Filing Petition for Permission to Remove Child from County.

West's California Judicial Council Forms ADOPT-216, Verification Of Compliance With Hague Adoption Convention Attachment.

Treatises and Practice Aids

Witkin, California Summary 10th Parent and Child § 81, Removal or Concealment Of Child Pending Adoption.

§ 8911. Conditions of placement; filing of petition

As a condition of placement, the prospective adoptive parents shall file a petition to adopt the child under Section 8912 within 30 days of placement. *(Stats.1992, c. 162 (A.B.2650), § 10, operative Jan. 1, 1994.)*

Law Revision Commission Comments

Enactment [Revised Comment]

Section 8911 continues former Civil Code Section 226.50 without substantive change. See also Section 8542 ("prospective adoptive parent" defined). [23 Cal.L.Rev.Comm. Reports 1 (1993)].

Research References

Forms

West's California Judicial Council Forms ADOPT-216, Verification Of Compliance With Hague Adoption Convention Attachment.

Treatises and Practice Aids

Witkin, California Summary 10th Parent and Child § 140, Petition, Hearing, and Order.

§ 8912. Petition for adoption; notification of department; contents; guardianship petitions; order of adoption

(a) An international adoption or readoption request may be filed by a resident of this state in a county authorized by Section 8609.5. The court clerk shall immediately notify the department at Sacramento in writing of the pendency of the proceeding and of any subsequent action taken.

(b) The caption of the adoption petition shall contain the names of the petitioners, but not the child's name. The petition shall state the child's sex and date of birth. The name the child had before adoption shall appear in the joinder signed by the licensed adoption agency.

(c) If the child is the subject of a guardianship petition, the adoption petition shall so state and shall include the caption and docket number or have attached a copy of the letters of the guardianship or temporary guardianship. The petitioners shall notify the court of any petition for guardianship or temporary guardianship filed after the adoption petition. The guardianship proceeding shall be consolidated with the adoption proceeding.

(d) The order of adoption shall contain the child's adopted name, but not the name the child had before adoption.

(e) If the petitioner has entered into a postadoption contact agreement with the birth parent as set forth in Section 8616.5, the agreement, signed by the participating parties, shall be attached to and filed with the petition for adoption. *(Stats.1992, c. 162 (A.B.2650), § 10, operative Jan. 1, 1994. Amended by Stats.2004, c. 858 (S.B.1357), § 6; Stats.2012, c. 638 (A.B.1757), § 12.)*

Law Revision Commission Comments

Enactment [Revised Comment]

Section 8912 continues former Civil Code Section 226.52 without substantive change. In subdivision (a), the reference to an "action" has been changed to "proceeding" for consistency with other sections. See also Section 8518 ("department" defined).

For comparable provisions, see Sections 8714 (petition for agency adoption), 8802 (petition for independent adoption), 9000 (petition for stepparent adoption). [23 Cal.L.Rev.Comm. Reports 1 (1993)].

Research References

Forms

California Transactions Forms--Family Law § 6:139, Overview Of Intercountry Adoption.

West's California Judicial Council Forms JV-505, Statement Regarding Parentage (Juvenile).

West's California Judicial Council Forms ADOPT-200, Adoption Request.

West's California Judicial Council Forms ADOPT-215, Adoption Order.

West's California Judicial Council Forms ADOPT-216, Verification Of Compliance With Hague Adoption Convention Attachment.

Treatises and Practice Aids

Witkin, California Summary 10th Parent and Child § 71, Special Statutory Proceeding.

Witkin, California Summary 10th Parent and Child § 90, Effect Of Guardianship Proceeding.

Witkin, California Summary 10th Parent and Child § 95, Petition and Hearing.

Witkin, California Summary 10th Parent and Child § 96, Agreement and Order.

Witkin, California Summary 10th Parent and Child § 104, in General.

Witkin, California Summary 10th Parent and Child § 137, in General.

Witkin, California Summary 10th Parent and Child § 140, Petition, Hearing, and Order.

§ 8913. Adoptive parent and child; appearance before court

The prospective adoptive parents and the child proposed to be adopted shall appear before the court pursuant to Sections 8612 and 8613. *(Stats.1992, c. 162 (A.B.2650), § 10, operative Jan. 1, 1994.)*

Law Revision Commission Comments

Enactment [Revised Comment]

Section 8913 continues former Civil Code Sections 221.62 and 226.55 without substantive change. The reference to "prospective adoptive parents" has been substituted for "person or persons desiring to adopt a child." This is not a substantive change. See Section 8542 ("prospective adoptive parent" defined).

For comparable provisions, see Sections 8718 (appearance in agency adoption), 8823 (appearance in independent adoption), 9007 (appearance in stepparent adoption). [23 Cal.L.Rev.Comm. Reports 1 (1993)].

Research References

Forms

California Transactions Forms--Family Law § 6:139, Overview Of Intercountry Adoption.

Treatises and Practice Aids

Witkin, California Summary 10th Parent and Child § 95, Petition and Hearing.

Witkin, California Summary 10th Parent and Child § 140, Petition, Hearing, and Order.

§ 8914. Agency as party to petition; report of facts; submission to court

If the licensed adoption agency is a party to or joins in the adoption petition, it shall submit a full report of the facts of the case to the court. The department may also submit a report. *(Stats.1992, c. 162 (A.B.2650), § 10, operative Jan. 1, 1994.)*

Law Revision Commission Comments

Enactment [Revised Comment]

Section 8914 continues former Civil Code Section 226.57 without substantive change. See also Sections 8518 ("department" defined), 8530 ("licensed adoption agency" defined).

For related provisions, see Sections 8715 (report of department or agency in agency adoption), 8807 (report of department or agency in independent adoption), 9001 (report of county welfare department or probation officer in stepparent adoption). [23 Cal.L.Rev.Comm. Reports 1 (1993)].

Research References

Forms

California Transactions Forms--Family Law § 6:13, Appearance in Person or by Counsel.

California Transactions Forms--Family Law § 6:139, Overview Of Intercountry Adoption.

Treatises and Practice Aids

Witkin, California Summary 10th Parent and Child § 95, Petition and Hearing.

Witkin, California Summary 10th Parent and Child § 139, Investigation and Report.

§ 8915. Report or findings of agency; copy to attorney or petitioner

When any report or findings are submitted to the court by a licensed adoption agency, a copy of the report or findings, whether favorable or unfavorable, shall be given to the petitioner's attorney in the proceeding, if the petitioner has an attorney of record, or to the petitioner. *(Stats.1992, c. 162 (A.B.2650), § 10, operative Jan. 1, 1994.)*

Law Revision Commission Comments

Enactment [Revised Comment]

Section 8915 continues former Civil Code Section 226.59 without change. See also Section 8530 ("licensed adoption agency" defined).

For comparable provisions, see Sections 8717 (copy of report in agency adoption), 8821 (copy of report in independent adoption). [23 Cal.L.Rev.Comm. Reports 1 (1993)].

Research References

Treatises and Practice Aids

Witkin, California Summary 10th Parent and Child § 139, Investigation and Report.

§ 8916. Withdrawal of petition; dismissal of proceedings; notification of department; agency report; recommendations; jurisdiction

(a) If the petitioners move to withdraw the adoption petition or to dismiss the proceeding, the court clerk shall immediately notify the department at Sacramento of the action. The licensed adoption agency shall file a full report with the court recommending a suitable plan for the child in every case where the petitioners desire to withdraw the adoption petition or where the licensed adoption agency recommends that the adoption petition be denied and shall appear before the court for the purpose of representing the child.

(b) Notwithstanding the petitioners' withdrawal or dismissal, the court may retain jurisdiction over the child for the purpose of making any order for the child's custody that the court deems to be in the child's best interest. *(Stats.1992, c. 162 (A.B.2650), § 10, operative Jan. 1, 1994.)*

Law Revision Commission Comments

Enactment [Revised Comment]

Section 8916 continues former Civil Code Section 226.60 without substantive change. In subdivision (a), the former reference to the "clerk of the court in which the proceeding is pending" has been shortened to the "court clerk" to eliminate surplus language. The reference to "orders" has been omitted as surplus. See Section 10 (singular includes plural). See also Sections 8518 ("department" defined), 8530 ("licensed adoption agency" defined).

For related provisions, see Sections 8719 (notice of withdrawal or dismissal in agency adoption), 8804 (notice of withdrawal or dismissal in independent adoption), 9006 (notice of withdrawal or dismissal in stepparent adoption). [23 Cal.L.Rev.Comm. Reports 1 (1993)].

Research References

Treatises and Practice Aids

Witkin, California Summary 10th Parent and Child § 140, Petition, Hearing, and Order.

§ 8917. Denial or withdrawal of petition; referral to court for review

(a) If the licensed adoption agency finds that the home of the petitioners is not suitable for the child or that the required agency consents are not available and the agency recommends that the petition be denied, or if the petitioners desire to withdraw the petition and the agency recommends that the petition be denied, the clerk upon receipt of the report of the licensed adoption agency shall immediately refer it to the court for review.

(b) Upon receipt of the report, the court shall set a date for a hearing of the petition and shall give reasonable notice of the hearing to the licensed adoption agency and the petitioners by certified mail, return receipt requested, to the address of each as shown in the proceeding.

(c) The licensed adoption agency shall appear to represent the child. *(Stats.1992, c. 162 (A.B.2650), § 10, operative Jan. 1, 1994.)*

Law Revision Commission Comments

Enactment [Revised Comment]

Section 8917 continues former Civil Code Section 226.64 without substantive change. The reference to the "county" clerk has been omitted. This is not a substantive change. The reference to the "superior" court has been omitted as surplus. See Section 200 (jurisdiction in superior court). See also Section 8530 ("licensed adoption agency" defined).

For comparable provisions, see Sections 8720 (unfavorable recommendation in agency adoption), 8822 (unfavorable recommendation in independent adoption). [23 Cal.L.Rev.Comm. Reports 1 (1993)].

Research References

Treatises and Practice Aids

Witkin, California Summary 10th Parent and Child § 85, Recommendation Of Department or Agency.

Witkin, California Summary 10th Parent and Child § 140, Petition, Hearing, and Order.

§ 8918. Hearing; recommendation of removal of child sustained; transfer of child to care of agency

At the hearing, if the court sustains the recommendation that the child be removed from the home of the petitioners because the licensed adoption agency has recommended denial or the petitioners desire to withdraw the petition or the court dismisses the petition and does not return the child to the child's parents, the court shall commit the child to the care of the licensed adoption agency for the agency to arrange adoptive placement or to make a suitable plan. *(Stats.1992, c. 162 (A.B.2650), § 10, operative Jan. 1, 1994.)*

Law Revision Commission Comments

Enactment [Revised Comment]

Section 8918 continues former Civil Code Section 226.66 without substantive change. See also Section 8530 ("licensed adoption agency" defined). [23 Cal.L.Rev.Comm. Reports 1 (1993)].

Research References

Treatises and Practice Aids

Witkin, California Summary 10th Parent and Child § 140, Petition, Hearing, and Order.

§ 8919. Adoptions finalized in foreign country; readoption of child in state; state-issued birth certificate

(a) Each state resident who adopts a child through an intercountry adoption that is finalized in a foreign country shall readopt the child in this state if it is required by the Department of Homeland Security. Except as provided in subdivision (c), the readoption shall include, but is not limited to, at least one postplacement in-home visit, the filing of the adoption petition, the intercountry adoption court report, accounting reports, the home study report, and the final adoption order. If the adoptive parents have already completed a home study as part of their adoption process, a copy of that study shall be submitted in lieu of a second home study. No readoption order shall be granted unless the court receives a copy of the home study report previously completed for the international finalized adoption by an adoption agency authorized to provide intercountry adoption services pursuant to Section 8900. The court shall consider the postplacement visit or visits and the previously completed home study when deciding whether to grant or deny the petition for readoption.

(b) Each state resident who adopts a child through an intercountry adoption that is finalized in a foreign country may readopt the child in this state. Except as provided in subdivision (c), the readoption shall meet the standards described in subdivision (a).

(c)(1) A state resident who adopts a child through an intercountry adoption that is finalized in a foreign country with adoption standards that meet or exceed those of this state, as certified by the State Department of Social Services, may readopt the child in this state according to this subdivision. The readoption shall include one postplacement in-home visit and the final adoption order.

(2) The petition to readopt may be granted if all of the following apply:

(A) The adoption was finalized in accordance with the laws of the foreign country.

(B) The resident has filed with the petition a copy of both of the following:

(i) The decree, order, or certificate of adoption that evidences finalization of the adoption in the foreign country.

(ii) The child's birth certificate and visa.

(C) A certified translation is included of all documents described in this paragraph that are not in English.

(3) If the court denies a petition for readoption, the court shall summarize its reasons for the denial on the record.

(d) The State Department of Social Services shall certify whether the adoption standards in the following countries meet or exceed those of this state:

(1) China

(2) Guatemala

(3) Kazakhstan

(4) Russia

(5) South Korea

(e) In addition to the requirement or option of the readoption process set forth in this section, each state resident who adopts a child through an intercountry adoption which is finalized in a foreign country may obtain a birth certificate in the State of California in accordance with the provisions of Section 102635 or 103450 of the Health and Safety Code. *(Added by Stats.1993, c. 219 (A.B.1500), § 203. Amended by Stats.2001, c. 353 (A.B.538), § 2; Stats.2006, c. 809 (S.B.1393), § 1; Stats.2007, c. 130 (A.B.299), § 92.)*

Law Revision Commission Comments

Enactment [Revised Comment]

Section 8919 continues former Civil Code Section 226.69 without substantive change. The references to a "decree" in the former section have been replaced by "order" for consistency with other sections. See, e.g., Section 8912 (adoption order). [23 Cal.L.Rev. Comm. Reports 1 (1993)].

Research References

Forms

California Transactions Forms--Family Law § 6:139, Overview Of Intercountry Adoption.

California Transactions Forms--Family Law § 6:142, Readoption Of Child Adopted in Foreign Country.

West's California Code Forms, Family § 7840, Comment Overview--Freedom from Parental Control.

West's California Judicial Council Forms ADOPT-200, Adoption Request.

West's California Judicial Council Forms ADOPT-216, Verification Of Compliance With Hague Adoption Convention Attachment.

Treatises and Practice Aids

Witkin, California Summary 10th Parent and Child § 97, Certificates Of Birth and Adoption.

Witkin, California Summary 10th Parent and Child § 137, in General.

§ 8920. Separation from sibling group through readoption; agreements for visitation; enforcement; best interests of child

(a) A child who was adopted as part of a sibling group and who has been separated from his or her sibling or siblings through readoption by a resident of this state may petition the court to enforce any agreement for visitation to which the separate adoptive families of the siblings subscribed prior to the child's readoption or to order visitation if no such agreement exists. The court may order that the agreement be enforced or grant visitation rights upon a finding that visitation is in the best interest of the child.

(b) In making a finding that enforcement of an existing agreement or the granting of visitation rights is in the best interest of the child under subdivision (a), the court shall take into consideration the nature and extent of the child's sibling relationship, including, but not limited to, whether the child was raised with a sibling in the same home, whether the child shares significant common experiences or has close and strong bonds with a sibling, and whether ongoing contact with a sibling is in the child's best interest, including the child's long-term interest.

(c) As used in this section, "sibling" means full-siblings or half-siblings.

(d) As used in this section, "readoption" means the process by which a child who belongs to a foreign-born sibling group that was adopted together through an intercountry adoption is subsequently adopted by a different set of adoptive parents who are residents of the state. *(Added by Stats.2003, c. 19 (S.B.169), § 1.)*

Research References

Treatises and Practice Aids

Witkin, California Summary 10th Parent and Child § 137, in General.

§ 8921. Services of adoption facilitator

An adoption facilitator shall not offer, provide, or facilitate any adoption service, as described in this chapter, in connection with a convention adoption unless it is registered and posts a bond pursuant to Section 8632.5, and is approved by the accrediting entity pursuant to Subpart F (commencing with Section 96.29) of Part 96 of Title 22 of the Code of Federal Regulations. *(Added by Stats.2007, c. 583 (S.B.703), § 7.)*

Research References

Treatises and Practice Aids

Witkin, California Summary 10th Parent and Child § 137, in General.

§ 8923. Complaint procedures

(a) A complaint against an accredited agency or approved person in connection with a convention adoption shall be filed according to the procedures set forth in Subpart J (commencing with Section 96.68) of Part 96 of Title 22 of the Code of Federal Regulations.

(b) Each private full-service adoption agency and noncustodial adoption agency licensed by the department under this chapter shall notify the department of any complaint filed against it pursuant to Subpart J (commencing with Section 96.68) of Part 96 of Title 22 of the Code of Federal Regulations.

(c) The department may revoke the license of any agency that fails to comply with the provisions of this chapter and Part 96 of Title 22 of the Code of Federal Regulations. *(Added by Stats.2007, c. 583 (S.B.703), § 8.)*

Research References

Treatises and Practice Aids

Witkin, California Summary 10th Parent and Child § 138, Powers and Duties Of Licensed Adoption Agencies.

§ 8924. Emigration of child to convention country

(a) For cases in which a child is emigrating from California to a convention country, an accredited agency or approved person providing any adoption service described in this chapter, shall perform all of the following:

(1) A background study on the child prepared in accordance with all requirements set forth in subdivisions (a) and (b) of Section 96.53 of Title 22 of the Code of Federal Regulations, Section 8706, and applicable state law.

(2) Consents are obtained in accordance with subdivision (c) of Section 96.53 of Title 22 of the Code of Federal Regulations and applicable state law.

(3) If the child is 12 years of age or older, the agency or person has given due consideration to the child's wishes or opinions before determining that an intercountry adoption is in the child's best interests and in accordance with applicable state law.

(4) Transmission to the United States Department of State or other competent authority, or accredited bodies of the convention country, of the child background study, proof that the necessary consents have been obtained, and the reasons for the determination that the placement is in the child's best interests.

(b) The accredited agency shall comply with all placement standards set forth in Section 96.54 of Title 22 of the Code of Federal Regulations for children emigrating from California to a convention country.

(c) The accredited agency shall keep the central authority of the convention country and the Secretary informed as necessary about the adoption process and the measures taken to complete it for children emigrating from California to a convention country, in accordance with all communication and coordination functions set forth in Section 96.55 of Title 22 of the Code of Federal Regulations.

(d) For all convention and nonconvention adoption cases involving children emigrating from California to a convention country, the agency, person, or public domestic authority providing adoption services shall report information to the Secretary in accordance with Part 99 of Title 22 of the Code of Federal Regulations. *(Added by Stats.2007, c. 583 (S.B. 703), § 9.)*

Research References

Forms

West's California Judicial Council Forms ADOPT-200, Adoption Request.

West's California Judicial Council Forms ADOPT-216, Verification Of Compliance With Hague Adoption Convention Attachment.

Treatises and Practice Aids

Witkin, California Summary 10th Parent and Child § 138, Powers and Duties Of Licensed Adoption Agencies.

§ 8925. Hague adoption certificate or custody declaration

A Hague adoption certificate or, in outgoing cases, a Hague custody declaration, obtained pursuant to Part 97 of Title 22 of the Code of Federal Regulations shall be recognized as a final valid adoption for purposes of all state and local laws. *(Added by Stats.2007, c. 583 (S.B.703), § 10.)*

Research References

Forms

West's California Judicial Council Forms ADOPT-200, Adoption Request.

West's California Judicial Council Forms ADOPT-216, Verification Of Compliance With Hague Adoption Convention Attachment.

Treatises and Practice Aids

Witkin, California Summary 10th Parent and Child § 140, Petition, Hearing, and Order.

CHAPTER 5. STEPPARENT ADOPTIONS

§ 9000. Petition for adoption; caption; contents; guardianship petition; order of adoption

(a) A stepparent desiring to adopt a child of the stepparent's spouse may for that purpose file a petition in the county in which the petitioner resides.

(b) A domestic partner, as defined in Section 297, desiring to adopt a child of his or her domestic partner may for that purpose file a petition in the county in which the petitioner resides.

(c) The caption of the adoption petition shall contain the names of the petitioners, but not the child's name. The petition shall state the child's sex and date of birth and the name the child had before adoption.

(d) If the child is the subject of a guardianship petition, the adoption petition shall so state and shall include the caption and docket number or have attached a copy of the letters of the guardianship or temporary guardianship. The petitioners shall notify the court of any petition for guardianship or temporary guardianship filed after the adoption petition. The guardianship proceeding shall be consolidated with the adoption proceeding.

(e) The order of adoption shall contain the child's adopted name, but not the name the child had before adoption.

(f) If the petitioner has entered into a postadoption contact agreement with the birth parent as set forth in Section 8616.5, the agreement, signed by the participating parties, shall be attached to and filed with the petition for adoption.

(g) For the purposes of this chapter, stepparent adoption includes adoption by a domestic partner, as defined in Section 297. *(Stats.1992, c. 162 (A.B.2650), § 10, operative Jan. 1, 1994. Amended by Stats.2001, c. 893 (A.B.25), § 5; Stats.2004, c. 858 (S.B.1357), § 7.)*

Law Revision Commission Comments

Enactment [Revised Comment]

Section 9000 continues former Civil Code Section 227.10 without substantive change. The reference to the "superior" court has been omitted as surplus. See Section 200 (jurisdiction in superior court).

For comparable provisions, see Sections 8714 (petition for agency adoption), 8802 (petition for independent adoption), 8912 (petition for intercountry adoption). [23 Cal.L.Rev.Comm. Reports 1 (1993)].

Commentary

Appellate Defenders, Inc. v. Cheri S., 35 Cal.App.4th 1819, 42 Cal.Rptr.2d 195 (1995), holds that an indigent parent has a right to appointed counsel in any proceeding that terminates his or her parental rights (cf. Section 7895), including proceedings invoking Family Code Sections 7822, 8604, and 9000. Relying on *In re Jacqueline H., 21 Cal.3d 170, 577 P.2d 683, 145 Cal.Rptr. 548 (1978)*, *Appellate Defenders* reasons that it is immaterial whether the proceeding is initiated by private parties or the state; the magnitude of the loss is identical. But see *In re Curtis S., 25 Cal.App.4th 687, 30 Cal.Rptr.2d 739 (1994), review denied 8/29/94*, (appointment of appellate counsel required only when parental rights of indigent parent have been terminated in a dependency proceeding).

In *Sharon S. v. Superior Court, 31 Cal.4th 417, 73 P.3d 554, 2 Cal.Rptr.3d 699 (2003)*, the California Supreme Court held that termination of a birth parent's rights is not mandatory in every adoption and that second-parent adoptions are valid under California laws regulating independent adoption. The court reasoned that relief from parental duties under § 8617 may be waived by the parties to an adoption.

The opportunity created by subsections (b) and (f) will largely involve same-sex-partner adoptions, because domestic partnership is limited to same-sex couples and couples in which one person is over the age of 62 and meets the eligibility criteria or social security old-age benefits. See Commentary to Family Code section 299.5

Research References

Forms

California Transactions Forms--Family Law § 6:108, Petition for Stepparent Adoption.

California Transactions Forms--Family Law § 6:112, Form Drafting Considerations.

West's California Code Forms, Family § 9000, Comment Overview--Stepparent Adoptions.

West's California Judicial Council Forms JV-505, Statement Regarding Parentage (Juvenile).

West's California Judicial Council Forms ADOPT-200, Adoption Request.

West's California Judicial Council Forms ADOPT-215, Adoption Order.

Treatises and Practice Aids

Witkin, California Summary 10th Husband and Wife § 33, Other Rights.

Witkin, California Summary 10th Parent and Child § 60, Action to Determine Mother and Child Relationship.

Witkin, California Summary 10th Parent and Child § 70, Types Of Adoption.

Witkin, California Summary 10th Parent and Child § 71, Special Statutory Proceeding.

Witkin, California Summary 10th Parent and Child § 72, Statutory Framework.
Witkin, California Summary 10th Parent and Child § 90, Effect Of Guardianship Proceeding.
Witkin, California Summary 10th Parent and Child § 95, Petition and Hearing.
Witkin, California Summary 10th Parent and Child § 96, Agreement and Order.
Witkin, California Summary 10th Parent and Child § 104, in General.
Witkin, California Summary 10th Parent and Child § 141, in General.
Witkin, California Summary 10th Parent and Child § 144, Procedure.
Witkin, California Summary 10th Parent and Child § 330, Who May Bring Action.
Witkin, California Summary 10th Parent and Child § 354, Statutory Right.

§ 9000.5. Procedures

(a) Stepparent adoptions where one of the spouses or partners gave birth to the child during the marriage or domestic partnership, including a registered domestic partnership or civil union from another jurisdiction, shall follow the procedure provided by this section. Unless otherwise provided in this section, the procedures for stepparent adoptions apply.

(b) The following are not required in stepparent adoptions under this section unless otherwise ordered by the court for good cause:

(1) A home investigation pursuant to Section 9001 or a home study.

(2) Costs incurred pursuant to Section 9002.

(3) A hearing pursuant to Section 9007.

(c) For stepparent adoptions filed under this section, the following shall be filed with the petition for adoption:

(1) A copy of the parties' marriage certificate, registered domestic partner certificate, or civil union from another jurisdiction.

(2) A copy of the child's birth certificate.

(3) Declarations by the parent who gave birth and the spouse or partner who is adopting explaining the circumstances of the child's conception in detail sufficient to identify whether there may be other persons with a claim to parentage of the child who is required to be provided notice of, or who must consent to, the adoption.

(d) The court may order a hearing to ascertain whether there are additional persons who must be provided notice of, or who must consent to, the adoption if it appears from the face of the pleadings and the evidence that proper notice or consent have not been provided.

(e) The court shall grant the stepparent adoption under this section upon finding both of the following:

(1) That the parent who gave birth and the spouse or partner who is adopting were married or in a domestic partnership, including a registered domestic partnership or civil union from another jurisdiction, at the time of the child's birth.

(2) Any other person with a claim to parentage of the child who is required to be provided notice of, or who must consent to, the adoption has been noticed or provided consent to the adoption. *(Added by Stats.2014, c. 636 (A.B.2344), § 3, eff. Jan. 1, 2015.)*

Research References

Forms

West's California Judicial Council Forms ADOPT-200, Adoption Request.
West's California Judicial Council Forms ADOPT-205, Declaration Confirming Parentage in Stepparent Adoption.
West's California Judicial Council Forms ADOPT-210, Adoption Agreement.
West's California Judicial Council Forms ADOPT-215, Adoption Order.

Treatises and Practice Aids

Witkin, California Summary 10th Parent and Child § 95, Petition and Hearing.
Witkin, California Summary 10th Parent and Child § 144, Procedure.
Witkin, California Summary 10th Parent and Child § 144A, (New) Procedure Where Child Born to Spouse or Partner During Marriage or Domestic Partnership.

§ 9001. Review of investigation and written report

(a) Except as provided in Section 9000.5, before granting or denying a stepparent adoption request, the court shall review and consider a written investigative report. The report in a stepparent adoption case shall not require a home study unless so ordered by the court upon request of an investigator or interested person, or on the court's own motion. "Home study" as used in this section means a physical investigation of the premises where the child is residing.

(b) At the time of filing the adoption request, the petitioner shall inform the court in writing if the petitioner is electing to have the investigation and written report completed by a licensed clinical social worker, a licensed marriage and family therapist, or a private licensed adoption agency, in which cases the petitioner shall not be required to pay any investigation fee pursuant to Section 9002 at the time of filing, but shall pay these fees directly to the investigator. Absent that notification, the court may, at the time of filing, collect an investigation fee pursuant to Section 9002, and may assign one of the following to complete the investigation: a probation officer, a qualified court investigator, or the county welfare department, if so authorized by the board of supervisors of the county where the action is pending.

(c) If a private licensed adoption agency conducts the investigation, it shall assign the investigation to a licensed clinical social worker or licensed marriage and family therapist associated with the agency. Any grievance regarding the investigation shall be directed to the licensing authority of the clinical social worker or marriage and family therapist, as applicable.

(d) Nothing in this section shall be construed to require the State Department of Social Services to issue regulations for stepparent adoptions. *(Stats.1992, c. 162 (A.B.2650), § 10, operative Jan. 1, 1994. Amended by Stats.1993, c. 219 (A.B.1500), § 204; Stats.2001, c. 353 (A.B.538), § 3; Stats. 2010, c. 588 (A.B.2020), § 8; Stats.2014, c. 636 (A.B.2344),*

§ 4, eff. Jan. 1, 2015; Stats.2016, c. 702 (A.B.2872), § 1, eff. Jan. 1, 2017.)

Law Revision Commission Comments

Enactment [Revised Comment]

Section 9001 continues former Civil Code Section 227.20 without substantive change. In subdivision (a), the reference to an "action" has been changed to "proceeding" for consistency with other sections. This is not a substantive change. See Section 110 ("proceeding" defined). See also Sections 8543 ("qualified court investigator" defined), 8548 ("stepparent adoption" defined).

For related provisions, see Sections 8712 (investigation in agency adoption), 8811 (investigation in independent adoption), 8908 (investigation in intercountry adoption). For other related provisions, see Sections 8715 (report of department or agency in agency adoption), 8807 (report of department or agency in independent adoption), 8914 (report of department or agency in intercountry adoption). [23 Cal.L.Rev.Comm. Reports 1 (1993)].

Research References

Forms

California Transactions Forms--Family Law § 6:13, Appearance in Person or by Counsel.
California Transactions Forms--Family Law § 6:104, Nature and Purpose Of Stepparent Adoption.
California Transactions Forms--Family Law § 6:109, Investigation Of Stepparent Adoption.
West's California Code Forms, Family § 9000, Comment Overview--Stepparent Adoptions.

Treatises and Practice Aids

Witkin, California Summary 10th Parent and Child § 62, Inquiry to Identify Natural Father.
Witkin, California Summary 10th Parent and Child § 95, Petition and Hearing.
Witkin, California Summary 10th Parent and Child § 144, Procedure.
Witkin, California Summary 10th Parent and Child § 144A, (New) Procedure Where Child Born to Spouse or Partner During Marriage or Domestic Partnership.

§ 9002. Costs

Except as provided in Section 9000.5, in a stepparent adoption, the prospective adoptive parent is liable for all reasonable costs incurred in connection with the stepparent adoption, including, but not limited to, costs incurred for the investigation required by Section 9001, up to a maximum of seven hundred dollars ($700). The court, probation officer, qualified court investigator, or county welfare department may defer, waive, or reduce the fee if its payment would cause economic hardship to the prospective adoptive parent detrimental to the welfare of the adopted child. *(Stats.1992, c. 162 (A.B.2650), § 10, operative Jan. 1, 1994. Amended by Stats.1993, c. 219 (A.B.1500), § 205; Stats.1993, c. 494 (A.B.1430), § 1; Stats.2001, c. 893 (A.B.25), § 6; Stats.2014, c. 636 (A.B.2344), § 5, eff. Jan. 1, 2015.)*

Law Revision Commission Comments

Enactment [Revised Comment]

Section 9002 continues former Civil Code Section 227.30 without substantive change. The first part of the first sentence has been revised to use the defined term "stepparent adoption" and to delete the phrase "stepparent adopting a child of his or her spouse." This is not a substantive change. See Section 8548 ("stepparent adoption" defined). Other language changes have been made for consistency with Sections 8716 and 8810. See also Sections 8542 ("prospective adoptive parent" defined), 8543 ("qualified court investigator" defined).

For related provisions, see Sections 8716 (fee for report in agency adoption), 8810 (fee for report in independent adoption). [23 Cal.L.Rev.Comm. Reports 1 (1993)].

Research References

Forms

California Transactions Forms--Family Law § 6:109, Investigation Of Stepparent Adoption.

Treatises and Practice Aids

Witkin, California Summary 10th Parent and Child § 144, Procedure.
Witkin, California Summary 10th Parent and Child § 144A, (New) Procedure Where Child Born to Spouse or Partner During Marriage or Domestic Partnership.

§ 9003. Consent of birth parents to adoption; execution; filing; out-of-state procedure; prima facie evidence of custody; minor birth parents

(a) In a stepparent adoption, the consent of either or both birth parents shall be signed in the presence of a notary public, court clerk, probation officer, qualified court investigator, authorized representative of a licensed adoption agency, or county welfare department staff member of any county of this state. The petitioner, petitioner's counsel, or person before whom the consent is signed shall immediately file the consent with the clerk of the court where the adoption request is filed. If the request has not been filed at the time the consent has been signed, the consent shall be filed simultaneously with the adoption request. Upon filing of the adoption request, the clerk shall immediately notify the probation officer or, at the option of the board of supervisors, the county welfare department of that county.

(b) If the birth parent of a child to be adopted is outside this state at the time of signing the consent, the consent may be signed before an authorized representative of an adoption agency licensed in the state or country where the consent is being signed, a notary, or other person authorized to perform notarial acts.

(c) The consent, when reciting that the person giving it is entitled to sole custody of the child and when acknowledged before any authorized witness specified in subdivision (a), is prima facie evidence of the right of the person signing the consent to the sole custody of the child and that person's sole right to consent.

(d) A birth parent who is a minor has the right to sign a consent for the adoption of the birth parent's child and the consent is not subject to revocation by reason of the minority. *(Stats.1992, c. 162 (A.B.2650), § 10, operative Jan. 1, 1994. Amended by Stats.1993, c. 219 (A.B.1500), § 206; Stats.2005, c. 627 (S.B.302), § 4; Stats.2011, c. 462 (A.B.687), § 8.)*

Law Revision Commission Comments

Enactment [Revised Comment]

Section 9003 continues former Civil Code Section 227.40 without substantive change. The first sentence of subdivision (a) has been revised to require consent of "birth parents" rather than "parents." This terminology is consistent with subdivision (d). The reference to the "superior" court has been omitted as surplus. See Section 200 (jurisdiction in superior court). The word "duly" formerly preceding "acknowledged" has been omitted as surplus. See also Sections 8512 ("birth parent" defined), 8543 ("qualified court investigator" defined), 8548 ("stepparent adoption" defined).

For related provisions, see Sections 8700 (consent to agency adoption), 8814 (consent to independent adoption). [23 Cal.L.Rev. Comm. Reports 1 (1993)].

Research References

Forms

California Transactions Forms--Family Law § 7:39, Adoption and Termination Of Parental Rights.
California Transactions Forms--Family Law § 6:105, Consent Of Custodial Parent.
California Transactions Forms--Family Law § 6:106, Consent Of Noncustodial Parent.
California Transactions Forms--Family Law § 6:115, Consent to Stepparent Adoption by Custodial Parent.
Nichols Cyclopedia of Legal Forms Annotated § 7:6, Statutory Provisions--Consent to Adoption.
West's California Judicial Council Forms ADOPT-210, Adoption Agreement.

Treatises and Practice Aids

Witkin, California Summary 10th Parent and Child § 142, Consent Of Birth Parents.

§ 9004. Consent form; notice; contents

In a stepparent adoption, the form prescribed by the department for the consent of the birth parent shall contain substantially the following notice:

"Notice to the parent who gives the child for adoption: If you and your child lived together at any time as parent and child, the adoption of your child through a stepparent adoption does not affect the child's right to inherit your property or the property of other blood relatives." *(Stats. 1992, c. 162 (A.B.2650), § 10, operative Jan. 1, 1994. Amended by Stats.2001, c. 893 (A.B.25), § 7.)*

Law Revision Commission Comments

Enactment [Revised Comment]

Section 9004 continues former Civil Code Section 227.44 without change. See also Sections 8512 ("birth parent" defined), 8518 ("department" defined), 8548 ("stepparent adoption" defined). [23 Cal.L.Rev.Comm. Reports 1 (1993)].

Research References

Forms

California Transactions Forms--Family Law § 6:114, Consent Of Noncustodial Parent.

Treatises and Practice Aids

Witkin, California Summary 10th Parent and Child § 142, Consent Of Birth Parents.

§ 9005. Withdrawal of consent; court approval; motion or petition; form; hearing; notice; probation officer, court investigator or welfare department report; court order; appeal

(a) Consent of the birth parent to the adoption of the child through a stepparent adoption may not be withdrawn except with court approval. Request for that approval may be made by motion, or a birth parent seeking to withdraw consent may file with the clerk of the court where the adoption petition is pending, a petition for approval of withdrawal of consent, without the necessity of paying a fee for filing the petition. The petition or motion shall be in writing, and shall set forth the reasons for withdrawal of consent, but otherwise may be in any form.

(b) The court clerk shall set the matter for hearing and shall give notice thereof to the probation officer, qualified court investigator, or county welfare department, to the prospective adoptive parent, and to the birth parent or parents by certified mail, return receipt requested, to the address of each as shown in the proceeding, at least 10 days before the time set for hearing.

(c) The probation officer, qualified court investigator, or county welfare department shall, before the hearing of the motion or petition for withdrawal, file a full report with the court and shall appear at the hearing to represent the interests of the child.

(d) At the hearing, the parties may appear in person or with counsel. The hearing shall be held in chambers, but the court reporter shall report the proceedings and, on court order, the fee therefor shall be paid from the county treasury. If the court finds that withdrawal of the consent to adoption is reasonable in view of all the circumstances and that withdrawal of the consent is in the child's best interest, the court shall approve the withdrawal of the consent. Otherwise the court shall withhold its approval. Consideration of the child's best interest shall include, but is not limited to, an assessment of the child's age, the extent of bonding with the prospective adoptive parent, the extent of bonding or the potential to bond with the birth parent, and the ability of the birth parent to provide adequate and proper care and guidance to the child. If the court approves the withdrawal of consent, the adoption proceeding shall be dismissed.

(e) A court order granting or withholding approval of a withdrawal of consent to an adoption may be appealed in the same manner as an order of the juvenile court declaring a person to be a ward of the juvenile court. *(Stats.1992, c. 162 (A.B.2650), § 10, operative Jan. 1, 1994. Amended by Stats. 1993, c. 219 (A.B.1500), § 207; Stats.2001, c. 893 (A.B.25), § 8.)*

Law Revision Commission Comments

Enactment [Revised Comment]

Section 9005 continues former Civil Code Section 227.46 without substantive change. The introductory phrase "once given" in the former provision has been omitted as surplus. The reference to the "superior" court has been omitted as surplus. See Section 200 (jurisdiction in superior court). In subdivision (b), the phrase "persons to whose adoption of the child the consent was given" has been changed to "prospective adoptive parent." See also Sections 8542 ("prospective adoptive parent" defined), 8543 ("qualified court investigator" defined).

For a comparable provision, see Section 8815 (motion or petition to withdraw consent in independent adoption). [23 Cal.L.Rev. Comm. Reports 1 (1993)].

Research References

Forms

California Transactions Forms--Family Law § 7:39, Adoption and Termination Of Parental Rights.

California Transactions Forms--Family Law § 6:110, Withdrawal Of Consent Once Given--Withdrawal or Dismissal Of Adoption Petition.

Treatises and Practice Aids

Witkin, California Summary 10th Parent and Child § 143, Withdrawal Of Consent.

§ 9006. Withdrawal of petition or dismissal by petitioner; notification of probation officer, court investigator or welfare department; consent refused by birth parent

(a) If the petitioner moves to withdraw the adoption petition or to dismiss the proceeding, the court clerk shall immediately notify the probation officer, qualified court investigator, or county welfare department of the action, unless a home investigation was not required pursuant to Section 9000.5.

(b) If a birth parent has refused to give the required consent, the adoption petition shall be dismissed. *(Stats. 1992, c. 162 (A.B.2650), § 10, operative Jan. 1, 1994. Amended by Stats.1993, c. 219 (A.B.1500), § 208; Stats.2014, c. 636 (A.B.2344), § 6, eff. Jan. 1, 2015.)*

Law Revision Commission Comments

Enactment [Revised Comment]

Section 9006 continues former Civil Code Section 227.50 without substantive change. In subdivision (a), the former reference to the "clerk of the court in which the proceeding is pending" has been shortened to the "court clerk" to eliminate surplus language. See also Sections 8512 ("birth parent" defined), 8543 ("qualified court investigator" defined).

For related provisions, see Sections 8719 (notice of withdrawal or dismissal in agency adoption), 8804 (notice of withdrawal or dismissal in independent adoption), 8916 (notice of withdrawal or dismissal in intercountry adoption). [23 Cal.L.Rev.Comm. Reports 1 (1993)].

Research References

Forms

California Transactions Forms--Family Law § 6:107, Adoption Without Consent Of Noncustodial Parent.

California Transactions Forms--Family Law § 6:110, Withdrawal Of Consent Once Given--Withdrawal or Dismissal Of Adoption Petition.

Treatises and Practice Aids

Witkin, California Summary 10th Parent and Child § 144, Procedure.

§ 9007. Prospective adoptive parents; appearance before court

Except as provided in Section 9000.5, the prospective adoptive parent and the child proposed to be adopted shall appear before the court pursuant to Sections 8612, 8613, and 8613.5. *(Stats.1992, c. 162 (A.B.2650), § 10, operative Jan. 1, 1994. Amended by Stats.2009, c. 492 (A.B.941), § 5; Stats. 2014, c. 636 (A.B.2344), § 7, eff. Jan. 1, 2015.)*

Law Revision Commission Comments

Enactment [Revised Comment]

Section 9007 continues former Civil Code Sections 221.62 and 227.60 without substantive change. The reference to "prospective adoptive parent" has been substituted for "person or persons desiring to adopt a child." This is not a substantive change. See Section 8542 ("prospective adoptive parent" defined).

For comparable provisions, see Sections 8718 (appearance in agency adoption), 8823 (appearance in independent adoption), 8913 (appearance in intercountry adoption). [23 Cal.L.Rev.Comm. Reports 1 (1993)].

Research References

Forms

California Transactions Forms--Family Law § 6:111, Hearing on Stepparent Adoption Petition.

West's California Code Forms, Family § 9000, Comment Overview--Stepparent Adoptions.

Treatises and Practice Aids

Witkin, California Summary 10th Parent and Child § 95, Petition and Hearing.

Witkin, California Summary 10th Parent and Child § 144A, (New) Procedure Where Child Born to Spouse or Partner During Marriage or Domestic Partnership.

CHAPTER 6. VACATION OF ADOPTION

§ 9100. Developmental disability or mental illness prior to adoption; setting aside decree or order of adoption; petition; limitation of action; notification of department

(a) If a child adopted pursuant to the law of this state shows evidence of a developmental disability or mental illness as a result of conditions existing before the adoption to an extent that the child cannot be relinquished to an adoption agency on the grounds that the child is considered unadoptable, and of which conditions the adoptive parents or parent had no knowledge or notice before the entry of the order of adoption, a petition setting forth those facts may be filed by the adoptive parents or parent with the court that granted the adoption petition. If these facts are proved to the satisfaction of the court, it may make an order setting aside the order of adoption.

(b) The petition shall be filed within five years after the entry of the order of adoption.

(c) The court clerk shall immediately notify the department at Sacramento of the petition. Within 60 days after the notice, the department shall file a full report with the court and shall appear before the court for the purpose of representing the adopted child. *(Stats.1992, c. 162 (A.B. 2650), § 10, operative Jan. 1, 1994.)*

Law Revision Commission Comments

Enactment [Revised Comment]

Section 9100 continues former Civil Code Section 228.10 without substantive change. References to a "decree" of adoption have been omitted as surplus. See Section 100 ("order" includes decree, as appropriate). The reference to the "superior" court has been omitted as surplus. See Section 200 (jurisdiction in superior court).

In subdivision (c), the former reference to "clerk of the superior court of the county wherein the action is brought" has been shortened to "court clerk" to eliminate surplus language and the "it shall be the duty" language has been replaced by "shall." See Section 12 ("shall" is mandatory). See also Section 8518 ("department" defined). [23 Cal.L.Rev.Comm. Reports 1 (1993)].

Commentary

In re Adoption of M.S., 181 Cal.App.4th 50, 103 Cal.Rptr.3d 715 (2010), holds that this section allows a court to set aside California adoptions only. It does not authorize a court to set aside a Ukrainian intercountry adoption.

Research References

Forms

West's California Code Forms, Family § 7630, Comment Overview--Determining Parent and Child Relationship.
West's California Code Forms, Family § 9100, Comment Overview--Vacation Of Adoption.

Treatises and Practice Aids

Witkin, California Summary 10th Constitutional Law § 789, Developmentally Disabled Persons.
Witkin, California Summary 10th Parent and Child § 53, Judgment.
Witkin, California Summary 10th Parent and Child § 72, Statutory Framework.
Witkin, California Summary 10th Parent and Child § 145, Child Unadoptable.
Witkin, California Summary 10th Parent and Child § 148, Limitation Of Actions.
Witkin, California Summary 10th Parent and Child § 638, Preferential Right Of Relatives.
Witkin, California Summary 10th Parent and Child § 148A, (New) Set-Aside Procedure.

§ 9101. Decree or order of adoption set aside; proceedings; care and custody of child

(a) If an order of adoption is set aside as provided in Section 9100, the court making the order shall direct the district attorney, the county counsel, or the county welfare department to take appropriate action under the Welfare and Institutions Code. The court may also make any order relative to the care, custody, or confinement of the child pending the proceeding the court sees fit.

(b) The county in which the proceeding for adoption was had is liable for the child's support until the child is able to support himself or herself. *(Stats.1992, c. 162 (A.B.2650), § 10, operative Jan. 1, 1994.)*

Law Revision Commission Comments

Enactment [Revised Comment]

Section 9101 continues former Civil Code Section 228.13 without substantive change. The reference to a "decree" of adoption has been omitted as surplus. See Section 100 ("order" includes decree, as appropriate). [23 Cal.L.Rev.Comm. Reports 1 (1993)].

Research References

Forms

West's California Code Forms, Family § 9100, Comment Overview--Vacation Of Adoption.

Treatises and Practice Aids

Witkin, California Summary 10th Parent and Child § 145, Child Unadoptable.

§ 9102. Limitation of actions; findings of fact; duty of department

(a) Except as provided in Section 9100, an action or proceeding of any kind to vacate, set aside, or otherwise nullify an order of adoption on any ground, except fraud, shall be commenced within one year after entry of the order.

(b) Except as provided in Section 9100, an action or proceeding of any kind to vacate, set aside, or nullify an order of adoption, based on fraud, shall be commenced within three years after entry of the order, or within 90 days of discovery of the fraud, whichever is earlier.

(c) In any action to set aside an order of adoption pursuant to this section or Section 9100, the court shall first determine whether the facts presented are legally sufficient to set aside the order of adoption. If the facts are not legally sufficient, the petition shall be denied. If the facts are legally sufficient, the court's final ruling on the matter shall take into consideration the best interests of the child, in conjunction with all other factors required by law.

(d) The department shall not be required under any circumstances to investigate a petition filed pursuant to this section or to represent a child who is the subject of a proceeding under this section. *(Stats.1992, c. 162 (A.B.2650), § 10, operative Jan. 1, 1994. Amended by Stats.1995, c. 567 (A.B.898), § 1; Stats.2000, c. 937 (A.B.2433), § 6; Stats.2011, c. 462 (A.B.687), § 9.)*

Law Revision Commission Comments

Enactment [Revised Comment]

Section 9102 continues former Civil Code Section 228.15 without substantive change. References to a "decree" of adoption have been omitted as surplus. See Section 100 ("order" includes decree, as appropriate). [23 Cal.L.Rev.Comm. Reports 1 (1993)].

Commentary

In re Adoption of B.C., 195 Cal.App.4th 913, 125 Cal.Rptr.3d 727 (2011), holds that subsection (b) *fraud* includes extrinsic and well as intrinsic fraud.

Research References

Forms

California Transactions Forms--Family Law § 6:89, Revocation Of Relinquishment After Filing Due to Fraud or Procedural Irregularity.
West's California Code Forms, Family § 7630, Comment Overview--Determining Parent and Child Relationship.
West's California Code Forms, Family § 9100, Comment Overview--Vacation Of Adoption.

Treatises and Practice Aids

Witkin, California Summary 10th Parent and Child § 53, Judgment.
Witkin, California Summary 10th Parent and Child § 145, Child Unadoptable.
Witkin, California Summary 10th Parent and Child § 148, Limitation Of Actions.
Witkin, California Summary 10th Parent and Child § 60A, (New) Lesbian Partner Who is Not Biological Mother Of Child.
Witkin, California Summary 10th Parent and Child § 638, Preferential Right Of Relatives.
Witkin, California Summary 10th Parent and Child § 148A, (New) Set-Aside Procedure.

CHAPTER 7. DISCLOSURE OF INFORMATION

§ 9200. Inspection of documents; authorization; fee; deletion of identification of birth parents; certificate of adoption

(a) The petition, relinquishment or consent, agreement, order, report to the court from any investigating agency, and any power of attorney and deposition filed in the office of the clerk of the court pursuant to this part is not open to inspection by any person other than the parties to the proceeding and their attorneys and the department, except upon the written authority of the judge of the superior court. A judge of the superior court may not authorize anyone to inspect the petition, relinquishment or consent, agreement, order, report to the court from any investigating agency, or power of attorney or deposition or any portion of any of these documents, except in exceptional circumstances and for good cause approaching the necessitous. The petitioner may be required to pay the expenses for preparing the copies of the documents to be inspected.

(b) Upon written request of any party to the proceeding and upon the order of any judge of the superior court, the clerk of the court shall not provide any documents referred to in this section for inspection or copying to any other person, unless the name of the child's birth parents or any information tending to identify the child's birth parents is deleted from the documents or copies thereof.

(c) Upon the request of the adoptive parents or the child, a clerk of the court may issue a certificate of adoption that states the date and place of adoption, the child's birth date, the names of the adoptive parents, and the name the child has taken. Unless the child has been adopted by a stepparent, the certificate shall not state the name of the child's birth parents. *(Stats.1992, c. 162 (A.B.2650), § 10, operative Jan. 1, 1994. Amended by Stats.2002, c. 784 (S.B.1316), § 114.)*

Law Revision Commission Comments

Enactment [Revised Comment]

Section 9200 continues former Civil Code Section 229.10 without substantive change. In subdivisions (a) and (b), references to the "action" have been changed to the "proceeding." See also Sections 8503 ("adoptive parent" defined), 8512 ("birth parent" defined), 8548 ("stepparent adoption" defined). [23 Cal.L.Rev.Comm. Reports 1 (1993)].

2002 Amendment

Section 9200 is amended to reflect elimination of the county clerk's role as ex officio clerk of the superior court. See former Gov't Code § 26800 (county clerk acting as clerk of superior court). The powers, duties, and responsibilities formerly exercised by the county clerk as ex officio clerk of the court are delegated to the court administrative or executive officer, and the county clerk is relieved of those powers, duties, and responsibilities. See Gov't Code §§ 69840 (powers, duties, and responsibilities of clerk of court and deputy clerk of court), 71620 (trial court personnel). [32 Cal.L.Rev.Comm. Reports 171 (2002)].

Research References

Treatises and Practice Aids

Witkin, California Summary 10th Parent and Child § 72, Statutory Framework.

Witkin, California Summary 10th Parent and Child § 89, Adoption Facilitators.

Witkin, California Summary 10th Parent and Child § 97, Certificates Of Birth and Adoption.

Witkin, California Summary 10th Parent and Child § 149, Confidentiality Of Records.

§ 9201. Adoption services; identification; adoption petitions; research

(a) Except as otherwise permitted or required by statute, neither the department nor a licensed adoption agency shall release information that would identify persons who receive, or have received, adoption services.

(b) Employees of the department and licensed adoption agencies shall release to the department at Sacramento any requested information, including identifying information, for the purposes of recordkeeping and monitoring, evaluation, and regulation of the provision of adoption services.

(c) Prior to the placement of a child for adoption, the department or licensed adoption agency may, upon the written request of both a birth and a prospective adoptive parent, arrange for contact between these birth and prospective adoptive parents that may include the sharing of identifying information regarding these parents.

(d) The department and any licensed adoption agency may, upon written authorization for the release of specified information by the subject of that information, share information regarding a prospective adoptive parent or birth parent with other social service agencies, including the department, other licensed adoption agencies, counties or licensed foster family agencies for purposes of approving a resource family pursuant to subparagraph (A) of paragraph (4) of subdivision (p) of Section 16519.5 of the Welfare and Institutions Code, or providers of health care as defined in Section 56.05 of the Civil Code.

(e) Notwithstanding any other law, the department and any licensed adoption agency may furnish information relating to an adoption petition or to a child in the custody of the department or any licensed adoption agency to the juvenile court, county welfare department, public welfare agency, private welfare agency licensed by the department, provider of foster care services, potential adoptive parent, or provider of health care as defined in Section 56.05 of the Civil Code, if it is believed the child's welfare will be promoted thereby.

(f) The department and any licensed adoption agency may make adoption case records, including identifying information, available for research purposes, provided that the research will not result in the disclosure of the identity of the child or the parties to the adoption to anyone other than the entity conducting the research. *(Stats.1992, c. 162 (A.B. 2650), § 10, operative Jan. 1, 1994. Amended by Stats.2000, c. 910 (A.B.2921), § 5; Stats.2006, c. 538 (S.B.1852), § 161; Stats.2016, c. 612 (A.B.1997), § 11, eff. Jan. 1, 2017.)*

Law Revision Commission Comments

Enactment [Revised Comment]

Section 9201 continues former Civil Code Section 229.20 without substantive change. See also Sections 8518 ("department" defined), 8530 ("licensed adoption agency" defined). [23 Cal.L.Rev.Comm. Reports 1 (1993)].

Research References

Treatises and Practice Aids

Witkin, California Summary 10th Parent and Child § 150, Confidentiality Of Information.

§ 9202. Medical report; request of adopted person or adoptive parents; access

(a) Notwithstanding any other law, the department or licensed adoption agency that made a medical report required by Section 8706, 8817, or 8909 shall provide a copy of the medical report, in the manner the department prescribes by regulation, to any of the following persons upon the person's request:

(1) A person who has been adopted pursuant to this part and who has attained the age of 18 years or who presents a certified copy of the person's marriage certificate.

(2) The adoptive parent of a person under the age of 18 years who has been adopted pursuant to this part.

(b) A person who is denied access to a medical report pursuant to regulations adopted pursuant to this section may petition the court for review of the reasonableness of the department's or licensed adoption agency's decision.

(c) The names and addresses of any persons contained in the report shall be removed unless the person requesting the report has previously received the information. *(Stats.1992, c. 162 (A.B.2650), § 10, operative Jan. 1, 1994. Amended by Stats.2000, c. 910 (A.B.2921), § 6.)*

Law Revision Commission Comments

Enactment [Revised Comment]

Section 9202 continues former Civil Code Section 229.30 without substantive change. This section has been substantially reorganized. The reference to the "superior" court has been omitted as surplus. See Section 200 (jurisdiction in superior court). See also Sections 8503 ("adoptive parent" defined), 8518 ("department" defined), 8530 ("licensed adoption agency" defined).

For related provision, see Section 8608 (regulations concerning form and content of medical reports). [23 Cal.L.Rev.Comm. Reports 1 (1993)].

Research References

Treatises and Practice Aids

Witkin, California Summary 10th Parent and Child § 149, Confidentiality Of Records.

§ 9202.5. Blood sample; access

(a) Notwithstanding any other law, the laboratory that is storing a blood sample pursuant to Section 8706, 8817, or 8909 shall provide access to the blood sample to only the following persons upon the person's request:

(1) A person who has been adopted pursuant to this part.

(2) The adoptive parent of a person under the age of 18 years who has been adopted pursuant to this part. The adoptive parent may receive access to the blood sample only after entry of the order of adoption.

(b) The birth parent or parents shall be given access to any DNA test results related to the blood sample on request.

(c) Except as provided in subdivision (b), no person other than the adoptive parent and the adopted child shall have access to the blood sample or any DNA test results related to the blood sample, unless the adoptive parent or the child authorizes another person or entity to have that access. *(Added by Stats.1996, c. 1053 (A.B.3241), § 4.)*

Research References

Treatises and Practice Aids

Witkin, California Summary 10th Parent and Child § 93, Medical Report on Child and Birth Parents.

§ 9203. Disclosure of identity of birth parents; application of section

(a) The department or a licensed adoption agency shall do the following:

(1) Upon the request of a person who has been adopted pursuant to this part and who has attained the age of 21 years, disclose the identity of the person's birth parent or parents and their most current address shown in the records of the department or licensed adoption agency, if the birth parent or parents have indicated consent to the disclosure in writing.

(2) Upon the request of the birth parent of a person who has been adopted pursuant to this part and who has attained the age of 21 years, disclose the adopted name of the adoptee and the adoptee's most current address shown in the records of the department or licensed adoption agency, if the adult adoptee has indicated in writing, pursuant to the registration program developed by the department, that the adult adoptee wishes the adult adoptee's name and address to be disclosed.

(3) Upon the request of the adoptive parent of a person under the age of 21 years who has been adopted pursuant to this part, disclose the identity of a birth parent and the birth parent's most current address shown in the records of the department or licensed adoption agency if the department or licensed adoption agency finds that a medical necessity or other extraordinary circumstances justify the disclosure.

(b) The department shall prescribe the form of the request required by this section. The form shall provide for an affidavit to be executed by the requester that to the best of the requester's knowledge the requester is an adoptee, the adoptee's birth parent, or the adoptee's adoptive parent. The department may adopt regulations requiring any additional means of identification from a requester that it deems necessary. The request shall advise an adoptee that if the adoptee consents, the adoptee's adoptive parents will be notified of the filing of the request before the release of the name and address of the adoptee's birth parent.

(c) Subdivision (a) is not applicable if a birth parent or an adoptee has indicated that he or she does not wish his or her name or address to be disclosed.

(d) Within 20 working days of receipt of a request for information pursuant to this section, the department shall either respond to the request or forward the request to a licensed adoption agency that was a party to the adoption.

(e) Notwithstanding any other law, the department shall announce the availability of the present method of arranging contact among an adult adoptee, the adult adoptee's birth parents, and adoptive parents authorized by Section 9204 utilizing a means of communication appropriate to inform the public effectively.

(f) The department or licensed adoption agency may charge a reasonable fee in an amount the department establishes by regulation to cover the costs of processing requests for information made pursuant to subdivision (a). The department or licensed adoption agency shall waive fees authorized by this section for any person who is receiving public assistance pursuant to Part 3 (commencing with Section 11000) of Division 9 of the Welfare and Institutions Code. The revenue resulting from the fees so charged shall be utilized by the department or licensed adoption agency to increase existing staff as needed to process these requests. Fees received by the department shall be deposited in the Adoption Information Fund. This revenue shall be in addition to any other funds appropriated in support of the state adoption program.

(g) This section applies only to adoptions in which the relinquishment for or consent to adoption was signed or the birth parent's rights were involuntarily terminated by court action on or after January 1, 1984. *(Stats.1992, c. 162 (A.B.2650), § 10, operative Jan. 1, 1994. Amended by Stats. 2000, c. 910 (A.B.2921), § 7.)*

Law Revision Commission Comments

Enactment [Revised Comment]

Section 9203 continues former Civil Code Section 229.40 without substantive change. This section has been substantially reorganized. See also Sections 8503 ("adoptive parent" defined), 8512 ("birth parent" defined), 8518 ("department" defined), 8530 ("licensed adoption agency" defined). [23 Cal.L.Rev.Comm. Reports 1 (1993)].

Research References

Forms

Nichols Cyclopedia of Legal Forms Annotated § 7:16, Voluntary Adoption Registries.

Treatises and Practice Aids

Witkin, California Summary 10th Parent and Child § 79, Adoption Information.

Witkin, California Summary 10th Parent and Child § 151, Request for Disclosure.

Witkin, California Summary 10th Parent and Child § 152, Contact Between Adoptees and Others.

§ 9203.1. Disclosure of adoption homestudy; form; time for response; fees

(a) The department or a licensed adoption agency shall, upon the request of a prospective adoptive parent, disclose an adoption homestudy and any updates to an adoption homestudy to a county or licensed foster family agency for the purpose of approving the prospective adoptive parent as a resource family pursuant to subparagraph (A) of paragraph (4) of subdivision (p) of Section 16519.5 of the Welfare and Institutions Code.

(b) The department shall prescribe the form of the request described in subdivision (a).

(c) The department or a licensed adoption agency shall respond to a request made pursuant to subdivision (a) within 20 working days of receiving it.

(d) The department or a licensed adoption agency may charge a fee to cover the reasonable costs of processing requests made pursuant to subdivision (a). The department or a licensed adoption agency shall waive fees authorized by this subdivision for any person who is receiving public assistance pursuant to Part 3 (commencing with Section 11000) of Division 9 of the Welfare and Institutions Code. *(Added by Stats.2016, c. 612 (A.B.1997), § 12, eff. Jan. 1, 2017.)*

§ 9204. Consent between adult adoptee and birth parents to arrange for contact between the parties

(a) Notwithstanding any other law, if an adult adoptee and the adult adoptee's birth parents have each filed a written consent with the department or licensed adoption agency, the department or licensed adoption agency may arrange for contact between those persons. Neither the department nor a licensed adoption agency may solicit, directly or indirectly, the execution of a written consent.

(b) The written consent authorized by this section shall be in a form prescribed by the department. *(Stats.1992, c. 162 (A.B.2650), § 10, operative Jan. 1, 1994.)*

Law Revision Commission Comments

Enactment [Revised Comment]

Section 9204 continues former Civil Code Section 229.50 without substantive change. In the first sentence of subdivision (a), "licensed agency" has been changed to "licensed adoption agency" for internal consistency and for consistency with the defined term. See also Sections 8503 ("adoptive parent" defined), 8512 ("birth parent" defined), 8518 ("department" defined), 8530 ("licensed adoption agency" defined). [23 Cal.L.Rev.Comm. Reports 1 (1993)].

Research References

Treatises and Practice Aids

Witkin, California Summary 10th Parent and Child § 152, Contact Between Adoptees and Others.

§ 9205. Contact with sibling; request; form

(a) Notwithstanding any other law, the department, county adoption agency, or licensed adoption agency that joined in the adoption petition shall release the names and addresses of siblings to one another if both of the siblings have attained 18 years of age and have filed the following with the department or agency:

(1) A current address.

(2) A written request for contact with any sibling whose existence is known to the person making the request.

(3) A written waiver of the person's rights with respect to the disclosure of the person's name and address to the sibling, if the person is an adoptee.

(b) Upon inquiry and proof that a person is the sibling of an adoptee who has filed a waiver pursuant to this section, the department, county adoption agency, or licensed adoption agency may advise the sibling that a waiver has been filed by the adoptee. The department, county adoption agency, or licensed adoption agency may charge a reasonable fee, not to exceed fifty dollars ($50), for providing the service required by this section.

(c) An adoptee may revoke a waiver filed pursuant to this section by giving written notice of revocation to the department or agency.

(d) The department shall adopt a form for the request authorized by this section. The form shall provide for an affidavit to be executed by a person seeking to employ the procedure provided by this section that, to the best of the person's knowledge, the person is an adoptee or sibling of an adoptee. The form also shall contain a notice of an adoptee's rights pursuant to subdivision (c) and a statement that information will be disclosed only if there is a currently valid waiver on file with the department or agency. The department may adopt regulations requiring any additional means of identification from a person making a request pursuant to this section as it deems necessary.

(e) The department, county adoption agency, or licensed adoption agency may not solicit the execution of a waiver authorized by this section. However, the department shall announce the availability of the procedure authorized by this section, utilizing a means of communication appropriate to inform the public effectively.

(f) Notwithstanding the age requirement described in subdivision (a), an adoptee or sibling who is under 18 years of age may file a written waiver of confidentiality for the release of his or her name, address, and telephone number pursuant to this section provided that, if an adoptee, the adoptive parent consents, and, if a sibling, the sibling's legal parent or guardian consents. If the sibling is under the jurisdiction of the dependency court and has no legal parent or guardian able or available to provide consent, the dependency court may provide that consent.

(g) Notwithstanding subdivisions (a) and (e), an adoptee or sibling who seeks contact with the other for whom no waiver is on file may petition the court to appoint a confidential intermediary. If the sibling being sought is the adoptee, the intermediary shall be the department, county adoption agency, or licensed adoption agency that provided adoption services as described in Section 8521 or 8533. If the sibling being sought was formerly under the jurisdiction of the juvenile court, but is not an adoptee, the intermediary shall be the department, the county child welfare agency that provided services to the dependent child, or the licensed adoption agency that provided adoption services to the sibling seeking contact, as appropriate. If the court finds that the agency that conducted the adoptee's adoption is unable, due to economic hardship, to serve as the intermediary, then the agency shall provide all records related to the adoptee or the sibling to the court and the court shall appoint an alternate confidential intermediary. The court shall grant the petition unless it finds that it would be detrimental to the adoptee or sibling with whom contact is sought. The intermediary shall have access to all records of the adoptee or the sibling and shall make all reasonable efforts to locate and attempt to obtain the consent of the adoptee, sibling, or adoptive or birth parent, as required to make the disclosure authorized by this section. The confidential intermediary shall notify any located adoptee, sibling, or adoptive or birth parent that consent is optional, not required by law, and does not affect the status of the adoption. If that individual denies the request for consent, the confidential intermediary shall not make any further attempts to obtain consent. The confidential intermediary shall use information found in the records of the adoptee or the sibling for authorized purposes only, and may not disclose that information without authorization. If contact is sought with an adoptee or sibling who is under 18 years of age, the confidential intermediary shall contact and obtain the consent of that child's legal parent before contacting the child. If the sibling is under 18 years of age, under the jurisdiction of the dependency court, and has no legal parent or guardian able or available to provide consent, the intermediary shall obtain that consent from the dependency court. If the adoptee is seeking information regarding a sibling who is known to be a dependent child of the juvenile court, the procedures set forth in subdivision (b) of Section 388 of the Welfare and Institutions Code shall be utilized. If the adoptee is foreign born and was the subject of an intercountry adoption as defined in Section 8527, the adoption agency may fulfill the reasonable efforts requirement by utilizing all information in the agency's case file, and any information received upon request from the foreign adoption agency that conducted the adoption, if any, to locate and attempt to obtain the consent of the adoptee, sibling, or adoptive or birth parent. If that information is neither in the agency's case file, nor received from the foreign adoption agency, or if the attempts to locate are unsuccessful, then the agency shall be relieved of any further obligation to search for the adoptee or the sibling.

(h) For purposes of this section, "sibling" means a biological sibling, half-sibling, or step-sibling of the adoptee.

(i) It is the intent of the Legislature that implementation of some or all of the changes made to Section 9205 of the Family Code by Chapter 386 of the Statutes of 2006 shall continue, to the extent possible.

(j) Beginning in the 2011–12 fiscal year, and each fiscal year thereafter, funding and expenditures for programs and activities under this section shall be in accordance with the requirements provided in Sections 30025 and 30026.5 of the Government Code. *(Stats.1992, c. 162 (A.B.2650), § 10, operative Jan. 1, 1994. Amended by Stats.2006, c. 386 (A.B.2488), § 1; Stats.2007, c. 130 (A.B.299), § 93; Stats. 2008, c. 759 (A.B.1279), § 15, eff. Sept. 30, 2008; Stats.2010, c. 725 (A.B.1612), § 2, eff. Oct. 19, 2010; Stats.2011, c. 8 (S.B.72), § 1, eff. March 24, 2011; Stats.2012, c. 35 (S.B. 1013), § 36, eff. June 27, 2012.)*

Law Revision Commission Comments

Enactment [Revised Comment]

Section 9205 continues former Civil Code Section 229.60 without substantive change. The provisions of subdivision (a) have been substantially revised. In subdivision (c), the reference to filing of a waiver has been substituted for the former reference to execution of a waiver. This is not a substantive change. In subdivision (e), the reference to the agency has been added. This is consistent with the remainder of this section and with Section 9204. See also Sections 8503 ("adoptive parent" defined), 8512 ("birth parent" defined), 8518 ("department" defined). [23 Cal.L.Rev.Comm. Reports 1 (1993)].

Research References

Forms

West's California Judicial Council Forms ADOPT-330, Request for Appointment Of Confidential Intermediary.

West's California Judicial Council Forms ADOPT-331, Order for Appointment Of Confidential Intermediary.

Treatises and Practice Aids

Witkin, California Summary 10th Parent and Child § 152, Contact Between Adoptees and Others.

§ 9206. Release of letters, photographs, or other items of personal property; requests; release form; fees

(a) Notwithstanding any other law, the department or licensed adoption agency shall release any letters, photographs, or other items of personal property in its possession to an adoptee, birth parent, or adoptive parent, upon written request. The material may be requested by any of the following persons:

(1) The adoptee, if the adoptee has attained the age of 18 years.

(2) The adoptive parent or parents, on behalf of an adoptee under the age of 18 years, as long as instructions to the contrary have not been made by the depositor.

(3) The birth parent or parents.

(b) Notwithstanding any other law, all identifying names and addresses shall be deleted from the letters, photographs, or items of personal property before delivery to the requester.

(c) Letters, photographs, and other items of personal property deposited on or after January 1, 1985, shall be accompanied by a release form or similar document signed by the person depositing the material, specifying to whom the material may be released. At its discretion, the department or licensed adoption agency may refuse for deposit items of personal property that, because of value or bulk, would pose storage problems.

(d) Notwithstanding subdivisions (a) and (b), only the following photographs deposited before January 1, 1985, shall be released:

(1) Photographs of the adoptee that have been requested by the adoptee.

(2) Photographs that have been deposited by the adoptee, the adoptive parent or parents, or the birth parent or parents, and for which there is a letter or other document on file indicating that person's consent to the release of the photographs.

(e) The department and licensed adoption agencies may charge a fee to cover the actual costs of any services required by this section in excess of normal postadoptive services provided by the department or agency. The department shall develop a fee schedule that shall be implemented by the department and licensed adoption agencies in assessing charges to the person who deposits the material or the person to whom the material is released. The fee may be waived by the department or licensed adoption agencies in cases in which it is established that a financial hardship exists.

(f) "Photograph" as used in this section means a photograph of the person depositing the photograph or the person making the request for the release. *(Stats.1992, c. 162 (A.B.2650), § 10, operative Jan. 1, 1994.)*

Law Revision Commission Comments

Enactment [Revised Comment]

Section 9206 continues former Civil Code Section 229.70 without substantive change. In subdivision (a), "or" has been substituted for "and" between the references to the department and the licensed adoption agency. These are not substantive changes. In subdivision (d), a reference to subdivision (b) has been added. This is not a substantive change. See also Sections 8503 ("adoptive parent" defined), 8512 ("birth parent" defined), 8518 ("department" defined), 8530 ("licensed adoption agency" defined). [23 Cal.L.Rev. Comm. Reports 1 (1993)].

Research References

Forms

California Transactions Forms--Family Law § 6:2, Governing Law.

Treatises and Practice Aids

Witkin, California Summary 10th Parent and Child § 153, Deposit and Release Of Personal Property.

§ 9208. Children of Indian ancestry; notice to Secretary of Interior

(a) The clerk of the superior court entering a final order of adoption concerning an Indian child shall provide the Secretary of the Interior or his or her designee with a copy of the order within 30 days of the date of the order, together with any information necessary to show the following:

(1) The name and tribal affiliation of the child.

(2) The names and addresses of the biological parents.

(3) The names and addresses of the adoptive parents.

(4) The identity of any agency having files or information relating to that adoptive placement.

(b) If the court records contain an affidavit of the biological parent or parents that their identity remain confidential, the court shall include that affidavit with the other information. *(Added by Stats.2006, c. 838 (S.B.678), § 13.)*

Research References

Forms

California Transactions Forms--Family Law § 6:143, Overview Of Indian Child Welfare Act (ICWA).

West's California Judicial Council Forms ADOPT-200, Adoption Request.

Treatises and Practice Aids

Witkin, California Summary 10th Parent and Child § 149, Confidentiality Of Records.

Witkin, California Summary 10th Parent and Child § 150, Confidentiality Of Information.

§ 9209. Children of Indian ancestry; adoptees who have reached age eighteen; access to information

(a) Upon application by an Indian individual who has reached the age of 18 years and who was the subject of an adoptive placement, the court which entered the final decree of adoption shall inform that individual of the tribal affiliation, if any, of the individual's biological parents and provide any other information as may be necessary to protect any rights flowing from the individual's tribal relationship, including, but not limited to, tribal membership rights or eligibility for federal or tribal programs or services available to Indians.

(b) If the court records contain an affidavit of the biological parent or parents that their identity remain confidential, the court shall inform the individual that the Secretary of the Interior may, upon request, certify to the individual's tribe that the individual's parentage and other circumstances of birth entitle the individual to membership under the criteria established by the tribe. *(Added by Stats.2006, c. 838 (S.B.678), § 14.)*

Research References

Treatises and Practice Aids

Witkin, California Summary 10th Parent and Child § 151, Request for Disclosure.

CHAPTER 8. ADOPTION PROCEEDINGS: CONFLICT OF LAWS

§ 9210. Actions commenced under this part; conditions required for California court jurisdiction; exceptions

(a) Except as otherwise provided in subdivisions (b) and (c), a court of this state has jurisdiction over a proceeding for the adoption of a minor commenced under this part if any of the following applies:

(1) Immediately before commencement of the proceeding, the minor lived in this state with a parent, a guardian, a prospective adoptive parent, or another person acting as parent, for at least six consecutive months, excluding periods of temporary absence, or, in the case of a minor under six months of age, lived in this state with any of those individuals from soon after birth and there is available in this state substantial evidence concerning the minor's present or future care.

(2) Immediately before commencement of the proceeding, the prospective adoptive parent lived in this state for at least six consecutive months, excluding periods of temporary absence, and there is available in this state substantial evidence concerning the minor's present or future care.

(3) The agency that placed the minor for adoption is located in this state and both of the following apply:

(A) The minor and the minor's parents, or the minor and the prospective adoptive parent, have a significant connection with this state.

(B) There is available in this state substantial evidence concerning the minor's present or future care.

(4) The minor and the prospective adoptive parent are physically present in this state and the minor has been abandoned or it is necessary in an emergency to protect the minor because the minor has been subjected to or threatened with mistreatment or abuse or is otherwise neglected.

(5) It appears that no other state would have jurisdiction under requirements substantially in accordance with paragraphs (1) to (4), inclusive, or another state has declined to exercise jurisdiction on the ground that this state is the more appropriate forum to hear a petition for adoption of the minor, and there is available in this state substantial evidence concerning the minor's present or future care.

(b) A court of this state may not exercise jurisdiction over a proceeding for adoption of a minor if at the time the petition for adoption is filed a proceeding concerning the custody or adoption of the minor is pending in a court of another state exercising jurisdiction substantially in conformity with this part, unless the proceeding is stayed by the court of the other state because this state is a more appropriate forum or for another reason.

(c) If a court of another state has issued a decree or order concerning the custody of a minor who may be the subject of a proceeding for adoption in this state, a court of this state may not exercise jurisdiction over a proceeding for adoption of the minor, unless both of the following apply:

(1) The requirements for modifying an order of a court of another state under this part are met, the court of another state does not have jurisdiction over a proceeding for adoption substantially in conformity with paragraphs (1) to (4), inclusive, of subdivision (a), or the court of another state has declined to assume jurisdiction over a proceeding for adoption.

(2) The court of this state has jurisdiction under this section over the proceeding for adoption.

(d) For purposes of subdivisions (b) and (c), "a court of another state" includes, in the case of an Indian child, a tribal court having and exercising jurisdiction over a custody proceeding involving the Indian child. *(Added by Stats.2002, c. 260 (S.B.1512), § 8. Amended by Stats.2003, c. 62 (S.B. 600), § 89; Stats.2006, c. 838 (S.B.678), § 15.)*

Research References

Treatises and Practice Aids

Witkin, California Summary 10th Parent and Child § 72, Statutory Framework.

Witkin, California Summary 10th Parent and Child § 91, Jurisdiction, Venue, and Conflict Of Laws.

§ 9212. Prospective adoptive parents residing outside of the state; applicability of §§ 9210 and 9211

(a) Sections 9210 and 9211 apply to interstate adoptions if the prospective adoptive parents reside outside of the state.

(b) This section shall become operative only if Assembly Bill 746 of the 2001–02 Regular Session is enacted.[1] If

Assembly Bill 746 is not enacted, the application of Sections 9210 and 9211 is not intended to expand jurisdiction to apply to interstate adoptions if the prospective adoptive parents reside outside of the state. *(Added by Stats.2002, c. 260 (S.B.1512), § 8. Amended by Stats.2003, c. 62 (S.B.600), § 90.)*

[1] Assembly Bill 746 was enacted as Stats.2002, c. 1112 (A.B.746).

Research References

Treatises and Practice Aids

Witkin, California Summary 10th Parent and Child § 91, Jurisdiction, Venue, and Conflict Of Laws.

Part 3

ADOPTION OF ADULTS AND MARRIED MINORS

CHAPTER 1. GENERAL PROVISIONS

§ 9300. Adoption of adults or married minors; authority

(a) An adult may be adopted by another adult, including a stepparent, as provided in this part.

(b) A married minor may be adopted in the same manner as an adult under this part. *(Stats.1992, c. 162 (A.B.2650), § 10, operative Jan. 1, 1994. Amended by Stats.1993, c. 266 (S.B.970), § 1.)*

Law Revision Commission Comments

Enactment [Revised Comment]

Section 9300 restates former Civil Code Section 230.10 without substantive change. [23 Cal.L.Rev.Comm. Reports 1 (1993)].

Research References

Forms

California Transactions Forms--Family Law § 6:2, Governing Law.

California Transactions Forms--Family Law § 6:4, Types Of Adoptions.

California Transactions Forms--Family Law § 6:7, Who May be Adopted.

California Transactions Forms--Family Law § 6:158, Governing Law--Venue and Procedure.

California Transactions Forms--Family Law § 6:164, Agreement Of Adult Adoption.

West's California Code Forms, Family § 9302 Form 2, Consent Of Spouse Of Adopted Adult.

Treatises and Practice Aids

Witkin, California Summary 10th Parent and Child § 70, Types Of Adoption.

Witkin, California Summary 10th Parent and Child § 72, Statutory Framework.

Witkin, California Summary 10th Parent and Child § 154, in General.

Witkin, California Summary 10th Parent and Child § 669A, (New) Review Hearings Just Before and After Minor Attains Age 18.

§ 9301. Consent of spouse of adoptive parent

A married person who is not lawfully separated from the person's spouse may not adopt an adult without the consent of the spouse, provided that the spouse is capable of giving that consent. *(Stats.1992, c. 162 (A.B.2650), § 10, operative Jan. 1, 1994.)*

Law Revision Commission Comments

Enactment [Revised Comment]

Section 9301 continues without substantive change the first sentence of the second paragraph of former Civil Code Section 230.20(a). [23 Cal.L.Rev.Comm. Reports 1 (1993)].

Research References

Forms

California Transactions Forms--Family Law § 6:9, Consent for Adoption Of Married Minor or Adult.

California Transactions Forms--Family Law § 6:163, Matters to Consider in Adoption Of Adult or Married Minor.

West's California Code Forms, Family § 9301, Comment Overview--Adoption Of Adults and Married Minors.

Treatises and Practice Aids

Witkin, California Summary 10th Parent and Child § 154, in General.

§ 9302. Consent of spouse of proposed adoptee; consent of others not required

(a) A married person who is not lawfully separated from the person's spouse may not be adopted without the consent of the spouse, provided that the spouse is capable of giving that consent.

(b) The consent of the parents of the proposed adoptee, of the department, or of any other person is not required. *(Stats.1992, c. 162 (A.B.2650), § 10, operative Jan. 1, 1994.)*

Law Revision Commission Comments

Enactment [Revised Comment]

Section 9302 continues without substantive change the last two sentences of the second paragraph of former Civil Code Section 230.20(a) and supersedes the second paragraph of former Civil Code Section 230.20(c). A reference to "proposed adoptee" has been substituted for "the person to be adopted" to eliminate surplus language. This is consistent with other sections in this part. See, e.g., Sections 9321, 9326–9327. A reference to "birth" parents has been omitted. This is not a substantive change. See Section 8512 ("birth parent" defined). See also Section 8518 ("department" defined). [23 Cal.L.Rev.Comm. Reports 1 (1993)].

Research References

Forms

California Transactions Forms--Family Law § 6:9, Consent for Adoption Of Married Minor or Adult.
California Transactions Forms--Family Law § 6:163, Matters to Consider in Adoption Of Adult or Married Minor.
West's California Code Forms, Family § 9301, Comment Overview--Adoption Of Adults and Married Minors.

Treatises and Practice Aids

Witkin, California Summary 10th Parent and Child § 154, in General.

§ 9303. Restrictions on adoption of more than one unrelated adult

(a) A person may not adopt more than one unrelated adult under this part within one year of the person's adoption of an unrelated adult, unless the proposed adoptee is the biological sibling of a person previously adopted pursuant to this part or unless the proposed adoptee is disabled or physically handicapped.

(b) A person may not adopt an unrelated adult under this part within one year of an adoption of another person under this part by the prospective adoptive parent's spouse, unless the proposed adoptee is a biological sibling of a person previously adopted pursuant to this part. *(Stats.1992, c. 162 (A.B.2650), § 10, operative Jan. 1, 1994.)*

Law Revision Commission Comments

Enactment [Revised Comment]

Section 9303 continues former Civil Code Section 230.12 without substantive change. A reference to "proposed adoptee" has been substituted for "the person to be adopted" to eliminate surplus language. This is consistent with other sections in this part. See, e.g., Sections 9321, 9326–9327. A reference to "biological sibling" has been substituted for "sibling by birth" for consistency with the language of Section 9205. The phrase "pursuant to this part" has been substituted for the former, narrower reference to "this section." This is not a substantive change. See also Section 8542 ("prospective adoptive parent" defined). [23 Cal.L.Rev.Comm. Reports 1 (1993)].

Research References

Forms

California Transactions Forms--Family Law § 6:6, Who May Adopt.
California Transactions Forms--Family Law § 6:159, Limitations on Adult Adoption.

Treatises and Practice Aids

Witkin, California Summary 10th Parent and Child § 154, in General.

§ 9304. Adoptee may take adoptive parent's family name

A person adopted pursuant to this part may take the family name of the adoptive parent. *(Stats.1992, c. 162 (A.B.2650), § 10, operative Jan. 1, 1994.)*

Law Revision Commission Comments

Enactment [Revised Comment]

Section 9304 continues the first sentence of former Civil Code Section 230.14 without substantive change. See also Section 8503 ("adoptive parent" defined).

For a comparable provision, see Section 8618 (name of adopted child). [23 Cal.L.Rev.Comm. Reports 1 (1993)].

Research References

Treatises and Practice Aids

Witkin, California Summary 10th Parent and Child § 154, in General.

§ 9305. Legal relationship of parent and child

After adoption, the adoptee and the adoptive parent or parents shall sustain towards each other the legal relationship of parent and child and have all the rights and are subject to all the duties of that relationship. *(Stats.1992, c. 162 (A.B.2650), § 10, operative Jan. 1, 1994.)*

Law Revision Commission Comments

Enactment [Revised Comment]

Section 9305 continues the last sentence of former Civil Code Section 230.14 without substantive change. See also Section 8503 ("adoptive parent" defined).

For a comparable provision, see Section 8616 (relationship in adoption of unmarried minors). [23 Cal.L.Rev.Comm. Reports 1 (1993)].

Commentary

Ehrenclou v. MacDonald, 117 Cal.App.4th 364, 12 Cal.Rptr.3d 411 (2004), review denied, held that two adults adopted by a trust beneficiary under Colorado adult adoption law were not the deceased trust beneficiary's "children then living" under a trust governed by California law because, unlike this section, the Colorado adult adoption statute gave the adoptees heir-at-law status, but did not create a parent-child relationship between the trust beneficiary and the adoptees.

Research References

Forms

California Transactions Forms--Family Law § 6:17, Legal Relationship Following Adoption Of Married Minor or Adult.
California Transactions Forms--Family Law § 6:18, Intestate Succession Rights.
California Transactions Forms--Family Law § 6:161, Estate Planning Considerations.

Treatises and Practice Aids

Witkin, California Summary 10th Parent and Child § 154, in General.

§ 9306. Birth parents; relief of parental duties; exception

(a) Except as provided in subdivision (b), the birth parents of a person adopted pursuant to this part are, from the time of the adoption, relieved of all parental duties towards, and all responsibility for, the adopted person, and have no right over the adopted person.

(b) Where an adult is adopted by the spouse of a birth parent, the parental rights and responsibilities of that birth parent are not affected by the adoption. *(Stats.1992, c. 162 (A.B.2650), § 10, operative Jan. 1, 1994. Amended by Stats. 1993, c. 266 (S.B.970), § 2.)*

Law Revision Commission Comments

Enactment [Revised Comment]

Subdivision (a) of Section 9306 continues former Civil Code Section 230.16 without substantive change. The reference to "birth" parents has been added. This is consistent with Section 8617. See also Section 8512 ("birth parent" defined).

For a comparable provision, see Section 8617 (responsibility of birth parents of unmarried minors). [23 Cal.L.Rev.Comm. Reports 1 (1993)].

Research References

Forms

California Transactions Forms--Family Law § 6:17, Legal Relationship Following Adoption Of Married Minor or Adult.

California Transactions Forms--Family Law § 6:161, Estate Planning Considerations.

Treatises and Practice Aids

Witkin, California Summary 10th Parent and Child § 154, in General.

§ 9307. Open and public hearing

A hearing with regard to adoption under Chapter 2 (commencing with Section 9320) or termination of a parent and child relationship under Chapter 3 (commencing with Section 9340) may, in the discretion of the court, be open and public. *(Stats.1992, c. 162 (A.B.2650), § 10, operative Jan. 1, 1994.)*

Law Revision Commission Comments

Enactment [Revised Comment]

Section 9307 continues former Civil Code Section 230.20(d) without substantive change. [23 Cal.L.Rev.Comm. Reports 1 (1993)].

Research References

Forms

California Transactions Forms--Family Law § 6:12, Conduct Of Hearing.

Treatises and Practice Aids

Witkin, California Summary 10th Parent and Child § 155, Procedure for Adoption.

Witkin, California Summary 10th Parent and Child § 156, Procedure for Terminating Adoption.

CHAPTER 2. PROCEDURE FOR ADULT ADOPTION

§ 9320. Adoption agreement; execution; content

(a) An adult may adopt another adult who is younger, except the spouse of the prospective adoptive parent, by an adoption agreement approved by the court, as provided in this chapter.

(b) The adoption agreement shall be in writing, executed by the prospective adoptive parent and the proposed adoptee, and shall state that the parties agree to assume toward each other the legal relationship of parent and child and to have all of the rights and be subject to all of the duties and responsibilities of that relationship. *(Stats.1992, c. 162 (A.B.2650), § 10, operative Jan. 1, 1994.)*

Law Revision Commission Comments

Enactment [Revised Comment]

Section 9320 continues the first paragraph of former Civil Code Section 230.20(a) without substantive change. The former language describing the court and the method of approving an adoption agreement has been omitted as surplus. References to "prospective adoptive parent" have been substituted for references to "person adopting" and "adopting person." These are not substantive changes. See Section 8542 ("prospective adoptive parent" defined). A reference to "proposed adoptee" has been substituted for "the person to be adopted" to eliminate surplus language. This is consistent with other sections in this part. See, e.g., Sections 9321, 9326–9327. [23 Cal.L.Rev.Comm. Reports 1 (1993)].

Research References

Forms

California Transactions Forms--Family Law § 6:6, Who May Adopt.

California Transactions Forms--Family Law § 6:7, Who May be Adopted.

California Transactions Forms--Family Law § 6:9, Consent for Adoption Of Married Minor or Adult.

California Transactions Forms--Family Law § 6:159, Limitations on Adult Adoption.

California Transactions Forms--Family Law § 6:160, Adoption Agreement--Petition for Approval Of Adoption Agreement.

California Transactions Forms--Family Law § 6:163, Matters to Consider in Adoption Of Adult or Married Minor.

California Transactions Forms--Family Law § 6:164, Agreement Of Adult Adoption.

California Transactions Forms--Family Law § 6:165, Petition for Adoption (Adult).

West's California Code Forms, Family § 9320, Comment Overview--Procedure for Adult Adoption.

Treatises and Practice Aids

Witkin, California Summary 10th Parent and Child § 71, Special Statutory Proceeding.

Witkin, California Summary 10th Parent and Child § 72, Statutory Framework.

Witkin, California Summary 10th Parent and Child § 154, in General.

Witkin, California Summary 10th Parent and Child § 155, Procedure for Adoption.

§ 9321. Petition for approval of adoption agreement; filing; contents of petition

(a) The prospective adoptive parent and the proposed adoptee may file in the county in which either person resides a petition for approval of the adoption agreement.

(b) The petition for approval of the adoption agreement shall state all of the following:

(1) The length and nature of the relationship between the prospective adoptive parent and the proposed adoptee.

(2) The degree of kinship, if any.

(3) The reason the adoption is sought.

(4) A statement as to why the adoption would be in the best interest of the prospective adoptive parent, the proposed adoptee, and the public.

(5) The names and addresses of any living birth parents or adult children of the proposed adoptee.

(6) Whether the prospective adoptive parent or the prospective adoptive parent's spouse has previously adopted any other adult and, if so, the name of the adult, together with the date and place of the adoption. *(Stats.1992, c. 162 (A.B. 2650), § 10, operative Jan. 1, 1994.)*

Law Revision Commission Comments

Enactment [Revised Comment]

Subdivision (a) of Section 9321 continues the first sentence of former Civil Code Section 230.20(b) without substantive change. Subdivision (b) continues former Civil Code Section 230.20(f)(1) without substantive change. References to "prospective adoptive parent" have been substituted for references to "adopting person" and "person seeking to adopt." These are not substantive changes. See Section 8542 ("prospective adoptive parent" defined). In subdivision (a), "proposed adoptee" has been substituted for "person to be adopted" to eliminate surplus language and to conform with the remainder of the section. The reference to the "superior" court has been omitted as surplus. See Section 200 (jurisdiction in superior court). See also Section 8512 ("birth parent" defined). [23 Cal.L.Rev.Comm. Reports 1 (1993)].

Research References

Forms

California Transactions Forms--Family Law § 6:9, Consent for Adoption Of Married Minor or Adult.
California Transactions Forms--Family Law § 6:158, Governing Law--Venue and Procedure.
California Transactions Forms--Family Law § 6:160, Adoption Agreement--Petition for Approval Of Adoption Agreement.
California Transactions Forms--Family Law § 6:163, Matters to Consider in Adoption Of Adult or Married Minor.
California Transactions Forms--Family Law § 6:165, Petition for Adoption (Adult).
West's California Code Forms, Family § 9320, Comment Overview--Procedure for Adult Adoption.

Treatises and Practice Aids

Witkin, California Summary 10th Parent and Child § 155, Procedure for Adoption.

§ 9321.5. Petitions for adult adoption; filing; residents; nonresidents; venue

(a) Notwithstanding Section 9321, a person who is a resident of this state may file a petition for adult adoption with the court in any of the following:

(1) The county in which the prospective adoptive parent resides.

(2) The county in which the proposed adoptee was born or resides at the time the petition was filed.

(3) The county in which an office of the public or private agency that placed the proposed adoptee for foster care or adoption as a minor or dependent child is located.

(b) A petitioner who is not a resident of this state may file a petition for adult adoption with the court in a county specified in paragraph (3) of subdivision (a). *(Formerly § 9213, added by Stats.2011, c. 462 (A.B.687), § 10. Renumbered § 9321.5 and amended by Stats.2012, c. 162 (S.B.1171), § 48.)*

Research References

Treatises and Practice Aids

Witkin, California Summary 10th Parent and Child § 155, Procedure for Adoption.

§ 9322. Setting matter for hearing

When the petition for approval of the adoption agreement is filed, the court clerk shall set the matter for hearing. *(Stats.1992, c. 162 (A.B.2650), § 10, operative Jan. 1, 1994.)*

Law Revision Commission Comments

Enactment [Revised Comment]

Section 9322 restates without substantive change the first part of the second sentence of former Civil Code Section 230.20(b). [23 Cal.L.Rev.Comm. Reports 1 (1993)].

Research References

Forms

West's California Code Forms, Family § 9320, Comment Overview--Procedure for Adult Adoption.

Treatises and Practice Aids

Witkin, California Summary 10th Parent and Child § 155, Procedure for Adoption.

§ 9323. Notice of hearing; appearances and objections of interested persons

The court may require notice of the time and place of the hearing to be served on any other interested person and any interested person may appear and object to the proposed adoption. *(Stats.1992, c. 162 (A.B.2650), § 10, operative Jan. 1, 1994.)*

Law Revision Commission Comments

Enactment [Revised Comment]

Section 9323 continues the third sentence of former Civil Code Section 230.20(b) without substantive change. A reference to "prospective adoptive parent" has been substituted for "adopting person." This is not a substantive change. See Section 8542 ("prospective adoptive parent" defined). A reference to "proposed adoptee" has been substituted for "person to be adopted" to eliminate surplus language. This is consistent with other sections in this part. See, e.g., Sections 9321, 9326–9327. [23 Cal.L.Rev. Comm. Reports 1 (1993)].

Research References

Forms

West's California Code Forms, Family § 9320, Comment Overview--Procedure for Adult Adoption.

Treatises and Practice Aids

Witkin, California Summary 10th Parent and Child § 155, Procedure for Adoption.

§ 9324. Mandatory appearances by prospective adoptive parent and proposed adoptee; exceptions

Both the prospective adoptive parent and the proposed adoptee shall appear at the hearing in person, unless an appearance is impossible, in which event an appearance may be made for either or both of the persons by counsel, empowered in writing to make the appearance. *(Stats.1992, c. 162 (A.B.2650), § 10, operative Jan. 1, 1994.)*

Law Revision Commission Comments

Enactment [Revised Comment]

Section 9324 continues the last part of the second sentence of former Civil Code Section 230.20(b) without change. A reference to "prospective adoptive parent" has been substituted for "person adopting." This is not a substantive change. See Section 8542 ("prospective adoptive parent" defined). A reference to "proposed adoptee" has been substituted for "person to be adopted" to eliminate surplus language. This is consistent with other sections in this part. See, e.g., Sections 9321, 9326–9327. [23 Cal.L.Rev. Comm. Reports 1 (1993)].

Research References

Forms

California Transactions Forms--Family Law § 6:167, Power Of Attorney for Counsel to Appear on Behalf Of Party to Adoption Of Adult or Married Minor.

Treatises and Practice Aids

Witkin, California Summary 10th Parent and Child § 155, Procedure for Adoption.

§ 9325. Investigation and report

No investigation or report to the court by any public officer or agency is required, but the court may require the county probation officer or the department to investigate the circumstances of the proposed adoption and report thereon, with recommendations, to the court before the hearing. *(Stats. 1992, c. 162 (A.B.2650), § 10, operative Jan. 1, 1994.)*

Law Revision Commission Comments

Enactment [Revised Comment]

Section 9325 continues the last sentence of former Civil Code Section 230.20(b) without change. See also Section 8518 ("department" defined). [23 Cal.L.Rev.Comm. Reports 1 (1993)].

Research References

Forms

California Transactions Forms--Family Law § 6:158, Governing Law--Venue and Procedure.

West's California Code Forms, Family § 9320, Comment Overview--Procedure for Adult Adoption.

Treatises and Practice Aids

Witkin, California Summary 10th Parent and Child § 155, Procedure for Adoption.

§ 9326. Notice of hearing of proposed adoption of developmentally disabled adult

The prospective adoptive parent shall mail or personally serve notice of the hearing and a copy of the petition to the director of the regional center for the developmentally disabled, established pursuant to Chapter 5 (commencing with Section 4620) of Division 4.5 of the Welfare and Institutions Code, and to any living birth parents or adult children of the proposed adoptee, at least 30 days before the day of the hearing on an adoption petition in any case in which both of the following conditions exist:

(a) The proposed adoptee is an adult with developmental disabilities.

(b) The prospective adoptive parent is a provider of board and care, treatment, habilitation, or other services to persons with developmental disabilities or is a spouse or employee of a provider. *(Stats.1992, c. 162 (A.B.2650), § 10, operative Jan. 1, 1994.)*

Law Revision Commission Comments

Enactment [Revised Comment]

Section 9326 continues former Civil Code Section 230.20(e) without substantive change. A reference to "prospective adoptive parent" has been substituted for "person seeking to adopt." This is not a substantive change. See Section 8542 ("prospective adoptive parent" defined). See also Section 8512 ("birth parent" defined). [23 Cal.L.Rev.Comm. Reports 1 (1993)].

Research References

Forms

California Transactions Forms--Family Law § 6:158, Governing Law--Venue and Procedure.

Treatises and Practice Aids

Witkin, California Summary 10th Parent and Child § 155, Procedure for Adoption.

§ 9327. Report on proposed adoption of developmentally disabled adult

If the prospective adoptive parent is a provider of board and care, treatment, habilitation, or other services to persons with developmental disabilities, or is a spouse or employee of a provider, and seeks to adopt an unrelated adult with developmental disabilities, the regional center for the developmentally disabled notified pursuant to Section 9326 shall file a written report with the court regarding the suitability of the proposed adoption in meeting the needs of the proposed adoptee and regarding any known previous adoption by the prospective adoptive parent. *(Stats.1992, c. 162 (A.B.2650), § 10, operative Jan. 1, 1994.)*

Law Revision Commission Comments

Enactment [Revised Comment]

Section 9327 continues former Civil Code Section 230.20(f)(2) without substantive change. References to "prospective adoptive parent" have been substituted for references to "person seeking to adopt" and "the petitioner." These are not substantive changes. See Section 8542 ("prospective adoptive parent" defined). [23 Cal.L.Rev.Comm. Reports 1 (1993)].

Research References

Forms

California Transactions Forms--Family Law § 6:158, Governing Law--Venue and Procedure.

West's California Code Forms, Family § 9320, Comment Overview--Procedure for Adult Adoption.

Treatises and Practice Aids

Witkin, California Summary 10th Parent and Child § 155, Procedure for Adoption.

§ 9328. Hearing; order of adoption or denial of petitions

(a) At the hearing the court shall examine the parties, or the counsel of any party not present in person.

(b) If the court is satisfied that the adoption will be in the best interests of the persons seeking the adoption and in the public interest and that there is no reason why the petition should not be granted, the court shall approve the adoption agreement and make an order of adoption declaring that the person adopted is the child of the adoptive parent. Otherwise, the court shall withhold approval of the agreement and deny the petition.

(c) In determining whether or not the adoption of any person pursuant to this part is in the best interests of the persons seeking the adoption or the public interest, the court may consider evidence, oral or written, whether or not it is in conformity with the Evidence Code. *(Stats.1992, c. 162 (A.B.2650), § 10, operative Jan. 1, 1994.)*

Law Revision Commission Comments

Enactment [Revised Comment]

Section 9328 continues the first and last paragraphs of former Civil Code Section 230.20(c) without substantive change. In subdivision (b), "persons seeking the adoption" has been substituted for "parties" to conform with subdivision (c). The defined term "adoptive parent" has been substituted for "person adopting [the child]." This is not a substantive change. See Section 8503 ("adoptive parent" defined). In subdivision (c), a reference to this part has been substituted for the former reference to this subdivision. This is not a substantive change. [23 Cal.L.Rev.Comm. Reports 1 (1993)].

Research References

Forms

California Transactions Forms--Family Law § 6:5, Issues Common to All Types Of Adoptions.
California Transactions Forms--Family Law § 6:164, Agreement Of Adult Adoption.
West's California Code Forms, Family § 9320, Comment Overview--Procedure for Adult Adoption.

Treatises and Practice Aids

Witkin, California Summary 10th Parent and Child § 155, Procedure for Adoption.

CHAPTER 3. PROCEDURE FOR TERMINATING ADULT ADOPTION

§ 9340. Filing of petition; contents of petition; consent to termination; order

(a) Any person who has been adopted under this part may, upon written notice to the adoptive parent, file a petition to terminate the relationship of parent and child. The petition shall state the name and address of the petitioner, the name and address of the adoptive parent, the date and place of the adoption, and the circumstances upon which the petition is based.

(b) If the adoptive parent consents in writing to the termination, an order terminating the relationship of parent and child may be issued by the court without further notice.

(c) If the adoptive parent does not consent in writing to the termination, a written response shall be filed within 30 days of the date of mailing of the notice, and the matter shall be set for hearing. The court may require an investigation by the county probation officer or the department. *(Stats.1992, c. 162 (A.B.2650), § 10, operative Jan. 1, 1994.)*

Law Revision Commission Comments

Enactment [Revised Comment]

Section 9340 continues former Civil Code Section 230.20(g) without substantive change. In subdivision (a), a reference to this part has been substituted for the former reference to this section. This is not a substantive change. A reference to the "verified" response has been omitted as surplus. See Section 212 (pleadings to be verified). See also Sections 8503 ("adoptive parent" defined), 8518 ("department" defined). [23 Cal.L.Rev.Comm. Reports 1 (1993)].

Research References

Forms

California Transactions Forms--Family Law § 6:2, Governing Law.
California Transactions Forms--Family Law § 6:158, Governing Law--Venue and Procedure.
California Transactions Forms--Family Law § 6:162, Termination Of Adoption.

Treatises and Practice Aids

Witkin, California Summary 10th Parent and Child § 72, Statutory Framework.
Witkin, California Summary 10th Parent and Child § 156, Procedure for Terminating Adoption.

Division 14

FAMILY LAW FACILITATOR ACT

§ 10000. Short title

This division shall be known and may be cited as the Family Law Facilitator Act. *(Added by Stats.1996, c. 957 (A.B.1058), § 9.)*

Research References

Forms

California Practice Guide: Rutter Family Law Forms Form 1:32, Glossary Of Common Family Law Terms, Phrases and Concepts (Enclosure to Form 1:31).

Treatises and Practice Aids

Witkin, California Summary 10th Husband and Wife § 3, Statutory Framework.

Witkin, California Summary 10th Parent and Child § 383, in General.

§ 10001. Legislative findings and declarations

(a) The Legislature finds and declares the following:

(1) Child and spousal support are serious legal obligations. The entry of a child support order is frequently delayed while parents engage in protracted litigation concerning custody and visitation. The current system for obtaining child and spousal support orders is suffering because the family courts are unduly burdened with heavy case loads and do not have sufficient personnel to meet increased demands on the courts.

(2) Reports to the Legislature regarding the family law pilot projects in the Superior Courts of the Counties of Santa Clara and San Mateo indicate that the pilot projects have provided a cost-effective and efficient method for the courts to process family law cases that involve unrepresented litigants with issues concerning child support, spousal support, and health insurance.

(3) The reports to the Legislature further indicate that the pilot projects in both counties have been successful in making the process of obtaining court orders concerning child support, spousal support, and health insurance more accessible to unrepresented parties. Surveys conducted by both counties indicate a high degree of satisfaction with the services provided by the pilot projects.

(4) There is a compelling state interest in having a speedy, conflict-reducing system for resolving issues of child support, spousal support, and health insurance that is cost-effective and accessible to families that cannot afford legal representation.

(b) Therefore, it is the intent of the Legislature to make the services provided in the family law pilot projects in the Counties of Santa Clara and San Mateo available to unrepresented parties in the superior courts of all California counties. *(Added by Stats.1996, c. 957 (A.B.1058), § 9.)*

§ 10002. Family law facilitator office; appointment of facilitator

Each superior court shall maintain an office of the family law facilitator. The office of the family law facilitator shall be staffed by an attorney licensed to practice law in this state who has mediation or litigation experience, or both, in the field of family law. The family law facilitator shall be appointed by the superior court. *(Added by Stats.1996, c. 957 (A.B.1058), § 9.)*

§ 10003. Application of division

This division shall apply to all actions or proceedings for temporary or permanent child support, spousal support, health insurance, child custody, or visitation in a proceeding for dissolution of marriage, nullity of marriage, legal separation, or exclusive child custody, or pursuant to the Uniform Parentage Act (Part 3 (commencing with Section 7600) of Division 12) or the Domestic Violence Prevention Act (Division 10 (commencing with Section 6200)). *(Added by Stats.1996, c. 957 (A.B.1058), § 9. Amended by Stats.1999, c. 652 (S.B.240), § 12.)*

§ 10004. Facilitator services

Services provided by the family law facilitator shall include, but are not limited to, the following: providing educational materials to parents concerning the process of establishing parentage and establishing, modifying, and enforcing child support and spousal support in the courts; distributing necessary court forms and voluntary declarations of paternity; providing assistance in completing forms; preparing support schedules based upon statutory guidelines; and providing referrals to the local child support agency, family court services, and other community agencies and resources that provide services for parents and children. In counties where a family law information center exists, the family law facilitator shall provide assistance on child support issues. *(Added by Stats.1996, c. 957 (A.B.1058), § 9. Amended by Stats.1999, c. 652 (S.B.240), § 13.)*

§ 10005. Additional facilitator duties

(a) By local rule, the superior court may designate additional duties of the family law facilitator, which may include, but are not limited to, the following:

(1) Meeting with litigants to mediate issues of child support, spousal support, and maintenance of health insurance, subject to Section 10012. Actions in which one or both of the parties are unrepresented by counsel shall have priority.

(2) Drafting stipulations to include all issues agreed to by the parties, which may include issues other than those specified in Section 10003.

(3) If the parties are unable to resolve issues with the assistance of the family law facilitator, prior to or at the hearing, and at the request of the court, the family law facilitator shall review the paperwork, examine documents, prepare support schedules, and advise the judge whether or not the matter is ready to proceed.

(4) Assisting the clerk in maintaining records.

(5) Preparing formal orders consistent with the court's announced order in cases where both parties are unrepresented.

(6) Serving as a special master in proceedings and making findings to the court unless he or she has served as a mediator in that case.

(7) Providing the services specified in Section 10004 concerning the issues of child custody and visitation as they relate to calculating child support, if funding is provided for that purpose.

(b) If staff and other resources are available and the duties listed in subdivision (a) have been accomplished, the duties of the family law facilitator may also include the following:

(1) Assisting the court with research and any other responsibilities that will enable the court to be responsive to the litigants' needs.

(2) Developing programs for bar and community outreach through day and evening programs, video recordings, and other innovative means that will assist unrepresented and financially disadvantaged litigants in gaining meaningful access to family court. These programs shall specifically include information concerning underutilized legislation, such as expedited child support orders (Chapter 5 (commencing with Section 3620) of Part 1 of Division 9), and preexisting, court-sponsored programs, such as supervised visitation and appointment of attorneys for children. *(Added by Stats.1996, c. 957 (A.B.1058), § 9. Amended by Stats.1997, c. 599 (A.B.573), § 45; Stats.1999, c. 652 (S.B.240), § 13.5; Stats.2009, c. 88 (A.B.176), § 39.)*

Law Revision Commission Comments

2009 Amendment

Subdivision (a)(7) of Section 10005 is deleted as obsolete. Former Division 15 was repealed by 1999 Cal. Stat. 1004, § 6.

Subdivision (b)(2) is amended to reflect advances in recording technology and for consistency of terminology. For a similar reform, see 2002 Cal. Stat. ch. 1068 (replacing numerous references to "audiotape" in Civil Discovery Act with either "audio technology," "audio recording," or "audio record," as context required). [37 Cal. L. Revision Comm'n Reports 211 (2007)].

§ 10006. Access to court hearing; protocol

The court shall adopt a protocol wherein all litigants, both unrepresented by counsel and represented by counsel, have ultimate access to a hearing before the court. *(Added by Stats.1996, c. 957 (A.B.1058), § 9.)*

§ 10007. Cost to parties

The court shall provide the family law facilitator at no cost to the parties. *(Added by Stats.1996, c. 957 (A.B.1058), § 9.)*

§ 10008. Child support obligations; services provided; services of facilitator

(a) Except as provided in subdivision (b), nothing in this chapter shall be construed to apply to a child for whom services are provided or required to be provided by a local child support agency pursuant to Section 17400.

(b) In cases in which the services of the local child support agency are provided pursuant to Section 17400, either parent may utilize the services of the family law facilitator that are specified in Section 10004. In order for a custodial parent who is receiving the services of the local child support agency pursuant to Section 17400 to utilize the services specified in Section 10005 relating to support, the custodial parent must obtain written authorization from the local child support agency. It is not the intent of the Legislature in enacting this section to limit the duties of local child support agencies with respect to seeking child support payments or to in any way limit or supersede other provisions of this code respecting temporary child support. *(Added by Stats.1996, c. 957 (A.B.1058), § 9. Amended by Stats.2000, c. 808 (A.B.1358), § 78, eff. Sept. 28, 2000.)*

§ 10010. Standards for office

The Judicial Council shall adopt minimum standards for the office of the family law facilitator and any forms or rules of court that are necessary to implement this division. *(Added by Stats.1996, c. 957 (A.B.1058), § 9.)*

§ 10011. Title IV–D funding; federal approval

The Director of the State Department of Social Services shall seek approval from the United States Department of Health and Human Services, Office of Child Support Enforcement, to utilize funding under Title IV–D of the Social Security Act [1] for the services provided pursuant to this division. *(Added by Stats.1996, c. 957 (A.B.1058), § 9.)*

[1] See 42 U.S.C.A. § 651 et seq.

§ 10012. Domestic violence history; separate meetings with parties

(a) In a proceeding in which mediation is required pursuant to paragraph (1) of subdivision (a) of Section 10005, where there has been a history of domestic violence between the parties or where a protective order as defined in Section 6218 is in effect, at the request of the party alleging domestic violence in a written declaration under penalty of perjury or protected by the order, the family law facilitator shall meet with the parties separately and at separate times.

(b) Any intake form that the office of the family law facilitator requires the parties to complete before the commencement of mediation shall state that, if a party alleging domestic violence in a written declaration under penalty of perjury or a party protected by a protective order so requests, the mediator will meet with the parties separately and at separate times. *(Added by Stats.1996, c. 957 (A.B.1058), § 9.)*

§ 10013. Facilitator; attorney-client relationship; notice

The family law facilitator shall not represent any party. No attorney-client relationship is created between a party and the family law facilitator as a result of any information or services provided to the party by the family law facilitator. The family law facilitator shall give conspicuous notice that no attorney-client relationship exists between the facilitator, its staff, and the family law litigant. The notice shall include the advice that the absence of an attorney-client relationship means that communications between the party and the family law facilitator are not privileged and that the family law facilitator may provide services to the other party. *(Added by Stats.1999, c. 652 (S.B.240), § 14.)*

§ 10014. Person employed or supervised by facilitator; public comments; ethical requirements

A person employed by, or directly supervised by, the family law facilitator shall not make any public comment about a pending or impending proceeding in the court as provided by paragraph (9) of subdivision (B) of Canon 3 of the Code of Judicial Ethics. All persons employed by or directly supervised by the family law facilitator shall be provided a copy of paragraph (9) of subdivision (B) of Canon 3 of the Code of Judicial Ethics, and shall be required to sign an acknowledgment that he or she is aware of its provisions. *(Added by Stats.1999, c. 652 (S.B.240), § 15.)*

§ 10015. Forms

The Judicial Council shall create any necessary forms to advise the parties of the types of services provided, that there is no attorney-client relationship, that the family law facilitator is not responsible for the outcome of any case, that the family law facilitator does not represent any party and will not appear in court on the party's behalf, and that the other party may also be receiving information and services from the family law facilitator. *(Added by Stats.1999, c. 652 (S.B.240), § 15.5.)*

Research References

Forms

West's California Judicial Council Forms FL-940, Office Of the Family Law Facilitator Disclosure.

Division 17

SUPPORT SERVICES

CHAPTER 1. DEPARTMENT OF CHILD SUPPORT SERVICES

ARTICLE 1. GENERAL

§ 17000. Definitions

The definitions contained in this section, and definitions applicable to Division 9 (commencing with Section 3500), shall govern the construction of this division, unless the context requires otherwise.

(a) "Child support debt" means the amount of money owed as child support pursuant to a court order.

(b) "Child support order" means any court order for the payment of a set or determinable amount of support by a parent or a court order requiring a parent to provide for health insurance coverage. "Child support order" includes any court order for spousal support or for medical support to the extent these obligations are to be enforced by a single state agency for child support under Title IV–D.

(c) "Court" means any superior court of this state and any court or tribunal of another state that has jurisdiction to determine the liability of persons for the support of another person.

(d) "Court order" means any judgment, decree, or order of any court of this state that orders the payment of a set or determinable amount of support by a parent. It does not include any order or decree of any proceeding in which a court did not order support.

(e) "Department" means the Department of Child Support Services.

(f) "Dependent child" means any of the following:

(1) Any person under 18 years of age who is not emancipated, self-supporting, married, or a member of the armed forces of the United States.

(2) Any unmarried person who is at least 18 years of age but who has not reached his or her 19th birthday, is not emancipated, and is a student regularly attending high school or a program of vocational or technical training designed to train that person for gainful employment.

(g) "Director" means the Director of Child Support Services or his or her authorized representative.

(h) "Local child support agency" means the new county department of child support services created pursuant to this chapter and with which the department has entered into a cooperative agreement, to secure child and spousal support, medical support, and determine paternity. Local child support agency includes county programs in multiple counties that have been consolidated into a single agency pursuant to subdivision (a) of Section 17304.

(i) "Parent" means the natural or adoptive father or mother of a dependent child, and includes any person who has an enforceable obligation to support a dependent child.

(j) "Public assistance" means any amount paid under the California Work Opportunity and Responsibility to Kids Act (Chapter 2 (commencing with Section 11200) of Part 3 of Division 9 of the Welfare and Institutions Code), or any Medi–Cal benefit, for the benefit of any dependent child or the caretaker of a child.

(k) "Public assistance debt" means any amount paid under the California Work Opportunity and Responsibility to Kids Act, contained in Chapter 2 (commencing with Section 11200) of Part 3 of Division 9 of the Welfare and Institutions Code, for the benefit of any dependent child or the caretaker of a child for whom the department is authorized to seek recoupment under this division, subject to applicable federal law.

(*l*) "Title IV–D" or "IV-D" means Part D of Title IV of the federal Social Security Act (42 U.S.C. Sec. 651 et seq.). *(Added by Stats.1999, c. 478 (A.B.196), § 1. Amended by Stats.1999, c. 480 (S.B.542), § 5; Stats.2000, c. 808 (A.B. 1358), § 78.3, eff. Sept. 28, 2000; Stats.2003, c. 308 (A.B.738), § 3.)*

Commentary

Relying on the final sentence of subsection (b) and subsection (*l*), *In re Marriage of Lamoure, 198 Cal.App.4th 807, 132 Cal.Rptr.3d 1 (2011), review denied*, holds that a parent who has requested enforcement by the Department of Child Support Services (DCSS) may collect spousal support as well as child support arrearages under the Financial Institution Data Match provisions (§ 17453 et seq.). Enforcement need not be originally initiated by the DCSS; nor need the parent be receiving public assistance. All that is required is that the support obligee have requested DCSS enforcement and the obligor have been ordered to send all support payments to DCSS (§ 17400(a)).

Research References

Forms

California Practice Guide: Rutter Family Law Forms Form 1:32, Glossary Of Common Family Law Terms, Phrases and Concepts (Enclosure to Form 1:31).

West's California Code Forms, Family § 4200, Comment Overview--Child Support Orders to Parents.

West's California Code Forms, Family § 4500, Comment Overview--Enforcement Of Support Orders.

West's California Code Forms, Family § 5230, Comment Overview--Earnings Assignment Order.

Treatises and Practice Aids

Witkin, California Summary 10th Husband and Wife § 3, Statutory Framework.
Witkin, California Summary 10th Husband and Wife § 308, Background and Scope.
Witkin, California Summary 10th Husband and Wife § 310, Local Child Support Agency.
Witkin, California Summary 10th Parent and Child § 2, The Family Code.
Witkin, California Summary 10th Parent and Child § 383, in General.

ARTICLE 2. ORGANIZATION

§ 17200. Creation and duties

The Department of Child Support Services is hereby created within the California Health and Human Services Agency. The department shall administer all services and perform all functions necessary to establish, collect, and distribute child support. *(Added by Stats.1999, c. 478 (A.B. 196), § 1.)*

Research References

Forms

California Transactions Forms--Family Law § 3:3, Child Support.
California Transactions Forms--Family Law § 3:21, Jurisdiction for Orders to Pay Child Support.

Treatises and Practice Aids

Witkin, California Summary 10th Husband and Wife § 309, State Department Of Child Support Services.

§ 17202. Title IV–D state plan administration; state plan functions

(a) The department is hereby designated the single organizational unit whose duty it shall be to administer the Title IV–D state plan for securing child and spousal support, medical support, and determining paternity. State plan functions shall be performed by other agencies as required by law, by delegation of the department, or by cooperative agreements.

(b) The department shall appoint the local child support agency, as defined in Section 17304, or any other entity receiving federal tax information in performance of its child support duties as its designee for purposes of paragraph (26) of subdivision (b) of Section 11105 of the Penal Code.

(c) For purposes of this section, "federal tax information" is as defined in Section 1044 of the Government Code. *(Added by Stats.1999, c. 478 (A.B.196), § 1. Amended by Stats.2017, c. 19 (A.B.111), § 7, eff. June 27, 2017.)*

Research References

Treatises and Practice Aids

Witkin, California Summary 10th Husband and Wife § 309, State Department Of Child Support Services.

§ 17204. Director and administrative units

The department consists of the director and such division or other administrative units as the director may find necessary. *(Added by Stats.1999, c. 478 (A.B.196), § 1.)*

Research References

Treatises and Practice Aids

Witkin, California Summary 10th Husband and Wife § 309, State Department Of Child Support Services.

§ 17206. Structure and staff

The department shall ensure that there is an adequate organizational structure and sufficient staff to perform functions delegated to any governmental unit relating to Part D (commencing with Section 651) of Subchapter 4 of Chapter 7 of Title 42 of the United States Code, including a sufficient number of attorneys to ensure that all requirements of due process are satisfied in the establishment and enforcement of child support orders. *(Added by Stats.1999, c. 478 (A.B.196), § 1.)*

§ 17208. Cost reduction; speed and efficiency; enforcement through local agencies; federal funds; administrative service fee

(a) The department shall reduce the cost of, and increase the speed and efficiency of, child support enforcement operations. It is the intent of the Legislature to operate the child support enforcement program through local child support agencies without a net increase in state General Fund or county general fund costs, considering all increases to the General Fund as a result of increased collections and welfare recoupment.

(b) The department shall maximize the use of federal funds available for the costs of administering a child support services department, and to the maximum extent feasible, obtain funds from federal financial incentives for the efficient collection of child support, to defray the remaining costs of administration of the department consistent with effective and efficient support enforcement.

(c) Effective October 1, 2010, the Department of Child Support Services shall impose an administrative service fee in the amount of twenty-five dollars ($25) on a never-assisted custodial party receiving services from the California child support program for order establishment, enforcement, and collection services provided. The annual amount of child support payments collected on behalf of the custodial party must be five hundred dollars ($500) or more before an administrative service fee is imposed pursuant to this subdivision. The fee shall be deducted from the custodial party's collection payment at the time the collection payments for that year have reached levels specified by the department. *(Added by Stats.1999, c. 478 (A.B.196), § 1. Amended by Stats.2009–2010, 4th Ex.Sess., c. 4 (A.B.4), § 1, eff. July 28, 2009.)*

§ 17210. Local agency accessibility

The department shall ensure that the local child support agency offices and services are reasonably accessible throughout the counties, and shall establish systems for informing the public, including custodial and noncustodial parents of dependent children, of its services and operations. *(Added by Stats.1999, c. 478 (A.B.196), § 1.)*

§ 17211. Child Support Assurance Demonstration Project; county demonstration projects to provide employment and training services to nonsupporting noncustodial parents

The department shall administer the Child Support Assurance Demonstration Project established by Article 5 (commencing with Section 18241) of Chapter 3.3 of Part 6 of the Welfare and Institutions Code, and the county demonstration projects to provide employment and training services to nonsupporting noncustodial parents authorized by Section 18205.5 of the Welfare and Institutions Code. However, the department may contract with the State Department of Social Services to continue development and implementation of these demonstration projects until they have been fully implemented. After the demonstration projects have been fully implemented, the department shall consult with the State Department of Social Services on the administration of the projects. The contracts for evaluation of the demonstration projects shall continue to be maintained by the State Department of Social Services. The department shall be responsible for the final evaluation of the projects. *(Added by Stats.1999, c. 478 (A.B.196), § 1. Amended by Stats.1999, c. 480 (S.B.542), § 6.)*

§ 17212. Privacy rights; confidentiality of records

(a) It is the intent of the Legislature to protect individual rights of privacy, and to facilitate and enhance the effectiveness of the child and spousal support enforcement program, by ensuring the confidentiality of support enforcement and child abduction records, and to thereby encourage the full and frank disclosure of information relevant to all of the following:

(1) The establishment or maintenance of parent and child relationships and support obligations.

(2) The enforcement of the child support liability of absent parents.

(3) The enforcement of spousal support liability of the spouse or former spouse to the extent required by the state plan under Section 17604 and Part 6 (commencing with Section 5700.101) of Division 9.

(4) The location of absent parents.

(5) The location of parents and children abducted, concealed, or detained by them.

(b)(1) Except as provided in subdivision (c), all files, applications, papers, documents, and records established or maintained by any public entity pursuant to the administration and implementation of the child and spousal support enforcement program established pursuant to Part D (commencing with Section 651) of Subchapter IV of Chapter 7 of Title 42 of the United States Code and this division, shall be confidential, and shall not be open to examination or released for disclosure for any purpose not directly connected with the administration of the child and spousal support enforcement program. No public entity shall disclose any file, application, paper, document, or record, or the information contained therein, except as expressly authorized by this section.

(2) In no case shall information be released or the whereabouts of one party or the child disclosed to another party, or to the attorney of any other party, if a protective order has been issued by a court or administrative agency with respect to the party, a good cause claim under Section 11477.04 of the Welfare and Institutions Code has been approved or is pending, or the public agency responsible for establishing paternity or enforcing support has reason to believe that the release of the information may result in physical or emotional harm to the party or the child. When a local child support agency is prohibited from releasing information pursuant to this subdivision, the information shall be omitted from any pleading or document to be submitted to the court and this subdivision shall be cited in the pleading or other document as the authority for the omission. The information shall be released only upon an order of the court pursuant to paragraph (6) of subdivision (c).

(3) Notwithstanding any other law, a proof of service filed by the local child support agency shall not disclose the address where service of process was accomplished. Instead, the local child support agency shall keep the address in its own records. The proof of service shall specify that the address is on record at the local child support agency and that the address may be released only upon an order from the court pursuant to paragraph (6) of subdivision (c). The local child support agency shall, upon request by a party served, release to that person the address where service was effected.

(c) Disclosure of the information described in subdivision (b) is authorized as follows:

(1) All files, applications, papers, documents, and records as described in subdivision (b) shall be available and may be used by a public entity for all administrative, civil, or criminal investigations, actions, proceedings, or prosecutions conducted in connection with the administration of the child and spousal support enforcement program approved under Part D (commencing with Section 651) of Subchapter IV of Chapter 7 of Title 42 of the United States Code and to the county welfare department responsible for administering a program operated under a state plan pursuant to Part A, Subpart 1 or 2 of Part B, or Part E of Subchapter IV of Chapter 7 of Title 42 of the United States Code.

(2) A document requested by a person who wrote, prepared, or furnished the document may be examined by or disclosed to that person or his or her designee.

(3) The payment history of an obligor pursuant to a support order may be examined by or released to the court, the obligor, or the person on whose behalf enforcement actions are being taken or that person's designee.

(4) An income and expense declaration of either parent may be released to the other parent for the purpose of establishing or modifying a support order.

(5) Public records subject to disclosure under the California Public Records Act (Chapter 3.5 (commencing with Section 6250) of Division 7 of Title 1 of the Government Code) may be released.

(6) After a noticed motion and a finding by the court, in a case in which establishment or enforcement actions are being taken, that release or disclosure to the obligor or obligee is required by due process of law, the court may order a public entity that possesses an application, paper, document, or record as described in subdivision (b) to make that item available to the obligor or obligee for examination or copying, or to disclose to the obligor or obligee the contents of that item. Article 9 (commencing with Section 1040) of Chapter 4 of Division 8 of the Evidence Code shall not be applicable to proceedings under this part. At any hearing of a motion filed pursuant to this section, the court shall inquire of the local child support agency and the parties appearing at the hearing if there is reason to believe that release of the requested information may result in physical or emotional harm to a party. If the court determines that harm may occur, the court shall issue any protective orders or injunctive orders restricting the use and disclosure of the information as are necessary to protect the individuals.

(7) To the extent not prohibited by federal law or regulation, information indicating the existence or imminent threat of a crime against a child, or location of a concealed, detained, or abducted child or the location of the concealing, detaining, or abducting person, may be disclosed to any district attorney, any appropriate law enforcement agency, or to any state or county child protective agency, or may be used in any judicial proceedings to prosecute that crime or to protect the child.

(8) The social security number, most recent address, and the place of employment of the absent parent may be released to an authorized person as defined in Section 653(c) of Title 42 of the United States Code, only if the authorized person has filed a request for the information, and only if the information has been provided to the California Parent Locator Service by the federal Parent Locator Service pursuant to Section 653 of Title 42 of the United States Code.

(9) A parent's or relative's name, social security number, most recent address, telephone number, place of employment, or other contact information may be released to a county child welfare agency or county probation department pursuant to subdivision (c) of Section 17506.

(d)(1) "Administration and implementation of the child and spousal support enforcement program," as used in this division, means the carrying out of the state and local plans for establishing, modifying, and enforcing child support obligations, enforcing spousal support orders, and determining paternity pursuant to Part D (commencing with Section 651) of Subchapter IV of Chapter 7 of Title 42 of the United States Code and this article.

(2) For purposes of this division, "obligor" means any person owing a duty of support.

(3) As used in this division, "putative parent" shall refer to any person reasonably believed to be the parent of a child for whom the local child support agency is attempting to establish paternity or establish, modify, or enforce support pursuant to Section 17400.

(e) Any person who willfully, knowingly, and intentionally violates this section is guilty of a misdemeanor.

(f) Nothing in this section shall be construed to compel the disclosure of information relating to a deserting parent who is a recipient of aid under a public assistance program for which federal aid is paid to this state, if that information is required to be kept confidential by the federal law or regulations relating to the program. *(Added by Stats.1999, c. 478 (A.B.196), § 1. Amended by Stats.1999, c. 653 (A.B.380), § 12; Stats.2000, c. 808 (A.B.1358), § 79, eff. Sept. 28, 2000; Stats.2001, c. 755 (S.B.943), § 10, eff. Oct. 12, 2001; Stats. 2012, c. 637 (A.B.1751), § 2; Stats.2014, c. 772 (S.B.1460), § 2, eff. Jan. 1, 2015; Stats.2015, c. 493 (S.B.646), § 7, eff. Jan. 1, 2016; Stats.2016, c. 474 (A.B.2882), § 11, eff. Jan. 1, 2017.)*

Research References

Treatises and Practice Aids

Witkin, California Summary 10th Husband and Wife § 314, Acquisition and Confidentiality Of Information.

ARTICLE 3. DIRECTOR OF CHILD SUPPORT SERVICES

§ 17300. Appointment; salary; deputies

With the consent of the Senate, the Governor shall appoint, to serve at his or her pleasure, an executive officer who shall be director of the department. In making the appointment the Governor shall consider training, demonstrated ability, experience, and leadership in organized child support enforcement administration. The director shall receive the salary provided for by Chapter 6 (commencing with Section 11550), Part 1, Division 3, Title 2 of the Government Code.

The Governor also may appoint, to serve at his or her pleasure, not to exceed two chief deputy directors of the department, and one deputy director of the department. The salaries of the chief deputy directors and the deputy director shall be fixed in accordance with law. *(Added by Stats.1999, c. 478 (A.B.196), § 1. Amended by Stats.1999, c. 480 (S.B.542), § 6.5.)*

Research References

Treatises and Practice Aids

Witkin, California Summary 10th Husband and Wife § 309, State Department Of Child Support Services.

§ 17302. Duties

The director shall do all of the following:

(a) Be responsible for the management of the department.

(b) Administer all federal and state laws and regulations pertaining to the administration of child support enforcement obligations.

(c) Perform all duties as may be prescribed by law, and any other administrative and executive duties imposed by law.

(d) Observe, and report to the Governor, the Legislature, and the public on, the conditions of child support enforcement activities throughout the state pursuant to subdivision (e) of Section 17602. *(Added by Stats.1999, c. 478 (A.B.196), § 1. Amended by Stats.1999, c. 480 (S.B.542), § 7.)*

Research References

Treatises and Practice Aids

Witkin, California Summary 10th Husband and Wife § 309, State Department Of Child Support Services.

§ 17303. Legislative findings and declarations

The Legislature finds and declares all of the following:

(a) Title IV–D of the federal Social Security Act, contained in Part D (commencing with Section 651) of Subchapter 4 of Chapter 7 of Title 42 of the United States Code, requires that there be a single state agency for child support enforcement. California's child support enforcement system is extremely complex, involving numerous state and local agencies. The state's system was divided between the State Department of Social Services, the Attorney General's office, the Franchise Tax Board, the Employment Development Department, the Department of Motor Vehicles, and the 58 county district attorneys' offices.

(b) The lack of coordination and integration between state and local child support agencies has been a major impediment to getting support to the children of this state. An effective child support enforcement program must have strong leadership and effective state oversight and management to best serve the needs of the children of the state.

(c) The state would benefit by centralizing its obligation to hold counties responsible for collecting support. Oversight would be best accomplished by direct management by the state.

(d) A single state agency for child support enforcement with strong leadership and direct accountability for local child support agencies will benefit the taxpayers of the state by reducing the inefficiencies introduced by involving multiple layers of government in child support enforcement operations. *(Added by Stats.1999, c. 478 (A.B.196), § 1.)*

Research References

Treatises and Practice Aids

Witkin, California Summary 10th Husband and Wife § 309, State Department Of Child Support Services.

§ 17304. County departments of child support services; duties; criminal enforcement; state plan for local agency functions; cooperative agreements; consolidation; oversight responsibility; district attorney responsibility, assets, and staff; administrators

To address the concerns stated by the Legislature in Section 17303, each county shall establish a new county department of child support services. Each department is also referred to in this division as the local child support agency. The local child support agency shall be separate and independent from any other county department and shall be responsible for promptly and effectively establishing, modifying, and enforcing child support obligations, including medical support, enforcing spousal support orders established by a court of competent jurisdiction, and determining paternity in the case of a child born out of wedlock. The local child support agency shall refer all cases requiring criminal enforcement services to the district attorney and the district attorney shall prosecute those cases, as appropriate. If a district attorney fails to comply with this section, the director shall notify the Attorney General and the Attorney General shall take appropriate action to secure compliance. The director shall be responsible for implementing and administering all aspects of the state plan that direct the functions to be performed by the local child support agencies relating to their Title IV–D operations. In developing the new system, all of the following shall apply:

(a) The director shall negotiate and enter into cooperative agreements with county and state agencies to carry out the requirements of the state plan and provide services relating to the establishment of paternity or the establishment, modification, or enforcement of child support obligations as required pursuant to Section 654 of Title 42 of the United States Code. The cooperative agreements shall require that the local child support agencies are reasonably accessible to the citizens of each county and are visible and accountable to the public for their activities. The director, in consultation with the impacted counties, may consolidate the local child support agencies, or any function of the agencies, in more than one county into a single local child support agency, if the director determines that the consolidation will increase the efficiency of the state Title IV–D program and each county has at least one local child support office accessible to the public.

(b) The director shall have direct oversight and supervision of the Title IV–D operations of the local child support agency, and no other local or state agency shall have any authority over the local child support agency as to any function relating to its Title IV–D operations. The local child support agency shall be responsible for the performance of child support enforcement activities required by law and regulation in a manner prescribed by the department. The administrator of the local child support agency shall be responsible for reporting to and responding to the director on all aspects of the child support program.

(c) Nothing in this section prohibits the local child support agency, with the prior approval of the director, from entering into cooperative arrangements with other county departments, as necessary to carry out the responsibilities imposed by this section pursuant to plans of cooperation submitted to the department and approved by the director. The local child support agency may not enter into a cooperative agreement or contract with any county department or independently elected official, including the office of the district attorney, to run, supervise, manage, or oversee the Title IV–D functions of the local child support agency. Until September 1, 2004, the local child support agency may enter into a cooperative agreement or contract of restricted scope and duration with a district attorney to utilize individual attorneys as necessary to carry out limited attorney services. Any cooperative agreement or contract for the attorney services shall be subject to approval by the department and contingent upon a written finding by the department that either the relatively small size of the local child support agency program, or other serious programmatic needs, arising as a result of the transition make it most efficient and cost-effective to contract for limited attorney services. The department shall ensure that any cooperative agreement or contract for attorney services provides that all attorneys be supervised by, and report directly to, the local child support agency, and comply with all state and federal child support laws and regulations. The office of the Legislative Analyst shall review and assess the efficiency and effectiveness of that cooperative agreement or contract, and shall report its findings to the Legislature by January 1, 2004. Within 60 days of receipt of a plan of cooperation or contract from the local child support agency, the department shall either approve the plan of cooperation or contract or notify the agency that the plan is denied. If an agency is notified that the plan is denied, the agency shall have the opportunity to resubmit a revised plan of cooperation or contract. If the director fails to respond in writing within 60 days of receipt, the plan shall otherwise be deemed approved. Nothing in this section shall be deemed an approval of program costs relative to the cooperative arrangements entered into by the counties with other county departments.

(d) In order to minimize the disruption of services provided and to capitalize on the expertise of employees, the director shall create a program that builds on existing staff and facilities to the fullest extent possible. All assets of the family support division in the district attorney's office shall become assets of the local child support agency.

(e)(1)(A) Except as provided in subparagraph (B), all employees and other personnel who serve the office of the district attorney and perform child support collection and enforcement activities shall become the employees and other personnel of the county child support agency at their existing or equivalent classifications, and at their existing salaries and benefits that include, but are not limited to, accrued and unused vacation, sick leave, personal leave, and health and pension plans.

(B) The Title IV–D director is entitled to become an employee of the local child support agency or may be selected as the administrator pursuant to the provisions of subdivision (f).

(2) Permanent employees of the office of the district attorney on the effective date of this chapter shall be deemed qualified, and no other qualifications shall be required for employment or retention in the county child support agency. Probationary employees on the effective date of this chapter shall retain their probationary status and rights, and shall not be deemed to have transferred, so as to require serving a new probationary period.

(3) Employment seniority of an employee of the office of the district attorney on the effective date of this chapter shall be counted toward seniority in the county child support agency and all time spent in the same, equivalent, or higher classification shall be counted toward classification seniority.

(4) An employee organization that has been recognized as the representative or exclusive representative of an established appropriate bargaining unit of employees who perform child support collection and enforcement activities shall continue to be recognized as the representative or exclusive representative of the same employees of the county.

(5) An existing memorandum of understanding or agreement between the county or the office of the district attorney and the employee organization shall remain in effect and be fully binding on the parties involved for the term of the agreement.

(6) Nothing in this section shall be construed to limit the rights of employees or employee organizations to bargain in good faith on matters of wages, hours, or other terms and conditions of employment, including the negotiation of workplace standards within the scope of bargaining as authorized by state and federal law.

(7)(A) Except as provided in subparagraph (B), a public agency shall, in implementing programs affected by the act of addition or amendment of this chapter to this code, perform program functions exclusively through the use of merit civil service employees of the public agency.

(B) Prior to transition from the district attorney to the local child support agency under Section 17305, the district attorney may continue existing contracts and their renewals, as appropriate. After the transition under Section 17305, any contracting out of program functions shall be approved by the director consistent with Section 31000 and following of the Government Code, except as otherwise provided in subdivision (c) with regard to attorney services. The director shall approve or disapprove a proposal to contract out within 60 days. Failure of the director to respond to a request to contract out within 60 days after receipt of the request shall be deemed approval, unless the director submits an extension to respond, which in no event shall be longer than 30 days.

(f) The administrator of the local child support agency shall be an employee of the county selected by the board of supervisors, or in the case of a city and county, selected by the mayor, pursuant to the qualifications established by the department. The administrator may hire staff, including attorneys, to fulfill the functions required by the agency and in conformity with any staffing requirements adopted by the department, including all those set forth in Section 17306. All staff shall be employees of the county and shall comply with all local, state, and federal child support laws, regulations, and directives. *(Added by Stats.1999, c. 478 (A.B.196), § 1. Amended by Stats.1999, c. 480 (S.B.542), § 8; Stats. 2000, c. 808 (A.B.1358), § 80, eff. Sept. 28, 2000; Stats.2001, c. 755 (S.B.943), § 11, eff. Oct. 12, 2001.)*

Research References

Forms

California Transactions Forms--Family Law § 3:3, Child Support.
California Transactions Forms--Family Law § 3:21, Jurisdiction for Orders to Pay Child Support.
West's California Judicial Council Forms FL-684, Request for Order and Supporting Declaration (Governmental).

Treatises and Practice Aids

Witkin, California Summary 10th Husband and Wife § 308, Background and Scope.
Witkin, California Summary 10th Husband and Wife § 309, State Department Of Child Support Services.
Witkin, California Summary 10th Husband and Wife § 310, Local Child Support Agency.

§ 17305. Transition from district attorney to local agency

(a) In order to achieve an orderly and timely transition to the new system with minimal disruption of services, the director shall begin the transition from the office of the district attorney to the local child support agencies pursuant to Section 17304, commencing January 1, 2001. The director shall transfer the appropriate number of counties, equaling at least 50 percent of the statewide caseload into the new system by January 1, 2002. The transition shall be completed by January 1, 2003. A county that has appointed an administrator for the local child support agency and has complied with the requirements of subdivision (b) may transition prior to January 1, 2001, subject to the approval of the director. In determining the order in which counties will be transferred from the office of the district attorney to the local child support agencies, the director shall do all of the following:

(1) Consider the performance of the counties in establishing and collecting child support.

(2) Minimize the disruption of the services provided by the counties.

(3) Optimize the chances of a successful transition.

(b) In order to achieve an orderly transition with minimal disruption of services, a county shall submit a plan of transition which shall be approved by the department prior to transition.

(c) The director shall consult with the district attorney to achieve an orderly transition and to minimize the disruption of services. Each district attorney shall cooperate in the transition as requested by the director.

(d) To minimize any disruption of services provided under the child support enforcement program during the transition, each district attorney shall:

(1) Continue to be designated the single organizational unit whose duty it shall be to administer the Title IV–D state plan for securing child and spousal support, medical support, and determining paternity for that county until such time as the county is notified by the director that the county has been transferred pursuant to subdivision (a) or sooner under Section 17602.

(2) At a minimum, maintain all levels of funding, staffing, and services as of January 1, 1999, to administer the Title IV–D state plan for securing child and spousal support, medical support, and determining paternity. If the director determines that a district attorney has lowered the funding, staffing, or services of the child support enforcement program, the director may withhold part or all state and federal funds, including incentive funds, from the district attorney. Before the director withholds part of or all state and federal funds, including incentive funds, the district attorney shall have the opportunity to demonstrate good cause for any reductions in funding, staffing, or services. Good cause exceptions for reductions shall include, but not be limited to, natural staff attrition and caseload changes. *(Added by Stats.1999, c. 478 (A.B.196), § 1. Amended by Stats.1999, c. 480 (S.B.542), § 9.)*

Research References

Treatises and Practice Aids

Witkin, California Summary 10th Husband and Wife § 310, Local Child Support Agency.

§ 17306. Legislative findings and declarations; uniform forms, policies, and procedures for local agencies

(a) The Legislature finds and declares all of the following:

(1) While the State Department of Social Services has had statutory authority over the child support system, the locally elected district attorneys have operated their county programs with a great deal of autonomy.

(2) District attorneys have operated the child support programs with different forms, procedures, and priorities, making it difficult to adequately evaluate and modify performance statewide.

(3) Problems collecting child support reflect a fundamental lack of leadership and accountability in the collection program. These management problems have cost California taxpayers and families billions of dollars.

(b) The director shall develop uniform forms, policies, and procedures to be employed statewide by all local child support agencies. Pursuant to this subdivision, the director shall:

(1) Adopt uniform procedures and forms.

(2) Establish standard caseworker to case staffing ratios, adjusted as appropriate to meet the varying needs of local programs.

(3) Establish standard attorney to caseworker ratios, adjusted as appropriate to meet the varying needs of local programs.

(4) Institute a consistent statewide policy on the appropriateness of closing cases to ensure that, without relying solely on federal minimum requirements, all cases are fully and pragmatically pursued for collections prior to closing.

(5) Evaluate the best practices for the establishment, enforcement, and collection of child support, for the purpose of determining which practices should be implemented statewide in an effort to improve performance by local child support agencies. In evaluating the best practices, the director shall review existing practices in better performing counties within California, as well as practices implemented by other state Title IV–D programs nationwide.

(6) Evaluate the best practices for the management of effective child support enforcement operations for the purpose of determining what management structure should be implemented statewide in an effort to improve the establishment, enforcement, and collection of child support by local child support agencies, including an examination of the need for attorneys in management level positions. In evaluating the best practices, the director shall review existing practices in better performing counties within California, as well as practices implemented by other state Title IV–D programs nationwide.

(7) Set priorities for the use of specific enforcement mechanisms for use by local child support agencies. As part of establishing these priorities, the director shall set forth caseload processing priorities to target enforcement efforts and services in a way that will maximize collections and avoid welfare dependency.

(8) Develop uniform training protocols, require periodic training of all child support staff, and conduct training sessions as appropriate.

(9) Review and approve annual budgets submitted by the local child support agencies to ensure each local child support agency operates an effective and efficient program that complies with all federal and state laws, regulations, and directives, including the directive to hire sufficient staff.

(c) The director shall submit any forms intended for use in court proceedings to the Judicial Council for approval at least six months prior to the implementation of the use of the forms.

(d) In adopting the forms, policies, and procedures, the director shall consult with appropriate organizations representing stakeholders in California, such as the California State Association of Counties, labor organizations, custodial and noncustodial parent advocates, child support commissioners, family law facilitators, and the appropriate committees of the Legislature.

(e)(1)(A) Notwithstanding the Administrative Procedure Act, Chapter 3.5 (commencing with Section 11340) of Part 1 of Division 3 of Title 2 of the Government Code, through December 31, 2007, the department may implement the applicable provisions of this division through child support services letters or similar instructions from the director.

(B) The department shall adopt regulations implementing the forms, policies, and procedures established pursuant to this section. The director may delay implementation of any of these regulations in any county for any time as the director deems necessary for the smooth transition and efficient operation of a local child support agency, but implementation shall not be delayed beyond the time at which the transition to the new county department of child support services is completed. The department may adopt regulations to implement this division in accordance with the Administrative Procedure Act. The adoption of any emergency regulation filed with the Office of Administrative Law on or before December 31, 2007, shall be deemed to be an emergency and necessary for the immediate preservation of the public peace, health, and safety or general welfare. These emergency regulations shall remain in effect for no more than 180 days.

(2) It is the intent of the Legislature that the amendments to paragraph (1) of this subdivision made by Assembly Bill 3032 of the 2001–02 Regular Session shall be retroactive to June 30, 2002. *(Added by Stats.1999, c. 478 (A.B.196), § 1. Amended by Stats.1999, c. 480 (S.B.542), § 10; Stats.2001, c. 111 (A.B.429), § 2, eff. July 30, 2001; Stats.2002, c. 927 (A.B.3032), § 3.5; Stats.2004, c. 806 (A.B.2358), § 2; Stats. 2016, c. 474 (A.B.2882), § 12, eff. Jan. 1, 2017.)*

§ 17307. Legislative findings and declarations with respect to authority and discretion of Department of Child Support Services to prevent, correct, or remedy effects of changes in timing of receipt of child support payments resulting solely from initial implementation of federally required State Disbursement Unit

(a) The Legislature hereby finds and declares that the Department of Child Support Services has the authority and discretion to prevent, correct, or remedy the effects of changes in the timing of the receipt of child support payments resulting solely from the initial implementation of the federally required State Disbursement Unit. This authority shall not be construed to supplant existing statutory appropriation and technology project approval processes, limits, and requirements.

(b) The Legislature hereby finds and declares that this section is declaratory of existing law. *(Added by Stats.2006, c. 75 (A.B.1808), § 6, eff. July 12, 2006.)*

§ 17308. Automated child support system

The director shall assume responsibility for implementing and managing all aspects of a single statewide automated child support system that will comply with state and federal requirements. The director may delegate responsibility to, or enter into an agreement with, any agency or entity that it deems necessary to satisfy this requirement. *(Added by Stats.1999, c. 478 (A.B.196), § 1.)*

§ 17309. State Disbursement Unit

Effective October 1, 1998, the state shall operate a State Disbursement Unit as required by federal law (42 U.S.C. Secs. 654 (27), 654a(g), and 654b). *(Added by Stats.1999, c. 478 (A.B.196), § 1. Amended by Stats.2003, c. 387 (A.B.739), § 10.)*

Research References

Treatises and Practice Aids

Witkin, California Summary 10th Husband and Wife § 253, Rights and Obligations Of Employer.

Witkin, California Summary 10th Husband and Wife § 313, Payment to County by Court and Referral.

§ 17309.5. Employers required to make child support payments by electronic fund transfer; election to make payments; definitions

(a) An employer who is required to withhold and, by electronic fund transfer, pay tax pursuant to Section 19011 of the Revenue and Taxation Code or Section 13021 of the Unemployment Insurance Code, shall make child support payments to the State Disbursement Unit by electronic fund transfer. All child support payments required to be made to the State Disbursement Unit shall be remitted to the State Disbursement Unit by electronic fund transfer pursuant to Division 11 (commencing with Section 11101) of the Commercial Code.

(b) An employer not required to make payment to the State Disbursement Unit pursuant to paragraph (a), may elect to make payment by electronic fund transfer under the following conditions:

(1) The election shall be made in a form, and shall contain information, as prescribed by the Director of the Department of Child Support Services, and shall be subject to approval of the department.

(2) The election may be terminated upon written request to the Department of Child Support Services.

(c) For the purposes of this section:

(1) "Electronic fund transfer" means any transfer of funds, other than a transaction originated by check, draft, or similar paper instrument, that is initiated through an electronic terminal, telephonic instrument, or computer or magnetic tape, so as to order, instruct, or authorize a financial institution to debit or credit an account. Electronic fund transfers shall be accomplished by an automated clearinghouse debit, an automated clearinghouse credit, or by Federal Reserve Wire Transfer (Fedwire).

(2) "Automated clearinghouse" means any federal reserve bank, or an organization established in agreement with the National Automated Clearinghouse Association, that operates as a clearinghouse for transmitting or receiving entries between banks or bank accounts and which authorizes an electronic transfer of funds between these banks or bank accounts.

(3) "Automated clearinghouse debit" means a transaction in which the state, through its designated depository bank, originates an automated clearinghouse transaction debiting the person's bank account and crediting the state's bank account for the amount of tax. Banking costs incurred for the automated clearinghouse debit transaction shall be paid by the state.

(4) "Automated clearinghouse credit" means an automated clearinghouse transaction in which the person through his or her own bank, originates an entry crediting the state's bank account and debiting his or her own bank account. Banking costs incurred for the automated clearinghouse credit transaction charged to the state shall be paid by the person originating the credit.

(5) "Fedwire transfer" means any transaction originated by a person and utilizing the national electronic payment system to transfer funds through the federal reserve banks, when that person debits his or her own bank account and credits the state's bank account. Electronic fund transfers pursuant to this section may be made by Fedwire only if payment cannot, for good cause, be made according to subdivision (a), and the use of Fedwire is preapproved by the department. Banking costs incurred for the Fedwire transaction charged to the person and to the state shall be paid by the person originating the transaction. *(Added by Stats.2004, c. 806 (A.B.2358), § 3.)*

Research References

Treatises and Practice Aids

Witkin, California Summary 10th Husband and Wife § 313, Payment to County by Court and Referral.

§ 17310. Regulations and general policies

(a) The director shall formulate, adopt, amend, or repeal regulations and general policies affecting the purposes, responsibilities, and jurisdiction of the department that are consistent with law and necessary for the administration of the state plan for securing child support and enforcing spousal support orders and determining paternity.

(b) Notwithstanding any other provision of law, all regulations, including, but not limited to, regulations of the State Department of Social Services and the State Department of Health Services, relating to child support enforcement shall remain in effect and shall be fully enforceable by the department. The department may readopt, amend, or repeal the regulations in accordance with Section 17312 as necessary and appropriate. *(Added by Stats.1999, c. 478 (A.B.196), § 1. Amended by Stats.1999, c. 480 (S.B.542), § 11.)*

§ 17311. Establishment and operation of Child Support Payment Trust Fund; legislative intent; General Fund loan

(a) The Child Support Payment Trust Fund is hereby created in the State Treasury. The department shall administer the fund.

(b)(1) The state may deposit child support payments received by the State Disbursement Unit, including those amounts that result in overpayment of child support, into the Child Support Payment Trust Fund, for the purpose of processing and providing child support payments. Notwithstanding Section 13340 of the Government Code, the fund is continuously appropriated for the purposes of disbursing child support payments from the State Disbursement Unit.

(2) The state share of the interest and other earnings that accrue on the fund shall be available to the department and used to offset the following General Fund costs in this order:

(A) Any transfers made to the Child Support Payment Trust Fund from the General Fund.

(B) The cost of administering the State Disbursement Unit, subject to appropriation by the Legislature.

(C) Other child support program activities, subject to appropriation by the Legislature.

(c) The department may establish and administer a revolving account in the Child Support Payment Trust Fund in an amount not to exceed six hundred million dollars ($600,000,000) to ensure the timely disbursement of child support. This amount may be adjusted by the Director of Finance upon notification of the Legislature as required, to meet payment timeframes required under federal law.

(d) It is the intent of the Legislature to provide transfers from the General Fund to provide startup funds for the Child Support Payment Trust Fund so that, together with the balances transferred pursuant to Section 17311.7, the Child Support Payment Trust Fund will have sufficient cash on hand to make all child support payments within the required timeframes.

(e) Notwithstanding any other law, an ongoing loan shall be made available from the General Fund, from funds not otherwise appropriated, to the Child Support Payment Trust Fund, not to exceed one hundred fifty million dollars ($150,000,000) to ensure the timely disbursement of child support payments when funds have not been recorded to the Child Support Payment Trust Fund or due to other fund liabilities, including, but not limited to, Internal Revenue Service negative adjustments to tax intercept payments. Whenever an adjustment of this amount is required to meet payment timeframes under federal law, the amount shall be adjusted after approval of the Director of Finance. In conjunction with the Department of Finance and the Controller's office, the department shall establish repayment procedures to ensure the outstanding loan balance does not exceed the average daily cash needs. The ongoing evaluation of the fund as detailed in these procedures shall occur no less frequently than monthly.

(f) Notwithstanding any other law, the Controller may use the moneys in the Child Support Payment Trust Fund for loans to the General Fund as provided in Sections 16310 and 16381 of the Government Code. However, interest shall be paid on all moneys loaned to the General Fund from the Child Support Payment Trust Fund. Interest payable shall be computed at a rate determined by the Pooled Money Investment Board to be the current earning rate of the fund from which loaned. This subdivision does not authorize any transfer that will interfere with the carrying out of the object for which the Child Support Payment Trust Fund was created. *(Added by Stats.2003, c. 387 (A.B.739), § 11. Amended by Stats.2005, c. 78 (S.B.68), § 6, eff. July 19, 2005; Stats.2009–2010, 3rd Ex.Sess., c. 9 (A.B.13), § 4, eff. Feb. 20, 2009.)*

§ 17311.5. Trust agreement to receive or disburse child support collections; provisions of agreement; approved investment securities

(a) The department may enter into a trust agreement with a trustee or fiscal intermediary to receive or disburse child support collections. The trust agreement may contain provisions the department deems reasonable and proper for the security of the child support payments. Any trust accounts created by the trust agreements may be held outside the State Treasury.

(b) For the 2012–13 fiscal year only, trust account moneys may be invested in any of the types of securities listed in Section 16430 of the Government Code or alternatives offering comparable security, including, but not limited to, mutual funds and money market funds. This subdivision does not authorize investments or transfers that would interfere with carrying out the objective for which the Child Support Payment Trust Fund was created. *(Added by Stats.2003, c. 387 (A.B.739), § 12. Amended by Stats.2012, c. 47 (S.B.1041), § 1, eff. June 27, 2012.)*

§ 17311.7. Closeout activities to ensure accounting; audits

(a) Upon the transfer of collection and disbursement activities from each county to the State Disbursement Unit, the auditor and controller of each county shall perform closeout activities as directed by the Department of Child Support Services to ensure accounting for all collections, obligations, and payments. All child support collections remaining undisbursed and interest earned on these funds shall be transferred to the Department of Child Support Services for deposit in the Child Support Payment Trust Fund. The local child support agency director and auditor and controller shall perform these activities based on guidelines provided by the department and shall certify the results of these activities in a report submitted to the department within one year of transfer of collection and distribution functions to the state.

(b) The department may contract for the audit of each county report submitted under subdivision (a). Each audit shall be completed within one year after the receipt of the report from the county. *(Added by Stats.2003, c. 387 (A.B.739), § 13.)*

§ 17312. Regulations, orders, or standards

(a) The department shall adopt regulations, orders, or standards of general application to implement, interpret, or make specific the law enforced by the department. Regulations, orders, and standards shall be adopted, amended, or repealed by the director only in accordance with Chapter 3.5 (commencing with Section 11340) of Part 1 of Division 3 of Title 2 of the Government Code.

(b) In adopting regulations, the department shall strive for clarity of language that may be readily understood by those administering public social services or subject to those regulations.

(c) The rules of the department need not specify or include the detail of forms, reports, or records, but shall include the essential authority by which any person, agency, organization, association, or institution subject to the supervision or investigation of the department is required to use, submit, or maintain the forms, reports, or records.

(d) The department's regulations and other materials shall be made available pursuant to the California Code of Regulations and in the same manner as are materials of the State Department of Social Services under the provisions of Section 205.70 of Title 45 of the Code of Federal Regulations. *(Added by Stats.1999, c. 478 (A.B.196), § 1. Amended by Stats.1999, c. 480 (S.B.542), § 12.)*

§ 17314. Staff; regional state administrators

(a) Subject to the State Civil Service Act (Part 2 (commencing with Section 18500) of Division 5 of Title 2 of the Government Code), the director shall appoint any assistants and other employees that are necessary for the administration of the affairs of the department and shall prescribe their duties and, subject to the approval of the Department of Finance, fix their salaries.

(b) As the director adopts a plan for a local child support agency to assume responsibility for child support enforcement activities in any county served by a district attorney pursuant to Section 17304, the director shall hire a sufficient number of regional state administrators to oversee the local child support agencies to ensure compliance with all state and federal laws and regulations. The regions shall be divided based on the total caseload of each local child support agency. The responsibilities of the regional state administrators shall include all of the following:

(1) Conducting regular and comprehensive site visits to the local child support agencies assigned to their region and preparing quarterly reports to be submitted to the department. The local child support agencies shall fully cooperate with all reasonable requests made by the regional state administrators, including providing all requested data on the local child support agency's program.

(2) Notifying a local child support agency of any potential or actual noncompliance with any state or federal law or regulation by the agency and working with the local child support agency to develop an immediate plan to ensure compliance.

(3) Participating in program monitoring teams as set forth in subdivision (c) of Section 17602.

(4) Participating in meetings with all regional state administrators and the director on at least a monthly basis to promote statewide uniformity as to the functions and structure of the local child support agencies. The regional state administrators may recommend proposals for approval and adoption by the director to achieve this goal.

(5) Responding to requests for management or technical assistance regarding program operations by local child support agencies. *(Added by Stats.1999, c. 478 (A.B.196), § 1.)*

§ 17316. Involvement with agency supervised by department

No person, while holding the office of director, shall be a trustee, manager, director, or other officer or employee of any agency performing any function supervised by the department or any institution that is subject to examination, inspection, or supervision by the department. *(Added by Stats.1999, c. 478 (A.B.196), § 1.)*

§ 17318. Application of Government Code § 11000 et seq.

Except as otherwise expressly provided, Part 1 (commencing with Section 11000) of Division 3 of Title 2 of the Government Code, as it may be added to or amended from time to time, shall apply to the conduct of the department. *(Added by Stats.1999, c. 478 (A.B.196), § 1.)*

§ 17320. Temporary Assistance to Needy Families grant; federal penalties

The department shall coordinate with the State Department of Social Services to avoid the imposition of any federal penalties that cause a reduction in the state's Temporary Assistance to Needy Families grant, payable pursuant to Section 603(a)(1) of Title 42 of the United States Code. *(Added by Stats.1999, c. 478 (A.B.196), § 1.)*

§ 17325. Direct deposit of child support payments; qualifying account; requirements; definitions

(a)(1) Notwithstanding any other law, if child support payments are directly deposited to an account of the recipient's choice, as authorized under the federal Electronic Fund Transfer Act (EFTA) (15 U.S.C. Sec. 1693 et seq.), the payments may only be deposited to an account that meets the requirements of a qualifying account, as defined in paragraph (2), for deposit of child support payments.

(2) For purposes of this section, a "qualifying account" is one of the following:

(A) A demand deposit or savings account at an insured financial institution in the name of the person entitled to the receipt of child support payments.

(B) A prepaid card account that meets all of the following:

(i) The account is held at an insured financial institution.

(ii) The account is set up to meet the requirements for passthrough deposit or share insurance so that the funds accessible through the account are eligible for insurance for the benefit of the person entitled to the receipt of child support payments by the Federal Deposit Insurance Corporation in accordance with Part 330 of Title 12 of the Code of Federal Regulations, or the National Credit Union Share Insurance Fund in accordance with Part 745 of Title 12 of the Code of Federal Regulations.

(iii) The account is not attached to any credit or overdraft feature that is automatically repaid from the account after delivery of the payment.

(iv) The issuer of the card complies with all of the requirements, and provides the holder of the card with all of the consumer protections, that apply to a payroll card account under the rules implementing the EFTA or other rules subsequently adopted under the EFTA that apply to prepaid card accounts.

(3) A person or entity that issues a prepaid card or maintains or manages a prepaid card account that does not comply with paragraph (2) shall not accept or facilitate the direct deposit of child support payments to the prepaid card account.

(b) For purposes of this section, the department shall not be held liable for authorizing a direct deposit of child support payments into a prepaid card account designated by the recipient that does not comply with paragraph (2) of subdivision (a). The department has no obligation to determine whether an account at the financial institution of the recipient's choice is a qualifying account as described in subdivision (a).

(c) For the purposes of this section, the following definitions shall apply:

(1) "Financial institution" means a state or national bank, a state or federal savings and loan association, a mutual savings bank, or a state or federal credit union.

(2) "Issuer" means a person or entity that issues a prepaid card.

(3) "Payroll card account" shall have the same meaning as that term is defined in the regulations implementing the EFTA.

(4) "Prepaid card" or "prepaid card account" means either of the following:

(A) A card, code, or other means of access to funds of a recipient that is usable at multiple, unaffiliated merchants for goods or services, or usable at automated teller machines.

(B) The same as those terms or related terms are defined in the regulations adopted under the EFTA regarding general use reloadable cards. *(Added by Stats.2014, c. 180 (A.B. 2252), § 1, eff. Jan. 1, 2015. Amended by Stats.2014, c. 720 (A.B.1614), § 1, eff. Jan. 1, 2015; Stats.2015, c. 416 (A.B. 1519), § 2, eff. Jan. 1, 2016.)*

ARTICLE 4. STATEWIDE REGISTRY FOR CHILD SUPPORT

§ 17390. Legislative findings and declarations; utilization of California Child Support Enforcement System or its replacement

(a) The Legislature finds and declares that there is no single statewide database containing statistical data regarding child support orders.

(b) The California Child Support Enforcement System or its replacement may be utilized to provide a single statewide registry of all child support orders in California, including orders for cases under Title IV–D of the Social Security Act [1] and all cases with child support orders. *(Added by Stats.2016, c. 474 (A.B.2882), § 13, eff. Jan. 1, 2017.)*

[1] See 42 U.S.C.A. § 651 et seq.

§ 17391. Development of implementation plan for Statewide Child Support Registry; duties of clerks of court and department

(a) The department shall develop an implementation plan for the Statewide Child Support Registry. The Statewide Child Support Registry shall be operated by the agency responsible for operation of the California Child Support Enforcement System or its replacement. The Statewide Child Support Registry shall include storage and data retrieval of the data elements specified in Section 17392 for all California child support orders. The Statewide Child Support Registry will operate to ensure that all data in the Statewide Child Support Registry can be accessed and integrated for statistical analysis and reporting purposes with all child support order data contained in the California Child Support Enforcement System.

(b) Each clerk of the court shall provide the information specified in Section 17392 within 20 days to the department or the Statewide Child Support Registry from each new or modified child support order, including child support arrearage orders.

(c) The department shall maintain a system for compiling the child support data received from the clerks of the court, ensure that all child support data received from the clerks of the court are entered into the Statewide Child Support Registry within five business days of receipt in the Statewide Child Support Registry, and ensure that the Statewide Child Support Registry is fully implemented statewide.

(d) The department shall provide aggregate data on a periodic basis on the data maintained by the Statewide Child Support Registry to the Judicial Council, the appropriate agencies of the executive branch, and the Legislature for statistical analysis and review. The data shall not include individual identifying information for specific cases.

(e) Any information maintained by the Statewide Child Support Registry received from clerks of the court shall be provided to local child support agencies, the courts, and others as provided by law. *(Added by Stats.2016, c. 474 (A.B.2882), § 13, eff. Jan. 1, 2017.)*

§ 17392. Development of forms necessary for implementation of Statewide Child Support Registry; information to be transmitted

(a) The Judicial Council shall develop any forms that may be necessary to implement the Statewide Child Support Registry. The forms may be in electronic form or in hardcopy, as appropriate. The forms shall be developed so as not to delay implementation, and shall be available no later than 30 days prior to the implementation, of the Statewide Child Support Registry.

(b) The information transmitted from the clerks of the court to the Statewide Child Support Registry shall include all of the following:

(1) Any information required under federal law.

(2) Any other information the department and the Judicial Council find appropriate. *(Added by Stats.2016, c. 474 (A.B.2882), § 13, eff. Jan. 1, 2017.)*

§ 17393. Development of forms necessary for implementation or article

The Judicial Council shall develop the forms necessary to implement this article. *(Added by Stats.2016, c. 474 (A.B. 2882), § 13, eff. Jan. 1, 2017.)*

CHAPTER 2. CHILD SUPPORT ENFORCEMENT

ARTICLE 1. SUPPORT OBLIGATIONS

§ 17400. Local child support agencies; responsibilities; authorized actions; forms; venue

(a) Each county shall maintain a local child support agency, as specified in Section 17304, that shall have the responsibility for promptly and effectively establishing, modifying, and enforcing child support obligations, including medical support, enforcing spousal support orders established by a court of competent jurisdiction, and determining paternity in the case of a child born out of wedlock. The local child support agency shall take appropriate action, including criminal action in cooperation with the district attorneys, to establish, modify, and enforce child support and, if appropriate, enforce spousal support orders if the child is receiving public assistance, including Medi–Cal, and, if requested, shall take the same actions on behalf of a child who is not receiving public assistance, including Medi–Cal.

(b)(1) Notwithstanding Sections 25203 and 26529 of the Government Code, attorneys employed within the local child support agency may direct, control, and prosecute civil actions and proceedings in the name of the county in support of child support activities of the Department of Child Support Services and the local child support agency.

(2) Notwithstanding any other law, and except for pleadings or documents required to be signed under penalty of perjury, a local child support agency may substitute original signatures with any form of electronic signatures, including, but not limited to, typed, digital, or facsimile images of signatures, digital signatures, or other computer-generated signatures, on pleadings filed for the purpose of establishing, modifying, or enforcing paternity, child support, or medical support. Any substituted signature used by a local child support agency shall have the same effect as an original signature, including, but not limited to, the requirements of Section 128.7 of the Code of Civil Procedure.

(3) Notwithstanding any other law, effective July 1, 2016, a local child support agency may electronically file pleadings signed by an agent of the local child support agency under penalty of perjury. An original signed pleading shall be executed prior to, or on the same day as, the day of electronic filing. Original signed pleadings shall be maintained by the local child support agency for the period of time prescribed by subdivision (a) of Section 68152 of the Government Code. A local child support agency may maintain the original signed pleading by way of an electronic copy in the Statewide Automated Child Support System. The Judicial Council, by July 1, 2016, shall develop rules to implement this subdivision.

(c) Actions brought by the local child support agency to establish paternity or child support or to enforce child support obligations shall be completed within the time limits set forth by federal law. The local child support agency's responsibility applies to spousal support only if the spousal support obligation has been reduced to an order of a court of competent jurisdiction. In any action brought for modification or revocation of an order that is being enforced under Title IV–D of the Social Security Act (42 U.S.C. Sec. 651 et seq.), the effective date of the modification or revocation shall be as prescribed by federal law (42 U.S.C. Sec. 666(a)(9)), or any subsequent date.

(d)(1) The Judicial Council, in consultation with the department, the Senate Committee on Judiciary, the Assembly Committee on Judiciary, and a legal services organization providing representation on child support matters, shall develop simplified summons, complaint, and answer forms for any action for support brought pursuant to this section or Section 17404. The Judicial Council may combine the summons and complaint in a single form.

(2) The simplified complaint form shall provide notice of the amount of child support that is sought pursuant to the guidelines set forth in Article 2 (commencing with Section 4050) of Chapter 2 of Part 2 of Division 9 based upon the income or income history of the support obligor as known to the local child support agency. If the support obligor's income or income history is unknown to the local child support agency, the complaint shall inform the support obligor that income shall be presumed to be the amount of the minimum wage, at 40 hours per week, established by the Industrial Welfare Commission pursuant to Section 1182.11 of the Labor Code unless information concerning the support obligor's income is provided to the court. The complaint form shall be accompanied by a proposed judgment. The complaint form shall include a notice to the support obligor that the proposed judgment will become effective if he or she fails to file an answer with the court within 30 days of service. Except as provided in paragraph (2) of subdivision (a) of Section 17402, if the proposed judgment is entered by the court, the support order in the proposed judgment shall be effective as of the first day of the month following the filing of the complaint.

(3)(A) The simplified answer form shall be written in simple English and shall permit a defendant to answer and raise defenses by checking applicable boxes. The answer form shall include instructions for completion of the form and instructions for proper filing of the answer.

(B) The answer form shall be accompanied by a blank income and expense declaration or simplified financial statement and instructions on how to complete the financial forms. The answer form shall direct the defendant to file the completed income and expense declaration or simplified financial statement with the answer, but shall state that the answer will be accepted by a court without the income and expense declaration or simplified financial statement.

(C) The clerk of the court shall accept and file answers, income and expense declarations, and simplified financial statements that are completed by hand provided they are legible.

(4)(A) The simplified complaint form prepared pursuant to this subdivision shall be used by the local child support agency or the Attorney General in all cases brought under this section or Section 17404.

(B) The simplified answer form prepared pursuant to this subdivision shall be served on all defendants with the simplified complaint. Failure to serve the simplified answer form on all defendants shall not invalidate any judgment obtained. However, failure to serve the answer form may be used as evidence in any proceeding under Section 17432 of this code or Section 473 of the Code of Civil Procedure.

(C) The Judicial Council shall add language to the governmental summons, for use by the local child support agency with the governmental complaint to establish parental relationship and child support, informing defendants that a blank answer form should have been received with the summons and additional copies may be obtained from either the local child support agency or the superior court clerk.

(e) In any action brought or enforcement proceedings instituted by the local child support agency pursuant to this section for payment of child or spousal support, an action to recover an arrearage in support payments may be maintained by the local child support agency at any time within the period otherwise specified for the enforcement of a support judgment, notwithstanding the fact that the child has attained the age of majority.

(f) The county shall undertake an outreach program to inform the public that the services described in subdivisions (a) to (c), inclusive, are available to persons not receiving public assistance. There shall be prominently displayed in every public area of every office of the agencies established by this section a notice, in clear and simple language prescribed by the Director of Child Support Services, that the services provided in subdivisions (a) to (c), inclusive, are provided to all individuals, whether or not they are recipients of public assistance.

(g)(1) In any action to establish a child support order brought by the local child support agency in the performance of duties under this section, the local child support agency may make a motion for an order effective during the pendency of that action, for the support, maintenance, and education of the child or children that are the subject of the action. This order shall be referred to as an order for temporary support. This order has the same force and effect as a like or similar order under this code.

(2) The local child support agency shall file a motion for an order for temporary support within the following time limits:

(A) If the defendant is the mother, a presumed father under Section 7611, or any father if the child is at least six months old when the defendant files his or her answer, the time limit is 90 days after the defendant files an answer.

(B) In any other case in which the defendant has filed an answer prior to the birth of the child or not more than six months after the birth of the child, then the time limit is nine months after the birth of the child.

(3) If more than one child is the subject of the action, the limitation on reimbursement shall apply only as to those children whose parental relationship and age would bar recovery were a separate action brought for support of that child or those children.

(4) If the local child support agency fails to file a motion for an order for temporary support within the time limits specified in this section, the local child support agency shall be barred from obtaining a judgment of reimbursement for any support provided for that child during the period between the date the time limit expired and the date the motion was filed, or, if no motion is filed, when a final judgment is entered.

(5) Except as provided in Section 17304, nothing in this section prohibits the local child support agency from entering into cooperative arrangements with other county departments as necessary to carry out the responsibilities imposed by this section pursuant to plans of cooperation with the departments approved by the Department of Child Support Services.

(6) Nothing in this section otherwise limits the ability of the local child support agency from securing and enforcing orders for support of a spouse or former spouse as authorized under any other law.

(h) As used in this article, "enforcing obligations" includes, but is not limited to, all of the following:

(1) The use of all interception and notification systems operated by the department for the purpose of aiding in the enforcement of support obligations.

(2) The obtaining by the local child support agency of an initial order for child support that may include medical support or that is for medical support only, by civil or criminal process.

(3) The initiation of a motion or order to show cause to increase an existing child support order, and the response to a motion or order to show cause brought by an obligor parent to decrease an existing child support order, or the initiation of a motion or order to show cause to obtain an order for medical support, and the response to a motion or order to show cause brought by an obligor parent to decrease or terminate an existing medical support order, without regard to whether the child is receiving public assistance.

(4) The response to a notice of motion or order to show cause brought by an obligor parent to decrease an existing spousal support order if the child or children are residing with the obligee parent and the local child support agency is also enforcing a related child support obligation owed to the obligee parent by the same obligor.

(5) The referral of child support delinquencies to the department under subdivision (c) of Section 17500 in support of the local child support agency.

(i) As used in this section, "out of wedlock" means that the biological parents of the child were not married to each other at the time of the child's conception.

(j)(1) The local child support agency is the public agency responsible for administering wage withholding for current support for the purposes of Title IV–D of the Social Security Act (42 U.S.C. Sec. 651 et seq.).

(2) Nothing in this section limits the authority of the local child support agency granted by other sections of this code or otherwise granted by law.

(k) In the exercise of the authority granted under this article, the local child support agency may intervene, pursuant to subdivision (b) of Section 387 of the Code of Civil Procedure, by ex parte application, in any action under this code, or other proceeding in which child support is an issue or a reduction in spousal support is sought. By notice of motion, order to show cause, or responsive pleading served upon all parties to the action, the local child support agency may request any relief that is appropriate that the local child support agency is authorized to seek.

(*l*) The local child support agency shall comply with all regulations and directives established by the department that set time standards for responding to requests for assistance in locating noncustodial parents, establishing paternity, establishing child support awards, and collecting child support payments.

(m) As used in this article, medical support activities that the local child support agency is authorized to perform are limited to the following:

(1) The obtaining and enforcing of court orders for health insurance coverage.

(2) Any other medical support activity mandated by federal law or regulation.

(n)(1) Notwithstanding any other law, venue for an action or proceeding under this division shall be determined as follows:

(A) Venue shall be in the superior court in the county that is currently expending public assistance.

(B) If public assistance is not currently being expended, venue shall be in the superior court in the county where the child who is entitled to current support resides or is domiciled.

(C) If current support is no longer payable through, or enforceable by, the local child support agency, venue shall be in the superior court in the county that last provided public assistance for actions to enforce arrearages assigned pursuant to Section 11477 of the Welfare and Institutions Code.

(D) If subparagraphs (A), (B), and (C) do not apply, venue shall be in the superior court in the county of residence of the support obligee.

(E) If the support obligee does not reside in California, and subparagraphs (A), (B), (C), and (D) do not apply, venue shall be in the superior court of the county of residence of the obligor.

(2) Notwithstanding paragraph (1), if the child becomes a resident of another county after an action under this part has been filed, venue may remain in the county where the action was filed until the action is completed.

(*o*) The local child support agency of one county may appear on behalf of the local child support agency of any other county in an action or proceeding under this part.
(Added by Stats.1999, c. 478 (A.B.196), § 1. Amended by Stats.1999, c. 480 (S.B.542), § 13; Stats.1999, c. 980 (A.B. 1671), § 14.2; Stats.2000, c. 808 (A.B.1358), § 81, eff. Sept. 28, 2000; Stats.2001, c. 111 (A.B.429), § 3, eff. July 30, 2001; Stats.2002, c. 927 (A.B.3032), § 3.7; Stats.2003, c. 225 (A.B. 1752), § 3, eff. Aug. 11, 2003; Stats.2004, c. 339 (A.B.1704), § 6; Stats.2007, c. 249 (S.B.523), § 3; Stats.2015, c. 416 (A.B.1519), § 3, eff. Jan. 1, 2016; Stats.2016, c. 474 (A.B. 2882), § 14, eff. Jan. 1, 2017.)

Commentary

The registration of a foreign divorce decree does not give the county standing to initiate a child support enforcement proceeding unless the registration includes a proper request for enforcement services. If a family is receiving public assistance, the welfare department providing public assistance may request enforcement services; if not, the support obligee must request those services. *Codoni v. Codoni, 103 Cal.App.4th 18, 126 Cal.Rptr.2d 423 (2002).*

When the county seeks reimbursement from parents for public assistance provided to their children, *Clark v. Superior Court, 62 Cal.App.4th 576, 73 Cal.Rptr.2d 53 (1998)*, holds that due process does not require that indigent parents be provided court-appointed counsel at public expense. But see *County of Ventura v. Tillett, 133 Cal.App.3d 105, 183 Cal.Rptr. 741 (1982), cert. denied, 460 U.S. 1051 (1983)* (contra). Compare *Salas v. Cortez, 24 Cal.3d 22, 593 P.2d 226, 154 Cal.Rptr. 529 (1979)* (requiring appointed counsel for indigents in paternity actions).

County of Yuba v. Savedra, 78 Cal.App.4th 1311, 93 Cal.Rptr.2d 524 (2000), holds that it was error for the trial court to decline to enter a child support judgment before presentation of evidence of the defaulting parent's income when that parent had received notice satisfying subsection (d)(2) (former Welfare and Institutions Code § 11475.1) in that it specified (1) the amount sought and (2) that the proposed judgment would become effective if the defendant failed to file an answer.

Research References

Forms

California Practice Guide: Rutter Family Law Forms Form 1:32, Glossary Of Common Family Law Terms, Phrases and Concepts (Enclosure to Form 1:31).
West's California Code Forms, Family § 4250, Comment Overview--Child Support Commissioners.
West's California Judicial Council Forms FL-415, Findings and Order Regarding Contempt (Family Law--Domestic Violence Prevention--Uniform Parentage--Governmental).
West's California Judicial Council Forms FL-560, Ex Parte Application for Transfer and Order (UIFSA).
West's California Judicial Council Forms FL-600, Summons and Complaint or Supplemental Complaint Regarding Parental Obligations.
West's California Judicial Council Forms FL-605, Notice and Acknowledgment Of Receipt.
West's California Judicial Council Forms FL-610, Answer to Complaint or Supplemental Complaint Regarding Parental Obligations.
West's California Judicial Council Forms FL-615, Stipulation for Judgment or Supplemental Judgment Regarding Parental Obligations and Judgment.
West's California Judicial Council Forms FL-616, Declaration for Amended Proposed Judgment.
West's California Judicial Council Forms FL-620, Request to Enter Default Judgment (Governmental).
West's California Judicial Council Forms FL-625, Stipulation and Order.
West's California Judicial Council Forms FL-627, Order for Genetic (Parentage) Testing.
West's California Judicial Council Forms FL-630, Judgment Regarding Parental Obligations.
West's California Judicial Council Forms FL-632, Notice Regarding Payment Of Support.
West's California Judicial Council Forms FL-634, Notice Of Change Of Responsibility for Managing Child Support Case.
West's California Judicial Council Forms FL-635, Notice Of Entry Of Judgment and Proof Of Service by Mail (Governmental).
West's California Judicial Council Forms FL-640, Notice and Motion to Cancel (Set Aside) Support Order Based on Presumed Income.
West's California Judicial Council Forms FL-643, Declaration Of Obligor's Income During Judgment Period--Presumed Income Set--Aside Request.
West's California Judicial Council Forms FL-646, Response Of District Attorney to Notice Of Intent to Take Independent Action to Enforce Support Order.
West's California Judicial Council Forms FL-650, Statement for Registration Of California Support Order.
West's California Judicial Council Forms FL-660, Ex Parte Motion by District Attorney and Declaration for Joinder Of Other Parent.
West's California Judicial Council Forms FL-670, Notice Of Motion for Judicial Review Of License Denial.
West's California Judicial Council Forms FL-675, Order After Judicial Review Of License Denial.
West's California Judicial Council Forms FL-678, Order Determining Claim Of Exemption or Third-Party Claim.
West's California Judicial Council Forms FL-683, Order to Show Cause.
West's California Judicial Council Forms FL-684, Request for Order and Supporting Declaration (Governmental).
West's California Judicial Council Forms FL-687, Order After Hearing.
West's California Judicial Council Forms FL-688, Short Form Order After Hearing (Governmental).
West's California Judicial Council Forms FL-692, Minutes and Order or Judgment.
West's California Judicial Council Forms FL-640-INFO, Information Sheet for Notice and Motion to Cancel (Set Aside) Support Order Based on Presumed Income.

Treatises and Practice Aids

Witkin, California Summary 10th Husband and Wife § 12B, (New) Amount Of Filing Fees.
Witkin, California Summary 10th Husband and Wife § 257, Alternative Procedure in Title IV-D Cases.
Witkin, California Summary 10th Husband and Wife § 259, Procedure.
Witkin, California Summary 10th Husband and Wife § 270, Registration by Local Child Support Agency.
Witkin, California Summary 10th Husband and Wife § 308, Background and Scope.
Witkin, California Summary 10th Husband and Wife § 310, Local Child Support Agency.
Witkin, California Summary 10th Husband and Wife § 317, Nature Of Proceedings.
Witkin, California Summary 10th Husband and Wife § 319, Venue.
Witkin, California Summary 10th Husband and Wife § 322, Allocation Of Dependency Exemption.
Witkin, California Summary 10th Husband and Wife § 324, Pleadings.
Witkin, California Summary 10th Husband and Wife § 325, Consolidation Of Claims.
Witkin, California Summary 10th Husband and Wife § 326, Time and Notice Requirements.
Witkin, California Summary 10th Husband and Wife § 330, Relief from Order Based on Presumed Income.
Witkin, California Summary 10th Husband and Wife § 333, Temporary Support.
Witkin, California Summary 10th Husband and Wife § 334, in General.
Witkin, California Summary 10th Parent and Child § 57, Order for Genetic Testing.
Witkin, California Summary 10th Parent and Child § 200, Commission Of Crime.
Witkin, California Summary 10th Parent and Child § 304, Notice Of Hearing.
Witkin, California Summary 10th Parent and Child § 384, Information Required.
Witkin, California Summary 10th Parent and Child § 414, Stipulated Support Agreements.
Witkin, California Summary 10th Parent and Child § 416, Application and Order.
Witkin, California Summary 10th Parent and Child § 517, Collection Procedure.

§ 17400.5. Disabled obligors receiving SSI/SSP or social security disability insurance benefits; duty of local child support agency under certain circumstances to move to modify child support obligations

If an obligor has an ongoing child support order being enforced by a local child support agency pursuant to Title IV–

D of the Social Security Act and the obligor is disabled, meets the SSI resource test, and is receiving Supplemental Security Income/State Supplemental Payments (SSI/SSP) or, but for excess income as described in Section 416.1100 et seq. of Part 416 of Title 20 of the Code of Federal Regulations, would be eligible to receive as SSI/SSP, pursuant to Section 12200 of the Welfare and Institutions Code, and the obligor has supplied the local child support agency with proof of his or her eligibility for, and, if applicable, receipt of, SSI/SSP or Social Security Disability Insurance benefits, then the local child support agency shall prepare and file a motion to modify the support obligation within 30 days of receipt of verification from the noncustodial parent or any other source of the receipt of SSI/SSP or Social Security Disability Insurance benefits. The local child support agency shall serve the motion on both the noncustodial parent and custodial person and any modification of the support order entered pursuant to the motion shall be effective as provided in Section 3653 of the Family Code. *(Added by Stats.2001, c. 651 (A.B.891), § 3. Amended by Stats.2002, c. 787 (S.B. 1798), § 1.)*

Research References

Treatises and Practice Aids

Witkin, California Summary 10th Husband and Wife § 310, Local Child Support Agency.

§ 17401. Residence or work address information; establishment or enforcement action by agency

If the parent who is receiving support enforcement services provides to the local child support agency substantial, credible, information regarding the residence or work address of the support obligor, the agency shall initiate an establishment or enforcement action and serve the defendant, if service is required, within 60 days and inform the parent in writing when those actions have been taken. If the address or any other information provided by the support obligee is determined by the local child support agency to be inaccurate and if, after reasonable diligence, the agency is unable to locate and serve the support obligor within that 60–day period, the local child support agency shall inform the support obligee in writing of those facts. The requirements of this section shall be in addition to the time standards established by the Department of Child Support Services pursuant to subdivision (*l*) of Section 17400. *(Added by Stats.1999, c. 653 (A.B.380), § 14. Amended by Stats.2000, c. 808 (A.B.1358), § 83, eff. Sept. 28, 2000; Stats.2001, c. 755 (S.B.943), § 12, eff. Oct. 12, 2001.)*

Research References

Treatises and Practice Aids

Witkin, California Summary 10th Husband and Wife § 326, Time and Notice Requirements.

§ 17401.5. Child support service hearings; notice and information

(a) All of the following shall include notice of, and information about, the child support service hearings available pursuant to Section 17801, provided that there is federal financial participation available as set forth in subdivision (j) of Section 17801:

(1) The booklet required by subdivision (a) of Section 17434.

(2) Any notice required by subdivision (c) or (h) of Section 17406.

(b) To the extent not otherwise required by law, the local child support agency shall provide notice of, and information about, the child support services hearings available pursuant to Section 17801 in any regularly issued notices to custodial and noncustodial parents subject to Section 17400, provided that there is federal financial participation available as set forth in subdivision (e) of Section 17801.

Notice of and information about the child support service hearings and the child support complaint resolution process required under Section 17800 shall be easily accessible and shall be provided in a single section of the booklet. *(Formerly § 17401, added by Stats.1999, c. 803 (A.B.472), § 1. Renumbered § 17401.5 and amended by Stats.2000, c. 808 (A.B.1358), § 84, eff. Sept. 28, 2000.)*

§ 17402. CalWORKs aid due to separation from or desertion of child; noncustodial parent obligation to county

(a) In any case of separation or desertion of a parent or parents from a child or children that results in aid under Chapter 2 (commencing with Section 11200) of Part 3 of Division 9 of the Welfare and Institutions Code being granted to that family, the noncustodial parent or parents shall be obligated to the county for an amount equal to the amount specified in an order for the support and maintenance of the family issued by a court of competent jurisdiction.

(b) The local child support agency shall take appropriate action pursuant to this section as provided in subdivision (*l*) of Section 17400. The local child support agency may establish liability for child support as provided in subdivision (a) when public assistance was provided by another county or by other counties.

(c) The amount of the obligation established for each parent with a liability under subdivision (a) shall be determined by using the appropriate child support guideline currently in effect and shall be computed as follows:

(1) If one parent remains as a custodial parent, the support shall be computed according to the guideline.

(2) If the parents reside together and neither father nor mother remains as a custodial parent, the guideline support shall be computed by combining the noncustodial parents' incomes. The combined incomes shall be used as the high earner's net monthly disposable income in the guideline formula. Income shall not be attributed to the caretaker or governmental agency. The amount of guideline support resulting shall be proportionately shared between the noncustodial parents based upon their net monthly disposable incomes.

(3) If the parents reside apart and neither father nor mother remains as a custodial parent, the guideline support shall be computed separately for each parent by treating each parent as a noncustodial parent. Income shall not be attributed to the caretaker or government agency.

(d) A parent shall pay the amount of support specified in the support order to the local child support agency. *(Added by Stats.1999, c. 478 (A.B.196), § 1. Amended by Stats.1999, c. 653 (A.B.380), § 15; Stats.2000, c. 808 (A.B.1358), § 84.3, eff. Sept. 28, 2000; Stats.2004, c. 305 (A.B.2669), § 5.)*

Commentary

A noncustodial parent must pay the total amount of child support arrearages to the county, not merely the amount necessary for reimbursement of AFDC benefits paid on behalf of his child. Any amount in excess of AFDC benefits must be paid by the county to the child's family. *County of Alameda v. Johnson, 28 Cal.App.4th 259, 33 Cal.Rptr.2d 483 (1994)*; accord, *County of Orange v. Dabbs, 29 Cal.App.4th 999, 35 Cal.Rptr.2d 79 (1994), review denied 1/19/95.*

Ohio v. Barron, 52 Cal.App.4th 62, 60 Cal.Rptr.2d 342 (1997), holds that subsection (a)(2), which requires certain noncustodial parents to pay child support arrearages in excess of public welfare benefits paid by the state, does not violate the constitutional guarantees of due process or equal protection.

County of Santa Clara v. Perry, 18 Cal.4th 435, 956 P.2d 1191, 75 Cal.Rptr.2d 738 (1998), holds that Family Code § 4009 means exactly what it says: A child support order may be made retroactive only to the date of filing the notice of motion or order to show cause for establishment or modification of a child support order. Moreover, *Perry* holds that § 4009 applies equally to support orders in paternity actions brought by the district attorney. However, *County v. Riverside v. Burt, 78 Cal.App.4th 28, 92 Cal.Rptr.2d 619 (2000)*, holds that *Perry, supra,* does not apply to cases in which reimbursement is sought for public assistance payments on behalf of a child. In such case, reimbursement is subject only to the three-year statute of limitations (Civil Code § 338) and the parent's reasonable ability to pay. Effectively, *Burt* holds that Welfare and Institutions Code § 11350 (amended and reenacted as Family Code § 17402, effective January 1, 2000) provides an alternative path for reimbursement in public assistance cases. Family Code § 17402 adds a one-year statute of limitations: the period may not exceed one year from the filing of the petition or complaint.

When the county seeks reimbursement from parents for public assistance provided to their children, *Clark v. Superior Court, 62 Cal.App.4th 576, 73 Cal.Rptr.2d 53 (1998),* holds that due process does not require that indigent parents be provided court-appointed counsel at public expense. But see *County of Ventura v. Tillett, 133 Cal.App.3d 105, 183 Cal.Rptr. 741 (1982), cert. denied, 460 U.S. 1051 (1983)* (contra). Compare *Salas v. Cortez, 24 Cal.3d 22, 593 P.2d 226, 154 Cal.Rptr. 529 (1979)* (requiring appointed counsel for indigents in paternity actions).

County of San Diego v. Lamb, 63 Cal.App.4th 845, 73 Cal.Rptr.2d 912 (1998), review denied August 12, 1998, holds that subsection (a) does not authorize a county to seek reimbursement from the "noncustodial parent" of a minor child who receives benefits on behalf of the minor's own child. But see *County of San Bernadino v. Martinez, 51 Cal.App.4th 600, 59 Cal.Rptr.2d 142 (1996)* (contra).

Research References

Forms

West's California Code Forms, Family § 4500, Comment Overview--Enforcement Of Support Orders.

West's California Judicial Council Forms FL-415, Findings and Order Regarding Contempt (Family Law--Domestic Violence Prevention--Uniform Parentage--Governmental).

West's California Judicial Council Forms FL-600, Summons and Complaint or Supplemental Complaint Regarding Parental Obligations.

West's California Judicial Council Forms FL-615, Stipulation for Judgment or Supplemental Judgment Regarding Parental Obligations and Judgment.

West's California Judicial Council Forms FL-620, Request to Enter Default Judgment (Governmental).

West's California Judicial Council Forms FL-625, Stipulation and Order.

West's California Judicial Council Forms FL-630, Judgment Regarding Parental Obligations.

West's California Judicial Council Forms FL-684, Request for Order and Supporting Declaration (Governmental).

West's California Judicial Council Forms FL-687, Order After Hearing.

West's California Judicial Council Forms FL-688, Short Form Order After Hearing (Governmental).

Treatises and Practice Aids

Witkin, California Summary 10th Husband and Wife § 4, Definitions.

Witkin, California Summary 10th Husband and Wife § 340, Aid to Aged, Blind, and Disabled.

Witkin, California Summary 10th Husband and Wife § 343, CalWORKs Aid.

Witkin, California Summary 10th Parent and Child § 304, Notice Of Hearing.

Witkin, California Summary 10th Parent and Child § 383, in General.

Witkin, California Summary 10th Parent and Child § 512, Illustrations.

Witkin, California Summary 10th Parent and Child § 517, Collection Procedure.

§ 17402.1. Remittance to the department of federal and state public assistance child support payments; promulgation of regulations

(a) Each local child support agency shall, on a monthly basis, remit to the department both the federal and state public assistance child support payments received pursuant to Section 17402.

(b) The department shall promulgate regulations to implement this section. *(Added by Stats.2001, c. 111 (A.B.429), § 4, eff. July 30, 2001.)*

§ 17404. Procedure in actions, including parties, joinder, issues, parentage, pleading, notice, modification of order, forms, etc.

(a) Notwithstanding any other statute, in any action brought by the local child support agency for the support of a minor child or children, the action may be prosecuted in the name of the county on behalf of the child, children, or a parent of the child or children. The parent who has requested or is receiving support enforcement services of the local child support agency shall not be a necessary party to the action but may be subpoenaed as a witness. Except as provided in subdivision (e), in an action under this section there shall be no joinder of actions, or coordination of actions, or cross-complaints, and the issues shall be limited strictly to the question of parentage, if applicable, and child support, including an order for medical support. A final determination of parentage may be made in any action under this section as an incident to obtaining an order for support. An action for support or parentage pursuant to this section shall not be delayed or stayed because of the pendency of any other action between the parties.

(b) Judgment in an action brought pursuant to this section, and in an action brought pursuant to Section 17402, if at issue, may be rendered pursuant to a noticed motion, that shall inform the defendant that in order to exercise his or her right to trial, he or she must appear at the hearing on the motion.

If the defendant appears at the hearing on the motion, the court shall inquire of the defendant if he or she desires to subpoena evidence and witnesses, if parentage is at issue and genetic tests have not already been conducted whether he or she desires genetic tests, and if he or she desires a trial. If the defendant's answer is in the affirmative, a continuance shall be granted to allow the defendant to exercise those rights. A continuance shall not postpone the hearing to more than 90 days from the date of service of the motion. If a continuance is granted, the court may make an order for temporary support without prejudice to the right of the court to make an order for temporary support as otherwise allowed by law.

(c) In any action to enforce a spousal support order the action may be pled in the name of the county in the same manner as an action to establish a child support obligation. The same restrictions on joinder of actions, coordination of actions, cross-complaints, and delay because of the pendency of any other action as relates to actions to establish a child support obligation shall also apply to actions to enforce a spousal support order.

(d) Nothing contained in this section shall be construed to prevent the parties from bringing an independent action under other provisions of this code and litigating the issues of support, custody, visitation, or protective orders. In that event, any support, custody, visitation, or protective order issued by the court in an action pursuant to this section shall be filed in the action commenced under the other provisions of this code and shall continue in effect until modified by a subsequent order of the court. To the extent that the orders conflict, the court order last issued shall supersede all other orders and be binding upon all parties in that action.

(e)(1) After a support order, including a temporary support order and an order for medical support only, has been entered in an action brought pursuant to this section, the parent who has requested or is receiving support enforcement services of the local child support agency shall become a party to the action brought pursuant to this section, only in the manner and to the extent provided by this section, and only for the purposes allowed by this section.

(2) Notice of the parent's status as a party shall be given to the parent by the local child support agency in conjunction with the notice required by subdivision (e) of Section 17406. The complaint shall contain this notice. Service of the complaint on the parent in compliance with Section 1013 of the Code of Civil Procedure, or as otherwise provided by law, shall constitute compliance with this section. In all actions commenced under the procedures and forms in effect on or before December 31, 1996, the parent who has requested or is receiving support enforcement services of the local child support agency shall not become a party to the action until he or she is joined as a party pursuant to an ex parte application or noticed motion for joinder filed by the local child support agency or a noticed motion filed by either parent. The local child support agency shall serve a copy of any order for joinder of a parent obtained by the local child support agency's application on both parents in compliance with Section 1013 of the Code of Civil Procedure.

(3) Once both parents are parties to an action brought pursuant to this section in cases where Title IV–D services are currently being provided, the local child support agency shall be required, within five days of receipt, to mail the nonmoving party in the action all pleadings relating solely to the support issue in the action that have been served on the local child support agency by the moving party in the action, as provided in subdivision (f) of Section 17406. There shall be a rebuttable presumption that service on the local child support agency consistent with the provisions of this paragraph constitutes valid service on the nonmoving party. Where this procedure is used to effectuate service on the nonmoving party, the pleadings shall be served on the local child support agency not less than 30 days prior to the hearing.

(4) The parent who has requested or is receiving support enforcement services of the local child support agency is a party to an action brought under this section for issues relating to the support, custody, and visitation of a child, and for restraining orders, and for no other purpose. The local child support agency shall not be required to serve or receive service of papers, pleadings, or documents, or participate in, or attend any hearing or proceeding relating to issues of custody or visitation, except as otherwise required by law. Orders concerning custody and visitation may be made in an action pursuant to this subdivision only if orders concerning custody and visitation have not been previously made by a court of competent jurisdiction in this state or another state and the court has jurisdiction and is the proper venue for custody and visitation determinations. All issues regarding custody and visitation shall be heard and resolved in the manner provided by this code. Except as otherwise provided by law, the local child support agency shall control support and parentage litigation brought pursuant to this section, and the manner, method, and procedures used in establishing parentage and in establishing and enforcing support obligations unless and until the parent who requested or is receiving support enforcement services has requested in writing that the local child support agency close his or her case and the case has been closed in accordance with state and federal regulation or policy.

(f)(1) A parent who has requested or is receiving support enforcement services of the local child support agency may take independent action to modify a support order made pursuant to this section while support enforcement services are being provided by the local child support agency. The parent shall serve the local child support agency with notice of any action filed to modify the support order and provide the local child support agency with a copy of the modified order within 15 calendar days after the date the order is issued.

(2) A parent who has requested or is receiving support enforcement services of the local child support agency may take independent action to enforce a support order made pursuant to this section while support enforcement services are being provided by the local child support agency with the written consent of the local child support agency. At least 30 days prior to filing an independent enforcement action, the parent shall provide the local child support agency with

written notice of the parent's intent to file an enforcement action that includes a description of the type of enforcement action the parent intends to file. Within 30 days of receiving the notice, the local child support agency shall either provide written consent for the parent to proceed with the independent enforcement action or notify the parent that the local child support agency objects to the parent filing the proposed independent enforcement action. The local child support agency may object only if the local child support agency is currently using an administrative or judicial method to enforce the support obligation or if the proposed independent enforcement action would interfere with an investigation being conducted by the local child support agency. If the local child support agency does not respond to the parent's written notice within 30 days, the local child support agency shall be deemed to have given consent.

(3) The court shall order that all payments of support shall be made to the local child support agency in any action filed under this section by the parent who has requested, or is receiving, support enforcement services of the local child support agency unless support enforcement services have been terminated by the local child support agency by case closure as provided by state and federal law. Any order obtained by a parent prior to support enforcement services being terminated in which the local child support agency did not receive proper notice pursuant to this section shall be voidable upon the motion of the local child support agency.

(g) Any notice from the local child support agency requesting a meeting with the support obligor for any purpose authorized under this section shall contain a statement advising the support obligor of his or her right to have an attorney present at the meeting.

(h) For the purpose of this section, "a parent who is receiving support enforcement services" includes a parent who has assigned his or her rights to support pursuant to Section 11477 of the Welfare and Institutions Code.

(i) The Judicial Council shall develop forms to implement this section. *(Added by Stats.1999, c. 478 (A.B.196), § 1. Amended by Stats.1999, c. 480 (S.B.542), § 14; Stats.2000, c. 808 (A.B.1358), § 84.5, eff. Sept. 28, 2000; Stats.2001, c. 755 (S.B.943), § 13, eff. Oct. 12, 2001.)*

Commentary

Plumas County Child Support Services v. Rodriquez, 161 Cal.App.4th 1021, 76 Cal.Rptr.3d 1 (2008), holds that a county has no authority under this section to seek child support on behalf of non-parent relatives who are supporting a child and sharing their home with him, unless there is a contractual agreement between the parents and the relatives. See also section 3951(a), which provides that a parent is not required to compensate a relative for voluntary support of a child without an agreement for compensation.

County of Santa Clara v. Perry, 18 Cal.4th 435, 956 P.2d 1191, 75 Cal.Rptr.2d 738 (1998), holds that Family Code Section 4009 applies to original support orders as well as to orders modifying support, and it equally applies to support orders in paternity actions brought by the district attorney (local child support agency). Thus, for many children born out of wedlock, the support obligation of the noncustodial parent may be made retroactive only to the establishment of paternity. However, *County v. Riverside v. Burt, 78 Cal.App.4th 28, 92 Cal.Rptr.2d 619 (2000)* holds that *Perry, supra,* does not apply to cases in which reimbursement is sought for public assistance payments on behalf of a child. In such case, reimbursement is subject only to the three-year statute of limitations (Civil Code § 338) and the parent's reasonable ability to pay. Effectively, *Burt* holds that Welfare and Institutions Code § 11350 (amended and reenacted as Family Code § 17402, effective January 1, 2000) provides an alternative path for reimbursement in public assistance cases. Family Code § 17402 adds a one-year statute of limitations: the period may not exceed one year from the filing of the petition or complaint.

When the county seeks reimbursement from parents for public assistance provided to their children, *Clark v. Superior Court, 62 Cal.App.4th 576, 73 Cal.Rptr.2d 53 (1998),* holds that due process does not require that indigent parents be provided court-appointed counsel at public expense. But see *County of Ventura v. Tillett, 133 Cal.App.3d 105, 183 Cal.Rptr. 741 (1982) cert. denied, 460 U.S. 1051 (1983)* (contra). Compare *Salas v. Cortez, 24 Cal.3d 22, 593 P.2d 226, 154 Cal.Rptr. 529 (1979)* (requiring appointed counsel for indigents in paternity actions).

Research References

Forms

California Transactions Forms--Family Law § 3:2, Child Custody.

West's California Judicial Council Forms FL-334, Declaration Regarding Address Verification--Postjudgment Request to Modify a Child Custody, Visitation, or Child Support Order.

West's California Judicial Council Forms FL-415, Findings and Order Regarding Contempt (Family Law--Domestic Violence Prevention--Uniform Parentage--Governmental).

West's California Judicial Council Forms FL-600, Summons and Complaint or Supplemental Complaint Regarding Parental Obligations.

West's California Judicial Council Forms FL-610, Answer to Complaint or Supplemental Complaint Regarding Parental Obligations.

West's California Judicial Council Forms FL-620, Request to Enter Default Judgment (Governmental).

West's California Judicial Council Forms FL-625, Stipulation and Order.

West's California Judicial Council Forms FL-630, Judgment Regarding Parental Obligations.

West's California Judicial Council Forms FL-645, Notice to District Attorney Of Intent to Take Independent Action to Enforce Support Order.

West's California Judicial Council Forms FL-646, Response Of District Attorney to Notice Of Intent to Take Independent Action to Enforce Support Order.

West's California Judicial Council Forms FL-660, Ex Parte Motion by District Attorney and Declaration for Joinder Of Other Parent.

West's California Judicial Council Forms FL-661, Notice Of Motion and Declaration for Joinder Of Other Parent in Governmental Action.

West's California Judicial Council Forms FL-662, Responsive Declaration to Motion for Joinder Of Other Parent.

West's California Judicial Council Forms FL-663, Stipulation and Order for Joinder Of Other Parent (Governmental).

West's California Judicial Council Forms FL-684, Request for Order and Supporting Declaration (Governmental).

West's California Judicial Council Forms FL-687, Order After Hearing.

West's California Judicial Council Forms FL-688, Short Form Order After Hearing (Governmental).

West's California Judicial Council Forms FL-661-INFO, Information Sheet for Notice Of Motion and Declaration for Joinder Of Other Parent in Governmental Action.

West's California Judicial Council Forms FL-662-INFO, Information Sheet for Responsive Declaration to Motion for Joinder Of Other Parent--Consent Order Of Joinder.

Treatises and Practice Aids

Witkin, California Summary 10th Husband and Wife § 314, Acquisition and Confidentiality Of Information.
Witkin, California Summary 10th Husband and Wife § 317, Nature Of Proceedings.
Witkin, California Summary 10th Husband and Wife § 320, in General.
Witkin, California Summary 10th Husband and Wife § 321, Custody and Visitation.
Witkin, California Summary 10th Husband and Wife § 322, Allocation Of Dependency Exemption.
Witkin, California Summary 10th Husband and Wife § 323, Party Status Of Parents.
Witkin, California Summary 10th Husband and Wife § 326, Time and Notice Requirements.
Witkin, California Summary 10th Husband and Wife § 327, Hearing.
Witkin, California Summary 10th Husband and Wife § 332, Appeal.
Witkin, California Summary 10th Husband and Wife § 383, Temporary Custody and Visitation.
Witkin, California Summary 10th Parent and Child § 304, Notice Of Hearing.
Witkin, California Summary 10th Parent and Child § 363, Applicability Of Family Code Custody Provisions.

§ 17404.1. Pleading pursuant to Uniform Interstate Family Support Act; summons or order to show cause; proposed judgment; service; set aside of portion of judgment

(a) Upon receipt of a petition or comparable pleading pursuant to Part 6 (commencing with Section 5700.101) of Division 9, the local child support agency or petitioner may either (1) request the issuance of a summons or (2) request the court to issue an order requiring the respondent to appear personally at a specified time and place to show cause why an order should not be issued as prayed in the petition or comparable pleading on file.

(b) The respondent may also be served with a proposed judgment consistent with the relief sought in the petition or other comparable pleading. If the respondent's income or income history is unknown to the local child support agency, the local child support agency may serve a form of proposed judgment with the petition and other documents on the respondent that shall inform the respondent that income shall be presumed to be the amount of the state minimum wage, at 40 hours per week, unless information concerning the respondent's income is provided to the court. The respondent shall also receive notice that the proposed judgment will become effective if he or she fails to file a response with the court within 30 days after service.

(c) If a summons is issued for a petition or comparable pleading pursuant to Part 6 (commencing with Section 5700.101) of Division 9, the local child support agency or petitioner shall cause a copy of the summons, petition, and other documents to be served upon the respondent according to law.

(d) If an order to show cause is issued on a petition or comparable pleading pursuant to Part 6 (commencing with Section 5700.101) of Division 9 requiring the respondent to appear at a specified time and place to respond to the petition, a copy of the order to show cause, the petition, and other documents shall be served upon the respondent at least 15 days prior to the hearing.

(e) A petition or comparable pleading served upon a respondent in accordance with this section shall be accompanied by a blank responsive form that shall permit the respondent to answer the petition and raise any defenses by checking applicable boxes and by a blank income and expense declaration or simplified financial statement together with instructions for completion of the forms.

(f) In any action pursuant to Part 6 (commencing with Section 5700.101) of Division 9 in which the judgment was obtained pursuant to presumed income, as set forth in this section, the court may set aside that part of the judgment or order concerning the amount of child support to be paid on the grounds specified and in the manner set forth in Section 17432. *(Added by Stats.2015, c. 493 (S.B.646), § 8, eff. Jan. 1, 2016.)*

§ 17404.2. Pleading pursuant to Uniform Interstate Family Support Act; jurisdiction; transfer to appropriate court or state

(a) If, prior to filing, a petition or comparable pleading pursuant to Part 6 (commencing with Section 5700.101) of Division 9 is received by the local child support agency or the superior court and the county in which the pleadings are received is not the appropriate jurisdiction for trial of the action, the court or the local child support agency shall forward the pleadings and any accompanying documents to the appropriate court of this state or to the jurisdiction of another state without filing the pleadings or order of the court, and shall notify the petitioner, the California Central Registry, and the local child support agency of the receiving county where and when the pleading was sent.

(b) If, after a petition or comparable pleading has been filed with the superior court of a county pursuant to Part 6 (commencing with Section 5700.101) of Division 9, it appears that the respondent is not or is no longer a resident of the county in which the action has been filed, upon ex parte application by the local child support agency or petitioner, the court shall transfer the action to the appropriate court of this state or to the appropriate jurisdiction of another state and shall notify the petitioner, the respondent, the California Central Registry, and the local child support agency of the receiving county where and when the pleading was sent.

(c) If, after entry of an order by a court of this state or an order of another state registered in a court of this state for enforcement or modification pursuant to Part 6 (commencing with Section 5700.101) of Division 9, it appears that the respondent is not or is no longer a resident of the county in which the foreign order has been registered, upon ex parte application by the local child support agency of the transferring or receiving county or the petitioner, the court shall transfer the registered order and all documents subsequently filed in that action to the appropriate court of this state and shall notify the petitioner, the respondent, the California Central Registry, and the local child support agency of the transferring and receiving county where and when the registered order and all other appropriate documents were sent. Transfer of certified copies of documents shall meet the requirements of this section.

(d) If, in an action initiated in a court of this state pursuant to Part 6 (commencing with Section 5700.101) of Division 9 or a predecessor law for interstate enforcement of support, the petitioner is no longer a resident of the county in which the action has been filed, upon ex parte application by the petitioner or the local child support agency, the court shall transfer the action to the appropriate court of this state and shall notify the responding jurisdiction where and when the action was transferred.

(e) Notwithstanding subdivisions (b) and (c), if the respondent becomes a resident of another county or jurisdiction after an action or registered order has been filed pursuant to Part 6 (commencing with Section 5700.101) of Division 9, the action may remain in the county where the action was filed until the action is completed. *(Added by Stats.2015, c. 493 (S.B.646), § 9, eff. Jan. 1, 2016.)*

§ 17404.3. Hearings by telephone, audiovisual means or other electronic means; adoption of rules

Hearings by telephone, audiovisual means, or other electronic means shall be permitted in child support cases in which the local child support agency is providing child support services. The Judicial Council shall adopt court rules implementing this provision and subdivision (f) of Section 5700.316 on or before July 1, 2016. *(Added by Stats.2015, c. 493 (S.B.646), § 10, eff. Jan. 1, 2016.)*

Research References

Treatises and Practice Aids

Witkin, California Summary 10th Husband and Wife § 327, Hearing.

§ 17404.4. Issuance of notice to change payee on support order; filing of notice

In exercising the jurisdiction under Section 5700.319, either the department or the local child support agency may issue a notice to change payee on a support order issued in this state, upon request from the support enforcement agency of another state where a custodial party has either assigned the right to receive support or has requested support enforcement services. Notice of the administrative change of payee shall be filed with the court in which the order was issued or last registered. *(Added by Stats.2015, c. 493 (S.B.646), § 11, eff. Jan. 1, 2016.)*

§ 17405. Local child support agency; interview of custodial parent

In carrying out duties under this article, the local child support agency shall interview the custodial parent within 10 business days of opening a child support case. This interview shall solicit financial and all other information about the noncustodial parent. This information shall be acted upon immediately. The local child support agency shall reinterview the custodial parent as needed. *(Added by Stats.1999, c. 652 (S.B.240), § 16.)*

Research References

Treatises and Practice Aids

Witkin, California Summary 10th Husband and Wife § 314, Acquisition and Confidentiality Of Information.

§ 17406. Attorney-client relationship between Attorney General or local agency and any person; stipulated order resolving complaint for paternity or support; notice; civil action against noncustodial parent

(a) In all actions involving paternity or support, including, but not limited to, other proceedings under this code, and under Division 9 (commencing with Section 10000) of the Welfare and Institutions Code, the local child support agency and the Attorney General represent the public interest in establishing, modifying, and enforcing support obligations. No attorney-client relationship shall be deemed to have been created between the local child support agency or Attorney General and any person by virtue of the action of the local child support agency or the Attorney General in carrying out these statutory duties.

(b) Subdivision (a) is declaratory of existing law.

(c) In all requests for services of the local child support agency or Attorney General pursuant to Section 17400 relating to actions involving paternity or support, not later than the same day an individual makes a request for these services in person, and not later than five working days after either (1) a case is referred for services from the county welfare department, (2) receipt of a request by mail for an application for services, or (3) an individual makes a request for services by telephone, the local child support agency or Attorney General shall give notice to the individual requesting services or on whose behalf services have been requested that the local child support agency or Attorney General does not represent the individual or the children who are the subject of the case, that no attorney-client relationship exists between the local child support agency or Attorney General and those persons, and that no such representation or relationship shall arise if the local child support agency or Attorney General provides the services requested. Notice shall be in bold print and in plain English and shall be translated into the language understandable by the recipient when reasonable. The notice shall include the advice that the absence of an attorney-client relationship means that communications from the recipient are not privileged and that the local child support agency or Attorney General may provide support enforcement services to the other parent in the future.

(d) The local child support agency or Attorney General shall give the notice required pursuant to subdivision (c) to all recipients of services under Section 17400 who have not otherwise been provided that notice, not later than the date of the next annual notice required under Section 11476.2 of the Welfare and Institutions Code. This notice shall include notification to the recipient of services under Section 17400 that the recipient may inspect the clerk's file at the office of the clerk of the court, and that, upon request, the local child support agency, or, if appropriate, the Attorney General, will furnish a copy of the most recent order entered in the case.

(e) The local child support agency or, if appropriate, the Attorney General shall serve a copy of the complaint for paternity or support, or both, on recipients of support services under Section 17400, as specified in paragraph (2) of subdivision (e) of Section 17404. A notice shall accompany the complaint that informs the recipient that the local child support agency or Attorney General may enter into a stipulated order resolving the complaint, and that the recipient shall assist the prosecuting attorney, by sending all information on the noncustodial parent's earnings and assets to the prosecuting attorney.

(f)(1)(A) The local child support agency or Attorney General shall provide written notice to recipients of services under Section 17400 of the initial date and time, and purpose of every hearing in a civil action for paternity or support.

(B) Once the parent who has requested or is receiving support enforcement services becomes a party to the action pursuant to subdivision (e) of Section 17404, in lieu of the above, the local child support agency or Attorney General shall serve on a parent all pleadings relating to paternity or support that have been served on the local child support agency by the other parent. The pleading shall be accompanied by a notice.

(C) The notice provided subject to subparagraphs (A) and (B) shall include the following language:

IMPORTANT NOTICE

It may be important that you attend the hearing. The local child support agency does not represent you or your children. You may have information about the other parent, such as information about his or her income or assets that will not be presented to the court unless you attend the hearing. You have the right to attend the hearing and to be heard in court and tell the court what you think the court should do with the child support order. This hearing could change your rights or your children's rights to support.

(2) The notice shall state the purpose of the hearing or be attached to the motion or other pleading which caused the hearing to be scheduled.

(3) The notice shall be provided separate from all other material and shall be in at least 14–point type. The failure of the local child support agency or Attorney General to provide the notice required pursuant to subparagraph (A) of paragraph (1) does not affect the validity of any order.

(4)(A) The notice required pursuant to subparagraph (A) of paragraph (1) shall be provided not later than seven calendar days prior to the hearing, or, if the local child support agency or Attorney General receives notice of the hearing less than seven days prior to the hearing, within two days of the receipt by the local child support agency or Attorney General of the notice of the hearing.

(B) Service of the notice and the pleadings required pursuant to subparagraph (B) of paragraph (1) shall be completed not later than five days after receipt of the pleadings served on the local child support agency by the parent.

(5) The local child support agency or Attorney General shall, in order to implement this subdivision, make reasonable efforts to ensure that the local child support agency or Attorney General has current addresses for all parties to the child support action.

(g) The local child support agency or Attorney General shall give notice to recipients of services under Section 17400 of every order obtained by the local child support agency or Attorney General that establishes or modifies the support obligation for the recipient or the children who are the subject of the order, by sending a copy of the order to the recipient. The notice shall be made within the time specified by federal law after the order has been filed. The local child support agency or Attorney General shall also give notice to these recipients of every order obtained in any other jurisdiction that establishes or modifies the support obligation for the recipient or the children who are the subject of the order, and which is received by the local child support agency or Attorney General, by sending a copy of the order to the recipient within the timeframe specified by federal law after the local child support agency or Attorney General has received a copy of the order. In any action enforced under Part 6 (commencing with Section 5700.101) of Division 9, the notice shall be made in compliance with the requirements of that chapter. The failure of the local child support agency or Attorney General to comply with this subdivision does not affect the validity of any order.

(h) The local child support agency or Attorney General shall give notice to the noncustodial parent against whom a civil action is filed that the local child support agency or Attorney General is not the attorney representing any individual, including, but not limited to, the custodial parent, the child, or the noncustodial parent.

(i) Nothing in this section shall be construed to preclude any person who is receiving services under Section 17400 from filing and prosecuting an independent action to establish, modify, and enforce an order for current support on behalf of himself or herself or a child if that person is not receiving public assistance.

(j) A person who is receiving services under Section 17400 but who is not currently receiving public assistance on his or her own behalf or on behalf of a child shall be asked to execute, or consent to, any stipulation establishing or modifying a support order in any action in which that person is named as a party, before the stipulation is filed. The local child support agency or Attorney General may not submit to the court for approval a stipulation to establish or modify a support order in the action without first obtaining the signatures of all parties to the action, their attorneys of record, or persons authorized to act on their behalf. Any stipulation approved by the court in violation of this subdivision shall be void.

(k) The local child support agency or Attorney General may not enter into a stipulation that reduces the amount of past due support, including interest and penalties accrued pursuant to an order of current support, on behalf of a person who is receiving support enforcement services under Section 17400 and who is owed support arrearages that exceed unreimbursed public assistance paid to the recipient of the support enforcement services, without first obtaining the consent of the person who is receiving services under Section 17400 on his or her own behalf or on behalf of the child.

(*l*) The notices required in this section shall be provided in the following manner:

(1) In all cases in which the person receiving services under Section 17400 resides in California, notice shall be provided by mailing the item by first-class mail to the last known address of, or personally delivering the item to, that person.

(2) In all actions enforced under Part 6 (commencing with Section 5700.101) of Division 9, unless otherwise specified, notice shall be provided by mailing the item by first-class mail to the initiating court.

(m) Notwithstanding any other provision of this section, the notices provided for pursuant to subdivisions (c) to (g), inclusive, are not required in foster care cases. *(Added by Stats.1999, c. 478 (A.B.196), § 1. Amended by Stats.1999, c. 480 (S.B.542), § 15; Stats.2000, c. 808 (A.B.1358), § 84.7, eff. Sept. 28, 2000; Stats.2001, c. 176 (S.B.210), § 6; Stats.2004, c. 339 (A.B.1704), § 7; Stats.2015, c. 493 (S.B.646), § 12, eff. Jan. 1, 2016.)*

Commentary

Carlson v. Eassa, 54 Cal.App.4th 684, 62 Cal.Rptr.2d 884 (1997), holds that a stipulated URESA judgment is void when the district attorney (local child support agency) settles a child support arrearage claim without obtaining a party's subsection (j) consent.

Research References

Forms

West's California Judicial Council Forms FL-334, Declaration Regarding Address Verification--Postjudgment Request to Modify a Child Custody, Visitation, or Child Support Order.
West's California Judicial Council Forms FL-560, Ex Parte Application for Transfer and Order (UIFSA).
West's California Judicial Council Forms FL-600, Summons and Complaint or Supplemental Complaint Regarding Parental Obligations.
West's California Judicial Council Forms FL-605, Notice and Acknowledgment Of Receipt.
West's California Judicial Council Forms FL-615, Stipulation for Judgment or Supplemental Judgment Regarding Parental Obligations and Judgment.
West's California Judicial Council Forms FL-616, Declaration for Amended Proposed Judgment.
West's California Judicial Council Forms FL-627, Order for Genetic (Parentage) Testing.
West's California Judicial Council Forms FL-635, Notice Of Entry Of Judgment and Proof Of Service by Mail (Governmental).
West's California Judicial Council Forms FL-646, Response Of District Attorney to Notice Of Intent to Take Independent Action to Enforce Support Order.
West's California Judicial Council Forms FL-650, Statement for Registration Of California Support Order.
West's California Judicial Council Forms FL-660, Ex Parte Motion by District Attorney and Declaration for Joinder Of Other Parent.
West's California Judicial Council Forms FL-670, Notice Of Motion for Judicial Review Of License Denial.
West's California Judicial Council Forms FL-675, Order After Judicial Review Of License Denial.
West's California Judicial Council Forms FL-678, Order Determining Claim Of Exemption or Third-Party Claim.
West's California Judicial Council Forms FL-683, Order to Show Cause.
West's California Judicial Council Forms FL-684, Request for Order and Supporting Declaration (Governmental).
West's California Judicial Council Forms FL-688, Short Form Order After Hearing (Governmental).
West's California Judicial Council Forms FL-692, Minutes and Order or Judgment.
West's California Judicial Council Forms FL-697, Declaration for Default or Uncontested Judgment.

Treatises and Practice Aids

Witkin, California Summary 10th Husband and Wife § 317, Nature Of Proceedings.
Witkin, California Summary 10th Husband and Wife § 318, Agency's Representation Of Public Interest.
Witkin, California Summary 10th Husband and Wife § 326, Time and Notice Requirements.
Witkin, California Summary 10th Husband and Wife § 328, Agreement, Stipulation, or Compromise.
Witkin, California Summary 10th Husband and Wife § 334, in General.

§ 17407. Support order or support-related order; appeal taken or opposed by Attorney General; expenses

(a) If the Attorney General is of the opinion that a support order or support-related order is erroneous and presents a question of law warranting an appeal, or that an order is sound and should be defended on appeal, in the public interest the Attorney General may:

(1) Perfect or oppose an appeal to the proper appellate court if the order was issued by a court of this state.

(2) If the order was issued in another state, cause an appeal to be taken or opposed in the other state.

(b) In either case, expenses of the appeal may be paid on order of the Attorney General from funds appropriated for the Office of the Attorney General. *(Added by Stats.1999, c. 652 (S.B.240), § 17.)*

Research References

Treatises and Practice Aids

Witkin, California Summary 10th Husband and Wife § 332, Appeal.

§ 17407.5. State reciprocity; declaration; full force and effect unless specified condition is met

A declaration of state reciprocity issued by the Attorney General on or before December 31, 2015, and a declaration issued pursuant to subdivision (b) of Section 5700.308, shall remain in full force and effect unless one of the following occurs:

(a) The declaration is revoked or declared invalid by the Attorney General, in consultation with the department, or by the other party to the reciprocity agreement.

(b) The declaration is superseded by a subsequent federal bilateral agreement with the other party.

(c) The declaration is superseded by the other party's ratification of or accession to the Hague Convention on the International Recovery of Child Support and Other Forms of Family Maintenance. *(Added by Stats.2015, c. 493 (S.B.646), § 13, eff. Jan. 1, 2016.)*

§ 17408. Consolidation of multiple court files; consolidation of orders

(a) Notwithstanding Section 17404, upon noticed motion of the local child support agency, the superior court may consolidate or combine support or reimbursement arrearages owed by one obligor to one obligee in two or more court files into a single court file, or combine or consolidate two or more orders for current child support into a single court file. A motion to consolidate may be made by a local child support agency only if it is seeking to enforce the orders being consolidated. The motion shall be filed only in the court file the local child support agency is seeking to have designated as the primary file.

(b) Orders may be consolidated regardless of the nature of the underlying action, whether initiated under the Welfare and Institutions Code, this code, or another law. Orders for support shall not be consolidated unless the children involved have the same mother and father and venue is proper pursuant to Section 17400.

(c) Upon consolidation of orders, the court shall designate which court file the support orders are being consolidated into the primary file, and which court files are subordinate. Upon consolidation, the court shall order the local child support agency to file a notice in the subordinate court actions indicating the support orders in those actions were consolidated into the primary file. The notice shall state the date of the consolidation, the name of the court, and the primary file number.

(d) Upon consolidation of orders, the superior court shall not issue further orders pertaining to support in a subordinate court file; and all enforcement and modification of support orders shall occur in the primary court action.

(e) After consolidation of court orders, a single wage assignment for current support and arrearages may be issued when possible. *(Added by Stats.1999, c. 478 (A.B.196), § 1.)*

Research References

Forms

West's California Judicial Council Forms FL-920, Notice Of Consolidation.

Treatises and Practice Aids

Witkin, California Summary 10th Husband and Wife § 325, Consolidation Of Claims.

§ 17410. Voluntary declaration of paternity

In any action filed by the local child support agency pursuant to Section 17402 or 17404, the local child support agency shall provide the mother and the alleged father the opportunity to voluntarily acknowledge paternity by signing a paternity declaration as described in Section 7574 prior to a hearing or trial where the paternity of a minor child is at issue. The opportunity to voluntarily acknowledge paternity may be provided either before or after an action pursuant to Section 17402 or 17404 is filed and served upon the alleged father. For the purpose of meeting the requirements of this section, the local child support agency may afford the defendant an opportunity to enter into a stipulation for judgment of paternity after an action for paternity has been filed in lieu of the voluntary declaration of paternity. *(Added by Stats.1999, c. 478 (A.B.196), § 1.)*

Research References

Treatises and Practice Aids

Witkin, California Summary 10th Husband and Wife § 320, in General.

Witkin, California Summary 10th Husband and Wife § 343, CalWORKs Aid.

§ 17412. Voluntary declaration of paternity; child support action

(a) Notwithstanding any other law, an action for child support may be brought by the local child support agency on behalf of a minor child or caretaker parent based upon a voluntary declaration of paternity as provided in Chapter 3 (commencing with Section 7570) of Part 2 of Division 12.

(b) Except as provided in Sections 7576 and 7577, the voluntary declaration of paternity shall be given the same force and effect as a judgment for paternity entered by a court of competent jurisdiction. The court shall make appropriate orders for support of the minor child based upon the voluntary declaration of paternity unless evidence is presented that the voluntary declaration of paternity has been rescinded by the parties or set aside by a court as provided in Section 7575.

(c) The Judicial Council shall develop the forms and procedures necessary to implement this section. *(Added by Stats.1999, c. 478 (A.B.196), § 1.)*

Research References

Treatises and Practice Aids

Witkin, California Summary 10th Husband and Wife § 320, in General.

§ 17414. Parentage stipulation

In any action or proceeding brought by the local child support agency to establish parentage pursuant to Section 17400, the court shall enter a judgment establishing parentage upon the filing of a written stipulation between the parties provided that the stipulation is accompanied by a written advisement and waiver of rights which is signed by the defendant. The written advisement and waiver of rights shall be developed by the Judicial Council. *(Added by Stats.1999, c. 478 (A.B.196), § 1.)*

Research References

Treatises and Practice Aids

Witkin, California Summary 10th Husband and Wife § 328, Agreement, Stipulation, or Compromise.

§ 17415. Public assistance application where parent absent or parentage not established; welfare department referral to local child support agency

(a) It shall be the duty of the county welfare department to refer all cases in which a parent is absent from the home, or in which the parents are unmarried and parentage has not been established by the completion and filing of a voluntary declaration of paternity pursuant to Section 7573 or a court of competent jurisdiction, to the local child support agency immediately at the time the application for public assistance, including Medi–Cal benefits, or certificate of eligibility, is signed by the applicant or recipient, except as provided in Section 17552 and Sections 11477 and 11477.04 of the Welfare and Institutions Code. If an applicant is found to be ineligible, the applicant shall be notified in writing that the referral of the case to the local child support agency may be terminated at the applicant's request. The county welfare department shall cooperate with the local child support agency and shall make available all pertinent information pursuant to Section 17505.

(b) Upon referral from the county welfare department, the local child support agency shall investigate the question of nonsupport or paternity and shall take all steps necessary to obtain child support for the needy child, enforce spousal support as part of the state plan under Section 17604, and determine paternity in the case of a child born out of wedlock. Upon the advice of the county welfare department that a child is being considered for adoption, the local child support agency shall delay the investigation and other actions with respect to the case until advised that the adoption is no longer under consideration. The granting of public assistance or Medi–Cal benefits to an applicant shall not be delayed or contingent upon investigation by the local child support agency.

(c) In cases where Medi–Cal benefits are the only assistance provided, the local child support agency shall provide child and spousal support services unless the recipient of the services notifies the local child support agency that only services related to securing health insurance benefits are requested.

(d) Whenever a court order has been obtained, any contractual agreement for support between the local child support agency or the county welfare department and the noncustodial parent shall be deemed null and void to the extent that it is not consistent with the court order.

(e) Whenever a family that has been receiving public assistance, including Medi–Cal, ceases to receive assistance, including Medi–Cal, the local child support agency shall, to the extent required by federal regulations, continue to enforce support payments from the noncustodial parent until the individual on whose behalf the enforcement efforts are made sends written notice to the local child support agency requesting that enforcement services be discontinued.

(f) The local child support agency shall, when appropriate, utilize reciprocal arrangements adopted with other states in securing support from an absent parent. In individual cases where utilization of reciprocal arrangements has proven ineffective, the local child support agency may forward to the Attorney General a request to utilize federal courts in order to obtain or enforce orders for child or spousal support. If reasonable efforts to collect amounts assigned pursuant to Section 11477 of the Welfare and Institutions Code have failed, the local child support agency may request that the case be forwarded to the United States Treasury Department for collection in accordance with federal regulations. The Attorney General, when appropriate, shall forward these requests to the Secretary of Health and Human Services, or a designated representative. *(Added by Stats.1999, c. 478 (A.B.196), § 1. Amended by Stats.1999, c. 480 (S.B.542), § 16; Stats.2001, c. 463 (A.B.1449), § 1; Stats.2014, c. 29 (S.B.855), § 1, eff. June 20, 2014.)*

Implementation

For implementation relating to Stats.2001, c. 463 (A.B.1449), see § 6 of that Act.

Research References

Treatises and Practice Aids

Witkin, California Summary 10th Husband and Wife § 312, Referral to Agency by County Welfare Department.

§ 17416. Agency agreement with noncustodial parent

(a) In any case where the local child support agency has undertaken enforcement of support, the local child support agency may enter into an agreement with the noncustodial parent, on behalf of a minor child or children, a spouse, or former spouse for the entry of a judgment without action determining paternity, if applicable, and for periodic child and spousal support payments based on the noncustodial parent's reasonable ability to pay or, if for spousal support, an amount previously ordered by a court of competent jurisdiction. An agreement for entry of a judgment under this section may be executed prior to the birth of the child and may include a provision that the judgment is not to be entered until after the birth of the child.

(b) A judgment based on the agreement shall be entered only if one of the following requirements is satisfied:

(1) The noncustodial parent is represented by legal counsel and the attorney signs a certificate stating: "I have examined the proposed judgment and have advised my client concerning his or her rights in connection with this matter and the consequences of signing or not signing the agreement for the entry of the judgment and my client, after being so advised, has agreed to the entry of the judgment."

(2) A judge of the court in which the judgment is to be entered, after advising the noncustodial parent concerning his or her rights in connection with the matter and the consequences of agreeing or not agreeing to the entry of the judgment, makes a finding that the noncustodial parent has appeared before the judge and the judge has determined that under the circumstances of the particular case the noncustodial parent has willingly, knowingly, and intelligently waived his or her due process rights in agreeing to the entry of the judgment.

(c) The clerk shall file the agreement, together with any certificate of the attorney or finding of the court, without the payment of any fees or charges. If the requirements of this section are satisfied, the court shall enter judgment thereon without action. The provisions of Article 4 (commencing with Section 4200) of Chapter 2 of Part 2 of Division 9 or Chapter 4 (commencing with Section 4350) of Part 3 of Division 9 shall apply to the judgment. A judgment for support so entered may be enforced by any means by which any other judgment for support may be enforced.

(d) Upon request of the local child support agency in any case under this section, the clerk shall set the matter for hearing by the court. The hearing shall be held within 10 days after the clerk receives the request. The local child support agency may require the person who signed the agreement for the entry of judgment to attend the hearing by process of subpoena in the same manner as the attendance of a witness in a civil action may be required. The presence of the person who signed the agreement for entry of judgment at the hearing shall constitute the presence of the person in court at the time the order is pronounced for the purposes of Section 1209.5 of the Code of Civil Procedure if the court makes the findings required by paragraph (2) of subdivision (b).

(e) The local child support agency shall cause the following to be served, in the manner specified in Section 415.10, 415.20, 415.30, or 415.40 of the Code of Civil Procedure, upon the person who signed the agreement for entry of the judgment and shall file proof of service thereof with the court:

(1) A copy of the judgment as entered.

(2) If the judgment includes an order for child or spousal support payments, a notice stating the substance of the following: "The court has continuing authority to make an order increasing or decreasing the amount of the child or spousal support payments. You have the right to request that the court order the child and spousal support payments be decreased or eliminated entirely."

(f) An order for child and spousal support included in a judgment entered under this section may be modified or revoked as provided in Article 1 (commencing with Section 3650) of Chapter 6 of Part 1 of Division 9 and in (1) Article 1 (commencing with Section 4000) of Chapter 2 of Part 2 of Division 9 or (2) Chapter 2 (commencing with Section 4320) and Chapter 3 (commencing with Section 4330) of Part 3 of Division 9. The court may modify the order to make the support payments payable to a different person.

(g) For the purposes of this section, in making a determination of the noncustodial parent's reasonable ability to pay, any relevant circumstances set out in Section 4005 shall be considered.

(h) After arrest and before plea or trial, or after conviction or plea of guilty, under Section 270 of the Penal Code, if the defendant appears before the court in which the criminal action is pending and the requirements of paragraph (1) or (2) of subdivision (b) have been satisfied, the court may suspend proceedings or sentence in the criminal action, but this does not limit the later institution of a civil or criminal action or limit the use of any other procedures available to enforce the judgment entered pursuant to this section.

(i) Nothing in this section applies to a case where a civil action has been commenced. *(Added by Stats.1999, c. 478 (A.B.196), § 1.)*

Research References

Treatises and Practice Aids

Witkin, California Summary 10th Husband and Wife § 328, Agreement, Stipulation, or Compromise.

§ 17418. Number of children; computation of support

In enforcing the provisions of this division, the local child support agency shall inquire of both the custodial and noncustodial parent as to the number of minor children each is legally obligated to support. The local child support agency shall consider the needs of all of these children in computing the level of support requested to be ordered by the court. *(Added by Stats.1999, c. 478 (A.B.196), § 1.)*

Research References

Treatises and Practice Aids

Witkin, California Summary 10th Husband and Wife § 310, Local Child Support Agency.

§ 17420. Earnings assignment order for support

After judgment in any court action brought to enforce the support obligation of a noncustodial parent pursuant to the provisions of this division, the court shall issue an earnings assignment order for support pursuant to Chapter 8 (commencing with Section 5200) of Part 5 of Division 9. *(Added by Stats.1999, c. 478 (A.B.196), § 1.)*

Research References

Treatises and Practice Aids

Witkin, California Summary 10th Husband and Wife § 310, Local Child Support Agency.

§ 17422. Medical insurance form; health insurance coverage

(a) The state medical insurance form required in Article 1 (commencing with Section 3750) of Chapter 7 of Part 1 of Division 9 shall include, but shall not be limited to, all of the following:

(1) The parent or parents' names, addresses, and social security numbers.

(2) The name and address of each parent's place of employment.

(3) The name or names, addresses, policy number or numbers, and coverage type of the medical insurance policy or policies of the parents, if any.

(4) The name, CalWORKs case number, social security number, and Title IV–E foster care case number or Medi–Cal case numbers of the parents and children covered by the medical insurance policy or policies.

(b)(1) In any action brought or enforcement proceeding instituted by the local child support agency under this division for payment of child or spousal support, a completed state medical insurance form shall be obtained and sent by the local child support agency to the State Department of Health Services in the manner prescribed by the State Department of Health Services.

(2) Where it has been determined under Section 3751 that health insurance coverage is not available at no or reasonable cost, the local child support agency shall seek a provision in the support order that provides for health insurance coverage should it become available at no or reasonable cost.

(3) Health insurance coverage shall be considered reasonable in cost if the cost to the responsible parent providing medical support does not exceed 5 percent of his or her gross income. In applying the 5 percent for the cost of health insurance, the cost is the difference between self-only and family coverage. If the obligor is entitled to a low-income adjustment as provided in paragraph (7) of subdivision (b) of Section 4055, health insurance shall not be enforced, unless the court determines that not requiring medical support would be unjust and inappropriate in the particular case. As used in this section, "health insurance coverage" also includes providing for the delivery of health care services by a fee for service, health maintenance organization, preferred provider organization, or any other type of health care delivery system under which medical services could be provided to the dependent child or children of an absent parent.

(c)(1) The local child support agency shall request employers and other groups offering health insurance coverage that is being enforced under this division to notify the local child support agency if there has been a lapse in insurance coverage. The local child support agency shall be responsible for forwarding information pertaining to the health insurance policy secured for the dependent children for whom the local child support agency is enforcing the court-ordered medical support to the custodial parent.

(2) The local child support agency shall periodically communicate with the State Department of Health Services to determine if there have been lapses in health insurance coverage for public assistance applicants and recipients. The State Department of Health Services shall notify the local child support agency when there has been a lapse in court-ordered insurance coverage.

(3) The local child support agency shall take appropriate action, civil or criminal, to enforce the obligation to obtain health insurance when there has been a lapse in insurance coverage or failure by the responsible parent to obtain insurance as ordered by the court.

(4) The local child support agency shall inform all individuals upon their application for child support enforcement services that medical support enforcement services are available. *(Added by Stats.1999, c. 478 (A.B.196), § 1. Amended by Stats.2000, c. 119 (S.B.2045), § 3; Stats.2002, c. 927 (A.B.3032), § 4; Stats.2010, c. 103 (S.B.580), § 4.)*

Research References

Forms

West's California Judicial Council Forms FL-684, Request for Order and Supporting Declaration (Governmental).

Treatises and Practice Aids

Witkin, California Summary 10th Husband and Wife § 310, Local Child Support Agency.

Witkin, California Summary 10th Parent and Child § 304, Notice Of Hearing.

Witkin, California Summary 10th Parent and Child § 415, in General.

§ 17424. Medical insurance form; submission

(a) A parent who has been served with a medical insurance form shall complete and return the form to the local child support agency's office within 20 calendar days of the date the form was served.

(b) The local child support agency shall send the completed medical insurance form to the department in the manner prescribed by the department. *(Added by Stats.1999, c. 478 (A.B.196), § 1.)*

§ 17428. Supplemental complaint and judgment

In any action or judgment brought or obtained pursuant to Section 17400, 17402, 17404, or 17416, a supplemental complaint may be filed, pursuant to Section 464 of the Code of Civil Procedure and Section 2330.1, either before or after a final judgment, seeking a judgment or order of paternity or support for a child of the mother and father of the child whose paternity and support are already in issue before the court. A supplemental judgment entered in the proceedings shall include, when appropriate and requested in the supplemental complaint, an order establishing or modifying support for all children named in the original or supplemental actions in conformity with the statewide uniform guideline for child support. A supplemental complaint for paternity or support of children may be filed without leave of court either before or after final judgment in the underlying action. Service of the supplemental summons and complaint shall be made in the manner provided for the initial service of a summons by the Code of Civil Procedure. *(Added by Stats.1999, c. 478 (A.B.196), § 1.)*

Research References

Forms

West's California Judicial Council Forms FL-600, Summons and Complaint or Supplemental Complaint Regarding Parental Obligations.

West's California Judicial Council Forms FL-640, Notice and Motion to Cancel (Set Aside) Support Order Based on Presumed Income.

West's California Judicial Council Forms FL-643, Declaration Of Obligor's Income During Judgment Period--Presumed Income Set--Aside Request.

West's California Judicial Council Forms FL-640-INFO, Information Sheet for Notice and Motion to Cancel (Set Aside) Support Order Based on Presumed Income.

Treatises and Practice Aids

Witkin, California Summary 10th Husband and Wife § 324, Pleadings.

§ 17430. Default judgment; amendment

(a) Notwithstanding any other provision of law, in any action filed by the local child support agency pursuant to Section 17400, 17402, or 17404, a judgment shall be entered without hearing, without the presentation of any other evidence or further notice to the defendant, upon the filing of proof of service by the local child support agency evidencing that more than 30 days have passed since the simplified summons and complaint, proposed judgment, blank answer, blank income and expense declaration, and all notices required by this division were served on the defendant.

(b) If the defendant fails to file an answer with the court within 30 days of having been served as specified in subdivision (d) of Section 17400, or at any time before the default judgment is entered, the proposed judgment filed with the original summons and complaint shall be conformed by the court as the final judgment and a copy provided to the local child support agency, unless the local child support agency has filed a declaration and amended proposed judgment pursuant to subdivision (c).

(c) If the local child support agency receives additional financial information within 30 days of service of the complaint and proposed judgment on the defendant and the additional information would result in a support order that is different from the amount in the proposed judgment, the local child support agency shall file a declaration setting forth the additional information and an amended proposed judgment. The declaration and amended proposed judgment shall be served on the defendant in compliance with Section 1013 of the Code of Civil Procedure or otherwise as provided by law. The defendant's time to answer or otherwise appear shall be extended to 30 days from the date of service of the declaration and amended proposed judgment.

(d) Upon entry of the judgment, the clerk of the court shall provide a conformed copy of the judgment to the local child support agency. The local child support agency shall mail by first-class mail, postage prepaid, a notice of entry of judgment by default and a copy of the judgment to the defendant to the address where he or she was served with the summons and complaint and last known address if different from that address. *(Added by Stats.1999, c. 478 (A.B.196), § 1. Amended by Stats.1999, c. 480 (S.B.542), § 17; Stats. 1999, c. 652 (S.B.240), § 17.5; Stats.2000, c. 808 (A.B.1358), § 85, eff. Sept. 28, 2000; Stats.2002, c. 927 (A.B.3032), § 5.)*

Commentary

Interpreting subsection (a), *County of Yuba v. Savedra, 78 Cal. App.4th 1311, 93 Cal.Rptr.2d 524 (2000)*, holds that it was error for the trial court to decline to enter a child support judgment before presentation of evidence of the defaulting parent's income when that parent had received notice satisfying Family Code § 17400 (d)(2) (former Welfare and Institutions Code § 11475.1) in that it specified (1) the amount sought and (2) that the proposed judgment would become effective if the defendant failed to file an answer.

Research References

Forms

West's California Judicial Council Forms FL-600, Summons and Complaint or Supplemental Complaint Regarding Parental Obligations.

West's California Judicial Council Forms FL-620, Request to Enter Default Judgment (Governmental).

West's California Judicial Council Forms FL-625, Stipulation and Order.

West's California Judicial Council Forms FL-630, Judgment Regarding Parental Obligations.

West's California Judicial Council Forms FL-635, Notice Of Entry Of Judgment and Proof Of Service by Mail (Governmental).

West's California Judicial Council Forms FL-640, Notice and Motion to Cancel (Set Aside) Support Order Based on Presumed Income.

West's California Judicial Council Forms FL-643, Declaration Of Obligor's Income During Judgment Period--Presumed Income Set--Aside Request.

West's California Judicial Council Forms FL-640-INFO, Information Sheet for Notice and Motion to Cancel (Set Aside) Support Order Based on Presumed Income.

Treatises and Practice Aids

Witkin, California Summary 10th Husband and Wife § 329, Entry Of Default.

§ 17432. Setting aside part of judgment or order concerning amount of child support to be paid

(a) In any action filed by the local child support agency pursuant to Section 17400, 17402, or 17404, the court may, on any terms that may be just, set aside that part of the judgment or order concerning the amount of child support to be paid. This relief may be granted after the six- month time limit of Section 473 of the Code of Civil Procedure has elapsed, based on the grounds, and within the time limits, specified in this section.

(b) This section shall apply only to judgments or orders for support that were based upon presumed income as specified in subdivision (d) of Section 17400 and that were entered after the entry of the default of the defendant under Section 17430. This section shall apply only to the amount of support ordered and not that portion of the judgment or order concerning the determination of parentage.

(c) The court may set aside the child support order contained in a judgment described in subdivision (b) if the defendant's income was substantially different for the period of time during which judgment was effective compared with the income the defendant was presumed to have. A "substantial difference" means that amount of income that would result in an order for support that deviates from the order entered by default by 10 percent or more.

(d) Application for relief under this section shall be filed together with an income and expense declaration or simplified financial statement or other information concerning income for any relevant years. The Judicial Council may combine the application for relief under this section and the proposed answer into a single form.

(e) The burden of proving that the actual income of the defendant deviated substantially from the presumed income shall be on the party seeking to set aside the order.

(f) A motion for relief under this section shall be filed within one year of the first collection of money by the local child support agency or the obligee. The one-year time period shall run from the date that the local child support agency receives the first collection.

(g) Within three months from the date the local child support agency receives the first collection for any order established using presumed income, the local child support agency shall check all appropriate sources for income information, and if income information exists, the local child support agency shall make a determination whether the order qualifies for set aside under this section. If the order qualifies for set aside, the local child support agency shall bring a motion for relief under this section.

(h) In all proceedings under this section, before granting relief, the court shall consider the amount of time that has passed since the entry of the order, the circumstances surrounding the defendant's default, the relative hardship on the child or children to whom the duty of support is owed, the caretaker parent, and the defendant, and other equitable factors that the court deems appropriate.

(i) If the court grants the relief requested, the court shall issue a new child support order using the appropriate child support guidelines currently in effect. The new order shall have the same commencement date as the order set aside.

(j) The Judicial Council shall review and modify any relevant forms for purposes of this section. Any modifications to the forms shall be effective July 1, 2005. Prior to the implementation of any modified Judicial Council forms, the local child support agency or custodial parent may file any request to set aside a default judgment under this section using Judicial Council Form FL–680 entitled "Notice of Motion (Governmental)" and form FL–684 entitled "Request for Order and Supporting Declaration (Governmental)." *(Added by Stats.1999, c. 478 (A.B.196), § 1. Amended by Stats.2002, c. 927 (A.B.3032), § 6; Stats.2003, c. 225 (A.B.1752), § 4, eff. Aug. 11, 2003; Stats.2004, c. 339 (A.B. 1704), § 8.)*

Commentary

Of course, a default child support judgment is absolutely void for lack of personal jurisdiction over the defendant when service of the summons and complaint was fraudulent. In such case, dismissal of a motion to enforce is mandatory. *County of San Diego v. Gorham, 186 Cal.App.4th 1215, 113 Cal.Rptr.3d 147 (2010)* (defendant was incarcerated on the date summons was purported to have been served personally at his home address).

Research References

Forms

West's California Judicial Council Forms FL-640, Notice and Motion to Cancel (Set Aside) Support Order Based on Presumed Income.

West's California Judicial Council Forms FL-643, Declaration Of Obligor's Income During Judgment Period--Presumed Income Set--Aside Request.

West's California Judicial Council Forms FL-640-INFO, Information Sheet for Notice and Motion to Cancel (Set Aside) Support Order Based on Presumed Income.

Treatises and Practice Aids

Witkin, California Summary 10th Husband and Wife § 306, in General.

Witkin, California Summary 10th Husband and Wife § 330, Relief from Order Based on Presumed Income.

§ 17433. Relief from default judgment; mistaken identity; remedies

In any action in which a judgment or order for support was entered after the entry of the default of the defendant under Section 17430, the court shall relieve the defendant from that judgment or order if the defendant establishes that he or she was mistakenly identified in the order or in any subsequent documents or proceedings as the person having an obligation to provide support. The defendant shall also be entitled to the remedies specified in subdivisions (d) and (e) of Section 17530 with respect to any actions taken to enforce that judgment or order. This section is only intended to apply where an order has been entered against a person who is not the support obligor named in the judgment or order. *(Added by Stats.1999, c. 653 (A.B.380), § 16. Amended by Stats.2000, c. 808 (A.B.1358), § 85.3, eff. Sept. 28, 2000.)*

Research References

Treatises and Practice Aids

Witkin, California Summary 10th Husband and Wife § 306, in General.

Witkin, California Summary 10th Husband and Wife § 331, Relief from Order Based on Mistaken Identity.

§ 17433.5. Interest accruing on obligation for current child, spousal, family, or medical support due in a given month

In any action enforced pursuant to this article, no interest shall accrue on an obligation for current child, spousal, family, or medical support due in a given month until the first day of the following month. *(Added by Stats.2006, c. 75 (A.B.1808), § 7, eff. July 12, 2006.)*

§ 17434. Booklet about support; toll-free information hotline

(a) The department shall publish a booklet describing the proper procedures and processes for the collection and payment of child and spousal support. The booklet shall be written in language understandable to the lay person and shall direct the reader to obtain the assistance of the local child support agency, the family law facilitator, or legal counsel where appropriate. The department may contract on a competitive basis with an organization or individual to write the booklet.

(b) The department shall have primary responsibility for the design and development of the contents of the booklet. The department shall solicit comment regarding the content of the booklet from the Director of the Administrative Office of the Courts. The department shall verify the appropriateness and accuracy of the contents of the booklet with at least one representative of each of the following organizations:

(1) A local child support agency.

(2) The State Attorney General's office.

(3) A community organization that advocates for the rights of custodial parents.

(4) A community organization that advocates for the rights of supporting parents.

(c) Upon receipt of booklets on support collection, each county welfare department shall provide a copy to each head of household whose application for public assistance under Division 9 (commencing with Section 10000) of the Welfare and Institutions Code has been approved and for whom support rights have been assigned pursuant to Section 11477 of the Welfare and Institutions Code. The department shall provide copies of the booklet to local child support agencies for distribution, and to any person upon request. The department shall also distribute the booklets to all superior courts. Upon receipt of those booklets, each clerk of the court shall provide two copies of the booklet to the petitioner or plaintiff in any action involving the support of a minor child. The moving party shall serve a copy of the booklet on the responding party.

(d) The department shall expand the information provided under its toll-free information hotline in response to inquiries regarding the process and procedures for collection and payment of child and spousal support. This toll-free number shall be advertised as providing information on child and spousal support. The hotline personnel shall not provide legal consultation or advice, but shall provide only referral services.

(e) The department shall maintain a file of referral sources to provide callers to the telephone hotline with the following information specific to the county in which the caller resides:

(1) The location and telephone number of the local child support agency, the county welfare office, the family law facilitator, and any other government agency that handles child and spousal support matters.

(2) The telephone number of the local bar association for referral to attorneys in family law practice.

(3) The name and telephone number of at least one organization that advocates the payment of child and spousal support or the name and telephone number of at least one organization that advocates the rights of supporting parents, if these organizations exist in the county. *(Added by Stats. 1999, c. 478 (A.B.196), § 1. Amended by Stats.2000, c. 808 (A.B.1358), § 86, eff. Sept. 28, 2000; Stats.2016, c. 474 (A.B.2882), § 15, eff. Jan. 1, 2017.)*

Research References

Treatises and Practice Aids

Witkin, California Summary 10th Husband and Wife § 310, Local Child Support Agency.

§ 17440. United States military and National Guard service members; modification of child support; form; motion by local child support agency

(a) The Department of Child Support Services shall work with all branches of the United States military and the

National Guard to ensure that information is made available regarding the rights and abilities of activated service members to have their support orders modified based on a change in income resulting from their activation, or other change of circumstance affecting the child support calculation, or to have a portion of their child support arrearages compromised pursuant to Section 17560.

(b) No later than 90 days after the effective date of this section, the department shall develop a form for completion by the service member that will allow the local child support agency to proceed with a motion for modification without the service member being required to appear. The form shall contain only the information necessary for the local child support agency to proceed with the motion.

(c) Within five business days of receipt of a properly completed form, the local child support agency shall bring a motion to modify the support order. The local child support agency shall bring the motion if the change in circumstances would result in any change in the dollar amount of the support order.

(d) The department shall work with the United States military to have this form and the form developed pursuant to Section 3651 distributed at all mobilization stations or other appropriate locations to ensure timely notification to all activated personnel of their rights and responsibilities. *(Added by Stats.2005, c. 154 (S.B.1082), § 4, eff. Aug. 30, 2005.)*

Research References

Treatises and Practice Aids

Witkin, California Summary 10th Husband and Wife § 288A, (New) Activation and Out-Of-State Deployment Of Military Service Member.

ARTICLE 1.5. DELINQUENT CHILD SUPPORT OBLIGATIONS AND FINANCIAL INSTITUTION DATA MATCH

§ 17450. Definitions; manner of collecting child support delinquencies; return or retention; delegation of functions to Franchise Tax Board; letter of agreement and interagency agreement between department and Franchise Tax Board

(a) For purposes of this article:

(1) "Child support delinquency" means a delinquency defined in subdivision (c) of Section 17500.

(2) "Earnings" shall include the items described in Section 5206.

(b)(1) When a delinquency is submitted to the department pursuant to subdivision (c) of Section 17500, the amount of the child support delinquency shall be collected by the department in any manner authorized under state or federal law.

(2) Any compensation, fee, commission, expense, or any other fee for service incurred by the department in the collection of a child support delinquency authorized under this article shall not be an obligation of, or collected from, the obligated parent.

(c)(1) The department may return or allow a local child support agency to retain a child support delinquency for a specified purpose for collection where the department determines that the return or retention of the delinquency for the purpose so specified will enhance the collectibility of the delinquency. The department shall establish a process whereby a local child support agency may request and shall be allowed to withdraw, rescind, or otherwise recall the submittal of an account that has been submitted.

(2) If an obligor is disabled, meets the federal Supplemental Security Income resource test, and is receiving Supplemental Security Income/State Supplementary Payments (SSI/SSP), or, but for excess income as described in Section 416.1100 and following of Part 416 of Title 20 of the Code of Federal Regulations, would be eligible to receive as SSI/SSP, pursuant to Section 12200 of the Welfare and Institutions Code, and the obligor has supplied the local child support agency with proof of his or her eligibility for, and, if applicable, receipt of, SSI/SSP or Social Security Disability Insurance benefits, then the child support delinquency shall not be referred to the department for collection, and, if referred, shall be withdrawn, rescinded, or otherwise recalled from the department by the local child support agency. The department shall not take any collection action, or if the local child support agency has already taken collection action, shall cease collection actions in the case of a disabled obligor when the delinquency is withdrawn, rescinded, or otherwise recalled by the local child support agency in accordance with the process established as described in paragraph (1).

(d) It is the intent of the Legislature that when the California Child Support Enforcement System (CSE) is fully operational, any statutes that should be modified based upon the status of the system shall be revised. During the development and implementation of CSE, the department, as the Title IV–D agency, may, through appropriate interagency agreement, delegate any and all of the functions or procedures specified in this article to the Franchise Tax Board. The Franchise Tax Board shall perform those functions or procedures as specified in Sections 19271 to 19275, inclusive, of the Revenue and Taxation Code until such time as the director, by letter to the executive officer of the Franchise Tax Board, revokes such delegation of Title IV–D functions. Sections 19271 to 19275, inclusive, of the Revenue and Taxation Code shall be effective for these purposes until the revocation of delegation to the Franchise Tax Board.

(e) Consistent with the development and implementation of the California Child Support Enforcement System, the Franchise Tax Board and the department shall enter into a letter of agreement and an interagency agreement whereby the department shall assume responsibility for collection of child support delinquencies and the Financial Institution Data Match System as set forth in this article. The letter of agreement and interagency agreement shall, at a minimum, set forth all of the following:

(1) Contingent upon the enactment of the Budget Act, and staffing authorization from the Department of Finance and the Department of Human Resources, the department shall assume responsibility for leadership and staffing of the collection of child support delinquencies and the Financial Institution Data Match System.

(2) All employees and other personnel who staff or provide support for the collection of child support delinquencies and the Financial Institution Data Match System at the Franchise Tax Board shall become the employees of the department at their existing or equivalent classification, salaries, and benefits.

(3) Any other provisions necessary to ensure continuity of function and meet or exceed existing levels of service, including, but not limited to, agreements for continued use of automated systems used by the Franchise Tax Board to locate child support obligors and their assets. *(Added by Stats.2004, c. 806 (A.B.2358), § 6. Amended by Gov.Reorg.Plan No. 1 of 2011, § 31, eff. Sept. 9, 2011, operative July 1, 2012; Stats.2012, c. 665 (S.B.1308), § 13; Stats.2016, c. 474 (A.B.2882), § 16, eff. Jan. 1, 2017.)*

Commentary

Under subsection (c)(2), the bank account of a disabled child support obligor is exempt from levy for child support arrearages when his sole income is from Social Security Disability Insurance (SSDI) benefits and he would have been eligible for Supplemental Security Income/State Supplementary Payments (SSI/SSP) but for his SSDI benefits. *In re Marriage of Hopkins, 173 Cal.App.4th 281, 92 Cal.Rptr.3d 570 (2009).*

Relying on subsections (b) and (*l*) of section 17000, *In re Marriage of Lamoure, 198 Cal.App.4th 807, 132 Cal.Rptr.3d 1 (2011), review denied,* holds that a parent who has requested enforcement by the Department of Child Support Services (DCSS) may collect spousal support as well as child support arrearages under the Financial Institution Data Match provisions (§ 17453 et seq.). Enforcement need not be originally initiated by the DCSS; nor need the parent be receiving public assistance. Under subsection (a) of this section, all that is required is that the support obligee have requested DCSS enforcement and the obligor have been ordered to send all support payments to DCSS.

Research References

Treatises and Practice Aids

Witkin, California Summary 10th Husband and Wife § 337, Collection by Department.

Witkin, California Summary 10th Parent and Child § 518, Financial Evaluation.

§ 17452. Tax return information available to department; no obligation or liability incurred; privacy and confidentiality

(a) Subject to state and federal privacy and information security laws, the Franchise Tax Board shall make tax return information available to the department, upon request, for the purpose of collecting child support delinquencies referred to the department.

(b) For purposes of this article, the Franchise Tax Board shall incur no obligation or liability to any person arising from any of the following:

(1) Furnishing information to the department as required by this section.

(2) Failing to disclose to a taxpayer or accountholder that the name, address, social security number, or other taxpayer identification number or other identifying information of that person was included in the data exchange with the department required by this section.

(3) Any other action taken in good faith to comply with the requirements of this section.

(c) It is the intent of the Legislature that any provision of income tax return information by the Franchise Tax Board to the department pursuant to this article shall be done in accordance with the privacy and confidential information laws of this state and of the United States, and to the satisfaction of the Franchise Tax Board. *(Added by Stats. 2004, c. 806 (A.B.2358), § 6.)*

Research References

Treatises and Practice Aids

Witkin, California Summary 10th Husband and Wife § 337, Collection by Department.

§ 17453. Financial Institution Data Match System; guidelines; governmental access and misuse of information; compilation of records; identifying information; no obligation or liability incurred; notification of certain circumstances of obligors of past-due support; cost reimbursement

(a) The department, in coordination with financial institutions doing business in this state, shall operate a Financial Institution Data Match System utilizing automated data exchanges to the maximum extent feasible. The Financial Institution Data Match System shall be implemented and maintained pursuant to guidelines prescribed by the department. These guidelines shall include a structure by which financial institutions, or their designated data-processing agents, shall receive from the department the file or files of past-due support obligors compiled in accordance with subdivision (c), so that the institution shall match with its own list of accountholders to identify past-due support obligor accountholders at the institution. To the extent allowed by the federal Personal Responsibility and Work Opportunity Reconciliation Act of 1996 (P.L. 104–193),[1] the guidelines shall include an option by which financial institutions without the technical ability to process the data exchange, or without the ability to employ a third-party data processor to process the data exchange, may forward to the department a list of all accountholders and their social security numbers, so that the department shall match that list with the file or files of past-due support obligors compiled in accordance with subdivision (c).

(b) The Financial Institution Data Match System shall not be subject to any limitation set forth in Chapter 20 (commencing with Section 7460) of Division 7 of Title 1 of the Government Code. However, any use of the information provided pursuant to this section for any purpose other than the enforcement and collection of a child support delinquency, as set forth in Section 17450, shall be a violation of Section 17212.

(c)(1) Until implementation of the California Child Support Automation System, each county shall compile a file of support obligors with judgments and orders that are being enforced by local child support agencies pursuant to Section 17400, and who are past due in the payment of their support obligations. The file shall be compiled, updated, and forwarded to the department, in accordance with the guidelines prescribed by the department.

(2) The department shall compile a file of obligors with support arrearages from requests made by other states for administrative enforcement in interstate cases, in accordance with federal requirements pursuant to paragraph 14 of subsection (a) of Section 666 of Title 42 of the United States Code. The file shall include, to the extent possible, the obligor's address.

(d) To effectuate the Financial Institution Data Match System, financial institutions subject to this section shall do all of the following:

(1) Provide to the department on a quarterly basis, the name, record address and other addresses, social security number or other taxpayer identification number, and other identifying information for each noncustodial parent who maintains an account at the institution and who owes past-due support, as identified by the department by name and social security number or other taxpayer identification number.

(2) Except as provided in subdivision (j), in response to a notice or order to withhold issued by the department, withhold from any accounts of the obligor the amount of any past-due support stated on the notice or order and transmit the amount to the department in accordance with Section 17454.

(e) Unless otherwise required by applicable law, a financial institution furnishing a report or providing information to the department pursuant to this section shall not disclose to a depositor, accountholder, codepositor, or coaccountholder, that the name, address, social security number, or other taxpayer identification number or other identifying information of that person has been received from, or furnished to, the department.

(f) A financial institution shall incur no obligation or liability to any person arising from any of the following:

(1) Furnishing information to the department as required by this section.

(2) Failing to disclose to a depositor, accountholder, codepositor, or coaccountholder, that the name, address, social security number, or other taxpayer identification number or other identifying information of that person was included in the data exchange with the department required by this section.

(3) Withholding or transmitting any assets in response to a notice or order to withhold issued by the department as a result of the data exchange. This paragraph shall not preclude any liability that may result if the financial institution does not comply with subdivision (b) of Section 17456.

(4) Any other action taken in good faith to comply with the requirements of this section.

(g)(1) With respect to files compiled under paragraph (1) of subdivision (c), the department shall forward to the counties, in accordance with guidelines prescribed by the department, information obtained from the financial institutions pursuant to this section. No county shall use this information for directly levying on any account. Each county shall keep the information confidential as provided by Section 17212.

(2) With respect to files compiled under paragraph (2) of subdivision (c), the amount collected by the department shall be deposited and distributed to the referring state in accordance with Section 17458.

(h) For those noncustodial parents owing past-due support for which there is a match under paragraph (1) of subdivision (d), the amount past due as indicated on the file or files compiled pursuant to subdivision (c) at the time of the match shall be a delinquency under this article for the purposes of the department taking any collection action pursuant to Section 17454.

(i) A child support delinquency need not be referred to the department for collection if a jurisdiction outside this state is enforcing the support order.

(j)(1) Each county shall notify the department upon the occurrence of the circumstances described in the following subparagraphs with respect to an obligor of past-due support:

(A) A court has ordered an obligor to make scheduled payments on a child support arrearages obligation and the obligor is in compliance with that order.

(B) An earnings assignment order or an order/notice to withhold income that includes an amount for past-due support has been served on the obligated parent's employer and earnings are being withheld pursuant to the earnings assignment order or an order/notice to withhold income.

(C) At least 50 percent of the obligated parent's earnings are being withheld for support.

(2) Notwithstanding Section 704.070 of the Code of Civil Procedure, if any of the conditions set forth in paragraph (1) exist, the assets of an obligor held by a financial institution are subject to levy as provided by paragraph (2) of subdivision (d). However, the first three thousand five hundred dollars ($3,500) of an obligor's assets are exempt from collection under this subdivision without the obligor having to file a claim of exemption.

(3) If any of the conditions set forth in paragraph (1) exist, an obligor may apply for a claim of exemption pursuant to Article 2 (commencing with Section 703.510) of Chapter 4 of Division 2 of Title 9 of Part 2 of the Code of Civil Procedure for an amount that is less than or equal to the total amount levied. The sole basis for a claim of exemption under this subdivision shall be the financial hardship for the obligor and the obligor's dependents.

(4) For the purposes of a claim of exemption made pursuant to paragraph (3), Section 688.030 of the Code of Civil Procedure shall not apply.

(5) For claims of exemption made pursuant to paragraph (3), the local child support agency responsible for enforcement of the obligor's child support order shall be the levying officer for the purpose of compliance with the provisions set forth in Article 2 (commencing with Section 703.510) of Chapter 4 of Division 2 of Title 9 of Part 2 of the Code of Civil Procedure except for the release of property required by subdivision (e) of Section 703.580 of the Code of Civil Procedure.

(6) The local child support agency shall notify the department within two business days of the receipt of a claim of exemption from an obligor. The department shall direct the financial institution subject to the order to withhold to hold any funds subject to the order pending notification by the department to remit or release the amounts held.

(7) The superior court in the county in which the local child support agency enforcing the support obligation is located shall have jurisdiction to determine the amount of exemption to be allowed. The court shall consider the needs of the obligor, the obligee, and all persons the obligor is required to support, and all other relevant circumstances in determining whether to allow any exemption pursuant to this subdivision. The court shall give effect to its determination by an order specifying the extent to which the amount levied is exempt.

(8) Within two business days of receipt of an endorsed copy of a court order issued pursuant to subdivision (e) of Section 703.580 of the Code of Civil Procedure, the local child support agency shall provide the department with a copy of the order. The department shall instruct the financial institution to remit or release the obligor's funds in accordance with the court's order.

(k) Out of any money received from the federal government for the purpose of reimbursing financial institutions for their actual and reasonable costs incurred in complying with this section, the state shall reimburse those institutions. To the extent that money is not provided by the federal government for that purpose, the state shall not reimburse financial institutions for their costs in complying with this section.

(*l*) For purposes of this section:

(1) "Account" means any demand deposit account, share or share draft account, checking or negotiable withdrawal order account, savings account, time deposit account, or a money market mutual fund account, whether or not the account bears interest.

(2) "Financial institution" has the same meaning as defined in paragraph (1) of subsection (d) of Section 669A of Title 42 of the United States Code. *(Added by Stats.2004, c. 806 (A.B.2358), § 6.)*

[1] See 42 U.S.C.A. § 601 et seq.

Commentary

In re Marriage of Lamoure, 198 Cal.App.4th 807, 132 Cal.Rptr.3d 1 (2011), review denied, held that a court order is not required under the Financial Institution Data Match provisions in order for the Department of Child Support Services to levy on a support obligor's Individual Retirement Account in order to recover child and spousal support arrearages. *Lamoure* also sustains a trial court's denial of a hardship exemption under subsection (j) of this section.

Research References

Treatises and Practice Aids

Witkin, California Summary 10th Husband and Wife § 314, Acquisition and Confidentiality Of Information.

Witkin, California Summary 10th Husband and Wife § 337, Collection by Department.

§ 17454. Request for depository institution to provide designated address for receiving notices to withhold; liability for failure to withhold; withholding delinquency and interest by depository institution from credits or things of value

(a) At least 45 days before sending a notice to withhold, the department shall request that a depository institution provide the department with a designated address for receiving notices to withhold.

(b) Once the depository institution has specified a designated address pursuant to subdivision (a), the department shall send all notices to that address unless the depository institution provides notification of another address. The department shall send all notices to withhold to a new designated address 30 days after notification.

(c) If a notice to withhold is mailed to the branch where the account is located or principal banking office, the depository institution shall be liable for a failure to withhold only to the extent that the accounts can be identified in information normally maintained at that location in the ordinary course of business.

(d) The department may by notice, served by magnetic media, electronic transmission, or other electronic technology, require any depository institution, as defined in the Federal Reserve Act (12 U.S.C.A. Sec. 461 (b)(1)(A)), that the department, in its sole discretion, has reason to believe may have in its possession, or under its control, any credits or other personal property or other things of value, belonging to a child support obligor, to withhold, from the credits or other personal property or other things of value, the amount of any child support delinquency, and interest, due from an obligor and transmit that amount withheld to the department at the times that it may designate, but not less than 10 business days from receipt of the notice. The notice shall state the amount due from the obligor and shall be delivered or transmitted to the branch or office reported pursuant to subdivision (a), or other address designated by that depository institution for purposes of the department serving notice by magnetic media, electronic transmission, or other electronic technology.

(e) For purposes of this section, the term "address" shall include telephone or modem number, facsimile number, or any other number designated by the depository institution to receive data by electronic means. *(Added by Stats.2004, c. 806 (A.B.2358), § 6.)*

Commentary

In re Marriage of Lamoure, 198 Cal.App.4th 807, 132 Cal.Rptr.3d 1 (2011), review denied, held that a court order is not required under the Financial Institution Data Match provisions in order for the Department of Child Support Services to levy on a support obligor's Individual Retirement Account in order to recover child and spousal support arrearages.

§ 17456. Compliance without legal or equitable action; deposit accounts or accounts to be withheld; notice to each person named on account; contents and service charge

(a) Any person required to withhold and transmit any amount pursuant to this article shall comply with the requirement without resort to any legal or equitable action in a court of law or equity. Any person paying to the department any amount required by it to be withheld is not liable therefore to the person from whom withheld unless the amount withheld is refunded to the withholding agent. However, if a depository institution, as defined in the Federal Reserve Act (12 U.S.C.A. Sec. 461(b)(1)(A)) withholds and pays to the department pursuant to this article any moneys held in a deposit account in which the delinquent obligor and another person or persons have an interest, or in an account held in the name of a third party or parties in which the delinquent obligor is ultimately determined to have no interest, the depository institution paying those moneys to the department is not liable therefore to any of the persons who have an interest in the account, unless the amount withheld is refunded to the withholding agent.

(b) In the case of a deposit account or accounts for which this notice to withhold applies, the depository institution shall send a notice by first-class mail to each person named on the account or accounts included in the notice from the department, provided that a current address for each person is available to the institution. This notice shall inform each person as to the reason for the hold placed on the account or accounts, the amount subject to being withheld, and the date by which this amount is to be remitted to the department. An institution may assess the account or accounts of each person receiving this notice a reasonable service charge not to exceed three dollars ($3). *(Added by Stats.2004, c. 806 (A.B.2358), § 6.)*

Commentary

In re Marriage of Lamoure, 198 Cal.App.4th 807, 132 Cal.Rptr.3d 1 (2011), review denied, held that a court order is not required under the Financial Institution Data Match provisions in order for the Department of Child Support Services to levy on a support obligor's Individual Retirement Account in order to recover child and spousal support arrearages.

§ 17460. Reciprocal agreements with other states; exchange of information with Internal Revenue Service; interagency agreements; cost reimbursement and funding

(a) As necessary, the department shall seek reciprocal agreements with other states to improve its ability to collect child support payments from out-of-state obligated parents on behalf of custodial parents residing in California. The department may pursue agreements with the Internal Revenue Service, as permitted by federal law, to improve collections of child support delinquencies from out-of-state obligated parents through cooperative agreements with the service.

(b) The California Child Support Enforcement System shall, for purposes of this article, include the capacity to interface and exchange information, if feasible, with the Internal Revenue Service, to enable the immediate reporting and tracking of obligated parent information.

(c) The department shall enter into any interagency agreements that are necessary for the implementation of this article. State departments and boards shall cooperate with the department to the extent necessary for the implementation of this article. Out of any money received from the federal government for the purpose of reimbursing state departments and boards for their actual and reasonable costs incurred in complying with this section, the department shall reimburse those departments and boards. To the extent that money is not provided by the federal government for that purpose, and subject to the annual Budget Act, the state shall fund departments and boards for their costs in complying with this section. *(Added by Stats.2004, c. 806 (A.B.2358), § 6. Amended by Stats.2016, c. 474 (A.B.2882), § 18, eff. Jan. 1, 2017.)*

ARTICLE 2. COLLECTIONS AND ENFORCEMENT

§ 17500. Responsibility of department and local child support agency for collection and enforcement; administering wage withholding; submission of delinquencies; delinquency existing at time case is opened

(a) In carrying out its obligations under Title IV–D of the Social Security Act (42 U.S.C. Sec. 651 et seq.), the department and the local child support agency shall have the responsibility for promptly and effectively collecting and enforcing child support obligations.

(b) The department and the local child support agency are the public agencies responsible for administering wage withholding for the purposes of Title IV–D of the Social Security Act (42 U.S.C. Sec. 651 et seq.).

(c) Except as provided in Section 17450, the local child support agency shall submit child support delinquencies to the department for purposes of supplementing the collection efforts of the local child support agencies. Submissions shall be in the form and manner and at the time prescribed by the department. Collection shall be made by the department in accordance with Section 17450. For purposes of this subdivision, "child support delinquency" means an arrearage or otherwise past due amount that accrues when an obligor fails to make any court-ordered support payment when due, which is more than 60 days past due, and the aggregate amount of which exceeds one hundred dollars ($100).

(d) If a child support delinquency exists at the time a case is opened by the local child support agency, the responsibility for the collection of the child support delinquency shall be submitted to the department no later than 30 days after receipt of the case by the local child support agency. *(Added by Stats.1999, c. 478 (A.B.196), § 1. Amended by Stats.1999, c. 480 (S.B.542), § 18; Stats.2001, c. 111 (A.B.429), § 5, eff. July 30, 2001; Stats.2001, c. 651 (A.B.891), § 4; Stats.2004, c. 339 (A.B.1704), § 9; Stats.2004, c. 806 (A.B.2358), § 4.)*

Research References

Treatises and Practice Aids

Witkin, California Summary 10th Husband and Wife § 308, Background and Scope.

Witkin, California Summary 10th Husband and Wife § 310, Local Child Support Agency.

Witkin, California Summary 10th Husband and Wife § 337, Collection by Department.

§ 17502. Inability to deliver child support payments due to inability to locate obligee

A local child support agency that is collecting child support payments on behalf of a child and who is unable to deliver the payments to the obligee because the local child support agency is unable to locate the obligee shall make all reasonable efforts to locate the obligee for a period of six months. If the local child support agency is unable to locate the obligee within the six-month period, it shall return the undeliverable payments to the obligor, with written notice advising the obligor that (a) the return of the funds does not relieve the obligor of the support order, and (b) the obligor should consider placing the funds aside for purposes of child support in case the obligee appears and seeks collection of the undistributed amounts. No interest shall accrue on any past-due child support amount for which the obligor made payment to the local child support agency for six consecutive months, or on any amounts due thereafter until the obligee is located, provided that the local child support agency returned the funds to the obligor because the local child support agency was unable to locate the obligee and, when the obligee was located, the obligor made full payment for all past-due child support amounts. *(Added by Stats.1999, c. 478 (A.B. 196), § 1. Amended by Stats.2004, c. 806 (A.B.2358), § 5.)*

Research References

Treatises and Practice Aids

Witkin, California Summary 10th Husband and Wife § 310, Local Child Support Agency.

§ 17504. First fifty dollars collected in month; payment to aid recipients

The first fifty dollars ($50) of any amount of child support collected in a month in payment of the required support obligation for that month shall be paid to a recipient of aid under Article 2 (commencing with Section 11250) of Chapter 2 of Part 3 of Division 9 of the Welfare and Institutions Code, except recipients of foster care payments under Article 5 (commencing with Section 11400) of Chapter 2 of Part 3 of Division 9 of the Welfare and Institutions Code shall not be considered income or resources of the recipient family, and shall not be deducted from the amount of aid to which the family would otherwise be eligible. The local child support agency in each county shall ensure that payments are made to recipients as required by this section. *(Added by Stats.1999, c. 478 (A.B.196), § 1. Amended by Stats.2000, c. 808 (A.B.1358), § 86.3, eff. Sept. 28, 2000; Stats.2001, c. 159 (S.B.662), § 90.)*

Research References

Treatises and Practice Aids

Witkin, California Summary 10th Husband and Wife § 310, Local Child Support Agency.

§ 17504.1. CalWORKs recipients or former recipients; notice of amount of assigned support payments made on behalf of recipient, former recipient, or family member

On a monthly basis, the local child support agency shall provide to any CalWORKs recipient or former recipient for whom an assignment pursuant to subdivision (a) of Section 11477 of the Welfare and Institutions Code is currently effective, a notice of the amount of assigned support payments made on behalf of the recipient or former recipient or any other family member for whom public assistance is received. *(Added by Stats.2016, c. 474 (A.B.2882), § 19, eff. Jan. 1, 2017.)*

§ 17505. State and local agencies, cooperation with local child support agencies in enforcement of support obligations; information on location of children, location and property of parents

(a) All state, county, and local agencies shall cooperate with the local child support agency (1) in the enforcement of any child support obligation or to the extent required under the state plan under Part 6 (commencing with Section 5700.101) of Division 9, Section 270 of the Penal Code, and Section 17604, and (2) the enforcement of spousal support orders and in the location of parents or putative parents. The local child support agency may enter into an agreement with and shall secure from a municipal, county, or state law enforcement agency, pursuant to that agreement, state summary criminal record information through the California Law Enforcement Telecommunications System. This subdivision applies irrespective of whether the children are or are not receiving aid to families with dependent children. All state, county, and local agencies shall cooperate with the district attorney in implementing Chapter 8 (commencing with Section 3130) of Part 2 of Division 8 concerning the location, seizure, and recovery of abducted, concealed, or detained minor children.

(b) On request, all state, county, and local agencies shall supply the local child support agency of any county in this state or the California Parent Locator Service with all information on hand relative to the location, income, or property of any parents, putative parents, spouses, or former spouses, notwithstanding any other provision of law making the information confidential, and with all information on hand relative to the location and prosecution of any person who has, by means of false statement or representation or by impersonation or other fraudulent device, obtained aid for a child under this chapter.

(c) The California Child Support Automation System, or its replacement, shall be entitled to the same cooperation and information provided to the California Parent Locator Service, to the extent allowed by law. The California Child Support Automation System, or its replacement, shall be allowed access to criminal offender record information only to the extent that access is allowed by law.

(d) Information exchanged between the California Parent Locator Service or the California Child Support Automation System, or its replacement, and state, county, or local agencies as specified in Sections 653(c)(4) and 666(c)(1)(D) of Title 42 of the United State Code shall be through automated processes to the maximum extent feasible. *(Added by Stats.1999, c. 478 (A.B.196), § 1. Amended by Stats. 2000, c. 808 (A.B.1358), § 87, eff. Sept. 28, 2000; Stats.2012, c. 637 (A.B.1751), § 3; Stats.2015, c. 493 (S.B.646), § 14, eff. Jan. 1, 2016.)*

Research References

Treatises and Practice Aids

Witkin, California Summary 10th Parent and Child § 246, Custodial Parent Entitled to Obtain Child Support Despite Violation.

Witkin, California Summary 10th Parent and Child § 269, Locating Missing Party or Child.

§ 17506. California Parent Locator Service and Central Registry; California Child Support Enforcement System

(a) There is in the department a California Parent Locator Service and Central Registry that shall collect and disseminate all of the following, with respect to any parent, putative parent, spouse, or former spouse:

(1) The full and true name of the parent together with any known aliases.

(2) Date and place of birth.

(3) Physical description.

(4) Social security number.

(5) Employment history and earnings.

(6) Military status and Veterans Administration or military service serial number.

(7) Last known address, telephone number, and date thereof.

(8) Driver's license number, driving record, and vehicle registration information.

(9) Criminal, licensing, and applicant records and information.

(10)(A) Any additional location, asset, and income information, including income tax return information obtained pursuant to Section 19548 of the Revenue and Taxation Code, and to the extent permitted by federal law, the address, telephone number, and social security number obtained from a public utility, cable television corporation, a provider of electronic digital pager communication, or a provider of mobile telephony services that may be of assistance in locating the parent, putative parent, abducting, concealing, or detaining parent, spouse, or former spouse, in establishing a parent and child relationship, in enforcing the child support liability of the absent parent, or enforcing the spousal support liability of the spouse or former spouse to the extent required by the state plan pursuant to Section 17604.

(B) For purposes of this subdivision, "income tax return information" means all of the following regarding the taxpayer:

(i) Assets.

(ii) Credits.

(iii) Deductions.

(iv) Exemptions.

(v) Identity.

(vi) Liabilities.

(vii) Nature, source, and amount of income.

(viii) Net worth.

(ix) Payments.

(x) Receipts.

(xi) Address.

(xii) Social security number.

(b) Pursuant to a letter of agreement entered into between the Department of Child Support Services and the Department of Justice, the Department of Child Support Services shall assume responsibility for the California Parent Locator Service and Central Registry. The letter of agreement shall, at a minimum, set forth all of the following:

(1) Contingent upon funding in the Budget Act, the Department of Child Support Services shall assume responsibility for leadership and staff of the California Parent Locator Service and Central Registry commencing July 1, 2003.

(2) All employees and other personnel who staff or provide support for the California Parent Locator Service and Central Registry shall, at the time of the transition, at their option, become the employees of the Department of Child Support Services at their existing or equivalent classification, salaries, and benefits.

(3) Until the department's automation system for the California Parent Locator Service and Central Registry functions is fully operational, the department shall use the automation system operated by the Department of Justice.

(4) Any other provisions necessary to ensure continuity of function and meet or exceed existing levels of service.

(c) To effectuate the purposes of this section, the California Child Support Enforcement System and the California Parent Locator Service and Central Registry shall utilize the federal Parent Locator Service to the extent necessary, and may request and shall receive from all departments, boards, bureaus, or other agencies of the state, or any of its political subdivisions, and those entities shall provide, that assistance and data that will enable the Department of Child Support Services and other public agencies to carry out their powers and duties to locate parents, spouses, and former spouses, and to identify their assets, to establish parent-child relationships, and to enforce liability for child or spousal support, and for any other obligations incurred on behalf of children, and shall also provide that information to any local child support agency in fulfilling the duties prescribed in Section 270 of the Penal Code, and in Chapter 8 (commencing with Section 3130) of Part 2 of Division 8 of this code, relating to abducted, concealed, or detained children and to any county child welfare agency or county probation department in fulfilling the duties prescribed in Article 5.5 (commencing with Section 290.1) of Chapter 2 of Part 1 of Division 2 of the Welfare and Institutions Code, and prescribed in Article 6 (commencing with Section 300) of Chapter 2 of Part 1 of Division 2 of the Welfare and Institutions Code to identify, locate, and notify parents or relatives of children who are the subject of juvenile court proceedings, to establish parent and child relationships pursuant to Section 316.2 of the Welfare and Institutions Code, and to assess the appropriateness of placement of a child with a noncustodial parent pursuant to Section 361.2 of the Welfare and Institutions Code. Consistent with paragraph (1) of subdivision (e) of Section 309 of, and paragraph (2) of subdivision (d) of Section 628 of, the Welfare and Institutions Code, in order for county child welfare and probation departments to carry out their duties to identify and locate all grandparents, adult siblings, and other adult relatives of the child as defined in paragraph (2) of subdivision (f) of Section 319 of the Welfare and Institutions Code, including any other adult relatives suggested by the parents, county personnel are permitted to request and receive information from the California Parent Locator Service and Federal Parent Locator Service. County child welfare agencies and probation departments shall be entitled to the information described in this subdivision regardless of whether an all-county letter or similar instruction is issued pursuant to subparagraph (C) of paragraph (8) of subdivision (c) of Section 11478.1 of the Welfare and Institutions Code. The California Child Support Enforcement System shall be entitled to the same cooperation and information as the California Parent Locator Service and Central Registry to the extent allowed by law. The California Child Support Enforcement System shall be allowed access to criminal record information only to the extent that access is allowed by state and federal law.

(d)(1) To effectuate the purposes of this section, and notwithstanding any other law, regulation, or tariff, and to the extent permitted by federal law, the California Parent Locator Service and Central Registry and the California Child Support Enforcement System may request and shall receive from public utilities, as defined in Section 216 of the Public Utilities Code, customer service information, including the full name, address, telephone number, date of birth, employer name and address, and social security number of customers of the public utility, to the extent that this information is stored within the computer database of the public utility.

(2) To effectuate the purposes of this section, and notwithstanding any other law, regulation, or tariff, and to the extent permitted by federal law, the California Parent Locator Service and Central Registry and the California Child Support Enforcement System may request and shall receive from cable television corporations, as defined in Section 216.4 of the Public Utilities Code, the providers of electronic digital pager communication, as defined in Section 629.51 of the Penal Code, and the providers of mobile telephony services,

as defined in Section 224.4 of the Public Utilities Code, customer service information, including the full name, address, telephone number, date of birth, employer name and address, and social security number of customers of the cable television corporation, customers of the providers of electronic digital pager communication, and customers of the providers of mobile telephony services.

(3) In order to protect the privacy of utility, cable television, electronic digital pager communication, and mobile telephony service customers, a request to a public utility, cable television corporation, provider of electronic digital pager communication, or provider of mobile telephony services for customer service information pursuant to this section shall meet the following requirements:

(A) Be submitted to the public utility, cable television corporation, provider of electronic digital pager communication, or provider of mobile telephony services in writing, on a transmittal document prepared by the California Parent Locator Service and Central Registry or the California Child Support Enforcement System and approved by all of the public utilities, cable television corporations, providers of electronic digital pager communication, and providers of mobile telephony services. The transmittal shall be deemed to be an administrative subpoena for customer service information.

(B) Have the signature of a representative authorized by the California Parent Locator Service and Central Registry or the California Child Support Enforcement System.

(C) Contain at least three of the following data elements regarding the person sought:

(i) First and last name, and middle initial, if known.

(ii) Social security number.

(iii) Driver's license number.

(iv) Birth date.

(v) Last known address.

(vi) Spouse's name.

(D) The California Parent Locator Service and Central Registry and the California Child Support Enforcement System shall ensure that each public utility, cable television corporation, provider of electronic digital pager communication services, and provider of mobile telephony services has at all times a current list of the names of persons authorized to request customer service information.

(E) The California Child Support Enforcement System and the California Parent Locator Service and Central Registry shall ensure that customer service information supplied by a public utility, cable television corporation, provider of electronic digital pager communication, or provider of mobile telephony services is applicable to the person who is being sought before releasing the information pursuant to subdivision (d).

(4) During the development of the California Child Support Enforcement System, the department shall determine the necessity of additional locate sources, including those specified in this section, based upon the cost-effectiveness of those sources.

(5) The public utility, cable television corporation, electronic digital pager communication provider, or mobile telephony service provider may charge a fee to the California Parent Locator Service and Central Registry or the California Child Support Enforcement System for each search performed pursuant to this subdivision to cover the actual costs to the public utility, cable television corporation, electronic digital pager communication provider, or mobile telephony service provider for providing this information.

(6) No public utility, cable television corporation, electronic digital pager communication provider, or mobile telephony service provider or official or employee thereof, shall be subject to criminal or civil liability for the release of customer service information as authorized by this subdivision.

(e) Notwithstanding Section 14203 of the Penal Code, any records established pursuant to this section shall be disseminated only to the Department of Child Support Services, the California Child Support Enforcement System, the California Parent Locator Service and Central Registry, the parent locator services and central registries of other states as defined by federal statutes and regulations, a local child support agency of any county in this state, and the federal Parent Locator Service. The California Child Support Enforcement System shall be allowed access to criminal offender record information only to the extent that access is allowed by law.

(f)(1) At no time shall any information received by the California Parent Locator Service and Central Registry or by the California Child Support Enforcement System be disclosed to any person, agency, or other entity, other than those persons, agencies, and entities specified pursuant to Section 17505, this section, or any other provision.

(2) This subdivision shall not otherwise affect discovery between parties in any action to establish, modify, or enforce child, family, or spousal support, that relates to custody or visitation.

(g)(1) The Department of Justice, in consultation with the Department of Child Support Services, shall promulgate rules and regulations to facilitate maximum and efficient use of the California Parent Locator Service and Central Registry. Upon implementation of the California Child Support Enforcement System, the Department of Child Support Services shall assume all responsibility for promulgating rules and regulations for use of the California Parent Locator Service and Central Registry.

(2) The Department of Child Support Services, the Public Utilities Commission, the cable television corporations, providers of electronic digital pager communication, and the providers of mobile telephony services shall develop procedures for obtaining the information described in subdivision (c) from public utilities, cable television corporations, providers of electronic digital pager communication, and providers of mobile telephony services and for compensating the public utilities, cable television corporations, providers of electronic digital pager communication, and providers of mobile telephony services for providing that information.

(h) The California Parent Locator Service and Central Registry may charge a fee not to exceed eighteen dollars ($18) for any service it provides pursuant to this section that is not performed or funded pursuant to Section 651 and following of Title 42 of the United States Code.

(i) This section shall be construed in a manner consistent with the other provisions of this article. *(Added by Stats. 1999, c. 478 (A.B.196), § 1. Amended by Stats.1999, c. 652 (S.B.240), § 18; Stats.2002, c. 759 (A.B.3033), § 2; Stats. 2003, c. 62 (S.B.600), § 91; Stats.2004, c. 806 (A.B.2358), § 7; Stats.2006, c. 198 (A.B.3073), § 1; Stats.2012, c. 637 (A.B. 1751), § 4; Stats.2014, c. 437 (S.B.1066), § 3, eff. Jan. 1, 2015; Stats.2014, c. 772 (S.B.1460), § 3.5, eff. Jan. 1, 2015; Stats. 2016, c. 474 (A.B.2882), § 20, eff. Jan. 1, 2017.)*

Research References

Treatises and Practice Aids

Witkin, California Summary 10th Husband and Wife § 251, Issuance Of Order.

Witkin, California Summary 10th Parent and Child § 269, Locating Missing Party or Child.

Witkin, California Summary 10th Parent and Child § 427, Collection Of Information About Support Obligations.

Witkin, California Summary 10th Parent and Child § 555, Investigation, Detention, and Release.

Witkin, California Summary 10th Parent and Child § 576, in General.

Witkin, California Summary 10th Parent and Child § 585, in General.

Witkin, California Summary 10th Parent and Child § 603, Identification Of Presumed or Alleged Fathers.

Witkin, California Summary 10th Parent and Child § 637, Priority Right Of Noncustodial Parent.

Witkin, California Summary 10th Parent and Child § 763, Investigation, Release, and Conditions.

§ 17508. Employment Development Department; access to information

(a) The Employment Development Department shall, when requested by the Department of Child Support Services local child support agency, the federal Parent Locator Service, or the California Parent Locator Service, provide access to information collected pursuant to Division 1 (commencing with Section 100) of the Unemployment Insurance Code to the requesting department or agency for purposes of administering the child support enforcement program, and for purposes of verifying employment of applicants and recipients of aid under this chapter or CalFresh under Chapter 10 (commencing with Section 18900) of Part 6 of Division 9 of the Welfare and Institutions Code.

(b)(1) To the extent possible, the Employment Development Department shall share information collected under Sections 1088.5 and 1088.8 of the Unemployment Insurance Code immediately upon receipt. This sharing of information may include electronic means.

(2) This subdivision shall not authorize the Employment Development Department to share confidential information with any individuals not otherwise permitted by law to receive the information or preclude batch runs or comparisons of data. *(Added by Stats.1999, c. 478 (A.B.196), § 1. Amended by Stats.1999, c. 652 (S.B.240), § 19; Stats.2000, c. 808 (A.B.1358), § 88, eff. Sept. 28, 2000; Stats.2011, c. 227 (A.B.1400), § 4; Stats.2016, c. 474 (A.B.2882), § 21, eff. Jan. 1, 2017.)*

Research References

Treatises and Practice Aids

Witkin, California Summary 10th Husband and Wife § 314, Acquisition and Confidentiality Of Information.

§ 17509. Information compare; obligor employment and earning withholding order

Once the statewide automated system is fully implemented, the Department of Child Support Services shall periodically compare Employment Development Department information collected under Division 1 (commencing with Section 100) of the Unemployment Insurance Code to child support obligor records and identify cases where the obligor is employed but there is no earning withholding order in effect. The department shall immediately notify local child support agencies in those cases. *(Added by Stats.1999, c. 652 (S.B.240), § 20.)*

Research References

Treatises and Practice Aids

Witkin, California Summary 10th Husband and Wife § 314, Acquisition and Confidentiality Of Information.

§ 17510. Workers' compensation notification project

To assist local agencies in child support enforcement activities, the department shall operate a workers' compensation notification project based on information received pursuant to Section 138.5 of the Labor Code or any other source of information. *(Added by Stats.1999, c. 478 (A.B.196), § 1.)*

Research References

Treatises and Practice Aids

Witkin, California Summary 10th Husband and Wife § 314, Acquisition and Confidentiality Of Information.

§ 17512. Employment and income information from employer or labor organization

(a) Upon receipt of a written request from a local child support agency enforcing the obligation of parents to support their children pursuant to Section 17400, or from an agency of another state enforcing support obligations pursuant to Section 654 of Title 42 of the United States Code, every employer, as specified in Section 5210, and every labor organization shall cooperate with and provide relevant employment and income information that they have in their possession to the local child support agency or other requesting agency for the purpose of establishing, modifying, or enforcing the support obligation. No employer or labor organization shall incur any liability for providing this information to the local child support agency or other requesting agency.

(b) Relevant employment and income information shall include, but not be limited to, all of the following:

(1) Whether a named person has or has not been employed by an employer or whether a named person has or has not been employed to the knowledge of the labor organization.

(2) The full name of the employee or member or the first and middle initial and last name of the employee or member.

(3) The employee's or member's last known residence address.

(4) The employee's or member's date of birth.

(5) The employee's or member's social security number.

(6) The dates of employment.

(7) All earnings paid to the employee or member and reported as W–2 compensation in the prior tax year and the employee's or member's current basic rate of pay.

(8) Other earnings, as specified in Section 5206, paid to the employee or member.

(9) Whether dependent health insurance coverage is available to the employee through employment or membership in the labor organization.

(c) The local child support agency or other agency shall notify the employer and labor organization of the local child support agency case file number in making a request pursuant to this section. The written request shall include at least three of the following elements regarding the person who is the subject of the inquiry: (A) first and last name and middle initial, if known; (B) social security number; (C) driver's license number; (D) birth date; (E) last known address; or (F) spouse's name.

(d) The local child support agency or other requesting agency shall send a notice that a request for this information has been made to the last known address of the person who is the subject of the inquiry.

(e) An employer or labor organization that fails to provide relevant employment information to the local child support agency or other requesting agency within 30 days of receiving a request pursuant to subdivision (a) may be assessed a civil penalty of a maximum of one thousand dollars ($1,000), plus attorneys' fees and costs. Proceedings to impose the civil penalty shall be commenced by the filing and service of an order to show cause.

(f) "Labor organization," for the purposes of this section means a labor organization as defined in Section 1117 of the Labor Code or any related benefit trust fund covered under the federal Employee Retirement Income Security Act of 1974 (Chapter 18 (commencing with Section 1001) of Title 29 of the United States Code).

(g) Any reference to the local child support agency in this section shall apply only when the local child support agency is otherwise ordered or required to act pursuant to existing law. Nothing in this section shall be deemed to mandate additional enforcement or collection duties upon the local child support agency beyond those imposed under existing law on the effective date of this section. *(Added by Stats.1999, c. 478 (A.B.196), § 1.)*

Research References

Treatises and Practice Aids

Witkin, California Summary 10th Husband and Wife § 314, Acquisition and Confidentiality Of Information.

§ 17514. Child abduction records

(a) It is the intent of the Legislature to protect individual rights of privacy, and to facilitate and enhance the effectiveness of the child abduction and recovery programs, by ensuring the confidentiality of child abduction records, and to thereby encourage the full and frank disclosure of information relevant to all of the following:

(1) The establishment or maintenance of parent and child relationships and support obligations.

(2) The enforcement of the child support liability of absent parents.

(3) The enforcement of spousal support liability of the spouse or former spouse to the extent required by the state plan under Section 17400, and Chapter 6 (commencing with Section 4800) of Part 5 of Division 9.

(4) The location of absent parents.

(5) The location of parents and children abducted, concealed, or detained by them.

(b)(1) Except as provided in this subdivision, all files, applications, papers, documents, and records, established or maintained by any public entity for the purpose of locating an abducted child, locating a person who has abducted a child, or prosecution of a person who has abducted a child shall be confidential, and shall not be open to examination or released for disclosure for any purpose not directly connected with locating or recovering the abducted child or abducting person or prosecution of the abducting person.

(2) Except as provided in subdivision (c), no public entity shall disclose any file, application, paper document, or record described in this section, or the information contained therein.

(c)(1) All files, applications, papers, documents, and records as described in subdivision (b) shall be available and may be used by a public entity for all administrative, civil, or criminal investigations, actions, proceedings, or prosecution conducted in connection with the child abduction or prosecution of the abducting person.

(2) A document requested by a person who wrote, prepared, or furnished the document may be examined by or disclosed to that person or his or her designee.

(3) Public records subject to disclosure under Chapter 3.5 (commencing with Section 6250) of Division 7 of Title 1 of the Government Code may be released.

(4) After a noticed motion and a finding by the court, in a case in which child recovery or abduction prosecution actions are being taken, that release or disclosure is required by due process of law, the court may order a public entity that possesses an application, paper, document, or record described in this subdivision to make that item available to the defendant or other party for examination or copying, or to disclose to an appropriate person the contents of that item. Article 9 (commencing with Section 1040) of Chapter 4 of Division 8 of the Evidence Code shall not be applicable to proceedings under this part.

(5) To the extent not prohibited by federal law or regulation, information indicating the existence or imminent threat of a crime against a minor child, or location of a concealed or abducted child or the location of the concealing or abducting person, may be disclosed to any appropriate law enforcement agency, or to any state or county child protective agency, or may be used in any judicial proceedings to prosecute that crime or to protect the child.

(6) Information may be released to any state or local agency for the purposes connected with establishing, modifying, and enforcing child support obligations, enforcing spousal support orders, and determining paternity as required by Part D (commencing with Section 651) of Subchapter IV of Chapter 7 of Title 42 of the United States Code and this article. *(Added by Stats.1999, c. 478 (A.B.196), § 1.)*

Research References

Treatises and Practice Aids

Witkin, California Summary 10th Parent and Child § 193, California Criminal Statutes.

§ 17516. Social service benefits use for support obligation

In no event shall public social service benefits, as defined in Section 10051 of the Welfare and Institutions Code, or benefits paid pursuant to Title XVI of the Social Security Act [1] be employed to satisfy a support obligation. *(Added by Stats.1999, c. 478 (A.B.196), § 1.)*

[1] See 42 U.S.C.A. § 1381 et seq.

Research References

Treatises and Practice Aids

Witkin, California Summary 10th Husband and Wife § 334, in General.

§ 17518. Unemployment compensation benefits

(a) As authorized by subdivision (d) of Section 704.120 of the Code of Civil Procedure, the following actions shall be taken in order to enforce support obligations that are not being met. Whenever a support judgment or order has been rendered by a court of this state against an individual who is entitled to any unemployment compensation benefits or unemployment compensation disability benefits, the local child support agency may file a certification of support judgment or support order with the Department of Child Support Services, verifying under penalty of perjury that there is or has been a judgment or an order for support with sums overdue thereunder. The department shall periodically present and keep current, by deletions and additions, a list of the certified support judgments and orders and shall periodically notify the Employment Development Department of individuals certified as owing support obligations.

(b) If the Employment Development Department determines that an individual who owes support may have a claim for unemployment compensation disability insurance benefits under a voluntary plan approved by the Employment Development Department in accordance with Chapter 6 (commencing with Section 3251) of Part 2 of Division 1 of the Unemployment Insurance Code, the Employment Development Department shall immediately notify the voluntary plan payer. When the department notifies the Employment Development Department of changes in an individual's support obligations, the Employment Development Department shall promptly notify the voluntary plan payer of these changes. The Employment Development Department shall maintain and keep current a record of individuals who owe support obligations who may have claims for unemployment compensation or unemployment compensation disability benefits.

(c) Notwithstanding any other law, the Employment Development Department shall withhold the amounts specified below from the unemployment compensation benefits or unemployment compensation disability benefits of individuals with unmet support obligations. The Employment Development Department shall forward the amounts to the Department of Child Support Services for distribution to the appropriate certifying county.

(d) Notwithstanding any other law, during the payment of unemployment compensation disability benefits to an individual, with respect to whom the Employment Development Department has notified a voluntary plan payer that the individual has a support obligation, the voluntary plan payer shall withhold the amounts specified below from the individual's unemployment compensation disability benefits and shall forward the amounts to the appropriate certifying county.

(e) The amounts withheld in subdivisions (c) and (d) shall be equal to 25 percent of each weekly unemployment compensation benefit payment or periodic unemployment compensation disability benefit payment, rounded down to the nearest whole dollar, which is due the individual identified on the certified list. However, the amount withheld may be reduced to a lower whole dollar amount through a written agreement between the individual and the local child support agency or through an order of the court.

(f) The department shall ensure that the appropriate certifying county shall resolve any claims for refunds in the amounts overwithheld by the Employment Development Department or voluntary plan payer.

(g) No later than the time of the first withholding, the individuals who are subject to the withholding shall be notified by the payer of benefits of all of the following:

(1) That his or her unemployment compensation benefits or unemployment compensation disability benefits have been reduced by a court-ordered support judgment or order pursuant to this section.

(2) The address and telephone number of the local child support agency that submitted the certificate of support judgment or order.

(3) That the support order remains in effect even though he or she is unemployed or disabled unless it is modified by court order, and that if the amount withheld is less than the monthly support obligation, an arrearage will accrue.

(h) The individual may ask the appropriate court for an equitable division of the individual's unemployment compensation or unemployment compensation disability amounts withheld to take into account the needs of all the persons the individual is required to support.

(i) The Department of Child Support Services and the Employment Development Department shall enter into any agreements necessary to carry out this section.

(j) For purposes of this section, "support obligations" means the child and related spousal support obligations that are being enforced pursuant to a plan described in Section 454 of the Social Security Act and as that section may hereafter be amended. However, to the extent "related spousal support obligation" may not be collected from unemployment compensation under federal law, those obligations shall not be included in the definition of support obligations under this section. *(Added by Stats.1999, c. 478 (A.B.196), § 1. Amended by Stats.2000, c. 808 (A.B.1358), § 89, eff. Sept. 28, 2000.)*

Research References

Treatises and Practice Aids

Witkin, California Summary 10th Husband and Wife § 334, in General.

§ 17520. License applicants; compliance with support orders; license issuance, renewal, and suspension; review

(a) As used in this section:

(1) "Applicant" means a person applying for issuance or renewal of a license.

(2) "Board" means an entity specified in Section 101 of the Business and Professions Code, the entities referred to in Sections 1000 and 3600 of the Business and Professions Code, the State Bar, the Bureau of Real Estate, the Department of Motor Vehicles, the Secretary of State, the Department of Fish and Wildlife, and any other state commission, department, committee, examiner, or agency that issues a license, certificate, credential, permit, registration, or any other authorization to engage in a business, occupation, or profession, or to the extent required by federal law or regulations, for recreational purposes. This term includes all boards, commissions, departments, committees, examiners, entities, and agencies that issue a license, certificate, credential, permit, registration, or any other authorization to engage in a business, occupation, or profession. The failure to specifically name a particular board, commission, department, committee, examiner, entity, or agency that issues a license, certificate, credential, permit, registration, or any other authorization to engage in a business, occupation, or profession does not exclude that board, commission, department, committee, examiner, entity, or agency from this term.

(3) "Certified list" means a list provided by the local child support agency to the Department of Child Support Services in which the local child support agency verifies, under penalty of perjury, that the names contained therein are support obligors found to be out of compliance with a judgment or order for support in a case being enforced under Title IV–D of the federal Social Security Act.

(4) "Compliance with a judgment or order for support" means that, as set forth in a judgment or order for child or family support, the obligor is no more than 30 calendar days in arrears in making payments in full for current support, in making periodic payments in full, whether court ordered or by agreement with the local child support agency, on a support arrearage, or in making periodic payments in full, whether court ordered or by agreement with the local child support agency, on a judgment for reimbursement for public assistance, or has obtained a judicial finding that equitable estoppel as provided in statute or case law precludes enforcement of the order. The local child support agency is authorized to use this section to enforce orders for spousal support only when the local child support agency is also enforcing a related child support obligation owed to the obligee parent by the same obligor, pursuant to Sections 17400 and 17604.

(5) "License" includes membership in the State Bar, and a certificate, credential, permit, registration, or any other authorization issued by a board that allows a person to engage in a business, occupation, or profession, or to operate a commercial motor vehicle, including appointment and commission by the Secretary of State as a notary public. "License" also includes any driver's license issued by the Department of Motor Vehicles, any commercial fishing license issued by the Department of Fish and Wildlife, and to the extent required by federal law or regulations, any license used for recreational purposes. This term includes all licenses, certificates, credentials, permits, registrations, or any other authorization issued by a board that allows a person to engage in a business, occupation, or profession. The failure to specifically name a particular type of license, certificate, credential, permit, registration, or other authorization issued by a board that allows a person to engage in a business, occupation, or profession, does not exclude that license, certificate, credential, permit, registration, or other authorization from this term.

(6) "Licensee" means a person holding a license, certificate, credential, permit, registration, or other authorization issued by a board, to engage in a business, occupation, or profession, or a commercial driver's license as defined in Section 15210 of the Vehicle Code, including an appointment and commission by the Secretary of State as a notary public. "Licensee" also means a person holding a driver's license issued by the Department of Motor Vehicles, a person holding a commercial fishing license issued by the Department of Fish and Game, and to the extent required by federal law or regulations, a person holding a license used for recreational purposes. This term includes all persons holding a license, certificate, credential, permit, registration, or any other authorization to engage in a business, occupation, or profession, and the failure to specifically name a particular type of license, certificate, credential, permit, registration, or other authorization issued by a board does not exclude that person from this term. For licenses issued to an entity that is not an individual person, "licensee" includes an individual who is either listed on the license or who qualifies for the license.

(b) The local child support agency shall maintain a list of those persons included in a case being enforced under Title IV–D of the federal Social Security Act against whom a support order or judgment has been rendered by, or registered in, a court of this state, and who are not in compliance with that order or judgment. The local child support agency shall submit a certified list with the names, social security numbers, and last known addresses of these persons and the name, address, and telephone number of the local child support agency who certified the list to the department. The local child support agency shall verify, under penalty of perjury, that the persons listed are subject to an order or judgment for the payment of support and that these persons are not in compliance with the order or judgment. The local child support agency shall submit to the department an updated certified list on a monthly basis.

(c) The department shall consolidate the certified lists received from the local child support agencies and, within 30 calendar days of receipt, shall provide a copy of the consolidated list to each board that is responsible for the regulation of licenses, as specified in this section.

(d) On or before November 1, 1992, or as soon thereafter as economically feasible, as determined by the department, all boards subject to this section shall implement procedures to accept and process the list provided by the department, in accordance with this section. Notwithstanding any other law, all boards shall collect social security numbers or individual taxpayer identification numbers from all applicants for the purposes of matching the names of the certified list provided by the department to applicants and licensees and of responding to requests for this information made by child support agencies.

(e)(1) Promptly after receiving the certified consolidated list from the department, and prior to the issuance or renewal of a license, each board shall determine whether the applicant is on the most recent certified consolidated list provided by the department. The board shall have the authority to withhold issuance or renewal of the license of an applicant on the list.

(2) If an applicant is on the list, the board shall immediately serve notice as specified in subdivision (f) on the applicant of the board's intent to withhold issuance or renewal of the license. The notice shall be made personally or by mail to the applicant's last known mailing address on file with the board. Service by mail shall be complete in accordance with Section 1013 of the Code of Civil Procedure.

(A) The board shall issue a temporary license valid for a period of 150 days to any applicant whose name is on the certified list if the applicant is otherwise eligible for a license.

(B) Except as provided in subparagraph (D), the 150–day time period for a temporary license shall not be extended. Except as provided in subparagraph (D), only one temporary license shall be issued during a regular license term and it shall coincide with the first 150 days of that license term. As this paragraph applies to commercial driver's licenses, "license term" shall be deemed to be 12 months from the date the application fee is received by the Department of Motor Vehicles. A license for the full or remainder of the license term shall be issued or renewed only upon compliance with this section.

(C) In the event that a license or application for a license or the renewal of a license is denied pursuant to this section, any funds paid by the applicant or licensee shall not be refunded by the board.

(D) This paragraph shall apply only in the case of a driver's license, other than a commercial driver's license. Upon the request of the local child support agency or by order of the court upon a showing of good cause, the board shall extend a 150–day temporary license for a period not to exceed 150 extra days.

(3)(A) The department may, when it is economically feasible for the department and the boards to do so as determined by the department, in cases where the department is aware that certain child support obligors listed on the certified lists have been out of compliance with a judgment or order for support for more than four months, provide a supplemental list of these obligors to each board with which the department has an interagency agreement to implement this paragraph. Upon request by the department, the licenses of these obligors shall be subject to suspension, provided that the licenses would not otherwise be eligible for renewal within six months from the date of the request by the department. The board shall have the authority to suspend the license of any licensee on this supplemental list.

(B) If a licensee is on a supplemental list, the board shall immediately serve notice as specified in subdivision (f) on the licensee that his or her license will be automatically suspended 150 days after notice is served, unless compliance with this section is achieved. The notice shall be made personally or by mail to the licensee's last known mailing address on file with the board. Service by mail shall be complete in accordance with Section 1013 of the Code of Civil Procedure.

(C) The 150–day notice period shall not be extended.

(D) In the event that any license is suspended pursuant to this section, any funds paid by the licensee shall not be refunded by the board.

(E) This paragraph shall not apply to licenses subject to annual renewal or annual fee.

(f) Notices shall be developed by each board in accordance with guidelines provided by the department and subject to approval by the department. The notice shall include the address and telephone number of the local child support agency that submitted the name on the certified list, and shall emphasize the necessity of obtaining a release from that local child support agency as a condition for the issuance, renewal, or continued valid status of a license or licenses.

(1) In the case of applicants not subject to paragraph (3) of subdivision (e), the notice shall inform the applicant that the board shall issue a temporary license, as provided in subparagraph (A) of paragraph (2) of subdivision (e), for 150 calendar days if the applicant is otherwise eligible and that upon expiration of that time period the license will be denied unless the board has received a release from the local child support agency that submitted the name on the certified list.

(2) In the case of licensees named on a supplemental list, the notice shall inform the licensee that his or her license will continue in its existing status for no more than 150 calendar days from the date of mailing or service of the notice and thereafter will be suspended indefinitely unless, during the 150–day notice period, the board has received a release from the local child support agency that submitted the name on the certified list. Additionally, the notice shall inform the licensee that any license suspended under this section will remain so until the expiration of the remaining license term, unless the board receives a release along with applications and fees, if applicable, to reinstate the license during the license term.

(3) The notice shall also inform the applicant or licensee that if an application is denied or a license is suspended pursuant to this section, any funds paid by the applicant or licensee shall not be refunded by the board. The Department of Child Support Services shall also develop a form that the applicant shall use to request a review by the local child support agency. A copy of this form shall be included with every notice sent pursuant to this subdivision.

(g)(1) Each local child support agency shall maintain review procedures consistent with this section to allow an applicant to have the underlying arrearage and any relevant defenses investigated, to provide an applicant information on the process of obtaining a modification of a support order, or to provide an applicant assistance in the establishment of a payment schedule on arrearages if the circumstances so warrant.

(2) It is the intent of the Legislature that a court or local child support agency, when determining an appropriate payment schedule for arrearages, base its decision on the facts of the particular case and the priority of payment of child support over other debts. The payment schedule shall also recognize that certain expenses may be essential to enable an obligor to be employed. Therefore, in reaching its decision, the court or the local child support agency shall consider both of these goals in setting a payment schedule for arrearages.

(h) If the applicant wishes to challenge the submission of his or her name on the certified list, the applicant shall make a timely written request for review to the local child support agency who certified the applicant's name. A request for review pursuant to this section shall be resolved in the same manner and timeframe provided for resolution of a complaint pursuant to Section 17800. The local child support agency shall immediately send a release to the appropriate board and the applicant, if any of the following conditions are met:

(1) The applicant is found to be in compliance or negotiates an agreement with the local child support agency for a payment schedule on arrearages or reimbursement.

(2) The applicant has submitted a request for review, but the local child support agency will be unable to complete the review and send notice of its findings to the applicant within the time specified in Section 17800.

(3) The applicant has filed and served a request for judicial review pursuant to this section, but a resolution of that review will not be made within 150 days of the date of service of notice pursuant to subdivision (f). This paragraph applies only if the delay in completing the judicial review process is not the result of the applicant's failure to act in a reasonable, timely, and diligent manner upon receiving the local child support agency's notice of findings.

(4) The applicant has obtained a judicial finding of compliance as defined in this section.

(i) An applicant is required to act with diligence in responding to notices from the board and the local child support agency with the recognition that the temporary license will lapse or the license suspension will go into effect after 150 days and that the local child support agency and, where appropriate, the court must have time to act within that period. An applicant's delay in acting, without good cause, which directly results in the inability of the local child support agency to complete a review of the applicant's request or the court to hear the request for judicial review within the 150–day period shall not constitute the diligence required under this section which would justify the issuance of a release.

(j) Except as otherwise provided in this section, the local child support agency shall not issue a release if the applicant is not in compliance with the judgment or order for support. The local child support agency shall notify the applicant in writing that the applicant may, by filing an order to show cause or notice of motion, request any or all of the following:

(1) Judicial review of the local child support agency's decision not to issue a release.

(2) A judicial determination of compliance.

(3) A modification of the support judgment or order.

The notice shall also contain the name and address of the court in which the applicant shall file the order to show cause or notice of motion and inform the applicant that his or her name shall remain on the certified list if the applicant does not timely request judicial review. The applicant shall comply with all statutes and rules of court regarding orders to show cause and notices of motion.

This section shall not be deemed to limit an applicant from filing an order to show cause or notice of motion to modify a support judgment or order or to fix a payment schedule on arrearages accruing under a support judgment or order or to obtain a court finding of compliance with a judgment or order for support.

(k) The request for judicial review of the local child support agency's decision shall state the grounds for which review is requested and judicial review shall be limited to those stated grounds. The court shall hold an evidentiary hearing within 20 calendar days of the filing of the request for review. Judicial review of the local child support agency's decision shall be limited to a determination of each of the following issues:

(1) Whether there is a support judgment, order, or payment schedule on arrearages or reimbursement.

(2) Whether the petitioner is the obligor covered by the support judgment or order.

(3) Whether the support obligor is or is not in compliance with the judgment or order of support.

(4)(A) The extent to which the needs of the obligor, taking into account the obligor's payment history and the current circumstances of both the obligor and the obligee, warrant a conditional release as described in this subdivision.

(B) The request for judicial review shall be served by the applicant upon the local child support agency that submitted the applicant's name on the certified list within seven calendar days of the filing of the petition. The court has the authority to uphold the action, unconditionally release the license, or conditionally release the license.

(C) If the judicial review results in a finding by the court that the obligor is in compliance with the judgment or order for support, the local child support agency shall immediately send a release in accordance with subdivision (*l*) to the appropriate board and the applicant. If the judicial review results in a finding by the court that the needs of the obligor warrant a conditional release, the court shall make findings of fact stating the basis for the release and the payment necessary to satisfy the unrestricted issuance or renewal of the license without prejudice to a later judicial determination of the amount of support arrearages, including interest, and shall specify payment terms, compliance with which are necessary to allow the release to remain in effect.

(*l*) The department shall prescribe release forms for use by local child support agencies. When the obligor is in compliance, the local child support agency shall mail to the applicant and the appropriate board a release stating that the applicant is in compliance. The receipt of a release shall serve to notify the applicant and the board that, for the purposes of this section, the applicant is in compliance with the judgment or order for support. Any board that has received a release from the local child support agency pursuant to this subdivision shall process the release within five business days of its receipt.

If the local child support agency determines subsequent to the issuance of a release that the applicant is once again not in compliance with a judgment or order for support, or with the terms of repayment as described in this subdivision, the local child support agency may notify the board, the obligor, and the department in a format prescribed by the department that the obligor is not in compliance.

The department may, when it is economically feasible for the department and the boards to develop an automated process for complying with this subdivision, notify the boards in a manner prescribed by the department, that the obligor is once again not in compliance. Upon receipt of this notice, the board shall immediately notify the obligor on a form prescribed by the department that the obligor's license will be suspended on a specific date, and this date shall be no longer than 30 days from the date the form is mailed. The obligor shall be further notified that the license will remain suspended until a new release is issued in accordance with subdivision (h). Nothing in this section shall be deemed to limit the obligor from seeking judicial review of suspension pursuant to the procedures described in subdivision (k).

(m) The department may enter into interagency agreements with the state agencies that have responsibility for the administration of boards necessary to implement this section, to the extent that it is cost effective to implement this section. These agreements shall provide for the receipt by the other state agencies and boards of federal funds to cover that portion of costs allowable in federal law and regulation and incurred by the state agencies and boards in implementing this section. Notwithstanding any other provision of law, revenue generated by a board or state agency shall be used to fund the nonfederal share of costs incurred pursuant to this section. These agreements shall provide that boards shall reimburse the department for the nonfederal share of costs incurred by the department in implementing this section. The boards shall reimburse the department for the nonfederal share of costs incurred pursuant to this section from moneys collected from applicants and licensees.

(n) Notwithstanding any other law, in order for the boards subject to this section to be reimbursed for the costs incurred in administering its provisions, the boards may, with the approval of the appropriate department director, levy on all licensees and applicants a surcharge on any fee or fees collected pursuant to law, or, alternatively, with the approval of the appropriate department director, levy on the applicants or licensees named on a certified list or supplemental list, a special fee.

(*o*) The process described in subdivision (h) shall constitute the sole administrative remedy for contesting the issuance of a temporary license or the denial or suspension of a license under this section. The procedures specified in the administrative adjudication provisions of the Administrative Procedure Act (Chapter 4.5 (commencing with Section 11400) and Chapter 5 (commencing with Section 11500) of Part 1 of Division 3 of Title 2 of the Government Code) shall not apply to the denial, suspension, or failure to issue or renew a license or the issuance of a temporary license pursuant to this section.

(p) In furtherance of the public policy of increasing child support enforcement and collections, on or before November 1, 1995, the State Department of Social Services shall make a report to the Legislature and the Governor based on data collected by the boards and the district attorneys in a format prescribed by the State Department of Social Services. The report shall contain all of the following:

(1) The number of delinquent obligors certified by district attorneys under this section.

(2) The number of support obligors who also were applicants or licensees subject to this section.

(3) The number of new licenses and renewals that were delayed, temporary licenses issued, and licenses suspended subject to this section and the number of new licenses and renewals granted and licenses reinstated following board receipt of releases as provided by subdivision (h) by May 1, 1995.

(4) The costs incurred in the implementation and enforcement of this section.

(q) Any board receiving an inquiry as to the licensed status of an applicant or licensee who has had a license denied or suspended under this section or has been granted a temporary license under this section shall respond only that the license was denied or suspended or the temporary license was issued pursuant to this section. Information collected pursuant to this section by any state agency, board, or department shall be subject to the Information Practices Act of 1977 (Chapter 1 (commencing with Section 1798) of Title 1.8 of Part 4 of Division 3 of the Civil Code).

(r) Any rules and regulations issued pursuant to this section by any state agency, board, or department may be adopted as emergency regulations in accordance with the rulemaking provisions of the Administrative Procedure Act (Chapter 3.5 (commencing with Section 11340) of Part 1 of Division 3 of Title 2 of the Government Code). The adoption of these regulations shall be deemed an emergency and necessary for the immediate preservation of the public peace, health, and safety, or general welfare. The regulations shall become effective immediately upon filing with the Secretary of State.

(s) The department and boards, as appropriate, shall adopt regulations necessary to implement this section.

(t) The Judicial Council shall develop the forms necessary to implement this section, except as provided in subdivisions (f) and (*l*).

(u) The release or other use of information received by a board pursuant to this section, except as authorized by this section, is punishable as a misdemeanor.

(v) The State Board of Equalization shall enter into interagency agreements with the department and the Franchise Tax Board that will require the department and the

Franchise Tax Board to maximize the use of information collected by the State Board of Equalization, for child support enforcement purposes, to the extent it is cost effective and permitted by the Revenue and Taxation Code.

(w)(1) The suspension or revocation of any driver's license, including a commercial driver's license, under this section shall not subject the licensee to vehicle impoundment pursuant to Section 14602.6 of the Vehicle Code.

(2) Notwithstanding any other law, the suspension or revocation of any driver's license, including a commercial driver's license, under this section shall not subject the licensee to increased costs for vehicle liability insurance.

(x) If any provision of this section or the application thereof to any person or circumstance is held invalid, that invalidity shall not affect other provisions or applications of this section which can be given effect without the invalid provision or application, and to this end the provisions of this section are severable.

(y) All rights to administrative and judicial review afforded by this section to an applicant shall also be afforded to a licensee. *(Added by Stats.1999, c. 654 (A.B.370), § 3.5. Amended by Stats.2001, c. 755 (S.B.943), § 14, eff. Oct. 12, 2001; Stats.2013, c. 352 (A.B.1317), § 79, eff. Sept. 26, 2013, operative July 1, 2013; Stats.2014, c. 752 (S.B.1159), § 10, eff. Jan. 1, 2015.)*

Commentary

Suspension of a driver's license under this section (formerly Welfare and Institutions Code § 11350.6) does not violate a support obligor's constitutional right to equal protection or to travel. *Tolces v. Trask, 76 Cal.App.4th 285, 90 Cal.Rptr.2d 294 (1999).*

Research References

Forms

West's California Judicial Council Forms FL-670, Notice Of Motion for Judicial Review Of License Denial.

Treatises and Practice Aids

Witkin, California Summary 10th Husband and Wife § 331, Relief from Order Based on Mistaken Identity.
Witkin, California Summary 10th Husband and Wife § 338, Nonissuance, Nonrenewal, or Suspension Of License.
Witkin, California Summary 10th Parent and Child § 245, in General.
Witkin, California Summary 10th Parent and Child § 248, Supreme Court Decisions Resolving Conflict.

§ 17521. Order to show cause or notice of motion for judicial review of district attorney's decision; appropriate court

The order to show cause or notice of motion described in subdivision (j) of Section 17520 shall be filed and heard in the superior court. *(Added by Stats.1999, c. 653 (A.B.380), § 17. Amended by Stats.2002, c. 784 (S.B.1316), § 115.)*

Law Revision Commission Comments

2002 Amendment

Section 17521 is amended to reflect unification of the municipal and superior courts pursuant to Article VI, Section 5(e), of the California Constitution. [32 Cal.L.Rev.Comm. Reports 172 (2002)].

§ 17522. Delinquent support obligors; collection or lien enforcement by levy

(a) Notwithstanding any other law, if any support obligor is delinquent in the payment of support for at least 30 days and the local child support agency is enforcing the support obligation pursuant to Section 17400, the local child support agency may collect the delinquency or enforce any lien by levy served on all persons having in their possession, or who will have in their possession or under their control, any credits or personal property belonging to the delinquent support obligor, or who owe any debt to the obligor at the time they receive the notice of levy.

(b) A levy may be issued by a local child support agency for a support obligation that accrued under a court order or judgment if the obligor had notice of the accrued support arrearage as provided in this section, and did not make a timely request for review.

(c) The notice requirement shall be satisfied by the local child support agency sending a statement of support arrearages to the obligor at the obligor's last known address by first-class mail, postage prepaid. The notice shall advise the obligor of the amount of the support arrearage. The notice shall advise the obligor that the obligor may have the arrearage determination reviewed by administrative procedures and state how the review may be obtained. The local child support agency shall conduct the review pursuant to this section in the same manner and timeframe provided for resolution of a complaint pursuant to Section 17800. The notice shall also advise the obligor of his or her right to seek a judicial determination of arrearages pursuant to Section 17526 and shall include a form to be filed with the court to request a judicial determination of arrearages. If the obligor requests an administrative review of the arrearage determination within 20 days from the date the notice was mailed to the obligor, the local child support agency may not issue the levy for a disputed amount of support until the administrative review procedure is completed.

(d) If the obligor requests a judicial determination of the arrearages within 20 days from the date the notice was mailed to the obligor, the local child support agency shall not issue the levy for a disputed amount of support until the judicial determination is complete.

(e) Any person upon whom a levy has been served having in his or her possession or under his or her control any credits or personal property belonging to the delinquent support obligor or owing any debts to the delinquent support obligor at the time of receipt of the levy or coming into his or her possession or under his or her control within one year of receipt of the notice of levy, shall surrender the credits or personal property to the local child support agency or pay to the local child support agency the amount of any debt owing the delinquent support obligor within 10 days of service of the levy, and shall surrender the credits or personal property, or the amount of any debt owing to the delinquent support obligor coming into his or her own possession or control within one year of receipt of the notice of levy within 10 days of the date of coming into possession or control of the credits or personal property or the amount of any debt owing to the delinquent support obligor.

(f) Any person who surrenders any credits or personal property or pays the debts owing the delinquent support obligor to the local child support agency pursuant to this section shall be discharged from any obligation or liability to the delinquent support obligor to the extent of the amount paid to the local child support agency as a result of the levy.

(g) If the levy is made on a deposit or credits or personal property in the possession or under the control of a bank, savings and loan association, or other financial institution as defined by Section 669A(d)(1) of Title 42 of the United States Code, the notice of levy may be delivered or mailed to a centralized location designated by the bank, savings and loan association, or other financial institution pursuant to Section 689.040 of the Code of Civil Procedure.

(h) Any person who is served with a levy pursuant to this section and who fails or refuses to surrender any credits or other personal property or pay any debts owing to the delinquent support obligor shall be liable in his or her own person or estate to the local child support agency in an amount equal to the value of the credits or other personal property or in the amount of the levy, up to the amount specified in the levy.

(i) If any amount required to be paid pursuant to a levy under this section is not paid when due, the local child support agency may issue a warrant for enforcement of any lien and for the collection of any amount required to be paid to the local child support agency under this section. The warrant shall be directed to any sheriff, marshal, or the Department of the California Highway Patrol and shall have the same force and effect as a writ of execution. The warrant shall be levied and sale made pursuant to it in the manner and with the same force and effect as a levy and sale pursuant to a writ of execution. The local child support agency may pay or advance to the levying officer the same fees, commissions, and expenses for his or her services under this section as are provided by law for similar services pursuant to a writ of execution, except for those fees and expenses for which a district attorney is exempt by law from paying. The local child support agency, and not the court, shall approve the fees for publication in a newspaper.

(j) The fees, commissions, expenses, and the reasonable costs associated with the sale of property levied upon by warrant or levy pursuant to this section, including, but not limited to, appraisers' fees, auctioneers' fees, and advertising fees are an obligation of the support obligor and may be collected from the obligor by virtue of the warrant or levy or in any other manner as though these items were support payments delinquent for at least 30 days. *(Added by Stats. 1999, c. 478 (A.B.196), § 1. Amended by Stats.2001, c. 755 (S.B.943), § 15, eff. Oct. 12, 2001.)*

Research References

Treatises and Practice Aids

Witkin, California Summary 10th Husband and Wife § 262, in General.

Witkin, California Summary 10th Husband and Wife § 335, Levy by Agency.

§ 17522.5. Issuance of levy or notice to withhold; liquidation of asset by person, financial institution, or securities intermediary in possession or control of financial asset; manner of liquidation and transfer of proceeds; value of financial assets exceeding total amount of support due; instructions for liquidation by obligor

(a) Notwithstanding Section 8112 of the Commercial Code and Section 700.130 of the Code of Civil Procedure, when a local child support agency pursuant to Section 17522, or the department pursuant to Section 17454 or 17500, issues a levy upon, or requires by notice any employer, person, political officer or entity, or depository institution to withhold the amount of, as applicable, a financial asset for the purpose of collecting a delinquent child support obligation, the person, financial institution, or securities intermediary (as defined in Section 8102 of the Commercial Code) in possession or control of the financial asset shall liquidate the financial asset in a commercially reasonable manner within 20 days of the issuance of the levy or the notice to withhold. Within five days of liquidation, the person, financial institution, or securities intermediary shall transfer to the State Disbursement Unit, established under Section 17309, the proceeds of the liquidation, less any reasonable commissions or fees, or both, which are charged in the normal course of business.

(b) If the value of the financial assets exceed the total amount of support due, the obligor may, within 10 days after the service of the levy or notice to withhold upon the person, financial institution, or securities intermediary, instruct the person, financial institution, or securities intermediary who possesses or controls the financial assets as to which financial assets are to be sold to satisfy the obligation for delinquent support. If the obligor does not provide instructions for liquidation, the person, financial institution, or securities intermediary who possesses or controls the financial assets shall liquidate the financial assets in a commercially reasonable manner and in an amount sufficient to cover the obligation for delinquent child support, and any reasonable commissions or fees, or both, which are charged in the normal course of business, beginning with the financial assets purchased most recently.

(c) For the purposes of this section, a financial asset shall include, but not be limited to, an uncertificated security, certificated security, or security entitlement (as defined in Section 8102 of the Commercial Code), security (as defined in Section 8103 of the Commercial Code), or a securities account (as defined in Section 8501 of the Commercial Code). *(Added by Stats.2003, c. 225 (A.B.1752), § 5, eff. Aug. 11, 2003. Amended by Stats.2004, c. 806 (A.B.2358), § 8; Stats.2016, c. 474 (A.B.2882), § 22, eff. Jan. 1, 2017.)*

Research References

Treatises and Practice Aids

Witkin, California Summary 10th Husband and Wife § 335, Levy by Agency.

§ 17523. Lien for child support against personal property; perfection; priority; enforcement

(a) Notwithstanding any other provision of law, if a support obligor is delinquent in the payment of support and the local child support agency is enforcing the support obligation pursuant to Section 17400 or 17402, a lien for child support shall arise against the personal property of the support obligor in either of the following circumstances:

(1) By operation of law for all amounts of overdue support, regardless of whether the amounts have been adjudicated or otherwise determined.

(2) When either a court having continuing jurisdiction or the local child support agency determines a specific amount of arrearages is owed by the support obligor.

(b) The lien for child support shall be perfected by filing a notice of child support lien with the Secretary of State pursuant to Section 697.510 of the Code of Civil Procedure. Once filed, the child support lien shall have the same priority, force, and effect as a judgment lien on personal property pursuant to Article 3 (commencing with Section 697.510) of Chapter 2 of Division 2 of Article 9 of the Code of Civil Procedure.

(c) For purposes of this section, the following definitions shall apply:

(1) "Notice of child support lien" means a document filed with the Secretary of State that substantially complies with the requirements of Section 697.530 of the Code of Civil Procedure.

(2) "Support obligor is delinquent in payment of support" means that the support obligor has failed to make payment equal to one month's support obligation.

(3) "Personal property" means that property that is subject to attachment by a judgment lien pursuant to Section 697.530 of the Code of Civil Procedure.

(d) Nothing in this section shall affect the priority of any of the following interests:

(1) State tax liens as set forth in Article 2 (commencing with Section 7170) of Division 7 of Title 1 of the Government Code.

(2) Liens or security interests as set forth in Article 3 (commencing with Section 697.510) of Chapter 2 of Division 2 of Article 9 of the Code of Civil Procedure.

(e) As between competing child support liens and state tax liens, a child support lien arising under this section shall have priority over a state tax lien if (1) the child support lien is filed with the Secretary of State, (2) the notice of child support lien is filed in an action or proceeding in which the obligor may become entitled to property or money judgment, or (3) the levy for child support on personal property is made, before a notice of state tax lien is filed with the Secretary of State pursuant to Section 7171 of the Government Code or filed in an action or proceeding in accordance with Section 7173 of the Government Code.

(f) A personal property lien for child support arising in another state may be enforced in the same manner and to the same extent as a personal property lien arising in this state. *(Added by Stats.1999, c. 980 (A.B.1671), § 15.)*

Research References

Treatises and Practice Aids

Witkin, California Summary 10th Husband and Wife § 336, Lien on Personal Property.

§ 17523.5. Lien for child support against real property; digitized or digital electronic record

(a)(1) Notwithstanding any other law, in connection with the duty of the department and the local child support agency to promptly and effectively collect and enforce child support obligations under Title IV–D, the transmission, filing, and recording of a lien record by departmental and local child support agency staff that arises pursuant to subdivision (a) of Section 4506 of this code or Section 697.320 of the Code of Civil Procedure against the real property of a support obligor in the form of a digital or a digitized electronic record shall be permitted and governed only by this section.

(2) A facsimile signature that complies with the requirements of paragraph (2) of subdivision (b) of Section 27201 of the Government Code shall be accepted on any document relating to a lien that is filed or recorded pursuant to this section.

(3) The department and the local child support agency may use the California Child Support Enforcement System to transmit, file, and record a lien record under this section.

(b) Nothing in this section shall be construed to require a county recorder to establish an electronic recording delivery system or to enter into a contract with an entity to implement this section.

(c) For purposes of this section, the following terms have the following meanings:

(1) "Digital electronic record" means a record containing information that is created, generated, sent, communicated, received, or stored by electronic means, but not created in original paper form.

(2) "Digitized electronic record" means a scanned image of the original paper document. *(Added by Stats.2007, c. 441 (S.B.892), § 2. Amended by Stats.2016, c. 474 (A.B.2882), § 23, eff. Jan. 1, 2017.)*

§ 17524. Statement of arrearages

(a) Upon making application to the local child support agency for child support enforcement services pursuant to Section 17400, every applicant shall be requested to give the local child support agency a statement of arrearages stating whether any support arrearages are owed. If the applicant alleges arrearages are owed, the statement shall be signed under penalty of perjury.

(b) For all cases opened by the district attorney or local child support agency after December 31, 1995, the local child support agency shall enforce only arrearages declared under penalty of perjury pursuant to subdivision (a), arrearages accrued after the case was opened, or arrearages determined by the court in the child support action. Arrearages may be determined by judgment, noticed motion, renewal of judgment, or registration of the support order.

(c) For all cases opened by the district attorney on or before December 31, 1995, the local child support agency shall enforce only arrearages that have been based upon a statement of arrearages signed under penalty of perjury or where the local child support agency has some other reasonable basis for believing the amount of claimed arrearages to be correct. *(Added by Stats.1999, c. 478 (A.B.196), § 1.)*

Research References

Forms

West's California Judicial Council Forms FL-420, Declaration Of Support Arrearage.

West's California Judicial Council Forms FL-421, Attachment to Declaration Of Support Arrearage (Family Law--Domestic Violence Prevention--Uniform Parentage Act).

Treatises and Practice Aids

Witkin, California Summary 10th Husband and Wife § 334, in General.

§ 17525. Notice of support delinquency; contents

(a) Whenever a state or local governmental agency issues a notice of support delinquency, the notice shall state the date upon which the amount of the delinquency was calculated, and shall notify the obligor that the amount calculated may, or may not, include accrued interest. This requirement shall not be imposed until the local child support agency has instituted the California Child Support Enforcement System implemented and maintained by the Department of Child Support Services pursuant to Section 17308. The notice shall further notify the obligor of his or her right to an administrative determination of arrears by requesting that the local child support agency review the arrears, but that payments on arrears continue to be due and payable unless and until the local child support agency notifies the obligor otherwise. A state agency shall not be required to suspend enforcement of any arrearages as a result of the obligor's request for an administrative determination of arrears, unless the agency receives notification of a suspension pursuant to subdivision (b) of Section 17526.

(b) For purposes of this section, "notice of support delinquency" means a notice issued to a support obligor that includes a specific statement of the amount of delinquent support due and payable.

(c) This section shall not require a state or local entity to calculate the amount of a support delinquency, except as otherwise required by law. *(Added by Stats.1999, c. 654 (A.B.370), § 4. Amended by Stats.2000, c. 808 (A.B.1358), § 90, eff. Sept. 28, 2000; Stats.2001, c. 755 (S.B.943), § 16, eff. Oct. 12, 2001; Stats.2016, c. 474 (A.B.2882), § 24, eff. Jan. 1, 2017.)*

Research References

Treatises and Practice Aids

Witkin, California Summary 10th Husband and Wife § 334, in General.

§ 17526. Statement of arrearages; review

(a) Upon request of an obligor or obligee, the local child support agency shall review the amount of arrearages alleged in a statement of arrearages that may be submitted to the local child support agency by an applicant for child support enforcement services. The local child support agency shall complete the review in the same manner and pursuant to the same timeframes as a complaint submitted pursuant to Section 17800. In the review, the local child support agency shall consider all evidence and defenses submitted by either parent on the issues of the amount of support paid or owed.

(b) The local child support agency may, in its discretion, suspend enforcement or distribution of arrearages if it believes there is a substantial probability that the result of the administrative review will result in a finding that there are no arrearages.

(c) Any party to an action involving child support enforcement services of the local child support agency may request a judicial determination of arrearages. The party may request an administrative review of the alleged arrearages prior to requesting a judicial determination of arrearages. The local child support agency shall complete the review in the same manner and pursuant to the same timeframes specified in subdivision (a). Any motion to determine arrearages filed with the court shall include a monthly breakdown showing amounts ordered and amounts paid, in addition to any other relevant information.

(d) A county that submits a claim for reimbursement as a state-mandated local program of costs incurred with respect to the administrative review of alleged child support arrearages under this section shall be ineligible for state subventions or, to the extent permitted by federal law, state-administered federal subventions, for child support in the amount of any local costs under this section. *(Added by Stats.1999, c. 478 (A.B.196), § 1. Amended by Stats.2001, c. 755 (S.B.943), § 17, eff. Oct. 12, 2001; Stats.2002, c. 927 (A.B.3032), § 6.5.)*

Research References

Forms

West's California Judicial Council Forms FL-420, Declaration Of Support Arrearage.

West's California Judicial Council Forms FL-421, Attachment to Declaration Of Support Arrearage (Family Law--Domestic Violence Prevention--Uniform Parentage Act).

West's California Judicial Council Forms FL-626, Stipulation and Order Waiving Unassigned Arrears (Governmental).

West's California Judicial Council Forms FL-676, Request for Judicial Determination Of Support Arrearages or Adjustment Of Arrearages Due to Incarceration or Involuntary Institutionalization.

Treatises and Practice Aids

Witkin, California Summary 10th Husband and Wife § 334, in General.

§ 17528. Public Employees' Retirement System; withholding overdue support obligations

(a) As authorized by subdivision (c) of Section 704.110 of the Code of Civil Procedure, the following actions shall be taken in order to enforce support obligations that are not being met:

(1) Within 18 months of implementation of the California Child Support Enforcement System (CSE), or its replacement as prescribed by former Section 10815 of the Welfare and Institutions Code, and certification of CSE or its replacement by the United States Department of Health and Human Services, the department shall compile a file of all support judgments and orders that are being enforced by local child support agencies pursuant to Section 17400 that have sums overdue by at least 60 days or by an amount equal to 60 days of support.

(2) The file shall contain the name and social security number of the person who owes overdue support, the amount of overdue support as of the date the file is created, the name of the county in which the support obligation is being enforced by the local child support agency, and any other information that is deemed necessary by the department and the Public Employees' Retirement System.

(3) The department shall provide the certified file to the Public Employees' Retirement System for the purpose of matching the names in the file with members and beneficiaries of the Public Employees' Retirement System that are

entitled to receive Public Employees' Retirement System benefits. The department and the Public Employees' Retirement System shall work cooperatively to develop an interface in order to match the names in their respective electronic data processing systems. The interface required to intercept benefits that are payable periodically shall be done as soon as it is technically feasible.

(4) The department shall update the certified file no less than on a monthly basis to add new cases within the local child support agencies or existing cases that become delinquent and to delete persons who are no longer delinquent. The department shall provide the updated file no less than on a monthly basis to the Public Employees' Retirement System.

(5) Information contained in the certified file provided to the Public Employees' Retirement System by the department and the local child support agencies and information provided by the Public Employees' Retirement System to the department shall be used exclusively for child support enforcement purposes and may not be used for any other purpose.

(b) Notwithstanding any other law, the Public Employees' Retirement System shall withhold the amount certified from the benefits and refunds to be distributed to members with overdue support obligations or from benefits to be distributed to beneficiaries with overdue support obligations. If the benefits are payable periodically, the amount withheld pursuant to this section shall not exceed the amount permitted to be withheld for an earnings withholding order for support under Section 706.052 of the Code of Civil Procedure.

(c) The Public Employees' Retirement System shall forward the amounts withheld pursuant to subdivision (b) within 10 days of withholding to the department for distribution to the appropriate county.

(d) On an annual basis, the department shall notify individuals with overdue support obligations that PERS benefits or PERS contribution refunds may be intercepted for the purpose of enforcing family support obligations.

(e) No later than the time of the first withholding, the Public Employees' Retirement System shall send those persons subject to withholding the following:

(1) Notice that his or her benefits or retirement contribution refund have been reduced by payment on a support judgment pursuant to this section.

(2) A form developed by the department that the applicant shall use to request either a review by the local child support agency or a court hearing, as appropriate.

(f) The notice shall include the address and telephone number of the local child support agency that is enforcing the support obligation pursuant to Section 17400, and shall specify that the form requesting either a review by the local child support agency or a court hearing must be received by the local child support agency within 20 days of the date of the notice.

(g) The form shall include instructions that are designed to enable the member or beneficiary to obtain a review or a court hearing as appropriate on his or her own behalf. The form shall specify that if the member or beneficiary disputes the amount of support arrearages certified by the local child support agency pursuant to this section, he or she may request a review by the local child support agency.

(h) The department shall develop procedures that are consistent with this section to be used by each local child support agency in conducting the requested review. The local child support agency shall complete the review in accordance with the procedures developed by the department and shall notify the member or beneficiary of the result of the review within 20 days of receiving the request for review. The notification of review results shall include a request for hearing form and shall inform the member or beneficiary that if he or she returns the completed request for hearing form within 20 days of the date of the notice of review results, the local child support agency shall calendar the matter for court review. If the local child support agency cannot complete the review within 20 days, the local child support agency shall calendar the matter for hearing as specified in subdivision (k).

(i) The form specified in subdivision (g) shall also notify the member or beneficiary that he or she may request a court hearing to claim an exemption of any benefit not payable periodically by returning the completed form to the local child support agency within 20 days. If the local child support agency receives a timely request for a hearing for a claim of exemption, the local child support agency shall calendar a court hearing. The amount of the exemption, if any, shall be determined by the court in accordance with the procedures set forth in Section 703.070 of the Code of Civil Procedure.

(j) If the local child support agency receives the form requesting either a review by the local child support agency or a court hearing within the 20 days specified in subdivision (f), the local child support agency shall not distribute the amount intercepted until the review by the local child support agency or the court hearing is completed. If the local child support agency determines that all or a portion of the member's or beneficiary's benefits were intercepted in error, or if the court determines that any amount of the benefits are exempt, the local child support agency shall refund any amount determined to be exempt or intercepted in excess of the correct amount to the member or beneficiary within 10 days of determination that a refund is due.

(k) Any hearing properly requested pursuant to this section shall be calendared by the local child support agency. The hearing shall be held within 20 days from the date that the local child support agency receives the request for hearing. The local child support agency shall provide notice of the time and place for hearing by first-class mail no later than five days prior to the hearing.

(*l*) Nothing in this section shall limit any existing rights of the member or beneficiary, including, but not limited to, the right to seek a determination of arrearages or other appropriate relief directly from the court. However, if the procedures of this section are not utilized by the member or beneficiary, the court may not require the local child support agency to refund any money that was distributed to the child support obligee prior to the local child support agency receiving notice of a court determination that a refund is due to the member or beneficiary.

(m) The Department of Child Support Services and the Public Employees' Retirement System shall enter into any agreement necessary to implement this section which shall include provisions for the department to provide funding to the Public Employees' Retirement System to develop, implement, and maintain the intercept process described in this section.

(n) The Public Employees' Retirement System shall not assess service charges on members or beneficiaries in order to recover any administrative costs resulting from complying with this section. *(Added by Stats.1999, c. 478 (A.B.196), § 1. Amended by Stats.2016, c. 474 (A.B.2882), § 25, eff. Jan. 1, 2017.)*

Research References

Treatises and Practice Aids

Witkin, California Summary 10th Husband and Wife § 334, in General.

§ 17530. Support enforcement action; allegation of error due to mistaken identity; administrative and judicial remedies; penalty

(a) Notwithstanding any other provision of law, this section shall apply to any actions taken to enforce a judgment or order for support entered as a result of action filed by the local child support agency pursuant to Section 17400, 17402, or 17404, where it is alleged that the enforcement actions have been taken in error against a person who is not the support obligor named in the judgment or order.

(b) Any person claiming that any support enforcement actions have been taken against that person, or his or her wages or assets, in error, shall file a claim of mistaken identity with the local child support agency. The claim shall include verifiable information or documentation to establish that the person against whom the enforcement actions have been taken is not the person named in the support order or judgment. The local child support agency shall resolve a claim of mistaken identity submitted pursuant to this section in the same manner and time frames provided for resolution of a complaint pursuant to Section 17800.

(c) If the local child support agency determines that a claim filed pursuant to this section is meritorious, or if the court enters an order pursuant to Section 17433, the agency shall immediately take the steps necessary to terminate all enforcement activities with respect to the claimant, to return to the claimant any assets seized, to terminate any levying activities or attachment or assignment orders, to release any license renewal or application being withheld pursuant to Section 17520, to return any sums paid by the claimant pursuant to the judgment or order, including sums paid to any federal, state, or local government, but excluding sums paid directly to the support obligee, and to ensure that all other enforcement agencies and entities cease further actions against the claimant. With respect to a claim filed under this section, the local child support agency shall also provide the claimant with a statement certifying that the claimant is not the support obligor named in the support order or judgment, which statement shall be prima facie evidence of the claimant's identity in any subsequent enforcement proceedings or actions with respect to that support order or judgment.

(d) If the local child support agency rejects a claim pursuant to this section, or if the agency, after finding a claim to be meritorious, fails to take any of the remedial steps provided in subdivision (c), the claimant may file an action with the superior court to establish his or her mistaken identity or to obtain the remedies described in subdivision (c), or both.

(e) Filing a false claim pursuant to this section shall be a misdemeanor.

(f) This section shall become operative on April 1, 2000. *(Added by Stats.1999, c. 653 (A.B.380), § 18, operative April 1, 2000. Amended by Stats.2001, c. 755 (S.B.943), § 18, eff. Oct. 12, 2001.)*

Research References

Treatises and Practice Aids

Witkin, California Summary 10th Husband and Wife § 331, Relief from Order Based on Mistaken Identity.

§ 17531. Closure of a child support case; summary criminal history information in case; deletion or purging of file

When a local child support agency closes a child support case containing summary criminal history information, the local child support agency shall delete or purge from the file and destroy any documents or information concerning or arising from offenses for or of which the parent has been arrested, charged, or convicted, other than offenses related to the parent's having failed to provide support for minor children, no later than four years and four months, or any other timeframe that is consistent with federal regulations controlling child support records retention, after the date the local child support agency closes the case. *(Added by Stats.2000, c. 808 (A.B.1358), § 91, eff. Sept. 28, 2000.)*

Research References

Treatises and Practice Aids

Witkin, California Summary 10th Husband and Wife § 314, Acquisition and Confidentiality Of Information.

§ 17540. Payment of county claims for federal and state reimbursement; waiver of time limitation

(a)(1) Commencing July 1, 2000, the department shall pay only those county claims for federal or state reimbursement under this division which are filed with the department within nine months of the end of the calendar quarter in which the costs are paid. A claim filed after that time may only be paid if the claim falls within the exceptions set forth in federal law.

(2) The department may change the nine-month limitation specified in paragraph (1), as deemed necessary by the department to comply with federal changes which affect time limits for filing a claim.

(b)(1) The department may waive the time limit imposed by subdivision (a) if the department determines there was good cause for a county's failure to file a claim or claims within the time limit.

(2)(A) For purposes of this subdivision, "good cause" means circumstances which are beyond the county's control, including acts of God and documented action or inaction by the state or federal government.

(B) "Circumstances beyond the county's control" do not include neglect or failure on the part of the county or any of its offices, officers, or employees.

(C) A county shall request a waiver of the time limit imposed by this section for good cause in accordance with regulations adopted and promulgated by the department.

(3) The department's authority to waive the time limit under this subdivision shall be subject to the availability of funds and shall not apply to claims submitted more than 18 months after the end of the calendar quarter in which costs were paid. *(Added by Stats.2000, c. 808 (A.B.1358), § 92, eff. Sept. 28, 2000.)*

§ 17550. Establishment of regulations by which the local child support agency may compromise parents' liability for public assistance debt in cases of separation or desertion of parent from child; conditions

(a) The Department of Child Support Services, in consultation with the State Department of Social Services, shall establish regulations by which the local child support agency, in any case of separation or desertion of a parent from a child that results in aid under Chapter 2 (commencing with Section 11200) of Part 3 of Division 9 of the Welfare and Institutions Code being granted to the child, may compromise the obligor parent or parents' liability for public assistance debt, including interest thereon, owed to the state where the child for whom public assistance was paid is residing with the obligor parent, and all of the following conditions are met:

(1) The obligor parent establishes one of the following:

(A) The child has been adjudged a dependent of the court under Section 300 of the Welfare and Institutions Code and the child has been reunified with the obligor parent pursuant to a court order.

(B) The child received public assistance while living with a guardian or relative caregiver and the child has been returned to the custody of the obligor parent, provided that the obligor parent for whom the debt compromise is being considered was the parent with whom the child resided prior to the child's placement with the guardian or relative caregiver.

(2) The obligor parent, for whom the debt compromise is being considered, has an income less than 250 percent of the current federal poverty level.

(3) The local child support agency, pursuant to regulations set forth by the department, has determined that the compromise is necessary for the child's support.

(b) Prior to compromising an obligor parent's liability for debt incurred for either AFDC–FC payments provided to a child pursuant to Section 11400 of the Welfare and Institutions Code, or incurred for CalWORKs payments provided on behalf of a child, the local child support agency shall consult with the county child welfare department.

(c) Nothing in this section relieves an obligor, who has not been reunified with his or her child, of any liability for public assistance debt.

(d) For the purposes of this section, the following definitions apply:

(1) "Guardian" means the legal guardian of the child, who assumed care and control of the child while the child was in the guardian's control, and who is not a biological or adoptive parent.

(2) "Relative caregiver" means a relative as defined in subdivision (c) of Section 11362 of the Welfare and Institutions Code, who assumed primary responsibility for the child while the child was in the relative's care and control, and who is not a biological or adoptive parent.

(e) The department shall promulgate all necessary regulations pursuant to this section on or before October 1, 2002, including regulations that set forth guidelines to be used by the local child support agency when compromising public assistance debt. *(Added by Stats.2001, c. 463 (A.B.1449), § 2.)*

Implementation

For implementation relating to the availability of federal financial participation, see Stats.2001, c. 463 (A.B.1449), § 6.

Research References

Treatises and Practice Aids

Witkin, California Summary 10th Husband and Wife § 328, Agreement, Stipulation, or Compromise.

§ 17552. Regulations concerning determinations whether or not best interests of child or nonminor require case to be referred to local child support agency for child support services in situations resulting in foster care assistance, CalWORKs or Kin–GAP payments, or other specified aid; determination factors; review; nonminor dependents

(a) The State Department of Social Services, in consultation with the Department of Child Support Services, shall promulgate regulations by which the county child welfare department, in any case of separation or desertion of a parent or parents from a child that results in foster care assistance payments under Section 11400 of, or a voluntary placement under Section 11401.1 of, or the payments for a minor child placed in the same home as a minor or nonminor dependent parent under Section 11401.4 of, the Welfare and Institution Code, or CalWORKs payments to a caretaker relative of a child who comes within the jurisdiction of the juvenile court under Section 300, 601, or 602 of the Welfare and Institutions Code, who has been removed from the parental home and placed with the caretaker relative by court order, and who is under the supervision of the county child welfare agency or probation department under Section 11250 of, or Kin–GAP payments under Article 4.5 (commencing with Section 11360) or Article 4.7 (commencing with Section 11385) of, or aid under subdivision (c) of Section 10101 of, the Welfare and Institutions Code, shall determine whether it is in the best interests of the child or nonminor to have the case referred to the local child support agency for child support services. If reunification services are not offered or are terminated, the case may be referred to the local child support agency, unless the child's permanent plan is legal guardianship with a relative who is receiving Kin–GAP and the payment of support by the parent may compromise the stability of the current placement with the related guardian, or the permanent plan is transitional foster care for the nonminor under Section 11403 of the Welfare and Institutions Code. In making the determination, the department regulations shall provide the factors the county child welfare department shall consider, including:

(1) Whether the payment of support by the parent will pose a barrier to the proposed reunification, in that the payment of support will compromise the parent's ability to meet the requirements of the parent's reunification plan.

(2) Whether the payment of support by the parent will pose a barrier to the proposed reunification in that the payment of support will compromise the parent's current or future ability to meet the financial needs of the child.

(b) The department regulations shall provide that, where the county child welfare department determines that it is not in the best interests of the child to seek a support order against the parent, the county child welfare department shall refrain from referring the case to the local child support agency. The regulations shall define those circumstances in which it is not in the best interest of the child to refer the case to the local child support agency.

(c) The department regulations shall provide, where the county child welfare department determines that it is not in the child's best interest to have his or her case referred to the local child support agency, the county child welfare department shall review that determination periodically to coincide with the redetermination of AFDC–FC eligibility under Section 11401. 5 of, or the CalWORKs eligibility under Section 11265 of, or Kin–GAP eligibility under Article 4.5 (commencing with Section 11360) or Article 4.7 (commencing with Section 11385) of Chapter 2 of Part 3 of Division 9 of, the Welfare and Institutions Code, and shall refer the child's case to the local child support agency upon a determination that, due to a change in the child's circumstances, it is no longer contrary to the child's best interests to have his or her case referred to the local child support agency.

(d) The State Department of Social Services shall promulgate all necessary regulations pursuant to this section on or before October 1, 2002.

(e) Notwithstanding any other provision of law, a nonminor dependent, as described in subdivision (v) of Section 11400 of the Welfare and Institutions Code, who is over 19 years of age, is not a child for purposes of referral to the local child support agency for collection or enforcement of child support.

(f) Notwithstanding any other law, a minor or a nonminor dependent, as defined in subdivision (v) of Section 11400 of the Welfare and Institutions Code, who has a minor child placed in the same licensed or approved facility pursuant to Section 11401.4 of the Welfare and Institutions Code is not a parent for purposes of referral to the local child support agency for collection or enforcement of child support. *(Added by Stats.2001, c. 463 (A.B.1449), § 3. Amended by Stats.2005, c. 198 (A.B.1743), § 1; Stats.2010, c. 559 (A.B.12), § 2; Stats.2011, c. 459 (A.B.212), § 1, eff. Oct. 4, 2011; Stats.2012, c. 846 (A.B.1712), § 2.)*

Research References

Treatises and Practice Aids

Witkin, California Summary 10th Husband and Wife § 312, Referral to Agency by County Welfare Department.

Witkin, California Summary 10th Parent and Child § 515, Other Costs.

Witkin, California Summary 10th Parent and Child § 517, Collection Procedure.

§ 17555. Appropriations in annual Budget Act for purpose of augmenting funding for collection responsibilities; requirements; legislative intent

(a) Any appropriation made available in the annual Budget Act for the purposes of augmenting funding for local child support agencies in the furtherance of their revenue collection responsibilities shall be subject to all of the following requirements:

(1) Each local child support agency shall submit to the department an early intervention plan with all components to take effect upon receipt of their additional allocation as a result of this proposal.

(2) Funds shall be distributed to counties based on their performance on the following two federal performance measures:

(A) Measure 3: Collections on Current Support.

(B) Measure 4: Cases with Collections on Arrears.

(3) A local child support agency shall be required to use and ensure that 100 percent of the new funds allocated are dedicated to maintaining caseworker staffing levels in order to stabilize child support collections.

(4) At the end of each fiscal year that this augmentation is in effect, the department shall provide a report on the cost-effectiveness of this augmentation, including an assessment of caseload changes over time.

(b) It is the intent of the Legislature to review the results of this augmentation and the level of related appropriation during the legislative budget review process. *(Added by Stats.2009–2010, 4th Ex.Sess., c. 4 (A.B.4), § 2, eff. July 28, 2009. Amended by Stats.2010, c. 725 (A.B.1612), § 3, eff. Oct. 19, 2010; Stats.2012, c. 728 (S.B.71), § 38.)*

§ 17560. Arrears collection enhancement process; development of program; acceptance of offers in compromise

Text of section as amended by Stats.2008, c. 759 (A.B.1279), § 16, eff. Sept. 30, 2008.

Section 17560 was added by Stats.2003, c. 225 (A.B.1752), § 6, eff. Aug. 11, 2003, amended by Stats.2005, c. 154 (S.B.1082), § 5, eff. Aug. 30, 2005; Stats.2006, c. 75 (A.B.1808), § 8, eff. July 12, 2006, and repealed by its own terms, operative July 1, 2008. Therefore, this section was not in effect from July 1, 2008 until Sept. 30, 2008.

Stats.2008, c. 759 (A.B.1279), § 16, might be given effect as a new addition of this section; but see Government Code § 9609.

(a) The department shall establish and operate a statewide compromise of arrears program pursuant to which the department may accept offers in compromise of child support arrears and interest accrued thereon owed to the state for reimbursement of aid paid pursuant to Chapter 2 (commencing with Section 11200) of Part 3 of Division 9 of the Welfare and Institutions Code. The program shall operate uniformly across California and shall take into consideration the needs of the children subject to the child support order and the obligor's ability to pay.

(b) If the obligor owes current child support, the offer in compromise shall require the obligor to be in compliance with the current support order for a set period of time before any arrears and interest accrued thereon may be compromised.

(c) Absent a finding of good cause, or a determination by the director that it is in the best interest of the state to do otherwise, any offer in compromise entered into pursuant to this section shall be rescinded, all compromised liabilities shall be reestablished notwithstanding any statute of limitations that otherwise may be applicable, and no portion of the amount offered in compromise may be refunded, if either of the following occurs:

(1) The department or local child support agency determines that the obligor did any of the following acts regarding the offer in compromise:

(A) Concealed from the department or local child support agency any income, assets, or other property belonging to the obligor or any reasonably anticipated receipt of income, assets, or other property.

(B) Intentionally received, withheld, destroyed, mutilated, or falsified any information, document, or record, or intentionally made any false statement, relating to the financial conditions of the obligor.

(2) The obligor fails to comply with any of the terms and conditions of the offer in compromise.

(d) Pursuant to subdivision (k) of Section 17406, in no event may the administrator, director, or director's designee within the department, accept an offer in compromise of any child support arrears owed directly to the custodial party unless that party consents to the offer in compromise in writing and participates in the agreement. Prior to giving consent, the custodial party shall be provided with a clear written explanation of the rights with respect to child support arrears owed to the custodial party and the compromise thereof.

(e) Subject to the requirements of this section, the director shall delegate to the administrator of a local child support agency the authority to compromise an amount of child support arrears up to five thousand dollars ($5,000), and may delegate additional authority to compromise up to an amount determined by the director to support the effective administration of the offers in compromise program.

(f) For an amount to be compromised under this section, the following conditions shall exist:

(1)(A) The administrator, director or director's designee within the department determines that acceptance of an offer in compromise is in the best interest of the state and that the compromise amount equals or exceeds what the state can expect to collect for reimbursement of aid paid pursuant to Chapter 2 (commencing with Section 11200) of Part 3 of Division 9 of the Welfare and Institutions Code in the absence of the compromise, based on the obligor's ability to pay.

(B) Acceptance of an offer in compromise shall be deemed to be in the best interest of the state, absent a finding of good cause to the contrary, with regard to arrears that accrued as a result of a decrease in income when an obligor was a reservist or member of the National Guard, was activated to United States military service, and failed to modify the support order to reflect the reduction in income. Good cause to find that the compromise is not in the best interest of the state shall include circumstances in which the service member's failure to seek, or delay in seeking, the modification were not reasonable under the circumstances faced by the service member. The director, no later than 90 days after the effective date of the act adding this subparagraph, shall establish rules that compromise, at a minimum, the amount of support that would not have accrued had the order been modified to reflect the reduced income earned during the period of active military service.

(2) Any other terms and conditions that the director establishes that may include, but may not be limited to, paying current support in a timely manner, making lump-sum payments, and paying arrears in exchange for compromise of interest owed.

(3) The obligor shall provide evidence of income and assets, including, but not limited to, wage stubs, tax returns, and bank statements as necessary to establish all of the following:

(A) That the amount set forth in the offer in compromise of arrears owed is the most that can be expected to be paid or collected from the obligor's present assets or income.

(B) That the obligor does not have reasonable prospects of acquiring increased income or assets that would enable the obligor to satisfy a greater amount of the child support arrears than the amount offered, within a reasonable period of time.

(C) That the obligor has not withheld payment of child support in anticipation of the offers in compromise program.

(g) A determination by the administrator, director or the director's designee within the department that it would not be in the best interest of the state to accept or rescind an offer in compromise in satisfaction of child support arrears shall be final and not subject to the provisions of Chapter 5 (commencing with Section 17800) of Division 17, or subject to judicial review.

(h) Any offer in compromise entered into pursuant to this section shall be filed with the appropriate court. The local child support agency shall notify the court if the compromise is rescinded pursuant to subdivision (c).

(i) Any compromise of child support arrears pursuant to this section shall maximize to the greatest extent possible the state's share of the federal performance incentives paid pursuant to the Child Support Performance and Incentive Act of 1998 [1] and shall comply with federal law.

(j) The department shall ensure uniform application of this section across the state. *(Amended by Stats.2008, c. 759 (A.B.1279), § 16, eff. Sept. 30, 2008.)*

[1] Child Support Performance and Incentive Act of 1998 (Pub.L. 105–200, July 16, 1998, 112 Stat. 645). Public law sections classified to U.S.C.A., see USCA–Tables.

§ 17561. Annual report on implementation of California Child Support Automation System; joint production by Office of the Chief Information Officer and Department of Child Support Services; contents

The Office of the Chief Information Officer and the Department of Child Support Services, beginning in 2010, shall jointly produce an annual report to be submitted on March 1, to the appropriate policy and fiscal committees of the Legislature on the ongoing implementation of the California Child Support Automation System (CCSAS), including all of the following components:

(a) A clear breakdown of funding elements for past, current, and future years.

(b) Descriptions of active functionalities and a description of their usefulness in child support collections by local child support agencies.

(c) A review of current considerations relative to federal law and policy.

(d) A policy narrative on future, planned changes to the CCSAS and how those changes will advance activities for workers, collections for the state, and payments for recipient families. *(Added by Stats.2009–2010, 4th Ex.Sess., c. 4 (A.B.4), § 3, eff. July 28, 2009.)*

ARTICLE 3. PROGRAM COMPLIANCE

§ 17600. Legislative findings and declarations; county reporting requirements

(a) The Legislature finds and declares all of the following:

(1) The Legislative Analyst has found that county child support enforcement programs provide a net increase in revenues to the state.

(2) The state has a fiscal interest in ensuring that county child support enforcement programs perform efficiently.

(3) The state does not provide information to counties on child support enforcement programs, based on common denominators that would facilitate comparison of program performance.

(4) Providing this information would allow county officials to monitor program performance and to make appropriate modifications to improve program efficiency.

(5) This information is required for effective management of the child support program.

(b) Except as provided in this subdivision commencing with the 1998–99 fiscal year, and for each fiscal year thereafter, each county that is participating in the state incentive program described in Section 17704 shall provide to the department, and the department shall compile from this county child support information, monthly and annually, all of the following performance-based data, as established by the federal incentive funding system, provided that the department may revise the data required by this paragraph in order to conform to the final federal incentive system data definitions:

(1) One of the following data relating to paternity establishment, as required by the department, provided that the department shall require all counties to report on the same measurement:

(A) The total number of children in the caseload governed by Part D (commencing with Section 451) of Title IV of the federal Social Security Act (42 U.S.C. Sec. 651 et seq.), as of the end of the federal fiscal year, who were born to unmarried parents for whom paternity was established or acknowledged, and the total number of children in that caseload, as of the end of the preceding federal fiscal year, who were born to unmarried parents.

(B) The total number of minor children who were born in the state to unmarried parents for whom paternity was established or acknowledged during a federal fiscal year, and the total number of children in the state born to unmarried parents during the preceding calendar year.

(2) The number of cases governed by Part D (commencing with Section 451) of Title IV of the federal Social Security Act (42 U.S.C. Sec. 651 et seq.) during the federal fiscal year and the total number of those cases with support orders.

(3) The total dollars collected during the federal fiscal year for current support in cases governed by Part D (commencing with Section 451) of Title IV of the federal Social Security Act (42 U.S.C. Sec. 651 et seq.) and the total number of dollars owing for current support during that federal fiscal year in cases governed by those provisions.

(4) The total number of cases for the federal fiscal year governed by Part D (commencing with Section 451) of Title IV of the federal Social Security Act (42 U.S.C. Sec. 651 et seq.) in which payment was being made toward child support arrearages and the total number of cases for that fiscal year governed by these federal provisions that had child support arrearages.

(5) The total number of dollars collected and expended during a federal fiscal year in cases governed by Part D (commencing with Section 451) of Title IV of the federal Social Security Act (42 U.S.C. Sec. 651 et seq.).

(6) The total amount of child support dollars collected during a federal fiscal year, and, if and when required by federal law, the amount of these collections broken down by collections distributed on behalf of current recipients of federal Temporary Assistance for Needy Families block grant funds or federal foster care funds, on behalf of former recipients of federal Temporary Assistance for Needy Families block grant funds or federal foster care funds, or on behalf of persons who have never been recipients of these federal funds.

(c) In addition to the information required by subdivision (b), the department shall collect, on a monthly basis, from each county that is participating in the state incentive program described in Section 17704, information on the local child support agency for each federal fiscal year, and shall report semiannually on all of the following performance measurements:

(1) The percentage of cases with collections of current support. This percentage shall be calculated by dividing the number of cases with an order for current support by the number of those cases with collections of current support. The number of cases with support collected shall include only the number of cases actually receiving a collection, not the number of payments received. Cases with a medical support order that do not have an order for current support may not be counted.

(2) The average amount collected per case for all cases with collections.

(3) The percentage of cases that had a support order established during the period. A support order shall be counted as established only when the appropriate court has issued an order for child support, including an order for temporary child support, or an order for medical support.

(4) The total cost of administering the local child support agency, including the federal, state, and county share of the costs, and the federal and state incentives received by each county. The total cost of administering the program shall be broken down by the following:

(A) The direct costs of the program, broken down further by total employee salaries and benefits, a list of the number of employees broken down into at least the following categories: attorneys, administrators, caseworkers, investigators, and clerical support; contractor costs; space charges; and payments to other county agencies. Employee salaries and numbers need only be reported in the annual report.

(B) The indirect costs, showing all overhead charges.

(5) In addition, the local child support agency shall report monthly on measurements developed by the department that provide data on the following:

(A) Locating obligors.

(B) Obtaining and enforcing medical support.

(C) Providing customer service.

(D) Any other measurements that the director determines to be an appropriate determination of a local child support agency's performance.

(6) A county may apply for an exemption from any or all of the reporting requirements of this subdivision for a fiscal year by submitting an application for the exemption to the department at least three months prior to the commencement of the fiscal year or quarter for which the exemption is sought. A county shall provide a separate justification for each data element under this subdivision for which the county is seeking an exemption and the cost to the county of providing the data. The department may not grant an exemption for more than one year. The department may grant a single exemption only if both of the following conditions are met:

(A) The county cannot compile the data being sought through its existing automated system or systems.

(B) The county cannot compile the data being sought through manual means or through an enhanced automated system or systems without significantly harming the child support collection efforts of the county.

(d) After implementation of the statewide automated system, in addition to the information required by subdivision (b), the Department of Child Support Services shall collect, on a monthly basis, from each county that is participating in the state incentive program described in Section 17704, information on the county child support enforcement program beginning with the 1998–99 fiscal year or a later fiscal year, as appropriate, and for each subsequent fiscal year, and shall report semiannually on all of the following measurements:

(1) For each of the following support collection categories, the number of cases with support collected shall include only the number of cases actually receiving a collection, not the number of payments received.

(A)(i) The number of cases with collections for current support.

(ii) The number of cases with arrears collections only.

(iii) The number of cases with both current support and arrears collections.

(B) For cases with current support only due:

(i) The number of cases in which the full amount of current support owed was collected.

(ii) The number of cases in which some amount of current support, but less than the full amount of support owed, was collected.

(iii) The number of cases in which no amount of support owed was collected.

(C) For cases in which arrears only were owed:

(i) The number of cases in which all arrears owed were collected.

(ii) The number of cases in which some amount of arrears, but less than the full amount of arrears owed, were collected.

(iii) The number of cases in which no amount of arrears owed were collected.

(D) For cases in which both current support and arrears are owed:

(i) The number of cases in which the full amount of current support and arrears owed were collected.

(ii) The number of cases in which some amount of current support and arrears, but less than the full amount of support owed, were collected.

(iii) The number of cases in which no amount of support owed was collected.

(E) The total number of cases in which an amount was due for current support only.

(F) The total number of cases in which an amount was due for both current support and arrears.

(G) The total number of cases in which an amount was due for arrears only.

(H) For cases with current support due, the number of cases without orders for medical support and the number of cases with an order for medical support.

(2) The number of alleged fathers or obligors who were served with a summons and complaint to establish paternity or a support order, and the number of alleged fathers or obligors for whom it is required that paternity or a support order be established. In order to be counted under this

paragraph, the alleged father or obligor shall be successfully served with process. An alleged father shall be counted under this paragraph only once if he is served with process simultaneously for both a paternity and a support order proceeding for the same child or children. For purposes of this paragraph, a support order shall include a medical support order.

(3) The number of new asset seizures or successful initial collections on a wage assignment for purposes of child support collection. For purposes of this paragraph, a collection made on a wage assignment shall be counted only once for each wage assignment issued.

(4) The number of children requiring paternity establishment and the number of children for whom paternity has been established during the period. Paternity may only be established once for each child. Any child for whom paternity is not at issue shall not be counted in the number of children for whom paternity has been established. For this purpose, paternity is not at issue if the parents were married and neither parent challenges paternity or a voluntary paternity declaration has been executed by the parents prior to the local child support agency obtaining the case and neither parent challenges paternity.

(5) The number of cases requiring that a support order be established and the number of cases that had a support order established during the period. A support order shall be counted as established only when the appropriate court has issued an order for child support, including an order for temporary child support, or an order for medical support.

(6) The total cost of administering the local child support agency, including the federal, state, and county share of the costs and the federal and state incentives received by each county. The total cost of administering the program shall be broken down by the following:

(A) The direct costs of the program, broken down further by total employee salaries and benefits, a list of the number of employees broken down into at least the following categories: attorneys, administrators, caseworkers, investigators, and clerical support; contractor costs; space charges; and payments to other county agencies. Employee salaries and numbers need only be reported in the annual report.

(B) The indirect costs, showing all overhead charges.

(7) The total child support collections due, broken down by current support, interest on arrears, and principal, and the total child support collections that have been collected, broken down by current support, interest on arrears, and principal.

(8) The actual case status for all cases in the county child support enforcement program. Each case shall be reported in one case status only. If a case falls within more than one status category, it shall be counted in the first status category of the list set forth below in which it qualifies. The following shall be the case status choices:

(A) No support order, location of obligor parent required.

(B) No support order, alleged obligor parent located and paternity required.

(C) No support order, location and paternity not at issue but support order must be established.

(D) Support order established with current support obligation and obligor is in compliance with support obligation.

(E) Support order established with current support obligation, obligor is in arrears, and location of obligor is necessary.

(F) Support order established with current support obligation, obligor is in arrears, and location of obligor's assets is necessary.

(G) Support order established with current support obligation, obligor is in arrears, and no location of obligor or obligor's assets is necessary.

(H) Support order established with current support obligation, obligor is in arrears, the obligor is located, but the local child support agency has established satisfactorily that the obligor has no income or assets and no ability to earn.

(I) Support order established with current support obligation and arrears, obligor is paying the current support and is paying some or all of the interest on the arrears, but is paying no principal.

(J) Support order established for arrears only and obligor is current in repayment obligation.

(K) Support order established for arrears only, obligor is not current in arrears repayment schedule, and location of obligor is required.

(L) Support order established for arrears only, obligor is not current in arrears repayment schedule, and location of obligor's assets is required.

(M) Support order established for arrears only, obligor is not current in arrears repayment schedule, and no location of obligor or obligor's assets is required.

(N) Support order established for arrears only, obligor is not current in arrears repayment, and the obligor is located, but the local child support agency has established satisfactorily that the obligor has no income or assets and no ability to earn.

(O) Support order established for arrears only and obligor is repaying some or all of the interest, but no principal.

(P) Other, if necessary, to be defined in the regulations promulgated under subdivision (e).

(e) Upon implementation of the statewide automated system, or at the time that the department determines that compliance with this subdivision is possible, whichever is earlier, each county that is participating in the state incentive program described in Section 17704 shall collect and report, and the department shall compile for each participating county, information on the county child support program in each fiscal year, all of the following data, in a manner that facilitates comparison of counties and the entire state, except that the department may eliminate or modify the requirement to report any data mandated to be reported pursuant to this subdivision if the department determines that the local child support agencies are unable to accurately collect and report the information or that collecting and reporting of the data by the local child support agencies will be onerous:

(1) The number of alleged obligors or fathers who receive CalWORKs benefits, CalFresh benefits, and Medi–Cal benefits.

(2) The number of obligors or alleged fathers who are in state prison or county jail.

(3) The number of obligors or alleged fathers who do not have a social security number.

(4) The number of obligors or alleged fathers whose address is unknown.

(5) The number of obligors or alleged fathers whose complete name, consisting of at least a first and last name, is not known by the local child support agency.

(6) The number of obligors or alleged fathers who filed a tax return with the Franchise Tax Board in the last year for which a data match is available.

(7) The number of obligors or alleged fathers who have no income reported to the Employment Development Department during the third quarter of the fiscal year.

(8) The number of obligors or alleged fathers who have income between one dollar ($1) and five hundred dollars ($500) reported to the Employment Development Department during the third quarter of the fiscal year.

(9) The number of obligors or alleged fathers who have income between five hundred one dollars ($501) and one thousand five hundred dollars ($1,500) reported to the Employment Development Department during the third quarter of the fiscal year.

(10) The number of obligors or alleged fathers who have income between one thousand five hundred one dollars ($1,501) and two thousand five hundred dollars ($2,500) reported to the Employment Development Department during the third quarter of the fiscal year.

(11) The number of obligors or alleged fathers who have income between two thousand five hundred one dollars ($2,501) and three thousand five hundred dollars ($3,500) reported to the Employment Development Department during the third quarter of the fiscal year.

(12) The number of obligors or alleged fathers who have income between three thousand five hundred one dollars ($3,501) and four thousand five hundred dollars ($4,500) reported to the Employment Development Department during the third quarter of the fiscal year.

(13) The number of obligors or alleged fathers who have income between four thousand five hundred one dollars ($4,501) and five thousand five hundred dollars ($5,500) reported to the Employment Development Department during the third quarter of the fiscal year.

(14) The number of obligors or alleged fathers who have income between five thousand five hundred one dollars ($5,501) and six thousand five hundred dollars ($6,500) reported to the Employment Development Department during the third quarter of the fiscal year.

(15) The number of obligors or alleged fathers who have income between six thousand five hundred one dollars ($6,501) and seven thousand five hundred dollars ($7,500) reported to the Employment Development Department during the third quarter of the fiscal year.

(16) The number of obligors or alleged fathers who have income between seven thousand five hundred one dollars ($7,501) and nine thousand dollars ($9,000) reported to the Employment Development Department during the third quarter of the fiscal year.

(17) The number of obligors or alleged fathers who have income exceeding nine thousand dollars ($9,000) reported to the Employment Development Department during the third quarter of the fiscal year.

(18) The number of obligors or alleged fathers who have two or more employers reporting earned income to the Employment Development Department during the third quarter of the fiscal year.

(19) The number of obligors or alleged fathers who receive unemployment benefits during the third quarter of the fiscal year.

(20) The number of obligors or alleged fathers who receive state disability benefits during the third quarter of the fiscal year.

(21) The number of obligors or alleged fathers who receive workers' compensation benefits during the third quarter of the fiscal year.

(22) The number of obligors or alleged fathers who receive Social Security Disability Insurance benefits during the third quarter of the fiscal year.

(23) The number of obligors or alleged fathers who receive Supplemental Security Income/State Supplementary Program for the Aged, Blind and Disabled benefits during the third quarter of the fiscal year.

(f) The department, in consultation with the Legislative Analyst's Office, the Judicial Council, the California Family Support Council, and child support advocates, shall develop regulations to ensure that all local child support agencies report the data required by this section uniformly and consistently throughout California.

(g) For each federal fiscal year, the department shall provide the information for all participating counties to each member of a county board of supervisors, county executive officer, local child support agency, and the appropriate policy committees and fiscal committees of the Legislature on or before June 30, of each fiscal year. The department shall provide data semiannually, based on the federal fiscal year, on or before December 31, of each year. The department shall present the information in a manner that facilitates comparison of county performance.

(h) For purposes of this section, "case" means a noncustodial parent, whether mother, father, or putative father, who is, or eventually may be, obligated under law for support of a child or children. For purposes of this definition, a noncustodial parent shall be counted once for each family that has a dependent child he or she may be obligated to support.

(i) This section shall be operative only for as long as Section 17704 requires participating counties to report data to the department. *(Added by Stats.1999, c. 478 (A.B.196), § 1. Amended by Stats.1999, c. 480 (S.B.542), § 20; Stats. 2002, c. 927 (A.B.3032), § 7; Stats.2003, c. 308 (A.B.738), § 4; Stats.2004, c. 183 (A.B.3082), § 96; Stats.2011, c. 227 (A.B.1400), § 5.)*

Operative Effect

By its own terms, this section is operative only for as long as Family Code Section 17704 requires participating counties to report data to the department.

Research References

Treatises and Practice Aids

Witkin, California Summary 10th Husband and Wife § 310, Local Child Support Agency.

§ 17601. Performance data to be provided to Legislature

The department shall provide to the Legislature actual performance data on child support collections within 60 days of the end of each quarter. This data shall include all comparative data for managing program performance currently provided to local child support agencies, including national, state, and local performance data, as available. The department shall prominently post the data on its Web site, and shall require all local child support agency Web sites to prominently post a link to the state Web site. The department shall update the Legislature during the annual budget subcommittee hearing process, commencing in 2008, on the state and local progress on child support federal performance measures and collections. *(Added by Stats.2007, c. 177 (S.B.84), § 1, eff. Aug. 24, 2007.)*

§ 17602. Performance standards for local agencies

(a) The department shall adopt the federal minimum standards as the baseline standard of performance for the local child support agencies and work in consultation with the local child support agencies to develop program performance targets on an annual federal fiscal year basis. The performance measures shall include, at a minimum, the federal performance measures and the state performance measures, as described in subdivision (c) of Section 17600. The program performance targets shall represent ongoing improvement in the performance measures for each local child support agency, as well as the department's statewide performance level.

(b) In determining the performance measures in subdivision (a), the department shall consider the total amount of uncollected child support arrearages that are realistically collectible. The director shall analyze, in consultation with local child support agencies and child support advocates, the current amount of uncollected child support arrearages statewide and in each county to determine the amount of child support that may realistically be collected. The director shall consider, in conducting the analysis, factors that may influence collections, including demographic factors such as welfare caseload, levels of poverty and unemployment, rates of incarceration of obligors, and age of delinquencies. The director shall use this analysis to establish program priorities as provided in paragraph (7) of subdivision (b) of Section 17306.

(c) The department shall use the performance-based data, and the criteria for that data, as set forth in Section 17600 to determine a local child support agency's performance measures for the quarter.

(d) The director shall adopt a three phase process to be used statewide when a local child support agency is out of compliance with the performance standards adopted pursuant to subdivision (a), or the director determines that the local child support agency is failing in a substantial manner to comply with any provision of the state plan, the provisions of this code, the requirements of federal law, the regulations of the department, or the cooperative agreement. The director shall adopt policies as to the implementation of each phase, including requirements for measurement of progress and improvement which shall be met as part of the performance improvement plan specified in paragraphs (1) and (2), in order to avoid implementation of the next phase of compliance. The director shall not implement any of these phases until July 1, 2001, or until six months after a local child support agency has completed its transition from the office of the district attorney to the new county department of child support services, whichever is later. The phases shall include the following:

(1) Phase I: Development of a performance improvement plan that is prepared jointly by the local child support agency and the department, subject to the department's final approval. The plan shall provide performance expectations and goals for achieving compliance with the state plan and other state and federal laws and regulations that must be reviewed and assessed within specific timeframes in order to avoid execution of Phase II.

(2) Phase II: Onsite investigation, evaluation and oversight of the local child support agency by the department. The director shall appoint program monitoring teams to make site visits, conduct educational and training sessions, and help the local child support agency identify and attack problem areas. The program monitoring teams shall evaluate all aspects of the functions and performance of the local child support agency, including compliance with state and federal laws and regulations. Based on these investigations and evaluations, the program monitoring team shall develop a final performance improvement plan and shall oversee implementation of all recommendations made in the plan. The local child support agency shall adhere to all recommendations made by the program monitoring team. The plan shall provide performance expectations and compliance goals that must be reviewed and assessed within specific timeframes in order to avoid execution of Phase III.

(3) Phase III: The director shall assume, either directly or through agreement with another entity, responsibility for the management of the child and spousal support enforcement program in the county until the local child support agency provides reasonable assurances to the director of its intention and ability to comply. During the period of state management responsibility, the director or his or her authorized representative shall have all of the powers and responsibilities of the local child support agency concerning the administration of the program. The local child support agency shall be responsible for providing any funds as may be necessary for the continued operation of the program. If the local child support agency fails or refuses to provide these funds, including a sufficient amount to reimburse any and all costs incurred by the department in managing the program, the Controller may deduct an amount certified by the director as necessary for the continued operation of the program by the department from any state or federal funds payable to the county for any purpose.

(e) The director shall report in writing to the Legislature semiannually, beginning July 1, 2001, on the status of the state child support enforcement program. The director shall submit data semiannually to the Legislature, the Governor, and the public, on the progress of all local child support agencies in each performance measure, including identification of the local child support agencies that are out of compliance, the performance measures that they have failed to satisfy, and the performance improvement plan that is being taken for each. *(Added by Stats.1999, c. 478 (A.B.196), § 1. Amended by Stats.1999, c. 480 (S.B.542), § 21; Stats. 2002, c. 927 (A.B.3032), § 8; Stats.2003, c. 308 (A.B.738), § 5.)*

§ 17604. Agency noncompliance with state plan; reduced federal funding

(a)(1) If at any time the director considers any public agency, that is required by law, by delegation of the department, or by cooperative agreement to perform functions relating to the state plan for securing child and spousal support and determining paternity, to be failing in a substantial manner to comply with any provision of the state plan, the director shall put that agency on written notice to that effect.

(2) The state plan concerning spousal support shall apply only to spousal support included in a child support order.

(3) In this chapter the term spousal support shall include support for a former spouse.

(b) After receiving notice, the public agency shall have 45 days to make a showing to the director of full compliance or set forth a compliance plan that the director finds to be satisfactory.

(c) If the director determines that there is a failure on the part of that public agency to comply with the provisions of the state plan, or to set forth a compliance plan that the director finds to be satisfactory, or if the state certifies to the director that the public agency is not in conformity with applicable merit system standards under Part 2.5 (commencing with Section 19800) of Division 5 of Title 2 of the Government Code, and that sanctions are necessary to secure compliance, the director shall withhold part or all of state and federal funds, including incentive funds, from that public agency until the public agency shall make a showing to the director of full compliance.

(d) After sanctions have been invoked pursuant to subdivision (c), if the director determines that there remains a failure on the part of the public agency to comply with the provisions of the state plan, the director may remove that public agency from performing any part or all of the functions relating to the state plan.

(e) In the event of any other audit or review that results in the reduction or modification of federal funding for the program under Part D (commencing with Section 652) of Subchapter IV of Title 42 of the United States Code, the sanction shall be assessed against those counties specifically cited in the federal findings in the amount cited in those findings.

(f) The department shall establish a process whereby any county assessed a portion of any sanction may appeal the department's decision.

(g) Nothing in this section shall be construed as relieving the board of supervisors of the responsibility to provide funds necessary for the continued operation of the state plan as required by law. *(Added by Stats.1999, c. 478 (A.B.196), § 1. Amended by Stats.1999, c. 480 (S.B.542), § 21.5; Stats.2000, c. 808 (A.B.1358), § 93, eff. Sept. 28, 2000; Stats.2013, c. 427 (A.B.1062), § 1.)*

Research References

Treatises and Practice Aids

Witkin, California Summary 10th Husband and Wife § 310, Local Child Support Agency.

ARTICLE 4. PROGRAM COSTS

§ 17701. Quality assurance and performance improvement program; minimum requirements; promulgation of regulations

(a) There is established within California's child support program a quality assurance and performance improvement program, pursuant to which local child support agencies, in partnership with the Department of Child Support Services, shall monitor and measure program performance and compliance, and ensure the implementation of actions necessary to meet state and federal requirements and to continuously improve the quality of child support program services.

(b) Under the direction and oversight of the department, each local child support agency shall implement a quality assurance and performance improvement program that shall include, at a minimum, all of the following:

(1) An annual planning process that incorporates statewide standards and requirements, and establishes local performance goals that the department and local agency agree are appropriate.

(2) The inclusion of local performance goals and other performance-related measures in the local child support agency's Plan of Cooperation agreement with the department.

(3) Implementation of actions necessary to promote the delivery of enhanced program services and improved performance.

(4) An ongoing self-assessment process that evaluates progress in achieving performance improvement and compliance with program requirements.

(5) Regular and ongoing oversight by the department, including onsite reviews and the provision of technical assistance.

(c) The department shall promulgate regulations to implement this section. *(Added by Stats.2003, c. 308 (A.B.738), § 6.)*

§ 17702. Assessment of county and state compliance with child support laws and regulations; eligibility for state incentives

(a) The department shall assess, at least once every three years, each county's compliance with federal and state child support laws and regulations in effect for the time period being reviewed, using a statistically valid sample of cases. Counties found to be out of compliance shall be assessed annually, until they are found to be in compliance. The information for the assessment shall be based on reviews conducted and reports produced by either state or county staff, as determined by the department.

In addition, in order to meet federal self-assessment requirements, the department shall conduct an annual assessment of the state's compliance, using a statistically valid statewide sample of cases.

(b) A county shall be eligible for the state incentives under Section 17704 only if the department determines that the county is in compliance with all federal and state laws and regulations or if the county has a corrective action plan in place that has been certified by the department pursuant to this subdivision. If a county is determined not to be in compliance the county shall develop and submit a corrective action plan to the department. The department shall certify a corrective action plan if the department determines that the plan will put the county into compliance with federal and state laws and regulations. A county shall be eligible for state incentives under Section 17704 only for any quarter the county remains in compliance with a corrective action plan that has been certified by the department.

(c) Counties under a corrective action plan shall be assessed on a quarterly basis until the department determines that they are in compliance with federal and state child support program requirements. *(Added by Stats.1999, c. 478 (A.B.196), § 1. Amended by Stats.2003, c. 308 (A.B.738), § 7.)*

§ 17702.5. Child Support Collections Recovery Fund

(a) The Child Support Collections Recovery Fund is hereby created in the State Treasury, and shall be administered by the department for the purposes specified in subdivision (c).

(b) Except as otherwise provided in this section, the fund shall consist of both of the following:

(1) All public moneys transferred by public agencies to the department for deposit into the fund, as permitted under Section 304.30 of Title 45 of the Code of Federal Regulations or any other applicable federal statutes.

(2) Any interest that accrues on amounts in the fund.

(c) Upon appropriation by the Legislature, all moneys in the fund shall be used to make payments or advances to local child support agencies of the federal share of administrative payments for costs incurred pursuant to this article.

(d) Upon repeal of this section, the Legislature intends that any moneys remaining in the fund shall be returned to the federal agency that provides federal financial participation to the department. *(Added by Stats.2001, c. 111 (A.B.429), § 7, eff. July 30, 2001.)*

§ 17703. Child Support Services Advance Fund; purpose; payments

(a) A revolving fund in the State Treasury is hereby created to be known as the Child Support Services Advance Fund. All moneys deposited into the fund are for the purpose of making a consolidated payment or advance to counties, state agencies, or other governmental entities, comprised of the state and federal share of costs associated with the programs administered by the Department of Child Support Services, inclusive of the payment of refunds. In addition, the fund may be used for the purpose of making a consolidated payment to any payee, comprised of the state and federal shares of local assistance costs associated with the programs administered by the Department of Child Support Services.

(b) Payments or advances of funds to counties, state agencies, or other governmental agencies and other payees doing business with the state that are properly chargeable to appropriations or other funds in the State Treasury, may be made by a Controller's warrant drawn against the Child Support Services Advance Fund. For every warrant so issued, a remittance advice shall be issued by the Department of Child Support Services to identify the purposes and amounts for which it was drawn.

(c) The amounts to be transferred to the Child Support Services Advance Fund at any time shall be determined by the department, and, upon order of the Controller, shall be transferred from the funds and appropriations otherwise properly chargeable.

(d) Refunds of amounts disbursed from the Child Support Services Advance Fund shall, on order of the Controller, be deposited in the Child Support Services Advance Fund, and, on order of the Controller, shall be transferred therefrom to the funds and appropriations from which those amounts were originally derived. Claims for amounts erroneously deposited into the Child Support Services Advance Fund shall be submitted by the department to the Controller who, if he or she approves the claims, shall draw a warrant in payment thereof against the Child Support Services Advance Fund.

(e) All amounts increasing the cash balance in the Child Support Services Advance Fund, that were derived from the cancellation of warrants issued therefrom, shall, on order of the Controller, be transferred to the appropriations from which the amounts were originally derived. *(Added by Stats.2000, c. 108 (A.B.2876), § 2, eff. July 10, 2000.)*

§ 17704. State and federal child support incentives

(a) For the 1998–99 fiscal year the department shall pay to each county a child support incentive payment. Every county shall receive the federal child support incentive. A county shall receive the state child support incentive if it elects to do both of the following:

(1) Comply with the reporting requirements of Section 17600 while federal financial participation is available for collecting and reporting data.

(2) Comply with federal and state child support laws and regulations, or has a corrective action plan certified by the department pursuant to Section 17702. The combined federal and state incentive payment shall be 13.6 percent of distributed collections. If the amount appropriated by the Legislature for the state incentives is less than the amount necessary to satisfy each county's actual incentives pursuant to this section, each county shall receive its proportional share of incentives.

(b)(1) Beginning July 1, 1999, the department shall pay to each county a child support incentive for child support collections. Every county shall receive the federal child support incentive. The combined federal and state incentive payments shall be 13.6 percent of distributed collections. In addition to the federal child support incentive, each county may also receive a state child support incentive. A county shall receive the state child support incentive if it elects to do both of the following:

(A) Comply with the reporting requirements of Section 17600 while federal financial participation is available for collecting and reporting data.

(B) Be in compliance with federal and state child support laws and regulations, or have a performance improvement plan certified by the department pursuant to Section 17702.

(2)(A) For purposes of paragraph (1), the federal incentive component shall be each county's share of the child support incentive payments that the state receives from the federal government, based on the county's collections.

(B)(i) Effective July 1, 1999, and annually thereafter, state funds appropriated for child support incentives shall first be used to fund the administrative costs incurred by local child support agencies in administering the child support program, excluding automation costs as set forth in Section 10085 of the Welfare and Institutions Code, after subtracting all federal financial participation for administrative costs and all federal child support incentives received by the state and passed on to the local child support agencies. The department shall allocate sufficient resources to each local child support agency to fully fund the remaining administrative costs of its budget as approved by the director pursuant to paragraph (9) of subdivision (b) of Section 17306, subject to the appropriation of funding in the annual Budget Act. No later than January 1, 2000, the department shall identify allowable administrative costs that may be claimed for reimbursement from the state, which shall be limited to reasonable amounts in relation to the scope of services and the total funds available. If the total amount of administrative costs claimed in any year exceeds the amount appropriated in the Budget Act, the amount provided to local child support agencies shall be reduced by the percentage necessary to ensure that projected General Fund expenditures do not exceed the amount authorized in the Budget Act.

(ii) Effective July 1, 2001, and annually thereafter, after allowable administrative costs are funded under clause (i), the department shall use any remaining unallocated incentive funds appropriated from the prior fiscal year which are hereby reappropriated to implement an incentive program that rewards up to 10 local child support agencies in each year, based on their performance or increase in performance on one or more of the federal performance standards set forth in Section 458 of the federal Social Security Act (42 U.S.C. Sec. 658), or state performance standards set forth in subdivision (a) of Section 17602, as determined by the department. The department shall determine the number of local agencies that receive state incentive funds under this program, subject to a maximum of 10 agencies and shall determine the amount received by each local agency based on the availability of funds and each local child support agency's proportional share based on the performance standard or standards used.

(iii) Any funds received pursuant to this subdivision shall be used only for child support enforcement activities.

(c) Each county shall continue to receive its federal child support incentive funding whether or not it elects to participate in the state child support incentive funding program.

(d) The department shall provide incentive funds pursuant to this section only during any fiscal year in which funding is provided for that purpose in the Budget Act. *(Added by Stats.1999, c. 478 (A.B.196), § 1. Amended by Stats.1999, c. 480 (S.B.542), § 23; Stats.2001, c. 111 (A.B.429), § 8, eff. July 30, 2001; Stats.2002, c. 927 (A.B.3032), § 10; Stats.2003, c. 308 (A.B.738), § 8.)*

§ 17706. Counties with 10 best performance standards; additional incentives

(a) It is the intent of the Legislature to encourage counties to elevate the visibility and significance of the child support enforcement program in the county. To advance this goal, effective July 1, 2000, the counties with the 10 best performance standards pursuant to clause (ii) of subparagraph (B) of paragraph (2) of subdivision (b) of Section 17704 shall receive an additional 5 percent of the state's share of those counties' collections that are used to reduce or repay aid that is paid pursuant to Article 6 (commencing with Section 11450) of Chapter 2 of Part 3 of Division 9 of the Welfare and Institutions Code. The counties shall use the increased recoupment for child support-related activities that may not be eligible for federal child support funding under Part D of Title IV of the Social Security Act, including, but not limited to, providing services to parents to help them better support their children financially, medically, and emotionally.

(b) The operation of subdivision (a) shall be suspended for the 2002–03, 2003–04, 2004–05, 2005–06, 2006–07, 2007–08, 2008–09, 2009–10, 2010–11, 2011–12, 2012–13, 2013–14, 2014–15, 2015–16, * * * 2016–17, 2017–18, and 2018–19 fiscal years. *(Added by Stats.1999, c. 478 (A.B.196), § 1. Amended by Stats.1999, c. 480 (S.B.542), § 24; Stats.2001, c. 111 (A.B.429), § 9, eff. July 30, 2001; Stats.2002, c. 1022 (A.B.444), § 1, eff. Sept. 28, 2002; Stats.2003–2004, 1st Ex.Sess., c. 7 (S.B.24), § 1, eff. May 5, 2003; Stats.2006, c. 75 (A.B.1808), § 9, eff. July 12, 2006; Stats.2007, c. 177 (S.B.84), § 2, eff. Aug. 24, 2007; Stats.2008, c. 759 (A.B.1279), § 17, eff. Sept. 30, 2008; Stats.2009, c. 140 (A.B.1164), § 67; Stats.2012, c. 47 (S.B.1041), § 2, eff. June 27, 2012; Stats.2015, c. 20*

(S.B.79), § 2, eff. June 24, 2015; Stats.2017, c. 24 (S.B.89), § 4, eff. June 27, 2017.)

§ 17708. Data submitted to department

(a) This section shall apply to any county that elects to participate in the state incentive program described in Section 17704.

(b) Each participating county child support enforcement program shall provide the data required by Section 17600 to the department on a quarterly basis. The data shall be provided no later than 15 days after the end of each quarter.

(c) On and after July 1, 1998, a county shall be required to comply with the provisions of this section only during fiscal years in which funding is provided for that purpose in the Budget Act. *(Added by Stats.1999, c. 478 (A.B.196), § 1. Amended by Stats.2001, c. 755 (S.B.943), § 19, eff. Oct. 12, 2001.)*

§ 17710. Administrative expenditures

(a) Each county shall be responsible for any administrative expenditures for administering the child support program not covered by federal and state funds.

(b) Notwithstanding subdivision (a), effective July 1, 1991, to June 30, 1992, inclusive, counties shall pay the nonfederal share of the administrative costs of conducting the reviews required under former Section 15200.8 of the Welfare and Institutions Code from the savings counties will obtain as a result of the reduction in the maximum aid payments specified in Section 11450. Effective July 1, 1992, to June 30, 1993, inclusive, the state shall pay the nonfederal share of administrative costs of conducting the reviews required under former Section 15200.8 of the Welfare and Institutions Code. Funding for county costs after June 30, 1993, shall be subject to the availability of funds in the annual Budget Act. *(Added by Stats.1999, c. 478 (A.B.196), § 1. Amended by Stats.1999, c. 479 (A.B.150), § 1, eff. Sept. 27, 1999, operative Jan. 1, 2000; Stats.1999, c. 480 (S.B.542), § 24.5; Stats.2016, c. 474 (A.B. 2882), § 26, eff. Jan. 1, 2017.)*

§ 17712. Child support commissioners and family law facilitators; Judicial Council costs

Notwithstanding subdivision (a) of Section 17708, and to the extent funds are appropriated by the annual Budget Act, funds shall be provided to the Judicial Council for the nonfederal share of costs for the costs of child support commissioners pursuant to Section 4251 and family law facilitators pursuant to Division 14 (commencing with Section 10000). The Judicial Council shall distribute the funds to the counties for the purpose of matching federal funds for the costs of child support commissioners and family law facilitators and related costs. Funds distributed pursuant to this section may also be used to offset the nonfederal share of costs incurred by the Judicial Council for performing the duties specified in Sections 4252 and 10010. *(Added by Stats.1999, c. 478 (A.B.196), § 1.)*

§ 17714. Excess funds

(a)(1) Any funds paid to a county pursuant to this chapter prior to June 30, 1999, which exceed the county's cost of administering the child support program of the local child support agency pursuant to Section 17400 to that date, hereafter referred to as "excess funds," shall be expended by the county only upon that program. All these excess funds shall be deposited by the county into a special fund established by the county for this purpose.

(2) Performance incentive funds shall include, but not be limited to, incentive funds paid pursuant to Section 17704, and performance incentive funds paid pursuant to Section 14124.93 of the Welfare and Institutions Code and all interest earned on deposits in the special fund. Performance incentive funds shall not include funds paid pursuant to Section 17706. Performance incentive funds shall be expended by the county only upon that program. All performance incentive funds shall be deposited by the county into a special fund established by the county for this purpose.

(b) All excess funds and performance incentive funds shall be expended by the county on the support enforcement program of the local child support agency within two fiscal years following the fiscal year of receipt of the funds by the county. Except as provided in subdivision (c), any excess funds or performance incentive funds paid pursuant to this chapter since July 1, 1992, that the department determines have not been spent within the required two-year period shall revert to the state General Fund, and shall be distributed by the department only to counties that have complied with this section. The formula for distribution shall be based on the number of CalWORKs cases within each county.

(c) A county that submits to the department a written plan approved by that county's local child support agency for the expenditure of excess funds or performance incentive funds shall be exempted from the requirements of subdivision (b), if the department determines that the expenditure will be cost-effective, will maximize federal funds, and the expenditure plan will require more than the time provided for in subdivision (b) to expend the funds. Once the department approves a plan pursuant to this subdivision, funds received by a county and designated for an expenditure in the plan shall not be expended by the county for any other purpose.

(d) Nothing in this section shall be construed to nullify the recovery and reversion to the General Fund of unspent incentive funds as provided in Section 6 of Chapter 479 of the Statutes of 1999. *(Added by Stats.1999, c. 478, § 1. Amended by Stats.2000, c. 808 (A.B.1358), § 94, eff. Sept. 28, 2000; Stats.2001, c. 755 (S.B.943), § 20, eff. Oct. 12, 2001.)*

CHAPTER 5. COMPLAINT RESOLUTION

§ 17800. Process; forms and procedures; complaint time limitations

Each local child support agency shall maintain a complaint resolution process. The department shall specify by regulation, no later than July 1, 2001, uniform forms and procedures that each local child support agency shall use in resolving all complaints received from custodial and noncustodial parents. A complaint shall be made within 90 days after the custodial or noncustodial parent affected knew or should have known of the child support action complained of. The local child support agency shall provide a written resolution of the complaint within 30 days of the receipt of the complaint. The director of the local child support agency may extend the period for resolution of the complaint an additional 30 days in accordance with the regulations adopted pursuant to Section 17804. *(Added by Stats.1999, c. 803 (A.B.472), § 2. Amended by Stats.2001, c. 755 (S.B.943), § 21, eff. Oct. 12, 2001.)*

Research References

Treatises and Practice Aids

Witkin, California Summary 10th Husband and Wife § 315, Complaint Resolution by Agency.

Witkin, California Summary 10th Husband and Wife § 331, Relief from Order Based on Mistaken Identity.

Witkin, California Summary 10th Husband and Wife § 334, in General.

§ 17801. State hearing

(a) A custodial or noncustodial parent who is dissatisfied with the local child support agency's resolution of a complaint shall be accorded an opportunity for a state hearing when any one or more of the following actions or failures to take action by the department or the local child support agency is claimed by the parent:

(1) An application for child support services has been denied or has not been acted upon within the required timeframe.

(2) The child support services case has been acted upon in violation of state or federal law or regulation or department letter ruling, or has not yet been acted upon within the required timeframe, including services for the establishment, modification, and enforcement of child support orders and child support accountings.

(3) Child support collections have not been distributed or have been distributed or disbursed incorrectly, or the amount of child support arrears, as calculated by the department or the local child support agency is inaccurate. The amount of the court order for support, including current support and arrears, is not subject to a state hearing under this section.

(4) The child support agency's decision to close a child support case.

(b) Prior to requesting a hearing pursuant to subdivision (a), the custodial or noncustodial parent shall exhaust the complaint resolution process required in Section 17800, unless the local child support agency has not, within the 30–day period required by that section, submitted a written resolution of the complaint. If the custodial or noncustodial parent does not receive that timely written resolution he or she may request a hearing pursuant to subdivision (a).

(c) A hearing shall be provided under subdivision (a) when the request for a hearing is made within 90 days after receiving the written notice of resolution required in Section 17800 or, if no written notice of resolution is provided within 30 days from the date the complaint was made, within 90 days after making the complaint.

(d)(1) A hearing under subdivision (a) shall be set to commence within 45 days after the request is received by the state hearing office, and at least 10 days prior to the hearing, all parties shall be given written notice of the time and place of the hearing. Unless the time period is waived by the complainant, the proposed hearing decision shall be rendered by the state hearing office within 75 days after the request for a state hearing is received by the state hearing office. The department shall have 15 days from the date the proposed decision is rendered to act upon the decision. When a hearing is postponed, continued, or reopened with the consent of the complainant, the time for issuance of the decision, and action on the decision by the department, shall be extended for a period of time consistent with the postponement, continuance, or reopening.

(2) For purposes of this subdivision, the "state hearing office" refers to the division of the office or agency designated by the department to carry out state hearings, that conducts those state hearings.

(e) To the extent not inconsistent with this section, hearings under subdivision (a) shall be provided in the same manner in which hearings are provided in Sections 10950 to 10967 of the Welfare and Institutions Code and the State Department of Social Services' regulations implementing and interpreting those sections.

(f) Pendency of a state hearing shall not affect the obligation to comply with an existing child support order.

(g) Any child support determination that is subject to the jurisdiction of the superior court and that is required by law to be addressed by motion, order to show cause, or appeal under this code shall not be subject to a state hearing under this section. The director shall, by regulation, specify and exclude from the subject matter jurisdiction of state hearings provided under subdivision (a), grievances arising from a child support case in the superior court which must, by law, be addressed by motion, order to show cause, or appeal under this code.

(h) The local child support agency shall comply with, and execute, every decision of the director rendered pursuant to this section.

(i) The director shall contract with the State Department of Social Services or the Office of Administrative Hearings for the provision of state hearings in accordance with this section.

(j) This section shall be implemented only to the extent that there is federal financial participation available at the child support funding rate set forth in Section 655(a)(2) of Title 42 of the United States Code. *(Added by Stats.1999, c. 803 (A.B.472), § 2. Amended by Stats.2002, c. 927 (A.B. 3032), § 10.5; Stats.2016, c. 474 (A.B.2882), § 27, eff. Jan. 1, 2017.)*

Implementation

Implementation of this section, see subd. (j).

Research References

Treatises and Practice Aids

Witkin, California Summary 10th Husband and Wife § 315, Complaint Resolution by Agency.

§ 17803. Director's final decision; review in superior court; fees and costs

The custodial or noncustodial parent, within one year after receiving notice of the director's final decision, may file a petition with the superior court, under Section 1094.5 of the Code of Civil Procedure, praying for a review of the entire proceedings in the matter, upon questions of law involved in the case. The review, if granted, shall be the exclusive remedy available to the custodial or noncustodial parent for review of the director's decision. The director shall be the sole respondent in the proceedings. No filing fee shall be required for the filing of a petition pursuant to this section. Any such petition to the superior court shall be entitled to a preference in setting a date for hearing on the petition. No bond shall be required in the case of any petition for review, nor in any appeal therefrom. The custodial or noncustodial parent shall be entitled to reasonable attorney's fees and costs, if he or she obtains a decision in his or her favor. *(Added by Stats.1999, c. 803 (A.B.472), § 2.)*

Commentary

L.K. v. Golightly, 199 Cal.App.4th 641, 131 Cal.Rptr.3d 159 (2011), review denied, holds that a trial court properly dismissed a child support obligee's tort action against a child support services department, because this section provides that the exclusive remedy for departmental mishandling of the obligee's child support account is a petition for review under Code of Civil Procedure section 1094.5.

Research References

Treatises and Practice Aids

Witkin, California Summary 10th Husband and Wife § 315, Complaint Resolution by Agency.

§ 17804. Time frames for process establishment and state hearing requirement implementation

Each local child support agency shall establish the complaint resolution process specified in Section 17800. The department shall implement the state hearing requirements specified in Section 17801 no later than July 1, 2001. *(Added by Stats.1999, c. 803 (A.B.472), § 2. Amended by Stats.2001, c. 755 (S.B.943), § 22, eff. Oct. 12, 2001.)*

Division 20

PILOT PROJECTS

Part 1

FAMILY LAW PILOT PROJECTS

CHAPTER 1. GENERAL PROVISIONS

§ 20000. Legislative findings and declarations

(a) The Legislature finds and declares the following:

(1) Child and spousal support are serious legal obligations. In addition, children are frequently left in limbo while their parents engage in protracted litigation concerning custody and visitation. The current system for obtaining child and spousal support orders is suffering because the family courts are unduly burdened with heavy case loads and personnel insufficient to meet the needs of increased demands on the courts.

(2) There is a compelling state interest in the development of a child and spousal support system that is cost-effective and accessible to families with middle or low incomes.

(3) There is a compelling state interest in first implementing such a system on a small scale.

(4) There is a compelling state interest in the development of a speedy, conflict-reducing method of resolving custody and visitation disputes.

(b) Therefore, it is the intent of the Legislature in enacting this part to provide a means for experimenting with and evaluating procedural innovations with significant potential to improve the California child and spousal support systems, and the system for mediation, evaluation, and litigation of custody and visitation disputes. *(Added by Stats.1993, c. 219 (A.B.1500), § 210.)*

Law Revision Commission Comments

Enactment [Revised Comment]

Section 20000 continues former Civil Code Section 4760 without substantive change. [23 Cal.L.Rev.Comm. Reports 1 (1993)].

Research References

Treatises and Practice Aids

Witkin, California Summary 10th Husband and Wife § 3, Statutory Framework.

§ 20001. Authorization of pilot projects; superior courts of Santa Clara and San Mateo Counties

The Superior Courts of the Counties of Santa Clara and San Mateo may conduct pilot projects pursuant to this part. Chapter 2 (commencing with Section 20010) shall govern the San Mateo County Pilot Project, and Chapter 3 (commencing with Section 20030) shall govern the Santa Clara County Pilot Project. *(Added by Stats.1993, c. 219 (A.B.1500), § 210.)*

Law Revision Commission Comments

Enactment [Revised Comment]

Section 20001 continues former Civil Code Section 4761 without substantive change. [23 Cal.L.Rev.Comm. Reports 1 (1993)].

§ 20002. Duration of projects

The duration of the pilot projects shall be two years. *(Added by Stats.1993, c. 219 (A.B.1500), § 210.)*

Law Revision Commission Comments

Enactment [Revised Comment]

Section 20002 continues former Civil Code Sections 4762 and 4780 without substantive change. [23 Cal.L.Rev.Comm. Reports 1 (1993)].

CHAPTER 2. SAN MATEO COUNTY PILOT PROJECT

§ 20010. San Mateo County Pilot Project; hearings subject to project

The San Mateo County Pilot Project shall apply to hearings on motions for temporary child support, temporary spousal support, and temporary health insurance issuable in proceedings under this code, where at least one party is unrepresented by counsel. *(Added by Stats.1993, c. 219 (A.B.1500), § 210.)*

Law Revision Commission Comments

Enactment [Revised Comment]

Section 20010 continues former Civil Code Section 4763 without substantive change. A reference to motions for temporary support or health insurance in "proceedings under this code" has been substituted for the former reference to proceedings under "this part," (meaning the former Family Law Act (former Part 5 (commencing with former Section 4000) of Division 4 of the Civil Code) and references to proceedings under Civil Code Section 7000 *et seq.* (Uniform Parentage Act) and former Code of Civil Procedure Section 540 *et seq.* (Domestic Violence Prevention Act). These are not substantive changes, since all the proceedings formerly referred to are contained in the Family Code. [23 Cal.L.Rev.Comm. Reports 1 (1993)].

§ 20011. Motions for temporary orders; time for hearing

Motions for temporary orders under this chapter shall be heard as soon as practicable, consistent with the rules governing other civil actions. *(Added by Stats.1993, c. 219 (A.B.1500), § 210.)*

Law Revision Commission Comments

Enactment [Revised Comment]

Section 20011 continues former Civil Code Section 4764 without substantive change. The reference to "this chapter" corrects what appears to have been an incorrect reference in the former Civil Code section. [23 Cal.L.Rev.Comm. Reports 1 (1993)].

§ 20012. Family Law Evaluator; duties

The court shall appoint a Family Law Evaluator, who shall be available to assist parties. By local rule the superior court may designate the duties of the Family Law Evaluator, which may include, but are not limited to, the following:

(a) Requiring litigants in actions which involve temporary child support, temporary spousal support, and temporary maintenance of health insurance in which at least one litigant is unrepresented, to meet with the Family Law Evaluator prior to the support hearing.

(b) Preparing support schedules based on standardized formulae accessed through existing up-to-date computer technology.

(c) Drafting stipulations to include all issues agreed to by the parties.

(d) Prior to, or at, any hearing pursuant to this chapter, reviewing the paperwork by the court, advising the judge whether or not the matter is ready to proceed, and making a recommendation to the court regarding child support, spousal support, and health insurance.

(e) Assisting the clerk in maintaining records.

(f) Preparing a formal order consistent with the court's announced oral order, unless one of the parties is represented by an attorney.

(g) Assisting the court with research and any other responsibilities which will enable the court to be responsive to the litigants' needs. *(Added by Stats.1993, c. 219 (A.B.1500), § 210.)*

Law Revision Commission Comments

Enactment [Revised Comment]

Section 20012 continues former Civil Code Section 4765 without substantive change. [23 Cal.L.Rev.Comm. Reports 1 (1993)].

§ 20013. Family Law Evaluator; cost to parties

The court shall provide the Family Law Evaluator at no cost to the parties. *(Added by Stats.1993, c. 219 (A.B.1500), § 210.)*

Law Revision Commission Comments

Enactment [Revised Comment]

Section 20013 continues former Civil Code Section 4766 without change. [23 Cal.L.Rev.Comm. Reports 1 (1993)].

§ 20014. Unrepresented party; evaluator requirement notice; stamped pleadings service

The clerk shall stamp all moving papers in which a party is not represented by counsel with a notice of a requirement to see the Family Law Evaluator. The unrepresented party shall serve the stamped pleadings on the other party. *(Added by Stats.1993, c. 219 (A.B.1500), § 210.)*

Law Revision Commission Comments

Enactment [Revised Comment]

Section 20014 continues former Civil Code Section 4767 without change. [23 Cal.L.Rev.Comm. Reports 1 (1993)].

§ 20015. Court hearing access; protocol adoption

The court shall adopt a protocol wherein all litigants, both unrepresented by counsel and represented by counsel, have ultimate access to a hearing before the court. *(Added by Stats.1993, c. 219 (A.B.1500), § 210.)*

Law Revision Commission Comments

Enactment [Revised Comment]

Section 20015 continues former Civil Code Section 4768 without change. [23 Cal.L.Rev.Comm. Reports 1 (1993)].

§ 20016. Informational booklet; publication option

The court may elect to publish a low-cost booklet describing this program. *(Added by Stats.1993, c. 219 (A.B.1500), § 210.)*

Law Revision Commission Comments

Enactment [Revised Comment]

Section 20016 continues former Civil Code Section 4769 without change. [23 Cal.L.Rev.Comm. Reports 1 (1993)].

§ 20017. Family Law Evaluator; licensure as attorney

The Family Law Evaluator shall be an attorney, licensed to practice in this state. *(Added by Stats.1993, c. 219 (A.B.1500), § 210.)*

Law Revision Commission Comments

Enactment [Revised Comment]

Section 20017 continues former Civil Code Section 4770 without change. [23 Cal.L.Rev.Comm. Reports 1 (1993)].

§ 20018. Temporary child support orders; compliance with uniform guidelines; basis in economic evidence

Orders for temporary support issued pursuant to this chapter shall comply with the statewide uniform guideline set forth in Article 2 (commencing with Section 4050) of Chapter 2 of Part 2 of Division 9 and shall be based on the economic evidence supplied by the parties or otherwise available to the court. *(Added by Stats.1993, c. 219 (A.B.1500), § 210.)*

Law Revision Commission Comments

Enactment [Revised Comment]

Section 20018 continues former Civil Code Section 4771 without substantive change. Language has been revised to conform to terminology of the statewide uniform guideline. The reference to "this chapter" corrects what appears to have been an incorrect reference in the former Civil Code section. [23 Cal.L.Rev.Comm. Reports 1 (1993)].

§ 20019. Child custody and visitation contested; mediation pursuant to § 3170

Where it appears from a party's application for an order under this chapter or otherwise in the proceedings that the custody of, or visitation with, a minor child is contested, the court shall set those issues for mediation pursuant to Section 3170. The pendency of the mediation proceedings shall not delay a hearing on any other matter for which a temporary order is required, including child support, and a separate hearing, if required, shall be scheduled respecting the custody and visitation issues following mediation in accordance with Section 3170. However, the court may grant a continuance for good cause shown. *(Added by Stats.1993, c. 219 (A.B. 1500), § 210.)*

Law Revision Commission Comments

Enactment [Revised Comment]

Section 20019 continues former Civil Code Section 4772 without substantive change. The reference to "this chapter" corrects what appears to have been an incorrect reference in the former Civil Code section. References to Section 3170 have been substituted for broader references to former Civil Code Section 4607. These are not substantive changes. [23 Cal.L.Rev.Comm. Reports 1 (1993)].

§ 20020. Contested proceedings; documents to be provided to the court

In a contested proceeding for temporary child or spousal support under this chapter, both the moving party and the responding party shall provide all of the following documents to the Family Law Evaluator, and to the court at the time of the hearing:

(a) Copies of the last two federal and state income tax returns filed.

(b) Paycheck stubs for all paychecks received in the four months immediately prior to the hearing. *(Added by Stats. 1993, c. 219 (A.B.1500), § 210.)*

Law Revision Commission Comments

Enactment [Revised Comment]

Section 20020 continues former Civil Code Section 4773 without change. The reference to "this chapter" corrects what appears to have been an incorrect reference in the former Civil Code section. [23 Cal.L.Rev.Comm. Reports 1 (1993)].

§ 20021. Contested proceedings; failure to provide documents; sanctions

A party who fails to submit documents to the court as required by Section 20020 may, in the court's discretion, not be granted the relief requested, or the court may impose evidentiary sanctions. *(Added by Stats.1993, c. 219 (A.B. 1500), § 210.)*

Law Revision Commission Comments

Enactment [Revised Comment]

Section 20021 continues former Civil Code Section 4774 without substantive change. A reference to Section 20020 has been substituted for the former reference to "this section." This is not a substantive change, since Section 20020 is the section requiring the submission of documents. [23 Cal.L.Rev.Comm. Reports 1 (1993)].

§ 20022. Tax return; review by other party; examination

The tax return submitted pursuant to Section 20020 may be reviewed by the other party. A party may be examined by the other party as to the contents of the tax return. *(Added by Stats.1993, c. 219 (A.B.1500), § 210.)*

Law Revision Commission Comments

Enactment [Revised Comment]

Section 20022 continues former Civil Code Section 4775 without substantive change. A reference to Section 20020 has been substituted for the former reference to "this section." This is not a substantive change, since Section 20020 is the section requiring the submission of the tax return. [23 Cal.L.Rev.Comm. Reports 1 (1993)].

§ 20023. Children for whom services are to be provided by district attorney pursuant to Welfare and Institutions Code section; limited waiver

(a) Except as provided in subdivision (c):

(1) Nothing in this chapter shall be construed to apply to a child for whom services are provided or required to be provided by a district attorney pursuant to Section 11475.5 of the Welfare and Institutions Code.[1]

(2) The court shall not hear or enter any order under this chapter in a matter involving such a child.

(b) Any order entered contrary to the provisions of subdivision (a) is void and without legal effect.

(c) For purposes of enabling a custodial parent receiving assistance under Chapter 2 (commencing with Section 11200) of Part 3 of Division 9 of the Welfare and Institutions Code to participate in a pilot project authorized by this chapter, the district attorney, upon the request of the custodial parent, may execute a limited waiver of the obligation or representation under Section 11475.1 of the Welfare and Institutions Code. These limited waivers shall be signed by both the district attorney and custodial parent and shall only permit the custodial parent to participate in the proceedings under this chapter. It is not the intent of the Legislature in enacting this section to limit the duties of district attorneys with respect to seeking child support payments or to in any way limit or supersede other provisions of this code respecting temporary child support. *(Added by Stats.1993, c. 219 (A.B.1500), § 210.)*

[1] So in chaptered copy. See Welfare and Institutions Code § 11475.1.

Law Revision Commission Comments

Enactment [Revised Comment]

Section 20023 continues former Civil Code Section 4776 without substantive change. In the second sentence of subdivision (c), the reference to "this chapter" corrects what appears to have been an incorrect reference in the former Civil Code section. In the last sentence of subdivision (c), a reference to "this code" has been substituted for the narrower reference to "this part," meaning the former Family Law Act (former Part 5 (commencing with former Section 4000) of Division 4 of the Civil Code). This is not a substantive change. See also Section 20010 (application of San Mateo County Pilot Project). [23 Cal.L.Rev.Comm. Reports 1 (1993)].

§ 20026. Pilot project; litigants served; savings and costs

(a) It is estimated that under the pilot project authorized by this chapter, approximately 2,200 litigants will be served annually and that the following savings will occur:

(1) The program would save 520 hours, or 65 days, of court time per year.

(2) There would be a concomitant saving of time by litigants due to the expedited proceedings and, in addition, there would be a saving to litigants of wages that would otherwise be lost due to time off from work.

(b) The estimated costs of the pilot project are as follows:

(1) The salaries of the Family Law Evaluator and any staff necessary for the evaluator to carry out his or her functions.

(2) The cost of a booklet, if any, describing the program.

(c) There would be no cost for the following:

(1) Computers, printers, or other equipment. This equipment is already available in the family law department.

(2) Training for the Family Law Evaluator or his or her staff. They will be trained by already existing judicial personnel. *(Added by Stats.1993, c. 219 (A.B.1500), § 210.)*

Law Revision Commission Comments

Enactment [Revised Comment]

Section 20026 continues former Civil Code Section 4778.5 without change. [23 Cal.L.Rev.Comm. Reports 1 (1993)].

CHAPTER 3. SANTA CLARA COUNTY PILOT PROJECT

§ 20030. Santa Clara County Pilot Project

The Superior Court of the County of Santa Clara may conduct a pilot project pursuant to this chapter. *(Added by Stats.1993, c. 219 (A.B.1500), § 210.)*

Law Revision Commission Comments

Enactment [Revised Comment]

Section 20030 continues former Civil Code Section 4779 without substantive change. [23 Cal.L.Rev.Comm. Reports 1 (1993)].

§ 20031. Pilot project; hearings subject to project

The pilot project applies to all hearings, for temporary or permanent child or spousal support, modifications thereof, health insurance, custody, or visitation in a proceeding for dissolution of marriage, nullity of marriage, legal separation of the parties, exclusive custody, or pursuant to the Uniform Parentage Act (Part 3 (commencing with Section 7600) of Division 12). *(Added by Stats.1993, c. 219 (A.B.1500), § 210.)*

Law Revision Commission Comments

Enactment [Revised Comment]

Section 20031 continues former Civil Code Section 4781 without substantive change. A reference to a proceeding for "dissolution of marriage, nullity of marriage, legal separation of the parties, [and] exclusive custody" has been substituted for the former reference to a proceeding under "this part," meaning the former Family Law Act (former Part 5 (commencing with former Civil Code Section 4000) of Division 4). This is not a substantive change. [23 Cal.L.Rev.Comm. Reports 1 (1993)].

§ 20032. Contested proceedings; hearing date; duty and failure to provide documents to the court; notices; continuance

(a) Each and every hearing in a proceeding described in Section 20031 in which child or spousal support is at issue, including related contempt matters, shall be set by the clerk of the court for hearing within 30 days of filing.

(b) At any hearing in which child or spousal support is at issue, each party, both moving and responding, shall bring to the hearing, copies of the last two federal and state income tax returns filed by the party and pay stubs from the last four full months immediately preceding the hearing received by the party, and shall serve those documents on the opposing party at least five days in advance of the hearing date. Willful failure to comply with these requirements or any of the requirements of this pilot project may result in a citation for contempt under Title 5 (commencing with Section 1209) of Part 3 of the Code of Civil Procedure, or in the court's discretion, the court may refuse to grant relief requested or may impose evidentiary sanctions on a party who fails to submit these documents. The clerk shall cause to be placed on the face sheet of any moving papers for child or spousal support at the time of filing, a notice informing the parties of the requirements of this section. The notice shall also inform the parties that prior to the hearing, they must meet with the Attorney-Mediator pursuant to Section 20034. That meeting may occur in advance of the hearing dates by agreement of the parties, or on the day of the hearing.

(c) No continuance of any hearing involving child or spousal support shall be granted by a court without an order setting an interim support level unless the parties stipulate otherwise or the court finds good cause therefor. *(Added by Stats.1993, c. 219 (A.B.1500), § 210.)*

Law Revision Commission Comments

Enactment [Revised Comment]

Section 20032 continues former Civil Code Section 4782 without substantive change. In subdivision (a), a reference to "a proceeding described in Section 20031" has been substituted for the former references to "this part," meaning the former Family Law Act (former Part 5 (commencing with former Civil Code Section 4000) of Division 4) and to former Civil Code Section 7000 *et seq.* (Uniform Parentage Act). This is not a substantive change. See Section 20031 & Comment. [23 Cal.L.Rev.Comm. Reports 1 (1993)].

§ 20033. Income and Expense Declaration use; suspension

The court may pass a local rule that suspends the use of the Income and Expense Declaration mandated by California Rule of Court 1285.50 [1] in some or all proceedings during the pendency of the pilot project, provided that substitute forms are developed and adopted to solicit substantially the same information in a simplified format. The court may, notwithstanding the adoption of a local form, require the use of the Income and Expense Declaration mandated by California Rule of Court 1285.50 [1] in appropriate cases on the motion of either party or on the court's own motion. *(Added by Stats.1993, c. 219 (A.B.1500), § 210.)*

[1] California Rules of Court, Rule 1285.50 was repealed eff. Jan. 1, 2003. See West's Judicial Council Forms Pamphlet for mandatory and optional forms adopted and approved by the Judicial Council.

Law Revision Commission Comments

Enactment [Revised Comment]

Section 20033 continues former Civil Code Section 4783 without substantive change. [23 Cal.L.Rev.Comm. Reports 1 (1993)].

§ 20034. Attorney–Mediator; licensure and experience; duties; litigant hearing access

(a) An attorney, known as an Attorney–Mediator, shall be hired to assist the court in resolving child and spousal support disputes, to develop community outreach programs, and to undertake other duties as assigned by the court.

(b) The Attorney–Mediator shall be an attorney, licensed to practice in this state, with mediation or litigation experience, or both, in the field of family law.

(c) By local rule, the superior court may designate the duties of the Attorney–Mediator, which may include, but are not limited to, the following:

(1) Meeting with litigants to mediate issues of child support, spousal support, and maintenance of health insurance. Actions in which one or both of the parties are unrepresented by counsel shall have priority.

(2) Preparing support schedules based on statutory guidelines accessed through existing up-to-date computer technology.

(3) Drafting stipulations to include all issues agreed to by the parties, which may include issues other than those specified in Section 20031.

(4) If the parties are unable to resolve issues with the assistance of the Attorney–Mediator, prior to or at the hearing, and at the request of the court, the Attorney–Mediator shall review the paperwork, examine documents, prepare support schedules, and advise the judge whether or not the matter is ready to proceed.

(5) Assisting the clerk in maintaining records.

(6) Preparing formal orders consistent with the court's announced order in cases where both parties are unrepresented.

(7) Serving as a special master to hearing proceedings and making findings to the court unless he or she has served as a mediator in that case.

(8) Assisting the court with research and any other responsibilities that will enable the court to be responsive to the litigants' needs.

(9) Developing programs for bar and community outreach through day and evening programs, video recordings, and other innovative means that will assist unrepresented and financially disadvantaged litigants in gaining meaningful access to family court. These programs shall specifically include information concerning underutilized legislation, such as expedited temporary support orders (Chapter 5 (commencing with Section 3620) of Part 1 of Division 9), modification of support orders (Article 3 (commencing with Section 3680) of Chapter 6 of Part 1 of Division 9), and preexisting, court-sponsored programs, such as supervised visitation and appointment of attorneys for children.

(d) The court shall develop a protocol wherein all litigants, both unrepresented by counsel and represented by counsel, have ultimate access to a hearing before the court. *(Added by Stats.1993, c. 219 (A.B.1500), § 210. Amended by Stats. 2009, c. 88 (A.B.176), § 40.)*

Law Revision Commission Comments

2009 Amendment

Enactment [Revised Comment]

Section 20034 continues former Civil Code Section 4784 without substantive change. [23 Cal.L.Rev.Comm. Reports 1 (1993)].

Subdivision (c)(9) of Section 20034 is amended to reflect advances in recording technology and for consistency of terminology. For a similar reform, see 2002 Cal. Stat. ch. 1068 (replacing numerous references to "audiotape" in Civil Discovery Act with either "audio technology," "audio recording," or "audio record," as context required). [37 Cal. L. Revision Comm'n Reports 211 (2007)].

§ 20035. Temporary child support orders; compliance with uniform guidelines; basis in economic evidence

Orders for temporary support issued pursuant to this chapter shall comply with the statewide uniform guideline set forth in Article 2 (commencing with Section 4050) of Chapter 2 of Part 2 of Division 9 and shall be based on the economic evidence supplied by the parties or otherwise available to the court. *(Added by Stats.1993, c. 219 (A.B.1500), § 210.)*

Law Revision Commission Comments

Enactment [Revised Comment]

Section 20035 continues former Civil Code Section 4785 without substantive change. Language has been revised to conform to terminology of the statewide uniform guideline. The reference to "this chapter" corrects what appears to have been an incorrect reference in the former Civil Code section. [23 Cal.L.Rev.Comm. Reports 1 (1993)].

§ 20036. Pilot project proceedings; exemption; judicial order

Upon motion by either party or on the court's own motion, any proceeding that would otherwise fall within this pilot project may by judicial order be exempted from its requirements. *(Added by Stats.1993, c. 219 (A.B.1500), § 210.)*

Law Revision Commission Comments

Enactment [Revised Comment]

Section 20036 continues former Civil Code Section 4786 without substantive change. [23 Cal.L.Rev.Comm. Reports 1 (1993)].

§ 20037. Children for whom services are to be provided by district attorney pursuant to Welfare and Institutions Code § 11475.1; limited waiver

(a) Except as provided in subdivision (c):

(1) Nothing in this chapter shall be construed to apply to a child for whom services are provided or required to be provided by a district attorney pursuant to Section 11475.1 of the Welfare and Institutions Code.

(2) The court shall not hear or enter any order under this chapter in a matter involving such a child.

(b) Any order entered contrary to subdivision (a) is void and without legal effect.

(c) For purposes of enabling a custodial parent receiving assistance under Chapter 2 (commencing with Section 11200) of Part 3 of Division 9 of the Welfare and Institutions Code to participate in a pilot project authorized by this chapter, the district attorney, upon the request of the custodial parent, may execute a limited waiver of the obligation of representation under Section 11475.1 of the Welfare and Institutions Code. These limited waivers shall be signed by both the district attorney and custodial parent and shall only permit the custodial parent to participate in the proceedings under this chapter. It is not the intent of the Legislature in enacting this section to limit the duties of district attorneys with respect to seeking child support payments or to in any way limit or supersede other provisions of this code respecting temporary child support. *(Added by Stats.1993, c. 219 (A.B.1500), § 210.)*

Law Revision Commission Comments

Enactment [Revised Comment]

Section 20037 continues former Civil Code Section 4787 without substantive change. In subdivision (c), a reference to "this code" has been substituted for the narrower reference to "this part," meaning the former Family Law Act (former Part 5 (commencing with former Section 4000) of Division 4 of the Civil Code). This is not a substantive change. [23 Cal.L.Rev.Comm. Reports 1 (1993)].

§ 20038. Mediation orientation class; mediation agreements; Early Resolution Project; extended evaluation; judicial settlement conference; trial

(a) In any case where either party has filed a motion regarding a custody or visitation dispute and has not yet scheduled an appointment for the mediation orientation class by the time of the hearing on the order to show cause, the court shall order all parties to go to Family Court Services that day to schedule an appointment. The mediation orientation shall be scheduled within 14 days. Mediation orientation shall be conducted by Family Court Services and shall include general information on the effect of separation and dissolution on children and parents, the developmental and emotional needs of children in those circumstances, time-sharing considerations and various options concerning legal and physical custody of children, the effect of exposure to domestic violence and extreme conflict on children and parents, the nature of the mediation process and other Family Court Services procedures, and related community resources.

(b) After the mediation orientation, the parties may elect to utilize private mental health professionals, in which case the parties or the court may modify the fast track time guidelines provided for in this section.

(c) If, after orientation, either party requests mediation, and both parties complete Family Court Services mediation petitions, an appointment shall be scheduled within four weeks after both petitions are submitted and both parties shall attend the mediation as scheduled.

(d) At the mediation, if the parties agree to all of the issues regarding custody or visitation, the mediator shall memorialize the agreement in writing, and shall mail copies of the document to the attorneys and parents. Unless written objections to the agreement are sent to Family Court Services within 20 days of mailing the agreement, it will be submitted to the court and become a court order. A copy of the order shall be sent with proof of service to the parties and attorneys by the Family Court.

(e) If mediation is completed and there are remaining disputes, the mediator shall write a memorandum of any partial agreement and shall outline the remaining disputes which shall be sent to the attorneys and parties acting in propria persona. The mediator shall refer the parties to the Early Resolution Project. The parties shall meet and confer within 14 days of the referral to determine if a solution can be formulated. If there are remaining issues to be settled after the meeting, an early resolution judicial conference shall be scheduled within 30 days of the request of either party.

(f) At the early resolution conference, the judge may take stipulations resolving the issues of custody or visitation. The judge may also request the staff of Family Court Services to provide assessments and expedited evaluations to be held on the same day as the conference, in which case the judge, upon stipulation of the parties, may also order a hearing as soon as the same day on the issues. The judge may also order counseling, a mental health special master, psychological testing, or an extended evaluation by Family Court Services or a private evaluator on some or all issues.

(g) When the court at the early resolution judicial conference orders an extended evaluation, the parties shall complete all paperwork, submit deposits to Family Court Services, or both, within five days of the early resolution judicial conference. An evaluator shall be assigned to the case within 10 days thereafter.

(h) Evaluation shall be completed within 60 days of assignment to the evaluator, and the evaluator shall submit a report and recommendations which include a proposed order resolving all disputed issues. This report shall be served by certified mail on the attorneys of record, or on the parties if they are appearing in propria persona. If there are objections to the proposed order, the parties shall file written objections, meet with the evaluator within 30 days of service of the report, and serve a copy of the order on Family Court Services within the 30-day period. If a stipulation is reached, it shall be filed with the court. If a dispute remains, a judicial settlement conference shall be scheduled within 14 days of the meeting with the evaluator. Parties, counsel, and the evaluator shall be present at this judicial settlement conference. If there is no resolution at this settlement conference, a trial shall be set within 30 days from the settlement conference by the settlement conference judge. If no objections are filed, Family Court Services shall file the proposed order with the court, and it shall become the court's order.

(i) For good cause shown, all deadlines in this section may be altered by the court. *(Added by Stats.1993, c. 219 (A.B.1500), § 210.)*

Law Revision Commission Comments

Enactment [Revised Comment]

Section 20038 continues former Civil Code Section 4788 without substantive change. [23 Cal.L.Rev.Comm. Reports 1 (1993)].

§ 20040. Informational booklet; publication

The court may elect to publish a low-cost booklet describing the program. *(Added by Stats.1993, c. 219 (A.B.1500), § 210.)*

Law Revision Commission Comments

Enactment [Revised Comment]

Section 20040 continues former Civil Code Section 4790 without change. [23 Cal.L.Rev.Comm. Reports 1 (1993)].

§ 20041. Child-related programs; coordination by court

The court shall centralize, augment, and coordinate all presently existing programs under the court's supervision that relate to children, including, but not limited to, mental health special masters, appointment of attorneys for children, supervised visitation, and other supporting personnel. *(Added by Stats.1993, c. 219 (A.B.1500), § 210.)*

Law Revision Commission Comments

Enactment [Revised Comment]

Section 20041 continues former Civil Code Section 4791 without substantive change. [23 Cal.L.Rev.Comm. Reports 1 (1993)].

§ 20043. Pilot project; litigants served; savings and costs; income

(a) It is estimated for Santa Clara County's participation in the pilot project authorized by this chapter, that 4,000 litigants will be served annually, and that the following savings will occur:

(1) With an estimated 20 percent reduction in the use of court time over the current system, the county would save approximately 178 hours per year of court time, or approximately 22 workdays per year.

(2) With an estimated cost savings in incomes of judges, court reporters, clerks, bailiffs, and sheriffs, the project is expected to save approximately twenty thousand dollars ($20,000) per year. Cases involving child support obligations which the district attorney's office was required to handle in one participating county, for the 1989–90 fiscal year, number 2,461. The average time spent on a typical child support order is approximately five hours. There is a potential of 12,500 man-hours per year that could be saved, resulting in a savings of three hundred sixty-seven thousand eight hundred seventy-five dollars ($367,875) per year in attorney salaries alone. This does not take into consideration costs for documents, filing, and other district attorney personnel.

(3) The average savings personally to litigants who otherwise would require private representation would be from fifty dollars ($50) to two hundred fifty dollars ($250) per hour of court time and other preparation work.

(b) The satisfaction of participating parties will be determined by requiring the litigants using the pilot project to fill out a simple exit poll. The response of at least 70 percent of those questionnaires will be analyzed to decide whether the program has been deemed satisfactory by the participants.

(c) The estimated cost of the program is as follows:

(1) The estimated salary for an Attorney-Mediator is sixty thousand dollars ($60,000) to sixty-five thousand dollars ($65,000) per year, plus an additional 25 percent of salary to cover the costs of benefits for that position. In addition, there may be other costs connected with this position for support staff at the court.

(2) The costs of exit polling and any informational materials to be handed out to the public by the Attorney-Mediator is undetermined and cannot be estimated.

(d) The estimated income to cover the costs of this program will be as follows:

(1) There are approximately 10,000 dissolution of marriage petitions filed in Santa Clara County each year. Of those cases, approximately one-third of them have responses filed. At the present time, it costs one hundred sixty-five dollars ($165) to have a petition for dissolution of marriage filed and one hundred twenty-seven dollars ($127) to have a response filed, for a cost differential of thirty-eight dollars ($38). By equalizing the response fee with the petition fee, income generated would be approximately one hundred twenty-five thousand four hundred dollars ($125,400) per

year. This does not include the cost of fourteen dollars ($14) for each responsive declaration filed to a motion or order to show cause, the annual number of which is significantly greater than 3,300. It is estimated that an additional fifty thousand dollars ($50,000) per year could be generated by equalizing the responsive fees to a motion or order to show cause with the filing of those motions. These fees generated would more than offset the costs of the program.

(2) It is also anticipated that the Attorney-Mediator will develop public information and outreach programs which will be paid for by any excess revenue generated from the pilot project and ultimately will result in savings to the public and the court. The public will save by not having to pay attorneys for certain information regarding child support matters, and the court will save by not having to educate the public from the bench, thus expediting the handling of support and custody cases.

(e) The cost of computers, printers, and other equipment will be defrayed by contributions. *(Added by Stats.1993, c. 219 (A.B.1500), § 210.)*

Law Revision Commission Comments

Enactment [Revised Comment]

Section 20043 continues former Civil Code Section 4793 without change. [23 Cal.L.Rev.Comm. Reports 1 (1993)].

CONSTITUTION OF THE STATE OF CALIFORNIA 1879

ARTICLE I. DECLARATION OF RIGHTS

§ 31. Discrimination based on race, sex, color, ethnicity, or national origin; gender-based qualifications in public employment, education, or contracting

Sec. 31. (a) The State shall not discriminate against, or grant preferential treatment to, any individual or group on the basis of race, sex, color, ethnicity, or national origin in the operation of public employment, public education, or public contracting.

(b) This section shall apply only to action taken after the section's effective date.

(c) Nothing in this section shall be interpreted as prohibiting bona fide qualifications based on sex which are reasonably necessary to the normal operation of public employment, public education, or public contracting.

(d) Nothing in this section shall be interpreted as invalidating any court order or consent decree which is in force as of the effective date of this section.

(e) Nothing in this section shall be interpreted as prohibiting action which must be taken to establish or maintain eligibility for any federal program, where ineligibility would result in a loss of federal funds to the State.

(f) For the purposes of this section, "State" shall include, but not necessarily be limited to, the State itself, any city, county, city and county, public university system, including the University of California, community college district, school district, special district, or any other political subdivision or governmental instrumentality of or within the State.

(g) The remedies available for violations of this section shall be the same, regardless of the injured party's race, sex, color, ethnicity, or national origin, as are otherwise available for violations of then-existing California antidiscrimination law.

(h) This section shall be self-executing. If any part or parts of this section are found to be in conflict with federal law or the United States Constitution, the section shall be implemented to the maximum extent that federal law and the United States Constitution permit. Any provision held invalid shall be severable from the remaining portions of this section. *(Added by Initiative Measure (Prop. 209, approved Nov. 5, 1996, eff. Nov. 6, 1996).)*

Research References

Treatises and Practice Aids

Witkin, California Summary 10th Constitutional Law § 967, Proposition 209: Affirmative Action Prohibited.

Witkin, California Summary 10th Constitutional Law § 971, Other Decisions.

Witkin, California Summary 10th Constitutional Law § 974, California Cases.

§ 32. Public Safety and Rehabilitation Act of 2016

SEC. 32. (a) The following provisions are hereby enacted to enhance public safety, improve rehabilitation, and avoid the release of prisoners by federal court order, notwithstanding anything in this article or any other provision of law:

(1) Parole Consideration: Any person convicted of a nonviolent felony offense and sentenced to state prison shall be eligible for parole consideration after completing the full term for his or her primary offense.

(A) For purposes of this section only, the full term for the primary offense means the longest term of imprisonment imposed by the court for any offense, excluding the imposition of an enhancement, consecutive sentence, or alternative sentence.

(2) Credit Earning: The Department of Corrections and Rehabilitation shall have authority to award credits earned for good behavior and approved rehabilitative or educational achievements.

(b) The Department of Corrections and Rehabilitation shall adopt regulations in furtherance of these provisions, and the Secretary of the Department of Corrections and Rehabilitation shall certify that these regulations protect and enhance public safety. *(Added by Initiative Measure (Prop. 57, § 3, approved Nov. 8, 2016, eff. Nov. 9, 2016).)*

RELATED CALIFORNIA STATUTES
BUSINESS AND PROFESSIONS CODE

Division 2

HEALING ARTS

CHAPTER 1. GENERAL PROVISIONS

ARTICLE 15. SEXUAL ORIENTATION CHANGE EFFORTS

§ 865. Definitions

For the purposes of this article, the following terms shall have the following meanings:

(a) "Mental health provider" means a physician and surgeon specializing in the practice of psychiatry, a psychologist, a psychological assistant, intern, or trainee, a licensed marriage and family therapist, a registered marriage and family therapist, intern, or trainee, a licensed educational psychologist, a credentialed school psychologist, a licensed clinical social worker, an associate clinical social worker, a licensed professional clinical counselor, a registered clinical counselor, intern, or trainee, or any other person designated as a mental health professional under California law or regulation.

(b)(1) "Sexual orientation change efforts" means any practices by mental health providers that seek to change an individual's sexual orientation. This includes efforts to change behaviors or gender expressions, or to eliminate or reduce sexual or romantic attractions or feelings toward individuals of the same sex.

(2) "Sexual orientation change efforts" does not include psychotherapies that: (A) provide acceptance, support, and understanding of clients or the facilitation of clients' coping, social support, and identity exploration and development, including sexual orientation-neutral interventions to prevent or address unlawful conduct or unsafe sexual practices; and (B) do not seek to change sexual orientation. *(Added by Stats.2012, c. 835 (S.B.1172), § 2.)*

§ 865.1. Prohibited actions

Under no circumstances shall a mental health provider engage in sexual orientation change efforts with a patient under 18 years of age. *(Added by Stats.2012, c. 835 (S.B. 1172), § 2.)*

Research References

Treatises and Practice Aids

Witkin, California Summary 10th Parent and Child § 289, in General.

§ 865.2. Unprofessional conduct of mental health provider; disciplinary action

Any sexual orientation change efforts attempted on a patient under 18 years of age by a mental health provider shall be considered unprofessional conduct and shall subject a mental health provider to discipline by the licensing entity for that mental health provider. *(Added by Stats.2012, c. 835 (S.B.1172), § 2.)*

CHAPTER 13. LICENSED MARRIAGE AND FAMILY THERAPISTS

ARTICLE 1. REGULATION

§ 4980.397. Applicants for licensure; required examinations; time for California law and ethics examination; eligibility for clinical examination

(a) Effective January 1, 2016, an applicant for licensure as a marriage and family therapist shall pass the following two examinations as prescribed by the board:

(1) A California law and ethics examination.

(2) A clinical examination.

(b) Upon registration with the board, a marriage and family therapist intern shall, within the first year of registration, take an examination on California law and ethics.

(c) A registrant may take the clinical examination only upon meeting all of the following requirements:

(1) Completion of all required supervised work experience.

(2) Completion of all education requirements.

(3) Passage of the California law and ethics examination.

(d) This section shall become operative on January 1, 2016. *(Added by Stats.2011, c. 387 (S.B.704), § 2, operative*

Jan. 1, 2013. Amended by Stats.2012, c. 799 (S.B.1575), § 26, operative Jan. 1, 2014; Stats.2013, c. 473 (S.B.821), § 22, operative Jan. 1, 2016.)

§ 4980.398. Passing scores required on specified examinations

(a) Each applicant who had previously taken and passed the standard written examination but had not passed the clinical vignette examination shall also obtain a passing score on the clinical examination in order to be eligible for licensure.

(b) An applicant who had previously failed to obtain a passing score on the standard written examination shall obtain a passing score on the California law and ethics examination and the clinical examination.

(c) An applicant who had obtained eligibility for the standard written examination shall take the California law and ethics examination and the clinical examination.

(d) This section shall become operative on January 1, 2016. *(Added by Stats.2011, c. 387 (S.B.704), § 3, operative Jan. 1, 2013. Amended by Stats.2012, c. 799 (S.B.1575), § 27, operative Jan. 1, 2014; Stats.2013, c. 473 (S.B.821), § 23, operative Jan. 1, 2016.)*

§ 4980.399. California law and ethics examination; participation prior to registration renewal; retaking examination; failure to pass within first renewal period; issuance of subsequent registration number

(a) Except as provided in subdivision (a) of Section 4980.398, each applicant and registrant shall obtain a passing score on a board-administered California law and ethics examination in order to qualify for licensure.

(b) A registrant shall participate in a board-administered California law and ethics examination prior to his or her registration renewal.

(c) Notwithstanding subdivision (b), an applicant who holds a registration eligible for renewal, with an expiration date no later than June 30, 2016, and who applies for renewal of that registration between January 1, 2016, and June 30, 2016, shall, if eligible, be allowed to renew the registration without first participating in the California law and ethics examination. These applicants shall participate in the California law and ethics examination in the next renewal cycle, and shall pass the examination prior to licensure or issuance of a subsequent registration number, as specified in this section.

(d) If an applicant fails the California law and ethics examination, he or she may retake the examination, upon payment of the required fees, without further application except as provided in subdivision (e).

(e) If a registrant fails to obtain a passing score on the California law and ethics examination described in subdivision (a) within his or her renewal period on or after the operative date of this section, he or she shall complete, at a minimum, a 12–hour course in California law and ethics in order to be eligible to participate in the California law and ethics examination. Registrants shall only take the 12–hour California law and ethics course once during a renewal period. The 12–hour law and ethics course required by this section shall be taken through a continuing education provider as specified by the board by regulation, a county, state or governmental entity, or a college or university.

(f) The board shall not issue a subsequent registration number unless the registrant has passed the California law and ethics examination.

(g) Notwithstanding subdivision (f), an applicant who holds or has held a registration, with an expiration date no later than January 1, 2017, and who applies for a subsequent registration number between January 1, 2016, and January 1, 2017, shall, if eligible, be allowed to obtain the subsequent registration number without first passing the California law and ethics examination. These applicants shall pass the California law and ethics examination during the next renewal period or prior to licensure, whichever occurs first.

(h) This section shall become operative on January 1, 2016. *(Added by Stats.2011, c. 387 (S.B.704), § 4, operative Jan. 1, 2013. Amended by Stats.2012, c. 799 (S.B.1575), § 28, operative Jan. 1, 2014; Stats.2013, c. 473 (S.B.821), § 24, operative Jan. 1, 2016; Stats.2014, c. 316 (S.B.1466), § 18, eff. Jan. 1, 2015, operative Jan. 1, 2016; Stats.2015, c. 426 (S.B.800), § 38, eff. Jan. 1, 2016.)*

Division 3

PROFESSIONS AND VOCATIONS GENERALLY

CHAPTER 4. ATTORNEYS

ARTICLE 8.5. FEE AGREEMENTS

§ 6146. Limitations; periodic payments

(a) An attorney shall not contract for or collect a contingency fee for representing any person seeking damages in connection with an action for injury or damage against a health care provider based upon such person's alleged professional negligence in excess of the following limits:

(1) Forty percent of the first fifty thousand dollars ($50,000) recovered.

(2) Thirty-three and one-third percent of the next fifty thousand dollars ($50,000) recovered.

(3) Twenty-five percent of the next five hundred thousand dollars ($500,000) recovered.

(4) Fifteen percent of any amount on which the recovery exceeds six hundred thousand dollars ($600,000).

The limitations shall apply regardless of whether the recovery is by settlement, arbitration, or judgment, or whether the person for whom the recovery is made is a responsible adult, an infant, or a person of unsound mind.

(b) If periodic payments are awarded to the plaintiff pursuant to Section 667.7 of the Code of Civil Procedure, the court shall place a total value on these payments based upon the projected life expectancy of the plaintiff and include this amount in computing the total award from which attorney's fees are calculated under this section.

(c) For purposes of this section:

(1) "Recovered" means the net sum recovered after deducting any disbursements or costs incurred in connection with prosecution or settlement of the claim. Costs of medical care incurred by the plaintiff and the attorney's office-overhead costs or charges are not deductible disbursements or costs for such purpose.

(2) "Health care provider" means any person licensed or certified pursuant to Division 2 (commencing with Section 500), or licensed pursuant to the Osteopathic Initiative Act, or the Chiropractic Initiative Act, or licensed pursuant to Chapter 2.5 (commencing with Section 1440) of Division 2 of the Health and Safety Code; and any clinic, health dispensary, or health facility, licensed pursuant to Division 2 (commencing with Section 1200) of the Health and Safety Code. "Health care provider" includes the legal representatives of a health care provider.

(3) "Professional negligence" is a negligent act or omission to act by a health care provider in the rendering of professional services, which act or omission is the proximate cause of a personal injury or wrongful death, provided that the services are within the scope of services for which the provider is licensed and which are not within any restriction imposed by the licensing agency or licensed hospital. *(Added by Stats.1975, 2nd Ex.Sess., c. 1, p. 3967, § 24.2. Amended by Stats.1975, 2nd Ex.Sess., c. 2, p. 3989, § 1.185, eff. Sept. 24, 1975, operative Dec. 12, 1975; Stats.1981, c. 714, p. 2580, § 23; Stats.1987, c. 1498, § 2.)*

Research References

Forms

Cal. Transaction Forms - Bus. Transactions § 13:73, Independent Contractor Agreement for Outside Attorney--Contingency Fee Arrangement.

Cal. Transaction Forms - Bus. Transactions § 18:18, Approval and Limitation Of Attorney's Fees.

West's California Code Forms, Civil § 893 Form 1, Affirmative Defense--Rent Skimming.

Treatises and Practice Aids

Witkin, California Summary 10th Constitutional Law § 633, General Rule.

Witkin, California Summary 10th Contracts § 684, Miscellaneous Substantive Rights.

Witkin, California Summary 10th Torts § 942, Statutory Provisions.

Witkin, California Summary 10th Torts § 943, Constitutionality.

Witkin, California Summary 10th Torts § 944, Hybrid Action.

Witkin, California Summary 10th Torts § 945, Computation Of Fee.

Witkin, California Summary 10th Torts § 970, Attorneys' Fees When Periodic Payments Are Awarded.

Witkin, California Summary 10th Torts § 1046, in General.

Witkin, California Summary 10th Wills and Probate § 1070, in General.

§ 6147. Contingency fee contracts; duplicate copy; contents; effect of noncompliance; recovery of workers' compensation benefits

(a) An attorney who contracts to represent a client on a contingency fee basis shall, at the time the contract is entered into, provide a duplicate copy of the contract, signed by both the attorney and the client, or the client's guardian or representative, to the plaintiff, or to the client's guardian or representative. The contract shall be in writing and shall include, but is not limited to, all of the following:

(1) A statement of the contingency fee rate that the client and attorney have agreed upon.

(2) A statement as to how disbursements and costs incurred in connection with the prosecution or settlement of the claim will affect the contingency fee and the client's recovery.

(3) A statement as to what extent, if any, the client could be required to pay any compensation to the attorney for related matters that arise out of their relationship not covered by their contingency fee contract. This may include any amounts collected for the plaintiff by the attorney.

(4) Unless the claim is subject to the provisions of Section 6146, a statement that the fee is not set by law but is negotiable between attorney and client.

(5) If the claim is subject to the provisions of Section 6146, a statement that the rates set forth in that section are the maximum limits for the contingency fee agreement, and that the attorney and client may negotiate a lower rate.

(b) Failure to comply with any provision of this section renders the agreement voidable at the option of the plaintiff, and the attorney shall thereupon be entitled to collect a reasonable fee.

(c) This section shall not apply to contingency fee contracts for the recovery of workers' compensation benefits.

(d) This section shall become operative on January 1, 2000. *(Added by Stats.1993, c. 982 (S.B.645), § 5, operative Jan. 1, 1997. Amended by Stats.1994, c. 479 (A.B.3219), § 3, operative Jan. 1, 1997; Stats.1996, c. 1104 (A.B.2787), § 9, operative Jan. 1, 2000.)*

Research References

Forms

Cal. Transaction Forms - Bus. Transactions § 13:73, Independent Contractor Agreement for Outside Attorney--Contingency Fee Arrangement.

Cal. Transaction Forms - Bus. Transactions § 13:74, Letter Agreement for Independent Contractor Arrangement With Outside Attorney.

California Transactions Forms--Family Law § 6:50, Independent Adoption Retainer Agreement.

West's California Code Forms, Family § 2031 Form 1, Attorney's Fees Agreement.

West's California Code Forms, Probate § 10830, 10831 Form 1, Petition for Fixing and Allowing Compensation Of Personal Representative or Attorney for Personal Representative at Time Of Final Distribution.

Treatises and Practice Aids

Witkin, California Summary 10th Torts § 945, Computation Of Fee.

Witkin, California Summary 10th Wills and Probate § 534, Nature Of Allowance.

§ 6147.5. Contingency fee contracts; recovery of claims between merchants

(a) Sections 6147 and 6148 shall not apply to contingency fee contracts for the recovery of claims between merchants as defined in Section 2104 of the Commercial Code, arising from the sale or lease of goods or services rendered, or money loaned for use, in the conduct of a business or profession if the merchant contracting for legal services employs 10 or more individuals.

(b) (1) In the instances in which no written contract for legal services exists as permitted by subdivision (a), an attorney shall not contract for or collect a contingency fee in excess of the following limits:

(A) Twenty percent of the first three hundred dollars ($300) collected.

(B) Eighteen percent of the next one thousand seven hundred dollars ($1,700) collected.

(C) Thirteen percent of sums collected in excess of two thousand dollars ($2,000).

(2) However, the following minimum charges may be charged and collected:

(A) Twenty-five dollars ($25) in collections of seventy-five dollars ($75) to one hundred twenty-five dollars ($125).

(B) Thirty-three and one-third percent of collections less than seventy-five dollars ($75). *(Added by Stats.1990, c. 713 (S.B.2606), § 1.)*

Research References

Forms

Cal. Transaction Forms - Bus. Transactions § 18:18, Approval and Limitation Of Attorney's Fees.

§ 6148. Contracts for services in cases not coming within § 6147; bills rendered by attorney; contents; failure to comply

(a) In any case not coming within Section 6147 in which it is reasonably foreseeable that total expense to a client, including attorney fees, will exceed one thousand dollars ($1,000), the contract for services in the case shall be in writing. At the time the contract is entered into, the attorney shall provide a duplicate copy of the contract signed by both the attorney and the client, or the client's guardian or representative, to the client or to the client's guardian or representative. The written contract shall contain all of the following:

(1) Any basis of compensation including, but not limited to, hourly rates, statutory fees or flat fees, and other standard rates, fees, and charges applicable to the case.

(2) The general nature of the legal services to be provided to the client.

(3) The respective responsibilities of the attorney and the client as to the performance of the contract.

(b) All bills rendered by an attorney to a client shall clearly state the basis thereof. Bills for the fee portion of the bill shall include the amount, rate, basis for calculation, or other method of determination of the attorney's fees and costs. Bills for the cost and expense portion of the bill shall clearly identify the costs and expenses incurred and the amount of the costs and expenses. Upon request by the client, the attorney shall provide a bill to the client no later than 10 days following the request unless the attorney has provided a bill to the client within 31 days prior to the request, in which case the attorney may provide a bill to the client no later than 31 days following the date the most recent bill was provided. The client is entitled to make similar requests at intervals of no less than 30 days following the initial request. In providing responses to client requests for billing information, the attorney may use billing data that is currently effective on the date of the request, or, if any fees or costs to that date cannot be accurately determined, they shall be described and estimated.

(c) Failure to comply with any provision of this section renders the agreement voidable at the option of the client, and the attorney shall, upon the agreement being voided, be entitled to collect a reasonable fee.

(d) This section shall not apply to any of the following:

(1) Services rendered in an emergency to avoid foreseeable prejudice to the rights or interests of the client or where a writing is otherwise impractical.

(2) An arrangement as to the fee implied by the fact that the attorney's services are of the same general kind as previously rendered to and paid for by the client.

(3) If the client knowingly states in writing, after full disclosure of this section, that a writing concerning fees is not required.

(4) If the client is a corporation.

(e) This section applies prospectively only to fee agreements following its operative date.

(f) This section shall become operative on January 1, 2000. *(Added by Stats.1993, c. 982 (S.B.645), § 6, operative Jan. 1, 1997. Amended by Stats.1994, c. 479 (A.B.3219), § 5, operative Jan. 1, 1997; Stats.1996, c. 1104 (A.B.2787), § 11, operative Jan. 1, 2000.)*

Research References

Forms

California Transactions Forms--Business Entities § 3:75, Establishment Of Attorney/Client Relationship.

California Transactions Forms--Business Entities § 3:76, Contents Of Fee Agreement.

California Transactions Forms--Business Entities § 3:82, Attorney/Client Fee Agreement With Retainer.

California Transactions Forms--Business Entities § 3:83, Engagement Letter.

California Transactions Forms--Business Entities § 3:84, Hourly Rate Fee Agreement Between Attorney and Client.

California Transactions Forms--Business Entities § 3:85, Attorney-Client Hourly Rate Fee Rate Letter Agreement.

California Transactions Forms--Estate Planning § 1:51, Statutory Requirements.
California Transactions Forms--Family Law § 1:15, Establishment Of Attorney/Client Relationship.
California Transactions Forms--Family Law § 1:16, Contents Of Fee Agreement.
California Transactions Forms--Family Law § 4:17, Establishment Of Attorney/Client Relationship.
California Transactions Forms--Family Law § 4:18, Contents Of Fee Agreement.
California Transactions Forms--Family Law § 6:39, Advising Prospective Adoptive Parents.
California Transactions Forms--Family Law § 6:45, Matters to Consider in Initial Interview and Representation Of Adoptive Parents.
California Transactions Forms--Family Law § 6:50, Independent Adoption Retainer Agreement.

Treatises and Practice Aids

Witkin, California Summary 10th Wills and Probate § 528, Percentage Of Value Of Estate.

§ 6149. Written fee contract as confidential communication

A written fee contract shall be deemed to be a confidential communication within the meaning of subdivision (e) of Section 6068 and of Section 952 of the Evidence Code. *(Added by Stats.1986, c. 475, § 8.)*

§ 6149.5. Third-party liability claim; settlement by insurer; notice to claimant; effect on action or defense

(a) Upon the payment of one hundred dollars ($100) or more in settlement of any third-party liability claim the insurer shall provide written notice to the claimant if both of the following apply:

(1) The claimant is a natural person.

(2) The payment is delivered to the claimant's lawyer or other representative by draft, check, or otherwise.

(b) For purposes of this section, "written notice" includes providing to the claimant a copy of the cover letter sent to the claimant's attorney or other representative that accompanied the settlement payment.

(c) This section shall not create any cause of action for any person against the insurer based upon the insurer's failure to provide the notice to a claimant required by this section. This section shall not create a defense for any party to any cause of action based upon the insurer's failure to provide this notice. *(Added by Stats.1994, c. 479 (A.B.3219), § 6.)*

ARTICLE 13. ARBITRATION OF ATTORNEYS' FEES

§ 6200. Establishment of system and procedure; arbitration and mediation; application of article; voluntary or mandatory nature; rules; immunity of arbitrator and mediator; powers of arbitrator; confidentiality of mediation

(a) The board of trustees shall, by rule, establish, maintain, and administer a system and procedure for the arbitration, and may establish, maintain, and administer a system and procedure for mediation of disputes concerning fees, costs, or both, charged for professional services by members of the State Bar or by members of the bar of other jurisdictions. The rules may include provision for a filing fee in the amount as the board may, from time to time, determine.

(b) This article shall not apply to any of the following:

(1) Disputes where a member of the State Bar of California is also admitted to practice in another jurisdiction or where an attorney is only admitted to practice in another jurisdiction, and he or she maintains no office in the State of California, and no material portion of the services were rendered in the State of California.

(2) Claims for affirmative relief against the attorney for damages or otherwise based upon alleged malpractice or professional misconduct, except as provided in subdivision (a) of Section 6203.

(3) Disputes where the fee or cost to be paid by the client or on his or her behalf has been determined pursuant to statute or court order.

(c) Unless the client has agreed in writing to arbitration under this article of all disputes concerning fees, costs, or both, arbitration under this article shall be voluntary for a client and shall be mandatory for an attorney if commenced by a client. Mediation under this article shall be voluntary for an attorney and a client.

(d) The board of trustees shall adopt rules to allow arbitration and mediation of attorney fee and cost disputes under this article to proceed under arbitration and mediation systems sponsored by local bar associations in this state. Rules of procedure promulgated by local bar associations are subject to review by the board or a committee designated by the board to ensure that they provide for a fair, impartial, and speedy hearing and award.

(e) In adopting or reviewing rules of arbitration under this section, the board shall provide that the panel shall include one attorney member whose area of practice is either, at the option of the client, civil law, if the attorney's representation involved civil law, or criminal law, if the attorney's representation involved criminal law, as follows:

(1) If the panel is composed of three members the panel shall include one attorney member whose area of practice is either, at the option of the client, civil or criminal law, and shall include one lay member.

(2) If the panel is composed of one member, that member shall be an attorney whose area of practice is either, at the option of the client, civil or criminal law.

(f) In any arbitration or mediation conducted pursuant to this article by the State Bar or by a local bar association, pursuant to rules of procedure approved by the board of trustees, an arbitrator or mediator, as well as the arbitrating association and its directors, officers, and employees, shall have the same immunity which attaches in judicial proceedings.

(g) In the conduct of arbitrations under this article the arbitrator or arbitrators may do all of the following:

(1) Take and hear evidence pertaining to the proceeding.

(2) Administer oaths and affirmations.

(3) Issue subpoenas for the attendance of witnesses and the production of books, papers, and documents pertaining to the proceeding.

(h) Participation in mediation is a voluntary consensual process, based on direct negotiations between the attorney and his or her client, and is an extension of the negotiated settlement process. All discussions and offers of settlement are confidential and shall not be disclosed pursuant to any state law, including, but not limited to, the California Public Records Act (Chapter 3.5 (commencing with Section 6250) of Division 7 of Title 1 of the Government Code), and may not be disclosed in any subsequent arbitration or other proceedings. *(Added by Stats.1978, c. 719, p. 2249, § 1. Amended by Stats.1984, c. 825, § 1; Stats.1989, c. 1416, § 1; Stats.1990, c. 483 (S.B.2066), § 5; Stats.1990, c. 1020 (A.B.2682), § 2; Stats.1993, c. 1262 (A.B.1272), § 1; Stats.1994, c. 479 (A.B. 3219), § 8; Stats.1996, c. 1104 (A.B.2787), § 12; Stats.2009, c. 54 (S.B.544), § 1; Stats.2011, c. 417 (S.B.163), § 55; Stats.2015, c. 537 (S.B.387), § 17, eff. Jan. 1, 2016.)*

Commentary

In *Schatz v. Allen, Matkins, Leck, Gamble, & Mallory, LLP, 45 Cal.4th 557, 87 Cal.Rptr.3d 700, 198 P.3d 1109 (2009)*, the California Supreme Court held that a client who chooses arbitration under this article may not invoke the section 6204 right to a trial de novo after the conclusion of arbitration, if doing so would defeat an attorney's motion to compel contractual arbitration under the California Arbitration Act (Code of Civil Procedure § 1280 et seq.).

Research References

Forms

California Practice Guide: Rutter Family Law Forms Form 1:14, Attorney Fees and Costs Agreement.

California Transactions Forms--Business Entities § 3:76, Contents Of Fee Agreement.

California Transactions Forms--Business Entities § 3:86, Engagement Letter for Outside General Counsel Services--With Founder's Conflict Waiver.

Cal. Transaction Forms - Bus. Transactions § 14:2, ADR Methods, Definitions, and Distinctions.

Cal. Transaction Forms - Bus. Transactions § 14:90, Agreement to Arbitrate All Differences Arising Out Of Contract.

Cal. Transaction Forms - Bus. Transactions § 14:91, Commercial Arbitration Agreement--Negotiation and Mediation Prerequisite.

Cal. Transaction Forms - Bus. Transactions § 14:92, Arbitration Agreement--Submission Of All Disputes to Arbitration.

Cal. Transaction Forms - Bus. Transactions § 13:73, Independent Contractor Agreement for Outside Attorney--Contingency Fee Arrangement.

Cal. Transaction Forms - Bus. Transactions § 14:79.70, State Bar Of California--Notice Of Client's Right to Arbitrate.

Cal. Transaction Forms - Bus. Transactions § 14:79.80, State Bar Of California--Request for Arbitration Of a Fee Dispute.

Cal. Transaction Forms - Bus. Transactions § 14:79.90, State Bar Of California--Rules Of Procedure for Fee Arbitrations and the Enforcement Of Awards.

California Transactions Forms--Estate Planning § 1:54, Drafting Principles.

California Transactions Forms--Family Law § 6:50, Independent Adoption Retainer Agreement.

California Transactions Forms--Family Law § 7:53, Fee Agreement for Surrogacy Client.

26 West's Legal Forms § 1:3, Statutes Mandating or Encouraging Alternative Dispute Resolution.

West's California Code Forms, Civil Procedure § 284 Form 9, Attorneys--Petition After Attorney-Client Fee Dispute Arbitration Award--Official Form.

West's California Code Forms, Civil Procedure § 284 Form 10, Attorneys--Information Regarding Rights After Attorney-Client Fee Dispute Arbitration Award--Official Form.

West's California Code Forms, Civil Procedure § 284 Form 11, Attorneys--Rejection Of Award and Request for Trial After Attorney-Client Fee Arbitration (Alternative Dispute Resolution)--Official Form.

West's California Code Forms, Family § 2031 Form 1, Attorney's Fees Agreement.

West's California Judicial Council Forms SC-101, Attorney Fee Dispute (After Arbitration) (Attachment to Plaintiff's Claim and Order to Go to Small Claims Court).

West's California Judicial Council Forms SC-132, Attorney-Client Fee Dispute (Attachment to Notice Of Entry Of Judgment).

West's California Judicial Council Forms ADR-103, Petition to Confirm, Correct, or Vacate Attorney-Client Fee Arbitration Award (Alternative Dispute Resolution).

West's California Judicial Council Forms ADR-104, Rejection Of Award and Request for Trial After Attorney-Client Fee Arbitration.

West's California Judicial Council Forms ADR-105, Information Regarding Rights After Attorney-Client Fee Arbitration.

West's California Judicial Council Forms SC-202A, Decision on Attorney-Client Fee Dispute (Small Claims).

Treatises and Practice Aids

Witkin, California Summary 10th Torts § 174, Persons Engaged in Alternative Dispute Resolution.

§ 6201. Notice to client and State Bar; stay of action; right to arbitration; waiver by client

(a) The rules adopted by the board of trustees shall provide that an attorney shall forward a written notice to the client prior to or at the time of service of summons or claim in an action against the client, or prior to or at the commencement of any other proceeding against the client under a contract between attorney and client which provides for an alternative to arbitration under this article, for recovery of fees, costs, or both. The written notice shall be in the form that the board of trustees prescribes, and shall include a statement of the client's right to arbitration under this article. Failure to give this notice shall be a ground for the dismissal of the action or other proceeding. The notice shall not be required, however, prior to initiating mediation of the dispute.

The rules adopted by the board of trustees shall provide that the client's failure to request arbitration within 30 days after receipt of notice from the attorney shall be deemed a waiver of the client's right to arbitration under the provisions of this article.

(b) If an attorney, or the attorney's assignee, commences an action in any court or any other proceeding and the client is entitled to maintain arbitration under this article, and the dispute is not one to which subdivision (b) of Section 6200 applies, the client may stay the action or other proceeding by serving and filing a request for arbitration in accordance with the rules established by the board of trustees pursuant to subdivision (a) of Section 6200. The request for arbitration shall be served and filed prior to the filing of an answer in the action or equivalent response in the other proceeding; failure to so request arbitration prior to the filing of an answer or equivalent response shall be deemed a waiver of the client's right to arbitration under the provisions of this article if notice of the client's right to arbitration was given pursuant to subdivision (a).

(c) Upon filing and service of the request for arbitration, the action or other proceeding shall be automatically stayed until the award of the arbitrators is issued or the arbitration is otherwise terminated. The stay may be vacated in whole or in part, after a hearing duly noticed by any party or the court, if and to the extent the court finds that the matter is not appropriate for arbitration under the provisions of this article. The action or other proceeding may thereafter proceed subject to the provisions of Section 6204.

(d) A client's right to request or maintain arbitration under the provisions of this article is waived by the client commencing an action or filing any pleading seeking either of the following:

(1) Judicial resolution of a fee dispute to which this article applies.

(2) Affirmative relief against the attorney for damages or otherwise based upon alleged malpractice or professional misconduct.

(e) If the client waives the right to arbitration under this article, the parties may stipulate to set aside the waiver and to proceed with arbitration. *(Added by Stats.1978, c. 719, p. 2249, § 1. Amended by Stats.1979, c. 878, p. 3062, § 1; Stats.1982, c. 979, p. 3557, § 1; Stats.1984, c. 825, § 2; Stats.1989, c. 1416, § 2; Stats.1990, c. 483 (S.B.2066), § 6; Stats.1993, c. 1262 (A.B.1272), § 2; Stats.1994, c. 479 (A.B. 3219), § 9; Stats.1996, c. 1104 (A.B.2787), § 13; Stats.2011, c. 417 (S.B.163), § 56.)*

Commentary

Relying on this section, the California Supreme Court held that a client who chooses arbitration under this article may not invoke the section 6204 right to a trial de novo after the conclusion of arbitration, if doing so would defeat an attorney's motion to compel contractual arbitration under the California Arbitration Act (Code of Civil Procedure § 1280 et seq.). *Schatz v. Allen, Matkins, Leck, Gamble, & Mallory, LLP, 45 Cal.4th 557, 87 Cal.Rptr.3d 700, 198 P.3d 1109 (2009).*

Research References

Forms

California Transactions Forms--Estate Planning § 1:54, Drafting Principles.

West's California Judicial Council Forms CM-180, Notice Of Stay Of Proceedings.

§ 6202. Disclosure of attorney–client communication or attorney's work product; limitation

The provisions of Article 3 (commencing with Section 950) of Chapter 4 of Division 8 of the Evidence Code shall not prohibit the disclosure of any relevant communication, nor shall the provisions of Chapter 4 (commencing with Section 2018.010) of Title 4 of Part 4 of the Code of Civil Procedure be construed to prohibit the disclosure of any relevant work product of the attorney in connection with: (a) an arbitration hearing or mediation pursuant to this article; (b) a trial after arbitration; or (c) judicial confirmation, correction, or vacation of an arbitration award. In no event shall such disclosure be deemed a waiver of the confidential character of such matters for any other purpose. *(Added by Stats.1978, c. 719, p. 2249, § 1. Amended by Stats.1982, c. 979, p. 3558, § 2; Stats.1984, c. 825, § 3; Stats.1996, c. 1104 (A.B.2787), § 14; Stats.2004, c. 182 (A.B.3081), § 1, operative July 1, 2005.)*

Law Revision Commission Comments

2004 Amendment

Section 6202 is amended to reflect nonsubstantive reorganization of the rules governing civil discovery. [33 Cal.L.Rev.Comm. Reports 971 (2003)].

§ 6203. Award; contents; damages and offset; fees and costs; finality of award; appellate fees and costs; attorney inactive status and penalties

(a) The award shall be in writing and signed by the arbitrators concurring therein. It shall include a determination of all the questions submitted to the arbitrators, the decision of which is necessary in order to determine the controversy. The award shall not include any award to either party for costs or attorney's fees incurred in preparation for or in the course of the fee arbitration proceeding, notwithstanding any contract between the parties providing for such an award or costs or attorney's fees. However, the filing fee paid may be allocated between the parties by the arbitrators. This section shall not preclude an award of costs or attorney's fees to either party by a court pursuant to subdivision (c) of this section or of subdivision (d) of Section 6204. The State Bar, or the local bar association delegated by the State Bar to conduct the arbitration, shall deliver to each of the parties with the award, an original declaration of service of the award.

Evidence relating to claims of malpractice and professional misconduct, shall be admissible only to the extent that those claims bear upon the fees, costs, or both, to which the attorney is entitled. The arbitrators shall not award affirmative relief, in the form of damages or offset or otherwise, for injuries underlying the claim. Nothing in this section shall be construed to prevent the arbitrators from awarding the client a refund of unearned fees, costs, or both previously paid to the attorney.

(b) Even if the parties to the arbitration have not agreed in writing to be bound, the arbitration award shall become binding upon the passage of 30 days after service of notice of the award, unless a party has, within the 30 days, sought a trial after arbitration pursuant to Section 6204. If an action has previously been filed in any court, any petition to confirm, correct, or vacate the award shall be to the court in which the action is pending, and may be served by mail on any party who has appeared, as provided in Chapter 4 (commencing with Section 1003) of Title 14 of Part 2 of the Code of Civil Procedure; otherwise it shall be in the same manner as provided in Chapter 4 (commencing with Section 1285) of Title 9 of Part 3 of the Code of Civil Procedure. If no action is pending in any court, the award may be confirmed, corrected, or vacated by petition to the court having jurisdiction over the amount of the arbitration award, but otherwise in the same manner as provided in Chapter 4 (commencing with Section 1285) of Title 9 of Part 3 of the Code of Civil Procedure.

(c) Neither party to the arbitration may recover costs or attorney's fees incurred in preparation for or in the course of the fee arbitration proceeding with the exception of the filing fee paid pursuant to subdivision (a) of this section. However, a court confirming, correcting, or vacating an award under this section may award to the prevailing party reasonable fees and costs incurred in obtaining confirmation, correction, or vacation of the award including, if applicable, fees and costs on appeal. The party obtaining judgment confirming, correcting, or vacating the award shall be the prevailing party except that, without regard to consideration of who the prevailing party may be, if a party did not appear at the arbitration hearing in the manner provided by the rules adopted by the board of trustees, that party shall not be entitled to attorney's fees or costs upon confirmation, correction, or vacation of the award.

(d)(1) In any matter arbitrated under this article in which the award is binding or has become binding by operation of law or has become a judgment either after confirmation under subdivision (c) or after a trial after arbitration under Section 6204, or in any matter mediated under this article, if: (A) the award, judgment, or agreement reached after mediation includes a refund of fees or costs, or both, to the client and (B) the attorney has not complied with that award, judgment, or agreement the State Bar shall enforce the award, judgment, or agreement by placing the attorney on involuntary inactive status until the refund has been paid.

(2) The State Bar shall provide for an administrative procedure to determine whether an award, judgment, or agreement should be enforced pursuant to this subdivision. An award, judgment, or agreement shall be so enforced if:

(A) The State Bar shows that the attorney has failed to comply with a binding fee arbitration award, judgment, or agreement rendered pursuant to this article.

(B) The attorney has not proposed a payment plan acceptable to the client or the State Bar.

However, the award, judgment, or agreement shall not be so enforced if the attorney has demonstrated that he or she (i) is not personally responsible for making or ensuring payment of the refund, or (ii) is unable to pay the refund.

(3) An attorney who has failed to comply with a binding award, judgment, or agreement shall pay administrative penalties or reasonable costs, or both, as directed by the State Bar. Penalties imposed shall not exceed 20 percent of the amount to be refunded to the client or one thousand dollars ($1,000), whichever is greater. Any penalties or costs, or both, that are not paid shall be added to the membership fee of the attorney for the next calendar year.

(4) The board shall terminate the inactive enrollment upon proof that the attorney has complied with the award, judgment, or agreement and upon payment of any costs or penalties, or both, assessed as a result of the attorney's failure to comply.

(5) A request for enforcement under this subdivision shall be made within four years from the date (A) the arbitration award was mailed, (B) the judgment was entered, or (C) the date the agreement was signed. In an arbitrated matter, however, in no event shall a request be made prior to 100 days from the date of the service of a signed copy of the award. In cases where the award is appealed, a request shall not be made prior to 100 days from the date the award has become final as set forth in this section. *(Added by Stats. 1978, c. 719, p. 2249, § 1. Amended by Stats.1982, c. 979, p. 3559, § 3; Stats.1984, c. 825, § 4; Stats.1989, c. 1416, § 3; Stats.1990, c. 483 (S.B.2066), § 7; Stats.1992, c. 1265 (S.B. 1405), § 5; Stats.1993, c. 1262 (A.B.1272), § 3; Stats.1996, c. 1104 (A.B.2787), § 15; Stats.2009, c. 54 (S.B.544), § 2; Stats.2011, c. 417 (S.B.163), § 57.)*

§ 6204. Agreement to be bound by award of arbitrator; trial after arbitration in absence of agreement; commencement of proceeding; prevailing party; effect of award and determination

(a) The parties may agree in writing to be bound by the award of arbitrators appointed pursuant to this article at any time after the dispute over fees, costs, or both, has arisen. In the absence of such an agreement, either party shall be entitled to a trial after arbitration if sought within 30 days, pursuant to subdivisions (b) and (c), except that if either party willfully fails to appear at the arbitration hearing in the manner provided by the rules adopted by the board of trustees, that party shall not be entitled to a trial after arbitration. The determination of willfulness shall be made by the court. The party who failed to appear at the arbitration shall have the burden of proving that the failure to appear was not willful. In making its determination, the court may consider any findings made by the arbitrators on the subject of a party's failure to appear.

(b) If there is an action pending, the trial after arbitration shall be initiated by filing a rejection of arbitration award and request for trial after arbitration in that action within 30 days after service of notice of the award. If the rejection of arbitration award has been filed by the plaintiff in the pending action, all defendants shall file a responsive pleading within 30 days following service upon the defendant of the rejection of arbitration award and request for trial after arbitration. If the rejection of arbitration award has been filed by the defendant in the pending action, all defendants shall file a responsive pleading within 30 days after the filing of the rejection of arbitration award and request for trial after arbitration. Service may be made by mail on any party who has appeared; otherwise service shall be made in the manner provided in Chapter 4 (commencing with Section 413.10) of Title 5 of Part 2 of the Code of Civil Procedure. Upon service and filing of the rejection of arbitration award, any stay entered pursuant to Section 6201 shall be vacated, without the necessity of a court order.

(c) If no action is pending, the trial after arbitration shall be initiated by the commencement of an action in the court having jurisdiction over the amount of money in controversy within 30 days after service of notice of the award. After the filing of such an action, the action shall proceed in accordance with the provisions of Part 2 (commencing with Section 307) of the Code of Civil Procedure, concerning civil actions generally.

(d) The party seeking a trial after arbitration shall be the prevailing party if that party obtains a judgment more favorable than that provided by the arbitration award, and in all other cases the other party shall be the prevailing party. The prevailing party may, in the discretion of the court, be entitled to an allowance for reasonable attorney's fees and costs incurred in the trial after arbitration, which allowance shall be fixed by the court. In fixing the attorney's fees, the court shall consider the award and determinations of the arbitrators, in addition to any other relevant evidence.

(e) Except as provided in this section, the award and determinations of the arbitrators shall not be admissible nor operate as collateral estoppel or res judicata in any action or proceeding. *(Added by Stats.1978, c. 719, p. 2249, § 1. Amended by Stats.1979, c. 878, p. 3063, § 2; Stats.1982, c. 979, p. 3559, § 4; Stats.1984, c. 825, § 5; Stats.1992, c. 1265 (S.B.1405), § 6; Stats.1996, c. 1104 (A.B.2787), § 16; Stats. 1998, c. 798 (A.B.1374), § 1; Stats.2009, c. 54 (S.B.544), § 3; Stats.2011, c. 417 (S.B.163), § 58.)*

Commentary

For extensive interpretation and application of this section, see *Giorgianni v. Crowley, 197 Cal.App.4th 1462, 129 Cal.Rptr.3d 546 (2011).*

In *Schatz v. Allen, Matkins, Leck, Gamble, & Mallory, LLP, 45 Cal.4th 557, 87 Cal.Rptr.3d 700, 198 P.3d 1109 (2009)*, the California Supreme Court held that a client who chooses arbitration under this article may not invoke this section's right to a trial de novo after the conclusion of arbitration, if doing so would defeat an attorney's motion to compel contractual arbitration under the California Arbitration Act (Code of Civil Procedure § 1280 et seq.).

§ 6204.5. Disqualification of arbitrator or mediator; notice of right to judicial relief

(a) The State Bar shall provide by rule for an appropriate procedure to disqualify an arbitrator or mediator upon request of either party.

(b) The State Bar, or the local bar association delegated by the State Bar to conduct the arbitration, shall deliver a notice to the parties advising them of their rights to judicial relief subsequent to the arbitration proceeding. *(Added by Stats. 1986, c. 475, § 9. Amended by Stats.1996, c. 1104 (A.B.2787), § 17.)*

§ 6206. Limitation of actions tolled; judicial resolution of disputes subject to arbitration; effect of bar on civil actions requesting same relief

The time for filing a civil action seeking judicial resolution of a dispute subject to arbitration under this article shall be tolled from the time an arbitration is initiated in accordance with the rules adopted by the board of trustees until (a) 30 days after receipt of notice of the award of the arbitrators, or (b) receipt of notice that the arbitration is otherwise terminated, whichever comes first. Arbitration may not be commenced under this article if a civil action requesting the same relief would be barred by any provision of Title 2 (commencing with Section 312) of Part 2 of the Code of Civil Procedure; provided that this limitation shall not apply to a request for arbitration by a client, pursuant to the provisions of subdivision (b) of Section 6201, following the filing of a civil action by the attorney. *(Added by Stats.1978, c. 719, p. 2249, § 1. Amended by Stats.1984, c. 825, § 6; Stats.2011, c. 417 (S.B.163), § 59.)*

Research References

Forms

Cal. Transaction Forms - Bus. Transactions § 14:90, Agreement to Arbitrate All Differences Arising Out Of Contract.

Cal. Transaction Forms - Bus. Transactions § 14:91, Commercial Arbitration Agreement--Negotiation and Mediation Prerequisite.

Cal. Transaction Forms - Bus. Transactions § 14:92, Arbitration Agreement--Submission Of All Disputes to Arbitration.

Cal. Transaction Forms - Bus. Transactions § 14:79.70, State Bar Of California--Notice Of Client's Right to Arbitrate.

Cal. Transaction Forms - Bus. Transactions § 14:79.80, State Bar Of California--Request for Arbitration Of a Fee Dispute.

Cal. Transaction Forms - Bus. Transactions § 14:79.90, State Bar Of California--Rules Of Procedure for Fee Arbitrations and the Enforcement Of Awards.

California Transactions Forms--Family Law § 6:50, Independent Adoption Retainer Agreement.

West's California Code Forms, Civil Procedure § 284 Form 9, Attorneys--Petition After Attorney-Client Fee Dispute Arbitration Award--Official Form.

West's California Code Forms, Civil Procedure § 284 Form 10, Attorneys--Information Regarding Rights After Attorney-Client Fee Dispute Arbitration Award--Official Form.

West's California Code Forms, Civil Procedure § 284 Form 11, Attorneys--Rejection Of Award and Request for Trial After Attorney-Client Fee Arbitration (Alternative Dispute Resolution)--Official Form.

CIVIL CODE

Division 1

PERSONS

Part 1

PERSONS WITH UNSOUND MIND

Law Revision Commission Comments

Repeal

Part 1 (commencing with Section 25) of Division 1 is replaced by a new Part 1 (commencing with Civil Code Section 38) (persons of unsound mind), by Civil Code Section 43.1 (child conceived but not yet born), by Code of Civil Procedure Section 340.4 (statute of limitations on pre-birth injury), and by Division 11 (commencing with Section 6500) of the Family Code (minors). [23 Cal.L.Rev.Comm. Reports 1 (1993)].

§ 38. Person without understanding; contract; necessaries; liability

A person entirely without understanding has no power to make a contract of any kind, but the person is liable for the reasonable value of things furnished to the person necessary for the support of the person or the person's family. *(Added by Stats.1992, c. 163 (A.B.2641), § 3, operative Jan. 1, 1994.)*

Law Revision Commission Comments

1992 Addition

Section 38 restates former Civil Code Section 38 without substantive change. [22 Cal.L.Rev.Comm. Reports 1 (1992)].

Research References

Forms

Cal. Transaction Forms - Bus. Transactions § 6:14, Persons Of Unsound Mind.
Cal. Transaction Forms - Bus. Transactions § 6:29, Undue Influence.
California Transactions Forms--Estate Planning § 13:2, Testamentary Capacity Versus Contractual Capacity.
California Transactions Forms--Estate Planning § 2:17, Definitions Of Capacity.
California Transactions Forms--Estate Planning § 11:48, Governing Contractual Provisions [CC §§ 1550 et seq., Fam C S721(B)].

Treatises and Practice Aids

Witkin, California Summary 10th Contracts § 50, in General.
Witkin, California Summary 10th Contracts § 52, Insanity Without Adjudication.
Witkin, California Summary 10th Contracts § 1021, Exception: Performing Defendant's Duty.
Witkin, California Summary 10th Sales § 233, Illustrations.
Witkin, California Summary 10th Wills and Probate § 953, in General.

§ 39. Conveyance or contract; rescission; rebuttable presumption

(a) A conveyance or other contract of a person of unsound mind, but not entirely without understanding, made before the incapacity of the person has been judicially determined, is subject to rescission, as provided in Chapter 2 (commencing with Section 1688) of Title 5 of Part 2 of Division 3.

(b) A rebuttable presumption affecting the burden of proof that a person is of unsound mind shall exist for purposes of this section if the person is substantially unable to manage his or her own financial resources or resist fraud or undue influence. Substantial inability may not be proved solely by isolated incidents of negligence or improvidence. *(Added by Stats.1992, c. 163 (A.B.2641), § 3, operative Jan. 1, 1994. Amended by Stats.1995, c. 842 (S.B.730), § 1.)*

Law Revision Commission Comments

1992 Addition

Section 39 restates former Civil Code Section 39 without substantive change. [22 Cal.L.Rev.Comm. Reports 1 (1992)].

Research References

Forms

Cal. Transaction Forms - Bus. Transactions § 6:14, Persons Of Unsound Mind.
Cal. Transaction Forms - Bus. Transactions § 6:29, Undue Influence.
Cal. Transaction Forms - Bus. Transactions § 15:5, Qualifications.
Cal. Transaction Forms - Bus. Transactions § 17:23, Other Circumstances Justifying Rescission.
Cal. Transaction Forms - Bus. Transactions § 17:24, Unsound Mind [Civ. Code, S39].
California Transactions Forms--Estate Planning § 13:2, Testamentary Capacity Versus Contractual Capacity.
California Transactions Forms--Estate Planning § 2:17, Definitions Of Capacity.
West's California Code Forms, Civil § 39 Form 1, Notice Of Rescission Of Incompetent's Contract.
West's California Code Forms, Civil § 39 Form 2, Complaint by Incompetent for Rescission.

Treatises and Practice Aids

Witkin, California Summary 10th Contracts § 50, in General.
Witkin, California Summary 10th Contracts § 55, Voidable Contracts.
Witkin, California Summary 10th Contracts § 57, Manic Depressive Psychosis.
Witkin, California Summary 10th Contracts § 935, Grounds for Rescission.
Witkin, California Summary 10th Husband and Wife § 161, Insanity.
Witkin, California Summary 10th Sales § 233, Illustrations.

Witkin, California Summary 10th Wills and Probate § 953, in General.

§ 40. Judicial determination of incapacity; powers; conservatorship

(a) Subject to Section 1871 of the Probate Code, and subject to Part 1 (commencing with Section 5000) of Division 5 of the Welfare and Institutions Code, after his or her incapacity has been judicially determined a person of unsound mind can make no conveyance or other contract, nor delegate any power or waive any right, until his or her restoration to capacity.

(b) Subject to Sections 1873 to 1876, inclusive, of the Probate Code, the establishment of a conservatorship under Division 4 (commencing with Section 1400) of the Probate Code is a judicial determination of the incapacity of the conservatee for the purposes of this section. *(Added by Stats.1992, c. 163 (A.B.2641), § 3, operative Jan. 1, 1994.)*

Law Revision Commission Comments

1992 Addition

Section 40 continues former Civil Code Section 40 without substantive change. [22 Cal.L.Rev.Comm. Reports 1 (1992)].

Research References

Forms

Cal. Transaction Forms - Bus. Transactions § 6:14, Persons Of Unsound Mind.
California Transactions Forms--Estate Planning § 2:17, Definitions Of Capacity.

Treatises and Practice Aids

Witkin, California Summary 10th Contracts § 50, in General.
Witkin, California Summary 10th Contracts § 53, in General.
Witkin, California Summary 10th Contracts § 54, Conservatee.
Witkin, California Summary 10th Contracts § 55, Voidable Contracts.
Witkin, California Summary 10th Sales § 233, Illustrations.
Witkin, California Summary 10th Wills and Probate § 953, in General.
Witkin, California Summary 10th Wills and Probate § 954, Limited or Temporary Conservatee.

§ 41. Civil liability; exemplary damages

A person of unsound mind, of whatever degree, is civilly liable for a wrong done by the person, but is not liable in exemplary damages unless at the time of the act the person was capable of knowing that the act was wrongful. *(Added by Stats.1992, c. 163 (A.B.2641), § 3, operative Jan. 1, 1994.)*

Law Revision Commission Comments

1992 Addition

Section 41 continues former Civil Code Section 41 without substantive change, insofar as former Section 41 related to a person of unsound mind. [22 Cal.L.Rev.Comm. Reports 1 (1992)].

Research References

Treatises and Practice Aids

Witkin, California Summary 10th Torts § 26, Mentally Disabled Persons.
Witkin, California Summary 10th Torts § 1353, Medicine.
Witkin, California Summary 10th Torts § 1580, in General.

Part 2

PERSONAL RIGHTS

§ 43. General personal rights

Besides the personal rights mentioned or recognized in the Government Code, every person has, subject to the qualifications and restrictions provided by law, the right of protection from bodily restraint or harm, from personal insult, from defamation, and from injury to his personal relations. *(Enacted in 1872. Amended by Stats.1953, c. 604, p. 1849, § 1.)*

Research References

Forms

West's California Code Forms, Civil § 43 Form 1, Complaint for False Imprisonment.
West's California Code Forms, Civil § 43 Form 3, Complaint for Invasion Of Privacy.

Treatises and Practice Aids

Witkin, California Summary 10th Real Property § 599, Other Acts and Powers Of Entity Are Not Affected.
Witkin, California Summary 10th Torts § 1, Definitions and Distinctions.

§ 43.1. Unborn child deemed existing person

A child conceived, but not yet born, is deemed an existing person, so far as necessary for the child's interests in the event of the child's subsequent birth. *(Added by Stats.1992, c. 163 (A.B.2641), § 4, operative Jan. 1, 1994.)*

Law Revision Commission Comments

1992 Addition

Section 43.1 continues the first part of former Civil Code Section 29 without substantive change. See also Code Civ.Proc. § 340.4 (statute of limitations for injury before birth). [22 Cal.L.Rev.Comm.Reports 1 (1992)].

Commentary

Interpreting Probate Code Section 6453 (b)(3), *Cheyanna M. v. A.C. Nielsen Co., 66 Cal.App.4th 855, 78 Cal.Rptr.2d 335 (1998),* holds that a posthumous child has standing to sue for the wrongful death of the child's biological father if the child can establish paternity through clear and convincing evidence. In other words, *Cheyanna M.* restricts the definition of "child" for purposes of Probate Code Section 6453 (b)(3) to children who are already born at the father's death; thus by definition it is impossible for a father to have held a posthumous child out as his own. *Cheyanna M.* invokes this section of the Civil Code, which seeks to advance the interests of unborn children who are ultimately born, as support for its holding.

Research References

Forms

West's California Code Forms, Civil § 43 Form 1, Complaint for False Imprisonment.

Treatises and Practice Aids

Witkin, California Summary 10th Torts § 728, Injury to Unborn Child.
Witkin, California Summary 10th Torts § 1393, Child Of Presumed Parent.
Witkin, California Summary 10th Wills and Probate § 87, Afterborn Heirs.
Witkin, California Summary 10th Wills and Probate § 232, Time When Class is Ascertained.
Witkin, California Summary 10th Workers' Compensation § 65, Fetal Injury in Workplace.

§ 43.4. Fraudulent promise to marry or cohabit not actionable

A fraudulent promise to marry or to cohabit after marriage does not give rise to a cause of action for damages. *(Added by Stats.1959, c. 381, p. 2306, § 1.)*

Research References

Forms

West's California Code Forms, Civil § 43 Form 1, Complaint for False Imprisonment.

Treatises and Practice Aids

Witkin, California Summary 10th Torts § 785, Promise Inducing Marriage: Damages.
Witkin, California Summary 10th Torts § 786, Promise to Support.

§ 43.5. Wrongs not actionable

No cause of action arises for:

(a) Alienation of affection.

(b) Criminal conversation.

(c) Seduction of a person over the age of legal consent.

(d) Breach of promise of marriage. *(Added by Stats.1939, c. 128, p. 1245, § 2.)*

Commentary

See generally *Askew v. Askew, 22 Cal.App.4th 942, 28 Cal.Rptr.2d 284 (1994)* (husband's claim for relief based on wife's "fraudulent" antenuptial assertion that she felt sexual desire for husband held nonactionable because husband's claim is essentially in the nature of a heart-balm proceeding prohibited by Section 43.5). On October 13, 1994, the Supreme Court depublished *Underwood v. Croy, 25 Cal.App.4th 281, 30 Cal.Rptr.2d 504 (1994)* (husband's cause of action against wife's counselor for negligent infliction of emotional distress caused by counselor having affair with wife is barred by one-year statute of limitations; husband's effort to plead cause of action for alienation of affections is barred by section 43.5). See also *Steve H. v. Wendy S., 57 Cal.App.4th 379, 67 Cal.Rptr.2d 90 (1997)* (barring former husband's action against former wife for intentional infliction of emotional distress caused by her attempt to sever bond with marital child she had misrepresented to be husband's biological child). On July 16, 1998, the Supreme Court, on stipulation of the parties, dismissed the petition for review and remanded *Steve H.* to the court of appeal.

Research References

Treatises and Practice Aids

Witkin, California Summary 10th Community Property § 272, Nature Of Theory.
Witkin, California Summary 10th Torts § 441, in General.
Witkin, California Summary 10th Torts § 442, Warrant Defective on Face.
Witkin, California Summary 10th Torts § 443, Arrest Of Wrong Person.
Witkin, California Summary 10th Torts § 723, Types Of Actions.
Witkin, California Summary 10th Torts § 724, Distinction: Professional Negligence.
Witkin, California Summary 10th Torts § 784, Promise Inducing Transfer: Restitution.
Witkin, California Summary 10th Torts § 786, Promise to Support.
Witkin, California Summary 10th Torts § 790, Representation Of Sterility.
Witkin, California Summary 10th Torts § 1046, in General.
Witkin, California Summary 10th Torts § 1047, Duty Provable, But Not Established.

§ 43.56. Foster parents; alienation of child's affection

No cause of action arises against a foster parent for alienation of affection of a foster child. *(Formerly § 43.55, added by Stats.1986, c. 1330, § 2, eff. Sept. 29, 1986. Amended by Stats.1988, c. 195, § 1, eff. June 16, 1988. Renumbered § 43.56 and amended by Stats.1990, c. 216 (S.B.2510), § 5.)*

§ 43.6. Immunity from liability; actions against parents on childbirth claims; defenses and damages in third party actions

(a) No cause of action arises against a parent of a child based upon the claim that the child should not have been conceived or, if conceived, should not have been allowed to have been born alive.

(b) The failure or refusal of a parent to prevent the live birth of his or her child shall not be a defense in any action against a third party, nor shall the failure or refusal be considered in awarding damages in any such action.

(c) As used in this section "conceived" means the fertilization of a human ovum by a human sperm. *(Added by Stats.1981, c. 331, § 1.)*

Research References

Treatises and Practice Aids

Witkin, California Summary 10th Torts § 981, No Cause Of Action Against Parent.

Witkin, California Summary 10th Torts § 982, Recovery Limited to Special Damages.

§ 44. Defamation

Defamation is effected by either of the following:

(a) Libel.

(b) Slander. *(Enacted in 1872. Amended by Stats.1980, c. 676, § 39.)*

Research References

Forms

Am. Jur. Pl. & Pr. Forms Libel and Slander § 1, Introductory Comments.

Treatises and Practice Aids

Witkin, California Summary 10th Torts § 529, Nature Of Tort.

§ 45. Libel

LIBEL, WHAT. Libel is a false and unprivileged publication by writing, printing, picture, effigy, or other fixed representation to the eye, which exposes any person to hatred, contempt, ridicule, or obloquy, or which causes him to be shunned or avoided, or which has a tendency to injure him in his occupation. *(Enacted in 1872.)*

Research References

Forms

West's California Code Forms, Civil Procedure § 1021.7 Form 2, Costs--Actions Against Peace Officers--Public Entities Employing Peace Officers--Defamation--Bad Faith--Declaration in Support Of Award Of Attorney's Fees.

Treatises and Practice Aids

Witkin, California Summary 10th Torts § 529, Nature Of Tort.

Witkin, California Summary 10th Torts § 530, Libel and Slander Distinguished.

Witkin, California Summary 10th Torts § 539, Statutory Definition.

Witkin, California Summary 10th Torts § 542, Charges Of Criminal Conduct.

Witkin, California Summary 10th Torts § 551, Statutory Definition.

Witkin, California Summary 10th Torts § 675, Special Damages Requirement.

§ 45a. Libel on its face; other actionable defamatory language

A libel which is defamatory of the plaintiff without the necessity of explanatory matter, such as an inducement, innuendo or other extrinsic fact, is said to be a libel on its face. Defamatory language not libelous on its face is not actionable unless the plaintiff alleges and proves that he has suffered special damage as a proximate result thereof. Special damage is defined in Section 48a of this code. *(Added by Stats.1945, c. 1489, p. 2762, § 1.)*

Research References

Forms

West's California Code Forms, Civil § 45 Form 1, Complaint for Libel--Libelous on Its Face.

West's California Code Forms, Civil § 45 Form 2, Complaint for Libel--Not Libelous on Its Face.

Treatises and Practice Aids

Witkin, California Summary 10th Torts § 541, California Doctrine Of Libel Per Se.

Witkin, California Summary 10th Torts § 675, Special Damages Requirement.

§ 46. Slander, false and unprivileged publications which constitute

Slander is a false and unprivileged publication, orally uttered, and also communications by radio or any mechanical or other means which:

1. Charges any person with crime, or with having been indicted, convicted, or punished for crime;

2. Imputes in him the present existence of an infectious, contagious, or loathsome disease;

3. Tends directly to injure him in respect to his office, profession, trade or business, either by imputing to him general disqualification in those respects which the office or other occupation peculiarly requires, or by imputing something with reference to his office, profession, trade, or business that has a natural tendency to lessen its profits;

4. Imputes to him impotence or a want of chastity; or

5. Which, by natural consequence, causes actual damage. *(Enacted in 1872. Amended by Stats.1945, c. 1489, p. 2762, § 2.)*

Research References

Forms

West's California Code Forms, Civil § 46 Form 1, Complaint for Slander--Charging Crime.

West's California Code Forms, Civil Procedure § 1021.7 Form 2, Costs--Actions Against Peace Officers--Public Entities Employing Peace Officers--Defamation--Bad Faith--Declaration in Support Of Award Of Attorney's Fees.

Treatises and Practice Aids

Witkin, California Summary 10th Torts § 529, Nature Of Tort.

Witkin, California Summary 10th Torts § 530, Libel and Slander Distinguished.

Witkin, California Summary 10th Torts § 551, Statutory Definition.

Witkin, California Summary 10th Torts § 552, Slander Per Se.

Witkin, California Summary 10th Torts § 553, Injury to Business or Professional Reputation.

§ 47. Privileged publication or broadcast

A privileged publication or broadcast is one made:

(a) In the proper discharge of an official duty.

(b) In any (1) legislative proceeding, (2) judicial proceeding, (3) in any other official proceeding authorized by law, or (4) in the initiation or course of any other proceeding authorized by law and reviewable pursuant to Chapter 2 (commencing with Section 1084) of Title 1 of Part 3 of the Code of Civil Procedure, except as follows:

(1) An allegation or averment contained in any pleading or affidavit filed in an action for marital dissolution or legal separation made of or concerning a person by or against whom no affirmative relief is prayed in the action shall not be a privileged publication or broadcast as to the person making

the allegation or averment within the meaning of this section unless the pleading is verified or affidavit sworn to, and is made without malice, by one having reasonable and probable cause for believing the truth of the allegation or averment and unless the allegation or averment is material and relevant to the issues in the action.

(2) This subdivision does not make privileged any communication made in furtherance of an act of intentional destruction or alteration of physical evidence undertaken for the purpose of depriving a party to litigation of the use of that evidence, whether or not the content of the communication is the subject of a subsequent publication or broadcast which is privileged pursuant to this section. As used in this paragraph, "physical evidence" means evidence specified in Section 250 of the Evidence Code or evidence that is property of any type specified in Chapter 14 (commencing with Section 2031.010) of Title 4 of Part 4 of the Code of Civil Procedure.

(3) This subdivision does not make privileged any communication made in a judicial proceeding knowingly concealing the existence of an insurance policy or policies.

(4) A recorded lis pendens is not a privileged publication unless it identifies an action previously filed with a court of competent jurisdiction which affects the title or right of possession of real property, as authorized or required by law.

(c) In a communication, without malice, to a person interested therein, (1) by one who is also interested, or (2) by one who stands in such a relation to the person interested as to afford a reasonable ground for supposing the motive for the communication to be innocent, or (3) who is requested by the person interested to give the information. This subdivision applies to and includes a communication concerning the job performance or qualifications of an applicant for employment, based upon credible evidence, made without malice, by a current or former employer of the applicant to, and upon request of, one whom the employer reasonably believes is a prospective employer of the applicant. This subdivision authorizes a current or former employer, or the employer's agent, to answer whether or not the employer would rehire a current or former employee. This subdivision shall not apply to a communication concerning the speech or activities of an applicant for employment if the speech or activities are constitutionally protected, or otherwise protected by Section 527.3 of the Code of Civil Procedure or any other provision of law.

(d)(1) By a fair and true report in, or a communication to, a public journal, of (A) a judicial, (B) legislative, or (C) other public official proceeding, or (D) of anything said in the course thereof, or (E) of a verified charge or complaint made by any person to a public official, upon which complaint a warrant has been issued.

(2) Nothing in paragraph (1) shall make privileged any communication to a public journal that does any of the following:

(A) Violates Rule 5-120 of the State Bar Rules of Professional Conduct.

(B) Breaches a court order.

(C) Violates any requirement of confidentiality imposed by law.

(e) By a fair and true report of (1) the proceedings of a public meeting, if the meeting was lawfully convened for a lawful purpose and open to the public, or (2) the publication of the matter complained of was for the public benefit. *(Enacted in 1872. Amended by Code Am.1873–74, c. 612, p. 184, § 11; Stats.1895, c. 163, p. 167, § 1; Stats.1927, c. 866, p. 1881, § 1; Stats.1945, c. 1489, p. 2763, § 3; Stats.1979, c. 184, p. 403, § 1; Stats.1990, c. 1491 (A.B.3765), § 1; Stats.1991, c. 432 (A.B.529), § 1; Stats.1992, c. 615 (S.B.1804), § 1; Stats. 1994, c. 364 (A.B.2778), § 1; Stats.1994, c. 700 (S.B.1457), § 2.5; Stats.1996, c. 1055 (S.B.1540), § 2; Stats.2002, c. 1029 (A.B.2868), § 1, eff. Sept. 28, 2002; Stats.2004, c. 182 (A.B.3081), § 4, operative July 1, 2005.)*

Law Revision Commission Comments

2004 Amendment

Subdivision (b) of Section 47 is amended to reflect nonsubstantive reorganization of the rules governing civil discovery. [33 Cal.L.Rev. Comm. Reports 977 (2003)].

Commentary

Jacob B. v. County of Shasta, 40 Cal.4th 948, 154 P.3d 1003, 56 Cal.Rptr.3d 477 (2007), held that the subsection (b) litigation privilege protects from tort liability a public official who, in the course of his duties, wrote a letter regarding a visitation proceeding. *Jacob B.* states that subsection (b) protects against all actions based on California's constitutional right of privacy as well as all tort actions, except for those founded on malicious prosecution.

Holland v. Jones, 210 Cal.App.4th 378, 148 Cal.Rptr.3d 550 (2012), held that this section protects statements made by a wife about her husband in a declaration she filed in their marital dissolution proceeding, and the statements could thus not be the basis for a defamation action.

Ramalingam v. Thompson, 151 Cal.App.4th 491, 60 Cal.Rptr.3d 11 (2007), held that a former wife's malpractice claim against a jointly retained neutral accountant, who communicated opinions about the parties' community property in their dissolution action, was barred by the subsection (b) litigation privilege.

Although Section 47 absolutely privileges defendant's allegedly false accusations of child abuse made in the parties' dissolution action, Section 47 does not bar plaintiff's cause of action for intentional infliction of emotional distress caused by defendant's filing of police report alleging child abuse in light of the more specific Child Abuse and Neglect Reporting Act (Penal Code Section 11164 et seq.), which grants only limited immunity for making a false report to persons who are not statutorily obliged to make such reports. *Begier v. Strom, 46 Cal.App.4th 877, 881–885, 54 Cal.Rptr.2d 158 (1996)*. Similarly, *Siam v. Kizilbash, 130 Cal.App.4th 1536, 31 Cal.Rptr.3d 368 (2005)*, holds that Penal Code § 11172(a), which imposes liability for knowingly filing a false report of child abuse, is constitutional and supplants the litigation privilege of subsection (b) of this section, which grants immunity for statements made in legislative, judicial, or other official proceedings. For holdings on the absolute character of the Section 47 privilege, see *Silberg v. Anderson, 50 Cal.3d 205, 786 P.2d 365, 266 Cal.Rptr. 638 (1990)* (Section 47 establishes an absolute privilege; disapproving "interest of justice" exception); *Gootee v. Lightner, 224 Cal.App.3d 587, 274 Cal.Rptr. 697 (1990)* (applying privilege to protect psychologist evaluating family from action by parent); *Laborde v. Aronson, 92 Cal.App.4th 459, 112 Cal.Rptr.2d 119 (2001)* (divorcing husband's tort claims against child custody evaluator barred by subsection (b) litigation privilege); *Howard v. Drapkin, 222 Cal.App.3d 843, 271 Cal.Rptr. 893 (1990)* (applying *Silberg* to grant immunity to independent psychologist performing child custody evaluation as neutral third party); and *Bergeron v. Boyd, 223 Cal.App.4th 877, 167 Cal.Rptr*

3d 426 (2014), review denied (applying Howard to grand immunity to a court-appointed child custody evaluator).

On April 23, 2003, the California Supreme Court granted review to *Smith v. M.D., 130 Cal.Rptr.2d 315 (2003)*, but on March 30, 2004, dismissed review and remanded the case to the court of appeal. The depublished opinion of the court of appeal purported to hold that the Child Abuse and Neglect Reporting Act does not apply to minors who report claimed sexual abuse and that such minors are therefore entitled to assert the absolute privilege of subsection (b) of this section.

On September 10, 2003, the California Supreme Court granted review to *Navarette v. Holland, 134 Cal.Rptr.2d 403 (2003)*, but on March 30, 2004, dismissed review and remanded the case to the court of appeal. The depublished opinion of the court of appeal purported to hold that a former wife's spousal abuse report to law enforcement officers was absolutely privileged under subsection (b), which barred husband's tort action based on allegation that wife lied to officers.

The Section 47 privilege applies to communications about a nonparty made to a court-appointed psychologist in a child custody investigation. *Obos v. Scripps Psychological Associates, 59 Cal. App.4th 103, 69 Cal.Rptr.2d 30 (1997)* (privileging communications made by psychologist about mother's boyfriend and therefore dismissing boyfriend's defamation suit against psychologist).

Statements made in prelitigation demand letters and telephone calls that are extraneous to threatened litigation are not protected by the litigation privilege of subsection (b). *Nguyen v. Proton Technology Corp., 69 Cal.App.4th 140, 81 Cal.Rptr.2d 392 (1999).*

On June 13, 2001, the California Supreme Court denied a petition for review and ordered depublication of *Randall v. Scovis, 105 Cal.Rptr.2d 32 (2001)*, which purported to hold that subsection (b) does not bar a grandparent's claim for invasion of his constitutional and statutory rights to privacy by an attorney's unlawful and unauthorized use of his confidential criminal records in a guardianship proceeding, but that the litigation privilege barred the grandparent's common law tort claims of negligent and intentional infliction of emotional distress.

A child's statements to police alleging that she was abused were absolutely privileged under subsection (b) because Penal Code § 11172, which allows damages for false reports of child abuse, does not apply to a victim's report of alleged child abuse. *Chabak v. Monroy, 154 Cal.App.4th 1502, 65 Cal.Rptr.3d 641 (2007).*

Lefebvre v. Lefebvre, 199 Cal.App.4th 696, 131 Cal.Rptr.3d 171 (2011), held that a trial court properly denied a wife's "anti-SLAPP" motion, under Code of Civil Procedure section 452.16, to strike her former husband's malicious prosecution complaint when the court conclusively determined, from the criminal trial record, that the wife's filing of criminal reports leading to the husband's arrest and trial were false and that their filing was an illegal activity. *Lefebvre* reasoned that making a false police report is not a constitutionally protected activity for purposes of section 452.16. Thus it was immaterial that the report might have been a privileged communication for purposes of the litigation privilege under subsection (b) of this section.

Research References

Forms

Cal. Transaction Forms - Bus. Transactions § 14:56, Characteristics Of Arbitration, Definitions, and Distinctions.

West's California Code Forms, Civil § 47 Form 7, Affirmative Defense to Defamation--Common Interest.

West's California Code Forms, Civil § 45 Form 1, Complaint for Libel--Libelous on Its Face.

West's California Code Forms, Civil § 47 Form 1, Affirmative Defense to Defamation--Official Duty Privilege.

West's California Code Forms, Civil § 47 Form 2, Affirmative Defense to Defamation--Official Proceeding Privilege.

West's California Code Forms, Civil § 47 Form 3, Affirmative Defense to Defamation--Interested Person Privilege.

West's California Code Forms, Civil § 47 Form 4, Affirmative Defense to Defamation--Report Of Official Proceeding Privilege.

West's California Code Forms, Civil § 47 Form 5, Affirmative Defense to Defamation--Report Of Public Meeting.

West's California Code Forms, Civil § 2924 Form 1, Notice Of Default--Under Mortgage.

West's California Code Forms, Civil § 1788.30 Form 1, Complaint for Unfair Debt Collection Practices.

West's California Code Forms, Education § 48918 Form 1, Notice Of Expulsion Hearing.

Treatises and Practice Aids

Witkin, California Summary 10th Agency and Employment § 285, Disclosure to State Auditor.

Witkin, California Summary 10th Community Property § 248, Tort Action for Concealment.

Witkin, California Summary 10th Equity § 108, Unlawful Practices.

Witkin, California Summary 10th Equity § 120, Health Care Practices.

Witkin, California Summary 10th Equity § 128, Statute Of Limitations and Defenses.

Witkin, California Summary 10th Insurance § 246, Conduct Of Litigation.

Witkin, California Summary 10th Insurance § 251, Traditional Tort Actions.

Witkin, California Summary 10th Real Property § 574, Single Family Dwellings, New Construction, and Vacancy Controls.

Witkin, California Summary 10th Security Transactions in Real Property § 144, in General.

Witkin, California Summary 10th Torts § 21, Tort Recovery Precluded by Public Policy: Perjury or False Defense.

Witkin, California Summary 10th Torts § 155, Proceedings Of Professional Society or Committee.

Witkin, California Summary 10th Torts § 186, Statutory Privileged Communications.

Witkin, California Summary 10th Torts § 455, Privilege.

Witkin, California Summary 10th Torts § 458, Collectors' Tactics.

Witkin, California Summary 10th Torts § 470, Other Torts Distinguished.

Witkin, California Summary 10th Torts § 473, No Defense Of Absolute Privilege.

Witkin, California Summary 10th Torts § 488, Action or Special Proceeding.

Witkin, California Summary 10th Torts § 495, Contractual Arbitration.

Witkin, California Summary 10th Torts § 501, Dismissal Reflecting on Merits.

Witkin, California Summary 10th Torts § 508, Some, But Not All, Claims or Amounts Supported by Probable Cause.

Witkin, California Summary 10th Torts § 528, Defense Of Absolute Privilege.

Witkin, California Summary 10th Torts § 548, Political Cartoons.

Witkin, California Summary 10th Torts § 562, Statutory Framework.

Witkin, California Summary 10th Torts § 563, Scope Of Privilege.

Witkin, California Summary 10th Torts § 564, in General.

Witkin, California Summary 10th Torts § 565, High Ranking Officials.

Witkin, California Summary 10th Torts § 566, Lower Ranking Officials.

Witkin, California Summary 10th Torts § 567, in General.

Witkin, California Summary 10th Torts § 569, Relevancy Limitation.

Witkin, California Summary 10th Torts § 571, Steps Before and After Trial.

Witkin, California Summary 10th Torts § 572, Quasi-Judicial Proceedings.

Witkin, California Summary 10th Torts § 573, Arbitration Proceedings.
Witkin, California Summary 10th Torts § 576, Proceedings in Foreign Country.
Witkin, California Summary 10th Torts § 577, Attorney Communications.
Witkin, California Summary 10th Torts § 578, Statements to Media.
Witkin, California Summary 10th Torts § 579, Legislative Proceedings.
Witkin, California Summary 10th Torts § 580, in General.
Witkin, California Summary 10th Torts § 581, Scope Of Privilege.
Witkin, California Summary 10th Torts § 582, Report to Police.
Witkin, California Summary 10th Torts § 584, Proceedings Reviewable by Mandamus.
Witkin, California Summary 10th Torts § 585, in General.
Witkin, California Summary 10th Torts § 586, Proceedings Within Privilege.
Witkin, California Summary 10th Torts § 587, Requirement that Statement be Fair and True.
Witkin, California Summary 10th Torts § 588, Limitations on Communications to Public Journals.
Witkin, California Summary 10th Torts § 589, Report Of Public Meeting.
Witkin, California Summary 10th Torts § 591, in General.
Witkin, California Summary 10th Torts § 592, in General.
Witkin, California Summary 10th Torts § 593, What Constitutes Malice.
Witkin, California Summary 10th Torts § 594, in General.
Witkin, California Summary 10th Torts § 596, Request for Information.
Witkin, California Summary 10th Torts § 597, Credit Report.
Witkin, California Summary 10th Torts § 599, No "Public Interest" Privilege for Media.
Witkin, California Summary 10th Torts § 617, Common Law Privilege.
Witkin, California Summary 10th Torts § 648, Absolute Privilege.
Witkin, California Summary 10th Torts § 661, Wiretapping and Electronic Eavesdropping.
Witkin, California Summary 10th Torts § 686, Privileges.
Witkin, California Summary 10th Torts § 757, Litigation Privilege.
Witkin, California Summary 10th Torts § 766, Other Privileges.
Witkin, California Summary 10th Torts § 792, Representation Of Paternity.
Witkin, California Summary 10th Torts § 822, Liability to Third Parties.
Witkin, California Summary 10th Torts § 148A, (New) Reporting by Financial Institutions.
Witkin, California Summary 10th Torts § 1569, Nature and Validity Of Penalties.

§ 48.7. Child abuse; prohibition against libel or slander action while charges pending; tolling of limitations; pleadings; demurrer; attorney fees and costs

(a) No person charged by indictment, information, or other accusatory pleading of child abuse may bring a civil libel or slander action against the minor, the parent or guardian of the minor, or any witness, based upon any statements made by the minor, parent or guardian, or witness which are reasonably believed to be in furtherance of the prosecution of the criminal charges while the charges are pending before a trial court. The charges are not pending within the meaning of this section after dismissal, after pronouncement of judgment, or during an appeal from a judgment.

Any applicable statute of limitations shall be tolled during the period that such charges are pending before a trial court.

(b) Whenever any complaint for libel or slander is filed which is subject to the provisions of this section, no responsive pleading shall be required to be filed until 30 days after the end of the period set forth in subdivision (a).

(c) Every complaint for libel or slander based on a statement that the plaintiff committed an act of child abuse shall state that the complaint is not barred by subdivision (a). A failure to include that statement shall be grounds for a demurrer.

(d) Whenever a demurrer against a complaint for libel or slander is sustained on the basis that the complaint was filed in violation of this section, attorney's fees and costs shall be awarded to the prevailing party.

(e) Whenever a prosecutor is informed by a minor, parent, guardian, or witness that a complaint against one of those persons has been filed which may be subject to the provisions of this section, the prosecutor shall provide that person with a copy of this section.

(f) As used in this section, child abuse has the meaning set forth in Section 11165 of the Penal Code. *(Added by Stats.1981, c. 253, § 1.)*

Research References

Forms

West's California Code Forms, Civil § 48.7 Form 1, Allegation in Complaint for Defamation--Child Abuse.

Treatises and Practice Aids

Witkin, California Summary 10th Torts § 145, Related Immunities.
Witkin, California Summary 10th Torts § 591, in General.

§ 49. Personal relations, acts forbidden by

The rights of personal relations forbid:

(a) The abduction or enticement of a child from a parent, or from a guardian entitled to its custody;

(b) The seduction of a person under the age of legal consent;

(c) Any injury to a servant which affects his ability to serve his master, other than seduction, abduction or criminal conversation. *(Enacted in 1872. Amended by Stats.1905, c. 70, p. 68, § 1; Stats.1939, c. 128, p. 1245, § 1; Stats.1939, c. 1103, p. 3037, § 5.)*

Research References

Forms

Am. Jur. Pl. & Pr. Forms Seduction § 1, Introductory Comments.
West's California Code Forms, Civil § 49 Form 1, Complaint for Abduction Of Child.
West's California Code Forms, Civil § 49 Form 2, Complaint by Employer for Injury to Domestic Employee.

Treatises and Practice Aids

Witkin, California Summary 10th Agency and Employment § 162, Torts.
Witkin, California Summary 10th Torts § 143, Subsequent Concealment Of Victim.
Witkin, California Summary 10th Torts § 192, Comparative Impairment Analysis.
Witkin, California Summary 10th Torts § 723, Types Of Actions.
Witkin, California Summary 10th Torts § 729, Abduction Of Child.

Witkin, California Summary 10th Torts § 755, Interference With Employment Relation.

§ 50. Force, right to use

Any necessary force may be used to protect from wrongful injury the person or property of oneself, or of a spouse, child, parent, or other relative, or member of one's family, or of a ward, servant, master, or guest. *(Enacted in 1872. Amended by Code Am.1873–74, c. 612, p. 184, § 12; Stats.2016, c. 50 (S.B.1005), § 4, eff. Jan. 1, 2017.)*

Research References

Treatises and Practice Aids

Witkin, California Summary 10th Torts § 417, Nature and Scope Of Privilege.

Witkin, California Summary 10th Torts § 419, Use Of Reasonable Force.

Witkin, California Summary 10th Torts § 1099, Person Committing Serious Felony.

Witkin, California Summary 10th Torts § 1141, No Duty to Comply With Criminal's Demand.

§ 51. Unruh Civil Rights Act; equal rights; business establishments; violations of federal Americans with Disabilities Act

(a) This section shall be known, and may be cited, as the Unruh Civil Rights Act.

(b) All persons within the jurisdiction of this state are free and equal, and no matter what their sex, race, color, religion, ancestry, national origin, disability, medical condition, genetic information, marital status, sexual orientation, citizenship, primary language, or immigration status are entitled to the full and equal accommodations, advantages, facilities, privileges, or services in all business establishments of every kind whatsoever.

(c) This section shall not be construed to confer any right or privilege on a person that is conditioned or limited by law or that is applicable alike to persons of every sex, color, race, religion, ancestry, national origin, disability, medical condition, marital status, sexual orientation, citizenship, primary language, or immigration status, or to persons regardless of their genetic information.

(d) Nothing in this section shall be construed to require any construction, alteration, repair, structural or otherwise, or modification of any sort whatsoever, beyond that construction, alteration, repair, or modification that is otherwise required by other provisions of law, to any new or existing establishment, facility, building, improvement, or any other structure, nor shall anything in this section be construed to augment, restrict, or alter in any way the authority of the State Architect to require construction, alteration, repair, or modifications that the State Architect otherwise possesses pursuant to other laws.

(e) For purposes of this section:

(1) "Disability" means any mental or physical disability as defined in Sections 12926 and 12926.1 of the Government Code.

(2)(A) "Genetic information" means, with respect to any individual, information about any of the following:

(i) The individual's genetic tests.

(ii) The genetic tests of family members of the individual.

(iii) The manifestation of a disease or disorder in family members of the individual.

(B) "Genetic information" includes any request for, or receipt of, genetic services, or participation in clinical research that includes genetic services, by an individual or any family member of the individual.

(C) "Genetic information" does not include information about the sex or age of any individual.

(3) "Medical condition" has the same meaning as defined in subdivision (i) of Section 12926 of the Government Code.

(4) "Religion" includes all aspects of religious belief, observance, and practice.

(5) "Sex" includes, but is not limited to, pregnancy, childbirth, or medical conditions related to pregnancy or childbirth. "Sex" also includes, but is not limited to, a person's gender. "Gender" means sex, and includes a person's gender identity and gender expression. "Gender expression" means a person's gender-related appearance and behavior whether or not stereotypically associated with the person's assigned sex at birth.

(6) "Sex, race, color, religion, ancestry, national origin, disability, medical condition, genetic information, marital status, sexual orientation, citizenship, primary language, or immigration status" includes a perception that the person has any particular characteristic or characteristics within the listed categories or that the person is associated with a person who has, or is perceived to have, any particular characteristic or characteristics within the listed categories.

(7) "Sexual orientation" has the same meaning as defined in subdivision (s) of Section 12926 of the Government Code.

(f) A violation of the right of any individual under the federal Americans with Disabilities Act of 1990 (Public Law 101–336) [1] shall also constitute a violation of this section.

(g) Verification of immigration status and any discrimination based upon verified immigration status, where required by federal law, shall not constitute a violation of this section.

(h) Nothing in this section shall be construed to require the provision of services or documents in a language other than English, beyond that which is otherwise required by other provisions of federal, state, or local law, including Section 1632. *(Added by Stats.1905, c. 413, p. 553, § 1. Amended by Stats.1919, c. 210, p. 309, § 1; Stats.1923, c. 235, p. 485, § 1; Stats.1959, c. 1866, p. 4424, § 1; Stats.1961, c. 1187, p. 2920, § 1; Stats.1974, c. 1193, p. 2568, § 1; Stats. 1987, c. 159, § 1; Stats.1992, c. 913 (A.B.1077), § 3; Stats. 1998, c. 195 (A.B.2702), § 1; Stats.2000, c. 1049 (A.B.2222), § 2; Stats.2005, c. 420 (A.B.1400), § 3; Stats.2011, c. 261 (S.B.559), § 3; Stats.2011, c. 719 (A.B.887), § 1.5; Stats.2015, c. 303 (A.B.731), § 25, eff. Jan. 1, 2016; Stats.2015, c. 282 (S.B.600), § 1, eff. Jan. 1, 2016.)*

[1] For public law sections classified to the U.S.C.A., see USCA–Tables.

Commentary

In *Koebke v. Bernardo Heights Country Club, 36 Cal.4th 824, 115 P.3d 1212, 31 Cal.Rptr.3d 565 (2005)*, the California Supreme Court held that marital status discrimination is cognizable under the Unruh Act. Relying on the Domestic Partner Rights and Responsibilities

Act of 2003, the Court additionally held that registered domestic partners are equivalent to spouses for purposes of the Unruh Act. Thus a business that denies spousal benefits to registered domestic partners impermissibly discriminates on the basis of marital status under the Unruh Act.

In 2005, the Act was amended to include discrimination on the basis of marital status and sexual orientation. Stats.2005, c. 420 (A.B.1400), § 3. When a medical clinic refused insemination services to a lesbian because of her sexual orientation, the California Supreme Court held that federal and state constitutional rights of religious freedom and free speech do not exempt physicians from complying with this act's prohibition of sexual orientation discrimination. *North Coast Women's Care Medical Group, Inc. v. Superior Court, 44 Cal.4th 1145, 81 Cal.Rptr.3d 708, 189 P.3d 959 (2008).*

Research References

Forms

West's California Code Forms, Civil § 51 Form 1, Complaint for Violation Of Unruh Civil Rights Act.

West's California Code Forms, Civil § 53 Form 1, Complaint to Declare Discriminatory Lease Provision Void.

West's California Code Forms, Civil § 83 Form 1, Complaint for Unlawful Refusal to Grant Dealership.

West's California Code Forms, Civil § 54.3 Form 1, Complaint for Interference With Rights Of Disabled Person.

West's California Code Forms, Civil § 55.54 Form 1, Notice Of Right to Stay and Early Evaluation Conference.

West's California Code Forms, Civil § 1747.80 Form 1, Complaint--Discriminatory Refusal to Issue Credit Card.

West's California Code Forms, Commercial § 2207 GENERAL COMMENT 5, When Doing Business Online, "Must Know Matters" for Both Sellers and Buyers.

West's California Code Forms, Government § 845 Form 1, Complaint for Violation Of Civil Rights and Wrongful Death.

Treatises and Practice Aids

Witkin, California Summary 10th Constitutional Law § 389, Exclusion Of Women from Membership.

Witkin, California Summary 10th Constitutional Law § 526, Religious Discrimination Against Advertisers.

Witkin, California Summary 10th Constitutional Law § 891, Insurance.

Witkin, California Summary 10th Constitutional Law § 892, Public Programs and Activities.

Witkin, California Summary 10th Constitutional Law § 895, Hate Crimes, Intimidation, and Threats Of Violence.

Witkin, California Summary 10th Constitutional Law § 897, Other Discrimination Statutes.

Witkin, California Summary 10th Constitutional Law § 898, in General.

Witkin, California Summary 10th Constitutional Law § 899, Business Establishments.

Witkin, California Summary 10th Constitutional Law § 903, Cult Awareness Network.

Witkin, California Summary 10th Constitutional Law § 904, Boy Scouts.

Witkin, California Summary 10th Constitutional Law § 905, in General.

Witkin, California Summary 10th Constitutional Law § 906, Business Discrimination.

Witkin, California Summary 10th Constitutional Law § 908, Housing Discrimination.

Witkin, California Summary 10th Constitutional Law § 910, Classification Based on Marital Status.

Witkin, California Summary 10th Constitutional Law § 912, Economic Criteria.

Witkin, California Summary 10th Constitutional Law § 914, Enforcement.

Witkin, California Summary 10th Constitutional Law § 915, Nature and Purpose Of Act.

Witkin, California Summary 10th Constitutional Law § 941, Other Prohibited Discrimination.

Witkin, California Summary 10th Constitutional Law § 945, in General.

Witkin, California Summary 10th Constitutional Law § 957, in General.

Witkin, California Summary 10th Constitutional Law § 908A, (New) Marital Status Discrimination.

Witkin, California Summary 10th Constitutional Law § 908B, (New) Sexual Orientation Discrimination.

Witkin, California Summary 10th Equity § 121, Rental Car Company Practices.

Witkin, California Summary 10th Insurance § 6, Governing Law.

Witkin, California Summary 10th Real Property § 116, Age.

Witkin, California Summary 10th Real Property § 201, California Statute.

Witkin, California Summary 10th Real Property § 683, Discrimination Against Children.

Witkin, California Summary 10th Secured Transactions in Personal Property § 80, Name Of Debtor.

Witkin, California Summary 10th Torts § 468, Gender-Related Violence.

Witkin, California Summary 10th Torts § 1131, Assault Involving Firearms.

§ 52.4. Civil action for damages arising from gender violence

(a) Any person who has been subjected to gender violence may bring a civil action for damages against any responsible party. The plaintiff may seek actual damages, compensatory damages, punitive damages, injunctive relief, any combination of those, or any other appropriate relief. A prevailing plaintiff may also be awarded attorney's fees and costs.

(b) An action brought pursuant to this section shall be commenced within three years of the act, or if the victim was a minor when the act occurred, within eight years after the date the plaintiff attains the age of majority or within three years after the date the plaintiff discovers or reasonably should have discovered the psychological injury or illness occurring after the age of majority that was caused by the act, whichever date occurs later.

(c) For purposes of this section, "gender violence" is a form of sex discrimination and means either of the following:

(1) One or more acts that would constitute a criminal offense under state law that has as an element the use, attempted use, or threatened use of physical force against the person or property of another, committed at least in part based on the gender of the victim, whether or not those acts have resulted in criminal complaints, charges, prosecution, or conviction.

(2) A physical intrusion or physical invasion of a sexual nature under coercive conditions, whether or not those acts have resulted in criminal complaints, charges, prosecution, or conviction.

(d) For purposes of this section, "gender" has the meaning set forth in Section 51.

(e) Notwithstanding any other laws that may establish the liability of an employer for the acts of an employee, this section does not establish any civil liability of a person because of his or her status as an employer, unless the employer personally committed an act of gender violence.

(Added by Stats.2002, c. 842 (A.B.1928), § 2. Amended by Stats.2015, c. 202 (A.B.830), § 1, eff. Jan. 1, 2016.)

Research References

Forms

West's California Code Forms, Civil § 52.4 Form 1, Complaint for Gender Violence.

Treatises and Practice Aids

Witkin, California Summary 10th Constitutional Law § 897, Other Discrimination Statutes.

Witkin, California Summary 10th Husband and Wife § 371, Civil Remedies.

Witkin, California Summary 10th Torts § 468, Gender-Related Violence.

§ 52.45. Civil action for damages arising from sexual orientation violence

(a) Any person who has been subjected to sexual orientation violence may bring a civil action for damages against any responsible party. The plaintiff may seek actual damages, compensatory damages, punitive damages, injunctive relief, any combination of those, or any other appropriate relief. A prevailing plaintiff may also be awarded attorney's fees and costs.

(b) An action brought pursuant to this section shall be commenced within three years of the act, or if the victim was a minor when the act occurred, within eight years after the date the plaintiff attains the age of majority or within three years after the date the plaintiff discovers or reasonably should have discovered the psychological injury or illness occurring after the age of majority that was caused by the act, whichever date occurs later.

(c) For purposes of this section, "sexual orientation violence" means one or more acts that would constitute a criminal offense under state law that has as an element the use, attempted use, or threatened use of physical force against the person or property of another, committed at least in part based on the sexual orientation of the victim, whether or not those acts have resulted in criminal complaints, charges, prosecution, or conviction.

(d) Notwithstanding any other laws that may establish the liability of an employer for the acts of an employee, this section does not establish any civil liability of a person because of his or her status as an employer, unless the employer personally committed an act of sexual orientation violence. *(Added by Stats.2015, c. 202 (A.B.830), § 2, eff. Jan. 1, 2016.)*

Research References

Treatises and Practice Aids

Witkin, California Summary 10th Constitutional Law § 897, Other Discrimination Statutes.

Witkin, California Summary 10th Torts § 468C, (New) Sexual Orientation Violence.

Division 2

PROPERTY

Part 1

PROPERTY IN GENERAL

Title 2

OWNERSHIP

CHAPTER 2. MODIFICATION OF OWNERSHIP

ARTICLE 1. INTERESTS IN PROPERTY

§ 678. Absolute or qualified ownership

OWNERSHIP, ABSOLUTE OR QUALIFIED. The ownership of property is either:

1. Absolute; or,
2. Qualified. *(Enacted in 1872.)*

Research References

Treatises and Practice Aids

Witkin, California Summary 10th Personal Property § 27, in General.

§ 679. Absolute ownership defined

WHEN ABSOLUTE. The ownership of property is absolute when a single person has the absolute dominion over it, and may use it or dispose of it according to his pleasure, subject only to general laws. *(Enacted in 1872.)*

Research References

Treatises and Practice Aids

Witkin, California Summary 10th Personal Property § 27, in General.

§ 680. Qualified ownership defined

The ownership of property is qualified:

1. When it is shared with one or more persons;
2. When the time of enjoyment is deferred or limited;

3. When the use is restricted. *(Enacted in 1872.)*

Research References

Treatises and Practice Aids

Witkin, California Summary 10th Personal Property § 27, in General.

§ 681. Several ownership defined

SEVERAL OWNERSHIP, WHAT. The ownership of property by a single person is designated as a sole or several ownership. *(Enacted in 1872.)*

Research References

Treatises and Practice Aids

Witkin, California Summary 10th Personal Property § 27, in General.

§ 682. Ownership by several persons; types

The ownership of property by several persons is either:

(a) Of joint interest.

(b) Of partnership interests.

(c) Of interests in common.

(d) Of community interest of spouses. *(Enacted in 1872. Amended by Stats.2016, c. 50 (S.B.1005), § 7, eff. Jan. 1, 2017.)*

Research References

Forms

California Transactions Forms--Family Law § 4:97, Tracing Of Assets.
California Transactions Forms--Family Law § 1:107, Living Expenses Paid Out Of Joint Account:.
California Transactions Forms--Family Law § 4:107, Living Expenses Paid Out Of Joint Account.

Treatises and Practice Aids

Witkin, California Summary 10th Personal Property § 27, in General.
Witkin, California Summary 10th Personal Property § 35, Coownership Of Automobile.
Witkin, California Summary 10th Real Property § 32, in General.

§ 682.1. Community property of spouses; subject to express declaration in transfer documents; application and operation of section

(a) Community property of spouses, when expressly declared in the transfer document to be community property with right of survivorship, and which may be accepted in writing on the face of the document by a statement signed or initialed by the grantees, shall, upon the death of one of the spouses, pass to the survivor, without administration, pursuant to the terms of the instrument, subject to the same procedures, as property held in joint tenancy. Prior to the death of either spouse, the right of survivorship may be terminated pursuant to the same procedures by which a joint tenancy may be severed. Part 1 (commencing with Section 5000) of Division 5 of the Probate Code and Chapter 2 (commencing with Section 13540), Chapter 3 (commencing with Section 13550), and Chapter 3.5 (commencing with Section 13560) of Part 2 of Division 8 of the Probate Code apply to this property.

(b) This section does not apply to a joint account in a financial institution to which Part 2 (commencing with Section 5100) of Division 5 of the Probate Code applies.

(c) This section shall become operative on July 1, 2001, and shall apply to instruments created on or after that date. *(Added by Stats.2000, c. 645 (A.B.2913), § 1, operative July 1, 2001. Amended by Stats.2016, c. 50 (S.B.1005), § 8, eff. Jan. 1, 2017.)*

Research References

Forms

California Real Estate Forms (Miller & Starr) § 1:133, Grant Deed.
California Real Estate Forms (Miller & Starr) § 1:134, Interspousal Grant Deed.
California Real Estate Forms (Miller & Starr) § 1:135, Quitclaim Deed.

Treatises and Practice Aids

Witkin, California Summary 10th Community Property § 157, Conversion to Community Property With Right Of Survivorship.
Witkin, California Summary 10th Community Property § 251, Disposition Of Community Property.
Witkin, California Summary 10th Wills and Probate § 76, Surviving Spouse's Share in Community and Quasi-Community Property.
Witkin, California Summary 10th Wills and Probate § 103, Testamentary Disposition Of Property.
Witkin, California Summary 10th Wills and Probate § 266, Community Property With Right Of Survivorship.
Witkin, California Summary 10th Wills and Probate § 319, Joint Tenancy With Former Spouse.

§ 683. Joint tenancy; definition; method of creation

(a) A joint interest is one owned by two or more persons in equal shares, by a title created by a single will or transfer, when expressly declared in the will or transfer to be a joint tenancy, or by transfer from a sole owner to himself or herself and others, or from tenants in common or joint tenants to themselves or some of them, or to themselves or any of them and others, or from spouses, when holding title as community property or otherwise to themselves or to themselves and others or to one of them and to another or others, when expressly declared in the transfer to be a joint tenancy, or when granted or devised to executors or trustees as joint tenants. A joint tenancy in personal property may be created by a written transfer, instrument, or agreement.

(b) Provisions of this section do not apply to a joint account in a financial institution if Part 2 (commencing with Section 5100) of Division 5 of the Probate Code applies to such account. *(Enacted in 1872. Amended by Stats.1929, c. 93, p. 172, § 1; Stats.1931, c. 1051, p. 2205, § 1; Stats.1935, c. 234, p. 912, § 1; Stats.1955, c. 178, p. 645, § 1; Stats.1983, c. 92, § 1, operative July 1, 1984; Stats.1989, c. 397, § 1, operative July 1, 1990; Stats.1990, c. 79 (A.B.759), § 1, operative July 1, 1991; Stats.2016, c. 50 (S.B.1005), § 9, eff. Jan. 1, 2017.)*

Law Revision Commission Comments

1983 Amendment

Section 683 is amended to add subdivision (b) to make clear that this section does not apply to a joint account in a credit union or an industrial loan company to which the newly enacted provisions of the Probate Code (Sections 5100–5407) apply. [16 Cal.L.Rev.Comm.Reports 129 (1982); 83 S.J. 3245].

1989 Amendment

Subdivision (c) of Section 683 is deleted to reflect the expansion of the California Multiple-Party Accounts Law to include banks, savings and loan associations, and other like organizations. See Prob.Code § 5128 ("financial institution" defined). Banks are now governed by subdivision (b). [20 Cal.L.Rev.Comm.Reports 145 (1990)].

1990 Amendment

Subdivision (b) of Section 683 is amended to correct a cross-reference. This is a technical, nonsubstantive change. [20 Cal.L.Rev.Comm.Reports 1001 (1990)].

Commentary

May the doctrine of equitable estoppel be invoked to avoid the Section 683 writing requirement? Compare *Byrne v. Laura, 52 Cal.App.4th 1054, 60 Cal.Rptr.2d 908 (1997), review denied May 28, 1997* (doctrine of equitable estoppel is available to enforce oral joint tenancy agreements) with *Estate of Siebert, 226 Cal.App.3d 338, 276 Cal.Rptr. 508 (1990)* (doctrine of equitable estoppel is not available to enforce oral joint tenancy agreements). For discussion of the doctrine of equitable estoppel, see Family Code Section 1611, Commentary.

A judgment lien on a real property interest held by a tenant in common survives a change in title to joint tenancy and the subsequent death of the debtor joint tenant; therefore, the lien remains valid and enforceable. *Dieden v. Schmidt, 104 Cal.App.4th 645, 128 Cal.Rptr.2d 365 (2002), review denied March 19, 2003.*

Research References

Forms

California Transactions Forms--Estate Planning § 1:20, Joint Tenancy.
California Transactions Forms--Estate Planning § 10:19, Joint Tenancy Property.
Nichols Cyclopedia of Legal Forms Annotated § 111:3, Personal Property.
West's California Code Forms, Civil § 683 Form 1, Deed--Joint Tenancy--Sole Owner to Self and Others.

Treatises and Practice Aids

Witkin, California Summary 10th Contracts § 343, California Codes.
Witkin, California Summary 10th Contracts § 400, Miscellaneous Provisions.
Witkin, California Summary 10th Personal Property § 30, Nature Of Joint Tenancy.
Witkin, California Summary 10th Personal Property § 33, Proceeds Of Joint Tenancy Property.
Witkin, California Summary 10th Real Property § 33, in General.
Witkin, California Summary 10th Real Property § 35, Creation Of Joint Tenancy.
Witkin, California Summary 10th Real Property § 36, Equitable Interest.
Witkin, California Summary 10th Real Property § 51, Lease.

§ 683.1. Joint tenancy; safe-deposit box

No contract or other arrangement made after the effective date of this section between any person, firm, or corporation engaged in the business of renting safe-deposit boxes and the renter or renters of a safe-deposit box, shall create a joint tenancy in or otherwise establish ownership in any of the contents of such safe-deposit box. Any such contract or other arrangement purporting so to do shall be to such extent void and of no effect. *(Added by Stats.1949, c. 1597, p. 2845, § 1.)*

Research References

Forms

California Transactions Forms--Estate Planning § 1:20, Joint Tenancy.
California Transactions Forms--Estate Planning § 10:19, Joint Tenancy Property.

Treatises and Practice Aids

Witkin, California Summary 10th Personal Property § 34, Safe Deposit Boxes.

§ 683.2. Joint tenancy; severance; right of survivorship; applicable law

(a) Subject to the limitations and requirements of this section, in addition to any other means by which a joint tenancy may be severed, a joint tenant may sever a joint tenancy in real property as to the joint tenant's interest without the joinder or consent of the other joint tenants by any of the following means:

(1) Execution and delivery of a deed that conveys legal title to the joint tenant's interest to a third person, whether or not pursuant to an agreement that requires the third person to reconvey legal title to the joint tenant.

(2) Execution of a written instrument that evidences the intent to sever the joint tenancy, including a deed that names the joint tenant as transferee, or of a written declaration that, as to the interest of the joint tenant, the joint tenancy is severed.

(b) Nothing in this section authorizes severance of a joint tenancy contrary to a written agreement of the joint tenants, but a severance contrary to a written agreement does not defeat the rights of a purchaser or encumbrancer for value in good faith and without knowledge of the written agreement.

(c) Severance of a joint tenancy of record by deed, written declaration, or other written instrument pursuant to subdivision (a) is not effective to terminate the right of survivorship of the other joint tenants as to the severing joint tenant's interest unless one of the following requirements is satisfied:

(1) Before the death of the severing joint tenant, the deed, written declaration, or other written instrument effecting the severance is recorded in the county where the real property is located.

(2) The deed, written declaration, or other written instrument effecting the severance is executed and acknowledged before a notary public by the severing joint tenant not earlier than three days before the death of that joint tenant and is recorded in the county where the real property is located not later than seven days after the death of the severing joint tenant.

(d) Nothing in subdivision (c) limits the manner or effect of:

(1) A written instrument executed by all the joint tenants that severs the joint tenancy.

(2) A severance made by or pursuant to a written agreement of all the joint tenants.

(3) A deed from a joint tenant to another joint tenant.

(e) Subdivisions (a) and (b) apply to all joint tenancies in real property, whether the joint tenancy was created before, on, or after January 1, 1985, except that in the case of the death of a joint tenant before January 1, 1985, the validity of a severance under subdivisions (a) and (b) is determined by the law in effect at the time of death. Subdivisions (c) and (d) do not apply to or affect a severance made before January 1, 1986, of a joint tenancy. *(Added by Stats.1984, c. 519, § 1. Amended by Stats.1985, c. 157, § 1.)*

Commentary

Interpreting subsection (c)(2), *Dorn v. Solomon, 57 Cal.App.4th 650, 67 Cal.Rptr.2d 311 (1997),* held that a quit claim deed of a separated spouse that was not timely filed in accordance with the filing requirements was ineffective to sever a joint tenancy and hence was ineffective to transfer a dying spouse's one-half interest to a third party; instead, the decedent spouse's interest passed to the surviving spouse by the joint tenancy right of survivorship. On March 9, 2000, the Court of Appeal granted a rehearing in *Patience v. Snyder, 93 Cal.Rptr.2d 265 (2000),* in which the court initially held that, for purposes of this section, a severance is not "recorded" until the recording fees are paid and the document is stamped by the recorder's office.

Research References

Forms

California Transactions Forms--Estate Planning § 1:15, Overview.
California Transactions Forms--Estate Planning § 1:21, Severing Joint Tenancies in Real Property.
California Transactions Forms--Estate Planning § 1:25, Joint Tenancy or Community Property Treatment Of Property in Revocable Trust.
California Transactions Forms--Estate Planning § 1:77, Matters to Consider Regarding Property Distribution.
California Transactions Forms--Estate Planning § 20:6, Property Passing Outside Of Will.
California Transactions Forms--Estate Planning § 10:19, Joint Tenancy Property.
California Transactions Forms--Estate Planning § 19:66, Determining Testator's Intent; Information Gathering.
California Transactions Forms--Estate Planning § 19:108, Special Precautions for Deathbed Wills.
West's California Code Forms, Civil § 683.2 Form 1, Deed--Severing Joint Tenancy--Joint Tenant to Others.

Treatises and Practice Aids

Witkin, California Summary 10th Real Property § 58, Joint Tenant's Conveyance to Self.
Witkin, California Summary 10th Real Property § 60, Nature and Purpose Of Statute.
Witkin, California Summary 10th Real Property § 61, Methods Of Severance.
Witkin, California Summary 10th Real Property § 62, Recordation.
Witkin, California Summary 10th Real Property § 63, Severance Under Statute is Not Transfer Of Property.

§ 684. Partnership interest defined

PARTNERSHIP INTEREST, WHAT. A partnership interest is one owned by several persons, in partnership, for partnership purposes. *(Enacted in 1872.)*

Research References

Forms

West's California Code Forms, Civil § 684 Form 1, Deed--Partnership.

§ 685. Interest in common defined

INTEREST IN COMMON, WHAT. An interest in common is one owned by several persons, not in joint ownership or partnership. *(Enacted in 1872.)*

Research References

Forms

California Transactions Forms--Estate Planning § 10:6, Tenancy in Common.
West's California Code Forms, Civil § 685 Form 1, Deed--Tenants in Common.

Treatises and Practice Aids

Witkin, California Summary 10th Real Property § 39, in General.

§ 686. Interest in common; interests excluded

WHAT INTERESTS ARE IN COMMON. Every interest created in favor of several persons in their own right is an interest in common, unless acquired by them in partnership, for partnership purposes, or unless declared in its creation to be a joint interest, as provided in Section 683, or unless acquired as community property. *(Enacted in 1872.)*

Research References

Forms

California Transactions Forms--Estate Planning § 10:6, Tenancy in Common.
California Transactions Forms--Estate Planning § 20:8, Class Devises.
West's California Code Forms, Civil § 685 Form 1, Deed--Tenants in Common.

Treatises and Practice Aids

Witkin, California Summary 10th Personal Property § 27, in General.
Witkin, California Summary 10th Real Property § 35, Creation Of Joint Tenancy.
Witkin, California Summary 10th Real Property § 39, in General.
Witkin, California Summary 10th Real Property § 40, Failure Of Joint Tenancy.

§ 687. Community property defined

Community property is property that is community property under Part 2 (commencing with Section 760) of Division 4 of the Family Code. *(Enacted in 1872. Amended by Stats.1992, c. 163 (A.B.2641), § 6, operative Jan. 1, 1994.)*

Law Revision Commission Comments

1992 Amendment

Section 687 is amended to adopt the definition of community property provided by Section 65 of the Family Code. Part 2 (commencing with Section 760) of Division 4 of the Family Code contains detailed rules that determine whether property is community or separate property. [22 Cal.L.Rev.Comm.Reports 1 (1992)].

Research References

Forms

California Transactions Forms--Estate Planning § 1:22, Community Property.
California Transactions Forms--Estate Planning § 3:75, Community Property.
California Transactions Forms--Estate Planning § 10:10, Community Property.

ARTICLE 2. CONDITIONS OF OWNERSHIP

Section

§ 710. Conditions in restraint of marriage

Conditions imposing restraints upon marriage, except upon the marriage of a minor, are void; but this does not affect limitations where the intent was not to forbid marriage, but only to give the use until marriage. *(Enacted in 1872. Amended by Code Am.1873–74, c. 612, p. 218, § 101.)*

Commentary

Estate of Guidotti, 90 Cal.App.4th 1403, 109 Cal.Rptr.2d 674 (2001), held that a clause in husband's testamentary trust giving his wife the trust income for life only if she does not remarry or cohabit is void under this section.

Research References

Forms

California Transactions Forms--Estate Planning § 19:4, Public Policy and Conditional Devises.

California Transactions Forms--Estate Planning § 20:13, Conditional Devises.

Treatises and Practice Aids

Witkin, California Summary 10th Real Property § 197, Void Condition Against Marriage.

Witkin, California Summary 10th Real Property § 198, Valid Limitation Until Marriage.

Division 3

OBLIGATIONS

Part 2

CONTRACTS

Title 1

NATURE OF A CONTRACT

CHAPTER 3. CONSENT

§ 1565. Essentials of consent

ESSENTIALS OF CONSENT. The consent of the parties to a contract must be:

1. Free;
2. Mutual; and,
3. Communicated by each to the other. *(Enacted in 1872.)*

Research References

Forms

Cal. Transaction Forms - Bus. Transactions § 8:2, Offer and Acceptance.

Cal. Transaction Forms - Bus. Transactions § 6:21, Acceptance.

Cal. Transaction Forms - Bus. Transactions § 6:26, Fraud and Misrepresentation.

Cal. Transaction Forms - Bus. Transactions § 6:23, Essentials Of Assent.

California Transactions Forms--Estate Planning § 11:48, Governing Contractual Provisions [CC §§ 1550 et seq., Fam C S721(B)].

California Transactions Forms--Family Law § 2:2, Contractual Nature.

Treatises and Practice Aids

Witkin, California Summary 10th Contracts § 116, in General.

Witkin, California Summary 10th Contracts § 187, Necessity Of Communication.

§ 1566. Consent not free; rescission

CONSENT, WHEN VOIDABLE. A consent which is not free is nevertheless not absolutely void, but may be rescinded by the parties, in the manner prescribed by the Chapter on Rescission. *(Enacted in 1872.)*

Research References

Forms

Cal. Transaction Forms - Bus. Transactions § 6:24, Defective Consent.

Cal. Transaction Forms - Bus. Transactions § 6:25, Mistake.

Cal. Transaction Forms - Bus. Transactions § 6:26, Fraud and Misrepresentation.

Cal. Transaction Forms - Bus. Transactions § 17:13, Unilateral Mistake.

Cal. Transaction Forms - Bus. Transactions § 17:23, Other Circumstances Justifying Rescission.

California Transactions Forms--Estate Planning § 11:48, Governing Contractual Provisions [CC §§ 1550 et seq., Fam C S721(B)].

West's California Code Forms, Civil § 1566 COMMENT, Consent Forms.

Treatises and Practice Aids

Witkin, California Summary 10th Contracts § 285, in General.

Witkin, California Summary 10th Contracts § 299, Fraud in Inception.
Witkin, California Summary 10th Contracts § 935, Grounds for Rescission.

§ 1567. Reality or freedom of consent; causes for defeating

APPARENT CONSENT, WHEN NOT FREE. An apparent consent is not real or free when obtained through:

1. Duress;
2. Menace;
3. Fraud;
4. Undue influence; or,
5. Mistake. *(Enacted in 1872.)*

Research References

Forms

Cal. Transaction Forms - Bus. Transactions § 6:24, Defective Consent.
Cal. Transaction Forms - Bus. Transactions § 6:25, Mistake.
Cal. Transaction Forms - Bus. Transactions § 17:13, Unilateral Mistake.
California Transactions Forms--Estate Planning § 11:48, Governing Contractual Provisions [CC §§ 1550 et seq., Fam C S721(B)].
California Transactions Forms--Family Law § 2:2, Contractual Nature.
Am. Jur. Pl & Pr Forms Duress and Undue Influence § 1, Introductory Comments.
West's California Code Forms, Civil § 1566 COMMENT, Consent Forms.

§ 1568. Consent obtained by cause defeating reality or freedom

WHEN DEEMED TO HAVE BEEN OBTAINED BY FRAUD, ETC. Consent is deemed to have been obtained through one of the causes mentioned in the last section only when it would not have been given had such cause not existed. *(Enacted in 1872.)*

Research References

Forms

West's California Code Forms, Civil § 1566 COMMENT, Consent Forms.

Treatises and Practice Aids

Witkin, California Summary 10th Contracts § 260, General Principle.

§ 1569. Duress

Duress consists in any of the following:

(a) Unlawful confinement of the person of the party, or of the spouse of such party, or of an ancestor, descendant, or adopted child of such party or spouse.

(b) Unlawful detention of the property of any such person.

(c) Confinement of such person, lawful in form, but fraudulently obtained, or fraudulently made unjustly harassing or oppressive. *(Enacted in 1872. Amended by Stats.2016, c. 50 (S.B.1005), § 11, eff. Jan. 1, 2017.)*

Research References

Forms

Cal. Transaction Forms - Bus. Transactions § 6:27, Duress.
Cal. Transaction Forms - Bus. Transactions § 6:24, Defective Consent.
Cal. Transaction Forms - Bus. Transactions § 17:14, Duress [Civ. Code, S1569].
Cal. Transaction Forms - Bus. Transactions § 17:15, Menace [Civ. Code, S1570].
California Transactions Forms--Family Law § 4:73, No Fraud, Duress, or Undue Influence.
Am. Jur. Pl & Pr Forms Duress and Undue Influence § 1, Introductory Comments.
West's California Code Forms, Civil § 1566 COMMENT, Consent Forms.
West's California Code Forms, Probate § 8250 Form 1, Contest Of Will and Objection to Probate.

Treatises and Practice Aids

Witkin, California Summary 10th Contracts § 309, Nature and Kinds Of Duress.

§ 1570. Menace

MENACE, WHAT. Menace consists in a threat:

1. Of such duress as is specified in Subdivisions 1 and 3 of the last section;

2. Of unlawful and violent injury to the person or property of any such person as is specified in the last section; or,

3. Of injury to the character of any such person. *(Enacted in 1872.)*

Research References

Forms

Cal. Transaction Forms - Bus. Transactions § 6:24, Defective Consent.
Cal. Transaction Forms - Bus. Transactions § 6:28, Menace.
Cal. Transaction Forms - Bus. Transactions § 17:15, Menace [Civ. Code, S1570].
West's California Code Forms, Civil § 1566 COMMENT, Consent Forms.

Treatises and Practice Aids

Witkin, California Summary 10th Contracts § 309, Nature and Kinds Of Duress.
Witkin, California Summary 10th Contracts § 311, in General.

§ 1571. Kinds of fraud

FRAUD, ACTUAL OR CONSTRUCTIVE. Fraud is either actual or constructive. *(Enacted in 1872.)*

Research References

Forms

Cal. Transaction Forms - Bus. Transactions § 6:24, Defective Consent.
Cal. Transaction Forms - Bus. Transactions § 6:26, Fraud and Misrepresentation.
Cal. Transaction Forms - Bus. Transactions § 17:16, Actual Fraud.
California Transactions Forms--Estate Planning § 2:24, Fraudulent Deceit; Duress or Coercion.
West's California Code Forms, Civil § 1566 COMMENT, Consent Forms.

Treatises and Practice Aids

Witkin, California Summary 10th Contracts § 285, in General.

§ 1572. Actual fraud

ACTUAL FRAUD, WHAT. Actual fraud, within the meaning of this Chapter, consists in any of the following acts, committed by a party to the contract, or with his connivance, with intent to deceive another party thereto, or to induce him to enter into the contract:

1. The suggestion, as a fact, of that which is not true, by one who does not believe it to be true;

2. The positive assertion, in a manner not warranted by the information of the person making it, of that which is not true, though he believes it to be true;

3. The suppression of that which is true, by one having knowledge or belief of the fact;

4. A promise made without any intention of performing it; or,

5. Any other act fitted to deceive. *(Enacted in 1872.)*

Research References

Forms

Cal. Transaction Forms - Bus. Transactions § 6:26, Fraud and Misrepresentation.
Cal. Transaction Forms - Bus. Transactions § 17:16, Actual Fraud.
West's California Code Forms, Probate § 8250 Form 1, Contest Of Will and Objection to Probate.

Treatises and Practice Aids

Witkin, California Summary 10th Contracts § 286, Elements: Traditional Listing.
Witkin, California Summary 10th Contracts § 287, Intentional Misrepresentation.
Witkin, California Summary 10th Contracts § 288, Negligent Misrepresentation.
Witkin, California Summary 10th Contracts § 290, Fraudulent Representation.
Witkin, California Summary 10th Contracts § 291, in General.
Witkin, California Summary 10th Contracts § 293, False Promise.
Witkin, California Summary 10th Contracts § 617, Royalty Contracts for Performance Of Copyrighted Musical Works.
Witkin, California Summary 10th Security Transactions in Real Property § 126, Action is Not to Recover Debt.
Witkin, California Summary 10th Torts § 767, Governing Statutes.
Witkin, California Summary 10th Torts § 793, in General.
Witkin, California Summary 10th Torts § 801, Reckless Misrepresentation.
Witkin, California Summary 10th Torts § 819, Tort as Form Of Deceit.
Witkin, California Summary 10th Torts § 820, Scope Of Tort.

§ 1573. Constructive fraud

CONSTRUCTIVE FRAUD. Constructive fraud consists:

1. In any breach of duty which, without an actually fraudulent intent, gains an advantage to the person in fault, or any one claiming under him, by misleading another to his prejudice, or to the prejudice of any one claiming under him; or,

2. In any such act or omission as the law specially declares to be fraudulent, without respect to actual fraud. *(Enacted in 1872.)*

Research References

Forms

Cal. Transaction Forms - Bus. Transactions § 6:26, Fraud and Misrepresentation.
Cal. Transaction Forms - Bus. Transactions § 17:17, Constructive Fraud.
California Transactions Forms--Estate Planning § 2:24, Fraudulent Deceit; Duress or Coercion.
West's California Code Forms, Probate § 8250 Form 1, Contest Of Will and Objection to Probate.

Treatises and Practice Aids

Witkin, California Summary 10th Contracts § 294, in General.
Witkin, California Summary 10th Contracts § 295, Confidential Relationship.
Witkin, California Summary 10th Torts § 767, Governing Statutes.

§ 1574. Actual fraud; question of fact

ACTUAL FRAUD A QUESTION OF FACT. Actual fraud is always a question of fact. *(Enacted in 1872.)*

Research References

Forms

Cal. Transaction Forms - Bus. Transactions § 6:24, Defective Consent.
Cal. Transaction Forms - Bus. Transactions § 6:26, Fraud and Misrepresentation.
Cal. Transaction Forms - Bus. Transactions § 17:16, Actual Fraud.
West's California Code Forms, Civil § 1566 COMMENT, Consent Forms.

Treatises and Practice Aids

Witkin, California Summary 10th Contracts § 286, Elements: Traditional Listing.

§ 1575. Undue influence

UNDUE INFLUENCE, WHAT. Undue influence consists:

1. In the use, by one in whom a confidence is reposed by another, or who holds a real or apparent authority over him, of such confidence or authority for the purpose of obtaining an unfair advantage over him;

2. In taking an unfair advantage of another's weakness of mind; or,

3. In taking a grossly oppressive and unfair advantage of another's necessities or distress. *(Enacted in 1872.)*

Research References

Forms

Cal. Transaction Forms - Bus. Transactions § 6:24, Defective Consent.
Cal. Transaction Forms - Bus. Transactions § 6:29, Undue Influence.
Cal. Transaction Forms - Bus. Transactions § 17:18, Undue Influence [Civ. Code, S1575].
California Transactions Forms--Estate Planning § 2:22, Definition Of Undue Influence.
Am. Jur. Pl & Pr Forms Duress and Undue Influence § 1, Introductory Comments.
West's California Code Forms, Civil § 1566 COMMENT, Consent Forms.
West's California Code Forms, Probate § 8250 Form 1, Contest Of Will and Objection to Probate.

Treatises and Practice Aids

Witkin, California Summary 10th Contracts § 57, Manic Depressive Psychosis.
Witkin, California Summary 10th Contracts § 316, Nature and Types.

Witkin, California Summary 10th Contracts § 321, No Confidential Relationship.

§ 1576. Kinds of mistake

MISTAKE, WHAT. Mistake may be either of fact or law. *(Enacted in 1872.)*

Research References

Forms

Cal. Transaction Forms - Bus. Transactions § 6:25, Mistake.
Cal. Transaction Forms - Bus. Transactions § 17:13, Unilateral Mistake.
West's California Code Forms, Civil § 1566 COMMENT, Consent Forms.

§ 1577. Mistake of fact

MISTAKE OF FACT. Mistake of fact is a mistake, not caused by the neglect of a legal duty on the part of the person making the mistake, and consisting in:

1. An unconscious ignorance or forgetfulness of a fact past or present, material to the contract; or,

2. Belief in the present existence of a thing material to the contract, which does not exist, or in the past existence of such a thing, which has not existed. *(Enacted in 1872.)*

Research References

Forms

Cal. Transaction Forms - Bus. Transactions § 6:24, Defective Consent.
Cal. Transaction Forms - Bus. Transactions § 6:25, Mistake.
Cal. Transaction Forms - Bus. Transactions § 17:13, Unilateral Mistake.
West's California Code Forms, Probate § 8250 Form 1, Contest Of Will and Objection to Probate.

Treatises and Practice Aids

Witkin, California Summary 10th Contracts § 260, General Principle.
Witkin, California Summary 10th Contracts § 262, in General.
Witkin, California Summary 10th Contracts § 269, Relief Denied.
Witkin, California Summary 10th Contracts § 270, Excusable Neglect.
Witkin, California Summary 10th Contracts § 282, Effect Of Plaintiff's Negligence.

§ 1578. Mistake of law

MISTAKE OF LAW. Mistake of law constitutes a mistake, within the meaning of this Article, only when it arises from:

1. A misapprehension of the law by all parties, all supposing that they knew and understood it, and all making substantially the same mistake as to the law; or,

2. A misapprehension of the law by one party, of which the others are aware at the time of contracting, but which they do not rectify. *(Enacted in 1872.)*

Research References

Forms

Cal. Transaction Forms - Bus. Transactions § 6:25, Mistake.
Cal. Transaction Forms - Bus. Transactions § 17:13, Unilateral Mistake.

Treatises and Practice Aids

Witkin, California Summary 10th Contracts § 272, in General.
Witkin, California Summary 10th Contracts § 274, Unilateral Mistake.
Witkin, California Summary 10th Wills and Probate § 724, Order.

§ 1579. Mistake of foreign law

MISTAKE OF FOREIGN LAWS. Mistake of foreign laws is a mistake of fact. *(Enacted in 1872.)*

Research References

Forms

Cal. Transaction Forms - Bus. Transactions § 6:24, Defective Consent.
West's California Code Forms, Civil § 1566 COMMENT, Consent Forms.

Treatises and Practice Aids

Witkin, California Summary 10th Contracts § 272, in General.

§ 1580. Mutuality of consent

MUTUALITY OF CONSENT. Consent is not mutual, unless the parties all agree upon the same thing in the same sense. But in certain cases defined by the Chapter on Interpretation, they are to be deemed so to agree without regard to the fact. *(Enacted in 1872.)*

Research References

Forms

Cal. Transaction Forms - Bus. Transactions § 6:23, Essentials Of Assent.
Cal. Transaction Forms - Bus. Transactions § 17:2, Necessity for Enforceable Contract.

§ 1581. Communication; consent

COMMUNICATION OF CONSENT. Consent can be communicated with effect, only by some act or omission of the party contracting, by which he intends to communicate it, or which necessarily tends to such communication. *(Enacted in 1872.)*

Research References

Forms

Cal. Transaction Forms - Bus. Transactions § 6:21, Acceptance.
Cal. Transaction Forms - Bus. Transactions § 6:23, Essentials Of Assent.

Treatises and Practice Aids

Witkin, California Summary 10th Contracts § 160, When Revocation Becomes Effective.
Witkin, California Summary 10th Contracts § 187, Necessity Of Communication.

§ 1582. Communication; acceptance of proposal

MODE OF COMMUNICATING ACCEPTANCE OF PROPOSAL. If a proposal prescribes any conditions concerning the communication of its acceptance, the proposer is not bound unless they are conformed to; but in other cases any reasonable and usual mode may be adopted. *(Enacted in 1872.)*

Research References

Forms

Cal. Transaction Forms - Bus. Transactions § 6:21, Acceptance.
West's California Code Forms, Civil § 1582 Form 1, Provision Specifying Method Of Communicating Acceptance.

Treatises and Practice Aids

Witkin, California Summary 10th Contracts § 160, When Revocation Becomes Effective.
Witkin, California Summary 10th Contracts § 189, Prescribed Manner or Reasonable Manner.
Witkin, California Summary 10th Contracts § 191, in General.

§ 1583. Communication; completion

WHEN COMMUNICATION DEEMED COMPLETE. Consent is deemed to be fully communicated between the parties as soon as the party accepting a proposal has put his acceptance in the course of transmission to the proposer, in conformity to the last section. *(Enacted in 1872.)*

Research References

Forms

West's California Code Forms, Civil § 1582 Form 1, Provision Specifying Method Of Communicating Acceptance.
West's California Code Forms, Commercial § 2206 Form 7, Buyer's Purchase Order.

Treatises and Practice Aids

Witkin, California Summary 10th Contracts § 160, When Revocation Becomes Effective.
Witkin, California Summary 10th Contracts § 177, Effective on Deposit in Mail.
Witkin, California Summary 10th Contracts § 189, Prescribed Manner or Reasonable Manner.
Witkin, California Summary 10th Contracts § 191, in General.

§ 1584. Acceptance of proposal; performing conditions or acceptance of consideration

ACCEPTANCE BY PERFORMANCE OF CONDITIONS. Performance of the conditions of a proposal, or the acceptance of the consideration offered with a proposal, is an acceptance of the proposal. *(Enacted in 1872.)*

Research References

Treatises and Practice Aids

Witkin, California Summary 10th Contracts § 195, Conduct as Acceptance.
Witkin, California Summary 10th Contracts § 199, Notification to Offeror.

§ 1585. Acceptance of proposal; absolute acceptance; qualified acceptance

ACCEPTANCE MUST BE ABSOLUTE. An acceptance must be absolute and unqualified, or must include in itself an acceptance of that character which the proposer can separate from the rest, and which will conclude the person accepting. A qualified acceptance is a new proposal. *(Enacted in 1872.)*

Research References

Forms

Cal. Transaction Forms - Bus. Transactions § 6:19, Rejection Of Offer.
Cal. Transaction Forms - Bus. Transactions § 6:21, Acceptance.
Cal. Transaction Forms - Bus. Transactions § 6:67, Unconditional Acceptance.
Cal. Transaction Forms - Bus. Transactions § 6:68, Conditional Acceptance.
Cal. Transaction Forms - Bus. Transactions § 6:71, Rejection and Counteroffer.
West's California Code Forms, Civil § 1582 Form 1, Provision Specifying Method Of Communicating Acceptance.

Treatises and Practice Aids

Witkin, California Summary 10th Contracts § 183, General Rule.
Witkin, California Summary 10th Contracts § 185, in General.

§ 1586. Revocation of proposal; time

REVOCATION OF PROPOSAL. A proposal may be revoked at any time before its acceptance is communicated to the proposer, but not afterwards. *(Enacted in 1872.)*

Research References

Forms

Cal. Transaction Forms - Bus. Transactions § 6:18, Revocation Of Offer.
Cal. Transaction Forms - Bus. Transactions § 6:66, Withdrawal Of Offer.
West's California Code Forms, Civil § 1587 Form 1, Notice Of Revocation Of Offer.

Treatises and Practice Aids

Witkin, California Summary 10th Contracts § 164, General Rule Of Revocability.

§ 1587. Revocation of proposal; method

A proposal is revoked by any of the following:

(a) By the communication of notice of revocation by the proposer to the other party, in the manner prescribed by Sections 1581 and 1583, before his or her acceptance has been communicated to the former.

(b) By the lapse of the time prescribed in the proposal for its acceptance or, if no time is prescribed, the lapse of a reasonable time without communication of the acceptance.

(c) By the failure of the acceptor to fulfill a condition precedent to acceptance.

(d) By the death or legal incapacity to make decisions of the proposer. *(Enacted in 1872. Amended by Stats.2014, c. 144 (A.B.1847), § 2, eff. Jan. 1, 2015.)*

Research References

Forms

California Real Estate Forms (Miller & Starr) § 1:23, Purchase and Sale Agreement--Residential Project.
California Real Estate Forms (Miller & Starr) § 1:33, Real Estate Purchase Contract and Receipt for Deposit--Income Property.
Cal. Transaction Forms - Bus. Transactions § 6:18, Revocation Of Offer.
Cal. Transaction Forms - Bus. Transactions § 24:57, Matters to Consider in Drafting Forms Regarding Acceptance and Prompt Shipment.
Am. Jur. Pl & Pr Forms Duress and Undue Influence § 1, Introductory Comments.

West's California Code Forms, Civil § 1587 Form 1, Notice Of Revocation Of Offer.

Treatises and Practice Aids

Witkin, California Summary 10th Contracts § 157, Lapse Of Prescribed or Reasonable Time.

Witkin, California Summary 10th Contracts § 158, Death or Incapacity Of Offeror or Offeree.

Witkin, California Summary 10th Contracts § 159, in General.

Witkin, California Summary 10th Contracts § 160, When Revocation Becomes Effective.

§ 1588. Ratification of voidable contract

RATIFICATION OF CONTRACT, VOID FOR WANT OF CONSENT. A contract which is voidable solely for want of due consent, may be ratified by a subsequent consent. *(Enacted in 1872.)*

Research References

Forms

Am. Jur. Pl & Pr Forms Duress and Undue Influence § 1, Introductory Comments.

§ 1589. Consent by acceptance of benefits

ASSUMPTION OF OBLIGATION BY ACCEPTANCE OF BENEFITS. A voluntary acceptance of the benefit of a transaction is equivalent to a consent to all the obligations arising from it, so far as the facts are known, or ought to be known, to the person accepting. *(Enacted in 1872.)*

Research References

Forms

Cal. Transaction Forms - Bus. Transactions § 16:9, Assumption Of Contract Obligations.

Treatises and Practice Aids

Witkin, California Summary 10th Contracts § 195, Conduct as Acceptance.

Witkin, California Summary 10th Contracts § 740, Liability Of Assignee.

§ 1590. Gifts in contemplation of marriage; recovery

Where either party to a contemplated marriage in this State makes a gift of money or property to the other on the basis or assumption that the marriage will take place, in the event that the donee refuses to enter into the marriage as contemplated or that it is given up by mutual consent, the donor may recover such gift or such part of its value as may, under all of the circumstances of the case, be found by a court or jury to be just. *(Added by Stats.1939, c. 128, p. 1245, § 3.)*

Research References

Forms

California Transactions Forms--Estate Planning § 7:2, Types Of Gifts.

Treatises and Practice Aids

Witkin, California Summary 10th Personal Property § 154, Revocation Of Gift in Contemplation Of Marriage.

Title 2

MANNER OF CREATING CONTRACTS

§ 1619. Express or implied contracts

A contract is either express or implied. *(Enacted in 1872.)*

Research References

Forms

Cal. Transaction Forms - Bus. Transactions § 6:5, Express, Implied, and Quasi.

Cal. Transaction Forms - Bus. Transactions § 12:23, Express Contracts.

Am. Jur. Pl. & Pr. Forms Restitution and Implied Contracts § 1, Introductory Comments.

§ 1620. Express contract defined

An express contract is one, the terms of which are stated in words. *(Enacted in 1872.)*

Research References

Forms

Cal. Transaction Forms - Bus. Transactions § 6:5, Express, Implied, and Quasi.

West's California Code Forms, Commercial § 2201 GENERAL COMMENT 2, Several Basic and Fundamental Contracting Principles.

Treatises and Practice Aids

Witkin, California Summary 10th Agency and Employment § 230, Enforceability Of Express Contract.

Witkin, California Summary 10th Contracts § 102, Express and Implied in Fact Contracts.

§ 1621. Implied contract defined

An implied contract is one, the existence and terms of which are manifested by conduct. *(Enacted in 1872.)*

Research References

Forms

Cal. Transaction Forms - Bus. Transactions § 6:5, Express, Implied, and Quasi.

Am. Jur. Pl. & Pr. Forms Restitution and Implied Contracts § 1, Introductory Comments.

Treatises and Practice Aids

Witkin, California Summary 10th Agency and Employment § 232, Totality Of Circumstances Test.

Witkin, California Summary 10th Contracts § 102, Express and Implied in Fact Contracts.

§ 1622. Oral contracts; authorization

All contracts may be oral, except such as are specially required by statute to be in writing. *(Enacted in 1872.)*

Research References

Forms

Cal. Transaction Forms - Bus. Transactions § 8:3, Statute Of Frauds.

Cal. Transaction Forms - Bus. Transactions § 8:7, Matters to Consider in Making Agreements Through Electronic Communications.

Cal. Transaction Forms - Bus. Transactions § 6:42, Contracts Required to be in Writing.

California Transactions Forms--Estate Planning § 11:47, Formalities.

§ 1623. Statute of frauds; enforcement of contract oral by reason of fraud

Where a contract, which is required by law to be in writing, is prevented from being put into writing by the fraud of a party thereto, any other party who is by such fraud led to believe that it is in writing, and acts upon such belief to his prejudice, may enforce it against the fraudulent party. *(Enacted in 1872.)*

Research References

Forms

Cal. Transaction Forms - Bus. Transactions § 6:42, Contracts Required to be in Writing.

Am. Jur. Pl. & Pr. Forms Contracts § 6, Complaint, Petition, or Declaration--Allegation--Enforceability Of Oral Contract Due to Defendant's Fraud.

§ 1624. Statute of frauds

(a) The following contracts are invalid, unless they, or some note or memorandum thereof, are in writing and subscribed by the party to be charged or by the party's agent:

(1) An agreement that by its terms is not to be performed within a year from the making thereof.

(2) A special promise to answer for the debt, default, or miscarriage of another, except in the cases provided for in Section 2794.

(3) An agreement for the leasing for a longer period than one year, or for the sale of real property, or of an interest therein; such an agreement, if made by an agent of the party sought to be charged, is invalid, unless the authority of the agent is in writing, subscribed by the party sought to be charged.

(4) An agreement authorizing or employing an agent, broker, or any other person to purchase or sell real estate, or to lease real estate for a longer period than one year, or to procure, introduce, or find a purchaser or seller of real estate or a lessee or lessor of real estate where the lease is for a longer period than one year, for compensation or a commission.

(5) An agreement that by its terms is not to be performed during the lifetime of the promisor.

(6) An agreement by a purchaser of real property to pay an indebtedness secured by a mortgage or deed of trust upon the property purchased, unless assumption of the indebtedness by the purchaser is specifically provided for in the conveyance of the property.

(7) A contract, promise, undertaking, or commitment to loan money or to grant or extend credit, in an amount greater than one hundred thousand dollars ($100,000), not primarily for personal, family, or household purposes, made by a person engaged in the business of lending or arranging for the lending of money or extending credit. For purposes of this section, a contract, promise, undertaking, or commitment to loan money secured solely by residential property consisting of one to four dwelling units shall be deemed to be for personal, family, or household purposes.

(b) Notwithstanding paragraph (1) of subdivision (a):

(1) An agreement or contract that is valid in other respects and is otherwise enforceable is not invalid for lack of a note, memorandum, or other writing and is enforceable by way of action or defense, provided that the agreement or contract is a qualified financial contract as defined in paragraph (2) and one of the following apply:

(A) There is, as provided in paragraph (3), sufficient evidence to indicate that a contract has been made.

(B) The parties thereto by means of a prior or subsequent written contract, have agreed to be bound by the terms of the qualified financial contract from the time they reached agreement (by telephone, by exchange of electronic messages, or otherwise) on those terms.

(2) For purposes of this subdivision, a "qualified financial contract" means an agreement as to which each party thereto is other than a natural person and that is any of the following:

(A) For the purchase and sale of foreign exchange, foreign currency, bullion, coin, or precious metals on a forward, spot, next-day value or other basis.

(B) A contract (other than a contract for the purchase of a commodity for future delivery on, or subject to the rules of, a contract market or board of trade) for the purchase, sale, or transfer of any commodity or any similar good, article, service, right, or interest that is presently or in the future becomes the subject of a dealing in the forward contract trade, or any product or byproduct thereof, with a maturity date more than two days after the date the contract is entered into.

(C) For the purchase and sale of currency, or interbank deposits denominated in United States dollars.

(D) For a currency option, currency swap, or cross-currency rate swap.

(E) For a commodity swap or a commodity option (other than an option contract traded on, or subject to the rules of, a contract market or board of trade).

(F) For a rate swap, basis swap, forward rate transaction, or an interest rate option.

(G) For a security-index swap or option, or a security or securities price swap or option.

(H) An agreement that involves any other similar transaction relating to a price or index (including, without limitation, any transaction or agreement involving any combination of the foregoing, any cap, floor, collar, or similar transaction with respect to a rate, commodity price, commodity index, security or securities price, security index, other price index, or loan price).

(I) An option with respect to any of the foregoing.

(3) There is sufficient evidence that a contract has been made in any of the following circumstances:

(A) There is evidence of an electronic communication (including, without limitation, the recording of a telephone call or the tangible written text produced by computer retrieval), admissible in evidence under the laws of this state, sufficient to indicate that in the communication a contract was made between the parties.

(B) A confirmation in writing sufficient to indicate that a contract has been made between the parties and sufficient against the sender is received by the party against whom enforcement is sought no later than the fifth business day after the contract is made (or any other period of time that the parties may agree in writing) and the sender does not receive, on or before the third business day after receipt (or the other period of time that the parties may agree in writing), written objection to a material term of the confirmation. For purposes of this subparagraph, a confirmation or an objection thereto is received at the time there has been an actual receipt by an individual responsible for the transaction or, if earlier, at the time there has been constructive receipt, which is the time actual receipt by that individual would have occurred if the receiving party, as an organization, had exercised reasonable diligence. For the purposes of this subparagraph, a "business day" is a day on which both parties are open and transacting business of the kind involved in that qualified financial contract that is the subject of confirmation.

(C) The party against whom enforcement is sought admits in its pleading, testimony, or otherwise in court that a contract was made.

(D) There is a note, memorandum, or other writing sufficient to indicate that a contract has been made, signed by the party against whom enforcement is sought or by its authorized agent or broker.

For purposes of this paragraph, evidence of an electronic communication indicating the making in that communication of a contract, or a confirmation, admission, note, memorandum, or writing is not insufficient because it omits or incorrectly states one or more material terms agreed upon, as long as the evidence provides a reasonable basis for concluding that a contract was made.

(4) For purposes of this subdivision, the tangible written text produced by telex, telefacsimile, computer retrieval, or other process by which electronic signals are transmitted by telephone or otherwise shall constitute a writing, and any symbol executed or adopted by a party with the present intention to authenticate a writing shall constitute a signing. The confirmation and notice of objection referred to in subparagraph (B) of paragraph (3) may be communicated by means of telex, telefacsimile, computer, or other similar process by which electronic signals are transmitted by telephone or otherwise, provided that a party claiming to have communicated in that manner shall, unless the parties have otherwise agreed in writing, have the burden of establishing actual or constructive receipt by the other party as set forth in subparagraph (B) of paragraph (3).

(c) This section does not apply to leases subject to Division 10 (commencing with Section 10101) of the Commercial Code.

(d) An electronic message of an ephemeral nature that is not designed to be retained or to create a permanent record, including, but not limited to, a text message or instant message format communication, is insufficient under this title to constitute a contract to convey real property, in the absence of a written confirmation that conforms to the requirements of subparagraph (B) of paragraph (3) of subdivision (b). *(Enacted in 1872. Amended by Code Am.1873–74, c. 612, p. 241, § 190; Code Am.1877–78, c. 165, p. 86, § 1; Stats.1905, c. 451, p. 610, § 1; Stats.1931, c. 1070, p. 2260, § 9; Stats.1937, c. 316, p. 695, § 2; Stats.1963, c. 814, p. 1843, § 1; Stats.1967, c. 52, p. 953, § 1; Stats.1983, c. 842, § 6, operative Jan. 1, 1985; Stats.1985, c. 1315, § 1; Stats. 1988, c. 1096, § 1; Stats.1988, c. 1368, § 1.5, operative Jan. 1, 1990; Stats.1998, c. 78 (S.B.1865), § 1; Stats.2014, c. 107 (A.B.2136), § 2, eff. Jan. 1, 2015.)*

Law Revision Commission Comments

1983 Amendment

Section 1624 is amended to delete the last portion of subdivision 6 (agreement to devise or bequeath property or to make any provision by will) which is superseded by Probate Code Section 150. [16 Cal.L.Rev.Comm.Reports 2301 (1982)].

Research References

Forms

California Real Estate Forms (Miller & Starr) § 1:17, Purchase and Sale Agreement--Unimproved Real Property--With Escrow Instructions.

California Real Estate Forms (Miller & Starr) § 1:18, Purchase and Sale Agreement--Raw Land.

California Real Estate Forms (Miller & Starr) § 1:19, Agreement for Purchase and Sale Of Realty--Build-To-Suit.

California Real Estate Forms (Miller & Starr) § 1:20, Purchase and Sale Agreement--Small Commercial Properties Subject to Tenant Leases.

California Real Estate Forms (Miller & Starr) § 1:21, Purchase and Sale Agreement--Commercial Property Subject to Tenant Leases.

California Real Estate Forms (Miller & Starr) § 1:22, Agreement Of Purchase and Sale--Multi-Property.

California Real Estate Forms (Miller & Starr) § 1:23, Purchase and Sale Agreement--Residential Project.

California Real Estate Forms (Miller & Starr) § 1:24, Combination Purchase and Option Agreement--Residential Lots Being Acquired from a Bankrupt Seller.

California Real Estate Forms (Miller & Starr) § 1:25, Purchase and Sale Agreement--Multi-Tenant Residential Property (With Lease-Back).

California Real Estate Forms (Miller & Starr) § 1:26, Purchase and Sale Agreement--Seller-Oriented Short Form.

California Real Estate Forms (Miller & Starr) § 1:27, Purchase and Sale Agreement--Multitenant Residential Property.

California Real Estate Forms (Miller & Starr) § 1:28, Purchase and Sale Agreement--Hotel.

California Real Estate Forms (Miller & Starr) § 1:29, Purchase and Sale Agreement--Seller Oriented With Seller Financing.

California Real Estate Forms (Miller & Starr) § 1:30, Planned Development Deposit Receipt and Agreement Of Sale.

California Real Estate Forms (Miller & Starr) § 1:31, Condominium Deposit Receipt and Agreement Of Sale.

California Real Estate Forms (Miller & Starr) § 1:32, Hotel Purchase and Sale Agreement With Escrow Instructions.

California Real Estate Forms (Miller & Starr) § 1:33, Real Estate Purchase Contract and Receipt for Deposit--Income Property.

California Real Estate Forms (Miller & Starr) § 1:34, Installment Land Sale Contract With Power Of Sale.

California Real Estate Forms (Miller & Starr) § 1:35, Purchase and Sale Agreement--Partially Constructed Project.

California Real Estate Forms (Miller & Starr) § 1:94, California Residential Purchase Agreement and Joint Escrow Instructions.
California Real Estate Forms (Miller & Starr) § 1:26.50, Purchase and Sale Agreement--Seller Oriented--Shopping Center.
Cal. Transaction Forms - Bus. Transactions § 3:4, Methods Of Transfer.
Cal. Transaction Forms - Bus. Transactions § 8:3, Statute Of Frauds.
Cal. Transaction Forms - Bus. Transactions § 8:4, Overview.
Cal. Transaction Forms - Bus. Transactions § 8:7, Matters to Consider in Making Agreements Through Electronic Communications.
Cal. Transaction Forms - Bus. Transactions § 6:42, Contracts Required to be in Writing.
Cal. Transaction Forms - Bus. Transactions § 6:43, Sufficiency Of the Writing and Subscription.
Cal. Transaction Forms - Bus. Transactions § 18:9, Written or Oral Agreement.
Cal. Transaction Forms - Bus. Transactions § 17:95, Modification Of Written Contracts [Civ. Code, S1697].
Cal. Transaction Forms - Bus. Transactions § 29:36, Instructions to Transfer Uncertificated Securities.
Cal. Transaction Forms - Bus. Transactions § 12:25, Oral Contracts.
Cal. Transaction Forms - Bus. Transactions § 19:12, Overview Of Suretyship Defenses.
Cal. Transaction Forms - Bus. Transactions § 21:12, Bailment Contracts.
Cal. Transaction Forms - Bus. Transactions § 21:22, Bailment Contract; Long Form.
Cal. Transaction Forms - Bus. Transactions § 24:84, Price Requirement.
Cal. Transaction Forms - Bus. Transactions § 24:85, Writing.
Cal. Transaction Forms - Bus. Transactions § 24:86, Contracts Between Merchants.
Cal. Transaction Forms - Bus. Transactions § 24:91, Other Exceptions.
California Transactions Forms--Estate Planning § 11:2, Formalities for Establishing Contract Concerning Will or Devise Made on or After January 1, 1985.
California Transactions Forms--Estate Planning § 11:40, Premarital Agreements Entered Into Before January 1, 1986.
California Transactions Forms--Estate Planning § 11:47, Formalities.
California Transactions Forms--Family Law § 4:22, Statute Of Frauds.
West's California Code Forms, Civil § 1624 Form 1, Affirmative Defense Of Statute Of Frauds.
West's California Code Forms, Civil § 1698 Form 1, Agreement--Modifying Written Agreement.
West's California Code Forms, Civil § 2307 Form 2, Ratification Of Agency.
West's California Code Forms, Commercial § 1206 Form 1, Memorandum Of Agreement for Sale Of Personal Property.
West's California Code Forms, Commercial § 2201 GENERAL COMMENT, Statute Of Frauds.

Treatises and Practice Aids

Witkin, California Summary 10th Agency and Employment § 75, in General.
Witkin, California Summary 10th Agency and Employment § 233, in General.
Witkin, California Summary 10th Contracts § 201, Waiver Of Defect in Acceptance.
Witkin, California Summary 10th Contracts § 343, California Codes.
Witkin, California Summary 10th Contracts § 344, Defense Waived If Not Asserted.
Witkin, California Summary 10th Contracts § 354, California Cases.
Witkin, California Summary 10th Contracts § 359, Who is Party to be Charged.
Witkin, California Summary 10th Contracts § 363, in General.
Witkin, California Summary 10th Contracts § 364, Commencement and Computation Of Period.
Witkin, California Summary 10th Contracts § 371, Contract Not to be Performed During Lifetime.
Witkin, California Summary 10th Contracts § 372, Scope Of Statute.
Witkin, California Summary 10th Contracts § 383, Qualified Financial Contract.
Witkin, California Summary 10th Contracts § 385, Scope Of Statute.
Witkin, California Summary 10th Contracts § 388, Equal Dignities Rule.
Witkin, California Summary 10th Contracts § 391, Liability Of Principal to Agent.
Witkin, California Summary 10th Contracts § 392, Nature and Effect Of Statute.
Witkin, California Summary 10th Contracts § 393, Oral Agreement to Lease.
Witkin, California Summary 10th Contracts § 395, Oral Finders Agreement.
Witkin, California Summary 10th Contracts § 397, Distinctions.
Witkin, California Summary 10th Contracts § 398, Contract to Loan Money or Extend Credit.
Witkin, California Summary 10th Contracts § 399, Marital and Premarital Agreements.
Witkin, California Summary 10th Contracts § 400, Miscellaneous Provisions.
Witkin, California Summary 10th Contracts § 414, Real Estate Broker's Authorization.
Witkin, California Summary 10th Contracts § 417, Qualified Financial Contract.
Witkin, California Summary 10th Contracts § 418, Personal Property Leases.
Witkin, California Summary 10th Real Property § 520, Execution and Delivery.
Witkin, California Summary 10th Security Transactions in Real Property § 108, Manner and Requisites Of Assumption.
Witkin, California Summary 10th Torts § 788, Representations Concerning Credit.

§ 1624.5. Written contract; sale of personal property exceeding $5000; exceptions

(a) Except in the cases described in subdivision (b), a contract for the sale of personal property is not enforceable by way of action or defense beyond five thousand dollars ($5,000) in amount or value of remedy unless there is some record, as defined in subdivision (m) of Section 1633.2, but solely to the extent permitted by applicable law, that indicates that a contract for sale has been made between the parties at a defined or stated price, reasonably identifies the subject matter, and is signed, including by way of electronic signature, as defined in subdivision (h) of Section 1633.2, but solely to the extent permitted by applicable law, by the party against whom enforcement is sought or by his or her authorized agent.

(b) Subdivision (a) does not apply to contracts governed by the Commercial Code, including contracts for the sale of goods (Section 2201 of the Commercial Code), contracts for the sale of securities (Section 8113 of the Commercial Code), and security agreements (Sections 9201 and 9203 of the Commercial Code).

(c) Subdivision (a) does not apply to a qualified financial contract as that term is defined in paragraph (2) of subdivision (b) of Section 1624 if either of the following exists:

(1) There is, as provided in paragraph (3) of subdivision (b) of Section 1624, sufficient evidence to indicate that a contract has been made.

(2) The parties thereto, by means of a prior or subsequent written contract, have agreed to be bound by the terms of the qualified financial contract from the time they reach agreement (by telephone, by exchange of electronic messages, or otherwise) on those terms. *(Added by Stats.2006, c. 254 (S.B.1481), § 1.)*

Application

For provision relating to application of Stats.2006, c. 254 (S.B.1481) to documents of title that are issued or bailments that arise before Jan. 1, 2007, see § 81 of that act.

Research References

Forms

Cal. Transaction Forms - Bus. Transactions § 6:42, Contracts Required to be in Writing.

Cal. Transaction Forms - Bus. Transactions § 30:19, Statute Of Frauds.

Treatises and Practice Aids

Witkin, California Summary 10th Contracts § 384, Sale Of Chose in Action Of $5,000 Value.

Witkin, California Summary 10th Sales § 32, Statute Of Frauds.

§ 1625. Written contracts; effect on negotiations or stipulations

The execution of a contract in writing, whether the law requires it to be written or not, supersedes all the negotiations or stipulations concerning its matter which preceded or accompanied the execution of the instrument. *(Enacted in 1872. Amended by Stats.1905, c. 451, p. 611, § 2.)*

Research References

Forms

Cal. Transaction Forms - Bus. Transactions § 6:42, Contracts Required to be in Writing.

California Transactions Forms--Family Law § 2:2, Contractual Nature.

Treatises and Practice Aids

Witkin, California Summary 10th Insurance § 30, Oral Contracts.

§ 1626. Written contracts; effective upon delivery

A contract in writing takes effect upon its delivery to the party in whose favor it is made, or to his agent. *(Enacted in 1872.)*

Research References

Forms

Cal. Transaction Forms - Bus. Transactions § 6:42, Contracts Required to be in Writing.

Treatises and Practice Aids

Witkin, California Summary 10th Insurance § 45, in General.

Title 4

UNLAWFUL CONTRACTS

§ 1667. "Unlawfulness" defined

That is not lawful which is:

1. Contrary to an express provision of law;

2. Contrary to the policy of express law, though not expressly prohibited; or,

3. Otherwise contrary to good morals. *(Enacted in 1872.)*

Research References

Forms

California Real Estate Forms (Miller & Starr) § 4:5, Construction Agreement--Cost Plus a Percentage Fee With a Guaranteed Maximum Price.

California Real Estate Forms (Miller & Starr) § 4:6, Construction Contract--Commercial Project--Fixed Price.

California Real Estate Forms (Miller & Starr) § 3:37, Continuing Guaranty.

California Real Estate Forms (Miller & Starr) § 3:38, Completion Guaranty.

California Real Estate Forms (Miller & Starr) § 3:57, Loan Purchase and Sale Agreement.

Cal. Transaction Forms - Bus. Transactions § 6:8, Void, Voidable, and Unenforceable.

Cal. Transaction Forms - Bus. Transactions § 6:45, Illegality.

Cal. Transaction Forms - Bus. Transactions § 17:21, Unlawfulness Of Contract [Civ. Code, S1667].

West's California Code Forms, Civil § 1667 Form 1, Affirmative Defense Of Unlawful Contract.

Treatises and Practice Aids

Witkin, California Summary 10th Community Property § 32, Agreements Violating Public Policy.

Witkin, California Summary 10th Contracts § 426, Loan to Gambler.

Witkin, California Summary 10th Contracts § 451, in General.

Witkin, California Summary 10th Contracts § 672, Meaning Of Term "Negligent" in C.C. 1668.

Witkin, California Summary 10th Husband and Wife § 59, Fault Theory Eliminated for Dissolution.

Witkin, California Summary 10th Insurance § 47, Validity.

§ 1668. Contracts contrary to policy of law

All contracts which have for their object, directly or indirectly, to exempt anyone from responsibility for his own fraud, or willful injury to the person or property of another, or violation of law, whether willful or negligent, are against the policy of the law. *(Enacted in 1872.)*

Research References

Forms

Cal. Transaction Forms - Bus. Transactions § 6:45, Illegality.

Cal. Transaction Forms - Bus. Transactions § 21:9, Contractual Limits on Bailee's Liability.

Cal. Transaction Forms - Bus. Transactions § 17:21, Unlawfulness Of Contract [Civ. Code, S1667].
Cal. Transaction Forms - Bus. Transactions § 20:12, Validity Of Indemnity Agreements Providing for Indemnification for Indemnitee's Own Negligence.
West's California Code Forms, Civil § 1667 Form 1, Affirmative Defense Of Unlawful Contract.
West's California Code Forms, Commercial § 2719 Form 3, Alternate Form Of Contractual Modification or Limitation Of Remedies.
West's California Code Forms, Commercial § 2316 Form 13, Liquidation Of Damages for Breach Of Warranty.
West's California Code Forms, Commercial § 2719 GENERAL COMMENT, Modification or Limitation Of Noncontractual Remedies.

Treatises and Practice Aids

Witkin, California Summary 10th Contracts § 304, Representations Made by Party.
Witkin, California Summary 10th Contracts § 422, Liberal Rule Of Severability.
Witkin, California Summary 10th Contracts § 660, California Code.
Witkin, California Summary 10th Contracts § 662, Medicine.
Witkin, California Summary 10th Contracts § 663, Automobiles.
Witkin, California Summary 10th Contracts § 664, Employment.
Witkin, California Summary 10th Contracts § 665, Other Areas.
Witkin, California Summary 10th Contracts § 666, Statutory Prohibitions.
Witkin, California Summary 10th Contracts § 671, Valid Despite C.C. 1668.
Witkin, California Summary 10th Contracts § 672, Meaning Of Term "Negligent" in C.C. 1668.
Witkin, California Summary 10th Contracts § 675, "Sole Remedy" Provision in Employment Contract.
Witkin, California Summary 10th Contracts § 671A, (New) Distinction: "Any Negligent Act" Does Not Include Gross Negligence.
Witkin, California Summary 10th Equity § 123, Other Practices.
Witkin, California Summary 10th Insurance § 100, in General.
Witkin, California Summary 10th Insurance § 226, in General.
Witkin, California Summary 10th Insurance § 324, in General.
Witkin, California Summary 10th Sales § 94, Where Warranty is Fraudulent.
Witkin, California Summary 10th Torts § 231, Insurance Coverage.
Witkin, California Summary 10th Torts § 767, Governing Statutes.
Witkin, California Summary 10th Torts § 812, in General.

§ 1669. Restraint of marriage

Every contract in restraint of the marriage of any person, other than a minor, is void. *(Added by Stats.1977, c. 198, p. 718, § 1, operative July 1, 1978.)*

Law Revision Commission Comments

1977 Addition

Section 1669 continues without change former Section 1676. [13 Cal.L.Rev.Comm. Reports 1735 (1976)].

Research References

Forms

Cal. Transaction Forms - Bus. Transactions § 6:45, Illegality.

Treatises and Practice Aids

Witkin, California Summary 10th Contracts § 619, Contract Restraining Marriage.

§ 1669.5. Minor victim of unlawful sex act; payment of money or other consideration; application; district attorney enforcement; deposit to State Children's Trust Fund

(a) Any contract for the payment of money or other consideration to a minor who has been alleged to be the victim of an unlawful sex act, or to his or her legal representative, by the alleged perpetrator of that unlawful sex act, or his or her legal representative, entered into on or after the time of the alleged unlawful sex act, and providing for any payments to be made more than one year after the date of the execution of the contract, is void as contrary to public policy. A district attorney may bring an action or intervene in any action to enjoin enforcement of any contract which is in violation of this section.

(b) This section does not apply after the date of the final judgment in a criminal case against the alleged perpetrator for the unlawful sex act described in subdivision (a).

(c) This section does not apply to a contract for the payment of money or other consideration made from a nonrevocable trust established for the benefit of the minor if the alleged perpetrator has no direct or indirect access to, or control over, the trust.

(d) This section does not apply to an alleged perpetrator of an unlawful sex act against a minor to the extent he or she agrees to pay, or is required by court order to pay, child support for that minor upon a dissolution or legal separation.

(e) For purposes of this section, "unlawful sex act," means a felony sex offense committed against a minor.

(f) Notwithstanding subdivision (a), any contract declared void as contrary to public policy under this section may still be enforced by a district attorney against the payor, and the proceeds thereof shall be deposited in the State Children's Trust Fund pursuant to Section 18969 of the Welfare and Institutions Code. *(Added by Stats.1993–94, 1st Ex.Sess., c. 54 (S.B.35), § 1, eff. Nov. 30, 1994.)*

Research References

Treatises and Practice Aids

Witkin, California Summary 10th Contracts § 641, Contract to Pay Child Sex Victim.

§ 1669.7. Contract for consideration for providing information obtained as a result of witnessing a crime; validity; civil actions

A contract for the payment of money or other consideration in violation of Section 132.5 of the Penal Code is void as contrary to public policy. The Attorney General or the district attorney of the county in which a violation of Section 132.5 of the Penal Code occurs may bring a civil action, or intervene in any civil action, to enjoin the enforcement of a contract that violates that section. *(Added by Stats.1994, c. 869 (S.B.1999), § 1.)*

Research References

Treatises and Practice Aids

Witkin, California Summary 10th Contracts § 636, Contracts Involving Evidence.

§ 1670. Construction contract with public agency; disputes; resolution

Any dispute arising from a construction contract with a public agency, which contract contains a provision that one party to the contract or one party's agent or employee shall decide any disputes arising under that contract, shall be resolved by submitting the dispute to independent arbitration, if mutually agreeable, otherwise by litigation in a court of competent jurisdiction. *(Added by Stats.1978, c. 1374, p. 4556, § 1.)*

Research References

Forms

California Real Estate Forms (Miller & Starr) § 3:7, Promissory Note.
California Real Estate Forms (Miller & Starr) § 3:13, Promissory Note Secured by Construction Deed Of Trust.
California Real Estate Forms (Miller & Starr) § 3:20, Promissory Note--Conduit Loan.
California Real Estate Forms (Miller & Starr) § 3:78, Promissory Note--Line Of Credit.

Treatises and Practice Aids

Witkin, California Summary 10th Contracts § 948, Routine Waiver Invalid.
Witkin, California Summary 10th Contracts § 995, California Law.

§ 1670.5. Unconscionable contract or clause of contract; finding as matter of law; remedies

(a) If the court as a matter of law finds the contract or any clause of the contract to have been unconscionable at the time it was made the court may refuse to enforce the contract, or it may enforce the remainder of the contract without the unconscionable clause, or it may so limit the application of any unconscionable clause as to avoid any unconscionable result.

(b) When it is claimed or appears to the court that the contract or any clause thereof may be unconscionable the parties shall be afforded a reasonable opportunity to present evidence as to its commercial setting, purpose, and effect to aid the court in making the determination. *(Added by Stats.1979, c. 819, p. 2827, § 3, eff. Sept. 19, 1979.)*

Research References

Forms

Cal. Transaction Forms - Bus. Transactions § 6:46, Unconscionability.
Cal. Transaction Forms - Bus. Transactions § 1:72, Trend Toward Balance and Conciliation Between Parties.
Cal. Transaction Forms - Bus. Transactions § 12:21, Employment Contracts Generally.
Cal. Transaction Forms - Bus. Transactions § 12:51, Disputes Included and Excluded from Arbitration.
West's California Code Forms, Commercial § 1304 Form 3, Standards Of Good Faith--Statements by Agents or Employees.
West's California Code Forms, Commercial § 2714 Form 3, Clause Limiting Remedy for Breach Of Warranty.
West's California Code Forms, Commercial § 2715 Form 2, Clauses Excluding Incidental and Consequential Damages Of Buyer.
West's California Code Forms, Commercial § 2719 Form 3, Alternate Form Of Contractual Modification or Limitation Of Remedies.
West's California Code Forms, Commercial § 1203 Form 5, Standards Of Good Faith--Statements by Agents or Employees.
West's California Code Forms, Commercial § 2302 GENERAL COMMENT, Unconscionable Contract or Clause.

Treatises and Practice Aids

Witkin, California Summary 10th Contracts § 322, Alternate Approaches.
Witkin, California Summary 10th Contracts § 330, Commercial Code and California Statute.
Witkin, California Summary 10th Contracts § 332, in General.
Witkin, California Summary 10th Contracts § 339, Bank Depositor's Signature Card.
Witkin, California Summary 10th Contracts § 341, Employment Contract Terminating Commissions.
Witkin, California Summary 10th Contracts § 541, Fees Against Credit Card Customers.
Witkin, California Summary 10th Contracts § 827, Excuse Of Condition or Equitable Relief.
Witkin, California Summary 10th Equity § 40, Unconscionable Contract.
Witkin, California Summary 10th Sales § 7, Adoption in California.
Witkin, California Summary 10th Sales § 91, Strict Construction.
Witkin, California Summary 10th Sales § 207, Agreement Limiting Consequential Damages.
Witkin, California Summary 10th Sales § 296, Consumers Legal Remedies Act.

Part 3

OBLIGATIONS IMPOSED BY LAW

§ 1708.5.5. Sexual battery by adult in position of authority over minor; consent as defense

(a) Notwithstanding Section 3515, consent shall not be a defense in any civil action under Section 1708.5 if the person who commits the sexual battery is an adult who is in a position of authority over the minor.

(b) For purposes of this section, an adult is in a "position of authority" if he or she, by reason of that position, is able to exercise undue influence over a minor. A "position of authority" includes, but is not limited to, a natural parent, stepparent, foster parent, relative, partner of any such parent or relative, caretaker, youth leader, recreational director, athletic manager, coach, teacher, counselor, therapist, religious leader, doctor, employee of one of those aforementioned persons, or coworker.

(c) For purposes of this section, "undue influence" has the same meaning as in Section 15610.70 of the Welfare and Institutions Code. *(Added by Stats.2015, c. 128 (S.B.14), § 1, eff. Jan. 1, 2016.)*

Research References

Treatises and Practice Aids

Witkin, California Summary 10th Torts § 382, Statutory Actions.

Witkin, California Summary 10th Torts § 386, Nature Of Defense.

§ 1708.6. Liability for tort of domestic violence

(a) A person is liable for the tort of domestic violence if the plaintiff proves both of the following elements:

(1) The infliction of injury upon the plaintiff resulting from abuse, as defined in subdivision (a) of Section 13700 of the Penal Code.

(2) The abuse was committed by the defendant, a person having a relationship with the plaintiff as defined in subdivision (b) of Section 13700 of the Penal Code.

(b) A person who commits an act of domestic violence upon another is liable to that person for damages, including, but not limited to, general damages, special damages, and punitive damages pursuant to Section 3294.

(c) The court, in an action pursuant to this section, may grant to a prevailing plaintiff equitable relief, an injunction, costs, and any other relief that the court deems proper, including reasonable attorney's fees.

(d) The rights and remedies provided in this section are in addition to any other rights and remedies provided by law.

(e) The time for commencement of an action under this section is governed by Section 340.15 of the Code of Civil Procedure. *(Added by Stats.2002, c. 193 (A.B.1933), § 2.)*

Commentary

When a complaint alleged a continuing course of domestic violence throughout a long marriage, *Pugliese v. Superior Court, 146 Cal.App.4th 1444, 53 Cal.Rptr.3d 681 (2007), review denied April 11, 2007,* held that the trial court erred in interpreting the three-year statute of limitations of section 340.15 of the Code of Civil Procedure to bar damages for incidents of domestic violence occurring more than three years prior to timely filing of a complaint. Relying on the language subsection (a)(1) of section 340.15, the court reasoned that the three-year limitation runs from the *last* act of domestic violence and included all acts of continuing domestic violence. The court additionally relied upon the doctrine of "continuing tort" and the history of the enactment of this section.

Research References

Forms

West's California Code Forms, Civil § 1708.6 Form 1, Complaint--For Domestic Violence.

Treatises and Practice Aids

Witkin, California Summary 10th Husband and Wife § 371, Civil Remedies.

Witkin, California Summary 10th Torts § 467, Domestic Violence.

§ 1708.9. Interference with persons attempting to enter or exit school grounds or health facility prohibited; exception for parents or guardians; injunctive relief, damages, and civil penalties; constitutionally protected activities

(a) It is unlawful for any person, except a parent or guardian acting toward his or her minor child, to commit any of the following acts:

(1) By force, threat of force, or physical obstruction that is a crime of violence, to intentionally injure, intimidate, interfere with, or attempt to injure, intimidate, or interfere with, any person attempting to enter or exit a facility.

(2) By nonviolent physical obstruction, to intentionally injure, intimidate, interfere with, or attempt to injure, intimidate, or interfere with, any person attempting to enter or exit a facility.

(b) For purposes of this section:

(1) "Facility" means any public or private school grounds, as described in subdivision (a) of Section 626.8 of the Penal Code, or any health facility, as described in Section 1250 of the Health and Safety Code.

(2) To "interfere" means to restrict a person's freedom of movement.

(3) To "intimidate" means to place a person in reasonable apprehension of bodily harm to himself, herself, or another person.

(4) "Nonviolent" means conduct that would not constitute a crime of violence.

(5) "Physical obstruction" means rendering ingress to or egress from a facility impassable to another person, or rendering passage to or from a facility unreasonably difficult or hazardous to another person.

(c) A person aggrieved by a violation of subdivision (a) may bring a civil action to enjoin the violation, for compensatory and punitive damages, for injunctive relief, and for the cost of suit and reasonable attorney's and expert witness' fees. With respect to compensatory damages, the plaintiff may elect, at any time prior to the rendering of a final judgment, to recover, in lieu of actual damages, an award of statutory damages in the amount of five thousand dollars ($5,000) per violation of paragraph (1) of subdivision (a), and one thousand dollars ($1,000) per violation of paragraph (2) of subdivision (a).

(d) The Attorney General, a district attorney, or a city attorney may bring a civil action to enjoin a violation of subdivision (a), for compensatory damages to persons or entities aggrieved by the violation, and for the imposition of a civil penalty against each respondent. The civil penalty for a violation of paragraph (1) of subdivision (a) shall not exceed fifteen thousand dollars ($15,000), or twenty-five thousand dollars ($25,000) for a second or subsequent violation. The civil penalty for a violation of paragraph (2) of subdivision (a) shall not exceed five thousand dollars ($5,000), or twenty-five thousand dollars ($25,000) for a second or subsequent violation.

(e) This section shall not be construed to impair the right to engage in any constitutionally protected activity, including, but not limited to, speech, protest, or assembly.

(f) The adoption of the act that added this section is an exercise of the police power of the state for purposes of protecting the health, safety, and welfare of the people of California, and this section shall be liberally construed to effectuate that purpose.

(g) This section shall not be construed to restrict, inhibit, prevent, or bring a chilling effect upon any actions by a person that are reasonable under the circumstances to protect, secure, provide safety to, or prevent illness in any child or adult in a facility. *(Added by Stats.2014, c. 852 (A.B.1256), § 2, eff. Jan. 1, 2015.)*

Research References

Treatises and Practice Aids

Witkin, California Summary 10th Torts § 463A, (New) Interference With Access to School Grounds or Health Facility.

§ 1714.4. Knowingly assisting child support obligor escape, evade, or avoid paying court-ordered or court-approved child support; application to financial institutions

(a) Any person or business entity that knowingly assists a child support obligor who has an unpaid child support obligation to escape, evade, or avoid paying court-ordered or court-approved child support shall be liable for three times the value of the assistance provided, such as the fair market value of the obligor's assets transferred or hidden. The maximum liability imposed by this section shall not exceed the entire child support obligation due. Any funds or assets collected pursuant to this section shall be paid to the child support obligee, and shall not reduce the amount of the unpaid child support obligation. Upon the satisfaction of the unpaid child support obligation, this section shall not apply.

(b) For purposes of this section, actions taken to knowingly assist a child support obligor to escape, evade, or avoid paying court-ordered or court-approved child support include, with actual knowledge of the child support obligation, helping to hide or transfer assets of the child support obligor.

(c) This section shall not apply to a financial institution unless the financial institution has actual knowledge of the child support obligation and, with that knowledge, knowingly assists the obligor to escape, evade, or avoid paying the child support obligation. However, a financial institution with knowledge of an asset transfer has no duty to inquire into the rightfulness of the transaction, nor shall it be deemed to have knowingly assisted an obligor to escape, evade, or avoid paying the child support obligation if that assistance is provided by an employee or agent of the financial institution acting outside the terms and conditions of employment or agency without the actual knowledge of the financial institution. *(Added by Stats.2006, c. 820 (A.B.2440), § 2.)*

Commentary

Cabral v. Martins, 177 Cal.App.4th 471, 99 Cal.Rptr.3d 394 (2009), review denied, held that a custodial parent's child-support-evasion cause of action against a support obligor's attorneys was predicated on protected activity under Code of Civil Procedure § 425.16, the anti-SLAPP statute, and thus was subject to a special motion to strike.

Research References

Treatises and Practice Aids

Witkin, California Summary 10th Parent and Child § 390A, (New) Liability Of Person Assisting Evasion.

Witkin, California Summary 10th Torts § 1463, Firearms and Ammunition.

§ 1714.41. Knowingly assisting a child support obligor to escape, evade, or avoid paying child support; included actions

(a) Any person or business entity that knowingly assists a child support obligor who has an unpaid child support obligation to escape, evade, or avoid paying court-ordered or court-approved child support shall be liable for three times the value of the assistance provided, such as the fair market value of the assets transferred or hidden, or the amount of the wages or other compensation paid to the child support obligor but not reported. The maximum liability imposed by this section shall not exceed the entire child support obligation due. Any funds or assets collected pursuant to this section shall be paid to the child support obligee, and shall not reduce the amount of the unpaid child support obligation. Upon the satisfaction of the unpaid child support obligation, this section shall not apply.

(b) For purposes of this section, actions taken to knowingly assist a child support obligor to escape, evade, or avoid paying court-ordered or court-approved child support include, but are not limited to, any of the following actions taken when the individual or entity knew or should have known of the child support obligation:

(1) Hiring or employing the child support obligor as an employee in a trade or business and failing to timely file a report of new employees with the California New Employee Registry maintained by the Employment Development Department.

(2) Engaging the child support obligor as a service provider and failing to timely file a report with the Employment Development Department as required by Section 1088.8 of the Unemployment Insurance Code.

(3) When engaged in a trade or business, paying wages or other forms of compensation for services rendered by a child support obligor that are not reported to the Employment Development Department as required, including, but not limited to, payment in cash or via barter or trade. *(Added by Stats.2006, c. 820 (A.B.2440), § 3.)*

Commentary

Cabral v. Martins, 177 Cal.App.4th 471, 99 Cal.Rptr.3d 394 (2009), review denied, held that a custodial parent's child-support-evasion cause of action against a support obligor's attorneys was predicated on protected activity under Code of Civil Procedure § 425.16, the anti-SLAPP statute, and thus was subject to a special motion to strike.

Research References

Treatises and Practice Aids

Witkin, California Summary 10th Parent and Child § 390A, (New) Liability Of Person Assisting Evasion.

Part 4

OBLIGATIONS ARISING FROM PARTICULAR TRANSACTIONS

Title 2

CREDIT SALES

CHAPTER 2. CREDIT TRANSACTIONS REGARDING WOMEN

§ 1812.30. Denial of credit to person regardless of marital status; prohibition; conditions; reporting agency

(a) No person, regardless of marital status, shall be denied credit in his or her own name if the earnings and other property over which he or she has management and control are such that a person of the opposite sex managing and controlling the same amount of earnings and other property would receive credit.

(b) No person, regardless of marital status, managing and controlling earnings and other property shall be offered credit on terms less favorable than those offered to a person of the opposite sex seeking the same type of credit and managing and controlling the same amount of earnings and other property.

(c) No unmarried person shall be denied credit if his or her earnings and other property are such that a married person managing and controlling the same amount of earnings and other property would receive credit.

(d) No unmarried person shall be offered credit on terms less favorable than those offered to a married person managing and controlling the same amount of earnings and other property.

(e) For accounts established after January 1, 1977 or for accounts in existence on January 1, 1977 where information on that account is received after January 1, 1977, a credit reporting agency which in its normal course of business receives information on joint credit accounts identifying the persons responsible for such accounts, or receives information which reflects the participation of both spouses, shall: (1) at the time such information is received file such information separately under the names of each person or spouse, or file such information in another manner which would enable either person or spouse to automatically gain access to the credit history without having in any way to list or refer to the name of the other person, and (2) provide access to all information about the account in the name of each person or spouse.

(f) For all accounts established prior to January 1, 1977, a credit reporting agency shall at any time upon the written or personal request of a person who is or has been married, verify the contractual liability, liability by operation of law, or authorized use by such person, of joint credit accounts appearing in the file of the person's spouse or former spouse, and, if applicable, shall file such information separately and thereafter continue to do so under the names of each person responsible for the joint account or in another manner which would enable either person responsible for the joint account to automatically gain access to the credit history without having in any way to list or refer to the name of the other person.

(g) For the purposes of this chapter "credit" means obtainment of money, property, labor, or services on a deferred-payment basis.

(h) For the purposes of this chapter, earnings shall include, but not be limited to, spousal, family, and child support payments, pensions, social security, disability or survivorship benefits. Spousal, family, and child support payments shall be considered in the same manner as earnings from salary, wages, or other sources where the payments are received pursuant to a written agreement or court decree to the extent that the reliability of such payments is established. The factors which a creditor may consider in evaluating the reliability of such payments are the length of time payments have been received; the regularity of receipt; and whether full or partial payments have been made.

(i) Nothing in this chapter shall be construed to prohibit a person from: (1) utilizing an evaluation of the reliability of earnings provided that such an evaluation is applied to persons without regard to their sex or marital status; or (2) inquiring into and utilizing an evaluation of the obligations for which community property is liable pursuant to the Family Code for the sole purpose of determining the creditor's rights and remedies with respect to the particular extension of credit, provided that such is done with respect to all applicants without regard to their sex; or (3) utilizing any other relevant factors or methods in determining whether to extend credit to an applicant provided that such factors or methods are applicable to all applicants without regard to their sex or marital status. For the purpose of this subdivision, the fact that an applicant is of childbearing age is not a relevant factor.

(j) Credit applications for the obtainment of money, goods, labor, or services shall clearly specify that the applicant, if married, may apply for a separate account. *(Added by Stats.1973, c. 999, p. 1987, § 1. Amended by Stats.1975, c. 332, p. 778, § 1; Stats.1976, c. 1361, p. 6203, § 1; Stats.1992, c. 163 (A.B.2641), § 11, operative Jan. 1, 1994.)*

Law Revision Commission Comments

1992 Amendment

Section 1812.30 is amended to add a reference to "family" support in subdivision (h) and to replace the reference to the former Civil Code provisions in subdivision (i) with a reference to the Family Code. [22 Cal.L.Rev.Comm.Reports 1 (1992)].

Research References

Forms

27A West's Legal Forms § 11:34, Charge Account and Installment Credit Agreements--State Notice Requirements.

West's California Code Forms, Civil § 1812.31 Form 1, Complaint for Wrongful Denial Of Credit.

Treatises and Practice Aids

Witkin, California Summary 10th Constitutional Law § 897, Other Discrimination Statutes.

Witkin, California Summary 10th Husband and Wife § 22, Statutory Prohibitions.

Witkin, California Summary 10th Husband and Wife § 23, Remedies and Penalties.

Witkin, California Summary 10th Husband and Wife § 24, Permissible Evaluations and Credit Reports.

§ 1812.31. Right of action; damages; individual and class suits

(a) Whoever violates Section 1812.30 shall be liable to the aggrieved person in an amount equal to the sum of any actual damages sustained by such person acting either in an individual capacity or as a representative of a class.

(b) Whoever violates Section 1812.30 shall be liable to the aggrieved person for punitive damages in an amount not greater than ten thousand dollars ($10,000), as determined by the court, in addition to any actual damages provided in subdivision (a); provided, however, that in pursuing the recovery allowed under this subdivision, the aggrieved person may proceed only in an individual capacity and not as a representative of a class.

(c) Notwithstanding subdivision (b), whoever violates Section 1812.30 may be liable for punitive damages in the case of a class action in such amount as the court may allow, except that as to each member of the class no minimum recovery shall be applicable, and the total recovery in such action shall not exceed the lesser of one hundred thousand dollars ($100,000) or one percent (1%) of the net worth of the creditor. In determining the amount of the award in any class action, the court shall consider, among other relevant factors, the amount of any actual damages awarded, the frequency and persistence of violations, the resources of the creditor, the number of persons adversely affected, and the extent to which the creditor's violation was intentional. *(Added by Stats.1973, c. 999, p. 1987, § 1. Amended by Stats.1975, c. 332, p. 779, § 2.)*

Research References

Forms

West's California Code Forms, Civil § 1812.31 Form 1, Complaint for Wrongful Denial Of Credit.

Treatises and Practice Aids

Witkin, California Summary 10th Husband and Wife § 23, Remedies and Penalties.

§ 1812.32. Injunction

Any person, corporation, firm, partnership, joint stock company, or any other association or organization which violates or proposes to violate this chapter may be enjoined by any court of competent jurisdiction. Actions for injunction under this section may be prosecuted by the Attorney General or any district attorney, county counsel, city attorney, or city prosecutor in this state in the name of the people of the State of California or by any person denied credit or offered credit in violation of Section 1812.30. *(Added by Stats.1975, c. 332, p. 780, § 3.)*

Research References

Forms

West's California Code Forms, Civil § 1812.31 Form 1, Complaint for Wrongful Denial Of Credit.

Treatises and Practice Aids

Witkin, California Summary 10th Husband and Wife § 22, Statutory Prohibitions.

Witkin, California Summary 10th Husband and Wife § 23, Remedies and Penalties.

§ 1812.33. Civil penalties; precedence of action; distribution of proceeds

(a) Any person who intentionally violates any injunction issued pursuant to this chapter shall be liable for a civil penalty not to exceed two thousand five hundred dollars ($2,500) for each day that such person violates the injunction.

(b) The civil penalty prescribed by this section shall be assessed and recovered in a civil action brought in the name of the people of the State of California by the Attorney General or by any district attorney, county counsel, or city attorney in any court of competent jurisdiction. An action brought pursuant to this section to recover such civil penalties shall take special precedence over all civil matters on the calendar of the court except those matters to which equal precedence on the calendar is granted by law.

(c) If such an action is brought by the Attorney General, one-half of the penalty collected pursuant to this section shall be paid to the treasurer of the county in which the judgment was entered, and one-half to the State Treasurer. If brought by a district attorney or county counsel, the entire amount of the penalty collected shall be paid to the treasurer of the county in which the judgment was entered. If brought by a city attorney or city prosecutor, one-half of the penalty shall be paid to the treasurer of the county in which the judgment was entered and one-half to the city. *(Added by Stats.1975, c. 332, p. 780, § 4.)*

Research References

Treatises and Practice Aids

Witkin, California Summary 10th Husband and Wife § 23, Remedies and Penalties.

§ 1812.34. Costs and attorney fees

Any person denied credit or offered credit in violation of Section 1812.30 who brings an action pursuant to Section 1812.31 or 1812.32 of this code may petition the court for award of costs and reasonable attorney's fees which the court shall award if the action is successful. *(Added by Stats.1975, c. 332, p. 781, § 5.)*

Research References

Forms

West's California Code Forms, Civil § 1812.31 Form 1, Complaint for Wrongful Denial Of Credit.

Treatises and Practice Aids

Witkin, California Summary 10th Husband and Wife § 23, Remedies and Penalties.

§ 1812.35. Commencement of action; limitations

Any action commenced pursuant to Section 1812.31 shall be commenced within two years from the date on which the person is denied credit or is offered credit in violation of Section 1812.30. *(Added by Stats.1975, c. 332, p. 781, § 6.)*

Research References

Forms

West's California Code Forms, Civil § 1812.31 Form 1, Complaint for Wrongful Denial Of Credit.

Treatises and Practice Aids

Witkin, California Summary 10th Husband and Wife § 23, Remedies and Penalties.

Title 5
HIRING

CHAPTER 2. HIRING OF REAL PROPERTY

§ 1941.5. Tenant protected by restraining order against non-tenant; change of locks on dwelling unit; definitions

(a) This section shall apply if a person who is restrained from contact with the protected tenant under a court order or is named in a police report is not a tenant of the same dwelling unit as the protected tenant.

(b) A landlord shall change the locks of a protected tenant's dwelling unit upon written request of the protected tenant not later than 24 hours after the protected tenant gives the landlord a copy of a court order or police report, and shall give the protected tenant a key to the new locks.

(c)(1) If a landlord fails to change the locks within 24 hours, the protected tenant may change the locks without the landlord's permission, notwithstanding any provision in the lease to the contrary.

(2) If the protected tenant changes the locks pursuant to this subdivision, the protected tenant shall do all of the following:

(A) Change the locks in a workmanlike manner with locks of similar or better quality than the original lock.

(B) Notify the landlord within 24 hours that the locks have been changed.

(C) Provide the landlord with a key by any reasonable method agreed upon by the landlord and protected tenant.

(3) This subdivision shall apply to leases executed on or after the date the act that added this section takes effect.

(d) For the purposes of this section, the following definitions shall apply:

(1) "Court order" means a court order lawfully issued within the last 180 days pursuant to Section 527.6 of the Code of Civil Procedure, Part 3 (commencing with Section 6240), Part 4 (commencing with Section 6300), or Part 5 (commencing with Section 6400) of Division 10 of the Family Code, Section 136.2 of the Penal Code, or Section 213.5 of the Welfare and Institutions Code.

(2) "Locks" means any exterior lock that provides access to the dwelling.

(3) "Police report" means a written report, written within the last 180 days, by a peace officer employed by a state or local law enforcement agency acting in his or her official capacity, stating that the protected tenant or a household member has filed a report alleging that the protected tenant or the household member is a victim of domestic violence, sexual assault, or stalking.

(4) "Protected tenant" means a tenant who has obtained a court order or has a copy of a police report.

(5) "Tenant" means tenant, subtenant, lessee, or sublessee. *(Added by Stats.2010, c. 626 (S.B.782), § 2.)*

Research References

Treatises and Practice Aids

Witkin, California Summary 10th Real Property § 619, Nature Of Duty.

§ 1941.6. Tenant protected by restraining order against another tenant; change of locks on dwelling unit; liability regarding person excluded; definitions

(a) This section shall apply if a person who is restrained from contact with a protected tenant under a court order is a tenant of the same dwelling unit as the protected tenant.

(b) A landlord shall change the locks of a protected tenant's dwelling unit upon written request of the protected tenant not later than 24 hours after the protected tenant gives the landlord a copy of a court order that excludes from the dwelling unit the restrained person referred to in subdivision (a). The landlord shall give the protected tenant a key to the new locks.

(c)(1) If a landlord fails to change the locks within 24 hours, the protected tenant may change the locks without the landlord's permission, notwithstanding any provision in the lease to the contrary.

(2) If the protected tenant changes the locks pursuant to this subdivision, the protected tenant shall do all of the following:

(A) Change the locks in a workmanlike manner with locks of similar or better quality than the original lock.

(B) Notify the landlord within 24 hours that the locks have been changed.

(C) Provide the landlord with a key by any reasonable method agreed upon by the landlord and protected tenant.

(3) This subdivision shall apply to leases executed on or after the date the act that added this section takes effect.

(d) Notwithstanding Section 789.3, if the locks are changed pursuant to this section, the landlord is not liable to a person excluded from the dwelling unit pursuant to this section.

(e) A person who has been excluded from a dwelling unit under this section remains liable under the lease with all other tenants of the dwelling unit for rent as provided in the lease.

(f) For the purposes of this section, the following definitions shall apply:

(1) "Court order" means a court order lawfully issued within the last 180 days pursuant to Section 527.6 of the Code of Civil Procedure, Part 3 (commencing with Section 6240), Part 4 (commencing with Section 6300), or Part 5 (commencing with Section 6400) of Division 10 of the Family Code, Section 136.2 of the Penal Code, or Section 213.5 of the Welfare and Institutions Code.

(2) "Locks" means any exterior lock that provides access to the dwelling.

(3) "Protected tenant" means a tenant who has obtained a court order.

(4) "Tenant" means tenant, subtenant, lessee, or sublessee. *(Added by Stats.2010, c. 626 (S.B.782), § 3.)*

Research References

Treatises and Practice Aids

Witkin, California Summary 10th Real Property § 619, Nature Of Duty.

§ 1941.7. Obligation of lessor to repair dilapidation relating to presence of mold; notice; authority to enter dwelling unit for repair

(a) An obligation shall not arise under Section 1941 or 1942 to repair a dilapidation relating to the presence of mold pursuant to paragraph (13) of subdivision (a) of Section 17920.3 of the Health and Safety Code until the lessor has notice of the dilapidation or if the tenant is in violation of Section 1941.2.

(b) A landlord may enter a dwelling unit to repair a dilapidation relating to the presence of mold pursuant to paragraph (13) of subdivision (a) of Section 17920.3 of the Health and Safety Code provided the landlord complies with the provisions of Section 1954. *(Added by Stats.2015, c. 720 (S.B.655), § 1, eff. Jan. 1, 2016.)*

Research References

Treatises and Practice Aids

Witkin, California Summary 10th Real Property § 619, Nature Of Duty.

Division 4

GENERAL PROVISIONS

Part 1

RELIEF

Title 2

COMPENSATORY RELIEF

CHAPTER 1. DAMAGES IN GENERAL

ARTICLE 3. EXEMPLARY DAMAGES

§ 3294. Exemplary damages; when allowable; definitions

(a) In an action for the breach of an obligation not arising from contract, where it is proven by clear and convincing evidence that the defendant has been guilty of oppression, fraud, or malice, the plaintiff, in addition to the actual damages, may recover damages for the sake of example and by way of punishing the defendant.

(b) An employer shall not be liable for damages pursuant to subdivision (a), based upon acts of an employee of the employer, unless the employer had advance knowledge of the unfitness of the employee and employed him or her with a conscious disregard of the rights or safety of others or authorized or ratified the wrongful conduct for which the damages are awarded or was personally guilty of oppression, fraud, or malice. With respect to a corporate employer, the advance knowledge and conscious disregard, authorization, ratification or act of oppression, fraud, or malice must be on the part of an officer, director, or managing agent of the corporation.

(c) As used in this section, the following definitions shall apply:

(1) "Malice" means conduct which is intended by the defendant to cause injury to the plaintiff or despicable conduct which is carried on by the defendant with a willful and conscious disregard of the rights or safety of others.

(2) "Oppression" means despicable conduct that subjects a person to cruel and unjust hardship in conscious disregard of that person's rights.

(3) "Fraud" means an intentional misrepresentation, deceit, or concealment of a material fact known to the defendant with the intention on the part of the defendant of thereby depriving a person of property or legal rights or otherwise causing injury.

(d) Damages may be recovered pursuant to this section in an action pursuant to Chapter 4 (commencing with Section 377.10) of Title 3 of Part 2 of the Code of Civil Procedure based upon a death which resulted from a homicide for which the defendant has been convicted of a felony, whether or not the decedent died instantly or survived the fatal injury for some period of time. The procedures for joinder and consolidation contained in Section 377.62 of the Code of Civil Procedure shall apply to prevent multiple recoveries of punitive or exemplary damages based upon the same wrongful act.

(e) The amendments to this section made by Chapter 1498 of the Statutes of 1987 apply to all actions in which the initial trial has not commenced prior to January 1, 1988. *(Enacted in 1872. Amended by Stats.1905, c. 463, p. 621, § 1; Stats.1980, c. 1242, p. 4217, § 1; Stats.1982, c. 174, § 1; Stats.1983, c. 408, § 1; Stats.1987, c. 1498, § 5; Stats.1988, c. 160, § 17; Stats.1992, c. 178 (S.B.1496), § 5.)*

Law Revision Commission Comments

1992 Amendment

Section 3294 is amended to revise section references. These revisions are technical, nonsubstantive changes. [22 Cal.L.Rev.Comm.Reports 895 (1992)].

Commentary

Applying Family Code § 1101 (h), *In re Marriage of Rossi, 90 Cal.App.4th 34, 108 Cal.Rptr.2d 270 (2001)*, holds that a spouse's intentional concealment of community property lottery winnings constituted fraud under subsection (c)(3) and justified a trial court award of 100 percent of the winnings to the other spouse.

Research References

Forms

California Transactions Forms--Family Law § 2:9, Remedies for False Disclosure.

California Transactions Forms--Family Law § 2:81, Potential Community Assets and Obligations.

7 West's Federal Forms § 11125, Complaint--Sale Of Vessel.

2B West's Federal Forms § 8:23, Answer to Complaint for Patent Infringement and Unfair Competition.

West's California Code Forms, Civil § 3294 Form 1, Allegation in Complaint--Exemplary Damages.

West's California Code Forms, Civil § 798.86 Form 1, Allegation Of Statutory Penalty--Mobilehome Residency Law.

West's California Code Forms, Civil Procedure § 128.5 Form 4, Frivolous Actions or Delaying Tactics--Notice Of Motion for Order Assessing Punitive Damages.

West's California Code Forms, Civil Procedure § 128.5 Form 5, Frivolous Actions or Delaying Tactics--Declaration for Order Assessing Punitive Damages.

West's California Code Forms, Civil Procedure § 425.13 Form 1, Pleadings--Notice Of Motion to Add Claim for Punitive Damages--Professional Negligence Of Health Care Provider.

West's California Code Forms, Civil Procedure § 425.13 Form 2, Pleadings--Claim for Punitive Damages--Professional Negligence Of Health Care Provider.

West's California Code Forms, Civil Procedure § 425.13 Form 3, Pleadings--Order Allowing Claim for Punitive Damages--Professional Negligence Of Health Care Provider.

West's California Code Forms, Civil Procedure § 425.14 Form 1, Pleadings--Order Allowing Claim for Punitive Damages Against Religious Corporation.

West's California Code Forms, Family § 1100, Comment Overview--Community Personal Property.

West's California Code Forms, Insurance § 790.03 Form 1, Complaint for Unreasonably and in Bad Faith Withholding Payment.

Treatises and Practice Aids

Witkin, California Summary 10th Community Property § 134, Action for Breach Of Duty.

Witkin, California Summary 10th Constitutional Law § 950, Damages and Penalties.

Witkin, California Summary 10th Contracts § 876, No Award in Contract Case.

Witkin, California Summary 10th Equity § 63, in General.

Witkin, California Summary 10th Insurance § 240, in General.

Witkin, California Summary 10th Insurance § 242, Punitive Damages.

Witkin, California Summary 10th Insurance § 254, Abrogation Of Royal Globe in Moradi-Shalal.

Witkin, California Summary 10th Real Property § 715, Tenant's Remedies.

Witkin, California Summary 10th Real Property § 789, Actions and Penalties.

Witkin, California Summary 10th Torts § 164, Report Regarding Threat Of Violence on School Grounds.

Witkin, California Summary 10th Torts § 230, No Punitive Damages.

Witkin, California Summary 10th Torts § 663, Capturing Impression Of Personal or Familial Activity.

Witkin, California Summary 10th Torts § 952, Punitive Damages.

Witkin, California Summary 10th Torts § 1031, Financial Injury.

Witkin, California Summary 10th Torts § 1036, Fear Of Contracting Disease.

Witkin, California Summary 10th Torts § 1550, No Double Recovery.

Witkin, California Summary 10th Torts § 1559, Nature and Purpose Of Award.

Witkin, California Summary 10th Torts § 1571, Recovery Of Both Penalty and Punitive Damages.

Witkin, California Summary 10th Torts § 1572, Requirement Of Actual Malice.

Witkin, California Summary 10th Torts § 1574, Nature Of Problem and Earlier Cases.

Witkin, California Summary 10th Torts § 1576, Rule is Retroactive.

Witkin, California Summary 10th Torts § 1578, in General.

Witkin, California Summary 10th Torts § 1579, Recovery by Public Entities.

Witkin, California Summary 10th Torts § 1581, General Rule Of Nonliability.

Witkin, California Summary 10th Torts § 1582, Act Authorized or Ratified.

Witkin, California Summary 10th Torts § 1585, Codification Of Rules.

Witkin, California Summary 10th Torts § 1586, Personal Torts.

Witkin, California Summary 10th Torts § 1592, Breach by Surety.

Witkin, California Summary 10th Torts § 1593, in General.

Witkin, California Summary 10th Torts § 1596, Job Discrimination Action.

Witkin, California Summary 10th Torts § 1599, Alternative Contract or Tort Actions.

Witkin, California Summary 10th Torts § 1600, in General.

Witkin, California Summary 10th Torts § 1602, Substantial Probability that Plaintiff Will Prevail.

Witkin, California Summary 10th Torts § 1605, Action Against Religious Corporation.

Witkin, California Summary 10th Torts § 1607, Nature Of Requirement.

Witkin, California Summary 10th Torts § 1615, in General.

Witkin, California Summary 10th Torts § 1618, Discovery Of Financial Condition.

Witkin, California Summary 10th Torts § 1686, Statutory Remedies.

Witkin, California Summary 10th Torts § 1713, Quasi-Contractual Recovery.

Part 2

SPECIAL RELATIONS OF DEBTOR AND CREDITOR

Title 2

VOID AND VOIDABLE TRANSFERS AND UNDERTAKINGS

CHAPTER 1. UNIFORM VOIDABLE TRANSACTIONS ACT

§ 3439. Short title

This chapter may be cited as the Uniform Voidable Transactions Act. *(Added by Stats.1986, c. 383, § 2. Amended by Stats.2015, c. 44 (S.B.161), § 3, eff. Jan. 1, 2016.)*

Research References

Forms

California Transactions Forms--Business Entities § 3:27, Agreement to Incorporate Partnership.

California Transactions Forms--Business Entities § 16:19, Liability for Contributions.

California Transactions Forms--Business Entities § 13:68, Continued Existence Of Dissolved Corporation.

California Transactions Forms--Business Entities § 21:24, Fraudulent Transfers.

California Transactions Forms--Business Entities § 21:36, Checklist Of Matters to Consider in Drafting LLP Agreement.

California Transactions Forms--Business Entities § 18:119, Notice to Limited Partners Of Approval Of Merger or Conversion--Uniform Limited Partnership Act.

California Transactions Forms--Business Entities § 23:137, Distribution Defined; Distributions Of Public Benefit and Religious Corporations Assets.

California Transactions Forms--Business Entities § 23:138, Distribution Of Mutual Benefit Corporation Assets.

Cal. Transaction Forms - Bus. Transactions § 6:26, Fraud and Misrepresentation.

Cal. Transaction Forms - Bus. Transactions § 3:21, Overview.

Cal. Transaction Forms - Bus. Transactions § 3:23, Uniform Fraudulent Transfers Act.

Cal. Transaction Forms - Bus. Transactions § 30:117, Fraudulent Transfers.

California Transactions Forms--Estate Planning § 18:6, Fraudulent and Other Invalid Trusts.

California Transactions Forms--Estate Planning § 6:42, Right to Disclaim and Waiver Of Right.

California Transactions Forms--Estate Planning § 11:35, Agreement Entered Into on or After January 1, 1985.

Am. Jur. Pl. & Pr. Forms Fraudulent Conveyances § 1, Introductory Comments.

West's California Code Forms, Civil § 3439.07 Form 1, Complaint to Set Aside Fraudulent Conveyance.

West's California Code Forms, Commercial DIV 6 INTRO, Bulk Sales.

West's California Code Forms, Commercial § 10308 Form 1, Clause Reciting Reason for Lessor's Retention Of Leased Goods.

West's California Code Forms, Corporations § 500 Form 1, Resolution Of Directors--Declaring Cash Dividend on Common Stock.

West's California Code Forms, Family § 850, Comment Overview--Transmutation by Agreement or Transfer.

West's California Code Forms, Probate § 9653 Form 1, Petition by Creditor for Order Directing Personal Representative to Commence Action for Recovery Of Property Wrongfully Transferred by Decedent.

Treatises and Practice Aids

Witkin, California Summary 10th Contracts § 294, in General.

Witkin, California Summary 10th Contracts § 711, Conformity With Federal Statutes.

Witkin, California Summary 10th Corporations § 184, Unlawful Dividends or Purchases Of Shares.

Witkin, California Summary 10th Corporations § 289, Distributions to Members Prohibited.

Witkin, California Summary 10th Partnership § 1, Statutes Affecting Partnerships.

Witkin, California Summary 10th Partnership § 87, Capital Account and Contributions.

Witkin, California Summary 10th Partnership § 120, Rights and Privileges Of Dissenting Limited Partners.

Witkin, California Summary 10th Partnership § 156, Capital Contributions.

Witkin, California Summary 10th Partnership § 210, (New) Contributions.

Witkin, California Summary 10th Partnership § 121AAA, (New) Rights and Privileges Of Dissenting Limited Partners.

Witkin, California Summary 10th Real Property § 2, Uniform Laws and Model Acts.

Witkin, California Summary 10th Sales § 214, in General.

Witkin, California Summary 10th Sales § 228, Applicability Of Fraudulent Transfer Act.

Witkin, California Summary 10th Torts § 1607, Nature Of Requirement.

Witkin, California Summary 10th Wills and Probate § 333, Right to Disclaim and Waiver.

Witkin, California Summary 10th Wills and Probate § 478, Duty to Recover Property.

§ 3439.01. Definitions

As used in this chapter the following definitions are applicable:

(a) "Asset" means property of a debtor, but the term does not include the following:

(1) Property to the extent it is encumbered by a valid lien.

(2) Property to the extent it is generally exempt under nonbankruptcy law.

(3) An interest in property held in tenancy by the entireties to the extent it is not subject to process by a creditor holding a claim against only one tenant.

(b) "Claim," except as used in "claim for relief," means a right to payment, whether or not the right is reduced to judgment, liquidated, unliquidated, fixed, contingent, matured, unmatured, disputed, undisputed, legal, equitable, secured, or unsecured.

(c) "Creditor" means a person that has a claim, and includes an assignee of a general assignment for the benefit of creditors, as defined in Section 493.010 of the Code of Civil Procedure, of a debtor.

(d) "Debt" means liability on a claim.

(e) "Debtor" means a person that is liable on a claim.

(f) "Electronic" means relating to technology having electrical, digital, magnetic, wireless, optical, electromagnetic, or similar capabilities.

(g) "Lien" means a charge against or an interest in property to secure payment of a debt or performance of an obligation, and includes a security interest created by agreement, a judicial lien obtained by legal or equitable process or proceedings, a common-law lien, or a statutory lien.

(h) "Organization" means a person other than an individual.

(i) "Person" means an individual, partnership, corporation, limited liability company, association, government or governmental subdivision, instrumentality or agency, business trust, estate, trust, business or nonprofit entity, or other legal entity.

(j) "Property" means anything that may be the subject of ownership.

(k) "Record" means information that is inscribed on a tangible medium or that is stored in an electronic or other medium and is retrievable in perceivable form.

(*l*) "Sign" means, with present intent to authenticate or adopt a record, to either (1) execute or adopt a tangible symbol, or (2) attach to or logically associate with the record an electronic symbol, sound, or process.

(m) "Transfer" means every mode, direct or indirect, absolute or conditional, voluntary or involuntary, of disposing of or parting with an asset or an interest in an asset, and includes payment of money, release, lease, license, and creation of a lien or other encumbrance.

(n) "Valid lien" means a lien that is effective against the holder of a judicial lien subsequently obtained by legal or equitable process or proceedings. *(Added by Stats.1986, c. 383, § 2. Amended by Stats.1994, c. 1010 (S.B.2053), § 55; Stats.2015, c. 44 (S.B.161), § 4, eff. Jan. 1, 2016.)*

Commentary

When the Uniform Fraudulent Transfer Act is inapplicable because a transferred property interest does not satisfy the subsection (a) definition of "asset" in that it has no value given its encumbrance by lien and by the amount of the homestead exemption, nevertheless a creditor may impose a resulting trust on the transferred property when the transferee was intended to have only a legal interest and the transferor intended to retain the beneficial interest. In such case, the resulting trust attaches to the entire property. *Fidelity National Title Insurance Company v. Schroeder, 179 Cal.App.4th 834, 101 Cal.Rptr.3d 854 (2009).*

Mejia v. Reed, 31 Cal.4th 657, 74 P.3d 166, 3 Cal.Rptr.3d 390 (2003), holds that the Uniform Fraudulent Transfer Act applies to property transfers made pursuant to marital settlement agreements. Thus a plaintiff in a pending paternity suit against a former husband could challenge, under this act, a transfer of property to his former wife under their marital settlement agreement.

Research References

Forms

California Real Estate Forms (Miller & Starr) § 3:37, Continuing Guaranty.
California Real Estate Forms (Miller & Starr) § 3:38, Completion Guaranty.
California Real Estate Forms (Miller & Starr) § 3:38.50, "Bad Boy" Guaranty.

§ 3439.02. Insolvency

(a) A debtor is insolvent if, at a fair valuation, the sum of the debtor's debts is greater than the sum of the debtor's assets.

(b) A debtor that is generally not paying the debtor's debts as they become due other than as a result of a bona fide dispute is presumed to be insolvent. The presumption imposes on the party against which the presumption is directed the burden of proving that the nonexistence of insolvency is more probable than its existence.

(c) Assets under this section do not include property that has been transferred, concealed, or removed with intent to hinder, delay, or defraud creditors or that has been transferred in a manner making the transfer voidable under this chapter.

(d) Debts under this section do not include an obligation to the extent it is secured by a valid lien on property of the debtor not included as an asset. *(Added by Stats.1986, c. 383, § 2. Amended by Stats.2015, c. 44 (S.B.161), § 5, eff. Jan. 1, 2016.)*

§ 3439.03. Value

Value is given for a transfer or an obligation if, in exchange for the transfer or obligation, property is transferred or an antecedent debt is secured or satisfied, but value does not include an unperformed promise made otherwise than in the ordinary course of the promisor's business to furnish support to the debtor or another person. *(Added by Stats.1986, c. 383, § 2.)*

§ 3439.04. Transfers voidable as to present and future creditors; factors to determining intent

(a) A transfer made or obligation incurred by a debtor is voidable as to a creditor, whether the creditor's claim arose before or after the transfer was made or the obligation was incurred, if the debtor made the transfer or incurred the obligation as follows:

(1) With actual intent to hinder, delay, or defraud any creditor of the debtor.

(2) Without receiving a reasonably equivalent value in exchange for the transfer or obligation, and the debtor either:

(A) Was engaged or was about to engage in a business or a transaction for which the remaining assets of the debtor were unreasonably small in relation to the business or transaction.

(B) Intended to incur, or believed or reasonably should have believed that the debtor would incur, debts beyond the debtor's ability to pay as they became due.

(b) In determining actual intent under paragraph (1) of subdivision (a), consideration may be given, among other factors, to any or all of the following:

(1) Whether the transfer or obligation was to an insider.

(2) Whether the debtor retained possession or control of the property transferred after the transfer.

(3) Whether the transfer or obligation was disclosed or concealed.

(4) Whether before the transfer was made or obligation was incurred, the debtor had been sued or threatened with suit.

(5) Whether the transfer was of substantially all the debtor's assets.

(6) Whether the debtor absconded.

(7) Whether the debtor removed or concealed assets.

(8) Whether the value of the consideration received by the debtor was reasonably equivalent to the value of the asset transferred or the amount of the obligation incurred.

(9) Whether the debtor was insolvent or became insolvent shortly after the transfer was made or the obligation was incurred.

(10) Whether the transfer occurred shortly before or shortly after a substantial debt was incurred.

(11) Whether the debtor transferred the essential assets of the business to a lienor that transferred the assets to an insider of the debtor.

(c) A creditor making a claim for relief under subdivision (a) has the burden of proving the elements of the claim for relief by a preponderance of the evidence. *(Added by Stats.1986, c. 383, § 2. Amended by Stats.2004, c. 50 (S.B. 1408), § 1; Stats.2015, c. 44 (S.B.161), § 6, eff. Jan. 1, 2016.)*

Commentary

Reversing the Bankruptcy Court, *In re Beverly, 374 B.R. 221 (U.S. Bankr. App. Pan., 9th Cir. 2007)*, held that a divorcing attorney's marital settlement agreement, which transferred nonexempt community property to his wife in exchange for an equivalent amount of his exempt community property retirement fund, was a fraudulent transfer under California Civil Code § 3439.04(a)(1) and therefore under 11 U.S.C. § 544(b). Thus, in the attorney's involuntary bankruptcy proceeding, the Bankruptcy Trustee could avoid the transfer and reach the attorney's community property interest in the nonexempt property.

Research References

Forms

California Transactions Forms--Business Entities § 21:24, Fraudulent Transfers.
Cal. Transaction Forms - Bus. Transactions § 3:23, Uniform Fraudulent Transfers Act.
West's California Code Forms, Civil § 3439.07 Form 1, Complaint to Set Aside Fraudulent Conveyance.

Treatises and Practice Aids

Witkin, California Summary 10th Community Property § 153, Authority to Transmute.

§ 3439.05. Transfers voidable as to present creditors

(a) A transfer made or obligation incurred by a debtor is voidable as to a creditor whose claim arose before the transfer was made or the obligation was incurred if the debtor made the transfer or incurred the obligation without receiving a reasonably equivalent value in exchange for the transfer or obligation and the debtor was insolvent at that time or the debtor became insolvent as a result of the transfer or obligation.

(b) A creditor making a claim for relief under subdivision (a) has the burden of proving the elements of the claim for relief by a preponderance of the evidence. *(Added by Stats.1986, c. 383, § 2. Amended by Stats.2015, c. 44 (S.B. 161), § 7, eff. Jan. 1, 2016.)*

Commentary

Mejia v. Reed, 31 Cal.4th 657, 74 P.3d 166, 3 Cal.Rptr.3d 390 (2003), held that in determining whether a defendant is insolvent under this section, his future child support obligation may not be included as a debt to be weighed against his assets. The court reasoned that support payments are usually paid from present earnings, not liquidation of preexisting assets, and the amount of the child support obligation is based on actual or imputed earnings.

Research References

Forms

California Transactions Forms--Business Entities § 21:24, Fraudulent Transfers.
Cal. Transaction Forms - Bus. Transactions § 3:23, Uniform Fraudulent Transfers Act.

§ 3439.06. When transfer is made or obligation is incurred

For the purposes of this chapter:

(a) A transfer is made:

(1) With respect to an asset that is real property other than a fixture, but including the interest of a seller or purchaser under a contract for the sale of the asset, when the transfer is so far perfected that a good faith purchaser of the asset from the debtor against which applicable law permits the transfer to be perfected cannot acquire an interest in the asset that is superior to the interest of the transferee; and

(2) With respect to an asset that is not real property or that is a fixture, when the transfer is so far perfected that a creditor on a simple contract cannot acquire a judicial lien otherwise than under this chapter that is superior to the interest of the transferee.

(b) If applicable law permits the transfer to be perfected as provided in subdivision (a) and the transfer is not so perfected before the commencement of an action for relief under this chapter, the transfer is deemed made immediately before the commencement of the action.

(c) If applicable law does not permit the transfer to be perfected as provided in subdivision (a), the transfer is made when it becomes effective between the debtor and the transferee.

(d) A transfer is not made until the debtor has acquired rights in the asset transferred.

(e) An obligation is incurred:

(1) If oral, when it becomes effective between the parties; or

(2) If evidenced by a record, when the record signed by the obligor is delivered to or for the benefit of the obligee. *(Added by Stats.1986, c. 383, § 2. Amended by Stats.2015, c. 44 (S.B.161), § 8, eff. Jan. 1, 2016.)*

Research References

Treatises and Practice Aids

Witkin, California Summary 10th Community Property § 153, Authority to Transmute.

§ 3439.07. Remedies of creditors

(a) In an action for relief against a transfer or obligation under this chapter, a creditor, subject to the limitations in Section 3439.08, may obtain:

(1) Avoidance of the transfer or obligation to the extent necessary to satisfy the creditor's claim.

(2) An attachment or other provisional remedy against the asset transferred or other property of the transferee in accordance with the procedures described in Title 6.5 (commencing with Section 481.010) of Part 2 of the Code of Civil Procedure, or as may otherwise be available under applicable law.

(3) Subject to applicable principles of equity and in accordance with applicable rules of civil procedure, the following:

(A) An injunction against further disposition by the debtor or a transferee, or both, of the asset transferred or other property of the transferee.

(B) Appointment of a receiver to take charge of the asset transferred or other property of the transferee.

(C) Any other relief the circumstances may require.

(b) If a creditor has commenced an action on a claim against the debtor, the creditor may attach the asset transferred or other property of the transferee if the remedy of attachment is available in the action under applicable law and the property is subject to attachment in the hands of the transferee under applicable law.

(c) If a creditor has obtained a judgment on a claim against the debtor, the creditor may levy execution on the asset transferred or its proceeds.

(d) A creditor who is an assignee of a general assignment for the benefit of creditors, as defined in Section 493.010 of the Code of Civil Procedure, may exercise any and all of the rights and remedies specified in this section if they are available to any one or more creditors of the assignor who are beneficiaries of the assignment, and, in that event (1) only to the extent the rights or remedies are so available and (2) only for the benefit of those creditors whose rights are asserted by the assignee. *(Added by Stats.1986, c. 383, § 2. Amended by Stats.2015, c. 44 (S.B.161), § 9, eff. Jan. 1, 2016.)*

Research References

Forms

Cal. Transaction Forms - Bus. Transactions § 3:23, Uniform Fraudulent Transfers Act.

Cal. Transaction Forms - Bus. Transactions § 16:66, Debtor's Right to Transfer Property by Assignment.

West's California Code Forms, Civil § 3439.07 Form 1, Complaint to Set Aside Fraudulent Conveyance.

Treatises and Practice Aids

Witkin, California Summary 10th Contracts § 711, Conformity With Federal Statutes.

§ 3439.08. Defenses, liability, and protection of transferee; burden of proof

(a) A transfer or obligation is not voidable under paragraph (1) of subdivision (a) of Section 3439.04, against a person that took in good faith and for a reasonably equivalent value given the debtor or against any subsequent transferee or obligee.

(b) To the extent a transfer is avoidable in an action by a creditor under paragraph (1) of subdivision (a) of Section 3439.07, the following rules apply:

(1) Except as otherwise provided in this section, the creditor may recover judgment for the value of the asset transferred, as adjusted under subdivision (c), or the amount necessary to satisfy the creditor's claim, whichever is less. The judgment may be entered against the following:

(A) The first transferee of the asset or the person for whose benefit the transfer was made.

(B) An immediate or mediate transferee of the first transferee, other than either of the following:

(i) A good faith transferee that took for value.

(ii) An immediate or mediate good faith transferee of a person described in clause (i).

(2) Recovery pursuant to paragraph (1) of subdivision (a), or subdivision (b), or subdivision (c) of Section 3439.07 of or from the asset transferred or its proceeds, or other property of the transferee, as applicable, by levy or otherwise, is available only against a person described in subparagraph (A) or (B) of paragraph (1).

(c) If the judgment under subdivision (b) is based upon the value of the asset transferred, the judgment shall be for an amount equal to the value of the asset at the time of the transfer, subject to adjustment as the equities may require.

(d) Notwithstanding voidability of a transfer or an obligation under this chapter, a good faith transferee or obligee is entitled, to the extent of the value given the debtor for the transfer or obligation, to the following:

(1) A lien on or a right to retain an interest in the asset transferred.

(2) Enforcement of an obligation incurred.

(3) A reduction in the amount of the liability on the judgment.

(e) A transfer is not voidable under paragraph (2) of subdivision (a) of Section 3439.04 or Section 3439.05 if the transfer results from either of the following:

(1) Termination of a lease upon default by the debtor when the termination is pursuant to the lease and applicable law.

(2) Enforcement of a lien in a noncollusive manner and in compliance with applicable law, including Division 9 (commencing with Section 9101) of the Commercial Code, other than a retention of collateral under Sections 9620 and 9621 of the Commercial Code and other than a voluntary transfer of the collateral by the debtor to the lienor in satisfaction of all or part of the secured obligation.

(f) The following rules determine the burden of proving matters referred to in this section:

(1) A party that seeks to invoke subdivision (a), (d), or (e) has the burden of proving the applicability of that subdivision.

(2) Except as otherwise provided in paragraph (3) or (4), the creditor has the burden of proving each applicable element of subdivision (b) or (c).

(3) The transferee has the burden of proving the applicability to the transferee of subparagraph (B) of paragraph (1) of subdivision (b).

(4) A party that seeks adjustment under subdivision (c) has the burden of proving the adjustment.

(g) The standard of proof required to establish matters referred to in this section is preponderance of the evidence. *(Added by Stats.1986, c. 383, § 2. Amended by Stats.1987, c. 40, § 1, eff. June 8, 1987; Stats.1999, c. 991 (S.B.45), § 9, operative July 1, 2001; Stats.2005, c. 34 (A.B.248), § 1, eff. July 7, 2005; Stats.2015, c. 44 (S.B.161), § 10, eff. Jan. 1, 2016.)*

Research References

Forms

Cal. Transaction Forms - Bus. Transactions § 3:23, Uniform Fraudulent Transfers Act.

§ 3439.09. Extinguishment of cause of action

A cause of action with respect to a transfer or obligation under this chapter is extinguished unless action is brought pursuant to subdivision (a) of Section 3439.07 or levy made as provided in subdivision (b) or (c) of Section 3439.07:

(a) Under paragraph (1) of subdivision (a) of Section 3439.04, not later than four years after the transfer was made or the obligation was incurred or, if later, not later than one year after the transfer or obligation was or could reasonably have been discovered by the claimant.

(b) Under paragraph (2) of subdivision (a) of Section 3439.04 or Section 3439.05, not later than four years after the transfer was made or the obligation was incurred.

(c) Notwithstanding any other provision of law, a cause of action under this chapter with respect to a transfer or obligation is extinguished if no action is brought or levy made within seven years after the transfer was made or the obligation was incurred. *(Added by Stats.1986, c. 383, § 2. Amended by Stats.2005, c. 34 (A.B.248), § 2, eff. July 7, 2005; Stats.2015, c. 44 (S.B.161), § 11, eff. Jan. 1, 2016.)*

Research References

Forms

California Transactions Forms--Business Entities § 21:24, Fraudulent Transfers.

Cal. Transaction Forms - Bus. Transactions § 3:23, Uniform Fraudulent Transfers Act.

§ 3439.10. Governing law

(a) In this section, the following rules determine a debtor's location:

(1) A debtor who is an individual is located at the individual's principal residence.

(2) A debtor that is an organization and has only one place of business is located at its place of business.

(3) A debtor that is an organization and has more than one place of business is located at its chief executive office.

(b) A claim in the nature of a claim under this chapter is governed by the local law of the jurisdiction in which the debtor is located when the transfer is made or the obligation is incurred. *(Added by Stats.2015, c. 44 (S.B.161), § 13, eff. Jan. 1, 2016.)*

§ 3439.12. Supplementary provisions

Unless displaced by the provisions of this chapter, the principles of law and equity, including the law merchant and the law relating to principal and agent, estoppel, laches, fraud, misrepresentation, duress, coercion, mistake, insolvency, or other validating or invalidating cause, supplement its provisions. *(Formerly § 3439.10, added by Stats.1986, c. 383, § 2. Renumbered § 3439.12 and amended by Stats.2015, c. 44 (S.B.161), § 12, eff. Jan. 1, 2016.)*

Research References

Forms

Cal. Transaction Forms - Bus. Transactions § 3:21, Overview.

Cal. Transaction Forms - Bus. Transactions § 3:23, Uniform Fraudulent Transfers Act.

West's California Code Forms, Civil § 3439.07 Form 1, Complaint to Set Aside Fraudulent Conveyance.

West's California Code Forms, Commercial DIV 6 INTRO, Bulk Sales.

West's California Code Forms, Commercial § 10308 Form 1, Clause Reciting Reason for Lessor's Retention Of Leased Goods.

West's California Code Forms, Corporations § 500 Form 1, Resolution Of Directors--Declaring Cash Dividend on Common Stock.

West's California Code Forms, Family § 850, Comment Overview--Transmutation by Agreement or Transfer.

§ 3439.13. Uniformity of application and construction

This chapter shall be applied and construed to effectuate its general purpose to make uniform the law with respect to the subject of this chapter among states enacting it. *(Formerly § 3439.11, added by Stats.1986, c. 383, § 2. Renumbered § 3439.13 and amended by Stats.2015, c. 44 (S.B.161), § 14, eff. Jan. 1, 2016.)*

§ 3439.14. Application; prior provisions; construction

(a) The changes to this chapter made by the act adding this subdivision apply only to a right of action that accrued, transfer made, or obligation incurred, on or after the effective date of that act.

(b) This chapter, and the other changes in the law made by Chapter 383 of the Statutes of 1986, apply only to transfers made or obligations incurred before the effective date of the act that added subdivision (a) and on or after January 1, 1987. As to transfers made or obligations incurred prior to January 1, 1987, the law in effect at the time the transfer was made or the obligation was incurred shall apply.

(c) Section 3439.06 shall determine the date that a transfer was made or obligation incurred.

(d) The provisions of this chapter, insofar as they are substantially the same as the provisions of this chapter in effect on December 31, 2015, shall be construed as restatements and continuations, and not as new enactments. *(Formerly § 3439.12, added by Stats.1987, c. 40, § 2, eff. June 8, 1987. Renumbered § 3439.14 and amended by Stats.2015, c. 44 (S.B.161), § 15, eff. Jan. 1, 2016.)*

CODE OF CIVIL PROCEDURE

Part 1

OF COURTS OF JUSTICE

Title 1

ORGANIZATION AND JURISDICTION

CHAPTER 1. COURTS OF JUSTICE IN GENERAL

§ 36. Motion for preference; party over 70 years of age; party under 14 years of age; medical reasons; interests of justice; time of trial

(a) A party to a civil action who is over 70 years of age may petition the court for a preference, which the court shall grant if the court makes both of the following findings:

(1) The party has a substantial interest in the action as a whole.

(2) The health of the party is such that a preference is necessary to prevent prejudicing the party's interest in the litigation.

(b) A civil action to recover damages for wrongful death or personal injury shall be entitled to preference upon the motion of any party to the action who is under 14 years of age unless the court finds that the party does not have a substantial interest in the case as a whole. A civil action subject to subdivision (a) shall be given preference over a case subject to this subdivision.

(c) Unless the court otherwise orders:

(1) A party may file and serve a motion for preference supported by a declaration of the moving party that all essential parties have been served with process or have appeared.

(2) At any time during the pendency of the action, a party who reaches 70 years of age may file and serve a motion for preference.

(d) In its discretion, the court may also grant a motion for preference that is accompanied by clear and convincing medical documentation that concludes that one of the parties suffers from an illness or condition raising substantial medical doubt of survival of that party beyond six months, and that satisfies the court that the interests of justice will be served by granting the preference.

(e) Notwithstanding any other provision of law, the court may in its discretion grant a motion for preference that is supported by a showing that satisfies the court that the interests of justice will be served by granting this preference.

(f) Upon the granting of such a motion for preference, the court shall set the matter for trial not more than 120 days from that date and there shall be no continuance beyond 120 days from the granting of the motion for preference except for physical disability of a party or a party's attorney, or upon a showing of good cause stated in the record. Any continuance shall be for no more than 15 days and no more than one continuance for physical disability may be granted to any party.

(g) Upon the granting of a motion for preference pursuant to subdivision (b), a party in an action based upon a health provider's alleged professional negligence, as defined in Section 364, shall receive a trial date not sooner than six months and not later than nine months from the date that the motion is granted. *(Added by Stats.1979, c. 151, p. 348, § 2. Amended by Stats.1981, c. 215, § 1; Stats.1988, c. 1237, § 1; Stats.1989, c. 913, § 1; Stats.1990, c. 428 (A.B.3811), § 1; Stats.2008, c. 218 (A.B.1949), § 1.)*

Research References

Forms

West's California Code Forms, Civil Procedure § 36(A) Form 1, Preferences--Civil Cases--Notice Of Motion for Preference by Party Exceeding Age 70.

West's California Code Forms, Civil Procedure § 36(A) Form 3, Preferences--Civil Cases--Order Granting Preference--Party Exceeding Age 70.

West's California Code Forms, Civil Procedure § 36(E) Form 1, Preferences--Civil Cases--Order Denying Preference.

Treatises and Practice Aids

Witkin, California Summary 10th Constitutional Law § 581, Discovery Of Medical Patient's Records.

Witkin, California Summary 10th Torts § 1603, Time Limits.

Witkin, California Summary 10th Wills and Probate § 578, Trial.

§ 36.5. Motion for preference; affidavit

An affidavit submitted in support of a motion for preference under subdivision (a) of Section 36 may be signed by the attorney for the party seeking preference based upon information and belief as to the medical diagnosis and prognosis of any party. The affidavit is not admissible for any purpose other than a motion for preference under subdivision (a) of Section 36. *(Added by Stats.1990, c. 1232 (A.B.3820), § 1.)*

Research References

Treatises and Practice Aids

§ 37. Preference; action for damages incurred during felony; time

(a) A civil action shall be entitled to preference, if the action is one in which the plaintiff is seeking damages which were alleged to have been caused by the defendant during the commission of a felony offense for which the defendant has been criminally convicted.

(b) The court shall endeavor to try the action within 120 days of the grant of preference. *(Added by Stats.1982, c. 514, p. 2297, § 1. Amended by Stats.1983, c. 938, § 1, eff. Sept. 20, 1983.)*

§ 38. Judicial district

Unless the provision or context otherwise requires, a reference in a statute to a judicial district means:

(a) As it relates to a court of appeal, the court of appeal district.

(b) As it relates to a superior court, the county.

(c) As it relates to a municipal court, the municipal court district.

(d) As it relates to a county in which there is no municipal court, the county. *(Added by Stats.1998, c. 931 (S.B.2139), § 20, eff. Sept. 28, 1998.)*

Law Revision Commission Comments

1998 Addition

Section 38 is intended for drafting convenience. See also Section 17 ("judicial district" includes city and county). Court of appeal districts and municipal court districts are constitutionally mandated. See Cal. Const. art. VI, §§ 3, 5. Superior court districts do not exist except in Los Angeles County. See Gov't Code §§ 69640–69650.

By operation of this section, in a county in which the superior and municipal courts have unified, a statutory reference to a judicial district means the county rather than a former municipal court district. This general rule is subject to exceptions. See, e.g., Gov't Code 71042.5 (preservation of judicial districts for purpose of publication). [28 Cal.L.Rev.Comm. Reports 51 (1998)].

CHAPTER 6. GENERAL PROVISIONS RESPECTING COURTS OF JUSTICE

ARTICLE 1. PUBLICITY OF PROCEEDINGS

§ 124. Public sittings; exceptions

Except as provided in Section 214 of the Family Code or any other provision of law, the sittings of every court shall be public. *(Enacted in 1872. Amended by Code Am.1880, c. 35, p. 36, § 1; Stats.1971, c. 762, p. 1510, § 2; Stats.1990, c. 1363 (A.B.3532), § 10, operative July 1, 1991; Stats.1992, c. 163 (A.B.2641), § 12, operative Jan. 1, 1994.)*

Law Revision Commission Comments

1992 Amendment

Section 124 is amended to substitute a reference to Family Code Section 214 for the former Civil Code references. Family Code Section 214 gives the court general authority to direct that the trial of any issue of fact joined in a proceeding under the Family Code be private and to exclude all persons except the officers of the court, the parties, their witnesses, and counsel. Section 124 also recognizes that other provisions of law may qualify the rule stated in Section 124 or provide a contrary rule.

Other provisions of the Family Code may provide more restrictive rules that prevail over the rule stated in Family Code Section 214 or may provide special rules concerning exclusion of the public from hearings under the Family Code that prevail over the general rule stated in Section 214. See Fam. Code § 214 Comment. [22 Cal.L.Rev.Comm.Reports 1 (1992)].

Research References

Treatises and Practice Aids

Witkin, California Summary 10th Constitutional Law § 423, Civil Trial.

ARTICLE 2. INCIDENTAL POWERS AND DUTIES OF COURTS

§ 128. Powers of courts; contempt orders; execution of sentence; stay pending appeal; orders affecting county government

(a) Every court shall have the power to do all of the following:

(1) To preserve and enforce order in its immediate presence.

(2) To enforce order in the proceedings before it, or before a person or persons empowered to conduct a judicial investigation under its authority.

(3) To provide for the orderly conduct of proceedings before it, or its officers.

(4) To compel obedience to its judgments, orders, and process, and to the orders of a judge out of court, in an action or proceeding pending therein.

(5) To control in furtherance of justice, the conduct of its ministerial officers, and of all other persons in any manner connected with a judicial proceeding before it, in every matter pertaining thereto.

(6) To compel the attendance of persons to testify in an action or proceeding pending therein, in the cases and manner provided in this code.

(7) To administer oaths in an action or proceeding pending therein, and in all other cases where it may be necessary in the exercise of its powers and duties.

(8) To amend and control its process and orders so as to make them conform to law and justice. An appellate court shall not reverse or vacate a duly entered judgment upon an agreement or stipulation of the parties unless the court finds both of the following:

(A) There is no reasonable possibility that the interests of nonparties or the public will be adversely affected by the reversal.

(B) The reasons of the parties for requesting reversal outweigh the erosion of public trust that may result from the nullification of a judgment and the risk that the availability of stipulated reversal will reduce the incentive for pretrial settlement.

(b) Notwithstanding Section 1211 or any other law, if an order of contempt is made affecting an attorney, his or her agent, investigator, or any person acting under the attorney's direction, in the preparation and conduct of any action or proceeding, the execution of any sentence shall be stayed pending the filing within three judicial days of a petition for extraordinary relief testing the lawfulness of the court's order, the violation of which is the basis of the contempt except for the conduct as may be proscribed by subdivision (b) of Section 6068 of the Business and Professions Code, relating to an attorney's duty to maintain respect due to the courts and judicial officers.

(c) Notwithstanding Section 1211 or any other law, if an order of contempt is made affecting a public safety employee acting within the scope of employment for reason of the employee's failure to comply with a duly issued subpoena or subpoena duces tecum, the execution of any sentence shall be stayed pending the filing within three judicial days of a petition for extraordinary relief testing the lawfulness of the court's order, a violation of which is the basis for the contempt.

As used in this subdivision, "public safety employee" includes any peace officer, firefighter, paramedic, or any other employee of a public law enforcement agency whose duty is either to maintain official records or to analyze or present evidence for investigative or prosecutorial purposes.

(d) Notwithstanding Section 1211 or any other law, if an order of contempt is made affecting the victim of a sexual assault, where the contempt consists of refusing to testify concerning that sexual assault, the execution of any sentence shall be stayed pending the filing within three judicial days of a petition for extraordinary relief testing the lawfulness of the court's order, a violation of which is the basis for the contempt.

As used in this subdivision, "sexual assault" means any act made punishable by Section 261, 262, 264.1, 285, 286, 288, 288a, or 289 of the Penal Code.

(e) Notwithstanding Section 1211 or any other law, if an order of contempt is made affecting the victim of domestic violence, where the contempt consists of refusing to testify concerning that domestic violence, the execution of any sentence shall be stayed pending the filing within three judicial days of a petition for extraordinary relief testing the lawfulness of the court's order, a violation of which is the basis for the contempt.

As used in this subdivision, the term "domestic violence" means "domestic violence" as defined in Section 6211 of the Family Code.

(f) Notwithstanding Section 1211 or any other provision of law, no order of contempt shall be made affecting a county government or any member of its governing body acting pursuant to its constitutional or statutory authority unless the court finds, based on a review of evidence presented at a hearing conducted for this purpose, that either of the following conditions exist:

(1) That the county has the resources necessary to comply with the order of the court.

(2) That the county has the authority, without recourse to voter approval or without incurring additional indebtedness, to generate the additional resources necessary to comply with the order of the court, that compliance with the order of the court will not expose the county, any member of its governing body, or any other county officer to liability for failure to perform other constitutional or statutory duties, and that compliance with the order of the court will not deprive the county of resources necessary for its reasonable support and maintenance. *(Added by Stats.1987, c. 3, § 2, eff. March 11, 1987, operative March 11, 1989. Amended by Stats.1991, c. 866 (A.B.363), § 1; Stats.1992, c. 163 (A.B.2641), § 13; Stats.1992, c. 697 (S.B.1559), § 2; Stats.1993, c. 219 (A.B. 1500), § 63.3; Stats.1999, c. 508 (A.B.1676), § 1.)*

Law Revision Commission Comments

1993 Amendment

Subdivision (e) of Section 128 is amended to substitute a reference to the Family Code provision defining "domestic violence." See Fam. Code § 6211 ("domestic violence" defined) & Comment. [23 Cal.L.Rev.Comm. Reports 1 (1993)].

Commentary

In re Rashad H., 78 Cal.App.4th 376, 92 Cal.Rptr.2d 723 (2000), held that none of the factors listed in subsection (a)(8) barred the court from accepting a proposed reversal, stipulated by the county and the aggrieved parent, of an order terminating parental rights when the parent did not receive proper notice of the Welfare and Institutions Code § 366.26 hearing, and his rights were terminated by judicial error.

Research References

Forms

Am. Jur. Pl. & Pr. Forms Process § 18, Introductory Comments.
West's California Code Forms, Civil Procedure § 128 Form 1, Powers Of Courts--Order Reversing or Vacating Judgment Based Upon Stipulation Of Parties.
West's California Code Forms, Civil Procedure § 1211 Form 1, Contempts--Declaration--Not in Court's Presence.
West's California Code Forms, Insurance § 11583 Form 1, Motion in Limine.

Treatises and Practice Aids

Witkin, California Summary 10th Husband and Wife § 372, Criminal Proceedings.
Witkin, California Summary 10th Wills and Probate § 348, Current Law: General Jurisdiction.
Witkin, California Summary 10th Wills and Probate § 874, Petition.
Witkin, California Summary 10th Wills and Probate § 898, Petition.

§ 128.5. Frivolous actions or delaying tactics; order for payment of expenses; punitive damages; sanctions

(a) A trial court may order a party, the party's attorney, or both, to pay the reasonable expenses, including attorney's fees, incurred by another party as a result of * * * actions or tactics, made in bad faith, that are frivolous or solely intended to cause unnecessary delay. This section also applies to judicial arbitration proceedings under Chapter 2.5 (commencing with Section 1141.10) of Title 3 of Part 3.

(b) For purposes of this section:

(1) "Actions or tactics" include, but are not limited to, the making or opposing of motions or the filing and service of a complaint, cross-complaint, answer, or other responsive

pleading. The mere filing of a complaint without service thereof on an opposing party does not constitute "actions or tactics" for purposes of this section.

(2) "Frivolous" means totally and completely without merit or for the sole purpose of harassing an opposing party.

(c) Expenses pursuant to this section shall not be imposed except on notice contained in a party's moving or responding papers or, on the court's own motion, after notice and opportunity to be heard. An order imposing expenses shall be in writing and shall recite in detail the action or tactic or circumstances justifying the order.

(d) In addition to any award pursuant to this section for * * * an action or tactic described in subdivision (a), the court may assess punitive damages against the plaintiff on a determination by the court that the plaintiff's action was an action maintained by a person convicted of a felony against the person's victim, or the victim's heirs, relatives, estate, or personal representative, for injuries arising from the acts for which the person was convicted of a felony, and that the plaintiff is guilty of fraud, oppression, or malice in maintaining the action.

(e) This section shall not apply to disclosures and discovery requests, responses, objections, and motions.

(f) Sanctions ordered pursuant to this section shall be ordered pursuant to the following conditions and procedures:

(1) If, after notice and a reasonable opportunity to respond, the court issues an order pursuant to subdivision (a), the court may, subject to the conditions stated below, impose an appropriate sanction upon the party, the party's attorneys, or both, for an action or tactic described in subdivision (a). In determining what sanctions, if any, should be ordered, the court shall consider whether a party seeking sanctions has exercised due diligence.

(A) A motion for sanctions under this section shall be made separately from other motions or requests and shall describe the specific alleged action or tactic, made in bad faith, that is frivolous or solely intended to cause unnecessary delay.

(B) If the alleged action or tactic is the making or opposing of a written motion or the filing and service of a complaint, cross-complaint, answer, or other responsive pleading that can be withdrawn or appropriately corrected, a notice of motion shall be served as provided in Section 1010, but shall not be filed with or presented to the court, unless 21 days after service of the motion or any other period as the court may prescribe, the challenged action or tactic is not withdrawn or appropriately corrected.

(C) If warranted, the court may award to the party prevailing on the motion the reasonable expenses and attorney's fees incurred in presenting or opposing the motion. Absent exceptional circumstances, a law firm shall be held jointly responsible for violations committed by its partners, associates, and employees.

(D) If the alleged action or tactic is the making or opposing of a written motion or the filing and service of a complaint, cross-complaint, answer, or other responsive pleading that can be withdrawn or appropriately corrected, the court on its own motion may enter an order describing the specific action or tactic, made in bad faith, that is frivolous or solely intended to cause unnecessary delay, and direct an attorney, law firm, or party to show cause why it has made an action or tactic as defined in subdivision (b), unless, within 21 days of service of the order to show cause, the challenged action or tactic is withdrawn or appropriately corrected.

* * * (2) An order for sanctions * * * pursuant to this section shall be * * * limited to what is sufficient to deter repetition of the action or tactic or comparable action or tactic by others similarly situated. Subject to the limitations in subparagraphs (A) and (B), the sanction may consist of, or include, directives of a nonmonetary nature, an order to pay a penalty into court, or, if imposed on motion and warranted for effective deterrence, an order directing payment to the movant of some or all of the reasonable attorney's fees and other expenses incurred as a direct result of the action or tactic described in subdivision (a).

(A) Monetary sanctions may not be awarded against a represented party for a violation of presenting a claim, defense, and other legal contentions that are warranted by existing law or by a nonfrivolous argument for the extension, modification, or reversal of existing law or the establishment of new law.

(B) Monetary sanctions may not be awarded on the court's motion unless the court issues its order to show cause before a voluntary dismissal or settlement of the claims made by or against the party that is, or whose attorneys are, to be sanctioned.

(g) A motion for sanctions brought by a party or a party's attorney primarily for an improper purpose, such as to harass or to cause unnecessary delay or needless increase in the cost of litigation, shall itself be subject to a motion for sanctions. It is the intent of the Legislature that courts shall vigorously use its sanction authority to deter the improper actions or tactics or comparable actions or tactics of others similarly situated.

(h) The liability imposed by this section is in addition to any other liability imposed by law for acts or omissions within the purview of this section.

* * *

(i) This section * * * applies to actions or tactics that were part of a civil case filed on or after January 1, * * * 2015. *(Added by Stats.1981, c. 762, § 1. Amended by Stats.1984, c. 355, § 1; Stats.1985, c. 296, § 1; Stats.1990, c. 887 (S.B.2766), § 1; Stats.1994, c. 1062 (A.B.3594), § 1; Stats.2014, c. 425 (A.B.2494), § 1, eff. Jan. 1, 2015; Stats.2017, c. 169 (A.B.984), § 1, eff. Aug. 7, 2017.)*

Commentary

In *Olmstead v. Arthur J. Gallagher & Co., 32 Cal.4th 804, 11 Cal.Rptr.3d 298, 86 P.3d 354 (2004)*, the California Supreme Court held that this section does not authorize courts to impose sanctions in any law suit initiated after December 31, 1994. Claims after that date are governed by § 128.7 and, in the event § 128.7 is repealed, by § 128.6.

A trial court may award Section 128.5 sanctions to a party represented by an attorney on a contingency fee basis. *In re Marriage of Adams, 52 Cal.App.4th 911, 60 Cal.Rptr.2d 811 (1997), review denied May 14, 1997.*

To avoid liability for "bad faith actions or tactics," an attorney who receives a privileged document through another's inadvertence must examine the document no more than necessary to determine that it is privileged; notify the party entitled to the privilege; and resolve the situation by agreement or by seeking guidance from the court. *State Compensation Insurance Fund v. WPS, Inc., 70 Cal.App.4th 644, 82 Cal.Rptr.2d 799 (1999).*

Abandonato v. Coldren, 41 Cal.App.4th 264, 48 Cal.Rptr.2d 429 (1996), holds that an attorney representing himself may be awarded attorney's fees as sanctions under this Section. But see *Argaman v. Ratan, 73 Cal.App.4th 1173, 86 Cal.Rptr.2d 917 (1999),* disagreeing with *Abandonato* and holding that an attorney representing himself may not be awarded a monetary discovery sanction under Code of Civil Procedure Section 2023 (b)(1) as compensation for misuse of the discovery process. See also *Trope v. Katz, 11 Cal.4th 274, 902 P.2d 259, 45 Cal.Rptr.2d 241 (1995)* (attorney representing himself may not recover attorney's fees because he has not incurred any obligation to another to pay fees; see Civil Code Section 1717).

In re Marriage of Reese and Guy, 73 Cal.App.4th 1214, 87 Cal.Rptr.2d 339 (1999), holds that the trial court may not grant sanctions under this section, which concerns frivolous actions or delaying tactics by a party or an attorney, when a motion for sanctions has been noticed under § 128.7, which concerns nonmeritorious papers filed by an unrepresented party or an attorney. The court reasoned that notice sought under one statute was inadequate to warn a party or attorney of sanctions sought under the other, because the two statutes are significantly different. This section requires a finding of bad faith, and § 128.7 does not.

Research References

Forms

Cal. Transaction Forms - Bus. Transactions § 14:82, Availability Of Sanctions.
Cal. Transaction Forms - Bus. Transactions § 14:86, Matters to Consider in Drafting Arbitration Clauses.
Environmental Insurance Litigation: Practice Forms § 4:5, Sample Notice Of Motion and Motion to Compel Further Responses and Production Of Documents.
West's California Code Forms, Civil Procedure § 128.5 Form 1, Frivolous Actions or Delaying Tactics--Notice Of Motion for Payment Of Costs and Attorney's Fees.
West's California Code Forms, Civil Procedure § 128.5 Form 4, Frivolous Actions or Delaying Tactics--Notice Of Motion for Order Assessing Punitive Damages.
West's California Code Forms, Civil Procedure § 128.7 Form 3, Frivolous Actions or Delaying Tactics--Order for Payment Of Costs and Attorney's Fees.

Treatises and Practice Aids

Witkin, California Summary 10th Husband and Wife § 8, in General.
Witkin, California Summary 10th Insurance § 101, Conduct Intended to Harm or Inherently Harmful.
Witkin, California Summary 10th Torts § 471, Action as Disfavored.
Witkin, California Summary 10th Torts § 487, Public Entity Cannot Sue.
Witkin, California Summary 10th Torts § 490, Order to Show Cause.
Witkin, California Summary 10th Torts § 496, Family Law Proceedings.
Witkin, California Summary 10th Torts § 508, Some, But Not All, Claims or Amounts Supported by Probable Cause.
Witkin, California Summary 10th Torts § 1606, Felon's Action Against Victim.

§ 128.7. Signature requirement for court papers; certification that specified conditions met; violations; sanctions; punitive damages

(a) Every pleading, petition, written notice of motion, or other similar paper shall be signed by at least one attorney of record in the attorney's individual name, or, if the party is not represented by an attorney, shall be signed by the party. Each paper shall state the signer's address and telephone number, if any. Except when otherwise provided by law, pleadings need not be verified or accompanied by affidavit. An unsigned paper shall be stricken unless omission of the signature is corrected promptly after being called to the attention of the attorney or party.

(b) By presenting to the court, whether by signing, filing, submitting, or later advocating, a pleading, petition, written notice of motion, or other similar paper, an attorney or unrepresented party is certifying that to the best of the person's knowledge, information, and belief, formed after an inquiry reasonable under the circumstances, all of the following conditions are met:

(1) It is not being presented primarily for an improper purpose, such as to harass or to cause unnecessary delay or needless increase in the cost of litigation.

(2) The claims, defenses, and other legal contentions therein are warranted by existing law or by a nonfrivolous argument for the extension, modification, or reversal of existing law or the establishment of new law.

(3) The allegations and other factual contentions have evidentiary support or, if specifically so identified, are likely to have evidentiary support after a reasonable opportunity for further investigation or discovery.

(4) The denials of factual contentions are warranted on the evidence or, if specifically so identified, are reasonably based on a lack of information or belief.

(c) If, after notice and a reasonable opportunity to respond, the court determines that subdivision (b) has been violated, the court may, subject to the conditions stated below, impose an appropriate sanction upon the attorneys, law firms, or parties that have violated subdivision (b) or are responsible for the violation. In determining what sanctions, if any, should be ordered, the court shall consider whether a party seeking sanctions has exercised due diligence.

(1) A motion for sanctions under this section shall be made separately from other motions or requests and shall describe the specific conduct alleged to violate subdivision (b). Notice of motion shall be served as provided in Section 1010, but shall not be filed with or presented to the court unless, within 21 days after service of the motion, or any other period as the court may prescribe, the challenged paper, claim, defense, contention, allegation, or denial is not withdrawn or appropriately corrected. If warranted, the court may award to the party prevailing on the motion the reasonable expenses and attorney's fees incurred in presenting or opposing the motion. Absent exceptional circumstances, a law firm shall be held jointly responsible for violations committed by its partners, associates, and employees.

(2) On its own motion, the court may enter an order describing the specific conduct that appears to violate subdivision (b) and directing an attorney, law firm, or party to show cause why it has not violated subdivision (b), unless, within 21 days of service of the order to show cause, the challenged paper, claim, defense, contention, allegation, or denial is withdrawn or appropriately corrected.

(d) A sanction imposed for violation of subdivision (b) shall be limited to what is sufficient to deter repetition of this conduct or comparable conduct by others similarly situated. Subject to the limitations in paragraphs (1) and (2), the sanction may consist of, or include, directives of a nonmonetary nature, an order to pay a penalty into court, or, if imposed on motion and warranted for effective deterrence, an order directing payment to the movant of some or all of the reasonable attorney's fees and other expenses incurred as a direct result of the violation.

(1) Monetary sanctions may not be awarded against a represented party for a violation of paragraph (2) of subdivision (b).

(2) Monetary sanctions may not be awarded on the court's motion unless the court issues its order to show cause before a voluntary dismissal or settlement of the claims made by or against the party that is, or whose attorneys are, to be sanctioned.

(e) When imposing sanctions, the court shall describe the conduct determined to constitute a violation of this section and explain the basis for the sanction imposed.

(f) In addition to any award pursuant to this section for conduct described in subdivision (b), the court may assess punitive damages against the plaintiff upon a determination by the court that the plaintiff's action was an action maintained by a person convicted of a felony against the person's victim, or the victim's heirs, relatives, estate, or personal representative, for injuries arising from the acts for which the person was convicted of a felony, and that the plaintiff is guilty of fraud, oppression, or malice in maintaining the action.

(g) This section shall not apply to disclosures and discovery requests, responses, objections, and motions.

(h) A motion for sanctions brought by a party or a party's attorney primarily for an improper purpose, such as to harass or to cause unnecessary delay or needless increase in the cost of litigation, shall itself be subject to a motion for sanctions. It is the intent of the Legislature that courts shall vigorously use its sanctions authority to deter that improper conduct or comparable conduct by others similarly situated.

(i) This section shall apply to a complaint or petition filed on or after January 1, 1995, and any other pleading, written notice of motion, or other similar paper filed in that matter. *(Added by Stats.1994, c. 1062 (A.B.3594), § 3. Amended by Stats.1998, c. 121 (S.B.1511), § 2; Stats.2002, c. 491 (S.B. 2009), § 1; Stats.2005, c. 706 (A.B.1742), § 9.)*

Application

For application of 2005 amendment, see Stats.2005, c. 706 (A.B.1742), § 41.

Commentary

In re Mark B., 149 Cal.App.4th 61, 56 Cal.Rptr.3d 697 (2007), held that a juvenile court or a juvenile court referee may, under this section, impose sanctions in a dependency proceeding.

In *Olmstead v. Arthur J. Gallagher & Co., 32 Cal.4th 804, 11 Cal.Rptr.3d 298, 86 P.3d 354 (2004)*, the California Supreme Court held that § 128.5 does not authorize courts to impose sanctions in any law suit initiated after December 31, 1994. Claims after that date are governed by this section and, in the event this section is repealed, by § 128.6.

In re Marriage of Reese and Guy, 73 Cal.App.4th 1214, 87 Cal.Rptr.2d 339 (1999), holds that the trial court may not grant sanctions under § 128.5, which concerns frivolous actions or delaying tactics by a party or an attorney, when a motion for sanctions has been noticed under this section, which concerns non-meritorious papers filed by an unrepresented party or an attorney. The court reasoned that notice sought under one statute was inadequate to warn a party or attorney of sanctions sought under the other, because the two statutes are significantly different. *Reese and Guy,* applying the letter of Civil Code § 2015.5, also held that the attorney practice of signing declarations under penalty of perjury on behalf of clients and witnesses is improper and impermissible, for the purpose of that section is to ensure that the declaration is truthful and that an untruthful declaration may be prosecuted as perjury.

In re Marriage of Falcone & Fyke, 164 Cal.App.4th 814, 79 Cal.Rptr.3d 588 (2008), held that a trial court, under this section and Family Code section 271, properly imposed $64,500 in sanctions against a self-represented ex-spouse, because she prosecuted a motion for contempt without any factual or legal basis and pursued a meritless motion for a new trial.

Burkle v. Burkle, 144 Cal.App.4th 387, 50 Cal.Rptr.3d 436 (2006), review denied Feb. 21, 2007, affirmed a trial court dismissal of a wife's civil action for intentional infliction of emotional distress arising from her husband's failure to comply with an interim support order in a pending dissolution proceeding, on the ground that bringing a separate action pertaining to a pending dissolution proceeding violates well-established California precedent prohibiting such separate actions, and concluded that the wife's contentions about the proper forum for her civil action were frivolous; therefore the trial court properly ordered, as sanctions, that the wife make substantial payments to her husband under Family Code section 271 and that the wife and her attorneys make substantial payments to the husband under this section.

Eichenbaum v. Alon, 106 Cal.App.4th 967, 131 Cal.Rptr.2d 296 (2003), holds that the trial court retains authority to impose sanctions under this section when a plaintiff voluntarily dismisses the complaint after defendant has filed a motion for sanctions.

Musaelian v. Adams, 45 Cal.4th 512, 198 P.3d 560, 87 Cal.Rptr.3d 475 (2009), held that attorney fees may not be awarded under this section as a sanction to an attorney representing himself because a self-representing attorney does not "incur" attorney fees within the meaning of subsection (d). Musaelian disapproves *Laborde v. Aronson, 92 Cal.App.4th 459, 112 Cal.Rptr.2d 119 (2001)* and *Abandonato v. Coldren, 41 Cal.App.4th 264, 48 Cal.Rptr.2d 429 (1995)*, which reached the opposite conclusion.

Research References

Forms

West's California Code Forms, Civil Procedure § 128.7 Form 1, Frivolous Actions or Delaying Tactics--Notice Of Motion for Order Requiring Payment Of Costs and Attorney's Fees.

West's California Code Forms, Civil Procedure § 128.7 Form 2, Frivolous Actions or Delaying Tactics--Declaration for Order Requiring Payment Of Costs and Attorney's Fees.

West's California Code Forms, Civil Procedure § 128.7 Form 3, Frivolous Actions or Delaying Tactics--Order for Payment Of Costs and Attorney's Fees.

West's California Code Forms, Civil Procedure § 128.7 Form 4, Frivolous Actions or Delaying Tactics--Order to Show Cause for Sanctions.

Treatises and Practice Aids

Witkin, California Summary 10th Parent and Child § 467, Power to Hear Cases.

Witkin, California Summary 10th Torts § 1606, Felon's Action Against Victim.

§ 130. Deceased minor victims of criminal acts; sealing of autopsy report and associated evidence

(a) Subject to the provisions of this section, when a child who is under 18 years of age is killed as a result of a criminal act and a person has been convicted and sentenced for the commission of that criminal act, or a person has been found to have committed that offense by the juvenile court and adjudged a ward of the juvenile court, upon the request of a qualifying family member of the deceased child, the autopsy report and evidence associated with the examination of the victim in the possession of a public agency, as defined in Section 6252 of the Government Code, shall be sealed and not disclosed, except that an autopsy report and evidence associated with the examination of the victim which has been sealed pursuant to this section may be disclosed, as follows:

(1) To law enforcement, prosecutorial agencies and experts hired by those agencies, public social service agencies, child death review teams, or the hospital that treated the child immediately prior to death, to be used solely for investigative, prosecutorial, or review purposes, and may not be disseminated further.

(2) To the defendant and the defense team in the course of criminal proceedings or related habeas proceedings, to be used solely for investigative, criminal defense, and review purposes, including review for the purpose of initiating any criminal proceeding or related habeas proceeding, and may not be disseminated further. The "defense team" includes, but is not limited to, all of the following: attorneys, investigators, experts, paralegals, support staff, interns, students, and state and privately funded legal assistance projects hired or consulted for the purposes of investigation, defense, appeal, or writ of habeas corpus on behalf of the person accused of killing the deceased child victim.

(3) To civil litigants in a cause of action related to the victim's death with a court order upon a showing of good cause and proper notice under Section 129, to be used solely to pursue the cause of action, and may not be disseminated further.

(b) Nothing in this section shall prohibit the use of autopsy reports and evidence in relation to court proceedings.

(c) Nothing in this section shall abrogate the rights of victims, their authorized representatives, or insurance carriers to request the release of information pursuant to subdivision (f) of Section 6254 of the Government Code. However, if a seal has been requested, an insurance carrier receiving items pursuant to a request under that subdivision is prohibited from disclosing the requested items except as necessary in the normal course of business. An insurance carrier shall not, under any circumstances, disclose to the general public items received pursuant to subdivision (f) of Section 6254 of the Government Code.

(d) This section may not be invoked by a qualifying family member who has been charged with or convicted of any act in furtherance of the victim's death. Upon the filing of those charges against a qualifying family member, any seal maintained at the request of that qualifying family member under this section shall be removed.

(e) A coroner or medical examiner shall not be liable for damages in a civil action for any reasonable act or omission taken in good faith in compliance with this section.

(f) If sealing of the autopsy report has been requested by a qualifying family member and another qualifying family member opposes sealing, the opposing party may request a hearing in the superior court in the county with jurisdiction over the crime leading to the child's death for a determination of whether the sealing should be maintained. The opposing party shall notify all other qualifying family members, the medical examiner's office that conducted the autopsy, and the district attorney's office with jurisdiction over the crime at least 10 court days in advance of the hearing. At the hearing, the court shall consider the interests of all qualifying family members, the protection of the memory of the deceased child, any evidence that the qualifying family member requesting the seal was involved in the crime that resulted in the death of the child, the public interest in scrutiny of the autopsy report or the performance of the medical examiner, any impact that unsealing would have on pending investigations or pending litigation, and any other relevant factors. Official information in the possession of a public agency necessary to the determination of the hearing shall be received in camera upon a proper showing. In its discretion, the court may, to the extent allowable by law and with good cause shown, restrict the dissemination of an autopsy report or evidence associated with the examination of a victim. This section shall not apply if a public agency has independently determined that the autopsy report may not be disclosed pursuant to subdivision (f) of Section 6254 of the Government Code because it is an investigative file. In that instance, nothing in this section shall preclude the application of Sections 6258 and 6259 of the Government Code.

(g) If a seal has been maintained pursuant to this section, a qualifying family member, or a biological or adoptive aunt, uncle, sibling, first cousin, child, or grandparent of the deceased child may request that the seal be removed. The request to remove the seal shall be adjudicated pursuant to subdivision (f), with the party requesting the removal of the seal being the opposing party.

(h) Nothing in this section shall limit the public access to information contained in the death certificate including: name, age, gender, race, date, time and location of death, the name of a physician reporting a death in a hospital, the name of the certifying pathologist, date of certification, burial information, and cause of death.

(i) When a medical examiner declines a request to provide a copy of an autopsy report that has been sealed pursuant to this section, the examiner shall cite this section as the reason for declining to provide a copy of the report.

(j) For purposes of this section:

(1) A "child who is under 18 years of age" does not include any child who comes within either of the following descriptions:

(A) He or she was a dependent child of the juvenile court pursuant to Section 300 of the Welfare and Institutions Code at the time of his or her death, or, pursuant to subdivision (b) of Section 10850.4 of the Welfare and Institutions Code, abuse or neglect is determined to have led to his or her death.

(B) He or she was residing in a state or county juvenile facility, or a private facility under contract with the state or county for the placement of juveniles, as a ward of the juvenile court pursuant to Section 602 of the Welfare and Institutions Code at the time of his or her death.

(2) "Evidence associated with the examination of a victim" means any object, writing, diagram, recording, computer file, photograph, video, DVD, CD, film, digital device, or other item that was collected during, or serves to document, the autopsy of a deceased child.

(3) "Qualifying family member" means the biological or adoptive parent, spouse, or legal guardian.

(k) Nothing in this section shall limit the discovery provisions set forth in Chapter 10 (commencing with Section 1054) of Title 6 of the Penal Code.

(*l*) Nothing in this section shall be construed to limit the authority of the court to seal records or restrict the dissemination of an autopsy report or evidence associated with the examination of a victim under case law, other statutory law, or the rules of court.

(m) The provisions of this section are severable. If any provision of this section or its application is held invalid, that invalidity shall not affect other provisions or applications that can be given effect without the invalid provision or application. *(Added by Stats.2010, c. 302 (S.B.5), § 3, eff. Sept. 27, 2010.)*

Research References

Forms

West's California Code Forms, Civil Procedure § 130 Form 1, Photographs--Notice Of Motion for Order Permitting Disclosure Of Sealed Autopsy Report and Evidence Associated With the Examination Of the Victim Related to a Deceased Child Victim.

Title 2

JUDICIAL OFFICERS

CHAPTER 3. DISQUALIFICATIONS OF JUDGES

§ 170.3. Proceedings; waiver; failure or refusal to withdraw

(a)(1) If a judge determines himself or herself to be disqualified, the judge shall notify the presiding judge of the court of his or her recusal and shall not further participate in the proceeding, except as provided in Section 170.4, unless his or her disqualification is waived by the parties as provided in subdivision (b).

(2) If the judge disqualifying himself or herself is the only judge or the presiding judge of the court, the notification shall be sent to the person having authority to assign another judge to replace the disqualified judge.

(b)(1) A judge who determines himself or herself to be disqualified after disclosing the basis for his or her disqualification on the record may ask the parties and their attorneys whether they wish to waive the disqualification, except where the basis for disqualification is as provided in paragraph (2). A waiver of disqualification shall recite the basis for the disqualification, and is effective only when signed by all parties and their attorneys and filed in the record.

(2) There shall be no waiver of disqualification if the basis therefor is either of the following:

(A) The judge has a personal bias or prejudice concerning a party.

(B) The judge served as an attorney in the matter in controversy, or the judge has been a material witness concerning that matter.

(3) The judge shall not seek to induce a waiver and shall avoid any effort to discover which lawyers or parties favored or opposed a waiver of disqualification.

(4) If grounds for disqualification are first learned of or arise after the judge has made one or more rulings in a proceeding, but before the judge has completed judicial action in a proceeding, the judge shall, unless the disqualification be waived, disqualify himself or herself, but in the absence of good cause the rulings he or she has made up to that time shall not be set aside by the judge who replaces the disqualified judge.

(c)(1) If a judge who should disqualify himself or herself refuses or fails to do so, any party may file with the clerk a written verified statement objecting to the hearing or trial before the judge and setting forth the facts constituting the grounds for disqualification of the judge. The statement shall be presented at the earliest practicable opportunity after discovery of the facts constituting the ground for disqualification. Copies of the statement shall be served on each party or his or her attorney who has appeared and shall be personally served on the judge alleged to be disqualified, or on his or her clerk, provided that the judge is present in the courthouse or in chambers.

(2) Without conceding his or her disqualification, a judge whose impartiality has been challenged by the filing of a written statement may request any other judge agreed upon by the parties to sit and act in his or her place.

(3) Within 10 days after the filing or service, whichever is later, the judge may file a consent to disqualification in which case the judge shall notify the presiding judge or the person authorized to appoint a replacement of his or her recusal as provided in subdivision (a), or the judge may file a written verified answer admitting or denying any or all of the allegations contained in the party's statement and setting forth any additional facts material or relevant to the question of disqualification. The clerk shall forthwith transmit a copy of the judge's answer to each party or his or her attorney who has appeared in the action.

(4) A judge who fails to file a consent or answer within the time allowed shall be deemed to have consented to his or her disqualification and the clerk shall notify the presiding judge or person authorized to appoint a replacement of the recusal as provided in subdivision (a).

(5) A judge who refuses to recuse himself or herself shall not pass upon his or her own disqualification or upon the sufficiency in law, fact, or otherwise, of the statement of disqualification filed by a party. In that case, the question of

disqualification shall be heard and determined by another judge agreed upon by all the parties who have appeared or, in the event they are unable to agree within five days of notification of the judge's answer, by a judge selected by the chairperson of the Judicial Council, or if the chairperson is unable to act, the vice chairperson. The clerk shall notify the executive officer of the Judicial Council of the need for a selection. The selection shall be made as expeditiously as possible. No challenge pursuant to this subdivision or Section 170.6 may be made against the judge selected to decide the question of disqualification.

(6) The judge deciding the question of disqualification may decide the question on the basis of the statement of disqualification and answer and any written arguments as the judge requests, or the judge may set the matter for hearing as promptly as practicable. If a hearing is ordered, the judge shall permit the parties and the judge alleged to be disqualified to argue the question of disqualification and shall for good cause shown hear evidence on any disputed issue of fact. If the judge deciding the question of disqualification determines that the judge is disqualified, the judge hearing the question shall notify the presiding judge or the person having authority to appoint a replacement of the disqualified judge as provided in subdivision (a).

(d) The determination of the question of the disqualification of a judge is not an appealable order and may be reviewed only by a writ of mandate from the appropriate court of appeal sought only by the parties to the proceeding. The petition for the writ shall be filed and served within 10 days after service of written notice of entry of the court's order determining the question of disqualification. If the notice of entry is served by mail, that time shall be extended as provided in subdivision (a) of Section 1013. *(Added by Stats.1984, c. 1555, § 7. Amended by Stats.1990, c. 910 (S.B.2316), § 1; Stats.2006, c. 567 (A.B.2303), § 4.)*

Commentary

A private judge's rulings in a marital dissolution proceeding were void when the judge was deemed, under subsection (c)(4), to have consented to disqualification because she failed to follow the procedure prescribed in this section for responding to a statement of disqualification. The rulings were void from the time the facts justifying disqualification arose, not merely from the time disqualification was established. *Hayward v. Superior Court of Napa County, 2 Cal.App.5th 10, 206 Cal.Rptr.3d 102 (2016), review denied.*

In re Marriage of M.A., 234 Cal.App.4th 894, 184 Cal.Rptr.3d 315 (2015), review denied, holds that postjudgment orders in a marriage dissolution were invalid when they were made by a commissioner who declined to entertain a husband's statement of disqualification. Failure to determine at or before a hearing the issue of disqualification renders the commissioner powerless to decide the merits or enter any order.

Research References

Forms

West's California Code Forms, Civil Procedure § 170.1 Form 1, Judicial Officers--Objection to Judge on Ground Of Disqualification.

West's California Code Forms, Civil Procedure § 170.3 Form 5, Judicial Officers--Order Disqualifying Judge After Hearing.

Treatises and Practice Aids

§ 170.4. Powers of disqualified judges

(a) A disqualified judge, notwithstanding his or her disqualification may do any of the following:

(1) Take any action or issue any order necessary to maintain the jurisdiction of the court pending the assignment of a judge not disqualified.

(2) Request any other judge agreed upon by the parties to sit and act in his or her place.

(3) Hear and determine purely default matters.

(4) Issue an order for possession prior to judgment in eminent domain proceedings.

(5) Set proceedings for trial or hearing.

(6) Conduct settlement conferences.

(b) Notwithstanding paragraph (5) of subdivision (c) of Section 170.3, if a statement of disqualification is untimely filed or if on its face it discloses no legal grounds for disqualification, the trial judge against whom it was filed may order it stricken.

(c)(1) If a statement of disqualification is filed after a trial or hearing has commenced by the start of voir dire, by the swearing of the first witness or by the submission of a motion for decision, the judge whose impartiality has been questioned may order the trial or hearing to continue, notwithstanding the filing of the statement of disqualification. The issue of disqualification shall be referred to another judge for decision as provided in subdivision (a) of Section 170.3, and if it is determined that the judge is disqualified, all orders and rulings of the judge found to be disqualified made after the filing of the statement shall be vacated.

(2) For the purposes of this subdivision, if (A) a proceeding is filed in a single judge court or has been assigned to a single judge for comprehensive disposition, and (B) the proceeding has been set for trial or hearing 30 or more days in advance before a judge whose name was known at the time, the trial or hearing shall be deemed to have commenced 10 days prior to the date scheduled for trial or hearing as to any grounds for disqualification known before that time.

(3) A party may file no more than one statement of disqualification against a judge unless facts suggesting new grounds for disqualification are first learned of or arise after the first statement of disqualification was filed. Repetitive statements of disqualification not alleging facts suggesting new grounds for disqualification shall be stricken by the judge against whom they are filed.

(d) Except as provided in this section, a disqualified judge shall have no power to act in any proceeding after his or her disqualification or after the filing of a statement of disqualification until the question of his or her disqualification has been determined. *(Added by Stats.1984, c. 1555, § 8.)*

Commentary

In re Marriage of M.A., 234 Cal.App.4th 894, 184 Cal.Rptr.3d 315 (2015), review denied, holds that postjudgment orders in a marriage dissolution were invalid when they were made by a commissioner who declined to entertain a husband's statement of disqualification. Failure to determine at or before a hearing the issue of disqualification renders the commissioner powerless to decide the merits or enter any order.

Part 2

OF CIVIL ACTIONS

Title 2

OF THE TIME OF COMMENCING CIVIL ACTIONS

CHAPTER 1. THE TIME OF COMMENCING ACTIONS IN GENERAL

§ 312. General limitations; special cases

Civil actions, without exception, can only be commenced within the periods prescribed in this title, after the cause of action shall have accrued, unless where, in special cases, a different limitation is prescribed by statute. *(Enacted in 1872. Amended by Stats.1897, c. 21, p. 16, § 1.)*

§ 313. Claims against local public entities

The general procedure for the presentation of claims as a prerequisite to commencement of actions for money or damages against the State of California, counties, cities, cities and counties, districts, local authorities, and other political subdivisions of the State, and against the officers, employees, and servants thereof, is prescribed by Division 3.6 (commencing with Section 810) of Title 1 of the Government Code. *(Added by Stats.1959, c. 1724, p. 4138, § 3. Amended by Stats.1963, c. 1715, p. 3396, § 9.)*

CHAPTER 2. THE TIME OF COMMENCING ACTIONS FOR THE RECOVERY OF REAL PROPERTY

§ 318. Seizin within five years; necessity

SEIZIN WITHIN FIVE YEARS, WHEN NECESSARY IN ACTION FOR REAL PROPERTY. No action for the recovery of real property, or for the recovery of the possession thereof, can be maintained, unless it appear that the plaintiff, his ancestor, predecessor, or grantor, was seized or possessed of the property in question, within five years before the commencement of the action. *(Enacted in 1872.)*

Research References

Forms

West's California Code Forms, Civil Procedure § 328 Form 1, Statute Of Limitations--Tolling--Real Property Actions.

Treatises and Practice Aids

Witkin, California Summary 10th Constitutional Law § 1166, Statute Of Limitations.

Witkin, California Summary 10th Real Property § 227, Continuous Possession.

Witkin, California Summary 10th Real Property § 229, Laches Does Not Bar Claim Of Adverse Possession.

Witkin, California Summary 10th Real Property § 233, Showing Of Seisin or Possession.

Witkin, California Summary 10th Real Property § 398, Right to Easement.

§ 319. Seizin within five years; necessity to action or defense; cases involving title, rents or profits

SUCH SEIZIN, WHEN NECESSARY IN ACTION OR DEFENSE ARISING OUT OF TITLE TO OR RENTS OF REAL PROPERTY. No cause of action, or defense to an action, arising out of the title to real property, or to rents or profits out of the same, can be effectual, unless it appear that the person prosecuting the action, or making the defense, or under whose title the action is prosecuted, or the defense is made, or the ancestor, predecessor, or grantor of such person was seized or possessed of the premises in question within five years before the commencement of the act in respect to which such action is prosecuted or defense made. *(Enacted in 1872.)*

Research References

Forms

West's California Code Forms, Civil Procedure § 328 Form 1, Statute Of Limitations--Tolling--Real Property Actions.

Treatises and Practice Aids

Witkin, California Summary 10th Constitutional Law § 1166, Statute Of Limitations.

Witkin, California Summary 10th Real Property § 227, Continuous Possession.

§ 320. Entry; sufficiency; one and five year limitation of actions

ENTRY ON REAL ESTATE. No entry upon real estate is deemed sufficient or valid as a claim, unless an action be commenced thereupon within one year after making such entry, and within five years from the time when the right to make it descended or accrued. *(Enacted in 1872.)*

Research References

Treatises and Practice Aids

Witkin, California Summary 10th Real Property § 343, Operative Date Of Provisions.

§ 321. Presumption of timely possession; presumption of subordinate occupation; adverse possession for five years

POSSESSION, WHEN PRESUMED. In every action for the recovery of real property, or the possession thereof, the person establishing a legal title to the property is presumed to have been possessed thereof within the time required by law, and the occupation of the property by any other person is deemed to have been under and in subordination to the legal title, unless it appear that the property has been held and possessed adversely to such legal title, for five years before the commencement of the action. *(Enacted in 1872.)*

Research References

Forms

West's California Code Forms, Civil § 811 Form 1, Complaint to Quiet Title--Disuse Of Easement Acquired by Prescription.

West's California Code Forms, Civil § 1007 Form 1, Complaint to Quiet Title Acquired by Prescription.

Treatises and Practice Aids

Witkin, California Summary 10th Real Property § 218, Vendor and Purchaser, Grantor and Grantee.

Witkin, California Summary 10th Real Property § 227, Continuous Possession.

§ 322. Occupation under claim of title founded upon written instrument or judgment; presumption of adverse possession after five years; tract divided into lots

OCCUPATION UNDER WRITTEN INSTRUMENT OR JUDGMENT, WHEN DEEMED ADVERSE. When it appears that the occupant, or those under whom he claims, entered into the possession of the property under claim of title, exclusive of other right, founding such claim upon a written instrument, as being a conveyance of the property in question, or upon the decree or judgment of a competent Court, and that there has been a continued occupation and possession of the property included in such instrument, decree, or judgment, or of some part of the property, under such claim, for five years, the property so included is deemed to have been held adversely, except that when it consists of a tract divided into lots, the possession of one lot is not deemed a possession of any other lot of the same tract. *(Enacted in 1872.)*

Research References

Forms

Am. Jur. Pl. & Pr. Forms Adverse Possession § 32, Statutory References--Color Of Title and Adverse Possession.

Treatises and Practice Aids

Witkin, California Summary 10th Real Property § 224, Sufficiency Of Possession.

Witkin, California Summary 10th Real Property § 227, Continuous Possession.

Witkin, California Summary 10th Real Property § 232, Constructive Adverse Possession.

§ 323. Adverse possession under claim of title founded upon written instrument or judgment defined

WHAT CONSTITUTES ADVERSE POSSESSION UNDER WRITTEN INSTRUMENT OR JUDGMENT. For the purpose of constituting an adverse possession by any person claiming a title founded upon a written instrument, or a judgment or decree, land is deemed to have been possessed and occupied in the following cases:

1. Where it has been usually cultivated or improved;
2. Where it has been protected by a substantial inclosure;
3. Where, although not inclosed, it has been used for the supply of fuel, or of fencing timber for the purposes of husbandry, or for pasturage, or for the ordinary use of the occupant;
4. Where a known farm or single lot has been partly improved, the portion of such farm or lot that may have been left not cleared, or not inclosed according to the usual course and custom of the adjoining country, shall be deemed to have been occupied for the same length of time as the part improved and cultivated. *(Enacted in 1872.)*

Research References

Forms

Am. Jur. Pl. & Pr. Forms Adverse Possession § 32, Statutory References--Color Of Title and Adverse Possession.

Treatises and Practice Aids

Witkin, California Summary 10th Real Property § 224, Sufficiency Of Possession.

§ 324. Occupation under claim of title; adverse possession of premises actually occupied

PREMISES ACTUALLY OCCUPIED UNDER CLAIM OF TITLE DEEMED TO BE HELD ADVERSELY. Where it appears that there has been an actual continued occupation of land, under a claim of title, exclusive of any other right, but not founded upon a written instrument, judgment, or decree, the land so actually occupied, and no other, is deemed to have been held adversely. *(Enacted in 1872.)*

Research References

Treatises and Practice Aids

Witkin, California Summary 10th Real Property § 226, Sufficiency Of Possession.

§ 325. Adverse possession; claim of title not founded upon written instrument, judgment, or decree; possession and occupancy of land; payment of taxes

(a) For the purpose of constituting an adverse possession by a person claiming title, not founded upon a written instrument, judgment, or decree, land is deemed to have been possessed and occupied in the following cases only:

(1) Where it has been protected by a substantial enclosure.

(2) Where it has been usually cultivated or improved.

(b) In no case shall adverse possession be considered established under the provision of any section of this code, unless it shall be shown that the land has been occupied and claimed for the period of five years continuously, and the party or persons, their predecessors and grantors, have timely paid all state, county, or municipal taxes that have been levied and assessed upon the land for the period of five years during which the land has been occupied and claimed. Payment of those taxes by the party or persons, their predecessors and grantors shall be established by certified records of the county tax collector. *(Enacted in 1872. Amended by Code Am.1877–78, c. 590, p. 99, § 1; Stats.2010, c. 55 (A.B.1684), § 1.)*

Research References

Forms

Am. Jur. Pl. & Pr. Forms Adverse Possession § 33, Statutory References--Payment Of Taxes and Adverse Possession.
West's California Code Forms, Civil § 1007 Form 1, Complaint to Quiet Title Acquired by Prescription.

Treatises and Practice Aids

Witkin, California Summary 10th Real Property § 226, Sufficiency Of Possession.
Witkin, California Summary 10th Real Property § 227, Continuous Possession.
Witkin, California Summary 10th Real Property § 230, in General.
Witkin, California Summary 10th Real Property § 402, Issues and Proof.

§ 326. Adverse possession; relation of landlord and tenant; effect

RELATION OF LANDLORD AND TENANT AS AFFECTING ADVERSE POSSESSION. When the relation of landlord and tenant has existed between any persons, the possession of the tenant is deemed the possession of the landlord until the expiration of five years from the termination of the tenancy, or, where there has been no written lease, until the expiration of five years from the time of the last payment of rent, notwithstanding that such tenant may have acquired another title, or may have claimed to hold adversely to his landlord. But such presumptions cannot be made after the periods herein limited. *(Enacted in 1872.)*

§ 327. Right of possession; death of person in possession; effect of descent

RIGHT OF POSSESSION NOT AFFECTED BY DESCENT CAST. The right of a person to the possession of real property is not impaired or affected by a descent cast in consequence of the death of a person in possession of such property. *(Enacted in 1872.)*

§ 328. Computation of time; exclusion of certain disabilities

If a person entitled to commence an action for the recovery of real property, or for the recovery of the possession thereof, or to make an entry or defense founded on the title to real property, or to rents or services out of the property, is, at the time title first descends or accrues, either under the age of majority or lacking legal capacity to make decisions, the time, not exceeding 20 years, during which the disability continues is not deemed a portion of the time in this chapter limited for the commencement of the action, or the making of the entry or defense, but the action may be commenced, or entry or defense made, within the period of five years after the disability shall cease, or after the death of the person entitled, who shall die under the disability. The action shall not be commenced, or entry or defense made, after that period. *(Enacted in 1872. Amended by Code Am.1903, c. 160, p. 177, § 1; Stats.1994, c. 1083 (S.B.1445), § 2; Stats.2014, c. 144 (A.B.1847), § 3, eff. Jan. 1, 2015.)*

Research References

Forms

West's California Code Forms, Civil Procedure § 328 Form 1, Statute Of Limitations--Tolling--Real Property Actions.

Treatises and Practice Aids

Witkin, California Summary 10th Real Property § 235, Disabilities.

CHAPTER 3. THE TIME OF COMMENCING ACTIONS OTHER THAN FOR THE RECOVERY OF REAL PROPERTY

§ 335. Periods of limitation

PERIODS OF LIMITATION PRESCRIBED. The periods prescribed for the commencement of actions other than for the recovery of real property, are as follows: *(Enacted in 1872.)*

Research References

Forms

West's California Code Forms, Civil Procedure § 352 Form 1, Statute Of Limitations--Tolling--Contract Actions.

West's California Code Forms, Civil Procedure § 352.1 Form 1, Statute Of Limitations--Tolling--Imprisonment--Contract Actions.

§ 335.1. Two years; actions for assault, battery, or injury to, or for death of, individual caused by wrongful act or neglect

Within two years: An action for assault, battery, or injury to, or for the death of, an individual caused by the wrongful act or neglect of another. *(Added by Stats.2002, c. 448 (S.B.688), § 2.)*

Research References

Forms

Am. Jur. Pl. & Pr. Forms Products Liability § 247.40, Answer and Affirmative Defenses--By Manufacturer--In Suit Against Municipal Corporation and Police Officers and Manufacturer --For Wrongful Death; Survival Action; Deprivation Of Rights.

West's California Code Forms, Civil Procedure § 335.1 Form 1, Statutes Of Limitation--Action for Assault, Battery, Injury, or Death on Another Due to Negligence--Two-Year Time Period.

West's California Code Forms, Civil Procedure § 340.10 Form 1, Statutes Of Limitation--Action for Personal Injury or Wrongful Death Of Another--Terrorist Victims Of September 11, 2001 Attacks--Two-Year Time Period.

Treatises and Practice Aids

Witkin, California Summary 10th Agency and Employment § 243, Nature and Scope Of Action.

Witkin, California Summary 10th Torts § 1379, Statute Of Limitations.

§ 336. Five years; mesne profits

Within five years:

(a) An action for mesne profits of real property.

(b) An action for violation of a restriction, as defined in Section 784 of the Civil Code. The period prescribed in this subdivision runs from the time the person seeking to enforce the restriction discovered or, through the exercise of reasonable diligence, should have discovered the violation. A failure to commence an action for violation of a restriction within the period prescribed in this subdivision does not waive the right to commence an action for any other violation of the restriction and does not, in itself, create an implication that the restriction is abandoned, obsolete, or otherwise unenforceable. This subdivision shall not bar commencement of an action for violation of a restriction before January 1, 2001, and until January 1, 2001, any other applicable statutory or common law limitation shall continue to apply to that action. *(Enacted in 1872. Amended by Code Am.1873–74, c. 383, p. 291, § 31; Stats.1953, c. 1153, p. 2652, § 1; Stats.1998, c. 14 (A.B.707), § 3.)*

Law Revision Commission Comments

1998 Amendment

Subdivision (b) is added to Section 336 to make clear that the statutory limitation period applicable to enforcement of a restriction is five years, consistent with the general statutes governing recovery of real property. *Cf.* Section 319 (five years). This ensures a uniform limitation period regardless of whether the restriction is in the form of a covenant, condition, negative easement, or equitable servitude. See Civ. Code § 784 ("restriction" defined); *cf.* 2 A. Bowman, Ogden's Revised California Real Property Law 23.25, at 1155, 23.32, at 1159 (1975) (five years).

For purposes of subdivision (b), the time when a homeowners' association is deemed to have knowledge of a violation of a restriction would be determined under general principles of imputed knowledge. See, e.g., Civ. Code § 2332. Thus an incorporated or unincorporated homeowner's association is deemed to have knowledge of a violation of a restriction when an appropriate officer or agent of the association has knowledge of the violation.

Under subdivision (b), a failure to enforce a violation within the limitation period should not alone be grounds to imply a waiver or abandonment of the restriction. However, such a failure may, combined with other circumstances, be grounds for waiver or estoppel or evidence of abandonment or obsolescence. See, e.g., Bryant v. Whitney, 178 Cal. 640, 174 P. 32 (1918) (waiver).

Subdivision (b) provides a two-year grace period to enable action on a violation that would become unenforceable upon enactment of this chapter and a shorter grace period for action on a violation that would become unenforceable within two years after enactment of this chapter. The two-year grace period does not operate to extend the time to act on a violation that would become unenforceable by operation of law apart from this chapter, either pursuant to case law limitations or applicable statutes of limitation. [28 Cal.L.Rev. Comm. Reports App. 4 (1998)].

Research References

Forms

West's California Code Forms, Civil Procedure § 336 Form 1, Statutes Of Limitation--Restrictions on Use Of Real Property--Discovery Of Violations.

Treatises and Practice Aids

Witkin, California Summary 10th Real Property § 123, Statute Of Limitations.

Witkin, California Summary 10th Real Property § 451, in General.

§ 336a. Six years; corporate obligations held by public; corporate mortgages, deeds of trust, etc.

Within six years. 1. An action upon any bonds, notes or debentures issued by any corporation or pursuant to permit of the Commissioner of Corporations, or upon any coupons issued with such bonds, notes or debentures, if such bonds, notes or debentures shall have been issued to or held by the public.

2. An action upon any mortgage, trust deed or other agreement pursuant to which such bonds, notes or debentures were issued. Nothing in this section shall apply to bonds or other evidences of indebtedness of a public district or corporation. *(Added by Stats.1935, c. 614, p. 1740, § 1.)*

§ 337. Four years; written contract; exception; book account; account stated based upon account in writing; balance of mutual, open and current account in writing; rescission of written contract

Within four years: 1. An action upon any contract, obligation or liability founded upon an instrument in writing, except as provided in Section 336a of this code; provided, that the time within which any action for a money judgment for the balance due upon an obligation for the payment of which a deed of trust or mortgage with power of sale upon real property or any interest therein was given as security, following the exercise of the power of sale in such deed of trust or mortgage, may be brought shall not extend beyond three months after the time of sale under such deed of trust or mortgage.

2. An action to recover (1) upon a book account whether consisting of one or more entries; (2) upon an account stated based upon an account in writing, but the acknowledgment of the account stated need not be in writing; (3) a balance due upon a mutual, open and current account, the items of which are in writing; provided, however, that where an account stated is based upon an account of one item, the time shall begin to run from the date of said item, and where an account stated is based upon an account of more than one item, the time shall begin to run from the date of the last item.

3. An action based upon the rescission of a contract in writing. The time begins to run from the date upon which the facts that entitle the aggrieved party to rescind occurred. Where the ground for rescission is fraud or mistake, the time does not begin to run until the discovery by the aggrieved party of the facts constituting the fraud or mistake. Where the ground for rescission is misrepresentation under Section 359 of the Insurance Code, the time does not begin to run until the representation becomes false. *(Enacted in 1872. Amended by Code Am.1873–74, c. 383, p. 291, § 32; Stats. 1906, c. 1, p. 5, § 1; Stats.1907, c. 323, p. 599, § 1; Stats.1917, c. 203, p. 299, § 1; Stats.1933, c. 790, p. 2116, § 1; Stats.1935, c. 614, p. 1740, § 2; Stats.1947, c. 809, p. 1923, § 1; Stats.1961, c. 589, p. 1735, § 6.)*

Research References

Forms

Cal. Transaction Forms - Bus. Transactions § 28:4, Availability Of Remedies.

Cal. Transaction Forms - Bus. Transactions § 19:42, Continuing Guaranty (Single Individual Guarantor).

Cal. Transaction Forms - Bus. Transactions § 19:52, Continuing Guaranty (Multiple Individual Guarantors).

Cal. Transaction Forms - Bus. Transactions § 19:63, Suretyship Waivers by Co-Borrowers (Single Lender).

Am. Jur. Pl. & Pr. Forms Products Liability § 247.40, Answer and Affirmative Defenses--By Manufacturer--In Suit Against Municipal Corporation and Police Officers and Manufacturer --For Wrongful Death; Survival Action; Deprivation Of Rights.

West's California Code Forms, Civil Procedure § 337 Form 1, Statutes Of Limitation--Rescission Of Written Contract--Discovery Fraud or Mistake.

West's California Code Forms, Civil Procedure § 337.1 Form 1, Statutes Of Limitation--Construction Of Real Property--Personal Injury Caused by Patent Deficiency.

West's California Code Forms, Commercial § 2725 GENERAL COMMENT, Statute Of Limitations in Contracts Of Sale.

West's California Code Forms, Commercial § 3118 GENERAL COMMENT, Statute Of Limitations.

Treatises and Practice Aids

Witkin, California Summary 10th Agency and Employment § 418, in General.

Witkin, California Summary 10th Community Property § 180, Personal Liability for Debts for Spouse's Necessaries.

Witkin, California Summary 10th Equity § 33, Defenses.

Witkin, California Summary 10th Insurance § 205, in General.

Witkin, California Summary 10th Insurance § 309, in General.

Witkin, California Summary 10th Real Property § 123, Statute Of Limitations.

Witkin, California Summary 10th Wills and Probate § 517, Action Against Decedent.

Witkin, California Summary 10th Wills and Probate § 986, Sureties.

§ 337a. "Book account" defined

The term "book account" means a detailed statement which constitutes the principal record of one or more transactions between a debtor and a creditor arising out of a contract or some fiduciary relation, and shows the debits and credits in connection therewith, and against whom and in favor of whom entries are made, is entered in the regular course of business as conducted by such creditor or fiduciary, and is kept in a reasonably permanent form and manner and is (1) in a bound book, or (2) on a sheet or sheets fastened in a book or to backing but detachable therefrom, or (3) on a card or cards of a permanent character, or is kept in any other reasonably permanent form and manner. *(Added by Stats.1959, c. 1010, p. 3034, § 1.)*

§ 337.1. Four years; actions for damages from persons performing or furnishing design, specifications, surveying, planning, supervision or observation of construction or construction of improvement to realty

(a) Except as otherwise provided in this section, no action shall be brought to recover damages from any person performing or furnishing the design, specifications, surveying, planning, supervision or observation of construction or construction of an improvement to real property more than four years after the substantial completion of such improvement for any of the following:

(1) Any patent deficiency in the design, specifications, surveying, planning, supervision or observation of construction or construction of an improvement to, or survey of, real property;

(2) Injury to property, real or personal, arising out of any such patent deficiency; or

(3) Injury to the person or for wrongful death arising out of any such patent deficiency.

(b) If, by reason of such patent deficiency, an injury to property or the person or an injury causing wrongful death occurs during the fourth year after such substantial completion, an action in tort to recover damages for such an injury or wrongful death may be brought within one year after the date on which such injury occurred, irrespective of the date of death, but in no event may such an action be brought more than five years after the substantial completion of construction of such improvement.

(c) Nothing in this section shall be construed as extending the period prescribed by the laws of this state for the bringing of any action.

(d) The limitation prescribed by this section shall not be asserted by way of defense by any person in actual possession or the control, as owner, tenant or otherwise, of such an improvement at the time any deficiency in such an improvement constitutes the proximate cause of the injury or death for which it is proposed to bring an action.

(e) As used in this section, "patent deficiency" means a deficiency which is apparent by reasonable inspection.

(f) Subdivisions (a) and (b) shall not apply to any owner-occupied single-unit residence. *(Added by Stats.1967, c. 1326, p. 3157, § 1.)*

Research References

Forms

West's California Code Forms, Civil Procedure § 337.1 Form 1, Statutes Of Limitation--Construction Of Real Property--Personal Injury Caused by Patent Deficiency.

Treatises and Practice Aids

Witkin, California Summary 10th Contracts § 981, Challenged Contract.

Witkin, California Summary 10th Torts § 1159, Former Owner's Liability for Improvement.

§ 337.15. Ten years; developer, contractor, architect, etc. of real property; latent deficiency in design, supervision, etc.; injury to property

(a) No action may be brought to recover damages from any person, or the surety of a person, who develops real property or performs or furnishes the design, specifications, surveying, planning, supervision, testing, or observation of construction or construction of an improvement to real property more than 10 years after the substantial completion of the development or improvement for any of the following:

(1) Any latent deficiency in the design, specification, surveying, planning, supervision, or observation of construction or construction of an improvement to, or survey of, real property.

(2) Injury to property, real or personal, arising out of any such latent deficiency.

(b) As used in this section, "latent deficiency" means a deficiency which is not apparent by reasonable inspection.

(c) As used in this section, "action" includes an action for indemnity brought against a person arising out of that person's performance or furnishing of services or materials referred to in this section, except that a cross-complaint for indemnity may be filed pursuant to subdivision (b) of Section 428.10 in an action which has been brought within the time period set forth in subdivision (a) of this section.

(d) Nothing in this section shall be construed as extending the period prescribed by the laws of this state for bringing any action.

(e) The limitation prescribed by this section shall not be asserted by way of defense by any person in actual possession or the control, as owner, tenant or otherwise, of such an improvement, at the time any deficiency in the improvement constitutes the proximate cause for which it is proposed to bring an action.

(f) This section shall not apply to actions based on willful misconduct or fraudulent concealment.

(g) The 10-year period specified in subdivision (a) shall commence upon substantial completion of the improvement, but not later than the date of one of the following, whichever first occurs:

(1) The date of final inspection by the applicable public agency.

(2) The date of recordation of a valid notice of completion.

(3) The date of use or occupation of the improvement.

(4) One year after termination or cessation of work on the improvement.

The date of substantial completion shall relate specifically to the performance or furnishing design, specifications, surveying, planning, supervision, testing, observation of construction or construction services by each profession or trade rendering services to the improvement. *(Added by Stats. 1971, c. 1569, p. 3149, § 1. Amended by Stats.1979, c. 373, p. 1265, § 49; Stats.1979, c. 571, p. 1797, § 1; Stats.1980, c. 676, § 63; Stats.1981, c. 88, § 1.)*

Research References

Forms

West's California Code Forms, Civil Procedure § 337.1 Form 1, Statutes Of Limitation--Construction Of Real Property--Personal Injury Caused by Patent Deficiency.

West's California Code Forms, Civil Procedure § 337.15 Form 1, Statute Of Limitations--Pleading--Real Property--Latent Design Deficiency--Fraudulent Concealment.

Treatises and Practice Aids

Witkin, California Summary 10th Contracts § 720, in General.
Witkin, California Summary 10th Contracts § 981, Challenged Contract.
Witkin, California Summary 10th Torts § 192, Comparative Impairment Analysis.
Witkin, California Summary 10th Torts § 1159, Former Owner's Liability for Improvement.
Witkin, California Summary 10th Torts § 1503, Vendor Of Tract Lots.

§ 337.2. Four years; breach of written lease and abandonment of property

Where a lease of real property is in writing, no action shall be brought under Section 1951.2 of the Civil Code more than four years after the breach of the lease and abandonment of the property, or more than four years after the termination of the right of the lessee to possession of the property, whichever is the earlier time. *(Added by Stats.1970, c. 89, p. 107, § 12, operative July 1, 1971.)*

Law Revision Commission Comments

1970 Addition

The four-year period provided in Section 337.2 is consistent with the general statute of limitations applicable to written contracts. See Section 337. Although the former law was not clear, it appears that, if the lessor terminated a lease because of the lessee's breach and evicted the lessee, his cause of action for the damages resulting from the loss of the rentals due under the lease did not accrue until the end of the original lease term. See De Hart v. Allen, 26 Cal.2d 829, 161 P.2d 453 (1945); Treff v. Gulko, 214 Cal. 591, 7 P.2d 697 (1932). Under Civil Code Section 1951.2, however, an aggrieved lessor may sue immediately for the damages resulting from the loss of the rentals that would have accrued under the lease. Accordingly, Section 337.2 relates the period of limitations to breach and abandonment or to termination of the right of the lessee to possession.

§ 337.5. Ten years; municipal general obligation bonds or coupons; judgments or decrees

Within 10 years:

(a) An action upon any general obligation bonds or coupons, not secured in whole or in part by a lien on real property, issued by any county, city and county, municipal corporation, district (including school districts), or other political subdivision of the State of California.

(b) An action upon a judgment or decree of any court of the United States or of any state within the United States. *(Added by Stats.1939, c. 724, p. 2255, § 1. Amended by Stats.1947, c. 626, p. 1634, § 1; Stats.1953, c. 1153, p. 2653, § 2; Stats.2010, c. 719 (S.B.856), § 7, eff. Oct. 19, 2010.)*

Commentary

Interpreting subsection (3) together with Section 351 (period of limitation tolled while defendant out of state) and 28 U.S.C. § 1738 (h)(3), *Trend v. Bell, 57 Cal.App.4th 1092, 68 Cal.Rptr.2d 54 (1997), review denied December 23, 1997,* held that a Montana child support judgment against a California defendant, which was no longer enforceable under Montana law, was nevertheless enforceable under California law. 28 U.S.C. § 1738 (h)(3) provides, as a matter of choice of law, that in an action to enforce arrears, the court shall apply the period of limitation of the forum state or the state that issued the order, whichever is longer.

§ 337.6. Municipal general obligation bonds or coupons; additional time

Notwithstanding the provisions of Section 337.5 of this code actions may be brought on bonds or coupons as set forth in subsection 2 of said section, against which the statute of limitations ran on or after August 27, 1937; provided, such actions are brought on or before June 30, 1959. Upon presentation for payment they shall be registered and payment shall not be made thereon until the next fiscal year following presentation unless available funds are sufficient to first pay obligations which are due or will become due from the same fund during the fiscal year of presentation and during the next succeeding six months. Interest shall not be paid on bonds or coupons registered for the purpose of this section. *(Added by Stats.1949, c. 1282, p. 2265, § 1. Amended by Stats.1957, c. 719, p. 1925, § 1.)*

§ 338. Three years

Within three years:

(a) An action upon a liability created by statute, other than a penalty or forfeiture.

(b) An action for trespass upon or injury to real property.

(c)(1) An action for taking, detaining, or injuring goods or chattels, including actions for the specific recovery of personal property.

(2) The cause of action in the case of theft, as described in Section 484 of the Penal Code, of an article of historical, interpretive, scientific, or artistic significance is not deemed to have accrued until the discovery of the whereabouts of the article by the aggrieved party, his or her agent, or the law enforcement agency that originally investigated the theft.

(3)(A) Notwithstanding paragraphs (1) and (2), an action for the specific recovery of a work of fine art brought against a museum, gallery, auctioneer, or dealer, in the case of an unlawful taking or theft, as described in Section 484 of the Penal Code, of a work of fine art, including a taking or theft by means of fraud or duress, shall be commenced within six years of the actual discovery by the claimant or his or her agent, of both of the following:

(i) The identity and the whereabouts of the work of fine art. In the case where there is a possibility of misidentification of the object of fine art in question, the identity can be satisfied by the identification of facts sufficient to determine that the work of fine art is likely to be the work of fine art that was unlawfully taken or stolen.

(ii) Information or facts that are sufficient to indicate that the claimant has a claim for a possessory interest in the work of fine art that was unlawfully taken or stolen.

(B) This paragraph shall apply to all pending and future actions commenced on or before December 31, 2017, including an action dismissed based on the expiration of statutes of limitation in effect prior to the date of enactment of this statute if the judgment in that action is not yet final or if the time for filing an appeal from a decision on that action has not expired, provided that the action concerns a work of fine art that was taken within 100 years prior to the date of enactment of this statute.

(C) For purposes of this paragraph:

(i) "Actual discovery," notwithstanding Section 19 of the Civil Code, does not include constructive knowledge imputed by law.

(ii) "Auctioneer" means an individual who is engaged in, or who by advertising or otherwise holds himself or herself out as being available to engage in, the calling for, the recognition of, and the acceptance of, offers for the purchase of goods at an auction as defined in subdivision (b) of Section 1812.601 of the Civil Code.

(iii) "Dealer" means a person who holds a valid seller's permit and who is actively and principally engaged in, or conducting the business of, selling works of fine art.

(iv) "Duress" means a threat of force, violence, danger, or retribution against an owner of the work of fine art in question, or his or her family member, sufficient to coerce a reasonable person of ordinary susceptibilities to perform an act that otherwise would not have been performed or to acquiesce to an act to which he or she would otherwise not have acquiesced.

(v) "Fine art" has the same meaning as defined in paragraph (1) of subdivision (d) of Section 982 of the Civil Code.

(vi) "Museum or gallery" shall include any public or private organization or foundation operating as a museum or gallery.

(4) Section 361 shall not apply to an action brought pursuant to paragraph (3).

(5) A party in an action to which paragraph (3) applies may raise all equitable and legal affirmative defenses and doctrines, including, without limitation, laches and unclean hands.

(d) An action for relief on the ground of fraud or mistake. The cause of action in that case is not deemed to have accrued until the discovery, by the aggrieved party, of the facts constituting the fraud or mistake.

(e) An action upon a bond of a public official except any cause of action based on fraud or embezzlement is not deemed to have accrued until the discovery, by the aggrieved party or his or her agent, of the facts constituting the cause of action upon the bond.

(f)(1) An action against a notary public on his or her bond or in his or her official capacity except that a cause of action based on malfeasance or misfeasance is not deemed to have accrued until discovery, by the aggrieved party or his or her agent, of the facts constituting the cause of action.

(2) Notwithstanding paragraph (1), an action based on malfeasance or misfeasance shall be commenced within one year from discovery, by the aggrieved party or his or her agent, of the facts constituting the cause of action or within three years from the performance of the notarial act giving rise to the action, whichever is later.

(3) Notwithstanding paragraph (1), an action against a notary public on his or her bond or in his or her official capacity shall be commenced within six years.

(g) An action for slander of title to real property.

(h) An action commenced under Section 17536 of the Business and Professions Code. The cause of action in that case shall not be deemed to have accrued until the discovery by the aggrieved party, the Attorney General, the district attorney, the county counsel, the city prosecutor, or the city attorney of the facts constituting grounds for commencing the action.

(i) An action commenced under the Porter–Cologne Water Quality Control Act (Division 7 (commencing with Section 13000) of the Water Code). The cause of action in that case shall not be deemed to have accrued until the discovery by the State Water Resources Control Board or a regional water quality control board of the facts constituting grounds for commencing actions under their jurisdiction.

(j) An action to recover for physical damage to private property under Section 19 of Article I of the California Constitution.

(k) An action commenced under Division 26 (commencing with Section 39000) of the Health and Safety Code. These causes of action shall not be deemed to have accrued until the discovery by the State Air Resources Board or by a district, as defined in Section 39025 of the Health and Safety Code, of the facts constituting grounds for commencing the action under its jurisdiction.

(*l*) An action commenced under Section 1602, 1615, or 5650.1 of the Fish and Game Code. These causes of action shall not be deemed to have accrued until discovery by the agency bringing the action of the facts constituting the grounds for commencing the action.

(m) An action challenging the validity of the levy upon a parcel of a special tax levied by a local agency on a per parcel basis.

(n) An action commencing under Section 51.7 of the Civil Code. *(Enacted in 1872. Amended by Stats.1921, c. 183, p. 192, § 1; Stats.1933, c. 306, p. 878, § 1; Stats.1935, c. 581, p. 1673, § 1; Stats.1943, c. 1025, p. 2963, § 1; Stats.1949, c. 1540, p. 2734, § 1; Stats.1957, c. 649, p. 1849, § 1; Stats.1972, c. 823, p. 1470, § 2; Stats.1981, c. 247, § 1, eff. July 21, 1981; Stats.1981, c. 494, § 2; Stats.1982, c. 340, p. 1642, § 1; Stats.1987, c. 1200, § 1; Stats.1987, c. 1201, § 1; Stats.1988, c. 1186, § 1; Stats.1989, c. 467, § 1; Stats.1990, c. 669 (A.B. 4049), § 1; Stats.1995, c. 238 (A.B.1174), § 1; Stats.1998, c. 342 (A.B.1933), § 1; Stats.2005, c. 123 (A.B.378), § 2; Stats.2005, c. 383 (S.B.1110), § 1.5; Stats.2006, c. 538 (S.B. 1852), § 62; Stats.2010, c. 691 (A.B.2765), § 2; Stats.2015, c. 683 (S.B.798), § 1, eff. Jan. 1, 2016.)*

Commentary

Relying in part on subsection (d), *Rubenstein v. Rubenstein, 81 Cal.App.4th 1131, 97 Cal.Rptr.2d 707 (2000)*, holds that the Family Code § 2122 (a) one-year limitation begins to run when the defrauded party discovers, or should have discovered, the *facts* constituting the alleged fraud, rather than the prior date on which that party merely suspects or asserts, without knowledge of the necessary facts, that she was defrauded. Compare Family Code § 1101 (action for breach of fiduciary duty may be commenced within three years of the date that petitioner had notice of the transaction or event for which the remedy is sought; and remedy for breach of fiduciary duty involving fraud is 100 percent of the asset undisclosed or transferred in breach of the fiduciary duty) and Family

Code § 2556 (no statute of limitations for division of an omitted or unadjudicated community estate asset or liability).

Research References

Forms

Cal. Transaction Forms - Bus. Transactions § 28:4, Availability Of Remedies.
California Transactions Forms--Estate Planning § 2:8, Conduct Of Practitioner to Limit Tolling Of Statute Of Limitations.
West's California Code Forms, Civil Procedure § 337.1 Form 1, Statutes Of Limitation--Construction Of Real Property--Personal Injury Caused by Patent Deficiency.
West's California Code Forms, Civil Procedure § 338(A) Form 1, Statutes Of Limitation--Liability Based on Statute--Action Challenging Validity Of Tax.
West's California Code Forms, Civil Procedure § 338(D) Form 1, Statutes Of Limitation--Action Based on Fraud or Mistake--Accrual--Discovery.
West's California Code Forms, Civil Procedure § 338(F) Form 1, Statutes Of Limitation--Action Based on Malfeasance or Misfeasance Of Notary Public--Accrual--Discovery.
West's California Code Forms, Commercial § 2725 GENERAL COMMENT, Statute Of Limitations in Contracts Of Sale.
West's California Code Forms, Government § 37101 Form 17, Mobile Home Rent Control Ordinance.

Treatises and Practice Aids

Witkin, California Summary 10th Agency and Employment § 360, in General.
Witkin, California Summary 10th Agency and Employment § 399, Wilful Failure.
Witkin, California Summary 10th Constitutional Law § 895, Hate Crimes, Intimidation, and Threats Of Violence.
Witkin, California Summary 10th Constitutional Law § 1011, Statutes Of Limitation on Attack.
Witkin, California Summary 10th Constitutional Law § 1166, Statute Of Limitations.
Witkin, California Summary 10th Husband and Wife § 343, CalWORKs Aid.
Witkin, California Summary 10th Insurance § 12, in General.
Witkin, California Summary 10th Insurance § 216, in General.
Witkin, California Summary 10th Personal Property § 42, Procedure in Escheating Property.
Witkin, California Summary 10th Personal Property § 123, Adverse Possession.
Witkin, California Summary 10th Real Property § 476, Statute Of Limitations.
Witkin, California Summary 10th Real Property § 594, Violation as Defense in Unlawful Detainer Action.
Witkin, California Summary 10th Real Property § 899, in General.
Witkin, California Summary 10th Sales § 213, Statute Of Limitations.
Witkin, California Summary 10th Taxation § 133, Rule.
Witkin, California Summary 10th Taxation § 232, Time Limits.
Witkin, California Summary 10th Torts § 702, Intangible Property.
Witkin, California Summary 10th Torts § 813, No General Duty to Investigate.
Witkin, California Summary 10th Workers' Compensation § 83, Statute Of Limitations.

§ 340. One year; (a) Statutory penalty or forfeiture to individual and state; (b) Statutory forfeiture or penalty to state; (c) Libel, slander, false imprisonment, seduction, forged or raised checks, injury to animals by feeder or veterinarian; (d) Damages for seizure; (e) Action by good faith buyer

Within one year:

(a) An action upon a statute for a penalty or forfeiture, if the action is given to an individual, or to an individual and the state, except if the statute imposing it prescribes a different limitation.

(b) An action upon a statute for a forfeiture or penalty to the people of this state.

(c) An action for libel, slander, false imprisonment, seduction of a person below the age of legal consent, or by a depositor against a bank for the payment of a forged or raised check, or a check that bears a forged or unauthorized endorsement, or against any person who boards or feeds an animal or fowl or who engages in the practice of veterinary medicine as defined in Section 4826 of the Business and Professions Code, for that person's neglect resulting in injury or death to an animal or fowl in the course of boarding or feeding the animal or fowl or in the course of the practice of veterinary medicine on that animal or fowl.

(d) An action against an officer to recover damages for the seizure of any property for a statutory forfeiture to the state, or for the detention of, or injury to property so seized, or for damages done to any person in making that seizure.

(e) An action by a good faith improver for relief under Chapter 10 (commencing with Section 871.1) of Title 10 of Part 2. The time begins to run from the date upon which the good faith improver discovers that the good faith improver is not the owner of the land upon which the improvements have been made. *(Enacted in 1872. Amended by Code Am.1873–74, c. 383, p. 292, § 34; Code Am.1875–76, c. 29, p. 89, § 1; Stats.1905, c. 258, p. 232, § 2; Stats.1929, c. 518, p. 896, § 1; Stats.1939, c. 1103, p. 3036, § 1; Stats.1949, c. 863, p. 1637, § 1; Stats.1953, c. 1382, p. 2959, § 1; Stats.1963, c. 1681, p. 3284, § 2; Stats.1968, c. 150, p. 373, § 1; Stats.1973, c. 20, p. 32, § 1; Stats.1982, c. 517, p. 2334, § 97; Stats.2002, c. 448 (S.B.688), § 3.)*

Law Revision Commission Comments

1973 Amendment

Section 340 is amended to reflect the fact that arrest and imprisonment in a civil action is no longer permitted. See CODE CIV.PROC. § 478 and Comment thereto. See also former GOVT. CODE § 26681 et seq. (liability of sheriff for escape of person held upon civil arrest). Cf. former CODE CIV.PROC. § 501 (liability of officer for escape).

1982 Amendment

Section 340 is amended to delete the reference to an undertaking in a criminal action. Undertakings of bail are no longer governed by Section 340. See People v. Burton, 146 Cal.App.2d Supp. 878, 305 P.2d 302 (1956). Other undertakings in criminal actions are governed by the same rules that apply to undertakings generally. See Section 337 (four-year statute of limitations). The other changes in Section 340 are technical. [16 Cal.L.Rev.Comm. Reports 501 (1982)].

Research References

Forms

West's California Code Forms, Civil Procedure § 364 Form 1, Malpractice Actions--Notice Of Intention to File Suit.
West's California Code Forms, Civil Procedure § 340.1 Form 4, Statute Of Limitations--Certificate Of Merit--Plaintiff's Attorney--No Consultation--Statute Of Limitations.

West's California Code Forms, Civil Procedure § 340.5 Form 1, Statute Of Limitations--Pleading--Professional Negligence Of Healthcare Provider--Reasonable.

West's California Code Forms, Civil Procedure § 340.7 Form 1, Statute Of Limitations--Pleading--Dalkon Shield Claimants Trust Claims.

West's California Code Forms, Civil Procedure § 871.3 Form 1, Good Faith Improver--Complaint for Relief.

Treatises and Practice Aids

Witkin, California Summary 10th Agency and Employment § 399, Wilful Failure.

Witkin, California Summary 10th Negotiable Instruments § 88, Enforcing the Provisions Of Division 4.

Witkin, California Summary 10th Negotiable Instruments § 130, Preclusion Period and Statute Of Limitations.

Witkin, California Summary 10th Real Property § 459, Nature and Scope Of Statute.

Witkin, California Summary 10th Real Property § 903, Federal Statutes.

Witkin, California Summary 10th Workers' Compensation § 83, Statute Of Limitations.

Witkin, California Summary 10th Workers' Compensation § 86, Action by Employee: Joinder or Intervention by Employer.

§ 340.1. Childhood sexual abuse; certificates of merit executed by attorney; violations; failure to file; name designation of defendant; periods of limitation; legislative intent

(a) In an action for recovery of damages suffered as a result of childhood sexual abuse, the time for commencement of the action shall be within eight years of the date the plaintiff attains the age of majority or within three years of the date the plaintiff discovers or reasonably should have discovered that psychological injury or illness occurring after the age of majority was caused by the sexual abuse, whichever period expires later, for any of the following actions:

(1) An action against any person for committing an act of childhood sexual abuse.

(2) An action for liability against any person or entity who owed a duty of care to the plaintiff, where a wrongful or negligent act by that person or entity was a legal cause of the childhood sexual abuse which resulted in the injury to the plaintiff.

(3) An action for liability against any person or entity where an intentional act by that person or entity was a legal cause of the childhood sexual abuse which resulted in the injury to the plaintiff.

(b)(1) No action described in paragraph (2) or (3) of subdivision (a) may be commenced on or after the plaintiff's 26th birthday.

(2) This subdivision does not apply if the person or entity knew or had reason to know, or was otherwise on notice, of any unlawful sexual conduct by an employee, volunteer, representative, or agent, and failed to take reasonable steps, and to implement reasonable safeguards, to avoid acts of unlawful sexual conduct in the future by that person, including, but not limited to, preventing or avoiding placement of that person in a function or environment in which contact with children is an inherent part of that function or environment. For purposes of this subdivision, providing or requiring counseling is not sufficient, in and of itself, to constitute a reasonable step or reasonable safeguard.

(c) Notwithstanding any other provision of law, any claim for damages described in paragraph (2) or (3) of subdivision (a) that is permitted to be filed pursuant to paragraph (2) of subdivision (b) that would otherwise be barred as of January 1, 2003, solely because the applicable statute of limitations has or had expired, is revived, and, in that case, a cause of action may be commenced within one year of January 1, 2003. Nothing in this subdivision shall be construed to alter the applicable statute of limitations period of an action that is not time barred as of January 1, 2003.

(d) Subdivision (c) does not apply to either of the following:

(1) Any claim that has been litigated to finality on the merits in any court of competent jurisdiction prior to January 1, 2003. Termination of a prior action on the basis of the statute of limitations does not constitute a claim that has been litigated to finality on the merits.

(2) Any written, compromised settlement agreement which has been entered into between a plaintiff and a defendant where the plaintiff was represented by an attorney who was admitted to practice law in this state at the time of the settlement, and the plaintiff signed the agreement.

(e) "Childhood sexual abuse" as used in this section includes any act committed against the plaintiff that occurred when the plaintiff was under the age of 18 years and that would have been proscribed by Section 266j of the Penal Code; Section 285 of the Penal Code; paragraph (1) or (2) of subdivision (b), or of subdivision (c), of Section 286 of the Penal Code; subdivision (a) or (b) of Section 288 of the Penal Code; paragraph (1) or (2) of subdivision (b), or of subdivision (c), of Section 288a of the Penal Code; subdivision (h), (i), or (j) of Section 289 of the Penal Code; Section 647.6 of the Penal Code; or any prior laws of this state of similar effect at the time the act was committed. Nothing in this subdivision limits the availability of causes of action permitted under subdivision (a), including causes of action against persons or entities other than the alleged perpetrator of the abuse.

(f) Nothing in this section shall be construed to alter the otherwise applicable burden of proof, as defined in Section 115 of the Evidence Code, that a plaintiff has in a civil action subject to this section.

(g) Every plaintiff 26 years of age or older at the time the action is filed shall file certificates of merit as specified in subdivision (h).

(h) Certificates of merit shall be executed by the attorney for the plaintiff and by a licensed mental health practitioner selected by the plaintiff declaring, respectively, as follows, setting forth the facts which support the declaration:

(1) That the attorney has reviewed the facts of the case, that the attorney has consulted with at least one mental health practitioner who is licensed to practice and practices in this state and who the attorney reasonably believes is knowledgeable of the relevant facts and issues involved in the particular action, and that the attorney has concluded on the basis of that review and consultation that there is reasonable

and meritorious cause for the filing of the action. The person consulted may not be a party to the litigation.

(2) That the mental health practitioner consulted is licensed to practice and practices in this state and is not a party to the action, that the practitioner is not treating and has not treated the plaintiff, and that the practitioner has interviewed the plaintiff and is knowledgeable of the relevant facts and issues involved in the particular action, and has concluded, on the basis of his or her knowledge of the facts and issues, that in his or her professional opinion there is a reasonable basis to believe that the plaintiff had been subject to childhood sexual abuse.

(3) That the attorney was unable to obtain the consultation required by paragraph (1) because a statute of limitations would impair the action and that the certificates required by paragraphs (1) and (2) could not be obtained before the impairment of the action. If a certificate is executed pursuant to this paragraph, the certificates required by paragraphs (1) and (2) shall be filed within 60 days after filing the complaint.

(i) Where certificates are required pursuant to subdivision (g), the attorney for the plaintiff shall execute a separate certificate of merit for each defendant named in the complaint.

(j) In any action subject to subdivision (g), no defendant may be served, and the duty to serve a defendant with process does not attach, until the court has reviewed the certificates of merit filed pursuant to subdivision (h) with respect to that defendant, and has found, in camera, based solely on those certificates of merit, that there is reasonable and meritorious cause for the filing of the action against that defendant. At that time, the duty to serve that defendant with process shall attach.

(k) A violation of this section may constitute unprofessional conduct and may be the grounds for discipline against the attorney.

(*l*) The failure to file certificates in accordance with this section shall be grounds for a demurrer pursuant to Section 430.10 or a motion to strike pursuant to Section 435.

(m) In any action subject to subdivision (g), no defendant may be named except by "Doe" designation in any pleadings or papers filed in the action until there has been a showing of corroborative fact as to the charging allegations against that defendant.

(n) At any time after the action is filed, the plaintiff may apply to the court for permission to amend the complaint to substitute the name of the defendant or defendants for the fictitious designation, as follows:

(1) The application shall be accompanied by a certificate of corroborative fact executed by the attorney for the plaintiff. The certificate shall declare that the attorney has discovered one or more facts corroborative of one or more of the charging allegations against a defendant or defendants, and shall set forth in clear and concise terms the nature and substance of the corroborative fact. If the corroborative fact is evidenced by the statement of a witness or the contents of a document, the certificate shall declare that the attorney has personal knowledge of the statement of the witness or of the contents of the document, and the identity and location of the witness or document shall be included in the certificate. For purposes of this section, a fact is corroborative of an allegation if it confirms or supports the allegation. The opinion of any mental health practitioner concerning the plaintiff shall not constitute a corroborative fact for purposes of this section.

(2) Where the application to name a defendant is made prior to that defendant's appearance in the action, neither the application nor the certificate of corroborative fact by the attorney shall be served on the defendant or defendants, nor on any other party or their counsel of record.

(3) Where the application to name a defendant is made after that defendant's appearance in the action, the application shall be served on all parties and proof of service provided to the court, but the certificate of corroborative fact by the attorney shall not be served on any party or their counsel of record.

(*o*) The court shall review the application and the certificate of corroborative fact in camera and, based solely on the certificate and any reasonable inferences to be drawn from the certificate, shall, if one or more facts corroborative of one or more of the charging allegations against a defendant has been shown, order that the complaint may be amended to substitute the name of the defendant or defendants.

(p) The court shall keep under seal and confidential from the public and all parties to the litigation, other than the plaintiff, any and all certificates of corroborative fact filed pursuant to subdivision (n).

(q) Upon the favorable conclusion of the litigation with respect to any defendant for whom a certificate of merit was filed or for whom a certificate of merit should have been filed pursuant to this section, the court may, upon the motion of a party or upon the court's own motion, verify compliance with this section by requiring the attorney for the plaintiff who was required by subdivision (h) to execute the certificate to reveal the name, address, and telephone number of the person or persons consulted with pursuant to subdivision (h) that were relied upon by the attorney in preparation of the certificate of merit. The name, address, and telephone number shall be disclosed to the trial judge in camera and in the absence of the moving party. If the court finds there has been a failure to comply with this section, the court may order a party, a party's attorney, or both, to pay any reasonable expenses, including attorney's fees, incurred by the defendant for whom a certificate of merit should have been filed.

(r) The amendments to this section enacted at the 1990 portion of the 1989–90 Regular Session shall apply to any action commenced on or after January 1, 1991, including any action otherwise barred by the period of limitations in effect prior to January 1, 1991, thereby reviving those causes of action which had lapsed or technically expired under the law existing prior to January 1, 1991.

(s) The Legislature declares that it is the intent of the Legislature, in enacting the amendments to this section enacted at the 1994 portion of the 1993–94 Regular Session, that the express language of revival added to this section by those amendments shall apply to any action commenced on or after January 1, 1991.

(t) Nothing in the amendments to this section enacted at the 1998 portion of the 1997–98 Regular Session is intended to create a new theory of liability.

(u) The amendments to subdivision (a) of this section, enacted at the 1998 portion of the 1997–98 Regular Session, shall apply to any action commenced on or after January 1, 1999, and to any action filed prior to January 1, 1999, and still pending on that date, including any action or causes of action which would have been barred by the laws in effect prior to January 1, 1999. Nothing in this subdivision is intended to revive actions or causes of action as to which there has been a final adjudication prior to January 1, 1999. *(Added by Stats.1986, c. 914, § 1. Amended by Stats.1990, c. 1578 (S.B.108), § 1; Stats.1994, c. 288 (A.B.2846), § 1; Stats.1998, c. 1032 (A.B.1651), § 1; Stats.1999, c. 120 (S.B.674), § 1; Stats.2002, c. 149 (S.B.1779), § 1.)*

Validity

This section was held unconstitutional in the decision of Perez v. Richard Roe 1 (App. 2 Dist. 2006) 52 Cal.Rptr.3d 762, 146 Cal.App.4th 171, as modified, review denied.

Commentary

Tietge v. Western Province of Servites, 55 Cal.App.4th 382, 64 Cal.Rptr.2d 53 (1997), review denied August 13, 1997, holds that a cause of action for child sexual abuse barred under an earlier one-year statute of limitations was revived by 1994 amendments to this section (subsection (a)), which extended the period in which an action may be brought to eight or more years after a child reaches majority.

A parent accused of sexual abuse of a child may not sue the child's therapist for malpractice; a psychotherapist's duty to exercise due care does not extend to the patient's parent in cases involving an adult patient's recovered memory of childhood sexual abuse when the therapist has not assumed such duty and the parent is not a patient of the therapist. *Trear v. Sills, 69 Cal.App.4th 1341, 82 Cal.Rptr.2d 281 (1999), review denied May 12, 1999.*

Research References

Forms

West's California Code Forms, Civil Procedure § 340.1 Form 1, Statute Of Limitations--Pleading--Personal Injury Damages for Childhood Sexual Abuse.

West's California Code Forms, Civil Procedure § 340.1 Form 2, Statute Of Limitations--Certificate Of Merit--Plaintiff's Attorney.

West's California Code Forms, Civil Procedure § 340.1 Form 4, Statute Of Limitations--Certificate Of Merit--Plaintiff's Attorney--No Consultation--Statute Of Limitations.

West's California Code Forms, Civil Procedure § 340.1 Form 5, Statute Of Limitations--Certificate Of Merit--Compliance--Notice Of Motion for Order Requiring Disclosure Of Consultant.

West's California Code Forms, Civil Procedure § 340.1 Form 7, Statute Of Limitations--Certificate Of Merit--Compliance--Notice Of Motion for Order Awarding Sanctions for Noncompliance.

West's California Code Forms, Civil Procedure § 340.1 Form 9, Statute Of Limitations--Childhood Sexual Abuse--Application to Amend Complaint--Substitution Of Defendant's Name for Fictitious Designation.

West's California Code Forms, Civil Procedure § 340.1 Form 10, Statute Of Limitations--Childhood Sexual Abuse--Certificate Of Corroborative Fact--Substitution Of Defendant's Name for Fictitious Designation.

West's California Code Forms, Civil Procedure § 340.1 Form 11, Statute Of Limitations--Childhood Sexual Abuse--Order Allowing Amendment Of Complaint--Substitution Of Defendant's Name for Fictitious Designation.

Treatises and Practice Aids

Witkin, California Summary 10th Torts § 913, False Diagnosis Of Recovered Memory.

§ 340.15. Action for damages suffered as result of domestic violence

(a) In any civil action for recovery of damages suffered as a result of domestic violence, the time for commencement of the action shall be the later of the following:

(1) Within three years from the date of the last act of domestic violence by the defendant against the plaintiff.

(2) Within three years from the date the plaintiff discovers or reasonably should have discovered that an injury or illness resulted from an act of domestic violence by the defendant against the plaintiff.

(b) As used in this section, "domestic violence" has the same meaning as defined in Section 6211 of the Family Code. *(Added by Stats.1995, c. 602 (S.B.924), § 1. Amended by Stats.1998, c. 123 (S.B.1939), § 1.)*

Commentary

This section, effective January 1, 1996, increases the statute of limitations from one year to three years. *Papenthien v. Papenthien, 120 F.3d 1025 (9th Cir. 1997).*

When a complaint alleged a continuing course of domestic violence throughout a long marriage, *Pugliese v. Superior Court, 146 Cal.App.4th 1444, 53 Cal.Rptr.3d 681 (2007), review denied April 11, 2007,* held that the trial court erred in interpreting the three-year statute of limitations to bar damages for domestic violence occurring more than three years prior to timely filing of the complaint. The court relied upon the language of subsection (a)(1), reasoning that the three-year limitation ran from the *last* act of domestic violence and included all such acts. The court additionally relied upon the doctrine of "continuing tort."

Research References

Forms

West's California Code Forms, Civil Procedure § 340.15 Form 1, Statutes Of Limitations--Pleading--Recovery Of Damages--Domestic Violence.

Treatises and Practice Aids

Witkin, California Summary 10th Torts § 467, Domestic Violence.

§ 340.3. Actions for damages against defendant arising from felony offense; limitation of actions; stay of judgment; restitution

(a) Unless a longer period is prescribed for a specific action, in any action for damages against a defendant based upon the defendant's commission of a felony offense for which the defendant has been convicted, the time for commencement of the action shall be within one year after judgment is pronounced.

(b)(1) Notwithstanding subdivision (a), an action for damages against a defendant based upon the defendant's commission of a felony offense for which the defendant has been convicted may be commenced within 10 years of the date on which the defendant is discharged from parole if the conviction was for any offense specified in paragraph (1), except voluntary manslaughter, (2), (3), (4), (5), (6), (7), (9), (16), (17), (20), (22), (25), (34), or (35) of subdivision (c) of Section 1192.7 of the Penal Code.

(2) No civil action may be commenced pursuant to paragraph (1) if any of the following applies:

(A) The defendant has received either a certificate of rehabilitation as provided in Chapter 3.5 (commencing with Section 4852.01) of Title 6 of Part 3 of the Penal Code or a pardon as provided in Chapter 1 (commencing with Section 4800) or Chapter 3 (commencing with Section 4850) of Title 6 of Part 3 of the Penal Code.

(B) Following a conviction for murder or attempted murder, the defendant has been paroled based in whole or in part upon evidence presented to the Board of Prison Terms that the defendant committed the crime because he or she was the victim of intimate partner battering.

(C) The defendant was convicted of murder or attempted murder in the second degree in a trial at which substantial evidence was presented that the person committed the crime because he or she was a victim of intimate partner battering.

(D) The defendant was unlawfully imprisoned or restrained but has been released from prison after successfully prosecuting a writ of habeas corpus pursuant to Chapter 1 (commencing with Section 1473) of Title 12 of Part 2 of the Penal Code.

(c) If the sentence or judgment is stayed, the time for the commencement of the action shall be tolled until the stay is lifted. For purposes of this section, a judgment is not stayed if the judgment is appealed or the defendant is placed on probation.

(d)(1) Subdivision (b) shall apply to any action commenced before, on, or after the effective date of this section, including any action otherwise barred by a limitation of time in effect prior to the effective date of this section, thereby reviving those causes of action that had lapsed or expired under the law in effect prior to the effective date of this section.

(2) Paragraph (1) does not apply to either of the following:

(A) Any claim that has been litigated to finality on the merits in any court of competent jurisdiction prior to January 1, 2003. For purposes of this section, termination of a prior action on the basis of the statute of limitations does not constitute a claim that has been litigated to finality on the merits.

(B) Any written, compromised settlement agreement that has been entered into between a plaintiff and a defendant if the plaintiff was represented by an attorney who was admitted to practice law in this state at the time of the settlement, and the plaintiff signed the agreement.

(e) Any restitution paid by the defendant to the victim shall be credited against any judgment, award, or settlement obtained pursuant to this section. Any judgment, award, or settlement obtained pursuant to an action under this section shall be subject to the provisions of Section 13963 of the Government Code. *(Added by Stats.1983, c. 938, § 2, eff. Sept. 20, 1983. Amended by Stats.2002, c. 633 (S.B.1887), § 1, eff. Sept. 18, 2002; Stats.2005, c. 215 (A.B.220), § 1; Stats. 2015, c. 465 (A.B.538), § 1, eff. Jan. 1, 2016.)*

Research References

Forms

West's California Code Forms, Civil Procedure § 340.3 Form 1, Statute Of Limitations--Pleading--Damages Arising from Felony Offense--Tolling--Stay Of Judgment Of Conviction.

§ 340.35. Causes of action involving sexual abuse of a minor; statutes of limitation

(a) This section shall apply if both of the following conditions are met:

(1) A complaint, information, or indictment was filed in a criminal case initiated pursuant to subdivision (f), (g), or (h) of Section 803 of the Penal Code.

(2) The case was dismissed or overturned pursuant to the United States Supreme Court's decision in Stogner v. California (2003) 156 L.Ed.2d 544.

(b) Unless a longer period is prescribed for a specific action, any action for damages against an individual for committing an act of childhood sexual abuse shall be commenced before January 1, 2006.

(c) This section shall apply to any action commenced before, on, or after the effective date of this section, including any action otherwise barred by a limitation of time in effect prior to the effective date of this section, thereby reviving those causes of action that had lapsed or expired under the law in effect prior to the effective date of this section.

(d) This section shall not apply to any of the following:

(1) Any claim against a person or entity other than the individual against whom a complaint, information, or indictment was filed as described in paragraph (1) of subdivision (a).

(2) Any claim that has been litigated to finality on the merits in any court of competent jurisdiction prior to the effective date of this section. For purposes of this section, termination of a prior action on the basis of the statute of limitations does not constitute a claim that has been "litigated to finality on the merits."

(3) Any written, compromised settlement agreement that has been entered into between a plaintiff and a defendant, if the plaintiff was represented by an attorney who was admitted to practice law in this state at the time of the settlement, and the plaintiff signed the agreement.

(e) Any restitution paid by the defendant to the victim shall be credited against any judgment, award, or settlement obtained pursuant to this section. Any judgment, award, or settlement obtained pursuant to an action under this section shall be subject to Section 13966.01 of the Government Code. *(Added by Stats.2004, c. 741 (S.B.1678), § 1.)*

§ 340.4. Minors; action for personal injuries before or during birth; limitation of actions

An action by or on behalf of a minor for personal injuries sustained before or in the course of his or her birth must be commenced within six years after the date of birth, and the time the minor is under any disability mentioned in Section 352 shall not be excluded in computing the time limited for the commencement of the action. *(Added by Stats.1992, c. 163 (A.B.2641), § 16, operative Jan. 1, 1994.)*

Law Revision Commission Comments

1992 Addition

Section 340.4 continues the last part of former Civil Code Section 29 without substantive change. [22 Cal.L.Rev.Comm.Reports 1 (1992)].

Research References

Treatises and Practice Aids

Witkin, California Summary 10th Torts § 728, Injury to Unborn Child.

§ 340.5. Action against health care provider; three years from injury or one year from discovery; exceptions; minors

In an action for injury or death against a health care provider based upon such person's alleged professional negligence, the time for the commencement of action shall be three years after the date of injury or one year after the plaintiff discovers, or through the use of reasonable diligence should have discovered, the injury, whichever occurs first. In no event shall the time for commencement of legal action exceed three years unless tolled for any of the following: (1) upon proof of fraud, (2) intentional concealment, or (3) the presence of a foreign body, which has no therapeutic or diagnostic purpose or effect, in the person of the injured person. Actions by a minor shall be commenced within three years from the date of the alleged wrongful act except that actions by a minor under the full age of six years shall be commenced within three years or prior to his eighth birthday whichever provides a longer period. Such time limitation shall be tolled for minors for any period during which parent or guardian and defendant's insurer or health care provider have committed fraud or collusion in the failure to bring an action on behalf of the injured minor for professional negligence.

For the purposes of this section:

(1) "Health care provider" means any person licensed or certified pursuant to Division 2 (commencing with Section 500) of the Business and Professions Code, or licensed pursuant to the Osteopathic Initiative Act, or the Chiropractic Initiative Act, or licensed pursuant to Chapter 2.5 (commencing with Section 1440) of Division 2 of the Health and Safety Code; and any clinic, health dispensary, or health facility, licensed pursuant to Division 2 (commencing with Section 1200) of the Health and Safety Code. "Health care provider" includes the legal representatives of a health care provider;

(2) "Professional negligence" means a negligent act or omission to act by a health care provider in the rendering of professional services, which act or omission is the proximate cause of a personal injury or wrongful death, provided that such services are within the scope of services for which the provider is licensed and which are not within any restriction imposed by the licensing agency or licensed hospital. *(Added by Stats.1970, c. 360, p. 772, § 1. Amended by Stats.1975, 2nd Ex.Sess., c. 1, p. 3969, § 25; Stats.1975, 2nd Ex.Sess., c. 2, p. 3991, § 1.192, eff. Sept. 24, 1975, operative Dec. 15, 1975.)*

Research References

Forms

West's California Code Forms, Civil Procedure § 364 Form 1, Malpractice Actions--Notice Of Intention to File Suit.

West's California Code Forms, Civil Procedure § 340.5 Form 1, Statute Of Limitations--Pleading--Professional Negligence Of Healthcare Provider--Reasonable.

West's California Code Forms, Civil Procedure § 340.5 Form 2, Statute Of Limitations--Pleading--Professional Negligence Of Health Care Provider--Tolling--Fraud--Concealment--Foreign Body.

West's California Code Forms, Civil Procedure § 340.5 Form 3, Statute Of Limitations--Pleading--Professional Negligence Of Health Care Provider--Tolling--Fraud--Collusion.

West's California Code Forms, Civil Procedure § 352.1 Form 1, Statute Of Limitations--Tolling--Imprisonment--Contract Actions.

Treatises and Practice Aids

Witkin, California Summary 10th Constitutional Law § 779, Invalid Classification.

Witkin, California Summary 10th Torts § 934, Ordinary Versus Professional Negligence.

Witkin, California Summary 10th Torts § 954, Extension Of Applicable Statute Of Limitations.

Witkin, California Summary 10th Torts § 1379, Statute Of Limitations.

Witkin, California Summary 10th Torts § 1687, Exception for Professional Negligence by Health Care Provider.

§ 340.6. Attorneys; wrongful professional act or omission; tolling of period

(a) An action against an attorney for a wrongful act or omission, other than for actual fraud, arising in the performance of professional services shall be commenced within one year after the plaintiff discovers, or through the use of reasonable diligence should have discovered, the facts constituting the wrongful act or omission, or four years from the date of the wrongful act or omission, whichever occurs first. If the plaintiff is required to establish his or her factual innocence for an underlying criminal charge as an element of his or her claim, the action shall be commenced within two years after the plaintiff achieves postconviction exoneration in the form of a final judicial disposition of the criminal case. Except for a claim for which the plaintiff is required to establish his or her factual innocence, in no event shall the time for commencement of legal action exceed four years except that the period shall be tolled during the time that any of the following exist:

(1) The plaintiff has not sustained actual injury.

(2) The attorney continues to represent the plaintiff regarding the specific subject matter in which the alleged wrongful act or omission occurred.

(3) The attorney willfully conceals the facts constituting the wrongful act or omission when such facts are known to the attorney, except that this subdivision shall toll only the four-year limitation.

(4) The plaintiff is under a legal or physical disability which restricts the plaintiff's ability to commence legal action.

(b) In an action based upon an instrument in writing, the effective date of which depends upon some act or event of the future, the period of limitations provided for by this section shall commence to run upon the occurrence of that act or event. *(Added by Stats.1977, c. 863, p. 2609, § 1. Amended by Stats.2009, c. 432 (A.B.316), § 2.)*

Commentary

Hensley v. Caietti, 13 Cal.App.4th 1165, 16 Cal.Rptr.2d 837 (1993), review denied 5/13/93, holds that this section bars a client's malpractice action arising out of a negotiated marital settlement agreement when client filed the action more than one year after sustaining actual injury (the date the client entered into the agreement, not the date of the judgment or the date the right to appeal was finally terminated) and engaging new counsel. *Hensley* emphasizes the importance of formal termination of the attorney-client relationship once that relationship has broken down. Compare *Bennett v. McCall, 19 Cal.App.4th 122, 23 Cal.Rptr.2d 268 (1993), review denied 12/30/93* (one-year statute of limitations began to run when husband sustained actual injury by paying a retainer to second attorney in order to cure first attorney's error in the marital property agreement, not when husband earlier entered the binding marital property agreement). *Hensley* and *Bennett* are discussed and distinguished by the California Supreme Court in *ITT Small Business Finance Corporation v. Niles, 9 Cal.4th 245, 255, 885 P.2d 965, 36 Cal.Rptr.2d 552 (1994)* (in malpractice action against former attorney based on negligence in preparing loan documents for client as a lender, where adequacy of documentation is subject of dispute, action accrues on entry of adverse judgment, settlement, or dismissal of underlying action). See also *O'Neill v. Tichy, 19 Cal.App.4th 114, 25 Cal.Rptr.2d 162 (1993), review denied 1/13/94* (despite client's knowledge of wrongful act or omission, subsection (a)(2) tolls the one-year statute of limitations so long as the attorney continues to represent the plaintiff on the same specific matter).

In *Beal Bank, SSB v. Arter and Hadden, LLP, 42 Cal.4th 503, 66 Cal.Rptr.3d 52, 167 P.3d 666 (2007)*, the California Supreme Court held that subsection (a)(2) tolling of the statute of limitations during an attorney's representation of a client ceases for a law firm when the attorney leaves the firm and takes the client with him.

Research References

Forms

California Transactions Forms--Estate Planning § 2:5, Necessity Of Privity Between Estate Planner and Ultimate Beneficiary.
California Transactions Forms--Estate Planning § 2:7, Statute Of Limitations; Tolling.
California Transactions Forms--Estate Planning § 2:8, Conduct Of Practitioner to Limit Tolling Of Statute Of Limitations.
California Transactions Forms--Estate Planning § 2:46, Matters to Consider to Avoid Malpractice.
California Transactions Forms--Estate Planning § 2:56, Letter Terminating Attorney-Client Relationship.
West's California Code Forms, Civil Procedure § 340.6 Form 1, Statute Of Limitations--Pleading--Professional Negligence Of Attorney--Tolling--Legal Disability.
West's California Code Forms, Civil Procedure § 340.6 Form 2, Statute Of Limitations--Pleading--Professional Negligence Of Attorney--Tolling--Discovery Of Facts.

§ 340.7. Dalkon Shield Claimants' Trust claims; tolling for bankruptcy of A.H. Robins Co.

(a) Notwithstanding Section 335.1, a civil action brought by, or on behalf of, a Dalkon Shield victim against the Dalkon Shield Claimants' Trust, shall be brought in accordance with the procedures established by A.H. Robins Company, Inc. Plan of Reorganization, and shall be brought within 15 years of the date on which the victim's injury occurred, except that the statute shall be tolled from August 21, 1985, the date on which the A.H. Robins Company filed for Chapter 11 Reorganization in Richmond, Virginia.

(b) This section applies regardless of when the action or claim shall have accrued or been filed and regardless of whether it might have lapsed or otherwise be barred by time under California law. However, this section shall only apply to victims who, prior to January 1, 1990, filed a civil action, a timely claim, or a claim that is declared to be timely under the sixth Amended and Restated Disclosure Statement filed pursuant to Section 1125 of the Federal Bankruptcy Code in re: A.H. Robins Company, Inc., dated March 28, 1988, U.S. Bankruptcy Court, Eastern District of Virginia (case number 85–01307–R). *(Added by Stats.1994, c. 107 (A.B.2855), § 1. Amended by Stats.2007, c. 130 (A.B.299), § 35; Stats.2008, c. 179 (S.B.1498), § 34.)*

§ 340.8. Exposure to hazardous materials or toxic substances; time for commencement of action; injury or illness; wrongful death actions; definitions

(a) In any civil action for injury or illness based upon exposure to a hazardous material or toxic substance, the time for commencement of the action shall be no later than either two years from the date of injury, or two years after the plaintiff becomes aware of, or reasonably should have become aware of, (1) an injury, (2) the physical cause of the injury, and (3) sufficient facts to put a reasonable person on inquiry notice that the injury was caused or contributed to by the wrongful act of another, whichever occurs later.

(b) In an action for the wrongful death of any plaintiff's decedent, based upon exposure to a hazardous material or toxic substance, the time for commencement of an action shall be no later than either (1) two years from the date of the death of the plaintiff's decedent, or (2) two years from the first date on which the plaintiff is aware of, or reasonably should have become aware of, the physical cause of the death and sufficient facts to put a reasonable person on inquiry notice that the death was caused or contributed to by the wrongful act of another, whichever occurs later.

(c) For purposes of this section:

(1) A "civil action for injury or illness based upon exposure to a hazardous material or toxic substance" does not include an action subject to Section 340.2 or 340.5.

(2) Media reports regarding the hazardous material or toxic substance contamination do not, in and of themselves, constitute sufficient facts to put a reasonable person on inquiry notice that the injury or death was caused or contributed to by the wrongful act of another.

(d) Nothing in this section shall be construed to limit, abrogate, or change the law in effect on the effective date of this section with respect to actions not based upon exposure to a hazardous material or toxic substance. *(Added by Stats.2003, c. 873 (S.B.331), § 1.)*

Research References

Forms

West's California Code Forms, Civil Procedure § 340.8 Form 1, Statutes Of Limitation--Action for Personal Injury or Wrongful Death--Toxic Injuries--Two-Year Time Period.

§ 340.9. Northridge earthquake insurance claims

(a) Notwithstanding any other provision of law or contract, any insurance claim for damages arising out of the Northridge earthquake of 1994 which is barred as of the effective date of this section solely because the applicable statute of limitations has or had expired is hereby revived and a cause of action thereon may be commenced provided that the action is commenced within one year of the effective date of this section. This subdivision shall only apply to cases in which an insured contacted an insurer or an insurer's representative prior to January 1, 2000, regarding potential Northridge earthquake damage.

(b) Any action pursuant to this section commenced prior to, or within one year from, the effective date of this section shall not be barred based upon this limitations period.

(c) Nothing in this section shall be construed to alter the applicable limitations period of an action that is not time barred as of the effective date of this section.

(d) This section shall not apply to either of the following:

(1) Any claim that has been litigated to finality in any court of competent jurisdiction prior to the effective date of this section.

(2) Any written compromised settlement agreement which has been made between an insurer and its insured where the insured was represented by counsel admitted to the practice of law in California at the time of the settlement, and who signed the agreement. *(Added by Stats.2000, c. 1090 (S.B. 1899), § 1.)*

Research References

Forms

West's California Code Forms, Civil Procedure § 340.9 Form 1, Statutes Of Limitation--Northridge Earthquake Insurance Claims--Revival Of Barred Claims.

Treatises and Practice Aids

Witkin, California Summary 10th Constitutional Law § 1291, Insurance Contracts.
Witkin, California Summary 10th Insurance § 12, in General.
Witkin, California Summary 10th Insurance § 251, Traditional Tort Actions.
Witkin, California Summary 10th Insurance § 309, in General.
Witkin, California Summary 10th Insurance § 317, Notice and Proof Of Loss.

§ 340.10. "Terrorist victim" defined; statute of limitations for actions brought for injury or death to terrorist victim

(a) For purposes of this section, "terrorist victim" means any individual who died or was injured as a consequence of the terrorist-related aircraft crashes of September 11, 2001, including persons who were present at the World Trade Center in New York City, New York, the Pentagon in Arlington, Virginia, or at the site of the crash at Shanksville, Pennsylvania, or in the immediate aftermath of the terrorist-related aircraft crashes of September 11, 2001, including members of the flight crew and passengers on American Airlines Flight 11, American Airlines Flight 77, United Airlines Flight 175, and United Airlines Flight 93, and who suffered physical harm or death as a result of any of the crashes, as defined in Section 40101 of Title 49 of the United States Code and the related, applicable regulations, other than an individual identified by the Attorney General of the United States as a participant or conspirator in the terrorist-related aircraft crashes, or a representative or heir of such an individual.

(b) The statute of limitations for injury or death set forth in Section 335.1 shall apply to any action brought for injury to, or for the death of, any terrorist victim described in subdivision (a) and caused by the wrongful act or neglect of another, regardless of whether that action lapsed or was otherwise barred by time under California law predating the passage of this section and Section 335.1. *(Added by Stats.2002, c. 448 (S.B.688), § 4.)*

Research References

Forms

West's California Code Forms, Civil Procedure § 340.10 Form 1, Statutes Of Limitation--Action for Personal Injury or Wrongful Death Of Another--Terrorist Victims Of September 11, 2001 Attacks--Two-Year Time Period.

§ 341. Six months; officer for seizure as tax collector; stock sold for delinquent assessment; vacation of act of trustees of dissolved corporation

Within six months:

An action against an officer, or officer de facto:

1. To recover any goods, wares, merchandise, or other property, seized by any such officer in his official capacity as tax collector, or to recover the price or value of any goods, wares, merchandise, or other personal property so seized, or for damages for the seizure, detention, sale of, or injury to any goods, wares, merchandise, or other personal property seized, or for damages done to any person or property in making any such seizure.

2. To recover stock sold for a delinquent assessment, as provided in section three hundred forty-seven of the Civil Code.[1]

3. To set aside or invalidate any action taken or performed by a majority of the trustees of any corporation heretofore or hereafter dissolved by operation of law, including the revivor of any such corporation. *(Enacted in 1872. Amended by Code Am.1873–74, c. 383, p. 292, § 35; Stats. 1917, c. 217, p. 381, § 1.)*

[1] Now Corporations Code § 423.

§ 341.5. Actions challenging the constitutionality of state funding for municipalities, school districts, special districts, or local agencies; commencement

Notwithstanding any other provision of law, any action or proceeding in which a county, city, city and county, school district, special district, or any other local agency is a plaintiff or petitioner, that is brought against the State of California challenging the constitutionality of any statute relating to state funding for counties, cities, cities and counties, school districts, special districts, or other local agencies, shall be commenced within 90 days of the effective date of the statute at issue in the action. For purposes of this section, "State of California" means the State of California itself, or any of its agencies, departments, commissions, boards, or public officials. *(Added by Stats.1994, c. 155 (A.B.860), § 1, eff. July 11,*

1994. Amended by Stats.1994, c. 156 (S.B.2127), § 1, eff. July 11, 1994.)

§ 341a. Ninety days; recovery or conversion of personal property, baggage, etc., left at hotel, hospital, boarding house, etc.

All civil actions for the recovery or conversion of personal property, wearing apparel, trunks, valises or baggage alleged to have been left at a hotel, hospital, rest home, sanitarium, boarding house, lodging house, furnished apartment house, or furnished bungalow court, shall be begun within 90 days from and after the date of the departure of the owner of said personal property, wearing apparel, trunks, valises or baggage from said hotel, hospital, rest home, sanitarium, boarding house, lodging house, furnished apartment house, or furnished bungalow court. *(Added by Stats.1921, c. 152, p. 150, § 1. Amended by Stats.1927, c. 826, p. 1657, § 1; Stats.1943, c. 405, p. 1930, § 1.)*

Research References

Treatises and Practice Aids

Witkin, California Summary 10th Personal Property § 168, Liability: In General.

§ 342. Actions against public entities

An action against a public entity upon a cause of action for which a claim is required to be presented in accordance with Chapter 1 (commencing with Section 900) and Chapter 2 (commencing with Section 910) of Part 3 of Division 3.6 of Title 1 of the Government Code must be commenced within the time provided in Section 945.6 of the Government Code. *(Added by Stats.1963, c. 1715, p. 3394, § 4.)*

Law Revision Commission Comments

1963 Addition

This section is placed among the limitation of actions provisions of the Code of Civil Procedure so that the statute of limitations applicable to actions upon claims against public entities may be discovered by looking at either this section or the appropriate section of the Government Code.

§ 343. Four years; relief not otherwise provided for

ACTIONS FOR RELIEF NOT HEREINBEFORE PROVIDED FOR. An action for relief not hereinbefore provided for must be commenced within four years after the cause of action shall have accrued. *(Enacted in 1872.)*

Research References

Forms

California Transactions Forms--Business Entities § 20:21, Right to Final Accounting.

Am. Jur. Pl. & Pr. Forms Products Liability § 247.40, Answer and Affirmative Defenses--By Manufacturer--In Suit Against Municipal Corporation and Police Officers and Manufacturer --For Wrongful Death; Survival Action; Deprivation Of Rights.

Treatises and Practice Aids

Witkin, California Summary 10th Community Property § 264, Judicially Developed Rules.

Witkin, California Summary 10th Community Property § 276, Illustrations: Recovery Allowed.

Witkin, California Summary 10th Corporations § 9, Nature Of Doctrine.

Witkin, California Summary 10th Equity § 33, Defenses.

Witkin, California Summary 10th Taxation § 293, Procedure.

Witkin, California Summary 10th Trusts § 137, Limitations and Laches.

§ 344. Balance upon mutual, open and current account; accrual of cause

WHERE CAUSE OF ACTION ACCRUES ON MUTUAL ACCOUNT. In an action brought to recover a balance due upon a mutual, open, and current account, where there have been reciprocal demands between the parties, the cause of action is deemed to have accrued from the time of the last item proved in the account on either side. *(Enacted in 1872.)*

§ 345. Actions in name of state or county; applicability of chapter; support of patients at state or county hospitals; four year limit

The limitations prescribed in this chapter apply to actions brought in the name of the state or county or for the benefit of the state or county, in the same manner as to actions by private parties. Accounts for the support of patients at state or county hospitals are book accounts as defined in Section 337a, and actions on them may be commenced at any time within four years after the last date of service or the last date of payment. *(Enacted in 1872. Amended by Stats.1905, c. 381, p. 487, § 1; Stats.1921, c. 475, p. 722, § 1; Stats.1943, c. 177, p. 1071, § 1; Stats.1984, c. 797, § 1.)*

§ 346. Action to redeem mortgage; effect of five years adverse possession

ACTION TO REDEEM A MORTGAGE WITHOUT ACCOUNT OF RENTS AND PROFITS. An action to redeem a mortgage of real property, with or without an account of rents and profits, may be brought by the mortgagor or those claiming under him, against the mortgagee in possession, or those claiming under him, unless he or they have continuously maintained an adverse possession of the mortgaged premises for five years after breach of some condition of the mortgage. *(Enacted in 1872, unpublished Act of 1872.)*

§ 347. Action to redeem mortgage; multiple mortgagors or persons claiming under mortgagor

SAME, WHEN THERE ARE TWO OR MORE SUCH MORTGAGES. If there is more than one such mortgagor, or more than one person claiming under a mortgagor, some of whom are not entitled to maintain such an action under the provisions of this Chapter, any one of them who is entitled to maintain such an action may redeem therein a divided or undivided part of the mortgaged premises, according as his interest may appear and have an accounting, for a part of the rents and profits proportionate to his interest in the mortgaged premises, on payment of a part of the mortgage money, bearing the same proportion to the whole of such money as the value of his divided or undivided interest in the premises bears to the whole of such premises. *(Enacted in 1872, unpublished Act of 1872.)*

Research References

Treatises and Practice Aids

Witkin, California Summary 10th Security Transactions in Real Property § 234, Pro Tanto Redemption.

§ 348. No limitation; action to recover deposit of money or property; effect of insolvency

To actions brought to recover money or other property deposited with any bank, banker, trust company, building and loan association, or savings and loan society or evidenced by a certificate issued by an industrial loan company or credit union there is no limitation.

This section shall not apply to banks, bankers, trust companies, building and loan associations, industrial loan companies, credit unions, and savings and loan societies which have become insolvent and are in process of liquidation and in such cases the statute of limitations shall be deemed to have commenced to run from the beginning of the process of liquidation; provided, however, nothing herein contained shall be construed so as to relieve any stockholder of any banking corporation or trust company from stockholders' liability as shall at any time, be provided by law. *(Added by Code Am.1873–74, c. 383, p. 293, § 36. Amended by Stats. 1915, c. 411, p. 684, § 1; Stats.1917, c. 756, p. 1573, § 1; Stats.1955, c. 208, p. 677, § 1.)*

§ 348.5. No limitation; action upon bonds or coupons issued by State of California

An action upon any bonds or coupons issued by the State of California shall have no limitation. *(Added by Stats.2010, c. 719 (S.B.856), § 8, eff. Oct. 19, 2010.)*

CHAPTER 4. GENERAL PROVISIONS AS TO THE TIME OF COMMENCING ACTIONS

Section

§ 350. Action commenced with filing complaint

WHEN AN ACTION IS COMMENCED. An action is commenced, within the meaning of this Title, when the complaint is filed. *(Enacted in 1872.)*

§ 351. Absence from state; effect on limitation period

EXCEPTION, WHERE DEFENDANT IS OUT OF THE STATE. If, when the cause of action accrues against a person, he is out of the State, the action may be commenced within the term herein limited, after his return to the State, and if, after the cause of action accrues, he departs from the State, the time of his absence is not part of the time limited for the commencement of the action. *(Enacted in 1872.)*

Validity

This section was held unconstitutional, as violative of the commerce clause, with respect to residents who travel in the course of interstate commerce, in the decision of Filet Menu, Inc. v. Cheng (App. 2 Dist. 1999) 84 Cal.Rptr.2d 384, 71 Cal.App.4th 1276.

Commentary

Interpreting Section 351 together with 28 U.S.C. § 1738 (h)(3), *Trend v. Bell, 57 Cal.App.4th 1092, 68 Cal.Rptr.2d 54 (1997), review denied December 23, 1997,* held that a Montana child support judgment against a California defendant, which was no longer enforceable under Montana law, was nevertheless enforceable under California law. 28 U.S.C. § 1738 (h)(3) provides, as a matter of choice of law, that in an action to enforce arrears, the court shall apply the period of limitation of the forum state or the state that issued the order, whichever is longer.

Research References

Treatises and Practice Aids

Witkin, California Summary 10th Constitutional Law § 1300, in General; Dormant Commerce Clause.

Witkin, California Summary 10th Insurance § 205, in General.

Witkin, California Summary 10th Partnership § 69, Nature Of Limited Partnership.

§ 352. Disabilities of minority or lack of legal capacity to make decisions

(a) If a person entitled to bring an action, mentioned in Chapter 3 (commencing with Section 335) is, at the time the cause of action accrued either under the age of majority or lacking the legal capacity to make decisions, the time of the disability is not part of the time limited for the commencement of the action.

(b) This section shall not apply to an action against a public entity or public employee upon a cause of action for which a claim is required to be presented in accordance with Chapter 1 (commencing with Section 900) or Chapter 2 (commencing with Section 910) of Part 3, or Chapter 3 (commencing with Section 950) of Part 4, of Division 3.6 of Title 1 of the Government Code. This subdivision shall not apply to any claim presented to a public entity prior to January 1, 1971. *(Enacted in 1872. Amended by Stats.1959, c. 192, p. 2085, § 1; Stats.1970, c. 104, p. 323, § 1, operative Jan. 1, 1971; Stats.1975, c. 1241, p. 3187, § 1.5; Stats.1986, c. 1161, § 1; Stats.1994, c. 1083 (S.B.1445), § 4; Stats.2014, c. 144 (A.B.1847), § 4, eff. Jan. 1, 2015.)*

Law Revision Commission Comments

1970 Amendment

Subdivision (b) has been added so that Section 352, which operates to toll the statute of limitations for minors, insane persons, and prisoners, will not apply to the causes of action against a public entity or public employee described in this subdivision. Such actions are governed by the period of limitations specified in subdivision (a) of Section 945.6 of the Government Code. To safeguard the minor or incompetent from an inadvertent reliance on the tolling provision of Section 352, notice of rejection of his claim in the form provided in Government Code Section 913 is required to be given by the public entity. If notice is not given the claimant has two years from the accrual of his cause of action in which to sue. See Government Code Section 945.6(a).

Special exceptions for prisoners exist in both subdivision (b) of Section 945.6 and subdivision (c) of Section 950.6 of the Government Code, which toll the statute of limitations during the period of their civil disability.

The other general provisions of the Code of Civil Procedure relating to the time within which actions must be commenced—Sections 350, 351, 353–363—are applicable to actions against public entities and public employees. See Williams v. Los Angeles Metropolitan Transit Authority, 68 Cal.2d 599, 68 Cal.Rptr. 297, 440 P.2d 497 (1968). See also Government Code Sections 950.2 and 950.4.

Commentary

West Shield Investigations and Security Consultants v. Superior Court, 82 Cal.App.4th 935, 98 Cal.Rptr.2d 612 (2000), holds that this section has no application to an emancipated minor, because Family Code § 7050(e)(4) gives an emancipated minor the right "to sue and be sued."

Research References

Forms

California Transactions Forms--Estate Planning § 2:5, Necessity Of Privity Between Estate Planner and Ultimate Beneficiary.
West's California Code Forms, Civil Procedure § 352 Form 1, Statute Of Limitations--Tolling--Contract Actions.
West's California Code Forms, Civil Procedure § 340.4 Form 1, Statute Of Limitations--Pleading--Damages Arising from Personal Injuries at Birth.
West's California Code Forms, Civil Procedure § 340.5 Form 1, Statute Of Limitations--Pleading--Professional Negligence Of Healthcare Provider--Reasonable.
West's California Code Forms, Civil Procedure § 340.6 Form 1, Statute Of Limitations--Pleading--Professional Negligence Of Attorney--Tolling--Legal Disability.
West's California Code Forms, Civil Procedure § 366.2 Form 1, Statute Of Limitations--Death Of Persons--Defendants.

Treatises and Practice Aids

Witkin, California Summary 10th Insurance § 205, in General.

§ 352.1. Disability of imprisonment

(a) If a person entitled to bring an action, mentioned in Chapter 3 (commencing with Section 335), is, at the time the cause of action accrued, imprisoned on a criminal charge, or in execution under the sentence of a criminal court for a term less than for life, the time of that disability is not a part of the time limited for the commencement of the action, not to exceed two years.

(b) This section does not apply to an action against a public entity or public employee upon a cause of action for which a claim is required to be presented in accordance with Chapter 1 (commencing with Section 900) or Chapter 2 (commencing with Section 910) of Part 3, or Chapter 3 (commencing with Section 950) of Part 4, of Division 3.6 of Title 1 of the Government Code. This subdivision shall not apply to any claim presented to a public entity prior to January 1, 1971.

(c) This section does not apply to an action, other than an action to recover damages or that portion of an action that is for the recovery of damages, relating to the conditions of confinement, including an action brought by that person pursuant to Section 1983 of Title 42 of the United States Code. *(Added by Stats.1994, c. 1083 (S.B.1445), § 5.)*

Research References

Forms

West's California Code Forms, Civil Procedure § 340.5 Form 1, Statute Of Limitations--Pleading--Professional Negligence Of Healthcare Provider--Reasonable.
West's California Code Forms, Civil Procedure § 352.1 Form 1, Statute Of Limitations--Tolling--Imprisonment--Contract Actions.

§ 352.5. Action against person under order for restitution as condition of probation; tolling

If, after a cause of action accrues against a person, that person comes under an order for restitution as a condition of probation with respect to the specific act or omission giving rise to such person's liability, the time during which the order is in effect is not a part of the time limited for the commencement of such an action based upon that act or omission. *(Added by Stats.1976, c. 282, p. 589, § 1.)*

§ 353.1. Court assuming jurisdiction over attorney's practice; effect on limitation period

If a person entitled to bring an action or other proceeding, which action or other proceeding has not been filed or otherwise instituted, is represented by an attorney over whose practice a court of this state has assumed jurisdiction pursuant to Section 6180 or Section 6190 of the Business and Professions Code, and the application for the court to assume jurisdiction is filed prior to the expiration of the applicable statute of limitation or claim statute, the person shall have six months from the date of entry of the order assuming jurisdiction within which to file or otherwise institute the matter, if the applicable statute of limitation otherwise would have expired. *(Added by Stats.1983, c. 254, § 3.)*

§ 354. Disability during war; effect on limitation period

When a person is, by reason of the existence of a state of war, under a disability to commence an action, the time of the continuance of such disability is not part of the period limited for the commencement of the action whether such cause of action shall have accrued prior to or during the period of such disability. *(Enacted in 1872. Amended by Stats.1943, c. 151, p. 1043, § 1.)*

Research References

Forms

Am. Jur. Pl. & Pr. Forms War § 1, Introductory Comments.

§ 354.3. Recovery of Holocaust-era artwork from enumerated entities

(a) The following definitions govern the construction of this section:

(1) "Entity" means any museum or gallery that displays, exhibits, or sells any article of historical, interpretive, scientific, or artistic significance.

(2) "Holocaust-era artwork" means any article of artistic significance taken as a result of Nazi persecution during the period of 1929 to 1945, inclusive.

(b) Notwithstanding any other provision of law, any owner, or heir or beneficiary of an owner, of Holocaust-era artwork, may bring an action to recover Holocaust-era artwork from any entity described in paragraph (1) of subdivision (a). Subject to Section 410.10, that action may be brought in a superior court of this state, which court shall have jurisdiction over that action until its completion or resolution. Section 361 does not apply to this section.

(c) Any action brought under this section shall not be dismissed for failure to comply with the applicable statute of limitation, if the action is commenced on or before December 31, 2010. *(Added by Stats.2002, c. 332 (A.B.1758), § 2.)*

Validity

This section was held preempted by the foreign affairs doctrine in the decision of Von Saher v. Norton Simon Museum of Art at Pasadena, C.A.9 (Cal.)2010, 592 F.3d 954, certiorari denied 131 S.Ct. 3055, 564 U.S. 1037, 180 L.Ed.2d 885, on remand 862 F.Supp.2d 1044.

Research References

Forms

West's California Code Forms, Civil Procedure § 354.3 Form 1, Statutes Of Limitation--Holocaust Era Artwork--Claims Against Museums and Art Galleries.

§ 354.4. Armenian Genocide victims; insurance policy claims; waiver of statute of limitations

(a) The following definitions govern the construction of this section:

(1) "Armenian Genocide victim" means any person of Armenian or other ancestry living in the Ottoman Empire during the period of 1915 to 1923, inclusive, who died, was deported, or escaped to avoid persecution during that period.

(2) "Insurer" means an insurance provider doing business in the state, or whose contacts in the state satisfy the constitutional requirements for jurisdiction, that sold life, property, liability, health, annuities, dowry, educational, casualty, or any other insurance covering persons or property to persons in Europe or Asia at any time between 1875 and 1923.

(b) Notwithstanding any other provision of law, any Armenian Genocide victim, or heir or beneficiary of an Armenian Genocide victim, who resides in this state and has a claim arising out of an insurance policy or policies purchased or in effect in Europe or Asia between 1875 and 1923 from an insurer described in paragraph (2) of subdivision (a), may bring a legal action or may continue a pending legal action to recover on that claim in any court of competent jurisdiction in this state, which court shall be deemed the proper forum for that action until its completion or resolution.

(c) Any action, including any pending action brought by an Armenian Genocide victim or the heir or beneficiary of an Armenian Genocide victim, whether a resident or nonresident of this state, seeking benefits under the insurance policies issued or in effect between 1875 and 1923 shall not be dismissed for failure to comply with the applicable statute of limitation, provided the action is filed on or before December 31, 2016.

(d) The provisions of this section are severable. If any provision of this section or its application is held invalid, that invalidity shall not affect other provisions or applications that can be given effect without the invalid provision or application. *(Added by Stats.2000, c. 543 (S.B.1915), § 2, eff. Sept. 20, 2000. Amended by Stats.2011, c. 70 (A.B.173), § 1, eff. July 8, 2011.)*

Validity

For validity of this section, see Movsesian v. Victoria Versicherung AG, C.A.9 (Cal.)2012, 670 F.3d 1067, petition for certiorari denied, 133 S.Ct. 2795.

§ 354.45. Armenian Genocide victims; deposited and looted assets; waiver of statute of limitations

(a) For purposes of this section, the following terms have the following meanings:

(1) "Armenian Genocide victim" means any person of Armenian or other ancestry living in the Ottoman Empire during the period of 1890 to 1923, inclusive, who died, was injured in person or property, was deported, or escaped to avoid persecution during that period.

(2) "Bank" means any banking or financial institution, including any institution that issued bonds, that conducted business in Ottoman Turkey at any time during the period of 1890 to 1923, inclusive.

(3) "Deposited assets" means any and all cash, securities, bonds, gold, jewels or jewelry, or any other tangible or intangible items of personal property, or any documents indicating ownership or possessory interests in real, personal, or intangible property, that were deposited with and held by a bank.

(4) "Looted assets" means any and all personal, commercial, real, and intangible property, including cash, securities, gold, jewelry, businesses, artwork, equipment, and intellectual property, that was taken from the ownership or control of an individual, organization, or entity, by theft, forced transfer, or exploitation, during the period of 1890 to 1923, inclusive, by any person, organization, or entity acting on behalf of, or in furtherance of the acts of, the Turkish Government, that were received by and deposited with a bank.

(b) Notwithstanding any other law, any Armenian Genocide victim, or heir or beneficiary of an Armenian Genocide victim, who resides in this state and has a claim arising out of a failure of a bank to pay or turn over deposited assets, or to turn over looted assets, may bring an action or may continue a pending action, to recover on that claim in any court of competent jurisdiction in this state, which court shall be deemed the proper forum for that action until its completion or resolution.

(c) Any action, including any pending action brought by an Armenian Genocide victim, or the heir or beneficiary of an Armenian Genocide victim, who resides in this state, seeking payment for, or the return of, deposited assets, or the return of looted assets, shall not be dismissed for failure to comply with the applicable statute of limitation, if the action is filed on or before December 31, 2016.

(d) The provisions of this section are severable. If any provision of this section or its application is held invalid, that invalidity shall not affect other provisions or applications that can be given effect without the invalid provision or application. *(Added by Stats.2006, c. 443 (S.B.1524), § 2.)*

Validity

This section was recognized as preempted for conflicting with the federal government's resolution of wartime claims arising out of World War I in the decision of Deirmenjian v. Deutsche Bank, A.G., C.D.Cal.2007, 526 F.Supp.2d 1068.

§ 354.5. Holocaust victims; insurance policy claims purchased in Europe; legal action to recover on claims

(a) The following definitions govern the construction of this section:

(1) "Holocaust victim" means any person who was persecuted during the period of 1929 to 1945, inclusive, by Nazi Germany, its allies, or sympathizers.

(2) "Related company" means any parent, subsidiary, reinsurer, successor in interest, managing general agent, or affiliate company of the insurer.

(3) "Insurer" means an insurance provider doing business in the state, or whose contacts in the state satisfy the constitutional requirements for jurisdiction, that sold life, property, liability, health, annuities, dowry, educational, casualty, or any other insurance covering persons or property to persons in Europe at any time before 1945, directly or through a related company, whether the sale of the insurance occurred before or after the insurer and the related company became related.

(b) Notwithstanding any other provision of law, any Holocaust victim, or heir or beneficiary of a Holocaust victim, who resides in this state and has a claim arising out of an insurance policy or policies purchased or in effect in Europe before 1945 from an insurer described in paragraph (3) of subdivision (a), may bring a legal action to recover on that claim in any superior court of the state for the county in which the plaintiff or one of the plaintiffs resides, which court shall be vested with jurisdiction over that action until its completion or resolution.

(c) Any action brought by a Holocaust victim or the heir or beneficiary of a Holocaust victim, whether a resident or nonresident of this state, seeking proceeds of the insurance policies issued or in effect before 1945 shall not be dismissed for failure to comply with the applicable statute of limitation, provided the action is commenced on or before December 31, 2010. *(Added by Stats.1998, c. 43 (A.B.1334), § 2, eff. May 22, 1998. Amended by Stats.1999, c. 827 (A.B.600), § 1, eff. Oct. 10, 1999.)*

Validity

This statute was held preempted by United States foreign policy favoring settlement of such claims by International Commission on Holocaust Era Insurance Claims, in the decision of Steinberg v. International Com'n on Holocaust Era Ins. Claims (App. 2 Dist. 2005) 34 Cal.Rptr.3d 944, 133 Cal.App.4th 689.

Research References

Forms

West's California Code Forms, Civil Procedure § 354.5 Form 1, Statutes Of Limitation--Holocaust Victims--Claims for Insurance Policy Proceeds.

§ 354.6. Second World War slave or forced labor victims; heirs; actions for recovery of compensation; limitations

(a) As used in this section:

(1) "Second World War slave labor victim" means any person taken from a concentration camp or ghetto or diverted from transportation to a concentration camp or from a ghetto to perform labor without pay for any period of time between 1929 and 1945, by the Nazi regime, its allies and sympathizers, or enterprises transacting business in any of the areas occupied by or under control of the Nazi regime or its allies and sympathizers.

(2) 'Second World War forced labor victim" means any person who was a member of the civilian population conquered by the Nazi regime, its allies or sympathizers, or prisoner-of-war of the Nazi regime, its allies or sympathizers, forced to perform labor without pay for any period of time between 1929 and 1945, by the Nazi regime, its allies and sympathizers, or enterprises transacting business in any of the areas occupied by or under control of the Nazi regime or its allies and sympathizers.

(3) "Compensation" means the present value of wages and benefits that individuals should have been paid and damages for injuries sustained in connection with the labor performed. Present value shall be calculated on the basis of the market value of the services at the time they were performed, plus interest from the time the services were performed, compounded annually to date of full payment without diminution for wartime or postwar currency devaluation.

(b) Any Second World War slave labor victim, or heir of a Second World War slave labor victim, Second World War forced labor victim, or heir of a Second World War forced labor victim, may bring an action to recover compensation for labor performed as a Second World War slave labor victim or Second World War forced labor victim from any entity or successor in interest thereof, for whom that labor was performed, either directly or through a subsidiary or affiliate. That action may be brought in a superior court of this state, which court shall have jurisdiction over that action until its completion or resolution.

(c) Any action brought under this section shall not be dismissed for failure to comply with the applicable statute of limitation, if the action is commenced on or before December 31, 2010. *(Added by Stats.1999, c. 216 (S.B.1245), § 4, eff. July 28, 1999.)*

Validity

This statute was recognized as preempted by United States foreign policy favoring settlement of such claims by International Commission on Holocaust Era Insurance Claims, in the decision of Steinberg v. International Com'n on Holocaust Era Ins. Claims (App. 2 Dist. 2005) 34 Cal.Rptr.3d 944, 133 Cal.App.4th 689.

This section was held unconstitutional in the decision of In re World War II Era Japanese Forced Labor Litigation, N.D.Cal.2001, 164 F.Supp.2d 1160, 108 A.L.R.5th 743, affirmed 317 F.3d 1005, amended and superseded on denial of rehearing 324 F.3d 692, 192 A.L.R. Fed. 657, certiorari denied 124 S.Ct. 105, 540 U.S. 820, 157 L.Ed.2d 39, certiorari denied 124 S.Ct. 132, 540 U.S. 820, 157 L.Ed.2d 39, certiorari denied 124 S.Ct. 133, 540 U.S. 821, 157 L.Ed.2d 39.

Research References

Forms

West's California Code Forms, Civil Procedure § 354.6 Form 1, Statute Of Limitations--Second World War Slave or Forced Labor Victims--Claims for Compensation.

Treatises and Practice Aids

Witkin, California Summary 10th Constitutional Law § 1340, Supremacy Over State Law.

§ 354.7. Braceros, heirs or beneficiaries of braceros; right of action for recovery of savings fund amounts; limitations; severability of provisions

(a) The following definitions govern the construction of this section:

(1) "Bracero" means any person who participated in the labor importation program known as the Bracero program between January 1, 1942, and January 1, 1950, pursuant to agreements between the United States and Mexico.

(2) "Savings fund" means funds withheld from the wages of braceros as savings to be paid to braceros upon their return to Mexico.

(b) Notwithstanding any other provision of law, any bracero, or heir or beneficiary of a bracero, who has a claim arising out of a failure to pay or turn over savings fund amounts may bring a legal action or may continue a pending legal action to recover on that claim in any court of competent jurisdiction in this state, which court shall be deemed a proper forum for that action until its completion or resolution.

(c) Notwithstanding any other provision of law, any action brought by a bracero, or heir or beneficiary of a bracero, arising out of a failure to pay or turn over savings fund amounts shall not be dismissed for failure to comply with the otherwise applicable statute of limitations, provided the action is filed on or before December 31, 2005.

(d) The provisions of this section are severable. If any provision of this section or its application is held invalid, that invalidity shall not affect other provisions or applications that can be given effect without the invalid provision or application. *(Added by Stats.2002, c. 1070 (A.B.2913), § 2, eff. Sept. 29, 2002.)*

Research References

Forms

West's California Code Forms, Civil Procedure § 354.7 Form 1, Statute Of Limitations--Bracero Wage Claims (1942 to 1950).

§ 354.8. Torture, genocide, war crime, extrajudicial killing, crimes against humanity; limitations; application; fees and costs; severability

(a) Notwithstanding any other law, including, but not limited to Section 335.1, the following actions shall be commenced within 10 years:

(1) An action for assault, battery, or both, where the conduct constituting the assault or battery would also constitute any of the following:

(A) An act of torture, as described in Section 206 of the Penal Code.

(B) An act of genocide, as described in Section 1091(a) of Title 18 of the United States Code.

(C) A war crime, as defined in Section 2441 of Title 18 of the United States Code.

(D) An attempted extrajudicial killing, as defined in Section 3(a) of Public Law 102–256.

(E)(i) Crimes against humanity.

(ii) For purposes of this paragraph, "crimes against humanity" means any of the following acts as part of a widespread or systematic attack directed against a civil population, with knowledge of the attack:

(I) Murder.

(II) Extermination.

(III) Enslavement.

(IV) Forcible transfer of population.

(V) Arbitrary detention.

(VI) Rape, sexual slavery, enforced prostitution, forced pregnancy, enforced sterilization, or any other form of sexual violence of comparable gravity.

(VII) Persecution on political, race, national, ethnic, cultural, religious, or gender grounds.

(VIII) Enforced disappearance of persons.

(IX) Other inhuman acts of similar character intentionally causing great suffering, serious bodily injury, or serious mental injury.

(2) An action for wrongful death, where the death arises out of conduct constituting any of the acts described in paragraph (1), or where the death would constitute an extrajudicial killing, as defined in Section 3(a) of Public Law 102–256.

(3) An action for the taking of property in violation of international law, in which either of the following apply:

(A) That property, or any property exchanged for such property, is present in the United States in connection with a commercial activity carried on in the United States by a foreign state.

(B) That property, or any property exchanged for such property, is owned or operated by an agency or instrumentality of a foreign state and that agency or instrumentality is engaged in a commercial activity in the United States.

(4) An action seeking benefits under an insurance policy where the insurance claim arises out of any of the conduct described in paragraphs (1) to (3), inclusive.

(b) An action brought under this section shall not be dismissed for failure to comply with any previously applicable statute of limitations.

(c) Section 361 shall not apply to an action brought pursuant to this section if all or part of the unlawful act or acts out of which the action arises occurred in this state.

(d) A prevailing plaintiff may be awarded reasonable attorney's fees and litigation costs including, but not limited to, expert witness fees and expenses as part of the costs.

(e) This section shall apply to all actions commenced concerning an act described in paragraphs (1) to (4), inclusive, of subdivision (a), that occurs on or after January 1, 2016.

(f) The provisions of this section are severable. If any provision of this section or its application is held invalid, that invalidity shall not affect other provisions or applications that can be given effect without the invalid provision or application. *(Added by Stats.2015, c. 474 (A.B.15), § 2, eff. Jan. 1, 2016.)*

Research References

Forms

West's California Code Forms, Civil Procedure § 354.8 Form 1, Statute Of Limitations--Crimes Against Humanity.

§ 355. Reversal of judgment; limitation on new action

If an action is commenced within the time prescribed therefor, and a judgment therein for the plaintiff be reversed on appeal other than on the merits, a new action may be commenced within one year after the reversal. *(Enacted in 1872. Amended by Stats.1992, c. 178 (S.B.1496), § 7.)*

Law Revision Commission Comments

1992 Amendment

Section 355 is amended for conformity with the revised rules concerning litigation after death of a party. See Sections 377.10–377.62. This section is also revised to make clear that it does not apply where the judgment was reversed on the merits. See, e.g., Watterson v. Owens River Canal Co., 190 Cal. 88, 93, 210 P. 625 (1922); Schneider v. Schimmels, 256 Cal.App.2d 366, 370, 64 Cal.Rptr. 273 (1967). [22 Cal.L.Rev.Comm.Reports 895 (1992)].

§ 356. Injunction against commencement of action; effect on limitation period

PROVISION WHERE ACTION IS STAYED BY INJUNCTION. When the commencement of an action is stayed by injunction or statutory prohibition, the time of the continuance of the injunction or prohibition is not part of the time limited for the commencement of the action. *(Enacted in 1872.)*

Research References

Forms

West's California Code Forms, Civil Procedure § 340.5 Form 3, Statute Of Limitations--Pleading--Professional Negligence Of Health Care Provider--Tolling--Fraud--Collusion.

§ 357. Disability; necessity of existence when right of action accrued

DISABILITY MUST EXIST WHEN RIGHT OF ACTION ACCRUED. No person can avail himself of a disability, unless it existed when his right of action accrued. *(Enacted in 1872.)*

§ 358. Coexisting disabilities; effect on limitation period

WHEN TWO OR MORE DISABILITIES EXIST, ETC. When two or more disabilities coexist at the time the right of action accrues, the limitation does not attach until they are removed. *(Enacted in 1872.)*

§ 359. Corporate directors, stockholders or members; actions to recover penalty or forfeiture or enforce liability; inapplicability of title; limitation period

This title does not affect actions against directors, shareholders, or members of a corporation, to recover a penalty or forfeiture imposed, or to enforce a liability created by law; but such actions must be brought within three years after the discovery by the aggrieved party of the facts upon which the penalty or forfeiture attached, or the liability was created. *(Enacted in 1872. Amended by Stats.1978, c. 1305, p. 4265, § 1, operative Jan. 1, 1980.)*

Research References

Treatises and Practice Aids

Witkin, California Summary 10th Corporations § 9, Nature Of Doctrine.

Witkin, California Summary 10th Corporations § 102, in General.

§ 359.5. Principal and surety; performance bond; expiration of statute of limitations re obligations of principal; bar to action against principal or surety under bond

If the obligations under a surety bond are conditioned upon performance of the principal, the expiration of the statute of limitations with respect to the obligations of the principal, other than the obligations of the principal under the bond, shall also bar an action against the principal or surety under the bond, unless the terms of the bond provide otherwise. *(Added by Stats.1982, c. 106, § 1.)*

Research References

Forms

California Real Estate Forms (Miller & Starr) § 3:37, Continuing Guaranty.

California Real Estate Forms (Miller & Starr) § 3:38, Completion Guaranty.

California Real Estate Forms (Miller & Starr) § 3:38.50, "Bad Boy" Guaranty.

Cal. Transaction Forms - Bus. Transactions § 19:53, Continuing Guaranty (Multiple Individual Guarantors)--Loan Secured by Deed Of Trust.

§ 360. Acknowledgment or promise; payment on account; sufficiency to take case out of statute of limitations

No acknowledgment or promise is sufficient evidence of a new or continuing contract, by which to take the case out of the operation of this title, unless the same is contained in some writing, signed by the party to be charged thereby, provided that any payment on account of principal or interest due on a promissory note made by the party to be charged shall be deemed a sufficient acknowledgment or promise of a continuing contract to stop, from time to time as any such payment is made, the running of the time within which an action may be commenced upon the principal sum or upon any installment of principal or interest due on such note, and to start the running of a new period of time, but no such payment of itself shall revive a cause of action once barred. *(Enacted in 1872. Amended by Stats.1947, c. 1108, p. 2547, § 1; Stats.1955, c. 417, p. 874, § 1.)*

Research References

Forms

Cal. Transaction Forms - Bus. Transactions § 6:42, Contracts Required to be in Writing.
Cal. Transaction Forms - Bus. Transactions § 22:9, Waiver and Extinguishment.
California Transactions Forms--Family Law § 4:22, Statute Of Frauds.

Treatises and Practice Aids

Witkin, California Summary 10th Contracts § 240, Writing.
Witkin, California Summary 10th Contracts § 343, California Codes.
Witkin, California Summary 10th Contracts § 400, Miscellaneous Provisions.

§ 360.5. Waiver of statute of limitations; effective period; renewal

No waiver shall bar a defense to any action that the action was not commenced within the time limited by this title unless the waiver is in writing and signed by the person obligated. No waiver executed prior to the expiration of the time limited for the commencement of the action by this title shall be effective for a period exceeding four years from the date of expiration of the time limited for commencement of the action by this title and no waiver executed after the expiration of such time shall be effective for a period exceeding four years from the date thereof, but any such waiver may be renewed for a further period of not exceeding four years from the expiration of the immediately preceding waiver. Such waivers may be made successively. The provisions of this section shall not be applicable to any acknowledgment, promise or any form of waiver which is in writing and signed by the person obligated and given to any county to secure repayment of indigent aid or the repayment of moneys fraudulently or illegally obtained from the county. *(Added by Stats.1951, c. 1106, p. 2863, § 1. Amended by Stats.1953, c. 655, p. 1906, § 1.)*

Research References

Forms

California Real Estate Forms (Miller & Starr) § 3:8, Deed Of Trust, Security Agreement, and Fixture Filing With Assignment Of Rents and Agreements.
California Real Estate Forms (Miller & Starr) § 3:14, Construction Deed Of Trust, Security Agreement, and Fixture Filing With Assignment Of Rents and Agreements.
Cal. Transaction Forms - Bus. Transactions § 22:9, Waiver and Extinguishment.
West's California Code Forms, Civil Procedure § 360.5 Form 1, Statute Of Limitations--Pleading--Waiver Of Defense.

Treatises and Practice Aids

Witkin, California Summary 10th Real Property § 338, Ancient Mortgages and Deeds Of Trust.

§ 361. Effect of limitation laws of other states

LIMITATION LAWS OF OTHER STATES, EFFECT OF. When a cause of action has arisen in another State, or in a foreign country, and by the laws thereof an action thereon cannot there be maintained against a person by reason of the lapse of time, an action thereon shall not be maintained against him in this State, except in favor of one who has been a citizen of this State, and who has held the cause of action from the time it accrued. *(Enacted in 1872.)*

Research References

Forms

West's California Code Forms, Civil Procedure § 361 Form 1, Statute Of Limitations--Pleading--Other States Laws--Tolling--Resident Plaintiff.

Treatises and Practice Aids

Witkin, California Summary 10th Torts § 192, Comparative Impairment Analysis.

§ 362. Exemption of existing causes of action

EXISTING CAUSES OF ACTION NOT AFFECTED. This Title does not extend to actions already commenced, nor to cases where the time prescribed in any existing statute for acquiring a right or barring a remedy has fully run, but the laws now in force are applicable to such actions and cases, and are repealed subject to the provisions of this section. *(Enacted in 1872.)*

§ 363. "Action" defined

The word "action" as used in this Title is to be construed, whenever it is necessary so to do, as including a special proceeding of a civil nature. *(Enacted in 1872, unpublished Act of 1872.)*

CHAPTER 5. THE COMMENCEMENT OF ACTIONS BASED UPON PROFESSIONAL NEGLIGENCE

Section

§ 364. Notice of intention; time; law governing; fictitious name; effect of failure to comply

(a) No action based upon the health care provider's professional negligence may be commenced unless the defendant has been given at least 90 days' prior notice of the intention to commence the action.

(b) No particular form of notice is required, but it shall notify the defendant of the legal basis of the claim and the type of loss sustained, including with specificity the nature of the injuries suffered.

(c) The notice may be served in the manner prescribed in Chapter 5 (commencing with Section 1010) of Title 14 of Part 2.

(d) If the notice is served within 90 days of the expiration of the applicable statute of limitations, the time for the commencement of the action shall be extended 90 days from the service of the notice.

(e) The provisions of this section shall not be applicable with respect to any defendant whose name is unknown to the plaintiff at the time of filing the complaint and who is identified therein by a fictitious name, as provided in Section 474.

(f) For the purposes of this section:

(1) "Health care provider" means any person licensed or certified pursuant to Division 2 (commencing with Section 500) of the Business and Professions Code, or licensed pursuant to the Osteopathic Initiative Act, or the Chiropractic Initiative Act, or licensed pursuant to Chapter 2.5 (commencing with Section 1440) of Division 2 of the Health and Safety Code; and any clinic, health dispensary, or health facility, licensed pursuant to Division 2 (commencing with Section 1200) of the Health and Safety Code. "Health care provider" includes the legal representatives of a health care provider;

(2) "Professional negligence" means negligent act or omission to act by a health care provider in the rendering of professional services, which act or omission is the proximate cause of a personal injury or wrongful death, provided that such services are within the scope of services for which the provider is licensed and which are not within any restriction imposed by the licensing agency or licensed hospital. *(Added by Stats.1975, 2nd Ex.Sess., c. 1, p. 3970, § 25.5. Amended by Stats.1975, 2nd Ex.Sess., c. 2, p. 3992, § 1.193, eff. Sept. 24, 1975, operative Dec. 15, 1975.)*

Research References

Forms

West's California Code Forms, Civil Procedure § 364 Form 1, Malpractice Actions--Notice Of Intention to File Suit.

West's California Code Forms, Civil Procedure § 340.5 Form 1, Statute Of Limitations--Pleading--Professional Negligence Of Healthcare Provider--Reasonable.

West's California Code Forms, Civil Procedure § 340.5 Form 3, Statute Of Limitations--Pleading--Professional Negligence Of Health Care Provider--Tolling--Fraud--Collusion.

West's California Code Forms, Insurance § 11587 Form 1, Request for Explanation Of Medical Malpractice Insurance Rate.

Treatises and Practice Aids

Witkin, California Summary 10th Torts § 934, Ordinary Versus Professional Negligence.

Witkin, California Summary 10th Torts § 953, in General.

Witkin, California Summary 10th Torts § 954, Extension Of Applicable Statute Of Limitations.

Witkin, California Summary 10th Torts § 955, Government Tort Claim is Not Notice Of Intent to Sue.

Witkin, California Summary 10th Torts § 965, Intentional Torts.

§ 365. Failure to comply with chapter; effect

Failure to comply with this chapter shall not invalidate any proceedings of any court of this state, nor shall it affect the jurisdiction of the court to render a judgment therein. However, failure to comply with such provisions by any attorney at law shall be grounds for professional discipline and the State Bar of California shall investigate and take appropriate action in any such cases brought to its attention. *(Added by Stats.1975, 2nd Ex.Sess., c. 1, p. 3970, § 25.5.)*

Research References

Treatises and Practice Aids

Witkin, California Summary 10th Torts § 953, in General.

Title 3

OF THE PARTIES TO CIVIL ACTIONS

CHAPTER 2. MARRIED PERSON

§ 370. Married persons

A married person may be sued without his or her spouse being joined as a party, and may sue without his or her spouse being joined as a party in all actions. *(Enacted in 1872. Amended by Code Am.1873–74, c. 383, p. 293, § 37; Stats. 1913, c. 130, p. 217, § 1; Stats.1921, c. 110, p. 102, § 1; Stats.1975, c. 1241, p. 3187, § 2.)*

Research References

Treatises and Practice Aids

Witkin, California Summary 10th Husband and Wife § 18, in General.

Witkin, California Summary 10th Torts § 725, Personal Injury to Spouse.

§ 371. Spouses sued together; defense by spouse

If spouses are sued together, each may defend for his or her own right, but if one spouse neglects to defend, the other spouse may defend for that spouse's right also. *(Enacted in 1872. Amended by Stats.1975, c. 1241, p. 3187, § 3; Stats. 2016, c. 50 (S.B.1005), § 15, eff. Jan. 1, 2017.)*

Research References

Treatises and Practice Aids

Witkin, California Summary 10th Husband and Wife § 18, in General.

CHAPTER 3. DISABILITY OF PARTY

§ 372. Minors, persons who lack legal capacity to make decisions, or persons for whom conservator appointed; appearance by guardian, conservator or guardian ad litem; powers; disposition of moneys recovered; waiver of juvenile law rights

(a)(1) When a minor, a person who lacks legal capacity to make decisions, or a person for whom a conservator has been appointed is a party, that person shall appear either by a guardian or conservator of the estate or by a guardian ad litem appointed by the court in which the action or proceeding is pending, or by a judge thereof, in each case. A guardian ad litem may be appointed in any case when it is deemed by the court in which the action or proceeding is prosecuted, or by a judge thereof, expedient to appoint a guardian ad litem to represent the minor, person lacking legal capacity to make decisions, or person for whom a conservator has been appointed, notwithstanding that the person may have a guardian or conservator of the estate and may have appeared by the guardian or conservator of the estate. The guardian or conservator of the estate or guardian ad litem so appearing for any minor, person who lacks legal capacity to make decisions, or person for whom a conservator has been appointed shall have power, with the approval of the court in which the action or proceeding is pending, to compromise the same, to agree to the order or judgment to be entered therein for or against the ward or conservatee, and to satisfy any judgment or order in favor of the ward or conservatee or release or discharge any claim of the ward or conservatee pursuant to that compromise. Money or other property to be paid or delivered pursuant to the order or judgment for the benefit of a minor, person lacking legal capacity to make decisions, or person for whom a conservator has been appointed shall be paid and delivered as provided in Chapter 4 (commencing with Section 3600) of Part 8 of Division 4 of the Probate Code.

(2) Where reference is made in this section to "a person lacking legal competence to make decisions," the reference shall be deemed to include "a person for whom a conservator may be appointed."

(3) Nothing in this section, or in any other provision of this code, the Civil Code, the Family Code, or the Probate Code is intended by the Legislature to prohibit a minor from exercising an intelligent and knowing waiver of his or her constitutional rights in a proceeding under the Juvenile Court Law, Chapter 2 (commencing with Section 200) of Part 1 of Division 2 of the Welfare and Institutions Code.

(b)(1) Notwithstanding subdivision (a), a minor 12 years of age or older may appear in court without a guardian, counsel, or guardian ad litem, for the purpose of requesting or opposing a request for any of the following:

(A) An injunction or temporary restraining order or both to prohibit harassment pursuant to Section 527.6.

(B) An injunction or temporary restraining order or both against violence or a credible threat of violence in the workplace pursuant to Section 527.8.

(C) A protective order pursuant to Division 10 (commencing with Section 6200) of the Family Code.

(D) A protective order pursuant to Sections 7710 and 7720 of the Family Code.

The court may, either upon motion or in its own discretion, and after considering reasonable objections by the minor to the appointment of specific individuals, appoint a guardian ad litem to assist the minor in obtaining or opposing the order, provided that the appointment of the guardian ad litem does not delay the issuance or denial of the order being sought. In making the determination concerning the appointment of a particular guardian ad litem, the court shall consider whether the minor and the guardian have divergent interests.

(2) For purposes of this subdivision only, upon the issuance of an order pursuant to paragraph (1), if the minor initially appeared in court seeking an order without a guardian or guardian ad litem, and if the minor is residing with a parent or guardian, the court shall send a copy of the order to at least one parent or guardian designated by the minor, unless, in the discretion of the court, notification of a parent or guardian would be contrary to the best interest of the minor. The court is not required to send the order to more than one parent or guardian.

(3) The Judicial Council shall adopt forms by July 1, 1999, to facilitate the appointment of a guardian ad litem pursuant to this subdivision.

(c)(1) Notwithstanding subdivision (a), a minor may appear in court without a guardian ad litem in the following proceedings if the minor is a parent of the child who is the subject of the proceedings:

(A) Family court proceedings pursuant to Part 3 (commencing with Section 7600) of Division 12 of the Family Code.

(B) Dependency proceedings pursuant to Chapter 2 (commencing with Section 200) of Part 1 of Division 2 of the Welfare and Institutions Code.

(C) Guardianship proceedings for a minor child pursuant to Part 2 (commencing with Section 1500) of Division 4 of the Probate Code.

(D) Any other proceedings concerning child custody, visitation, or support.

(2) If the court finds that the minor parent is unable to understand the nature of the proceedings or to assist counsel in preparing the case, the court shall, upon its own motion or upon a motion by the minor parent or the minor parent's counsel, appoint a guardian ad litem. *(Enacted in 1872. Amended by Code Am.1873–74, c. 383, p. 294, § 38; Code Am.1880, c. 68, p. 63, § 2; Stats.1913, c. 202, p. 350, § 1; Stats.1933, c. 744, p. 1837, § 1; Stats.1939, c. 313, p. 1599, § 1; Stats.1951, c. 1737, p. 4097, § 43; Stats.1953, c. 1315, p. 2873, § 1; Stats.1961, c. 721, p. 1962, § 1; Stats.1963, c. 127,*

p. 803, § 4; Stats.1967, c. 1259, p. 3046, § 1; Stats.1979, c. 730, p. 2476, § 19, operative Jan. 1, 1981; Stats.1994, c. 1269 (A.B.2208), § 2; Stats.1996, c. 727 (A.B.2155), § 2; Stats. 1998, c. 706 (S.B.326), § 1, eff. Sept. 22, 1998; Stats.2008, c. 181 (S.B.1612), § 1; Stats.2014, c. 144 (A.B.1847), § 5, eff. Jan. 1, 2015.)

Law Revision Commission Comments

1978 Amendment

Recommendations relating to Guardianship-Conservatorship Law 14 Cal.L.Rev.Comm. Reports 501 (1978).

1979 Amendment

Section 372 is amended to change the reference in Section 372 to former Section 1510 of the Probate Code to reflect the revision and recodification of that provision. Other technical revisions to Section 372 are also made.

1994 Amendment

Section 372 is amended to add a reference to the Family Code to reflect the fact that provisions concerning the capacity of minors have been moved from the Civil Code to the Family Code. This is a technical, nonsubstantive change. [24 Cal.L.Rev.Comm. Reports 621 (1994)].

Commentary

See generally *Caballero v. Caballero, 27 Cal.App.4th 1139, 33 Cal.Rptr.2d 46 (1994)*, which holds that family court has jurisdiction to appoint a guardian ad litem to seek a legal separation for an incompetent spouse.

In an action by a former husband against the guardian ad litem appointed by the court to represent him, *McClintock v. West, 219 Cal.App.4th 540, 162 Cal.Rptr.3d 61 (2013)*, held that the guardian ad litem acted as an officer of the court and was therefore protected by the doctrine of quasi-judicial immunity. Former husband's legal malpractice action against the guardian ad litem failed because there was no attorney-client relationship between the husband the guardian.

In re James F., 42 Cal.4th 901, 70 Cal.Rptr.3d 358, 174 P.3d 180 (2008), held that a juvenile court's failure to explain to a parent the nature of the court's appointment of a guardian ad litem for the parent was harmless error because the mentally incompetent father suffered no prejudice from the error. In light of its decision in *James F.*, the California Supreme Court dismissed a petition for review of *In re Jacklyn S.*, in which the superseded opinion of the court of appeal, 58 Cal.Rptr.3d 321 (2007), held that a juvenile court's error in appointing a guardian ad litem for a parent without explaining the consequences of the appointment was harmless error when the appointment did not deprive the parent of notice, the opportunity to state her case, or the opportunity to express her wishes to the juvenile court.

In re Emily R., 80 Cal.App.4th 1344, 96 Cal.Rptr.2d 285 (2000), holds that a juvenile court need not appoint a guardian ad litem for a minor alleged father who did not appear in a dependency proceeding. *Emily R.* reasoned that the minor was not a party to the dependency proceeding because he had not appeared and asserted a position. Until such appearance, he was merely an "interested person" entitled only to notice of the proceedings. *Emily R.* further held when the address of an alleged father is unknown and cannot be determined with due diligence, due process is satisfied by notice by publication.

In re M.F., 161 Cal.App.4th 673, 74 Cal.Rptr.3d 383 (2008), review denied, vacated an order terminating a mother's parental rights because the juvenile court failed to appoint a guardian ad litem for the minor mother of a dependent child until the termination of reunification services, thereby compromising the mother's rights at important points in the proceedings.

In re A.C., 166 Cal.App.4th 146, 82 Cal.Rptr.3d 542 (2008), review denied, held that failure to appoint, in a dependency proceeding, a guardian ad litem for a parent for whom a conservator had been appointed, did not in itself violate the parent's due process rights when he received notice of the proceedings, attended most of them, and was represented throughout the hearings by court-appointed counsel.

Research References

Forms

Cal. Transaction Forms - Bus. Transactions § 18:6, Capacity.

Cal. Transaction Forms - Bus. Transactions § 18:16, Settlements that Require Court Approval.

West's California Code Forms, Civil Procedure § 372 Form 4, Parties--Order Approving Compromise Of Claim--Official Form.

West's California Code Forms, Civil Procedure § 372 Form 8, Parties--Notice Of Motion for Order Appointing Guardian Ad Litem for Minor 12 Years or Older to Assist Minor in Obtaining Protective Order.

West's California Code Forms, Civil Procedure § 372 Form 10, Parties--Application for and Appointment Of Guardian Ad Litem for Minor--Official Form.

West's California Code Forms, Probate § 3500 Form 1, Petition by Parent to Compromise Disputed Personal Injury Claim Of Minor Without a Guardian Of the Estate--Judicial Council Form MC-350.

West's California Code Forms, Probate § 2500-2507 Form 1, Petition by Guardian or Conservator to Approve Compromise Of Disputed Personal Injury Claim Of Minor or Incompetent Person--Judicial Council Form MC-350.

West's California Judicial Council Forms MC-350, Petition to Approve Compromise Of Disputed Claim or Pending Action or Disposition Of Proceeds Of Judgment for Minor or Person With a Disability.

West's California Judicial Council Forms MC-351, Order Approving Compromise Of Disputed Claim or Pending Action or Disposition Of Proceeds Of Judgment for Minor or Adult Person With a Disability.

West's California Judicial Council Forms MC-355, Order to Deposit Money Into Blocked Account.

West's California Judicial Council Forms MC-356, Receipt and Acknowledgment Of Order for the Deposit Of Money Into Blocked Account.

West's California Judicial Council Forms CIV-010, Application and Order for Appointment Of Guardian Ad Litem--Civil.

West's California Judicial Council Forms MC-350EX, Expedited Petition to Approve Compromise Of Disputed Claim or Pending Action or Disposition Of Proceeds Of Judgment for Minor or Person With a Disability.

West's California Judicial Council Forms MC-350(A-13B(5)), Medical Service Provider Attachment to Petition to Approve Compromise Of Claim or Action or Disposition Of Proceeds Of Judgment.

Treatises and Practice Aids

Witkin, California Summary 10th Husband and Wife § 77, Standing Of Guardian or Conservator.

Witkin, California Summary 10th Husband and Wife § 146, Proceedings.

Witkin, California Summary 10th Husband and Wife § 379, in General.

Witkin, California Summary 10th Parent and Child § 572, Appointment Of Guardian Ad Litem or Child Advocate.

Witkin, California Summary 10th Parent and Child § 577, Hearing.

Witkin, California Summary 10th Real Property § 67, Parties.

Witkin, California Summary 10th Wills and Probate § 374, Guardian Ad Litem.

Witkin, California Summary 10th Wills and Probate § 1014, Procedure for Court Approval.

§ 373. Guardian ad litem; appointment procedure

When a guardian ad litem is appointed, he or she shall be appointed as follows:

(a) If the minor is the plaintiff the appointment must be made before the summons is issued, upon the application of the minor, if the minor is 14 years of age or older, or, if under that age, upon the application of a relative or friend of the minor.

(b) If the minor is the defendant, upon the application of the minor, if the minor is 14 years of age or older, and the minor applies within 10 days after the service of the summons, or, if under that age or if the minor neglects to apply, then upon the application of a relative or friend of the minor, or of any other party to the action, or by the court on its own motion.

(c) If the person lacking legal competence to make decisions is a party to an action or proceeding, upon the application of a relative or friend of the person lacking legal competence to make decisions, or of any other party to the action or proceeding, or by the court on its own motion. *(Enacted in 1872. Amended by Code Am.1880, c. 68, p. 63, § 3; Stats.1933, c. 744, p. 1837, § 2; Stats.1971, c. 755, p. 1501, § 1; Stats.1980, c. 676, p. 1905, § 64; Stats.2014, c. 144 (A.B.1847), § 6, eff. Jan. 1, 2015.)*

Research References

Forms

California Transactions Forms--Family Law § 6:11, Initiating Proceeding Under Uniform Parentage Act [Fam C §§ 7600 to 7730].

West's California Code Forms, Civil Procedure § 373 Form 3, Parties--Petition for Appointment Of Guardian Ad Litem--Application by Minor.

West's California Code Forms, Civil Procedure § 116.410 Form 1, Small Claims Court--Order Appointing Guardian Ad Litem--Minor Under 14 Years.

West's California Judicial Council Forms FL-935, Application for and Appointment Of Guardian Ad Litem Of Minor--Family Law.

West's California Judicial Council Forms ADOPT-330, Request for Appointment Of Confidential Intermediary.

§ 373.5. Guardian ad litem; persons not ascertained, not in being or unknown; powers; expenses

If under the terms of a written instrument, or otherwise, a person or persons of a designated class who are not ascertained or who are not in being, or a person or persons who are unknown, may be or may become legally or equitably interested in any property, real or personal, the court in which any action, petition or proceeding of any kind relative to or affecting the property is pending, may, upon the representation of any party thereto, or of any person interested, appoint a suitable person to appear and act therein as guardian ad litem of the person or persons not ascertained, not in being, or who are unknown; and the judgment, order or decree in the proceedings, made after the appointment, shall be conclusive upon all persons for whom the guardian ad litem was appointed.

The guardian ad litem shall have power, with the approval of the court in which the action, petition or proceeding is pending, to compromise the same, to agree to the order or judgment to be entered therein for or against the persons for whom the guardian ad litem was appointed, and to satisfy any judgment or order in favor of the persons, or release, or discharge any claim of the persons pursuant to the compromise. The court shall have the same power with respect to the money or other property to be paid or delivered under such order or judgment as is provided in Section 372 of this code.

The reasonable expenses of the guardian ad litem, including compensation and counsel fees, shall be determined by the court and paid as it may order, either out of the property or by plaintiff or petitioner. If the expenses are to be paid by the plaintiff or petitioner, execution therefor may issue in the name of the guardian ad litem. *(Added by Stats.1949, c. 511, p. 869, § 1. Amended by Stats.1957, c. 976, p. 2217, § 1; Stats.1961, c. 435, p. 1503, § 1.)*

Research References

Treatises and Practice Aids

Witkin, California Summary 10th Trusts § 205, in General.

§ 374. Minor under age 12; appearance without counsel when accompanied by guardian ad litem; conditions

(a) A minor under 12 years of age, accompanied by a duly appointed and acting guardian ad litem, shall be permitted to appear in court without counsel for the limited purpose of requesting or opposing a request for (1) an injunction or temporary restraining order or both to prohibit harassment pursuant to Section 527.6, (2) an injunction or temporary restraining order or both against violence or a credible threat of violence in the workplace pursuant to Section 527.8, (3) a protective order pursuant to Division 10 (commencing with Section 6200) of the Family Code, or (4) a protective order pursuant to Sections 7710 and 7720 of the Family Code.

(b) In making the determination concerning appointment of a particular guardian ad litem for purposes of this section, the court shall consider whether the minor and the guardian have divergent interests.

(c) The Judicial Council shall adopt forms by July 1, 1999, to implement this section. The forms shall be designed to facilitate the appointment of the guardian ad litem for purposes of this section. *(Added by Stats.1998, c. 706 (S.B.326), § 2, eff. Sept. 22, 1998.)*

Research References

Treatises and Practice Aids

Witkin, California Summary 10th Husband and Wife § 373, in General.

Witkin, California Summary 10th Real Property § 122, Parties to Enforcement.

§ 374.5. Orders affecting minors; jurisdiction

A proceeding initiated by or brought against a minor for any of the injunctions or orders described in paragraph (1) of subdivision (b) of Section 372 or subdivision (a) of Section 374 shall be heard in the court assigned to hear those matters; except that, if the minor bringing the action or against whom the action is brought has previously been adjudged a dependent child or a ward of the juvenile court, the matter shall be heard in the juvenile court having jurisdiction over the minor. *(Added by Stats.1998, c. 706 (S.B.326), § 3, eff. Sept. 22, 1998.)*

§ 375. Disability of party; effect on action

An action or proceeding does not abate by the disability of a party. The court, on motion, shall allow the action or proceeding to be continued by or against the party's representative. *(Added by Stats.1992, c. 178 (S.B.1496), § 17.)*

Law Revision Commission Comments

1992 Addition

Section 375 restates part of former Section 385, but makes clear that substitution of the representative of a disabled person is mandatory rather than permissive. [22 Cal.L.Rev.Comm.Reports 895 (1992)].

Research References

Forms

Am. Jur. Pl. & Pr. Forms Parties § 196, Introductory Comments.
Am. Jur. Pl. & Pr. Forms Parties § 243, Introductory Comments.
West's California Code Forms, Civil § 49 Form 1, Complaint for Abduction Of Child.

§ 376. Parents; injuries to child; failure of one parent to join as plaintiff; service on parent not joining; illegitimate child; ward; parties defendant; death of child or ward; damages; consolidation of injury and death action

(a) The parents of a legitimate unmarried minor child, acting jointly, may maintain an action for injury to the child caused by the wrongful act or neglect of another. If either parent fails on demand to join as plaintiff in the action or is dead or cannot be found, then the other parent may maintain the action. The parent, if living, who does not join as plaintiff shall be joined as a defendant and, before trial or hearing of any question of fact, shall be served with summons either in the manner provided by law for the service of a summons in a civil action or by sending a copy of the summons and complaint by registered mail with proper postage prepaid addressed to that parent's last known address with request for a return receipt. If service is made by registered mail, the production of a return receipt purporting to be signed by the addressee creates a rebuttable presumption that the summons and complaint have been duly served. The presumption established by this section is a presumption affecting the burden of producing evidence. The respective rights of the parents to any award shall be determined by the court.

(b) A parent may maintain an action for such an injury to his or her illegitimate unmarried minor child if a guardian has not been appointed. Where a parent who does not have care, custody, or control of the child brings the action, the parent who has care, custody, or control of the child shall be served with the summons either in the manner provided by law for the serving of a summons in a civil action or by sending a copy of the summons and complaint by registered mail, with proper postage prepaid, addressed to the last known address of that parent, with request for a return receipt. If service is made by registered mail, the production of a return receipt purporting to be signed by the addressee creates a rebuttable presumption that the summons and complaint have been duly served. The presumption established by this section is a presumption affecting the burden of producing evidence. The respective rights of the parents to any award shall be determined by the court.

(c) The father of an illegitimate child who maintains an action under this section shall have acknowledged in writing prior to the child's injury, in the presence of a competent witness, that he is the father of the child, or, prior to the child's injury, have been judicially determined to be the father of the child.

(d) A parent of an illegitimate child who does not maintain an action under this section may be joined as a party thereto.

(e) A guardian may maintain an action for such an injury to his or her ward.

(f) An action under this section may be maintained against the person causing the injury. If any other person is responsible for the wrongful act or neglect, the action may also be maintained against the other person. The death of the child or ward does not abate the parents' or guardian's cause of action for the child's injury as to damages accruing before the child's death.

(g) In an action under this section, damages may be awarded that, under all of the circumstances of the case, may be just, except that:

(1) In an action maintained after the death of the child, the damages recoverable are as provided in Section 377.34.

(2) Where the person causing the injury is deceased, the damages recoverable in an action against the decedent's personal representative are as provided in Section 377.42.

(h) If an action arising out of the same wrongful act or neglect may be maintained pursuant to Section 377.60 for wrongful death of a child described in this section, the action authorized by this section may be consolidated therewith for trial as provided in Section 1048. *(Enacted in 1872. Amended by Code Am.1873–74, c. 383, p. 294, § 39; Stats.1939, 1939, c. 425, p. 1759, § 1; Stats.1949, c. 1380, p. 2400, § 3; Stats.1961, c. 657, p. 1868, § 4; Stats.1969, c. 1611, p. 3378, § 4, operative July 1, 1970; Stats.1975, c. 1241, p. 3187, § 4; Stats.1992, c. 178 (S.B.1496), § 18.)*

Law Revision Commission Comments

1992 Amendment

Section 376 is revised to correct cross-references, to add subdivision letters to the existing paragraphs, and to improve the wording. The word "ward" in subdivision (g)(1) has been omitted as surplus; this is a technical, nonsubstantive change.

Subdivision (h) is revised for consistency with Section 377.62. [22 Cal.L.Rev.Comm.Reports 895 (1992)].

Research References

Forms

West's California Code Forms, Civil Procedure § 376 Form 3, Parties--Notice Of Motion to Consolidate.

Treatises and Practice Aids

Witkin, California Summary 10th Torts § 23, Survival Of Tort Liability.

Witkin, California Summary 10th Torts § 726, Action by Parents.

CHAPTER 4. EFFECT OF DEATH

ARTICLE 6. WRONGFUL DEATH

§ 377.60. Persons with standing

A cause of action for the death of a person caused by the wrongful act or neglect of another may be asserted by any of the following persons or by the decedent's personal representative on their behalf:

(a) The decedent's surviving spouse, domestic partner, children, and issue of deceased children, or, if there is no surviving issue of the decedent, the persons, including the surviving spouse or domestic partner, who would be entitled to the property of the decedent by intestate succession.

(b) Whether or not qualified under subdivision (a), if they were dependent on the decedent, the putative spouse, children of the putative spouse, stepchildren, or parents. As used in this subdivision, "putative spouse" means the surviving spouse of a void or voidable marriage who is found by the court to have believed in good faith that the marriage to the decedent was valid.

(c) A minor, whether or not qualified under subdivision (a) or (b), if, at the time of the decedent's death, the minor resided for the previous 180 days in the decedent's household and was dependent on the decedent for one-half or more of the minor's support.

(d) This section applies to any cause of action arising on or after January 1, 1993.

(e) The addition of this section by Chapter 178 of the Statutes of 1992 was not intended to adversely affect the standing of any party having standing under prior law, and the standing of parties governed by that version of this section as added by Chapter 178 of the Statutes of 1992 shall be the same as specified herein as amended by Chapter 563 of the Statutes of 1996.

(f)(1) For the purpose of this section, "domestic partner" means a person who, at the time of the decedent's death, was the domestic partner of the decedent in a registered domestic partnership established in accordance with subdivision (b) of Section 297 of the Family Code.

(2) Notwithstanding paragraph (1), for a death occurring prior to January 1, 2002, a person may maintain a cause of action pursuant to this section as a domestic partner of the decedent by establishing the factors listed in paragraphs (1) to (6), inclusive, of subdivision (b) of Section 297 of the Family Code, as it read pursuant to Section 3 of Chapter 893 of the Statutes of 2001, prior to its becoming inoperative on January 1, 2005.

(3) The amendments made to this subdivision during the 2003–04 Regular Session of the Legislature are not intended to revive any cause of action that has been fully and finally adjudicated by the courts, or that has been settled, or as to which the applicable limitations period has run. *(Added by Stats.1992, c. 178 (S.B.1496), § 20. Amended by Stats.1996, c. 563 (S.B.392), § 1; Stats.1997, c. 13 (S.B.449), § 1, eff. May 23, 1997; Stats.2001, c. 893 (A.B.25), § 2; Stats.2004, c. 947 (A.B.2580), § 1.)*

Law Revision Commission Comments

1992 Addition

Section 377.60 restates subdivision (b) and the first part of the first sentence of subdivision (a) of former Section 377 without substantive change, except as discussed below. If the wrongdoer dies before or after the decedent, the cause of action provided in this section may be asserted against the personal representative of the wrongdoer. See Sections 377.20 (survival of cause of action), 377.40 (assertion of cause of action against decedent). See also Prob.Code § 6400 *et seq.* (intestate succession). Unlike other provisions of this chapter that relate to causes of action belonging to the decedent, this article relates to a cause of action for the decedent's wrongful death, which belongs not to the decedent, but to the persons specified in this section. Thus, the cause of action is not property in the estate of the decedent, and the authority of the personal representative to assert the cause of action is for administrative convenience only and is not for the benefit of creditors or other persons interested in the decedent's estate.

Subdivision (a) revises the language of former Section 377(b)(1) to refer specifically to the decedent's surviving spouse, children, and issue of deceased children, as proper parties plaintiff in a wrongful death action. This makes clear that, even if the decedent's estate is entirely community property, the decedent's children and issue of deceased children are proper parties plaintiff, along with the decedent's surviving spouse. This codifies Fiske v. Wilkie, 67 Cal.App.2d 440, 444, 154 P.2d 725 (1945). Under Probate Code Section 258, Section 377.60 is subject to the rules relating to the effect of homicide. This changes the rule of Marks v. Lyerla, 1 Cal.App.4th 556, 2 Cal.Rptr.2d 63 (1991).

For background, see *Standing To Sue for Wrongful Death,* 22 Cal.L.Revision Comm'n Reports 955 (1992). [22 Cal.L.Rev.Comm.Reports 895 (1992)].

Commentary

The requirements for claiming putative spouse status under subsection (b) are discussed in the commentary to Family Code §§ 300 and 2251.

Rosales v. Battle, 113 Cal.App.4th 1178, 7 Cal.Rptr.3d 13 (2003), review denied, holds that a surviving female companion, with whom decedent lived and had children in Mexico and who was legally characterized as his "concubine" under Mexican law, lacked standing to sue under this section because she was neither a surviving spouse nor an heir within the meaning of this section. She was not a "surviving spouse" because, under Mexican law, a concubine does not have *all* the rights and duties of a legal spouse. Although a concubine is an heir under Mexican law, she is not a person "entitled to the property of decedent by intestate succession" under California law. Effectively, *Rosales* interprets subsection (a) to refer only to the intestate succession law of California.

See *Smallwood v. American Trading & Transp. Co., 868 F.Supp. 280 (N.D.Cal.1995)* (children who lived with decedent, but who were unrelated to him and received less than one-half their support from him, had no claim under California wrongful death statute).

A father who has acknowledged and supported a child born out of wedlock may bring a wrongful death action because he is a person who would be entitled to take the deceased child's property by intestate succession (see Probate Code § 6452). *Lozano v. Scalier, 51 Cal.App.4th 843, 59 Cal.Rptr.2d 346 (1996).*

Interpreting Probate Code Section 6453, which limits application of the Uniform Parentage Act (Family Code Sections 7600–7730) to establish paternity when a putative father is deceased, *Cheyanna M. v. A.C. Nielsen Co., 66 Cal.App.4th 855, 78 Cal.Rptr.2d 335 (1998),* holds that a posthumous child has standing to sue for the wrongful death of the child's biological father if the child can establish paternity through clear and convincing evidence. In other words, *Cheyanna M.* restricts the definition of "child" for purposes of Probate Code Section 6453 (b)(3) to children who are already born at the father's death; thus by definition it is impossible for a father to have held a posthumous child out as his own. *Cheyanna M.* invokes Civil Code Section 43.1, which seeks to advance the interests of unborn children who are ultimately born, as support for its holding.

Phraner v. Cote Mart, Inc., 55 Cal.App.4th 166, 63 Cal.Rptr.2d 740 (1997), review denied August 27, 1997, holds that a child adopted away from her biological mother is not a "child" of the biological mother for purposes of this section even though the child and biological mother maintained a social relationship. Similarly, *Jackson v. Fitzgibbons, 127 Cal.App.4th 329, 25 Cal.Rptr.3d 478 (2005),* holds that a child lacks standing to bring a wrongful death action for the death of a parent when a juvenile court has terminated the parental rights of the child's parents.

Holding that subsection (f)(2) is constitutional, *Armijo v. Miles, 127 Cal.App.4th 1405, 26 Cal.Rptr.3d 623 (2005), review denied,* and *Bouley v. Long Beach Memorial Medical Center, 127 Cal.App.4th 601, 25 Cal.Rptr.3d 813 (2005),* allow an unregistered domestic partner to file a claim for the 2001 wrongful death of her partner.

Research References

Forms

California Transactions Forms--Family Law § 4:13, Surviving Cohabitant's Right to Sue for Wrongful Death, Loss Of Consortium, and Emotional Distress.
Am. Jur. Pl. & Pr. Forms Products Liability § 247.10. Complaint in Federal Court--Against Municipal Corporation and Police Officers--For Death; Survival Action; Deprivation Of Rights to Familial Relationships With Decedent; Cal. Civ. Code S52.1...
West's California Code Forms, Civil Procedure § 377.60 Form 1, Parties--Complaint--Wrongful Death Of Minor.
West's California Code Forms, Civil Procedure § 377.60 Form 2, Parties--Complaint--Wrongful Death Of Domestic Partner.

Treatises and Practice Aids

Witkin, California Summary 10th Husband and Wife § 33, Other Rights.
Witkin, California Summary 10th Torts § 948, Persons Who Did Not Sign: In General.
Witkin, California Summary 10th Torts § 1378, in General.
Witkin, California Summary 10th Torts § 1381, Scope Of Action.
Witkin, California Summary 10th Torts § 1382, No Action for Death Of Unborn Child.
Witkin, California Summary 10th Torts § 1385, in General.
Witkin, California Summary 10th Torts § 1389, Listed Persons Under Current Law.
Witkin, California Summary 10th Torts § 1390, Putative Spouse.
Witkin, California Summary 10th Torts § 1391, Domestic Partner.
Witkin, California Summary 10th Torts § 1393, Child Of Presumed Parent.
Witkin, California Summary 10th Torts § 1394, Other Persons.
Witkin, California Summary 10th Torts § 1397, Other Persons.
Witkin, California Summary 10th Torts § 1513, Physical Injury or Wrongful Death.
Witkin, California Summary 10th Torts § 1661, Wrongful Death.
Witkin, California Summary 10th Torts § 1683, No Recovery by Child.
Witkin, California Summary 10th Torts § 1690, Recovery Of Loss.
Witkin, California Summary 10th Wills and Probate § 521, Wrongful Death.
Witkin, California Summary 10th Workers' Compensation § 69, in General.

Title 3A

VEXATIOUS LITIGANTS

§ 391. Definitions

As used in this title, the following terms have the following meanings:

(a) "Litigation" means any civil action or proceeding, commenced, maintained or pending in any state or federal court.

(b) "Vexatious litigant" means a person who does any of the following:

(1) In the immediately preceding seven-year period has commenced, prosecuted, or maintained in propria persona at least five litigations other than in a small claims court that have been (i) finally determined adversely to the person or (ii) unjustifiably permitted to remain pending at least two years without having been brought to trial or hearing.

(2) After a litigation has been finally determined against the person, repeatedly relitigates or attempts to relitigate, in propria persona, either (i) the validity of the determination against the same defendant or defendants as to whom the litigation was finally determined or (ii) the cause of action, claim, controversy, or any of the issues of fact or law, determined or concluded by the final determination against the same defendant or defendants as to whom the litigation was finally determined.

(3) In any litigation while acting in propria persona, repeatedly files unmeritorious motions, pleadings, or other papers, conducts unnecessary discovery, or engages in other tactics that are frivolous or solely intended to cause unnecessary delay.

(4) Has previously been declared to be a vexatious litigant by any state or federal court of record in any action or proceeding based upon the same or substantially similar facts, transaction, or occurrence.

(c) "Security" means an undertaking to assure payment, to the party for whose benefit the undertaking is required to be furnished, of the party's reasonable expenses, including attorney's fees and not limited to taxable costs, incurred in or in connection with a litigation instituted, caused to be instituted, or maintained or caused to be maintained by a vexatious litigant.

(d) "Plaintiff" means the person who commences, institutes or maintains a litigation or causes it to be commenced, instituted or maintained, including an attorney at law acting in propria persona.

(e) "Defendant" means a person (including corporation, association, partnership and firm or governmental entity) against whom a litigation is brought or maintained or sought to be brought or maintained. *(Added by Stats.1963, c. 1471, p. 3088, § 1. Amended by Stats.1982, c. 517, p. 2335, § 98; Stats.1990, c. 621 (S.B.2675), § 1; Stats.1994, c. 587 (A.B. 3600), § 3.5.)*

Law Revision Commission Comments

1982 Amendment

Section 391 is amended to delete a provision duplicated in the Bond and Undertaking Law. See Section 995.710 (deposit in lieu of undertaking). The other changes in Section 391 are technical. [16 Cal.L.Rev.Comm. Reports 501 (1982)].

Commentary

A father of a child in long-term foster care, who sought to appeal from an order in a dependency proceeding and who had in 7 years brought at least 13 appeals or writ proceedings, all of which were decided against him, should be designated, under subsection (b)(1), a vexatious litigant and, under section 391.7, should be subject to a prefiling order, which an appellate court has authority to issue. *In re R.H., 170 Cal.App.4th 678, 88 Cal.Rptr.3d 650 (2009), review denied.*

Research References

Forms

West's California Code Forms, Civil Procedure § 391.7 Form 8, Vexatious Litigants--Prefiling Order--Official Form.

West's California Code Forms, Civil Procedure § 391.1 Form 1, Vexatious Litigants--Security for Costs--Notice Of Motion.

West's California Code Forms, Civil Procedure § 391.3 Form 1, Vexatious Litigants--Order for Deposit Of Security.

West's California Code Forms, Civil Procedure § 391.7 Form 1, Vexatious Litigants--Notice Of Motion for Prefiling Order Preventing Vexatious Litigant from Filing New Lawsuit Without Court Permission.

West's California Code Forms, Civil Procedure § 391.7 Form 3, Vexatious Litigants--Prefiling Order Preventing Vexatious Litigant from Filing New Lawsuit Without Court Permission.

West's California Code Forms, Civil Procedure § 389(B) Form 1, Parties--Order Dismissing Action Without Prejudice.

Treatises and Practice Aids

Witkin, California Summary 10th Constitutional Law § 792, Vexatious Litigant in Pro. Per.

Witkin, California Summary 10th Husband and Wife § 5, Generally Applicable Procedures.

Witkin, California Summary 10th Wills and Probate § 931, Vexatious Litigants.

Witkin, California Summary 10th Wills and Probate § 959A, (New) Vexatious Litigants.

§ 391.1. Motion for order requiring security; grounds

In any litigation pending in any court of this state, at any time until final judgment is entered, a defendant may move the court, upon notice and hearing, for an order requiring the plaintiff to furnish security or for an order dismissing the litigation pursuant to subdivision (b) of Section 391.3. The motion for an order requiring the plaintiff to furnish security shall be based upon the ground, and supported by a showing, that the plaintiff is a vexatious litigant and that there is not a reasonable probability that he or she will prevail in the litigation against the moving defendant. *(Added by Stats. 1963, c. 1471, p. 3038, § 1. Amended by Stats.1975, c. 381, p. 855, § 1; Stats.1990, c. 621 (S.B.2675), § 2; Stats.2012, c. 417 (A.B.2274), § 1.)*

Research References

Forms

West's California Code Forms, Civil Procedure § 391.1 Form 1, Vexatious Litigants--Security for Costs--Notice Of Motion.

§ 391.2. Scope of hearing; ruling not deemed determination of issues

At the hearing upon the motion the court shall consider any evidence, written or oral, by witnesses or affidavit, as may be material to the ground of the motion. Except for an order dismissing the litigation pursuant to subdivision (b) of Section 391.3, no determination made by the court in determining or ruling upon the motion shall be or be deemed to be a determination of any issue in the litigation or of the merits thereof. *(Added by Stats.1963, c. 1471, p. 3038, § 1. Amended by Stats.2012, c. 417 (A.B.2274), § 2.)*

§ 391.3. Order to furnish security; amount; dismissal of litigation

(a) Except as provided in subdivision (b), if, after hearing the evidence upon the motion, the court determines that the plaintiff is a vexatious litigant and that there is no reasonable probability that the plaintiff will prevail in the litigation against the moving defendant, the court shall order the plaintiff to furnish, for the benefit of the moving defendant, security in such amount and within such time as the court shall fix.

(b) If, after hearing evidence on the motion, the court determines that the litigation has no merit and has been filed for the purposes of harassment or delay, the court shall order the litigation dismissed. This subdivision shall only apply to litigation filed in a court of this state by a vexatious litigant subject to a prefiling order pursuant to Section 391.7 who was represented by counsel at the time the litigation was filed and who became in propria persona after the withdrawal of his or her attorney.

(c) A defendant may make a motion for relief in the alternative under either subdivision (a) or (b) and shall combine all grounds for relief in one motion. *(Added by Stats.1963, c. 1471, p. 3038, § 1. Amended by Stats.1982, c. 517, p. 2335, § 99; Stats.2012, c. 417 (A.B.2274), § 3.)*

Law Revision Commission Comments

1982 Amendment

Section 391.3 is amended to delete a provision duplicated in the Bond and Undertaking Law. See Sections 996.010 (undertaking in action or proceeding) and 996.030 (reduced undertaking). [16 Cal.L.Rev.Comm. Reports 501 (1982)].

§ 391.4. Dismissal for failure to furnish security

When security that has been ordered furnished is not furnished as ordered, the litigation shall be dismissed as to the defendant for whose benefit it was ordered furnished. *(Added by Stats.1963, c. 1471, p. 3038, § 1.)*

Research References

Forms

West's California Code Forms, Civil Procedure § 391.4 Form 1, Vexatious Litigants--Declaration for Dismissal Of Action.

Treatises and Practice Aids

§ 391.6. Stay of proceedings

Except as provided in subdivision (b) of Section 391.3, when a motion pursuant to Section 391.1 is filed prior to trial the litigation is stayed, and the moving defendant need not plead, until 10 days after the motion shall have been denied, or if granted, until 10 days after the required security has been furnished and the moving defendant given written notice thereof. When a motion pursuant to Section 391.1 is made at any time thereafter, the litigation shall be stayed for such period after the denial of the motion or the furnishing of the required security as the court shall determine. *(Added by Stats.1963, c. 1471, p. 3038, § 1. Amended by Stats.1975, c. 381, p. 855, § 2; Stats.2012, c. 417 (A.B.2274), § 4.)*

§ 391.7. Prefiling order prohibiting the filing of new litigation; contempt; conditions

(a) In addition to any other relief provided in this title, the court may, on its own motion or the motion of any party, enter a prefiling order which prohibits a vexatious litigant from filing any new litigation in the courts of this state in propria persona without first obtaining leave of the presiding justice or presiding judge of the court where the litigation is proposed to be filed. Disobedience of the order by a vexatious litigant may be punished as a contempt of court.

(b) The presiding justice or presiding judge shall permit the filing of that litigation only if it appears that the litigation has merit and has not been filed for the purposes of harassment or delay. The presiding justice or presiding judge may condition the filing of the litigation upon the furnishing of security for the benefit of the defendants as provided in Section 391.3.

(c) The clerk may not file any litigation presented by a vexatious litigant subject to a prefiling order unless the vexatious litigant first obtains an order from the presiding justice or presiding judge permitting the filing. If the clerk mistakenly files the litigation without the order, any party may file with the clerk and serve, or the presiding justice or presiding judge may direct the clerk to file and serve, on the plaintiff and other parties a notice stating that the plaintiff is a vexatious litigant subject to a prefiling order as set forth in subdivision (a). The filing of the notice shall automatically stay the litigation. The litigation shall be automatically dismissed unless the plaintiff within 10 days of the filing of that notice obtains an order from the presiding justice or presiding judge permitting the filing of the litigation as set forth in subdivision (b). If the presiding justice or presiding judge issues an order permitting the filing, the stay of the litigation shall remain in effect, and the defendants need not plead, until 10 days after the defendants are served with a copy of the order.

(d) For purposes of this section, "litigation" includes any petition, application, or motion other than a discovery motion, in a proceeding under the Family Code or Probate Code, for any order.

(e) The presiding justice or presiding judge of a court may designate a justice or judge of the same court to act on his or her behalf in exercising the authority and responsibilities provided under subdivisions (a) to (c), inclusive.

(f) The clerk of the court shall provide the Judicial Council a copy of any prefiling orders issued pursuant to subdivision (a). The Judicial Council shall maintain a record of vexatious litigants subject to those prefiling orders and shall annually disseminate a list of those persons to the clerks of the courts of this state. *(Added by Stats.1990, c. 621 (S.B.2675), § 3. Amended by Stats.2002, c. 1118 (A.B.1938), § 1; Stats.2011, c. 49 (S.B.731), § 1.)*

Commentary

A father of a child in long-term foster care, who sought to appeal from an order in a dependency proceeding and who had in 7 years brought at least 13 appeals or writ proceedings, all of which were decided against him, should be designated a vexatious litigant and should be subject to a prefiling order under this section, which order an appellate court has authority to issue. *In re R.H., 170 Cal.App.4th 678, 88 Cal.Rptr.3d 650 (2009), review denied.*

In re Marriage of Falcone & Fyke, 203 Cal.App.4th 964, 138 Cal.Rptr.3d 44 (2012), affirmed a trial court order awarding attorney fees, costs, and sanctions against a wife for taking a meritless appeal from a sanctions order and for misconduct in trying to obtain a trial continuance. *Falcone & Fyke* also found that the wife, who had previously filed at least 11 nonmeritorious appeals, was a vexatious litigant within the meaning of this section.

Research References

Forms

West's California Code Forms, Civil Procedure § 391.7 Form 3, Vexatious Litigants--Prefiling Order Preventing Vexatious Litigant from Filing New Lawsuit Without Court Permission.
West's California Code Forms, Civil Procedure § 391.7 Form 5, Vexatious Litigants--Notice Of Motion for Vexatious Litigant to File New Lawsuit.
West's California Code Forms, Civil Procedure § 391.7 Form 8, Vexatious Litigants--Prefiling Order--Official Form.
West's California Judicial Council Forms MC-700, Prefiling Order--Vexatious Litigant.
West's California Judicial Council Forms MC-701, Request to File New Litigation by Vexatious Litigant.
West's California Judicial Council Forms MC-702, Order to File New Litigation by Vexatious Litigant.

§ 391.8. Filing application to vacate prefiling order and remove name from Judicial Council's list

(a) A vexatious litigant subject to a prefiling order under Section 391.7 may file an application to vacate the prefiling order and remove his or her name from the Judicial Council's list of vexatious litigants subject to prefiling orders. The application shall be filed in the court that entered the prefiling order, either in the action in which the prefiling order was entered or in conjunction with a request to the presiding justice or presiding judge to file new litigation under Section 391.7. The application shall be made before the justice or judge who entered the order, if that justice or judge is available. If that justice or judge who entered the order is not available, the application shall be made before the presiding justice or presiding judge, or his or her designee.

(b) A vexatious litigant whose application under subdivision (a) was denied shall not be permitted to file another application on or before 12 months has elapsed after the date of the denial of the previous application.

(c) A court may vacate a prefiling order and order removal of a vexatious litigant's name from the Judicial Council's list of vexatious litigants subject to prefiling orders upon a showing of a material change in the facts upon which the order was granted and that the ends of justice would be served by vacating the order. *(Added by Stats.2011, c. 49 (S.B.731), § 2.)*

Research References

Forms

West's California Code Forms, Civil Procedure § 391.7 Form 9, Vexatious Litigants--Request to File New Litigation by Vexatious Litigant--Official Form.

West's California Judicial Council Forms MC-703, Application for Order to Vacate Prefiling Order and Remove Plaintiff/Petitioner from Judicial Council Vexatious Litigant List.

West's California Judicial Council Forms MC-704, Order on Application to Vacate Prefiling Order and Remove Plaintiff/Petitioner from Judicial Council Vexatious Litigant List.

Title 4

OF THE PLACE OF TRIAL, RECLASSIFICATION, AND COORDINATION OF CIVIL ACTIONS

CHAPTER 1. PLACE OF TRIAL

§ 392. Real property actions; proper court

(a) Subject to the power of the court to transfer actions and proceedings as provided in this title, the superior court in the county where the real property that is the subject of the action, or some part thereof, is situated, is the proper court for the trial of the following actions:

(1) For the recovery of real property, or of an estate or interest therein, or for the determination in any form, of that right or interest, and for injuries to real property.

(2) For the foreclosure of all liens and mortgages on real property.

(b) In the court designated as the proper court in subdivision (a), the proper court location for trial of a proceeding for an unlawful detainer, as defined in Section 1161, is the location where the court tries that type of proceeding that is nearest or most accessible to where the real property that is the subject of the action, or some part thereof, is situated. Otherwise any location of the superior court designated as the proper court in subdivision (a) is a proper court location for the trial. The court may specify by local rule the nearest or most accessible court location where the court tries that type of case. *(Enacted in 1872. Amended by Code Am.1875–76, c. 117, p. 90, § 1; Stats.1889, c. 342, p. 352, § 1; Stats.1907, c. 369, p. 700, § 1; Stats.1933, c. 744, p. 1837, § 3; Stats.1951, c. 869, p. 2383, § 1; Stats.1976, c. 73, p. 110, § 3; Stats.1998, c. 931 (S.B.2139), § 60, eff. Sept. 28, 1998; Stats.2002, c. 806 (A.B.3027), § 7.)*

Law Revision Commission Comments

1976 Amendment

Recommendations relating to partition of real and personal property. 13 Cal.L.Rev.Comm. Reports 401 (1975), 1691 (1976).

1998 Amendment

Section 392 is amended to reflect the elimination of the justice court. Cal. Const. art. VI, §§ 1, 5(b). In a county in which there is no municipal court, the superior court has jurisdiction of matters that would be within the subject matter jurisdiction of the municipal court. Cal. Const. art. VI, 10 (superior court jurisdiction); Code Civ. Proc. §§ 85, 85.1 (limited civil cases). [28 Cal.L.Rev.Comm. Reports 51 (1998)].

Research References

Forms

Am. Jur. Pl. & Pr. Forms Venue § 1, Introductory Comments.

Treatises and Practice Aids

Witkin, California Summary 10th Real Property § 728, Jurisdiction, Venue, and Process.

Witkin, California Summary 10th Trusts § 225, Venue.

§ 394. Actions by or against a city, county, city and county, or local agency; transfer of cases; proper court

(a) An action or proceeding against a county, or city and county, a city, or local agency, may be tried in the county, or city and county, or the county in which the city or local agency is situated, unless the action or proceeding is brought by a county, or city and county, a city, or local agency, in which case it may be tried in any county, or city and county, not a party thereto and in which the city or local agency is not situated. Except for actions initiated by the local child support agency pursuant to Section 17400, 17402, 17404, or 17416 of the Family Code, any action or proceeding brought by a county, city and county, city, or local agency within a certain county, or city and county, against a resident of another county, city and county, or city, or a corporation doing business in the latter, shall be, on motion of either party, transferred for trial to a county, or city and county, other than the plaintiff, if the plaintiff is a county, or city and county, and other than that in which the plaintiff is situated, if the plaintiff is a city, or a local agency, and other than that in which the defendant resides, or is doing business, or is situated. Whenever an action or proceeding is brought against a county, city and county, city, or local agency, in any county, or city and county, other than the defendant, if the defendant is a county, or city and county, or, if the defendant is a city, or local agency, other than that in which the defendant is situated, the action or proceeding must be, on motion of that defendant, transferred for trial to a county, or city and county, other than that in which the plaintiff, or any of the plaintiffs, resides, or is doing business, or is situated, and other than the plaintiff county, or city and county, or county in which that plaintiff city or local agency is situated, and other than the defendant county, or city and county, or county in which the defendant city or local agency is situated; provided, however, that any action or proceeding against the city, county, city and county, or local agency for injury occurring within the city, county, or city and county, or within the county in which the local agency is situated, to person or property or person and property caused by the negligence or alleged negligence of the city, county, city and county, local agency, or its agents or employees, shall be tried in that county, or city and county, or if a city is a defendant, in the city or in the county in which the city is situated, or if a local agency is a defendant, in the county in which the local agency is situated. In that action or proceeding, the parties thereto may, by stipulation in writing, or made in open court, and entered in the minutes, agree upon any county, or city and county, for the place of trial thereof. When the action or proceeding is one in which a jury is not of right, or in case a jury is waived, then in lieu of transferring the cause, the court in the original county may request the chairperson of the Judicial Council to assign a disinterested judge from a neutral county to hear that cause and all proceedings in connection therewith. When the action or proceeding is transferred to another county for trial, a witness required to respond to a subpoena for a hearing within the original county shall be compelled to attend hearings in the county to which the cause is transferred. If the demand for transfer is made by one party and the opposing party does not consent thereto, the additional costs of the nonconsenting party occasioned by the transfer of the cause, including living and traveling expenses of the nonconsenting party and material witnesses, found by the court to be material, and called by the nonconsenting party, not to exceed five dollars ($5) per day each in excess of witness fees and mileage otherwise allowed by law, shall be assessed by the court hearing the cause against the party requesting the transfer. To the extent of that excess, those costs shall be awarded to the nonconsenting party regardless of the outcome of the trial. This section shall apply to actions or proceedings now pending or hereafter brought.

(b) For the purposes of this section, "local agency" shall mean any governmental district, board, or agency, or any other local governmental body or corporation, but shall not include the State of California or any of its agencies, departments, commissions, or boards. *(Enacted in 1872. Amended by Stats.1881, c. 30, p. 23, § 1; Stats.1891, c. 61, p. 56, § 1; Stats.1907, c. 369, p. 700, § 2; Stats.1915, c. 434, p. 721, § 1; Stats.1921, c. 382, p. 573, § 1; Stats.1929, c. 112, p. 198, § 1; Stats.1931, c. 942, p. 1948, § 1; Stats.1933, c. 744, p. 1838, § 5; Stats.1970, c. 604, p. 1184, § 1; Stats.1971, c. 957, p. 1865, § 1; Stats.1994, c. 1269 (A.B.2208), § 2.2; Stats.2002, c. 784 (S.B.1316), § 52; Stats.2002, c. 927 (A.B.3032), § 1.)*

Law Revision Commission Comments

2002 Amendment

Subdivision (b) of Section 394 is deleted to reflect unification of the municipal and superior courts pursuant to Article VI, Section 5(e), of the California Constitution. [32 Cal.L.Rev.Comm. Reports 116 (2002)].

Research References

Forms

West's California Code Forms, Civil Procedure § 394 Form 1, Place Of Trial--Actions by or Against a City or County--Notice Of Motion for Change Of Venue.

West's California Code Forms, Civil Procedure § 394 Form 3, Place Of Trial--Order Transferring Case.

Treatises and Practice Aids

Witkin, California Summary 10th Constitutional Law § 1204, Jurisdiction and Venue.

Witkin, California Summary 10th Equity § 148, Action and Temporary Relief.

§ 395. Actions generally; proper court; waiver

(a) Except as otherwise provided by law and subject to the power of the court to transfer actions or proceedings as provided in this title, the superior court in the county where the defendants or some of them reside at the commencement of the action is the proper court for the trial of the action. If the action is for injury to person or personal property or for death from wrongful act or negligence, the superior court in either the county where the injury occurs or the injury causing death occurs or the county where the defendants, or some of them reside at the commencement of the action, is a proper court for the trial of the action. In a proceeding for dissolution of marriage, the superior court in the county where either the petitioner or respondent has been a resident for three months next preceding the commencement of the proceeding is the proper court for the trial of the proceeding. In a proceeding for nullity of marriage or legal separation of the parties, the superior court in the county where either the petitioner or the respondent resides at the commencement of the proceeding is the proper court for the trial of the proceeding. In a proceeding to enforce an obligation of support under Section 3900 of the Family Code, the superior court in the county where the child resides is the proper court for the trial of the action. In a proceeding to establish and enforce a foreign judgment or court order for the support of a minor child, the superior court in the county where the child resides is the proper court for the trial of the action. Subject to subdivision (b), if a defendant has contracted to perform an obligation in a particular county, the superior court in the county where the obligation is to be performed, where the contract in fact was entered into, or where the defendant or any defendant resides at the commencement of the action is a proper court for the trial of an action founded on that obligation, and the county where the obligation is incurred is the county where it is to be performed, unless there is a special contract in writing to the contrary. If none of the defendants reside in the state or if they reside in the state and the county where they reside is unknown to the plaintiff, the action may be tried in the superior court in any county that the plaintiff may designate in his or her complaint, and, if the defendant is about to depart from the state, the action may be tried in the superior court in any county where either of the parties reside or service is made. If any person is improperly joined as a defendant or has been made a defendant solely for the purpose of having the action tried in the superior court in the county where he or she resides, his or her residence shall not be considered in determining the proper place for the trial of the action.

(b) Subject to the power of the court to transfer actions or proceedings as provided in this title, in an action arising from an offer or provision of goods, services, loans or extensions of credit intended primarily for personal, family or household use, other than an obligation described in Section 1812.10 or

Section 2984.4 of the Civil Code, or an action arising from a transaction consummated as a proximate result of either an unsolicited telephone call made by a seller engaged in the business of consummating transactions of that kind or a telephone call or electronic transmission made by the buyer or lessee in response to a solicitation by the seller, the superior court in the county where the buyer or lessee in fact signed the contract, where the buyer or lessee resided at the time the contract was entered into, or where the buyer or lessee resides at the commencement of the action is the proper court for the trial of the action. In the superior court designated in this subdivision as the proper court, the proper court location for trial of a case is the location where the court tries that type of case that is nearest or most accessible to where the buyer or lessee resides, where the buyer or lessee in fact signed the contract, where the buyer or lessee resided at the time the contract was entered into, or where the buyer or lessee resides at the commencement of the action. Otherwise, any location of the superior court designated as the proper court in this subdivision is a proper court location for the trial. The court may specify by local rule the nearest or most accessible court location where the court tries that type of case.

(c) Any provision of an obligation described in subdivision (b) waiving that subdivision is void and unenforceable. *(Enacted in 1872. Amended by Stats.1907, c. 369, p. 700, § 3; Stats.1911, c. 421, p. 847, § 1; Stats.1933, c. 744, p. 1840, § 6; Stats.1939, c. 981, p. 2733, § 1; Stats.1951, c. 869, p. 2384, § 3; Stats.1955, c. 832, p. 1447, § 1; Stats.1969, c. 1608, p. 3344, § 11, operative Jan. 1, 1970; Stats.1970, c. 75, p. 88, § 1; Stats.1971, c. 1640, p. 3540, § 1; Stats.1972, c. 1117, § 1; Stats.1972, c. 1118, § 3; Stats.1972, c. 1119, § 3; Stats.1976, c. 610, p. 1460, § 1; Stats.1991, c. 228 (A.B.1889), § 3; Stats. 1992, c. 163 (A.B.2641), § 17, operative Jan. 1, 1994; Stats. 1994, c. 1269 (A.B.2208), § 2.4; Stats.1998, c. 473 (A.B.2134), § 1; Stats.1998, c. 931 (S.B.2139), § 62, eff. Sept. 28, 1998; Stats.1998, c. 931 (S.B.2139), § 62.5, eff. Sept. 28, 1998, operative Jan. 1, 1999; Stats.2002, c. 806 (A.B.3027), § 8.)*

Law Revision Commission Comments

1992 Amendment

Subdivision (a) of Section 395 is amended to substitute a reference to the Family Code provision that replaced the former Civil Code provision. The part of the fourth sentence of subdivision (a) relating to an action to determine parental relations has been deleted because it was inconsistent with and in effect replaced by Family Code Section 7620(b). [22 Cal.L.Rev.Comm.Reports 1 (1992)].

1998 Amendment

Section 395 is amended to reflect the elimination of the justice court. Cal. Const. art. VI, §§ 1, 5(b). In a county in which there is no municipal court, the superior court has jurisdiction of matters that would be within the subject matter jurisdiction of the municipal court. Cal. Const. art. VI, 10 (superior court jurisdiction); Code Civ. Proc. §§ 85, 85.1 (limited civil cases). [28 Cal.L.Rev.Comm. Reports 51 (1998)].

Research References

Forms

West's California Code Forms, Civil Procedure § 394 Form 3, Place Of Trial--Order Transferring Case.

West's California Code Forms, Civil Procedure § 585.5 Form 1, Judgments--Default--Notice Of Motion to Set Aside Default and Default Judgment and for Leave to Defend Action.

West's California Code Forms, Commercial § 1301 Form 6, Clause Selecting Applicable Forum.

West's California Code Forms, Corporations § 800 Form 5, Complaint for Breach Of Contract (Alter Ego).

Treatises and Practice Aids

Witkin, California Summary 10th Constitutional Law § 951, Judicial Enforcement.

Witkin, California Summary 10th Husband and Wife § 73, Residence and Venue.

Witkin, California Summary 10th Husband and Wife § 146, Proceedings.

Witkin, California Summary 10th Husband and Wife § 170, Venue, Limitations, Parties, and Pleadings.

Witkin, California Summary 10th Torts § 5, Classification Of Torts.

Witkin, California Summary 10th Torts § 525, Action Disregarding Venue Statutes.

Witkin, California Summary 10th Trusts § 225, Venue.

§ 396. Superior court lacking jurisdiction of appeal or petition; transfer to court having jurisdiction

(a) No appeal or petition filed in the superior court shall be dismissed solely because the appeal or petition was not filed in the proper state court.

(b) If the superior court lacks jurisdiction of an appeal or petition, and a court of appeal or the Supreme Court would have jurisdiction, the appeal or petition shall be transferred to the court having jurisdiction upon terms as to costs or otherwise as may be just, and proceeded with as if regularly filed in the court having jurisdiction. *(Added by Stats.2008, c. 56 (S.B.1182), § 2.)*

Law Revision Commission Comments

2008 Addition

Section 396 requires a superior court to transfer an appeal or petition over which the superior court lacks jurisdiction to an appellate court that has jurisdiction. The provision continues a policy that requires transfer and prohibits dismissal of a cause simply because it was filed in the wrong court. See, e.g., former Section 396 (2002 Cal. Stat. ch. 806, § 9); Gov't Code § 68915; see Friends of Mammoth v. Bd. of Supervisors, 8 Cal.3d 247, 268–69, 502 P.2d 1049, 104 Cal.Rptr. 761 (1972); Morgan v. Somervell, 40 Cal.App.2d 398, 400, 104 P.2d 866 (1940). [37 Cal.L.Rev.Comm. Reports 195 (2007)].

2008 Repeal of former § 396

Section 396 is repealed due to trial court unification. The provision directed a court not to dismiss but to transfer a case if the court lacked subject matter jurisdiction and another state court would have such jurisdiction. The provision was often invoked when a municipal court transferred a case outside its jurisdiction to the superior court, or vice versa. See, e.g., Walker v. Superior Court, 53 Cal.3d 257, 807 P.2d 418, 279 Cal.Rptr. 576 (1991); Cal. Employment Stabilization Comm'n v. Municipal Court, 62 Cal.App.2d 781, 145 P.2d 361 (1944). After unification of the municipal and superior courts, it no longer served that purpose.

There was a split of authority regarding whether the provision authorized a superior court lacking jurisdiction to transfer a case to a court of appeal or the state Supreme Court. Compare TrafficSchoolOnline, Inc. v. Superior Court, 89 Cal.App.4th 222, 225, 107 Cal.Rptr.2d 412 (2001) ("[T]he superior court is not vested with the authority by Code of Civil Procedure Section 396 to transfer a case to the Court of Appeal or the Supreme Court."), with Padilla v. Dep't of Alcoholic Beverage Control, 43 Cal.App.4th 1151, 1154, 51 Cal.Rptr.2d 133 (1996) (Transfer requirement of Section 396 applies "in the case of proceedings filed in the superior court which, by statute, may be filed only in the Supreme Court or the Court of Appeal."); see also Pajaro Valley Water Mgmt. Agency v. McGrath, 128 Cal.App.4th 1093, 1104 n.4, 27 Cal.Rptr.3d 741 (2005) ("It is possible, though a point of disagreement, that [Section 396] retains vitality as empowering the superior court to transfer cases within the exclusive original jurisdiction of the appellate courts." (emphasis in original)).

Consistent with the key policy of deciding a case on its merits even if it is filed in the wrong tribunal, new Section 396 makes clear that if a superior court lacks jurisdiction of a matter and a state appellate court would have jurisdiction, the superior court must transfer the matter instead of dismissing it. [37 Cal.L.Rev.Comm. Reports 195 (2007)].

Research References

Forms

West's California Code Forms, Civil Procedure § 396 Form 1, Place Of Trial--Appeal or Petition--Superior Court Lacks Jurisdiction--Notice Of Motion to Transfer Appeal or Petition to the Court Of Appeal.

§ 396a. Specified actions or proceedings; statement of jurisdictional facts; transfers; consent to retention of case

In a case that is subject to Sections 1812.10 and 2984.4 of the Civil Code, or subdivision (b) of Section 395 of the Code of Civil Procedure, or in an action or proceeding for an unlawful detainer as defined in Section 1161 of the Code of Civil Procedure:

(a) The plaintiff shall state facts in the complaint, verified by the plaintiff's oath, or the oath of the plaintiff's attorney, or in an affidavit of the plaintiff or of the plaintiff's attorney filed with the complaint, showing that the action has been commenced in the proper superior court and the proper court location for the trial of the action or proceeding, and showing that the action is subject to the provisions of Sections 1812.10 and 2984.4 of the Civil Code or subdivision (b) of Section 395 of the Code of Civil Procedure, or is an action for an unlawful detainer. When the affidavit is filed with the complaint, a copy thereof shall be served with the summons. Except as provided in this section, if the complaint or affidavit is not filed pursuant to this subdivision, no further proceedings may occur in the action or proceeding, except to dismiss the action or proceeding without prejudice. However, the court may, on terms that are just, permit the affidavit to be filed after the filing of the complaint, and a copy of the affidavit shall be served on the defendant and the time to answer or otherwise plead shall date from that service.

(b) If it appears from the complaint or affidavit, or otherwise, that the superior court or court location where the action or proceeding is commenced is not the proper court or court location for the trial, the court where the action or proceeding is commenced, or a judge thereof, shall, whenever that fact appears, transfer it to the proper court or court location, on its own motion, or on motion of the defendant, unless the defendant consents in writing, or in open court (consent in open court being entered in the minutes of the court), to the keeping of the action or proceeding in the court or court location where commenced. If that consent is given, the action or proceeding may continue in the court or court location where commenced. Notwithstanding Section 1801.1 and subdivision (f) of Section 2983.7 of the Civil Code, that consent may be given by a defendant who is represented by counsel at the time the consent is given, and if an action or proceeding is subject to subdivision (b) of Section 395 or is for an unlawful detainer, that consent may only be given by a defendant who is represented by counsel at the time the consent is given.

(c) In any case where the transfer of the action or proceeding is ordered under subdivision (a) or (b), if summons is served prior to the filing of the action or proceeding in the superior court or court location to which it is transferred, as to any defendant, so served, who has not appeared in the action or proceeding, the time to answer or otherwise plead shall date from service upon that defendant of written notice of the filing.

(d) If it appears from the complaint or affidavit of the plaintiff that the superior court and court location where the action or proceeding is commenced are a proper court and court location for the trial thereof, all proper proceedings may be had, and the action or proceeding may be tried in that court at that location.

(e) A motion for a transfer of the action or proceeding to a different superior court may be made as in other cases, within the time, upon the grounds, and in the manner provided in this title, and if upon that motion it appears that the action or proceeding is not pending in the proper court, or should for other cause be transferred, the action or proceeding shall be ordered transferred as provided in this title.

If any action or proceeding is ordered transferred to another court as provided in this section, proceedings shall be had, and the costs and fees shall be paid, as provided in Sections 398 and 399.

(f) If a motion is made for transfer of an action or proceeding to a different court location within the same superior court as provided in this section, proceedings shall be had as provided by local rules of the superior court. *(Added by Stats.1933, c. 744, p. 1841, § 8. Amended by Stats.1935, c. 722, p. 1948, § 2; Stats.1937, c. 97, p. 336, § 1; Stats.1949, c. 1286, p. 2270, § 3; Stats.1951, c. 869, p. 2386, § 5; Stats.1970, c. 725, p. 1353, § 3; Stats.1976, c. 1288, p. 5763, § 11; Stats.1982, c. 38, p. 75, § 1; Stats.1998, c. 931 (S.B.2139), § 65, eff. Sept. 28, 1998; Stats.2002, c. 806 (A.B.3027), § 10; Stats.2007, c. 263 (A.B.310), § 5.)*

Law Revision Commission Comments

1998 Amendment

Section 396a is amended to accommodate unification of the municipal and superior courts in a county. Cal. Const. art. VI, § 5(e). It is also amended to reflect elimination of the justice court. Cal. Const. art. VI, §§ 1, 5(b). Formerly, each county had one or more municipal courts and a superior court, and Section 396a applied to matters commenced in the municipal courts. A limited civil case is equivalent to a matter within the original jurisdiction of the municipal court under former law, so Section 396a as amended continues the effect of former law. *Cf.* Sections 85, 85.1 (limited civil cases). [28 Cal.L.Rev.Comm. Reports 51 (1998)].

2007 Amendment

Subdivision (b) of Section 396a is amended to delete the reference to a "docket," because courts no longer maintain a record denominated a "docket" in civil cases. Actions taken in open court are now recorded in the minutes of a superior court. See Gov't Code § 69844 (minutes of superior court); see also Copley Press v. Superior Court, 6 Cal.App.4th 106, 110, 7 Cal.Rptr.2d 841 (1992). [35 Cal.L.Rev. Comm. Reports 219 (2005)].

§ 396b. Trial in court having jurisdiction of subject matter but not proper court; transfer; domestic relations cases; retention of cause for convenience of witnesses; time to file response upon denial of motion for transfer

(a) Except as otherwise provided in Section 396a, if an action or proceeding is commenced in a court having jurisdiction of the subject matter thereof, other than the court designated as the proper court for the trial thereof, under this title, the action may, notwithstanding, be tried in the court where commenced, unless the defendant, at the time he or she answers, demurs, or moves to strike, or, at his or her option, without answering, demurring, or moving to strike and within the time otherwise allowed to respond to the complaint, files with the clerk, a notice of motion for an order transferring the action or proceeding to the proper court, together with proof of service, upon the adverse party, of a copy of those papers. Upon the hearing of the motion the court shall, if it appears that the action or proceeding was not commenced in the proper court, order the action or proceeding transferred to the proper court.

(b) In its discretion, the court may order the payment to the prevailing party of reasonable expenses and attorney's fees incurred in making or resisting the motion to transfer whether or not that party is otherwise entitled to recover his or her costs of action. In determining whether that order for expenses and fees shall be made, the court shall take into consideration (1) whether an offer to stipulate to change of venue was reasonably made and rejected, and (2) whether the motion or selection of venue was made in good faith given the facts and law the party making the motion or selecting the venue knew or should have known. As between the party and his or her attorney, those expenses and fees shall be the personal liability of the attorney not chargeable to the party. Sanctions shall not be imposed pursuant to this subdivision except on notice contained in a party's papers, or on the court's own noticed motion, and after opportunity to be heard.

(c) The court in a proceeding for dissolution of marriage or legal separation or under the Uniform Parentage Act (Part 3 (commencing with Section 7600) of Division 12 of the Family Code) may, prior to the determination of the motion to transfer, consider and determine motions for allowance of temporary spousal support, support of children, and counsel fees and costs, and motions to determine custody of and visitation with children, and may make all necessary and proper orders in connection therewith.

(d) In any case, if an answer is filed, the court may consider opposition to the motion to transfer, if any, and may retain the action in the county where commenced if it appears that the convenience of the witnesses or the ends of justice will thereby be promoted.

(e) If the motion to transfer is denied, the court shall allow the defendant time to move to strike, demur, or otherwise plead if the defendant has not previously filed a response. *(Added by Stats.1933, c. 744, p. 1842, § 8a. Amended by Stats.1939, c. 149, p. 1263, § 1; Stats.1951, c. 869, p. 2387, § 6; Stats.1969, c. 345, p. 720, § 1; Stats.1969, c. 1608, p. 3345, § 12; Stats.1969, c. 1609, p. 3360, § 28, operative Jan. 1, 1970; Stats.1974, c. 1369, p. 2964, § 2; Stats.1981, c. 122, p. 856, § 1; Stats.1982, c. 704, p. 2856, § 1; Stats.1983, c. 1167, § 1; Stats.1989, c. 1416, § 11; Stats.1989, c. 1417, § 3.5; Stats.1992, c. 163 (A.B.2641), § 18, operative Jan. 1, 1994; Stats.2005, c. 706 (A.B.1742), § 10.)*

Application

For application of 2005 amendment, see Stats.2005, c. 706 (A.B.1742), § 41.

Law Revision Commission Comments

1992 Amendment

Subdivision (c) of Section 396b is amended to conform to the language of the Family Code. [22 Cal.L.Rev.Comm.Reports 1 (1992)].

Retention of venue for convenience of witnesses; recommendation and study. Cal.Law Revision Comm. (1957) Vol. 1, p. L-5.

Research References

Forms

West's California Code Forms, Civil Procedure § 397 Form 2, Place Of Trial--Notice Of Motion for Change Of Venue.

West's California Code Forms, Civil Procedure § 396B Form 1, Place Of Trial--Notice Of Motion to Transfer Action Where Court Has Jurisdiction.

Treatises and Practice Aids

Witkin, California Summary 10th Husband and Wife § 73, Residence and Venue.

Witkin, California Summary 10th Real Property § 728, Jurisdiction, Venue, and Process.

§ 397. Change of place of trial; grounds

The court may, on motion, change the place of trial in the following cases:

(a) When the court designated in the complaint is not the proper court.

(b) When there is reason to believe that an impartial trial cannot be had therein.

(c) When the convenience of witnesses and the ends of justice would be promoted by the change.

(d) When from any cause there is no judge of the court qualified to act.

(e) When a proceeding for dissolution of marriage has been filed in the county in which the petitioner has been a resident for three months next preceding the commencement of the proceeding, and the respondent at the time of the commencement of the proceeding is a resident of another county in this state, to the county of the respondent's residence when the ends of justice would be promoted by the change. If a motion to change the place of trial is made pursuant to this paragraph, the court may, prior to the determination of such motion, consider and determine motions for allowance of temporary spousal support, support of children, temporary restraining orders, attorneys' fees, and costs, and make all necessary and proper orders in connection therewith. *(Enacted in 1872. Amended by Stats.1907, c. 369, p. 701, § 5; Stats.1933, c. 744, p. 1843, § 9; Stats.1955, c. 832, p. 1448, § 2; Stats.1969, c. 1608, p. 3346, § 13, operative Jan. 1, 1970; Stats.1992, c. 163 (A.B.2641), § 19, operative Jan. 1, 1994.)*

Law Revision Commission Comments

1992 Amendment

The subdivisions of Section 397 are redesignated and subdivision (e) is amended to more closely conform to the language of Sections 259(f) and 396b(c). [22 Cal.L.Rev.Comm.Reports 1 (1992)].

Research References

Forms

California Practice Guide: Rutter Family Law Forms Form 4:22, Request for Order to Transfer Venue.
West's California Code Forms, Civil Procedure § 397 Form 2, Place Of Trial--Notice Of Motion for Change Of Venue.

Treatises and Practice Aids

Witkin, California Summary 10th Husband and Wife § 73, Residence and Venue.

§ 397.5. Proceedings related to continuation of marriage; transfer from county

In any proceeding for dissolution or nullity of marriage or legal separation of the parties under the Family Code, where it appears that both petitioner and respondent have moved from the county rendering the order, the court may, when the ends of justice and the convenience of the parties would be promoted by the change, order that the proceedings be transferred to the county of residence of either party. *(Added by Stats.1971, c. 1210, p. 2328, § 7. Amended by Stats.1980, c. 234, p. 477, § 2; Stats.1994, c. 1269 (A.B.2208), § 2.6.)*

Law Revision Commission Comments

1994 Amendment

Section 397.5 is amended to correct a reference to the former Family Law Act (former Civ. Code § 4000 *et seq.*) and to conform to Family Code terminology. This is a technical, nonsubstantive change. [24 Cal.L.Rev.Comm. Reports 621 (1994)].

Research References

Treatises and Practice Aids

Witkin, California Summary 10th Husband and Wife § 73, Residence and Venue.
Witkin, California Summary 10th Husband and Wife § 146, Proceedings.
Witkin, California Summary 10th Husband and Wife § 170, Venue, Limitations, Parties, and Pleadings.
Witkin, California Summary 10th Parent and Child § 285, in General.

Title 5

JURISDICTION AND SERVICE OF PROCESS

CHAPTER 1. JURISDICTION AND FORUM

ARTICLE 2. FORUM

§ 410.30. Stay or dismissal of action; general appearance

(a) When a court upon motion of a party or its own motion finds that in the interest of substantial justice an action should be heard in a forum outside this state, the court shall stay or dismiss the action in whole or in part on any conditions that may be just.

(b) The provisions of Section 418.10 do not apply to a motion to stay or dismiss the action by a defendant who has made a general appearance. *(Added by Stats.1969, c. 1610, p. 3363, § 3, operative July 1, 1970. Amended by Stats.1972, c. 601, § 1; Stats.1986, c. 968, § 4, eff. Sept. 22, 1986; Stats. 1972, c. 601, § 1, operative Jan. 1, 1992.)*

Commentary

In re Marriage of Taschen, 134 Cal.App.4th 681, 36 Cal.Rptr.3d 286 (2005), review denied, reads this section literally and consequently holds that a petitioner, as well as a respondent, in a dissolution action may bring a motion to dismiss for forum non conveniens even though there have been no changed circumstances since the petitioner initially filed for dissolution.

Research References

Forms

California Practice Guide: Rutter Family Law Forms Form 4:26, Request for Order to Stay or Dismiss on Ground Of Inconvenient Forum.
West's California Code Forms, Civil Procedure § 418.10 Form 4, Objection to Jurisdiction--Notice Of Motion to Quash Service--Inconvenient Forum.
West's California Code Forms, Probate § 4540 Form 1, Petition Relating to Acts and Transactions Of Attorney-In-Fact Under Power Of Attorney.

Treatises and Practice Aids

Witkin, California Summary 10th Trusts § 218, Bases Of Jurisdiction.
Witkin, California Summary 10th Wills and Probate § 875, Hearing, Determination, and Appeal.
Witkin, California Summary 10th Wills and Probate § 899, Hearing, Determination, and Appeal.

Title 6

OF THE PLEADINGS IN CIVIL ACTIONS

CHAPTER 2. PLEADINGS DEMANDING RELIEF

ARTICLE 1. GENERAL PROVISIONS

§ 425.16. Anti–SLAPP motion

(a) The Legislature finds and declares that there has been a disturbing increase in lawsuits brought primarily to chill the valid exercise of the constitutional rights of freedom of speech and petition for the redress of grievances. The Legislature finds and declares that it is in the public interest to encourage continued participation in matters of public significance, and that this participation should not be chilled through abuse of the judicial process. To this end, this section shall be construed broadly.

(b)(1) A cause of action against a person arising from any act of that person in furtherance of the person's right of petition or free speech under the United States Constitution or the California Constitution in connection with a public issue shall be subject to a special motion to strike, unless the court determines that the plaintiff has established that there is a probability that the plaintiff will prevail on the claim.

(2) In making its determination, the court shall consider the pleadings, and supporting and opposing affidavits stating the facts upon which the liability or defense is based.

(3) If the court determines that the plaintiff has established a probability that he or she will prevail on the claim, neither that determination nor the fact of that determination shall be admissible in evidence at any later stage of the case, or in any subsequent action, and no burden of proof or degree of proof otherwise applicable shall be affected by that determination in any later stage of the case or in any subsequent proceeding.

(c)(1) Except as provided in paragraph (2), in any action subject to subdivision (b), a prevailing defendant on a special motion to strike shall be entitled to recover his or her attorney's fees and costs. If the court finds that a special motion to strike is frivolous or is solely intended to cause unnecessary delay, the court shall award costs and reasonable attorney's fees to a plaintiff prevailing on the motion, pursuant to Section 128.5.

(2) A defendant who prevails on a special motion to strike in an action subject to paragraph (1) shall not be entitled to attorney's fees and costs if that cause of action is brought pursuant to Section 6259, 11130, 11130.3, 54960, or 54960.1 of the Government Code. Nothing in this paragraph shall be construed to prevent a prevailing defendant from recovering attorney's fees and costs pursuant to subdivision (d) of Section 6259, or Section 11130.5 or 54960.5, of the Government Code.

(d) This section shall not apply to any enforcement action brought in the name of the people of the State of California by the Attorney General, district attorney, or city attorney, acting as a public prosecutor.

(e) As used in this section, "act in furtherance of a person's right of petition or free speech under the United States or California Constitution in connection with a public issue" includes: (1) any written or oral statement or writing made before a legislative, executive, or judicial proceeding, or any other official proceeding authorized by law, (2) any written or oral statement or writing made in connection with an issue under consideration or review by a legislative, executive, or judicial body, or any other official proceeding authorized by law, (3) any written or oral statement or writing made in a place open to the public or a public forum in connection with an issue of public interest, or (4) any other conduct in furtherance of the exercise of the constitutional right of petition or the constitutional right of free speech in connection with a public issue or an issue of public interest.

(f) The special motion may be filed within 60 days of the service of the complaint or, in the court's discretion, at any later time upon terms it deems proper. The motion shall be scheduled by the clerk of the court for a hearing not more than 30 days after the service of the motion unless the docket conditions of the court require a later hearing.

(g) All discovery proceedings in the action shall be stayed upon the filing of a notice of motion made pursuant to this section. The stay of discovery shall remain in effect until notice of entry of the order ruling on the motion. The court, on noticed motion and for good cause shown, may order that specified discovery be conducted notwithstanding this subdivision.

(h) For purposes of this section, "complaint" includes "cross-complaint" and "petition," "plaintiff" includes "cross-complainant" and "petitioner," and "defendant" includes "cross-defendant" and "respondent."

(i) An order granting or denying a special motion to strike shall be appealable under Section 904.1.

(j)(1) Any party who files a special motion to strike pursuant to this section, and any party who files an opposition to a special motion to strike, shall, promptly upon so filing, transmit to the Judicial Council, by e-mail or facsimile, a copy of the endorsed, filed caption page of the motion or opposition, a copy of any related notice of appeal or petition for a writ, and a conformed copy of any order issued pursuant to this section, including any order granting or denying a special motion to strike, discovery, or fees.

(2) The Judicial Council shall maintain a public record of information transmitted pursuant to this subdivision for at least three years, and may store the information on microfilm or other appropriate electronic media. *(Added by Stats.1992, c. 726 (S.B.1264), § 2. Amended by Stats.1993, c. 1239 (S.B.9), § 1; Stats.1997, c. 271 (S.B.1296), § 1; Stats.1999, c. 960 (A.B.1675), § 1, eff. Oct. 10, 1999; Stats.2005, c. 535 (A.B.1158), § 1, eff. Oct. 5, 2005; Stats.2009, c. 65 (S.B.786), § 1; Stats.2010, c. 328 (S.B.1330), § 34; Stats.2014, c. 71 (S.B.1304), § 17, eff. Jan. 1, 2015.)*

Commentary

Cabral v. Martins, 177 Cal.App.4th 471, 99 Cal.Rptr.3d 394 (2009), review denied, held that a custodial parent's child-support-evasion cause of action against a support obligor's attorneys was predicated on protected activity under Code of Civil Procedure § 425.16, the anti-SLAPP statute, and thus was subject to a special motion to strike.

Lefebvre v. Lefebvre, 199 Cal.App.4th 696, 131 Cal.Rptr.3d 171 (2011), held that a trial court properly denied a wife's motion to strike her former husband's malicious prosecution complaint when the court conclusively determined that the wife's filing of criminal reports leading to the husband's arrest and trial were false and that their filing was an illegal activity. *Lefebvre* reasoned that making a false police report is not constitutionally protected for purposes of this section. Thus it was immaterial that the report might have been a privileged communication for purposes of the litigation privilege under Civil Code section 47(b).

Chodos v. Cole, 210 Cal.App.4th 692, 148 Cal.Rptr.3d 451 (2012), review denied, holds that a cross-complaint by an attorney against other attorneys for indemnity with respect to a claim of attorney malpractice in handling a marital dissolution is indistinguishable from a client's claim of attorney malpractice and therefore the anti-SLAPP statute is not applicable to the attorney's cross-complaint.

Dwight R. v. Christy B., 212 Cal.App.4th 697, 151 Cal.Rptr.3d 406 (2013), review denied, holds that a father's section 42 U.S.C. § 1983 claims against a therapist for allegedly conspiring to falsely accuse him of sexually abusing his daughter were properly stricken as a SLAPP lawsuit under this section.

Research References

Forms

West's California Code Forms, Civil § 47 Form 1, Affirmative Defense to Defamation--Official Duty Privilege.
West's California Code Forms, Civil § 47 Form 2, Affirmative Defense to Defamation--Official Proceeding Privilege.
West's California Code Forms, Civil § 47 Form 3, Affirmative Defense to Defamation--Interested Person Privilege.
West's California Code Forms, Civil § 47 Form 4, Affirmative Defense to Defamation--Report Of Official Proceeding Privilege.
West's California Code Forms, Civil § 47 Form 5, Affirmative Defense to Defamation--Report Of Public Meeting.
West's California Code Forms, Civil Procedure § 425.16 Form 1, Pleadings--Notice Of Motion to Strike Complaint Infringing on Party's Right Of Petition or Free Speech.

Treatises and Practice Aids

Witkin, California Summary 10th Insurance § 311, Defense Of Fraud.
Witkin, California Summary 10th Torts § 469, Nature Of Tort.
Witkin, California Summary 10th Torts § 507, Judgment or Ruling in Prior Proceeding.
Witkin, California Summary 10th Torts § 510, Action Against Attorney.
Witkin, California Summary 10th Torts § 521, Ulterior Purpose.
Witkin, California Summary 10th Torts § 567, in General.

§ 425.17. Legislative findings and declarations regarding California Anti-SLAPP Law; application of § 425.16

(a) The Legislature finds and declares that there has been a disturbing abuse of Section 425.16, the California Anti–SLAPP Law, which has undermined the exercise of the constitutional rights of freedom of speech and petition for the redress of grievances, contrary to the purpose and intent of Section 425.16. The Legislature finds and declares that it is in the public interest to encourage continued participation in matters of public significance, and that this participation should not be chilled through abuse of the judicial process or Section 425.16.

(b) Section 425.16 does not apply to any action brought solely in the public interest or on behalf of the general public if all of the following conditions exist:

(1) The plaintiff does not seek any relief greater than or different from the relief sought for the general public or a class of which the plaintiff is a member. A claim for attorney's fees, costs, or penalties does not constitute greater or different relief for purposes of this subdivision.

(2) The action, if successful, would enforce an important right affecting the public interest, and would confer a significant benefit, whether pecuniary or nonpecuniary, on the general public or a large class of persons.

(3) Private enforcement is necessary and places a disproportionate financial burden on the plaintiff in relation to the plaintiff's stake in the matter.

(c) Section 425.16 does not apply to any cause of action brought against a person primarily engaged in the business of selling or leasing goods or services, including, but not limited to, insurance, securities, or financial instruments, arising from any statement or conduct by that person if both of the following conditions exist:

(1) The statement or conduct consists of representations of fact about that person's or a business competitor's business operations, goods, or services, that is made for the purpose of obtaining approval for, promoting, or securing sales or leases of, or commercial transactions in, the person's goods or services, or the statement or conduct was made in the course of delivering the person's goods or services.

(2) The intended audience is an actual or potential buyer or customer, or a person likely to repeat the statement to, or otherwise influence, an actual or potential buyer or customer, or the statement or conduct arose out of or within the context of a regulatory approval process, proceeding, or investigation, except where the statement or conduct was made by a telephone corporation in the course of a proceeding before the California Public Utilities Commission and is the subject of a lawsuit brought by a competitor, notwithstanding that the conduct or statement concerns an important public issue.

(d) Subdivisions (b) and (c) do not apply to any of the following:

(1) Any person enumerated in subdivision (b) of Section 2 of Article I of the California Constitution or Section 1070 of the Evidence Code, or any person engaged in the dissemination of ideas or expression in any book or academic journal, while engaged in the gathering, receiving, or processing of information for communication to the public.

(2) Any action against any person or entity based upon the creation, dissemination, exhibition, advertisement, or other similar promotion of any dramatic, literary, musical, political, or artistic work, including, but not limited to, a motion picture or television program, or an article published in a newspaper or magazine of general circulation.

(3) Any nonprofit organization that receives more than 50 percent of its annual revenues from federal, state, or local government grants, awards, programs, or reimbursements for services rendered.

(e) If any trial court denies a special motion to strike on the grounds that the action or cause of action is exempt pursuant to this section, the appeal provisions in subdivision (i) of Section 425.16 and paragraph (13) of subdivision (a) of Section 904.1 do not apply to that action or cause of action. *(Added by Stats.2003, c. 338 (S.B.515), § 1. Amended by Stats.2011, c. 296 (A.B.1023), § 36.5.)*

Commentary

Cabral v. Martins, 177 Cal.App.4th 471, 99 Cal.Rptr.3d 394 (2009), review denied, held that a custodial parent's child-support-evasion cause of action against a support obligor's attorneys was predicated on protected activity under Code of Civil Procedure § 425.16, the anti-SLAPP statute, and thus was subject to a special motion to strike.

Research References

Forms

West's California Code Forms, Civil Procedure § 425.16 Form 1, Pleadings--Notice Of Motion to Strike Complaint Infringing on Party's Right Of Petition or Free Speech.

Treatises and Practice Aids

Witkin, California Summary 10th Insurance § 311, Defense Of Fraud.

§ 425.18. SLAPPback actions; motion to strike; limitations periods; discovery; remedies

(a) The Legislature finds and declares that a SLAPPback is distinguishable in character and origin from the ordinary malicious prosecution action. The Legislature further finds and declares that a SLAPPback cause of action should be treated differently, as provided in this section, from an ordinary malicious prosecution action because a SLAPPback is consistent with the Legislature's intent to protect the valid exercise of the constitutional rights of free speech and petition by its deterrent effect on SLAPP (strategic lawsuit against public participation) litigation and by its restoration of public confidence in participatory democracy.

(b) For purposes of this section, the following terms have the following meanings:

(1) "SLAPPback" means any cause of action for malicious prosecution or abuse of process arising from the filing or maintenance of a prior cause of action that has been dismissed pursuant to a special motion to strike under Section 425.16.

(2) "Special motion to strike" means a motion made pursuant to Section 425.16.

(c) The provisions of subdivisions (c), (f), (g), and (i) of Section 425.16, and paragraph (13) of subdivision (a) of Section 904.1, shall not apply to a special motion to strike a SLAPPback.

(d)(1) A special motion to strike a SLAPPback shall be filed within any one of the following periods of time, as follows:

(A) Within 120 days of the service of the complaint.

(B) At the court's discretion, within six months of the service of the complaint.

(C) At the court's discretion, at any later time in extraordinary cases due to no fault of the defendant and upon written findings of the court stating the extraordinary case and circumstance.

(2) The motion shall be scheduled by the clerk of the court for a hearing not more than 30 days after the service of the motion unless the docket conditions of the court require a later hearing.

(e) A party opposing a special motion to strike a SLAPPback may file an ex parte application for a continuance to obtain necessary discovery. If it appears that facts essential to justify opposition to that motion may exist, but cannot then be presented, the court shall grant a reasonable continuance to permit the party to obtain affidavits or conduct discovery or may make any other order as may be just.

(f) If the court finds that a special motion to strike a SLAPPback is frivolous or solely intended to cause unnecessary delay, the court shall award costs and reasonable attorney's fees to a plaintiff prevailing on the motion, pursuant to Section 128.5.

(g) Upon entry of an order denying a special motion to strike a SLAPPback claim, or granting the special motion to strike as to some but less than all causes of action alleged in a complaint containing a SLAPPback claim, an aggrieved party may, within 20 days after service of a written notice of the entry of the order, petition an appropriate reviewing court for a peremptory writ.

(h) A special motion to strike may not be filed against a SLAPPback by a party whose filing or maintenance of the prior cause of action from which the SLAPPback arises was illegal as a matter of law.

(i) This section does not apply to a SLAPPback filed by a public entity. *(Added by Stats.2005, c. 535 (A.B.1158), § 2, eff. Oct. 5, 2005.)*

Commentary

Cabral v. Martins, 177 Cal.App.4th 471, 99 Cal.Rptr.3d 394 (2009), review denied, held that a custodial parent's child-support-evasion cause of action against a support obligor's attorneys was predicated on protected activity under Code of Civil Procedure § 425.16, the anti-SLAPP statute, and thus was subject to a special motion to strike.

Research References

Forms

West's California Code Forms, Civil Procedure § 425.18 Form 1, Pleadings--Notice Of Motion to Strike SLAPPback Cause Of Action.

Treatises and Practice Aids

Witkin, California Summary 10th Torts § 469, Nature Of Tort.
Witkin, California Summary 10th Torts § 517, Nature Of Tort.

CHAPTER 8. VARIANCE—MISTAKES IN PLEADINGS AND AMENDMENTS

§ 473. Amendments permitted by court; enlargement of time to answer or demur; continuance, costs; relief from judgment, etc., taken by mistake, inadvertence, surprise, or excusable neglect; vacating default judgment; compensatory costs and legal fees; penalties; clerical mistakes in judgment or order; relief

(a)(1) The court may, in furtherance of justice, and on any terms as may be proper, allow a party to amend any pleading or proceeding by adding or striking out the name of any party, or by correcting a mistake in the name of a party, or a mistake in any other respect; and may, upon like terms, enlarge the time for answer or demurrer. The court may likewise, in its discretion, after notice to the adverse party, allow, upon any terms as may be just, an amendment to any pleading or proceeding in other particulars; and may upon like terms allow an answer to be made after the time limited by this code.

(2) When it appears to the satisfaction of the court that the amendment renders it necessary, the court may postpone the trial, and may, when the postponement will by the

amendment be rendered necessary, require, as a condition to the amendment, the payment to the adverse party of any costs as may be just.

(b) The court may, upon any terms as may be just, relieve a party or his or her legal representative from a judgment, dismissal, order, or other proceeding taken against him or her through his or her mistake, inadvertence, surprise, or excusable neglect. Application for this relief shall be accompanied by a copy of the answer or other pleading proposed to be filed therein, otherwise the application shall not be granted, and shall be made within a reasonable time, in no case exceeding six months, after the judgment, dismissal, order, or proceeding was taken. However, in the case of a judgment, dismissal, order, or other proceeding determining the ownership or right to possession of real or personal property, without extending the six-month period, when a notice in writing is personally served within the State of California both upon the party against whom the judgment, dismissal, order, or other proceeding has been taken, and upon his or her attorney of record, if any, notifying that party and his or her attorney of record, if any, that the order, judgment, dismissal, or other proceeding was taken against him or her and that any rights the party has to apply for relief under the provisions of Section 473 of the Code of Civil Procedure shall expire 90 days after service of the notice, then the application shall be made within 90 days after service of the notice upon the defaulting party or his or her attorney of record, if any, whichever service shall be later. No affidavit or declaration of merits shall be required of the moving party. Notwithstanding any other requirements of this section, the court shall, whenever an application for relief is made no more than six months after entry of judgment, is in proper form, and is accompanied by an attorney's sworn affidavit attesting to his or her mistake, inadvertence, surprise, or neglect, vacate any (1) resulting default entered by the clerk against his or her client, and which will result in entry of a default judgment, or (2) resulting default judgment or dismissal entered against his or her client, unless the court finds that the default or dismissal was not in fact caused by the attorney's mistake, inadvertence, surprise, or neglect. The court shall, whenever relief is granted based on an attorney's affidavit of fault, direct the attorney to pay reasonable compensatory legal fees and costs to opposing counsel or parties. However, this section shall not lengthen the time within which an action shall be brought to trial pursuant to Section 583.310.

(c)(1) Whenever the court grants relief from a default, default judgment, or dismissal based on any of the provisions of this section, the court may do any of the following:

(A) Impose a penalty of no greater than one thousand dollars ($1,000) upon an offending attorney or party.

(B) Direct that an offending attorney pay an amount no greater than one thousand dollars ($1,000) to the State Bar Client Security Fund.

(C) Grant other relief as is appropriate.

(2) However, where the court grants relief from a default or default judgment pursuant to this section based upon the affidavit of the defaulting party's attorney attesting to the attorney's mistake, inadvertence, surprise, or neglect, the relief shall not be made conditional upon the attorney's payment of compensatory legal fees or costs or monetary penalties imposed by the court or upon compliance with other sanctions ordered by the court.

(d) The court may, upon motion of the injured party, or its own motion, correct clerical mistakes in its judgment or orders as entered, so as to conform to the judgment or order directed, and may, on motion of either party after notice to the other party, set aside any void judgment or order. *(Enacted in 1872. Amended by Code Am.1873–74, c. 383, p. 302, § 60; Code Am.1880, c. 14, p. 2, § 3; Stats.1917, c. 159, p. 242, § 1; Stats.1933, c. 744, p. 1851, § 34; Stats.1961, c. 722, p. 1965, § 1; Stats.1981, c. 122, p. 857, § 2; Stats.1988, c. 1131, § 1; Stats.1991, c. 1003 (S.B.882), § 1; Stats.1992, c. 427 (A.B.3355), § 16; Stats.1992, c. 876 (A.B.3296), § 4; Stats.1996, c. 60 (S.B.52), § 1.)*

Commentary

When a plaintiff's action was dismissed as a sanction for failure to respond to discovery, and the plaintiff subsequently sought subsection (b) relief from judgment, supported by her attorney's declaration acknowledging that the dismissal was the result of his negligence, the trial court was required either to grant the relief or make a finding that the dismissal was not caused by the attorney's negligence. The trial court erred in denying relief without making any finding. *Rodriguez v. Brill, 234 Cal.App.4th 715, 184 Cal.Rptr.3d 265 (2015).*

Subsection (b) provides two types of relief from attorney error. The first, discretionary relief, is available for many types of orders. The second, mandatory relief, is available only for defaults, default judgments, and dismissals. *Martin Potts and Associates, Inc. v. Corsair, LLC., 244 Cal.App.4th 432, 197 Cal.Rptr.3d 856 (2016)*, holds that the affidavit requirement for mandatory relief does not require an attorney to state the reasons for his "mistake, inadvertence, surprise or neglect."

Henderson v. Pacific Gas & Electric Co., 187 Cal.App.4th 215, 113 Cal.Rptr.3d 692 (2010), sustains a trial court's denial of discretionary or mandatory relief under subsection (b) because the court could reasonably conclude, in the exercise of its discretionary power, that an attorney's reliance on a paralegal to file opposition papers to a motion for summary judgment was not excusable neglect, and because mandatory relief is not available for summary judgments.

An attorney's failure to appear for trial on reserved jurisdiction issues justified setting aside the resulting judgment, which was in the nature of a default judgment, under subsection (b). *In re Marriage of Hock & Gordon–Hock, 80 Cal.App.4th 1438, 96 Cal.Rptr.2d 546 (2000)*. See also Family Code § 2124 ("the negligence of an attorney shall not be imputed to client to bar an order setting aside a judgment, unless . . . "). However, the holding of *Marriage of Hock & Gordon–Hock* was explicitly rejected in *Vandermoon v. Sanwong, 142 Cal.App.4th 315, 47 Cal.Rptr.3d 772 (2006), review denied Nov. 15, 2006*, which affirmed a trial court's judgment that the attorney's affidavit provision of subsection (b) was inapplicable. *Vandermoon* held that the provision does not apply to a judgment entered after an uncontested trial in which the defendant and his attorney failed to appear because the judgment was not a "default" or "default judgment," which *Vandermoon* defined as "defendant's failure to answer a complaint," and "a judgment entered after defendant failed to answer," respectively.

Invoking Family Code § 2123, *In re Marriage of Heggie, 99 Cal.App.4th 28, 120 Cal.Rptr.2d 707 (2002)*, holds that a stipulated dissolution judgment may not be set aside under this section or Family Code § 2121 solely because of inequality in the distribution of community property attributable to a postjudgment increase in the value of community property stock.

County of Los Angeles v. Sheldon P., 102 Cal.App.4th 1337, 126 Cal.Rptr.2d 35 (2002), review denied January 15, 2003, holds that the trial court erred in granting a county's motion to set aside a voluntary declaration of paternity under this section without notice to the voluntary declarant, as required by Code of Civil Procedure § 389(a) and basic notions of due process.

Hu v. Fang, 104 Cal.App.4th 61, 127 Cal.Rptr.2d 756 (2002), holds that, for purposes of granting a subsection (b) motion to set aside a default judgment for mistake, a paralegal's mistake is attributable to the attorney responsible for supervising the paralegal.

Research References

Forms

California Practice Guide: Rutter Family Law Forms Form 16:1, Request for Order to Set Aside Judgment (Family Code S2120 et seq.).

California Real Estate Forms (Miller & Starr) § 2:18.30, Office Lease--Medical.

Cal. Transaction Forms - Bus. Transactions § 14:58, Offers to Compromise.

West's California Code Forms, Civil Procedure § 473 Form 4, Pleadings--Notice Of Motion to Amend Pleading.

West's California Code Forms, Civil Procedure § 473 Form 7, Pleadings--Notice Of Motion to Correct Judgment.

West's California Code Forms, Civil Procedure § 473 Form 9, Pleadings--Notice Of Motion to Set Aside Default and Judgment Taken Thereon.

West's California Code Forms, Civil Procedure § 998 Form 1, Offer Of Plaintiff to Compromise.

West's California Code Forms, Civil Procedure § 1008 Form 1, Motions and Orders--New Application for Order After Prior Refusal--Declaration Supporting New Application.

West's California Code Forms, Civil Procedure § 473 Form 13, Pleadings--Order Vacating Default and Permitting Filing Of Answer--Attorney Fault--Sanctions.

West's California Code Forms, Civil Procedure § 473 Form 14, Pleadings--Notice Of Motion to Set Aside Void Judgment.

West's California Code Forms, Civil Procedure § 473 Form 16, Pleadings--Notice Of Judgment or Order Determining Ownership Of Real or Personal Property.

West's California Code Forms, Civil Procedure § 595.2 Form 1, Trial--Stipulation for Continuance--Order.

West's California Code Forms, Civil Procedure § 1285.4 Form 1, Arbitration--Petition to Confirm Award Of Arbitrators.

West's California Code Forms, Civil Procedure § 1141.22 Form 1, Judicial Arbitration--Rule 3.825--Notice Of Motion to Vacate Judgment (Award Of Arbitrator).

West's California Code Forms, Family § 3690, Comment Overview--Relief from Order.

West's California Code Forms, Government § 911.4 Form 1, Application to Present Late Claim.

West's California Judicial Council Forms FL-280, Request for Hearing and Application to Set Aside Voluntary Declaration Of Paternity.

West's California Judicial Council Forms FL-281, Information Sheet for Completing Request for Hearing and Application to Set Aside Voluntary Declaration Of Paternity.

West's California Judicial Council Forms FL-285, Responsive Declaration to Application to Set Aside Voluntary Declaration Of Paternity.

West's California Judicial Council Forms FL-290, Order After Hearing on Motion to Set Aside Voluntary Declaration Of Paternity.

West's California Judicial Council Forms SC-114, Request to Amend Claim Before Hearing (Small Claims).

Treatises and Practice Aids

Witkin, California Summary 10th Agency and Employment § 320, Appeal by Defendant Who Defaults.

Witkin, California Summary 10th Community Property § 240, Former Interlocutory Decree Law.

Witkin, California Summary 10th Community Property § 243, Grounds and Time Limits.

Witkin, California Summary 10th Constitutional Law § 1209, Award Of Litigation Expenses.

Witkin, California Summary 10th Equity § 124A, (New) Retroactive Application Of Proposition 64.

Witkin, California Summary 10th Husband and Wife § 15, in General.

Witkin, California Summary 10th Husband and Wife § 72, Abatement Of Proceeding on Death.

Witkin, California Summary 10th Husband and Wife § 108, Former Two-Judgment Procedure.

Witkin, California Summary 10th Husband and Wife § 116, Development Of Law.

Witkin, California Summary 10th Husband and Wife § 128, Judgment.

Witkin, California Summary 10th Husband and Wife § 180, in General.

Witkin, California Summary 10th Husband and Wife § 218, Express Advance Waiver.

Witkin, California Summary 10th Husband and Wife § 243, Request in Petition.

Witkin, California Summary 10th Husband and Wife § 307, Grounds and Time Limits.

Witkin, California Summary 10th Husband and Wife § 330, Relief from Order Based on Presumed Income.

Witkin, California Summary 10th Husband and Wife § 352, in General.

Witkin, California Summary 10th Insurance § 297, Action Defended by Insured.

Witkin, California Summary 10th Parent and Child § 34, Rescinding or Setting Aside Declaration.

Witkin, California Summary 10th Parent and Child § 47, Where Presumption Of Paternity Applies.

Witkin, California Summary 10th Parent and Child § 67, Thirty-Day Requirement.

Witkin, California Summary 10th Parent and Child § 388, Hearing and Order After Hearing.

Witkin, California Summary 10th Real Property § 856, Statutes Of Limitations.

Witkin, California Summary 10th Real Property § 858, Expedited Proceedings.

Witkin, California Summary 10th Security Transactions in Real Property § 180, Determining Fair Value.

Witkin, California Summary 10th Torts § 76, Time Of Settlement.

Witkin, California Summary 10th Torts § 970, Attorneys' Fees When Periodic Payments Are Awarded.

Witkin, California Summary 10th Torts § 1749, Judgment by Default.

Witkin, California Summary 10th Wills and Probate § 409, New Trial and Relief from Default.

Witkin, California Summary 10th Wills and Probate § 496, Exchange Of Property.

Witkin, California Summary 10th Wills and Probate § 497, Authority to Grant Option.

Witkin, California Summary 10th Wills and Probate § 498, Exercise Of Option Given in Will.

Witkin, California Summary 10th Wills and Probate § 504, Order and Lease.

Witkin, California Summary 10th Wills and Probate § 548, Admission to Probate.

Witkin, California Summary 10th Wills and Probate § 579, Orders and Judgment.

Witkin, California Summary 10th Wills and Probate § 582, Hearing and Determination.

Witkin, California Summary 10th Wills and Probate § 645, Right to Bring Action.

Witkin, California Summary 10th Wills and Probate § 690, Overbid and Confirmation.

Witkin, California Summary 10th Wills and Probate § 697, Confirmation or Vacation Of Sale.
Witkin, California Summary 10th Wills and Probate § 728, Correction Of Order.
Witkin, California Summary 10th Workers' Compensation § 388, Service by Board.
Witkin, California Summary 10th Workers' Compensation § 408, Procedure.

Title 7

OTHER PROVISIONAL REMEDIES IN CIVIL ACTIONS

CHAPTER 3. INJUNCTION

§ 525. Definition; grant; enforcement

An injunction is a writ or order requiring a person to refrain from a particular act. It may be granted by the court in which the action is brought, or by a judge thereof; and when granted by a judge, it may be enforced as an order of the court. *(Enacted in 1872. Amended by Code Am.1880, c. 15, p. 3, § 3; Stats.1907, c. 272, p. 340, § 1.)*

Research References

Forms

West's California Code Forms, Civil § 51 Form 1, Complaint for Violation Of Unruh Civil Rights Act.
West's California Code Forms, Civil § 809 Form 1, Complaint for Interference With Easement.
West's California Code Forms, Civil § 810 Form 1, Complaint by Owner Of Servient Tenement for Possession Of Land.
West's California Code Forms, Civil § 834 Form 1, Complaint for Injunctive Relief for Cutting Down Jointly Owned Trees.
West's California Code Forms, Civil § 1921 Form 1, Complaint for Failure to Provide Publication on Adjustable Rate Mortgages.
West's California Code Forms, Civil § 2929 Form 1, Complaint to Enjoin Waste Of Mortgaged Property.
West's California Code Forms, Civil § 3491 Form 1, Complaint--Enjoin Public Nuisance.
West's California Code Forms, Civil § 52.1 Form 1, Complaint for Violation Of Civil Rights.
West's California Code Forms, Civil § 52.1 Form 2, Order Granting Preliminary Injunction for Violation Of Civil Rights.
West's California Code Forms, Civil § 52.4 Form 1, Complaint for Gender Violence.
West's California Code Forms, Civil § 52.5 Form 1, Complaint for Human Trafficking.
West's California Code Forms, Civil § 52.7 Form 1, Complaint for Unlawful Subcutaneous Implanting.
West's California Code Forms, Civil § 3420 COMMENT, Complaint--Injunctive Relief.
West's California Code Forms, Civil § 789.3 Form 1, Complaint by Tenant Against Landlord for Wrongful Termination Of Utility Services.
West's California Code Forms, Civil § 841.4 Form 1, Complaint by Adjoining Landowner to Abate Spite Fence.
West's California Code Forms, Civil § 1940.9 Form 2, Complaint for Failure to Disclose Multiple Servicing Of Meters.
West's California Code Forms, Civil § 2954.6 Form 2, Complaint for Failure to Give Notice Of Private Mortgage Insurance Requirements.
West's California Code Forms, Civil § 2955.5 Form 1, Complaint for Improper Hazard Insurance Requirement.
West's California Code Forms, Civil § 798.52 Form 1, Complaint to Enjoin Enforcement Of Unlawful Mobile-Home Park Rule.
West's California Code Forms, Civil § 798.88 Form 1, Petition to Enjoin Continuing Violations Of Mobile-Home Park Rules.
West's California Code Forms, Civil § 1798.46 Form 1, Complaint for Injunction for Withholding Personal Information Records.
West's California Code Forms, Civil § 1798.93 Form 1, Complaint for Identity Theft.
West's California Code Forms, Family § 7501 Form 1, Notice Of Motion and Supporting Declaration for Order Restraining Change Of Residence Of Child.

§ 526. Cases in which authorized; restrictions on grant

(a) An injunction may be granted in the following cases:

(1) When it appears by the complaint that the plaintiff is entitled to the relief demanded, and the relief, or any part thereof, consists in restraining the commission or continuance of the act complained of, either for a limited period or perpetually.

(2) When it appears by the complaint or affidavits that the commission or continuance of some act during the litigation would produce waste, or great or irreparable injury, to a party to the action.

(3) When it appears, during the litigation, that a party to the action is doing, or threatens, or is about to do, or is procuring or suffering to be done, some act in violation of the rights of another party to the action respecting the subject of the action, and tending to render the judgment ineffectual.

(4) When pecuniary compensation would not afford adequate relief.

(5) Where it would be extremely difficult to ascertain the amount of compensation which would afford adequate relief.

(6) Where the restraint is necessary to prevent a multiplicity of judicial proceedings.

(7) Where the obligation arises from a trust.

(b) An injunction cannot be granted in the following cases:

(1) To stay a judicial proceeding pending at the commencement of the action in which the injunction is demanded, unless the restraint is necessary to prevent a multiplicity of proceedings.

(2) To stay proceedings in a court of the United States.

(3) To stay proceedings in another state upon a judgment of a court of that state.

(4) To prevent the execution of a public statute by officers of the law for the public benefit.

(5) To prevent the breach of a contract the performance of which would not be specifically enforced, other than a contract in writing for the rendition of personal services from one to another where the promised service is of a special, unique, unusual, extraordinary, or intellectual character, which gives it peculiar value, the loss of which cannot be reasonably or adequately compensated in damages in an action at law, and where the compensation for the personal services is as follows:

(A) As to contracts entered into on or before December 31, 1993, the minimum compensation provided in the contract for the personal services shall be at the rate of six thousand dollars ($6,000) per annum.

(B) As to contracts entered into on or after January 1, 1994, the criteria of clause (i) or (ii), as follows, are satisfied:

(i) The compensation is as follows:

(I) The minimum compensation provided in the contract shall be at the rate of nine thousand dollars ($9,000) per annum for the first year of the contract, twelve thousand dollars ($12,000) per annum for the second year of the contract, and fifteen thousand dollars ($15,000) per annum for the third to seventh years, inclusive, of the contract.

(II) In addition, after the third year of the contract, there shall actually have been paid for the services through and including the contract year during which the injunctive relief is sought, over and above the minimum contractual compensation specified in subclause (I), the amount of fifteen thousand dollars ($15,000) per annum during the fourth and fifth years of the contract, and thirty thousand dollars ($30,000) per annum during the sixth and seventh years of the contract. As a condition to petitioning for an injunction, amounts payable under this clause may be paid at any time prior to seeking injunctive relief.

(ii) The aggregate compensation actually received for the services provided under a contract that does not meet the criteria of subparagraph (A), is at least 10 times the applicable aggregate minimum amount specified in subclauses (I) and (II) of clause (i) through and including the contract year during which the injunctive relief is sought. As a condition to petitioning for an injunction, amounts payable under this subparagraph may be paid at any time prior to seeking injunctive relief.

(C) Compensation paid in any contract year in excess of the minimums specified in clauses (i) and (ii) of subparagraph (B) shall apply to reduce the compensation otherwise required to be paid under those provisions in any subsequent contract years. However, an injunction may be granted to prevent the breach of a contract entered into between any nonprofit cooperative corporation or association and a member or stockholder thereof, in respect to any provision regarding the sale or delivery to the corporation or association of the products produced or acquired by the member or stockholder.

(6) To prevent the exercise of a public or private office, in a lawful manner, by the person in possession.

(7) To prevent a legislative act by a municipal corporation.

(Enacted in 1872. Amended by Stats.1907, c. 272, p. 341, § 2; Stats.1919, c. 224, p. 325, § 1; Stats.1925, c. 408, p. 828, § 1; Stats.1992, c. 177 (S.B.1459), § 2; Stats.1993, c. 836 (S.B.487), § 2.)

Research References

Forms

Am. Jur. Pl. & Pr. Forms Waste § 1, Introductory Comments.

West's California Code Forms, Civil § 54.3 Form 1, Complaint for Interference With Rights Of Disabled Person.

Treatises and Practice Aids

Witkin, California Summary 10th Constitutional Law § 98, in General.

Witkin, California Summary 10th Equity § 37, Other Contracts.

Witkin, California Summary 10th Equity § 51, Nature and Purpose Of Statute.

Witkin, California Summary 10th Equity § 52, Option to Pay is Insufficient.

Witkin, California Summary 10th Trusts § 123, Enjoining Threatened Breach.

Witkin, California Summary 10th Trusts § 232, Orders and Appeal.

§ 527. Grants before judgment upon verified complaint or affidavits; service; notice; procedures; application; fees

(a) A preliminary injunction may be granted at any time before judgment upon a verified complaint, or upon affidavits if the complaint in the one case, or the affidavits in the other, show satisfactorily that sufficient grounds exist therefor. No preliminary injunction shall be granted without notice to the opposing party.

(b) A temporary restraining order or a preliminary injunction, or both, may be granted in a class action, in which one or more of the parties sues or defends for the benefit of numerous parties upon the same grounds as in other actions, whether or not the class has been certified.

(c) No temporary restraining order shall be granted without notice to the opposing party, unless both of the following requirements are satisfied:

(1) It appears from facts shown by affidavit or by the verified complaint that great or irreparable injury will result to the applicant before the matter can be heard on notice.

(2) The applicant or the applicant's attorney certifies one of the following to the court under oath:

(A) That within a reasonable time prior to the application the applicant informed the opposing party or the opposing party's attorney at what time and where the application would be made.

(B) That the applicant in good faith attempted but was unable to inform the opposing party and the opposing party's attorney, specifying the efforts made to contact them.

(C) That for reasons specified the applicant should not be required to so inform the opposing party or the opposing party's attorney.

(d) In case a temporary restraining order is granted without notice in the contingency specified in subdivision (c):

(1) The matter shall be made returnable on an order requiring cause to be shown why a preliminary injunction should not be granted, on the earliest day that the business of the court will admit of, but not later than 15 days or, if good cause appears to the court, 22 days from the date the temporary restraining order is issued.

(2) The party who obtained the temporary restraining order shall, within five days from the date the temporary restraining order is issued or two days prior to the hearing, whichever is earlier, serve on the opposing party a copy of the complaint if not previously served, the order to show cause stating the date, time, and place of the hearing, any affidavits to be used in the application, and a copy of the points and authorities in support of the application. The court may for good cause, on motion of the applicant or on its own motion, shorten the time required by this paragraph for service on the opposing party.

(3) When the matter first comes up for hearing, if the party who obtained the temporary restraining order is not ready to proceed, or if the party has failed to effect service as required by paragraph (2), the court shall dissolve the temporary restraining order.

(4) The opposing party is entitled to one continuance for a reasonable period of not less than 15 days or any shorter period requested by the opposing party, to enable the opposing party to meet the application for a preliminary injunction. If the opposing party obtains a continuance under this paragraph, the temporary restraining order shall remain in effect until the date of the continued hearing.

(5) Upon the filing of an affidavit by the applicant that the opposing party could not be served within the time required by paragraph (2), the court may reissue any temporary restraining order previously issued. The reissued order shall be made returnable as provided by paragraph (1), with the time for hearing measured from the date of reissuance. No fee shall be charged for reissuing the order.

(e) The opposing party may, in response to an order to show cause, present affidavits relating to the granting of the preliminary injunction, and if the affidavits are served on the applicant at least two days prior to the hearing, the applicant shall not be entitled to any continuance on account thereof. On the day the order is made returnable, the hearing shall take precedence over all other matters on the calendar of the day, except older matters of the same character, and matters to which special precedence may be given by law. When the cause is at issue it shall be set for trial at the earliest possible date and shall take precedence over all other cases, except older matters of the same character, and matters to which special precedence may be given by law.

(f) Notwithstanding failure to satisfy the time requirements of this section, the court may nonetheless hear the order to show cause why a preliminary injunction should not be granted if the moving and supporting papers are served within the time required by Section 1005 and one of the following conditions is satisfied:

(1) The order to show cause is issued without a temporary restraining order.

(2) The order to show cause is issued with a temporary restraining order, but is either not set for hearing within the time required by paragraph (1) of subdivision (d), or the party who obtained the temporary restraining order fails to effect service within the time required by paragraph (2) of subdivision (d).

(g) This section does not apply to an order issued under the Family Code.

(h) As used in this section:

(1) "Complaint" means a complaint or a cross-complaint.

(2) "Court" means the court in which the action is pending. *(Enacted in 1872. Amended by Stats.1895, c. 49, p. 51, § 1; Stats.1907, c. 272, p. 341, § 3; Stats.1911, c. 42, p. 59, § 1; Stats.1963, c. 878, p. 2125, § 2; Stats.1970, c. 488, p. 969, § 1; Stats.1977, c. 720, § 1; Stats.1978, c. 346, § 1; Stats. 1979, c. 129, p. 316, § 1; Stats.1979, c. 795, p. 2707, § 7, operative July 1, 1980; Stats.1981, c. 182, p. 1100, § 1; Stats.1982, c. 812, p. 3100, § 1; Stats.1992, c. 163 (A.B.2641), § 23, operative Jan. 1, 1994; Stats.1993, c. 583 (A.B.284), § 1; Stats.1994, c. 587 (A.B.3600), § 5; Stats.1995, c. 796 (S.B.45), § 6; Stats.2000, c. 688 (A.B.1669), § 4.)*

Law Revision Commission Comments

1992 Amendment

Section 527 is amended to delete provisions that applied only to orders described in Family Code Section 240, which are now governed by Part 4 (commencing with Section 240) of Division 2 of the Family Code, not by this section.

The provision formerly in subdivision (b) is continued in Family Code Section 245. The new language in subdivision (b) makes clear that the section does not apply to an order described in Family Code Section 240. The provisions of Section 527 that applied to the orders described in Family Code Section 240 have been duplicated in Part 4 (commencing with Section 240) of Division 2 of the Family Code. [22 Cal.L.Rev.Comm.Reports 1 (1992)].

1994 Amendment

Paragraph (1) of subdivision (d) of Section 527 is amended to increase from five to seven days the additional time the court may for good cause allow to hear an order to show cause with a temporary restraining order. This permits a court that hears such matters one day a week to extend the hearing until the next regular day for hearing.

A provision is added in paragraph (2) of subdivision (d) to require the moving papers to be served within five days after issuance of the temporary restraining order or two days before the hearing, whichever is earlier. Although paragraph (2) permits the order to show cause to be served less than 15 days before the hearing (the general requirement for a notice of motion under Section 1005), the short time permitted for service is ameliorated by paragraph (4) of subdivision (d) which gives the opposing party the right to a continuance to prepare for the hearing.

A provision is added in paragraph (2) of subdivision (d) to include a copy of the order to show cause with the documents that must be served. A copy of the complaint must be served only if not previously served. (The former second sentence of subdivision (a), which required a copy of the complaint or of the affidavits on which the "injunction" was granted to be served if not previously served, is deleted. Neither a preliminary nor a permanent injunction may be granted without notice.) Paragraph (2) of subdivision (d) requires the order to show cause to state the date, time, and place of the hearing. This is consistent with Section 1010 (notice of motion must state when it will be made).

A provision is added in paragraph (2) of subdivision (d) to give the court authority to shorten the time for service. This is consistent with Family Code Section 243. The requirement of good cause for shortening time is taken from Rule 305 of the California Rules of Court.

A provision is added in paragraph (4) of subdivision (d) to provide that if the opposing party obtains a continuance, the temporary restraining order is continued in effect until the hearing. This codifies the rule of International Molders & Allied Workers Union, Local 164 v. Superior Court, 70 Cal.App.3d 395, 407, 138 Cal.Rptr. 794 (1977).

Paragraph (5) is added to subdivision (d) to give the court authority to reissue a temporary restraining order not served within the required time. This is consistent with McDonald v. Superior Court, 18 Cal.App.2d 652, 655–56, 64 P.2d 738 (1937), and with Family Code Section 245.

Subdivision (f) is added to make clear that if the time requirements of this section are not satisfied or if the order to show cause is issued without a temporary restraining order, the court may still hear the matter if the papers are served within the time provided by Section 1005 for a notice of motion (15 days, with additional time if mailed). This changes the result in McDonald v. Superior Court, *supra*, and treats an order to show cause without a temporary restraining order the same as a notice of motion for a preliminary injunction without a temporary restraining order. See Gilbert & Kaplan, *Injunctions*, in 2 California Civil Procedure Before Trial § 39.43 (Cal. Cont. Ed. Bar 3d ed. 1992).

The other revisions to Section 527 are technical. [24 Cal.L.Rev. Comm. Reports 603 (1994)].

Research References

Forms

West's California Code Forms, Civil § 798.88 Form 1, Petition to Enjoin Continuing Violations Of Mobile-Home Park Rules.

West's California Code Forms, Civil Procedure § 527 Form 5, Injunction--Notice Of Motion for Preliminary Injunction.

West's California Code Forms, Civil Procedure § 530 Form 1, Injunction--Notice Of Motion for Preliminary Injunction Against Diversion Of Water.

West's California Judicial Council Forms CD-200, Temporary Restraining Order.

West's California Judicial Council Forms RC-200, Ex Parte Order Appointing Receiver and Order to Show Cause and Temporary Restraining Order--Rents, Issues, and Profits.

West's California Judicial Council Forms RC-210, Order Confirming Appointment Of Receiver and Preliminary Injunction--Rents, Issues, and Profits.

West's California Judicial Council Forms RC-300, Order to Show Cause and Temporary Restraining Order--Rents, Issues, and Profits.

West's California Judicial Council Forms RC-310, Order Appointing Receiver After Hearing and Preliminary Injunction--Rents, Issues, and Profits.

West's California Judicial Council Forms CIV-025, Application and Order for Reissuance Of Order to Show Cause and Temporary Restraining Order.

Treatises and Practice Aids

Witkin, California Summary 10th Constitutional Law § 371, Restrictions on Motion Pictures and Plays.

Witkin, California Summary 10th Constitutional Law § 397, by Labor Organizations.

Witkin, California Summary 10th Constitutional Law § 656, Restraining Criminal Nuisance.

Witkin, California Summary 10th Husband and Wife § 371, Civil Remedies.

Witkin, California Summary 10th Parent and Child § 453, Jurisdiction Over Adults.

§ 527.6. Harassment; temporary restraining order and order after hearing; procedure; allegations or threats of violence; support person; costs and attorney fees; punishment; confidentiality of information relating to minors

(a)(1) A person who has suffered harassment as defined in subdivision (b) may seek a temporary restraining order and an order after hearing prohibiting harassment as provided in this section.

(2) A minor, under 12 years of age, accompanied by a duly appointed and acting guardian ad litem, shall be permitted to appear in court without counsel for the limited purpose of requesting or opposing a request for a temporary restraining order or order after hearing, or both, under this section as provided in Section 374.

(b) For purposes of this section:

(1) "Course of conduct" is a pattern of conduct composed of a series of acts over a period of time, however short, evidencing a continuity of purpose, including following or stalking an individual, making harassing telephone calls to an individual, or sending harassing correspondence to an individual by any means, including, but not limited to, the use of public or private mails, interoffice mail, facsimile, or email. Constitutionally protected activity is not included within the meaning of "course of conduct."

(2) "Credible threat of violence" is a knowing and willful statement or course of conduct that would place a reasonable person in fear for his or her safety or the safety of his or her immediate family, and that serves no legitimate purpose.

(3) "Harassment" is unlawful violence, a credible threat of violence, or a knowing and willful course of conduct directed at a specific person that seriously alarms, annoys, or harasses the person, and that serves no legitimate purpose. The course of conduct must be that which would cause a reasonable person to suffer substantial emotional distress, and must actually cause substantial emotional distress to the petitioner.

(4) "Petitioner" means the person to be protected by the temporary restraining order and order after hearing and, if the court grants the petition, the protected person.

(5) "Respondent" means the person against whom the temporary restraining order and order after hearing are sought and, if the petition is granted, the restrained person.

(6) "Temporary restraining order" and "order after hearing" mean orders that include any of the following restraining orders, whether issued ex parte or after notice and hearing:

(A) An order enjoining a party from harassing, intimidating, molesting, attacking, striking, stalking, threatening, sexually assaulting, battering, abusing, telephoning, including, but not limited to, making annoying telephone calls, as described in Section 653m of the Penal Code, destroying personal property, contacting, either directly or indirectly, by mail or otherwise, or coming within a specified distance of, or disturbing the peace of, the petitioner. On a showing of good cause, in an order issued pursuant to this subparagraph in connection with an animal owned, possessed, leased, kept, or held by the petitioner, or residing in the residence or household of the petitioner, the court may do either or both of the following:

(i) Grant the petitioner exclusive care, possession, or control of the animal.

(ii) Order the respondent to stay away from the animal and refrain from taking, transferring, encumbering, concealing, molesting, attacking, striking, threatening, harming, or otherwise disposing of the animal.

(B) An order enjoining a party from specified behavior that the court determines is necessary to effectuate orders described in subparagraph (A).

(7) "Unlawful violence" is any assault or battery, or stalking as prohibited in Section 646.9 of the Penal Code, but does not include lawful acts of self-defense or defense of others.

(c) In the discretion of the court, on a showing of good cause, a temporary restraining order or order after hearing issued under this section may include other named family or household members.

(d) Upon filing a petition for orders under this section, the petitioner may obtain a temporary restraining order in accordance with Section 527, except to the extent this section provides an inconsistent rule. The temporary restraining order may include any of the restraining orders described in paragraph (6) of subdivision (b). A temporary restraining order may be issued with or without notice, based on a declaration that, to the satisfaction of the court, shows reasonable proof of harassment of the petitioner by the respondent, and that great or irreparable harm would result to the petitioner.

(e) A request for the issuance of a temporary restraining order without notice under this section shall be granted or denied on the same day that the petition is submitted to the court. If the petition is filed too late in the day to permit effective review, the order shall be granted or denied on the next day of judicial business in sufficient time for the order to be filed that day with the clerk of the court.

(f) A temporary restraining order issued under this section shall remain in effect, at the court's discretion, for a period not to exceed 21 days, or, if the court extends the time for hearing under subdivision (g), not to exceed 25 days, unless otherwise modified or terminated by the court.

(g) Within 21 days, or, if good cause appears to the court, 25 days from the date that a petition for a temporary order is granted or denied, a hearing shall be held on the petition. If a request for a temporary order is not made, the hearing shall be held within 21 days, or, if good cause appears to the court, 25 days, from the date that the petition is filed.

(h) The respondent may file a response that explains, excuses, justifies, or denies the alleged harassment, or may file a cross-petition under this section.

(i) At the hearing, the judge shall receive any testimony that is relevant, and may make an independent inquiry. If the judge finds by clear and convincing evidence that unlawful harassment exists, an order shall issue prohibiting the harassment.

(j)(1) In the discretion of the court, an order issued after notice and hearing under this section may have a duration of no more than five years, subject to termination or modification by further order of the court either on written stipulation filed with the court or on the motion of a party. The order may be renewed, upon the request of a party, for a duration of no more than five additional years, without a showing of any further harassment since the issuance of the original order, subject to termination or modification by further order of the court either on written stipulation filed with the court or on the motion of a party. A request for renewal may be brought any time within the three months before the order expires.

(2) The failure to state the expiration date on the face of the form creates an order with a duration of three years from the date of issuance.

(3) If an action is filed for the purpose of terminating or modifying a protective order before the expiration date specified in the order by a party other than the protected party, the party who is protected by the order shall be given notice, pursuant to subdivision (b) of Section 1005, of the proceeding by personal service or, if the protected party has satisfied the requirements of Chapter 3.1 (commencing with Section 6205) of Division 7 of Title 1 of the Government Code, by service on the Secretary of State. If the party who is protected by the order cannot be notified before the hearing for modification or termination of the protective order, the court shall deny the motion to modify or terminate the order without prejudice or continue the hearing until the party who is protected can be properly noticed and may, upon a showing of good cause, specify another method for service of process that is reasonably designed to afford actual notice to the protected party. The protected party may waive his or her right to notice if he or she is physically present in court and does not challenge the sufficiency of the notice.

(k) This section does not preclude either party from representation by private counsel or from appearing on the party's own behalf.

(*l*) In a proceeding under this section, if there are allegations of unlawful violence or credible threats of violence, a support person may accompany a party in court and, if the party is not represented by an attorney, may sit with the party at the table that is generally reserved for the party and the party's attorney. The support person is present to provide moral and emotional support for a person who alleges he or she is a victim of violence. The support person is not present as a legal adviser and may not provide legal advice. The support person may assist the person who alleges he or she is a victim of violence in feeling more confident that he or she will not be injured or threatened by the other party during the proceedings if the person who alleges he or she is a victim of violence and the other party are required to be present in close proximity. This subdivision does not preclude the court from exercising its discretion to remove the support person from the courtroom if the court believes the support person is prompting, swaying, or influencing the party assisted by the support person.

(m) Upon the filing of a petition under this section, the respondent shall be personally served with a copy of the petition, temporary restraining order, if any, and notice of hearing of the petition. Service shall be made at least five days before the hearing. The court may for good cause, on motion of the petitioner or on its own motion, shorten the time for service on the respondent.

(n) A notice of hearing under this section shall notify the respondent that if he or she does not attend the hearing, the court may make orders against him or her that could last up to five years.

(*o*) The respondent shall be entitled, as a matter of course, to one continuance, for a reasonable period, to respond to the petition.

(p)(1) Either party may request a continuance of the hearing, which the court shall grant on a showing of good cause. The request may be made in writing before or at the hearing, or orally at the hearing. The court may also grant a continuance on its own motion.

(2) If the court grants a continuance, any temporary restraining order that has been granted shall remain in effect until the end of the continued hearing, unless otherwise ordered by the court. In granting a continuance, the court may modify or terminate a temporary restraining order.

(q)(1) If a respondent named in a restraining order issued after a hearing has not been served personally with the order but has received actual notice of the existence and substance of the order through personal appearance in court to hear the terms of the order from the court, additional proof of service is not required for enforcement of the order.

(2) If the respondent named in a temporary restraining order is personally served with the order and notice of hearing with respect to a restraining order or protective order based on the temporary restraining order, but the respondent does not appear at the hearing, either personally or by an attorney, and the terms and conditions of the restraining order or protective order issued at the hearing are identical to the temporary restraining order, except for the duration of the order, the restraining order or protective order issued at the hearing may be served on the respondent by first-class mail sent to the respondent at the most current address for the respondent available to the court.

(3) The Judicial Council form for temporary orders issued pursuant to this subdivision shall contain a statement in substantially the following form:

"If you have been personally served with this temporary restraining order and notice of hearing, but you do not appear at the hearing either in person or by a lawyer, and a restraining order that is the same as this temporary restraining order except for the expiration date is issued at the hearing, a copy of the restraining order will be served on you by mail at the following address: ______.

If that address is not correct or you wish to verify that the temporary restraining order was converted to a restraining order at the hearing without substantive change and to find out the duration of that order, contact the clerk of the court."

(4) If information about a minor has been made confidential pursuant to subdivision (v), the notice shall identify the information, specifically, that has been made confidential and shall include a statement that disclosure or misuse of that information is punishable as a contempt of court.

(r)(1) Information on a temporary restraining order or order after hearing relating to civil harassment issued by a court pursuant to this section shall be transmitted to the Department of Justice in accordance with either paragraph (2) or (3).

(2) The court shall order the petitioner or the attorney for the petitioner to deliver a copy of an order issued under this section, or reissuance, extension, modification, or termination of the order, and any subsequent proof of service, by the close of the business day on which the order, reissuance, extension, modification, or termination was made, to a law enforcement agency having jurisdiction over the residence of the petitioner and to any additional law enforcement agencies within the court's discretion as are requested by the petitioner.

(3) Alternatively, the court or its designee shall transmit, within one business day, to law enforcement personnel all information required under subdivision (b) of Section 6380 of the Family Code regarding any order issued under this section, or a reissuance, extension, modification, or termination of the order, and any subsequent proof of service, by either one of the following methods:

(A) Transmitting a physical copy of the order or proof of service to a local law enforcement agency authorized by the Department of Justice to enter orders into the California Law Enforcement Telecommunications System (CLETS).

(B) With the approval of the Department of Justice, entering the order or proof of service into CLETS directly.

(4) Each appropriate law enforcement agency shall make available information as to the existence and current status of orders issued under this section to law enforcement officers responding to the scene of reported harassment.

(5) An order issued under this section shall, on request of the petitioner, be served on the respondent, whether or not the respondent has been taken into custody, by any law enforcement officer who is present at the scene of reported harassment involving the parties to the proceeding. The petitioner shall provide the officer with an endorsed copy of the order and a proof of service that the officer shall complete and send to the issuing court.

(6) Upon receiving information at the scene of an incident of harassment that a protective order has been issued under this section, or that a person who has been taken into custody is the subject of an order, if the protected person cannot produce a certified copy of the order, a law enforcement officer shall immediately attempt to verify the existence of the order.

(7) If the law enforcement officer determines that a protective order has been issued but not served, the officer

shall immediately notify the respondent of the terms of the order and shall at that time also enforce the order. Verbal notice of the terms of the order shall constitute service of the order and is sufficient notice for purposes of this section and for purposes of Section 29825 of the Penal Code. Verbal notice shall include the information required pursuant to paragraph (4) of subdivision (q).

(s) The prevailing party in an action brought * * * pursuant to this section may be awarded court costs and attorney's fees, if any.

(t) Willful disobedience of a temporary restraining order or order after hearing granted * * * pursuant to this section is punishable pursuant to Section 273.6 of the Penal Code.

(u)(1) A person subject to a protective order issued * * * pursuant to this section shall not own, possess, purchase, receive, or attempt to purchase or receive a firearm or ammunition while the protective order is in effect.

(2) The court shall order a person subject to a protective order issued * * * pursuant to this section to relinquish any firearms he or she owns or possesses pursuant to Section 527.9.

(3) A person who owns, possesses, purchases, or receives, or attempts to purchase or receive, a firearm or ammunition while the protective order is in effect is punishable pursuant to Section 29825 of the Penal Code.

(v)(1) A minor or the minor's legal guardian may petition the court to have information regarding the minor obtained when issuing an order pursuant to this section, including, but not limited to, the minor's name, address, and the circumstances surrounding the protective order with respect to that minor, be kept confidential.

(2) The court may order the information specified in paragraph (1) be kept confidential if the court expressly finds all of the following:

(A) The minor's right to privacy overcomes the right of public access to the information.

(B) There is a substantial probability that the minor's interest will be prejudiced if the information is not kept confidential.

(C) The order to keep the information confidential is narrowly tailored.

(D) No less restrictive means exist to protect the minor's privacy.

(3) If the request is granted, except as provided in paragraph (4), information regarding the minor shall be maintained in a confidential case file and shall not become part of the public file in the proceeding or any other civil proceeding. Disclosure or misuse of that information is punishable as civil contempt of court with a fine of up to one thousand dollars ($1,000). An order of civil contempt under this paragraph shall not include imprisonment.

(4)(A) Confidential information about a minor who is protected by an order issued pursuant to this section shall be made available to law enforcement pursuant to subdivision (r), to the extent necessary and only for the purpose of enforcing the order.

(B) To the extent necessary for the enforcement of the order and to allow the respondent to comply with and respond to the order, confidential information shall be included in the notice sent to the respondent pursuant to this section.

(w) This section does not apply to any action or proceeding covered by Title 1.6C (commencing with Section 1788) of Part 4 of Division 3 of the Civil Code or by Division 10 (commencing with Section 6200) of the Family Code. This section does not preclude a petitioner from using other existing civil remedies.

(x)(1) The Judicial Council shall develop forms, instructions, and rules relating to matters governed by this section. The petition and response forms shall be simple and concise, and their use by parties in actions brought pursuant to this section is mandatory.

(2) A temporary restraining order or order after hearing relating to civil harassment issued by a court pursuant to this section shall be issued on forms adopted by the Judicial Council and that have been approved by the Department of Justice pursuant to subdivision (i) of Section 6380 of the Family Code. However, the fact that an order issued by a court pursuant to this section was not issued on forms adopted by the Judicial Council and approved by the Department of Justice shall not, in and of itself, make the order unenforceable.

(y) There is no filing fee for a petition that alleges that a person has inflicted or threatened violence against the petitioner, stalked the petitioner, or acted or spoken in any other manner that has placed the petitioner in reasonable fear of violence, and that seeks a protective or restraining order restraining stalking, future violence, or threats of violence, in an action brought pursuant to this section. A fee shall not be paid for a subpoena filed in connection with a petition alleging these acts. A fee shall not be paid for filing a response to a petition alleging these acts.

(z)(1) Subject to paragraph (4) of subdivision (b) of Section 6103.2 of the Government Code, there shall not be a fee for the service of process by a sheriff or marshal of a protective or restraining order to be issued, if either of the following conditions apply:

(A) The protective or restraining order issued pursuant to this section is based upon stalking, as prohibited by Section 646.9 of the Penal Code.

(B) The protective or restraining order issued pursuant to this section is based upon unlawful violence or a credible threat of violence.

(2) The Judicial Council shall prepare and develop forms for persons who wish to avail themselves of the services described in this subdivision. *(Added by Stats.2013, c. 158 (A.B.499), § 2, operative July 1, 2014. Amended by Stats.2015, c. 401 (A.B.494), § 1, eff. Jan. 1, 2016; Stats.2015, c. 411 (A.B.1081), § 1.5, eff. Jan. 1, 2016; Stats.2016, c. 86 (S.B. 1171), § 24, eff. Jan. 1, 2017; Stats.2017, c. 384 (A.B.953), § 1, eff. Jan. 1, 2018.)*

Commentary

Applying subsection (i), *Krug v. Maschmeier, 172 Cal.App.4th 796, 91 Cal.Rptr.3d 452 (2009)*, holds that the court may award a prevailing defendant court costs and attorney fees without finding that the action for injunctive relief was filed frivolously or in bad faith.

entity requesting the order, the judge shall receive evidence concerning the employer's decision to retain, terminate, or otherwise discipline the respondent. If the judge finds by clear and convincing evidence that the respondent engaged in unlawful violence or made a credible threat of violence, an order shall issue prohibiting further unlawful violence or threats of violence.

(k)(1) In the discretion of the court, an order issued after notice and hearing under this section may have a duration of not more than three years, subject to termination or modification by further order of the court either on written stipulation filed with the court or on the motion of a party. These orders may be renewed, upon the request of a party, for a duration of not more than three years, without a showing of any further violence or threats of violence since the issuance of the original order, subject to termination or modification by further order of the court either on written stipulation filed with the court or on the motion of a party. The request for renewal may be brought at any time within the three months before the expiration of the order.

(2) The failure to state the expiration date on the face of the form creates an order with a duration of three years from the date of issuance.

(3) If an action is filed for the purpose of terminating or modifying a protective order prior to the expiration date specified in the order by a party other than the protected party, the party who is protected by the order shall be given notice, pursuant to subdivision (b) of Section 1005, of the proceeding by personal service or, if the protected party has satisfied the requirements of Chapter 3.1 (commencing with Section 6205) of Division 7 of Title 1 of the Government Code, by service on the Secretary of State. If the party who is protected by the order cannot be notified prior to the hearing for modification or termination of the protective order, the court shall deny the motion to modify or terminate the order without prejudice or continue the hearing until the party who is protected can be properly noticed and may, upon a showing of good cause, specify another method for service of process that is reasonably designed to afford actual notice to the protected party. The protected party may waive his or her right to notice if he or she is physically present in court and does not challenge the sufficiency of the notice.

(*l*) This section does not preclude either party from representation by private counsel or from appearing on his or her own behalf.

(m) Upon filing of a petition under this section, the respondent shall be personally served with a copy of the petition, temporary restraining order, if any, and notice of hearing of the petition. Service shall be made at least five days before the hearing. The court may, for good cause, on motion of the petitioner or on its own motion, shorten the time for service on the respondent.

(n) A notice of hearing under this section shall notify the respondent that, if he or she does not attend the hearing, the court may make orders against him or her that could last up to three years.

(*o*) The respondent shall be entitled, as a matter of course, to one continuance, for a reasonable period, to respond to the petition.

(p)(1) Either party may request a continuance of the hearing, which the court shall grant on a showing of good cause. The request may be made in writing before or at the hearing or orally at the hearing. The court may also grant a continuance on its own motion.

(2) If the court grants a continuance, any temporary restraining order that has been granted shall remain in effect until the end of the continued hearing, unless otherwise ordered by the court. In granting a continuance, the court may modify or terminate a temporary restraining order.

(q)(1) If a respondent, named in a restraining order issued under this section after a hearing, has not been served personally with the order but has received actual notice of the existence and substance of the order through personal appearance in court to hear the terms of the order from the court, no additional proof of service is required for enforcement of the order.

(2) If the respondent named in a temporary restraining order is personally served with the order and notice of hearing with respect to a restraining order or protective order based on the temporary restraining order, but the person does not appear at the hearing, either personally or by an attorney, and the terms and conditions of the restraining order or protective order issued at the hearing are identical to the temporary restraining order, except for the duration of the order, then the restraining order or protective order issued at the hearing may be served on the person by first-class mail sent to that person at the most current address for the person available to the court.

(3) The Judicial Council form for temporary orders issued pursuant to this subdivision shall contain a statement in substantially the following form:

"If you have been personally served with this temporary restraining order and notice of hearing, but you do not appear at the hearing either in person or by a lawyer, and a restraining order that is the same as this restraining order except for the expiration date is issued at the hearing, a copy of the order will be served on you by mail at the following address: ____.

If that address is not correct or you wish to verify that the temporary restraining order was converted to a restraining order at the hearing without substantive change and to find out the duration of that order, contact the clerk of the court."

(r)(1) Information on a temporary restraining order or order after hearing relating to workplace violence issued by a court pursuant to this section shall be transmitted to the Department of Justice in accordance with either paragraph (2) or (3).

(2) The court shall order the petitioner or the attorney for the petitioner to deliver a copy of any order issued under this section, or a reissuance, extension, modification, or termination of the order, and any subsequent proof of service, by the close of the business day on which the order, reissuance, extension, modification, or termination was made, to each law enforcement agency having jurisdiction over the residence of the petitioner and to any additional law enforcement

agencies within the court's discretion as are requested by the petitioner.

(3) Alternatively, the court or its designee shall transmit, within one business day, to law enforcement personnel all information required under subdivision (b) of Section 6380 of the Family Code regarding any order issued under this section, or a reissuance, extension, modification, or termination of the order, and any subsequent proof of service, by either one of the following methods:

(A) Transmitting a physical copy of the order or proof of service to a local law enforcement agency authorized by the Department of Justice to enter orders into the California Law Enforcement Telecommunications System (CLETS).

(B) With the approval of the Department of Justice, entering the order or proof of service into CLETS directly.

(4) Each appropriate law enforcement agency shall make available information as to the existence and current status of these orders to law enforcement officers responding to the scene of reported unlawful violence or a credible threat of violence.

(5) At the request of the petitioner, an order issued under this section shall be served on the respondent, regardless of whether the respondent has been taken into custody, by any law enforcement officer who is present at the scene of reported unlawful violence or a credible threat of violence involving the parties to the proceedings. The petitioner shall provide the officer with an endorsed copy of the order and proof of service that the officer shall complete and send to the issuing court.

(6) Upon receiving information at the scene of an incident of unlawful violence or a credible threat of violence that a protective order has been issued under this section, or that a person who has been taken into custody is the subject of an order, if the petitioner or the protected person cannot produce an endorsed copy of the order, a law enforcement officer shall immediately attempt to verify the existence of the order.

(7) If the law enforcement officer determines that a protective order has been issued but not served, the officer shall immediately notify the respondent of the terms of the order and obtain the respondent's address. The law enforcement officer shall at that time also enforce the order, but may not arrest or take the respondent into custody for acts in violation of the order that were committed prior to the verbal notice of the terms and conditions of the order. The law enforcement officer's verbal notice of the terms of the order shall constitute service of the order and constitutes sufficient notice for the purposes of this section and for the purposes of Section 29825 of the Penal Code. The petitioner shall mail an endorsed copy of the order to the respondent's mailing address provided to the law enforcement officer within one business day of the reported incident of unlawful violence or a credible threat of violence at which a verbal notice of the terms of the order was provided by a law enforcement officer.

(s)(1) A person subject to a protective order issued under this section shall not own, possess, purchase, receive, or attempt to purchase or receive a firearm or ammunition while the protective order is in effect.

(2) The court shall order a person subject to a protective order issued under this section to relinquish any firearms he or she owns or possesses pursuant to Section 527.9.

(3) Every person who owns, possesses, purchases or receives, or attempts to purchase or receive a firearm or ammunition while the protective order is in effect is punishable pursuant to Section 29825 of the Penal Code.

(t) Any intentional disobedience of any temporary restraining order or order after hearing granted under this section is punishable pursuant to Section 273.6 of the Penal Code.

(u) This section shall not be construed as expanding, diminishing, altering, or modifying the duty, if any, of an employer to provide a safe workplace for employees and other persons.

(v)(1) The Judicial Council shall develop forms, instructions, and rules for relating to matters governed by this section. The forms for the petition and response shall be simple and concise, and their use by parties in actions brought pursuant to this section shall be mandatory.

(2) A temporary restraining order or order after hearing relating to unlawful violence or a credible threat of violence issued by a court pursuant to this section shall be issued on forms adopted by the Judicial Council of California and that have been approved by the Department of Justice pursuant to subdivision (i) of Section 6380 of the Family Code. However, the fact that an order issued by a court pursuant to this section was not issued on forms adopted by the Judicial Council and approved by the Department of Justice shall not, in and of itself, make the order unenforceable.

(w) There is no filing fee for a petition that alleges that a person has inflicted or threatened violence against an employee of the petitioner, or stalked the employee, or acted or spoken in any other manner that has placed the employee in reasonable fear of violence, and that seeks a protective or restraining order restraining stalking or future violence or threats of violence, in any action brought pursuant to this section. No fee shall be paid for a subpoena filed in connection with a petition alleging these acts. No fee shall be paid for filing a response to a petition alleging these acts.

(x)(1) Subject to paragraph (4) of subdivision (b) of Section 6103.2 of the Government Code, there shall be no fee for the service of process by a sheriff or marshal of a temporary restraining order or order after hearing to be issued pursuant to this section if either of the following conditions applies:

(A) The temporary restraining order or order after hearing issued pursuant to this section is based upon stalking, as prohibited by Section 646.9 of the Penal Code.

(B) The temporary restraining order or order after hearing issued pursuant to this section is based on unlawful violence or a credible threat of violence.

(2) The Judicial Council shall prepare and develop forms for persons who wish to avail themselves of the services described in this subdivision. *(Added by Stats.1993–94, 1st Ex.Sess., c. 29 (A.B.68), § 2, eff. Nov. 30, 1994. Amended by Stats.1998, c. 581 (A.B.2801), § 3; Stats.1999, c. 661 (A.B. 825), § 2; Stats.2000, c. 688 (A.B.1669), § 6; Stats.2002, c. 1008 (A.B.3028), § 3; Stats.2003, c. 498 (S.B.226), § 3;*

Stats.2005, c. 467 (A.B.429), § 1; Stats.2006, c. 476 (A.B. 2695), § 2; Stats.2010, c. 178 (S.B.1115), § 21, operative Jan. 1, 2012; Stats.2010, c. 572 (A.B.1596), § 2, operative Jan. 1, 2012; Stats.2011, c. 285 (A.B.1402), § 2; Stats.2011, c. 101 (A.B.454), § 2; Stats.2012, c. 162 (S.B.1171), § 13; Stats. 2015, c. 411 (A.B.1081), § 2, eff. Jan. 1, 2016.)

Research References

Forms

Cal. Transaction Forms - Bus. Transactions § 12:9, Provision Of Sanitary, Safe, and Healthy Workplace.

West's California Code Forms, Civil Procedure § 527.8 Form 1, Injunction--Workplace Violence--Petition for Workplace Violence Restraining Orders (Workplace Violence Prevention)--Official Form.

West's California Code Forms, Civil Procedure § 527.6 Form 16, Injunction--Order to Show Cause (Workplace Violence) and Temporary Restraining Order (CLETS)--Official Form.

West's California Code Forms, Civil Procedure § 425.10 Form 1, Pleadings--Complaint--Negligence Action.

West's California Code Forms, Civil Procedure § 430.10 Form 1, Pleadings--Demurrer.

West's California Judicial Council Forms WV-100, Petition for Workplace Violence Restraining Orders.

West's California Judicial Council Forms WV-109, Notice Of Court Hearing.

West's California Judicial Council Forms WV-110, Temporary Restraining Order.

West's California Judicial Council Forms WV-115, Request to Continue Court Hearing and Reissue Temporary Restraining Order.

West's California Judicial Council Forms WV-116, Notice Of New Hearing Date and Order on Reissuance.

West's California Judicial Council Forms WV-130, Workplace Violence Restraining Order After Hearing.

West's California Judicial Council Forms WV-200, Proof Of Personal Service.

West's California Judicial Council Forms WV-250, Proof Of Service Of Response by Mail.

West's California Judicial Council Forms WV-260, Proof Of Service Of Order After Hearing by Mail.

West's California Judicial Council Forms WV-700, Request to Renew Restraining Order.

West's California Judicial Council Forms WV-710, Notice Of Hearing to Renew Restraining Order.

West's California Judicial Council Forms WV-720, Response to Request to Renew Restraining Order.

West's California Judicial Council Forms WV-730, Order Renewing Workplace Violence Restraining Order.

West's California Judicial Council Forms WV-100-INFO, How Do I Get an Order to Prohibit Workplace Violence?

West's California Judicial Council Forms WV-115-INFO, How to Ask for a New Hearing Date.

West's California Judicial Council Forms WV-120-INFO, How Can I Respond to a Petition for Workplace Violence Restraining Orders?

Treatises and Practice Aids

Witkin, California Summary 10th Agency and Employment § 246, Policy Delineated in Constitution, Statute, Regulation, or Rule.

Witkin, California Summary 10th Agency and Employment § 375, Work Violence Safety Act.

Witkin, California Summary 10th Husband and Wife § 371, Civil Remedies.

Witkin, California Summary 10th Husband and Wife § 387, Electronic Transmission and Recording Of Data.

Witkin, California Summary 10th Parent and Child § 519, Nature Of Dependency Proceedings.

Witkin, California Summary 10th Torts § 496B, (New) Petition to Enjoin Workplace Violence or Threats.

§ 527.85. Officers authorized to maintain order on school campus or facility; threat of violence made off school campus; temporary restraining order and order after hearing; violation of restraining order

(a) Any chief administrative officer of a postsecondary educational institution, or an officer or employee designated by the chief administrative officer to maintain order on the school campus or facility, a student of which has suffered a credible threat of violence made off the school campus or facility from any individual which can reasonably be construed to be carried out or to have been carried out at the school campus or facility, may, with the written consent of the student, seek a temporary restraining order and an order after hearing on behalf of the student and, at the discretion of the court, any number of other students at the campus or facility who are similarly situated.

(b) For purposes of this section, the following definitions apply:

(1) "Chief administrative officer" means the principal, president, or highest ranking official of the postsecondary educational institution.

(2) "Course of conduct" means a pattern of conduct composed of a series of acts over a period of time, however short, evidencing a continuity of purpose, including any of the following:

(A) Following or stalking a student to or from school.

(B) Entering the school campus or facility.

(C) Following a student during school hours.

(D) Making telephone calls to a student.

(E) Sending correspondence to a student by any means, including, but not limited to, the use of the public or private mails, interoffice mail, facsimile, or computer email.

(3) "Credible threat of violence" means a knowing and willful statement or course of conduct that would place a reasonable person in fear for his or her safety, or the safety of his or her immediate family, and that serves no legitimate purpose.

(4) "Petitioner" means the chief administrative officer, or his or her designee, who petitions under subdivision (a) for a temporary restraining order and order after hearing.

(5) "Postsecondary educational institution" means a private institution of vocational, professional, or postsecondary education.

(6) "Respondent" means the person against whom the temporary restraining order and order after hearing are sought and, if the petition is granted, the restrained person.

(7) "Student" means an adult currently enrolled in or applying for admission to a postsecondary educational institution.

(8) "Temporary restraining order" and "order after hearing" mean orders that include any of the following restraining orders, whether issued ex parte, or after notice and hearing:

(A) An order enjoining a party from harassing, intimidating, molesting, attacking, striking, stalking, threatening, sexually assaulting, battering, abusing, telephoning, including, but not limited to, making annoying telephone calls as described in Section 653m of the Penal Code, destroying personal property, contacting, either directly or indirectly, by mail or otherwise, or coming within a specified distance of, or disturbing the peace of, the student.

(B) An order enjoining a party from specified behavior that the court determines is necessary to effectuate orders described in subparagraph (A).

(9) "Unlawful violence" means any assault or battery, or stalking as prohibited in Section 646.9 of the Penal Code, but shall not include lawful acts of self-defense or defense of others.

(c) This section does not permit a court to issue a temporary restraining order or order after hearing prohibiting speech or other activities that are constitutionally protected, or otherwise protected by Section 527.3 or any other provision of law.

(d) In the discretion of the court, on a showing of good cause, a temporary restraining order or order after hearing issued under this section may include other named family or household members of the student, or other students at the campus or facility.

(e) Upon filing a petition under this section, the petitioner may obtain a temporary restraining order in accordance with subdivision (a) of Section 527, if the petitioner also files a declaration that, to the satisfaction of the court, shows reasonable proof that a student has suffered a credible threat of violence made off the school campus or facility by the respondent, and that great or irreparable harm would result to the student. The temporary restraining order may include any of the protective orders described in paragraph (8) of subdivision (b).

(f) A request for the issuance of a temporary restraining order without notice under this section shall be granted or denied on the same day that the petition is submitted to the court, unless the petition is filed too late in the day to permit effective review, in which case the order shall be granted or denied on the next day of judicial business in sufficient time for the order to be filed that day with the clerk of the court.

(g) A temporary restraining order granted under this section shall remain in effect, at the court's discretion, for a period not to exceed 21 days, or if the court extends the time for hearing under subdivision (h), not to exceed 25 days, unless otherwise modified or terminated by the court.

(h) Within 21 days, or if good cause appears to the court, within 25 days, from the date that a petition for a temporary order is granted or denied, a hearing shall be held on the petition. If no request for temporary orders is made, the hearing shall be held within 21 days, or if good cause appears to the court, 25 days, from the date the petition is filed.

(i) The respondent may file a response that explains, excuses, justifies, or denies the alleged credible threats of violence.

(j) At the hearing, the judge shall receive any testimony that is relevant and may make an independent inquiry. Moreover, if the respondent is a current student of the entity requesting the order, the judge shall receive evidence concerning the decision of the postsecondary educational institution decision to retain, terminate, or otherwise discipline the respondent. If the judge finds by clear and convincing evidence that the respondent made a credible threat of violence off the school campus or facility, an order shall be issued prohibiting further threats of violence.

(k)(1) In the discretion of the court, an order issued after notice and hearing under this section may have a duration of not more than three years, subject to termination or modification by further order of the court either on written stipulation filed with the court or on the motion of a party. These orders may be renewed, upon the request of a party, for a duration of not more than three years, without a showing of any further violence or threats of violence since the issuance of the original order, subject to termination or modification by further order of the court either on written stipulation filed with the court or on the motion of a party. The request for renewal may be brought at any time within the three months before the expiration of the order.

(2) The failure to state the expiration date on the face of the form creates an order with a duration of three years from the date of issuance.

(3) If an action is filed for the purpose of terminating or modifying a protective order prior to the expiration date specified in the order by a party other than the protected party, the party who is protected by the order shall be given notice, pursuant to subdivision (b) of Section 1005, of the proceeding by personal service or, if the protected party has satisfied the requirements of Chapter 3.1 (commencing with Section 6205) of Division 7 of Title 1 of the Government Code, by service on the Secretary of State. If the party who is protected by the order cannot be notified prior to the hearing for modification or termination of the protective order, the court shall deny the motion to modify or terminate the order without prejudice or continue the hearing until the party who is protected can be properly noticed and may, upon a showing of good cause, specify another method for service of process that is reasonably designed to afford actual notice to the protected party. The protected party may waive his or her right to notice if he or she is physically present in court and does not challenge the sufficiency of the notice.

(*l*) This section does not preclude either party from representation by private counsel or from appearing on his or her own behalf.

(m) Upon filing of a petition under this section, the respondent shall be personally served with a copy of the petition, temporary restraining order, if any, and notice of hearing of the petition. Service shall be made at least five days before the hearing. The court may, for good cause, on motion of the petitioner or on its own motion, shorten the time for service on the respondent.

(n) A notice of hearing under this section shall notify the respondent that if he or she does not attend the hearing, the court may make orders against him or her that could last up to three years.

(*o*) The respondent shall be entitled, as a matter of course, to one continuance, for a reasonable period, to respond to the petition.

(p)(1) Either party may request a continuance of the hearing, which the court shall grant on a showing of good cause. The request may be made in writing before or at the hearing or orally at the hearing. The court may also grant a continuance on its own motion.

(2) If the court grants a continuance, any temporary restraining order that has been granted shall remain in effect until the end of the continued hearing, unless otherwise ordered by the court. In granting a continuance, the court may modify or terminate a temporary restraining order.

(q)(1) If a respondent, named in an order issued under this section after a hearing, has not been served personally with the order but has received actual notice of the existence and substance of the order through personal appearance in court to hear the terms of the order from the court, no additional proof of service is required for enforcement of the order.

(2) If the respondent named in a temporary restraining order is personally served with the order and notice of hearing with respect to a restraining order or protective order based on the temporary restraining order, but the respondent does not appear at the hearing, either personally or by an attorney, and the terms and conditions of the restraining order or protective order issued at the hearing are identical to the temporary restraining order, except for the duration of the order, then the restraining order or protective order issued at the hearing may be served on the respondent by first-class mail sent to that person at the most current address for the respondent available to the court.

(3) The Judicial Council form for temporary orders issued pursuant to this subdivision shall contain a statement in substantially the following form:

"If you have been personally served with a temporary restraining order and notice of hearing, but you do not appear at the hearing either in person or by a lawyer, and a restraining order that is the same as this temporary restraining order except for the expiration date is issued at the hearing, a copy of the order will be served on you by mail at the following address:____.

If that address is not correct or you wish to verify that the temporary restraining order was converted to a restraining order at the hearing without substantive change and to find out the duration of that order, contact the clerk of the court."

(r)(1) Information on a temporary restraining order or order after hearing relating to schoolsite violence issued by a court pursuant to this section shall be transmitted to the Department of Justice in accordance with either paragraph (2) or (3).

(2) The court shall order the petitioner or the attorney for the petitioner to deliver a copy of any order issued under this section, or a reissuance, extension, modification, or termination of the order, and any subsequent proof of service, by the close of the business day on which the order, reissuance, or termination of the order, and any proof of service, was made, to each law enforcement agency having jurisdiction over the residence of the petition and to any additional law enforcement agencies within the court's discretion as are requested by the petitioner.

(3) Alternatively, the court or its designee shall transmit, within one business day, to law enforcement personnel all information required under subdivision (b) of Section 6380 of the Family Code regarding any order issued under this section, or a reissuance, extension, modification, or termination of the order, and any subsequent proof of service, by either one of the following methods:

(A) Transmitting a physical copy of the order or proof of service to a local law enforcement agency authorized by the Department of Justice to enter orders into the California Law Enforcement Telecommunications System (CLETS).

(B) With the approval of the Department of Justice, entering the order of proof of service into CLETS directly.

(4) Each appropriate law enforcement agency shall make available information as to the existence and current status of these orders to law enforcement officers responding to the scene of reported unlawful violence or a credible threat of violence.

(5) At the request of the petitioner, an order issued under this section shall be served on the respondent, regardless of whether the respondent has been taken into custody, by any law enforcement officer who is present at the scene of reported unlawful violence or a credible threat of violence involving the parties to the proceedings. The petitioner shall provide the officer with an endorsed copy of the order and proof of service that the officer shall complete and send to the issuing court.

(6) Upon receiving information at the scene of an incident of unlawful violence or a credible threat of violence that a protective order has been issued under this section, or that a person who has been taken into custody is the subject of an order, if the petitioner or the protected person cannot produce an endorsed copy of the order, a law enforcement officer shall immediately attempt to verify the existence of the order.

(7) If the law enforcement officer determines that a protective order has been issued but not served, the officer shall immediately notify the respondent of the terms of the order and obtain the respondent's address. The law enforcement officer shall at that time also enforce the order, but may not arrest or take the respondent into custody for acts in violation of the order that were committed prior to the verbal notice of the terms and conditions of the order. The law enforcement officer's verbal notice of the terms of the order shall constitute service of the order and constitutes sufficient notice for the purposes of this section, and Section 29825 of the Penal Code. The petitioner shall mail an endorsed copy of the order to the respondent's mailing address provided to the law enforcement officer within one business day of the reported incident of unlawful violence or a credible threat of violence at which a verbal notice of the terms of the order was provided by a law enforcement officer.

(s)(1) A person subject to a protective order issued under this section shall not own, possess, purchase, receive, or attempt to purchase or receive a firearm or ammunition while the protective order is in effect.

(2) The court shall order a person subject to a protective order issued under this section to relinquish any firearms he or she owns or possesses pursuant to Section 527.9.

(3) Every person who owns, possesses, purchases, or receives, or attempts to purchase or receive a firearm or ammunition while the protective order is in effect is punishable pursuant to Section 29825 of the Penal Code.

(t) Any intentional disobedience of any temporary restraining order or order after hearing granted under this section is punishable pursuant to Section 273.6 of the Penal Code.

(u) This section shall not be construed as expanding, diminishing, altering, or modifying the duty, if any, of a postsecondary educational institution to provide a safe environment for students and other persons.

(v)(1) The Judicial Council shall develop forms, instructions, and rules relating to matters governed by this section. The forms for the petition and response shall be simple and concise, and their use by parties in actions brought pursuant to this section shall be mandatory.

(2) A temporary restraining order or order after hearing relating to unlawful violence or a credible threat of violence issued by a court pursuant to this section shall be issued on forms adopted by the Judicial Council that have been approved by the Department of Justice pursuant to subdivision (i) of Section 6380 of the Family Code. However, the fact that an order issued by a court pursuant to this section was not issued on forms adopted by the Judicial Council and approved by the Department of Justice shall not, in and of itself, make the order unenforceable.

(w) There is no filing fee for a petition that alleges that a person has threatened violence against a student of the petitioner, or stalked the student, or acted or spoken in any other manner that has placed the student in reasonable fear of violence, and that seeks a protective or restraining order restraining stalking or future threats of violence, in any action brought pursuant to this section. No fee shall be paid for a subpoena filed in connection with a petition alleging these acts. No fee shall be paid for filing a response to a petition alleging these acts.

(x)(1) Subject to paragraph (4) of subdivision (b) of Section 6103.2 of the Government Code, there shall be no fee for the service of process by a sheriff or marshal of a temporary restraining order or order after hearing to be issued pursuant to this section if either of the following conditions applies:

(A) The temporary restraining order or order after hearing issued pursuant to this section is based upon stalking, as prohibited by Section 646.9 of the Penal Code.

(B) The temporary restraining order or order after hearing issued pursuant to this section is based upon a credible threat of violence.

(2) The Judicial Council shall prepare and develop forms for persons who wish to avail themselves of the services described in this subdivision. *(Added by Stats.2009, c. 566 (S.B.188), § 1. Amended by Stats.2010, c. 178 (S.B.1115), § 22, operative Jan. 1, 2012; Stats.2010, c. 572 (A.B.1596), § 4, operative Jan. 1, 2012; Stats.2011, c. 285 (A.B.1402), § 3; Stats.2011, c. 101 (A.B.454), § 3; Stats.2012, c. 162 (S.B. 1171), § 14; Stats.2015, c. 411 (A.B.1081), § 3, eff. Jan. 1, 2016.)*

Research References

Forms

West's California Judicial Council Forms SV-100, Petition for Private Postsecondary School Violence Restraining Orders.

West's California Judicial Council Forms SV-110, Temporary Restraining Order.

West's California Judicial Council Forms SV-115, Request to Continue Court Hearing and Reissue Temporary Restraining Order.

West's California Judicial Council Forms SV-116, Notice Of New Hearing Date and Order on Reissuance.

West's California Judicial Council Forms SV-120, Response to Petition for Private Postsecondary School Violence Restraining Orders.

West's California Judicial Council Forms SV-130, Private Postsecondary School Violence Restraining Order After Hearing.

West's California Judicial Council Forms SV-200, Proof Of Personal Service.

West's California Judicial Council Forms SV-250, Proof Of Service Of Response by Mail.

West's California Judicial Council Forms SV-260, Proof Of Service Of Order After Hearing by Mail.

West's California Judicial Council Forms SV-700, Request to Renew Restraining Order.

West's California Judicial Council Forms SV-710, Notice Of Hearing to Renew Restraining Order.

West's California Judicial Council Forms SV-720, Response to Request to Renew Restraining Order.

West's California Judicial Council Forms SV-730, Order Renewing Private Postsecondary School Violence Restraining Order.

West's California Judicial Council Forms WV-120, Response to Petition for Workplace Violence Restraining Orders.

West's California Judicial Council Forms SV-100-INFO, How Do I Get an Order to Prohibit Private Postsecondary School Violence?

West's California Judicial Council Forms SV-115-INFO, How to Ask for a New Hearing Date.

West's California Judicial Council Forms SV-120-INFO, How Can I Respond to a Petition for Private Postsecondary School Violence Restraining Orders?

Treatises and Practice Aids

Witkin, California Summary 10th Husband and Wife § 387, Electronic Transmission and Recording Of Data.

§ 527.9. Relinquishment of firearms; persons subject to protective orders

(a) A person subject to a temporary restraining order or injunction issued pursuant to Section 527.6, 527.8, or 527.85 or subject to a restraining order issued pursuant to Section 136.2 of the Penal Code, or Section 15657.03 of the Welfare and Institutions Code, shall relinquish the firearm pursuant to this section.

(b) Upon the issuance of a protective order against a person pursuant to subdivision (a), the court shall order that person to relinquish any firearm in that person's immediate possession or control, or subject to that person's immediate possession or control, within 24 hours of being served with the order, either by surrendering the firearm to the control of local law enforcement officials, or by selling the firearm to a licensed gun dealer, as specified in Article 1 (commencing with Section 26700) and Article 2 (commencing with Section 26800) of Chapter 2 of Division 6 of Title 4 of Part 6 of the

Penal Code. A person ordered to relinquish any firearm pursuant to this subdivision shall file with the court a receipt showing the firearm was surrendered to the local law enforcement agency or sold to a licensed gun dealer within 48 hours after receiving the order. In the event that it is necessary to continue the date of any hearing due to a request for a relinquishment order pursuant to this section, the court shall ensure that all applicable protective orders described in Section 6218 of the Family Code remain in effect or bifurcate the issues and grant the permanent restraining order pending the date of the hearing.

(c) A local law enforcement agency may charge the person subject to the order or injunction a fee for the storage of any firearm relinquished pursuant to this section. The fee shall not exceed the actual cost incurred by the local law enforcement agency for the storage of the firearm. For purposes of this subdivision, "actual cost" means expenses directly related to taking possession of a firearm, storing the firearm, and surrendering possession of the firearm to a licensed dealer as defined in Section 26700 of the Penal Code or to the person relinquishing the firearm.

(d) The restraining order requiring a person to relinquish a firearm pursuant to subdivision (b) shall state on its face that the respondent is prohibited from owning, possessing, purchasing, or receiving a firearm while the protective order is in effect and that the firearm shall be relinquished to the local law enforcement agency for that jurisdiction or sold to a licensed gun dealer, and that proof of surrender or sale shall be filed with the court within a specified period of receipt of the order. The order shall also state on its face the expiration date for relinquishment. Nothing in this section shall limit a respondent's right under existing law to petition the court at a later date for modification of the order.

(e) The restraining order requiring a person to relinquish a firearm pursuant to subdivision (b) shall prohibit the person from possessing or controlling any firearm for the duration of the order. At the expiration of the order, the local law enforcement agency shall return possession of any surrendered firearm to the respondent, within five days after the expiration of the relinquishment order, unless the local law enforcement agency determines that (1) the firearm has been stolen, (2) the respondent is prohibited from possessing a firearm because the respondent is in any prohibited class for the possession of firearms, as defined in Chapter 2 (commencing with Section 29800) and Chapter 3 (commencing with Section 29900) of Division 9 of Title 4 of Part 6 of the Penal Code and Sections 8100 and 8103 of the Welfare and Institutions Code, or (3) another successive restraining order is issued against the respondent under this section. If the local law enforcement agency determines that the respondent is the legal owner of any firearm deposited with the local law enforcement agency and is prohibited from possessing any firearm, the respondent shall be entitled to sell or transfer the firearm to a licensed dealer as defined in Section 26700 of the Penal Code. If the firearm has been stolen, the firearm shall be restored to the lawful owner upon his or her identification of the firearm and proof of ownership.

(f) The court may, as part of the relinquishment order, grant an exemption from the relinquishment requirements of this section for a particular firearm if the respondent can show that a particular firearm is necessary as a condition of continued employment and that the current employer is unable to reassign the respondent to another position where a firearm is unnecessary. If an exemption is granted pursuant to this subdivision, the order shall provide that the firearm shall be in the physical possession of the respondent only during scheduled work hours and during travel to and from his or her place of employment. In any case involving a peace officer who as a condition of employment and whose personal safety depends on the ability to carry a firearm, a court may allow the peace officer to continue to carry a firearm, either on duty or off duty, if the court finds by a preponderance of the evidence that the officer does not pose a threat of harm. Prior to making this finding, the court shall require a mandatory psychological evaluation of the peace officer and may require the peace officer to enter into counseling or other remedial treatment program to deal with any propensity for domestic violence.

(g) During the period of the relinquishment order, a respondent is entitled to make one sale of all firearms that are in the possession of a local law enforcement agency pursuant to this section. A licensed gun dealer, who presents a local law enforcement agency with a bill of sale indicating that all firearms owned by the respondent that are in the possession of the local law enforcement agency have been sold by the respondent to the licensed gun dealer, shall be given possession of those firearms, at the location where a respondent's firearms are stored, within five days of presenting the local law enforcement agency with a bill of sale. *(Added by Stats.2003, c. 498 (S.B.226), § 4. Amended by Stats.2006, c. 474 (A.B.2129), § 1; Stats.2010, c. 178 (S.B. 1115), § 23, operative Jan. 1, 2012; Stats.2010, c. 572 (A.B. 1596), § 5, operative Jan. 1, 2012; Stats.2011, c. 285 (A.B. 1402), § 4.)*

Law Revision Commission Comments

2011 Amendment

Subdivisions (b), (c), and (e) of Section 527.9 (as it reads in 2010 Cal. Stat. ch. 572, § 5) are amended to reflect nonsubstantive reorganization of the statutes governing control of deadly weapons. [41 Cal.L.Rev.Comm. Reports 135 (2011)].

Research References

Forms

West's California Code Forms, Civil Procedure § 527.6 Form 10, Injunction--Request to Continue Court Hearing and to Reissue Temporary Restraining Order (CLETS-TCH) (Civil Harassment Prevention)--Official Form.

West's California Code Forms, Civil Procedure § 527.6 Form 18, Injunction--How Can I Respond to a Request for Civil Harassment Restraining Orders? (Civil Harassment Prevention)--Official Form.

West's California Judicial Council Forms CH-100, Request for Civil Harassment Restraining Orders.

West's California Judicial Council Forms CH-110, Temporary Restraining Order.

West's California Judicial Council Forms CH-120, Response to Request for Civil Harassment Restraining Orders.

West's California Judicial Council Forms CH-130, Civil Harassment Restraining Order After Hearing.

West's California Judicial Council Forms CH-800, Proof Of Firearms Turned In, Sold, or Stored (Civil Harassment Prevention).

West's California Judicial Council Forms EA-100, Request for Elder or Dependent Adult Abuse Restraining Orders.

West's California Judicial Council Forms EA-110, Temporary Restraining Order.
West's California Judicial Council Forms SV-100, Petition for Private Postsecondary School Violence Restraining Orders.
West's California Judicial Council Forms SV-110, Temporary Restraining Order.
West's California Judicial Council Forms SV-120, Response to Petition for Private Postsecondary School Violence Restraining Orders.
West's California Judicial Council Forms SV-130, Private Postsecondary School Violence Restraining Order After Hearing.
West's California Judicial Council Forms SV-800, Proof Of Firearms Turned In, Sold, or Stored (Private Postsecondary School Violence Prevention).
West's California Judicial Council Forms WV-100, Petition for Workplace Violence Restraining Orders.
West's California Judicial Council Forms WV-110, Temporary Restraining Order.
West's California Judicial Council Forms WV-120, Response to Petition for Workplace Violence Restraining Orders.
West's California Judicial Council Forms WV-130, Workplace Violence Restraining Order After Hearing.
West's California Judicial Council Forms WV-800, Proof Of Firearms Turned In, Sold, or Stored (Workplace Violence Prevention).
West's California Judicial Council Forms SV-120-INFO, How Can I Respond to a Petition for Private Postsecondary School Violence Restraining Orders?
West's California Judicial Council Forms WV-120-INFO, How Can I Respond to a Petition for Workplace Violence Restraining Orders?

§ 527.10. Addresses or locations of persons protected under court order; prohibition upon certain enjoined parties from acting to obtain such information

(a) The court shall order that any party enjoined pursuant to Section 527.6, 527.8, or 527.85 be prohibited from taking any action to obtain the address or location of any protected person, unless there is good cause not to make that order.

(b) The Judicial Council shall develop forms necessary to effectuate this section. *(Added by Stats.2005, c. 472 (A.B. 978), § 1. Amended by Stats.2010, c. 572 (A.B.1596), § 3, operative Jan. 1, 2012.)*

Research References

Treatises and Practice Aids

Witkin, California Summary 10th Husband and Wife § 371, Civil Remedies.

§ 528. Grant after answer; notice; order to show cause; temporary restraint

An injunction cannot be allowed after the defendant has answered, unless upon notice, or upon an order to show cause; but in such case the defendant may be restrained until the decision of the Court or Judge granting or refusing the injunction. *(Enacted in 1872.)*

§ 529. Undertaking; objection; insufficiency; dissolution of injunction; exceptions

(a) On granting an injunction, the court or judge must require an undertaking on the part of the applicant to the effect that the applicant will pay to the party enjoined any damages, not exceeding an amount to be specified, the party may sustain by reason of the injunction, if the court finally decides that the applicant was not entitled to the injunction. Within five days after the service of the injunction, the person enjoined may object to the undertaking. If the court determines that the applicant's undertaking is insufficient and a sufficient undertaking is not filed within the time required by statute, the order granting the injunction must be dissolved.

(b) This section does not apply to any of the following persons:

(1) Either spouse against the other in a proceeding for legal separation or dissolution of marriage.

(2) The applicant for an order described in Division 10 (commencing with Section 6200) of the Family Code.

(3) A public entity or officer described in Section 995.220. *(Enacted in 1872. Amended by Code Am.1873–74, c. 624, p. 405, § 1; Code Am.1880, c. 64, p. 62, § 1; Stats.1907, c. 272, p. 342, § 4; Stats.1931, c. 140, p. 201, § 1; Stats.1933, c. 744, p. 1858, § 66; Stats.1979, c. 795, p. 2710, § 9, operative July 1, 1980; Stats.1982, c. 517, p. 2340, § 123; Stats.1992, c. 163 (A.B.2641), § 25, operative Jan. 1, 1994; Stats.1993, c. 219 (A.B.1500), § 63.7.)*

Law Revision Commission Comments

1982 Amendment

Section 529 is amended for consistency with the Bond and Undertaking Law. See Sections 995.220 (undertaking not required of public entity or officer), 995.310 (sureties on undertaking), 995.920 (grounds for objection), 995.930 (manner of making objection), 995.950 (hearing on objection), 995.960 (determination of sufficiency of undertaking). Unlike Section 995.930, Section 529 requires objection to an undertaking to be made within 5 days after service of the injunction, rather than within 10 days after service of the undertaking. The other changes in Section 529 are technical. [16 Cal.L.Rev.Comm. Reports 501 (1982)].

1992 Amendment [Revised Comment]

Subdivision (b) of Section 529 is amended to refer to the Family Code provisions that replaced the Code of Civil Procedure and Civil Code provisions. The reference to "applicant" has been substituted for the former reference to "plaintiff." This is not a substantive change. [23 Cal.L.Rev.Comm. Reports 1 (1993)].

Commentary

When a wife was not the debtor spouse, *In re Marriage of Guasch, 201 Cal.App.4th 942, 134 Cal.Rptr.3d 358 (2011)*, affirmed a judgment granting a wife's motion to quash a judgment creditor's writ of execution and enjoining further enforcement against community property, without requiring the wife to post an undertaking under this section. *Guasch* declined to read the requirement of this section into Family Code 2010, upon which the trial court relied in granting the wife relief.

Research References

Forms

West's California Code Forms, Civil § 52.1 Form 2, Order Granting Preliminary Injunction for Violation Of Civil Rights.
West's California Code Forms, Commercial § 8315 Form 1, Demand for Surrender Of Security.
West's California Judicial Council Forms RC-200, Ex Parte Order Appointing Receiver and Order to Show Cause and Temporary Restraining Order--Rents, Issues, and Profits.
West's California Judicial Council Forms RC-210, Order Confirming Appointment Of Receiver and Preliminary Injunction--Rents, Issues, and Profits.

West's California Judicial Council Forms RC-300, Order to Show Cause and Temporary Restraining Order--Rents, Issues, and Profits.

West's California Judicial Council Forms RC-310, Order Appointing Receiver After Hearing and Preliminary Injunction--Rents, Issues, and Profits.

§ 532. Application to dissolve or modify; opposition; bond for dissolution or modification; damages; attorney's fees

(a) If an injunction is granted without notice to the person enjoined, the person may apply, upon reasonable notice to the judge who granted the injunction, or to the court in which the action was brought, to dissolve or modify the injunction. The application may be made upon the complaint or the affidavit on which the injunction was granted, or upon affidavit on the part of the person enjoined, with or without the answer. If the application is made upon affidavits on the part of the person enjoined, but not otherwise, the person against whom the application is made may oppose the application by affidavits or other evidence in addition to that on which the injunction was granted.

(b) In all actions in which an injunction or restraining order has been or may be granted or applied for, to prevent the diversion, pending the litigation, of water used, or to be used, for irrigation or domestic purposes only, if it is made to appear to the court that great damage will be suffered by the person enjoined, in case the injunction is continued, and that the person in whose behalf it issued can be fully compensated for any damages suffered by reason of the continuance of the acts enjoined during the pendency of the litigation, the court in its discretion, may dissolve or modify the injunction. The dissolution or modification shall be subject to the person enjoined giving a bond in such amount as may be fixed by the court or judge, conditioned that the enjoined person will pay all damages which the person in whose behalf the injunction issued may suffer by reason of the continuance, during the litigation, of the acts complained of. Upon the trial the amount of the damages must be ascertained, and in case judgment is rendered for the person in whose behalf the injunction was granted, the amount fixed as damages must be included in the judgment, together with reasonable attorney's fees. In any proceedings to enforce the liability on the bond, the amount of the damages as fixed in the judgment is conclusive. *(Enacted in 1872. Amended by Stats.1887, c. 188, p. 241; Stats.1907, c. 272, p. 342, § 7; Stats.1982, c. 517, p. 2341, § 125.)*

Law Revision Commission Comments

1982 Amendment

Section 532 is amended for consistency with the Bond and Undertaking Law. See Sections 995.910 (objections to bonds) and 996.410 (enforcement of liability on bond). The other changes in Section 532 are technical. [16 Cal.L.Rev.Comm. Reports 501 (1982)].

Research References

Forms

West's California Code Forms, Civil Procedure § 532 Form 1, Injunction--Notice Of Motion to Modify or Vacate Injunction Granted Without Notice.

§ 533. Modification or dissolution of injunction or temporary restraining order

In any action, the court may on notice modify or dissolve an injunction or temporary restraining order upon a showing that there has been a material change in the facts upon which the injunction or temporary restraining order was granted, that the law upon which the injunction or temporary restraining order was granted has changed, or that the ends of justice would be served by the modification or dissolution of the injunction or temporary restraining order. *(Added by Stats. 1995, c. 796 (S.B.45), § 8.)*

Commentary

Loeffler v. Medina, 174 Cal.App.4th 1495, 95 Cal.Rptr.3d 343 (2009), holds that this section sets forth the applicable standard for a trial court considering whether to terminate a domestic violence restraining order under the Domestic Violence Prevention Act (Family Code sections 6200–6409.)

Research References

Treatises and Practice Aids

Witkin, California Summary 10th Husband and Wife § 384, Orders After Notice and Hearing.

Title 8

OF THE TRIAL AND JUDGMENT IN CIVIL ACTIONS

CHAPTER 1. JUDGMENT IN GENERAL

Section

§ 580. Relief granted; no answer; limited civil case

(a) The relief granted to the plaintiff, if there is no answer, cannot exceed that demanded in the complaint, in the statement required by Section 425.11, or in the statement provided for by Section 425.115; but in any other case, the court may grant the plaintiff any relief consistent with the case made by the complaint and embraced within the issue. The court may impose liability, regardless of whether the theory upon which liability is sought to be imposed involves legal or equitable principles.

(b) Notwithstanding subdivision (a), the following types of relief may not be granted in a limited civil case:

(1) Relief exceeding the maximum amount in controversy for a limited civil case as provided in Section 85, exclusive of attorney's fees, interest, and costs.

(2) A permanent injunction, except as otherwise authorized by statute.

(3) A determination of title to real property.

(4) Declaratory relief, except as authorized by Section 86.

(Enacted in 1872. Amended by Stats.1993, c. 456 (A.B.58), § 8; Stats.1995, c. 796 (S.B.45), § 9; Stats.1998, c. 931 (S.B.2139), § 78, eff. Sept. 28, 1998; Stats.2006, c. 86 (A.B. 2126), § 1; Stats.2007, c. 43 (S.B.649), § 5.)

Law Revision Commission Comments

1998 Amendment

Section 580 is amended to accommodate unification of the municipal and superior courts in a county. Cal. Const. art. VI, § 5(e).

The last sentence of subdivision (a) continues former Section 86(c) without substantive change.

Subdivision (b)(1) makes explicit that although the jurisdiction of a unified superior court includes matters in which the amount in controversy exceeds the maximum for a limited civil case as provided in Section 85, the court cannot grant substantive relief exceeding that maximum in a limited civil case. Formerly, each county had one or more municipal courts and a superior court, and the jurisdictional limit of the municipal courts constrained the relief awardable in matters tried in those courts. *See* Stokus v. Marsh, 217 Cal.App.3d 647, 653, 266 Cal.Rptr. 90 (1990) ("we view the jurisdictional limit of Code of Civil Procedure section 86 as applying to the substantive judgment and not the award of costs, including reasonable attorneys' fees"); Bakkebo v. Municipal Court, 124 Cal.App.3d 229, 235, 177 Cal.Rptr. 239 (1981) ("Since the substantive demand is the touchstone of jurisdiction it follows that if the recovery on that demand is within the jurisdiction of the municipal court, that court retains jurisdiction to award costs and attorney fees even though those items, when added to the substantive portion of the judgment, aggregate an amount in excess of the jurisdictional limit."); *see also* Section 396 ("In any case where the lack of jurisdiction is due solely to an excess in the amount of the demand, the excess may be remitted and the action may continue in the court where it is pending."). A limited civil case is equivalent to a matter within the original jurisdiction of the municipal court under former law, so Section 580(b)(1) as amended continues and codifies the effect of former law.

Similarly, subdivisions (b)(2)-(b)(5) reflect and preserve limitations on the types of equitable relief awardable in a municipal court. See R. Weil & I. Brown, Jr., California Practice Guide: Civil Procedure Before Trial, *Jurisdiction and Venue* 3:12–3:18.1, at 3–6 to 3–7 (1997). *See also* St. James Church of Christ Holiness v. Superior Court, 135 Cal.App.2d 352, 362, 287 P.2d 387 (1955) (municipal court lacks jurisdiction to grant permanent injunction); Pasadena Inv. Co. v. Peerless Casualty Co., 134 Cal.App.2d Supp. 902, 286 P.2d 1014 (1955) (municipal court lacks jurisdiction to grant declaratory relief). On enforcement of orders under the Family Code, see Fam. Code 200, 290; *In re* Marriage of Lackey, 143 Cal.App.3d 698, 191 Cal.Rptr. 309 (1983).

Cf. Sections 85, 85.1 (limited civil cases). [28 Cal.L.Rev.Comm. Reports App. 7 (1998)].

2006 Amendment

Section 580 is amended to authorize the enforcement of a Family Code judgment in a limited civil case. The change would affect two judgment enforcement procedures: (1) a creditor's suit (Sections 708.210-708.270), and (2) a lien filed against a judgment debtor's interest in a pending case (Sections 708.410-708.480).

Other judgment enforcement procedures, which do not give rise to enforcement in a limited civil case, are not affected by the amendment. Those procedures fall into one of the following categories:

(1) A procedure conducted without a court hearing. See Sections 697.310-697.410 (judgment lien on real property), 697.510-697.670 (judgment lien on personal property), 699.010-701.830 (execution), 708.010-708.030 (written interrogatory or inspection demand), 712.010-716.030 (enforcement of writ of possession or sale).

(2) A procedure conducted in the same court that entered the judgment to be enforced (or in a court of the same or higher jurisdiction). See Sections 708.110-708.205 (debtor examination), 708.310-708.320 (charging order), 708.510-708.560 (assignment order), 708.610-708.630 (appointment of receiver), 708.710-708.795 (enforcement against obligation of public entity), 708.910-708.930 (enforcement against franchise), 709.020 (action against nonvested property interest).

(3) A special proceeding under the Probate Code. See Sections 709.010 (enforcement against debtor's interest as beneficiary of trust), 709.030 (enforcement against debtor's interest in guardianship or conservatorship estate).

The changes to subdivision (a) are nonsubstantive. [35 Cal.L.Rev. Comm. Reports 175 (2005)].

2007 Amendment

Subdivision (b) of Section 580 is amended to clarify its interrelationship with provisions such as Business and Professions Code Section 12606, under which a court in a limited civil case is authorized to grant relief that might be considered a permanent injunction (e.g., an order to destroy property packed in misleading containers). See also Bus. & Prof. Code § 12606.2; Food & Agric. Code §§ 25564, 29733, 43039, 59289. [36 Cal.L.Rev.Comm. Reports 305 (2006)].

Commentary

In re Marriage of Andresen, 28 Cal.App.4th 873, 34 Cal.Rptr.2d 147 (1994), review denied, held that a default judgment did not go beyond the scope of a wife's petition, which listed assets and liabilities but did not include their values or request any particular disposition, reasoning that the husband had adequate notice that the petition requested distribution of the assets and liabilities listed in the petition.

Although a default judgment ordinarily cannot dispose of property not listed in a petition for dissolution or attached property declaration, *In re Marriage of Eustice, 242 Cal.App.4th 1291, 195 Cal.Rptr.3d 876 (2015)*, held that a property disposition was not void for lack of notice when the husband appeared by filing a response listing assets and liabilities and was served with the wife's preliminary declaration of disclosure before the default was entered.

Research References

Forms

California Real Estate Forms (Miller & Starr) § 3:8, Deed Of Trust, Security Agreement, and Fixture Filing With Assignment Of Rents and Agreements.

California Real Estate Forms (Miller & Starr) § 3:14, Construction Deed Of Trust, Security Agreement, and Fixture Filing With Assignment Of Rents and Agreements.

California Real Estate Forms (Miller & Starr) § 3:21, Deed Of Trust, Assignment Of Rents, Security Agreement and Fixture Filing--Conduit Loan.

California Real Estate Forms (Miller & Starr) § 3:34, Short Form DEed Of Trust and Assignment Of Rents.

California Real Estate Forms (Miller & Starr) § 3:35, Long Form DEed Of Trust and Assignment Of Rents.

Cal. Transaction Forms - Bus. Transactions § 19:42, Continuing Guaranty (Single Individual Guarantor).
Cal. Transaction Forms - Bus. Transactions § 19:52, Continuing Guaranty (Multiple Individual Guarantors).
West's California Code Forms, Civil Procedure § 580 COMMENT, Judgment--Relief Granted--Default Proceeding.

Treatises and Practice Aids

Witkin, California Summary 10th Husband and Wife § 243, Request in Petition.
Witkin, California Summary 10th Husband and Wife § 274, Default Award.
Witkin, California Summary 10th Torts § 1749, Judgment by Default.

§ 580a. Action for deficiency judgment after foreclosure or trustee's sale; complaint; appraisal; deficiency computed on basis of fair market value; limitation of actions; necessity of sale

Whenever a money judgment is sought for the balance due upon an obligation for the payment of which a deed of trust or mortgage with power of sale upon real property or any interest therein was given as security, following the exercise of the power of sale in such deed of trust or mortgage, the plaintiff shall set forth in his or her complaint the entire amount of the indebtedness which was secured by the deed of trust or mortgage at the time of sale, the amount for which the real property or interest therein was sold and the fair market value thereof at the date of sale and the date of that sale. Upon the application of either party made at least 10 days before the time of trial the court shall, and upon its own motion the court at any time may, appoint one of the probate referees provided for by law to appraise the property or the interest therein sold as of the time of sale. The referee shall file his or her appraisal with the clerk and that appraisal shall be admissible in evidence. The referee shall take and subscribe an oath to be attached to the appraisal that he or she has truly, honestly and impartially appraised the property to the best of his or her knowledge and ability. Any referee so appointed may be called and examined as a witness by any party or by the court itself. The court must fix the compensation of the referee in an amount as determined by the court to be reasonable, but those fees shall not exceed similar fees for similar services in the community where the services are rendered, which may be taxed and allowed in like manner as other costs. Before rendering any judgment the court shall find the fair market value of the real property, or interest therein sold, at the time of sale. The court may render judgment for not more than the amount by which the entire amount of the indebtedness due at the time of sale exceeded the fair market value of the real property or interest therein sold at the time of sale with interest thereon from the date of the sale; provided, however, that in no event shall the amount of the judgment, exclusive of interest after the date of sale, exceed the difference between the amount for which the property was sold and the entire amount of the indebtedness secured by the deed of trust or mortgage. Any such action must be brought within three months of the time of sale under the deed of trust or mortgage. No judgment shall be rendered in any such action until the real property or interest therein has first been sold pursuant to the terms of the deed of trust or mortgage, unless the real property or interest therein has become valueless. *(Added by Stats.1933, c. 642, p. 1672, § 4. Reenacted by Stats.1935, c. 650, p. 1805, § 4. Amended by Stats.1968, c. 450, p. 1070, § 2; Stats.1970, c. 1282, p. 2320, § 1, eff. July 1, 1971; Stats.1982, c. 1535, p. 5965, § 1; Stats.1988, c. 1199, § 6, operative July 1, 1989.)*

Law Revision Commission Comments

1988 Amendment

Section 580a is amended to correct terminology. See Prob.Code §§ 400–453 (probate referees). [19 Cal.L.Rev.Comm. Reports 103.5 (1988)].

Research References

Forms

California Real Estate Forms (Miller & Starr) § 3:7, Promissory Note.
California Real Estate Forms (Miller & Starr) § 3:8, Deed Of Trust, Security Agreement, and Fixture Filing With Assignment Of Rents and Agreements.
California Real Estate Forms (Miller & Starr) § 3:9, Assignment Of Lessor's Interest in Leases and Seller's Interest in Contracts for Sale.
California Real Estate Forms (Miller & Starr) § 3:13, Promissory Note Secured by Construction Deed Of Trust.
California Real Estate Forms (Miller & Starr) § 3:14, Construction Deed Of Trust, Security Agreement, and Fixture Filing With Assignment Of Rents and Agreements.
California Real Estate Forms (Miller & Starr) § 3:20, Promissory Note--Conduit Loan.
California Real Estate Forms (Miller & Starr) § 3:22, Assignment Of Leases and Rents--Conduit Loans.
California Real Estate Forms (Miller & Starr) § 3:29, Exceptions to Non-Recourse Guaranty--Conduit Loan.
California Real Estate Forms (Miller & Starr) § 3:30, Environmental Indemnity--Conduit Loan.
California Real Estate Forms (Miller & Starr) § 3:37, Continuing Guaranty.
California Real Estate Forms (Miller & Starr) § 3:38, Completion Guaranty.
California Real Estate Forms (Miller & Starr) § 3:40, Assignment Of Membership Interest.
California Real Estate Forms (Miller & Starr) § 3:38.50, "Bad Boy" Guaranty.
California Transactions Forms--Business Entities § 21:18, Agreements to be Liable.
Cal. Transaction Forms - Bus. Transactions § 19:13, Authority to Waive Suretyship Defenses.
Cal. Transaction Forms - Bus. Transactions § 19:14, Language Required to Waive Defenses.
Cal. Transaction Forms - Bus. Transactions § 19:42, Continuing Guaranty (Single Individual Guarantor).
Cal. Transaction Forms - Bus. Transactions § 19:52, Continuing Guaranty (Multiple Individual Guarantors).
Cal. Transaction Forms - Bus. Transactions § 19:53, Continuing Guaranty (Multiple Individual Guarantors)--Loan Secured by Deed Of Trust.
Cal. Transaction Forms - Bus. Transactions § 19:54, Guaranty Of Payment and Completion (Real Estate).
Cal. Transaction Forms - Bus. Transactions § 19:57, Guaranty Of Indebtedness by Subsidiary Of Debtor.
Cal. Transaction Forms - Bus. Transactions § 19:63, Suretyship Waivers by Co-Borrowers (Single Lender).
Cal. Transaction Forms - Bus. Transactions § 20:39, Indemnity Agreement: Note and Deed Of Trust.
Cal. Transaction Forms - Bus. Transactions § 30:125, Mixed Collateral.

Cal. Transaction Forms - Bus. Transactions § 19:44.10, Limited Continuing Guaranty (Trust Guarantor)--Liability Limited to Specified Maximum Including Amount Paid Under Other Guarantees.

West's California Code Forms, Civil § 891 Form 1, Complaint for Rent Skimming--By Seller.

West's California Code Forms, Civil § 891 Form 2, Complaint for Rent Skimming--By Mortgagee or Beneficiary Of Deed Of Trust.

West's California Code Forms, Civil § 891 Form 3, Complaint for Rent Skimming--By Tenant.

West's California Code Forms, Civil Procedure § 580A Form 1, Judgment--Allegation in Complaint for Deficiency After Exercise Of Power Of Sale.

West's California Code Forms, Civil Procedure § 580A Form 2, Judgment--Application for Appointment Of Appraiser--Complaint for Deficiency.

Treatises and Practice Aids

Witkin, California Summary 10th Contracts § 681, Waivers by Mortgagors.

Witkin, California Summary 10th Security Transactions in Real Property § 125, Security is Not Mortgage.

Witkin, California Summary 10th Security Transactions in Real Property § 132, in General.

Witkin, California Summary 10th Security Transactions in Real Property § 136, Mixed Collateral: Real and Personal Property.

Witkin, California Summary 10th Security Transactions in Real Property § 179, Nature and Scope Of Statutes.

Witkin, California Summary 10th Security Transactions in Real Property § 181, Sold-Out Junior Lienor.

Witkin, California Summary 10th Security Transactions in Real Property § 183, Waiver Of Protection.

Witkin, California Summary 10th Security Transactions in Real Property § 184, Distinctions.

Witkin, California Summary 10th Security Transactions in Real Property § 203, Where Purported Guarantor is Principal.

Witkin, California Summary 10th Security Transactions in Real Property § 204, Waiver Of Defenses.

Witkin, California Summary 10th Security Transactions in Real Property § 207, Constitutionality Of Restrictions.

Witkin, California Summary 10th Security Transactions in Real Property § 210, Waiver Of Lien.

Witkin, California Summary 10th Security Transactions in Real Property § 211, Breach Of Environmental Provision.

§ 580b. Contract of sale; deed of trust or mortgage; credit transaction; chattel mortgage; no deficiency to be owed or collected and deficiency judgments prohibited; exception for liability of guarantor, pledgor, or other surety

(a) Except as provided in subdivision (c), no deficiency shall be owed or collected, and no deficiency judgment shall lie, for any of the following:

(1) After a sale of real property or an estate for years therein for failure of the purchaser to complete his or her contract of sale.

(2) Under a deed of trust or mortgage given to the vendor to secure payment of the balance of the purchase price of that real property or estate for years therein.

(3) Under a deed of trust or mortgage on a dwelling for not more than four families given to a lender to secure repayment of a loan that was used to pay all or part of the purchase price of that dwelling, occupied entirely or in part by the purchaser. For purposes of subdivision (b), a loan described in this paragraph is a "purchase money loan."

(b) No deficiency shall be owed or collected, and no deficiency judgment shall lie, on a loan, refinance, or other credit transaction (collectively, a "credit transaction") that is used to refinance a purchase money loan, or subsequent refinances of a purchase money loan, except to the extent that in a credit transaction the lender or creditor advances new principal (hereafter "new advance") that is not applied to an obligation owed or to be owed under the purchase money loan, or to fees, costs, or related expenses of the credit transaction. A new credit transaction shall be deemed to be a purchase money loan except as to the principal amount of a new advance. For purposes of this section, any payment of principal shall be deemed to be applied first to the principal balance of the purchase money loan, and then to the principal balance of a new advance, and interest payments shall be applied to any interest due and owing. This subdivision applies only to credit transactions that are executed on or after January 1, 2013.

(c) The fact that no deficiency shall be owed or collected under the circumstances set forth in subdivisions (a) and (b) does not affect the liability that a guarantor, pledgor, or other surety might otherwise have with respect to the deficiency, or that might otherwise be satisfied in whole or in part from other collateral pledged to secure the obligation that is the subject of the deficiency.

(d) When both a chattel mortgage and a deed of trust or mortgage have been given to secure payment of the balance of the combined purchase price of both real and personal property, no deficiency judgment shall lie under any one thereof if no deficiency judgment would lie under the deed of trust or mortgage on the real property or estate for years therein. *(Added by Stats.1933, c. 642, p. 1673, § 5. Reenacted and amended by Stats.1935, c. 650, p. 1806, § 5. Amended by Stats.1935, c. 680, p. 1869, § 1; Stats.1949, c. 1599, p. 2846, § 1; Stats.1963, c. 2158, p. 4500, § 1; Stats. 1989, c. 698, § 12; Stats.2012, c. 64 (S.B.1069), § 1; Stats. 2013, c. 65 (S.B.426), § 2; Stats.2014, c. 71 (S.B.1304), § 18, eff. Jan. 1, 2015.)*

Research References

Forms

California Real Estate Forms (Miller & Starr) § 3:7, Promissory Note.

California Real Estate Forms (Miller & Starr) § 3:8, Deed Of Trust, Security Agreement, and Fixture Filing With Assignment Of Rents and Agreements.

California Real Estate Forms (Miller & Starr) § 3:9, Assignment Of Lessor's Interest in Leases and Seller's Interest in Contracts for Sale.

California Real Estate Forms (Miller & Starr) § 3:13, Promissory Note Secured by Construction Deed Of Trust.

California Real Estate Forms (Miller & Starr) § 3:14, Construction Deed Of Trust, Security Agreement, and Fixture Filing With Assignment Of Rents and Agreements.

California Real Estate Forms (Miller & Starr) § 3:20, Promissory Note--Conduit Loan.

California Real Estate Forms (Miller & Starr) § 3:22, Assignment Of Leases and Rents--Conduit Loans.

California Real Estate Forms (Miller & Starr) § 3:29, Exceptions to Non-Recourse Guaranty--Conduit Loan.

California Real Estate Forms (Miller & Starr) § 3:30, Environmental Indemnity--Conduit Loan.

California Real Estate Forms (Miller & Starr) § 3:37, Continuing Guaranty.
California Real Estate Forms (Miller & Starr) § 3:38, Completion Guaranty.
California Real Estate Forms (Miller & Starr) § 3:40, Assignment Of Membership Interest.
California Real Estate Forms (Miller & Starr) § 3:38.50, "Bad Boy" Guaranty.
Cal. Transaction Forms - Bus. Transactions § 19:13, Authority to Waive Suretyship Defenses.
Cal. Transaction Forms - Bus. Transactions § 19:14, Language Required to Waive Defenses.
Cal. Transaction Forms - Bus. Transactions § 19:42, Continuing Guaranty (Single Individual Guarantor).
Cal. Transaction Forms - Bus. Transactions § 19:52, Continuing Guaranty (Multiple Individual Guarantors).
Cal. Transaction Forms - Bus. Transactions § 19:53, Continuing Guaranty (Multiple Individual Guarantors)--Loan Secured by Deed Of Trust.
Cal. Transaction Forms - Bus. Transactions § 19:54, Guaranty Of Payment and Completion (Real Estate).
Cal. Transaction Forms - Bus. Transactions § 19:57, Guaranty Of Indebtedness by Subsidiary Of Debtor.
Cal. Transaction Forms - Bus. Transactions § 19:63, Suretyship Waivers by Co-Borrowers (Single Lender).
Cal. Transaction Forms - Bus. Transactions § 30:125, Mixed Collateral.
West's California Code Forms, Civil Procedure § 580A Form 1, Judgment--Allegation in Complaint for Deficiency After Exercise Of Power Of Sale.

Treatises and Practice Aids

Witkin, California Summary 10th Contracts § 72, Deficiency Judgment.
Witkin, California Summary 10th Contracts § 902, Resale Price as Evidence.
Witkin, California Summary 10th Equity § 29, Action by Vendor.
Witkin, California Summary 10th Equity § 175, Risk Of Loss.
Witkin, California Summary 10th Sales § 253, Exceptions: Mobilehome or Motor Vehicle.
Witkin, California Summary 10th Security Transactions in Real Property § 16, Equitable Mortgage Not Established.
Witkin, California Summary 10th Security Transactions in Real Property § 17, Effect Of Equitable Mortgage.
Witkin, California Summary 10th Security Transactions in Real Property § 25, Rights Of Defaulting Purchaser.
Witkin, California Summary 10th Security Transactions in Real Property § 33, Conflict Of Laws.
Witkin, California Summary 10th Security Transactions in Real Property § 74, in General.
Witkin, California Summary 10th Security Transactions in Real Property § 125, Security is Not Mortgage.
Witkin, California Summary 10th Security Transactions in Real Property § 136, Mixed Collateral: Real and Personal Property.
Witkin, California Summary 10th Security Transactions in Real Property § 175, in General.
Witkin, California Summary 10th Security Transactions in Real Property § 179, Nature and Scope Of Statutes.
Witkin, California Summary 10th Security Transactions in Real Property § 182, Nature and Purpose Of Statute.
Witkin, California Summary 10th Security Transactions in Real Property § 183, Waiver Of Protection.
Witkin, California Summary 10th Security Transactions in Real Property § 184, Distinctions.
Witkin, California Summary 10th Security Transactions in Real Property § 185, Standard Transactions.
Witkin, California Summary 10th Security Transactions in Real Property § 186, Variations on Standard Transaction.
Witkin, California Summary 10th Security Transactions in Real Property § 187, Transactions in Nature Of Deficiency Judgment.
Witkin, California Summary 10th Security Transactions in Real Property § 188, Contract Of Sale.
Witkin, California Summary 10th Security Transactions in Real Property § 189, What Are Not Purchase Money Mortgages.
Witkin, California Summary 10th Security Transactions in Real Property § 190, Third-Party Lenders.
Witkin, California Summary 10th Security Transactions in Real Property § 191, Construction Loan on Owned Land.
Witkin, California Summary 10th Security Transactions in Real Property § 192, in General.
Witkin, California Summary 10th Security Transactions in Real Property § 193, Exception for Subordinated Junior Lien.
Witkin, California Summary 10th Security Transactions in Real Property § 194, True Guaranty.
Witkin, California Summary 10th Security Transactions in Real Property § 195, Purported Guaranty.
Witkin, California Summary 10th Security Transactions in Real Property § 196, Action on Indorsement.
Witkin, California Summary 10th Security Transactions in Real Property § 197, in General.
Witkin, California Summary 10th Security Transactions in Real Property § 198, Bad Faith Waste.
Witkin, California Summary 10th Security Transactions in Real Property § 199, in General.
Witkin, California Summary 10th Security Transactions in Real Property § 204, Waiver Of Defenses.
Witkin, California Summary 10th Security Transactions in Real Property § 207, Constitutionality Of Restrictions.
Witkin, California Summary 10th Security Transactions in Real Property § 211, Breach Of Environmental Provision.
Witkin, California Summary 10th Security Transactions in Real Property § 215, Erroneous Payoff Statement.
Witkin, California Summary 10th Security Transactions in Real Property § 207A, (New) Nonjudicial Sale: C.C.P. 580e (Short Sale).

§ 580c. Mortgage foreclosure or trustee's sale; liability for actual costs and reasonable fees

In all cases where existing deeds of trust or mortgages are judicially foreclosed, unless a different amount is set up in the mortgage or deed of trust, and in all cases of mortgages and deeds of trust executed after this act takes effect, the mortgagor or trustor may be required to pay only such amount as trustee's or attorney's fees for processing the judicial foreclosure as the court may find reasonable and also the actual cost of publishing, recording, mailing and posting notices, litigation guarantee, and litigation cost of suit. *(Added by Stats.1933, c. 642, p. 1673, § 6. Re-enacted by Stats.1935, c. 650, p. 1806, § 6. Amended by Stats.1984, c. 1730, § 6.)*

Research References

Treatises and Practice Aids

Witkin, California Summary 10th Security Transactions in Real Property § 125, Security is Not Mortgage.

§ 580d. Real property or estate for years sold under power of sale; no deficiency to be owed or collected and deficiency judgments prohibited; exception for liability of guarantor, pledgor, or other surety

(a) Except as provided in subdivision (b), no deficiency shall be owed or collected, and no deficiency judgment shall be rendered for a deficiency on a note secured by a deed of trust or mortgage on real property or an estate for years therein executed in any case in which the real property or estate for years therein has been sold by the mortgagee or trustee under power of sale contained in the mortgage or deed of trust.

(b) The fact that no deficiency shall be owed or collected under the circumstances set forth in subdivision (a) does not affect the liability that a guarantor, pledgor, or other surety might otherwise have with respect to the deficiency, or that might otherwise be satisfied in whole or in part from other collateral pledged to secure the obligation that is the subject of the deficiency.

(c) This section does not apply to a deed of trust, mortgage, or other lien given to secure the payment of bonds or other evidences of indebtedness authorized or permitted to be issued by the Commissioner of Business Oversight or which is made by a public utility subject to the Public Utilities Act (Part 1 (commencing with Section 201) of Division 1 of the Public Utilities Code). *(Added by Stats.1940, Ex.Sess., c. 29, p. 84, § 2. Amended by Stats.1989, c. 698, § 13; Stats.2013, c. 65 (S.B.426), § 3; Stats.2014, c. 71 (S.B.1304), § 19, eff. Jan. 1, 2015; Stats.2014, c. 401 (A.B.2763), § 14, eff. Jan. 1, 2015.)*

Commentary

A former wife who received, as part of a dissolution judgment, a promissory note secured by deeds of trust and who, after her husband's default on the note, collected a portion of the debt through a nonjudicial trustee's sale of the property, may not subsequently obtain a deficiency judgment for the remaining debt. *In re Marriage of Oropallo, 68 Cal.App.4th 997, 80 Cal.Rptr.2d 669 (1998),* holds that this Section precludes a deficiency judgment unless the creditor has used the remedy of judicial foreclosure.

Research References

Forms

California Real Estate Forms (Miller & Starr) § 3:7, Promissory Note.
California Real Estate Forms (Miller & Starr) § 3:8, Deed Of Trust, Security Agreement, and Fixture Filing With Assignment Of Rents and Agreements.
California Real Estate Forms (Miller & Starr) § 3:9, Assignment Of Lessor's Interest in Leases and Seller's Interest in Contracts for Sale.
California Real Estate Forms (Miller & Starr) § 3:13, Promissory Note Secured by Construction Deed Of Trust.
California Real Estate Forms (Miller & Starr) § 3:14, Construction Deed Of Trust, Security Agreement, and Fixture Filing With Assignment Of Rents and Agreements.
California Real Estate Forms (Miller & Starr) § 3:20, Promissory Note--Conduit Loan.
California Real Estate Forms (Miller & Starr) § 3:21, Deed Of Trust, Assignment Of Rents, Security Agreement and Fixture Filing--Conduit Loan.
California Real Estate Forms (Miller & Starr) § 3:22, Assignment Of Leases and Rents--Conduit Loans.
California Real Estate Forms (Miller & Starr) § 3:29, Exceptions to Non-Recourse Guaranty--Conduit Loan.
California Real Estate Forms (Miller & Starr) § 3:30, Environmental Indemnity--Conduit Loan.
California Real Estate Forms (Miller & Starr) § 3:36, Contingent Interest Agreement.
California Real Estate Forms (Miller & Starr) § 3:37, Continuing Guaranty.
California Real Estate Forms (Miller & Starr) § 3:38, Completion Guaranty.
California Real Estate Forms (Miller & Starr) § 3:40, Assignment Of Membership Interest.
California Real Estate Forms (Miller & Starr) § 3:55, Subordination, Nondisturbance, and Attornment Agreement.
California Real Estate Forms (Miller & Starr) § 3:66, Deed in Lieu Of Foreclosure--Transfer Agreement.
California Real Estate Forms (Miller & Starr) § 3:75, Third-Party Waivers--Deed Of Trust.
California Real Estate Forms (Miller & Starr) § 3:38.50, "Bad Boy" Guaranty.
Cal. Transaction Forms - Bus. Transactions § 19:13, Authority to Waive Suretyship Defenses.
Cal. Transaction Forms - Bus. Transactions § 19:14, Language Required to Waive Defenses.
Cal. Transaction Forms - Bus. Transactions § 19:42, Continuing Guaranty (Single Individual Guarantor).
Cal. Transaction Forms - Bus. Transactions § 19:52, Continuing Guaranty (Multiple Individual Guarantors).
Cal. Transaction Forms - Bus. Transactions § 19:53, Continuing Guaranty (Multiple Individual Guarantors)--Loan Secured by Deed Of Trust.
Cal. Transaction Forms - Bus. Transactions § 19:54, Guaranty Of Payment and Completion (Real Estate).
Cal. Transaction Forms - Bus. Transactions § 19:57, Guaranty Of Indebtedness by Subsidiary Of Debtor.
Cal. Transaction Forms - Bus. Transactions § 19:63, Suretyship Waivers by Co-Borrowers (Single Lender).
Cal. Transaction Forms - Bus. Transactions § 20:39, Indemnity Agreement: Note and Deed Of Trust.
Cal. Transaction Forms - Bus. Transactions § 27:21, Subrogation.
Cal. Transaction Forms - Bus. Transactions § 30:125, Mixed Collateral.
Cal. Transaction Forms - Bus. Transactions § 19:44.10, Limited Continuing Guaranty (Trust Guarantor)--Liability Limited to Specified Maximum Including Amount Paid Under Other Guarantees.
West's California Code Forms, Civil § 891 Form 1, Complaint for Rent Skimming--By Seller.
West's California Code Forms, Civil § 891 Form 2, Complaint for Rent Skimming--By Mortgagee or Beneficiary Of Deed Of Trust.
West's California Code Forms, Civil § 891 Form 3, Complaint for Rent Skimming--By Tenant.
West's California Code Forms, Commercial DIV 5 INTRO, Letters Of Credit.

Treatises and Practice Aids

Witkin, California Summary 10th Constitutional Law § 624, Clarification Of Existing Law.
Witkin, California Summary 10th Security Transactions in Real Property § 132, in General.
Witkin, California Summary 10th Security Transactions in Real Property § 136, Mixed Collateral: Real and Personal Property.
Witkin, California Summary 10th Security Transactions in Real Property § 179, Nature and Scope Of Statutes.
Witkin, California Summary 10th Security Transactions in Real Property § 181, Sold-Out Junior Lienor.
Witkin, California Summary 10th Security Transactions in Real Property § 184, Distinctions.
Witkin, California Summary 10th Security Transactions in Real Property § 195, Purported Guaranty.
Witkin, California Summary 10th Security Transactions in Real Property § 197, in General.
Witkin, California Summary 10th Security Transactions in Real Property § 198, Bad Faith Waste.

Witkin, California Summary 10th Security Transactions in Real Property § 199, in General.
Witkin, California Summary 10th Security Transactions in Real Property § 200, Where Additional Security is Given.
Witkin, California Summary 10th Security Transactions in Real Property § 201, Where Part Of Note Unsecured.
Witkin, California Summary 10th Security Transactions in Real Property § 202, in General.
Witkin, California Summary 10th Security Transactions in Real Property § 203, Where Purported Guarantor is Principal.
Witkin, California Summary 10th Security Transactions in Real Property § 204, Waiver Of Defenses.
Witkin, California Summary 10th Security Transactions in Real Property § 205, Action by Sold-Out Junior Lienor.
Witkin, California Summary 10th Security Transactions in Real Property § 206, Defense Of Action to Enjoin Sale.
Witkin, California Summary 10th Security Transactions in Real Property § 207, Constitutionality Of Restrictions.
Witkin, California Summary 10th Security Transactions in Real Property § 210, Waiver Of Lien.
Witkin, California Summary 10th Security Transactions in Real Property § 211, Breach Of Environmental Provision.
Witkin, California Summary 10th Security Transactions in Real Property § 207A, (New) Nonjudicial Sale: C.C.P. 580e (Short Sale).

§ 580e. Deficiency collection and judgment following short sale with consent of trustee or mortgagee prohibited; circumstances; exception for fraud; non-application of section; waivers void and against public policy

(a)(1) No deficiency shall be owed or collected, and no deficiency judgment shall be requested or rendered for any deficiency upon a note secured solely by a deed of trust or mortgage for a dwelling of not more than four units, in any case in which the trustor or mortgagor sells the dwelling for a sale price less than the remaining amount of the indebtedness outstanding at the time of sale, in accordance with the written consent of the holder of the deed of trust or mortgage, provided that both of the following have occurred:

(A) Title has been voluntarily transferred to a buyer by grant deed or by other document of conveyance that has been recorded in the county where all or part of the real property is located.

(B) The proceeds of the sale have been tendered to the mortgagee, beneficiary, or the agent of the mortgagee or beneficiary, in accordance with the parties' agreement.

(2) In circumstances not described in paragraph (1), when a note is not secured solely by a deed of trust or mortgage for a dwelling of not more than four units, no judgment shall be rendered for any deficiency upon a note secured by a deed of trust or mortgage for a dwelling of not more than four units, if the trustor or mortgagor sells the dwelling for a sale price less than the remaining amount of the indebtedness outstanding at the time of sale, in accordance with the written consent of the holder of the deed of trust or mortgage. Following the sale, in accordance with the holder's written consent, the voluntary transfer of title to a buyer by grant deed or by other document of conveyance recorded in the county where all or part of the real property is located, and the tender to the mortgagee, beneficiary, or the agent of the mortgagee or beneficiary of the sale proceeds, as agreed, the rights, remedies, and obligations of any holder, beneficiary, mortgagee, trustor, mortgagor, obligor, obligee, or guarantor of the note, deed of trust, or mortgage, and with respect to any other property that secures the note, shall be treated and determined as if the dwelling had been sold through foreclosure under a power of sale contained in the deed of trust or mortgage for a price equal to the sale proceeds received by the holder, in the manner contemplated by Section 580d.

(b) A holder of a note shall not require the trustor, mortgagor, or maker of the note to pay any additional compensation, aside from the proceeds of the sale, in exchange for the written consent to the sale.

(c) If the trustor or mortgagor commits either fraud with respect to the sale of, or waste with respect to, the real property that secures the deed of trust or mortgage, this section shall not limit the ability of the holder of the deed of trust or mortgage to seek damages and use existing rights and remedies against the trustor or mortgagor or any third party for fraud or waste.

(d)(1) This section shall not apply if the trustor or mortgagor is a corporation, limited liability company, limited partnership, or political subdivision of the state.

(2) This section shall not apply to any deed of trust, mortgage, or other lien given to secure the payment of bonds or other evidence of indebtedness authorized, or permitted to be issued, by the Commissioner of Corporations, or that is made by a public utility subject to the Public Utilities Act (Part 1 (commencing with Section 201) of Division 1 of the Public Utilities Code).

(e) Any purported waiver of subdivision (a) or (b) shall be void and against public policy. *(Added by Stats.2010, c. 701 (S.B.931), § 1. Amended by Stats.2011, c. 82 (S.B.458), § 1, eff. July 15, 2011.)*

Research References

Treatises and Practice Aids

Witkin, California Summary 10th Security Transactions in Real Property § 185, Standard Transactions.
Witkin, California Summary 10th Security Transactions in Real Property § 207A, (New) Nonjudicial Sale: C.C.P. 580e (Short Sale).

CHAPTER 1.5. DISMISSAL FOR DELAY IN PROSECUTION

ARTICLE 1. DEFINITIONS AND GENERAL PROVISIONS

§ 583.161. Petition for separation or dissolution of marriage, nullity, or termination of domestic partnership, or petition filed under the Uniform Parentage Act; existence of child support, child custody, visitation, or spousal support orders, personal conduct restraining order, or bifurcated case; dismissal prohibited

A petition filed pursuant to Section 299, 2250, 2330, or 7600 of the Family Code shall not be dismissed pursuant to this chapter if any of the following conditions exist:

(a) An order for child support or an order regarding child custody or visitation has been issued in connection with the proceeding and the order has not been (1) terminated by the court or (2) terminated by operation of law pursuant to Sections 3022, 3900, 3901, 4007, and 4013 of the Family Code.

(b) An order for spousal support has been issued in connection with the proceeding and the order has not been terminated by the court.

(c) A personal conduct restraining order has been issued pursuant to the Domestic Violence Prevention Act (Division 10 (commencing with Section 6200) of the Family Code) and the order has not been terminated by operation of law or by the court.

(d) An issue in the case has been bifurcated and one of the following has occurred:

(1) A separate trial has been conducted pursuant to Section 2337 of the Family Code.

(2) A separate trial has been conducted pursuant to the California Rules of Court. *(Added by Stats.1986, c. 366, § 2. Amended by Stats.1992, c. 163 (A.B.2641), § 26, operative Jan. 1, 1994; Stats.1993, c. 219 (A.B.1500), § 65; Stats.1994, c. 1269 (A.B.2208), § 3; Stats.2013, c. 40 (A.B.522), § 1.)*

Law Revision Commission Comments

1992 Amendment [Revised Comment]

Section 583.161 is amended to substitute references to the Family Code provisions that replaced the former Civil Code provisions and to conform it to Family Code Section 3601. [23 Cal.L.Rev.Comm. Reports 1 (1993)].

Commentary

County of Orange v. Quinn, 97 Cal.App.4th 956, 118 Cal.Rptr.2d 833 (2002), holds that, despite the apparent restriction of this section to marital dissolution cases, by virtue of Family Code § 3600, the exception to the five-year dismissal rule expressed in this section and in Family Code § 3601 applies to any case in which continuing pendente lite child support has been ordered. Compare *County of Orange v. Rosales, 99 Cal.App.4th 1214, 121 Cal.Rptr.2d 788 (2002)* (once father's parental rights were terminated, there was no "continuing child support order" and county's child support action was subject to dismissal five years after filing of claim).

In re Marriage of Dunmore, 45 Cal.App.4th 1372, 53 Cal.Rptr.2d 450 (1996), review denied August 28, 1996, holds that subsection (c) protection against dismissal extends as well to a bifurcated uncontested proceeding in which a trial court dissolved the parties' marital status and reserved judgment over unresolved economic issues.

CHAPTER 5. TRIAL BY COURT

§ 632. Statement of decision

In superior courts, upon the trial of a question of fact by the court, written findings of fact and conclusions of law shall not be required. The court shall issue a statement of decision explaining the factual and legal basis for its decision as to each of the principal controverted issues at trial upon the request of any party appearing at the trial. The request must be made within 10 days after the court announces a tentative decision unless the trial is concluded within one calendar day or in less than eight hours over more than one day in which event the request must be made prior to the submission of the matter for decision. The request for a statement of decision shall specify those controverted issues as to which the party is requesting a statement of decision. After a party has requested the statement, any party may make proposals as to the content of the statement of decision.

The statement of decision shall be in writing, unless the parties appearing at trial agree otherwise; however, when the trial is concluded within one calendar day or in less than 8 hours over more than one day, the statement of decision may be made orally on the record in the presence of the parties. *(Enacted in 1872. Amended by Code Am.1873–74, c. 383, p. 312, § 79; Stats.1933, c. 744, p. 1876, § 105; Stats.1951, c. 1737, p. 4116, § 92, operative Jan. 1, 1952; Stats.1959, c. 637, p. 2613, § 1; Stats.1968, c. 716, p. 1417, § 1, operative Jan. 1, 1969; Stats.1969, c. 339, p. 713, § 1; Stats.1975, c. 301, § 2; Stats.1977, c. 1257, p. 4763, § 22, eff. Jan. 3, 1977; Stats.1981, c. 900, p. 3425, § 1; Stats.1987, c. 207, § 1; Stats.1998, c. 931 (S.B.2139), § 84, eff. Sept. 28, 1998; Stats.2002, c. 784 (S.B.1316), § 64.)*

Law Revision Commission Comments

1975 Amendment

Section 632 is amended to require the court to state in its announcement of intended decision or in its findings, if findings are requested, which findings are based primarily on evidence obtained at a view pursuant to Section 651. In addition, the court must state its observations at the view which support the indicated findings. This provision changes the rule as stated in Gates v. McKinnon, 18 Cal.2d 179, 114 P.2d 576 (1941), that an appellate court will assume that the evidence acquired at a view by the trial judge is sufficient to sustain the findings. See also South Santa Clara Valley Water Cons. Dist. v. Johnson, 231 Cal.App.2d 388, 41 Cal.Rptr. 846 (1964); Stegner v. Bahr & Ledoyen, Inc., 126 Cal.App.2d 220, 272 P.2d 106 (1954); Orchard v. Cecil F. White Ranches, Inc., 97 Cal.App.2d 35, 217 P.2d 143 (1950); Estate of Sullivan, 86 Cal.App.2d 890, 195 P.2d 894 (1948); Chatterton v. Boone, 81 Cal.App.2d 943, 185 P.2d 610 (1947). If the court does not state that a finding is primarily supported by evidence obtained at a view and also state the observations supporting the finding, the finding will not be sustained by the appellate court in the absence of substantial evidence in the record to support it.

1998 Amendment

Section 632 is amended to reflect the elimination of the justice court. Cal. Const. art. VI, §§ 1, 5(b). [28 Cal.L.Rev.Comm. Reports 51 (1998)].

2002 Amendment

Section 632 is amended to reflect unification of the municipal and superior courts pursuant to Article VI, Section 5(e), of the California Constitution. [32 Cal.L.Rev.Comm. Reports 125 (2002)].

Commentary

When parties waive a statement of decision, whether expressly or by not requesting one in a timely manner, appellate courts reviewing the judgment must presume that the trial court made all factual findings necessary to support the judgment so long as there was sufficient evidence to support such findings. A party who does not request a statement of decision may not argue that the trial court failed to make any finding required to support its decision. *In re Marriage of Condon, 62 Cal.App.4th 533, 73 Cal.Rptr.2d 33 (1998).* This is known as "the doctrine of implied findings."

A.G. v. C.S., 246 Cal.App.4th 1269, 201 Cal.Rptr.3d 552 (2016), held that the doctrine of implied findings applies when the parties do not request a statement of decision and rely on a settled statement instead of a reporter's transcript, and the settled statement does not expressly state that it serves as the trial court's statement of decision. Applying the doctrine of implied findings, the court of appeal concluded that a trial court's award of sole custody to a father was supported by an implied finding that the award was in the best interest of the children, when there was sufficient evidence to make that finding.

But compare In re Marriage of Fingert, 221 Cal.App.3d 1575, 271 Cal.Rptr. 389 (1990), review denied, where the appellate court declined to apply the implied findings doctrine when the appeal was based on a settled statement of facts, the trial court's decision, and the reasons for the trial court's decision. *Fingert* concluded that the settled statement provided it with the necessary information to decide the appeal. Accord, *In re Marriage of Seaman & Menjou, 1 Cal.App.4th 1489, 2 Cal.Rptr.2d 690 (1991), review denied.*

Research References

Forms

Am. Jur. Pl. & Pr. Forms Trial § 496, Introductory Comments.
West's California Code Forms, Civil Procedure § 632 Form 1, Trial--Request for Statement Of Decision.
West's California Code Forms, Civil Procedure § 632 Form 3, Trial--Waiver Of Statement Of Decision.
West's California Code Forms, Civil Procedure § 632 Form 6, Trial--Notice Of Motion for Order Deeming Statement Of Decision Waived.
West's California Code Forms, Family § 3022, Comment Overview--Order for Custody.
West's California Judicial Council Forms UD-110, Judgment--Unlawful Detainer.

Treatises and Practice Aids

Witkin, California Summary 10th Community Property § 241, Statutory Requirement Of Division.
Witkin, California Summary 10th Husband and Wife § 107, Statement Of Decision.
Witkin, California Summary 10th Parent and Child § 218, Statutory Rule.
Witkin, California Summary 10th Parent and Child § 285, in General.
Witkin, California Summary 10th Wills and Probate § 472, Summary Determination Of Disputes.
Witkin, California Summary 10th Wills and Probate § 998, Summary Determination Of Disputes.

CHAPTER 6. OF REFERENCES AND TRIALS BY REFEREES

§ 638. Appointment of referee; agreement of parties

A referee may be appointed upon the agreement of the parties filed with the clerk, or judge, or entered in the minutes, or upon the motion of a party to a written contract or lease that provides that any controversy arising therefrom shall be heard by a referee if the court finds a reference agreement exists between the parties:

(a) To hear and determine any or all of the issues in an action or proceeding, whether of fact or of law, and to report a statement of decision.

(b) To ascertain a fact necessary to enable the court to determine an action or proceeding.

(c) In any matter in which a referee is appointed pursuant to this section, a copy of the order shall be forwarded to the office of the presiding judge. The Judicial Council shall, by rule, collect information on the use of these referees. The Judicial Council shall also collect information on fees paid by the parties for the use of referees to the extent that information regarding those fees is reported to the court. The Judicial Council shall report thereon to the Legislature by July 1, 2003. This subdivision shall become inoperative on January 1, 2004. *(Enacted in 1872. Amended by Stats. 1933, c. 744, p. 1877, § 107; Stats.1951, c. 1737, p. 4117, § 93, operative Jan. 1, 1952; Stats.1982, c. 440, p. 1810, § 1; Stats.1984, c. 350, § 1; Stats.2000, c. 644 (A.B.2912), § 1; Stats.2001, c. 44 (S.B.562), § 5; Stats.2002, c. 1008 (A.B. 3028), § 4.)*

Law Revision Commission Comments

2001 Amendment

Section 638 is amended to delete the reference to a "docket," because courts no longer maintain a record denominated a "docket" in civil cases. Formerly, justice courts maintained a docket in civil cases, which was a record of actions taken in open court, as well as documents filed and other proceedings in the case. See former Gov't Code 71614 (1953 Cal. Stat. ch. 206, 1, repealed by 1977 Cal. Stat. ch. 1257, 71) (judge of justice court shall keep a book denominated a "docket"), 71614.5 (1959 Cal. Stat. ch. 671, 2, repealed by 1977 Cal. Stat. ch. 1257, 72) (clerk or judge of justice court shall keep the "docket" and other records of the court). Now actions taken in open court are recorded in the minutes of a superior court. Gov't Code 69844; see also Copley Press v. Superior Court, 6 Cal.App.4th 106, 110, 7 Cal.Rptr.2d 841 (1992). Documents filed or lodged and other proceedings in a civil case are recorded in the register of actions. See Gov't Code 69845 (clerk of superior court may keep a register of actions), 69845.5 (alternative to maintaining register of actions in superior court). Because the minutes are the proper record for reflecting an agreement in open court, and Section 638 already refers to the minutes, the reference to the "docket" may be deleted without substituting a reference to the register of actions.

A technical change is also made for conformity with preferred drafting style. [30 Cal.L.Rev.Comm. Reports 479 (2000)].

Research References

Forms

Alternative Dispute Resolution with Forms § 24:13, Appointment.
Alternative Dispute Resolution with Forms § 24:14, Private Judging Distinguished from Other Alternative Dispute Resolution Procedures.
California Real Estate Forms (Miller & Starr) § 3:55, Subordination, Nondisturbance, and Attornment Agreement.
Cal. Transaction Forms - Bus. Transactions § 14:57, Choosing Arbitration.

Cal. Transaction Forms - Bus. Transactions § 10:82, Agreement Between Production Company and Writer for Motion Picture.
Cal. Transaction Forms - Bus. Transactions § 19:44.10, Limited Continuing Guaranty (Trust Guarantor)--Liability Limited to Specified Maximum Including Amount Paid Under Other Guarantees.
California Transactions Forms--Estate Planning § 1:54, Drafting Principles.
California Transactions Forms--Family Law § 2:73, Special Masters.
California Transactions Forms--Family Law § 3:16, Identifying Areas Of Parental Decision Making and Participation.
California Transactions Forms--Family Law § 3:59, Basis for Modification Of Physical Custody.
California Transactions Forms--Family Law § 3:87, Appointment Of a Special Master.
California Transactions Forms--Family Law § 5:25, Special Master.
California Transactions Forms--Family Law § 5:30, Parenting Agreement Providing for Joint Legal and Joint Physical Custody Where Both Partners Are Biological Parents Of Child.
California Transactions Forms--Family Law § 5:31, Parenting Agreement Providing for Joint Legal and Sole Physical Custody Where Both Partners Are Biological Parents Of Child.
26 West's Legal Forms § 2:85, Private Judging.
Am. Jur. Pl. & Pr. Forms References § 1, Introductory Comments.
Am. Jur. Pl. & Pr. Forms References § 15, Introductory Comments.
UCC Legal Forms § 9:1050, Foreclosure Sale Agreement--Sample.
West's California Code Forms, Civil Procedure § 638 Form 4, Trial--Order Appointing Referee (Alternative Dispute Resolution)--Official Form.
West's California Code Forms, Civil Procedure § 638 Form 5, Trial--Notice Of Motion for Reference--Contract Cases.
West's California Judicial Council Forms ADR-109, Stipulation or Motion for Order Appointing Referee.
West's California Judicial Council Forms ADR-110, Order Appointing Referee.

Treatises and Practice Aids

Witkin, California Summary 10th Husband and Wife § 107, Statement Of Decision.
Witkin, California Summary 10th Wills and Probate § 597, Powers Of Probate Referee.
Witkin, California Summary 10th Wills and Probate § 998, Summary Determination Of Disputes.

§ 639. Appointment of referee

(a) When the parties do not consent, the court may, upon the written motion of any party, or of its own motion, appoint a referee in the following cases pursuant to the provisions of subdivision (b) of Section 640:

(1) When the trial of an issue of fact requires the examination of a long account on either side; in which case the referees may be directed to hear and decide the whole issue, or report upon any specific question of fact involved therein.

(2) When the taking of an account is necessary for the information of the court before judgment, or for carrying a judgment or order into effect.

(3) When a question of fact, other than upon the pleadings, arises upon motion or otherwise, in any stage of the action.

(4) When it is necessary for the information of the court in a special proceeding.

(5) When the court in any pending action determines that it is necessary for the court to appoint a referee to hear and determine any and all discovery motions and disputes relevant to discovery in the action and to report findings and make a recommendation thereon.

(b) In a discovery matter, a motion to disqualify an appointed referee pursuant to Section 170.6 shall be made to the court by a party either:

(A) Within 10 days after notice of the appointment, or if the party has not yet appeared in the action, a motion shall be made within 10 days after the appearance, if a discovery referee has been appointed for all discovery purposes.

(B) At least five days before the date set for hearing, if the referee assigned is known at least 10 days before the date set for hearing and the discovery referee has been assigned only for limited discovery purposes.

(c) When a referee is appointed pursuant to paragraph (5) of subdivision (a), the order shall indicate whether the referee is being appointed for all discovery purposes in the action.

(d) All appointments of referees pursuant to this section shall be by written order and shall include the following:

(1) When the referee is appointed pursuant to paragraph (1), (2), (3), or (4) of subdivision (a), a statement of the reason the referee is being appointed.

(2) When the referee is appointed pursuant to paragraph (5) of subdivision (a), the exceptional circumstances requiring the reference, which must be specific to the circumstances of the particular case.

(3) The subject matter or matters included in the reference.

(4) The name, business address, and telephone number of the referee.

(5) The maximum hourly rate the referee may charge and, at the request of any party, the maximum number of hours for which the referee may charge. Upon the written application of any party or the referee, the court may, for good cause shown, modify the maximum number of hours subject to any findings as set forth in paragraph (6).

(6)(A) Either a finding that no party has established an economic inability to pay a pro rata share of the referee's fee or a finding that one or more parties has established an economic inability to pay a pro rata share of the referee's fees and that another party has agreed voluntarily to pay that additional share of the referee's fee. A court shall not appoint a referee at a cost to the parties if neither of these findings is made.

(B) In determining whether a party has established an inability to pay the referee's fees under subparagraph (A), the court shall consider only the ability of the party, not the party's counsel, to pay these fees. If a party is proceeding in forma pauperis, the party shall be deemed by the court to have an economic inability to pay the referee's fees. However, a determination of economic inability to pay the fees shall not be limited to parties that proceed in forma pauperis. For those parties who are not proceeding in forma pauperis, the court, in determining whether a party has established an inability to pay the fees, shall consider, among other things, the estimated cost of the referral and the impact of the proposed fees on the party's ability to proceed with the litigation.

(e) In any matter in which a referee is appointed pursuant to paragraph (5) of subdivision (a), a copy of the order appointing the referee shall be forwarded to the office of the presiding judge of the court. The Judicial Council shall, by rule, collect information on the use of these references and the reference fees charged to litigants, and shall report thereon to the Legislature by July 1, 2003. This subdivision shall become inoperative on January 1, 2004. *(Enacted in 1872. Amended by Stats.1933, c. 744, p. 1877, § 108; Stats. 1951, c. 1737, p. 4117, § 94, operative Jan. 1, 1952; Stats.1977, c. 1257, p. 4764, § 23, eff. Jan. 3, 1977; Stats.1981, c. 299, p. 1429, § 1; Stats.2000, c. 644 (A.B.2912), § 2; Stats.2000, c. 1011 (S.B.2153), § 1.5; Stats.2001, c. 362 (S.B.475), § 1.)*

Commentary

Ruisi v. Thierot, 53 Cal.App.4th 1197, 62 Cal.Rptr.2d 766 (1997), review denied June 11, 1997, holds that a trial court's reference of "any and all issues regarding custody" to a special master without the consent of both parties is overly broad and not authorized by this section. Similarly, *Settlemire v. Superior Court, 105 Cal.App.4th 666, 129 Cal.Rptr.2d 560 (2003)*, holds that, when one party refused to stipulate to the assigned commissioner, the trial court erred in assigning an order to show cause involving various family law issues to a commissioner "for a hearing, and findings on any matter of fact upon which information is required by the Court" without stating the specific facts the court wanted the commissioner to decide. Applying this section, *Settlemire* reasoned that the broad order was an improper delegation of judicial duties and directed the court to vacate the broad order and enter a new order specifying the factual issues to be decided by the commissioner.

Research References

Forms

California Transactions Forms--Family Law § 2:73, Special Masters.
West's California Code Forms, Civil Procedure § 639 Form 3, Trial--Combined Order Appointing a Referee and for Payment Of Referee's Fee.
West's California Code Forms, Civil Procedure § 639 Form 1, Trial--Notice Of Motion for Reference.

Treatises and Practice Aids

Witkin, California Summary 10th Husband and Wife § 201, Case Management Plan.
Witkin, California Summary 10th Parent and Child § 281, Recommendations.
Witkin, California Summary 10th Wills and Probate § 371, General Rules Of Practice.

§ 640. Selection of referees

(a) The court shall appoint as referee or referees the person or persons, not exceeding three, agreed upon by the parties.

(b) If the parties do not agree on the selection of the referee or referees, each party shall submit to the court up to three nominees for appointment as referee and the court shall appoint one or more referees, not exceeding three, from among the nominees against whom there is no legal objection. If no nominations are received from any of the parties, the court shall appoint one or more referees, not exceeding three, against whom there is no legal objection, or the court may appoint a court commissioner of the county where the cause is pending as a referee.

(c) Participation in the referee selection procedure pursuant to this section does not constitute a waiver of grounds for objection to the appointment of a referee under Section 641 or 641.2. *(Enacted in 1872. Amended by Stats.1913, c. 166, p. 246, § 1; Stats.1933, c. 744, p. 1877, § 109; Stats.1951, c. 1737, p. 4117, § 95, operative Jan. 1, 1952; Stats.1975, c. 1240, § 6, operative July 1, 1976; Stats.2000, c. 644 (A.B.2912), § 3.)*

Law Revision Commission Comments

1975 Amendment

The portion of Section 640 relating to the residence of referees in eminent domain proceedings is deleted because it serves no useful purpose and tends unnecessarily to complicate eminent domain law. The last sentence is deleted as unnecessary. See Cal.Const., Art. XII, § 23a and Pub.Util.Code §§ 1401–1421.

Research References

Forms

Cal. Transaction Forms - Bus. Transactions § 10:82, Agreement Between Production Company and Writer for Motion Picture.
Cal. Transaction Forms - Bus. Transactions § 19:44.10, Limited Continuing Guaranty (Trust Guarantor)--Liability Limited to Specified Maximum Including Amount Paid Under Other Guarantees.

§ 640.5. Judicial Council report on the practice and cost of referring discovery disputes to outside referees

It is the intent of the Legislature that the practice and cost of referring discovery disputes to outside referees be thoroughly reviewed. Therefore, in addition to the requirements of subdivision (e) of Section 639, the Judicial Council shall collect information from the trial courts on the use of referees in discovery matters pursuant to either Sections 638 and 639. The collected data shall include information on the number of referees, the cost to the parties, and the time spent by the discovery referee. The Judicial Council shall report thereon to the Legislature by July 1, 2003. *(Added by Stats.2001, c. 362 (S.B.475), § 2.)*

§ 641. Objections to referee; grounds

A party may object to the appointment of any person as referee, on one or more of the following grounds:

(a) A want of any of the qualifications prescribed by statute to render a person competent as a juror, except a requirement of residence within a particular county in the state.

(b) Consanguinity or affinity, within the third degree, to either party, or to an officer of a corporation which is a party, or to any judge of the court in which the appointment shall be made.

(c) Standing in the relation of guardian and ward, conservator and conservatee, master and servant, employer and clerk, or principal and agent, to either party; or being a member of the family of either party; or a partner in business with either party; or security on any bond or obligation for either party.

(d) Having served as a juror or been a witness on any trial between the same parties.

(e) Interest on the part of the person in the event of the action, or in the main question involved in the action.

(f) Having formed or expressed an unqualified opinion or belief as to the merits of the action.

(g) The existence of a state of mind in the potential referee evincing enmity against or bias toward either party. *(Enacted in 1872. Amended by Stats.1897, c. 69, p. 60, § 2; Stats.1907, c. 378, p. 714, § 1; Stats.1933, c. 744, p. 1878, § 110; Stats.1951, c. 1737, p. 4118, § 96, operative Jan. 1, 1952; Stats.1979, c. 730, p. 2477, § 22, operative Jan. 1, 1981; Stats.1997, c. 724 (A.B.1172), § 1; Stats.2000, c. 644 (A.B. 2912), § 4.)*

Law Revision Commission Comments

1979 Amendment

Section 641 is amended to add the reference to conservator and conservatee in subdivision 3.

§ 641.2. Environmental actions; objection to referee on grounds of technical qualifications

In any action brought under Article 8 (commencing with Section 12600) of Chapter 6, Part 2, Division 3, Title 3[1] of the Government Code, a party may object to the appointment of any person as referee on the ground that the person is not technically qualified with respect to the particular subject matter of the proceeding. *(Added by Stats.1971, c. 1518, p. 2994, § 2. Amended by Stats.2000, c. 644 (A.B.2912), § 5.)*

[1] So in enrolled bill. Probably should read "Title 2".

Research References

Forms

West's California Code Forms, Civil Procedure § 641.2 Form 1, Trial--Objection to Appointment Of Referee--Environmental Actions.

§ 642. Objections to reference or to referee

Objections, if any, to a reference or to the referee or referees appointed by the court shall be made in writing, and must be heard and disposed of by the court, not by the referee. *(Added by Stats.2000, c. 644 (A.B.2912), § 7.)*

§ 643. Written report; time; objections

(a) Unless otherwise directed by the court, the referees or commissioner must report their statement of decision in writing to the court within 20 days after the hearing, if any, has been concluded and the matter has been submitted.

(b) A referee appointed pursuant to Section 638 shall report as agreed by the parties and approved by the court.

(c) A referee appointed pursuant to Section 639 shall file with the court a report that includes a recommendation on the merits of any disputed issue, a statement of the total hours spent and the total fees charged by the referee, and the referee's recommended allocation of payment. The referee shall serve the report on all parties. Any party may file an objection to the referee's report or recommendations within 10 days after the referee serves and files the report, or within another time as the court may direct. The objection shall be served on the referee and all other parties. Responses to the objections shall be filed with the court and served on the referee and all other parties within 10 days after the objection is served. The court shall review any objections to the report and any responses submitted to those objections and shall thereafter enter appropriate orders. Nothing in this section is intended to deprive the court of its power to change the terms of the referee's appointment or to modify or disregard the referee's recommendations, and this overriding power may be exercised at any time, either on the motion of any party for good cause shown or on the court's own motion. *(Enacted in 1872. Amended by Stats.1984, c. 350, § 2; Stats.2000, c. 644 (A.B.2912), § 8.)*

Research References

Forms

West's California Code Forms, Civil Procedure § 643 Form 1, Trial--Report Of Referee.

West's California Judicial Council Forms ADR-111, Report Of Referee.

§ 644. Effect of referee or commissioner's decision

(a) In the case of a consensual general reference pursuant to Section 638, the decision of the referee or commissioner upon the whole issue must stand as the decision of the court, and upon filing of the statement of decision with the clerk of the court, judgment may be entered thereon in the same manner as if the action had been tried by the court.

(b) In the case of all other references, the decision of the referee or commissioner is only advisory. The court may adopt the referee's recommendations, in whole or in part, after independently considering the referee's findings and any objections and responses thereto filed with the court. *(Enacted in 1872. Amended by Stats.1933, c. 744, p. 1878, § 111; Stats.1951, c. 1737, p. 4118, § 97, operative Jan. 1, 1952; Stats.1984, c. 350, § 3; Stats.2000, c. 644 (A.B.2912), § 9; Stats.2007, c. 263 (A.B.310), § 8.)*

Law Revision Commission Comments

2007 Amendment

Section 644 is amended to delete unnecessary language authorizing the judge to substitute for the clerk if there is no clerk. See Code Civ. Proc. § 167 (judge may perform any act court clerk may perform); Gov't Code §§ 69840–69848 (duties of clerk of superior court), 71620(b) (executive or administrative officer has authority of clerk of court). [35 Cal.L.Rev.Comm. Reports 219 (2006)].

Research References

Forms

Alternative Dispute Resolution with Forms § 24:14, Private Judging Distinguished from Other Alternative Dispute Resolution Procedures.

California Real Estate Forms (Miller & Starr) § 3:55, Subordination, Nondisturbance, and Attornment Agreement.

West's California Code Forms, Probate § 9837 Form 4. [Proposed] Order for Instructions and Approval Of Settlement Agreement [And Instructions to Distribute Estate Pursuant to Agreement] (Prob. Code §§ 9830, 9837, [11600, 11700] Code Of Civil...

West's California Code Forms, Probate § 17200(B)(6) Form 2, [Proposed] Order Approving Settlement Agreement [And Authorizing Distribution Of Trust Pursuant to Agreement] Prob. Code S17200(B)(6).

§ 645. Exception and review; decision as special verdict

The decision of the referee appointed pursuant to Section 638 or commissioner may be excepted to and reviewed in like manner as if made by the court. When the reference is to report the facts, the decision reported has the effect of a special verdict. *(Enacted in 1872. Amended by Stats.1984, c. 350, § 4; Stats.2000, c. 644 (A.B.2912), § 10.)*

Research References

Forms

California Real Estate Forms (Miller & Starr) § 3:55, Subordination, Nondisturbance, and Attornment Agreement.

26 West's Legal Forms § 2:85, Private Judging.

West's California Code Forms, Civil Procedure § 645 Form 1, Trial--Notice Of Alternative Motion to Set Aside Report Of Referee or for New Trial.

§ 645.1. Payment of referee's fees; court order

(a) When a referee is appointed pursuant to Section 638, the referee's fees shall be paid as agreed by the parties. If the parties do not agree on the payment of fees and request the matter to be resolved by the court, the court may order the parties to pay the referee's fees as set forth in subdivision (b).

(b) When a referee is appointed pursuant to Section 639, at any time after a determination of ability to pay is made as specified in paragraph (6) of subdivision (d) of Section 639, the court may order the parties to pay the fees of referees who are not employees or officers of the court at the time of appointment, as fixed pursuant to Section 1023, in any manner determined by the court to be fair and reasonable, including an apportionment of the fees among the parties. For purposes of this section, the term "parties" does not include parties' counsel. *(Added by Stats.1981, c. 299, p. 1430, § 2. Amended by Stats.2000, c. 644 (A.B.2912), § 11; Stats.2001, c. 159 (S.B.662), § 38.5.)*

Research References

Forms

Cal. Transaction Forms - Bus. Transactions § 19:44.10, Limited Continuing Guaranty (Trust Guarantor)--Liability Limited to Specified Maximum Including Amount Paid Under Other Guarantees.

West's California Code Forms, Civil Procedure § 639 Form 3, Trial--Combined Order Appointing a Referee and for Payment Of Referee's Fee.

Treatises and Practice Aids

Witkin, California Summary 10th Contracts § 337, Other Contract or Provision.

§ 645.2. Adoption of rules

The Judicial Council shall adopt all rules of court necessary to implement this chapter. *(Added by Stats.2000, c. 644 (A.B.2912), § 12.)*

Title 9

ENFORCEMENT OF JUDGMENTS

Division 1

DEFINITIONS AND GENERAL PROVISIONS

CHAPTER 3. PERIOD FOR ENFORCEMENT AND RENEWAL OF JUDGMENTS

ARTICLE 1. PERIOD FOR ENFORCEMENT OF JUDGMENTS

§ 683.010. Entry of judgment

Except as otherwise provided by statute or in the judgment, a judgment is enforceable under this title upon entry. *(Added by Stats.1982, c. 1364, p. 5073, § 2, operative July 1, 1983.)*

Law Revision Commission Comments

1982 Addition

Section 683.010 continues the substance of a portion of former Section 681. Nothing in Section 683.010 limits the authority of the court to stay enforcement of a judgment under any other applicable statutory provisions, such as Sections 916–923. See also Sections 117.7 (automatic stay of small claims court judgment), 1174(c) (delay of enforcement of certain unlawful detainer judgments). Section 683.010 does not apply to judgments under the Family Law Act (Section 683.310) or to a money judgment against a public entity (Section 683.320). [16 Cal.L.Rev.Comm. Reports 1207 (1982)].

Research References

Forms

West's California Code Forms, Family § 290, Comment Overview--Enforcement Of Judgments and Orders.

Treatises and Practice Aids

Witkin, California Summary 10th Husband and Wife § 5, Generally Applicable Procedures.

Witkin, California Summary 10th Parent and Child § 902, Restitution to Victim.

§ 683.020. Period of enforceability

Except as otherwise provided by statute, upon the expiration of 10 years after the date of entry of a money judgment or a judgment for possession or sale of property:

(a) The judgment may not be enforced.

(b) All enforcement procedures pursuant to the judgment or to a writ or order issued pursuant to the judgment shall cease.

(c) Any lien created by an enforcement procedure pursuant to the judgment is extinguished. *(Added by Stats.1982, c. 1364, p. 5073, § 2, operative July 1, 1983.)*

Law Revision Commission Comments

1982 Addition

Section 683.020 supersedes the first sentence of former Section 681 (which provided a 10-year enforcement period). Unless the judgment is renewed by action (see Section 683.050) or pursuant to Article 2 (commencing with Section 683.110), a judgment is enforceable only for 10 years; at the end of this period, enforcement of the judgment is barred and any liens created by the enforcement process are extinguished. No further action, including levy, sale, collection, or delivery pursuant to the judgment, or pursuant to a writ or order issued to enforce the judgment, may take place. The rule announced in Alonso Inv. Corp. v. Doff, 17 Cal.3d 539, 541–43, 551 P.2d 1243, 131 Cal.Rptr. 411 (1976), permitting the enforcement of a writ of execution after the expiration of the 10-year period if the writ had been timely issued, is not continued, subject to an exception where the judgment is renewed. See Section 683.200 (continuation of enforcement procedures upon renewal).

Section 683.020 applies only to money judgments and judgments for the possession or sale of property. Accordingly, other judgments—such as those governed by Section 717.010—are not subject to the 10-year rule of Section 683.020. Section 683.030 provides a special rule applicable to money judgments payable in installments. See also Sections 683.310 (judgments under Family Law Act excluded from this chapter), 683.320 (money judgment against public entity excluded from this chapter). As to judgments entered prior to the operative date of this section, see Section 694.030.

Unlike former Section 681, the 10-year period provided by Section 683.020 is not extended because enforcement of the judgment has been stayed or enjoined by court order or by operation of law. Nor is the 10-year period tolled for any reason. The statement in Nutt v. Nutt, 247 Cal.App.2d 166, 168, 55 Cal.Rptr. 380 (1966)—that the absence from the state of the judgment debtor and the debtor's property tolls the running of the time to seek a writ of execution under former Section 681—does not apply to this chapter. However, a judgment may be used as an offset after the expiration of the 10-year period if the claim of the judgment debtor (against which the judgment is offset) existed during the 10-year period during which the judgment was enforceable. See Section 431.70 and the Comment thereto. The judgment creditor may also be able to bring an action on the judgment after the 10-year enforcement period of this section has expired if the statute of limitations provided by Section 337.5 has not yet run. See Section 683.050 and the Comment thereto. [16 Cal.L.Rev.Comm. Reports 1207 (1982)].

Research References

Treatises and Practice Aids

Witkin, California Summary 10th Parent and Child § 902, Restitution to Victim.

§ 683.030. Period of enforceability; money judgments payable in installments

If a money judgment is payable in installments, the 10-year period of enforceability prescribed by Section 683.020 runs as to each installment from the date the installment becomes due and runs as to costs from the date the costs are added to the judgment pursuant to Section 685.090. *(Added by Stats.1982, c. 1364, p. 5073, § 2, operative July 1, 1983.)*

Law Revision Commission Comments

1982 Addition

Section 683.030 codifies case law concerning the time within which installment judgments may be enforced. Cf. Wolfe v. Wolfe, 30 Cal.2d 1, 4, 180 P.2d 345 (1947) (installment judgment for support). For provisions authorizing installment judgments, see Civil Code § 3347 (installment payment of damages caused by slayer in a duel); Code Civ.Proc. §§ 85 (installment payment of municipal or justice court money judgment), 117 (time of payment of small claims court money judgment), 667.7 (periodic payment of certain future damages); Labor Code §§ 5801, 5806 (installment payment of workers' compensation award); Penal Code § 1205 (installment payment of fine); Veh. Code § 16380 (installment payment of vehicle accident damage judgment). Some installment judgments are not governed by this chapter. See Sections 683.310 (spousal or child support), 683.320 (money judgment against public entity). As to judgments entered prior to the operative date of this section, see Section 694.030. [16 Cal.L.Rev.Comm. Reports 1208 (1982)].

§ 683.040. Application more than 10 years after entry or renewal; affidavit

If the judgment creditor applies for a writ for the enforcement of a judgment and the application is made more than 10 years after the date the judgment was entered or renewed, the application shall be accompanied by an affidavit of a person having knowledge of the facts stating facts showing that the issuance of the writ sought in the application is not barred under this chapter. A copy of the affidavit shall be attached to the writ when issued. *(Added by Stats.1982, c. 1364, p. 5073, § 2, operative July 1, 1983.)*

Law Revision Commission Comments

1982 Addition

Section 683.040 establishes a new requirement designed to provide information to the court clerk and levying officer when a writ of execution, possession, or sale is sought more than 10 years after the judgment was entered or renewed. Where the judgment is a money judgment payable in installments, the affidavit will be sufficient if it states that the 10-year limitation period (Section 683.030) has not run as to the installment or installments covered by the application for the writ. Section 683.040 does not apply to a judgment for child or spousal support; Civil Code Section 4380 requires the creditor to obtain a court order to enforce support obligations that are more than 10 years overdue. See Section 683.310. See also Civil Code Section 4383. As to the period of enforcement of a money judgment against a public entity, see Section 683.320 and Gov't Code §§ 965.5, 970.1. [16 Cal.L.Rev.Comm. Reports 1209 (1982)].

§ 683.050. Judgment creditor's right to bring action; limitations

Nothing in this chapter limits any right the judgment creditor may have to bring an action on a judgment, but any such action shall be commenced within the period prescribed by Section 337.5. *(Added by Stats.1982, c. 1364, p. 5073, § 2, operative July 1, 1983.)*

Law Revision Commission Comments

1982 Addition

Section 683.050 makes clear that the 10-year period of enforcement prescribed by Section 683.020 and the renewal procedure provided by Article 2 (commencing with Section 683.110) do not affect the right to bring an action on a judgment. The limitation period for commencing the action is prescribed by Section 337.5. The 10-year period provided by Section 683.020 and the 10-year statute of limitations provided by Section 337.5 are not coterminous. The period prescribed in Section 683.020 commences on the date of entry and is not tolled for any reason. The statute of limitations commences to run when the judgment is final (see Turner v. Donovan, 52 Cal.App.2d 236, 126 P.2d 187 (1942)) and may be tolled such as by the debtor's absence from the state (see Section 351). See also Section 683.220 (action on renewed judgment). [16 Cal.L.Rev.Comm. Reports 1210 (1982)].

ARTICLE 2. RENEWAL OF JUDGMENTS

Section

§ 683.110. Period of enforceability; extension; renewal of judgment

(a) The period of enforceability of a money judgment or a judgment for possession or sale of property may be extended by renewal of the judgment as provided in this article.

(b) A judgment shall not be renewed under this article if the application for renewal is filed within five years from the time the judgment was previously renewed under this article. *(Added by Stats.1982, c. 1364, p. 5073, § 2, operative July 1, 1983.)*

Law Revision Commission Comments

1982 Addition

Sections 683.110–683.220 provide a new procedure for renewing judgments. This procedure is drawn from the procedure for enforcing sister state money judgments (Sections 1710.10–1710.65). Renewal under this article permits enforcement of a judgment beyond the 10-year period prescribed by Section 683.020. This procedure supersedes the procedure under former Section 685 pursuant to which a judgment could be enforced upon noticed motion after the expiration of 10 years in the discretion of the court upon a showing of the reasons for failure to enforce the judgment during the first 10 years. This article does not require the judgment creditor to demonstrate diligence in enforcing the judgment, but if renewal is not accomplished within 10 years after entry of the judgment, the judgment becomes unenforceable. See Sections 683.020, 683.130(a). See also Section 683.050 (right of action on judgment preserved). This article does not apply to a judgment under the Family Law Act (Section 683.310) or to a money judgment against a public entity (Section 683.320).

By preventing the renewal of a judgment more often than once every five years, subdivision (b) of Section 683.110 prevents the judgment creditor from renewing a judgment more frequently merely to compound the interest on the judgment. Renewal has the effect of compounding the interest on the judgment, since interest accrues on the total amount of the judgment as renewed (Sections 680.300, 685.010(a), 695.210) and the judgment as renewed includes accrued interest on the date of filing the application for renewal (Sections 683.150(b), 685.010(a), 695.210). [16 Cal.L.Rev.Comm. Reports 1210 (1982)].

Research References

Forms

West's California Code Forms, Civil Procedure § 683.140 Form 1, Enforcement Of Judgments--Application for and Renewal Of Judgment--Official Form.

Treatises and Practice Aids

Witkin, California Summary 10th Husband and Wife § 248, in General.

§ 683.120. Application for renewal; effect

(a) The judgment creditor may renew a judgment by filing an application for renewal of the judgment with the court in which the judgment was entered.

(b) Except as otherwise provided in this article, the filing of the application renews the judgment in the amount determined under Section 683.150 and extends the period of enforceability of the judgment as renewed for a period of 10 years from the date the application is filed.

(c) In the case of a money judgment payable in installments, for the purposes of enforcement and of any later renewal, the amount of the judgment as renewed shall be treated as a lump-sum money judgment entered on the date the application is filed. *(Added by Stats.1982, c. 1364, p. 5074, § 2, operative July 1, 1983.)*

Law Revision Commission Comments

1982 Addition

Under Section 683.120 the enforceability of the judgment is extended until 10 years from the date the application for renewal is filed. Renewal under this article does not result in entry of a new judgment as would be the case where an action is brought on a California or sister state judgment or where a California judgment is entered on the basis of a sister state judgment. See Sections 683.050 (right of action on judgment preserved), 1710.25, 1710.35 (entry of California judgment on basis of sister state judgment).

Subdivision (c) makes clear that the application for renewal of an installment judgment reduces past due amounts of principal (including allowed costs) and interest (see Section 683.150) to a lump sum enforceable for an additional 10 years. Only those past due amounts that are not barred by the 10-year period of enforceability may be renewed. See Sections 683.030, 683.130(b), 683.150(c), (d). Future installments continue to accrue under the judgment as originally entered or as modified according to its terms.

This renewal procedure does not apply to the enforcement of judgments for support. See Section 683.310. See also Civil Code §§ 4380, 4384. [16 Cal.L.Rev.Comm. Reports 1211 (1982)].

§ 683.130. Application for renewal

(a) In the case of a lump-sum money judgment or a judgment for possession or sale of property, the application for renewal of the judgment may be filed at any time before the expiration of the 10–year period of enforceability provided by Section 683.020 or, if the judgment is a renewed judgment, at any time before the expiration of the 10–year period of enforceability of the renewed judgment provided by Section 683.120.

(b) In the case of a money judgment payable in installments, the application for renewal of the judgment may be filed:

(1) If the judgment has not previously been renewed, at any time as to past due amounts that at the time of filing are not barred by the expiration of the 10–year period of enforceability provided by Sections 683.020 and 683.030.

(2) If the judgment has previously been renewed, within the time specified by subdivision (a) as to the amount of the judgment as previously renewed and, as to any past due amounts that became due and payable after the previous renewal, at any time before the expiration of the 10–year period of enforceability provided by Sections 683.020 and 683.030. *(Added by Stats.1982, c. 1364, p. 5074, § 2, operative July 1, 1983. Amended by Stats.1991, c. 110 (S.B.101), § 14; Stats.1992, c. 163 (A.B.2641), § 30, operative Jan. 1, 1994; Stats.1992, c. 718 (A.B.568), § 4; Stats.1993, c. 219 (A.B. 1500), § 66; Stats.1993, c. 876 (S.B.1068), § 8, eff. Oct. 6, 1993; Stats.2000, c. 808 (A.B.1358), § 4, eff. Sept. 28, 2000.)*

Law Revision Commission Comments

1982 Addition

Subdivision (a) of Section 683.130 prescribes the general rule that renewal may be accomplished at any time when the judgment is still enforceable. See also Section 683.210 (renewal permitted during stay of enforcement). Renewal may take place during the initial 10-year period of enforcement (see Section 683.020) or during any subsequent renewal period (see subdivision (b) of Section 683.120). There is no limit on the number of renewals.

Subdivision (b) states a special application of the general rule to installment judgments. Renewal as to any installment must take place within 10 years after the installment becomes due. See Section 683.030 (time for enforcement of installment judgment). Subdivision (b) governs the type of installment judgments listed in the Comment to Section 683.030. When an installment judgment is renewed as to past due amounts, the renewed judgment is a lump-sum judgment (see subdivision (c) of Section 683.120) which thereafter is governed by subdivision (a) of Section 683.130 as to the amount of the renewed judgment. See also Section 683.150. Costs are included in the principal amount of the renewed judgment only if added to the judgment within the 10-year period. See Section 683.030.

This section does not apply to the enforcement of judgments for support. See Section 683.310. See also Civil Code §§ 4380, 4384. As to the renewal of judgments entered prior to the operative date of this section, see Section 694.030. [16 Cal.L.Rev.Comm. Reports 1213 (1982)].

2000 Amendment

Subdivision (c) of Section 683.130 is deleted as unnecessary because it duplicates rules in the Family Code. See Fam. Code §4502. This is not a substantive change. The exemption from renewal requirements for support orders in subdivision (c)(1) is unnecessary because Section 683.310 makes clear that this chapter does not apply to judgments or orders made or entered under the Family Code. Reimbursement for child support under Family Code Section 17402 is treated in the same fashion, as provided in Family Code Section 4502(a). The second sentence of subdivision (c)(1) is misplaced in this section pertaining to the time for filing an application for renewal. The period of enforceability of support orders is governed by Family Code Section 4502(a). The optional renewal procedure in Family Code Section 4502(b) continues the substance of subdivision (c)(2) of this section. See also Fam. Code §290 (methods of enforcement). [30 Cal.L.Rev.Comm. Reports 717 (2000)].

Commentary

Family Code § 291, which subjects judgments "for possession or sale of property" to this section's 10–year time limit for renewal, does not apply to Family Code money judgments. *In re Marriage of Wilcox, 124 Cal.App.4th 492, 21 Cal.Rptr.3d 315 (2004).*

See *In re Marriage of Garcia, 67 Cal.App.4th 693, 79 Cal.Rptr.2d 242 (1998),* holding that Family Code Section 4502, which makes child, family and spousal support orders infinitely enforceable, may not be applied retroactively to orders made before its effective date. Pre–1993 orders are instead controlled by former Civil Code Section 4383, which provided that arrears could be collected for 10 years as of right and at the discretion at the court thereafter.

§ 683.140. Application for renewal; execution; contents

The application for renewal of the judgment shall be executed under oath and shall include all of the following:

(a) The title of the court where the judgment is entered and the cause and number of the action.

(b) The date of entry of the judgment and of any renewals of the judgment and where entered in the records of the court.

(c) The name and address of the judgment creditor and the name and last known address of the judgment debtor. However, the judgment creditor shall omit the name of a judgment debtor from the application for a writ of execution if the liability of that judgment debtor has ceased with regard to the judgment, including either of the following occurrences:

(1) The judgment debtor has obtained a discharge of the judgment pursuant to Title 11 of the United States Code and notice thereof has been filed with the court.

(2) The judgment creditor files an acknowledgment of satisfaction of judgment with regard to the judgment debtor pursuant to Chapter 1 (commencing with Section 724.010) of Division 5.

(d) In the case of a money judgment, the information necessary to compute the amount of the judgment as renewed. In the case of a judgment for possession or sale of property, a description of the performance remaining due. *(Added by Stats.1982, c. 1364, p. 5074, § 2, operative July 1, 1983. Amended by Stats.2013, c. 176 (S.B.551), § 1.)*

Law Revision Commission Comments

1982 Addition

Section 683.140 sets forth the contents of the application for renewal of a judgment. It is drawn in part from Section 1710.15 (application for entry of judgment based on sister state judgment). As to the amount of the judgment as renewed, see Section 683.150. [16 Cal.L.Rev.Comm. Reports 1214 (1982)].

Research References

Forms

West's California Judicial Council Forms EJ-190, Application for and Renewal Of Judgment.

§ 683.150. Entry of renewal; amount of judgment as renewed

(a) Upon the filing of the application, the court clerk shall enter the renewal of the judgment in the court records.

(b) The fee for filing an application for renewal of judgment is as provided in subdivision (b) of Section 70626 of the Government Code.

(c) In the case of a money judgment, the entry of renewal shall show the amount of the judgment as renewed. Except as provided in subdivisions (d) and (e), this amount is the amount required to satisfy the judgment on the date of the filing of the application for renewal and includes the fee for the filing of the application for renewal.

(d) In the case of a money judgment payable in installments not previously renewed, the amount of the judgment as renewed is the total of the past due installments, the costs added to the judgment pursuant to Section 685.090, and the accrued interest, which remains unsatisfied and is enforceable on the date of the filing of the application for renewal and includes the fee for the filing of the application for renewal.

(e) In the case of a money judgment payable in installments previously renewed, the amount of the judgment as renewed under the latest renewal is the total of the following which remains unsatisfied and is enforceable on the date of the filing of the application for the latest renewal:

(1) The amount of the judgment as renewed under the previous renewal.

(2) The past due installments that became due and payable after the previous renewal.

(3) The costs that have been added to the judgment pursuant to Section 685.090 after the previous renewal.

(4) The interest that has accrued on the amounts described in paragraphs (1), (2), and (3) since the last renewal.

(5) The fee for filing the application for renewal.

(f) In the case of a judgment for possession or sale of property, the entry of renewal shall describe the performance remaining due. *(Added by Stats.1982, c. 1364, p. 5074, § 2, operative July 1, 1983. Amended by Stats.2005, c. 75 (A.B. 145), § 36, eff. July 19, 2005, operative Jan. 1, 2006.)*

Law Revision Commission Comments

1982 Addition

Section 683.150 requires that the court clerk enter the renewal of the judgment based on the application. The entry of the renewal by the court clerk is a ministerial act. In the case of a money judgment payable in installments, past due installments and costs that are not enforceable on the date of filing the application for renewal may not be renewed. See Section 683.030 (period of enforceability). [16 Cal.L.Rev.Comm. Reports 1215 (1982)].

§ 683.160. Notice; service; filing proof of service

(a) The judgment creditor shall serve a notice of renewal of the judgment on the judgment debtor. Service shall be made personally or by first-class mail and proof of service shall be filed with the court clerk. The notice shall be in a form prescribed by the Judicial Council and shall inform the judgment debtor that the judgment debtor has 30 days within which to make a motion to vacate or modify the renewal.

(b) Until proof of service is filed pursuant to subdivision (a), no writ may be issued, nor may any enforcement proceedings be commenced to enforce the judgment, except to the extent that the judgment would be enforceable had it not been renewed. *(Added by Stats.1982, c. 1364, p. 5074, § 2, operative July 1, 1983. Amended by Stats.1985, c. 41, § 4; Stats.1988, c. 900, § 5.)*

Law Revision Commission Comments

1982 Addition

Subdivision (a) of Section 683.160 is derived from subdivision (a) of Section 1710.30 and a portion of subdivision (b) of Section 1710.40 pertaining to sister state judgments. Under Section 683.150, the entry and filing of the renewal is a ministerial act. The judgment debtor is protected, however, by the provisions for notice under Section 683.160 and the opportunity to seek an order vacating or modifying the renewal pursuant to Section 683.170.

Subdivision (b) is designed to prevent enforcement after the 10-year period in a case where the judgment creditor has failed to serve notice of renewal on the judgment debtor. See also Section 683.040 (application for writ after 10 years). The notice of renewal may be served after the 10-year period has expired if the application for renewal is timely filed, and the judgment is enforceable after proof of service of the notice of renewal is filed unless the renewal is vacated. [16 Cal.L.Rev.Comm. Reports 1215 (1982)].

1985 Amendment

Subdivision (a) of Section 683.160 is amended to delete the reference to a repealed statutory form and substitute a reference to the form prepared by the Judicial Council. [18 Cal.L.Rev.Comm. Reports 361 (1985)].

Research References

Forms

West's California Judicial Council Forms EJ-195, Notice Of Renewal Of Judgment.

§ 683.170. Vacation of renewal

(a) The renewal of a judgment pursuant to this article may be vacated on any ground that would be a defense to an action on the judgment, including the ground that the amount of the renewed judgment as entered pursuant to this article is incorrect, and shall be vacated if the application for renewal was filed within five years from the time the judgment was previously renewed under this article.

(b) Not later than 30 days after service of the notice of renewal pursuant to Section 683.160, the judgment debtor may apply by noticed motion under this section for an order of the court vacating the renewal of the judgment. The notice of motion shall be served on the judgment creditor. Service shall be made personally or by mail.

(c) Upon the hearing of the motion, the renewal may be ordered vacated upon any ground provided in subdivision (a), and another and different renewal may be entered, including, but not limited to, the renewal of the judgment in a different amount if the decision of the court is that the judgment creditor is entitled to renewal in a different amount. *(Added by Stats.1982, c. 1364, p. 5075, § 2, operative July 1, 1983.)*

Law Revision Commission Comments

1982 Addition

Section 683.170 is derived from Section 1710.40 pertaining to sister state judgments. If it is determined at the hearing that the amount of the judgment as renewed (Section 683.150) is not correct, the court may order renewal in the correct amount pursuant to subdivision (c). On the other hand, if the court determines that the judgment has been fully satisfied or offset, the renewal should be vacated. If a motion to vacate is not made within the time stated in subdivision (b), the judgment remains enforceable in the amount stated in the entry of renewal. See Section 683.150. But nothing in this section affects or limits any remedies otherwise available to the judgment debtor after the time for making a motion to vacate has expired. [16 Cal.L.Rev.Comm. Reports 1216 (1982)].

§ 683.180. Judgment liens; effect of renewal

(a) If a judgment lien on an interest in real property has been created pursuant to a money judgment and the judgment is renewed pursuant to this article, the duration of the judgment lien is extended until 10 years from the date of the filing of the application for renewal if, before the expiration of the judgment lien, a certified copy of the application for renewal is recorded with the county recorder of the county where the real property subject to the judgment lien is located.

(b) A judgment lien on an interest in real property that has been transferred subject to the lien is not extended pursuant to subdivision (a) if the transfer was recorded before the application for renewal was filed unless both of the following requirements are satisfied:

(1) A copy of the application for renewal is personally served on the transferee.

(2) Proof of such service is filed with the court clerk within 90 days after the filing of the application for renewal. *(Added by Stats.1982, c. 1364, p. 5076, § 2, operative July 1, 1983. Amended by Stats.1983, c. 155, § 9.5, eff. June 30, 1983, operative July 1, 1983.)*

Law Revision Commission Comments

1982 Addition

Section 683.180 provides a special procedure for extending the duration of a judgment lien on an interest in real property. See generally Article 2 (commencing with Section 697.310) of Chapter 2 of Division 2 (judgment liens on interests in real property). As to renewal of a judgment lien on real property under a judgment for support or against a health care provider, see Section 697.320. Section 683.180 does not apply to judgment liens under judgments for support. See Section 683.310. See also Civil Code §§ 4380, 4384.

Extension of the judgment lien for an additional 10 years under this section is analogous to the result obtained where a judgment in an action on a money judgment is recorded while a judgment lien under the original judgment is still in effect. See Provisor v. Nelson, 234 Cal.App.2d Supp. 876, 44 Cal.Rptr. 894 (1965). The priority of the judgment lien on an interest in real property remains the same, but the extension adds 10 years to the life of the lien dating from the time the application for renewal is filed. See also Section 697.030 (duration of liens). The judgment lien is extended only if the certified copy of the application for renewal is recorded while the judgment lien is still in effect. If the judgment lien is not so extended, the judgment creditor may record an abstract of the renewed judgment to obtain a new judgment lien dating from the recording of such abstract. As provided in subdivision (b), if the interest in real property has been transferred subject to the lien and the transfer has been recorded, an extension pursuant to this section extends the lien on the property in the hands of the transferee only if the transferee is served notice of the renewal and proof of service is filed within the prescribed time. [16 Cal.L.Rev.Comm. Reports 1217 (1982)].

§ 683.190. Liens other than judgment liens; effect of renewal

If a lien (other than a judgment lien on an interest in real property or an execution lien) has been created by an enforcement procedure pursuant to a judgment and the judgment is renewed pursuant to this article, the duration of the lien is extended, subject to any other limitations on its duration under this title, until 10 years from the date of the filing of the application for renewal of the judgment if, before the expiration of the lien, a certified copy of the application for renewal is served on or filed with the same person and in the same manner as the notice or order that created the lien. *(Added by Stats.1982, c. 1364, p. 5076, § 2, operative July 1, 1983.)*

Law Revision Commission Comments

1982 Addition

Section 683.190 permits the continuation of liens, except for judgment liens on interests in real property and execution liens, both of which are governed by other provisions. Under Section 683.199, however, a lien of limited duration, such as a judgment lien on personal property (five years), is not increased in duration but is permitted to continue past the 10-year period specified in Section 683.020. See Section 697.510 (duration of judgment lien on personal property). A judgment lien on real property is continued by recording a certified copy of the application for renewal as provided in Section 683.180. An execution lien is continued by filing with the levying officer under Section 683.200. However, other liens governed by the general rule that the lien exists as long as the judgment is enforceable (see Section 697.030) are increased in duration pursuant to Section 683.190. [16 Cal.L.Rev.Comm. Reports 1218 (1982)].

§ 683.200. Enforcement proceedings; continuance

If a judgment is renewed pursuant to this article, any enforcement proceeding previously commenced pursuant to the judgment or to a writ or order issued pursuant to the judgment that would have ceased pursuant to Section 683.020 had the judgment not been renewed may be continued, subject to any other limitations provided in this title, if, before the expiration of the prior 10-year period of enforceability, a certified copy of the application for renewal of the judgment is filed with the levying officer, receiver, or other officer acting pursuant to such writ or order or, in other cases, is filed in the enforcement proceeding. *(Added by Stats.1982, c. 1364, p. 5076, § 2, operative July 1, 1983.)*

Law Revision Commission Comments

1982 Addition

Section 683.200 permits the continuation of enforcement proceedings under this title that would otherwise have ceased because of the expiration of the period of enforceability. See Section 683.020. For example, a sale of real property pursuant to a writ of execution may proceed after the expiration of 10 years from the date of entry of the judgment if the judgment is renewed within the time allowed and a certified copy of the application for renewal is filed with the levying officer in charge of the sale before the expiration of the 10-year period. Likewise, an examination proceeding may continue if the certified copy of the application for renewal is filed with the court that is to conduct the examination. [16 Cal.L.Rev.Comm. Reports 1219 (1982)].

§ 683.210. Stay of enforcement

A judgment may be renewed notwithstanding any stay of enforcement of the judgment, but the renewal of the judgment does not affect the stay of enforcement. *(Added by Stats.1982, c. 1364, p. 5076, § 2, operative July 1, 1983.)*

Validity

For validity of this section, see In re Lobherr, Bkrtcy.C.D.Cal.2002, 282 B.R. 912.

Law Revision Commission Comments

1982 Addition

Section 683.210 permits the judgment creditor to obtain an extension of the enforceability of a judgment even though a stay of enforcement is in effect. Renewal may be necessary if a judgment is temporarily stayed during the time that the 10-year enforcement period prescribed by Section 683.020 is running out. Renewal during a stay of enforcement does not affect the stay, but merely prevents the termination of the period of enforceability. [16 Cal.L.Rev. Comm. Reports 1219 (1982)].

§ 683.220. Application filing date; commencement of period for bringing action

If a judgment is renewed pursuant to this article, the date of the filing of the application for renewal shall be deemed to be the date that the period for commencing an action on the renewed judgment commences to run under Section 337.5. *(Added by Stats.1982, c. 1364, p. 5076, § 2, operative July 1, 1983.)*

Law Revision Commission Comments

1982 Addition

Section 683.220 gives the judgment creditor a right to bring an action on a renewed judgment comparable to that which would have existed had the judgment creditor earlier resorted to an action on the judgment instead of the renewal procedure provided by this article. See Section 683.050 (right of action on judgment preserved). [16 Cal.L.Rev.Comm. Reports 1219 (1982)].

ARTICLE 3. APPLICATION OF CHAPTER

§ 683.310. Judgments under Family Code; application of chapter

Except as otherwise provided in the Family Code, this chapter does not apply to a judgment or order made or entered pursuant to the Family Code. *(Added by Stats.1982, c. 1364, p. 5077, § 2, operative July 1, 1983. Amended by Stats.1991, c. 110 (S.B.101), § 15; Stats.1992, c. 163 (A.B. 2641), § 31, operative Jan. 1, 1994; Stats.2000, c. 808 (A.B. 1358), § 5, eff. Sept. 28, 2000.)*

Law Revision Commission Comments

1992 Amendment

Section 683.310 is amended to substitute a reference to the Family Code section that replaced the former Civil Code section and to substitute "a judgment or order made or entered pursuant to the Family Code" for the former reference to the former Family Law Act. Family Code Section 4502 provides that a judgment for child, family, or spousal support may be renewed in the manner specified in Article 2 (commencing with Section 683.110) of Chapter 3 of Title 9 of Part 2 of the Code of Civil Procedure. The methods of enforcement of a judgment or order made or entered pursuant to the Family Code are prescribed by Family Code Sections 290 and 291. [22 Cal.L.Rev.Comm.Reports 1 (1992)].

2000 Amendment

Section 683.310 is amended to accommodate other exceptions in the Family Code concerning enforcement of judgments and the likelihood of future revisions in the Family Code. This is a technical, nonsubstantive change. Family Code Section 4502 provides an important exception, making the ministerial renewal scheme under the Enforcement of Judgments Law available as an option for support judgments. Moreover, Family Code Section 291 makes this chapter applicable to enforceability and renewal of judgments for possession or sale entered under the Family Code. [30 Cal.L.Rev.Comm.Reports 717 (2000)].

Commentary

Family Code § 291, which subjects judgments "for possession or sale of property" to the Code of Civil Procedure § 683.130 10-year time limit for renewal, does not apply to Family Code money judgments. *In re Marriage of Wilcox, 124 Cal.App.4th 492, 21 Cal.Rptr.3d 315 (2004).*

§ 683.320. Money judgments against public entities

This chapter does not apply to a money judgment against a public entity that is subject to Section 965.5 or 970.1 of the Government Code. *(Added by Stats.1982, c. 1364, p. 5077, § 2, operative July 1, 1983.)*

Law Revision Commission Comments

1982 Addition

Section 683.320 recognizes that the period of enforceability of a money judgment against the state or a local public entity is governed by provisions of the Government Code. But see Gov't Code § 965.9 (judgment against the Regents of the University of California). The period of enforceability of a money judgment against a public entity may not be extended using the renewal procedure under Sections 683.110–683.220. This does not, however, affect the right to bring an action on the judgment. See Sections 337.5 and 683.050. See also Sections 695.050 (enforcement of money judgment against public entity), 712.070 (enforcement of nonmoney judgment against public entity). [16 Cal.L.Rev.Comm. Reports 1220 (1982)].

CHAPTER 5. INTEREST AND COSTS

§ 685.010. Rate of interest

(a) Interest accrues at the rate of 10 percent per annum on the principal amount of a money judgment remaining unsatisfied.

(b) The Legislature reserves the right to change the rate of interest provided in subdivision (a) at any time to a rate of less than 10 percent per annum, regardless of the date of entry of the judgment or the date any obligation upon which the judgment is based was incurred. A change in the rate of interest may be made applicable only to the interest that accrues after the operative date of the statute that changes the rate. *(Added by Stats.1982, c. 1364, p. 5080, § 2, operative July 1, 1983.)*

Research References

Treatises and Practice Aids

Witkin, California Summary 10th Agency and Employment § 666, Interest on Back Pay Award.
Witkin, California Summary 10th Negotiable Instruments § 47, Additional Liability to Payee or Payee's Assignee.
Witkin, California Summary 10th Torts § 1650, Prejudgment Interest is Not Element Of Damages.
Witkin, California Summary 10th Wills and Probate § 525, Statutory Framework.
Witkin, California Summary 10th Wills and Probate § 651, Interest.
Witkin, California Summary 10th Wills and Probate § 999, Liability for Breach Of Fiduciary Duty.

§ 685.020. Interest; commencement of accrual

(a) Except as provided in subdivision (b), interest commences to accrue on a money judgment on the date of entry of the judgment.

(b) Unless the judgment otherwise provides, if a money judgment is payable in installments, interest commences to accrue as to each installment on the date the installment becomes due. *(Added by Stats.1982, c. 1364, p. 5080, § 2, operative July 1, 1983. Amended by Stats.1983, c. 155, § 10, eff. June 30, 1983, operative July 1, 1983.)*

Law Revision Commission Comments

1983 Amendment

Subdivision (a) of Section 685.020 continues the general rule as to the time postjudgment interest commences to run. See former Section 682.2, Section 1033; Dixon Mobile Homes, Inc. v. Walters, 48 Cal.App.3d 964, 122 Cal.Rptr. 202 (1975). See also Sections 695.210 and 724.010 (amount to satisfy a judgment).

Subdivision (b) codifies the rule concerning accrual of interest on support judgments payable in installments and extends the rule to other judgments payable in installments. See, e.g., Huellmantel v. Huellmantel, 124 Cal. 583, 589–90, 57 P. 582 (1899); In re Marriage of Hoffee, 60 Cal.App.3d 337, 131 Cal.Rptr. 637 (1976). The introductory clause of subdivision (b) also recognizes that in certain circumstances the court may have the authority to order that interest accrues from the date of entry of a judgment rendered in an amount certain but payable in installments. See Section 85 (municipal or justice court may fix terms and conditions of payment of money judgment), 117 (small claims court may fix terms and conditions of payment).

Section 685.020 does not affect the rules that determine the extent to which prejudgment interest is to be included in a judgment. See Section 685.110. [16 Cal.L.Rev.Comm. Reports 2193 (1982)].

Commentary

The 2002 amendment of Family Code § 155, which exempts support orders from the operation of subsection (b) of this section, was intended to abrogate the installment-payment holding of *Dupont v. Dupont, 88 Cal.App.4th 192, 105 Cal.Rptr.2d 607 (2001). Dupont* sustained the conclusion of the trial court that a 1978 child support order requiring a former spouse to pay child support and spousal support arrearages of $9,000 at the rate of $15 monthly was an installment judgment within the meaning of subsection (b). Thus, interest began to accrue with respect to each installment as each installment became due. In other words, interest did not accrue on the entire $9,000 judgment from the date that the 1978 order was entered. Under the 2002 amendment of Family Code § 155, interest accrues on an order requiring the payment of support arrearages from the time the order was entered.

In re Marriage of McClellan, 130 Cal.App.4th 247, 30 Cal.Rptr.3d 5 (2005), holds that the 2000 amendment to Family Code § 155 applies retroactively because it clarified, rather than altered, existing law. Accordingly, it applies in calculating the interest due on child support arrearages that were the subject of arrearage orders entered before the amendment took effect.

In re Marriage of Hubner, 124 Cal.App.4th 1082, 22 Cal.Rptr.3d 549 (2004), holds that statutory interest on unpaid child support accrues from the period each payment originally came due during the period in which the trial court erroneously suspended the parent's child support obligation.

Research References

Forms

West's California Code Forms, Civil Procedure § 685.070 Form 1, Enforcement Of Judgments--Memorandum Of Costs After Judgment, Acknowledgment Of Credit, and Declaration Of Accrued Interest--Official Form.

Treatises and Practice Aids

Witkin, California Summary 10th Husband and Wife § 4, Definitions.

§ 685.030. Money judgments; satisfaction in full; accrual of interest; writ of execution

(a) If a money judgment is satisfied in full pursuant to a writ under this title, interest ceases to accrue on the judgment:

(1) If the proceeds of collection are paid in a lump sum, on the date of levy.

(2) If the money judgment is satisfied pursuant to an earnings withholding order, on the date and in the manner provided in Section 706.024 or Section 706.028.

(3) In any other case, on the date the proceeds of sale or collection are actually received by the levying officer.

(b) If a money judgment is satisfied in full other than pursuant to a writ under this title, interest ceases to accrue on the date the judgment is satisfied in full.

(c) If a money judgment is partially satisfied pursuant to a writ under this title or is otherwise partially satisfied, interest ceases to accrue as to the part satisfied on the date the part is satisfied.

(d) For the purposes of subdivisions (b) and (c), the date a money judgment is satisfied in full or in part is the earliest of the following times:

(1) The date satisfaction is actually received by the judgment creditor.

(2) The date satisfaction is tendered to the judgment creditor or deposited in court for the judgment creditor.

(3) The date of any other performance that has the effect of satisfaction.

(e) The clerk of a court may enter in the Register of Actions a writ of execution on a money judgment as returned wholly satisfied when the judgment amount, as specified on the writ, is fully collected and only an interest deficit of no more than ten dollars ($10) exists, due to automation of the continual daily interest accrual calculation. *(Added by Stats. 1982, c. 1364, p. 5080, § 2, operative July 1, 1983. Amended by Stats.1991, c. 1090 (A.B.1484), § 4.5; Stats.1992, c. 283 (S.B.1372), § 1, eff. July 21, 1992; Stats.1998, c. 931 (S.B. 2139), § 88, eff. Sept. 28, 1998; Stats.2001, c. 812 (A.B.223), § 4.)*

Law Revision Commission Comments

1992 Amendment

Subdivision (a) of Section 685.030 is amended to recognize the special rules applicable to cessation of interest with regard to collections by wage garnishment. See Sections 706.024 (amount required to satisfy earnings withholding order), 706.028 (final earnings withholding order for costs and interest). [21 Cal.L.Rev.Comm.Reports 135 (1991)].

1998 Amendment

Subdivision (e) of Section 685.030 is amended to accommodate unification of the municipal and superior courts in a county. Cal. Const. art. VI, § 5(e). It is also amended to reflect elimination of the justice court. Cal. Const. art. VI, §§ 1, 5(b). A limited civil case is equivalent to a matter within the original jurisdiction of the municipal court under former law, so Section 685.030 as amended continues the effect of former law. See Section 85 (limited civil cases) & Comment. [28 Cal.L.Rev.Comm. Reports 51 (1998)].

2001 Amendment

Subdivision (e) of Section 685.030 is amended to eliminate the difference in treatment between limited and unlimited civil cases.

For the register of actions in superior court, see Gov't Code 69845, 69845.5. For the register of actions in municipal court, see Code Civ. Proc. 1052, 1052.1.

A technical change is also made for conformity with preferred drafting style. [30 Cal.L.Rev.Comm. Reports 443 (2000)].

§ 685.040. Costs; attorney's fees

The judgment creditor is entitled to the reasonable and necessary costs of enforcing a judgment. Attorney's fees incurred in enforcing a judgment are not included in costs collectible under this title unless otherwise provided by law. Attorney's fees incurred in enforcing a judgment are included as costs collectible under this title if the underlying judgment includes an award of attorney's fees to the judgment creditor pursuant to subparagraph (A) of paragraph (10) of subdivision (a) of Section 1033.5. *(Added by Stats.1982, c. 1364, p. 5081, § 2, operative July 1, 1983. Amended by Stats.1992, c. 1348 (A.B.2616), § 3.)*

Research References

Forms

West's California Code Forms, Civil Procedure § 685.070 Form 1, Enforcement Of Judgments--Memorandum Of Costs After Judgment, Acknowledgment Of Credit, and Declaration Of Accrued Interest--Official Form.

Division 2

ENFORCEMENT OF MONEY JUDGMENTS

CHAPTER 1. GENERAL PROVISIONS

ARTICLE 1. PROPERTY SUBJECT TO ENFORCEMENT OF MONEY JUDGMENT

§ 695.010. Property subject to enforcement generally

(a) Except as otherwise provided by law, all property of the judgment debtor is subject to enforcement of a money judgment.

(b) If property of the judgment debtor was attached in the action but was transferred before entry of the money judgment in favor of the judgment creditor, the property is subject to enforcement of the money judgment so long as the attachment lien remains effective. *(Added by Stats.1982, c. 1364, p. 5103, § 2, operative July 1, 1983. Amended by Stats.1984, c. 538, § 17.)*

Law Revision Commission Comments

1982 Addition

Section 695.010 supersedes the first portion of subdivision (a) of former Section 688. The reference in former law to "any interest" in property and the enumeration of types of property subject to enforcement is not continued; all property of the judgment debtor, regardless of type or interest, is subject to enforcement of a money judgment unless an exception is provided by law. See also Civil Code §§ 1390.3, 1390.4 (enforcement against property subject to general power of appointment).

Some property that is not the judgment debtor's may also be subject to enforcement of a money judgment against the judgment debtor. See Section 695.020 (community property). For provisions governing liens on property that is transferred, see Sections 697.390 (judgment lien on real property), 697.610 (judgment lien on personal property), 697.720–697.750 (execution lien). The introductory clause of Section 695.010 recognizes that some property of the judgment debtor is by law not subject to enforcement of a money judgment despite the general rule stated in Section 695.010. Property that is exempt by statute without the need to make an exemption claim is not subject to enforcement of a money judgment unless a particular exemption provision otherwise provides. See Section 703.030(b) (general rule). See also Sections 704.110(c) (public retirement plan benefits), 704.113 (public vacation credit), 704.115(c) (private retirement plan benefits), 706.052 (wage garnishment). Property of a public entity is not subject to enforcement of a money judgment under this division. See Section 695.050; Gov't Code §§ 965.5, 970.1. Property that is not transferable is generally not subject to enforcement. See Section 695.030. Certain property held in a fiduciary capacity may not be subject to enforcement. See, e.g., Civil Code § 986(a)(6) (amounts held for payment of artists); Educ.Code § 21116 (educational endowment property); Health & Saf.Code § 32508 (hospital endowment property); Labor Code § 270.5 (property held by logging employer as fund for wages). Specific property may be made not subject to enforcement by other statutes. See, e.g., Civil Code § 765 (estate at will); Health & Saf.Code § 7925 (cemetery funds); Labor Code § 4901 (workers' compensation). Federal law protects certain property from enforcement. See, e.g., 42 U.S.C. § 407 (social security).

Property of the judgment debtor that is by law not subject to enforcement of a money judgment may not be reached by any enforcement process, whether execution or otherwise. Certain property of the judgment debtor may be subject to enforcement by some, but not all, enforcement procedures. See, e.g., Section 699.720 (property not subject to execution but subject to other enforcement procedures. [16 Cal.L.Rev.Comm. Reports 1265 (1982)].

1984 Amendment

Subdivision (b) is added to Section 695.010 to make clear that property attached in the action is subject to enforcement even though it has been transferred. See Section 488.500 (attachment lien). Such property may be levied upon under a writ of execution after judgment without the need to bring a separate action to foreclose the lien. See Section 699.710 (property subject to execution). See also Section 697.340 (judgment lien does not reach real property transferred before judgment.) [17 Cal.L.Rev.Comm.Reports 1002 (1983)].

Commentary

Ventura County Department of Child Support Services v. Brown, 117 Cal.App.4th 144, 11 Cal.Rptr.3d 489 (2004), relying on Probate Code

§ 15305(c), holds that when there is an enforceable child support judgment against a trust beneficiary, which the trustee refuses to satisfy, a trial court may overcome the trustee's discretion and order the trustee to satisfy the past due and ongoing child support obligations of the beneficiary directly from the trust. The analysis and rationale of *Brown* would seem to apply equally to spousal support judgments.

Research References

Forms

Cal. Transaction Forms - Bus. Transactions § 22:14, Landlord's Lien.

§ 695.020. Community property

(a) Community property is subject to enforcement of a money judgment as provided in the Family Code.

(b) Unless the provision or context otherwise requires, if community property that is subject to enforcement of a money judgment is sought to be applied to the satisfaction of a money judgment:

(1) Any provision of this division that applies to the property of the judgment debtor or to obligations owed to the judgment debtor also applies to the community property interest of the spouse of the judgment debtor and to obligations owed to the other spouse that are community property.

(2) Any provision of this division that applies to property in the possession or under the control of the judgment debtor also applies to community property in the possession or under the control of the spouse of the judgment debtor. *(Added by Stats.1982, c. 1364, p. 5103, § 2, operative July 1, 1983. Amended by Stats.1983, c. 155, § 12, eff. June 30, 1983, operative July 1, 1983; Stats.1992, c. 163 (A.B.2641), § 33, operative Jan. 1, 1994.)*

Law Revision Commission Comments

1982 Addition

Section 695.020 recognizes the rule that community property, including the interest of a nondebtor spouse, is generally subject to enforcement of a money judgment. For exceptions to this rule, see Civil Code Section 5100 et seq. [16 Cal.L.Rev.Comm. Reports 1266 (1982)].

1983 Amendment

Subdivision (b)(1) is amended to correct a typographical error. [16 Cal.L.Rev.Comm.Reports 2194 (1982)].

1992 Amendment

Subdivision (a) of Section 695.020 is amended to substitute a reference to the Family Code for the reference to the former Civil Code provisions. [22 Cal.L.Rev.Comm.Reports 1 (1992)].

§ 695.030. Non-assignable and non-transferable property; interest in trust; cause of action for money or property

(a) Except as otherwise provided by statute, property of the judgment debtor that is not assignable or transferable is not subject to enforcement of a money judgment.

(b) The following property is subject to enforcement of a money judgment:

(1) An interest in a trust, to the extent provided by law.

(2) A cause of action for money or property that is the subject of a pending action or special proceeding. *(Added by Stats.1982, c. 1364, p. 5103, § 2, operative July 1, 1983. Amended by Stats.1986, c. 820, § 17, operative July 1, 1987.)*

Law Revision Commission Comments

1986 Amendment

Section 695.030 is amended to delete "spendthrift" from subdivision (b)(1) in recognition that trusts other than "spendthrift" trusts may be not assignable or transferable. See e.g., Prob.Code § 15302 (trust for support). [18 Cal.L.Rev.Comm. Reports 765 (1985)].

Commentary

Ventura County Department of Child Support Services v. Brown, 117 Cal.App.4th 144, 11 Cal.Rptr.3d 489 (2004), relying on Probate Code § 15305(c), holds that when there is an enforceable child support judgment against a trust beneficiary, which the trustee refuses to satisfy, a trial court may overcome the trustee's discretion and order the trustee to satisfy the past due and ongoing child support obligations of the beneficiary directly from the trust. The analysis and rationale of *Brown* would seem to apply equally to spousal support judgments.

Research References

Treatises and Practice Aids

Witkin, California Summary 10th Trusts § 23, Other Provisions Governing Trusts.

§ 695.035. Lessee's interest in real property; provisions in lease for termination or modification upon involuntary transfer or assignment

(a) A lessee's interest in real property may be applied to the satisfaction of a money judgment in any of the following circumstances:

(1) If the lessee has the right voluntarily to sublet the property or assign the interest in the lease.

(2) If the lessee has the right voluntarily to sublet the property or assign the interest in the lease subject to standards or conditions and the purchaser at the execution sale or other assignee agrees to comply with the standards or conditions that would have had to be complied with had the lessee voluntarily sublet the property or assigned the interest in the lease.

(3) If the lessee has the right voluntarily to sublet the property or assign the interest in the lease with the consent of the lessor, in which case the obligation of the lessor to consent to the assignment is subject to the same standard that would apply had the lessee voluntarily sublet the property or assigned the interest in the lease.

(4) In any other case, if the lessor consents in writing.

(b) A provision in a lease for the termination or modification of the lease upon an involuntary transfer or assignment of the lessee's interest is ineffective to the extent that such provision would prevent the application of the lessee's interest to the satisfaction of the money judgment under subdivision (a). *(Added by Stats.1982, c. 1364, p. 5104, § 2, operative July 1, 1983.)*

§ 695.040. Exempt property; release

Property that is not subject to enforcement of a money judgment may not be levied upon or in any other manner applied to the satisfaction of a money judgment. If property that is not subject to enforcement of a money judgment has been levied upon, the property may be released pursuant to the claim of exemption procedure provided in Article 2 (commencing with Section 703.510) of Chapter 4. *(Added by Stats.1982, c. 1364, p. 5104, § 2, operative July 1, 1983.)*

Law Revision Commission Comments

1982 Addition

Section 695.040 is comparable to Section 703.510(b) (release of property exempt without making a claim). [16 Cal.L.Rev.Comm. Reports 1269 (1982)].

§ 695.050. Money judgment against public entity

A money judgment against a public entity is not enforceable under this division if the money judgment is subject to Chapter 1 (commencing with Section 965) of, or Article 1 (commencing with Section 970) of Chapter 2 of, Part 5 of Division 3.6 of Title 1 of the Government Code. *(Added by Stats.1982, c. 1364, p. 5104, § 2, operative July 1, 1983.)*

Law Revision Commission Comments

1982 Addition

Section 695.050 continues existing law. See Government Code Sections 965.5(b) (state) and 970.1(b) (local public entities). See also Sections 683.320 and Comment to that section (period for enforcement of judgment), 712.070 (nonmoney judgments). [16 Cal.L.Rev.Comm. Reports 1269 (1982)].

§ 695.060. License to engage in business, profession or activity

Except as provided in Section 708.630, a license issued by a public entity to engage in any business, profession, or activity is not subject to enforcement of a money judgment. *(Added by Stats.1982, c. 1364, p. 5104, § 2, operative July 1, 1983.)*

§ 695.070. Transfer or encumbrance of property subject to lien

(a) Notwithstanding the transfer or encumbrance of property subject to a lien created under this division, if the property remains subject to the lien after the transfer or encumbrance, the money judgment may be enforced against the property in the same manner and to the same extent as if it had not been transferred or encumbered.

(b) If the judgment debtor dies after the transfer of property that remains subject to a lien created under this division, the money judgment may be enforced against the property as provided in subdivision (a). *(Added by Stats. 1982, c. 1364, p. 5104, § 2, operative July 1, 1983. Amended by Stats.1989, c. 1416, § 22.)*

Law Revision Commission Comments

1989 Amendment

Section 695.070 is amended to clarify the manner of enforcement of a money judgment against property of a decedent in a situation where the property was transferred during the judgment debtor's lifetime subject to an enforcement lien. For provisions relating to continuation of liens after transfer, see Sections 697.390 (judgment line on real property), 697.610 (judgment lien on personal property), 697.720–697.750 (execution lien), 697.920 (other liens).

Under subdivision (b), the judgment creditor may enforce the money judgment against the transferred property after the judgment debtor's death using any appropriate procedure available before death. Thus, the death of the judgment debtor has no effect on the judgment creditor's remedies against property that was transferred subject to an enforcement lien. The judgment creditor may use a writ of execution, any other applicable enforcement procedure provided in this division, or an action against the owner of the property to foreclose the lien. Enforcement under this section may proceed only against the property subject to the lien and only in the amount of the lien on the transferred property, as is the case when enforcing a lien on transferred property while the judgment debtor is alive. See Sections 695.210 (amount required to satisfy judgment), 697.010 (amount of lien). As to enforcement of a judgment against property in the decedent's estate, see Code Civ.Proc. § 686.020 (enforcement against property in deceased judgment debtor's estate is governed by Probate Code); Prob.Code §§ 9300–9304 (enforcement of claims established by judgment). [20 Cal.L.Rev.Comm.Reports 233 (1990)].

ARTICLE 2. AMOUNT TO SATISFY MONEY JUDGMENT

§ 695.210. Amount required

The amount required to satisfy a money judgment is the total amount of the judgment as entered or renewed with the following additions and subtractions:

(a) The addition of costs added to the judgment pursuant to Section 685.090.

(b) The addition of interest added to the judgment as it accrues pursuant to Sections 685.010 to 685.030, inclusive.

(c) The subtraction of the amount of any partial satisfactions of the judgment.

(d) The subtraction of the amount of any portion of the judgment that is no longer enforceable. *(Added by Stats. 1982, c. 1364, p. 5105, § 2, operative July 1, 1983. Amended by Stats.1992, c. 848 (S.B.1614), § 8, eff. Sept. 22, 1992; Stats.1993, c. 876 (S.B.1068), § 9, eff. Oct. 6, 1993.)*

Law Revision Commission Comments

1982 Addition

Section 695.210 is new. For a related provision, see Section 680.300 ("principal amount of the judgment" defined). See also Section 577.5 (amount to be computed and stated in dollars and cents, rejecting fractions). [16 Cal.L.Rev.Comm. Reports 1270 (1982)].

Research References

Treatises and Practice Aids

Witkin, California Summary 10th Husband and Wife § 250, Definitions.

§ 695.211. Interest accrual on arrearages; notice; statement of account; required contents

(a) Every money judgment or order for child support shall provide notice that interest on arrearages accrues at the legal rate.

(b) The notice provisions required by this section shall be incorporated in the appropriate Judicial Council forms.

(c) Upon implementation of the California Child Support Automation System prescribed in Chapter 4 (commencing with Section 10080) of Part 1 of Division 9 of the Welfare and Institutions Code and certification of the California Child Support Automation System by the United States Department of Health and Human Services, whenever a statement of account is issued by the local child support agency in any child support action, the statement shall include a statement of an amount of current support, arrears, and interest due. *(Added by Stats.1994, c. 959 (A.B.3072), § 1, eff. Sept. 28, 1994. Amended by Stats.2000, c. 808 (A.B.1358), § 10, eff. Sept. 28, 2000.)*

Commentary

See generally *In re Marriage of Perez, 35 Cal.App.4th 77, 41 Cal.Rptr.2d 377 (1995)* (trial court's reduction of child support arrearages and forgiveness of interest due on arrearages were impermissible retroactive modifications within the meaning of Section 3651 (c) and they also ran afoul of the principles articulated in Family Code Section 4502 and Code of Civil Procedure Sections 695.211 and 695.221); and *In re Marriage of Hamer, 81 Cal.App.4th 712, 97 Cal.Rptr.2d 195 (2000)* (trial court improperly held that former wife waived her right to collect the full amount of spousal and child support due under the judgment of dissolution by accepting former husband's payment of lesser amounts).

§ 695.220. Crediting of money received

Money received in satisfaction of a money judgment, except a money judgment for support, is to be credited as follows:

(a) The money is first to be credited against the amounts described in subdivision (b) of Section 685.050 that are collected by the levying officer.

(b) Any remaining money is next to be credited against any fee due the court pursuant to Section 6103.5 or 68511.3 of the Government Code, which are to be remitted to the court by the levying officer.

(c) Any remaining money is next to be credited against the accrued interest that remains unsatisfied.

(d) Any remaining money is to be credited against the principal amount of the judgment remaining unsatisfied. If the judgment is payable in installments, the remaining money is to be credited against the matured installments in the order in which they matured. *(Added by Stats.1982, c. 1364, p. 5105, § 2, operative July 1, 1983. Amended by Stats.1992, c. 848 (S.B.1614), § 9, eff. Sept. 22, 1992; Stats.1993, c. 158 (A.B.392), § 3.2, eff. July 21, 1993; Stats.1993, c. 876 (S.B. 1068), § 10, eff. Oct. 6, 1993; Stats.1993, c. 909 (S.B.15), § 1; Stats.1994, c. 146 (A.B.3601), § 25; Stats.1994, c. 75 (A.B. 1702), § 1, eff. May 20, 1994.)*

Law Revision Commission Comments

1982 Addition

Section 695.220 is drawn from a portion of former Section 682.1 (writ of execution issued on money judgment), but Section 695.220 applies to any money received in satisfaction of the judgment not just that received pursuant to a levy of execution. See also the Comment to Section 724.010. [16 Cal.L.Rev.Comm. Reports 1270 (1982)].

§ 695.221. Crediting of money judgment for support

Satisfaction of a money judgment for support shall be credited as follows:

(a) The money shall first be credited against the current month's support.

(b) Any remaining money shall next be credited against the principal amount of the judgment remaining unsatisfied. If the judgment is payable in installments, the remaining money shall be credited against the matured installments in the order in which they matured.

(c) Any remaining money shall be credited against the accrued interest that remains unsatisfied.

(d) In cases enforced pursuant to Part D (commencing with Section 651) of Subchapter 4 of Chapter 7 of Title 42 of the United States Code, if a lump-sum payment is collected from a support obligor who has money judgments for support owing to more than one family, after the implementation of the California Child Support Automation System (CCSAS), all support collected shall be distributed pursuant to guidelines developed by the State Department of Child Support Services.

(e) Notwithstanding subdivisions (a), (b), and (c), a collection received as a result of a federal tax refund offset shall first be credited against the principal amount of past due support that has been assigned to the state pursuant to Section 11477 of the Welfare and Institutions Code and federal law and then any interest due on that past due support, prior to the principal amount of any other past due support remaining unsatisfied and then any interest due on that past due support.

(f) If federal law does not permit states to adopt the same order of distribution for the pre- and post-assistance child support arrears effective October 1, 1998, the following shall be the order of distribution of child support collections through September 30, 2000, except for federal tax refund offset collections, for child support received for families and children who are former recipients of Aid to Families with Dependent Children (AFDC) program benefits or former recipients of Temporary Assistance for Needy Families (TANF) program benefits:

(1) The money shall first be credited against the current month's support.

(2) Any remaining money shall next be credited against interest that accrued on arrearages owed to the family or children since leaving the AFDC program or the TANF program and then the arrearages.

(3) Any remaining money shall next be credited against interest that accrued on arrearages owed during the time the family or children received benefits under the AFDC program or the TANF program and then the arrearages.

(4) Any remaining money shall next be credited against interest that accrued on arrearages owed to the family or children prior to receiving benefits from the AFDC program or the TANF program and then the arrearages.

(g) If federal law does permit states to adopt the same order of distribution for the pre- and post-assistance child support arrears effective October 1, 1998, or effective October 1, 2000, whichever comes first, the following shall be the order of distribution of child support collections, except for federal tax refund offset collections, for child support received for families and children who are former recipients of

AFDC program benefits or former recipients of TANF program benefits:

(1) The money shall first be credited against the current month's support.

(2) Any remaining money shall next be credited against the principal amount of the arrearages owed to the family or children since leaving the AFDC program or the TANF program and then the interest that accrued on those arrearages.

(3) Any remaining money shall next be credited against the principal amount of the arrearages owed to the family or children prior to receiving benefits from the AFDC program or the TANF program and then the interest that accrued on those arrearages.

(4) Any remaining money shall next be credited against the principal amount of the arrearages owed during the time the family or children received benefits under the AFDC program or the TANF program and then the interest that accrued on those arrearages.

(h) This section shall become operative on January 1, 2009. *(Added by Stats.2004, c. 305 (A.B.2669), § 2, operative Jan. 1, 2009.)*

Commentary

See generally *In re Marriage of Perez, 35 Cal.App.4th 77, 41 Cal.Rptr.2d 377 (1995)* (trial court's reduction of child support arrearages and forgiveness of interest due on arrearages were impermissible retroactive modifications within the meaning of Section 3651 (c) and they also ran afoul of the principles articulated in Family Code Section 4502 and Code of Civil Procedure Sections 695.211 and 695.221); and *In re Marriage of Hamer, 81 Cal.App.4th 712, 97 Cal.Rptr.2d 195 (2000)* (trial court improperly held that former wife waived her right to collect the full amount of spousal and child support due under the judgment of dissolution by accepting former husband's payment of lesser amounts).

Social security "child's insurance benefits" payable on account of the disability or retirement of the noncustodial parent are not payments received in satisfaction of a money judgment for support within the meaning of this section. Although Family Code Section 4054 provides that social security "child's insurance benefits" payable on account of the disability or retirement of the noncustodial parent shall be credited against the amount of child support otherwise payable by the noncustodial parent, current benefits may not be applied against child support arrearages. *In re Marriage of Robinson, 65 Cal.App.4th 93, 76 Cal.Rptr.2d 134 (1998).*

Research References

Treatises and Practice Aids

Witkin, California Summary 10th Parent and Child § 393, Crediting Federal Retirement or Disability Payments.

CHAPTER 2. LIENS

ARTICLE 2. JUDGMENT LIEN ON REAL PROPERTY

§ 697.320. Judgment for support payable in installments; judgment against health care provider requiring periodic payments; creation and duration

(a) A judgment lien on real property is created under this section by recording an abstract, a notice of support judgment, an interstate lien form promulgated by the federal Secretary of Health and Human Services pursuant to Section 652(a)(11) of Title 42 of the United States Code, or a certified copy of either of the following money judgments with the county recorder:

(1) A judgment for child, family, or spousal support payable in installments.

(2) A judgment entered pursuant to Section 667.7 (judgment against health care provider requiring periodic payments).

(b) Unless the money judgment is satisfied or the judgment lien is released, a judgment lien created under paragraph (1) of subdivision (a) or by recording an interstate lien form, as described in subdivision (a), continues during the period the judgment remains enforceable. Unless the money judgment is satisfied or the judgment lien is released, a judgment lien created under paragraph (2) of subdivision (a) continues for a period of 10 years from the date of its creation. The duration of a judgment lien created under paragraph (2) of subdivision (a) may be extended any number of times by recording, during the time the judgment lien is in existence, a certified copy of the judgment in the manner provided in this section for the initial recording; this rerecording has the effect of extending the duration of the judgment lien created under paragraph (2) of subdivision (a) until 10 years from the date of the rerecording. *(Added by Stats.1982, c. 1364, p. 5107, § 2, operative July 1, 1983. Amended by Stats.1986, c. 946, § 2; Stats.1992, c. 163 (A.B.2641), § 34, operative Jan. 1, 1994; Stats.1993, c. 876 (S.B.1068), § 12, eff. Oct. 6, 1993; Stats.1997, c. 599 (A.B. 573), § 3; Stats.2002, c. 927 (A.B.3032), § 1.5.)*

Law Revision Commission Comments

1992 Amendment

Subdivision (a)(1) of Section 697.320 is amended to make clear that Section 697.320 applies to a judgment for family support. See Fam. Code § 4501 (family support order is enforceable in same manner and to same extent as child support order). See also Section 680.145 ("child support" includes family support). [22 Cal.L.Rev.Comm.Reports 1 (1992)].

Commentary

A former husband's judgment-based obligation to maintain life insurance was neither a money judgment nor a support obligation for which his former wife could obtain a judgment lien under this section. *Guess v. Bernhardson, 242 Cal.App.4th 821, 195 Cal.Rptr.3d 349 (2015), review denied.*

Research References

Forms

West's California Judicial Council Forms FL-480, Abstract Of Support Judgment.

Treatises and Practice Aids

Witkin, California Summary 10th Husband and Wife § 267, Judgment Lien.

CHAPTER 5. WAGE GARNISHMENT

ARTICLE 1. SHORT TITLE; DEFINITIONS

§ 706.010. Short title

This chapter shall be known and may be cited as the "Wage Garnishment Law." *(Added by Stats.1982, c. 1364, p. 5172, § 2, operative July 1, 1983.)*

Law Revision Commission Comments

1982 Addition

Section 706.010 substitutes the more descriptive term "Wage Garnishment Law" for the term "Employees' Earnings Protection Law" used in former Section 723.010. [16 Cal.L.Rev.Comm. Reports 1442 (1982)].

Research References

Forms

Cal. Transaction Forms - Bus. Transactions § 16:88, Assignment Of Wages or Salary (General).

Cal. Transaction Forms - Bus. Transactions § 16:94, Assignor's Revocation Of Assignment Of Wages or Salary.

California Transactions Forms--Estate Planning § 18:36, Disclaimers as Protective Device.

Am. Jur. Pl. & Pr. Forms Attachment and Garnishment § 1, Introductory Comments.

Am. Jur. Pl. & Pr. Forms Attachment and Garnishment § 207, Introductory Comments.

§ 706.011. Definitions

As used in this chapter:

(a) "Disposable earnings" means the portion of an individual's earnings that remains after deducting all amounts required to be withheld by law.

(b) "Earnings" means compensation payable by an employer to an employee for personal services performed by such employee, whether denominated as wages, salary, commission, bonus, or otherwise.

(c) "Earnings withholding order for elder or dependent adult financial abuse" means an earnings withholding order, made pursuant to Article 5 (commencing with Section 706.100) and based on a money judgment in an action for elder or adult dependent financial abuse under Section 15657.5 of the Welfare and Institutions Code.

(d) "Earnings assignment order for support" means an order, made pursuant to Chapter 8 (commencing with Section 5200) of Part 5 of Division 9 of the Family Code or Section 3088 of the Probate Code, which requires an employer to withhold earnings for support.

(e) "Employee" means a public officer and any individual who performs services subject to the right of the employer to control both what shall be done and how it shall be done.

(f) "Employer" means a person for whom an individual performs services as an employee.

(g) "Judgment creditor," as applied to the state, means the specific state agency seeking to collect a judgment or tax liability.

(h) "Judgment debtor" includes a person from whom the state is seeking to collect a tax liability under Article 4 (commencing with Section 706.070), whether or not a judgment has been obtained on such tax liability.

(i) "Person" includes an individual, a corporation, a partnership or other unincorporated association, a limited liability company, and a public entity. *(Added by Stats.1982, c. 1364, p. 5172, § 2, operative July 1, 1983. Amended by Stats.1990, c. 1493 (A.B.3974), § 30.5; Stats.1992, c. 163 (A.B.2641), § 45, operative Jan. 1, 1994; Stats.1994, c. 1010 (S.B.2053), § 61; Stats.2010, c. 64 (A.B.2619), § 1, operative Jan. 1, 2012; Stats.2012, c. 474 (A.B.1775), § 1, operative July 1, 2013.)*

Law Revision Commission Comments

1992 Amendment

Section 706.011 is amended to conform to the terminology of the Family Code and to substitute references to the Family Code provisions that replaced the former Civil Code provisions. See Chapter 8 (commencing with Section 5200) of Part 5 of Division 9 of the Family Code (earnings assignment order for support). The term "wage assignment for support" in former subdivision (g) has been replaced by "earnings assignment for support" in new subdivision (b), and other subdivisions have been redesignated to keep the definitions in alphabetical order. [22 Cal.L.Rev.Comm.Reports 1 (1992)].

Research References

Treatises and Practice Aids

Witkin, California Summary 10th Husband and Wife § 250, Definitions.

ARTICLE 2. GENERAL PROVISIONS

Section

§ 706.020. Application of chapter

Except for an earning assignment order for support, the earnings of an employee shall not be required to be withheld by an employer for payment of a debt by means of any judicial procedure other than pursuant to this chapter. *(Added by Stats.1982, c. 1364, p. 5173, § 2, operative July 1, 1983. Amended by Stats.1992, c. 163 (A.B.2641), § 46, operative Jan. 1, 1994.)*

Law Revision Commission Comments

1982 Addition

Section 706.020 makes clear that, with the exception of wage assignments for support (defined in subdivision (g) of Section 706.011), the Wage Garnishment Law is the exclusive judicial method of compelling an employer to withhold earnings. The section continues former Section 723.020. Attachment of earnings before judgment is abolished by Section 487.020(c). For provisions relating to voluntary wage assignments, see Labor Code Section 300. This chapter has no effect on judgment collection procedures that do not involve the withholding of an employee's earnings. However, where an employee's earnings are sought to be garnished, the creditor must comply with the provisions of this chapter. This rule applies to public entities as well as private persons. This chapter, for example, imposes limitations on the state's ability to garnish wages for tax delinquencies pursuant to its warrant and notice procedures. See Article 4 (commencing with Section 706.070).

The Wage Garnishment Law has no effect on matters that are preempted by federal law, such as federal bankruptcy proceedings and federal tax collection procedures. E.g., I.R.C. § 6334(c). Nor does this chapter apply to deductions which an employer is authorized by statute to make for such items as insurance premiums and payments to health, welfare, or pension plans. See, e.g., Gov't Code §§ 1156–1158, Labor Code §§ 224, 300. Finally, this chapter does not affect the procedures for the examination of a debtor of the judgment debtor provided in Article 2 (commencing with Section 708.110) of Chapter 6. See also Comment to Section 706.154. [16 Cal.L.Rev.Comm. Reports 1443 (1982)].

1992 Amendment

Section 706.020 is amended to conform to the terminology of the Family Code. See Chapter 8 (commencing with Section 5200) of Part 5 of Division 9 of the Family Code (earnings assignment order for support). "Earnings assignment order for support" is defined in Section 706.011. [22 Cal.L.Rev.Comm.Reports 1 (1992)].

§ 706.021. Procedure for levy of execution upon employee earnings

Notwithstanding any other provision of this title, a levy of execution upon the earnings of an employee shall be made by service of an earnings withholding order upon the employer in accordance with this chapter. *(Added by Stats.1982, c. 1364, p. 5173, § 2, operative July 1, 1983.)*

Law Revision Commission Comments

1982 Addition

Section 706.021 continues former Section 723.021 except that a reference to "this title" is substituted for the reference to former Section 688 in the introductory clause. Section 706.021 makes clear that a levy of execution on earnings is made as provided in this chapter rather than under Chapter 3 (commencing with Section 699.010). [16 Cal.L.Rev.Comm. Reports 1444 (1982)].

§ 706.022. Withholding period, defined; amount withheld; employer liability for amounts withheld and paid prior to service of order

(a) As used in this section, "withholding period" means the period which commences on the 10th day after service of an earnings withholding order upon the employer and which continues until the earliest of the following dates:

(1) The date the employer has withheld the full amount required to satisfy the order.

(2) The date of termination specified in a court order served on the employer.

(3) The date of termination specified in a notice of termination served on the employer by the levying officer.

(4) The date of termination of a dormant or suspended earnings withholding order as determined pursuant to Section 706.032.

(b) Except as otherwise provided by statute, an employer shall withhold the amounts required by an earnings withholding order from all earnings of the employee payable for any pay period of the employee which ends during the withholding period.

(c) An employer is not liable for any amounts withheld and paid over to the levying officer pursuant to an earnings withholding order prior to service upon the employer pursuant to paragraph (2) or (3) of subdivision (a). *(Added by Stats.1982, c. 1364, p. 5173, § 2, operative July 1, 1983. Amended by Stats.1989, c. 263, § 1; Stats.1992, c. 283 (S.B.1372), § 5, eff. July 21, 1992.)*

Law Revision Commission Comments

1992 Amendment

Subdivision (a)(1) of Section 706.022 is amended for conformity with Section 706.024 (amount required to satisfy earnings withholding order). Subdivision (a)(4) is added to reflect the automatic termination of earnings withholding orders under Section 706.032.

The remainder of this Comment is drawn from the Comment to Section 706.022 as enacted in 1982, with revisions to reflect the amendment of this section in 1989. See 1982 Cal.Stat. ch. 1364, § 2; 1989 Cal.Stat. ch. 263, § 1.

Section 706.022 states the basic rules governing the employer's duty to withhold pursuant to an earnings withholding order.

Subdivision (b) requires the employer to withhold from all earnings of an employee payable for any pay period of such employee which *ends* during the "withholding period." The "withholding period" is described in subdivision (a). It should be noted that *only* earnings for a pay period ending during the withholding period are subject to levy. Earnings for prior periods, even though still in the possession of the employer, are not subject to the order. An employer may not, however, defer or accelerate any payment of earnings to an employee with the intent to defeat or diminish the satisfaction of a judgment pursuant to this chapter. See Section 706.153.

Under subdivision (a), the withholding period generally commences 10 calendar days (not working or business days) after service of an earnings withholding order is completed. See Section 706.101 (when service completed). For example, if an order is served on Friday, the withholding period would commence on the second following Monday. See Section 12 (computation of time). The 10-day delay affords the employer time to process the order within its organization, i.e., deliver the order to the employer's bookkeeper, make bookkeeping adjustments, and so on.

The introductory clause to subdivision (b) recognizes certain exceptions to the general rule stated in subdivision (b). An employer is not generally required to withhold pursuant to two orders at the same time, except in special cases involving withholding orders for support or taxes. Thus, an ordinary earnings withholding order served when an earlier order is in place will not be given effect. See Section 706.023 (priority of orders) & Comment. See also Section 706.104(a) (no withholding if debtor not employed and no earnings due).

The withholding period does not end until the first of the events described in paragraphs (1) through (4) of subdivision (a) occurs. The employer has a *continuing* duty to withhold during the withholding period. See also Section 706.032 (termination of dormant or suspended order).

Paragraph (1) requires the employer to stop withholding when the full amount required to satisfy the earnings withholding order has been withheld. See Section 706.024 (amount required to satisfy order).

Paragraph (2) reflects the fact that the court may order the termination of the earnings withholding order. See Section 706.105(g). Of course, in some situations, the court will only modify the prior order, and the employer then must comply with the order as modified for the remainder of the withholding period.

Paragraph (3) requires the employer to stop withholding when served with a notice of termination. See Section 706.101 (manner of service). A notice of termination is served (1) where the levying officers is notified of the satisfaction of the judgment or (2) where the judgment debtor has claimed an exemption for the entire amount of earnings but the judgment creditor has failed within the time allowed to file with the levying officer a notice of opposition to claim of exemption and a notice of the hearing on the exemption. See Sections 706.027 (satisfaction of judgment), 706.105(f) (grounds for termination of withholding order in exemption proceeding). The levying officer may also serve a notice of termination where the order has been dormant or suspended for 180 days. See Section 706.032 (termination for dormancy or suspension).

Paragraph (4) recognizes the special rule for termination of earnings withholding orders that have been dormant or suspended for a period of 180 days. See Section 706.032 & Comment.

The judgment creditor has an affirmative duty to inform the levying officer of the satisfaction of the judgment. See Section 706.027.

Service of an order for the collection of state taxes suspends the duty of an employer to withhold pursuant to a prior order (other than an order for support). See Section 706.077 (tax orders). However, this is only a suspension. After the tax order is satisfied, if the withholding period for the prior order has not ended, the employer must again withhold pursuant to the prior order. See Section 706.032 (termination in case of suspension for 180 days by supervening order).

Similarly, the duty to withhold is not terminated by the layoff, discharge, or suspension of an employee and, if the employee is rehired or returns to work during the withholding period, the employer must resume withholding pursuant to the order. See Section 706.032 (termination in case of dormancy for 180 days).

The termination of certain types of orders—orders for the collection of state taxes and support orders—is governed by separate rules. See Sections 706.030 (support orders), 706.078 (tax orders).

Sometimes an order will be terminated without the employer's prior knowledge. Subdivision (c) makes clear that an employer will not be subject to liability for having withheld and paid over amounts pursuant to an order prior to service of a written notice of termination of the order. In such a case, the employee must look to the judgment creditor for the recovery of amounts previously paid to the judgment creditor. See Section 706.154 (employer entitled to rely on documents actually served). See also Section 706.105(i) (recovery from levying officer or judgment creditor of amounts received after order terminated).

An earnings withholding order may also be affected by federal bankruptcy proceedings. See Comment to Section 706.020. [21 Cal.L.Rev.Comm.Reports 135 (1991)].

Research References

Forms

Cal. Transaction Forms - Bus. Transactions § 16:94, Assignor's Revocation Of Assignment Of Wages or Salary.

West's California Judicial Council Forms WG-002, Earnings Withholding Order (Wage Garnishment).

§ 706.023. Multiple earnings withholding orders; earnings withholding orders for elder or dependent adult financial abuse

Except as otherwise provided in this chapter:

(a) An employer shall comply with the first earnings withholding order served upon the employer.

(b) If the employer is served with two or more earnings withholding orders on the same day, the employer shall comply with the order issued pursuant to the judgment first entered. If two or more orders served on the same day are based on judgments entered upon the same day, the employer shall comply with whichever one of the orders the employer selects.

(c) If an earnings withholding order is served while an employer is required to comply with another earnings withholding order with respect to the earnings of the same employee, the subsequent order is ineffective and the employer shall not withhold earnings pursuant to the subsequent order, except as provided in subdivision (d).

(d) Notwithstanding any other provisions of this section, a withholding order for elder or dependent adult financial abuse has priority over any other earning withholding order except for a withholding order for support under Section 706.030 and a withholding order for taxes under Section 706.072.

(1) An employer upon whom a withholding order for elder or dependent adult financial abuse is served shall withhold and pay over earnings of the employee pursuant to that order notwithstanding the requirements of another earnings withholding order except as provided in paragraph (2).

(2) An employer shall not withhold earnings of an employee pursuant to an earnings withholding order for elder or dependent adult financial abuse if a withholding order for support or for taxes is in effect or if a prior withholding order for elder or dependent adult financial abuse is in effect. In that case, the subsequent withholding order for elder or dependent financial abuse is ineffective.

(3) When an employer is required to cease withholding earnings pursuant to a prior earnings withholding order, the employer shall notify the levying officer who served the prior earnings withholding order that a supervening earnings withholding order for elder or dependent financial abuse is in effect. *(Added by Stats.1982, c. 1364, p. 5173, § 2, operative July 1, 1983. Amended by Stats.2010, c. 64 (A.B.2619), § 2, operative Jan. 1, 2012.)*

Research References

Forms

West's California Judicial Council Forms WG-030, Earnings Withholding Order for Elder or Dependent Adult Financial Abuse (Wage Garnishment).

§ 706.024. Amount required to satisfy earnings withholding order; discretionary notice; accrual of interest

(a) The amount required to satisfy an earnings withholding order is the total amount required to satisfy the writ of execution on the date the order is issued, with the following additions and subtractions:

(1) The addition of the statutory fee for service of the order and any other statutory fees for performing duties under the order.

(2) The addition of costs added to the order pursuant to Section 685.090.

(3) The subtraction of the amount of any partial satisfactions.

(4) The addition of daily interest accruing after issuance of the order, as adjusted for partial satisfactions.

(b) From time to time the levying officer, in the levying officer's discretion, may give written notice to the employer of the amount required to satisfy the earnings withholding order and the employer shall determine the total amount to withhold based upon the levying officer's notice, notwithstanding a different amount stated in the order originally served on the employer.

(c) If the full amount required to satisfy the earnings withholding order as stated in the order or in the levying officer's notice under subdivision (b) is withheld from the judgment debtor's earnings, interest ceases to accrue on that amount. *(Added by Stats.1992, c. 283 (S.B.1372), § 6, eff. July 21, 1992.)*

Law Revision Commission Comments

1992 Addition

Section 706.024 is new. This section provides for adjustment of the total amount required to satisfy an earnings withholding order. Since an active order continues in force until it is satisfied, full satisfaction of the judgment may not occur unless the total amount due as stated in the order as issued is adjusted as provided in subdivision (a).

See also Sections 685.030 (accrual of interest and satisfaction), 685.050 (costs and interest under writ), 685.090(c) (costs added to writ or order after issuance), 695.210 (amount required to satisfy money judgment), 699.520(e) (amount enforceable under writ of execution), 706.101(c) (notice by first class mail). [21 Cal.L.Rev.Comm.Reports 135 (1991)].

§ 706.025. Payments to levying officer

(a) Except as provided in subdivision (b), the amount required to be withheld pursuant to an earnings withholding order shall be paid monthly to the levying officer not later than the 15th day of each month. The initial monthly payment shall include all amounts required to be withheld from the earnings of the employee during the preceding calendar month up to the close of the employee's pay period ending closest to the last day of that month, and thereafter each monthly payment shall include amounts withheld from the employee's earnings for services rendered in the interim up to the close of the employee's pay period ending closest to the last day of the preceding calendar month.

(b) The employer may elect to pay the amounts withheld to the levying officer more frequently than monthly. If the employer so elects, payment of the amount withheld from the employee's earnings for each pay period shall be made not later than 10 days after the close of the pay period. *(Added by Stats.1982, c. 1364, p. 5173, § 2, operative July 1, 1983.)*

Law Revision Commission Comments

1982 Addition

Section 706.025 specifies when the amounts withheld pursuant to an earnings withholding order must be paid over to the levying officer. As to payment to the employee if an exemption claim is allowed, see Section 706.105(i). Regardless whether payment is required, the employer is required to send an employer's return to the levying officer. See Sections 706.104 and 706.126. Section 706.025 continues former Section 723.025. [16 Cal.L.Rev.Comm. Reports 1448 (1982)].

§ 706.026. Levying officer; receipt, accounting, and payment of amounts received; electronic filing

(a) The levying officer shall receive and account for all amounts paid by the employer pursuant to Section 706.025 and shall pay the amounts so received over to the person entitled thereto at least once every 30 days.

(b) At least once every two years, the levying officer shall file an accounting with the court, as provided by Section 699.560, for all amounts collected under the earnings withholding order, including costs and interest added to the amount due. Subject to the limitations in subdivision (c) of Section 263, the levying officer may electronically file the accounting with the court, pursuant to Chapter 2 (commencing with Section 263) of Title 4 of Part 1. *(Added by Stats.1982, c. 1364, p. 5174, § 2, operative July 1, 1983. Amended by Stats.1992, c. 283 (S.B.1372), § 7, eff. July 21, 1992; Stats.2010, c. 680 (A.B.2394), § 12.)*

Law Revision Commission Comments

1982 Addition

Section 706.026 continues subdivision (a) of former Section 723.026. The remainder of former Section 723.026 (which in effect extended the time for return of the writ of execution) has not been continued because this portion is no longer necessary in view of Section 699.560 which extends generally the time for return of writs of execution. [16 Cal.L.Rev.Comm. Reports 1449 (1982)].

1992 Amendment

Subdivision (b) is added to Section 706.026 to provide for an accounting to the court of activities under an earnings withholding order. See Section 680.160 ("court" defined). This account is in the nature of a return on a writ and is required whether or not the writ has been returned. See Section 699.560 (return of writ of execution). When the earnings withholding order terminates, the levying officer is to make a supplemental return on the writ. See Section 706.033 (supplemental return).

The change in subdivision (a) is a technical, nonsubstantive change intended to conform the language of this section to Section 706.025. [21 Cal.L.Rev.Comm.Reports 135 (1991)].

§ 706.027. Notice of satisfaction of judgment

If the judgment pursuant to which the earnings withholding order is issued is satisfied before the order otherwise terminates pursuant to Section 706.022, the judgment creditor shall promptly notify the levying officer who shall promptly terminate the order by serving a notice of termination on the employer. *(Added by Stats.1982, c. 1364, p. 5174, § 2, operative July 1, 1983.)*

Law Revision Commission Comments

1982 Addition

Section 706.027 continues former Section 723.027 and requires the judgment creditor to give notice of satisfaction of the judgment to the levying officer if the earnings withholding order has not yet terminated. See Section 706.022 (withholding period). In some cases, the employer will be aware of the satisfaction by virtue of the employer's having withheld the amount necessary to satisfy the judgment. See Section 706.022(a) (2). In this case, Section 706.027 does not apply. However, the judgment may be satisfied by additional payments from the debtor or through other debt collection procedures instituted by the judgment creditor. If this is the case, Section 706.027 applies, and the judgment creditor has the duty to notify the levying officer promptly of the satisfaction so that the levying officer may serve a notice of termination on the employer. Service of the notice of termination is to be made on the person, and at the address, indicated in the employer's return. See Sections 706.101(c) and 706.126(b) (6). As to the general duty of a creditor to furnish a debtor a satisfaction of judgment, see Chapter 1 (commencing with Section 724.010) of Division 5. Failure to perform the duty imposed by this section may make the judgment creditor liable in an action for abuse of process. See White Lighting Co. v. Wolfson, 68 Cal.2d 336, 347–51, 438 P.2d 345, 351–54, 66 Cal.Rptr. 697, 703–06 (1968). [16 Cal.L.Rev.Comm. Reports 1449 (1982)].

Research References

Forms

Cal. Transaction Forms - Bus. Transactions § 16:94, Assignor's Revocation Of Assignment Of Wages or Salary.

§ 706.028. Final earnings withholding order for costs and interest

(a) "Final earnings withholding order for costs and interest" means an earnings withholding order for the collection only of unsatisfied costs and interest, which is issued after an earlier earnings withholding order has been returned satisfied.

(b) After the amount stated as owing in a prior earnings withholding order is paid, the judgment creditor may obtain a final earnings withholding order for costs and interest to collect amounts of costs and interest that were not collected under the prior earnings withholding order.

(c) A final earnings withholding order for costs and interest shall be enforced in the same manner as other earnings withholding orders.

(d) Satisfaction of the amount stated as owing in a final earnings withholding order for costs and interest is equivalent to satisfaction of the money judgment. For this purpose, interest ceases to accrue on the date of issuance of the final earnings withholding order and no additional costs may be added after that date, except for the statutory fee for service of the order and any other statutory fees for performing duties under the order. *(Added by Stats.1992, c. 283 (S.B. 1372), § 9, eff. July 21, 1992.)*

Law Revision Commission Comments

1992 Addition

Section 706.028 is new. This section provides for a final earnings withholding order for costs and interest and supersedes former Section 706.028 (subsequent order for costs and interest). The new "final order" differs from the "subsequent order" under former law since it permits a full satisfaction of the money judgment through wage garnishment by stopping the running of interest on the remaining balance due on the judgment (which balance comprises earlier costs and interest). The amount stated as due on a final earnings withholding order may be increased only by statutory costs. See Gov't Code §§ 26746 (disbursement fee), 26750 (fee for service and other duties under earnings withholding order). In other respects, as provided in subdivision (c), a final earnings withholding order is treated the same as any other earnings withholding order.

If the principal amount of the judgment is not fully satisfied before an earnings withholding order is terminated, another order may be issued to collect the balance due on the judgment pursuant to this chapter. See Section 706.102 (issuance of earnings withholding order). This later earnings withholding order is distinct from a final earnings withholding order for costs and interest provided by this section.

A final earnings withholding order is not available where the full amount due on the judgment has been collected under the initial earnings withholding order pursuant to the optional procedure set forth in Section 706.024. [21 Cal.L.Rev.Comm.Reports 135 (1991)].

§ 706.029. Service of order creating lien; duration

Service of an earnings withholding order creates a lien upon the earnings of the judgment debtor that are required to be withheld pursuant to the order and upon all property of the employer subject to the enforcement of a money judgment in the amount required to be withheld pursuant to such order. The lien continues for a period of one year from the date the earnings of the judgment debtor become payable unless the amount required to be withheld pursuant to the order is paid as required by law. *(Added by Stats.1982, c. 1364, p. 5174, § 2, operative July 1, 1983.)*

Research References

Forms

Am. Jur. Pl. & Pr. Forms Attachment and Garnishment § 230, Introductory Comments.

Treatises and Practice Aids

Witkin, California Summary 10th Husband and Wife § 249, in General.

§ 706.030. Withholding order for support; operation with earnings withholding order

(a) A "withholding order for support" is an earnings withholding order issued on a writ of execution to collect delinquent amounts payable under a judgment for the support of a child, or spouse or former spouse, of the judgment debtor. A withholding order for support shall be denoted as such on its face.

(b) The local child support agency may issue a withholding order for support on a notice of levy pursuant to Section 17522 of the Family Code to collect a support obligation.

(1) When the local child support agency issues a withholding order for support, a reference in this chapter to a levying officer is deemed to mean the local child support agency who issues the withholding order for support.

(2) Service of a withholding order for support issued by the local child support agency may be made by first-class mail or in any other manner described in Section 706.101. Service of a withholding order for support issued by the local child support agency is complete when it is received by the employer or a person described in paragraph (1) or (2) of subdivision (a) of Section 706.101, or if service is by first-class mail, service is complete as specified in Section 1013.

(3) The local child support agency shall serve upon the employer the withholding order for support, a copy of the order, and a notice informing the support obligor of the effect of the order and of his or her right to hearings and remedies provided in this chapter and in the Family Code. The notice shall be accompanied by the forms necessary to obtain an administrative review and a judicial hearing and instructions on how to file the forms. Within 10 days from the date of service, the employer shall deliver to the support obligor a copy of the withholding order for support, the forms to obtain an administrative review and judicial hearing, and the notice. If the support obligor is no longer employed by the employer and the employer does not owe the support obligor any earnings, the employer shall inform the local child support agency that the support obligor is no longer employed by the employer.

(4) An employer who fails to comply with paragraph (3) shall be subject to a civil penalty of five hundred dollars ($500) for each occurrence.

(5) The local child support agency shall provide for an administrative review to reconsider or modify the amount to be withheld for arrearages pursuant to the withholding order for support, if the support obligor requests a review at any time after service of the withholding order. The local child support agency shall provide the review in the same manner and timeframes provided for resolution of a complaint pursuant to Section 17800 of the Family Code. The local child support agency shall notify the employer if the review results in any modifications to the withholding order for support. If the local child support agency cannot complete the administrative review within 30 calendar days of receipt of the complaint, the local child support agency shall notify the employer to suspend withholding any disputed amount pending the completion of the review and the determination by the local child support agency.

(6) Nothing in this section prohibits the support obligor from seeking a judicial determination of arrearages pursuant to subdivision (c) of Section 17256 of the Family Code or from filing a motion for equitable division of earnings pursuant to Section 706.052 either prior to or after the administrative review provided by this section. Within five business days after receiving notice of the obligor having filed for judicial relief pursuant to this section, the local child support agency shall notify the employer to suspend withholding any disputed amount pending a determination by the court. The employer shall then adjust the withholding within not more than nine days of receiving the notice from the local child support agency.

(c) Notwithstanding any other provision of this chapter:

(1) An employer shall continue to withhold pursuant to a withholding order for support until the earliest of the dates specified in paragraph (1), (2), or (3) of subdivision (a) of Section 706.022, except that a withholding order for support shall automatically terminate one year after the employment of the employee by the employer terminates.

(2) A withholding order for support has priority over any other earnings withholding order. An employer upon whom a withholding order for support is served shall withhold and pay over earnings of the employee pursuant to that order notwithstanding the requirements of another earnings withholding order.

(3) Subject to paragraph (2) and to Article 3 (commencing with Section 706.050), an employer shall withhold earnings pursuant to both a withholding order for support and another earnings withholding order simultaneously.

(4) An employer who willfully fails to withhold and forward support pursuant to a valid earnings withholding order for support issued and served upon the employer pursuant to this chapter is liable to the support obligee, as defined in Section 5214 of the Family Code, for the amount of support not withheld, forwarded, or otherwise paid to the support obligee.

(5) Notwithstanding any other provision of law, an employer shall send all earnings withheld pursuant to a withholding order for support to the levying officer or the State Disbursement Unit as described in Section 17309 of the Family Code within the time period specified by federal law.

(6) Once the State Disbursement Unit as described in Section 17309 of the Family Code is operational, all support payments made pursuant to an earnings withholding order shall be made to that unit.

(7) Earnings withheld pursuant to an earnings withholding order for support shall be credited toward satisfaction of a support judgment as specified in Section 695.221. *(Added by Stats.1982, c. 1364, p. 5174, § 2, operative July 1, 1983. Amended by Stats.1992, c. 283 (S.B.1372), § 10, eff. July 21, 1992; Stats.1997, c. 599 (A.B.573), § 5; Stats.2000, c. 808 (A.B.1358), § 17, eff. Sept. 28, 2000; Stats.2001, c. 755 (S.B.943), § 1, eff. Oct. 12, 2001; Stats.2003, c. 387 (A.B.739), § 1.)*

Law Revision Commission Comments

1982 Addition

Section 706.030 continues former Section 723.030 and provides special rules for an earnings withholding order to enforce a judgment for delinquent support payments for a child or spouse or former spouse of the judgment debtor. An earnings withholding order for support is given a different effect than other withholding orders: It is effective until the employer has withheld the full amount specified in the order or he is served with a notice of termination, in which case the date of termination will be specified in the notice. See subdivision (b) (1). Thus, the withholding order for support does not terminate 100 days after service (it may, of course, be modified). The withholding order for support is subject to special exemption rules (see Section 706.052). Even when in effect, it does not necessarily preclude withholding on either a prior or subsequent earnings withholding order. If not earlier terminated, the withholding order for support automatically terminates one year after the employment of the employee terminates. Thus, for example, if the employee returns to work for the same employer within one year from the date his employment terminated, the employer must withhold pursuant to the withholding order for support. On the other hand, if the employee does not return to work until more than one year from the date his employment terminated, the order expires at the end of the year, and nothing is withheld pursuant to the order when the employee returns to work.

The earnings withholding order for support is given priority over any other earnings withholding order. But see Section 706.031 (wage assignment for support given priority). However, a prior earnings withholding order remains in effect, and a judgment creditor may still obtain an earnings withholding order even where there is already in effect a prior earnings withholding order for support.

Thus, where there are two earnings withholding orders in effect—one for support and one for another obligation—the amount withheld for support is deducted from the employee's earnings first. The amount, if any, that may be withheld pursuant to the other earnings withholding order is determined by subtracting the amount withheld pursuant to the withholding order for support from the amount that otherwise could be withheld pursuant to the other earnings withholding order. See Sections 706.077, 706.050, and 706.051 and the Comments thereto. [16 Cal.L.Rev.Comm. Reports 1452 (1982)].

1992 Amendment

Section 706.030(b)(1) is amended to correct the cross-reference to Section 706.022 (as amended by 1989 Cal.Stat. ch. 263, § 1). This is a technical, nonsubstantive change. [21 Cal.L.Rev.Comm.Reports 135 (1991)].

Research References

Forms

West's California Judicial Council Forms WG-004, Earnings Withholding Order for Support.

Treatises and Practice Aids

Witkin, California Summary 10th Husband and Wife § 262, in General.

Witkin, California Summary 10th Husband and Wife § 335, Levy by Agency.

Witkin, California Summary 10th Trusts § 164, in General.

§ 706.031. Earnings assignment order for support; operation with earnings withholding order

(a) Nothing in this chapter affects an earnings assignment order for support.

(b) An earnings assignment order for support shall be given priority over any earnings withholding order. An employer upon whom an earnings assignment order for support is served shall withhold and pay over the earnings of the employee pursuant to the assignment order notwithstanding the requirements of any earnings withholding order. When an employer is required to cease withholding earnings pursuant to an earnings withholding order, the employer shall notify the levying officer who served the earnings withholding order that a supervening earnings assignment order for support is in effect.

(c) Subject to subdivisions (b), (d), and (e), an employer shall withhold earnings of an employee pursuant to both an earnings assignment order for support and an earnings withholding order.

(d) The employer shall withhold pursuant to an earnings withholding order only to the extent that the sum of the amount withheld pursuant to any earnings assignment order for support and the amount withheld pursuant to the earnings withholding order does not exceed the amount that may be withheld under Article 3 (commencing with Section 706.050).

(e) The employer shall withhold pursuant to an earnings withholding order for taxes only to the extent that the sum of the amount withheld pursuant to any earnings assignment order for support and the amount withheld pursuant to the earnings withholding order for taxes does not exceed the amount that may be withheld under Article 4 (commencing with Section 706.070). *(Added by Stats.1982, c. 1364, p. 5175, § 2, operative July 1, 1983. Amended by Stats.1992, c. 163 (A.B.2641), § 47, operative Jan. 1, 1994.)*

Law Revision Commission Comments

1982 Addition

Section 706.031 continues former Section 723.031 and states the effect of a wage assignment for support (defined in subdivision (g) of Section 706.011) on an earnings withholding order.

Subdivision (a) makes clear that nothing in this chapter affects the wage assignment for support, and subdivision (b) makes clear that the wage assignment has priority over any earnings withholding order, including a withholding order for support under Section 706.030. Under subdivision (b), the employer is required to notify the levying officer who earlier served an earnings withholding order if that order is completely superseded by the wage assignment. It should be noted that "levying officer" includes the state agency where a withholding order for taxes is superseded. See Section 706.073.

Subdivisions (b) and (d) of Section 706.031 make clear that, where any wage assignment for support is in effect, the amount withheld from the debtor's earnings pursuant to any such wage assignment is deducted from the amount that otherwise would be withheld under Section 706.050 on an earnings withholding order to enforce an ordinary money judgment or that otherwise would be withheld where a portion of the debtor's earnings have been determined to be exempt under Section 706.051. Suppose, for example, that a wage assignment for support is in effect which requires that $40 per week be withheld. Assume that Section 706.050 limits the amount that may be withheld to $56. To determine the maximum amount that may be withheld pursuant to the earnings withholding order (absent any exemption allowed under Section 706.051), the $40 withheld pursuant to the wage assignment for support is subtracted from the $56, leaving $16 as the maximum amount that may be withheld pursuant to the earnings withholding order. For a special rule applicable when the earnings withholding order is on a judgment for delinquent amounts payable for child or spousal support, see Sections 706.030 and 706.052. The rule stated in subdivision (d) of Section 706.031 is required to avoid conflict with the federal Consumer Credit Protection Act. That act requires that the amount withheld pursuant to any wage assignment for support be included in determining whether any amount may be withheld pursuant to an earnings withholding order on an ordinary judgment. See subdivision (c) of Section 302 of the act, 15 U.S.C. § 1672(c) (1970) ("garnishment" means "any legal or equitable procedure through which the earnings of any individual are required to be withheld for payment of any debt") and [1969–1973 Transfer Binder] Lab.L.Rep. (CCH) para. 30.813.

Under subdivision (e), the amount that could be withheld pursuant to a withholding order for taxes would be computed in the same manner as for an ordinary earnings withholding order pursuant to Section 706.050 unless the withholding order for taxes is obtained under Section 706.076. [16 Cal.L.Rev.Comm. Reports 1454 (1982)].

1992 Amendment

Section 706.031 is amended to conform to the terminology of the Family Code. See Chapter 8 (commencing with Section 5200) of Part 5 of Division 9 of the Family Code (earnings assignment order for support). "Earnings assignment order for support" is defined in Section 706.011. [22 Cal.L.Rev.Comm.Reports 1 (1992)].

Research References

Forms

West's California Judicial Council Forms FL-435, Earnings Assignment Order for Spousal or Partner Support.

Treatises and Practice Aids

Witkin, California Summary 10th Husband and Wife § 249, in General.

Witkin, California Summary 10th Husband and Wife § 254, Priorities.

§ 706.032. Termination of earnings withholding orders

(a) Except as otherwise provided by statute:

(1) If withholding under an earnings withholding order ceases because the judgment debtor's employment has terminated, the earnings withholding order terminates at the conclusion of a continuous 180-day period during which no amounts are withheld under the order.

(2) If withholding under an earnings withholding order ceases because the judgment debtor's earnings are subject to an order or assignment with higher priority, the earnings withholding order terminates at the conclusion of a continuous two-year period during which no amounts are withheld under the order.

(b) If an earnings withholding order has terminated pursuant to subdivision (a), the employer shall return the order to the levying officer along with a statement of the reasons for returning the order. *(Added by Stats.1992, c. 283 (S.B.1372), § 11, eff. July 21, 1992.)*

Law Revision Commission Comments

1992 Addition

Section 706.032 is new. This section provides for the automatic termination of dormant or suspended earnings withholding orders in favor of general creditors. If the debtor leaves employment after an earnings withholding order has become effective, the duty to withhold continues for 180 days under subdivision (a)(1). If the debtor returns to work during this period, the employer is required to resume withholding pursuant to the order. If withholding under a general creditor's earnings withholding order is suspended because of withholding under an earnings withholding order or assignment for support or an earnings withholding order for taxes, the suspended order remains in effect until two years have elapsed with no withholding. See Sections 706.030 (support orders), 706.031 (wage assignment for support), 706.078 (tax orders).

The employer has a duty under subdivision (b) to determine whether an earnings withholding order has terminated under subdivision (a) and to return the order to the levying officer.

For a special rule concerning termination of earnings withholding orders for support, see Section 706.030(b)(1). For a special rule concerning termination of earnings withholding orders for taxes, see Section 706.078(c).

If the debtor is not employed and no earnings are due when the withholding period would begin under Section 706.022, the service of the order is ineffective and is not subject to the 180-day rule or two-year rule in this section. See Section 706.104(a). [22 Cal.L.Rev.Comm.Reports 987 (1992)].

Research References

Forms

Cal. Transaction Forms - Bus. Transactions § 16:94, Assignor's Revocation Of Assignment Of Wages or Salary.

§ 706.033. Return of writ before earnings withholding order terminates; supplemental return on writ

If the writ is returned before the earnings withholding order terminates, on termination of the earnings withholding order the levying officer shall make a supplemental return on the writ. The supplemental return shall contain the same information as an original return pursuant to Section 699.560. *(Added by Stats.1992, c. 283 (S.B.1372), § 12, eff. July 21, 1992.)*

Law Revision Commission Comments

1992 Addition

Section 706.033 is new. This section provides explicit authority for making a supplemental return on a writ where withholding under an earnings withholding order continues after the writ is returned. See also Section 706.026 (account of levying officer for amounts collected). [21 Cal.L.Rev.Comm.Reports 135 (1991)].

§ 706.034. Deduction from employee earnings for payments made in accordance with earnings withholding order

The employer may deduct from the earnings of the employee the sum of one dollar and fifty cents ($1.50) for each payment made in accordance with an earnings withholding order issued pursuant to this chapter. *(Added by Stats.1997, c. 137 (A.B.519), § 1. Amended by Stats.2004, c. 520 (A.B.2530), § 1.)*

ARTICLE 3. RESTRICTIONS ON EARNINGS WITHHOLDING

§ 706.050. Maximum amount of disposable earnings of an individual judgment debtor subject to levy

(a) Except as otherwise provided in this chapter, the maximum amount of disposable earnings of an individual judgment debtor for any workweek that is subject to levy under an earnings withholding order shall not exceed the lesser of the following:

(1) Twenty–five percent of the individual's disposable earnings for that week.

(2) Fifty percent of the amount by which the individual's disposable earnings for that week exceed 40 times the state minimum hourly wage in effect at the time the earnings are payable. If a judgment debtor works in a location where the local minimum hourly wage is greater than the state minimum hourly wage, the local minimum hourly wage in effect at the time the earnings are payable shall be used for the calculation made pursuant to this paragraph.

(b) For any pay period other than weekly, the following multipliers shall be used to determine the maximum amount of disposable earnings subject to levy under an earnings withholding order that is proportional in effect to the calculation described in paragraph (2) of subdivision (a), except as specified in paragraph (1):

(1) For a daily pay period, the amounts shall be identical to the amounts described in subdivision (a).

(2) For a biweekly pay period, multiply the applicable hourly minimum wage by 80 work hours.

(3) For a semimonthly pay period, multiply the applicable hourly minimum wage by 86 ⅔ work hours.

(4) For a monthly pay period, multiply the applicable hourly minimum wage by 173 ⅓ work hours.

(c) This section shall become operative on July 1, 2016. *(Added by Stats.2015, c. 800 (S.B.501), § 2, eff. Jan. 1, 2016, operative July 1, 2016.)*

Research References

Treatises and Practice Aids

Witkin, California Summary 10th Trusts § 164, in General.

§ 706.051. Amount necessary for support of judgment debtor or family; exemption

(a) For the purposes of this section, "family of the judgment debtor" includes the spouse or former spouse of the judgment debtor.

(b) Except as provided in subdivision (c), the portion of the judgment debtor's earnings that the judgment debtor proves is necessary for the support of the judgment debtor or the judgment debtor's family supported in whole or in part by the judgment debtor is exempt from levy under this chapter.

(c) The exemption provided in subdivision (b) is not available if any of the following exceptions applies:

(1) The debt was incurred pursuant to an order or award for the payment of attorney's fees under Section 2030, 3121, or 3557 of the Family Code.

(2) The debt was incurred for personal services rendered by an employee or former employee of the judgment debtor.

(3) The order is a withholding order for support under Section 706.030.

(4) The order is one governed by Article 4 (commencing with Section 706.070) (state tax order). *(Added by Stats.1982, c. 1364, p. 5175, § 2, operative July 1, 1983. Amended by Stats.2011, c. 694 (A.B.1388), § 1.)*

Research References

Forms

West's California Judicial Council Forms WG-026, Claim Of Exemption and Financial Declaration (State Tax Liability).

Treatises and Practice Aids

Witkin, California Summary 10th Trusts § 164, in General.

§ 706.052. Disposable earnings and earnings withheld pursuant to earning assignment order for support; exemption; equitable division of earnings by court

(a) Except as provided in subdivision (b), one-half of the disposable earnings (as defined by Section 1672 of Title 15 of the United States Code) of the judgment debtor, plus any amount withheld from the judgment debtor's earnings pursuant to any earnings assignment order for support, is exempt from levy under this chapter where the earnings withholding order is a withholding order for support under Section 706.030.

(b) Except as provided in subdivision (c), upon motion of any interested party, the court shall make an equitable division of the judgment debtor's earnings that takes into account the needs of all the persons the judgment debtor is required to support and shall effectuate such division by an order determining the amount to be withheld from the judgment debtor's earnings pursuant to the withholding order for support.

(c) An order made under subdivision (b) may not authorize the withholding of an amount in excess of the amount that may be withheld for support under federal law under Section 1673 of Title 15 of the United States Code. *(Added by Stats.1982, c. 1364, p. 5176, § 2, operative July 1, 1983. Amended by Stats.1992, c. 163 (A.B.2641), § 48, operative Jan. 1, 1994.)*

Law Revision Commission Comments

1982 Addition

Section 706.052 continues former Section 723.052 except that subdivision (c) is added to reflect that the court's authority under subdivision (b) is limited by the maximum amounts that may be withheld under federal law. See 15 U.S.C. § 1673(b) (2) (Supp. 1979).

Subdivision (a) of Section 706.052 prescribes the exemption applicable to a wage garnishment for the collection of delinquent child or spousal support payments except in cases where the court has made an equitable division pursuant to subdivision (b). The judgment debtor's earnings that are subject to the 50 percent exemption under subdivision (a) are "disposable earnings" as defined by the federal Consumer Credit Protection Act, 15 U.S.C. § 1672 (1976). Unlike federal law, however, subdivision (a) protects the same amount of earnings regardless of whether the judgment debtor is supporting a present and a former spouse or is more than 12 weeks delinquent. Federal law permits garnishment of 50 percent of the employee's earnings if the employee is supporting a spouse or dependent other than the person who caused the garnishment and 60 percent if the employee is not supporting such additional persons; these percentages are increased to 55 percent and 65 percent, respectively, if the support payments are more than 12 weeks delinquent. See 15 U.S.C. § 1673(b) (2) (Supp.1979).

Subdivision (a) also makes clear that, in applying the 50 percent exemption, the amount withheld from the earnings of the judgment debtor pursuant to any wage assignment for support (defined in subdivision (g) of Section 706.011) is included in computing the 50 percent of the judgment debtor's earnings that may be withheld. For example, if 30 percent of the judgment debtor's earnings are withheld pursuant to a wage assignment for support, an additional 20 percent may be withheld pursuant to the earnings withholding order for the collection of delinquent amounts payable for child or spousal support.

Subdivision (b) makes the 50 percent standard provided by subdivision (a) subject to the power of the court to make an order that more or less of the judgment debtor's earnings be withheld where the earnings withholding order is issued to collect delinquent child or spousal support payments. Subdivision (c) makes clear that the court may not order the withholding of an amount in excess of that permitted by federal law. This maximum amount varies depending upon whether the judgment debtor is supporting more than one person or is more than 12 weeks delinquent. The authority of the court to make an equitable division of the judgment debtor's earnings between, for example, the debtor and a former spouse, or between a former spouse and a present family, is based on decisions under a former statute. See, e.g., Rankins v. Rankins, 52 Cal.App.2d 231, 126 P.2d 125 (1942).

Under this section, an employer who receives an earnings withholding order for support will know that 50 percent of disposable earnings is to be withheld unless the employer is served with a court order requiring a greater or lesser amount to be withheld.

For rules relating to the priority to be given a withholding order for support, see Section 706.030. [16 Cal.L.Rev.Comm. Reports 1457 (1982)].

1992 Amendment

Subdivision (a) of Section 706.052 is amended to conform to the terminology of the Family Code. See Chapter 8 (commencing with Section 5200) of Part 5 of Division 9 of the Family Code (earnings assignment order for support). "Earnings assignment order for support" is defined in Section 706.011. [22 Cal.L.Rev.Comm.Reports 1 (1992)].

Research References

Forms

West's California Judicial Council Forms FL-460, Qualified Domestic Relations Order for Support.

West's California Judicial Council Forms WG-004, Earnings Withholding Order for Support.

West's California Judicial Council Forms WG-030, Earnings Withholding Order for Elder or Dependent Adult Financial Abuse (Wage Garnishment).

Treatises and Practice Aids

Witkin, California Summary 10th Husband and Wife § 334, in General.

Witkin, California Summary 10th Parent and Child § 416, Application and Order.

ARTICLE 5. PROCEDURE FOR EARNINGS WITHHOLDING ORDERS AND EXEMPTION CLAIMS

§ 706.109. Earnings withholding order; issuance against spouse of judgment debtor

An earnings withholding order may not be issued against the earnings of the spouse of the judgment debtor except by court order upon noticed motion. *(Added by Stats.1984, c. 1671, § 20.)*

Research References

Treatises and Practice Aids

Witkin, California Summary 10th Community Property § 177, General Rule.

Title 13

APPEALS IN CIVIL ACTIONS

CHAPTER 2. STAY OF ENFORCEMENT AND OTHER PROCEEDINGS

§ 917.7. Appeal; stay of proceedings as to judgment or order affecting custody

The perfecting of an appeal shall not stay proceedings as to those provisions of a judgment or order which award, change, or otherwise affect the custody, including the right of visitation, of a minor child in any civil action, in an action filed under the Juvenile Court Law, or in a special proceeding, or the provisions of a judgment or order for the temporary exclusion of a party from a dwelling, as provided in the Family Code. However, the trial court may in its discretion stay execution of these provisions pending review on appeal or for any other period or periods that it may deem appropriate. Further, in the absence of a writ or order of a reviewing court providing otherwise, the provisions of the judgment or order allowing, or eliminating restrictions against, removal of the minor child from the state are stayed by operation of law for a period of seven calendar days from the entry of the judgment or order by a juvenile court in a dependency hearing, or for a period of 30 calendar days from the entry of judgment or order by any other trial court. The periods during which these provisions allowing, or eliminating restrictions against, removal of the minor child from the state are stayed, are subject to further stays as ordered by the trial court or by the juvenile court pursuant to this section. An order directing the return of a child to a sister state or country, including any order effectuating that return, made in a proceeding brought pursuant to the Uniform Child Custody Jurisdiction and Enforcement Act (Part 3 (commencing with Section 3400) of Division 8 of the Family Code), the Parental Kidnapping Prevention Act of 1980 (28 U.S.C. Sec. 1738A), or the Hague Convention on the Civil Aspects of International Child Abduction (implemented pursuant to the International Child Abduction Remedies Act (42 U.S.C. Secs. 11601–11610)) is not a judgment or order which awards, changes, or otherwise affects the custody of a minor child within the meaning of this section, and therefore is not subject to the automatic stay provisions of this section. *(Added by Stats.1968, c. 385, p. 818, § 2. Amended by Stats.1971, c. 1210, p. 2328, § 9; Stats.1981, c. 714, p. 2596, § 70; Stats.1992, c. 163 (A.B.2641), § 55, operative Jan. 1, 1994; Stats.1993, c. 219 (A.B.1500), § 69.5; Stats.1999, c. 346 (S.B.518), § 1; Stats.2001, c. 48 (S.B.1151), § 1.)*

Law Revision Commission Comments

1992 Amendment [Revised Comment]

Section 917.7 is amended to substitute a reference to the Family Code for the reference to former Civil Code Section 4359. A general reference to "a dwelling" has been substituted for the former reference to specific dwellings. This allows the Family Code provisions relating to exclusion from a dwelling to control the details of this type of order. This is not a substantive change, but prevents a conflict from arising in the future where one statute is amended without making a similar revision to the other. For provisions of the Family Code relating to the exclusion of a party from a dwelling, see, e.g., Fam. Code §§ 6321 (ex parte order), 6340 (order after notice and hearing), 6360 (order included in judgment). [23 Cal.L.Rev. Comm. Reports 1 (1993)].

Research References

Forms

West's California Code Forms, Civil Procedure § 917.7 Form 1, Appeals--Custody Of Minor--Notice Of Motion for Stay Of Proceedings.

West's California Code Forms, Civil Procedure § 917.7 Form 2, Appeals--Order Staying Change Of Custody Of Minor.

Treatises and Practice Aids

Witkin, California Summary 10th Parent and Child § 190, Appeal.

Witkin, California Summary 10th Parent and Child § 192, Other Federal Acts.

Witkin, California Summary 10th Parent and Child § 288, Appeal.
Witkin, California Summary 10th Parent and Child § 351, in General.
Witkin, California Summary 10th Parent and Child § 361, Issuance by Appellate Court.
Witkin, California Summary 10th Parent and Child § 374, Appellate Court Proceeding.
Witkin, California Summary 10th Wills and Probate § 402, Effect Of Appeal.

§ 917.75. Perfecting of an appeal; stay of enforcement

The perfecting of an appeal shall not stay enforcement of the judgment or order of the trial court awarding attorney's fees or costs, or both, if the judgment or order appealed from was rendered in a proceeding under the Family Code, unless an undertaking is given in a sum and upon conditions fixed by the trial court. *(Added by Stats.2014, c. 95 (A.B.2154), § 1, eff. Jan. 1, 2015.)*

Title 14

OF MISCELLANEOUS PROVISIONS

CHAPTER 4. MOTIONS AND ORDERS

§ 1005. Written notice for motions; service and filing of moving and supporting papers

(a) Written notice shall be given, as prescribed in subdivisions (b) and (c), for the following motions:

(1) Notice of Application and Hearing for Writ of Attachment under Section 484.040.

(2) Notice of Application and Hearing for Claim and Delivery under Section 512.030.

(3) Notice of Hearing for Claim of Exemption under Section 706.105.

(4) Motion to Quash Summons pursuant to subdivision (b) of Section 418.10.

(5) Motion for Determination of Good Faith Settlement pursuant to Section 877.6.

(6) Hearing for Discovery of Peace Officer Personnel Records pursuant to Section 1043 of the Evidence Code.

(7) Notice of Hearing of Third–Party Claim pursuant to Section 720.320.

(8) Motion for an Order to Attend Deposition more than 150 miles from deponent's residence pursuant to Section 2025.260.

(9) Notice of Hearing of Application for Relief pursuant to Section 946.6 of the Government Code.

(10) Motion to Set Aside Default or Default Judgment and for Leave to Defend Actions pursuant to Section 473.5.

(11) Motion to Expunge Notice of Pendency of Action pursuant to Section 405.30.

(12) Motion to Set Aside Default and for Leave to Amend pursuant to Section 585.5.

(13) Any other proceeding under this code in which notice is required and no other time or method is prescribed by law or by court or judge.

(b) Unless otherwise ordered or specifically provided by law, all moving and supporting papers shall be served and filed at least 16 court days before the hearing. The moving and supporting papers served shall be a copy of the papers filed or to be filed with the court. However, if the notice is served by mail, the required 16–day period of notice before the hearing shall be increased by five calendar days if the place of mailing and the place of address are within the State of California, 10 calendar days if either the place of mailing or the place of address is outside the State of California but within the United States, and 20 calendar days if either the place of mailing or the place of address is outside the United States, and if the notice is served by facsimile transmission, express mail, or another method of delivery providing for overnight delivery, the required 16–day period of notice before the hearing shall be increased by two calendar days. Section 1013, which extends the time within which a right may be exercised or an act may be done, does not apply to a notice of motion, papers opposing a motion, or reply papers governed by this section. All papers opposing a motion so noticed shall be filed with the court and a copy served on each party at least nine court days, and all reply papers at least five court days before the hearing.

The court, or a judge thereof, may prescribe a shorter time.

(c) Notwithstanding any other provision of this section, all papers opposing a motion and all reply papers shall be served by personal delivery, facsimile transmission, express mail, or other means consistent with Sections 1010, 1011, 1012, and 1013, and reasonably calculated to ensure delivery to the other party or parties not later than the close of the next business day after the time the opposing papers or reply papers, as applicable, are filed. This subdivision applies to the service of opposition and reply papers regarding motions for summary judgment or summary adjudication, in addition to the motions listed in subdivision (a).

The court, or a judge thereof, may prescribe a shorter time. *(Enacted in 1872. Amended by Code Am.1880, c. 23, p. 13, § 2; Stats.1907, c. 326, p. 601, § 1; Stats.1919, c. 195, p. 289, § 1; Stats.1933, c. 744, p. 1897, § 175; Stats.1935 c. 658, p. 1816, § 1; Stats.1935, c. 722, p. 1966, § 27; Stats.1951, c. 1737, p. 4132, § 132, operative Jan. 1, 1952; Stats.1963, c. 878, p. 2126, § 3; Stats.1980, c. 196, p. 418, § 1; Stats.1981, c. 197, p. 1121, § 1; Stats.1984, c. 352, § 2; Stats.1986, c. 246, § 1; Stats.1989, c. 693, § 6; Stats.1990, c. 1491 (A.B.3765), § 7; Stats.1991, c. 1090 (A.B.1484), § 5; Stats.1992, c. 339 (S.B. 1409), § 2; Stats.1993, c. 456 (A.B.58), § 14.5; Stats.1997, c. 571 (A.B.1088), § 1.3; Stats.1998, c. 932 (A.B.1094), § 18; Stats.1999, c. 43 (A.B.1132), § 1; Stats.2002, c. 806 (A.B. 3027), § 16; Stats.2004, c. 182 (A.B.3081), § 13; Stats.2004, c. 171 (A.B.3078), § 3; Stats.2005, c. 294 (A.B.333), § 3.)*

Law Revision Commission Comments

2005 Amendment

Subdivision (a) of Section 1005 is amended to reflect nonsubstantive reorganization of the rules governing civil discovery. See 2004 Cal. Stat. ch. 182. [35 Cal.L.Rev.Comm. Reports 77 (2005)].

Research References

Forms

California Practice Guide: Rutter Family Law Forms Form 5:15, Stipulation Waiving Time for Hearing, Acknowledgment Of Service Of Notice Of Request for Order and Order Thereon.
West's California Code Forms, Civil § 3080.09 Form 1, Application for Substitution Of Undertaking for Livestock.
West's California Code Forms, Civil Procedure § 527 Form 3, Injunction--Temporary Restraining Order and Order to Show Cause.
West's California Code Forms, Civil Procedure § 527 Form 5, Injunction--Notice Of Motion for Preliminary Injunction.
West's California Code Forms, Government § 946.6 Form 1, Petition for Order Seeking Relief from Claims Statute--Action Against Local Public Entity.
West's California Judicial Council Forms FL-320, Responsive Declaration to Request for Order.
West's California Judicial Council Forms FL-685, Response to Governmental Notice Of Motion or Order to Show Cause.

Treatises and Practice Aids

Witkin, California Summary 10th Real Property § 78, Division Of Property.
Witkin, California Summary 10th Torts § 84, Notice or Application.

§ 1008. Application to reconsider and modify or revoke prior order; affidavit; noncompliance; revocation of order; contempt; appeal

(a) When an application for an order has been made to a judge, or to a court, and refused in whole or in part, or granted, or granted conditionally, or on terms, any party affected by the order may, within 10 days after service upon the party of written notice of entry of the order and based upon new or different facts, circumstances, or law, make application to the same judge or court that made the order, to reconsider the matter and modify, amend, or revoke the prior order. The party making the application shall state by affidavit what application was made before, when and to what judge, what order or decisions were made, and what new or different facts, circumstances, or law are claimed to be shown.

(b) A party who originally made an application for an order which was refused in whole or part, or granted conditionally or on terms, may make a subsequent application for the same order upon new or different facts, circumstances, or law, in which case it shall be shown by affidavit what application was made before, when and to what judge, what order or decisions were made, and what new or different facts, circumstances, or law are claimed to be shown. For a failure to comply with this subdivision, any order made on a subsequent application may be revoked or set aside on ex parte motion.

(c) If a court at any time determines that there has been a change of law that warrants it to reconsider a prior order it entered, it may do so on its own motion and enter a different order.

(d) A violation of this section may be punished as a contempt and with sanctions as allowed by Section 128.7. In addition, an order made contrary to this section may be revoked by the judge or commissioner who made it, or vacated by a judge of the court in which the action or proceeding is pending.

(e) This section specifies the court's jurisdiction with regard to applications for reconsideration of its orders and renewals of previous motions, and applies to all applications to reconsider any order of a judge or court, or for the renewal of a previous motion, whether the order deciding the previous matter or motion is interim or final. No application to reconsider any order or for the renewal of a previous motion may be considered by any judge or court unless made according to this section.

(f) For the purposes of this section, an alleged new or different law shall not include a later enacted statute without a retroactive application.

(g) An order denying a motion for reconsideration made pursuant to subdivision (a) is not separately appealable. However, if the order that was the subject of a motion for reconsideration is appealable, the denial of the motion for reconsideration is reviewable as part of an appeal from that order.

(h) This section applies to all applications for interim orders. *(Added by Stats.1978, c. 631, § 2. Amended by Stats.1992, c. 460 (S.B.1805), § 4; Stats.1998, c. 200 (S.B. 1556), § 2; Stats.2011, c. 78 (A.B.1067), § 1.)*

Commentary

A trial court order denying a subsection (b) renewed motion is not an appealable order. *Tate v. Wilburn, 184 Cal.App.4th 150, 109 Cal.Rptr.3d 18 (2010), review denied*.

In *Le Francois v. Goel, 35 Cal.4th 1094, 29 Cal.Rptr.3d 249, 112 P.3d 636 (2005)*, the California Supreme Court held that a trial court has inherent authority to correct an erroneous interim order on its own motion, even though this section would preclude a party from filing a motion for reconsideration. Even when a party files a motion that fails to satisfy the requirements of this section, and filing of the motion stimulates the trial court to review and recognize the error of its prior final order, the court has inherent power to correct the prior final order so long as its recognition of error does not rely on or mention additional evidence alleged in the improper motion for reconsideration. *In re Marriage of Barthold, 158 Cal.App.4th 1301, 70 Cal.Rptr.3d 691 (2008)*.

In re Marriage of Oliverez, 238 Cal.App.4th 1242, 190 Cal.Rptr.3d 436 (2015), holds that a trial judge erred in reconsidering and reversing another judge's order that a marital settlement agreement was unenforceable, when reversal was based only on disagreement with the original judge's ruling, not based on new evidence, law, or facts, and there was no evidence that the original judge was not available to hear the reconsideration motion.

Research References

Forms

Environmental Insurance Litigation: Practice Forms § 1:14, Insurer's Notice Of Motion and Motion for Reconsideration (With Supporting Memorandum and Declaration) (Owned Property Exclusion and Absence Of Third Party Property Damage).
West's California Code Forms, Civil Procedure § 473 Form 9, Pleadings--Notice Of Motion to Set Aside Default and Judgment Taken Thereon.
West's California Code Forms, Civil Procedure § 1008 Form 1, Motions and Orders--New Application for Order After Prior Refusal--Declaration Supporting New Application.
West's California Code Forms, Civil Procedure § 1008 Form 2, Motions and Orders--Application to Set Aside Order Obtained Without Prior Refusal Disclosure.

West's California Code Forms, Civil Procedure § 437C Form 1, Summary Judgment--Notice Of Motion for Summary Judgment or Summary Adjudication--By Plaintiff.

Treatises and Practice Aids

Witkin, California Summary 10th Constitutional Law § 143, in General.
Witkin, California Summary 10th Husband and Wife § 207, Modification.
Witkin, California Summary 10th Husband and Wife § 384, Orders After Notice and Hearing.
Witkin, California Summary 10th Insurance § 275, Inception and Duration Of Duty.
Witkin, California Summary 10th Parent and Child § 58, Grant or Denial.
Witkin, California Summary 10th Parent and Child § 662, Nature and Purpose.

CHAPTER 5. NOTICES, AND FILING AND SERVICE OF PAPERS

§ 1010.6. Electronic service of documents; local rules for electronic filing; uniform rules

(a) A document may be served electronically in an action filed with the court as provided in this section, in accordance with rules adopted pursuant to subdivision (e).

(1) For purposes of this section:

(A) "Electronic service" means service of a document, on a party or other person, by either electronic transmission or electronic notification. Electronic service may be performed directly by a party or other person, by an agent of a party or other person, including the * * * party or other person's attorney, or through an electronic filing service provider.

(B) "Electronic transmission" means the transmission of a document by electronic means to the electronic service address at or through which a party or other person has authorized electronic service.

(C) "Electronic notification" means the notification of the party or other person that a document is served by sending an electronic message to the electronic address at or through which the party or other person has authorized electronic service, specifying the exact name of the document served, and providing a hyperlink at which the served document may be viewed and downloaded.

(2)* * * (A)(i) For cases filed on or before December 31, 2018, if a document may be served by mail, express mail, overnight delivery, or facsimile transmission, electronic service of the document is not authorized unless a party or other person has agreed to accept electronic service * * * in that * * * specific action or the court has ordered electronic service on a represented party or other represented person under subdivision (c) or (d).

(ii) For cases filed on or after January 1, 2019, if a document may be served by mail, express mail, overnight delivery, or facsimile transmission, electronic service of the document is not authorized unless a party or other person has expressly consented to receive electronic service in that specific action or the court has ordered electronic service on a represented party or other represented person under subdivision (c) or (d). Express consent to electronic service may be accomplished either by (I) serving a notice on all the parties and filing the notice with the court, or (II) manifesting affirmative consent through electronic means with the court or the court's electronic filing service provider, and concurrently providing the party's electronic address with that consent for the purpose of receiving electronic service. The act of electronic filing shall not be construed as express consent.

(B) If a document is required to be served by certified or registered mail, electronic service of the document is not authorized.

(3) In any action in which a party or other person has agreed or provided express consent, as applicable, to accept electronic service under paragraph (2), or in which the court has ordered electronic service on a represented party or other represented person under subdivision (c) or (d), the court may electronically serve any document issued by the court that is not required to be personally served in the same manner that parties electronically serve documents. The electronic service of documents by the court shall have the same legal effect as service by mail, except as provided in paragraph (4).

(4)(A) * * * If a document may be served by mail, express mail, overnight delivery, or facsimile transmission, electronic service of that document is deemed complete at the time of the electronic transmission of the document or at the time that the electronic notification of service of the document is sent.

* * * (B) Any period of notice, or any right or duty to do any act or make any response within any period or on a date certain after the service of the document, which time period or date is prescribed by statute or rule of court, shall be extended after service by electronic means by two court days, but the extension shall not apply to extend the time for filing any of the following:

(i) A notice of intention to move for new trial.

(ii) A notice of intention to move to vacate judgment under Section 663a.

(iii) A notice of appeal.

(C) This extension applies in the absence of a specific exception provided by any other statute or rule of court.

(5) Any document that is served electronically between 12:00 a.m. and 11:59:59 p.m. on a court day shall be deemed served on that court day. Any document that is served electronically on a noncourt day shall be deemed served on the next court day.

(6) A party or other person who has provided express consent to accept service electronically may withdraw consent at any time by completing and filing with the court the appropriate Judicial Council form. The Judicial Council shall create the form by January 1, 2019.

(7) Consent, or the withdrawal of consent, to receive electronic service may only be completed by a party or other person entitled to service or that person's attorney.

(8) Confidential or sealed records shall be electronically served through encrypted methods to ensure that the documents are not improperly disclosed.

(b) A trial court may adopt local rules permitting electronic filing of documents, subject to rules adopted pursuant to subdivision (e) and the following conditions:

(1) A document that is filed electronically shall have the same legal effect as an original paper document.

(2)(A) When a document to be filed requires the signature of any person, not under penalty of perjury, * * * the document shall be deemed to have been signed by * * * the person who filed the document electronically.

(B) When a document to be filed requires the signature, under penalty of perjury, of any person, the document shall be deemed to have been signed by that person if filed electronically and if * * * either of the following conditions is satisfied:

* * * (i) The person has signed a printed form of the document * * * before, or on the same day as, the date of filing. The attorney or other person filing the document represents, by the act of filing, that the declarant has complied with this section. The attorney or other person filing the document shall maintain the printed form of the document bearing the original signature until final disposition of the case, as defined in subdivision (c) of Section 68151 of the Government Code, and make it available for review and copying upon the request of the court or any party to the action or proceeding in which it is filed.

(ii) The person has signed the document using a computer or other technology pursuant to the procedure set forth in a rule of court adopted by the Judicial Council by January 1, 2019.

(3) Any document * * * received electronically * * * by the court between 12:00 a.m. and 11:59:59 p.m. on a court day shall be deemed * * * filed on that court day. Any document that is received electronically on a noncourt day shall be deemed filed on the next court day.

(4) The court receiving a document filed electronically shall issue a confirmation that the document has been received and filed. The confirmation shall serve as proof that the document has been filed.

(5) Upon electronic filing of a complaint, petition, or other document that must be served with a summons, a trial court, upon request of the party filing the action, shall issue a summons with the court seal and the case number. The court shall keep the summons in its records and may electronically transmit a copy of the summons to the requesting party. Personal service of a printed form of the electronic summons shall have the same legal effect as personal service of an original summons. If a trial court plans to electronically transmit a summons to the party filing a complaint, the court shall immediately, upon receipt of the complaint, notify the attorney or party that a summons will be electronically transmitted to the electronic address given by the person filing the complaint.

(6) The court shall permit a party or attorney to file an application for waiver of court fees and costs, in lieu of requiring the payment of the filing fee, as part of the process involving the electronic filing of a document. The court shall consider and determine the application in accordance with Article 6 (commencing with Section 68630) of Chapter 2 of Title 8 of the Government Code and shall not require the party or attorney to submit any documentation other than that set forth in Article 6 (commencing with Section 68630) of Chapter 2 of Title 8 of the Government Code. Nothing in this section shall require the court to waive a filing fee that is not otherwise waivable.

(7) A fee, if any, charged by the court, an electronic filing manager, or an electronic filing service provider to process a payment for filing fees and other court fees shall not exceed the costs incurred in processing the payment.

(c) If a trial court adopts rules conforming to subdivision (b), it may provide by order that all parties to an action file and serve documents electronically in a class action, a consolidated action, a group of actions, a coordinated action, or an action that is deemed complex under Judicial Council rules, provided that the trial court's order does not cause undue hardship or significant prejudice to any party in the action.

(d) * * * A trial court may, by local rule * * *, require electronic filing and service in civil actions * * *, subject to the requirements * * * and conditions stated in subdivision (b), the rules adopted * * * by the Judicial Council under subdivision (f), and the following conditions:

(1) The court shall have the ability to maintain the official court record in electronic format for all cases where electronic filing is required.

(2) The court and the parties shall have access to more than one electronic filing service provider capable of electronically filing documents with the court or to electronic filing access directly through the court. The court may charge fees of no more than the actual cost of the electronic filing and service of the documents. Any fees charged by an electronic filing service provider shall be reasonable. The court, an electronic filing manager, or an electronic filing service provider shall waive any fees charged if the court deems a waiver appropriate, including in instances where a party has received a fee waiver.

(3) The court shall have a procedure for the filing of nonelectronic documents in order to prevent the program from causing undue hardship or significant prejudice to any party in an action, including, but not limited to, unrepresented parties. The Judicial Council shall make a form available to allow a party to seek an exemption from mandatory electronic filing and service on the grounds provided in this paragraph.

* * *

(4) Unrepresented persons are exempt from mandatory electronic filing and service.

(5) Until January 1, 2019, a local child support agency, as defined in subdivision (h) of Section 17000 of the Family Code, is exempt from a trial court's mandatory electronic filing and service requirements, unless the Department of Child Support Services and the local child support agency

determine it has the capacity and functionality to comply with the trial court's mandatory electronic filing and service requirements.

(e) The Judicial Council shall adopt uniform rules for the electronic filing and service of documents in the trial courts of the state, which shall include statewide policies on vendor contracts, privacy, and access to public records, and rules relating to the integrity of electronic service. These rules shall conform to the conditions set forth in this section, as amended from time to time.

(f) The Judicial Council shall * * * adopt uniform rules to permit the mandatory electronic filing and service of documents for specified civil actions in the trial courts of the state, which shall * * * include statewide policies on vendor contracts, privacy, access to public records, unrepresented parties, parties with fee waivers, hardships, reasonable exceptions to electronic filing, and rules relating to the integrity of electronic service. These rules shall conform to the conditions set forth in this section, as amended from time to time.

* * *

(g)(1) The Judicial Council shall adopt uniform rules to implement this subdivision as soon as practicable, but no later than June 30, 2019.

(2) Any system for the electronic filing and service of documents, including any information technology applications, Internet Web sites, and Web-based applications, used by an electronic service provider or any other vendor or contractor that provides an electronic filing and service system to a trial court, regardless of the case management system used by the trial court, shall satisfy both of the following requirements:

(A) The system shall be accessible to individuals with disabilities, including parties and attorneys with disabilities, in accordance with Section 508 of the federal Rehabilitation Act of 1973 (29 U.S.C. Sec. 794d), as amended, the regulations implementing that act set forth in Part 1194 of Title 36 of the Code of Federal Regulations and Appendices A, C, and D of that part, and the federal Americans with Disabilities Act of 1990 (42 U.S.C. Sec. 12101 et seq.).

(B) The system shall comply with the Web Content Accessibility Guidelines 2.0 at a Level AA success criteria.

(3) A vendor or contractor that provides an electronic filing and service system to a trial court shall comply with paragraph (2) as soon as practicable, but no later than June 30, 2019. Commencing on * * * June 27, 2017, the vendor or contractor shall provide an accommodation to an individual with a disability in accordance with subparagraph (D) of paragraph (4).

(4) A trial court that contracts with an entity for the provision of a system for electronic filing and service of documents shall require the entity, in the trial court's contract with the entity, to do all of the following:

(A) Test and verify that the entity's system complies with this subdivision and provide the verification to the Judicial Council no later than June 30, 2019.

(B) Respond to, and resolve, any complaints regarding the accessibility of the system that are brought to the attention of the entity.

(C) Designate a lead individual to whom any complaints concerning accessibility may be addressed and post the individual's name and contact information on the entity's Internet Web site.

(D) Provide to an individual with a disability, upon request, an accommodation to enable the individual to file and serve documents electronically at no additional charge for any time period that the entity is not compliant with paragraph (2) of this subdivision. Exempting an individual with a disability from mandatory electronic filing and service of documents shall not be deemed an accommodation unless the person chooses that as an accommodation. The vendor or contractor shall clearly state in its Internet Web site that an individual with a disability may request an accommodation and the process for submitting a request for an accommodation.

(5) A trial court that provides electronic filing and service of documents directly to the public shall comply with this subdivision to the same extent as a vendor or contractor that provides electronic filing and services to a trial court.

(6)(A) The Judicial Council shall submit four reports to the appropriate committees of the Legislature relating to the trial courts that have implemented a system of electronic filing and service of documents. The first report is due by June 30, 2018; the second report is due by December 31, 2019; the third report is due by December 31, 2021; and the fourth report is due by December 31, 2023.

(B) The Judicial Council's reports shall include all of the following information:

(i) The name of each court that has implemented a system of electronic filing and service of documents.

(ii) A description of the system of electronic filing and service.

(iii) The name of the entity or entities providing the system.

(iv) A statement as to whether the system complies with this subdivision and, if the system is not fully compliant, a description of the actions that have been taken to make the system compliant.

(7) An entity that contracts with a trial court to provide a system for electronic filing and service of documents shall cooperate with the Judicial Council by providing all information, and by permitting all testing, necessary for the Judicial Council to prepare its reports to the Legislature in a complete and timely manner. *(Added by Stats.1999, c. 514 (S.B.367), § 1. Amended by Stats.2001, c. 824 (A.B.1700), § 10.5; Stats.2005, c. 300 (A.B.496), § 5; Stats.2010, c. 156 (S.B.1274), § 1; Stats.2011, c. 296 (A.B.1023), § 40; Stats. 2012, c. 320 (A.B.2073), § 1; Stats.2016, c. 461 (A.B.2244), § 1, eff. Jan. 1, 2017; Stats.2017, c. 17 (A.B.103), § 5, eff. June 27, 2017; Stats.2017, c. 319 (A.B.976), § 2, eff. Jan. 1, 2018.)*

Research References

Forms

West's California Judicial Council Forms POS-040, Proof Of Service--Civil.

Treatises and Practice Aids

Witkin, California Summary 10th Wills and Probate § 378, Hearings.

§ 1013a. Service by mail; proof

Proof of service by mail may be made by one of the following methods:

(1) An affidavit setting forth the exact title of the document served and filed in the cause, showing the name and residence or business address of the person making the service, showing that he or she is a resident of or employed in the county where the mailing occurs, that he or she is over the age of 18 years and not a party to the cause, and showing the date and place of deposit in the mail, the name and address of the person served as shown on the envelope, and also showing that the envelope was sealed and deposited in the mail with the postage thereon fully prepaid.

(2) A certificate setting forth the exact title of the document served and filed in the cause, showing the name and business address of the person making the service, showing that he or she is an active member of the State Bar of California and is not a party to the cause, and showing the date and place of deposit in the mail, the name and address of the person served as shown on the envelope, and also showing that the envelope was sealed and deposited in the mail with the postage thereon fully prepaid.

(3) An affidavit setting forth the exact title of the document served and filed in the cause, showing (A) the name and residence or business address of the person making the service, (B) that he or she is a resident of, or employed in, the county where the mailing occurs, (C) that he or she is over the age of 18 years and not a party to the cause, (D) that he or she is readily familiar with the business' practice for collection and processing of correspondence for mailing with the United States Postal Service, (E) that the correspondence would be deposited with the United States Postal Service that same day in the ordinary course of business, (F) the name and address of the person served as shown on the envelope, and the date and place of business where the correspondence was placed for deposit in the United States Postal Service, and (G) that the envelope was sealed and placed for collection and mailing on that date following ordinary business practices. Service made pursuant to this paragraph, upon motion of a party served, shall be presumed invalid if the postal cancellation date or postage meter date on the envelope is more than one day after the date of deposit for mailing contained in the affidavit.

(4) In case of service by the clerk of a court of record, a certificate by that clerk setting forth the exact title of the document served and filed in the cause, showing the name of the clerk and the name of the court of which he or she is the clerk, and that he or she is not a party to the cause, and showing the date and place of deposit in the mail, the name and address of the person served as shown on the envelope, and also showing that the envelope was sealed and deposited in the mail with the postage thereon fully prepaid. This form of proof is sufficient for service of process in which the clerk or deputy clerk signing the certificate places the document for collection and mailing on the date shown thereon, so as to cause it to be mailed in an envelope so sealed and so addressed on that date following standard court practices. Service made pursuant to this paragraph, upon motion of a party served and a finding of good cause by the court, shall be deemed to have occurred on the date of postage cancellation or postage meter imprint as shown on the envelope if that date is more than one day after the date of deposit for mailing contained in the certificate. *(Added by Stats.1931, c. 739, p. 1534, § 3. Amended by Stats.1953, c. 1110, p. 2606, § 1; Stats.1955, c. 779, p. 1379, § 1; Stats.1959, c. 345, p. 2268, § 1; Stats.1972, c. 601, p. 1065, § 3; Stats.1972, c. 1083, p. 2019, § 1; Stats.1973, c. 302, p. 718, § 1; Stats.1974, c. 282, p. 546, § 3, eff. May 28, 1974; Stats.1980, c. 196, p. 419, § 3; Stats.1987, c. 190, § 1; Stats.1988, c. 160, § 18; Stats.1995, c. 576 (A.B.1225), § 4.)*

Research References

Forms

West's California Code Forms, Civil Procedure § 595.2 Form 1, Trial--Stipulation for Continuance--Order.

West's California Code Forms, Corporations § 317 Form 1, Defendants' Notice Of Application to Court for Indemnity.

West's California Code Forms, Government § 913 Form 1, Notice Of Action Taken.

West's California Code Forms, Probate § 1211 Form 1, Notice Of Hearing (Probate)--Judicial Council Form DE-120.

West's California Judicial Council Forms FL-334, Declaration Regarding Address Verification--Postjudgment Request to Modify a Child Custody, Visitation, or Child Support Order.

West's California Judicial Council Forms FL-335, Proof Of Service by Mail.

West's California Judicial Council Forms FL-686, Proof Of Service by Mail.

West's California Judicial Council Forms JV-310, Proof Of Service Under Section 366.26 Of the Welfare and Institutions Code.

West's California Judicial Council Forms DAL-012, Proof Of Service--Disability Access Litigation.

West's California Judicial Council Forms MIL-184, Order for Dismissal (Military Personnel) (Pen. Code, §§ 17(B), 1170.9(H)).

West's California Judicial Council Forms POS-030, Proof Of Service by First-Class Mail--Civil.

West's California Judicial Council Forms POS-040, Proof Of Service--Civil.

West's California Judicial Council Forms FL-335-INFO, Information Sheet for Proof Of Service by Mail.

Treatises and Practice Aids

Witkin, California Summary 10th Wills and Probate § 397, Proof Of Giving Notice.

§ 1013b. Proof of electronic service

(a) Proof of electronic service may be made by any of the following methods:

(1) An affidavit setting forth the exact title of the document served and filed in the cause, showing the name and residence or business address of the person making the service, showing that he or she is a resident of or employed in the county where the filing occurs, and that he or she is over the age of 18 years.

(2) A certificate setting forth the exact title of the document served and filed in the cause, showing the name and business address of the person making the service, and showing that he or she is an active member of the State Bar of California.

(3) An affidavit setting forth the exact title of the document served and filed in the cause, showing (A) the name and residence or business address of the person making the service, (B) that he or she is a resident of, or employed in, the county where the filing occurs, (C) that he or she is over the age of 18 years, (D) that he or she is readily familiar with the business' practice for filing electronically, and (E) that the document would be electronically filed that same day in the

ordinary course of business following ordinary business practices.

(4) In case of service by the clerk of a court of record, a certificate by that clerk setting forth the exact title of the document served and filed in the cause, showing the name of the clerk and the name of the court of which he or she is the clerk.

(b) Proof of electronic service shall include all of the following:

(1) The electronic service address and the residence or business address of the person making the electronic service.

(2) The date of electronic service.

(3) The name and electronic service address of the person served.

(4) A statement that the document was served electronically.

(c) Proof of electronic service shall be signed as provided in subparagraph (B) of paragraph (2) of subdivision (b) of Section 1010.6.

(d) Proof of electronic service may be in electronic form and may be filed electronically with the court. *(Added by Stats.2017, c. 319 (A.B.976), § 4, eff. Jan. 1, 2018.)*

§ 1015. Service; nonresident party; service on clerk or attorney

When a plaintiff or a defendant, who has appeared, resides out of the state, and has no attorney in the action or proceeding, the service may be made on the clerk of the court, for that party. But in all cases where a party has an attorney in the action or proceeding, the service of papers, when required, must be upon the attorney instead of the party, except service of subpoenas, of writs, and other process issued in the suit, and of papers to bring the party into contempt. If the sole attorney for a party is removed or suspended from practice, then the party has no attorney within the meaning of this section. If the party's sole attorney has no known office in this state, notices and papers may be served by leaving a copy thereof with the clerk of the court, unless the attorney has filed in the cause an address of a place at which notices and papers may be served on the attorney, in which event they may be served at that place. *(Enacted in 1872. Amended by Stats.1907, c. 327, p. 602, § 4; Stats.1933, c. 744, p. 1899, § 179; Stats.1951, c. 1737, p. 4133, § 136, operative Jan. 1, 1952; Stats.2007, c. 263 (A.B.310), § 12.)*

Law Revision Commission Comments

2007 Amendment

Section 1015 is amended to delete unnecessary language authorizing the judge to substitute for the clerk if there is no clerk. See Code Civ. Proc. § 167 (judge may perform any act court clerk may perform); Gov't Code §§ 69840–69848 (duties of clerk of superior court), 71620(b) (executive or administrative officer has authority of clerk of court).

Section 1015 is also amended to make stylistic revisions and make the statute gender neutral. [35 Cal.L.Rev.Comm. Reports 219 (2006)].

Research References

Treatises and Practice Aids

Witkin, California Summary 10th Workers' Compensation § 353, Appearance and Representation.

§ 1016. Service; process to bring party into contempt; inapplicability of certain sections

PRECEDING PROVISIONS NOT TO APPLY TO PROCEEDING TO BRING PARTY INTO CONTEMPT. The foregoing provisions of this Chapter do not apply to the service of a summons or other process, or of any paper to bring a party into contempt. *(Enacted in 1872.)*

CHAPTER 7. GENERAL PROVISIONS

§ 1048. Consolidation of actions; separate trial of any cause of action, or of any separate issues, or causes of action or issues

(a) When actions involving a common question of law or fact are pending before the court, it may order a joint hearing or trial of any or all the matters in issue in the actions; it may order all the actions consolidated and it may make such orders concerning proceedings therein as may tend to avoid unnecessary costs or delay.

(b) The court, in furtherance of convenience or to avoid prejudice, or when separate trials will be conducive to expedition and economy, may order a separate trial of any cause of action, including a cause of action asserted in a cross-complaint, or of any separate issue or of any number of causes of action or issues, preserving the right of trial by jury required by the Constitution or a statute of this state or of the United States. *(Enacted in 1872. Amended by Stats.1927, c. 320, p. 531, § 1; Stats.1971, c. 244, p. 392, § 58, operative July 1, 1972.)*

Commentary

Although a tort claim may be consolidated with a *pending* dissolution action in appropriate circumstances, *Sosnick v. Sosnick, 71 Cal.App.4th 1335, 84 Cal.Rptr.2d 700 (1999),* holds that the divorce court lacks jurisdiction to consolidate a former wife's tort claim against her former husband with a closed dissolution action.

Research References

Forms

Am. Jur. Pl. & Pr. Forms Actions § 2, Introductory Comments.
Am. Jur. Pl. & Pr. Forms Actions § 87, Introductory Comments.
West's Cal. Code Forms, Bus. & Prof. § 475 COMMENT, Administrative Procedure Act.
West's California Code Forms, Civil Procedure § 1048 Form 1, General Practice Provisions--Notice Of Motion to Consolidate Actions.
West's California Code Forms, Civil Procedure § 1048 Form 2, General Practice Provisions--Notice Of Motion to Sever Actions.
West's California Code Forms, Civil Procedure § 418.10 Form 1, Objection to Jurisdiction--Notice Of Motion to Quash Service for Lack Of Jurisdiction.

West's California Judicial Council Forms FL-920, Notice Of Consolidation.

Treatises and Practice Aids

Witkin, California Summary 10th Constitutional Law § 1219, in General.

Witkin, California Summary 10th Husband and Wife § 68, in General.

Witkin, California Summary 10th Real Property § 736, Trial.

Witkin, California Summary 10th Torts § 1357, Adoption Of Doctrine.

Part 3

OF SPECIAL PROCEEDINGS OF A CIVIL NATURE

Title 3

OF SUMMARY PROCEEDINGS

CHAPTER 4. SUMMARY PROCEEDINGS FOR OBTAINING POSSESSION OF REAL PROPERTY IN CERTAIN CASES

§ 1161.3. Termination of lease prohibited based upon acts of domestic violence, sexual assault, stalking, human trafficking, or abuse of elder or dependent adult; exceptions; limitation of landlord liability to other tenants; definition; forms

(a) Except as provided in subdivision (b), a landlord shall not terminate a tenancy or fail to renew a tenancy based upon an act or acts against a tenant or a tenant's household member that constitute domestic violence as defined in Section 6211 of the Family Code, sexual assault as defined in Section 1219, stalking as defined in Section 1708.7 of the Civil Code or Section 646.9 of the Penal Code, human trafficking as defined in Section 236.1 of the Penal Code, or abuse of an elder or a dependent adult as defined in Section 15610.07 of the Welfare and Institutions Code, if both of the following apply:

(1) The act or acts of domestic violence, sexual assault, stalking, human trafficking, or abuse of an elder or a dependent adult have been documented by one of the following:

(A) A temporary restraining order, emergency protective order, or protective order lawfully issued within the last 180 days pursuant to Section 527.6, Part 3 (commencing with Section 6240), Part 4 (commencing with Section 6300), or Part 5 (commencing with Section 6400) of Division 10 of the Family Code, Section 136.2 of the Penal Code, or Section 213.5 or 15657.03 of the Welfare and Institutions Code that protects the tenant or household member from domestic violence, sexual assault, stalking, human trafficking, or abuse of an elder or a dependent adult.

(B) A copy of a written report, written within the last 180 days, by a peace officer employed by a state or local law enforcement agency acting in his or her official capacity, stating that the tenant or household member has filed a report alleging that he or she or the household member is a victim of domestic violence, sexual assault, stalking, human trafficking, or abuse of an elder or a dependent adult.

(2) The person against whom the protection order has been issued or who was named in the police report of the act or acts of domestic violence, sexual assault, stalking, human trafficking, or abuse of an elder or dependent adult is not a tenant of the same dwelling unit as the tenant or household member.

(b) A landlord may terminate or decline to renew a tenancy after the tenant has availed himself or herself of the protections afforded by subdivision (a) if both of the following apply:

(1) Either of the following:

(A) The tenant allows the person against whom the protection order has been issued or who was named in the police report of the act or acts of domestic violence, sexual assault, stalking, human trafficking, or abuse of an elder or a dependent adult to visit the property.

(B) The landlord reasonably believes that the presence of the person against whom the protection order has been issued or who was named in the police report of the act or acts of domestic violence, sexual assault, stalking, human trafficking, or abuse of an elder or dependent adult poses a physical threat to other tenants, guests, invitees, or licensees, or to a tenant's right to quiet possession pursuant to Section 1927 of the Civil Code.

(2) The landlord previously gave at least three days' notice to the tenant to correct a violation of paragraph (1).

(c) Notwithstanding any provision in the lease to the contrary, the landlord shall not be liable to any other tenants for any action that arises due to the landlord's compliance with this section.

(d) For the purposes of this section, "tenant" means tenant, subtenant, lessee, or sublessee.

(e) The Judicial Council shall, on or before July 1, 2014, develop a new form or revise an existing form that may be used by a party to assert in the responsive pleading the grounds set forth in this section as an affirmative defense to an unlawful detainer action. *(Added by Stats.2010, c. 626 (S.B.782), § 4. Amended by Stats.2012, c. 516 (S.B.1403), § 2; Stats.2013, c. 130 (S.B.612), § 3.)*

Research References

Treatises and Practice Aids

Witkin, California Summary 10th Real Property § 683A, (New) Domestic Violence, Sexual Assault, Stalking, Human Trafficking, or Elder Abuse Against Tenant.

Title 5

OF CONTEMPTS

§ 1209. Acts or omissions constituting; stay of sentence pending appeal

(a) The following acts or omissions in respect to a court of justice, or proceedings therein, are contempts of the authority of the court:

(1) Disorderly, contemptuous, or insolent behavior toward the judge while holding the court, tending to interrupt the due course of a trial or other judicial proceeding.

(2) A breach of the peace, boisterous conduct, or violent disturbance, tending to interrupt the due course of a trial or other judicial proceeding.

(3) Misbehavior in office, or other willful neglect or violation of duty by an attorney, counsel, clerk, sheriff, coroner, or other person, appointed or elected to perform a judicial or ministerial service.

(4) Abuse of the process or proceedings of the court, or falsely pretending to act under authority of an order or process of the court.

(5) Disobedience of any lawful judgment, order, or process of the court.

(6) Willful disobedience by a juror of a court admonishment related to the prohibition on any form of communication or research about the case, including all forms of electronic or wireless communication or research.

(7) Rescuing any person or property in the custody of an officer by virtue of an order or process of that court.

(8) Unlawfully detaining a witness or party to an action while going to, remaining at, or returning from the court where the action is on the calendar for trial.

(9) Any other unlawful interference with the process or proceedings of a court.

(10) Disobedience of a subpoena duly served, or refusing to be sworn or answer as a witness.

(11) When summoned as a juror in a court, neglecting to attend or serve as a juror, or improperly conversing with a party to an action to be tried at the court, or with any other person, in relation to the merits of the action, or receiving a communication from a party or other person in respect to the action, without immediately disclosing the communication to the court.

(12) Disobedience by an inferior tribunal or judicial officer of the lawful judgment, order, or process of a superior court, or proceeding in an action or special proceeding contrary to law, after the action or special proceeding is removed from the jurisdiction of the inferior tribunal or judicial officer.

(b) A speech or publication reflecting upon or concerning a court or an officer thereof shall not be treated or punished as a contempt of the court unless made in the immediate presence of the court while in session and in such a manner as to actually interfere with its proceedings.

(c) Notwithstanding Section 1211 or any other law, if an order of contempt is made affecting an attorney, his or her agent, investigator, or any person acting under the attorney's direction, in the preparation and conduct of an action or proceeding, the execution of any sentence shall be stayed pending the filing within three judicial days of a petition for extraordinary relief testing the lawfulness of the court's order, the violation of which is the basis of the contempt, except for conduct proscribed by subdivision (b) of Section 6068 of the Business and Professions Code, relating to an attorney's duty to maintain respect due to the courts and judicial officers.

(d) Notwithstanding Section 1211 or any other law, if an order of contempt is made affecting a public safety employee acting within the scope of employment for reason of the employee's failure to comply with a duly issued subpoena or subpoena duces tecum, the execution of any sentence shall be stayed pending the filing within three judicial days of a petition for extraordinary relief testing the lawfulness of the court's order, a violation of which is the basis for the contempt.

As used in this subdivision, "public safety employee" includes any peace officer, firefighter, paramedic, or any other employee of a public law enforcement agency whose duty is either to maintain official records or to analyze or present evidence for investigative or prosecutorial purposes. *(Enacted in 1872. Amended by Stats.1891, c. 9, p. 6, § 1; Stats.1907, c. 255, p. 319, § 1; Stats.1939, c. 979, p. 2731, § 1; Stats.1975, c. 836, p. 1896, § 2; Stats.1982, c. 510, p. 2286, § 2; Stats.2011, c. 181 (A.B.141), § 3.)*

Commentary

The sanction of contempt for willfully disobeying a court order outside the presence of the court ("indirect contempt") cannot be imposed unless the order is in writing, either as a court order or as set forth in the court's minutes. *In re Marcus, 138 Cal.App.4th 1009, 41 Cal.Rptr.3d 861 (2006).*

Under former California law, a criminal contempt sentence of incarceration could not constitutionally be imposed on a parent who chose not to seek employment or earn money, although required to do so by a child support order. The California Supreme Court disapproved this long standing rule in *Moss v. Superior Court, 17 Cal.4th 396, 950 P.2d 59, 71 Cal.Rptr.2d 215 (1998),* which held that a parent who willfully fails to seek and accept employment may be held in criminal contempt. Additionally, inability to comply with a child support order is an affirmative defense, and thus the petitioner need not prove the nonsupporting parent's ability to pay.

In *Turner v. Rogers, 564 U.S. 431, 131 S. Ct. 2507, 180 L.Ed.2d 452 (2011)*, the United States Supreme Court held that the Due Process Clause of the Fourteenth Amendment requires the state to provide counsel to an indigent parent threatened, at a civil contempt hearing, with incarceration for failure to pay child support unless the other parent is not represented by counsel and the state provides alternative procedures that assure a fair determination of the incarceration-related question of whether the support obligor is able to comply with the support order.

Research References

Forms

West's California Code Forms, Civil Procedure § 1211 Form 1, Contempts--Declaration--Not in Court's Presence.
West's California Judicial Council Forms FL-411, Affidavit Of Facts Constituting Contempt.
West's California Judicial Council Forms FL-415, Findings and Order Regarding Contempt (Family Law--Domestic Violence Prevention--Uniform Parentage--Governmental).

Treatises and Practice Aids

Witkin, California Summary 10th Constitutional Law § 895, Hate Crimes, Intimidation, and Threats Of Violence.
Witkin, California Summary 10th Equity § 149, Decision and Order.
Witkin, California Summary 10th Parent and Child § 437, Contempt Proceedings.
Witkin, California Summary 10th Parent and Child § 744, Conditions.
Witkin, California Summary 10th Workers' Compensation § 14, Powers.

§ 1209.5. Noncompliance with order for care or support of child

When a court of competent jurisdiction makes an order compelling a parent to furnish support or necessary food, clothing, shelter, medical attendance, or other remedial care for his or her child, proof that the order was made, filed, and served on the parent or proof that the parent was present in court at the time the order was pronounced and proof that the parent did not comply with the order is prima facie evidence of a contempt of court. *(Added by Stats.1955, c. 1359, p. 2444, § 1. Amended by Stats.1961, c. 1307, p. 3087, § 1, eff. July 10, 1961; Stats.1992, c. 163 (A.B.2641), § 57, operative Jan. 1, 1994.)*

Law Revision Commission Comments

1992 Amendment

Section 1209.5 is amended to make clear that it applies to an order directed to a mother as well as to a father. This is not a substantive change. See Code Civ.Proc. § 17 (masculine gender includes the feminine). [22 Cal.L.Rev.Comm.Reports 1 (1992)].

Commentary

In *Turner v. Rogers, 564 U.S. 431, 131 S. Ct. 2507, 180 L.Ed.2d 452 (2011)*, the United States Supreme Court held that the Due Process Clause of the Fourteenth Amendment requires the state to provide counsel to an indigent parent threatened, at a civil contempt hearing, with incarceration for failure to pay child support unless the other parent is not represented by counsel and the state provides alternative procedures that assure a fair determination of the incarceration-related question of whether the support obligor is able to comply with the support order.

In *Hicks v. Feiock, 485 U.S. 624 (1988)*, the United States Supreme Court held that this section's imposition on the support obligor of the burden of proof on the issue of ability to pay is unconstitutional in a criminal, as opposed to a civil, contempt proceeding.

Under former California law, a criminal contempt sentence of incarceration could not constitutionally be imposed on a parent who chose not to seek employment or earn money, although required to do so by a child support order. The California Supreme Court disapproved this long standing rule in *Moss v. Superior Court, 17 Cal.4th 396, 950 P.2d 59, 71 Cal.Rptr.2d 215 (1998),* which held that a parent who willfully fails to seek and accept employment may be held in criminal contempt. Additionally, inability to comply with a child support order is an affirmative defense, and thus the petitioner need not prove the nonsupporting parent's ability to pay. *In re Ivey, 85 Cal.App.4th 793, 102 Cal.Rptr.2d 447 (2000)*, extends the affirmative defense rule of *Moss* to an order requiring the father to pay pendente lite attorney's fees and expert fees to the mother in a child custody and support proceeding.

As an additional enforcement mechanism, a federal district court may require a defendant to comply with a state child support order as a condition of supervised release. However, a federal court may not alter the terms of the state order. *United States v. Lakatos, 241 F.3d 690 (9th Cir. 2001)*.

Research References

Treatises and Practice Aids

Witkin, California Summary 10th Parent and Child § 437, Contempt Proceedings.

§ 1210. Re-entry after ejectment; alias process after conviction; undertaking for appeal

Every person dispossessed or ejected from any real property by the judgment or process of any court of competent jurisdiction, who, not having right so to do, reenters into or upon or takes possession of the real property, or induces or procures any person not having right so to do, or aids or abets such a person therein, is guilty of a contempt of the court by which the judgment was rendered or from which the process issued. Upon a conviction for contempt the court must immediately issue an alias process, directed to the proper officer, and requiring the officer to restore possession to the party entitled under the original judgment or process, or to the party's lessee, grantee, or successor in interest. No appeal from the order directing the issuance of an alias writ of possession stays the execution of the writ, unless an undertaking is executed on the part of the appellant to the effect that the appellant will not commit or suffer to be committed any waste on the property, and if the order is affirmed, or the appeal dismissed, the appellant will pay the value of the use and occupation of the property from the time of the unlawful reentry until the delivery of the possession of the property, pursuant to the judgment or order, not exceeding a sum to be fixed by the judge of the court by which the order for the alias writ was made. *(Enacted in 1872. Amended by Stats.1893, c. 198, p. 281, § 1; Stats.1907, c. 255, p. 320, § 2; Stats.1982, c. 517, p. 2362, § 179.)*

Law Revision Commission Comments

1982 Amendment

Section 1210 is amended to delete provisions duplicated in the Bond and Undertaking Law. See Sections 995.310 (sureties on undertaking) and 995.320 (contents of undertaking). The other changes in Section 1210 are technical. [16 Cal.L.Rev.Comm. Reports 501 (1982)].

§ 1211. Summary punishment; order; affidavit or statement of facts; compliance by filing of form

(a) When a contempt is committed in the immediate view and presence of the court, or of the judge at chambers, it may be punished summarily; for which an order must be made, reciting the facts as occurring in such immediate view and presence, adjudging that the person proceeded against is thereby guilty of a contempt, and that he or she be punished as therein prescribed.

When the contempt is not committed in the immediate view and presence of the court, or of the judge at chambers, an affidavit shall be presented to the court or judge of the facts constituting the contempt, or a statement of the facts by the referees or arbitrators, or other judicial officers.

(b) In family law matters, filing of the Judicial Council form entitled "Order to Show Cause and Affidavit for Contempt (Family Law)" shall constitute compliance with this section. *(Enacted in 1872. Amended by Stats.1933, c. 745, p. 1906, § 11; Stats.1951, c. 1737, p. 4141, § 162, operative Jan. 1, 1952; Stats.1995, c. 904 (A.B.965), § 1; Stats.2001, c. 754 (A.B.1697), § 1.)*

Commentary

The sanction of contempt for willfully disobeying a court order outside the presence of the court ("indirect contempt") cannot be imposed unless the order is in writing, either as a court order or as set forth in the court's minutes. *In re Marcus, 138 Cal.App.4th 1009, 41 Cal.Rptr.3d 861 (2006).*

Research References

Forms

West's California Code Forms, Civil Procedure § 1211 Form 1, Contempts--Declaration--Not in Court's Presence.
West's California Judicial Council Forms FL-411, Affidavit Of Facts Constituting Contempt.

§ 1211.5. Affidavit or statement of facts; rules for construction, amendment and review

At all stages of all proceedings, the affidavit or statement of facts, as the case may be, required by Section 1211 shall be construed, amended, and reviewed according to the followings[1] rules:

(a) If no objection is made to the sufficiency of such affidavit or statement during the hearing on the charges contained therein, jurisdiction of the subject matter shall not depend on the averments of such affidavit or statement, but may be established by the facts found by the trial court to have been proved at such hearing, and the court shall cause the affidavit or statement to be amended to conform to proof.

(b) The court may order or permit amendment of such affidavit or statement for any defect or insufficiency at any stage of the proceedings, and the trial of the person accused of contempt shall continue as if the affidavit or statement had been originally filed as amended, unless substantial rights of such person accused would be prejudiced thereby, in which event a reasonable postponement, not longer than the ends of justice require, may be granted.

(c) No such affidavit or statement is insufficient, nor can the trial, order, judgment, or other proceeding thereon be affected by reason of any defect or imperfection in matter of form which does not prejudice a substantial right of the person accused on the merits. No order or judgment of conviction of contempt shall be set aside, nor new trial granted, for any error as to any matter of pleading in such affidavit or statement, unless, after an examination of the entire cause, including the evidence, the court shall be of the opinion that the error complained of has resulted in a miscarriage of justice. *(Added by Stats.1970, c. 1264, p. 2282, § 1.)*

[1] So in chaptered copy.

Research References

Forms

West's California Judicial Council Forms FL-410, Order to Show Cause and Affidavit for Contempt.
West's California Judicial Council Forms FL-411, Affidavit Of Facts Constituting Contempt.
West's California Judicial Council Forms FL-412, Affidavit Of Facts Constituting Contempt.

§ 1212. Warrant of attachment; issuance; order to show cause; warrant of commitment

When the contempt is not committed in the immediate view and presence of the court or judge, a warrant of attachment may be issued to bring the person charged to answer, or, without a previous arrest, a warrant of commitment may, upon notice, or upon an order to show cause, be granted; and no warrant of commitment can be issued without such previous attachment to answer, or such notice or order to show cause. *(Enacted in 1872. Amended by Stats.1933, c. 745, p. 1906, § 12; Stats.1951, c. 1737, p. 4141, § 163, operative Jan. 1, 1952.)*

§ 1213. Warrant of attachment; endorsement for undertaking

Whenever a warrant of attachment is issued pursuant to this title the court or judge must direct, by an endorsement on the warrant, that the person charged may give an undertaking for the person's appearance in an amount to be specified in such endorsement. *(Enacted in 1872. Amended by Stats. 1933, c. 745, p. 1906, § 13; Stats.1951, c. 1737, p. 4142, § 164, operative Jan. 1, 1952; Stats.1982, c. 517, p. 2362, § 179.5.)*

Law Revision Commission Comments

1982 Amendment

Section 1213 is amended to substitute the more accurate reference to an undertaking for the misleading reference to "bail." The other changes in Section 1213 are technical. [16 Cal.L.Rev.Comm. Reports 501 (1982)].

§ 1214. Warrant of attachment; execution

Upon executing the warrant of attachment, the officer executing the warrant must keep the person in custody, bring him before the court or judge, and detain him until an order be made in the premises, unless the person arrested entitle himself to be discharged, as provided in the next section. *(Enacted in 1872. Amended by Stats.1933, c. 745, p. 1906, § 14; Stats.1951, c. 1737, p. 4142, § 165, operative Jan. 1, 1952.)*

§ 1215. Discharge on undertaking

The person arrested must be discharged from the arrest upon executing and delivering to the officer, at any time before the return day of the warrant, an undertaking to the effect that the person arrested will appear on the return of the warrant and abide the order of the court or judge thereupon. *(Enacted in 1872. Amended by Stats.1933, c. 745, p. 1907, § 15; Stats.1951, c. 1737, p. 4142, § 166, operative Jan. 1, 1952; Stats.1982, c. 517, p. 2362, § 180.)*

Law Revision Commission Comments

1982 Amendment

Section 1215 is amended to delete the reference to "bail" and to delete provisions duplicated in the Bond and Undertaking Law. See Sections 995.310 (sureties on undertaking) and 995.320 (contents of undertaking). [16 Cal.L.Rev.Comm. Reports 501 (1982)].

§ 1216. Warrant of attachment; undertaking; return

The officer must return the warrant of arrest and undertaking, if any, received by him from the person arrested, by the return day specified therein. *(Enacted in 1872.)*

§ 1217. Trial

When the person arrested has been brought up or appeared, the court or judge must proceed to investigate the charge, and must hear any answer which the person arrested may make to the same, and may examine witnesses for or against him, for which an adjournment may be had from time to time if necessary. *(Enacted in 1872. Amended by Stats.1933, c. 745, p. 1907, § 16; Stats.1951, c. 1737, p. 4142, § 167, operative Jan. 1, 1952).*

§ 1218. Determination of guilt; punishment; restrictions on enforcement of orders by party in contempt; action for contempt of domestic violence prevention order

(a) Upon the answer and evidence taken, the court or judge shall determine whether the person proceeded against is guilty of the contempt charged, and if it be adjudged that he or she is guilty of the contempt, a fine may be imposed on him or her not exceeding one thousand dollars ($1,000), payable to the court, or he or she may be imprisoned not exceeding five days, or both. In addition, a person who is subject to a court order as a party to the action, or any agent of this person, who is adjudged guilty of contempt for violating that court order may be ordered to pay to the party initiating the contempt proceeding the reasonable attorney's fees and costs incurred by this party in connection with the contempt proceeding.

(b) Any party, who is in contempt of a court order or judgment in a dissolution of marriage, dissolution of domestic partnership, or legal separation action, shall not be permitted to enforce such an order or judgment, by way of execution or otherwise, either in the same action or by way of a separate action, against the other party. This restriction shall not affect nor apply to the enforcement of child or spousal support orders.

(c) In any court action in which a party is found in contempt of court for failure to comply with a court order pursuant to the Family Code, the court shall order the following:

(1) Upon a first finding of contempt, the court shall order the contemner to perform community service of up to 120 hours, or to be imprisoned up to 120 hours, for each count of contempt.

(2) Upon the second finding of contempt, the court shall order the contemner to perform community service of up to 120 hours, in addition to ordering imprisonment of the contemner up to 120 hours, for each count of contempt.

(3) Upon the third or any subsequent finding of contempt, the court shall order both of the following:

(A) The court shall order the contemner to serve a term of imprisonment of up to 240 hours, and to perform community service of up to 240 hours, for each count of contempt.

(B) The court shall order the contemner to pay an administrative fee, not to exceed the actual cost of the contemner's administration and supervision, while assigned to a community service program pursuant to this paragraph.

(4) The court shall take parties' employment schedules into consideration when ordering either community service or imprisonment, or both.

(d) Pursuant to Section 1211 and this section, a district attorney or city attorney may initiate and pursue a court action for contempt against a party for failing to comply with a court order entered pursuant to the Domestic Violence Protection Act (Division 10 (commencing with Section 6200) of the Family Code). Any attorney's fees and costs ordered by the court pursuant to subdivision (a) against a party who is adjudged guilty of contempt under this subdivision shall be paid to the Office of Emergency Services' account established for the purpose of funding domestic violence shelter service providers pursuant to subdivision (f) of Section 13823.15 of the Penal Code. *(Enacted in 1872. Amended by Stats.1933, c. 745, p. 1907, § 17; Stats.1951, c. 1737, p. 4142, § 168, operative Jan. 1, 1952; Stats.1968, c. 938, p. 1788, § 2; Stats.1977, c. 1257, p. 4770, § 39, eff. Jan. 3, 1977; Stats.1983, c. 1092, § 72, eff. Sept. 27, 1983, operative Jan. 1, 1984; Stats.1988, c. 969, § 2; Stats.1993, c. 745 (S.B.788), § 1; Stats.1993, c. 746 (A.B.934), § 1; Stats.1994, c. 368 (A.B. 2911), § 1; Stats.1994, c. 1269 (A.B.2208), § 3.3; Stats.1995, c. 576 (A.B.1225), § 5.5; Stats.2000, c. 808 (A.B.1358), § 20, eff. Sept. 28, 2000; Stats.2005, c. 75 (A.B.145), § 44, eff. July 19, 2005, operative Jan. 1, 2006; Stats.2005, c. 631 (S.B.720), § 1; Stats.2010, c. 618 (A.B.2791), § 3; Stats.2013, c. 352 (A.B.1317), § 56, eff. Sept. 26, 2013, operative July 1, 2013.)*

Commentary

In *Turner v. Rogers, 564 U.S. 431, 131 S. Ct. 2507, 180 L.Ed.2d 452 (2011)*, the United States Supreme Court held that the Due Process Clause of the Fourteenth Amendment requires the state to provide counsel to an indigent parent threatened, at a civil contempt hearing, with incarceration for failure to pay child support unless the other parent is not represented by counsel and the state provides alternative procedures that assure a fair determination of the incarceration-related question of whether the support obligor is able to comply with the support order.

Goold v. Superior Court, 145 Cal.App.4th 1, 51 Cal.Rptr.3d 455 (2006), sustained a trial court's award to a wife of attorney's fees under subsection (a) and imposition on her husband of 360 hours in custody under subsection (c), after finding the husband in contempt for repeatedly violating Family Code section 2040 restraining orders prohibiting either spouse from encumbering or transferring property during dissolution proceedings.

Monterey County v. Banuelos, 82 Cal.App.4th 1299, 98 Cal.Rptr.2d 710 (2000), holds that post–1993 amendments to Family Code § 150 enlarged the definition of "child support" to include amounts owed to individuals or the county for current support or arrearages, and subsection (c) of this section was accordingly amended to make it consistent with the enlarged definition of child support. Thus, a court may issue a seek-work order under § 290 when a county attempts to recover child support arrearages or reimbursement for public assistance. See commentary to Family Code § 290.

Rickley v. Goodfriend, 207 Cal.App.4th 1528, 145 Cal.Rptr.3d 13 (2012), review denied, holds that an attorney who represented herself and her spouse as plaintiffs in a contempt proceeding may be entitled to attorney fees under this section, so long as she and her co-plaintiff spouse had an attorney-client relationship with respect to the action. The issue was whether, for purposes of the action, the husband consulted his wife in her professional capacity and she provided him with legal advice.

Research References

Forms

West's California Code Forms, Civil Procedure § 1218 Form 1, Contempts--Order Holding Party in Contempt.
West's California Code Forms, Civil Procedure § 1218 Form 2, Contempts--Notice Of Motion for Order Awarding Attorney's Fees.
West's California Code Forms, Civil Procedure § 1218 Form 4, Contempts--Order Awarding Attorney's Fees.
West's California Judicial Council Forms FL-415, Findings and Order Regarding Contempt (Family Law--Domestic Violence Prevention--Uniform Parentage--Governmental).

Treatises and Practice Aids

Witkin, California Summary 10th Equity § 149, Decision and Order.
Witkin, California Summary 10th Husband and Wife § 205, Contempt.
Witkin, California Summary 10th Husband and Wife § 253, Rights and Obligations Of Employer.
Witkin, California Summary 10th Husband and Wife § 258, Nature Of Remedy.
Witkin, California Summary 10th Husband and Wife § 343, CalWORKs Aid.
Witkin, California Summary 10th Husband and Wife § 362, Integrated Agreement.
Witkin, California Summary 10th Husband and Wife § 373, in General.
Witkin, California Summary 10th Parent and Child § 285, in General.
Witkin, California Summary 10th Parent and Child § 417, Provision and Termination Of Coverage.

§ 1218.5. Child, family, or spousal support; contempt for failure to pay; separate counts; limitation of actions

(a) If the contempt alleged is for failure to pay child, family, or spousal support, each month for which payment has not been made in full may be alleged as a separate count of contempt and punishment imposed for each count proven.

(b) If the contempt alleged is the failure to pay child, family, or spousal support, the period of limitations for commencing a contempt action is three years from the date that the payment was due. If the action before the court is enforcement of another order under the Family Code, the period of limitations for commencing a contempt action is two years from the time that the alleged contempt occurred. *(Added by Stats.1994, c. 1269 (A.B.2208), § 3.5.)*

Commentary

Under former California law, a criminal contempt sentence of incarceration could not constitutionally be imposed on a parent who chose not to seek employment or earn money, although required to do so by a child support order. The California Supreme Court disapproved this long standing rule in *Moss v. Superior Court, 17 Cal.4th 396, 950 P.2d 59, 71 Cal.Rptr.2d 215 (1998)*, which held that a parent who willfully fails to seek and accept employment may be held in criminal contempt. Additionally, inability to comply with a child support order is an affirmative defense, and thus the petitioner need not prove the nonsupporting parent's ability to pay.

Relying on subsection (a), *In re Marriage of Rice & Eaton, 204 Cal.App.4th 1073, 139 Cal.Rptr.3d 518 (2012)*, held that when the Department of Child Support Services (DCSS) brought a contempt action against a father for failing to pay court-ordered child support and did not include all of the claims known to DCSS, the mother could bring her own motion for contempt based on the omitted claims.

Research References

Treatises and Practice Aids

Witkin, California Summary 10th Husband and Wife § 205, Contempt.
Witkin, California Summary 10th Husband and Wife § 258, Nature Of Remedy.
Witkin, California Summary 10th Husband and Wife § 259, Procedure.
Witkin, California Summary 10th Parent and Child § 285, in General.

§ 1219. Imprisonment to compel performance of acts; exemptions; definitions

(a) Except as provided in subdivisions (b) and (c), if the contempt consists of the omission to perform an act which is yet in the power of the person to perform, he or she may be imprisoned until he or she has performed it, and in that case the act shall be specified in the warrant of commitment.

(b) Notwithstanding any other law, a court shall not imprison or otherwise confine or place in custody the victim of a sexual assault or domestic violence crime for contempt if the contempt consists of refusing to testify concerning that sexual assault or domestic violence crime. Before finding a victim of a domestic violence crime in contempt as described in this section, the court may refer the victim for consultation with a domestic violence counselor. All communications between the victim and the domestic violence counselor that occur as a result of that referral shall remain confidential under Section 1037.2 of the Evidence Code.

(c) Notwithstanding any other law, a court shall not imprison, hold in physical confinement, or otherwise confine or place in custody a minor for contempt if the contempt consists of the minor's failure to comply with a court order pursuant to subdivision (b) of Section 601 of, or Section 727 of, the Welfare and Institutions Code, if the minor was adjudged a ward of the court on the ground that he or she is a person described in subdivision (b) of Section 601 of the Welfare and Institutions Code. Upon a finding of contempt of court, the court may issue any other lawful order, as necessary, to secure the minor's attendance at school.

(d) As used in this section, the following terms have the following meanings:

(1) "Sexual assault" means any act made punishable by Section 261, 262, 264.1, 285, 286, 288, 288a, or 289 of the Penal Code.

(2) "Domestic violence" means "domestic violence" as defined in Section 6211 of the Family Code.

(3) "Domestic violence counselor" means "domestic violence counselor" as defined in subdivision (a) of Section 1037.1 of the Evidence Code.

(4) "Physical confinement" has the same meaning as defined in subdivision (d) of Section 726 of the Welfare and Institutions Code. *(Enacted in 1872. Amended by Stats. 1980, c. 676, § 68; Stats.1984, c. 1644, § 2; Stats.1991, c. 866 (A.B.363), § 4; Stats.1992, c. 163 (A.B.2641), § 58, operative Jan. 1, 1994; Stats.1993, c. 219 (A.B.1500), § 69.7; Stats.2008, c. 49 (S.B.1356), § 1; Stats.2009, c. 35 (S.B.174), § 3; Stats.2012, c. 510 (A.B.2051), § 1; Stats.2014, c. 70 (S.B. 1296), § 1, eff. Jan. 1, 2015.)*

Law Revision Commission Comments

1992 Amendment [Revised Comment]

Subdivision (d)(2) of Section 1219 is amended to substitute a reference to the Family Code provision defining "domestic violence." The Family Code definition is the same as the definition formerly included in this provision, except that the Family Code provision applies to children. See Fam. Code § 6211 ("domestic violence" defined) & Comment. For the special provisions applicable to child witnesses, see Code Civ. Proc. 1219.5 (referral to probation officer where minor in contempt); Penal Code §§ 1346–1348.5 (examination of child victims of abuse). [23 Cal.L.Rev.Comm. Reports 1 (1993)].

Commentary

In *Turner v. Rogers, 564 U.S. 431, 131 S. Ct. 2507, 180 L.Ed.2d 452 (2011)*, the United States Supreme Court held that the Due Process Clause of the Fourteenth Amendment requires the state to provide counsel to an indigent parent threatened, at a civil contempt hearing, with incarceration for failure to pay child support unless the other parent is not represented by counsel and the state provides alternative procedures that assure a fair determination of the incarceration-related question of whether the support obligor is able to comply with the support order.

Under former California law, a criminal contempt sentence of incarceration could not constitutionally be imposed on a parent who chose not to seek employment or earn money, although required to do so by a child support order. The California Supreme Court disapproved this long standing rule in *Moss v. Superior Court, 17 Cal.4th 396, 950 P.2d 59, 71 Cal.Rptr.2d 215 (1998)*, which held that a parent who willfully fails to seek and accept employment may be held in criminal contempt. Additionally, inability to comply with a child support order is an affirmative defense, and thus the petitioner need not prove the nonsupporting parent's ability to pay.

§ 1219.5. Minors under 16 years of age; refusal to take oath; referral to probation officer; meeting with victim advocate; placement outside minor's home; sanctions

(a) Except as provided in subdivision (d), in any case in which a contempt consists of the refusal of a minor under 16 years of age to take the oath or to testify, before imposing any sanction for the contempt, the court shall first refer the matter to the probation officer in charge of matters coming before the juvenile court for a report and recommendation as to the appropriateness of the imposition of a sanction. The probation officer shall prepare and file the report and recommendation within the time directed by the court. In making the report and recommendation, the probation officer shall consider factors such as the maturity of the minor, the reasons for the minor's refusal to take the oath or to testify, the probability that available sanctions will affect the decision of the minor not to take the oath or not to testify, the potential impact on the minor of his or her testimony, the potential impact on the pending litigation of the minor's unavailability as a witness, and the appropriateness of the various available sanctions in the minor's case. The court shall consider the report and recommendation in imposing a sanction in the case.

(b) A victim of a sex crime who is subject to subdivision (a) shall meet with a victim advocate, as defined in Section 679.04 of the Penal Code, unless the court, for good cause, finds that it is not in the best interest of the victim.

(c) In any case in which the court orders the minor to be placed outside of his or her home, the placement shall be in the least restrictive setting available. Except as provided in subdivision (e), the court shall not order the minor to be placed in a secure facility unless other placements have been made and the minor has fled the custody and control of the person under the control of whom he or she has been placed or has persistently refused to obey the reasonable and proper orders or directions of the person under the control of whom he or she has been placed.

(d) The court may impose a sanction for contempt prior to receipt of the report and recommendation required by subdivision (a) if the court enters a finding, supported by specific facts stated on the record, that the minor would be likely to flee if released before the receipt of the report and recommendation.

(e) The court may order the minor placed in a secure facility without first attempting the nonsecure placement required by subdivision (c) if the court enters a finding, supported by specific facts stated on the record, that the minor would be likely to flee if released to nonsecure placement as a prerequisite to secure confinement. *(Added by Stats.1984, c. 1643, § 1. Amended by Stats.2012, c. 223 (S.B.1248), § 1.)*

Research References

Treatises and Practice Aids

Witkin, California Summary 10th Parent and Child § 284, Trial.

§ 1220. Nonappearance; alias warrant; enforcement of undertaking; damages

When the warrant of arrest has been returned served, if the person arrested does not appear on the return day, the court or judge may issue another warrant of arrest or may order the undertaking to be enforced, or both. If the undertaking is enforced, the measure of damages is the extent of the loss or injury sustained by the aggrieved party by reason of the misconduct for which the warrant was issued. *(Enacted in 1872. Amended by Stats.1933, c. 745, p. 1907, § 18; Stats. 1951, c. 1737, p. 2143, § 169, operative Jan. 1, 1952; Stats. 1982, c. 517, p. 2362, § 181.)*

Law Revision Commission Comments

1982 Amendment

Section 1220 is amended to delete a provision duplicated in the Bond and Undertaking Law and for consistency with the provisions of the Law. See Sections 996.410–996.495 (liability of principal and sureties) and 996.460 (judgment of liability). [16 Cal.L.Rev.Comm. Reports 501 (1982)].

§ 1221. Illness for excuse for not bringing in prisoner; unnecessary restraint

Whenever, by the provisions of this title, an officer is required to keep a person arrested on a warrant of attachment in custody, and to bring him before a court or judge, the inability, from illness or otherwise, of the person to attend, is a sufficient excuse for not bringing him up; and the officer must not confine a person arrested upon the warrant in a prison, or otherwise restrain him of personal liberty, except so far as may be necessary to secure his personal attendance. *(Enacted in 1872. Amended by Stats.1933, c. 745, p. 1907, § 19; Stats.1951, c. 1737, p. 4143, § 170, operative Jan. 1, 1952.)*

§ 1222. Conclusiveness of judgments and orders

The judgment and orders of the court or judge, made in cases of contempt, are final and conclusive. *(Enacted in 1872. Amended by Stats.1933, c. 745, p. 1908, § 20; Stats. 1951, c. 1737, p. 4143, § 171, operative Jan. 1, 1952.)*

Commentary

Section 1222 has been construed by California courts to bar ordinary review; thus an incarcerated contemner must file a petition for writ of habeas corpus. *In re Buckely, 10 Cal.3d 237, 258–259, 514 P.2d 1201, 110 Cal.Rptr. 121 (1973)*. Similarly, because the order is final and conclusive, California courts have concluded that it may not be amended, nor may a proceeding which resulted in an annulled order be remanded for further proceedings. *In re John F. Baroldi, 189 Cal.App.3d 101, 234 Cal.Rptr. 286 (1987)*. Nevertheless, *In re Kreitman, 40 Cal.App.4th 750, 47 Cal.Rptr.2d 595 (1995)*, remanded to the trial court a 210 day contempt order, which unlawfully exceeded the 180 day limit permissible without waiver of a jury trial, and directed the trial court to reduce the unlawful 210 day order to the 180 day federal constitutional limit.

Title 8

CHANGE OF NAMES

§ 1275. Jurisdiction

Applications for change of names must be determined by the Superior Courts. *(Enacted in 1872. Amended by Code Am.1880, c. 113, p. 117, § 1; Stats.1983, c. 486, § 1.)*

Research References

Forms

West's California Judicial Council Forms NC-100, Petition for Change Of Name.

West's California Judicial Council Forms NC-110, Attachment to Petition for Change Of Name.

West's California Judicial Council Forms NC-200, Petition for Change Of Name and Gender.

West's California Judicial Council Forms NC-220, Order to Show Cause for Change Of Name.

West's California Judicial Council Forms NC-110G, Supplemental Attachment to Petition for Change Of Name (Declaration Of Guardian).

Treatises and Practice Aids

Witkin, California Summary 10th Husband and Wife § 20, After Judgment Of Dissolution or Nullity.

Witkin, California Summary 10th Parent and Child § 46, in General.

Witkin, California Summary 10th Personal Property § 24, Right to Change Name.

Witkin, California Summary 10th Personal Property § 25A, (New) Right to Maintain or Change Name Following Marriage or Domestic Partnership Registration.

§ 1276. Application or petition; venue; contents

(a) All applications for change of names shall be made to the superior court of the county where the person whose name is proposed to be changed resides, except as specified in subdivision (e), either (1) by petition signed by the person or, if the person is under 18 years of age, either by one of the person's parents, or by any guardian of the person, or if both parents are dead and there is no guardian of the person, then by some near relative or friend of the person or (2) as provided in Section 7638 of the Family Code.

The petition or pleading shall specify the place of birth and residence of the person, his or her present name, the name proposed, and the reason for the change of name.

(b) In a proceeding for a change of name commenced by the filing of a petition, if the person whose name is to be changed is under 18 years of age, the petition shall, if neither parent of the person has signed the petition, name, as far as known to the person proposing the name change, the parents of the person and their place of residence, if living, or if neither parent is living, near relatives of the person, and their place of residence.

(c) In a proceeding for a change of name commenced by the filing of a petition, if the person whose name is proposed to be changed is under 18 years of age and the petition is signed by only one parent, the petition shall specify the address, if known, of the other parent if living. If the petition is signed by a guardian, the petition shall specify the name and address, if known, of the parent or parents, if living, or the grandparents, if the addresses of both parents are unknown or if both parents are deceased, of the person whose name is proposed to be changed.

(d) In a proceeding for a change of name commenced by the filing of a petition, if the person whose name is proposed to be changed is 12 years of age or older, has been relinquished to an adoption agency by his or her parent or parents, and has not been legally adopted, the petition shall be signed by the person and the adoption agency to which the person was relinquished. The near relatives of the person and their place of residence shall not be included in the petition unless they are known to the person whose name is proposed to be changed.

(e) All petitions for the change of the name of a minor submitted by a guardian appointed by the juvenile court or the probate court shall be made in the appointing court.

(f) If the petition is signed by a guardian, the petition shall specify relevant information regarding the guardianship, the likelihood that the child will remain under the guardian's care until the child reaches the age of majority, and information suggesting that the child will not likely be returned to the custody of his or her parents. *(Enacted in 1872. Amended by Code Am.1877–78, c. 413, p. 110, § 1; Code Am.1880, c. 113, p. 117, § 2; Stats.1885, c. 128, p. 112, § 1; Stats.1929, c. 710, p. 1260, § 1; Stats.1945, c. 842, p. 1540, § 1; Stats.1961, c. 1817, p. 3864, § 1; Stats.1970, c. 651, p. 1276, § 1; Stats.1971, c. 1748, p. 3748, § 30; Stats.1975, c. 1241, p. 3192, § 9; Stats.1989, c. 1105, § 9; Stats.1992, c. 163 (A.B.2641), § 59, operative Jan. 1, 1994; Stats.2000, c. 111 (A.B.2155), § 1; Stats.2006, c. 567 (A.B.2303), § 10.)*

Law Revision Commission Comments

1992 Amendment

Section 1276 is amended to substitute a reference to the Family Code provision that replaced former Civil Code Section 7007(d). [22 Cal.L.Rev.Comm.Reports 1 (1992)].

Research References

Forms

West's California Code Forms, Civil Procedure § 1276 Form 1, Change Of Name--Petition for Change Of Name (Change Of Name)--Official Form.

Treatises and Practice Aids

Witkin, California Summary 10th Parent and Child § 109, in General.

Witkin, California Summary 10th Parent and Child § 292, Common Law Rule Against Change.

Witkin, California Summary 10th Personal Property § 24, Right to Change Name.

§ 1277. Orders to show cause; publication or posting; petitions for minors; exemptions; service of notice

Section operative until Sept. 1, 2018. See, also, § 1277 operative Sept. 1, 2018.

(a)(1) If a proceeding for a change of name is commenced by the filing of a petition, except as provided in subdivisions (b), (c), and (e), the court shall thereupon make an order reciting the filing of the petition, the name of the person by whom it is filed, and the name proposed. The order shall direct all persons interested in the matter to appear before the court at a time and place specified, which shall be not less than 6 weeks nor more than 12 weeks from the time of making the order, unless the court orders a different time, to show cause why the application for change of name should not be granted. The order shall direct all persons interested in the matter to make known any objection that they may have to the granting of the petition for change of name by filing a written objection, which includes the reasons for the objection, with the court at least two court days before the matter is scheduled to be heard and by appearing in court at the hearing to show cause why the petition for change of name should not be granted. The order shall state that, if no written objection is timely filed, the court may grant the petition without a hearing. If the petition seeks to conform the petitioner's name to * * * the petitioner's gender identity and no objection is timely filed, the court shall grant the petition without a hearing.

(2) A copy of the order to show cause shall be published pursuant to Section 6064 of the Government Code in a newspaper of general circulation to be designated in the order published in the county. If a newspaper of general circulation is not published in the county, a copy of the order to show cause shall be posted by the clerk of the court in three of the most public places in the county in which the court is located, for a like period. Proof shall be made to the satisfaction of the court of this publication or posting at the time of the hearing of the application.

(3) Four weekly publications shall be sufficient publication of the order to show cause. If the order is published in a daily newspaper, publication once a week for four successive weeks shall be sufficient.

(4) If a petition has been filed for a minor by a parent and the other parent, if living, does not join in consenting thereto, the petitioner shall cause, not less than 30 days before the hearing, to be served notice of the time and place of the hearing or a copy of the order to show cause on the other parent pursuant to Section 413.10, 414.10, 415.10, or 415.40. If notice of the hearing cannot reasonably be accomplished pursuant to Section 415.10 or 415.40, the court may order that notice be given in a manner that the court determines is reasonably calculated to give actual notice to the nonconsenting parent. In that case, if the court determines that notice by publication is reasonably calculated to give actual notice to the nonconsenting parent, the court may determine that publication of the order to show cause pursuant to this subdivision is sufficient notice to the nonconsenting parent.

(5) If the petition for a change of name is sought in order to conform the petitioner's name to * * * the petitioner's gender identity, the action for a change of name is exempt from the requirement for publication of the order to show cause under this subdivision.

(b)(1) If the petition for a change of name alleges a reason or circumstance described in paragraph (2), and the petitioner has established that * * * the petitioner is an active participant in the address confidentiality program created pursuant to Chapter 3.1 (commencing with Section 6205) of Division 7 of Title 1 of the Government Code, and that the name * * * the petitioner is seeking to acquire is on file with the Secretary of State, the action for a change of name is exempt from the requirement for publication of the order to show cause under subdivision (a), and the petition and the order of the court shall, in lieu of reciting the proposed name, indicate that the proposed name is confidential and is on file with the Secretary of State pursuant to the provisions of the address confidentiality program.

(2) The procedure described in paragraph (1) applies to petitions alleging any of the following reasons or circumstances:

(A) To avoid domestic violence, as defined in Section 6211 of the Family Code.

(B) To avoid stalking, as defined in Section 646.9 of the Penal Code.

(C) The petitioner is, or is filing on behalf of, a victim of sexual assault, as defined in Section 1036.2 of the Evidence Code.

(3) For any petition under this subdivision, the current legal name of the petitioner shall be kept confidential by the court and shall not be published or posted in the court's calendars, indexes, or register of actions, as required by Article 7 (commencing with Section 69840) of Chapter 5 of Title 8 of the Government Code, or by any means or in any public forum, including a hardcopy or an electronic copy, or any other type of public media or display.

(4) Notwithstanding paragraph (3), the court may, at the request of the petitioner, issue an order reciting the name of the petitioner at the time of the filing of the petition and the new legal name of the petitioner as a result of the court's granting of the petition.

(5) A petitioner may request that the court file the petition and any other papers associated with the proceeding under seal. The court may consider the request at the same time as the petition for name change, and may grant the request in any case in which the court finds that all of the following factors apply:

(A) There exists an overriding interest that overcomes the right of public access to the record.

(B) The overriding interest supports sealing the record.

(C) A substantial probability exists that the overriding interest will be prejudiced if the record is not sealed.

(D) The proposed order to seal the records is narrowly tailored.

(E) No less restrictive means exist to achieve the overriding interest.

(c) A proceeding for a change of name for a witness participating in the state Witness Relocation and Assistance Program established by Title 7.5 (commencing with Section 14020) of Part 4 of the Penal Code who has been approved for the change of name by the program is exempt from the requirement for publication of the order to show cause under subdivision (a).

(d) If an application for change of name is brought as part of an action under the Uniform Parentage Act (Part 3 (commencing with Section 7600) of Division 12 of the Family Code), whether as part of a petition or cross-complaint or as a separate order to show cause in a pending action thereunder, service of the application shall be made upon all other parties to the action in a like manner as prescribed for the service of a summons, as set forth in Article 3 (commencing with Section 415.10) of Chapter 4 of Title 5 of Part 2. Upon the setting of a hearing on the issue, notice of the hearing shall be given to all parties in the action in a like manner and within the time limits prescribed generally for the type of hearing (whether trial or order to show cause) at which the issue of the change of name is to be decided.

(e) If a guardian files a petition to change the name of * * * the guardian's minor ward pursuant to Section 1276:

(1) The guardian shall provide notice of the hearing to any living parent of the minor by personal service at least 30 days before the hearing.

(2) If either or both parents are deceased or cannot be located, the guardian shall cause, not less than 30 days before the hearing, to be served a notice of the time and place of the hearing or a copy of the order to show cause on the child's grandparents, if living, pursuant to Section 413.10, 414.10, 415.10, or 415.40.

(f) This section shall become operative on July 1, 2014, shall become inoperative on September 1, 2018, and shall be repealed on January 1, 2019. *(Added by Stats.2013, c. 651 (A.B.1121), § 2, operative July 1, 2014. Amended by Stats. 2014, c. 49 (S.B.545), § 1, eff. Jan. 1, 2015; Stats.2015, c. 303 (A.B.731), § 41, eff. Jan. 1, 2016; Stats.2017, c. 853 (S.B.179), § 3, eff. Jan. 1, 2018.)*

Inoperative Date and Repeal

For inoperative date and repeal of this section, see its terms.

Research References

Forms

West's California Judicial Council Forms NC-120, Order to Show Cause for Change Of Name (Change Of Name).

West's California Judicial Council Forms NC-121, Proof Of Service Of Order to Show Cause.

West's California Judicial Council Forms NC-400, Confidential Cover Sheet-Name Change Proceeding Under Address Confidentiality Program (Safe at Home).

West's California Judicial Council Forms NC-410, Application to File Documents Under Seal in Name Change Proceeding Under Address Confidentiality Program (Safe at Home).

West's California Judicial Council Forms NC-420, Declaration in Support Of Application to File Documents Under Seal in Name Change Proceeding Under Address Confidentiality Program (Safe at Home).

West's California Judicial Council Forms NC-425, Order on Application to File Documents Under Seal in Name Change Proceeding Under Address Confidentiality Program (Safe at Home).

West's California Judicial Council Forms NC-400-INFO, Information Sheet for Name Change Proceedings Under Address Confidentiality Program (Safe at Home).

Treatises and Practice Aids

Witkin, California Summary 10th Parent and Child § 46, in General.

§ 1277. Orders to show cause; publication or posting; petitions for minors; exemptions; service of notice

Section operative Sept. 1, 2018. See, also, § 1277 operative until Sept. 1, 2018.

(a)(1) If a proceeding for a change of name is commenced by the filing of a petition, except as provided in subdivisions (b), (c), and (e), or Section 1277.5, the court shall thereupon make an order reciting the filing of the petition, the name of the person by whom it is filed, and the name proposed. The order shall direct all persons interested in the matter to appear before the court at a time and place specified, which shall be not less than 6 weeks nor more than 12 weeks from the time of making the order, unless the court orders a different time, to show cause why the application for change of name should not be granted. The order shall direct all persons interested in the matter to make known any objection that they may have to the granting of the petition for change of name by filing a written objection, which includes the reasons for the objection, with the court at least two court days before the matter is scheduled to be heard and by appearing in court at the hearing to show cause why the petition for change of name should not be granted. The order shall state that, if no written objection is timely filed, the court may grant the petition without a hearing.

(2) A copy of the order to show cause shall be published pursuant to Section 6064 of the Government Code in a newspaper of general circulation to be designated in the order published in the county. If a newspaper of general circulation is not published in the county, a copy of the order to show cause shall be posted by the clerk of the court in three of the most public places in the county in which the court is located, for a like period. Proof shall be made to the satisfaction of the court of this publication or posting at the time of the hearing of the application.

(3) Four weekly publications shall be sufficient publication of the order to show cause. If the order is published in a daily newspaper, publication once a week for four successive weeks shall be sufficient.

(4) If a petition has been filed for a minor by a parent and the other parent, if living, does not join in consenting thereto, the petitioner shall cause, not less than 30 days before the hearing, to be served notice of the time and place of the hearing or a copy of the order to show cause on the other parent pursuant to Section 413.10, 414.10, 415.10, or 415.40. If notice of the hearing cannot reasonably be accomplished pursuant to Section 415.10 or 415.40, the court may order that notice be given in a manner that the court determines is reasonably calculated to give actual notice to the nonconsenting parent. In that case, if the court determines that notice by publication is reasonably calculated to give actual notice to the nonconsenting parent, the court may determine that publication of the order to show cause pursuant to this subdivision is sufficient notice to the nonconsenting parent.

(b)(1) If the petition for a change of name alleges a reason or circumstance described in paragraph (2), and the petitioner has established that the petitioner is an active participant in the address confidentiality program created pursuant to Chapter 3.1 (commencing with Section 6205) of Division 7 of Title 1 of the Government Code, and that the name the petitioner is seeking to acquire is on file with the Secretary of State, the action for a change of name is exempt from the requirement for publication of the order to show cause under subdivision (a), and the petition and the order of the court shall, in lieu of reciting the proposed name, indicate that the proposed name is confidential and is on file with the Secretary of State pursuant to the provisions of the address confidentiality program.

(2) The procedure described in paragraph (1) applies to petitions alleging any of the following reasons or circumstances:

(A) To avoid domestic violence, as defined in Section 6211 of the Family Code.

(B) To avoid stalking, as defined in Section 646.9 of the Penal Code.

(C) The petitioner is, or is filing on behalf of, a victim of sexual assault, as defined in Section 1036.2 of the Evidence Code.

(3) For any petition under this subdivision, the current legal name of the petitioner shall be kept confidential by the court and shall not be published or posted in the court's calendars, indexes, or register of actions, as required by Article 7 (commencing with Section 69840) of Chapter 5 of Title 8 of the Government Code, or by any means or in any public forum, including a hardcopy or an electronic copy, or any other type of public media or display.

(4) Notwithstanding paragraph (3), the court may, at the request of the petitioner, issue an order reciting the name of the petitioner at the time of the filing of the petition and the new legal name of the petitioner as a result of the court's granting of the petition.

(5) A petitioner may request that the court file the petition and any other papers associated with the proceeding under seal. The court may consider the request at the same time as the petition for name change, and may grant the request in any case in which the court finds that all of the following factors apply:

(A) There exists an overriding interest that overcomes the right of public access to the record.

(B) The overriding interest supports sealing the record.

(C) A substantial probability exists that the overriding interest will be prejudiced if the record is not sealed.

(D) The proposed order to seal the records is narrowly tailored.

(E) No less restrictive means exist to achieve the overriding interest.

(c) A proceeding for a change of name for a witness participating in the state Witness Relocation and Assistance Program established by Title 7.5 (commencing with Section 14020) of Part 4 of the Penal Code who has been approved for the change of name by the program is exempt from the requirement for publication of the order to show cause under subdivision (a).

(d) If an application for change of name is brought as part of an action under the Uniform Parentage Act (Part 3 (commencing with Section 7600) of Division 12 of the Family Code), whether as part of a petition or cross-complaint or as a separate order to show cause in a pending action thereunder, service of the application shall be made upon all other parties to the action in a like manner as prescribed for the service of a summons, as set forth in Article 3 (commencing with Section 415.10) of Chapter 4 of Title 5 of Part 2. Upon the setting of a hearing on the issue, notice of the hearing shall be given to all parties in the action in a like manner and within the time limits prescribed generally for the type of hearing (whether trial or order to show cause) at which the issue of the change of name is to be decided.

(e) If a guardian files a petition to change the name of the guardian's minor ward pursuant to Section 1276:

(1) The guardian shall provide notice of the hearing to any living parent of the minor by personal service at least 30 days before the hearing.

(2) If either or both parents are deceased or cannot be located, the guardian shall cause, not less than 30 days before the hearing, to be served a notice of the time and place of the hearing or a copy of the order to show cause on the child's grandparents, if living, pursuant to Section 413.10, 414.10, 415.10, or 415.40.

(f) This section shall become operative on September 1, 2018. *(Added by Stats.2017, c. 853 (S.B.179), § 4, eff. Jan. 1, 2018, operative Sept. 1, 2018.)*

§ 1277.5. Petition for change of name to conform petitioner's name to petitioner's gender identity; objections; exemptions; hearings

Section operative Sept. 1, 2018.

(a)(1) If a proceeding for a change of name to conform the petitioner's name to the petitioner's gender identity is commenced by the filing of a petition, the court shall thereupon make an order reciting the filing of the petition, the name of the person by whom it is filed, and the name proposed. The order shall direct all persons interested in the matter to make known any objection to the change of name by filing a written objection, which includes any reasons for the objection, within six weeks of the making of the order, and shall state that if no objection showing good cause to oppose the name change is timely filed, the court shall, without hearing, enter the order that the change of name is granted.

(2) The proceeding for a change of name to conform the petitioner's name to the petitioner's gender identity is exempt from any requirement for publication.

(b) A hearing date shall not be set in the proceeding unless an objection is timely filed and shows good cause for opposing the name change. Objections based solely on concerns over the petitioner's actual gender identity shall not constitute good cause. At the hearing, the court may examine under oath any of the petitioners, remonstrants, or other persons touching the petition or application, and may make an order changing the name or dismissing the petition or application as the court may deem right and proper.

(c) This section shall become operative on September 1, 2018. *(Added by Stats.2017, c. 853 (S.B.179), § 5, eff. Jan. 1, 2018, operative Sept. 1, 2018.)*

§ 1278. Hearings; orders without hearings

Section operative until Sept. 1, 2018. See, also, § 1278 operative Sept. 1, 2018.

(a)(1) Except as provided in subdivisions (c) and (d), the petition or application shall be heard at the time designated by the court, only if objections are filed by a person who can, in those objections, show to the court good cause against the change of name. At the hearing, the court may examine on oath any of the petitioners, remonstrants, or other persons touching the petition or application, and may make an order changing the name, or dismissing the petition or application, as the court may seem right and proper.

(2) If no objection is filed at least two court days before the date set for hearing, the court may, without hearing, enter the order that the change of name is granted. If the petition seeks to conform the petitioner's name to * * * the petitioner's gender identity and no objection is timely filed, the court shall grant the petition without a hearing.

(b) If the provisions of subdivision (b) of Section 1277 apply, the court shall not disclose the proposed name unless the court finds by clear and convincing evidence that the allegations of domestic violence, stalking, sexual assault, or gender identity in the petition are false.

(c) If the application for a change of name is brought as part of an action under the Uniform Parentage Act (Part 3 (commencing with Section 7600) of Division 12 of the Family Code), the hearing on the issue of the change of name shall be conducted pursuant to statutes and rules of court governing those proceedings, whether the hearing is conducted upon an order to show cause or upon trial.

(d) If the petition for a change of name is filed by a guardian on behalf of a minor ward, the court shall first find that the ward is likely to remain in the guardian's care until the age of majority and that the ward is not likely to be returned to the custody of * * * the parents. Upon making those findings, the court shall consider the petition and may grant the petition only if it finds that the proposed name change is in the best interest of the child.

(e) This section shall become operative on July 1, 2014, shall become inoperative on September 1, 2018, and shall be repealed on January 1, 2019. *(Added by Stats.2013, c. 651 (A.B.1121), § 4, operative July 1, 2014. Amended by Stats. 2017, c. 853 (S.B.179), § 6, eff. Jan. 1, 2018.)*

Inoperative Date and Repeal

For inoperative date and repeal of this section, see its terms.

Research References

Forms

West's California Judicial Council Forms NC-130, Decree Changing Name (Change Of Name).

West's California Judicial Council Forms NC-230, Decree Changing Name and Gender.

West's California Judicial Council Forms NC-400, Confidential Cover Sheet-Name Change Proceeding Under Address Confidentiality Program (Safe at Home).

West's California Judicial Council Forms NC-130G, Decree Changing Name (Change Of Name Of Minor by Guardian).

West's California Judicial Council Forms NC-400-INFO, Information Sheet for Name Change Proceedings Under Address Confidentiality Program (Safe at Home).

Treatises and Practice Aids

Witkin, California Summary 10th Parent and Child § 46, in General.

§ 1278. Hearings; orders without hearings

Section operative Sept. 1, 2018. See, also, § 1278 operative until Sept. 1, 2018.

(a)(1) Except as provided in subdivisions (c) and (d), the petition or application shall be heard at the time designated by the court, only if objections are filed by a person who can, in those objections, show to the court good cause against the change of name. At the hearing, the court may examine on oath any of the petitioners, remonstrants, or other persons touching the petition or application, and may make an order changing the name, or dismissing the petition or application, as the court may deem right and proper.

(2) If no objection is filed at least two court days before the date set for hearing, the court may, without hearing, enter the order that the change of name is granted.

(b) If the provisions of subdivision (b) of Section 1277 apply, the court shall not disclose the proposed name unless the court finds by clear and convincing evidence that the allegations of domestic violence, stalking, or sexual assault in the petition are false.

(c) If the application for a change of name is brought as part of an action under the Uniform Parentage Act (Part 3 (commencing with Section 7600) of Division 12 of the Family Code), the hearing on the issue of the change of name shall be conducted pursuant to statutes and rules of court governing those proceedings, whether the hearing is conducted upon an order to show cause or upon trial.

(d) If the petition for a change of name is filed by a guardian on behalf of a minor ward, the court shall first find that the ward is likely to remain in the guardian's care until the age of majority and that the ward is not likely to be returned to the custody of the parents. Upon making those findings, the court shall consider the petition and may grant the petition only if it finds that the proposed name change is in the best interest of the child.

(e) This section shall become operative on September 1, 2018. *(Added by Stats.2017, c. 853 (S.B.179), § 7, eff. Jan. 1, 2018, operative Sept. 1, 2018.)*

§ 1278.5. Petitions relating to minors; absence of consent of both parents

In any proceeding pursuant to this title in which a petition has been filed to change the name of a minor, and both parents, if living, do not join in consent, the court may deny the petition in whole or in part if it finds that any portion of the proposed name change is not in the best interest of the child. *(Added by Stats.1996, c. 1061 (S.B.1033), § 2. Amended by Stats.2006, c. 567 (A.B.2303), § 13.)*

§ 1279.5. Name change; common law right; state prisoners, parolees and probationers; registered sex offenders

Section operative until Sept. 1, 2018. See, also, § 1279.5 operative Sept. 1, 2018.

(a) Except as provided in subdivision (b), (c), (d), or (e), nothing in this title shall be construed to abrogate the common law right of any person to change his or her name.

(b) Notwithstanding any other law, no person imprisoned in the state prison and under the jurisdiction of the Director of Corrections shall be allowed to file a petition for change of name pursuant to Section 1276, except as permitted at the discretion of the Director of Corrections.

(c) A court shall deny a petition for a name change pursuant to Section 1276 made by a person who is under the jurisdiction of the Department of Corrections, unless that person's parole agent or probation officer grants prior written approval. Before granting that approval, the parole agent or probation officer shall determine that the name change will not pose a security risk to the community.

(d) Notwithstanding any other law, a court shall deny a petition for a name change pursuant to Section 1276 made by a person who is required to register as a sex offender under Section 290 of the Penal Code, unless the court determines that it is in the best interest of justice to grant the petition and that doing so will not adversely affect the public safety. If a petition for a name change is granted for an individual required to register as a sex offender, the individual shall, within five working days, notify the chief of police of the city in which he or she is domiciled, or the sheriff of the county if he or she is domiciled in an unincorporated area, and additionally with the chief of police of a campus of a University of California or California State University if he or she is domiciled upon the campus or in any of its facilities.

(e) For the purpose of this section, the court shall use the California Law Enforcement Telecommunications System (CLETS) and Criminal Justice Information System (CJIS) to determine whether or not an applicant for a name change is under the jurisdiction of the Department of Corrections or is required to register as a sex offender pursuant to Section 290 of the Penal Code. Each person applying for a name change shall declare under penalty of perjury that he or she is not under the jurisdiction of the Department of Corrections or is required to register as a sex offender pursuant to Section 290 of the Penal Code. If a court is not equipped with CLETS or CJIS, the clerk of the court shall contact an appropriate local law enforcement agency, which shall determine whether or not the petitioner is under the jurisdiction of the Department of Corrections or is required to register as a sex offender pursuant to Section 290 of the Penal Code.

(f) This section shall become inoperative on September 1, 2018, and, as of January 1, 2019, is repealed. *(Added by Stats.1974, c. 1235, p. 2681, § 3. Amended by Stats.1975, c. 1070, p. 2616, § 3; Stats.1992, c. 163 (A.B.2641), § 62, operative Jan. 1, 1994; Stats.1994, c. 557 (A.B.2782), § 1; Stats.1996, c. 730 (A.B.2359), § 1; Stats.1997, c. 821 (A.B. 290), § 1, eff. Oct. 9, 1997; Stats.2006, c. 567 (A.B.2303), § 14; Stats.2017, c. 856 (S.B.310), § 2, eff. Jan. 1, 2018.)*

Inoperative Date and Repeal

For inoperative date and repeal of this section, see its terms.

Law Revision Commission Comments

1992 Amendment

Former subdivision (b) of Section 1279.5 is continued in Section 1279.6 without substantive change. [22 Cal.L.Rev.Comm.Reports 1 (1992)].

Research References

Treatises and Practice Aids

Witkin, California Summary 10th Personal Property § 24, Right to Change Name.

§ 1279.5. Name change; common law right; state prisoners; parolees and probationers; registered sex offenders

Section operative Sept. 1, 2018. See, also, § 1279.5 operative until Sept. 1, 2018.

(a) Except as provided in subdivision (e) or (f), this title does not abrogate the common law right of a person to change his or her name.

(b) A person under the jurisdiction of the Department of Corrections and Rehabilitation or sentenced to county jail has the right to petition the court to obtain a name or gender change pursuant to this title or Article 7 (commencing with Section 103425) of Chapter 11 of Part 1 of Division 102 of the Health and Safety Code.

(c) A person under the jurisdiction of the Department of Corrections and Rehabilitation shall provide a copy of the petition for a name change to the department, in a manner prescribed by the department, at the time the petition is filed. A person sentenced to county jail shall provide a copy of the petition for name change to the sheriff's department, in a manner prescribed by the department, at the time the petition is filed.

(d) In all documentation of a person under the jurisdiction of the Department of Corrections and Rehabilitation or imprisoned within a county jail, the new name of a person who obtains a name change shall be used, and prior names shall be listed as an alias.

(e) Notwithstanding any other law, a court shall deny a petition for a name change pursuant to this title made by a person who is required to register as a sex offender under Section 290 of the Penal Code, unless the court determines that it is in the best interest of justice to grant the petition and that doing so will not adversely affect the public safety. If a petition for a name change is granted for an individual required to register as a sex offender, the individual shall, within five working days, notify the chief of police of the city in which he or she is domiciled, or the sheriff of the county if he or she is domiciled in an unincorporated area, and additionally with the chief of police of a campus of a University of California or California State University if he or she is domiciled upon the campus or in any of its facilities.

(f) For the purpose of this section, the court shall use the California Law Enforcement Telecommunications System (CLETS) and Criminal Justice Information System (CJIS) to determine whether or not an applicant for a name change is required to register as a sex offender pursuant to Section 290 of the Penal Code. Each person applying for a name change shall declare under penalty of perjury that he or she is not required to register as a sex offender pursuant to Section 290 of the Penal Code. If a court is not equipped with CLETS or CJIS, the clerk of the court shall contact an appropriate local law enforcement agency, which shall determine whether or not the petitioner is required to register as a sex offender pursuant to Section 290 of the Penal Code.

(g) This section shall become operative on September 1, 2018. *(Added by Stats.2017, c. 856 (S.B.310), § 3, eff. Jan. 1, 2018, operative Sept. 1, 2018.)*

§ 1279.6. Trade or business; doing business or providing services; prohibitions

No person engaged in a trade or business of any kind or in the provision of a service of any kind shall do any of the following:

(a) Refuse to do business with a person, or refuse to provide the service to a person, regardless of the person's marital status, because he or she has chosen to use or regularly uses his or her birth name, former name, or name adopted upon solemnization of marriage or registration of domestic partnership.

(b) Impose, as a condition of doing business with a person, or as a condition of providing the service to a person, a requirement that the person, regardless of his or her marital status, use a name other than his or her birth name, former name, or name adopted upon solemnization of marriage or registration of domestic partnership, if the person has chosen to use or regularly uses that name. *(Added by Stats.1992, c. 163 (A.B.2641), § 63, operative Jan. 1, 1994. Amended by Stats.2007, c. 567 (A.B.102), § 3.)*

Law Revision Commission Comments

1992 Addition

Section 1279.6 continues without substantive change former subdivision (b) of Code of Civil Procedure Section 1279.5, former Civil Code Section 4362(d), and former Civil Code Section 4457(d). [22 Cal.L.Rev.Comm.Reports 1 (1992)].

Research References

Treatises and Practice Aids

Witkin, California Summary 10th Husband and Wife § 21, in Business Transactions.

Witkin, California Summary 10th Husband and Wife § 33, Other Rights.

Witkin, California Summary 10th Personal Property § 23, in General.

CORPORATIONS CODE

Title 2

PARTNERSHIPS

CHAPTER 5. UNIFORM PARTNERSHIP ACT OF 1994

ARTICLE 4. RELATIONS OF PARTNERS TO EACH OTHER AND TO PARTNERSHIP

§ 16401. Partner accounts; share of profits; reimbursements; conduct of partnership business; becoming a partner

(a) Each partner is deemed to have an account that is subject to both of the following:

(1) Credited with an amount equal to the money plus the value of any other property, net of the amount of any liabilities, the partner contributes to the partnership and the partner's share of the partnership profits.

(2) Subject to Sections 16306 and 16957, charged with an amount equal to the money plus the value of any other property, net of the amount of any liabilities, distributed by the partnership to the partner and the partner's share of the partnership losses.

(b) Each partner is entitled to an equal share of the partnership profits and, subject to Sections 16306 and 16957, is chargeable with a share of the partnership losses in proportion to the partner's share of the profits.

(c) A partnership shall reimburse a partner for payments made and indemnify a partner for liabilities incurred by the partner in the ordinary course of the business of the partnership or for the preservation of its business or property.

(d) A partnership shall reimburse a partner for an advance to the partnership beyond the amount of capital the partner agreed to contribute.

(e) A payment or advance made by a partner that gives rise to a partnership obligation under subdivision (c) or (d) constitutes a loan to the partnership that accrues interest from the date of the payment or advance.

(f) Each partner has equal rights in the management and conduct of the partnership business.

(g) A partner may use or possess partnership property only on behalf of the partnership.

(h) A partner is not entitled to remuneration for services performed for the partnership, except for reasonable compensation for services rendered in winding up the business of the partnership.

(i) A person may become a partner only with the consent of all of the partners.

(j) A difference arising as to a matter in the ordinary course of business of a partnership may be decided by a majority of the partners. An act outside the ordinary course of business of a partnership and an amendment to the partnership agreement may be undertaken only with the consent of all of the partners.

(k) This section does not affect the obligations of a partnership to other persons under Section 16301. *(Added by Stats.1996, c. 1003 (A.B.583), § 2.)*

Research References

Forms

California Transactions Forms--Business Entities § 15:6, Centralized Management.

California Transactions Forms--Business Entities § 17:9, Acquisition Of Partnership Interest and Capital Contributions.

California Transactions Forms--Business Entities § 19:3, Rights Of Assignee.

California Transactions Forms--Business Entities § 19:5, Sale Of Interest by Partnership.

California Transactions Forms--Business Entities § 19:6, Agreement Admitting New Partner in General Partnership.

California Transactions Forms--Business Entities § 19:13, Agreement for Sale Of Partnership Interest With Consent by Remaining Partners.

California Transactions Forms--Business Entities § 17:10, Partnership Property.

California Transactions Forms--Business Entities § 17:12, Management Of Partnership Business.

California Transactions Forms--Business Entities § 17:14, Allocations, Distributions, Compensation and Benefits.

California Transactions Forms--Business Entities § 17:23, Transfer Of Partnership Interests.

California Transactions Forms--Business Entities § 17:24, Dissolution and Winding up.

California Transactions Forms--Business Entities § 17:41, Simple Partnership Agreement for Definite Term.

California Transactions Forms--Business Entities § 17:70, General Provision.

California Transactions Forms--Business Entities § 17:88, Equal Authority to Conduct Business.

California Transactions Forms--Business Entities § 17:89, Control by Majority in Number.

California Transactions Forms--Business Entities § 20:23, Rights Of RUPA General Partners.

California Transactions Forms--Business Entities § 20:29, Transfer Of Partnership Interest.

California Transactions Forms--Business Entities § 19:104, Structuring the Gift.

California Transactions Forms--Business Entities § 17:106, Division Of Duties.

California Transactions Forms--Business Entities § 17:120, for Specified Partners.
California Transactions Forms--Business Entities § 17:148, Payment and Indemnification Of Partnership for Separate Debts Of Partners.
California Transactions Forms--Business Entities § 17:151, Equal Sharing Of Profits and Losses.
California Transactions Forms--Business Entities § 17:166, Approval Of All Partners.
West's California Code Forms, Corporations § 200 Form 3, Checklist Of Factors to be Considered in Determining the Form Of Organization Of a Business Enterprise--Forms Of Business Organizations--General Partnership.

Treatises and Practice Aids

Witkin, California Summary 10th Equity § 181, Illustrations: Partnership Cases.
Witkin, California Summary 10th Partnership § 16, Organization.
Witkin, California Summary 10th Partnership § 27, Nature and Acquisition Of Property.
Witkin, California Summary 10th Partnership § 33, Rights and Entitlements Of Partners.
Witkin, California Summary 10th Partnership § 34, Actions Between Partners.
Witkin, California Summary 10th Partnership § 48, Effect Of Dissolution.

§ 16402. Distributions in kind

A partner has no right to receive, and may not be required to accept, a distribution in kind. *(Added by Stats.1996, c. 1003 (A.B.583), § 2.)*

Research References

Forms

California Transactions Forms--Business Entities § 17:14, Allocations, Distributions, Compensation and Benefits.

Treatises and Practice Aids

Witkin, California Summary 10th Partnership § 33, Rights and Entitlements Of Partners.
Witkin, California Summary 10th Partnership § 34, Actions Between Partners.

§ 16403. Books and records; right of access

(a) A partnership shall keep its books and records, if any, in writing or in any other form capable of being converted into clearly legible tangible form, at its chief executive office.

(b) A partnership shall provide partners and their agents and attorneys access to its books and records. It shall provide former partners and their agents and attorneys access to books and records pertaining to the period during which they were partners. The right of access provides the opportunity to inspect and copy books and records during ordinary business hours. A partnership may impose a reasonable charge, covering the costs of labor and material, for copies of documents furnished.

(c) Each partner and the partnership shall furnish to a partner, and to the legal representative of a deceased partner or partner under legal disability, both of the following, which may be transmitted by electronic transmission by the partnership (subdivision (4) of Section 16101):

(1) Without demand, any information concerning the partnership's business and affairs reasonably required for the proper exercise of the partner's rights and duties under the partnership agreement or this chapter; and

(2) On demand, any other information concerning the partnership's business and affairs, except to the extent the demand or the information demanded is unreasonable or otherwise improper under the circumstances. *(Added by Stats.1996, c. 1003 (A.B.583), § 2. Amended by Stats.2004, c. 254 (S.B.1306), § 45.)*

Research References

Forms

California Transactions Forms--Business Entities § 2:3, Fiduciary Duty Considerations.
California Transactions Forms--Business Entities § 17:6, Overview Of Partnership Agreement.
California Transactions Forms--Business Entities § 17:15, Books and Records; Accounting.
California Transactions Forms--Business Entities § 17:41, Simple Partnership Agreement for Definite Term.
California Transactions Forms--Business Entities § 21:39, Complex Partnership Agreement for Legal LLP Based on Units.
California Transactions Forms--Business Entities § 17:113, Keeping and Inspecting Account Books.
California Transactions Forms--Business Entities § 17:114, Access to and Right to Audit Books and Papers.
California Transactions Forms--Business Entities § 17:118, Accounting to Heirs or Representatives Of Deceased Partner.
California Transactions Forms--Business Entities § 12:35.40, Filings With Secretary Of State.

Treatises and Practice Aids

Witkin, California Summary 10th Community Property § 133, Statutory Requirement.
Witkin, California Summary 10th Corporations § 42, Inspection Of Records.
Witkin, California Summary 10th Partnership § 19, Partnership Agreement.
Witkin, California Summary 10th Partnership § 33, Rights and Entitlements Of Partners.
Witkin, California Summary 10th Partnership § 34, Actions Between Partners.
Witkin, California Summary 10th Wills and Probate § 487, Decedent's Partnership Business.

§ 16404. Fiduciary duties

(a) The fiduciary duties a partner owes to the partnership and the other partners are the duty of loyalty and the duty of care set forth in subdivisions (b) and (c).

(b) A partner's duty of loyalty to the partnership and the other partners includes all of the following:

(1) To account to the partnership and hold as trustee for it any property, profit, or benefit derived by the partner in the conduct and winding up of the partnership business or derived from a use by the partner of partnership property or information, including the appropriation of a partnership opportunity.

(2) To refrain from dealing with the partnership in the conduct or winding up of the partnership business as or on behalf of a party having an interest adverse to the partnership.

(3) To refrain from competing with the partnership in the conduct of the partnership business before the dissolution of the partnership.

(c) A partner's duty of care to the partnership and the other partners in the conduct and winding up of the partnership business is limited to refraining from engaging in grossly negligent or reckless conduct, intentional misconduct, or a knowing violation of law.

(d) A partner shall discharge the duties to the partnership and the other partners under this chapter or under the partnership agreement and exercise any rights consistently with the obligation of good faith and fair dealing.

(e) A partner does not violate a duty or obligation under this chapter or under the partnership agreement merely because the partner's conduct furthers the partner's own interest.

(f) A partner may lend money to and transact other business with the partnership, and as to each loan or transaction, the rights and obligations of the partner regarding performance or enforcement are the same as those of a person who is not a partner, subject to other applicable law.

(g) This section applies to a person winding up the partnership business as the personal or legal representative of the last surviving partner as if the person were a partner. *(Added by Stats.1996, c. 1003 (A.B.583), § 2.)*

Research References

Forms

California Transactions Forms--Business Entities § 2:3, Fiduciary Duty Considerations.
California Transactions Forms--Business Entities § 17:6, Overview Of Partnership Agreement.
California Transactions Forms--Business Entities § 20:1, General Partnership Defined; Governing Law.
California Transactions Forms--Business Entities § 17:13, Fiduciary Duties Of Partners.
California Transactions Forms--Business Entities § 17:15, Books and Records; Accounting.
California Transactions Forms--Business Entities § 17:21, Consequences Of Dissociation; Statement Of Dissociation.
California Transactions Forms--Business Entities § 20:25, Fiduciary Duties Of RUPA General Partners.
California Transactions Forms--Business Entities § 19:112, Consequences Of Dissociation.
California Transactions Forms--Business Entities § 17:110, Fiduciary Duties Of Partners.
California Transactions Forms--Business Entities § 17:186, Expulsion Of Partner Generally.
West's California Code Forms, Corporations § 200 Form 3, Checklist Of Factors to be Considered in Determining the Form Of Organization Of a Business Enterprise--Forms Of Business Organizations--General Partnership.

Treatises and Practice Aids

Witkin, California Summary 10th Community Property § 133, Statutory Requirement.
Witkin, California Summary 10th Partnership § 15, Statutory Development.
Witkin, California Summary 10th Partnership § 19, Partnership Agreement.
Witkin, California Summary 10th Partnership § 30, Fiduciary Relationship.
Witkin, California Summary 10th Partnership § 31, Good Faith and Fair Dealing.
Witkin, California Summary 10th Partnership § 32, Permissible Partner Activity.
Witkin, California Summary 10th Partnership § 34, Actions Between Partners.
Witkin, California Summary 10th Partnership § 43, Expulsion.
Witkin, California Summary 10th Partnership § 44, Effect Of Dissociation.
Witkin, California Summary 10th Partnership § 62, Statutory Development.
Witkin, California Summary 10th Partnership § 121A, (New) Adoption and Effect.

§ 16405. Breach of partnership agreement; violation of duty; action by partnership against partner

(a) A partnership may maintain an action against a partner for a breach of the partnership agreement, or for the violation of a duty to the partnership, causing harm to the partnership.

(b) A partner may maintain an action against the partnership or another partner for legal or equitable relief, with or without an accounting as to partnership business, to do any of the following:

(1) Enforce the partner's rights under the partnership agreement.

(2) Enforce the partner's rights under this chapter, including all of the following:

(A) The partner's rights under Section 16401, 16403, or 16404.

(B) The partner's right on dissociation to have the partner's interest in the partnership purchased pursuant to Section 16701 or 16701.5, or to enforce any other right under Article 6 (commencing with Section 16601) or 7 (commencing with Section 16701).

(C) The partner's right to compel a dissolution and winding up of the partnership business under Section 16801 or enforce any other right under Article 8 (commencing with Section 16801).

(3) Enforce the rights and otherwise protect the interests of the partner, including rights and interests arising independently of the partnership relationship.

(c) The accrual of, and any time limitation on, a right of action for a remedy under this section is governed by other law. A right to an accounting upon a dissolution and winding up does not revive a claim barred by law. *(Added by Stats.1996, c. 1003 (A.B.583), § 2.)*

Research References

Forms

California Transactions Forms--Business Entities § 17:18, Actions Against Partners and Partnership.
California Transactions Forms--Business Entities § 19:113, Buyout Of Dissociated Partner.
West's California Code Forms, Corporations § 200 Form 3, Checklist Of Factors to be Considered in Determining the Form Of Organization Of a Business Enterprise--Forms Of Business Organizations--General Partnership.

Treatises and Practice Aids

Witkin, California Summary 10th Partnership § 23, Distinct Entity.
Witkin, California Summary 10th Partnership § 34, Actions Between Partners.
Witkin, California Summary 10th Partnership § 45, Buyout Of Dissociating Partner's Interest.

Witkin, California Summary 10th Partnership § 46, in General.

§ 16406. Continuation of partnership after expiration or completion

(a) If a partnership for a definite term or particular undertaking is continued, without an express agreement, after the expiration of the term or completion of the undertaking, the rights and duties of the partners remain the same as they were at the expiration or completion, so far as is consistent with a partnership at will.

(b) If the partners, or those of them who habitually acted in the business during the term or undertaking, continue the business without any settlement or liquidation of the partnership, they are presumed to have agreed that the partnership will continue. *(Added by Stats.1996, c. 1003 (A.B.583), § 2.)*

Research References

Forms

California Transactions Forms--Business Entities § 17:8, Duration Of Partnership.

California Transactions Forms--Business Entities § 17:24, Dissolution and Winding up.

California Transactions Forms--Business Entities § 17:61, Partnership for Definite Term With Election to Terminate.

California Transactions Forms--Business Entities § 20:22, General Partnership Terms Under RUPA.

Treatises and Practice Aids

Witkin, California Summary 10th Partnership § 30, Fiduciary Relationship.

Witkin, California Summary 10th Partnership § 33, Rights and Entitlements Of Partners.

ARTICLE 5. TRANSFEREES AND CREDITORS OF PARTNER

§ 16503. Transfer of transferable interest; effects

(a) A transfer, in whole or in part, of a partner's transferable interest in the partnership is permissible. However, a transfer does not do either of the following:

(1) By itself cause the partner's dissociation or a dissolution and winding up of the partnership business.

(2) As against the other partners or the partnership, entitle the transferee, during the continuance of the partnership, to participate in the management or conduct of the partnership business, to require access to information concerning partnership transactions, or to inspect or copy the partnership books or records.

(b) A transferee of a partner's transferable interest in the partnership has a right to all of the following:

(1) To receive, in accordance with the transfer, distributions to which the transferor would otherwise be entitled.

(2) To receive upon the dissolution and winding up of the partnership business, in accordance with the transfer, the net amount otherwise distributable to the transferor.

(3) To seek under paragraph (6) of Section 16801 a judicial determination that it is equitable to wind up the partnership business.

(c) In a dissolution and winding up, a transferee is entitled to an account of partnership transactions only from the date of the latest account agreed to by all of the partners.

(d) Upon transfer, the transferor retains the rights and duties of a partner other than the interest in distributions transferred.

(e) A partnership need not give effect to a transferee's rights under this section until it has notice of the transfer.

(f) A transfer of a partner's transferable interest in the partnership in violation of a restriction on transfer contained in the partnership agreement is ineffective as to a person having notice of the restriction at the time of transfer. *(Added by Stats.1996, c. 1003 (A.B.583), § 2.)*

Research References

Forms

California Transactions Forms--Business Entities § 19:2, Right to Sell Partnership Interest.

California Transactions Forms--Business Entities § 19:3, Rights Of Assignee.

California Transactions Forms--Business Entities § 19:61, Assignment Of Deceased Partner's Interest.

California Transactions Forms--Business Entities § 19:71, Purpose Of Buy-Sell Agreements.

California Transactions Forms--Business Entities § 17:23, Transfer Of Partnership Interests.

California Transactions Forms--Business Entities § 17:33, Termination Of Partnership for Tax Purposes.

California Transactions Forms--Business Entities § 17:41, Simple Partnership Agreement for Definite Term.

California Transactions Forms--Business Entities § 19:57, Transfer to Heirs at Death.

California Transactions Forms--Business Entities § 20:29, Transfer Of Partnership Interest.

California Transactions Forms--Business Entities § 17:103, Restriction on Assignment Of Partnership Interest.

California Transactions Forms--Business Entities § 17:166, Approval Of All Partners.

Cal. Transaction Forms - Bus. Transactions § 16:36, Assignment Of Ownership Interests in Partnerships, Limited Liability Companies, and Corporations.

Cal. Transaction Forms - Bus. Transactions § 16:56, Partnership Interest.

California Transactions Forms--Estate Planning § 9:44, Impact on Valuation Discounts for Partnerships and LLCS.

California Transactions Forms--Estate Planning § 9:46, Impact on Valuation Discounts for Partnerships and LLCS.

California Transactions Forms--Estate Planning § 20:51, Specific Devise Of General Partnership.

West's California Code Forms, Corporations § 200 Form 3, Checklist Of Factors to be Considered in Determining the Form Of Organization Of a Business Enterprise--Forms Of Business Organizations--General Partnership.

Treatises and Practice Aids

Witkin, California Summary 10th Community Property § 133, Statutory Requirement.

Witkin, California Summary 10th Partnership § 28, Interest Of Partner.

EDUCATION CODE

Title 1

GENERAL EDUCATION CODE PROVISIONS

Division 1

GENERAL EDUCATION CODE PROVISIONS

Part 13

STATE TEACHERS' RETIREMENT SYSTEM

CHAPTER 12. COMMUNITY PROPERTY

§ 22650. Marriage dissolution or legal separation; rights of nonmember spouses and nonmember registered domestic partners; termination or separation of domestic partnership

(a) This chapter establishes the power of a court in a dissolution of marriage or legal separation action with respect to community property rights in accounts with the plan under this part and establishes and defines the rights of nonmember spouses and nonmember registered domestic partners in the plan under this part.

(b) For purposes of this chapter, the termination, dissolution, or nullity of a registered domestic partnership, or the legal separation of partners in a registered domestic partnership, as provided in Section 299 of the Family Code, shall be treated in the same manner as a dissolution of marriage or legal separation of a member and his or her spouse. *(Added by Stats.1993, c. 893 (A.B.1796), § 2. Amended by Stats.1996, c. 634 (S.B.2041), § 118; Stats.1998, c. 965 (A.B.2765), § 59; Stats.2004, c. 912 (A.B.2233), § 6; Stats.2005, c. 418 (S.B. 973), § 4.)*

Research References

Forms

Nichols Cyclopedia of Legal Forms Annotated § 100:4, Dissolution or Termination Of Marital Relationship, Generally.

§ 22651. Nonmember spouse; treatment of domestic partner as nonmember spouse

(a) For purposes of this chapter and Section 23300, "nonmember spouse" means a member's spouse or former spouse, and also includes a member's registered domestic partner or former registered domestic partner, who is being or has been awarded a community property interest in the service credit, accumulated retirement contributions, accumulated Defined Benefit Supplement account balance, or benefits of the member under this part.

(b) For purposes of this chapter and Section 23300, a member's registered domestic partner or former registered domestic partner who is being or has been awarded a community property interest in the service credit, accumulated retirement contributions, accumulated Defined Benefit Supplement account balance, or benefits of the member under this part shall be treated in the same manner as a nonmember spouse.

(c) A nonmember spouse shall not be considered a member based upon his or her receipt of any of the following being awarded to the nonmember spouse as a result of legal separation or dissolution of marriage:

(1) A separate account of service credit and accumulated retirement contributions, a retirement allowance, or an interest in the member's retirement allowance under the Defined Benefit Program.

(2) A separate account based on the member's Defined Benefit Supplement account balance, a retirement benefit, or an interest in the member's retirement benefit under the Defined Benefit Supplement Program. *(Added by Stats.1993, c. 893 (A.B.1796), § 2. Amended by Stats.1996, c. 634 (S.B.2041), § 119; Stats.1998, c. 965 (A.B.2765), § 60; Stats. 2000, c. 74 (A.B.1509), § 33; Stats.2000, c. 1021 (A.B.2700), § 18; Stats.2004, c. 912 (A.B.2233), § 7; Stats.2005, c. 418 (S.B.973), § 5.)*

§ 22652. Court orders; division of contributions and service credits; community property rights

(a) Upon the legal separation or dissolution of marriage of a member, other than a retired member, the court shall include in the judgment or a court order the date on which the parties separated.

(b) The court may order in the judgment or court order that the member's accumulated retirement contributions and service credit under the Defined Benefit Program, or the member's Defined Benefit Supplement account balance, or both, under this part that are attributable to periods of service during the marriage be divided into two separate and distinct accounts in the name of the member and the nonmember spouse, respectively. Any service credit and accumulated retirement contributions under the Defined Benefit Program and any accumulated Defined Benefit Supplement account balance under this part that are not explicitly awarded by the judgment or court order shall be deemed the exclusive property of the member under the Defined Benefit Program or the Defined Benefit Supplement Program, as applicable.

(c) The determination of the court of community property rights pursuant to this section shall be consistent with this chapter and shall address the rights of the nonmember spouse under this part, including, but not limited to, the following:

(1) The right to a retirement allowance under the Defined Benefit Program and, if applicable, a retirement benefit under the Defined Benefit Supplement Program.

(2) The right to a refund of accumulated retirement contributions under the Defined Benefit Program and the return of the accumulated Defined Benefit Supplement account balance that were awarded to the nonmember spouse.

(3) The right to redeposit all or a portion of accumulated retirement contributions previously refunded to the member which the member is eligible to redeposit pursuant to Sections 23200 to 23203, inclusive, and shall specify the shares of the redeposit amount awarded to the member and the nonmember spouse.

(4) The right to purchase additional service credit that the member is eligible to purchase pursuant to Sections 22800 to 22810, inclusive, and shall specify the shares of the additional service credit awarded to the member and the nonmember spouse. *(Added by Stats.1993, c. 893 (A.B.1796), § 2. Amended by Stats.1998, c. 965 (A.B.2765), § 61; Stats.2000, c. 74 (A.B.1509), § 34; Stats.2000, c. 1020 (A.B.820), § 1, operative July 1, 2001; Stats.2000, c. 1021 (A.B.2700), § 19.5.)*

§ 22653. Status of nonmember spouse; limitation of rights and benefits

(a) The nonmember spouse who is awarded a separate account under this part pursuant to Section 22652 is not a member of the Defined Benefit Program based on that award. The nonmember spouse is entitled only to rights and benefits based on that award explicitly established by this chapter.

(b) This section shall not be construed to limit any right arising from the account of a nonmember spouse under this part that exists because the nonmember spouse is or was employed to perform creditable service subject to coverage by the Defined Benefit Program. *(Added by Stats.1993, c. 893 (A.B.1796), § 2. Amended by Stats.1996, c. 634 (S.B.2041), § 120; Stats.1998, c. 965 (A.B.2765), § 62.)*

§ 22655. Retirement allowance or retirement annuity; community property rights of nonmember spouse; rights upon death

(a) Upon the legal separation or dissolution of marriage of a retired member, the court may include in the judgment or court order a determination of the community property rights of the parties in the retired member's retirement allowance and, if applicable, retirement benefit under this part consistent with this section. Upon election under subparagraph (B) of paragraph (3) of subdivision (a) of Section 2610 of the Family Code, the court order awarding the nonmember spouse a community property share in the retirement allowance or retirement benefit, or both, of a retired member shall be consistent with this section.

(b) If the court does not award the entire retirement allowance or retirement benefit under this part to the retired member and the retired member is receiving a retirement allowance that has not been modified pursuant to Section 24300 or 24300.1, a single life annuity pursuant to Section 25011 or 25018, or a member only annuity described in paragraph (1) of subdivision (a) of Sections 25011.1 and 25018.1, the court shall require only that the system pay the nonmember spouse, by separate warrant, his or her community property share of the retired member's retirement allowance or retirement benefit, or both, under this part.

(c) If the court does not award the entire retirement allowance or retirement benefit under this part to the retired member and the retired member is receiving an allowance that has been actuarially modified pursuant to Section 24300 or 24300.1, or a joint and survivor annuity pursuant to Section 25011, 25011.1, 25018, or 25018.1, the court shall order only one of the following:

(1) The retired member, shall maintain the retirement allowance or joint and survivor annuity, or both, under this part without change.

(2) The retired member shall cancel the option that modified the retirement allowance under this part pursuant to Section 24322 and elect a new joint and survivor option or designate a new beneficiary or both, and the system shall pay the nonmember spouse, by separate warrant, his or her community property share of the retirement allowance payable to the retired member, the option beneficiary, or both.

(3) The retired member shall cancel the joint and survivor annuity under which the retirement benefit is being paid pursuant to Section 24324, and elect a new joint and survivor annuity or designate a new annuity beneficiary or both, based on the actuarial equivalent of the member's canceled annuity, and the system shall pay the nonmember spouse, by separate warrant, his or her community property share of the retirement benefit payable to the retired member, the annuity beneficiary, or both.

(4) The retired member shall take the action specified in both paragraphs (2) and (3).

(5) The retired member shall cancel the option that modified the retirement allowance under this part pursuant

to Section 24322 and elect an unmodified retirement allowance and the system shall pay the nonmember spouse, by separate warrant, his or her community property share of the retired member's retirement allowance under this part.

(6) The retired member shall cancel, pursuant to Section 24324, the joint and survivor annuity under which the retirement benefit is being paid, and elect a single life annuity, and the system shall pay the nonmember spouse, by separate warrant, his or her community property share of the retirement benefit payable to the retired member.

(7) The retired member shall take the action specified in both paragraphs (5) and (6).

(d) If the option beneficiary or annuity beneficiary or both under this part, other than the nonmember spouse, predeceases the retired member, the court shall order the retired member to designate a new option beneficiary pursuant to Section 24323, or a new annuity beneficiary pursuant to Section 24324 and shall order the system to pay the nonmember spouse, by separate warrant, his or her share of the community property interest in the retirement allowance or retirement benefit payable to the retired member or the new option beneficiary or annuity beneficiary or each of them.

(e) The right of the nonmember spouse to receive his or her community property share of the retired member's retirement allowance or retirement benefit or both under this section shall terminate upon the death of the nonmember spouse. However, the nonmember spouse may designate a beneficiary under the Defined Benefit Program and a payee under the Defined Benefit Supplement Program to receive his or her community property share of the retired member's accumulated retirement contributions and accumulated Defined Benefit Supplement account balance under this part in the event that there are remaining accumulated retirement contributions and a balance of credits in the member's Defined Benefit Supplement account to be paid upon the death of the nonmember spouse. *(Added by Stats.1993, c. 893 (A.B.1796), § 2. Amended by Stats.1994, c. 1269 (A.B. 2208), § 5; Stats.1996, c. 634 (S.B.2041), § 122; Stats.1998, c. 965 (A.B.2765), § 63; Stats.2000, c. 74 (A.B.1509), § 35; Stats.2000, c. 1021 (A.B.2700), § 20; Stats.2006, c. 655 (S.B.1466), § 9; Stats.2014, c. 755 (S.B.1220), § 16, eff. Jan. 1, 2015.)*

Law Revision Commission Comments

1994 Amendment

Section 22655 is amended to correct a cross-reference to Family Code Section 2610. This is a technical, nonsubstantive change. [24 Cal.L.Rev.Comm.Reports ___ (1994), Annual Report for 1994, App. 5].

§ 22656. Judgments or orders; conditions for binding effect

No judgment or court order issued pursuant to this chapter is binding on the system with respect to the Defined Benefit Program or the Defined Benefit Supplement Program until the system has been joined as a party to the action and has been served with a certified copy of the judgment or court order. *(Added by Stats.1993, c. 893 (A.B.1796), § 2. Amended by Stats.1996, c. 634 (S.B.2041), § 122.5; Stats.1998, c. 965 (A.B.2765), § 64; Stats.2000, c. 74 (A.B.1509), § 36; Stats. 2000, c. 1021 (A.B.2700), § 21.)*

§ 22657. Nonmember spouse; applicable statutory provisions

(a) The following provisions shall apply to a nonmember spouse as if he or she were a member under this part: Sections 22107, 22306, 22906, and 23802, subdivisions (a) and (b) of Section 24600, and Sections 24601, 24602, 24603, 24605, 24606, 24607, 24608, 24611, 24612, 24613, 24616, 24617, 25009, 25010, 25011, 25011.1, 25013, 25020, 25021, and 25022.

(b) Notwithstanding subdivision (a), this section shall not be construed to establish any right for the nonmember spouse under this part that is not explicitly established in Sections 22650 to 22655, inclusive, and Sections 22658 to 22665, inclusive. *(Added by Stats.1993, c. 893 (A.B.1796), § 2. Amended by Stats.1996, c. 634 (S.B.2041), § 123; Stats.1998, c. 965 (A.B.2765), § 65; Stats.2002, c. 375 (A.B.2982), § 5; Stats.2006, c. 655 (S.B.1466), § 10.)*

§ 22658. Accounts of nonmember spouse; administration; separation

(a) A separate account awarded to a nonmember spouse pursuant to Section 22652 shall be administered independently of the member's account.

(b) An accumulated [1] Defined Benefit Supplement account balance, accumulated retirement contributions, service credit, and final compensation attributable to a separate account of a nonmember spouse under this part shall not be combined in any way or for any purpose with the accumulated Defined Benefit Supplement account balance, accumulated retirement contributions, service credit, and final compensation of any other separate account of the nonmember spouse.

(c) An accumulated [1] Defined Benefit Supplement account balance, accumulated retirement contributions, service credit, and final compensation attributable to the separate account of a nonmember spouse shall not be combined in any way or for any purpose with the accumulated Defined Benefit Supplement account balance, accumulated retirement contributions, service credit, and final compensation of an account that exists under this part because the nonmember spouse is employed or has been employed to perform creditable service subject to coverage under the Defined Benefit Program or the Defined Benefit Supplement Program. *(Added by Stats. 1993, c. 893 (A.B.1796), § 2. Amended by Stats.1996, c. 634 (S.B.2041), § 123.5; Stats.1998, c. 965 (A.B.2765), § 66; Stats.2000, c. 74 (A.B.1509), § 37.)*

[1] So in enrolled bill.

§ 22659. Information from nonmember spouse

Upon being awarded a separate account or an interest in the retirement allowance or retirement benefit of a retired member under this part, a nonmember spouse shall provide the system with proof of his or her date of birth, social security number, and any other information requested by the system, in the form and manner requested by the system. *(Added by Stats.1993, c. 893 (A.B.1796), § 2. Amended by Stats.1996, c. 634 (S.B.2041), § 124; Stats.1998, c. 965 (A.B.2765), § 67; Stats.2000, c. 74 (A.B.1509), § 38; Stats. 2000, c. 1021 (A.B.2700), § 22.)*

§ 22660. Beneficiary of nonmember spouse; modification of allowance

(a) The nonmember spouse who is awarded a separate account under this part shall have the right to designate, pursuant to Sections 23300 to 23304, inclusive, a beneficiary or beneficiaries to receive the accumulated retirement contributions under the Defined Benefit Program and to designate a payee to receive the remaining balance of payments for a period-certain annuity, or the accumulated Defined Benefit Supplement account balance under the Defined Benefit Supplement Program remaining in the separate account of the nonmember spouse on his or her date of death, and any accrued allowance or accrued benefit under the Defined Benefit Supplement Program that is attributable to the separate account of the nonmember spouse and that is unpaid on the date of the death of the nonmember spouse.

(b) This section shall not be construed to provide the nonmember spouse with any right to elect to modify a retirement allowance under Section 24300 or 24300.1, or to elect a joint and survivor annuity under the Defined Benefit Supplement Program. *(Added by Stats.1993, c. 893 (A.B. 1796), § 2. Amended by Stats.1998, c. 965 (A.B.2765), § 68; Stats.2000, c. 74 (A.B.1509), § 39; Stats.2000, c. 1021 (A.B. 2700), § 23; Stats.2001, c. 159 (S.B.662), § 59; Stats.2006, c. 655 (S.B.1466), § 11; Stats.2017, c. 298 (A.B.1325), § 3, eff. Jan. 1, 2018.)*

§ 22661. Accumulated retirement contributions; nonmember spouse's right to refund; lump-sum payment; mode of deposit and notice

(a) The nonmember spouse who is awarded a separate account under this part shall have the right to a refund of the accumulated retirement contributions in the account under the Defined Benefit Program, and a return of the Defined Benefit Supplement account balance, of the nonmember spouse under this part.

(b) The nonmember spouse shall file an application on a form provided by the system to obtain a refund or lump-sum payment.

(c) Except as provided in subdivision (i), the refund of accumulated retirement contributions in the account under the Defined Benefit Program and the return of the accumulated Defined Benefit Supplement account balance under this part are effective when the system deposits in the United States mail an initial warrant drawn in favor of the nonmember spouse and addressed to the latest address for the nonmember spouse on file with the system.

(d) Except as provided in subdivision (i), if the nonmember spouse has elected on a form provided by the system to transfer all or a specified portion of the accumulated retirement contributions or accumulated Defined Benefit Supplement account balance that are eligible for direct trustee-to-trustee transfer to the trustee of a qualified plan under Section 402 of the Internal Revenue Code of 1986 (26 U.S.C. Sec. 402), deposit in the United States mail of a notice that the requested transfer has been made constitutes a refund of the nonmember spouse's accumulated retirement contributions as defined in Section 22161.5 or the return of the accumulated Defined Benefit Supplement account balance. This subdivision shall not apply to a nonmember domestic partner, consistent with Section 402 of the Internal Revenue Code.

(e) The nonmember spouse is deemed to have permanently waived all rights and benefits pertaining to the service credit, accumulated retirement contributions, and accumulated Defined Benefit Supplement account balance under this part when the refund and lump-sum payment become effective.

(f) The nonmember spouse may not cancel a refund or lump-sum payment under this part after it is effective.

(g) The nonmember spouse shall not have a right to elect to redeposit the refunded accumulated retirement contributions under this part after the refund is effective, to redeposit under Section 22662 or purchase additional service credit under Section 22663 after the refund becomes effective, or to redeposit the accumulated Defined Benefit Supplement account balance after the lump-sum payment becomes effective.

(h) If the total service credit in the separate account of the nonmember spouse under the Defined Benefit Program, including service credit purchased under Sections 22662 and 22663, is less than two and one-half years, the system shall refund the accumulated retirement contributions in the account.

(i) The mode of deposit described in subdivision (c) and the mode of notice described in subdivision (d) are subject to Section 22337. *(Added by Stats.1993, c. 893 (A.B.1796), § 2. Amended by Stats.1994, c. 933 (A.B.3171), § 38, eff. Sept. 28, 1994; Stats.1996, c. 634 (S.B.2041), § 125; Stats.1998, c. 965 (A.B.2765), § 69; Stats.2000, c. 74 (A.B.1509), § 40; Stats. 2000, c. 1021 (A.B.2700), § 24; Stats.2004, c. 912 (A.B.2233), § 8; Stats.2007, c. 513 (A.B.1432), § 1; Stats.2009, c. 304 (S.B.634), § 4; Stats.2013, c. 459 (A.B.989), § 3.)*

§ 22662. Accumulated retirement contributions refunded to members; redeposit by nonmember spouse

The nonmember spouse who is awarded a separate account under the Defined Benefit Program may redeposit accumulated retirement contributions previously refunded to the member in accordance with the determination of the court pursuant to Section 22652.

(a) The nonmember spouse may redeposit under the Defined Benefit Program only those accumulated retirement contributions that were previously refunded to the member and in which the court has determined the nonmember spouse has a community property interest.

(b) The nonmember spouse shall inform the system in writing of his or her intent to redeposit within 180 days after the judgment or court order that specifies the redeposit rights of the nonmember spouse is entered. Except as provided in subdivision (g), the nonmember spouse's election to redeposit shall be made on a form provided by the system within 30 days after the system mails an election form and the billing.

(c) If the nonmember spouse elects to redeposit under the Defined Benefit Program, he or she shall repay all or a portion of the member's refunded accumulated retirement contributions that were awarded to the nonmember spouse and shall pay regular interest from the date of the refund to the date payment of the redeposit is completed.

(d) All payments shall be received by the system before the effective date of the nonmember spouse's retirement under this part. If any payment due because of the election is not received at the system's headquarters office within 120 days of its due date, the election shall be canceled and any payments made under the election shall be returned to the nonmember spouse.

(e) The right of the nonmember spouse to redeposit shall be subject to Section 23203.

(f) The member shall not have a right to redeposit the share of the nonmember spouse in the previously refunded accumulated retirement contributions under this part whether or not the nonmember spouse elects to redeposit. However, any accumulated retirement contributions previously refunded under this part and not explicitly awarded to the nonmember spouse under this part by the judgment or court order shall be deemed the exclusive property of the member.

(g) The measurement of time within which the election to redeposit described in subdivision (b) shall be made is subject to Section 22337. *(Added by Stats.1993, c. 893 (A.B.1796), § 2. Amended by Stats.1996, c. 634 (S.B.2041), § 126; Stats.1998, c. 965 (A.B.2765), § 70; Stats.2000, c. 74 (A.B. 1509), § 41; Stats.2000, c. 1020 (A.B.820), § 2, operative July 1, 2001; Stats.2000, c. 1021 (A.B.2700), § 25.5; Stats.2005, c. 351 (A.B.224), § 7; Stats.2013, c. 558 (A.B.1379), § 8; Stats.2013, c. 459 (A.B.989), § 4; Stats.2014, c. 755 (S.B. 1220), § 17, eff. Jan. 1, 2015.)*

§ 22663. Additional service credit; purchase by nonmember spouse

The nonmember spouse who is awarded a separate account under this part has the right to purchase additional service credit in accordance with the determination of the court pursuant to Section 22652.

(a) The nonmember spouse may purchase only the service credit that the court, pursuant to Section 22652, has determined to be the community property interest of the nonmember spouse.

(b) The nonmember spouse shall inform the system in writing of his or her intent to purchase additional service credit within 180 days after the date the judgment or court order addressing the right of the nonmember spouse to purchase additional service credit is entered. Except as provided in subdivision (f), the nonmember spouse shall elect to purchase additional service credit on a form provided by the system within 30 days after the system mails an election form and billing.

(c) If the nonmember spouse elects to purchase additional service credit, he or she shall pay, prior to retirement under this part, all contributions with respect to the additional service at the contribution rate for additional service credit in effect at the time of election and regular interest from July 1 of the year following the year upon which contributions are based.

(1)(A) The nonmember spouse shall purchase additional service credit by paying the required contributions and interest in one lump sum, or in not more than 120 monthly installments, provided that no installment, except the final installment, is less than twenty-five dollars ($25). Regular interest shall be charged on the monthly, unpaid balance if the nonmember spouse pays in installments.

(B) If any payment due, because of the election, is not received at the system's headquarters office within 120 days of its due date, the election shall be canceled and any payments made under the election shall be returned to the nonmember spouse.

(2) The contributions shall be based on the member's compensation earnable in the most recent school year during which the member was employed, preceding the date of separation established by the court pursuant to Section 22652.

(3) All payments of contributions and interest shall be received by the system before the effective date of the retirement of the nonmember spouse.

(d) The nonmember spouse does not have a right to purchase additional service credit under this part after the effective date of a refund of the accumulated retirement contributions in the separate account of the nonmember spouse.

(e) The member does not have a right to purchase the community property interest of the nonmember spouse of additional service credit under this part whether or not the nonmember spouse elects to purchase the additional service credit. However, any additional service credit eligible for purchase that is not explicitly awarded to the nonmember spouse by the judgment or court order shall be deemed the exclusive property of the member.

(f) The measurement of time within which the election to purchase additional service credit described in subdivision (b) shall be made is subject to Section 22337. *(Added by Stats.1993, c. 893 (A.B.1796), § 2. Amended by Stats.1996, c. 634 (S.B.2041), § 127; Stats.1998, c. 965 (A.B.2765), § 71; Stats.2003, c. 859 (S.B.627), § 7; Stats.2004, c. 912 (A.B. 2233), § 9; Stats.2005, c. 351 (A.B.224), § 8; Stats.2013, c. 558 (A.B.1379), § 9; Stats.2013, c. 459 (A.B.989), § 5; Stats.2014, c. 755 (S.B.1220), § 18, eff. Jan. 1, 2015.)*

§ 22664. Service retirement allowance for nonmember spouse; conditions for retirement for service; limitations; calculation of allowance; increases; nonmember spouse of member subject to the California Public Employees' Pension Reform Act of 2013

The nonmember spouse who is awarded a separate account shall have the right to a service retirement allowance and, if applicable, a retirement benefit under this part.

(a) The nonmember spouse shall be eligible to retire for service under this part if the following conditions are satisfied:

(1) The member had at least five years of credited service during the period of marriage, at least one year of which had been performed subsequent to the most recent refund to the member of accumulated retirement contributions. The credited service may include service credited to the account of the member as of the date of the dissolution or legal separation, previously refunded service, out-of-state service, and permissive service credit that the member is eligible to purchase at the time of the dissolution or legal separation.

(2) The nonmember spouse has at least two and one-half years of credited service in his or her separate account.

(3) The nonmember spouse has attained 55 years of age or more.

(b) A service retirement allowance of a nonmember spouse under this part shall become effective upon a date designated by the nonmember spouse, provided:

(1) The requirements of subdivision (a) are satisfied.

(2) The nonmember spouse has filed an application for service retirement on a properly executed form provided by the system, that is executed no earlier than six months before the effective date of the retirement allowance.

(3) The effective date is no earlier than the first day of the month that the application is received at the system's headquarters office and the effective date is after the date the judgment or court order pursuant to Section 22652 was entered.

(c)(1) Upon service retirement at normal retirement age under this part, the nonmember spouse shall receive a retirement allowance that shall consist of an annual allowance payable in monthly installments equal to 2 percent of final compensation for each year of credited service.

(2) If the nonmember spouse's retirement is effective at less than normal retirement age and between early retirement age under this part and normal retirement age, the retirement allowance shall be reduced by one-half of 1 percent for each full month, or fraction of a month, that will elapse until the nonmember spouse would have reached normal retirement age.

(3) If the nonmember spouse's service retirement is effective at an age greater than normal retirement age and is effective on or after January 1, 1999, the percentage of final compensation for each year of credited service shall be determined pursuant to the following table:

Age at Retirement	Percentage
60 ¼	2.033
60 ½	2.067
60 ¾	2.10
61	2.133
61 ¼	2.167
61 ½	2.20
61 ¾	2.233
62	2.267
62 ¼	2.30
62 ½	2.333
62 ¾	2.367
63 and over	2.40

(4) In computing the retirement allowance of the nonmember spouse, the age of the nonmember spouse on the last day of the month that the retirement allowance begins to accrue shall be used.

(5) Final compensation, for purposes of calculating the service retirement allowance of the nonmember spouse under this subdivision, shall be calculated according to the definition of final compensation in Section 22134, 22134.5, or 22135, whichever is applicable, and shall be based on the member's compensation earnable up to the date the parties separated, as established in the judgment or court order pursuant to Section 22652. The nonmember spouse shall not be entitled to use any other calculation of final compensation.

(d) Upon service retirement under this part, the nonmember spouse shall receive a retirement benefit based on an amount equal to the balance of credits in the nonmember spouse's Defined Benefit Supplement account on the date the retirement benefit becomes payable.

(1) A retirement benefit shall be a lump-sum payment, or an annuity payable in monthly installments, or a combination of both a lump-sum payment and an annuity, as elected by the nonmember spouse on the application for a retirement benefit. A retirement benefit paid as an annuity under this chapter shall be subject to Sections 22660, 25011, and 25011.1.

(2) Upon distribution of the entire retirement benefit in a lump-sum payment, no other benefit shall be payable to the nonmember spouse or the nonmember spouse's beneficiary under the Defined Benefit Supplement Program.

(e) If the member is or was receiving a disability allowance under this part with an effective date before or on the date the parties separated as established in the judgment or court order pursuant to Section 22652, or at any time applies for and receives a disability allowance with an effective date that is before or coincides with the date the parties separated as established in the judgment or court order pursuant to Section 22652, the nonmember spouse shall not be eligible to retire until after the disability allowance of the member terminates. If the member who is or was receiving a disability allowance returns to employment to perform creditable service subject to coverage under the Defined Benefit Program or has his or her allowance terminated under Section 24015, the nonmember spouse may not be paid a retirement allowance until at least six months after termination of the disability allowance and the return of the member to employment to perform creditable service subject to coverage under the Defined Benefit Program, or the termination of the disability allowance and the employment or self-employment of the member in any capacity, notwithstanding Section 22132. If at the end of the six-month period, the member has not had a recurrence of the original disability or has not had his or her earnings fall below the amounts described in Section 24015, the nonmember spouse may be paid a retirement allowance if all other eligibility requirements are met.

(1) The retirement allowance of the nonmember spouse under this subdivision shall be calculated as follows: the disability allowance the member was receiving, exclusive of the portion for dependent children, shall be divided between the share of the member and the share of the nonmember spouse. The share of the nonmember spouse shall be the amount obtained by multiplying the disability allowance, exclusive of the portion for dependent children, by the years of service credited to the separate account of the nonmember spouse, including service projected to the date of separation, and dividing by the projected service of the member. The nonmember spouse's retirement allowance shall be the lesser of the share of the nonmember spouse under this subdivision or the retirement allowance under subdivision (c).

(2) The share of the member shall be the total disability allowance reduced by the share of the nonmember spouse.

The share of the member shall be considered the disability allowance of the member for purposes of Section 24213.

(f) The nonmember spouse who receives a retirement allowance is not a retired member under this part. However, the allowance of the nonmember spouse shall be increased by application of the improvement factor and shall be eligible for the application of supplemental increases and other benefit maintenance provisions under this part, including, but not limited to, Sections 24412 and 24415 based on the same criteria used for the application of these benefit maintenance increases to the service retirement allowances of members.

(g) Paragraphs (1) to (3), inclusive, of subdivision (c) shall not apply to a nonmember spouse of a member subject to the California Public Employees' Pension Reform Act of 2013. For a person who is a nonmember spouse of a member subject to the California Public Employees' Pension Reform Act of 2013 and is awarded a separate account, the retirement allowance shall equal the percentage of final compensation for each year of credited service that is equal to the percentage specified in Section 24202.6 based on the age of the nonmember spouse on the effective date of the allowance. *(Added by Stats.1993, c. 893 (A.B.1796), § 2. Amended by Stats.1996, c. 634 (S.B.2041), § 128; Stats.1998, c. 965 (A.B.2765), § 72.5; Stats.1999, c. 939 (S.B.1074), § 43; Stats. 2000, c. 74 (A.B.1509), § 42; Stats.2000, c. 1021 (A.B.2700), § 26; Stats.2001, c. 803 (S.B.501), § 6; Stats.2002, c. 375 (A.B.2982), § 6; Stats.2006, c. 655 (S.B.1466), § 12; Stats. 2008, c. 751 (A.B.1389), § 4, eff. Sept. 30, 2008; Stats.2013, c. 558 (A.B.1379), § 10; Stats.2013, c. 559 (A.B.1381), § 13; Stats.2014, c. 755 (S.B.1220), § 19, eff. Jan. 1, 2015; Stats. 2016, c. 218 (S.B.1352), § 15, eff. Jan. 1, 2017.)*

§ 22665. Service credit awarded in judgment or court order; calculation of retirement or disability allowance

The system shall include the service credit awarded to a nonmember spouse in the judgment or court order to determine the eligibility of a member for a retirement or disability allowance under this part. That portion of awarded service credit based on previously refunded accumulated retirement contributions or on permissive service credit may not be used by the member for eligibility requirements until the member has redeposited or purchased his or her portion of the service credit. The member's service retirement allowance shall be calculated based on the service credit in the member's account on the effective date of service retirement. *(Added by Stats.1993, c. 893 (A.B.1796), § 2. Amended by Stats.1996, c. 634 (S.B.2041), § 129; Stats.1998, c. 965 (A.B.2765), § 73; Stats.2000, c. 74 (A.B.1509), § 43.)*

§ 22666. Terminable interest doctrine; legislative intent

It is the intent of the Legislature to abolish any remaining application of the terminable interest doctrine in California relating to the division of public retirement benefits of a member in the event of dissolution of marriage or death if the division is made under this chapter. *(Added by Stats.1993, c. 893 (A.B.1796), § 2.)*

EVIDENCE CODE

Division 5

BURDEN OF PROOF; BURDEN OF PRODUCING EVIDENCE; PRESUMPTIONS AND INFERENCES

CHAPTER 3. PRESUMPTIONS AND INFERENCES

ARTICLE 4. PRESUMPTIONS AFFECTING THE BURDEN OF PROOF

§ 662. Owner of legal title to property is owner of beneficial title

The owner of the legal title to property is presumed to be the owner of the full beneficial title. This presumption may be rebutted only by clear and convincing proof. *(Stats.1965, c. 299, § 2, operative Jan. 1, 1967.)*

Law Revision Commission Comments

Section 662 codifies a common law presumption recognized in the California cases. The presumption may be overcome only by clear and convincing proof. Olson v. Olson, 4 Cal.2d 434, 437, 49 P.2d 827, 828 (1935); Rench v. McMullen, 82 Cal.App.2d 872, 187 P.2d 111 (1947). [7 Cal.L.Rev.Comm. Reports 1 (1965)].

Commentary

In re Marriage of Valli, 58 Cal.4th 1396, 324 P.2d 274, 171 Cal.Rptr.3d 454 (2014), held that the presumption arising under this section from the form of title, a common law presumption, is inapplicable when it conflicts with the transmutation statutes. Justice Chin's concurrence in *Valli* further considers the relationship between the common law title presumption and California community property law. *Valli* also held that spousal purchases from a third party are subject to the transmutation requirements of Family Code section 852, that is, in order to give up any property interest he would otherwise have based on the character of the purchase funds, a spouse must expressly declare in writing that he is giving up any interest he may have in the purchased asset. Thus when Frankie Valli used community property funds to purchase a life insurance policy on his life and had his spouse named as the owner of the policy, the policy remained community property because Frankie did not expressly declare in writing that he was giving up any interest he had in the policy. *Valli overrules In re Summers, 332 F.3d 1240 (9th Cir. 2003)* and *In re Marriage of Brooks & Robinson, 169 Cal.App.4th 176, 86 Cal.Rptr.3d 624 (2008)*, to the extent that they hold that spousal purchases from third parties are not subject to the requirements of Family Code section 852 or that they are subject to the presumption of this section.

In re Marriage of Haines, 33 Cal.App.4th 277, 39 Cal.Rptr.2d 673 (1995), holds that Evidence Code Section 662 does not apply in family law proceedings insofar as its application would be inconsistent with the presumption of undue influence that arises from the Family Code Section 721 principle that the spouses have a confidential relationship in their transactions with each other. See also *In re Marriage of Barneson, 69 Cal.App.4th 583, 81 Cal.Rptr.2d 726 (1999)*, which holds that a husband's written order to "transfer" shares of stock to his wife's name did not satisfy the Family Code Section 852(a) requirement of an "express declaration" of transmutation because the word "transfer" does not necessarily imply a change in ownership. *Barneson* reasons that Evidence Code Section 662 does not apply when it conflicts with the presumption of undue influence that may arise in spousal transactions. Similarly, *In re Marriage of Delaney, 111 Cal.App.4th 991, 4 Cal.Rptr.3d 378 (2003)*, applies the holding of *Haines, supra,* to a spouse's routine transfer of his separate property home into joint tenancy in connection with the couple's application for a home improvement loan. *Delaney* requires that the spouse who benefited from the transfer by gaining a property interest show that the transfer "was freely and voluntarily made, with full knowledge of all the facts, and with a complete understanding of the effect of a transfer from his unencumbered separate interest to a joint interest." For additional presumption of undue influence cases, see Commentary to Family Code section 721.

Research References

Treatises and Practice Aids

Witkin, California Summary 10th Community Property § 275, Nature Of Relief.
Witkin, California Summary 10th Trusts § 324, in General.
Witkin, California Summary 10th Trusts § 326, Promise to Reconvey to Transferor.

§ 663. Ceremonial marriage

A ceremonial marriage is presumed to be valid. *(Stats. 1965, c. 299, § 2, operative Jan. 1, 1967.)*

Law Revision Commission Comments

Section 663 codifies a common law presumption recognized in the California cases. Estate of Hughson, 173 Cal. 448, 160 Pac. 548 (1916); Wilcox v. Wilcox, 171 Cal. 770, 155 Pac. 95 (1916); Freeman S.S. Co. v. Pillsbury, 172 F.2d 321 (9th Cir.1949). [7 Cal.L.Rev. Comm. Reports 1 (1965)].

Research References

Treatises and Practice Aids

Witkin, California Summary 10th Husband and Wife § 54, Presumption Of Valid Marriage from Proof Of Solemnization.

§ 667. Death of person not heard from in five years

A person not heard from in five years is presumed to be dead. *(Stats.1965, c. 299, § 2, operative Jan. 1, 1967. Amended by Stats.1983, c. 201, § 1.)*

Law Revision Commission Comments

1965 Enactment

Section 667 restates and supersedes the presumption in subdivision 26 of Code of Civil Procedure Section 1963. [7 Cal.L.Rev.Comm. Reports 1 (1965)].

1983 Amendment

Section 667 is amended to adopt a five-year missing period. This period is consistent with Probate Code Section 1301 (administration of estates of persons missing five years) and Civil Code Sections 4401(2), 4425(b) (five-year absence in bigamy situations). Except for the change in the duration of the missing period from seven to five years, the amendment of Section 667 has no effect on the case law interpreting this section. [16 Cal.L.Rev.Comm. Reports 105 (1982)].

Research References

Treatises and Practice Aids

Witkin, California Summary 10th Wills and Probate § 369, Presumption and Order.

Division 8

PRIVILEGES

CHAPTER 4. PARTICULAR PRIVILEGES

ARTICLE 3. LAWYER–CLIENT PRIVILEGE

§ 950. Lawyer

As used in this article, "lawyer" means a person authorized, or reasonably believed by the client to be authorized, to practice law in any state or nation. *(Stats.1965, c. 299, § 2, operative Jan. 1, 1967.)*

Law Revision Commission Comments

"Lawyer" is defined to include a person "reasonably believed by the client to be authorized" to practice law. Since the privilege is intended to encourage full disclosure, the client's reasonable belief that the person he is consulting is an attorney is sufficient to justify application of the privilege. See 8 Wigmore, Evidence § 2302 (McNaughton rev. 1961), and cases there cited in note 1. See also McCormick, Evidence § 92 (1954).

There is no requirement that the lawyer be licensed to practice in a jurisdiction that recognizes the lawyer-client privilege. Legal transactions frequently cross state and national boundaries and require consultation with attorneys from many different jurisdictions. When a California resident travels outside the State and has occasion to consult a lawyer during such travel, or when a lawyer from another state or nation participates in a transaction involving a California client, the client should be entitled to assume that his communications will be given as much protection as they would be if he consulted a California lawyer in California. A client should not be forced to inquire about the jurisdictions where the lawyer is authorized to practice and whether such jurisdictions recognize the lawyer-client privilege before he may safely communicate with the lawyer. [7 Cal.L.Rev.Comm. Reports 1 (1965)].

Research References

Forms

California Transactions Forms--Business Entities § 15:56, Employment Agreement for Employee-Shareholder.

Environmental Insurance Litigation: Practice Forms § 2:16. Sample Memorandum in Opposition to Plaintiff Insured's Motion to Compel Further Responses and Production Of Documents...

West's California Code Forms, Government § 54954 Form 1, Ordinance Fixing Time and Place for Holding Regular Meetings.

Treatises and Practice Aids

Witkin, California Summary 10th Wills and Probate § 20, Transfer Of Documents.

§ 951. Client

As used in this article, "client" means a person who, directly or through an authorized representative, consults a lawyer for the purpose of retaining the lawyer or securing legal service or advice from him in his professional capacity, and includes an incompetent (a) who himself so consults the lawyer or (b) whose guardian or conservator so consults the lawyer in behalf of the incompetent. *(Stats.1965, c. 299, § 2, operative Jan. 1, 1967.)*

Law Revision Commission Comments

Under Section 951, public entities have a privilege insofar as communications made in the course of the lawyer-client relationship are concerned. This codifies existing law. See Holm v. Superior Court, 42 Cal.2d 500, 267 P.2d 1025 (1954). Likewise, such unincorporated organizations as labor unions, social clubs, and fraternal societies have a lawyer-client privilege when the organization (rather than its individual members) is the client. See Evidence Code § 175 (defining "person") and § 200 (defining "public entity"). [7 Cal.L.Rev.Comm. Reports 1 (1965)].

§ 952. Confidential communication between client and lawyer

As used in this article, "confidential communication between client and lawyer" means information transmitted between a client and his or her lawyer in the course of that relationship and in confidence by a means which, so far as the client is aware, discloses the information to no third persons other than those who are present to further the interest of the client in the consultation or those to whom disclosure is reasonably necessary for the transmission of the information or the accomplishment of the purpose for which the lawyer is consulted, and includes a legal opinion formed and the advice given by the lawyer in the course of that relationship. *(Stats.1965, c. 299, § 2, operative Jan. 1, 1967. Amended by Stats.1967, c. 650, p. 2006, § 3; Stats.1994, c. 186 (A.B.2662), § 1; Stats.1994, c. 587 (A.B.3600), § 9; Stats.2002, c. 72 (S.B.2061), § 3.)*

Law Revision Commission Comments

1965 Amendment

The requirement that the communication be made in the course of the lawyer-client relationship and be confidential is in accord with existing law. See City & County of San Francisco v. Superior Court, 37 Cal.2d 227, 234–235, 231 P.2d 26, 29–30 (1951).

Confidential communications also include those made to third parties—such as the lawyer's secretary, a physician, or similar expert—for the purpose of transmitting such information to the lawyer because they are "reasonably necessary for the transmission of the information." This codifies existing law. See, *e.g.,* City & County of San Francisco v. Superior Court, *supra* (communication to a physician); Loftin v. Glaser, Civil No. 789604 (L.A.Super.Ct., July 23, 1964) (communication to an accountant), as reported in Los Angeles Daily Journal Report Section, August 25, 1964 (memorandum opinion of Judge Philbrick McCoy).

A lawyer at times may desire to have a client reveal information to an expert consultant in order that the lawyer may adequately advise his client. The inclusion of the words "or the accomplishment of the purpose for which the lawyer is consulted" assures that these communications, too, are within the scope of the privilege. This part of the definition may change existing law. Himmelfarb v. United States, 175 F.2d 924, 938–939 (9th Cir.1949), applying California law, held that the presence of an accountant during a lawyer-client consultation destroyed the privilege, but no California case directly in point has been found. Of course, if the expert consultant is acting merely as a conduit for communications from the client to the attorney, the doctrine of City & County of San Francisco v. Superior Court, *supra,* applies and the communication would be privileged under existing law as well as under this section. See also Evidence Code § 912(d) and the Comment thereto.

The words "other than those who are present to further the interest of the client in the consultation" indicate that a communication to a lawyer is nonetheless confidential even though it is made in the presence of another person—such as a spouse, parent, business associate, or joint client—who is present to further the interest of the client in the consultation. These words refer, too, to another person and his attorney who may meet with the client and his attorney in regard to a matter of joint concern. This may change existing law, for the presence of a third person sometimes has been held to destroy the confidential character of the consultation, even where the third person was present because of his concern for the welfare of the client. See Attorney-Client Privilege in California, 10 Stan. L. Rev 297, 308 (1958), and authorities there cited in notes 67–71. See also Himmelfarb v. United States, *supra*. [7 Cal.L.Rev.Comm. Reports 1 (1965)].

1967 Amendment

The express inclusion of "a legal opinion" in the last clause will preclude a possible construction of this section that would leave the attorney's uncommunicated legal opinion—which includes his impressions and conclusions—unprotected by the privilege. Such a construction would virtually destroy the privilege. [8 Cal.L.Rev. Comm. Reports 101 (1967)].

2002 Amendment

Section 952 is amended to delete the last sentence concerning confidentiality of electronic communications, because this rule is generalized in Section 917(b)-(c) applicable to all confidential communication privileges. [31 Cal.L.Rev.Comm. Reports 258 (2002)].

Research References

Forms

Cal. Transaction Forms - Bus. Transactions § 6:51, Attorney-Client Privilege.

California Transactions Forms--Estate Planning § 19:57, Maintaining Confidentiality.

California Transactions Forms--Family Law § 1:132, Signature by Attorneys.

California Transactions Forms--Family Law § 4:128, Signature by Attorneys.

Environmental Insurance Litigation: Practice Forms § 4:8, Opposition to Motion to Compel Production Of Documents.

Environmental Insurance Litigation: Practice Forms APP A, Fall 2016 Survey for Environmental Insurance Litigation: Forms.

Environmental Insurance Litigation: Practice Forms § 2:14, Sample Notice Of Motion and Motion to Compel Production Of Documents (Insurers Attacking Policyholders' Claims Of Attorney Work Product and Attorney Client Privilege).

Treatises and Practice Aids

Witkin, California Summary 10th Parent and Child § 788, Duty to Provide Counsel.

§ 953. Holder of the privilege

As used in this article, "holder of the privilege" means:

(a) The client, if the client has no guardian or conservator.

(b) A guardian or conservator of the client, if the client has a guardian or conservator.

(c) The personal representative of the client if the client is dead, including a personal representative appointed pursuant to Section 12252 of the Probate Code.

(d) A successor, assign, trustee in dissolution, or any similar representative of a firm, association, organization, partnership, business trust, corporation, or public entity that is no longer in existence. *(Stats.1965, c. 299, § 2, operative Jan. 1, 1967. Amended by Stats.2009, c. 8 (A.B.1163), § 1.)*

Law Revision Commission Comments

Under subdivisions (a) and (b), the guardian of a client is the holder of the privilege if the client has a guardian, and the client becomes the holder of the privilege when he no longer has a guardian. For example, if an underage client or his guardian consults a lawyer, the guardian is the holder of the privilege under subdivision (b) until the guardianship is terminated; thereafter, the client himself is the holder of the privilege. The present California law is uncertain. The statutes do not deal with the problem, and no appellate decision has discussed it.

Under subdivision (c), the personal representative of a client is the holder of the privilege when the client is dead. He may either claim or waive the privilege on behalf of the deceased client. This may be a change in California law. Under existing law, it seems probable that the privilege survives the death of the client and that no one can waive it after the client's death. See Collette v. Sarrasin, 184 Cal. 283, 289, 193 Pac. 571, 573 (1920). Hence, the privilege apparently is recognized even when it would be clearly to the interest of the estate of the deceased client to waive it. Under Section 953, however, the personal representative of a deceased client may waive the privilege. The purpose underlying the privilege—to provide a client with the assurance of confidentiality—does not require the recognition of the privilege when to do so is detrimental to his interest or to the interests of his estate. [7 Cal.L.Rev.Comm. Reports 1 (1965)].

2009 Amendment

Subdivision (a) of Section 953 is amended to revise a gender reference.

Subdivision (c) is amended to make clear that a personal representative holds the decedent's lawyer-client privilege at any time while the personal representative has duties as a personal representative, including, without limitation, during any subsequent estate administration. See, e.g., Prob. Code § 12252 (appointment of personal representative for subsequent administration of estate); see also Prob. Code § 58 (personal representative). The personal representative holds the privilege during any action asserted, commenced, continued, or defended by a personal representative. See Code Civ. Proc. §§ 377.30 (commencement of surviving action by personal representative), 377.31 (continuation of surviving action by personal representative), 377.40 (defense by personal representative of surviving action), 377.60 (assertion by personal representative of wrongful death action); Prob. Code §§ 9000–9399 (creditor claims against estate). [38 Cal. L. Revision Comm'n Reports 163 (2008)].

Research References

Forms

West's California Code Forms, Probate § 2584 Form 1, Order Authorizing Conservator to Make Gifts.

Treatises and Practice Aids

Witkin, California Summary 10th Insurance § 11, Conservatorship and Liquidation.

Witkin, California Summary 10th Wills and Probate § 744, Administration After Discharge.

§ 954. Lawyer-client privilege

Subject to Section 912 and except as otherwise provided in this article, the client, whether or not a party, has a privilege to refuse to disclose, and to prevent another from disclosing, a confidential communication between client and lawyer if the privilege is claimed by:

(a) The holder of the privilege;

(b) A person who is authorized to claim the privilege by the holder of the privilege; or

(c) The person who was the lawyer at the time of the confidential communication, but such person may not claim the privilege if there is no holder of the privilege in existence or if he is otherwise instructed by a person authorized to permit disclosure.

The relationship of attorney and client shall exist between a law corporation as defined in Article 10 (commencing with Section 6160) of Chapter 4 of Division 3 of the Business and Professions Code and the persons to whom it renders professional services, as well as between such persons and members of the State Bar employed by such corporation to render services to such persons. The word "persons" as used in this subdivision includes partnerships, corporations, limited liability companies, associations and other groups and entities. *(Stats.1965, c. 299, § 2, operative Jan. 1, 1967. Amended by Stats.1968, c. 1375, p. 2695, § 2; Stats.1994, c. 1010 (S.B.2053), § 104.)*

Law Revision Commission Comments

Section 954 is the basic statement of the lawyer-client privilege. Exceptions to this privilege are stated in Sections 956–962.

Persons entitled to claim the privilege. The persons entitled to claim the privilege are specified in subdivisions (a), (b), and (c). See Evidence Code § 953 for the definition of "holder of the privilege."

Eavesdroppers. Under Section 954, the lawyer-client privilege can be asserted to prevent *anyone* from testifying to a confidential communication. Thus, clients are protected against the risk of disclosure by eavesdroppers and other wrongful interceptors of confidential communications between lawyer and client. Probably no such protection was provided prior to the enactment of Penal Code Sections 653i and 653j. See People v. Castiel, 153 Cal.App.2d 653, 315 P.2d 79 (1957). See also Attorney-Client Privilege in California, 10 Stan. L. Rev 297, 310–312 (1958), and cases there cited in note 84.

Penal Code Section 653j makes evidence obtained by *electronic* eavesdropping or recording in violation of the section inadmissible in "any judicial, administrative, legislative, or other proceeding." The section also provides a criminal penalty and contains definitions and exceptions. Penal Code Section 653i makes it a felony to eavesdrop by an electronic or other device upon a conversation between a person in custody of a public officer or on public property and that person's lawyer, religious advisor, or physician.

Section 954 is consistent with Penal Code Sections 653i and 653j but provides broader protection, for it protects against disclosure of confidential communications by anyone who obtained knowledge of the communication without the client's consent. See also Evidence Code § 912 (when disclosure with client's consent constitutes a waiver of the privilege). The use of the privilege to prevent testimony by eavesdroppers and those to whom the communication was wrongfully disclosed does not, however, affect the rule that the making of the communication under circumstances where others could easily overhear it is evidence that the client did not intend the communication to be confidential. See Sharon v. Sharon, 79 Cal. 633, 677, 22 Pac. 26, 39 (1889).

Termination of privilege. The privilege may be claimed by a person listed in Section 954, or the privileged information excluded by the presiding officer under Section 916, only if there is a holder of the privilege in existence. Hence, the privilege ceases to exist when the client's estate is finally distributed and his personal representative is discharged. This is apparently a change in California law. Under the existing law, it seems likely that the privilege continues to exist indefinitely after the client's death and that no one has authority to waive the privilege. See Collette v. Sarrasin, 184 Cal. 283, 193 Pac. 571 (1920). See generally Paley v. Superior Court, 137 Cal.App.2d 450, 290 P.2d 617 (1955), and discussion of the analogous situation in connection with the physician-patient privilege in Tentative Recommendation and a Study Relating to the Uniform Rules of Evidence (Article V. Privileges), 6 Cal.Law Revision Comm'n, Rep., Rec. & Studies 201, 408–410 (1964). Although there is good reason for maintaining the privilege while the estate is being administered—particularly if the estate is involved in litigation—there is little reason to preserve secrecy at the expense of excluding relevant evidence after the estate is wound up and the representative is discharged. [7 Cal.L.Rev.Comm. Reports 1 (1965)].

Research References

Forms

Cal. Transaction Forms - Bus. Transactions § 6:51, Attorney-Client Privilege.

California Transactions Forms--Estate Planning § 19:57, Maintaining Confidentiality.

Environmental Insurance Litigation: Practice Forms § 4:8, Opposition to Motion to Compel Production Of Documents.

§ 955. When lawyer required to claim privilege

The lawyer who received or made a communication subject to the privilege under this article shall claim the privilege whenever he is present when the communication is sought to be disclosed and is authorized to claim the privilege under subdivision (c) of Section 954. *(Stats.1965, c. 299, § 2, operative Jan. 1, 1967.)*

Law Revision Commission Comments

The obligation of the lawyer to claim the privilege on behalf of the client, unless otherwise instructed by a person authorized to permit disclosure, is consistent with Section 6068(e) of the Business and Professions Code. [7 Cal.L.Rev.Comm. Reports 1 (1965)].

Research References

Forms

Cal. Transaction Forms - Bus. Transactions § 6:51, Attorney-Client Privilege.

§ 956. Exception: Crime or fraud; applicability to legal services for lawful cannabis–related activities

(a) There is no privilege under this article if the services of the lawyer were sought or obtained to enable or aid anyone to commit or plan to commit a crime or a fraud.

(b) This exception to the privilege granted by this article shall not apply to legal services rendered in compliance with state and local laws on medicinal cannabis or adult-use cannabis, and confidential communications provided for the purpose of rendering those services are confidential communications between client and lawyer, as defined in Section 952, provided the lawyer also advises the client on conflicts with respect to federal law. *(Stats.1965, c. 299, § 2, operative Jan. 1, 1967. Amended by Stats.2017, c. 530 (A.B.1159), § 2, eff. Jan. 1, 2018.)*

Law Revision Commission Comments

California now recognizes this exception. Abbott v. Superior Court, 78 Cal.App.2d 19, 177 P.2d 317 (1947). *Cf.* Nowell v. Superior Court, 223 Cal.App.2d 652, 36 Cal.Rptr. 21 (1963). [7 Cal.L.Rev.Comm. Reports 1 (1965)].

Research References

Treatises and Practice Aids

Witkin, California Summary 10th Torts § 661, Wiretapping and Electronic Eavesdropping.

§ 956.5. Exception: Prevention of criminal act likely to result in death or substantial bodily harm

There is no privilege under this article if the lawyer reasonably believes that disclosure of any confidential communication relating to representation of a client is necessary to prevent a criminal act that the lawyer reasonably believes is likely to result in the death of, or substantial bodily harm to, an individual. *(Added by Stats.1993, c. 982 (S.B.645), § 8. Amended by Stats.2003, c. 765 (A.B.1101), § 2, operative July 1, 2004; Stats.2004, c. 183 (A.B.3082), § 94.)*

§ 957. Exception: Parties claiming through deceased client

There is no privilege under this article as to a communication relevant to an issue between parties all of whom claim through a deceased client, regardless of whether the claims are by testate or intestate succession, nonprobate transfer, or inter vivos transaction. *(Stats.1965, c. 299, § 2, operative Jan. 1, 1967. Amended by Stats.2009, c. 8 (A.B.1163), § 2.)*

Law Revision Commission Comments

The lawyer-client privilege does not apply to a communication relevant to an issue between parties all of whom claim through a deceased client. Under existing law, all must claim through the client by testate or intestate succession in order for this exception to be applicable; a claim by inter vivos transaction apparently is not within the exception. Paley v. Superior Court, 137 Cal.App.2d 450, 457–460, 290 P.2d 617, 621–623 (1955). Section 957 extends this exception to include inter vivos transactions.

The traditional exception for litigation between claimants by testate or intestate succession is based on the theory that claimants in privity with the estate claim *through* the client, not adversely, and the deceased client presumably would want his communications disclosed in litigation between such claimants so that his desires in regard to the disposition of his estate might be correctly ascertained and carried out. This rationale is equally applicable where one or more of the parties is claiming by inter vivos transaction as, for example, in an action between a party who claims under a deed (executed by a client in full possession of his faculties) and a party who claims under a will executed while the client's mental stability was dubious. See the discussion in Tentative Recommendation and a Study Relating to the Uniform Rules of Evidence (Article V. Privileges), 6 Cal.Law Revision Comm'n, Rep., Rec. & Studies 201, 392–396 (1964). [7 Cal.L.Rev.Comm. Reports 1 (1965)].

2009 Amendment

Section 957 is amended to clarify that the exception is applicable to parties who all claim through a deceased client, including a person who claims through a nonprobate transfer. [38 Cal. L. Revision Comm'n Reports 163 (2008)].

Research References

Forms

California Transactions Forms--Estate Planning § 19:57, Maintaining Confidentiality.

§ 958. Exception: Breach of duty arising out of lawyer-client relationship

There is no privilege under this article as to a communication relevant to an issue of breach, by the lawyer or by the client, of a duty arising out of the lawyer-client relationship. *(Stats.1965, c. 299, § 2, operative Jan. 1, 1967.)*

Law Revision Commission Comments

This exception has not been recognized by a holding in any California case, although dicta in several opinions indicate that it would be recognized if the question were presented in a proper case. People v. Tucker, 61 Cal.2d 828, 40 Cal.Rptr. 609, 395 P.2d 449 (1964); Henshall v. Coburn, 177 Cal. 50, 169 Pac. 1014 (1917); Pacific Tel. & Tel. Co. v. Fink, 141 Cal.App.2d 332, 335, 296 P.2d 843, 845 (1956); Fleschler v. Strauss, 15 Cal.App.2d 735, 60 P.2d 193 (1936). See generally Witkin, California Evidence § 419 (1958).

It would be unjust to permit a client either to accuse his attorney of a breach of duty and to invoke the privilege to prevent the attorney from bringing forth evidence in defense of the charge or to refuse to pay his attorney's fee and invoke the privilege to defeat the attorney's claim. Thus, for example, if the defendant in a criminal action claims that his lawyer did not provide him with an adequate defense, communications between the lawyer and client relevant to that issue are not privileged. See People v. Tucker, 61 Cal.2d 828, 40 Cal.Rptr. 609, 395 P.2d 449 (1964). The duty involved must, of course, be one arising out of the lawyer-client relationship, *e.g.,* the duty of the lawyer to exercise reasonable diligence on behalf of his client, the duty of the lawyer to care faithfully and account for his client's property, or the client's duty to pay for the lawyer's services. [7 Cal.L.Rev.Comm. Reports 1 (1965)].

§ 959. Exception: Lawyer as attesting witness

There is no privilege under this article as to a communication relevant to an issue concerning the intention or competence of a client executing an attested document of which the lawyer is an attesting witness, or concerning the execution or attestation of such a document. *(Stats.1965, c. 299, § 2, operative Jan. 1, 1967.)*

Law Revision Commission Comments

This exception relates to the type of communication about which an attesting witness would testify. The mere fact that an attorney acts as an attesting witness should not destroy the lawyer-client privilege as to all statements made concerning the document attested; but the privilege should not prohibit the lawyer from performing the duties expected of an attesting witness. Under existing law, the attesting witness exception is broader, having been used as a device to obtain information which the lawyer who is an attesting witness received in his capacity as a lawyer rather than as an attesting witness. See In re Mullin, 110 Cal. 252, 42 Pac. 645 (1895). [7 Cal.L.Rev.Comm. Reports 1 (1965)].

§ 960. Exception: Intention of deceased client concerning writing affecting property interest

There is no privilege under this article as to a communication relevant to an issue concerning the intention of a client, now deceased, with respect to a deed of conveyance, will, or other writing, executed by the client, purporting to affect an interest in property. *(Stats.1965, c. 299, § 2, operative Jan. 1, 1967.)*

Law Revision Commission Comments

Although the attesting witness exception stated in Section 959 is limited to information of the kind to which one would expect an attesting witness to testify, there is merit to having an exception that applies to all dispositive instruments. A client ordinarily would desire his lawyer to communicate his true intention with regard to a dispositive instrument if the instrument itself leaves the matter in doubt and the client is deceased. Likewise, the client ordinarily would desire his attorney to testify to communications relevant to the validity of such instruments after the client dies. Accordingly, two additional exceptions—Sections 960 and 961—are provided for this purpose. These exceptions have been recognized by the California decisions only in cases where the lawyer is an attesting witness. See the Comment to Evidence Code § 959. [7 Cal.L.Rev.Comm. Reports 1 (1965)].

§ 961. Exception: Validity of writing affecting property interest

There is no privilege under this article as to a communication relevant to an issue concerning the validity of a deed of conveyance, will, or other writing, executed by a client, now deceased, purporting to affect an interest in property. *(Stats. 1965, c. 299, § 2, operative Jan. 1, 1967.)*

Law Revision Commission Comments

See the Comment to Section 960. [7 Cal.L.Rev.Comm. Reports 1 (1965)].

§ 962. Exception: Joint clients

Where two or more clients have retained or consulted a lawyer upon a matter of common interest, none of them, nor the successor in interest of any of them, may claim a privilege under this article as to a communication made in the course of that relationship when such communication is offered in a civil proceeding between one of such clients (or his successor in interest) and another of such clients (or his successor in interest). *(Stats.1965, c. 299, § 2, operative Jan. 1, 1967.)*

Law Revision Commission Comments

This section states existing law. Clyne v. Brock, 82 Cal.App.2d 958, 965, 188 P.2d 263, 267 (1947); Croce v. Superior Court, 21 Cal.App.2d 18, 68 P.2d 369 (1937). See also Harris v. Harris, 136 Cal. 379, 69 Pac. 23 (1902). [7 Cal.L.Rev.Comm. Reports 1 (1965)].

Research References

Forms

California Transactions Forms--Business Entities § 15:56, Employment Agreement for Employee-Shareholder.

California Transactions Forms--Business Entities § 20:13, Fiduciary Obligations Of Attorney for Dissolved Partnership.

California Transactions Forms--Estate Planning § 20:4, Separate and Community Property.

Environmental Insurance Litigation: Practice Forms § 4:8, Opposition to Motion to Compel Production Of Documents.

West's California Code Forms, Government § 54954 Form 1, Ordinance Fixing Time and Place for Holding Regular Meetings.

ARTICLE 4. PRIVILEGE NOT TO TESTIFY AGAINST SPOUSE

§ 970. Spouse's privilege not to testify against spouse; exceptions

Except as otherwise provided by statute, a married person has a privilege not to testify against his spouse in any proceeding. *(Stats.1965, c. 299, § 2, operative Jan. 1, 1967.)*

Law Revision Commission Comments

Under this article, a married person has two privileges: (1) a privilege not to testify against his spouse in any proceeding (Section 970) and (2) a privilege not to be called as a witness in any proceeding to which his spouse is a party (Section 971).

The privileges under this article are not as broad as the privilege provided by existing law. Under existing law, a married person has a privilege to prevent his spouse from testifying against him, but only the witness spouse has a privilege under this article. Under the existing law, a married person may refuse to testify *for* the other spouse, but no such privilege exists under this article. For a discussion of the reasons for these changes in existing law, see the Law Revision Commission's Comment to Code of Civil Procedure Section 1881 (superseded by the Evidence Code).

The rationale of the privilege provided by Section 970 not to testify against one's spouse is that such testimony would seriously disturb or disrupt the marital relationship. Society stands to lose more from such disruption than it stands to gain from the testimony which would be available if the privilege did not exist. The privilege is based in part on a previous recommendation and study of the California Law Revision Commission. See 1 Cal.Law Revision Comm'n, Rep., Rec. & Studies, Recommendation and Study Relating to the Marital "For and Against" Testimonial Privilege at F–1 (1957). [7 Cal.L.Rev. Comm. Reports 1 (1965)].

Commentary

Jurcoane v. Superior Court, 93 Cal.App.4th 886, 113 Cal.Rptr.2d 483 (2001), holds that a magistrate erred in denying wife's assertion of the marital privilege on the ground that the spouses no longer had a viable marital relationship. *Jurcoane* reasons that there is no statutory basis for such an exception to the marital privilege.

Interpreting § 972(e)(2), *People v. Sinohui, 28 Cal.4th 205, 47 P.3d 629, 120 Cal.Rptr.2d 783 (2002)*, holds that a court may compel spousal testimony even though no accusatory pleading charges a defendant with a crime against a spouse so long as the defendant commits a crime against a third party in the course of committing a crime against a spouse and the two crimes are part of a continuous course of criminal conduct and are logically related to each other.

Research References

Forms

California Transactions Forms--Family Law § 4:14, Domestic Violence and Restraining Orders.

§ 971. Privilege not to be called as a witness against spouse

Except as otherwise provided by statute, a married person whose spouse is a party to a proceeding has a privilege not to be called as a witness by an adverse party to that proceeding without the prior express consent of the spouse having the privilege under this section unless the party calling the spouse does so in good faith without knowledge of the marital relationship. *(Stats.1965, c. 299, § 2, operative Jan. 1, 1967.)*

Law Revision Commission Comments

The privilege of a married person not to be called as a witness against his spouse is somewhat similar to the privilege given the defendant in a criminal case not to be called as a witness (Section 930). This privilege is necessary to avoid the prejudicial effect. For example, of the prosecution's calling the defendant's wife as a witness, thus forcing her to object before the jury. The privilege not to be called as a witness does not apply, however, in a proceeding where the other spouse is not a party. Thus, a married person may be called as a witness in a grand jury proceeding because his spouse is not a party to that proceeding, but the witness in the grand jury proceeding may claim the privilege under Section 970 to refuse to answer a question that would compel him to testify *against* his spouse. [7 Cal.L.Rev.Comm. Reports 1 (1965)].

Commentary

Jurcoane v. Superior Court, 93 Cal.App.4th 886, 113 Cal.Rptr.2d 483 (2001), holds that a magistrate erred in denying wife's assertion of the marital privilege on the ground that the spouses no longer had a viable marital relationship. *Jurcoane* reasons that there is no statutory basis for such an exception to the marital privilege.

Interpreting § 972(e)(2), *People v. Sinohui, 28 Cal.4th 205, 47 P.3d 629, 120 Cal.Rptr.2d 783 (2002)*, holds that a court may compel spousal testimony even though no accusatory pleading charges a defendant with a crime against a spouse so long as the defendant commits a crime against a third party in the course of committing a crime against a spouse and the two crimes are part of a continuous course of criminal conduct and are logically related to each other.

Research References

Forms

California Transactions Forms--Family Law § 4:14, Domestic Violence and Restraining Orders.

§ 972. Exceptions to privilege

A married person does not have a privilege under this article in:

(a) A proceeding brought by or on behalf of one spouse against the other spouse.

(b) A proceeding to commit or otherwise place his or her spouse or his or her spouse's property, or both, under the control of another because of the spouse's alleged mental or physical condition.

(c) A proceeding brought by or on behalf of a spouse to establish his or her competence.

(d) A proceeding under the Juvenile Court Law, Chapter 2 (commencing with Section 200) of Part 1 of Division 2 of the Welfare and Institutions Code.

(e) A criminal proceeding in which one spouse is charged with:

(1) A crime against the person or property of the other spouse or of a child, parent, relative, or cohabitant of either, whether committed before or during marriage.

(2) A crime against the person or property of a third person committed in the course of committing a crime against the person or property of the other spouse, whether committed before or during marriage.

(3) Bigamy.

(4) A crime defined by Section 270 or 270a of the Penal Code.

(f) A proceeding resulting from a criminal act which occurred prior to legal marriage of the spouses to each other regarding knowledge acquired prior to that marriage if prior to the legal marriage the witness spouse was aware that his or her spouse had been arrested for or had been formally charged with the crime or crimes about which the spouse is called to testify.

(g) A proceeding brought against the spouse by a former spouse so long as the property and debts of the marriage have not been adjudicated, or in order to establish, modify, or enforce a child, family or spousal support obligation arising from the marriage to the former spouse; in a proceeding brought against a spouse by the other parent in order to establish, modify, or enforce a child support obligation for a child of a nonmarital relationship of the spouse; or in a proceeding brought against a spouse by the guardian of a child of that spouse in order to establish, modify, or enforce a child support obligation of the spouse. The married person does not have a privilege under this subdivision to refuse to provide information relating to the issues of income, expenses, assets, debts, and employment of either spouse, but may assert the privilege as otherwise provided in this article if other information is requested by the former spouse, guardian, or other parent of the child.

Any person demanding the otherwise privileged information made available by this subdivision, who also has an obligation to support the child for whom an order to estabish[1] , modify, or enforce child support is sought, waives his or her marital privilege to the same extent as the spouse as provided in this subdivision. *(Stats.1965, c. 299, § 2, operative Jan. 1, 1967. Amended by Stats.1975, c. 71, p. 132, § 2; Stats.1982, c. 256, p. 833, § 1; Stats.1983, c. 244, § 1; Stats.1986, c. 769, § 1, eff. Sept. 15, 1986; Stats.1989, c. 1359, § 9.7.)*

[1] So in enrolled bill.

Law Revision Commission Comments

The exceptions to the privileges under this article are similar to those contained in Code of Civil Procedure Section 1881(1) and Penal Code Section 1322, both of which are superseded by the

Evidence Code. However, the exceptions in this section have been drafted so that they are consistent with those provided in Article 5 (commencing with Section 980) of this chapter (the privilege for confidential marital communications).

A discussion of comparable exceptions may be found in the Comments to the sections in Article 5 of this chapter. [7 Cal.L.Rev. Comm. Reports 1 (1965)].

Commentary

Jurcoane v. Superior Court, 93 Cal.App.4th 886, 113 Cal.Rptr.2d 483 (2001), holds that a magistrate erred in denying wife's assertion of the marital privilege on the ground that the spouses no longer had a viable marital relationship. *Jurcoane* reasons that there is no statutory basis for such an exception to the marital privilege

Interpreting subsection (e)(2), *People v. Sinohui, 28 Cal.4th 205, 47 P.3d 629, 120 Cal.Rptr.2d 783 (2002)*, holds that a court may compel spousal testimony even though no accusatory pleading charges a defendant with a crime against a spouse so long as the defendant commits a crime against a third party in the course of committing a crime against a spouse and the two crimes are part of a continuous course of criminal conduct and are logically related to each other.

For purposes of subsection (e)(1), a foster child is a "child." *Dunn v. Superior Court, 21 Cal.App.4th 721, 26 Cal.Rptr.2d 365 (1993), review denied 3/30/94.*

Research References

Treatises and Practice Aids

Witkin, California Summary 10th Parent and Child § 620, Privileges.
Witkin, California Summary 10th Parent and Child § 873, Privileges.

§ 973. Waiver of privilege

(a) Unless erroneously compelled to do so, a married person who testifies in a proceeding to which his spouse is a party, or who testifies against his spouse in any proceeding, does not have a privilege under this article in the proceeding in which such testimony is given.

(b) There is no privilege under this article in a civil proceeding brought or defended by a married person for the immediate benefit of his spouse or of himself and his spouse. *(Stats.1965, c. 299, § 2, operative Jan. 1, 1967.)*

ARTICLE 5. PRIVILEGE FOR CONFIDENTIAL MARITAL COMMUNICATIONS

§ 980. Confidential spousal communication privilege

Subject to Section 912 and except as otherwise provided in this article, a spouse (or his or her guardian or conservator when he or she has a guardian or conservator), whether or not a party, has a privilege during the marital or domestic partnership relationship and afterwards to refuse to disclose, and to prevent another from disclosing, a communication if he or she claims the privilege and the communication was made in confidence between him or her and the other spouse while they were spouses. *(Stats.1965, c. 299, § 2, operative Jan. 1, 1967. Amended by Stats.2016, c. 86 (S.B.1171), § 125, eff. Jan. 1, 2017; Stats.2016, c. 50 (S.B.1005), § 34, eff. Jan. 1, 2017.)*

Law Revision Commission Comments

Section 980 is the basic statement of the privilege for confidential marital communications. Exceptions to this privilege are stated in Sections 981–987.

Who can claim the privilege. Under Section 980, both spouses are the holders of the privilege and either spouse may claim it. Under existing law, the privilege *may* belong only to the nontestifying spouse inasmuch as Code of Civil Procedure Section 1881(1), superseded by the Evidence Code, provides: "[N]or can either . . . be, *without the consent of the other,* examined as to any communication made by one to the other during the marriage." (Emphasis added.) It is likely, however, that Section 1881(1) would be construed to grant the privilege to both spouses. See In re De Neef, 42 Cal.App.2d 691, 109 P.2d 741 (1941). *But see* People v. Keller, 165 Cal.App.2d 419, 423–424, 332 P.2d 174, 176 (1958) (dictum).

A guardian of an incompetent spouse may claim the privilege on behalf of that spouse. However, when a spouse is dead, no one can claim the privilege for him; the privilege, if it is to be claimed at all, can be claimed only by or on behalf of the surviving spouse.

Termination of marriage. The privilege may be claimed as to confidential communications made during a marriage even though the marriage has been terminated at the time the privilege is claimed. This states existing law. Code Civ.Proc. § 1881(1) (superseded by the Evidence Code); People v. Mullings, 83 Cal. 138, 23 Pac. 229 (1890). Free and open communication between spouses would be unduly inhibited if one of the spouses could be compelled to testify as to the nature of such communications after the termination of the marriage.

Eavesdroppers. The privilege may be asserted to prevent testimony by anyone, including eavesdroppers. To a limited extent, this constitutes a change in California law. See the Comment to Evidence Code § 954. See generally People v. Peak, 66 Cal.App.2d 894, 153 P.2d 464 (1944); People v. Morhar, 78 Cal.App. 380, 248 Pac. 975 (1926); People v. Mitchell, 61 Cal.App. 569, 215 Pac. 117 (1923). Section 980 also changes the existing law which permits a third party, to whom one of the spouses had revealed a confidential communication, to testify concerning it. People v. Swaile, 12 Cal.App. 192, 195–196, 107 Pac. 134, 137 (1909); People v. Chadwick, 4 Cal.App. 63, 72, 87 Pac. 384, 387, 388 (1906). See also Wolfle v. United States, 291 U.S. 7 (1934). Under Section 912, such conduct would constitute a waiver of the privilege only as to the spouse who makes the disclosure. [7 Cal.L.Rev.Comm. Reports 1 (1965)].

Commentary

Riverside County Sheriff's Dept. v. Zigman, 169 Cal.App.4th 763, 87 Cal.Rptr.3d 358 (2008), review denied, held that the marital communication privilege does not apply in the administrative investigations and proceedings of a law enforcement agency.

See generally *People v. Badgett, 10 Cal.4th 330, 895 P.2d 877, 41 Cal.Rptr.2d 635 (1995)* (evidence supported trial court determination that defendant and witness had not contracted a valid Texas common law marriage and thus the defendant could not assert the privilege for confidential marriage communications in order to bar the testimony of witness).

Research References

Forms

California Transactions Forms--Family Law § 4:14, Domestic Violence and Restraining Orders.

Treatises and Practice Aids

Witkin, California Summary 10th Husband and Wife § 151, Relation Back Theory.

§ 981. Exception: Crime or fraud

There is no privilege under this article if the communication was made, in whole or in part, to enable or aid anyone to commit or plan to commit a crime or a fraud. *(Stats.1965, c. 299, § 2, operative Jan. 1, 1967.)*

Law Revision Commission Comments

California recognizes this as an exception to the lawyer-client privilege, but it does not appear to have been recognized in the California cases dealing with the confidential marital communications privilege. Nonetheless, the exception does not seem so broad that it would impair the values that the privilege is intended to preserve; in many cases, the evidence which would be admissible under this exception will be vital in order to do justice between the parties to a lawsuit. This exception would not, of course, infringe on the privileges accorded to a married person under Sections 970 and 971.

It is important to note that the exception provided by Section 981 is quite limited. It does not permit disclosure of communications that merely reveal a plan to commit a crime or fraud; it permits disclosure only of communications made to *enable* or *aid* anyone to commit or plan to commit a crime or fraud. Thus, unless the communication is for the purpose of obtaining assistance in the commission of the crime or fraud or in furtherance thereof, it is not made admissible by the exception provided in this section. *Cf.* People v. Pierce, 61 Cal.2d 879, 40 Cal.Rptr. 845, 395 P.2d 893 (1964) (husband and wife who conspire only between themselves against others cannot claim immunity from prosecution for conspiracy on the basis of their marital status). [7 Cal.L.Rev.Comm. Reports 1 (1965)].

§ 982. Commitment or similar proceedings

There is no privilege under this article in a proceeding to commit either spouse or otherwise place him or his property, or both, under the control of another because of his alleged mental or physical condition. *(Stats.1965, c. 299, § 2, operative Jan. 1, 1967.)*

Law Revision Commission Comments

Sections 982 and 983 express existing law. Code Civ.Proc. § 1881(1) (superseded by the Evidence Code). Commitment and competency proceedings are undertaken for the benefit of the subject person. Frequently, much or all of the evidence bearing on a spouse's competency or lack of competency will consist of communications to the other spouse. It would be undesirable to permit either spouse to invoke a privilege to prevent the presentation of this vital information inasmuch as these proceedings are of such vital importance both to society and to the spouse who is the subject of the proceedings. [7 Cal.L.Rev.Comm. Reports 1 (1965)].

§ 983. Competency proceedings

There is no privilege under this article in a proceeding brought by or on behalf of either spouse to establish his competence. *(Stats.1965, c. 299, § 2, operative Jan. 1, 1967.)*

Law Revision Commission Comments

See the Comment to Section 982. [7 Cal.L.Rev.Comm. Reports 1 (1965)].

§ 984. Proceeding between spouses

There is no privilege under this article in:

(a) A proceeding brought by or on behalf of one spouse against the other spouse.

(b) A proceeding between a surviving spouse and a person who claims through the deceased spouse, regardless of whether such claim is by testate or intestate succession or by inter vivos transaction. *(Stats.1965, c. 299, § 2, operative Jan. 1, 1967.)*

Law Revision Commission Comments

The exception to the marital communications privilege for litigation between the spouses states existing law. Code Civ.Proc. § 1881(1) (superseded by the Evidence Code). Section 984 extends the principle to cases where one of the spouses is dead and the litigation is between his successor and the surviving spouse. See generally Estate of Gillett, 73 Cal.App.2d 588, 166 P.2d 870 (1946). [7 Cal.L.Rev.Comm. Reports 1 (1965)].

§ 985. Criminal proceedings

There is no privilege under this article in a criminal proceeding in which one spouse is charged with:

(a) A crime committed at any time against the person or property of the other spouse or of a child of either.

(b) A crime committed at any time against the person or property of a third person committed in the course of committing a crime against the person or property of the other spouse.

(c) Bigamy.

(d) A crime defined by Section 270 or 270a of the Penal Code. *(Stats.1965, c. 299, § 2, operative Jan. 1, 1967. Amended by Stats.1975, c. 71, p. 133, § 3.)*

Law Revision Commission Comments

This exception restates with minor variations an exception that is recognized under existing law. Code Civ.Proc. § 1881(1) (superseded by the Evidence Code). Sections 985 and 986 together create an exception for all the proceedings mentioned in Section 1322 of the Penal Code (superseded by the Evidence Code). [7 Cal.L.Rev. Comm. Reports 1 (1965)].

Commentary

For discussion of the Rule 501 marital communication privilege of the Federal Rules of Evidence, see *United States v. Murphy, 65 F.3d 758 (9th Cir. 1995)* (holding that the federal privilege does not apply when the communication was made while the spouses were separated and their differences were irreconcilable).

§ 986. Juvenile court proceedings

There is no privilege under this article in a proceeding under the Juvenile Court Law, Chapter 2 (commencing with Section 200) of Part 1 of Division 2 of the Welfare and Institutions Code. *(Stats.1965, c. 299, § 2, operative Jan. 1, 1967. Amended by Stats.1982, c. 256, p. 833, § 2.)*

Law Revision Commission Comments

See the Comment to Section 985. [7 Cal.L.Rev.Comm. Reports 1 (1965)].

Research References

Treatises and Practice Aids

Witkin, California Summary 10th Parent and Child § 620, Privileges.
Witkin, California Summary 10th Parent and Child § 873, Privileges.

§ 987. Communication offered by spouse who is criminal defendant

There is no privilege under this article in a criminal proceeding in which the communication is offered in evidence by a defendant who is one of the spouses between whom the communication was made. *(Stats.1965, c. 299, § 2, operative Jan. 1, 1967.)*

Law Revision Commission Comments

This exception does not appear to have been recognized in any California case. Nonetheless, it is a desirable exception. When a married person is the defendant in a criminal proceeding and seeks to introduce evidence which is material to his defense, his spouse (or his former spouse) should not be privileged to withhold the information. [7 Cal.L.Rev.Comm. Reports 1 (1965)].

ARTICLE 6. PHYSICIAN–PATIENT PRIVILEGE

§ 990. Physician

As used in this article, "physician" means a person authorized, or reasonably believed by the patient to be authorized, to practice medicine in any state or nation. *(Stats.1965, c. 299, § 2, operative Jan. 1, 1967.)*

Law Revision Commission Comments

Defining "physician" to include a person "reasonably believed by the patient to be authorized" to practice medicine changes the existing law which requires that the physician be licensed. See Code Civ.Proc. § 1881(4) (superseded by the Evidence Code). But, if this privilege is to be recognized, it should protect the patient from reasonable mistakes as to unlicensed practitioners. The privilege also should be applicable to communications made to a physician authorized to practice in any state or nation. When a California resident travels outside the State and has occasion to visit a physician during such travel, or when a physician from another state or nation participates in the treatment of a person in California, the patient should be entitled to assume that his communications will be given as much protection as they would be if he consulted a California physician in California. A patient should not be forced to inquire about the jurisdictions where the physician is authorized to practice medicine and whether such jurisdictions recognize the physician-patient privilege before he may safely communicate with the physician. [7 Cal.L.Rev.Comm. Reports 1 (1965)].

§ 991. Patient

As used in this article, "patient" means a person who consults a physician or submits to an examination by a physician for the purpose of securing a diagnosis or preventive, palliative, or curative treatment of his physical or mental or emotional condition. *(Stats.1965, c. 299, § 2, operative Jan. 1, 1967.)*

§ 992. Confidential communication between patient and physician

As used in this article, "confidential communication between patient and physician" means information, including information obtained by an examination of the patient, transmitted between a patient and his physician in the course of that relationship and in confidence by a means which, so far as the patient is aware, discloses the information to no third persons other than those who are present to further the interest of the patient in the consultation or those to whom disclosure is reasonably necessary for the transmission of the information or the accomplishment of the purpose for which the physician is consulted, and includes a diagnosis made and the advice given by the physician in the course of that relationship. *(Stats.1965, c. 299, § 2, operative Jan. 1, 1967. Amended by Stats.1967, c. 650, p. 2006, § 4.)*

Law Revision Commission Comments

1967 Amendment

The express inclusion of "a diagnosis" in the last clause will preclude a possible construction of this section that would leave an uncommunicated diagnosis unprotected by the privilege. Such a construction would virtually destroy the privilege. [8 Cal.L.Rev. Comm. Reports 101 (1967)].

§ 993. Holder of the privilege

As used in this article, "holder of the privilege" means:

(a) The patient when he has no guardian or conservator.

(b) A guardian or conservator of the patient when the patient has a guardian or conservator.

(c) The personal representative of the patient if the patient is dead. *(Stats.1965, c. 299, § 2, operative Jan. 1, 1967.)*

Law Revision Commission Comments

A guardian of the patient is the holder of the privilege if the patient has a guardian. If the patient has separate guardians of his estate and of his person, either guardian may claim the privilege. The provision making the personal representative of the patient the holder of the privilege when the patient is dead may change California law. The existing law may be that the privilege survives the death of the patient in some cases and that no one can waive it on behalf of the patient. See the discussion in Tentative Recommendation and a Study Relating to the Uniform Rules of Evidence (Article V. Privileges), 6 Cal.Law Revision Comm'n, Rep., Rec. & Studies 201, 408–410 (1964). Sections 993 and 994 enable the personal representative to protect the interest of the patient's estate in the confidentiality of these statements and to waive the privilege when the estate would benefit by waiver. When the patient's estate has no interest in preserving confidentiality, or when the estate has been distributed and the representative discharged, the importance of providing complete access to information relevant to a particular proceeding should prevail over whatever remaining interest the decedent may have had in secrecy. [7 Cal.L.Rev.Comm. Reports 1 (1965)].

§ 994. Physician-patient privilege

Subject to Section 912 and except as otherwise provided in this article, the patient, whether or not a party, has a privilege to refuse to disclose, and to prevent another from disclosing, a confidential communication between patient and physician if the privilege is claimed by:

(a) The holder of the privilege;

(b) A person who is authorized to claim the privilege by the holder of the privilege; or

(c) The person who was the physician at the time of the confidential communication, but such person may not claim the privilege if there is no holder of the privilege in existence or if he or she is otherwise instructed by a person authorized to permit disclosure.

The relationship of a physician and patient shall exist between a medical or podiatry corporation as defined in the Medical Practice Act and the patient to whom it renders professional services, as well as between such patients and licensed physicians and surgeons employed by such corporation to render services to such patients. The word "persons" as used in this subdivision includes partnerships, corporations, limited liability companies, associations, and other groups and entities. *(Stats.1965, c. 299, § 2, operative Jan. 1, 1967. Amended by Stats.1968, c. 1375, p. 2696, § 3; Stats. 1980, c. 1313, p. 4532, § 12; Stats.1994, c. 1010 (S.B.2053), § 105.)*

Law Revision Commission Comments

This section, like Section 954 (lawyer-client privilege), is based on the premise that the privilege must be claimed by a person who is authorized to claim the privilege. If there is no claim of privilege by a person with authority to make the claim, the evidence is admissible. See the Comments to Evidence Code §§ 993 and 954.

For the reasons indicated in the Comment to Section 954, an eavesdropper or other interceptor of a communication privileged under this section is not permitted to testify to the communication. [7 Cal.L.Rev.Comm. Reports 1 (1965)].

Commentary

A sperm donor may not invoke this privilege in order to avoid discovery about his dealings with the sperm bank to which he sold sperm, because the sperm donor is not a patient of the sperm bank. *Johnson v. Superior Court, 80 Cal.App.4th 1050, 95 Cal.Rptr.2d 864 (2000)*. For further discussion of *Johnson*, see Family Code § 7613, Commentary.

§ 995. When physician required to claim privilege

The physician who received or made a communication subject to the privilege under this article shall claim the privilege whenever he is present when the communication is sought to be disclosed and is authorized to claim the privilege under subdivision (c) of Section 994. *(Stats.1965, c. 299, § 2, operative Jan. 1, 1967.)*

Law Revision Commission Comments

The obligation of the physician to claim the privilege on behalf of the patient, unless otherwise instructed by a person authorized to permit disclosure, is consistent with Section 2379 of the Business and Professions Code. [7 Cal.L.Rev.Comm. Reports 1 (1965)].

§ 996. Patient-litigant exception

There is no privilege under this article as to a communication relevant to an issue concerning the condition of the patient if such issue has been tendered by:

(a) The patient;

(b) Any party claiming through or under the patient;

(c) Any party claiming as a beneficiary of the patient through a contract to which the patient is or was a party; or

(d) The plaintiff in an action brought under Section 376 or 377 of the Code of Civil Procedure for damages for the injury or death of the patient. *(Stats.1965, c. 299, § 2, operative Jan. 1, 1967.)*

Law Revision Commission Comments

Section 996 provides that the physician-patient privilege does not exist in any proceeding in which an issue concerning the condition of the patient has been tendered by the patient. If the patient himself tenders the issue of his condition, he should not be able to withhold relevant evidence from the opposing party by the exercise of the physician-patient privilege.

A limited form of this exception is recognized by Code of Civil Procedure Section 1881(4) (superseded by the Evidence Code) which makes the privilege inapplicable in personal injury actions. This exception is also recognized in various types of administrative proceedings where the patient tenders the issue of his condition. *E.g.,* Labor Code §§ 4055, 5701, 5703, 6407, 6408 (proceedings before the Industrial Accident Commission). The exception provided by Section 996 applies not only to proceedings before the Industrial Accident Commission but also to any other proceeding where the patient tenders the issue of his condition. The exception in Section 996 also states existing law in applying the exception to other situations where the patient himself has raised the issue of his condition. In re Cathey, 55 Cal.2d 679, 690–692, 12 Cal.Rptr. 762, 768, 361 P.2d 426, 432 (1961) (prisoner in state medical facility waived physician-patient privilege by putting his mental condition in issue by application for habeas corpus); see also City & County of San Francisco v. Superior Court, 37 Cal.2d 227, 232, 231 P.2d 26, 28 (1951) (personal injury case).

Section 996 also provides that there is no privilege in an action brought under Section 377 of the Code of Civil Procedure (wrongful death). Under Code of Civil Procedure Section 1881(4) (superseded by the Evidence Code), a person authorized to bring the wrongful death action may consent to the testimony by the physician. As far as testimony by the physician is concerned, there is no reason why the rules of evidence should be different in a case where the patient brings the action and a case where someone else sues for the patient's wrongful death.

Section 996 also provides that there is no privilege in an action brought under Section 376 of the Code of Civil Procedure (parent's action for injury to child). In this case, as in a case under the wrongful death statute, the same rule of evidence should apply when the parent brings the action as applies when the child is the plaintiff. [7 Cal.L.Rev.Comm. Reports 1 (1965)].

Commentary

Invoking this section, *In re R.R., 187 Cal.App.4th 1264, 114 Cal.Rptr.3d 765 (2010)*, holds that in a child dependency proceeding, a parent who claims to have been drug-free for six years himself tenders the issue of past drug use and thus forfeits the patient-physician privilege as to past drug use.

By disclosing sexual abuse by a parent to authorities or by submitting to a forensic medical examination, a child does not tender her medical condition, within the meaning of subsection (a), in dependency litigation. Nor did a social services agency become a party within the meaning of subsection (b) when it filed a dependency petition alleging the child was sexually abused by a parent. *Karen P. v. Superior Court, 200 Cal.App.4th 908, 133 Cal.Rptr.3d 67 (2011).*

§ 997. Exception: crime or tort

There is no privilege under this article if the services of the physician were sought or obtained to enable or aid anyone to commit or plan to commit a crime or a tort or to escape detection or apprehension after the commission of a crime or a tort. *(Stats.1965, c. 299, § 2, operative Jan. 1, 1967.)*

Law Revision Commission Comments

This section is considerably broader in scope than Section 956 which provides that the lawyer-client privilege does not apply when the communication was made to enable anyone to commit or plan to commit a crime or a *fraud*. Section 997 creates an exception to the physician-patient privilege where the services of the physician were sought or obtained to enable or aid anyone to commit or plan to commit a crime or a *tort,* or to escape detection or apprehension after commission of a crime or a *tort*. People seldom, if ever, consult their physicians in regard to matters which might subsequently be determined to be a tort, and there is no desirable end to be served by encouraging such communications. On the other hand, people often consult lawyers about matters which may later turn out to be torts and it is desirable to encourage discussion of such matters with lawyers. Whether the exception provided by Section 997 now exists in California has not been determined in any decided case, but it probably would be recognized in an appropriate case in view of the similar court-created exception to the lawyer-client privilege. See the Comment to Evidence Code § 956. [7 Cal.L.Rev.Comm. Reports 1 (1965)].

§ 998. Criminal proceeding

There is no privilege under this article in a criminal proceeding. *(Stats.1965, c. 299, § 2, operative Jan. 1, 1967.)*

§ 999. Communication relating to patient condition in proceeding to recover damages; good cause

There is no privilege under this article as to a communication relevant to an issue concerning the condition of the patient in a proceeding to recover damages on account of the conduct of the patient if good cause for disclosure of the communication is shown. *(Stats.1965, c. 299, § 2, operative Jan. 1, 1967. Amended by Stats.1975, c. 318, p. 764, § 1.)*

§ 1000. Parties claiming through deceased patient

There is no privilege under this article as to a communication relevant to an issue between parties all of whom claim through a deceased patient, regardless of whether the claims are by testate or intestate succession or by inter vivos transaction. *(Stats.1965, c. 299, § 2, operative Jan. 1, 1967.)*

Law Revision Commission Comments

See the Comment to Section 957. [7 Cal.L.Rev.Comm. Reports 1 (1965)].

§ 1001. Breach of duty arising out of physician-patient relationship

There is no privilege under this article as to a communication relevant to an issue of breach, by the physician or by the patient, of a duty arising out of the physician-patient relationship. *(Stats.1965, c. 299, § 2, operative Jan. 1, 1967.)*

Law Revision Commission Comments

See the Comment to Section 658. [7 Cal.L.Rev.Comm. Reports 1 (1965)].

§ 1002. Intention of deceased patient concerning writing affecting property interest

There is no privilege under this article as to a communication relevant to an issue concerning the intention of a patient, now deceased, with respect to a deed of conveyance, will, or other writing, executed by the patient, purporting to affect an interest in property. *(Stats.1965, c. 299, § 2, operative Jan. 1, 1967.)*

Law Revision Commission Comments

Existing law provides exceptions virtually coextensive with those provided in Sections 1002 and 1003. Code Civ.Proc. § 1881(4) (superseded by the Evidence Code). See the Comment to Section 960. [7 Cal.L.Rev.Comm. Reports 1 (1965)].

§ 1003. Validity of writing affecting property interest

There is no privilege under this article as to a communication relevant to an issue concerning the validity of a deed of conveyance, will, or other writing, executed by a patient, now deceased, purporting to affect an interest in property. *(Stats. 1965, c. 299, § 2, operative Jan. 1, 1967.)*

Law Revision Commission Comments

See the Comment to Section 1002. [7 Cal.L.Rev.Comm. Reports 1 (1965)].

§ 1004. Commitment or similar proceeding

There is no privilege under this article in a proceeding to commit the patient or otherwise place him or his property, or both, under the control of another because of his alleged mental or physical condition. *(Stats.1965, c. 299, § 2, operative Jan. 1, 1967.)*

Law Revision Commission Comments

This exception covers not only commitments of mentally ill persons but also such cases as the appointment of a conservator under Probate Code Section 1751. In these cases, the proceedings are being conducted for the benefit of the patient and he should not have a privilege to withhold evidence that the court needs in order to act properly for his welfare. There is no similar exception in existing law. McClenahan v. Keyes, 188 Cal. 574, 584, 206 Pac. 454, 458 (1922) (dictum). *But see* 35 Ops.Cal.Atty.Gen. 226 (1960), regarding the unavailability of the present physician-patient privilege where the physician acts pursuant to court appointment for the explicit purpose of giving testimony. [7 Cal.L.Rev.Comm. Reports 1 (1965)].

§ 1005. Proceeding to establish competence

There is no privilege under this article in a proceeding brought by or on behalf of the patient to establish his competence. *(Stats.1965, c. 299, § 2, operative Jan. 1, 1967.)*

Law Revision Commission Comments

This exception is new to California law. When a patient has placed his mental condition in issue by instituting a proceeding to establish his competence, he should not be permitted to withhold the most vital evidence relating thereto. [7 Cal.L.Rev.Comm. Reports 1 (1965)].

§ 1006. Required report

There is no privilege under this article as to information that the physician or the patient is required to report to a public employee, or as to information required to be recorded in a public office, if such report or record is open to public inspection. *(Stats.1965, c. 299, § 2, operative Jan. 1, 1967.)*

Law Revision Commission Comments

This exception is not recognized by existing law. However, no valid purpose is served by preventing the use of relevant information when the law requiring the information to be reported to a public office does not restrict disclosure. [7 Cal.L.Rev.Comm. Reports 1 (1965)].

§ 1007. Proceeding to terminate right, license or privilege

There is no privilege under this article in a proceeding brought by a public entity to determine whether a right, authority, license, or privilege (including the right or privilege to be employed by the public entity or to hold a public office) should be revoked, suspended, terminated, limited, or conditioned. *(Stats.1965, c. 299, § 2, operative Jan. 1, 1967.)*

ARTICLE 7. PSYCHOTHERAPIST–PATIENT PRIVILEGE

§ 1010. Psychotherapist

As used in this article, "psychotherapist" means a person who is, or is reasonably believed by the patient to be:

(a) A person authorized to practice medicine in any state or nation who devotes, or is reasonably believed by the patient to devote, a substantial portion of his or her time to the practice of psychiatry.

(b) A person licensed as a psychologist under Chapter 6.6 (commencing with Section 2900) of Division 2 of the Business and Professions Code.

(c) A person licensed as a clinical social worker under * * * Chapter 14 (commencing with Section * * * 4991) of Division 2 of the Business and Professions Code, when he or she is engaged in applied psychotherapy of a nonmedical nature.

(d) A person who is serving as a school psychologist and holds a credential authorizing that service issued by the state.

(e) A person licensed as a marriage and family therapist under Chapter 13 (commencing with Section 4980) of Division 2 of the Business and Professions Code.

(f) A person registered as a psychological assistant who is under the supervision of a licensed psychologist or board certified psychiatrist as required by Section 2913 of the Business and Professions Code, or a person registered as * * * an associate marriage and family therapist * * * who is under the supervision of a licensed marriage and family therapist, a licensed clinical social worker, a licensed psychologist, or a licensed physician and surgeon certified in psychiatry, as specified in Section 4980.44 of the Business and Professions Code.

(g) A person registered as an associate clinical social worker who is under supervision as specified in Section 4996.23 of the Business and Professions Code.

(h) A person registered with the Board of Psychology as a registered psychologist who is under the supervision of a licensed psychologist or board certified psychiatrist.

(i) A psychological intern as defined in Section 2911 of the Business and Professions Code who is under the supervision of a licensed psychologist or board certified psychiatrist.

(j) A trainee, as defined in subdivision (c) of Section 4980.03 of the Business and Professions Code, who is fulfilling his or her supervised practicum required by subparagraph (B) of paragraph (1) of subdivision (d) of Section 4980.36 of, or subdivision (c) of Section 4980.37 of, the Business and Professions Code and is supervised by a licensed psychologist, a board certified psychiatrist, a licensed clinical social worker, a licensed marriage and family therapist, or a licensed professional clinical counselor.

(k) A person licensed as a registered nurse pursuant to Chapter 6 (commencing with Section 2700) of Division 2 of the Business and Professions Code, who possesses a master's degree in psychiatric-mental health nursing and is listed as a psychiatric-mental health nurse by the Board of Registered Nursing.

(*l*) An advanced practice registered nurse who is certified as a clinical nurse specialist pursuant to Article 9 (commencing with Section 2838) of Chapter 6 of Division 2 of the Business and Professions Code and who participates in expert clinical practice in the specialty of psychiatric-mental health nursing.

(m) A person rendering mental health treatment or counseling services as authorized pursuant to Section 6924 of the Family Code.

(n) A person licensed as a professional clinical counselor under Chapter 16 (commencing with Section 4999.10) of Division 2 of the Business and Professions Code.

(*o*) A person registered as * * * an associate professional clinical counselor * * * who is under the supervision of a licensed professional clinical counselor, a licensed marriage and family therapist, a licensed clinical social worker, a licensed psychologist, or a licensed physician and surgeon certified in psychiatry, as specified in Sections 4999.42 to 4999.46, inclusive, of the Business and Professions Code.

(p) A clinical counselor trainee, as defined in subdivision (g) of Section 4999.12 of the Business and Professions Code, who is fulfilling his or her supervised practicum required by paragraph (3) of subdivision (c) of Section 4999.32 of, or paragraph (3) of subdivision (c) of Section 4999.33 of, the Business and Professions Code, and is supervised by a licensed psychologist, a board-certified psychiatrist, a licensed clinical social worker, a licensed marriage and family therapist, or a licensed professional clinical counselor. *(Stats. 1965, c. 299, § 2, operative Jan. 1, 1967. Amended by Stats.1967, c. 1677, p. 4211, § 3; Stats.1970, c. 1396, p. 2624, § 1.5; Stats.1970, c. 1397, p. 2626, § 1.5; Stats.1972, c. 888, p. 1584, § 1; Stats.1974, c. 546, p. 1359, § 16; Stats.1983, c. 928, § 8; Stats.1987, c. 724, § 1; Stats.1988, c. 488, § 1; Stats. 1989, c. 1104, § 37; Stats.1990, c. 662 (A.B.3613), § 1; Stats.1992, c. 308 (A.B.3035), § 2; Stats.1994, c. 1270 (A.B. 2659), § 1; Stats.2001, c. 142 (S.B.716), § 1; Stats.2001, c. 420 (A.B.1253), § 1, eff. Oct. 2, 2001; Stats.2001, c. 420 (A.B.1253), § 1.5, eff. Oct. 2, 2001, operative Jan. 1, 2002; Stats.2009, c. 26 (S.B.33), § 21; Stats.2011, c. 381 (S.B.146), § 21; Stats.2015, c. 529 (A.B.1374), § 4, eff. Jan. 1, 2016; Stats.2016, c. 86 (S.B.1171), § 126, eff. Jan. 1, 2017; Stats. 2017, c. 573 (S.B.800), § 75, eff. Jan. 1, 2018.)*

Law Revision Commission Comments

A "psychotherapist" is defined to include only a person who is or who is reasonably believed to be a psychiatrist or who is a California certified psychologist (see Bus. & Prof.Code § 2900 et seq.). See the Comment to Section 990. [7 Cal.L.Rev.Comm. Reports 1 (1965)].

Research References

Forms

California Transactions Forms--Family Law § 3:16, Identifying Areas Of Parental Decision Making and Participation.

Treatises and Practice Aids

Witkin, California Summary 10th Contracts § 45, Minor Needing Mental Health Treatment.

§ 1010.5. Privileged communication between patient and educational psychologist

A communication between a patient and an educational psychologist, licensed under Article 5 (commencing with Section 4986) of Chapter 13 of Division 2 of the Business and Professions Code, shall be privileged to the same extent, and subject to the same limitations, as a communication between a patient and a psychotherapist described in subdivisions (c), (d), and (e) of Section 1010. *(Added by Stats.1985, c. 545, § 1.)*

§ 1011. Patient

As used in this article, "patient" means a person who consults a psychotherapist or submits to an examination by a psychotherapist for the purpose of securing a diagnosis or preventive, palliative, or curative treatment of his mental or emotional condition or who submits to an examination of his mental or emotional condition for the purpose of scientific research on mental or emotional problems. *(Stats.1965, c. 299, § 2, operative Jan. 1, 1967.)*

§ 1012. Confidential communication between patient and psychotherapist

As used in this article, "confidential communication between patient and psychotherapist" means information, including information obtained by an examination of the patient, transmitted between a patient and his psychotherapist in the course of that relationship and in confidence by a means which, so far as the patient is aware, discloses the information to no third persons other than those who are present to further the interest of the patient in the consultation, or those to whom disclosure is reasonably necessary for the transmission of the information or the accomplishment of the purpose for which the psychotherapist is consulted, and includes a diagnosis made and the advice given by the psychotherapist in the course of that relationship. *(Stats. 1965, c. 299, § 2, operative Jan. 1, 1967. Amended by Stats.1967, c. 650, p. 2006, § 5; Stats.1970, c. 1396, p. 2625, § 2; Stats.1970, c. 1397, p. 2627, § 2.)*

Law Revision Commission Comments

1965 Enactment

See the Comment to Section 992. [7 Cal.L.Rev.Comm. Reports 1 (1965)].

1967 Amendment

The express inclusion of "a diagnosis" in the last clause will preclude a possible construction of this section that would leave an uncommunicated diagnosis unprotected by the privilege. Such a construction would virtually destroy the privilege. [8 Cal.L.Rev. Comm. Reports 101 (1967)].

1970 Amendment

Section 1012 is amended to add "including other patients present at joint therapy" in order to foreclose the possibility that the section would be construed not to embrace marriage counseling, family counseling, and other forms of group therapy. However, it should be noted that communications made in the course of joint therapy are within the privilege only if they are made "in confidence" and "by a means which . . . discloses the information to no third persons other than those . . . to whom disclosure is reasonably necessary for . . . the accomplishment of the purpose for which the psychotherapist is consulted." The making of a communication that meets these two requirements in the course of joint therapy would not amount to a waiver of the privilege. See Evidence Code Section 912(c) and (d).

The other amendments are technical and conform the language of Section 1012 to that of Section 992, the comparable section relating to the physician-patient privilege. Deletion of the words "or examination" makes no substantive change since "consultation" is broad enough to cover an examination. See Section 992. Substitution of "for which the psychotherapist is consulted" for "of the consultation or examination" adopts the broader language used in subdivision (d) of Section 912 and in Section 992. [9 Cal.L.Rev. Comm. Reports 153 (1969)].

Research References

Treatises and Practice Aids

Witkin, California Summary 10th Parent and Child § 620, Privileges.
Witkin, California Summary 10th Parent and Child § 873, Privileges.
Witkin, California Summary 10th Parent and Child § 939, Other Conditions.

§ 1013. Holder of the privilege

As used in this article, "holder of the privilege" means:

(a) The patient when he has no guardian or conservator.

(b) A guardian or conservator of the patient when the patient has a guardian or conservator.

(c) The personal representative of the patient if the patient is dead. *(Stats.1965, c. 299, § 2, operative Jan. 1, 1967.)*

Law Revision Commission Comments

See the Comment to Section 993. [7 Cal.L.Rev.Comm. Reports 1 (1965)].

§ 1014. Psychotherapist-patient privilege; application to individuals and entities

Subject to Section 912 and except as otherwise provided in this article, the patient, whether or not a party, has a privilege to refuse to disclose, and to prevent another from disclosing, a confidential communication between patient and psychotherapist if the privilege is claimed by:

(a) The holder of the privilege.

(b) A person who is authorized to claim the privilege by the holder of the privilege.

(c) The person who was the psychotherapist at the time of the confidential communication, but the person may not claim the privilege if there is no holder of the privilege in existence or if he or she is otherwise instructed by a person authorized to permit disclosure.

The relationship of a psychotherapist and patient shall exist between a psychological corporation as defined in Article 9 (commencing with Section 2995) of Chapter 6.6 of Division 2 of the Business and Professions Code, a marriage and family therapist corporation as defined in Article 6 (commencing with Section 4987.5) of Chapter 13 of Division 2 of the Business and Professions Code, a licensed clinical social workers corporation as defined in Article 5 (commencing with Section 4998) of Chapter 14 of Division 2 of the Business and Professions Code, or a professional clinical counselor corporation as defined in Article 7 (commencing with Section 4999.123) of Chapter 16 of Division 2 of the Business and Professions Code, and the patient to whom it renders professional services, as well as between those patients and psychotherapists employed by those corporations to render services to those patients. The word "persons" as used in this subdivision includes partnerships, corporations, limited liability companies, associations, and other groups and entities. *(Stats.1965, c. 299, § 2, operative Jan. 1, 1967. Amended by Stats.1969, c. 1436, p. 2943, § 1; Stats.1972, c. 1286, p. 2569, § 6; Stats.1989, c. 1104, § 38; Stats.1990, c. 605 (S.B.2245), § 1; Stats.1994, c. 1010 (S.B. 2053), § 106; Stats.2002, c. 1013 (S.B.2026), § 78; Stats.2011, c. 381 (S.B.146), § 22.)*

Commentary

Mansell v. Otto, 108 Cal.App.4th 265, 133 Cal.Rptr.2d 276 (2003), holds that a crime victim could not state a claim for invasion of her right to privacy, under this section or under the constitutional right of privacy, for unauthorized reading of her mental health records by members of a criminal defense team, when her medical and psychiatric records were obtained through normal judicial process.

Research References

Treatises and Practice Aids

Witkin, California Summary 10th Constitutional Law § 423, Civil Trial.

Witkin, California Summary 10th Parent and Child § 284, Trial.

Witkin, California Summary 10th Parent and Child § 873, Privileges.

§ 1015. When psychotherapist required to claim privilege

The psychotherapist who received or made a communication subject to the privilege under this article shall claim the privilege whenever he is present when the communication is sought to be disclosed and is authorized to claim the privilege under subdivision (c) of Section 1014. *(Stats.1965, c. 299, § 2, operative Jan. 1, 1967.)*

Law Revision Commission Comments

See the Comment to Section 995. [7 Cal.L.Rev.Comm. Reports 1 (1965)].

§ 1016. Exception: Patient-litigant exception

There is no privilege under this article as to a communication relevant to an issue concerning the mental or emotional condition of the patient if such issue has been tendered by:

(a) The patient;

(b) Any party claiming through or under the patient;

(c) Any party claiming as a beneficiary of the patient through a contract to which the patient is or was a party; or

(d) The plaintiff in an action brought under Section 376 or 377 of the Code of Civil Procedure for damages for the injury or death of the patient. *(Stats.1965, c. 299, § 2, operative Jan. 1, 1967.)*

Law Revision Commission Comments

See the Comment to Section 996. [7 Cal.L.Rev.Comm. Reports 1 (1965)].

Research References

Treatises and Practice Aids

Witkin, California Summary 10th Parent and Child § 620, Privileges.

§ 1017. Exception: Psychotherapist appointed by court or board of prison terms

(a) There is no privilege under this article if the psychotherapist is appointed by order of a court to examine the patient, but this exception does not apply where the psychotherapist is appointed by order of the court upon the request of the lawyer for the defendant in a criminal proceeding in order to provide the lawyer with information needed so that he or she may advise the defendant whether to enter or withdraw a plea based on insanity or to present a defense based on his or her mental or emotional condition.

(b) There is no privilege under this article if the psychotherapist is appointed by the Board of Prison Terms to examine a patient pursuant to the provisions of Article 4 (commencing with Section 2960) of Chapter 7 of Title 1 of Part 3 of the Penal Code. *(Stats.1965, c. 299, § 2, operative Jan. 1, 1967. Amended by Stats.1967, c. 650, p. 2007, § 6; Stats.1987, c. 687, § 1.)*

Law Revision Commission Comments

1965 Enactment

Section 1017 provides an exception to the psychotherapist-patient privilege if the psychotherapist is appointed by order of a court to examine the patient. Generally, where the relationship of psychotherapist and patient is created by court order, there is not a sufficiently confidential relationship to warrant extending the privilege to communications made in the course of that relationship. Moreover, when the psychotherapist is appointed by the court, it is most often for the purpose of having the psychotherapist testify concerning his conclusions as to the patient's condition. It would be inappropriate to have the privilege apply in this situation. See generally 35 Ops.Cal.Atty.Gen. 226 (1960), regarding the unavailability of the present physician-patient privilege under these circumstances.

On the other hand, it is essential that the privilege apply where the psychotherapist is appointed by order of the court to provide the defendant's lawyer with information needed so that he may advise the defendant whether to enter a plea based on insanity or to present a defense based on his mental or emotional condition. If the defendant determines not to tender the issue of his mental or emotional condition, the privilege will protect the confidentiality of the communication between him and his court-appointed psychotherapist. If, however, the defendant determines to tender this issue—by a plea of not guilty by reason of insanity, by presenting a defense based on his mental or emotional condition, or by raising the question of his sanity at the time of the trial—the exceptions provided in Sections 1016 and 1023 make the privilege unavailable to prevent disclosure of the communications between the defendant and the psychotherapist. [7 Cal.L.Rev.Comm. Reports 1 (1965)].

1967 Amendment

The words "or withdraw" are added to Section 1017 to make it clear that the psychotherapist-patient privilege applies in a case where the defendant in a criminal proceeding enters a plea based on insanity, submits to an examination by a court-appointed psychotherapist, and later withdraws the plea based on insanity prior to the trial on that issue. In such case, since the defendant does not tender an issue based on his mental or emotional condition at the trial, the privilege should remain applicable. Of course, if the defendant determines to go to trial on the plea based on insanity, the psychotherapist-patient privilege will not be applicable. See Section 1016.

It should be noted that violation of the constitutional right to counsel may require the exclusion of evidence that is not privileged under this article; and, even in cases where this constitutional right is not violated, the protection that this right affords may require certain procedural safeguards in the examination procedure and a limiting instruction if the psychotherapist's testimony is admitted. See In re Spencer, 63 Cal.2d 400, 46 Cal.Rptr. 753, 406 P.2d 33 (1965).

It is important to recognize that the attorney-client privilege may provide protection in some cases where an exception to the psychotherapist-patient privilege is applicable. See Section 952 and the *Comment* thereto. See also Sections 912(d) and 954 and the *Comments* thereto. [8 Cal.L.Rev.Comm. Reports 101 (1967)].

Research References

Treatises and Practice Aids

Witkin, California Summary 10th Parent and Child § 284, Trial.
Witkin, California Summary 10th Parent and Child § 620, Privileges.

§ 1018. Exception: Crime or tort

There is no privilege under this article if the services of the psychotherapist were sought or obtained to enable or aid anyone to commit or plan to commit a crime or a tort or to escape detection or apprehension after the commission of a crime or a tort. *(Stats.1965, c. 299, § 2, operative Jan. 1, 1967.)*

Law Revision Commission Comments

See the Comment to Section 997. [7 Cal.L.Rev.Comm. Reports 1 (1965)].

§ 1019. Exception: Parties claiming through deceased patient

There is no privilege under this article as to a communication relevant to an issue between parties all of whom claim through a deceased patient, regardless of whether the claims are by testate or intestate succession or by inter vivos transaction. *(Stats.1965, c. 299, § 2, operative Jan. 1, 1967.)*

Law Revision Commission Comments

See the Comment to Section 957. [7 Cal.L.Rev.Comm. Reports 1 (1965)].

§ 1020. Exception: Breach of duty arising out of psychotherapist-patient relationship

There is no privilege under this article as to a communication relevant to an issue of breach, by the psychotherapist or by the patient, of a duty arising out of the psychotherapist-patient relationship. *(Stats.1965, c. 299, § 2, operative Jan. 1, 1967.)*

Law Revision Commission Comments

See the Comment to Section 958. [7 Cal.L.Rev.Comm. Reports 1 (1965)].

§ 1021. Exception: Intention of deceased patient concerning writing affecting property interest

There is no privilege under this article as to a communication relevant to an issue concerning the intention of a patient, now deceased, with respect to a deed of conveyance, will, or other writing, executed by the patient, purporting to affect an interest in property. *(Stats.1965, c. 299, § 2, operative Jan. 1, 1967.)*

Law Revision Commission Comments

See the Comment to Section 1002. [7 Cal.L.Rev.Comm. Reports 1 (1965)].

§ 1022. Exception: Validity of writing affecting property interest

There is no privilege under this article as to a communication relevant to an issue concerning the validity of a deed of conveyance, will, or other writing, executed by a patient, now deceased, purporting to affect an interest in property. *(Stats. 1965, c. 299, § 2, operative Jan. 1, 1967.)*

Law Revision Commission Comments

See the Comment to Section 1002. [7 Cal.L.Rev.Comm. Reports 1 (1965)].

§ 1023. Exception: Proceeding to determine sanity of criminal defendant

There is no privilege under this article in a proceeding under Chapter 6 (commencing with Section 1367) of Title 10 of Part 2 of the Penal Code initiated at the request of the defendant in a criminal action to determine his sanity. *(Stats.1965, c. 299, § 2, operative Jan. 1, 1967.)*

Law Revision Commission Comments

Section 1023 is included to make it clear that the psychotherapist-patient privilege does not apply when the defendant raises the issue of his sanity at the time of trial. The section probably is unnecessary because the exception provided by Section 1016 is broad enough to cover this situation. [7 Cal.L.Rev.Comm. Reports 1 (1965)].

§ 1024. Exception: Patient dangerous to himself or others

There is no privilege under this article if the psychotherapist has reasonable cause to believe that the patient is in such mental or emotional condition as to be dangerous to himself or to the person or property of another and that disclosure of the communication is necessary to prevent the threatened danger. *(Stats.1965, c. 299, § 2, operative Jan. 1, 1967.)*

Law Revision Commission Comments

This section provides a narrower exception to the psychotherapist-patient privilege than the comparable exceptions provided by Section 982 (privilege for confidential marital communications) and Section 1004 (physician-patient privilege). Although this exception might inhibit the relationship between the patient and his psychotherapist to a limited extent, it is essential that appropriate action be taken if the psychotherapist becomes convinced during the course of treatment that the patient is a menace to himself or others and the patient refuses to permit the psychotherapist to make the disclosure necessary to prevent the threatened danger. [7 Cal.L.Rev.Comm. Reports 1 (1965)].

Research References

Treatises and Practice Aids

Witkin, California Summary 10th Parent and Child § 873, Privileges.
Witkin, California Summary 10th Torts § 1050, in General.

§ 1025. Exception: Proceeding to establish competence

There is no privilege under this article in a proceeding brought by or on behalf of the patient to establish his competence. *(Stats.1965, c. 299, § 2, operative Jan. 1, 1967.)*

Law Revision Commission Comments

See the Comment to Section 1005. [7 Cal.L.Rev.Comm. Reports 1 (1965)].

§ 1026. Exception: Required report

There is no privilege under this article as to information that the psychotherapist or the patient is required to report to a public employee or as to information required to be recorded in a public office, if such report or record is open to public inspection. *(Stats.1965, c. 299, § 2, operative Jan. 1, 1967.)*

Law Revision Commission Comments

See the Comment to Section 1006. [7 Cal.L.Rev.Comm. Reports 1 (1965)].

§ 1027. Exception: Child under 16 victim of crime

There is no privilege under this article if all of the following circumstances exist:

(a) The patient is a child under the age of 16.

(b) The psychotherapist has reasonable cause to believe that the patient has been the victim of a crime and that disclosure of the communication is in the best interest of the child. *(Added by Stats.1970, c. 1397, p. 2627, § 3.)*

Law Revision Commission Comments

1970 Addition

Section 1027 provides an exception to the psychotherapist-patient privilege that is analogous to the exception provided by Section 1024 (patient dangerous to himself or others). The exception provided by Section 1027 is necessary to permit court disclosure of communications to a psychotherapist by a child who has been the victim of a crime (such as child abuse) in a proceeding in which the commission of such crime is a subject of inquiry. Although the exception provided by Section 1027 might inhibit the relationship between the patient and his psychotherapist to a limited extent, it is essential that appropriate action be taken if the psychotherapist becomes convinced during the course of treatment that the patient is the victim of a crime and that disclosure of the communication would be in the best interest of the child.

The text of both 1970 additions was identical. [9 Cal.L.Rev. Comm. Reports 137 (1970)].

ARTICLE 8. CLERGY PENITENT PRIVILEGES

§ 1030. Member of the clergy

As used in this article, a "member of the clergy" means a priest, minister, religious practitioner, or similar functionary of a church or of a religious denomination or religious organization. *(Stats.1965, c. 299, § 2, operative Jan. 1, 1967. Amended by Stats.2002, c. 806 (A.B.3027), § 19.)*

Law Revision Commission Comments

Clergyman is broadly defined in this section. [7 Cal.L.Rev.Comm. Reports 1 (1965)].

§ 1031. Penitent

As used in this article, "penitent" means a person who has made a penitential communication to a member of the clergy. *(Stats.1965, c. 299, § 2, operative Jan. 1, 1967. Amended by Stats.2002, c. 806 (A.B.3027), § 20.)*

Law Revision Commission Comments

This section defines "penitent" by incorporating the definitions in Sections 1030 and 1032. [7 Cal.L.Rev.Comm. Reports 1 (1965)].

§ 1032. Penitential communication

As used in this article, "penitential communication" means a communication made in confidence, in the presence of no third person so far as the penitent is aware, to a member of the clergy who, in the course of the discipline or practice of the clergy member's church, denomination, or organization, is authorized or accustomed to hear those communications and, under the discipline or tenets of his or her church, denomination, or organization, has a duty to keep those communications secret. *(Stats.1965, c. 299, § 2, operative Jan. 1, 1967. Amended by Stats.2002, c. 806 (A.B.3027), § 21.)*

Law Revision Commission Comments

Under existing law, the communication must be a "confession." Code Civ.Proc. § 1881(3) (superseded by the Evidence Code). Section 1032 extends the protection that traditionally has been provided only to those persons whose religious practice involves "confessions." [7 Cal.L.Rev.Comm. Reports 1 (1965)].

§ 1033. Privilege of penitent

Subject to Section 912, a penitent, whether or not a party, has a privilege to refuse to disclose, and to prevent another from disclosing, a penitential communication if he or she claims the privilege. *(Stats.1965, c. 299, § 2, operative Jan. 1, 1967. Amended by Stats.2002, c. 806 (A.B.3027), § 22.)*

Law Revision Commission Comments

This section provides the penitent with a privilege to refuse to disclose, and to prevent another from disclosing, a penitential communication. Because of the definition of "penitential communication," Section 1033 provides a broader privilege than the existing law.

Section 1033 differs from Code of Civil Procedure Section 1881(3) (superseded by the Evidence Code) in that Section 1881(3) gives a penitent a privilege only to prevent a clergyman from disclosing the communication. Literally, Section 1881(3) does not give the penitent himself the right to refuse disclosure. However, similar privilege statutes have been held to grant a privilege both to refuse to disclose and to prevent the other communicant from disclosing the privileged statement. See City & County of San Francisco v. Superior Court, 37 Cal.2d 227, 236, 231 P.2d 26, 31 (1951) (attorney-client privilege); Verdelli v. Gray's Harbor Commercial Co., 115 Cal. 517, 525–526, 47 Pac. 364, 366 (1897) ("a client cannot be compelled to disclose communications which his attorney cannot be permitted to disclose"). Hence, it is likely that Section 1881 (3) would be similarly construed.

Section 1033 also protects against disclosure by eavesdroppers. In this respect, the section provides the same scope of protection that is provided by the other confidential communication privileges. See the Comment to Section 954. [7 Cal.L.Rev.Comm. Reports 1 (1965)].

§ 1034. Privilege of clergy

Subject to Section 912, a member of the clergy, whether or not a party, has a privilege to refuse to disclose a penitential communication if he or she claims the privilege. *(Stats.1965, c. 299, § 2, operative Jan. 1, 1967. Amended by Stats.2002, c. 806 (A.B.3027), § 23.)*

Law Revision Commission Comments

This section provides the clergyman with a privilege in his own right. Moreover, he may claim this privilege even if the penitent has waived the privilege granted him by Section 1033.

There may be several reasons for granting clergyman the traditional priest-penitent privilege. At least one underlying reason seems to be that the law will not compel a clergyman to violate—nor punish him for refusing to violate—the tenets of his church which require him to maintain secrecy as to confidential statements made to him in the course of his religious duties. See generally 8 Wigmore, Evidence §§ 2394–2396 (McNaughton rev. 1961).

The clergyman is under no legal compulsion to claim the privilege. Hence, a penitential communication will be admitted if the clergyman fails to claim the privilege and the penitent is deceased, incompetent, absent, or fails to claim the privilege. This probably changes existing law; but, if so, the change is desirable. For example, if a murderer had confessed the crime to a clergyman, the clergyman might under some circumstances (*e.g.*, if the murderer has died) decline to claim the privilege and instead, give the evidence on behalf of an innocent third party who had been indicted for the crime. The extent to which a clergyman should keep secret or reveal penitential communications is not an appropriate subject for legislation; the matter is better left to the discretion of the individual clergyman involved and the discipline of the religious body of which he is a member. [7 Cal.L.Rev.Comm. Reports 1 (1965)].

ARTICLE 8.5. SEXUAL ASSAULT COUNSELOR–VICTIM PRIVILEGE

§ 1035. Victim

As used in this article, "victim" means a person who consults a sexual assault counselor for the purpose of securing advice or assistance concerning a mental, physical, or emotional condition caused by a sexual assault. *(Added by Stats.1980, c. 917, p. 2916, § 2. Amended by Stats.2006, c. 689 (S.B.1743), § 4.)*

§ 1035.2. Sexual assault counselor

As used in this article, "sexual assault counselor" means any of the following:

(a) A person who is engaged in any office, hospital, institution, or center commonly known as a rape crisis center, whose primary purpose is the rendering of advice or assistance to victims of sexual assault and who has received a certificate evidencing completion of a training program in the counseling of sexual assault victims issued by a counseling center that meets the criteria for the award of a grant established pursuant to Section 13837 of the Penal Code and who meets one of the following requirements:

(1) Is a psychotherapist as defined in Section 1010; has a master's degree in counseling or a related field; or has one year of counseling experience, at least six months of which is in rape crisis counseling.

(2) Has 40 hours of training as described below and is supervised by an individual who qualifies as a counselor under paragraph (1). The training, supervised by a person qualified under paragraph (1), shall include, but not be limited to, the following areas:

(A) Law.

(B) Medicine.

(C) Societal attitudes.

(D) Crisis intervention and counseling techniques.

(E) Role playing.

(F) Referral services.

(G) Sexuality.

(b) A person who is employed by any organization providing the programs specified in Section 13835.2 of the Penal Code, whether financially compensated or not, for the purpose of counseling and assisting sexual assault victims, and who meets one of the following requirements:

(1) Is a psychotherapist as defined in Section 1010; has a master's degree in counseling or a related field; or has one year of counseling experience, at least six months of which is in rape assault counseling.

(2) Has the minimum training for sexual assault counseling required by guidelines established by the employing agency pursuant to subdivision (c) of Section 13835.10 of the Penal Code, and is supervised by an individual who qualifies as a counselor under paragraph (1). The training, supervised by a person qualified under paragraph (1), shall include, but not be limited to, the following areas:

(A) Law.

(B) Victimology.

(C) Counseling.

(D) Client and system advocacy.

(E) Referral services. *(Added by Stats.1980, c. 917, p. 2916, § 2. Amended by Stats.1983, c. 580, § 1; Stats.1983, c. 1072, § 1; Stats.1990, c. 1342 (S.B.2501), § 1; Stats.2006, c. 689 (S.B.1743), § 5.)*

§ 1035.4. Confidential communication between the sexual assault counselor and the victim; disclosure

As used in this article, "confidential communication between the sexual assault counselor and the victim" means information transmitted between the victim and the sexual assault counselor in the course of their relationship and in confidence by a means which, so far as the victim is aware, discloses the information to no third persons other than those who are present to further the interests of the victim in the consultation or those to whom disclosures are reasonably necessary for the transmission of the information or an accomplishment of the purposes for which the sexual assault counselor is consulted. The term includes all information regarding the facts and circumstances involving the alleged sexual assault and also includes all information regarding the victim's prior or subsequent sexual conduct, and opinions regarding the victim's sexual conduct or reputation in sexual matters.

The court may compel disclosure of information received by the sexual assault counselor which constitutes relevant evidence of the facts and circumstances involving an alleged sexual assault about which the victim is complaining and which is the subject of a criminal proceeding if the court determines that the probative value outweighs the effect on the victim, the treatment relationship, and the treatment services if disclosure is compelled. The court may also compel disclosure in proceedings related to child abuse if the court determines the probative value outweighs the effect on the victim, the treatment relationship, and the treatment services if disclosure is compelled.

When a court is ruling on a claim of privilege under this article, the court may require the person from whom disclosure is sought or the person authorized to claim the privilege, or both, to disclose the information in chambers out of the presence and hearing of all persons except the person authorized to claim the privilege and such other persons as the person authorized to claim the privilege is willing to have present. If the judge determines that the information is privileged and must not be disclosed, neither he or she nor any other person may ever disclose, without the consent of a person authorized to permit disclosure, what was disclosed in the course of the proceedings in chambers.

If the court determines certain information shall be disclosed, the court shall so order and inform the defendant. If the court finds there is a reasonable likelihood that particular information is subject to disclosure pursuant to the balancing test provided in this section, the following procedure shall be followed:

(1) The court shall inform the defendant of the nature of the information which may be subject to disclosure.

(2) The court shall order a hearing out of the presence of the jury, if any, and at the hearing allow the questioning of the sexual assault counselor regarding the information which the court has determined may be subject to disclosure.

(3) At the conclusion of the hearing, the court shall rule which items of information, if any, shall be disclosed. The court may make an order stating what evidence may be introduced by the defendant and the nature of questions to be permitted. The defendant may then offer evidence pursuant to the order of the court. Admission of evidence concerning the sexual conduct of the complaining witness is subject to Sections 352, 782, and 1103. *(Added by Stats.1980, c. 917, p. 2916, § 2. Amended by Stats.1983, c. 1072, § 2.)*

§ 1035.6. Holder of the privilege

As used in this article, "holder of the privilege" means:

(a) The victim when such person has no guardian or conservator.

(b) A guardian or conservator of the victim when the victim has a guardian or conservator.

(c) The personal representative of the victim if the victim is dead. *(Added by Stats.1980, c. 917, p. 2916, § 2.)*

§ 1035.8. Sexual assault counselor privilege

A victim of a sexual assault, whether or not a party, has a privilege to refuse to disclose, and to prevent another from disclosing, a confidential communication between the victim and a sexual assault counselor if the privilege is claimed by any of the following:

(a) The holder of the privilege;

(b) A person who is authorized to claim the privilege by the holder of the privilege; or

(c) The person who was the sexual assault counselor at the time of the confidential communication, but that person may not claim the privilege if there is no holder of the privilege in existence or if he or she is otherwise instructed by a person authorized to permit disclosure. *(Added by Stats.1980, c. 917, p. 2916, § 2. Amended by Stats.2006, c. 689 (S.B.1743), § 6.)*

§ 1036. Claim of privilege by sexual assault counselor

The sexual assault counselor who received or made a communication subject to the privilege under this article shall claim the privilege if he or she is present when the communication is sought to be disclosed and is authorized to claim the privilege under subdivision (c) of Section 1035.8. *(Added by Stats.1980, c. 917, p. 2916, § 2. Amended by Stats.2006, c. 689 (S.B.1743), § 7.)*

§ 1036.2. Sexual assault

As used in this article, "sexual assault" includes all of the following:

(a) Rape, as defined in Section 261 of the Penal Code.

(b) Unlawful sexual intercourse, as defined in Section 261.5 of the Penal Code.

(c) Rape in concert with force and violence, as defined in Section 264.1 of the Penal Code.

(d) Rape of a spouse, as defined in Section 262 of the Penal Code.

(e) Sodomy, as defined in Section 286 of the Penal Code, except a violation of subdivision (e) of that section.

(f) A violation of Section 288 of the Penal Code.

(g) Oral copulation, as defined in Section 288a of the Penal Code, except a violation of subdivision (e) of that section.

(h) Sexual penetration, as defined in Section 289 of the Penal Code.

(i) Annoying or molesting a child under 18, as defined in Section 647a of the Penal Code.

(j) Any attempt to commit any of the above acts. *(Added by Stats.1980, c. 917, p. 2916, § 2. Amended by Stats.1988, c. 102, § 1; Stats.2001, c. 854 (S.B.205), § 4.)*

ARTICLE 8.7. DOMESTIC VIOLENCE COUNSELOR–VICTIM PRIVILEGE

§ 1037. Victim

As used in this article, "victim" means any person who suffers domestic violence, as defined in Section 1037.7. *(Added by Stats.1986, c. 854, § 1.)*

Research References

Treatises and Practice Aids

Witkin, California Summary 10th Husband and Wife § 371, Civil Remedies.

§ 1037.1. Domestic violence counselor; qualifications; domestic violence victim service organization

(a)(1) As used in this article, "domestic violence counselor" means a person who is employed by a domestic violence victim service organization, as defined in this article, whether financially compensated or not, for the purpose of rendering advice or assistance to victims of domestic violence and who has at least 40 hours of training as specified in paragraph (2).

(2) The 40 hours of training shall be supervised by an individual who qualifies as a counselor under paragraph (1), and who has at least one year of experience counseling domestic violence victims for the domestic violence victim service organization. The training shall include, but need not be limited to, the following areas: history of domestic violence, civil and criminal law as it relates to domestic violence, the domestic violence victim-counselor privilege and other laws that protect the confidentiality of victim records and information, societal attitudes towards domestic violence, peer counseling techniques, housing, public assistance and other financial resources available to meet the financial needs of domestic violence victims, and referral services available to domestic violence victims.

(3) A domestic violence counselor who has been employed by the domestic violence victim service organization for a period of less than six months shall be supervised by a domestic violence counselor who has at least one year of experience counseling domestic violence victims for the domestic violence victim service organization.

(b) As used in this article, "domestic violence victim service organization" means * * * either of the following:

(1) A nongovernmental organization or entity that provides shelter, programs, or services to victims of domestic violence and their children, including, but not limited to, either of the following:

(A) Domestic violence shelter-based programs, as described in Section 18294 of the Welfare and Institutions Code.

(B) Other programs with the primary mission to provide services to victims of domestic violence whether or not that program exists in an agency that provides additional services.

(2) Programs on the campus of a public or private institution of higher education with the primary mission to provide support or advocacy services to victims of domestic violence. *(Added by Stats.1986, c. 854, § 1. Amended by Stats.1990, c. 1342 (S.B.2501), § 2; Stats.2007, c. 206 (S.B. 407), § 2; Stats.2017, c. 178 (S.B.331), § 1, eff. Jan. 1, 2018.)*

§ 1037.2. Confidential communication; compulsion of disclosure by court; claim of privilege

(a) As used in this article, "confidential communication" means any information, including, but not limited to, written or oral communication, transmitted between the victim and the counselor in the course of their relationship and in confidence by a means which, so far as the victim is aware, discloses the information to no third persons other than those who are present to further the interests of the victim in the consultation or those to whom disclosures are reasonably necessary for the transmission of the information or an accomplishment of the purposes for which the domestic violence counselor is consulted. The term includes all information regarding the facts and circumstances involving all incidences of domestic violence, as well as all information about the children of the victim or abuser and the relationship of the victim with the abuser.

(b) The court may compel disclosure of information received by a domestic violence counselor which constitutes relevant evidence of the facts and circumstances involving a crime allegedly perpetrated against the victim or another household member and which is the subject of a criminal proceeding, if the court determines that the probative value of the information outweighs the effect of disclosure of the information on the victim, the counseling relationship, and the counseling services. The court may compel disclosure if the victim is either dead or not the complaining witness in a criminal action against the perpetrator. The court may also compel disclosure in proceedings related to child abuse if the court determines that the probative value of the evidence outweighs the effect of the disclosure on the victim, the counseling relationship, and the counseling services.

(c) When a court rules on a claim of privilege under this article, it may require the person from whom disclosure is sought or the person authorized to claim the privilege, or both, to disclose the information in chambers out of the presence and hearing of all persons except the person authorized to claim the privilege and such other persons as the person authorized to claim the privilege consents to have present. If the judge determines that the information is privileged and shall not be disclosed, neither he nor she nor any other person may disclose, without the consent of a person authorized to permit disclosure, any information disclosed in the course of the proceedings in chambers.

(d) If the court determines that information shall be disclosed, the court shall so order and inform the defendant in the criminal action. If the court finds there is a reasonable likelihood that any information is subject to disclosure pursuant to the balancing test provided in this section, the procedure specified in subdivisions (1), (2), and (3) of Section 1035.4 shall be followed. *(Added by Stats.1986, c. 854, § 1. Amended by Stats.2007, c. 206 (S.B.407), § 3.)*

§ 1037.3. Child abuse; reporting

Nothing in this article shall be construed to limit any obligation to report instances of child abuse as required by Section 11166 of the Penal Code. *(Added by Stats.1986, c. 854, § 1.)*

§ 1037.4. Holder of the privilege

As used in this article, "holder of the privilege" means:

(a) The victim when he or she has no guardian or conservator.

(b) A guardian or conservator of the victim when the victim has a guardian or conservator, unless the guardian or conservator is accused of perpetrating domestic violence against the victim. *(Added by Stats.1986, c. 854, § 1. Amended by Stats.2007, c. 206 (S.B.407), § 4.)*

§ 1037.5. Privilege of refusal to disclose communication; claimants

A victim of domestic violence, whether or not a party to the action, has a privilege to refuse to disclose, and to prevent another from disclosing, a confidential communication between the victim and a domestic violence counselor in any proceeding specified in Section 901 if the privilege is claimed by any of the following persons:

(a) The holder of the privilege.

(b) A person who is authorized to claim the privilege by the holder of the privilege.

(c) The person who was the domestic violence counselor at the time of the confidential communication. However, that person may not claim the privilege if there is no holder of the privilege in existence or if he or she is otherwise instructed by a person authorized to permit disclosure. *(Added by Stats.1986, c. 854, § 1. Amended by Stats.2007, c. 206 (S.B.407), § 5.)*

§ 1037.6. Claim of privilege by counselor

The domestic violence counselor who received or made a communication subject to the privilege granted by this article shall claim the privilege whenever he or she is present when the communication is sought to be disclosed and he or she is authorized to claim the privilege under subdivision (c) of Section 1037.5. *(Added by Stats.1986, c. 854, § 1.)*

§ 1037.7. Domestic violence

As used in this article, "domestic violence" means "domestic violence" as defined in Section 6211 of the Family Code. *(Added by Stats.1993, c. 219 (A.B.1500), § 77.4.)*

Law Revision Commission Comments

1993 Addition

Section 1037.7 substitutes a reference to the Family Code provision defining "domestic violence" for the definitions of "abuse," "domestic violence," and "family or household member" in the former section. This is not a substantive change, since the Family Code definition of "domestic violence" continues the substance of the omitted definitions. See Fam. Code § 6211 ("domestic violence" defined) & Comment. See also Fam. Code §§ 6203 ("abuse" defined), 6209 ("cohabitant" and "former cohabitant" defined). [23 Cal.L.Rev.Comm. Reports 1 (1993)].

§ 1037.8. Notice; limitations on confidential communications

A domestic violence counselor shall inform a domestic violence victim of any applicable limitations on confidentiality of communications between the victim and the domestic violence counselor. This information may be given orally. *(Added by Stats.2002, c. 629 (S.B.1735), § 1.)*

Division 9

EVIDENCE AFFECTED OR EXCLUDED BY EXTRINSIC POLICIES

CHAPTER 2. MEDIATION

§ 1115. Definitions

For purposes of this chapter:

(a) "Mediation" means a process in which a neutral person or persons facilitate communication between the disputants to assist them in reaching a mutually acceptable agreement.

(b) "Mediator" means a neutral person who conducts a mediation. "Mediator" includes any person designated by a mediator either to assist in the mediation or to communicate with the participants in preparation for a mediation.

(c) "Mediation consultation" means a communication between a person and a mediator for the purpose of initiating, considering, or reconvening a mediation or retaining the mediator. *(Added by Stats.1997, c. 772 (A.B.939), § 3.)*

Law Revision Commission Comments

1997 Addition

Subdivision (a) of Section 1115 is drawn from Code of Civil Procedure Section 1775.1. To accommodate a wide range of mediation styles, the definition is broad, without specific limitations on format. For example, it would include a mediation conducted as a number of sessions, only some of which involve the mediator. The definition focuses on the nature of a proceeding, not its label. A proceeding may be a "mediation" for purposes of this chapter, even though it is denominated differently.

Under subdivision (b), a mediator must be neutral. The neutrality requirement is drawn from Code of Civil Procedure Section 1775.1. An attorney or other representative of a party is not neutral and so does not qualify as a "mediator" for purposes of this chapter.

A "mediator" may be an individual, group of individuals, or entity. See Section 175 ("person" defined). See also Section 10 (singular includes the plural). This definition of mediator encompasses not only the neutral person who takes the lead in conducting a mediation, but also any neutral who assists in the mediation, such as a case-developer, interpreter, or secretary. The definition focuses on a person's role, not the person's title. A person may be a "mediator" under this chapter even though the person has a different title, such as "ombudsperson." Any person who meets the definition of "mediator" must comply with Section 1121 (mediator reports and communications), which generally prohibits a mediator from reporting to a court or other tribunal concerning the mediated dispute.

Subdivision (c) is drawn from former Section 1152.5, which was amended in 1996 to explicitly protect mediation intake communications. See 1996 Cal. Stat. ch. 174, § 1. Subdivision (c) is not limited to communications to retain a mediator. It also encompasses contacts concerning whether to mediate, such as where a mediator contacts a disputant because another disputant desires to mediate, and contacts concerning initiation or recommencement of mediation, such as where a case-developer meets with a disputant before mediation.

For the scope of this chapter, see Section 1117. [1997–98 Annual Report, 27 Cal.L.Rev.Comm. Reports App. 5 (1997)].

Research References

Forms

Alternative Dispute Resolution with Forms § 4:7, Rules Excluding Evidence Of Settlement Negotiations or Compromise Offers.
Alternative Dispute Resolution with Forms § 4:9, Statutes Making Mediation Proceedings Confidential.
Alternative Dispute Resolution with Forms APP. D, Uniform Mediation Act.
California Practice Guide: Rutter Family Law Forms Form 1:32, Glossary Of Common Family Law Terms, Phrases and Concepts (Enclosure to Form 1:31).
Cal. Transaction Forms - Bus. Transactions § 14:30, Confidentiality Of Negotiations.
Cal. Transaction Forms - Bus. Transactions § 14:50, Confidentiality Of Mediation Process.
Cal. Transaction Forms - Bus. Transactions § 14:51, Enforceability Of Written Settlement Agreement Reached in Mediation.
Cal. Transaction Forms - Bus. Transactions § 14:52, Enforceability Of Oral Settlement Agreement Reached in Mediation.
Cal. Transaction Forms - Bus. Transactions § 14:53, Matters to Consider in Drafting Mediation Clauses.
Cal. Transaction Forms - Bus. Transactions § 14:54, Mediation Clause.
Cal. Transaction Forms - Bus. Transactions § 14:98, Mini-Trial.
Cal. Transaction Forms - Bus. Transactions § 18:28, Methods Of Reaching Settlement.
Cal. Transaction Forms - Bus. Transactions § 14:103, Mini-Trial.
26 West's Legal Forms § 2:22, Confidentiality.
26 West's Legal Forms APP. 2B, Uniform Mediation Act.
West's California Code Forms, Commercial § 1301 Form 8, Clause Providing for Mandatory Mediation.
West's California Code Forms, Commercial § 1105 Form 5, Clause Providing for Mandatory Mediation.

Treatises and Practice Aids

Witkin, California Summary 10th Community Property § 237, Final Declaration.
Witkin, California Summary 10th Real Property § 125, Alternative Dispute Resolution.

§ 1116. Effect of chapter

(a) Nothing in this chapter expands or limits a court's authority to order participation in a dispute resolution proceeding. Nothing in this chapter authorizes or affects the enforceability of a contract clause in which parties agree to the use of mediation.

(b) Nothing in this chapter makes admissible evidence that is inadmissible under Section 1152 or any other statute. *(Added by Stats.1997, c. 772 (A.B.939), § 3.)*

Law Revision Commission Comments

1997 Addition

Subdivision (a) of Section 1116 establishes guiding principles for applying this chapter.

Subdivision (b) continues the first sentence of former Section 1152.5(c) without substantive change. [1997–98 Annual Report, 27 Cal.L.Rev.Comm. Reports App. 5 (1997)].

§ 1117. Application of chapter

(a) Except as provided in subdivision (b), this chapter applies to a mediation as defined in Section 1115.

(b) This chapter does not apply to either of the following:

(1) A proceeding under Part 1 (commencing with Section 1800) of Division 5 of the Family Code or Chapter 11

(commencing with Section 3160) of Part 2 of Division 8 of the Family Code.

(2) A settlement conference pursuant to Rule 3.1380 of the California Rules of Court. *(Added by Stats.1997, c. 772 (A.B.939), § 3. Amended by Stats.2007, c. 130 (A.B.299), § 84.)*

Law Revision Commission Comments

1997 Addition

Under subdivision (a) of Section 1117, mediation confidentiality and the other safeguards of this chapter apply to a broad range of mediations. See Section 1115 Comment.

Subdivision (b) sets forth two exceptions. Section 1117(b)(1) continues without substantive change former Section 1152.5(b). Special confidentiality rules apply to a proceeding in family conciliation court or a mediation of child custody or visitation issues. See Section 1040; Fam. Code §§ 1818, 3177.

Section 1117(b)(2) establishes that a court settlement conference is not a mediation within the scope of this chapter. A settlement conference is conducted under the aura of the court and is subject to special rules. [1997–98 Annual Report, 27 Cal.L.Rev.Comm. Reports App. 5 (1997)].

Research References

Forms

Cal. Transaction Forms - Bus. Transactions § 14:50, Confidentiality Of Mediation Process.

§ 1118. Oral agreements

An oral agreement "in accordance with Section 1118" means an oral agreement that satisfies all of the following conditions:

(a) The oral agreement is recorded by a court reporter or reliable means of audio recording.

(b) The terms of the oral agreement are recited on the record in the presence of the parties and the mediator, and the parties express on the record that they agree to the terms recited.

(c) The parties to the oral agreement expressly state on the record that the agreement is enforceable or binding, or words to that effect.

(d) The recording is reduced to writing and the writing is signed by the parties within 72 hours after it is recorded. *(Added by Stats.1997, c. 772 (A.B.939), § 3. Amended by Stats.2009, c. 88 (A.B.176), § 35; Stats.2010, c. 328 (S.B. 1330), § 64.)*

Law Revision Commission Comments

1997 Addition

Section 1118 establishes a procedure for orally memorializing an agreement, in the interest of efficiency. Provisions permitting use of that procedure for certain purposes include Sections 1121 (mediator reports and communications), 1122 (disclosure by agreement), 1123 (written settlement agreements reached through mediation), and 1124 (oral agreements reached through mediation). See also Section 1125 (when mediation ends). For guidance on authority to bind a litigant, see Williams v. Saunders, 55 Cal.App.4th 1158, 64 Cal. Rptr.2d 571 (1997) ("The litigants' direct participation tends to ensure that the settlement is the result of their mature reflection and deliberate assent.") [1997–98 Annual Report, 27 Cal.L.Rev.Comm. Reports App. 5 (1997)].

2009 Amendment

Section 1118 is amended to reflect advances in recording technology and for consistency of terminology. For a similar reform, see 2002 Cal. Stat. ch. 1068 (replacing numerous references to "audiotape" in Civil Discovery Act with either "audio technology," "audio recording," or "audio record," as context required). [37 Cal. L. Revision Comm'n Reports 211 (2007)].

Research References

Forms

Alternative Dispute Resolution with Forms § 4:7, Rules Excluding Evidence Of Settlement Negotiations or Compromise Offers.
Cal. Transaction Forms - Bus. Transactions § 14:50, Confidentiality Of Mediation Process.
Cal. Transaction Forms - Bus. Transactions § 14:51, Enforceability Of Written Settlement Agreement Reached in Mediation.
Cal. Transaction Forms - Bus. Transactions § 14:52, Enforceability Of Oral Settlement Agreement Reached in Mediation.
Cal. Transaction Forms - Bus. Transactions § 18:21, Admissibility Of Settlement Offers and Negotiations.
Cal. Transaction Forms - Bus. Transactions § 18:28, Methods Of Reaching Settlement.
Cal. Transaction Forms - Bus. Transactions § 18:51.30, Settlement Agreement Following Mediation Of Disputes Subject to Pending Litigation.
26 West's Legal Forms APP. 2B, Uniform Mediation Act.

§ 1119. Written or oral communications during mediation process; admissibility

Except as otherwise provided in this chapter:

(a) No evidence of anything said or any admission made for the purpose of, in the course of, or pursuant to, a mediation or a mediation consultation is admissible or subject to discovery, and disclosure of the evidence shall not be compelled, in any arbitration, administrative adjudication, civil action, or other noncriminal proceeding in which, pursuant to law, testimony can be compelled to be given.

(b) No writing, as defined in Section 250, that is prepared for the purpose of, in the course of, or pursuant to, a mediation or a mediation consultation, is admissible or subject to discovery, and disclosure of the writing shall not be compelled, in any arbitration, administrative adjudication, civil action, or other noncriminal proceeding in which, pursuant to law, testimony can be compelled to be given.

(c) All communications, negotiations, or settlement discussions by and between participants in the course of a mediation or a mediation consultation shall remain confidential. *(Added by Stats.1997, c. 772 (A.B.939), § 3.)*

Law Revision Commission Comments

1997 Addition

Subdivision (a) of Section 1119 continues without substantive change former Section 1152.5(a)(1), except that its protection explicitly applies in a subsequent arbitration or administrative adjudication, as well as in any civil action or proceeding. See Section 120 ("civil action" includes civil proceedings). In addition, the protection of Section 1119(a) extends to oral communications made for the purpose of or pursuant to a mediation, not just oral communications made in the course of the mediation.

Subdivision (b) continues without substantive change former Section 1152.5(a)(2), except that its protection explicitly applies in a subsequent arbitration or administrative adjudication, as well as in any civil action or proceeding. See Section 120 ("civil action" includes civil proceedings). In addition, subdivision (b) expressly encompasses any type of "writing" as defined in Section 250, regardless of whether the representations are on paper or on some other medium.

Subdivision (c) continues former Section 1152.5(a)(3) without substantive change. A mediation is confidential notwithstanding the presence of an observer, such as a person evaluating or training the mediator or studying the mediation process.

See Sections 1115(a) ("mediation" defined), 1115(c) ("mediation consultation" defined). See also Section 703.5 (testimony by a judge, arbitrator, or mediator).

For examples of specialized mediation confidentiality provisions, see Bus. & Prof. Code §§ 467.4–467.5 (community dispute resolution programs), 6200 (attorney-client fee disputes); Code Civ. Proc. §§ 1297.371 (international commercial disputes), 1775.10 (civil action mediation in participating courts); Fam. Code §§ 1818 (family conciliation court), 3177 (child custody); Food & Agric. Code § 54453 (agricultural cooperative bargaining associations); Gov't Code §§ 11420.20–11420.30 (administrative adjudication), 12984–12985 (housing discrimination), 66032–66033 (land use); Ins. Code § 10089.80 (earthquake insurance); Lab. Code § 65 (labor disputes); Welf. & Inst. Code § 350 (dependency mediation). See also Cal. Const. art. I, § 1 (right to privacy); Garstang v. Superior Court, 39 Cal.App.4th 526, 46 Cal.Rptr.2d 84, 88 (1995) (constitutional right of privacy protected communications made during mediation sessions before an ombudsperson). [1997–98 Annual Report, 27 Cal.L.Rev. Comm. Reports App. 5 (1997)].

Commentary

Applying this section and section 1120(a), *Lappe v. Superior Court, 232 Cal.App.4th 774, 181 Cal.Rptr.3d 510 (2014), review denied*, holds that the mediation confidentiality provisions do not apply to mandatory financial disclosure declarations required under Family Law Code section 2100 et seq. because they are not "prepared for the purpose of" or "pursuant to" a mediation. Thus *Lappe* limits the scope of the mediation privilege to writings and statements that would not have existed "but for" mediation. Additionally, the court held that because section 1119(b) does not apply to declarations of disclosure, the contractual provisions of the parties' stipulation regarding the confidentiality of the declarations of disclosure were an impermissible attempt to preclude the court from receiving the declarations into evidence.

Applying this section and section 1123(a) and (b), *In re Marriage of Daly & Oyster, 228 Cal.App.4th 505, 175 Cal.Rptr.3d 364 (2014)*, held that a stipulated judgment achieved in mediation and admitted in a dissolution proceeding that was dismissed for lack of prosecution, was admissible in a later dissolution proceeding because the stipulated judgment clearly reflected the parties' intention that it be disclosable and enforceable.

Relying on subsections (a) and (b) of this section and section 1126, *Amis v. Greenberg Taurig LLP, 235 Cal.App.4th 331, 185 Cal.Rptr.3d 322 (2015), review denied*, affirmed summary judgment for a law firm in their client's legal malpractice action, which arose from a mediated settlement agreement, because the malpractice claim necessarily required inferences about the content of confidential attorney communication with the client during mediation.

Research References

Forms

Alternative Dispute Resolution with Forms § 4:9, Statutes Making Mediation Proceedings Confidential.
Cal. Transaction Forms - Bus. Transactions § 14:50, Confidentiality Of Mediation Process.
Cal. Transaction Forms - Bus. Transactions § 18:19, Confidentiality Provisions.
Cal. Transaction Forms - Bus. Transactions § 18:21, Admissibility Of Settlement Offers and Negotiations.
26 West's Legal Forms § 2:22, Confidentiality.
26 West's Legal Forms APP. 2B, Uniform Mediation Act.
West's California Code Forms, Civil Procedure § 998 Form 1, Offer Of Plaintiff to Compromise.
West's California Code Forms, Commercial § 1301 COMMENT 1, Alternative Dispute Resolution and Dispute Management.
West's California Code Forms, Commercial § 1105 COMMENT 1, Alternative Dispute Resolution.

Treatises and Practice Aids

Witkin, California Summary 10th Husband and Wife § 10, Imposition Of Award as Sanction.

§ 1120. Evidence otherwise admissible

(a) Evidence otherwise admissible or subject to discovery outside of a mediation or a mediation consultation shall not be or become inadmissible or protected from disclosure solely by reason of its introduction or use in a mediation or a mediation consultation.

(b) This chapter does not limit any of the following:

(1) The admissibility of an agreement to mediate a dispute.

(2) The effect of an agreement not to take a default or an agreement to extend the time within which to act or refrain from acting in a pending civil action.

(3) Disclosure of the mere fact that a mediator has served, is serving, will serve, or was contacted about serving as a mediator in a dispute.

(4) The admissibility of declarations of disclosure required by Sections 2104 and 2105 of the Family Code, even if prepared for the purpose of, in the course of, or pursuant to, a mediation or a mediation consultation. *(Added by Stats. 1997, c. 772 (A.B.939), § 3. Amended by Stats.2017, c. 60 (S.B.217), § 1, eff. Jan. 1, 2018.)*

Law Revision Commission Comments

1997 Addition

Subdivision (a) of Section 1120 continues former Section 1152.5(a)(6) without change. It limits the scope of Section 1119 (mediation confidentiality), preventing parties from using a mediation as a pretext to shield materials from disclosure.

Subdivision (b)(1) makes explicit that Section 1119 does not restrict admissibility of an agreement to mediate. Subdivision (b)(2) continues former Section 1152.5(e) without substantive change, but also includes an express exception for extensions of litigation deadlines. Subdivision (b)(3) makes clear that Section 1119 does not preclude a disputant from obtaining basic information about a mediator's track record, which may be significant in selecting an impartial mediator. Similarly, mediation participants may express their views on a mediator's performance, so long as they do not disclose anything said or done at the mediation.

See Sections 1115(a) ("mediation" defined), 1115(b) ("mediator" defined), 1115(c) ("mediation consultation" defined). [1997–98 Annual Report, 27 Cal.L.Rev.Comm. Reports App. 5 (1997)].

Commentary

Applying this section and section 1119(b), *Lappe v. Superior Court, 232 Cal.App.4th 774, 181 Cal.Rptr.3d 510 (2014), review denied,* holds that the mediation confidentiality provisions do not apply to mandatory financial disclosure declarations required under Family Law Code section 2100 et seq., because they are not "prepared for the purpose of" or "pursuant to" a mediation. Thus *Lappe* limits the scope of the mediation privilege to writings and statements that would not have existed "but for" mediation. Additionally, the court held that because section 1119(b) does not apply to declarations of disclosure, the contractual provisions of the parties' stipulation regarding the confidentiality of the declarations of disclosure were an impermissible attempt to preclude the court from receiving the declarations into evidence.

Research References

Forms

Cal. Transaction Forms - Bus. Transactions § 14:50, Confidentiality Of Mediation Process.

26 West's Legal Forms APP. 2B, Uniform Mediation Act.

§ 1121. Mediator's reports and findings

Neither a mediator nor anyone else may submit to a court or other adjudicative body, and a court or other adjudicative body may not consider, any report, assessment, evaluation, recommendation, or finding of any kind by the mediator concerning a mediation conducted by the mediator, other than a report that is mandated by court rule or other law and that states only whether an agreement was reached, unless all parties to the mediation expressly agree otherwise in writing, or orally in accordance with Section 1118. *(Added by Stats.1997, c. 772 (A.B.939), § 3.)*

Law Revision Commission Comments

1997 Addition

Section 1121 continues the first sentence of former Section 1152.6 without substantive change, except to make clear that (1) the section applies to all submissions, not just filings, (2) the section is not limited to court proceedings but rather applies to all types of adjudications, including arbitrations and administrative adjudications, (3) the section applies to any report or statement of opinion, however denominated, and (4) neither a mediator nor anyone else may submit the prohibited information. The section does not prohibit a mediator from providing a mediation participant with feedback on the dispute in the course of the mediation.

Rather, the focus is on preventing coercion. As Section 1121 recognizes, a mediator should not be able to influence the result of a mediation or adjudication by reporting or threatening to report to the decisionmaker on the merits of the dispute or reasons why mediation failed to resolve it. Similarly, a mediator should not have authority to resolve or decide the mediated dispute, and should not have any function for the adjudicating tribunal with regard to the dispute, except as a non-decisionmaking neutral. See Section 1117 (scope of chapter), which excludes settlement conferences from this chapter.

The exception to Section 1121 (permitting submission and consideration of a mediator's report where "all parties to the mediation expressly agree" in writing) is modified to allow use of the oral procedure in Section 1118 (recorded oral agreement) and to permit making of the agreement at any time, not just before the mediation. A mediator's report to a court may disclose mediation communications only if all parties to the mediation agree to the reporting and all persons who participate in the mediation agree to the disclosure. See Section 1122 (disclosure by agreement).

The second sentence of former Section 1152.6 is continued without substantive change in Section 1117 (scope of chapter), except that Section 1117 excludes proceedings under Part 1 (commencing with Section 1800) of Division 5 of the Family Code, as well as proceedings under Chapter 11 (commencing with Section 3160) of Part 2 of Division 8 of the Family Code.

See Sections 1115(a) ("mediation" defined), 1115(b) ("mediator" defined). See also Sections 703.5 (testimony by a judge, arbitrator, or mediator), 1127 (attorney's fees), 1128 (irregularity in proceedings). [1997–98 Annual Report, 27 Cal.L.Rev.Comm. Reports App. 5 (1997)].

Research References

Forms

Cal. Transaction Forms - Bus. Transactions § 14:50, Confidentiality Of Mediation Process.

26 West's Legal Forms APP. 2B, Uniform Mediation Act.

§ 1122. Communications or writings; conditions to admissibility

(a) A communication or a writing, as defined in Section 250, that is made or prepared for the purpose of, or in the course of, or pursuant to, a mediation or a mediation consultation, is not made inadmissible, or protected from disclosure, by provisions of this chapter if either of the following conditions is satisfied:

(1) All persons who conduct or otherwise participate in the mediation expressly agree in writing, or orally in accordance with Section 1118, to disclosure of the communication, document, or writing.

(2) The communication, document, or writing was prepared by or on behalf of fewer than all the mediation participants, those participants expressly agree in writing, or orally in accordance with Section 1118, to its disclosure, and the communication, document, or writing does not disclose anything said or done or any admission made in the course of the mediation.

(b) For purposes of subdivision (a), if the neutral person who conducts a mediation expressly agrees to disclosure, that agreement also binds any other person described in subdivision (b) of Section 1115. *(Added by Stats.1997, c. 772 (A.B.939), § 3.)*

Law Revision Commission Comments

1997 Addition

Section 1122 supersedes former Section 1152.5(a)(4) and part of former Section 1152.5(a)(2), which were unclear regarding precisely whose agreement was required for admissibility or disclosure of mediation communications and documents.

Subdivision (a)(1) states the general rule that mediation documents and communications may be admitted or disclosed only upon agreement of all participants, including not only parties but also the mediator and other nonparties attending the mediation (e.g., a disputant not involved in litigation, a spouse, an accountant, an insurance representative, or an employee of a corporate affiliate). Agreement must be express, not implied. For example, parties cannot be deemed to have agreed in advance to disclosure merely because they agreed to participate in a particular dispute resolution program.

Subdivision (a)(2) facilitates admissibility and disclosure of unilaterally prepared materials, but it only applies so long as those materials may be produced in a manner revealing nothing about the mediation discussion. Materials that necessarily disclose mediation communications may be admitted or disclosed only upon satisfying the general rule of subdivision (a)(1).

Mediation materials that satisfy the requirements of subdivisions (a)(1) or (a)(2) are not necessarily admissible or subject to disclosure. Although the provisions on mediation confidentiality do not bar admissibility or disclosure, there may be other bases for exclusion.

Subdivision (b) makes clear that if the person who takes the lead in conducting a mediation agrees to disclosure, it is unnecessary to seek out and obtain assent from each assistant to that person, such as a case developer, interpreter, or secretary.

For exceptions to Section 1122, see Sections 1123 (written settlement agreements reached through mediation) and 1124 (oral agreements reached through mediation) & Comments.

See Section 1115(a) ("mediation" defined), 1115(c) ("mediation consultation" defined). See also Sections 703.5 (testimony by a judge, arbitrator, or mediator), 1119 (mediation confidentiality), 1121 (mediator reports and communications). [1997–98 Annual Report, 27 Cal.L.Rev.Comm. Reports App. 5 (1997)].

Research References

Forms

Cal. Transaction Forms - Bus. Transactions § 14:50, Confidentiality Of Mediation Process.

26 West's Legal Forms APP. 2B, Uniform Mediation Act.

§ 1123. Written settlement agreements; conditions to admissibility

A written settlement agreement prepared in the course of, or pursuant to, a mediation, is not made inadmissible, or protected from disclosure, by provisions of this chapter if the agreement is signed by the settling parties and any of the following conditions are satisfied:

(a) The agreement provides that it is admissible or subject to disclosure, or words to that effect.

(b) The agreement provides that it is enforceable or binding or words to that effect.

(c) All parties to the agreement expressly agree in writing, or orally in accordance with Section 1118, to its disclosure.

(d) The agreement is used to show fraud, duress, or illegality that is relevant to an issue in dispute. *(Added by Stats.1997, c. 772 (A.B.939), § 3.)*

Law Revision Commission Comments

1997 Addition

Section 1123 consolidates and clarifies provisions governing written settlements reached through mediation. For guidance on binding a disputant to a written settlement agreement, see Williams v. Saunders, 55 Cal.App.4th 1158, 64 Cal.Rptr.2d 571 (1997) ("The litigants' direct participation tends to ensure that the settlement is the result of their mature reflection and deliberate assent.").

As to an executed written settlement agreement, subdivision (a) continues part of former Section 1152.5(a)(2). See also Ryan v. Garcia, 27 Cal.App.4th 1006, 1012, 33 Cal.Rptr.2d 158, 162 (1994) (Section 1152.5 "provides a simple means by which settlement agreements executed during mediation can be made admissible in later proceedings," i.e., the "parties may consent, as part of a writing, to subsequent admissibility of the agreement").

Subdivision (b) is new. It is added due to the likelihood that parties intending to be bound will use words to that effect, rather than saying their agreement is intended to be admissible or subject to disclosure.

As to fully executed written settlement agreements, subdivision (c) supersedes former Section 1152.5(a)(4). To facilitate enforceability of such agreements, disclosure pursuant to subdivision (c) requires only agreement of the parties. Agreement of the mediator and other mediation participants is not necessary. Subdivision (c) is thus an exception to the general rule governing disclosure of mediation communications by agreement. See Section 1122.

Subdivision (d) continues former Section 1152.5(a)(5) without substantive change.

A written settlement agreement that satisfies the requirements of subdivision (a), (b), (c), or (d) is not necessarily admissible or subject to disclosure. Although the provisions on mediation confidentiality do not bar admissibility or disclosure, there may be other bases for exclusion.

See Section 1115(a) ("mediation" defined). [1997–98 Annual Report, 27 Cal.L.Rev.Comm. Reports App. 5 (1997)].

Commentary

Applying section 1119 and subsections (a) and (b) of this section, *In re Marriage of Daly & Oyster, 228 Cal.App.4th 505, 175 Cal.Rptr.3d 364 (2014)*, held that a stipulated judgment reached in mediation and admitted in a dissolution proceeding that was dismissed for lack of prosecution, was admissible in a later dissolution proceeding because the stipulated judgment clearly reflected the parties' intention that it be disclosable and enforceable.

Research References

Forms

Cal. Transaction Forms - Bus. Transactions § 14:51, Enforceability Of Written Settlement Agreement Reached in Mediation.

Cal. Transaction Forms - Bus. Transactions § 18:21, Admissibility Of Settlement Offers and Negotiations.

Cal. Transaction Forms - Bus. Transactions § 18:28, Methods Of Reaching Settlement.

Cal. Transaction Forms - Bus. Transactions § 18:73, Admissibility Of Agreement Reached Through Mediation.

Cal. Transaction Forms - Bus. Transactions § 18:51.30, Settlement Agreement Following Mediation Of Disputes Subject to Pending Litigation.

26 West's Legal Forms APP. 2B, Uniform Mediation Act.

West's California Code Forms, Commercial § 1301 COMMENT 1, Alternative Dispute Resolution and Dispute Management.

West's California Code Forms, Commercial § 1105 COMMENT 1, Alternative Dispute Resolution.

§ 1124. Oral agreements; conditions to admissibility

An oral agreement made in the course of, or pursuant to, a mediation is not made inadmissible, or protected from disclosure, by the provisions of this chapter if any of the following conditions are satisfied:

(a) The agreement is in accordance with Section 1118.

(b) The agreement is in accordance with subdivisions (a), (b), and (d) of Section 1118, and all parties to the agreement expressly agree, in writing or orally in accordance with Section 1118, to disclosure of the agreement.

(c) The agreement is in accordance with subdivisions (a), (b), and (d) of Section 1118, and the agreement is used to show fraud, duress, or illegality that is relevant to an issue in dispute. *(Added by Stats.1997, c. 772 (A.B.939), § 3.)*

Law Revision Commission Comments

1997 Addition

Section 1124 sets forth specific circumstances under which mediation confidentiality is inapplicable to an oral agreement reached through mediation. Except in those circumstances, Sections 1119 (mediation confidentiality) and 1124 codify the rule of Ryan v. Garcia, 27 Cal.App.4th 1006, 33 Cal.Rptr.2d 158 (1994) (mediation confidentiality applies to oral statement of settlement terms), and reject the contrary approach of Regents of University of California v. Sumner, 42 Cal.App.4th 1209, 50 Cal.Rptr.2d 200 (1996) (mediation confidentiality does not protect oral statement of settlement terms).

Subdivision (a) of Section 1124 facilitates enforcement of an oral agreement that is recorded and memorialized in writing in accordance with Section 1118. For guidance in applying subdivision (a), see Section 1125 (when mediation ends) & Comment.

Subdivision (b) parallels Section 1123(c).

Subdivision (c) parallels Section 1123(d).

An oral agreement that satisfies the requirements of subdivision (a), (b), or (c) is not necessarily admissible or subject to disclosure. Although the provisions on mediation confidentiality do not bar admissibility or disclosure, there may be other bases for exclusion. For guidance on binding a disputant to a settlement agreement, see Williams v. Saunders, 55 Cal.App.4th 1158, 64 Cal.Rptr.2d 571 (1997) ("The litigants' direct participation tends to ensure that the settlement is the result of their mature reflection and deliberate assent.").

See Section 1115(a) ("mediation" defined). [1997–98 Annual Report, 27 Cal.L.Rev.Comm. Reports App. 5 (1997)].

Research References

Forms

Alternative Dispute Resolution with Forms § 4:7, Rules Excluding Evidence Of Settlement Negotiations or Compromise Offers.

Cal. Transaction Forms - Bus. Transactions § 14:52, Enforceability Of Oral Settlement Agreement Reached in Mediation.

Cal. Transaction Forms - Bus. Transactions § 18:21, Admissibility Of Settlement Offers and Negotiations.

26 West's Legal Forms APP. 2B, Uniform Mediation Act.

§ 1125. End of mediation; satisfaction of conditions

(a) For purposes of confidentiality under this chapter, a mediation ends when any one of the following conditions is satisfied:

(1) The parties execute a written settlement agreement that fully resolves the dispute.

(2) An oral agreement that fully resolves the dispute is reached in accordance with Section 1118.

(3) The mediator provides the mediation participants with a writing signed by the mediator that states that the mediation is terminated, or words to that effect, which shall be consistent with Section 1121.

(4) A party provides the mediator and the other mediation participants with a writing stating that the mediation is terminated, or words to that effect, which shall be consistent with Section 1121. In a mediation involving more than two parties, the mediation may continue as to the remaining parties or be terminated in accordance with this section.

(5) For 10 calendar days, there is no communication between the mediator and any of the parties to the mediation relating to the dispute. The mediator and the parties may shorten or extend this time by agreement.

(b) For purposes of confidentiality under this chapter, if a mediation partially resolves a dispute, mediation ends when either of the following conditions is satisfied:

(1) The parties execute a written settlement agreement that partially resolves the dispute.

(2) An oral agreement that partially resolves the dispute is reached in accordance with Section 1118.

(c) This section does not preclude a party from ending a mediation without reaching an agreement. This section does not otherwise affect the extent to which a party may terminate a mediation. *(Added by Stats.1997, c. 772 (A.B. 939), § 3.)*

Law Revision Commission Comments

1997 Addition

By specifying when a mediation ends, Section 1125 provides guidance on which communications are protected by Section 1119 (mediation confidentiality).

Under subdivision (a)(1), if mediation participants reach an oral compromise and reduce it to a written settlement fully resolving their dispute, confidentiality extends until the agreement is signed by all the parties. For guidance on binding a disputant to a settlement agreement, see Williams v. Saunders, 55 Cal.App.4th 1158, 64 Cal.Rptr.2d 571 (1997) ("The litigants' direct participation tends to ensure that the settlement is the result of their mature reflection and deliberate assent.").

Subdivision (a)(2) applies where mediation participants fully resolve their dispute by an oral agreement that is recorded and memorialized in writing in accordance with Section 1118. The mediation is over upon completion of that procedure, and the confidentiality protections of this chapter do not apply to any later proceedings, such as attempts to further refine the content of the agreement. See Section 1124 (oral agreements reached through mediation). Subdivisions (a)(3) and (a)(4) are drawn from Rule 14 of the American Arbitration Association's Commercial Mediation Rules (as amended, Jan. 1, 1992). Subdivision (a)(5) applies where an affirmative act terminating a mediation for purposes of this chapter does not occur.

Subdivision (b) applies where mediation partially resolves a dispute, such as when the disputants resolve only some of the issues (e.g., contract, but not tort, liability) or when only some of the disputants settle.

Subdivision (c) limits the effect of Section 1125.

See Sections 1115(a) ("mediation" defined), 1115(b) ("mediator" defined). [1997–98 Annual Report, 27 Cal.L.Rev.Comm. Reports App. 5 (1997)].

Research References

Forms

Cal. Transaction Forms - Bus. Transactions § 14:50, Confidentiality Of Mediation Process.

Cal. Transaction Forms - Bus. Transactions § 14:53, Matters to Consider in Drafting Mediation Clauses.

Cal. Transaction Forms - Bus. Transactions § 14:54, Mediation Clause.

Cal. Transaction Forms - Bus. Transactions § 14:47, Scheduling.

Cal. Transaction Forms - Bus. Transactions § 14:105, Arbitration-Mediation.

26 West's Legal Forms APP. 2B, Uniform Mediation Act.

§ 1126. Protections before and after mediation ends

Anything said, any admission made, or any writing that is inadmissible, protected from disclosure, and confidential under this chapter before a mediation ends, shall remain inadmissible, protected from disclosure, and confidential to the same extent after the mediation ends. *(Added by Stats.1997, c. 772 (A.B.939), § 3.)*

Law Revision Commission Comments

1997 Addition

Section 1126 clarifies that mediation materials are confidential not only during a mediation, but also after the mediation ends pursuant to Section 1125 (when mediation ends).

See Section 1115(a) ("mediation" defined). [1997–98 Annual Report, 27 Cal.L.Rev.Comm. Reports App. 5 (1997)].

Commentary

Relying on this section and subsections (a) and (b) of section 1119, *Amis v. Greenberg Taurig LLP, 235 Cal.App.4th 331, 185 Cal.Rptr.3d 322 (2015), review denied*, affirmed summary judgment for a law firm in a legal malpractice action based on the law firm's communications during mediation.

Research References

Forms

Cal. Transaction Forms - Bus. Transactions § 14:50, Confidentiality Of Mediation Process.

§ 1127. Attorney's fees and costs

If a person subpoenas or otherwise seeks to compel a mediator to testify or produce a writing, as defined in Section 250, and the court or other adjudicative body determines that the testimony or writing is inadmissible under this chapter, or protected from disclosure under this chapter, the court or adjudicative body making the determination shall award reasonable attorney's fees and costs to the mediator against the person seeking the testimony or writing. *(Added by Stats.1997, c. 772 (A.B.939), § 3.)*

Law Revision Commission Comments

1997 Addition

Section 1127 continues former Section 1152.5(d) without substantive change, except to clarify that either a court or another adjudicative body (e.g., an arbitrator or an administrative tribunal) may award the fees and costs. Because Section 1115 (definitions) defines "mediator" to include not only the neutral person who takes the lead in conducting a mediation, but also any neutral who assists in the mediation, fees are available regardless of the role played by the person subjected to discovery.

See Section 1115(b) ("mediator" defined). [1997–98 Annual Report, 27 Cal.L.Rev.Comm. Reports App. 5 (1997)].

Research References

Forms

Cal. Transaction Forms - Bus. Transactions § 14:50, Confidentiality Of Mediation Process.

§ 1128. Subsequent trials; references to mediation

Any reference to a mediation during any subsequent trial is an irregularity in the proceedings of the trial for the purposes of Section 657 of the Code of Civil Procedure. Any reference to a mediation during any other subsequent noncriminal proceeding is grounds for vacating or modifying the decision in that proceeding, in whole or in part, and granting a new or further hearing on all or part of the issues, if the reference materially affected the substantial rights of the party requesting relief. *(Added by Stats.1997, c. 772 (A.B.939), § 3.)*

Law Revision Commission Comments

1997 Addition

Section 1128 is drawn from Code of Civil Procedure Section 1775.12. The first sentence makes it an irregularity to refer to a mediation in a subsequent civil trial; the second sentence extends that rule to other noncriminal proceedings, such as an administrative adjudication. An appropriate situation for invoking this section is where a party urges the trier of fact to draw an adverse inference from an adversary's refusal to disclose mediation communications.

See Section 1115 ("mediation" defined). [1997–98 Annual Report, 27 Cal.L.Rev.Comm. Reports App. 5 (1997)].

Research References

Forms

Alternative Dispute Resolution with Forms § 4:9, Statutes Making Mediation Proceedings Confidential.

Cal. Transaction Forms - Bus. Transactions § 14:50, Confidentiality Of Mediation Process.

26 West's Legal Forms § 2:22, Confidentiality.

West's California Code Forms, Commercial § 1301 Form 8, Clause Providing for Mandatory Mediation.

West's California Code Forms, Commercial § 1105 Form 5, Clause Providing for Mandatory Mediation.

Division 10

HEARSAY EVIDENCE

Law Revision Commission Comments

Division 10 contains the hearsay rule and the most commonly used exceptions to the rule. Other exceptions may be found in other statutes scattered throughout the codes. Under the Evidence Code, the hearsay objection is met if the evidence offered falls within any of the exceptions to the hearsay rule. But the fact that the hearsay objection is overcome does not necessarily make the evidence admissible. All other exclusionary rules apply and may require exclusion of the evidence. [7 Cal.L.Rev.Comm. Reports 1 (1965)].

CHAPTER 2. EXCEPTIONS TO THE HEARSAY RULE

ARTICLE 11. FAMILY HISTORY

§ 1310. Statement concerning declarant's own family history

(a) Subject to subdivision (b), evidence of a statement by a declarant who is unavailable as a witness concerning his own birth, marriage, divorce, a parent and child relationship, relationship by blood or marriage, race, ancestry, or other similar fact of his family history is not made inadmissible by the hearsay rule, even though the declarant had no means of acquiring personal knowledge of the matter declared.

(b) Evidence of a statement is inadmissible under this section if the statement was made under circumstances such as to indicate its lack of trustworthiness. *(Stats.1965, c. 299, § 2, operative Jan. 1, 1967. Amended by Stats.1975, c. 1244, p. 3202, § 15.)*

Law Revision Commission Comments

Section 1310 provides a hearsay exception for a statement concerning the declarant's own family history. It restates in substance and supersedes Section 1870(4) of the Code of Civil Procedure. Section 1870(4), however, requires that the declarant be dead whereas unavailability of the declarant for any of the reasons specified in Section 240 makes the statement admissible under Section 1310.

The statement is not admissible if it was made under circumstances such as to indicate its lack of trustworthiness. The requirement is similar to the requirement of existing case law that the statement be made at a time when no controversy existed as to the matters stated. See, *e.g.,* Estate of Walden, 166 Cal. 446, 137 Pac. 35 (1913); Estate of Nidever, 181 Cal.App.2d 367, 5 Cal.Rptr. 343 (1960). However, the language of Section 1310 permits the judge to consider the declarant's motives to tell the truth as well as his reasons to deviate therefrom in determining whether the statement is sufficiently trustworthy to be admitted as evidence. [7 Cal.L.Rev.Comm. Reports 1 (1965)].

§ 1311. Statement concerning family history of another

(a) Subject to subdivision (b), evidence of a statement concerning the birth, marriage, divorce, death, parent and child relationship, race, ancestry, relationship by blood or marriage, or other similar fact of the family history of a person other than the declarant is not made inadmissible by the hearsay rule if the declarant is unavailable as a witness and:

(1) The declarant was related to the other by blood or marriage; or

(2) The declarant was otherwise so intimately associated with the other's family as to be likely to have had accurate information concerning the matter declared and made the statement (i) upon information received from the other or from a person related by blood or marriage to the other or (ii) upon repute in the other's family.

(b) Evidence of a statement is inadmissible under this section if the statement was made under circumstances such as to indicate its lack of trustworthiness. *(Stats.1965, c. 299, § 2, operative Jan. 1, 1967. Amended by Stats.1975, c. 1244, p. 3202, § 16.)*

Law Revision Commission Comments

Section 1311 provides a hearsay exception for a statement concerning the family history of another. Paragraph (1) of subdivision (a) restates in substance existing law as found in Section 1870(4) of the Code of Civil Procedure which it supersedes. Paragraph (2) is new to California law, but it is a sound extension of the present law to cover a situation where the declarant was a family housekeeper or doctor or so close a friend as to be included by the family in discussions of its family history.

There are two limitations on admissibility of a statement under Section 1311. *First,* a statement is admissible only if the declarant is unavailable as a witness within the meaning of Section 240. (Section 1870(4) requires that the declarant be deceased in order for his statement to be admissible.) *Second,* a statement is not admissible if it was made under circumstances such as to indicate its lack of trustworthiness. For a discussion of this requirement, see the Comment to Evidence Code § 1310. [7 Cal.L.Rev.Comm. Reports 1 (1965)].

§ 1312. Entries in family records and the like

Evidence of entries in family Bibles or other family books or charts, engravings on rings, family portraits, engravings on urns, crypts, or tombstones, and the like, is not made inadmissible by the hearsay rule when offered to prove the birth, marriage, divorce, death, parent and child relationship, race, ancestry, relationship by blood or marriage, or other similar fact of the family history of a member of the family by blood or marriage. *(Stats.1965, c. 299, § 2, operative Jan. 1, 1967. Amended by Stats.1975, c. 1244, p. 3202, § 17.)*

Law Revision Commission Comments

Section 1312 restates the substance of and supersedes the provisions of Code of Civil Procedure Section 1870(13). [7 Cal.L.Rev. Comm. Reports 1 (1965)].

§ 1313. Reputation in family concerning family history

Evidence of reputation among members of a family is not made inadmissible by the hearsay rule if the reputation concerns the birth, marriage, divorce, death, parent and child relationship, race, ancestry, relationship by blood or marriage, or other similar fact of the family history of a member of the family by blood or marriage. *(Stats.1965, c. 299, § 2, operative Jan. 1, 1967. Amended by Stats.1975, c. 1244, p. 3202, § 18.)*

Law Revision Commission Comments

Section 1313 restates the substance of and supersedes the provisions of Code of Civil Procedure Sections 1852 and 1870(11). See Estate of Connors, 53 Cal.App.2d 484, 128 P.2d 200 (1942); Estate of Newman, 34 Cal.App.2d 706, 94 P.2d 356 (1939). However, Section 1870(11) requires the family reputation in question to have existed "previous to the controversy." This qualification is not included in Section 1313 because it is unlikely that a family reputation on a matter of pedigree would be influenced by the existence of a controversy even though the declaration of an individual member of the family, covered in Sections 1310 and 1311, might be.

The family reputation admitted under Section 1313 is necessarily multiple hearsay. If, however, such reputation were inadmissible because of the hearsay rule, and if direct statements of pedigree were inadmissible because they are based on such reputation (as most of them are), the courts would be virtually helpless in determining matters of pedigree. See Tentative Recommendation and a Study Relating to the Uniform Rules of Evidence (Article VIII. Hearsay Evidence), 6 Cal.Law Revision Comm'n, Rep., Rec. & Studies Appendix at 548 (1964). [7 Cal.L.Rev.Comm. Reports 1 (1965)].

§ 1314. Reputation in community concerning family history

Evidence of reputation in a community concerning the date or fact of birth, marriage, divorce, or death of a person resident in the community at the time of the reputation is not made inadmissible by the hearsay rule. *(Stats.1965, c. 299, § 2, operative Jan. 1, 1967.)*

Law Revision Commission Comments

Section 1314 restates what has been held to be existing law under Code of Civil Procedure Section 1963(30) with respect to proof of the fact of marriage. See People v. Vogel, 46 Cal.2d 798, 299 P.2d 850 (1956); Estate of Baldwin, 162 Cal. 471, 123 Pac. 267 (1912). However, Section 1314 has no counterpart in California law insofar as proof of the date or fact of birth, divorce, or death is concerned, since proof of such facts by reputation is presently limited to reputation in the family. See Estate of Heaton, 135 Cal. 385, 67 Pac. 321 (1902). [7 Cal.L.Rev.Comm. Reports 1 (1965)].

Research References

Treatises and Practice Aids

Witkin, California Summary 10th Husband and Wife § 53, in General.

§ 1315. Church records concerning family history

Evidence of a statement concerning a person's birth, marriage, divorce, death, parent and child relationship, race, ancestry, relationship by blood or marriage, or other similar fact of family history which is contained in a writing made as a record of a church, religious denomination, or religious society is not made inadmissible by the hearsay rule if:

(a) The statement is contained in a writing made as a record of an act, condition, or event that would be admissible as evidence of such act, condition, or event under Section 1271; and

(b) The statement is of a kind customarily recorded in connection with the act, condition, or event recorded in the writing. *(Stats.1965, c. 299, § 2, operative Jan. 1, 1967. Amended by Stats.1975, c. 1244, p. 3203, § 19.)*

Law Revision Commission Comments

Church records generally are admissible as business records under the provisions of Section 1271. Under Section 1271, such records would be admissible to prove the occurrence of the church activity—the baptism, confirmation, or marriage—recorded in the writing. However, it is unlikely that Section 1271 would permit such records to be used as evidence of the age or relationship of the participants, for the business records act has been held to authorize business records to be used to prove only facts known personally to the recorder of the information or to other employees of the business. Patek & Co. v. Vineberg, 210 Cal.App.2d 20, 23, 26 Cal.Rptr. 293, 294 (1962) (hearing denied); People v. Williams, 187 Cal.App.2d 355, 9 Cal.Rptr. 722 (1960); Gough v. Security Trust & Sav. Bank, 162 Cal.App.2d 90, 327 P.2d 555 (1958).

Section 1315 permits church records to be used to prove certain additional information. Facts of family history, such as birth dates, relationships, marital histories, etc., that are ordinarily reported to church authorities and recorded in connection with the church's baptismal, confirmation, marriage, and funeral records may be proved by such records under Section 1315.

Section 1315 continues in effect and supersedes the provisions of Code of Civil Procedure Section 1919a without, however, the special and cumbersome authentication procedure specified in Code of Civil Procedure Section 1919b. Under Section 1315, church records may be authenticated in the same manner that other business records are authenticated. [7 Cal.L.Rev.Comm. Reports 1 (1965)].

§ 1316. Marriage, baptismal and similar certificates

Evidence of a statement concerning a person's birth, marriage, divorce, death, parent and child relationship, race, ancestry, relationship by blood or marriage, or other similar fact of family history is not made inadmissible by the hearsay rule if the statement is contained in a certificate that the maker thereof performed a marriage or other ceremony or administered a sacrament and:

(a) The maker was a clergyman, civil officer, or other person authorized to perform the acts reported in the certificate by law or by the rules, regulations, or requirements of a church, religious denomination, or religious society; and

(b) The certificate was issued by the maker at the time and place of the ceremony or sacrament or within a reasonable time thereafter. *(Stats.1965, c. 299, § 2, operative Jan. 1, 1967. Amended by Stats.1975, c. 1244, p. 3203, § 20.)*

Law Revision Commission Comments

Section 1316 provides a hearsay exception for marriage, baptismal, and similar certificates. This exception is somewhat broader than that found in Sections 1919a and 1919b of the Code of Civil Procedure (superseded by Evidence Code Sections 1315 and 1316). Sections 1919a and 1919b are limited to church records and, hence, with respect to marriages, to those performed by clergymen. Moreover, they establish an elaborate and detailed authentication procedure, whereas certificates made admissible by Section 1316 need meet only the general authentication requirement of Section 1401. [7 Cal.L.Rev.Comm. Reports 1 (1965)].

GOVERNMENT CODE

Title 2

GOVERNMENT OF THE STATE OF CALIFORNIA

Division 3

EXECUTIVE DEPARTMENT

Part 2.8

DEPARTMENT OF FAIR EMPLOYMENT AND HOUSING

CHAPTER 6. DISCRIMINATION PROHIBITED

ARTICLE 1. UNLAWFUL PRACTICES, GENERALLY

§ 12945.2. Family care and medical leave; definitions; conditions; unlawful employment practices

(a) Except as provided in subdivision (b), it shall be an unlawful employment practice for any employer, as defined in paragraph (2) of subdivision (c), to refuse to grant a request by any employee with more than 12 months of service with the employer, and who has at least 1,250 hours of service with the employer during the previous 12–month period, to take up to a total of 12 workweeks in any 12–month period for family care and medical leave. Family care and medical leave requested pursuant to this subdivision shall not be deemed to have been granted unless the employer provides the employee, upon granting the leave request, a guarantee of employment in the same or a comparable position upon the termination of the leave. The commission shall adopt a regulation specifying the elements of a reasonable request.

(b) Notwithstanding subdivision (a), it shall not be an unlawful employment practice for an employer to refuse to grant a request for family care and medical leave by an employee if the employer employs less than 50 employees within 75 miles of the worksite where that employee is employed.

(c) For purposes of this section:

(1) "Child" means a biological, adopted, or foster child, a stepchild, a legal ward, or a child of a person standing in loco parentis who is either of the following:

(A) Under 18 years of age.

(B) An adult dependent child.

(2) "Employer" means either of the following:

(A) Any person who directly employs 50 or more persons to perform services for a wage or salary.

(B) The state, and any political or civil subdivision of the state and cities.

(3) "Family care and medical leave" means any of the following:

(A) Leave for reason of the birth of a child of the employee, the placement of a child with an employee in connection with the adoption or foster care of the child by the employee, or the serious health condition of a child of the employee.

(B) Leave to care for a parent or a spouse who has a serious health condition.

(C) Leave because of an employee's own serious health condition that makes the employee unable to perform the functions of the position of that employee, except for leave taken for disability on account of pregnancy, childbirth, or related medical conditions.

(4) "Employment in the same or a comparable position" means employment in a position that has the same or similar duties and pay that can be performed at the same or similar geographic location as the position held prior to the leave.

(5) "FMLA" means the federal Family and Medical Leave Act of 1993 (P.L. 103–3).[1]

(6) "Health care provider" means any of the following:

(A) An individual holding either a physician's and surgeon's certificate issued pursuant to Article 4 (commencing with Section 2080) of Chapter 5 of Division 2 of the Business and Professions Code, an osteopathic physician's and surgeon's certificate issued pursuant to Article 4.5 (commencing with Section 2099.5) of Chapter 5 of Division 2 of the Business and Professions Code, or an individual duly licensed as a physician, surgeon, or osteopathic physician or surgeon in another state or jurisdiction, who directly treats or supervises the treatment of the serious health condition.

(B) Any other person determined by the United States Secretary of Labor to be capable of providing health care services under the FMLA.

(7) "Parent" means a biological, foster, or adoptive parent, a stepparent, a legal guardian, or other person who stood in loco parentis to the employee when the employee was a child.

(8) "Serious health condition" means an illness, injury, impairment, or physical or mental condition that involves either of the following:

(A) Inpatient care in a hospital, hospice, or residential health care facility.

(B) Continuing treatment or continuing supervision by a health care provider.

(d) An employer shall not be required to pay an employee for any leave taken pursuant to subdivision (a), except as required by subdivision (e).

(e) An employee taking a leave permitted by subdivision (a) may elect, or an employer may require the employee, to substitute, for leave allowed under subdivision (a), any of the employee's accrued vacation leave or other accrued time off during this period or any other paid or unpaid time off negotiated with the employer. If an employee takes a leave because of the employee's own serious health condition, the employee may also elect, or the employer may also require the employee, to substitute accrued sick leave during the period of the leave. However, an employee shall not use sick leave during a period of leave in connection with the birth, adoption, or foster care of a child, or to care for a child, parent, or spouse with a serious health condition, unless mutually agreed to by the employer and the employee.

(f)(1) During any period that an eligible employee takes leave pursuant to subdivision (a) or takes leave that qualifies as leave taken under the FMLA, the employer shall maintain and pay for coverage under a "group health plan," as defined in Section 5000(b)(1) of the Internal Revenue Code, [2] for the duration of the leave, not to exceed 12 workweeks in a 12–month period, commencing on the date leave taken under the FMLA commences, at the level and under the conditions coverage would have been provided if the employee had continued in employment continuously for the duration of the leave. Nothing in the preceding sentence shall preclude an employer from maintaining and paying for coverage under a "group health plan" beyond 12 workweeks. An employer may recover the premium that the employer paid as required by this subdivision for maintaining coverage for the employee under the group health plan if both of the following conditions occur:

(A) The employee fails to return from leave after the period of leave to which the employee is entitled has expired.

(B) The employee's failure to return from leave is for a reason other than the continuation, recurrence, or onset of a serious health condition that entitles the employee to leave under subdivision (a) or other circumstances beyond the control of the employee.

(2) Any employee taking leave pursuant to subdivision (a) shall continue to be entitled to participate in employee health plans for any period during which coverage is not provided by the employer under paragraph (1), employee benefit plans, including life insurance or short-term or long-term disability or accident insurance, pension and retirement plans, and supplemental unemployment benefit plans to the same extent and under the same conditions as apply to an unpaid leave taken for any purpose other than those described in subdivision (a). In the absence of these conditions an employee shall continue to be entitled to participate in these plans and, in the case of health and welfare employee benefit plans, including life insurance or short-term or long-term disability or accident insurance, or other similar plans, the employer may, at * * * the employer's discretion, require the employee to pay premiums, at the group rate, during the period of leave not covered by any accrued vacation leave, or other accrued time off, or any other paid or unpaid time off negotiated with the employer, as a condition of continued coverage during the leave period. However, the nonpayment of premiums by an employee shall not constitute a break in service, for purposes of longevity, seniority under any collective bargaining agreement, or any employee benefit plan. For purposes of pension and retirement plans, an employer shall not be required to make plan payments for an employee during the leave period, and the leave period shall not be required to be counted for purposes of time accrued under the plan. However, an employee covered by a pension plan may continue to make contributions in accordance with the terms of the plan during the period of the leave.

(g) During a family care and medical leave period, the employee shall retain employee status with the employer, and the leave shall not constitute a break in service, for purposes of longevity, seniority under any collective bargaining agreement, or any employee benefit plan. An employee returning from leave shall return with no less seniority than the employee had when the leave commenced, for purposes of layoff, recall, promotion, job assignment, and seniority-related benefits such as vacation.

(h) If the employee's need for a leave pursuant to this section is foreseeable, the employee shall provide the employer with reasonable advance notice of the need for the leave.

(i) If the employee's need for leave pursuant to this section is foreseeable due to a planned medical treatment or supervision, the employee shall make a reasonable effort to schedule the treatment or supervision to avoid disruption to the operations of the employer, subject to the approval of the health care provider of the individual requiring the treatment or supervision.

(j)(1) An employer may require that an employee's request for leave to care for a child, a spouse, or a parent who has a serious health condition be supported by a certification issued by the health care provider of the individual requiring care. That certification shall be sufficient if it includes all of the following:

(A) The date on which the serious health condition commenced.

(B) The probable duration of the condition.

(C) An estimate of the amount of time that the health care provider believes the employee needs to care for the individual requiring the care.

(D) A statement that the serious health condition warrants the participation of a family member to provide care during a period of the treatment or supervision of the individual requiring care.

(2) Upon expiration of the time estimated by the health care provider in subparagraph (C) of paragraph (1), the employer may require the employee to obtain recertification, in accordance with the procedure provided in paragraph (1), if additional leave is required.

(k)(1) An employer may require that an employee's request for leave because of the employee's own serious health condition be supported by a certification issued by * * * the employee's health care provider. That certification shall be sufficient if it includes all of the following:

(A) The date on which the serious health condition commenced.

(B) The probable duration of the condition.

(C) A statement that, due to the serious health condition, the employee is unable to perform the function of * * * the employee's position.

(2) The employer may require that the employee obtain subsequent recertification regarding the employee's serious health condition on a reasonable basis, in accordance with the procedure provided in paragraph (1), if additional leave is required.

(3)(A) In any case in which the employer has reason to doubt the validity of the certification provided pursuant to this section, the employer may require, at the employer's expense, that the employee obtain the opinion of a second health care provider, designated or approved by the employer, concerning any information certified under paragraph (1).

(B) The health care provider designated or approved under subparagraph (A) shall not be employed on a regular basis by the employer.

(C) In any case in which the second opinion described in subparagraph (A) differs from the opinion in the original certification, the employer may require, at the employer's expense, that the employee obtain the opinion of a third health care provider, designated or approved jointly by the employer and the employee, concerning the information certified under paragraph (1).

(D) The opinion of the third health care provider concerning the information certified under paragraph (1) shall be considered to be final and shall be binding on the employer and the employee.

(4) As a condition of an employee's return from leave taken because of the employee's own serious health condition, the employer may have a uniformly applied practice or policy that requires the employee to obtain certification from * * * the employee's health care provider that the employee is able to resume work. Nothing in this paragraph shall supersede a valid collective bargaining agreement that governs the return to work of that employee.

(*l*) It shall be an unlawful employment practice for an employer to refuse to hire, or to discharge, fine, suspend, expel, or discriminate against, any individual because of any of the following:

(1) An individual's exercise of the right to family care and medical leave provided by subdivision (a).

(2) An individual's giving information or testimony as to * * * the individual's own family care and medical leave, or another person's family care and medical leave, in any inquiry or proceeding related to rights guaranteed under this section.

(m) This section shall not be construed to require any changes in existing collective bargaining agreements during the life of the contract, or until January 1, 1993, whichever occurs first.

(n) The amendments made to this section by Chapter 827 of the Statutes of 1993 shall not be construed to require any changes in existing collective bargaining agreements during the life of the contract, or until February 5, 1994, whichever occurs first.

(*o*) This section shall be construed as separate and distinct from Section 12945.

(p) Leave provided for pursuant to this section may be taken in one or more periods. The 12–month period during which 12 workweeks of leave may be taken under this section shall run concurrently with the 12–month period under the FMLA, and shall commence the date leave taken under the FMLA commences.

(q) In any case in which both parents entitled to leave under subdivision (a) are employed by the same employer, the employer shall not be required to grant leave in connection with the birth, adoption, or foster care of a child that would allow the parents family care and medical leave totaling more than the amount specified in subdivision (a).

(r)(1) Notwithstanding subdivision (a), an employer may refuse to reinstate an employee returning from leave to the same or a comparable position if all of the following apply:

(A) The employee is a salaried employee who is among the highest paid 10 percent of the employer's employees who are employed within 75 miles of the worksite at which that employee is employed.

(B) The refusal is necessary to prevent substantial and grievous economic injury to the operations of the employer.

(C) The employer notifies the employee of the intent to refuse reinstatement at the time the employer determines the refusal is necessary under subparagraph (B).

(2) In any case in which the leave has already commenced, the employer shall give the employee a reasonable opportunity to return to work following the notice prescribed by subparagraph (C).

(s) Leave taken by an employee pursuant to this section shall run concurrently with leave taken pursuant to the FMLA, except for any leave taken under the FMLA for disability on account of pregnancy, childbirth, or related medical conditions. The aggregate amount of leave taken under this section or the FMLA, or both, except for leave taken for disability on account of pregnancy, childbirth, or related medical conditions, shall not exceed 12 workweeks in a 12–month period. An employee is entitled to take, in addition to the leave provided for under this section and the FMLA, the leave provided for in Section 12945, if the employee is otherwise qualified for that leave.

(t) It shall be an unlawful employment practice for an employer to interfere with, restrain, or deny the exercise of, or the attempt to exercise, any right provided under this section. *(Added by Stats.1991, c. 462 (A.B.77), § 4. Amended by Stats.1992, c. 427 (A.B.3355), § 49; Stats.1993, c. 827 (A.B.1460), § 1, eff. Oct. 5, 1993; Stats.1994, c. 146 (A.B. 3601), § 68; Stats.2011, c. 678 (A.B.592), § 2; Stats.2017, c. 799 (A.B.1556), § 11, eff. Jan. 1, 2018.)*

[1] For public law sections classified to the U.S.C.A., see USCA–Tables.

[2] Internal Revenue Code sections are in Title 26 of the U.S.C.A.

Research References

Forms

California Transactions Forms--Business Entities § 15:56, Employment Agreement for Employee-Shareholder.

Treatises and Practice Aids

Witkin, California Summary 10th Agency and Employment § 421, California Law.

Witkin, California Summary 10th Constitutional Law § 942, in General.

Witkin, California Summary 10th Constitutional Law § 943, Requirements for Taking Leave.

Witkin, California Summary 10th Constitutional Law § 944, Unlawful Employment Practices.

Division 5

PERSONNEL

Part 2

STATE CIVIL SERVICE

CHAPTER 10. PROHIBITIONS AND OFFENSES

ARTICLE 2. DISCRIMINATION

§ 19702.3. Family care leave; exercise of rights; giving information or testimony in inquiry

(a) An appointing authority shall not refuse to hire, and shall not discharge, suspend, expel, or discriminate against, any individual because of any of the following:

(1) An individual's exercise of the right to family care leave provided by subdivision (a) of Section 12945.2.

(2) An individual's giving information or testimony as to his or her own family care leave, or another person's family care leave, in any inquiry or proceeding related to rights guaranteed under Section 12945.2.

(b) This section shall not be construed to require any changes in existing collective bargaining agreements during the life of the contract, or until January 1, 1993, whichever occurs first. *(Added by Stats.1991, c. 462 (A.B.77), § 5. Amended by Stats.1994, c. 1232 (A.B.3619), § 1.)*

Research References

Forms

California Transactions Forms--Business Entities § 15:56, Employment Agreement for Employee-Shareholder.

Treatises and Practice Aids

Witkin, California Summary 10th Agency and Employment § 421, California Law.

Witkin, California Summary 10th Constitutional Law § 942, in General.

Witkin, California Summary 10th Constitutional Law § 944, Unlawful Employment Practices.

Part 3

PUBLIC EMPLOYEES' RETIREMENT SYSTEM

CHAPTER 13. RETIREMENT BENEFITS

ARTICLE 2. COMMUNITY PROPERTY

§ 21290. Marriage dissolutions or legal separations; accounts for accumulated contributions and service credits; rights of nonmembers

(a) Upon the legal separation or dissolution of marriage of a member, the court shall include in the judgment or a court order the date on which the parties separated.

(b) If the community property is divided in accordance with paragraph (3) of subdivision (a) of Section 2610 of the Family Code, the court shall order that the accumulated contributions and service credit attributable to periods of service during the marriage be divided into two separate and distinct accounts in the name of the member and the nonmember, respectively. Any service credit or accumulated contributions that are not explicitly awarded by the judgment or court order shall be deemed the exclusive property of the member.

(c) The court shall address the rights of the nonmember to the following:

(1) The right to a retirement allowance, and the consequent right to elect an optional settlement and designate a beneficiary.

(2) The right to a refund of accumulated contributions.

(3) The right to redeposit accumulated contributions that are eligible for redeposit by the member under Sections 20750 and 20752.

(4) The right to purchase service credit that is eligible for purchase by the member under Article 4 (commencing with Section 20990) and Article 5 (commencing with Section 21020) of Chapter 11.

(5) The right to designate a beneficiary to receive his or her accumulated contributions payable where death occurs prior to retirement.

(6) The right to designate a beneficiary for any unpaid allowance payable at the time of the nonmember's death.

(7) The right to elect coverage in the Second Tier for that member service that is subject to the Second Tier, provided that the election is made within one year of the establishment of the nonmember account or prior to the nonmember's retirement, whichever occurs first. Immediately upon establishment of a nonmember account, the board shall provide, by certified mail, the necessary form and information so that the election may be made.

(d) In the capacity of nonmember, he or she shall not be entitled to any disability or industrial disability retirement allowance, any basic death benefit, any special death benefit, any monthly allowance for survivors of a member or retired person, any insurance benefit, or retired member lump-sum death benefit. No survivor continuance allowance shall be payable to a survivor of a nonmember.

(e)(1) A nonmember whose account is credited with service subject to the Second Tier benefits provided in Section 21076 or 21077 may make an irrevocable election, to be filed with the board, to have his or her Second Tier service credited under Section 21354.1, if the following conditions are met:

(A) The member is employed by the state on or after January 1, 2000.

(B) If eligible, the member has made the election provided in subdivision (a) of Section 21073.7 at the time of the nonmember's election.

(2) An election under this subdivision shall be effective the first of the month following the date the election is received by the system. An election under this subdivision may be made at any time prior to the retirement of the nonmember or prior to payment of a refund of the accumulated contributions in the separate account of the nonmember. A nonmember who makes the election under this subdivision shall make the contributions specified in Section 21073.1.

(3) The term "member" as used in this subdivision means the person from whose account the Second Tier service that is credited to the separate account of the nonmember was derived. *(Added by Stats.1995, c. 379 (S.B.541), § 2. Amended by Stats.1998, c. 485 (A.B.2803), § 88; Stats.1998, c. 932 (A.B.1094), § 33; Stats.2001, c. 21 (S.B.54), § 11, eff. June 25, 2001.)*

Operative Effect

Section 37 of Stats.2001, c. 21 (S.B.54), provides that, other than the provisions of Section 1, the provisions of that Act shall be operative retroactively to January 1, 2000.

Operation of provisions of Part 3 which are not in conformity with Internal Revenue Code § 415, see Government Code § 21762.

Research References

Treatises and Practice Aids

Witkin, California Summary 10th Community Property § 68, Statutory Abrogation Of Rule.

Witkin, California Summary 10th Community Property § 72, in General.

§ 21291. Nonmember

"Nonmember," as used in this article, means the spouse or former spouse of a member, who as a result of petitioning the court for the division of community property, has been awarded a distinct and separate account reflecting specific credited service and accumulated contributions. *(Added by Stats.1995, c. 379 (S.B.541), § 2.)*

Operative Effect

Operation of provisions of Part 3 which are not in conformity with Internal Revenue Code § 415, see Government Code § 21762.

§ 21291.5. Spouse or domestic partner not alternate payee

Notwithstanding any other provision of this article, a spouse or registered domestic partner who is not an alternate payee, as defined in Section 414(p)(8) of the Internal Revenue Code (26 U.S.C. Sec. 401 et seq.) shall not receive a distribution until the member separates from employment. *(Added by Stats.2005, c. 418 (S.B.973), § 13.)*

Operative Effect

Operation of provisions of Part 3 which are not in conformity with Internal Revenue Code § 415, see Government Code § 21762.

§ 21292. Refund of accumulated contributions; rights of nonmember; effect of refund; redeposit of refunded accumulations

(a) The nonmember who is awarded a separate account shall have the right to a refund of the accumulated contributions in the separate account of the nonmember.

(b) The nonmember shall file an application on a form provided by this system to obtain the refund.

(c) The refund shall be effective when this system deposits in the United States mail an initial warrant drawn in favor of the nonmember and addressed to the latest address for the nonmember on file with this system.

(d) The nonmember is deemed to have permanently waived all rights in this system and all rights to any future retirement benefits pertaining to the service credit accumulated contributions, or both, when the refund becomes effective.

(e) The nonmember may not cancel a refund once it has become effective.

(f) The nonmember shall have no right to elect to redeposit the refunded accumulated contributions from the nonmember's account after the refund is effective, and shall have no right to redeposit under Section 20750 or 20752, or to purchase service credit under Article 4 (commencing with Section 20990) or Article 5 (commencing with Section 21020) of Chapter 11 after the refund becomes effective.

(g) If at the time of the marriage dissolution or legal separation, the member does not have the necessary minimum credited service to retire, the nonmember shall receive a refund of the accumulated contributions placed in the nonmember's account. *(Added by Stats.1995, c. 379 (S.B. 541), § 2.)*

Operative Effect

Operation of provisions of Part 3 which are not in conformity with Internal Revenue Code § 415, see Government Code § 21762.

§ 21293. Redeposit of previously refunded accumulated contributions; death of nonmember

(a) The nonmember who is awarded a separate account may redeposit accumulated contributions previously refunded to the member in accordance with the determination of the court required by Section 21290.

(b) The nonmember may redeposit only those accumulated contributions that were previously refunded to the member and that the court has determined to be the community property interest of the nonmember in the accumulated contributions.

(c) If the nonmember elects to redeposit, he or she shall repay the accumulated contributions pursuant to Section 20750 or Section 20752.

(d) An election to redeposit shall be considered an election to repay all accumulated contributions previously refunded that the nonmember is entitled to redeposit.

(e) The right of the nonmember to redeposit is subject to the regulations of the board.

(f) The member has no right to redeposit the share of the nonmember in the previously refunded accumulated contributions unless the nonmember has permanently waived all rights in the system by effecting a refund of accumulated contributions pursuant to Section 21292. However, any right to redeposit previously refunded accumulated contributions not explicitly awarded to the nonmember by the judgment or court order shall be deemed the exclusive property of the member.

(g) If the nonmember elected to redeposit upon retirement and has subsequently died, prior to completing the redeposit, the board shall file a claim against the estate of the decedent to recover benefit payments that exceeded those for which payment was made. *(Added by Stats.1995, c. 379 (S.B.541), § 2. Amended by Stats.2003, c. 855 (S.B.268), § 8.)*

Operative Effect

Operation of provisions of Part 3 which are not in conformity with Internal Revenue Code § 415, see Government Code § 21762.

§ 21294. Purchase of service credit by nonmember; death of nonmember

(a) The nonmember shall have the right to purchase service credit pursuant to the determination of the court required by Section 21290.

(b) The nonmember may purchase only that service credit that the court, pursuant to Section 21290 has determined to be the community property interest of the nonmember spouse.

(c) If the nonmember elects to purchase service credit, he or she shall pay, prior to retirement, the contributions and interest required by Article 4 (commencing with Section 20990) and Article 5 (commencing with Section 21020) of Chapter 11 and pursuant to the regulations of the board.

(d) The nonmember shall have no right to purchase the service credit after the effective date of a refund of the accumulated contributions in the separate account of the nonmember.

(e) The member has no right to purchase the community property interest of the nonmember of the service credit unless the nonmember has permanently waived all rights in the system by effecting a refund of accumulated contributions pursuant to Section 21292. However, any service credit eligible for purchase that is not explicitly awarded to the nonmember by the judgment or court order shall be deemed the exclusive property of the member.

(f) If the nonmember elected to purchase service credits upon retirement and has subsequently died, prior to completing the purchase, the board shall file a claim against the estate of the deceased to recover benefit payments that exceeded those for which payment was made. *(Added by Stats.1995, c. 379 (S.B.541), § 2. Amended by Stats.2003, c. 855 (S.B.268), § 9.)*

Operative Effect

Operation of provisions of Part 3 which are not in conformity with Internal Revenue Code § 415, see Government Code § 21762.

§ 21295. Retirement of nonmember

A nonmember shall be retired upon his or her written application to the board if all of the following conditions are met:

(a) The nonmember has attained the minimum age prescribed by the applicable service retirement formula of the member.

(b) On the date of marriage dissolution or legal separation, the member had sufficient credited service to retire for service.

(c) On the date of application, the member has attained minimum retirement age to receive a service retirement allowance. *(Added by Stats.1995, c. 379 (S.B.541), § 2.)*

Operative Effect

Operation of provisions of Part 3 which are not in conformity with Internal Revenue Code § 415, see Government Code § 21762.

§ 21296. Effective date of retirement; accrual of retirement allowance

Retirement shall be effective and the retirement allowance shall begin to accrue as of the date designated in the nonmember's application as the effective date of retirement, or the day following the date of court order dividing the community property of the member and nonmember, if later. If the retirement application is not received within nine months of the requested effective date, in no event shall the retirement become effective or the retirement allowance begin to accrue earlier than the first day of the month in which the nonmember's application is received at an office of the board or by an employee of this system designated by the board, or, if the nonmember has been incompetent to act on his or her own behalf continuously from the date of dissolution or legal separation, one year prior to the month in which an application by the guardian of his or her estate is so received. An application for retirement may only be filed by or for a nonmember who is living on the date the application is actually received by this system. The effective date of a nonmember application for retirement received more than nine months after the requested effective date shall be determined in accordance with Section 20160. *(Added by Stats.1995, c. 379 (S.B.541), § 2. Amended by Stats.2009, c. 130 (A.B.966), § 30.)*

Operative Effect

Operation of provisions of Part 3 which are not in conformity with Internal Revenue Code § 415, see Government Code § 21762.

§ 21297. Final compensation

For a nonmember, "final compensation" means the highest average annual compensation earnable by the member during the three consecutive years, or one year where applicable, prior to the date of dissolution of marriage or legal separation. The nonmember may designate an earlier period to be used where the time period of the nonmember's marriage to the member and membership correspond. *(Added by Stats. 1995, c. 379 (S.B.541), § 2.)*

Operative Effect

Operation of provisions of Part 3 which are not in conformity with Internal Revenue Code § 415, see Government Code § 21762.

§ 21298. Calculation of retirement allowance

(a) A nonmember entitled to receive a retirement allowance shall receive a retirement allowance based on the service retirement formula applicable to the service credited to the nonmember.

(b) The retirement allowance shall consist of a pension and an annuity, the latter of which shall be derived from the nonmember's accumulated contributions. The nonmember's retirement allowance, based upon the service credited by the employer and the nonmember's effective date of retirement, shall be subject to all cost-of-living increases, ad hoc increases, and increases provided by Section 21337 or 21337.1.

(c) If, prior to the nonmember's retirement, there is any increase in the service retirement formula that applies to service credited to the nonmember, that increase shall apply to the applicable service credited to the nonmember, provided that the same increase also applies to the applicable service credited to the member from whose account the nonmember's service was derived. *(Added by Stats.1995, c. 379 (S.B.541), § 2. Amended by Stats.1996, c. 906 (S.B.1859), § 148; Stats.2001, c. 21 (S.B.54), § 12, eff. June 25, 2001; Stats.2001, c. 793 (A.B.1683), § 21.)*

Operative Effect

Operation of provisions of Part 3 which are not in conformity with Internal Revenue Code § 415, see Government Code § 21762.

INSURANCE CODE

Division 1

GENERAL RULES GOVERNING INSURANCE

Part 1

THE CONTRACT

CHAPTER 4. THE POLICY

ARTICLE 1. DEFINITION AND SCOPE

§ 381.5. Domestic partners; coverage

(a) Every policy issued, amended, delivered, or renewed in this state shall provide coverage for the registered domestic partner of an insured or policyholder that is equal to, and subject to the same terms and conditions as, the coverage provided to a spouse of an insured or policyholder. A policy may not offer or provide coverage for a registered domestic partner if it is not equal to the coverage provided for the spouse of an insured or policyholder. This subdivision applies to all forms of insurance regulated by this code.

(b) A policy subject to this section that is issued, amended, delivered, or renewed in this state on or after January 1, 2005, shall be deemed to provide coverage for registered domestic partners that is equal to the coverage provided to a spouse of an insured or policyholder.

(c) It is the intent of the Legislature that, for purposes of this section, "terms," "conditions," and "coverage" do not include instances of differential treatment of domestic partners and spouses under federal law. *(Added by Stats.2004, c. 488 (A.B.2208), § 3.)*

Research References

Treatises and Practice Aids

Witkin, California Summary 10th Husband and Wife § 33, Other Rights.

Witkin, California Summary 10th Insurance § 48, Governing Rules and Principles.

Division 2

CLASSES OF INSURANCE

Part 2

LIFE AND DISABILITY INSURANCE

CHAPTER 1. THE CONTRACT

ARTICLE 1. GENERAL PROVISIONS

§ 10110.3. Issuing life insurance policy to applicant that insures life of applicant's spouse

(a) An insurer may not issue an individual life insurance policy to an applicant that insures the life of the applicant's spouse unless the applicant's spouse has signed the policy application or has otherwise been notified in advance of the issuance of the policy.

(b) This section shall apply to policies of individual life insurance with face amounts exceeding fifty thousand dollars ($50,000) that are issued on or after July 1, 2004. *(Added by Stats.2003, c. 115 (A.B.1083), § 1.)*

Research References

Treatises and Practice Aids

Witkin, California Summary 10th Insurance § 78, in General.

PENAL CODE

Part 1

OF CRIMES AND PUNISHMENTS

Title 9

OF CRIMES AGAINST THE PERSON INVOLVING SEXUAL ASSAULT, AND CRIMES AGAINST PUBLIC DECENCY AND GOOD MORALS

CHAPTER 2. ABANDONMENT AND NEGLECT OF CHILDREN

§ 270. Failure to provide; parent; punishment; effect of custody; evidence; applicability of section; artificial insemination; treatment by spiritual means

If a parent of a minor child willfully omits, without lawful excuse, to furnish necessary clothing, food, shelter or medical attendance, or other remedial care for his or her child, he or she is guilty of a misdemeanor punishable by a fine not exceeding two thousand dollars ($2,000), or by imprisonment in the county jail not exceeding one year, or by both such fine and imprisonment. If a court of competent jurisdiction has made a final adjudication in either a civil or a criminal action that a person is the parent of a minor child and the person has notice of such adjudication and he or she then willfully omits, without lawful excuse, to furnish necessary clothing, food, shelter, medical attendance or other remedial care for his or her child, this conduct is punishable by imprisonment in the county jail not exceeding one year or in a state prison for a determinate term of one year and one day, or by a fine not exceeding two thousand dollars ($2,000), or by both such fine and imprisonment. This statute shall not be construed so as to relieve such parent from the criminal liability defined herein for such omission merely because the other parent of such child is legally entitled to the custody of such child nor because the other parent of such child or any other person or organization voluntarily or involuntarily furnishes such necessary food, clothing, shelter or medical attendance or other remedial care for such child or undertakes to do so.

Proof of abandonment or desertion of a child by such parent, or the omission by such parent to furnish necessary food, clothing, shelter or medical attendance or other remedial care for his or her child is prima facie evidence that such abandonment or desertion or omission to furnish necessary food, clothing, shelter or medical attendance or other remedial care is willful and without lawful excuse.

The court, in determining the ability of the parent to support his or her child, shall consider all income, including social insurance benefits and gifts.

The provisions of this section are applicable whether the parents of such child are or were ever married or divorced, and regardless of any decree made in any divorce action relative to alimony or to the support of the child. A child conceived but not yet born is to be deemed an existing person insofar as this section is concerned.

The husband of a woman who bears a child as a result of artificial insemination shall be considered the father of that child for the purpose of this section, if he consented in writing to the artificial insemination.

If a parent provides a minor with treatment by spiritual means through prayer alone in accordance with the tenets and practices of a recognized church or religious denomination, by a duly accredited practitioner thereof, such treatment shall constitute "other remedial care", as used in this section. *(Enacted in 1872. Amended by Stats.1905, c. 568, p. 758, § 1; Stats.1909, c. 159, p. 258, § 1; Stats.1915, c. 374, p. 572, § 1; Stats.1917, c. 168, p. 252, § 1; Stats.1921, c. 911, p. 1723, § 1; Stats.1923, c. 284, p. 592, § 1; Stats.1925, c. 325, p. 544, § 1; Stats.1931, c. 696, p. 1438, § 1; Stats.1939, c. 1001, p. 2783, § 1; Stats.1955, c. 753, p. 1247, § 1; Stats.1957, c. 139, p. 742, § 32; Stats.1957, c. 1855, p. 3255, § 1; Stats.1965, c. 496, p. 1805, § 1; Stats.1968, c. 235, p. 546, § 2; Stats.1971, c. 1587, p. 3202, § 1; Stats.1974, c. 893, p. 1892, § 1; Stats.1976, c. 673, p. 1661, § 1; Stats.1983, c. 1092, § 259, eff. Sept. 27, 1983, operative Jan. 1, 1984; Stats.1984, c. 1432, § 1.)*

Commentary

In re Gruntz, 202 F.3d 1074 (9th Cir. en banc 2000), holds that an automatic stay in bankruptcy does not enjoin a state criminal prosecution for willful failure to pay child support.

People v. Moore, 65 Cal.App.4th 933, 76 Cal.Rptr.2d 872 (1998), holds that the prosecution has the burden of proving beyond a reasonable doubt that a parent's failure to support a child was "willful."

Research References

Forms

West's California Code Forms, Family § 7630, Comment Overview--Determining Parent and Child Relationship.

Treatises and Practice Aids

Witkin, California Summary 10th Constitutional Law § 203, Other Exceptions.

Witkin, California Summary 10th Parent and Child § 13, Nature and Effect Of Classification.

Witkin, California Summary 10th Parent and Child § 14, Child Of Artificial Insemination is Legitimate.

Witkin, California Summary 10th Parent and Child § 26, Constitutional Challenges.

Witkin, California Summary 10th Parent and Child § 53, Judgment.

Witkin, California Summary 10th Parent and Child § 55, Appeal.

Witkin, California Summary 10th Parent and Child § 290, in General.

Witkin, California Summary 10th Parent and Child § 291, Prayer Treatment for Child.

Witkin, California Summary 10th Parent and Child § 438, Criminal Prosecution.

Witkin, California Summary 10th Parent and Child § 484, Receipt, Deposit, and Disbursements Of Money.

Witkin, California Summary 10th Torts § 1382, No Action for Death Of Unborn Child.

§ 270.1. Parent or guardian of chronic truant; failure to reasonably supervise and encourage school attendance deemed misdemeanor; punishment; deferred entry of judgment program; funding; punishment under other provisions; declaration of eligibility or ineligibility for program

(a) A parent or guardian of a pupil of six years of age or more who is in kindergarten or any of grades 1 to 8, inclusive, and who is subject to compulsory full-time education or compulsory continuation education, whose child is a chronic truant as defined in Section 48263.6 of the Education Code, who has failed to reasonably supervise and encourage the pupil's school attendance, and who has been offered language accessible support services to address the pupil's truancy, is guilty of a misdemeanor punishable by a fine not exceeding two thousand dollars ($2,000), or by imprisonment in a county jail not exceeding one year, or by both that fine and imprisonment. A parent or guardian guilty of a misdemeanor under this subdivision may participate in the deferred entry of judgment program defined in subdivision (b).

(b) A superior court may establish a deferred entry of judgment program that includes the components listed in paragraphs (1) to (7), inclusive, to adjudicate cases involving parents or guardians of elementary school pupils who are chronic truants as defined in Section 48263.6 of the Education Code:

(1) A dedicated court calendar.

(2) Leadership by a judge of the superior court in that county.

(3) Meetings, scheduled and held periodically, with school district representatives designated by the chronic truant's school district of enrollment. Those representatives may include school psychologists, school counselors, teachers, school administrators, or other educational service providers deemed appropriate by the school district.

(4) Service referrals for parents or guardians, as appropriate to each case that may include, but are not limited to, all of the following:

(A) Case management.

(B) Mental and physical health services.

(C) Parenting classes and support.

(D) Substance abuse treatment.

(E) Child care and housing.

(5) A clear statement that, in lieu of trial, the court may grant deferred entry of judgment with respect to the current crime or crimes charged if the defendant pleads guilty to each charge and waives time for the pronouncement of judgment and that, upon the defendant's compliance with the terms and conditions set forth by the court and agreed to by the defendant upon the entry of his or her plea, and upon the motion of the prosecuting attorney, the court will dismiss the charge or charges against the defendant and the same procedures specified for successful completion of a drug diversion program or a deferred entry of judgment program pursuant to Section 851.90 and the provisions of Section 1203.4 shall apply.

(6) A clear statement that failure to comply with any condition under the program may result in the prosecuting attorney or the court making a motion for entry of judgment, whereupon the court will render a finding of guilty to the charge or charges pled, enter judgment, and schedule a sentencing hearing as otherwise provided in this code.

(7) An explanation of criminal record retention and disposition resulting from participation in the deferred entry of judgment program and the defendant's rights relative to answering questions about his or her arrest and deferred entry of judgment following successful completion of the program.

(c) Funding for the deferred entry of judgment program pursuant to this section shall be derived solely from nonstate sources.

(d) A parent or guardian of an elementary school pupil who is a chronic truant, as defined in Section 48263.6 of the Education Code, may not be punished for a violation of both this section and the provisions of Section 272 that involve criminal liability for parents and guardians of truant children.

(e) If any district attorney chooses to charge a defendant with a violation of subdivision (a) and the defendant is found by the prosecuting attorney to be eligible or ineligible for deferred entry of judgment, the prosecuting attorney shall file with the court a declaration in writing, or state for the record, the grounds upon which that determination is based. *(Added by Stats.2010, c. 647 (S.B.1317), § 2.)*

§ 270.5. Duty to accept minor into parent's home or provide alternative shelter; request of child protection agency; lawful excuse

(a) Every parent who refuses, without lawful excuse, to accept his or her minor child into the parent's home, or, failing to do so, to provide alternative shelter, upon being requested to do so by a child protective agency and after being informed of the duty imposed by this statute to do so, is guilty of a misdemeanor and shall be punished by a fine of not more than five hundred dollars ($500).

(b) For purposes of this section, "child protective agency" means a police or sheriff's department, a county probation department, or a county welfare department.

(c) For purposes of this section, "lawful excuse" shall include, but not be limited to, a reasonable fear that the minor child's presence in the home will endanger the safety of the parent or other persons residing in the home. *(Added by Stats.1984, c. 1616, § 1.)*

Research References

Treatises and Practice Aids

Witkin, California Summary 10th Parent and Child § 290, in General.

§ 270.6. Willful violation of court order to pay spousal support; punishment

If a court of competent jurisdiction has made a temporary or permanent order awarding spousal support that a person must pay, the person has notice of that order, and he or she then leaves the state with the intent to willfully omit, without lawful excuse, to furnish the spousal support, he or she is punishable by imprisonment in a county jail for a period not exceeding one year, a fine not exceeding two thousand dollars ($2,000), or both that imprisonment and fine. *(Added by Stats.2002, c. 410 (S.B.1399), § 1.)*

§ 270a. Failure to provide support for spouse; punishment

Every individual who has sufficient ability to provide for his or her spouse's support, or who is able to earn the means of such spouse's support, who willfully abandons and leaves his or her spouse in a destitute condition, or who refuses or neglects to provide such spouse with necessary food, clothing, shelter, or medical attendance, unless by such spouse's conduct the individual was justified in abandoning such spouse, is guilty of a misdemeanor. *(Added by Stats.1907, c. 74, p. 91, § 1. Amended by Stats.1909, c. 159, p. 258, § 2; Stats.1957, c. 139, p. 743, § 33; Stats.1957, c. 1855, p. 3255, § 2; Stats.1976, c. 1170, p. 5250, § 1.)*

Research References

Treatises and Practice Aids

Witkin, California Summary 10th Husband and Wife § 36, Mutual Obligations.

Witkin, California Summary 10th Parent and Child § 484, Receipt, Deposit, and Disbursements Of Money.

§ 270b. Undertaking to provide support; suspension of proceedings or sentence; proceedings on breach of undertaking

After arrest and before plea or trial, or after conviction or plea of guilty and before sentence under either Section 270 or 270a, if the defendant shall appear before the court and enter into an undertaking with sufficient sureties to the people of the State of California in such penal sum as the court may fix, to be approved by the court, and conditioned that the defendant will pay to the person having custody of such child or to such spouse, such sum per month as may be fixed by the court in order to thereby provide such minor child or such spouse as the case may be, with necessary food, shelter, clothing, medical attendance, or other remedial care, then the court may suspend proceedings or sentence therein; and such undertaking is valid and binding for two years, or such lesser time which the court shall fix; and upon the failure of defendant to comply with such undertaking, the defendant may be ordered to appear before the court and show cause why further proceedings should not be had in such action or why sentence should not be imposed, whereupon the court may proceed with such action, or pass sentence, or for good cause shown may modify the order and take a new undertaking and further suspend proceedings or sentence for a like period. *(Added by Stats.1907, c. 74, p. 92, § 2. Amended by Stats.1909, c. 159, p. 259, § 3; Stats.1931, c. 645, p. 1386, § 1; Stats.1976, c. 1170, p. 5250, § 2.)*

§ 270c. Failure of adult child to provide for indigent parent

Except as provided in Chapter 2 (commencing with Section 4410) of Part 4 of Division 9 of the Family Code, every adult child who, having the ability so to do, fails to provide necessary food, clothing, shelter, or medical attendance for an indigent parent, is guilty of a misdemeanor. *(Added by Stats.1909, c. 113, p. 166, § 1. Amended by Stats.1955, c. 613, p. 1103, § 3; Stats.1992, c. 163 (A.B.2641), § 102, operative Jan. 1, 1994.)*

Law Revision Commission Comments

1992 Amendment

Section 270c is amended to substitute a reference to the Family Code provisions that replaced former Civil Code Section 206.5. [22 Cal.L.Rev.Comm.Reports 1 (1992)].

Research References

Treatises and Practice Aids

Witkin, California Summary 10th Husband and Wife § 340, Aid to Aged, Blind, and Disabled.

Witkin, California Summary 10th Parent and Child § 376, Civil and Criminal Liability.

Witkin, California Summary 10th Parent and Child § 484, Receipt, Deposit, and Disbursements Of Money.

§ 270d. Fine; disposition

In any case where there is a conviction and sentence under the provisions of either Section 270 or Section 270a, should a fine be imposed, such fine shall be directed by the court to be paid in whole or in part to the spouse of the defendant or guardian or custodian of the child or children of such defendant, except as follows:

If the children are receiving public assistance, all fines, penalties or forfeitures imposed and all funds collected from the defendant shall be paid to the county department. Money so paid shall be applied first to support for the calendar month following its receipt by the county department and any balance remaining shall be applied to future needs, or be treated as reimbursement for past support furnished from public assistance funds. *(Added by Stats.1911, c. 379, p. 687, § 1. Amended by Stats.1963, c. 834, p. 2033, § 2; Stats.1974, c. 893, p. 1893, § 2.)*

§ 270e. Evidence of marriage, domestic partnership, or parenthood; confidential communications; competency of spouse as witness; proof of willfulness

No other evidence shall be required to prove marriage or registered domestic partnership of spouses, or that a person is the lawful father or mother of a child or children, than is or shall be required to prove such facts in a civil action. In all prosecutions under either Section 270a or 270 of this code, Sections 970, 971, and 980 of the Evidence Code do not apply, and both spouses or domestic partners shall be competent to testify to any and all relevant matters, including the fact of marriage or registered domestic partnership and the parentage of a child or children. Proof of the abandonment and nonsupport of a spouse, or of the omission to furnish necessary food, clothing, shelter, or of medical attendance for a child or children is prima facie evidence that such abandonment and nonsupport or omission to furnish necessary food, clothing, shelter, or medical attendance is willful. In any prosecution under Section 270, it shall be competent for the people to prove nonaccess of husband to wife or any other fact establishing nonpaternity of a husband. In any prosecution pursuant to Section 270, the final establishment of paternity or nonpaternity in another proceeding shall be admissible as evidence of paternity or nonpaternity. *(Added by Stats.1911, c. 379, c. 688, § 1. Amended by Stats.1955, c. 948, p. 1834, § 1; Stats.1957, c. 1855, p. 3256, § 3; Stats.1965, c. 299, p. 1367, § 138, operative Jan. 1, 1967; Stats.1976, c. 1170, p. 5250, § 3; Stats.2016, c. 50 (S.B.1005), § 68, eff. Jan. 1, 2017.)*

Law Revision Commission Comments

1965 Amendment

The revision of Section 270e merely inserts a reference to the pertinent sections of the Evidence Code. [7 Cal.L.Rev.Comm. Reports 362 (1965)].

Research References

Treatises and Practice Aids

Witkin, California Summary 10th Husband and Wife § 36, Mutual Obligations.

§ 270f. Report by parent of failure to support; investigation and action by district attorney

Where, under the provisions of this chapter, a report is filed by a parent of a child with the district attorney averring:

(1) That the other parent has failed to provide necessary support and

(2) That neither the child in need of assistance nor another on his behalf is receiving public assistance, the district attorney shall immediately investigate the verity of such report and determine the defaulting parent's location and financial ability to provide the needed support, and upon a finding that the report is true shall immediately take all steps necessary to obtain support for the child in need of assistance. *(Added by Stats.1965, c. 496, p. 1806, § 2. Amended by Stats.1974, c. 893, p. 1893, § 3.)*

§ 270g. Review of reports

A review of each report filed with the district attorney under Section 270f shall be made at 90-day intervals unless the support payments have been legally terminated, the parties involved are permanently located beyond county jurisdiction, or the defaulting parent is complying with the provisions of this chapter. *(Added by Stats.1965, c. 496, p. 1806, § 3. Amended by Stats.1974, c. 893, p. 1894, § 4.)*

§ 270h. Support order included in order granting probation; issuance of execution; assignment of wages

In any case where there is a conviction under either Section 270 or 270a and there is an order granting probation which includes an order for support, the court may:

(a) Issue an execution on the order for the support payments that accrue during the time the probation order is in effect, in the same manner as on a judgment in a civil action for support payments. This remedy shall apply only when there is no existing civil order of this state or a foreign court order that has been reduced to a judgment of this state for support of the same person or persons included in the probation support order.

(b) Issue an earnings assignment order for support pursuant to Chapter 8 (commencing with Section 5200) of Part 5 of Division 9 of the Family Code as a condition of probation. This remedy shall apply only when there is no existing civil order for support of the same person or persons included in the probation support order upon which an assignment order has been entered pursuant to Chapter 8 (commencing with Section 5200) of Part 5 of Division 9 of the Family Code or pursuant to former Chapter 5 (commencing with Section 4390) of Title 1.5 of Part 5 of Division 4 of the Civil Code.

These remedies are in addition to any other remedies available to the court. *(Added by Stats.1969, c. 1202, p. 2342, § 1. Amended by Stats.1971, c. 1587, p. 3203, § 2; Stats.1991, c. 1091 (A.B.1487), § 118; Stats.1992, c. 163 (A.B.2641), § 103, operative Jan. 1, 1994.)*

Law Revision Commission Comments

1992 Amendment

The first sentence of subdivision (b) of Section 270h is amended to substitute a reference to the Family Code provisions that replaced the former Civil Code provisions. The second sentence of subdivision (b) is amended to add a reference to the Family Code provisions that replaced the former Civil Code provisions. The terminology used in subdivision (b) has been revised to conform to the terminology of the Family Code. See Fam. Code § 5208 ("earnings assignment order for support"). [22 Cal.L.Rev.Comm.Reports 1 (1992)].

§ 271. Desertion of child under 14 with intent to abandon; punishment

Every parent of any child under the age of 14 years, and every person to whom any such child has been confided for nurture, or education, who deserts such child in any place whatever with intent to abandon it, is punishable by imprisonment pursuant to subdivision (h) of Section 1170 or in the county jail not exceeding one year or by fine not exceeding one thousand dollars ($1,000) or by both. *(Enacted in 1872. Amended by Stats.1909, c. 190, p. 297, § 1; Stats.1945, c. 250, p. 713, § 1; Stats.1983, c. 1092, § 260, eff. Sept. 27, 1983, operative Jan. 1, 1984; Stats.2011, c. 15 (A.B.109), § 306, eff. April 4, 2011, operative Oct. 1, 2011.)*

§ 271a. Abandonment or failure to maintain child under 14; false representation that child is orphan; punishment

Every person who knowingly and willfully abandons, or who, having ability so to do, fails or refuses to maintain his or her minor child under the age of 14 years, or who falsely, knowing the same to be false, represents to any manager, officer or agent of any orphan asylum or charitable institution for the care of orphans, that any child for whose admission into that asylum or institution application has been made is an orphan, is punishable by imprisonment pursuant to subdivision (h) of Section 1170, or in the county jail not exceeding one year, or by fine not exceeding one thousand dollars ($1,000), or by both. *(Added by Stats.1905, c. 568, p. 758, § 2. Amended by Stats.1909, c. 190, p. 297, § 2; Stats.1983, c. 1092, § 261, eff. Sept. 27, 1983, operative Jan. 1, 1984; Stats.2011, c. 15 (A.B.109), § 307, eff. April 4, 2011, operative Oct. 1, 2011.)*

§ 271.5. Safe-surrender sites; parents or other individuals surrendering custody of baby

(a) No parent or other individual having lawful custody of a minor child 72 hours old or younger may be prosecuted for a violation of Section 270, 270.5, 271, or 271a if he or she voluntarily surrenders physical custody of the child to personnel on duty at a safe-surrender site.

(b) For purposes of this section, "safe-surrender site" has the same meaning as defined in paragraph (1) of subdivision (a) of Section 1255.7 of the Health and Safety Code.

(c)(1) For purposes of this section, "lawful custody" has the same meaning as defined in subdivision (j) of Section 1255.7 of the Health and Safety Code.

(2) For purposes of this section, "personnel" has the same meaning as defined in paragraph (3) of subdivision (a) of Section 1255.7 of the Health and Safety Code. *(Added by Stats.2000, c. 824 (S.B.1368), § 2. Amended by Stats.2003, c. 150 (S.B.139), § 2; Stats.2004, c. 103 (S.B.1413), § 2; Stats.2005, c. 279 (S.B.1107), § 3; Stats.2005, c. 625 (S.B.116), § 2; Stats.2007, c. 130 (A.B.299), § 186.)*

§ 272. Contributing to delinquency of persons under 18 years; persuading, luring, or transporting minors 12 years of age or younger

(a)(1) Every person who commits any act or omits the performance of any duty, which act or omission causes or tends to cause or encourage any person under the age of 18 years to come within the provisions of Section 300, 601, or 602 of the Welfare and Institutions Code or which act or omission contributes thereto, or any person who, by any act or omission, or by threats, commands, or persuasion, induces or endeavors to induce any person under the age of 18 years or any ward or dependent child of the juvenile court to fail or refuse to conform to a lawful order of the juvenile court, or to do or to perform any act or to follow any course of conduct or to so live as would cause or manifestly tend to cause that person to become or to remain a person within the provisions of Section 300, 601, or 602 of the Welfare and Institutions Code, is guilty of a misdemeanor and upon conviction thereof shall be punished by a fine not exceeding two thousand five hundred dollars ($2,500), or by imprisonment in the county jail for not more than one year, or by both fine and imprisonment in a county jail, or may be released on probation for a period not exceeding five years.

(2) For purposes of this subdivision, a parent or legal guardian to any person under the age of 18 years shall have the duty to exercise reasonable care, supervision, protection, and control over their minor child.

(b)(1) An adult stranger who is 21 years of age or older, who knowingly contacts or communicates with a minor who is under 14 years of age, who knew or reasonably should have known that the minor is under 14 years of age, for the purpose of persuading and luring, or transporting, or attempting to persuade and lure, or transport, that minor away from the minor's home or from any location known by the minor's parent, legal guardian, or custodian, to be a place where the minor is located, for any purpose, without the express consent of the minor's parent or legal guardian, and with the intent to avoid the consent of the minor's parent or legal guardian, is guilty of an infraction or a misdemeanor, subject to subdivision (d) of Section 17.

(2) This subdivision shall not apply in an emergency situation.

(3) As used in this subdivision, the following terms are defined to mean:

(A) "Emergency situation" means a situation where the minor is threatened with imminent bodily harm, emotional harm, or psychological harm.

(B) "Contact" or "communication" includes, but is not limited to, the use of a telephone or the Internet, as defined in Section 17538 of the Business and Professions Code.

(C) "Stranger" means a person of casual acquaintance with whom no substantial relationship exists, or an individual with whom a relationship has been established or promoted for the primary purpose of victimization, as defined in subdivision (e) of Section 6600 of the Welfare and Institutions Code.

(D) "Express consent" means oral or written permission that is positive, direct, and unequivocal, requiring no inference or implication to supply its meaning.

(4) This section shall not be interpreted to criminalize acts of persons contacting minors within the scope and course of their employment, or status as a volunteer of a recognized civic or charitable organization.

(5) This section is intended to protect minors and to help parents and legal guardians exercise reasonable care, supervision, protection, and control over minor children. *(Added by Stats.1961, c. 1616, p. 3503, § 3. Amended by Stats.1972, c. 579, p. 1005, § 34; Stats.1976, c. 1068, p. 4740, § 1; Stats. 1976, c. 1125, p. 5037, § 16; Stats.1979, c. 373, p. 1349, § 237; Stats.1988, c. 1256, § 2, eff. Sept. 26, 1988; Stats.2000, c. 621 (A.B.2021), § 1; Stats.2001, c. 159 (S.B.662), § 161; Stats. 2005, c. 461 (A.B.33), § 1.)*

Research References

Forms

California Transactions Forms--Family Law § 3:14, Fiscal Responsibility and Liability Issues.

Treatises and Practice Aids

Witkin, California Summary 10th Parent and Child § 440, Original Statute and Revision.
Witkin, California Summary 10th Parent and Child § 539, Serious Physical Harm.
Witkin, California Summary 10th Parent and Child § 636, Criminal Records Check and Fingerprint Clearance.
Witkin, California Summary 10th Parent and Child § 876, Consent to Search.

§ 273. Paying or receiving money or thing of value to parent for placement for, or consent to, adoption of child

(a) It is a misdemeanor for any person or agency to pay, offer to pay, or to receive money or anything of value for the placement for adoption or for the consent to an adoption of a child. This subdivision shall not apply to any fee paid for adoption services provided by the State Department of Social Services, a licensed adoption agency, adoption services providers, as defined in Section 8502 of the Family Code, or an attorney providing adoption legal services.

(b) This section shall not make it unlawful to pay or receive the maternity-connected medical or hospital and necessary living expenses of the mother preceding and during confinement as an act of charity, as long as the payment is not contingent upon placement of the child for adoption, consent to the adoption, or cooperation in the completion of the adoption.

(c) It is a misdemeanor punishable by imprisonment in a county jail not exceeding one year or by a fine not exceeding two thousand five hundred dollars ($2,500) for any parent to obtain the financial benefits set forth in subdivision (b) with the intent to receive those financial benefits where there is an intent to do either of the following:

(1) Not complete the adoption.

(2) Not consent to the adoption.

(d) It is a misdemeanor punishable by imprisonment in a county jail not exceeding one year or by a fine not exceeding two thousand five hundred dollars ($2,500) for any parent to obtain the financial benefits set forth in subdivision (b) from two or more prospective adopting families or persons, if either parent does both of the following:

(1) Knowingly fails to disclose to those families or persons that there are other prospective adopting families or persons interested in adopting the child, with knowledge that there is an obligation to disclose that information.

(2) Knowingly accepts the financial benefits set forth in subdivision (b) if the aggregate amount exceeds the reasonable maternity-connected medical or hospital and necessary living expenses of the mother preceding and during the pregnancy.

(e) Any person who has been convicted previously of an offense described in subdivision (c) or (d), who is separately tried and convicted of a subsequent violation of subdivision (c) or (d), is guilty of a public offense punishable by imprisonment in a county jail or in the state prison.

(f) Nothing in this section shall be construed to prohibit the prosecution of any person for a misdemeanor or felony pursuant to Section 487 or any other provision of law in lieu of prosecution pursuant to this section. *(Added by Stats.1967, c. 1088, p. 2723, § 1. Amended by Stats.1990, c. 1492 (A.B.4288), § 1; Stats.1993, c. 377 (S.B.244), § 1; Stats.1997, c. 185 (S.B.122), § 1.)*

Research References

Forms

California Transactions Forms--Family Law § 6:2, Governing Law.
California Transactions Forms--Family Law § 6:20, Financial Assistance to Birth Parents.

Treatises and Practice Aids

Witkin, California Summary 10th Parent and Child § 22, Where Intended Mother is Genetic Mother.

Witkin, California Summary 10th Parent and Child § 87, Private Adoptions.

§ 273a. Willful harm or injury to child; endangering person or health; punishment; conditions of probation

(a) Any person who, under circumstances or conditions likely to produce great bodily harm or death, willfully causes or permits any child to suffer, or inflicts thereon unjustifiable physical pain or mental suffering, or having the care or custody of any child, willfully causes or permits the person or health of that child to be injured, or willfully causes or permits that child to be placed in a situation where his or her person or health is endangered, shall be punished by imprisonment in a county jail not exceeding one year, or in the state prison for two, four, or six years.

(b) Any person who, under circumstances or conditions other than those likely to produce great bodily harm or death, willfully causes or permits any child to suffer, or inflicts thereon unjustifiable physical pain or mental suffering, or having the care or custody of any child, willfully causes or permits the person or health of that child to be injured, or willfully causes or permits that child to be placed in a situation where his or her person or health may be endangered, is guilty of a misdemeanor.

(c) If a person is convicted of violating this section and probation is granted, the court shall require the following minimum conditions of probation:

(1) A mandatory minimum period of probation of 48 months.

(2) A criminal court protective order protecting the victim from further acts of violence or threats, and, if appropriate, residence exclusion or stay-away conditions.

(3)(A) Successful completion of no less than one year of a child abuser's treatment counseling program approved by the probation department. The defendant shall be ordered to begin participation in the program immediately upon the grant of probation. The counseling program shall meet the criteria specified in Section 273.1. The defendant shall produce documentation of program enrollment to the court within 30 days of enrollment, along with quarterly progress reports.

(B) The terms of probation for offenders shall not be lifted until all reasonable fees due to the counseling program have been paid in full, but in no case shall probation be extended beyond the term provided in subdivision (a) of Section 1203.1. If the court finds that the defendant does not have the ability to pay the fees based on the defendant's changed circumstances, the court may reduce or waive the fees.

(4) If the offense was committed while the defendant was under the influence of drugs or alcohol, the defendant shall abstain from the use of drugs or alcohol during the period of probation and shall be subject to random drug testing by his or her probation officer.

(5) The court may waive any of the above minimum conditions of probation upon a finding that the condition would not be in the best interests of justice. The court shall state on the record its reasons for any waiver. *(Added by Stats.1905, c. 568, p. 759, § 5. Amended by Stats.1963, c. 783, p. 1811, § 1; Stats.1965, c. 697, p. 2091, § 1; Stats.1976, c. 1139, p. 5108, § 165, operative July 1, 1977; Stats.1980, c. 1117, p. 3590, § 4; Stats.1984, c. 1423, § 2, eff. Sept. 26, 1984; Stats.1993, c. 1253 (A.B.897), § 1; Stats.1994, c. 1263 (A.B. 1328), § 3; Stats.1996, c. 1090 (A.B.3215), § 1; Stats.1997, c. 134 (A.B.273), § 1.)*

Research References

Treatises and Practice Aids

Witkin, California Summary 10th Agency and Employment § 424, Jurors, Witnesses, and Victims.

Witkin, California Summary 10th Parent and Child § 200, Commission Of Crime.

Witkin, California Summary 10th Parent and Child § 290, in General.

Witkin, California Summary 10th Parent and Child § 291, Prayer Treatment for Child.

Witkin, California Summary 10th Torts § 1077, Statutory Duty.

§ 273ab. Assault resulting in death, comatose state, or paralysis of child under 8; imprisonment

(a) Any person, having the care or custody of a child who is under eight years of age, who assaults the child by means of force that to a reasonable person would be likely to produce great bodily injury, resulting in the child's death, shall be punished by imprisonment in the state prison for 25 years to life. Nothing in this section shall be construed as affecting the applicability of subdivision (a) of Section 187 or Section 189.

(b) Any person, having the care or custody of a child who is under eight years of age, who assaults the child by means of force that to a reasonable person would be likely to produce great bodily injury, resulting in the child becoming comatose due to brain injury or suffering paralysis of a permanent nature, shall be punished by imprisonment in the state prison for life with the possibility of parole. As used in this subdivision, "paralysis" means a major or complete loss of motor function resulting from injury to the nervous system or to a muscular mechanism. *(Added by Stats.1993–94, 1st Ex.Sess., c. 47 (A.B.27), § 1, eff. Nov. 30, 1994. Amended by Stats.1996, c. 460 (A.B.2258), § 2; Stats.2010, c. 300 (A.B. 1280), § 1.)*

Research References

Treatises and Practice Aids

Witkin, California Summary 10th Agency and Employment § 424, Jurors, Witnesses, and Victims.

§ 273b. Children under 16; placement in courtroom or vehicle with adult offender; restriction

No child under the age of 16 years shall be placed in any courtroom, or in any vehicle for transportation to any place, in company with adults charged with or convicted of crime, except in the presence of a proper official. *(Added by Stats.1905, c. 568, p. 760, § 6. Amended by Stats.1941, c. 106, p. 1081, § 8; Stats.1987, c. 828, § 13.5.)*

§ 273c. Prosecution instituted by society for prevention of cruelty to children; fines, penalties and forfeitures payable to society

All fines, penalties, and forfeitures imposed and collected under the provisions of Sections 270, 271, 271a, 273a, and 273b, or under the provisions of any law relating to, or affecting, children, in every case where the prosecution is instituted or conducted by a society incorporated under the laws of this state for the prevention of cruelty to children, inure to such society in aid of the purposes for which it is incorporated. *(Added by Stats.1905, c. 568, p. 760, § 7. Amended by Stats.1987, c. 828, § 14.)*

§ 273d. Corporal punishment or injury of child; felony; punishment; enhancement for prior conviction; conditions of probation

(a) Any person who willfully inflicts upon a child any cruel or inhuman corporal punishment or an injury resulting in a traumatic condition is guilty of a felony and shall be punished by imprisonment pursuant to subdivision (h) of Section 1170 for two, four, or six years, or in a county jail for not more than one year, by a fine of up to six thousand dollars ($6,000), or by both that imprisonment and fine.

(b) Any person who is found guilty of violating subdivision (a) shall receive a four-year enhancement for a prior conviction of that offense provided that no additional term shall be imposed under this subdivision for any prison term or term imposed under the provisions of subdivision (h) of Section 1170 served prior to a period of 10 years in which the defendant remained free of both the commission of an offense that results in a felony conviction and prison custody or custody in a county jail under the provisions of subdivision (h) of Section 1170.

(c) If a person is convicted of violating this section and probation is granted, the court shall require the following minimum conditions of probation:

(1) A mandatory minimum period of probation of 36 months.

(2) A criminal court protective order protecting the victim from further acts of violence or threats, and, if appropriate, residence exclusion or stay-away conditions.

(3)(A) Successful completion of no less than one year of a child abuser's treatment counseling program. The defendant shall be ordered to begin participation in the program immediately upon the grant of probation. The counseling program shall meet the criteria specified in Section 273.1. The defendant shall produce documentation of program enrollment to the court within 30 days of enrollment, along with quarterly progress reports.

(B) The terms of probation for offenders shall not be lifted until all reasonable fees due to the counseling program have been paid in full, but in no case shall probation be extended beyond the term provided in subdivision (a) of Section 1203.1. If the court finds that the defendant does not have the ability to pay the fees based on the defendant's changed circumstances, the court may reduce or waive the fees.

(4) If the offense was committed while the defendant was under the influence of drugs or alcohol, the defendant shall abstain from the use of drugs or alcohol during the period of probation and shall be subject to random drug testing by his or her probation officer.

(5) The court may waive any of the above minimum conditions of probation upon a finding that the condition would not be in the best interests of justice. The court shall state on the record its reasons for any waiver. *(Added by Stats.1945, c. 1312, p. 2462, § 1. Amended by Stats.1957, c. 1342, p. 2673, § 1; Stats.1965, c. 1271, p. 3146, § 4; Stats.1976, c. 1139, p. 5109, § 166, operative July 1, 1977; Stats.1977, c. 908, p. 2780, § 1; Stats.1977, c. 912, p. 2786, § 2; Stats.1980, c. 1117, p. 3590, § 5; Stats.1984, c. 1423, § 3, eff. Sept. 26, 1984; Stats.1987, c. 415, § 1; Stats.1993, c. 607 (S.B.529), § 1; Stats.1996, c. 1090 (A.B.3215), § 2; Stats.1997, c. 134 (A.B.273), § 2; Stats.1999, c. 662 (S.B.218), § 8; Stats.2004, c. 229 (S.B.1104), § 14, eff. Aug. 16, 2004; Stats.2011, c. 15 (A.B.109), § 312, eff. April 4, 2011, operative Oct. 1, 2011; Stats.2011–2012, 1st Ex.Sess., c. 12 (A.B.17), § 8, eff. Sept. 21, 2011, operative Oct. 1, 2011.)*

Research References

Treatises and Practice Aids

Witkin, California Summary 10th Constitutional Law § 769, Crimes.

Witkin, California Summary 10th Parent and Child § 200, Commission Of Crime.

Witkin, California Summary 10th Parent and Child § 290, in General.

§ 273e. Places of questionable repute; minors not to deliver messages, etc., or enter

Every telephone, special delivery company or association, and every other corporation or person engaged in the delivery of packages, letters, notes, messages, or other matter, and every manager, superintendent, or other agent of such person, corporation, or association, who sends any minor in the employ or under the control of any such person, corporation, association, or agent, to the keeper of any house of prostitution, variety theater, or other place of questionable repute, or to any person connected with, or any inmate of, such house, theater, or other place, or who permits such minor to enter such house, theater, or other place, is guilty of a misdemeanor. *(Added by Stats.1905, c. 568, p. 760, § 9.)*

§ 273f. Sending minors to immoral places

Any person, whether as parent, guardian, employer, or otherwise, and any firm or corporation, who as employer or otherwise, shall send, direct, or cause to be sent or directed to any saloon, gambling house, house of prostitution, or other immoral place, any minor, is guilty of a misdemeanor. *(Added by Stats.1907, c. 294, p. 565, § 2. Amended by Stats.1972, c. 579, p. 1006, § 35.)*

§ 273g. Degrading, immoral, or vicious practices or habitual drunkenness in presence of children

Any person who in the presence of any child indulges in any degrading, lewd, immoral or vicious habits or practices, or who is habitually drunk in the presence of any child in his care, custody or control, is guilty of a misdemeanor. *(Added by Stats.1907, c. 413, p. 756, § 1.)*

Validity

This section was held unconstitutional in the decision of People v. Perreault (Super. 1960), 5 Cal.Rptr. 849, 182 Cal.App.2d Supp. 843.

§ 273h. Sentence to work on public roads; payment of earnings to wife or to guardian of children, etc.

In all prosecutions under the provisions of either section 270, section 270a, section 270b, section 271 or section 271a, of this code, where a conviction is had and sentence of imprisonment in the county jail or in the city jail is imposed, the court may direct that the person so convicted shall be compelled to work upon the public roads or highways, or any other public work, in the county or in the city where such conviction is had, during the term of such sentence. And it shall be the duty of the board of supervisors of the county where such person is imprisoned in the county jail, and of the city council of the city where such person is imprisoned in the city jail, where such conviction and sentence are had and where such work is performed by a person under sentence to the county jail or to the city jail, to allow and order the payment out of any funds available, to the wife or to the guardian, or to the custodian of a child or children, or to an organization, or to an individual, appointed by the court as trustee, at the end of each calendar month, for the support of such wife or children, a sum not to exceed two dollars for each day's work of such person so imprisoned. *(Added by Stats.1911, c. 379, p. 688, § 1. Amended by Stats.1927, c. 243, p. 433, § 1.)*

§ 273i. Publication of information describing or depicting child or relating to child with intent that information be used to commit crime against child; punishment; definitions; injunction

(a) Any person who publishes information describing or depicting a child, the physical appearance of a child, the location of a child, or locations where children may be found with the intent that another person imminently use the information to commit a crime against a child and the information is likely to aid in the imminent commission of a crime against a child, is guilty of a misdemeanor, punishable by imprisonment in a county jail for not more than one year, a fine of not more than one thousand dollars ($1,000), or by both a fine and imprisonment.

(b) For purposes of this section, "publishes" means making the information available to another person through any medium, including, but not limited to, the Internet, the World Wide Web, or e-mail.

(c) For purposes of this section, "child" means a person who is 14 years of age or younger.

(d) For purposes of this section, "information" includes, but is not limited to, an image, film, filmstrip, photograph, negative, slide, photocopy, videotape, video laser disc, or any other computer-generated image.

(e) Any parent or legal guardian of a child about whom information is published in violation of subdivision (a) may seek a preliminary injunction enjoining any further publication of that information. *(Added by Stats.2008, c. 423 (A.B.534), § 1.)*

§ 273j. Notification of public safety agency of death of child; notification of law enforcement of missing child; penalties

(a)(1) Any parent or guardian having the care, custody, or control of a child under 14 years of age who knows or should have known that the child has died shall notify a public safety agency, as defined in Section 53102 of the Government Code, within 24 hours of the time that the parent or guardian knew or should have known that the child has died.

(2) This subdivision shall not apply when a child is otherwise under the immediate care of a physician at the time of death, or if a public safety agency, a coroner, or a medical examiner is otherwise aware of the death.

(b)(1) Any parent or guardian having the care, custody, or control of a child under 14 years of age shall notify law enforcement within 24 hours of the time that the parent or guardian knows or should have known that the child is a missing person and there is evidence that the child is a person at risk, as those terms are defined in Section 14215.

(2) This subdivision shall not apply if law enforcement is otherwise aware that the child is a missing person.

(c) A violation of this section is a misdemeanor punishable by imprisonment in a county jail for not more than one year, or by a fine not exceeding one thousand dollars ($1,000), or by both that fine and imprisonment.

(d) Nothing in this section shall preclude prosecution under any other provision of law. *(Added by Stats.2012, c. 805 (A.B.1432), § 2. Amended by Stats.2014, c. 437 (S.B. 1066), § 8, eff. Jan. 1, 2015.)*

§ 273.1. Treatment programs for child abusers convicted of specified sections

(a) Any treatment program to which a child abuser convicted of a violation of Section 273a or 273d is referred as a condition of probation shall meet the following criteria:

(1) Substantial expertise and experience in the treatment of victims of child abuse and the families in which abuse and violence have occurred.

(2) Staff providing direct service are therapists licensed to practice in this state or are under the direct supervision of a therapist licensed to practice in this state.

(3) Utilization of a treatment regimen designed to specifically address the offense, including methods of preventing and breaking the cycle of family violence, anger management, and parenting education that focuses, among other things, on means of identifying the developmental and emotional needs of the child.

(4) Utilization of group and individual therapy and counseling, with groups no larger than 12 persons.

(5) Capability of identifying substance abuse and either treating the abuse or referring the offender to a substance abuse program, to the extent that the court has not already done so.

(6) Entry into a written agreement with the defendant that includes an outline of the components of the program, the attendance requirements, a requirement to attend group session free of chemical influence, and a statement that the defendant may be removed from the program if it is determined that the defendant is not benefiting from the program or is disruptive to the program.

(7) The program may include, on the recommendation of the treatment counselor, family counseling. However, no child victim shall be compelled or required to participate in the program, including family counseling, and no program may condition a defendant's enrollment on participation by the child victim. The treatment counselor shall privately

advise the child victim that his or her participation is voluntary.

(b) If the program finds that the defendant is unsuitable, the program shall immediately contact the probation department or the court. The probation department or court shall either recalendar the case for hearing or refer the defendant to an appropriate alternative child abuser's treatment counseling program.

(c) Upon request by the child abuser's treatment counseling program, the court shall provide the defendant's arrest report, prior incidents of violence, and treatment history to the program.

(d) The child abuser's treatment counseling program shall provide the probation department and the court with periodic progress reports at least every three months that include attendance, fee payment history, and program compliance. The program shall submit a final evaluation that includes the program's evaluation of the defendant's progress, and recommendation for either successful or unsuccessful termination of the program.

(e) The defendant shall pay for the full costs of the treatment program, including any drug testing. However, the court may waive any portion or all of that financial responsibility upon a finding of an inability to pay. Upon the request of the defendant, the court shall hold a hearing to determine the defendant's ability to pay for the treatment program. At the hearing the court may consider all relevant information, but shall consider the impact of the costs of the treatment program on the defendant's ability to provide food, clothing, and shelter for the child injured by a violation of Section 273a or 273d. If the court finds that the defendant is unable to pay for any portion of the costs of the treatment program, its reasons for that finding shall be stated on the record. In the event of this finding, the program fees or a portion thereof shall be waived.

(f) All programs accepting referrals of child abusers pursuant to this section shall accept offenders for whom fees have been partially or fully waived. However, the court shall require each qualifying program to serve no more than its proportionate share of those offenders who have been granted fee waivers, and require all qualifying programs to share equally in the cost of serving those offenders with fee waivers. *(Added by Stats.1996, c. 1090 (A.B.3215), § 3. Amended by Stats.1997, c. 17 (S.B.947), § 95.)*

§ 273.4. Female genital mutilation; additional punishment

(a) If the act constituting a felony violation of subdivision (a) of Section 273a was female genital mutilation, as defined in subdivision (b), the defendant shall be punished by an additional term of imprisonment in the state prison for one year, in addition and consecutive to the punishment prescribed by Section 273a.

(b) "Female genital mutilation" means the excision or infibulation of the labia majora, labia minora, clitoris, or vulva, performed for nonmedical purposes.

(c) Nothing in this section shall preclude prosecution under Section 203, 205, or 206 or any other provision of law. *(Added by Stats.1996, c. 790 (A.B.2125), § 4. Amended by Stats.2011, c. 15 (A.B.109), § 308, eff. April 4, 2011, operative Oct. 1, 2011; Stats.2011, c. 39 (A.B.117), § 12, eff. June 30, 2011, operative Oct. 1, 2011.)*

§ 273.5. Willful infliction of corporal injury; violation; punishment

(a) Any person who willfully inflicts corporal injury resulting in a traumatic condition upon a victim described in subdivision (b) is guilty of a felony, and upon conviction thereof shall be punished by imprisonment in the state prison for two, three, or four years, or in a county jail for not more than one year, or by a fine of up to six thousand dollars ($6,000), or by both that fine and imprisonment.

(b) Subdivision (a) shall apply if the victim is or was one or more of the following:

(1) The offender's spouse or former spouse.

(2) The offender's cohabitant or former cohabitant.

(3) The offender's fiancé or fiancée, or someone with whom the offender has, or previously had, an engagement or dating relationship, as defined in paragraph (10) of subdivision (f) of Section 243.

(4) The mother or father of the offender's child.

(c) Holding oneself out to be the spouse of the person with whom one is cohabiting is not necessary to constitute cohabitation as the term is used in this section.

(d) As used in this section, "traumatic condition" means a condition of the body, such as a wound, or external or internal injury, including, but not limited to, injury as a result of strangulation or suffocation, whether of a minor or serious nature, caused by a physical force. For purposes of this section, "strangulation" and "suffocation" include impeding the normal breathing or circulation of the blood of a person by applying pressure on the throat or neck.

(e) For the purpose of this section, a person shall be considered the father or mother of another person's child if the alleged male parent is presumed the natural father under Sections 7611 and 7612 of the Family Code.

(f)(1) Any person convicted of violating this section for acts occurring within seven years of a previous conviction under subdivision (a), or subdivision (d) of Section 243, or Section 243.4, 244, 244.5, or 245, shall be punished by imprisonment in a county jail for not more than one year, or by imprisonment in the state prison for two, four, or five years, or by both imprisonment and a fine of up to ten thousand dollars ($10,000).

(2) Any person convicted of a violation of this section for acts occurring within seven years of a previous conviction under subdivision (e) of Section 243 shall be punished by imprisonment in the state prison for two, three, or four years, or in a county jail for not more than one year, or by a fine of up to ten thousand dollars ($10,000), or by both that imprisonment and fine.

(g) If probation is granted to any person convicted under subdivision (a), the court shall impose probation consistent with the provisions of Section 1203.097.

(h) If probation is granted, or the execution or imposition of a sentence is suspended, for any defendant convicted under subdivision (a) who has been convicted of any prior offense specified in subdivision (f), the court shall impose one of the following conditions of probation:

(1) If the defendant has suffered one prior conviction within the previous seven years for a violation of any offense specified in subdivision (f), it shall be a condition of probation, in addition to the provisions contained in Section 1203.097, that he or she be imprisoned in a county jail for not less than 15 days.

(2) If the defendant has suffered two or more prior convictions within the previous seven years for a violation of any offense specified in subdivision (f), it shall be a condition of probation, in addition to the provisions contained in Section 1203.097, that he or she be imprisoned in a county jail for not less than 60 days.

(3) The court, upon a showing of good cause, may find that the mandatory imprisonment required by this subdivision shall not be imposed and shall state on the record its reasons for finding good cause.

(i) If probation is granted upon conviction of a violation of subdivision (a), the conditions of probation may include, consistent with the terms of probation imposed pursuant to Section 1203.097, in lieu of a fine, one or both of the following requirements:

(1) That the defendant make payments to a battered women's shelter, up to a maximum of five thousand dollars ($5,000), pursuant to Section 1203.097.

(2)(A) That the defendant reimburse the victim for reasonable costs of counseling and other reasonable expenses that the court finds are the direct result of the defendant's offense.

(B) For any order to pay a fine, make payments to a battered women's shelter, or pay restitution as a condition of probation under this subdivision, the court shall make a determination of the defendant's ability to pay. An order to make payments to a battered women's shelter shall not be made if it would impair the ability of the defendant to pay direct restitution to the victim or court-ordered child support. If the injury to a person who is married or in a registered domestic partnership is caused in whole or in part by the criminal acts of his or her spouse or domestic partner in violation of this section, the community property may not be used to discharge the liability of the offending spouse or domestic partner for restitution to the injured spouse or domestic partner, required by Section 1203.04, as operative on or before August 2, 1995, or Section 1202.4, or to a shelter for costs with regard to the injured spouse or domestic partner and dependents, required by this section, until all separate property of the offending spouse or domestic partner is exhausted.

(j) Upon conviction under subdivision (a), the sentencing court shall also consider issuing an order restraining the defendant from any contact with the victim, which may be valid for up to 10 years, as determined by the court. It is the intent of the Legislature that the length of any restraining order be based upon the seriousness of the facts before the court, the probability of future violations, and the safety of the victim and his or her immediate family. This protective order may be issued by the court whether the defendant is sentenced to state prison or county jail, or if imposition of sentence is suspended and the defendant is placed on probation.

(k) If a peace officer makes an arrest for a violation of this section, the peace officer is not required to inform the victim of his or her right to make a citizen's arrest pursuant to subdivision (b) of Section 836. *(Added by Stats.1977, c. 912, p. 2786, § 3. Amended by Stats.1980, c. 1117, p. 3589, § 3; Stats.1985, c. 563, § 1; Stats.1987, c. 415, § 2; Stats.1988, c. 576, § 1, eff. Aug. 26, 1988; Stats.1990, c. 680 (A.B.2632), § 1; Stats.1992, c. 163 (A.B.2641), § 104; Stats.1992, c. 183 (S.B.1545), § 1; Stats.1992, c. 184 (A.B.2439), § 3; Stats. 1993, c. 219 (A.B.1500), § 216.4; Stats.1993–94, 1st Ex.Sess., c. 28 (A.B.93), § 2, eff. Nov. 30, 1994; Stats.1996, c. 1075 (S.B.1444), § 15; Stats.1996, c. 1077 (A.B.2898), § 16; Stats. 1999, c. 660 (S.B.563), § 2; Stats.1999, c. 662 (S.B.218), § 9.5; Stats.2000, c. 287 (S.B.1955), § 5; Stats.2003, c. 262 (A.B.134), § 1; Stats.2007, c. 582 (A.B.289), § 1; Stats.2011, c. 129 (S.B.430), § 2; Stats.2012, c. 867 (S.B.1144), § 16; Stats.2013, c. 763 (A.B.16), § 1; Stats.2014, c. 71 (S.B.1304), § 117, eff. Jan. 1, 2015; Stats.2016, c. 50 (S.B.1005), § 69, eff. Jan. 1, 2017.)*

Law Revision Commission Comments

1993 Amendment

Subdivision (d) of Section 273.5 is amended to substitute a reference to the Family Code provisions that replaced former Civil Code Section 7004. [23 Cal.L.Rev.Comm. Reports 1 (1993)].

Commentary

A person may be convicted of willfully inflicting corporal injury upon the parent of his child even though the parental rights of both parents have been terminated. *People v. Mora, 51 Cal.App.4th 1349, 59 Cal.Rptr.2d 801 (1996).*

For purposes of Section 273.5, a defendant may simultaneously cohabit with two or more persons in different residences so long as he has lived with each person for a significant period of time and he maintains a substantial ongoing relationship with each person. *People v. Moore, 44 Cal.App.4th 1323, 45 Cal.App.4th 1232C, 52 Cal.Rptr.2d 256 (1996).*

People v. Ward, 62 Cal.App.4th 122, 72 Cal.Rptr.2d 531 (1998), holds that the subsection (a) phrase "any person who willfully inflicts [traumatic corporal injury] upon any person who is the mother or father or his or her child" does not include a man who inflicts traumatic corporal injury upon a woman pregnant with his unborn child.

People v. Jackson, 77 Cal.App.4th 574, 91 Cal.Rptr.2d 805 (2000), review denied April 19, 2000, holds that this section is not violated when a victim's injuries result from an attempt to escape confinement, rather than from direct physical assault by a defendant.

With respect to a defendant who was convicted under this section of willfully inflicting corporal injury on his wife, *People v. Jungers, 127 Cal.App.4th 698, 25 Cal.Rptr.3d 873 (2005), review denied,* held that, as a condition of probation, the trial court reasonably prohibited defendant from initiating any contact with his wife, and that the prohibition did not violate defendant's constitutional rights of privacy or free association.

When a father was convicted and sent to prison under this section for corporal injury to a spouse or cohabitant, a subsection (j) post-conviction criminal protective order could not limit the father's contact with his children in the absence of evidence that the father had inflicted corporal injury on the children. *People v. Delarosarauda, 227 Cal.App.4th 205, 173 Cal.Rptr.3d 512 (2014), review denied.*

Research References

Forms

West's California Judicial Council Forms CR-160, Criminal Protective Order--Domestic Violence (CLETS - Cpo).
West's California Judicial Council Forms CR-165, Notice Of Termination Of Protective Order in Criminal Proceeding (CLETS).

Treatises and Practice Aids

Witkin, California Summary 10th Agency and Employment § 50, Denial for Conviction Of Crime.
Witkin, California Summary 10th Agency and Employment § 424, Jurors, Witnesses, and Victims.
Witkin, California Summary 10th Constitutional Law § 769, Crimes.
Witkin, California Summary 10th Husband and Wife § 372, Criminal Proceedings.
Witkin, California Summary 10th Torts § 439, Arrest by Private Person.

§ 273.6. Intentional and knowing violation of court order to prevent harassment, disturbing the peace, or threats or acts of violence; penalties

(a) Any intentional and knowing violation of a protective order, as defined in Section 6218 of the Family Code, or of an order issued pursuant to Section 527.6, 527.8, or 527.85 of the Code of Civil Procedure, or Section 15657.03 of the Welfare and Institutions Code, is a misdemeanor punishable by a fine of not more than one thousand dollars ($1,000), or by imprisonment in a county jail for not more than one year, or by both that fine and imprisonment.

(b) In the event of a violation of subdivision (a) that results in physical injury, the person shall be punished by a fine of not more than two thousand dollars ($2,000), or by imprisonment in a county jail for not less than 30 days nor more than one year, or by both that fine and imprisonment. However, if the person is imprisoned in a county jail for at least 48 hours, the court may, in the interest of justice and for reasons stated on the record, reduce or eliminate the 30–day minimum imprisonment required by this subdivision. In determining whether to reduce or eliminate the minimum imprisonment pursuant to this subdivision, the court shall consider the seriousness of the facts before the court, whether there are additional allegations of a violation of the order during the pendency of the case before the court, the probability of future violations, the safety of the victim, and whether the defendant has successfully completed or is making progress with counseling.

(c) Subdivisions (a) and (b) shall apply to the following court orders:

(1) Any order issued pursuant to Section 6320 or 6389 of the Family Code.

(2) An order excluding one party from the family dwelling or from the dwelling of the other.

(3) An order enjoining a party from specified behavior that the court determined was necessary to effectuate the order described in subdivision (a).

(4) Any order issued by another state that is recognized under Part 5 (commencing with Section 6400) of Division 10 of the Family Code.

(d) A subsequent conviction for a violation of an order described in subdivision (a), occurring within seven years of a prior conviction for a violation of an order described in subdivision (a) and involving an act of violence or "a credible threat" of violence, as defined in subdivision (c) of Section 139, is punishable by imprisonment in a county jail not to exceed one year, or pursuant to subdivision (h) of Section 1170.

(e) In the event of a subsequent conviction for a violation of an order described in subdivision (a) for an act occurring within one year of a prior conviction for a violation of an order described in subdivision (a) that results in physical injury to a victim, the person shall be punished by a fine of not more than two thousand dollars ($2,000), or by imprisonment in a county jail for not less than six months nor more than one year, by both that fine and imprisonment, or by imprisonment pursuant to subdivision (h) of Section 1170. However, if the person is imprisoned in a county jail for at least 30 days, the court may, in the interest of justice and for reasons stated in the record, reduce or eliminate the six-month minimum imprisonment required by this subdivision. In determining whether to reduce or eliminate the minimum imprisonment pursuant to this subdivision, the court shall consider the seriousness of the facts before the court, whether there are additional allegations of a violation of the order during the pendency of the case before the court, the probability of future violations, the safety of the victim, and whether the defendant has successfully completed or is making progress with counseling.

(f) The prosecuting agency of each county shall have the primary responsibility for the enforcement of orders described in subdivisions (a), (b), (d), and (e).

(g)(1) Every person who owns, possesses, purchases, or receives a firearm knowing he or she is prohibited from doing so by the provisions of a protective order as defined in Section 136.2 of this code, Section 6218 of the Family Code, or Section 527.6, 527.8, or 527.85 of the Code of Civil Procedure, or Section 15657.03 of the Welfare and Institutions Code, shall be punished under Section 29825.

(2) Every person subject to a protective order described in paragraph (1) shall not be prosecuted under this section for owning, possessing, purchasing, or receiving a firearm to the extent that firearm is granted an exemption pursuant to subdivision (f) of Section 527.9 of the Code of Civil Procedure, or subdivision (h) of Section 6389 of the Family Code.

(h) If probation is granted upon conviction of a violation of subdivision (a), (b), (c), (d), or (e), the court shall impose probation consistent with Section 1203.097, and the conditions of probation may include, in lieu of a fine, one or both of the following requirements:

(1) That the defendant make payments to a battered women's shelter or to a shelter for abused elder persons or dependent adults, up to a maximum of five thousand dollars ($5,000), pursuant to Section 1203.097.

(2) That the defendant reimburse the victim for reasonable costs of counseling and other reasonable expenses that the court finds are the direct result of the defendant's offense.

(i) For any order to pay a fine, make payments to a battered women's shelter, or pay restitution as a condition of probation under subdivision (e), the court shall make a determination of the defendant's ability to pay. In no event shall any order to make payments to a battered women's shelter be made if it would impair the ability of the defendant to pay direct restitution to the victim or court-ordered child support. Where the injury to a married person is caused in whole or in part by the criminal acts of his or her spouse in violation of this section, the community property may not be used to discharge the liability of the offending spouse for restitution to the injured spouse, required by Section 1203.04, as operative on or before August 2, 1995, or Section 1202.4, or to a shelter for costs with regard to the injured spouse and dependents, required by this section, until all separate property of the offending spouse is exhausted. *(Added by Stats.1979, c. 795, p. 2713, § 12, operative July 1, 1980. Amended by Stats.1981, c. 182, p. 1104, § 5; Stats.1982, c. 423, p. 1775, § 2; Stats.1983, c. 1092, § 262, eff. Sept. 27, 1983, operative Jan. 1, 1984; Stats.1985, c. 1387, § 1; Stats. 1986, c. 10, § 1, eff. Feb. 28, 1986; Stats.1988, c. 674, § 1, eff. Aug. 27, 1988; Stats.1989, c. 1105, § 12; Stats.1990, c. 411 (A.B.3973), § 8, eff. July 25, 1990; Stats.1992, c. 163 (A.B. 2641), § 105; Stats.1992, c. 184 (A.B.2439), § 4; Stats.1992, c. 1209 (A.B.2762), §§ 1, 2; Stats.1993, c. 219 (A.B.1500), § 216.5; Stats.1993, c. 583 (A.B.284), § 5; Stats.1993–94, 1st Ex.Sess., c. 28 (A.B.93), § 3, eff. Nov. 30, 1994; Stats.1993–94, 1st Ex.Sess., c. 29 (A.B.68), § 3.5, eff. Nov. 30, 1994; Stats. 1994, c. 873 (S.B.739), § 2.3; Stats.1996, c. 904 (A.B.2224), § 5; Stats.1996, c. 1077 (A.B.2898), § 17.1; Stats.1999, c. 561 (A.B.59), § 5; Stats.1999, c. 662 (S.B.218), § 12.5; Stats.2001, c. 816 (A.B.731), § 4; Stats.2003, c. 498 (S.B.226), § 7; Stats.2009, c. 566 (S.B.188), § 2; Stats.2010, c. 709 (S.B.1062), § 10; Stats.2010, c. 178 (S.B.1115), § 55, operative Jan. 1, 2012; Stats.2011, c. 285 (A.B.1402), § 13; Stats.2011, c. 15 (A.B.109), § 310, eff. April 4, 2011, operative Jan. 1, 2012; Stats.2013, c. 76 (A.B.383), § 145.7.)*

Law Revision Commission Comments

1993 Amendment

Subdivision (a) of Section 273.6 is amended to substitute a reference to the Family Code for the references to the former provisions in the Civil Code and Code of Civil Procedure. The specific description of the orders to which this section is applicable have been omitted. This is not a substantive change, since Section 6218 of the Family Code describes substantially the same orders. [23 Cal.L.Rev.Comm. Reports 1 (1993)].

2010 Amendment

Subdivision (g) of Section 273.6 is amended to reflect nonsubstantive reorganization of the statutes governing control of deadly weapons. [38 Cal.L.Rev.Comm. Reports 217 (2009)].

2013 Amendment

Subdivision (g) of Section 273.6 is amended to incorporate language that was chaptered out due to a conflict between two bills that amended the section in 2010. See SB 1062 (Strickland), 2010 Cal. Stat. ch. 709, §§ 10, 28; SB 1115 (Committee on Public Safety), 2010 Cal. Stat. ch. 178, §§ 55, 108; Gov't Code § 9605 (specifying how to resolve conflict between two bills that amend same section). [41 Cal.L.Rev.Comm. Reports 135 (2011)].

Research References

Treatises and Practice Aids

Witkin, California Summary 10th Husband and Wife § 6, Order in Summons.

Witkin, California Summary 10th Husband and Wife § 112, Contents Of Judgment.

Witkin, California Summary 10th Husband and Wife § 372, Criminal Proceedings.

Witkin, California Summary 10th Husband and Wife § 386, in General.

Witkin, California Summary 10th Husband and Wife § 388, Service Of Order.

§ 273.65. Intentional and knowing violations of restraining and protective orders relating to minors adjudged to be dependent children of the juvenile court; offense; penalties

(a) Any intentional and knowing violation of a protective order issued pursuant to Section 213.5, 304, or 362.4 of the Welfare and Institutions Code is a misdemeanor punishable by a fine of not more than one thousand dollars ($1,000), or by imprisonment in a county jail for not more than one year, or by both the fine and imprisonment.

(b) In the event of a violation of subdivision (a) which results in physical injury, the person shall be punished by a fine of not more than two thousand dollars ($2,000), or by imprisonment in a county jail for not less than 30 days nor more than one year, or by both the fine and imprisonment. However, if the person is imprisoned in a county jail for at least 48 hours, the court may, in the interests of justice and for reasons stated on the record, reduce or eliminate the 30–day minimum imprisonment required by this subdivision. In determining whether to reduce or eliminate the minimum imprisonment pursuant to this subdivision, the court shall consider the seriousness of the facts before the court, whether there are additional allegations of a violation of the order during the pendency of the case before the court, the probability of future violations, the safety of the victim, and whether the defendant has successfully completed or is making progress with counseling.

(c) Subdivisions (a) and (b) shall apply to the following court orders:

(1) An order enjoining any party from molesting, attacking, striking, threatening, sexually assaulting, battering, harassing, contacting repeatedly by mail with the intent to harass, or disturbing the peace of the other party, or other named family and household members.

(2) An order excluding one party from the family dwelling or from the dwelling of the other.

(3) An order enjoining a party from specified behavior which the court determined was necessary to effectuate the order under subdivision (a).

(d) A subsequent conviction for a violation of an order described in subdivision (a), occurring within seven years of a prior conviction for a violation of an order described in subdivision (a) and involving an act of violence or "a credible threat" of violence, as defined in subdivision (c) of Section 139, is punishable by imprisonment in a county jail not to exceed one year, or pursuant to subdivision (h) of Section 1170.

(e) In the event of a subsequent conviction for a violation of an order described in subdivision (a) for an act occurring within one year of a prior conviction for a violation of an order described in subdivision (a) which results in physical injury to the same victim, the person shall be punished by a fine of not more than two thousand dollars ($2,000), or by imprisonment in a county jail for not less than six months nor more than one year, by both that fine and imprisonment, or by imprisonment pursuant to subdivision (h) of Section 1170. However, if the person is imprisoned in a county jail for at least 30 days, the court may, in the interests of justice and for reasons stated in the record, reduce or eliminate the six-month minimum imprisonment required by this subdivision. In determining whether to reduce or eliminate the minimum imprisonment pursuant to this subdivision, the court shall consider the seriousness of the facts before the court, whether there are additional allegations of a violation of the order during the pendency of the case before the court, the probability of future violations, the safety of the victim, and whether the defendant has successfully completed or is making progress with counseling.

(f) The prosecuting agency of each county shall have the primary responsibility for the enforcement of orders issued pursuant to subdivisions (a), (b), (d), and (e).

(g) The court may order a person convicted under this section to undergo counseling, and, if appropriate, to complete a batterer's treatment program.

(h) If probation is granted upon conviction of a violation of subdivision (a), (b), or (c), the conditions of probation may include, in lieu of a fine, one or both of the following requirements:

(1) That the defendant make payments to a battered women's shelter, up to a maximum of five thousand dollars ($5,000), pursuant to Section 1203.097.

(2) That the defendant reimburse the victim for reasonable costs of counseling and other reasonable expenses that the court finds are the direct result of the defendant's offense.

(i) For any order to pay a fine, make payments to a battered women's shelter, or pay restitution as a condition of probation under subdivision (e), the court shall make a determination of the defendant's ability to pay. In no event shall any order to make payments to a battered women's shelter be made if it would impair the ability of the defendant to pay direct restitution to the victim or court-ordered child support. *(Added by Stats.1996, c. 1139 (A.B.2647), § 2. Amended by Stats.2011, c. 15 (A.B.109), § 311, eff. April 4, 2011, operative Oct. 1, 2011.)*

§ 273.7. Malicious disclosure of location of trafficking shelter or domestic violence shelter; misdemeanor; definitions; exemption for attorney-client communications

(a) Any person who maliciously publishes, disseminates, or otherwise discloses the location of any trafficking shelter or domestic violence shelter or any place designated as a trafficking shelter or domestic violence shelter, without the authorization of that trafficking shelter or domestic violence shelter, is guilty of a misdemeanor.

(b)(1) For purposes of this section, "domestic violence shelter" means a confidential location that provides emergency housing on a 24-hour basis for victims of sexual assault, spousal abuse, or both, and their families.

(2) For purposes of this section, "trafficking shelter" means a confidential location that provides emergency housing on a 24-hour basis for victims of human trafficking, including any person who is a victim under Section 236.1.

(3) Sexual assault, spousal abuse, or both, include, but are not limited to, those crimes described in Sections 240, 242, 243.4, 261, 261.5, 262, 264.1, 266, 266a, 266b, 266c, 266f, 273.5, 273.6, 285, 288, and 289.

(c) Nothing in this section shall apply to confidential communications between an attorney and his or her client. *(Added by Stats.1988, c. 840, § 1. Amended by Stats.1994, c. 1188 (S.B.59), § 4; Stats.2005, c. 240 (A.B.22), § 9; Stats. 2006, c. 538 (S.B.1852), § 499.)*

Research References

Treatises and Practice Aids

Witkin, California Summary 10th Husband and Wife § 372, Criminal Proceedings.

§ 273.75. Criminal history search; prior restraining orders

(a) On any charge involving acts of domestic violence as defined in subdivisions (a) and (b) of Section 13700 of the Penal Code or Sections 6203 and 6211 of the Family Code, the district attorney or prosecuting city attorney shall perform or cause to be performed, by accessing the electronic databases enumerated in subdivision (b), a thorough investigation of the defendant's history, including, but not limited to, prior convictions for domestic violence, other forms of violence or weapons offenses and any current protective or restraining order issued by any civil or criminal court. This information shall be presented for consideration by the court (1) when setting bond or when releasing a defendant on his or her own recognizance at the arraignment, if the defendant is in custody, (2) upon consideration of any plea agreement, and (3) when issuing a protective order pursuant to Section 136.2 of the Penal Code, in accordance with subdivision (h) of that section. In determining bail or release upon a plea agreement, the court shall consider the safety of the victim, the victim's children, and any other person who may be in danger if the defendant is released.

(b) For purposes of this section, the district attorney or prosecuting city attorney shall search or cause to be searched the following databases, when readily available and reasonably accessible:

(1) The California Sex and Arson Registry (CSAR).

(2) The Supervised Release File.

(3) State summary criminal history information maintained by the Department of Justice pursuant to Section 11105 of the Penal Code.

(4) The Federal Bureau of Investigation's nationwide database.

(5) Locally maintained criminal history records or databases.

However, a record or database need not be searched if the information available in that record or database can be obtained as a result of a search conducted in another record or database.

(c) If the investigation required by this section reveals a current civil protective or restraining order or a protective or restraining order issued by another criminal court and involving the same or related parties, and if a protective or restraining order is issued in the current criminal proceeding, the district attorney or prosecuting city attorney shall send relevant information regarding the contents of the order issued in the current criminal proceeding, and any information regarding a conviction of the defendant, to the other court immediately after the order has been issued. When requested, the information described in this subdivision may be sent to the appropriate family, juvenile, or civil court. When requested, and upon a showing of a compelling need, the information described in this section may be sent to a court in another state. *(Added by Stats.2001, c. 572 (S.B.66), § 4. Amended by Stats.2008, c. 86 (A.B.1771), § 2; Stats. 2014, c. 54 (S.B.1461), § 10, eff. Jan. 1, 2015.)*

CHAPTER 2.5. SPOUSAL ABUSERS

§ 273.8. Legislative findings

The Legislature hereby finds that spousal abusers present a clear and present danger to the mental and physical well-being of the citizens of the State of California. The Legislature further finds that the concept of vertical prosecution, in which a specially trained deputy district attorney, deputy city attorney, or prosecution unit is assigned to a case after arraignment and continuing to its completion, is a proven way of demonstrably increasing the likelihood of convicting spousal abusers and ensuring appropriate sentences for those offenders. In enacting this chapter, the Legislature intends to support increased efforts by district attorneys' and city attorneys' offices to prosecute spousal abusers through organizational and operational techniques that have already proven their effectiveness in selected cities and counties in this and other states. *(Added by Stats.1985, c. 1122, § 1. Amended by Stats.1994, c. 599 (A.B.801), § 2, eff. Sept. 16, 1994.)*

Research References

Treatises and Practice Aids

Witkin, California Summary 10th Husband and Wife § 372, Criminal Proceedings.

§ 273.81. Spousal abuser prosecution program; appropriation, allocation, and award of funds; guidelines for grant awards; matching funds

(a) There is hereby established in the Department of Justice a program of financial and technical assistance for district attorneys' or city attorneys' offices, designated the Spousal Abuser Prosecution Program. All funds appropriated to the Department of Justice for the purposes of this chapter shall be administered and disbursed by the Attorney General, and shall to the greatest extent feasible, be coordinated or consolidated with any federal or local funds that may be made available for these purposes.

The Department of Justice shall establish guidelines for the provision of grant awards to proposed and existing programs prior to the allocation of funds under this chapter. These guidelines shall contain the criteria for the selection of agencies to receive funding and the terms and conditions upon which the Department of Justice is prepared to offer grants pursuant to statutory authority. The guidelines shall not constitute rules, regulations, orders, or standards of general application.

(b) The Attorney General may allocate and award funds to cities or counties, or both, in which spousal abuser prosecution units are established or are proposed to be established in substantial compliance with the policies and criteria set forth in this chapter.

(c) The allocation and award of funds shall be made upon application executed by the county's district attorney or by the city's attorney and approved by the county board of supervisors or by the city council. Funds disbursed under this chapter shall not supplant local funds that would, in the absence of the California Spousal Abuser Prosecution Program, be made available to support the prosecution of spousal abuser cases. Local grant awards made under this program shall not be subject to review as specified in Section 10295 of the Public Contract Code.

(d) Local government recipients shall provide 20 percent matching funds for every grant awarded under this program. *(Added by Stats.1985, c. 1122, § 1. Amended by Stats.1987, c. 828, § 15; Stats.1994, c. 599 (A.B.801), § 3, eff. Sept. 16, 1994.)*

§ 273.82. Enhanced prosecution efforts and resources

Spousal abuser prosecution units receiving funds under this chapter shall concentrate enhanced prosecution efforts and resources upon individuals identified under selection criteria set forth in Section 273.83. Enhanced prosecution efforts and resources shall include, but not be limited to, all of the following:

(a)(1) Vertical prosecutorial representation, whereby the prosecutor who, or prosecution unit that, makes all major court appearances on that particular case through its conclusion, including bail evaluation, preliminary hearing, significant law and motion litigation, trial, and sentencing.

(2) Vertical counselor representation, whereby a trained domestic violence counselor maintains liaison from initial court appearances through the case's conclusion, including the sentencing phase.

(b) The assignment of highly qualified investigators and prosecutors to spousal abuser cases. "Highly qualified" for the purposes of this chapter means any of the following:

(1) Individuals with one year of experience in the investigation and prosecution of felonies.

(2) Individuals with at least two years of experience in the investigation and prosecution of misdemeanors.

(3) Individuals who have attended a program providing domestic violence training as approved by the Office of Emergency Services or the Department of Justice.

(c) A significant reduction of caseloads for investigators and prosecutors assigned to spousal abuser cases.

(d) Coordination with local rape victim counseling centers, spousal abuse services programs, and victim-witness assistance programs. That coordination shall include, but not be limited to: referrals of individuals to receive client services; participation in local training programs; membership and participation in local task forces established to improve communication between criminal justice system agencies and community service agencies; and cooperating with individuals serving as liaison representatives of local rape victim counseling centers, spousal abuse victim programs, and victim-witness assistance programs. *(Added by Stats.1985, c. 1122, § 1. Amended by Stats.1987, c. 828, § 16; Stats.1994, c. 599 (A.B.801), § 4, eff. Sept. 16, 1994; Stats.2003, c. 229 (A.B. 1757), § 2.4; Stats.2010, c. 618 (A.B.2791), § 191; Stats.2013, c. 352 (A.B.1317), § 403, eff. Sept. 26, 2013, operative July 1, 2013.)*

§ 273.83. Individuals subject to spousal abuser prosecution effort; selection of cases

(a) An individual shall be the subject of a spousal abuser prosecution effort who is under arrest for any act or omission described in subdivisions (a) and (b) of Section 13700.

(b) In applying the spousal abuser selection criteria set forth in subdivision (a), a district attorney or city attorney shall not reject cases for filing exclusively on the basis that there is a family or personal relationship between the victim and the alleged offender.

(c) In exercising the prosecutorial discretion granted by Section 273.85, the district attorney or city attorney shall consider the number and seriousness of the offenses currently charged against the defendant. *(Added by Stats.1985, c. 1122, § 1. Amended by Stats.1994, c. 599 (A.B.801), § 5, eff. Sept. 16, 1994.)*

§ 273.84. Policies; pretrial release, sentence, and reduction of time between arrest and disposition of charge

Each district attorney's or city attorney's office establishing a spousal abuser prosecution unit and receiving state support under this chapter shall adopt and pursue the following policies for spousal abuser cases:

(a) All reasonable prosecutorial efforts shall be made to resist the pretrial release of a charged defendant meeting spousal abuser selection criteria.

(b) All reasonable prosecutorial efforts shall be made to persuade the court to impose the most severe authorized sentence upon a person convicted after prosecution as a spousal abuser. In the prosecution of an intrafamily sexual abuse case, discretion may be exercised as to the type and nature of sentence recommended to the court.

(c) All reasonable prosecutorial efforts shall be made to reduce the time between arrest and disposition of charge against an individual meeting spousal abuser criteria. *(Added by Stats.1985, c. 1122, § 1. Amended by Stats.1994, c. 599 (A.B.801), § 6, eff. Sept. 16, 1994; Stats.2000, c. 135 (A.B. 2539), § 131.)*

§ 273.85. Adherence to selection criteria; quarterly submission of information

(a) The selection criteria set forth in Section 273.84 shall be adhered to for each spousal abuser case unless, in the reasonable exercise of prosecutor's discretion, extraordinary circumstances require departure from those policies in order to promote the general purposes and intent of this chapter.

(b) Each district attorney's and city attorney's office establishing a spousal abuser prosecution unit and receiving state support under this chapter shall submit the following information, on a quarterly basis, to the Department of Justice:

(1) The number of spousal abuser cases referred to the district attorney's or city attorney's office for possible filing.

(2) The number of spousal abuser cases filed for prosecution.

(3) The number of spousal abuser cases taken to trial.

(4) The number of spousal abuser cases tried that resulted in conviction. *(Added by Stats.1985, c. 1122, § 1. Amended by Stats.1994, c. 599 (A.B.801), § 7, eff. Sept. 16, 1994.)*

§ 273.86. Characterization of defendant as spousal abuser

The characterization of a defendant as a "spousal abuser" as defined by this chapter shall not be communicated to the trier of fact. *(Added by Stats.1985, c. 1122, § 1.)*

§ 273.87. Use of federal funds; implementation of chapter

The Department of Justice is encouraged to utilize Federal Victims of Crimes Act (VOCA) funds or any other federal funds that may become available in order to implement this chapter. *(Added by Stats.1985, c. 1122, § 1. Amended by Stats.1994, c. 599 (A.B.801), § 8, eff. Sept. 16, 1994.)*

§ 273.88. Administrative costs; limit

Administrative costs incurred by the Department of Justice pursuant to the Spousal Abuser Prosecution Program shall not exceed 5 percent of the total funds allocated for the program. *(Added by Stats.1994, c. 599 (A.B.801), § 9, eff. Sept. 16, 1994.)*

CHAPTER 4. CHILD ABDUCTION

Section

§ 277. Definitions

The following definitions apply for the purposes of this chapter:

(a) "Child" means a person under the age of 18 years.

(b) "Court order" or "custody order" means a custody determination decree, judgment, or order issued by a court of competent jurisdiction, whether permanent or temporary, initial or modified, that affects the custody or visitation of a child, issued in the context of a custody proceeding. An order, once made, shall continue in effect until it expires, is modified, is rescinded, or terminates by operation of law.

(c) "Custody proceeding" means a proceeding in which a custody determination is an issue, including, but not limited to, an action for dissolution or separation, dependency, guardianship, termination of parental rights, adoption, paternity, except actions under Section 11350 or 11350.1 of the Welfare and Institutions Code, or protection from domestic violence proceedings, including an emergency protective order pursuant to Part 3 (commencing with Section 6240) of Division 10 of the Family Code.

(d) "Lawful custodian" means a person, guardian, or public agency having a right to custody of a child.

(e) A "right to custody" means the right to the physical care, custody, and control of a child pursuant to a custody order as defined in subdivision (b) or, in the absence of a court order, by operation of law, or pursuant to the Uniform Parentage Act contained in Part 3 (commencing with Section 7600) of Division 12 of the Family Code. Whenever a public agency takes protective custody or jurisdiction of the care, custody, control, or conduct of a child by statutory authority or court order, that agency is a lawful custodian of the child and has a right to physical custody of the child. In any subsequent placement of the child, the public agency continues to be a lawful custodian with a right to physical custody of the child until the public agency's right of custody is terminated by an order of a court of competent jurisdiction or by operation of law.

(f) In the absence of a court order to the contrary, a parent loses his or her right to custody of the child to the other parent if the parent having the right to custody is dead, is unable or refuses to take the custody, or has abandoned his or her family. A natural parent whose parental rights have been terminated by court order is no longer a lawful custodian and no longer has a right to physical custody.

(g) "Keeps" or "withholds" means retains physical possession of a child whether or not the child resists or objects.

(h) "Visitation" means the time for access to the child allotted to any person by court order.

(i) "Person" includes, but is not limited to, a parent or an agent of a parent.

(j) "Domestic violence" means domestic violence as defined in Section 6211 of the Family Code.

(k) "Abduct" means take, entice away, keep, withhold, or conceal. *(Added by Stats.1996, c. 988 (A.B.2936), § 9.)*

Commentary

In *People v. Ryan, 76 Cal.App.4th 1304, 91 Cal.Rptr.2d 160 (1999), review denied March 29, 2000,* the court of appeal sustained defendant father's conviction under § 278 because there was sufficient evidence of refusal to take custody and abandonment to support a finding that defendant had no "right to custody" of the child within the meaning of subsections (e) and (f) of this section.

Research References

Treatises and Practice Aids

Witkin, California Summary 10th Parent and Child § 193, California Criminal Statutes.

§ 278. Noncustodial persons; detainment or concealment of child from legal custodian; punishment

Every person, not having a right to custody, who maliciously takes, entices away, keeps, withholds, or conceals any child with the intent to detain or conceal that child from a lawful custodian shall be punished by imprisonment in a county jail not exceeding one year, a fine not exceeding one thousand dollars ($1,000), or both that fine and imprisonment, or by imprisonment pursuant to subdivision (h) of Section 1170 for two, three, or four years, a fine not exceeding ten thousand dollars ($10,000), or both that fine and imprisonment. *(Added by Stats.1996, c. 988 (A.B.2936), § 9. Amended by Stats.2011, c. 15 (A.B.109), § 313, eff. April 4, 2011, operative Oct. 1, 2011.)*

Commentary

Absent a court order affecting custody, Family Code Section 3010 provides that the mother and a man presumed to be the father under Family Code Section 7611 have an equal right to custody of an unemancipated minor child. On March 9, 1999, the Supreme Court denied review and depublished *People v. Zeghtchanian, 79 Cal.Rptr.2d 866 (1998),* in which the Court of Appeal held that when a parent is prosecuted under Section 278, the prosecution bears the burden of showing that the parent does not have a right to custody of the child and that the parent took the child from a person or agency that had "lawful custody" of the child. *Zeghtchanian* also purported to hold that the invalidity of a custody order may be asserted as a defense to a Section 278 prosecution.

Compare *People v. Ryan, 76 Cal.App.4th 1304, 91 Cal.Rptr.2d 160 (1999), review denied March 29, 2000,* where the court of appeal sustained defendant father's conviction under this section, because there was sufficient evidence of refusal to take custody and abandonment to support a finding that defendant had no "right to custody" of the child under § 277 (e) and (f).

Research References

Forms

California Transactions Forms--Family Law § 3:9, Statutory Custody Definitions.

Treatises and Practice Aids

Witkin, California Summary 10th Parent and Child § 193, California Criminal Statutes.

Witkin, California Summary 10th Torts § 729, Abduction Of Child.

§ 278.5. Deprivation of custody of child or right to visitation; punishment

(a) Every person who takes, entices away, keeps, withholds, or conceals a child and maliciously deprives a lawful custodian of a right to custody, or a person of a right to visitation, shall be punished by imprisonment in a county jail not exceeding one year, a fine not exceeding one thousand dollars ($1,000), or both that fine and imprisonment, or by imprisonment pursuant to subdivision (h) of Section 1170 for 16 months, or two or three years, a fine not exceeding ten thousand dollars ($10,000), or both that fine and imprisonment.

(b) Nothing contained in this section limits the court's contempt power.

(c) A custody order obtained after the taking, enticing away, keeping, withholding, or concealing of a child does not constitute a defense to a crime charged under this section. *(Added by Stats.1996, c. 988 (A.B.2936), § 9. Amended by Stats.2011, c. 15 (A.B.109), § 314, eff. April 4, 2011, operative Oct. 1, 2011.)*

Commentary

People v. Mehaisin, 101 Cal.App.4th 958, 124 Cal.Rptr.2d 683 (2002), review denied November 20, 2002, held that a father convicted under this section of withholding his children from their lawful custodian was not entitled to the § 278.7 defense of necessity because he was not a person "with a right to custody of the child" within the meaning of that section and he failed to comply with the reporting provisions of that section.

People v. Lazarevich, 124 Cal.App.4th 140, 21 Cal.Rptr.3d 1 (2004), review denied, sustains the application of this section to a nonresident defendant father who withheld his children, harboring them outside of the country, and maliciously deprived the lawful custodian, a California resident, of her right to custody. *Lazarevich* reasoned that prosecution in California under California law did not violate due process because defendant was a party to the California child custody order and, when the order was entered, the former version of Section 279 gave him fair warning that he might be prosecuted in California for violation of the order.

In *People v. Neidinger, 40 Cal.4th 67, 51 Cal.Rptr.3d 45, 146 P.3d 502 (2006),* the California Supreme Court held that a defendant charged under subsection (a) had only to raise a reasonable doubt about the applicability of the statute in light of subsection (a) of section 278.7, because the defendant had a right to custody of the child and acted under a good faith reasonable belief that the child would suffer immediate injury if he left the child with the other person.

Research References

Forms

California Transactions Forms--Family Law § 3:9, Statutory Custody Definitions.

Treatises and Practice Aids

Witkin, California Summary 10th Husband and Wife § 6, Order in Summons.

Witkin, California Summary 10th Parent and Child § 193, California Criminal Statutes.

Witkin, California Summary 10th Parent and Child § 244, in General.

§ 278.6. Sentencing; relevant factors and circumstances; aggravation; mitigation; expenses and costs in recovering child

(a) At the sentencing hearing following a conviction for a violation of Section 278 or 278.5, or both, the court shall consider any relevant factors and circumstances in aggravation, including, but not limited to, all of the following:

(1) The child was exposed to a substantial risk of physical injury or illness.

(2) The defendant inflicted or threatened to inflict physical harm on a parent or lawful custodian of the child or on the child at the time of or during the abduction.

(3) The defendant harmed or abandoned the child during the abduction.

(4) The child was taken, enticed away, kept, withheld, or concealed outside the United States.

(5) The child has not been returned to the lawful custodian.

(6) The defendant previously abducted or threatened to abduct the child.

(7) The defendant substantially altered the appearance or the name of the child.

(8) The defendant denied the child appropriate education during the abduction.

(9) The length of the abduction.

(10) The age of the child.

(b) At the sentencing hearing following a conviction for a violation of Section 278 or 278.5, or both, the court shall consider any relevant factors and circumstances in mitigation, including, but not limited to, both of the following:

(1) The defendant returned the child unharmed and prior to arrest or issuance of a warrant for arrest, whichever is first.

(2) The defendant provided information and assistance leading to the child's safe return.

(c) In addition to any other penalties provided for a violation of Section 278 or 278.5, a court shall order the defendant to pay restitution to the district attorney for any costs incurred in locating and returning the child as provided in Section 3134 of the Family Code, and to the victim for those expenses and costs reasonably incurred by, or on behalf of, the victim in locating and recovering the child. An award made pursuant to this section shall constitute a final judgment and shall be enforceable as such. *(Added by Stats.1996, c. 988 (A.B.2936), § 9.)*

Research References

Treatises and Practice Aids

Witkin, California Summary 10th Parent and Child § 193, California Criminal Statutes.

§ 278.7. Exception; belief of bodily injury or emotional harm; report by person taking or concealing child; confidentiality

(a) Section 278.5 does not apply to a person with a right to custody of a child who, with a good faith and reasonable belief that the child, if left with the other person, will suffer immediate bodily injury or emotional harm, takes, entices away, keeps, withholds, or conceals that child.

(b) Section 278.5 does not apply to a person with a right to custody of a child who has been a victim of domestic violence who, with a good faith and reasonable belief that the child, if left with the other person, will suffer immediate bodily injury or emotional harm, takes, entices away, keeps, withholds, or conceals that child. "Emotional harm" includes having a parent who has committed domestic violence against the parent who is taking, enticing away, keeping, withholding, or concealing the child.

(c) The person who takes, entices away, keeps, withholds, or conceals a child shall do all of the following:

(1) Within a reasonable time from the taking, enticing away, keeping, withholding, or concealing, make a report to the office of the district attorney of the county where the child resided before the action. The report shall include the name of the person, the current address and telephone number of the child and the person, and the reasons the child was taken, enticed away, kept, withheld, or concealed.

(2) Within a reasonable time from the taking, enticing away, keeping, withholding, or concealing, commence a custody proceeding in a court of competent jurisdiction consistent with the federal Parental Kidnapping Prevention Act (Section 1738A, Title 28, United States Code) or the Uniform Child Custody Jurisdiction Act (Part 3 (commencing with Section 3400) of Division 8 of the Family Code).

(3) Inform the district attorney's office of any change of address or telephone number of the person and the child.

(d) For the purposes of this article, a reasonable time within which to make a report to the district attorney's office is at least 10 days and a reasonable time to commence a custody proceeding is at least 30 days. This section shall not preclude a person from making a report to the district attorney's office or commencing a custody proceeding earlier than those specified times.

(e) The address and telephone number of the person and the child provided pursuant to this section shall remain confidential unless released pursuant to state law or by a court order that contains appropriate safeguards to ensure the safety of the person and the child. *(Added by Stats.1996, c. 988 (A.B.2936), § 9.)*

Commentary

In *People v. Neidinger, 40 Cal.4th 67, 51 Cal.Rptr.3d 45, 146 P.3d 502 (2006)*, the California Supreme Court held that a defendant charged under section 278.5(a) had only to raise a reasonable doubt about the applicability of that section in light of subsection (a) of this section, because the defendant had a right to custody of the child and acted under a good faith reasonable belief that the child would suffer immediate injury if he left the child with the other person.

People v. Mehaisin, 101 Cal.App.4th 958, 124 Cal.Rptr.2d 683 (2002), review denied November 20, 2002, held that a father convicted under § 278.5 of withholding his children from their lawful custodian was not entitled to this section's defense of necessity because he was not a person "with a right to custody of the child" within the meaning of this section and he failed to comply with the reporting provisions of this section.

Research References

Treatises and Practice Aids

Witkin, California Summary 10th Parent and Child § 270, Risk Of Abduction and Missing Person Check.

§ 279. Jurisdiction; persons not residents or present in state at time of offense

A violation of Section 278 or 278.5 by a person who was not a resident of, or present in, this state at the time of the alleged offense is punishable in this state, whether the intent to commit the offense is formed within or outside of this state, if any of the following apply:

(a) The child was a resident of, or present in, this state at the time the child was taken, enticed away, kept, withheld, or concealed.

(b) The child thereafter is found in this state.

(c) A lawful custodian or a person with a right to visitation is a resident of this state at the time the child was taken, enticed away, kept, withheld, or concealed. *(Added by Stats.1996, c. 988 (A.B.2936), § 9.)*

Commentary

People v. Lazarevich, 124 Cal.App.4th 140, 21 Cal.Rptr.2d 1 (2004), review denied, sustains the application of Section 278.5 to a non-resident defendant father who withheld his children, harboring them outside of the country, and maliciously deprived the lawful custodian, a California resident, of her right to custody. *Lazarevich* reasoned that prosecution in California under California law did not violate due process because defendant was a party to the California child custody order and, when the order was entered, the former version of this section gave him fair warning that he might be prosecuted in California for violation of the order.

§ 279.1. Continuation of offenses

The offenses enumerated in Sections 278 and 278.5 are continuous in nature, and continue for as long as the minor child is concealed or detained. *(Added by Stats.1996, c. 988 (A.B.2936), § 9.)*

Research References

Treatises and Practice Aids

Witkin, California Summary 10th Parent and Child § 193, California Criminal Statutes.

§ 279.5. Bail; considerations

When a person is arrested for an alleged violation of Section 278 or 278.5, the court, in setting bail, shall take into consideration whether the child has been returned to the lawful custodian, and if not, shall consider whether there is an increased risk that the child may not be returned, or the defendant may flee the jurisdiction, or, by flight or concealment, evade the authority of the court. *(Added by Stats.1996, c. 988 (A.B.2936), § 9.)*

§ 279.6. Protective custody; circumstances; procedures; conflicting custodial orders; court hearing and enforcement

(a) A law enforcement officer may take a child into protective custody under any of the following circumstances:

(1) It reasonably appears to the officer that a person is likely to conceal the child, flee the jurisdiction with the child, or, by flight or concealment, evade the authority of the court.

(2) There is no lawful custodian available to take custody of the child.

(3) There are conflicting custody orders or conflicting claims to custody and the parties cannot agree which party should take custody of the child.

(4) The child is an abducted child.

(b) When a law enforcement officer takes a child into protective custody pursuant to this section, the officer shall do one of the following:

(1) Release the child to the lawful custodian of the child, unless it reasonably appears that the release would cause the child to be endangered, abducted, or removed from the jurisdiction.

(2) Obtain an emergency protective order pursuant to Part 3 (commencing with Section 6240) of Division 10 of the Family Code ordering placement of the child with an interim custodian who agrees in writing to accept interim custody.

(3) Release the child to the social services agency responsible for arranging shelter or foster care.

(4) Return the child as ordered by a court of competent jurisdiction.

(c) Upon the arrest of a person for a violation of Section 278 or 278.5, a law enforcement officer shall take possession of an abducted child who is found in the company of, or under the control of, the arrested person and deliver the child as directed in subdivision (b).

(d) Notwithstanding any other law, when a person is arrested for an alleged violation of Section 278 or 278.5, the court shall, at the time of the arraignment or thereafter, order that the child shall be returned to the lawful custodian by or on a specific date, or that the person show cause on that date why the child has not been returned as ordered. If conflicting custodial orders exist within this state, or between this state and a foreign state, the court shall set a hearing within five court days to determine which court has jurisdiction under the laws of this state and determine which state has subject matter jurisdiction to issue a custodial order under the laws of this state, the Uniform Child Custody Jurisdiction Act (Part 3 (commencing with Section 3400) of Division 8 of the Family Code), or federal law, if applicable. At the conclusion of the hearing, or if the child has not been returned as ordered by the court at the time of arraignment, the court shall enter an order as to which custody order is valid and is to be enforced. If the child has not been returned at the conclusion of the hearing, the court shall set a date within a reasonable time by which the child shall be returned to the lawful custodian, and order the defendant to comply by this date, or to show cause on that date why he or she has not returned the child as directed. The court shall only enforce its order, or any subsequent orders for the return of the child, under subdivision (a) of Section 1219 of the Code of Civil Procedure, to ensure that the child is promptly placed with the lawful custodian. An order adverse to either the prosecution or defense is reviewable by a writ of mandate or prohibition addressed to the appropriate court. *(Added by Stats.1996, c. 988 (A.B.2936), § 9.)*

Research References

Treatises and Practice Aids

Witkin, California Summary 10th Parent and Child § 193, California Criminal Statutes.

Witkin, California Summary 10th Parent and Child § 269, Locating Missing Party or Child.

§ 280. Violations of specified adoption proceedings; punishment

Every person who willfully causes or permits the removal or concealment of any child in violation of Section 8713, 8803, or 8910 of the Family Code shall be punished as follows:

(a) By imprisonment in a county jail for not more than one year if the child is concealed within the county in which the adoption proceeding is pending or in which the child has been placed for adoption, or is removed from that county to a place within this state.

(b) By imprisonment pursuant to subdivision (h) of Section 1170, or by imprisonment in a county jail for not more than one year, if the child is removed from that county to a place outside of this state. *(Added by Stats.1996, c. 988 (A.B.2936), § 9. Amended by Stats.2011, c. 15 (A.B.109), § 315, eff. April 4, 2011, operative Oct. 1, 2011.)*

Research References

Forms

California Transactions Forms--Family Law § 6:2, Governing Law.

California Transactions Forms--Family Law § 6:90, Adoptive Placement Agreement.

Treatises and Practice Aids

Witkin, California Summary 10th Parent and Child § 81, Removal or Concealment Of Child Pending Adoption.

Witkin, California Summary 10th Parent and Child § 193, California Criminal Statutes.

CHAPTER 5. BIGAMY, INCEST, AND THE CRIME AGAINST NATURE

Section

§ 281. "Bigamy" defined; evidence necessary to support proof

(a) Every person having a spouse living, who marries or enters into a registered domestic partnership with any other person, except in the cases specified in Section 282, is guilty of bigamy.

(b) Upon a trial for bigamy, it is not necessary to prove either of the marriages or registered domestic partnerships by the register, certificate, or other record evidence thereof, but the marriages or registered domestic partnerships may be proved by evidence which is admissible to prove a marriage or registered domestic partnership in other cases; and when the second marriage or registered domestic partnership took place out of this state, proof of that fact, accompanied with proof of cohabitation thereafter in this state, is sufficient to sustain the charge. *(Enacted in 1872. Amended by Stats. 1987, c. 828, § 17; Stats.1989, c. 897, § 18; Stats.2016, c. 50 (S.B.1005), § 70, eff. Jan. 1, 2017.)*

Research References

Treatises and Practice Aids

Witkin, California Summary 10th Husband and Wife § 156, Bigamy.

§ 282. Bigamy; exceptions

Section 281 does not extend to any of the following:

(a) To any person by reason of any former marriage or former registered domestic partnership whose spouse by such marriage or registered domestic partnership has been absent for five successive years without being known to such person within that time to be living.

(b) To any person by reason of any former marriage, or any former registered domestic partnership, which has been pronounced void, annulled, or dissolved by the judgment of a competent court. *(Enacted in 1872. Amended by Stats.1987, c. 828, § 18; Stats.2016, c. 50 (S.B.1005), § 71, eff. Jan. 1, 2017.)*

§ 283. Bigamy; punishment

Bigamy is punishable by a fine not exceeding ten thousand dollars ($10,000) or by imprisonment in a county jail not exceeding one year or in the state prison. *(Enacted in 1872. Amended by Stats.1905, c. 272, p. 245, § 1; Stats.1949, c. 1252, p. 2205, § 1; Stats.1976, c. 1139, p. 5110, § 172, operative July 1, 1977; Stats.1983, c. 1092, § 264, eff. Sept. 27, 1983, operative Jan. 1, 1984.)*

§ 284. Marrying or entering into registered domestic partnership with another's spouse; scienter; punishment

Every person who knowingly and willfully marries or enters into a registered domestic partnership with the spouse of another, in any case in which such spouse would be punishable under the provisions of this chapter, is punishable by a fine not less than five thousand dollars ($5,000), or by imprisonment pursuant to subdivision (h) of Section 1170. *(Enacted in 1872. Amended by Stats.1905, c. 272, p. 245, § 2; Stats.1976, c. 1139, p. 5110, § 173, operative July 1, 1977; Stats.2011, c. 15 (A.B.109), § 316, eff. April 4, 2011, operative Oct. 1, 2011; Stats.2016, c. 50 (S.B.1005), § 72, eff. Jan. 1, 2017.)*

§ 285. Incest

Persons being within the degrees of consanguinity within which marriages are declared by law to be incestuous and void, who intermarry with each other, or who being 14 years of age or older, commit fornication or adultery with each other, are punishable by imprisonment in the state prison. *(Enacted in 1872. Amended by Stats.1921, c. 101, p. 96, § 1; Stats.1976, c. 1139, p. 5110, § 174, operative July 1, 1977; Stats.2005, c. 477 (S.B.33), § 1.)*

Research References

Treatises and Practice Aids

Witkin, California Summary 10th Husband and Wife § 155, Incest.

Title 15

MISCELLANEOUS CRIMES

CHAPTER 1.5. INVASION OF PRIVACY

§ 633.6. Domestic violence restraining order; permission to record prohibited communications by perpetrator

(a) Notwithstanding the provisions of this chapter, and in accordance with federal law, upon the request of a victim of domestic violence who is seeking a domestic violence restraining order, a judge issuing the order may include a provision in the order that permits the victim to record any prohibited communication made to him or her by the perpetrator.

(b) Notwithstanding the provisions of this chapter, and in accordance with federal law, a victim of domestic violence who is seeking a domestic violence restraining order from a court, and who reasonably believes that a confidential communication made to him or her by the perpetrator may contain evidence germane to that restraining order, may record that communication for the exclusive purpose and use of providing that evidence to the court.

(c) The Judicial Council shall amend its domestic violence prevention application and order forms to incorporate the provisions of this section. *(Added by Stats.1999, c. 367 (A.B.207), § 1. Amended by Stats.2017, c. 191 (A.B.413), § 2, eff. Jan. 1, 2018.)*

Title 17

RIGHTS OF VICTIMS AND WITNESSES OF CRIME

§ 679.05. Right to have domestic violence or abuse advocates present at interviews with law enforcement authorities; notice

(a) A victim of domestic violence or abuse, as defined in Sections 6203 or 6211 of the Family Code, or Section 13700 of the Penal Code, has the right to have a domestic violence advocate and a support person of the victim's choosing present at any interview by law enforcement authorities, prosecutors, or defense attorneys. However, the support person may be excluded from an interview by law enforcement or the prosecutor if the law enforcement authority or the prosecutor determines that the presence of that individual would be detrimental to the purpose of the interview. As used in this section, "domestic violence advocate" means either a person employed by a program specified in Section 13835.2 for the purpose of rendering advice or assistance to victims of domestic violence, or a domestic violence counselor, as defined in Section 1037.1 of the Evidence Code. Prior to being present at any interview conducted by law enforcement authorities, prosecutors, or defense attorneys, a domestic violence advocate shall advise the victim of any applicable limitations on the confidentiality of communications between the victim and the domestic violence advocate.

(b)(1) Prior to the commencement of the initial interview by law enforcement authorities or the prosecutor pertaining to any criminal action arising out of a domestic violence incident, a victim of domestic violence or abuse, as defined in Section 6203 or 6211 of the Family Code, or Section 13700 of this code, shall be notified orally or in writing by the attending law enforcement authority or prosecutor that the victim has the right to have a domestic violence advocate and a support person of the victim's choosing present at the interview or contact. This subdivision applies to investigators and agents employed or retained by law enforcement or the prosecutor.

(2) At the time the victim is advised of his or her rights pursuant to paragraph (1), the attending law enforcement authority or prosecutor shall also advise the victim of the right to have a domestic violence advocate and a support person present at any interview by the defense attorney or investigators or agents employed by the defense attorney.

(c) An initial investigation by law enforcement to determine whether a crime has been committed and the identity of the suspects shall not constitute a law enforcement interview for purposes of this section. *(Added by Stats.2004, c. 159 (S.B.1441), § 1. Amended by Stats.2005, c. 279 (S.B.1107), § 6; Stats.2005, c. 22 (S.B.1108), § 149; Stats.2007, c. 206 (S.B.407), § 6.)*

§ 679.10. Victim of qualifying criminal activity under Immigration and Nationality Act provision; certification of victim helpfulness; use of Form I–918 Supplement B

(a) For purposes of this section, a "certifying entity" is any of the following:

(1) A state or local law enforcement agency.

(2) A prosecutor.

(3) A judge.

(4) Any other authority that has responsibility for the detection or investigation or prosecution of a qualifying crime or criminal activity.

(5) Agencies that have criminal detection or investigative jurisdiction in their respective areas of expertise, including, but not limited to, child protective services, the Department of Fair Employment and Housing, and the Department of Industrial Relations.

(b) For purposes of this section, a "certifying official" is any of the following:

(1) The head of the certifying entity.

(2) A person in a supervisory role who has been specifically designated by the head of the certifying entity to issue Form I–918 Supplement B certifications on behalf of that agency.

(3) A judge.

(4) Any other certifying official defined under Section 214.14 (a)(2) of Title 8 of the Code of Federal Regulations.

(c) "Qualifying criminal activity" means qualifying criminal activity pursuant to Section 101(a)(15)(U)(iii) of the federal Immigration and Nationality Act which includes, but is not limited to, the following crimes:

(1) Rape.

(2) Torture.

(3) Human trafficking.

(4) Incest.

(5) Domestic violence.

(6) Sexual assault.

(7) Abusive sexual conduct.

(8) Prostitution.

(9) Sexual exploitation.

(10) Female genital mutilation.

(11) Being held hostage.

(12) Peonage.

(13) Perjury.

(14) Involuntary servitude.

(15) Slavery.

(16) Kidnaping.[1]

(17) Abduction.

(18) Unlawful criminal restraint.

(19) False imprisonment.

(20) Blackmail.

(21) Extortion.

(22) Manslaughter.

(23) Murder.

(24) Felonious assault.

(25) Witness tampering.

(26) Obstruction of justice.

(27) Fraud in foreign labor contracting.

(28) Stalking.

(d) A "qualifying crime" includes criminal offenses for which the nature and elements of the offenses are substantially similar to the criminal activity described in subdivision (c), and the attempt, conspiracy, or solicitation to commit any of those offenses.

(e) Upon the request of the victim or victim's family member, a certifying official from a certifying entity shall certify victim helpfulness on the Form I–918 Supplement B certification, when the victim was a victim of a qualifying criminal activity and has been helpful, is being helpful, or is likely to be helpful to the detection or investigation or prosecution of that qualifying criminal activity.

(f) For purposes of determining helpfulness pursuant to subdivision (e), there is a rebuttable presumption that a victim is helpful, has been helpful, or is likely to be helpful to the detection or investigation or prosecution of that qualifying criminal activity, if the victim has not refused or failed to provide information and assistance reasonably requested by law enforcement.

(g) The certifying official shall fully complete and sign the Form I–918 Supplement B certification and, regarding victim helpfulness, include specific details about the nature of the crime investigated or prosecuted and a detailed description of the victim's helpfulness or likely helpfulness to the detection or investigation or prosecution of the criminal activity.

(h) A certifying entity shall process a Form I–918 Supplement B certification within 90 days of request, unless the noncitizen is in removal proceedings, in which case the certification shall be processed within 14 days of request.

(i) A current investigation, the filing of charges, and a prosecution or conviction are not required for the victim to request and obtain the Form I–918 Supplement B certification from a certifying official.

(j) A certifying official may only withdraw the certification if the victim refuses to provide information and assistance when reasonably requested.

(k) A certifying entity is prohibited from disclosing the immigration status of a victim or person requesting the Form I–918 Supplement B certification, except to comply with federal law or legal process, or if authorized by the victim or person requesting the Form I–918 Supplement B certification.

(*l*) A certifying entity that receives a request for a Form I–918 Supplement B certification shall report to the Legislature, on or before January 1, 2017, and annually thereafter, the number of victims that requested Form I–918 Supplement B certifications from the entity, the number of those certification forms that were signed, and the number that were denied. A report pursuant to this subdivision shall comply with Section 9795 of the Government Code. *(Added by Stats.2015, c. 721 (S.B.674), § 1, eff. Jan. 1, 2016. Amended by Stats.2016, c. 86 (S.B.1171), § 227, eff. Jan. 1, 2017.)*

[1] So in enrolled bill.

§ 679.11. Certification of victim cooperation; human trafficking victims; form; disclosure of immigration status

(a) For purposes of this section, a "certifying entity" is any of the following:

(1) A state or local law enforcement agency.

(2) A prosecutor.

(3) A judge.

(4) The Department of Industrial Relations.

(5) Any other state or local government agencies that have criminal, civil, or administrative investigative or prosecutorial authority relating to human trafficking.

(b) For purposes of this section, a "certifying official" is any of the following:

(1) The head of the certifying entity.

(2) A person in a supervisory role who has been specifically designated by the head of the certifying entity to issue Form I–914 Supplement B declarations on behalf of that agency.

(3) A judge.

(4) Any other certifying official defined under Section 214.14(a)(2) of Title 8 of the Code of Federal Regulations.

(c) "Human trafficking" means "severe forms of trafficking in persons" pursuant to Section 7102 of Title 22 of the United States Code and includes either of the following:

(1) Sex trafficking in which a commercial sex act is induced by force, fraud, or coercion, or in which the person induced to perform such act has not attained 18 years of age.

(2) The recruitment, harboring, transportation, provision, or obtaining of a person for labor or services, through the use of force, fraud, or coercion for the purpose of subjection to involuntary servitude, peonage, debt bondage, or slavery.

(d) "Human trafficking" also includes criminal offenses for which the nature and elements of the offenses are substantially similar to the criminal activity described in subdivision (c), and the attempt, conspiracy, or solicitation to commit any of those offenses.

(e) Upon the request of the victim or victim's family member, a certifying official from a certifying entity shall certify victim cooperation on the Form I–914 Supplement B declaration, when the victim was a victim of human trafficking and has been cooperative, is being cooperative, or is likely to be cooperative to the investigation or prosecution of human trafficking.

(f) For purposes of determining cooperation pursuant to subdivision (e), there is a rebuttable presumption that a victim is cooperative, has been cooperative, or is likely to be cooperative to the investigation or prosecution of human trafficking, if the victim has not refused or failed to provide information and assistance reasonably requested by law enforcement.

(g) The certifying official shall fully complete and sign the Form I–914 Supplement B declaration and, regarding victim cooperation, include specific details about the nature of the crime investigated or prosecuted and a detailed description of the victim's cooperation or likely cooperation to the detection, investigation, or prosecution of the criminal activity.

(h) A certifying entity shall process a Form I–914 Supplement B declaration within 90 days of request, unless the noncitizen is in removal proceedings, in which case the declaration shall be processed within 14 days of request.

(i) A current investigation, the filing of charges, or a prosecution or conviction is not required for the victim to request and obtain the Form I–914 Supplement B declaration from a certifying official.

(j) A certifying official may only withdraw the certification if the victim refuses to provide information and assistance when reasonably requested.

(k) A certifying entity is prohibited from disclosing the immigration status of a victim or person requesting the Form I–914 Supplement B declaration, except to comply with federal law or legal process, or if authorized by the victim or person requesting the Form I–914 Supplement B declaration.

(*l*) A certifying entity that receives a request for a Form I–914 Supplement B declaration shall report to the Legislature, on or before January 1, 2018, and annually thereafter, the number of victims who requested Form I–914 Supplement B declarations from the entity, the number of those declaration forms that were signed, and the number that were denied. A report pursuant to this subdivision shall comply with Section 9795 of the Government Code. *(Added by Stats.2016, c. 749 (A.B.2027), § 1, eff. Jan. 1, 2017.)*

Part 2

OF CRIMINAL PROCEDURE

Title 6

PLEADINGS AND PROCEEDINGS BEFORE TRIAL

CHAPTER 2.65. CHILD ABUSE AND NEGLECT COUNSELING

§ 1000.12. Legislative intent; referral to counseling or psychological treatment in lieu of prosecution; deferral of judgment in lieu of trial; dismissal of charges; eligibility standards

(a) It is the intent of the Legislature that nothing in this chapter deprive a prosecuting attorney of the ability to prosecute any person who is suspected of committing any crime in which a minor is a victim of an act of physical abuse or neglect to the fullest extent of the law, if the prosecuting attorney so chooses.

(b) In lieu of prosecuting a person suspected of committing any crime, involving a minor victim, of an act of physical abuse or neglect, the prosecuting attorney may refer that person to the county department in charge of public social services or the probation department for counseling or psychological treatment and such other services as the department deems necessary. The prosecuting attorney shall seek the advice of the county department in charge of public social services or the probation department in determining whether or not to make the referral.

(c) This section shall not apply to any person who is charged with sexual abuse or molestation of a minor victim, or any sexual offense involving force, violence, duress, menace, or fear of immediate and unlawful bodily injury on the minor victim or another person. *(Added by Stats.1983, c. 804, § 2. Amended by Stats.1985, c. 1262, § 1; Stats.1993–94, 1st Ex.Sess., c. 49 (S.B.38), § 1; Stats.1995, c. 935 (S.B.816), § 3; Stats.2005, c. 477 (S.B.33), § 3.)*

§ 1000.17. Administrative cost of referral and expense of counseling; payment

If the person is referred pursuant to this chapter he or she shall be responsible for paying the administrative cost of the referral and the expense of such counseling as determined by the county department responsible for public social services or the probation department. The administrative cost of the referral shall not exceed one hundred dollars ($100) for any person referred pursuant to this chapter for an offense punishable as a felony and shall not exceed fifty dollars ($50) for any person referred pursuant to the chapter for an offense punishable as a misdemeanor. The department shall take into consideration the ability of the referred party to pay and no such person shall be denied counseling services because of his or her inability to pay. *(Added by Stats.1983, c. 804, § 2.)*

Title 8

OF JUDGMENT AND EXECUTION

CHAPTER 1. THE JUDGMENT

§ 1203.097. Terms of probation for crimes of domestic violence

(a) If a person is granted probation for a crime in which the victim is a person defined in Section 6211 of the Family Code, the terms of probation shall include all of the following:

(1) A minimum period of probation of 36 months, which may include a period of summary probation as appropriate.

(2) A criminal court protective order protecting the victim from further acts of violence, threats, stalking, sexual abuse, and harassment, and, if appropriate, containing residence exclusion or stay-away conditions.

(3) Notice to the victim of the disposition of the case.

(4) Booking the defendant within one week of sentencing if the defendant has not already been booked.

(5)(A) A minimum payment by the defendant of a fee of five hundred dollars ($500) to be disbursed as specified in this paragraph. If, after a hearing in open court, the court finds that the defendant does not have the ability to pay, the court may reduce or waive this fee. If the court exercises its discretion to reduce or waive the fee, it shall state the reason on the record.

(B) Two-thirds of the moneys deposited with the county treasurer pursuant to this section shall be retained by counties and deposited in the domestic violence programs special fund created pursuant to Section 18305 of the Welfare and Institutions Code, to be expended for the purposes of Chapter 5 (commencing with Section 18290) of Part 6 of Division 9 of the Welfare and Institutions Code. Of the moneys deposited in the domestic violence programs special fund, no more than 8 percent may be used for administrative costs, as specified in Section 18305 of the Welfare and Institutions Code.

(C) The remaining one-third of the moneys shall be transferred, once a month, to the Controller for deposit in equal amounts in the Domestic Violence Restraining Order Reimbursement Fund and in the Domestic Violence Training and Education Fund, which are hereby created, in an amount equal to one-third of funds collected during the preceding month. Moneys deposited into these funds pursuant to this section shall be available upon appropriation by the Legislature and shall be distributed each fiscal year as follows:

(i) Funds from the Domestic Violence Restraining Order Reimbursement Fund shall be distributed to local law enforcement or other criminal justice agencies for state-mandated local costs resulting from the notification requirements set forth in subdivision (b) of Section 6380 of the Family Code, based on the annual notification from the Department of Justice of the number of restraining orders issued and registered in the state domestic violence restraining order registry maintained by the Department of Justice, for the development and maintenance of the domestic violence restraining order databank system.

(ii) Funds from the Domestic Violence Training and Education Fund shall support a statewide training and education program to increase public awareness of domestic violence and to improve the scope and quality of services provided to the victims of domestic violence. Grants to support this program shall be awarded on a competitive basis and be administered by the State Department of Public Health, in consultation with the statewide domestic violence coalition, which is eligible to receive funding under this section.

(D) The fee imposed by this paragraph shall be treated as a fee, not as a fine, and shall not be subject to reduction for time served as provided pursuant to Section 1205 or 2900.5.

(E) The fee imposed by this paragraph may be collected by the collecting agency, or the agency's designee, after the termination of the period of probation, whether probation is terminated by revocation or by completion of the term.

(6) Successful completion of a batterer's program, as defined in subdivision (c), or if none is available, another appropriate counseling program designated by the court, for a period not less than one year with periodic progress reports by the program to the court every three months or less and weekly sessions of a minimum of two hours class time duration. The defendant shall attend consecutive weekly sessions, unless granted an excused absence for good cause by the program for no more than three individual sessions during the entire program, and shall complete the program within 18 months, unless, after a hearing, the court finds good cause to modify the requirements of consecutive attendance or completion within 18 months.

(7)(A)(i) The court shall order the defendant to comply with all probation requirements, including the requirements to attend counseling, keep all program appointments, and pay program fees based upon the ability to pay.

(ii) The terms of probation for offenders shall not be lifted until all reasonable fees due to the counseling program have been paid in full, but in no case shall probation be extended beyond the term provided in subdivision (a) of Section 1203.1. If the court finds that the defendant does not have the ability to pay the fees based on the defendant's changed circumstances, the court may reduce or waive the fees.

(B) Upon request by the batterer's program, the court shall provide the defendant's arrest report, prior incidents of violence, and treatment history to the program.

(8) The court also shall order the defendant to perform a specified amount of appropriate community service, as designated by the court. The defendant shall present the court with proof of completion of community service and the court shall determine if the community service has been satisfactorily completed. If sufficient staff and resources are available, the community service shall be performed under the jurisdiction of the local agency overseeing a community service program.

(9) If the program finds that the defendant is unsuitable, the program shall immediately contact the probation department or the court. The probation department or court shall either recalendar the case for hearing or refer the defendant to an appropriate alternative batterer's program.

(10)(A) Upon recommendation of the program, a court shall require a defendant to participate in additional sessions throughout the probationary period, unless it finds that it is not in the interests of justice to do so, states its reasons on the record, and enters them into the minutes. In deciding whether the defendant would benefit from more sessions, the court shall consider whether any of the following conditions exists:

(i) The defendant has been violence free for a minimum of six months.

(ii) The defendant has cooperated and participated in the batterer's program.

(iii) The defendant demonstrates an understanding of and practices positive conflict resolution skills.

(iv) The defendant blames, degrades, or has committed acts that dehumanize the victim or puts at risk the victim's safety, including, but not limited to, molesting, stalking, striking, attacking, threatening, sexually assaulting, or battering the victim.

(v) The defendant demonstrates an understanding that the use of coercion or violent behavior to maintain dominance is unacceptable in an intimate relationship.

(vi) The defendant has made threats to harm anyone in any manner.

(vii) The defendant has complied with applicable requirements under paragraph (6) of subdivision (c) or subparagraph (C) to receive alcohol counseling, drug counseling, or both.

(viii) The defendant demonstrates acceptance of responsibility for the abusive behavior perpetrated against the victim.

(B) The program shall immediately report any violation of the terms of the protective order, including any new acts of violence or failure to comply with the program requirements, to the court, the prosecutor, and, if formal probation has been ordered, to the probation department. The probationer shall file proof of enrollment in a batterer's program with the court within 30 days of conviction.

(C) Concurrent with other requirements under this section, in addition to, and not in lieu of, the batterer's program, and unless prohibited by the referring court, the probation department or the court may make provisions for a defendant to use his or her resources to enroll in a chemical dependency program or to enter voluntarily a licensed chemical dependency recovery hospital or residential treatment program that has a valid license issued by the state to provide alcohol or drug services to receive program participation credit, as determined by the court. The probation department shall document evidence of this hospital or residential treatment participation in the defendant's program file.

(11) The conditions of probation may include, in lieu of a fine, but not in lieu of the fund payment required under paragraph (5), one or more of the following requirements:

(A) That the defendant make payments to a battered women's shelter, up to a maximum of five thousand dollars ($5,000).

(B) That the defendant reimburse the victim for reasonable expenses that the court finds are the direct result of the defendant's offense.

For any order to pay a fine, to make payments to a battered women's shelter, or to pay restitution as a condition of probation under this subdivision, the court shall make a determination of the defendant's ability to pay. Determination of a defendant's ability to pay may include his or her future earning capacity. A defendant shall bear the burden of demonstrating lack of his or her ability to pay. Express findings by the court as to the factors bearing on the amount of the fine shall not be required. In no event shall any order to make payments to a battered women's shelter be made if it would impair the ability of the defendant to pay direct restitution to the victim or court-ordered child support. When the injury to a married person is caused, in whole or in part, by the criminal acts of his or her spouse in violation of this section, the community property shall not be used to discharge the liability of the offending spouse for restitution to the injured spouse, as required by Section 1203.04, as operative on or before August 2, 1995, or Section 1202.4, or to a shelter for costs with regard to the injured spouse, until all separate property of the offending spouse is exhausted.

(12) If it appears to the prosecuting attorney, the court, or the probation department that the defendant is performing unsatisfactorily in the assigned program, is not benefiting from counseling, or has engaged in criminal conduct, upon request of the probation officer, the prosecuting attorney, or on its own motion, the court, as a priority calendar item, shall hold a hearing to determine whether further sentencing should proceed. The court may consider factors, including, but not limited to, any violence by the defendant against the former or a new victim while on probation and noncompliance with any other specific condition of probation. If the court finds that the defendant is not performing satisfactorily in the assigned program, is not benefiting from the program, has not complied with a condition of probation, or has engaged in criminal conduct, the court shall terminate the defendant's participation in the program and shall proceed with further sentencing.

(b) If a person is granted formal probation for a crime in which the victim is a person defined in Section 6211 of the Family Code, in addition to the terms specified in subdivision (a), all of the following shall apply:

(1) The probation department shall make an investigation and take into consideration the defendant's age, medical history, employment and service records, educational background, community and family ties, prior incidents of violence, police report, treatment history, if any, demonstrable motivation, and other mitigating factors in determining which batterer's program would be appropriate for the defendant. This information shall be provided to the batterer's program if it is requested. The probation department shall also determine which community programs the defendant would benefit from and which of those programs would accept the defendant. The probation department shall report its findings and recommendations to the court.

(2) The court shall advise the defendant that the failure to report to the probation department for the initial investigation, as directed by the court, or the failure to enroll in a specified program, as directed by the court or the probation department, shall result in possible further incarceration. The court, in the interests of justice, may relieve the defendant from the prohibition set forth in this subdivision based upon the defendant's mistake or excusable neglect. Application for this relief shall be filed within 20 court days of the missed deadline. This time limitation may not be extended. A copy of any application for relief shall be served on the office of the prosecuting attorney.

(3) After the court orders the defendant to a batterer's program, the probation department shall conduct an initial assessment of the defendant, including, but not limited to, all of the following:

(A) Social, economic, and family background.

(B) Education.

(C) Vocational achievements.

(D) Criminal history.

(E) Medical history.

(F) Substance abuse history.

(G) Consultation with the probation officer.

(H) Verbal consultation with the victim, only if the victim desires to participate.

(I) Assessment of the future probability of the defendant committing murder.

(4) The probation department shall attempt to notify the victim regarding the requirements for the defendant's participation in the batterer's program, as well as regarding available victim resources. The victim also shall be informed that attendance in any program does not guarantee that an abuser will not be violent.

(c) The court or the probation department shall refer defendants only to batterer's programs that follow standards outlined in paragraph (1), which may include, but are not limited to, lectures, classes, group discussions, and counseling. The probation department shall design and implement an approval and renewal process for batterer's programs and shall solicit input from criminal justice agencies and domestic violence victim advocacy programs.

(1) The goal of a batterer's program under this section shall be to stop domestic violence. A batterer's program shall consist of the following components:

(A) Strategies to hold the defendant accountable for the violence in a relationship, including, but not limited to, providing the defendant with a written statement that the defendant shall be held accountable for acts or threats of domestic violence.

(B) A requirement that the defendant participate in ongoing same-gender group sessions.

(C) An initial intake that provides written definitions to the defendant of physical, emotional, sexual, economic, and verbal abuse, and the techniques for stopping these types of abuse.

(D) Procedures to inform the victim regarding the requirements for the defendant's participation in the intervention program as well as regarding available victim resources. The victim also shall be informed that attendance in any program does not guarantee that an abuser will not be violent.

(E) A requirement that the defendant attend group sessions free of chemical influence.

(F) Educational programming that examines, at a minimum, gender roles, socialization, the nature of violence, the dynamics of power and control, and the effects of abuse on children and others.

(G) A requirement that excludes any couple counseling or family counseling, or both.

(H) Procedures that give the program the right to assess whether or not the defendant would benefit from the program and to refuse to enroll the defendant if it is determined that the defendant would not benefit from the program, so long as the refusal is not because of the defendant's inability to pay. If possible, the program shall suggest an appropriate alternative program.

(I) Program staff who, to the extent possible, have specific knowledge regarding, but not limited to, spousal abuse, child abuse, sexual abuse, substance abuse, the dynamics of violence and abuse, the law, and procedures of the legal system.

(J) Program staff who are encouraged to utilize the expertise, training, and assistance of local domestic violence centers.

(K) A requirement that the defendant enter into a written agreement with the program, which shall include an outline of the contents of the program, the attendance requirements, the requirement to attend group sessions free of chemical influence, and a statement that the defendant may be removed from the program if it is determined that the defendant is not benefiting from the program or is disruptive to the program.

(L) A requirement that the defendant sign a confidentiality statement prohibiting disclosure of any information obtained through participating in the program or during group sessions regarding other participants in the program.

(M) Program content that provides cultural and ethnic sensitivity.

(N) A requirement of a written referral from the court or probation department prior to permitting the defendant to enroll in the program. The written referral shall state the number of minimum sessions required by the court.

(O) Procedures for submitting to the probation department all of the following uniform written responses:

(i) Proof of enrollment, to be submitted to the court and the probation department and to include the fee determined to be charged to the defendant, based upon the ability to pay, for each session.

(ii) Periodic progress reports that include attendance, fee payment history, and program compliance.

(iii) Final evaluation that includes the program's evaluation of the defendant's progress, using the criteria set forth in subparagraph (A) of paragraph (10) of subdivision (a), and recommendation for either successful or unsuccessful termination or continuation in the program.

(P) A sliding fee schedule based on the defendant's ability to pay. The batterer's program shall develop and utilize a sliding fee scale that recognizes both the defendant's ability to pay and the necessity of programs to meet overhead expenses. An indigent defendant may negotiate a deferred payment schedule, but shall pay a nominal fee, if the defendant has the ability to pay the nominal fee. Upon a hearing and a finding by the court that the defendant does not have the financial ability to pay the nominal fee, the court shall waive this fee. The payment of the fee shall be made a condition of probation if the court determines the defendant has the present ability to pay the fee. The fee shall be paid during the term of probation unless the program sets other conditions. The acceptance policies shall be in accordance with the scaled fee system.

(2) The court shall refer persons only to batterer's programs that have been approved by the probation department pursuant to paragraph (5). The probation department shall do both of the following:

(A) Provide for the issuance of a provisional approval, provided that the applicant is in substantial compliance with applicable laws and regulations and an urgent need for approval exists. A provisional approval shall be considered an authorization to provide services and shall not be considered a vested right.

(B) If the probation department determines that a program is not in compliance with standards set by the department, the department shall provide written notice of the noncompliant areas to the program. The program shall submit a written plan of corrections within 14 days from the date of the written notice on noncompliance. A plan of correction shall include, but not be limited to, a description of each corrective action and timeframe for implementation. The department shall review and approve all or any part of the plan of correction and notify the program of approval or disapproval in writing. If the program fails to submit a plan of correction or fails to implement the approved plan of correction, the department shall consider whether to revoke or suspend approval and, upon revoking or suspending approval, shall have the option to cease referrals of defendants under this section.

(3) No program, regardless of its source of funding, shall be approved unless it meets all of the following standards:

(A) The establishment of guidelines and criteria for education services, including standards of services that may include lectures, classes, and group discussions.

(B) Supervision of the defendant for the purpose of evaluating the person's progress in the program.

(C) Adequate reporting requirements to ensure that all persons who, after being ordered to attend and complete a program, may be identified for either failure to enroll in, or failure to successfully complete, the program or for the successful completion of the program as ordered. The program shall notify the court and the probation department, in writing, within the period of time and in the manner specified by the court of any person who fails to complete the program. Notification shall be given if the program determines that the defendant is performing unsatisfactorily or if the defendant is not benefiting from the education, treatment, or counseling.

(D) No victim shall be compelled to participate in a program or counseling, and no program may condition a defendant's enrollment on participation by the victim.

(4) In making referrals of indigent defendants to approved batterer's programs, the probation department shall apportion these referrals evenly among the approved programs.

(5) The probation department shall have the sole authority to approve a batterer's program for probation. The program shall be required to obtain only one approval but shall renew that approval annually.

(A) The procedure for the approval of a new or existing program shall include all of the following:

(i) The completion of a written application containing necessary and pertinent information describing the applicant program.

(ii) The demonstration by the program that it possesses adequate administrative and operational capability to operate a batterer's treatment program. The program shall provide documentation to prove that the program has conducted batterer's programs for at least one year prior to application. This requirement may be waived under subparagraph (A) of paragraph (2) if there is no existing batterer's program in the city, county, or city and county.

(iii) The onsite review of the program, including monitoring of a session to determine that the program adheres to applicable statutes and regulations.

(iv) The payment of the approval fee.

(B) The probation department shall fix a fee for approval not to exceed two hundred fifty dollars ($250) and for approval renewal not to exceed two hundred fifty dollars ($250) every year in an amount sufficient to cover its costs in administering the approval process under this section. No fee shall be charged for the approval of local governmental entities.

(C) The probation department has the sole authority to approve the issuance, denial, suspension, or revocation of approval and to cease new enrollments or referrals to a batterer's program under this section. The probation department shall review information relative to a program's performance or failure to adhere to standards, or both. The probation department may suspend or revoke an approval issued under this subdivision or deny an application to renew an approval or to modify the terms and conditions of approval, based on grounds established by probation, including, but not limited to, either of the following:

(i) Violation of this section by any person holding approval or by a program employee in a program under this section.

(ii) Misrepresentation of any material fact in obtaining the approval.

(6) For defendants who are chronic users or serious abusers of drugs or alcohol, standard components in the program shall include concurrent counseling for substance abuse and violent behavior, and in appropriate cases, detoxification and abstinence from the abused substance.

(7) The program shall conduct an exit conference that assesses the defendant's progress during his or her participation in the batterer's program.

(d) An act or omission relating to the approval of a batterer's treatment programs under paragraph (5) of subdivision (c) is a discretionary act pursuant to Section 820.2 of the Government Code. *(Added by Stats.2003, c. 431 (A.B. 352), § 2, operative Jan. 1, 2007. Amended by Stats.2006, c. 476 (A.B.2695), § 6, operative Jan. 1, 2010; Stats.2007, c. 483 (S.B.1039), § 43, operative Jan. 1, 2010; Stats.2010, c. 132 (A.B.2011), § 1, eff. Aug. 13, 2010; Stats.2012, c. 511 (A.B. 2094), § 1; Stats.2012, c. 628 (A.B.1165), § 1.5; Stats.2013, c. 59 (S.B.514), § 3; Stats.2013, c. 76 (A.B.383), § 153; Stats. 2013, c. 144 (A.B.139), § 2.)*

Research References

Forms

West's California Code Forms, Family § 6340, Comment Overview--Issuance Of Orders After Notice and Hearing.

West's California Judicial Council Forms CR-160, Criminal Protective Order--Domestic Violence (CLETS - Cpo).

West's California Judicial Council Forms CR-165, Notice Of Termination Of Protective Order in Criminal Proceeding (CLETS).

Treatises and Practice Aids

Witkin, California Summary 10th Husband and Wife § 384, Orders After Notice and Hearing.

§ 1203.098. Batterers' intervention program facilitators; requirements

(a) Unless otherwise provided, a person who works as a facilitator in a batterers' intervention program that provides programs for batterers pursuant to subdivision (c) of Section 1203.097 shall complete the following requirements before being eligible to work as a facilitator in a batterers' intervention program:

(1) Forty hours of basic core training. A minimum of eight hours of this instruction shall be provided by a shelter-based or shelter- approved trainer. The core curriculum shall include the following components:

(A) A minimum of eight hours in basic domestic violence knowledge focusing on victim safety and the role of domestic violence shelters in a community-coordinated response.

(B) A minimum of eight hours in multicultural, cross-cultural, and multiethnic diversity and domestic violence.

(C) A minimum of four hours in substance abuse and domestic violence.

(D) A minimum of four hours in intake and assessment, including the history of violence and the nature of threats and substance abuse.

(E) A minimum of eight hours in group content areas focusing on gender roles and socialization, the nature of violence, the dynamics of power and control, and the effects of abuse on children and others as required by Section 1203.097.

(F) A minimum of four hours in group facilitation.

(G) A minimum of four hours in domestic violence and the law, ethics, all requirements specified by the probation department pursuant to Section 1203.097, and the role of batterers' intervention programs in a coordinated-community response.

(H) Any person that provides documentation of coursework, or equivalent training, that he or she has satisfactorily completed, shall be exempt from that part of the training that was covered by the satisfactorily completed coursework.

(I) The coursework that this person performs shall count toward the continuing education requirement.

(2) Fifty-two weeks or no less than 104 hours in six months, as a trainee in an approved batterers' intervention program with a minimum of a two-hour group each week. A training program shall include at least one of the following:

(A) Cofacilitation internship in which an experienced facilitator is present in the room during the group session.

(B) Observation by a trainer of the trainee conducting a group session via a one-way mirror.

(C) Observation by a trainer of the trainee conducting a group session via a video or audio recording.

(D) Consultation or supervision twice a week in a six-month program or once a week in a 52–week program.

(3) An experienced facilitator is one who has the following qualifications:

(A) Documentation on file, approved by the agency, evidencing that the experienced facilitator has the skills needed to provide quality supervision and training.

(B) Documented experience working with batterers for three years, and a minimum of two years working with batterers' groups.

(C) Documentation by January 1, 2003, of coursework or equivalent training that demonstrates satisfactory completion of the 40–hour basic core training.

(b) A facilitator of a batterers' intervention program shall complete, as a minimum continuing education requirement, 16 hours annually of continuing education in either domestic violence or a related field with a minimum of eight hours in domestic violence.

(c) A person or agency with a specific hardship may request the probation department, in writing, for an extension of time to complete the training or to complete alternative training options.

(d)(1) An experienced facilitator, as defined in paragraph (3) of subdivision (a), is not subject to the supervision requirements of this section, if he or she meets the requirements of subparagraph (C) of paragraph (3) of subdivision (a).

(2) This section does not apply to a person who provides batterers' treatment through a jail education program if the person in charge of that program determines that the person providing treatment has adequate education or training in domestic violence or a related field.

(e) A person who satisfactorily completes the training requirements of a county probation department whose training program is equivalent to or exceeds the training requirements of this act shall be exempt from the training requirements of this act. *(Added by Stats.2000, c. 544 (A.B.1886), § 1. Amended by Stats.2009, c. 88 (A.B.176), § 74; Stats. 2010, c. 328 (S.B.1330), § 165.)*

Law Revision Commission Comments

2009 Amendment

Subdivision (a)(2)(C) of Section 1203.098 is amended to reflect advances in recording technology and for consistency of terminology. For a similar reform, see 2002 Cal. Stat. ch. 1068 (replacing numerous references to "audiotape" in Civil Discovery Act with either "audio technology," "audio recording," or "audio record," as context required). [37 Cal. L. Revision Comm'n Reports 211 (2007)].

Title 12

OF SPECIAL PROCEEDINGS OF A CRIMINAL NATURE

CHAPTER 1. OF THE WRIT OF HABEAS CORPUS

§ 1473.5. Circumstances under which writ of habeas corpus may be prosecuted relating to evidence of intimate partner battering and its effects; limitation to violent felonies; expert testimony; grounds for denial; legislative intent

(a) A writ of habeas corpus also may be prosecuted on the basis that competent and substantial expert testimony relating to intimate partner battering and its effects, within the meaning of Section 1107 of the Evidence Code, was not presented to the trier of fact at the trial court proceedings and is of such substance that, had the competent and substantial expert testimony been presented, there is a reasonable probability, sufficient to undermine confidence in the judgment of conviction or sentence, that the result of the proceedings would have been different. Sections 1260 to 1262, inclusive, apply to the prosecution of a writ of habeas corpus pursuant to this section. As used in this section, "trial court proceedings" means those court proceedings that occur from the time the accusatory pleading is filed until and including judgment and sentence.

(b) This section is limited to violent felonies as specified in subdivision (c) of Section 667.5 that were committed before August 29, 1996, and that resulted in judgments of conviction or sentence after a plea or trial as to which expert testimony admissible pursuant to Section 1107 of the Evidence Code may be probative on the issue of culpability.

(c) A showing that expert testimony relating to intimate partner battering and its effects was presented to the trier of fact is not a bar to granting a petition under this section if that expert testimony was not competent or substantial. The burden of proof is on the petitioner to establish a sufficient showing that competent and substantial expert testimony, of a nature which would be competent using prevailing understanding of intimate partner battering and its effects, was not presented to the trier of fact, and had that evidence been presented, there is a reasonable probability that the result of the proceedings would have been different.

(d) If a petitioner for habeas corpus under this section has previously filed a petition for writ of habeas corpus, it is grounds for denial of the new petition if a court determined on the merits in the prior petition that the omission of expert testimony relating to battered women's syndrome or intimate partner battering and its effects at trial was not prejudicial and did not entitle the petitioner to the writ of habeas corpus.

(e) For purposes of this section, the changes that become effective on January 1, 2005, are not intended to expand the uses or applicability of expert testimony on battering and its effects that were in effect immediately prior to that date in criminal cases. *(Added by Stats.2001, c. 858 (S.B.799), § 1. Amended by Stats.2003, c. 136 (S.B.784), § 1; Stats.2004, c. 609 (S.B.1385), § 2; Stats.2008, c. 146 (A.B.2306), § 1; Stats.2012, c. 803 (A.B.593), § 1.)*

Part 3

OF IMPRISONMENT AND THE DEATH PENALTY

Title 1

IMPRISONMENT OF MALE PRISONERS IN STATE PRISONS

CHAPTER 3. CIVIL RIGHTS OF PRISONERS

ARTICLE 2. PRISONERS AS WITNESSES

§ 2625. Termination of parental rights or dependency proceedings; other actions affecting parental or marital rights; notice; right to appear; order for temporary removal; appearance by videoconference; prisoners sentenced to death

(a) For the purposes of this section only, the term "prisoner" includes any individual in custody in a state prison, the California Rehabilitation Center, or a county jail, or who is a ward of the Department of the Youth Authority or who, upon a verdict or finding that the individual was insane at the time of committing an offense, or mentally incompetent to be tried or adjudged to punishment, is confined in a state hospital for the care and treatment of the mentally disordered or in any other public or private treatment facility.

(b) In any proceeding brought under Part 4 (commencing with Section 7800) of Division 12 of the Family Code, and Section 366.26 of the Welfare and Institutions Code, where the proceeding seeks to terminate the parental rights of any prisoner, or any proceeding brought under Section 300 of the Welfare and Institutions Code, where the proceeding seeks to adjudicate the child of a prisoner a dependent child of the court, the superior court of the county in which the proceeding is pending, or a judge thereof, shall order notice of any court proceeding regarding the proceeding transmitted to the prisoner.

(c) Service of notice shall be made pursuant to Section 7881 or 7882 of the Family Code or Section 290.2, 291, or 294 of the Welfare and Institutions Code, as appropriate.

(d) Upon receipt by the court of a statement from the prisoner or his or her attorney indicating the prisoner's desire to be present during the court's proceedings, the court shall issue an order for the temporary removal of the prisoner from the institution, and for the prisoner's production before the court. No proceeding may be held under Part 4 (commencing with Section 7800) of Division 12 of the Family Code or Section 366.26 of the Welfare and Institutions Code and no petition to adjudge the child of a prisoner a dependent child of the court pursuant to subdivision (a), (b), (c), (d), (e), (f), (i), or (j) of Section 300 of the Welfare and Institutions Code may be adjudicated without the physical presence of the prisoner or the prisoner's attorney, unless the court has before it a knowing waiver of the right of physical presence signed by the prisoner or an affidavit signed by the warden, superintendent, or other person in charge of the institution, or his or her designated representative stating that the prisoner has, by express statement or action, indicated an intent not to appear at the proceeding.

(e) In any other action or proceeding in which a prisoner's parental or marital rights are subject to adjudication, an order for the prisoner's temporary removal from the institution and for the prisoner's production before the court may be made by the superior court of the county in which the action or proceeding is pending, or by a judge thereof. A copy of the order shall be transmitted to the warden, superintendent, or other person in charge of the institution not less than 15 days before the order is to be executed. The order shall be executed by the sheriff of the county in which it shall be made, whose duty it shall be to bring the prisoner before the proper court, to keep the prisoner safely, and when the prisoner's presence is no longer required, to return the prisoner to the institution from which he or she was taken. The expense of executing the order shall be a proper charge against, and shall be paid by, the county in which the order shall be made.

The order shall be to the following effect:

County of _________ (as the case may be).

The people of the State of California to the warden of _________:

An order having been made this day by me, that (name of prisoner) be produced in this court as a party in the case of _________, you are commanded to deliver (name of prisoner) into the custody of _________ for the purpose of (recite purposes).

Dated this _________ day of _________, 20___.

(f) When a prisoner is removed from the institution pursuant to this section, the prisoner shall remain in the constructive custody of the warden, superintendent, or other person in charge of the institution.

(g) A prisoner who is a parent of a child involved in a dependency hearing described in this section and who has either waived his or her right to physical presence at the hearing pursuant to subdivision (d) or who has not been ordered before the court may, at the court's discretion, in order to facilitate the parent's participation, be given the opportunity to participate in the hearing by videoconference, if that technology is available, and if that participation otherwise complies with the law. If videoconferencing technology is not available, teleconferencing may be utilized to facilitate parental participation. Because of the significance of dependency court hearings for parental rights and children's long-term care, physical attendance by the parent at the hearings is preferred to participation by videoconference or teleconference. This subdivision shall not be construed to limit a prisoner's right to physically attend a dependency hearing as provided in this section. This section does not authorize the use of videoconference or teleconference to replace in-person family visits with prisoners.

(h) It is the intent of the Legislature to maintain internal job placement opportunities and preserve earned privileges for prisoners, and prevent the removal of prisoners subject to this section from court-ordered courses as a result of their participation in the proceedings described in this section.

(i) Notwithstanding any other law, a court may not order the removal and production of a prisoner sentenced to death, whether or not that sentence is being appealed, in any action or proceeding in which the prisoner's parental rights are subject to adjudication. *(Added by Stats.1974, c. 1462, p. 3199, § 1. Amended by Stats.1976, c. 1376, p. 6262, § 2; Stats.1983, c. 301, § 1; Stats.1991, c. 820 (S.B.475), § 1; Stats.1992, c. 163 (A.B.2641), § 110, operative Jan. 1, 1994; Stats.1996, c. 805 (A.B.1325), § 1; Stats.2002, c. 65 (A.B. 2336), § 1; Stats.2004, c. 20 (A.B.44), § 1, eff. March 5, 2004; Stats.2010, c. 482 (S.B.962), § 1.)*

Law Revision Commission Comments

1992 Amendment

Section 2625 is amended to substitute references to the Family Code provisions that replaced the former Civil Code provisions. The word "proceeding" has been substituted for "action" in various places in this section for consistency with the Family Code. See, e.g., Fam. Code § 7802 ("proceeding" to have minor child declared free from custody and control of either or both parents). [22 Cal.L.Rev.Comm.Reports 1 (1992)].

Commentary

Section 2625 does not require that an incarcerated parent be present at a Welfare and Institutions Code Section 366.26 guardianship hearing unless the issue at the hearing is the termination of parental rights. *In re Barry W., 21 Cal.App.4th 358, 26 Cal.Rptr.2d 161 (1993)*. *In re Jesusa V., 32 Cal.4th 588, 10 Cal.Rptr.3d 205, 85 P.3d 2 (2004)*, held that in a biological father's appeal from a dependency proceeding concerning the dependency and placement of a child whose mother was hospitalized because she had been beaten and raped by appellant, now incarcerated and absent from the hearing, subsection (e) could not properly be invoked by appellant because the dependency proceeding did not terminate his parental rights. However, subsection (d) was properly invoked. Although appellant's attorney was present at the hearing, the Supreme Court interpreted the clause providing that no petition to adjudge the child of a prisoner a dependent child "may be adjudicated without the physical presence of the prisoner or the prisoner's attorney" in the conjunctive, that is, to require the presence of both, and disapproved all cases holding to the contrary. Nevertheless, *Jesusa* concluded that the error was harmless because appellant was not prejudiced by his absence from the hearing. *In re Iris R., 131 Cal.App.4th 337, 32 Cal.Rptr.3d 146 (2005)*, holds that a mother's absence from a hearing at which her children were declared dependent under Welfare and Institutions Code § 300(g) because she was incarcerated did not violate her statutory right to be present at the dependency proceeding because subsection (d) of this section does not include Welfare and Institutions Code § 300(g), and any due process violation arising from her absence was harmless.

Compare *In re M.M., 236 Cal.App.4th 935, 187 Cal.Rptr.3d 19 (2015)*, which held that a trial court violated a mother's subsection (d) right to be present at a contested jurisdiction and disposition hearing when her absence was not harmless error because the outcome of the case might have been altered by her testimony.

In re Maria S., 60 Cal.App.4th 1309, 71 Cal.Rptr.2d 30 (1998), holds that a father's inability to appear at a permanent plan hearing because of his incarceration in a federal prison does not unconstitutionally deprive him of his right to participate in such hearing because *California* does not prevent him from appearing. Section 2625 only provides a right to appear for California state prisoners. For further discussion of *Maria S.*, see Commentary to Welfare and Institutions Code Section 366.26.

On July 23, 2002, the court of appeal granted a rehearing to *In re Alexander B., 121 Cal.Rptr.2d 512 (2002)*, which originally held that, under this section, when a juvenile court has been notified that an incarcerated parent wishes to attend a Welfare and Institutions Code § 366.26 hearing, it must either arrange for the parent's presence at the hearing or obtain the parent's signed waiver of the right to be physically present. Nevertheless, the first judgment of the court of appeal concluded that the juvenile court's failure to comply with the requirements of the section was harmless error because the parent, who was represented by counsel at the hearing that resulted in an order terminating her parental rights, failed to demonstrate that any prejudice resulted from her absence at the hearing.

Research References

Forms

West's California Judicial Council Forms JV-450, Order for Prisoner's Appearance at Hearing Affecting Parental Rights.

West's California Judicial Council Forms JV-451, Prisoner's Statement Regarding Appearance at Hearing Affecting Parental Rights.

Treatises and Practice Aids

Witkin, California Summary 10th Husband and Wife § 76, in General.

Witkin, California Summary 10th Parent and Child § 12, Parental or Marital Rights Of Prisoners.

Witkin, California Summary 10th Parent and Child § 343, Conduct Of Hearing.

Witkin, California Summary 10th Parent and Child § 595, Limitations on Continuances.

Witkin, California Summary 10th Parent and Child § 646, Incarcerated or Institutionalized Parent or Guardian.

Part 4

PREVENTION OF CRIMES AND APPREHENSION OF CRIMINALS

Title 5

LAW ENFORCEMENT RESPONSE TO DOMESTIC VIOLENCE

CHAPTER 1. GENERAL PROVISIONS

§ 13700. Definitions

As used in this title:

(a) "Abuse" means intentionally or recklessly causing or attempting to cause bodily injury, or placing another person in reasonable apprehension of imminent serious bodily injury to himself or herself, or another.

(b) "Domestic violence" means abuse committed against an adult or a minor who is a spouse, former spouse, cohabitant, former cohabitant, or person with whom the suspect has had a child or is having or has had a dating or engagement relationship. For purposes of this subdivision, "cohabitant" means two unrelated adult persons living together for a substantial period of time, resulting in some permanency of relationship. Factors that may determine whether persons are cohabiting include, but are not limited to, (1) sexual relations between the parties while sharing the same living quarters, (2) sharing of income or expenses, (3) joint use or ownership of property, (4) whether the parties hold themselves out as spouses, (5) the continuity of the relationship, and (6) the length of the relationship.

(c) "Officer" means any officer or employee of a local police department or sheriff's office, and any peace officer of the Department of the California Highway Patrol, the Department of Parks and Recreation, the University of California Police Department, or the California State University and College Police Departments, as defined in Section 830.2, a peace officer of the Department of General Services of the City of Los Angeles, as defined in subdivision (c) of Section 830.31, a housing authority patrol officer, as defined in subdivision (d) of Section 830.31, a peace officer as defined in subdivisions (a) and (b) of Section 830.32, or a peace officer as defined in subdivision (a) of Section 830.33.

(d) "Victim" means a person who is a victim of domestic violence. *(Added by Stats.1984, c. 1609, § 3. Amended by Stats.1992, c. 1136 (S.B.1541), § 9; Stats.1993, c. 1229 (A.B.224), § 3; Stats.1993, c. 1230 (A.B.2250), § 1.5; Gov. Reorg.Plan No. 1 of 1995, § 57, eff. July 12, 1995; Stats.1996, c. 305 (A.B.3103), § 58; Stats.1999, c. 659 (S.B.355), § 5; Stats.2002, c. 534 (A.B.2826), § 2; Stats.2004, c. 250 (S.B. 1391), § 3; Stats.2014, c. 559 (S.B.1154), § 2, eff. Jan. 1, 2015; Stats.2016, c. 50 (S.B.1005), § 75, eff. Jan. 1, 2017.)*

Commentary

People v. Therman, 236 Cal.App.4th 1276, 187 Cal.Rptr.3d 492 (2015), affirmed a criminal protective order prohibiting defendant from contacting his spouse for five years, based on his no-contest plea to felony false imprisonment of his spouse, because the plea supported a finding that the conviction involved abuse and domestic violence within the meaning of this section.

Research References

Forms

West's California Code Forms, Civil § 1708.6 Form 1, Complaint--For Domestic Violence.

Treatises and Practice Aids

Witkin, California Summary 10th Husband and Wife § 372, Criminal Proceedings.
Witkin, California Summary 10th Torts § 467, Domestic Violence.
Witkin, California Summary 10th Wills and Probate § 304A, (New) in General.

§ 13701. Written policies and standards; development, adoption, and implementation; availability to public; consultations with experts

(a) Every law enforcement agency in this state shall develop, adopt, and implement written policies and standards for officers' responses to domestic violence calls by January 1, 1986. These policies shall reflect that domestic violence is alleged criminal conduct. Further, they shall reflect existing policy that a request for assistance in a situation involving domestic violence is the same as any other request for assistance where violence has occurred.

(b) The written policies shall encourage the arrest of domestic violence offenders if there is probable cause that an offense has been committed. These policies also shall require the arrest of an offender, absent exigent circumstances, if there is probable cause that a protective order issued under Chapter 4 (commencing with Section 2040) of Part 1 of Division 6, Division 10 (commencing with Section 6200), or Chapter 6 (commencing with Section 7700) of Part 3 of Division 12, of the Family Code, or Section 136.2 of this code, or by a court of any other state, a commonwealth, territory, or insular possession subject to the jurisdiction of the United States, a military tribunal, or a tribe has been violated. These policies shall discourage, when appropriate, but not prohibit, dual arrests. Peace officers shall make reasonable efforts to identify the dominant aggressor in any incident. The dominant aggressor is the person determined to be the most significant, rather than the first, aggressor. In identifying the dominant aggressor, an officer shall consider the intent of the law to protect victims of domestic violence from continuing abuse, the threats creating fear of physical injury, the history of domestic violence between the persons involved, and whether either person acted in self-defense. These arrest policies shall be developed, adopted, and implemented by July 1, 1996. Notwithstanding subdivision (d), law enforcement agencies shall develop these policies with the input of local domestic violence agencies.

(c) These existing local policies and those developed shall be in writing and shall be available to the public upon request and shall include specific standards for the following:

(1) Felony arrests.

(2) Misdemeanor arrests.

(3) Use of citizen arrests.

(4) Verification and enforcement of temporary restraining orders when (A) the suspect is present and (B) the suspect has fled.

(5) Verification and enforcement of stay-away orders.

(6) Cite and release policies.

(7) Emergency assistance to victims, such as medical care, transportation to a shelter, or a hospital for treatment when necessary, and police standbys for removing personal property and assistance in safe passage out of the victim's residence.

(8) Assisting victims in pursuing criminal options, such as giving the victim the report number and directing the victim to the proper investigation unit.

(9) Furnishing written notice to victims at the scene, including, but not limited to, all of the following information:

(A) A statement informing the victim that despite official restraint of the person alleged to have committed domestic violence, the restrained person may be released at any time.

(B) A statement that, "For further information about a shelter you may contact ____."

(C) A statement that, "For information about other services in the community, where available, you may contact ____."

(D) A statement that, "For information about the California Victims' Compensation Program, you may contact 1–800–777–9229."

(E) A statement informing the victim of domestic violence that he or she may ask the district attorney to file a criminal complaint.

(F) A statement informing the victim of the right to go to the superior court and file a petition requesting any of the following orders for relief:

(i) An order restraining the attacker from abusing the victim and other family members.

(ii) An order directing the attacker to leave the household.

(iii) An order preventing the attacker from entering the residence, school, business, or place of employment of the victim.

(iv) An order awarding the victim or the other parent custody of or visitation with a minor child or children.

(v) An order restraining the attacker from molesting or interfering with minor children in the custody of the victim.

(vi) An order directing the party not granted custody to pay support of minor children, if that party has a legal obligation to do so.

(vii) An order directing the defendant to make specified debit payments coming due while the order is in effect.

(viii) An order directing that either or both parties participate in counseling.

(G) A statement informing the victim of the right to file a civil suit for losses suffered as a result of the abuse, including medical expenses, loss of earnings, and other expenses for injuries sustained and damage to property, and any other related expenses incurred by the victim or any agency that shelters the victim.

(H) In the case of an alleged violation of subdivision (e) of Section 243 or Section 261, 261.5, 262, 273.5, 286, 288a, or 289, a "Victims of Domestic Violence" card which shall include, but is not limited to, the following information:

(i) The names and phone numbers of or local county hotlines for, or both the phone numbers of and local county hotlines for, local shelters for battered women and rape victim counseling centers within the county, including those centers specified in Section 13837, and their 24–hour counseling service telephone numbers.

(ii) A simple statement on the proper procedures for a victim to follow after a sexual assault.

(iii) A statement that sexual assault by a person who is known to the victim, including sexual assault by a person who is the spouse of the victim, is a crime.

(iv) A statement that domestic violence or assault by a person who is known to the victim, including domestic violence or assault by a person who is the spouse of the victim, is a crime.

(I) A statement informing the victim that strangulation may cause internal injuries and encouraging the victim to seek medical attention.

(10) Writing of reports.

(d) In the development of these policies and standards, each local department is encouraged to consult with domestic violence experts, such as the staff of the local shelter for battered women and their children. Departments may use the response guidelines developed by the commission in developing local policies. *(Added by Stats.1984, c. 1609, § 3. Amended by Stats.1985, c. 668, § 1; Stats.1990, c. 1692 (A.B.4237), § 3; Stats.1991, c. 999 (S.B.835), § 2; Stats.1995, c. 246 (S.B.591), § 4; Stats.1998, c. 698 (A.B.1201), § 2; Stats.1998, c. 701 (A.B.2172), § 2; Stats.1998, c. 702 (A.B. 2177), § 3.3; Stats.1999, c. 661 (A.B.825), § 11; Stats.2000, c. 1001 (S.B.1944), § 5; Stats.2013, c. 28 (S.B.71), § 47, eff. June 27, 2013; Stats.2013, c. 161 (A.B.81), § 1, eff. Aug. 27, 2013; Stats.2014, c. 71 (S.B.1304), § 133, eff. Jan. 1, 2015; Stats. 2017, c. 331 (S.B.40), § 1, eff. Jan. 1, 2018.)*

Research References

Treatises and Practice Aids

Witkin, California Summary 10th Torts § 435, When Arrest is Authorized.

§ 13702. Written policies and standards for dispatchers' response to domestic calls

Every law enforcement agency in this state shall develop, adopt, and implement written policies and standards for dispatchers' response to domestic violence calls by July 1, 1991. These policies shall reflect that calls reporting threatened, imminent, or ongoing domestic violence, and the violation of any protection order, including orders issued pursuant to Section 136.2, and restraining orders, shall be ranked among the highest priority calls. Dispatchers are not required to verify the validity of the protective order before responding to the request for assistance. *(Added by Stats. 1990, c. 1692 (A.B.4237) § 4.)*

CHAPTER 2. RESTRAINING ORDERS

§ 13710. Record of orders; enforceability of terms and conditions; service to party to be restrained

(a)(1) Law enforcement agencies shall maintain a complete and systematic record of all protection orders with respect to domestic violence incidents, including orders which have not yet been served, issued pursuant to Section 136.2, restraining orders, and proofs of service in effect. This shall be used to inform law enforcement officers responding to domestic violence calls of the existence, terms, and effective dates of protection orders in effect.

(2) The police department of a community college or school district described in subdivision (a) or (b) of Section 830.32 shall notify the sheriff or police chief of the city in whose jurisdiction the department is located of any protection order served by the department pursuant to this section.

(b) The terms and conditions of the protection order remain enforceable, notwithstanding the acts of the parties, and may be changed only by order of the court.

(c) Upon request, law enforcement agencies shall serve the party to be restrained at the scene of a domestic violence incident or at any time the party is in custody. *(Added by Stats.1984, c. 1609, § 3. Amended by Stats.1986, c. 1183, § 2, eff. Sept. 26, 1986; Stats.1990, c. 1692 (A.B.4237), § 5; Stats.1999, c. 659 (S.B.355), § 6; Stats.2013, c. 28 (S.B.71), § 48, eff. June 27, 2013; Stats.2013, c. 161 (A.B.81), § 2, eff. Aug. 27, 2013.)*

Research References

Treatises and Practice Aids

Witkin, California Summary 10th Husband and Wife § 372, Criminal Proceedings.

§ 13711. Protection order; application for or issuance; pamphlet to person to be protected; contents

Whenever a protection order with respect to domestic violence incidents, including orders issued pursuant to Section 136.2 and restraining orders, is applied for or issued, it shall be the responsibility of the clerk of the superior court to distribute a pamphlet to the person who is to be protected by the order that includes the following:

(a) Information as specified in subdivision (i) of Section 13701.

(b) Notice that it is the responsibility of the victim to request notification of an inmate's release.

(c) Notice that the terms and conditions of the protection order remain enforceable, notwithstanding any acts of the parties, and may be changed only by order of the court.

(d) Notice that the protection order is enforceable in any state, in a commonwealth, territory, or insular possession subject to the jurisdiction of the United States, or on a reservation, and general information about agencies in other jurisdictions that may be contacted regarding enforcement of a protective order issued by a court of this state. *(Added by Stats.1990, c. 1692 (A.B.4237) § 6. Amended by Stats.1998, c. 702 (A.B.2177), § 4; Stats.1999, c. 661 (A.B.825), § 12.)*

CHAPTER 4. DATA COLLECTION

§ 13730. Recordation system for domestic violence calls; annual report; incident report form

(a) Each law enforcement agency shall develop a system, by January 1, 1986, for recording all domestic violence-related calls for assistance made to the department, including whether weapons are involved, or whether the incident involved strangulation or suffocation. All domestic violence-related calls for assistance shall be supported with a written incident report, as described in subdivision (c), identifying the domestic violence incident. Monthly, the total number of domestic violence calls received and the numbers of those cases involving weapons or strangulation or suffocation shall be compiled by each law enforcement agency and submitted to the Attorney General.

(b) The Attorney General shall report annually to the Governor, the Legislature, and the public the total number of domestic violence-related calls received by California law enforcement agencies, the number of cases involving weapons, the number of cases involving strangulation or suffocation, and a breakdown of calls received by agency, city, and county.

(c) Each law enforcement agency shall develop an incident report form that includes a domestic violence identification code by January 1, 1986. In all incidents of domestic violence, a report shall be written and shall be identified on the face of the report as a domestic violence incident. The report shall include at least all of the following:

(1) A notation of whether the officer or officers who responded to the domestic violence call observed any signs that the alleged abuser was under the influence of alcohol or a controlled substance.

(2) A notation of whether the officer or officers who responded to the domestic violence call determined if any law enforcement agency had previously responded to a domestic violence call at the same address involving the same alleged abuser or victim.

(3) A notation of whether the officer or officers who responded to the domestic violence call found it necessary, for the protection of the peace officer or other persons present, to inquire of the victim, the alleged abuser, or both, whether a firearm or other deadly weapon was present at the

location, and, if there is an inquiry, whether that inquiry disclosed the presence of a firearm or other deadly weapon. Any firearm or other deadly weapon discovered by an officer at the scene of a domestic violence incident shall be subject to confiscation pursuant to Division 4 (commencing with Section 18250) of Title 2 of Part 6.

(4) A notation of whether there were indications that the incident involved strangulation or suffocation. This includes whether any witness or victim reported any incident of strangulation or suffocation, whether any victim reported symptoms of strangulation or suffocation, or whether the officer observed any signs of strangulation or suffocation. *(Added by Stats.1984, c. 1609, § 3. Amended by Stats.1993, c. 1230 (A.B.2250), § 2; Stats.1995, c. 965 (S.B.132), § 2; Stats.2001, c. 483 (A.B.469), § 1; Stats.2010, c. 178 (S.B. 1115), § 94, operative Jan. 1, 2012; Stats.2013, c. 28 (S.B.71), § 49, eff. June 27, 2013; Stats.2013, c. 161 (A.B.81), § 3, eff. Aug. 27, 2013; Stats.2017, c. 331 (S.B.40), § 2, eff. Jan. 1, 2018.)*

Law Revision Commission Comments

2010 Amendment

Subdivision (c) of Section 13730 is amended to reflect nonsubstantive reorganization of the statutes governing control of deadly weapons. [38 Cal.L.Rev.Comm. Reports 217 (2009)].

Research References

Treatises and Practice Aids

Witkin, California Summary 10th Husband and Wife § 388, Service Of Order.

§ 13731. Domestic violence data regional clearinghouse; San Diego Association of Governments

(a) The San Diego Association of Governments may serve as the regional clearinghouse for criminal justice data involving domestic violence. The association may obtain monthly crime statistics from all law enforcement agencies in San Diego County. These law enforcement agencies may include their domestic violence supplements in the monthly crime reports that are supplied to the association. The association may obtain client-based data regarding clients or victims of domestic violence who seek protection in San Diego County shelters.

(b) Contingent upon the appropriation of funds therefor, the association shall do all of the following:

(1) Create a standardized, uniform intake form, to be referred to as a Compilation of Research and Evaluation Intake Instrument, also known as C.O.R.E., for use in San Diego County's domestic violence shelters. This form shall be completed and ready to use in the field for data collection purposes not later than March 31, 1997. The C.O.R.E. intake form shall be standardized to compile the same information from all clients for all shelters.

(2) Collect and analyze the standardized, uniform intake form in order to compile information including, but not limited to, victim sociodemographic characteristics, descriptions of domestic violence incidents pertaining to each victim and services needed by domestic violence shelter clients within San Diego County.

(3) Use the collected client-based data to describe the nature and scope of violence from the perspective of domestic violence shelter clients and to determine the service needs of clients and what gaps in service delivery exist, so that resources can be appropriately targeted and allocated. All data supplied to the association shall be stripped of any information regarding the personal identity of an individual to protect the privacy of domestic violence shelter clients.

(4) Establish an advisory committee in order to facilitate the research effort and to assess the value of the research project. The advisory committee shall consist of representation from the shelters, as well as members of the San Diego County Domestic Violence Council, local justice administrators, and the principal investigator. The advisory committee shall meet at least four times before April 30, 1999, to review the progress of the research, including research methodology, data collection instruments, preliminary analyses, and work product as they are drafted. Advisory committee members shall evaluate the final research product in terms of applicability and utility of findings and recommendations. *(Added by Stats.1996, c. 375 (A.B.2448), § 2. Amended by Stats.2001, c. 745 (S.B.1191), § 163, eff. Oct. 12, 2001.)*

§ 13732. Legislative findings and declarations regarding the connection between domestic violence and child abuse

(a) The Legislature finds and declares that a substantial body of research demonstrates a strong connection between domestic violence and child abuse. However, despite this connection, child abuse and domestic violence services and agencies often fail to coordinate appropriately at the local level. It is the intent of the Legislature in enacting this section to improve preventative and supportive services to families experiencing violence in order to prevent further abuse of children and the victims of domestic violence. It is the further intent of this section that child protective services agencies develop a protocol which clearly sets forth the criteria for a child protective services response to a domestic violence related incident in a home in which a child resides.

(b) Commencing January 1, 2003, child protective services agencies, law enforcement, prosecution, child abuse and domestic violence experts, and community-based organizations serving abused children and victims of domestic violence shall develop, in collaboration with one another, protocols as to how law enforcement and child welfare agencies will cooperate in their response to incidents of domestic violence in homes in which a child resides. The requirements of this section shall not apply to counties where protocols consistent with this section already have been developed. *(Added by Stats.2002, c. 187 (S.B.1745), § 3.)*

Title 5.3

FAMILY JUSTICE CENTERS

§ 13750. Establishment of family justice centers; definitions

(a) A city, county, city and county, or community-based nonprofit organization may each establish a multiagency, multidisciplinary family justice center to assist victims of domestic violence, sexual assault, elder or dependent adult abuse, and human trafficking, to ensure that victims of abuse are able to access all needed services in one location in order to enhance victim safety, increase offender accountability, and improve access to services for victims of domestic violence, sexual assault, elder or dependent adult abuse, and human trafficking.

(b) For purposes of this title, the following terms have the following meanings:

(1) "Abuse" has the same meaning as set forth in Section 6203 of the Family Code.

(2) "Domestic violence" has the same meaning as set forth in Section 6211 of the Family Code.

(3) "Sexual assault" means an act or attempt made punishable by Section 220, 261, 261.5, 262, 264.1, 266c, 269, 285, 286, 288, 288.5, 288a, 289, or 647.6.

(4) "Elder or dependent adult abuse" means an act made punishable by Section 368.

(5) "Human trafficking" has the same meaning as set forth in Section 236.1.

(c) For purposes of this title, family justice centers shall be defined as multiagency, multidisciplinary service centers where public and private agencies assign staff members on a full-time or part-time basis in order to provide services to victims of domestic violence, sexual assault, elder or dependent adult abuse, or human trafficking from one location in order to reduce the number of times victims must tell their story, reduce the number of places victims must go for help, and increase access to services and support for victims and their children. Staff members at a family justice center may be comprised of, but are not limited to, the following:

(1) Law enforcement personnel.

(2) Medical personnel.

(3) District attorneys and city attorneys.

(4) Victim–witness program personnel.

(5) Domestic violence shelter service staff.

(6) Community–based rape crisis, domestic violence, and human trafficking advocates.

(7) Social service agency staff members.

(8) Child welfare agency social workers.

(9) County health department staff.

(10) City or county welfare and public assistance workers.

(11) Nonprofit agency counseling professionals.

(12) Civil legal service providers.

(13) Supervised volunteers from partner agencies.

(14) Other professionals providing services.

(d) Nothing in this section is intended to abrogate existing laws regarding privacy or information sharing. Family justice center staff members shall comply with the laws governing their respective professions.

(e) Victims of crime shall not be denied services on the grounds of criminal history. No criminal history search shall be conducted of a victim at a family justice center without the victim's written consent unless the criminal history search is pursuant to a criminal investigation.

(f) Victims of crime shall not be required to participate in the criminal justice system or cooperate with law enforcement in order to receive counseling, medical care, or other services at a family justice center.

(g)(1) Each family justice center shall consult with community-based domestic violence, sexual assault, elder or dependent adult abuse, and human trafficking agencies in partnership with survivors of violence and abuse and their advocates in the operations process of the family justice center, and shall establish procedures for the ongoing input, feedback, and evaluation of the family justice center by survivors of violence and abuse and community-based crime victim service providers and advocates.

(2) Each family justice center shall develop policies and procedures, in collaboration with local community-based crime victim service providers and local survivors of violence and abuse, to ensure coordinated services are provided to victims and to enhance the safety of victims and professionals at the family justice center who participate in affiliated survivor-centered support or advocacy groups. Each family justice center shall maintain a formal client feedback, complaint, and input process to address client concerns about services provided or the conduct of any family justice center professionals, agency partners, or volunteers providing services in the family justice center.

(h)(1) Each family justice center shall maintain a client consent policy and shall be in compliance with all state and federal laws protecting the confidentiality of the types of information and documents that may be in a victim's file, including, but not limited to, medical, legal, and victim counselor records. Each family justice center shall have a designated privacy officer to develop and oversee privacy policies and procedures consistent with state and federal privacy laws and the Fair Information Practice Principles promulgated by the United States Department of Homeland Security. At no time shall a victim be required to sign a client consent form to share information in order to access services.

(2) Each family justice center is required to obtain informed, written, reasonably time limited, consent from the victim before sharing information obtained from the victim with any staff member or agency partner, except as provided in paragraphs (3) and (4).

(3) A family justice center is not required to obtain consent from the victim before sharing information obtained from the victim with any staff member or agency partner if the person is a mandated reporter, a peace officer, or a member of the prosecution team and is required to report or disclose specific information or incidents. These persons shall inform the victim that they may share information obtained from the victim without the victim's consent.

(4) Each family justice center is required to inform the victim that information shared with staff members or partner agencies at a family justice center may be shared with law enforcement professionals without the victim's consent if

there is a mandatory duty to report, or the client is a danger to himself or herself, or others. Each family justice center shall obtain written acknowledgment that the victim has been informed of this policy.

(5) Consent by a victim for sharing information within a family justice center pursuant to this section shall not be construed as a universal waiver of any existing evidentiary privilege that makes confidential any communications or documents between the victim and any service provider, including, but not limited to, any lawyer, advocate, sexual assault or domestic violence counselor as defined in Section 1035.2 or 1037.1 of the Evidence Code, human trafficking caseworker as defined in Section 1038.2 of the Evidence Code, therapist, doctor, or nurse. Any oral or written communication or any document authorized by the victim to be shared for the purposes of enhancing safety and providing more effective and efficient services to the victim of domestic violence, sexual assault, elder or dependent adult abuse, or human trafficking shall not be disclosed to any third party, unless that third-party disclosure is authorized by the victim, or required by other state or federal law or by court order.

(i) An individual staff member, volunteer, or agency that has victim information governed by this section shall not be required to disclose that information unless the victim has consented to the disclosure or it is otherwise required by other state or federal law or by court order.

(j) A disclosure of information consented to by the victim in a family justice center, made for the purposes of clinical assessment, risk assessment, safety planning, or service delivery, shall not be deemed a waiver of any privilege or confidentiality provision contained in Sections 2263, 2918, 4982, and 6068 of the Business and Professions Code, the lawyer-client privilege protected by Article 3 (commencing with Section 950) of Chapter 4 of Division 8 of the Evidence Code, the physician-patient privilege protected by Article 6 (commencing with Section 990) of Chapter 4 of Division 8 of the Evidence Code, the psychotherapist-patient privilege protected by Article 7 (commencing with Section 1010) of Chapter 4 of Division 8 of the Evidence Code, the sexual assault counselor-victim privilege protected by Article 8.5 (commencing with Section 1035) of Chapter 4 of Division 8 of the Evidence Code, or the domestic violence counselor-victim privilege protected by Article 8.7 (commencing with Section 1037) of Chapter 4 of Division 8 of the Evidence Code. *(Added by Stats.2014, c. 85 (A.B.1623), § 1, eff. Jan. 1, 2015.)*

Research References

Treatises and Practice Aids

Witkin, California Summary 10th Husband and Wife § 371, Civil Remedies.

Witkin, California Summary 10th Parent and Child § 4A, (New) Federal Programs and Services for Alien Children.

§ 13751. Mandatory training programs

Each family justice center established pursuant to subdivision (a) of Section 13750 shall maintain a formal training program with mandatory training for all staff members, volunteers, and agency professionals of not less than eight hours per year on subjects, including, but not limited to, privileges and confidentiality, information sharing, risk assessment, safety planning, victim advocacy, and high-risk case response. *(Added by Stats.2014, c. 85 (A.B.1623), § 1, eff. Jan. 1, 2015.)*

Title 6

CALIFORNIA COUNCIL ON CRIMINAL JUSTICE

CHAPTER 3. CRIMINAL JUSTICE PLANNING

§ 13823.4. Family Violence Prevention Program; funding; information and materials

(a) The Legislature finds the problem of family violence to be of serious and increasing magnitude. The Legislature also finds that acts of family violence often result in other crimes and social problems.

(b) There is in the Office of Emergency Services, a Family Violence Prevention Program. This program shall provide financial and technical assistance to local domestic and family violence centers in implementing family violence prevention programs.

The goals and functions of the program shall include all of the following:

(1) Promotion of community involvement through public education geared specifically toward reaching and educating the friends and neighbors of members of violent families.

(2) Development and dissemination of model protocols for the training of criminal justice system personnel in domestic violence intervention and prevention.

(3) Increasing citizen involvement in family violence prevention.

(4) Identification and testing of family violence prevention models.

(5) Replication of successful models, as appropriate, through the state.

(6) Identification and testing of domestic violence model protocols and intervention systems in major service delivery institutions.

(7) Development of informational materials and seminars to enable emulation or adaptation of the models by other communities.

(8) Provision of domestic violence prevention education and skills to students in schools.

(c) The Director of Emergency Services shall allocate funds to local centers meeting the criteria for funding that shall be established by the Office of Emergency Services in consultation with practitioners and experts in the field of family violence prevention. All centers receiving funds pursuant to this section shall have had an ongoing recognized program, supported by either public or private funds, dealing with an aspect of family violence, for at least two years prior to the date specified for submission of applications for funding pursuant to this section. All centers funded pursuant to this section shall utilize volunteers to the greatest extent possible.

The centers may seek, receive, and make use of any funds which may be available from all public and private sources to augment any state funds received pursuant to this section. Sixty percent of the state funds received pursuant to this section shall be used to develop and implement model program protocols and materials. Forty percent of the state funds received pursuant to this section shall be allocated to programs to disseminate model program protocols and materials. Dissemination shall include training for domestic violence agencies in California. Each of the programs funded under this section shall focus on no more than two targeted areas. These targeted model areas shall be determined by the Office of Emergency Services in consultation with practitioners and experts in the field of domestic violence, using the domestic violence model priorities survey of the California Alliance Against Domestic Violence.

Centers receiving funding shall provide matching funds of at least 10 percent of the funds received pursuant to this section.

(d) The Office of Emergency Services shall develop and disseminate throughout the state information and materials concerning family violence prevention, including, but not limited to, a procedures manual on prevention models. The Office of Emergency Services shall also establish a resource center for the collection, retention, and distribution of educational materials related to family violence and its prevention. *(Added by Stats.1985, c. 250, § 1, eff. July 26, 1985. Amended by Stats.1988, c. 1371, § 3; Stats.2003, c. 229 (A.B.1757), § 35; Stats.2010, c. 618 (A.B.2791), § 221; Stats. 2013, c. 352 (A.B.1317), § 432, eff. Sept. 26, 2013, operative July 1, 2013.)*

Research References

Treatises and Practice Aids

Witkin, California Summary 10th Husband and Wife § 372, Criminal Proceedings.

PROBATE CODE

Division 1

PRELIMINARY PROVISIONS AND DEFINITIONS

Law Revision Commission Comments

1990 Enactment

This division supersedes Division 1 (commencing with Section 1) of the repealed Probate Code. Division 1 of the repealed Probate Code was enacted upon recommendation of the California Law Revision Commission. See Tentative Recommendation Relating to Wills and Intestate Succession, 16 Cal.L.Revision Comm'n Reports 2301 (1982). See also Report of Senate Committee on Judiciary on Assembly Bills 25 and 68, 17 Cal.L.Revision Comm'n Reports 867–68 (1984). Division 1 was thereafter revised upon recommendations of the California Law Revision Commission. See Recommendation Relating to Revision of Wills and Intestate Succession Law, 17 Cal.L.Revision Comm'n Reports 537 (1984); Communication of Law Revision Commission Concerning Assembly Bill 2290, 18 Cal.L.Revision Comm'n Reports 77, 78–79 (1986); Recommendation Relating to Preliminary Provisions and Definitions of the Probate Code, 18 Cal.L.Revision Comm'n Reports 1807 (1986); Recommendation Proposing the Trust Law, 18 Cal.L.Revision Comm'n Reports 501, 779–80 (1986); Communication from California Law Revision Commission Concerning Assembly Bill 2625, 18 Cal.L.Revision Comm'n Reports 1743, 1745 (1986); Communication from California Law Revision Commission Concerning Assembly Bill 2652, 18 Cal.L.Revision Comm'n Reports 1763, 1765–66 (1986); Comments to Conforming Revisions and Repeals, 19 Cal.L.Revision Comm'n Reports 391, 393–94 (1988); Comments to Conforming Revisions and Repeals, 19 Cal.L.Revision Comm'n Reports 1031, 1041 (1988); Communication from the California Law Revision Commission Concerning Assembly Bill 2841, 19 Cal.L.Revision Comm'n Reports 1201, 1207–09 (1988). [20 Cal.L.Rev.Comm.Reports 1001 (1990)].

Part 2

DEFINITIONS

§ 26. Child

"Child" means any individual entitled to take as a child under this code by intestate succession from the parent whose relationship is involved. *(Stats.1990, c. 79 (A.B.759), § 14, operative July 1, 1991.)*

Law Revision Commission Comments

1990 Enactment

Section 26 continues Section 26 of the repealed Probate Code without change. The context may require that a word or phrase used in a particular section be given a meaning different from the definition provided in this part. Also special definitions may be used for a particular portion of the code that differ from those provided in this part. See Section 20.

Section 26 is comparable to Section 1–201(3) of the Uniform Probate Code (1987). As to the construction of provisions drawn from uniform acts, see Section 2. "Child" is limited to the persons who are entitled to take as a child by intestate succession. The definition of "child" in Section 26 applies unless the provision or context otherwise requires. See Section 20.

Although under Section 26 a stepchild or foster child is not included within the meaning of "child" only on the basis of that relationship, a stepchild or foster child may be included if the relationship began during the person's minority, continued throughout the parties' joint lifetimes, and it is established by clear and convincing evidence that the stepparent or foster parent would have adopted the person but for a legal barrier. See Section 6408. [Repealed, see now, Probate Code § 6454.] See also Sections 54 (definition of "parent"), 6152 (parent-child relationship for purposes of construing will).

Background on Section 26 of Repealed Code

Section 26 was a new provision added by 1983 Cal.Stat. ch. 842 § 21 and amended by 1984 Cal.Stat. ch. 892 § 4 and 1987 Cal.Stat. ch. 923 § 12. The 1984 amendment deleted the last clause of the section which excluded from the definition of "child" any person "who is only a stepchild, a foster child, a grandchild, or any more remote descendant." The amendment did not make a substantive change; the deleted language was omitted because it was unnecessary and was confusing. Deletion of the last clause from Section 26 made it clearer that a stepchild or foster child may be included within the definition of "child" when the requirements of Section 6408 are met. See Report of Senate Committee on Judiciary on Assembly Bills 25 and 68, 17 Cal.L.Revision Comm'n Reports 867 (1984); Communication of Law Revision Commission Concerning Assembly Bill 2290, 18 Cal.L.Revision Comm'n Reports 77, 78–79 (1986). The 1987 amendment replaced "includes" with "means." This made clear that "child" is limited to the persons who are entitled to take as a child by intestate succession. See Recommendation Relating to Preliminary Provisions and Definitions of the Probate Code, 18 Cal.L.Revision Comm'n Reports 1807, 1812–13, 1819 (1986). For background on the provisions of this division, see the Comment to this division under the division heading. [20 Cal.L.Rev.Comm.Reports 1001 (1990)].

Commentary

Estate of Furia, 103 Cal.App.4th 1, 126 Cal.Rptr.2d 384 (2002), holds that a child equitably adopted by a stepparent may not inherit property from the stepparent's parent, whose will leaves the property to her children's surviving issue, because the doctrine of equitable adoption creates only a contractual right to receive property from an intestate decedent; the doctrine does not make a person a "child" or "issue," as defined by Probate Code §§ 26 or 50.

Research References

Forms

California Transactions Forms--Estate Planning § 6:7, Persons Included in Class.

California Transactions Forms--Estate Planning § 6:60, Distribution as Provided in Prob C § 240.
California Transactions Forms--Estate Planning § 6:66, Devise to Children Living at Testator's Death.

Treatises and Practice Aids

Witkin, California Summary 10th Wills and Probate § 49, Persons and Entities.
Witkin, California Summary 10th Wills and Probate § 95, Foster or Stepchildren.

§ 28. Community property

"Community property" means:

(a) Community property heretofore or hereafter acquired during marriage by a married person while domiciled in this state.

(b) All personal property wherever situated, and all real property situated in this state, heretofore or hereafter acquired during the marriage by a married person while domiciled elsewhere, that is community property, or a substantially equivalent type of marital property, under the laws of the place where the acquiring spouse was domiciled at the time of its acquisition.

(c) All personal property wherever situated, and all real property situated in this state, heretofore or hereafter acquired during the marriage by a married person in exchange for real or personal property, wherever situated, that is community property, or a substantially equivalent type of marital property, under the laws of the place where the acquiring spouse was domiciled at the time the property so exchanged was acquired. *(Stats.1990, c. 79 (A.B.759), § 14, operative July 1, 1991.)*

Law Revision Commission Comments

1990 Enactment

Section 28 continues Section 28 of the repealed Probate Code without substantive change. The context may require that a word or phrase used in a particular section be given a meaning different from the definition provided in this part. Also special definitions may be used for a particular portion of the code that differ from those provided in this part. See Section 20.

Subdivision (a) is consistent with Civil Code Sections 687 and 5110. Under subdivisions (b) and (c), community property acquired while domiciled in another community property jurisdiction is treated as community property in California even though the property might not have been community if acquired while domiciled in California. For example, property is community property under subdivision (b) if it is the income of separate property and the income of separate property is community property under the laws of the place where the spouse owning the separate property is domiciled at the time the income is earned. Thus, subdivisions (b) and (c) ensure generally comparable treatment of the property in California to that given it in the other community property jurisdiction and fills a gap in the quasi-community property law. See Section 66 ("quasi-community property" defined). Section 28 applies whether the property is acquired before or after the operative date of the section. The reference in subdivisions (b) and (c) to substantially equivalent types of marital property is intended to cover possible adoption in other jurisdictions of the Uniform Marital Property Act (1983) or other laws establishing a community property regime. See also Section 68 ("real property" defined).

Background on Section 28 of Repealed Code

Section 28 was a new provision added by 1983 Cal.Stat. ch. 842 § 21. See Report of Senate Committee on Judiciary on Assembly Bills 25 and 68, 17 Cal.L.Revision Comm'n Reports 867 (1984). For background on the provisions of this division, see the Comment to this division under the division heading. [20 Cal.L.Rev.Comm.Reports 1001 (1990)].

Research References

Forms

California Transactions Forms--Estate Planning § 1:22, Community Property.
California Transactions Forms--Estate Planning § 10:4, Community Property.
California Transactions Forms--Estate Planning § 3:75, Community Property.
California Transactions Forms--Estate Planning § 19:18, Community Property.
California Transactions Forms--Estate Planning § 19:19, Quasi-Community Property.

Treatises and Practice Aids

Witkin, California Summary 10th Community Property § 253, Where California Law Applies.
Witkin, California Summary 10th Wills and Probate § 25, Major Changes.
Witkin, California Summary 10th Wills and Probate § 50, Legal and Financial Terms.
Witkin, California Summary 10th Wills and Probate § 76, Surviving Spouse's Share in Community and Quasi-Community Property.
Witkin, California Summary 10th Wills and Probate § 264, Definitions.

§ 32. Devise

"Devise," when used as a noun, means a disposition of real or personal property by will, and, when used as a verb, means to dispose of real or personal property by will. *(Stats.1990, c. 79 (A.B.759), § 14, operative July 1, 1991.)*

Law Revision Commission Comments

1990 Enactment

Section 32 continues Section 32 of the repealed Probate Code without change. This section is the same in substance as Section 1–201(7) of the Uniform Probate Code (1987). As to the construction of provisions drawn from uniform acts, see Section 2. The context may require that a word or phrase used in a particular section be given a meaning different from the definition provided in this part. Also special definitions may be used for a particular portion of the code that differ from those provided in this part. See Section 20. [20 Cal.L.Rev.Comm.Reports 1001 (1990)].

Background on Section 32 of Repealed Code

Section 32 was a new provision added by 1983 Cal.Stat. ch. 842 § 21. For background on the provisions of this division, see the Comment to this division under the division heading. [20 Cal.L.Rev.Comm.Reports 1001 (1990)].

Research References

Forms

California Transactions Forms--Estate Planning § 6:1, Definitions.
California Transactions Forms--Estate Planning § 19:1, Will Defined.
California Transactions Forms--Estate Planning § 20:1, Definitions; Current Use Of Terms.

California Transactions Forms--Estate Planning § 19:64, Words Given Their Ordinary Meaning; Technical Words.

Treatises and Practice Aids

Witkin, California Summary 10th Wills and Probate § 50, Legal and Financial Terms.
Witkin, California Summary 10th Wills and Probate § 241, Nature and Classification.

§ 37. Domestic partner

(a) "Domestic partner" means one of two persons who have filed a Declaration of Domestic Partnership with the Secretary of State pursuant to Division 2.5 (commencing with Section 297) of the Family Code, provided that the domestic partnership has not been terminated pursuant to Section 299 of the Family Code.

(b) Notwithstanding Section 299 of the Family Code, if a domestic partnership is terminated by the death of one of the parties and Notice of Termination was not filed by either party prior to the date of death of the decedent, the domestic partner who survives the deceased is a surviving domestic partner, and shall be entitled to the rights of a surviving domestic partner as provided in this code. *(Added by Stats.2001, c. 893 (A.B.25), § 13.)*

Research References

Forms

West's California Code Forms, Probate § 1820 Form 1, Petition for Appointment Of Probate Conservator--Judicial Council Form GC-310.

Treatises and Practice Aids

Witkin, California Summary 10th Wills and Probate § 49, Persons and Entities.
Witkin, California Summary 10th Wills and Probate § 438, Surviving Spouse or Domestic Partner.

§ 44. Heir

"Heir" means any person, including the surviving spouse, who is entitled to take property of the decedent by intestate succession under this code. *(Stats.1990, c. 79 (A.B.759), § 14, operative July 1, 1991.)*

Law Revision Commission Comments

1990 Enactment

Section 44 continues Section 44 of the repealed Probate Code without substantive change. The context may require that a word or phrase used in a particular section be given a meaning different from the definition provided in this part. Also, special definitions may be used for a particular portion of the code that differ from those provided in this part. See Section 20.

Section 44 is the same in substance as Section 1–201(17) of the Uniform Probate Code (1987). As to the construction of provisions drawn from uniform acts, see Section 2. See also Section 78 ("surviving spouse" defined). As to a surviving spouse's waiver of rights at death, see Sections 140–147.

Background on Section 44 of Repealed Code

Section 44 was a new provision added by 1983 Cal.Stat. ch. 842 § 21. For background on the provisions of this division, see the Comment to this division under the division heading. [20 Cal.L.Rev.Comm.Reports 1001 (1990)].

Research References

Forms

California Transactions Forms--Estate Planning § 6:1, Definitions.
California Transactions Forms--Estate Planning § 6:7, Persons Included in Class.
California Transactions Forms--Estate Planning § 1:18, Property Subject to Probate; Intestacy.
California Transactions Forms--Estate Planning § 6:60, Distribution as Provided in Prob C § 240.

Treatises and Practice Aids

Witkin, California Summary 10th Wills and Probate § 49, Persons and Entities.

§ 50. Issue

"Issue" of a person means all his or her lineal descendants of all generations, with the relationship of parent and child at each generation being determined by the definitions of child and parent. *(Stats.1990, c. 79 (A.B.759), § 14, operative July 1, 1991.)*

Law Revision Commission Comments

1990 Enactment

Section 50 continues Section 50 of the repealed Probate Code without change. This section is the same in substance as Section 1–201(21) of the Uniform Probate Code (1987). As to the construction of provisions drawn from uniform acts, see Section 2. See also Section 6408 (parent-child relationship for determination of rights under intestate succession). The context may require that a word or phrase used in a particular section be given a meaning different from the definition provided in this part. Also, special definitions may be used for a particular portion of the code that differ from those provided in this part. See Section 20.

Background on Section 50 of Repealed Code

Section 50 was a new provision added by 1983 Cal.Stat. ch. 842 § 21. For background on the provisions of this division, see the Comment to this division under the division heading. [20 Cal.L.Rev.Comm.Reports 1001 (1990)].

Commentary

Estate of Furia, 103 Cal.App.4th 1, 126 Cal.Rptr.2d 384 (2002), holds that a child equitably adopted by a stepparent may not inherit property from the stepparent's parent, whose will leaves the property to her children's surviving issue, because the doctrine of equitable adoption creates only a contractual right to receive property from an intestate decedent; the doctrine does not make a person a "child" or "issue," as defined by Probate Code §§ 26 or 50.

Ehrenclou v. MacDonald, 117 Cal.App.4th 364, 12 Cal.Rptr.3d 411 (2004), review denied, held that two adults adopted by a trust beneficiary under Colorado adult adoption law were not the deceased trust beneficiary's "children then living" under a trust governed by California law, because the Colorado adult adoption statute gave the adoptees heir-at-law status, but did not create a parent-child relationship between the trust beneficiary and the adoptees.

Research References

Forms

California Transactions Forms--Estate Planning § 6:7, Persons Included in Class.
California Transactions Forms--Estate Planning § 6:60, Distribution as Provided in Prob C § 240.

California Transactions Forms--Estate Planning § 21:19, Accumulation Trust for Children.

Treatises and Practice Aids

Witkin, California Summary 10th Wills and Probate § 49, Persons and Entities.

Witkin, California Summary 10th Wills and Probate § 81, Grandparents or Issue Of Grandparents.

Witkin, California Summary 10th Wills and Probate § 95, Foster or Stepchildren.

Witkin, California Summary 10th Wills and Probate § 219, in General.

Witkin, California Summary 10th Wills and Probate § 263, Revised Statute.

§ 59. Predeceased spouse

"Predeceased spouse" means a person who died before the decedent while married to the decedent, except that the term does not include any of the following:

(a) A person who obtains or consents to a final decree or judgment of dissolution of marriage from the decedent or a final decree or judgment of annulment of their marriage, which decree or judgment is not recognized as valid in this state, unless they (1) subsequently participate in a marriage ceremony purporting to marry each to the other or (2) subsequently live together as spouses.

(b) A person who, following a decree or judgment of dissolution or annulment of marriage obtained by the decedent, participates in a marriage ceremony to a third person.

(c) A person who was a party to a valid proceeding concluded by an order purporting to terminate all marital property rights. *(Stats.1990, c. 79 (A.B.759), § 14, operative July 1, 1991. Amended by Stats.2016, c. 50 (S.B.1005), § 76, eff. Jan. 1, 2017.)*

Law Revision Commission Comments

1990 Enactment

Section 59 continues Section 59 of the repealed Probate Code without change. The context may require that a word or phrase used in a particular section be given a meaning different from the definition provided in this part. Also special definitions may be used for a particular portion of the code that differ from those provided in this part. See Section 20.

Section 59 is consistent with Section 78 ("surviving spouse" defined). See the Comment to Section 78. Under Section 59, it is possible that the decedent may have more than one predeceased spouse. For California provisions relating to annulment of marriage, see Title 2 (commencing with Section 4400) of Part 5 of the Civil Code (judicial determination of void or voidable marriage). As to a surviving spouse's waiver of rights at death, see Sections 140–147.

Background on Section 59 of Repealed Code

Section 59 was a new provision added by 1984 Cal.Stat. ch. 892 § 6. See Recommendation Relating to Revision of Wills and Intestate Succession Law, 17 Cal.L.Revision Comm'n Reports 537, 546, 547–48 (1984). For background on the provisions of this division, see the Comment to this division under the division heading. [20 Cal.L.Rev.Comm.Reports 1001 (1990)].

Research References

Treatises and Practice Aids

Witkin, California Summary 10th Wills and Probate § 49, Persons and Entities.

Witkin, California Summary 10th Wills and Probate § 84, Nature and Scope Of Statute.

§ 66. Quasi-community property

"Quasi-community property" means the following property, other than community property as defined in Section 28:

(a) All personal property wherever situated, and all real property situated in this state, heretofore or hereafter acquired by a decedent while domiciled elsewhere that would have been the community property of the decedent and the surviving spouse if the decedent had been domiciled in this state at the time of its acquisition.

(b) All personal property wherever situated, and all real property situated in this state, heretofore or hereafter acquired in exchange for real or personal property, wherever situated, that would have been the community property of the decedent and the surviving spouse if the decedent had been domiciled in this state at the time the property so exchanged was acquired. *(Stats.1990, c. 79 (A.B.759), § 14, operative July 1, 1991.)*

Law Revision Commission Comments

1990 Enactment

Section 66 continues Section 66 of the repealed Probate Code without substantive change. The context may require that a word or phrase used in a particular section be given a meaning different from the definition provided in this part. Also special definitions may be used for a particular portion of the code that differ from those provided in this part. See Section 20.

Community property under the laws of another jurisdiction is classified as community rather than quasi-community property. See Section 28 ("community property" defined) and the Comment thereto. See also Section 68 ("real property" defined). For background on the definition of "quasi-community property," see Recommendation and Study Relating to Rights of Surviving Spouse in Property Acquired by Decedent While Domiciled Elsewhere, 1 Cal.L.Revision Comm'n Reports E–1 (1957); Recommendation and Study Relating to Inter Vivos Marital Property Rights in Property Acquired While Domiciled Elsewhere, 3 Cal.L.Revision Comm'n Reports I–1 (1961); Recommendation Relating to Quasi–Community Property, 9 Cal.L.Revision Comm'n Reports 113 (1969).

Background on Section 66 of Repealed Code

Section 66 was added by 1983 Cal.Stat. ch. 842 § 21. The section continued the substance of portions of former Probate Code Section 201.5 (repealed by 1983 Cal.Stat. ch. 842 § 19), except that community property under the laws of another jurisdiction was classified by Sections 28 and 66 as community rather than quasi-community property. For background on the provisions of this division, see the Comment to this division under the division heading. [20 Cal.L.Rev.Comm.Reports 1001 (1990)].

Research References

Forms

California Transactions Forms--Estate Planning § 1:26, Quasi-Community Property; Separate Property.

California Transactions Forms--Estate Planning § 10:5, Quasi-Community Property.

California Transactions Forms--Estate Planning § 3:75, Community Property.

California Transactions Forms--Estate Planning § 19:19, Quasi-Community Property.

Treatises and Practice Aids

Witkin, California Summary 10th Community Property § 34, Personal Property Brought to California.
Witkin, California Summary 10th Community Property § 252, Former Law and Corrective Legislation.
Witkin, California Summary 10th Community Property § 253, Where California Law Applies.
Witkin, California Summary 10th Wills and Probate § 50, Legal and Financial Terms.
Witkin, California Summary 10th Wills and Probate § 76, Surviving Spouse's Share in Community and Quasi-Community Property.
Witkin, California Summary 10th Wills and Probate § 264, Definitions.

§ 78. Surviving spouse

"Surviving spouse" does not include any of the following:

(a) A person whose marriage to, or registered domestic partnership with, the decedent has been dissolved or annulled, unless, by virtue of a subsequent marriage or registered domestic partnership, the person is married to, or in a registered domestic partnership with, the decedent at the time of death.

(b) A person who obtains or consents to a final decree or judgment of dissolution of marriage or termination of registered domestic partnership from the decedent or a final decree or judgment of annulment of their marriage or termination of registered domestic partnership, which decree or judgment is not recognized as valid in this state, unless they (1) subsequently participate in a marriage ceremony purporting to marry each to the other or (2) subsequently live together as spouses.

(c) A person who, following a decree or judgment of dissolution or annulment of marriage or registered domestic partnership obtained by the decedent, participates in a marriage ceremony with a third person.

(d) A person who was a party to a valid proceeding concluded by an order purporting to terminate all marital or registered domestic partnership property rights. *(Stats.1990, c. 79 (A.B.759), § 14, operative July 1, 1991. Amended by Stats.2016, c. 50 (S.B.1005), § 78, eff. Jan. 1, 2017.)*

Law Revision Commission Comments

1990 Enactment

Section 78 continues Section 78 of the repealed Probate Code without change. The context may require that a word or phrase used in a particular section be given a meaning different from the definition provided in this part. Also, special definitions may be used for a particular portion of the code that differ from those provided in this part. See Section 20.

Section 78 is drawn from Section 2–802 of the Uniform Probate Code (1987). As to the construction of provisions drawn from uniform acts, see Section 2. See also Section 40 ("heir" defined). Subdivisions (b) and (c) address the problem of a divorce or annulment which is not recognized in California, and apply an estoppel principle against the surviving spouse. These provisions are consistent with prior California law. See, e.g., Spellens v. Spellens, 49 Cal.2d 210, 317 P.2d 613 (1957) (estoppel to deny validity of marriage); Estate of Atherley, 44 Cal.App.3d 758, 764, 119 Cal.Rptr. 41 (1975) (recognizing principle but declining to apply it). See also Sections 36 ("dissolution of marriage" defined), 59 ("predeceased spouse" defined) and the Comments to those sections. As to a surviving spouse's waiver of rights at death, see Sections 140–147. For California provisions relating to annulment of marriage, see Title 2 (commencing with Section 4400) of Part 5 of the Civil Code (judicial determination of void or voidable marriage).

Background on Section 78 of Repealed Code

Interpreting subsection (d), *Estate of Lahey, 76 Cal.App.4th 1056, 91 Cal.Rptr.2d 30 (1999), review denied March 1, 2000,* holds that a decedent's spouse who had obtained a judgment of legal separation, which stated that there were no items of community property subject to disposition by the court, terminated all support rights, and terminated the court's jurisdiction to order support, was an "order purporting to terminate all marital property rights" within the meaning of this section.

Section 78 was a new provision added by 1983 Cal.Stat. ch. 842 § 21. For background on the provisions of this division, see the Comment to this division under the division heading. [20 Cal.L.Rev.Comm.Reports 1001 (1990)].

Commentary

A person may be a "lawful spouse" for purposes of the Family Code, but not a "surviving spouse" for purposes of the Probate Code. When a spouse dies in the interlocutory period after entry of an order terminating all marital property rights but before the end of the six-month waiting period after which the dissolution decree becomes final, the survivor is not a "surviving spouse" for purposes of subsection (d). *Estate of McDaniel, 161 Cal.App.4th 458, 73 Cal. Rptr.3d 907 (2008).* "Being married opens enormous opportunities for Social Security recipients. . . The financial advantages of marriage can be so great that most committed couples in their 60s or older who've been in a long term relationship should at least consider tying the knot." Lange, *Optimizing Social Security Benefits for Unmarried Couples*, Trusts & Estates (Sept. 2014), p. 40.

Irvin v. CCERA, 13 Cal.App.5th 162, 220 Cal.Rptr.3d 510 (2017), declined to adopt the subsection (d) exclusion of a legally separated spouse from the definition of "surviving spouse," and instead held that a legally separated spouse is a "surviving spouse" for the purpose of receiving continuance pension benefits under the County Employees Retirement Law of 1937 (Government Code § 31450 et seq.).

Research References

Forms

California Transactions Forms--Estate Planning § 6:27, Omitted Spouse Statute.
California Transactions Forms--Estate Planning § 6:30, Effect Of Dissolution or Annulment Of Marriage.

Treatises and Practice Aids

Witkin, California Summary 10th Husband and Wife § 147, Effect Of Judgment.
Witkin, California Summary 10th Wills and Probate § 49, Persons and Entities.
Witkin, California Summary 10th Wills and Probate § 119, Amendment and Revocation.
Witkin, California Summary 10th Wills and Probate § 177, Dissolution or Annulment Of Marriage.
Witkin, California Summary 10th Wills and Probate § 318, Transfer to Former Spouse.
Witkin, California Summary 10th Wills and Probate § 319, Joint Tenancy With Former Spouse.

Division 2

GENERAL PROVISIONS

Part 1

EFFECT OF DEATH OF MARRIED PERSON ON COMMUNITY AND QUASI–COMMUNITY PROPERTY

Law Revision Commission Comments

1990 Enactment

This part supersedes Part 1 (commencing with Section 100) of Division 2 of the repealed Probate Code. The superseded part was enacted upon recommendation of the California Law Revision Commission. See Tentative Recommendation Relating to Wills and Intestate Succession, 16 Cal.L.Revision Comm'n Reports 2301 (1982). See also Report of Senate Committee on Judiciary on Assembly Bills 25 and 68, 17 Cal.L.Revision Comm'n Reports 867, 868–69 (1984). Technical and substantive revisions were made as a result of a subsequent recommendation. See Recommendation Relating to Revision of Wills and Intestate Succession Law, 17 Cal.L.Revision Comm'n Reports 537 (1984). See also Communication of Law Revision Commission Concerning Assembly Bill 2290, 18 Cal.L.Revision Comm'n Reports 77, 79–84 (1986). [20 Cal.L.Rev.Comm.Reports 1001 (1990)].

§ 100. Community property

(a) Upon the death of a person who is married or in a registered domestic partnership, one-half of the community property belongs to the surviving spouse and the other one-half belongs to the decedent.

(b) Notwithstanding subdivision (a), spouses may agree in writing to divide their community property on the basis of a non pro rata division of the aggregate value of the community property or on the basis of a division of each individual item or asset of community property, or partly on each basis. Nothing in this subdivision shall be construed to require this written agreement in order to permit or recognize a non pro rata division of community property. *(Stats.1990, c. 79 (A.B.759), § 14, operative July 1, 1991. Amended by Stats. 1998, c. 682 (A.B.2069), § 2; Stats.2016, c. 50 (S.B.1005), § 79, eff. Jan. 1, 2017.)*

Law Revision Commission Comments

1990 Enactment

Section 100 continues Section 100 of the repealed Probate Code without change. The decedent's half of the community property is subject to the testamentary disposition of the decedent (Section 6101) and, in the absence of testamentary disposition, goes to the surviving spouse (Section 6401). But see Section 103 (effect on community property where married persons die simultaneously). As to the allocation of debts between the estate and the surviving spouse, see Sections 11440–11446. As to the liability of the surviving spouse for debts of the deceased spouse chargeable against community property, see Sections 13550–13554. See also Sections 28 ("community property" defined), 104 (community property held in revocable trust). This part applies only where the decedent died on or after January 1, 1985. See Section 105. As to the application of any amendments made after that date, see Section 3.

Background on Section 100 of Repealed Code

Section 100 was added by 1983 Cal.Stat. ch. 842 § 22. Section 100 restated a portion of former Probate Code Section 201 (repealed by 1983 Cal.Stat. ch. 842 § 19) without substantive change. For background on the provisions of this part, see the Comment to this part under the part heading. [20 Cal.L.Rev.Comm.Reports 1001 (1990)].

Commentary

Despite the plain language of subsection (a), a decedent may explicitly or implicitly force his surviving spouse to elect between her community property rights and her claims under the decedent's will. *Estate of Dunphy, 147 Cal. 95, 81 P. 315 (1905)*; *Estate of Wolfe, 48 Cal.2d. 570, 311 P.2d 476 (1957)*. Contrast Section 142 which requires a signed writing for a waiver of community property rights. When a surviving spouse asserts community property rights, paragraph (b) facilitates agreements for a non pro-rata division of community property.

A testator is presumed to know that his testamentary power does not extend to his spouse's share of the community property, and he is presumed to intend to dispose of his share only. Thus, absent indication to the contrary, the surviving spouse may assert both her Section 100 community property rights and her claims under the decedent spouse's will. *Estate of Prager, 166 Cal. 450, 137 P.37 (1913)*; *Estate of Richter, 12 Cal.App.4th 1361, 16 Cal.Rptr.2d 108 (1993)*. The survivor is required to elect between the two only when decedent's will clearly shows that the decedent intended that the testamentary gifts to the surviving spouse be taken in lieu of her community property interests. In such case, an election is required in order to effectuate the decedent's testamentary plan. *Estate of Prager*, supra. The will may expressly require an election. *Dunphy*, supra. Or the will may implicitly require an election, as when the decedent's will purports to exercise complete dominion over property that is in fact community property. For example, the decedent may assert, albeit erroneously, that certain community property is his separate property. In such case, putting the survivor to an election effectively enforces the decedent's legal misunderstanding. See, for example, *In re Stewart, 74 Cal. 98, 103, 15 P. 445 (1887)*; *Estate of Kennedy, 135 Cal.App.3d 676, 681, 185 Cal.Rptr. 540 (1982)*; *Wolfe*, supra; *Estate of Moore, 62 Cal.App. 265, 268–269, 216 P. 981 (1923)*.

See also Probate Code Sections 21300–21322, regulating "no contest" clauses, that is, provisions in an instrument penalizing any beneficiary who brings a legal proceeding to upset the instrument or a provision thereof. In *Burch v. George, 7 Cal.4th 246, 866 P.2d 92, 27 Cal.Rptr.2d 165 (1994)*, a sharply divided Supreme Court purported to hold that a no contest clause in decedent husband's trust forced his surviving wife to an election either to take the testamentary gifts under the trust or to assert her community property rights in the trust property. The dissenting justices argued that the assertion of community property rights is not an attack upon an instrument, but rather an assertion of independent ownership rights. Yet close reading of *Burch v. George* suggests that it is fundamentally an election case. Before his death, decedent established an inter vivos trust with testamentary provisions. In the preliminary recitals, he stated that all property placed in the trust was entirely his separate property, even though some of it was at least arguably community property. His surviving spouse sought to determine whether her assertion of community property rights in the trust property would violate the no contest clause. The majority concluded that it would because the separate property recital of decedent's trust together with the fact that he placed community property in the trust implicitly put the surviving spouse to an election. Thus, even in the absence of a no contest clause, the majority's conclusion would seem to compel a finding that the survivor was put to an election, that is, that she could either claim her community property rights or she could take decedent's gifts under the trust, but she could not do both. In this sense, the discussion of the no contest clause is gratuitous and unnecessary. Thus *Burch v. George* should be read to hold, rather narrowly, that when a surviving spouse is already forced to an election based on the other facts of the case, a no contest clause will trigger a forfeiture of testamentary gifts to the survivor if she initiates a proceeding to assert her community property rights. Compare *Estate of Richter, 12 Cal.App.4th 1361, 16 Cal.Rptr.2d 108 (1993)* (widow's proposed petition to determine the community property assets in deceased husband's estate would not violate no contest clause of husband's will when will did not purport to dispose of particular assets or of community property, but instead referred only to "residue of my estate"). For further discussion of the interpretation of no contest clauses, see the Commentary to Probate Code Section 21303.

Research References

Forms

California Transactions Forms--Estate Planning § 1:21, Severing Joint Tenancies in Real Property.
California Transactions Forms--Estate Planning § 1:22, Community Property.
California Transactions Forms--Estate Planning § 1:23, Aggregate or Asset-By-Asset Division Of Community Property.
California Transactions Forms--Estate Planning § 1:25, Joint Tenancy or Community Property Treatment Of Property in Revocable Trust.
California Transactions Forms--Estate Planning § 1:26, Quasi-Community Property; Separate Property.
California Transactions Forms--Estate Planning § 1:77, Matters to Consider Regarding Property Distribution.
California Transactions Forms--Estate Planning § 1:81, Memorandum to Married Clients Regarding Property Characterization.
California Transactions Forms--Estate Planning § 10:4, Community Property.
California Transactions Forms--Estate Planning § 20:4, Separate and Community Property.
California Transactions Forms--Estate Planning § 3:75, Community Property.
California Transactions Forms--Estate Planning § 6:27, Omitted Spouse Statute.
California Transactions Forms--Estate Planning § 10:18, Property Passing to Spouse.
California Transactions Forms--Estate Planning § 18:32, Non Pro Rata Allocation Of Community Property.
California Transactions Forms--Estate Planning § 19:16, Overview.
California Transactions Forms--Estate Planning § 19:18, Community Property.
California Transactions Forms--Estate Planning § 9:164, Property Agreement to Permit Non Pro Rata Division Of Community Property.
California Transactions Forms--Estate Planning § 9:193, Property Agreement for Aggregate Theory Of Community Property.

Treatises and Practice Aids

Witkin, California Summary 10th Community Property § 253, Where California Law Applies.
Witkin, California Summary 10th Wills and Probate § 76, Surviving Spouse's Share in Community and Quasi-Community Property.
Witkin, California Summary 10th Wills and Probate § 103, Testamentary Disposition Of Property.
Witkin, California Summary 10th Wills and Probate § 265, Disposition.
Witkin, California Summary 10th Wills and Probate § 321, Case Law Development.
Witkin, California Summary 10th Wills and Probate § 820, Survivor's Election.
Witkin, California Summary 10th Wills and Probate § 824, Property Of Deceased Spouse.
Witkin, California Summary 10th Wills and Probate § 829, Nature Of Proceeding.
Witkin, California Summary 10th Wills and Probate § 830, Petition.
Witkin, California Summary 10th Wills and Probate § 832, Orders.

§ 101. Quasi-community property

(a) Upon the death of a person who is married or in a registered domestic partnership, and is domiciled in this state, one-half of the decedent's quasi-community property belongs to the surviving spouse and the other one-half belongs to the decedent.

(b) Notwithstanding subdivision (a), spouses may agree in writing to divide their quasi-community property on the basis of a non pro rata division of the aggregate value of the quasi-community property, or on the basis of a division of each individual item or asset of quasi-community property, or partly on each basis. Nothing in this subdivision shall be construed to require this written agreement in order to permit or recognize a non pro rata division of quasi-community property. *(Stats.1990, c. 79 (A.B.759), § 14, operative July 1, 1991. Amended by Stats.1998, c. 682 (A.B.2069), § 3; Stats.2016, c. 50 (S.B.1005), § 80, eff. Jan. 1, 2017.)*

Law Revision Commission Comments

1990 Enactment

Section 101 continues Section 101 of the repealed Probate Code without change. The decedent's half of the quasi-community property is subject to the testamentary disposition of the decedent (Section 6101) and, in the absence of testamentary disposition, goes to the surviving spouse (Section 6401). But see Section 103 (effect on quasi-community property where married persons die simultaneously). See also Section 66 ("quasi-community property" defined). As to the allocation of debts between the estate and the surviving spouse, see Sections 11440–11446. As to the liability of the surviving spouse for debts of the deceased spouse chargeable against quasi-community property, see Sections 13550–13554. This part applies only where the decedent died on or after January 1, 1985. See Section 105. As to the application of any amendments made after that date, see Section 3.

The California Law Revision Commission made a series of recommendations concerning the subject matter of this section. See Recommendation and Study Relating to Rights of Surviving Spouse in Property Acquired by Decedent While Domiciled Elsewhere, 1 Cal.L.Revision Comm'n Reports E–1 (1957); Recommendation and Study Relating to Inter Vivos Marital Property Rights in Property Acquired While Domiciled Elsewhere, 3 Cal.L.Revision Comm'n Reports I–1 (1961); Recommendation Relating to Quasi–Community Property, 9 Cal.L.Revision Comm'n Reports 113 (1969).

Background on Section 101 of Repealed Code

Section 101 was added by 1983 Cal.Stat. ch. 842 § 22. Section 101 restated a portion of former Probate Code Section 201.5 (repealed by

1983 Cal.Stat. ch. 842 § 19) without substantive change. For background on the provisions of this part, see the Comment to this part under the part heading. [20 Cal.L.Rev.Comm.Reports 1001 (1990)].

Research References

Forms

California Transactions Forms--Estate Planning § 1:25, Joint Tenancy or Community Property Treatment Of Property in Revocable Trust.
California Transactions Forms--Estate Planning § 1:26, Quasi-Community Property; Separate Property.
California Transactions Forms--Estate Planning § 1:77, Matters to Consider Regarding Property Distribution.
California Transactions Forms--Estate Planning § 1:81, Memorandum to Married Clients Regarding Property Characterization.
California Transactions Forms--Estate Planning § 10:5, Quasi-Community Property.
California Transactions Forms--Estate Planning § 20:4, Separate and Community Property.
California Transactions Forms--Estate Planning § 3:75, Community Property.
California Transactions Forms--Estate Planning § 6:27, Omitted Spouse Statute.
California Transactions Forms--Estate Planning § 18:32, Non Pro Rata Allocation Of Community Property.
California Transactions Forms--Estate Planning § 19:16, Overview.
California Transactions Forms--Estate Planning § 19:18, Community Property.
California Transactions Forms--Estate Planning § 19:19, Quasi-Community Property.

Treatises and Practice Aids

Witkin, California Summary 10th Community Property § 252, Former Law and Corrective Legislation.
Witkin, California Summary 10th Community Property § 253, Where California Law Applies.
Witkin, California Summary 10th Community Property § 255, Restoration Of Property Transferred Inter Vivos.
Witkin, California Summary 10th Wills and Probate § 50, Legal and Financial Terms.
Witkin, California Summary 10th Wills and Probate § 74, in General.
Witkin, California Summary 10th Wills and Probate § 76, Surviving Spouse's Share in Community and Quasi-Community Property.
Witkin, California Summary 10th Wills and Probate § 103, Testamentary Disposition Of Property.
Witkin, California Summary 10th Wills and Probate § 265, Disposition.
Witkin, California Summary 10th Wills and Probate § 267, Restoration Of Quasi-Community Property.
Witkin, California Summary 10th Wills and Probate § 295, Wills, Trusts, and Intestate Succession.
Witkin, California Summary 10th Wills and Probate § 321, Case Law Development.
Witkin, California Summary 10th Wills and Probate § 404, Title to Decedent's Property.
Witkin, California Summary 10th Wills and Probate § 405, Probate and Administration.
Witkin, California Summary 10th Wills and Probate § 820, Survivor's Election.
Witkin, California Summary 10th Wills and Probate § 824, Property Of Deceased Spouse.
Witkin, California Summary 10th Wills and Probate § 829, Nature Of Proceeding.
Witkin, California Summary 10th Wills and Probate § 830, Petition.
Witkin, California Summary 10th Wills and Probate § 832, Orders.
Witkin, California Summary 10th Wills and Probate § 901, Former Law Of Guardianship.

§ 102. Transfer of quasi-community property; restoration of decedent's estate; requirements

(a) The decedent's surviving spouse may require the transferee of property in which the surviving spouse had an expectancy under Section 101 at the time of the transfer to restore to the decedent's estate one-half of the property if the transferee retains the property or, if not, one-half of its proceeds or, if none, one-half of its value at the time of transfer, if all of the following requirements are satisfied:

(1) The decedent died domiciled in this state.

(2) The decedent made a transfer of the property to a person other than the surviving spouse without receiving in exchange a consideration of substantial value and without the written consent or joinder of the surviving spouse.

(3) The transfer is any of the following types:

(A) A transfer under which the decedent retained at the time of death the possession or enjoyment of, or the right to income from, the property.

(B) A transfer to the extent that the decedent retained at the time of death a power, either alone or in conjunction with any other person, to revoke or to consume, invade, or dispose of the principal for the decedent's own benefit.

(C) A transfer whereby property is held at the time of the decedent's death by the decedent and another with right of survivorship.

(b) Nothing in this section requires a transferee to restore to the decedent's estate any life insurance, accident insurance, joint annuity, or pension payable to a person other than the surviving spouse.

(c) All property restored to the decedent's estate under this section belongs to the surviving spouse pursuant to Section 101 as though the transfer had not been made. *(Stats.1990, c. 79 (A.B.759), § 14, operative July 1, 1991.)*

Law Revision Commission Comments

1990 Enactment

Section 102 continues Section 102 of the repealed Probate Code without change. This section provides that the property shall be restored to the decedent's estate rather than that the surviving spouse may recover it directly from the transferee. This is to make the property available to creditors of the decedent to the extent that it would have been available to them if no inter vivos transfer had been made.

The provision of Section 102 that only one-half of the property transferred is to be restored is applied when the decedent dies intestate as well as when the decedent dies testate. This is because the decedent has manifested an intention to deprive the surviving spouse of the property. The intent of the intestate decedent should be given effect to the extent he or she could have accomplished the same result by will.

Paragraph (2) of subdivision (a) provides that a transfer may be set aside only if the decedent made it without receiving in exchange a consideration of "substantial" value. Where the consideration is not substantial and the transfer is set aside, no provision is made for return of the insubstantial consideration given by the transferee when property transferred is required to be restored. It is not expected that a transfer will be set aside under the statute if the transferee gave a consideration equal to one-half or more of the value of the property received. Thus, in cases in which the transfer is set aside, the one-half which the transferee keeps will be at least equal in value to any consideration given. Paragraph (3) of subdivision (a) is drawn from Uniform Probate Code Section 2–202(1) (1987) and Idaho Code Section 15–2–202 (1979). Subdivision (b) is drawn from a portion of Uniform Probate Code Section 2–202 (1987). As to the construction of provisions drawn from uniform acts, see Section 2.

Subdivision (c) provides that all of the property restored to the estate belongs to the surviving spouse pursuant to Section 101. Such property is, in effect, the one-half which the surviving spouse could have claimed against the decedent's will. The one-half which the transferee is permitted to retain is, in effect, the one-half which the decedent could have given to the transferee by will. The surviving spouse is entitled to all of the first half.

Section 102 is limited in application to transfers made at a time when the surviving spouse has an expectancy under Section 101—i.e., at a time when the transferor is domiciled in California. This is to avoid the application of the statute to transfers made before the transferor moved here, when the transferor could not reasonably have anticipated that the transfer would later be subjected to California law.

This part applies only where the decedent died on or after January 1, 1985. See Section 105. As to the application of any amendments made after that date, see Section 3.

The California Law Revision Commission made a recommendation which resulted in the enactment of a statutory provision (former Probate Code Section 201.8) on the subject matter of this section. See Recommendation and Study Relating to Rights of Surviving Spouse in Property Acquired by Decedent While Domiciled Elsewhere, 1 Cal.L.Revision Comm'n Reports E–1 (1957). With respect to Section 201.8, see the discussion, infra, under "Background on Section 102 of Repealed Code."

Background on Section 102 of Repealed Code

Section 102 was added by 1983 Cal.Stat. ch. 842 § 22. Subdivisions (a) and (b) superseded the first sentence of former Probate Code Section 201.8 (repealed by 1983 Cal.Stat. ch. 842 § 19). Subdivision (c) restated the last sentence of former Section 201.8 without substantive change.

The second sentence of former Section 201.8 which required the surviving spouse to elect to take under or against the decedent's will was not continued. Under the law as revised in 1983, the rule for quasi-community property was the same as for community property: The surviving spouse no longer was forced to an election unless the decedent's will expressly so provides or unless such a requirement should be implied to avoid thwarting the testator's apparent intent. See 7 B. Witkin, Summary of California Law Wills and Probate §§ 21–22, at 5542–44 (8th ed. 1974).

Paragraph (3) of subdivision (a) of Section 102 replaced the provision of former Probate Code Section 201.8 that required as a condition of recapture that the decedent had a "substantial quantum of ownership or control of the property at death."

For background on the provisions of this part, see the Comment to this part under the part heading. [20 Cal.L.Rev.Comm.Reports 1001 (1990)].

Research References

Forms

California Transactions Forms--Estate Planning § 1:25, Joint Tenancy or Community Property Treatment Of Property in Revocable Trust.

California Transactions Forms--Estate Planning § 1:26, Quasi-Community Property; Separate Property.

California Transactions Forms--Estate Planning § 1:77, Matters to Consider Regarding Property Distribution.

Treatises and Practice Aids

Witkin, California Summary 10th Community Property § 252, Former Law and Corrective Legislation.

Witkin, California Summary 10th Community Property § 255, Restoration Of Property Transferred Inter Vivos.

Witkin, California Summary 10th Wills and Probate § 76, Surviving Spouse's Share in Community and Quasi-Community Property.

Witkin, California Summary 10th Wills and Probate § 267, Restoration Of Quasi-Community Property.

Witkin, California Summary 10th Wills and Probate § 295, Wills, Trusts, and Intestate Succession.

Witkin, California Summary 10th Wills and Probate § 405, Probate and Administration.

§ 103. Simultaneous death; community or quasi-community property

Except as provided by Section 224, if spouses die leaving community or quasi-community property and it cannot be established by clear and convincing evidence that one spouse survived the other:

(a) One-half of the community property and one-half of the quasi-community property shall be administered or distributed, or otherwise dealt with, as if one spouse had survived and as if that one-half belonged to that spouse.

(b) The other one-half of the community property and the other one-half of the quasi-community property shall be administered or distributed, or otherwise dealt with, as if the other spouse had survived and as if that one-half belonged to that spouse. *(Stats.1990, c. 79 (A.B.759), § 14, operative July 1, 1991. Amended by Stats.2016, c. 50 (S.B.1005), § 81, eff. Jan. 1, 2017.)*

Law Revision Commission Comments

1990 Enactment

Section 103 continues Section 103 of the repealed Probate Code without substantive change. The introductory clause recognizes that Section 224 governs the disposition of life or accident insurance benefits where one spouse is the insured and the other the beneficiary, even if the source of the insurance premiums was community property. This section, insofar as it is the same in substance as a provision of the Uniform Simultaneous Death Act (1953), is to be so construed and interpreted as to effectuate the general purpose to make uniform the law in those states which enact that act. See Section 2 (general provision relating to construction of provisions drawn from uniform acts). See also Sections 230–234 (proceeding to determine whether one spouse survived the other). This part applies only where the decedent died on or after January 1, 1985. See Section 105. As to the application of any amendments made after that date, see Section 3.

Background on Section 103 of Repealed Code

Section 103 was added by 1983 Cal.Stat. ch. 842 § 22. The section superseded the first paragraph of former Probate Code Section 296.4 (repealed by 1983 Cal.Stat. ch. 842 § 20) and extended to quasi-community property the rule formerly applicable only to community property. For background on the provisions of this part, see the Comment to this part under the part heading. [20 Cal.L.Rev.Comm.Reports 1001 (1990)].

Research References

Forms

California Transactions Forms--Estate Planning § 6:23, Simultaneous Death.

Treatises and Practice Aids

Witkin, California Summary 10th Wills and Probate § 76, Surviving Spouse's Share in Community and Quasi-Community Property.
Witkin, California Summary 10th Wills and Probate § 79, Issue Of Decedent.
Witkin, California Summary 10th Wills and Probate § 80, Parents or Issue Of Parents.
Witkin, California Summary 10th Wills and Probate § 81, Grandparents or Issue Of Grandparents.
Witkin, California Summary 10th Wills and Probate § 265, Disposition.
Witkin, California Summary 10th Wills and Probate § 289, Revised Statute.
Witkin, California Summary 10th Wills and Probate § 290, Rules Of Survival.

Part 2

SURVIVING SPOUSE'S RIGHT IN CALIFORNIA REAL PROPERTY OF NONDOMICILIARY DECEDENT

Law Revision Commission Comments

1990 Enactment

This part supersedes Part 2 (commencing with Section 120) of Division 2 of the repealed Probate Code. The superseded part was enacted upon recommendation of the California Law Revision Commission. See Tentative Recommendation Relating to Wills and Intestate Succession, 16 Cal.L.Revision Comm'n Reports 2301 (1982). [20 Cal.L.Rev.Comm.Reports 1001 (1990)].

§ 120. Nondomiciliary decedent; real property within state; surviving spouse's right; effect of will

If a married person dies not domiciled in this state and leaves a valid will disposing of real property in this state which is not the community property of the decedent and the surviving spouse, the surviving spouse has the same right to elect to take a portion of or interest in such property against the will of the decedent as though the property were located in the decedent's domicile at death. *(Stats.1990, c. 79 (A.B.759), § 14, operative July 1, 1991.)*

Law Revision Commission Comments

1990 Enactment

Section 120 continues Section 120 of the repealed Probate Code without substantive change. This section gives the surviving spouse the same protected interest in California as the surviving spouse would have under the law of the decedent's domicile. See also Section 68 ("real property" defined).

The California Law Revision Commission made a recommendation which resulted in the enactment of a statutory provision (former Probate Code Section 201.6, repealed by 1983 Cal.Stat. ch. 842 § 19) on the subject matter of this section. See Recommendation and Study Relating to Rights of Surviving Spouse in Property Acquired by Decedent While Domiciled Elsewhere, 1 Cal.L.Revision Comm'n Reports E–1 (1957).

Background on Section 120 of Repealed Code

Section 120 was added by 1983 Cal.Stat. ch. 842 § 22. The section restated former Probate Code Section 201.6 (repealed by 1983 Cal.Stat. ch. 842 § 19) without substantive change. For background on the provisions of this part, see the Comment to this part under the part heading. [20 Cal.L.Rev.Comm.Reports 1001 (1990)].

Research References

Forms

California Transactions Forms--Estate Planning § 19:16, Overview.
California Transactions Forms--Estate Planning § 19:19, Quasi-Community Property.

Treatises and Practice Aids

Witkin, California Summary 10th Community Property § 1, Community Property System.
Witkin, California Summary 10th Community Property § 252, Former Law and Corrective Legislation.
Witkin, California Summary 10th Community Property § 254, Will Of California Property by Nondomiciled Testator.
Witkin, California Summary 10th Wills and Probate § 74, in General.
Witkin, California Summary 10th Wills and Probate § 272, Surviving Spouse Of Nondomiciliary Decedent.

Part 3

CONTRACTUAL ARRANGEMENTS RELATING TO RIGHTS AT DEATH

Law Revision Commission Comments

1990 Enactment

This part supersedes Part 3 (commencing with Section 140) of Division 2 of the repealed Probate Code. The superseded part was enacted upon recommendation of the California Law Revision Commission. See Tentative Recommendation Relating to Wills and Intestate Succession, 16 Cal.L.Revision Comm'n Reports 2301, 2347–51, 2375–81 (1982). See also Report of Senate Committee on Judiciary on Assembly Bills 25 and 68, 17 Cal.L.Revision Comm'n Reports 867, 869–70 (1984); Communication of Law Revision Commission Concerning Assembly Bill 2290, 18 Cal.L.Revision Comm'n Reports 77, 79–82 (1986). [20 Cal.L.Rev.Comm.Reports 1001 (1990)].

CHAPTER 1. SURVIVING SPOUSE'S WAIVER OF RIGHTS

Application

Limited applicability of Chapter 1 before Jan. 1, 1985, see Probate Code § 147.

§ 140. Waiver

As used in this chapter, "waiver" means a waiver by the surviving spouse of any of the rights listed in subdivision (a) of Section 141, whether signed before or during marriage. *(Stats.1990, c. 79 (A.B.759), § 14, operative July 1, 1991.)*

Law Revision Commission Comments

1990 Enactment

Section 140 continues Section 140 of the repealed Probate Code without change. This chapter has no effect on waivers, agreements, or property settlements made prior to January 1, 1985 (the date this chapter of the repealed Probate Code first became operative). See Section 147. As to the application of any amendments made after that date, see Section 3. As to premarital property agreements, see Section 147 and the Comment thereto.

Background on Section 140 of Repealed Code

Section 140 was a new provision added by 1983 Cal.Stat. ch. 842 § 22 and amended by 1984 Cal.Stat. ch. 892 § 8. The 1984 amendment made a clarifying, nonsubstantive revision. For background on the provisions of this part, see the Comment to this part under the part heading. [20 Cal.L.Rev.Comm.Reports 1001 (1990)].

Research References

Forms

California Transactions Forms--Estate Planning § 6:28, Exceptions to Omitted Spouse Statute.
California Transactions Forms--Estate Planning § 6:99, Omitted Spouse Made Valid Agreement Waiving Right to Share in Decedent's Estate.
California Transactions Forms--Estate Planning § 11:49, Introduction and Definition [Prob C § 140].
California Transactions Forms--Estate Planning § 11:50, Rights Of Surviving Spouse that May be Waived [Prob C § 141].
California Transactions Forms--Estate Planning § 11:51, Requirements.
California Transactions Forms--Estate Planning § 11:52, Enforceability Under Probate Code § 143.
California Transactions Forms--Estate Planning § 11:53, Enforceability Under Probate Code § 144.
California Transactions Forms--Estate Planning § 19:15, Waiver Of Family Protection.

Treatises and Practice Aids

Witkin, California Summary 10th Community Property § 29, Lack Of Independent Counsel.
Witkin, California Summary 10th Wills and Probate § 25, Major Changes.
Witkin, California Summary 10th Wills and Probate § 27, Major Changes.
Witkin, California Summary 10th Wills and Probate § 277, in General.
Witkin, California Summary 10th Wills and Probate § 309, Nature and Scope Of Statute.
Witkin, California Summary 10th Wills and Probate § 322, Nature and Scope Of Statute.
Witkin, California Summary 10th Wills and Probate § 325, Alteration or Revocation.
Witkin, California Summary 10th Wills and Probate § 788, Express Release or Waiver.

§ 141. Rights which may be waived

(a) The right of a surviving spouse to any of the following may be waived in whole or in part by a waiver under this chapter:

(1) Property that would pass from the decedent by intestate succession.

(2) Property that would pass from the decedent by testamentary disposition in a will executed before the waiver.

(3) A probate homestead.

(4) The right to have exempt property set aside.

(5) Family allowance.

(6) The right to have an estate set aside under Chapter 6 (commencing with Section 6600) of Part 3 of Division 6.

(7) The right to elect to take community or quasi-community property against the decedent's will.

(8) The right to take the statutory share of an omitted spouse.

(9) The right to be appointed as the personal representative of the decedent's estate.

(10) An interest in property that is the subject of a nonprobate transfer on death under Part 1 (commencing with Section 5000) of Division 5.

(b) Nothing in this chapter affects or limits the waiver or manner of waiver of rights other than those referred to in subdivision (a), including, but not limited to, the right to property that would pass from the decedent to the surviving spouse by nonprobate transfer upon the death of the decedent, such as the survivorship interest under a joint tenancy, a Totten trust account, or a pay-on-death account. *(Stats.1990, c. 79 (A.B.759), § 14, operative July 1, 1991. Amended by Stats.1992, c. 51 (A.B.1719), § 2.)*

Law Revision Commission Comments

1990 Enactment

Section 141 continues Section 141 of the repealed Probate Code without substantive change. This section is drawn in part from the first sentence of Section 2–204 of the Uniform Probate Code (1987). As to the construction of provisions drawn from uniform acts, see Section 2.

Paragraphs (1) and (2) of subdivision (a) permit waiver of property, interests, or benefits that would pass to the spouse making the waiver by intestate succession or by virtue of a will of the other spouse executed before the waiver.

Paragraphs (3), (4), and (5) are the same in substance as provisions found in Section 2–204 of the Uniform Probate Code (1987) and are consistent with prior California case law. See, e.g., Estate of Howe, 81 Cal.App.2d 95, 183 P.2d 329 (1947) (probate homestead); In re Estate of Fulton, 15 Cal.App.2d 202, 59 P.2d 508 (1936) (exempt property); Estate of Brooks, 28 Cal.2d 748, 171 P.2d 724 (1946) (family allowance). As to the construction of provisions drawn from uniform acts, see Section 2.

Paragraph (6) is consistent with prior California case law. See Soares v. Steidtmann, 130 Cal.App.2d 401, 278 P.2d 953 (1955).

Paragraph (7) is comparable to the provision in Section 2–204 of the Uniform Probate Code (1987) for waiver of the elective share under the Uniform Probate Code. As to the construction of provisions drawn from uniform acts, see Section 2. Paragraph (7) is consistent with prior California case law. See 7 B. Witkin, Summary of California Law Wills and Probate § 20, at 5541 (8th ed. 1974).

Paragraph (8) is included to make clear that a spouse may waive the right to claim as an omitted spouse under Section 6560. Paragraph (9) is consistent with Section 8440 (waiver of right to appointment by executor).

Subdivision (b) makes clear that this chapter applies only to the waiver of the rights listed in subdivision (a). The law applicable to the waiver of other rights is not affected by this chapter. See, e.g., Civil Code §§ 5200–5317. See also Section 80 ("Totten trust account" defined). As to pay-on-death accounts, see also Division 5 (commencing with Section 5100) (multiple-party accounts in financial institutions).

This chapter has no effect on waivers, agreements, or property settlements made prior to January 1, 1985 (the date this chapter of the repealed Probate Code first became operative). See Section 147. As to the application of any amendments made after that date, see Section 3. As to premarital property agreements, see Section 147 and the Comment thereto.

1992 Amendment

Paragraph (10) is added to Section 141(a) for purposes of cross-referencing the provisions on nonprobate transfers. See also Section 5013 (waiver or agreement that affects rights in community property). [21 Cal.L.Rev.Comm.Reports 163 (1991)].

Background on Section 141 of Repealed Code

Section 141 was a new provision added by 1983 Cal.Stat. ch. 842 § 22 and amended by 1987 Cal.Stat. ch. 923 § 19. The 1987 amendment revised a cross-reference to another statute and made other nonsubstantive revisions. For background on the provisions of this part, see the Comment to this part under the part heading. [20 Cal.L.Rev.Comm.Reports 1001 (1990)].

Research References

Forms

California Transactions Forms--Estate Planning § 1:26, Quasi-Community Property; Separate Property.
California Transactions Forms--Estate Planning § 11:50, Rights Of Surviving Spouse that May be Waived [Prob C § 141].
California Transactions Forms--Estate Planning § 11:53, Enforceability Under Probate Code § 144.
California Transactions Forms--Estate Planning § 11:62, Matters to Include in Spousal Waiver.
California Transactions Forms--Estate Planning § 11:72, Spousal Waiver.
California Transactions Forms--Estate Planning § 19:15, Waiver Of Family Protection.
California Transactions Forms--Family Law § 1:27, Complete Agreement.
Nichols Cyclopedia of Legal Forms Annotated § 100:40, Premarital Agreement--Community Property--California.
West's California Code Forms, Family § 1611 Form 1, Premarital Agreement.

Treatises and Practice Aids

Witkin, California Summary 10th Contracts § 680, Other Rights.
Witkin, California Summary 10th Wills and Probate § 277, in General.
Witkin, California Summary 10th Wills and Probate § 322, Nature and Scope Of Statute.
Witkin, California Summary 10th Wills and Probate § 788, Express Release or Waiver.

§ 142. Requirement of writing; enforceability; defenses

(a) A waiver under this chapter shall be in writing and shall be signed by the surviving spouse.

(b) Subject to subdivision (c), a waiver under this chapter is enforceable only if it satisfies the requirements of subdivision (a) and is enforceable under either Section 143 or Section 144.

(c) Enforcement of the waiver against the surviving spouse is subject to the same defenses as enforcement of a contract, except that:

(1) Lack of consideration is not a defense to enforcement of the waiver.

(2) A minor intending to marry may make a waiver under this chapter as if married, but the waiver becomes effective only upon the marriage. *(Stats.1990, c. 79 (A.B.759), § 14, operative July 1, 1991.)*

Law Revision Commission Comments

1990 Enactment

Section 142 continues Section 142 of the repealed Probate Code without change. Subdivision (a) requires that a waiver be in writing and be signed by the surviving spouse in order to be effective under this chapter. See also Sections 143–145 (enforcement of waiver), 146 (alteration, amendment, or revocation of waiver).

Subdivisions (b) and (c) make clear that enforcement of the waiver is subject to the same defenses as enforcement of a contract, but lack of consideration is not a defense and a minor intending to marry is treated as an emancipated minor (Civil Code § 63). The surviving spouse can raise the defense of lack of capacity to contract. See Civil Code § 1556 (unsound mind or deprived of civil rights). The defense of lack of consent because of duress, menace, fraud, undue influence, or mistake (Civil Code §§ 1565–1579) also is available. But see the Comment to Section 143.

This chapter has no effect on waivers, agreements, or property settlements made prior to January 1, 1985 (the date this chapter of the repealed Probate Code first became operative). See Section 147. As to the application of any amendments made after that date, see Section 3. As to premarital property agreements, see Section 147 and the Comment thereto.

Background on Section 142 of Repealed Code

Section 142 was a new provision added by 1983 Cal.Stat. ch. 842 § 22 and amended by 1984 Cal.Stat. ch. 892 § 9. Subdivision (a) was enacted in 1983; subdivisions (b) and (c) were added to Section 142 by the 1984 amendment. For background on the provisions of this part, see the Comment to this part under the part heading. [20 Cal.L.Rev.Comm.Reports 1001 (1990)].

Commentary

In re Estate of Will, 170 Cal.App.4th 902, 88 Cal.Rptr.3d 502 (2009), review denied, held that although a premarital agreement did not satisfy current Family Code section 1615 (c), it was independently enforceable as a waiver of inheritance rights when it satisfied Probate Code sections 140–147, which set out the Probate Code requirements for an enforceable surviving spouse's waiver of death rights. Thus a surviving wife, who married decedent-husband after he had written his final will, was barred from claiming that she was an "omitted spouse" under Probate Code section 21611(c).

Research References

Forms

California Transactions Forms--Estate Planning § 6:28, Exceptions to Omitted Spouse Statute.
California Transactions Forms--Estate Planning § 11:51, Requirements.
California Transactions Forms--Estate Planning § 19:15, Waiver Of Family Protection.

Treatises and Practice Aids

Witkin, California Summary 10th Wills and Probate § 323, Requisites and Defenses.

Witkin, California Summary 10th Wills and Probate § 324, Enforcement.

§ 143. Enforceability

(a) Subject to Section 142, a waiver is enforceable under this section unless the surviving spouse proves either of the following:

(1) A fair and reasonable disclosure of the property or financial obligations of the decedent was not provided to the surviving spouse prior to the signing of the waiver unless the surviving spouse waived such a fair and reasonable disclosure after advice by independent legal counsel.

(2) The surviving spouse was not represented by independent legal counsel at the time of signing of the waiver.

(b) Subdivision (b) of Section 721 of the Family Code does not apply if the waiver is enforceable under this section. *(Stats.1990, c. 79 (A.B.759), § 14, operative July 1, 1991. Amended by Stats.1992, c. 163 (A.B.2641), § 120, operative Jan. 1, 1994.)*

Law Revision Commission Comments

1990 Enactment

Section 143 continues Section 143 of the repealed Probate Code without change. This section establishes the basic standards of enforceability for a waiver.

The court shall enforce the waiver unless the surviving spouse proves either (or both) of the following:

(1) The surviving spouse was not provided a fair and reasonable disclosure of property (absent a waiver of such disclosure after advice by independent legal counsel).

(2) The surviving spouse was not represented by independent legal counsel at the time of execution.

By satisfying the conditions of disclosure and independent counsel, the parties can have certainty that their affairs will be governed in an agreed upon manner. If these conditions are not satisfied (for example, counsel may not have been sought at all or the surviving spouse may not have been separately represented), a waiver may still be enforceable under Section 144 (waiver enforceable in discretion of court).

The disclosure required under subdivision (a)(1) includes a disclosure both of the property and of the financial obligations of the decedent. Information concerning financial obligations may be important in determining whether the rights described in Section 141 should be waived.

The introductory clause of Section 143 makes clear that enforcement of a waiver under Section 143 is subject to the same defenses as enforcement of a contract. See Section 142(c). However, the requirement of representation by independent legal counsel and disclosure or waiver of disclosure on the advice of independent legal counsel should permit enforcement of the waiver against a claim of undue influence, duress, or mistake, except where the surviving spouse lacked sound mind or there was some type of duress, mistake, or fraud that the independent counsel and disclosure requirements do not protect against. Thus, parties who want more assurance that the waiver is enforceable should obtain independent legal counsel despite the added expense. See Rothschild, Antenuptial and Postnuptial Agreements, in 2 California Marital Dissolution Practice § 29.2, at 1174–75, § 29.4, at 1176–77 (Cal.Cont.Ed.Bar 1983); Wolfe & Hellman, Handling Surviving Spouse's Share of Marital Property, in California Will Drafting Practice §§ 5.31–5.33, at 205–07 (Cal.Cont.Ed.Bar 1982). However, even if the requirements of Section 143 are not satisfied, the waiver may be enforceable under Section 144.

Subdivision (b) makes clear that the fiduciary standards normally applicable to spouses pursuant to Civil Code Section 5103 do not apply if the waiver is enforceable under Section 143.

This chapter has no effect on waivers, agreements, or property settlements made prior to January 1, 1985 (the date this chapter of the repealed Probate Code first became operative). See Section 147. As to the application of any amendments made after that date, see Section 3. As to premarital property agreements, see Section 147 and the Comment thereto.

1992 Amendment

Subdivision (b) of Section 143 is amended to substitute a reference to the Family Code provision that replaced former Civil Code Section 5103. [22 Cal.L.Rev.Comm.Reports 1 (1992)].

Background on Section 143 of Repealed Code

Section 143 was a new provision added by 1983 Cal.Stat. ch. 842 § 22 and amended by 1984 Cal.Stat. ch. 892 § 10. The 1984 amendment made substantive and clarifying revisions. For background on the provisions of this part, see the Comment to this part under the part heading. [20 Cal.L.Rev.Comm.Reports 1001 (1990)].

Commentary

In re Estate of Will, 170 Cal.App.4th 902, 88 Cal.Rptr.3d 502 (2009), review denied, held that although a premarital agreement did not satisfy current Family Code section 1615 (c), it was independently enforceable as a waiver of inheritance rights when it satisfied Probate Code sections 140–147, which set out the Probate Code requirements for an enforceable surviving spouse's waiver of death rights. Thus a surviving wife, who married decedent-husband after he had written his final will, was barred from claiming that she was an "omitted spouse" under Probate Code section 21611(c).

Research References

Forms

California Transactions Forms--Estate Planning § 11:51, Requirements.

California Transactions Forms--Estate Planning § 11:52, Enforceability Under Probate Code § 143.

California Transactions Forms--Estate Planning § 19:15, Waiver Of Family Protection.

Treatises and Practice Aids

Witkin, California Summary 10th Community Property § 133, Statutory Requirement.

Witkin, California Summary 10th Husband and Wife § 39, in General.

Witkin, California Summary 10th Wills and Probate § 323, Requisites and Defenses.

Witkin, California Summary 10th Wills and Probate § 324, Enforcement.

Witkin, California Summary 10th Wills and Probate § 788, Express Release or Waiver.

§ 144. Enforceability under certain circumstances

(a) Except as provided in subdivision (b), subject to Section 142, a waiver is enforceable under this section if the court determines either of the following:

(1) The waiver at the time of signing made a fair and reasonable disposition of the rights of the surviving spouse.

(2) The surviving spouse had, or reasonably should have had, an adequate knowledge of the property and financial obligations of the decedent and the decedent did not violate the duty imposed by subdivision (b) of Section 721 of the Family Code.

(b) If, after considering all relevant facts and circumstances, the court finds that enforcement of the waiver pursuant to subdivision (a) would be unconscionable under the circumstances existing at the time enforcement is sought, the court may refuse to enforce the waiver, enforce the remainder of the waiver without the unconscionable provisions, or limit the application of the unconscionable provisions to avoid an unconscionable result.

(c) Except as provided in paragraph (2) of subdivision (a), subdivision (b) of Section 721 of the Family Code does not apply if the waiver is enforceable under this section. *(Stats. 1990, c. 79 (A.B.759), § 14, operative July 1, 1991. Amended by Stats.1992, c. 163 (A.B.2641), § 121, operative Jan. 1, 1994.)*

Law Revision Commission Comments

1990 Enactment

Section 144 continues Section 144 of the repealed Probate Code without change.

Under subdivision (a), a waiver that is not enforceable pursuant to Section 143 may be enforceable if it is shown that the waiver at the time of execution made a fair and reasonable disposition of the rights of the surviving spouse or the surviving spouse had, or reasonably should have had, an adequate knowledge of the property and the financial obligations of the other spouse.

Subdivision (b) provides a "safety valve" from the liberal standards of enforceability provided by subdivision (a). It permits the court to refuse to enforce all or a portion of the waiver if the court finds that enforcement would be "unconscionable" under the circumstances existing at the time enforcement is sought. Satisfaction of the standards of enforceability provided by subdivision (a) should insure in the vast majority of cases that the waiver was fairly made and properly enforceable. However, in the exceptional case, circumstances may have changed in a way that neither party may have contemplated and enforcement of the waiver in its entirety would now be unconscionable. In short, subdivision (b) provides a measure of flexibility. It should be emphasized, however, that this subdivision is not intended to apply in any but the extraordinary case and never applies where the conditions of Section 143 are met.

Subdivision (a)(2) and subdivision (c) of Section 144 make clear the extent to which the fiduciary standards normally applicable to spouses pursuant to Civil Code Section 5103 apply when the waiver is sought to be enforced under Section 144. See also Wolfe & Hellman, Handling Surviving Spouse's Share of Marital Property, in California Will Drafting Practice §§ 5.31–5.32, at 205–06 (Cal. Cont.Ed.Bar 1982).

The reference to Section 142 in the introductory clause of subdivision (a) makes clear that enforcement of the waiver against the surviving spouse is subject to the same defenses as enforcement of a contract. See the Comments to Sections 142 and 143.

This chapter has no effect on waivers, agreements, or property settlements made prior to January 1, 1985 (the date this chapter of the repealed Probate Code first became operative). See Section 147. As to the application of any amendments made after that date, see Section 3. As to premarital property agreements, see Section 147 and the Comment thereto.

1992 Amendment

Subdivisions (a)(2) and (c) of Section 144 are amended to substitute references to the Family Code provision that replaced former Civil Code Section 5103. [22 Cal.L.Rev.Comm.Reports 1 (1992)].

Background on Section 144 of Repealed Code

Section 144 was a new provision added by 1983 Cal.Stat. ch. 842 § 22 and amended by 1984 Cal.Stat. ch. 892 § 11. The 1984 amendment made substantive and clarifying revisions. For background on the provisions of this part, see the Comment to this part under the part heading. [20 Cal.L.Rev.Comm.Reports (1990)].

Commentary

In re Estate of Will, 170 Cal.App.4th 902, 88 Cal.Rptr.3d 502 (2009), review denied, held that although a premarital agreement did not satisfy current Family Code section 1615 (c), it was independently enforceable as a waiver of inheritance rights when it satisfied Probate Code sections 140–147, which set out the Probate Code requirements for an enforceable surviving spouse's waiver of death rights. Thus a surviving wife, who married decedent-husband after he had written his final will, was barred from claiming that she was an "omitted spouse" under Probate Code section 21611(c).

Research References

Forms

California Transactions Forms--Estate Planning § 11:51, Requirements.

California Transactions Forms--Estate Planning § 11:52, Enforceability Under Probate Code § 143.

California Transactions Forms--Estate Planning § 11:53, Enforceability Under Probate Code § 144.

California Transactions Forms--Estate Planning § 19:15, Waiver Of Family Protection.

Treatises and Practice Aids

Witkin, California Summary 10th Community Property § 133, Statutory Requirement.

Witkin, California Summary 10th Husband and Wife § 39, in General.

Witkin, California Summary 10th Wills and Probate § 323, Requisites and Defenses.

Witkin, California Summary 10th Wills and Probate § 324, Enforcement.

Witkin, California Summary 10th Wills and Probate § 788, Express Release or Waiver.

§ 145. Waiver of "all rights"

Unless the waiver or property settlement provides to the contrary, a waiver under this chapter of "all rights" (or equivalent language) in the property or estate of a present or prospective spouse, or a complete property settlement entered into after or in anticipation of separation or dissolution or annulment of marriage, is a waiver by the spouse of the rights described in subdivision (a) of Section 141. *(Stats. 1990, c. 79 (A.B.759), § 14, operative July 1, 1991.)*

Law Revision Commission Comments

1990 Enactment

Section 145 continues Section 145 of the repealed Probate Code without change. This section is drawn from the second sentence of Section 2–204 of the Uniform Probate Code (1987). As to the construction of provisions drawn from uniform acts, see Section 2. Nothing in Section 145 affects or limits the waiver or manner of waiver of rights other than those mentioned in subdivision (a) of Section 141. See Section 141(b) and the Comment thereto. This chapter has no effect on waivers, agreements, or property settlements made before January 1, 1985 (the date this chapter of the repealed Probate Code first became operative). See Section 147. As to the application of any amendments made after that date, see Section 3. As to the requirements for a property settlement made on or after January 1, 1985, insofar as the settlement affects rights listed in subdivision (a) of Section 141, see Section 147. As to premarital property agreements, see Section 147 and the Comment thereto.

Background on Section 145 of Repealed Code

Section 145 was added by 1983 Cal.Stat. ch. 842 § 22. The section superseded former Probate Code Section 80 (repealed by 1983 Cal.Stat. ch. 842 § 18). For background on the provisions of this part, see the Comment to this part under the part heading. [20 Cal.L.Rev.Comm.Reports 1001 (1990)].

Research References

Forms

California Transactions Forms--Estate Planning § 11:50, Rights Of Surviving Spouse that May be Waived [Prob C § 141].

California Transactions Forms--Estate Planning § 19:15, Waiver Of Family Protection.

Treatises and Practice Aids

Witkin, California Summary 10th Wills and Probate § 322, Nature and Scope Of Statute.

§ 146. Agreement; requirements

(a) As used in this section, "agreement" means a written agreement signed by each spouse or prospective spouse altering, amending, or revoking a waiver under this chapter.

(b) Except as provided in subdivisions (c) and (d) of Section 147, unless the waiver specifically otherwise provides, a waiver under this chapter may not be altered, amended, or revoked except by a subsequent written agreement signed by each spouse or prospective spouse.

(c) Subject to subdivision (d), the agreement is enforceable only if it satisfies the requirements of subdivision (b) and is enforceable under either subdivision (e) or subdivision (f).

(d) Enforcement of the agreement against a party to the agreement is subject to the same defenses as enforcement of any other contract, except that:

(1) Lack of consideration is not a defense to enforcement of the agreement.

(2) A minor intending to marry may enter into the agreement as if married, but the agreement becomes effective only upon the marriage.

(e) Subject to subdivision (d), an agreement is enforceable under this subdivision unless the party to the agreement against whom enforcement is sought proves either of the following:

(1) A fair and reasonable disclosure of the property or financial obligations of the other spouse was not provided to the spouse against whom enforcement is sought prior to the signing of the agreement unless the spouse against whom enforcement is sought waived such a fair and reasonable disclosure after advice by independent legal counsel.

(2) The spouse against whom enforcement is sought was not represented by independent legal counsel at the time of signing of the agreement.

(f) Subject to subdivisions (d) and (g), an agreement is enforceable under this subdivision if the court determines that the agreement at the time of signing made a fair and reasonable disposition of the rights of the spouses.

(g) If, after considering all relevant facts and circumstances, the court finds that enforcement of the agreement pursuant to subdivision (f) would be unconscionable under the circumstances existing at the time enforcement is sought, the court may refuse to enforce the agreement, enforce the remainder of the agreement without the unconscionable provisions, or limit the application of the unconscionable provisions to avoid an unconscionable result.

(h) Subdivision (b) of Section 721 of the Family Code does not apply if the agreement is enforceable under this section. *(Stats.1990, c. 79 (A.B.759), § 14, operative July 1, 1991. Amended by Stats.1992, c. 163 (A.B.2641), § 122, operative Jan. 1, 1994.)*

Law Revision Commission Comments

1990 Enactment

Section 146 continues Section 146 of the repealed Probate Code without change. This section prescribes the conditions that must be satisfied if the agreement to alter, amend, or revoke the waiver is to be enforceable. The provisions of Section 146 are consistent with those provided by Sections 142–144 for a waiver. Under subdivision (b), a waiver expressly may provide, for example, that it is revocable during the lifetime of the other spouse. See also, e.g., Wolfe & Hellman, Handling Surviving Spouse's Share of Marital Property, in California Will Drafting Practice §§ 5.34, 5.36, at 207–09 (Cal. Cont.Ed.Bar 1982).

Nothing in this chapter limits any right one spouse otherwise has to revoke a consent or election to disposition of his or her half of the community or quasi-community property under the will of the other spouse. See Section 147(d). This chapter has no effect on waivers, agreements, or property settlements made prior to January 1, 1985 (the date this chapter of the repealed Probate Code first became operative). See Section 147. As to the application of any amendments made after that date, see Section 3. As to premarital property agreements, see Section 147 and the Comment thereto.

1992 Amendment

Subdivision (h) of Section 146 is amended to substitute a reference to the Family Code provision that replaced former Civil Code Section 5103. [22 Cal.L.Rev.Comm.Reports 1 (1992)].

Background on Section 146 of Repealed Code

Section 146 was added by 1983 Cal.Stat. ch. 842 § 22 and amended by 1984 Cal.Stat. ch. 892 § 12. The section was extensively revised by the 1984 amendment. For background on the provisions of this part, see the Comment to this part under the part heading. [20 Cal.L.Rev.Comm.Reports 1001 (1990)].

Research References

Forms

California Transactions Forms--Estate Planning § 11:54, Revocation and Amendment Of Waiver by Agreement.

California Transactions Forms--Estate Planning § 11:63, Matters to Include in Agreement Revoking Spousal Waiver.

Treatises and Practice Aids

Witkin, California Summary 10th Community Property § 133, Statutory Requirement.

Witkin, California Summary 10th Husband and Wife § 39, in General.

Witkin, California Summary 10th Wills and Probate § 325, Alteration or Revocation.

§ 147. Waiver, agreement or property settlement; validity; validity or effect of premarital property agreement; right to dispose of community or quasi-community property

(a) Subject to subdivisions (c) and (d), a waiver, agreement, or property settlement made after December 31, 1984, is invalid insofar as it affects the rights listed in subdivision (a) of Section 141 unless it satisfies the requirements of this chapter.

(b) Nothing in this chapter affects the validity or effect of any waiver, agreement, or property settlement made prior to January 1, 1985, and the validity and effect of such waiver, agreement, or property settlement shall continue to be determined by the law applicable to the waiver, agreement, or settlement prior to January 1, 1985.

(c) Nothing in this chapter affects the validity or effect of any premarital property agreement, whether made prior to, on, or after January 1, 1985, insofar as the premarital property agreement affects the rights listed in subdivision (a) of Section 141, and the validity and effect of such premarital property agreement shall be determined by the law otherwise applicable to the premarital property agreement. Nothing in this subdivision limits the enforceability under this chapter of a waiver made under this chapter by a person intending to marry that is otherwise enforceable under this chapter.

(d) Nothing in this chapter limits any right one spouse otherwise has to revoke a consent or election to disposition of his or her half of the community or quasi-community property under the will of the other spouse. *(Stats.1990, c. 79 (A.B.759), § 14, operative July 1, 1991.)*

Law Revision Commission Comments

1990 Enactment

Section 147 continues Section 147 of the repealed Probate Code without change. Subdivision (a) makes clear that, absent a valid premarital property agreement, interspousal agreements or waivers of rights on death must satisfy the requirements of this chapter. See also Civil Code §§ 5300–5317 (Uniform Premarital Agreement Act). Under the Uniform Premarital Agreement Act, the parties to a premarital agreement may contract with respect to the disposition of property upon death, the making of a will, trust, or other arrangement to carry out the provisions of the agreement, the disposition of the death benefit from a life insurance policy, and other matters. See Civil Code § 5312. As to the requirements for execution of a premarital agreement under the Uniform Act, see Civil Code §§ 5311, 5314, 5315.

Subdivision (b) makes clear that the provisions of this chapter have no effect on waivers, agreements, or property settlements made prior to January 1, 1985 (the date this chapter of the repealed Probate Code first became operative). As to the application of any amendments made after that date, see Section 3. See also Section 141(b) (nothing in chapter affects or limits the waiver or manner of waiver of rights other than those referred to in subdivision (a) of Section 141).

Subdivision (c) makes two things clear. First, an enforceable agreement affecting rights listed in subdivision (a) of Section 141 may be made in a valid premarital property agreement. Second, a premarital waiver of rights listed in subdivision (a) also is enforceable under this chapter if the requirements of this chapter are satisfied.

Subdivision (d) makes clear that this chapter does not limit the right of a spouse to revoke a consent or election to disposition of his or her half of the community or quasi-community property under the will of the other spouse. See Wolfe & Hellman, Handling Surviving Spouse's Share of Marital Property, in California Will Drafting Practice §§ 5.31–5.34, at 205–08 (Cal.Cont.Ed.Bar 1982). See also the Comment to Section 146.

Background on Section 147 of Repealed Code

Section 147 was a new provision added by 1983 Cal.Stat. ch. 842 § 22. The section was amended by 1984 Cal.Stat. ch. 892 § 13 to add subdivisions (c) and (d). For background on the provisions of this part, see the Comment to this part under the part heading. [20 Cal.L.Rev.Comm.Reports 1001 (1990)].

Research References

Forms

California Transactions Forms--Estate Planning § 11:54, Revocation and Amendment Of Waiver by Agreement.

Treatises and Practice Aids

Witkin, California Summary 10th Wills and Probate § 322, Nature and Scope Of Statute.

Witkin, California Summary 10th Wills and Probate § 324, Enforcement.

Part 6

DISTRIBUTION AMONG HEIRS OR BENEFICIARIES

Law Revision Commission Comments

1990 Enactment

This part supersedes Part 6 (commencing with Section 240) of Division 2 of the repealed Probate Code. The superseded part was enacted upon recommendation of the California Law Revision Commission. See Recommendation Relating to Distribution Under a Will or Trust, 18 Cal.L.Revision Comm'n Reports 269 (1986); Communication Concerning Assembly Bill 196, 18 Cal.L.Revision Comm'n Reports 367, 369–70 (1986). See also Recommendation Relating to Revision of Wills and Intestate Succession Law, 17 Cal.L.Revision Comm'n Reports 537, 542–44, 549–50 (1984); Communication of Law Revision Commission Concerning Assembly Bill 2290, 18 Cal.L.Revision Comm'n Reports 77, 83–84 (1986); Tentative Recommendation Relating to Wills and Intestate Succession, 16 Cal.L.Revision Comm'n Reports 2301, 2338–40 (1982); Report of Senate Committee on Judiciary on Assembly Bills 25 and 68, 17 Cal.L.Revision Comm'n Reports 867, 871 (1984). [20 Cal.L.Rev.Comm.Reports 1001 (1990)].

CHAPTER 1. INTESTATE DISTRIBUTION SYSTEM

§ 240. Division into equal shares

If a statute calls for property to be distributed or taken in the manner provided in this section, the property shall be divided into as many equal shares as there are living members of the nearest generation of issue then living and deceased members of that generation who leave issue then living, each living member of the nearest generation of issue then living receiving one share and the share of each deceased member of that generation who leaves issue then living being divided in the same manner among his or her then living issue. *(Stats.1990, c. 79 (A.B.759), § 14, operative July 1, 1991.)*

Application

This section applicable to estates of decedents who died after Jan. 1, 1985, see Probate Code § 241.

Law Revision Commission Comments

1990 Enactment

Section 240 continues Section 240 of the repealed Probate Code without change. This section was drawn from Section 2–106 of the Uniform Probate Code (1987). As to the construction of provisions drawn from uniform acts, see Section 2. Under this section, the primary division of the estate takes place at the first generation having any living members. This changes the rule of Maud v. Catherwood, 67 Cal.App.2d 636, 155 P.2d 111 (1945). For sections applying Section 240, see Civil Code § 1389.4; Prob.Code §§ 6147, 6402, 6402.5. For an example of distribution under Section 240, see the Comment to Section 245. As to the effect of a disclaimer, see Section 282.

Section 240 applies only where the death of the decedent in the case of intestate succession or of the testator or trustor occurs on or after January 1, 1985; the law applicable prior to January 1, 1985, continues to apply where the death occurred before January 1, 1985. See Section 241. As to the application of any amendments made after that date, see Section 3.

Background on Section 240 of Repealed Code

Section 240 was a new provision added by 1983 Cal.Stat. ch. 842 § 22 and was amended by 1984 Cal.Stat. ch. 892 § 16 and 1985 Cal.Stat. ch. 982 § 6. The 1984 and 1985 amendments made substantive and clarifying revisions. For background on the provisions of this part, see the Comment to this part under the part heading. [20 Cal.L.Rev.Comm.Reports 1001 (1990)].

Research References

Forms

California Transactions Forms--Estate Planning § 6:8, Distribution Under Prob C § 240.
California Transactions Forms--Estate Planning § 20:9, Devises to Heirs.
California Transactions Forms--Estate Planning § 6:22, Antilapse Statutes.
California Transactions Forms--Estate Planning § 6:52, Matters to Consider in Drafting Class Gifts.
California Transactions Forms--Estate Planning § 6:60, Distribution as Provided in Prob C § 240.
California Transactions Forms--Estate Planning § 14:19, Married Couple's Living Trust With Bypass Trust Provisions, Remainder to Descendants.
California Transactions Forms--Estate Planning § 14:20, Unmarried Person's Living Trust.
California Transactions Forms--Estate Planning § 14:22, Trust for Minors Qualifying for Annual Gift Tax Exclusion.
California Transactions Forms--Estate Planning § 14:28, "Representation" Defined.
California Transactions Forms--Estate Planning § 18:54, Revocable Trust Agreement.
California Transactions Forms--Estate Planning § 20:15, Lapsed Devises.
California Transactions Forms--Estate Planning § 20:65, Residuary Devise to Heirs Per Capita.
California Transactions Forms--Estate Planning § 20:74, Direction Not to Apply Anti-Lapse Statute.
California Transactions Forms--Estate Planning § 6:105, Devise Lapses If Devisee Predeceases Testator.
California Transactions Forms--Estate Planning § 6:106, Requirement that Beneficiary Survive Decedent by Specified Period.
California Transactions Forms--Estate Planning § 19:100, Distribution to Issue.
California Transactions Forms--Estate Planning § 19:116, Will for Single Person.
California Transactions Forms--Estate Planning § 19:117, Will for Married Person.
California Transactions Forms--Estate Planning § 19:118, Will With Family Pot Trust.
California Transactions Forms--Estate Planning § 19:119, Pour-Over Will.
California Transactions Forms--Estate Planning § 19:146, Distribution Under Intestate Distribution System.

Treatises and Practice Aids

Witkin, California Summary 10th Real Property § 166, Death Of Appointee Before Appointment.
Witkin, California Summary 10th Wills and Probate § 25, Major Changes.
Witkin, California Summary 10th Wills and Probate § 75, Distribution Of Shares by Representation.
Witkin, California Summary 10th Wills and Probate § 79, Issue Of Decedent.
Witkin, California Summary 10th Wills and Probate § 80, Parents or Issue Of Parents.
Witkin, California Summary 10th Wills and Probate § 81, Grandparents or Issue Of Grandparents.
Witkin, California Summary 10th Wills and Probate § 84, Nature and Scope Of Statute.
Witkin, California Summary 10th Wills and Probate § 85, Apportionment Of Property Between Families.
Witkin, California Summary 10th Wills and Probate § 225, Express Intention or No Specification.
Witkin, California Summary 10th Wills and Probate § 261, Effect Of Lapsed Gift.
Witkin, California Summary 10th Wills and Probate § 263, Revised Statute.
Witkin, California Summary 10th Wills and Probate § 339, Effect Of Disclaimer.

CHAPTER 3. IDENTITY OF HEIRS

§ 249.5. Posthumous conception; child of decedent deemed born in decedent's lifetime; conditions

For purposes of determining rights to property to be distributed upon the death of a decedent, a child of the decedent conceived and born after the death of the decedent shall be deemed to have been born in the lifetime of the decedent, and after the execution of all of the decedent's testamentary instruments, if the child or his or her representative proves by clear and convincing evidence that all of the following conditions are satisfied:

(a) The decedent, in writing, specifies that his or her genetic material shall be used for the posthumous conception of a child of the decedent, subject to the following:

(1) The specification shall be signed by the decedent and dated.

(2) The specification may be revoked or amended only by a writing, signed by the decedent and dated.

(3) A person is designated by the decedent to control the use of the genetic material.

(b) The person designated by the decedent to control the use of the genetic material has given written notice by certified mail, return receipt requested, that the decedent's genetic material was available for the purpose of posthumous conception. The notice shall have been given to a person who has the power to control the distribution of either the decedent's property or death benefits payable by reason of the decedent's death, within four months of the date of issuance of a certificate of the decedent's death or entry of a judgment determining the fact of the decedent's death, whichever event occurs first.

(c) The child was in utero using the decedent's genetic material and was in utero within two years of the date of issuance of a certificate of the decedent's death or entry of a judgment determining the fact of the decedent's death, whichever event occurs first. This subdivision does not apply to a child who shares all of his or her nuclear genes with the person donating the implanted nucleus as a result of the application of somatic nuclear transfer technology commonly known as human cloning. *(Added by Stats.2004, c. 775 (A.B.1910), § 5. Amended by Stats.2005, c. 285 (A.B.204), § 1.)*

Research References

Forms

California Transactions Forms--Estate Planning § 6:11, Existence Of Relationship.

West's California Code Forms, Probate § 249.5 Form 1, Specification Of Donor's Intent that Genetic Material be Used for Posthumous Conception and Birth Of Donor's Child.

West's California Code Forms, Probate § 249.5 Form 2, Revocation or Amendment Of Specification for Use Of Genetic Material.

West's California Code Forms, Probate § 249.6(C) Form 1, Notice Of Nonintention to Use Genetic Material for Posthumous Conception Of a Child Of Decedent.

Treatises and Practice Aids

Witkin, California Summary 10th Parent and Child § 20, in General.

Witkin, California Summary 10th Parent and Child § 40, Child in Utero.

Witkin, California Summary 10th Parent and Child § 45, Semen Of Decedent.

Witkin, California Summary 10th Wills and Probate § 94, Parent and Child Relationship.

Witkin, California Summary 10th Wills and Probate § 719, Proceeding to Determine Heirship.

§ 249.6. Notice of genetic material available for posthumous conception; delay of distribution of property or payment of death benefits exceptions; liability; time to bring action

(a) Upon timely receipt of the notice required by Section 249.5 or actual knowledge by a person who has the power to control the distribution of either the decedent's property or death benefits payable by reason of the decedent's death, that person may not make a distribution of property or pay death benefits payable by reason of the decedent's death before two years following the date of issuance of a certificate of the decedent's death or entry of a judgment determining the fact of decedent's death, whichever event occurs first.

(b) Subdivision (a) does not apply to, and the distribution of property or the payment of benefits may proceed in a timely manner as provided by law with respect to, any property if the birth of a child or children of the decedent conceived after the death of the decedent will not have an effect on any of the following:

(1) The proposed distribution of the decedent's property.

(2) The payment of death benefits payable by reason of the decedent's death.

(3) The determination of rights to property to be distributed upon the death of the decedent.

(4) The right of any person to claim a probate homestead or probate family allowance.

(c) Subdivision (a) does not apply to, and the distribution of property or the payment of benefits may proceed in a timely manner as provided by law with respect to, any property if the person named in subdivision (a) of Section 249.5 sends written notice by certified mail, return receipt requested, that the person does not intend to use the genetic material for the posthumous conception of a child of a decedent. This notice shall be signed by the person named in paragraph (3) of subdivision (a) of Section 249.5 and at least one competent witness, and dated.

(d) A person who has the power to control the distribution of either the decedent's property or death benefits payable by reason of the decedent's death, shall incur no liability for making a distribution of property or paying death benefits if that person made a distribution of property or paid death benefits prior to receiving notice or acquiring actual knowledge of the existence of genetic material available for posthumous conception purposes or the written notice required by subdivision (b) of Section 249.5.

(e) Each person to whom payment, delivery, or transfer of the decedent's property is made is personally liable to a person who, pursuant to Section 249.5, has a superior right to the payment, delivery, or transfer of the decedent's property. The aggregate of the personal liability of a person shall not exceed the fair market value, valued as of the time of the transfer, of the property paid, delivered, or transferred to the person under this section, less the amount of any liens and encumbrances on that property at that time.

(f) In addition to any other liability a person may have pursuant to this section, any person who fraudulently secures the payment, delivery, or transfer of the decedent's property pursuant to this section shall be liable to the person having a superior right for three times the fair market value of the property.

(g) An action to impose liability under this section shall be barred three years after the distribution to the holder of the decedent's property, or three years after the discovery of fraud, whichever is later. The three-year period specified in this subdivision may not be tolled for any reason. *(Added by Stats.2004, c. 775 (A.B.1910), § 6. Amended by Stats.2005, c. 285 (A.B.204), § 2.)*

Research References

Forms

West's California Code Forms, Probate § 249.5 Form 1, Specification Of Donor's Intent that Genetic Material be Used for Posthumous Conception and Birth Of Donor's Child.
West's California Code Forms, Probate § 249.6(C) Form 1, Notice Of Nonintention to Use Genetic Material for Posthumous Conception Of a Child Of Decedent.

§ 249.7. Failure to give timely notice of genetic material available for posthumous conception; distribution of property or payment of death benefits not delayed; bar of claim for wrongful distribution

If the written notice required pursuant to Section 249.5 is not given in a timely manner to any person who has the power to control the distribution of either the decedent's property or death benefits payable by reason of the decedent's death, that person may make the distribution in the manner provided by law as if any child of the decedent conceived after the death of the decedent had predeceased the decedent without heirs. Any child of a decedent conceived after the death of the decedent, or that child's representative, shall be barred from making a claim against either the person making the distribution or the recipient of the distribution when the claim is based on wrongful distribution and written notice has not been given in a timely manner pursuant to Section 249.5 to the person making that distribution. *(Added by Stats.2004, c. 775 (A.B.1910), § 7.)*

Research References

Forms

West's California Code Forms, Probate § 249.5 Form 1, Specification Of Donor's Intent that Genetic Material be Used for Posthumous Conception and Birth Of Donor's Child.

§ 249.8. Petition by interested person requesting distribution of property or death benefits subject to delay; hearing and order

Notwithstanding Section 249.6, any interested person may file a petition in the manner prescribed in Section 248 or 17200 requesting a distribution of property of the decedent or death benefits payable by reason of decedent's death that are subject to the delayed distribution provisions of Section 249.6. The court may order distribution of all, or a portion of, the property or death benefits, if at the hearing it appears that distribution can be made without any loss to any interested person, including any loss, either actual or contingent, to a decedent's child who is conceived after the death of the decedent. The order for distribution shall be stayed until any bond required by the court is filed. *(Added by Stats.2004, c. 775 (A.B.1910), § 8. Amended by Stats.2005, c. 285 (A.B. 204), § 3.)*

Research References

Forms

California Transactions Forms--Estate Planning § 6:11, Existence Of Relationship.
West's California Code Forms, Probate § 249.5 Form 1, Specification Of Donor's Intent that Genetic Material be Used for Posthumous Conception and Birth Of Donor's Child.

Part 7

EFFECT OF HOMICIDE OR ABUSE OF AN ELDER OR DEPENDENT ADULT

Application

Part 7 applies to decedents killed on or after Jan. 1, 1985. See Probate Code § 257.

Law Revision Commission Comments

1990 Enactment

This part supersedes Part 7 (commencing with Section 250) of Division 2 of the repealed Probate Code. The superseded part was enacted upon recommendation of the California Law Revision Commission. See Tentative Recommendation Relating to Wills and Intestate Succession, 16 Cal.L.Revision Comm'n Reports 2301, 2346–47, 2382–85, 2509 (1982). See also Report of Senate Committee on Judiciary on Assembly Bills 25 and 68, 17 Cal.L.Revision Comm'n Reports 867, 870 (1984).

The Commission recommended legislation was originally enacted as Sections 200–206 of the repealed Probate Code (added by 1983 Cal.Stat. ch. 842 § 22). These provisions were repealed by 1984 Cal.Stat. ch. 527 § 1 and reenacted as Sections 250–256 of the repealed Probate Code by 1984 Cal.Stat. ch. 527 § 3. See Recommendation Relating to Recording Affidavit of Death, 17 Cal.L.Revision Comm'n Reports 493, 504–07 (1984). [20 Cal.L.Rev.Comm.Reports 1001 (1990)].

§ 251. Joint tenants; rights by survivorship

A joint tenant who feloniously and intentionally kills another joint tenant thereby effects a severance of the interest of the decedent so that the share of the decedent passes as the decedent's property and the killer has no rights by survivorship. This section applies to joint tenancies in real and personal property, joint and multiple-party accounts in financial institutions, and any other form of coownership with survivorship incidents. *(Stats.1990, c. 79 (A.B.759), § 14, operative July 1, 1991.)*

Law Revision Commission Comments

1990 Enactment

Section 251 continues Section 251 of the repealed Probate Code without change. This section is the same in substance as Section 2–803(b) of the Uniform Probate Code (1987) and is consistent with prior California law. See, e.g., Estate of Hart, 135 Cal.App.3d 684, 185 Cal.Rptr. 544 (1982); Johansen v. Pelton, 8 Cal.App.3d 625, 87 Cal.Rptr. 784 (1970). As to the construction of provisions drawn from uniform acts, see Section 2. This part applies only where the decedent was killed on or after January 1, 1985. See Section 257. As to the application of any amendments made after that date, see Section 3.

Background on Section 251 of Repealed Code

Section 251 was added by 1984 Cal.Stat. ch. 527 § 3. The section restated without substantive change former Probate Code Section 201 (enacted by 1983 Cal.Stat. ch. 842 § 22 and repealed by 1984

Cal.Stat. ch. 527 § 1). Former Probate Code Sections 200–206 (repealed by 1984 Cal.Stat. ch. 527 § 1) superseded former Probate Code Section 258 (repealed by 1983 Cal.Stat. ch. 842 § 19). For background on the provisions of this part, see the Comment to this part under the part heading. [20 Cal.L.Rev.Comm.Reports 1001 (1990)].

Commentary

See generally *Estate of Castiglioni, 40 Cal.App.4th 367, 47 Cal. Rptr.2d 288 (1995), review denied February 15, 1996* (when real property is held in joint tenancy and one joint tenant feloniously and intentionally kills the other, the joint tenancy is severed and the portion of property that passes as decedent's property must be calculated according to the principles of tracing and reimbursement of contributions ordinarily used in marital dissolution cases).

Research References

Treatises and Practice Aids

Witkin, California Summary 10th Real Property § 34, Right Of Survivorship.
Witkin, California Summary 10th Wills and Probate § 294, Nature and Scope Of Statute.
Witkin, California Summary 10th Wills and Probate § 296, Joint Tenancy.
Witkin, California Summary 10th Wills and Probate § 301, Other Acquisition Of Property or Benefit.

Part 17

LEGAL MENTAL CAPACITY

§ 810. Findings and declarations; capabilities of persons with mental or physical disorders; judicial determination; evidence

The Legislature finds and declares the following:

(a) For purposes of this part, there shall exist a rebuttable presumption affecting the burden of proof that all persons have the capacity to make decisions and to be responsible for their acts or decisions.

(b) A person who has a mental or physical disorder may still be capable of contracting, conveying, marrying, making medical decisions, executing wills or trusts, and performing other actions.

(c) A judicial determination that a person is totally without understanding, or is of unsound mind, or suffers from one or more mental deficits so substantial that, under the circumstances, the person should be deemed to lack the legal capacity to perform a specific act, should be based on evidence of a deficit in one or more of the person's mental functions rather than on a diagnosis of a person's mental or physical disorder. *(Added by Stats.1995, c. 842 (S.B.730), § 2. Amended by Stats.1998, c. 581 (A.B.2801), § 19.)*

Commentary

In re Marriage of Greenway, 217 Cal.App.4th 628, 158 Cal.Rptr.3d 364 (2013), review denied, holds that the standard for mental capacity to end a marriage is low and a husband's diagnosis of dementia did not require a determination under this section that he was of unsound mind or lacked mental capacity to end his marriage (section 811). Even the appointment of a conservator does not affect the capacity to marry (section 1900). Moreover, the court was not bound by the testimony of experts when the husband's testimony before the trial court provided sufficient evidence that he was mentally capable of exercising judgment and expressing a wish that his marriage be terminated on account of irreconcilable differences.

Research References

Forms

California Transactions Forms--Estate Planning § 8:8, Ethical Considerations.
California Transactions Forms--Estate Planning § 13:2, Testamentary Capacity Versus Contractual Capacity.
California Transactions Forms--Estate Planning § 13:3, Deficits in Mental Functions.
California Transactions Forms--Estate Planning § 2:16, Overview.
California Transactions Forms--Estate Planning § 2:18, Due Process in Competence Determinations Act.
California Transactions Forms--Estate Planning § 21:3, Trust Requirements.
California Transactions Forms--Estate Planning § 19:33, Requirement Of Testamentary Capacity.
California Transactions Forms--Estate Planning § 21:13, Matters to Consider in Drafting Testamentary Trust.
West's California Code Forms, Probate § 1891 Form 1, Petition for Exclusive Authority to Give Consent for Medical Treatment (Probate Conservatorship)--Judicial Council Form GC-380.

Treatises and Practice Aids

Witkin, California Summary 10th Contracts § 51, Capacity to Contract.
Witkin, California Summary 10th Husband and Wife § 43, Capacity Of Parties.
Witkin, California Summary 10th Husband and Wife § 59A, (New) Capacity to Terminate Marriage.
Witkin, California Summary 10th Wills and Probate § 8, in General.
Witkin, California Summary 10th Wills and Probate § 121, Test.

§ 811. Deficits in mental functions

(a) A determination that a person is of unsound mind or lacks the capacity to make a decision or do a certain act, including, but not limited to, the incapacity to contract, to make a conveyance, to marry, to make medical decisions, to execute wills, or to execute trusts, shall be supported by evidence of a deficit in at least one of the following mental functions, subject to subdivision (b), and evidence of a correlation between the deficit or deficits and the decision or acts in question:

(1) Alertness and attention, including, but not limited to, the following:

(A) Level of arousal or consciousness.

(B) Orientation to time, place, person, and situation.

(C) Ability to attend and concentrate.

(2) Information processing, including, but not limited to, the following:

(A) Short- and long-term memory, including immediate recall.

(B) Ability to understand or communicate with others, either verbally or otherwise.

(C) Recognition of familiar objects and familiar persons.

(D) Ability to understand and appreciate quantities.

(E) Ability to reason using abstract concepts.

(F) Ability to plan, organize, and carry out actions in one's own rational self-interest.

(G) Ability to reason logically.

(3) Thought processes. Deficits in these functions may be demonstrated by the presence of the following:

(A) Severely disorganized thinking.

(B) Hallucinations.

(C) Delusions.

(D) Uncontrollable, repetitive, or intrusive thoughts.

(4) Ability to modulate mood and affect. Deficits in this ability may be demonstrated by the presence of a pervasive and persistent or recurrent state of euphoria, anger, anxiety, fear, panic, depression, hopelessness or despair, helplessness, apathy or indifference, that is inappropriate in degree to the individual's circumstances.

(b) A deficit in the mental functions listed above may be considered only if the deficit, by itself or in combination with one or more other mental function deficits, significantly impairs the person's ability to understand and appreciate the consequences of his or her actions with regard to the type of act or decision in question.

(c) In determining whether a person suffers from a deficit in mental function so substantial that the person lacks the capacity to do a certain act, the court may take into consideration the frequency, severity, and duration of periods of impairment.

(d) The mere diagnosis of a mental or physical disorder shall not be sufficient in and of itself to support a determination that a person is of unsound mind or lacks the capacity to do a certain act.

(e) This part applies only to the evidence that is presented to, and the findings that are made by, a court determining the capacity of a person to do a certain act or make a decision, including, but not limited to, making medical decisions. Nothing in this part shall affect the decisionmaking process set forth in Section 1418.8 of the Health and Safety Code, nor increase or decrease the burdens of documentation on, or potential liability of, health care providers who, outside the judicial context, determine the capacity of patients to make a medical decision. *(Added by Stats.1996, c. 178 (S.B.1650), § 3. Amended by Stats.1998, c. 581 (A.B.2801), § 20.)*

Commentary

In re Marriage of Greenway, 217 Cal.App.4th 628, 158 Cal.Rptr.3d 364 (2013), review denied, holds that the standard for mental capacity to end a marriage is low and, pursuant to this section, a husband's diagnosis of dementia did not require a determination under this section that he was of unsound mind or lacked mental capacity to end his marriage. Even the appointment of a conservator does not affect the capacity to marry (section 1900). Moreover, the court was not bound by the testimony of experts when the husband's testimony before the trial court provided sufficient evidence that he was mentally capable of exercising judgment and expressing a wish that his marriage be terminated on account of irreconcilable differences.

Research References

Forms

California Transactions Forms--Estate Planning § 8:8, Ethical Considerations.
California Transactions Forms--Estate Planning § 1:32, Testamentary Capacity.
California Transactions Forms--Estate Planning § 13:2, Testamentary Capacity Versus Contractual Capacity.
California Transactions Forms--Estate Planning § 13:3, Deficits in Mental Functions.
California Transactions Forms--Estate Planning § 2:16, Overview.
California Transactions Forms--Estate Planning § 2:18, Due Process in Competence Determinations Act.
California Transactions Forms--Estate Planning § 2:19, Duty to Advocate for Client's Capacity; Obtaining Evidence Of Client's Capacity.
California Transactions Forms--Estate Planning § 21:3, Trust Requirements.
California Transactions Forms--Estate Planning § 8:33, Capacity Of Principal.
California Transactions Forms--Estate Planning § 19:33, Requirement Of Testamentary Capacity.
California Transactions Forms--Estate Planning § 21:13, Matters to Consider in Drafting Testamentary Trust.
West's California Code Forms, Probate § 1825 Form 1, Capacity Declaration--Conservatorship--Judicial Council Form GC-335.
West's California Code Forms, Probate § 3204 Form 2, Medical Declaration Of Patient's Physician.
West's California Judicial Council Forms GC-335, Capacity Declaration--Conservatorship.

Treatises and Practice Aids

Witkin, California Summary 10th Contracts § 51, Capacity to Contract.
Witkin, California Summary 10th Wills and Probate § 8, in General.
Witkin, California Summary 10th Wills and Probate § 9, Determining Legal Capacity.
Witkin, California Summary 10th Wills and Probate § 10, Consent to Medical Treatment.
Witkin, California Summary 10th Wills and Probate § 941, Investigation and Report.
Witkin, California Summary 10th Wills and Probate § 956, Determination by Court.
Witkin, California Summary 10th Wills and Probate § 995, Conservatee With Dementia.
Witkin, California Summary 10th Wills and Probate § 1064, Petition, Notice, and Hearing.
Witkin, California Summary 10th Wills and Probate § 304A, (New) in General.

Division 4

GUARDIANSHIP, CONSERVATORSHIP, AND OTHER PROTECTIVE PROCEEDINGS

Part 1

DEFINITIONS AND GENERAL PROVISIONS

Law Revision Commission Comments

1990 Enactment

This part supersedes Part 1 (commencing with Section 1400) of Division 4 of the repealed Probate Code. The superseded part was enacted upon recommendation of the California Law Revision Commission. See Recommendation Relating to Guardianship–Conservatorship Law, 14 Cal.L.Revision Comm'n Reports 501 (1978). For the Guardianship–Conservatorship Law as enacted in 1979 (Chapter 726 of the Statutes of 1979) with the revisions made by Chapters 89 and 246 of the Statutes of 1980, see Guardianship–Conservatorship Law, 15 Cal.L.Revision Comm'n Reports 451 (1980). [20 Cal.L.Rev.Comm. Reports 1001 (1990)].

CHAPTER 1. SHORT TITLE AND DEFINITIONS

§ 1400. Guardianship–Conservatorship Law

The portion of this division consisting of Part 1 (commencing with Section 1400), Part 2 (commencing with Section 1500), Part 3 (commencing with Section 1800), and Part 4 (commencing with Section 2100) may be cited as the Guardianship-Conservatorship Law. *(Stats.1990, c. 79 (A.B.759), § 14, operative July 1, 1991.)*

Law Revision Commission Comments

1990 Enactment

Section 1400 is a new provision, not found in the repealed Probate Code. For background on the provisions of this part, see the Comment to this part under the part heading. [20 Cal.L.Rev.Comm. Reports 1001 (1990)].

Research References

Forms

California Transactions Forms--Family Law § 6:2, Governing Law.

Am. Jur. Pl. & Pr. Forms Veterans and Veterans' Laws § 59, Introductory Comments.

Treatises and Practice Aids

Witkin, California Summary 10th Parent and Child § 63, in General.

Witkin, California Summary 10th Parent and Child § 311, Other Proceedings Stayed.

Witkin, California Summary 10th Parent and Child § 696, Continuing Jurisdiction.

Witkin, California Summary 10th Trusts § 2, in General.

Witkin, California Summary 10th Wills and Probate § 21, Adoption and Early Amendments.

Witkin, California Summary 10th Wills and Probate § 399, Trial.

Witkin, California Summary 10th Wills and Probate § 901, Former Law Of Guardianship.

Witkin, California Summary 10th Wills and Probate § 903, in General.

Witkin, California Summary 10th Wills and Probate § 905, Statutory Framework.

Witkin, California Summary 10th Wills and Probate § 906, Definitions.

Witkin, California Summary 10th Wills and Probate § 907, Rules Of Practice.

Witkin, California Summary 10th Wills and Probate § 910, General Notice Requirement.

Witkin, California Summary 10th Wills and Probate § 954, Limited or Temporary Conservatee.

Witkin, California Summary 10th Wills and Probate § 1006, Life Insurance and Other Benefits.

Witkin, California Summary 10th Wills and Probate § 1027, Determination and Order.

Witkin, California Summary 10th Wills and Probate § 1071, Disposition Of Proceeds.

Witkin, California Summary 10th Wills and Probate § 1072, Special Needs Trust.

§ 1401. Application of definitions

Unless the provision or context otherwise requires, the definitions in this chapter govern the construction of this division. *(Stats.1990, c. 79 (A.B.759), § 14, operative July 1, 1991.)*

Law Revision Commission Comments

1990 Enactment

Section 1401 restates Section 1400 of the repealed Probate Code without substantive change. For background on the provisions of this part, see the Comment to this part under the part heading. [20 Cal.L.Rev.Comm. Reports 1001 (1990)].

Research References

Treatises and Practice Aids

Witkin, California Summary 10th Wills and Probate § 48, Scope.

Witkin, California Summary 10th Wills and Probate § 906, Definitions.

§ 1403. Absentee

"Absentee" means either of the following:

(a) A member of a uniformed service covered by United States Code, Title 37, Chapter 10, who is determined thereunder by the secretary concerned, or by the authorized delegate thereof, to be in missing status as missing status is defined therein.

(b) An employee of the United States government or an agency thereof covered by United States Code, Title 5, Chapter 55, Subchapter VII, who is determined thereunder by the head of the department or agency concerned, or by the authorized delegate thereof, to be in missing status as missing status is defined therein. *(Stats.1990, c. 79 (A.B.759), § 14, operative July 1, 1991.)*

Law Revision Commission Comments

1990 Enactment

Section 1403 continues Section 1403 of the repealed Probate Code without change. "Secretary concerned" is defined in Section 1440. For background on the provisions of this part, see the Comment to this part under the part heading. [20 Cal.L.Rev.Comm. Reports 1001 (1990)].

Research References

Forms

West's California Code Forms, Probate § 1820 Form 1, Petition for Appointment Of Probate Conservator--Judicial Council Form GC-310.

Treatises and Practice Aids

Witkin, California Summary 10th Agency and Employment § 215, Revocation, Death, or Incapacity Of Principal.

Witkin, California Summary 10th Wills and Probate § 852, Revocation Of Authority Of Attorney-In-Fact.

Witkin, California Summary 10th Wills and Probate § 865, Power Not Revoked Until Notice.

Witkin, California Summary 10th Wills and Probate § 906, Definitions.

Witkin, California Summary 10th Wills and Probate § 948, Where Proposed Conservatee is Absentee.

Witkin, California Summary 10th Wills and Probate § 1052, Appointment Of Successor Conservator.

Witkin, California Summary 10th Wills and Probate § 1073, in General.

§ 1418. Court

"Court," when used in connection with matters in the guardianship or conservatorship proceeding, means the court in which such proceeding is pending. *(Stats.1990, c. 79 (A.B.759), § 14, operative July 1, 1991.)*

Law Revision Commission Comments

1990 Enactment

Section 1418 continues Section 1418 of the repealed Probate Code without change. This definition does not apply where the context otherwise requires. See Section 1401. For examples of where the context otherwise requires, see Sections 2216, 2803. For background on the provisions of this part, see the Comment to this part under the part heading. [20 Cal.L.Rev.Comm. Reports 1001 (1990)].

Research References

Treatises and Practice Aids

Witkin, California Summary 10th Wills and Probate § 906, Definitions.

§ 1419. Court investigator

"Court investigator" means the person referred to in Section 1454. *(Stats.1990, c. 79 (A.B.759), § 14, operative July 1, 1991.)*

Law Revision Commission Comments

1990 Enactment

Section 1419 continues Section 1419 of the repealed Probate Code without change. For background on the provisions of this part, see the Comment to this part under the part heading. [20 Cal.L.Rev. Comm. Reports 1001 (1990)].

§ 1419.5. Custodial parent

"Custodial parent" means the parent who either (a) has been awarded sole legal and physical custody of the child in another proceeding, or (b) with whom the child resides if there is currently no operative custody order. If the child resides with both parents, then they are jointly the custodial parent. *(Added by Stats.1993, c. 978 (S.B.305), § 1.)*

Research References

Treatises and Practice Aids

Witkin, California Summary 10th Wills and Probate § 906, Definitions.

Witkin, California Summary 10th Wills and Probate § 963, Joint Guardians or Conservators.

Witkin, California Summary 10th Wills and Probate § 965, Nominated Guardian.

§ 1420. Developmental disability

"Developmental disability" means a disability that originates before an individual attains 18 years of age, continues, or can be expected to continue, indefinitely, and constitutes a substantial handicap for the individual. As defined by the Director of Developmental Services, in consultation with the Superintendent of Public Instruction, this term includes intellectual disability, cerebral palsy, epilepsy, and autism. This term also includes handicapping conditions found to be closely related to intellectual disability or to require treatment similar to that required for individuals with an intellectual disability, but does not include other handicapping conditions that are solely physical in nature. *(Stats.1990, c. 79 (A.B.759), § 14, operative July 1, 1991. Amended by Stats.2012, c. 448 (A.B.2370), § 44; Stats.2012, c. 457 (S.B. 1381), § 44.)*

Law Revision Commission Comments

1990 Enactment

Section 1420 continues Section 1420 of the repealed Probate Code without substantive change. For background on the provisions of this part, see the Comment to this part under the part heading. [20 Cal.L.Rev.Comm. Reports 1001 (1990)].

Research References

Forms

West's California Code Forms, Probate § 1952 Form 1, Allegations for Petition for Authority to Consent to Sterilization Of Developmentally Disabled Adult.

Treatises and Practice Aids

Witkin, California Summary 10th Wills and Probate § 906, Definitions.

Witkin, California Summary 10th Wills and Probate § 912, When Conservatee or Ward is Developmentally Disabled.

Witkin, California Summary 10th Wills and Probate § 942, Assessment Of Developmentally Disabled Person.

Witkin, California Summary 10th Wills and Probate § 1054, in General.

§ 1424. Interested person

"Interested person" includes, but is not limited to:

(a) Any interested state, local, or federal entity or agency.

(b) Any interested public officer or employee of this state or of a local public entity of this state or of the federal government. *(Stats.1990, c. 79 (A.B.759), § 14, operative July 1, 1991.)*

Law Revision Commission Comments

1990 Enactment

Section 1424 continues Section 1424 of the repealed Probate Code without change. This section makes clear that a public officer or employee or a public entity may be an interested person for the purposes of this division. See also Section 1461 (notice to Director of Mental Health or Director of Developmental Services) and the Comment thereto. For background on the provisions of this part, see the Comment to this part under the part heading. [20 Cal.L.Rev.Comm. Reports 1001 (1990)].

Recommendations relating to revision of the guardianship-conservatorship law, 15 Cal.L.Rev.Comm. Reports 1463 (1980).

Research References

Treatises and Practice Aids

Witkin, California Summary 10th Wills and Probate § 906, Definitions.
Witkin, California Summary 10th Wills and Probate § 937, Who May File.
Witkin, California Summary 10th Wills and Probate § 943, in General.
Witkin, California Summary 10th Wills and Probate § 952, Procedure.
Witkin, California Summary 10th Wills and Probate § 955, Court Order Broadening Capacity.
Witkin, California Summary 10th Wills and Probate § 957, Procedure.
Witkin, California Summary 10th Wills and Probate § 972, Appointment Procedure.
Witkin, California Summary 10th Wills and Probate § 981, Change Of Venue.
Witkin, California Summary 10th Wills and Probate § 987, Request for Special Notice.
Witkin, California Summary 10th Wills and Probate § 994, Court Authorization Of Treatment.
Witkin, California Summary 10th Wills and Probate § 1001, Duty to Manage Estate.
Witkin, California Summary 10th Wills and Probate § 1018, Authorization by Court.
Witkin, California Summary 10th Wills and Probate § 1022, Leases.
Witkin, California Summary 10th Wills and Probate § 1031, Procedure.
Witkin, California Summary 10th Wills and Probate § 1035, Examination on Property Wrongfully Withheld.
Witkin, California Summary 10th Wills and Probate § 1036, in General.
Witkin, California Summary 10th Wills and Probate § 1037, Hearing and Objections.
Witkin, California Summary 10th Wills and Probate § 1049, Procedure for Removal.
Witkin, California Summary 10th Wills and Probate § 1052, Appointment Of Successor Conservator.
Witkin, California Summary 10th Wills and Probate § 1053, Transfer Of Property Out Of State.

§ 1430. Petition

"Petition" includes an application or request in the nature of a petition. *(Stats.1990, c. 79 (A.B.759), § 14, operative July 1, 1991.)*

Law Revision Commission Comments

1990 Enactment

Section 1430 continues Section 1430 of the repealed Probate Code without change. For background on the provisions of this part, see the Comment to this part under the part heading. For general provisions relating to petitions and other papers, see Sections 1020–1023. [20 Cal.L.Rev.Comm. Reports 1001 (1990)].

Research References

Treatises and Practice Aids

Witkin, California Summary 10th Wills and Probate § 906, Definitions.

§ 1431. Proceedings to establish a limited conservatorship

"Proceedings to establish a limited conservatorship" include proceedings to modify or revoke the powers or duties of a limited conservator. *(Stats.1990, c. 79 (A.B.759), § 14, operative July 1, 1991.)*

Law Revision Commission Comments

1990 Enactment

Section 1431 continues Section 1431 of the repealed Probate Code without change. For background on the provisions of this part, see the Comment to this part under the part heading. [20 Cal.L.Rev. Comm. Reports 1001 (1990)].

Research References

Treatises and Practice Aids

Witkin, California Summary 10th Wills and Probate § 906, Definitions.

§ 1440. Secretary concerned

"Secretary concerned" has the same meaning as provided in United States Code, Title 37, Section 101. *(Stats.1990, c. 79 (A.B.759), § 14, operative July 1, 1991.)*

Law Revision Commission Comments

1990 Enactment

Section 1440 continues Section 1440 of the repealed Probate Code without substantive change. For background on the provisions of this part, see the Comment to this part under the part heading. [20 Cal.L.Rev.Comm. Reports 1001 (1990)].

Research References

Treatises and Practice Aids

Witkin, California Summary 10th Wills and Probate § 948, Where Proposed Conservatee is Absentee.

§ 1446. Single-premium deferred annuity

"Single-premium deferred annuity" means an annuity offered by an admitted life insurer for the payment of a one-time lump-sum premium and for which the insurer neither assesses any initial charges or administrative fees against the premium paid nor exacts or assesses any penalty for withdrawal of any funds by the annuitant after a period of five years. *(Stats.1990, c. 79 (A.B.759), § 14, operative July 1, 1991.)*

Law Revision Commission Comments

1990 Enactment

Section 1446 continues Section 1446 of the repealed Probate Code without change. For background on the provisions of this part, see the Comment to this part under the part heading. [20 Cal.L.Rev. Comm. Reports 1001 (1990)].

Research References

Treatises and Practice Aids

Witkin, California Summary 10th Wills and Probate § 906, Definitions.

§ 1449. Indian child custody proceedings; definitions; membership in more than one tribe

(a) As used in this division, unless the context otherwise requires, the terms "Indian," "Indian child," "Indian child's tribe," "Indian custodian," "Indian tribe," "reservation," and "tribal court" shall be defined as provided in Section 1903 of the Indian Child Welfare Act (25 U.S.C. Sec. 1901 et seq.).

(b) When used in connection with an Indian child custody proceeding, the terms "extended family member" and "parent" shall be defined as provided in Section 1903 of the Indian Child Welfare Act (25 U.S.C. Sec. 1901 et seq.).

(c) "Indian child custody proceeding" means a "child custody proceeding" within the meaning of Section 1903 of the Indian Child Welfare Act (25 U.S.C. Sec. 1901 et seq.), including a voluntary or involuntary proceeding that may result in an Indian child's temporary or long-term foster care or guardianship placement if the parent or Indian custodian cannot have the child returned upon demand, termination of parental rights or adoptive placement.

(d) When an Indian child is a member of more than one tribe or is eligible for membership in more than one tribe, the court shall make a determination, in writing together with the reasons for it, as to which tribe is the Indian child's tribe for purposes of the Indian child custody proceeding. The court shall make that determination as follows:

(1) If the Indian child is or becomes a member of only one tribe, that tribe shall be designated as the Indian child's tribe, even though the child is eligible for membership in another tribe.

(2) If an Indian child is or becomes a member of more than one tribe, or is not a member of any tribe but is eligible for membership in more than one tribe, the tribe with which the child has the more significant contacts shall be designated as the Indian child's tribe. In determining which tribe the child has the more significant contacts with, the court shall consider, among other things, the following factors:

(A) The length of residence on or near the reservation of each tribe and frequency of contact with each tribe.

(B) The child's participation in activities of each tribe.

(C) The child's fluency in the language of each tribe.

(D) Whether there has been a previous adjudication with respect to the child by a court of one of the tribes.

(E) The residence on or near one of the tribes' reservations by the child parents, Indian custodian, or extended family members.

(F) Tribal membership of custodial parent or Indian custodian.

(G) Interest asserted by each tribe in response to the notice specified in Section 1460.2.

(H) The child's self-identification.

(3) If an Indian child becomes a member of a tribe other than the one designated by the court as the Indian child's tribe under paragraph (2), actions taken based on the court's determination prior to the child's becoming a tribal member shall continue to be valid. *(Added by Stats.2006, c. 838 (S.B.678), § 16.)*

Research References

Forms

West's California Code Forms, Probate § 1459.5 COMMENT, Application Of Federal Law to Proceedings Involving Children Of Indian Ancestry.

West's California Judicial Council Forms ICWA-030, Notice Of Child Custody Proceeding for Indian Child (Indian Child Welfare Act).

West's California Judicial Council Forms GC-210(CA), Guardianship Petition--Child Information Attachment.

West's California Judicial Council Forms ICWA-030(A), Attachment to Notice Of Child Custody Proceeding for Indian Child (Indian Child Welfare Act).

Treatises and Practice Aids

Witkin, California Summary 10th Wills and Probate § 915A, (New) Special Provisions Applicable to Indian Children.

CHAPTER 2. GENERAL PROVISIONS

§ 1452. Trial by jury

Except as otherwise specifically provided in this division, there is no right to trial by jury in proceedings under this division. *(Stats.1990, c. 79 (A.B.759), § 14, operative July 1, 1991.)*

Law Revision Commission Comments

1990 Enactment

Section 1452 continues Section 1452 of the repealed Probate Code without change. There is a right to a jury trial in a hearing on a petition for establishment of a conservatorship (see Section 1827), for termination of conservatorship (see Section 1863), and for modification of the powers of a limited conservator (Section 2351.5(c)). For background on the provisions of this part, see the Comment to this part under the part heading. [20 Cal.L.Rev.Comm. Reports 1001 (1990)].

Research References

Treatises and Practice Aids

Witkin, California Summary 10th Wills and Probate § 399, Trial.
Witkin, California Summary 10th Wills and Probate § 907, Rules Of Practice.
Witkin, California Summary 10th Wills and Probate § 943, in General.

§ 1453. Motion for new trial

A motion for a new trial may be made only in cases in which, under the provisions of this division, a right to jury trial is expressly granted, whether or not the case was tried by a jury. *(Stats.1990, c. 79 (A.B.759), § 14, operative July 1, 1991.)*

Law Revision Commission Comments

1990 Enactment

Section 1453 continues Section 1453 of the repealed Probate Code without change. For background on the provisions of this part, see the Comment to this part under the part heading. [20 Cal.L.Rev. Comm. Reports 1001 (1990)].

Research References

Treatises and Practice Aids

Witkin, California Summary 10th Wills and Probate § 907, Rules Of Practice.

§ 1454. Court investigator; appointment; qualifications

(a) The court shall appoint a court investigator when one is required for the purposes of a proceeding under this division. The person appointed as the court investigator shall be an officer or special appointee of the court with no personal or other beneficial interest in the proceeding.

(b) The person appointed as the court investigator shall have the following qualifications:

(1) The training or experience, or both, necessary (i) to make the investigations required under this division, (ii) to communicate with, assess, and deal with persons who are or may be the subject of proceedings under this division, and (iii) to perform the other duties required of a court investigator.

(2) A demonstrated sufficient knowledge of law so as to be able to inform conservatees and proposed conservatees of the nature and effect of a conservatorship proceeding and of their rights, to answer their questions, and to inform conservators concerning their powers and duties. *(Stats.1990, c. 79 (A.B.759), § 14, operative July 1, 1991.)*

Law Revision Commission Comments

1990 Enactment

Section 1454 continues Section 1454 of the repealed Probate Code without change. For background on the provisions of this part, see the Comment to this part under the part heading. See also Report of Assembly Committee on Judiciary on Assembly Bills Nos. 261 and 167, reprinted in 15 Cal.L.Revision Comm'n Reports 1061–67 (1980). [20 Cal.L.Rev.Comm. Reports 1001 (1990)].

Research References

Forms

California Transactions Forms--Estate Planning § 1:4, Loss Of Due Process Inherent in Probate Avoidance.
West's California Code Forms, Probate § 1454 Form 1, Order Appointing Court Investigator--Judicial Council Form GC-330.
West's California Code Forms, Probate § 4765 Form 1, Petition to Enforce Duties Of Attorney-In-Fact for Health Care.
West's California Judicial Council Forms GC-330, Order Appointing Court Investigator.
West's California Judicial Council Forms GC-331, Order Appointing Court Investigator (Review and Successor Conservator Investigations).
West's California Judicial Council Forms GC-332, Order Setting Biennial Review Investigation and Directing Status Report Before Review.

Treatises and Practice Aids

Witkin, California Summary 10th Wills and Probate § 874, Petition.
Witkin, California Summary 10th Wills and Probate § 898, Petition.
Witkin, California Summary 10th Wills and Probate § 907, Rules Of Practice.

§ 1455. Petitions for instructions, or grant of power or authority; persons authorized to file

Any petition for instructions or to grant a guardian or a conservator any power or authority under this division, which may be filed by a guardian or conservator, may also be filed by a person who petitions for the appointment of a guardian or conservator, including, but not limited to, a person who petitions under Section 2002 for transfer of conservatorship. *(Added by Stats.1996, c. 563 (S.B.392), § 5. Amended by Stats.2014, c. 553 (S.B.940), § 4, eff. Jan. 1, 2015, operative Jan. 1, 2016.)*

Law Revision Commission Comments

2014 Amendment

Section 1455 is amended to reflect the enactment of the California Conservatorship Jurisdiction Act (Section 1980 *et seq.*). [43 Cal. L.Rev.Comm. Reports 93 (2013)].

Research References

Treatises and Practice Aids

Witkin, California Summary 10th Wills and Probate § 907, Rules Of Practice.

§ 1456. Court-appointed attorneys, examiners and investigators; educational requirements

(a) In addition to any other requirements that are part of the judicial branch education program, on or before January 1, 2008, the Judicial Council shall adopt a rule of court that shall do all of the following:

(1) Specifies the qualifications of a court-employed staff attorney, examiner, and investigator, and any attorney appointed pursuant to Sections 1470 and 1471.

(2) Specifies the number of hours of education in classes related to conservatorships or guardianships that a judge who is regularly assigned to hear probate matters shall complete, upon assuming the probate assignment, and then over a three-year period on an ongoing basis.

(3) Specifies the number of hours of education in classes related to conservatorships or guardianships that a court-employed staff attorney, examiner, and investigator, and any attorney appointed pursuant to Sections 1470 and 1471 shall complete each year.

(4) Specifies the particular subject matter that shall be included in the education required each year.

(5) Specifies reporting requirements to ensure compliance with this section.

(b) In formulating the rule required by this section, the Judicial Council shall consult with interested parties, including, but not limited to, the California Judges Association, the California Association of Superior Court Investigators, the California Public Defenders Association, the County Counsels' Association of California, the State Bar of California, the National Guardianship Association, the Professional Fiduciary Association of California, the California Association of Public Administrators, Public Guardians and Public Conservators, a disability rights organization, and the Association of Professional Geriatric Care Managers. *(Added by Stats.2006, c. 493 (A.B.1363), § 3. Amended by Stats.2007, c. 553 (A.B.1727), § 2.)*

Research References

Forms

West's California Judicial Council Forms GC-010, Certification Of Attorney Concerning Qualifications for Court Appointment in Conservatorships or Guardianships (Probate--Guardianships and Conservatorships).

West's California Judicial Council Forms GC-011, Annual Certification Of Court-Appointed Attorney (Probate--Guardianships and Conservatorships).

§ 1456.2. Continuing education requirements; compliance by public conservator

On or before January 1, 2010, the public conservator shall comply with the continuing education requirements that are established by the California State Association of Public Administrators, Public Guardians, and Public Conservators. *(Added by Stats.2008, c. 237 (A.B.2343), § 2.)*

Research References

Treatises and Practice Aids

Witkin, California Summary 10th Wills and Probate § 971, Nature Of Office.

§ 1456.5. Compliance with filing requirements

Each court shall ensure compliance with the requirements of filing the inventory and appraisal and the accountings required by this division. Courts may comply with this section in either of the following ways:

(a) By placing on the court's calendar, at the time of the appointment of the guardian or conservator and at the time of approval of each accounting, a future hearing date to enable the court to confirm timely compliance with these requirements.

(b) By establishing and maintaining internal procedures to generate an order for appearance and consideration of appropriate sanctions or other actions if the guardian or conservator fails to comply with the requirements of this section. *(Added by Stats.2007, c. 553 (A.B.1727), § 3.)*

§ 1457. Nonprofessional conservators and guardians; educational program and training

In order to assist relatives and friends who may seek appointment as a nonprofessional conservator or guardian the Judicial Council shall, on or before January 1, 2008, develop a short educational program of no more than three hours that is user-friendly and shall make that program available free of charge to each proposed conservator and guardian and each court-appointed conservator and guardian who is not required to be licensed as a professional conservator or guardian pursuant to Chapter 6 (commencing with Section 6500) of Division 3 of the Business and Professions Code. The program may be available by video presentation or Internet access. *(Added by Stats.2006, c. 493 (A.B.1363), § 4. Amended by Stats.2007, c. 553 (A.B.1727), § 4.)*

Research References

Treatises and Practice Aids

Witkin, California Summary 10th Wills and Probate § 916, in General.

Witkin, California Summary 10th Wills and Probate § 947, Disclosures to Conservator.

§ 1459. Legislative findings and declarations; children of Indian ancestry

(a) The Legislature finds and declares the following:

(1) There is no resource that is more vital to the continued existence and integrity of recognized Indian tribes than their children, and the State of California has an interest in protecting Indian children who are members of, or are eligible for membership in, an Indian tribe. The state is committed to protecting the essential tribal relations and best interest of an Indian child by promoting practices, in accordance with the Indian Child Welfare Act (25 U.S.C. Sec. 1901 et seq.) and other applicable law, designed to prevent the child's involuntary out-of-home placement and, whenever such placement is necessary or ordered, by placing the child, whenever possible, in a placement that reflects the unique values of the child's tribal culture and is best able to assist the child in establishing, developing, and maintaining a political, cultural, and social relationship with the child's tribe and tribal community.

(2) It is in the interest of an Indian child that the child's membership in the child's Indian tribe and connection to the tribal community be encouraged and protected, regardless of whether or not the child is in the physical custody of an Indian parent or Indian custodian at the commencement of a child custody proceeding, the parental rights of the child's parents have been terminated, or where the child has resided or been domiciled.

(b) In all Indian child custody proceedings, as defined in the federal Indian Child Welfare Act, the court shall consider all of the findings contained in subdivision (a), strive to promote the stability and security of Indian tribes and families, comply with the federal Indian Child Welfare Act, and seek to protect the best interest of the child. Whenever an Indian child is removed from a foster care home or institution, guardianship, or adoptive placement for the purpose of further foster care, guardianship, or adoptive placement, placement of the child shall be in accordance with the Indian Child Welfare Act.

(c) A determination by an Indian tribe that an unmarried person, who is under the age of 18 years, is either (1) a member of an Indian tribe or (2) eligible for membership in an Indian tribe and a biological child of a member of an Indian tribe shall constitute a significant political affiliation with the tribe and shall require the application of the federal Indian Child Welfare Act to the proceedings.

(d) In any case in which this code or other applicable state or federal law provides a higher standard of protection to the rights of the parent or Indian custodian of an Indian child, or the Indian child's tribe, than the rights provided under the Indian Child Welfare Act, the court shall apply the higher state or federal standard.

(e) Any Indian child, the Indian child's tribe, or the parent or Indian custodian from whose custody the child has been removed, may petition the court to invalidate an action in an Indian child custody proceeding for foster care or guardianship placement or termination of parental rights if the action violated Sections 1911, 1912, and 1913 of the Indian Child Welfare Act. *(Added by Stats.2006, c. 838 (S.B.678), § 17.)*

Research References

Forms

West's California Code Forms, Probate § 1459 COMMENT, Guardianships for Children Of Indian Ancestry.

Treatises and Practice Aids

Witkin, California Summary 10th Parent and Child § 535, Placement Standards and Preferences.

Witkin, California Summary 10th Wills and Probate § 915A, (New) Special Provisions Applicable to Indian Children.

§ 1459.5. Application of federal law to proceedings involving children of Indian ancestry

(a) The Indian Child Welfare Act (25 U.S.C. Sec. 1901 et seq.) shall apply to the following guardianship or conservatorship proceedings under this division when the proposed ward or conservatee is an Indian child:

(1) In any case in which the petition is a petition for guardianship of the person and the proposed guardian is not the natural parent or Indian custodian of the proposed ward, unless the proposed guardian has been nominated by the natural parents pursuant to Section 1500 and the parents retain the right to have custody of the child returned to them upon demand.

(2) To a proceeding to have an Indian child declared free from the custody and control of one or both parents brought in a guardianship proceeding.

(3) In any case in which the petition is a petition for conservatorship of the person of a minor whose marriage has been dissolved, the proposed conservator is seeking physical custody of the minor, the proposed conservator is not the natural parent or Indian custodian of the proposed conservatee and the natural parent or Indian custodian does not retain the right to have custody of the child returned to them upon demand.

(b) When the Indian Child Welfare Act applies to a proceeding under this division, the court shall apply Sections 224.3 to 224.6, inclusive, and Sections 305.5, 361.31, and 361.7 of the Welfare and Institutions Code, and the following rules from the California Rules of Court, as they read on January 1, 2005:

(1) Paragraph (7) of subdivision (b) of Rule 1410.

(2) Subdivision (i) of Rule 1412.

(c) In the provisions cited in subdivision (b), references to social workers, probation officers, county welfare department, or probation department shall be construed as meaning the party seeking a foster care placement, guardianship, or adoption. *(Added by Stats.2006, c. 838 (S.B.678), § 18.)*

Research References

Forms

West's California Code Forms, Probate § 1459.5 COMMENT, Application Of Federal Law to Proceedings Involving Children Of Indian Ancestry.

West's California Judicial Council Forms ICWA-020, Parental Notification Of Indian Status.

West's California Judicial Council Forms ICWA-030, Notice Of Child Custody Proceeding for Indian Child (Indian Child Welfare Act).

West's California Judicial Council Forms ICWA-040, Notice Of Designation Of Tribal Representative and Notice Of Intervention in a Court Proceeding Involving an Indian Child.

West's California Judicial Council Forms ICWA-050, Notice Of Petition and Petition to Transfer Case Involving an Indian Child to Tribal Jurisdiction.

West's California Judicial Council Forms ICWA-060, Order on Petition to Transfer Case Involving an Indian Child to Tribal Jurisdiction.

West's California Judicial Council Forms GC-210(CA), Guardianship Petition--Child Information Attachment.

West's California Judicial Council Forms ICWA-030(A), Attachment to Notice Of Child Custody Proceeding for Indian Child (Indian Child Welfare Act).

Treatises and Practice Aids

Witkin, California Summary 10th Parent and Child § 522, Nature and Scope Of Indian Child Welfare Act.

Witkin, California Summary 10th Parent and Child § 524, Jurisdiction.

Witkin, California Summary 10th Wills and Probate § 915A, (New) Special Provisions Applicable to Indian Children.

CHAPTER 3. NOTICES

Section
1469. References to § 1220 deemed references to this chapter.

§ 1460. Notice of time and place; delivery; posting; special notice; dispensation

(a) Subject to Sections 1202 and 1203, if notice of hearing is required under this division but the applicable provision does not fix the manner of giving notice of hearing, the notice of the time and place of the hearing shall be given at least 15 days before the day of the hearing as provided in this section.

(b) Subject to subdivision (e), the petitioner, who includes, for * * * purposes of this section, a person filing a petition, report, or account, shall cause the notice of hearing to be * * * delivered pursuant to Section 1215, to each of the following persons:

(1) The guardian or conservator.

(2) The ward or the conservatee.

(3) The spouse of the ward or conservatee, if the ward or conservatee has a spouse, or the domestic partner of the conservatee, if the conservatee has a domestic partner.

(4) Any person who has requested special notice of the matter, as provided in Section 2700.

(5) For any hearing on a petition to terminate a guardianship, to accept the resignation of, or to remove the guardian, the persons described in subdivision (c) of Section 1510.

(6) For any hearing on a petition to terminate a conservatorship, to accept the resignation of, or to remove the conservator, the persons described in subdivision (b) of Section 1821.

(c) The clerk of the court shall cause the notice of the hearing to be posted as provided in Section 1230 if the posting is required by subdivision (c) of Section 2543.

(d) Except as provided in subdivision (e), * * * this section * * * does not excuse compliance with the requirements for notice to a person who has requested special notice pursuant to Chapter 10 (commencing with Section 2700) of Part 4.

(e) The court, for good cause, may dispense with the notice otherwise required to be given to a person as provided in this section. *(Stats.1990, c. 79 (A.B.759), § 14, operative July 1, 1991. Amended by Stats.1994, c. 806 (A.B.3686), § 8; Stats.1996, c. 862 (A.B.2751), § 5; Stats.2001, c. 893 (A.B.25), § 14; Stats.2017, c. 319 (A.B.976), § 26, eff. Jan. 1, 2018.)*

Law Revision Commission Comments

1990 Enactment

Section 1460 continues Section 1460 of the repealed Probate Code with revisions that permit the court for good cause to dispense with notice to a person who has requested special notice. A reference to Sections 1202 and 1203 has been substituted for the reference to Section 1462, the substance of former Section 1462 now being found in Sections 1202 and 1203. The phrase "other than the petitioner or persons joining in the petition" has been omitted from subdivision (b), this phrase being unnecessary in view of Section 1201. The reference in subdivision (c) to the courthouse of the county of the court where the proceedings are pending has been omitted as unnecessary in view of comparable provision in subdivision (a) of Section 1230.

For general provisions relating to notice of hearing, see Sections 1200–1221. Where the court determines that the notice otherwise required is insufficient under the particular circumstances, the court may require that further or additional notice be given. See Section 1202. The court may for good cause shorten or lengthen the 15–day notice required by this section. See Sections 1202, 1203. A petitioner need not give notice of himself or herself or to persons joining in the petition. See Section 1201.

The court may dispense with the required notice where good cause is shown. See subdivision (e). This authority permits the court to dispense with notice, for example, where the person specified to receive the notice is in such mental or physical condition that giving the person notice would be useless or detrimental to the person or where, after the exercise of reasonable diligence, the whereabouts of the person is unknown.

Any interested person may receive notice of hearing on all petitions or notice of hearing of certain specified matters by filing and serving a request for special notice under Section 2700. Subdivision (d) makes clear that the provisions of this section have no effect on the requirements for notice to a person who has requested special notice. See Section 2700 and the Comment thereto. However, subdivision (e) permits the court for good cause to dispense with notice to a person who has requested special notice.

Section 1460 does not deal with the effect of giving notice or the failure to receive notice. See Section 1260(c) (conclusiveness of order concerning notice) and the Comment thereto. Proof of the giving of notice must be made at or before the hearing as provided in Sections 1260–1265. For background on the provisions of this part, see the Comment to this part under the part heading. See also Report of Senate Committee on Judiciary on Assembly Bill No. 261, reprinted in 15 Cal.L.Revision Comm'n Reports 1097–99 (1980). [20 Cal.L.Rev.Comm. Reports 1001 (1990)].

Research References

Forms

West's California Code Forms, Probate § 1861 Form 1, Petition for Termination Of Conservatorship.

West's California Code Forms, Probate § 1874 Form 1, Petition for Order Authorizing Conservatee to Enter Into Transaction.

West's California Code Forms, Probate § 2213 Form 1, Petition for Order for Transfer Of Proceedings.

West's California Code Forms, Probate § 2329 Form 1, Petition for Reduction Of Bond.

West's California Code Forms, Probate § 2403 Form 1, Petition for Instructions (Or Confirmation).

West's California Code Forms, Probate § 2404 Form 1, Petition to Compel Payment Of Support.

West's California Code Forms, Probate § 2404 Form 3, Petition by Creditor to Compel Payment Of Debt.

West's California Code Forms, Probate § 2421 Form 1, Petition for Allowance.

West's California Code Forms, Probate § 2423 Form 1, Petition for Payment Of Surplus Income to Relatives Of Conservatee.

West's California Code Forms, Probate § 2450 Form 1, Petition to Withdraw or Limit Independent Powers Of Guardian or Conservator.

West's California Code Forms, Probate § 2456 Form 1, Petition for Order Conditioning Withdrawal Of Deposits in Financial Institution on Prior Authorization Of the Court.

West's California Code Forms, Probate § 2551 Form 1, Petition to Borrow Money and Encumber Real Property.

West's California Code Forms, Probate § 2553 Form 1, Petition to Lease Real Property.

West's California Code Forms, Probate § 2580 Form 1, Petition for Authority to Make Gifts.

West's California Code Forms, Probate § 2620 Form 1, [First/Second, Etc] Account for Guardianship or Conservatorship Estate and Petition for Settlement Of Account [And for Compensation].
West's California Code Forms, Probate § 2630 Form 2, Order Settling Final Account Of Guardian or Conservator.
West's California Code Forms, Probate § 2640 Form 1, Petition for Fees.
West's California Code Forms, Probate § 2651 Form 1, Petition for Removal Of Guardian or Conservator.
West's California Code Forms, Probate § 2682 Form 1, Petition for Appointment Of Successor Conservator.
West's California Code Forms, Probate § 3080 Form 1, Petition for Support; for Injunctive Orders; for Determination Of the Character Of Property; for an Accounting; for Employment Of Counsel; and for Attorney Fees and Costs.
West's California Code Forms, Probate § 277(C) Form 1, Petition for Order Authorizing Personal Representative to Disclaim.
West's California Code Forms, Probate § 2459(E) Form 1, Petition for Authorization for Guardian to Effect or Maintain in Force Contract Under Insurance Code Section 10112.
West's California Code Forms, Probate § 1460-1461 Form 1, Notice Of Hearing (Guardianship or Conservatorship)--Judicial Council Form GC-020.
West's California Code Forms, Probate § 1460-1461 Form 2, Order Dispensing With Notice--Judicial Council Form GC-021.
West's California Code Forms, Probate § 2500-2507 Form 1, Petition by Guardian or Conservator to Approve Compromise Of Disputed Personal Injury Claim Of Minor or Incompetent Person--Judicial Council Form MC-350.
West's California Judicial Council Forms GC-020, Notice Of Hearing--Guardianship or Conservatorship.
West's California Judicial Council Forms GC-021, Order Dispensing With Notice.
West's California Judicial Council Forms GC-255, Petition for Termination Of Guardianship.
West's California Judicial Council Forms GC-020(C), Clerk's Certificate Of Posting Notice Of Hearing--Guardianship or Conservatorship.
West's California Judicial Council Forms GC-020(P), Proof Of Personal Service Of Notice Of Hearing--Guardianship or Conservatorship.

Treatises and Practice Aids

Witkin, California Summary 10th Community Property § 169, Hearing and Incidental Proceedings.
Witkin, California Summary 10th Community Property § 170, Orders.
Witkin, California Summary 10th Real Property § 163, Procedure.
Witkin, California Summary 10th Wills and Probate § 336, Disclaimer for Minor, Conservatee, or Decedent.
Witkin, California Summary 10th Wills and Probate § 357, Notice.
Witkin, California Summary 10th Wills and Probate § 910, General Notice Requirement.
Witkin, California Summary 10th Wills and Probate § 914, Notice in Missing Person Proceedings.
Witkin, California Summary 10th Wills and Probate § 930, Termination Of Guardianship.
Witkin, California Summary 10th Wills and Probate § 949, Where Proposed Conservatee is Missing Person.
Witkin, California Summary 10th Wills and Probate § 952, Procedure.
Witkin, California Summary 10th Wills and Probate § 955, Court Order Broadening Capacity.
Witkin, California Summary 10th Wills and Probate § 957, Procedure.
Witkin, California Summary 10th Wills and Probate § 971, Nature Of Office.
Witkin, California Summary 10th Wills and Probate § 972, Appointment Procedure.
Witkin, California Summary 10th Wills and Probate § 981, Change Of Venue.
Witkin, California Summary 10th Wills and Probate § 987, Request for Special Notice.
Witkin, California Summary 10th Wills and Probate § 989, in General.
Witkin, California Summary 10th Wills and Probate § 990, Fixing Residence.
Witkin, California Summary 10th Wills and Probate § 1001, Duty to Manage Estate.
Witkin, California Summary 10th Wills and Probate § 1017, Procedure.
Witkin, California Summary 10th Wills and Probate § 1022, Leases.
Witkin, California Summary 10th Wills and Probate § 1026, Petition, Notice, and Hearing.
Witkin, California Summary 10th Wills and Probate § 1031, Procedure.
Witkin, California Summary 10th Wills and Probate § 1034, Objections and Independent Appraisal.
Witkin, California Summary 10th Wills and Probate § 1037, Hearing and Objections.
Witkin, California Summary 10th Wills and Probate § 1044, Procedure.
Witkin, California Summary 10th Wills and Probate § 1047, Order Authorizing Periodic Payments.
Witkin, California Summary 10th Wills and Probate § 1049, Procedure for Removal.
Witkin, California Summary 10th Wills and Probate § 1050, Resignation.
Witkin, California Summary 10th Wills and Probate § 1052, Appointment Of Successor Conservator.
Witkin, California Summary 10th Wills and Probate § 1058, Modification Of Powers.
Witkin, California Summary 10th Wills and Probate § 1071, Disposition Of Proceeds.
Witkin, California Summary 10th Wills and Probate § 915B, (New) Special Immigrant Juvenile Status Proceedings.

§ 1460.1. Children under 12 years of age; exceptions to notice requirements

Notwithstanding any other provision of this division, no notice is required to be given to any child under the age of 12 years if the court determines either of the following:

(a) Notice was properly given to a parent, guardian, or other person having legal custody of the minor, with whom the minor resides.

(b) The petition is brought by a parent, guardian, or other person having legal custody of the minor, with whom the minor resides. *(Added by Stats.1997, c. 724 (A.B.1172), § 9.)*

Research References

Forms

West's California Code Forms, Probate § 1460-1461 Form 1, Notice Of Hearing (Guardianship or Conservatorship)--Judicial Council Form GC-020.

Treatises and Practice Aids

Witkin, California Summary 10th Wills and Probate § 390, Other Persons.

Witkin, California Summary 10th Wills and Probate § 910, General Notice Requirement.

§ 1460.2. Knowledge that proposed ward or conservatee may be a child of Indian ancestry; notice to interested parties; requirements; time; proof

(a) If the court or petitioner knows or has reason to know that the proposed ward or conservatee may be an Indian child, notice shall comply with subdivision (b) in any case in which the Indian Child Welfare Act (25 U.S.C. Sec. 1901 et seq.) applies, as specified in Section 1459.5.

(b) Any notice sent under this section shall be sent to the minor's parent or legal guardian, Indian custodian, if any, and the Indian child's tribe, and shall comply with all of the following requirements:

(1) Notice shall be sent by registered or certified mail with return receipt requested. Additional notice by first-class mail is recommended, but not required.

(2) Notice to the tribe shall be to the tribal chairperson, unless the tribe has designated another agent for service.

(3) Notice shall be sent to all tribes of which the child may be a member or eligible for membership until the court makes a determination as to which tribe is the Indian child's tribe in accordance with subdivision (d) of Section 1449, after which notice need only be sent to the tribe determined to be the Indian child's tribe.

(4) Notice, to the extent required by federal law, shall be sent to the Secretary of the Interior's designated agent, the Sacramento Area Director, Bureau of Indian Affairs. If the identity or location of the Indian child's tribe is known, a copy of the notice shall also be sent directly to the Secretary of the Interior, unless the Secretary of the Interior has waived the notice in writing and the person responsible for giving notice under this section has filed proof of the waiver with the court.

(5) The notice shall include all of the following information:

(A) The name, birthdate, and birthplace of the Indian child, if known.

(B) The name of any Indian tribe in which the child is a member or may be eligible for membership, if known.

(C) All names known of the Indian child's biological parents, grandparents and great-grandparents or Indian custodians, including maiden, married, and former names or aliases, as well as their current and former addresses, birthdates, places of birth and death, tribal enrollment numbers, and any other identifying information, if known.

(D) A copy of the petition.

(E) A copy of the child's birth certificate, if available.

(F) The location, mailing address, and telephone number of the court and all parties notified pursuant to this section.

(G) A statement of the following:

(i) The absolute right of the child's parents, Indian custodians, and tribe to intervene in the proceeding.

(ii) The right of the child's parents, Indian custodians, and tribe to petition the court to transfer the proceeding to the tribal court of the Indian child's tribe, absent objection by either parent and subject to declination by the tribal court.

(iii) The right of the child's parents, Indian custodians, and tribe to, upon request, be granted up to an additional 20 days from the receipt of the notice to prepare for the proceeding.

(iv) The potential legal consequences of the proceedings on the future custodial rights of the child's parents or Indian custodians.

(v) That if the parents or Indian custodians are unable to afford counsel, counsel shall be appointed to represent the parents or Indian custodians pursuant to Section 1912 of the Indian Child Welfare Act (25 U.S.C. Sec. 1901 et seq.).

(vi) That the information contained in the notice, petition, pleading, and other court documents is confidential, so any person or entity notified shall maintain the confidentiality of the information contained in the notice concerning the particular proceeding and not reveal it to anyone who does not need the information in order to exercise the tribe's rights under the Indian Child Welfare Act (25 U.S.C. Sec. 1901 et seq.).

(c) Notice shall be sent whenever it is known or there is reason to know that an Indian child is involved, and for every hearing thereafter, including, but not limited to, the hearing at which a final adoption order is to be granted. After a tribe acknowledges that the child is a member or eligible for membership in the tribe, or after the Indian child's tribe intervenes in a proceeding, the information set out in subparagraphs (C), (D), (E), and (G) of paragraph (5) of subdivision (b) need not be included with the notice.

(d) Proof of the notice, including copies of notices sent and all return receipts and responses received, shall be filed with the court in advance of the hearing except as permitted under subdivision (e).

(e) No proceeding shall be held until at least 10 days after receipt of notice by the parent, Indian custodian, the tribe or the Bureau of Indian Affairs. The parent, Indian custodian, or the tribe shall, upon request, be granted up to 20 additional days to prepare for the proceeding. Nothing herein shall be construed as limiting the rights of the parent, Indian custodian, or tribe to 10 days' notice when a lengthier notice period is required by statute.

(f) With respect to giving notice to Indian tribes, a party shall be subject to court sanctions if that person knowingly and willfully falsifies or conceals a material fact concerning whether the child is an Indian child, or counsels a party to do so.

(g) The inclusion of contact information of any adult or child that would otherwise be required to be included in the notification pursuant to this section, shall not be required if that person is at risk of harm as a result of domestic violence, child abuse, sexual abuse, or stalking. *(Added by Stats.2006, c. 838 (S.B.678), § 19.)*

Research References

Forms

West's California Code Forms, Probate § 1459.5 COMMENT, Application Of Federal Law to Proceedings Involving Children Of Indian Ancestry.

Treatises and Practice Aids

Witkin, California Summary 10th Parent and Child § 529, Formal Requisites.

Witkin, California Summary 10th Wills and Probate § 915A, (New) Special Provisions Applicable to Indian Children.

§ 1461. Notice to director; conditions; certificate; limitations

(a) As used in this section, "director" means:

(1) The Director of State Hospitals when the state hospital referred to in subdivision (b) is under the jurisdiction of the State Department of State Hospitals.

(2) The Director of Developmental Services when the state hospital referred to in subdivision (b) is under the jurisdiction of the State Department of Developmental Services.

(b) Notice of the time and place of hearing on the petition, report, or account, and a copy of the petition, report, or account, shall be * * * delivered pursuant to Section 1215 to the director at the director's office in Sacramento or to the electronic address designated by the director for receipt of notice pursuant to this code, at least 15 days before the hearing if both of the following conditions exist:

(1) The ward or conservatee is or has been during the guardianship or conservatorship proceeding a patient in, or on leave from, a state hospital under the jurisdiction of the State Department of State Hospitals or the State Department of Developmental Services.

(2) The petition, report, or account is filed under any one or more of the following provisions: Section 1510, 1820, 1861, 2212, 2403, 2421, 2422, or 2423; Article 7 (commencing with Section 2540) of Chapter 6 of Part 4; Section 2580, 2592, or 2620; Chapter 9.5 (commencing with Section 2670) of Part 4; Section 3080 or 3088; or Chapter 3 (commencing with Section 3100) of Part 6. Notice under this section is not required in the case of an account pursuant to Section 2620 if the total guardianship or conservatorship assets are less than one thousand five hundred dollars ($1,500) and the gross annual income, exclusive of any public assistance income, is less than six thousand dollars ($6,000), and the ward or conservatee is not a patient in, or on leave or on outpatient status from, a state hospital at the time of the filing of the petition.

(c) If the ward or conservatee has been discharged from the state hospital, the director, upon ascertaining the facts, may file with the court a certificate stating that the ward or conservatee is not indebted to the state and waive the giving of further notices under this section. Upon the filing of the certificate of the director, compliance with this section thereafter is not required unless the certificate is revoked by the director and notice of the revocation is filed with the court.

(d) The statute of limitations does not run against any claim of the State Department of State Hospitals or the State Department of Developmental Services against the estate of the ward or conservatee for board, care, maintenance, or transportation with respect to an account that is settled without giving the notice required by this section. *(Stats. 1990, c. 79 (A.B.759), § 14, operative July 1, 1991. Amended by Stats.2012, c. 440 (A.B.1488), § 39, eff. Sept. 22, 2012; Stats.2017, c. 319 (A.B.976), § 27, eff. Jan. 1, 2018.)*

Law Revision Commission Comments

1990 Enactment

Section 1461 continues Section 1461 of the repealed Probate Code without substantive change. The exception for a petition, report, or account filed by the director in the introductory clause of subdivision (b) has been omitted as unnecessary in view of Section 1201.

The following provisions, listed in paragraph (2) of subdivision (b), require a notice in cases where the condition in paragraph (1) of subdivision (b) exists:

Section 1510 (petition for appointment of guardian)

Section 1820 (petition for appointment of conservator)

Section 1861 (petition for termination of conservatorship)

Section 2212 (petition for change of venue)

Section 2403 (authorization and instructions or approval and confirmation by court for guardian or conservator of estate)

Section 2421 (petition for allowance for ward or conservatee)

Section 2422 (petition for support of ward or conservatee out of the estate notwithstanding existence of person legally obligated to provide support)

Section 2423 (petition for payment of surplus income to relatives of conservatee)

Article 7 (commencing with Section 2540) of Chapter 6 of Part 4 (petitions for sales)

Section 2580 (substituted judgment)

Section 2592 (independent exercise of powers)

Section 2620 (presentation of account for settlement and allowance)

Chapter 9.5 (commencing with Section 2670) (appointment of successor guardian or conservator)

Sections 3080 and 3088 (enforcement of support for spouse who has conservator)

Chapter 3 (commencing with Section 3100) of Part 6 (special proceeding to authorize transaction involving community property)

For other provisions concerning notice to the Director of Mental Health or the Director of Developmental Services, see Sections 2611 (inventory and appraisal), 2621 (hearing on accounts). See also Section 1542 (notice of petition for nonrelative guardianship to Director of Social Services). Where the Director of Mental Health or the Director of Developmental Services is an interested person (Section 1424), a request for special notice may be filed under Section 2700. For general provisions relating to notice, see Sections 1200–1230. See also Sections 1260–1265 (proof of giving notice). For background on the provisions of this part, see the Comment to this part under the part heading. See also Recommendation Relating to Revision of the Guardianship–Conservatorship Law, 15 Cal.L.Revision Comm'n Reports 1463, 1473–74 (1980); Report of Assembly Committee on Judiciary on Assembly Bills Nos. 261 and 167, reprinted in 15 Cal.L.Revision Comm'n Reports 1061–67 (1980). [20 Cal.L.Rev.Comm. Reports 1001 (1990)].

Research References

Forms

West's California Code Forms, Probate § 2620 Form 1, [First/Second, Etc] Account for Guardianship or Conservatorship Estate and Petition for Settlement Of Account [And for Compensation].

Treatises and Practice Aids

Witkin, California Summary 10th Community Property § 164, Notice and Hearing.

Witkin, California Summary 10th Community Property § 169, Hearing and Incidental Proceedings.

Witkin, California Summary 10th Wills and Probate § 911, When Conservatee or Ward is State Hospital Patient.

Witkin, California Summary 10th Wills and Probate § 920, in General.
Witkin, California Summary 10th Wills and Probate § 939, in General.
Witkin, California Summary 10th Wills and Probate § 1033, in General.
Witkin, California Summary 10th Wills and Probate § 1052, Appointment Of Successor Conservator.

§ 1461.4. Regional center for developmentally disabled; notice of hearing and copy of petition; report and recommendation

(a) The petitioner shall * * * deliver pursuant to Section 1215 a notice of the hearing and a copy of the petition to the director of the regional center for the developmentally disabled at least 30 days before the day of the hearing on a petition for appointment in any case in which all of the following conditions exist:

(1) The proposed ward or conservatee has developmental disabilities.

(2) The proposed guardian or conservator is not the natural parent of the proposed ward or conservatee.

(3) The proposed guardian or conservator is a provider of board and care, treatment, habilitation, or other services to persons with developmental disabilities or is a spouse or employee of a provider.

(4) The proposed guardian or conservator is not a public entity.

(b) The regional center shall file a written report and recommendation with the court regarding the suitability of the petitioners to meet the needs of the proposed ward or conservatee in any case described in subdivision (a). *(Stats. 1990, c. 79 (A.B.759), § 14, operative July 1, 1991. Amended by Stats.2017, c. 319 (A.B.976), § 28, eff. Jan. 1, 2018.)*

Law Revision Commission Comments

1990 Enactment

Section 1461.4 continues Section 1461.4 of the repealed Probate Code without change. For background on the provisions of this part, see the Comment to this part under the part heading. [20 Cal.L.Rev.Comm. Reports 1001 (1990)].

Research References

Treatises and Practice Aids

Witkin, California Summary 10th Wills and Probate § 912, When Conservatee or Ward is Developmentally Disabled.
Witkin, California Summary 10th Wills and Probate § 939, in General.

§ 1461.5. Veterans Administration; notice of hearing on petition, report, account or inventory; time; conditions

Notice of the time and place of hearing on a petition, report, or account, and a notice of the filing of an inventory, together with a copy of the petition, report, inventory, or account, shall be * * * delivered pursuant to Section 1215 to the office of the Veterans Administration having jurisdiction over the area in which the court is located at least 15 days before the hearing, or within 15 days after the inventory is filed, if both of the following conditions exist:

(a) The guardianship or conservatorship estate consists or will consist wholly or in part of any of the following:

(1) Money received from the Veterans Administration.

(2) Revenue or profit from such money or from property acquired wholly or in part from such money.

(3) Property acquired wholly or in part with such money or from such property.

(b) The petition, report, inventory, or account is filed under any one or more of the following provisions: Section 1510, 1601, 1820, 1861, 1874, 2422, or 2423; Article 7 (commencing with Section 2540) of Chapter 6 of Part 4; Section 2570, 2571, 2580, 2592, 2610, 2613, or 2620; Chapter 8 (commencing with Section 2640) of Part 4; Chapter 9.5 (commencing with Section 2670) of Part 4; Section 3080 or 3088; or Chapter 3 (commencing with Section 3100) of Part 6. *(Stats.1990, c. 79 (A.B.759), § 14, operative July 1, 1991. Amended by Stats.2017, c. 319 (A.B.976), § 29, eff. Jan. 1, 2018.)*

Law Revision Commission Comments

1990 Enactment

Section 1461.5 continues Section 1461.5 of the repealed Probate Code without substantive change. The exception for a petition filed by the Veterans Administration in the introductory clause of the section has been omitted as unnecessary in view of Section 1201. For general provisions relating to notice, see Sections 1200–1230. See also Sections 1260–1265 (proof of giving notice). For the recommendation of the California Law Revision Commission that resulted in the repeal of the Uniform Veterans Guardianship Act and the enactment of this section of the repealed Probate Code, see Recommendation Relating to Uniform Veterans Guardianship Act, 15 Cal.L.Revision Comm'n Reports 1289 (1980). For additional background on the provisions of this part, see the Comment to this part under the part heading. See also Recommendation Relating to Revision of the Guardianship–Conservatorship Law, 15 Cal.L.Revision Comm'n Reports 1463, 1474 (1980). [20 Cal.L.Rev.Comm. Reports 1001 (1990)].

Research References

Treatises and Practice Aids

Witkin, California Summary 10th Community Property § 169, Hearing and Incidental Proceedings.
Witkin, California Summary 10th Wills and Probate § 913, Notice to Veterans Administration.
Witkin, California Summary 10th Wills and Probate § 920, in General.
Witkin, California Summary 10th Wills and Probate § 939, in General.
Witkin, California Summary 10th Wills and Probate § 1052, Appointment Of Successor Conservator.

§ 1461.7. Time and place of hearing on petition, report, or account; copies

Unless the court for good cause dispenses with such notice, notice of the time and place of the hearing on a petition, report, or account, together with a copy of the petition, report, or account, shall be given to the same persons who are required to be given notice under Section 2581 for the period and in the manner provided in this chapter if both of the following conditions exist:

(a) A conservator of the estate has been appointed under Article 5 (commencing with Section 1845) of Chapter 1 of Part 3 for a person who is missing and whose whereabouts is unknown.

(b) The petition, report, or account is filed in the conservatorship proceeding under any one or more of the following provisions:

(1) Section 1861 or 2423.

(2) Article 7 (commencing with Section 2540) of Chapter 6 of Part 4.

(3) Section 2570, 2571, 2580, 2592, or 2620.

(4) Chapter 8 (commencing with Section 2640) of Part 4.

(5) Chapter 9.5 (commencing with Section 2670) of Part 4.

(6) Chapter 3 (commencing with Section 3100) of Part 6. *(Stats.1990, c. 79 (A.B.759), § 14, operative July 1, 1991.)*

Law Revision Commission Comments

1990 Enactment

Section 1461.7 continues Section 1461.7 of the repealed Probate Code without change. For the recommendation of the California Law Revision Commission that resulted in the enactment of this section of the repealed Probate Code, see Recommendation Relating to Missing Persons, 16 Cal.L.Revision Comm'n Reports 105 (1982). For additional background on the provisions of this part, see the Comment to this part under the part heading. [20 Cal.L.Rev.Comm. Reports 1001 (1990)].

Research References

Treatises and Practice Aids

Witkin, California Summary 10th Wills and Probate § 914, Notice in Missing Person Proceedings.

Witkin, California Summary 10th Wills and Probate § 949, Where Proposed Conservatee is Missing Person.

§ 1467. Service by mail deemed complete

If service is made by mail pursuant to this division in the manner authorized in Section 415.30 of the Code of Civil Procedure, the service is complete on the date a written acknowledgment of receipt is executed. *(Stats.1990, c. 79 (A.B.759), § 14, operative July 1, 1991.)*

Law Revision Commission Comments

1990 Enactment

Section 1467 continues Section 1467 of the repealed Probate Code without change. This section makes clear that, when service is made under this division in the manner authorized in Section 415.30 of the Code of Civil Procedure, the service is complete on the date the acknowledgment of receipt is executed. This section does not include the requirement found in Section 415.30 that the acknowledgment be returned "to the sender." It is sufficient if proof is made that the person served (or a person authorized to acknowledge service on behalf of such person) did execute a written acknowledgment of receipt. For example, service is complete under Section 1467 if the written acknowledgment is returned to a person other than the sender.

This section applies only where service is made by mail in the manner authorized in Section 415.30. This section does not apply where a provision of this division merely requires that a notice or other paper be mailed. In the latter case, the applicable provision ordinarily is satisfied when the notice or other paper is deposited in the mail. See Section 1215.

For background on the provisions of this part, see the Comment to this part under the part heading. [20 Cal.L.Rev.Comm. Reports 1001 (1990)].

Research References

Treatises and Practice Aids

Witkin, California Summary 10th Wills and Probate § 910, General Notice Requirement.

§ 1469. References to § 1220 deemed references to this chapter

Where a provision of this division applies the provisions of this code applicable to personal representatives to proceedings under this division, a reference to Section 1220 in the provisions applicable to personal representatives shall be deemed to be a reference to this chapter. *(Stats.1990, c. 79 (A.B.759), § 14, operative July 1, 1991.)*

Law Revision Commission Comments

1990 Enactment

Section 1469 continues Section 1469 of the repealed Probate Code with the omission of the reference to Section 1230. The reference to Section 1230 has been omitted as unnecessary in view of the revision of Section 1460(c). Section 1469 ensures that the notice provisions contained in this chapter will be used in all proceedings under this division. Section 2543 adopts the procedures applicable to personal representatives for manner of sale for sales under this division. The manner of sale procedures applicable to the personal representative require giving of notice as provided in Section 1220 (notice provision applicable to proceedings with respect to estates of decedents). However, Section 1469 provides that notice is to be given under this chapter rather than as provided in that section. See also Section 2100 (law governing where no specific provision of this division applicable). For background on the provisions of this part, see the Comment to this part under the part heading. See also Report of Assembly Committee on Judiciary on Assembly Bills Nos. 261 and 167, reprinted in 15 Cal.L.Revision Comm'n Reports 1061, 1063–64 (1980); Comments to Conforming Revisions and Repeals, 19 Cal.L.Revision Comm'n Reports 391, 444 (1988). [20 Cal.L.Rev. Comm. Reports 1001 (1990)].

Research References

Forms

West's California Judicial Council Forms GC-020, Notice Of Hearing--Guardianship or Conservatorship.

West's California Judicial Council Forms GC-020(P), Proof Of Personal Service Of Notice Of Hearing--Guardianship or Conservatorship.

Treatises and Practice Aids

Witkin, California Summary 10th Wills and Probate § 910, General Notice Requirement.

Witkin, California Summary 10th Wills and Probate § 1017, Procedure.

CHAPTER 4. APPOINTMENT OF LEGAL COUNSEL

§ 1470. Discretionary appointment; compensation and expenses; source for payment

(a) The court may appoint private legal counsel for a ward, a proposed ward, a conservatee, or a proposed conservatee in any proceeding under this division if the court determines the person is not otherwise represented by legal counsel and that the appointment would be helpful to the resolution of the matter or is necessary to protect the person's interests.

(b) If a person is furnished legal counsel under this section, the court shall, upon conclusion of the matter, fix a reasonable sum for compensation and expenses of counsel. The sum may, in the discretion of the court, include compensation for services rendered, and expenses incurred, before the date of the order appointing counsel.

(c) The court shall order the sum fixed under subdivision (b) to be paid:

(1) If the person for whom legal counsel is appointed is an adult, from the estate of that person.

(2) If the person for whom legal counsel is appointed is a minor, by a parent or the parents of the minor or from the minor's estate, or any combination thereof, in any proportions the court deems just.

(3) If a ward or proposed ward is furnished legal counsel for a guardianship proceeding, upon its own motion or that of a party, the court shall determine whether a parent or parents of the ward or proposed ward or the estate of the ward or proposed ward is financially unable to pay all or a portion of the cost of counsel appointed pursuant to this section. Any portion of the cost of that counsel that the court finds the parent or parents or the estate of the ward or proposed ward is unable to pay shall be paid by the county. The Judicial Council shall adopt guidelines to assist in determining financial eligibility for county payment of counsel appointed by the court pursuant to this chapter.

(d) The court may make an order under subdivision (c) requiring payment by a parent or parents of the minor only after the parent or parents, as the case may be, have been given notice and the opportunity to be heard on whether the order would be just under the circumstances of the particular case. *(Stats.1990, c. 79 (A.B.759), § 14, operative July 1, 1991. Amended by Stats.1992, c. 572 (S.B.1455), § 1.5; Stats.2007, c. 719 (S.B.241), § 1.)*

Law Revision Commission Comments

1990 Enactment

Section 1470 continues Section 1470 of the repealed Probate Code without change. This section gives the court discretionary authority to appoint legal counsel in guardianship and conservatorship proceedings. The court's authority to appoint counsel in a guardianship proceeding involving custody of a minor is comparable to the court's authority to appoint counsel for a minor in a child custody proceeding under the Family Law Act. See Civil Code § 4606. As to the duty of the public defender to represent an indigent upon request or upon order of court, see Gov't Code § 27706. For background on the provisions of this part, see the Comment to this part under the part heading. [20 Cal.L.Rev.Comm. Reports 1001 (1990)].

1992 Amendment

Subdivision (b) of section 1470 is amended to make clear that, when legal counsel is appointed under this section, the court is not precluded from awarding compensation for legal services rendered, and expenses incurred, before the date of appointment.

Although Section 1470(b) provides that the court shall fix compensation of counsel "upon conclusion of the matter," this does not prevent the court from later making an award of compensation. See 1 W. Johnstone & S. House, California Conservatorships and Guardianships § 7.68, at 374–75 (Cal.Cont.Ed.Bar 1990). The "matter" to which Section 1470 refers is the particular matter for which counsel was appointed. See Section 1471.

Subdivision (b) deals with compensation of appointed counsel for a ward or conservatee. Section 1470 does not affect the right to compensation in cases not covered by the section. *Cf.* Estate of Moore, 258 Cal.App.2d 458, 65 Cal.Rptr. 831 (1968) (payment of attorney's fees of petitioner for conservatorship where another person appointed as conservator); *In re* Guardianship of Bundy, 44 Cal.App. 466, 186 P. 811 (1919) (payment of attorney's fees of petitioner for adult guardianship where proposed ward contested petition). [21 Cal.L.Rev.Comm. Reports 227 (1991)].

Commentary

Guardianship of Elan E., 85 Cal.App.4th 998, 102 Cal.Rptr.2d 528 (2000), review denied March 14, 2001, holds that the trial court erred in ordering grandparents to pay attorney's fees and court costs for their indigent grandchild, who was represented by court-appointed counsel. This section extends liability to a child's parents only.

Research References

Forms

California Transactions Forms--Estate Planning § 1:4, Loss Of Due Process Inherent in Probate Avoidance.

West's California Judicial Council Forms GC-010, Certification Of Attorney Concerning Qualifications for Court Appointment in Conservatorships or Guardianships (Probate--Guardianships and Conservatorships).

West's California Judicial Council Forms GC-011, Annual Certification Of Court-Appointed Attorney (Probate--Guardianships and Conservatorships).

Treatises and Practice Aids

Witkin, California Summary 10th Wills and Probate § 43, Major Changes.

Witkin, California Summary 10th Wills and Probate § 908, Discretionary Appointment.

Witkin, California Summary 10th Wills and Probate § 943, in General.

Witkin, California Summary 10th Wills and Probate § 1041, Failure to File Account.

§ 1471. Mandatory appointment; proceedings

(a) If a conservatee, proposed conservatee, or person alleged to lack legal capacity is unable to retain legal counsel and requests the appointment of counsel to assist in the particular matter, whether or not that person lacks or appears to lack legal capacity, the court shall, at or before the time of the hearing, appoint the public defender or private counsel to represent the interest of that person in the following proceedings under this division:

(1) A proceeding to establish or transfer a conservatorship or to appoint a proposed conservator.

(2) A proceeding to terminate the conservatorship.

(3) A proceeding to remove the conservator.

(4) A proceeding for a court order affecting the legal capacity of the conservatee.

(5) A proceeding to obtain an order authorizing removal of a temporary conservatee from the temporary conservatee's place of residence.

(b) If a conservatee or proposed conservatee does not plan to retain legal counsel and has not requested the court to appoint legal counsel, whether or not that person lacks or appears to lack legal capacity, the court shall, at or before the time of the hearing, appoint the public defender or private counsel to represent the interests of that person in any proceeding listed in subdivision (a) if, based on information contained in the court investigator's report or obtained from any other source, the court determines that the appointment would be helpful to the resolution of the matter or is necessary to protect the interests of the conservatee or proposed conservatee.

(c) In any proceeding to establish a limited conservatorship, if the proposed limited conservatee has not retained legal counsel and does not plan to retain legal counsel, the court shall immediately appoint the public defender or private counsel to represent the proposed limited conservatee. The proposed limited conservatee shall pay the cost for that legal service if he or she is able. This subdivision applies irrespective of any medical or psychological inability to attend the hearing on the part of the proposed limited conservatee as allowed in Section 1825. *(Stats.1990, c. 79 (A.B.759), § 14, operative July 1, 1991. Amended by Stats.2014, c. 553 (S.B.940), § 5, eff. Jan. 1, 2015, operative Jan. 1, 2016.)*

Law Revision Commission Comments

1990 Enactment

Section 1471 continues Section 1471 of the repealed Probate Code without substantive change. This section specifies those instances where appointment of counsel is required under this division. Compensation of counsel appointed under Section 1471 is governed by Section 1472.

Subdivision (b) requires appointment of legal counsel in the cases listed in subdivision (a) where the conservatee or proposed conservatee does not request the appointment but the court determines that the appointment would be helpful to the resolution of the matter or is necessary to protect the interests of the conservatee or proposed conservatee. Although the court is given discretionary authority under Section 1470 to appoint legal counsel where the court determines that the appointment would be helpful to the resolution of the matter or is necessary to protect a person's interests, the appointment under Section 1471(b) is mandatory and makes Section 1472 applicable. Sections 1471–1472 permit appointment of the public defender, compensation of legal counsel by the county in cases where the person furnished counsel is determined by the court to lack the ability to pay, and installment payments. These provisions are not found in Section 1470 which provides for discretionary appointment of private legal counsel.

Appointment of the public defender or private counsel under Sections 1471–1472 is also required under some circumstances in a proceeding under Section 1852 (removal of conservator, restoration of conservatee's right to register to vote, making, modification, or revocation of order affecting conservatee's legal capacity, termination of conservatorship), 2357 (authorization of medical treatment for ward or conservatee), Chapter 3 (commencing with Section 3100) of Part 6 (transaction involving community property—Section 3140), or Part 7 (commencing with Section 3200) (authorization of medical treatment of an adult who does not have conservator of the person—Section 3205). See also Gov't Code § 27706 (duty of public defender to represent indigent person). For background on the provisions of this part, see the Comment to this part under the part heading. See also Report of Assembly Committee on Judiciary on Assembly Bills Nos. 261 and 167, reprinted in 15 Cal.L.Revision Comm'n Reports 1061, 1064–65 (1980). [20 Cal.L.Rev.Comm. Reports 1001 (1990)].

2014 Amendment

Section 1471 is amended to make clear that it applies when a conservatorship is transferred under the California Conservatorship Jurisdiction Act (Sections 1980–2024).

The section is also amended to replace "such" with "that," in conformity with California drafting practices. [43 Cal.L.Rev.Comm. Reports 93 (2013)].

Research References

Forms

West's California Code Forms, Probate § 3204 Form 2, Medical Declaration Of Patient's Physician.

West's California Judicial Council Forms GC-010, Certification Of Attorney Concerning Qualifications for Court Appointment in Conservatorships or Guardianships (Probate--Guardianships and Conservatorships).

West's California Judicial Council Forms GC-011, Annual Certification Of Court-Appointed Attorney (Probate--Guardianships and Conservatorships).

Treatises and Practice Aids

Witkin, California Summary 10th Community Property § 164, Notice and Hearing.

Witkin, California Summary 10th Wills and Probate § 909, Mandatory Appointment.

Witkin, California Summary 10th Wills and Probate § 1055, Procedure.

§ 1472. Mandatory appointment; compensation and expenses; determination by court; source for payment

(a) If a person is furnished legal counsel under Section 1471:

(1) The court shall, upon conclusion of the matter, fix a reasonable sum for compensation and expenses of counsel and shall make a determination of the person's ability to pay all or a portion of that sum. The sum may, in the discretion of the court, include compensation for services rendered, and expenses incurred, before the date of the order appointing counsel.

(2) If the court determines that the person has the ability to pay all or a portion of the sum, the court shall order the conservator of the estate or, if none, the person, to pay in any installments and in any manner the court determines to be reasonable and compatible with the person's financial ability.

(3) In a proceeding under Chapter 3 (commencing with Section 3100) of Part 6 for court authorization of a proposed transaction involving community property, the court may order payment out of the proceeds of the transaction.

(4) If a conservator is not appointed for the person furnished legal counsel, the order for payment may be enforced in the same manner as a money judgment.

(b) If the court determines that a person furnished private counsel under Section 1471 lacks the ability to pay all or a portion of the sum determined under paragraph (1) of subdivision (a), the county shall pay the sum to the private counsel to the extent the court determines the person is unable to pay.

(c) The payment ordered by the court under subdivision (a) shall be made to the county if the public defender has been appointed or if private counsel has been appointed to perform the duties of the public defender and the county has compensated that counsel. In the case of other court-appointed counsel, the payment shall be made to that counsel. *(Stats.1990, c. 79 (A.B.759), § 14, operative July 1, 1991. Amended by Stats.1992, c. 572 (S.B.1455), § 2.)*

Law Revision Commission Comments

1990 Enactment

Section 1472 continues Section 1472 of the repealed Probate Code without substantive change. The reference to homestead property in subdivision (a)(3) has been omitted because the statutory proceeding referred to in that paragraph applies only to community property.

Section 1472 applies where legal counsel is appointed under Section 1471. This section also applies where legal counsel is appointed under Section 1852 (removal of conservator, restoration of conservatee's right to register to vote, making, modification, or revocation of order affecting conservatee's legal capacity, termination of conservatorship), 2357 (authorization of medical treatment for ward or conservatee), 3140 (transaction involving community property) or 3205 (authorization of medical treatment for adult without conservator). For background on the provisions of this part, see the Comment to this part under the part heading. See also Report of Assembly Committee on Judiciary on Assembly Bills Nos. 261 and 167, reprinted in 15 Cal.L.Revision Comm'n Reports 1061, 1065 (1980). [20 Cal.L.Rev.Comm. Reports 1001 (1990)].

1992 Amendment

Paragraph (1) of subdivision (a) of Section 1472 is amended to make clear that, when legal counsel is appointed under Section 1471, the court is not precluded from awarding compensation for legal services rendered, and expenses incurred, before the date of appointment.

Although Section 1472(a)(1) provides that the court shall fix compensation of counsel "upon conclusion of the matter," this does not prevent the court from later making an award of compensation. See 1 W. Johnstone & S. House, California Conservatorships and Guardianships § 6.57, at 291–92 (Cal.Cont.Ed.Bar 1990). The "matter" to which Section 1472 refers is the particular matter for which counsel was appointed. See Section 1471.

Section 1472 deals with compensation of counsel appointed under Section 1471. The section does not affect the right to compensation in cases not covered by the section. *Cf.* Estate of Moore, 258 Cal.App.2d 458, 65 Cal.Rptr. 831 (1968) (payment of attorney's fees of petitioner for conservatorship where another person appointed as conservator); *In re* Guardianship of Bundy, 44 Cal.App. 466, 186 P. 811 (1919) (payment of attorney's fees of petitioner for adult guardianship where proposed ward contested petition). [21 Cal. L.Rev.Comm. Reports 227 (1991)].

Research References

Treatises and Practice Aids

Witkin, California Summary 10th Community Property § 164, Notice and Hearing.

Witkin, California Summary 10th Wills and Probate § 43, Major Changes.

Witkin, California Summary 10th Wills and Probate § 909, Mandatory Appointment.

§ 1474. Matters involving children of Indian ancestry

If an Indian custodian or biological parent of an Indian child lacks the financial ability to retain counsel and requests the appointment of counsel in proceedings described in Section 1459.5, the provisions of subsection (b) of Section 1912 of the Indian Child Welfare Act (25 U.S.C. Sec. 1901 et seq.) and Section 23.13 of Title 25 of the Code of Federal Regulations are applicable. *(Added by Stats.2006, c. 838 (S.B.678), § 20.)*

Research References

Forms

West's California Code Forms, Probate § 1459.5 COMMENT, Application Of Federal Law to Proceedings Involving Children Of Indian Ancestry.

Treatises and Practice Aids

Witkin, California Summary 10th Wills and Probate § 915A, (New) Special Provisions Applicable to Indian Children.

CHAPTER 5. TRANSITIONAL PROVISIONS

§ 1488. Nomination by adult of guardian for such adult deemed nomination of conservator

If before January 1, 1981, an adult has in a signed writing nominated a person to serve as guardian if a guardian is in the future appointed for such adult, such nomination shall be deemed to be a nomination of a conservator. This section applies whether or not the signed writing was executed in the same manner as a witnessed will so long as the person signing the writing had at the time the writing was signed sufficient capacity to form an intelligent preference. *(Stats.1990, c. 79 (A.B.759), § 14, operative July 1, 1991.)*

Law Revision Commission Comments

1990 Enactment

Section 1488 continues Section 1488 of the repealed Probate Code without substantive change. This section ensures that a nomination of a guardian made under former Probate Code Section 1463 (repealed by 1979 Cal.Stat. ch. 726, § 1) will be given effect under Section 1810. Under Section 1810, a conservator may be nominated in a signed writing whether or not the writing is executed in the same manner as a witnessed will. The second sentence of Section 1488 applies the same standard to a signed writing made under pre–1979 law and purporting to nominate a guardian, even though the writing may not have met the stricter requirement of former Probate Code Section 1463. For background on the provisions of this part, see the Comment to this part under the part heading.

§ 1489. Appointment of guardian by parent or other person for a minor; effect

If, before January 1, 1981, a parent or other person has in a signed writing appointed a person to serve as the guardian of the person or estate or both of a minor, or as the guardian of the property the minor receives from or by designation of the person making the appointment, such appointment shall be deemed to be a nomination of a guardian if the requirements of Section 1500 or 1501 are satisfied and, in such case, shall be given the same effect it would have under Section 1500 or 1501, as the case may be, if made on or after January 1, 1981.

This section applies whether or not the signed writing is a will or deed so long as the person signing the writing had at the time the writing was signed sufficient capacity to form an intelligent preference. *(Stats.1990, c. 79 (A.B.759), § 14, operative July 1, 1991.)*

Law Revision Commission Comments

1990 Enactment

Section 1489 continues Section 1489 of the repealed Probate Code without substantive change. This section ensures that appointment of a testamentary guardian made under former Section 1402 or 1403 (provisions repealed by 1979 Cal.Stat. ch. 726, § 1) will be given effect as a nomination of a guardian under Sections 1500 and 1501. See also Section 1514(c)–(d); Civil Code § 4600.

Under Sections 1500 and 1501, a guardian may be nominated in a signed writing whether or not the writing is a will or deed. See Section 1502 and the Comment thereto. The second sentence of Section 1489 applies the same standard to a signed writing made prior to January 1, 1981, and purporting to appoint a guardian, even though the writing may not have met the stricter requirements of former Section 1402 or 1403 (provisions repealed by 1979 Cal.Stat. ch. 726, § 1). As to the application of any amendments made after that date, see Section 3. For background on the provisions of this part, see the Comment to this part under the part heading. [20 Cal.L.Rev.Comm. Reports 1001 (1990)].

§ 1490. References in statutes

Except as set forth in Section 1510.1, when used in any statute of this state with reference to an adult or to the person of a married minor, "guardian" means the conservator of that adult or the conservator of the person in the case of the married minor. *(Stats.1990, c. 79 (A.B.759), § 14, operative July 1, 1991. Amended by Stats.2015, c. 694 (A.B.900), § 2, eff. Jan. 1, 2016; Stats.2016, c. 86 (S.B.1171), § 244, eff. Jan. 1, 2017.)*

Law Revision Commission Comments

1990 Enactment

Section 1490 continues subdivision (a) of Section 1490 of the repealed Probate Code without change. This section recognizes that through inadvertence some conforming changes may not have been made in sections containing references made obsolete by enactment of this division in 1979. Subdivisions (b) and (c) of Section 1490 of the repealed Probate Code are omitted as unnecessary. See Sections 22 (defining "account in an insured credit union"), 23 (defining "account in an insured savings and loan association"), 1403 (defining "absentee"), 1440 (defining "secretary concerned"), 1446 (defining "single-premium deferred annuity"). For background on the provisions of this part, see the Comment to this part under the part heading. [20 Cal.L.Rev. Comm. Reports 1001 (1990)].

Part 2

GUARDIANSHIP

Law Revision Commission Comments

1990 Enactment

This part supersedes Part 2 (commencing with Section 1500) of Division 4 of the repealed Probate Code. The superseded part was enacted upon recommendation of the California Law Revision Commission. See Recommendation Relating to Guardianship–Conservatorship Law, 14 Cal.L.Revision Comm'n Reports 501 (1978). For the Guardianship–Conservatorship Law as enacted in 1979 (Chapter 726 of the Statutes of 1979) with the revisions made by Chapters 89 and 246 of the Statutes of 1980, see Guardianship–Conservatorship Law, 15 Cal.L.Revision Comm'n Reports 451 (1980). [20 Cal.L.Rev.Comm. Reports 1001 (1990)].

CHAPTER 1. ESTABLISHMENT OF GUARDIANSHIP

ARTICLE 1. NOMINATION OF GUARDIAN

§ 1500. Nomination of guardian of person or estate or both by parent

Subject to Section 1502, a parent may nominate a guardian of the person or estate, or both, of a minor child in either of the following cases:

(a) Where the other parent nominates, or consents in writing to the nomination of, the same guardian for the same child.

(b) Where, at the time the petition for appointment of the guardian is filed, either (1) the other parent is dead or lacks legal capacity to consent to the nomination or (2) the consent of the other parent would not be required for an adoption of the child. *(Stats.1990, c. 79 (A.B.759), § 14, operative July 1, 1991.)*

Law Revision Commission Comments

1990 Enactment

Section 1500 continues Section 1500 of the repealed Probate Code without substantive change. As to the effect to be given to a nomination under this section, see Section 1514. See also Civil Code Section 4600 (consideration in proceeding where there is at issue the custody of a minor child of a nomination of a guardian of the person of the child by a parent). As to providing in the nomination for the powers of the guardian, see Section 2108. See also Sections 300–301 (trust company as guardian of estate), 2104 (nonprofit charitable corporation as guardian).

A nomination under Section 1500 is subject to Section 1502, which requires that the nomination be made in the petition for appointment of the guardian or at the hearing on the petition or in a writing signed either before or after the petition is filed. See Section 1502 and the Comment thereto.

An appointment of a guardian for a minor under the law before January 1, 1981, is deemed to be a nomination of a guardian. Section 1489.

For background on the provisions of this part, see the Comment to this part under the part heading. [20 Cal.L.Rev.Comm. Reports 1001 (1990)].

Research References

Forms

California Transactions Forms--Estate Planning § 6:15, Minors' Capacity to Take Devised Property.

California Transactions Forms--Estate Planning § 6:16, Guardian Of Person.

California Transactions Forms--Estate Planning § 6:17, Guardian Of Estate or Of Property.

California Transactions Forms--Estate Planning § 6:53, Matters to Consider in Drafting Gifts to Minors.
California Transactions Forms--Estate Planning § 6:73, Appointment Of Guardian Of Person Of Minor Child and Statement Of Desire that Same Person be Appointed Guardian Of Minor's Estate.
California Transactions Forms--Estate Planning § 6:74, Appointment Of Guardian Of Person and Estate Of Minor Children.
California Transactions Forms--Estate Planning § 6:77, Use Of Child's Estate by Guardian Of Person.
California Transactions Forms--Estate Planning § 19:93, Nomination Of Guardian.
California Transactions Forms--Estate Planning § 19:94, Appointment Of Guardian Of Person.
California Transactions Forms--Estate Planning § 19:95, Appointment Of Guardian Of Estate.
California Transactions Forms--Family Law § 5:3, Rights Of Nonparents Generally.
California Transactions Forms--Family Law § 5:4, Rights Of De Facto Parents.
West's California Code Forms, Probate § 1510 Form 1, Petition for Appointment Of Guardian Of Estate Of Minor--Judicial Council Form GC-210.
West's California Code Forms, Probate § 1510 Form 2, Consent Of Guardian, Nomination and Waiver Of Notice--Judicial Council Form GC-211.
West's California Code Forms, Probate § 1514 Form 1, Order Appointing Guardian Of Minor--Judicial Council Form GC-240.
West's California Code Forms, Probate § 2651 Form 1, Petition for Removal Of Guardian or Conservator.
West's California Code Forms, Probate § 1500-1502 Form 1, Nomination Of Guardian.
West's California Code Forms, Probate § 1500-1502 Form 2, Probate Guardianship Pamphlet--Judicial Council Form GC-205.
West's California Judicial Council Forms GC-211, Consent Of Guardian, Nomination, and Waiver Of Notice.

Treatises and Practice Aids

Witkin, California Summary 10th Parent and Child § 63, in General.
Witkin, California Summary 10th Parent and Child § 209, Nomination Of Guardian by Parent.
Witkin, California Summary 10th Parent and Child § 311, Other Proceedings Stayed.
Witkin, California Summary 10th Parent and Child § 363, Applicability Of Family Code Custody Provisions.
Witkin, California Summary 10th Parent and Child § 493, Persons Entitled to Inspect Records.
Witkin, California Summary 10th Parent and Child § 696, Continuing Jurisdiction.
Witkin, California Summary 10th Wills and Probate § 916, in General.
Witkin, California Summary 10th Wills and Probate § 917, Nomination.
Witkin, California Summary 10th Wills and Probate § 919, Content and Form.
Witkin, California Summary 10th Wills and Probate § 920, in General.
Witkin, California Summary 10th Wills and Probate § 924, Factors Considered in Appointment.
Witkin, California Summary 10th Wills and Probate § 926, Determination and Order.
Witkin, California Summary 10th Wills and Probate § 965, Nominated Guardian.
Witkin, California Summary 10th Wills and Probate § 984, Exceptions and Waiver.
Witkin, California Summary 10th Wills and Probate § 1048, Causes for Removal.
Witkin, California Summary 10th Wills and Probate § 959C, (New) Exclusions and Limitations.

§ 1500.1. Consent by Indian child's parent; requirements

(a) Notwithstanding any other section in this part, and in accordance with Section 1913 of the Indian Child Welfare Act (25 U.S.C. Sec. 1901 et seq.), consent to nomination of a guardian of the person or of a guardian of the person and the estate given by an Indian child's parent is not valid unless both of the following occur:

(1) The consent is executed in writing at least 10 days after the child's birth and recorded before a judge.

(2) The judge certifies that the terms and consequences of the consent were fully explained in detail in English and were fully understood by the parent or that they were interpreted into a language that the parent understood.

(b) The parent of an Indian child may withdraw his or her consent to guardianship for any reason at any time prior to the issuance of letters of guardianship and the child shall be returned to the parent. *(Added by Stats.2006, c. 838 (S.B. 678), § 21.)*

Research References

Forms

West's California Code Forms, Probate § 1811 Form 1, Nomination Of Conservator by Spouse/Domestic Partner or Parent.
West's California Code Forms, Probate § 1459.5 COMMENT, Application Of Federal Law to Proceedings Involving Children Of Indian Ancestry.

Treatises and Practice Aids

Witkin, California Summary 10th Wills and Probate § 917, Nomination.
Witkin, California Summary 10th Wills and Probate § 915A, (New) Special Provisions Applicable to Indian Children.

§ 1501. Nomination of guardian for property received by minor

Subject to Section 1502, a parent or any other person may nominate a guardian for property that a minor receives from or by designation of the nominator (whether before, at the time of, or after the nomination) including, but not limited to, property received by the minor by virtue of a gift, deed, trust, will, succession, insurance, or benefits of any kind. *(Stats. 1990, c. 79 (A.B.759), § 14, operative July 1, 1991.)*

Law Revision Commission Comments

1990 Enactment

Section 1501 continues Section 1501 of the repealed Probate Code without change. As to the effect to be given to a nomination under this section, see Section 1514. As to the powers and duties of the guardian, see Section 2109. See also Sections 300–301 (trust company as guardian of estate), 2104 (nonprofit charitable corporation as guardian).

A nomination under Section 1501 is subject to Section 1502, which requires that the nomination be made in the petition for appointment of the guardian or at the hearing on the petition or in a writing signed either before or after the petition is filed. See Section 1502 and the Comment thereto.

Section 1501 covers all property received from or by designation of the person making the nomination, and includes such property as proceeds from an insurance policy. This changes the rule of Estate of Welfer, 110 Cal.App.2d 262, 242 P.2d 655 (1952). Under Section

1501, a person may nominate a guardian for the proceeds of a life insurance policy owned by the nominator on the life of the nominator or on the life of a person surviving the nominator.

Where a parent attempts to nominate a general guardian of the estate of a child as authorized by Section 1500, but the nomination does not satisfy the requirements of Section 1500 because written consent of the other parent is required but not obtained, the nomination may nevertheless satisfy the requirements of Section 1501 and permit appointment of a guardian with respect to the property of the nominating parent that the child takes from that parent. See Guardianship of Joaquin, 168 Cal.App.2d 99, 335 P.2d 507 (1959).

For background on the provisions of this part, see the Comment to this part under the part heading. [20 Cal.L.Rev.Comm. Reports 1001 (1990)].

Research References

Forms

California Transactions Forms--Estate Planning § 6:16, Guardian Of Person.
California Transactions Forms--Estate Planning § 6:17, Guardian Of Estate or Of Property.
California Transactions Forms--Estate Planning § 6:73, Appointment Of Guardian Of Person Of Minor Child and Statement Of Desire that Same Person be Appointed Guardian Of Minor's Estate.
California Transactions Forms--Estate Planning § 6:75, Appointment Of Guardian Of Specific Property.
West's California Code Forms, Probate § 1510 Form 1, Petition for Appointment Of Guardian Of Estate Of Minor--Judicial Council Form GC-210.
West's California Code Forms, Probate § 1510 Form 2, Consent Of Guardian, Nomination and Waiver Of Notice--Judicial Council Form GC-211.
West's California Code Forms, Probate § 1514 Form 1, Order Appointing Guardian Of Minor--Judicial Council Form GC-240.
West's California Code Forms, Probate § 2651 Form 1, Petition for Removal Of Guardian or Conservator.
West's California Code Forms, Probate § 1500-1502 Form 1, Nomination Of Guardian.

Treatises and Practice Aids

Witkin, California Summary 10th Wills and Probate § 917, Nomination.
Witkin, California Summary 10th Wills and Probate § 919, Content and Form.
Witkin, California Summary 10th Wills and Probate § 920, in General.
Witkin, California Summary 10th Wills and Probate § 924, Factors Considered in Appointment.
Witkin, California Summary 10th Wills and Probate § 926, Determination and Order.
Witkin, California Summary 10th Wills and Probate § 984, Exceptions and Waiver.
Witkin, California Summary 10th Wills and Probate § 1048, Causes for Removal.

§ 1502. Manner of nomination; time effective; subsequent legal incapacity or death of nominator

(a) A nomination of a guardian under this article may be made in the petition for the appointment of the guardian or at the hearing on the petition or in a writing signed either before or after the petition for the appointment of the guardian is filed.

(b) The nomination of a guardian under this article is effective when made except that a writing nominating a guardian under this article may provide that the nomination becomes effective only upon the occurrence of such specified condition or conditions as are stated in the writing, including but not limited to such conditions as the subsequent legal incapacity or death of the person making the nomination.

(c) Unless the writing making the nomination expressly otherwise provides, a nomination made under this article remains effective notwithstanding the subsequent legal incapacity or death of the person making the nomination. *(Stats.1990, c. 79 (A.B.759), § 14, operative July 1, 1991.)*

Law Revision Commission Comments

1990 Enactment

Section 1502 continues Section 1502 of the repealed Probate Code without change. Subdivision (b) makes clear that a writing making a nomination under this article may specify one or more conditions the occurrence of which makes the nomination become effective. Absent such specification, the nomination is effective, unless revoked, when made. Subdivision (c) makes clear that death or subsequent lack of legal capacity does not make the nomination ineffective unless the writing making the nomination expressly otherwise provides. For background on the provisions of this part, see the Comment to this part under the part heading. [20 Cal.L.Rev.Comm. Reports 1001 (1990)].

Research References

Forms

California Transactions Forms--Estate Planning § 6:16, Guardian Of Person.
California Transactions Forms--Estate Planning § 6:17, Guardian Of Estate or Of Property.
California Transactions Forms--Estate Planning § 6:73, Appointment Of Guardian Of Person Of Minor Child and Statement Of Desire that Same Person be Appointed Guardian Of Minor's Estate.
California Transactions Forms--Estate Planning § 6:74, Appointment Of Guardian Of Person and Estate Of Minor Children.
California Transactions Forms--Estate Planning § 6:77, Use Of Child's Estate by Guardian Of Person.
California Transactions Forms--Estate Planning § 19:93, Nomination Of Guardian.
West's California Code Forms, Probate § 1500-1502 Form 1, Nomination Of Guardian.
West's California Judicial Council Forms GC-211, Consent Of Guardian, Nomination, and Waiver Of Notice.

Treatises and Practice Aids

Witkin, California Summary 10th Wills and Probate § 917, Nomination.

ARTICLE 2. APPOINTMENT OF GUARDIAN GENERALLY

§ 1510. Petition for appointment; contents

(a) A relative or other person on behalf of the minor, or the minor if 12 years of age or older, may file a petition for the appointment of a guardian of the minor. A relative may file a petition for the appointment of a guardian under this section regardless of the relative's immigration status.

(b) The petition shall request that a guardian of the person or estate of the minor, or both, be appointed, shall specify the name and address of the proposed guardian and the name and date of birth of the proposed ward, and shall state that the appointment is necessary or convenient.

(c) The petition shall set forth, so far as is known to the petitioner, the names and addresses of all of the following:

(1) The parents of the proposed ward.

(2) The person having legal custody of the proposed ward and, if that person does not have the care of the proposed ward, the person having the care of the proposed ward.

(3) The relatives of the proposed ward within the second degree.

(4) In the case of a guardianship of the estate, the spouse of the proposed ward.

(5) Any person nominated as guardian for the proposed ward under Section 1500 or 1501.

(6) In the case of a guardianship of the person involving an Indian child, any Indian custodian and the Indian child's tribe.

(d) If the petitioner or proposed guardian is a professional fiduciary, as described in Section 2340, who is required to be licensed under the Professional Fiduciaries Act (Chapter 6 (commencing with Section 6500) of Division 3 of the Business and Professions Code), the petition shall include the following:

(1) The petitioner's or proposed guardian's proposed hourly fee schedule or another statement of his or her proposed compensation from the estate of the proposed ward for services performed as a guardian. The petitioner's or proposed guardian's provision of a proposed hourly fee schedule or another statement of his or her proposed compensation, as required by this paragraph, shall not preclude a court from later reducing the petitioner's or proposed guardian's fees or other compensation.

(2) Unless a petition for appointment of a temporary guardian that contains the statements required by this paragraph is filed together with a petition for appointment of a guardian, both of the following:

(A) A statement of the petitioner's or proposed guardian's license information.

(B) A statement explaining who engaged the petitioner or proposed guardian or how the petitioner or proposed guardian was engaged to file the petition for appointment of a guardian or to agree to accept the appointment as guardian and what prior relationship the petitioner or proposed guardian had with the proposed ward or the proposed ward's family or friends.

(e) If the proposed ward is a patient in or on leave of absence from a state institution under the jurisdiction of the State Department of State Hospitals or the State Department of Developmental Services and that fact is known to the petitioner or proposed guardian, the petition shall state that fact and name the institution.

(f) The petition shall state, so far as is known to the petitioner or proposed guardian, whether or not the proposed ward is receiving or is entitled to receive benefits from the Veterans Administration and the estimated amount of the monthly benefit payable by the Veterans Administration for the proposed ward.

(g) If the petitioner or proposed guardian has knowledge of any pending adoption, juvenile court, marriage dissolution, domestic relations, custody, or other similar proceeding affecting the proposed ward, the petition shall disclose the pending proceeding.

(h) If the petitioners or proposed guardians have accepted or intend to accept physical care or custody of the child with intent to adopt, whether formed at the time of placement or formed subsequent to placement, the petitioners or proposed guardians shall so state in the guardianship petition, whether or not an adoption petition has been filed.

(i) If the proposed ward is or becomes the subject of an adoption petition, the court shall order the guardianship petition consolidated with the adoption petition, and the consolidated case shall be heard and decided in the court in which the adoption is pending.

(j) If the proposed ward is or may be an Indian child, the petition shall state that fact. *(Stats.1990, c. 79 (A.B.759), § 14, operative July 1, 1991. Amended by Stats.1992, c. 1064 (S.B.1445), § 1; Stats.2006, c. 838 (S.B.678), § 22; Stats. 2008, c. 534 (S.B.1726), § 12; Stats.2012, c. 440 (A.B.1488), § 40, eff. Sept. 22, 2012; Stats.2012, c. 845 (S.B.1064), § 2; Stats.2013, c. 248 (A.B.1339), § 1.)*

Law Revision Commission Comments

1990 Enactment

Section 1510 continues Section 1510 of the repealed Probate Code without change. For general provisions relating to petitions and other papers, see Sections 1020–1023. See also Sections 1021 (petition to be verified), 1041 (clerk to set petition for hearing), 1512 (amendment of petition to disclose newly discovered proceeding affecting custody). For background on the provisions of this part, see the Comment to this part under the part heading. See also Recommendation Relating to the Uniform Veterans Guardianship

Act, 15 Cal.L.Revision Comm'n Reports 1289, 1299 (1980). [20 Cal.L.Rev.Comm. Reports 1001 (1990)].

Commentary

Suleman v. Superior Court, 180 Cal.App.4th 1287, 103 Cal.Rptr.3d 651 (2010), restrictively defines "other person"' for purposes of subsection (a).

Guardianship of Vaughan, 207 Cal.App.4th 1055, 144 Cal.Rptr.3d 216 (2012), held that when grandchildren have been residing with their grandparents for over a year, Family Code section 3041(c) does not require a showing that the children were abandoned by their parent in order for a trial court to grant the grandparents' petition for a probate guardianship under this section and section 1514.

Research References

Forms

California Transactions Forms--Estate Planning § 6:16, Guardian Of Person.

California Transactions Forms--Family Law § 6:41, Initiating the Adoption.

California Transactions Forms--Family Law § 6:47, Matters to Consider in Drafting Petition for Independent Adoption Of Unmarried Minor.

California Transactions Forms--Family Law § 6:108, Petition for Stepparent Adoption.

West's California Code Forms, Probate § 1510 Form 1, Petition for Appointment Of Guardian Of Estate Of Minor--Judicial Council Form GC-210.

West's California Code Forms, Probate § 1510 Form 3, Declaration Under Uniform Child Custody Jurisdiction and Enforcement Act (UCCJEA)-Judicial Council Form FL-105/GC-120.

West's California Code Forms, Probate § 2357 Form 1, Petition for Order Directing Medical Treatment for Ward or Conservatee.

West's California Code Forms, Probate § 1459.5 COMMENT, Application Of Federal Law to Proceedings Involving Children Of Indian Ancestry.

West's California Code Forms, Probate § 1460-1461 Form 1, Notice Of Hearing (Guardianship or Conservatorship)--Judicial Council Form GC-020.

West's California Judicial Council Forms GC-120, Declaration Under Uniform Child Custody Jurisdiction and Enforcement Act (UCCJEA).

West's California Judicial Council Forms GC-210, Petition for Appointment Of Guardian Of Minor.

West's California Judicial Council Forms GC-120(A), Attachment to Declaration Under Uniform Child Custody Jurisdiction and Enforcement Act (UCCJEA).

West's California Judicial Council Forms GC-210(P), Petition for Appointment Of Guardian Of the Person.

West's California Judicial Council Forms GC-210(CA), Guardianship Petition--Child Information Attachment.

West's California Judicial Council Forms GC-210(PE), Petition to Extend Guardianship Of the Person.

West's California Judicial Council Forms FL-105/GC-120, Declaration Under Uniform Child Custody Jurisdiction and Enforcement Act (UCCJEA).

West's California Judicial Council Forms FL-105(A)/GC-120(A), Attachment to Declaration Under Uniform Child Custody Jurisdiction and Enforcement Act (UCCJEA).

Treatises and Practice Aids

Witkin, California Summary 10th Parent and Child § 220, Illustrations: Guardianship Cases.

Witkin, California Summary 10th Wills and Probate § 910, General Notice Requirement.

Witkin, California Summary 10th Wills and Probate § 918, Who May File.

Witkin, California Summary 10th Wills and Probate § 919, Content and Form.

Witkin, California Summary 10th Wills and Probate § 915A, (New) Special Provisions Applicable to Indian Children.

Witkin, California Summary 10th Wills and Probate § 915B, (New) Special Immigrant Juvenile Status Proceedings.

Witkin, California Summary 10th Wills and Probate § 970A, (New) Professional Fiduciaries Act.

§ 1510.1. Appointment of guardian for unmarried individual between 18 and 21 years of age; findings regarding special immigrant juvenile status; rights as an adult; adoption of rules and forms for implementation

(a)(1) With the consent of the proposed ward, the court may appoint a guardian of the person for an unmarried individual who is 18 years of age or older, but who has not yet attained 21 years of age, in connection with a petition to make the necessary findings regarding special immigrant juvenile status pursuant to subdivision (b) of Section 155 of the Code of Civil Procedure.

(2) A petition for guardianship of the person of a proposed ward who is 18 years of age or older, but who has not yet attained 21 years of age, may be filed by a relative or any other person on behalf of the proposed ward, or the proposed ward.

(b)(1) At the request of, or with the consent of, the ward, the court may extend an existing guardianship of the person for a ward past 18 years of age, for purposes of allowing the ward to complete the application process with the United States Citizenship and Immigration Services for classification as a special immigrant juvenile pursuant to Section 1101(a)(27)(J) of Title 8 of the United States Code.

(2) A relative or any other person on behalf of a ward, or the ward, may file a petition to extend the guardianship of the person for a period of time not to extend beyond the ward reaching 21 years of age.

(c) This section does not authorize the guardian to abrogate any of the rights that a person who has attained 18 years of age may have as an adult under state law, including, but not limited to, decisions regarding the ward's medical treatment, education, or residence, without the ward's express consent.

(d) For purposes of this division, the terms "child," "minor," and "ward" include an unmarried individual who is younger than 21 years of age and who, pursuant to this section, consents to the appointment of a guardian or extension of a guardianship after he or she attains 18 years of age.

(e) The Judicial Council shall, by July 1, 2016, adopt any rules and forms needed to implement this section. *(Added by Stats.2015, c. 694 (A.B.900), § 3, eff. Jan. 1, 2016. Amended by Stats.2016, c. 86 (S.B.1171), § 245, eff. Jan. 1, 2017.)*

Research References

Forms

West's California Judicial Council Forms GC-210, Petition for Appointment Of Guardian Of Minor.

West's California Judicial Council Forms GC-240, Order Appointing Guardian Of Minor.

West's California Judicial Council Forms GC-210(P), Petition for Appointment Of Guardian Of the Person.

West's California Judicial Council Forms GC-210(PE), Petition to Extend Guardianship Of the Person.

Treatises and Practice Aids

Witkin, California Summary 10th Wills and Probate § 930, Termination Of Guardianship.

Witkin, California Summary 10th Wills and Probate § 915B, (New) Special Immigrant Juvenile Status Proceedings.

§ 1511. Notice of hearing

(a) Except as provided in subdivisions (f) and (g), at least 15 days before the hearing on the petition for the appointment of a guardian, notice of the time and place of the hearing shall be given as provided in subdivisions (b), (c), (d), and (e) of this section. The notice shall be accompanied by a copy of the petition. The court shall not shorten the time for giving the notice of hearing under this section.

(b) Notice shall be served in the manner provided in Section 415.10 or 415.30 of the Code of Civil Procedure, or in any manner authorized by the court, on all of the following persons:

(1) The proposed ward if 12 years of age or older.

(2) Any person having legal custody of the proposed ward, or serving as guardian of the estate of the proposed ward.

(3) The parents of the proposed ward.

(4) Any person nominated as a guardian for the proposed ward under Section 1500 or 1501.

(c) Notice shall be * * * delivered pursuant to Section 1215 to the addresses stated in the petition, or in any manner authorized by the court, to all of the following:

(1) The spouse named in the petition.

(2) The relatives named in the petition, except that if the petition is for the appointment of a guardian of the estate only the court may dispense with the giving of notice to any one or more or all of the relatives.

(3) The person having the care of the proposed ward if other than the person having legal custody of the proposed ward.

(d) If notice is required by Section 1461 or * * * 1542 to be given to the Director of State Hospitals or the Director of Developmental Services or the Director of Social Services, notice shall be * * * delivered pursuant to Section 1215 as * * * required.

(e) If the petition states that the proposed ward is receiving or is entitled to receive benefits from the Veterans Administration, notice shall be * * * delivered pursuant to Section 1215 to the office of the Veterans Administration referred to in Section 1461.5.

(f) Unless the court orders otherwise, notice shall not be given to any of the following:

(1) The parents or other relatives of a proposed ward who has been relinquished to a licensed adoption agency.

(2) The parents of a proposed ward who has been judicially declared free from their custody and control.

(g) Notice need not be given to any person if the court so orders upon a determination of either of the following:

(1) The person cannot with reasonable diligence be given the notice.

(2) The giving of the notice would be contrary to the interest of justice.

(h) Before the appointment of a guardian is made, proof shall be made to the court that each person entitled to notice under this section either:

(1) Has been given notice as required by this section.

(2) Has not been given notice as required by this section because the person cannot with reasonable diligence be given the notice or because the giving of notice to that person would be contrary to the interest of justice.

(i) If notice is required by Section 1460.2 to be given to an Indian custodian or tribe, notice shall be mailed as * * * required. *(Stats.1990, c. 79 (A.B.759), § 14, operative July 1, 1991. Amended by Stats.1992, c. 1064 (S.B.1445), § 2; Stats.1996, c. 563 (S.B.392), § 6; Stats.2006, c. 838 (S.B.678), § 23; Stats.2012, c. 440 (A.B.1488), § 41, eff. Sept. 22, 2012; Stats.2017, c. 319 (A.B.976), § 30, eff. Jan. 1, 2018.)*

Law Revision Commission Comments

1990 Enactment

Section 1511 continues Section 1511 of the repealed Probate Code without substantive change. The provision that the court may not shorten the time for giving the notice of hearing has been added to Section 1511, but this provision continues a provision formerly found in the introductory clause of subdivision (a) of Section 1462 of the repealed Probate Code. The phrase "other than the petitioner or persons joining in the petition" has been omitted from two places in the section. This phrase is unnecessary in view of Section 1201.

Subdivision (a) requires that notice be given at least 15 days before the hearing, and this time may not be shortened by the court. If there is urgency, a temporary guardian may be appointed under Section 2250. For general provisions relating to notice of hearing, see Sections 1200–1221, 1460–1469. See also Sections 1260–1265 (proof of giving notice). For general provisions relating to hearings and orders, see Sections 1040–1050. For background on the provisions of this part, see the Comment to this part under the part heading. See also Recommendation Relating to the Uniform Veterans Guardianship Act, 15 Cal.L.Revision Comm'n Reports 1289, 1299–300 (1980); Report of Assembly Committee on Judiciary on Assembly Bills Nos. 261 and 167, reprinted in 15 Cal.L.Revision Comm'n Reports 1061, 1067 (1980). [20 Cal.L.Rev.Comm. Reports 1001 (1990)].

Research References

Forms

Am. Jur. Pl. & Pr. Forms Guardian and Ward § 72, Introductory Comments.

West's California Code Forms, Probate § 1510 Form 1, Petition for Appointment Of Guardian Of Estate Of Minor--Judicial Council Form GC-210.

West's California Code Forms, Probate § 2352 Form 1, Change Of Residence Notice--Judicial Council Form GC-080.

West's California Code Forms, Probate § 1459.5 COMMENT, Application Of Federal Law to Proceedings Involving Children Of Indian Ancestry.

West's California Code Forms, Probate § 1460-1461 Form 2, Order Dispensing With Notice--Judicial Council Form GC-021.

West's California Judicial Council Forms DE-120, Notice Of Hearing--Decedent's Estate or Trust.

West's California Judicial Council Forms GC-020, Notice Of Hearing--Guardianship or Conservatorship.

West's California Judicial Council Forms GC-505, Forms You Need to Ask the Court to Appoint a Guardian Of the Person (Probate--Guardianships and Conservatorships).

West's California Judicial Council Forms GC-510, What is "Proof Of Service" in a Guardianship? (Probate--Guardianships and Conservatorships).

West's California Judicial Council Forms GC-020(P), Proof Of Personal Service Of Notice Of Hearing--Guardianship or Conservatorship.

Treatises and Practice Aids

Witkin, California Summary 10th Wills and Probate § 920, in General.

Witkin, California Summary 10th Wills and Probate § 921, When Notice is Not Required.

Witkin, California Summary 10th Wills and Probate § 975, Appointment.

Witkin, California Summary 10th Wills and Probate § 990, Fixing Residence.

Witkin, California Summary 10th Wills and Probate § 915A, (New) Special Provisions Applicable to Indian Children.

§ 1512. Amendment of petition to disclose newly discovered proceeding affecting custody

Within 10 days after the petitioner in the guardianship proceeding becomes aware of any proceeding not disclosed in the guardianship petition affecting the custody of the proposed ward (including any adoption, juvenile court, marriage dissolution, domestic relations, or other similar proceeding affecting the proposed ward), the petitioner shall amend the guardianship petition to disclose the other proceeding. *(Stats.1990, c. 79 (A.B.759), § 14, operative July 1, 1991.)*

Law Revision Commission Comments

1990 Enactment

Section 1512 continues Section 1512 of the repealed Probate Code without change. The purpose of this section is to alert the court to any other proceeding affecting custody of the proposed ward that was not disclosed in the initial guardianship petition. See also Section 1510(h) (consolidation of guardianship petition with adoption petition). For background on the provisions of this part, see the Comment to this part under the part heading. [20 Cal.L.Rev.Comm. Reports 1001 (1990)].

Research References

Forms

West's California Judicial Council Forms GC-120, Declaration Under Uniform Child Custody Jurisdiction and Enforcement Act (UCCJEA).

West's California Judicial Council Forms GC-120(A), Attachment to Declaration Under Uniform Child Custody Jurisdiction and Enforcement Act (UCCJEA).

West's California Judicial Council Forms FL-105/GC-120, Declaration Under Uniform Child Custody Jurisdiction and Enforcement Act (UCCJEA).

West's California Judicial Council Forms FL-105(A)/GC-120(A), Attachment to Declaration Under Uniform Child Custody Jurisdiction and Enforcement Act (UCCJEA).

Treatises and Practice Aids

Witkin, California Summary 10th Wills and Probate § 919, Content and Form.

§ 1513. Investigation; filing of report and recommendation concerning proposed guardianship; contents of report; confidentiality; application of section

(a) Unless waived by the court, a court investigator, probation officer, or domestic relations investigator shall make an investigation and file with the court a report and recommendation concerning each proposed guardianship of the person or guardianship of the estate. Investigations where the proposed guardian is a relative shall be made by a court investigator. Investigations where the proposed guardian is a nonrelative shall be made by the county agency designated to investigate potential dependency. The report for the guardianship of the person shall include, but need not be limited to, an investigation and discussion of all of the following:

(1) A social history of the guardian.

(2) A social history of the proposed ward, including, to the extent feasible, an assessment of any identified developmental, emotional, psychological, or educational needs of the proposed ward and the capability of the petitioner to meet those needs.

(3) The relationship of the proposed ward to the guardian, including the duration and character of the relationship, where applicable, the circumstances whereby physical custody of the proposed ward was acquired by the guardian, and a statement of the proposed ward's attitude concerning the proposed guardianship, unless the statement of the attitude is affected by the proposed ward's developmental, physical, or emotional condition.

(4) The anticipated duration of the guardianship and the plans of both natural parents and the proposed guardian for the stable and permanent home for the child. The court may waive this requirement for cases involving relative guardians.

(b) If the proposed ward is or may be described by Section 300 of the Welfare and Institutions Code, the court may refer the matter to the local child welfare services agency to initiate an investigation of the referral pursuant to Sections 328 and 329 of the Welfare and Institutions Code and to report the findings of that investigation to the court. Pending completion of the investigation, the court may take any reasonable steps it deems appropriate to protect the child' s safety, including, but not limited to, appointment of a temporary guardian or issuance of a temporary restraining order. If dependency proceedings are initiated, the guardianship proceedings shall be stayed in accordance with Section 304 of the Welfare and Institutions Code. Nothing in this section shall affect the applicability of Section 16504 or 16506 of the Welfare and Institutions Code. If a dependency proceeding is not initiated, the probate court shall retain jurisdiction to hear the guardianship matter.

(c) Prior to ruling on the petition for guardianship, the court shall read and consider all reports submitted pursuant to this section, which shall be reflected in the minutes or stated on the record. Any person who reports to the court pursuant to this section may be called and examined by any party to the proceeding.

(d) All reports authorized by this section are confidential and shall only be made available to persons who have been served in the proceedings or their attorneys. The clerk of the court shall make provisions to limit access to the reports exclusively to persons entitled to receipt. The reports shall be made available to all parties entitled to receipt no less than three court days before the hearing on the guardianship petition.

(e) For the purpose of writing either report authorized by this section, the person making the investigation and report shall have access to the proposed ward's school records, probation records, and public and private social services records, and to an oral or written summary of the proposed ward's medical records and psychological records prepared by any physician, psychologist, or psychiatrist who made or who is maintaining those records. The physician, psychologist, or psychiatrist shall be available to clarify information regarding these records pursuant to the investigator's responsibility to gather and provide information for the court.

(f) This section does not apply to guardianships resulting from a permanency plan for a dependent child pursuant to Section 366.26 of the Welfare and Institutions Code.

(g) For purposes of this section, a "relative" means a person who is a spouse, parent, stepparent, brother, sister, stepbrother, stepsister, half-brother, half-sister, uncle, aunt, niece, nephew, first cousin, or any person denoted by the prefix "grand" or "great," or the spouse of any of these persons, even after the marriage has been terminated by death or dissolution.

(h) In an Indian child custody proceeding, any person making an investigation and report shall consult with the Indian child's tribe and include in the report information provided by the tribe. *(Stats.1990, c. 79 (A.B.759), § 14, operative July 1, 1991. Amended by Stats.1992, c. 572 (S.B.1455), § 3; Stats.1993, c. 59 (S.B.443), § 16, eff. June 30, 1993; Stats.1996, c. 563 (S.B.392), § 7; Stats.2002, c. 784 (S.B.1316), § 576; Stats.2006, c. 838 (S.B.678), § 24; Stats. 2012, c. 638 (A.B.1757), § 14.)*

Law Revision Commission Comments

1990 Enactment

Section 1513 continues Section 1513 of the repealed Probate Code without substantive change. See also Section 1454 (court investigator), 1543 (report on suitability of guardian). For background on the provisions of this part, see the Comment to this part under the part heading. [20 Cal.L.Rev.Comm. Reports 1001 (1990)].

2002 Amendment

Subdivision (d) of Section 1513 is amended to reflect elimination of the county clerk's role as ex officio clerk of the superior court. See former Gov't Code § 26800 (county clerk acting as clerk of superior court). The powers, duties, and responsibilities formerly exercised by the county clerk as ex officio clerk of the court are delegated to the court administrative or executive officer, and the county clerk is relieved of those powers, duties, and responsibilities. See Gov't Code §§ 69840 (powers, duties, and responsibilities of clerk of court and deputy clerk of court), 71620 (trial court personnel). [32 Cal.L.Rev. Comm. Reports 516 (2002)].

Commentary

In re Guardianship of Christian G., 195 Cal.App.4th 581, 124 Cal.Rptr.3d 642 (2011), held that a probate court erred in failing to refer a guardian case brought by a child's paternal uncle to a county child protective agency when it became apparent that the uncle's allegations about the child's father indicated that the father was an unfit parent.

Tracy A. v. Superior Court, 117 Cal.App.4th 1309, 12 Cal.Rptr.3d 684 (2004), holds that a probate court's practice of denying parties and their attorneys copies of confidential reports prepared for guardianship hearings is inconsistent with subsection (d), which contemplates that parties and their attorneys will, upon request, be furnished with such reports.

Research References

Forms

West's California Code Forms, Probate § 1516 Form 1, Confidential Guardianship Screening Report--Judicial Council Form GC-212.

West's California Code Forms, Probate § 1459.5 COMMENT, Application Of Federal Law to Proceedings Involving Children Of Indian Ancestry.

West's California Code Forms, Probate § 1514.5 COMMENT, Confidential Information from Family Law Court.

Treatises and Practice Aids

Witkin, California Summary 10th Wills and Probate § 922, Investigation and Report.

Witkin, California Summary 10th Wills and Probate § 915A, (New) Special Provisions Applicable to Indian Children.

§ 1513.1. Assessments

(a) Each court or county shall assess (1) the parent, parents, or other person charged with the support and maintenance of the ward or proposed ward, and (2) the guardian, proposed guardian, or the estate of the ward or proposed ward, for court or county expenses incurred for any investigation or review conducted by the court investigator, probation officer, or domestic relations investigator. Subject to Section 68631 of the Government Code, the court may order reimbursement to the court or to the county in the amount of the assessment, unless the court finds that all or any part of the assessment would impose a hardship on the ward or the ward's estate. A county may waive any or all of an assessment against the guardianship on the basis of hardship. There shall be a rebuttable presumption that the assessment would impose a hardship if the ward is receiving Medi-Cal benefits.

(b) Any amount chargeable as state-mandated local costs incurred by a county for the cost of the investigation or review shall be reduced by any assessments actually collected by the county pursuant to subdivision (a) during that fiscal year. *(Stats.1990, c. 79 (A.B.759), § 14, operative July 1, 1991. Amended by Stats.1991, c. 82 (S.B.896), § 4, eff. June 30, 1991, operative July 1, 1991; Stats.1996, c. 563 (S.B.392), § 8; Stats.2002, c. 1008 (A.B.3028), § 27; Stats.2003, c. 62 (S.B. 600), § 242; Stats.2014, c. 913 (A.B.2747), § 27.5, eff. Jan. 1, 2015.)*

Law Revision Commission Comments

1990 Enactment

Section 1513.1 continues Section 1513.1 of the repealed Probate Code without substantive change. For background on the provisions of this part, see the Comment to this part under the part heading.

1991 Amendment

Section 1513.1 is amended to delete subdivision (a) and language in subdivision (b) relating to determination by the Controller of the statewide average cost per investigation or review by the court investigator, probation officer, or domestic relations officer incurred by each county. This requirement was deleted from Section 1513.1 of the repealed Probate Code by 1990 Cal.Stat. ch. 1208. This amendment preserves the effect of that legislation. [20 Cal.L.Rev. Comm. Reports 1001 (1990)].

Research References

Treatises and Practice Aids

Witkin, California Summary 10th Wills and Probate § 922, Investigation and Report.

§ 1513.2. Status report; form; contents; confidentiality

(a) To the extent resources are available, the court shall implement procedures, as described in this section, to ensure that every guardian annually completes and returns to the court a status report, including the statement described in subdivision (b). A guardian who willfully submits any material information required by the form which he or she knows to be false shall be guilty of a misdemeanor. Not later than one month * * * before the date the status report is required to be returned, the clerk of the court shall * * * deliver a notice pursuant to Section 1215 to the guardian informing the guardian that he or she is required to complete and return the status report to the court. The clerk shall enclose with the letter a blank status report form for the guardian to complete and return * * *. If the status report is not completed and returned as required, or if the court finds, after a status report has been completed and returned, that further information is needed, the court shall attempt to obtain the information required in the report from the guardian or other sources. If the court is unable to obtain this information within 30 days after the date the status report is due, the court shall either order the guardian to make himself or herself available to the investigator for purposes of investigation of the guardianship, or to show cause why the guardian should not be removed.

(b) The Judicial Council shall develop a form for the status report. The form shall include the following statement: "A guardian who willfully submits any material information required by this form which he or she knows to be false is guilty of a misdemeanor." The form shall request information the Judicial Council deems necessary to determine the status of the guardianship, including, but not limited to, the following:

(1) The guardian's present address and electronic address.

(2) The name and birth date of the child under guardianship.

(3) The name of the school in which the child is enrolled, if any.

(4) If the child is not in the guardian's home, the name, relationship, address, electronic address, and telephone number of the person or persons with whom the child resides.

(5) If the child is not in the guardian's home, why the child was moved.

(c) The report authorized by this section is confidential and shall only be made available to persons who have been served in the proceedings or their attorneys. The clerk of the court shall implement procedures for the limitation of the report exclusively to persons entitled to its receipt.

* * * *(Added by Stats.2002, c. 1115 (A.B.3036), § 2. Amended by Stats.2017, c. 319 (A.B.976), § 31, eff. Jan. 1, 2018.)*

Research References

Forms

West's California Code Forms, Probate § 1514 Form 1, Order Appointing Guardian Of Minor--Judicial Council Form GC-240.

West's California Code Forms, Probate § 1516 Form 1, Confidential Guardianship Screening Report--Judicial Council Form GC-212.

West's California Code Forms, Probate § 1513.2 Form 1, Confidential Guardianship Status Report--Judicial Council Form GC 251.

West's California Judicial Council Forms GC-251, Confidential Guardianship Status Report.

Treatises and Practice Aids

Witkin, California Summary 10th Wills and Probate § 929, Annual Status Report.

§ 1514. Appointment of guardian

(a) Upon hearing of the petition, if it appears necessary or convenient, the court may appoint a guardian of the person or estate of the proposed ward or both.

(b)(1) In appointing a guardian of the person, the court is governed by Chapter 1 (commencing with Section 3020) and Chapter 2 (commencing with Section 3040) of Part 2 of Division 8 of the Family Code, relating to custody of a minor.

(2) Except as provided in Section 2105, a minor's parent may not be appointed as a guardian of the person of the minor.

(c) The court shall appoint a guardian nominated under Section 1500 insofar as the nomination relates to the guardianship of the estate unless the court determines that the nominee is unsuitable. If the nominee is a relative, the nominee's immigration status alone shall not constitute unsuitability.

(d) The court shall appoint the person nominated under Section 1501 as guardian of the property covered by the nomination unless the court determines that the nominee is unsuitable. If the person so appointed is appointed only as guardian of the property covered by the nomination, the letters of guardianship shall so indicate.

(e) Subject to subdivisions (c) and (d), in appointing a guardian of the estate:

(1) The court is to be guided by what appears to be in the best interest of the proposed ward, taking into account the proposed guardian's ability to manage and to preserve the estate as well as the proposed guardian's concern for and interest in the welfare of the proposed ward.

(2) If the proposed ward is of sufficient age to form an intelligent preference as to the person to be appointed as guardian, the court shall give consideration to that preference in determining the person to be so appointed. *(Stats.1990, c. 79 (A.B.759), § 14, operative July 1, 1991. Amended by Stats.1992, c. 163 (A.B.2641), § 123, operative Jan. 1, 1994; Stats.2011, c. 102 (A.B.458), § 1; Stats.2012, c. 845 (S.B. 1064), § 3.)*

Law Revision Commission Comments

1990 Enactment

Section 1514 continues Section 1514 of the repealed Probate Code without change. See also Sections 300–301 (trust company as guardian of estate), 2104 (nonprofit charitable corporation as guardian), 2750 (granting letters, other than temporary letters, an appealable order), 2752 (effect of reversal of order appointing guardian). For general provisions relating to hearings and orders, see Sections 1040–1050.

Subdivision (b) applies only to a guardian of the person of a minor. If a person is to be appointed as guardian of both the person and of the estate, the requirement of subdivision (b) governs the appointment. Subdivision (b) incorporates by reference Section 4600 of the Civil Code, which applies to any proceeding where there is at issue the custody of a minor, including a guardianship proceeding. See, e.g., Guardianship of Marino, 30 Cal.App.3d 952, 106 Cal.Rptr. 655 (1973).

Subdivision (d) permits appointment of a person nominated as guardian of the person and estate of a minor in the court's discretion if the appointment of such person is permitted under the standard provided in Civil Code Section 4600. But, even though the person nominated as a guardian of the person and estate is not appointed as guardian of the person, the court must nevertheless appoint the nominee as the guardian of the estate unless the court determines that the nominee is unsuitable.

Subdivision (e) provides standards for appointing a guardian of the general estate of a minor. See also Section 2650 (conflict of interest, conviction of felony, or gross immorality as causes for removal of guardian). Insolvency or bankruptcy of guardian of estate also is cause for removal. See Section 2650. A guardian of the general estate may coexist with a guardian as to particular property nominated under Section 1501, with the latter controlling the property received from the person making the nomination. Section 2109. However, no new guardian of the general estate may be appointed when an existing guardian of the general estate is serving unless the existing guardian is removed or the appointment is vacated. See Guardianship of Kimball, 80 Cal.App.2d 884, 182 P.2d 612 (1947).

When a nominated guardian is granted additional powers in the nomination and is appointed by the court, the order of appointment shall include a grant of the additional powers to the guardian unless the court for good cause determines otherwise. See Section 2108. As to the powers and duties of a guardian of particular property, see Section 2109.

Section 1510 permits a minor 14 years of age or older to petition as a party in a guardianship proceeding for the appointment of his or her own guardian and requires that the proposed guardian be specified in the petition. Civil Code Section 4600 requires the court to consider and give due weight to the minor's preference concerning the minor's custody. And subdivision (e) of Section 1514 requires the court to consider the minor's preference as to the person to be appointed as guardian of the estate.

If a guardian of the estate is nominated under Section 1500 or 1501, the provisions of subdivision (e) are subject to subdivisions (c) and (d), so that the court must appoint the nominee unless the court determines that the nominee is unsuitable. In such a case, the court is not bound by the requirements of subdivision (e). The court may thus disregard the minor's preference, although nothing precludes the court from taking it into account in determining whether the nominee is unsuitable. See also Civil Code Section 4600 (consideration in proceeding where there is at issue the custody of a minor child of a nomination of a guardian of the person of the child by a parent).

For background on the provisions of this part, see the Comment to this part under the part heading. [20 Cal.L.Rev.Comm. Reports 1001 (1990)].

1992 Amendment

Subdivision (b) of Section 1514 is amended to substitute references to the Family Code provisions that replaced the former Civil Code provision. [22 Cal.L.Rev.Comm. Reports 1 (1992)].

Commentary

A parent had no constitutional right to appointed counsel in a guardianship hearing under this section when there was no indication that the appointed guardian, who was the parent's brother, might later seek to adopt the child and there were no findings in the guardianship proceeding that might lead to a termination of the parent's parental rights. *Guardianship of H.C., 198 Cal.App.4th 1235, 130 Cal.Rptr.3d 316 (2011).*

Guardianship of Vaughan, 207 Cal.App.4th 1055, 144 Cal.Rptr.3d 216 (2012), held that when grandchildren have been residing with their grandparents for over a year, Family Code section 3041(c) does not require a showing that the children were abandoned by their parent in order for a trial court to grant the grandparents' petition for a probate guardianship under this section 1510 and this section.

For an expansive reading of subsection (a) ("whenever necessary or convenient"), see *Guardianship of Olivia J., 84 Cal.App.4th 1146, 101 Cal.Rptr.2d 364 (2000)*, which held that the trial court should not have dismissed, without a hearing on the merits, a guardianship proceeding brought by a former same-sex domestic partner who alleged that parental custody would be detrimental to the child because the child's parent would cause the child psychological harm by terminating the child's relationship with the former same-sex partner, and thus an award of custody to the same-sex partner would be necessary to serve the best interests of the child.

With respect to subsection (b), see generally Commentary to Family Code section 3041.

Research References

Forms

California Transactions Forms--Estate Planning § 6:17, Guardian Of Estate or Of Property.

California Transactions Forms--Estate Planning § 19:95, Appointment Of Guardian Of Estate.

West's California Code Forms, Probate § 1510 Form 1, Petition for Appointment Of Guardian Of Estate Of Minor--Judicial Council Form GC-210.

West's California Code Forms, Probate § 1514 Form 1, Order Appointing Guardian Of Minor--Judicial Council Form GC-240.

West's California Judicial Council Forms GC-240, Order Appointing Guardian Of Minor.

Treatises and Practice Aids

Witkin, California Summary 10th Parent and Child § 218, Statutory Rule.

Witkin, California Summary 10th Parent and Child § 220, Illustrations: Guardianship Cases.

Witkin, California Summary 10th Parent and Child § 363, Applicability Of Family Code Custody Provisions.

Witkin, California Summary 10th Parent and Child § 451, in General.

Witkin, California Summary 10th Wills and Probate § 924, Factors Considered in Appointment.

Witkin, California Summary 10th Wills and Probate § 926, Determination and Order.

Witkin, California Summary 10th Wills and Probate § 967, in General.

Witkin, California Summary 10th Wills and Probate § 969, Statewide Registry.

§ 1514.5. Information available for probate guardianship proceeding and guardianship investigator regarding best interest of child; confidentiality

Notwithstanding any other provision of law, except provisions of law governing the retention and storage of data, a family law court shall, upon request from the court in any county hearing a probate guardianship matter proceeding before the court pursuant to this part, provide to the court all available information the court deems necessary to make a determination regarding the best interest of a child, as described in Section 3011 of the Family Code, who is the subject of the proceeding. The information shall also be released to a guardianship investigator, as provided in subdivision (a) of Section 1513, acting within the scope of his or her duties in that proceeding. Any information released pursuant to this section that is confidential pursuant to any other provision of law shall remain confidential and may not be released, except to the extent necessary to comply with this section. No records shared pursuant to this section may be disclosed to any party in a case unless the party requests the agency or court that originates the record to release these records and the request is granted. In counties that provide confidential family law mediation, or confidential dependency mediation, those mediations are not covered by this section. *(Added by Stats.2004, c. 574 (A.B.2228), § 2.)*

Research References

Forms

California Transactions Forms--Estate Planning § 6:16, Guardian Of Person.

West's California Code Forms, Probate § 1514.5 COMMENT, Confidential Information from Family Law Court.

Treatises and Practice Aids

Witkin, California Summary 10th Parent and Child § 276, Report.

Witkin, California Summary 10th Wills and Probate § 922, Investigation and Report.

§ 1515. No guardian of person for married minor

Notwithstanding any other provision of this part, no guardian of the person may be appointed for a minor who is married or whose marriage has been dissolved. This section does not apply in the case of a minor whose marriage has been adjudged a nullity. *(Stats.1990, c. 79 (A.B.759), § 14, operative July 1, 1991.)*

Law Revision Commission Comments

1990 Enactment

Section 1515 continues Section 1515 of the repealed Probate Code without substantive change. A conservator of the person may be appointed where necessary for a minor who is married or whose marriage has been dissolved. See Section 1800.3(b). Nothing in Section 1515 precludes appointment of a guardian of the estate of a married minor. For background on the provisions of this part, see the Comment to this part under the part heading. [20 Cal.L.Rev. Comm. Reports 1001 (1990)].

Research References

Forms

California Transactions Forms--Estate Planning § 6:16, Guardian Of Person.

Treatises and Practice Aids

Witkin, California Summary 10th Wills and Probate § 916, in General.

§ 1516. Petitions for guardianship of the person; delivery of notice of hearing and copy of petition; screening of guardians; application of section

(a) In each case involving a petition for guardianship of the person, the petitioner shall * * * deliver pursuant to Section 1215 a notice of the hearing and a copy of the petition, at least 15 days * * * before the hearing, to the local agency designated by the board of supervisors to investigate guardianships for the court. The local social services agency providing child protection services shall screen the name of the guardian for prior referrals of neglect or abuse of minors. The results of this screening shall be provided to the court.

(b) This section does not apply to guardianships resulting from a permanency plan for a dependent child pursuant to Section 366.25 of the Welfare and Institutions Code. *(Stats. 1990, c. 79 (A.B.759), § 14, operative July 1, 1991. Amended by Stats.2017, c. 319 (A.B.976), § 32, eff. Jan. 1, 2018.)*

Law Revision Commission Comments

1990 Enactment

Section 1516 continues Section 1516 of the repealed Probate Code without substantive change. The phrase "having jurisdiction over the case" is omitted as unnecessary in view of the definition of "court" found in Section 1418. For background on the provisions of this part, see the Comment to this part under the part heading. [20 Cal.L.Rev.Comm. Reports 1001 (1990)].

Research References

Forms

West's California Code Forms, Probate § 1516 Form 1, Confidential Guardianship Screening Report--Judicial Council Form GC-212.

West's California Judicial Council Forms GC-212, Confidential Guardian Screening Form.

Treatises and Practice Aids

Witkin, California Summary 10th Wills and Probate § 920, in General.

§ 1516.5. Proceeding to have child declared free from custody and control of one or both parents

(a) A proceeding to have a child declared free from the custody and control of one or both parents may be brought in accordance with the procedures specified in Part 4 (commencing with Section 7800) of Division 12 of the Family Code within an existing guardianship proceeding, in an adoption action, or in a separate action filed for that purpose, if all of the following requirements are satisfied:

(1) One or both parents do not have the legal custody of the child.

(2) The child has been in the physical custody of the guardian for a period of not less than two years.

(3) The court finds that the child would benefit from being adopted by his or her guardian. In making this determination, the court shall consider all factors relating to the best interest of the child, including, but not limited to, the nature and extent of the relationship between all of the following:

(A) The child and the birth parent.

(B) The child and the guardian, including family members of the guardian.

(C) The child and any siblings or half siblings.

(b) The court shall appoint a court investigator or other qualified professional to investigate all factors enumerated in subdivision (a). The findings of the investigator or professional regarding those issues shall be included in the written report required pursuant to Section 7851 of the Family Code.

(c) The rights of the parent, including the rights to notice and counsel provided in Part 4 (commencing with Section 7800) of Division 12 of the Family Code, shall apply to actions brought pursuant to this section.

(d) This section does not apply to any child who is a dependent of the juvenile court or to any Indian child. *(Added by Stats.2003, c. 251 (S.B.182), § 11. Amended by Stats.2006, c. 838 (S.B.678), § 25; Stats.2010, c. 588 (A.B. 2020), § 9.)*

Commentary

In Guardianship of Ann S., 45 Cal.4th 1110, 90 Cal.Rptr.3d 701, 202 P.3d 1089 (2009), and *In re Charlotte D., 45 Cal.4th 1140, 90 Cal.Rptr.3d 724, 202 P.3d 1109 (2009)*, the California Supreme Court, held that this section does not on its face violate the substantive due process rights of parents by using the "best interest of the child" rather than the "parental unfitness" standard to terminate parental rights when a child has been in the physical custody of a guardian for not less than two years. The court reasoned that application of the parental unfitness standard is intended to protect a parent's custodial rights when a parent is exercising custody or the parent has demonstrated a full commitment to parental responsibility but his efforts to obtain custody have been thwarted. By contrast, a Probate guardianship suspends a parent's custodial rights, and a prolonged guardianship is generally inconsistent with a full commitment to parental responsibility. Nevertheless, the court indicated that the provision may be constitutionally challenged in its application to particular parents.

Adoption of Myah M., 201 Cal.App.4th 1518, 135 Cal.Rptr.3d 636 (2011), affirmed a trial court's termination of parental rights pursuant to this section when the parents stipulated to the paternal grandparents' guardianship four years earlier, the parents failed to demonstrate a commitment to parenting the child, and adoption by the grandparents would be in the best interests of the child. Under the circumstances, it was neither necessary to demonstrate parental unfitness nor to refer the case to the county child welfare agency.

In re Noreen G., 181 Cal.App.4th 1359, 105 Cal.Rptr.3d 521 (2010), review denied, held that the term "physical custody" is not unconstitutionally vague and that the trial court lacks jurisdiction to award visitation to persons whose parental rights have been terminated under this section.

Research References

Forms

West's California Code Forms, Probate § 1510 Form 1, Petition for Appointment Of Guardian Of Estate Of Minor--Judicial Council Form GC-210.

West's California Code Forms, Probate § 1459.5 COMMENT, Application Of Federal Law to Proceedings Involving Children Of Indian Ancestry.

Treatises and Practice Aids

Witkin, California Summary 10th Parent and Child § 307, Nature Of Action.

Witkin, California Summary 10th Parent and Child § 526, Determination Of Indian Status.

Witkin, California Summary 10th Wills and Probate § 926, Determination and Order.

§ 1517. Guardianships resulting from selection and implementation of a permanent plan; application of part; administration of funds for benefit of child

(a) This part does not apply to guardianships resulting from the selection and implementation of a permanent plan pursuant to Section 366.26 of the Welfare and Institutions Code. For those minors, Section 366.26 of the Welfare and Institutions Code and Division 3 (commencing with Rule 5.500) of Title Five of the California Rules of Court specify the exclusive procedures for establishing, modifying, and terminating legal guardianships. If no specific provision of the Welfare and Institutions Code or the California Rules of Court is applicable, the provisions applicable to the administration of estates under Part 4 (commencing with Section 2100) govern so far as they are applicable to like situations.

(b) This chapter shall not be construed to prevent a court that assumes jurisdiction of a minor child pursuant to Section 300 of the Welfare and Institutions Code, or a probate court, as appropriate, from issuing orders or making appointments, on motion of the child's counsel, consistent with Division 2 of the Welfare and Institutions Code or Divisions 4 to 6, inclusive, of the Probate Code necessary to ensure the appropriate administration of funds for the benefit of the child. Orders or appointments regarding those funds may continue after the court's jurisdiction is terminated pursuant to Section 391 of the Welfare and Institutions Code. *(Added by Stats.1991, c. 82 (S.B.896), § 6, eff. June 30, 1991, operative July 1, 1991. Amended by Stats.2008, c. 166 (A.B.3051), § 2.)*

Law Revision Commission Comments

1991 Addition

Section 1517 continues former Section 1517 which was added to the repealed Probate Code by 1990 Cal.Stat. ch. 1530. [20 Cal. L.Rev.Comm. Reports 2909 (1990)].

Research References

Treatises and Practice Aids

Witkin, California Summary 10th Parent and Child § 696, Continuing Jurisdiction.

Witkin, California Summary 10th Wills and Probate § 916, in General.

ARTICLE 3. NONRELATIVE GUARDIANSHIPS

Section

§ 1540. Application of article

This article does not apply in any of the following cases:

(a) Where the petition is for guardianship of the estate exclusively.

(b) Where the proposed guardian is a relative of the proposed ward.

(c) Where the Director of Developmental Services is appointed guardian pursuant to Article 7.5 (commencing with Section 416) of Chapter 2 of Part 1 of Division 1 of the Health and Safety Code.

(d) Where the director of the department designated by the board of supervisors to provide social services is appointed guardian.

(e) Where the public guardian is appointed guardian.

(f) Where the guardianship results from a permanency plan for a dependent child pursuant to Section 366.25 of the Welfare and Institutions Code. *(Stats.1990, c. 79 (A.B.759), § 14, operative July 1, 1991.)*

Law Revision Commission Comments

1990 Enactment

Section 1540 continues Section 1540 of the repealed Probate Code without substantive change. For background on the provisions of this part, see the Comment to this part under the part heading. [20 Cal.L.Rev.Comm. Reports 1001 (1990)].

Research References

Treatises and Practice Aids

Witkin, California Summary 10th Wills and Probate § 923, Additional Requirements for Nonrelative Guardianship.

§ 1541. Petition for guardianship; additional contents

In addition to the other required contents of the petition for appointment of a guardian, the petition shall include both of the following:

(a) A statement by the proposed guardian that, upon request by an agency referred to in Section 1543 for information relating to the investigation referred to in that section, the proposed guardian will promptly submit the information required.

(b) A disclosure of any petition for adoption by the proposed guardian of the minor who is the subject of the guardianship petition regardless of when or where filed.

(c) A statement whether or not the home of the proposed guardian is a licensed foster family home, a certified family home of a licensed foster family agency, or a resource family home approved by a county or a licensed foster family agency. *(Stats.1990, c. 79 (A.B.759), § 14, operative July 1, 1991. Amended by Stats.2016, c. 612 (A.B.1997), § 58, eff. Jan. 1, 2017.)*

Law Revision Commission Comments

1990 Enactment

Section 1541 continues Section 1541 of the repealed Probate Code without change. For cases in which this article does not apply, see Section 1540. For general provisions relating to petitions and other papers, see Sections 1020–1023. For background on the provisions of this part, see the Comment to this part under the part heading. [20 Cal.L.Rev.Comm. Reports 1001 (1990)].

Research References

Forms

California Transactions Forms--Estate Planning § 13:60, Revocation by Settlor.

Treatises and Practice Aids

Witkin, California Summary 10th Wills and Probate § 919, Content and Form.

Witkin, California Summary 10th Wills and Probate § 923, Additional Requirements for Nonrelative Guardianship.

§ 1542. Notice of hearing and copy of petition to director and local agency

In each case involving a petition for guardianship of the person, the petitioner shall * * * deliver pursuant to Section 1215 a notice of the hearing and a copy of the petition, at least 15 days * * * before the hearing, to the Director of Social Services at the director's office in Sacramento and to the local agency designated by the board of supervisors to investigate guardianships for the court. *(Stats.1990, c. 79 (A.B.759), § 14, operative July 1, 1991. Amended by Stats. 2017, c. 319 (A.B.976), § 33, eff. Jan. 1, 2018.)*

Law Revision Commission Comments

1990 Enactment

Section 1542 continues Section 1542 of the repealed Probate Code without change. For cases in which this article does not apply, see Section 1540. For general provisions relating to notice of hearing, see Sections 1200–1221, 1460–1469. See also Sections 1260–1265 (proof of giving notice). For background on the provisions of this part, see the Comment to this part under the part heading. [20 Cal.L.Rev.Comm. Reports 1001 (1990)].

Research References

Treatises and Practice Aids

Witkin, California Summary 10th Wills and Probate § 920, in General.

Witkin, California Summary 10th Wills and Probate § 923, Additional Requirements for Nonrelative Guardianship.

§ 1543. Suitability of proposed guardian for guardianship; report; confidentiality

(a) If the petition as filed or as amended states that an adoption petition has been filed, a report with respect to the suitability of the proposed guardian for guardianship shall be filed with the court by the agency investigating the adoption. In other cases, the local agency designated by the board of supervisors to provide public social services shall file a report with the court with respect to the proposed guardian of the same character required to be made with regard to an applicant for foster family home licensure, or, on and after January 1, 2020, resource family approval, as described in Section 16519.5 of the Welfare and Institutions Code.

(b) The report filed with the court pursuant to this section is confidential. The report may be considered by the court and shall be made available only to the persons who have been served in the proceeding and the persons who have appeared in the proceeding or their attorneys. The report may be received in evidence upon stipulation of counsel for all of those persons who are present at the hearing or, if a person is present at the hearing but is not represented by counsel, upon consent of that person. *(Stats.1990, c. 79 (A.B.759), § 14, operative July 1, 1991. Amended by Stats. 2016, c. 612 (A.B.1997), § 59, eff. Jan. 1, 2017.)*

Law Revision Commission Comments

1990 Enactment

Section 1543 continues Section 1543 of the repealed Probate Code without change. See also Section 1513 (investigation by court investigator, probation officer, or domestic relations investigator). For cases in which this article does not apply, see Section 1540. For background on the provisions of this part, see the Comment to this part under the part heading. [20 Cal.L.Rev.Comm. Reports 1001 (1990)].

Research References

Treatises and Practice Aids

Witkin, California Summary 10th Wills and Probate § 922, Investigation and Report.

Witkin, California Summary 10th Wills and Probate § 923, Additional Requirements for Nonrelative Guardianship.

CHAPTER 2. TERMINATION

§ 1600. Majority, death, adoption, or emancipation of ward

(a) A guardianship of the person or estate or both terminates when the ward attains majority unless, pursuant to Section 1510.1, the ward requests the extension of, or consents to the extension of, the guardianship of the person until the ward attains 21 years of age.

(b) A guardianship of the person terminates upon the death of the ward, the adoption of the ward, or upon the emancipation of the ward under Section 7002 of the Family Code. *(Stats.1990, c. 79 (A.B.759), § 14, operative July 1, 1991. Amended by Stats.1996, c. 862 (A.B.2751), § 6; Stats. 2015, c. 694 (A.B.900), § 4, eff. Jan. 1, 2016.)*

Law Revision Commission Comments

1990 Enactment

Section 1600 continues Section 1600 of the repealed Probate Code without change. The court retains jurisdiction of the guardianship proceeding despite the termination of the guardianship. See Section 2630. If a married minor needs protective supervision of the person, a petition for conservatorship of the person may be filed. See Section 1800.3. See also Section 1820(b) (filing petition for appointment of conservator during proposed conservatee's minority so appointment may be effective immediately upon minor becoming 18) and Section 2467 (powers and duties after death of ward). For background on the provisions of this part, see the Comment to this part under the part heading. [20 Cal.L.Rev.Comm. Reports 1001 (1990)].

Research References

Forms

California Transactions Forms--Estate Planning § 1:29, Options Involving Gifts to Minors.

California Transactions Forms--Estate Planning § 6:16, Guardian Of Person.

California Transactions Forms--Estate Planning § 6:17, Guardian Of Estate or Of Property.

West's California Code Forms, Probate § 1601 Form 1, Petition for Termination Of Guardianship--Judicial Council Form GC-255.

West's California Judicial Council Forms GC-255, Petition for Termination Of Guardianship.

Treatises and Practice Aids

Witkin, California Summary 10th Wills and Probate § 930, Termination Of Guardianship.

§ 1601. Court order; notice

Upon petition of the guardian, a parent, the minor ward, or, in the case of an Indian child custody proceeding, an Indian custodian or the ward's tribe, the court may make an order terminating the guardianship if the court determines that it is in the ward's best interest to terminate the guardianship. Upon petition of a ward who is 18 years of age or older, the court shall make an order terminating the guardianship. Notice of the hearing on the petition shall be given for the period and in the manner provided in Chapter 3 (commencing with Section 1460) of Part 1. *(Stats.1990, c. 79 (A.B.759), § 14, operative July 1, 1991. Amended by Stats. 2002, c. 1118 (A.B.1938), § 6; Stats.2006, c. 838 (S.B.678), § 26; Stats.2015, c. 694 (A.B.900), § 5, eff. Jan. 1, 2016.)*

Law Revision Commission Comments

1990 Enactment

Section 1601 continues Section 1601 of the repealed Probate Code without change. The court retains jurisdiction of the guardianship proceeding despite termination of the guardianship. See Section 2630. For general provisions, see Sections 1000–1004 (rules of practice), 1020–1023 (petitions and other papers), 1040–1050 (hearings and orders), 2103 (effect of final order). For general provisions relating to notice of hearing, see Sections 1200–1221, 1460–1469. See also Sections 1260–1265 (proof of giving notice), 2700–2702 (notice to persons who request special notice). For background on the provisions of this part, see the Comment to this part under the part heading. See also Report of Assembly Committee on Judiciary on Assembly Bills Nos. 261 and 167, reprinted in 15 Cal.L.Revision Comm'n Reports 1061, 1068 (1980). [20 Cal.L.Rev.Comm. Reports 1001 (1990)].

Commentary

In re Z.F., 248 Cal.App.4th 68, 203 Cal.Rptr.3d 319 (2016), held that a probate guardianship may be terminated when termination is shown by a preponderance of the evidence to be in the ward's best interests. Z.F. applied this standard to a juvenile court's termination, under Welfare and Institutions Code section 728, of a guardianship previously ordered by the court in a dependency proceeding.

This section requires that a parent show "overall fitness" as a parent in order to terminate a guardianship. The mere absence of the circumstances that initially gave rise to the guardianship does not suffice. *Guardianship of Kassandra H., 64 Cal.App.4th 1228, 75 Cal.Rptr.2d 668 (1998).* To the same effect, see *Guardianship of Sydney Simpson, 67 Cal.App.4th 914, 79 Cal.Rptr.2d 389 (1998), review denied February 24, 1999* (holding that this Section applies to the termination of a voluntary guardianship, and requires that the natural parent seeking to recover custody from the guardian show sufficient overall fitness to justify termination of the guardianship; it was error for the trial court to apply the Family Code Section 3041 substantive standard and burden of proof in a proceeding to terminate a voluntary guardianship).

Relying on the 2002 amendment to this section, which requires a court determination that it is "in the ward's best interest to terminate the guardianship," *Guardianship of L.V., 136 Cal.App.4th 481, 38 Cal.Rptr.3d 894 (2006), review denied,* holds that fit parents who can provide adequate food, clothing, and shelter do not have a constitutional right to have a guardianship terminated; rather the sole criterion is the best interest of the child. In *L.V.*, the child had done poorly with the parents but was thriving in all aspects with the guardians; moreover, the child, who was of the age and reasoning capacity to have her views considered, strongly opposed termination of the guardianship.

Research References

Forms

California Transactions Forms--Estate Planning § 6:16, Guardian Of Person.

California Transactions Forms--Estate Planning § 6:17, Guardian Of Estate or Of Property.

West's California Code Forms, Probate § 1601 Form 1, Petition for Termination Of Guardianship--Judicial Council Form GC-255.
West's California Code Forms, Probate § 2626 Form 1, Ex Parte Petition for Final Discharge and Order--Judicial Council Form DE-295/GC-395.
West's California Judicial Council Forms GC-255, Petition for Termination Of Guardianship.
West's California Judicial Council Forms GC-260, Order Terminating Guardianship.

Treatises and Practice Aids

Witkin, California Summary 10th Parent and Child § 698, Other Procedures.
Witkin, California Summary 10th Wills and Probate § 930, Termination Of Guardianship.
Witkin, California Summary 10th Wills and Probate § 1048, Causes for Removal.
Witkin, California Summary 10th Wills and Probate § 915A, (New) Special Provisions Applicable to Indian Children.

§ 1602. Visitation

(a) The Legislature hereby finds and declares that guardians perform a critical and important role in the lives of minors, frequently assuming a parental role and caring for a child when the child's parent or parents are unable or unwilling to do so.

(b) Upon making a determination that a guardianship should be terminated pursuant to Section 1601, the court may consider whether continued visitation between the ward and the guardian is in the ward's best interest. As part of the order of termination, the court shall have jurisdiction to issue an order providing for ongoing visitation between a former guardian and his or her former minor ward after the termination of the guardianship. The order granting or denying visitation may not be modified unless the court determines, based upon evidence presented, that there has been a significant change of circumstances since the court issued the order and that modification of the order is in the best interest of the child.

(c) A copy of the visitation order shall be filed in any court proceeding relating to custody of the minor. If a prior order has not been filed, and a proceeding is not pending relating to the custody of the minor in the court of any county, the visitation order may be used as the sole basis for opening a file in the court of the county in which the custodial parent resides. While a parent of the child has custody of the child, proceedings for modification of the visitation order shall be determined in a proceeding under the Family Code. *(Added by Stats.2004, c. 301 (A.B.2292), § 2.)*

Research References

Forms

West's California Code Forms, Probate § 1601 Form 1, Petition for Termination Of Guardianship--Judicial Council Form GC-255.
West's California Code Forms, Probate § 1601 Form 2, Order Terminating Guardianship--Judicial Council Form GC-260.
West's California Judicial Council Forms GC-260, Order Terminating Guardianship.

Treatises and Practice Aids

Witkin, California Summary 10th Wills and Probate § 930, Termination Of Guardianship.

CHAPTER 3. PERMANENT AND STABLE HOME

§ 1610. Legislative findings and declarations

(a) The Legislature finds and declares that it is in the best interests of children to be raised in a permanent, safe, stable, and loving environment.

(b) Unwarranted petitions, applications, or motions other than discovery motions after the guardianship has been established create an environment that can be harmful to children and are inconsistent with the goals of permanency, safety, and stability. *(Added by Stats.2002, c. 1118 (A.B. 1938), § 7. Amended by Stats.2006, c. 493 (A.B.1363), § 6.)*

Research References

Treatises and Practice Aids

Witkin, California Summary 10th Wills and Probate § 931, Vexatious Litigants.

§ 1611. Petitions without merit or intended to harass or annoy guardian

If a person files a petition for visitation, termination of the guardianship, or instruction to the guardian that is unmeritorious, or intended to harass or annoy the guardian, and the person has previously filed pleadings in the guardianship proceedings that were unmeritorious, or intended to harass or annoy the guardian, this petition shall be grounds for the court to determine that the person is a vexatious litigant for the purposes of Title 3a (commencing with Section 391) of Part 2 of the Code of Civil Procedure. For these purposes, the term "new litigation" shall include petitions for visitation, termination of the guardianship, or instruction to the guardian. *(Added by Stats.2002, c. 1118 (A.B.1938), § 7.)*

Research References

Treatises and Practice Aids

Witkin, California Summary 10th Wills and Probate § 931, Vexatious Litigants.

Part 3

CONSERVATORSHIP

Law Revision Commission Comments

1990 Enactment

This part supersedes Part 3 (commencing with Section 1800) of Division 4 of the repealed Probate Code. The superseded part was enacted upon recommendation of the California Law Revision Commission. See Recommendation Relating to Guardianship–Conservatorship Law, 14 Cal.L.Revision Comm'n Reports 501 (1978). For the Guardianship–Conservatorship Law as enacted in 1979 (Chapter 726 of the Statutes of 1979) with the revisions made by Chapters 89 and 246 of the Statutes of 1980, see Guardianship–Conservatorship Law, 15 Cal.L.Revision Comm'n Reports 451 (1980). [20 Cal.L.Rev.Comm. Reports 1001 (1990)].

CHAPTER 2. PERIODIC REVIEW OF CONSERVATORSHIP

§ 1851.2. Coordination

Each court shall coordinate investigations with the filing of accountings, so that investigators may review accountings before visiting conservatees, if feasible. *(Added by Stats.2007, c. 553 (A.B.1727), § 10.)*

Research References

Treatises and Practice Aids

Witkin, California Summary 10th Wills and Probate § 950, Periodic Review Of Conservatorship.

CHAPTER 4. LEGAL CAPACITY OF CONSERVATEE

ARTICLE 3. CAPACITY OF CONSERVATEE TO MARRY

§ 1900. Appointment of conservator; effect

The appointment of a conservator of the person or estate or both does not affect the capacity of the conservatee to marry or to enter into a registered domestic partnership. *(Stats.1990, c. 79 (A.B.759), § 14, operative July 1, 1991. Amended by Stats.2005, c. 418 (S.B.973), § 26.)*

Law Revision Commission Comments

1990 Enactment

Section 1900 continues Section 1900 of the repealed Probate Code without change. This section makes clear that appointment of a conservator under the Probate Code does not deprive the conservatee of capacity to marry. Cf. Conservatorship of Roulet, 23 Cal.3d 219, 228, 590 P.2d 1, 152 Cal.Rptr. 425 (1979) (one found to be gravely disabled under Lanterman–Petris–Short Act faces "possible loss" of right to marry). Whether the conservatee has capacity to marry is determined by the law that would be applicable had no conservatorship been established. See also Section 1901 (court determination of conservatee's capacity to marry). For background on the provisions of this part, see the Comment to this part under the part heading. See also Report of Assembly Committee on Judiciary on Assembly Bills Nos. 261 and 167, reprinted in 15 Cal.L.Revision Comm'n Reports 1061, 1075–76 (1980). [20 Cal.L.Rev.Comm. Reports 1001 (1990)].

Commentary

In re Marriage of Greenway, 217 Cal.App.4th 628, 158 Cal.Rptr.3d 364 (2013), review denied, relying on Probate Code sections 810 and 811, holds that the standard for mental capacity to end a marriage is low and a husband's diagnosis of dementia did not require a determination that he was of unsound mind or lacked mental capacity to end his marriage. Under this section, even the appointment of a conservator does not affect the capacity to marry. Moreover, the court was not bound by the testimony of experts when the husband's testimony before the trial court provided sufficient evidence that he was mentally capable of exercising judgment and expressing a wish that his marriage be terminated on account of irreconcilable differences.

Research References

Treatises and Practice Aids

Witkin, California Summary 10th Husband and Wife § 27, Establishment Of Domestic Partnership.

Witkin, California Summary 10th Husband and Wife § 43, Capacity Of Parties.

Witkin, California Summary 10th Wills and Probate § 958, Capacity to Marry.

Part 4

PROVISIONS COMMON TO GUARDIANSHIP AND CONSERVATORSHIP

Law Revision Commission Comments

1990 Enactment

This part supersedes Part 4 (commencing with Section 2100) of Division 4 of the repealed Probate Code. The superseded part was enacted upon recommendation of the California Law Revision Commission. See Recommendation Relating to Guardianship–Conservatorship Law, 14 Cal.L.Revision Comm'n Reports 501 (1978). See also Report of Assembly Committee on Judiciary on Assembly Bills Nos. 261 and 167, republished in 15 Cal.L.Revision Comm'n Reports 1061, 1076–89 (1980); Report of Senate Committee on Judiciary on Assembly Bill No. 261, republished in 15 Cal.L.Revision Comm'n Reports 1097, 1099 (1980); Communication from the California Law Revision Commission concerning Assembly Bill 158, 20 Cal.L.Revision Comm'n Reports 235 (1990). For the Guardianship–Conservatorship Law as enacted in 1979 (Chapter 726 of the Statutes of 1979) with the revisions made by Chapters 89 and 246 of the Statutes of 1980, see Guardianship–Conservatorship Law, 15 Cal.L.Revision Comm'n Reports 451 (1980). [20 Cal.L.Rev. Comm. Reports 1001 (1990)].

CHAPTER 2. JURISDICTION AND VENUE

ARTICLE 2. CHANGE OF VENUE

§ 2217. Transferred guardianship or conservatorship; notice of receipt; compliance; review; hearing by transferring court

(a) When an order has been made transferring venue to another county, the court transferring the matter shall set a hearing within two months to confirm receipt of the notification described in subdivision (b). If the notification has not been made, the transferring court shall make reasonable inquiry into the status of the matter.

(b) When a court receives the file of a transferred guardianship or conservatorship, the court:

(1) Shall send written notification of the receipt to the court that transferred the matter.

(2) Shall take proper action pursuant to ensure compliance by the guardian or conservator with the matters provided in Section 1456.5.

(3) If the case is a conservatorship, may conduct a review, including an investigation, as described in Sections 1851 to 1853, inclusive. *(Added by Stats.2007, c. 553 (A.B.1727), § 11.)*

Research References

Treatises and Practice Aids

Witkin, California Summary 10th Wills and Probate § 981, Change Of Venue.

CHAPTER 6. POWERS AND DUTIES OF GUARDIAN OR CONSERVATOR OF THE ESTATE

ARTICLE 4. ESTATE MANAGEMENT POWERS GENERALLY

§ 2451.5. Powers of guardian or conservator

The guardian or conservator may do any of the following:

(a) Contract for the guardianship or conservatorship, perform outstanding contracts, and, thereby, bind the estate.

(b) Purchase tangible personal property.

(c) Subject to the provisions of Chapter 8 (commencing with Section 2640), employ an attorney to advise and represent the guardian or conservator in all matters, including the conservatorship proceeding and all other actions or proceedings.

(d) Employ and pay the expense of accountants, investment advisers, agents, depositaries, and employees.

(e) Operate for a period of 45 days after the issuance of the letters of guardianship or conservatorship, at the risk of the estate, a business, farm, or enterprise constituting an asset of the estate. *(Added by Stats.2007, c. 553 (A.B.1727), § 16.)*

Research References

Treatises and Practice Aids

Witkin, California Summary 10th Wills and Probate § 1002, Exercise Of Powers Without Court Supervision.

CHAPTER 7. INVENTORY AND ACCOUNTS

ARTICLE 3. ACCOUNTS

§ 2620.1. Guidelines to be developed

The Judicial Council shall, by January 1, 2009, develop guidelines to assist investigators and examiners in reviewing accountings and detecting fraud. *(Added by Stats.2007, c. 553 (A.B.1727), § 21.)*

CHAPTER 8. COMPENSATION OF GUARDIAN, CONSERVATOR, AND ATTORNEY

§ 2647. Attorney fees

No attorney fees may be paid from the estate of the ward or conservatee without prior court order. The estate of the ward or conservatee is not obligated to pay attorney fees established by any engagement agreement or other contract until it has been approved by the court. This does not preclude an award of fees by the court pursuant to this chapter even if the contractual obligations are unenforceable pursuant to this section. *(Added by Stats.2007, c. 553 (A.B.1727), § 24.)*

Research References

Forms

West's California Code Forms, Probate § 1064 Form 1, Petition for Approval Of Account and for Compensation.

Treatises and Practice Aids

Witkin, California Summary 10th Wills and Probate § 1044, Procedure.

Part 5

PUBLIC GUARDIAN

Law Revision Commission Comments

1990 Enactment

This part supersedes Part 5 (commencing with Section 2900) of Division 4 of the repealed Probate Code. The superseded part was enacted upon recommendation of the California Law Revision Commission. See Recommendation Relating to Public Guardians and Administrators, 19 Cal.L.Revision Comm'n Reports 707 (1988). See also Communication from the California Law Revision Commission Concerning Assembly Bill 2841, 19 Cal.L.Revision Comm'n Reports 1201, 1228 (1988). For general provisions governing the office of the public guardian, formerly found in Welfare and Institutions Code Sections 8000–8005, 8008, and 8015, see Government Code Sections 27430–27436. [20 Cal.L.Rev.Comm.Reports 1001 (1990)].

CHAPTER 2. PREFILING INVESTIGATION BY PUBLIC GUARDIAN

§ 2910. Petition for appointment of public guardian as conservator; investigation; notice and service of process

(a) Upon a showing of probable cause to believe that a person is in substantial danger of abuse or neglect and needs a conservator of the person, the estate, or the person and estate for his or her own protection, the public guardian or the county's adult protective services agency may petition for either or both of the orders of the court provided in subdivision (b) in connection with his or her investigation to determine whether a petition for the appointment of the public guardian as conservator of the person, estate, or the person and estate of the person would be necessary or appropriate.

(b) The petition may request either or both of the following orders for the limited purposes of the investigation concerning a person:

(1) An order authorizing identified health care providers or organizations to provide private medical information about the person to the public guardian's authorized representatives.

(2) An order authorizing identified financial institutions or advisers, accountants, and others with financial information about the person to provide the information to the public guardian's authorized representatives.

(c) Notice of the hearing and a copy of the petition shall be served on the person who is the subject of the investigation in the manner and for the period required by Section 1460 or, on application of the public guardian contained in or accompanying the petition, on an expedited basis in the manner and for the period ordered by the court. The court may dispense with notice of the hearing only on a showing of facts demonstrating an immediate threat of substantial harm to the person if notice is given. *(Added by Stats.2007, c. 553 (A.B.1727), § 25.)*

Research References

Treatises and Practice Aids

Witkin, California Summary 10th Wills and Probate § 971, Nature Of Office.

§ 2911. Contents of order issued in response to petition

A court order issued in response to a public guardian's petition pursuant to Section 2910 shall do all of the following:

(a) Authorize health care providers to disclose a person's confidential medical information as permitted under California law, and also authorize disclosure of the information under federal medical privacy regulations enacted pursuant to the Health Insurance Portability and Accountability Act of 1996.

(b) Direct the public guardian or the adult protective services agency to keep the information acquired under the order confidential, except as disclosed in a judicial proceeding or as required by law enforcement or an authorized regulatory agency.

(c) Direct the public guardian or the adult protective services agency to destroy all copies of written information obtained under the order or give them to the person who was the subject of the investigation if a conservatorship proceeding is not commenced within 60 days after the date of the order. The court may extend this time period as the court finds to be in the subject's best interest. *(Added by Stats. 2007, c. 553 (A.B.1727), § 25.)*

Research References

Treatises and Practice Aids

Witkin, California Summary 10th Wills and Probate § 971, Nature Of Office.

CHAPTER 3. APPOINTMENT OF PUBLIC GUARDIAN

§ 2920. Application for appointment; court order; notice and hearing

(a) If any person domiciled in the county requires a guardian or conservator and there is no one else who is qualified and willing to act and whose appointment as guardian or conservator would be in the best interests of the person, then either of the following shall apply:

(1) The public guardian shall apply for appointment as guardian or conservator of the person, the estate, or the person and estate, if there is an imminent threat to the person's health or safety or the person's estate.

(2) The public guardian may apply for appointment as guardian or conservator of the person, the estate, or the person and estate in all other cases.

(b) The public guardian shall apply for appointment as guardian or conservator of the person, the estate, or the person and estate, if the court so orders. The court may make an order under this subdivision on motion of an interested person or on the court's own motion in a pending proceeding or in a proceeding commenced for that purpose. The court shall order the public guardian to apply for appointment as guardian or conservator of the person, the estate, or the person and estate, on behalf of any person domiciled in the county who appears to require a guardian or conservator, if it appears that there is no one else who is qualified and willing to act, and if that appointment as guardian or conservator appears to be in the best interests of the person. However, if prior to the filing of the petition for appointment it is discovered that there is someone else who is qualified and willing to act as guardian or conservator, the public guardian shall be relieved of the duty under the order. The court shall not make an order under this subdivision except after notice to the public guardian for the period and in the manner provided for in Chapter 3 (commencing with Section 1460) of Part 1, consideration of the alternatives, and a determination by the court that the appointment is necessary. The notice and hearing under this subdivision may be combined with the notice and hearing required for appointment of a guardian or conservator.

(c) The public guardian shall begin an investigation within two business days of receiving a referral for conservatorship or guardianship. *(Stats.1990, c. 79 (A.B.759), § 14, operative July 1, 1991. Amended by Stats.2006, c. 493 (A.B.1363), § 32.)*

Law Revision Commission Comments

1990 Enactment

Section 2920 continues Section 2920 of the repealed Probate Code without change. For general provisions, see Sections 1000–1004 (rules of practice), 1020–1023 (petitions and other papers), 1040–1050 (hearings and orders), 2103 (effect of final order). For general provisions relating to notice of hearing, see Sections 1200–1221, 1460–1469. See also Sections 1260–1265 (proof of giving notice).

Section 2920 applies even though a person may be institutionalized in a facility in another county if the person is domiciled in the county of the public guardian. Even though there may be other persons qualified and willing to act, their appointment may not be in the best interest of the ward or conservatee. This could occur, for example, where a neutral party is needed because of family disputes. In such a situation, a public guardian is not liable for failure to take possession or control of property that is beyond the public guardian's ability to possess or control. See Section 2944 (immunity of public guardian).

The court may order appointment of the public guardian only after notice to the public guardian and a determination that the appointment is necessary. The determination of necessity may require the court to ascertain whether there is any other alternative to public guardianship, and whether the public guardianship is simply being sought as a convenience or as a strategic litigation device by the parties involved. Alternative means of resolving the situation, besides appointment of the public guardian, could include such options as use of a private guardian or appointment of a guardian ad litem, in an appropriate case.

Subdivision (b) permits the special notice to the public guardian and hearing under this subdivision to be combined with a general notice and hearing for appointment of a guardian or conservator, in the interest of procedural efficiency.

Background on Section 2920 of Repealed Code

Section 2920 was added by 1988 Cal.Stat. ch. 1199 § 72. The section superseded the first, second, and a portion of the third sentences of former Welfare and Institutions Code Section 8006. For background on the provisions of this part, see the Comment to this part under the part heading. [20 Cal.L.Rev.Comm.Reports 1001 (1990)].

Research References

Treatises and Practice Aids

Witkin, California Summary 10th Wills and Probate § 936, Court's Discretion and Statutory Preference.
Witkin, California Summary 10th Wills and Probate § 971, Nature Of Office.
Witkin, California Summary 10th Wills and Probate § 972, Appointment Procedure.

§ 2921. Persons under jurisdiction of Department of State Hospitals or Department of Developmental Services; consent to application

An application of the public guardian for guardianship or conservatorship of the person, the estate, or the person and estate, of a person who is under the jurisdiction of the State Department of State Hospitals or the State Department of Developmental Services shall not be granted without the written consent of the department having jurisdiction of the person. *(Stats.1990, c. 79 (A.B.759), § 14, operative July 1, 1991. Amended by Stats.2012, c. 440 (A.B.1488), § 50, eff. Sept. 22, 2012.)*

Law Revision Commission Comments

1990 Enactment

Section 2921 continues Section 2921 of the repealed Probate Code without change.

Background on Section 2921 of Repealed Code

Section 2921 was added by 1988 Cal.Stat. ch. 1199 § 72. The section restated former Welfare and Institutions Code Section 8007 without substantive change. For background on the provisions of this part, see the Comment to this part under the part heading. [20 Cal.L.Rev.Comm.Reports 1001 (1990)].

Research References

Treatises and Practice Aids

Witkin, California Summary 10th Wills and Probate § 972, Appointment Procedure.

§ 2922. Letters; bond and oath

If the public guardian is appointed as guardian or conservator:

(a) Letters shall be issued in the same manner and by the same proceedings as letters are issued to other persons. Letters may be issued to "the public guardian" of the county without naming the public guardian.

(b) The official bond and oath of the public guardian are in lieu of the guardian or conservator's bond and oath on the grant of letters. *(Stats.1990, c. 79 (A.B.759), § 14, operative July 1, 1991.)*

Law Revision Commission Comments

1990 Enactment

Section 2922 continues Section 2922 of the repealed Probate Code without change. Letters issued to "the public guardian" are sufficient to enable a successor public guardian to act without issuance of new letters. Gov't Code § 27433 (termination of authority of public guardian). See also Section 52 ("letters" defined). The public guardian is allowed a share of the cost of the bond as an expense of administration. See Section 2942(c).

Background on Section 2922 of Repealed Code

Section 2922 was added by 1988 Cal.Stat. ch. 1199 § 72. The section restated the third and fourth sentences of former Welfare and Institutions Code Section 8006 with the addition of authority to issue letters to "the public guardian." For background on the provisions of this part, see the Comment to this part under the part heading. [20 Cal.L.Rev.Comm.Reports 1001 (1990)].

Research References

Treatises and Practice Aids

Witkin, California Summary 10th Wills and Probate § 972, Appointment Procedure.

§ 2923. Continuing education requirements

On or before January 1, 2008, the public guardian shall comply with the continuing education requirements that are established by the California State Association of Public Administrators, Public Guardians, and Public Conservators. *(Added by Stats.2006, c. 493 (A.B.1363), § 33.)*

CHAPTER 4. ADMINISTRATION BY PUBLIC GUARDIAN

Section

§ 2940. Funds; deposit or investment

All funds coming into the custody of the public guardian shall be deposited or invested in the same manner and subject to the same terms and conditions as deposit or investment by the public administrator of money in an estate pursuant to Article 3 (commencing with Section 7640) of Chapter 4 of Part 1 of Division 7. *(Stats.1990, c. 79 (A.B.759), § 14, operative July 1, 1991.)*

Law Revision Commission Comments

1990 Enactment

Section 2940 continues Section 2940 of the repealed Probate Code without change. This section cross-refers to comparable provisions of the public administrator statute.

Background on Section 2940 of Repealed Code

Section 2940 was added by 1988 Cal.Stat. ch. 1199 § 72. The section superseded former Welfare and Institutions Code Section 8009. For background on the provisions of this part, see the Comment to this part under the part heading. [20 Cal.L.Rev.Comm.Reports 1001 (1990)].

Research References

Treatises and Practice Aids

Witkin, California Summary 10th Wills and Probate § 974, Administration Of Estate.

§ 2941. Private attorneys; cost of employment

The public guardian may, if necessary and in the public guardian's discretion, employ private attorneys where the cost of employment can be defrayed out of estate funds or where satisfactory pro bono or contingency fee arrangements can be made. *(Stats.1990, c. 79 (A.B.759), § 14, operative July 1, 1991.)*

Law Revision Commission Comments

1990 Enactment

Section 2941 continues Section 2941 of the repealed Probate Code without change.

Background on Section 2941 of Repealed Code

Section 2941 was added by 1988 Cal.Stat. ch. 1199 § 72. The section restated former Welfare and Institutions Code Section 8010 with the addition of reference to satisfactory pro bono or contingency fee arrangements. For background on the provisions of this part, see the Comment to this part under the part heading. [20 Cal.L.Rev.Comm.Reports 1001 (1990)].

Research References

Treatises and Practice Aids

Witkin, California Summary 10th Wills and Probate § 974, Administration Of Estate.

§ 2942. Payments from estate

The public guardian shall be paid from the estate of the ward or conservatee for all of the following:

(a) Reasonable expenses incurred in the execution of the guardianship or conservatorship.

(b) Compensation for services of the public guardian and the attorney of the public guardian, and for the filing and processing services of the county clerk or the clerk of the superior court, in the amount the court determines is just and reasonable. In determining what constitutes just and reasonable compensation, the court shall, among other factors, take into consideration the actual costs of the services provided, the amount of the estate involved, the special value of services provided in relation to the estate, and whether the compensation requested might impose an economic hardship on the estate. Nothing in this section shall require a public guardian to base a request for compensation upon an hourly rate of service.

(c) An annual bond fee in the amount of twenty-five dollars ($25) plus one-fourth of 1 percent of the amount of an estate greater than ten thousand dollars ($10,000). The amount charged shall be deposited in the county treasury. This subdivision does not apply if the ward or conservatee is eligible for Social Security Supplemental Income benefits. *(Stats.1990, c. 79 (A.B.759), § 14, operative July 1, 1991. Amended by Stats.1994, c. 472 (A.B.2725), § 2; Stats.1998, c. 103 (S.B.1487), § 2; Stats.1999, c. 866 (A.B.1152), § 1.)*

Law Revision Commission Comments

1990 Enactment

Section 2942 continues Section 2942 of the repealed Probate Code without change. Subdivision (c) is comparable to Section 7621(d) (public administrator).

Background on Section 2942 of Repealed Code

Section 2942 was added by 1988 Cal.Stat. ch. 1199 § 72. Subdivisions (a) and (b) of Section 2942 restated former Welfare and Institutions Code Section 8013 without substantive change. Subdivision (c) was new. For background on the provisions of this part, see the Comment to this part under the part heading. [20 Cal.L.Rev.Comm.Reports 1001 (1990)].

Research References

Treatises and Practice Aids

Witkin, California Summary 10th Wills and Probate § 972, Appointment Procedure.

Witkin, California Summary 10th Wills and Probate § 973, Temporary Possession or Control Of Property.

Witkin, California Summary 10th Wills and Probate § 974, Administration Of Estate.

§ 2943. Appraisal of inventory property; sale of residence

(a) Notwithstanding subdivision (c) of Section 2610, the property described in the inventory may be appraised by the public guardian and need not be appraised by a probate referee if the public guardian files with the inventory an appraisal showing that the estimated value of the property in the estate does not exceed the amount prescribed in Section 13100.

(b) If the conservator seeks authority pursuant to subdivision (b) of Section 2540 to sell the conservatee's personal residence, whether or not it is real property, or if the conservator seeks authority pursuant to Section 2590 to sell the conservatee's real property, valued in excess of ten thousand dollars ($10,000), or an item of personal property valued in excess of ten thousand dollars ($10,000) that is not a security sold pursuant to subdivision (a) of Section 2544, that property shall be appraised by a probate referee. *(Stats.1990, c. 79 (A.B.759), § 14, operative July 1, 1991. Amended by Stats.1996, c. 86 (A.B.2146), § 3.)*

Law Revision Commission Comments

1990 Enactment

Section 2943 continues Section 2943 of the repealed Probate Code without change.

Background on Section 2943 of Repealed Code

Section 2943 was added by 1988 Cal.Stat. ch. 1199 § 72. The section superseded former Welfare and Institutions Code Section 8011. For background on the provisions of this part, see the Comment to this part under the part heading. [20 Cal.L.Rev.Comm.Reports 1001 (1990)].

Research References

Treatises and Practice Aids

Witkin, California Summary 10th Wills and Probate § 974, Administration Of Estate.

Witkin, California Summary 10th Wills and Probate § 1015, in General.
Witkin, California Summary 10th Wills and Probate § 1029, Purpose and Effect Of Authorization.

§ 2944. Liability for failure to take possession

The public guardian is not liable for failing to take possession or control of property that is beyond the ability of the public guardian to possess or control. *(Stats.1990, c. 79 (A.B.759), § 14, operative July 1, 1991.)*

Law Revision Commission Comments

1990 Enactment

Section 2944 continues Section 2944 of the repealed Probate Code without change. Cf. Section 7601(b) (duty of public administrator).

Background on Section 2944 of Repealed Code

Section 2944 was a new provision added by 1988 Cal.Stat. ch. 1199 § 72. For background on the provisions of this part, see the Comment to this part under the part heading. [20 Cal.L.Rev.Comm.Reports 1001 (1990)].

Research References

Treatises and Practice Aids

Witkin, California Summary 10th Wills and Probate § 973, Temporary Possession or Control Of Property.

CHAPTER 5. FINANCIAL ABUSE OF MENTALLY IMPAIRED ELDERS

ARTICLE 1. GENERAL

§ 2950. Legislative intent; coordination with existing programs

(a) It is the intent of the Legislature to do all of the following:

(1) Reduce the incidence of financial abuse perpetrated against mentally impaired elder adults.

(2) Minimize monetary losses to mentally impaired elder adults as a result of financial abuse.

(3) Facilitate timely intervention by law enforcement, in collaboration with the public guardian, to effectively protect mentally impaired elder adult victims of financial abuse, and to recover their assets.

(b) Any peace officer or public guardian of a county that has both of the following, as determined by the public guardian of that county, may take the actions authorized by this chapter:

(1) The existence of sufficient law enforcement personnel with expertise in the assessment of competence.

(2) The existence of a law enforcement unit devoted to investigating elder financial abuse and the enforcement of laws applicable to elder abuse.

(c) This chapter shall be coordinated with existing mandated programs affecting financial abuse of mentally impaired elders that are administered by the adult protective services agency of the county. *(Added by Stats.2000, c. 813 (S.B. 1742), § 1.)*

Research References

Treatises and Practice Aids

Witkin, California Summary 10th Wills and Probate § 973, Temporary Possession or Control Of Property.

§ 2951. Definitions

The definitions contained in this section shall govern the construction of this chapter, unless the context requires otherwise.

(a) "Declaration" means a document that substantially complies with the requirements of Section 2954, and is signed by both a peace officer and a supervisor from the county's adult protective services agency and provided to the public guardian in accordance with subdivision (b) of Section 2952.

(b) "Elder person" means any person residing in this state, 65 years of age or older.

(c) "Financial abuse" means a situation described in Section 15610.30 of the Welfare and Institutions Code.

(d) "Financial abuse POST training" means an elder financial abuse training course certified by the Commission on Peace Officer Standards and Training.

(e) "Financial institution" means any bank, savings and loan, thrift, industrial loan company, credit union, or any branch of any of these institutions doing business in the state, as defined by provisions of the Financial Code.

(f) "Peace officer" means a sheriff, deputy sheriff, municipal police officer, or a peace officer authorized under subdivision (b) of Section 830.1 of the Penal Code, duly sworn under the requirements of state law, who satisfies any of the following requirements:

(1) The sheriff, deputy sheriff, municipal police officer, or peace officer authorized under subdivision (b) of Section 830.1 of the Penal Code has completed or participated as a lecturer in a financial abuse POST training program within the last 36 months. The completion of the course may be satisfied by telecourse, video training tape, or other instruction. The training shall, at a minimum, address relevant elder abuse laws, recognition of financial abuse and fraud, assessment of mental competence in accordance with the standards set forth in Part 17 (commencing with Section 810) of the Probate Code, reporting requirements and procedures for the investigation of financial abuse and related crimes, including neglect, and civil and criminal procedures for the protection of victims. The course may be presented as part of a training program that includes other subjects or courses.

(2) The sheriff, deputy sheriff, municipal police officer, or peace officer authorized under subdivision (b) of Section 830.1 of the Penal Code, has consulted with a sheriff, deputy sheriff, municipal police officer, or peace officer authorized under subdivision (b) of Section 830.1 of the Penal Code, who satisfies the requirements of paragraph (1) concerning the declaration defined in subdivision (a) and obtained the signature of that sheriff, deputy sheriff, municipal police officer, or peace officer authorized under subdivision (b) of Section 830.1 of the Penal Code on a declaration that

substantially complies with the form described in Section 2954.

(g) "Property" means all personal property and real property of every kind belonging to, or alleged to belong to, the elder. *(Added by Stats.2000, c. 813 (S.B.1742), § 1.)*

ARTICLE 2. ESTATE PROTECTION

§ 2952. Issuance of declaration by peace officer; certificate of authority; standardized form; authority and responsibility; liabilities for actions under certificate; expiration; investigation by county adult protective services agency

(a) A peace officer may issue a declaration, as provided in Section 2954, concerning an elder person if all of the following conditions are satisfied:

(1) There is probable cause to believe that the elder person is substantially unable to manage his or her financial resources or to resist fraud or undue influence.

(2) There exists a significant danger that the elder person will lose all or a portion of his or her property as a result of fraud or misrepresentations or the mental incapacity of the elder person.

(3) There is probable cause to believe that a crime is being committed against the elder person.

(4) The crime is connected to the inability of the elder person to manage his or her financial resources or to resist fraud or undue influence, and that inability is the result of deficits in the elder person's mental functions.

(5) The peace officer has consulted with an individual qualified to perform a mental status examination.

(b) If the requirements of subdivision (a) are satisfied, the peace officer may provide a signed declaration to the public guardian of the county. The declaration provided by the peace officer under this subdivision shall be signed by both the peace officer and a supervisor from the county's adult protective services agency. The declaration shall be transmitted to the public guardian within 24 hours of its being signed, and may be transmitted by facsimile.

(c)(1) Upon receiving a signed declaration from a peace officer, the public guardian is authorized to rely on the information contained in the declaration to take immediate possession or control of any real or personal property belonging to the elder person referred to in the declaration, including any property that is held jointly between the elder person and a third party that is subject to loss, injury, waste, or misappropriation, and may issue a written recordable certification of that fact pursuant to this section. The written recordable certification shall substantially comply with the following form:

"CERTIFICATE OF AUTHORITY

THIS IS AN OFFICIAL CERTIFICATE ENTITLING THE PUBLIC GUARDIAN TO TAKE POSSESSION OF ANY AND ALL PROPERTY BELONGING TO THE FOLLOWING INDIVIDUAL:

(Name of Victim) ________

This Certificate of Authority has been issued by the Public Guardian pursuant to and in compliance with the Financial Abuse of Mentally Impaired Elders statute, Chapter 4 (commencing with Section 2950) of Part 5 of Division 4 of the California Probate Code. Under California law, this Certificate of Authority authorizes the Public Guardian to take possession or control of property belonging to the above-named individual.

SPECIAL NOTE TO FINANCIAL INSTITUTIONS:

State law requires that upon receiving a copy of this Certificate of Authority, financial institutions shall provide the public guardian with information concerning property held by the above-named individual and surrender the property to the Public Guardian if requested.

This Certificate of Authority shall only be valid when signed and dated by the Public Guardian or a deputy Public Guardian of the County of _____ and affixed with the official seal of the Public Guardian below.

Signature of Public Guardian:

Date:

Official Seal"

(2) The mere issuance of the declaration provided by this section shall not require the public guardian to take possession or control of property and shall not require the public guardian to make a determination that the requirements for the appointment of a conservator are satisfied.

(3) The authority provided to the public guardian in paragraph (1) includes the authority to deny use of, access to, or prohibit residency in the home of the elder, by anyone who does not have a written rental agreement or other legal right to the use of, or access to, the residence, and, subject to the requirements of subdivision (b) of Section 2900, the authority to terminate the occupancy of anyone living in the home of the elder person, and the authority to remove that occupant residing therein.

(4) The public guardian shall serve, or cause to be served, a copy of the certification issued pursuant to this section on the elder person by mail within 24 hours of the execution of the certification, or as soon thereafter as is practical, in the manner provided in Chapter 4 (commencing with Section 413.10) of Title 5 of Part 2 of the Code of Civil Procedure.

(5) Receipt of a certification issued under this section constitutes sufficient acquittance to financial institutions and others in possession of an elder person's property to provide information and surrender property of the elder person to the public guardian. Any financial institution or other person who provides information or surrenders property pursuant to this section shall be discharged from any liability for any act

or omission of the public guardian with respect to the property.

(6) A public guardian acting in good faith is not liable when taking possession or control of property pursuant to this section.

(7) A certification issued pursuant to this section is valid for 15 days after the date of issuance. Upon ex parte petition to the superior court, the public guardian may seek additional 15–day certifications. The court shall grant that petition only if it determines that the additional certification is necessary to protect the elder from financial abuse and the elder's property from loss, injury, waste, or misappropriation.

(d)(1) If the public guardian takes possession of an elder person's property pursuant to this section, the public guardian shall attempt to find agents pursuant to the use of durable powers of attorney or successor trustees nominated in trust instruments, or other persons having legal authority under existing legal instruments, to manage the elder person's estate.

(2) If the public guardian is unable to find any appropriate person to manage the elder person's estate pursuant to paragraph (1), the public guardian shall attempt to find appropriate family members willing to manage the elder person's estate. If no documents exist appointing appropriate fiduciaries, the public guardian shall follow the priorities set forth in Article 2 (commencing with Section 1810) of Chapter 1 of Part 3.

(3) The public guardian shall take the steps described in paragraphs (1) and (2) within 15 days of taking possession of an elder person's property pursuant to this section.

(e) Nothing in this section prevents the county's adult protective services agency from conducting an investigation regarding the elder person named in the declaration and providing appropriate services, in coordination with any actions taken with the public guardian under this section or an investigation conducted by law enforcement regarding the elder person. *(Added by Stats.2000, c. 813 (S.B.1742), § 1. Amended by Stats.2001, c. 232 (A.B.1517), § 3.)*

§ 2953. Petition for costs and fees; duties of public guardian; petition for order to quash certification

(a)(1) A public guardian who has taken possession or control of the property of an elder person pursuant to this chapter is entitled to petition a court of competent jurisdiction for the reasonable costs incurred by the public guardian for the protection of the person or the property, together with reasonable fees for services, including, but not limited to, reasonable attorneys' fees. These fees shall be payable from the estate of the elder person if the person is not deemed competent by the court and if any of the following apply:

(A) The public guardian or someone else is appointed as the temporary or general conservator of the estate.

(B) An attorney-in-fact, under a durable power of attorney, or a trustee, takes steps, or is notified of the need to take steps, to protect the estate of the elder person.

(C) An action is brought against the alleged financial abuser by the elder person, his or her conservator, a trustee, a fiduciary, or a successor in interest of the elder person, arising from a harm that the public guardian taking charge was intended to prevent or minimize.

(2) Any costs incurred by the public guardian pursuant to paragraph (1) shall be compensable as provided in Section 2902. Fees collected by the public guardian pursuant to this chapter shall be used for the activities described in this chapter.

(b) When a public guardian has taken possession or control of the property of an elder person pursuant to this chapter, the public guardian shall exercise reasonable care to ensure that the reasonable living expenses and legitimate debts of the elder person are addressed as well as is practical under the circumstances.

(c) Any person identified as a victim in a declaration described in Section 2954 may bring an ex parte petition in the superior court for an order quashing the certification issued by the public guardian as provided in subdivision (c) of Section 2952.

(1) Upon request by the petitioner, the court may defer filing fees related to the petition, and order the public guardian to authorize the release of funds from a financial institution to reimburse the petitioner the filing fees from assets belonging to the petitioner, but shall waive filing fees if the petitioner meets the standards of eligibility established by subparagraph (A) or (B) of paragraph (6) of subdivision (a) of Section 68511.3 of the Government Code for the waiver of a filing fee.

(2) The court shall quash the certification if the court determines that there is insufficient evidence to justify the imposition on the alleged victim's civil liberties caused by the certification.

(3) If the court determines that there is sufficient evidence to justify the imposition on the alleged victim's civil liberties caused by the certification, the court may, in its discretion, do one or more of the following:

(A) Order disbursements from the alleged victim's assets, as are reasonably needed to address the alleged victim's needs.

(B) Appoint a temporary conservator of the alleged victim's estate, where the facts before the court would be sufficient for the appointment of a temporary conservator under Section 2250.

(C) Deny the petition.

(D) Award reasonable attorney's fees to the respondent's attorney from the victim's estate. *(Added by Stats.2000, c. 813 (S.B.1742), § 1. Amended by Stats.2001, c. 232 (A.B. 1517), § 4.)*

§ 2954. Form of declaration

A declaration issued by a peace officer under this chapter shall not be valid unless it substantially complies with the following form:

DECLARATION

PRINT OR TYPE

1. My name is: ______________________.
   My badge number is: ________________.
   My office address and telephone number are:

____
____
____

2. I am a duly sworn peace officer presently employed by ____ _______________________________, in the County of _______________________________, in the State of California.

4. There is probable cause to believe that:

(a) _______________________________ (Victim) is substantially unable to manage his or her financial resources or to resist fraud or undue influence, and

(b) There exists a significant danger the victim will lose all or a portion of his or her property as a result of fraud or misrepresentations or the mental incapacity of the victim, and

(c) There is probable cause to believe that a crime is being committed against the victim, and

(d) The crime is connected to the victim's inability to manage his or her financial resources or to resist fraud or undue influence, and

(e) The victim suffers from that inability as a result of deficits in one or more of the following mental functions:

INSTRUCTIONS TO PEACE OFFICER: CHECK ALL BOXES THAT APPLY:

[A] ALERTNESS AND ATTENTION

☐ 1. Levels of arousal. (Lethargic, responds only to vigorous and persistent stimulation, stupor.)

☐ 2. Orientation. Person ________ Time ________ (day, date, month, season, year), Place ________ (address, town, state), Situation ________ (why am I here?).

☐ 3. Ability to attend and concentrate. (Give detailed answers from memory, mental ability required to thread a needle.)

[B] INFORMATION PROCESSING

Ability to:

☐ 1. Remember, i.e., short- and long-term memory, immediate recall. (Deficits reflected by: forgets question before answering, cannot recall names, relatives, past presidents, events of past 24 hours.)

☐ 2. Understand and communicate either verbally or otherwise. (Deficits reflected by: inability to comprehend questions, follow instructions, use words correctly or name objects; nonsense words.)

☐ 3. Recognize familiar objects and persons. (Deficits reflected by: inability to recognize familiar faces, objects, etc.)

☐ 4. Understand and appreciate quantities. (Perform simple calculations.)

☐ 5. Reason using abstract concepts. (Grasp abstract aspects of his or her situation; interpret idiomatic expressions or proverbs.)

☐ 6. Plan, organize, and carry out actions (assuming physical ability) in one's own rational self-interest. (Break complex tasks down into simple steps and carry them out.)

☐ 7. Reason logically.

[C] THOUGHT DISORDERS

☐ 1. Severely disorganized thinking. (Rambling, nonsensical, incoherent, or nonlinear thinking.)

☐ 2. Hallucinations. (Auditory, visual, olfactory.)

☐ 3. Delusions. (Demonstrably false belief maintained without or against reason or evidence.)

☐ 4. Uncontrollable or intrusive thoughts. (Unwanted compulsive thoughts, compulsive behavior.)

[D] ABILITY TO MODULATE MOOD AND AFFECT

Pervasive and persistent or recurrent emotional state which appears severely inappropriate in degree to the patient's circumstances. Encircle the inappropriate mood(s):

Anger	Euphoria	Helplessness
Anxiety	Depression	Apathy
Fear	Hopelessness	Indifference
Panic	Despair	

5. The property at risk is identified as, but not limited to, the following:

Bank account located at: _______________________________
(name, telephone number, and address of the bank branch)

Account number(s): _______________________________

Securities/other funds located at: _______________________________
(name, telephone number, and address of financial institution)

Account number(s): _______________________________

Real property located at: _______________________________
(address)

Automobile described as: _______________________________
(make, model/color)
____
(license plate number and state)

Other property described as: _______________________________

Other property located at: _______________________________

6. A criminal investigation will ☐ will not ☐ be commenced against: _______________________________
(name, address, and telephone number)
for alleged financial abuse.

BLOCKS 1, 2, AND 3 MUST BE CHECKED IN ORDER FOR THIS DECLARATION TO BE VALID:

☐ 1. I am a peace officer in the county identified above.

☐ 2. I have consulted concerning this case with a supervisor in the county's adult protective services agency who has signed below, indicating that he or she concurs that, based on the information I provided to him or her, or based on information he or she obtained independently, this declaration is warranted under the circumstances.

☐ 3. I have consulted concerning this case with an individual qualified to perform a mental status examination.

____
Signature of Declarant Peace Officer

____
Date

____
Signature of Concurring Adult Protective Services Supervisor

(Added by Stats.2000, c. 813 (S.B.1742), § 1.)

Research References

Treatises and Practice Aids

Witkin, California Summary 10th Wills and Probate § 973, Temporary Possession or Control Of Property.

§ 2955. Powers of public guardian to undertake other proceedings

Nothing in this chapter shall prohibit or restrict a public guardian from undertaking any other proceeding authorized by law. *(Added by Stats.2000, c. 813 (S.B.1742), § 1.)*

Part 8

OTHER PROTECTIVE PROCEEDINGS

Law Revision Commission Comments

1990 Enactment

This part supersedes Part 8 (commencing with Section 3300) of Division 4 of the repealed Probate Code. The superseded part was enacted upon recommendation of the California Law Revision Commission. See Recommendation Relating to Guardianship–Conservatorship Law, 14 Cal.L.Revision Comm'n Reports 501 (1978). For the Guardianship–Conservatorship Law as enacted in 1979 with the revisions made by Chapters 89 and 246 of the Statutes of 1980, see Guardianship–Conservatorship Law, 15 Cal.L.Revision Comm'n Reports 451 (1980). [20 Cal.L.Rev.Comm.Reports 1001 (1990)].

CHAPTER 1. GENERAL PROVISIONS

§ 3300. Accounting by parent to minor for money received

A parent who receives any money or property belonging to a minor under any provision of this part shall account to the minor for the money or other property when the minor reaches the age of majority. *(Stats.1990, c. 79 (A.B.759), § 14, operative July 1, 1991.)*

Law Revision Commission Comments

1990 Enactment

Section 3300 continues Section 3300 of the repealed Probate Code without change. For background on the provisions of this part, see the Comment to this part under the part heading. [20 Cal.L.Rev.Comm.Reports 1001 (1990)].

Research References

Forms

California Transactions Forms--Estate Planning § 1:29, Options Involving Gifts to Minors.

Treatises and Practice Aids

Witkin, California Summary 10th Insurance § 214, Award and Review.

Witkin, California Summary 10th Parent and Child § 297, Protection Of Minor.

Witkin, California Summary 10th Wills and Probate § 1066, in General.

§ 3303. Effect on Uniform Transfers to Minors Act

Nothing in this part limits the provisions of the California Uniform Transfers to Minors Act, Part 9 (commencing with Section 3900). *(Stats.1990, c. 79 (A.B.759), § 14, operative July 1, 1991.)*

Law Revision Commission Comments

1990 Enactment

Section 3303 continues Section 3303 of the repealed Probate Code without change. Although this part does not limit the California Uniform Transfers to Minors Act, some provisions of this part supplement that act. See Sections 3412(b), 3413(b), 3602(c)(2), 3611(e). For background on this section, see Recommendation Relating to Uniform Transfers to Minors Act, 17 Cal.L.Revision Comm'n Reports 601 (1984). For background on the provisions of this part, see the Comment to this part under the part heading. [20 Cal.L.Rev.Comm.Reports 1001 (1990)].

CHAPTER 2. MONEY OR PROPERTY BELONGING TO MINOR

ARTICLE 1. TOTAL ESTATE NOT IN EXCESS OF $5,000

§ 3400. Total estate of minor; deductions

(a) As used in this article, "total estate of the minor" includes both the money and other property belonging to the minor and the money and other property belonging to the guardianship estate, if any, of the minor.

(b) In computing the "total estate of the minor" for the purposes of this article, all of the following shall be deducted:

(1) "Custodial property" held pursuant to the California Uniform Transfers to Minors Act, Part 9 (commencing with Section 3900).

(2) Any money or property subject to court order pursuant to subdivision (c) of Section 3602 or Article 2 (commencing with Section 3610) of Chapter 4. *(Stats.1990, c. 79 (A.B.759), § 14, operative July 1, 1991.)*

Law Revision Commission Comments

1990 Enactment

Section 3400 continues Section 3400 of the repealed Probate Code without change. For background on the provisions of this part, see the Comment to this part under the part heading. [20 Cal.L.Rev.Comm.Reports 1001 (1990)].

Research References

Forms

California Transactions Forms--Estate Planning § 6:15, Minors' Capacity to Take Devised Property.

California Transactions Forms--Estate Planning § 6:53, Matters to Consider in Drafting Gifts to Minors.

California Transactions Forms--Estate Planning § 6:79, Distribution Of Minor's Bequest to Parents.

California Transactions Forms--Estate Planning § 10:34, Multiple Party Accounts.
West's California Code Forms, Probate § 3410 COMMENT, Court Ordered Transfer Of Money Belonging to a Minor.

Treatises and Practice Aids

Witkin, California Summary 10th Parent and Child § 297, Protection Of Minor.
Witkin, California Summary 10th Wills and Probate § 1066, in General.
Witkin, California Summary 10th Wills and Probate § 1067, Small Estate.
Witkin, California Summary 10th Wills and Probate § 1068, Money Belonging to Minor.
Witkin, California Summary 10th Wills and Probate § 1071, Disposition Of Proceeds.

§ 3401. Delivery of money or property to parent

(a) Where a minor does not have a guardian of the estate, money or other property belonging to the minor may be paid or delivered to a parent of the minor entitled to the custody of the minor to be held in trust for the minor until the minor reaches majority if the requirements of subdivision (c) are satisfied.

(b) Where the minor has a guardian of the estate, all the money and other property belonging to the guardianship estate may be paid or delivered to a parent entitled to the custody of the minor to be held in trust for the minor until the minor reaches majority if the requirements of subdivision (c) are satisfied.

(c) This section applies only if both of the following requirements are satisfied:

(1) The total estate of the minor, including the money and other property to be paid or delivered to the parent, does not exceed five thousand dollars ($5,000) in value.

(2) The parent to whom the money or other property is to be paid or delivered gives the person making the payment or delivery written assurance, verified by the oath of such parent, that the total estate of the minor, including the money or other property to be paid or delivered to the parent, does not exceed five thousand dollars ($5,000) in value. *(Stats. 1990, c. 79 (A.B.759), § 14, operative July 1, 1991.)*

Law Revision Commission Comments

1990 Enactment

Section 3401 continues Section 3401 of the repealed Probate Code without change. For background on the provisions of this part, see the Comment to this part under the part heading.

Subdivision (a) applies only where the minor has no guardian of the estate. If the minor has a guardian of the estate, the money is paid to the guardian, not to a parent. However, subdivision (b) permits the entire guardianship estate to be paid over to a parent without the need for a court order when the requirements of subdivision (c) are satisfied. Such payment does not avoid the need for termination of the guardianship by the court. See Section 2626. [20 Cal.L.Rev.Comm.Reports 1001 (1990)].

Research References

Forms

California Transactions Forms--Estate Planning § 6:15, Minors' Capacity to Take Devised Property.
California Transactions Forms--Estate Planning § 6:53, Matters to Consider in Drafting Gifts to Minors.
California Transactions Forms--Estate Planning § 6:79, Distribution Of Minor's Bequest to Parents.
California Transactions Forms--Estate Planning § 20:10, Devises to Minors.
West's California Code Forms, Probate § 3401 Form 1, Declaration by Parent Under Probate Code S3401.
West's California Code Forms, Probate § 6240 Form 1, California Statutory Will.

Treatises and Practice Aids

Witkin, California Summary 10th Wills and Probate § 1067, Small Estate.

§ 3402. Written receipt of parent; effect

The written receipt of the parent giving the written assurance under Section 3401 shall be an acquittance of the person making the payment of money or delivery of other property pursuant to this article. *(Stats.1990, c. 79 (A.B.759), § 14, operative July 1, 1991.)*

Law Revision Commission Comments

1990 Enactment

Section 3402 continues Section 3402 of the repealed Probate Code without change. For background on the provisions of this part, see the Comment to this part under the part heading. [20 Cal.L.Rev.Comm.Reports 1001 (1990)].

Research References

Forms

West's California Code Forms, Probate § 3401 Form 1, Declaration by Parent Under Probate Code S3401.

Treatises and Practice Aids

Witkin, California Summary 10th Wills and Probate § 1067, Small Estate.

ARTICLE 2. PROPERTY IN THE FORM OF MONEY

§ 3410. Application of article; computation of money belonging to minor

(a) This article applies to both of the following cases:

(1) Where the minor has a guardian of the estate and the sole asset of the guardianship estate is money.

(2) Where the minor has no guardian of the estate and there is money belonging to the minor.

(b) This article does not apply to, and there shall be excluded in computing "money belonging to the minor" for the purpose of this article, all of the following:

(1) Money or property which is or will be held as "custodial property" pursuant to the California Uniform Transfers to Minors Act, Part 9 (commencing with Section 3900).

(2) Any money or property subject to court order pursuant to subdivision (c) of Section 3602 or Article 2 (commencing with Section 3610) of Chapter 4. *(Stats.1990, c. 79 (A.B.759), § 14, operative July 1, 1991.)*

Law Revision Commission Comments

1990 Enactment

Section 3410 continues Section 3410 of the repealed Probate Code without change. For background on the provisions of this part, see the Comment to this part under the part heading. [20 Cal.L.Rev.Comm.Reports 1001 (1990)].

Research References

Forms

West's California Code Forms, Probate § 3401 Form 1, Declaration by Parent Under Probate Code S3401.

West's California Code Forms, Probate § 3410 COMMENT, Court Ordered Transfer Of Money Belonging to a Minor.

Treatises and Practice Aids

Witkin, California Summary 10th Parent and Child § 297, Protection Of Minor.

Witkin, California Summary 10th Wills and Probate § 1066, in General.

Witkin, California Summary 10th Wills and Probate § 1068, Money Belonging to Minor.

§ 3411. Filing of petition; venue

(a) A parent of a minor entitled to custody of the minor, the guardian of the estate of the minor, or the person holding the money belonging to the minor may file a petition requesting that the court make an order under this article.

(b) The petition shall be filed in the superior court of:

(1) The county where the minor resides if the minor has no guardian of the estate.

(2) The county having jurisdiction of the guardianship estate if the minor has a guardian of the estate. *(Stats.1990, c. 79 (A.B.759), § 14, operative July 1, 1991.)*

Law Revision Commission Comments

1990 Enactment

Section 3411 continues Section 3411 of the repealed Probate Code without change. For general provisions, see 1020–1023 (petitions and other papers). For background on the provisions of this part, see the Comment to this part under the part heading. [20 Cal.L.Rev.Comm.Reports 1001 (1990)].

Research References

Treatises and Practice Aids

Witkin, California Summary 10th Wills and Probate § 1068, Money Belonging to Minor.

§ 3412. Court-ordered termination of guardianship where sole asset of guardianship estate is money; additional orders within court's discretion

If the minor has a guardian of the estate and the sole asset of the guardianship estate is money, the court may order that the guardianship of the estate be terminated and, if the court so orders, the court in its discretion shall also order any one or more of the following:

(a) That the money be deposited in an insured account in a financial institution in this state, or in a single-premium deferred annuity, subject to withdrawal only upon authorization of the court.

(b) That all or any part of the money be transferred to a custodian for the benefit of the minor under the California Uniform Transfers to Minors Act, Part 9 (commencing with Section 3900).

(c) If the money of the guardianship estate does not exceed twenty thousand dollars ($20,000), that the money be held on any other condition that the court in its discretion determines to be in the best interests of the minor.

(d) If the money of the guardianship estate does not exceed five thousand dollars ($5,000), that all or any part of the money be paid to a parent of the minor, without bond, upon the terms and under the conditions specified in Article 1 (commencing with Section 3400).

(e) That the remaining balance of any money paid or to be paid be deposited with the county treasurer, if all of the following conditions are met:

(1) The county treasurer has been authorized by the county board of supervisors to handle the deposits.

(2) The county treasurer shall receive and safely keep all money deposited with the county treasurer pursuant to this subdivision, shall pay the money out only upon the order of the court, and shall credit each estate with the interest earned by the funds deposited less the county treasurer's actual cost authorized to be recovered under Section 27013 of the Government Code.

(3) The county treasurer and sureties on the official bond of the county treasurer are responsible for the safekeeping and payment of the money.

(4) The county treasurer shall ensure that the money deposited is to earn interest or dividends, or both, at the highest rate which the county can reasonably obtain as a prudent investor.

(5) Funds so deposited with the county treasurer shall only be invested or deposited in compliance with the provisions governing the investment or deposit of state funds set forth in Chapter 5 (commencing with Section 16640) of Part 2 of Division 4 of Title 2 of the Government Code, the investment or deposit of county funds set forth in Chapter 4 (commencing with Section 53600) of Part 1 of Division 2 of Title 5 of the Government Code, or as authorized under Chapter 6 (commencing with Section 2400) of Part 4. *(Stats.1990, c. 79 (A.B.759), § 14, operative July 1, 1991. Amended by Stats. 1991, c. 413 (A.B.934), § 1; Stats.2004, c. 67 (A.B.1851), § 1.)*

Law Revision Commission Comments

1990 Enactment

Section 3412 continues Section 3412 of the repealed Probate Code with the substitution of language that requires money to be deposited in an insured account in a financial institution in this state for the former language listing various financial institution accounts. This section applies only where the minor has a guardian of the estate. Where the minor has no guardian of the estate, Section 3413 applies. Section 3412 is comparable to Section 3611 (money received pursuant to compromise or judgment). For general provisions relating to hearings and orders, see Sections 1040–1050. For background on the provisions of this part, see the Comment to this part under the part heading.

Where the money of the guardianship estate does not exceed $5,000, the court, in its discretion, may make an order under subdivision (a), (b), (c), or (d). Where the money exceeds $5,000 but does not exceed $20,000, the court has discretion to make an order under subdivision (a), (b), or (c). Where the money exceeds $20,000, the court may make an order only under subdivision (a) or (b).

Where the total estate of the minor (as defined in Section 3400) does not exceed $5,000, money of the guardianship estate may be paid directly to a parent under Section 3401 without obtaining a court order under this article, or a petition may be filed under this article to obtain a court order under Section 3412. This article provides a guardian who is reluctant to turn over the money to a parent to hold in trust for the minor with the alternative of requesting that the court order the amount be deposited or invested under subdivision (a) of Section 3412. [20 Cal.L.Rev.Comm.Reports 1001 (1990)].

Research References

Forms

West's California Code Forms, Probate § 3410 COMMENT, Court Ordered Transfer Of Money Belonging to a Minor.

Treatises and Practice Aids

Witkin, California Summary 10th Wills and Probate § 1068, Money Belonging to Minor.

§ 3413. Order of court if no guardianship exists

If the minor has no guardian of the estate and there is money belonging to the minor, the court may order that a guardian of the estate be appointed and that the money be paid to the guardian or the court may order any one or more of the following:

(a) That the money be deposited in an insured account in a financial institution in this state, or in a single-premium deferred annuity, subject to withdrawal only upon authorization of the court.

(b) That all or any part of the money be transferred to a custodian for the benefit of the minor under the California Uniform Transfers to Minors Act, Part 9 (commencing with Section 3900).

(c) If the money belonging to the minor does not exceed twenty thousand dollars ($20,000), that the money be held on any other condition that the court in its discretion determines to be in the best interests of the minor.

(d) If the money belonging to the minor does not exceed five thousand dollars ($5,000), that all or any part of the money be paid to a parent of the minor, without bond, upon the terms and under the conditions specified in Article 1 (commencing with Section 3400).

(e) That the remaining balance of any money paid or to be paid be deposited with the county treasurer, if all of the following conditions are met:

(1) The county treasurer has been authorized by the county board of supervisors to handle the deposits.

(2) The county treasurer shall receive and safely keep all money deposited with the county treasurer pursuant to this subdivision, shall pay the money out only upon the order of the court, and shall credit each estate with the interest earned by the funds deposited less the county treasurer's actual cost authorized to be recovered under Section 27013 of the Government Code.

(3) The county treasurer and sureties on the official bond of the county treasurer are responsible for the safekeeping and payment of the money.

(4) The county treasurer shall ensure that the money deposited is to earn interest or dividends, or both, at the highest rate which the county can reasonably obtain as a prudent investor.

(5) Funds so deposited with the county treasurer shall only be invested or deposited in compliance with the provisions governing the investment or deposit of state funds set forth in Chapter 5 (commencing with Section 16640) of Part 2 of Division 4 of Title 2 of the Government Code, the investment or deposit of county funds set forth in Chapter 4 (commencing with Section 53600) of Part 1 of Division 2 of Title 5 of the Government Code, or as authorized under Chapter 6 (commencing with Section 2400) of Part 4. *(Stats.1990, c. 79 (A.B.759), § 14, operative July 1, 1991. Amended by Stats. 1991, c. 413 (A.B.934), § 2; Stats.2004, c. 67 (A.B.1851), § 2.)*

Law Revision Commission Comments

1990 Enactment

Section 3413 continues Section 3413 of the repealed Probate Code with the substitution of language that requires money to be deposited in an insured account in a financial institution in this state for the former language listing various financial institution accounts. This section applies only where the minor does not have a guardian of the estate. Where the minor has a guardian of the estate, Section 3412 applies. Section 3413 is similar to Section 3412. See the Comment to Section 3412. For background on the provisions of this part, see the Comment to this part under the part heading. [20 Cal.L.Rev.Comm.Reports 1001 (1990)].

Research References

Forms

California Transactions Forms--Estate Planning § 6:15, Minors' Capacity to Take Devised Property.

West's California Code Forms, Probate § 3401 Form 1, Declaration by Parent Under Probate Code S3401.

West's California Code Forms, Probate § 3410 COMMENT, Court Ordered Transfer Of Money Belonging to a Minor.

Treatises and Practice Aids

Witkin, California Summary 10th Wills and Probate § 1068, Money Belonging to Minor.

CHAPTER 3. COMPROMISE BY PARENT OF MINOR'S DISPUTED CLAIM

§ 3500. Parental right to compromise minor's claim

(a) When a minor has a disputed claim for damages, money, or other property and does not have a guardian of the estate, the following persons have the right to compromise, or to execute a covenant not to sue on or a covenant not to enforce judgment on, the claim, unless the claim is against such person or persons:

(1) Either parent if the parents of the minor are not living separate and apart.

(2) The parent having the care, custody, or control of the minor if the parents of the minor are living separate and apart.

(b) The compromise or covenant is valid only after it has been approved, upon the filing of a petition, by the superior court of either of the following counties:

(1) The county where the minor resides when the petition is filed.

(2) Any county where suit on the claim or matter properly could be brought.

(c) Any money or other property to be paid or delivered for the benefit of the minor pursuant to the compromise or covenant shall be paid and delivered in the manner and upon the terms and conditions specified in Chapter 4 (commencing with Section 3600).

(d) A parent having the right to compromise the disputed claim of the minor under this section may execute a full release and satisfaction, or execute a covenant not to sue on or a covenant not to enforce judgment on the disputed claim, after the money or other property to be paid or delivered has been paid or delivered as provided in subdivision (c). If the court orders that all or any part of the money to be paid under the compromise or covenant be deposited in an insured account in a financial institution in this state, or in a single-premium deferred annuity, the release and satisfaction or covenant is not effective for any purpose until the money has been deposited as directed in the order of the court. *(Stats.1990, c. 79 (A.B.759), § 14, operative July 1, 1991.)*

Law Revision Commission Comments

1990 Enactment

Section 3500 continues Section 3500 of the repealed Probate Code with the substitution of language that requires money to be deposited in an insured account in a financial institution in this state for the former language listing various financial institution accounts. The provision of Section 3500 which permits approval by the superior court in any county in which suit could be brought on the claim or matter is consistent with Section 2505 (compromise by guardian or conservator). For background on the provisions of this part, see the Comment to this part under the part heading.

Where the minor has a guardian of the estate, the guardian (rather than the parent) has authority to compromise the claim. See Sections 2500–2507. If the claim is the subject of pending litigation, the minor must appear in the action either by a guardian of the estate or by a guardian ad litem, and in such case Section 372 of the Code of Civil Procedure provides for compromise of the claim. [20 Cal.L.Rev.Comm.Reports 1001 (1990)].

Research References

Forms

Cal. Transaction Forms - Bus. Transactions § 18:6, Capacity.
Cal. Transaction Forms - Bus. Transactions § 18:16, Settlements that Require Court Approval.
West's California Code Forms, Probate § 3500 Form 1, Petition by Parent to Compromise Disputed Personal Injury Claim Of Minor Without a Guardian Of the Estate--Judicial Council Form MC-350.
West's California Code Forms, Probate § 3600 COMMENT, Disposition Of Compromise or Judgment Amount on Behalf Of an Incompetent Person Without a Conservator Of the Estate.
West's California Code Forms, Probate § 2500-2507 Form 1, Petition by Guardian or Conservator to Approve Compromise Of Disputed Personal Injury Claim Of Minor or Incompetent Person--Judicial Council Form MC-350.
West's California Judicial Council Forms MC-350, Petition to Approve Compromise Of Disputed Claim or Pending Action or Disposition Of Proceeds Of Judgment for Minor or Person With a Disability.
West's California Judicial Council Forms MC-351, Order Approving Compromise Of Disputed Claim or Pending Action or Disposition Of Proceeds Of Judgment for Minor or Adult Person With a Disability.
West's California Judicial Council Forms MC-350EX, Expedited Petition to Approve Compromise Of Disputed Claim or Pending Action or Disposition Of Proceeds Of Judgment for Minor or Person With a Disability.
West's California Judicial Council Forms MC-350(A-13B(5)), Medical Service Provider Attachment to Petition to Approve Compromise Of Claim or Action or Disposition Of Proceeds Of Judgment.

Treatises and Practice Aids

Witkin, California Summary 10th Contracts § 49, Parent's Agreement to Arbitrate.
Witkin, California Summary 10th Parent and Child § 297, Protection Of Minor.
Witkin, California Summary 10th Wills and Probate § 1014, Procedure for Court Approval.
Witkin, California Summary 10th Wills and Probate § 1066, in General.
Witkin, California Summary 10th Wills and Probate § 1069, Parent's Compromise Of Minor's Claim.

CHAPTER 4. MONEY OR PROPERTY PAID OR DELIVERED PURSUANT TO COMPROMISE OR JUDGMENT FOR MINOR OR DISABLED PERSON

Application

For application of this chapter, see Probate Code § 3600.

ARTICLE 1. GENERAL PROVISIONS

Application

For application of this chapter, see Probate Code § 3600.

§ 3600. Application of chapter

This chapter applies whenever both of the following conditions exist:

(a) A court (1) approves a compromise of, or the execution of a covenant not to sue on or a covenant not to enforce judgment on, a minor's disputed claim, (2) approves a compromise of a pending action or proceeding to which a minor or person with a disability is a party, or (3) gives judgment for a minor or person with a disability.

(b) The compromise, covenant, or judgment provides for the payment or delivery of money or other property for the benefit of the minor or person with a disability. *(Stats.1990, c. 79 (A.B.759), § 14, operative July 1, 1991. Amended by Stats.2004, c. 67 (A.B.1851), § 3.)*

Law Revision Commission Comments

1990 Enactment

Section 3600 continues Section 3600 of the repealed Probate Code without change. The reference in this section to "incompetent person" includes "a person for whom a conservator may be appointed." See Section 3603. For background on the provisions of this part, see the Comment to this part under the part heading. [20 Cal.L.Rev.Comm.Reports 1001 (1990)].

Research References

Forms

Cal. Transaction Forms - Bus. Transactions § 18:31, Delivery and Disposition Of Settlement Proceeds.

California Transactions Forms--Estate Planning § 17:2, Types Of Special Needs Trusts.

California Transactions Forms--Estate Planning § 17:13, Overview [Prob. Code §§ 3600 to 3613].

California Transactions Forms--Estate Planning § 17:14, Person With a Disability.

California Transactions Forms--Estate Planning § 17:15, Required Findings [Prob C § 3604(B)].

California Transactions Forms--Estate Planning § 17:32, Medi-Cal Reimbursement Claims.

California Transactions Forms--Estate Planning § 17:34, Notice.

California Transactions Forms--Estate Planning § 17:41, Types Of Special Needs Trusts Requiring Payback Provisions (Self-Settled Trusts Established on or After October 1, 1993).

West's California Code Forms, Probate § 3401 Form 1, Declaration by Parent Under Probate Code S3401.

West's California Code Forms, Probate § 3500 Form 1, Petition by Parent to Compromise Disputed Personal Injury Claim Of Minor Without a Guardian Of the Estate--Judicial Council Form MC-350.

West's California Code Forms, Probate § 3500 Form 2, Order Authorizing Parent to Compromise Claim Of Minor Without Guardian--Judicial Council Form MC-351.

West's California Code Forms, Probate § 3410 COMMENT, Court Ordered Transfer Of Money Belonging to a Minor.

West's California Code Forms, Probate § 3600 COMMENT, Disposition Of Compromise or Judgment Amount on Behalf Of an Incompetent Person Without a Conservator Of the Estate.

West's California Judicial Council Forms MC-355, Order to Deposit Money Into Blocked Account.

West's California Judicial Council Forms MC-356, Receipt and Acknowledgment Of Order for the Deposit Of Money Into Blocked Account.

Treatises and Practice Aids

Witkin, California Summary 10th Parent and Child § 297, Protection Of Minor.

Witkin, California Summary 10th Wills and Probate § 1004, Deposit Of Money or Property.

Witkin, California Summary 10th Wills and Probate § 1014, Procedure for Court Approval.

Witkin, California Summary 10th Wills and Probate § 1025, Nature Of Doctrine.

Witkin, California Summary 10th Wills and Probate § 1026, Petition, Notice, and Hearing.

Witkin, California Summary 10th Wills and Probate § 1066, in General.

Witkin, California Summary 10th Wills and Probate § 1069, Parent's Compromise Of Minor's Claim.

Witkin, California Summary 10th Wills and Probate § 1070, in General.

Witkin, California Summary 10th Wills and Probate § 380C, (New) Trusts.

Witkin, California Summary 10th Wills and Probate § 380E, (New) Specified Proceedings.

§ 3601. Order directing payment of expenses, costs and fees

(a) The court making the order or giving the judgment referred to in Section 3600, as a part thereof, shall make a further order authorizing and directing that reasonable expenses, medical or otherwise and including reimbursement to a parent, guardian, or conservator, costs, and attorney's fees, as the court shall approve and allow therein, shall be paid from the money or other property to be paid or delivered for the benefit of the minor or person with a disability.

(b) The order required by subdivision (a) may be directed to the following:

(1) A parent of the minor, the guardian ad litem, or the guardian of the estate of the minor or the conservator of the estate of the person with a disability.

(2) The payer of any money to be paid pursuant to the compromise, covenant, or judgment for the benefit of the minor or person with a disability. *(Stats.1990, c. 79 (A.B. 759), § 14, operative July 1, 1991. Amended by Stats.2004, c. 67 (A.B.1851), § 4.)*

Application

For application of this chapter, see Probate Code § 3600.

Law Revision Commission Comments

1990 Enactment

Section 3601 continues Section 3601 of the repealed Probate Code without change. The reference in this section to "incompetent person" includes "a person for whom a conservator may be appointed." See Section 3603. For background on the provisions of this part, see the Comment to this part under the part heading.

Under subdivision (b)(2), the court may order the payer of the money to pay the expenses, costs, and fees approved and allowed by the court directly to the persons entitled thereto. For example, under subdivision (b), the court may either:

(1) Order pursuant to paragraph (1) that the money be paid to the guardian or conservator of the estate who is further ordered to pay the expenses, costs, and fees approved and allowed by the court to the persons entitled thereto; or

(2) Order pursuant to paragraph (2) that the payer of the money pay such expenses, costs, and fees directly to the persons entitled thereto and the remaining balance to the guardian or conservator of the estate or as otherwise provided in Article 2 (commencing with Section 3610). [20 Cal.L.Rev.Comm.Reports 1001 (1990)].

Research References

Forms

Cal. Transaction Forms - Bus. Transactions § 18:18, Approval and Limitation Of Attorney's Fees.

Cal. Transaction Forms - Bus. Transactions § 18:31, Delivery and Disposition Of Settlement Proceeds.

West's California Code Forms, Probate § 3500 Form 1, Petition by Parent to Compromise Disputed Personal Injury Claim Of Minor Without a Guardian Of the Estate--Judicial Council Form MC-350.

Treatises and Practice Aids

Witkin, California Summary 10th Wills and Probate § 1070, in General.

§ 3602. Disposition of remaining balance

(a) If there is no guardianship of the estate of the minor or conservatorship of the estate of the person with a disability, the remaining balance of the money and other property, after payment of all expenses, costs, and fees as approved and allowed by the court under Section 3601, shall be paid, delivered, deposited, or invested as provided in Article 2 (commencing with Section 3610).

(b) Except as provided in subdivisions (c) and (d), if there is a guardianship of the estate of the minor or conservatorship of the estate of the person with a disability, the remaining balance of the money and other property, after payment of all expenses, costs, and fees as approved and allowed by the court under Section 3601, shall be paid or delivered to the guardian or conservator of the estate. Upon application of the guardian or conservator, the court making the order or giving the judgment referred to in Section 3600 or the court in which the guardianship or conservatorship proceeding is pending may, with or without notice, make an order that all or part of the money paid or to be paid to the guardian or conservator under this subdivision be deposited or invested as provided in Section 2456.

(c) Upon ex parte petition of the guardian or conservator or upon petition of any person interested in the guardianship or conservatorship estate, the court making the order or giving the judgment referred to in Section 3600 may for good cause shown order one or more of the following:

(1) That all or part of the remaining balance of money not become a part of the guardianship or conservatorship estate and instead be deposited in an insured account in a financial institution in this state, or in a single-premium deferred annuity, subject to withdrawal only upon authorization of the court.

(2) If there is a guardianship of the estate of the minor, that all or part of the remaining balance of money and other property not become a part of the guardianship estate and instead be transferred to a custodian for the benefit of the minor under the California Uniform Transfers to Minors Act, Part 9 (commencing with Section 3900).

(3) That all or part of the remaining balance of money and other property not become a part of the guardianship estate and, instead, be transferred to the trustee of a trust which is either created by, or approved of, in the order or judgment described in Section 3600. This trust shall be revocable by the minor upon attaining 18 years of age, and shall contain other terms and conditions, including, but not limited to, terms and conditions concerning trustee's accounts and trustee's bond, as the court determines to be necessary to protect the minor's interests.

(d) Upon petition of the guardian, conservator, or any person interested in the guardianship or conservatorship estate, the court making the order or giving the judgment referred to in Section 3600 may order that all or part of the remaining balance of money not become a part of the guardianship or conservatorship estate and instead be paid to a special needs trust established under Section 3604 for the benefit of the minor or person with a disability.

(e) If the petition is by a person other than the guardian or conservator, notice of hearing on a petition under subdivision (c) shall be given for the period and in the manner provided in Chapter 3 (commencing with Section 1460) of Part 1.

(f) Notice of the time and place of hearing on a petition under subdivision (d), and a copy of the petition, shall be * * * delivered pursuant to Section 1215 to the State Director of Health Care Services, the Director of State Hospitals, and the Director of Developmental Services at the office of each director in Sacramento at least 15 days before the hearing. *(Stats.1990, c. 79 (A.B.759), § 14, operative July 1, 1991. Amended by Stats.1992, c. 355 (A.B.3328), § 2; Stats.1996, c. 563 (S.B.392), § 18; Stats.2004, c. 67 (A.B. 1851), § 5; Stats.2012, c. 440 (A.B.1488), § 54, eff. Sept. 22, 2012; Stats.2017, c. 319 (A.B.976), § 59, eff. Jan. 1, 2018.)*

Application

For application of this chapter, see Probate Code § 3600.

Law Revision Commission Comments

1990 Enactment

Section 3602 continues Section 3602 of the repealed Probate Code with the substitution of language that requires money to be deposited in an insured account in a financial institution in this state for the former language listing various financial institution accounts. The reference in this section to "incompetent person" includes "a person for whom a conservator may be appointed." See Section 3603. For general provisions relating to notice of hearing, see Sections 1200–1221. See also Sections 1260–1265 (proof of giving notice). For background on the provisions of this part, see the Comment to this part under the part heading.

Paragraph (2) of subdivision (c) gives the court the alternative of ordering that all or any part of the money and other property be transferred to a custodian to be subject to the California Uniform Transfers to Minors Act. This alternative gives the custodian more flexibility in handling money (by avoiding the need for court authorization for any withdrawal) and permits a custodian to handle other property (rather than requiring it in every case to become a part of the guardianship estate).

Nothing in the California Uniform Transfers to Minors Act gives a custodian under that act any authority to settle or release a claim of the minor against a third party. Only a guardian of the estate (Prob.Code §§ 2500–2507) or guardian ad litem or other person authorized under another law (see, e.g., Code Civ.Proc. § 372; Prob.Code § 3500) to act for the minor may settle or release such a claim. See Uniform Transfers to Minors Act § 8 comment (1986). [20 Cal.L.Rev.Comm.Reports 1001 (1990)].

1992 Amendment

Section 3602 is amended to add authority for the court to order that money of a minor or incompetent person be paid to a special needs trust established under Section 3604. As provided in Section 3604(d), before payment to the trustee, liens authorized by the Welfare and Institutions Code must first be satisfied. See, e.g., Welf. & Inst.Code §§ 7282.1, 14124.71–14124.76, 17109, 17403. [22 Cal.L.Rev.Comm.Reports 989 (1992)].

Research References

Forms

Cal. Transaction Forms - Bus. Transactions § 18:31, Delivery and Disposition Of Settlement Proceeds.

California Transactions Forms--Estate Planning § 17:16, Court's Continuing Jurisdiction.

West's California Code Forms, Probate § 3600 COMMENT, Disposition Of Compromise or Judgment Amount on Behalf Of an Incompetent Person Without a Conservator Of the Estate.

Treatises and Practice Aids

Witkin, California Summary 10th Wills and Probate § 1067, Small Estate.

Witkin, California Summary 10th Wills and Probate § 1068, Money Belonging to Minor.

Witkin, California Summary 10th Wills and Probate § 1071, Disposition Of Proceeds.

Witkin, California Summary 10th Wills and Probate § 1072, Special Needs Trust.

§ 3603. Reference to "person with a disability"

Where reference is made in this chapter to a "person with a disability," the reference shall be deemed to include the following:

(a) A person for whom a conservator may be appointed.

(b) Any of the following persons, subject to the provisions of Section 3613:

(1) A person who meets the definition of disability as defined in Section 1382c(a)(3) of Title 42 of the United States Code, or as defined in Section 416(i)(1) of Title II of the federal Social Security Act (42 U.S.C. Sec. 401 et seq.) and regulations implementing that act, as set forth in Part 416.905 of Title 20 of the Federal Code of Regulations.

(2) A person who meets the definition of disability as defined in paragraphs (1), (2), and (3) of subsection (d) of Section 423 of Title II of the federal Social Security Act (42 U.S.C. Sec. 401 et seq.) and regulations implementing that act, as set forth in Part 404.1505 of Title 20 of the Federal Code of Regulations.

(3) A minor who meets the definition of disability, as set forth in Part 416.906 of Title 20 of the Federal Code of Regulations.

(4) A person with a developmental disability, as defined in Section 4512 of the Welfare and Institutions Code. *(Stats. 1990, c. 79 (A.B.759), § 14, operative July 1, 1991. Amended by Stats.2004, c. 67 (A.B.1851), § 6.)*

Application

For application of this chapter, see Probate Code § 3600.

Law Revision Commission Comments

1990 Enactment

Section 3603 continues Section 3603 of the repealed Probate Code without substantive change. For background on the provisions of this part, see the Comment to this part under the part heading. [20 Cal.L.Rev.Comm.Reports 1001 (1990)].

Research References

Forms

California Transactions Forms--Estate Planning § 17:14, Person With a Disability.

Treatises and Practice Aids

Witkin, California Summary 10th Wills and Probate § 1070, in General.

§ 3604. Payment to special needs trust; petition for order; trust requirements; jurisdiction of court; court orders

(a)(1) If a court makes an order under Section 3602 or 3611 that money of a minor or person with a disability be paid to a special needs trust, the terms of the trust shall be reviewed and approved by the court and shall satisfy the requirements of this section. The trust is subject to continuing jurisdiction of the court, and is subject to court supervision to the extent determined by the court. The court may transfer jurisdiction to the court in the proper county for commencement of a proceeding as determined under Section 17005.

(2) If the court referred to in subdivision (a) could have made an order under Section 3602 or 3611 to place that money into a special needs trust, but that order was not requested, a parent, guardian, conservator, or other interested person may petition a court that exercises jurisdiction pursuant to Section 800 for that order. In doing so, notice shall be provided pursuant to subdivisions (e) and (f) of Section 3602, or subdivision (c) of Section 3611, and that notice shall be given at least 15 days before the hearing.

(b) A special needs trust may be established and continued under this section only if the court determines all of the following:

(1) That the minor or person with a disability has a disability that substantially impairs the individual's ability to provide for the individual's own care or custody and constitutes a substantial handicap.

(2) That the minor or person with a disability is likely to have special needs that will not be met without the trust.

(3) That money to be paid to the trust does not exceed the amount that appears reasonably necessary to meet the special needs of the minor or person with a disability.

(c) If at any time it appears (1) that any of the requirements of subdivision (b) are not satisfied or the trustee refuses without good cause to make payments from the trust for the special needs of the beneficiary, and (2) that the State Department of Health Care Services, the State Department of State Hospitals, the State Department of Developmental Services, or a county or city and county in this state has a claim against trust property, that department, county, or city and county may petition the court for an order terminating the trust.

(d) A court order under Section 3602 or 3611 for payment of money to a special needs trust shall include a provision that all statutory liens in favor of the State Department of Health Care Services, the State Department of State Hospitals, the State Department of Developmental Services, and any county or city and county in this state shall first be satisfied. *(Added by Stats.1992, c. 355 (A.B.3328), § 3.*

Amended by Stats.2004, c. 67 (A.B.1851), § 7; Stats.2012, c. 440 (A.B.1488), § 55, eff. Sept. 22, 2012.)

Application

For application of this chapter, see Probate Code § 3600.

Law Revision Commission Comments

1992 Addition

Section 3604 is new. The section permits personal injury damages or settlement proceeds for a disabled minor or incompetent person to be delivered to a trustee of a special needs trust. In approving the terms of the trust, the court may, for example, require periodic accountings, court approval for certain kinds of investments, or the giving of a surety bond.

If the personal injury case is concluded in another jurisdiction, e.g., in federal court, a petition for supervision of the trust may be filed in the proper superior court as provided in Section 17200. [22 Cal.L.Rev.Comm.Reports 989 (1992)].

Research References

Forms

California Transactions Forms--Estate Planning § 17:15, Required Findings [Prob C § 3604(B)].
California Transactions Forms--Estate Planning § 17:16, Court's Continuing Jurisdiction.
California Transactions Forms--Estate Planning § 17:17, Provisions Required for Medi-Cal Qualification.
California Transactions Forms--Estate Planning § 17:43, Litigation Settlement Trust Introductory Paragraph.
West's California Code Forms, Probate § 3500 Form 1, Petition by Parent to Compromise Disputed Personal Injury Claim Of Minor Without a Guardian Of the Estate--Judicial Council Form MC-350.
West's California Code Forms, Probate § 3500 Form 2, Order Authorizing Parent to Compromise Claim Of Minor Without Guardian--Judicial Council Form MC-351.
West's California Code Forms, Probate § 3600 COMMENT, Disposition Of Compromise or Judgment Amount on Behalf Of an Incompetent Person Without a Conservator Of the Estate.

Treatises and Practice Aids

Witkin, California Summary 10th Wills and Probate § 43, Major Changes.
Witkin, California Summary 10th Wills and Probate § 622, Claims Under Specific Statutes.
Witkin, California Summary 10th Wills and Probate § 1071, Disposition Of Proceeds.
Witkin, California Summary 10th Wills and Probate § 1072, Special Needs Trust.

§ 3605. Statutes of limitation; death of beneficiary; notice of death; payment of claims; application of section

(a) This section applies only to a special needs trust established under Section 3604 on or after January 1, 1993.

(b) While the special needs trust is in existence, the statute of limitations otherwise applicable to claims of the State Department of Health Care Services, the State Department of State Hospitals, the State Department of Developmental Services, and any county or city and county in this state is tolled. Notwithstanding any provision in the trust instrument, at the death of the special needs trust beneficiary or on termination of the trust, the trust property is subject to claims of the State Department of Health Care Services, the State Department of State Hospitals, the State Department of Developmental Services, and any county or city and county in this state to the extent authorized by law as if the trust property is owned by the beneficiary or is part of the beneficiary's estate.

(c) At the death of the special needs trust beneficiary or on termination of the trust, the trustee shall give notice of the beneficiary's death or the trust termination, in the manner provided in Section 1215, to all of the following:

(1) The State Department of Health Care Services, the State Department of State Hospitals, and the State Department of Developmental Services, addressed to the director of that department at the Sacramento office of the director.

(2) Any county or city and county in this state that has made a written request to the trustee for notice, addressed to that county or city and county at the address specified in the request.

(d) Failure to give the notice required by subdivision (c) prevents the running of the statute of limitations against the claim of the department, county, or city and county not given the notice.

(e) The department, county, or city and county has four months after notice is given in which to make a claim with the trustee. If the trustee rejects the claim, the department, county, or city and county making the claim may petition the court for an order under Chapter 3 (commencing with Section 17200) of Part 5 of Division 9, directing the trustee to pay the claim. A claim made under this subdivision shall be paid as a preferred claim prior to any other distribution. If trust property is insufficient to pay all claims under this subdivision, the trustee shall petition the court for instructions and the claims shall be paid from trust property as the court deems just.

(f) If trust property is distributed before expiration of four months after notice is given without payment of the claim, the department, county, or city and county has a claim against the distributees to the full extent of the claim, or each distributee's share of trust property, whichever is less. The claim against distributees includes interest at a rate equal to that earned in the Pooled Money Investment Account, Article 4.5 (commencing with Section 16480) of Chapter 3 of Part 2 of Division 4 of Title 2 of the Government Code, from the date of distribution or the date of filing the claim, whichever is later, plus other accruing costs as in the case of enforcement of a money judgment. *(Added by Stats.1992, c. 355 (A.B. 3328), § 4. Amended by Stats.2012, c. 440 (A.B.1488), § 56, eff. Sept. 22, 2012.)*

Application

For application of this chapter, see Probate Code § 3600.

Law Revision Commission Comments

1992 Addition

Section 3605 is new. Section 3605 permits reimbursement from special needs trusts established under Section 3604, but only on termination of the trust. Section 3605 does not affect other trusts, including special needs trusts to receive damages or settlement proceeds established pursuant to court order before the operative date of this section.

A court order under subdivision (e) directing the trustee to pay the claim or denying the claim is appealable. Section 17207.

Except for statutory liens ordered paid under subdivision (d) of Section 3604, all reimbursement rights of public agencies are deferred while the special needs trust is in existence. On the death of the special needs trust beneficiary or on termination of the trust, trust property may become subject to reimbursement claims under federal or state law. See, e.g., 42 U.S.C. § 1396p(b)(1)(B) (Medicaid); Welf. & Inst.Code §§ 7276, 7513–7513.2 (state hospital costs), 14009.5 (Medi–Cal), 17109, 17403 (counties). For this purpose and only this purpose, the trust property is treated as the beneficiary's property or as property of the beneficiary's estate.

On termination of a special needs trust, the normal rules governing distribution of property are applicable, subject to the claims reimbursement provisions of this section. See Section 15410 (disposition of property on trust termination). [22 Cal.L.Rev.Comm.Reports 989 (1992)].

Research References

Forms

California Transactions Forms--Estate Planning § 17:17, Provisions Required for Medi-Cal Qualification.
California Transactions Forms--Estate Planning § 17:34, Notice.
California Transactions Forms--Estate Planning § 17:44, Payback Provisions Required in Self-Funded Special Needs Trusts.
West's California Code Forms, Probate § 3500 Form 2, Order Authorizing Parent to Compromise Claim Of Minor Without Guardian--Judicial Council Form MC-351.

Treatises and Practice Aids

Witkin, California Summary 10th Wills and Probate § 43, Major Changes.
Witkin, California Summary 10th Wills and Probate § 622, Claims Under Specific Statutes.
Witkin, California Summary 10th Wills and Probate § 1072, Special Needs Trust.

ARTICLE 2. DISPOSITION OF MONEY OR OTHER PROPERTY WHERE NO GUARDIANSHIP OR CONSERVATORSHIP

Application

For application of this chapter, see Probate Code § 3600.

§ 3610. Disposition of remaining balance

When money or other property is to be paid or delivered for the benefit of a minor or person with a disability under a compromise, covenant, order or judgment, and there is no guardianship of the estate of the minor or conservatorship of the estate of the person with a disability, the remaining balance of the money and other property (after payment of all expenses, costs, and fees as approved and allowed by the court under Section 3601) shall be paid, delivered, deposited, or invested as provided in this article. *(Stats.1990, c. 79 (A.B.759), § 14, operative July 1, 1991. Amended by Stats. 2004, c. 67 (A.B.1851), § 8.)*

Application

For application of this chapter, see Probate Code § 3600.

Law Revision Commission Comments

1990 Enactment

Section 3610 continues Section 3610 of the repealed Probate Code without change. This section makes clear that this article applies only where there is not an existing guardianship or conservatorship of the estate. The section is consistent with subdivision (a) of Section 3602. For provisions relating to the authority of a parent, guardian, conservator, or guardian ad litem to compromise claims and actions, see Sections 2500–2507 and 3500 and Code of Civil Procedure Sections 372 and 373.5. The reference in Section 3610 to "incompetent person" includes "a person for whom a conservator may be appointed." See Section 3603. For background on the provisions of this part, see the Comment to this part under the part heading. [20 Cal.L.Rev.Comm.Reports 1001 (1990)].

Research References

Forms

Cal. Transaction Forms - Bus. Transactions § 18:31, Delivery and Disposition Of Settlement Proceeds.
West's California Code Forms, Probate § 3600 COMMENT, Disposition Of Compromise or Judgment Amount on Behalf Of an Incompetent Person Without a Conservator Of the Estate.

Treatises and Practice Aids

Witkin, California Summary 10th Wills and Probate § 1067, Small Estate.
Witkin, California Summary 10th Wills and Probate § 1068, Money Belonging to Minor.
Witkin, California Summary 10th Wills and Probate § 1071, Disposition Of Proceeds.

§ 3611. Order of court

In any case described in Section 3610, the court making the order or giving the judgment referred to in Section 3600 shall, upon application of counsel for the minor or person with a disability, order any one or more of the following:

(a) That a guardian of the estate or conservator of the estate be appointed and that the remaining balance of the money and other property be paid or delivered to the person so appointed.

(b) That the remaining balance of any money paid or to be paid be deposited in an insured account in a financial institution in this state, or in a single-premium deferred annuity, subject to withdrawal only upon the authorization of the court, and that the remaining balance of any other property delivered or to be delivered be held on conditions the court determines to be in the best interest of the minor or person with a disability.

(c) After a hearing by the court, that the remaining balance of any money and other property be paid to a special needs trust established under Section 3604 for the benefit of the minor or person with a disability. Notice of the time and place of the hearing and a copy of the petition shall be mailed to the State Director of Health Care Services, the Director of State Hospitals, and the Director of Developmental Services at the office of each director in Sacramento at least 15 days before the hearing.

(d) If the remaining balance of the money to be paid or delivered does not exceed twenty thousand dollars ($20,000), that all or any part of the money be held on any other conditions the court in its discretion determines to be in the best interest of the minor or person with a disability.

(e) If the remaining balance of the money and other property to be paid or delivered does not exceed five thousand dollars ($5,000) in value and is to be paid or delivered for the benefit of a minor, that all or any part of the money and the other property be paid or delivered to a parent of the minor, without bond, upon the terms and under the conditions specified in Article 1 (commencing with Section 3400) of Chapter 2.

(f) If the remaining balance of the money and other property to be paid or delivered is to be paid or delivered for the benefit of the minor, that all or any part of the money and other property be transferred to a custodian for the benefit of the minor under the California Uniform Transfers to Minors Act, Part 9 (commencing with Section 3900).

(g) That the remaining balance of the money and other property be paid or delivered to the trustee of a trust which is created by, or approved of, in the order or judgment referred to in Section 3600. This trust shall be revocable by the minor upon attaining the age of 18 years, and shall contain other terms and conditions, including, but not limited to, terms and conditions concerning trustee's accounts and trustee's bond, as the court determines to be necessary to protect the minor's interests.

(h) That the remaining balance of any money paid or to be paid be deposited with the county treasurer, if all of the following conditions are met:

(1) The county treasurer has been authorized by the county board of supervisors to handle the deposits.

(2) The county treasurer shall receive and safely keep all money deposited with the county treasurer pursuant to this subdivision, shall pay the money out only upon the order of the court, and shall credit each estate with the interest earned by the funds deposited less the county treasurer's actual cost authorized to be recovered under Section 27013 of the Government Code.

(3) The county treasurer and sureties on the official bond of the county treasurer are responsible for the safekeeping and payment of the money.

(4) The county treasurer shall ensure that the money deposited is to earn interest or dividends, or both, at the highest rate which the county can reasonably obtain as a prudent investor.

(5) Funds so deposited with the county treasurer shall only be invested or deposited in compliance with the provisions governing the investment or deposit of state funds set forth in Chapter 5 (commencing with Section 16640) of Part 2 of Division 4 of Title 2 of the Government Code, the investment or deposit of county funds set forth in Chapter 4 (commencing with Section 53600) of Part 1 of Division 2 of Title 5 of the Government Code, or as authorized under Chapter 6 (commencing with Section 2400) of Part 4.

(i) That the remaining balance of the money and other property be paid or delivered to the person with a disability. *(Stats.1990, c. 79 (A.B.759), § 14, operative July 1, 1991. Amended by Stats.1991, c. 413 (A.B.934), § 3; Stats.1992, c. 355 (A.B.3328), § 5; Stats.1993, c. 978 (S.B.305), § 4; Stats. 1996, c. 563 (S.B.392), § 19; Stats.2004, c. 67 (A.B.1851), § 9; Stats.2012, c. 440 (A.B.1488), § 57, eff. Sept. 22, 2012.)*

Application

For application of this chapter, see Probate Code § 3600.

Law Revision Commission Comments

1990 Enactment

Section 3611 continues Section 3611 of the repealed Probate Code with the substitution of language that requires money to be deposited in an insured account in a financial institution in this state for the former language listing various financial institution accounts. Where the money and other property to be paid or delivered does not exceed $5,000 and is for the benefit of a minor, the court, in its discretion, may make an order under subdivision (a), (b), (c), (d), or (e). Where the amount exceeds $5,000 but does not exceed $20,000, the court has discretion to make an order under subdivision (a), (b), (c), or (e), but not under subdivision (d). Where the amount exceeds $20,000, the court may make an order under subdivision (a), (b), or (e). See also Section 3401 (direct payment to parent without court order). The reference in Section 3611 to "incompetent person" includes "a person for whom a conservator may be appointed." See Section 3603. For background on the provisions of this part, see the Comment to this part under the part heading. [20 Cal.L.Rev.Comm.Reports 1001 (1990)].

1992 Amendment

Section 3611 is amended to add subdivision (c) to permit money of a minor or incompetent person to be paid to the trustee of a special needs trust established under Section 3604. Before payment or delivery to the trust, all statutory liens in favor of the Department of Health Services, Department of Mental Health. Department of Developmental Services, and any county or city and county in this state must first be satisfied. See Section 3604(d); Welf. & Inst.Code §§ 7282.1, 14124.71–14124.76, 17109, 17403. [22 Cal.L.Rev.Comm.Reports 989 (1992)].

1993 Amendment

Subdivision (c) of Section 3611 is amended to require a hearing before the court may order money to be paid to a special needs trust under this section, and to require notice to affected state agencies. This amendment conforms Section 3611(c) to Section 3602(f). [23 Cal.L.Rev.Comm. Reports 901 (1993) (Annual Report, App. 4)].

Research References

Forms

West's California Code Forms, Probate § 3500 Form 1, Petition by Parent to Compromise Disputed Personal Injury Claim Of Minor Without a Guardian Of the Estate--Judicial Council Form MC-350.

West's California Code Forms, Probate § 3500 Form 2, Order Authorizing Parent to Compromise Claim Of Minor Without Guardian--Judicial Council Form MC-351.

West's California Code Forms, Probate § 3600 COMMENT, Disposition Of Compromise or Judgment Amount on Behalf Of an Incompetent Person Without a Conservator Of the Estate.

Treatises and Practice Aids

Witkin, California Summary 10th Wills and Probate § 1071, Disposition Of Proceeds.

Witkin, California Summary 10th Wills and Probate § 1072, Special Needs Trust.

§ 3612. Continuing jurisdiction until minor reaches majority; continuing jurisdiction over trust of person with a disability who reaches majority

(a) Notwithstanding any other provision of law and except to the extent the court orders otherwise, the court making the order under Section 3611 shall have continuing jurisdiction of the money and other property paid, delivered, deposited, or invested under this article until the minor reaches 18 years of age.

(b) Notwithstanding subdivision (a), the trust of an individual who meets the definition of a person with a disability under paragraph (3) of subdivision (b) of Section 3603 and who reaches 18 years of age, shall continue and be under continuing court jurisdiction until terminated by the court. *(Stats.1990, c. 79 (A.B.759), § 14, operative July 1, 1991. Amended by Stats.2004, c. 67 (A.B.1851), § 10.)*

Application

For application of this chapter, see Probate Code § 3600.

Law Revision Commission Comments

1990 Enactment

Section 3612 continues Section 3612 of the repealed Probate Code without change. For background on the provisions of this part, see the Comment to this part under the part heading. [20 Cal.L.Rev.Comm.Reports 1001 (1990)].

Research References

Forms

West's California Code Forms, Probate § 3500 Form 2, Order Authorizing Parent to Compromise Claim Of Minor Without Guardian--Judicial Council Form MC-351.

Treatises and Practice Aids

Witkin, California Summary 10th Wills and Probate § 1071, Disposition Of Proceeds.

§ 3613. Orders or judgments with respect to adults who have capacity to consent

Notwithstanding any other provision of this chapter, a court may not make an order or give a judgment pursuant to Section 3600, 3601, 3602, 3610, or 3611 with respect to an adult who has the capacity within the meaning of Section 812 to consent to the order and who has no conservator of the estate with authority to make that decision, without the express consent of that person. *(Added by Stats.2004, c. 67 (A.B.1851), § 11.)*

Application

For application of this chapter, see Probate Code § 3600.

Research References

Forms

California Transactions Forms--Estate Planning § 17:13, Overview [Prob. Code §§ 3600 to 3613].

California Transactions Forms--Estate Planning § 17:14, Person With a Disability.

California Transactions Forms--Estate Planning § 17:15, Required Findings [Prob C § 3604(B)].

Treatises and Practice Aids

Witkin, California Summary 10th Wills and Probate § 1070, in General.

CHAPTER 5. PROPERTY OF ABSENT FEDERAL PERSONNEL

Law Revision Commission Comments

1994 Amendment

The chapter heading is amended since the power of attorney provisions in Article 4 (commencing with Section 3720) are not restricted to personal property. [24 Cal.L.Rev.Comm.Reports 323 (1994)].

ARTICLE 1. DEFINITIONS

§ 3700. Meaning of terms used in chapter

As used in this chapter:

(a) "Absentee" is defined in Section 1403.

(b) "Certificate of missing status" means the official written report complying with Section 1283 of the Evidence Code and showing the determination of the secretary of the military department or the head of the department or agency concerned or the delegate of the secretary or head that the absentee is in missing status.

(c) "Eligible spouse" means the spouse of an absentee who has not commenced an action or proceeding for judicial or legal separation, annulment, adjudication of nullity, or dissolution of the marriage of the spouse and the absentee.

(d) "Family of an absentee" means an eligible spouse, if any, or if no eligible spouse, the child or children of an absentee, equally, or if no child or children, the parent or parents of an absentee, equally, provided these persons are dependents of the absentee as defined in Section 401 of Title 37 of the United States Code, and the guardian of the estate or conservator of the estate of any person bearing such relationship to the absentee.

(e) "Secretary concerned" is defined in Section 1440. *(Stats.1990, c. 79 (A.B.759), § 14, operative July 1, 1991.)*

Law Revision Commission Comments

1990 Enactment

Section 3700 continues Section 3700 of the repealed Probate Code without substantive change. The reference to "divorce" is omitted as unnecessary in view of Section 36 ("dissolution of marriage" includes divorce). For background on this section, see Recommendation Relating to Missing Persons, 16 Cal.L.Revision Comm'n Reports 105, 124–25 (1982). [20 Cal.L.Rev.Comm.Reports 1001 (1990)].

Research References

Forms

Am. Jur. Pl. & Pr. Forms Absentees § 1, Introductory Comments.

Treatises and Practice Aids

Witkin, California Summary 10th Wills and Probate § 1073, in General.

Witkin, California Summary 10th Wills and Probate § 1074, Court Proceeding to Set Aside Property.

ARTICLE 2. COURT PROCEEDING TO SET ASIDE PERSONAL PROPERTY OF ABSENTEE

§ 3701. Setting aside personal property of absentee

Upon petition as provided in this chapter, the court may set aside to the family of an absentee personal property of the absentee situated in this state for the purpose of managing, controlling, encumbering, selling, or conveying, or otherwise engaging in any transaction with respect to the property, if the court determines that to do so will be in the best interest of the absentee, including the interest of the absentee in providing for shelter, food, health care, education, transportation, or the maintenance of a reasonable and adequate standard of living for the family of the absentee. The absentee's interest in the property set aside shall not exceed twenty thousand dollars ($20,000). *(Stats.1990, c. 79 (A.B. 759), § 14, operative July 1, 1991.)*

Law Revision Commission Comments

1990 Enactment

Section 3701 continues Section 3701 of the repealed Probate Code without change. The authority for the court to provide support for the absentee's family is consistent with the original purpose of the legislation, which was not only to avoid "prejudice to the estates of such missing persons," but also to avoid "difficulty and hardship to their families [caused] by their inability to consummate transactions, such as to sell property, withdraw funds, cash checks, transfer securities and the like, upon which the families are dependent." 1972 Cal.Stat. ch. 988 § 9. [20 Cal.L.Rev.Comm.Reports 1001 (1990)].

Research References

Treatises and Practice Aids

Witkin, California Summary 10th Wills and Probate § 1073, in General.

§ 3702. Persons authorized to petition

A petition that personal property of an absentee be set aside as provided in this chapter may be filed by any of the following persons:

(a) A person in whose favor the personal property of the absentee may be set aside.

(b) A person to whom the absentee has issued a general power of attorney while serving in the armed forces of the United States or while an employee of any agency or department of the United States, provided the power of attorney was valid and effective at the time issued, regardless whether it has expired or terminated. *(Stats.1990, c. 79 (A.B.759), § 14, operative July 1, 1991.)*

Law Revision Commission Comments

1990 Enactment

Section 3702 continues Section 3702 of the repealed Probate Code without change. [20 Cal.L.Rev.Comm.Reports 1001 (1990)].

Research References

Treatises and Practice Aids

Witkin, California Summary 10th Wills and Probate § 1074, Court Proceeding to Set Aside Property.

§ 3703. Contents of petition

(a) The petition shall contain all of the following:

(1) A statement that the petition is filed under this chapter.

(2) In its caption, the last known military rank or grade and the social security account number of the absentee.

(3) A specific description and estimate of the value of all of the absentee's property, wherever situated (including all sums due the absentee from the United States).

(4) A designation of the property to be set aside, and the facts establishing that setting aside the property is necessary and in the best interest of the absentee.

(5) If the property is to be set aside for the benefit of the spouse of the absentee, an allegation that the spouse is an eligible spouse.

(6) So far as known to the petitioner, the names and addresses of all persons comprising the family of the absentee, and an allegation whether a guardian of the estate or a conservator of the estate of any member of the family of the absentee has been appointed.

(b) There shall be attached to the petition a certificate of missing status. The certificate of missing status shall be received as evidence of that fact and the court shall not determine the status of the absentee inconsistent with the status shown in the certificate. *(Stats.1990, c. 79 (A.B.759), § 14, operative July 1, 1991.)*

Law Revision Commission Comments

1990 Enactment

Section 3703 continues Section 3703 of the repealed Probate Code without substantive change. For general provisions relating to petitions and other papers, see Sections 1020–1023. For background on this section, see Recommendation Relating to Missing Persons, 16 Cal.L.Revision Comm'n Reports 105, 125–26 (1982). [20 Cal.L.Rev.Comm.Reports 1001 (1990)].

Research References

Treatises and Practice Aids

Witkin, California Summary 10th Wills and Probate § 1074, Court Proceeding to Set Aside Property.

§ 3704. Notice of hearing

(a) Notice of the nature of the proceedings and the time and place of the hearing shall be given by the petitioner at least 15 days before the hearing date by all of the following means:

(1) By * * * delivery pursuant to Section 1215, together with a copy of the petition, to all persons comprising the family of the absentee.

(2) By delivery by a method that would be sufficient for service of summons in a civil action, together with a copy of the petition, to the secretary concerned or to the head of the United States department or agency concerned.

(3) By publication pursuant to Section 6061 of the Government Code in a newspaper of general circulation in the county in which the proceedings will be held.

(b) If notice to an officer or agency of this state or of the United States * * * is required under Section 1461 or * * * 1822 upon petition for appointment of a conservator, * * * notice shall be given of the petition under this chapter. *(Stats.1990, c. 79 (A.B.759), § 14, operative July 1, 1991.*

Amended by Stats.2017, c. 319 (A.B.976), § 60, eff. Jan. 1, 2018.)

Law Revision Commission Comments

1990 Enactment

Section 3704 continues Section 3704 of the repealed Probate Code without change. For general provisions relating to notice of hearing, see Sections 1200–1221. See also Sections 1260–1265 (proof of giving notice). [20 Cal.L.Rev.Comm.Reports 1001 (1990)].

Research References

Treatises and Practice Aids

Witkin, California Summary 10th Wills and Probate § 1074, Court Proceeding to Set Aside Property.

§ 3705. Hearing and order

(a) Upon the hearing of the petition, any officer or agency of this state or the United States or the authorized delegate of the officer or agency, or any relative or friend of the absentee, may appear and support or oppose the petition.

(b) If the court determines that the allegations of the petition are true and correct, the court may order set aside to the family of the absentee personal property of the absentee situated in this state (excluding any sums due the absentee from the United States) in which the absentee's interest does not exceed twenty thousand dollars ($20,000). The property set aside shall be specified in the order.

(c) No bond shall be required of any person to whom property of the absentee has been set aside by order of the court pursuant to this chapter. *(Stats.1990, c. 79 (A.B.759), § 14, operative July 1, 1991.)*

Law Revision Commission Comments

1990 Enactment

Section 3705 continues Section 3705 of the repealed Probate Code without substantive change. For general provisions, see Sections 1000–1004 (rules of practice), 1040–1050 (hearings and orders). [20 Cal.L.Rev.Comm.Reports 1001 (1990)].

Research References

Treatises and Practice Aids

Witkin, California Summary 10th Wills and Probate § 1074, Court Proceeding to Set Aside Property.

§ 3706. Jurisdiction of court; amount

A determination by the court that the value of all of the absentee's property, wherever situated, exceeds twenty thousand dollars ($20,000) or that the absentee owns or has an interest in real property, wherever situated, does not deprive the court of jurisdiction to set aside to the family of the absentee personal property of the absentee situated in this state in which the absentee's interest does not exceed twenty thousand dollars ($20,000), and the court shall order set aside such personal property to the family of the absentee if the court finds that all of the other provisions of this chapter have been complied with. The property set aside shall be specified in the order. *(Stats.1990, c. 79 (A.B.759), § 14, operative July 1, 1991.)*

Law Revision Commission Comments

1990 Enactment

Section 3706 continues Section 3706 of the repealed Probate Code without substantive change. [20 Cal.L.Rev.Comm.Reports 1001 (1990)].

Research References

Treatises and Practice Aids

Witkin, California Summary 10th Wills and Probate § 1073, in General.

§ 3707. Joint tenancy property

For the purposes of this chapter, any property or interest therein or lien thereon that the absentee holds as joint tenant shall be included in determining the property of the absentee and its value. The joint tenancy interest may be set aside to the family of the absentee as provided in this chapter but may only be set aside to a member of the absentee's family who was a joint tenant with the absentee in the property. *(Stats.1990, c. 79 (A.B.759), § 14, operative July 1, 1991.)*

Law Revision Commission Comments

1990 Enactment

Section 3707 continues Section 3707 of the repealed Probate Code without change. [20 Cal.L.Rev.Comm.Reports 1001 (1990)].

Research References

Treatises and Practice Aids

Witkin, California Summary 10th Wills and Probate § 1073, in General.

§ 3708. Accounting

(a) Within six months after the absentee has returned to the controllable jurisdiction of the military department or civilian agency or department concerned, or within six months after the determination of death of the absentee by the secretary concerned or the head of the department or agency concerned or the delegate of the secretary or head, the former absentee or the personal representative of the deceased absentee may, by motion in the same proceeding, require the person or persons to whom the property of the absentee was set aside to account for the property and the proceeds, if any. The time of return to the controllable jurisdiction of the military department or civilian department or agency concerned or the determination of the time of death of the absentee shall be determined by the court under 37 United States Code, Section 556, or 5 United States Code, Section 5566. An official written report or record of the military department or civilian department or agency that the absentee has returned to its controllable jurisdiction or is deceased shall be received as evidence of that fact.

(b) This section does not in any manner derogate the finality and conclusiveness of any order, judgment, or decree previously entered in the proceeding. *(Stats.1990, c. 79 (A.B.759), § 14, operative July 1, 1991.)*

Law Revision Commission Comments

1990 Enactment

Section 3708 continues Section 3708 of the repealed Probate Code without change. [20 Cal.L.Rev.Comm.Reports 1001 (1990)].

Research References

Treatises and Practice Aids

Witkin, California Summary 10th Wills and Probate § 1074, Court Proceeding to Set Aside Property.

ARTICLE 3. MANAGEMENT AND DISPOSITION OF PERSONAL PROPERTY OF ABSENTEE WITHOUT COURT PROCEEDING

Law Revision Commission Comments

1990 Enactment

This article supersedes Article 3 (commencing with Section 3710) of Chapter 5 of Part 8 of Division 4 of the repealed Probate Code. The superseded article was enacted upon recommendation of the California Law Revision Commission. See Recommendation Relating to Missing Persons, 16 Cal.L.Revision Comm'n Reports 105, 126–28 (1982). [20 Cal.L.Rev.Comm.Reports 1001 (1990)].

§ 3710. Transactions relating to absentee's personal property

The family of an absentee may collect, receive, dispose of, or engage in any transaction relating to the absentee's personal property situated in this state without any judicial proceeding if all the following conditions are satisfied:

(a) The absentee owns no real property situated in this state.

(b) The aggregate value of all of the absentee's personal property situated in this state is five thousand dollars ($5,000) or less, excluding any money owed the absentee by the United States.

(c) The family of the absentee needs to dispose of such personal property to provide for shelter, food, health care, education, transportation, or the maintenance of a reasonable and adequate standard of living for the family of the absentee. *(Stats.1990, c. 79 (A.B.759), § 14, operative July 1, 1991.)*

Law Revision Commission Comments

1990 Enactment

Section 3710 continues Section 3710 of the repealed Probate Code without substantive change. For background on the provisions of this article, see the Comment to this article under the article heading. [20 Cal.L.Rev.Comm.Reports 1001 (1990)].

Research References

Treatises and Practice Aids

Witkin, California Summary 10th Wills and Probate § 834, Special Property Interests and Benefits.
Witkin, California Summary 10th Wills and Probate § 1075, Management and Disposition Without Court Proceeding.

§ 3711. Transfer of property; certificate; affidavit

(a) If the conditions set forth in Section 3710 are satisfied, the family of the absentee may have any evidence of interest, indebtedness, or right attributable to the absentee's personal property transferred to the family of the absentee, or transferred to the person to whom the property is to be sold or transferred by the family of the absentee, upon furnishing the person (including any governmental body) having custody of the property both of the following:

(1) A certificate of missing status.

(2) An affidavit stating under oath that the provisions of this article are applicable and that the aggregate value of all property received pursuant to this affidavit, together with all other property previously received under this article, does not exceed five thousand dollars ($5,000).

(b) The receipt of a certificate of missing status and affidavit under subdivision (a) constitutes sufficient acquittance for any payment of money or delivery of property made pursuant to this article and fully discharges the recipient from any further liability concerning the money or property without the necessity of inquiring into the truth of any of the facts stated in the affidavit. *(Stats.1990, c. 79 (A.B.759), § 14, operative July 1, 1991.)*

Law Revision Commission Comments

1990 Enactment

Section 3711 continues Section 3711 of the repealed Probate Code without change. For background on the provisions of this article, see the Comment to this article under the article heading. [20 Cal.L.Rev.Comm.Reports 1001 (1990)].

Research References

Treatises and Practice Aids

Witkin, California Summary 10th Wills and Probate § 1075, Management and Disposition Without Court Proceeding.

§ 3712. Limitation of actions

The time within which an absentee may commence an action against any person who executes an affidavit and receives property pursuant to this article commences to run on the earlier of the following dates:

(a) Ninety days after the absentee returns to the United States after the termination of the condition that caused the classification of an absentee.

(b) Two years after the termination of the condition that caused the classification of an absentee. *(Stats.1990, c. 79 (A.B.759), § 14, operative July 1, 1991.)*

Law Revision Commission Comments

1990 Enactment

Section 3712 continues Section 3712 of the repealed Probate Code with the substitution of "United States" for "continental United States." For background on the provisions of this article, see the Comment to this article under the article heading. [20 Cal.L.Rev.Comm.Reports 1001 (1990)].

Research References

Treatises and Practice Aids

Witkin, California Summary 10th Wills and Probate § 1075, Management and Disposition Without Court Proceeding.

ARTICLE 4. ABSENTEE'S POWER OF ATTORNEY

§ 3720. Termination of power; liability for relying or acting on power

If an absentee executed a power of attorney that expires during the period that occasions absentee status, the power of attorney continues in full force and effect until 30 days after the absentee status is terminated. Any person who acts in reliance upon the power of attorney when accompanied by a copy of a certificate of missing status is not liable for relying and acting upon the power of attorney. *(Stats.1990, c. 79 (A.B.759), § 14, operative July 1, 1991.)*

Law Revision Commission Comments

1990 Enactment

Section 3720 continues Section 3720 of the repealed Probate Code without substantive change. For background on this section, see Recommendation Relating to Missing Persons, 16 Cal.L.Revision Comm'n Reports 105, 128 (1982). [20 Cal.L.Rev.Comm.Reports 1001 (1990)].

Research References

Treatises and Practice Aids

Witkin, California Summary 10th Wills and Probate § 1076, Absentee's Power Of Attorney.

§ 3721. Actual knowledge of principal's death or incapacity while absent; revocation by absent principal

For the purposes of Chapter 5 (commencing with Section 4300) of Part 2 of Division 4.5, in the case of a principal who is an absentee, an attorney-in-fact or third person shall be deemed to be without actual knowledge of the following:

(a) The principal's death or incapacity while the absentee continues in missing status and until the attorney-in-fact or third person receives notice of the determination of the absentee's death by the secretary concerned or the head of the department or agency concerned or the delegate of the secretary or head.

(b) Revocation by the principal during the period described in subdivision (a). *(Added by Stats.1994, c. 307 (S.B.1907), § 14.)*

Law Revision Commission Comments

1994 Addition

Section 3721 continues without substantive change the part of Civil Code Section 2357 that related to powers of attorney involving federal absentees. References to "attorney-in-fact or third person" have been substituted for the former references to "person" for clarity and conformity with the language of the Power of Attorney Law.

See also Sections 1403 ("absentee" defined), 1440 ("secretary concerned" defined), 4014 ("attorney-in-fact" defined), 4026 ("principal" defined), 4034 ("third person" defined). [24 Cal.L.Rev.Comm.Reports 323 (1994)].

Research References

Treatises and Practice Aids

Witkin, California Summary 10th Wills and Probate § 839, Enactment Of Revised Law.
Witkin, California Summary 10th Wills and Probate § 865, Power Not Revoked Until Notice.
Witkin, California Summary 10th Wills and Probate § 1076, Absentee's Power Of Attorney.

§ 3722. Dissolution of marriage, annulment or legal separation; absentee's spouse acting as attorney-in-fact

If after the absentee executes a power of attorney, the principal's spouse who is the attorney-in-fact commences a proceeding for dissolution, annulment, or legal separation, or a legal separation is ordered, the attorney-in-fact's authority is revoked. This section is in addition to the provisions of Sections 4154 and 4697. *(Added by Stats.1994, c. 307 (S.B.1907), § 15. Amended by Stats.1999, c. 658 (A.B.891), § 26, operative July 1, 2000.)*

Law Revision Commission Comments

1994 Addition

Section 3722 continues the part of former subdivision (f) of Civil Code Section 2355 relating to the effect of a legal separation and the filing of a petition for dissolution, nullity, or legal separation in the case of federal absentees. The reference in former law to contrary provisions "in writing" is omitted because it is unnecessary; powers of attorney are required to be in writing and the Power of Attorney Law permits variation of default rules in the power of attorney. See Sections 4022 ("power of attorney" defined), 4101 (priority of provisions of power of attorney).

See also Sections 1403 ("absentee" defined), 4014 ("attorney-in-fact" defined), 4022 ("power of attorney" defined). [24 Cal.L.Rev.Comm.Reports 323 (1994)].

1999 Amendment

Section 3722 is amended to refer to a corresponding section concerning advance health care directives.

See also Sections 1403 ("absentee" defined), 4014 ("attorney-in-fact" defined), 4022 ("power of attorney" defined). [29 Cal.L.Rev. Comm. Reports 1 (1999)].

Research References

Treatises and Practice Aids

Witkin, California Summary 10th Wills and Probate § 839, Enactment Of Revised Law.
Witkin, California Summary 10th Wills and Probate § 852, Revocation Of Authority Of Attorney-In-Fact.
Witkin, California Summary 10th Wills and Probate § 1076, Absentee's Power Of Attorney.

CHAPTER 6. REMOVAL OF PROPERTY OF NONRESIDENT

§ 3800. Petition; filing; conservatorship transferred to another state

(a) If a nonresident has a duly appointed, qualified, and acting guardian, conservator, committee, or comparable fiduciary in the place of residence and if no proceeding for guardianship or conservatorship of the nonresident is pending or contemplated in this state, the nonresident fiduciary may petition to have property owned by the nonresident removed to the place of residence.

(b) The petition for removal of property of the nonresident shall be filed in the superior court of the county in which the nonresident is or has been temporarily present or in which the property of the nonresident, or the principal part thereof, is located.

(c) If a conservatorship was transferred from this state to another state pursuant to Article 3 (commencing with Section 2001) of Chapter 8 of Part 3, the foreign conservator may remove the conservatee's personal property from this state without seeking a petition under this chapter. *(Stats.1990, c. 79 (A.B.759), § 14, operative July 1, 1991. Amended by Stats.2014, c. 553 (S.B.940), § 27, eff. Jan. 1, 2015, operative Jan. 1, 2016.)*

Law Revision Commission Comments

1990 Enactment

Section 3800 continues Section 3800 of the repealed Probate Code without substantive change. For general provisions relating to petitions and other papers, see Sections 1020–1023. See also Sections 1260–1265 (proof of giving notice). [20 Cal.L.Rev.Comm.Reports 1001 (1990)].

2014 Amendment

Section 3800 is amended to reflect the enactment of the California Conservatorship Jurisdiction Act (Section 1980 *et seq.*). [43 Cal. L.Rev.Comm. Reports 93 (2013)].

Research References

Treatises and Practice Aids

Witkin, California Summary 10th Wills and Probate § 1053, Transfer Of Property Out Of State.
Witkin, California Summary 10th Wills and Probate § 1077, Property Of Nonresident.

§ 3801. Notice

(a) The petition shall be made upon 15 days' notice, by * * * delivery pursuant to Section 1215, to all of the following persons:

(1) The personal representative or other person in whose possession the property may be.

(2) Persons in this state, known to the petitioner, who are obligated to pay a debt, perform an obligation, or issue a security to the nonresident or the estate of the nonresident.

(b) The petition shall be made upon * * * additional notice, if any, as the court may order. *(Stats.1990, c. 79 (A.B.759), § 14, operative July 1, 1991. Amended by Stats. 2017, c. 319 (A.B.976), § 61, eff. Jan. 1, 2018.)*

Law Revision Commission Comments

1990 Enactment

Section 3801 continues Section 3801 of the repealed Probate Code without substantive change. For general provisions relating to notice of hearing, see Sections 1200–1221. See also Sections 1260–1265 (proof of giving notice). [20 Cal.L.Rev.Comm.Reports 1001 (1990)].

Research References

Treatises and Practice Aids

Witkin, California Summary 10th Wills and Probate § 1077, Property Of Nonresident.

§ 3802. Certificate of nonresident fiduciary

(a) The nonresident fiduciary shall produce and file one of the following certificates:

(1) A certificate that the fiduciary is entitled, by the laws of the place of appointment of the fiduciary, to the possession of the estate of the nonresident. The certificate shall be under the hand of the clerk and seal of the court from which the appointment of the fiduciary was derived and shall show a transcript of the record of appointment and that the fiduciary has entered upon the discharge of the duties of the fiduciary.

(2) A certificate that the fiduciary is entitled, by the laws of the place of residence, to custody of the estate of the nonresident, without the appointment of any court. The certificate shall be under the hand of the clerk and seal of either (i) the court in the place of residence having jurisdiction of estates of persons that have a guardian, conservator, committee, or comparable fiduciary or (ii) the highest court in the place of residence.

(b) In the case of a foreign country, the certificate shall be accompanied by a final statement certifying the genuineness of the signature and official position of (1) the court clerk making the original certificate or (2) any foreign official who has certified either the genuineness of the signature and official position of the court clerk making the original certificate or the genuineness of the signature and official position of another foreign official who has executed a similar certificate in a chain of such certificates beginning with a certificate of the genuineness of the signature and official position of the clerk making the original certificate. The final statement may be made only by a secretary of an embassy or legation, consul general, consul, vice consul, or consular agent of the United States, or a diplomatic or consular official of the foreign country assigned or accredited to the United States. *(Stats.1990, c. 79 (A.B.759), § 14, operative July 1, 1991.)*

Law Revision Commission Comments

1990 Enactment

Section 3802 continues Section 3802 of the repealed Probate Code without change. Subdivision (b) (persons who may attest certificate in foreign country) is consistent with Evidence Code Section 1530 (statement certifying genuineness of attestation to accuracy of copy of a writing). [20 Cal.L.Rev.Comm.Reports 1001 (1990)].

Research References

Treatises and Practice Aids

Witkin, California Summary 10th Wills and Probate § 1077, Property Of Nonresident.

§ 3803. Order for removal

(a) Upon the petition, if the court determines that removal of the property will not conflict with any restriction or limitation on the property or impair the right of the nonresident to the property or the rights of creditors or claimants in this state, the court shall make an order granting to the nonresident fiduciary leave to remove the property of the nonresident to the place of residence unless good cause to the contrary is shown.

(b) The order is authority to the fiduciary to sue for and receive the property in his or her own name for the use and benefit of the nonresident.

(c) The order is a discharge of the personal representative or other person in whose possession the property may be at the time the order is made and of the person obligated to pay a debt, perform an obligation, or issue a security to the nonresident or the estate of the nonresident, upon filing with the clerk of the court the receipt of the nonresident fiduciary for the property and transmitting a duplicate receipt, or a certified copy of the receipt, to the court, if any, from which the nonresident fiduciary received his or her appointment. *(Stats.1990, c. 79 (A.B.759), § 14, operative July 1, 1991.)*

Law Revision Commission Comments

1990 Enactment

Section 3803 continues Section 3803 of the repealed Probate Code without substantive change. For general provisions, see Sections 1000–1004 (rules of practice), 1040–1050 (hearings and orders). [20 Cal.L.Rev.Comm.Reports 1001 (1990)].

Research References

Treatises and Practice Aids

Witkin, California Summary 10th Wills and Probate § 1077, Property Of Nonresident.

Part 9

CALIFORNIA UNIFORM TRANSFERS TO MINORS ACT

Application

Application of part to transfers made on or after January 1, 1985, see Probate Code §§ 3922, 3923.

Law Revision Commission Comments

1990 Enactment

This part supersedes Part 9 (commencing with Section 3900) of Division 4 of the repealed Probate Code. The superseded part was enacted upon recommendation of the California Law Revision Commission. See Recommendation Relating to Uniform Transfers to Minors Act, 17 Cal.L.Revision Comm'n Reports 601 (1984). See also Report of Senate Committee on Judiciary on Assembly Bill 2492, 18 Cal.L.Revision Comm'n Reports 105 (1986). As to the construction of provisions drawn from uniform acts, see Section 2. See also the Comments of the Uniform Law Commissioners to the Uniform Transfers to Minors Act (1986). [20 Cal.L.Rev.Comm.Reports 1001 (1990)].

§ 3900. Short title

This part may be cited as the "California Uniform Transfers to Minors Act." *(Stats.1990, c. 79 (A.B.759), § 14, operative July 1, 1991.)*

Law Revision Commission Comments

1990 Enactment

Section 3900 continues Section 3900 of the repealed Probate Code without change. This section is the same as Section 24 of the Uniform Transfers to Minors Act (1986).

Background on Section 3900 of Repealed Code

Section 3900 was a new provision added by 1984 Cal.Stat. ch. 243 § 9. For background on the provisions of this part, see the Comment to this part under the part heading. [20 Cal.L.Rev.Comm.Reports 1001 (1990)].

Research References

Forms

Cal. Transaction Forms - Bus. Transactions § 26:30, Drafting Signature Cards.

California Transactions Forms--Estate Planning § 1:29, Options Involving Gifts to Minors.

California Transactions Forms--Estate Planning § 6:18, Custodian Under Uniform Transfers to Minors Act.

California Transactions Forms--Estate Planning § 6:78, Devise to Custodian for Child Who is Minor at Testator's Death Under California Uniform Transfers to Minors Act.

California Transactions Forms--Estate Planning § 7:39, California Uniform Transfers to Minors Act.

California Transactions Forms--Estate Planning § 10:21, Life Insurance Generally.

California Transactions Forms--Estate Planning § 10:23, Third Party or Irrevocable Trust as Owner Of Life Insurance Policy.

California Transactions Forms--Estate Planning § 10:34, Multiple Party Accounts.

California Transactions Forms--Estate Planning § 13:64, Methods Of Distribution.

California Transactions Forms--Estate Planning § 14:24, Incorporation Of CUTMA.
California Transactions Forms--Estate Planning § 14:52, Limited Power to Designate Remainder Beneficiaries.
California Transactions Forms--Estate Planning § 14:58, Provisions Typically Requested by Corporate Trustees.
California Transactions Forms--Estate Planning § 18:53, Irrevocable Asset Protection Discretionary Trust for Children With Spendthrift Provisions.
California Transactions Forms--Estate Planning § 18:54, Revocable Trust Agreement.
California Transactions Forms--Estate Planning § 20:10, Devises to Minors.
California Transactions Forms--Estate Planning § 21:19, Accumulation Trust for Children.
California Transactions Forms--Estate Planning § 21:22, Trust Provision for Spouse With Remainder to Issue Partly Outright and Partly in Trust.
California Transactions Forms--Estate Planning § 21:23, Trust Provision for Spouse With Secondary Trust for Children and General Power Of Appointment.
California Transactions Forms--Estate Planning § 21:24, Trust Provision for Children With Limited Powers Of Appointment.
California Transactions Forms--Estate Planning § 19:134, Determining Manner Of Distribution to Minors and Others.
Am. Jur. Pl. & Pr. Forms Gifts § 23, Introductory Comments.
West's California Code Forms, Probate § 3500 Form 1, Petition by Parent to Compromise Disputed Personal Injury Claim Of Minor Without a Guardian Of the Estate--Judicial Council Form MC-350.
West's California Code Forms, Probate § 6240 Form 1, California Statutory Will.

Treatises and Practice Aids

Witkin, California Summary 10th Parent and Child § 297, Protection Of Minor.
Witkin, California Summary 10th Personal Property § 140, Transfers to Minors Act.
Witkin, California Summary 10th Trusts § 113, Loans and Distributions to Beneficiaries.
Witkin, California Summary 10th Wills and Probate § 2, Uniform and Model Acts.
Witkin, California Summary 10th Wills and Probate § 27, Major Changes.
Witkin, California Summary 10th Wills and Probate § 250, Devise Subject to Uniform Transfers to Minors Act.
Witkin, California Summary 10th Wills and Probate § 736, Deposit With County Treasurer.
Witkin, California Summary 10th Wills and Probate § 795, Authority Of Fiduciaries.
Witkin, California Summary 10th Wills and Probate § 1066, in General.

§ 3901. Definitions

In this part:

(a) "Adult" means an individual who has attained the age of 18 years.

(b) "Benefit plan" means an employer's plan for the benefit of an employee or partner.

(c) "Broker" means a person lawfully engaged in the business of effecting transactions in securities or commodities for the person's own account or for the account of others.

(d) "Conservator" means a person appointed or qualified by a court to act as general, limited, or temporary guardian of a minor's property or a person legally authorized to perform substantially the same functions.

(e) "Court" means the superior court.

(f) "Custodial property" means (1) any interest in property transferred to a custodian under this part and (2) the income from and proceeds of that interest in property.

(g) "Custodian" means a person so designated under Section 3909 or a successor or substitute custodian designated under Section 3918.

(h) "Financial institution" means a bank, trust company, savings institution, or credit union, chartered and supervised under state or federal law or an industrial loan company licensed and supervised under the laws of this state.

(i) "Legal representative" means an individual's personal representative or conservator.

(j) "Member of the minor's family" means the minor's parent, stepparent, spouse, grandparent, brother, sister, uncle, or aunt, whether of the whole or half blood or by adoption.

(k) "Minor" means:

(1) Except as provided in paragraph (2), an individual who has not attained the age of 18 years.

(2) When used with reference to the beneficiary for whose benefit custodial property is held or is to be held, an individual who has not attained the age at which the custodian is required under Sections 3920 and 3920.5 to transfer the custodial property to the beneficiary.

(*l*) "Person" means an individual, corporation, organization, or other legal entity.

(m) "Personal representative" means an executor, administrator, successor personal representative, or special administrator of a decedent's estate or a person legally authorized to perform substantially the same functions.

(n) "State" includes any state of the United States, the District of Columbia, the Commonwealth of Puerto Rico, and any territory or possession subject to the legislative authority of the United States.

(*o*) "Transfer" means a transaction that creates custodial property under Section 3909.

(p) "Transferor" means a person who makes a transfer under this part.

(q) "Trust company" means a financial institution, corporation, or other legal entity, authorized to exercise general trust powers. *(Stats.1990, c. 79 (A.B.759), § 14, operative July 1, 1991.)*

Law Revision Commission Comments

1990 Enactment

Section 3901 continues Section 3901 of the repealed Probate Code without change. This section is the same in substance as Section 1 of the Uniform Transfers to Minors Act (1986), except as indicated below.

Section 3901 differs from the Uniform Transfers to Minors Act in the following respects:

(1) Definition of "adult." "Adult" is defined in subdivision (a) to mean an individual who has attained the age of 18 years. This is consistent with Civil Code Sections 25 and 27. One effect of this definition is that an individual custodian (other than a transferor-custodian) must be 18 years of age or older. See Section 3909. This minimum age requirement does not apply where the transferor is the

custodian (see Section 3909); a transferor may be a custodian without regard to age so long as the transferor has the capacity to make the transfer. Accordingly, if the minor can make an effective transfer of the property under the law relating to emancipation or competence to make a will, gift, or other transfer, a minor may transfer the property to a custodian for his or her own benefit or for the benefit of another minor. For example, Civil Code Section 63 permits an emancipated minor to make a will, gift, or other transfer. This authorizes an emancipated minor to make a transfer to a custodian for the minor's own benefit or for the benefit of another minor and also to serve as the custodian for custodial property the minor transfers under this part for the benefit of another minor.

The definition of "adult" is also used to determine persons who may file petitions under this part. See Section 3918, subdivision (d) ("adult member of the minor's family" may petition the court to designate a successor custodian), subdivision (f) ("adult member of the minor's family" may petition the court to remove the custodian for cause and to designate a successor custodian or to require the custodian to give appropriate bond), Section 3919(a) ("adult member of minor's family" may petition for accounting or determination of custodian's liability).

(2) Definition of "court." "Court" is defined in subdivision (e) to mean "the superior court."

(3) Definition of "financial institution." Subdivision (h) expands the Uniform Act definition of "financial institution" to include "an industrial loan company licensed and supervised under the laws of this state."

(4) Definition of "minor." "Minor" is defined in subdivision (k) to mean an individual who has not attained the age of 18 years (consistent with Civil Code § 25), except that the term "minor" may include an older individual under some circumstances when the term is used with reference to the beneficiary for whose benefit custodial property is held or is to be held. See Sections 3920, 3920.5. When used with reference to a beneficiary for whose benefit custodial property is held or is to be held, "minor" is defined in subdivision (k)(2) as an individual who has not attained the age at which the custodial property is to be transferred to the beneficiary. This age depends upon the type of transfer and whether the transfer specifically provides for the custodianship to continue until the minor attains an age older than 18 years of age. See Sections 3920 and 3920.5 and the Comments thereto. Where a custodianship may continue until a specified age older than 18, the custodianship may be established after the beneficiary has attained the age of 18 and may continue for so long as is specifically provided but not longer than the maximum duration permitted for a custodianship created by that type of transfer.

The definition of "benefit plan" in subdivision (b) is intentionally very broad and is meant to cover any contract, plan, system, account, or trust, such as a pension plan, retirement plan, death benefit plan, deferred compensation plan, employment agency arrangement, or stock bonus, option, or profit sharing plan.

The definition of "conservator" in subdivision (d) conforms to the Uniform Transfers to Minors Act. For California purposes, the term means the guardian of the estate of the minor, if the minor has not attained the age of 18 years (Prob.Code § 1600) and the conservator of the estate if the "minor" has attained the age of 18 years (Prob.Code § 1800.3).

The definition of "custodial property" in subdivision (f) encompasses every conceivable legal or equitable interest in property of any kind, including real property and tangible or intangible personal property. The term is intended, for example, to include joint interests with right of survivorship and beneficial interests in land trusts, as well as all other intangible interests in property. Contingent or expectancy interests such as the designation as a beneficiary under insurance policies or benefit plans become "custodial property" only if the designation is irrevocable, or when it becomes so, but this part specifically authorizes the "nomination" of a future custodian as beneficiary of such interests (see Section 3903). Proceeds of custodial property, both immediate and remote, are themselves custodial property.

Custodial property is defined without reference to the physical location of the property, even if it has one. No useful purpose would be served by restricting the application of this part to, for example, real estate "located in this state," since a conveyance recorded in the state of the property's location, if done with proper formalities, should be effective even if that state has not enacted the Uniform Transfers to Minors Act. The rights, duties and powers of the custodian should be determined by reference to the law of the state under which the custodianship is created, assuming there is sufficient nexus under Section 3902 between that state and the transferor, the minor, or the custodian.

The definition of "transfer" in subdivision (*o*) reflects the application of this part not only to gifts, but also to distributions from trusts and estates, obligors of the minor, and transfers of the minor's own assets to a custodianship by the legal representative of a minor, all of which are permitted by this part.

"Transferor" as defined in subdivision (p) includes not only the maker of a gift (i.e., a donor in the usual sense), but also fiduciaries and obligors who control or own property that is the subject of the transfer. Nothing requires that a transferor be an "adult." See discussion, supra, this Comment.

Only entities authorized to exercise "general" trust powers qualify as "trust companies" under subdivision (q); the authority to exercise only limited fiduciary responsibilities, such as the authority to accept Individual Retirement Account deposits, is not sufficient.

Background on Section 3901 of Repealed Code

Section 3901 was added by 1984 Cal.Stat. ch. 243 § 9. Section 3901 superseded former Civil Code Section 1155 (repealed by 1984 Cal.Stat. ch. 243 § 1) which provided definitions for the former California Uniform Gifts to Minors Act. To reflect the broader scope and the unlimited types of property to which the new California Uniform Transfers to Minors Act applies, a number of definitional changes were from the old California Uniform Gifts to Minors Act. For background on the provisions of this part, see the Comment to this part under the part heading.

Several definitions in the old Uniform Act specifically applicable to limited types of property (cash, securities, and insurance policies) covered before the expansion of the scope of the Uniform Act were omitted as unnecessary. These omitted definitions included the definitions of "bank," "issuer," "life or endowment insurance policies and annuity contracts," "savings and loan association," "security," and "transfer agent." No change in the meaning or construction of those terms as used in this part was intended by such omissions. See Uniform Transfers to Minors Act § 1 comment (1986). The substantive effect of the definition of "[l]ife or endowment insurance policies and annuity contracts" in the old Act was superseded by Section 3901(f) and subdivision (b)(2) of Section 3912 (right to retain property transferred to custodian) and subdivision (c) of Section 3912 (right to invest in or pay premiums on insurance or endowment policies). The definition of "insured financial institution" was omitted because the prudent person rule of Section 3912(b) may dictate the use of insured institutions or depositories, without having the Act so specify. See Uniform Transfers to Minors Act § 1 comment (1986).

The principal changes or additions to the remaining definitions contained in former Civil Code Section 1155 are discussed below.

Subdivision (a). Subdivision (a), defining "adult," continued subdivision (a) of former Section 1155 of the Civil Code. The requirement of former law—Civil Code Section 1156(a) (repealed by 1984 Cal.Stat. ch. 243 § 1)—that the donor be an "adult" was not continued.

Subdivision (b). The definition of "benefit plan" was new and drawn from the Uniform Transfers to Minors Act § 1(2).

Subdivision (d). The term "conservator" was defined instead of "guardian" to conform to the Uniform Transfers to Minors Act § 1(4).

Subdivision (e). The definition of "court" continued the definition of former Civil Code § 1155(d).

Subdivision (f). The definition of "custodial property" was generalized to conform to the Uniform Transfers to Minors Act § 1(6).

Subdivision (h). The definition of "financial institution" continued a provision of the definition of former Civil Code § 1155(g).

Subdivision (j). The definition of "member of the minor's family" expanded the definition under former Civil Code Section 1155 to include the minor's stepparent and spouse.

Subdivision (k). When used with reference to a beneficiary for whose benefit custodial property is held or is to be held, "minor" was defined as an individual who has not attained the age at which the custodial property is to be transferred to the beneficiary. Under former Civil Code Section 1155(m), the age of termination of the custodianship had been lowered from 21 to 18 (1972 Cal.Stat. ch. 579 § 11) to conform to the lowering of the age of majority from 21 to 18 (1971 Cal.Stat. ch. 1748 § 23).

Subdivision (m). The new definition of "personal representative" was based upon that definition in Section 1–201(30) of the Uniform Probate Code (1987). This definition was the same in substance as the Uniform Transfers to Minors Act § 1(13).

Subdivision (*o*). The new definition of "transfer" was necessary to reflect the application of the Act not only to gifts, but also to distributions from trusts and estates, obligors of the minor, and transfers of the minor's own assets to a custodianship by the legal representative of a minor, all of which are permitted by the Uniform Transfers to Minors Act and under this part.

Subdivision (p). The new definition of "transferor" was required because the term includes not only the maker of a gift, i.e., a donor in the usual sense, but also fiduciaries and obligors who control or own property that is the subject of the transfer.

Subdivision (q). The new definition of "trust company" replaced the definition of former Civil Code Section 1155 (which defined a trust company by reference to Financial Code Sections 107 and 109). [20 Cal.L.Rev.Comm.Reports 1001 (1990)].

Research References

Forms

California Transactions Forms--Estate Planning § 6:18, Custodian Under Uniform Transfers to Minors Act.

California Transactions Forms--Estate Planning § 6:78, Devise to Custodian for Child Who is Minor at Testator's Death Under California Uniform Transfers to Minors Act.

California Transactions Forms--Estate Planning § 7:39, California Uniform Transfers to Minors Act.

California Transactions Forms--Estate Planning § 19:47, Appointment Of Custodian.

West's California Code Forms, Probate § 3918 Form 1, Petition for Order Designating Successor Custodian.

West's California Code Forms, Probate § 3918 Form 2, Petition for Removal Of Custodian and Designation Of Successor Custodian.

Treatises and Practice Aids

Witkin, California Summary 10th Personal Property § 140, Transfers to Minors Act.

Witkin, California Summary 10th Personal Property § 141, Nature and Scope Of Act.

Witkin, California Summary 10th Personal Property § 142, in General.

Witkin, California Summary 10th Personal Property § 143, Selection, Removal, and Successor.

Witkin, California Summary 10th Personal Property § 144, Who May Make Transfer.

Witkin, California Summary 10th Personal Property § 145, Manner Of Making Transfer.

Witkin, California Summary 10th Personal Property § 150, Termination Of Custodianship.

§ 3902. Application of part

(a) This part applies to a transfer that refers to this part in the designation under subdivision (a) of Section 3909 by which the transfer is made if at the time of the transfer, the transferor, the minor, or the custodian is a resident of this state or the custodial property is located in this state. The custodianship so created remains subject to this part despite a subsequent change in residence of a transferor, the minor, or the custodian, or the removal of custodial property from this state.

(b) A person designated as custodian under this part is subject to personal jurisdiction in this state with respect to any matter relating to the custodianship.

(c) A transfer that purports to be made and which is valid under the Uniform Transfers to Minors Act, the Uniform Gifts to Minors Act, or a substantially similar act, of another state is governed by the law of the designated state and may be executed and is enforceable in this state if at the time of the transfer, the transferor, the minor, or the custodian is a resident of the designated state or the custodial property is located in the designated state. *(Stats.1990, c. 79 (A.B.759), § 14, operative July 1, 1991.)*

Law Revision Commission Comments

1990 Enactment

Section 3902 continues Section 3902 of the repealed Probate Code without change. This section is the same as Section 2 of the Uniform Transfers to Minors Act (1986). The section attempts to resolve uncertainties and conflicts-of-law questions that have frequently arisen because of the former non-uniformity of Uniform Gifts to Minors Act (1966) in the various states and which may continue to arise during the transition from the Uniform Gifts to Minors Act to the Uniform Transfers to Minors Act.

The creation of a custodianship must invoke the law of a particular state because of the form of the transfer required under subdivision (a) of Section 3909. Section 3902 provides that a choice of the California Uniform Transfers to Minors Act is appropriate and effective if any of the nexus factors specified in subdivision (a) exists at the time of the transfer. The California Uniform Transfers to Minors Act continues to govern, and subdivision (b) makes the custodian subject to personal jurisdiction in the courts of this state for the duration of the custodianship, despite subsequent relocation of the parties or the property.

Subdivision (c) recognizes that residents of California may elect to have the law of another state apply to a transfer. That choice is valid if a nexus with the chosen state exists at the time of the transfer. If personal jurisdiction can be obtained in California under other law apart from the California Uniform Transfers to Minors Act, the custodianship may be enforced in a California court, which is directed to apply the law of the state elected by the transferor.

If the choice of law under subdivision (a) or (c) is ineffective because of the absence of the required nexus, the transfer may still be effective under the Uniform Transfers to Minors Act of another state with which a nexus does exist. See Uniform Transfers to Minors Act § 21 (1986) (Prob.Code § 3922).

Background on Section 3902 of Repealed Code

Section 3902 was a new provision added by 1984 Cal.Stat. ch. 243 § 9. For background on the provisions of this part, see the

Comment to this part under the part heading. [20 Cal.L.Rev.Comm.Report 1001 (1990)].

Research References

Forms

California Transactions Forms--Estate Planning § 7:39, California Uniform Transfers to Minors Act.

Treatises and Practice Aids

Witkin, California Summary 10th Personal Property § 141, Nature and Scope Of Act.

Witkin, California Summary 10th Personal Property § 142, in General.

§ 3903. Nomination of custodian; creation of custodial property

(a) A person having the right to designate the recipient of property transferable upon the occurrence of a future event may revocably nominate a custodian to receive the property for a minor beneficiary upon the occurrence of the event by naming the custodian followed in substance by the words: "as custodian for ______________ (Name of Minor) under the California Uniform Transfers to Minors Act." The nomination may name one or more persons as substitute custodians to whom the property must be transferred, in the order named, if the first nominated custodian dies before the transfer or is unable, declines, or is ineligible to serve. The nomination may be made in a will, a trust, a deed, an instrument exercising a power of appointment, or in a writing designating a beneficiary of contractual rights which is registered with or delivered to the payor, issuer, or other obligor of the contractual rights.

(b) A custodian nominated under this section must be a person to whom a transfer of property of that kind may be made under subdivision (a) of Section 3909.

(c) The nomination of a custodian under this section does not create custodial property until the nominating instrument becomes irrevocable or a transfer to the nominated custodian is completed under Section 3909. Unless the nomination of a custodian has been revoked, upon the occurrence of the future event, the custodianship becomes effective, and the custodian shall enforce a transfer of the custodial property pursuant to Section 3909. *(Stats.1990, c. 79 (A.B.759), § 14, operative July 1, 1991.)*

Law Revision Commission Comments

1990 Enactment

Section 3903 continues Section 3903 of the repealed Probate Code without change. This section is the same as Section 3 of the Uniform Transfers to Minors Act (1986).

Section 3903 permits a future custodian for a minor to be nominated to receive a distribution under a will or trust, or as a beneficiary of a power of appointment, or of contractual rights such as a life or endowment insurance policy, annuity contract, P.O.D. account, benefit plan, or similar future payment right. Nomination of a future custodian does not constitute a "transfer" under this Act and does not create custodial property. If it did, the nomination and beneficiary designation would have to be permanent, since a "transfer" is irrevocable and indefeasibly vests ownership of the interest in the minor under subdivision (b) of Section 3911. Instead, Section 3903 permits a revocable beneficiary designation that takes effect only when the donor dies or when a lifetime transfer to the custodian for the minor beneficiary occurs, such as a distribution under an inter vivos trust. However, an unrevoked nomination under Section 3903 is binding on a personal representative or trustee (see subdivision (b) of Section 3905) and on insurance companies and other obligors who contract to pay in the future (see subdivision (b) of Section 3907).

The person making the nomination may name contingent or successive future custodians to serve, in the order named, in the event that the person first nominated dies, or is unable, declines, or is ineligible to serve. Such a substitute future custodian is a custodian "nominated ... under Section 3903" to whom the transfer must be made under subdivision (b) of Section 3905 and subdivision (b) of Section 3907.

Any person nominated as future custodian may decline to serve before the transfer occurs and may resign at any time after the transfer. See Section 3918.

The transferor may designate one or more persons as successor custodians to serve, in the designated order of priority, in case the custodian originally designated or a prior successor custodian is unable, declines, or is ineligible to serve or resigns, dies, becomes incapacitated, or is removed. See Section 3918(b).

Background on Section 3903 of Repealed Code

Section 3903 was a new provision added by 1984 Cal.Stat. ch. 243 § 9. No provision like Section 3903 was included in the former California statute. But see former Probate Code Section 6340 (repealed by 1984 Cal.Stat. ch. 243 § 10) which permitted a person to designate in his or her will the custodian to receive property devised under the will to a minor to be transferred to a designated custodian for the benefit of a minor. For background on the provisions of this part, see the Comment to this part under the part heading. [20 Cal.L.Rev.Comm.Reports 1001 (1990)].

Research References

Forms

California Transactions Forms--Estate Planning § 1:29, Options Involving Gifts to Minors.

California Transactions Forms--Estate Planning § 6:15, Minors' Capacity to Take Devised Property.

California Transactions Forms--Estate Planning § 6:18, Custodian Under Uniform Transfers to Minors Act.

California Transactions Forms--Estate Planning § 6:53, Matters to Consider in Drafting Gifts to Minors.

California Transactions Forms--Estate Planning § 6:78, Devise to Custodian for Child Who is Minor at Testator's Death Under California Uniform Transfers to Minors Act.

California Transactions Forms--Estate Planning § 7:40, Form Drafting Principles.

California Transactions Forms--Estate Planning § 7:42, Matters to Consider When Making Transfer Under California Uniform Transfers to Minors Act.

California Transactions Forms--Estate Planning § 7:43, Nomination Of Custodian.

West's California Code Forms, Probate § 3909 Form 1, Creation Of Custodial Property.

Treatises and Practice Aids

Witkin, California Summary 10th Personal Property § 142, in General.

Witkin, California Summary 10th Personal Property § 143, Selection, Removal, and Successor.

Witkin, California Summary 10th Personal Property § 145, Manner Of Making Transfer.

Witkin, California Summary 10th Personal Property § 150, Termination Of Custodianship.

§ 3904. Transfer by gift or exercise of power of appointment

A person may make a transfer by irrevocable gift to, or the irrevocable exercise of a power of appointment in favor of, a custodian for the benefit of a minor pursuant to Section 3909. *(Stats.1990, c. 79 (A.B.759), § 14, operative July 1, 1991.)*

Law Revision Commission Comments

1990 Enactment

Section 3904 continues Section 3904 of the repealed Probate Code without change. This section is the same as Section 4 of the Uniform Transfers to Minors Act (1986).

To emphasize the different kinds of transfers that create presently effective custodianships under this Act, they are separately described in Sections 3904, 3905, 3906, and 3907. Section 3904 covers not only the traditional lifetime gift but also an irrevocable exercise of a power of appointment in favor of a custodian, as distinguished from the exercise of a power in a revocable instrument that results only in the nomination of a future custodian under Section 3903.

A custodianship created under this section will terminate upon the minor's attainment of the age of 18 unless the transfer specifies a later time. In the case of the traditional lifetime transfer, the custodianship cannot be continued after the time the beneficiary attains 21 years of age. This limitation satisfies the requirements of Section 2503(c) of the Internal Revenue Code which permits "minority trusts" to continue in effect until age 21. In the case of an irrevocable exercise of a power of appointment in favor of a custodian, the custodianship cannot be continued after the time the beneficiary attains 25 years of age. See Section 3920 and 3920.5 and the Comments thereto. A custodianship created under this section may be created for a beneficiary who has already attained the age of 18 if the transfer provides that the custodianship is to continue until the beneficiary attains a specified age older than 18. See Section 3901(k).

Background on Section 3904 of Repealed Code

Section 3904 was added by 1984 Cal.Stat. ch. 243 § 9. Section 3904 in part corresponded to subdivision (a) of former Civil Code Section 1156 (repealed by 1984 Cal.Stat. ch. 243 § 1) but was broader than that provision which covered only the traditional lifetime gift. Section 3904 did not continue the requirement of former Civil Code Section 1156 that the donor be an "adult person." See the Comment to subdivision (a) of Section 3901. See also Report of Senate Committee on Judiciary on Assembly Bill 2492, 18 Cal.L.Revision Comm'n Reports 105, 108 (1986). For background on the provisions of this part, see the Comment to this part under the part heading. [20 Cal.L.Rev.Comm.Reports 1001 (1990)].

Research References

Forms

California Transactions Forms--Estate Planning § 6:18, Custodian Under Uniform Transfers to Minors Act.

Treatises and Practice Aids

Witkin, California Summary 10th Personal Property § 144, Who May Make Transfer.

Witkin, California Summary 10th Personal Property § 150, Termination Of Custodianship.

§ 3905. Transfer authorized by will or trust

(a) A personal representative or trustee may make an irrevocable transfer pursuant to Section 3909 to a custodian for the benefit of a minor as authorized in the governing will or trust.

(b) If the testator or settlor has nominated a custodian under Section 3903 to receive the custodial property, the transfer shall be made to that person.

(c) If the testator or settlor has not nominated a custodian under Section 3903, or all persons so nominated as custodian die before the transfer or are unable, decline, or are ineligible to serve, the personal representative or the trustee, as the case may be, shall designate the custodian from among those eligible to serve as custodian for property of that kind under subdivision (a) of Section 3909. *(Stats.1990, c. 79 (A.B.759), § 14, operative July 1, 1991.)*

Law Revision Commission Comments

1990 Enactment

Section 3905 continues Section 3905 of the repealed Probate Code without change. This section is the same as Section 5 of the Uniform Transfers to Minors Act (1986). The section includes not only a testamentary disposition but also makes clear that a trustee may make a transfer to a custodian for the benefit of a minor as authorized in the governing trust. Section 3905 also authorizes the personal representative or trustee to designate the custodian whenever the settlor or testator fails to make a nomination or whenever a future custodian nominated under Section 3903 (and any alternate named) fails to qualify. See also Section 3918.

A custodianship created under this section will terminate upon the minor's attainment of the age of 18 unless a later time is specified in the will or trust and in the transfer, but in no event does the custodianship continue after the time the minor attains 25 years of age. See Section 3920 and 3920.5 and the Comments thereto. A custodianship created under this section may be created for a beneficiary who has already attained age 18 if the will or trust provides that the custodianship is to continue until the beneficiary attains a specified age older than 18. See Section 3901(k).

Background on Section 3905 of Repealed Code

Section 3905 was added by 1984 Cal.Stat. ch. 243 § 9. Former Probate Code Section 6340 (repealed by 1984 Cal.Stat. ch. 243 § 10) permitted a testator to devise any kind of property to a custodian subject to the California Uniform Gifts to Minors Act. Section 3905 expanded the authorization of former Probate Code Section 6340 to include not only a testamentary disposition but also to make clear that a trustee may make a transfer to a custodian for the benefit of a minor as authorized in the governing trust. See also Report of Senate Committee on Judiciary on Assembly Bill 2492, 18 Cal.L.Revision Comm'n Reports 105, 108 (1986). For background on the provisions of this part, see the Comment to this part under the part heading. [20 Cal.L.Rev.Comm.Reports 1001 (1990)].

Research References

Forms

California Transactions Forms--Estate Planning § 6:18, Custodian Under Uniform Transfers to Minors Act.

California Transactions Forms--Estate Planning § 19:47, Appointment Of Custodian.

Treatises and Practice Aids

Witkin, California Summary 10th Personal Property § 144, Who May Make Transfer.

Witkin, California Summary 10th Personal Property § 150, Termination Of Custodianship.

Witkin, California Summary 10th Trusts § 215, Disposition Of Property on Termination.

§ 3906. Other transfer by fiduciary

(a) Subject to subdivision (c), a personal representative or trustee may make an irrevocable transfer to another adult or trust company as custodian for the benefit of a minor pursuant to Section 3909, in the absence of a will or under a will or trust that does not contain an authorization to do so.

(b) Subject to subdivision (c), a conservator may make an irrevocable transfer to another adult or trust company as custodian for the benefit of the minor pursuant to Section 3909.

(c) A transfer under subdivision (a) or (b) may be made only if all of the following requirements are satisfied:

(1) The personal representative, trustee, or conservator considers the transfer to be in the best interest of the minor.

(2) The transfer is not prohibited by or inconsistent with provisions of the applicable will, trust agreement, or other governing instrument. For the purposes of this subdivision, a spendthrift provision (such as that described in Section 15300) shall not prohibit or be inconsistent with the transfer.

(3) The transfer is authorized by the court if it exceeds ten thousand dollars ($10,000) in value; provided, however, that such court authorization shall not be required when the transfer is to a custodian who is either (A) a trust company or (B) an individual designated as a trustee by the terms of a trust instrument which does not require a bond. *(Stats.1990, c. 79 (A.B.759), § 14, operative July 1, 1991. Amended by Stats.1996, c. 862 (A.B.2751), § 13.)*

Law Revision Commission Comments

1990 Enactment

Section 3906 continues Section 3906 of the repealed Probate Code without change. This section is the same as Section 6 of the Uniform Transfers to Minors Act (1986).

Section 3906 permits custodianships to be used as guardianship substitutes, even though not specifically authorized by the person whose property is the subject of the transfer. Subdivision (a) permits the personal representative of a decedent's estate or a trustee to transfer estate property to a custodian for the benefit of a minor in the absence of a will or under a will or trust that does not contain an authorization to do so. Subdivision (b) permits the guardian of the estate of a minor to transfer the minor's own property to a new or existing custodianship for the purpose of convenience or economies of administration.

A custodianship may be created under this section even though not specifically authorized by the transferor, the testator, or the settlor of the trust if three tests are satisfied. First, the fiduciary making the transfer must determine in good faith and in his or her fiduciary capacity that a custodianship will be in the best interest of the minor. Second, a custodianship may not be prohibited by, or inconsistent with, the terms of any governing instrument. Inconsistent terms would include, for example, a spendthrift clause in a governing trust, provisions terminating a governing trust for the minor's benefit at a time other than the time of the minor's age of majority, and provisions for mandatory distributions of income or principal at specific times or periodic intervals. Provisions for other outright distributions or bequests would not be inconsistent with the creation of a custodianship under this section. Third, the amount of property transferred (as measured by its value) must be of such relatively small amount ($10,000 or less in value) that the lack of court supervision and the typically stricter investment standards that would apply to a guardianship will not be important. However, if the property is of greater value, transfer to a custodian may still be made if the court approves and if the other two tests are met.

The custodianship created under this section without express authority in the governing instrument will terminate upon the minor's attainment of the age of 18, the same age at which a guardianship of the estate would end. See Section 3920 and the Comment thereto.

Background on Section 3906 of Repealed Code

Section 3906 was a new provision added by 1984 Cal.Stat. ch. 243 § 9. See also Report of Senate Committee on Judiciary on Assembly Bill 2492, 18 Cal.L.Revision Comm'n Reports 105, 108 (1986). For background on the provisions of this part, see the Comment to this part under the part heading. [20 Cal.L.Rev.Comm.Reports 1001 (1990)].

Research References

Forms

California Transactions Forms--Estate Planning § 6:18, Custodian Under Uniform Transfers to Minors Act.

California Transactions Forms--Estate Planning § 13:64, Methods Of Distribution.

California Transactions Forms--Estate Planning § 21:19, Accumulation Trust for Children.

California Transactions Forms--Estate Planning § 21:22, Trust Provision for Spouse With Remainder to Issue Partly Outright and Partly in Trust.

California Transactions Forms--Estate Planning § 21:23, Trust Provision for Spouse With Secondary Trust for Children and General Power Of Appointment.

California Transactions Forms--Estate Planning § 21:24, Trust Provision for Children With Limited Powers Of Appointment.

Treatises and Practice Aids

Witkin, California Summary 10th Personal Property § 144, Who May Make Transfer.

Witkin, California Summary 10th Personal Property § 150, Termination Of Custodianship.

Witkin, California Summary 10th Trusts § 113, Loans and Distributions to Beneficiaries.

Witkin, California Summary 10th Trusts § 215, Disposition Of Property on Termination.

§ 3907. Transfer by obligor

(a) Subject to subdivisions (b) and (c), a person not subject to Section 3905 or 3906 who holds property of, or owes a liquidated debt to, a minor not having a conservator may make an irrevocable transfer to a custodian for the benefit of the minor pursuant to Section 3909.

(b) If a person having the right to do so under Section 3903 has nominated a custodian under that section to receive the custodial property, the transfer shall be made to that person.

(c) If no custodian has been nominated under Section 3903, or all persons so nominated as custodian die before the transfer or are unable, decline, or are ineligible to serve, a transfer under this section may be made to an adult member of the minor's family or to a trust company unless the property exceeds ten thousand dollars ($10,000) in value. *(Stats.1990, c. 79 (A.B.759), § 14, operative July 1, 1991.)*

Law Revision Commission Comments

1990 Enactment

Section 3907 continues Section 3907 of the repealed Probate Code without change. This section is the same as Section 7 of the Uniform Transfers to Minors Act (1986).

Like Section 3906, Section 3907 permits a custodianship to be established as a substitute for a guardianship to receive payments due a minor from sources other than estates, trusts, and existing guardianships covered by Sections 3905 and 3906. For example, a tort judgment debtor of a minor, a bank holding a joint or P.O.D. account of which a minor is the surviving payee, or an insurance company holding life insurance policy or benefit plan proceeds payable to a minor may create a custodianship under this section.

Use of this section is mandatory when a future custodian has been nominated under Section 3903 as a named beneficiary of an insurance policy, benefit plan, deposit account, or the like, because the original owner of the property specified a custodianship (and a future custodian) to receive the property. If that custodian (or any alternate named) is not available, if none was nominated, or none could have been nominated (as in the case of a tort judgment payable to the minor), this section is permissive and does not preclude the obligor from requiring the establishment of a guardianship of the estate to receive payment. The section merely allows the obligor to transfer to a custodian unless the property exceeds the stated value in which case a guardian of the estate must be appointed to receive it or some other procedure used (See Sections 3410–3413, 3600–3612).

Background on Section 3907 of Repealed Code

Section 3907 was a new provision added by 1984 Cal.Stat. ch. 243 § 9. For background on the provisions of this part, see the Comment to this part under the part heading. [20 Cal.L.Rev.Comm.Reports 1001 (1990)].

Research References

Treatises and Practice Aids

Witkin, California Summary 10th Personal Property § 144, Who May Make Transfer.

§ 3908. Acknowledgment of delivery

A written acknowledgment of delivery by a custodian constitutes a sufficient receipt and discharge for custodial property transferred to the custodian pursuant to this part. *(Stats.1990, c. 79 (A.B.759), § 14, operative July 1, 1991.)*

Law Revision Commission Comments

1990 Enactment

Section 3908 continues Section 3908 of the repealed Probate Code without change. This section is the same as Section 8 of the Uniform Transfers to Minors Act (1986).

Section 3908 discharges transferors from further responsibility for custodial property delivered to and receipted for by the custodian. See also Section 3916 which protects transferors and other third parties dealing with custodians. A discharge or release for a donative transfer is not necessary. But see Section 3402 (effect of written receipt of parent).

Section 3908 does not authorize an existing custodian, or a custodian to whom an obligor makes a transfer under Section 3907, to settle or release a claim of the minor against a third party. Only a guardian, guardian ad litem or other person authorized under other law to act for the minor may release such a claim. See the Comment to Section 3602.

Background on Section 3908 of Repealed Code

Section 3908 was a new provision added by 1984 Cal.Stat. ch. 243 § 9. For background on the provisions of this part, see the Comment to this part under the part heading. [20 Cal.L.Rev.Comm.Reports 1001 (1990)].

Research References

Treatises and Practice Aids

Witkin, California Summary 10th Personal Property § 145, Manner Of Making Transfer.

§ 3909. Creation of custodial property; designation of initial custodian; control

(a) Custodial property is created and a transfer is made whenever any of the following occurs:

(1) An uncertificated security or a certificated security in registered form is either:

(A) Registered in the name of the transferor, an adult other than the transferor, or a trust company, followed in substance by the words:

"as custodian for ______________________
(Name of Minor)
under the California Uniform Transfers to Minors Act."

(B) Delivered if in certificated form, or any document necessary for the transfer of an uncertificated security is delivered, together with any necessary endorsement to an adult other than the transferor or to a trust company as custodian, accompanied by an instrument in substantially the form set forth in subdivision (b).

(2) Money is paid or delivered, or a security held in the name of a broker, financial institution, or its nominee is transferred, to a broker or financial institution for credit to an account in the name of the transferor, an adult other than the transferor, or a trust company, followed in substance by the words:

"as custodian for ______________________
(Name of Minor)
under the California Uniform Transfers to Minors Act."

(3) The ownership of a life or endowment insurance policy or annuity contract is either:

(A) Registered with the issuer in the name of the transferor, an adult other than the transferor, or a trust company, followed in substance by the words:

"as custodian for ______________________
(Name of Minor)
under the California Uniform Transfers to Minors Act."

(B) Assigned in a writing delivered to an adult other than the transferor or to a trust company whose name in the assignment is followed in substance by the words:

"as custodian for ______________________
(Name of Minor)
under the California Uniform Transfers to Minors Act."

(4) An irrevocable exercise of a power of appointment or an irrevocable present right to future payment under a contract is the subject of a written notification delivered to the payor, issuer, or other obligor that the right is transferred to the transferor, an adult other than the transferor, or a trust company, whose name in the notification is followed in substance by the words:

"as custodian for ______________________
(Name of Minor)
under the California Uniform Transfers to Minors Act."

(5) An interest in real property is recorded in the name of the transferor, an adult other than the transferor, or a trust company, followed in substance by the words:

"as custodian for ______________________
(Name of Minor)
under the California Uniform Transfers to Minors Act."

(6) A certificate of title issued by a department or agency of a state or of the United States which evidences title to tangible personal property is either:

(A) Issued in the name of the transferor, an adult other than the transferor, or a trust company, followed in substance by the words:

"as custodian for ______________________
(Name of Minor)
under the California Uniform Transfers to Minors Act."

(B) Delivered to an adult other than the transferor or to a trust company, endorsed to that person followed in substance by the words:

"as custodian for ______________________
(Name of Minor)
under the California Uniform Transfers to Minors Act."

(7) An interest in any property not described in paragraphs (1) through (6) is transferred to an adult other than the transferor or to a trust company by a written instrument in substantially the form set forth in subdivision (b).

(b) An instrument in the following form satisfies the requirements of subparagraph (B) of paragraph (1) and paragraph (7) of subdivision (a):

"TRANSFER UNDER THE CALIFORNIA UNIFORM TRANSFERS TO MINORS ACT

I, ______________________________________
(Name of Transferor or Name and Representative Capacity if a Fiduciary)
hereby transfer to ______________________,
(Name of Custodian)
as custodian for ______________________
(Name of Minor)
under the California Uniform Transfers to Minors Act, the following:
(insert a description of the custodial property sufficient to identify it).

Dated: ______________

____
(Signature)

______________ acknowledges receipt of the
(Name of Custodian)
property described above as custodian for the minor named above under the California Uniform Transfers to Minors Act.

Dated: ______________

______________________________"
(Signature of Custodian)

(c) A transferor shall place the custodian in control of the custodial property as soon as practicable. *(Stats.1990, c. 79 (A.B.759), § 14, operative July 1, 1991. Amended by Stats. 1991, c. 1055 (S.B.271), § 17.)*

Law Revision Commission Comments

1990 Enactment

Section 3909 continues Section 3909 of the repealed Probate Code without change. It is the same in substance as Section 9 of the Uniform Transfers to Minors Act (1986).

Subdivision (a) describes how the property is to be transferred and persons eligible to serve as custodian:

Paragraph (1) of subdivision (a) permits a transfer of securities in registered form to be accomplished without registering the transfer in the name of the custodian. This permits securities to be held by custodians in street names. Although the transferor may serve as the custodian when the security is registered in the name of the custodian under subparagraph (A) of paragraph (1), the transferor may not serve as a custodian if the security is transferred in the manner provided in subparagraph (B) of paragraph (1).

Paragraph (3) of subdivision (a) covers the irrevocable transfer of ownership of life and endowment insurance policies and annuity contracts. It provides for registration with the issuer in the name of the custodian (in which case the transferor is eligible to serve as custodian) or for an assignment in writing delivered to the custodian (in which case the transferor is not eligible to serve as custodian).

Paragraph (4) of subdivision (a) covers the irrevocable exercise of a power of appointment and the irrevocable present assignment of future payments rights (such as royalties, interest and principal payments under a promissory note, or beneficial interests under life or endowment or annuity insurance contracts or benefit plans). The payor, issuer, or obligor may require additional formalities such as completion of a specific assignment form and an endorsement, but the transfer is effective upon delivery of the notification to the payor, issuer, or other obligor that the right is transferred to the custodian. Compare Section 3903 and the Comment thereto for the procedure for revocably "nominating" a future custodian as a beneficiary of a power of appointment or such payment rights.

Paragraph (5) of subdivision (a) provides the exclusive method for the transfer of real property, including a disposition made by a will. The transfer of an interest in real property must be recorded in the name of the custodian in order that the transfer be an effective transfer.

Paragraph (6) of subdivision (a) covers the transfer of tangible personal property (such as automobiles and aircraft) subject to registration of ownership with a state or federal agency. Either registration of the transfer in the name of the custodian (in which case the transferor is eligible to serve as custodian) or delivery of the endorsed certificate in registerable form (in which case the transferor is not eligible to serve as custodian) makes the transfer effective.

Paragraph (7) of subdivision (a) is a residual classification, covering all property not otherwise covered in the preceding paragraphs. Examples would include partnership interests and tangible personal property not subject to title certificates. The transferor is not eligible to be a custodian of property transferred under paragraph (7).

Execution of the acceptance by the custodian on the form of transfer document set forth in subdivision (b) is sufficient to satisfy the requirements of subparagraph (B) of paragraph (1) and paragraph (7) of subdivision (a). While such a form of written acceptance is not specifically required in the case of registered securities under subdivision (a)(1), money under subdivision (a)(2), insurance contracts or interests under subdivision (a)(3) or (4), real estate under subdivision (a)(5), or titled personal property under subdivision (a)(6), it is certainly the better and recommended practice to obtain the acknowledgment, consent, and acceptance of the designated custodian on the instrument of transfer or otherwise.

Failure of the transferor to comply with subdivision (c) does not affect the validity of a transfer. See Section 3911(a).

1991 Amendment

Subdivision (a)(2) of Section 3909 is amended to make a technical revision to fill a gap in the statute. The amendment covers the situation where a security held in the name of a broker, financial institution, or its nominee is to be transferred to a broker or financial institution for credit to an account in the name of the transferor, an adult other than the transferor, or a trust company, as custodian for a designated minor. [20 Cal.L.Rev.Comm.Reports 2907 (1990)].

Background on Section 3909 of Repealed Code

Section 3909 was added by 1984 Cal.Stat. ch. 243 § 9 and was amended by 1989 Cal.Stat. ch. 544 § 3. Section 3909 provided more detailed rules than former Civil Code Section 1156 (repealed by 1984 Cal.Stat. ch. 243 § 1) concerning the manner of creating custodial property and effecting the transfer. The 1989 amendment revised the former reference in the introductory clause of subdivision (b) to refer to "subparagraph (B)" rather than "subparagraph (A)"; this corrected an obvious error and made the provision conform to the Uniform Transfers to Minors Act (1986). See also Communication from the California Law Revision Commission Concerning Assembly Bill 158, 20 Cal.L.Revision Comm'n Reports 235 (1990). For background on the provisions of this part, see the Comment to this part under the part heading.

Subdivision (a) of Section 3909 superseded subdivision (a) of former Civil Code Section 1156. Paragraph (1) of subdivision (a) continued the substance of paragraphs (1) and (2) of subdivision (a) of former Section 1156 relating to securities and also permitted a transfer of securities in registered form to be accomplished without registering the transfer in the name of the custodian. Paragraph (2) of subdivision (a) continued the substance of paragraph (3) of subdivision (a) of former Civil Code Section 1156 relating to money credited to a custodial account. Paragraph (3) of subdivision (a) superseded paragraph (4) of subdivision (a) of former Civil Code Section 1156. Paragraph (4) of subdivision (a) was a new provision. Paragraph (5) of subdivision (a) changed the former law which required that the transfer be made "by executing and delivering in the appropriate manner a deed, assignment, or similar instrument" to the custodian. Former Civil Code § 1156(a)(5). Paragraph (6) of subdivision (a) was a new provision. Paragraph (7) of subdivision (a) was comparable to paragraph (6) of subdivision (a) of former Civil Code Section 1156; but, unlike the former California law, the transferor was not eligible to be a custodian of property transferred under paragraph (7) of subdivision (a) of Section 3909.

Former California law did not provide for the form for a transfer document such as is provided in subdivision (b) of Section 3909 except for the gift of a security not in registered form under former Civil Code Section 1156(a)(2). [20 Cal.L.Rev.Comm.Reports 1001 (1990)].

Research References

Forms

California Transactions Forms--Estate Planning § 6:18, Custodian Under Uniform Transfers to Minors Act.

California Transactions Forms--Estate Planning § 6:78, Devise to Custodian for Child Who is Minor at Testator's Death Under California Uniform Transfers to Minors Act.

California Transactions Forms--Estate Planning § 7:39, California Uniform Transfers to Minors Act.

California Transactions Forms--Estate Planning § 7:40, Form Drafting Principles.

California Transactions Forms--Estate Planning § 7:42, Matters to Consider When Making Transfer Under California Uniform Transfers to Minors Act.

California Transactions Forms--Estate Planning § 7:44, Transfer Of Certificated or Uncertificated Securities or Tangible Personal Property Not Subject to Title Certification to Custodian for Minor.

West's California Code Forms, Probate § 3909 Form 1, Creation Of Custodial Property.

Treatises and Practice Aids

Witkin, California Summary 10th Personal Property § 141, Nature and Scope Of Act.

Witkin, California Summary 10th Personal Property § 142, in General.

Witkin, California Summary 10th Personal Property § 143, Selection, Removal, and Successor.

Witkin, California Summary 10th Personal Property § 144, Who May Make Transfer.

Witkin, California Summary 10th Personal Property § 145, Manner Of Making Transfer.

§ 3910. Single custodianship

A transfer may be made only for one minor, and only one person may be the custodian. All custodial property held under this part by the same custodian for the benefit of the same minor constitutes a single custodianship. *(Stats.1990, c. 79 (A.B.759), § 14, operative July 1, 1991.)*

Law Revision Commission Comments

1990 Enactment

Section 3910 continues Section 3910 of the repealed Probate Code without change. This section is the same in substance as Section 10 of the Uniform Transfers to Minors Act (1986).

Under Section 3910, additional transfers at different times and from different sources may be made to an existing custodian for the minor and do not create multiple custodianships. For the purpose of consolidating assets in a single custodianship, an existing custodian may be named as successor custodian by another custodian for the same minor who resigns under Section 3918. Note, however, that these results are limited to transfers made "under this part." Gifts previously made under the California Uniform Gifts to Minors Act or under the Uniform Gifts to Minors Act or Uniform Transfers to Minors Act of another state must be treated as separate custodianships, even though the same custodian and minor are involved, because of possible differences in the age of distribution and custodian's powers under those other Acts. But see Section 3923 (transfers made before January 1, 1985).

Even when all transfers to a single custodian are made "under this part" and a single custodianship results, custodial property transferred under Sections 3906 and 3907 or under Section 3412, 3413, 3602, or 3611 may have to be accounted for separately from property transferred under or pursuant to Section 3903, 3904, or 3905 because the custodianship may terminate sooner with respect to the former property. See Sections 3920 and 3920.5 and the Comments thereto.

Background on Section 3910 of Repealed Code

Section 3910 was added by 1984 Cal.Stat. ch. 243 § 9. The first sentence of Section 3910 continued subdivision (b) of former Civil Code Section 1156 (repealed by 1984 Cal.Stat. ch. 243 § 1). The second sentence of Section 3910 stated what was implicit in the former law. See Report of Senate Committee on Judiciary on Assembly Bill 2942, 18 Cal.L.Revision Comm'n Reports 105, 110 (1986). For background on the provisions of this part, see the Comment to this part under the part heading. [20 Cal.L.Rev.Comm.Reports 1001 (1990)].

Research References

Forms

California Transactions Forms--Estate Planning § 6:18, Custodian Under Uniform Transfers to Minors Act.

West's California Code Forms, Probate § 3909 Form 1, Creation Of Custodial Property.

Treatises and Practice Aids

Witkin, California Summary 10th Personal Property § 142, in General.

§ 3911. Validity and effect of transfer

(a) The validity of a transfer made in a manner prescribed in this part is not affected by any of the following:

(1) Failure of the transferor to comply with subdivision (c) of Section 3909.

(2) Designation of an ineligible custodian, except designation of the transferor in the case of property for which the transferor is ineligible to serve as custodian under subdivision (a) of Section 3909.

(3) Death or incapacity of a person nominated under Section 3903 or designated under Section 3909 as custodian, or the disclaimer of the office by that person.

(b) A transfer made pursuant to Section 3909 is irrevocable, and the custodial property is indefeasibly vested in the minor, but the custodian has all the rights, powers, duties, and authority provided in this part, and neither the minor nor the minor's legal representative has any right, power, duty, or authority with respect to the custodial property except as provided in this part.

(c) By making a transfer, the transferor incorporates in the disposition all the provisions of this part and grants to the custodian, and to any third person dealing with a person designated as custodian, the respective powers, rights, and immunities provided in this part.

(d) A person is not precluded from being a custodian for a minor under this part with respect to some property because the person is a conservator of the minor with respect to other property.

(e) A person who is the conservator of the minor is not precluded from being a custodian for a minor under this part because the custodial property has or will be transferred to the custodian from the guardianship estate of the minor. In such case, for the purposes of Section 3909, the custodian shall be deemed to be "an adult other than the transferor."

(f) In the cases described in subdivisions (d) and (e), with respect to the property transferred to the custodian, this part applies to the extent it would apply if the person to whom the custodial property is transferred were not and had not been a conservator of the minor. *(Stats.1990, c. 79 (A.B.759), § 14, operative July 1, 1991.)*

Law Revision Commission Comments

1990 Enactment

Section 3911 continues Section 3911 of the repealed Probate Code without change. Subdivisions (a), (b), and (c) are the same as Section 11 of the Uniform Transfers to Minors Act (1986). The transferor's designation of himself or herself as custodian of property for which the transferor is not eligible to serve as custodian under subdivision (a) of Section 3909 makes the transfer ineffective. See the Comment to Section 3909. For a list of the immunities enjoyed by third persons under subdivision (c), see Section 3916 and the Comment thereto.

Subdivisions (d), (e), and (f) are not included in the Uniform Transfers to Minors Act. These subdivisions are included in Section 3911 to make clear that (1) a person serving as guardian of the estate of the minor may also serve as custodian under this part and in this case the custodial property does not become a part of the guardianship estate and (2) property may be transferred from a guardianship estate to the person who serves as guardian to be held by that person as custodian under this part and in such case the property is no longer a part of the guardianship estate but instead is governed solely by this part.

Background on Section 3911 of Repealed Code

Section 3911 was added by 1984 Cal.Stat. ch. 243 § 9. Subdivision (a) of Section 3911 generally continued the substance of the last portion of subdivision (c) of former Civil Code Section 1156 (repealed by 1984 Cal.Stat. ch. 243 § 1). The balance of Section 3911 generally continued former Civil Code Section 1157 (repealed by 1984 Cal.Stat. ch. 243 § 1) with a number of necessary, and perhaps significant, changes required by the new kinds of property subject to custodianship. Former Civil Code Section 1157 provided that a transfer made in accordance with its terms "conveys to the minor indefeasibly vested legal title to the custodial property." Because equitable interests in property may be the subject of a transfer under this Act, the reference to "legal title" was deleted, but no change concerning the effect or finality of the transfer was intended. However, subdivision (b) of Section 3911 qualified the rights of the minor in the property by making them subject to "the rights, powers, duties, and authority" of the custodian under this part, a concept that may have been implicit and intended in former Civil Code Section 1157, but was not expressed. For background on the provisions of this part, see the Comment to this part under the part heading. [20 Cal.L.Rev.Comm.Reports 1001 (1990)].

Research References

Forms

California Transactions Forms--Estate Planning § 7:39, California Uniform Transfers to Minors Act.

California Transactions Forms--Estate Planning § 7:42, Matters to Consider When Making Transfer Under California Uniform Transfers to Minors Act.

Treatises and Practice Aids

Witkin, California Summary 10th Personal Property § 140, Transfers to Minors Act.

Witkin, California Summary 10th Personal Property § 142, in General.

Witkin, California Summary 10th Personal Property § 146, Effect Of Transfer.

§ 3912. Duties of custodians; standard of care; records

(a) A custodian shall do all of the following:

(1) Take control of custodial property.

(2) Register or record title to custodial property if appropriate.

(3) Collect, hold, manage, invest, and reinvest custodial property.

(b) In dealing with custodial property, a custodian shall observe the standard of care that would be observed by a prudent person dealing with property of another and is not limited by any other statute restricting investments by fiduciaries except that:

(1) If a custodian is not compensated for his or her services, the custodian is not liable for losses to custodial property unless they result from the custodian's bad faith,

intentional wrongdoing, or gross negligence, or from the custodian's failure to maintain the standard of prudence in investing the custodial property provided in this section.

(2) A custodian, in the custodian's discretion and without liability to the minor or the minor's estate, may retain any custodial property received from a transferor.

(c) A custodian may invest in or pay premiums on life insurance or endowment policies on (1) the life of the minor only if the minor or the minor's estate is the sole beneficiary or (2) the life of another person in whom the minor has an insurable interest only to the extent that the minor, the minor's estate, or the custodian in the capacity of custodian, is the irrevocable beneficiary.

(d) A custodian at all times shall keep custodial property separate and distinct from all other property in a manner sufficient to identify it clearly as custodial property of the minor. Custodial property consisting of an undivided interest is so identified if the minor's interest is held as a tenant in common and is fixed. Custodial property subject to recordation is so identified if it is recorded, and custodial property subject to registration is so identified if it is either registered, or held in an account designated, in the name of the custodian, followed in substance by the words:

"as a custodian for ______________________
(Name of Minor)

under the California Uniform Transfers to Minors Act."

(e) A custodian shall keep records of all transactions with respect to custodial property, including information necessary for the preparation of the minor's tax returns, and shall make them available for inspection at reasonable intervals by a parent or legal representative of the minor or by the minor if the minor has attained the age of 14 years. *(Stats.1990, c. 79 (A.B.759), § 14, operative July 1, 1991.)*

Law Revision Commission Comments

1990 Enactment

Section 3912 continues Section 3912 of the repealed Probate Code without change. This section is the same in substance as Section 12 of the Uniform Transfers to Minors Act (1986) except as indicated below.

Subdivision (b) does not include the provision of the Uniform Transfers to Minors Act which specifically provides a slightly higher standard for professional fiduciaries. However, in determining what constitutes "the standard of care that would be observed by a prudent person dealing with the property of another" under subdivision (b), a professional custodian (such as a trust company or the trust department of a bank) is held to a greater standard of care based on its presumed expertise than a lay custodian. Cf. Estate of Beach, 15 Cal.3d 623, 542 P.2d 994, 125 Cal.Rptr. 570 (1975) (executor). See also the Comments to Sections 2401 (guardian or conservator) and 16040 (trustee).

No provision comparable to subdivision (b)(1) is found in the Uniform Transfers to Minors Act. This provision is included because it is likely to reflect the desires of the transferor who makes a transfer to a custodian who serves without compensation.

Subdivision (d) includes a provision of the Uniform Transfers to Minors Act requiring that custodial property consisting of an undivided interest be held as a tenant in common. This provision permits the custodian to invest custodial property in common trust funds, mutual funds, or in a proportional interest in a "jumbo" certificate of deposit. Investment in property held in joint tenancy with right of survivorship is not permitted, but this does not preclude a transfer of such an interest to a custodian, and the custodian is authorized under subdivision (b) to retain a joint tenancy interest so received.

Subdivision (e) includes the requirement of the Uniform Transfers to Minors Act that income tax information be maintained and made available for preparation of the minor's tax returns. Because the custodianship is not a separate legal entity or taxpayer, the minor's tax identification number should be used to identify all custodial property accounts.

Background on Section 3912 of Repealed Code

Section 3912 was added by 1984 Cal.Stat. ch. 243 § 9. For background on the provisions of this part, see the Comment to this part under the part heading. See also Report of Senate Committee on Judiciary on Assembly Bill 2492, 18 Cal.L.Revision Comm'n Reports 105, 110–11 (1986).

Subdivision (a) expanded subdivision (a) of former Civil Code Section 1158 (repealed by 1984 Cal.Stat. ch. 243 § 1) to include the duties to take control and appropriately register or record custodial property in the name of the custodian.

Subdivision (b) restated and made somewhat stricter the prudent man fiduciary standard for the custodian, since Section 3912 cast the standard in terms of a prudent person "dealing with property of another" rather than one "who is seeking a reasonable income and preservation of his capital," as under subdivision (e) of former Civil Code Section 1158. Subdivision (b)(1) of Section 3912 continued subdivision (e) of former Civil Code Section 1159 (repealed by 1984 Cal.Stat. ch. 243 § 1)—a special immunity from liability for the custodian for losses to custodial property where the custodian is not compensated.

Subdivision (e) of former Civil Code Section 1158 permitted a custodian to retain any security received, without the obligation to diversify investment. Subdivision (b)(2) of Section 3912 extended that rule to any property received.

Subdivision (c) of Section 3912 was a new provision.

Subdivision (d) generally continued subdivision (g) of former Civil Code Section 1158, but added the provision requiring that custodial property consisting of an undivided interest be held as a tenant in common.

Subdivision (e) continued subdivision (h) of former Civil Code Section 1158, but added the requirement that income tax information be maintained and made available for preparation of the minor's tax returns. [20 Cal.L.Rev.Comm.Reports 1001 (1990)].

Research References

Forms

California Transactions Forms--Estate Planning § 1:29, Options Involving Gifts to Minors.

California Transactions Forms--Estate Planning § 6:18, Custodian Under Uniform Transfers to Minors Act.

California Transactions Forms--Estate Planning § 6:78, Devise to Custodian for Child Who is Minor at Testator's Death Under California Uniform Transfers to Minors Act.

California Transactions Forms--Estate Planning § 7:39, California Uniform Transfers to Minors Act.

Treatises and Practice Aids

Witkin, California Summary 10th Personal Property § 147, Duties and Compensation Of Custodian.

Witkin, California Summary 10th Personal Property § 148, Powers Of Custodian.

§ 3913. Rights, powers, and authority of custodians over custodial property; liability

(a) A custodian, acting in a custodial capacity, has all the rights, powers, and authority over custodial property that unmarried adult owners have over their own property, but a custodian may exercise those rights, powers, and authority in that capacity only.

(b) This section does not relieve a custodian from liability for breach of Section 3912. *(Stats.1990, c. 79 (A.B.759), § 14, operative July 1, 1991.)*

Law Revision Commission Comments

1990 Enactment

Section 3913 continues Section 3913 of the repealed Probate Code without change. This section is the same in substance as Section 13 of the Uniform Transfers to Minors Act (1986).

Subdivision (a) replaces the specific list of custodian's powers contained in the former Uniform Gifts to Minors Act. The Uniform Law Commissioners decided not to expand that list to try to deal with all forms of property now covered by the Uniform Transfers to Minors Act and not to specify all powers that might be appropriate for each kind of property, nor to refer to an existing body of state law, such as a statutory provision stating powers of a trustee, since such powers would not be uniform. Instead, this provision grants the custodian the very broad and general powers of an unmarried adult owner of the property, subject to the prudent person rule and to the duties of segregation and record keeping specified in Section 3912. (See subdivision (b) of Section 3913). This approach permits the Uniform Transfers to Minors Act to be self-contained and more readily understandable by volunteer, non-professional fiduciaries, who most often serve as custodians. It is intended that the authority granted includes the powers most often suggested for custodians, such as the power to borrow, whether at interest or interest free, the power to invest in common trust funds, and the power to enter contracts that extend beyond the termination of the custodianship.

Subdivision (a) further specifies that the custodian's power or incidents of ownership in custodial property such as insurance policies may be exercised only in the capacity as custodian. This provision is intended to prevent the exercise of those powers for the direct or indirect benefit of the custodian, so as to avoid as nearly as possible the result that a custodian who dies while holding an insurance policy on his or her own life for the benefit of a minor will have the policy taxed in his estate. See I.R.C. § 2042. But compare Terriberry v. United States, 517 F.2d 286 (5th Cir.1975) cert. denied, 424 U.S. 977 (1976); Rose v. United States, 511 F.2d 259 (5th Cir.1975).

Background on Section 3913 of Repealed Code

Section 3913 was added by 1984 Cal.Stat. ch. 243 § 9. Subdivision (a) replaced the specific list of custodian's powers contained in subdivisions (f), (i), and (j) of former Civil Code Section 1158 (repealed by 1984 Cal.Stat. ch. 243 § 1). For background on the provisions of this part, see the Comment to this part under the part heading. [20 Cal.L.Rev.Comm.Reports 1001 (1990)].

Research References

Forms

California Transactions Forms--Estate Planning § 1:29, Options Involving Gifts to Minors.

California Transactions Forms--Estate Planning § 6:18, Custodian Under Uniform Transfers to Minors Act.

California Transactions Forms--Estate Planning § 7:39, California Uniform Transfers to Minors Act.

Treatises and Practice Aids

Witkin, California Summary 10th Personal Property § 148, Powers Of Custodian.

§ 3914. Use of custodial property

(a) A custodian may deliver or pay to the minor or expend for the minor's benefit as much of the custodial property as the custodian considers advisable for the use and benefit of the minor, without court order and without regard to (1) the duty or ability of the custodian personally, or of any other person, to support the minor or (2) any other income or property of the minor which may be applicable or available for that purpose.

(b) On petition of an interested person or the minor if the minor has attained the age of 14 years, the court may order the custodian to deliver or pay to the minor or expend for the minor's benefit so much of the custodial property as the court considers advisable for the use and benefit of the minor.

(c) A delivery, payment, or expenditure under this section is in addition to, not in substitution for, and does not affect, any obligation of a person to support the minor.

(d) In lieu of the powers and duties described in subdivision (a), a transferor who is also the custodian may elect to govern his or her custodial powers and duties under this subdivision. If such election is made, the custodian shall not pay over to the minor for expenditure by the minor, and shall not expend for the minor's use or benefit, any part of the custodial property for any purpose prior to the time specified in Section 3920, except by order of the court upon a showing that the expenditure is necessary for the support, maintenance, or education of the minor. When the powers and duties of the custodian are governed by this subdivision, the transferor-custodian shall file with the clerk of the court a declaration in substantially the following form:

Declaration Under the California Uniform Transfers to Minors Act

I, ______________________________,
(Name of Transferor-Custodian)

as custodian for ______________________
(Name of Minor)

under the California Uniform Transfers to Minors Act, hereby irrevocably elect to be governed under subdivision (d) of Section 3914 of the Probate Code in my custodial capacity over the following described property

____

______________________________________.
(Description of Custodial Property)

I declare under penalty of perjury that the foregoing is true and correct.

Dated: _______________, 19___

____
(Signature of Transferor-Custodian)

(Stats.1990, c. 79 (A.B.759), § 14, operative July 1, 1991.)

Law Revision Commission Comments

1990 Enactment

Section 3914 continues Section 3914 of the repealed Probate Code without change. Subdivisions (a), (b), and (c) are the same as Section 14 of the Uniform Transfers to Minors Act (1986). Subdivision (d) is not included in the Uniform Act.

The "use and benefit" standard in subdivisions (a) and (b) is intended to avoid the implication that the custodial property can be used only for the required support of the minor. The "use and benefit" standard permits, for example, payment of the minor's legally enforceable obligations such as tax or child support obligations or tort claims. Custodial property can be reached by levy of a judgment creditor in any event, so there is no reason not to permit custodian or court-ordered expenditures for enforceable claims.

An "interested person" authorized to file a petition under subdivision (b) includes not only the parent or conservator or guardian of the minor and a transferor or a transferor's legal representative, but also a public agency or official with custody of the minor and a third party to whom the minor owes legally enforceable debts.

The Internal Revenue Service has taken the position that the income from custodial property, to the extent it is used for the support of the minor-donee, is includable in the gross income of any person who is legally obligated to support the minor-donee, whether or not that person or parent is serving as the custodian. Rev.Rul. 56–484, 1956–2 C.B. 23; Rev.Rul. 59–357, 1959–2 C.B. 212. However, Treasury Regulation § 1.662(a)–4 (1980) provides that the term "legal obligation" includes a legal obligation to support another person if, and only if, the obligation is not affected by the adequacy of the dependent's own resources. Thus, if under local law a parent may use the resources of a child for the child's support in lieu of supporting the child himself or herself, no obligation of support exists, whether or not income is actually used for support, at least if the child's resources are adequate. See 3 B. Bittker, Federal Taxation of Income, Estates and Gifts § 80.4.4 (1981). For this reason, subdivision (c) specifies that distributions or expenditures may be made for the minor without regard to the duty or ability of any other person to support the minor and that distributions or expenditures are not in substitution for, and shall not affect, the obligation of any person to support the minor.

Subdivision (d) of Section 3914 is a provision not found in the Uniform Transfers to Minors Act. This provision permits a transferor who is also a custodian to elect to eliminate the authority of the custodian to distribute property for the minor's use or benefit except pursuant to a court order. The section was added to the California statute in an effort to solve the tax problems that may arise when the transferor makes a transfer to a minor under the Act and designates himself or herself as custodian. For a discussion of the provision, see Review of Selected 1965 Code Legislation 52–53 (Cal.Cont.Ed.Bar 1965).

Background on Section 3914 of Repealed Code

Section 3914 was added by 1984 Cal.Stat. ch. 243 § 9. For background on the provisions of this part, see the Comment to this part under the part heading.

Subdivisions (a) and (b) continued subdivisions (b) and (c) of former Civil Code Section 1158 (repealed by 1984 Cal.Stat. ch. 243 § 1), with two changes. The standard for expenditure of custodial property was revised to substitute "for the use and benefit of the minor" for the language "for the support, maintenance, education, and benefit of the minor" used in former Section 1158. Subdivision (b) expanded the authority to file a petition under former Civil Code Section 1158 to permit a petition to be filed by "an interested person."

Subdivision (c) was a new provision. Subdivision (d) continued the substance of former Civil Code Section 1158.5 (repealed by 1984 Cal.Stat. ch. 243 § 1). [20 Cal.L.Rev.Comm.Reports 1001 (1990)].

Research References

Forms

California Transactions Forms--Estate Planning § 1:29, Options Involving Gifts to Minors.

California Transactions Forms--Estate Planning § 6:18, Custodian Under Uniform Transfers to Minors Act.

California Transactions Forms--Estate Planning § 6:78, Devise to Custodian for Child Who is Minor at Testator's Death Under California Uniform Transfers to Minors Act.

California Transactions Forms--Estate Planning § 7:47, Transferor-Custodian's Declaration Of Election that Court Order be Required for Payment to or Expenditure for Minor.

West's California Code Forms, Probate § 3914 Form 1, Petition for Order Directing Custodian to Deliver Custodial Property to Minor.

West's California Code Forms, Probate § 3914 Form 2, Declaration Under the California Uniform Transfers to Minors Act.

Treatises and Practice Aids

Witkin, California Summary 10th Personal Property § 140, Transfers to Minors Act.

Witkin, California Summary 10th Personal Property § 148, Powers Of Custodian.

§ 3915. Custodian's expenses, compensation and bond

(a) A custodian is entitled to reimbursement from custodial property for reasonable expenses incurred in the performance of the custodian's duties.

(b) Except for one who is a transferor under Section 3904, a custodian has a noncumulative election during each calendar year to charge reasonable compensation for services performed during that year.

(c) Except as provided in subdivision (f) of Section 3918, a custodian need not give a bond. *(Stats.1990, c. 79 (A.B.759), § 14, operative July 1, 1991.)*

Law Revision Commission Comments

1990 Enactment

Section 3915 continues Section 3915 of the repealed Probate Code without change. This section is the same as Section 15 of the Uniform Transfers to Minors Act (1986). Compensation may be determined by agreement, by a provision in a will (see Section 6345), by reference to a statute, or by a court order. To prevent abuse, the provision for permissive compensation is denied to a custodian who is also the donor of the custodial property.

The custodian's election to charge compensation must be exercised (although the compensation need not be actually paid) at least annually or it lapses and may not be exercised later. This provision is intended to avoid imputed income to the custodian who waives compensation, and also to avoid the accumulation of a large unanticipated claim for compensation exercisable at termination of the custodianship.

Background on Section 3915 of Repealed Code

Section 3915 was added by 1984 Cal.Stat. ch. 243 § 9. Section 3915 superseded former Civil Code Section 1159 (repealed by 1984 Cal.Stat. ch. 243 § 1). For background on the provisions of this part, see the Comment to this part under the part heading.

Section 3915 did not continue the statement in the former section that a custodian may act without compensation for services, since that concept is implied in the provision in Section 3915 that a custodian has an "election" to be compensated.

Section 3915 omits as surplusage the standard contained in subdivision (c) of former Civil Code Section 1159 for determining "reasonable compensation" which included, "in the order stated," a direction by the donor, statutes governing compensation of custodians or guardians, or court order. This was an optional provision of the Uniform Gifts to Minors Act (1966) and was not continued in the Uniform Transfers to Minors Act (1986). While compensation of custodians became a more likely occurrence and a more important issue under the Uniform Transfers to Minors Act because property requiring increased management may be subject to custodianship under the Act, compensation can still be determined by agreement, by a provision in a will (see Section 6345), by reference to a statute or by court order, without the need to so state in the Uniform Transfers to Minors Act. [20 Cal.L.Rev.Comm.Reports 1001 (1990)].

Research References

Forms

California Transactions Forms--Estate Planning § 1:29, Options Involving Gifts to Minors.

California Transactions Forms--Estate Planning § 6:18, Custodian Under Uniform Transfers to Minors Act.

California Transactions Forms--Estate Planning § 7:40, Form Drafting Principles.

California Transactions Forms--Estate Planning § 7:42, Matters to Consider When Making Transfer Under California Uniform Transfers to Minors Act.

Treatises and Practice Aids

Witkin, California Summary 10th Personal Property § 142, in General.

Witkin, California Summary 10th Personal Property § 147, Duties and Compensation Of Custodian.

§ 3916. Exemption of third person from liability

A third person in good faith and without court order may act on the instructions of, or otherwise deal with, any person purporting to make a transfer or purporting to act in the capacity of a custodian and, in the absence of knowledge, is not responsible for determining any of the following:

(a) The validity of the purported custodian's designation.

(b) The propriety of, or the authority under this part for, any act of the purported custodian.

(c) The validity or propriety under this part of any instrument or instructions executed or given either by the person purporting to make a transfer or by the purported custodian.

(d) The propriety of the application of any property of the minor delivered to the purported custodian. *(Stats.1990, c. 79 (A.B.759), § 14, operative July 1, 1991.)*

Law Revision Commission Comments

1990 Enactment

Section 3916 continues Section 3916 of the repealed Probate Code without change. This section is the same as Section 16 of the Uniform Transfers to Minors Act (1986).

Because Section 3916 refers to any custodian, and "custodian" is defined to include successor custodians (subdivision (g) of Section 3901), a successor custodian appointed by the minor is included among those upon whom third persons may rely. Similarly, because Section 3916 protects any "third person," it is not necessary to specify in Section 3916 or in subdivision (c) of Section 3911 that the protection extends to any "issuer, transfer agent, bank, life insurance company, broker, or other person or financial institution," as did former Civil Code Section 1160. See the definition of "person" in Section 3901(*l*).

Section 3916 does not alter the requirements for bona fide purchaser or holder in due course status under other law for persons who acquire from a custodial property subject to recordation or registration.

Background on Section 3916 of Repealed Code

Section 3916 was added by 1984 Cal.Stat. ch. 243 § 9. For background on the provisions of this part, see the Comment to this part under the part heading.

Section 3916 carried forward, but shortened and simplified, former Civil Code Section 1160 (repealed by 1984 Cal.Stat. ch. 243 § 1), with no substantive change intended. The former section permitted a 14–year old minor to appoint a successor custodian and specifically provided that third parties were entitled to rely on the appointment. Because Section 3916 referred to any custodian, and "custodian" was defined to include successor custodians (subdivision (g) of Section 3901), a successor custodian appointed by the minor was included among those upon whom third parties may rely.

Section 3916 excluded from its protection persons with "knowledge" of the irregularity of a transaction, a concept not expressed but probably implied in former Civil Code Section 1160. See, e.g., State ex rel. Paden v. Carrel, 597 S.W.2d 167 (Mo.App.1980), disapproving the pledge of custodial property to secure a personal loan to the custodian. [20 Cal.L.Rev.Comm.Reports 1001 (1990)].

Research References

Treatises and Practice Aids

Witkin, California Summary 10th Personal Property § 148, Powers Of Custodian.

§ 3917. Liability to third persons

(a) A claim based on (1) a contract entered into by a custodian acting in a custodial capacity, (2) an obligation arising from the ownership or control of custodial property, or (3) a tort committed during the custodianship, may be asserted against the custodial property by proceeding against the custodian in the custodial capacity, whether or not the custodian or the minor is personally liable therefor.

(b) A custodian is not personally liable for either of the following:

(1) On a contract properly entered into in the custodial capacity unless the custodian fails to reveal that capacity and to identify the custodianship in the contract.

(2) For an obligation arising from control of custodial property or for a tort committed during the custodianship unless the custodian is personally at fault.

(c) A minor is not personally liable for an obligation arising from ownership of custodial property or for a tort committed during the custodianship unless the minor is personally at fault. *(Stats.1990, c. 79 (A.B.759), § 14, operative July 1, 1991.)*

Law Revision Commission Comments

1990 Enactment

Section 3917 continues Section 3917 of the repealed Probate Code without change. This section is the same as Section 17 of the Uniform Transfers to Minors Act (1986) and is based upon Section 5–428 of the Uniform Probate Code (1987), relating to limitations on the liability of conservators.

Some forms of custodial property can give rise to liabilities as well as benefits (e.g., general partnership interests, interests in real estate or business proprietorships, automobiles, etc.). Section 3917 is included to protect the minor and other assets the minor might have or acquire from such liabilities, since the minor is unable to disclaim a transfer to a custodian for the minor's benefit. Similar protection for the custodian is necessary so as not to discourage nonprofessional or uncompensated persons from accepting the office. Therefore, this section generally limits the claims of third parties to recourse against the custodial property, as third parties dealing with a trust are generally limited to recourse against the trust corpus.

The custodian incurs personal liability only as provided in subdivision (b) for actual fault or for failure to disclose the custodial capacity "in the contract" when contracting with third parties. In oral contracts, oral disclosure of the custodial capacity is sufficient.

The minor, on the other hand, incurs personal liability under subdivision (c) only for actual fault.

When custodial property is subjected to claims of third parties under this section, the minor or the minor's legal representative, if not a party to the action by which the claim is successfully established, may seek to recover the loss from the custodian in a separate action. See Section 3919 and the Comment thereto.

Background on Section 3917 of Repealed Code

Section 3917 was a new provision added by 1984 Cal.Stat. ch. 243 § 9. For background on the provisions of this part, see the Comment to this part under the part heading. Section 3917 appears to have been consistent with prior California law concerning the tort liability of a guardian. See Campbell v. Bradbury, 179 Cal. 364, 176 P. 685 (1918). But the provision may have restricted the liability under prior law of the custodian who makes a contract in the custodial capacity. See Hall v. Jameson, 151 Cal. 606, 91 P. 518 (1907) (trustee personally liable on contract unless contract stipulates trustee not liable). But see Prob. Code § 18000 (unless contract otherwise provides, trustee not personally liable on contract properly entered into in the trustee's fiduciary capacity in the course of administration of the trust unless the trustee fails to reveal the trustee's representative capacity or identify the trust in the contract). [20 Cal.L.Rev.Comm.Reports 1001 (1990)].

Research References

Forms

West's California Code Forms, Probate § 3919 Form 1, Petition for Accounting.

Treatises and Practice Aids

Witkin, California Summary 10th Personal Property § 149, Liability to Third Persons.

§ 3918. Substitute and successor custodians

(a) A person nominated under Section 3903 or designated under Section 3909 as custodian may decline to serve by delivering a valid disclaimer under Part 8 (commencing with Section 260) of Division 2 to the person who made the nomination or to the transferor or the transferor's legal representative. If the event giving rise to a transfer has not occurred and no substitute custodian able, willing, and eligible to serve was nominated under Section 3903, the person who made the nomination may nominate a substitute custodian under Section 3903; otherwise the transferor or the transferor's legal representative shall designate a substitute custodian at the time of the transfer, in either case from among the persons eligible to serve as custodian for that kind of property under subdivision (a) of Section 3909. The custodian so designated has the rights of a successor custodian.

(b) A custodian at any time may designate a trust company or an adult other than a transferor under Section 3904 as successor custodian by executing and dating an instrument of designation before a subscribing witness other than the successor. If the instrument of designation does not contain or is not accompanied by the resignation of the custodian, the designation of the successor does not take effect until the custodian resigns, dies, becomes incapacitated, or is removed. The transferor may designate one or more persons as successor custodians to serve, in the designated order of priority, in case the custodian originally designated or a prior successor custodian is unable, declines, or is ineligible to serve or resigns, dies, becomes incapacitated, or is removed. The designation either (1) shall be made in the same transaction and by the same document by which the transfer is made or (2) shall be made by executing and dating a separate instrument of designation before a subscribing witness other than a successor as a part of the same transaction and contemporaneously with the execution of the document by which the transfer is made. The designation is made by setting forth the successor custodian's name, followed in substance by the words: "is designated [first, second, etc., where applicable] successor custodian." A successor custodian designated by the transferor may be a trust company or an adult other than a transferor under Section 3904. A successor custodian effectively designated by the transferor has priority over a successor custodian designated by a custodian.

(c) A custodian may resign at any time by delivering written notice to the minor if the minor has attained the age of 14 years and to the successor custodian and by delivering the custodial property to the successor custodian.

(d) If the transferor has not effectively designated a successor custodian, and a custodian is ineligible, dies, or becomes incapacitated without having effectively designated a successor and the minor has attained the age of 14 years, the minor may designate as successor custodian, in the manner prescribed in subdivision (b), an adult member of the minor's family, a conservator of the minor, or a trust company. If the minor has not attained the age of 14 years or fails to act within 60 days after the ineligibility, death, or incapacity, the conservator of the minor becomes successor custodian. If the minor has no conservator or the conservator declines to act, the transferor, the legal representative of the transferor or of the custodian, an adult member of the minor's family, or any other interested person may petition the court to designate a successor custodian.

(e) A custodian who declines to serve under subdivision (a) or resigns under subdivision (c), or the legal representative of a deceased or incapacitated custodian, as soon as practicable, shall put the custodial property and records in the possession and control of the successor custodian. The successor custodian by action may enforce the obligation to deliver custodial property and records and becomes responsible for each item as received.

(f) A transferor, the legal representative of a transferor, an adult member of the minor's family, a guardian of the person of the minor, the conservator of the minor, or the minor if the minor has attained the age of 14 years, may petition the court to remove the custodian for cause and to designate a successor custodian other than a transferor under Section 3904 or to require the custodian to give appropriate bond.

(g) At least 15 days before the hearing on a petition under subdivision (d) or (f), the petitioner shall deliver notice * * * pursuant to Section 1215 to each of the following persons:

(1) The minor.

(2) The parent or parents of the minor.

(3) The transferor.

(h) Upon consideration of the petition under subdivision (d) or (f), the court may grant the relief that the court finds to be in the best interests of the minor. *(Stats.1990, c. 79 (A.B.759), § 14, operative July 1, 1991. Amended by Stats.*

1992, c. 871 (A.B.2975), § 7; Stats.2017, c. 319 (A.B.976), § 62, eff. Jan. 1, 2018.)

Law Revision Commission Comments

1990 Enactment

Section 3918 continues Section 3918 of the repealed Probate Code without change. This section is the same in substance as Section 18 of the Uniform Transfers to Minors Act (1986) with the addition of subdivision (g) and the addition of provisions authorizing the transferor to designate a successor custodian. See also Section 3901(d) ("conservator" includes a guardian).

Background on Section 3918 of Repealed Code

Section 3918 was added by 1984 Cal.Stat. ch. 243 § 9 and was amended by 1985 Cal.Stat. ch. 90 § 1 and 1988 Cal.Stat. ch. 1199 § 73.5. For background on the provisions of this part, see the Comment to this part under the part heading. Section 3918 tracked but condensed former Civil Code Section 1161 (repealed by 1984 Cal.Stat. ch. 243 § 1).

Enactment of the Uniform Transfers to Minors Act broadened the category of persons the initial custodian may designate as successor custodian from an adult member of the minor's family, the guardian of the minor, or a trust company to include any adult other than the donor. However, the minor's designation remained limited to an adult member of the minor's family (expanded to include a spouse and a stepparent, see subdivision (j) of Section 3901), the guardian of the minor's estate, or a trust company. Subdivision (g) of Section 3918 continued subdivision (h) of former Civil Code Section 1161 (repealed by 1984 Cal.Stat. ch. 243 § 1). See also Sections 3905(c), 3907(c).

The 1985 amendment added provisions authorizing the transferor to designate a successor custodian. The language of the 1985 amendment was drawn in part from portions of former Civil Code Section 1161. For background on this amendment, see 18 Cal.L.Revision Comm'n Reports at 218 (1986).

The 1988 amendment substituted a reference in subdivision (a) to Part 8 of Division 2 in place of the former reference to Division 2.5, to reflect a change in the numbering of the provisions to which reference was made. [20 Cal.L.Rev.Comm.Reports 1001 (1990)].

Research References

Forms

California Transactions Forms--Estate Planning § 1:95, Nomination Of Successor Custodian.
California Transactions Forms--Estate Planning § 6:18, Custodian Under Uniform Transfers to Minors Act.
California Transactions Forms--Estate Planning § 7:39, California Uniform Transfers to Minors Act.
California Transactions Forms--Estate Planning § 7:40, Form Drafting Principles.
California Transactions Forms--Estate Planning § 7:42, Matters to Consider When Making Transfer Under California Uniform Transfers to Minors Act.
California Transactions Forms--Estate Planning § 7:45, Custodian's Resignation and Designation Of Successor.
West's California Code Forms, Probate § 3909 Form 1, Creation Of Custodial Property.
West's California Code Forms, Probate § 3918 Form 1, Petition for Order Designating Successor Custodian.
West's California Code Forms, Probate § 3918 Form 2, Petition for Removal Of Custodian and Designation Of Successor Custodian.

Treatises and Practice Aids

Witkin, California Summary 10th Personal Property § 142, in General.
Witkin, California Summary 10th Personal Property § 143, Selection, Removal, and Successor.
Witkin, California Summary 10th Personal Property § 145, Manner Of Making Transfer.

§ 3919. Petition for accounting; determination of liability of custodian; removal of custodian

(a) A minor who has attained the age of 14 years, the minor's guardian of the person or legal representative, an adult member of the minor's family, a transferor, or a transferor's legal representative may petition the court for any of the following:

(1) An accounting by the custodian or the custodian's legal representative.

(2) A determination of responsibility, as between the custodial property and the custodian personally, for claims against the custodial property unless the responsibility has been adjudicated in an action under Section 3917 to which the minor or the minor's legal representative was a party.

(b) A successor custodian may petition the court for an accounting by the predecessor custodian.

(c) The court, in a proceeding under this part or in any other proceeding, may require or permit the custodian or the custodian's legal representative to account.

(d) If a custodian is removed under subdivision (f) of Section 3918, the court shall require an accounting and order delivery of the custodial property and records to the successor custodian and the execution of all instruments required for transfer of the custodial property.

(e) The right to petition for an accounting shall continue for one year after the filing of a final accounting by the custodian or the custodian's legal representative and delivery of the custodial property to the minor or the minor's estate. *(Stats.1990, c. 79 (A.B.759), § 14, operative July 1, 1991.)*

Law Revision Commission Comments

1990 Enactment

Section 3919 continues Section 3919 of the repealed Probate Code without change. This section is the same as Section 19 of the Uniform Transfers to Minors Act (1986) with the addition of subdivision (e). The introductory clause of subdivision (a) states the persons who may require an accounting by the custodian. Subdivision (a) also gives the same parties (other than a successor custodian) the right to seek recovery from the custodian for loss or diminution of custodial property resulting from successful claims by third persons under Section 3917, unless that issue has already been adjudicated in an action under that section to which the minor was a party.

Subdivision (b) authorizes but does not obligate a successor custodian to seek an accounting by the predecessor custodian. Since the minor and other persons mentioned in subdivision (a) may also seek an accounting from the predecessor at any time, it is anticipated that the exercise of this right by the successor should be rare.

Property in a single custodianship may be distributable at different times, so separate accounting for custodial property (depending on the time of distribution) may be required. See the Comment to Section 3910.

Background on Section 3919 of Repealed Code

Section 3919 was added by 1984 Cal.Stat. ch. 243 § 9. The section carried forward former Civil Code Section 1162 (repealed by 1984 Cal.Stat. ch. 243 § 1), but expanded the class of parties who could require an accounting by the custodian. Subdivisions (c) and (d) continued the substance of subdivision (b) of former Civil Code Section 1162. Subdivision (e) continued the second sentence of subdivision (a) of former Civil Code Section 1162. For background on the provisions of this part, see the Comment to this part under the part heading. [20 Cal.L.Rev.Comm.Reports 1001 (1990)].

Research References

Forms

Cal. Transaction Forms - Bus. Transactions § 26:30, Drafting Signature Cards.

California Transactions Forms--Estate Planning § 1:29, Options Involving Gifts to Minors.

West's California Code Forms, Probate § 3918 Form 2, Petition for Removal Of Custodian and Designation Of Successor Custodian.

West's California Code Forms, Probate § 3919 Form 1, Petition for Accounting.

Treatises and Practice Aids

Witkin, California Summary 10th Personal Property § 147, Duties and Compensation Of Custodian.

§ 3920. Termination of custodianship

The custodian shall transfer in an appropriate manner the custodial property to the minor or to the minor's estate upon the earlier of the following:

(a) The minor's attainment of 18 years of age unless the time of transfer of the custodial property to the minor is delayed under Section 3920.5 to a time after the time the minor attains the age of 18 years.

(b) The time specified in the transfer pursuant to Section 3909 if the time of transfer of the custodial property to the minor is delayed under Section 3920.5 to a time after the time the minor attains the age of 18 years.

(c) The minor's death. *(Stats.1990, c. 79 (A.B.759), § 14, operative July 1, 1991.)*

Law Revision Commission Comments

1990 Enactment

Section 3920 continues Section 3920 of the repealed Probate Code without change. This section is drawn from Section 20 of the Uniform Transfers to Minors Act (1986). Subdivision (a) establishes the age of termination as 18 years unless the time of transfer of custodial property to the minor is delayed under Section 3920.5.

Background on Section 3920 of Repealed Code

Section 3920 was added by 1984 Cal.Stat. ch. 243 § 9. Sections 3920 and 3920.5 superseded subdivision (d) of former Civil Code Section 1158 (repealed by 1984 Cal.Stat. ch. 243 § 1). See Report of Senate Committee on Judiciary on Assembly Bill 2492, 18 Cal.L.Revision Comm'n Reports 105, 111 (1986). For background on the provisions of this part, see the Comment to this part under the part heading. [20 Cal.L.Rev.Comm.Reports 1001 (1990)].

Research References

Forms

Cal. Transaction Forms - Bus. Transactions § 26:30, Drafting Signature Cards.

California Transactions Forms--Estate Planning § 1:29, Options Involving Gifts to Minors.

California Transactions Forms--Estate Planning § 6:18, Custodian Under Uniform Transfers to Minors Act.

California Transactions Forms--Estate Planning § 7:39, California Uniform Transfers to Minors Act.

California Transactions Forms--Estate Planning § 14:24, Incorporation Of CUTMA.

California Transactions Forms--Estate Planning § 19:47, Appointment Of Custodian.

Treatises and Practice Aids

Witkin, California Summary 10th Personal Property § 147, Duties and Compensation Of Custodian.

Witkin, California Summary 10th Personal Property § 150, Termination Of Custodianship.

§ 3920.5. Delay in transfer of custodial property until after minor attains age eighteen; transfers not specifying age

(a) Subject to the requirements and limitations of this section, the time for transfer to the minor of custodial property transferred under or pursuant to Section 3903, 3904, 3905, or 3906, may be delayed until a specified time after the time the minor attains the age of 18 years, which time shall be specified in the transfer pursuant to Section 3909.

(b) To specify a delayed time for transfer to the minor of the custodial property, the words

"as custodian for ______________
(Name of Minor)
until age ______________
(Age for Delivery of Property to Minor)
under the California Uniform Transfers to Minors Act" shall be substituted in substance for the words
"as custodian for ______________
(Name of Minor)
under the California Uniform Transfers to Minors Act" in making the transfer pursuant to Section 3909.

(c) The time for transfer to the minor of custodial property transferred under or pursuant to Section 3903 or 3905 may be delayed under this section only if the governing will or trust or nomination provides in substance that the custodianship is to continue until the time the minor attains a specified age, which time may not be later than the time the minor attains 25 years of age, and in that case the governing will or trust or nomination shall determine the time to be specified in the transfer pursuant to Section 3909.

(d) The time for transfer to the minor of custodial property transferred by the irrevocable exercise of a power of appointment under Section 3904 may be delayed under this section only if the transfer pursuant to Section 3909 provides in substance that the custodianship is to continue until the time the minor attains a specified age, which time may not be later than the time the minor attains 25 years of age.

(e) The time for transfer to the minor of custodial property transferred by irrevocable gift under Section 3904 may be delayed under this section only if the transfer pursuant to Section 3909 provides in substance that the custodianship is to continue until the time the minor attains a specified age, which time may not be later than the time the minor attains 21 years of age.

(f) The time for transfer to the minor of custodial property transferred by a trustee under Section 3906 may be delayed under this section only if the transfer pursuant to Section 3909 provides that the custodianship is to continue until a specified time not later than the time the minor attains 25 years of age or the time of termination of all present beneficial interests of the minor in the trust from which the custodial property was transferred, whichever is to occur first.

(g) If the transfer pursuant to Section 3909 does not specify any age, the time for the transfer of the custodial property to the minor under Section 3920 is the time when the minor attains 18 years of age.

(h) If the transfer pursuant to Section 3909 provides in substance that the duration of the custodianship is for a time longer than the maximum time permitted by this section for the duration of a custodianship created by that type of transfer, the custodianship shall be deemed to continue only until the time the minor attains the maximum age permitted by this section for the duration of a custodianship created by that type of transfer. *(Stats.1990, c. 79 (A.B.759), § 14, operative July 1, 1991. Amended by Stats.1996, c. 862 (A.B.2751), § 14.)*

Law Revision Commission Comments

1990 Enactment

Section 3920.5 continues Section 3920.5 of the repealed Probate Code without change. There is no provision under the Uniform Transfers to Minors Act (1986) for choice as to the age at which custodial property shall be transferred to the minor. Likewise, there was no such provision under prior California law. Section 3920.5 gives this choice since many transferors who specifically authorize a custodianship wish to preserve the custodianship as long as possible. This is most likely to be the case, for example, where the custodial property is intended to be preserved and used to finance a college education. Continuing the custodianship past the age of 18 permits the donor to avoid the expense of preparing a trust instrument to create a trust that otherwise would be required in order to retain the property under custodial management until the young person reaches the specified age.

The custodian is required to transfer the property to the minor when the minor attains the age of 18 years unless the transfer pursuant to Section 3909 specifies a later time. See Section 3920.

Subdivision (c) permits the custodianship to continue until not later than the time the minor attains the age of 25 years where the transfer is made pursuant to a provision in a will or trust that provides that the custodianship is to continue until the specified age, not later than the time the beneficiary attains the age of 25. A custodianship may be established pursuant to a provision in a will or trust that provides that the custodianship is to continue until a specified age after age 18 even though the beneficiary has attained an age older than 18 but younger than the specified age at which the custodianship is to terminate. See Section 3901(k).

Subdivision (d) permits the custodianship to continue until not later than the time the minor attains the age of 25 years where the custodial property is transferred by the irrevocable exercise of a power of appointment under Section 3904 if the transfer specifies that the custodianship is to continue until the specified age.

Subdivision (e) permits the custodianship to continue until not later than the time the minor attains the age of 21 years where the custodial property is transferred by a lifetime gift. The 21–year maximum duration of the custodianship is consistent with the Internal Revenue Code which permits "minority trusts" under Section 2503(c) of the Internal Revenue Code to continue in effect until age 21.

Section 3920.5 does not provide for continuance beyond age 18 of a custodianship created under or pursuant to Sections 3412, 3413, 3602, 3611, 3906, or 3907. These custodianships terminate at age 18 because they are substitutes for a guardianship that otherwise would terminate at that time (see Section 1600). And, in the cases where Section 3920.5 permits the custodianship to continue after the minor attains the age of 18 years, if the transfer pursuant to Section 3909 does not specify any age, the custodianship terminates when the minor attains 18 years of age. See subdivision (f) of Section 3920.5.

Subdivision (g) validates a transfer that specifies a maximum time for the duration of the custodianship that is longer than permitted by Section 3920.5 by reducing the duration of the custodianship to the maximum duration permitted for a custodianship created by that type of transfer.

Because property in a single custodianship may be distributable at different times, separate accounting for custodial property by source may be required. See the Comment to Section 3910.

Background on Section 3920.5 of Repealed Code

Section 3920.5 was a new provision added by 1984 Cal.Stat. ch. 243 § 9. See Report of Senate Committee on Judiciary on Assembly Bill 2492, 18 Cal.L.Revision Comm'n Reports 105, 111–13 (1986). For background on the provisions of this part, see the Comment to this part under the part heading. [20 Cal.L.Rev.Comm.Reports 1001 (1990)].

Research References

Forms

Cal. Transaction Forms - Bus. Transactions § 26:30, Drafting Signature Cards.

California Transactions Forms--Estate Planning § 1:29, Options Involving Gifts to Minors.

California Transactions Forms--Estate Planning § 6:18, Custodian Under Uniform Transfers to Minors Act.

California Transactions Forms--Estate Planning § 7:39, California Uniform Transfers to Minors Act.

California Transactions Forms--Estate Planning § 14:24, Incorporation Of CUTMA.

California Transactions Forms--Estate Planning § 19:47, Appointment Of Custodian.

California Transactions Forms--Estate Planning § 20:10, Devises to Minors.

California Transactions Forms--Estate Planning § 20:43, General Pecuniary Devise to Custodian for Minor.

Treatises and Practice Aids

Witkin, California Summary 10th Personal Property § 140, Transfers to Minors Act.

Witkin, California Summary 10th Personal Property § 150, Termination Of Custodianship.

§ 3921. Proceedings on petition; place

Subject to the power of the court to transfer actions and proceedings as provided in the Code of Civil Procedure, a petition filed under this part shall be heard and proceedings thereon held in the superior court in the proper county, which shall be determined as follows:

(a) If the minor resides in this state, in either of the following counties:

(1) Where the minor resides.

(2) Where the custodian resides.

(b) If the minor does not reside within this state, in any of the following counties:

(1) Where the transferor resides.

(2) Where the custodian resides.

(3) Where the estate of a deceased or legally incapacitated custodian is being administered.

(4) Where a parent of the minor resides.

(c) If neither the minor, nor the transferor, nor any parent resides within this state, and no estate of a deceased or legally incapacitated custodian is being administered within this state, in any county. *(Stats.1990, c. 79 (A.B.759), § 14, operative July 1, 1991.)*

Law Revision Commission Comments

1990 Enactment

Section 3921 continues Section 3921 of the repealed Probate Code without change. No comparable provision is included in the Uniform Transfers to Minors Act (1986). Even where the custodian resides in this state, the venue is proper in any county if neither the minor, nor the transferor, nor any parent reside in this state, and no estate of a deceased or legally incapacitated custodian is being administered in this state.

Background on Section 3921 of Repealed Code

Section 3921 was added by 1984 Cal.Stat. ch. 243 § 9. The section continued and expanded the venue provision of former Civil Code Section 1162.5 (repealed by 1984 Cal.Stat. ch. 243 § 1). The former provision was liberalized to add the county where the custodian resides as a proper county, whether or not the minor resides in this state. For background on the provisions of this part, see the Comment to this part under the part heading. [20 Cal.L.Rev.Comm.Reports 1001 (1990)].

Research References

Treatises and Practice Aids

Witkin, California Summary 10th Personal Property § 140, Transfers to Minors Act.

Witkin, California Summary 10th Personal Property § 141, Nature and Scope Of Act.

§ 3922. Transfers made under Uniform Gifts to Minors Act or Uniform Transfers to Minors Act of other state

This part applies to a transfer within the scope of Section 3902 made on or after January 1, 1985, if either of the following requirements is satisfied:

(a) The transfer purports to have been made under the California Uniform Gifts to Minors Act.

(b) The instrument by which the transfer purports to have been made uses in substance the designation "as custodian under the Uniform Gifts to Minors Act" or "as custodian under the Uniform Transfers to Minors Act" of any other state, and the application of this part is necessary to validate the transfer. *(Stats.1990, c. 79 (A.B.759), § 14, operative July 1, 1991.)*

Law Revision Commission Comments

1990 Enactment

Section 3922 continues Section 3922 of the repealed Probate Code without change. This section is the same as Section 21 of the Uniform Transfers to Minors Act (1986). The section has two purposes. First, it operates as a "savings clause" to validate transfers made on or after January 1, 1985 (the effective date of the California Uniform Transfers to Minors Act) which mistakenly refer to the California Uniform Gifts to Minors Act rather than to the California Uniform Transfers to Minors Act. Second, it validates transfers attempted under the Uniform Gifts to Minors Act (1966) of another state which would not permit transfers from that source or of property of that kind or under the Uniform Transfers to Minors Act of another state with no nexus to the transaction, provided in each case that California has a sufficient nexus to the transaction under Section 3902.

Background on Section 3922 of Repealed Code

Section 3922 was a new provision added by 1984 Cal.Stat. ch. 243 § 9. For background on the provisions of this part, see the Comment to this part under the part heading. [20 Cal.L.Rev.Comm.Reports 1001 (1990)].

Research References

Treatises and Practice Aids

Witkin, California Summary 10th Personal Property § 141, Nature and Scope Of Act.

§ 3923. Effect on existing custodianships

(a) As used in this section, "California Uniform Gifts to Minors Act" means former Article 4 (commencing with Section 1154) of Chapter 3 of Title 4 of Part 4 of Division 2 of the Civil Code.

(b) Any transfer of custodial property, as now defined in this part, made before January 1, 1985, is validated, notwithstanding that there was no specific authority in the California Uniform Gifts to Minors Act for the coverage of custodial property of that kind or for a transfer from that source at the time the transfer was made.

(c) This part applies to all transfers made before January 1, 1985, in a manner and form prescribed in the California Uniform Gifts to Minors Act, except insofar as the application impairs constitutionally vested rights.

(d) To the extent that this part, by virtue of subdivision (c), does not apply to transfers made in a manner prescribed in the California Uniform Gifts to Minors Act or to the powers, duties, and immunities conferred by transfers in that manner upon custodians and persons dealing with custodians, the repeal of the California Uniform Gifts to Minors Act does not affect those transfers or those powers, duties, and immunities. *(Stats.1990, c. 79 (A.B.759), § 14, operative July 1, 1991.)*

Law Revision Commission Comments

1990 Enactment

Section 3923 continues Section 3923 of the repealed Probate Code without change. Subdivision (b) is the same as subsection (a) of Section 22 of the Uniform Transfers to Minors Act (1986). This subdivision attempts to validate any transfer of custodial property made before the effective date of enactment of this part of the repealed Probate Code, notwithstanding that there was no specific authority in California law for the coverage of custodial property of that kind or for a transfer from that source at the time the transfer was made. The subdivision would, for example, validate a transfer from an intervivos trust by a trustee to a custodianship pursuant to an express provision in the trust instrument giving the trustee that authority. It was not clear under prior law that such a transfer created a valid custodianship.

Subdivision (c) is the same as subsection (b) of Section 22 of the Uniform Transfers to Minors Act (1986), except that subdivision (c) does not contain the language of Section 22(b) relating to extending the duration of custodianships in existence on the operative date. The omitted language is unnecessary because custodianships created under the California Uniform Gifts to Minors Act will still terminate at age 18 under this part. See Sections 3920, 3920.5. Subdivision (c) makes this part apply to all transfers made before January 1, 1985, in the manner and form prescribed in the California Uniform Gifts to Minors Act, except insofar as the application impairs constitutionally vested rights. This provision avoids having two bodies of law in force—one applicable to prior custodianships and the other to custodianships created under this part—for 18 more years until all custodianships created under the California Uniform Gifts to Minors Act have terminated. As to the application of any amendments made after that date, see Section 3.

Subdivision (d) is the same as the second sentence of Section 27 of the Uniform Transfers to Minors Act (1986). It preserves prior law for matters not governed by this part.

Background on Section 3923 of Repealed Code

Section 3923 was a new provision added by 1984 Cal.Stat. ch. 243 § 9. See Report of Senate Committee on Judiciary on Assembly Bill 2492, 18 Cal.L. Revision Comm'n Reports 105, 113 (1986). For background on the provisions of this part, see the Comment to this part under the part heading. [20 Cal.L.Rev.Comm.Reports 1001 (1990)].

Research References

Treatises and Practice Aids

Witkin, California Summary 10th Personal Property § 141, Nature and Scope Of Act.

§ 3925. Part not exclusive

This part shall not be construed as providing an exclusive method for making gifts or other transfers to minors. *(Stats.1990, c. 79 (A.B.759), § 14, operative July 1, 1991.)*

Law Revision Commission Comments

1990 Enactment

Section 3925 continues Section 3925 of the repealed Probate Code without change. No comparable provision is found in the Uniform Transfers to Minors Act (1986).

Background on Section 3925 of Repealed Code

Section 3925 was added by 1984 Cal.Stat. ch. 243 § 9. The section continued the substance of subdivision (b) of former Civil Code Section 1163 (repealed by 1984 Cal.Stat. ch. 243 § 1). For background on the provisions of this part, see the Comment to this part under the part heading. [20 Cal.L.Rev.Comm.Reports 1001 (1990)].

Research References

Forms

California Transactions Forms--Estate Planning § 6:18, Custodian Under Uniform Transfers to Minors Act.

California Transactions Forms--Estate Planning § 6:78, Devise to Custodian for Child Who is Minor at Testator's Death Under California Uniform Transfers to Minors Act.

California Transactions Forms--Estate Planning § 7:39, California Uniform Transfers to Minors Act.

California Transactions Forms--Estate Planning § 13:64, Methods Of Distribution.

California Transactions Forms--Estate Planning § 19:134, Determining Manner Of Distribution to Minors and Others.

Treatises and Practice Aids

Witkin, California Summary 10th Personal Property § 141, Nature and Scope Of Act.

Division 5

NONPROBATE TRANSFERS

Part 1

PROVISIONS RELATING TO EFFECT OF DEATH

CHAPTER 1. GENERAL PROVISIONS

§ 5000. Written instruments; compliance with requirements for execution of will; rights of creditors

(a) A provision for a nonprobate transfer on death in an insurance policy, contract of employment, bond, mortgage, promissory note, certificated or uncertificated security, account agreement, custodial agreement, deposit agreement, compensation plan, pension plan, individual retirement plan, employee benefit plan, trust, conveyance, deed of gift, revocable transfer on death deed, marital property agreement, or other written instrument of a similar nature is not invalid because the instrument does not comply with the requirements for execution of a will, and this code does not invalidate the instrument.

(b) Included within subdivision (a) are the following:

(1) A written provision that moneys or other benefits due to, controlled by, or owned by a decedent before death shall be paid after the decedent's death to a person whom the decedent designates either in the instrument or in a separate writing, including a will, executed either before or at the same time as the instrument, or later.

(2) A written provision that moneys due or to become due under the instrument shall cease to be payable in the event of the death of the promisee or the promisor before payment or demand.

(3) A written provision that any property controlled by or owned by the decedent before death that is the subject of the instrument shall pass to a person whom the decedent designates either in the instrument or in a separate writing, including a will, executed either before or at the same time as the instrument, or later.

(c) Nothing in this section limits the rights of creditors under any other law. *(Stats.1990, c. 79 (A.B.759), § 14, operative July 1, 1991. Amended by Stats.2015, c. 293 (A.B.139), § 8, eff. Jan. 1, 2016.)*

Law Revision Commission Comments

1990 Enactment

Section 5000 is a new provision that restates Section 160 of the repealed Probate Code without substantive change. Section 160 was a new provision added by 1983 Cal.Stat. ch. 842, § 22. Section 160 was enacted upon recommendation of the California Law Revision Commission. See Tentative Recommendation Relating to Wills and Intestate Succession, 16 Cal.L. Revision Comm'n Reports 2301, 2350–51, 2381–82 (1982). Section 5000 adopts the substance of

Section 6–201 of the Uniform Probate Code (1987). As to the construction of provisions drawn from uniform acts, see Section 2.

Section 5000 differs from Section 160 of the repealed Probate Code in several respects:

(1) References to a certificated or uncertificated security, account agreement, custodial agreement, compensation plan, individual retirement plan, employee benefit plan, deed of gift, and marital property agreement have been added in Section 5000. The reference to a "marital property agreement" includes an agreement made during marriage as well as a premarital contract. The reference to profit-sharing plans is omitted for conformity with Section 6–201 of the Uniform Probate Code (1987).

(2) The examples in subdivision (b) of Section 5000 have been revised to include a separate writing executed before the instrument containing the written transfer provision.

(3) The phrase "or other written instrument of a similar nature" has been substituted in subdivision (a) of Section 5000 for the language "or any other written instrument effective as a contract, gift, conveyance, or trust" (which was found in the introductory portion of subdivision (a) of Section 160 of the repealed Probate Code). The Supreme Court of Washington read the replaced language to relieve against the delivery requirement of the law of deeds. See In re Estate of O'Brien, 109 Wash.2d 913, 749 P.2d 154 (1988). The substitution of the language in subdivision (a) makes clear that Section 5000 does not have this effect. See First Nat'l Bank of Minot v. Bloom, 264 N.W.2d 208, 212 (N.D.1978), in which the Supreme Court of North Dakota held that "nothing in ... the Uniform Probate Code [provision] eliminates the necessity of delivery of a deed to effectuate a conveyance from one living person to another."

An instrument making a transfer under this section does not have to be executed in compliance with the formalities for a will; nor does the instrument have to be probated, nor does the personal representative have any power or duty with respect to the property transferred. See also Section 6321 (designation of trustee named or to be named in will as primary or contingent beneficiary, payee, or owner of insurance or employee benefits need not comply with the formalities for execution of a will). The Uniform Probate Code language that any provision referred to in this section is "deemed to be nontestamentary" has been replaced by the language making the provision "not invalid because the instrument does not comply with the requirements for execution of a will." This change is nonsubstantive.

The sole purpose of this section is to prevent the transfers covered by the section from being treated as testamentary. This section does not invalidate other arrangements by negative implication. Thus, this section does not affect an oral trust to hold personal property at death for named persons, an arrangement given specific recognition by Section 15207. [20 Cal.L.Rev.Comm.Reports 1001 (1990)].

1992 Supplementary Comment

Section 5000 is intended broadly to validate written instruments that provide for nonprobate transfers on death. The listing in the section of types of written instruments is not exclusive, and the section also would validate, for example, a nonprobate transfer provision in a partnership agreement, stock redemption plan, buy-sell agreement, power of appointment, and the like.

Note. Section 5000 is unchanged. It is set out here for convenience of reference, together with a supplementary comment. [21 Cal.L.Rev.Comm.Reports 163 (1991)].

2015 Amendment

Section 5000 is revised to make explicit its application to a revocable TOD deed. See Section 5614 (revocable transfer on death deed). This is a specific instance of the general principle stated in the section. [36 Cal.L.Rev.Comm. Reports 103 (2006)].

Commentary

See generally *Estate of Petersen, 28 Cal.App.4th 1742, 34 Cal. Rptr.2d 449 (1994)* (unambiguous provision of community-funded annuity contract effected a nonprobate death transfer by right of survivorship; in contrast, statement of "joint account" for money market funds was insufficient to create a nonprobate right of survivorship).

Research References

Forms

California Transactions Forms--Estate Planning § 1:2, Probate System.
California Transactions Forms--Estate Planning § 1:6, Revocable Living Trust as Centerpiece.
California Transactions Forms--Estate Planning § 1:15, Overview.
California Transactions Forms--Estate Planning § 1:18, Property Subject to Probate; Intestacy.
California Transactions Forms--Estate Planning § 1:19, Nonprobate Transfers Under Prob C S5000.
California Transactions Forms--Estate Planning § 1:77, Matters to Consider Regarding Property Distribution.
California Transactions Forms--Estate Planning § 10:4, Community Property.
California Transactions Forms--Estate Planning § 20:6, Property Passing Outside Of Will.
California Transactions Forms--Estate Planning § 9:77, Beneficiary Designations Of Community Property Interests in Plan or IRA [Prob C §§ 5000 et seq.].
California Transactions Forms--Estate Planning § 1:106, Revocable Grant Deed.
California Transactions Forms--Estate Planning § 10:14, Formalities Required.
California Transactions Forms--Estate Planning § 10:20, Contract Rights.
California Transactions Forms--Estate Planning § 10:26, Employee Benefits.
California Transactions Forms--Estate Planning § 11:50, Rights Of Surviving Spouse that May be Waived [Prob C § 141].
California Transactions Forms--Estate Planning § 19:66, Determining Testator's Intent; Information Gathering.
West's California Judicial Council Forms FL-347, Bifurcation Of Status Of Marriage or Domestic Partnership--Attachment.

Treatises and Practice Aids

Witkin, California Summary 10th Community Property § 251, Disposition Of Community Property.
Witkin, California Summary 10th Husband and Wife § 88, Order in Summons.
Witkin, California Summary 10th Husband and Wife § 105, Statutory Rule.
Witkin, California Summary 10th Wills and Probate § 25, Major Changes.
Witkin, California Summary 10th Wills and Probate § 106, Obligation Terminable on Death.
Witkin, California Summary 10th Wills and Probate § 108, Pay-On-Death Provisions.
Witkin, California Summary 10th Wills and Probate § 266, Community Property With Right Of Survivorship.
Witkin, California Summary 10th Wills and Probate § 295, Wills, Trusts, and Intestate Succession.
Witkin, California Summary 10th Wills and Probate § 305, Recommendation and Enactment.
Witkin, California Summary 10th Wills and Probate § 306, Authorized Transfers.
Witkin, California Summary 10th Wills and Probate § 307, Rights and Liabilities Of Holder.

Witkin, California Summary 10th Wills and Probate § 309, Nature and Scope Of Statute.
Witkin, California Summary 10th Wills and Probate § 310, Consent.
Witkin, California Summary 10th Wills and Probate § 318, Transfer to Former Spouse.
Witkin, California Summary 10th Wills and Probate § 322, Nature and Scope Of Statute.
Witkin, California Summary 10th Wills and Probate § 360, in General.
Witkin, California Summary 10th Wills and Probate § 405, Probate and Administration.

§ 5002. Restrictions imposed by terms of the instrument

Notwithstanding any other provision of this part, a holder of property under an instrument of a type described in Section 5000 is not required to receive, hold, or transfer the property in compliance with a provision for a nonprobate transfer on death executed by a person who has an interest in the property if either (1) the person is not authorized by the terms of the instrument to execute a provision for transfer of the property, or (2) the provision for transfer of the property does not otherwise satisfy the terms of the instrument. *(Added by Stats.1992, c. 51 (A.B.1719), § 4.)*

Law Revision Commission Comments

1992 Addition

Section 5002 is added to make clear that this part is not a substantive grant of authority for a person to enforce a nonprobate transfer of the person's interest in property where such a transfer is not authorized by the terms of the instrument under which the property is held. Thus, for example, a nonemployee spouse under an employee benefit plan, or a nonowner spouse under an insurance policy, is not authorized by this part to direct a nonprobate transfer of the spouse's community property interest, if any, in the plan or policy. Although this chapter does not authorize execution of a provision for such a nonprobate transfer, the holder of the property may be required by federal law, by other state law, or by the terms of the instrument itself to recognize the property interest of a spouse. [21 Cal.L.Rev.Comm.Reports 163 (1991)].

Research References

Treatises and Practice Aids

Witkin, California Summary 10th Wills and Probate § 43, Major Changes.
Witkin, California Summary 10th Wills and Probate § 307, Rights and Liabilities Of Holder.

§ 5003. Protection of property; exceptions; notice

(a) A holder of property under an instrument of a type described in Section 5000 may transfer the property in compliance with a provision for a nonprobate transfer on death that satisfies the terms of the instrument, whether or not the transfer is consistent with the beneficial ownership of the property as between the person who executed the provision for transfer of the property and other persons having an interest in the property or their successors, and whether or not the transfer is consistent with the rights of the person named as beneficiary.

(b) Except as provided in this subdivision, no notice or other information shown to have been available to the holder of the property affects the right of the holder to the protection provided by subdivision (a). The protection provided by subdivision (a) does not extend to a transfer made after either of the following events:

(1) The holder of the property has been served with a contrary court order.

(2) The holder of the property has been served with a written notice of a person claiming an adverse interest in the property. However, this paragraph does not apply to a pension plan to the extent the transfer is a periodic payment pursuant to the plan.

(c) The protection provided by this section does not affect the rights of the person who executed the provision for transfer of the property and other persons having an interest in the property or their successors in disputes among themselves concerning the beneficial ownership of the property.

(d) The protection provided by this section is not exclusive of any protection provided the holder of the property by any other provision of law.

(e) A person shall not serve notice under paragraph (2) of subdivision (b) in bad faith. If the court in an action or proceeding relating to the rights of the parties determines that a person has served notice under paragraph (2) of subdivision (b) in bad faith, the court shall award against the person the cost of the action or proceeding, including a reasonable attorney's fee, and the damages caused by the service. *(Added by Stats.1992, c. 51 (A.B.1719), § 5. Amended by Stats.2001, c. 417 (A.B.873), § 7.)*

Law Revision Commission Comments

1992 Addition

Section 5003 is drawn from portions of Section 5405 (protection of financial institution under California Multiple–Party Accounts Law). A holder of property that is the subject of a nonprobate transfer is not obligated to ascertain the respective separate, community, and quasi-community property interests in the property of participant and nonparticipant, or employee and nonemployee, or covered and noncovered, or insured and noninsured, spouses. Unless the holder of property has been served with a contrary court order or notice of an adverse claim, the holder may transfer the property in accordance with the terms of the instrument, and any adverse rights of a spouse or beneficiaries must be asserted against the estate of the person who executed the instrument or against the beneficiary, not against the holder of the property. See Sections 5012 (community property rights independent of transfer obligation), 5021 (transfer without consent)

For the manner and proof of service, see Part 2 (commencing with Section 1200) of Division 3. [21 Cal.L.Rev.Comm.Reports 163 (1991)].

2001 Amendment

Subdivision (a) of Section 5003 is amended to make clear that the section applies where a nonprobate transfer has been caused to fail by operation of Section 5600.

Subdivision (e) provides for compensation where a person serves a bad faith notice of a contrary claim to property held for the purpose of a nonprobate transfer. This provision is similar to Section 13541(d) (compensation where notice slanders title to community property after spouse's death). [28 Cal.L.Rev.Comm. Reports 599 (1998)].

Research References

Treatises and Practice Aids

Witkin, California Summary 10th Wills and Probate § 43, Major Changes.
Witkin, California Summary 10th Wills and Probate § 307, Rights and Liabilities Of Holder.

Witkin, California Summary 10th Wills and Probate § 309, Nature and Scope Of Statute.
Witkin, California Summary 10th Wills and Probate § 311, Revocation Of Consent.

CHAPTER 2. NONPROBATE TRANSFERS OF COMMUNITY PROPERTY

ARTICLE 1. GENERAL PROVISIONS

§ 5010. Written consent

As used in this chapter, "written consent" to a provision for a nonprobate transfer of community property on death includes a written joinder in such a provision. *(Added by Stats.1992, c. 51 (A.B.1719), § 6.)*

Law Revision Commission Comments

1992 Addition [Revised Comment]

Section 5010 is intended for drafting convenience. Written joinder in a provision for a nonprobate transfer includes joint action by both spouses in writing. A written consent, to be effective, need not satisfy the statutory requirements for a transmutation. See Section 5022 (written consent not a transmutation). A written consent becomes irrevocable on death of either spouse. Section 5030 (revocability of written consent).

It should be noted that the validity of a purported written consent is subject to relevant common law and statutory defenses, including but not limited to fraud, undue influence, misrepresentation, and violation of the special fiduciary duty applicable in transactions between spouses. See, e.g., Civ.Code § 5103. [22 Cal.L.Rev.Comm.Reports 985 (1992)].

Research References

Forms

California Transactions Forms--Estate Planning § 10:28, Differences Between Qualified Retirement Plans and IRAs.
California Transactions Forms--Estate Planning § 11:35, Agreement Entered Into on or After January 1, 1985.

Treatises and Practice Aids

Witkin, California Summary 10th Community Property § 136, in General.
Witkin, California Summary 10th Community Property § 138, Permissible Transactions.
Witkin, California Summary 10th Community Property § 156, Estate Planning Transactions.
Witkin, California Summary 10th Wills and Probate § 43, Major Changes.
Witkin, California Summary 10th Wills and Probate § 265, Disposition.
Witkin, California Summary 10th Wills and Probate § 305, Recommendation and Enactment.
Witkin, California Summary 10th Wills and Probate § 308, Recommendation and Enactment.
Witkin, California Summary 10th Wills and Probate § 309, Nature and Scope Of Statute.
Witkin, California Summary 10th Wills and Probate § 310, Consent.
Witkin, California Summary 10th Wills and Probate § 320C, (New) Effect Of Deed.

§ 5011. Rights of parties in nonprobate transfers; application of chapter

Notwithstanding any other provision of this part, the rights of the parties in a nonprobate transfer of community property on death are subject to all of the following:

(a) The terms of the instrument under which the nonprobate transfer is made.

(b) A contrary state statute specifically applicable to the instrument under which the nonprobate transfer is made.

(c) A written expression of intent of a party in the provision for transfer of the property or in a written consent to the provision. *(Added by Stats.1992, c. 51 (A.B.1719), § 6.)*

Law Revision Commission Comments

1992 Addition

Section 5011 establishes the principle that the rules in this chapter only apply in the absence of other governing provisions

Subdivision (a) recognizes that the terms of the instrument may define the rights of the parties. See also Section 5012 (community property rights independent of transfer obligation).

Subdivision (b) makes clear that the general rules set out in this chapter are not intended to override other state statutes that are narrowly drawn to govern rights under specific named instruments. It should also be noted that this chapter cannot override preempting federal law. See, e.g., Ablamis v. Roper, 937 F.2d 1450 (9th Cir.1991) (ERISA precludes testamentary disposition of community property interest of nonparticipant spouse).

Subdivision (c) makes clear that an expression of intent of the spouses in directing a nonprobate transfer of their interests in community property prevails over the default rules in this chapter. [21 Cal.L.Rev.Comm.Reports 163 (1991)].

Commentary

See generally *Estate of Petersen, 28 Cal.App.4th 1742, 34 Cal. Rptr.2d 449 (1994)* (unambiguous provision of community-funded annuity contract effected a nonprobate death transfer by right of survivorship; in contrast, statement of "joint account" for money market funds was insufficient to create a nonprobate right of survivorship).

Research References

Treatises and Practice Aids

Witkin, California Summary 10th Wills and Probate § 309, Nature and Scope Of Statute.
Witkin, California Summary 10th Wills and Probate § 310, Consent.

§ 5012. Holders of § 5000 instruments; application of chapter

A provision of this chapter concerning rights between a married person and the person's spouse in community property is relevant only to controversies between the person and spouse and their successors and does not affect the obligation of a holder of community property under an instrument of a type described in Section 5000 to hold, receive, or transfer the property in compliance with a provision for a nonprobate transfer on death, or the protection provided the holder by Section 5003. *(Added by Stats.1992, c. 51 (A.B.1719), § 6.)*

Law Revision Commission Comments

1992 Addition

Section 5012 is drawn from Section 5201 (multiple-party accounts). [21 Cal.L.Rev.Comm.Reports 163 (1991)].

Research References

Treatises and Practice Aids

Witkin, California Summary 10th Wills and Probate § 309, Nature and Scope Of Statute.

§ 5013. Waivers or other instruments or agreements affecting rights in community property

Nothing in this chapter limits the effect of a surviving spouse's waiver of rights in community property under Chapter 1 (commencing with Section 140) of Part 3 of Division 2 or other instrument or agreement that affects a married person's interest in community property. *(Added by Stats.1992, c. 51 (A.B.1719), § 6.)*

Law Revision Commission Comments

1992 Addition

Section 5013 recognizes alternate procedures for releasing rights of a surviving spouse in community property.

Waiver of a joint and survivor annuity or survivor's benefits under the federal Retirement Equity Act of 1984 is not a transmutation. Civ.Code § 5110.740 (estate planning instruments). [21 Cal.L.Rev.Comm.Reports 163 (1991)].

Research References

Forms

California Transactions Forms--Estate Planning § 11:49, Introduction and Definition [Prob C § 140].

Treatises and Practice Aids

Witkin, California Summary 10th Wills and Probate § 309, Nature and Scope Of Statute.

§ 5014. Application of chapter; transitional rules

(a) Except as provided in subdivision (b), this chapter applies to a provision for a nonprobate transfer of community property on the death of a married person, regardless of whether the provision for transfer of the property was executed by the person, or written consent to the provision for transfer of the property was given by the person's spouse, before, on, or after January 1, 1993.

(b) Subdivision (c) of Section 5030 does not apply, and the applicable law in effect on the date of death does apply, to revocation of a written consent given by a spouse who died before January 1, 1993. *(Added by Stats.1992, c. 51 (A.B.1719), § 6.)*

Law Revision Commission Comments

1992 Addition

Section 5014 is an exception to the rule stated in Section 3 (general transitional provision). To the extent this chapter changes the law governing the rights of successors of a person who gives written consent to a nonprobate transfer by the person's spouse, this chapter does not seek to apply the change in law to rights that vested as a result of a death that occurred before the operative date of the chapter. [21 Cal.L.Rev.Comm.Reports 163 (1991)].

Research References

Treatises and Practice Aids

Witkin, California Summary 10th Community Property § 156, Estate Planning Transactions.

Witkin, California Summary 10th Wills and Probate § 309, Nature and Scope Of Statute.

§ 5015. Fraud, undue influence, duress, mistake, or other invalidating causes

Nothing in this chapter limits the application of principles of fraud, undue influence, duress, mistake, or other invalidating cause to a written consent to a provision for a nonprobate transfer of community property on death. *(Added by Stats. 1992, c. 51 (A.B.1719), § 6.)*

Research References

Treatises and Practice Aids

Witkin, California Summary 10th Wills and Probate § 309, Nature and Scope Of Statute.

ARTICLE 2. CONSENT TO NONPROBATE TRANSFER

§ 5020. Written consent requirement

A provision for a nonprobate transfer of community property on death executed by a married person without the written consent of the person's spouse (1) is not effective as to the nonconsenting spouse's interest in the property and (2) does not affect the nonconsenting spouse's disposition on death of the nonconsenting spouse's interest in the community property by will, intestate succession, or nonprobate transfer. *(Added by Stats.1992, c. 51 (A.B.1719), § 6.)*

Law Revision Commission Comments

1992 Addition

Section 5020 is comparable to Civil Code Section 5125(b). It codifies the case law rule that the statutory community property gift limitations apply to nonprobate transfers such as beneficiary designations in trusts and accounts. See, e.g., Tyre v. Aetna Life Ins. Co., 54 Cal.2d 399, 353 P.2d 725, 6 Cal.Rptr. 13 (1960) (beneficiary designation in life insurance policy); Yiatchos v. Yiatchos, 376 U.S. 306 (1964) (beneficiary designation for United States Savings Bonds).

It should be noted that while Section 5020 makes clear that a nonconsenting spouse retains full dispositional rights over the spouse's community property interest (subject to overriding governing principles as provided in Section 5011), this does not imply that a consenting spouse loses these rights. A written consent is revocable during the spouse's lifetime, and a revocation and contrary disposition may be made by will. See Section 5031 (form and service of revocation).

Section 5020 does not affect the principle that a holder of property may transfer the property as specified in the instrument. Section 5003 (protection of holder of property). But the actions of the holder do not affect rights between the spouses and their successors.

See Section 5012 (community property rights independent of transfer obligation). [21 Cal.L.Rev.Comm.Reports 163 (1991)].

Research References

Forms

California Transactions Forms--Estate Planning § 10:4, Community Property.
California Transactions Forms--Estate Planning § 9:77, Beneficiary Designations Of Community Property Interests in Plan or IRA [Prob C §§ 5000 et seq.].
California Transactions Forms--Estate Planning § 10:14, Formalities Required.

Treatises and Practice Aids

Witkin, California Summary 10th Wills and Probate § 310, Consent.

§ 5021. Transfers without written consent

(a) In a proceeding to set aside a nonprobate transfer of community property on death made pursuant to a provision for transfer of the property executed by a married person without the written consent of the person's spouse, the court shall set aside the transfer as to the nonconsenting spouse's interest in the property, subject to terms and conditions or other remedies that appear equitable under the circumstances of the case, taking into account the rights of all interested persons.

(b) Nothing in subdivision (a) affects any additional remedy the nonconsenting spouse may have against the person's estate for a nonprobate transfer of community property on death without the spouse's written consent. *(Added by Stats.1992, c. 51 (A.B.1719), § 6.)*

Law Revision Commission Comments

1992 Addition

Subdivision (a) of Section 5021 is consistent with the rule applicable to present gifts of community property at termination of the marriage by dissolution or death. See, e.g., Ballinger v. Ballinger, 9 Cal.2d 330, 70 P.2d 629 (1937); In re Marriage of Stephenson, 162 Cal.App.3d 1057, 209 Cal.Rptr. 383 (1984). It implements the concept that a nonprobate transfer is a will substitute, and that a person has the right to direct a transfer of the person's one-half interest in the community property at death, with or without the spouse's consent. See, e.g., Sections 100–102 (effect of death of married person on community and quasi-community property), 6101 (property which may be disposed of by will).

Under subdivision (a) the court has discretion to fashion an appropriate order, depending on the circumstances of the case. The order may, for example, provide for recovery of the value of the property rather than the particular item, or aggregate property received by a beneficiary instead of imposing a division by item.

Subdivision (b) makes clear that this section does not provide the exclusive remedy where a person has directed a nonprobate transfer of community property without the written consent of the other spouse. It may be proper, for example and without limitation, simply to allow the surviving spouse, instead of or in addition to proceeding against the beneficiary of the nonprobate asset, to proceed against the decedent's estate for an offset for the value of the property transferred out of the share of the decedent, or to give the surviving spouse a right of reimbursement. [21 Cal.L.Rev.Comm.Reports 163 (1991)].

Commentary

Estate of Miramontes–Najera, 118 Cal.App.4th 750, 13 Cal.Rptr.3d 240 (2004), holds that subsection (a) codifies the case law "item" rule of death distribution. Under the item rule, a spouse is entitled to one-half of each and every community property asset and may recover his or her one-half interest in any inter vivos gift of community property made by the other spouse without his or her consent, even though he or she is otherwise receiving one-half or more of the aggregate community property.

Research References

Forms

California Transactions Forms--Estate Planning § 9:77, Beneficiary Designations Of Community Property Interests in Plan or IRA [Prob C §§ 5000 et seq.].
California Transactions Forms--Estate Planning § 10:14, Formalities Required.

Treatises and Practice Aids

Witkin, California Summary 10th Community Property § 138, Permissible Transactions.
Witkin, California Summary 10th Wills and Probate § 310, Consent.

§ 5022. Written consent not a transmutation; exception

(a) Except as provided in subdivision (b), a spouse's written consent to a provision for a nonprobate transfer of community property on death is not a transmutation of the consenting spouse's interest in the property.

(b) This chapter does not apply to a spouse's written consent to a provision for a nonprobate transfer of community property on death that satisfies Section 852 of the Family Code. Such a consent is a transmutation and is governed by the law applicable to transmutations. *(Added by Stats.1992, c. 51 (A.B.1719), § 6. Amended by Stats.1993, c. 219 (A.B.1500), § 224.3.)*

Law Revision Commission Comments

1992 Addition

Section 5022 is consistent with the result in Estate of MacDonald, 51 Cal.3d 262, 794 P.2d 911, 272 Cal.Rptr. 153 (1990). A consent to a nonprobate transfer is in effect a consent to a future gift of the person's interest in community property, and is subject to the legal incidents provided in this chapter. Until the gift is complete, however, it remains community property and is part of the community estate for purposes of division of property at dissolution of marriage until the consent becomes irrevocable by the death of either spouse. See Section 5030 (revocability of written consent). However, if the consent specifies a clear intent to transmute the property, the expression of intent controls over this section.

See Section 5011(c) (governing provision of consent). [21 Cal.L.Rev.Comm.Reports 163 (1991)].

1993 Amendment

Subdivision (b) of Section 5022 is amended to substitute the reference to the Family Code section that replaced the former Civil Code section. [23 Cal.L.Rev.Comm. Reports 1 (1993)].

Research References

Forms

California Transactions Forms--Estate Planning § 10:4, Community Property.
California Transactions Forms--Estate Planning § 9:77, Beneficiary Designations Of Community Property Interests in Plan or IRA [Prob C §§ 5000 et seq.].

California Transactions Forms--Estate Planning § 10:14, Formalities Required.

Treatises and Practice Aids

Witkin, California Summary 10th Community Property § 156, Estate Planning Transactions.

Witkin, California Summary 10th Wills and Probate § 310, Consent.

§ 5023. Modifications

(a) As used in this section "modification" means revocation of a provision for a nonprobate transfer on death in whole or part, designation of a different beneficiary, or election of a different benefit or payment option. As used in this section, "modification" does not mean, and this section does not apply to, the exercise of a power of appointment under a trust.

(b) If a married person executes a provision for a nonprobate transfer of community property on death with the written consent of the person's spouse and thereafter executes a modification of the provision for transfer of the property without written consent of the spouse, the modification is effective as to the person's interest in the community property and has the following effect on the spouse's interest in the community property:

(1) If the person executes the modification during the spouse's lifetime, the modification revokes the spouse's previous written consent to the provision for transfer of the property.

(2) If the person executes the modification after the spouse's death, the modification does not affect the spouse's previous written consent to the provision for transfer of the property, and the spouse's interest in the community property is subject to the nonprobate transfer on death as consented to by the spouse.

(3) If a written expression of intent of a party in the provision for transfer of the property or in the written consent to the provision for transfer of the property authorizes the person to execute a modification after the spouse's death, the spouse's interest in the community property is deemed transferred to the married person on the spouse's death, and the modification is effective as to both the person's and the spouse's interests in the community property. *(Added by Stats.1992, c. 51 (A.B.1719), § 6. Amended by Stats.1993, c. 527 (A.B.908), § 3.)*

Law Revision Commission Comments

1992 Addition

Subdivision (a) of Section 5023 includes election of a different benefit or payment option among the types of modification covered by the section because the choice of benefit or payment options can substantially affect the rights of the parties. For example, rights can be substantially altered by selection of a life expectancy as opposed to term payout on a pension plan, or by selection of a cash benefit, annuity, or reinvestment option in a life insurance policy.

Subdivision (b)(1) treats a modification of a nonprobate transfer during the lifetimes of the spouses as a new nonprobate transfer, as to which the living spouse may consent if so desired. If the spouse does not have legal capacity to consent at the time, consent may be obtained through substituted judgment procedures. See Section 2580 (substituted judgment). Failure of consent to the changed terms during the spouse's lifetime revokes the original consent to the nonprobate transfer, and the spouse's interest ultimately passes with the spouse's estate or as otherwise disposed of by the spouse. See Section 5032 (effect of revocation). It should be noted that a modification is subject to the right of the decedent to make a contrary disposition by will. Section 5031 (form and service of revocation).

Under subdivision (b)(2), a modification by the surviving spouse after the death of the other spouse does not affect the nonprobate transfer of the community property interest of the deceased spouse as consented to by the deceased spouse. In effect, the consent is itself a nonprobate transfer which becomes irrevocable on the death of the spouse. See Section 5030 (revocability of consent). The deceased spouse's interest in the community property is transferred as consented to by the deceased spouse, unless by the terms of the consent the deceased spouse has authorized the surviving spouse to make modifications in the nonprobate transfer. See subdivision (b)(3). This is a special instance of the rule stated in Section 5011 that a nonprobate transfer of community property on death is governed by overriding principles, including a written expression of intent. [21 Cal.L.Rev.Comm.Reports 163 (1991)].

Research References

Forms

California Transactions Forms--Estate Planning § 10:4, Community Property.

California Transactions Forms--Estate Planning § 9:77, Beneficiary Designations Of Community Property Interests in Plan or IRA [Prob C §§ 5000 et seq.].

California Transactions Forms--Estate Planning § 10:14, Formalities Required.

California Transactions Forms--Estate Planning § 10:50, IRA Beneficiary Designation for Distribution Outright to Beneficiary.

Treatises and Practice Aids

Witkin, California Summary 10th Wills and Probate § 310, Consent.

ARTICLE 3. REVOCATION OF CONSENT

§ 5030. Revocability of written consent

(a) A spouse's written consent to a provision for a nonprobate transfer of community property on death is revocable during the marriage.

(b) On termination of the marriage by dissolution or on legal separation, the written consent is revocable and the community property is subject to division under Division 7 (commencing with Section 2500) of the Family Code or other disposition on order within the jurisdiction of the court.

(c) On the death of either spouse, the written consent is irrevocable. *(Added by Stats.1992, c. 51 (A.B.1719), § 6. Amended by Stats.1993, c. 219 (A.B.1500), § 224.5.)*

Law Revision Commission Comments

1992 Addition

Section 5030 is subject to express terms to the contrary. See Section 5011 (governing provision of instrument, law, or consent). If the consent is part of a mutual estate plan, nothing in this section precludes enforcement of the mutual estate plan by appropriate remedies, including an injunction affecting revocation.

Subdivision (c), to the extent it relates to the death of the consenting spouse, overrules the effect of Estate of MacDonald, 51

Cal.3d 262, 794 P.2d 911, 272 Cal.Rptr. 153 (1990). The consent of a spouse to disposition of the spouse's one-half interest in the community property is subject to a contrary disposition in the spouse's will. Section 5031. The spouse's personal representative may not revoke the consent to a nonprobate transfer and impose a different estate plan on the spouse's property.

The surviving spouse may modify a provision for a nonprobate transfer of community property previously consented to by the deceased spouse to the extent provided in Section 5023.

It should be noted that these changes in the law are subject to Section 5014 (transitional provision). [21 Cal.L.Rev.Comm.Reports 163 (1991)].

1993 Amendment

Subdivision (b) of Section 5030 is amended to substitute the reference to the Family Code sections that replaced the former Civil Code section. [23 Cal.L.Rev.Comm. Reports 1 (1993)].

Research References

Forms

California Transactions Forms--Estate Planning § 9:77, Beneficiary Designations Of Community Property Interests in Plan or IRA [Prob C §§ 5000 et seq.].

California Transactions Forms--Estate Planning § 10:14, Formalities Required.

Treatises and Practice Aids

Witkin, California Summary 10th Community Property § 156, Estate Planning Transactions.

Witkin, California Summary 10th Wills and Probate § 309, Nature and Scope Of Statute.

Witkin, California Summary 10th Wills and Probate § 311, Revocation Of Consent.

§ 5031. Form and service of revocation

(a) If a married person executes a provision for a nonprobate transfer of community property on death with the written consent of the person's spouse, the consenting spouse may revoke the consent by a writing, including a will, that identifies the provision for transfer of the property being revoked, and that is served on the married person before the married person's death.

(b) Revocation of a spouse's written consent to a provision for a nonprobate transfer of community property on death does not affect the authority of the holder of the property to transfer the property in compliance with the provision for transfer of the property to the extent provided in Section 5003. *(Added by Stats.1992, c. 51 (A.B.1719), § 6.)*

Law Revision Commission Comments

1992 Addition

Section 5031 is consistent with subdivision (c) of Section 5030 (written consent irrevocable on death). Under this section any specific and served writing is sufficient, including a document purporting to be a will, whether or not admitted to probate. The will provision would change existing law as to life insurance by allowing the beneficiary designation to be overridden by an express provision in a will.

For the manner and proof of service, see Part 2 (commencing with Section 1200) of Division 3. This section is subject to a contrary provision in the instrument, and the instrument may include terms that specify the manner of revocation of consent. Section 5011 (governing provision of instrument, law, or consent). [21 Cal.L.Rev.Comm.Reports 163 (1991)].

Research References

Forms

California Transactions Forms--Estate Planning § 9:77, Beneficiary Designations Of Community Property Interests in Plan or IRA [Prob C §§ 5000 et seq.].

California Transactions Forms--Estate Planning § 10:49, Will Provision Regarding Retirement Plan.

Treatises and Practice Aids

Witkin, California Summary 10th Wills and Probate § 311, Revocation Of Consent.

§ 5032. Revocations; effect on transfers

On revocation of a spouse's written consent to a nonprobate transfer of community property on death, the property passes in the same manner as if the consent had not been given. *(Added by Stats.1992, c. 51 (A.B.1719), § 6.)*

Law Revision Commission Comments

1992 Addition

Section 5032 governs the substantive rights of the spouses in the community property notwithstanding overriding contractual and legal requirements that bind a holder of the community property. See Sections 5003 (protection of holder of property), 5012 (community property rights independent of transfer obligation). However, this section is subject to contrary terms of the instrument and to overriding law governing the obligation of a holder of community property to deal with the property under the particular type of instrument. See Section 5011 (governing provision of instrument, law, or consent).

For rights of a spouse who has not given written consent, see Section 5020 (written consent required). [21 Cal.L.Rev.Comm.Reports 163 (1991)].

Research References

Forms

California Transactions Forms--Estate Planning § 10:4, Community Property.

California Transactions Forms--Estate Planning § 10:14, Formalities Required.

California Transactions Forms--Estate Planning § 10:28, Differences Between Qualified Retirement Plans and IRAs.

Treatises and Practice Aids

Witkin, California Summary 10th Wills and Probate § 311, Revocation Of Consent.

CHAPTER 3. NONPROBATE TRANSFER TO FORMER SPOUSE

Operative Effect

For operative effect and application of Chapter 3, see Probate Code § 5048.

§ 5040. Nonprobate transfer to former spouse executed before or during marriage or registered domestic partnership; failure of transfer due to dissolution or annulment of marriage or termination of registered domestic partnership; situations that do not cause a nonprobate transfer to fail; rights of subsequent purchaser

(a) Except as provided in subdivision (b), a nonprobate transfer to the transferor's former spouse, in an instrument executed by the transferor before or during the marriage or registered domestic partnership, fails if, at the time of the transferor's death, the former spouse is not the transferor's surviving spouse as defined in Section 78, as a result of the dissolution or annulment of the marriage or termination of registered domestic partnership. A judgment of legal separation that does not terminate the status of spouses is not a dissolution for purposes of this section.

(b) Subdivision (a) does not cause a nonprobate transfer to fail in any of the following cases:

(1) The nonprobate transfer is not subject to revocation by the transferor at the time of the transferor's death.

(2) There is clear and convincing evidence that the transferor intended to preserve the nonprobate transfer to the former spouse.

(3) A court order that the nonprobate transfer be maintained on behalf of the former spouse is in effect at the time of the transferor's death.

(c) Where a nonprobate transfer fails by operation of this section, the instrument making the nonprobate transfer shall be treated as it would if the former spouse failed to survive the transferor.

(d) Nothing in this section affects the rights of a subsequent purchaser or encumbrancer for value in good faith who relies on the apparent failure of a nonprobate transfer under this section or who lacks knowledge of the failure of a nonprobate transfer under this section.

(e) As used in this section, "nonprobate transfer" means a provision, other than a provision of a life insurance policy, of either of the following types:

(1) A provision of a type described in Section 5000.

(2) A provision in an instrument that operates on death, other than a will, conferring a power of appointment or naming a trustee. *(Formerly § 5600, added by Stats.2001, c. 417 (A.B.873), § 9, operative Jan. 1, 2002. Renumbered § 5040 and amended by Stats.2015, c. 293 (A.B.139), § 12, eff. Jan. 1, 2016. Amended by Stats.2016, c. 50 (S.B.1005), § 83, eff. Jan. 1, 2017.)*

Operative Effect

For operative effect and application of Chapter 3, see Probate Code § 5048.

Law Revision Commission Comments

2001 Addition

Subdivision (a) of Section 5600 establishes the general rule that a nonprobate transfer to a former spouse fails if, at the time of the transferor's death, the former spouse is not the transferor's surviving spouse, due to the dissolution or annulment of their marriage. "Dissolution or annulment" does not include legal separation. This is consistent with the law governing wills. See Sections 6122(d), 6227. "Surviving spouse" is defined in Section 78. "Nonprobate transfer" does not include life insurance. See subdivision (e).

Paragraph (1) of subdivision (b) provides that a nonprobate transfer to a former spouse does not fail by operation of subdivision (a) if, at the time of the transferor's death, the nonprobate transfer is not subject to revocation by the transferor. This precludes operation of subdivision (a) where a nonprobate transfer is irrevocable on execution, or later becomes irrevocable by the transferor (for reasons other than the death or incapacity of the transferor). The irrevocability of a trust can be established by certification of the trust's contents. See Section 18100.5.

Paragraph (2) of subdivision (b) provides that a nonprobate transfer to a former spouse does not fail on the transferor's death if there is clear and convincing evidence that the transferor intended to preserve the nonprobate transfer. For example, if after divorcing, the transferor modified the beneficiary terms of a trust without changing the designation of the former spouse as primary beneficiary, this might be sufficiently clear and convincing evidence of the transferor's intent to preserve the nonprobate transfer to the former spouse so as to prevent the operation of subdivision (a).

Subdivision (c) governs the effect of failure of a nonprobate transfer under this section. For the effect of a failed nonprobate transfer of property, see Section 21111. For the effect of a failure of a trustee designation, see Section 15660.

Subdivision (d) makes clear that nothing in this section affects the rights of a good faith purchaser or encumbrancer for value who relies on the apparent failure of a nonprobate transfer under this section or who lacks knowledge of the failure of a nonprobate transfer under this section. For the purpose of this subdivision, "knowledge" of the failure of a nonprobate transfer includes both actual knowledge and constructive knowledge through recordation of a judgment of dissolution or annulment or other relevant document. See Civ. Code 1213 (recordation as constructive notice to subsequent purchasers and mortgagees). The rights of a subsequent purchaser or encumbrancer are also protected if the purchaser or encumbrancer relies on an affidavit or declaration executed under Section 5602. The remedy for a person injured by a transaction with a subsequent purchaser or encumbrancer for value is against the transacting former spouse and not against the purchaser or encumbrancer.

In general, Section 5003 protects a property holder from liability for transferring the property according to the terms of the instrument making the nonprobate transfer, even if the nonprobate transfer has failed by operation of subdivision (a).

This section may be preempted by federal laws with respect to employer-provided benefits. See Egelhoff v. Egelhoff, 532 U.S. 141, 121 S. Ct. 1322 (2001) (ERISA preempts state law revoking spouse's rights as beneficiary of employer-provided life insurance). It is therefore especially important on dissolution or annulment of marriage to review beneficiary designations for employer-provided benefits. [31 Cal.L.Rev.Comm. Reports 76 (2001)].

2015 Addition

Section 5040 continues former Section 5600 without change. [36 Cal.L.Rev.Comm. Reports 103 (2006)].

Research References

Forms

California Transactions Forms--Estate Planning § 10:34, Multiple Party Accounts.

Treatises and Practice Aids

Witkin, California Summary 10th Husband and Wife § 105, Statutory Rule.

Witkin, California Summary 10th Negotiable Instruments § 79, Ownership Of Account.

Witkin, California Summary 10th Wills and Probate § 317, in General.

Witkin, California Summary 10th Wills and Probate § 318, Transfer to Former Spouse.

Witkin, California Summary 10th Wills and Probate § 320, Real Property Affidavit.

§ 5042. Joint tenancy created before or during marriage or registered domestic partnership severed if former spouse not decedent's surviving spouse; situations where joint tenancy is not severed

(a) Except as provided in subdivision (b), a joint tenancy between the decedent and the decedent's former spouse, created before or during the marriage or registered domestic partnership, is severed as to the decedent's interest if, at the time of the decedent's death, the former spouse is not the decedent's surviving spouse as defined in Section 78, as a result of the dissolution or annulment of the marriage or registered domestic partnership. A judgment of legal separation that does not terminate the status of spouses is not a dissolution for purposes of this section.

(b) Subdivision (a) does not sever a joint tenancy in either of the following cases:

(1) The joint tenancy is not subject to severance by the decedent at the time of the decedent's death.

(2) There is clear and convincing evidence that the decedent intended to preserve the joint tenancy in favor of the former spouse.

(c) Nothing in this section affects the rights of a subsequent purchaser or encumbrancer for value in good faith who relies on an apparent severance under this section or who lacks knowledge of a severance under this section.

(d) For purposes of this section, property held in "joint tenancy" includes property held as community property with right of survivorship, as described in Section 682.1 of the Civil Code. *(Formerly § 5601, added by Stats.2001, c. 417 (A.B. 873), § 9, operative Jan. 1, 2002. Renumbered § 5042 and amended by Stats.2015, c. 293 (A.B.139), § 13, eff. Jan. 1, 2016. Amended by Stats.2016, c. 50 (S.B.1005), § 84, eff. Jan. 1, 2017.)*

Operative Effect

For operative effect and application of Chapter 3, see Probate Code § 5048.

Law Revision Commission Comments

2001 Addition

Subdivision (a) of Section 5601 establishes the general rule that a joint tenancy between a decedent and the decedent's former spouse is severed if, at the time of the decedent's death, the former spouse is not the decedent's surviving spouse, due to the dissolution or annulment of their marriage. "Dissolution or annulment" does not include legal separation. This is consistent with the law governing wills. See Sections 6122(d), 6227. "Surviving spouse" is defined in Section 78. This effectively reverses the common law rule that dissolution or annulment of marriage does not sever a joint tenancy between spouses. See, e.g., Estate of Layton, 44 Cal.App.4th 1337, 52 Cal.Rptr.2d 251 (1996).

Note that property acquired during marriage in joint tenancy form is presumed to be community property on dissolution of marriage or legal separation. See Fam. Code 2581. See also *In re* Marriage of Hilke, 4 Cal.4th 215, 841 P.2d 891, 14 Cal.Rptr.2d 371 (1992) (community property presumption applies after death of former spouse if court has entered judgment dissolving marriage and reserved jurisdiction over property matters). This section does not affect the community property presumption and does not affect property characterized as community property under that presumption.

This section applies to both real and personal property joint tenancies, and affects property rights that depend on the law of joint tenancy. See, e.g., Veh. Code 4150.5, 5600.5 (property passes as though in joint tenancy). This section does not affect United States Savings Bonds, which are subject to federal regulation. See Conrad v. Conrad, 66 Cal.App.2d 280, 284–85, 152 P.2d 221, 223 (1944) (federal law controls).

The method provided in this section for severing a joint tenancy is not exclusive. See, e.g., Civ. Code 683.2.

Where a joint tenancy involves three or more joint tenants, severance by operation of this section converts the decedent's interest into a tenancy in common, but does not sever the joint tenancy as between the other joint tenants. For example, husband, wife, and a third person create a joint tenancy during husband and wife's marriage to each other. On husband's death, wife is not husband's surviving spouse and the joint tenancy is severed by operation of this section. Husband's one third interest becomes a tenancy in common and does not pass by survivorship. The remaining two thirds remain in joint tenancy as between the third person and the former wife.

Paragraph (1) of subdivision (b) provides that a joint tenancy is not severed by operation of subdivision (a) if the joint tenancy is not subject to severance by the decedent (for reasons other than the decedent's death). For example, if the decedent is subject to a court order or binding agreement prohibiting severance of the joint tenancy by the decedent, then the joint tenancy is not severed by operation of subdivision (a).

Subdivision (c) makes clear that nothing in this section affects the rights of a good faith purchaser or encumbrancer who relies on an apparent severance by operation of this section or who lacks knowledge of a severance by operation of this section. For the purpose of this subdivision, "knowledge" of a severance of joint tenancy includes both actual knowledge and constructive knowledge through recordation of a judgment of dissolution or annulment or other relevant document. See Civ. Code 1213 (recordation as constructive notice to subsequent purchasers and mortgagees). The rights of a subsequent purchaser or encumbrancer are also protected if the purchaser or encumbrancer relies on an affidavit or declaration executed under Section 5602. The remedy for a person injured by a transaction with a subsequent purchaser or encumbrancer is against the transacting joint tenant and not against the purchaser or encumbrancer. [31 Cal.L.Rev.Comm. Reports 78 (2001)].

2015 Addition

Section 5042 continues former Section 5601 without change. [36 Cal.L.Rev.Comm. Reports 103 (2006)].

Research References

Treatises and Practice Aids

Witkin, California Summary 10th Community Property § 15, Nature and Effect.

Witkin, California Summary 10th Community Property § 157, Conversion to Community Property With Right Of Survivorship.

Witkin, California Summary 10th Community Property § 221, Effect Of Party's Death After Dissolution But Before Division.

Witkin, California Summary 10th Real Property § 54, Agreement With Other Joint Tenant.

Witkin, California Summary 10th Wills and Probate § 317, in General.

Witkin, California Summary 10th Wills and Probate § 319, Joint Tenancy With Former Spouse.

Witkin, California Summary 10th Wills and Probate § 320, Real Property Affidavit.

§ 5044. Rights of purchaser or encumbrancer of real property who relies on affidavit or declaration

(a) Nothing in this chapter affects the rights of a purchaser or encumbrancer of real property for value who in good faith relies on an affidavit or a declaration under penalty of perjury under the laws of this state that states all of the following:

(1) The name of the decedent.

(2) The date and place of the decedent's death.

(3) A description of the real property transferred to the affiant or declarant by an instrument making a nonprobate transfer or by operation of joint tenancy survivorship.

(4) Either of the following, as appropriate:

(A) The affiant or declarant is the surviving spouse of the decedent.

(B) The affiant or declarant is not the surviving spouse of the decedent, but the rights of the affiant or declarant to the described property are not affected by Section 5040 or 5042.

(b) A person relying on an affidavit or declaration made pursuant to subdivision (a) has no duty to inquire into the truth of the matters stated in the affidavit or declaration.

(c) An affidavit or declaration made pursuant to subdivision (a) may be recorded. *(Formerly § 5602, added by Stats.2001, c. 417 (A.B.873), § 9, operative Jan. 1, 2002. Renumbered § 5044 and amended by Stats.2015, c. 293 (A.B.139), § 14, eff. Jan. 1, 2016.)*

Operative Effect

For operative effect and application of Chapter 3, see Probate Code § 5048.

Law Revision Commission Comments

2001 Addition

Section 5602 provides a procedure for certifying that a person's rights to real property transferred on the death of a spouse or former spouse, by an instrument making a nonprobate transfer or by operation of joint tenancy survivorship, are not affected by this part. See also Code Civ. Proc. 2015.5 (certification or declaration under penalty of perjury); Prob. Code 210–212 (recording evidence of death affecting title to real property). [28 Cal.L.Rev.Comm. Reports 599 (1998)].

2015 Addition

Section 5044 continues former Section 5602 without change. [36 Cal.L.Rev.Comm. Reports 103 (2006)].

Research References

Treatises and Practice Aids

Witkin, California Summary 10th Wills and Probate § 320, Real Property Affidavit.

§ 5046. Court authority to order dissolution or annulment of marriage to maintain former spouse as beneficiary or preserve joint tenancy

Nothing in this chapter is intended to limit the court's authority to order a party to a dissolution or annulment of marriage to maintain the former spouse as a beneficiary on any nonprobate transfer described in this chapter, or to preserve a joint tenancy in favor of the former spouse. *(Formerly § 5603, added by Stats.2001, c. 417 (A.B.873), § 9, operative Jan. 1, 2002. Renumbered § 5046 and amended by Stats.2015, c. 293 (A.B.139), § 15, eff. Jan. 1, 2016.)*

Operative Effect

For operative effect and application of Chapter 3, see Probate Code § 5048.

Law Revision Commission Comments

2001 Addition

Section 5603 clarifies the effect of this part. [31 Cal.L.Rev.Comm. Reports 79 (2001)].

2015 Addition

Section 5046 continues former Section 5603 without change. [36 Cal.L.Rev.Comm. Reports 103 (2006)].

Research References

Treatises and Practice Aids

Witkin, California Summary 10th Wills and Probate § 317, in General.

§ 5048. Operative date and application

(a) This chapter, formerly Part 4 (commencing with Section 5600), is operative on January 1, 2002.

(b) Except as provided in subdivision (c), this chapter applies to an instrument making a nonprobate transfer or creating a joint tenancy whether executed before, on, or after the operative date of this chapter.

(c) Sections 5040 and 5042 do not apply, and the applicable law in effect before the operative date of this chapter applies, to an instrument making a nonprobate transfer or creating a joint tenancy in either of the following circumstances:

(1) The person making the nonprobate transfer or creating the joint tenancy dies before the operative date of this chapter.

(2) The dissolution of marriage or other event that terminates the status of the nonprobate transfer beneficiary or joint tenant as a surviving spouse occurs before the operative date of this chapter. *(Formerly § 5604, added by Stats.2001, c. 417 (A.B.873), § 9, operative Jan. 1, 2002. Renumbered § 5048 and amended by Stats.2015, c. 293 (A.B.139), § 16, eff. Jan. 1, 2016.)*

Law Revision Commission Comments

2001 Addition

Section 5604 governs the application of this part.

Under subdivision (c), where a dissolution of marriage, or other event terminating a person's status as a decedent's surviving spouse occurs before January 1, 2000, that person's rights as a nonprobate transfer beneficiary or joint tenant of the decedent are not affected by Section 5600 or 5601. See Section 78 ("surviving spouse" defined). [31 Cal.L.Rev.Comm. Reports 79 (2001)].

2015 Addition

Section 5048 continues former Section 5604 without change. [36 Cal.L.Rev.Comm. Reports 103 (2006)].

Research References

Treatises and Practice Aids

Witkin, California Summary 10th Wills and Probate § 317, in General.

Part 2

MULTIPLE–PARTY ACCOUNTS

Law Revision Commission Comments

1990 Enactment

This part supersedes Part 1 (commencing with Section 5100) of Division 5 the repealed Probate Code. The superseded part was enacted upon recommendation of the California Law Revision Commission. See Recommendation Relating to Multiple–Party Accounts in Financial Institutions, 20 Cal.L.Revision Comm'n Reports 95 (1990). See also Communication from the California Law Revision Commission Concerning Senate Bill 985, 20 Cal.L.Revision Comm'n Reports 247 (1990).

For an earlier Commission recommendation which resulted in enactment of a statute covering credit unions and industrial loan companies, see Recommendation Relating to Nonprobate Transfers, 16 Cal.L.Revision Comm'n Reports 129 (1982). See also 17 Cal.L.Revision Comm'n Reports 823 (1984) (legislative history). For an earlier recommendation, see Recommendation Relating to Non–Probate Transfers, 15 Cal.L.Revision Comm'n Reports 1605 (1980). See also 16 Cal.L.Revision Comm'n Reports 2026 (1982) (legislative history). [20 Cal.L.Rev.Comm.Reports 1001 (1990)].

CHAPTER 1. SHORT TITLE AND DEFINITIONS

Application

Application of Part 2 to accounts in existence on or established after July 1, 1990, see Probate Code § 5205.

ARTICLE 1. SHORT TITLE

§ 5100. Short title

This part may be cited as the California Multiple-Party Accounts Law. *(Stats.1990, c. 79 (A.B.759), § 14, operative July 1, 1991.)*

Law Revision Commission Comments

1990 Enactment

Section 5100 continues Section 5100 of the repealed Probate Code without change.

Background on Section 5100 of Repealed Code

Section 5100 was a new provision added by 1983 Cal.Stat. ch. 92 § 5. For background on the provisions of this part, see the Comment to this part under the part heading. [20 Cal.L.Rev.Comm.Reports 1001 (1990)].

Research References

Forms

California Transactions Forms--Estate Planning § 10:19, Joint Tenancy Property.

California Transactions Forms--Estate Planning § 10:34, Multiple Party Accounts.

Treatises and Practice Aids

Witkin, California Summary 10th Community Property § 22, Community Property.

Witkin, California Summary 10th Community Property § 157, Conversion to Community Property With Right Of Survivorship.

Witkin, California Summary 10th Negotiable Instruments § 77, Nature and Purpose Of Statutes.

Witkin, California Summary 10th Negotiable Instruments § 79, Ownership Of Account.

Witkin, California Summary 10th Personal Property § 30, Nature Of Joint Tenancy.

Witkin, California Summary 10th Trusts § 8, Nature Of Trust.

Witkin, California Summary 10th Wills and Probate § 37, Major Changes.

Witkin, California Summary 10th Wills and Probate § 108, Pay-On-Death Provisions.

Witkin, California Summary 10th Wills and Probate § 266, Community Property With Right Of Survivorship.

Witkin, California Summary 10th Wills and Probate § 305, Recommendation and Enactment.

Witkin, California Summary 10th Wills and Probate § 405, Probate and Administration.

ARTICLE 2. DEFINITIONS

§ 5120. Application of definitions

Unless the provision or context otherwise requires, the definitions in this article govern the construction of this part. *(Stats.1990, c. 79 (A.B.759), § 14, operative July 1, 1991.)*

Law Revision Commission Comments

1990 Enactment

Section 5120 continues Section 5120 of the repealed Probate Code without change. Section 5120 is consistent with the introductory clause of Uniform Probate Code Section 6–101 (1987). As to the construction of provisions drawn from uniform acts, see Section 2.

Background on Section 5120 of Repealed Code

Section 5120 was added by 1989 Cal.Stat. ch. 397 § 25. The section restated without substantive change the introductory portion of former Probate Code Section 5101 (repealed by 1989 Cal.Stat. ch. 397 § 24). For background on the provisions of this part, see the Comment to this part under the part heading. [20 Cal.L.Rev.Comm.Reports 1001 (1990)].

Research References

Forms

West's California Code Forms, Probate § 6602 Form 1, Petition to Set Aside Small Estate.

Treatises and Practice Aids

Witkin, California Summary 10th Negotiable Instruments § 79, Ownership Of Account.
Witkin, California Summary 10th Wills and Probate § 781, Nature Of Right.
Witkin, California Summary 10th Wills and Probate § 794, Property Excluded from Estate.

§ 5122. Account

(a) "Account" means a contract of deposit of funds between a depositor and a financial institution, and includes a checking account, savings account, certificate of deposit, share account, and other like arrangement.

(b) "Account" does not include:

(1) An account established for deposit of funds of a partnership, joint venture, or other association for business purposes.

(2) An account controlled by one or more persons as the duly authorized agent or trustee for a corporation, unincorporated association, or charitable or civic organization.

(3) A regular fiduciary or trust account where the relationship is established other than by deposit agreement.

(4) An account established for the deposit of funds of the estate of a ward, conservatee, or decedent. *(Stats.1990, c. 79 (A.B.759), § 14, operative July 1, 1991.)*

Law Revision Commission Comments

1990 Enactment

Section 5122 continues Section 5122 of the repealed Probate Code without change. Subdivision (a) is the same in substance as subsection (1) of Section 6–101 of the Uniform Probate Code (1987). Paragraphs (1)–(3) of subdivision (b) are the same in substance as the second sentence of subsection (5) of Section 6–101 of the Uniform Probate Code (1987). As to the construction of provisions drawn from uniform acts, see Section 2.

Background on Section 5122 of Repealed Code

Section 5122 was added by 1989 Cal.Stat. ch. 397 § 25. Subdivision (a) restated subdivision (a) of former Probate Code Section 5101 (repealed by 1989 Cal.Stat. ch. 397 § 24) without change. Paragraphs (1)–(3) of subdivision (b) restated the second sentence of subdivision (e) of former Section 5101 without substantive change. Paragraph (4) of subdivision (b) was new and superseded the third sentence of subdivision (g) of former Section 5101. The new paragraph made clear that the rules applicable to an account established for funds of a guardianship, conservatorship, or decedent's estate are not affected by this part. For background on the provisions of this part, see the Comment to this part under the part heading. [20 Cal.L.Rev.Comm.Reports 1001 (1990)].

Research References

Treatises and Practice Aids

Witkin, California Summary 10th Community Property § 22, Community Property.
Witkin, California Summary 10th Negotiable Instruments § 78, Definitions.
Witkin, California Summary 10th Negotiable Instruments § 79, Ownership Of Account.
Witkin, California Summary 10th Wills and Probate § 310, Consent.

§ 5124. Agent

"Agent" means a person who has a present right, subject to request, to payment from an account as an attorney in fact under a power of attorney. *(Stats.1990, c. 79 (A.B.759), § 14, operative July 1, 1991.)*

Law Revision Commission Comments

1990 Enactment

Section 5124 continues Section 5124 of the repealed Probate Code without change. See also Section 5204 (special power of attorney with respect to accounts at financial institutions).

Background on Section 5124 of Repealed Code

Section 5124 was a new provision added by 1989 Cal.Stat. ch. 397 § 25. For background on the provisions of this part, see the Comment to this part under the part heading. [20 Cal.L.Rev.Comm.Reports 1001 (1990)].

§ 5126. Beneficiary

"Beneficiary" means a person named in a Totten trust account as one for whom a party to the account is named as trustee. *(Stats.1990, c. 79 (A.B.759), § 14, operative July 1, 1991.)*

Law Revision Commission Comments

1990 Enactment

Section 5126 continues Section 5126 of the repealed Probate Code without change. The section is the same in substance as subsection (2) of Section 6–101 of the Uniform Probate Code (1987). As to the construction of provisions drawn from uniform acts, see Section 2. See also Section 80 (defining "Totten trust account"). As used in this part, "trustee" means the trustee of a Totten trust account.

Background on Section 5126 of Repealed Code

Section 5126 was added by 1989 Cal.Stat. ch. 397 § 25. The section restated subdivision (b) of former Probate Code Section 5101 (repealed by 1989 Cal.Stat. ch. 397 § 24) without substantive change. For background on the provisions of this part, see the Comment to this part under the part heading. [20 Cal.L.Rev.Comm.Reports 1001 (1990)].

§ 5128. Financial institution

"Financial institution" includes:

(a) A financial institution as defined in Section 40.

(b) An industrial loan company as defined in Section 18003 of the Financial Code. *(Stats.1990, c. 79 (A.B.759), § 14, operative July 1, 1991.)*

Law Revision Commission Comments

1990 Enactment

Section 5128 continues Section 5128 of the repealed Probate Code without change. Subdivision (a), read with the definition of "financial institution" in Section 40, is comparable to subsection (3) of Section 6–101 of the Uniform Probate Code (1987). As to the construction of provisions drawn from uniform acts, see Section 2.

Background on Section 5128 of Repealed Code

Section 5128 was added by 1989 Cal.Stat. ch. 397 § 25. The section superseded subdivision (c) of former Probate Code Section 5101 (repealed by 1989 Cal.Stat. ch. 397 § 24). The term "financial institution" as defined in subdivision (c) of former Section 5101 was limited to credit unions and industrial loan companies. The new definition in Section 5128 applied as well to banks, savings and loan associations, and other like organizations, by force of Section 40 defining "financial institution." For background on the provisions of this part, see the Comment to this part under the part heading. [20 Cal.L.Rev.Comm.Reports 1001 (1990)].

Research References

Forms

California Transactions Forms--Estate Planning § 10:34, Multiple Party Accounts.

Treatises and Practice Aids

Witkin, California Summary 10th Negotiable Instruments § 77, Nature and Purpose Of Statutes.

Witkin, California Summary 10th Negotiable Instruments § 78, Definitions.

Witkin, California Summary 10th Personal Property § 32, Unilateral Severance.

§ 5130. Joint account

"Joint account" means an account payable on request to one or more of two or more parties whether or not mention is made of any right of survivorship. *(Stats.1990, c. 79 (A.B. 759), § 14, operative July 1, 1991.)*

Law Revision Commission Comments

1990 Enactment

Section 5130 continues Section 5130 of the repealed Probate Code without change. The section is the same in substance as subsection (4) of Section 6–101 of the Uniform Probate Code (1987). As to the construction of provisions drawn from uniform acts, see Section 2.

The definition of "joint account" embraces all of the following:

(1) *Joint account with right of survivorship.* See Sections 5301(a), 5302(a).

(2) *Joint account without right of survivorship.* This is a special type of joint account where there is clear and convincing evidence of an intent not to have survivorship. The terms of the account may include an express statement making clear that there is no survivorship right (see subdivision (a) of Section 5302) or the account may be designated as a "tenancy in common" account (see Section 5306).

(3) *Joint account held by a husband and wife with right of survivorship that cannot be changed by will.* This is a joint account held by a husband and wife that is not specifically designated in the account agreement as a "community property" account and there is no clear and convincing evidence of an intent that there be no survivorship right. The statute creates a presumption that if the parties to an account are married to each other, whether or not they are so described in the deposit agreement, their net contribution to the account is presumed to be and remain their community property. See Section 5305. The rules stated in Sections 5301(a) and 5302(a) apply to this type of joint account, including a rule that the right of survivorship of the surviving spouse cannot be changed by will. However, if the deposit agreement or the terms of the account *clearly indicates an intent that there be no survivorship right,* either spouse can designate one or more P.O.D. payees (or Totten trust beneficiaries) to take that spouse's share of the account upon the death of that spouse and, absent such a designation, the share of the deceased spouse becomes a part of the estate of the deceased spouse.

(4) *Joint account held by husband and wife that is specifically designated as a "community property" account.* This is a joint account held by a husband and wife that is specifically designated in the account agreement as a "community property" account. Section 5307 provides that this type of account is governed by the rules that apply to community property generally. Accordingly, unless the parties have agreed otherwise, the right of survivorship of the surviving spouse can be changed by will (deceased spouse by will devises his or her one-half share of the account to a person other than the surviving spouse). Also, the deposit agreement or the terms of the account can include, for example, a provision that the one-half share of a spouse will pass on the death of that spouse to one or more P.O.D. payees (or Totten trust beneficiaries) upon the death of that spouse. On the other hand, absent a contrary agreement or a contrary disposition, the surviving spouse will take the one-half share of the deceased spouse as community property.

Background on Section 5130 of Repealed Code

Section 5130 was added by 1989 Cal.Stat. ch. 397 § 25. The section continued subdivision (d) of former Probate Code Section 5101 (repealed by 1989 Cal.Stat. ch. 397 § 24) without change. For background on the provisions of this part, see the Comment to this part under the part heading. [20 Cal.L.Rev.Comm.Reports 1001 (1990)].

Research References

Forms

California Transactions Forms--Estate Planning § 10:34, Multiple Party Accounts.

Treatises and Practice Aids

Witkin, California Summary 10th Negotiable Instruments § 78, Definitions.

§ 5132. Multiple-party account

A "multiple-party account" is any of the following types of account:

(a) A joint account.

(b) A P.O.D. account.

(c) A Totten trust account. *(Stats.1990, c. 79 (A.B.759), § 14, operative July 1, 1991.)*

Law Revision Commission Comments

1990 Enactment

Section 5132 continues Section 5132 of the repealed Probate Code without change. The section is the same in substance as the first sentence of subsection (5) of Section 6–101 of the Uniform Probate Code (1987). As to the construction of provisions drawn from uniform acts, see Section 2. See also Section 5204 (special power of attorney with respect to accounts at financial institutions). As to types of joint accounts, see the Comment to Section 5130.

Background on Section 5132 of Repealed Code

Section 5132 was added by 1989 Cal.Stat. ch. 397 § 25. The section restated the first sentence of subdivision (e) of former Probate Code Section 5101 (repealed by 1989 Cal.Stat. ch. 397 § 24) without substantive change. For background on the provisions of this part, see the Comment to this part under the part heading. [20 Cal.L.Rev.Comm.Reports 1001 (1990)].

Research References

Treatises and Practice Aids

Witkin, California Summary 10th Negotiable Instruments § 78, Definitions.

Witkin, California Summary 10th Wills and Probate § 360, in General.

§ 5134. Net contribution

(a) "Net contribution" of a party to an account as of any given time is the sum of all of the following:

(1) All deposits thereto made by or for the party, less all withdrawals made by or for the party that have not been paid to or applied to the use of any other party.

(2) A pro rata share of any interest or dividends earned, whether or not included in the current balance.

(3) Any proceeds of deposit life insurance added to the account by reason of the death of the party whose net contribution is in question.

(b) In the absence of proof otherwise:

(1) Only parties who have a present right of withdrawal shall be considered as having a net contribution.

(2) The net contribution of each of the parties having a present right of withdrawal is deemed to be an equal amount.

(c) It is the intent of the Legislature in enacting this section to provide a definition for the purpose of determining ownership interests in an account as between the parties to the account, and not as between the parties and the financial institution. *(Stats.1990, c. 79 (A.B.759), § 14, operative July 1, 1991.)*

Law Revision Commission Comments

1990 Enactment

Section 5134 continues Section 5134 of the repealed Probate Code without change.

Subdivision (a) is the same in substance as subsection (6) of Section 6–101 of the Uniform Probate Code (1987). As to the construction of provisions drawn from uniform acts, see Section 2. As may be seen from an examination of the provisions of this part, "net contribution" as defined in subdivision (a) has no application to the financial institution-depositor relationship. Rather, it is relevant only to controversies that may arise between parties to a multiple-party account. Subdivision (c), which is not found in the Uniform Probate Code (1987), makes this clear.

Subdivision (b) is not found in the Uniform Probate Code (1987). This subdivision provides a clear rule concerning the amount of "net contribution" in the absence of proof of a different amount.

Background on Section 5134 of Repealed Code

Section 5134 was added by 1989 Cal.Stat. ch. 397 § 25. The section restated the substance of subdivision (f) of former Probate Code Section 5101 (repealed by 1989 Cal.Stat. ch. 397 § 24) with the substitution of "whether or not included in the current balance" for the former phrase "included in the current balance" and with the addition of subdivision (c). For background on the provisions of this part, see the Comment to this part under the part heading. [20 Cal.L.Rev.Comm.Reports 1001 (1990)].

Research References

Forms

California Transactions Forms--Estate Planning § 10:34, Multiple Party Accounts.

§ 5136. Party

(a) "Party" means a person who, by the terms of the account, has a present right, subject to request, to payment from a multiple-party account other than as an agent.

(b) A P.O.D. payee is a party, by reason of being a P.O.D. payee, only after the account becomes payable to the payee by reason of surviving all persons named as original payees.

(c) A beneficiary of a Totten trust account is a party, by reason of being a beneficiary, only after the account becomes payable to the beneficiary by reason of surviving all persons named as trustees. *(Stats.1990, c. 79 (A.B.759), § 14, operative July 1, 1991.)*

Law Revision Commission Comments

1990 Enactment

Section 5136 continues Section 5136 of the repealed Probate Code without change. This section is similar to subsection (7) of Section 6–101 of the Uniform Probate Code (1987). As to the construction of provisions drawn from uniform acts, see Section 2.

The phrase "other than as an agent" in subdivision (a) makes clear that the person named as an agent (attorney in fact under a power of attorney) is not a "party" for the purposes of this part. See Section 5124 (defining "agent"). A P.O.D. payee or a Totten trust beneficiary is a party under subdivision (a) if the payee or beneficiary has, by the terms of the account, a present right, subject to request, to payment from the account other than as an agent.

Background on Section 5136 of Repealed Code

Section 5136 was added by 1989 Cal.Stat. ch. 397 § 25. The section restated the substance of subdivision (g) of former Probate Code Section 5101 (repealed by 1989 Cal.Stat. ch. 397 § 24) with the following revisions:

(1) Section 5136 omitted the third sentence of former subdivision (g) (defining "party" to include a guardian, conservator, personal representative, or assignee, including a levying creditor, of a party). This part does not apply to an account established for the deposit of funds of the estate of a ward, conservatee, or decedent. See Section 5122(b)(4).

(2) Section 5136 omitted the portion of the last sentence of former subdivision (g) relating to "a person identified as a trustee of an account for another whether or not a beneficiary is named," this portion being unnecessary. Insofar as this language applied to the trustee of a Totten trust account, it was unnecessary in view of subdivision (a) of Section 5136 which applied to any person, including a trustee of a Totten trust, who has a present right to payment. Insofar as this language applied to a regular trust account under a testamentary trust or a trust agreement that has significance apart from the account, it was unnecessary because this statute does not apply to such a trustee. See Section 5122(b)(3). See also Section 80 (defining "Totten trust account").

(3) Section 5136 revised the remaining portion of the last sentence of former subdivision (g) to conform to the language used in subdivision (b) of Section 5136.

For background on the provisions of this part, see the Comment to this part under the part heading. [20 Cal.L.Rev.Comm.Reports 1001 (1990)].

Research References

Treatises and Practice Aids

Witkin, California Summary 10th Negotiable Instruments § 78, Definitions.

§ 5138. Payment

"Payment" of sums on deposit includes all of the following:

(a) A withdrawal, including payment on check or other directive of a party.

(b) A pledge of sums of deposit.

(c) A setoff, reduction, or other disposition of all or part of an account pursuant to a pledge. *(Stats.1990, c. 79 (A.B.759), § 14, operative July 1, 1991.)*

Law Revision Commission Comments

1990 Enactment

Section 5138 continues Section 5138 of the repealed Probate Code without change. The section is the same in substance as subsection (8) of Section 6–101 of the Uniform Probate Code (1987). As to the construction of provisions drawn from uniform acts, see Section 2.

Background on Section 5138 of Repealed Code

Section 5138 was added by 1989 Cal.Stat. ch. 397 § 25. The section continued subdivision (h) of former Probate Code Section 5101 (repealed by 1989 Cal.Stat. ch. 397 § 24) without substantive change. For background on the provisions of this part, see the Comment to this part under the part heading. [20 Cal.L.Rev.Comm.Reports 1001 (1990)].

§ 5139. P.O.D.

"P.O.D." means pay on death. *(Stats.1990, c. 79 (A.B. 759), § 14, operative July 1, 1991.)*

Law Revision Commission Comments

1990 Enactment

Section 5139 continues Section 5139 of the repealed Probate Code without change. See also Sections 5140 ("P.O.D. account"), 5142 ("P.O.D. payee"). No comparable provision is found in the Uniform Probate Code (1987).

Background on Section 5139 of Repealed Code

Section 5139 was a new provision added by 1989 Cal.Stat. ch. 397 § 25. For background on the provisions of this part, see the Comment to this part under the part heading. [20 Cal.L.Rev.Comm.Reports 1001 (1990)].

Research References

Forms

California Transactions Forms--Estate Planning § 10:34, Multiple Party Accounts.

§ 5140. P.O.D. account

"P.O.D. account" means any of the following:

(a) An account payable on request to one person during the person's lifetime and on the person's death to one or more P.O.D. payees.

(b) An account payable on request to one or more persons during their lifetimes and on the death of all of them to one or more P.O.D. payees. *(Stats.1990, c. 79 (A.B.759), § 14, operative July 1, 1991.)*

Law Revision Commission Comments

1990 Enactment

Section 5140 continues Section 5140 of the repealed Probate Code without change. The section is the same in substance as subsection (10) of Section 6–101 of the Uniform Probate Code (1987). As to the construction of provisions drawn from uniform acts, see Section 2.

Background on Section 5140 of Repealed Code

Section 5140 was added by 1989 Cal.Stat. ch. 397 § 25. The section continued subdivision (i) of former Probate Code Section 5101 (repealed by 1989 Cal.Stat. ch. 397 § 24) without substantive change. For background on the provisions of this part, see the Comment to this part under the part heading. [20 Cal.L.Rev.Comm.Reports 1001 (1990)].

Research References

Forms

California Transactions Forms--Estate Planning § 6:41, Definition and Creation Of Interest.

California Transactions Forms--Estate Planning § 10:34, Multiple Party Accounts.

Treatises and Practice Aids

Witkin, California Summary 10th Negotiable Instruments § 78, Definitions.

Witkin, California Summary 10th Wills and Probate § 50, Legal and Financial Terms.

§ 5142. P.O.D. payee

"P.O.D. payee" means a person designated on a P.O.D. account as one to whom the account is payable on request after the death of one or more persons. *(Stats.1990, c. 79 (A.B.759), § 14, operative July 1, 1991.)*

Law Revision Commission Comments

1990 Enactment

Section 5142 continues Section 5142 of the repealed Probate Code without change. The section is the same as subsection (11) of Section 6–101 of the Uniform Probate Code (1987). As to the construction of provisions drawn from uniform acts, see Section 2.

Background on Section 5142 of Repealed Code

Section 5142 was added by 1989 Cal.Stat. ch. 397 § 25. The section continued subdivision (j) of former Probate Code Section 5101 (repealed by 1989 Cal.Stat. ch. 397 § 24) without change. For background on the provisions of this part, see the Comment to this part under the part heading. [20 Cal.L.Rev.Comm.Reports 1001 (1990)].

Research References

Forms

California Transactions Forms--Estate Planning § 10:34, Multiple Party Accounts.

Treatises and Practice Aids

Witkin, California Summary 10th Negotiable Instruments § 78, Definitions.

§ 5144. Proof of death

"Proof of death" includes any of the following:

(a) An original or attested or certified copy of a death certificate.

(b) A record or report that is prima facie evidence of death under Section 103550 of the Health and Safety Code, Sections 1530 to 1532, inclusive, of the Evidence Code, or another statute of this state. *(Stats.1990, c. 79 (A.B.759), § 14, operative July 1, 1991. Amended by Stats.1996, c. 1023 (S.B.1497), § 400, eff. Sept. 29, 1996.)*

Law Revision Commission Comments

1990 Enactment

Section 5144 continues Section 5144 of the repealed Probate Code without change. The section is consistent with subsection (9) of Section 6–101 of the Uniform Probate Code (1987). As to the construction of provisions drawn from uniform acts, see Section 2.

Background on Section 5144 of Repealed Code

Section 5144 was added by 1989 Cal.Stat. ch. 397 § 25. The section continued subdivision (k) of former Probate Code Section 5101 (repealed by 1989 Cal.Stat. ch. 397 § 24) without substantive change. For background on the provisions of this part, see the Comment to this part under the part heading. [20 Cal.L.Rev.Comm.Reports 1001 (1990)].

§ 5146. Receives (order or notice received by institution)

Except to the extent the terms of the account or deposit agreement expressly provide otherwise, a financial institution "receives" an order or notice under this part when it is received by the particular office or branch office of the financial institution where the account is carried. *(Stats. 1990, c. 79 (A.B.759), § 14, operative July 1, 1991.)*

Law Revision Commission Comments

1990 Enactment

Section 5146 continues Section 5146 of the repealed Probate Code without change. No comparable provision is found in the Uniform Probate Code (1987).

Background on Section 5146 of Repealed Code

Section 5146 was added by 1989 Cal.Stat. ch. 397 § 25. The section continued subdivision (*l*) of former Probate Code Section 5101 (repealed by 1989 Cal.Stat. ch. 397 § 24) with the addition of the introductory clause to make clear that the terms of the account or deposit agreement may expressly provide when an order or notice is "received." For background on the provisions of this part, see the Comment to this part under the part heading. [20 Cal.L.Rev.Comm.Reports 1001 (1990)].

§ 5148. Request

"Request" means a proper request for withdrawal, including a check or order for payment, that complies with all conditions of the account (including special requirements concerning necessary signatures) and regulations of the financial institution; but, if the financial institution conditions withdrawal or payment on advance notice, for purposes of this part the request for withdrawal or payment is treated as immediately effective and a notice of intent to withdraw is treated as a request for withdrawal. *(Stats.1990, c. 79 (A.B.759), § 14, operative July 1, 1991.)*

Law Revision Commission Comments

1990 Enactment

Section 5148 continues Section 5148 of the repealed Probate Code without change. The section is the same in substance as subsection (12) of Section 6–101 of the Uniform Probate Code (1987). As to the construction of provisions drawn from uniform acts, see Section 2. Various signature requirements may be involved in order to meet the withdrawal requirements of the account. A "request" involves compliance with these requirements. A "party" is one (other than an agent) to whom an account is presently payable without regard for whose signature may be required for a "request." See Section 5136.

Background on Section 5148 of Repealed Code

Section 5148 was added by 1989 Cal.Stat. ch. 397 § 25. The section restated subdivision (m) of former Probate Code Section 5101 (repealed by 1989 Cal.Stat. ch. 397 § 24) without substantive change. For background on the provisions of this part, see the Comment to this part under the part heading. [20 Cal.L.Rev.Comm.Reports 1001 (1990)].

§ 5150. Sums on deposit

"Sums on deposit" means both of the following:

(a) The balance payable on an account, including interest and dividends earned, whether or not included in the current balance.

(b) Any life insurance proceeds added to the account by reason of the death of a party. *(Stats.1990, c. 79 (A.B.759), § 14, operative July 1, 1991.)*

Law Revision Commission Comments

1990 Enactment

Section 5150 continues Section 5150 of the repealed Probate Code without change. The section is the same in substance as subsection (13) of Section 6–101 of the Uniform Probate Code (1987). As to the construction of provisions drawn from uniform acts, see Section 2.

Background on Section 5150 of Repealed Code

Section 5150 was added by 1989 Cal.Stat. ch. 397 § 25. The section continued subdivision (n) of former Probate Code Section 5101 (repealed by 1989 Cal.Stat. ch. 397 § 24) without substantive change. The language "whether or not included in the current balance" was added to cover the situation where interest or dividends have been earned but have not yet been credited to the account. For background on the provisions of this part, see the Comment to this part under the part heading. [20 Cal.L.Rev.Comm.Reports 1001 (1990)].

§ 5152. Withdrawal

"Withdrawal" includes payment to a third person pursuant to a check or other directive of a party or an agent. *(Stats.1990, c. 79 (A.B.759), § 14, operative July 1, 1991.)*

Law Revision Commission Comments

1990 Enactment

Section 5152 continues Section 5152 of the repealed Probate Code without change. See Section 5124 (defining "agent"). See also Section 5204 (special power of attorney with respect to accounts at financial institutions). Section 5152 is the same in substance as subsection (15) of Section 6–101 of the Uniform Probate Code (1987), except that the UPC provision does not include the reference to payment to "an agent." As to the construction of provisions drawn from uniform acts, see Section 2.

Background on Section 5152 of Repealed Code

Section 5152 was added by 1989 Cal.Stat. ch. 397 § 25. The section continued subdivision (p) of former Probate Code Section 5101 (repealed by 1989 Cal.Stat. ch. 397 § 24) with the addition of the reference to payment to "an agent." For background on the provisions of this part, see the Comment to this part under the part heading. [20 Cal.L.Rev.Comm.Reports 1001 (1990)].

CHAPTER 2. GENERAL PROVISIONS

Application

Application of Part 2 to accounts in existence on or established after July 1, 1990, see Probate Code § 5205.

§ 5201. Application of provisions concerning beneficial ownership and liability of financial institutions

(a) The provisions of Chapter 3 (commencing with Section 5301) concerning beneficial ownership as between parties, or as between parties and P.O.D. payees or beneficiaries of multiple-party accounts, are relevant only to controversies between these persons and their creditors and other successors, and have no bearing on the power of withdrawal of these persons as determined by the terms of account contracts.

(b) The provisions of Chapter 4 (commencing with Section 5401) govern the liability of financial institutions who make payments pursuant to that chapter. *(Stats.1990, c. 79 (A.B. 759), § 14, operative July 1, 1991.)*

Law Revision Commission Comments

1990 Enactment

Section 5201 continues Section 5201 of the repealed Probate Code without change. The section is the same in substance as Section 6–102 of the Uniform Probate Code (1987). As to the construction of provisions drawn from uniform acts, see Section 2. Nothing in this part affects set off rights of financial institutions. See generally Kruger v. Wells Fargo Bank, 11 Cal.3d 352, 357, 521 P.2d 441, 113 Cal.Rptr. 449 (1974) (right of setoff is "based upon general principles of equity").

Background on Section 5201 of Repealed Code

Section 5201 was added by 1983 Cal.Stat. ch. 92 § 5. For background on the provisions of this part, see the Comment to this part under the part heading. [20 Cal.L.Rev.Comm.Reports 1001 (1990)].

Research References

Treatises and Practice Aids

Witkin, California Summary 10th Negotiable Instruments § 79, Ownership Of Account.

§ 5202. Fraudulent transfers

Nothing in this part affects the law relating to transfers in fraud of creditors. *(Stats.1990, c. 79 (A.B.759), § 14, operative July 1, 1991.)*

Law Revision Commission Comments

1990 Enactment

Section 5202 continues Section 5202 of the repealed Probate Code without change. No comparable provision is found in the Uniform Probate Code (1987).

Background on Section 5202 of Repealed Code

Section 5202 was added by 1983 Cal.Stat. ch. 92 § 5. For background on the provisions of this part, see the Comment to this part under the part heading. [20 Cal.L.Rev.Comm.Reports 1001 (1990)].

Research References

Treatises and Practice Aids

Witkin, California Summary 10th Negotiable Instruments § 79, Ownership Of Account.

§ 5203. Words used to create accounts; effect of different wording

(a) Words in substantially the following form in a signature card, passbook, contract, or instrument evidencing an account, or words to the same effect, executed before, on, or after July 1, 1990, create the following accounts:

(1) Joint account: "This account or certificate is owned by the named parties. Upon the death of any of them, ownership passes to the survivor(s)."

(2) P.O.D. account with single party: "This account or certificate is owned by the named party. Upon the death of that party, ownership passes to the named pay-on-death payee(s)."

(3) P.O.D. account with multiple parties: "This account or certificate is owned by the named parties. Upon the death of any of them, ownership passes to the survivor(s). Upon the death of all of them, ownership passes to the named pay-on-death payee(s)."

(4) Joint account of spouses with right of survivorship: "This account or certificate is owned by the named parties, who are spouses, and is presumed to be their community property. Upon the death of either of them, ownership passes to the survivor."

(5) Community property account of spouses: "This account or certificate is the community property of the named parties who are spouses. The ownership during lifetime and after the death of a spouse is determined by the law applicable to community property generally and may be affected by a will."

(6) Tenancy in common account: "This account or certificate is owned by the named parties as tenants in common. Upon the death of any party, the ownership interest of that party passes to the named pay-on-death payee(s) of that party or, if none, to the estate of that party."

(b) Use of the form language provided in this section is not necessary to create an account that is governed by this part. If the contract of deposit creates substantially the same relationship between the parties as an account created using the form language provided in this section, this part applies to the same extent as if the form language had been used. *(Stats.1990, c. 79 (A.B.759), § 14, operative July 1, 1991. Amended by Stats.2016, c. 86 (S.B.1171), § 249, eff. Jan. 1, 2017; Stats.2016, c. 50 (S.B.1005), § 85, eff. Jan. 1, 2017.)*

Law Revision Commission Comments

1990 Enactment

Section 5203 continues Section 5203 of the repealed Probate Code without change. The section provides form language for multiple-party accounts, but does not require use of the form language. Accordingly, the account agreement for existing accounts need not be changed to conform to the form language provided in this section. Also, accounts may be established after this section becomes operative using forms that were used under the law in effect before this section was enacted. For the form language to establish a special power of attorney for account transactions, see Section 5204(c). Section 5203 is drawn in part from a Wisconsin statute. See Wis.Stat.Ann. § 705.02 (West 1981 & Supp.1988).

A contract of deposit that does not use the form language for a particular kind of account is nevertheless governed by this part if the contract of deposit provides for substantially the same relationship between the parties. For example, an account held by two persons as "joint tenants with right of survivorship" is treated as a joint account under this part. Likewise, an account payable on request to one or more of two or more parties is treated as a joint account under this part even though no mention is made of any right of survivorship unless the terms of the account or deposit agreement otherwise provide. See Section 5130 ("joint account" defined). An account treated as a joint account belongs to the parties in proportion to their net contributions and passes to the survivors unless there is clear and convincing evidence of a different intent. See Sections 5301 (ownership during lifetime), 5302 (right of survivorship). But see Sections 5306 (tenancy in common accounts), 5307 (account expressly described as "community property" account).

A party to a "tenancy in common" account can designate a P.O.D. beneficiary to receive that tenant's share of the account upon the tenant's death, and the provisions of this part are applicable with respect to the P.O.D. designation. Likewise, although the rights during lifetime and upon death of the parties to an account expressly described as a "community property" account are governed by the law applicable to community property generally, either spouse on the "community property" account can designate a P.O.D. beneficiary to receive that spouse's one-half share of the account upon the death of that spouse, and the provisions of this part are applicable with respect to the P.O.D. designation. See also the discussion in the Comment to Section 5130.

Section 5203 does not provide form language for a Totten trust account (as defined in Section 80), since the P.O.D. account serves the same function. However, a Totten trust account is authorized and is governed by the provisions of this part that apply to Totten trust accounts.

Background on Section 5203 of Repealed Code

Section 5203 was added by 1989 Cal.Stat. ch. 397 § 26. For background on the provisions of this part, see the Comment to this part under the part heading. [20 Cal.L.Rev.Comm.Reports 1001 (1990)].

Research References

Forms

California Transactions Forms--Estate Planning § 10:53, Joint Account.

California Transactions Forms--Estate Planning § 10:54, Pod Account With Single Party.

California Transactions Forms--Estate Planning § 10:55, Pod Account With Multiple Parties.

California Transactions Forms--Estate Planning § 10:56, Joint Account Of Husband and Wife With Right Of Survivorship.

California Transactions Forms--Estate Planning § 10:57, Community Property Account Of Husband and Wife.

California Transactions Forms--Estate Planning § 10:58, Tenancy in Common Account.

Treatises and Practice Aids

Witkin, California Summary 10th Wills and Probate § 310, Consent.

§ 5204. Special power of attorney; institution liability upon reliance on validity; records for accounting; attorney liability; application of other laws

(a) In addition to a power of attorney otherwise authorized by law, a special power of attorney is authorized under this section to apply to one or more accounts at a financial institution or to one or more contracts with a financial institution concerning safe deposit services. For the purposes of this section, "account" includes checking accounts, savings accounts, certificates of deposit, savings certificates, and any other depository relationship with the financial institution.

(b) The special power of attorney under this section shall:

(1) Be in writing.

(2) Be signed by the person or persons giving the power of attorney.

(3) Explicitly identify the attorney-in-fact or attorneys-in-fact, the financial institution, and the accounts or contracts subject to the power.

(c) The special power of attorney shall contain language in substantially the following form:

"WARNING TO PERSON EXECUTING THIS DOCUMENT: This is an important legal document. It creates a power of attorney that provides the person you designate as your attorney-in-fact with the broad powers it sets forth. You have the right to terminate this power of attorney. If there is anything about this form that you do not understand, you should ask a lawyer to explain it to you."

(d) In addition to the language required by subdivision (c), special powers of attorney that are or may be durable shall also contain substantially the following language:

"These powers of attorney shall continue even if you later become disabled or incapacitated."

(e) The power of attorney granted under this section shall endure as between the grantor and grantee of the power until the earliest of the following occurs:

(1) Revocation by the grantor of the power.

(2) Termination of the account.

(3) Death of the grantor of the power.

(4) In the case of a nondurable power of attorney, appointment of a guardian or conservator of the estate of the grantor of the power.

(f) A financial institution may rely in good faith upon the validity of the power of attorney granted under this section and is not liable to the principal or any other person for doing so if (1) the power of attorney is on file with the financial institution and the transaction is made by the attorney-in-fact named in the power of attorney, (2) the power of attorney appears on its face to be valid, and (3) the financial institution has convincing evidence of the identity of the person signing the power of attorney as principal.

(g) For the purposes of subdivision (f), "convincing evidence" requires both of the following:

(1) Reasonable reliance on a document that satisfies the requirement of Section 4751.

(2) The absence of any information, evidence, or other circumstances that would lead a reasonable person to believe that the person signing the power of attorney as principal is not the individual he or she claims to be.

(h) The protection provided by subdivision (f) does not extend to payments made after written notice is received by the financial institution as to any of the events of termination of the power under subdivision (e) if the financial institution has had a reasonable time to act on the notice. No other notice or any other information shown to have been available to the financial institution shall affect its right to the protection provided by this subdivision.

(i) The attorney-in-fact acting under the power of attorney granted under this section shall maintain books or records to permit an accounting of the acts of the attorney-in-fact if an accounting is requested by a legal representative of the grantor of the power.

(j) The attorney-in-fact acting under a power of attorney granted under this section is liable for any disbursement other than a disbursement to or for the benefit of the grantor of the power, unless the grantor has authorized the disbursement in writing.

(k) Nothing in this section limits the use or effect of any other form of power of attorney for transactions with a financial institution. Nothing in this section creates an implication that a financial institution is liable for acting in reliance upon a power of attorney under circumstances where the requirements of subdivision (f) are not satisfied. Nothing in this section affects any immunity that may otherwise exist apart from this section.

(*l*) Nothing in this section prevents the attorney-in-fact from also being designated as a P.O.D. payee.

(m) Except as otherwise provided in this section, the Power of Attorney Law, Division 4.5 (commencing with Section 4000) shall not apply to a special power of attorney under this section. Section 4130 and Part 5 (commencing with Section 4900) of Division 4.5 shall apply to a special power of attorney under this section. *(Stats.1990, c. 79 (A.B.759), § 14, operative July 1, 1991. Amended by Stats. 1994, c. 307 (S.B.1907), § 17; Stats.1995, c. 300 (S.B.984), § 15, eff. Aug. 3, 1995.)*

Law Revision Commission Comments

1990 Enactment

Section 5204 continues Section 5204 of the repealed Probate Code without substantive change. Naming a person as agent—technically giving the person named as agent a power of attorney with respect to account transactions—is commonly used for convenience and permits the agent to make withdrawals from the account. Even though the account is presently payable to the agent, the account belongs to the parties to the account, and the power of attorney gives the agent no ownership or survivorship right in the account.

1994 Amendment

Subdivision (f)(1) of Section 5204 is amended to substitute a reference to the provision of the Power of Attorney Law that replaced the former Civil Code section. [24 Cal.L.Rev.Comm.Reports 323 (1994)].

Background on Section 5204 of Repealed Code

Section 5204 was a new provision added by 1989 Cal.Stat. ch. 397 § 27. For background on the provisions of this part, see the Comment to this part under the part heading. [20 Cal.L.Rev.Comm.Reports 1001 (1990)].

Research References

Forms

Cal. Transaction Forms - Bus. Transactions § 26:29, Powers Of Attorney.

Cal. Transaction Forms - Bus. Transactions § 26:37, Special Power Of Attorney for Deposit Accounts.

Cal. Transaction Forms - Bus. Transactions § 26:39, Notice Of Postdating [Cal. Com. Code, S4401].

California Transactions Forms--Estate Planning § 8:49, Financial Institutions.

California Transactions Forms--Estate Planning § 8:57, Attorney-Drafted Durable Power Of Attorney for Asset Management.

California Transactions Forms--Estate Planning § 10:34, Multiple Party Accounts.

§ 5205. Application; accounts in existence on July 1, 1990

This part applies to accounts in existence on July 1, 1990, and accounts thereafter established. *(Stats.1990, c. 79 (A.B. 759), § 14, operative July 1, 1991.)*

Law Revision Commission Comments

1990 Enactment

Section 5205 is a new provision that continues the substance of 1989 Cal.Stat. ch. 397, § 41. [20 Cal.L.Rev.Comm.Reports 1001 (1990)].

CHAPTER 3. OWNERSHIP BETWEEN PARTIES AND THEIR CREDITORS AND SUCCESSORS

Application

Application of Part 2 to accounts in existence on or established after July 1, 1990, see Probate Code § 5205.

§ 5301. Lifetime ownership; excess withdrawal; claim to recover ownership interest in excess withdrawal; P.O.D. accounts; Totten trusts

(a) An account belongs, during the lifetime of all parties, to the parties in proportion to the net contributions by each, unless there is clear and convincing evidence of a different intent.

(b) If a party makes an excess withdrawal from an account, the other parties to the account shall have an ownership interest in the excess withdrawal in proportion to the net contributions of each to the amount on deposit in the account immediately following the excess withdrawal, unless there is clear and convincing evidence of a contrary agreement between the parties.

(c) Only a living party, or a conservator, guardian, or agent acting on behalf of a living party, shall be permitted to make a claim to recover the living party's ownership interest in an excess withdrawal, pursuant to subdivision (b). A court may, at its discretion, and in the interest of justice, reduce any recovery under this section to reflect funds withdrawn and applied for the benefit of the claiming party.

(d) In the case of a P.O.D. account, the P.O.D. payee has no rights to the sums on deposit during the lifetime of any party, unless there is clear and convincing evidence of a different intent.

(e) In the case of a Totten trust account, the beneficiary has no rights to the sums on deposit during the lifetime of any party, unless there is clear and convincing evidence of a different intent. If there is an irrevocable trust, the account belongs beneficially to the beneficiary.

(f) For purposes of this section, "excess withdrawal" means the amount of a party's withdrawal that exceeds that party's net contribution on deposit in the account immediately preceding the withdrawal. *(Stats.1990, c. 79 (A.B.759), § 14, operative July 1, 1991. Amended by Stats.2012, c. 235 (A.B.1624), § 1.)*

Law Revision Commission Comments

1990 Enactment

Section 5301 continues Section 5301 of the repealed Probate Code without substantive change. Section 5301 is the same in substance as Section 6–103 of the Uniform Probate Code (1987). As to the construction of provisions drawn from uniform acts, see Section 2. The presumption under subdivision (a) that an account belongs to the parties during their lifetimes in proportion to the net contributions by each changed the rule under former law. Under former law, if the joint account provided for rights of survivorship, the account was presumed to be a joint tenancy and each joint tenant was presumed to have an equal interest in the account. Wallace v. Riley, 23 Cal.App.2d 654, 667, 74 P.2d 807 (1937).

Where there are several parties to an account and the account is one where there is no survivorship right among the parties (as where the terms of the account specifically provide that there is no survivorship right among the parties or the account is expressly designated as a "tenancy in common" account), any party may designate a P.O.D. payee (or Totten trust beneficiary) to take that party's share of the account upon the death of that party. The language "unless there is clear and convincing evidence of a different intent" in subdivisions (b) and (c) makes this clear. See also Sections 5305 (presumption that sum on deposit in joint account of married persons is community property), 5307 (account expressly described as "community property" account).

A party to a "community property" account may designate a P.O.D. payee to take that spouse's one-half interest in the account when that spouse dies. Under Section 5301, unless there is clear and convincing evidence of a different intent, the P.O.D. payee has no rights to the sums on deposit during the lifetime of the spouse naming the P.O.D. beneficiary.

Background on Section 5301 of Repealed Code

Section 5301 was added by 1983 Cal.Stat. ch. 92 § 5 and was amended by 1989 Cal.Stat. ch. 397 § 28. The 1989 amendment made no substantive change; it merely simplified the language of the section. For background on the provisions of this part, see the Comment to this part under the part heading. [20 Cal.L.Rev.Comm.Reports 1001 (1990)].

2012 Amendment

Subdivision (a) of Section 5301 is amended to avoid the implication that the net contribution rule is used only to determine the ownership interests of the parties in sums remaining on deposit. See Section 5150 ("sums on deposit" defined). The net contribution rule is used also to determine whether a party has withdrawn from the account an amount in excess of the party's ownership interest. The amendment reverses the holding of *Lee v. Yang*, 111 Cal. App. 4th 481, 3 Cal. Rptr. 3d 819 (2003) (withdrawing party owns funds withdrawn from joint account regardless of source of funds). In the absence of proof otherwise, the net contribution to an account of each of the parties having a present right of withdrawal is deemed to be an equal amount. Section 5134 ("net contribution" defined). [42 Cal.L.Rev.Comm. Reports 411 (2012)].

Research References

Forms

California Transactions Forms--Estate Planning § 10:34, Multiple Party Accounts.

Treatises and Practice Aids

Witkin, California Summary 10th Negotiable Instruments § 79, Ownership Of Account.

§ 5302. Sums remaining upon death of party

Subject to Section 5040:

(a) Sums remaining on deposit at the death of a party to a joint account belong to the surviving party or parties as against the estate of the decedent unless there is clear and convincing evidence of a different intent. If there are two or more surviving parties, their respective ownerships during lifetime are in proportion to their previous ownership interests under Section 5301 augmented by an equal share for each survivor of any interest the decedent may have owned in the account immediately before the decedent's death; and the right of survivorship continues between the surviving parties.

(b) If the account is a P.O.D. account:

(1) On death of one of two or more parties, the rights to any sums remaining on deposit are governed by subdivision (a).

(2) On death of the sole party or of the survivor of two or more parties, (A) any sums remaining on deposit belong to the P.O.D. payee or payees if surviving, or to the survivor of them if one or more die before the party, (B) if two or more P.O.D. payees survive, any sums remaining on deposit belong to them in equal and undivided shares unless the terms of the account or deposit agreement expressly provide for different shares, and (C) if two or more P.O.D. payees survive, there is no right of survivorship in the event of death of a P.O.D. payee thereafter unless the terms of the account or deposit agreement expressly provide for survivorship between them.

(c) If the account is a Totten trust account:

(1) On death of one of two or more trustees, the rights to any sums remaining on deposit are governed by subdivision (a).

(2) On death of the sole trustee or the survivor of two or more trustees, (A) any sums remaining on deposit belong to the person or persons named as beneficiaries, if surviving, or to the survivor of them if one or more die before the trustee, unless there is clear and convincing evidence of a different intent, (B) if two or more beneficiaries survive, any sums remaining on deposit belong to them in equal and undivided shares unless the terms of the account or deposit agreement expressly provide for different shares, and (C) if two or more beneficiaries survive, there is no right of survivorship in event of death of any beneficiary thereafter unless the terms of the account or deposit agreement expressly provide for survivorship between them.

(d) In other cases, the death of any party to a multiparty account has no effect on beneficial ownership of the account other than to transfer the rights of the decedent as part of the decedent's estate.

(e) A right of survivorship arising from the express terms of the account or under this section, a beneficiary designation in a Totten trust account, or a P.O.D. payee designation, cannot be changed by will. *(Stats.1990, c. 79 (A.B.759), § 14, operative July 1, 1991. Amended by Stats.2001, c. 417 (A.B.873), § 8; Stats.2015, c. 293 (A.B.139), § 9, eff. Jan. 1, 2016.)*

Law Revision Commission Comments

1990 Enactment

Section 5302 continues Section 5302 of the repealed Probate Code without change. The section is the same in substance as Section 6–104 of the Uniform Probate Code (1987), except that Section 5302 omits the UPC requirement that the intent that there be no rights of survivorship exist "at the time the account is created." Thus, under Section 5302, the intention to negate survivorship may be shown to have existed after the time of creation of the account, although the evidence must be clear and convincing. This is consistent with the rule under subdivision (a) of Section 5303 that rights of survivorship are determined by the form of the account at the death of a party. Under Section 5303, a party having the right of withdrawal can eliminate survivorship rights, for example, by closing out the account having the survivorship rights and opening a new account without survivorship rights. See the Comment to Section 5303. As to the construction of provisions drawn from uniform acts, see Section 2.

Subdivision (a) creates a right of survivorship in a joint account whether or not the account is described as a "joint tenancy" or mentions any right of survivorship. See Section 5130. The right of survivorship created by subdivision (a) may be rebutted by clear and convincing evidence of a different intent. This strengthens survivorship rights, since under prior law the presumption of survivorship arising from the joint tenancy form of the account could be overcome by a preponderance of the evidence. See Schmedding v. Schmedding, 240 Cal.App.2d 312, 315–16, 49 Cal.Rptr. 523 (1966) (presumption rebuttable); Evid.Code § 115 (except as otherwise provided by law, burden of proof requires preponderance of evidence); Comment to Evid.Code § 606 (ordinarily party against whom a rebuttable presumption operates must overcome the presumption by a preponderance of the evidence). To rebut the right of survivorship where no right of survivorship is desired, the parties to a joint account may, for example, establish a "JOINT ACCOUNT—NO SURVIVORSHIP."

Rights of survivorship are determined by the form of the account at the death of a party. See subdivision (a) of Section 5303. Under that subdivision, a party having the right of withdrawal can eliminate survivorship rights, for example, by closing out the account having the survivorship rights and opening a new account without survivorship rights. See the Comment to Section 5303.

Paragraph (2)(B) of subdivision (b), and paragraph (2)(B) of subdivision (c), are clarifying provisions not found in the Uniform Probate Code (1987). These provisions are drawn from the law of Maine. See Me.Rev.Stat.Ann. tit. 18–A, § 6–104 (West 1981).

Community funds may be deposited in an account held jointly by one of the spouses and a third person, with the other spouse not being a party to the account. Also community funds may be deposited in an account by one spouse as a trustee for a beneficiary who is not the other spouse or in a P.O.D. account where the P.O.D. payee is not the other spouse. In any of these cases, upon the death of the spouse who is a party to the account, the non-party spouse may recover his or her half interest in the community funds in preference to the survivorship rights of the third person. See Section 100. See also Section 6101 (formerly Section 201); Mazman v. Brown, 12 Cal.App.2d 272, 55 P.2d 539 (1936) (Former Probate Code Section 201 applied to nonprobate transfers with testamentary effect such as life insurance).

Even though the funds in a multiple-party account may be community funds under Section 5305, the financial institution may rely on the form of the account as a joint account, P.O.D. account, or Totten trust account and may make payment pursuant to Chapter 4 (commencing with Section 5401), and is protected from liability in so doing. See Section 5405. The nature of the property rights in such funds is to be determined among the competing claimants, and the financial institution has no interest in this controversy. See Section 5201.

Subdivision (c) codifies the judicially-recognized rule that, in the case of a tentative or "Totten" trust, the sums on deposit vest in the designated beneficiary on the death of the trustee. See 7 B. Witkin, Summary of California Law Trusts § 17, at 5379 (8th ed. 1974). However, subdivision (c) strengthens the rights of the beneficiary by permitting the trust to be attacked only by "clear and convincing" evidence that survivorship was not intended. Under prior California law, a tentative or "Totten" trust could be defeated by circumstantial and often flimsy evidence, making its use unreliable. Id. § 18, at 5380–82.

The rule stated in subdivision (d) applies to an account where there is clear and convincing evidence of an intent not to have a right of survivorship and the decedent has not designated a P.O.D. payee, such as a case where the terms of the account expressly provide that there is no right of survivorship or where the account is expressly described in the deposit agreement as a "tenancy in common" account (Section 5306). In a case where the rule stated in subdivision (d) applies, only the decedent's interest in the account becomes a part of the decedent's estate. A party to a "tenancy in common" account may, of course, designate a P.O.D. payee for the party's interest in the account, in which case upon the party's death the party's interest in the account is paid to the P.O.D. payee rather than to the party's estate. In the case of an account expressly designated in the deposit agreement as a "community property" account, either spouse may designate a P.O.D. payee for that spouse's interest, thereby making clear that the other spouse has no survivorship right to that interest, or may provide expressly in the deposit agreement that there is no survivorship right or may make a disposition of the interest in his or her will, in which case the rule in subdivision (d) applies.

Subdivision (e) changes the rule applicable to a tentative or "Totten" trust under prior California law by preventing revocation or modification of the trust by will. See Brucks v. Home Fed. Sav. & Loan Ass'n, 36 Cal.2d 845, 852–53, 228 P.2d 545 (1951) (testamentary plan wholly inconsistent with terms of tentative trust revokes the trust).

Nothing in Section 5302 prevents the court, for example, from enforcing a promise by the surviving beneficiary to share the account funds with someone else. Cf. Jarkieh v. Badagliacco, 75 Cal.App.2d 505, 170 P.2d 994 (1946).

2001 Amendment

Section 5302 is amended to make clear that the transfer on death of funds in a multiple party account is subject to Section 5600, which causes a nonprobate transfer to a former spouse to fail if the former spouse is not the transferor's surviving spouse. See Section 5600 (effect of dissolution of marriage on nonprobate transfer). [28 Cal.L.Rev.Comm. Reports 599 (1998)].

Background on Section 5302 of Repealed Code

Section 5302 was added by 1983 Cal.Stat. ch. 92 § 5 and was amended by 1989 Cal.Stat. ch. 397 § 29. The 1989 amendment made technical, nonsubstantive revisions to conform to language used in other provisions of this part. For background on the provisions of this part, see the Comment to this part under the part heading. [20 Cal.L.Rev.Comm.Reports 1001 (1990)].

2015 Amendment

Section 5302 is amended to reflect the renumbering of former Section 5600 as Section 5040. [36 Cal.L.Rev.Comm. Reports 103 (2006)].

Commentary

See generally *Estate of Petersen, 28 Cal.App.4th 1742, 34 Cal. Rptr.2d 449 (1994)* (unambiguous provision of community-funded annuity contract effected a nonprobate death transfer by right of survivorship; in contrast, statement of "joint account" for money market funds was insufficient to create a nonprobate right of survivorship).

Research References

Forms

California Transactions Forms--Estate Planning § 10:34, Multiple Party Accounts.

California Transactions Forms--Estate Planning § 19:66, Determining Testator's Intent; Information Gathering.

Treatises and Practice Aids

Witkin, California Summary 10th Negotiable Instruments § 79, Ownership Of Account.

Witkin, California Summary 10th Wills and Probate § 108, Pay-On-Death Provisions.

Witkin, California Summary 10th Wills and Probate § 274, Nature and Scope Of Statute.

Witkin, California Summary 10th Wills and Probate § 310, Consent.

§ 5303. Survivorship determined by form of account at death; methods for change of terms; effect of withdrawals

(a) The provisions of Section 5302 as to rights of survivorship are determined by the form of the account at the death of a party.

(b) Once established, the terms of a multiple-party account can be changed only by any of the following methods:

(1) Closing the account and reopening it under different terms.

(2) Presenting to the financial institution a modification agreement that is signed by all parties with a present right of withdrawal. If the financial institution has a form for this purpose, it may require use of the form.

(3) If the provisions of the terms of the account or deposit agreement provide a method of modification of the terms of the account, complying with those provisions.

(4) As provided in subdivision (c) of Section 5405.

(c) During the lifetime of a party, the terms of the account may be changed as provided in subdivision (b) to eliminate or to add rights of survivorship. Withdrawal of funds from the account by a party also eliminates rights of survivorship with respect to the funds withdrawn to the extent of the withdrawing party's net contribution to the account. *(Stats.1990, c. 79 (A.B.759), § 14, operative July 1, 1991. Amended by Stats. 2012, c. 235 (A.B.1624), § 2.)*

Law Revision Commission Comments

1990 Enactment

Section 5303 continues Section 5303 of the repealed Probate Code without change.

Subdivision (a) is the same as the first sentence of Section 6–105 of the Uniform Probate Code (1987). As to the construction of provisions drawn from uniform acts, see Section 2.

Subdivision (b) is substituted for the remainder of the Uniform Probate Code section and is drawn from Georgia law. See Ga.Code Ann. § 7–1–814 (1989). Paragraph (3) of subdivision (b) permits a change in the terms of a multiple-party account by complying with a method of modification provided in the terms of the account or deposit agreement. Accordingly, for example, if the terms of the account or deposit agreement permit a party to the account to change a P.O.D. beneficiary or to substitute a new party to a joint account for an original party to the account, the change would be effective to give the right of survivorship to the new beneficiary or new party to the joint account. The requirement of paragraph (1) that the account be closed and reopened under different terms would not apply where the modification is made under paragraph (2) or (3) of subdivision (b).

Under subdivision (a), rights of survivorship are determined by the form of the account at the death of a party. Subdivision (c) makes clear that the terms of the account that can be changed include terms relating to rights of survivorship. For example, under subdivision (b), a party having the right of withdrawal can eliminate survivorship rights by closing out the account having the survivorship rights and opening a new account without survivorship rights. Withdrawal of the funds from the account will not, however, change the other rights of the parties to the moneys withdrawn. See Sections 5301 (ownership during lifetime), 5305 (presumption of community property). See also the Comment to Section 5305.

Merely changing the terms of the account to eliminate survivorship rights does not affect the right of the financial institution to make payments in accordance with the terms of the account in effect at the time payment is made. See also Section 5405.

Section 5303 does not affect the presumption established by Section 5305 (funds of married persons who are parties to joint account presumed to be community property). See also Section 5405 (notice to financial institution from party that withdrawals should not be permitted).

Background on Section 5303 of Repealed Code

Section 5303 was added by 1983 Cal.Stat. ch. 92 § 5 and amended by 1984 Cal.Stat. ch. 452 § 7 and 1989 Cal.Stat. ch. 397 § 30. The 1984 amendment added subdivision (b)(4). The 1989 amendment added subdivision (c), a clarifying, nonsubstantive provision. For background on the provisions of this part, see the Comment to this part under the part heading. [20 Cal.L.Rev.Comm.Reports 1001 (1990)].

2012 Amendment

Section 5303 is amended to make clear that, although a party may sever the right of survivorship in a joint account by withdrawal of funds, the severance is limited in the case of an overwithdrawal. A party's ownership interest in an account, and the concomitant power to terminate a right of survivorship by withdrawing funds from the account, is determined by the party's net contribution to the account. See Section 5301 (ownership during lifetime). This codifies the rule in *Estate of Propst*, 50 Cal. 3d 448, 461–62, 268 Cal. Rptr. 114, 788 P.2d 628 (1990) ("Accordingly, we hold that in the absence of prior agreement, a joint tenant of personal property may unilaterally sever his or her own interest from the joint tenancy and thereby nullify the right of survivorship, as to that interest, of the other joint tenant or tenants without their consent."). [34 Cal.L.Rev.Comm. Reports 199 (2004)].

Research References

Treatises and Practice Aids

Witkin, California Summary 10th Negotiable Instruments § 79, Ownership Of Account.

Witkin, California Summary 10th Negotiable Instruments § 80, Protection Of Financial Institutions.

Witkin, California Summary 10th Personal Property § 32, Unilateral Severance.

§ 5304. Transfers not testamentary; necessity of writing

Any transfers resulting from the application of Section 5302 are effective by reason of the account contracts involved and this part and are not to be considered as testamentary. The right under this part of a surviving party to a joint account, or of a beneficiary, or of a P.O.D. payee, to the sums on deposit on the death of a party to a multiple-party account shall not be denied, abridged, or affected because such right has not been created by a writing executed in accordance with the laws of this state prescribing the requirements to effect a valid testamentary disposition of property. *(Stats.1990, c. 79 (A.B.759), § 14, operative July 1, 1991.)*

Law Revision Commission Comments

1990 Enactment

Section 5304 continues Section 5304 of the repealed Probate Code without change. The first sentence is the same as the first portion of Section 6–106 of the Uniform Probate Code (1987). As to the construction of provisions drawn from uniform acts, see Section 2. The remainder of the Uniform Probate Code section is omitted. The second sentence of Section 5304 is comparable to New Jersey law. See N.J.Stat.Ann. § 17:16I–14 (West 1984). The purpose of Section 5304 is to make clear that the effectiveness of transfers under this part is not to be determined by the requirements for a will.

A transfer under this part is effective by reason of the provisions of this part and the terms of the account or deposit agreement. This transfer avoids the need for a probate proceeding to accomplish a transfer. However, the transfer does not affect rights otherwise provided by law. Also, for example, Section 5304 has no effect on a surviving spouse's right to his or her share of community funds deposited in a multiple-party account under which a third person has a survivorship right upon the death of the other spouse. See the Comment to Section 5302.

Background on Section 5304 of Repealed Code

Section 5304 was added by 1983 Cal.Stat. ch. 92 § 5. The section was drawn from portions of then-existing Financial Code Sections 852.5, 7604.5, 11203.5, 14854.5, and 18318.5 (pay-on-death transfers nontestamentary). For background on the provisions of this part, see the Comment to this part under the part heading. [20 Cal.L.Rev.Comm.Reports 1001 (1990)].

Research References

Treatises and Practice Aids

Witkin, California Summary 10th Negotiable Instruments § 79, Ownership Of Account.

Witkin, California Summary 10th Wills and Probate § 108, Pay-On-Death Provisions.

§ 5305. Married parties; community property; presumption; rebuttal; change of survivorship right, beneficiary, or payee by will

(a) Notwithstanding Sections 5301 to 5303, inclusive, if parties to an account are married to each other, whether or not they are so described in the deposit agreement, their net contribution to the account is presumed to be and remain their community property.

(b) Notwithstanding Sections 2581 and 2640 of the Family Code, the presumption established by this section is a presumption affecting the burden of proof and may be rebutted by proof of either of the following:

(1) The sums on deposit that are claimed to be separate property can be traced from separate property unless it is proved that the married persons made a written agreement that expressed their clear intent that the sums be their community property.

(2) The married persons made a written agreement, separate from the deposit agreement, that expressly provided that the sums on deposit, claimed not to be community property, were not to be community property.

(c) Except as provided in Section 5307, a right of survivorship arising from the express terms of the account or under Section 5302, a beneficiary designation in a Totten trust account, or a P.O.D. payee designation, may not be changed by will.

(d) Except as provided in subdivisions (b) and (c), a multiple-party account created with community property funds does not in any way alter community property rights. *(Stats.1990, c. 79 (A.B.759), § 14, operative July 1, 1991. Amended by Stats.1992, c. 163 (A.B.2641), § 131, operative Jan. 1, 1994; Stats.1993, c. 219 (A.B.1500), § 224.7.)*

Law Revision Commission Comments

1990 Enactment

The introductory clause of subdivision (b) makes clear that the rule stated in subdivision (b) prevails over the rules stated in Civil Code Sections 4800.1 and 4800.2 with respect to the division of a joint account upon dissolution of marriage or legal separation as well as for all other purposes. Compare Section 5307 (account expressly described as "community property" account).

Paragraph (1) of subdivision (b) specifies one of the two methods of rebutting the presumption—the source-of-funds or tracing rule. If the person having the burden of proof can trace separate funds into a joint account, the presumption of community property is overcome and the funds retain their separate character. If separate funds have been commingled with community funds but remain ascertainable or traceable into a proportionate share of the account, the funds retain their separate character. On the other hand, if separate and community funds are so commingled that the party having the burden of proving that the funds are separate cannot meet that burden, then the entire account is treated as community property. See generally 7 B. Witkin, Summary of California Law Community Property §§ 33–34, at 5126–28 (8th ed. 1974). Even though the separate funds can still be traced, nothing prevents the married persons from making an agreement that expresses their clear intent that the funds be community property. If the person claiming that such an agreement was made proves that fact by a preponderance of the evidence, the agreement is given effect as provided in the last clause of paragraph (1).

Section 5305 continues Section 5305 of the repealed Probate Code without change. There is no comparable provision in the Uniform Probate Code (1987).

Section 5305 applies to "accounts" (defined in Section 5122), not just "multiple-party accounts" (defined in Section 5132). Thus, the presumption of community property applies, for example, to a husband and wife who have funds on deposit in a partnership account.

Section 5305 does not affect or limit the right of the financial institution to make payments pursuant to Sections 5401–5407 and the deposit agreement. See Section 5201. For this reason, Section 5305 does not affect the definiteness and certainty that the financial institution must have in order to be induced to make payments from the account and, at the same time, the section preserves the rights of the parties, creditors, and successors that arise out of the nature of the funds—community or separate—in the account.

The presumption created by Section 5305 is one affecting the burden of proof. See also Evid.Code § 606 ("The effect of a presumption affecting the burden of proof is to impose upon the party against whom it operates the burden of proof as to the nonexistence of the presumed fact"). This requires proof that the funds of married persons in a joint account are not community property. Subdivision (b) of Section 5305 specifies the proof that must be made to rebut the presumption that the property is community property.

Paragraph (2) of subdivision (b) specifies the other method by which the presumption may be rebutted: The spouses may expressly agree that the sums on deposit are not community property. But lay persons often do not understand the detailed provisions of the deposit agreement, and those provisions may not reflect the intent of the spouses as to the character of the property in the joint account. For this reason, paragraph (2) provides that the character of the property as community property is not changed unless there is an agreement—separate from the deposit agreement—expressly providing, for example, that the sums on deposit are not community property or that such sums are the separate property of one or both of the spouses. This scheme gives the spouses the necessary flexibility to change the character of the property where that is their intention but, at the same time, protects the spouses against unintentionally changing community property into separate property merely by signing a deposit agreement that would have that unintended effect.

The presumption created by Section 5305 does not affect the provisions of Sections 5302, 5402, and 5405 that permit prompt payment of the sums on deposit in a joint account to the surviving spouse. The prompt payment provisions are most useful where the estate is small and payment to the surviving spouse will avoid the expense and delay of probate. Yet, because the presumption created by Section 5305 governs the rights between the spouses and their successors, claimants who wish to show that the funds are community funds will find it easier to do so.

During the lifetimes of the married persons, the terms of the contract of deposit may be changed as provided in Section 5303 to eliminate or to add rights of survivorship. If there is a survivorship right in the surviving spouse at the time of the other spouse's death, the surviving spouse takes the share of the deceased spouse in the joint account by right of survivorship. See subdivision (c) of Section 5305. If there is no survivorship right in the surviving spouse at the time of the other spouse's death and the joint account consists of community property, the will of the deceased spouse may dispose of the deceased spouse's share of the account. See also Section 5307 (account expressly described in account agreement as a "community property" account is governed by law governing community property generally).

If a spouse has the unilateral right to withdraw funds from the joint account, that spouse may terminate all rights of survivorship by withdrawing the funds from the account and depositing them in another account that does not give the spouses rights of survivorship. Either spouse could then dispose of his or her share of the funds in the new account by will. One spouse may not, however, deprive the other spouse of community property rights by unilateral action with respect to funds in a joint account created with community property funds. For example, if a spouse withdraws community property funds from a joint account and deposits the funds withdrawn in an account in his or her name, this does not change the community property interest of the other spouse in the funds so deposited. See subdivision (d). See also Section 5307 (account expressly described in account agreement as a "community property" account is governed by law governing community property generally).

Likewise, for example, if the funds in a joint account of a married couple have their source in the separate property of the wife, the husband can eliminate survivorship rights by closing out the account and opening another account in his own name, but absent an agreement of the husband and wife this would not change the ownership interest of the wife in the funds withdrawn. See Section 5301 (joint account belongs, during the lifetime of all parties, to the parties in proportion to the net contributions of each to the sums on deposit, unless there is clear and convincing evidence of a different intent).

Community property funds on deposit in a multiple-party account are not subject to testamentary disposition by the deceased depositor. See subdivision (c). This is consistent with the general Uniform Probate Code rule stated in subdivision (e) of Section 5302. If a right to dispose of community property in a multiple-party account by will is desired to be retained, that objective can be accomplished by the two spouses establishing a joint account with the express provision that no right of survivorship arises upon the death of one of the spouses.

1992 Amendment [Revised Comment]

Subdivision (b) of Section 5305 is amended to substitute references to the Family Code provisions that replaced the former Civil Code provisions. [23 Cal.L.Rev.Comm. Reports 1 (1993)].

Background on Section 5305 of Repealed Code

Section 5305 was added by 1983 Cal.Stat. ch. 92 § 5 and amended by 1989 Cal.Stat. ch. 397 § 31. The 1989 amendment made the following revisions:

(1) References to Civil Code Sections 4800.1 and 4800.2 were added to the introductory clause of subdivision (b).

(2) Paragraph (1) of subdivision (b) was revised to require that the community property agreement be in writing. This is consistent with paragraph (2) of subdivision (b) and with Civil Code Section 5110.730.

With respect to the spouses and those claiming under them, Section 5305 reversed the presumption under former law that community funds deposited into a joint account with right of survivorship are presumed to be converted into true joint tenancy funds and to lose their character as community property. See In re Estate of McCoin, 9 Cal.App.2d 480, 50 P.2d 114 (1935). See also Griffith, Community Property in Joint Tenancy Form, 14 Stan. L. Rev 87, 91–93 (1961). The former presumption was inconsistent with the general belief of married persons. Married persons generally believe that community funds deposited in a joint tenancy account remain community property. See Griffith, supra at 90, 95, 106–109. The presumption created by Section 5305 is consistent with this general belief.

For background on the provisions of this part, see the Comment to this part under the part heading. [20 Cal.L.Rev.Comm.Reports 1001 (1990)].

Commentary

See generally *Estate of Petersen, 28 Cal.App.4th 1742, 34 Cal. Rptr.2d 449 (1994)* (unambiguous provision of community-funded annuity contract effected a nonprobate death transfer by right of survivorship; in contrast, statement of "joint account" for money market funds was insufficient to create a nonprobate right of survivorship).

Marriage of Brandes, 239 Cal.App.4th 1461, 192 Cal.Rptr.3d 1 (2015), applied this section to allow a spouse to trace funds held in a jointly titled bank account to his separate property deposits and consequently to claim, as his separate property, stock purchased with those funds.

Research References

Forms

California Transactions Forms--Estate Planning § 10:34, Multiple Party Accounts.

Treatises and Practice Aids

Witkin, California Summary 10th Community Property § 22, Community Property.

Witkin, California Summary 10th Negotiable Instruments § 79, Ownership Of Account.

§ 5306. Tenancy in common; right of survivorship

For the purposes of this chapter, if an account is expressly described in the deposit agreement as a "tenancy in common" account, no right of survivorship arises from the terms of the account or under Section 5302 unless the terms of the account or deposit agreement expressly provide for survivorship. *(Stats.1990, c. 79 (A.B.759), § 14, operative July 1, 1991.)*

Law Revision Commission Comments

1990 Enactment

Section 5306 continues Section 5306 of the repealed Probate Code without change. There is no comparable provision in the Uniform Probate Code (1987). The purpose of Section 5306 is to preserve the effect of a tenancy in common account. A right of survivorship may exist in a "tenancy in common" account, for example, where a party to the account designates a P.O.D. beneficiary to receive that tenant's share of the account upon the tenant's death.

Background on Section 5306 of Repealed Code

Section 5306 was added by 1983 Cal.Stat. ch. 92 § 5 and amended by 1989 Cal.Stat. ch. 397 § 32. The 1989 amendment made the section applicable to all tenancy in common accounts, whenever established, and added an exception where the terms of the account or deposit agreement expressly provide for survivorship. For background on the provisions of this part, see the Comment to this part under the part heading. [20 Cal.L.Rev.Comm.Reports 1001 (1990)].

Research References

Forms

California Transactions Forms--Estate Planning § 10:6, Tenancy in Common.

California Transactions Forms--Estate Planning § 10:34, Multiple Party Accounts.

Treatises and Practice Aids

Witkin, California Summary 10th Negotiable Instruments § 79, Ownership Of Account.

§ 5307. Community property account

For the purposes of this chapter, except to the extent the terms of the account or deposit agreement expressly provide otherwise, if the parties to an account are married to each other and the account is expressly described in the account agreement as a "community property" account, the ownership of the account during lifetime and after the death of a spouse is governed by the law governing community property generally. *(Stats.1990, c. 79 (A.B.759), § 14, operative July 1, 1991.)*

Law Revision Commission Comments

1990 Enactment

Section 5307 continues Section 5307 of the repealed Probate Code without change. The section deals with the situation where a joint account held by a husband and wife is specifically designated in the account agreement as a "community property" account. Section 5307 makes clear that this type of account is governed by the rules that apply to community property generally. Accordingly, unless the parties have agreed otherwise, the right of survivorship of the surviving spouse can be changed by will (deceased spouse by will devises his or her one-half share of the account to a person other than the surviving spouse). Also, the deposit agreement or the terms of the account can include, for example, a provision that the one-half share of a spouse will pass on the death of that spouse to one or more P.O.D. payees (or Totten trust beneficiaries) upon the death of that spouse. On the other hand, absent a contrary agreement or a contrary disposition, the surviving spouse will take the one-half share of the deceased spouse as community property.

Background on Section 5307 of Repealed Code

Section 5307 was a new provision added by 1989 Cal.Stat. ch. 397 § 33. For background on the provisions of this part, see the Comment to this part under the part heading. [20 Cal.L.Rev.Comm.Reports 1001 (1990)].

CHAPTER 4. PROTECTION OF FINANCIAL INSTITUTION

Application

Application of Part 2 to accounts in existence on or established after July 1, 1990, see Probate Code § 5205.

§ 5401. Entry; payment; multiple signatures for transactions; requirements regarding net contributions of party; liens, etc.

(a) Financial institutions may enter into multiple-party accounts to the same extent that they may enter into single-party accounts. Any multiple-party account may be paid, on request and according to its terms, to any one or more of the parties or agents.

(b) The terms of the account or deposit agreement may require the signatures of more than one of the parties to a multiple-party account during their lifetimes or of more than one of the survivors after the death of any one of them on any check, check endorsement, receipt, notice of withdrawal, request for withdrawal, or withdrawal order. In such case, the financial institution shall pay the sums on deposit only in accordance with such terms, but those terms do not limit the right of the sole survivor or of all of the survivors to receive the sums on deposit.

(c) A financial institution is not required to do any of the following pursuant to Section 5301, 5303, or any other provision of this part:

(1) Inquire as to the source of funds received for deposit to a multiple-party account, or inquire as to the proposed application of any sum withdrawn from an account, for purposes of establishing net contributions.

(2) Determine any party's net contribution.

(3) Limit withdrawals or any other use of an account based on the net contribution of any party, whether or not the financial institution has actual knowledge of each party's contribution.

(d) All funds in an account, unless otherwise agreed in writing by the financial institution and the parties to the account, remain subject to liens, security interests, rights of setoff, and charges, notwithstanding the determination or allocation of net contributions with respect to the parties. *(Stats.1990, c. 79 (A.B.759), § 14, operative July 1, 1991. Amended by Stats.2012, c. 235 (A.B.1624), § 3.)*

Law Revision Commission Comments

1990 Enactment

Section 5401 continues Section 5401 of the repealed Probate Code without change. Subdivision (a) is the same as the first two sentences of Section 6–108 of the Uniform Probate Code (1987) with the addition of the clarifying phrase "and according to its terms." Paragraph (1) of subdivision (c) is the same in substance as the last sentence of Section 6–108 of the Uniform Probate Code (1987). As to the construction of provisions drawn from uniform acts, see Section 2.

Background on Section 5401 of Repealed Code

Section 5401 was added by 1983 Cal.Stat. ch. 92 § 5 and was amended by 1989 Cal.Stat. ch. 397 § 34. Subdivision (a) was a new provision. Subdivision (b) was drawn from portions of then-existing Financial Code Sections 852, 7603, 11204, and 14854 (second sentence). The 1989 amendment added the reference to agents in subdivision (a). See Section 5124 (defining "agent"). See also Section 5204 (special power of attorney with respect to accounts at financial institutions). The 1989 amendment also added paragraphs (2) and (3) to subdivision (c) and added subdivision (d). For background on the provisions of this part, see the Comment to this part under the part heading. [20 Cal.L.Rev.Comm.Reports 1001 (1990)].

2012 Amendment

Subdivision (c) of Section 5401 is amended to state expressly that a financial institution has no duty with respect to tracing net contributions of a party under either Section 5301 (ownership during lifetime) or 5303 (right of survivorship and terms of account). This is not a change in, but is declarative of, existing law. [34 Cal.L.Rev.Comm. Reports 199 (2004)].

A husband and wife opened a joint account. Later the name of the wife's sister was added to the account and she subsequently withdrew all the funds. After the wife died, the husband's claim against the bank was upheld under Section 5303(b) because his wife's sister's name was added to the account without his written consent. As long as the bank pays a proper party to a multiple party account, it is not liable for paying more than the party's beneficial ownership. But the bank is liable if it pays someone who has no right of withdrawal at all because the person was not added to the account in accordance with Section 5303. The present Section only protects financial institutions for payments paid "to any one or more of the parties or agents." A bank will not be liable if it permits one party to withdraw more than his or her beneficial interest in the account; that is a matter to be resolved between the parties. Thus the designation of the parties to an account is of critical importance. *Stevens v. Tri Counties Bank, 177 Cal.App.4th 236, 99 Cal.Rptr.3d 188 (3d Dist. 2009).*

Research References

Forms

California Transactions Forms--Estate Planning § 1:26, Quasi-Community Property; Separate Property.

California Transactions Forms--Estate Planning § 10:34, Multiple Party Accounts.

Treatises and Practice Aids

Witkin, California Summary 10th Negotiable Instruments § 80, Protection Of Financial Institutions.

§ 5402. Payment of sums in joint account; personal representative or heir of deceased party

Any sums in a joint account may be paid, on request and according to its terms, to any party without regard to whether any other party is incapacitated or deceased at the time the payment is demanded; but payment may not be made to the personal representative or heirs of a deceased party unless proof of death is presented to the financial institution showing that the decedent was the last surviving party or unless there is no right of survivorship under Section 5302. *(Stats.1990, c. 79 (A.B.759), § 14, operative July 1, 1991.)*

Law Revision Commission Comments

1990 Enactment

Section 5402 continues Section 5402 of the repealed Probate Code without change. The section is the same in substance as Section 6–109 of the Uniform Probate Code (1987). As to the construction of provisions drawn from uniform acts, see Section 2.

Background on Section 5402 of Repealed Code

Section 5402 was a new provision added by 1983 Cal.Stat. ch. 92 § 5. For background on the provisions of this part, see the Comment to this part under the part heading. [20 Cal.L.Rev.Comm.Reports 1001 (1990)].

Research References

Forms

California Transactions Forms--Estate Planning § 10:34, Multiple Party Accounts.

§ 5403. Payment of P.O.D. account; personal representative or heir of deceased payee

Any P.O.D. account may be paid, on request and according to its terms, to any original party to the account. Payment may be made, on request, to the P.O.D. payee or to the personal representative or heirs of a deceased P.O.D. payee upon presentation to the financial institution of proof of death showing that the P.O.D. payee survived all persons named as original payees. Payment may be made to the personal representative or heirs of a deceased original payee if proof of death is presented to the financial institution showing that the deceased original payee was the survivor of all other persons named on the account either as an original payee or as P.O.D. payee. *(Stats.1990, c. 79 (A.B.759), § 14, operative July 1, 1991.)*

Law Revision Commission Comments

1990 Enactment

Section 5403 continues Section 5403 of the repealed Probate Code without change. The section is the same in substance as Section 6–110 of the Uniform Probate Code (1987). As to the construction of provisions drawn from uniform acts, see Section 2.

Background on Section 5403 of Repealed Code

Section 5403 was a new provision added by 1983 Cal.Stat. ch. 92 § 5. For background on the provisions of this part, see the Comment to this part under the part heading. [20 Cal.L.Rev.Comm.Reports 1001 (1990)].

Research References

Forms

California Transactions Forms--Estate Planning § 10:34, Multiple Party Accounts.

§ 5404. Totten trust account; payment; deceased trustee

Any Totten trust account may be paid, on request and according to its terms, to any trustee. Unless the financial institution has received written notice that the beneficiary has a vested interest not dependent upon surviving the trustee, payment may be made to the personal representative or heirs of a deceased trustee if proof of death is presented to the financial institution showing that the deceased trustee was the survivor of all other persons named on the account either as trustee or beneficiary. A Totten trust account may be paid to a beneficiary or beneficiaries or the personal representative or heirs of a beneficiary or beneficiaries if proof of death is presented to the financial institution showing that the beneficiary or beneficiaries survived all persons named as trustees. *(Stats.1990, c. 79 (A.B.759), § 14, operative July 1, 1991.)*

Law Revision Commission Comments

1990 Enactment

Section 5404 continues Section 5404 of the repealed Probate Code without change. The section is the same in substance as Section 6–111 of the Uniform Probate Code (1987). As to the construction of provisions drawn from uniform acts, see Section 2.

Background on Section 5404 of Repealed Code

Section 5404 was a new provision added by 1983 Cal.Stat. ch. 92 § 5 and amended by 1989 Cal.Stat. ch. 397 § 35. The 1989 amendment substituted "Totten trust account" in place of "trust account." See Section 80 (defining "Totten trust account"). For background on the provisions of this part, see the Comment to this part under the part heading. [20 Cal.L.Rev.Comm.Reports 1001 (1990)].

Research References

Forms

California Transactions Forms--Estate Planning § 10:34, Multiple Party Accounts.

§ 5405. Payment as discharge of financial institution from claims

(a) Payment made pursuant to Section 5401, 5402, 5403, or 5404 discharges the financial institution from all claims for amounts so paid whether or not the payment is consistent with the beneficial ownership of the account as between parties, P.O.D. payees, or beneficiaries, or their successors.

(b) The protection provided by subdivision (a) does not extend to payments made after the financial institution has been served with a court order restraining payment. No other notice or any other information shown to have been available to a financial institution shall affect its right to the protection provided by subdivision (a).

(c) Unless the notice is withdrawn by a subsequent writing, after receipt of a written notice from any party that withdrawals in accordance with the terms of the account, other than a checking account, share draft account, or other similar third-party payment instrument, should not be permitted, except with the signatures of more than one of the parties during their lifetimes or of more than one of the survivors after the death of any one of the parties, the financial institution may only pay the sums on deposit in accordance with the written instructions pending determination of the rights of the parties or their successors. No liability shall attach to the financial institution for complying with the terms of any written notice provided pursuant to this subdivision.

(d) The protection provided by this section has no bearing on the rights of parties in disputes between themselves or their successors concerning the beneficial ownership of funds in, or withdrawn from, multiple-party accounts and is in addition to, and not exclusive of, any protection provided the financial institution by any other provision of law. *(Stats. 1990, c. 79 (A.B.759), § 14, operative July 1, 1991.)*

Law Revision Commission Comments

1990 Enactment

Section 5405 continues Section 5405 of the repealed Probate Code without change. The section is drawn in part from Section 6–112 of the Uniform Probate Code (1987). Subdivision (a) is the same in substance as a portion of the Uniform Probate Code section. Subdivision (b) is substituted for the comparable portion of the Uniform Probate Code section. Subdivision (d) is the same in substance as the comparable portion of the Uniform Probate Code section. Receipt of notice under this section must be at the particular office or branch office where the account is carried unless the terms of the account or deposit agreement expressly provide otherwise. See Section 5146. As to the construction of provisions drawn from uniform acts, see Section 2.

Background on Section 5405 of Repealed Code

Section 5405 was added by 1983 Cal.Stat. ch. 92 § 5 and amended by 1984 Cal.Stat. ch. 452 § 8. Subdivision (a) was new. Subdivision (b) was drawn from then-existing Financial Code Sections 852.5, 7604.5, 11203.5, 14854.5, and 18318.5 relating to service of a court order restraining payment. Subdivision (c) was drawn from portions of Financial Code Sections 852 and 7603. Subdivision (d) was new. The 1984 amendment rewrote subdivision (c). For background on the provisions of this part, see the Comment to this part under the part heading. [20 Cal.L.Rev.Comm.Reports 1001 (1990)].

Research References

Forms

California Transactions Forms--Estate Planning § 10:34, Multiple Party Accounts.

Treatises and Practice Aids

Witkin, California Summary 10th Negotiable Instruments § 80, Protection Of Financial Institutions.

§ 5406. Trust account; payment same as Totten trust account in absence of notice to contrary

The provisions of this chapter that apply to the payment of a Totten trust account apply to an account in the name of one or more parties as trustee for one or more other persons if the financial institution has no other or further notice in writing that the account is not a Totten trust account as defined in Section 80. *(Stats.1990, c. 79 (A.B.759), § 14, operative July 1, 1991.)*

Law Revision Commission Comments

1990 Enactment

Section 5406 continues Section 5406 of the repealed Probate Code without change. The section permits a financial institution to treat an account in trust form as a Totten trust account (defined in Section 80) if it is unknown to the financial institution that the funds on deposit are subject to a trust created other than by the deposit of the funds in the account in trust form. If the financial institution does not have the additional information, the financial institution is protected from liability if it pays the account as provided in this chapter. See Section 5405. However, Section 5406 does not affect the rights as between the parties to the account, the beneficiary, or their successors. See Sections 5201, 5301(c), 5302(c).

Background on Section 5406 of Repealed Code

Section 5406 was added by 1983 Cal.Stat. ch. 92 § 5 and was amended by 1989 Cal.Stat. ch. 397 § 36. The section was drawn from a portion of Financial Code Section 853. The 1989 amendment substituted a reference to Section 80 (defining "Totten trust account") in place of the former reference to Section 5101. The 1989 amendment also required the notice that the account is not a Totten trust account to be in writing. This was consistent with a requirement also found in Financial Code Sections 853 and 6853. For background on the provisions of this part, see the Comment to this part under the part heading. [20 Cal.L.Rev.Comm.Reports 1001 (1990)].

Research References

Treatises and Practice Aids

Witkin, California Summary 10th Negotiable Instruments § 76, Deposit in Trust.

§ 5407. Payment to minor

If a financial institution is required or permitted to make payment pursuant to this chapter to a person who is a minor:

(a) If the minor is a party to a multiple-party account, payment may be made to the minor or to the minor's order, and payment so made is a valid release and discharge of the financial institution, but this subdivision does not apply if the account is to be paid to the minor because the minor was designated as a P.O.D. payee or as a beneficiary of a Totten trust account.

(b) In cases where subdivision (a) does not apply, payment shall be made pursuant to the California Uniform Transfers to Minors Act (Part 9 (commencing with Section 3900) of Division 4), or as provided in Chapter 2 (commencing with Section 3400) of Part 8 of Division 4. *(Stats.1990, c. 79 (A.B.759), § 14, operative July 1, 1991.)*

Law Revision Commission Comments

1990 Enactment

Section 5407 continues Section 5407 of the repealed Probate Code without change. Under the Uniform Transfers to Minors Act, if there has been no nomination of a custodian, $10,000 or less may be transferred to an adult member of the minor's family or to a trust company without the need for a court order. See Section 3907. In addition, the court may order that all or part of the money be paid to a custodian under the Uniform Act for the benefit of the minor. See Section 3413.

Background on Section 5407 of Repealed Code

Section 5407 was added by 1983 Cal.Stat. ch. 92 § 5 and amended by 1989 Cal.Stat. ch. 397 § 37. Subdivision (a) was consistent with Section 850 of the Financial Code. Subdivision (b) was new. The 1989 amendment authorized payment pursuant to the Uniform Transfers to Minors Act. For background on the provisions of this part, see the Comment to this part under the part heading. [20 Cal.L.Rev.Comm.Reports 1001 (1990)].

Research References

Forms

California Transactions Forms--Estate Planning § 10:34, Multiple Party Accounts.

Part 4

REVOCABLE TRANSFER ON DEATH DEED

Repeal

For repeal of Part 4, see Probate Code § 5600.

Law Revision Commission Comments

2015 Repeal

Former Sections 5600–5604 are continued without change, other than renumbering, in Chapter 3 (commencing with Section 5040) of Part 1. The sections are relocated to make room for new Part 4 (commencing with Section 5600), relating to the revocable TOD deed. [36 Cal.L.Rev.Comm. Reports 103 (2006)].

CHAPTER 1. GENERAL PROVISIONS

Repeal

For repeal of Part 4, see Probate Code § 5600.

ARTICLE 1. PRELIMINARY PROVISIONS

Repeal

For repeal of Part 4, see Probate Code § 5600.

§ 5600. Application; duration of part

(a) This part applies to a revocable transfer on death deed made by a transferor who dies on or after January 1, 2016, whether the deed was executed or recorded before, on, or after January 1, 2016.

(b) Nothing in this part invalidates an otherwise valid transfer under Section 5602.

(c) This part shall remain in effect only until January 1, 2021, and as of that date is repealed, unless a later enacted statute, that is enacted before January 1, 2021, deletes or extends that date. The repeal of this part pursuant to this subdivision shall not affect the validity or effect of a revocable transfer on death deed that is executed before January 1, 2021, and shall not affect the authority of the transferor to revoke a transfer on death deed by recording a signed and notarized instrument that is substantially in the form specified in Section 5644. *(Added by Stats.2015, c. 293 (A.B.139), § 17, eff. Jan. 1, 2016.)*

Law Revision Commission Comments

2015 Addition

Section 5600 implements the general rule that a new provision of the Probate Code applies retroactively. See Section 3. However, this part does not interfere with rights of a decedent's successors acquired by reason of the decedent's death before the operative date of this part. An instrument of a decedent who dies before the operative date of this part, or an instrument of a decedent who dies after the operative date of this part that was not executed in compliance with this part, is governed by other law. See Sections 3(g) (application of old law), 5602 (effect on other forms of transfer).

Former Sections 5600–5604, relating to a nonprobate transfer to a former spouse, are continued without change, other than renumbering, in Chapter 3 (commencing with Section 5040) of Part 1. The sections are relocated to make room for new Part 4 (commencing with Section 5600), relating to the revocable TOD deed. [36 Cal.L.Rev.Comm. Reports 103 (2006)].

Research References

Forms

California Transactions Forms--Estate Planning § 10:34, Multiple Party Accounts.
California Transactions Forms--Estate Planning § 10:19.50, Deed Transfers on Death.
California Transactions Forms--Estate Planning § 10:47.75, Revocation Of Revocable Transfer on Death (TOD) Deed.

Treatises and Practice Aids

Witkin, California Summary 10th Negotiable Instruments § 79, Ownership Of Account.
Witkin, California Summary 10th Real Property § 258A, (New) Revocable Transfer on Death Deed.
Witkin, California Summary 10th Wills and Probate § 2, Uniform and Model Acts.
Witkin, California Summary 10th Wills and Probate § 305, Recommendation and Enactment.
Witkin, California Summary 10th Wills and Probate § 317, in General.
Witkin, California Summary 10th Wills and Probate § 318, Transfer to Former Spouse.
Witkin, California Summary 10th Wills and Probate § 320, Real Property Affidavit.
Witkin, California Summary 10th Wills and Probate § 405, Probate and Administration.
Witkin, California Summary 10th Wills and Probate § 320A, (New) in General.
Witkin, California Summary 10th Wills and Probate § 320B, (New) Execution and Revocation.

§ 5602. Use of other methods of conveying real property

This part does not preclude use of any other method of conveying real property that is permitted by law and that has the effect of postponing enjoyment of the property until the death of the owner. *(Added by Stats.2015, c. 293 (A.B.139), § 17, eff. Jan. 1, 2016.)*

Repeal

For repeal of Part 4, see Probate Code § 5600.

Law Revision Commission Comments

2015 Addition

Section 5602 recognizes the possibility of other devices that may achieve an effect similar to the revocable TOD deed, such as a revocable deed under *Tennant v. John Tennant Memorial Home*, 167 Cal. 570, 140 P. 242 (1914), or another instrument under Section 5000 (nonprobate transfer). [44 Cal.L.Rev.Comm. Reports 573 (2015) [2015–16 AR Appx. 5]]

Research References

Forms

California Transactions Forms--Estate Planning § 10:19.50, Deed Transfers on Death.

Treatises and Practice Aids

Witkin, California Summary 10th Wills and Probate § 320, Real Property Affidavit.
Witkin, California Summary 10th Wills and Probate § 320A, (New) in General.

§ 5604. Application of other provisions relating to revocable transfer on death deeds

(a) Except as provided in subdivision (b), nothing in this part affects the application to a revocable transfer on death deed of any other statute governing a nonprobate transfer on death, including, but not limited to, any of the following provisions that by its terms or intent would apply to a nonprobate transfer on death:

(1) Division 2 (commencing with Section 100).

(2) Part 1 (commencing with Section 5000) of this division.

(3) Division 10 (commencing with Section 20100).

(4) Division 11 (commencing with Section 21101).

(b) Notwithstanding subdivision (a), a provision of another statute governing a nonprobate transfer on death does not apply to a revocable transfer on death deed to the extent this part provides a contrary rule. *(Added by Stats.2015, c. 293 (A.B.139), § 17, eff. Jan. 1, 2016.)*

Repeal

For repeal of Part 4, see Probate Code § 5600.

Law Revision Commission Comments

2015 Addition

Section 5604 makes clear that the revocable TOD deed law is supplemented by general statutory provisions governing a nonprobate transfer. The specific cross-references in this section are illustrative and not exclusive. General provisions referenced in this section include effect of death on community property, establishing and reporting fact of death, simultaneous death, effect of homicide or abuse, disclaimer, provisions relating to effect of death, nonprobate transfers of community property, nonprobate transfer to former spouse, proration of taxes, rules for interpretation of instruments, and limitations on transfers to drafters.

This part may in some instances limit the effect of a provision otherwise applicable to a nonprobate transfer on death. [44 Cal. L.Rev.Comm. Reports 573 (2015) [2015–16 AR Appx. 5]]

Research References

Treatises and Practice Aids

Witkin, California Summary 10th Wills and Probate § 317, in General.
Witkin, California Summary 10th Wills and Probate § 320A, (New) in General.

ARTICLE 2. DEFINITIONS

Repeal

For repeal of Part 4, see Probate Code § 5600.

§ 5606. Construction of part

Unless the provision or context otherwise requires, the definitions in this article govern the construction of this part. *(Added by Stats.2015, c. 293 (A.B.139), § 17, eff. Jan. 1, 2016.)*

Repeal

For repeal of Part 4, see Probate Code § 5600.

Law Revision Commission Comments

2015 Addition

Although Section 5606 limits the application of these definitions, a defined term may also be used in another statute in its defined sense. See, e.g., Section 5000(a) (nonprobate transfer includes revocable TOD deed).

The definitions in this article are supplemented by those in Part 2 (commencing with Section 20) of Division 1. See, e.g., Sections 24 (beneficiary), 28 (community property), 39 (fiduciary), 45 (instrument), 48 (interested person), 56 (person), 58 (personal representative), 62 (property), 68 (real property), 81 (transferor), 81.5 (transferee), 82 (trust), 84 (trustee), 88 (will). [36 Cal.L.Rev.Comm. Reports 103 (2006)].

Research References

Treatises and Practice Aids

Witkin, California Summary 10th Wills and Probate § 320A, (New) in General.

§ 5608. "Beneficiary" defined

"Beneficiary" means a person named in a revocable transfer on death deed as transferee of the property. *(Added by Stats.2015, c. 293 (A.B.139), § 17, eff. Jan. 1, 2016.)*

Repeal

For repeal of Part 4, see Probate Code § 5600.

Law Revision Commission Comments

2015 Addition

Section 5608 is a specific application of Section 24 ("beneficiary" defined). The beneficiary must be identified by name. Section 5622 (beneficiary). [36 Cal.L.Rev.Comm. Reports 103 (2006)].

Research References

Forms

California Transactions Forms--Estate Planning § 10:19.50, Deed Transfers on Death.

Treatises and Practice Aids

Witkin, California Summary 10th Wills and Probate § 320B, (New) Execution and Revocation.

§ 5610. "Real property" defined

"Real property" means any of the following:

(a) Real property improved with not less than one nor more than four residential dwelling units.

(b) A condominium unit, including the limited common elements allocated to the exclusive use thereof that form an integral part of the condominium unit.

(c) A single tract of agricultural real estate consisting of 40 acres or less that is improved with a single-family residence. *(Added by Stats.2015, c. 293 (A.B.139), § 17, eff. Jan. 1, 2016.)*

Repeal

For repeal of Part 4, see Probate Code § 5600.

Law Revision Commission Comments

2015 Addition

Section 5610 supplements the definition of real property found in Section 68 ("real property" includes leasehold). [44 Cal.L.Rev. Comm. Reports 573 (2015) [2015–16 AR Appx. 5]]

Research References

Treatises and Practice Aids

Witkin, California Summary 10th Wills and Probate § 320B, (New) Execution and Revocation.

§ 5612. "Recorded" defined

"Recorded" has the meaning provided in Section 1170 of the Civil Code. *(Added by Stats.2015, c. 293 (A.B.139), § 17, eff. Jan. 1, 2016.)*

Repeal

For repeal of Part 4, see Probate Code § 5600.

Law Revision Commission Comments

2015 Addition

Section 5612 adopts the rule that an instrument is deemed to be recorded when, being duly acknowledged or proved and certified, it is deposited in the recorder's office, with the proper officer, for record. See Civ. Code § 1170 (recorded). This definition applies to variants of the term defined, including "of record," "recordation," and the like. [36 Cal.L.Rev.Comm. Reports 103 (2006)].

Research References

Forms

California Transactions Forms--Estate Planning § 10:19.50, Deed Transfers on Death.

§ 5614. "Revocable transfer on death deed" defined

(a) "Revocable transfer on death deed" means an instrument created pursuant to this part that does all of the following:

(1) Makes a donative transfer of real property to a named beneficiary.

(2) Operates on the transferor's death.

(3) Remains revocable until the transferor's death.

(b) A revocable transfer on death deed may also be known as a "revocable TOD deed." *(Added by Stats.2015, c. 293 (A.B.139), § 17, eff. Jan. 1, 2016.)*

Repeal

For repeal of Part 4, see Probate Code § 5600.

Law Revision Commission Comments

2015 Addition

Section 5614 adopts revocable TOD deed terminology, rather than "beneficiary deed" terminology used in some jurisdictions that have enacted comparable legislation.

A revocable TOD deed may be made for real property of the types described in Section 5610 ("real property" defined).

The beneficiary must be identified by name in a revocable TOD deed. See Section 5622 (beneficiary).

A revocable TOD deed creates no rights in the beneficiary until the death of the transferor, and is revocable until that time. See Sections 5630 (revocability) and 5650 (effect during transferor's life).

For a revocable TOD deed statutory form, see Section 5642. For construction of a revocable TOD deed, see Part 1 (commencing with Section 21101) of Division 11 (rules for interpretation of instruments). [44 Cal.L.Rev.Comm. Reports 573 (2015) [2015–16 AR Appx. 5]]

Research References

Treatises and Practice Aids

Witkin, California Summary 10th Real Property § 258A, (New) Revocable Transfer on Death Deed.

Witkin, California Summary 10th Wills and Probate § 50, Legal and Financial Terms.

Witkin, California Summary 10th Wills and Probate § 320A, (New) in General.

Witkin, California Summary 10th Wills and Probate § 320B, (New) Execution and Revocation.

§ 5616. "Transferor" defined

"Transferor" means an owner of real property who makes a revocable transfer on death deed of the property. *(Added by Stats.2015, c. 293 (A.B.139), § 17, eff. Jan. 1, 2016.)*

Repeal

For repeal of Part 4, see Probate Code § 5600.

Law Revision Commission Comments

2015 Addition

Section 5616 is a specific application of Section 81 ("transferor" defined). [36 Cal.L.Rev.Comm. Reports 103 (2006)].

Research References

Treatises and Practice Aids

Witkin, California Summary 10th Wills and Probate § 320B, (New) Execution and Revocation.

CHAPTER 2. EXECUTION AND REVOCATION

Repeal

For repeal of Part 4, see Probate Code § 5600.

ARTICLE 1. EXECUTION

Repeal

For repeal of Part 4, see Probate Code § 5600.

§ 5620. Who may make revocable transfer on death deed

An owner of real property who has the capacity to contract may make a revocable transfer on death deed of the property. *(Added by Stats.2015, c. 293 (A.B.139), § 17, eff. Jan. 1, 2016.)*

Repeal

For repeal of Part 4, see Probate Code § 5600.

Law Revision Commission Comments

2015 Addition

Section 5620 specifies the capacity that is required for execution of a revocable transfer on death deed. [44 Cal.L.Rev.Comm. Reports 573 (2015) [2015–16 AR Appx. 5]]

Research References

Treatises and Practice Aids

Witkin, California Summary 10th Wills and Probate § 320A, (New) in General.

Witkin, California Summary 10th Wills and Probate § 320B, (New) Execution and Revocation.

§ 5622. Identification of beneficiary

The transferor shall identify the beneficiary by name in a revocable transfer on death deed. *(Added by Stats.2015, c. 293 (A.B.139), § 17, eff. Jan. 1, 2016.)*

Repeal

For repeal of Part 4, see Probate Code § 5600.

Law Revision Commission Comments

2015 Addition

Subdivision (a) of Section 5622 makes explicit the requirement that a beneficiary be identified by name in the instrument. A class gift is not permissible.

A beneficiary must survive the transferor in order to take an interest under this section. Section 5652(b)(2). [44 Cal.L.Rev.Comm. Reports 573 (2015) [2015–16 AR Appx. 5]]

Research References

Forms

California Transactions Forms--Estate Planning § 10:19.50, Deed Transfers on Death.

Treatises and Practice Aids

Witkin, California Summary 10th Wills and Probate § 320B, (New) Execution and Revocation.

§ 5624. Signature, date and acknowledgment

A revocable transfer on death deed is not effective unless the transferor signs and dates the deed and acknowledges the deed before a notary public. *(Added by Stats.2015, c. 293 (A.B.139), § 17, eff. Jan. 1, 2016.)*

Repeal

For repeal of Part 4, see Probate Code § 5600.

Law Revision Commission Comments

2015 Addition

Section 5624 prescribes execution requirements. A revocable TOD deed is not invalid because it does not comply with the requirements for execution of a will. See Section 5000(a) (provision for nonprobate transfer on death in written instrument).

A properly executed revocable TOD deed is ineffective unless recorded within 60 days after it is executed. See Section 5626 (recordation, delivery, and acceptance). [44 Cal.L.Rev.Comm. Reports 573 (2015) [2015–16 AR Appx. 5]]

Research References

Treatises and Practice Aids

Witkin, California Summary 10th Wills and Probate § 320B, (New) Execution and Revocation.

§ 5626. Recording; delivery to beneficiary not required; acceptance by beneficiary not required

(a) A revocable transfer on death deed is not effective unless the deed is recorded on or before 60 days after the date it was executed.

(b) The transferor is not required to deliver a revocable transfer on death deed to the beneficiary during the transferor's life.

(c) The beneficiary is not required to accept a revocable transfer on death deed from the transferor during the transferor's life. *(Added by Stats.2015, c. 293 (A.B.139), § 17, eff. Jan. 1, 2016.)*

Repeal

For repeal of Part 4, see Probate Code § 5600.

Law Revision Commission Comments

2015 Addition

Subdivision (a) of Section 5626 requires recordation of the revocable TOD deed, but does not require recordation by the transferor—an agent or other person authorized by the transferor may record the instrument. The deed is considered recorded for purposes of this section when it is deposited for record with the county recorder. See Section 5612 ("record" defined).

Subdivision (b) makes clear that delivery of a revocable TOD deed is not necessary, notwithstanding a Law Revision Commission Comment to Section 5000 to the effect that Section 5000 does not relieve against the delivery requirement of the law of deeds. The recordation requirement for a revocable TOD deed makes delivery unnecessary. Consideration is not required for a revocable TOD deed. See Civ. Code § 1040.

Subdivision (c) states the rule that, unlike an inter vivos deed, a revocable TOD deed does not require acceptance. Acceptance of a donative transfer is presumed. Disclaimer procedures are available to a beneficiary. See Sections 267, 279 (disclaimer).

A revocable TOD deed has no effect, and confers no rights on the beneficiary, until the transferor's death. See Section 5650 (effect during transferor's life). [44 Cal.L.Rev.Comm. Reports 573 (2015) [2015–16 AR Appx. 5]]

Research References

Forms

California Transactions Forms--Estate Planning § 10:19.50, Deed Transfers on Death.

Treatises and Practice Aids

Witkin, California Summary 10th Wills and Probate § 320B, (New) Execution and Revocation.

§ 5628. Effect of multiple recordings for same property

(a) If a revocable transfer on death deed is recorded for the same property for which another revocable transfer on death deed is recorded, the later executed deed is the operative instrument and its recordation revokes the earlier executed deed.

(b) Revocation of a revocable transfer on death deed does not revive an instrument earlier revoked by recordation of that deed. *(Added by Stats.2015, c. 293 (A.B.139), § 17, eff. Jan. 1, 2016.)*

Repeal

For repeal of Part 4, see Probate Code § 5600.

Law Revision Commission Comments

2015 Addition

Subdivision (a) of Section 5628 gives effect to the last executed of revocable TOD deeds recorded before the transferor's death. A revocable TOD deed is executed by signing, dating, and acknowledging before a notary public. See Section 5624 (execution). Execution is complete when the transferor acknowledges the deed before a notary public, not when the deed is signed and dated.

Under subdivision (b), recordation of a revocable TOD deed has the effect of revoking an earlier executed revocable TOD deed, regardless of the order of recordation of the deeds. Subsequent revocation of the later executed recorded deed does not revive an earlier executed deed. Instead, the property passes under failed transfer principles. See Section 21111 (failed transfer). [36 Cal.L.Rev. Comm. Reports 103 (2006)].

Research References

Treatises and Practice Aids

Witkin, California Summary 10th Wills and Probate § 320B, (New) Execution and Revocation.

ARTICLE 2. REVOCATION

Repeal

For repeal of Part 4, see Probate Code § 5600.

§ 5630. Who may revoke revocable transfer on death deed

A transferor who has the capacity to contract may revoke a revocable transfer on death deed at any time. *(Added by Stats.2015, c. 293 (A.B.139), § 17, eff. Jan. 1, 2016.)*

Repeal

For repeal of Part 4, see Probate Code § 5600.

Law Revision Commission Comments

2015 Addition

Section 5630 states the rule that a transfer on death deed is revocable. The transferor's right of revocation may be subject to a contractual or court ordered limitation.

A TOD deed may be revocable in some circumstances even though the transferor lacks capacity. The transferor's agent under a durable power of attorney may not revoke a TOD deed unless expressly authorized. See Section 4264(f) (power of attorney). If the transferor's conservator seeks to revoke a TOD deed, the transferor's estate plan must be taken into account under general principles of substituted judgment, and notice must be given to the beneficiary. See Sections 2580–2586 (guardianship and conservatorship). [44 Cal.L.Rev.Comm. Reports 573 (2015) [2015–16 AR Appx. 5]].

Research References

Treatises and Practice Aids

Witkin, California Summary 10th Wills and Probate § 320A, (New) in General.

Witkin, California Summary 10th Wills and Probate § 320B, (New) Execution and Revocation.

§ 5632. Execution and recording of revocation

(a) An instrument revoking a revocable transfer on death deed shall be executed and recorded before the transferor's death in the same manner as execution and recordation of a revocable transfer on death deed.

(b) Joinder, consent, or agreement of, or notice to, the beneficiary is not required for revocation of a revocable transfer on death deed. *(Added by Stats.2015, c. 293 (A.B.139), § 17, eff. Jan. 1, 2016.)*

Repeal

For repeal of Part 4, see Probate Code § 5600.

Law Revision Commission Comments

2015 Addition

Under subdivision (a) of Section 5632 a revoking instrument must be signed, dated, acknowledged, and recorded by the transferor or a person acting at the transferor's direction. See Sections 5624 (execution), 5626 (recordation).

Subdivision (b) implements the principle that creation and recordation of a revocable TOD deed creates no rights in the beneficiary. See Section 5650 (effect during transferor's life). [36 Cal.L.Rev. Comm. Reports 103 (2006)].

Research References

Treatises and Practice Aids

Witkin, California Summary 10th Wills and Probate § 320B, (New) Execution and Revocation.

ARTICLE 3. STATUTORY FORMS

Repeal

For repeal of Part 4, see Probate Code § 5600.

§ 5642. Form of revocable transfer on death deed

A revocable transfer on death deed shall be substantially in the following form.

(a) The first page of the form shall be substantially the following:

SIMPLE REVOCABLE TRANSFER ON DEATH (TOD) DEED
(California Probate Code Section 5642)

Recording Requested By:
When Recorded Mail This Deed To
Name:
Address:
Assessor's Parcel Number: Space Above For Recorder's Use

This document is exempt from documentary transfer tax under Rev. & Tax. Code § 11930. This document is exempt from preliminary change of ownership report under Rev. & Tax. Code § 480.3.

IMPORTANT NOTICE: THIS DEED MUST BE RECORDED ON OR BEFORE 60 DAYS AFTER THE DATE IT IS SIGNED AND NOTARIZED

Use this deed to transfer the residential property described below directly to your named beneficiaries when you die. YOU SHOULD CAREFULLY READ ALL OF THE INFORMATION ON THE OTHER PAGES OF THIS FORM. You may wish to consult an attorney before using this deed. It may have results that you do not want. Provide only the information asked for in the form. DO NOT INSERT ANY OTHER INFORMATION OR INSTRUCTIONS. This form MUST be RECORDED on or before 60 days after the date it is signed and notarized or it will not be effective.

PROPERTY DESCRIPTION

Print the legal description of the residential property affected by this deed:

____

BENEFICIARY(IES)

Print the FULL NAME(S) of the person(s) who will receive the property on your death (DO NOT use general terms like "my children") and state the RELATIONSHIP that each named person has to you (spouse, son, daughter, friend, etc.):

____

____

____

TRANSFER ON DEATH

I transfer all of my interest in the described property to the named beneficiary(ies) on my death. I may revoke this deed. When recorded, this deed revokes any TOD deed that I made before signing this deed.

Sign and print your name below (your name should exactly match the name shown on your title documents):

__________________________________ Date _________________________

NOTE: This deed only transfers MY ownership share of the property. The deed does NOT transfer the share of any co-owner of the property. Any co-owner who wants to name a TOD beneficiary must execute and RECORD a SEPARATE deed.

ACKNOWLEDGMENT OF NOTARY

A notary public or other officer completing this certificate verifies only the identity of the individual who signed the document to which this certificate is attached, and not the truthfulness, accuracy, or validity of that document.

State of California)
County of ________________)

On ____________________________ before me, (here insert name and title of the officer), personally appeared _____________________________, who proved to me on the basis of satisfactory evidence to be the person(s) whose name(s) is/are subscribed to the within instrument and acknowledged to me that he/she/they executed the same in his/her/their authorized capacity(ies), and that by his/her/their signature(s) on the instrument the person(s), or the entity upon behalf of which the person(s) acted, executed the instrument.

I certify under PENALTY OF PERJURY under the laws of the State of California that the foregoing paragraph is true and correct.

WITNESS my hand and official seal.

Signature __________________________________
(Seal)

(b) Subsequent pages of a form executed under this section shall be in substantially the following form:

COMMON QUESTIONS ABOUT THE USE OF THIS FORM

WHAT DOES THE TOD DEED DO? When you die, the identified property will transfer to your named beneficiary without probate. The TOD deed has no effect until you die. You can revoke it at any time.

CAN I USE THIS DEED TO TRANSFER BUSINESS PROPERTY? This deed can only be used to transfer (1) a parcel of property that contains one to four residential dwelling units, (2) a condominium unit, or (3) a parcel of agricultural land of 40 acres or less, which contains a single-family residence.

HOW DO I USE THE TOD DEED? Complete this form. Have it notarized. RECORD the form in the county where the property is located. The form MUST be recorded on or before 60 days after the date you sign it or the deed has no effect.

IS THE "LEGAL DESCRIPTION" OF THE PROPERTY NECESSARY? Yes.

HOW DO I FIND THE "LEGAL DESCRIPTION" OF THE PROPERTY? This information may be on the deed you received when you became an owner of the property. This information may also be available in the office of the county recorder for the county where the property is located. If you are not absolutely sure, consult an attorney.

HOW DO I "RECORD" THE FORM? Take the completed and notarized form to the county recorder for the county in which the property is located. Follow the instructions given by the county recorder to make the form part of the official property records.

WHAT IF I SHARE OWNERSHIP OF THE PROPERTY? This form only transfers YOUR share of the property. If a co-owner also wants to name a TOD beneficiary, that co-owner must complete and RECORD a separate form.

CAN I REVOKE THE TOD DEED IF I CHANGE MY MIND? Yes. You may revoke the TOD deed at any time. No one, including your beneficiary, can prevent you from revoking the deed.

HOW DO I REVOKE THE TOD DEED? There are three ways to revoke a recorded TOD deed: (1) Complete, have notarized, and RECORD a revocation form. (2) Create, have notarized, and RECORD a new TOD deed. (3) Sell or give away the property, or transfer it to a trust, before your death and RECORD the deed. A TOD deed can only affect property that you own when you die. A TOD deed cannot be revoked by will.

CAN I REVOKE A TOD DEED BY CREATING A NEW DOCUMENT THAT DISPOSES OF THE PROPERTY (FOR EXAMPLE, BY CREATING A NEW TOD DEED OR BY ASSIGNING THE PROPERTY TO A TRUST)? Yes, but only if the new document is RECORDED. To avoid any doubt, you may wish to RECORD a TOD deed revocation form before creating the new instrument. A TOD deed cannot be revoked by will, or by purporting to leave the subject property to anyone via will.

IF I SELL OR GIVE AWAY THE PROPERTY DESCRIBED IN A TOD DEED, WHAT HAPPENS WHEN I DIE? If the deed or other document used to transfer your property is RECORDED before your death, the TOD deed will have no effect. If the transfer document is not RECORDED before your death, the TOD deed will take effect.

I AM BEING PRESSURED TO COMPLETE THIS FORM. WHAT SHOULD I DO? Do NOT complete this form unless you freely choose to do so. If you are being pressured to dispose of your property in a way that you do not want, you may want to alert a family member, friend, the district attorney, or a senior service agency.

DO I NEED TO TELL MY BENEFICIARY ABOUT THE TOD DEED? No. But secrecy can cause later complications and might make it easier for others to commit fraud.

WHAT DOES MY BENEFICIARY NEED TO DO WHEN I DIE? Your beneficiary must RECORD evidence of your death (Prob. Code § 210), and file a change in ownership notice (Rev. & Tax. Code § 480). If you received Medi-Cal benefits, your beneficiary must notify the State Department of Health Care Services of your death and provide a copy of your death certificate (Prob. Code § 215).

WHAT IF I NAME MORE THAN ONE BENEFICIARY? Your beneficiaries will become co-owners in equal shares as tenants in common. If you want a different result, you should not use this form.

HOW DO I NAME BENEFICIARIES? You MUST name your beneficiaries individually, using each beneficiary's FULL name. You MAY NOT use general terms to describe beneficiaries, such as "my children." For each beneficiary that you name, you should briefly state that person's relationship to you (for example, my spouse, my son, my daughter, my friend, etc.).

WHAT IF A BENEFICIARY DIES BEFORE I DO? If all beneficiaries die before you, the TOD deed has no effect. If a beneficiary dies before you, but other beneficiaries survive you, the share of the deceased beneficiary will be divided equally between the surviving beneficiaries. If that is not the result you want, you should not use the TOD deed.

WHAT IS THE EFFECT OF A TOD DEED ON PROPERTY THAT I OWN AS JOINT TENANCY OR COMMUNITY PROPERTY WITH RIGHT OF SURVIVORSHIP? If you are the first joint tenant or spouse to die, the deed is VOID and has no effect. The property transfers to your joint tenant or surviving spouse and not according to this deed. If you are the last joint tenant or spouse to die, the deed takes effect and controls the ownership of your property when you die. If you do not want these results, do not use this form. The deed does NOT transfer the share of a co-owner of the property. Any co-owner who wants to name a TOD beneficiary must complete and RECORD a SEPARATE deed.

CAN I ADD OTHER CONDITIONS ON THE FORM? No. If you do, your beneficiary may need to go to court to clear title.

IS PROPERTY TRANSFERRED BY THE TOD DEED SUBJECT TO MY DEBTS? Yes.

DOES THE TOD DEED HELP ME TO AVOID GIFT AND ESTATE TAXES? No.

HOW DOES THE TOD DEED AFFECT PROPERTY TAXES? The TOD deed has no effect on your property taxes until your death. At that time, property tax law applies as it would to any other change of ownership.

DOES THE TOD DEED AFFECT MY ELIGIBILITY FOR MEDI–CAL? No.

AFTER MY DEATH, WILL MY HOME BE LIABLE FOR REIMBURSEMENT OF THE STATE FOR MEDI–CAL EXPENDITURES? Your home may be liable for reimbursement. If you have questions, you should consult an attorney.

(Added by Stats.2015, c. 293 (A.B.139), § 17, eff. Jan. 1, 2016.)

Repeal

For repeal of Part 4, see Probate Code § 5600.

Law Revision Commission Comments

2015 Addition

Section 5642 provides a form for creation of a revocable TOD deed. [44 Cal.L.Rev.Comm. Reports 573 (2015) [2015–16 AR Appx. 5]]

Research References

Forms

California Transactions Forms--Estate Planning § 10:47.50, Simple Revocable Transfer on Death (TOD) Deed.

Treatises and Practice Aids

Witkin, California Summary 10th Wills and Probate § 320A, (New) in General.

Witkin, California Summary 10th Wills and Probate § 320B, (New) Execution and Revocation.

§ 5644. Form of instrument revoking revocable transfer on death deed

A transferor may revoke a revocable transfer on death deed by an instrument in substantially the following form:

Revocation of
Revocable Transfer on Death (TOD) Deed
(California Probate Code Section 5600)

Recording Requested By:

When Recorded Mail This Deed To
Name:
Address:
Assessor's Parcel Number: Space Above For Recorder's Use

This deed revocation is exempt from documentary transfer tax under Rev. & Tax. Code § 11930. This deed revocation is exempt from preliminary change of ownership report under Rev. & Tax. Code § 480.3.

IMPORTANT NOTICE: THIS FORM MUST BE RECORDED TO BE EFFECTIVE

This revocation form MUST be RECORDED before your death or it will not be effective. This revocation form only affects a transfer on death deed that YOU made. A transfer on death deed made by a co-owner of your property is not affected by this revocation form. A co-owner who wants to revoke a transfer on death deed that he/she made must complete and RECORD a SEPARATE revocation form.

PROPERTY DESCRIPTION

Print the legal description of the property affected by this revocation:

____

REVOCATION

I revoke any TOD deed to transfer the described property that I executed before executing this form.

SIGNATURE AND DATE

Sign and print your name below (your name should exactly match the name shown on your title documents):

____________________ Date ________________

ACKNOWLEDGMENT OF NOTARY

A notary public or other officer completing this certificate verifies only the identity of the individual who signed the document to which this certificate is attached, and not the truthfulness, accuracy, or validity of that document.

State of California)
County of ____________)

On ____________________ before me, (here insert name and title of the officer), personally appeared ________________, who proved to me on the basis of satisfactory evidence to be the person(s) whose name(s) is/are subscribed to the within instrument and acknowledged to me that he/she/they executed the same in his/her/their authorized capacity(ies), and that by his/her/their signature(s) on the instrument the person(s), or the entity upon behalf of which the person(s) acted, executed the instrument.

I certify under PENALTY OF PERJURY under the laws of the State of California that the foregoing paragraph is true and correct.

WITNESS my hand and official seal.

Signature ________________________
(Seal)

(Added by Stats.2015, c. 293 (A.B.139), § 17, eff. Jan. 1, 2016.)

Repeal

For repeal of Part 4, see Probate Code § 5600.

Law Revision Commission Comments

2015 Addition

Section 5644 provides a form for revocation of a revocable TOD deed. Use of the form is not mandatory, since other recorded instruments may revoke a TOD deed. See Sections 5628 (multiple deeds), 5660 (conflicting dispositive instruments). [44 Cal.L.Rev. Comm. Reports 573 (2015) [2015–16 AR Appx. 5]]

Research References

Forms

California Transactions Forms--Estate Planning § 10:47.75, Revocation Of Revocable Transfer on Death (TOD) Deed.

Treatises and Practice Aids

Witkin, California Summary 10th Wills and Probate § 320A, (New) in General.

Witkin, California Summary 10th Wills and Probate § 320B, (New) Execution and Revocation.

CHAPTER 3. EFFECT

Repeal

For repeal of Part 4, see Probate Code § 5600.

ARTICLE 1. GENERAL PROVISIONS

Repeal

For repeal of Part 4, see Probate Code § 5600.

§ 5650. Effect on ownership rights

During the transferor's life, execution and recordation of a revocable transfer on death deed:

(a) Does not affect the ownership rights of the transferor, and the transferor or the transferor's agent or other fiduciary may convey, assign, contract, encumber, or otherwise deal with the property, and the property is subject to process of the transferor's creditors, as if no revocable transfer on death deed were executed or recorded.

(b) Does not create any legal or equitable right in the beneficiary, and the property is not subject to process of the beneficiary's creditors.

(c) Does not transfer or convey any right, title, or interest in the property. *(Added by Stats.2015, c. 293 (A.B.139), § 17, eff. Jan. 1, 2016.)*

Repeal

For repeal of Part 4, see Probate Code § 5600.

Law Revision Commission Comments

2015 Addition

Section 5650 makes clear that a revocable TOD deed is effective only on the transferor's death and not before. A revocable TOD deed remains revocable until that time. See Section 5630 (revocability).

The transferor's execution and recordation of a revocable TOD deed has no effect on the ability of the transferor's creditors to subject the property to an involuntary lien or execution of a judgment.

The reference to the transferor's agent or other fiduciary in subdivision (a) includes a conservator. The authority of the fiduciary is subject to the qualification that the specific transaction entered into on behalf of the transferor must be within the scope of the fiduciary's authority. See, e.g., Section 4264(f) (power of attorney).

Subdivision (b) makes clear that the transferor's execution and recordation of a revocable TOD deed does not enable the creditors of a beneficiary to subject the property to an involuntary lien or execution of a judgment. The beneficiary is not entitled to notice of a trustee's sale, nor is the beneficiary's consent required to enable the transferor to refinance.

The beneficiary's joinder, consent, or agreement to any transaction by the transferor is unnecessary and irrelevant. If an obligation of the beneficiary incurred before the transferor's death attaches to the property on the transferor's death as a result of the doctrine of after-acquired title, that obligation is subordinate to any limitations on the transferor's interest in the property. See Sections 5652 (effect at death), 5670 (priority of secured creditor of transferor).

Subdivision (c) reinforces the concept that a revocable TOD deed does not effectuate a transfer before the transferor's death. Creation of a revocable TOD deed should not have the effect of a default on a loan secured by the property, since it is not a disposition of the property. [36 Cal.L.Rev.Comm. Reports 103 (2006)].

Research References

Treatises and Practice Aids

Witkin, California Summary 10th Wills and Probate § 320A, (New) in General.

Witkin, California Summary 10th Wills and Probate § 320C, (New) Effect Of Deed.

§ 5652. Rules for transfer of interest in property on transferor's death

(a) A revocable transfer on death deed transfers all of the transferor's interest in the property on the transferor's death according to the following rules:

(1) Subject to the beneficiary's right to disclaim the transfer, the interest in the property is transferred to the beneficiary in accordance with the deed.

(2) The interest of a beneficiary is contingent on the beneficiary surviving the transferor. Notwithstanding Section 21110, the interest of a beneficiary that fails to survive the transferor lapses.

(3) Except as provided in paragraph (4), if there is more than one beneficiary, they take the property as tenants in common, in equal shares.

(4) If there is more than one beneficiary, the share of a beneficiary that lapses or fails for any reason is transferred to the others in equal shares.

(b) Property is transferred by a revocable transfer on death deed subject to any limitation on the transferor's interest that is of record at the transferor's death, including, but not limited to, a lien, encumbrance, easement, lease, or other instrument affecting the transferor's interest, whether recorded before or after recordation of the revocable transfer on death deed. The holder of rights under that instrument may enforce those rights against the property notwithstanding its transfer by the revocable transfer on death deed.

(c) A revocable transfer on death deed transfers the property without covenant or warranty of title. *(Added by Stats.2015, c. 293 (A.B.139), § 17, eff. Jan. 1, 2016.)*

Repeal

For repeal of Part 4, see Probate Code § 5600.

Law Revision Commission Comments

2015 Addition

Under subdivision (a) of Section 5652, whatever interest the transferor owned at death in the property passes to the beneficiary. It should be noted, however, that this provision is not limited to the fee interest. If the transferor's ownership interest is a less than fee interest, the transferor's entire less than fee ownership interest passes to the beneficiary on the transferor's death.

Subdivision (b) conditions a transfer to a beneficiary on the beneficiary surviving the transferor.

Under subdivision (b), a beneficiary takes only what the transferor has at death. This is a specific application of the general rule that recordation of a revocable TOD deed does not affect the transferor's ownership rights or ability to deal with the property until death. See Section 5650 (effect during transferor's life). Likewise, if an obligation of the beneficiary attaches to the property as a result of the doctrine of after-acquired title, that obligation is subordinate to any limitations on the transferor's interest in the property, and a transfer by the beneficiary financed by a purchase money mortgage is subject to the priority of a recorded encumbrance on the transferor's interest notwithstanding Civil Code Section 2898 (priority of purchase money encumbrance).

Subdivision (c) emphasizes the point that a revocable TOD deed is basically a quitclaim, passing whatever interest the transferor had at death to the beneficiary. [44 Cal.L.Rev.Comm. Reports 573 (2015) [2015–16 AR Appx. 5]]

Research References

Treatises and Practice Aids

Witkin, California Summary 10th Wills and Probate § 320C, (New) Effect Of Deed.

§ 5654. Medi–Cal eligibility

(a) For the purpose of determination of eligibility for health care under Chapter 7 (commencing with Section 14000) or Chapter 8 (commencing with Section 14200) of Part 3 of Division 9 of the Welfare and Institutions Code, execution and recordation of a revocable transfer on death deed is not a lifetime transfer of the property.

(b) Property transferred by a revocable transfer on death deed is subject to claims of the State Department of Health Care Services to the extent authorized by law. *(Added by Stats.2015, c. 293 (A.B.139), § 17, eff. Jan. 1, 2016.)*

Repeal

For repeal of Part 4, see Probate Code § 5600.

Law Revision Commission Comments

2015 Addition

Subdivision (a) of Section 5654 is a specific application of the general rule that execution and recordation of a revocable TOD deed divests the transferor of no interest in the property, and invests the beneficiary with no rights in the property, during the transferor's life. Section 5650 (effect during transferor's life).

Subdivision (b) is consistent with case law interpretation of the meaning and purpose of Welfare and Institutions Code Section 14009.5, providing for reimbursement to the state for Medi–Cal payments made during the decedent's life. See Bonta v. Burke, 98 Cal. App. 4th 788, 120 Cal. Rptr. 2d 72 (2002). [36 Cal.L.Rev.Comm. Reports 103 (2006)].

§ 5656. Application of property taxation and documentary transfer tax provisions

For the purpose of application of the property taxation and documentary transfer tax provisions of the Revenue and Taxation Code:

(a) Execution and recordation of, or revocation of, a revocable transfer on death deed of real property is not a change in ownership of the property and does not require declaration or payment of a documentary transfer tax or filing of a preliminary change of ownership report.

(b) Transfer of real property on the death of the transferor by a revocable transfer on death deed is a change in ownership of the property. *(Added by Stats.2015, c. 293 (A.B.139), § 17, eff. Jan. 1, 2016.)*

Repeal

For repeal of Part 4, see Probate Code § 5600.

Law Revision Commission Comments

2015 Addition

Section 5656 prescribes the effect of a revocable TOD deed or its revocation for purposes of property tax reassessment and documentary transfer taxation.

Under subdivision (a), mere recordation or revocation of a revocable TOD deed is not a transfer or change in ownership for taxation purposes. This is an application of existing law. See, e.g., Rev. & Tax Code §§ 480.3 (application of preliminary change of ownership requirement), 11930 (exemption from documentary transfer tax).

Under subdivision (b), a change in ownership pursuant to a revocable TOD deed does not occur until the transferor's death. The TOD beneficiary is responsible for filing the change in ownership statement required by Revenue and Taxation Code Section 480. See Section 5680 (beneficiary rights and duties). Although a transfer of property by a revocable TOD deed is a change in ownership for reassessment purposes, the transfer may qualify for exclusion under the Revenue and Taxation Code, depending on the nature of the parties to the transfer. See, e.g., Rev. & Tax. Code §§ 62–63.1. [36 Cal.L.Rev.Comm. Reports 103 (2006)].

Research References

Treatises and Practice Aids

Witkin, California Summary 10th Wills and Probate § 320C, (New) Effect Of Deed.

ARTICLE 2. OTHER INSTRUMENTS AND FORMS OF TENURE

Section

Repeal

For repeal of Part 4, see Probate Code § 5600.

§ 5660. Multiple instruments disposing of same property; operative instrument

If a revocable transfer on death deed recorded on or before 60 days after the date it was executed and another instrument both purport to dispose of the same property:

(a) If the other instrument is not recorded before the transferor's death, the revocable transfer on death deed is the operative instrument.

(b) If the other instrument is recorded before the transferor's death and makes a revocable disposition of the property, the later executed of the revocable transfer on death deed or the other instrument is the operative instrument.

(c) If the other instrument is recorded before the transferor's death and makes an irrevocable disposition of the property, the other instrument and not the revocable transfer on death deed is the operative instrument. *(Added by Stats.2015, c. 293 (A.B.139), § 17, eff. Jan. 1, 2016.)*

Repeal

For repeal of Part 4, see Probate Code § 5600.

Law Revision Commission Comments

2015 Addition

Section 5660 establishes the general rules governing a conflicting disposition of property that is subject to a recorded revocable TOD deed. A revocable TOD deed has no effect unless recorded. Section 5626 (recordation, delivery, and acceptance). A conflicting instrument may not affect a revocable TOD deed under this section unless recorded before the transferor's death.

This section does not apply if the transferor revokes a recorded revocable TOD deed before death. See Section 5630 (revocability).

Absent a total disposition of the property before death, the revocable TOD deed passes property subject to conflicting interests of record. See Section 5652 (effect at death). [36 Cal.L.Rev.Comm. Reports 103 (2006)].

Research References

Treatises and Practice Aids

Witkin, California Summary 10th Wills and Probate § 320A, (New) in General.

Witkin, California Summary 10th Wills and Probate § 320C, (New) Effect Of Deed.

§ 5664. Property held in joint tenancy or as community property with right of survivorship

If, at the time of the transferor's death, title to the property described in the revocable transfer on death deed is held in joint tenancy or as community property with right of survivorship, the revocable transfer on death deed is void. The transferor's interest in the property is governed by the right of survivorship and not by the revocable transfer on death deed. *(Added by Stats.2015, c. 293 (A.B.139), § 17, eff. Jan. 1, 2016.)*

Repeal

For repeal of Part 4, see Probate Code § 5600.

Law Revision Commission Comments

2015 Addition

Section 5664 addresses the effect of a revocable TOD deed that purports to transfer property held, at the time of the transferor's death, in joint tenancy or community property with a right of survivorship. [44 Cal.L.Rev.Comm. Reports 573 (2015) [2015–16 AR Appx. 5]]

Research References

Forms

California Transactions Forms--Estate Planning § 10:19.50, Deed Transfers on Death.

Treatises and Practice Aids

Witkin, California Summary 10th Wills and Probate § 320C, (New) Effect Of Deed.

§ 5666. Provisions applicable to revocable transfer on death deed of community property

(a) Chapter 2 (commencing with Section 5010) of Part 1 applies to a revocable transfer on death deed of community property.

(b) For the purpose of application of Chapter 2 (commencing with Section 5010) of Part 1 to a revocable transfer on death deed of community property, written consent to the deed, revocation of written consent to the deed, or modification of the deed, is ineffective unless recorded within the time required by that chapter for execution or service of the written consent, revocation, or modification. *(Added by Stats.2015, c. 293 (A.B.139), § 17, eff. Jan. 1, 2016.)*

Repeal

For repeal of Part 4, see Probate Code § 5600.

Law Revision Commission Comments

2015 Addition

Subdivision (a) of Section 5666 incorporates the general statutes governing the rights of spouses in a nonprobate transfer of community property. This is a specific application of the rule that general provisions of Part 1 of this division governing a nonprobate transfer apply to a revocable TOD deed. Section 5604(a)(2) (effect of other law).

Under the rules governing a nonprobate transfer of community property, a person has the power of disposition at death of the person's interest in community property without the joinder of the person's spouse.

Subdivision (b) makes clear that the general statute governing the rights of spouses in a nonprobate transfer of community property is qualified by the recording requirement in the case of a revocable TOD deed of community property. This is a specific application of the rule that general provisions of Part 1 of this division governing a nonprobate transfer are subject to a contrary rule in the revocable TOD deed law. See Section 5604(b); see also Section 5011(b) (rights of parties subject to "contrary state statute specifically applicable to instrument under which nonprobate transfer is made").

A third party that acts in reliance on apparent spousal rights under a revocable TOD deed is protected in that reliance. Section 5682 (bona fide purchaser protection). [44 Cal.L.Rev.Comm. Reports 573 (2015) [2015–16 AR Appx. 5]]

Research References

Treatises and Practice Aids

Witkin, California Summary 10th Wills and Probate § 320C, (New) Effect Of Deed.

§ 5668. Provisions applicable to revocable transfer on death deed of community property with right of survivorship

A revocable transfer on death deed of community property with right of survivorship is subject to Section 5666, relating to a revocable transfer on death deed of community property. *(Added by Stats.2015, c. 293 (A.B.139), § 17, eff. Jan. 1, 2016.)*

Repeal

For repeal of Part 4, see Probate Code § 5600.

Law Revision Commission Comments

2015 Addition

Section 5668 addresses the effect of a revocable TOD deed on community property with right of survivorship. See Civ. Code § 682.1 (community property with right of survivorship). [44 Cal.L.Rev. Comm. Reports 573 (2015) [2015–16 AR Appx. 5]]

Research References

Treatises and Practice Aids

Witkin, California Summary 10th Wills and Probate § 320C, (New) Effect Of Deed.

ARTICLE 3. CREDITORS

Repeal

For repeal of Part 4, see Probate Code § 5600.

§ 5670. Creditor of transferor has priority over creditor of beneficiary

Notwithstanding any other statute governing priorities among creditors, a creditor of the transferor whose right is evidenced at the time of the transferor's death by an encumbrance or lien of record on property transferred by a revocable transfer on death deed has priority against the property over a creditor of the beneficiary, regardless of whether the beneficiary's obligation was created before or after the transferor's death and regardless of whether the obligation is secured or unsecured, voluntary or involuntary, recorded or unrecorded. *(Added by Stats.2015, c. 293 (A.B.139), § 17, eff. Jan. 1, 2016.)*

Repeal

For repeal of Part 4, see Probate Code § 5600.

Law Revision Commission Comments

2015 Addition

Section 5670 makes clear that a creditor of the transferor has priority over a creditor of the beneficiary, at least to the extent the transferor's creditor has a lien or encumbrance of record at the time of the transferor's death. Thus the doctrine of after-acquired title (Civ. Code §§ 1106, 2930) does not create a priority in the beneficiary's creditors, even if the right of the transferor's creditor was created after the interest of the beneficiary's creditor. Likewise, the priority given by statute to a purchase money encumbrance by the beneficiary's transferee does not override the general priority of an encumbrance of record by a creditor of the transferor. See Civ. Code § 2898 (priority of purchase money encumbrance). [36 Cal.L.Rev. Comm. Reports 103 (2006)].

Research References

Treatises and Practice Aids

Witkin, California Summary 10th Wills and Probate § 320A, (New) in General.

Witkin, California Summary 10th Wills and Probate § 320D, (New) Rights Of Creditors and Enforcement Of Liability.

§ 5672. Liability of beneficiary for unsecured debts of transferor

Each beneficiary is personally liable to the extent provided in Section 5674 for the unsecured debts of the transferor. Any such debt may be enforced against the beneficiary in the same manner as it could have been enforced against the transferor if the transferor had not died. In any action based on the debt, the beneficiary may assert any defense, cross-complaint, or setoff that would have been available to the transferor if the transferor had not died. Nothing in this section permits enforcement of a claim that is barred under Part 4 (commencing with Section 9000) of Division 7. Section 366.2 of the Code of Civil Procedure applies in an action under this section. *(Added by Stats.2015, c. 293 (A.B.139), § 17, eff. Jan. 1, 2016.)*

Repeal

For repeal of Part 4, see Probate Code § 5600.

Law Revision Commission Comments

2015 Addition

Section 5672 is drawn from Section 13204, relating to the liability of a decedent's successor who takes real property of small value under the affidavit procedure. A beneficiary who wishes to avoid the liability imposed by this section may commence a probate proceeding and return the property to the estate under Section 5676. See Section 5674 (limitation on liability). See also Section 275 (disclaimer). [36 Cal.L.Rev.Comm. Reports 103 (2006)].

Research References

Treatises and Practice Aids

Witkin, California Summary 10th Wills and Probate § 320D, (New) Rights Of Creditors and Enforcement Of Liability.

§ 5674. Exceptions to beneficiary liability; aggregate personal liability of beneficiary

(a) A beneficiary is not liable under Section 5672 if proceedings for the administration of the transferor's estate are commenced and the beneficiary satisfies the requirements of Section 5676.

(b) The aggregate of the personal liability of a beneficiary under Section 5672 shall not exceed the sum of the following:

(1) The fair market value at the time of the transferor's death of the property received by the beneficiary pursuant to the revocable transfer on death deed, less the amount of any liens and encumbrances on the property at that time.

(2) The net income the beneficiary received from the property.

(3) If the property has been disposed of, interest on the fair market value of the property from the date of disposition at the rate payable on a money judgment. For the purposes of this paragraph, "fair market value of the property" has the same meaning as defined in paragraph (2) of subdivision (a) of Section 5676. *(Added by Stats.2015, c. 293 (A.B.139), § 17, eff. Jan. 1, 2016.)*

Repeal

For repeal of Part 4, see Probate Code § 5600.

Law Revision Commission Comments

2015 Addition

Section 5674 is drawn from Section 13207, relating to limitation of liability of a decedent's successor who takes real property of small value under the affidavit procedure. [36 Cal.L.Rev.Comm. Reports 103 (2006)].

Research References

Treatises and Practice Aids

Witkin, California Summary 10th Wills and Probate § 320D, (New) Rights Of Creditors and Enforcement Of Liability.

§ 5676. Proceedings for administration of transferor's estate commenced; beneficiary's liability to estate

(a) Subject to subdivisions (b), (c), and (d), if proceedings for the administration of the transferor's estate are commenced, each beneficiary is liable for:

(1) The restitution to the transferor's estate of the property the beneficiary received pursuant to the revocable transfer on death deed if the beneficiary still has the property, together with (A) the net income the beneficiary received from the property and (B) if the beneficiary encumbered the property after the transferor's death, the amount necessary to satisfy the balance of the encumbrance as of the date the property is restored to the estate.

(2) The restitution to the transferor's estate of the fair market value of the property if the beneficiary no longer has the property, together with (A) the net income the beneficiary received from the property prior to disposing of it and (B) interest from the date of disposition at the rate payable on a money judgment on the fair market value of the property. For the purposes of this paragraph, the "fair market value of the property" is the fair market value, determined as of the time of the disposition of the property, of the property the beneficiary received pursuant to the revocable transfer on death deed, less the amount of any liens and encumbrances on the property at the time of the transferor's death.

(b) Subject to subdivision (c), if proceedings for the administration of the transferor's estate are commenced and a beneficiary made a significant improvement to the property received by the beneficiary pursuant to the revocable transfer on death deed, the beneficiary is liable for whichever of the following the transferor's estate elects:

(1) The restitution of the property, as improved, to the estate of the transferor upon the condition that the estate reimburse the beneficiary for (A) the amount by which the improvement increases the fair market value of the property restored, determined as of the time of restitution, and (B) the amount paid by the beneficiary for principal and interest on any liens or encumbrances that were on the property at the time of the transferor's death.

(2) The restoration to the transferor's estate of the fair market value of the property, determined as of the time of the transferor's death, less the amount of any liens and encumbrances on the property at that time, together with interest on the net amount at the rate payable on a money judgment running from the time of the transferor's death.

(c) The property and amount required to be restored to the estate under this section shall be reduced by any property or amount paid by the beneficiary to satisfy a liability under Section 5672.

(d) An action to enforce the liability under this section may be brought only by the personal representative of the estate of the transferor. Whether or not the personal representative brings an action under this section, the personal representative may enforce the liability only to the extent of the beneficiary's liability under Section 5672. The reasonable cost of proceeding under this section shall be reimbursed as an extraordinary service under Sections 10801 and 10811. Action under this section is optional. A personal representative is never required to act under this section.

(e) An action to enforce the liability under this section is forever barred three years after the transferor's death. The three-year period specified in this subdivision is not tolled for any reason. Nothing in this subdivision affects the requirements of Section 215, any law that may toll the limitations period for the commencement of a Medi–Cal estate recovery action, or the time for commencement of an action by the State Department of Health Care Services under Section 14009.5 of the Welfare and Institutions Code.

(f) If property is restored to the transferor's estate under this section, that property shall be treated as a specific gift and any proceeds remaining from the sale of the property after the payment of claims shall be returned to the beneficiary. *(Added by Stats.2015, c. 293 (A.B.139), § 17, eff. Jan. 1, 2016.)*

Repeal

For repeal of Part 4, see Probate Code § 5600.

Law Revision Commission Comments

2015 Addition

Section 5676 is drawn from Section 13206, relating to restoration of property to the estate by a decedent's successor who takes real property of small value under the affidavit procedure.

Subdivision (d) makes clear that liability for restitution of property to the estate under this section is limited to satisfaction of creditor claims, regardless of whether restitution under this section is made voluntarily or pursuant to a court proceeding. Any surplus belongs to the beneficiary.

Subdivision (f) makes clear that the beneficiary of revocable TOD-deeded property that is restored to the transferor's estate under this section is the beneficiary of a specific gift for purposes of abatement under Section 21402. [44 Cal.L.Rev.Comm. Reports 573 (2015) [2015–16 AR Appx. 5]]

Research References

Treatises and Practice Aids

Witkin, California Summary 10th Wills and Probate § 320D, (New) Rights Of Creditors and Enforcement Of Liability.

CHAPTER 4. EFFECTUATION OF TRANSFER

Repeal

For repeal of Part 4, see Probate Code § 5600.

§ 5680. Establishment of transferor's death; change in ownership statement; notice to Director of Health Care Services; liability for estate and generation-skipping transfer taxes

(a) The beneficiary may establish the fact of the transferor's death under the procedure provided in Chapter 2 (commencing with Section 210) of Part 4 of Division 2. For the purpose of this subdivision, the beneficiary is a person empowered by statute to act on behalf of the transferor or the transferor's estate within the meaning of Section 103526 of the Health and Safety Code.

(b) For the purpose of filing the change in ownership statement required by Section 480 of the Revenue and Taxation Code, the beneficiary is a transferee of real property by reason of death.

(c) For the purpose of giving the notice to the Director of Health Care Services provided for in Section 215, the beneficiary is a beneficiary of the transferor.

(d) The beneficiary is liable to the transferor's estate for prorated estate and generation-skipping transfer taxes to the extent provided in Division 10 (commencing with Section 20100). *(Added by Stats.2015, c. 293 (A.B.139), § 17, eff. Jan. 1, 2016.)*

Repeal

For repeal of Part 4, see Probate Code § 5600.

Law Revision Commission Comments

2015 Addition

Subdivision (a) of Section 5680 establishes that a beneficiary may record an affidavit of death of the transferor to effectuate the transfer. See Section 212 (recordation is prima facie evidence of death to extent it "identifies real property located in county, title to which is affected by death"). Subdivision (a) authorizes the named beneficiary to obtain a certified copy of the transferor's death certificate under Health and Safety Code Section 103526 for the purpose of effectuating the transfer by revocable TOD deed.

Subdivision (b) cross-references the duty imposed on the beneficiary to file a change of ownership statement with the country recorder or assessor within 150 days after the transferor's death. See Rev. & Tax. Code § 480.

Subdivision (c) cross-references the duty imposed on the beneficiary to give the Director of Health Services notice of the death of a transferor who has received Medi–Cal benefits. See Section 215.

Subdivision (d) is a specific application of Division 10 (commencing with Section 20100), relating to proration of taxes. The beneficiary of a nonprobate transfer, such as a revocable TOD deed, is liable for a pro rata share of estate and generation-skipping transfer taxes paid by the transferor's estate. See Sections 20100 *et seq.* (proration of estate tax), 20200 *et seq.* (proration of tax on generation-skipping transfer).

A beneficiary may disclaim the property under Section 275 (disclaimer). [36 Cal.L.Rev.Comm. Reports 103 (2006)].

Research References

Treatises and Practice Aids

Witkin, California Summary 10th Wills and Probate § 320A, (New) in General.

Witkin, California Summary 10th Wills and Probate § 320E, (New) Effectuation Of Transfer.

§ 5682. Rights and protections of beneficiary same as distributee from estate; conditions

If both of the following conditions are satisfied, a person dealing with a beneficiary of a revocable transfer on death deed of real property shall have the same rights and protections as the person would have if the beneficiary had been named as a distributee of the property in an order for distribution of the transferor's estate that had become final:

(a) The person acted in good faith and for a valuable consideration.

(b) An affidavit of death was recorded for the property under Chapter 2 (commencing with Section 210) of Part 4 of Division 2. *(Added by Stats.2015, c. 293 (A.B.139), § 17, eff. Jan. 1, 2016.)*

Repeal

For repeal of Part 4, see Probate Code § 5600.

Law Revision Commission Comments

2015 Addition

Section 5682 is drawn from Section 13203(a) (affidavit procedure for real property of small value). [36 Cal.L.Rev.Comm. Reports 103 (2006)].

Research References

Treatises and Practice Aids

Witkin, California Summary 10th Wills and Probate § 320E, (New) Effectuation Of Transfer.

CHAPTER 5. CONTEST

Section
5696. Fraud, undue influence, duress, mistake, or other invalidating causes; petition by conservator or guardian of transferor.

Repeal

For repeal of Part 4, see Probate Code § 5600.

§ 5690. Action for disqualification of beneficiary; person who may file; county for proceedings; lis pendens

(a)(1) An action for the disqualification of a beneficiary under Part 3.7 (commencing with Section 21360) of Division 11 may be brought to contest the validity of a transfer of property by a revocable transfer on death deed.

(2) An action to contest the validity of a transfer of property by a revocable transfer on death deed may be filed by the transferor's personal representative or an interested person under Part 19 (commencing with Section 850) of Division 2.

(b) The proper county for a contest proceeding is the proper county for proceedings concerning administration of the transferor's estate, whether or not proceedings concerning administration of the transferor's estate have been commenced at the time of the contest.

(c) On commencement of a contest proceeding, the contestant may record a lis pendens in the county in which the revocable transfer on death deed is recorded. *(Added by Stats.2015, c. 293 (A.B.139), § 17, eff. Jan. 1, 2016.)*

Repeal

For repeal of Part 4, see Probate Code § 5600.

Law Revision Commission Comments

2015 Addition

Section 5690 incorporates the procedure of Sections 850–859, relating to a conveyance or transfer of property claimed to belong to a decedent or other person. A person adversely affected by a revocable TOD deed has standing to contest the transfer. *Cf.* Section 48 ("interested person" defined).

Grounds for contest may include but are not limited to lack of capacity of the transferor (Section 5620), improper execution or recordation (Sections 5624–5626), invalidating cause for consent to a transfer of community property (Section 5015), and transfer to a disqualified person (Section 21380). See also Section 5696 (fraud, undue influence, duress, mistake, or other invalidating cause).

The proper county for proceedings for administration of a decedent's estate is the county of the decedent's domicile or, in the case of a nondomiciliary, the county of the decedent's death or, if the decedent died outside the state, where property of the decedent is located. Prob. Code §§ 7051, 7052.

Recordation of a lis pendens within 120 days after the transferor's death preserves remedies for the contestant. See Section 5694 (remedies). [44 Cal.L.Rev.Comm. Reports 573 (2015) [2015–16 AR Appx. 5]]

Research References

Treatises and Practice Aids

Witkin, California Summary 10th Wills and Probate § 320A, (New) in General.

Witkin, California Summary 10th Wills and Probate § 320F, (New) Contest Of Validity Of Transfer.

§ 5692. Time for commencing action; accrual of limitations period

(a) A contest proceeding pursuant to Section 5690 shall not be commenced before the transferor's death.

(b) For the purposes of the applicable limitations period, a contest proceeding accrues on the date of the transferor's death. *(Added by Stats.2015, c. 293 (A.B.139), § 17, eff. Jan. 1, 2016.)*

Repeal

For repeal of Part 4, see Probate Code § 5600.

Law Revision Commission Comments

2015 Addition

Subdivision (a) of Section 5692 limits the contest of a revocable TOD deed to a post-death challenge. A challenge before the transferor's death would be premature since a revocable TOD deed may be revoked at any time before the transfer occurs by reason of the transferor's death. However, the transferor's conservator may seek to revoke a revocable TOD deed pursuant to substituted judgment principles. See Section 5630 (revocability) & Comment and Section 5696(b); see also Sections 2580–2586 (substituted judgment).

Subdivision (b) provides that the limitations period for contesting a TOD deed commences on the transferor's death. [44 Cal.L.Rev. Comm. Reports 573 (2015) [2015–16 AR Appx. 5]]

Research References

Treatises and Practice Aids

Witkin, California Summary 10th Wills and Probate § 320F, (New) Contest Of Validity Of Transfer.

§ 5694. Determination of invalid transfer; relief

If the court in a contest proceeding determines that a transfer of property by a revocable transfer on death deed is invalid, the court shall order the following relief:

(a) If the proceeding was commenced and a lis pendens was recorded within 120 days after the transferor's death, the court shall void the deed and order transfer of the property to the person entitled to it.

(b) If the proceeding was not commenced and a lis pendens was not recorded within 120 days after the transferor's death, the court shall grant appropriate relief but the court order shall not affect the rights in the property of a purchaser or encumbrancer for value and in good faith acquired before commencement of the proceeding and recordation of a lis pendens. *(Added by Stats.2015, c. 293 (A.B.139), § 17, eff. Jan. 1, 2016.)*

Repeal

For repeal of Part 4, see Probate Code § 5600.

Law Revision Commission Comments

2015 Addition

The 120–day period under Section 5694 represents a balance between the 40–day period applicable to disposition of an estate without administration under Sections 13100 (affidavit procedure for collection or transfer of personal property) and 13151 (court order determining succession to property), and the six month period applicable to the affidavit procedure for real property of small value under Section 13200. [44 Cal.L.Rev.Comm. Reports 573 (2015) [2015–16 AR Appx. 5]]

Research References

Treatises and Practice Aids

Witkin, California Summary 10th Wills and Probate § 320F, (New) Contest Of Validity Of Transfer.

§ 5696. Fraud, undue influence, duress, mistake, or other invalidating causes; petition by conservator or guardian of transferor

(a) Nothing in this chapter limits the application of principles of fraud, undue influence, duress, mistake, or other invalidating cause to a transfer of property by a revocable transfer on death deed.

(b) Notwithstanding subdivision (a) of Section 5692, the conservator or guardian of a transferor may, before the transferor's death, petition the court for invalidation of a revocable transfer on death deed executed by the transferor. *(Added by Stats.2015, c. 293 (A.B.139), § 17, eff. Jan. 1, 2016.)*

Repeal

For repeal of Part 4, see Probate Code § 5600.

Law Revision Commission Comments

2015 Addition

Subdivision (a) of Section 5696 is drawn from Section 5015 (nonprobate transfer of community property).

Subdivision (b) is new. [44 Cal.L.Rev.Comm. Reports 573 (2015) [2015–16 AR Appx. 5]]

Research References

Treatises and Practice Aids

Witkin, California Summary 10th Wills and Probate § 320F, (New) Contest Of Validity Of Transfer.

Division 6

WILLS AND INTESTATE SUCCESSION

Part 1

WILLS

Law Revision Commission Comments

1990 Enactment

This part supersedes Part 1 (commencing with Section 6100) of Division 6 the repealed Probate Code. The superseded part was enacted upon recommendation of the California Law Revision Commission. See Tentative Recommendation Relating to Wills and Intestate Succession, 16 Cal.L.Revision Comm'n Reports 2301 (1982). See also Report of Senate Committee on Judiciary on Assembly Bills 25 and 68, 17 Cal.L. Revision Comm'n Reports 867, 870–79 (1984). [20 Cal.L.Rev.Comm.Reports 1001 (1990)].

CHAPTER 3. REVOCATION AND REVIVAL

§ 6122. Dissolution or annulment of marriage; provisions revoked; other change in circumstances

(a) Unless the will expressly provides otherwise, if after executing a will the testator's marriage is dissolved or annulled, the dissolution or annulment revokes all of the following:

(1) Any disposition or appointment of property made by the will to the former spouse.

(2) Any provision of the will conferring a general or special power of appointment on the former spouse.

(3) Any provision of the will nominating the former spouse as executor, trustee, conservator, or guardian.

(b) If any disposition or other provision of a will is revoked solely by this section, it is revived by the testator's remarriage to the former spouse.

(c) In case of revocation by dissolution or annulment:

(1) Property prevented from passing to a former spouse because of the revocation passes as if the former spouse failed to survive the testator.

(2) Other provisions of the will conferring some power or office on the former spouse shall be interpreted as if the former spouse failed to survive the testator.

(d) For purposes of this section, dissolution or annulment means any dissolution or annulment which would exclude the spouse as a surviving spouse within the meaning of Section 78. A decree of legal separation which does not terminate the status of spouses is not a dissolution for purposes of this section.

(e) Except as provided in Section 6122.1, no change of circumstances other than as described in this section revokes a will.

(f) Subdivisions (a) to (d), inclusive, do not apply to any case where the final judgment of dissolution or annulment of marriage occurs before January 1, 1985. That case is governed by the law in effect prior to January 1, 1985. *(Stats.1990, c. 79 (A.B.759), § 14, operative July 1, 1991. Amended by Stats.2001, c. 893 (A.B.25), § 50; Stats.2002, c. 664 (A.B.3034), § 179; Stats.2016, c. 50 (S.B.1005), § 86, eff. Jan. 1, 2017.)*

Law Revision Commission Comments

1990 Enactment

Section 6122 continues Section 6122 of the repealed Probate Code without change. This section is the same in substance as Section 2–508 of the Uniform Probate Code (1987). As to the construction of provisions drawn from uniform acts, see Section 2. This section changed the former case law rule that dissolution or annulment of marriage had no effect on the will of either spouse. See In re Estate of Patterson, 64 Cal.App. 643, 646, 222 P. 374 (1923) cert. denied, 266 U.S. 594 (1925); 7 B. Witkin, Summary of California Law Wills and Probate § 150, at 5666 (8th ed. 1974). See also Section 36 ("dissolution of marriage" defined), Civil Code § 4352 (required notice in judgment of dissolution or nullity). For a comparable provision, see Section 6226 (California statutory will).

Subdivision (f) limits the application of subdivisions (a)–(d) to cases where the final judgment of dissolution or annulment of marriage occurs on or after the date this section of the repealed Probate Code first become operative.

Background on Section 6122 of Repealed Code

Section 6122 was added by 1983 Cal.Stat. ch. 842 § 55 and was amended by 1984 Cal.Stat. ch. 892 § 23. For background on the provisions of this part, see the Comment to this part under the part heading. The 1984 amendment added subdivision (f). See Communication of Law Revision Commission Concerning Assembly Bill 2290, 18 Cal.L.Revision Comm'n 77, 86 (1986). [20 Cal.L.Rev.Comm.Reports 1001 (1990)].

Commentary

Extending the literal letter of Section 6122, *Estate of Hermon, 39 Cal.App.4th 1525, 46 Cal.Rptr.2d 577 (1995), review denied February 15, 1996,* holds that dissolution of marriage automatically revokes not only will bequests to a "spouse" but also to a "spouse's children" and "spouse's issue." This analysis follows Uniform Probate Code Section 2–804, not adopted in California, which provides that dissolution revokes bequests to former spouses and the relatives of former spouses.

Moving a step beyond *Hermon*, *Estate of Jones, 122 Cal.App.4th 326, 18 Cal.Rptr.3d 637 (2004)*, applies the rule that *Hermon* adopted for a class gift to a testamentary gift to two specifically named stepchildren.

Research References

Forms

California Transactions Forms--Estate Planning § 2:14, Failure to Properly Designate Disposition Of Assets, Provide for Pretermitted Heirs, and Plan for Dissolution Of Marriage.
California Transactions Forms--Estate Planning § 22:9, Overview.
California Transactions Forms--Estate Planning § 6:30, Effect Of Dissolution or Annulment Of Marriage.
California Transactions Forms--Estate Planning § 6:51, Matters to Consider in Drafting Dispositions to Beneficiaries.
California Transactions Forms--Estate Planning § 19:42, Nature and Purpose; Governing Law.
California Transactions Forms--Estate Planning § 22:15, Revocation as a Result Of Dissolution or Annulment.
California Transactions Forms--Estate Planning § 6:100, Spouse Omitted If Marriage is Terminated by Dissolution or Annulment.
West's California Code Forms, Probate § 8250 Form 1, Contest Of Will and Objection to Probate.
West's California Code Forms, Probate § 8270 Form 1, Petition for Revocation Of Probate Of Will.

Treatises and Practice Aids

Witkin, California Summary 10th Wills and Probate § 25, Major Changes.
Witkin, California Summary 10th Wills and Probate § 173, in General.
Witkin, California Summary 10th Wills and Probate § 177, Dissolution or Annulment Of Marriage.
Witkin, California Summary 10th Wills and Probate § 317, in General.

§ 6122.1. Domestic partnership of testator; revocation by termination

(a) Unless the will expressly provides otherwise, if after executing a will the testator's domestic partnership is terminated, the termination revokes all of the following:

(1) Any disposition or appointment of property made by the will to the former domestic partner.

(2) Any provision of the will conferring a general or special power of appointment on the former domestic partner.

(3) Any provision of the will nominating the former domestic partner as executor, trustee, conservator, or guardian.

(b) If any disposition or other provision of a will is revoked solely by this section, it is revived by the testator establishing another domestic partnership with the former domestic partner.

(c) In case of revocation by termination of a domestic partnership:

(1) Property prevented from passing to a former domestic partner because of the revocation passes as if the former domestic partner failed to survive the testator.

(2) Other provisions of the will conferring some power or office on the former domestic partner shall be interpreted as if the former domestic partner failed to survive the testator.

(d) This section shall apply only to wills executed on or after January 1, 2002. *(Added by Stats.2001, c. 893 (A.B.25), § 51.)*

Application

For application of this section, see its terms.

Research References

Forms

California Transactions Forms--Estate Planning § 2:14, Failure to Properly Designate Disposition Of Assets, Provide for Pretermitted Heirs, and Plan for Dissolution Of Marriage.
California Transactions Forms--Estate Planning § 22:9, Overview.
California Transactions Forms--Estate Planning § 6:51, Matters to Consider in Drafting Dispositions to Beneficiaries.
California Transactions Forms--Estate Planning § 6:30.50, Effect Of Termination Of Domestic Partnership.
California Transactions Forms--Estate Planning § 22:15.50, Revocation as a Result Of Termination Of a Domestic Partnership.

Treatises and Practice Aids

Witkin, California Summary 10th Wills and Probate § 173, in General.
Witkin, California Summary 10th Wills and Probate § 177, Dissolution or Annulment Of Marriage.
Witkin, California Summary 10th Wills and Probate § 178, Termination Of Domestic Partnership.

Part 2

INTESTATE SUCCESSION

Law Revision Commission Comments

1990 Enactment

This part supersedes Part 2 (commencing with Section 6400) of Division 6 the repealed Probate Code. The superseded part was enacted upon recommendation of the California Law Revision Commission. See Tentative Recommendation Relating to Wills and Intestate Succession, 16 Cal.L.Revision Comm'n Reports 2301 (1982). See also Report of Senate Committee on Judiciary on Assembly Bills 25 and 68, 17 Cal.L.Revision Comm'n Reports 867, 871–83 (1984). [20 Cal.L.Rev.Comm.Reports 1001 (1990)].

CHAPTER 1. INTESTATE SUCCESSION GENERALLY

§ 6400. Property subject to intestacy provisions

Any part of the estate of a decedent not effectively disposed of by will passes to the decedent's heirs as prescribed in this part. *(Stats.1990, c. 79 (A.B.759), § 14, operative July 1, 1991.)*

Law Revision Commission Comments

1990 Enactment

Section 6400 continues Section 6400 of the repealed Probate Code without change. This section is the same in substance as Section 2–101 of the Uniform Probate Code (1987). As to the construction of provisions drawn from uniform acts, see Section 2. The section does not apply if the decedent died before January 1, 1985. See Section 6414(a). As to the application of any amendments made after that date, see Section 3. If the decedent died before January 1, 1985, see Section 6414(b), (c). See also Section 6404 (escheat).

Background on Section 6400 of Repealed Code

Section 6400 was added by 1983 Cal.Stat. ch. 842 § 55. The section superseded former Probate Code Section 200 (repealed by 1983 Cal.Stat. ch. 842 § 19) and the first portion of former Probate Code Section 220 (repealed by 1983 Cal.Stat. ch. 842 § 19). For background on the provisions of this part, see the Comment to this part under the part heading. [20 Cal.L.Rev.Comm.Reports 1001 (1990)].

Research References

Forms

California Transactions Forms--Estate Planning § 6:1, Definitions.

California Transactions Forms--Estate Planning § 6:2, Who May be Beneficiary Under Will.

California Transactions Forms--Estate Planning § 1:18, Property Subject to Probate; Intestacy.

California Transactions Forms--Estate Planning § 10:3, Separate Property.

California Transactions Forms--Estate Planning § 2:14, Failure to Properly Designate Disposition Of Assets, Provide for Pretermitted Heirs, and Plan for Dissolution Of Marriage.

California Transactions Forms--Estate Planning § 6:65, Beneficiaries Determined Under Laws Of Intestate Succession.

California Transactions Forms--Estate Planning § 19:62, Preference for Interpretation that Prevents Intestacy.

California Transactions Forms--Estate Planning § 19:96, Overview; Avoiding Intestacy.

California Transactions Forms--Estate Planning § 19:98, No-Contest Provision.

West's California Code Forms, Probate § 10951 Form 1, Final Account and Petition for Settlement Of Final Account and for Final Distribution.

West's California Code Forms, Probate § 11620 Form 1, Petition for Preliminary Distribution.

Treatises and Practice Aids

Witkin, California Summary 10th Torts § 1389, Listed Persons Under Current Law.

Witkin, California Summary 10th Wills and Probate § 74, in General.

Witkin, California Summary 10th Wills and Probate § 99, Nature and Scope Of Statute.

§ 6401. Surviving spouse; intestate share; community or quasi-community property; separate property

(a) As to community property, the intestate share of the surviving spouse is the one-half of the community property that belongs to the decedent under Section 100.

(b) As to quasi-community property, the intestate share of the surviving spouse is the one-half of the quasi-community property that belongs to the decedent under Section 101.

(c) As to separate property, the intestate share of the surviving spouse is as follows:

(1) The entire intestate estate if the decedent did not leave any surviving issue, parent, brother, sister, or issue of a deceased brother or sister.

(2) One–half of the intestate estate in the following cases:

(A) Where the decedent leaves only one child or the issue of one deceased child.

(B) Where the decedent leaves no issue, but leaves a parent or parents or their issue or the issue of either of them.

(3) One–third of the intestate estate in the following cases:

(A) Where the decedent leaves more than one child.

(B) Where the decedent leaves one child and the issue of one or more deceased children.

(C) Where the decedent leaves issue of two or more deceased children. *(Stats.1990, c. 79 (A.B.759), § 14, operative July 1, 1991. Amended by Stats.2002, c. 447 (A.B.2216), § 1, operative July 1, 2003; Stats.2014, c. 913 (A.B.2747), § 32, eff. Jan. 1, 2015.)*

Law Revision Commission Comments

1990 Enactment

Section 6401 continues Section 6401 of the repealed Probate Code without substantive change. As to a surviving spouse's waiver of rights at death, see Sections 140–147.

Upon the death of a married person, one-half of the decedent's quasi-community property belongs to the surviving spouse (Section 101); in the case of intestate succession, the other one-half of the decedent's quasi-community property, which belongs to the decedent (Section 101), goes to the surviving spouse under subdivision (b) of Section 6401. The quasi-community property recaptured under Section 102 does not belong to the decedent even though the property is restored to the decedent's estate; rather it is property that belongs to the surviving spouse. See Section 102 and the Comment thereto. Accordingly, the surviving spouse does not take the recaptured property by intestate succession. See also Section 66 (defining "quasi-community property").

Community property and quasi-community property that passes to the surviving spouse under subdivisions (a) and (b) is subject to Section 13502 (election to have community and quasi-community property administered) and Sections 13540–13542 (right of surviving spouse to deal with and dispose of community and quasi-community real property). As to the liability of the surviving spouse for debts of the deceased spouse, see Sections 13550–13554.

This section does not apply if the decedent died before January 1, 1985. See Section 6414(a). As to amendments made after that date, see Section 3. If the decedent died before January 1, 1985, see Section 6414(b), (c).

For background on this section, see Recommendation and Study Relating to Rights of Surviving Spouse in Property Acquired by Decedent While Domiciled Elsewhere, 1 Cal.L.Revision Comm'n Reports E–1 (1957); Recommendation and Study Relating to Inter Vivos Marital Property Rights in Property Acquired While Domiciled Elsewhere, 3 Cal.L.Revision Comm'n Reports I–1 (1961); Recommendation Relating to Quasi–Community Property, 9 Cal.L.Revision Comm'n Reports 113 (1969).

Background on Section 6401 of Repealed Code

Section 6401 was added by 1983 Cal.Stat. ch. 842 § 55 and was amended by 1984 Cal.Stat. ch. 892 § 40. Subdivision (a) of Section 6401 was the same in substance as a portion of former Probate Code Section 201 (repealed by 1983 Cal.Stat. ch. 842 § 19). Subdivision (b) was the same in substance as a portion of former Probate Code Section 201.5 (repealed by 1983 Cal.Stat. ch. 842 § 19). Subdivision (c) continued the rules under former law that determined the share the surviving spouse received of the decedent's separate estate. See former Prob.Code §§ 221, 223, 224 (repealed by 1983 Cal.Stat. ch. 842 § 19). The 1984 amendment made a nonsubstantive technical change. See Recommendation Relating to Revision of Wills and Intestate Succession Law, 17 Cal.L.Revision Comm'n Reports 537 (1984). For background on the provisions of this part, see the Comment to this part under the part heading. [20 Cal.L.Rev.Comm.Reports 1001 (1990)].

Research References

Forms

California Transactions Forms--Estate Planning § 1:22, Community Property.
California Transactions Forms--Estate Planning § 1:26, Quasi-Community Property; Separate Property.
California Transactions Forms--Estate Planning § 1:36, Conflicts Between Clients.
California Transactions Forms--Estate Planning § 1:77, Matters to Consider Regarding Property Distribution.
California Transactions Forms--Estate Planning § 10:4, Community Property.
California Transactions Forms--Estate Planning § 10:5, Quasi-Community Property.
California Transactions Forms--Estate Planning § 10:18, Property Passing to Spouse.
California Transactions Forms--Estate Planning § 19:19, Quasi-Community Property.
West's California Code Forms, Probate § 13502(A) Form 1, Election to Subject Spousal Property to Estate Administration.

Treatises and Practice Aids

Witkin, California Summary 10th Community Property § 251, Disposition Of Community Property.
Witkin, California Summary 10th Community Property § 252, Former Law and Corrective Legislation.
Witkin, California Summary 10th Community Property § 253, Where California Law Applies.
Witkin, California Summary 10th Wills and Probate § 76, Surviving Spouse's Share in Community and Quasi-Community Property.
Witkin, California Summary 10th Wills and Probate § 77, in General.
Witkin, California Summary 10th Wills and Probate § 78, Surviving Spouse or Domestic Partner.
Witkin, California Summary 10th Wills and Probate § 84, Nature and Scope Of Statute.
Witkin, California Summary 10th Wills and Probate § 96, Out Of Wedlock Children.
Witkin, California Summary 10th Wills and Probate § 233, in General.
Witkin, California Summary 10th Wills and Probate § 265, Disposition.
Witkin, California Summary 10th Wills and Probate § 659, Order Of Abatement.
Witkin, California Summary 10th Wills and Probate § 793, Definitions.
Witkin, California Summary 10th Wills and Probate § 818, Property Passing Without Administration.

§ 6402. Intestate estate not passing to surviving spouse

Except as provided in Section 6402.5, the part of the intestate estate not passing to the surviving spouse, under Section 6401, or the entire intestate estate if there is no surviving spouse, passes as follows:

(a) To the issue of the decedent, the issue taking equally if they are all of the same degree of kinship to the decedent, but if of unequal degree those of more remote degree take in the manner provided in Section 240.

(b) If there is no surviving issue, to the decedent's parent or parents equally.

(c) If there is no surviving issue or parent, to the issue of the parents or either of them, the issue taking equally if they are all of the same degree of kinship to the decedent, but if of unequal degree those of more remote degree take in the manner provided in Section 240.

(d) If there is no surviving issue, parent or issue of a parent, but the decedent is survived by one or more grandparents or issue of grandparents, to the grandparent or grandparents equally, or to the issue of those grandparents if there is no surviving grandparent, the issue taking equally if they are all of the same degree of kinship to the decedent, but if of unequal degree those of more remote degree take in the manner provided in Section 240.

(e) If there is no surviving issue, parent or issue of a parent, grandparent or issue of a grandparent, but the decedent is survived by the issue of a predeceased spouse, to that issue, the issue taking equally if they are all of the same degree of kinship to the predeceased spouse, but if of unequal degree those of more remote degree take in the manner provided in Section 240.

(f) If there is no surviving issue, parent or issue of a parent, grandparent or issue of a grandparent, or issue of a predeceased spouse, but the decedent is survived by next of kin, to the next of kin in equal degree, but where there are two or more collateral kindred in equal degree who claim through different ancestors, those who claim through the nearest ancestor are preferred to those claiming through an ancestor more remote.

(g) If there is no surviving next of kin of the decedent and no surviving issue of a predeceased spouse of the decedent, but the decedent is survived by the parents of a predeceased spouse or the issue of those parents, to the parent or parents equally, or to the issue of those parents if both are deceased, the issue taking equally if they are all of the same degree of kinship to the predeceased spouse, but if of unequal degree those of more remote degree take in the manner provided in Section 240. *(Stats.1990, c. 79 (A.B.759), § 14, operative July 1, 1991. Amended by Stats.2002, c. 447 (A.B.2216), § 2, operative July 1, 2003; Stats.2014, c. 913 (A.B.2747), § 32.5, eff. Jan. 1, 2015.)*

Law Revision Commission Comments

1990 Enactment

Section 6402 continues Section 6402 of the repealed Probate Code without substantive change. Except to the extent indicated below, subdivisions (a)–(d) are the same in substance as Section 2–103 of the Uniform Probate Code (1987). As to the construction of provisions drawn from uniform acts, see Section 2.

Under subdivision (d), grandchildren or more remote lineal descendants of the grandparents of the deceased take ahead of great-grandparents. Subdivision (d) does not adopt the scheme of paragraph (4) of Section 2–103 of the Uniform Probate Code (1987). (Under that provision of the Uniform Probate Code, half of the estate goes to paternal grandparents or to the issue of the paternal grandparents if both are deceased, and the other half goes to maternal grandparents or to the issue of the maternal grandparents if both are deceased.)

If there are no takers under Sections 6401–6402.5, the decedent's estate escheats to the state. See Section 6404.

This section does not apply if the decedent died before January 1, 1985. See Section 6414(a). As to the application of any amendments made after that date, see Section 3. If the decedent died before January 1, 1985, see Section 6414(b), (c).

Background on Section 6402 of Repealed Code

Section 6402 was added by 1983 Cal.Stat. ch. 842 § 55 and was amended by 1984 Cal.Stat. ch. 892 § 41 and 1985 Cal.Stat. ch. 982 § 19. Subdivision (a) was consistent with former Probate Code Section 222 (repealed by 1983 Cal.Stat. ch. 842 § 19) except that the rule of representation was changed. See Section 240 and the Comment thereto. Subdivisions (b) and (c) were consistent with former Probate Code Section 225 (repealed by 1983 Cal.Stat. ch. 842 § 19) except for the new rule of representation.

Subdivisions (d), (e), (f), and (g) superseded former Probate Code Section 226 (repealed by 1983 Cal.Stat. ch. 842 § 19) and a portion of former Probate Code Section 229 (repealed by 1983 Cal.Stat. ch. 842 § 19). Subdivision (d) was consistent with former Probate Code Section 226 (repealed by 1983 Cal.Stat. ch. 842 § 19) pursuant to which the estate went to the next of kin, except that under subdivision (d) grandchildren or more remote lineal descendants of the grandparents of the deceased took ahead of great-grandparents. By way of contrast, under former Section 226 great-grandparents (related in the third degree) took ahead of grandchildren of the deceased's grandparents (fourth degree). Subdivision (e) was drawn from former Probate Code Section 229 (repealed by 1983 Cal.Stat. ch. 842 § 19) and gave the decedent's stepchildren and issue of deceased stepchildren a right to inherit if there is no one to inherit under subdivisions (a) through (d). Subdivision (f) was drawn from former Probate Code Section 226 (repealed by 1983 Cal.Stat. ch. 842 § 19). Subdivision (g) was drawn from former Section 229 and gave parents and issue of deceased parents of a predeceased spouse of the decedent a right to inherit if there is no one to inherit under subdivisions (a) through (f). See also Section 6402.5 (succession to the portion of the decedent's estate attributable to the decedent's predeceased spouse). The 1984 amendment made a nonsubstantive technical change. See Communication of Law Revision Commission Concerning Assembly Bill 2290, 18 Cal.L.Revision Comm'n Reports 77, 89 (1986). See also Recommendation Relating to Revision of Wills and Intestate Succession Law, 17 Cal.L.Revision Comm'n Reports 537 (1984). The 1985 amendment substituted the references to Section 240 for the former references to taking "by representation." This change was nonsubstantive. See Communication Concerning Assembly Bill 196, 18 Cal.L.Revision Comm'n Reports 367, 375 (1986). See also Recommendation Relating to Distribution Under a Will or Trust, 18 Cal.L.Revision Comm'n Reports 269, 284–85 (1986). For background on the provisions of this part, see the Comment to this part under the part heading. [20 Cal.L.Rev.Comm.Reports 1001 (1990)].

Commentary

Although a father abandoned his wife and in-utero son, for whom he acknowledged paternity but never paid any child support, under subsection (b) he was still entitled to share the deceased son's intestate estate with the child's mother. *Estate of Shellenbarger, 169 Cal.App.4th 894, 86 Cal.Rptr.3d 862 (2008), review denied.*

Jackson v. Fitzgibbons, 127 Cal.App.4th 329, 25 Cal.Rptr.3d 478 (2005), holds that a child lacks standing to bring a Code of Civil Procedure § 377.60 action for the wrongful death of a parent when a juvenile court has terminated the parental rights of the child's parents; in such case this section and Probate Code § 6450 and 6451 are also inapplicable.

Research References

Forms

California Transactions Forms--Estate Planning § 1:77, Matters to Consider Regarding Property Distribution.

California Transactions Forms--Estate Planning § 6:13, Conditions Preventing Parent from Inheriting from a Child.

Treatises and Practice Aids

Witkin, California Summary 10th Torts § 1393, Child Of Presumed Parent.

Witkin, California Summary 10th Wills and Probate § 77, in General.

Witkin, California Summary 10th Wills and Probate § 79, Issue Of Decedent.

Witkin, California Summary 10th Wills and Probate § 80, Parents or Issue Of Parents.

Witkin, California Summary 10th Wills and Probate § 81, Grandparents or Issue Of Grandparents.

Witkin, California Summary 10th Wills and Probate § 82, Next Of Kin.

Witkin, California Summary 10th Wills and Probate § 84, Nature and Scope Of Statute.

Witkin, California Summary 10th Wills and Probate § 85, Apportionment Of Property Between Families.

Witkin, California Summary 10th Wills and Probate § 96, Out Of Wedlock Children.

Witkin, California Summary 10th Wills and Probate § 97, Adopted Children.

Witkin, California Summary 10th Wills and Probate § 659, Order Of Abatement.

Witkin, California Summary 10th Wills and Probate § 793, Definitions.

§ 6402.5. Predeceased spouse; portion of decedent's estate attributable to decedent's predeceased spouse

(a) For purposes of distributing real property under this section if the decedent had a predeceased spouse who died not more than 15 years before the decedent and there is no surviving spouse or issue of the decedent, the portion of the decedent's estate attributable to the decedent's predeceased spouse passes as follows:

(1) If the decedent is survived by issue of the predeceased spouse, to the surviving issue of the predeceased spouse; if they are all of the same degree of kinship to the predeceased spouse they take equally, but if of unequal degree those of

more remote degree take in the manner provided in Section 240.

(2) If there is no surviving issue of the predeceased spouse but the decedent is survived by a parent or parents of the predeceased spouse, to the predeceased spouse's surviving parent or parents equally.

(3) If there is no surviving issue or parent of the predeceased spouse but the decedent is survived by issue of a parent of the predeceased spouse, to the surviving issue of the parents of the predeceased spouse or either of them, the issue taking equally if they are all of the same degree of kinship to the predeceased spouse, but if of unequal degree those of more remote degree take in the manner provided in Section 240.

(4) If the decedent is not survived by issue, parent, or issue of a parent of the predeceased spouse, to the next of kin of the decedent in the manner provided in Section 6402.

(5) If the portion of the decedent's estate attributable to the decedent's predeceased spouse would otherwise escheat to the state because there is no kin of the decedent to take under Section 6402, the portion of the decedent's estate attributable to the predeceased spouse passes to the next of kin of the predeceased spouse who shall take in the same manner as the next of kin of the decedent take under Section 6402.

(b) For purposes of distributing personal property under this section if the decedent had a predeceased spouse who died not more than five years before the decedent, and there is no surviving spouse or issue of the decedent, the portion of the decedent's estate attributable to the decedent's predeceased spouse passes as follows:

(1) If the decedent is survived by issue of the predeceased spouse, to the surviving issue of the predeceased spouse; if they are all of the same degree of kinship to the predeceased spouse they take equally, but if of unequal degree those of more remote degree take in the manner provided in Section 240.

(2) If there is no surviving issue of the predeceased spouse but the decedent is survived by a parent or parents of the predeceased spouse, to the predeceased spouse's surviving parent or parents equally.

(3) If there is no surviving issue or parent of the predeceased spouse but the decedent is survived by issue of a parent of the predeceased spouse, to the surviving issue of the parents of the predeceased spouse or either of them, the issue taking equally if they are all of the same degree of kinship to the predeceased spouse, but if of unequal degree those of more remote degree take in the manner provided in Section 240.

(4) If the decedent is not survived by issue, parent, or issue of a parent of the predeceased spouse, to the next of kin of the decedent in the manner provided in Section 6402.

(5) If the portion of the decedent's estate attributable to the decedent's predeceased spouse would otherwise escheat to the state because there is no kin of the decedent to take under Section 6402, the portion of the decedent's estate attributable to the predeceased spouse passes to the next of kin of the predeceased spouse who shall take in the same manner as the next of kin of the decedent take under Section 6402.

(c) For purposes of disposing of personal property under subdivision (b), the claimant heir bears the burden of proof to show the exact personal property to be disposed of to the heir.

(d) For purposes of providing notice under any provision of this code with respect to an estate that may include personal property subject to distribution under subdivision (b), if the aggregate fair market value of tangible and intangible personal property with a written record of title or ownership in the estate is believed in good faith by the petitioning party to be less than ten thousand dollars ($10,000), the petitioning party need not give notice to the issue or next of kin of the predeceased spouse. If the personal property is subsequently determined to have an aggregate fair market value in excess of ten thousand dollars ($10,000), notice shall be given to the issue or next of kin of the predeceased spouse as provided by law.

(e) For the purposes of disposing of property pursuant to subdivision (b), "personal property" means that personal property in which there is a written record of title or ownership and the value of which in the aggregate is ten thousand dollars ($10,000) or more.

(f) For the purposes of this section, the "portion of the decedent's estate attributable to the decedent's predeceased spouse" means all of the following property in the decedent's estate:

(1) One-half of the community property in existence at the time of the death of the predeceased spouse.

(2) One-half of any community property, in existence at the time of death of the predeceased spouse, which was given to the decedent by the predeceased spouse by way of gift, descent, or devise.

(3) That portion of any community property in which the predeceased spouse had any incident of ownership and which vested in the decedent upon the death of the predeceased spouse by right of survivorship.

(4) Any separate property of the predeceased spouse which came to the decedent by gift, descent, or devise of the predeceased spouse or which vested in the decedent upon the death of the predeceased spouse by right of survivorship.

(g) For the purposes of this section, quasi-community property shall be treated the same as community property.

(h) For the purposes of this section:

(1) Relatives of the predeceased spouse conceived before the decedent's death but born thereafter inherit as if they had been born in the lifetime of the decedent.

(2) A person who is related to the predeceased spouse through two lines of relationship is entitled to only a single share based on the relationship which would entitle the person to the larger share. *(Stats.1990, c. 79 (A.B.759), § 14, operative July 1, 1991.)*

Law Revision Commission Comments

1990 Enactment

Section 6402.5 continues Section 6402.5 of the repealed Probate Code without change. This section does not apply if the decedent died before January 1, 1985. See Section 6414(a). As to the application of any amendments made after that date, see Section 3. If the decedent died before January 1, 1985, see Section 6414(b), (c).

Background on Section 6402.5 of Repealed Code

Section 6402.5 was added by 1983 Cal.Stat. ch. 842 § 55 and was amended by 1985 Cal.Stat. ch. 982 § 20 and 1986 Cal.Stat. ch. 873 § 1. As enacted in 1983, the section continued the substance of subdivisions (a), (b), and (e) of former Probate Code Section 229 (repealed by 1983 Cal.Stat. ch. 842 § 19) with the following changes:

(1) The application of Section 6402.5 was limited to real property and the section applied only where the predeceased spouse died not more than 15 years before the decedent. Former Section 229 was not so limited. The rules for determining what constitutes "the portion of the decedent's estate attributable to the decedent's predeceased spouse" were the same as under subdivision (b) of former Section 229.

(2) The provisions of Section 6402.5 relating to taking by representation were consistent with the general provisions relating to taking by representation. See Section 240.

(3) Paragraph (4) of subdivision (b) of former Section 229 was not continued. The omitted provision was made obsolete by 1980 Cal.Stat. ch. 119, which provided that property set aside as a probate homestead for a surviving spouse shall in no case be set aside beyond the lifetime of the surviving spouse; after the 1980 enactment, the probate homestead is not a part of the estate of that spouse when that spouse dies.

(4) Subdivision (c), now subdivision (g), was included in Section 6402.5 to make clear that quasi-community real property (see Section 66) is to be treated the same as community real property for the purposes of this section. Former Section 229 contained no provision that dealt specifically with quasi-community property.

(5) The special rule provided in subdivision (c) of former Section 229 was not continued. Insofar as the property described in that subdivision is a "portion of the decedent's estate attributable to the decedent's predeceased spouse" and the spouse died not more than 15 years before the decedent, the property is governed by the general provisions of Section 6402.5.

(6) Subdivision (d) of former Section 229 was superseded by subdivisions (e) and (g) of Section 6402.

The 1985 amendment substituted the references to Section 240 for the former reference to taking "by representation." This change was nonsubstantive. See Recommendation Relating to Distribution Under a Will or Trust, 18 Cal.L.Revision Comm'n Reports 269, 285–87 (1986). The 1986 amendment made the section applicable to personal property. For background on the provisions of this part, see the Comment to this part under the part heading. [20 Cal.L.Rev.Comm.Reports 1001 (1990)].

Commentary

For discussion of the history and content of the "ancestral property" provisions, of which Section 6402.5 is the latest version, see *Estate of Newman, 25 Cal.App.4th 472, 30 Cal.Rptr.2d 547 (1994)* (under predecessor provision, Probate Code Section 229, which is identical to the current provision on the issue presented, where the source of the property in decedent's estate was the separate property of the predeceased spouse, the "source rule" is applied to property transmuted from separate property to community property during the life of the predeceased spouse; thus the predeceased spouse's former separate property was improperly treated as community property for purposes of distribution under this statute, and the correct result was that decedent's entire estate go entirely to predeceased wife's blood relatives).

Research References

Forms

California Transactions Forms--Estate Planning § 1:77, Matters to Consider Regarding Property Distribution.

California Transactions Forms--Estate Planning § 19:96, Overview; Avoiding Intestacy.

Treatises and Practice Aids

Witkin, California Summary 10th Community Property § 50, Veteran's Insurance.

Witkin, California Summary 10th Wills and Probate § 25, Major Changes.

Witkin, California Summary 10th Wills and Probate § 31, Major Changes.

Witkin, California Summary 10th Wills and Probate § 77, in General.

Witkin, California Summary 10th Wills and Probate § 83, Former Law.

Witkin, California Summary 10th Wills and Probate § 84, Nature and Scope Of Statute.

Witkin, California Summary 10th Wills and Probate § 85, Apportionment Of Property Between Families.

Witkin, California Summary 10th Wills and Probate § 233, in General.

Witkin, California Summary 10th Wills and Probate § 303, in General.

§ 6403. Failure to survive decedent by 120 hours; deemed predeceased; application of section

(a) A person who fails to survive the decedent by 120 hours is deemed to have predeceased the decedent for the purpose of intestate succession, and the heirs are determined accordingly. If it cannot be established by clear and convincing evidence that a person who would otherwise be an heir has survived the decedent by 120 hours, it is deemed that the person failed to survive for the required period. The requirement of this section that a person who survives the decedent by 120 hours does not apply if the application of the 120-hour survival requirement would result in the escheat of property to the state.

(b) This section does not apply to the case where any of the persons upon whose time of death the disposition of property depends died before January 1, 1990, and such case continues to be governed by the law applicable before January 1, 1990. *(Stats.1990, c. 79 (A.B.759), § 14, operative July 1, 1991.)*

Law Revision Commission Comments

1990 Enactment

Section 6403 continues Section 6403 of the repealed Probate Code without substantive change. The section is the same in substance as Section 2–104 of the Uniform Probate Code (1987) insofar as that section relates to taking by intestate succession. As to the construction of provisions drawn from uniform acts, see Section 2.

Where Section 6403 applies, the 120–hour survival requirement is used to determine whether one person survived another for the purposes of Sections 103 (simultaneous death of husband and wife) and 234 (proceedings to determine survival).

For a provision governing disposition of community property and quasi-community property where a married person does not survive his or her spouse, see Section 103. See also Sections 230–234 (proceeding to determine whether one person survived another).

Section 6403 does not apply if the decedent died before January 1, 1985. See Section 6414(a). As to the application of any amendments made after that date, see Section 3. If the decedent died before January 1, 1985, see Section 6414(b), (c).

Background on Section 6403 of Repealed Code

Section 6403 was a new provision added by 1983 Cal.Stat. ch. 842 § 55 and amended by 1989 Cal.Stat. ch. 544 § 5 to provide a 120–hour survival rule. See Recommendation Relating to 120–Hour Survival Requirement, 20 Cal.L.Revision Commission Reports 21 (1990); see also Communication from the California Law Revision Commission Concerning Assembly Bill 158, 20 Cal.L.Revision Commission Reports 235, 236 (1990). For background on the provisions of this part, see the Comment to this part under the part heading. [20 Cal.L.Rev.Comm.Reports 1001 (1990)].

Research References

Forms

California Transactions Forms--Estate Planning § 6:21, Devisee's Failure to Survive.

California Transactions Forms--Estate Planning § 6:23, Simultaneous Death.

California Transactions Forms--Estate Planning § 19:97, Survivorship Requirements.

California Transactions Forms--Estate Planning § 14:10, "End Of the World" Provisions.

Treatises and Practice Aids

Witkin, California Summary 10th Wills and Probate § 37, Major Changes.

Witkin, California Summary 10th Wills and Probate § 74, in General.

Witkin, California Summary 10th Wills and Probate § 289, Revised Statute.

Witkin, California Summary 10th Wills and Probate § 291, Authorized Purposes.

Witkin, California Summary 10th Wills and Probate § 99, Nature and Scope Of Statute.

§ 6404. Application of escheat provisions

Part 4 (commencing with Section 6800) (escheat) applies if there is no taker of the intestate estate under the provisions of this part. *(Stats.1990, c. 79 (A.B.759), § 14, operative July 1, 1991.)*

Law Revision Commission Comments

1990 Enactment

Section 6404 continues Section 6404 of the repealed Probate Code without change. This section is comparable to Section 2–105 of the Uniform Probate Code (1987). As to the construction of provisions drawn from uniform acts, see Section 2. For provisions relating to escheat, see Sections 6800–6806. See also Code Civ.Proc. §§ 1300–1615 (unclaimed property). Section 6404 does not apply if the decedent died before January 1, 1985. See Section 6414(a). As to the application of any amendments made after that date, see Section 3. If the decedent died before January 1, 1985, see Section 6414(b), (c).

Background on Section 6404 of Repealed Code

Section 6404 was a new provision added by 1983 Cal.Stat. ch. 842 § 55. For background on the provisions of this part, see the Comment to this part under the part heading. [20 Cal.L.Rev.Comm.Report 1001 (1990)].

Research References

Forms

Cal. Transaction Forms - Bus. Transactions § 23:4, Unclaimed Property.

California Transactions Forms--Estate Planning § 1:18, Property Subject to Probate; Intestacy.

§ 6406. Relatives of halfblood

Except as provided in Section 6451, relatives of the halfblood inherit the same share they would inherit if they were of the whole blood. *(Stats.1990, c. 79 (A.B.759), § 14, operative July 1, 1991. Amended by Stats.1993, c. 529 (A.B.1137), § 3.)*

Law Revision Commission Comments

1990 Enactment

Section 6406 continues Section 6406 of the repealed Probate Code without change. This section is the same as Section 2–107 of the Uniform Probate Code (1987). As to the construction of provisions drawn from uniform acts, see Section 2. See also Section 6152 (construction of wills). Section 6406 does not apply if the decedent died before January 1, 1985. See Section 6414(a). As to the application of any amendments made after that date, see Section 3. If the decedent died before January 1, 1985, see Section 6414(b), (c).

1993 Amendment

Section 6406 is amended to recognize the exception in Section 6451. This amendment is clarifying. [23 Cal.L.Rev.Comm. Reports 901 (1993) (Annual Report, App. 9)].

Background on Section 6406 of Repealed Code

Section 6406 was added by 1983 Cal.Stat. ch. 842 § 55. The section superseded former Probate Code Section 254 (repealed by 1983 Cal.Stat. ch. 842 § 19). Under former Section 254, halfblood relatives of the decedent who were not of the blood of an ancestor of the decedent were excluded from inheriting property of the decedent which had come to the decedent from such ancestor. Section 6406 eliminated this rule and puts halfbloods on the same footing as wholeblood relatives of the decedent. For background on the provisions of this part, see the Comment to this part under the part heading. [20 Cal.L.Rev.Comm.Reports 1001 (1990)].

Research References

Treatises and Practice Aids

Witkin, California Summary 10th Wills and Probate § 86, Relatives Of Half Blood.

Witkin, California Summary 10th Wills and Probate § 303, in General.

Witkin, California Summary 10th Wills and Probate § 304A, (New) in General.

§ 6407. Unborn relatives of decedent

Relatives of the decedent conceived before the decedent's death but born thereafter inherit as if they had been born in the lifetime of the decedent. *(Stats.1990, c. 79 (A.B.759), § 14, operative July 1, 1991.)*

Law Revision Commission Comments

1990 Enactment

Section 6407 continues Section 6407 of the repealed Probate Code without change. This section is the same in substance as Section 2–108 of the Uniform Probate Code (1987). As to the construction of provisions drawn from uniform acts, see Section 2. Section 6407 is consistent with Civil Code Section 29. See also Section 6150(c) (person conceived before but born after a testator's death or after time the devise is to take effect in enjoyment takes if answering the class description). Section 6407 does not apply if the decedent died before January 1, 1985. See Section 6414(a). As to the application of any amendments made after that date, see Section 3. If the decedent died before January 1, 1985, see Section 6414(b), (c).

Background on Section 6407 of Repealed Code

Section 6407 was added by 1983 Cal.Stat. ch. 842 § 55. The section superseded the second sentence of former Probate Code Section 250 (repealed by 1983 Cal.Stat. ch. 842 § 19). For background on the provisions of this part, see the Comment to this part under the part heading. [20 Cal.L.Rev.Comm.Reports 1001 (1990)].

Research References

Treatises and Practice Aids

Witkin, California Summary 10th Parent and Child § 45, Semen Of Decedent.
Witkin, California Summary 10th Wills and Probate § 87, Afterborn Heirs.
Witkin, California Summary 10th Wills and Probate § 232, Time When Class is Ascertained.
Witkin, California Summary 10th Wills and Probate § 303, in General.
Witkin, California Summary 10th Wills and Probate § 304A, (New) in General.

CHAPTER 2. PARENT AND CHILD RELATIONSHIP

§ 6450. Relationship existence

Subject to the provisions of this chapter, a relationship of parent and child exists for the purpose of determining intestate succession by, through, or from a person in the following circumstances:

(a) The relationship of parent and child exists between a person and the person's natural parents, regardless of the marital status of the natural parents.

(b) The relationship of parent and child exists between an adopted person and the person's adopting parent or parents. *(Added by Stats.1993, c. 529 (A.B.1137), § 5.)*

Law Revision Commission Comments

1993 Addition

Section 6450 continues former Section 6408(a) without substantive change. The language "[s]ubject to the provisions of this chapter" is placed in the introductory clause because Sections 6451, 6452, and 6454 modify the relationship of parent and child between an adopted person and the person's adopting parent or parents, as well as the relationship of parent and child between a person and the person's natural parents. See also Section 6453 (establishing natural parent-child relationship). In former Section 6408, application of the "except" clause was limited to the relationship of parent and child between a person and the person's natural parents.

The definitions of "child" (Section 26), "issue" (Section 50), and "parent" (Section 54) adopt the rules set out in this chapter. See also Section 6152 (construction of wills). [23 Cal.L.Rev.Comm. Reports 901 (1993) (Annual Report, App. 9)].

Commentary

Jackson v. Fitzgibbons, 127 Cal.App.4th 329, 25 Cal.Rptr.3d 478 (2005), holds that a child lacks standing to bring a Code of Civil Procedure § 377.60 action for the wrongful death of a parent when a juvenile court has terminated the parental rights of the child's parents; in such case this section and Probate Code §§ 6451 and 6402 are also inapplicable.

Ehrenclou v. MacDonald, 117 Cal.App.4th 364, 12 Cal.Rptr.3d 411 (2004), review denied, held that two adults adopted by a trust beneficiary under Colorado adult adoption law were not the deceased trust beneficiary's "children then living" under a trust governed by California law, because the Colorado adult adoption statute gave the adoptees heir-at-law status, but did not create a parent-child relationship between the trust beneficiary and the adoptees.

Research References

Forms

California Transactions Forms--Estate Planning § 6:11, Existence Of Relationship.
California Transactions Forms--Estate Planning § 6:52, Matters to Consider in Drafting Class Gifts.
California Transactions Forms--Estate Planning § 19:116, Will for Single Person.
California Transactions Forms--Estate Planning § 19:144, Adopted Persons Included.
California Transactions Forms--Estate Planning § 19:145, Adopted Persons Excluded.
California Transactions Forms--Family Law § 6:18, Intestate Succession Rights.

Treatises and Practice Aids

Witkin, California Summary 10th Parent and Child § 75, Equitable Adoption.
Witkin, California Summary 10th Parent and Child § 76, Nature and Effect Of Adoption.
Witkin, California Summary 10th Wills and Probate § 45, Major Changes.
Witkin, California Summary 10th Wills and Probate § 92, Revision.
Witkin, California Summary 10th Wills and Probate § 93, in General.
Witkin, California Summary 10th Wills and Probate § 94, Parent and Child Relationship.
Witkin, California Summary 10th Wills and Probate § 97, Adopted Children.
Witkin, California Summary 10th Wills and Probate § 229, Adopted Children.
Witkin, California Summary 10th Wills and Probate § 281, Nature and Scope Of Statute.
Witkin, California Summary 10th Wills and Probate § 303, in General.
Witkin, California Summary 10th Wills and Probate § 388, Heirs and Devisees.
Witkin, California Summary 10th Wills and Probate § 304A, (New) in General.

§ 6451. Adoption

(a) An adoption severs the relationship of parent and child between an adopted person and a natural parent of the adopted person unless both of the following requirements are satisfied:

(1) The natural parent and the adopted person lived together at any time as parent and child, or the natural parent was married to or cohabiting with the other natural parent at the time the person was conceived and died before the person's birth.

(2) The adoption was by the spouse of either of the natural parents or after the death of either of the natural parents.

(b) Neither a natural parent nor a relative of a natural parent, except for a wholeblood brother or sister of the adopted person or the issue of that brother or sister, inherits from or through the adopted person on the basis of a parent and child relationship between the adopted person and the natural parent that satisfies the requirements of paragraphs (1) and (2) of subdivision (a), unless the adoption is by the spouse or surviving spouse of that parent.

(c) For the purpose of this section, a prior adoptive parent and child relationship is treated as a natural parent and child relationship. *(Added by Stats.1993, c. 529 (A.B.1137), § 5.)*

Law Revision Commission Comments

1993 Addition [Revised Comment]

Section 6451 continues the substance of subdivisions (b) and (c) of former Section 6408.

In case of an adoption coming within subdivision (a), the adopted child may inherit from or through the adoptive parent, and also from or through the natural parent who gave up the child for adoption or through the natural parent who died preceding the adoption. The following examples indicate in various situations whether an adopted child or the issue of an adopted child may inherit from or through the child's natural parent.

Example 1. Child never lived with either mother or father. Both parents relinquish child for adoption. The adopted child's relationship with both natural parents' families is severed. The requirements of subdivision (a)(1) are not satisfied.

Example 2. Child's mother and father were married or lived together as a family. Child lives with mother and father. Father dies. Mother relinquishes child for adoption. For the purpose of inheritance, the adopted child remains a member of both the deceased father's family and of the relinquishing mother's family. The requirement of subdivision (a) is satisfied because the adoption was "after the death of either of the natural parents."

Example 3. Child's mother and father were married or lived together as a family until father died. Child lives with mother but not father because father died prior to child's birth. Mother relinquishes child for adoption. For the purpose of inheritance, the adopted child remains a member of both the deceased father's family and of the relinquishing mother's family. Child remains a member of the deceased father's family because the father died before the birth of the child (satisfying the subdivision (a)(1) requirement) and the adoption was after the death of the father (satisfying the subdivision (a)(2) requirement).

Under subdivision (a), a non-stepparent adoption severs the relationship between the adopted person and his or her natural "parent." Thus, for example, if a person is adopted by only one adopting parent, that severs the parent-child relationship between the adopted person and his or her natural parent of the same gender as the adopting parent. The parent-child relationship continues to exist between the adopted person and his or her other natural parent.

In case of an adoption described in subdivision (b), the natural relatives cannot inherit from the adopted child, even though under Section 6450(a) the child could inherit from the natural relatives.

In subdivision (b), the reference to inheritance on the basis of a parent-child relationship "that satisfies the requirements of paragraphs (1) and (2) of subdivision (a)" is added to make clear that, for a wholeblood brother or sister to inherit from or through the adoptee, the requirements of these two paragraphs must be satisfied. Under these two paragraphs, the relationship of parent and child does not exist between an adopted person and the person's natural parent unless the living-together or other requirements of paragraph (1) of subdivision (a) are satisfied, and the adoption was after the death of either natural parent. This changes the rule of *In re* Estate of Reedy, 22 Cal.Rptr.2d 478 (1993), *petition for hearing in California Supreme Court filed*. If the adoption was by the spouse of either natural parent, by its terms subdivision (b) does not apply.

Subdivision (b) omits the reference to the adoptee's "issue" that was in the parenthetical "except" clause in subdivision (c) of former Section 6408. The former reference to "issue" was unnecessary. Issue of the adoptee do not inherit from or through the adoptee on the basis of a parent-child relationship between the adoptee and the adoptee's parents. Rather they inherit from or through the adoptee on the basis of the parent-child relationship between themselves and the adoptee.

Subdivision (c) is new, and makes clear that, for the purpose of this section, a prior adoptive parent and child relationship is treated as a natural parent and child relationship. Thus, for example, if a person is adopted by one set of parents, and later is adopted by a second set of parents, the second adoption severs the parent-child relationship between the adoptee and the first set of adoptive parents unless paragraphs (1) and (2) of subdivision (a) are satisfied, substituting "adoptive" for "natural" in those paragraphs. This is a clarification, and may be a change in prior law.

"Wholeblood" relatives were defined in *In re* Estate of Belshaw, 190 Cal. 278, 285, 212 P. 13 (1923), to mean persons having both natural parents in common. One effect of subdivision (c) is to broaden "wholeblood" in subdivision (b) to include adoptive siblings in an appropriate case. For example, assume a person, *P,* is born to two parents, a brother, *B,* is born to the same two parents, and a half-sister, *S,* is born to the mother and later adopted by the father. *B* is a wholeblood sibling of *P* because they have both natural parents in common. For the purpose of inheritance, *S* is treated as a wholeblood sibling of *P,* because under subdivision (c) the effect of the adoption is to treat *S* as the natural child of the adopting father. If *P* is later adopted by two adopting parents, under subdivision (b) the adoption cuts off inheritance by most of *P's* natural relatives, except that both *B* and *S* may inherit from or through *P* if the requirements of paragraphs (1) and (2) of subdivision (a) are satisfied. [23 Cal.L.Rev.Comm. Reports 1009 (1993)].

Commentary

Newman v. Wells Fargo Bank, 14 Cal.4th 126, 926 P.2d 969, 59 Cal.Rptr.2d 2 (1996), holds that absent an expression of contrary intent in the instrument, the law in effect at the time of the execution of a will or testamentary trust determines whether a child adopted out of the family by stepparent adoption is included within the beneficiary class of "children" or "issue." The current subsection (a)(2) exception for stepparent adoptions was enacted in 1985 and hence may not be retroactively applied to testamentary instruments executed before 1985. *Estate of Dye, 92 Cal.App.4th 966, 112 Cal.Rptr.2d 362 (2001),* sustains a probate court ruling that a decedent's adopted-out sons or their issue per stirpes could take a share of the decedent's lapsed estate under this section, which permits adopted-out children to take in intestacy from their natural parents when adoption was by a step-parent.

Phraner v. Cote Mart, Inc., 55 Cal.App.4th 166, 63 Cal.Rptr.2d 740 (1997), review denied August 27, 1997, holds that a child adopted away from her biological mother is not a "child" of the biological mother for purposes of Code of Civil Procedure Section 377.60, specifying who may bring a wrongful death action, even though the child and biological mother maintained a social relationship.

Jackson v. Fitzgibbons, 127 Cal.App.4th 329, 25 Cal.Rptr.3d 478 (2005), holds that a child lacks standing to bring a Code of Civil Procedure § 377.60 action for the wrongful death of a parent when a juvenile court has terminated the parental rights of the child's parents; in such case this section and Probate Code §§ 6450 and 6402 are also inapplicable.

Research References

Forms

California Transactions Forms--Estate Planning § 6:12, Natural Parents Of Adopted Child.
California Transactions Forms--Estate Planning § 6:52, Matters to Consider in Drafting Class Gifts.
California Transactions Forms--Estate Planning § 19:101, Adopted Children and Stepchildren.
California Transactions Forms--Family Law § 6:18, Intestate Succession Rights.
California Transactions Forms--Family Law § 6:114, Consent Of Noncustodial Parent.

Treatises and Practice Aids

Witkin, California Summary 10th Wills and Probate § 86, Relatives Of Half Blood.
Witkin, California Summary 10th Wills and Probate § 96, Out Of Wedlock Children.
Witkin, California Summary 10th Wills and Probate § 97, Adopted Children.

§ 6452. Conditions preventing a parent from inheriting from or through a child

(a) A parent does not inherit from or through a child on the basis of the parent and child relationship if any of the following apply:

(1) The parent's parental rights were terminated and the parent-child relationship was not judicially reestablished.

(2) The parent did not acknowledge the child.

(3) The parent left the child during the child's minority without an effort to provide for the child's support or without communication from the parent, for at least seven consecutive years that continued until the end of the child's minority, with the intent on the part of the parent to abandon the child. The failure to provide support or to communicate for the prescribed period is presumptive evidence of an intent to abandon.

(b) A parent who does not inherit from or through the child as provided in subdivision (a) shall be deemed to have predeceased the child, and the intestate estate shall pass as otherwise required under Section 6402. *(Added by Stats. 2013, c. 39 (A.B.490), § 2.)*

Research References

Forms

California Transactions Forms--Estate Planning § 6:13, Conditions Preventing Parent from Inheriting from a Child.
California Transactions Forms--Estate Planning § 6:52, Matters to Consider in Drafting Class Gifts.

Treatises and Practice Aids

Witkin, California Summary 10th Torts § 1394, Other Persons.
Witkin, California Summary 10th Wills and Probate § 80, Parents or Issue Of Parents.
Witkin, California Summary 10th Wills and Probate § 96, Out Of Wedlock Children.

§ 6453. Natural parents

For the purpose of determining whether a person is a "natural parent" as that term is used in this chapter:

(a) A natural parent and child relationship is established where that relationship is presumed and not rebutted pursuant to the Uniform Parentage Act (Part 3 (commencing with Section 7600) of Division 12 of the Family Code).

(b) A natural parent and child relationship may be established pursuant to any other provisions of the Uniform Parentage Act, except that the relationship may not be established by an action under subdivision (c) of Section 7630 of the Family Code unless any of the following conditions exist:

(1) A court order was entered during the father's lifetime declaring paternity.

(2) Paternity is established by clear and convincing evidence that the father has openly held out the child as his own.

(3) It was impossible for the father to hold out the child as his own and paternity is established by clear and convincing evidence.

(c) A natural parent and child relationship may be established pursuant to Section 249.5. *(Added by Stats.1993, c. 529 (A.B.1137), § 5. Amended by Stats.2004, c. 775 (A.B.1910), § 9.)*

Law Revision Commission Comments

1993 Addition [Revised Comment]

Subdivision (a) and paragraphs (1) and (2) of subdivision (b) of Section 6453 continue the substance of former Section 6408(f), except that former Section 6408(f)(2) required the father to have "openly and notoriously held out the child as his own." Paragraph (2) of subdivision (b) of Section 6453 omits "and notoriously," and merely requires the father to have "openly held out" the child as his own. [23 Cal.L.Rev.Comm. Reports 1009 (1993)].

Commentary

A child born out of wedlock's claim to be an heir was accepted by the probate court on the basis of a preponderance of the evidence that the decedent held out the child as his own. The appellate court reversed. Under paragraph (b)(2) "clear and convincing evidence" was required. The reference to Family Code Section 7600 in paragraph (a) did not apply here because the "presumed father was deceased." See Family Code Section 7630(c). *In re Estate of Chambers, 175 Cal.App.4th 891, 96 Cal.Rptr.3d 651 (2d Dist. 2009).*

Estate of Burden, 146 Cal.App.4th 1021, 53 Cal.Rptr.3d 390 (2007), review denied May 9, 2007, interpreting subsection (b)(2), held that "openly held child out as his own" is satisfied by a father's acknowledgment of a child, that is, by his written or oral admission of being the child's parent. No formal written acknowledgement is necessary.

Estate of Britel, 236 Cal.App.4th 127, 186 Cal.Rptr 3d 321 (2015), review denied, held that a father's private acknowledgment of paternity did not satisfy subsection (b)(2) where acknowledgment was limited to the mother on condition that it be kept secret and to a close friend, who was later told that the pregnancy was terminated. The court reasoned that since intestacy statutes are intended to carry out decedent's likely intent concerning estate distribution, the father's desire to conceal his paternity indicated his intent not to include his son as heir.

Interpreting subsection (b)(3), *Cheyanna M. v. A.C. Nielsen Co., 66 Cal.App.4th 855, 78 Cal.Rptr.2d 335 (1998),* holds that a posthumous child has standing to sue for the wrongful death of the child's biological father if the child can establish paternity through clear and convincing evidence. In other words, *Cheyanna M.* restricts the definition of "child" for purposes of subsection (b)(3) to children who are already born at the father's death; thus by definition it is impossible for a father to have held a posthumous child out as his own.

Weir v. Ferreira, 59 Cal.App.4th 1509, 70 Cal.Rptr.2d 33 (1997), review denied March 25, 1998, holds that principles of res judicata and collateral estoppel bar a decedent's son from challenging ward's right to inherit as decedent's issue after dissolution judgment expressly found that the ward was a child of decedent's marriage.

Research References

Forms

California Transactions Forms--Estate Planning § 6:11, Existence Of Relationship.
California Transactions Forms--Estate Planning § 6:52, Matters to Consider in Drafting Class Gifts.

Treatises and Practice Aids

Witkin, California Summary 10th Wills and Probate § 94, Parent and Child Relationship.

§ 6454. Foster parent or stepparent

For the purpose of determining intestate succession by a person or the person's issue from or through a foster parent or stepparent, the relationship of parent and child exists between that person and the person's foster parent or stepparent if both of the following requirements are satisfied:

(a) The relationship began during the person's minority and continued throughout the joint lifetimes of the person and the person's foster parent or stepparent.

(b) It is established by clear and convincing evidence that the foster parent or stepparent would have adopted the person but for a legal barrier. *(Added by Stats.1993, c. 529 (A.B.1137), § 5.)*

Law Revision Commission Comments

1993 Addition

Section 6454 continues the substance of former Section 6408(e). Section 6454 applies, for example, where a foster child or stepchild is not adopted because a parent of the child refuses to consent to the adoption. See also Estate of Lind, 209 Cal.App.3d 1424, 257 Cal.Rptr. 853 (2d Dist.1989), review denied; Estate of Claffey, 209 Cal.App.3d 254, 257 Cal.Rptr. 197 (1989).

In the introductory clause of Section 6454, "issue" is substituted for "descendants" in former Section 6408(e). This change is nonsubstantive, and is for consistency with other provisions in this part. See, e.g., Sections 6401, 6402, 6402.5, 6451, 6452, 6455.

Even though the requirements of Section 6454 are satisfied, the natural parent may continue to inherit from the child under Section 6450(a). The foster parent or stepparent may not inherit from the child: Subdivision (b) of Section 6450 does not apply because the adoption was not completed, and Section 6454 does not apply because the section applies only to inheritance by the foster child or stepchild or the child's issue "from" or "through" a foster parent or stepparent, not to inheritance "by" a foster parent or stepparent. The child, however, may inherit both from the natural parent under Section 6450(a), and from the foster parent or stepparent under Section 6454. [23 Cal.L.Rev.Comm. Reports 901 (1993) (Annual Report, App. 9)].

Commentary

Must the subsection (b) "legal barrier" exist continuously until the decedent's death? Resolving a conflict among the courts of appeal, *Estate of Joseph, 17 Cal.4th 203, 949 P.2d 472, 70 Cal.Rptr.2d 619 (1998),* holds that a child may not take in intestacy from a foster parent or stepparent unless the foster parent or stepparent would have adopted the child except for a legal barrier that continued until the parent's death.

Research References

Forms

California Transactions Forms--Estate Planning § 2:14, Failure to Properly Designate Disposition Of Assets, Provide for Pretermitted Heirs, and Plan for Dissolution Of Marriage.
California Transactions Forms--Estate Planning § 6:14, Foster or Stepparent.
California Transactions Forms--Estate Planning § 6:52, Matters to Consider in Drafting Class Gifts.
California Transactions Forms--Estate Planning § 19:101, Adopted Children and Stepchildren.

Treatises and Practice Aids

Witkin, California Summary 10th Wills and Probate § 49, Persons and Entities.
Witkin, California Summary 10th Wills and Probate § 95, Foster or Stepchildren.

§ 6455. Equitable adoption; application

Nothing in this chapter affects or limits application of the judicial doctrine of equitable adoption for the benefit of the child or the child's issue. *(Added by Stats.1993, c. 529 (A.B.1137), § 5.)*

Law Revision Commission Comments

1993 Addition

Section 6455 continues the substance of subdivision (g) of former Section 6408. "Issue" is substituted in Section 6455 for "descendants" in former Section 6408(g). This change is nonsubstantive, and is for consistency with other provisions in this part. See, e.g., Sections 6401, 6402, 6402.5, 6451, 6452, 6454.

Concerning equitable adoption, see Estate of Wilson, 111 Cal. App.3d 242, 168 Cal.Rptr. 533 (1980). [23 Cal.L.Rev.Comm. Reports 901 (1993) (Annual Report, App. 9)].

Commentary

Estate of Furia, 103 Cal.App.4th 1, 126 Cal.Rptr.2d 384 (2002), holds that a child equitably adopted by a stepparent may not inherit property from the stepparent's parent, whose will leaves the property to her children's surviving issue, because the doctrine of equitable adoption creates only a contractual right to receive property from an intestate decedent; the doctrine does not make a person a "child" or "issue," as defined by Probate Code §§ 26 or 50.

Estate of Ford, 32 Cal.4th 160, 8 Cal.Rptr.3d 541, 82 P.3d 747 (2004), holds that a person claiming to be an "equitably adopted child" for purposes of intestate succession must prove decedent's intention to adopt by clear and convincing evidence. *Ford* declines to recognize an estoppel arising merely from the existence of a familial relationship.

Research References

Forms

California Transactions Forms--Estate Planning § 6:11, Existence Of Relationship.
California Transactions Forms--Estate Planning § 14:31, Issue Defined, Including "Technotots".

Treatises and Practice Aids

Witkin, California Summary 10th Parent and Child § 75, Equitable Adoption.
Witkin, California Summary 10th Wills and Probate § 95, Foster or Stepchildren.

Witkin, California Summary 10th Wills and Probate § 97, Adopted Children.

Part 3

FAMILY PROTECTION

Law Revision Commission Comments

1990 Enactment

This part supersedes Part 3 (commencing with Section 6500) of Division 6 [of] the repealed Probate Code. The superseded part was enacted upon recommendation of the California Law Revision Commission. See Tentative Recommendation Relating to Wills and Intestate Succession, 16 Cal.L.Revision Comm'n Reports 2301 (1982). See also Report of Senate Committee on Judiciary on Assembly Bills 25 and 68, 17 Cal.L.Revision Comm'n Reports 867, 871–83 (1984). [20 Cal.L.Rev.Comm.Reports 1001 (1990)].

CHAPTER 1. TEMPORARY POSSESSION OF FAMILY DWELLING AND EXEMPT PROPERTY

§ 6500. Possession of family dwelling; exempt property; duration

Until the inventory is filed and for a period of 60 days thereafter, or for such other period as may be ordered by the court for good cause on petition therefor, the decedent's surviving spouse and minor children are entitled to remain in possession of the family dwelling, the wearing apparel of the family, the household furniture, and the other property of the decedent exempt from enforcement of a money judgment. *(Stats.1990, c. 79 (A.B.759), § 14, operative July 1, 1991.)*

Law Revision Commission Comments

1990 Enactment

Section 6500 continues Section 6500 of the repealed Probate Code without change. See also Code Civ.Proc. §§ 695.010–695.070, 703.010–704.995, 706.050–706.051 (property exempt from enforcement of money judgment). Other exemptions are listed in the Comment to Code of Civil Procedure Section 703.010. As to a surviving spouse's waiver of rights at death, see Sections 140–147. For background on this section, see Recommendation Relating to Probate Homestead, 15 Cal.L.Revision Comm'n Reports 401, 420 (1980).

Background on Section 6500 of Repealed Code

Section 6500 was added by 1983 Cal.Stat. ch. 842 § 55. The section continued the substance of subdivision (a) of former Probate Code Section 660 (repealed by 1983 Cal.Stat. ch. 842 § 39). For background on the provisions of this part, see the Comment to this part under the part heading. [20 Cal.L.Rev.Comm.Reports 1001 (1990)].

Research References

Forms

California Transactions Forms--Estate Planning § 19:6, Law Governing Meaning and Effect Of Will.

California Transactions Forms--Estate Planning § 19:7, Overview.

California Transactions Forms--Estate Planning § 19:8, Exempt Property.

California Transactions Forms--Estate Planning § 18:31, Homestead Exemption.

Treatises and Practice Aids

Witkin, California Summary 10th Wills and Probate § 56, Interpretation and Construction Of Instrument.

Witkin, California Summary 10th Wills and Probate § 295, Wills, Trusts, and Intestate Succession.

Witkin, California Summary 10th Wills and Probate § 475, Right and Duty.

Witkin, California Summary 10th Wills and Probate § 765, Temporary Possession Of Dwelling and Exempt Property.

Witkin, California Summary 10th Wills and Probate § 791, Murder Of Decedent.

§ 6501. Petition for order

A petition for an order under Section 6500 may be filed by any interested person. Notice of the hearing on the petition shall be given as provided in Section 1220. *(Stats.1990, c. 79 (A.B.759), § 14, operative July 1, 1991.)*

Law Revision Commission Comments

1990 Enactment

Section 6501 continues Section 6501 of the repealed Probate Code without change. For general provisions, see Sections 1000–1004 (rules of practice), 1020–1023 (petitions and other papers), 1040–1050 (hearings and orders). For general provisions relating to notice of hearing, see Sections 1200–1221. See also Sections 1250–1252 (request for special notice), 1260–1265 (proof of giving notice). The requirement that notice be given as provided in Section 1220 does not apply to a particular notice where the notice was delivered, mailed, posted, or first published before July 1, 1991. In such a case, the applicable law in effect before July 1, 1991, continues to apply to the giving of the notice. Section 1200(c). As to the application of any amendments made after that date, see Section 3. See also Section 48 ("interested person" defined).

Background on Section 6501 of Repealed Code

Section 6501 was a new provision added by 1983 Cal.Stat. ch. 842 § 55 and was amended by 1987 Cal.Stat. ch. 923 § 87. The section was drawn from former Probate Code Section 662 (probate homestead) (repealed by 1983 Cal.Stat. ch. 842 § 39). The 1987 amendment (1) revised the cross-reference to the procedure for mailing notice of the hearing and (2) deleted the provision requiring the clerk to set the petition for hearing, this provision being unnecessary in view of Section 1285 which is a general provision that imposes this duty on the clerk. As to the 1987 amendment, see Communication from California Law Revision Commission Concerning Assembly Bill 708, 19 Cal.L.Revision Comm'n Reports 545, 560 (1988); Comments to Conforming Revisions and Repeals, 19 Cal.L.Revision Comm'n Reports 391, 449 (1988). For background on the provisions of this part, see the Comment to this part under the part heading. [20 Cal.L.Rev.Comm.Reports 1001 (1990)].

Research References

Forms

West's California Code Forms, Probate § 6501 Form 1, Petition for Order Authorizing Extended Temporary Possession Of Family Dwelling and Other Exempt Property by Decedent's Family.

Treatises and Practice Aids

Witkin, California Summary 10th Wills and Probate § 765, Temporary Possession Of Dwelling and Exempt Property.

CHAPTER 2. SETTING ASIDE EXEMPT PROPERTY OTHER THAN FAMILY DWELLING

§ 6510. Exempt property; setting apart by court

Upon the filing of the inventory or at any subsequent time during the administration of the estate, the court in its discretion may on petition therefor set apart all or any part of the property of the decedent exempt from enforcement of a money judgment, other than the family dwelling, to any one or more of the following:

(a) The surviving spouse.

(b) The minor children of the decedent. *(Stats.1990, c. 79 (A.B.759), § 14, operative July 1, 1991.)*

Law Revision Commission Comments

1990 Enactment

Section 6510 continues Section 6510 of the repealed Probate Code without change. This section permits, for example, the minor children to receive the furniture and household furnishings for a probate homestead set apart for the use of the minor children. See the Comment to Section 6521. See also the Comment to Section 6500 for a listing of provisions relating to property exempt from enforcement of a money judgment. As to a surviving spouse's waiver of rights at death, see Sections 140–147.

Background on Section 6510 of Repealed Code

Section 6510 was added by 1983 Cal.Stat. ch. 842 § 55. The section continued the substance of a portion of subdivision (b) of former Probate Code Section 660 (repealed by 1983 Cal.Stat. ch. 842 § 39), except that Section 6510 permitted the court to award the exempt property to the decedent's minor children even where there is a surviving spouse, while the former section permitted an award to the minor children only in case of the death of the surviving spouse. This change in the former law adopted the rule as to a probate homestead under former Probate Code Section 661 (repealed by 1983 Cal.Stat. ch. 842 § 39), the substance of which is continued in Section 6521, and applied it to property exempt from a money judgment other than the family dwelling. For background on the provisions of this part, see the Comment to this part under the part heading. [20 Cal.L.Rev.Comm.Reports 1001 (1990)].

Research References

Forms

California Transactions Forms--Estate Planning § 19:8, Exempt Property.

California Transactions Forms--Estate Planning § 6:32, Exceptions to Omitted Child Statute.

West's California Code Forms, Probate § 6510 Form 1, Petition for Order Setting Apart Exempt Property Other Than Family Dwelling.

Treatises and Practice Aids

Witkin, California Summary 10th Wills and Probate § 766, Setting Aside Exempt Property.

§ 6511. Petition; notice

A petition for an order under Section 6510 may be filed by any interested person. Notice of the hearing on the petition shall be given as provided in Section 1220. *(Stats.1990, c. 79 (A.B.759), § 14, operative July 1, 1991.)*

Law Revision Commission Comments

1990 Enactment

Section 6511 continues Section 6511 of the repealed Probate Code without change. For general provisions, see Sections 1000–1004 (rules of practice), 1020–1023 (petitions and other papers), 1040–1050 (hearings and orders). For general provisions relating to notice of hearing, see Sections 1200–1221. See also Sections 1250–1252 (request for special notice), 1260–1265 (proof of giving notice). The requirement that notice be given as provided in Section 1220 does not apply to a particular notice where the notice was delivered, mailed, posted, or first published before July 1, 1991. In such a case, the applicable law in effect before July 1, 1991, continues to apply to the giving of the notice. Section 1200(c). As to the application of any amendments made after that date, see Section 3. See also Section 48 ("interested person" defined). As to the right to appeal from an order under this section, see Section 7240 and the Comment thereto.

Background on Section 6511 of Repealed Code

Section 6511 was a new provision added by 1983 Cal.Stat. ch. 842 § 55 and was amended by 1987 Cal.Stat. ch. 923 § 88. The section was drawn from former Probate Code Section 662 (probate homestead) (repealed by 1983 Cal.Stat. ch. 842 § 39). The 1987 amendment (1) revised the cross-reference to the procedure for mailing notice of the hearing and (2) deleted the provision requiring the clerk to set the petition for hearing, this provision being unnecessary in view of Section 1285 (now Section 1041), a general provision that imposes this duty on the clerk. As to the 1987 amendment, see Communication from California Law Revision Commission Concerning Assembly Bill 708, 19 Cal.L.Revision Comm'n Reports 545, 560 (1988); Comments to Conforming Revisions and Repeals, 19 Cal.L.Revision Comm'n Reports 391, 449 (1988). [20 Cal.L.Rev.Comm.Reports 1001 (1990)].

Research References

Forms

West's California Code Forms, Probate § 6510 Form 1, Petition for Order Setting Apart Exempt Property Other Than Family Dwelling.

Treatises and Practice Aids

Witkin, California Summary 10th Wills and Probate § 766, Setting Aside Exempt Property.

CHAPTER 3. SETTING ASIDE PROBATE HOMESTEAD

Section

Law Revision Commission Comments

1990 Enactment

This chapter supersedes Chapter 3 (commencing with Section 6520) of Part 3 of Division 6 of the repealed Probate Code. The superseded chapter was enacted upon recommendation of the California Law Revision Commission. See Recommendation Relating to Probate Homestead, 15 Cal.L.Revision Comm'n Reports 401 (1980). See also Recommendation and Study Relating to Rights of Surviving Spouse in Property Acquired by Decedent While Domiciled Elsewhere, 1 Cal.L.Revision Comm'n Reports E–1 (1957); Recommendation and Study Relating to Inter Vivos Marital Property Rights in Property Acquired While Domiciled Elsewhere, 3

Cal.L.Revision Comm'n Reports I–1 (1961). [20 Cal.L.Rev.Comm.Reports 1001 (1990)].

§ 6520. Authority; setting aside probate homestead

Upon the filing of the inventory or at any subsequent time during the administration of the estate, the court in its discretion may on petition therefor select and set apart one probate homestead in the manner provided in this chapter. *(Stats.1990, c. 79 (A.B.759), § 14, operative July 1, 1991.)*

Law Revision Commission Comments

1990 Enactment

Section 6520 continues Section 6520 of the repealed Probate Code without change. Under this section, establishment of a probate homestead is discretionary with the court. The factors to be used by the court in exercising discretion are set forth in Section 6523.

Background on Section 6520 of Repealed Code

Section 6520 was added by 1983 Cal.Stat. ch. 842 § 55. The section continued the substance of a portion of subdivision (b) of former Probate Code Section 660 (repealed by 1983 Cal.Stat. ch. 842 § 39). For background on the provisions of this chapter, see the Comment to this chapter under the chapter heading. [20 Cal.L.Rev.Comm.Reports 1001 (1990)].

Research References

Forms

California Transactions Forms--Estate Planning § 19:3, Legislative Control Over Testation.
California Transactions Forms--Estate Planning § 19:9, Probate Homestead.
West's California Code Forms, Probate § 6520 Form 1, Petition for Order Setting Apart Probate Homestead to Surviving Spouse.
West's California Code Forms, Probate § 6602 Form 1, Petition to Set Aside Small Estate.

Treatises and Practice Aids

Witkin, California Summary 10th Wills and Probate § 767, Statutory Development.
Witkin, California Summary 10th Wills and Probate § 769, Petition.
Witkin, California Summary 10th Wills and Probate § 781, Nature Of Right.
Witkin, California Summary 10th Wills and Probate § 782, Petition to Set Aside.
Witkin, California Summary 10th Wills and Probate § 784, Order.

§ 6521. Persons for whose use homestead shall be set apart

The probate homestead shall be set apart for the use of one or more of the following persons:

(a) The surviving spouse.

(b) The minor children of the decedent. *(Stats.1990, c. 79 (A.B.759), § 14, operative July 1, 1991.)*

Law Revision Commission Comments

1990 Enactment

Section 6521 continues Section 6521 of the repealed Probate Code without change. This section permits the probate homestead to be set apart for minor children of the decedent even if there is a surviving spouse. This may be desirable, for example, if the minor children live apart from the surviving spouse or where the minor children are not children of the surviving spouse. As to a surviving spouse's waiver of rights at death, see Section 140–147.

Background on Section 6521 of Repealed Code

Section 6521 was added by 1983 Cal.Stat. ch. 842 § 55. The section continued subdivision (a) of former Probate Code Section 661 (repealed by 1983 Cal.Stat. ch. 842 § 39). For background on the provisions of this chapter, see the Comment to this chapter under the chapter heading. [20 Cal.L.Rev.Comm.Reports 1001 (1990)].

Research References

Forms

California Transactions Forms--Estate Planning § 19:9, Probate Homestead.
California Transactions Forms--Estate Planning § 6:32, Exceptions to Omitted Child Statute.
West's California Code Forms, Probate § 6520 Form 1, Petition for Order Setting Apart Probate Homestead to Surviving Spouse.

Treatises and Practice Aids

Witkin, California Summary 10th Wills and Probate § 769, Petition.

§ 6522. Property out of which selected; preference

(a) The probate homestead shall be selected out of the following property, giving first preference to the community and quasi-community property of, or property owned in common by, the decedent and the person entitled to have the homestead set apart:

(1) If the homestead is set apart for the use of the surviving spouse or for the use of the surviving spouse and minor children, out of community property or quasi-community property.

(2) If the homestead is set apart for the use of the surviving spouse or for the use of the minor children or for the use of the surviving spouse and minor children, out of property owned in common by the decedent and the persons entitled to have the homestead set apart, or out of the separate property of the decedent or, if the decedent was not married at the time of death, out of property owned by the decedent.

(b) The probate homestead shall not be selected out of property the right to possession of which is vested in a third person unless the third person consents thereto. As used in this subdivision, "third person" means a person whose right to possession of the property (1) existed at the time of the death of the decedent or came into existence upon the death of the decedent and (2) was not created by testate or intestate succession from the decedent. *(Stats.1990, c. 79 (A.B.759), § 14, operative July 1, 1991. Amended by Stats.1990, c. 710 (S.B.1775), § 17, operative July 1, 1991.)*

Law Revision Commission Comments

1990 Enactment

Section 6522 continues Section 6522 of the repealed Probate Code without change. This section does not require that the probate homestead be selected out of real property. The probate homestead may be selected out of personal property such as a mobilehome. Under Section 6522, the court may select a homestead out of separate property of the decedent despite the availability of community or quasi-community property or property held in common by the decedent and the person in whose use the homestead is set apart. However, the court must give preference to property other than the separate property of the decedent for selection as a probate homestead.

Subdivision (b) limits the property from which the homestead may be selected. A probate homestead may not be created on property of which a third person has the right to possession, whether by partial ownership, lease, or otherwise, without the person's consent. The probate homestead can affect the possessory rights only of testate and intestate successors of the decedent. See also Sections 28 ("community property" defined), 66 ("quasi-community property" defined). As to a surviving spouse's waiver of rights at death, see Sections 140–147.

1990 Amendment

Section 6522 (enacted as a part of the new Probate Code by 1990 Cal.Stat. ch. 79 § 14) was amended by 1990 Cal.Stat. ch. 710 § 17 to remove any implication that the decedent's separate property may not be used for a probate homestead for both the surviving spouse and the minor children. [20 Cal.L.Rev.Comm.Reports 1001 (1990)].

Background on Section 6522 of Repealed Code

Section 6522 was added by 1983 Cal.Stat. ch. 842 § 55. The section continued subdivisions (b) and (c) of former Probate Code Section 661 (repealed by 1983 Cal.Stat. ch. 842 § 39). For background on the provisions of this chapter, see the Comment to this chapter under the chapter heading. [20 Cal.L.Rev.Comm.Reports 1001 (1990)].

Research References

Forms

West's California Code Forms, Probate § 6520 Form 1, Petition for Order Setting Apart Probate Homestead to Surviving Spouse.

Treatises and Practice Aids

Witkin, California Summary 10th Real Property § 53, Homestead.
Witkin, California Summary 10th Wills and Probate § 770, Available Property.

§ 6523. Facts considered; conditions

(a) In selecting and setting apart the probate homestead, the court shall consider the needs of the surviving spouse and minor children, the liens and encumbrances on the property, the claims of creditors, the needs of the heirs or devisees of the decedent, and the intent of the decedent with respect to the property in the estate and the estate plan of the decedent as expressed in inter vivos and testamentary transfers or by other means.

(b) The court, in light of subdivision (a) and other relevant considerations as determined by the court in its discretion, shall:

(1) Select as a probate homestead the most appropriate property available that is suitable for that use, including in addition to the dwelling itself such adjoining property as appears reasonable.

(2) Set the probate homestead so selected apart for such a term and upon such conditions (including, but not limited to, assignment by the homestead recipient of other property to the heirs or devisees of the property set apart as a homestead) as appear proper. *(Stats.1990, c. 79 (A.B.759), § 14, operative July 1, 1991.)*

Law Revision Commission Comments

1990 Enactment

Section 6523 continues Section 6523 of the repealed Probate Code without change. Under this section, the court has broad discretion in selecting the probate homestead and may take into account a wide variety of factors in exercising its discretion. This section expressly authorizes the court to condition the homestead on any terms that appear proper to the court. The court may select the homestead out of the separate property of the decedent but must give a preference to community or quasi-community property or of other property held in common by the decedent and the person for whose use the homestead is set apart. See Section 6522 and the Comment thereto. The court must select the most appropriate property as the homestead and is not limited to the existing dwelling. The court is not limited to existing lots or parcels, but must set apart only so much of the property as is reasonable under the circumstances of the case. As to a surviving spouse's waiver of rights at death, see Sections 140–147.

Background on Section 6523 of Repealed Code

Section 6523 was added by 1983 Cal.Stat. ch. 842 § 55. The section continued former Probate Code Section 664 (repealed by 1983 Cal.Stat. ch. 842 § 39). For background on the provisions of this chapter, see the Comment to this chapter under the chapter heading. [20 Cal.L.Rev.Comm.Reports 1001 (1990)].

Research References

Treatises and Practice Aids

Witkin, California Summary 10th Wills and Probate § 771, Factors to be Considered.

§ 6524. Period; rights of parties

The property set apart as a probate homestead shall be set apart only for a limited period, to be designated in the order, and in no case beyond the lifetime of the surviving spouse, or, as to a child, beyond its minority. Subject to the probate homestead right, the property of the decedent remains subject to administration including testate and intestate succession. The rights of the parties during the period for which the probate homestead is set apart are governed, to the extent applicable, by the Legal Estates Principal and Income Law, Chapter 2.6 (commencing with Section 731) of Title 2 of Part 1 of Division 2 of the Civil Code. *(Stats.1990, c. 79 (A.B.759), § 14, operative July 1, 1991.)*

Law Revision Commission Comments

1990 Enactment

Section 6524 continues Section 6524 of the repealed Probate Code without change. This section requires that the probate homestead be set apart only for a limited period, regardless whether the homestead is selected out of the separate property of the decedent or otherwise. Under this section, the property set aside as a probate homestead remains subject to administration. The testate or intestate successors of the decedent or other successors to the property set aside as a probate homestead take the property subject to the probate homestead right. Any portion of the probate homestead that is the property of the person for whom the homestead was set apart remains vested in the person at the termination of the probate homestead right. The rights of the homestead recipients and remaindermen are governed by the Legal Estates Principal and Income Law, but the court setting apart the homestead may vary the requirements of that law where appropriate to do so. See Civil Code § 731.04. As to the rights of creditors during and after administration, see Section 6526.

Background on Section 6524 of Repealed Code

Section 6524 was added by 1983 Cal.Stat. ch. 842 § 55. The section continued subdivision (d) of former Probate Code Section 661 (repealed by 1983 Cal.Stat. ch. 842 § 39). For background on the provisions of this chapter, see the Comment to this chapter under the chapter heading. [20 Cal.L.Rev.Comm.Reports 1001 (1990)].

Research References

Forms

California Transactions Forms--Estate Planning § 19:9, Probate Homestead.
California Transactions Forms--Estate Planning § 19:10, Family Allowance.
West's California Code Forms, Probate § 6520 Form 1, Petition for Order Setting Apart Probate Homestead to Surviving Spouse.

Treatises and Practice Aids

Witkin, California Summary 10th Wills and Probate § 769, Petition.
Witkin, California Summary 10th Wills and Probate § 772, Liability Of Property.

§ 6525. Petition; notice

(a) A petition to select and set apart a probate homestead may be filed by any interested person.

(b) Notice of the hearing on the petition shall be given as provided in Section 1220 to all of the following persons:

(1) Each person listed in Section 1220.

(2) Each known heir whose interest in the estate would be affected by the petition.

(3) Each known devisee whose interest in the estate would be affected by the petition. *(Stats.1990, c. 79 (A.B.759), § 14, operative July 1, 1991.)*

Law Revision Commission Comments

1990 Enactment

Section 6525 restates Section 6525 of the repealed Probate Code with the addition of the requirement that notice of the hearing be given to each known heir or devisee whose interest in the estate would be affected by the petition. See Section 1206 (notice to known heirs or known devisees). For general provisions, see Sections 1000–1004 (rules of practice), 1020–1023 (petitions and other papers), 1040–1050 (hearings and orders). For general provisions relating to notice of hearing, see Sections 1200–1221. See also Sections 1250–1252 (request for special notice), 1260–1265 (proof of giving notice). The requirement that notice be given as provided in Section 1220 does not apply to a particular notice where the notice was delivered, mailed, posted, or first published before July 1, 1991. In such a case, the applicable law in effect before July 1, 1991, continues to apply to the giving of the notice. Section 1200(c). As to the application of any amendments made after that date, see Section 3. See also Section 48 ("interested person" defined). As to the right to appeal from an order under this chapter, see Section 7240 and the Comment thereto.

Background on Section 6525 of Repealed Code

Section 6525 was added by 1983 Cal.Stat. ch. 842 § 55 and was amended by 1987 Cal.Stat. ch. 923 § 89. The section continued the substance of former Probate Code Section 662 (repealed by 1983 Cal.Stat. ch. 842 § 39). The 1987 amendment (1) revised the cross-reference to the procedure for mailing notice of the hearing and (2) deleted the provision requiring the clerk to set the petition for hearing, this provision being unnecessary in view of Section 1285 which is a general provision that imposes this duty on the clerk. As to the 1987 amendment, see Communication from California Law Revision Commission Concerning Assembly Bill 708, 19 Cal.L.Revision Comm'n Reports 545, 560 (1988); Comments to Conforming Revisions and Repeals, 19 Cal.L.Revision Comm'n Reports 391, 449 (1988). For background on the provisions of this chapter, see the Comment to this chapter under the chapter heading. [20 Cal.L.Rev.Comm.Reports 1001 (1990)].

Research References

Forms

West's California Code Forms, Probate § 6520 Form 1, Petition for Order Setting Apart Probate Homestead to Surviving Spouse.

Treatises and Practice Aids

Witkin, California Summary 10th Wills and Probate § 769, Petition.

§ 6526. Liability for claims against estate; homestead exemption

(a) Property of the decedent set apart as a probate homestead is liable for claims against the estate of the decedent, subject to the probate homestead right. The probate homestead right in property of the decedent is liable for claims that are secured by liens and encumbrances on the property at the time of the decedent's death but is exempt to the extent of the homestead exemption as to any claim that would have been subject to a homestead exemption at the time of the decedent's death under Article 4 (commencing with Section 704.710) of Chapter 4 of Division 2 of Title 9 of Part 2 of the Code of Civil Procedure.

(b) The probate homestead right in the property of the decedent is not liable for claims against the person for whose use the probate homestead is set apart.

(c) Property of the decedent set apart as a probate homestead is liable for claims against the testate or intestate successors of the decedent or other successors to the property after administration, subject to the probate homestead right. *(Stats.1990, c. 79 (A.B.759), § 14, operative July 1, 1991.)*

Law Revision Commission Comments

1990 Enactment

Section 6526 continues Section 6526 of the repealed Probate Code without change. Subdivision (a) sets the rules governing liability of probate homestead property for debts of the decedent. The first sentence makes clear that such property may be used to satisfy debts of the decedent, but any sale is subject to the probate homestead right of occupancy by the person for whose use the homestead is set apart. This codifies the rule of In re Estate of Tittel, 139 Cal. 149, 72 P. 909 (1903). The second sentence recognizes the common law rule that the probate homestead does not affect prior liens and encumbrances. See, e.g., In re Estate of McCauley, 50 Cal. 544 (1875); In re Estate of Huelsman, 127 Cal. 275, 59 P. 776 (1899). However, the court may select as a probate homestead property not subject to liens and encumbrances or property whose liens and encumbrances will be discharged in probate. See Section 6523 (discretion of court). Preexisting liens and encumbrances on the property may be satisfied out of the probate homestead right. If the property would have been exempt from enforcement of a claim secured by a lien or encumbrance at the time of the decedent's death, however, the homestead recipient may claim a homestead exemption for the probate homestead right.

Subdivision (b) states the rule governing liability of the probate homestead right for debts of the person for whose use the homestead is set apart. Subdivision (b) creates an absolute exemption for the probate homestead right, both as to prior and subsequently incurred debts, regardless of liens created on the probate homestead right. Subdivision (b) does not preclude a creditor of the person for whose use the probate homestead is set apart from reaching any interest in the property the person may have apart from the probate homestead right; this may occur where the homestead was selected out of community property of or property held in common by the decedent and the person for whose use the homestead is set apart. In such a situation, the exemption from execution for a dwelling may be available to the person for whose use the homestead is set apart to protect his or her property interest.

Subdivision (c) states the rule governing liability of probate homestead property for debts of the heirs or devisees or other persons who may have acquired the property through administration. The probate homestead property is subject to administration and devolves as any other property, subject to the right of use of the homestead by the persons for whose use it is set apart. See Section 6524. Under subdivision (c) of Section 6526, the remainder interest but not the probate homestead right is subject to claims of creditors.

Background on Section 6526 of Repealed Code

Section 6526 was added by 1983 Cal.Stat. ch. 842 § 55. The section continued former Probate Code Section 663 (repealed by 1983 Cal.Stat. ch. 842 § 39). For background on the provisions of this chapter, see the Comment to this chapter under the chapter heading. [20 Cal.L.Rev.Comm.Reports 1001 (1990)].

Research References

Forms

California Transactions Forms--Estate Planning § 19:9, Probate Homestead.

West's California Code Forms, Probate § 6520 Form 1, Petition for Order Setting Apart Probate Homestead to Surviving Spouse.

West's California Code Forms, Probate § 6520 Form 2, Order Setting Apart Probate Homestead to Surviving Spouse.

Treatises and Practice Aids

Witkin, California Summary 10th Wills and Probate § 772, Liability Of Property.

§ 6527. Modification, terms and conditions; termination; petition for order; notice of hearing

(a) The court may by order modify the term or conditions of the probate homestead right or terminate the probate homestead right at any time prior to entry of an order for final distribution of the decedent's estate if in the court's discretion to do so appears appropriate under the circumstances of the case.

(b) A petition for an order under this section may be filed by any of the following:

(1) The person for whose use the probate homestead is set apart.

(2) The testate or intestate successors of the decedent or other successors to the property set apart as a probate homestead.

(3) Persons having claims secured by liens or encumbrances on the property set apart as a probate homestead.

(c) Notice of the hearing on the petition shall be given to all the persons listed in subdivision (b) as provided in Section 1220. *(Stats.1990, c. 79 (A.B.759), § 14, operative July 1, 1991.)*

Law Revision Commission Comments

1990 Enactment

Section 6527 continues Section 6527 of the repealed Probate Code without change. This section gives the court authority to modify the probate homestead right until the entry of an order for final distribution in recognition of the possibility of changed circumstances. For general provisions, see Sections 1000–1004 (rules of practice), 1020–1023 (petitions and other papers), 1040–1050 (hearings and orders). For general provisions relating to notice of hearing, see Sections 1200–1221. See also Sections 1250–1252 (request for special notice), 1260–1265 (proof of giving notice). See also Section 48 ("interested person" defined).

Background on Section 6527 of Repealed Code

Section 6527 was added by 1983 Cal.Stat. ch. 842 § 55 and was amended by 1987 Cal.Stat. ch. 923 § 90 and 1988 Cal.Stat. ch. 1199 § 77.5. The section continued the substance of former Probate Code Section 665 (repealed by 1983 Cal.Stat. ch. 842 § 39) with the addition of subdivision (c). The 1987 amendment (1) revised the cross-reference to the procedure for mailing notice of the hearing and (2) deleted the provision formerly in subdivision (c) excusing giving notice to oneself, this provision now being generalized in Section 1201. As to the 1987 amendment, see Communication from California Law Revision Commission Concerning Assembly Bill 708, 19 Cal.L.Revision Comm'n Reports 545, 561 (1988); Comments to Conforming Revisions and Repeals, 19 Cal.L.Revision Comm'n Reports 391, 450 (1988). The 1988 amendment conformed terminology to revisions made to the Probate Code in 1988. As to the 1988 amendment, see Comments to Conforming Revisions and Repeals, 19 Cal.L.Revision Comm'n Reports 1031, 1090 (1988). For background on the provisions of this chapter, see the Comment to this chapter under the chapter heading. [20 Cal.L.Rev.Comm.Reports 1001 (1990)].

Research References

Forms

California Transactions Forms--Estate Planning § 19:9, Probate Homestead.

Treatises and Practice Aids

Witkin, California Summary 10th Wills and Probate § 773, Modification or Termination.

§ 6528. Relationship to existing law

Nothing in this chapter terminates or otherwise affects a declaration of homestead by, or for the benefit of, a surviving spouse or minor child of the decedent with respect to the community, quasi-community, or common interest of the surviving spouse or minor child in property in the decedent's estate. This section is declaratory of, and does not constitute a change in, existing law. *(Stats.1990, c. 79 (A.B.759), § 14, operative July 1, 1991.)*

Law Revision Commission Comments

1990 Enactment

Section 6528 continues Section 6528 of the repealed Probate Code without change. This section makes clear the relationship between the probate homestead law and the declared homestead law. See Code Civ.Proc. §§ 704.910–704.990 (declared homestead). Although there is no longer a right of survivorship created by a declaration of homestead (1980 Cal.Stat. ch. 119, § 22), in the sense that the survivor no longer takes the decedent's interest in the property over a contrary testamentary disposition, a homestead declaration made by or for the benefit of a survivor nonetheless remains effective as to the survivor's interest in the property, notwithstanding dictum to the contrary in Estate of Grigsby, 134 Cal.App.3d 611, 184 Cal.Rptr. 886 (1982).

Background on Section 6528 of Repealed Code

Section 6528 was a new provision added by 1983 Cal.Stat. ch. 842 § 55. For background on the provisions of this chapter, see the Comment to this chapter under the chapter heading. [20 Cal.L.Rev.Comm.Reports 1001 (1990)].

Research References

Treatises and Practice Aids

Witkin, California Summary 10th Wills and Probate § 768, Relationship Between Probate Homestead and Declared Homestead.

CHAPTER 4. FAMILY ALLOWANCE

§ 6540. Persons entitled to allowance

(a) The following are entitled to such reasonable family allowance out of the estate as is necessary for their maintenance according to their circumstances during administration of the estate:

(1) The surviving spouse of the decedent.

(2) Minor children of the decedent.

(3) Adult children of the decedent who are physically or mentally incapacitated from earning a living and were actually dependent in whole or in part upon the decedent for support.

(b) The following may be given such reasonable family allowance out of the estate as the court in its discretion determines is necessary for their maintenance according to their circumstances during administration of the estate:

(1) Other adult children of the decedent who were actually dependent in whole or in part upon the decedent for support.

(2) A parent of the decedent who was actually dependent in whole or in part upon the decedent for support.

(c) If a person otherwise eligible for family allowance has a reasonable maintenance from other sources and there are one or more other persons entitled to a family allowance, the family allowance shall be granted only to those who do not have a reasonable maintenance from other sources. *(Stats. 1990, c. 79 (A.B.759), § 14, operative July 1, 1991.)*

Law Revision Commission Comments

1990 Enactment

Section 6540 continues Section 6540 of the repealed Probate Code without change. The right of a surviving spouse to a family allowance may be waived in whole or in part, whether the waiver is executed before or during marriage. See Sections 140–147. As to the priority of the family allowance, see Section 11420. See also Sections 21400–21406 (abatement of shares of beneficiaries).

Background on Section 6540 of Repealed Code

Section 6540 was added by 1983 Cal.Stat. ch. 842 § 55. Subdivision (a) continued the substance of subdivision (a) of former Probate Code Section 680 (repealed by 1983 Cal.Stat. ch. 842 § 39). Subdivision (b) continued the substance of subdivision (b) of former Probate Code Section 680, with the addition of discretionary authority for the court to award family allowance to a parent of the decedent who was actually dependent in whole or in part on the decedent for support. Subdivision (c) continued the substance of former Probate Code Section 682 (repealed by 1983 Cal.Stat. ch. 842 § 39). For background on the provisions of this part, see the Comment to this part under the part heading. [20 Cal.L.Rev.Comm.Reports 1001 (1990)].

Commentary

Parson v. Parson, 49 Cal.App.4th 537, 56 Cal.Rptr.2d 686 (1996), review denied December 18, 1996, holds that, for purposes of this section, the decedent's estate does not include decedent's revocable living trust.

Research References

Forms

California Transactions Forms--Estate Planning § 1:2, Probate System.
California Transactions Forms--Estate Planning § 19:3, Legislative Control Over Testation.
California Transactions Forms--Estate Planning § 6:32, Exceptions to Omitted Child Statute.
California Transactions Forms--Estate Planning § 19:10, Family Allowance.
California Transactions Forms--Estate Planning § 19:80, Overview.
California Transactions Forms--Estate Planning § 21:20, Surviving Spouse's Trust Income Withheld to Extent Of Family Allowance.
California Transactions Forms--Estate Planning § 9:151, IRD is Principal for Trust Accounting Purposes.
West's California Code Forms, Probate § 6541 Form 1, Petition for Family Allowance.

Treatises and Practice Aids

Witkin, California Summary 10th Wills and Probate § 25, Major Changes.
Witkin, California Summary 10th Wills and Probate § 50, Legal and Financial Terms.
Witkin, California Summary 10th Wills and Probate § 774, Statutory Development.
Witkin, California Summary 10th Wills and Probate § 775, Mandatory Allowance.
Witkin, California Summary 10th Wills and Probate § 776, Discretionary Allowance.
Witkin, California Summary 10th Wills and Probate § 777, Limitations.
Witkin, California Summary 10th Wills and Probate § 779, Procedure.

§ 6541. Grant or modification; petition; hearing; notice

(a) The court may grant or modify a family allowance on petition of any interested person.

(b) With respect to an order for the family allowance provided for in subdivision (a) of Section 6540:

(1) Before the inventory is filed, the order may be made or modified either (A) ex parte or (B) after notice of the hearing on the petition has been given as provided in Section 1220.

(2) After the inventory is filed, the order may be made or modified only after notice of the hearing on the petition has been given as provided in Section 1220.

(c) An order for the family allowance provided in subdivision (b) of Section 6540 may be made only after notice of the hearing on the petition has been given as provided in Section 1220 to all of the following persons:

(1) Each person listed in Section 1220.

(2) Each known heir whose interest in the estate would be affected by the petition.

(3) Each known devisee whose interest in the estate would be affected by the petition. *(Stats.1990, c. 79 (A.B.759), § 14, operative July 1, 1991.)*

Law Revision Commission Comments

1990 Enactment

Section 6541 continues Section 6541 of the repealed Probate Code without substantive change. See also Section 1206 (notice to known heirs or known devisees). For general provisions, see Sections 1000–1004 (rules of practice), 1020–1023 (petitions and other papers), 1040–1050 (hearings and orders). For general provisions relating to notice of hearing, see Sections 1200–1221. See also Sections 1250–1252 (request for special notice), 1260–1265 (proof of giving notice). The notice provisions referred to in Section 6541 do not apply to a particular notice where the notice was delivered, mailed, posted, or first published before July 1, 1991. In such a case, the applicable law in effect before July 1, 1991, continues to apply to the giving of the notice. Section 1200(c). As to the application of any amendments made after that date, see Section 3. See also Section 48 ("interested person" defined).

Background on Section 6541 of Repealed Code

Section 6541 was added by 1983 Cal.Stat. ch. 842 § 55 and was amended by 1987 Cal.Stat. ch. 923 § 91. The section continued the substance of a portion of former Probate Code Section 681 (repealed by 1983 Cal.Stat. ch. 842 § 39). The 1987 amendments revised the provisions relating to notice. As to the 1987 amendment, see Communication from California Law Revision Commission Concerning Assembly Bill 708, 19 Cal.L.Revision Comm'n Reports 545, 561 (1988); Comments to Conforming Revisions and Repeals, 19 Cal.L.Revision Comm'n Reports 391, 450 (1988). For background on the provisions of this part, see the Comment to this part under the part heading. [20 Cal.L.Rev.Comm.Reports 1001 (1990)].

Research References

Forms

West's California Code Forms, Probate § 6541 Form 1, Petition for Family Allowance.

West's California Code Forms, Probate § 6541 Form 3, Petition to Modify Order for Family Allowance by Reducing or Terminating Allowance.

Treatises and Practice Aids

Witkin, California Summary 10th Wills and Probate § 779, Procedure.

§ 6542. Commencement; retroactive allowances

A family allowance commences on the date of the court's order or such other time as may be provided in the court's order, whether before or after the date of the order, as the court in its discretion determines, but the allowance may not be made retroactive to a date earlier than the date of the decedent's death. *(Stats.1990, c. 79 (A.B.759), § 14, operative July 1, 1991.)*

Law Revision Commission Comments

1990 Enactment

Section 6542 continues Section 6542 of the repealed Probate Code without change.

Background on Section 6542 of Repealed Code

Section 6542 was added by 1983 Cal.Stat. ch. 842 § 55. The section codified the previously existing practice. The prohibition against an order which is retroactive to a date earlier to a date earlier than the date of decedent's death continued the substance of a portion of subdivision (c) of former Probate Code Section 680 (repealed by 1983 Cal.Stat. ch. 842 § 39). For background on the provisions of this part, see the Comment to this part under the part heading. [20 Cal.L.Rev.Comm.Reports 1001 (1990)].

Research References

Forms

West's California Code Forms, Probate § 6541 Form 2, Order for Family Allowance.

Treatises and Practice Aids

Witkin, California Summary 10th Wills and Probate § 778, Commencement and Termination.

§ 6543. Termination; limitation; continuation

(a) A family allowance shall terminate no later than the entry of the order for final distribution of the estate or, if the estate is insolvent, no later than one year after the granting of letters.

(b) Subject to subdivision (a), a family allowance shall continue until modified or terminated by the court or until such time as the court may provide in its order. *(Stats.1990, c. 79 (A.B.759), § 14, operative July 1, 1991.)*

Law Revision Commission Comments

1990 Enactment

Section 6543 restates Section 6543 of the repealed Probate Code without substantive change. The phrase "entry of the order for final distribution of the estate" has been substituted for "final settlement of the estate." See also Section 12203 (continuation of administration of the estate in order to pay family allowance).

Background on Section 6543 of Repealed Code

Section 6543 was added by 1983 Cal.Stat. ch. 842 § 55. Subdivision (a) continued portions of former Probate Code Section 680 (repealed by 1983 Cal.Stat. ch. 842 § 39). Subdivision (b) continued a portion of the first sentence of subdivision (a) of former Probate Code Section 681 (repealed by 1983 Cal.Stat. ch. 842 § 39). The authority in subdivision (b) for the court to make an order terminating a family allowance or to include a termination date in its original order was new, but was implied under the former sections. For background on the provisions of this part, see the Comment to this part under the part heading. [20 Cal.L.Rev.Comm.Reports 1001 (1990)].

Research References

Forms

California Transactions Forms--Estate Planning § 19:10, Family Allowance.

West's California Code Forms, Probate § 6541 Form 2, Order for Family Allowance.

Treatises and Practice Aids

Witkin, California Summary 10th Wills and Probate § 25, Major Changes.

Witkin, California Summary 10th Wills and Probate § 740, Continuance Of Administration.

Witkin, California Summary 10th Wills and Probate § 778, Commencement and Termination.

§ 6544. Costs

The costs of proceedings under this chapter shall be paid by the estate as expenses of administration. *(Stats.1990, c. 79 (A.B.759), § 14, operative July 1, 1991.)*

Law Revision Commission Comments

1990 Enactment

Section 6544 continues Section 6544 of the repealed Probate Code without change.

Background on Section 6544 of Repealed Code

Section 6544 was added by 1983 Cal.Stat. ch. 842 § 55. The section continued the substance of former Probate Code Section 683 (repealed by 1983 Cal.Stat. ch. 842 § 39). For background on the provisions of this part, see the Comment to this part under the part heading. [20 Cal.L.Rev.Comm.Reports 1001 (1990)].

Research References

Treatises and Practice Aids

Witkin, California Summary 10th Wills and Probate § 400, Costs.
Witkin, California Summary 10th Wills and Probate § 779, Procedure.

§ 6545. Perfection of appeal; stay of proceedings

Notwithstanding Chapter 2 (commencing with Section 916) of Title 13 of Part 2 of the Code of Civil Procedure, the perfecting of an appeal from an order made under this chapter does not stay proceedings under this chapter or the enforcement of the order appealed from if the person in whose favor the order is made gives an undertaking in double the amount of the payment or payments to be made to that person. The undertaking shall be conditioned that if the order appealed from is modified or reversed so that the payment or any part thereof to the person proves to have been unwarranted, the payment or part thereof shall, unless deducted from any preliminary or final distribution ordered in favor of the person, be repaid and refunded into the estate within 30 days after the court so orders following the modification or reversal, together with interest and costs. *(Stats.1990, c. 79 (A.B.759), § 14, operative July 1, 1991.)*

Law Revision Commission Comments

1990 Enactment

Section 6545 continues Section 6545 of the repealed Probate Code without change. Concerning enforcement of liability on the undertaking, see Code Civ.Proc. §§ 996.410–996.495.

Background on Section 6545 of Repealed Code

Section 6545 was added by 1983 Cal.Stat. ch. 842 § 55. The section continued the substance of a portion of former Probate Code Section 684 (repealed by 1983 Cal.Stat. ch. 842 § 39). For background on the requirement of an undertaking, see Recommendation Relating to Statutory Bonds and Undertakings, 16 Cal.L.Revision Comm'n Reports 501, 610 (1982). For background on the provisions of this part, see the Comment to this part under the part heading. [20 Cal.L.Rev.Comm.Reports 1001 (1990)].

Research References

Forms

California Transactions Forms--Estate Planning § 1:2, Probate System.
California Transactions Forms--Estate Planning § 19:3, Legislative Control Over Testation.
California Transactions Forms--Estate Planning § 19:7, Overview.

Treatises and Practice Aids

Witkin, California Summary 10th Wills and Probate § 779, Procedure.

CHAPTER 6. SMALL ESTATE SET-ASIDE

Section

Application

Provisions applicable to decedents who died on or after July 1, 1987, see Probate Code § 6614.

Law Revision Commission Comments

1990 Enactment

This chapter supersedes Chapter 6 (commencing with Section 6600) of Part 3 of Division 6 of the repealed Probate Code. The superseded chapter was enacted upon recommendation of the California Law Revision Commission. See Recommendation Relating to Small Estate Set-Aside, 18 Cal.L.Revision Comm'n Reports 1101 (1986). See also Communication from California Law Revision Commission Concerning Assembly Bill 2625, 18 Cal.L.Revision Comm'n Reports 1743, 1750–53 (1986). The Commission, in cooperation with California Continuing Education of the Bar, published the recommended legislation as enacted with official comments. See Selected 1986 Trust and Probate Legislation, 18 Cal.L.Revision Comm'n Reports 1201, 1597–1621 (1986). [20 Cal.L.Rev.Comm.Reports 1001 (1990)].

§ 6600. Decedent's estate defined

(a) Subject to subdivision (b), for the purposes of this chapter, "decedent's estate" means all the decedent's personal property, wherever located, and all the decedent's real property located in this state.

(b) For the purposes of this chapter:

(1) Any property or interest or lien thereon which, at the time of the decedent's death, was held by the decedent as a joint tenant, or in which the decedent had a life or other interest terminable upon the decedent's death, shall be excluded in determining the estate of the decedent or its value.

(2) A multiple-party account to which the decedent was a party at the time of the decedent's death shall be excluded in

determining the estate of the decedent or its value, whether or not all or a portion of the sums on deposit are community property, to the extent that the sums on deposit belong after the death of the decedent to a surviving party, P.O.D. payee, or beneficiary. As used in this paragraph, the terms "multiple-party account," "party," "P.O.D. payee," and "beneficiary" have the meanings given those terms in Article 2 (commencing with Section 5120) of Chapter 1 of Part 2 of Division 5. *(Stats.1990, c. 79 (A.B.759), § 14, operative July 1, 1991.)*

Law Revision Commission Comments

1990 Enactment

Section 6600 continues Section 6600 of the repealed Probate Code without substantive change. As to a surviving spouse's waiver of rights at death, see Sections 140–47.

As defined in subdivision (a), "decedent's estate" is not limited to probate assets. The term includes all personal property, wherever located, and all real property located in this state, excluding the property described in subdivision (b). Subdivision (a) requires, for example, that the decedent's one-half share of the community and quasi-community property be included in determining the decedent's estate or its value, whether or not the decedent's interest is set apart to the surviving spouse under Sections 13650–13660, unless the interest is excluded in determining the estate of the decedent under subdivision (b) as would be the case, for example, if the property is held in joint tenancy. This is consistent with prior law. Estate of Pezzola, 112 Cal.App.3d 752, 169 Cal.Rptr. 464 (1980).

Subdivision (b) excludes any interest that terminates at death in determining the estate of the decedent or its value. If the interest is one that passes to another on the death of the decedent by virtue of a joint tenancy, a pay-on-death provision, or a contractual provision that provides that the interest is to be transferred or paid to another upon the death of the decedent, subdivision (b)(1) requires that the value of the interest be excluded in determining the estate of the decedent or its value. For example, if there is a policy of insurance on the decedent's life and the proceeds are payable to a named beneficiary (not to the decedent's estate), the insurance proceeds are excluded in determining the estate of the decedent or its value. Similarly, for example, if the decedent has a retirement plan that provides benefits to a surviving spouse, those benefits are excluded in determining the estate of the decedent or its value. Subdivision (b) also excludes, for example, life interests in trusts and life estates. See O. McCarroll, 1 California Decedent Estate Administration Supplement § 3.24, at 84–85 (Cal.Cont.Ed.Bar 1985).

This section does not apply if the decedent died before July 1, 1987. See Section 6614. As to the application of any amendments made after that date, see Section 3. A reference to a provision of the former statute is deemed to be a reference to the comparable provisions of this chapter. See Section 6615.

Background on Section 6600 of Repealed Code

Section 6600 was added by 1986 Cal.Stat. ch. 783 § 23 and amended by 1989 Cal.Stat. ch. 397 § 38. Subdivision (a) was a new provision that defined "decedent's estate." This definition replaced the phrase "the whole estate" used in former Probate Code Section 640 (repealed by 1986 Cal.Stat. ch. 783 § 9). Subdivision (a) made clear that real property located outside California is not included in determining the estate of the decedent or its value. The rule under former law was unclear. See Broll, Summary Administration, in 1 California Decedent Estate Administration § 3.24, at 129 (Cal. Cont.Ed.Bar 1971). Apparently real property outside California was not included under former law, since former Section 644 required "an inventory and appraisement to be prepared in the manner prescribed by law and filed within such time as the court may allow," and an inventory and appraisement does not include real property located outside California.

Subdivision (b) continued former Probate Code Section 647 (repealed by 1986 Cal.Stat. ch. 783 § 9) without substantive change. As to paragraph (2) of subdivision (b), see Recommendation Relating to Nonprobate Transfers, 16 Cal.L.Revision Comm'n Reports 129, 159 (1982).

The 1989 amendment conformed a reference to the definitional provisions to the renumbering of those provisions made by 1989 Cal.Stat. ch. 397. For background on the provisions of this chapter, see the Comment to this chapter under the chapter heading. [20 Cal.L.Rev.Comm.Reports 1001 (1990)].

Research References

Forms

California Transactions Forms--Estate Planning § 19:7, Overview.
California Transactions Forms--Estate Planning § 11:50, Rights Of Surviving Spouse that May be Waived [Prob C § 141].
California Transactions Forms--Estate Planning § 19:12, Small Estate Set-Aside.
California Transactions Forms--Estate Planning § 19:15, Waiver Of Family Protection.
West's California Code Forms, Probate § 6602 Form 1, Petition to Set Aside Small Estate.

Treatises and Practice Aids

Witkin, California Summary 10th Wills and Probate § 108, Pay-On-Death Provisions.
Witkin, California Summary 10th Wills and Probate § 322, Nature and Scope Of Statute.
Witkin, California Summary 10th Wills and Probate § 780, Statutory Development.
Witkin, California Summary 10th Wills and Probate § 781, Nature Of Right.
Witkin, California Summary 10th Wills and Probate § 782, Petition to Set Aside.
Witkin, California Summary 10th Wills and Probate § 783, Notice and Hearing.
Witkin, California Summary 10th Wills and Probate § 819, Property Subject to Administration.

§ 6601. Minor child

As used in this chapter, "minor child" means a child of the decedent who was under the age of 18 at the time of the decedent's death and who survived the decedent. *(Stats. 1990, c. 79 (A.B.759), § 14, operative July 1, 1991.)*

Law Revision Commission Comments

1990 Enactment

Section 6601 continues Section 6601 of the repealed Probate Code without change. This determination whether a child is a minor is made at the time of the death of the decedent. This section does not apply if the decedent died before July 1, 1987. See Section 6614. As to the application of any amendments made after that date, see Section 3. A reference to a provision of the former statute is deemed to be a reference to the comparable provisions of this chapter. See Section 6615.

Background on Section 6601 of Repealed Code

Section 6601 was a new provision added by 1986 Cal.Stat. ch. 783 § 23. The section changed the rule under former Probate Code Section 645 (repealed by 1986 Cal.Stat. ch. 783 § 9) that, if the other statutory requirements were satisfied, the court could order that the estate be set aside "to such child or children of the decedent as may then be minors." The apparent result of this provision was that a child who was a minor at the time of the decedent's death was deprived of the right to a small estate set aside if the order was not made while the child was still a minor. The definition under Section 6601 avoided this result. For background on the provisions of this chapter, see the Comment to this chapter under the chapter heading. [20 Cal.L.Rev.Comm.Reports 1001 (1990)].

Research References

Forms

California Transactions Forms--Estate Planning § 19:12, Small Estate Set-Aside.

West's California Code Forms, Probate § 6602 Form 1, Petition to Set Aside Small Estate.

Treatises and Practice Aids

Witkin, California Summary 10th Wills and Probate § 781, Nature Of Right.

§ 6602. Petition requesting order to set aside estate; maximum value

A petition may be filed under this chapter requesting an order setting aside the decedent's estate to the decedent's surviving spouse and minor children, or one or more of them, as provided in this chapter, if the net value of the decedent's estate, over and above all liens and encumbrances at the date of death and over and above the value of any probate homestead interest set apart out of the decedent's estate under Section 6520, does not exceed twenty thousand dollars ($20,000). *(Stats.1990, c. 79 (A.B.759), § 14, operative July 1, 1991.)*

Law Revision Commission Comments

1990 Enactment

Section 6602 continues Section 6602 of the repealed Probate Code without change. The purpose of this chapter is to insure the support of the dependent surviving spouse and minor children (or any one or more of them) when the breadwinner is taken by death leaving but a small estate. This right to have a small estate set aside effectively forecloses the rights of a third person to inherit or otherwise receive a part of that estate under the decedent's will. Estate of Pezzola, 112 Cal.App.3d 752, 169 Cal.Rptr. 464 (1980). Section 6602 limits the use of this chapter to a case where the decedent's estate, less liens and encumbrances and the value of any probate homestead interest, does not exceed $20,000. See also Section 6600 (defining "decedent's estate") and the Comment thereto. As to a surviving spouse's waiver of rights at death, see Sections 140–147.

This section does not apply if the decedent died before July 1, 1987. See Section 6614. As to the application of any amendments made after that date, see Section 3. A reference to a provision of the former statute is deemed to be a reference to the comparable provisions of this chapter. See Section 6615.

Background on Section 6602 of Repealed Code

Section 6602 was added by 1986 Cal.Stat. ch. 783 § 23. The section superseded former Probate Code Section 640 (repealed by 1986 Cal.Stat. ch. 783 § 9). For background on the provisions of this chapter, see the Comment to this chapter under the chapter heading. [20 Cal.L.Rev.Comm.Reports 1001 (1990)].

Research References

Forms

California Transactions Forms--Estate Planning § 19:12, Small Estate Set-Aside.

West's California Code Forms, Probate § 6602 Form 1, Petition to Set Aside Small Estate.

Treatises and Practice Aids

Witkin, California Summary 10th Wills and Probate § 781, Nature Of Right.

Witkin, California Summary 10th Wills and Probate § 380B, (New) Decedents' Estates.

§ 6603. Venue

The petition shall be filed in the superior court of a county in which the estate of the decedent may be administered. *(Stats.1990, c. 79 (A.B.759), § 14, operative July 1, 1991.)*

Law Revision Commission Comments

1990 Enactment

Section 6603 continues Section 6603 of the repealed Probate Code without change. This section specifies the county in which the petition is to be filed. The section is consistent with a provision of Section 13650 (determination or confirmation of property passing or belonging to surviving spouse). This section does not apply if the decedent died before July 1, 1987. See Section 6614. As to the application of any amendments made after that date, see Section 3. A reference to a provision of the former statute is deemed to be a reference to the comparable provisions of this chapter. See Section 6615.

Background on Section 6603 of Repealed Code

Section 6603 was a new provision added by 1986 Cal.Stat. ch. 783 § 23. For background on the provisions of this chapter, see the Comment to this chapter under the chapter heading. [20 Cal.L.Rev.Comm.Reports 1001 (1990)].

Research References

Forms

West's California Code Forms, Probate § 6602 Form 1, Petition to Set Aside Small Estate.

Treatises and Practice Aids

Witkin, California Summary 10th Wills and Probate § 782, Petition to Set Aside.

§ 6604. Contents of petition

(a) The petition shall allege that this chapter applies and request that an order be made setting aside the estate of the decedent as provided in this chapter.

(b) The petition shall include the following:

(1) If proceedings for administration of the estate are not pending, the facts necessary to determine the county in which the estate of the decedent may be administered.

(2) The name, age, address, and relation to the decedent of each heir and devisee of the decedent, so far as known to the petitioner.

(3) A specific description and estimate of the value of the decedent's estate and a list of all liens and encumbrances at the date of death.

(4) A specific description and estimate of the value of any of the decedent's real property located outside this state that passed to the surviving spouse and minor children of the decedent, or any one or more of them, under the will of the decedent or by intestate succession.

(5) A specific description and estimate of the value of any of the decedent's property described in subdivision (b) of Section 6600 that passed to the surviving spouse and minor children of the decedent, or any one or more of them, upon the death of the decedent.

(6) A designation of any property as to which a probate homestead is set apart out of the decedent's estate under Section 6520.

(7) A statement of any unpaid liabilities for expenses of the last illness, funeral charges, and expenses of administration.

(8) The requested disposition of the estate of the decedent under this chapter and the considerations that justify the requested disposition. *(Stats.1990, c. 79 (A.B.759), § 14, operative July 1, 1991.)*

Law Revision Commission Comments

1990 Enactment

Section 6604 continues Section 6604 of the repealed Probate Code without substantive change. Paragraph (1) of subdivision (b) implements Section 6603 (venue). Paragraph (2) of subdivision (b) is designed to implement the provision for giving notice of the hearing on the petition under this chapter. See Section 6607. Paragraph (7) of subdivision (b) is consistent with subdivision (d) of Section 6609 (court shall ensure that expenses of last illness, funeral charges, and expenses of administration are paid).

Paragraph (8) of subdivision (b) requires that the petition contain the information necessary so that the court may make an appropriate order under Section 6609. If the court makes an order under Section 6609, the court may set aside the small estate to the surviving spouse and minor children of the decedent, or to any one or more of them. See the Comment to 6609. The petition, for example, may request that the small estate be set aside to one of the minor children and that the other minor children and the spouse be excluded, or it may request that the small estate be set aside in unequal shares to the minor children. In determining whether to make such an order, the court must take into account the various considerations listed in subdivision (b) of Section 6609.

For general provisions, see Sections 1020–1023 (petitions and other papers). This section does not apply if the decedent died before July 1, 1987. See Section 6614. As to the application of any amendments made after that date, see Section 3. A reference to a provision of the former statute is deemed to be a reference to the comparable provisions of this chapter. See Section 6615.

Background on Section 6604 of Repealed Code

Section 6604 was added by 1986 Cal.Stat. ch. 783 § 23. Subdivision (a) continued the first portion of the first sentence of former Probate Code Section 641 (repealed by 1986 Cal.Stat. ch. 783 § 9) without substantive change. Subdivision (b) superseded the last sentence of former Section 641 which specified the contents of the petition. Paragraphs (1) and (2) of subdivision (b) were new. Paragraphs (3), (4), and (5) of subdivision (b) superseded the provision of former Probate Code Section 641 that required that the petition include "a specific description and an estimate of the value of all of the decedent's property" and "a list of all liens and encumbrances at the date of death." Paragraph (6) of subdivision (b) continued a requirement of former Probate Code Section 641 without substantive change. Paragraphs (7) and (8) of subdivision (b) were new. For background on the provisions of this chapter, see the Comment to this chapter under the chapter heading. [20 Cal.L.Rev.Comm.Reports 1001 (1990)].

Research References

Forms

West's California Code Forms, Probate § 6602 Form 1, Petition to Set Aside Small Estate.

Treatises and Practice Aids

Witkin, California Summary 10th Wills and Probate § 782, Petition to Set Aside.

§ 6605. Procedure for filing petition; time for filing

(a) If proceedings for the administration of the estate of the decedent are pending, a petition under this chapter shall be filed in those proceedings without the payment of an additional fee.

(b) If proceedings for the administration of the estate of the decedent have not yet been commenced, a petition under this chapter may be filed concurrently with a petition for the probate of the decedent's will or for administration of the estate of the decedent, or, if no petition for probate or for administration is being filed, a petition under this chapter may be filed independently.

(c) A petition may be filed under this chapter at any time prior to the entry of the order for final distribution of the estate. *(Stats.1990, c. 79 (A.B.759), § 14, operative July 1, 1991.)*

Law Revision Commission Comments

1990 Enactment

Section 6605 continues Section 6605 of the repealed Probate Code without substantive change. This section does not apply if the decedent died before July 1, 1987. See Section 6614. As to the application of any amendments made after that date, see Section 3. A reference to a provision of the former statute is deemed to be a reference to the comparable provisions of this chapter. See Section 6615.

Background on Section 6605 of Repealed Code

Section 6605 was added by 1986 Cal.Stat. ch. 783 § 23. Subdivisions (a) and (b) continued the substance of portions of former Probate Code Section 641 (repealed by 1986 Cal.Stat. ch. 783 § 9) with language added to subdivision (a) to provide that a petition under this chapter may be filed in a pending probate proceeding "without the payment of an additional fee." The added language was drawn from Section 13652 (determination or confirmation of property passing or belonging to surviving spouse). Subdivision (c), which permitted a petition to be filed at any time prior to the final distribution of the estate, replaced the provision of former Section 641 which permitted a petition to be "filed at any time before the hearing on the petition for probate of the will or for letters of administration or after the filing of the inventory." For background on the provisions of this chapter, see the Comment to this chapter under the chapter heading. [20 Cal.L.Rev.Comm.Reports 1001 (1990)].

Research References

Treatises and Practice Aids

Witkin, California Summary 10th Wills and Probate § 782, Petition to Set Aside.

§ 6606. Who may file

(a) A petition may be filed under this chapter by any of the following:

(1) The person named in the will of the decedent as executor.

(2) The surviving spouse of the decedent.

(3) The guardian of a minor child of the decedent.

(4) A child of the decedent who was a minor at the time the decedent died.

(5) The personal representative if a personal representative has been appointed for the decedent's estate.

(b) The guardian of a minor child of the decedent may file the petition without authorization or approval of the court in which the guardianship proceeding is pending. *(Stats.1990, c. 79 (A.B.759), § 14, operative July 1, 1991.)*

Law Revision Commission Comments

1990 Enactment

Section 6606 continues Section 6606 of the repealed Probate Code without substantive change. Paragraph (4) of subdivision (a) recognizes that the court is authorized to set aside a small estate to a child who is a minor at the time of the decedent's death (as distinguished from a requirement that the child be a minor at the time the petition is filed or the time the court order under this chapter is made or some other time). See Section 6609(c). See also Section 6601 (defining "minor child"). Subdivision (b) is consistent with Section 13650(c) (determination or confirmation of property passing or belonging to surviving spouse). See also Section 13051(a) (collection or transfer of small estate without administration). As to a surviving spouse's waiver of rights at death, see Sections 140–147.

This section does not apply if the decedent died before July 1, 1987. See Section 6614. As to the application of any amendments made after that date, see Section 3. A reference to a provision of the former statute is deemed to be a reference to the comparable provisions of this chapter. See Section 6615.

Background on Section 6606 of Repealed Code

Section 6606 was added by 1986 Cal.Stat. ch. 783 § 23. The section continued the provisions of former Probate Code Section 641 (repealed by 1986 Cal.Stat. ch. 783 § 9) that described the persons authorized to file a petition and added paragraph (4) of subdivision (a) and all of subdivision (b), which were new provisions. For background on the provisions of this chapter, see the Comment to this chapter under the chapter heading. [20 Cal.L.Rev.Comm.Reports 1001 (1990)].

Research References

Forms

California Transactions Forms--Estate Planning § 19:12, Small Estate Set-Aside.

West's California Code Forms, Probate § 6602 Form 1, Petition to Set Aside Small Estate.

Treatises and Practice Aids

Witkin, California Summary 10th Wills and Probate § 782, Petition to Set Aside.

§ 6607. Notice of hearing; concurrent with hearing of petition for probate or administration

(a) Where proceedings for the administration of the estate of the decedent are not pending when the petition is filed under this chapter and the petition under this chapter is not joined with a petition for the probate of the decedent's will or for administration of the estate of the decedent, the petitioner shall give notice of the hearing on the petition as provided in Section 1220 to (1) each person named as executor in the decedent's will and to (2) each heir or devisee of the decedent, if known to the petitioner. A copy of the petition shall be sent with the notice of hearing to the surviving spouse, each child, and each devisee who is not petitioning.

(b) If the petition under this chapter is filed with a petition for the probate of the decedent's will or with a petition for administration of the estate of the deceased spouse, notice of the hearing on the petition shall be given to the persons and in the manner prescribed by Section 8003 and shall be included in the notice required by that section.

(c) If proceedings for the administration of the estate of the decedent are pending when the petition is filed under this chapter and the hearing of the petition for probate of the will or administration of the estate of the decedent is set for a day more than 15 days after the filing of the petition filed under this chapter, the petition under this chapter shall be set for hearing at the same time as the petition for probate of the will or for administration of the estate, and notice of hearing on the petition filed under this chapter shall be given by the petitioner as provided in Section 1220. If the hearing of the petition for probate of the will or for administration of the estate is not set for hearing for a day more than 15 days after the filing of the petition under this chapter, (1) the petition filed under this chapter shall be set for hearing at least 15 days after the date on which it is filed, (2) notice of the hearing on the petition filed under this chapter shall be given by the petitioner as provided in Section 1220, and (3) if the petition for probate of the will or for administration of the estate has not already been heard, that petition shall be continued until that date and heard at the same time unless the court otherwise orders. *(Stats.1990, c. 79 (A.B.759), § 14, operative July 1, 1991.)*

Law Revision Commission Comments

1990 Enactment

Section 6607 continues Section 6607 of the repealed Probate Code without substantive change. See also Section 1206 (notice to known heirs or known devisees). Subdivision (b) is comparable to subdivision (a) of Section 13655 (determination or confirmation of property passing or belonging to surviving spouse). For general provisions relating to notice of hearing, see Sections 1200–1221. See also Sections 1250–1252 (request for special notice), 1260–1265 (proof of giving notice). This section does not apply if the decedent died before July 1, 1987. See Section 6614. As to the application of any amendments made after that date, see Section 3. A reference to a provision of the former statute is deemed to be a reference to the comparable provisions of this chapter. See Section 6615.

The notice provisions referred to in Section 6607 do not apply to a particular notice where the notice was delivered, mailed, posted, or first published before July 1, 1991. In such a case, the applicable law in effect before July 1, 1991, continues to apply to the giving of the notice. See Section 1200(c).

Background on Section 6607 of Repealed Code

Section 6607 was added by 1986 Cal.Stat. ch. 783 § 23 and was amended by 1987 Cal.Stat. ch. 923 § 92 and 1988 Cal.Stat. ch. 1199 § 78. Subdivision (a) continued the substance of subdivision (a) of former Probate Code Section 643 (repealed by 1986 Cal.Stat. ch. 783 § 9) but specified the persons to whom the notice of hearing is to be mailed in place of the reference to former Section 1200.5 contained in former Section 643 and added the requirement that a copy of the petition be mailed with the notice of hearing given to the surviving spouse, each child, and each devisee, who is not petitioning. Subdivision (b) superseded former Probate Code Section 642 (repealed by 1986 Cal.Stat. ch. 783 § 9). Subdivision (c) continued subdivision (b) of former Probate Code Section 643 (repealed by 1986 Cal.Stat. ch. 783 § 9) without substantive change but with the addition of the phrase "unless the court otherwise orders" at the end of the subdivision. The 1987 amendment revised the provisions relating to notice. As to the 1987 amendment, see Communication from California Law Revision Commission Concerning Assembly Bill 708, 19 Cal.L.Revision Comm'n Reports 545, 561–62 (1988); Comments to Conforming Revisions and Repeals, 19 Cal.L.Revision Comm'n Reports 391, 450 (1988). The 1988 amendment corrected section references and conformed terminology to revisions made in the Probate Code in 1988. As to the 1988 amendment, see Comments to Conforming Revisions and Repeals, 19 Cal.L.Revision Comm'n Reports 1031, 1090 (1988). For background on the provisions of this chapter, see the Comment to this chapter under the chapter heading. [20 Cal.L.Rev.Comm.Reports 1001 (1990)].

Research References

Forms

West's California Code Forms, Probate § 6602 Form 1, Petition to Set Aside Small Estate.

Treatises and Practice Aids

Witkin, California Summary 10th Wills and Probate § 783, Notice and Hearing.

§ 6608. Inventory and appraisal; filing

If a petition is filed under this chapter, the personal representative, or the petitioner if no personal representative has been appointed, shall file with the clerk of the court, prior to the hearing of the petition, an inventory and appraisal made as provided in Part 3 (commencing with Section 8800) of Division 7. The personal representative or the petitioner, as the case may be, may appraise the assets which a personal representative could appraise under Section 8901. *(Stats. 1990, c. 79 (A.B.759), § 14, operative July 1, 1991.)*

Law Revision Commission Comments

1990 Enactment

Section 6608 continues Section 6608 of the repealed Probate Code without substantive change. This section does not apply if the decedent died before July 1, 1987. See Section 6614. As to the application of any amendments made after that date, see Section 3. A reference to a provision of the former statute is deemed to be a reference to the comparable provisions of this chapter. See Section 6615.

Background on Section 6608 of Repealed Code

Section 6608 was added by 1986 Cal.Stat. ch. 783 § 23 and was amended by 1988 Cal.Stat. ch. 1199 § 78.5. The section continued the requirement of former Probate Code Section 644 (repealed by 1986 Cal.Stat. ch. 783 § 9) that an inventory and appraisement be filed. The former provision was revised to conform to the then existing provisions relating to inventory and appraisement. See former Probate Code Sections 600–611 (repealed by 1988 Cal.Stat. ch. 1199 § 51). The requirement that the inventory and appraisement be filed before the hearing of the petition was substituted for the requirement of former Section 644 that the inventory and appraisement be filed within such time as the court may allow. The 1988 amendment corrected section references and conformed terminology to revisions made in the Probate Code in 1988. As to the 1988 amendment, see Comments to Conforming Revisions and Repeals, 19 Cal.L.Revision Comm'n Reports 1031, 1090 (1988). For background on the provisions of this chapter, see the Comment to this chapter under the chapter heading. [20 Cal.L.Rev.Comm.Reports 1001 (1990)].

Research References

Forms

West's California Code Forms, Probate § 6602 Form 1, Petition to Set Aside Small Estate.

Treatises and Practice Aids

Witkin, California Summary 10th Wills and Probate § 592, Requirement Of Inventory and Appraisal.

Witkin, California Summary 10th Wills and Probate § 783, Notice and Hearing.

§ 6609. Determination of whether to make order; assignment of estate; unpaid liabilities; title to property

(a) If the court determines that the net value of the decedent's estate, over and above all liens and encumbrances at the date of death of the decedent and over and above the value of any probate homestead interest set apart out of the decedent's estate under Section 6520, does not exceed twenty thousand dollars ($20,000) as of the date of the decedent's death, the court shall make an order under this section unless the court determines that making an order under this section would be inequitable under the circumstances of the particular case.

(b) In determining whether to make an order under this section, the court shall consider the needs of the surviving spouse and minor children, the liens and encumbrances on the property of the decedent's estate, the claims of creditors, the needs of the heirs or devisees of the decedent, the intent of the decedent with respect to the property in the estate and the estate plan of the decedent as expressed in inter vivos and testamentary transfers or by other means, and any other relevant considerations. If the surviving spouse has remarried at the time the petition is heard, it shall be presumed that the needs of the surviving spouse do not justify the setting aside of the small estate, or any portion thereof, to the surviving spouse. This presumption is a presumption affecting the burden of proof.

(c) Subject to subdivision (d), if the court makes an order under this section, the court shall assign the whole of the decedent's estate, subject to all liens and encumbrances on property in the estate at the date of the decedent's death, to the surviving spouse and the minor children of the decedent, or any one or more of them.

(d) If there are any liabilities for expenses of the last illness, funeral charges, or expenses of administration that are unpaid at the time the court makes an order under this section, the court shall make such orders as are necessary so that those unpaid liabilities are paid.

(e) Title to property in the decedent's estate vests absolutely in the surviving spouse, minor children, or any or all of them, as provided in the order, subject to all liens and encumbrances on property in the estate at the date of the decedent's death, and there shall be no further proceedings in the administration of the decedent's estate unless additional property in the decedent's estate is discovered. *(Stats.1990, c. 79 (A.B.759), § 14, operative July 1, 1991.)*

Law Revision Commission Comments

1990 Enactment

Section 6609 continues Section 6609 of the repealed Probate Code without substantive change. The court may decline to set aside a small estate if the court determines that it would be inequitable to do so. An appeal may be taken from an order made under this section. See Section 7240.

The court may assign the estate to the minor child or minor children of the decedent even if there is a surviving spouse. This may be desirable, for example, if the minor children live apart from the surviving spouse or where the minor children are not children of the surviving spouse. In this respect, Section 6609 is consistent with Section 6510 (setting aside exempt property other than family dwelling) and Section 6521 (setting apart probate homestead).

The court may assign the estate to a surviving spouse even if the surviving spouse has remarried. Permitting the small estate to be set aside to a surviving spouse, whether or not remarried, makes Section 6609 consistent with Section 6510 (setting aside exempt property other than family dwelling) and Section 6521 (setting apart probate homestead). The last two sentences of subdivision (b) place on the remarried surviving spouse the burden of proof to establish the need for the small estate set aside.

Subdivision (b) specifies matters to be considered in determining whether to make an order under the section. Under some circumstances, the court may order that the small estate be set aside to one of the minor children and that the other minor children and the spouse be excluded, or that the small estate be set aside in unequal shares to the minor children, or that the small estate be set aside to the surviving spouse and that the minor children be excluded. In determining the assignment to make, the court must take into account the various considerations listed in subdivision (b). See also Section 6604(b)(8) (petition must include the requested disposition of the decedent's estate and the considerations justifying the requested disposition).

Under subdivision (d), the court may set aside a small estate whether or not expenses of last illness, funeral charges, and expenses of administration have been paid, but the court must make an appropriate order to ensure that they will be paid.

For general provisions, see Sections 1000–1004 (rules of practice), 1040–1050 (hearings and orders). This section does not apply if the decedent died before July 1, 1987. See Section 6614. As to the application of any amendments made after that date, see Section 3. A reference to a provision of the former statute is deemed to be a reference to the comparable provisions of this chapter. See Section 6615.

Background on Section 6609 of Repealed Code

Section 6609 was added by 1986 Cal.Stat. ch. 783 § 23. The section superseded former Probate Code Section 645 (repealed by 1986 Cal.Stat. ch. 783 § 9).

Section 6609 made these significant substantive changes in the former law:

(1) Under Section 6609, the court may decline to set aside a small estate if the court determines that it would be inequitable to do so. Under former Section 645, the court had no discretion; the court was required to set aside the small estate if the court made the findings prescribed by that section.

(2) Under Section 6609, the court may assign the estate to the minor child or minor children of the decedent even if there is a surviving spouse. Former law did not permit the small estate to be assigned to the minor child or children if there was an unmarried surviving spouse.

(3) Under Section 6609, the court may assign the estate to a surviving spouse even if the surviving spouse has remarried. Under former Section 645, the small estate could be set aside only to a "surviving spouse who has not theretofore remarried."

Subdivision (b) of Section 6609, which specifies matters to be considered in determining whether to make an order under the section, was a new provision drawn from subdivision (a) of Section 6523 which specifies matters to be considered in selecting and setting apart a probate homestead.

The word "mortgages," which was found in former Section 645, was omitted as unnecessary, mortgages being included within the phrase "liens and encumbrances."

Subdivision (d) of Section 6609 superseded the portion of the first sentence of former Section 645 that required expenses of last illness, funeral charges, and expenses of administration to be paid before the court could set aside a small estate. Under subdivision (d), the court may set aside a small estate whether or not such expenses have been paid, but the court must make an appropriate order to ensure that they will be paid.

Subdivision (e) of Section 6609 continued the last sentence of former Section 645, revised to reflect the new authority of the court to assign the small estate to one or more of the minor children of the decedent where there is a surviving spouse.

For background on the provisions of this chapter, see the Comment to this chapter under the chapter heading. [20 Cal.L.Rev.Comm.Reports 1001 (1990)].

Research References

Forms

California Transactions Forms--Estate Planning § 19:12, Small Estate Set-Aside.
West's California Code Forms, Probate § 6602 Form 1, Petition to Set Aside Small Estate.
West's California Code Forms, Probate § 6602 Form 2, Order Setting Aside Small Estate.

Treatises and Practice Aids

Witkin, California Summary 10th Wills and Probate § 784, Order.
Witkin, California Summary 10th Wills and Probate § 785, Personal Liability for Unsecured Debts.

§ 6610. Effect of order

Upon becoming final, an order under Section 6609 shall be conclusive on all persons, whether or not they are then in being. *(Stats.1990, c. 79 (A.B.759), § 14, operative July 1, 1991.)*

Law Revision Commission Comments

1990 Enactment

Section 6610 continues Section 6610 of the repealed Probate Code without change. This section gives the order the same effect as an order under Section 13657 (effect of order determining or confirming property passing or belonging to surviving spouse). For general provisions, see Sections 1040–1050 (hearings and orders). This section does not apply if the decedent died before July 1, 1987. See Section 6614. As to the application of any amendments made after that date, see Section 3. A reference to a provision of the former statute is deemed to be a reference to the comparable provisions of this chapter. See Section 6615.

Background on Section 6610 of Repealed Code

Section 6610 was added by 1986 Cal.Stat. ch. 783 § 23. The section superseded former Probate Code Section 645.1 (repealed by 1986 Cal.Stat. ch. 783 § 9). The language in former Section 645.1 referring to fraud or the erroneously assumed deceased appearing has been omitted from Section 6610 as unnecessary. The omission of this language make no substantive change in the effect of the section. See McMillan v. Boese, 45 Cal.App.2d 764, 115 P.2d 37 (1941). For background on the provisions of this chapter, see the Comment to this chapter under the chapter heading. [20 Cal.L.Rev.Comm.Reports 1001 (1990)].

Research References

Treatises and Practice Aids

Witkin, California Summary 10th Wills and Probate § 784, Order.

§ 6611. Unsecured debts; liability; actions and proceedings

(a) Subject to the limitations and conditions specified in this section, the person or persons in whom title vested pursuant to Section 6609 are personally liable for the unsecured debts of the decedent.

(b) The personal liability of a person under this section does not exceed the fair market value at the date of the decedent's death of the property title to which vested in that person pursuant to Section 6609, less the total of all of the following:

(1) The amount of any liens and encumbrances on that property.

(2) The value of any probate homestead interest set apart under Section 6520 out of that property.

(3) The value of any other property set aside under Section 6510 out of that property.

(c) In any action or proceeding based upon an unsecured debt of the decedent, the surviving spouse of the decedent, the child or children of the decedent, or the guardian of the minor child or children of the decedent, may assert any defense, cross-complaint, or setoff which would have been available to the decedent if the decedent had not died.

(d) If proceedings are commenced in this state for the administration of the estate of the decedent and the time for filing claims has commenced, any action upon the personal liability of a person under this section is barred to the same extent as provided for claims under Part 4 (commencing with Section 9000) of Division 7, except as to the following:

(1) Creditors who commence judicial proceedings for the enforcement of the debt and serve the person liable under this section with the complaint therein prior to the expiration of the time for filing claims.

(2) Creditors who have or who secure an acknowledgment in writing of the person liable under this section that that person is liable for the debts.

(3) Creditors who file a timely claim in the proceedings for the administration of the estate of the decedent.

(e) Section 366.2 of the Code of Civil Procedure applies in an action under this section. *(Stats.1990, c. 79 (A.B.759), § 14, operative July 1, 1991. Amended by Stats.1990, c. 140 (S.B.1855), § 4.1, operative July 1, 1991; Stats.1992, c. 178 (S.B.1496), § 32.)*

Law Revision Commission Comments

1990 Enactment

Section 6611 continues Section 6611 of the repealed Probate Code without substantive change. The personal liability of a person who takes only a share or portion of the decedent's estate is limited to the net value of the share or portion (fair market value less liens and encumbrances and any probate homestead or exempt property set apart out of the share), rather than the net value of the entire estate.

Subdivision (e) is drawn from Section 13552 (liability for debts of deceased spouse). The subdivision is a limitation on the one-year limitation period of subdivision (c) where estate proceedings are commenced, and provides the same period as for creditors' claims in estate proceedings generally.

This section does not apply if the decedent died before July 1, 1987. See Section 6614. As to the application of any amendments made after that date, see Section 3. A reference to a provision of the former statute is deemed to be a reference to the comparable provisions of this chapter. See Section 6615.

1990 Amendment

Section 6611 (enacted as a part of the new Probate Code by 1990 Cal.Stat. ch. 79 § 14) was amended by 1990 Cal.Stat. ch. 140 § 4.1 to delete former subdivision (c), which conflicted with Code of Civil Procedure Section 353 (statute of limitations), and to make clear that the general one-year statute of limitations applicable to all causes of action against a decedent is applicable to liability for the decedent's debts under Section 6611. For background on the 1990 amendment, see Recommendation Relating to Notice to Creditors in Estate Administration, 20 Cal.L.Revision Comm'n Reports 507 (1990). [20 Cal.L.Rev.Comm.Reports 1001 (1990)].

1992 Amendment

Section 6611 is amended to revise a section reference. This revision is a technical, nonsubstantive change. [22 Cal.L.Rev.Comm.Reports 895 (1992)].

Background on Section 6611 of Repealed Code

Section 6611 was added by 1986 Cal.Stat. ch. 783 § 23 and was amended by 1987 Cal.Stat. ch. 923 § 92.5. The section continued former Probate Code Section 645.3 (repealed by 1986 Cal.Stat. ch. 783 § 9) without substantive change, except as follows:

(1) Subdivision (b) of Section 6611 made clear that the personal liability of a person who takes only a share or portion of the decedent's estate is limited to the net value of the share or portion (fair market value less liens and encumbrances and any probate homestead or exempt property set apart out of the share), rather than the net value of the entire estate.

(2) Subdivision (e) of Section 6611 was new.

The 1987 amendment revised the provisions relating to notice. As to the 1987 amendment, see Communication from California Law Revision Commission Concerning Assembly Bill 708, 19 Cal.L.Revision Comm'n Reports 545, 560 (1988); Comments to Conforming Revisions and Repeals, 19 Cal.L.Revision Comm'n Reports 391, 450 (1988). For background on the provisions of this chapter, see the Comment to this chapter under the chapter heading. [20 Cal.L.Rev.Comm.Reports 1001 (1990)].

Research References

Forms

California Transactions Forms--Estate Planning § 19:12, Small Estate Set-Aside.

Treatises and Practice Aids

Witkin, California Summary 10th Wills and Probate § 785, Personal Liability for Unsecured Debts.

§ 6612. Determinations not to make order under § 6609; action on petition for probate or administration

If a petition filed under this chapter is filed with a petition for the probate of the decedent's will or for administration of the estate of the decedent and the court determines not to make an order under Section 6609, the court shall act on the petition for probate of the decedent's will or for administration of the estate of the decedent in the same manner as if no petition had been filed under this chapter, and the estate shall then be administered in the same manner as if no petition had been filed under this chapter. *(Stats.1990, c. 79 (A.B.759), § 14, operative July 1, 1991.)*

Law Revision Commission Comments

1990 Enactment

Section 6612 continues Section 6612 of the repealed Probate Code without change. Under Section 6609, the court is required to deny a petition filed under this chapter if the decedent's estate is not a small estate (see Sections 6600, 6609), or if there is neither a surviving spouse nor a minor child. The court also may decline to order a small estate set-aside when it would be inequitable to do so. See Section 6609.

For general provisions, see Sections 1000–1004 (rules of practice), 1020–1023 (petitions and other papers), 1040–1050 (hearings and orders). This section does not apply if the decedent died before July 1, 1987. See Section 6614. As to the application of any amendments made after that date, see Section 3. A reference to a provision of the former statute is deemed to be a reference to the comparable provisions of this chapter. See Section 6615.

Background on Section 6612 of Repealed Code

Section 6612 was added by 1986 Cal.Stat. ch. 783 § 23. The section was drawn from former Probate Code Section 646 (repealed by 1986 Cal.Stat. ch. 783 § 9) but the language of the former section was revised to recognize that the court has discretion to deny a petition filed under this chapter. See Section 6609. For background on the provisions of this chapter, see the Comment to this chapter under the chapter heading. [20 Cal.L.Rev.Comm.Reports 1001 (1990)].

Research References

Forms

West's California Code Forms, Probate § 6602 Form 1, Petition to Set Aside Small Estate.

Treatises and Practice Aids

Witkin, California Summary 10th Wills and Probate § 784, Order.

§ 6613. Attorney's fees

The attorney's fees for services performed in connection with the filing of a petition and the obtaining of a court order under this chapter shall be determined by private agreement between the attorney and the client and are not subject to approval by the court. If there is no agreement between the attorney and the client concerning the attorney's fees for services performed in connection with the filing of a petition and obtaining of a court order under this chapter and there is a dispute concerning the reasonableness of the attorney's fees for those services, a petition may be filed with the court in the same proceeding requesting that the court determine the reasonableness of the attorney's fees for those services. If there is an agreement between the attorney and the client concerning the attorney's fees for services performed in connection with the filing of a petition and obtaining a court order under this chapter and there is a dispute concerning the meaning of the agreement, a petition may be filed with the court in the same proceeding requesting that the court determine the dispute. *(Stats.1990, c. 79 (A.B.759), § 14, operative July 1, 1991.)*

Law Revision Commission Comments

1990 Enactment

Section 6613 continues Section 6613 of the repealed Probate Code without substantive change. This section is the same as Section 13660 (petition for determination or confirmation of property passing or belonging to surviving spouse). Section 6613 continues former law and practice but gives the probate court authority to determine disputes concerning the attorney's fee for services performed in connection with the filing of a petition and the obtaining of a court order under this chapter. The court has no jurisdiction to determine disputes concerning attorney's fees for other services, such as termination of joint tenancies, collection of insurance, and the like.

For general provisions, see Sections 1000–1004 (rules of practice), 1020–1023 (petitions and other papers), 1040–1050 (hearings and orders). For general provisions relating to notice of hearing, see Sections 1200–1221. See also Sections 1250–1252 (request for special notice), 1260–1265 (proof of giving notice). This section does not apply if the decedent died before July 1, 1987. See Section 6614. As to the application of any amendments made after that date, see Section 3. A reference to a provision of the former statute is deemed to be a reference to the comparable provisions of this chapter. See Section 6615.

Background on Section 6613 of Repealed Code

Section 6613 was a new provision added by 1986 Cal.Stat. ch. 783 § 23. For background on the provisions of this chapter, see the Comment to this chapter under the chapter heading. [20 Cal.L.Rev.Comm.Reports 1001 (1990)].

Research References

Treatises and Practice Aids

Witkin, California Summary 10th Wills and Probate § 31, Major Changes.

Witkin, California Summary 10th Wills and Probate § 786, Attorneys' Fees.

§ 6614. Application of law

Sections 6600 to 6613, inclusive, do not apply if the decedent died before July 1, 1987. If the decedent died before July 1, 1987, the case continues to be governed by the law applicable to the case prior to July 1, 1987. *(Stats.1990, c. 79 (A.B.759), § 14, operative July 1, 1991.)*

Application

For law applicable if decedent died before July 1, 1987, see Probate Code § 6615 and Law Revision Commission Comments under heading and sections of this chapter.

Law Revision Commission Comments

1990 Enactment

Section 6614 continues Section 6614 of the repealed Probate Code without substantive change. This section makes clear that Sections 6600–6613 do not apply if the decedent died before July 1, 1987, the operative date of those sections. If the decedent died before that date, the right to a small estate set-aside is determined under the law that was applicable prior to July 1, 1987. The application of Sections 6600 to 6613 does not apply if the decedent died before July 1, 1987 because in a case where the decedent died before that date there was a right to have a small estate set-aside. Under Sections 6600 to 6613, the court may decline to order a small estate set-aside when it would be inequitable to do so. See Section 6609.

Background on Section 6614 of Repealed Code

Section 6614 was added by 1986 Cal.Stat. ch. 783 § 23. The section superseded former Probate Code Section 647.5 (repealed by 1986 Cal.Stat. ch. 783 § 9). For background on the provisions of this chapter, see the Comment to this chapter under the chapter heading. [20 Cal.L.Rev.Comm.Reports 1001 (1990)].

§ 6615. References to former sections deemed references to comparable provisions of this chapter

A reference in any statute of this state or in a written instrument, including a will or trust, to a provision of former Sections 640 to 647.5, inclusive, repealed by Chapter 783 of the Statutes of 1986, shall be deemed to be a reference to the comparable provisions of this chapter. *(Stats.1990, c. 79 (A.B.759), § 14, operative July 1, 1991.)*

Law Revision Commission Comments

1990 Enactment

Section 6615 continues Section 6615 of the repealed Probate Code without substantive change. This section makes clear that, after the operative date of this chapter of the repealed Probate Code (July 1, 1987), a reference in a statute or written instrument to a provision of former law will be deemed to be a reference to the comparable provision of this chapter.

Background on Section 6615 of Repealed Code

Section 6615 was a new provision added by 1986 Cal.Stat. ch. 783 § 23. The section was drawn from former Probate Code Section 1490 and from former Probate Code Section 649.6 (repealed by 1986 Cal.Stat. ch. 783 § 9). For background on the provisions of this chapter, see the Comment to this chapter under the chapter heading. [20 Cal.L.Rev.Comm.Reports 1001 (1990)].

Part 4

ESCHEAT OF DECEDENT'S PROPERTY

Law Revision Commission Comments

1990 Enactment

This part supersedes Part 4 (commencing with Section 6800) of Division 6 of the repealed Probate Code. The superseded part was enacted upon recommendation of the California Law Revision Commission. See Tentative Recommendation Relating to Wills and Intestate Succession, 16 Cal.L.Revision Comm'n Reports 2301 (1982). See also Recommendation Relating to Escheat, 8 Cal.L.Revision Comm'n Reports 1001 (1967). [20 Cal.L.Rev.Comm.Reports 1001 (1990)].

§ 6800. Failure to leave person to take by testate or intestate succession; escheat

(a) If a decedent, whether or not the decedent was domiciled in this state, leaves no one to take the decedent's estate or any portion thereof by testate succession, and no one other than a government or governmental subdivision or agency to take the estate or a portion thereof by intestate succession, under the laws of this state or of any other jurisdiction, the same escheats at the time of the decedent's death in accordance with this part.

(b) Property that escheats to the state under this part, whether held by the state or its officers, is subject to the same charges and trusts to which it would have been subject if it had passed by succession and is also subject to the provisions of Title 10 (commencing with Section 1300) of Part 3 of the Code of Civil Procedure relating to escheated estates. *(Stats. 1990, c. 79 (A.B.759), § 14, operative July 1, 1991.)*

Law Revision Commission Comments

1990 Enactment

Section 6800 continues Section 6800 of the repealed Probate Code without substantive change.

Background on Section 6800 of Repealed Code

Section 6800 was added by 1983 Cal.Stat. ch. 842 § 55. The section continued the substance of subdivisions (a) and (b) of former Probate Code Section 231 (repealed by 1983 Cal.Stat. ch. 842 § 19). For background on the provisions of this part, see the Comment to this part under the part heading. [20 Cal.L.Rev.Comm.Reports 1001 (1990)].

Research References

Forms

Cal. Transaction Forms - Bus. Transactions § 23:4, Unclaimed Property.

Treatises and Practice Aids

Witkin, California Summary 10th Wills and Probate § 99, Nature and Scope Of Statute.
Witkin, California Summary 10th Wills and Probate § 102, Benefits Distributable from Certain Trusts.

§ 6801. Real property

Real property in this state escheats to this state in accordance with Section 6800. *(Stats.1990, c. 79 (A.B.759), § 14, operative July 1, 1991.)*

Law Revision Commission Comments

1990 Enactment

Section 6801 continues Section 6801 of the repealed Probate Code without change.

Background on Section 6801 of Repealed Code

Section 6801 was added by 1983 Cal.Stat. ch. 842 § 55. The section continued former Probate Code Section 232 (repealed by 1983 Cal.Stat. ch. 842 § 19). For background on the provisions of this part, see the Comment to this part under the part heading. [20 Cal.L.Rev.Comm.Reports 1001 (1990)].

Research References

Treatises and Practice Aids

Witkin, California Summary 10th Wills and Probate § 100, Real and Tangible Personal Property.

§ 6802. Personal property

All tangible personal property owned by the decedent, wherever located at the decedent's death, that was customarily kept in this state prior to the decedent's death, escheats to this state in accordance with Section 6800. *(Stats.1990, c. 79 (A.B.759), § 14, operative July 1, 1991.)*

Law Revision Commission Comments

1990 Enactment

Section 6802 continues Section 6802 of the repealed Probate Code without change.

Background on Section 6802 of Repealed Code

Section 6802 was added by 1983 Cal.Stat. ch. 842 § 55. The section continued former Probate Code Section 233 (repealed by 1983 Cal.Stat. ch. 842 § 19). For background on the provisions of this part, see the Comment to this part under the part heading. [20 Cal.L.Rev.Comm.Reports 1001 (1990)].

Research References

Treatises and Practice Aids

Witkin, California Summary 10th Wills and Probate § 100, Real and Tangible Personal Property.

§ 6803. Personal property subject to control of superior court of state; property going to another jurisdiction

(a) Subject to subdivision (b), all tangible personal property owned by the decedent that is subject to the control of a superior court of this state for purposes of administration under this code escheats to this state in accordance with Section 6800.

(b) The property described in subdivision (a) does not escheat to this state but goes to another jurisdiction if the other jurisdiction claims the property and establishes all of the following:

(1) The other jurisdiction is entitled to the property under its law.

(2) The decedent customarily kept the property in that jurisdiction prior to the decedent's death.

(3) This state has the right to escheat and take tangible personal property being administered as part of a decedent's estate in that jurisdiction if the decedent customarily kept the property in this state prior to the decedent's death. *(Stats. 1990, c. 79 (A.B.759), § 14, operative July 1, 1991.)*

Law Revision Commission Comments

1990 Enactment

Section 6803 continues Section 6803 of the repealed Probate Code without substantive change. The words "and disposition" have been omitted as unnecessary, "administration" covering "disposition" as well as all other aspects of administration of a decedent's estate.

Background on Section 6803 of Repealed Code

Section 6803 was added by 1983 Cal.Stat. ch. 842 § 55 and was amended by 1988 Cal.Stat. ch. 1199 § 79. The section continued former Probate Code Section 234 (repealed by 1983 Cal.Stat. ch. 842 § 19). The 1988 amendment corrected a section reference. As to the 1988 amendment, see Comments to Conforming Revisions and Repeals, 19 Cal.L.Revision Comm'n Reports 1031, 1091 (1988). For background on the provisions of this part, see the Comment to this part under the part heading. [20 Cal.L.Rev.Comm.Reports 1001 (1990)].

Research References

Treatises and Practice Aids

Witkin, California Summary 10th Wills and Probate § 100, Real and Tangible Personal Property.

§ 6804. Intangible property

All intangible property owned by the decedent escheats to this state in accordance with Section 6800 if the decedent was domiciled in this state at the time of the decedent's death. *(Stats.1990, c. 79 (A.B.759), § 14, operative July 1, 1991.)*

Law Revision Commission Comments

1990 Enactment

Section 6804 continues Section 6804 of the repealed Probate Code without change.

Background on Section 6804 of Repealed Code

Section 6804 was added by 1983 Cal.Stat. ch. 842 § 55. The section continued former Probate Code Section 235 (repealed by 1983 Cal.Stat. ch. 842 § 19). For background on the provisions of this part, see the Comment to this part under the part heading. [20 Cal.L.Rev.Comm.Reports 1001 (1990)].

Research References

Treatises and Practice Aids

Witkin, California Summary 10th Wills and Probate § 101, Intangible Property.

§ 6805. Intangible property subject to control of superior court of state; property going to another jurisdiction

(a) Subject to subdivision (b), all intangible property owned by the decedent that is subject to the control of a superior court of this state for purposes of administration under this code escheats to this state in accordance with Section 6800 whether or not the decedent was domiciled in this state at the time of the decedent's death.

(b) The property described in subdivision (a) does not escheat to this state but goes to another jurisdiction if the other jurisdiction claims the property and establishes all of the following:

(1) The other jurisdiction is entitled to the property under its laws.

(2) The decedent was domiciled in that jurisdiction at the time of the decedent's death.

(3) This state has the right to escheat and take intangible property being administered as part of a decedent's estate in that jurisdiction if the decedent was domiciled in this state at the time of the decedent's death. *(Stats.1990, c. 79 (A.B. 759), § 14, operative July 1, 1991.)*

Law Revision Commission Comments

1990 Enactment

Section 6805 continues Section 6805 of the repealed Probate Code without substantive change. The words "and disposition" have been omitted as unnecessary, "administration" covering "disposition" as well as all other aspects of administration of a decedent's estate.

Background on Section 6805 of Repealed Code

Section 6805 was added by 1983 Cal.Stat. ch. 842 § 55 and was amended by 1988 Cal.Stat. ch. 1199 § 79.5. The section continued former Probate Code Section 236 (repealed by 1983 Cal.Stat. ch. 842 § 19). The 1988 amendment corrected a section reference. As to the 1988 amendment, see Comments to Conforming Revisions and Repeals, 19 Cal.L.Revision Comm'n Reports 1031, 1091 (1988). For background on the provisions of this part, see the Comment to this part under the part heading. [20 Cal.L.Rev.Comm.Reports 1001 (1990)].

Research References

Treatises and Practice Aids

Witkin, California Summary 10th Wills and Probate § 101, Intangible Property.

§ 6806. Property distributable from trusts; benefit plans; reversion to trust or fund from which distributable

Notwithstanding any other provision of law, a benefit consisting of money or other property distributable from a trust established under a plan providing health and welfare, pension, vacation, severance, retirement benefit, death benefit, unemployment insurance or similar benefits does not pass to or escheat to the state under this part but goes to the trust or fund from which it is distributable, subject to the provisions of Section 1521 of the Code of Civil Procedure. However, if such plan has terminated and the trust or fund has been distributed to the beneficiaries thereof prior to distribution of such benefit from the estate, such benefit passes to the state and escheats to the state under this part. *(Stats.1990, c. 79 (A.B.759), § 14, operative July 1, 1991.)*

Law Revision Commission Comments

1990 Enactment

Section 6806 continues Section 6806 of the repealed Probate Code without substantive change.

Background on Section 6806 of Repealed Code

Section 6806 was added by 1983 Cal.Stat. ch. 842 § 55. The section continued subdivision (c) of former Probate Code Section 231 (repealed by 1983 Cal.Stat. ch. 842 § 19). For background on the provisions of this part, see the Comment to this part under the part heading. [20 Cal.L.Rev.Comm.Reports 1001 (1990)].

Research References

Treatises and Practice Aids

Witkin, California Summary 10th Agency and Employment § 403, Nature Of Funds.

Witkin, California Summary 10th Wills and Probate § 102, Benefits Distributable from Certain Trusts.

Division 7

ADMINISTRATION OF ESTATES OF DECEDENTS

Part 1

GENERAL PROVISIONS

CHAPTER 1. PASSAGE OF DECEDENT'S PROPERTY

Law Revision Commission Comments

1990 Enactment

This chapter supersedes Chapter 1 of Part 1 (commencing with Section 7000) of Division 7 of the repealed Probate Code. The superseded chapter was enacted upon recommendation of the California Law Revision Commission. See Recommendation Relating to Rules of Procedure in Probate, 19 Cal.L.Revision Comm'n Reports 917 (1988). [20 Cal.L.Rev.Comm.Reports 1001 (1990)].

§ 7000. Passage to devisee or intestate heirs

Subject to Section 7001, title to a decedent's property passes on the decedent's death to the person to whom it is devised in the decedent's last will or, in the absence of such a devise, to the decedent's heirs as prescribed in the laws governing intestate succession. *(Stats.1990, c. 79 (A.B.759), § 14, operative July 1, 1991.)*

Law Revision Commission Comments

1990 Enactment

Section 7000 continues Section 7000 of the repealed Probate Code without change. The decedent's heirs are determined as provided in Part 2 (commencing with Section 6400) of Division 6 (intestate succession). The rule stated in Section 7000 is subject to limitations. See Section 7001 and the Comment thereto.

Background on Section 7000 of Repealed Code

Section 7000 was added by 1988 Cal.Stat. ch. 1199 § 80.5. The section restated the first part of former Probate Code Section 300 (repealed by 1988 Cal.Stat. ch. 1199 § 40) without substantive change. For background on the provisions of this chapter, see the Comment to this chapter under the chapter heading. [20 Cal.L.Rev.Comm.Reports 1001 (1990)].

Research References

Forms

California Transactions Forms--Estate Planning § 1:2, Probate System.

California Transactions Forms--Estate Planning § 1:6, Revocable Living Trust as Centerpiece.

California Transactions Forms--Estate Planning § 1:18, Property Subject to Probate; Intestacy.

California Transactions Forms--Estate Planning § 1:19, Nonprobate Transfers Under Prob C S5000.

Treatises and Practice Aids

Witkin, California Summary 10th Parent and Child § 509, No Third-Party Action for Redaction.

Witkin, California Summary 10th Real Property § 491B, (New) Notice Of Transfer Fee.

Witkin, California Summary 10th Trusts § 260, in General.

Witkin, California Summary 10th Wills and Probate § 1, Legislative Power Over Inheritance.

Witkin, California Summary 10th Wills and Probate § 100, Real and Tangible Personal Property.

Witkin, California Summary 10th Wills and Probate § 101, Intangible Property.

Witkin, California Summary 10th Wills and Probate § 402, Effect Of Appeal.

Witkin, California Summary 10th Wills and Probate § 404, Title to Decedent's Property.

Witkin, California Summary 10th Wills and Probate § 448, in General.

Witkin, California Summary 10th Wills and Probate § 519, Decedent's Cause Of Action.

Witkin, California Summary 10th Wills and Probate § 612, in General.

Witkin, California Summary 10th Wills and Probate § 618, in General.

Witkin, California Summary 10th Wills and Probate § 793, Definitions.

Witkin, California Summary 10th Wills and Probate § 819, Property Subject to Administration.

Witkin, California Summary 10th Wills and Probate § 829, Nature Of Proceeding.

Witkin, California Summary 10th Wills and Probate § 960, Governing Law.

§ 7001. Administration of decedent's property; rights of beneficiaries and creditors

The decedent's property is subject to administration under this code, except as otherwise provided by law, and is subject to the rights of beneficiaries, creditors, and other persons as provided by law. *(Stats.1990, c. 79 (A.B.759), § 14, operative July 1, 1991.)*

Law Revision Commission Comments

1990 Enactment

Section 7001 continues Section 7001 of the repealed Probate Code without change. Administration of the decedent's estate includes possession by the personal representative, control by the court, sale and other disposition of the property, charges of administration, and payment of debts and family allowance. The requirement of administration is subject to exceptions. See, e.g., Sections 5000 (contract rights), 5100–5407 (multiple party accounts), 13000–13660 (disposition without administration), 15000–18201 (trusts), and the law governing joint tenancy. For provisions relating to the rights of beneficiaries, creditors, and others, see, e.g., Sections 100–105 (effect of death of married person on community and quasi-community property), 260–295 (disclaimers), 6146–6147 (lapsed gifts), 6510–6511 (exempt property), 6520–6528 (probate homestead), 6540–6545 (family allowance), 6560–6573 (omitted spouse and children), 6600–6615 (small estate set-aside), 21400–21406 (abatement).

Background on Section 7001 of Repealed Code

Section 7001 was added by 1988 Cal.Stat. ch. 1199 § 80.5. The section restated the last part of former Probate Code Section 300 (repealed by 1988 Cal.Stat. ch. 1199 § 40) without substantive change. For background on the provisions of this chapter, see the Comment to this chapter under the chapter heading. [20 Cal.L.Rev.Comm.Reports 1001 (1990)].

Research References

Forms

California Transactions Forms--Estate Planning § 1:2, Probate System.

California Transactions Forms--Estate Planning § 1:6, Revocable Living Trust as Centerpiece.

California Transactions Forms--Estate Planning § 1:18, Property Subject to Probate; Intestacy.

California Transactions Forms--Estate Planning § 1:19, Nonprobate Transfers Under Prob C S5000.

California Transactions Forms--Estate Planning § 19:25, Pour-Over Wills.

Treatises and Practice Aids

Witkin, California Summary 10th Wills and Probate § 404, Title to Decedent's Property.

Witkin, California Summary 10th Wills and Probate § 405, Probate and Administration.

Witkin, California Summary 10th Wills and Probate § 519, Decedent's Cause Of Action.

Part 2

OPENING ESTATE ADMINISTRATION

Law Revision Commission Comments

1990 Enactment

This part supersedes Part 2 (commencing with Section 8000) of Division 7 of the repealed Probate Code. The superseded part was enacted upon recommendation of the California Law Revision Commission. See Recommendation Relating to Opening Estate Administration, 19 Cal.L.Revision Comm'n Reports 787 (1988). See also Communication from the California Law Revision Commission Concerning Assembly Bill 2841, 19 Cal.L.Revision Comm'n Reports 1201, 1231–35 (1988); Communication from the California Law Revision Commission Concerning Assembly Bill 158, 20 Cal.L.Revision Comm'n Reports 235, 236 (1990). [20 Cal.L.Rev.Comm.Reports 1001 (1990)].

CHAPTER 4. APPOINTMENT OF PERSONAL REPRESENTATIVE

ARTICLE 1. GENERAL PROVISIONS

Section

§ 8400. Power to administer estate; appointment effective upon issuance of letters; named executor; funeral expenses; preservation of estate

(a) A person has no power to administer the estate until the person is appointed personal representative and the appointment becomes effective. Appointment of a personal representative becomes effective when the person appointed is issued letters.

(b) Subdivision (a) applies whether or not the person is named executor in the decedent's will, except that a person named executor in the decedent's will may, before the appointment is made or becomes effective, pay funeral expenses and take necessary measures for the maintenance and preservation of the estate.

(c) The order appointing a personal representative shall state in capital letters on the first page of the order, in at least 12–point type, the following: "WARNING: THIS APPOINTMENT IS NOT EFFECTIVE UNTIL LETTERS HAVE ISSUED." *(Stats.1990, c. 79 (A.B.759), § 14, operative July 1, 1991. Amended by Stats.1996, c. 862 (A.B.2751), § 16.)*

Law Revision Commission Comments

1990 Enactment

Section 8400 continues Section 8400 of the repealed Probate Code without change. Letters may not be issued until the person appointed takes the oath of office and gives any required bond. See Section 8403 (oath) and Article 5 (commencing with Section 8480) (bond). It should be noted that a petitioner for appointment as personal representative may deliver or deposit property of the decedent in the petitioner's possession in a controlled account. See Section 8401. A person named executor in the will is under no duty to defend a contest of the will until appointment as executor. See Section 8250 (summons). See also Sections 300–301 (trust company as personal representative), 9605 (appointment does not discharge any claim the decedent has against personal representative).

Background on Section 8400 of Repealed Code

Section 8400 was added by 1988 Cal.Stat. ch. 1199 § 81.5. The section restated former Probate Code Section 400 (repealed by 1988 Cal.Stat. ch. 1199 § 43) without substantive change. For background on the provisions of this part, see the Comment to this part under the part heading. [20 Cal.L.Rev.Comm.Reports 1001 (1990)].

Research References

Forms

California Transactions Forms--Estate Planning § 1:2, Probate System.
California Transactions Forms--Estate Planning § 19:71, Statutory Qualifications.
California Transactions Forms--Estate Planning § 19:81, General Court Supervision.
California Transactions Forms--Estate Planning § 19:111, Retention by Attorney.
West's California Code Forms, Probate § 8006 Form 1, Order for Probate--Judicial Council Form DE-140.
West's California Code Forms, Probate § 8405 Form 1, Letters--Judicial Council Form DE-150.
West's California Code Forms, Probate § 9703 Form 1, Application for Order Requiring Deposit Of Funds and Assets Of Estate (And for Order for Reduced Bond).
West's California Judicial Council Forms DE-140, Order for Probate.

Treatises and Practice Aids

Witkin, California Summary 10th Wills and Probate § 66, Ancillary Administration.
Witkin, California Summary 10th Wills and Probate § 415, in General.
Witkin, California Summary 10th Wills and Probate § 431, in General.

§ 8401. Petitioner for appointment; deposit of property in institution; written receipt; withdrawal; liability of institution

(a) Notwithstanding Section 8400, a petitioner for appointment as personal representative may deliver property in the petitioner's possession to a trust company or financial institution for deposit, or allow a trust company or financial institution to retain on deposit property already in its possession, as provided in Chapter 3 (commencing with Section 9700) of Part 5.

(b) The petitioner shall obtain and file with the court a written receipt including the agreement of the trust company or financial institution that the property on deposit, including any earnings thereon, shall not be allowed to be withdrawn except on order of the court.

(c) In receiving and retaining property under this section, the trust company or financial institution is protected to the same extent as though it had received the property from a person who had been appointed personal representative. *(Stats.1990, c. 79 (A.B.759), § 14, operative July 1, 1991.)*

Law Revision Commission Comments

1990 Enactment

Section 8401 continues Section 8401 of the repealed Probate Code without change. See also Section 8483 (reduction of bond by deposit of assets).

Background on Section 8401 of Repealed Code

Section 8401 was added by 1988 Cal.Stat. ch. 1199 § 81.5. The section restated subdivision (b) of former Probate Code Section 541.1 (repealed by 1988 Cal.Stat. ch. 1199 § 48) and extended the coverage of the section to include "personal property" in addition to "money" and "securities." Section 8401 was amended by 1989 Cal.Stat. ch. 544 § 6 to refer to the procedures in Sections 9700–9705 for depositing money in an insured account in a financial institution and depositing personal property with a trust company. This continued a provision of former Section 541.1(b). For background on the provisions of this part, see the Comment to this part under the part heading. [20 Cal.L.Rev.Comm.Reports 1001 (1990)].

Research References

Forms

West's California Code Forms, Probate § 9703 Form 1, Application for Order Requiring Deposit Of Funds and Assets Of Estate (And for Order for Reduced Bond).

Treatises and Practice Aids

Witkin, California Summary 10th Wills and Probate § 415, in General.

§ 8402. Persons ineligible for appointment; minors; incapable persons; grounds for removal existing; non-U.S. residents; surviving business partner

(a) Notwithstanding any other provision of this chapter, a person is not competent to act as personal representative in any of the following circumstances:

(1) The person is under the age of majority.

(2) The person is subject to a conservatorship of the estate or is otherwise incapable of executing, or is otherwise unfit to execute, the duties of the office.

(3) There are grounds for removal of the person from office under Section 8502.

(4) The person is not a resident of the United States.

(5) The person is a surviving business partner of the decedent and an interested person objects to the appointment.

(b) Paragraphs (4) and (5) of subdivision (a) do not apply to a person named as executor or successor executor in the decedent's will. *(Stats.1990, c. 79 (A.B.759), § 14, operative July 1, 1991. Amended by Stats.2016, c. 703 (A.B.2881), § 19, eff. Jan. 1, 2017.)*

Law Revision Commission Comments

1990 Enactment

Section 8402 continues Section 8402 of the repealed Probate Code without change. Paragraph (3) of subdivision (a) enables the court to deny appointment of a personal representative if the personal representative would be subject to removal, for example, for a conflict of interest that is sufficient to require removal. This would reverse the result in cases such as Estate of Backer, 164 Cal.App.3d 1159, 211 Cal.Rptr. 163 (1985). For contest of appointment, see Section 8004.

Background on Section 8402 of Repealed Code

Section 8402 was added by 1988 Cal.Stat. ch. 1199 § 81.5. Paragraph (a)(1) restated a provision of former Probate Code Section 401 (repealed by 1988 Cal.Stat. ch. 1199 § 43) without substantive change. Paragraph (a)(2) superseded the remainder of former Section 401. Paragraph (a)(3) was a new provision. Paragraph (a)(4) and subdivision (b) restated former Probate Code Section 420 (repealed by 1988 Cal.Stat. ch. 1199 § 45) without substantive change. Paragraph (a)(5) and subdivision (b) restated former Probate Code Section 421 (repealed by 1988 Cal.Stat. ch. 1199 § 45) without substantive change. For background on the provisions of this part, see the Comment to this part under the part heading. [20 Cal.L.Rev.Comm.Reports 1001 (1990)].

Research References

Forms

California Transactions Forms--Estate Planning § 19:71, Statutory Qualifications.

California Transactions Forms--Estate Planning § 19:75, Attorney as Executor.

Treatises and Practice Aids

Witkin, California Summary 10th Wills and Probate § 433, Competency and Qualifications.

Witkin, California Summary 10th Wills and Probate § 434, Testator's Direction or Intention.

Witkin, California Summary 10th Wills and Probate § 436, in General.

Witkin, California Summary 10th Wills and Probate § 440, Nominee Of Person Entitled.

Witkin, California Summary 10th Wills and Probate § 444, Any Other Person.

§ 8403. Oath

(a) Before letters are issued, the personal representative shall take and subscribe an oath to perform, according to law, the duties of the office. The oath may be taken and dated on or after the time the petition for appointment as personal representative is signed, and may be filed with the clerk at any time after the petition is granted.

(b) The oath constitutes an acceptance of the office and shall be attached to or endorsed on the letters. *(Stats.1990, c. 79 (A.B.759), § 14, operative July 1, 1991.)*

Law Revision Commission Comments

1990 Enactment

Section 8403 continues Section 8403 of the repealed Probate Code without change. The requirement of an oath may be satisfied by a written affirmation. See Code Civ.Proc. § 2015.6. See also Adams v. Sharp, 61 Cal.2d 775, 394 P.2d 943, 40 Cal.Rptr. 255 (1964) (oath taken out of state).

Background on Section 8403 of Repealed Code

Section 8403 was added by 1988 Cal.Stat. ch. 1199 § 81.5. The section restated former Probate Code Section 540 (repealed by 1988 Cal.Stat. ch. 1199 § 48) but permitted the oath to be signed at the time the petition is signed. For background on the provisions of this part, see the Comment to this part under the part heading. [20 Cal.L.Rev.Comm.Reports 1001 (1990)].

Research References

Forms

West's California Code Forms, Probate § 8405 Form 1, Letters--Judicial Council Form DE-150.

West's California Judicial Council Forms DE-150, Letters.

Treatises and Practice Aids

Witkin, California Summary 10th Wills and Probate § 446, Letters and Oath.

§ 8404. Statement of duties and liabilities of personal representative; acknowledgment of receipt; form of statement; supersedure by law

(a) Before letters are issued, the personal representative (other than a trust company or a public administrator) shall file an acknowledgment of receipt of a statement of duties and liabilities of the office of personal representative. The statement shall be in the form prescribed by the Judicial Council.

(b) The court may by local rule require the acknowledgment of receipt to include the personal representative's birth date and driver's license number, if any, provided that the court ensures their confidentiality.

(c) The statement of duties and liabilities prescribed by the Judicial Council does not supersede the law on which the statement is based. *(Stats.1990, c. 79 (A.B.759), § 14, operative July 1, 1991. Amended by Stats.1994, c. 806 (A.B.3686), § 26.)*

Law Revision Commission Comments

1990 Enactment

Section 8404 continues Section 8404 of the repealed Probate Code with the following revisions:

(1) Subdivision (a) has been revised to except the public administrator from the requirement of filing an acknowledgment of receipt of the statement of duties and liabilities.

(2) The second sentence of subdivision (a) has been revised to eliminate the reference to the form provided in former subdivision (c).

(3) The form stating the personal representative's duties and liabilities in former subdivision (c) has been omitted because the form was superseded by the Judicial Council Form DE 147 (July 1, 1989).

Although the statement of duties and liabilities must be in the form prescribed by the Judicial Council, the attorney for the personal representative may supplement, explain, or otherwise address the subject matter separately, where appropriate.

Background on Section 8404 of Repealed Code

Section 8404 was added by 1988 Cal.Stat. ch. 1199 § 81.5. The section was a new provision drawn from general instructions given to personal representatives by a number of courts. Section 8404 was amended by 1989 Cal.Stat. ch. 21 § 17 to amend item 4 in subdivision (c) to conform with Section 8800. See Communication from the California Law Revision Commission Concerning Assembly Bill 156, 20 Cal.L.Revision Comm'n Reports 227, 230 (1990). For background on the provisions of this part, see the Comment to this part under the part heading. [20 Cal.L.Rev.Comm.Reports 1001 (1990)].

Research References

Forms

West's California Code Forms, Probate § 8404 Form 1, Duties and Liabilities Of Personal Representative--Judicial Council Form DE-147.
West's California Judicial Council Forms DE-147, Duties and Liabilities Of Personal Representative.
West's California Judicial Council Forms DE-147S, Confidential Supplement to Duties and Liabilities Of Personal Representative.

Treatises and Practice Aids

Witkin, California Summary 10th Wills and Probate § 35, Major Changes.
Witkin, California Summary 10th Wills and Probate § 447, Statement Of Duties and Liabilities.

§ 8405. Letters; contents

Letters shall be signed by the clerk under the seal of the court and shall include:

(a) The county from which the letters are issued.

(b) The name of the person appointed as personal representative and whether the personal representative is an executor, administrator, administrator with the will annexed, or special administrator.

(c) A notation whether the personal representative is authorized to act under the Independent Administration of Estates Act (Part 6 (commencing with Section 10400) of Division 7), and if so authorized whether the independent administration authority includes or excludes the power to do any of the following:

(1) Sell real property.

(2) Exchange real property.

(3) Grant an option to purchase real property.

(4) Borrow money with the loan secured by an encumbrance upon real property. *(Stats.1990, c. 79 (A.B.759), § 14, operative July 1, 1991.)*

Law Revision Commission Comments

1990 Enactment

Section 8405 continues Section 8405 of the repealed Probate Code with the addition of the requirement in subdivision (c) that the letters include a notation whether the independent administration authority includes or excludes the power to borrow money with the loan secured by an encumbrance upon real property. This is consistent with subdivision (c) of Section 10452 of the repealed Probate Code, which is superseded by subdivision (c) of Section 8405, and with subdivision (b) of Section 10501. The Judicial Council may prescribe the form of letters. See Section 1001 (Judicial Council and local court rules). See also Section 10454 (new letters to be issued when court orders limits or revokes independent administration authority).

Background on Section 8405 of Repealed Code

Section 8405 was added by 1988 Cal.Stat. ch. 1199 § 81.5. The section superseded former Probate Code Sections 500, 501, and 502 (provisions repealed by 1988 Cal.Stat. ch. 1199 § 47). The section was amended by 1989 Cal.Stat. ch. 21 § 18 to conform with Sections 10403 (limited authority) and 10452 (endorsement on letters) of the repealed Probate Code. See Communication from the California Law Revision Commission Concerning Assembly Bill 156, 20 Cal.L.Revision Comm'n Reports 227, 230 (1990). For background on the provisions of this part, see the Comment to this part under the part heading. [20 Cal.L.Rev.Comm.Reports 1001 (1990)].

Research References

Forms

California Transactions Forms--Estate Planning § 19:81, General Court Supervision.
West's California Judicial Council Forms DE-150, Letters.

Treatises and Practice Aids

Witkin, California Summary 10th Wills and Probate § 446, Letters and Oath.
Witkin, California Summary 10th Wills and Probate § 749, Order, Letters, and Bond.
Witkin, California Summary 10th Wills and Probate § 750, Petition to Revoke or Limit Authority.

ARTICLE 2. EXECUTORS

§ 8420. Right to appointment as personal representative

The person named as executor in the decedent's will has the right to appointment as personal representative. *(Stats. 1990, c. 79 (A.B.759), § 14, operative July 1, 1991.)*

Law Revision Commission Comments

1990 Enactment

Section 8420 continues Section 8420 of the repealed Probate Code without change. This section is an express statement of the concept that the named executor has first priority for appointment as personal representative. The section does not apply if the person named is not qualified for appointment under Section 8402 (qualifications) or has waived the right to appointment. See also Section 9605 (appointment does not discharge any claim the decedent has against personal representative).

Background on Section 8420 of Repealed Code

Section 8420 was a new provision added by 1988 Cal.Stat. ch. 1199 § 81.5. Cf. former Probate Code Section 407 (repealed by 1988 Cal.Stat. ch. 1199 § 43). For background on the provisions of this part, see the Comment to this part under the part heading. [20 Cal.L.Rev.Comm.Reports 1001 (1990)].

Research References

Forms

West's California Code Forms, Probate § 8440 Form 1, Named Executor's Declination to Act and Nomination Of Proposed Personal Representative; Attachment 3f(1)(C), (D) to Petition for Probate.

Treatises and Practice Aids

Witkin, California Summary 10th Wills and Probate § 434, Testator's Direction or Intention.

§ 8421. Person apparently intended as executor by will; right to appointment as personal representative

If a person is not named as executor in a will but it appears by the terms of the will that the testator intended to commit the execution of the will and the administration of the estate to the person, the person is entitled to appointment as personal representative in the same manner as if named as executor. *(Stats.1990, c. 79 (A.B.759), § 14, operative July 1, 1991.)*

Law Revision Commission Comments

1990 Enactment

Section 8421 continues Section 8421 of the repealed Probate Code without change.

Background on Section 8421 of Repealed Code

Section 8421 was added by 1988 Cal.Stat. ch. 1199 § 81.5. The section restated former Probate Code Section 402 (repealed by 1988 Cal.Stat. ch. 1199 § 43) without substantive change. For background on the provisions of this part, see the Comment to this part under the part heading. [20 Cal.L.Rev.Comm.Reports 1001 (1990)].

Research References

Treatises and Practice Aids

Witkin, California Summary 10th Wills and Probate § 434, Testator's Direction or Intention.

§ 8422. Power in will to designate executor or coexecutor; bond; designation; executor authority to name coexecutor or successor

(a) The testator may by will confer on a person the power to designate an executor or coexecutor, or successor executor or coexecutor. The will may provide that the persons so designated may serve without bond.

(b) A designation shall be in writing and filed with the court. Unless the will provides otherwise, if there are two or more holders of the power to designate, the designation shall be unanimous, unless one of the holders of the power is unable or unwilling to act, in which case the remaining holder or holders may exercise the power.

(c) Except as provided in this section, an executor does not have authority to name a coexecutor, or a successor executor or coexecutor. *(Stats.1990, c. 79 (A.B.759), § 14, operative July 1, 1991.)*

Law Revision Commission Comments

1990 Enactment

Section 8422 continues Section 8422 of the repealed Probate Code without change. An executor designated under this section must be appointed by the court. See Section 8400 (appointment necessary).

Background on Section 8422 of Repealed Code

Section 8422 was added by 1988 Cal.Stat. ch. 1199 § 81.5. The section restated former Probate Code Section 403 (repealed by 1988 Cal.Stat. ch. 1199 § 43) without substantive change. For background on the provisions of this part, see the Comment to this part under the part heading. [20 Cal.L.Rev.Comm.Reports 1001 (1990)].

Research References

Forms

California Transactions Forms--Estate Planning § 19:71, Statutory Qualifications.

Treatises and Practice Aids

Witkin, California Summary 10th Wills and Probate § 435, Power to Designate Executor.

§ 8423. Trust company named as executor; sale to, merger with, etc., another trust company

If the executor named in the will is a trust company that has sold its business and assets to, has consolidated or merged with, or is in any manner provided by law succeeded by, another trust company, the court may, and to the extent required by the Banking Law (Division 1 (commencing with Section 99) of the Financial Code) shall, appoint the successor trust company as executor. *(Stats.1990, c. 79 (A.B.759), § 14, operative July 1, 1991.)*

Law Revision Commission Comments

1990 Enactment

Section 8423 continues Section 8423 of the repealed Probate Code without change. A trust company is an entity that has qualified to engage in and conduct a trust business in this state. A trust company may act as an executor. See Sections 83, 300; Fin.Code § 1580.

Background on Section 8423 of Repealed Code

Section 8423 was added by 1988 Cal.Stat. ch. 1199 § 81.5. The section restated former Probate Code Section 404 (repealed by 1988 Cal.Stat. ch. 1199 § 43) without substantive change. For background on the provisions of this part, see the Comment to this part under the part heading. [20 Cal.L.Rev.Comm.Reports 1001 (1990)].

Research References

Forms

California Transactions Forms--Estate Planning § 19:74, Alternate Executor.

Treatises and Practice Aids

Witkin, California Summary 10th Wills and Probate § 433, Competency and Qualifications.

§ 8424. Minor named as executor

(a) If a person named as executor is under the age of majority and there is another person named as executor, the other person may be appointed and may administer the estate until the majority of the minor, who may then be appointed as coexecutor.

(b) If a person named as executor is under the age of majority and there is no other person named as executor, another person may be appointed as personal representative, but the court may revoke the appointment on the majority of the minor, who may then be appointed as executor. *(Stats. 1990, c. 79 (A.B.759), § 14, operative July 1, 1991.)*

Law Revision Commission Comments

1990 Enactment

Section 8424 continues Section 8424 of the repealed Probate Code without change. The court may exercise its discretion under this section.

Background on Section 8424 of Repealed Code

Section 8424 was added by 1988 Cal.Stat. ch. 1199 § 81.5. The section restated without substantive change the portion of former Probate Code Section 405 (repealed by 1988 Cal.Stat. ch. 1199 § 43) that related to a minor named as executor. For background on the provisions of this part, see the Comment to this part under the part heading. [20 Cal.L.Rev.Comm.Reports 1001 (1990)].

Research References

Forms

California Transactions Forms--Estate Planning § 19:71, Statutory Qualifications.

Treatises and Practice Aids

Witkin, California Summary 10th Wills and Probate § 434, Testator's Direction or Intention.

§ 8425. Court appointment of fewer than all persons named in will as executors; authority of appointees

If the court does not appoint all the persons named in the will as executors, those appointed have the same authority to act in every respect as all would have if appointed. *(Stats. 1990, c. 79 (A.B.759), § 14, operative July 1, 1991.)*

Law Revision Commission Comments

1990 Enactment

Section 8425 continues Section 8425 of the repealed Probate Code without change.

Background on Section 8425 of Repealed Code

Section 8425 was added by 1988 Cal.Stat. ch. 1199 § 81.5. The section restated former Probate Code Section 408 (repealed by 1988 Cal.Stat. ch. 1199 § 43) without substantive change. For background on the provisions of this part, see the Comment to this part under the part heading. [20 Cal.L.Rev.Comm.Reports 1001 (1990)].

Research References

Forms

California Transactions Forms--Estate Planning § 19:71, Statutory Qualifications.

Treatises and Practice Aids

Witkin, California Summary 10th Wills and Probate § 434, Testator's Direction or Intention.

ARTICLE 3. ADMINISTRATORS WITH THE WILL ANNEXED

§ 8440. Appointment as personal representative; no executor named; named executors waive right or are unwilling or unable

An administrator with the will annexed shall be appointed as personal representative if no executor is named in the will or if the sole executor or all the executors named in the will have waived the right to appointment or are for any reason unwilling or unable to act. *(Stats.1990, c. 79 (A.B.759), § 14, operative July 1, 1991.)*

Law Revision Commission Comments

1990 Enactment

Section 8440 continues Section 8440 of the repealed Probate Code without change. A person named as an executor may be unwilling or unable to act because the person is dead or incompetent, renounces or fails to petition for appointment, fails to appear and qualify, or dies or is removed from office after appointment and before the completion of administration.

No executor of a deceased executor is, as such, authorized to administer the estate of the first testator. Section 8522 (vacancy where no personal representatives remain). However, the deceased executor may have the power to designate a successor executor. See Section 8422 (power to designate executor). And the executor of the deceased executor may qualify independently for appointment as an administrator with the will annexed under this section. See also Sections 300–301 (trust company as personal representative), 9605 (appointment does not discharge any claim the decedent has against personal representative).

Background on Section 8440 of Repealed Code

Section 8440 was added by 1988 Cal.Stat. ch. 1199 § 81.5. The section superseded former Probate Code Section 406 (repealed by 1988 Cal.Stat. ch. 1199 § 43). For background on the provisions of this part, see the Comment to this part under the part heading. [20 Cal.L.Rev.Comm.Reports 1001 (1990)].

Research References

Forms

California Transactions Forms--Estate Planning § 19:72, Corporate Versus Individual Executor.

West's California Code Forms, Probate § 8440 Form 1, Named Executor's Declination to Act and Nomination Of Proposed Personal Representative; Attachment 3f(1)(C), (D) to Petition for Probate.

Treatises and Practice Aids

Witkin, California Summary 10th Wills and Probate § 430, Administrator With Will Annexed.

Witkin, California Summary 10th Wills and Probate § 583, Who May Petition.

§ 8441. Priority for appointment

(a) Except as provided in subdivision (b), persons and their nominees are entitled to appointment as administrator with the will annexed in the same order of priority as for appointment of an administrator.

(b) A person who takes under the will has priority over a person who does not, but the court in its discretion may give priority to a person who does not take under the will if the person is entitled to a statutory interest that is a substantially greater portion of the estate than the devise to the person who takes under the will and the priority appears appropriate under the circumstances. A person who takes more than 50 percent of the value of the estate under the will or the person's nominee, or the nominee of several persons who together take more than 50 percent of the value of the estate under the will, has priority over other persons who take under the will. *(Stats.1990, c. 79 (A.B.759), § 14, operative July 1, 1991.)*

Law Revision Commission Comments

1990 Enactment

Section 8441 continues Section 8441 of the repealed Probate Code without change. For priority for appointment of an administrator, see Section 8461. Subdivision (b) gives priority to devisees, who need not be entitled to succeed to all or part of the estate under the law of succession in order to have priority. However, subdivision (b) also gives the court discretion to disregard the priority of a devisee in an appropriate case where another person would take a substantial statutory intestate or omitted heir share. See also Sections 140–147 (surviving spouse's waiver of rights at death), 9605 (appointment does not discharge claim decedent has against personal representative).

Background on Section 8441 of Repealed Code

Section 8441 was added by 1988 Cal.Stat. ch. 1199 § 81.5. The section superseded the second and third sentences of former Probate Code Section 409 (repealed by 1988 Cal.Stat. ch. 1199 § 43). The express references to nominees were new. For background on the provisions of this part, see the Comment to this part under the part heading. [20 Cal.L.Rev.Comm.Reports 1001 (1990)].

Research References

Forms

West's California Code Forms, Probate § 8440 Form 1, Named Executor's Declination to Act and Nomination Of Proposed Personal Representative; Attachment 3f(1)(C), (D) to Petition for Probate.

Treatises and Practice Aids

Witkin, California Summary 10th Wills and Probate § 430, Administrator With Will Annexed.

Witkin, California Summary 10th Wills and Probate § 442, Public Administrator.

§ 8442. Authority over estate

(a) Subject to subdivision (b), an administrator with the will annexed has the same authority over the decedent's estate as an executor named in the will would have.

(b) If the will confers a discretionary power or authority on an executor that is not conferred by law and the will does not extend the power or authority to other personal representatives, the power or authority shall not be deemed to be conferred on an administrator with the will annexed, but the court in its discretion may authorize the exercise of the power or authority. *(Stats.1990, c. 79 (A.B.759), § 14, operative July 1, 1991.)*

Law Revision Commission Comments

1990 Enactment

Section 8442 continues Section 8442 of the repealed Probate Code without change. The acts of the administrator with the will annexed are as effectual for all purposes as the acts of an executor would be.

Background on Section 8442 of Repealed Code

Section 8442 was added by 1988 Cal.Stat. ch. 1199 § 81.5. The section restated the first sentence of former Probate Code Section 409 (repealed by 1988 Cal.Stat. ch. 1199 § 43), with the addition of court discretion to permit exercise of a discretionary power or authority. For background on the provisions of this part, see the Comment to this part under the part heading. [20 Cal.L.Rev.Comm.Reports 1001 (1990)].

Research References

Treatises and Practice Aids

Witkin, California Summary 10th Wills and Probate § 430, Administrator With Will Annexed.

Witkin, California Summary 10th Wills and Probate § 462, Vacancy Of All Representatives.

ARTICLE 4. ADMINISTRATORS

Section

§ 8460. Intestate decedent; appointment of administrator; number

(a) If the decedent dies intestate, the court shall appoint an administrator as personal representative.

(b) The court may appoint one or more persons as administrator. *(Stats.1990, c. 79 (A.B.759), § 14, operative July 1, 1991.)*

Law Revision Commission Comments

1990 Enactment

Section 8460 continues Section 8460 of the repealed Probate Code without change. See also Section 9605 (appointment does not discharge any claim decedent has against personal representative).

Background on Section 8460 of Repealed Code

Section 8460 was added by 1988 Cal.Stat. ch. 1199 § 81.5. The section restated the introductory portion of subdivision (a) of former Probate Code Section 422 (repealed by 1988 Cal.Stat. ch. 1199 § 45) without substantive change. For background on the provisions of this part, see the Comment to this part under the part heading. [20 Cal.L.Rev.Comm.Reports 1001 (1990)].

Research References

Treatises and Practice Aids

Witkin, California Summary 10th Wills and Probate § 436, in General.

§ 8461. Persons entitled to appointment; priority

Subject to the provisions of this article, a person in the following relation to the decedent is entitled to appointment as administrator in the following order of priority:

(a) Surviving spouse or domestic partner as defined in Section 37.

(b) Children.

(c) Grandchildren.

(d) Other issue.

(e) Parents.

(f) Brothers and sisters.

(g) Issue of brothers and sisters.

(h) Grandparents.

(i) Issue of grandparents.

(j) Children of a predeceased spouse or domestic partner.

(k) Other issue of a predeceased spouse or domestic partner.

(*l*) Other next of kin.

(m) Parents of a predeceased spouse or domestic partner.

(n) Issue of parents of a predeceased spouse or domestic partner.

(*o*) Conservator or guardian of the estate acting in that capacity at the time of death who has filed a first account and is not acting as conservator or guardian for any other person.

(p) Public administrator.

(q) Creditors.

(r) Any other person. *(Stats.1990, c. 79 (A.B.759), § 14, operative July 1, 1991. Amended by Stats.1990, c. 710 (S.B.1775), § 20, operative July 1, 1991; Stats.2001, c. 893 (A.B.25), § 53.)*

Law Revision Commission Comments

1990 Enactment

Section 8461 continues Section 8461 of the repealed Probate Code without change. The general order of priority prescribed in Section 8461 is subject to limitation in the succeeding sections of this article. See, e.g., Sections 8462 (priority of relatives), 8463 (surviving spouse). A person appointed must be legally competent. See Section 8402 (qualifications). See also Sections 140–147 (surviving spouse's waiver of rights at death), 300–301 (trust company as personal representative), 12252 (appointment where subsequent administration necessary after personal representative has been discharged), 12513 (priority of sister state personal representative).

1990 Amendment

Section 8461 (enacted as a part of the new Probate Code by 1990 Cal.Stat. ch. 79 § 14) was amended by 1990 Cal.Stat. ch. 710 § 20. The amendment revised subdivision (*o*) to limit the priority for a conservator or guardian of the estate to the case where a first account has been filed (Section 2620) and the conservator or guardian is not acting in that capacity for any other person. See also Section 8469 (court discretion to give priority to conservator or guardian where requirements of Section 8461 not met). For background on the 1990 amendment, see Recommendation Relating to Priority of Conservator or Guardian for Appointment as Administrator, 20 Cal.L.Revision Comm'n Reports 607 (1990). [20 Cal.L.Rev.Comm.Reports 1001 (1990)].

Background on Section 8461 of Repealed Code

Section 8461 was added by 1988 Cal.Stat. ch. 1199 § 81.5. The section restated a portion of subdivision (a) of former Probate Code Section 422 (repealed by 1988 Cal.Stat. ch. 1199 § 45), with the addition of subdivisions (d), (g), (h), and (i) to reflect changes in the law governing intestate succession. See Section 6402 (intestate share of heirs other than surviving spouse). Section 8461 was amended by 1989 Cal.Stat. ch. 544 § 8 to conform the priorities for appointment as administrator more closely to the priorities to take from the decedent by intestate succession. See Section 6402. For background on the provisions of this part, see the Comment to this part under the part heading. [20 Cal.L.Rev.Comm.Reports 1001 (1990)].

Commentary

Estate of Lewis, 184 Cal.App.4th 507, 108 Cal.Rptr.3d 800 (2010), holds that a probate court abused its discretion in appointing the public administrator to administer a deceased father's estate instead of the biological mother and legal guardian of the father's two children, as required by this section and Probate Code § 8464, in the absence of a finding that the mother was not competent to act as the personal representative.

Estate of Garrett, 159 Cal.App.4th 831, 71 Cal.Rptr.3d 864 (2008), review denied, holds that an estranged wife living apart from her husband at the time of his death has a surviving spouse's priority under this section, even though the wife once filed an action to dissolve her marriage to decedent, which action was dismissed for lack of prosecution. *Garrett* interprets section 8463 to include only an action for dissolution *pending* at the time of decedent's death.

Research References

Forms

West's California Code Forms, Probate § 12404 Form 1, Petition for Probate or Administration Of Estate Of Missing Person.

Treatises and Practice Aids

Witkin, California Summary 10th Husband and Wife § 33, Other Rights.

Witkin, California Summary 10th Wills and Probate § 78, Surviving Spouse or Domestic Partner.

Witkin, California Summary 10th Wills and Probate § 367, Petition.

Witkin, California Summary 10th Wills and Probate § 419, Procedure.

Witkin, California Summary 10th Wills and Probate § 426, Procedure for Appointment.

Witkin, California Summary 10th Wills and Probate § 430, Administrator With Will Annexed.

Witkin, California Summary 10th Wills and Probate § 436, in General.

Witkin, California Summary 10th Wills and Probate § 437, Statutory Priority.

Witkin, California Summary 10th Wills and Probate § 438, Surviving Spouse or Domestic Partner.

Witkin, California Summary 10th Wills and Probate § 439, Relatives.

Witkin, California Summary 10th Wills and Probate § 441, Guardian or Conservator Of Person Entitled.

Witkin, California Summary 10th Wills and Probate § 442, Public Administrator.

Witkin, California Summary 10th Wills and Probate § 443, Creditor.

Witkin, California Summary 10th Wills and Probate § 444, Any Other Person.

Witkin, California Summary 10th Wills and Probate § 455, Substitution Of Person With Higher Priority.

Witkin, California Summary 10th Wills and Probate § 462, Vacancy Of All Representatives.

§ 8462. Surviving spouse or domestic partner, relative, or relative of predeceased spouse or domestic partner; conditions of priority

The surviving spouse or domestic partner of the decedent, a relative of the decedent, or a relative of a predeceased spouse or domestic partner of the decedent, has priority under Section 8461 only if one of the following conditions is satisfied:

(a) The surviving spouse, domestic partner, or relative is entitled to succeed to all or part of the estate.

(b) The surviving spouse, domestic partner, or relative either takes under the will of, or is entitled to succeed to all or part of the estate of, another deceased person who is entitled to succeed to all or part of the estate of the decedent. *(Stats.1990, c. 79 (A.B.759), § 14, operative July 1, 1991. Amended by Stats.2001, c. 893 (A.B.25), § 54.)*

Law Revision Commission Comments

1990 Enactment

Section 8462 continues Section 8462 of the repealed Probate Code without change. See also Sections 140–147 (surviving spouse's waiver of rights at death).

Background on Section 8462 of Repealed Code

Section 8462 was added by 1988 Cal.Stat. ch. 1199 § 81.5. The section restated subdivision (b) of former Probate Code Section 422 (repealed by 1988 Cal.Stat. ch. 1199 § 45) with the addition of language recognizing the priority of relatives of a predeceased spouse and the expansion of subdivision (b) to include any relative of the decedent who satisfies the prescribed conditions. For background on the provisions of this part, see the Comment to this part under the part heading. [20 Cal.L.Rev.Comm.Reports 1001 (1990)].

Research References

Treatises and Practice Aids

Witkin, California Summary 10th Husband and Wife § 33, Other Rights.

Witkin, California Summary 10th Wills and Probate § 438, Surviving Spouse or Domestic Partner.

Witkin, California Summary 10th Wills and Probate § 439, Relatives.

§ 8463. Surviving spouse; living apart and party to action for separate maintenance, annulment, or dissolution; priority

If the surviving spouse is a party to an action for separate maintenance, annulment, or dissolution of the marriage of the decedent and the surviving spouse, and was living apart from the decedent on the date of the decedent's death, the surviving spouse has priority next after brothers and sisters and not the priority prescribed in Section 8461. *(Stats.1990, c. 79 (A.B.759), § 14, operative July 1, 1991.)*

Law Revision Commission Comments

1990 Enactment

Section 8463 continues Section 8463 of the repealed Probate Code without change. There is an inherent conflict of interest between the surviving spouse and other heirs of the decedent in the situation described in this section. As to the surviving spouse's waiver of rights at death, see Sections 140–147.

Background on Section 8463 of Repealed Code

Section 8463 was added by 1988 Cal.Stat. ch. 1199 § 81.5. The section superseded subdivision (a)(6) and the second paragraph of subdivision (a)(1) of former Probate Code Section 422 (repealed by 1988 Cal.Stat. ch. 1199 § 45). For background on the provisions of this part, see the Comment to this part under the part heading. [20 Cal.L.Rev.Comm.Reports 1001 (1990)].

Commentary

Estate of Garrett, 159 Cal.App.4th 831, 71 Cal.Rptr.3d 864 (2008), review denied, holds that an estranged wife living apart from her husband at the time of his death has a surviving spouse's priority under section 8461, even though the wife once filed an action to dissolve her marriage to decedent, which action was dismissed for lack of prosecution. *Garrett* interprets this section to include only an action for dissolution *pending* at the time of decedent's death.

Research References

Treatises and Practice Aids

Witkin, California Summary 10th Wills and Probate § 27, Major Changes.

Witkin, California Summary 10th Wills and Probate § 438, Surviving Spouse or Domestic Partner.

§ 8464. Minor; appointment of guardian or conservator

If a person otherwise entitled to appointment as administrator is a person under the age of majority or a person for whom a guardian or conservator of the estate has been appointed, the court in its discretion may appoint the guardian or conservator or another person entitled to appointment. *(Stats.1990, c. 79 (A.B.759), § 14, operative July 1, 1991.)*

Law Revision Commission Comments

1990 Enactment

Section 8464 continues Section 8464 of the repealed Probate Code without change.

Background on Section 8464 of Repealed Code

Section 8464 was added by 1988 Cal.Stat. ch. 1199 § 81.5. The section restated former Probate Code Section 426 (repealed by 1988 Cal.Stat. ch. 1199 § 45) without substantive change. For background on the provisions of this part, see the Comment to this part under the part heading. [20 Cal.L.Rev.Comm.Reports 1001 (1990)].

Estate of Lewis, 184 Cal.App.4th 507, 108 Cal.Rptr.3d 80 (2010), holds that a probate court abused its discretion in appointing the public administrator to administer a deceased father's estate instead of the biological mother and legal guardian of the father's two children, as required by this section and Probate Code § 8461, in the absence of a finding that the mother was not competent to act as the personal representative.

Research References

Treatises and Practice Aids

Witkin, California Summary 10th Wills and Probate § 441, Guardian or Conservator Of Person Entitled.

§ 8465. Appointment of nominated persons; priority; considerations; nominees required to obtain a bond; resignation upon cessation of California residency; submission to jurisdiction of court

(a) The court may appoint as administrator a person nominated by any of the following persons:

(1) A person otherwise entitled to appointment.

(2) A person who would otherwise be entitled for appointment but who is ineligible for appointment under paragraph (4) of subdivision (a) of Section 8402 because he or she is not a resident of the United States.

(3) The guardian or conservator of the estate of a person otherwise entitled to appointment. The nomination shall be made in writing and filed with the court.

(b) If a person making a nomination for appointment of an administrator is the surviving spouse or domestic partner, child, grandchild, other issue, parent, brother or sister, or grandparent of the decedent, the nominee has priority next after those in the class of the person making the nomination.

(c) If a person making a nomination for appointment of an administrator is other than a person described in subdivision (b), the court in its discretion may appoint either the nominee or a person of a class lower in priority to that of the person making the nomination, but other persons of the class of the person making the nomination have priority over the nominee.

(d) If a person making a nomination for appointment of an administrator is a person described in paragraph (2) of subdivision (a), the court shall not appoint a nominee who is not a California resident to act as administrator. For California residents nominated under paragraph (2) of subdivision (a), the court shall consider whether the nominee is capable of faithfully executing the duties of the office. The court may in its discretion deny the appointment and appoint another person. In determining whether to appoint the nominee, the factors the court may consider include, but are not limited to, the following:

(1) Whether the nominee has a conflict of interest with the heirs or any other interested party.

(2) Whether the nominee had a business or personal relationship with the decedent or decedent's family before the decedent's death.

(3) Whether the nominee is engaged in or acting on behalf of an individual, a business, or other entity that solicits heirs to obtain the person's nomination for appointment as administrator.

(4) Whether the nominee has been appointed as a personal representative in any other estate.

(e) If the court decides to appoint a nominee under the circumstances described in subdivision (d), the court shall require the nominee to obtain bond, unless the court orders otherwise for good cause. Any order for good cause must be supported by specific findings of fact, and shall consider the need for the protection of creditors, heirs, and any other interested parties. Before waiving a bond, the court shall consider all other alternatives, including, but not limited to, the deposit of property in the estate pursuant to Chapter 3 (commencing with Section 9700) of Part 5 on the condition that the property, including any earnings thereon, will not be withdrawn except on authorization of the court. The waiver of all of the heirs of the requirement of a bond shall not constitute good cause.

(f) If the appointed nominee ceases to be a California resident following his or her appointment, he or she shall be deemed to have resigned as administrator for the purposes of Article 7 (commencing with Section 8520). The court shall not lose jurisdiction of the proceeding by any resignation under this subdivision.

(g) By accepting appointment as personal representative, the nominee shall submit personally to the jurisdiction of the court. *(Stats.1990, c. 79 (A.B.759), § 14, operative July 1, 1991. Amended by Stats.2001, c. 893 (A.B.25), § 55; Stats. 2012, c. 635 (A.B.1670), § 1; Stats.2015, c. 54 (A.B.548), § 1, eff. Jan. 1, 2016.)*

Law Revision Commission Comments

1990 Enactment

Section 8465 continues Section 8465 of the repealed Probate Code without change. The nominee is not entitled to appointment unless legally competent. See Section 8402 (qualifications).

Background on Section 8465 of Repealed Code

Section 8465 was added by 1988 Cal.Stat. ch. 1199 § 81.5. The section restated without substantive change provisions found in former Probate Code Section 423 (repealed by 1988 Cal.Stat. ch. 1199 § 45). "Grandparent" and "issue" were added to subdivision (b) consistent with Section 8461 (priority for appointment). For background on the provisions of this part, see the Comment to this part under the part heading. [20 Cal.L.Rev.Comm.Reports 1001 (1990)].

Research References

Treatises and Practice Aids

Witkin, California Summary 10th Husband and Wife § 33, Other Rights.
Witkin, California Summary 10th Wills and Probate § 440, Nominee Of Person Entitled.

§ 8466. Creditor; court denial of appointment

If a person whose only priority is that of a creditor claims appointment as administrator, the court in its discretion may deny the appointment and appoint another person. *(Stats. 1990, c. 79 (A.B.759), § 14, operative July 1, 1991.)*

Law Revision Commission Comments

1990 Enactment

Section 8466 continues Section 8466 of the repealed Probate Code without change. Any person appointed under this section must be legally competent. See Section 8402 (qualifications). See also Section 9605 (appointment of person as personal representative does not discharge any claim the decedent has against the person).

Background on Section 8466 of Repealed Code

Section 8466 was added by 1988 Cal.Stat. ch. 1199 § 81.5. The section restated the last portion of former Probate Code Section 425 (repealed by 1988 Cal.Stat. ch. 1199 § 45) but omitted the requirement that there be a request of another creditor before the court may appoint another person. For background on the provisions of this part, see the Comment to this part under the part heading. [20 Cal.L.Rev.Comm.Reports 1001 (1990)].

Research References

Treatises and Practice Aids

Witkin, California Summary 10th Wills and Probate § 443, Creditor.

§ 8467. Persons with equal priority

If several persons have equal priority for appointment as administrator, the court may appoint one or more of them, or if such persons are unable to agree, the court may appoint the public administrator or a disinterested person in the same or the next lower class of priority as the persons who are unable to agree. *(Stats.1990, c. 79 (A.B.759), § 14, operative July 1, 1991.)*

Law Revision Commission Comments

1990 Enactment

Section 8467 continues Section 8467 of the repealed Probate Code without change.

Background on Section 8467 of Repealed Code

Section 8467 was added by 1988 Cal.Stat. ch. 1199 § 81.5. The section restated the first portion of former Probate Code Section 425 (repealed by 1988 Cal.Stat. ch. 1199 § 45), with the addition of authority to appoint the public administrator or a disinterested person where there is a conflict between persons of equal priority. For background on the provisions of this part, see the Comment to this part under the part heading. [20 Cal.L.Rev.Comm.Reports 1001 (1990)].

Research References

Treatises and Practice Aids

Witkin, California Summary 10th Wills and Probate § 436, in General.

§ 8468. Failure to claim appointment

If persons having priority fail to claim appointment as administrator, the court may appoint any person who claims appointment. *(Stats.1990, c. 79 (A.B.759), § 14, operative July 1, 1991.)*

Law Revision Commission Comments

1990 Enactment

Section 8468 continues Section 8468 of the repealed Probate Code without change. A person appointed under this section must be legally competent. See Section 8402 (qualifications).

Background on Section 8468 of Repealed Code

Section 8468 was added by 1988 Cal.Stat. ch. 1199 § 81.5. The section restated former Probate Code Section 427 (repealed by 1988 Cal.Stat. ch. 1199 § 45) without substantive change. For background on the provisions of this part, see the Comment to this part under the part heading. [20 Cal.L.Rev.Comm.Reports 1001 (1990)].

Research References

Treatises and Practice Aids

Witkin, California Summary 10th Wills and Probate § 444, Any Other Person.

§ 8469. Conservator or guardian serving at time of death; priority; petition; notice

(a) For good cause, the court may allow the priority given by Section 8461 to a conservator or guardian of the estate of the decedent serving in that capacity at the time of death that has not filed a first account, or that is acting as guardian or conservator for another person, or both.

(b) If the petition for appointment as administrator requests the court to allow the priority permitted by subdivision (a), the petitioner shall, in addition to the notice otherwise required by statute, deliver notice of the hearing * * * pursuant to Section 1215 to the public administrator. *(Added by Stats.1990, c. 710 (S.B.1775), § 21, operative July 1, 1991. Amended by Stats.2017, c. 319 (A.B.976), § 68, eff. Jan. 1, 2018.)*

Law Revision Commission Comments

1990 Addition

Section 8469 was added to the new Probate Code by 1990 Cal.Stat. ch. 710 § 21. The section permits the court to allow the priority given by Section 8461 to a conservator or guardian of the estate of the decedent serving in that capacity at the time of death, notwithstanding that the conservator or guardian fails to satisfy the other requirements of Section 8461. For background on this section, see Recommendation Relating to Priority of Conservator or Guardian for Appointment as Administrator, 20 Cal.L.Revision Comm'n Reports 607 (1990). [20 Cal.L.Rev.Comm.Reports 1001 (1990)].

Research References

Treatises and Practice Aids

Witkin, California Summary 10th Wills and Probate § 437, Statutory Priority.

Part 9

PAYMENT OF DEBTS

Law Revision Commission Comments

1990 Enactment

This part supersedes Part 9 (commencing with Section 11400) of Division 7 of the repealed Probate Code. The superseded part was enacted upon recommendation of the California Law Revision Commission. See *Recommendation Relating to Creditor Claims Against Decedent's Estate,* 19 Cal.L.Revision Comm'n Reports 299 (1988). [20 Cal.L.Rev.Comm.Reports 1001 (1990)].

CHAPTER 3. ALLOCATION OF DEBTS BETWEEN ESTATE AND SURVIVING SPOUSE

§ 11440. Petition to allocate debt

If it appears that a debt of the decedent has been paid or is payable in whole or in part by the surviving spouse, or that a debt of the surviving spouse has been paid or is payable in whole or in part from property in the decedent's estate, the personal representative, the surviving spouse, or a beneficiary may, at any time before an order for final distribution is made, petition for an order to allocate the debt. *(Stats.1990, c. 79 (A.B.759), § 14, operative July 1, 1991.)*

Law Revision Commission Comments

1990 Enactment

Section 11440 continues Section 11440 of the repealed Probate Code without change. Under this section, a petition may be made for allocation of a debt of the decedent or of the surviving spouse even though the creditor has not made a claim and the debt has not been established under Part 4 (commencing with Section 9000). In this respect, the term "debt" is used in this section more broadly than the definition in Section 11401 ("debt" defined). For general provisions relating to petitions and other papers, see Sections 1020–1023. This part does not apply in any proceeding for administration of a decedent's estate commenced before July 1, 1988. See Section 11405. As to the application of any amendments made after that date, see Section 3.

Background on Section 11440 of Repealed Code

Section 11440 was added by 1987 Cal.Stat. ch. 923 § 93. The section combined subdivision (a) of former Probate Code Section 980 (repealed by 1987 Cal.Stat. ch. 923 § 48.6) with portions of former Probate Code Sections 704.2 and 704.4 (claim by surviving spouse) (provisions repealed by 1987 Cal.Stat. ch. 923 § 37), but allowed the petition to be made at any time before the court order for final distribution. [20 Cal.L.Rev.Comm.Reports 1001 (1990)].

Research References

Forms

West's California Code Forms, Probate § 11440 Form 1, Petition to Allocate Debts When There is No Agreement Between Personal Representative and Surviving Spouse.

Treatises and Practice Aids

Witkin, California Summary 10th Wills and Probate § 655, in General.

§ 11441. Contents of petition

The petition shall include a statement of all of the following:

(a) All debts of the decedent and surviving spouse known to the petitioner that are alleged to be subject to allocation and whether paid in whole or part or unpaid.

(b) The reason why the debts should be allocated.

(c) The proposed allocation and the basis for allocation alleged by the petitioner. *(Stats.1990, c. 79 (A.B.759), § 14, operative July 1, 1991.)*

Law Revision Commission Comments

1990 Enactment

Section 11441 continues Section 11441 of the repealed Probate Code without change. The term "debt" is used in this section more broadly than the definition in Section 11401 ("debt" defined). See the Comment to Section 11440. For general provisions relating to petitions and other papers, see Sections 1020–1023. This part does not apply in any proceeding for administration of a decedent's estate commenced before July 1, 1988. See Section 11405. As to the application of any amendments made after that date, see Section 3.

Background on Section 11441 of Repealed Code

Section 11441 was added by 1987 Cal.Stat. ch. 923 § 93. The section combined subdivision (b) of former Probate Code Section 980 (repealed by 1987 Cal.Stat. ch. 923 § 48.6) and portions of former Probate Code Sections 704.2 and 704.4 (provisions repealed by 1987 Cal.Stat. ch. 923 § 37). [20 Cal.L.Rev.Comm.Reports 1001 (1990)].

Research References

Forms

West's California Code Forms, Probate § 11440 Form 1, Petition to Allocate Debts When There is No Agreement Between Personal Representative and Surviving Spouse.

Treatises and Practice Aids

Witkin, California Summary 10th Wills and Probate § 655, in General.

§ 11442. Value of separate and community property affecting allocation where no inventory and appraisal provided; show cause order

If it appears from the petition that allocation would be affected by the value of the separate property of the surviving spouse and any community property and quasi-community property not administered in the estate and if an inventory and appraisal of the property has not been provided by the surviving spouse, the court shall make an order to show cause why the information should not be provided. *(Stats.1990, c. 79 (A.B.759), § 14, operative July 1, 1991.)*

Law Revision Commission Comments

1990 Enactment

Section 11442 continues Section 11442 of the repealed Probate Code without change. For general provisions relating to hearings and orders, see Sections 1040–1050. This part does not apply in any proceeding for administration of a decedent's estate commenced before July 1, 1988. See Section 11405. As to the application of any amendments made after that date, see Section 3.

Background on Section 11442 of Repealed Code

Section 11442 was added by 1987 Cal.Stat. ch. 923 § 93. The section restated subdivision (c) of former Probate Code Section 980 (repealed by 1987 Cal.Stat. ch. 923 § 48.6) without substantive change and superseded portions of former Probate Code Sections 704.2 and 704.4 (provisions repealed by 1987 Cal.Stat. ch. 923 § 37). [20 Cal.L.Rev.Comm.Reports 1001 (1990)].

Research References

Forms

West's California Code Forms, Probate § 11440 Form 1, Petition to Allocate Debts When There is No Agreement Between Personal Representative and Surviving Spouse.

Treatises and Practice Aids

Witkin, California Summary 10th Wills and Probate § 655, in General.

§ 11443. Notice of hearing on show cause order

The petitioner shall give notice of the hearing as provided in Section 1220, together with a copy of the petition and the order to show cause, if any. *(Stats.1990, c. 79 (A.B.759), § 14, operative July 1, 1991.)*

Law Revision Commission Comments

1990 Enactment

Section 11443 continues Section 11443 of the repealed Probate Code without change. For general provisions, see Sections 1200–1230 (notice of hearing), 1250–1252 (request for special notice), 1260–1265 (proof of giving of notice). This part does not apply in any proceeding for administration of a decedent's estate commenced before July 1, 1988. See Section 11405. As to the application of any amendments made after that date, see Section 3.

Background on Section 11443 of Repealed Code

Section 11443 was added by 1987 Cal.Stat. ch. 923 § 93. The section superseded subdivision (d) of former Probate Code Section 980 (repealed by 1987 Cal.Stat. ch. 923 § 48.6) and incorporated general service of notice procedures. [20 Cal.L.Rev.Comm.Reports 1001 (1990)].

Research References

Forms

West's California Code Forms, Probate § 11440 Form 1, Petition to Allocate Debts When There is No Agreement Between Personal Representative and Surviving Spouse.

Treatises and Practice Aids

Witkin, California Summary 10th Wills and Probate § 655, in General.

§ 11444. Allocation of debt

(a) The personal representative and the surviving spouse may provide for allocation by agreement and, on a determination by the court that the agreement substantially protects the rights of interested persons, the allocation provided in the agreement shall be ordered by the court.

(b) In the absence of an agreement, each debt subject to allocation shall first be characterized by the court as separate or community, in accordance with the laws of the state applicable to marital dissolution proceedings. Following that characterization, the debt or debts shall be allocated as follows:

(1) Separate debts of either spouse shall be allocated to that spouse's separate property assets, and community debts shall be allocated to the spouses' community property assets.

(2) If a separate property asset of either spouse is subject to a secured debt that is characterized as that spouse's separate debt, and the net equity in that asset available to satisfy that secured debt is less than that secured debt, the unsatisfied portion of that secured debt shall be treated as an unsecured separate debt of that spouse and allocated to the net value of that spouse's other separate property assets.

(3) If the net value of either spouse's separate property assets is less than that spouse's unsecured separate debt or debts, the unsatisfied portion of the debt or debts shall be allocated to the net value of that spouse's one-half share of the community property assets. If the net value of that spouse's one-half share of the community property assets is less than that spouse's unsatisfied unsecured separate debt or debts, the remaining unsatisfied portion of the debt or debts shall be allocated to the net value of the other spouse's one-half share of the community property assets.

(4) If a community property asset is subject to a secured debt that is characterized as a community debt, and the net equity in that asset available to satisfy that secured debt is less than that secured debt, the unsatisfied portion of that secured debt shall be treated as an unsecured community debt and allocated to the net value of the other community property assets.

(5) If the net value of the community property assets is less than the unsecured community debt or debts, the unsatisfied portion of the debt or debts shall be allocated equally between the separate property assets of the decedent and the surviving spouse. If the net value of either spouse's separate property assets is less than that spouse's share of the unsatisfied portion of the unsecured community debt or debts, the remaining unsatisfied portion of the debt or debts shall be allocated to the net value of the other spouse's separate property assets.

(c) For purposes of this section:

(1) The net value of either spouse's separate property asset shall refer to its fair market value as of the date of the decedent's death, minus the date-of-death balance of any liens and encumbrances on that asset that have been characterized as that spouse's separate debts.

(2) The net value of a community property asset shall refer to its fair market value as of the date of the decedent's death, minus the date-of-death balance of any liens and encumbrances on that asset that have been characterized as community debts.

(3) In the case of a nonrecourse debt, the amount of that debt shall be limited to the net equity in the collateral, based on the fair market value of the collateral as of the date of the decedent's death, that is available to satisfy that debt. For the purposes of this paragraph, "nonrecourse debt" means a debt for which the debtor's obligation to repay is limited to the collateral securing the debt, and for which a deficiency judgment against the debtor is not permitted by law.

(d) Notwithstanding the foregoing provisions of this section, the court may order a different allocation of debts between the decedent's estate and the surviving spouse if the court finds a different allocation to be equitable under the circumstances.

(e) Nothing contained in this section is intended to impair or affect the rights of third parties. If a personal representative or the surviving spouse incurs any damages or expense, including attorney's fees, on account of the nonpayment of a debt that was allocated to the other party pursuant to subdivision (b), or as the result of a debt being misallocated due to fraud or intentional misrepresentation by the other party, the party incurring damages shall be entitled to recover from the other party for damages or expense deemed reasonable by the court that made the allocation. *(Stats. 1990, c. 79 (A.B.759), § 14, operative July 1, 1991. Amended by Stats.2001, c. 72 (S.B.668), § 1.)*

Law Revision Commission Comments

1990 Enactment

Section 11444 continues Section 11444 of the repealed Probate Code without change. This section makes clear that allocation of liability is to be based on rules applicable to liability of marital property for debts during marriage. See Civil Code Sections 5120.010–5122. This part does not apply in any proceeding for administration of a decedent's estate commenced before July 1, 1988. See Section 11405. As to the application of any amendments made after that date, see Section 3.

Background on Section 11444 of Repealed Code

Section 11444 was added by 1987 Cal.Stat. ch. 923 § 93. The section combined subdivision (e) of former Probate Code Section 980 (repealed by 1987 Cal.Stat. ch. 923 § 48.6) and a portion of former Probate Code Section 713.5 (repealed by 1987 Cal.Stat. ch. 923 § 37). [20 Cal.L.Rev.Comm.Reports 1001 (1990)].

Research References

Forms

West's California Code Forms, Probate § 11440 Form 1, Petition to Allocate Debts When There is No Agreement Between Personal Representative and Surviving Spouse.

West's California Code Forms, Probate § 11445 Form 1, Order to Allocate Debts.

West's California Code Forms, Probate § 19324 COMMENT, Allocation Of Debts Between Trust and Surviving Spouse.

Treatises and Practice Aids

Witkin, California Summary 10th Trusts § 285, Allocation Of Debts.

Witkin, California Summary 10th Wills and Probate § 655, in General.

Witkin, California Summary 10th Wills and Probate § 656, Allocation Rules.

§ 11445. Payment of allocated shares; court order

On making a determination as provided in this chapter, the court shall make an order that:

(a) Directs the personal representative to make payment of the amounts allocated to the estate by payment to the surviving spouse or creditors.

(b) Directs the personal representative to charge amounts allocated to the surviving spouse against any property or interests of the surviving spouse that are in the possession or control of the personal representative. To the extent that property or interests of the surviving spouse in the possession or control of the personal representative are insufficient to satisfy the allocation, the court order shall summarily direct the surviving spouse to pay the allocation to the personal representative. *(Stats.1990, c. 79 (A.B.759), § 14, operative July 1, 1991.)*

Law Revision Commission Comments

1990 Enactment

Section 11445 continues Section 11445 of the repealed Probate Code without change. For general provisions relating to hearings and orders, see Sections 1040–1050. See also Section 7240 (order appealable). This part does not apply in any proceeding for administration of a decedent's estate commenced before July 1, 1988. See Section 11405. As to the application of any amendments made after that date, see Section 3.

Background on Section 11445 of Repealed Code

Section 11445 was added by 1987 Cal.Stat. ch. 923 § 93. The section combined subdivision (f) of former Probate Code Section 980 (repealed by 1987 Cal.Stat. ch. 923 § 48.6) and a portion of former Probate Code Section 713.5 (repealed by 1987 Cal.Stat. ch. 923 § 37). [20 Cal.L.Rev.Comm.Reports 1001 (1990)].

Research References

Forms

West's California Code Forms, Probate § 11445 Form 1, Order to Allocate Debts.

Treatises and Practice Aids

Witkin, California Summary 10th Wills and Probate § 655, in General.

§ 11446. Last illness and funeral expenses

Notwithstanding any other statute, funeral expenses and expenses of last illness shall be charged against the estate of the decedent and shall not be allocated to, or charged against the community share of, the surviving spouse, whether or not the surviving spouse is financially able to pay the expenses and whether or not the surviving spouse or any other person is also liable for the expenses. *(Stats.1990, c. 79 (A.B.759), § 14, operative July 1, 1991.)*

Law Revision Commission Comments

1990 Enactment

Section 11446 continues Section 11446 of the repealed Probate Code without change. This part does not apply in any proceeding for administration of a decedent's estate commenced before July 1, 1988. See Section 11405. As to the application of any amendments made after that date, see Section 3.

Background on Section 11446 of Repealed Code

Section 11446 was added by 1987 Cal.Stat. ch. 923 § 93. The section restated former Probate Code Section 951.1 (repealed by 1987 Cal.Stat. ch. 923 § 48) without substantive change. [20 Cal.L.Rev.Comm.Reports 1001 (1990)].

Research References

Forms

California Transactions Forms--Estate Planning § 3:64, Funeral Expenses.

West's California Code Forms, Probate § 11440 Form 1, Petition to Allocate Debts When There is No Agreement Between Personal Representative and Surviving Spouse.

Treatises and Practice Aids

Witkin, California Summary 10th Wills and Probate § 655, in General.

Witkin, California Summary 10th Wills and Probate § 657, Liability for Funeral Expenses.

Witkin, California Summary 10th Wills and Probate § 823, Debts Of Deceased Spouse.

Division 8

DISPOSITION OF ESTATE WITHOUT ADMINISTRATION

Law Revision Commission Comments

1990 Enactment

This division supersedes Division 8 (commencing with Section 13000) of the repealed Probate Code. The superseded division was enacted upon recommendation of the California Law Revision Commission. See Recommendation Relating to Distribution of Estate Without Administration, 18 Cal.L.Revision Comm'n Reports 1005 (1986); Communication from California Law Revision Commission Concerning Assembly Bill 2625, 18 Cal.L.Revision Comm'n Reports 1743 (1986). The Commission, in cooperation with California Continuing Education of the Bar, published the recommended legislation as enacted with official comments. See Selected 1986 Trust and Probate Legislation, 18 Cal.L.Revision Comm'n Reports 1201, 1503–96 (1986).

Legislation enacted to effectuate an earlier Commission recommendation made significant improvements in the law relating to the distribution of estates without administration. See Recommendation Relating to Distribution of Estates Without Administration, 17 Cal.L.Revision Comm'n Reports 421 (1984). See also Report of Senate Committee on Judiciary on Assembly Bill 2270, 18 Cal.L.Revision Comm'n Reports 63, 64–65 (1986). [20 Cal.L.Rev.Comm.Reports 1001 (1990)].

Part 2

PASSAGE OF PROPERTY TO SURVIVING SPOUSE WITHOUT ADMINISTRATION

CHAPTER 1. GENERAL PROVISIONS

Section
13502. Property subject to administration upon election of surviving spouse.

§ 13500. Spouse dying intestate; surviving spouse; administration not necessary

Except as provided in this chapter, when a spouse dies intestate leaving property that passes to the surviving spouse under Section 6401, or dies testate and by his or her will devises all or a part of his or her property to the surviving spouse, the property passes to the survivor subject to the provisions of Chapter 2 (commencing with Section 13540) and Chapter 3 (commencing with Section 13550), and no administration is necessary. *(Stats.1990, c. 79 (A.B.759), § 14, operative July 1, 1991. Amended by Stats.2016, c. 50 (S.B.1005), § 89, eff. Jan. 1, 2017.)*

Law Revision Commission Comments

1990 Enactment

Section 13500 continues Section 13500 of the repealed Probate Code without change. As to a surviving spouse's waiver of rights, see Sections 140–147.

Background on Section 13500 of Repealed Code

Section 13500 was added by 1986 Cal.Stat. ch. 783 § 24. The section restated subdivision (a) of former Probate Code Section 649.1 (repealed by 1986 Cal.Stat. ch. 783 § 9) without substantive change. For background on the provisions of this division, see the Comment to this division under the division heading. [20 Cal.L.Rev.Comm.Reports 1001 (1990)].

Commentary

Estate of Bonanno, 165 Cal.App.4th 7, 80 Cal.Rptr.3d 560 (2008), held that an estranged wife was estopped from asserting her right under this section to have decedent spouse's property pass to her without administration when she had allowed and benefited from years of administration by an estate administrator. *Bonanno* reasoned that allowing her to do so would be unfair to the administrator and the estate's attorney, who expected to receive payment for the value of their services based on the value of all the property, including the surviving spouse's share.

Research References

Forms

California Transactions Forms--Estate Planning § 1:22, Community Property.
California Transactions Forms--Estate Planning § 1:26, Quasi-Community Property; Separate Property.
California Transactions Forms--Estate Planning § 10:3, Separate Property.
California Transactions Forms--Estate Planning § 10:18, Property Passing to Spouse.
West's California Code Forms, Probate § 13502(A) Form 1, Election to Subject Spousal Property to Estate Administration.

Treatises and Practice Aids

Witkin, California Summary 10th Community Property § 250, Probate Code Revision.
Witkin, California Summary 10th Community Property § 251, Disposition Of Community Property.
Witkin, California Summary 10th Wills and Probate § 21, Adoption and Early Amendments.
Witkin, California Summary 10th Wills and Probate § 27, Major Changes.
Witkin, California Summary 10th Wills and Probate § 31, Major Changes.
Witkin, California Summary 10th Wills and Probate § 405, Probate and Administration.
Witkin, California Summary 10th Wills and Probate § 770, Available Property.
Witkin, California Summary 10th Wills and Probate § 792, Statutory Framework.
Witkin, California Summary 10th Wills and Probate § 794, Property Excluded from Estate.
Witkin, California Summary 10th Wills and Probate § 818, Property Passing Without Administration.

§ 13501. Property subject to administration

Except as provided in Chapter 6 (commencing with Section 6600) of Division 6 and in Part 1 (commencing with Section 13000) of this division, the following property of the decedent is subject to administration under this code:

(a) Property passing to someone other than the surviving spouse under the decedent's will or by intestate succession.

(b) Property disposed of in trust under the decedent's will.

(c) Property in which the decedent's will limits the surviving spouse to a qualified ownership. For the purposes of this subdivision, a devise to the surviving spouse that is conditioned on the spouse surviving the decedent by a specified period of time is not a "qualified ownership" interest if the specified period of time has expired. *(Stats.1990, c. 79 (A.B.759), § 14, operative July 1, 1991.)*

Law Revision Commission Comments

1990 Enactment

Section 13501 continues Section 13501 of the repealed Probate Code without substantive change. Administration of property described in Section 13501 may be avoided under Part 1 (commencing with Section 13000) (collection or transfer of small estate without administration) if the requirements of that part are satisfied. See also Chapter 6 (commencing with Section 6600) of Part 3 of Division 6 (small estate set-aside). As to a surviving spouse's waiver of rights, see Sections 140–147.

Background on Section 13501 of Repealed Code

Section 13501 was added by 1986 Cal.Stat. ch. 783 § 24. The section restated former Probate Code Section 649.3 (repealed by 1986 Cal.Stat. ch. 783 § 9) without substantive change. The section was amended by 1987 Cal.Stat. ch. 923 § 96 to revise a cross reference. The section was again amended by 1988 Cal.Stat. ch. 1199 § 100.5 to correct section references. For background on the provisions of this division, see the Comment to this division under the division heading. [20 Cal.L.Rev.Comm.Reports 1001 (1990)].

Research References

Forms

California Transactions Forms--Estate Planning § 10:18, Property Passing to Spouse.
West's California Code Forms, Probate § 13502(A) Form 1, Election to Subject Spousal Property to Estate Administration.

Treatises and Practice Aids

Witkin, California Summary 10th Community Property § 251, Disposition Of Community Property.

Witkin, California Summary 10th Wills and Probate § 819, Property Subject to Administration.

§ 13502. Property subject to administration upon election of surviving spouse

(a) Upon the election of the surviving spouse or the personal representative, guardian of the estate, or conservator of the estate of the surviving spouse, all or a portion of the following property may be administered under this code:

(1) The one-half of the community property that belongs to the decedent under Section 100, the one-half of the quasi-community property that belongs to the decedent under Section 101, and the separate property of the decedent.

(2) The one-half of the community property that belongs to the surviving spouse under Section 100 and the one-half of the quasi-community property that belongs to the surviving spouse under Section 101.

(b) The election shall be made by a writing specifically evidencing the election filed in the proceedings for the administration of the estate of the deceased spouse within four months after the issuance of letters, or within any further time that the court may allow upon a showing of good cause, and before entry of an order under Section 13656. *(Stats. 1990, c. 79 (A.B.759), § 14, operative July 1, 1991.)*

Law Revision Commission Comments

1990 Enactment

Section 13502 continues Section 13502 of the repealed Probate Code without substantive change. The surviving spouse may elect to probate only a portion of the surviving spouse's one-half of the community or quasi-community property. This permits, for example, probate of all of a block of stock that is community property without the need to probate the surviving spouse's one-half share of the other community property. As to a surviving spouse's waiver of rights, see Sections 140–147.

Background on Section 13502 of Repealed Code

Section 13502 was added by 1986 Cal.Stat. ch. 783 § 24 and was amended by 1988 Cal.Stat. ch. 1199 § 101. The section continued subdivisions (b) and (c) of former Probate Code Section 649.1 (repealed by 1986 Cal.Stat. ch. 783 § 9) with the addition of language in the introductory portion of subdivision (a) that makes clear that "all or a portion" of the described property of the deceased spouse or the surviving spouse may be administered. This language made clear that the surviving spouse may elect to have administered only a portion of the surviving spouse's one-half of the community or quasi-community property. This was consistent with the practice under prior law. The language also recognized the practice in some cases under former law of probating less than all of the property of the deceased spouse in the estate of the deceased spouse. The 1988 amendment corrected terminology and section references. For background on the provisions of this division, see the Comment to this division under the division heading. [20 Cal.L.Rev.Comm.Report 1001 (1990)].

Research References

Forms

California Transactions Forms--Estate Planning § 10:18, Property Passing to Spouse.

West's California Code Forms, Probate § 10951 Form 1, Final Account and Petition for Settlement Of Final Account and for Final Distribution.

West's California Code Forms, Probate § 13503 Form 1, Election and Agreement to Transfer to Trustee.

West's California Code Forms, Probate § 13502(A) Form 1, Election to Subject Spousal Property to Estate Administration.

Treatises and Practice Aids

Witkin, California Summary 10th Community Property § 251, Disposition Of Community Property.

Witkin, California Summary 10th Parent and Child § 302, Estate Planning and Probate.

Witkin, California Summary 10th Wills and Probate § 731, in General.

Witkin, California Summary 10th Wills and Probate § 820, Survivor's Election.

Witkin, California Summary 10th Wills and Probate § 823, Debts Of Deceased Spouse.

Witkin, California Summary 10th Wills and Probate § 829, Nature Of Proceeding.

Witkin, California Summary 10th Wills and Probate § 1026, Petition, Notice, and Hearing.

CHAPTER 3. LIABILITY FOR DEBTS OF DECEASED SPOUSE

§ 13550. Personal liability for debts chargeable against property

Except as provided in Sections 11446, 13552, 13553, and 13554, upon the death of a married person, the surviving spouse is personally liable for the debts of the deceased spouse chargeable against the property described in Section 13551 to the extent provided in Section 13551. *(Stats.1990, c. 79 (A.B.759), § 14, operative July 1, 1991.)*

Law Revision Commission Comments

1990 Enactment

Section 13550 continues Section 13550 of the repealed Probate Code without change.

Background on Section 13550 of Repealed Code

Section 13550 was added by 1986 Cal.Stat. ch. 783 § 24 and was amended by 1988 Cal.Stat. ch. 1199 § 102. The section continued subdivision (a) of former Probate Code Section 649.4 (repealed by 1986 Cal.Stat. ch. 783 § 9) without substantive change. The 1988 amendment corrected a section reference. For background on the provisions of this division, see the Comment to this division under the division heading. [20 Cal.L.Rev.Comm.Reports 1001 (1990)].

Research References

Forms

California Transactions Forms--Estate Planning § 10:18, Property Passing to Spouse.

Treatises and Practice Aids

Witkin, California Summary 10th Community Property § 250, Probate Code Revision.

Witkin, California Summary 10th Community Property § 251, Disposition Of Community Property.

Witkin, California Summary 10th Trusts § 286, Liability Of Surviving Spouse.

Witkin, California Summary 10th Wills and Probate § 266, Community Property With Right Of Survivorship.

Witkin, California Summary 10th Wills and Probate § 624, Claim on Cause Of Action.
Witkin, California Summary 10th Wills and Probate § 792, Statutory Framework.
Witkin, California Summary 10th Wills and Probate § 818, Property Passing Without Administration.
Witkin, California Summary 10th Wills and Probate § 821, Real Property.
Witkin, California Summary 10th Wills and Probate § 822, Securities.
Witkin, California Summary 10th Wills and Probate § 823, Debts Of Deceased Spouse.
Witkin, California Summary 10th Wills and Probate § 824, Property Of Deceased Spouse.

§ 13551. Limitation of liability

The liability imposed by Section 13550 shall not exceed the fair market value at the date of the decedent's death, less the amount of any liens and encumbrances, of the total of the following:

(a) The portion of the one-half of the community and quasi-community property belonging to the surviving spouse under Sections 100 and 101 that is not exempt from enforcement of a money judgment and is not administered in the estate of the deceased spouse.

(b) The portion of the one-half of the community and quasi-community property belonging to the decedent under Sections 100 and 101 that passes to the surviving spouse without administration.

(c) The separate property of the decedent that passes to the surviving spouse without administration. *(Stats.1990, c. 79 (A.B.759), § 14, operative July 1, 1991.)*

Law Revision Commission Comments

1990 Enactment

Section 13551 continues Section 13551 of the repealed Probate Code without change.

Background on Section 13551 of Repealed Code

Section 13551 was added by 1986 Cal.Stat. ch. 783 § 24. The section continued the substance of subdivision (b) of former Probate Code Section 649.4 (repealed by 1986 Cal.Stat. ch. 783 § 9) without substantive change but with the addition of language to make clear that (1) "value" means fair market value and (2) the value of property belonging to the surviving spouse that is administered in the estate of the deceased spouse is excluded in determining the extent of the liability of the surviving spouse. See Section 13502(a) (election to administer only a portion of the community and quasi-community property that belongs to the surviving spouse). For background on the provisions of this division, see the Comment to this division under the division heading. [20 Cal.L.Rev.Comm.Reports 1001 (1990)].

Commentary

When a marital settlement agreement provided for continuing spousal support payments to a former wife after a decedent's death, the decedent's surviving spouse was personally liable, under this section, for the continuing support payments to the extent of the fair market value (less encumbrances) at the time of decedent's death of the real property held in joint tenancy by the decedent and surviving spouse. *Kircher v. Kircher, 189 Cal.App.4th 1105, 117 Cal.Rptr.3d 254 (2010), review denied.*

Research References

Forms

California Transactions Forms--Estate Planning § 10:18, Property Passing to Spouse.

Treatises and Practice Aids

Witkin, California Summary 10th Wills and Probate § 823, Debts Of Deceased Spouse.

Division 9

TRUST LAW

Law Revision Commission Comments

1990 Enactment

This division supersedes Division 9 (commencing with Section 15000) of the repealed Probate Code. The superseded division was enacted upon recommendation of the California Law Revision Commission. See Recommendation Proposing the Trust Law, 18 Cal.L.Revision Comm'n Reports 501 (1986). See also Communication from California Law Revision Commission Concerning Assembly Bill 2652, 18 Cal.L.Revision Comm'n Reports 1763 (1986). The Commission, in cooperation with California Continuing Education of the Bar, published the Trust Law as enacted with official comments. See Selected 1986 Trust and Probate Legislation, 18 Cal.L.Revision Comm'n Reports 1201, 1207–499 (1986).

After this division was enacted, revisions were made upon recommendation of the Law Revision Commission. See Recommendation Relating to Technical Revisions in the Trust Law, 18 Cal.L.Revision Comm'n Reports 1823 (1986); Communication from the California Law Revision Commission Concerning Assembly Bill 362, 19 Cal.L.Revision Comm'n Reports 541 (1988); Comments to Conforming Revisions and Repeals, 19 Cal.L.Revision Comm'n Reports 1031, 1097–98 (1988); Recommendation Relating to Trustees' Fees, 20 Cal.L.Revision Comm'n Reports 185 (1990). [20 Cal.L.Rev.Comm.Reports 1001 (1990)].

Part 2

CREATION, VALIDITY, MODIFICATION, AND TERMINATION OF TRUSTS

Application

Application of Division, see Probate Code § 15001.

CHAPTER 2. RESTRICTIONS ON VOLUNTARY AND INVOLUNTARY TRANSFERS

Application

Application of Division, see Probate Code § 15001.

§ 15305. Claims for child or spousal support

(a) As used in this section, "support judgment" means a money judgment for support of the trust beneficiary's spouse or former spouse or minor child.

(b) If the beneficiary has the right under the trust to compel the trustee to pay income or principal or both to or for the benefit of the beneficiary, the court may, to the extent that the court determines it is equitable and reasonable under the circumstances of the particular case, order the trustee to satisfy all or part of the support judgment out of all or part of those payments as they become due and payable, presently or in the future.

(c) Whether or not the beneficiary has the right under the trust to compel the trustee to pay income or principal or both to or for the benefit of the beneficiary, the court may, to the extent that the court determines it is equitable and reasonable under the circumstances of the particular case, order the trustee to satisfy all or part of the support judgment out of all or part of future payments that the trustee, pursuant to the exercise of the trustee's discretion, determines to make to or for the benefit of the beneficiary.

(d) This section applies to a support judgment notwithstanding any provision in the trust instrument. *(Stats.1990, c. 79 (A.B.759), § 14, operative July 1, 1991.)*

Law Revision Commission Comments

1990 Enactment

Section 15305 continues Section 15305 of the repealed Probate Code without change.

This section is drawn in part from a provision of Wisconsin law relating to enforcement of child support. See Wis.Stat.Ann. § 701.06(4) (West 1981). Section 15305 reflects the same public policy as Section 157(a) of the Restatement (Second) of Trusts (1957). To obtain relief under Section 15305, the judgment creditor under the support judgment must file a petition with the court under Section 709.010 of the Code of Civil Procedure. For general provisions relating to petitions and other papers, see Sections 1020–1023, 17201; see also Sections 1021 (petition to be verified), 1041 (clerk to set petition for hearing). For general provisions relating to notice of hearing, see Sections 1200–1221, 15802–15804, 17100–17105, 17203–17205; see also Sections 1260–1265 (proof of giving notice). For general provisions relating to hearings and orders, see Sections 1040–1050, 17000–17006, 17201–17202, 17206–17207; see also Section 15308.

Although a trust is a spendthrift trust or a trust for support, the interest of the beneficiary can be reached in satisfaction of a money judgment against the beneficiary for child or spousal support. In some cases a spendthrift clause may be construed as not intended to exclude the beneficiary's dependents. Even if the clause is construed as applicable to claims of the dependents for support, it is against public policy to give full effect to the provision. A provision in the trust is not effective to exempt the trust from enforcement of a judgment for support of a minor child or support of a spouse or former spouse. See subdivision (b). As a general rule, the beneficiary should not be permitted to have the enjoyment of the interest under the trust while neglecting to support his or her dependents. It is a matter for the exercise of discretion by the court as to how much of the amount payable to the beneficiary under the trust should be applied for such support and how much the beneficiary should receive. Even though the beneficiary's spouse has obtained an order directing the beneficiary to pay a specified amount for support, the spouse cannot compel the trustee to pay the full amount ordered unless the court determines that it is equitable and reasonable under the circumstances of the particular case to compel the trustee to make the payment. The result is much the same as though the trust were created not solely for the benefit of the beneficiary, but also for the benefit of the beneficiary's dependents. Cf. Estate of Johnston, 252 Cal.App.2d 923, 927–30, 60 Cal.Rptr. 852 (1967) (discussion of public policy in light of former Civil Code § 859).

Background on Section 15305 of Repealed Code

Section 15305 was a new provision added by 1986 Cal.Stat. ch. 820 § 40. The section changed prior California law. Code of Civil Procedure Section 709.010 (prior to its amendment by 1986 Cal.Stat. ch. 820 § 18) included a provision giving the court discretion to divide periodic payments to a beneficiary from a trust (including a spendthrift trust) between the beneficiary and the person or persons entitled to child or spousal support from the beneficiary. The amount that could be applied to child or spousal support was limited to the amount that could have been applied to child or spousal support on a like amount of earnings. This provision was removed from Section 709.010, leaving Section 15305 to govern this situation. Apart from the provision in Code of Civil Procedure Section 709.010, under prior law child or spousal support was not a preferred claim against the interest of a trust beneficiary, and the support claimant was treated the same as any other creditor. See, e.g., In re Lawrence's Estate, 267 Cal.App.2d 77, 82–83, 72 Cal.Rptr. 851 (1968) (former wife); Canfield v. Security–First Nat'l Bank, 8 Cal.App.2d 277, 288–89, 48 P.2d 133 (1935) (former wife); San Diego Trust & Sav. Bank v. Heustis, 121 Cal.App. 675, 683–94, 10 P.2d 158 (1932) (estranged wife); Estate of Johnston, 252 Cal. App.2d 923, 928–29, 60 Cal.Rptr. 852 (1967) (minor child); but see Parscal v. Parscal, 148 Cal.App.3d 1098, 1104–05, 196 Cal.Rptr. 462 (1983) (child support enforceable against beneficiary's interest in trust created by beneficiary's employers under a collective bargaining agreement where employer's contributions based on employee's hours of work); cf. Estate of Lackmann, 156 Cal.App.2d 674, 678–83, 320 P.2d 186 (1958) (state institution in which beneficiary of a spendthrift trust was an inmate permitted to reach the beneficiary's interest). For background on the provisions of this division, see the Comment to this division under the division heading. [20 Cal.L.Rev.Comm.Reports 1001 (1990)].

Commentary

Pratt v. Ferguson, 3 Cal.App.5th 102, 206 Cal.Rptr.3d 895 (2016), holds that this section gives the trial court discretion to order a trustee to make distributions of income and principal to satisfy child support orders despite spendthrift and shutoff clauses in the trust instrument and without regard to whether the trustor intended to benefit the child.

Research References

Forms

California Transactions Forms--Estate Planning § 18:9, No Protection Against Child and Spousal Support.

California Transactions Forms--Estate Planning § 12:55, Claims for Child or Spousal Support.

California Transactions Forms--Estate Planning § 12:58, General Claims Of Creditors.

California Transactions Forms--Estate Planning § 14:15, Spendthrift Provisions.

California Transactions Forms--Estate Planning § 18:12, Extent Of Protection.

Treatises and Practice Aids

Witkin, California Summary 10th Trusts § 154, Rights Of Favored Creditors.

Witkin, California Summary 10th Trusts § 161, Claims for Child or Spousal Support.

Witkin, California Summary 10th Trusts § 164, in General.

Part 4

TRUST ADMINISTRATION

CHAPTER 1. DUTIES OF TRUSTEES

ARTICLE 2. TRUSTEE'S STANDARD OF CARE

§ 16040. Standard of care; modification by trust instrument; exceptions

(a) The trustee shall administer the trust with reasonable care, skill, and caution under the circumstances then prevailing that a prudent person acting in a like capacity would use in the conduct of an enterprise of like character and with like aims to accomplish the purposes of the trust as determined from the trust instrument.

(b) The settlor may expand or restrict the standard provided in subdivision (a) by express provisions in the trust instrument. A trustee is not liable to a beneficiary for the trustee's good faith reliance on these express provisions.

(c) This section does not apply to investment and management functions governed by the Uniform Prudent Investor Act, Article 2.5 (commencing with Section 16045). *(Stats. 1990, c. 79 (A.B.759), § 14, operative July 1, 1991. Amended by Stats.1995, c. 63 (S.B.222), § 4.)*

Law Revision Commission Comments

1990 Enactment

Section 16040 continues Section 16040 of the repealed Probate Code without change. Subdivision (a) provides a general standard of care for administration of the trust; subdivision (b) provides the standard of care applicable to investment and management of trust property.

An expert trustee is held to the standard of care of other experts. See the discussions in Estate of Collins, 72 Cal.App.3d 663, 673, 139 Cal.Rptr. 644 (1977); Coberly v. Superior Court, 231 Cal.App.2d 685, 689, 42 Cal.Rptr. 64 (1965); Estate of Beach, 15 Cal.3d 623, 635, 542 P.2d 994, 125 Cal.Rptr. 570 (1975) (bank as executor); see also Section 16014 (duty to use special skills); Comment to Section 2401 (standard of care applicable to professional guardian or conservator of estate); Comment to Section 3912 (standard of care applicable to professional fiduciary acting as custodian under California Uniform Transfers to Minors Act). The last sentence of subdivision (b) reflects the portfolio approach for judging investment decisions.

1995 Amendment

Section 16040 is amended for harmony with the new Uniform Prudent Investor Act, Article 2.5 (commencing with Section 16045). This section provides a general standard of care that applies where the special, more detailed rule applicable to investments and management of trust property does not apply, such as determining whether to make discretionary distributions, communicating with beneficiaries, and relations with creditors. See subdivision (c).

The portfolio rule formerly provided by subdivision (b) is restated in Section 16047. Former subdivision (c) has been redesignated as subdivision (b) and revised to delete the reference to former subdivision (b). For a special rule protecting the trustee's good-faith reliance on trust provisions concerning investments, see Section 16046 (prudent investor rule). [25 Cal.L.Rev.Comm. Reports 543, 673 (1995)].

Background on Section 16040 of Repealed Code

Section 16040 was added by 1986 Cal.Stat. ch. 820 § 40. For background on the provisions of this division, see the Comment to this division under the division heading.

Subdivision (a) is drawn from subdivision (a)(1) of former Civil Code Section 2261 (repealed by 1986 Cal.Stat. ch. 820 § 7) which applied to investment and management decisions. This subdivision superseded the "ordinary care and diligence" standard that was provided in former Civil Code Section 2259 (repealed by 1986 Cal.Stat. ch. 820 § 7).

Subdivision (b) restated subdivision (a)(1) of former Civil Code Section 2261 without substantive change. The former reference to attaining the goals of the trustor was changed to refer to accomplishing the purposes of the trust.

Subdivision (c) restated subdivision (a)(2) of former Civil Code Section 2261 without substantive change. [20 Cal.L.Rev.Comm.Reports 1001 (1990)].

Research References

Forms

California Transactions Forms--Business Entities § 23:16, Separate Charitable Trust Entities.

California Transactions Forms--Estate Planning § 21:4, Naming and Powers Of Trustee.

California Transactions Forms--Estate Planning § 12:29, Duty to Preserve and Manage Trust Property.

California Transactions Forms--Estate Planning § 12:37, Sources Of Power.

Treatises and Practice Aids

Witkin, California Summary 10th Community Property § 133, Statutory Requirement.

Witkin, California Summary 10th Husband and Wife § 39, in General.

Witkin, California Summary 10th Trusts § 75, in General.

Witkin, California Summary 10th Trusts § 79, Nature and Scope Of Rule.

Witkin, California Summary 10th Trusts § 91, Nature and Scope Of Powers.

Witkin, California Summary 10th Trusts § 118, Liability for Acts Of Agent.

ARTICLE 2.5. UNIFORM PRUDENT INVESTOR ACT

§ 16047. Standard of care; investments and management; considerations

(a) A trustee shall invest and manage trust assets as a prudent investor would, by considering the purposes, terms, distribution requirements, and other circumstances of the trust. In satisfying this standard, the trustee shall exercise reasonable care, skill, and caution.

(b) A trustee's investment and management decisions respecting individual assets and courses of action must be evaluated not in isolation, but in the context of the trust portfolio as a whole and as a part of an overall investment strategy having risk and return objectives reasonably suited to the trust.

(c) Among circumstances that are appropriate to consider in investing and managing trust assets are the following, to the extent relevant to the trust or its beneficiaries:

(1) General economic conditions.

(2) The possible effect of inflation or deflation.

(3) The expected tax consequences of investment decisions or strategies.

(4) The role that each investment or course of action plays within the overall trust portfolio.

(5) The expected total return from income and the appreciation of capital.

(6) Other resources of the beneficiaries known to the trustee as determined from information provided by the beneficiaries.

(7) Needs for liquidity, regularity of income, and preservation or appreciation of capital.

(8) An asset's special relationship or special value, if any, to the purposes of the trust or to one or more of the beneficiaries.

(d) A trustee shall make a reasonable effort to ascertain facts relevant to the investment and management of trust assets.

(e) A trustee may invest in any kind of property or type of investment or engage in any course of action or investment strategy consistent with the standards of this chapter. *(Added by Stats.1995, c. 63 (S.B.222), § 6.)*

Law Revision Commission Comments

1995 Addition

Section 16047 is generally the same in substance as Section 2(a)-(e) of the Uniform Prudent Investor Act (1994). Subdivisions (a)-(c) of Section 16047 replace the portfolio investment rule of former subdivision (b) of Section 16040. Subdivision (a) is also the same in substance as the first paragraph and subsection (a) of Section 227 of Restatement (Third) of Trusts: Prudent Investor Rule (1992).

The second sentence of subdivision (a) states the basic elements of prudence. Thus, where "prudence" is used in this article, it includes "reasonable care, skill, and caution." These elements are delineated in the Restatement:

[Care]

The duty of care requires the trustee to exercise reasonable effort and diligence in making and monitoring investments for the trust, with attention to the trust's objectives. The trustee has a related duty of care in keeping informed of rights and opportunities associated with those investments....

[Skill]

The exercise of care alone is not sufficient, however, because a trustee is liable for losses resulting from failure to use the skill of an individual of ordinary intelligence. This is so despite the careful use of all the skill of which the particular trustee is capable.

On the other hand, if follows from the requirement of care as well as from sound policy that, if the trustee possesses a degree of skill greater than that of an individual of ordinary intelligence, the trustee is liable for a loss that results from failure to make reasonably diligent use of that skill....

[Caution]

In addition to the duty to use care and skill, the trustee must exercise the caution of a prudent investor managing similar funds for similar purposes. In the absence of contrary provisions in the terms of the trust, this requirement of caution requires the trustee to invest with a view both to safety of the capital and to securing a reasonable return....

Restatement (Third) of Trusts: Prudent Investor Rule § 227 comments d & e (1992). For a full discussion, see *id.* § 227, comments & Reporter's Notes (1992).

Subdivision (d) is new to the code. Subdivision (e) replaces former Section 16223 ("The trustee has the power to invest in any kind of property, whether real, personal, or mixed."). This subdivision, like its predecessor, makes clear that there are no categorical restrictions on proper investments. Any form of investment is permissible in the absence of a prohibition in the trust instrument or an overriding duty. This subdivision is intended to permit investment in investment company shares, mutual funds, index funds, and other modern vehicles for collective investments. While investment in these funds is not forbidden merely because discretion over the fund is delegated to others, the trustee is ultimately subject to fiduciary standards under this chapter in making the investment. See also Sections 62 ("property" defined), 16053 (language invoking standard of Uniform Prudent Investor Act), 16202 (exercise of powers is subject to duties), 16203 (trust instrument that incorporates the powers provided in former Section 1120.2 of the repealed Probate Code).

Statutes pertaining to legal investments appear in other codes. See, e.g., Fin. Code §§ 1561.1 (funds provided services by trust company or affiliate), 1564 (common trust funds); Gov't Code §§ 971.2, 17202, 61673; Harb. & Nav. Code §§ 6331, 6931; Health and Safety Code §§ 33663, 34369, 37649, 52040, 52053.5; Pub. Res. Code § 26026; Sts. & Hy. Code §§ 8210, 25371, 30241, 30242, 31173; Water Code §§ 9526, 20064.

Section 2(f) of the Uniform Prudent Investor Act (1994) has been omitted from Section 16047 because it is unnecessary. The same general rule is provided by Section 16014 (duty to use special skills). An expert trustee is held to the standard of care of other experts. See the discussions in Estate of Collins, 72 Cal.App.3d 663, 673, 139 Cal.Rptr. 644 (1977); Coberly v. Superior Court, 231 Cal.App.2d 685, 689, 42 Cal.Rptr. 64 (1965); Estate of Beach, 15 Cal.3d 623, 635, 542 P.2d 994, 125 Cal.Rptr. 570 (1975) (bank as executor); see also Section 2401 Comment (standard of care applicable to professional guardian or conservator of estate); Section 3912 Comment (standard of care applicable to professional fiduciary acting as custodian under California Uniform Transfers to Minors Act). [25 Cal.L.Rev.Comm. Reports 673 (1995)].

Research References

Forms

California Transactions Forms--Business Entities § 23:16, Separate Charitable Trust Entities.

California Transactions Forms--Estate Planning § 21:4, Naming and Powers Of Trustee.

California Transactions Forms--Estate Planning § 12:31, Compliance With Prudent Investor Rule.

California Transactions Forms--Estate Planning § 12:149, Standard for Investment.

Treatises and Practice Aids

Witkin, California Summary 10th Community Property § 133, Statutory Requirement.

Witkin, California Summary 10th Husband and Wife § 39, in General.

Witkin, California Summary 10th Trusts § 80, Standard Of Care.

Witkin, California Summary 10th Trusts § 91, Nature and Scope Of Powers.

Witkin, California Summary 10th Trusts § 105, Investments.

Witkin, California Summary 10th Trusts § 173, Law Revision Commission Comments.

Witkin, California Summary 10th Trusts § 185, Non-Income-Producing Assets.

Division 11

CONSTRUCTION OF WILLS, TRUSTS, AND OTHER INSTRUMENTS

Part 1

RULES FOR INTERPRETATION OF INSTRUMENTS

CHAPTER 1. GENERAL PROVISIONS

§ 21110. Transferee's death; taking by representation; contrary intent in instrument

(a) Subject to subdivision (b), if a transferee is dead when the instrument is executed, or fails or is treated as failing to survive the transferor or until a future time required by the instrument, the issue of the deceased transferee take in the transferee's place in the manner provided in Section 240. A transferee under a class gift shall be a transferee for the purpose of this subdivision unless the transferee's death occurred before the execution of the instrument and that fact was known to the transferor when the instrument was executed.

(b) The issue of a deceased transferee do not take in the transferee's place if the instrument expresses a contrary intention or a substitute disposition. A requirement that the initial transferee survive the transferor or survive for a specified period of time after the death of the transferor constitutes a contrary intention. A requirement that the initial transferee survive until a future time that is related to the probate of the transferor's will or administration of the estate of the transferor constitutes a contrary intention.

(c) As used in this section, "transferee" means a person who is kindred of the transferor or kindred of a surviving, deceased, or former spouse of the transferor. *(Added by Stats.1994, c. 806 (A.B.3686), § 41. Amended by Stats.2002, c. 138 (A.B.1784), § 19.)*

Law Revision Commission Comments

2002 Amendment

Subdivision (b) of Section 21110 is amended to avoid the implication that a specific period of time is the only expression of survival that constitutes a contrary intention. While an expression of that type may well indicate an intention that the antilapse statute not apply, other survival requirements in an instrument may also be sufficient to override the antilapse statute.

In applying the provision of subdivision (b) relating to a substitute gift, care must be taken not to ascribe to the transferor too readily or too broadly an intention to override the antilapse statute, the purpose of which is to lessen the risk of serious oversight by the transferor. For example, by providing a substitute taker, the transferor may very well intend to override the antilapse statute in the ordinary case. If, however, the substitute taker has also predeceased the transferor, the transferor may have intended that the antilapse statute should apply to the first taker.

Section 21110 does not make a substitute gift in the case of a class gift where a person otherwise answering the description of the class was dead when the instrument was executed and that fact was known to the transferor. It is consistent with Estate of Steidl, 89 Cal.App.2d 488, 201 P.2d 58 (1948) (antilapse statute applied where class member died before testator but after execution of will).

Subdivision (c) makes the antilapse statute apply not only to kindred of the transferor but also to kindred of a surviving, deceased, or former spouse of the transferor. Thus, if the transferor were to make a transfer to a stepchild who predeceased the transferor, Section 21110 will make a substitute gift to issue of the predeceased stepchild. The term "kindred" was taken from former Section 92 (repealed by 1983 Cal. Stat. ch. 842, § 18) and refers to persons related by blood. In re Estate of Sowash, 62 Cal.App. 512, 516, 217 P. 123 (1923). In addition, an adoptee is generally kindred of the adoptive family and not of the natural relatives. See Section 21115 (halfbloods, adopted persons, persons born out of wedlock, stepchildren, and foster children, plus issue of such persons, as "kindred" or "issue"). See also Estate of Goulart, 222 Cal.App.2d 808, 35 Cal.Rptr. 465 (1963).

As to when a transferee is treated as having predeceased the transferor, see Sections 220 (simultaneous death), 282 (effect of disclaimer), 250 (effect of feloniously and intentionally killing decedent), 6122 & 5600 (effect of dissolution of marriage), See also Sections 230–234 (proceeding to determine survival), 240 (manner of taking by representation). [31 Cal.L.Rev.Comm. Reports 197 (2001)].

Research References

Forms

California Transactions Forms--Estate Planning § 6:7, Persons Included in Class.

California Transactions Forms--Estate Planning § 21:6, Modification and Revocation Of Trust.

California Transactions Forms--Estate Planning § 6:21, Devisee's Failure to Survive.

California Transactions Forms--Estate Planning § 6:22, Antilapse Statutes.

California Transactions Forms--Estate Planning § 6:31, Omitted Child Statutes.

California Transactions Forms--Estate Planning § 6:51, Matters to Consider in Drafting Dispositions to Beneficiaries.

California Transactions Forms--Estate Planning § 19:48, "120-Hour" Survival Requirement.

California Transactions Forms--Estate Planning § 20:15, Lapsed Devises.

California Transactions Forms--Estate Planning § 20:74, Direction Not to Apply Anti-Lapse Statute.

California Transactions Forms--Estate Planning § 6:105, Devise Lapses If Devisee Predeceases Testator.

California Transactions Forms--Estate Planning § 6:106, Requirement that Beneficiary Survive Decedent by Specified Period.

California Transactions Forms--Estate Planning § 6:107, Devise Not to Lapse on Death Of Beneficiary Before Death Of Testator.

California Transactions Forms--Estate Planning § 19:116, Will for Single Person.

Treatises and Practice Aids

Witkin, California Summary 10th Wills and Probate § 29, Major Changes.

Witkin, California Summary 10th Wills and Probate § 214, Statutory Rules.

Witkin, California Summary 10th Wills and Probate § 252, California Statute.

Witkin, California Summary 10th Wills and Probate § 261, Effect Of Lapsed Gift.

Witkin, California Summary 10th Wills and Probate § 263, Revised Statute.

Witkin, California Summary 10th Wills and Probate § 291, Authorized Purposes.

Witkin, California Summary 10th Wills and Probate § 295, Wills, Trusts, and Intestate Succession.

Witkin, California Summary 10th Wills and Probate § 388, Heirs and Devisees.

§ 21112. Issue; conditions

A condition in a transfer of a present or future interest that refers to a person's death "with" or "without" issue, or to a person's "having" or "leaving" issue or no issue, or a condition based on words of similar import, is construed to refer to that person's being dead at the time the transfer takes effect in enjoyment and to that person either having or not having, as the case may be, issue who are alive at the time of enjoyment. *(Added by Stats.1994, c. 806 (A.B.3686), § 41. Amended by Stats.2002, c. 138 (A.B.1784), § 21.)*

Law Revision Commission Comments

2002 Amendment

The amendment to Section 21112 is technical. The 1994 enactment of Section 21112 extended former Section 6149 (wills) to trusts and other instruments. See also Section 21101 (application of part).

The section overrules California's much criticized theory of indefinite failure of issue established by *In re* Estate of Carothers, 161 Cal. 588, 119 P. 926 (1911). See generally 12 B. Witkin, Summary of California Law *Wills and Probate* §§ 279–80, at 310–12 (9th ed. 1990). Section 6149 adopts the majority view of the Restatement of Property. See Witkin, *id.* § 280, at 310–12; Annot., 26 A.L.R.3d 407 (1969); Restatement of Property § 269 (1940). Under Section 21112, if the transfer is "to *A* for life, remainder to *B* and *B*'s heirs, but if *B* dies without issue, then to *C*," the transfer is read as meaning "if *B* dies before *A* without issue living at the death of *A*." If *B* survives *A*, whether or not *B* then has living issue, *B* takes the transfer absolutely. If *B* predeceases *A* with issue then living but at the time of *A*'s subsequent death *B* does not have living issue, the transfer goes to *C*. [31 Cal.L.Rev.Comm. Reports 200 (2001)].

Research References

Treatises and Practice Aids

Witkin, California Summary 10th Wills and Probate § 220, Where Distribution or Possession is Postponed.

§ 21114. Transfers to heirs; designated persons

(a) If a statute or an instrument provides for transfer of a present or future interest to, or creates a present or future interest in, a designated person's "heirs," "heirs at law," "next of kin," "relatives," or "family," or words of similar import, the transfer is to the persons, including the state under Section 6800, and in the shares that would succeed to the designated person's intestate estate under the intestate succession law of the transferor's domicile, if the designated person died when the transfer is to take effect in enjoyment. If the designated person's surviving spouse is living but is remarried at the time the transfer is to take effect in enjoyment, the surviving spouse is not an heir of the designated person for purposes of this section.

(b) As used in this section, "designated person" includes the transferor. *(Added by Stats.1994, c. 806 (A.B.3686), § 41. Amended by Stats.2002, c. 138 (A.B.1784), § 23.)*

Law Revision Commission Comments

2002 Amendment

Section 21114 is amended to conform to Uniform Probate Code Section 2–711 (1993). The amendment clarifies a number of issues:

(1) Application of the section to interests acquired by operation of law.

(2) Application of escheat principles.

(3) Application of the law of another state, based on the transferor's domicile.

(4) Elimination of the special rule for ancestral property.

The 1994 enactment of Section 21114 extended former Section 6151 (wills) to trusts and other instruments. See also Section 21101 (application of part). The former section was drawn from Section 2514 of the Pennsylvania Consolidated Statutes, Title 20, and established a special rule for a class gift to an indefinite class such as the transferor's or another designated person's "heirs," "next of kin," "relative," "family," and the like. As Section 21114 applies to a transfer of a future interest, the section is consistent with Section 21109 in that Section 21114 establishes a constructional preference against early vesting. However, Section 21114 differs from Section 21109 in that one who does not survive until the future interest takes effect in enjoyment is not deemed a member of the indefinite class described in Section 21114 (such as "heirs"), is therefore not a "transferee" under the class gift, and no substitute gift will be made by the antilapse statute (Section 21110). If the transfer of a future interest is to a more definite class such as "children," one coming within that description who fails to survive until the transfer takes effect in enjoyment does not take under the instrument (Section 21109) but may nonetheless be a "deceased transferee" under the antilapse statute (Section 21110) permitting substitution of the deceased transferee's issue. See Sections 21109 & 21110 Comments. See also Section 21115(c)(3) (rules for determining persons who would be heirs of transferor or other person).

By postponing the determination of class membership until the gift takes effect in enjoyment where the class is indefinite (e.g., to "heirs"), Section 21114 should reduce the uncertainty of result under prior law. See Halbach, *Future Interests: Express and Implied Conditions of Survival*, 49 Cal. L. Rev. 297, 317–20 (1961). Section 21114 is consistent with *Estate of Easter*, 24 Cal.2d 191, 148 P.2d 601 (1944). [31 Cal.L.Rev.Comm. Reports 201 (2001)].

Research References

Forms

California Transactions Forms--Estate Planning § 6:6, Distinction Between Class and Individual Gifts.

California Transactions Forms--Estate Planning § 6:7, Persons Included in Class.

California Transactions Forms--Estate Planning § 20:9, Devises to Heirs.

California Transactions Forms--Estate Planning § 6:52, Matters to Consider in Drafting Class Gifts.

California Transactions Forms--Estate Planning § 6:65, Beneficiaries Determined Under Laws Of Intestate Succession.

Treatises and Practice Aids

Witkin, California Summary 10th Real Property § 14, Interest Passing.

Witkin, California Summary 10th Wills and Probate § 228, in General.

Witkin, California Summary 10th Wills and Probate § 233, in General.

Witkin, California Summary 10th Wills and Probate § 234, Time When Heirs Are Ascertained.

Witkin, California Summary 10th Wills and Probate § 261, Effect Of Lapsed Gift.

§ 21115. Halfbloods, adoptees, persons born out of wedlock, stepchildren and foster children; inclusion; intestate succession

(a) Except as provided in subdivision (b), halfbloods, adopted persons, persons born out of wedlock, stepchildren, foster children, and the issue of these persons when appropriate to the class, are included in terms of class gift or relationship in accordance with the rules for determining relationship and inheritance rights for purposes of intestate succession.

(b) In construing a transfer by a transferor who is not the natural parent, a person born to the natural parent shall not be considered the child of that parent unless the person lived while a minor as a regular member of the household of the natural parent or of that parent's parent, brother, sister, spouse, or surviving spouse. In construing a transfer by a transferor who is not the adoptive parent, a person adopted by the adoptive parent shall not be considered the child of that parent unless the person lived while a minor (either before or after the adoption) as a regular member of the household of the adopting parent or of that parent's parent, brother, sister, or surviving spouse.

(c) Subdivisions (a) and (b) shall also apply in determining:

(1) Persons who would be kindred of the transferor or kindred of a surviving, deceased, or former spouse of the transferor under Section 21110.

(2) Persons to be included as issue of a deceased transferee under Section 21110.

(3) Persons who would be the transferor's or other designated person's heirs under Section 21114.

(d) The rules for determining intestate succession under this section are those in effect at the time the transfer is to take effect in enjoyment. *(Added by Stats.1994, c. 806 (A.B.3686), § 41. Amended by Stats.2002, c. 138 (A.B.1784), § 24.)*

Law Revision Commission Comments

2002 Amendment

Subdivision (d) is added to Section 21115 for consistency with the choice of law rules of Section 21114. The 1994 enactment of Section 21115 extended former Section 6152 (wills) to trusts and other instruments. See also Section 21101 (application of part).

Subdivision (a) is drawn from Section 2–611 of the Uniform Probate Code (1987). As to the construction of provisions drawn from uniform acts, see Section 2. To the extent that California cases had addressed the matter, subdivision (a) is consistent with prior California law. See 12 B. Witkin, Summary of California Law *Wills and Probate* §§ 287–90, at 320–23 (9th ed. 1990). For the rules for determining relationship and inheritance rights for purposes of intestate succession, see Sections 6406, 6408. Under some circumstances stepchildren and foster children are included in terms of class gift or relationship pursuant to the rules for intestate succession. See Section 6408 (when stepchild or foster child treated the same as adopted child).

Subdivision (b) precludes the adoption of a person (often an adult) solely for the purpose of permitting the adoptee to take under the testamentary instrument of another. Subdivision (b) also construes a transfer to exclude a child born out of wedlock (where the transferor is not the parent) if the child never lives while a minor as a regular member of the parent's household. A child is included in class gift terminology in the transferor's instrument if the child lived while a minor or as a regular member of the household of the parent's spouse or surviving spouse. As a result, a child born of a marital relationship will almost always be included in the class, consistent with the transferor's likely intent.

Subdivision (c) makes clear that the rules stated in subdivisions (a) and (b) apply for the purposes of the antilapse statute (Section 21110) and in construing transfers (Section 21114). [31 Cal.L.Rev. Comm. Reports 203 (2001)].

Commentary

Applying subsection (b), *Estate of DeLoreto, 118 Cal.App.4th 1048, 13 Cal.Rptr.3d 513 (2004)*, concluded that persons who were adopted as adults by testator's now deceased child, were not "grandchildren" within the meaning of testator's will. *DeLoreto* additionally holds that this section applies, as a rule of construction, to determine a testator's intent even though it was enacted after the testator's death

Research References

Forms

California Transactions Forms--Estate Planning § 6:7, Persons Included in Class.

California Transactions Forms--Estate Planning § 20:9, Devises to Heirs.

California Transactions Forms--Estate Planning § 6:22, Antilapse Statutes.

California Transactions Forms--Estate Planning § 6:52, Matters to Consider in Drafting Class Gifts.

California Transactions Forms--Estate Planning § 19:101, Adopted Children and Stepchildren.

California Transactions Forms--Estate Planning § 19:116, Will for Single Person.

California Transactions Forms--Estate Planning § 19:143, General Provision.

California Transactions Forms--Estate Planning § 19:144, Adopted Persons Included.

California Transactions Forms--Estate Planning § 19:145, Adopted Persons Excluded.

California Transactions Forms--Family Law § 6:19, Testate Succession Rights.

West's California Code Forms, Probate § 248 Form 1, Petition to Determine Identity Of Heirs.

Treatises and Practice Aids

Witkin, California Summary 10th Wills and Probate § 27, Major Changes.

Witkin, California Summary 10th Wills and Probate § 93, in General.

Witkin, California Summary 10th Wills and Probate § 117, Definitions and Rules Of Construction.

Witkin, California Summary 10th Wills and Probate § 228, in General.

Witkin, California Summary 10th Wills and Probate § 229, Adopted Children.

Witkin, California Summary 10th Wills and Probate § 230, Adopted Adults.

Witkin, California Summary 10th Wills and Probate § 231, Out Of Wedlock Children.

Witkin, California Summary 10th Wills and Probate § 233, in General.

Witkin, California Summary 10th Wills and Probate § 263, Revised Statute.

Part 3

NO CONTEST CLAUSE

§ 21310. Definitions

As used in this part:

(a) "Contest" means a pleading filed with the court by a beneficiary that would result in a penalty under a no contest clause, if the no contest clause is enforced.

(b) "Direct contest" means a contest that alleges the invalidity of a protected instrument or one or more of its terms, based on one or more of the following grounds:

(1) Forgery.

(2) Lack of due execution.

(3) Lack of capacity.

(4) Menace, duress, fraud, or undue influence.

(5) Revocation of a will pursuant to Section 6120, revocation of a trust pursuant to Section 15401, or revocation of an instrument other than a will or trust pursuant to the procedure for revocation that is provided by statute or by the instrument.

(6) Disqualification of a beneficiary under Section 6112, 21350, or 21380.

(c) "No contest clause" means a provision in an otherwise valid instrument that, if enforced, would penalize a beneficiary for filing a pleading in any court.

(d) "Pleading" means a petition, complaint, cross-complaint, objection, answer, response, or claim.

(e) "Protected instrument" means all of the following instruments:

(1) The instrument that contains the no contest clause.

(2) An instrument that is in existence on the date that the instrument containing the no contest clause is executed and is expressly identified in the no contest clause, either individually or as part of an identifiable class of instruments, as being governed by the no contest clause. *(Added by Stats.2008, c. 174 (S.B.1264), § 2, operative Jan. 1, 2010. Amended by Stats.2010, c. 620 (S.B.105), § 5.)*

Law Revision Commission Comments

2008 Addition

Section 21310 is new. Subdivision (a) continues part of the substance of former Section 21300(b).

Subdivision (b)(1)–(5) continues the substance of former Section 21300(b), except that mistake and misrepresentation are no longer included as separate grounds for a direct contest.

Subdivision (b)(6) is consistent with former Sections 21306(a)(3) and 21307(c).

Subdivision (c) continues the substance of former Section 21300(d).

Subdivision (d) restates the substance of former Section 21305(f).

Subdivision (e) is new. Subdivision (e)(1) provides that a protected instrument includes an instrument that contains a no contest clause. That may include an instrument that expressly incorporates or republishes a no contest clause in another instrument. Subdivision (e)(2) is similar to former Section 21305(a)(3). [38 Cal.L.Rev. Comm. Reports apx 5 (2008)].

2010 Amendment

Section 21310 is amended to correct a reference to former Section 21350. [38 Cal.L.Rev.Comm. Reports 107 (2008)].

Commentary

For general discussion of former Section 21300, see *Burch v. George, 7 Cal.4th 246, 27 Cal.Rptr.2d 165 (1994). Burch v. George* is explained and analyzed in the Commentary to Probate Code Sections 100 and 21311.

Applying subsections (b) and (c) of former section 21300, *Johnson v. Greenelsh, 47 Cal.4th 598, 100 Cal.Rptr.3d 622, 217 P.3d 1194 (2009)*, held that a trustee's challenge to a surviving spouse's mental capacity to exercise managerial rights under a family trust is not an attack on the trust itself so long as it does not seek to alter the estate plan established by the trust. *Johnson* held that the challenged documents were not "instruments" within the meaning of Probate Code section 45 and therefore the challenge was not a "direct contest." The challenge was not an "indirect contest'" because the trustee's claims did not conflict with any of the provisions of the trust. Moreover, the trustee's claims were consistent with her fiduciary obligations as a trustee under Probate Code sections 16000, 16002 and 16006.

Research References

Forms

California Transactions Forms--Estate Planning § 2:34, Overview.
California Transactions Forms--Estate Planning § 2:36, Criteria for Use Of No-Contest Clauses in Estate Planning Documents.
California Transactions Forms--Estate Planning § 6:34, Contest Provisions Generally.
California Transactions Forms--Estate Planning § 6:35, Enforcing No-Contest Provisions.
California Transactions Forms--Estate Planning § 6:57, Matters to Consider in Drafting No-Contest Clause.
California Transactions Forms--Estate Planning § 18:33, One-Year Statute Of Limitations.
California Transactions Forms--Estate Planning § 19:98, No-Contest Provision.
California Transactions Forms--Estate Planning § 21:15, Basic Testamentary Trust.
California Transactions Forms--Estate Planning § 6:116, No-Contest Clause for Will.
California Transactions Forms--Estate Planning § 6:117, No-Contest Clause for Trust.

Treatises and Practice Aids

Witkin, California Summary 10th Trusts § 23, Other Provisions Governing Trusts.
Witkin, California Summary 10th Wills and Probate § 561, Statutory Framework.
Witkin, California Summary 10th Wills and Probate § 562, Determination Whether Act Constitutes Contest.
Witkin, California Summary 10th Wills and Probate § 563, Validity and Effect Of Clause.
Witkin, California Summary 10th Wills and Probate § 564, Strict Construction.

Witkin, California Summary 10th Wills and Probate § 565, in General.
Witkin, California Summary 10th Wills and Probate § 566, Forgery.
Witkin, California Summary 10th Wills and Probate § 567, Revocation.
Witkin, California Summary 10th Wills and Probate § 568, Benefit to Interested Person.
Witkin, California Summary 10th Wills and Probate § 569, Invalid Donative Transfer.
Witkin, California Summary 10th Wills and Probate § 570, Claim Of Creditor.
Witkin, California Summary 10th Wills and Probate § 571, Property Claimed Independent Of Instrument.
Witkin, California Summary 10th Wills and Probate § 572, Action to Determine Character, Title, or Ownership Of Property.
Witkin, California Summary 10th Wills and Probate § 573, Challenge to Validity Of Another Instrument.
Witkin, California Summary 10th Wills and Probate § 574, Challenge on Ground Of Duress and Undue Influence.
Witkin, California Summary 10th Wills and Probate § 575, Procedural Challenges.
Witkin, California Summary 10th Wills and Probate § 576, Public Policy Limitations.
Witkin, California Summary 10th Wills and Probate § 560A, (New) Revised No Contest Clause Statutes.

§ 21311. Enforcement of clause

(a) A no contest clause shall only be enforced against the following types of contests:

(1) A direct contest that is brought without probable cause.

(2) A pleading to challenge a transfer of property on the grounds that it was not the transferor's property at the time of the transfer. A no contest clause shall only be enforced under this paragraph if the no contest clause expressly provides for that application.

(3) The filing of a creditor's claim or prosecution of an action based on it. A no contest clause shall only be enforced under this paragraph if the no contest clause expressly provides for that application.

(b) For the purposes of this section, probable cause exists if, at the time of filing a contest, the facts known to the contestant would cause a reasonable person to believe that there is a reasonable likelihood that the requested relief will be granted after an opportunity for further investigation or discovery. *(Added by Stats.2008, c. 174 (S.B.1264), § 2, operative Jan. 1, 2010.)*

Law Revision Commission Comments

2008 Addition

Section 21311 is new.

Subdivision (a)(1) generalizes the probable cause exception provided in former Sections 21306 and 21307, so that it applies to all direct contests.

For a direct contest based on Section 6112 or 21350, the probable cause exception requires only that the contestant show probable cause that a beneficiary is a witness described in Section 6112(c) or a "disqualified person" under Section 21350.5.

Subdivision (a)(2) restates the substance of former Section 21305(a)(2). It provides for enforcement of a no contest clause in response to a pleading that contests a transfer of property on the ground that the property was not subject to the transferor's dispositional control at the time of the transfer. Probable cause is not a defense to the enforcement of a no contest clause under this provision.

Subdivision (a)(3) continues former Section 21305(a)(1) without substantive change. Probable cause is not a defense to the enforcement of a no contest clause under this provision.

Subdivision (b) restates the reasonable cause exception provided in former Sections 21306, with two exceptions:

(1) The former standard referred only to the contestant's factual contentions. By contrast, subdivision (b) refers to the granting of relief, which requires not only the proof of factual contentions but also a legally sufficient ground for the requested relief.

(2) The former standard required only that success be "likely." One court interpreted that standard as requiring only that a contest be "legally tenable."' In re Estate of Gonzalez, 102 Cal.App.4th 1296, 1304, 126 Cal.Rptr.2d 332 (2002). Subdivision (a) imposes a higher standard. There must be a "reasonable likelihood" that the requested relief will be granted. The term "reasonable likelihood" has been interpreted to mean more than merely possible, but less than "more probable than not." See Alvarez v. Superior Ct., 154 Cal.App.4th 642, 653 n.4, 64 Cal.Rptr.3d 854 (2007) (construing Penal Code § 938.1); People v. Proctor, 4 Cal.4th 499, 523, 15 Cal.Rptr.2d 340 (1992) (construing Penal Code § 1033). See Section 21310(b) ("direct contest" defined). [38 Cal.L.Rev.Comm. Reports apx 5 (2008)].

Commentary

This section states the general California rule that a no contest clause is enforceable according to its terms. Although the California Supreme Court commented extensively on the no contest clause sections in *Burch v. George, 7 Cal.4th 246, 27 Cal.Rptr.2d 165 (1994)*, that discussion must be read in context. In *Burch v. George*, a sharply divided Supreme Court purported to hold that a no contest clause in decedent husband's trust forced his surviving wife to an election either to take the testamentary gifts under the trust or to assert her community property rights in the trust property. The dissenting justices argued that the assertion of community property rights is not an attack upon an instrument, but rather an assertion of independent ownership rights. Additionally, they pointed out that Section 21304 requires that a no contest clause be strictly construed. Yet close reading of *Burch v. George* suggests that it is fundamentally an election case. Before his death, decedent established an inter vivos trust with testamentary provisions. In the preliminary recitals, he stated that all property placed in the trust was entirely his separate property, even though some of it was at least arguably community property. His surviving spouse, pursuant to Section 21320, sought to determine whether her initiation of a proceeding to claim her community property rights in the trust property would violate the no contest clause. The majority concluded that it would violate the no contest clause because the separate property recital of decedent's trust together with the fact that he placed community property in the trust implicitly put the surviving spouse to an election. Thus, even in the absence of a no contest clause, the majority's conclusion would seem to compel a finding that the survivor was put to an election, that is, that she could either claim her community property rights or she could take decedent's gifts under the trust, but that she could not do both. In this sense, the discussion of the no contest clause is gratuitous and unnecessary. Thus *Burch v. George* should be read to hold, rather narrowly, that when a surviving spouse is already forced to an election based on the other facts of the case, a no contest clause will trigger a forfeiture of testamentary gifts to the survivor if the survivor initiates a proceeding to assert her community property rights. On its facts, *Burch v George* merely treats the no contest clause as the enforcement mechanism of an independently created obligation to elect. As such, it should probably not be read to prescribe general interpretive rules for no contest clauses.

Relying on *Burch v. George*, *Genger v. Delsol, 56 Cal.App.4th 1410, 66 Cal.Rptr.2d 527 (1997)*, holds that a widow's action to set aside a stock redemption agreement included in an integrated estate plan would violate a no contest clause because it would frustrate the decedent's estate plan. Also relying on *Burch v. George, Estate of Pittman, 63 Cal.App.4th 290, 73 Cal.Rptr.2d 622 (1998), review denied July 22, 1998,* held that an attempt by the beneficiaries of the decedent wife to have assets in a testamentary trust recharacterized as community property, where the testamentary trust had systemically characterized all the assets as either the community property or the separate property of the spouses, constituted a will contest and thus violated the no contest clause of the trust. *Pittman* pointed out that the beneficiaries could have avoided forfeiture by using Section 21320 to determine whether their attempt would be deemed a violation of the trust's no contest clause.

Safai v. Safai, 164 Cal.App.4th 233, 78 Cal.Rptr.3d 759 (2008), held that claims made on behalf of a child by the child's guardian ad litem, appointed pursuant to section 1003(a), against a deceased parent's trust would not violate the trust's no contest clause because a minor cannot *voluntarily* participate in a trust contest.

Perrin v. Lea, 164 Cal.App.4th 1239, 79 Cal.Rptr.3d 885 (2008), held that a petition to invalidate amendments to a deceased parent's trust, pursued on behalf of children by a guardian ad litem, would not violate the trust's no contest clause because the clause did not specifically state that it applied to trust amendments.

For further discussion of no contest clauses, see Commentary to Probate Code section 100.

Research References

Forms

California Transactions Forms--Estate Planning § 2:34, Overview.

Treatises and Practice Aids

Witkin, California Summary 10th Wills and Probate § 565, in General.
Witkin, California Summary 10th Wills and Probate § 566, Forgery.
Witkin, California Summary 10th Wills and Probate § 570, Claim Of Creditor.
Witkin, California Summary 10th Wills and Probate § 572, Action to Determine Character, Title, or Ownership Of Property.
Witkin, California Summary 10th Wills and Probate § 560A, (New) Revised No Contest Clause Statutes.

§ 21312. Construction of clause

In determining the intent of the transferor, a no contest clause shall be strictly construed. *(Added by Stats.2008, c. 174 (S.B.1264), § 2, operative Jan. 1, 2010.)*

Law Revision Commission Comments

2008 Addition

Section 21312 continues former Section 21304 without change. [37 Cal.L.Rev.Comm. Reports 359 (2007)].

Research References

Forms

California Transactions Forms--Estate Planning § 2:34, Overview.
California Transactions Forms--Estate Planning § 6:34, Contest Provisions Generally.
California Transactions Forms--Estate Planning § 6:57, Matters to Consider in Drafting No-Contest Clause.

Treatises and Practice Aids

Witkin, California Summary 10th Wills and Probate § 564, Strict Construction.
Witkin, California Summary 10th Wills and Probate § 560A, (New) Revised No Contest Clause Statutes.

§ 21313. Legislative intent; codification; common law

This part is not intended as a complete codification of the law governing enforcement of a no contest clause. The common law governs enforcement of a no contest clause to the extent this part does not apply. *(Added by Stats.2008, c. 174 (S.B.1264), § 2, operative Jan. 1, 2010.)*

Law Revision Commission Comments

2008 Addition

Section 21313 continues former Section 21301 without change. [37 Cal.L.Rev.Comm. Reports 359 (2007)].

Commentary

For general discussion of former Section 21301, see *Burch v. George, 7 Cal.4th 246, 27 Cal.Rptr.2d 165 (1994). Burch v. George* is explained and analyzed in the Commentary to Probate Code Sections 100 and 21311.

Research References

Forms

California Transactions Forms--Estate Planning § 2:34, Overview.
California Transactions Forms--Estate Planning § 6:26, Drafting Disinheritance Provisions.
California Transactions Forms--Estate Planning § 6:35, Enforcing No-Contest Provisions.
California Transactions Forms--Estate Planning § 6:57, Matters to Consider in Drafting No-Contest Clause.
California Transactions Forms--Estate Planning § 6:116, No-Contest Clause for Will.

Treatises and Practice Aids

Witkin, California Summary 10th Wills and Probate § 561, Statutory Framework.
Witkin, California Summary 10th Wills and Probate § 560A, (New) Revised No Contest Clause Statutes.

§ 21314. Contrary provision in instrument; application of part

This part applies notwithstanding a contrary provision in the instrument. *(Added by Stats.2008, c. 174 (S.B.1264), § 2, operative Jan. 1, 2010.)*

Law Revision Commission Comments

2008 Addition

Section 21314 continues former Section 21302 without change. [37 Cal.L.Rev.Comm. Reports 359 (2007)].

Research References

Forms

California Transactions Forms--Estate Planning § 2:34, Overview.
California Transactions Forms--Estate Planning § 6:35, Enforcing No-Contest Provisions.
California Transactions Forms--Estate Planning § 6:57, Matters to Consider in Drafting No-Contest Clause.
California Transactions Forms--Estate Planning § 19:98, No-Contest Provision.

California Transactions Forms--Estate Planning § 6:116, No-Contest Clause for Will.

Treatises and Practice Aids

Witkin, California Summary 10th Wills and Probate § 561, Statutory Framework.
Witkin, California Summary 10th Wills and Probate § 560A, (New) Revised No Contest Clause Statutes.

§ 21315. Application of part to any instrument executed

(a) This part applies to any instrument, whenever executed, that became irrevocable on or after January 1, 2001.

(b) This part does not apply to an instrument that became irrevocable before January 1, 2001. *(Added by Stats.2008, c. 174 (S.B.1264), § 2, operative Jan. 1, 2010.)*

Law Revision Commission Comments

2008 Addition

Section 21315 is new. It is similar in effect to the application date provisions of former Section 21305. Section 3 may further limit the application of this chapter to an instrument that became irrevocable prior to the operative date of the chapter. See Section 3(d)–(f), (h). An instrument that is not governed by this chapter would be governed by the law that applied to the instrument prior to the operative date of this chapter. See Section 3(g). [37 Cal.L.Rev. Comm. Reports 359 (2007)].

Research References

Forms

California Transactions Forms--Estate Planning § 2:34, Overview.
California Transactions Forms--Estate Planning § 2:36, Criteria for Use Of No-Contest Clauses in Estate Planning Documents.
California Transactions Forms--Estate Planning § 6:34, Contest Provisions Generally.
California Transactions Forms--Estate Planning § 6:35, Enforcing No-Contest Provisions.
California Transactions Forms--Estate Planning § 6:57, Matters to Consider in Drafting No-Contest Clause.
California Transactions Forms--Estate Planning § 19:98, No-Contest Provision.
California Transactions Forms--Estate Planning § 21:15, Basic Testamentary Trust.
California Transactions Forms--Estate Planning § 6:116, No-Contest Clause for Will.
California Transactions Forms--Estate Planning § 6:117, No-Contest Clause for Trust.

Treatises and Practice Aids

Witkin, California Summary 10th Wills and Probate § 560A, (New) Revised No Contest Clause Statutes.

Part 6

FAMILY PROTECTION: OMITTED SPOUSES AND CHILDREN

Application

Part 6 is not applicable where decedent died before Jan. 1, 1998, see Probate Code § 21630. For provisions applicable to estates of decedents who died before Jan. 1, 1998, see Chapter 5, Probate Code § 6560 et seq.

CHAPTER 1. GENERAL PROVISIONS

Section

Application

Part 6 is not applicable where decedent died before Jan. 1, 1998, see Probate Code § 21630. For provisions applicable to estates of decedents who died before Jan. 1, 1998, see Chapter 5, Probate Code § 6560 et seq.

§ 21600. Application of part

This part shall apply to property passing by will through a decedent's estate or by a trust, as defined in Section 82, that becomes irrevocable only on the death of the settlor. *(Added by Stats.1997, c. 724 (A.B.1172), § 34.)*

Application

Part 6 is not applicable where decedent died before Jan. 1, 1998, see Probate Code § 21630. For provisions applicable to estates of decedents who died before Jan. 1, 1998, see Chapter 5, Probate Code § 6560 et seq.

Research References

Forms

California Transactions Forms--Estate Planning § 19:7, Overview.
California Transactions Forms--Estate Planning § 2:14, Failure to Properly Designate Disposition Of Assets, Provide for Pretermitted Heirs, and Plan for Dissolution Of Marriage.
California Transactions Forms--Estate Planning § 22:9, Overview.
California Transactions Forms--Estate Planning § 6:27, Omitted Spouse Statute.
California Transactions Forms--Estate Planning § 6:56, Matters to Consider in Drafting Disinheritance Clause.
California Transactions Forms--Estate Planning § 6:94, Omission Of Specific Heir.
California Transactions Forms--Estate Planning § 19:13, Protection from Unintentional Disinheritance.
California Transactions Forms--Estate Planning § 22:13, Revocation as Result Of Application Of Statute Governing Omitted Spouse.
California Transactions Forms--Estate Planning § 22:14, Revocation as Result Of Application Of Statute Governing Omitted Child.
California Transactions Forms--Estate Planning § 22:16, Partial Revocation.

Treatises and Practice Aids

Witkin, California Summary 10th Trusts § 250, Liability to Omitted Spouse or Child.
Witkin, California Summary 10th Wills and Probate § 273, in General.
Witkin, California Summary 10th Wills and Probate § 274, Nature and Scope Of Statute.
Witkin, California Summary 10th Wills and Probate § 280, in General.

§ 21601. Definitions

(a) For purposes of this part, "decedent's testamentary instruments" means the decedent's will or revocable trust.

(b) "Estate" as used in this part shall include a decedent's probate estate and all property held in any revocable trust that becomes irrevocable on the death of the decedent. *(Added by Stats.1997, c. 724 (A.B.1172), § 34.)*

Application

Part 6 is not applicable where decedent died before Jan. 1, 1998, see Probate Code § 21630. For provisions applicable to estates of decedents who died before Jan. 1, 1998, see Chapter 5, Probate Code § 6560 et seq.

Research References

Forms

California Transactions Forms--Estate Planning § 6:27, Omitted Spouse Statute.
California Transactions Forms--Estate Planning § 6:28, Exceptions to Omitted Spouse Statute.
California Transactions Forms--Estate Planning § 6:29, Manner Of Satisfying Omitted Spouse's Share.
California Transactions Forms--Estate Planning § 6:31, Omitted Child Statutes.
California Transactions Forms--Estate Planning § 6:32, Exceptions to Omitted Child Statute.
California Transactions Forms--Estate Planning § 6:33, Manner Of Satisfying Omitted Child's Share.
California Transactions Forms--Estate Planning § 19:13, Protection from Unintentional Disinheritance.
California Transactions Forms--Estate Planning § 22:13, Revocation as Result Of Application Of Statute Governing Omitted Spouse.

Treatises and Practice Aids

Witkin, California Summary 10th Wills and Probate § 274, Nature and Scope Of Statute.
Witkin, California Summary 10th Wills and Probate § 281, Nature and Scope Of Statute.

CHAPTER 2. OMITTED SPOUSES

Application

Part 6 is not applicable where decedent died before Jan. 1, 1998, see Probate Code § 21630. For provisions applicable to estates of decedents who died before Jan. 1, 1998, see Chapter 5, Probate Code § 6560 et seq.

§ 21610. Share of omitted spouse

Except as provided in Section 21611, if a decedent fails to provide in a testamentary instrument for the decedent's surviving spouse who married the decedent after the execution of all of the decedent's testamentary instruments, the omitted spouse shall receive a share in the decedent's estate, consisting of the following property in said estate:

(a) The one-half of the community property that belongs to the decedent under Section 100.

(b) The one-half of the quasi-community property that belongs to the decedent under Section 101.

(c) A share of the separate property of the decedent equal in value to that which the spouse would have received if the decedent had died without having executed a testamentary instrument, but in no event is the share to be more than one-half the value of the separate property in the estate. *(Added by Stats.1997, c. 724 (A.B.1172), § 34.)*

Application

Part 6 is not applicable where decedent died before Jan. 1, 1998, see Probate Code § 21630. For provisions applicable to estates of decedents who died before Jan. 1, 1998, see Chapter 5, Probate Code § 6560 et seq.

Commentary

Estate of Wilson, 211 Cal.App.4th 1284, 150 Cal.Rptr.3d 699 (2012), review denied, held that domestic partnership agreements that satisfy the requirements of Family Code sections 1600-1617 and were made after the enactment of statutes providing domestic partners with essentially the same property rights as spouses, are not automatically invalidated by the partner's subsequent same-sex marriage. Thus, a pre-registration California domestic partnership agreement in which the parties waived any interest in each other's estate and that required a signed writing to terminate the agreement, was not revoked by the parties' subsequent same-sex marriage. Although the surviving spouse was an omitted spouse for purposes of this section, under section 21611(c) he waived his right to any interest in the decedent spouse's estate in the domestic partnership agreement.

Research References

Forms

California Transactions Forms--Estate Planning § 19:3, Legislative Control Over Testation.
California Transactions Forms--Estate Planning § 2:14, Failure to Properly Designate Disposition Of Assets, Provide for Pretermitted Heirs, and Plan for Dissolution Of Marriage.
California Transactions Forms--Estate Planning § 6:27, Omitted Spouse Statute.
California Transactions Forms--Estate Planning § 6:28, Exceptions to Omitted Spouse Statute.
California Transactions Forms--Estate Planning § 6:29, Manner Of Satisfying Omitted Spouse's Share.
California Transactions Forms--Estate Planning § 6:96, Omission Of Existing Spouse.
California Transactions Forms--Estate Planning § 6:97, Omission Of Future Spouse.
California Transactions Forms--Estate Planning § 6:99, Omitted Spouse Made Valid Agreement Waiving Right to Share in Decedent's Estate.
California Transactions Forms--Estate Planning § 19:13, Protection from Unintentional Disinheritance.
California Transactions Forms--Estate Planning § 19:30, Republication by Codicil.
California Transactions Forms--Estate Planning § 22:13, Revocation as Result Of Application Of Statute Governing Omitted Spouse.

Treatises and Practice Aids

Witkin, California Summary 10th Wills and Probate § 25, Major Changes.
Witkin, California Summary 10th Wills and Probate § 161, Republication Of Valid Will.
Witkin, California Summary 10th Wills and Probate § 273, in General.
Witkin, California Summary 10th Wills and Probate § 274, Nature and Scope Of Statute.

§ 21611. Spouse not to receive share; circumstances

The spouse shall not receive a share of the estate under Section 21610 if any of the following is established:

(a) The decedent's failure to provide for the spouse in the decedent's testamentary instruments was intentional and that intention appears from the testamentary instruments.

(b) The decedent provided for the spouse by transfer outside of the estate passing by the decedent's testamentary instruments and the intention that the transfer be in lieu of a provision in said instruments is shown by statements of the decedent or from the amount of the transfer or by other evidence.

(c) The spouse made a valid agreement waiving the right to share in the decedent's estate. *(Added by Stats.1997, c. 724 (A.B.1172), § 34.)*

Application

Part 6 is not applicable where decedent died before Jan. 1, 1998, see Probate Code § 21630. For provisions applicable to estates of decedents who died before Jan. 1, 1998, see Chapter 5, Probate Code § 6560 et seq.

Commentary

In re Estate of Will, 170 Cal.App.4th 902, 88 Cal.Rptr.3d 502 (2009), review denied, held that although a premarital agreement did not satisfy current Family Code section 1615(c), it was independently enforceable as a waiver of inheritance rights when it satisfied Probate Code sections 140–147, which set out the Probate Code requirements for an enforceable surviving spouse's waiver of death rights. Thus a surviving wife, who married decedent-husband after he had written his final will, was barred from claiming that she was an "omitted spouse" under subsection (c).

Estate of Wilson, 211 Cal.App.4th 1284, 150 Cal.Rptr.3d 699 (2012), review denied, held that domestic partnership agreements that satisfy the requirements of Family Code sections 1600-1617 and were made after the enactment of statutes providing domestic partners with essentially the same property rights as spouses, are not automatically invalidated by the partner's subsequent same-sex marriage. Thus, a pre-registration California domestic partnership agreement in which the parties waived any interest in each other's estate and that required a signed writing to terminate the agreement, was not revoked by the parties' subsequent same-sex marriage. Although the surviving spouse was an omitted spouse for purposes of section 21610, under section 21611(c), he waived his right to any interest in the decedent spouse's estate in the domestic partnership agreement.

Research References

Forms

California Transactions Forms--Estate Planning § 2:14, Failure to Properly Designate Disposition Of Assets, Provide for Pretermitted Heirs, and Plan for Dissolution Of Marriage.
California Transactions Forms--Estate Planning § 6:27, Omitted Spouse Statute.
California Transactions Forms--Estate Planning § 6:28, Exceptions to Omitted Spouse Statute.
California Transactions Forms--Estate Planning § 6:94, Omission Of Specific Heir.
California Transactions Forms--Estate Planning § 6:95, Omission Of Heir Provided for by Transfer Outside Of Testamentary Instrument.
California Transactions Forms--Estate Planning § 6:96, Omission Of Existing Spouse.
California Transactions Forms--Estate Planning § 6:98, Omitted Spouse Provided for by Transfer Outside Of Testamentary Instrument.
California Transactions Forms--Estate Planning § 6:99, Omitted Spouse Made Valid Agreement Waiving Right to Share in Decedent's Estate.
California Transactions Forms--Estate Planning § 11:50, Rights Of Surviving Spouse that May be Waived [Prob C § 141].
California Transactions Forms--Estate Planning § 19:14, Exceptions to Pretermission.
California Transactions Forms--Estate Planning § 19:99, Disinheritance Provision.
California Transactions Forms--Estate Planning § 22:13, Revocation as Result Of Application Of Statute Governing Omitted Spouse.
California Transactions Forms--Estate Planning § 6:102, Omission Of Child Born or Adopted After Execution Of Instrument.
California Transactions Forms--Estate Planning § 19:121, Contemplated Marriage Not to Revoke Will.

Treatises and Practice Aids

Witkin, California Summary 10th Wills and Probate § 277, in General.

§ 21612. Manner of satisfying share of omitted spouse; intention of decedent

(a) Except as provided in subdivision (b), in satisfying a share provided by this chapter:

(1) The share will first be taken from the decedent's estate not disposed of by will or trust, if any.

(2) If that is not sufficient, so much as may be necessary to satisfy the share shall be taken from all beneficiaries of decedent's testamentary instruments in proportion to the value they may respectively receive. The proportion of each beneficiary's share that may be taken pursuant to this subdivision shall be determined based on values as of the date of the decedent's death.

(b) If the obvious intention of the decedent in relation to some specific gift or devise or other provision of a testamentary instrument would be defeated by the application of subdivision (a), the specific devise or gift or provision may be exempted from the apportionment under subdivision (a), and a different apportionment, consistent with the intention of the decedent, may be adopted. *(Formerly § 26112, added by Stats.1997, c. 724 (A.B.1172), § 34. Renumbered § 21612 and amended by Stats.2003, c. 32 (A.B.167), § 17.)*

Application

Part 6 is not applicable where decedent died before Jan. 1, 1998, see Probate Code § 21630. For provisions applicable to estates of decedents who died before Jan. 1, 1998, see Chapter 5, Probate Code § 6560 et seq.

Law Revision Commission Comments

2003 Renumbered and Amended

Former Section 26112 is renumbered as 21612. It was incorrectly numbered on enactment. See 1997 Cal. Stat. ch. 724, § 34.

Subdivision (a)(2) of Section 21612 is amended to make clear that it is the proportionate obligation of each beneficiary, rather than the total amount of the obligation, that is determined based on the date of death valuation. Thus for example if there are two beneficiaries entitled to receive property valued equally as of the date of death, the proportionate amount that will be taken from each is one-half the value of property distributed to each, regardless of the relative value of the property on the date of the distribution.

In a case where the share of the omitted spouse is partially satisfied pursuant to subdivision (a)(1), the obligation of the beneficiaries for the remainder abates proportionately. Thus if half the share of the omitted spouse is satisfied pursuant to subdivision (a)(1), the amount for which each of the beneficiaries is otherwise responsible pursuant to subdivision (a)(2) is reduced by half. [33 Cal.L.Rev.Comm. Reports 150 (2003)].

Research References

Forms

California Transactions Forms--Estate Planning § 2:14, Failure to Properly Designate Disposition Of Assets, Provide for Pretermitted Heirs, and Plan for Dissolution Of Marriage.
California Transactions Forms--Estate Planning § 6:29, Manner Of Satisfying Omitted Spouse's Share.

Treatises and Practice Aids

Witkin, California Summary 10th Wills and Probate § 27, Major Changes.
Witkin, California Summary 10th Wills and Probate § 276, Satisfaction Of Share.
Witkin, California Summary 10th Wills and Probate § 282, Satisfaction Of Share.
Witkin, California Summary 10th Wills and Probate § 658, in General.

CHAPTER 3. OMITTED CHILDREN

Application

Part 6 is not applicable where decedent died before Jan. 1, 1998, see Probate Code § 21630. For provisions applicable to estates of decedents who died before Jan. 1, 1998, see Chapter 5, Probate Code § 6560 et seq.

§ 21620. Child born or adopted after execution of will; share in estate

Except as provided in Section 21621, if a decedent fails to provide in a testamentary instrument for a child of decedent born or adopted after the execution of all of the decedent's testamentary instruments, the omitted child shall receive a share in the decedent's estate equal in value to that which the child would have received if the decedent had died without having executed any testamentary instrument. *(Added by Stats.1997, c. 724 (A.B.1172), § 34.)*

Application

Part 6 is not applicable where decedent died before Jan. 1, 1998, see Probate Code § 21630. For provisions applicable to estates of decedents who died before Jan. 1, 1998, see Chapter 5, Probate Code § 6560 et seq.

Commentary

Estate of Mowry, 107 Cal.App.4th 338, 131 Cal.Rptr.2d 855 (2003), review denied June 11, 2003, affirmed a trial court determination that a child adopted before the execution of the adoptive father's will was not an omitted heir within the meaning of this section.

Research References

Forms

California Transactions Forms--Estate Planning § 19:3, Legislative Control Over Testation.
California Transactions Forms--Estate Planning § 2:14, Failure to Properly Designate Disposition Of Assets, Provide for Pretermitted Heirs, and Plan for Dissolution Of Marriage.
California Transactions Forms--Estate Planning § 6:31, Omitted Child Statutes.
California Transactions Forms--Estate Planning § 6:32, Exceptions to Omitted Child Statute.
California Transactions Forms--Estate Planning § 6:33, Manner Of Satisfying Omitted Child's Share.
California Transactions Forms--Estate Planning § 6:68, Afterborn Children to Participate in Devise.
California Transactions Forms--Estate Planning § 19:13, Protection from Unintentional Disinheritance.
California Transactions Forms--Estate Planning § 22:14, Revocation as Result Of Application Of Statute Governing Omitted Child.
California Transactions Forms--Estate Planning § 6:101, Omission Of Living Child.
California Transactions Forms--Estate Planning § 6:102, Omission Of Child Born or Adopted After Execution Of Instrument.

Treatises and Practice Aids

Witkin, California Summary 10th Wills and Probate § 25, Major Changes.
Witkin, California Summary 10th Wills and Probate § 280, in General.
Witkin, California Summary 10th Wills and Probate § 281, Nature and Scope Of Statute.
Witkin, California Summary 10th Wills and Probate § 283, in General.

§ 21621. Child not to receive share; circumstances

A child shall not receive a share of the estate under Section 21620 if any of the following is established:

(a) The decedent's failure to provide for the child in the decedent's testamentary instruments was intentional and that intention appears from the testamentary instruments.

(b) The decedent had one or more children and devised or otherwise directed the disposition of substantially all the estate to the other parent of the omitted child.

(c) The decedent provided for the child by transfer outside of the estate passing by the decedent's testamentary instruments and the intention that the transfer be in lieu of a provision in said instruments is show by statements of the decedent or from the amount of the transfer or by other evidence. *(Added by Stats.1997, c. 724 (A.B.1172), § 34.)*

Application

Part 6 is not applicable where decedent died before Jan. 1, 1998, see Probate Code § 21630. For provisions applicable to estates of decedents who died before Jan. 1, 1998, see Chapter 5, Probate Code § 6560 et seq.

Research References

Forms

California Transactions Forms--Estate Planning § 2:14, Failure to Properly Designate Disposition Of Assets, Provide for Pretermitted Heirs, and Plan for Dissolution Of Marriage.

California Transactions Forms--Estate Planning § 6:31, Omitted Child Statutes.

California Transactions Forms--Estate Planning § 6:32, Exceptions to Omitted Child Statute.

California Transactions Forms--Estate Planning § 6:33, Manner Of Satisfying Omitted Child's Share.

California Transactions Forms--Estate Planning § 6:94, Omission Of Specific Heir.

California Transactions Forms--Estate Planning § 6:95, Omission Of Heir Provided for by Transfer Outside Of Testamentary Instrument.

California Transactions Forms--Estate Planning § 19:14, Exceptions to Pretermission.

California Transactions Forms--Estate Planning § 19:99, Disinheritance Provision.

California Transactions Forms--Estate Planning § 22:14, Revocation as Result Of Application Of Statute Governing Omitted Child.

California Transactions Forms--Estate Planning § 6:101, Omission Of Living Child.

California Transactions Forms--Estate Planning § 6:103, Omission Of Child Provided for by Transfer Outside Of Testamentary Instrument.

California Transactions Forms--Estate Planning § 6:104, Disposition Of Estate to Parent Of Omitted Child.

Treatises and Practice Aids

Witkin, California Summary 10th Wills and Probate § 283, in General.

§ 21622. Decedent's erroneous belief or lack of knowledge; child's share of estate

If, at the time of the execution of all of decedent's testamentary instruments effective at the time of decedent's death, the decedent failed to provide for a living child solely because the decedent believed the child to be dead or was unaware of the birth of the child, the child shall receive a share in the estate equal in value to that which the child would have received if the decedent had died without having executed any testamentary instruments. *(Added by Stats. 1997, c. 724 (A.B.1172), § 34.)*

Application

Part 6 is not applicable where decedent died before Jan. 1, 1998, see Probate Code § 21630. For provisions applicable to estates of decedents who died before Jan. 1, 1998, see Chapter 5, Probate Code § 6560 et seq.

Research References

Forms

California Transactions Forms--Estate Planning § 6:31, Omitted Child Statutes.

California Transactions Forms--Estate Planning § 19:13, Protection from Unintentional Disinheritance.

California Transactions Forms--Estate Planning § 6:102, Omission Of Child Born or Adopted After Execution Of Instrument.

Treatises and Practice Aids

Witkin, California Summary 10th Wills and Probate § 281, Nature and Scope Of Statute.

§ 21623. Manner of satisfying share of omitted child; intention of decedent

(a) Except as provided in subdivision (b), in satisfying a share provided by this chapter:

(1) The share will first be taken from the decedent's estate not disposed of by will or trust, if any.

(2) If that is not sufficient, so much as may be necessary to satisfy the share shall be taken from all beneficiaries of decedent's testamentary instruments in proportion to the value they may respectively receive. The proportion of each beneficiary's share that may be taken pursuant to this subdivision shall be determined based on values as of the date of the decedent's death.

(b) If the obvious intention of the decedent in relation to some specific gift or devise or other provision of a testamentary instrument would be defeated by the application of subdivision (a), the specific devise or gift or provision of a testamentary instrument may be exempted from the apportionment under subdivision (a), and a different apportionment, consistent with the intention of the decedent, may be adopted. *(Added by Stats.1997, c. 724 (A.B.1172), § 34. Amended by Stats.2003, c. 32 (A.B.167), § 16.)*

Application

Part 6 is not applicable where decedent died before Jan. 1, 1998, see Probate Code § 21630. For provisions applicable to estates of decedents who died before Jan. 1, 1998, see Chapter 5, Probate Code § 6560 et seq.

Law Revision Commission Comments

2003 Amendment

Subdivision (a)(2) of Section 21623 is amended to make clear that it is the proportionate obligation of each beneficiary, rather than the total amount of the obligation, that is determined based on the date of death valuation. Thus for example if there are two beneficiaries entitled to receive property valued equally as of the date of death, the proportionate amount that will be taken from each is one-half the value of property distributed to each, regardless of the relative value of the property on the date of the distribution.

In a case where the share of the omitted child is partially satisfied pursuant to subdivision (a)(1), the obligation of the beneficiaries for the remainder abates proportionately. Thus if half the share of the omitted child is satisfied pursuant to subdivision (a)(1), the amount for which each of the beneficiaries is otherwise responsible pursuant to subdivision (a)(2) is reduced by half. [33 Cal.L.Rev.Comm. Reports 167 (2003)].

Research References

Forms

California Transactions Forms--Estate Planning § 2:14, Failure to Properly Designate Disposition Of Assets, Provide for Pretermitted Heirs, and Plan for Dissolution Of Marriage.

California Transactions Forms--Estate Planning § 6:33, Manner Of Satisfying Omitted Child's Share.

California Transactions Forms--Estate Planning § 6:68, Afterborn Children to Participate in Devise.

California Transactions Forms--Estate Planning § 22:13, Revocation as Result Of Application Of Statute Governing Omitted Spouse.

California Transactions Forms--Estate Planning § 22:14, Revocation as Result Of Application Of Statute Governing Omitted Child.

Treatises and Practice Aids

Witkin, California Summary 10th Wills and Probate § 27, Major Changes.

Witkin, California Summary 10th Wills and Probate § 276, Satisfaction Of Share.

Witkin, California Summary 10th Wills and Probate § 282, Satisfaction Of Share.

Witkin, California Summary 10th Wills and Probate § 658, in General.

CHAPTER 4. APPLICABILITY

Application

For provisions applicable to estates of decedents who died before Jan. 1, 1998, see Chapter 5, Probate Code § 6560 et seq.

§ 21630. Decedent's death before January 1, 1998; application of part

This part does not apply if the decedent died before January 1, 1998. The law applicable prior to January 1, 1998, applies if the decedent died before January 1, 1998. *(Added by Stats.1997, c. 724 (A.B.1172), § 34.)*

Application

For provisions applicable to estates of decedents who died before Jan. 1, 1998, see Chapter 5, Probate Code § 6560 et seq.

Research References

Forms

California Transactions Forms--Estate Planning § 2:14, Failure to Properly Designate Disposition Of Assets, Provide for Pretermitted Heirs, and Plan for Dissolution Of Marriage.

California Transactions Forms--Estate Planning § 6:27, Omitted Spouse Statute.

California Transactions Forms--Estate Planning § 6:28, Exceptions to Omitted Spouse Statute.

California Transactions Forms--Estate Planning § 6:29, Manner Of Satisfying Omitted Spouse's Share.

California Transactions Forms--Estate Planning § 6:31, Omitted Child Statutes.

California Transactions Forms--Estate Planning § 6:32, Exceptions to Omitted Child Statute.

California Transactions Forms--Estate Planning § 6:33, Manner Of Satisfying Omitted Child's Share.

California Transactions Forms--Estate Planning § 6:56, Matters to Consider in Drafting Disinheritance Clause.

California Transactions Forms--Estate Planning § 6:94, Omission Of Specific Heir.

California Transactions Forms--Estate Planning § 6:96, Omission Of Existing Spouse.

California Transactions Forms--Estate Planning § 19:13, Protection from Unintentional Disinheritance.

California Transactions Forms--Estate Planning § 22:13, Revocation as Result Of Application Of Statute Governing Omitted Spouse.

California Transactions Forms--Estate Planning § 22:14, Revocation as Result Of Application Of Statute Governing Omitted Child.

Treatises and Practice Aids

Witkin, California Summary 10th Trusts § 250, Liability to Omitted Spouse or Child.

Witkin, California Summary 10th Wills and Probate § 273, in General.

Witkin, California Summary 10th Wills and Probate § 280, in General.

Part 7

CONTRACTS REGARDING TESTAMENTARY OR INTESTATE SUCCESSION

§ 21700. Contract to make will or devise; establishment; effect of execution of joint will or mutual wills; applicable law

(a) A contract to make a will or devise or other instrument, or not to revoke a will or devise or other instrument, or to die intestate, if made after the effective date of this statute, can be established only by one of the following:

(1) Provisions of a will or other instrument stating the material provisions of the contract.

(2) An expressed reference in a will or other instrument to a contract and extrinsic evidence proving the terms of the contract.

(3) A writing signed by the decedent evidencing the contract.

(4) Clear and convincing evidence of an agreement between the decedent and the claimant or a promise by the decedent to the claimant that is enforceable in equity.

(5) Clear and convincing evidence of an agreement between the decedent and another person for the benefit of the claimant or a promise by the decedent to another person for the benefit of the claimant that is enforceable in equity.

(b) The execution of a joint will or mutual wills does not create a presumption of a contract not to revoke the will or wills.

(c) A contract to make a will or devise or other instrument, or not to revoke a will or devise or other instrument, or to die intestate, if made prior to the effective date of this section, shall be construed under the law applicable to the contract prior to the effective date of this section. *(Added by Stats.2000, c. 17 (A.B.1491), § 8.)*

Commentary

A "Marvin" oral cohabitation agreement asserted after the death of one of the cohabitants is not subject to the requirements of the statute. *Byrne v. Laura, 52 Cal.App.4th 1054, 60 Cal.Rptr.2d 908 (1997), review denied May 28, 1997.* For discussion of "Marvin" agreements, see Family Code Section 2251, Commentary. For discussion of equitable exceptions to writing requirements, see Family Code Section 1611, Commentary.

Research References

Forms

California Transactions Forms--Estate Planning § 11:3, Formalities for Establishing Contract Concerning Will or Devise Made Before January 1, 1985.

California Transactions Forms--Estate Planning § 11:4, Contract as Distinct from Will Itself.

California Transactions Forms--Estate Planning § 11:6, Effect Of Oral Contracts and Equitable Estoppel.

California Transactions Forms--Estate Planning § 11:9, Application to Trusts.

California Transactions Forms--Estate Planning § 11:10, Joint Wills.

California Transactions Forms--Estate Planning § 11:11, Mutual or Reciprocal Wills.

California Transactions Forms--Estate Planning § 19:23, Joint and Mutual Wills; Contract to Make Will or Not Revoke Will.

California Transactions Forms--Estate Planning § 19:102, No Contract Provision.

Treatises and Practice Aids

Witkin, California Summary 10th Contracts § 409, in General.

Witkin, California Summary 10th Equity § 31, Quasi-Specific Performance by Constructive Trust.

Witkin, California Summary 10th Wills and Probate § 25, Major Changes.

Witkin, California Summary 10th Wills and Probate § 112, Joint Will Without Contract.

Witkin, California Summary 10th Wills and Probate § 326, Contracts Concerning Will or Succession.

Witkin, California Summary 10th Wills and Probate § 562, Determination Whether Act Constitutes Contest.

VEHICLE CODE

Division 9

CIVIL LIABILITY

CHAPTER 2. CIVIL LIABILITY OF PERSONS SIGNING LICENSE APPLICATIONS OF MINORS

§ 17700. Minor defined

For the purposes of this chapter, all persons under 18 years of age are minors. *(Stats.1959, c. 3, p. 1658, § 17700. Amended by Stats.1959, c. 1996, p. 4629, § 21; Stats.1971, c. 1748, p. 3765, § 60, operative March 4, 1972.)*

Research References

Treatises and Practice Aids

Witkin, California Summary 10th Torts § 1256, Signer Of Driver's License.

§ 17701. Signature by parents, guardian, or person having custody; child as dependent or ward of the court

No application for a driver's license shall be granted by the department to any minor unless it is signed and verified by the father and mother of such minor, if both father and mother are living and have custody of the minor.

If only one parent is living or has custody, the application shall be signed and verified by that parent.

If neither parent is living or has custody, the application shall be signed and verified by the guardian, or if there is no guardian, by a person having custody of the minor.

If the minor is a dependent or ward of the court, the application may be signed by a grandparent, sibling over the age of 18 years, aunt, uncle, or foster parent with whom the minor resides. The probation officer or child protective services worker acting as an officer of the court, on behalf of a child, may also sign and verify the application of a minor who is a dependent or ward of the court, if the minor files proof of financial responsibility as provided in Article 1 (commencing with Section 16430) of Chapter 3 of Division 7 at the time of application. Prior to signing the application, the probation officer or child protective services worker shall notify the foster parents or other responsible party of his or her intent to sign and verify the application. *(Stats.1959, c. 3, p. 1658, § 17701. Amended by Stats.1967, c. 485, p. 1692, § 1; Stats.1970, c. 166, p. 409, § 3; Stats.1992, c. 865 (A.B.2691), § 2.)*

Research References

Treatises and Practice Aids

Witkin, California Summary 10th Torts § 1256, Signer Of Driver's License.

§ 17702. Signature by adult spouse

If a minor under the age of 18 years is married, the application may be signed and verified by the adult spouse of the minor or by the parents of either spouse or in lieu of the signature, the minor may file proof of financial responsibility, as defined in Section 16430. *(Stats.1959, c. 3, p. 1658, § 17702. Amended by Stats.1984, c. 144, § 209; Stats.1992, c. 974 (S.B.1600), § 12, eff. Sept. 28, 1992.)*

Research References

Treatises and Practice Aids

Witkin, California Summary 10th Torts § 1256, Signer Of Driver's License.

§ 17703. Nonresident signers

If the person or persons required to sign and verify the application of a minor are not residents of this state, the application shall be signed and verified by a person residing within this state who has custody of the minor, or the department may accept an application signed and verified by the minor and accompanied by proof of financial responsibility, as defined in Section 16430. *(Stats.1959, c. 3, p. 1658, § 17703. Amended by Stats.1959, c. 1048, p. 3090, § 5; Stats.1984, c. 144, § 210; Stats.1992, c. 974 (S.B.1600), § 13, eff. Sept. 28, 1992.)*

§ 17704. Failure of proof

If, at any time during the minority of the person who has given proof of financial responsibility, as defined in Section 16430, the proof fails, the department shall immediately cancel the license until proof of the licensee's continued financial responsibility has been given or until the minor has otherwise complied with the requirements of this code relative to the issuance of a driver's license. *(Stats.1959, c. 3, p. 1659, § 17704. Amended by Stats.1959, c. 1048, p. 3090, § 6; Stats.1992, c. 974 (S.B.1600), § 14, eff. Sept. 28, 1992.)*

§ 17705. Application verified by minor only

If the person who is required to sign and verify the application of a minor gives his or her written consent, or the minor is emancipated other than by marriage, the department may accept an application signed and verified only by the minor and accompanied by proof of financial responsibility, as defined in Section 16430. The person giving the consent to but not signing or verifying the application shall not be subject to the civil liability specified in Sections 17707 and 17708 merely by reason of having given consent. *(Stats.1959, c. 3, p. 1659, § 17705. Amended by Stats.1959, c. 1048, p. 3090, § 7; Stats.1992, c. 974 (S.B.1600), § 15, eff. Sept. 28, 1992.)*

Research References

Treatises and Practice Aids

Witkin, California Summary 10th Torts § 1259, Termination Of Liability.

§ 17706. Minor's negligence imputed to employer

(a) If the person who is required by the provisions of this code to sign and verify the application of a minor gives his written consent, the department may accept an application signed and verified by the minor and his employer, but in such case the department shall issue to the minor only a driver's license restricted to the operation of vehicles by the minor within the scope of his employment by the employer, unless the employer in writing authorizes the issuance of an unrestricted driver's license.

(b) The person giving his consent to, but not signing or verifying, the application as provided in this section shall not be subject to the civil liability specified in Sections 17707 and 17708 merely by reason of having given such consent. *(Stats.1959, c. 3, p. 1659, § 17706.)*

Research References

Treatises and Practice Aids

Witkin, California Summary 10th Torts § 1256, Signer Of Driver's License.

§ 17707. Minor's negligence; exceptions

Any civil liability of a minor arising out of his driving a motor vehicle upon a highway during his minority is hereby imposed upon the person who signed and verified the application of the minor for a license and the person shall be jointly and severally liable with the minor for any damages proximately resulting from the negligent or wrongful act or omission of the minor in driving a motor vehicle, except that an employer signing the application shall be subject to the provisions of this section only if an unrestricted driver's license has been issued to the minor pursuant to the employer's written authorization.

No liability may be imposed under this section or under Section 17708 on the state or county, or on a probation officer or child protective services worker acting as an officer of the court for damages caused solely by the negligence or willful misconduct of a minor driver whose application for a driver's license was signed by the child protective services worker or probation officer while the minor was a dependent or ward of the court. *(Stats.1959, c. 3, p. 1659, § 17707. Amended by Stats.1967, c. 702, p. 2075, § 9; Stats.1992, c. 865 (A.B.2691), § 3.)*

Law Revision Commission Comments

1967 Amendment

This amendment to section 17707 merely substitutes the term that has been used in Vehicle Code Section 17001 and in sections 17150–17159 for that which appeared in section 17707. The substitution has been made in order to make it clear that the same meaning is intended. No substantive change is made by the revision.

Research References

Treatises and Practice Aids

Witkin, California Summary 10th Torts § 1256, Signer Of Driver's License.

Witkin, California Summary 10th Torts § 1257, Minor Driving With Permission.

Witkin, California Summary 10th Torts § 1258, Nature and Scope Of Liability.

Witkin, California Summary 10th Torts § 1260, Statutory Development.

§ 17708. Liability of parent or guardian

Any civil liability of a minor, whether licensed or not under this code, arising out of his driving a motor vehicle upon a highway with the express or implied permission of the parents or the person or guardian having custody of the minor is hereby imposed upon the parents, person, or guardian and the parents, person, or guardian shall be jointly and severally liable with the minor for any damages proximately resulting from the negligent or wrongful act or omission of the minor in driving a motor vehicle. *(Stats.1959, c. 3, p. 1659, § 17708. Amended by Stats.1967, c. 702, p. 2075, § 10.)*

Law Revision Commission Comments

1967 Amendment

The same reasons which justify the deletion of the provisions for imputed contributory negligence from section 17150 justify the removal of the similar provisions from section 17708. The language of the section has been revised to conform to that use in section 17707.

Research References

Treatises and Practice Aids

Witkin, California Summary 10th Torts § 1257, Minor Driving With Permission.

Witkin, California Summary 10th Torts § 1258, Nature and Scope Of Liability.

§ 17709. Limit of liability

(a) No person, or group of persons collectively, shall incur liability for a minor's negligent or wrongful act or omission under Sections 17707 and 17708 in any amount exceeding fifteen thousand dollars ($15,000) for injury to or death of one person as a result of any one accident or, subject to the limit as to one person, exceeding thirty thousand dollars ($30,000) for injury to or death of all persons as a result of any one accident or exceeding five thousand dollars ($5,000) for damage to property of others as a result of any one accident.

(b) No person is liable under Section 17707 or 17708 for damages imposed for the sake of example and by way of punishing the minor. Nothing in this subdivision makes any person immune from liability for damages imposed for the sake of example and by way of punishing him for his own wrongful conduct. *(Stats.1959, c. 3, p. 1660, § 17709. Amended by Stats.1963, c. 403, p. 1211, § 3; Stats.1967, c. 702, p. 2076, § 11.5; Stats.1967, c. 862, p. 2308, § 11, operative July 1, 1968.)*

Research References

Treatises and Practice Aids

Witkin, California Summary 10th Torts § 1258, Nature and Scope Of Liability.
Witkin, California Summary 10th Torts § 1261, Limited Liability.
Witkin, California Summary 10th Torts § 1580, in General.

§ 17710. Minor agent or servant

The person signing a minor's application for a license is not liable under this chapter for a negligent or wrongful act or omission of the minor committed when the minor is acting as the agent or servant of any person. *(Stats.1959, c. 3, p. 1660, § 17710. Amended by Stats.1967, c. 702, p. 2076, § 12.)*

Law Revision Commission Comments

1967 Amendment

This amendment merely conforms the section to section 17707 as amended.

Research References

Treatises and Practice Aids

Witkin, California Summary 10th Torts § 1256, Signer Of Driver's License.

§ 17711. Release from liability

Any person who has signed and verified the application of a minor for a driver's license or any employer who has authorized the issuance of a license to a minor and who desires to be relieved from the joint and several liability imposed by reason of having signed and verified such application, may file a verified application with the department requesting that the license of the minor be canceled. The department shall cancel the license, except as provided in subdivision (e) of Section 17712. Thereafter, the person shall be relieved from the liability imposed under this chapter by reason of having signed and verified the original application on account of any subsequent willful misconduct or negligent operation of a motor vehicle by the minor. *(Stats. 1959, c. 3, p. 1660, § 17711. Amended by Stats.1976, c. 645, p. 1595, § 2.)*

Research References

Treatises and Practice Aids

Witkin, California Summary 10th Torts § 1259, Termination Of Liability.

§ 17712. Cancellation of license; transfer of liability

(a) The department, upon receipt of satisfactory evidence of the death of the father and mother or the person or guardian who signed and verified the application of any minor under Section 17701 or any employer who signed and verified the application of any minor under subdivision (a) of Section 17706, shall cancel the license, except as provided in subdivision (e).

(b) The department, upon receipt of the verified application of a person who has given written consent to the issuance of a license to a minor as prescribed in Sections 17705 and 17706, for the cancellation of such minor's license, shall cancel the license, except as provided in subdivision (e).

(c) The department, upon receipt of satisfactory evidence that there has been a change of custody of a minor licensed under Chapter 1 (commencing with Section 12500) of Division 6, and upon written request by the person to whom custody has been transferred, shall cancel the license.

(d) The department, upon receipt of satisfactory evidence showing that any minor to whom was issued a license pursuant to Section 17706, has left the employ of the employer who signed and verified the application for the license, shall cancel the license, except as provided in subdivision (e).

(e) The department, upon written request by the person to whom custody of a minor has been transferred, shall transfer the liability imposed under this chapter to such person upon receipt of such person's written verified application for acceptance of liability. Upon receipt, by the department, of such application for acceptance of liability, the person who had signed and verified the application of the minor for the driver's license presently held by the minor shall be relieved from the liability imposed under this chapter. If such application for acceptance of liability is on file with the department prior to the receipt of a request for cancellation by the person who had signed the application of the minor for a driver's license, the license issued under such application shall not be canceled so long as the license is otherwise valid. If, however, such application for acceptance of liability is not on file with the department prior to the receipt of a request for cancellation by the person who had signed the application of the minor for a driver's license, the license issued under such application shall be canceled. *(Stats.1959, c. 3, p. 1660, § 17712. Amended by Stats.1965, c. 466, p. 1772, § 1; Stats.1976, c. 645, p. 1595, § 3.)*

Research References

Treatises and Practice Aids

Witkin, California Summary 10th Torts § 1259, Termination Of Liability.

§ 17714. Limitation of double liability

In the event, in one or more actions, judgment is rendered against a defendant under this chapter based upon the negligent or wrongful act or omission of a minor in the operation of a vehicle, and also by reason of such act or omission rendered against such defendant under Article 2 (commencing with Section 17150) of Chapter 1 of Division 9, then such judgment or judgments shall not be cumulative but recovery shall be limited to the amount specified in Section 17709. *(Stats.1959, c. 3, p. 1660, § 17714. Amended by Stats.1961, c. 58, p. 1010, § 39, eff. March 31, 1961; Stats. 1967, c. 702, p. 2076, § 13.)*

Law Revision Commission Comments

1967 Amendment

This amendment merely conforms the section to sections 17707 and 17708 as amended.

Research References

Treatises and Practice Aids

Witkin, California Summary 10th Torts § 1258, Nature and Scope Of Liability.

Witkin, California Summary 10th Torts § 1261, Limited Liability.

WELFARE AND INSTITUTIONS CODE

GENERAL PROVISIONS

§ 17.1. Residence of minor or nonminor dependent

Unless otherwise provided under the provisions of this code, to the extent not in conflict with federal law, the residence of a minor person, or a nonminor dependent, as described in subdivision (v) of Section 11400, shall be determined by the following rules:

(a) The residence of the parent with whom a child maintains his or her place of abode or the residence of any individual who has been appointed legal guardian or the individual who has been given the care or custody by a court of competent jurisdiction, determines the residence of the child.

(b) Wherever in this section it is provided that the residence of a child is determined by the residence of the person who has custody, "custody" means the legal right to custody of the child unless that right is held jointly by two or more persons, in which case "custody" means the physical custody of the child by one of the persons sharing the right to custody.

(c) The residence of a foundling shall be deemed to be that of the county in which the child is found.

(d) If the residence of the child is not determined under subdivision (a), (b), (c), or (e), the county in which the child is living shall be deemed the county of residence, if and when the child has had a physical presence in the county for one year.

(e) If the child has been declared permanently free from the custody and control of his or her parents, his or her residence is the county in which the court issuing the order is situated.

(f) If a nonminor dependent under the dependency jurisdiction or transition jurisdiction of the juvenile court is placed in a planned permanent living arrangement, as described in subdivision (i) of Section 366.3, the county in which the nonminor dependent is living may be deemed the county of residence, if and when the nonminor dependent has had a continuous physical presence in the county for one year as a nonminor dependent and the nonminor dependent expressed his or her intent to remain in that county.

(g) If a nonminor dependent's dependency jurisdiction has been resumed, or transition jurisdiction assumed or resumed by the juvenile court that retained general jurisdiction pursuant to subdivision (b) of Section 303, as a result of the filing of a petition pursuant to subdivision (e) of Section 388, following the granting of the petition, the county in which the nonminor dependent is living at the time the petition was filed may be deemed the county of residence, if and when the nonminor dependent establishes that he or she has had a continuous physical presence in the county for one year and has expressed his or her intent to remain in that county. The period of continuous physical presence in the county shall include any period of continuous residence in the county immediately prior to the filing of the petition. *(Added by Stats.1943, c. 713, p. 2473, § 1. Amended by Stats.1953, c. 1233, p. 2790, § 1; Stats.1975, c. 1129, p. 2772, § 1; Stats. 2012, c. 846 (A.B.1712), § 7.)*

Research References

Treatises and Practice Aids

Witkin, California Summary 10th Parent and Child § 456, Proper Court.

Witkin, California Summary 10th Parent and Child § 458, Conditions for Transfer.

Witkin, California Summary 10th Parent and Child § 459, Residence Of Child.

Witkin, California Summary 10th Parent and Child § 464, Continuing Jurisdiction Outside County.

Division 2

CHILDREN

Part 1

DELINQUENTS AND WARDS OF THE JUVENILE COURT

CHAPTER 2. JUVENILE COURT LAW

ARTICLE 1. GENERAL PROVISIONS

§ 200. Title of chapter

This chapter shall be known and may be cited as the "Arnold–Kennick Juvenile Court Law." *(Added by Stats. 1976, c. 1068, p. 4741, § 1.5.)*

Research References

Treatises and Practice Aids

Witkin, California Summary 10th Parent and Child § 2, The Family Code.

Witkin, California Summary 10th Parent and Child § 440, Original Statute and Revision.

Witkin, California Summary 10th Parent and Child § 497, Authorized Disclosure to Law Enforcement Agencies.

Witkin, California Summary 10th Parent and Child § 523, Definitions.

Witkin, California Summary 10th Parent and Child § 529, Formal Requisites.

Witkin, California Summary 10th Parent and Child § 572, Appointment Of Guardian Ad Litem or Child Advocate.

Witkin, California Summary 10th Parent and Child § 696, Continuing Jurisdiction.

Witkin, California Summary 10th Torts § 349, Particular Employees.

Witkin, California Summary 10th Torts § 368, Institution or Prosecution Of Judicial or Administrative Proceeding.

§ 201. Construction

The provisions of this chapter, insofar as they are substantially the same as existing statutory provisions relating to the same subject matter, shall be construed as restatements and continuations thereof, and not as new enactments. *(Added by Stats.1976, c. 1068, p. 4741, § 1.5.)*

Research References

Treatises and Practice Aids

Witkin, California Summary 10th Parent and Child § 440, Original Statute and Revision.

§ 202. Purpose; protective services; reunification with family; guidance for delinquents; accountability for objectives and results; punishment defined

(a) The purpose of this chapter is to provide for the protection and safety of the public and each minor under the jurisdiction of the juvenile court and to preserve and strengthen the minor's family ties whenever possible, removing the minor from the custody of his or her parents only when necessary for his or her welfare or for the safety and protection of the public. If removal of a minor is determined by the juvenile court to be necessary, reunification of the minor with his or her family shall be a primary objective. If the minor is removed from his or her own family, it is the purpose of this chapter to secure for the minor custody, care, and discipline as nearly as possible equivalent to that which should have been given by his or her parents. This chapter shall be liberally construed to carry out these purposes.

(b) Minors under the jurisdiction of the juvenile court who are in need of protective services shall receive care, treatment, and guidance consistent with their best interest and the best interest of the public. Minors under the jurisdiction of the juvenile court as a consequence of delinquent conduct shall, in conformity with the interests of public safety and protection, receive care, treatment, and guidance that is consistent with their best interest, that holds them accountable for their behavior, and that is appropriate for their circumstances. This guidance may include punishment that is consistent with the rehabilitative objectives of this chapter. If a minor has been removed from the custody of his or her parents, family preservation and family reunification are appropriate goals for the juvenile court to consider when determining the disposition of a minor under the jurisdiction of the juvenile court as a consequence of delinquent conduct when those goals are consistent with his or her best interests and the best interests of the public. When the minor is no longer a ward of the juvenile court, the guidance he or she received should enable him or her to be a law-abiding and productive member of his or her family and the community.

(c) It is also the purpose of this chapter to reaffirm that the duty of a parent to support and maintain a minor child continues, subject to the financial ability of the parent to pay, during any period in which the minor may be declared a ward of the court and removed from the custody of the parent.

(d) Juvenile courts and other public agencies charged with enforcing, interpreting, and administering the juvenile court law shall consider the safety and protection of the public, the importance of redressing injuries to victims, and the best interests of the minor in all deliberations pursuant to this chapter. Participants in the juvenile justice system shall hold themselves accountable for its results. They shall act in conformity with a comprehensive set of objectives established to improve system performance in a vigorous and ongoing manner. In working to improve system performance, the presiding judge of the juvenile court and other juvenile court judges designated by the presiding judge of the juvenile court shall take into consideration the recommendations contained in subdivision (e) of Standard 5.40 of Title 5 of the California Standards of Judicial Administration, contained in the California Rules of Court.

(e) As used in this chapter, "punishment" means the imposition of sanctions. It does not include retribution and shall not include a court order to place a child in foster care as defined by Section 727.3. Permissible sanctions may include any of the following:

(1) Payment of a fine by the minor.

(2) Rendering of compulsory service without compensation performed for the benefit of the community by the minor.

(3) Limitations on the minor's liberty imposed as a condition of probation or parole.

(4) Commitment of the minor to a local detention or treatment facility, such as a juvenile hall, camp, or ranch.

(5) Commitment of the minor to the Division of Juvenile Facilities, Department of Corrections and Rehabilitation.

(f) In addition to the actions authorized by subdivision (e), the juvenile court may, as appropriate, direct the offender to complete a victim impact class, participate in victim offender conferencing subject to the victim's consent, pay restitution to the victim or victims, and make a contribution to the victim restitution fund after all victim restitution orders and fines have been satisfied, in order to hold the offender accountable or restore the victim or community. *(Added by Stats.1984, c. 756, § 2. Amended by Stats.1989, c. 569, § 1, eff. Sept. 21, 1989; Stats.1998, c. 761 (S.B.2074), § 1; Stats.1999, c. 997 (A.B.575), § 1; Stats.2001, c. 830 (S.B.940), § 2; Stats.2007, c. 130 (A.B.299), § 242.)*

Commentary

In re Carmen M., 141 Cal.App.4th 478, 46 Cal.Rptr.3d 117 (2006), holds that subsection (a) of this section and subsection (a) of Section 362 suffice to authorize a juvenile court to order random drug tests to help a dependent child remain drug-free even though the child has not been found, under Section 359, to be a danger to herself or others as a result of drug use.

Research References

Treatises and Practice Aids

Witkin, California Summary 10th Parent and Child § 22, Where Intended Mother is Genetic Mother.

Witkin, California Summary 10th Parent and Child § 442, General Purposes.

Witkin, California Summary 10th Parent and Child § 874, Uncorroborated Testimony Of Accomplice.

Witkin, California Summary 10th Parent and Child § 884, Social Study.

Witkin, California Summary 10th Parent and Child § 912, Petition to Modify or Terminate Juvenile Court Jurisdiction.

Witkin, California Summary 10th Parent and Child § 942, Types Of Sanctions.

Witkin, California Summary 10th Parent and Child § 943, Invalid Commitment.

Witkin, California Summary 10th Parent and Child § 950, Youth Authority Act.

Witkin, California Summary 10th Parent and Child § 951, in General.

Witkin, California Summary 10th Parent and Child § 958, Punishment as Proper Purpose.

Witkin, California Summary 10th Parent and Child § 968, Detention in Adult Facility.

§ 202.5. Probation officers' duties deemed social service; governing authority

The duties of the probation officer, as described in this chapter with respect to minors alleged or adjudged to be described by Section 300, whether or not delegated pursuant to Section 272, shall be deemed to be social service as defined by Section 10051, and subject to the administration, supervision and regulations of the State Department of Social

Services. *(Added by Stats.1982, c. 978, § 3, eff. Sept. 13, 1982, operative July 1, 1982.)*

Research References

Treatises and Practice Aids

Witkin, California Summary 10th Parent and Child § 483, Juvenile Court Proceedings.

§ 203. Order adjudging minor ward of juvenile court; effect; proceedings

An order adjudging a minor to be a ward of the juvenile court shall not be deemed a conviction of a crime for any purpose, nor shall a proceeding in the juvenile court be deemed a criminal proceeding. *(Added by Stats.1976, c. 1068, p. 4741, § 1.5.)*

Research References

Treatises and Practice Aids

Witkin, California Summary 10th Parent and Child § 731, in General.
Witkin, California Summary 10th Parent and Child § 805, Presence at Trial.
Witkin, California Summary 10th Parent and Child § 946, Inapplicable Enhancements.
Witkin, California Summary 10th Workers' Compensation § 305, Particular Employees.

§ 204. Information available for juvenile court proceedings regarding best interest of child; confidentiality

Notwithstanding any other provision of law, except provisions of law governing the retention and storage of data, a family law court and a court hearing a probate guardianship matter shall, upon request from the juvenile court in any county, provide to the court all available information the court deems necessary to make a determination regarding the best interest of a child, as described in Section 202, who is the subject of a proceeding before the juvenile court pursuant to this division. The information shall also be released to a child protective services worker or juvenile probation officer acting within the scope of his or her duties in that proceeding. Any information released pursuant to this section that is confidential pursuant to any other provision of law shall remain confidential and may not be released, except to the extent necessary to comply with this section. No records shared pursuant to this section may be disclosed to any party in a case unless the party requests the agency or court that originates the record to release these records and the request is granted. In counties that provide confidential family law mediation, or confidential dependency mediation, those mediations are not covered by this section. *(Added by Stats. 2004, c. 574 (A.B.2228), § 3.)*

Research References

Treatises and Practice Aids

Witkin, California Summary 10th Parent and Child § 276, Report.
Witkin, California Summary 10th Parent and Child § 442, General Purposes.
Witkin, California Summary 10th Parent and Child § 497, Authorized Disclosure to Law Enforcement Agencies.

§ 204.5. Disclosure of minor's name

Notwithstanding any other provision of law, the name of a minor may be disclosed to the public if the minor is 14 years of age or older and found by the juvenile court to be a person described in Section 602 as a result of a sustained petition for the commission of any of the offenses listed in Section 667.5 of the Penal Code, or in subdivision (c) of Section 1192.7 of the Penal Code. *(Added by Stats.1994, c. 1019 (A.B.3309), § 1.)*

Research References

Treatises and Practice Aids

Witkin, California Summary 10th Parent and Child § 731, in General.

§ 205. Commitments; religious beliefs

All commitments to institutions or for placement in family homes under this chapter shall be, so far as practicable, either to institutions or for placement in family homes of the same religious belief as that of the person so committed or of his parents or to institutions affording opportunity for instruction in such religious belief. *(Added by Stats.1976, c. 1068, p. 4741, § 1.5.)*

Research References

Treatises and Practice Aids

Witkin, California Summary 10th Parent and Child § 442, General Purposes.

§ 206. Separate segregated facilities for habitual delinquents or truants; secure and nonsecure facilities; temporary custody; arrest record

Persons taken into custody and persons alleged to be within the description of Section 300, or persons adjudged to be such and made dependent children of the court pursuant to this chapter solely upon that ground, shall be provided by the board of supervisors with separate facilities segregated from persons either alleged or adjudged to come within the description of Section 601 or 602 except as provided in Section 16514. Separate segregated facilities may be provided in the juvenile hall or elsewhere.

The facilities required by this section shall, with regard to minors alleged or adjudged to come within Section 300, be nonsecure.

For the purposes of this section, the term "secure facility" means a facility which is designed and operated so as to insure that all entrances to, and exits from, the facility are under the exclusive control of the staff of the facility, whether or not the person being detained has freedom of movement within the perimeters of the facility, or which relies on locked rooms and buildings, fences, or physical restraints in order to control behavior of its residents. The term "nonsecure facility" means a facility that is not characterized by the use of physically restricting construction, hardware, and procedures and which provides its residents access to the surrounding community with minimal supervision. A facility shall not be deemed secure due solely to any of the following conditions: (1) the existence within the facility of a small room for the protection of individual residents from themselves or others; (2) the adoption of regulations establishing reasonable hours for residents to come and go from the facility based upon a sensible and fair balance between allowing residents free access to the community and providing the staff with sufficient authority to maintain order, limit unreasonable actions by residents, and to ensure that minors placed in their care do not come and go at all hours of the day and night or absent themselves at will for days at a time; and (3) staff control over ingress and egress no greater than that exercised by a prudent parent. The State Department of Social Services may adopt regulations governing the use of small rooms pursuant to this section.

No minor described in this section may be held in temporary custody in any building that contains a jail or lockup for the confinement of adults, unless, while in the building, the minor is under continuous supervision and is not permitted to come into or remain in contact with adults in custody in the building. In addition, no minor who is alleged to be within the description of Section 300 may be held in temporary custody in a building that contains a jail or lockup for the confinement of adults, unless the minor is under the direct and continuous supervision of a peace officer or other child protective agency worker, as specified in Section 11165.9 of the Penal Code, until temporary custody and detention of the minor is assumed pursuant to Section 309. However, if a child protective agency worker is not available to supervise the minor as certified by the law enforcement agency which has custody of the minor, a trained volunteer may be directed to supervise the minor. The volunteer shall be trained and function under the auspices of the agency which utilizes the volunteer. The minor may not remain under the supervision of the volunteer for more than three hours. A county which elects to utilize trained volunteers for the temporary supervision of minors shall adopt guidelines for the training of the volunteers which guidelines shall be approved by the State Department of Social Services. Each county which elects to utilize trained volunteers for the temporary supervision of minors shall report annually to the department on the number of volunteers utilized, the number of minors under their supervision, and the circumstances under which volunteers were utilized.

No record of the detention of such a person shall be made or kept by any law enforcement agency or the Department of Justice as a record of arrest. *(Added by Stats.1982, c. 978, § 3.8, eff. Sept. 13, 1982, operative July 1, 1982. Amended by Stats.1986, c. 1271, § 1; Stats.1987, c. 1485, § 1.5; Stats.1989, c. 913, § 2.)*

Research References

Treatises and Practice Aids

Witkin, California Summary 10th Parent and Child § 744, Conditions.

Witkin, California Summary 10th Parent and Child § 749, Segregation Of Classes Of Minors.

Witkin, California Summary 10th Parent and Child § 750, Segregation Of Minors and Adults.

§ 207. Place of detention; contact with other detainees; records; reports; disclosure

(a) A minor shall not be detained in any jail, lockup, juvenile hall, or other secure facility if he or she is taken into custody solely upon the ground that he or she is a person described by Section 213.3, or described by Section 601 or adjudged to be such or made a ward of the juvenile court solely upon that ground, except as provided in subdivision (b). If any such minor, other than a minor described in subdivision (b), is detained, he or she shall be detained in a sheltered-care facility or crisis resolution home as provided for in Section 654, or in a nonsecure facility provided for in subdivision (a), (b), (c), or (d) of Section 727.

(b) A minor taken into custody upon the ground that he or she is a person described in Section 601, or adjudged to be a ward of the juvenile court solely upon that ground, may be held in a secure facility, other than a facility in which adults are held in secure custody, in any of the following circumstances:

(1) For up to 12 hours after having been taken into custody for the purpose of determining if there are any outstanding wants, warrants, or holds against the minor in cases where the arresting officer or probation officer has cause to believe that the wants, warrants, or holds exist.

(2) For up to 24 hours after having been taken into custody, in order to locate the minor's parent or guardian as soon as possible and to arrange the return of the minor to his or her parent or guardian, with the exception of an out-of-state runaway who is being held pursuant to the Interstate Compact for Juveniles.[1]

(c) Any minor detained in juvenile hall pursuant to subdivision (b) shall not be permitted to come or remain in contact with any person detained on the basis that he or she has been taken into custody upon the ground that he or she is a person described in Section 602 or adjudged to be such or made a ward of the juvenile court upon that ground.

(d) Minors detained in juvenile hall pursuant to Sections 601 and 602 may be held in the same facility provided they are not permitted to come or remain in contact within that facility.

(e) Every county shall keep a record of each minor detained under subdivision (b), the place and length of time of the detention, and the reasons why the detention was necessary. Every county shall report this information to the Board of Corrections on a monthly basis, on forms to be provided by that agency.

The board shall not disclose the name of the detainee, or any personally identifying information contained in reports sent to the Division of Juvenile Justice under this subdivision. *(Added by Stats.1976, c. 1068, p. 4741, § 1.5. Amended by Stats.1977, c. 910, p. 2782, § 2; Stats.1977, c. 1241, p. 4180, § 1, eff. Oct. 1, 1977; Stats.1978, c. 1061, p. 3271, § 1, eff. Sept. 25, 1978; Stats.1979, c. 373, p. 1387, § 347; Stats.1986, c. 1271, § 2; Stats.1996, c. 12 (A.B.1397), § 2, eff. Feb. 14, 1996; Stats.2010, c. 96 (A.B.2350), § 1; Stats.2014, c. 70 (S.B.1296), § 2, eff. Jan. 1, 2015.)*

[1] See Welfare and Institutions Code § 1400.

Research References

Treatises and Practice Aids

Witkin, California Summary 10th Parent and Child § 743, in General.

Witkin, California Summary 10th Parent and Child § 744, Conditions.

Witkin, California Summary 10th Parent and Child § 749, Segregation Of Classes Of Minors.

Witkin, California Summary 10th Parent and Child § 755, Secure Detention Of Status Offender.

§ 207.1. Detention of minor in jail or lockup; conditions; implementation assistance; compliance exemptions; extensions; special purpose juvenile halls; evaluation and testing

(a) No court, judge, referee, peace officer, or employee of a detention facility shall knowingly detain any minor in a jail or lockup, except as provided in subdivision (b) or (d).

(b) Any minor who is alleged to have committed an offense described in subdivision (b), paragraph (2) of subdivision (d), or subdivision (e) of Section 707 whose case is transferred to a court of criminal jurisdiction pursuant to Section 707.1 after a finding is made that he or she is not a fit and proper subject to be dealt with under the juvenile court law, or any minor who has been charged directly in or transferred to a court of criminal jurisdiction pursuant to Section 707.01, may be detained in a jail or other secure facility for the confinement of adults if all of the following conditions are met:

(1) The juvenile court or the court of criminal jurisdiction makes a finding that the minor's further detention in the juvenile hall would endanger the safety of the public or would be detrimental to the other minors in the juvenile hall.

(2) Contact between the minor and adults in the facility is restricted in accordance with Section 208.

(3) The minor is adequately supervised.

(c) A minor who is either found not to be a fit and proper subject to be dealt with under the juvenile court law or who will be transferred to a court of criminal jurisdiction pursuant to Section 707.01, at the time of transfer to a court of criminal jurisdiction or at the conclusion of the fitness hearing, as the case may be, shall be entitled to be released on bail or on his or her own recognizance upon the same circumstances, terms, and conditions as an adult who is alleged to have committed the same offense.

(d)(1) A minor 14 years of age or older who is taken into temporary custody by a peace officer on the basis of being a person described by Section 602, and who, in the reasonable belief of the peace officer, presents a serious security risk of harm to self or others, may be securely detained in a law enforcement facility that contains a lockup for adults, if all of the following conditions are met:

(A) The minor is held in temporary custody for the purpose of investigating the case, facilitating release of the minor to a parent or guardian, or arranging transfer of the minor to an appropriate juvenile facility.

(B) The minor is detained in the law enforcement facility for a period that does not exceed six hours except as provided in subdivision (f).

(C) The minor is informed at the time he or she is securely detained of the purpose of the secure detention, of the length of time the secure detention is expected to last, and of the maximum six-hour period the secure detention is authorized to last. In the event an extension is granted pursuant to subdivision (f), the minor shall be informed of the length of time the extension is expected to last.

(D) Contact between the minor and adults confined in the facility is restricted in accordance with Section 208.

(E) The minor is adequately supervised.

(F) A log or other written record is maintained by the law enforcement agency showing the offense that is the basis for the secure detention of the minor in the facility, the reasons and circumstances forming the basis for the decision to place the minor in secure detention, and the length of time the minor was securely detained.

(2) Any other minor, other than a minor to which paragraph (1) applies, who is taken into temporary custody by a peace officer on the basis that the minor is a person described by Section 602 may be taken to a law enforcement facility that contains a lockup for adults and may be held in temporary custody in the facility for the purposes of investigating the case, facilitating the release of the minor to a parent or guardian, or arranging for the transfer of the minor to an appropriate juvenile facility. While in the law enforcement facility, the minor may not be securely detained and shall be supervised in a manner so as to ensure that there will be no contact with adults in custody in the facility. If the minor is held in temporary, nonsecure custody within the facility, the peace officer shall exercise one of the dispositional options authorized by Sections 626 and 626.5 without unnecessary delay and, in every case, within six hours.

(3) "Law enforcement facility," as used in this subdivision, includes a police station or a sheriff's station, but does not include a jail, as defined in subdivision (i).

(e) The Board of Corrections shall assist law enforcement agencies, probation departments, and courts with the implementation of this section by doing all of the following:

(1) The board shall advise each law enforcement agency, probation department, and court affected by this section as to its existence and effect.

(2) The board shall make available and, upon request, shall provide, technical assistance to each governmental agency that reported the confinement of a minor in a jail or lockup in calendar year 1984 or 1985. The purpose of this technical assistance is to develop alternatives to the use of jails or lockups for the confinement of minors. These alternatives may include secure or nonsecure facilities located apart from an existing jail or lockup, improved transportation or access to juvenile halls or other juvenile facilities, and other programmatic alternatives recommended by the board. The technical assistance shall take any form the board deems appropriate for effective compliance with this section.

(f)(1)(A) Under the limited conditions of inclement weather, acts of God, or natural disasters that result in the temporary unavailability of transportation, an extension of the six-hour maximum period of detention set forth in paragraph (2) of subdivision (d) may be granted to a county by the Board of Corrections. The extension may be granted only by the board, on an individual, case-by-case basis. If the extension is granted, the detention of minors under those conditions shall not exceed the duration of the special conditions, plus a period reasonably necessary to accomplish transportation of the minor to a suitable juvenile facility, not to exceed six hours after the restoration of available transportation.

(B) A county that receives an extension under this paragraph shall comply with the requirements set forth in subdivision (d). The county also shall provide a written report to the board that specifies when the inclement weather, act of God, or natural disaster ceased to exist, when transportation availability was restored, and when the minor was delivered to a suitable juvenile facility. If the minor was detained in excess of 24 hours, the board shall verify the information contained in the report.

(2) Under the limited condition of temporary unavailability of transportation, an extension of the six-hour maximum period of detention set forth in paragraph (2) of subdivision (d) may be granted by the board to an offshore law enforcement facility. The extension may be granted only by the board, on an individual, case-by-case basis. If the extension is granted, the detention of minors under those conditions shall extend only until the next available mode of transportation can be arranged.

An offshore law enforcement facility that receives an extension under this paragraph shall comply with the requirements set forth in subdivision (d). The facility also shall provide a written report to the board that specifies when the next mode of transportation became available, and when the minor was delivered to a suitable juvenile facility. If the minor was detained in excess of 24 hours, the board shall verify the information contained in the report.

(3) At least annually, the board shall review and report on extensions sought and granted under this subdivision. If, upon that review, the board determines that a county has sought one or more extensions resulting in the excessive confinement of minors in adult facilities, or that a county is engaged in a pattern and practice of seeking extensions, it shall require the county to submit a detailed explanation of the reasons for the extensions sought and an assessment of the need for a conveniently located and suitable juvenile facility. Upon receiving this information, the board shall make available, and the county shall accept, technical assistance for the purpose of developing suitable alternatives to the confinement of minors in adult lockups.

(g) Any county that did not have a juvenile hall on January 1, 1987, may establish a special purpose juvenile hall, as defined by the Board of Corrections, for the detention of minors for a period not to exceed 96 hours. Any county that had a juvenile hall on January 1, 1987, also may establish, in addition to the juvenile hall, a special purpose juvenile hall. The board shall prescribe minimum standards for that type of facility.

(h) No part of a building or a building complex that contains a jail may be converted or utilized as a secure juvenile facility unless all of the following criteria are met:

(1) The juvenile facility is physically, or architecturally, separate and apart from the jail or lockup such that there could be no contact between juveniles and incarcerated adults.

(2) Sharing of nonresidential program areas only occurs where there are written policies and procedures that assure that there is time-phased use of those areas that prevents contact between juveniles and incarcerated adults.

(3) The juvenile facility has a dedicated and separate staff from the jail or lockup, including management, security, and direct care staff. Staff who provide specialized services such as food, laundry, maintenance, engineering, or medical services, who are not normally in contact with detainees, or whose infrequent contacts occur under conditions of separation of juveniles and adults, may serve both populations.

(4) The juvenile facility complies with all applicable state and local statutory, licensing, and regulatory requirements for juvenile facilities of its type.

(i)(1) "Jail," as used in this chapter, means a locked facility administered by a law enforcement or governmental agency, the purpose of which is to detain adults who have been charged with violations of criminal law and are pending trial, or to hold convicted adult criminal offenders sentenced for less than one year.

(2) "Lockup," as used in this chapter, means any locked room or secure enclosure under the control of a sheriff or other peace officer that is primarily for the temporary confinement of adults upon arrest.

(3) "Offshore law enforcement facility," as used in this section, means a sheriff's station containing a lockup for adults that is located on an island located at least 22 miles from the California coastline.

(j) Nothing in this section shall be deemed to prevent a peace officer or employee of an adult detention facility or jail from escorting a minor into the detention facility or jail for the purpose of administering an evaluation, test, or chemical test pursuant to Section 23157 of the Vehicle Code, if all of the following conditions are met:

(1) The minor is taken into custody by a peace officer on the basis of being a person described by Section 602 and there is no equipment for the administration of the evaluation, test, or chemical test located at a juvenile facility within a reasonable distance of the point where the minor was taken into custody.

(2) The minor is not locked in a cell or room within the adult detention facility or jail, is under the continuous, personal supervision of a peace officer or employee of the detention facility or jail, and is not permitted to come in contact or remain in contact with in-custody adults.

(3) The evaluation, test, or chemical test administered pursuant to Section 23157 of the Vehicle Code is performed as expeditiously as possible, so that the minor is not delayed unnecessarily within the adult detention facility or jail. Upon completion of the evaluation, test, or chemical test, the minor shall be removed from the detention facility or jail as soon as reasonably possible. No minor shall be held in custody in an adult detention facility or jail under the authority of this paragraph in excess of two hours. *(Added by Stats.1995, c. 304 (A.B.904), § 2, eff. Aug. 3, 1995. Amended by Stats.1996, c. 12 (A.B.1397), § 3, eff. Feb. 14, 1996; Stats.1997, c. 17 (S.B.947), § 147; Stats.1998, c. 694 (S.B.2147), § 1.)*

Research References

Forms

West's California Judicial Council Forms JV-710, Juvenile Fitness Hearing Order.

Treatises and Practice Aids

Witkin, California Summary 10th Parent and Child § 746, Juvenile Halls.

Witkin, California Summary 10th Parent and Child § 751, in General.
Witkin, California Summary 10th Parent and Child § 752, Minor Transferred to Adult Criminal Court.
Witkin, California Summary 10th Parent and Child § 753, Minor in Temporary Custody.
Witkin, California Summary 10th Parent and Child § 754, Administration Of Evaluation or Test.
Witkin, California Summary 10th Parent and Child § 756, Inspection Of Facilities.
Witkin, California Summary 10th Parent and Child § 793, Involuntary Confession or Admission.
Witkin, California Summary 10th Parent and Child § 852, Detention Of Minor.

§ 207.2. Temporary custody

* * * A minor who is held in temporary custody in a law enforcement facility that contains a lockup for adults pursuant to subdivision (d) of Section 207.1 may be released to a parent, guardian, or responsible relative by the law enforcement agency operating the facility, or may at the discretion of the law enforcement agency be released into his or her own custody, provided that a minor released into his or her own custody is furnished, upon request, with transportation to his or her home or to the place where the minor was taken into custody.

* * * *(Added by Stats.1992, c. 429 (S.B.1274), § 2, eff. Aug. 3, 1992. Amended by Stats.2017, c. 678 (S.B.190), § 5, eff. Jan. 1, 2018.)*

Research References

Treatises and Practice Aids

Witkin, California Summary 10th Parent and Child § 518, Financial Evaluation.

§ 207.5. Misrepresentation or false identification to secure admission to facility; misdemeanor

Every person who misrepresents or falsely identifies himself or herself either verbally or by presenting any fraudulent written instrument to any probation officer, or to any superintendent, director, counselor, or employee of a juvenile hall, ranch, or camp for the purpose of securing admission to the premises or grounds of any juvenile hall, ranch, or camp, or to gain access to any minor detained therein, and who would not otherwise qualify for admission or access thereto, is guilty of a misdemeanor. *(Added by Stats.1981, c. 697, p. 2517, § 1. Amended by Stats.1998, c. 694 (S.B.2147), § 2.)*

Research References

Treatises and Practice Aids

Witkin, California Summary 10th Parent and Child § 746, Juvenile Halls.

§ 207.6. Detention of minor in jail or other secure facility for confinement of adults; conditions

A minor may be detained in a jail or other secure facility for the confinement of adults pursuant to subdivision (b) of Section 207.1 or paragraph (1) of subdivision (b) of Section 707.1 only if the court makes its findings on the record and, in addition, finds that the minor poses a danger to the staff, other minors in the juvenile facility, or to the public because of the minor's failure to respond to the disciplinary control of the juvenile facility, or because the nature of the danger posed by the minor cannot safely be managed by the disciplinary procedures of the juvenile facility. *(Added by Stats.2003, c. 332 (A.B.945), § 1.)*

Research References

Treatises and Practice Aids

Witkin, California Summary 10th Parent and Child § 751, in General.
Witkin, California Summary 10th Parent and Child § 852, Detention Of Minor.

§ 208. Detention or sentence to adult institutions; contact with adults; adults committed for sex offenses

(a) When any person under 18 years of age is detained in or sentenced to any institution in which adults are confined, it shall be unlawful to permit such person to come or remain in contact with such adults.

(b) No person who is a ward or dependent child of the juvenile court who is detained in or committed to any state hospital or other state facility shall be permitted to come or remain in contact with any adult person who has been committed to any state hospital or other state facility as a mentally disordered sex offender under the provisions of Article 1 (commencing with Section 6300) of Chapter 2 of Part 2 of Division 6, or with any adult person who has been charged in an accusatory pleading with the commission of any sex offense for which registration of the convicted offender is required under Section 290 of the Penal Code and who has been committed to any state hospital or other state facility pursuant to Section 1026 or 1370 of the Penal Code.

(c) As used in this section, "contact" does not include participation in supervised group therapy or other supervised treatment activities, participation in work furlough programs, or participation in hospital recreational activities which are directly supervised by employees of the hospital, so long as living arrangements are strictly segregated and all precautions are taken to prevent unauthorized associations.

(d) This section shall be operative January 1, 1998. *(Added by Stats.1993–94, 1st Ex.Sess., c. 23 (A.B.45), § 2, eff. Nov. 30, 1994, operative Jan. 1, 1998.)*

Research References

Treatises and Practice Aids

Witkin, California Summary 10th Parent and Child § 750, Segregation Of Minors and Adults.
Witkin, California Summary 10th Parent and Child § 752, Minor Transferred to Adult Criminal Court.
Witkin, California Summary 10th Parent and Child § 753, Minor in Temporary Custody.

§ 208.3. Placement of minor or ward in room confinement; guidelines; length of confinement; exceptions

(a) For purposes of this section, the following definitions * * * apply:

(1) "Juvenile facility" includes any of the following:

(A) A juvenile hall, as described in Section 850.

(B) A juvenile camp or ranch, as described in Article 24 (commencing with Section 880).

(C) A facility of the Department of Corrections and Rehabilitation, Division of Juvenile Facilities.

(D) A regional youth educational facility, as described in Section 894.

(E) A youth correctional center, as described in Article 9 (commencing with Section 1850) of Chapter 1 of Division 2.5.

(F) A juvenile regional facility as described in Section 5695.

(G) Any other local or state facility used for the confinement of minors or wards.

(2) "Minor" means a person who is any of the following:

(A) A person under 18 years of age.

(B) A person under the maximum age of juvenile court jurisdiction who is confined in a juvenile facility.

(C) A person under the jurisdiction of the Department of Corrections and Rehabilitation, Division of Juvenile Facilities.

(3) "Room confinement" means the placement of a minor or ward in a locked sleeping room or cell with minimal or no contact with persons other than correctional facility staff and attorneys. Room confinement does not include confinement of a minor or ward in a single-person room or cell for brief periods of locked room confinement necessary for required institutional operations.

(4) "Ward" means a person who has been declared a ward of the court pursuant to * * * Section 602.

(b) The placement of a minor or ward in room confinement shall be accomplished in accordance with the following guidelines:

(1) Room confinement shall not be used before other less restrictive options have been attempted and exhausted, unless attempting those options poses a threat to the safety or security of any minor, ward, or staff.

(2) Room confinement shall not be used for the purposes of punishment, coercion, convenience, or retaliation by staff.

(3) Room confinement shall not be used to the extent that it compromises the mental and physical health of the minor or ward.

(c) A minor or ward may be held up to four hours in room confinement. After the minor or ward has been held in room confinement for a period of four hours, staff shall do one or more of the following:

(1) Return the minor or ward to general population.

(2) Consult with mental health or medical staff.

(3) Develop an individualized plan that includes the goals and objectives to be met in order to reintegrate the minor or ward to general population.

(d) If room confinement must be extended beyond four hours, staff shall do the following:

(1) Document the reason for room confinement and the basis for the extension, the date and time the minor or ward was first placed in room confinement, and when he or she is eventually released from room confinement.

(2) Develop an individualized plan that includes the goals and objectives to be met in order to reintegrate the minor or ward to general population.

(3) Obtain documented authorization by the facility superintendent or his or her designee every four hours thereafter.

(e) This section is not intended to limit the use of single-person rooms or cells for the housing of minors or wards in juvenile facilities and does not apply to normal sleeping hours.

(f) This section does not apply to minors or wards in court holding facilities or adult facilities.

(g) * * * This section shall not be construed to conflict with any law providing greater or additional protections to minors or wards.

(h) This section does not apply during an extraordinary, emergency circumstance that requires a significant departure from normal institutional operations, including a natural disaster or facility-wide threat that poses an imminent and substantial risk of harm to multiple staff, minors, or wards. This exception shall apply for the shortest amount of time needed to address the imminent and substantial risk of harm.

(i) This section does not apply when a minor or ward is placed in a locked cell or sleeping room to treat and protect against the spread of a communicable disease for the shortest amount of time required to reduce the risk of infection, with the written approval of a licensed physician or nurse practitioner, when the minor or ward is not required to be in an infirmary for an illness. Additionally, this section does not apply when a minor or ward is placed in a locked cell or sleeping room for required extended care after medical treatment with the written approval of a licensed physician or nurse practitioner, when the minor or ward is not required to be in an infirmary for illness.

(j) This section shall become operative on January 1, 2018.

(Added by Stats.2016, c. 726 (S.B.1143), § 1, eff. Jan. 1, 2017, operative Jan. 1, 2018. Amended by Stats.2017, c. 561 (A.B.1516), § 263, eff. Jan. 1, 2018.)

§ 208.5. Minor attaining age 18 prior to or during detention or confinement in county institution established for housing juveniles; contact with juveniles until age 19; delivery to custody of sheriff or continued detention in juvenile facility

(a) Notwithstanding any other law, in any case in which a minor who is detained in or committed to a county institution established for the purpose of housing juveniles attains 18 years of age prior to or during the period of detention or confinement he or she may be allowed to come or remain in contact with those juveniles until 19 years of age, at which time he or she, upon the recommendation of the probation officer, shall be delivered to the custody of the sheriff for the remainder of the time he or she remains in custody, unless the juvenile court orders continued detention in a juvenile facility. If continued detention is ordered for a ward under the jurisdiction of the juvenile court who is 19 years of age or older but under 21 years of age, the detained person may be allowed to come into or remain in contact with any other person detained in the institution subject to the requirements of subdivision (b). The person shall be advised of his or her ability to petition the court for continued detention in a juvenile facility at the time of his or her attainment of 19 years of age. Notwithstanding any other law, the sheriff may allow the person to come into and remain in contact with other adults in the county jail or in any other county correctional facility in which he or she is housed.

(b) The county shall apply to the Corrections Standards Authority for approval of a county institution established for the purpose of housing juveniles as a suitable place for confinement before the institution is used for the detention or commitment of an individual under the jurisdiction of the juvenile court who is 19 years of age or older but under 21 years of age where the detained person will come into or remain in contact with persons under 18 years of age who are detained in the institution. The authority shall review and approve or deny the application of the county within 30 days of receiving notice of this proposed use. In its review, the authority shall take into account the available programming, capacity, and safety of the institution as a place for the combined confinement and rehabilitation of individuals under the jurisdiction of the juvenile court who are over 19 years of age and those who are under 19 years of age.
(Added by Stats.1984, c. 207, § 1. Amended by Stats.1986, c. 676, § 1; Stats.2007, c. 175 (S.B.81), § 18, eff. Aug. 24, 2007, operative Sept. 1, 2007.)

Research References

Treatises and Practice Aids

Witkin, California Summary 10th Parent and Child § 750, Segregation Of Minors and Adults.
Witkin, California Summary 10th Parent and Child § 943, Invalid Commitment.
Witkin, California Summary 10th Parent and Child § 968, Detention in Adult Facility.
Witkin, California Summary 10th Parent and Child § 976, (New) Violation Of Conditions Of Supervision.

§ 209. Inspection of juvenile detention facilities for suitability; minimum standards

(a)(1) The judge of the juvenile court of a county, or, if there is more than one judge, any of the judges of the juvenile court shall, at least annually, inspect any jail, juvenile hall, or special purpose juvenile hall that, in the preceding calendar year, was used for confinement, for more than 24 hours, of any minor.

(2) The judge shall promptly notify the operator of the jail, juvenile hall, or special purpose juvenile hall of any observed noncompliance with minimum standards for juvenile facilities adopted by the Board of State and Community Corrections under Section 210. Based on the facility's subsequent compliance with the provisions of subdivisions (d) and (e), the judge shall thereafter make a finding whether the facility is a suitable place for the confinement of minors and shall note the finding in the minutes of the court.

(3) The Board of State and Community Corrections shall conduct a biennial inspection of each jail, juvenile hall, lockup, or special purpose juvenile hall situated in this state that, during the preceding calendar year, was used for confinement, for more than 24 hours, of any minor. The board shall promptly notify the operator of any jail, juvenile hall, lockup, or special purpose juvenile hall of any noncompliance found, upon inspection, with any of the minimum standards for juvenile facilities adopted by the Board of State and Community Corrections under Section 210 or 210.2.

(4) If either a judge of the juvenile court or the board, after inspection of a jail, juvenile hall, special purpose juvenile hall, or lockup, finds that it is not being operated and maintained as a suitable place for the confinement of minors, the juvenile court or the board shall give notice of its finding to all persons having authority to confine minors pursuant to this chapter and commencing 60 days thereafter the facility shall not be used for confinement of minors until the time the judge or board, as the case may be, finds, after reinspection of the facility that the conditions that rendered the facility unsuitable have been remedied, and the facility is a suitable place for confinement of minors.

(5) The custodian of each jail, juvenile hall, special purpose juvenile hall, and lockup shall make any reports as may be requested by the board or the juvenile court to effectuate the purposes of this section.

(b)(1) The Board of State and Community Corrections may inspect any law enforcement facility that contains a lockup for adults and that it has reason to believe may not be in compliance with the requirements of subdivision (d) of Section 207.1 or with the certification requirements or standards adopted under Section 210.2. A judge of the juvenile court shall conduct an annual inspection, either in person or through a delegated member of the appropriate county or regional juvenile justice commission, of any law enforcement facility that contains a lockup for adults which, in the preceding year, was used for the secure detention of any minor. If the law enforcement facility is observed, upon inspection, to be out of compliance with the requirements of subdivision (d) of Section 207.1, or with any standard adopted under Section 210.2, the board or the judge shall promptly notify the operator of the law enforcement facility of the specific points of noncompliance.

(2) If either the judge or the board finds after inspection that the facility is not being operated and maintained in conformity with the requirements of subdivision (d) of Section 207.1 or with the certification requirements or standards adopted under Section 210.2, the juvenile court or the board shall give notice of its finding to all persons having authority to securely detain minors in the facility, and, commencing 60 days thereafter, the facility shall not be used for the secure detention of a minor until the time the judge or the board, as the case may be, finds, after reinspection, that the conditions that rendered the facility unsuitable have been remedied, and the facility is a suitable place for the confinement of minors in conformity with all requirements of law.

(3) The custodian of each law enforcement facility that contains a lockup for adults shall make any report as may be requested by the board or by the juvenile court to effectuate the purposes of this subdivision.

(c) The board shall collect biennial data on the number, place, and duration of confinements of minors in jails and lockups, as defined in subdivision (i) of Section 207.1, and shall publish biennially this information in the form as it deems appropriate for the purpose of providing public information on continuing compliance with the requirements of Section 207.1.

(d) Except as provided in subdivision (e), a juvenile hall, special purpose juvenile hall, law enforcement facility, or jail shall be unsuitable for the confinement of minors if it is not in compliance with one or more of the minimum standards for juvenile facilities adopted by the Board of State and Community Corrections under Section 210 or 210.2, and if, within 60 days of having received notice of noncompliance from the board or the judge of the juvenile court, the juvenile hall, special purpose juvenile hall, law enforcement facility, or jail has failed to file an approved corrective action plan with the Board of State and Community Corrections to correct the condition or conditions of noncompliance of which it has been notified. The corrective action plan shall outline how the juvenile hall, special purpose juvenile hall, law enforcement facility, or jail plans to correct the issue of noncompliance and give a reasonable timeframe, not to exceed 90 days, for resolution, that the board shall either approve or deny. In the event the juvenile hall, special purpose juvenile hall, law enforcement facility, or jail fails to meet its commitment to resolve noncompliance issues outlined in its corrective action plan, the board shall make a determination of suitability at its next scheduled meeting.

(e) If a juvenile hall is not in compliance with one or more of the minimum standards for juvenile facilities adopted by the Board of State and Community Corrections under Section 210, and where the noncompliance arises from sustained occupancy levels that are above the population capacity permitted by applicable minimum standards, the juvenile hall shall be unsuitable for the confinement of minors if the board or the judge of the juvenile court determines that conditions in the facility pose a serious risk to the health, safety, or welfare of minors confined in the facility. In making its determination of suitability, the board or the judge of the juvenile court shall consider, in addition to the noncompliance with minimum standards, the totality of conditions in the juvenile hall, including the extent and duration of overpopulation as well as staffing, program, physical plant, and medical and mental health care conditions in the facility. The Board of State and Community Corrections may develop guidelines and procedures for its determination of suitability in accordance with this subdivision and to assist counties in bringing their juvenile halls into full compliance with applicable minimum standards. This subdivision shall not be interpreted to exempt a juvenile hall from having to correct, in accordance with the provisions of subdivision (d), any minimum standard violations that are not directly related to overpopulation of the facility.

(f) In accordance with the federal Juvenile Justice and Delinquency Prevention Act of 2002 (42 U.S.C. Sec. 5601 et seq.), the Corrections Standards Authority shall inspect and collect relevant data from any facility that may be used for the secure detention of minors.

(g) All reports and notices of findings prepared by the Board of State and Community Corrections pursuant to this section shall be posted on the Board of State and Community Corrections' Internet Web site in a manner in which they are accessible to the public. *(Added by Stats.1992, c. 695 (S.B.97), § 27, eff. Sept. 15, 1992, operative July 1, 1995. Amended by Stats.1993, c. 59 (S.B.443), § 20, eff. June 30, 1993, operative July 1, 1995; Stats.1995, c. 304 (A.B.904), § 3, eff. Aug. 3, 1995; Stats.1996, c. 805 (A.B.1325), § 8; Stats. 1998, c. 694 (S.B.2147), § 3; Stats.2010, c. 157 (S.B.1447), § 1; Stats.2017, c. 17 (A.B.103), § 55, eff. June 27, 2017.)*

Research References

Treatises and Practice Aids

Witkin, California Summary 10th Parent and Child § 756, Inspection Of Facilities.

§ 210. Standards for juvenile halls

The Board of Corrections shall adopt minimum standards for the operation and maintenance of juvenile halls for the confinement of minors. *(Added by Stats.1976, c. 1068, p. 4741, § 1.5. Amended by Stats.1996, c. 12 (A.B.1397), § 5, eff. Feb. 14, 1996; Stats.1998, c. 694 (S.B.2147), § 4.)*

Research References

Treatises and Practice Aids

Witkin, California Summary 10th Parent and Child § 756, Inspection Of Facilities.

§ 210.1. Guidelines for operation and maintenance of nonsecure placement facilities

The Board of Corrections shall develop guidelines for the operation and maintenance of nonsecure placement facilities for persons alleged or found to be persons coming within the terms of Section 601 or 602. *(Added by Stats.1978, c. 1157, p. 3553, § 1, eff. Sept. 26, 1978. Amended by Stats.1996, c. 12 (A.B.1397), § 6, eff. Feb. 14, 1996.)*

Research References

Treatises and Practice Aids

Witkin, California Summary 10th Parent and Child § 756, Inspection Of Facilities.

§ 210.2. Standards for facilities containing adult lockups; certification

(a) The Board of Corrections shall adopt regulations establishing standards for law enforcement facilities which contain lockups for adults and which are used for the temporary, secure detention of minors upon arrest under subdivision (d) of Section 207.1. The standards shall identify appropriate conditions of confinement for minors in law enforcement facilities, including standards for places within a police station or sheriff's station where minors may be securely detained; standards regulating contact between minors and adults in custody in lockup, booking, or common areas; standards for the supervision of minors securely detained in these facilities; and any other related standard as the board deems appropriate to effectuate compliance with subdivision (d) of Section 207.1.

(b) Every person in charge of a law enforcement facility which contains a lockup for adults and which is used in any calendar year for the secure detention of any minor shall certify annually that the facility is in conformity with the regulations adopted by the board under subdivision (a). The certification shall be endorsed by the sheriff or chief of police of the jurisdiction in which the facility is located and shall be forwarded to and maintained by the board. The board may provide forms and instructions to local jurisdictions to facilitate compliance with this requirement. *(Added by Stats.1986, c. 1271, § 5. Amended by Stats.1996, c. 12 (A.B.1397), § 7, eff. Feb. 14, 1996.)*

Research References

Treatises and Practice Aids

Witkin, California Summary 10th Parent and Child § 756, Inspection Of Facilities.

§ 210.5. Tulare County Juvenile Facility; construction and operation; staffing ratios and housing capacity; review

The Legislature finds and declares that it is in the best public interest to encourage innovations in staffing ratios, maximization of housing unit size, and experimentation with innovative architectural designs and program components, designs, or operations in the operation and maintenance of new juvenile detention facilities. Therefore, to these ends, Tulare County, as a demonstration project, may undertake the construction and operation of a juvenile detention facility, to be known as the "Tulare County Juvenile Facility," that shall not be subject to laws or regulations governing staffing ratios and housing capacity for juvenile facilities except as provided in this section. Before the county proceeds with the construction and operation of the Tulare County Juvenile Facility, the schematics and the proposed staffing patterns of this project shall be subject to review and approval by the Board of Corrections, which shall consider the proposed regulations, applicable current case law, and appropriate juvenile correctional practices in order to determine the merits of the proposal and to ensure the safety and security of wards and the staff. Any review conducted by the Board of Corrections pursuant to this section shall consider community, inmate, and staff safety, and the extent to which the project makes the most efficient use of resources. In addition, progress reports and evaluative data regarding the success of the demonstration project shall be provided to the Board of Corrections by the county.

Nothing contained in this section shall affect the applicability of the provisions of the Labor Code. *(Added by Stats. 1996, c. 100 (A.B.2189), § 1, eff. July 1, 1996.)*

§ 210.6. Mechanical restraints

(a)(1) Mechanical restraints, including, but not limited to, handcuffs, chains, irons, straitjackets or cloth or leather restraints, or other similar items, may be used on a juvenile detained in or committed to a local secure juvenile facility, camp, ranch, or forestry camp, as established pursuant to Sections 850 and 881, during transportation outside of the facility only upon a determination made by the probation department, in consultation with the transporting agency, that the mechanical restraints are necessary to prevent physical harm to the juvenile or another person or due to a substantial risk of flight.

(2) If a determination is made that mechanical restraints are necessary, the least restrictive form of restraint shall be used consistent with the legitimate security needs of each juvenile.

(3) A county probation department that chooses to use mechanical restraints other than handcuffs on juveniles shall establish procedures for the documentation of their use, including the reasons for the use of those mechanical restraints.

(4) This subdivision does not apply to mechanical restraints used by medical care providers in the course of medical care or transportation.

(b)(1) Mechanical restraints may only be used during a juvenile court proceeding if the court determines that the individual juvenile's behavior in custody or in court establishes a manifest need to use mechanical restraints to prevent physical harm to the juvenile or another person or due to a substantial risk of flight.

(2) The burden to establish the need for mechanical restraints pursuant to paragraph (1) is on the prosecution.

(3) If the court determines that mechanical restraints are necessary, the least restrictive form of restraint shall be used and the reasons for the use of mechanical restraints shall be documented in the record. *(Added by Stats.2017, c. 660 (A.B.878), § 1, eff. Jan. 1, 2018.)*

§ 211. Commitment to correctional facilities

(a) No person under the age of 14 years shall be committed to a state prison or be transferred thereto from any other institution.

(b) Notwithstanding any other provision of law, no person under the age of 16 years shall be housed in any facility under the jurisdiction of the Department of Corrections. *(Added by Stats.1976, c. 1068, p. 4741, § 1.5. Amended by Stats.1994, c. 453 (A.B.560), § 2.7.)*

Research References

Treatises and Practice Aids

Witkin, California Summary 10th Parent and Child § 751, in General.

§ 212. Fees; expenses

There shall be no fee for filing a petition under this chapter nor shall any fees be charged by any public officer for his services in filing or serving papers or for the performance of any duty enjoined upon him by this chapter, except where the sheriff transports a person to a state institution. If the judge of the juvenile court orders that a ward or dependent child go to a state institution without being accompanied by an officer or that a ward or dependent child be taken to an institution by the probation officer of the county or parole officer of the institution or by some other suitable person, all expenses necessarily incurred therefor shall be allowed and paid in the same manner and from the same funds as such expenses would be allowed and paid were such transportation effected by the sheriff. *(Added by Stats.1976, c. 1068, p. 4741, § 1.5.)*

Research References

Treatises and Practice Aids

Witkin, California Summary 10th Parent and Child § 564, in General.

Witkin, California Summary 10th Parent and Child § 566, Notices, Citations, Warrants, and Subpenas.

Witkin, California Summary 10th Parent and Child § 771, in General.

§ 212.5. Electronic filing and service; conditions

Unless otherwise provided by law, a document in a juvenile court matter may be filed and served electronically as prescribed by Section 1010.6 of the Code of Civil Procedure, under the following conditions:

(a) Electronic service is authorized only if the county and the court permit electronic service.

(b)(1) On or before December 31, 2018, electronic service on a party or other person is permitted only if the party or other person has consented to accept electronic service in that specific action. A party or other person may subsequently withdraw its consent to electronic service.

(2) On or after January 1, 2019, electronic service on a party or other person is permitted only if the party or other person has expressly consented, as provided in Section 1010.6 of the Code of Civil Procedure. A party or other person may subsequently withdraw its consent to electronic service by completing the appropriate Judicial Council form.

(c) Consent, or the withdrawal of consent, to receive electronic service may be completed by a party or other person entitled to service, or that person's attorney.

(d) Electronic service shall be provided in the following manner:

(1) Electronic service is not permitted on any party or person who is under 10 years of age.

(2) Electronic service is not permitted on any party or person who is between 10 years of age and 15 years of age without the express consent of the minor and the minor's attorney.

(3) Electronic service shall be permitted on any party or person who is 16 to 18 years of age only if the minor, after consultation with his or her attorney, consents. By January 1, 2019, the Judicial Council shall develop a rule of court on the duties of the minor's attorney during the required consultation.

(4) Electronic service of psychological or medical documentation related to a minor shall not be permitted, other than the summary required pursuant to Section 16010 when included as part of a required report to the court.

(e) In the following matters, the party or other person shall be served by both electronic means and by other means specified by law if the document to be served is one of the following:

(1) A notice of hearing or an appellate advisement issued pursuant to subparagraph (A) of paragraph (3) of subdivision (*l*) of Section 366.26 for a hearing at which a social worker is recommending the termination of parental rights.

(2) A citation issued pursuant to Section 661.

(3) A notice of hearing pursuant to subdivision (d) of Section 777.

(f) If the minor is an Indian child or the court has reason to know that an Indian child is involved, service shall be made pursuant to Section 224.2.

(g) Electronic service and electronic filing shall be conducted in a manner that preserves and ensures the confidentiality of records by encryption.

(h) The requirements of this section shall be consistent with Section 1010.6 of the Code of Civil Procedure and rules of court adopted by the Judicial Council pursuant to that section. *(Added by Stats.2017, c. 319 (A.B.976), § 108, eff. Jan. 1, 2018.)*

§ 213. Contempt of court

Any willful disobedience or interference with any lawful order of the juvenile court or of a judge or referee thereof constitutes a contempt of court. *(Added by Stats.1976, c. 1068, p. 4741, § 1.5.)*

Commentary

The California Supreme Court has held that a juvenile court, as part of a reunification plan, has the power to order a parent to participate in a substance abuse program; however, the court may not use the contempt sanction as punishment solely because a parent has failed to satisfy a reunification condition. *In re Nolan W., 45 Cal.4th 1217, 91 Cal.Rptr.3d 140, 203 P.3d 454 (2009).*

Research References

Treatises and Practice Aids

Witkin, California Summary 10th Parent and Child § 453, Jurisdiction Over Adults.
Witkin, California Summary 10th Parent and Child § 469, Findings, Explanation, and Order.
Witkin, California Summary 10th Parent and Child § 589, Informality and Control by Court.
Witkin, California Summary 10th Parent and Child § 743, in General.
Witkin, California Summary 10th Parent and Child § 744, Conditions.
Witkin, California Summary 10th Parent and Child § 745, Limitations.

§ 213.3. Willful disobedience or interference with juvenile court order; detainment prohibited; orders to ensure school attendance

A person under 18 years of age shall not be detained in a secure facility, as defined in Section 206, solely upon the ground that he or she is in willful disobedience or interference with any lawful order of the juvenile court, if the basis of an order of contempt is the failure to comply with a court order pursuant to subdivision (b) of Section 601. Upon a finding of contempt of court, the court may issue any other lawful order, as necessary, to ensure the minor's school attendance. *(Added by Stats.2014, c. 70 (S.B.1296), § 3, eff. Jan. 1, 2015.)*

Research References

Treatises and Practice Aids

Witkin, California Summary 10th Parent and Child § 743, in General.
Witkin, California Summary 10th Parent and Child § 744, Conditions.
Witkin, California Summary 10th Parent and Child § 755, Secure Detention Of Status Offender.

§ 213.5. Proceedings to declare a minor child a dependent child; ex parte orders

(a) After a petition has been filed pursuant to Section 311 to declare a child a dependent child of the juvenile court, and until the time that the petition is dismissed or dependency is terminated, upon application in the manner provided by Section 527 of the Code of Civil Procedure or in the manner provided by Section 6300 of the Family Code, if related to domestic violence, the juvenile court has exclusive jurisdiction to issue ex parte orders (1) enjoining any person from molesting, attacking, striking, stalking, threatening, sexually assaulting, battering, harassing, telephoning, including, but not limited to, making annoying telephone calls as described in Section 653m of the Penal Code, destroying the personal property, contacting, either directly or indirectly, by mail or otherwise, coming within a specified distance of, or disturbing the peace of the child or any other child in the household; and (2) excluding any person from the dwelling of the person who has care, custody, and control of the child. A court may also issue an ex parte order enjoining any person from molesting, attacking, striking, stalking, threatening, sexually assaulting, battering, harassing, telephoning, including, but not limited to, making annoying telephone calls as described in Section 653m of the Penal Code, destroying the personal property, contacting, either directly or indirectly, by mail or otherwise, coming within a specified distance of, or disturbing the peace of any parent, legal guardian, or current caretaker of the child, regardless of whether the child resides with that parent, legal guardian, or current caretaker, upon application in the manner provided by Section 527 of the Code of Civil Procedure or, if related to domestic violence, in the manner provided by Section 6300 of the Family Code. A court may also issue an ex parte order enjoining any person from molesting, attacking, striking, stalking, threatening, sexually assaulting, battering, harassing, telephoning, including, but not limited to, making annoying telephone calls as described in Section 653m of the Penal Code, destroying the personal property, contacting, either directly or indirectly, by mail or otherwise, coming within a specified distance of, or disturbing the peace of the child's current or former social worker or court appointed special advocate, upon application in the manner provided by Section 527 of the Code of Civil Procedure. On a showing of good cause, in an ex parte order issued pursuant to this subdivision in connection with an animal owned, possessed, leased, kept, or held by a person protected by the restraining order, or residing in the residence or household of a person protected by the restraining order, the court may do either or both of the following:

(1) Grant the applicant exclusive care, possession, or control of the animal.

(2) Order the restrained person to stay away from the animal and refrain from taking, transferring, encumbering, concealing, molesting, attacking, striking, threatening, harming, or otherwise disposing of the animal.

(b) After a petition has been filed pursuant to Section 601 or 602 to declare a child a ward of the juvenile court, and until the time that the petition is dismissed or wardship is terminated, upon application in the manner provided by Section 527 of the Code of Civil Procedure or, if related to domestic violence, in the manner provided by Section 6300 of the Family Code, the juvenile court may issue ex parte orders (1) enjoining any person from molesting, attacking, striking, stalking, threatening, sexually assaulting, battering, harassing, telephoning, including, but not limited to, making annoying telephone calls as described in Section 653m of the Penal Code, destroying the personal property, contacting, either directly or indirectly, by mail or otherwise, coming within a specified distance of, or disturbing the peace of the child or any other child in the household; (2) excluding any person from the dwelling of the person who has care, custody, and control of the child; or (3) enjoining the child from contacting, threatening, stalking, or disturbing the peace of any person the court finds to be at risk from the conduct of the child, or with whom association would be detrimental to the child. A court may also issue an ex parte order enjoining any person from molesting, attacking, striking, stalking, threatening, sexually assaulting, battering, harassing, telephoning, including, but not limited to, making annoying telephone calls as described in Section 653m of the Penal Code, destroying the personal property, contacting, either directly or indirectly, by mail or otherwise, coming within a specified distance of, or disturbing the peace of any parent, legal guardian, or current caretaker of the child, regardless of whether the child resides with that parent, legal guardian, or current caretaker, upon application in the manner provided by Section 527 of the Code of Civil Procedure or, if related to domestic violence, in the manner provided by Section 6300 of the Family Code. A court may also issue an ex parte order enjoining any person from molesting, attacking, striking, stalking, threatening, sexually assaulting, battering, harassing, telephoning, including, but not limited to, making annoying telephone calls as described in Section 653m of the Penal Code, destroying the personal property, contacting, either directly or indirectly, by mail or otherwise, coming within a specified distance of, or disturbing the peace of the child's current or former probation officer or court appointed special advocate, upon application in the manner provided by Section 527 of the Code of Civil Procedure. On a showing of good cause, in an ex parte order issued pursuant to this subdivision in connection with an animal owned, possessed, leased, kept, or held by a person protected by the restraining order, or residing in the residence or household of a person protected by the restraining order, the court may do either or both of the following:

(1) Grant the applicant exclusive care, possession, or control of the animal.

(2) Order the respondent to stay away from the animal and refrain from taking, transferring, encumbering, concealing, molesting, attacking, striking, threatening, harming, or otherwise disposing of the animal.

(c)(1) If a temporary restraining order is granted without notice, the matter shall be made returnable on an order requiring cause to be shown why the order should not be granted, on the earliest day that the business of the court will permit, but not later than 21 days or, if good cause appears to the court, 25 days from the date the temporary restraining order is granted. The court may, on the motion of the person seeking the restraining order, or on its own motion, shorten the time for the service of the order to show cause on the person to be restrained.

(2) The respondent shall be entitled, as a matter of course, to one continuance, for a reasonable period, to respond to the petition.

(3) Either party may request a continuance of the hearing, which the court shall grant on a showing of good cause. The request may be made in writing before or at the hearing or orally at the hearing. The court may also grant a continuance on its own motion.

(4) If the court grants a continuance, any temporary restraining order that has been issued shall remain in effect until the end of the continued hearing, unless otherwise

ordered by the court. In granting a continuance, the court may modify or terminate a temporary restraining order.

(5) A hearing pursuant to this section may be held simultaneously with any regularly scheduled hearings held in proceedings to declare a child a dependent child or ward of the juvenile court pursuant to Section 300, 601, or 602, or subsequent hearings regarding the dependent child or ward.

(d)(1) The juvenile court may issue, upon notice and a hearing, any of the orders set forth in subdivisions (a), (b), and (c). A restraining order granted pursuant to this subdivision shall remain in effect, in the discretion of the court, no more than three years, unless otherwise terminated by the court, extended by mutual consent of all parties to the restraining order, or extended by further order of the court on the motion of any party to the restraining order.

(2) If an action is filed for the purpose of terminating or modifying a protective order prior to the expiration date specified in the order by a party other than the protected party, the party who is protected by the order shall be given notice, pursuant to subdivision (b) of Section 1005 of the Code of Civil Procedure, of the proceeding by personal service or, if the protected party has satisfied the requirements of Chapter 3.1 (commencing with Section 6205) of Division 7 of Title 1 of the Government Code, by service on the Secretary of State. If the party who is protected by the order cannot be notified prior to the hearing for modification or termination of the protective order, the juvenile court shall deny the motion to modify or terminate the order without prejudice or continue the hearing until the party who is protected can be properly noticed and may, upon a showing of good cause, specify another method for service of process that is reasonably designed to afford actual notice to the protected party. The protected party may waive his or her right to notice if he or she is physically present and does not challenge the sufficiency of the notice.

(e)(1) The juvenile court may issue an order made pursuant to subdivision (a), (b), or (d) excluding a person from a residence or dwelling. This order may be issued for the time and on the conditions that the court determines, regardless of which party holds legal or equitable title or is the lessee of the residence or dwelling.

(2) The court may issue an order under paragraph (1) only on a showing of all of the following:

(A) Facts sufficient for the court to ascertain that the party who will stay in the dwelling has a right under color of law to possession of the premises.

(B) That the party to be excluded has assaulted or threatens to assault the other party or any other person under the care, custody, and control of the other party, or any minor child of the parties or of the other party.

(C) That physical or emotional harm would otherwise result to the other party, to any person under the care, custody, and control of the other party, or to any minor child of the parties or of the other party.

(f) An order issued pursuant to subdivision (a), (b), (c), or (d) shall state on its face the date of expiration of the order.

(g) All data with respect to a juvenile court protective order, or extension, modification, or termination thereof, granted pursuant to subdivision (a), (b), (c), or (d), shall be transmitted by the court or its designee, within one business day, to law enforcement personnel by either one of the following methods:

(1) Transmitting a physical copy of the order to a local law enforcement agency authorized by the Department of Justice to enter orders into the California Law Enforcement Telecommunications System (CLETS).

(2) With the approval of the Department of Justice, entering the order into CLETS directly.

(h) Any willful and knowing violation of any order granted pursuant to subdivision (a), (b), (c), or (d) shall be a misdemeanor punishable under Section 273.65 of the Penal Code.

(i) A juvenile court restraining order related to domestic violence issued by a court pursuant to this section shall be issued on forms adopted by the Judicial Council of California and that have been approved by the Department of Justice pursuant to subdivision (i) of Section 6380 of the Family Code. However, the fact that an order issued by a court pursuant to this section was not issued on forms adopted by the Judicial Council and approved by the Department of Justice shall not, in and of itself, make the order unenforceable.

(j)(1) Prior to a hearing on the issuance or denial of an order under this part, a search shall be conducted as described in subdivision (a) of Section 6306 of the Family Code.

(2) Prior to deciding whether to issue an order under this part, the court shall consider the following information obtained pursuant to a search conducted under paragraph (1): any conviction for a violent felony specified in Section 667.5 of the Penal Code or a serious felony specified in Section 1192.7 of the Penal Code; any misdemeanor conviction involving domestic violence, weapons, or other violence; any outstanding warrant; parole or probation status; any prior restraining order; and any violation of a prior restraining order.

(3)(A) If the results of the search conducted pursuant to paragraph (1) indicate that an outstanding warrant exists against the subject of the search, the court shall order the clerk of the court to immediately notify, by the most effective means available, appropriate law enforcement officials of any information obtained through the search that the court determines is appropriate. The law enforcement officials notified shall take all actions necessary to execute any outstanding warrants or any other actions, as appropriate and as soon as practicable.

(B) If the results of the search conducted pursuant to paragraph (1) indicate that the subject of the search is currently on parole or probation, the court shall order the clerk of the court to immediately notify, by the most effective means available, the appropriate parole or probation officer of any information obtained through the search that the court determines is appropriate. The parole or probation officer notified shall take all actions necessary to revoke any parole or probation, or any other actions, with respect to the subject person, as appropriate and as soon as practicable.

(k) Upon making any order for custody or visitation pursuant to this section, the court shall follow the procedures specified in subdivisions (c) and (d) of Section 6323 of the Family Code. *(Added by Stats.1989, c. 1409, § 2. Amended by Stats.1996, c. 1138 (A.B.2154), § 1; Stats.1996, c. 1139 (A.B.2647), § 3.5; Stats.1998, c. 390 (S.B.2017), § 1; Stats. 1999, c. 661 (A.B.825), § 13; Stats.1999, c. 980 (A.B.1671), § 19.5; Stats.2001, c. 572 (S.B.66), § 5; Stats.2001, c. 713 (A.B.1129), § 1.5; Stats.2002, c. 664 (A.B.3034), § 229; Stats.2002, c. 1008 (A.B.3028), § 30; Stats.2003, c. 365 (A.B.1710), § 6; Stats.2005, c. 634 (A.B.519), § 1; Stats.2010, c. 572 (A.B.1596), § 25, operative Jan. 1, 2012; Stats.2011, c. 101 (A.B.454), § 5; Stats.2014, c. 54 (S.B.1461), § 17, eff. Jan. 1, 2015; Stats.2015, c. 303 (A.B.731), § 564, eff. Jan. 1, 2016; Stats.2015, c. 401 (A.B.494), § 2, eff. Jan. 1, 2016; Stats.2015, c. 411 (A.B.1081), § 7.5, eff. Jan. 1, 2016.)*

Commentary

In re C.Q., 219 Cal.App.4th 355, 161 Cal.Rptr.3d 719 (2013), review denied, reversed a permanent restraining order to the extent that it required a father to stay away from his children except during monitored visitation, when there was no evidence that failure to include the children in the order might jeopardize the safety of the children.

Interpreting subsection (b), *In re Cassandra B., 125 Cal.App.4th 199, 22 Cal.Rptr.3d 686 (2004), review denied*, holds that a juvenile court may issue a restraining order against a parent absent violent behavior or threats of violence when the parent was "molesting" the child by seeking unauthorized access and threatening to remove the child from the caregivers' home.

Research References

Forms

West's California Code Forms, Family § 6250, Comment Overview--Issuance and Effect Of Emergency Protective Order.
West's California Judicial Council Forms JV-245, Request for Restraining Order--Juvenile.
West's California Judicial Council Forms JV-250, Notice Of Hearing and Temporary Restraining Order--Juvenile.
West's California Judicial Council Forms JV-251, Application and Order for Reissuance Of Temporary Restraining Order--Juvenile.
West's California Judicial Council Forms JV-255, Restraining Order - Juvenile Order After Hearing.
West's California Judicial Council Forms JV-257, Change to Restraining Order After Hearing--Juvenile.

Treatises and Practice Aids

Witkin, California Summary 10th Husband and Wife § 376, Issuance and Effect.
Witkin, California Summary 10th Husband and Wife § 381, Criminal Background Search.
Witkin, California Summary 10th Husband and Wife § 387, Electronic Transmission and Recording Of Data.
Witkin, California Summary 10th Parent and Child § 370, in General.
Witkin, California Summary 10th Parent and Child § 451, in General.
Witkin, California Summary 10th Parent and Child § 453, Jurisdiction Over Adults.
Witkin, California Summary 10th Parent and Child § 637, Priority Right Of Noncustodial Parent.
Witkin, California Summary 10th Parent and Child § 653, Ex Parte Orders Pending Nullity or Dissolution Proceedings.
Witkin, California Summary 10th Parent and Child § 672, Child in Custody Of Parent or Guardian.
Witkin, California Summary 10th Parent and Child § 704, Miscellaneous Orders.
Witkin, California Summary 10th Parent and Child § 892, in General.

§ 213.6. Subsequent restraining orders or protective orders based upon prior temporary restraining order or emergency protective order; service of subsequent orders; statement regarding service in judicial forms

(a) If a person named in a temporary restraining order or emergency protective order issued under this part is personally served with the order and notice of hearing with respect to a subsequent restraining order or protective order based thereon, but the person does not appear at the hearing either in person or by counsel, and the terms and conditions of the restraining order or protective order are identical to those of the prior temporary restraining order, except for the duration of the order, the subsequent restraining order or protective order may be served on the person by first-class mail sent to that person at the most current address for the person available to the court.

(b) The judicial forms for temporary restraining orders or emergency protective orders issued under this part shall contain a statement in substantially the following form:

"If you have been personally served with a temporary restraining order or emergency protective order and notice of hearing, but you do not appear at the hearing either in person or by counsel, and a restraining order or protective order is issued at the hearing that does not differ from the prior temporary restraining order or protective order except with respect to the duration of the order, a copy of the order will be served upon you by mail at the following address: __________. If that address is not correct or if you wish to verify that the temporary order was made permanent without substantive change, call the clerk of the court at __________." *(Added by Stats.2003, c. 365 (A.B.1710), § 7.)*

Research References

Treatises and Practice Aids

Witkin, California Summary 10th Parent and Child § 453, Jurisdiction Over Adults.

§ 213.7. Addresses or locations of persons protected under court order; prohibition upon certain enjoined parties from acting to obtain such information

(a) The court shall order that any party enjoined pursuant to Section 213.5, 304, 362.4, or 726.5 be prohibited from taking any action to obtain the address or location of a protected party or a protected party's family members, caretakers, or guardian, unless there is good cause not to make that order.

(b) The Judicial Council shall promulgate forms necessary to effectuate this section. *(Added by Stats.2005, c. 472 (A.B.978), § 6.)*

Research References

Forms

West's California Judicial Council Forms JV-245, Request for Restraining Order--Juvenile.
West's California Judicial Council Forms JV-250, Notice Of Hearing and Temporary Restraining Order--Juvenile.

West's California Judicial Council Forms JV-255, Restraining Order - Juvenile Order After Hearing.

Treatises and Practice Aids

Witkin, California Summary 10th Husband and Wife § 371, Civil Remedies.

Witkin, California Summary 10th Parent and Child § 370, in General.

Witkin, California Summary 10th Parent and Child § 451, in General.

Witkin, California Summary 10th Parent and Child § 453, Jurisdiction Over Adults.

Witkin, California Summary 10th Parent and Child § 892, in General.

§ 214. Written promise to appear; failure to perform; misdemeanor

In each instance in which a provision of this chapter authorizes the execution by any person of a written promise to appear or to have any other person appear before the probation officer or before the juvenile court, any willful failure of such promissor to perform as promised constitutes a misdemeanor and is punishable as such if at the time of the execution of such written promise the promissor is given a copy of such written promise upon which it is clearly written that failure to appear or to have any other person appear as promised is punishable as a misdemeanor. *(Added by Stats.1976, c. 1068, p. 4741, § 1.5.)*

Research References

Treatises and Practice Aids

Witkin, California Summary 10th Parent and Child § 555, Investigation, Detention, and Release.

Witkin, California Summary 10th Parent and Child § 759, in General.

Witkin, California Summary 10th Parent and Child § 763, Investigation, Release, and Conditions.

§ 215. Probation officer or social worker; department of probation

As used in this chapter, unless otherwise specifically provided, the term "probation officer" or "social worker" shall include the juvenile probation officer or the person who is both the juvenile probation officer and the adult probation officer, and any social worker in a county welfare department or any social worker in a California Indian tribe or any out-of-state Indian tribe that has reservation land that extends into the state that has authority, pursuant to an agreement with the department concerning child welfare services or foster care payments under the Aid to Families with Dependent Children program when supervising dependent children of the juvenile court pursuant to Section 272 by order of the court under Section 300, and the term "department of probation" shall mean the department of juvenile probation or the department wherein the services of juvenile and adult probation are both performed. *(Added by Stats.1976, c. 1068, p. 4741, § 1.5. Amended by Stats.1995, c. 724 (A.B.1525), § 1.5; Stats.1998, c. 1054 (A.B.1091), § 1.)*

Research References

Treatises and Practice Aids

Witkin, California Summary 10th Parent and Child § 482, Appointment and Staff.

§ 216. Application of chapter to fugitive under 18

This chapter shall not apply:

(a) To any person who violates any law of this state defining a crime, and is at the time of such violation under the age of 18 years, if such person thereafter flees from this state. Any such person may be proceeded against in the manner otherwise provided by law for proceeding against persons accused of crime. Upon the return of such person to this state by extradition or otherwise, proceedings shall be commenced in the manner provided for in this chapter.

(b) To any person who violates any law of another state defining a crime, and is at the time of such violation under the age of 18 years, if such person thereafter flees from that state into this state. Any such person may be proceeded against as an adult in the manner provided in Chapter 4 (commencing with Section 1547) of Title 12 of Part 2 of the Penal Code. The magistrate shall, for purposes of detention, detain such person in juvenile hall if space is available. If no space is available in juvenile hall, the magistrate may detain such person in the county jail. *(Added by Stats.1976, c. 1068, p. 4741, § 1.5.)*

Research References

Treatises and Practice Aids

Witkin, California Summary 10th Parent and Child § 451, in General.

§ 217. Unclaimed personal property; use in programs designed to prevent delinquency; notification to owner

(a) The board of supervisors of any county or the governing body of any city may by ordinance provide that any personal property with a value of not more than five hundred dollars ($500) in the possession of the sheriff of the county or in the possession of the police department of the city which have been unclaimed for a period of at least 90 days may, instead of being sold at public auction to the highest bidder pursuant to the provisions of Section 2080.5 of the Civil Code, be turned over to the probation officer, to the welfare department of the county, or to any charitable or nonprofit organization which is authorized under its articles of incorporation to participate in a program or activity designed to prevent juvenile delinquency and which is exempt from income taxation under federal or state law, or both, for use in any program or activity designed to prevent juvenile delinquency.

(b) Before any property subject to this section is turned over to the probation officer, to the welfare department of the county, or to any charitable or nonprofit organization, the police department or sheriff's department shall notify the owner, if his or her identity is known or can be reasonably ascertained, that it possesses the property, and where the property may be claimed. The owner may be notified by mail, telephone, or by means of a notice published in a newspaper of general circulation which it determines is most likely to give notice to the owner of the property. *(Added by Stats.1976, c. 1068, p. 4741, § 1.5. Amended by Stats.1986, c. 865, § 1; Stats.1999, c. 233 (A.B.191), § 1.)*

Research References

Treatises and Practice Aids

Witkin, California Summary 10th Parent and Child § 487, Other Powers and Duties.

Witkin, California Summary 10th Personal Property § 39, Other Statutes Dealing With Unclaimed Property.

§ 218. Counsel; compensation and expenses

In any case in which, pursuant to this chapter, the court appoints counsel to represent any person who desires but is unable to employ counsel, counsel shall receive a reasonable sum for compensation and for necessary expenses, the amount of which shall be determined by the court, to be paid out of the general fund of the county. *(Added by Stats.1976, c. 1068, p. 4741, § 1.5.)*

Research References

Treatises and Practice Aids

Witkin, California Summary 10th Parent and Child § 788, Duty to Provide Counsel.

§ 218.5. Domestic violence training programs; participation by counsel; requirements

All counsel performing duties under this chapter, including, but not limited to, county counsel, court appointed counsel, or volunteer counsel, shall participate in mandatory training on domestic violence where available through existing programs at no additional cost to the county. The training shall meet the requirements of Section 16206. *(Added by Stats.1996, c. 1139 (A.B.2647), § 4.)*

§ 219. Workers' compensation for ward injured while doing rehabilitative work

The board of supervisors of a county may provide a ward of the juvenile court engaged in rehabilitative work without pay, under an assignment by order of the juvenile court to a work project in a county department, with workers' compensation benefits for injuries sustained while performing such rehabilitative work, in accordance with Section 3364.55 of the Labor Code. *(Added by Stats.1976, c. 1068, p. 4741, § 1.5.)*

Research References

Treatises and Practice Aids

Witkin, California Summary 10th Parent and Child § 942, Types Of Sanctions.

§ 219.5. Work providing access to personal information pertaining to private individuals; ineligibility of certain juvenile offenders

(a) No ward of the juvenile court or Department of the Youth Authority shall perform any function that provides access to personal information of private individuals, including, but not limited to: addresses; telephone numbers; health insurance, taxpayer, school, or employee identification numbers; mothers' maiden names; demand deposit account, debit card, credit card, savings or checking account numbers, PINs, or passwords; social security numbers; places of employment; dates of birth; state or government issued driver's license or identification numbers; alien registration numbers; government passport numbers; unique biometric data, such as fingerprints, facial scan identifiers, voice prints, retina or iris images, or other similar identifiers; unique electronic identification numbers; address or routing codes; and telecommunication identifying information or access devices.

(b) Subdivision (a) shall apply to a person who has been adjudicated to have committed an offense described by any of the following categories:

(1) An offense involving forgery or fraud.

(2) An offense involving misuse of a computer.

(3) An offense for which the person is required to register as a sex offender pursuant to Section 290 of the Penal Code.

(4) An offense involving any misuse of the personal or financial information of another person.

(c) If asked, any person who is a ward of the juvenile court or the Department of the Youth Authority, and who has access to any personal information, shall disclose that he or she is a ward of the juvenile court or the Department of the Youth Authority before taking any personal information from anyone.

(d) Any program involving the taking of personal information over the telephone by a person who is a ward of the juvenile court or the Department of the Youth Authority, shall be subject to random monitoring of those telephone calls.

(e) Any program involving the taking of personal information by a person who is a ward of the juvenile court or the Department of the Youth Authority shall provide supervision at all times of the ward's activities.

(f) This section shall not apply to wards in employment programs or public service facilities where incidental contact with personal information may occur. *(Added by Stats.1998, c. 551 (A.B.2649), § 3. Amended by Stats.2002, c. 196 (A.B.2456), § 3.)*

Research References

Treatises and Practice Aids

Witkin, California Summary 10th Parent and Child § 942, Types Of Sanctions.

§ 220. Abortions; conditions and restrictions; eligibility

No condition or restriction upon the obtaining of an abortion by a female detained in any local juvenile facility, pursuant to the Therapeutic Abortion Act (Article 2 (commencing with Section 123400) of Chapter 2 of Part 2 of Division 106 of the Health and Safety Code), other than those contained in that act, shall be imposed. Females found to be pregnant and desiring abortions, shall be permitted to determine their eligibility for an abortion pursuant to law, and if determined to be eligible, shall be permitted to obtain an abortion.

For the purposes of this section, "local juvenile facility" means any city, county, or regional facility used for the confinement of female juveniles for more than 24 hours.

The rights provided for females by this section shall be posted in at least one conspicuous place to which all females have access. *(Added by Stats.1976, c. 1068, p. 4741, § 1.5. Amended by Stats.1996, c. 1023 (S.B.1497), § 455, eff. Sept. 29, 1996.)*

Research References

Treatises and Practice Aids

Witkin, California Summary 10th Parent and Child § 761, Rights Of Minor.

§ 221. Female in state or local juvenile facility; use of materials for personal hygiene or birth control measures; family planning services; furnishing; operative date

(a) Any female confined in a state or local juvenile facility shall upon her request be allowed to continue to use materials necessary for (1) personal hygiene with regard to her menstrual cycle and reproductive system and (2) birth control measures as prescribed by her physician.

(b) Any female confined in a state or local juvenile facility shall upon her request be furnished by the confining state or local agency with information and education regarding prescription birth control measures.

(c) Family planning services shall be offered to each and every woman inmate at least 60 days prior to a scheduled release date. Upon request any woman inmate shall be furnished by the confining state or local agency with the services of a licensed physician, or she shall be furnished by the confining state or local agency or by any other agency which contracts with the confining state or local agency, with services necessary to meet her family planning needs at the time of her release.

(d) For the purposes of this section, "local juvenile facility" means any city, county, or regional facility used for the confinement of juveniles for more than 24 hours.

This section shall become operative on January 1, 1988. *(Added by Stats.1981, c. 618, p. 2367, § 2, operative Jan. 1, 1988.)*

Research References

Treatises and Practice Aids

Witkin, California Summary 10th Parent and Child § 761, Rights Of Minor.

§ 222. Pregnancy; determination; right of choice and services of any physician or surgeon

(a) A female in the custody of a local juvenile facility shall have the right to summon and receive the services of a physician and surgeon of her choice in order to determine whether she is pregnant. If she is found to be pregnant, she is entitled to a determination of the extent of the medical services needed by her and to the receipt of those services from the physician and surgeon of her choice. Expenses occasioned by the services of a physician and surgeon whose services are not provided by the facility shall be borne by the female.

(b) A ward who is known to be pregnant or in recovery from delivery shall not be restrained except as provided in Section 3407 of the Penal Code.

(c) For purposes of this section, "local juvenile facility" means a city, county, or regional facility used for the confinement of juveniles for more than 24 hours.

(d) The rights provided to females by this section shall be posted in at least one conspicuous place to which all female wards have access. *(Added by Stats.1976, c. 1068, p. 4741, § 1.5. Amended by Stats.2005, c. 608 (A.B.478), § 6; Stats. 2012, c. 726 (A.B.2530), § 4.)*

Research References

Treatises and Practice Aids

Witkin, California Summary 10th Parent and Child § 761, Rights Of Minor.

§ 223. Notice to parent or guardian of serious injury or offense committed against minor in state or county custody

(a)(1) The parents or guardians of any minor in the custody of the state or the county, if they can reasonably be located, shall be notified within 24 hours by the public officer responsible for the well-being of that minor, of any serious injury or serious offense committed against the minor, upon reasonable substantiation that a serious injury or offense has occurred.

(2) This section shall not apply if the minor requests that his or her parents or guardians not be informed and the chief probation officer or the Director of the Youth Authority, as appropriate, determines it would be in the best interest of the minor not to inform the parents or guardians.

(b) For purposes of this section, "serious offense" means any offense that is chargeable as a felony and that involves violence against another person. "Serious injury" means, for purposes of this section, any illness or injury that requires hospitalization, is potentially life threatening, or that potentially will permanently impair the use of a major body organ, appendage, or limb. *(Added by Stats.1998, c. 496 (S.B.2081), § 2.)*

Research References

Treatises and Practice Aids

Witkin, California Summary 10th Parent and Child § 941, Commitment Of Minor for Status Offense.

Witkin, California Summary 10th Parent and Child § 942, Types Of Sanctions.

§ 223.1. Suicide attempt by or serious injury to person in custody of Division of Juvenile Facilities; notice to appropriate party; information for ward's record

(a)(1) At least one individual who is a parent, guardian, or designated emergency contact of a person in the custody of the Division of Juvenile Facilities, if the individual can reasonably be located, shall be successfully notified within 24 hours by the public officer responsible for the well-being of that person, of any suicide attempt by the person, or any serious injury or serious offense committed against the person. In consultation with division staff, as appropriate, and with concurrence of the public officer responsible for the well-being of that person, the person may designate other persons who should be notified in addition to, or in lieu of, parents or guardians, of any suicide attempt by the person, or any serious injury or serious offense committed against the person.

(2) This section shall not apply if either of the following conditions is met:

(A) A minor requests that his or her parents, guardians, or other persons not be notified, and the director of the division facility, as appropriate, determines it would be in the best interest of the minor not to notify the parents, guardians, or other persons.

(B) A person 18 years of age or older does not consent to the notification.

(b) Upon intake of a person into a division facility, and again upon attaining 18 years of age while in the custody of the division, an appropriate staff person shall explain, using language clearly understandable to the person, all of the provisions of this section, including that the person has the right to (1) request that the information described in paragraph (1) of subdivision (a) not be provided to a parent or guardian, and (2) request that another person or persons in addition to, or in lieu of, a parent or guardian be notified. The division shall provide the person with forms and any information necessary to provide informed consent as to who shall be notified. Any designation made pursuant to paragraph (1) of subdivision (a), the consent to notify parents, guardians, or other persons, and the withholding of that consent, may be amended or revoked by the person, and shall be transferable among facilities.

(c) Staff of the division shall enter the following information into the ward's record, as appropriate, upon its occurrence:

(1) A minor's request that his or her parents, guardians, or other persons not be notified of an emergency pursuant to this section, and the determination of the relevant public officer on that request.

(2) The designation of persons who are emergency contacts, in lieu of parents or guardians, who may be notified pursuant to this section.

(3) The revocation or amendment of a designation or consent made pursuant to this section.

(4) A person's consent, or withholding thereof, to notify parents, guardians, or other persons pursuant to this section.

(d) For purposes of this section, the following terms have the following meanings:

(1) "Serious offense" means any offense that is chargeable as a felony and that involves violence against another person.

(2) "Serious injury" means any illness or injury that requires hospitalization, requires an evaluation for involuntary treatment for a mental health disorder or grave disability under the Lanterman–Petris–Short Act (Part 1 (commencing with Section 5000) of Division 5), is potentially life threatening, or that potentially will permanently impair the use of a major body organ, appendage, or limb.

(3) "Suicide attempt" means a self-inflicted destructive act committed with explicit or inferred intent to die. *(Added by Stats.2008, c. 522 (S.B.1250), § 1. Amended by Stats.2009, c. 140 (A.B.1164), § 185.)*

Research References

Treatises and Practice Aids

Witkin, California Summary 10th Parent and Child § 960, in General.

§ 224. Legislative findings and declarations; Indian child custody proceedings

(a) The Legislature finds and declares the following:

(1) There is no resource that is more vital to the continued existence and integrity of Indian tribes than their children, and the State of California has an interest in protecting Indian children who are members of, or are eligible for membership in, an Indian tribe. The state is committed to protecting the essential tribal relations and best interest of an Indian child by promoting practices, in accordance with the Indian Child Welfare Act (25 U.S.C. Sec. 1901 et seq.) and other applicable law, designed to prevent the child's involuntary out-of-home placement and, whenever that placement is necessary or ordered, by placing the child, whenever possible, in a placement that reflects the unique values of the child's tribal culture and is best able to assist the child in establishing, developing, and maintaining a political, cultural, and social relationship with the child's tribe and tribal community.

(2) It is in the interest of an Indian child that the child's membership in the child's Indian tribe and connection to the tribal community be encouraged and protected, regardless of whether the child is in the physical custody of an Indian parent or Indian custodian at the commencement of a child custody proceeding, the parental rights of the child's parents have been terminated, or where the child has resided or been domiciled.

(b) In all Indian child custody proceedings, as defined in the federal Indian Child Welfare Act the court shall consider all of the findings contained in subdivision (a), strive to promote the stability and security of Indian tribes and families, comply with the federal Indian Child Welfare Act, and seek to protect the best interest of the child. Whenever an Indian child is removed from a foster care home or institution, guardianship, or adoptive placement for the purpose of further foster care, guardianship, or adoptive placement, placement of the child shall be in accordance with the Indian Child Welfare Act.

(c) A determination by an Indian tribe that an unmarried person, who is under the age of 18 years, is either (1) a member of an Indian tribe or (2) eligible for membership in an Indian tribe and a biological child of a member of an Indian tribe shall constitute a significant political affiliation with the tribe and shall require the application of the federal Indian Child Welfare Act to the proceedings.

(d) In any case in which this code or other applicable state or federal law provides a higher standard of protection to the rights of the parent or Indian custodian of an Indian child, or the Indian child's tribe, than the rights provided under the Indian Child Welfare Act, the court shall apply the higher standard.

(e) Any Indian child, the Indian child's tribe, or the parent or Indian custodian from whose custody the child has been removed, may petition the court to invalidate an action in an Indian child custody proceeding for foster care or guardianship placement or termination of parental rights if the action violated Sections 1911, 1912, and 1913 of the Indian Child Welfare Act. *(Added by Stats.2006, c. 838 (S.B.678), § 29.)*

Commentary

In re Francisco D., 230 Cal.App.4th 73, 178 Cal.Rptr.3d 388 (2014), held that when a child was removed from his adoptive mother's care under section 300(j) because she abused the child's sister, the Indian Child Welfare Act had no application, despite the adoptive mother's tribal membership, when the child was neither a tribal member nor the biological child of a member.

Reading subsection (e) of this section together with section 224.1, *In re Michael A., 209 Cal.App.4th 661, 147 Cal.Rptr.3d 169 (2012)*, held that a grandmother with de facto parent status did not have standing to raise an Indian Child Welfare Act (ICWA) notice challenge to an order removing her grandchildren from her custody. See also Commentary to 25 U.S.C. §§ 1903 and 1914.

Research References

Treatises and Practice Aids

Witkin, California Summary 10th Parent and Child § 522, Nature and Scope Of Indian Child Welfare Act.

Witkin, California Summary 10th Parent and Child § 525, Existing Indian Family Doctrine.

Witkin, California Summary 10th Parent and Child § 526, Determination Of Indian Status.

Witkin, California Summary 10th Parent and Child § 537, Proceedings After Termination or Removal.

§ 224.1. Definitions; Indian child membership in more than one tribe

(a) As used in this division, unless the context requires otherwise, the terms "Indian," "Indian child," "Indian child's tribe," "Indian custodian," "Indian tribe," "reservation," and "tribal court" shall be defined as provided in Section 1903 of the Indian Child Welfare Act (25 U.S.C. Sec. 1901 et seq.).

(b) As used in connection with an Indian child custody proceeding, the term "Indian child" also means an unmarried person who is 18 years of age or over, but under 21 years of age, who is a member of an Indian tribe or eligible for membership in an Indian tribe and is the biological child of a member of an Indian tribe, and who is under the jurisdiction of the dependency court, unless that person or his or her attorney elects not to be considered an Indian child for purposes of the Indian child custody proceeding. All Indian child custody proceedings involving persons 18 years of age and older shall be conducted in a manner that respects the person's status as a legal adult.

(c) As used in connection with an Indian child custody proceeding, the terms "extended family member" and "parent" shall be defined as provided in Section 1903 of the Indian Child Welfare Act.

(d) "Indian child custody proceeding" means a "child custody proceeding" within the meaning of Section 1903 of the Indian Child Welfare Act, including a proceeding for temporary or long-term foster care or guardianship placement, termination of parental rights, preadoptive placement after termination of parental rights, or adoptive placement. "Indian child custody proceeding" does not include a voluntary foster care or guardianship placement if the parent or Indian custodian retains the right to have the child returned upon demand.

(e) If an Indian child is a member of more than one tribe or is eligible for membership in more than one tribe, the court shall make a determination, in writing together with the reasons for it, as to which tribe is the Indian child's tribe for purposes of the Indian child custody proceeding. The court shall make that determination as follows:

(1) If the Indian child is or becomes a member of only one tribe, that tribe shall be designated as the Indian child's tribe, even though the child is eligible for membership in another tribe.

(2) If an Indian child is or becomes a member of more than one tribe, or is not a member of any tribe but is eligible for membership in more than one tribe, the tribe with which the child has the more significant contacts shall be designated as the Indian child's tribe. In determining which tribe the child has the more significant contacts with, the court shall consider, among other things, the following factors:

(A) The length of residence on or near the reservation of each tribe and frequency of contact with each tribe.

(B) The child's participation in activities of each tribe.

(C) The child's fluency in the language of each tribe.

(D) Whether there has been a previous adjudication with respect to the child by a court of one of the tribes.

(E) Residence on or near one of the tribes' reservations by the child parents, Indian custodian or extended family members.

(F) Tribal membership of custodial parent or Indian custodian.

(G) Interest asserted by each tribe in response to the notice specified in Section 224.2.

(H) The child's self-identification.

(3) If an Indian child becomes a member of a tribe other than the one designated by the court as the Indian child's tribe under paragraph (2), actions taken based on the court's determination prior to the child's becoming a tribal member continue to be valid. *(Added by Stats.2006, c. 838 (S.B.678), § 30. Amended by Stats.2010, c. 468 (A.B.2418), § 1.)*

Commentary

Reading this section together with subsection (e) of section 224, *In re Michael A., 209 Cal.App.4th 661, 147 Cal.Rptr.3d 169 (2012)*, held that a grandmother with de facto parent status did not have standing to raise an Indian Child Welfare Act (ICWA) notice challenge to an order removing her grandchildren from her custody. See also Commentary to 25 U.S.C. §§ 1903 and 1914.

California provides a higher standard of protection for the rights of an Indian child's parents than does the federal Indian Child Welfare Act. Compare this section, Family Code section 170, and California Rules of Court, Rule 5.481 with 25 U.S.C. § 1903. Thus a trial court, a court-connected investigator, and a petitioner have an affirmative duty to inquire whether a child is or may be an Indian child in proceedings for foster care placement, guardianship, conservatorship, custody placement with a non-parent pursuant to Family Code section 3041, a declaration freeing a child from parental custody and control, termination of parental rights, or adoption. *In re Noreen G., 181 Cal.App.4th 1359, 105 Cal.Rptr.3d 521 (2010), review denied.*

Section 361(c)(6) has no application when a juvenile court removes an Indian child from the custody of one parent and places the child in the other parent's custody, because subsection (c) of this section does not include within the definition of an "Indian child custody proceeding" a proceeding in which custody is transferred from one parent to the other parent *In re J.B., 178 Cal.App.4th 751, 100 Cal.Rptr.3d 679 (2009).*

Research References

Forms

West's California Judicial Council Forms JV-466, Request to Return to Juvenile Court Jurisdiction and Foster Care.

West's California Judicial Council Forms JV-468, Confidential Information--Request to Return to Juvenile Court Jurisdiction and Foster Care.

West's California Judicial Council Forms JV-464-INFO, How to Ask to Return to Juvenile Court Jurisdiction and Foster Care.

Treatises and Practice Aids

Witkin, California Summary 10th Parent and Child § 523, Definitions.

Witkin, California Summary 10th Parent and Child § 526, Determination Of Indian Status.

Witkin, California Summary 10th Parent and Child § 896, General Requirements.

Witkin, California Summary 10th Parent and Child § 688A, (New) Tribal Customary Adoption.

§ 224.2. Matters involving an Indian child; notice to interested parties; time to notify; proof

(a) If the court, a social worker, or probation officer knows or has reason to know that an Indian child is involved, any notice sent in an Indian child custody proceeding under this code shall be sent to the minor's parents or legal guardian, Indian custodian, if any, and the minor's tribe and comply with all of the following requirements:

(1) Notice shall be sent by registered or certified mail with return receipt requested. Additional notice by first-class mail is recommended, but not required.

(2) Notice to the tribe shall be to the tribal chairperson, unless the tribe has designated another agent for service.

(3) Notice shall be sent to all tribes of which the child may be a member or eligible for membership, until the court makes a determination as to which tribe is the child's tribe in accordance with subdivision (d) of Section 224.1, after which notice need only be sent to the tribe determined to be the Indian child's tribe.

(4) Notice, to the extent required by federal law, shall be sent to the Secretary of the Interior's designated agent, the Sacramento Area Director, Bureau of Indian Affairs. If the identity or location of the parents, Indian custodians, or the minor's tribe is known, a copy of the notice shall also be sent directly to the Secretary of the Interior, unless the Secretary of the Interior has waived the notice in writing and the person responsible for giving notice under this section has filed proof of the waiver with the court.

(5) In addition to the information specified in other sections of this article, notice shall include all of the following information:

(A) The name, birthdate, and birthplace of the Indian child, if known.

(B) The name of the Indian tribe in which the child is a member or may be eligible for membership, if known.

(C) All names known of the Indian child's biological parents, grandparents, and great-grandparents, or Indian custodians, including maiden, married and former names or aliases, as well as their current and former addresses, birthdates, places of birth and death, tribal enrollment numbers, and any other identifying information, if known.

(D) A copy of the petition by which the proceeding was initiated.

(E) A copy of the child's birth certificate, if available.

(F) The location, mailing address, and telephone number of the court and all parties notified pursuant to this section.

(G) A statement of the following:

(i) The absolute right of the child's parents, Indian custodians, and tribe to intervene in the proceeding.

(ii) The right of the child's parents, Indian custodians, and tribe to petition the court to transfer the proceeding to the tribal court of the Indian child's tribe, absent objection by either parent and subject to declination by the tribal court.

(iii) The right of the child's parents, Indian custodians, and tribe to, upon request, be granted up to an additional 20 days from the receipt of the notice to prepare for the proceeding.

(iv) The potential legal consequences of the proceedings on the future custodial and parental rights of the child's parents or Indian custodians.

(v) That if the parents or Indian custodians are unable to afford counsel, counsel will be appointed to represent the parents or Indian custodians pursuant to Section 1912 of the Indian Child Welfare Act (25 U.S.C. Sec. 1901 et seq.).

(vi) That the information contained in the notice, petition, pleading, and other court documents is confidential, so any person or entity notified shall maintain the confidentiality of the information contained in the notice concerning the particular proceeding and not reveal it to anyone who does not need the information in order to exercise the tribe's rights under the Indian Child Welfare Act (25 U.S.C. Sec. 1901 et seq.).

(b) Notice shall be sent whenever it is known or there is reason to know that an Indian child is involved, and for every hearing thereafter, including, but not limited to, the hearing at which a final adoption order is to be granted, unless it is determined that the Indian Child Welfare Act (25 U.S.C. Sec. 1901 et seq.) does not apply to the case in accordance with Section 224.3. After a tribe acknowledges that the child is a member or eligible for membership in that tribe, or after a tribe intervenes in a proceeding, the information set out in subparagraphs (C), (D), (E), and (G) of paragraph (5) of subdivision (a) need not be included with the notice.

(c) Proof of the notice, including copies of notices sent and all return receipts and responses received, shall be filed with the court in advance of the hearing except as permitted under subdivision (d).

(d) No proceeding shall be held until at least 10 days after receipt of notice by the parent, Indian custodian, the tribe, or the Bureau of Indian Affairs, except for the detention hearing, provided that notice of the detention hearing shall be given as soon as possible after the filing of the petition initiating the proceeding and proof of the notice is filed with the court within 10 days after the filing of the petition. With the exception of the detention hearing, the parent, Indian custodian, or the tribe shall, upon request, be granted up to 20 additional days to prepare for that proceeding. Nothing herein shall be construed as limiting the rights of the parent, Indian custodian, or tribe to more than 10 days notice when a lengthier notice period is required by statute.

(e) With respect to giving notice to Indian tribes, a party shall be subject to court sanctions if that person knowingly and willfully falsifies or conceals a material fact concerning whether the child is an Indian child, or counsels a party to do so.

(f) The inclusion of contact information of any adult or child that would otherwise be required to be included in the notification pursuant to this section, shall not be required if that person is at risk of harm as a result of domestic violence, child abuse, sexual abuse, or stalking. *(Added by Stats.2006, c. 838 (S.B.678), § 31.)*

Commentary

In re Breanna S., 8 Cal.App.5th 636, 214 Cal.Rptr.3d 98 (2017), remanded a proceeding to terminate parental rights in order to provide proper notice, because the county department failed to provide the required information on the ICWA notice forms. That the children could not meet the blood percentage required for tribal membership did not render the error harmless because only the tribe could make membership determinations.

Applying subsections (a)(2) and (3) of this section, *In re J.T., 154 Cal.App.4th 986, 65 Cal.Rptr.3d 320 (2007)*, held that when a mother identified her possible Indian heritage as Sioux or Cherokee, the county family services agency was required to send notice under this section to all federally recognized Sioux and Cherokee tribes even though the agency had sent proper notice to the Bureau of Indian Affairs.

In re O.C., 5 Cal.App.5th 1173, 210 Cal.Rptr.3d 467 (2016), held that subsection (a)(3) was not satisfied when a father indicated that he had Pomo heritage, and notice was sent to only two Pomo Indians tribes, rather than all 22 Pomo-affiliated tribes.

In re Rayna N., 163 Cal.App.4th 262, 77 Cal.Rptr.3d 628 (2008), review denied, held that when a juvenile court fails to comply with the notice requirements of the Indian Child Welfare Act (25 USC § 1901 et seq.) or with the 2006 amendments, effective January 1, 2007, of the California statutes governing Indian child custody proceedings, subsection (d) of this section does not alter the established practice of limited reversal and remand for the purpose of complying with notice requirements.

In re J.M., 206 Cal.App.4th 375, 141 Cal.Rptr.3d 738 (2012), held that notice to an Indian tribe does not need to include information about a child's great-great-grandparents because neither subsection (5)(C) nor federal law requires information about lineal ancestors beyond a child's great-grandparents.

In re Charlotte V., 6 Cal.App.5th 51, 210 Cal.Rptr.3d 650 (2016), affirmed a trial court termination of a mother's parental rights, rejecting her claim that the Department of Children and Family Services violated the notice provisions of the ICWA by failing to provide a tribe with her child's cousin's information, because neither the ICWA nor California law requires the provision of information about non-lineal relatives.

In re J.L., 10 Cal.App.5th 913, 217 Cal.Rptr.3d 201 (2017), held that a mother's statement that she was not sure whether she had any Indian ancestry was insufficient to trigger the inquiry and notice provisions of the ICWA and the California corresponding Welfare and Institutions Code sections.

Research References

Forms

California Transactions Forms--Family Law § 3:4, Subject Matter Jurisdiction for Custody Determinations.

West's California Judicial Council Forms ICWA-030, Notice Of Child Custody Proceeding for Indian Child (Indian Child Welfare Act).

West's California Judicial Council Forms ICWA-030(A), Attachment to Notice Of Child Custody Proceeding for Indian Child (Indian Child Welfare Act).

Treatises and Practice Aids

Witkin, California Summary 10th Parent and Child § 524, Jurisdiction.

Witkin, California Summary 10th Parent and Child § 526, Determination Of Indian Status.

Witkin, California Summary 10th Parent and Child § 528, in General.

Witkin, California Summary 10th Parent and Child § 529, Formal Requisites.

Witkin, California Summary 10th Parent and Child § 531, Determining Adequacy Of Notice.

Witkin, California Summary 10th Parent and Child § 532, in General.

Witkin, California Summary 10th Parent and Child § 585, in General.

Witkin, California Summary 10th Parent and Child § 600, Petition and Notice Of Hearing.

Witkin, California Summary 10th Parent and Child § 610, Notice Of Hearing.

Witkin, California Summary 10th Parent and Child § 670, Notice Of Hearing.

Witkin, California Summary 10th Parent and Child § 681, Notice.

Witkin, California Summary 10th Parent and Child § 699, Notice.

Witkin, California Summary 10th Parent and Child § 712, Notice Of Appeal.

Witkin, California Summary 10th Parent and Child § 720, Notice Of Intent.

Witkin, California Summary 10th Parent and Child § 722, Writ Petition and Response.

Witkin, California Summary 10th Parent and Child § 725, Notice Of Intent and Record.

Witkin, California Summary 10th Parent and Child § 726, Writ Petition.

Witkin, California Summary 10th Parent and Child § 896, General Requirements.

Witkin, California Summary 10th Parent and Child § 288C, (New) Applicable Law.

§ 224.3. Determination whether child is an Indian child; considerations; scope of inquiry

(a) The court, county welfare department, and the probation department have an affirmative and continuing duty to inquire whether a child for whom a petition under Section 300, 601, or 602 is to be, or has been, filed is or may be an Indian child in all dependency proceedings and in any juvenile wardship proceedings if the child is at risk of entering foster care or is in foster care.

(b) The circumstances that may provide reason to know the child is an Indian child include, but are not limited to, the following:

(1) A person having an interest in the child, including the child, an officer of the court, a tribe, an Indian organization, a public or private agency, or a member of the child's extended family provides information suggesting the child is a member of a tribe or eligible for membership in a tribe or one or more of the child's biological parents, grandparents, or great-grandparents are or were a member of a tribe.

(2) The residence or domicile of the child, the child's parents, or Indian custodian is in a predominantly Indian community.

(3) The child or the child's family has received services or benefits from a tribe or services that are available to Indians from tribes or the federal government, such as the Indian Health Service.

(c) If the court, social worker, or probation officer knows or has reason to know that an Indian child is involved, the social worker or probation officer is required to make further inquiry regarding the possible Indian status of the child, and to do so as soon as practicable, by interviewing the parents, Indian custodian, and extended family members to gather the information required in paragraph (5) of subdivision (a) of Section 224.2, contacting the Bureau of Indian Affairs and the State Department of Social Services for assistance in identifying the names and contact information of the tribes in which the child may be a member or eligible for membership in and contacting the tribes and any other person that reasonably can be expected to have information regarding the child's membership status or eligibility.

(d) If the court, social worker, or probation officer knows or has reason to know that an Indian child is involved, the social worker or probation officer shall provide notice in accordance with paragraph (5) of subdivision (a) of Section 224.2.

(e)(1) A determination by an Indian tribe that a child is or is not a member of or eligible for membership in that tribe, or testimony attesting to that status by a person authorized by the tribe to provide that determination, shall be conclusive. Information that the child is not enrolled or eligible for enrollment in the tribe is not determinative of the child's membership status unless the tribe also confirms in writing that enrollment is a prerequisite for membership under tribal law or custom.

(2) In the absence of a contrary determination by the tribe, a determination by the Bureau of Indian Affairs that a child is or is not a member of or eligible for membership in that tribe is conclusive.

(3) If proper and adequate notice has been provided pursuant to Section 224.2, and neither a tribe nor the Bureau of Indian Affairs has provided a determinative response within 60 days after receiving that notice, the court may determine that the Indian Child Welfare Act (25 U.S.C. Sec. 1901 et seq.) does not apply to the proceedings, provided that the court shall reverse its determination of the inapplicability of the Indian Child Welfare Act and apply the act prospectively if a tribe or the Bureau of Indian Affairs subsequently confirms that the child is an Indian child.

(f) Notwithstanding a determination that the Indian Child Welfare Act does not apply to the proceedings made in accordance with subdivision (e), if the court, social worker, or probation officer subsequently receives any information required under paragraph (5) of subdivision (a) of Section 224.2 that was not previously available or included in the notice issued under Section 224.2, the social worker or probation officer shall provide the additional information to any tribes entitled to notice under paragraph (3) of subdivision (a) of Section 224.2 and the Bureau of Indian Affairs. *(Added by Stats.2006, c. 838 (S.B.678), § 32.)*

Commentary

With respect to ICWA notice requirements, *In re W.B., Jr., 55 Cal.4th 30, 281 P.3d 906, 144 Cal.Rptr.3d 843 (2012)*, distinguishes between dependency and delinquency proceedings. In all juvenile court proceedings, both dependency and delinquency, the court, social worker, or probation officer must inquire about the child's Indian status whenever the child is in foster care or conditions in the child's family may potentially require a foster care placement (subsection (a)). Notice to the tribes and other ICWA procedures must be provided only if the case is a "child custody proceeding," as defined in 25 U.S.C. section 1903(1). A case is a "child custody proceeding" if it will involve action taken to terminate parental rights or to place an Indian child in foster care or in an adoptive or preadoptive home or institution. Section 1903(1) specifically provides that any case involving placement of a child outside the home based upon an act that would be criminal if committed by an adult is *not* a "child custody proceeding."

When a dependent child's parent was adopted, the agency does not have a duty to investigate the parent's adoption records to determine whether the parent had Indian ancestry. *In re C.Y., 208 Cal.App.4th 34, 144 Cal.Rptr.3d 516 (2012)*.

As per subsection (e)(1), *In re D.N., 218 Cal.App.4th 1246, 161 Cal.Rptr.3d 151 (2013)*, held that the Choctaw Nation's determination that a person's children were ineligible for tribal membership is conclusive for purposes of the Indian Child Welfare Act.

Research References

Forms

West's California Judicial Council Forms ICWA-020, Parental Notification Of Indian Status.

West's California Judicial Council Forms ICWA-030, Notice Of Child Custody Proceeding for Indian Child (Indian Child Welfare Act).

West's California Judicial Council Forms ICWA-030(A), Attachment to Notice Of Child Custody Proceeding for Indian Child (Indian Child Welfare Act).

Treatises and Practice Aids

Witkin, California Summary 10th Parent and Child § 526, Determination Of Indian Status.

Witkin, California Summary 10th Parent and Child § 528, in General.

Witkin, California Summary 10th Parent and Child § 529, Formal Requisites.

Witkin, California Summary 10th Parent and Child § 531, Determining Adequacy Of Notice.

Witkin, California Summary 10th Parent and Child § 896, General Requirements.

§ 224.4. Intervention in proceedings by tribe

The Indian child's tribe and Indian custodian have the right to intervene at any point in an Indian child custody proceeding. *(Added by Stats.2006, c. 838 (S.B.678), § 33.)*

Research References

Forms

West's California Judicial Council Forms ICWA-040, Notice Of Designation Of Tribal Representative and Notice Of Intervention in a Court Proceeding Involving an Indian Child.

Treatises and Practice Aids

Witkin, California Summary 10th Parent and Child § 533, Participation by Indian Tribe.

§ 224.5. Full faith and credit to tribal proceedings and records

In an Indian child custody proceeding, the court shall give full faith and credit to the public acts, records, judicial proceedings, and judgments of any Indian tribe applicable to the proceeding to the same extent that such entities give full faith and credit to the public acts, records, judicial proceedings, and judgments of any other entity. *(Added by Stats. 2006, c. 838 (S.B.678), § 34.)*

Research References

Treatises and Practice Aids

Witkin, California Summary 10th Parent and Child § 522, Nature and Scope Of Indian Child Welfare Act.

Witkin, California Summary 10th Parent and Child § 694, Adoption Proceeding.

§ 224.6. Testimony of qualified expert witnesses; qualifications; participation at hearings; written reports and recommendations

(a) When testimony of a "qualified expert witness" is required in an Indian child custody proceeding, a "qualified expert witness" may include, but is not limited to, a social worker, sociologist, physician, psychologist, traditional tribal therapist and healer, tribal spiritual leader, tribal historian, or tribal elder, provided the individual is not an employee of the person or agency recommending foster care placement or termination of parental rights.

(b) In considering whether to involuntarily place an Indian child in foster care or to terminate the parental rights of the parent of an Indian child, the court shall:

(1) Require that a qualified expert witness testify regarding whether continued custody of the child by the parent or Indian custodian is likely to result in serious emotional or physical damage to the child.

(2) Consider evidence concerning the prevailing social and cultural standards of the Indian child's tribe, including that tribe's family organization and child-rearing practices.

(c) Persons with the following characteristics are most likely to meet the requirements for a qualified expert witness for purposes of Indian child custody proceedings:

(1) A member of the Indian child's tribe who is recognized by the tribal community as knowledgeable in tribal customs as they pertain to family organization and childrearing practices.

(2) Any expert witness having substantial experience in the delivery of child and family services to Indians, and extensive knowledge of prevailing social and cultural standards and childrearing practices within the Indian child's tribe.

(3) A professional person having substantial education and experience in the area of his or her specialty.

(d) The court or any party may request the assistance of the Indian child's tribe or Bureau of Indian Affairs agency serving the Indian child's tribe in locating persons qualified to serve as expert witnesses.

(e) The court may accept a declaration or affidavit from a qualified expert witness in lieu of testimony only if the parties have so stipulated in writing and the court is satisfied the stipulation is made knowingly, intelligently, and voluntarily. *(Added by Stats.2006, c. 838 (S.B.678), § 35.)*

Research References

Forms

California Transactions Forms--Family Law § 3:4, Subject Matter Jurisdiction for Custody Determinations.

California Transactions Forms--Family Law § 5:3, Rights Of Nonparents Generally.

Treatises and Practice Aids

Witkin, California Summary 10th Parent and Child § 218, Statutory Rule.

Witkin, California Summary 10th Parent and Child § 532, in General.

Witkin, California Summary 10th Parent and Child § 534, Out-Of-Home Placement or Guardianship.

Witkin, California Summary 10th Parent and Child § 536, Termination Of Parental Rights.

Witkin, California Summary 10th Parent and Child § 630, Bases for Removal.

Witkin, California Summary 10th Parent and Child § 689, in General.

Witkin, California Summary 10th Parent and Child § 288C, (New) Applicable Law.

Witkin, California Summary 10th Parent and Child § 348A, (New) Additional Findings for Indian Child.

ARTICLE 1.5. YOUTH BILL OF RIGHTS

§ 224.70. Definitions

For the purposes of this article:

(a) "Committed" means placed in a facility of the Division of Juvenile Facilities pursuant to a court order, independent of, or in connection with, other sentencing alternatives.

(b) "Detained" means held in secure confinement in a juvenile facility of the Division of Juvenile Facilities.

(c) "Extended family member" means any adult related to the youth by blood, adoption, or marriage, and any adult who has an established familial or mentoring relationship with the youth, including, but not limited to, godparents, clergy, teachers, neighbors, and family friends.

(d) "Facility of the Division of Juvenile Facilities" means a place of confinement that is operated by, or contracted for, the Department of Corrections and Rehabilitation, for the purpose of the detention or commitment of youth who are taken into custody and alleged to be within the description of Section 601 or 602 or who are adjudged to be a ward of the court.

(e) "Youth" means any person detained in a facility of the Division of Juvenile Facilities. *(Added by Stats.2007, c. 649 (S.B.518), § 2.)*

Research References

Treatises and Practice Aids

Witkin, California Summary 10th Constitutional Law § 897, Other Discrimination Statutes.

Witkin, California Summary 10th Parent and Child § 951, in General.

§ 224.71. Division of Juvenile Facilities; rights of youth confined in a juvenile facility

It is the policy of the state that all youth confined in a facility of the Division of Juvenile Facilities shall have the following rights:

(a) To live in a safe, healthy, and clean environment conducive to treatment and rehabilitation and where they are treated with dignity and respect.

(b) To be free from physical, sexual, emotional, or other abuse, or corporal punishment.

(c) To receive adequate and healthy food and water, sufficient personal hygiene items, and clothing that is adequate and clean.

(d) To receive adequate and appropriate medical, dental, vision, and mental health services.

(e) To refuse the administration of psychotropic and other medications consistent with applicable law or unless immediately necessary for the preservation of life or the prevention of serious bodily harm.

(f) To not be searched for the purpose of harassment or humiliation or as a form of discipline or punishment.

(g) To maintain frequent and continuing contact with parents, guardians, siblings, children, and extended family members, through visits, telephone calls, and mail.

(h) To make and receive confidential telephone calls, send and receive confidential mail, and have confidential visits with attorneys and their authorized representatives, ombudspersons and other advocates, holders of public office, state and federal court personnel, and legal service organizations.

(i) To have fair and equal access to all available services, placement, care, treatment, and benefits, and to not be subjected to discrimination or harassment on the basis of actual or perceived race, ethnic group identification, ancestry, national origin, color, religion, sex, sexual orientation, gender identity, mental or physical disability, or HIV status.

(j) To have regular opportunity for age-appropriate physical exercise and recreation, including time spent outdoors.

(k) To contact attorneys, ombudspersons and other advocates, and representatives of state or local agencies, regarding conditions of confinement or violations of rights, and to be free from retaliation for making these contacts or complaints.

(*l*) To participate in religious services and activities of their choice.

(m) To not be deprived of any of the following as a disciplinary measure: food, contact with parents, guardians, or attorneys, sleep, exercise, education, bedding, access to religious services, a daily shower, a drinking fountain, a toilet, medical services, reading material, or the right to send and receive mail.

(n) To receive a quality education that complies with state law, to attend age-appropriate school classes and vocational training, and to continue to receive educational services while on disciplinary or medical status.

(*o*) To attend all court hearings pertaining to them.

(p) To have counsel and a prompt probable cause hearing when detained on probation or parole violations.

(q) To make at least two free telephone calls within an hour after initially being placed in a facility of the Division of Juvenile Facilities following an arrest. *(Added by Stats.2007, c. 649 (S.B.518), § 2.)*

Research References

Treatises and Practice Aids

Witkin, California Summary 10th Parent and Child § 951, in General.

§ 224.72. Division of Juvenile Facilities; developmentally appropriate orientation; translations; copy of rights

(a) Every facility of the Division of Juvenile Facilities shall provide each youth who is placed in the facility with an age and developmentally appropriate orientation that includes an explanation and a copy of the rights of the youth, as specified in Section 224.71, and that addresses the youth's questions and concerns.

(b) Each facility of the Division of Juvenile Facilities shall post a listing of the rights provided by Section 224.71 in a conspicuous location. The Office of the Ombudspersons of the Division of Juvenile Facilities shall design posters and provide the posters to each Division of Juvenile Facilities facility subject to this subdivision. These posters shall include the toll-free telephone number of the Office of the Ombudspersons of the Division of Juvenile Facilities.

(c) Consistent with Chapter 17.5 (commencing with Section 7290) of Division 7 of Title 1 of the Government Code, on or before July 1, 2010, the division shall ensure the listing of rights and posters described in this section are translated into Spanish and other languages as determined necessary by the division.

(d) A copy of the rights of the youth shall be included in orientation packets provided to parents or guardians of wards. Copies of the rights of youth in English, Spanish, and other languages shall also be made available in the visiting areas of division facilities and, upon request, to parents or guardians. *(Added by Stats.2007, c. 649 (S.B.518), § 2. Amended by Stats.2008, c. 522 (S.B.1250), § 2.)*

Research References

Treatises and Practice Aids

Witkin, California Summary 10th Parent and Child § 951, in General.

§ 224.73. Division of Juvenile Facilities; youth safety, care, placement and services; non-discrimination

All facilities of the Division of Juvenile Facilities shall ensure the safety and dignity of all youth in their care and shall provide care, placement, and services to youth without discriminating on the basis of actual or perceived race, ethnic group identification, ancestry, national origin, color, religion, sex, sexual orientation, gender identity, mental or physical disability, or HIV status. *(Added by Stats.2007, c. 649 (S.B.518), § 2.)*

§ 224.74. Office of the Ombudspersons of the Division of Juvenile Facilities; duties

(a) The Office of the Ombudspersons of the Division of Juvenile Facilities shall do all of the following:

(1) Disseminate information on the rights of children and youth in the custody of the Division of Juvenile Facilities, as provided in Section 224.71, and the services provided by the office.

(2) Investigate and attempt to resolve complaints made by or on behalf of youth in the custody of the Division of Juvenile Facilities, related to their care, placement, or services, or in the alternative, refer appropriate complaints to another agency for investigation.

(3) Notify the complainant in writing of the intention to investigate or the decision to refer the complaint to another agency within 15 days of receiving the complaint. If the office declines to investigate a complaint, the office shall notify the complainant of the reason for this decision.

(4) Update the complainant on the progress of the investigation and notify the complainant in writing of the final outcome, steps taken during the investigation, basis for the decision, and any action to be taken as a result of the complaint.

(5) Document the number, source, origin, location, and nature of complaints.

(6) Provide a toll-free telephone number for the Office of the Ombudspersons of the Division of Juvenile Facilities.

(7) Compile and make available to the Legislature and the public all data collected over the course of the year, including, but not limited to, the number of contacts to the toll-free telephone number, the number of complaints made, the number of investigations performed by the office, the number of referrals made, the issues complained about, the number of sustained complaints, the actions taken as a result of sustained complaints, and the number of unresolved complaints, including the reasons the complaints could not be resolved.

(b)(1) The Office of the Ombudspersons of the Division of Juvenile Facilities, in consultation with youth advocate and support groups, and groups representing children, families, children's facilities, and other interested parties, shall develop, no later than July 1, 2008, standardized information explaining the rights specified in Section 224.71. The information developed shall be age-appropriate.

(2) The Office of the Ombudspersons of the Division of Juvenile Facilities and other interested parties may use the information developed in paragraph (1) in carrying out their responsibilities to inform youth of their rights provided under Section 224.71. *(Added by Stats.2007, c. 649 (S.B.518), § 2.)*

Research References

Treatises and Practice Aids

Witkin, California Summary 10th Parent and Child § 951, in General.

ARTICLE 5.5. NOTICES IN DEPENDENT CHILD PROCEEDINGS

§ 290.1. Child to be retained in custody; initial petition hearing; notice to interested parties; time to notify; contents; service

If the probation officer or social worker determines that the child shall be retained in custody, he or she shall immediately file a petition pursuant to Section 332 with the clerk of the juvenile court, who shall set the matter for hearing on the detention hearing calendar. The probation officer or social worker shall serve notice as prescribed in this section.

(a) Notice shall be given to the following persons whose whereabouts are known or become known prior to the initial petition hearing:

(1) The mother.

(2) The father or fathers, presumed and alleged.

(3) The legal guardian or guardians.

(4) The child, if the child is 10 years of age or older.

(5) Any known sibling of the child who is the subject of the hearing if that sibling either is the subject of a dependency proceeding or has been adjudged to be a dependent child of the juvenile court. If the sibling is 10 years of age or older, the sibling, the sibling's caregiver, and the sibling's attorney. If the sibling is under 10 years of age, the sibling's caregiver and the sibling's attorney. However, notice is not required to be given to any sibling whose matter is calendared in the same court on the same day.

(6) If there is no parent or guardian residing in California, or if the residence is unknown, then to any adult relative residing within the county, or, if none, the adult relative residing nearest the court.

(7) The attorney for the parent or parents, or legal guardian or guardians.

(8) The district attorney, if the district attorney has notified the clerk of the court that he or she wishes to receive the petition, containing the time, date, and place of the hearing.

(9) The probate department of the superior court that appointed the guardian, if the child is a ward of a guardian appointed pursuant to the Probate Code.

(b) No notice is required for a parent whose parental rights have been terminated.

(c) The notice shall be given as soon as possible after the filing of the petition.

(d) The notice of the initial petition hearing shall include all of the following:

(1) The date, time, and place of the hearing.

(2) The name of the child.

(3) A copy of the petition.

(e) Service of the notice shall be written or oral. If the person being served cannot read, notice shall be given orally.
* * *

(f) Notice shall not be served electronically under this section.

(g) If the probation officer or social worker knows or has reason to know that an Indian child is involved, notice shall be given in accordance with Section 224.2.

* * * *(Added by Stats.2002, c. 416 (S.B.1956), § 1. Amended by Stats.2003, c. 558 (A.B.579), § 1; Stats.2006, c. 838 (S.B.678), § 36; Stats.2015, c. 219 (A.B.879), § 1, eff. Jan. 1, 2016; Stats.2017, c. 319 (A.B.976), § 111, eff. Jan. 1, 2018.)*

Research References

Forms

West's California Judicial Council Forms EFS-005, E-Mail Notice Of Hearing: Consent, Withdrawal Of Consent, Address Change (Juvenile Dependency).

Treatises and Practice Aids

Witkin, California Summary 10th Parent and Child § 12, Parental or Marital Rights Of Prisoners.
Witkin, California Summary 10th Parent and Child § 529, Formal Requisites.
Witkin, California Summary 10th Parent and Child § 564, in General.
Witkin, California Summary 10th Parent and Child § 566, Notices, Citations, Warrants, and Subpenas.
Witkin, California Summary 10th Parent and Child § 570, in General.
Witkin, California Summary 10th Parent and Child § 576, in General.
Witkin, California Summary 10th Parent and Child § 585, in General.
Witkin, California Summary 10th Parent and Child § 587, Persons Entitled to be Present.
Witkin, California Summary 10th Parent and Child § 589, Informality and Control by Court.
Witkin, California Summary 10th Parent and Child § 600, Petition and Notice Of Hearing.
Witkin, California Summary 10th Parent and Child § 657, Filing, Setting for Hearing, and Notice.

§ 290.2. Initial petition hearing; petition filed

Upon the filing of a petition by a probation officer or social worker, the clerk of the juvenile court shall issue notice, to which shall be attached a copy of the petition, and he or she shall cause the same to be served as prescribed in this section.

(a) Notice shall be given to the following persons whose address is known or becomes known prior to the initial petition hearing:

(1) The mother.

(2) The father or fathers, presumed and alleged.

(3) The legal guardian or guardians.

(4) The child, if the child is 10 years of age or older.

(5) Any known sibling of the child who is the subject of the hearing if that sibling either is the subject of a dependency proceeding or has been adjudged to be a dependent child of the juvenile court. If the sibling is 10 years of age or older, the sibling, the sibling's caregiver, and the sibling's attorney. If the sibling is under 10 years of age, the sibling's caregiver and the sibling's attorney. However, notice is not required to be given to any sibling whose matter is calendared in the same court on the same day.

(6) If there is no parent or guardian residing in California, or, if the residence is unknown, to any adult relative residing within the county, or, if none, the adult relative residing nearest the court.

(7) Upon reasonable notification by counsel representing the child, parent, or guardian, the clerk of the court shall give notice to that counsel as soon as possible.

(8) The district attorney, if the district attorney has notified the clerk of the court that he or she wishes to receive the petition, containing the time, date, and place of the hearing.

(9) The probate department of the superior court that appointed the guardian, if the child is a ward of a guardian appointed pursuant to the Probate Code.

(b) Notice is not required for a parent whose parental rights have been terminated.

(c) Notice shall be served as follows:

(1) If the child is retained in custody, the notice shall be given to the persons required to be noticed as soon as possible, and at least five days before the hearing, unless the hearing is set to be heard in less than five days in which case notice shall be given at least 24 hours prior to the hearing.

(2) If the child is not retained in custody, the notice shall be given to those persons required to be noticed at least 10 days prior to the date of the hearing. If any person who is required to be given notice is known to reside outside of the county, the clerk of the juvenile court shall mail the notice and copy of the petition by first-class mail to that person as soon as possible after the filing of the petition and at least 10 days before the time set for hearing. Failure to respond to the notice is not cause for an arrest or detention. In the instance of a failure to appear after notice by first-class mail, the court shall direct that the notice and copy of the petition be personally served on all persons required to receive the notice and copy of the petition. For these purposes, personal service of the notice and copy of the petition outside of the county at least 10 days before the time set for hearing is equivalent to service by first-class mail. Service may be waived by any person by a voluntary appearance entered in the minutes of the court or by a written waiver of service filed with the clerk of the court at, or prior to, the hearing.
* * *

(3) Notice shall not be served electronically under this section.

(d) The notice of the initial petition hearing shall include all of the following:

(1) The date, time, and place of the hearing.

(2) The name of the child.

(3) A copy of the petition.

(e) If the court knows or has reason to know that an Indian child is involved, notice shall be given in accordance with Section 224.2.

* * * *(Added by Stats.2002, c. 416 (S.B.1956), § 1. Amended by Stats.2003, c. 558 (A.B.579), § 2; Stats.2006, c. 838 (S.B.678), § 37; Stats.2015, c. 219 (A.B.879), § 3, eff. Jan. 1, 2016; Stats.2016, c. 86 (S.B.1171), § 309, eff. Jan. 1, 2017; Stats.2017, c. 319 (A.B.976), § 113, eff. Jan. 1, 2018.)*

Commentary

In re Claudia S., 131 Cal.App.4th 236, 31 Cal.Rptr.3d 697 (2005), reversed all orders that resulted from improperly noticed dependency, disposition, and 6–month and 12–month hearings conducted in the absence of the children, their parents, and appointed counsel for the parents while the family was out of the country caring for the children's ill grandmother. The parents did not receive written notice of the dependency proceedings, as required by this section and due process.

Research References

Treatises and Practice Aids

Witkin, California Summary 10th Parent and Child § 12, Parental or Marital Rights Of Prisoners.

Witkin, California Summary 10th Parent and Child § 529, Formal Requisites.

Witkin, California Summary 10th Parent and Child § 566, Notices, Citations, Warrants, and Subpenas.

Witkin, California Summary 10th Parent and Child § 570, in General.

Witkin, California Summary 10th Parent and Child § 587, Persons Entitled to be Present.

Witkin, California Summary 10th Parent and Child § 600, Petition and Notice Of Hearing.

Witkin, California Summary 10th Parent and Child § 657, Filing, Setting for Hearing, and Notice.

§ 291. Jurisdictional hearing; notice of pretrial, adjudication or disposition

After the initial petition hearing, the clerk of the court shall cause the notice to be served in the following manner:

(a) Notice of the hearing shall be given to the following persons:

(1) The mother.

(2) The father or fathers, presumed and alleged.

(3) The legal guardian or guardians.

(4) The child, if the child is 10 years of age or older.

(5) Any known sibling of the child who is the subject of the hearing if that sibling either is the subject of a dependency proceeding or has been adjudged to be a dependent child of the juvenile court. If the sibling is 10 years of age or older, the sibling, the sibling's caregiver, and the sibling's attorney. If the sibling is under 10 years of age, the sibling's caregiver and the sibling's attorney. However, notice is not required to be given to any sibling whose matter is calendared in the same court on the same day.

(6) Each attorney of record unless counsel of record is present in court when the hearing is scheduled, then no further notice need be given.

(7) If there is no parent or guardian residing in California, or if the residence is unknown, then to any adult relative residing within the county, or, if none, the adult relative residing nearest the court.

(8) If the hearing is a dispositional hearing that is also serving as a permanency hearing pursuant to subdivision (f) of Section 361.5, notice shall be given to the current caregiver for the child, including foster parents, relative caregivers, preadoptive parents, nonrelative extended family members, and resource family. Any person notified may attend all hearings and may submit any information he or she deems relevant to the court in writing.

(b) No notice is required for a parent whose parental rights have been terminated.

(c) Notice shall be served as follows:

(1) If the child is detained, the notice shall be given to the persons required to be noticed as soon as possible, and at least five days before the hearing, unless the hearing is set less than five days and then at least 24 hours * * * <u>before</u> the hearing.

(2) If the child is not detained, the notice shall be given to those persons required to be noticed at least 10 days * * * <u>before</u> the date of the hearing.

(d) The notice shall include all of the following:

(1) The name and address of the person notified.

(2) The nature of the hearing.

(3) Each section and subdivision under which the proceeding has been initiated.

(4) The date, time, and place of the hearing.

(5) The name of the child upon whose behalf the petition has been brought.

(6) A statement that:

(A) If they fail to appear, the court may proceed without them.

(B) The child, parent, guardian, Indian custodian, or adult relative to whom notice is required to be given pursuant to paragraph (1), (2), (3), (4), or (7) of subdivision (a) is entitled to have an attorney present at the hearing.

(C) If the parent, guardian, Indian custodian, or adult relative noticed pursuant to paragraph (1), (2), (3), or (7) of subdivision (a) is indigent and cannot afford an attorney, and desires to be represented by an attorney, the parent, guardian, Indian custodian, or adult relative shall promptly notify the clerk of the juvenile court.

(D) If an attorney is appointed to represent the parent, guardian, Indian custodian, or adult relative, the represented person shall be liable for all or a portion of the costs to the extent of his or her ability to pay.

(E) The parent, guardian, Indian custodian, or adult relative may be liable for the costs of support of the child in any out-of-home placement.

(7) A copy of the petition.

(e) Service of the notice of the hearing shall be given in the following manner:

(1) If the child is detained and the persons required to be noticed are not present at the initial petition hearing, they

shall be noticed by personal service or by certified mail, return receipt requested.

(2) If the child is detained and the persons required to be noticed are present at the initial petition hearing, they shall be noticed by personal service * * *, by first-class mail, or by electronic service pursuant to Section 212.5.

(3) If the child is not detained, the persons required to be noticed shall be noticed by personal service * * *, by first-class mail, or by electronic service pursuant to Section 212.5, unless the person to be served is known to reside outside the county, in which case service shall be by first-class mail or by electronic service pursuant to Section 212.5.

* * *

(f) Any of the notices required to be given under this section or Sections 290.1 and 290.2 may be waived by a party in person or through his or her attorney, or by a signed written waiver filed on or before the date scheduled for the hearing.

(g) If the court knows or has reason to know that an Indian child is involved, notice shall be given in accordance with Section 224.2.

* * * *(Added by Stats.2002, c. 416 (S.B.1956), § 1. Amended by Stats.2003, c. 558 (A.B.579), § 3; Stats.2006, c. 838 (S.B.678), § 38; Stats.2007, c. 583 (S.B.703), § 20; Stats.2015, c. 219 (A.B.879), § 5, eff. Jan. 1, 2016; Stats.2016, c. 612 (A.B.1997), § 60, eff. Jan. 1, 2017; Stats.2017, c. 319 (A.B.976), § 115, eff. Jan. 1, 2018.)*

Commentary

In re Wilford J. Jr., 131 Cal.App.4th 742, 32 Cal.Rptr.3d 317 (2005), holds that a juvenile court's conversion of a noticed pretrial resolution conference into an unscheduled and unnoticed dependency jurisdiction hearing violated the parent's right to adequate notice under subsection (d)(2). However, the parent lost his right to challenge the juvenile court's jurisdictional order by appearing with counsel at the subsequent dispositional hearings without raising the issue.

Research References

Treatises and Practice Aids

Witkin, California Summary 10th Parent and Child § 12, Parental or Marital Rights Of Prisoners.
Witkin, California Summary 10th Parent and Child § 529, Formal Requisites.
Witkin, California Summary 10th Parent and Child § 566, Notices, Citations, Warrants, and Subpenas.
Witkin, California Summary 10th Parent and Child § 600, Petition and Notice Of Hearing.
Witkin, California Summary 10th Parent and Child § 610, Notice Of Hearing.
Witkin, California Summary 10th Parent and Child § 628, Legal Guardianship.
Witkin, California Summary 10th Parent and Child § 657, Filing, Setting for Hearing, and Notice.
Witkin, California Summary 10th Parent and Child § 664, in General.
Witkin, California Summary 10th Parent and Child § 682, Preliminary Assessment.

§ 292. Review hearing on retention by parent or guardian of child adjudged a dependent child; notice to interested parties; time to serve; method of service

The social worker or probation officer shall give notice of the review hearing held pursuant to Section 364 in the following manner:

(a) Notice of the hearing shall be given to the following persons:

(1) The mother.

(2) The presumed father or any father receiving services.

(3) The legal guardian or guardians.

(4) The child, if the child is 10 years of age or older.

(5) Any known sibling of the child who is the subject of the hearing if that sibling either is the subject of a dependency proceeding or has been adjudged to be a dependent child of the juvenile court. If the sibling is 10 years of age or older, the sibling, the sibling's caregiver, and the sibling's attorney. If the sibling is under 10 years of age, the sibling's caregiver and the sibling's attorney. However, notice is not required to be given to any sibling whose matter is calendared in the same court on the same day.

(6) Each attorney of record, if that attorney was not present at the time that the hearing was set by the court.

(b) No notice is required for a parent whose parental rights have been terminated.

(c) The notice of the hearing shall be served not earlier than 30 days, nor later than 15 days, before the hearing.

(d) The notice shall contain a statement regarding the nature of the hearing to be held and any change in the custody or status of the child being recommended by the supervising agency. The notice shall also include a statement that the child and the parent or parents or legal guardian or guardians have a right to be present at the hearing, to be represented by counsel at the hearing and the procedure for obtaining appointed counsel, and to present evidence regarding the proper disposition of the case. The notice shall also state that if the parent or parents or legal guardian or guardians fail to appear, the court may proceed without them.

(e) Service of the notice shall be by personal service, by first-class mail, or by certified mail * * * with return receipt requested, addressed to the last known address of the person to be noticed * * *, or by electronic service pursuant to Section 212.5.

(f) If the social worker or the probation officer knows or has reason to know that an Indian child is involved, notice shall be given in accordance with Section 224.2.

* * * *(Added by Stats.2002, c. 416 (S.B.1956), § 1. Amended by Stats.2003, c. 558 (A.B.579), § 4; Stats.2006, c. 838 (S.B.678), § 39; Stats.2015, c. 219 (A.B.879), § 7, eff. Jan. 1, 2016; Stats.2017, c. 319 (A.B.976), § 117, eff. Jan. 1, 2018.)*

Research References

Treatises and Practice Aids

Witkin, California Summary 10th Parent and Child § 529, Formal Requisites.
Witkin, California Summary 10th Parent and Child § 670, Notice Of Hearing.

§ 293. Review hearings held pursuant to § 366.21, 366.22, or 366.25

The social worker or probation officer shall give notice of the review hearings held pursuant to Section 366.21, 366.22, or 366.25 in the following manner:

(a) Notice of the hearing shall be given to the following persons:

(1) The mother.

(2) The presumed father or any father receiving services.

(3) The legal guardian or guardians.

(4) The child, if the child is 10 years of age or older.

(5) Any known sibling of the child who is the subject of the hearing if that sibling either is the subject of a dependency proceeding or has been adjudged to be a dependent child of the juvenile court. If the sibling is 10 years of age or older, the sibling, the sibling's caregiver, and the sibling's attorney. If the sibling is under 10 years of age, the sibling's caregiver and the sibling's attorney. However, notice is not required to be given to any sibling whose matter is calendared in the same court on the same day.

(6) In the case of a child removed from the physical custody of his or her parent or legal guardian, the current caregiver of the child, including the foster parents, relative caregivers, preadoptive parents, nonrelative extended family members, resource family, community care facility, or foster family agency having custody of the child. In a case in which a foster family agency is notified of the hearing pursuant to this section, and the child resides in a foster home certified by the foster family agency, the foster family agency shall provide timely notice of the hearing to the child's caregivers.

(7) Each attorney of record if that attorney was not present at the time that the hearing was set by the court.

(b) No notice is required for a parent whose parental rights have been terminated. On and after January 1, 2012, in the case of a nonminor dependent, as described in subdivision (v) of Section 11400, no notice is required for a parent.

(c) The notice of hearing shall be served not earlier than 30 days, nor later than 15 days, before the hearing.

(d) The notice shall contain a statement regarding the nature of the hearing to be held and any change in the custody or status of the child being recommended by the supervising agency. If the notice is to the child, parent or parents, or legal guardian or guardians, the notice shall also advise them of the right to be present, the right to be represented by counsel, the right to request counsel, and the right to present evidence. The notice shall also state that if the parent or parents or legal guardian or guardians fail to appear, the court may proceed without them.

(e) Service of the notice shall be by first-class mail addressed to the last known address of the person to be noticed * * *, by personal service * * *, or by electronic service pursuant to Section 212.5.

(f) Notice to the current caregiver of the child, including a foster parent, a relative caregiver, a preadoptive parent, a nonrelative extended family member, a resource family, a certified foster parent who has been approved for adoption, or the State Department of Social Services when it is acting as an adoption agency or by a county adoption agency, shall indicate that the person notified may attend all hearings or may submit any information he or she deems relevant to the court in writing.

(g) If the social worker or probation officer knows or has reason to know that an Indian child is involved, notice shall be given in accordance with Section 224.2.

* * * *(Added by Stats.2002, c. 416 (S.B.1956), § 1. Amended by Stats.2003, c. 558 (A.B.579), § 5; Stats.2004, c. 858 (S.B.1357), § 8; Stats.2006, c. 838 (S.B.678), § 40; Stats.2007, c. 583 (S.B.703), § 21; Stats.2010, c. 559 (A.B.12), § 6; Stats.2012, c. 35 (S.B.1013), § 40, eff. June 27, 2012; Stats.2015, c. 219 (A.B.879), § 9, eff. Jan. 1, 2016; Stats.2016, c. 612 (A.B.1997), § 62, eff. Jan. 1, 2017; Stats.2017, c. 319 (A.B.976), § 119, eff. Jan. 1, 2018.)*

Research References

Treatises and Practice Aids

Witkin, California Summary 10th Parent and Child § 12, Parental or Marital Rights Of Prisoners.

Witkin, California Summary 10th Parent and Child § 529, Formal Requisites.

Witkin, California Summary 10th Parent and Child § 670, Notice Of Hearing.

Witkin, California Summary 10th Parent and Child § 678, Twelve-Month Review.

Witkin, California Summary 10th Parent and Child § 679, Eighteen-Month Review.

§ 294. Selection and implementation hearings held pursuant to § 366.26

The social worker or probation officer shall give notice of a selection and implementation hearing held pursuant to Section 366.26 in the following manner:

(a) Notice of the hearing shall be given to the following persons:

(1) The mother.

(2) The fathers, presumed and alleged.

(3) The child, if the child is 10 years of age or older.

(4) Any known sibling of the child who is the subject of the hearing if that sibling either is the subject of a dependency proceeding or has been adjudged to be a dependent child of the juvenile court. If the sibling is 10 years of age or older, the sibling, the sibling's caregiver, and the sibling's attorney. If the sibling is under 10 years of age, the sibling's caregiver and the sibling's attorney. However, notice is not required to be given to any sibling whose matter is calendared in the same court on the same day.

(5) The grandparents of the child, if their address is known and if the parent's whereabouts are unknown.

(6) All counsel of record.

(7) To any unknown parent by publication, if ordered by the court pursuant to paragraph (2) of subdivision (g).

(8) The current caregiver of the child, including foster parents, relative caregivers, preadoptive parents, nonrelative extended family members, or resource family. Any person notified may attend all hearings and may submit any information he or she deems relevant to the court in writing.

(b) The following persons shall not be notified of the hearing:

(1) A parent who has relinquished the child to the State Department of Social Services, county adoption agency, or licensed adoption agency for adoption, and the relinquish-

ment has been accepted and filed with notice as required under Section 8700 of the Family Code.

(2) An alleged father who has denied paternity and has executed a waiver of the right to notice of further proceedings.

(3) A parent whose parental rights have been terminated.

(c)(1) Service of the notice shall be completed at least 45 days before the hearing date. Service is deemed complete at the time the notice is personally delivered to the person named in the notice or 10 days after the notice has been placed in the mail or sent by electronic mail, or at the expiration of the time prescribed by the order for publication.

(2) Service of notice in cases where publication is ordered shall be completed at least 30 days before the date of the hearing.

(d) Regardless of the type of notice required, or the manner in which it is served, once the court has made the initial finding that notice has properly been given to the parent, or to any person entitled to receive notice pursuant to this section, subsequent notice for any continuation of a Section 366.26 hearing may be by first-class mail to any last known address, by an order made pursuant to Section 296, * * * by electronic service pursuant to Section 212.5, or by any other means that the court determines is reasonably calculated, under any circumstance, to provide notice of the continued hearing. However, if the recommendation changes from the recommendation contained in the notice previously found to be proper, notice shall be provided to the parent, and to any person entitled to receive notice pursuant to this section, regarding that subsequent hearing.

(e) The notice shall contain the following information:

(1) The date, time, and place of the hearing.

(2) The right to appear.

(3) The parents' right to counsel.

(4) The nature of the proceedings.

(5) The recommendation of the supervising agency.

(6) A statement that, at the time of hearing, the court is required to select a permanent plan of adoption, legal guardianship, placement with a fit and willing relative, or another planned permanent living arrangement, as appropriate, for the child.

(f) Notice to the parents may be given in any one of the following manners:

(1) If the parent is present at the hearing at which the court schedules a hearing pursuant to Section 366.26, the court shall advise the parent of the date, time, and place of the proceedings, their right to counsel, the nature of the proceedings, and the requirement that at the proceedings the court shall select and implement a plan of adoption, legal guardianship, placement with a fit and willing relative, or another planned permanent living arrangement, as appropriate, for the child. The court shall direct the parent to appear for the proceedings and then direct that the parent be notified thereafter only by first-class mail to the parent's usual place of residence or business * * *, or by electronic service pursuant to Section 212.5.

(2) Certified mail, return receipt requested, to the parent's last known mailing address. This notice shall be sufficient if the child welfare agency receives a return receipt signed by the parent.

(3) Personal service to the parent named in the notice.

(4) Delivery to a competent person who is at least 18 years of age at the parent's usual place of residence or business, and thereafter * * * served on the parent named in the notice by first-class mail at the place where the notice was delivered or by electronic service pursuant to Section 212.5.

(5) If the residence of the parent is outside the state, service may be made as described in paragraph (1), (3), or (4) or by certified mail, return receipt requested.

(6) If the recommendation of the probation officer or social worker is legal guardianship, placement with a fit and willing relative, or another planned permanent living arrangement, as appropriate, service may be made by first-class mail to the parent's usual place of residence or business or by electronic service pursuant to Section 212.5. In the case of an Indian child, if the recommendation of the probation officer or social worker is tribal customary adoption, service may be made by first-class mail to the parent's usual place of residence or business. * * *

(7) If a parent's identity is known but his or her whereabouts are unknown and the parent cannot, with reasonable diligence, be served in any manner specified in paragraphs (1) to (6), inclusive, the petitioner shall file an affidavit with the court at least 75 days before the hearing date, stating the name of the parent and describing the efforts made to locate and serve the parent.

(A) If the court determines that there has been due diligence in attempting to locate and serve the parent and the probation officer or social worker recommends adoption, service shall be to that parent's attorney of record, if any, by certified mail, return receipt requested. If the parent does not have an attorney of record, the court shall order that service be made by publication of citation requiring the parent to appear at the date, time, and place stated in the citation, and that the citation be published in a newspaper designated as most likely to give notice to the parent. Publication shall be made once a week for four consecutive weeks. Whether notice is to the attorney of record or by publication, the court shall also order that notice be given to the grandparents of the child, if their identities and addresses are known, by first-class mail or by electronic service pursuant to Section 212.5.

(B) If the court determines that there has been due diligence in attempting to locate and serve the parent and the probation officer or social worker recommends legal guardianship, placement with a fit and willing relative, or another planned permanent living arrangement, as appropriate, no further notice is required to the parent, but the court shall order that notice be given to the grandparents of the child, if their identities and addresses are known, by first-class mail or by electronic service pursuant to Section 212.5.

(C) In any case where the residence of the parent becomes known, notice shall immediately be served upon the parent as provided for in either paragraph (2), (3), (4), (5), or (6).

(g)(1) If the identity of one or both of the parents, or alleged parents, of the child is unknown, or if the name of one or both parents is uncertain, then that fact shall be set forth in the affidavit filed with the court at least 75 days before the hearing date and the court, consistent with the provisions of Sections 7665 and 7666 of the Family Code, shall issue an order dispensing with notice to a natural parent or possible natural parent under this section if, after inquiry and a determination that there has been due diligence in attempting to identify the unknown parent, the court is unable to identify the natural parent or possible natural parent and no person has appeared claiming to be the natural parent.

(2) After a determination that there has been due diligence in attempting to identify an unknown parent pursuant to paragraph (1) and the probation officer or social worker recommends adoption, the court shall consider whether publication notice would be likely to lead to actual notice to the unknown parent. The court may order publication notice if, on the basis of all information before the court, the court determines that notice by publication is likely to lead to actual notice to the parent. If publication notice to an unknown parent is ordered, the court shall order the published citation to be directed to either the father or mother, or both, of the child, and to all persons claiming to be the father or mother of the child, naming and otherwise describing the child. An order of publication pursuant to this paragraph shall be based on an affidavit describing efforts made to identify the unknown parent or parents. Service made by publication pursuant to this paragraph shall require the unknown parent or parents to appear at the date, time, and place stated in the citation. Publication shall be made once a week for four consecutive weeks.

(3) If the court determines that there has been due diligence in attempting to identify one or both of the parents, or alleged parents, of the child and the probation officer or social worker recommends legal guardianship, placement with a fit and willing relative, or another planned permanent living arrangement, as appropriate, no further notice to the parent shall be required.

(h) * * * Notice to all counsel of record shall be by first-class mail * * * or by electronic service pursuant to Section 212.5.

* * *

(i) If the court knows or has reason to know that an Indian child is involved, notice shall be given in accordance with Section 224.2.

(j) Notwithstanding subdivision (a), if the attorney of record is present at the time the court schedules a hearing pursuant to Section 366.26, no further notice is required, except as required by subparagraph (A) of paragraph (7) of subdivision (f).

(k) This section shall also apply to children adjudged wards pursuant to Section 727.31.

(*l*) The court shall state the reasons on the record explaining why good cause exists for granting any continuance of a hearing held pursuant to Section 366.26 to fulfill the requirements of this section.

(m) * * * Notice of any hearing at which the county welfare department is recommending the termination of parental rights may only be served * * * electronically if notice is also given by another means of service provided for in this section.

* * * *(Added by Stats.2002, c. 416 (S.B.1956), § 1. Amended by Stats.2003, c. 558 (A.B.579), § 6; Stats.2004, c. 20 (A.B.44), § 2, eff. March 5, 2004; Stats.2005, c. 22 (S.B.1108), § 213; Stats.2005, c. 627 (S.B.302), § 5; Stats. 2006, c. 838 (S.B.678), § 41; Stats.2007, c. 583 (S.B.703), § 22; Stats.2009, c. 287 (A.B.1325), § 2, operative July 1, 2010; Stats.2012, c. 35 (S.B.1013), § 41, eff. June 27, 2012; Stats.2015, c. 219 (A.B.879), § 11, eff. Jan. 1, 2016; Stats.2016, c. 612 (A.B.1997), § 64, eff. Jan. 1, 2017; Stats.2017, c. 319 (A.B.976), § 121, eff. Jan. 1, 2018.)*

Commentary

In re Jasmine G., 127 Cal.App.4th 1109, 26 Cal.Rptr.3d 394 (2005), holds that a mother's due process rights were violated when her parental rights were terminated at a hearing for which the social service agency neglected to give her notice, as required by subsection (a). *Jasmine G.* characterized the failure to give notice as a "structural error" requiring automatic reversal of the termination order.

Research References

Forms

West's California Judicial Council Forms JV-305, Citation for Publication Under Welfare and Institutions Code Section 294.

Treatises and Practice Aids

Witkin, California Summary 10th Parent and Child § 12, Parental or Marital Rights Of Prisoners.
Witkin, California Summary 10th Parent and Child § 529, Formal Requisites.
Witkin, California Summary 10th Parent and Child § 610, Notice Of Hearing.
Witkin, California Summary 10th Parent and Child § 681, Notice.
Witkin, California Summary 10th Parent and Child § 695, Legal Guardianship.
Witkin, California Summary 10th Parent and Child § 899, Termination Of Parental Rights.
Witkin, California Summary 10th Parent and Child § 693E, (New) Reinstatement Of Parental Rights.

§ 295. Review hearings held pursuant to Sections 366.3 and 366.31, and termination of jurisdiction hearings held pursuant to Section 391

The social worker or probation officer shall give notice of review hearings held pursuant to Sections 366.3 and 366.31 and for termination of jurisdiction hearings held pursuant to Section 391 in the following manner:

(a) Notice of the hearing shall be given to the following persons:

(1) The mother.

(2) The presumed father.

(3) The legal guardian or guardians.

(4) The child, if the child is 10 years of age or older, or a nonminor dependent.

(5) Any known sibling of the child or nonminor dependent who is the subject of the hearing if that sibling either is the subject of a dependency proceeding or has been adjudged to be a dependent child of the juvenile court. If the sibling is 10 years of age or older, the sibling, the sibling's caregiver, and

the sibling's attorney. If the sibling is under 10 years of age, the sibling's caregiver and the sibling's attorney. However, notice is not required to be given to any sibling whose matter is calendared in the same court on the same day.

(6) The current caregiver of the child, including the foster parents, relative caregivers, preadoptive parents, nonrelative extended family members, resource family, community care facility, or foster family agency having physical custody of the child if a child is removed from the physical custody of the parents or legal guardian. The person notified may attend all hearings and may submit any information he or she deems relevant to the court in writing.

(7) The current caregiver of a nonminor dependent, as described in subdivision (v) of Section 11400. The person notified may attend all hearings and may submit for filing an original and eight copies of written information he or she deems relevant to the court. The court clerk shall provide the current parties and attorneys of record with a copy of the written information immediately upon receipt and complete, file, and distribute a proof of service.

(8) The attorney of record if that attorney of record was not present at the time that the hearing was set by the court.

(9) The alleged father or fathers, but only if the recommendation is to set a new hearing pursuant to Section 366.26.

(b) No notice shall be required for a parent whose parental rights have been terminated or for the parent of a nonminor dependent, as described in subdivision (v) of Section 11400, unless the parent is receiving court-ordered family reunification services pursuant to Section 361.6.

(c) The notice of the review hearing shall be served no earlier than 30 days, nor later than 15 days, before the hearing.

(d) The notice of the review hearing shall contain a statement regarding the nature of the hearing to be held, any recommended change in the custody or status of the child, and any recommendation that the court set a new hearing pursuant to Section 366.26 in order to select a more permanent plan.

(e) Service of notice shall be by first-class mail addressed to the last known address of the person to be provided * * * notice or by electronic service pursuant to Section 212.5. In the case of an Indian child, notice shall be by registered mail, return receipt requested.

(f) If the child is ordered into a permanent plan of legal guardianship, and subsequently a petition to terminate or modify the guardianship is filed, the probation officer or social worker shall serve notice of the petition not less than 15 court days * * * before the hearing on all persons listed in subdivision (a) and on the court that established legal guardianship if it is in another county.

(g) If the social worker or probation officer knows or has reason to know that an Indian child is involved, notice shall be given in accordance with Section 224.2.

* * * *(Added by Stats.2002, c. 416 (S.B.1956), § 1. Amended by Stats.2003, c. 558 (A.B.579), § 7; Stats.2006, c. 389 (S.B.1667), § 1; Stats.2006, c. 838 (S.B.678), § 42.5; Stats.2007, c. 583 (S.B.703), § 23; Stats.2010, c. 559 (A.B.12), § 6.5; Stats.2012, c. 846 (A.B.1712), § 11; Stats.2015, c. 219 (A.B.879), § 13, eff. Jan. 1, 2016; Stats.2016, c. 612 (A.B. 1997), § 66, eff. Jan. 1, 2017; Stats.2017, c. 319 (A.B.976), § 123, eff. Jan. 1, 2018.)*

Research References

Forms

West's California Judicial Council Forms JV-281, Notice Of Hearing--Nonminor Dependent Review Hearing / Other.

West's California Judicial Council Forms EFS-005, E-Mail Notice Of Hearing: Consent, Withdrawal Of Consent, Address Change (Juvenile Dependency).

Treatises and Practice Aids

Witkin, California Summary 10th Parent and Child § 697, Status Review Hearings.

Witkin, California Summary 10th Parent and Child § 699, Notice.

Witkin, California Summary 10th Parent and Child § 669A, (New) Review Hearings Just Before and After Minor Attains Age 18.

Witkin, California Summary 10th Parent and Child § 699B, (New) Status Review Hearings.

§ 296. Order requiring reappearance of any parent, child or guardian

Upon any hearing or rehearing under this article, the court may order the child or any parent or guardian, or Indian custodian of the child who is present in court, to again appear before the court, before the social worker or probation officer, or before the county financial officer at a time and place specified in the order. *(Added by Stats.2002, c. 416 (S.B.1956), § 1.)*

Research References

Treatises and Practice Aids

Witkin, California Summary 10th Parent and Child § 589, Informality and Control by Court.

Witkin, California Summary 10th Parent and Child § 681, Notice.

§ 297. Subsequent petitions; supplemental petitions; petitions for modification

(a) * * * A subsequent petition filed pursuant to * * * Section 342 shall be noticed pursuant to Sections 290.1 and 290.2, except that service may be delivered by electronic service pursuant to Section 212.5.

(b) Upon the filing of a supplemental petition pursuant to Section 387, the clerk of the juvenile court shall immediately set the matter for hearing within 30 days of the date of the filing, and the social worker or probation officer shall cause notice thereof to be served upon the persons required by, and in the manner prescribed by, Sections 290.1, 290.2, and 291, except that service may be delivered by electronic service pursuant to Section 212.5.

(c) If a petition for modification has been filed pursuant to Section 388, and it appears that the best interest of the child may be promoted by the proposed change of the order, the recognition of a sibling relationship, or the termination of jurisdiction, the court shall order that a hearing be held and shall give prior notice, or cause prior notice to be given, to the social worker or probation officer and to the child's attorney of record, or if there is no attorney of record for the child, to the child, and his or her parent or parents or legal guardian or guardians in the manner prescribed by Section 291 unless a different manner is prescribed by the court.

(d) If the court knows or has reason to know that an Indian child is involved, notice shall be given in accordance with Section 224.2.

(e) On and after January 1, 2012, if a petition for modification has been filed pursuant to subdivision (e) of Section 388 by a nonminor dependent, as described in subdivision (v) of Section 11400, no notice is required for a parent. *(Added by Stats.2002, c. 416 (S.B.1956), § 1. Amended by Stats.2006, c. 838 (S.B.678), § 43; Stats.2010, c. 559 (A.B.12), § 6.7; Stats.2017, c. 319 (A.B.976), § 125, eff. Jan. 1, 2018.)*

Research References

Treatises and Practice Aids

Witkin, California Summary 10th Parent and Child § 657, Filing, Setting for Hearing, and Notice.
Witkin, California Summary 10th Parent and Child § 664, in General.
Witkin, California Summary 10th Parent and Child § 668, Subsequent Petition.
Witkin, California Summary 10th Parent and Child § 693E, (New) Reinstatement Of Parental Rights.

ARTICLE 6. DEPENDENT CHILDREN—JURISDICTION

§ 300. Children subject to jurisdiction; legislative intent and declarations; "guardian" defined

A child who comes within any of the following descriptions is within the jurisdiction of the juvenile court which may adjudge that person to be a dependent child of the court:

(a) The child has suffered, or there is a substantial risk that the child will suffer, serious physical harm inflicted nonaccidentally upon the child by the child's parent or guardian. For purposes of this subdivision, a court may find there is a substantial risk of serious future injury based on the manner in which a less serious injury was inflicted, a history of repeated inflictions of injuries on the child or the child's siblings, or a combination of these and other actions by the parent or guardian that indicate the child is at risk of serious physical harm. For purposes of this subdivision, "serious physical harm" does not include reasonable and age-appropriate spanking to the buttocks if there is no evidence of serious physical injury.

(b)(1) The child has suffered, or there is a substantial risk that the child will suffer, serious physical harm or illness, as a result of the failure or inability of his or her parent or guardian to adequately supervise or protect the child, or the willful or negligent failure of the child's parent or guardian to adequately supervise or protect the child from the conduct of the custodian with whom the child has been left, or by the willful or negligent failure of the parent or guardian to provide the child with adequate food, clothing, shelter, or medical treatment, or by the inability of the parent or guardian to provide regular care for the child due to the parent's or guardian's mental illness, developmental disability, or substance abuse. A child shall not be found to be a person described by this subdivision solely due to the lack of an emergency shelter for the family. Whenever it is alleged that a child comes within the jurisdiction of the court on the basis of the parent's or guardian's willful failure to provide adequate medical treatment or specific decision to provide spiritual treatment through prayer, the court shall give deference to the parent's or guardian's medical treatment, nontreatment, or spiritual treatment through prayer alone in accordance with the tenets and practices of a recognized church or religious denomination, by an accredited practitioner thereof, and shall not assume jurisdiction unless necessary to protect the child from suffering serious physical harm or illness. In making its determination, the court shall consider (1) the nature of the treatment proposed by the parent or guardian, (2) the risks to the child posed by the course of treatment or nontreatment proposed by the parent or guardian, (3) the risk, if any, of the course of treatment being proposed by the petitioning agency, and (4) the likely success of the courses of treatment or nontreatment proposed by the parent or guardian and agency. The child shall continue to be a dependent child pursuant to this subdivision only so long as is necessary to protect the child from risk of suffering serious physical harm or illness.

(2) The Legislature finds and declares that a child who is sexually trafficked, as described in Section 236.1 of the Penal Code, or who receives food or shelter in exchange for, or who is paid to perform, sexual acts described in Section 236.1 or 11165.1 of the Penal Code, and whose parent or guardian failed to, or was unable to, protect the child, is within the description of this subdivision, and that this finding is declaratory of existing law. These children shall be known as commercially sexually exploited children.

(c) The child is suffering serious emotional damage, or is at substantial risk of suffering serious emotional damage, evidenced by severe anxiety, depression, withdrawal, or untoward aggressive behavior toward self or others, as a result of the conduct of the parent or guardian or who has no parent or guardian capable of providing appropriate care. A child shall not be found to be a person described by this subdivision if the willful failure of the parent or guardian to provide adequate mental health treatment is based on a sincerely held religious belief and if a less intrusive judicial intervention is available.

(d) The child has been sexually abused, or there is a substantial risk that the child will be sexually abused, as defined in Section 11165.1 of the Penal Code, by his or her parent or guardian or a member of his or her household, or the parent or guardian has failed to adequately protect the child from sexual abuse when the parent or guardian knew or reasonably should have known that the child was in danger of sexual abuse.

(e) The child is under the age of five years and has suffered severe physical abuse by a parent, or by any person known by the parent, if the parent knew or reasonably should have known that the person was physically abusing the child. For the purposes of this subdivision, "severe physical abuse" means any of the following: any single act of abuse which causes physical trauma of sufficient severity that, if left untreated, would cause permanent physical disfigurement, permanent physical disability, or death; any single act of sexual abuse which causes significant bleeding, deep bruising, or significant external or internal swelling; or more than one act of physical abuse, each of which causes bleeding, deep bruising, significant external or internal swelling, bone fracture, or unconsciousness; or the willful, prolonged failure to provide adequate food. A child shall not be removed from the physical custody of his or her parent or guardian on the basis of a finding of severe physical abuse unless the social worker has made an allegation of severe physical abuse pursuant to Section 332.

(f) The child's parent or guardian caused the death of another child through abuse or neglect.

(g) The child has been left without any provision for support; physical custody of the child has been voluntarily surrendered pursuant to Section 1255.7 of the Health and Safety Code and the child has not been reclaimed within the 14–day period specified in subdivision (g) of that section; the child's parent has been incarcerated or institutionalized and cannot arrange for the care of the child; or a relative or other adult custodian with whom the child resides or has been left is unwilling or unable to provide care or support for the child, the whereabouts of the parent are unknown, and reasonable efforts to locate the parent have been unsuccessful.

(h) The child has been freed for adoption by one or both parents for 12 months by either relinquishment or termination of parental rights or an adoption petition has not been granted.

(i) The child has been subjected to an act or acts of cruelty by the parent or guardian or a member of his or her household, or the parent or guardian has failed to adequately protect the child from an act or acts of cruelty when the parent or guardian knew or reasonably should have known that the child was in danger of being subjected to an act or acts of cruelty.

(j) The child's sibling has been abused or neglected, as defined in subdivision (a), (b), (d), (e), or (i), and there is a substantial risk that the child will be abused or neglected, as defined in those subdivisions. The court shall consider the circumstances surrounding the abuse or neglect of the sibling, the age and gender of each child, the nature of the abuse or neglect of the sibling, the mental condition of the parent or guardian, and any other factors the court considers probative in determining whether there is a substantial risk to the child.

It is the intent of the Legislature that this section not disrupt the family unnecessarily or intrude inappropriately into family life, prohibit the use of reasonable methods of parental discipline, or prescribe a particular method of parenting. Further, this section is not intended to limit the offering of voluntary services to those families in need of assistance but who do not come within the descriptions of this section. To the extent that savings accrue to the state from child welfare services funding obtained as a result of the enactment of the act that enacted this section, those savings shall be used to promote services which support family maintenance and family reunification plans, such as client transportation, out-of-home respite care, parenting training, and the provision of temporary or emergency in-home caretakers and persons teaching and demonstrating homemaking skills. The Legislature further declares that a physical disability, such as blindness or deafness, is no bar to the raising of happy and well-adjusted children and that a court's determination pursuant to this section shall center upon whether a parent's disability prevents him or her from exercising care and control. The Legislature further declares that a child whose parent has been adjudged a dependent child of the court pursuant to this section shall not be considered to be at risk of abuse or neglect solely because of the age, dependent status, or foster care status of the parent.

As used in this section, "guardian" means the legal guardian of the child. *(Added by Stats.1987, c. 1485, § 4, operative Jan. 1, 1989. Amended by Stats.1989, c. 913, § 3; Stats.1991, c. 1203 (S.B.1125), § 1.5; Stats.1992, c. 382 (S.B.1646), § 1; Stats.1996, c. 1082 (A.B.2679), § 1; Stats. 1996, c. 1084 (S.B.1516), § 1.5; Stats.1998, c. 1054 (A.B. 1091), § 2; Stats.2000, c. 824 (S.B.1368), § 3; Stats.2005, c. 625 (S.B.116), § 3; Stats.2005, c. 630 (S.B.500), § 1; Stats. 2014, c. 29 (S.B.855), § 64, eff. June 20, 2014; Stats.2015, c. 303 (A.B.731), § 566, eff. Jan. 1, 2016.)*

Commentary

In re Kaylee H., 205 Cal.App.4th 92, 139 Cal.Rptr.3d 867 (2012), held that a juvenile court abused its discretion in ordering a social worker to file a petition under this section to remove a child from the care and custody of her parents when the dependency petition was not necessary to protect the child, because the child was not in the custody of her parents but was instead under the temporary guardianship of a suitable and protective family member.

In re Mariah T., 159 Cal.App.4th 428, 71 Cal.Rptr.3d 542 (2008), held that subsection (a), which authorizes the juvenile court to assume dependency jurisdiction if the child "has suffered . . . or there is a substantial risk that the child will suffer serious physical harm" is not unconstitutionally vague, because "serious physical harm" has a well-established meaning.

In re N.M., 197 Cal.App.4th 159, 127 Cal.Rptr.3d 424 (2011), held that a father's agreement to a negotiated settlement in order to avoid a trial and required therapy for child abuse, was an implied waiver of his right to appeal the sufficiency of evidence supporting a juvenile court's finding of subsection (a) dependency jurisdiction.

A juvenile court lacked jurisdiction to order a minor to undergo section 369 blood transfusions against his will and over the objection of his parents when the state agency failed to file a juvenile dependency petition, pursuant to subsection (b) of this section, asserting that the minor was at substantial risk of suffering serious physical harm because of his parent's religiously-based refusal to provide him with necessary medical treatment. The minor also had not been taken in custody pursuant to section 305 and had not been adjudicated a dependent child. The court could not dispense with the statutory requirements in order to avoid stigma to the parents. *San Joaquin County Human Services Agency v. Marcus W.*, 185 Cal.App.4th 182, 110 Cal.Rptr.3d 232 (2010).

In re V.M., 191 Cal.App.4th 245, 119 Cal.Rptr.3d 589 (2010), held that a juvenile court erred in assuming subsection (b) dependency jurisdiction over a child who did not want to leave her grandparents to live with a father whom she felt she barely knew, because she had never been abused or neglected by anyone and was not at risk of being abused or neglected by anyone. The father's prior non-exercise of his parental role was not a statutory basis for dependency jurisdiction.

Similarly, *In re X.S.*, 190 Cal.App.4th 1154, 119 Cal.Rptr.3d 153 (2010), held that a juvenile court erred in asserting subsection (b) jurisdiction over a child whose father failed to provide for his child until the child was eight months old absent evidence that the father's failure to provide caused the child to suffer serious physical harm or created a substantial risk that the child would suffer serious physical harm.

Likewise, in a jurisdictional proceeding in which jurisdictional allegations had already been sustained against a physically abusive mother, the juvenile court erred in sustaining jurisdictional allegations against the incarcerated father based on his failure to provide the children with the necessities of life, when the evidence showed that, aside from the abuse, the children were adequately cared for and there was no evidence that the father could not arrange for their care. *In re M.R.*, 7 Cal.App.5th 886, 212 Cal.Rptr.3d 807 (2017).

In re B.T., 193 Cal.App.4th 685, 122 Cal.Rptr.3d 651 (2011), held that a juvenile court erred in asserting subsection (b) dependency over a child on the basis of the relationship between the child's adult mother and the child's father, who was a minor when the relationship began, absent any evidence that the mother was likely to abuse or neglect the child.

In re Daisy H., 192 Cal.App.4th 713, 120 Cal.Rptr.3d 709 (2011), held that a juvenile court erred in asserting dependency jurisdiction on the ground that the children were at risk of physical harm without sufficient evidence to support the finding.

Reversing and remanding a trial court's assumption of dependency jurisdiction, *In re D.M.*, 242 Cal.App.4th 634, 195 Cal.Rptr.3d 402 (2015), held that a mother's repeated spanking of a child on the buttocks with a bare hand or a sandal does not categorically establish "serious physical harm" under subsections (a), (b), or (j), without considering whether the spankings qualified as reasonable parental discipline.

In re Jonathan B., 235 Cal.App.4th 115, 185 Cal.Rptr.3d 308 (2015), reversed a jurisdictional finding against a mother, based on the father's physical abuse of the mother in the children's presence, when the father had not been violent against the mother for the last five years and the mother immediately reported the assault to the police. Subsection (a) was not satisfied because there was no evidence that the mother would knowingly expose the children to the father's violent conduct or that she would fail to protect them. Subsection (b) was not satisfied because there was no evidence that the children suffered serious physical harm.

In re Jesus M., 235 Cal.App.4th 104, 184 Cal.Rptr.3d 920 (2015), held that a father's persistent harassment of the custodial mother in violation of a restraining order did not support dependency jurisdiction, under subsection (b), and a resultant order detaining the children from the father, when the children were not at risk of physical harm. The mother's remedy was to seek sole legal and physical custody in Family Court. Alternatively, dependency jurisdiction might be sought under subsection (c).

In re D.P., 237 Cal.App.4th 911, 188 Cal.Rptr.3d 123 (2015), sustained a trial court finding of subsection (c) dependency, holding that where there was sufficient evidence that a child was at risk of suffering serious emotional harm, it was unnecessary to find that the child showed signs of serious emotional harm.

In re Roxanne B., 234 Cal.App.4th 916, 184 Cal.Rptr.3d 170 (2015), affirmed a jurisdictional finding of dependency with respect to a depressed teenager, because despite the parents' ostensible compliance with the care plan, the parents had failed to provide the child with mental health care in the past and the child remained deeply depressed.

In re Roberto C., 209 Cal.App.4th 1241, 147 Cal.Rptr.3d 505 (2012), held that the trial court did not abuse its discretion when it dismissed a dependency petition on the ground that while the child suffered brain injuries while in the care of a baby sitter, there was no evidence that the parents abused the child or knew that he was being abused.

In re Rebecca C., 228 Cal.App.4th 720, 175 Cal.Rptr.3d 264 (2014), reversed an order declaring a teenage daughter a dependent child based on her mother's drug abuse when there was no evidence that the mother's drug abuse endangered the child's health and safety or put her at risk of harm.

In re Noe F., 213 Cal.App.4th 358, 152 Cal.Rptr.3d 484 (2013), reversed a juvenile court's finding of jurisdiction under this section when the mother, who was incarcerated, identified two suitable placements for the child, either with the maternal or paternal grandmother.

The California Supreme Court granted review, 364 P.3d 411 (2016), to *In re Tyler R.*, 194 Cal.Rptr.3d 543 (2015), which had affirmed a juvenile court finding that a child was a dependent child and removing him from his mother's custody, when the severely disabled mother was unable to care for the child even though her family members were willing to care for the child. *Tyler R.* reasoned that, unlike subsection (g), which provides an exception to dependency jurisdiction when an incarcerated parent arranges for care of a child, subsection (a) makes no such exception.

Invoking subsection (b), *In re J.L.*, 226 Cal.App.4th 1429, 173 Cal.Rptr.3d 86 (2014), held that the juvenile court abused its discretion in dismissing a dependency proceeding when there was substantial and undisputed evidence that the often incarcerated mother left the child with a relative who physically and sexually abused her for two years.

Applying subsection (g), *In re Christopher M.*, 228 Cal.App.4th 1310, 175 Cal.Rptr.3d 837 (2014), reversed a jurisdictional order, finding no evidence that the father could not make arrangements for his son's care.

A person nominated as guardian of the child by a deceased parent is entitled to de facto parent status at the child's dependency proceeding. *In re Vanessa P.*, 38 Cal.App.4th 1763, 45 Cal.Rptr.2d 760 (1995), review denied January 31, 1996.

Applying subsection (b), *In re R.C.*, 210 Cal.App.4th 930, 148 Cal.Rptr.3d 835 (2012), affirmed the juvenile court's finding that it had jurisdiction in a dependency proceeding based on multiple incidents of domestic violence between the parents, which created a substantial risk that the children would suffer serious physical harm.

In re T.V., 217 Cal.App.4th 126, 157 Cal.Rptr.3d 693 (2013), held that evidence that a child's parents engaged in a pattern of domestic violence that was witnessed by their child was sufficient to support a juvenile court order removing the child from parental custody.

Interpreting subsection (b), *In re Heather A.*, 52 Cal.App.4th 183, 60 Cal.Rptr.2d 315 (1997), review denied March 12, 1997, held that the juvenile court properly removed daughters from their father's custody to protect them from possible physical injury and "secondary abuse" incident to the father's physical and verbal abuse of their stepmother. Interpreting subsection (d), *In re Karen R.*, 95 Cal.App.4th 84, 115 Cal.Rptr.2d 18 (2002), held that substantial evidence supported the juvenile court's finding that a child was sexually abused when the child had witnessed his parents beating his sister and had heard his sister report that their father raped her.

See *In re Clay W.*, 88 Cal.Rptr.2d 629 (1999), *review denied and depublished by the Supreme Court on November 23, 1999*, in which the depublished opinion of the court of appeal considers whether substantial evidence supported a finding that a parent had caused a child's injuries.

For discussion of the sufficiency of a petition alleging subsection (b) grounds, see *In re Alysha S.*, 51 Cal.App.4th 393, 58 Cal.Rptr.2d 494 (1996), review denied February 19, 1997. *Alysha S.* allowed the parent to argue for the first time on appeal that the dependency petition failed to state a claim under this section. *In re Shelley J., 68 Cal.App.4th 322, 79 Cal.Rptr.2d 922 (1998), review denied March 9, 1999,* declined to follow *Alysha S.* and held that a challenge to the sufficiency of dependency pleadings may not be raised for the first time on appeal.

The due process rights of the parent require an informal hearing and an opportunity to be heard prior to the appointment of a guardian ad litem for the parent in a § 300 hearing. *In re Sara D., 87 Cal.App.4th 661, 104 Cal.Rptr.2d 909 (2001)* (failure to provide parent with an opportunity to be heard prior to appointment of guardian ad litem for the parent constitutes reversible error).

In re R.T., 3 Cal.5th 622, 399 P.3d 1, 220 Cal.Rptr.3d 770 (2017), held that due process does not require a court to find parental unfitness or neglect before establishing dependency jurisdiction when a child has suffered or there is a substantial risk that a child will suffer serious physical harm or illness "as a result of the failure or inability of his or her parent...to adequately supervise or protect the child...."

Applying subsection (b), *In re Nicholas B., 88 Cal.App.4th 1126, 106 Cal.Rptr.2d 465 (2001)*, holds that a juvenile court may not make a finding of dependency when the dependency petition fails to allege a current substantial risk that the child will suffer serious harm due to the failure or inability of his parent to supervise or protect him. *In re Janet T., 93 Cal.App.4th 377, 113 Cal.Rptr.2d 163 (2001)*, held that the juvenile court erred in finding that there was jurisdiction over three children under this section when neither the dependency petition nor the social worker's reports alleged facts that would support a conclusion that the children were currently at substantial risk of serious harm or illness because of their mother's emotional problems or failure to ensure the children's regular school attendance. *In re S.D., 99 Cal.App.4th 1068, 121 Cal.Rptr.2d 518 (2002), review denied September 11, 2002*, held that the juvenile court erred in finding dependency jurisdiction on the ground that no parent was available to care for the child when there was neither allegation nor evidence that the incarcerated parent could not arrange for care of the child during her incarceration. *S.D.* additionally held that the parent could challenge dependency jurisdiction for the first time on appeal of an order terminating her parental rights because the jurisdictional order was the direct result of ineffective assistance of counsel.

In re K.S., 244 Cal.App.4th 327, 198 Cal.Rptr.3d 143 (2016), held that a juvenile court properly asserted subsection (c) dependency jurisdiction over a child and removed her from the mother's custody when the child was at risk of suffering severe emotional damage because the mother had repeatedly impeded the child's mental health treatment.

In re A.M., 187 Cal.App.4th 1380, 115 Cal.Rptr.3d 552 (2010), review denied, sustained a juvenile court's finding of dependency jurisdiction over a father's four children, under subsection (f), because he neglectfully caused his newborn child's death. In the case of *In re Ethan C., 54 Cal.4th 610, 143 Cal.Rptr.3d 565, 279 P.3d 1052 (2012)*, the California Supreme Court held that subsection (f) allows an initial adjudication of dependency when a child's parent caused the death of another child by failing to strap her in a car safety seat. Subsection (f) merely requires neglect; it does not require criminal neglect.

In re Anthony G., 194 Cal.App.4th 1060, 123 Cal.Rptr.3d 660 (2011), held that a juvenile court erred in finding subsection(g) dependency jurisdiction, which applies when to a child left with any provision of support, when a child's biological father was not providing support, but the child's mother and grandmother were providing adequate support.

Applying subsection (g), *D.M. v. Superior Court, 173 Cal.App.4th 1117, 93 Cal.Rptr.3d 418 (2009), review denied*, held that a child who caused the death of her family's pets, spent two months in juvenile hall awaiting a delinquency proceeding, and was then placed on informal probation for misdemeanor animal cruelty, was properly declared by a juvenile court to be a dependent child after the child's adoptive parents declined reunification services, leaving the child with no home and nowhere to go. The court rejected the parents' claim that their daughter should have been made a delinquent ward of the court in order to spare them the stigma of dependency proceedings.

In re P.A., 155 Cal.App.4th 1197, 66 Cal.Rptr.3d 783 (2007), held that a juvenile court properly declared a father's three children dependent under subsections (b) and (d) when the father had sexually abused his daughter and the father's presence in the home placed his two sons at risk of sexual abuse, even though the father was participating in counseling, the sons had not been abused, and they were unaware that their sister had been abused. The court of appeal reasoned that any younger sibling approaching the age at which a sibling was abused may be found at risk of abuse.

In re R.C., 196 Cal.App.4th 741, 126 Cal.Rptr.3d 418 (2011), held that a trial court erred in concluding that an unwed father's French kissing of the 12-year-old daughter of his son's mother did not constitute subsection (d) sexual abuse of the daughter.

Interpreting subsection (i), *In re D.C., 195 Cal.App.4th 1010, 124 Cal.Rptr.3d 795 (2011), review denied*, holds that a court's finding of dependency jurisdiction on the ground that the parent has subjected a child to an act of cruelty does not require a finding that the parent intended to harm the child.

In re Ashley B., 202 Cal.App.4th 968, 135 Cal.Rptr.3d 659 (2012), sustained a trial court's jurisdictional finding of dependency under subsection (j) based on the parent's abuse or neglect of the child's deceased three-month-old brother without making an express finding that the sibling's death resulted from parental abuse or neglect, when there was sufficient evidence to support an implied finding that the deceased sibling had been subject to neglect or abuse, as those terms are defined in subsections (a) and (b).

Resolving a conflict among the courts of appeal, *In re I.J., 56 Cal.4th 776, 299 P.3d 1254, 156 Cal.Rptr.3d (2013)*, held that a father's severe sexual abuse of one child is sufficient to support dependency jurisdiction over all his children, regardless of gender. Subsequently, the California Supreme Court, 301 P.3d 1175, 157 Cal.Rptr.3d 569 (2013), ordered the court of appeal to vacate its decision in *In re David R., 151 Cal.Rptr.3d 253 (2012)*, and to reconsider the cause is light of *In re I.J.* In *David R.*, the vacated decision of the court of appeal reversed a trial court order declaring a father's two-year-old son dependent, based upon a single incident in which the father molested the child's six-year-old sister, when there was no other evidence that the son was at substantial risk of being sexually abused by the father. On remand to Division One of the Second Appellate District, the court of appeal, in an unpublished opinion, reversed its decision and affirmed the trial's courts declaration that David R. was a dependent of the court because he was at substantial risk of sexual abuse (2013 WL 4630479). Nevertheless, shortly thereafter, the same court reversed a juvenile court order that declared a father's two sons dependents of the court because they were at substantial risk of being molested by the father, solely because the father had sexually molested an unrelated girl while fully clothed. *In re A.A, 164 Cal.Rptr.3d (2013)* (reasoning that sexual molestation of an unrelated girl while fully clothed did not suffice to support a finding that the sons were at substantial risk of sexual abuse). The California Supreme Court denied review and ordered that *A.A.* not be officially published.

In re Marquis H., 212 Cal.App.4th 718, 151 Cal.Rptr.3d 284 (2013), review denied, held that a juvenile court properly assumed jurisdiction over appellant's son, based on the appellant's abuse of the grandchildren who were in his custody, reasoning that subsection (a) does not limit jurisdiction to the particular circumstances described in that section.

In re Ethan G., 145 Cal.App.4th 692, 51 Cal.Rptr.3d 816 (2006), held that it was error, under section 362.1(a)(1)(B), to allow a father who sexually abused a child, found dependent under section 300 (b) and (d), to return to the family home so long as his conduct was monitored at all times. The court reasoned that monitored visitation cannot be effective to protect a child when an offending parent enjoys around-the-clock home contact.

In re E. H., 108 Cal.App.4th 659, 133 Cal.Rptr.2d 740 (2003), review denied July 16, 2003, holds that the trial court erred in dismissing a dependency petition on the mistaken theory that subsection (e) is inapplicable absent an identifiable child abuser, when the parents reasonably should have known that someone in their household was abusing the child.

In re Jasmin C., 106 Cal.App.4th 177, 130 Cal.Rptr.2d 558 (2003), holds that a juvenile court may not order a non-offending custodial parent to attend a parenting class where there is no substantial evidence that either the parent or the children would benefit from it.

In re Iris R., 131 Cal.App.4th 337, 32 Cal.Rptr.3d 146 (2005), holds that an incarcerated mother's absence from a hearing at which her children were declared dependent under subsection (g) did not violate any statutory right to be present at the dependency hearing because the language of Penal Code § 2625(d) does not include determinations made under Welfare and Institutions Code § 300(g), and any due process violation arising from her absence was harmless.

In re Vanessa M., 138 Cal.App.4th 1121, 41 Cal.Rptr.3d 909 (2006), holds that a juvenile court violated a father's due process rights in barring his testimony as an "evidence sanction" for his failure to appear for several court dates during a multi-day jurisdictional hearing, at the conclusion of which the court adjudged the father's daughter a dependent of the court and removed her from her father's custody.

Applying the doctrine of disentitlement, *In re E.M., 204 Cal. App.4th 467, 138 Cal.Rptr.3d 846 (2012)*, held that a mother who willfully left the jurisdiction with her children while a dependency petition was pending forfeited her right to appeal from the orders of the juvenile court.

In re Briana V., 236 Cal.App.4th 297, 186 Cal.Rptr.3d 397 (2015), held that the father's appeal of a jurisdictional order of dependency against him was non-justiciable when the jurisdictional finding against the mother was not being appealed, because the appeal would not affect the children's status as dependents nor would the finding against him have consequences for the father beyond the dependency proceedings.

Research References

Forms

California Transactions Forms--Family Law § 6:10, Initiating Proceeding Under Fam. Code, §§ 7800 et seq.
California Transactions Forms--Family Law § 6:97, Kinship Adoption.
California Transactions Forms--Family Law § 6:98, Form Drafting Considerations.
California Transactions Forms--Family Law § 6:100, Postadoption Contact Agreement [Form Adopt-310].
California Transactions Forms--Family Law § 6:139, Overview Of Intercountry Adoption.
West's California Code Forms, Family § 7840, Comment Overview--Freedom from Parental Control.
West's California Judicial Council Forms JV-100, Juvenile Dependency Petition (Version One) (Welfare and Institutions Code, S300 et seq.).
West's California Judicial Council Forms JV-110, Juvenile Dependency Petition (Version Two) (Welfare and Institutions Code, S300 et seq.).
West's California Judicial Council Forms JV-120, Serious Physical Harm (S300(a)).
West's California Judicial Council Forms JV-121, Failure to Protect (S300(B)).
West's California Judicial Council Forms JV-122, Serious Emotional Damage (S300(C)).
West's California Judicial Council Forms JV-123, Sexual Abuse (S300(D)).
West's California Judicial Council Forms JV-124, Severe Physical Abuse (S300(E)).
West's California Judicial Council Forms JV-125, Caused Another Child's Death Through Abuse or Neglect (S300(F)).
West's California Judicial Council Forms JV-126, No Provision for Support (S300(G)).
West's California Judicial Council Forms JV-127, Freed for Adoption (S300(H)).
West's California Judicial Council Forms JV-128, Cruelty (S300(i)).
West's California Judicial Council Forms JV-129, Abuse Of Sibling (S300(i)).
West's California Judicial Council Forms JV-150, Supplemental Petition for More Restrictive Placement (Attachment)(Welfare and Institutions Code, S387).
West's California Judicial Council Forms JV-550, Juvenile Court Transfer Orders.
West's California Judicial Council Forms JV-101(A), Additional Children Attachment (Juvenile Dependency Petition).

Treatises and Practice Aids

Witkin, California Summary 10th Parent and Child § 12, Parental or Marital Rights Of Prisoners.
Witkin, California Summary 10th Parent and Child § 48, Where No Presumption Applies.
Witkin, California Summary 10th Parent and Child § 63, in General.
Witkin, California Summary 10th Parent and Child § 80, Interstate Placement Of Children for Adoption.
Witkin, California Summary 10th Parent and Child § 109, in General.
Witkin, California Summary 10th Parent and Child § 113, Consideration Of Relatives and Foster Parents.
Witkin, California Summary 10th Parent and Child § 137, in General.
Witkin, California Summary 10th Parent and Child § 138, Powers and Duties Of Licensed Adoption Agencies.
Witkin, California Summary 10th Parent and Child § 171, Illustrations.
Witkin, California Summary 10th Parent and Child § 175, in General.
Witkin, California Summary 10th Parent and Child § 267, Jurisdiction and Venue.
Witkin, California Summary 10th Parent and Child § 274, Counsel for Parent.
Witkin, California Summary 10th Parent and Child § 276, Report.
Witkin, California Summary 10th Parent and Child § 300, Family Relationships.
Witkin, California Summary 10th Parent and Child § 311, Other Proceedings Stayed.
Witkin, California Summary 10th Parent and Child § 316, Statutory Ground.
Witkin, California Summary 10th Parent and Child § 325, Statutory Ground.
Witkin, California Summary 10th Parent and Child § 339, Effective Assistance Of Counsel.
Witkin, California Summary 10th Parent and Child § 353, Case Law.
Witkin, California Summary 10th Parent and Child § 355, Review on Appeal.
Witkin, California Summary 10th Parent and Child § 367, in General.
Witkin, California Summary 10th Parent and Child § 368, Where Issues Are Identical.
Witkin, California Summary 10th Parent and Child § 440, Original Statute and Revision.
Witkin, California Summary 10th Parent and Child § 447, Department and Staff.
Witkin, California Summary 10th Parent and Child § 449, Nature and Scope Of Jurisdiction: Three Classes Of Minors.

Witkin, California Summary 10th Parent and Child § 450, Dual Bases Of Jurisdiction.
Witkin, California Summary 10th Parent and Child § 451, in General.
Witkin, California Summary 10th Parent and Child § 452, Jurisdiction Retained After Majority.
Witkin, California Summary 10th Parent and Child § 456, Proper Court.
Witkin, California Summary 10th Parent and Child § 458, Conditions for Transfer.
Witkin, California Summary 10th Parent and Child § 462, Appeal from Transfer Order.
Witkin, California Summary 10th Parent and Child § 485, Reports.
Witkin, California Summary 10th Parent and Child § 494, Records Of Dependent Children.
Witkin, California Summary 10th Parent and Child § 500, Disclosure on Petition.
Witkin, California Summary 10th Parent and Child § 507, Sealed Records.
Witkin, California Summary 10th Parent and Child § 508, Unsealed Records.
Witkin, California Summary 10th Parent and Child § 509, No Third-Party Action for Redaction.
Witkin, California Summary 10th Parent and Child § 517, Collection Procedure.
Witkin, California Summary 10th Parent and Child § 520, Jurisdiction.
Witkin, California Summary 10th Parent and Child § 522, Nature and Scope Of Indian Child Welfare Act.
Witkin, California Summary 10th Parent and Child § 524, Jurisdiction.
Witkin, California Summary 10th Parent and Child § 526, Determination Of Indian Status.
Witkin, California Summary 10th Parent and Child § 538, Governing Law.
Witkin, California Summary 10th Parent and Child § 539, Serious Physical Harm.
Witkin, California Summary 10th Parent and Child § 540, in General.
Witkin, California Summary 10th Parent and Child § 541, Mental Illness and Substance Abuse.
Witkin, California Summary 10th Parent and Child § 542, Spiritual Treatment.
Witkin, California Summary 10th Parent and Child § 543, Serious Emotional Damage.
Witkin, California Summary 10th Parent and Child § 544, in General.
Witkin, California Summary 10th Parent and Child § 545, Abuse Of Sibling.
Witkin, California Summary 10th Parent and Child § 546, Severe Physical Abuse.
Witkin, California Summary 10th Parent and Child § 547, Causing Death Of Another Child.
Witkin, California Summary 10th Parent and Child § 548, Child Left Without Care or Support.
Witkin, California Summary 10th Parent and Child § 549, Child Freed for Adoption.
Witkin, California Summary 10th Parent and Child § 550, Child Cruelly Treated.
Witkin, California Summary 10th Parent and Child § 551, Sibling Abused or Neglected.
Witkin, California Summary 10th Parent and Child § 552, in General.
Witkin, California Summary 10th Parent and Child § 555, Investigation, Detention, and Release.
Witkin, California Summary 10th Parent and Child § 559, Medical Care.
Witkin, California Summary 10th Parent and Child § 562, Application to Social Worker.
Witkin, California Summary 10th Parent and Child § 564, in General.
Witkin, California Summary 10th Parent and Child § 565, Form and Content.
Witkin, California Summary 10th Parent and Child § 566, Notices, Citations, Warrants, and Subpenas.
Witkin, California Summary 10th Parent and Child § 567, Statutory Rights.
Witkin, California Summary 10th Parent and Child § 569, Protection Of Interests and Rights.
Witkin, California Summary 10th Parent and Child § 570, in General.
Witkin, California Summary 10th Parent and Child § 572, Appointment Of Guardian Ad Litem or Child Advocate.
Witkin, California Summary 10th Parent and Child § 576, in General.
Witkin, California Summary 10th Parent and Child § 577, Hearing.
Witkin, California Summary 10th Parent and Child § 579, in General.
Witkin, California Summary 10th Parent and Child § 583, Alleged Father.
Witkin, California Summary 10th Parent and Child § 585, in General.
Witkin, California Summary 10th Parent and Child § 587, Persons Entitled to be Present.
Witkin, California Summary 10th Parent and Child § 588, Persons Who May be Admitted.
Witkin, California Summary 10th Parent and Child § 592, Participation by District Attorney.
Witkin, California Summary 10th Parent and Child § 596, Disposition Where Burden Of Proof Not Met.
Witkin, California Summary 10th Parent and Child § 598, in General.
Witkin, California Summary 10th Parent and Child § 603, Identification Of Presumed or Alleged Fathers.
Witkin, California Summary 10th Parent and Child § 604, in General.
Witkin, California Summary 10th Parent and Child § 605, Rights Of Child, Parent, and Guardian.
Witkin, California Summary 10th Parent and Child § 607, Findings and Orders.
Witkin, California Summary 10th Parent and Child § 608, Nature and Purpose Of Hearing.
Witkin, California Summary 10th Parent and Child § 612, Discovery.
Witkin, California Summary 10th Parent and Child § 613, Commencement Of Hearing.
Witkin, California Summary 10th Parent and Child § 614, Determination by Admission, No Contest, or Submission.
Witkin, California Summary 10th Parent and Child § 615, in General.
Witkin, California Summary 10th Parent and Child § 616, Presumptions from Parental Misconduct.
Witkin, California Summary 10th Parent and Child § 617, in General.
Witkin, California Summary 10th Parent and Child § 618, Admissibility and Weight Of Social Study.
Witkin, California Summary 10th Parent and Child § 621, Immunity Of Witnesses.
Witkin, California Summary 10th Parent and Child § 622, Findings and Order.
Witkin, California Summary 10th Parent and Child § 623, Continuance Pending Disposition Hearing.
Witkin, California Summary 10th Parent and Child § 624, in General.
Witkin, California Summary 10th Parent and Child § 625, Preparation Of Social Study.
Witkin, California Summary 10th Parent and Child § 627, in General.

Witkin, California Summary 10th Parent and Child § 628, Legal Guardianship.
Witkin, California Summary 10th Parent and Child § 630, Bases for Removal.
Witkin, California Summary 10th Parent and Child § 637, Priority Right Of Noncustodial Parent.
Witkin, California Summary 10th Parent and Child § 642, in General.
Witkin, California Summary 10th Parent and Child § 643, Duration Of Services.
Witkin, California Summary 10th Parent and Child § 648, Parent or Guardian Absent, Unwilling, or Incapable.
Witkin, California Summary 10th Parent and Child § 650, Abuse, Neglect, or Abduction Of Child.
Witkin, California Summary 10th Parent and Child § 654, Power to Modify or Correct.
Witkin, California Summary 10th Parent and Child § 659, Sufficiency Of Evidence.
Witkin, California Summary 10th Parent and Child § 662, Nature and Purpose.
Witkin, California Summary 10th Parent and Child § 668, Subsequent Petition.
Witkin, California Summary 10th Parent and Child § 672, Child in Custody Of Parent or Guardian.
Witkin, California Summary 10th Parent and Child § 677, Scheduling Selection and Implementation Hearing.
Witkin, California Summary 10th Parent and Child § 691, Constitutionality Of Termination Procedure.
Witkin, California Summary 10th Parent and Child § 696, Continuing Jurisdiction.
Witkin, California Summary 10th Parent and Child § 700, Right to Appeal.
Witkin, California Summary 10th Parent and Child § 702, Appeal from Order Of Dismissal.
Witkin, California Summary 10th Parent and Child § 705, in General.
Witkin, California Summary 10th Parent and Child § 706, Waiver Of Appellate Review.
Witkin, California Summary 10th Parent and Child § 708, Counsel on Appeal.
Witkin, California Summary 10th Parent and Child § 709, in General.
Witkin, California Summary 10th Parent and Child § 712, Notice Of Appeal.
Witkin, California Summary 10th Parent and Child § 730, Truancy.
Witkin, California Summary 10th Parent and Child § 732, Criminal Intent and Capacity.
Witkin, California Summary 10th Parent and Child § 734, Procedure on Insanity Plea.
Witkin, California Summary 10th Parent and Child § 749, Segregation Of Classes Of Minors.
Witkin, California Summary 10th Parent and Child § 750, Segregation Of Minors and Adults.
Witkin, California Summary 10th Parent and Child § 763, Investigation, Release, and Conditions.
Witkin, California Summary 10th Parent and Child § 782, Statutory Rights.
Witkin, California Summary 10th Parent and Child § 821, Probation Officer's Report and Recommendation.
Witkin, California Summary 10th Parent and Child § 827, in General.
Witkin, California Summary 10th Parent and Child § 834, Orders.
Witkin, California Summary 10th Parent and Child § 898, Court Supervision Of Child.
Witkin, California Summary 10th Parent and Child § 452E, (New) Termination Of Jurisdiction Over Minor.
Witkin, California Summary 10th Parent and Child § 699A, (New) in General.
Witkin, California Summary 10th Parent and Child § 715A, (New) Abandoning Appeal.
Witkin, California Summary 10th Parent and Child § 899A, (New) Hearing Before Termination Of Jurisdiction.
Witkin, California Summary 10th Wills and Probate § 916, in General.
Witkin, California Summary 10th Wills and Probate § 920, in General.
Witkin, California Summary 10th Wills and Probate § 922, Investigation and Report.

§ 300.1. Dependent child freed for adoption; family reunification services

Notwithstanding subdivision (e) of Section 361 and Section 16507, family reunification services shall not be provided to a child adjudged a dependent pursuant to subdivision (h) of Section 300. *(Added by Stats.1987, c. 1485, § 6, operative Jan. 1, 1989. Amended by Stats.1998, c. 1054 (A.B.1091), § 3.)*

Research References

Treatises and Practice Aids

Witkin, California Summary 10th Parent and Child § 642, in General.

§ 300.2. Purpose of chapter

Notwithstanding any other provision of law, the purpose of the provisions of this chapter relating to dependent children is to provide maximum safety and protection for children who are currently being physically, sexually, or emotionally abused, being neglected, or being exploited, and to ensure the safety, protection, and physical and emotional well-being of children who are at risk of that harm. This safety, protection, and physical and emotional well-being may include provision of a full array of social and health services to help the child and family and to prevent reabuse of children. The focus shall be on the preservation of the family as well as the safety, protection, and physical and emotional well-being of the child. The provision of a home environment free from the negative effects of substance abuse is a necessary condition for the safety, protection and physical and emotional well-being of the child. Successful participation in a treatment program for substance abuse may be considered in evaluating the home environment. In addition, the provisions of this chapter ensuring the confidentiality of proceedings and records are intended to protect the privacy rights of the child. *(Added by Stats.1996, c. 1084 (S.B.1516), § 2. Amended by Stats.1999, c. 346 (S.B.518), § 2.)*

Commentary

Interpreting this section's emphasis on "the preservation of the family as well as the safety... of the child" and § 366.22(a), *Jennifer A. v. Superior Court, 117 Cal.App.4th 1322, 12 Cal.Rptr.3d 572 (2004)*, held that the juvenile court's finding, at an 18–month review hearing, that return to the mother would create a substantial risk of detriment to the physical or emotional well-being of children who had been removed from their mother's home because she once left them alone while she was working, was not supported by evidence of some drug test failures when there was neither evidence that the mother had a clinically significant substance abuse problem nor that her marijuana and alcohol use affected her parenting judgment and skills.

Relying on the language of this section, *In re Alexis E., 171 Cal.App.4th 438, 90 Cal.Rptr.3d 44 (2009)*, held that although a father's use of medical marijuana alone would not support a finding of dependency jurisdiction over the father's children, a juvenile court properly found dependency jurisdiction when the father had a history of marijuana use predating his physician's recommendation that he use medical marijuana, the children were exposed to marijuana smoke in the father's home, and the use of marijuana had a negative effect on his demeanor toward the children. Thus the juvenile court did not err in ordering drug counseling and testing.

Research References

Treatises and Practice Aids

Witkin, California Summary 10th Parent and Child § 452, Jurisdiction Retained After Majority.
Witkin, California Summary 10th Parent and Child § 519, Nature Of Dependency Proceedings.
Witkin, California Summary 10th Parent and Child § 538, Governing Law.
Witkin, California Summary 10th Parent and Child § 540, in General.
Witkin, California Summary 10th Torts § 247, Illustrations Finding No Liability.

§ 300.3. Child or nonminor whose jurisdiction is modified pursuant to specified provisions and placed in foster care; supervision

(a) Notwithstanding Section 215 or 272, or any other provision of law, a child or nonminor whose jurisdiction is modified pursuant to subdivision (b) of Section 607.2 or subdivision (i) of Section 727.2 and who is placed in foster care may be supervised by the probation department of the county in which the court with jurisdiction over the dependent is located, if the county protocol in that county requires it. In those counties, all case management, case plan review, and reporting functions as described in Sections 671 and 675 of Title 42 of the United States Code and contained in this article shall be performed by the probation officer for these dependents.

(b) This section shall become operative on January 1, 2012. *(Added by Stats.2010, c. 559 (A.B.12), § 7, operative Jan. 1, 2012. Amended by Stats.2011, c. 459 (A.B.212), § 6, eff. Oct. 4, 2011, operative Jan. 1, 2012.)*

Research References

Treatises and Practice Aids

Witkin, California Summary 10th Parent and Child § 450, Dual Bases Of Jurisdiction.

§ 300.5. Medical care; treatment by spiritual means

In any case in which a child is alleged to come within the provisions of Section 300 on the basis that he or she is in need of medical care, the court, in making that finding, shall give consideration to any treatment being provided to the child by spiritual means through prayer alone in accordance with the tenets and practices of a recognized church or religious denomination by an accredited practitioner thereof. *(Added by Stats.1978, c. 539, p. 1701, § 2. Amended by Stats.1998, c. 1054 (A.B.1091), § 4.)*

Research References

Treatises and Practice Aids

Witkin, California Summary 10th Parent and Child § 542, Spiritual Treatment.

§ 301. Program of supervision

(a) In any case in which a social worker, after investigation of an application for petition or other investigation he or she is authorized to make, determines that a child is within the jurisdiction of the juvenile court or will probably soon be within that jurisdiction, the social worker may, in lieu of filing a petition or subsequent to dismissal of a petition already filed, and with consent of the child's parent or guardian, undertake a program of supervision of the child. If a program of supervision is undertaken, the social worker shall attempt to ameliorate the situation that brings the child within, or creates the probability that the child will be within, the jurisdiction of Section 300 by providing or arranging to contract for all appropriate child welfare services pursuant to Sections 16506 and 16507.3, within the time periods specified in those sections. No further child welfare services shall be provided subsequent to these time limits. If the family has refused to cooperate with the services being provided, the social worker may file a petition with the juvenile court pursuant to Section 332. Nothing in this section shall be construed to prevent the social worker from filing a petition pursuant to Section 332 when otherwise authorized by law.

(b) The program of supervision of the child undertaken pursuant to this section may call for the child to obtain care and treatment for the misuse of, or addiction to, controlled substances from a county mental health service or other appropriate community agency.

(c) If the parent is a dependent, nonminor dependent, or ward of the juvenile court at the time that a social worker seeks to undertake a program of supervision pursuant to subdivision (a), including a voluntary family reunification program or a voluntary family maintenance program, and if counsel has been appointed for the parent pursuant to subdivision (c) of Section 317, the program of supervision shall not be undertaken until the parent has consulted with his or her counsel. In cases when a ward is not represented by counsel appointed in a dependency proceeding pursuant to subdivision (c) of Section 317, he or she shall be given the opportunity to confer with counsel appointed in the wardship proceeding pursuant to Section 634 or by counsel retained to represent the ward in the wardship proceeding. *(Formerly § 330, added by Stats.1976, c. 1068, p. 4766, § 8. Amended by Stats.1982, c. 978, § 13, eff. Sept. 13, 1982, operative July 1, 1982; Stats.1984, c. 1618, § 2; Stats.1984, c. 1635, § 94.5. Renumbered § 301 and amended by Stats.1991, c. 1203 (S.B.125), § 4. Amended by Stats.1998, c. 1054 (A.B.1091), § 5; Stats.2008, c. 132 (A.B.2483), § 1; Stats.2017, c. 666 (A.B.1371), § 1, eff. Jan. 1, 2018.)*

Research References

Treatises and Practice Aids

Witkin, California Summary 10th Parent and Child § 343, Conduct Of Hearing.
Witkin, California Summary 10th Parent and Child § 494, Records Of Dependent Children.
Witkin, California Summary 10th Parent and Child § 510, in General.
Witkin, California Summary 10th Parent and Child § 560, Intake Program.
Witkin, California Summary 10th Parent and Child § 563, Program Of Supervision.
Witkin, California Summary 10th Parent and Child § 627, in General.

Witkin, California Summary 10th Parent and Child § 698, Other Procedures.

§ 302. Assumption of jurisdiction regardless of custody by one or both parents; notice to parents; report of social worker; custodial rights

(a) A juvenile court may assume jurisdiction over a child described in Section 300 regardless of whether the child was in the physical custody of both parents or was in the sole legal or physical custody of only one parent at the time that the events or conditions occurred that brought the child within the jurisdiction of the court.

(b) Unless their parental rights have been terminated, both parents shall be notified of all proceedings involving the child. In any case where the social worker is required to provide a parent or guardian with notice of a proceeding at which the social worker intends to present a report, the social worker shall also provide both parents, whether custodial or noncustodial, or any guardian, or the counsel for the parent or guardian a copy of the report prior to the hearing, * * * by personal service, by first-class mail, or by electronic service pursuant to Section 212.5. The social worker shall not charge any fee for providing a copy of a report required by this subdivision. The social worker shall keep confidential the address of any parent who is known to be the victim of domestic violence.

(c) When a child is adjudged a dependent of the juvenile court, any issues regarding custodial rights between his or her parents shall be determined solely by the juvenile court, as specified in Sections 304, 361.2, and 362.4, so long as the child remains a dependent of the juvenile court.

(d) Any custody or visitation order issued by the juvenile court at the time the juvenile court terminates its jurisdiction pursuant to Section 362.4 regarding a child who has been previously adjudged to be a dependent child of the juvenile court shall be a final judgment and shall remain in effect after that jurisdiction is terminated. The order shall not be modified in a proceeding or action described in Section 3021 of the Family Code unless the court finds that there has been a significant change of circumstances since the juvenile court issued the order and modification of the order is in the best interests of the child. *(Formerly § 301, added by Stats.1987, c. 1485, § 7.5. Renumbered § 302 and amended by Stats. 1991, c. 1203 (S.B.1125), § 3. Amended by Stats.1996, c. 1139 (A.B.2647), § 5; Stats.1998, c. 1054 (A.B.1091), § 6; Stats. 2000, c. 921 (A.B.2464), § 1; Stats.2001, c. 854 (S.B.205), § 69; Stats.2017, c. 319 (A.B.976), § 126, eff. Jan. 1, 2018.)*

Commentary

Applying the final sentence of subsection (d) of this section, *Heidi S. v. David H., 1 Cal App.5th 1150, 205 Cal.Rptr.3d 335 (2016)*, held that a trial court did not abuse its discretion when it ruled that a mother's successful treatment of substance abuse constituted a change of circumstances warranting an incremental increase in her visitation rights, but not a change in custodial rights.

Applying subsection (d), *In re Marriage of David and Martha M., 140 Cal.App.4th 96, 44 Cal.Rptr.3d 388 (2006)*, holds that a family court erred in applying only the "best interests of the child" standard, rather than also applying the "changed circumstances" rule prescribed by subsection (d) in ordering modification of a juvenile court's exit order regarding child custody and visitation.

In re Cole Y., 233 Cal.App.4th 1444, 183 Cal.Rptr.3d 308 (2015), applying subsection (d), holds that a juvenile court does not have authority to condition a family court's modification of the juvenile court's exit order upon the father's completion of drug and parenting programs, because the decision to modify an exit order is within the province of the family court and then only upon application of the "significant change of circumstances" and "best interests of the child" standards.

Research References

Forms

California Transactions Forms--Family Law § 6:10, Initiating Proceeding Under Fam. Code, §§ 7800 et seq.

West's California Judicial Council Forms JV-200, Custody Order - Juvenile - Final Judgment.

West's California Judicial Council Forms JV-205, Visitation Order--Juvenile.

West's California Judicial Council Forms JV-206, Reasons for No or Supervised Visitation--Juvenile.

Treatises and Practice Aids

Witkin, California Summary 10th Parent and Child § 277, Investigation Of Child Sexual Abuse Allegations.

Witkin, California Summary 10th Parent and Child § 371, Modification Of Order.

Witkin, California Summary 10th Parent and Child § 494, Records Of Dependent Children.

Witkin, California Summary 10th Parent and Child § 520, Jurisdiction.

Witkin, California Summary 10th Parent and Child § 576, in General.

§ 303. Retention of jurisdiction

(a) The court may retain jurisdiction over any person who is found to be a ward or a dependent child of the juvenile court until the ward or dependent child attains * * * 21 years of age.

(b) * * * The court shall have within its jurisdiction any nonminor dependent, as defined in subdivision (v) of Section 11400. The court may terminate its dependency, delinquency, or transition jurisdiction over the nonminor dependent between the time the nonminor reaches the age of majority and 21 years of age. If the court terminates dependency, delinquency, or transition jurisdiction, the nonminor dependent shall remain under the general jurisdiction of the court in order to allow for a petition under subdivision (e) of Section 388.

(c) * * * A nonminor who has not yet attained 21 years of age and who exited foster care at or after the age of majority, may petition the court pursuant to subdivision (e) of Section 388 to resume dependency jurisdiction over himself or herself or to assume transition jurisdiction over himself or herself pursuant to Section 450.

(d)(1) Nothing in this code, including, but not limited to, Sections 340, 366.27, and 369.5, shall be construed to provide legal custody of a person who has attained 18 years of age to the county welfare or probation department or to otherwise abrogate any other rights that a person who has attained 18 years of age may have as an adult under California law. A nonminor dependent shall retain all of his or her legal decisionmaking authority as an adult. The nonminor shall enter into a mutual agreement for placement, as described in subdivision (u) of Section 11400, unless the nonminor dependent is incapable of making an informed agreement, or a voluntary reentry agreement, as described in subdivision (z) of Section 11400, for placement and care in which the nonminor consents to placement and care in a setting supervised by, and under the responsibility of, the county child welfare services department, the county probation department, or Indian tribe, tribal organization, or consortium of tribes that entered into an agreement pursuant to Section 10553.1.

(2) A nonminor dependent who remains under delinquency jurisdiction in order to complete his or her rehabilitative goals and is under a foster care placement order is not required to complete the mutual agreement as described in subdivision (u) of Section 11400. His or her adult decision-making authority may be limited by and subject to the care, supervision, custody, conduct, and maintenance orders as described in Section 727.

(e) Unless otherwise specified, the rights of a dependent child and the responsibilities of the county welfare or probation department, or tribe, and other entities, toward the child and family, shall also apply to nonminor dependents.

(f) The court shall assume transition jurisdiction pursuant to Section 450 over a person notwithstanding a court order vacating the underlying adjudication pursuant to Section 236.14 of the Penal Code. On or before January 1, 2019, the Judicial Council shall amend and adopt rules of court and develop appropriate forms to implement this subdivision. *(Formerly § 301, added by Stats.1976, c. 1068, p. 4759, § 6. Renumbered § 303 and amended by Stats.1987, c. 1485, § 7. Amended by Stats.2010, c. 559 (A.B.12), § 8; Stats.2011, c. 459 (A.B.212), § 7, eff. Oct. 4, 2011; Stats.2012, c. 846 (A.B.1712), § 12; Stats.2017, c. 707 (A.B.604), § 1, eff. Jan. 1, 2018.)*

Commentary

Invoking this section, *In re D.R. 155 Cal.App.4th 480, 66 Cal. Rptr.3d 151 (2007)*, held that a juvenile court erred in finding that it could not reinstate dependency jurisdiction over a mentally disabled child with a permanent plan of legal guardianship once the child reached the age of 18. Under this section, the court has discretion to retain dependency jurisdiction until a child reaches the age of 21.

Under this Section the juvenile court may retain jurisdiction over a dependent child who has attained the age of majority (18), but retention of jurisdiction must be based on foreseeable harm to the child's welfare. *In re Robert L., 68 Cal.App.4th 789, 80 Cal.Rptr.2d 578 (1998).* Finding that the children were not at risk of harm, *Robert L.* held that the juvenile court erred in retaining jurisdiction past the age of majority in order to continue foster care payments for the children so that they could attend college.

In re David B., 12 Cal.App.5th 633, 219 Cal.Rptr.3d 108 (2017), held that retention of jurisdiction under this section is derivative of dependency jurisdiction assumed by a court before a child reaches the age of 18. Thus, where a court dismissed a dependency petition filed just before a child reached 18 and the dismissal was appealed after the child's eighteenth birthday, the appeal was moot.

Research References

Forms

West's California Judicial Council Forms JV-466, Request to Return to Juvenile Court Jurisdiction and Foster Care.

West's California Judicial Council Forms JV-468, Confidential Information--Request to Return to Juvenile Court Jurisdiction and Foster Care.

West's California Judicial Council Forms JV-464-INFO, How to Ask to Return to Juvenile Court Jurisdiction and Foster Care.

Treatises and Practice Aids

Witkin, California Summary 10th Parent and Child § 452, Jurisdiction Retained After Majority.

Witkin, California Summary 10th Parent and Child § 458, Conditions for Transfer.

Witkin, California Summary 10th Parent and Child § 521, Termination Of Jurisdiction.

Witkin, California Summary 10th Parent and Child § 662, Nature and Purpose.

Witkin, California Summary 10th Parent and Child § 452F, (New) Termination Of Jurisdiction Over Nonminor.

Witkin, California Summary 10th Parent and Child § 669A, (New) Review Hearings Just Before and After Minor Attains Age 18.

Witkin, California Summary 10th Parent and Child § 699A, (New) in General.

Witkin, California Summary 10th Parent and Child § 699B, (New) Status Review Hearings.

Witkin, California Summary 10th Parent and Child § 899A, (New) Hearing Before Termination Of Jurisdiction.

§ 304. Custody of child; jurisdiction; review of records; restraining order

After a petition has been filed pursuant to Section 311, and until the time that the petition is dismissed or dependency is terminated, no other division of any superior court may hear proceedings pursuant to Part 2 (commencing with Section 3020) of Division 8 of the Family Code regarding the custody of the child or proceedings under Part 2 (commencing with Section 1500) of Division 4 of the Probate Code, except as otherwise authorized in this code, regarding the establishment of a guardianship for the child. While the child is under the jurisdiction of the juvenile court all issues regarding his or her custody shall be heard by the juvenile court. In deciding issues between the parents or between a parent and a guardian regarding custody of a child who has been adjudicated a dependent of the juvenile court, the juvenile court may review any records that would be available to the domestic relations division of a superior court hearing that matter. The juvenile court, on its own motion, may issue an order as provided for in Section 213.5, or as described in Section 6218 of the Family Code. The Judicial Council shall adopt forms for these restraining orders. These form orders shall not be confidential and shall be enforceable in the same manner as any other order issued pursuant to Division 10 (commencing with Section 6200) of the Family Code.

This section shall not be construed to divest the domestic relations division of a superior court from hearing any issues regarding the custody of a child when that child is no longer a dependent of the juvenile court. *(Added by Stats.1987, c. 1485, § 8. Amended by Stats.1989, c. 137, § 1; Stats.1992, c. 163 (A.B.2641), § 135, operative Jan. 1, 1994; Stats.1993, c. 219 (A.B.1500), § 225.5; Stats.1996, c. 1138 (A.B.2154), § 2; Stats.1996, c. 1139 (A.B.2647), § 6; Stats.1998, c. 1054 (A.B.1091), § 7.)*

Law Revision Commission Comments

1992 Amendment [Revised Comment]

Section 304 is amended to substitute references to the Family Code provisions that replaced the former Civil Code provisions. The reference to Family Code Section 6218 is broader than the former reference. Section 6218 includes an order restraining specific acts of abuse, excluding a party from a dwelling, and restraining additional behavior necessary to enforce the first two orders. The former reference did not include the order restraining additional behavior. [23 Cal.L.Rev.Comm. Reports 1 (1993)].

Research References

Forms

West's California Judicial Council Forms JV-200, Custody Order - Juvenile - Final Judgment.

West's California Judicial Council Forms JV-206, Reasons for No or Supervised Visitation--Juvenile.

West's California Judicial Council Forms JV-245, Request for Restraining Order--Juvenile.

West's California Judicial Council Forms JV-250, Notice Of Hearing and Temporary Restraining Order--Juvenile.

West's California Judicial Council Forms JV-255, Restraining Order - Juvenile Order After Hearing.

Treatises and Practice Aids

Witkin, California Summary 10th Husband and Wife § 387, Electronic Transmission and Recording Of Data.

Witkin, California Summary 10th Parent and Child § 369, Dependency Proceeding Pending.

Witkin, California Summary 10th Parent and Child § 450, Dual Bases Of Jurisdiction.

Witkin, California Summary 10th Parent and Child § 451, in General.

Witkin, California Summary 10th Parent and Child § 453, Jurisdiction Over Adults.

Witkin, California Summary 10th Parent and Child § 455, Concurrent and Exclusive Jurisdiction.

Witkin, California Summary 10th Parent and Child § 520, Jurisdiction.

Witkin, California Summary 10th Parent and Child § 628, Legal Guardianship.

Witkin, California Summary 10th Wills and Probate § 922, Investigation and Report.

Witkin, California Summary 10th Wills and Probate § 979, Jurisdiction.

§ 304.7. Continuing education and training requirements for judges

(a) The Judicial Council shall develop and implement standards for the education and training of all judges who conduct hearings pursuant to Section 300. The training shall include, but not be limited to, all of the following:

(1) A component relating to Section 300 proceedings for newly appointed or elected judges and an annual training session in Section 300 proceedings.

(2) Cultural competency and sensitivity relating to, and best practices for, providing adequate care to lesbian, gay, bisexual, and transgender youth.

(3) The information described in subdivision (d) of Section 16501.4.

(4) The information described in subdivision (i) of Section 16521.5.

(b) A commissioner or referee who is assigned to conduct hearings held pursuant to Section 300 shall meet the minimum standards for education and training established pursuant to subdivision (a), by July 31, 1998.

(c) The Judicial Council shall submit an annual report to the Legislature on compliance by judges, commissioners, and referees with the education and training standards described in subdivisions (a) and (b). *(Added by Stats.1996, c. 945 (S.B.1811), § 1. Amended by Stats.2013, c. 300 (A.B.868), § 3; Stats.2014, c. 71 (S.B.1304), § 180, eff. Jan. 1, 2015; Stats.2015, c. 534 (S.B.238), § 3, eff. Jan. 1, 2016; Stats.2017, c. 24 (S.B.89), § 10, eff. June 27, 2017.)*

Research References

Treatises and Practice Aids

Witkin, California Summary 10th Parent and Child § 447, Department and Staff.

ARTICLE 7. DEPENDENT CHILDREN—TEMPORARY CUSTODY AND DETENTION

Section

§ 305. Conditions allowing temporary custody without warrant

Any peace officer may, without a warrant, take into temporary custody a minor:

(a) When the officer has reasonable cause for believing that the minor is a person described in Section 300, and, in addition, that the minor has an immediate need for medical care, or the minor is in immediate danger of physical or sexual abuse, or the physical environment or the fact that the child is left unattended poses an immediate threat to the child's health or safety. In cases in which the child is left unattended, the peace officer shall first attempt to contact the child's parent or guardian to determine if the parent or guardian is able to assume custody of the child. If the parent or guardian cannot be contacted, the peace officer shall notify a social worker in the county welfare department to assume custody of the child.

(b) Who is in a hospital and release of the minor to a parent poses an immediate danger to the child's health or safety.

(c) Who is a dependent child of the juvenile court, or concerning whom an order has been made under Section 319, when the officer has reasonable cause for believing that the minor has violated an order of the juvenile court or has left any placement ordered by the juvenile court.

(d) Who is found in any street or public place suffering from any sickness or injury which requires care, medical treatment, hospitalization, or other remedial care. *(Added by Stats.1987, c. 1485, § 11. Amended by Stats.1988, c. 701, § 2, eff. Aug. 29, 1988; Stats.1988, c. 1075, § 1.)*

Research References

Treatises and Practice Aids

Witkin, California Summary 10th Parent and Child § 494, Records Of Dependent Children.

Witkin, California Summary 10th Parent and Child § 552, in General.

Witkin, California Summary 10th Parent and Child § 553, Disposition by Peace Officer.

Witkin, California Summary 10th Parent and Child § 559, Medical Care.

Witkin, California Summary 10th Parent and Child § 598, in General.

Witkin, California Summary 10th Parent and Child § 607, Findings and Orders.

Witkin, California Summary 10th Parent and Child § 643, Duration Of Services.

Witkin, California Summary 10th Parent and Child § 657, Filing, Setting for Hearing, and Notice.

Witkin, California Summary 10th Torts § 143, Subsequent Concealment Of Victim.

§ 305.5. Removal of Indian child from custody of parents by state or local authority; transfer of proceedings to tribal court

(a) If an Indian child, who is a ward of a tribal court or resides or is domiciled within a reservation of an Indian tribe that has exclusive jurisdiction over child custody proceedings as recognized in Section 1911 of Title 25 of the United States Code or reassumed exclusive jurisdiction over Indian child custody proceedings pursuant to Section 1918 of Title 25 of the United States Code, has been removed by a state or local authority from the custody of his or her parents or Indian custodian, the state or local authority shall provide notice of the removal to the tribe no later than the next working day following the removal and shall provide all relevant documentation to the tribe regarding the removal and the child's identity. If the tribe determines that the child is an Indian child, the state or local authority shall transfer the child custody proceeding to the tribe within 24 hours after receipt of written notice from the tribe of that determination.

(b) In the case of an Indian child who is not domiciled or residing within a reservation of an Indian tribe or who resides or is domiciled within a reservation of an Indian tribe that does not have exclusive jurisdiction over child custody proceedings pursuant to Section 1911 or 1918 of Title 25 of the United States Code, the court shall transfer the proceeding to the jurisdiction of the child's tribe upon petition of either parent, the Indian custodian, if any, or the child's tribe, unless the court finds good cause not to transfer. The court shall dismiss the proceeding or terminate jurisdiction only after receiving proof that the tribal court has accepted the transfer of jurisdiction. At the time that the court dismisses the proceeding or terminates jurisdiction, the court shall also make an order transferring the physical custody of the child to the tribal court.

(c)(1) If a petition to transfer proceedings as described in subdivision (b) is filed, the court shall find good cause to deny the petition if one or more of the following circumstances are shown to exist:

(A) One or both of the child's parents object to the transfer.

(B) The child's tribe does not have a "tribal court" as defined in Section 1910 of Title 25 of the United States Code.

(C) The tribal court of the child's tribe declines the transfer.

(2) Good cause not to transfer the proceeding may exist if:

(A) The evidence necessary to decide the case cannot be presented in the tribal court without undue hardship to the parties or the witnesses, and the tribal court is unable to mitigate the hardship by making arrangements to receive and consider the evidence or testimony by use of remote communication, by hearing the evidence or testimony at a location convenient to the parties or witnesses, or by use of other means permitted in the tribal court's rules of evidence or discovery.

(B) The proceeding was at an advanced stage when the petition to transfer was received and the petitioner did not file the petition within a reasonable time after receiving notice of the proceeding, provided the notice complied with Section 224.2. It shall not, in and of itself, be considered an unreasonable delay for a party to wait until reunification efforts have failed and reunification services have been terminated before filing a petition to transfer.

(C) The Indian child is over 12 years of age and objects to the transfer.

(D) The parents of the child over five years of age are not available and the child has had little or no contact with the child's tribe or members of the child's tribe.

(3) Socioeconomic conditions and the perceived adequacy of tribal social services or judicial systems may not be considered in a determination that good cause exists.

(4) The burden of establishing good cause to the contrary shall be on the party opposing the transfer. If the court believes, or any party asserts, that good cause to the contrary exists, the reasons for that belief or assertion shall be stated in writing and made available to all parties who are petitioning for the transfer, and the petitioner shall have the opportunity to provide information or evidence in rebuttal of the belief or assertion.

(5) Nothing in this section or Section 1911 or 1918 of Title 25 of the United States Code shall be construed as requiring a tribe to petition the Secretary of the Interior to reassume exclusive jurisdiction pursuant to Section 1918 of Title 25 of the United States Code prior to exercising jurisdiction over a proceeding transferred under subdivision (b).

(d) An Indian child's domicile or place of residence is determined by that of the parent, guardian, or Indian custodian with whom the child maintained his or her primary place of abode at the time the Indian child custody proceedings were initiated.

(e) If any petitioner in an Indian child custody proceeding has improperly removed the child from the custody of the parent or Indian custodian or has improperly retained custody after a visit or other temporary relinquishment of custody, the court shall decline jurisdiction over the petition and shall immediately return the child to his or her parent or Indian custodian, unless returning the child to the parent or Indian custodian would subject the child to a substantial and immediate danger or threat of danger.

(f) Nothing in this section shall be construed to prevent the emergency removal of an Indian child who is a ward of a tribal court or resides or is domiciled within a reservation of an Indian tribe, but is temporarily located off the reservation, from a parent or Indian custodian or the emergency placement of the child in a foster home or institution in order to prevent imminent physical damage or harm to the child. The state or local authority shall ensure that the emergency removal or placement terminates immediately when the removal or placement is no longer necessary to prevent imminent physical damage or harm to the child and shall expeditiously initiate an Indian child custody proceeding, transfer the child to the jurisdiction of the Indian child's tribe, or restore the child to the parent or Indian custodian, as may be appropriate.

(g) When an Indian child is transferred from a county juvenile court to an Indian tribe pursuant to subdivision (a), (b), or (f), the county shall, pursuant to Section 827.15, release the child case file to the tribe having jurisdiction. *(Added by Stats.1999, c. 275 (A.B.65), § 2, eff. Sept. 1, 1999. Amended by Stats.2006, c. 838 (S.B.678), § 44; Stats.2014, c. 772 (S.B.1460), § 8, eff. Jan. 1, 2015.)*

Research References

Forms

California Transactions Forms--Family Law § 3:4, Subject Matter Jurisdiction for Custody Determinations.

West's California Judicial Council Forms ICWA-050, Notice Of Petition and Petition to Transfer Case Involving an Indian Child to Tribal Jurisdiction.

West's California Judicial Council Forms ICWA-060, Order on Petition to Transfer Case Involving an Indian Child to Tribal Jurisdiction.

Treatises and Practice Aids

Witkin, California Summary 10th Parent and Child § 494, Records Of Dependent Children.

Witkin, California Summary 10th Parent and Child § 524, Jurisdiction.

Witkin, California Summary 10th Parent and Child § 554, Notice and Telephone Contact.

Witkin, California Summary 10th Parent and Child § 288C, (New) Applicable Law.

Witkin, California Summary 10th Parent and Child § 464A, (New) Transfer to Indian Tribe.

§ 305.6. Temporary custody without warrant; minor in hospital care; conditions requiring a warrant; filing of adoption request or guardianship petition following discharge; completion of Health Facility Minor Release Report

(a) Any peace officer may, without a warrant, take into temporary custody a minor who is in a hospital if the release of the minor to a prospective adoptive parent or a representative of a licensed adoption agency poses an immediate danger to the minor's health or safety.

(b) Notwithstanding subdivision (a) and Section 305, a peace officer shall not, without a warrant, take into temporary custody a minor who is in a hospital if all of the following conditions exist:

(1) The minor is a newborn who tested positive for illegal drugs or whose birth mother tested positive for illegal drugs.

(2) The minor is the subject of a proposed adoption and a Health Facility Minor Release Report, developed by the department, has been completed by the hospital, including the marking of the boxes applicable to an independent adoption or agency adoption planning, and signed by the placing birth parent or birth parents, as well as either the prospective adoptive parent or parents or an authorized representative of a licensed adoption agency, prior to the discharge of the birth parent or the minor from the hospital. The Health Facility Minor Release Report shall include a notice written in at least 14–point pica type, containing substantially all of the following statements:

(A) That the Health Facility Minor Release Report does not constitute consent to adoption of the minor by the prospective adoptive parent or parents, or any other person.

(B) That the Health Facility Minor Release Report does not constitute a relinquishment of parental rights for the purposes of adoption.

(C) That the birth parent or parents or any person authorized by the birth parent or parents may reclaim the minor at any time from the prospective adoptive parent or parents or any other person to whom the minor was released by the hospital, as provided in Section 8700, 8814.5, or 8815 of the Family Code.

(3) The release of the minor to a prospective adoptive parent or parents or an authorized representative of a licensed adoption agency does not pose an immediate danger to the minor.

(4) An attorney or an adoption agency has provided documentation stating that he or she, or the agency, is representing the prospective adoptive parent or parents for purposes of the adoption. In the case of an independent adoption, as defined in Section 8524 of the Family Code, the attorney or adoption agency shall provide documentation stating that the prospective adoptive parent or parents have been informed that the child may be eligible for benefits provided pursuant to the Adoption Assistance Program, as set forth in Chapter 2.1 (commencing with Section 16115) of Part 4 of Division 9, only if, at the time the adoption request is filed, the child has met the requirements to receive federal supplemental security income benefits pursuant to Subchapter XVI (commencing with Section 1381) of Chapter 7 of Title 42 of the United States Code, as determined and documented by the federal Social Security Administration.

(5) The prospective adoptive parent or parents or their representative, or an authorized representative of a licensed adoption agency, provides all of the following to the peace officer:

(A) A fully executed copy of the Health Facility Minor Release Report.

(B) A written form signed by either the prospective adoptive parent or parents or a representative of the licensed adoption agency, which shall include all of the following:

(i) A statement that the minor is the subject of a proposed adoption.

(ii) A declaration that the signer or signers will immediately notify the county child welfare agency pursuant to Section 11165.9 of the Penal Code if the adoption plan is terminated for any reason, and will not release the minor to the birth parent or parents or any designee of the birth parent or parents until the county child welfare agency or local law enforcement agency completes an investigation and determines that release of the minor to the birth parent or parents or a designee of the birth parent or parents will not create an immediate risk to the health or safety of the minor.

(iii) An agreement to provide a conformed copy of the adoption request or guardianship petition to the county child welfare agency within five business days after filing.

(iv) The names, identifying information, and contact information for the minor, for each prospective adoptive parent, and for each birth parent, to the extent that information is known. In the case of an agency adoption where no prospective adoptive parent or parents are identified at the time of the minor's release from the hospital, the licensed adoption agency may provide the information as it pertains to the licensed or certified foster home into which the agency intends to place the minor.

(c)(1) In every independent adoption proceeding under this section, the prospective adoptive parent or parents shall file with the court either an adoption request within 10 working days after execution of an adoption placement agreement, or a guardianship petition within 30 calendar days after the child's discharge from the hospital, whichever is earlier.

(2) If the adoption plan for a minor who was released from the hospital pursuant to subdivision (b) is terminated for any reason, the prospective adoptive parent or parents or licensed adoption agency shall immediately notify the county child welfare agency. The prospective adoptive parent or parents or licensed adoption agency may not release the minor into the physical custody of the birth parent or parents, or any designee of the birth parent or parents, until the county child welfare agency or local law enforcement agency completes an investigation and determines that release of the minor to the birth parent or parents or a designee of the birth parent or parents will not create an immediate risk to the health or safety of the minor.

(d) Upon request by a birth parent or parents of the minor newborn, the appropriate hospital personnel shall complete a Health Facility Minor Release Report and provide copies of the report to the birth parent or parents, and the person or persons who will receive physical custody of the child upon discharge pursuant to Section 1283 of the Health and Safety Code. Hospital personnel shall not refuse to complete a Health Facility Minor Release Report for any reason, even if the minor is ineligible for release at that time. However, nothing in this section shall be construed to require hospital personnel to release a minor contrary to the directives of a child welfare agency.

(e) Nothing in this section is intended to create a duty that requires law enforcement to investigate the prospective adoptive parent or parents. *(Formerly § 305.5, added by Stats.2002, c. 920 (A.B.2279), § 2. Renumbered § 305.6 and amended by Stats.2003, c. 568 (A.B.962), § 1. Amended by Stats.2010, c. 440 (A.B.973), § 1; Stats.2012, c. 35 (S.B.1013), § 43, eff. June 27, 2012; Stats.2016, c. 702 (A.B.2872), § 2, eff. Jan. 1, 2017.)*

Research References

Treatises and Practice Aids

Witkin, California Summary 10th Parent and Child § 552, in General.

§ 306. Social workers and Indian tribes; power to perform probation officer functions

(a) Any social worker in a county welfare department, or an Indian tribe that has entered into an agreement pursuant to Section 10553.1 while acting within the scope of his or her regular duties under the direction of the juvenile court and pursuant to subdivision (b) of Section 272, may do all of the following:

(1) Receive and maintain, pending investigation, temporary custody of a minor who is described in Section 300, and who has been delivered by a peace officer.

(2) Take into and maintain temporary custody of, without a warrant, a minor who has been declared a dependent child of the juvenile court under Section 300 or who the social worker has reasonable cause to believe is a person described in subdivision (b) or (g) of Section 300, and the social worker has reasonable cause to believe that the minor has an immediate need for medical care or is in immediate danger of physical or sexual abuse or the physical environment poses an immediate threat to the child's health or safety.

(b) Before taking a minor into custody, a social worker shall consider whether the child can remain safely in his or her residence. The consideration of whether the child can remain safely at home shall include, but not be limited to, the following factors:

(1) Whether there are any reasonable services available to the worker which, if provided to the minor's parent, guardian, caretaker, or to the minor, would eliminate the need to remove the minor from the custody of his or her parent, guardian, or caretaker.

(2) Whether a referral to public assistance pursuant to Chapter 2 (commencing with Section 11200) of Part 3, Chapter 7 (commencing with Section 14000) of Part 3, Chapter 1 (commencing with Section 17000) of Part 5, and Chapter 10 (commencing with Section 18900) of Part 6, of Division 9 would eliminate the need to take temporary custody of the minor. If those services are available they shall be utilized.

(3) Whether a nonoffending caretaker can provide for and protect the child from abuse and neglect and whether the alleged perpetrator voluntarily agrees to withdraw from the residence, withdraws from the residence, and is likely to remain withdrawn from the residence. *(Added by Stats.1987, c. 1485, § 13, operative Jan. 1, 1989. Amended by Stats.1988, c. 701, § 3, eff. Aug. 29, 1988; Stats.1989, c. 408, § 2; Stats.1994, c. 469 (A.B.1579), § 1; Stats.1995, c. 724 (A.B. 1525), § 3.)*

Research References

Treatises and Practice Aids

Witkin, California Summary 10th Parent and Child § 483, Juvenile Court Proceedings.

Witkin, California Summary 10th Parent and Child § 488, Social Workers.

Witkin, California Summary 10th Parent and Child § 494, Records Of Dependent Children.

Witkin, California Summary 10th Parent and Child § 552, in General.

Witkin, California Summary 10th Parent and Child § 604, in General.

Witkin, California Summary 10th Parent and Child § 607, Findings and Orders.

Witkin, California Summary 10th Parent and Child § 643, Duration Of Services.

§ 306.5. Placement of minor in custody with any siblings or half-siblings

In any case in which a social worker takes a minor into custody pursuant to Section 306, the social worker shall, to the extent that it is practical and appropriate, place the minor together with any siblings or half-siblings who are also detained or include in the report prepared pursuant to Section 319 a statement of his or her continuing efforts to place the siblings together or why those efforts are not appropriate. *(Added by Stats.2001, c. 747 (A.B.705), § 1.)*

Research References

Treatises and Practice Aids

Witkin, California Summary 10th Parent and Child § 552, in General.

Witkin, California Summary 10th Parent and Child § 604, in General.

§ 306.6. Indian child of tribe not recognized to have tribal status under federal law; tribal participation at hearings

(a) In a dependency proceeding involving a child who would otherwise be an Indian child, based on the definition contained in paragraph (4) of Section 1903 of the federal Indian Child Welfare Act (25 U.S.C. Sec. 1901 et seq.), but is not an Indian child based on status of the child's tribe, as defined in paragraph (8) of Section 1903 of the federal Indian Child Welfare Act (25 U.S.C. Sec. 1901 et seq.), the court may permit the tribe from which the child is descended to participate in the proceeding upon request of the tribe.

(b) If the court permits a tribe to participate in a proceeding, the tribe may do all of the following, upon consent of the court:

(1) Be present at the hearing.

(2) Address the court.

(3) Request and receive notice of hearings.

(4) Request to examine court documents relating to the proceeding.

(5) Present information to the court that is relevant to the proceeding.

(6) Submit written reports and recommendations to the court.

(7) Perform other duties and responsibilities as requested or approved by the court.

(c) If more than one tribe requests to participate in a proceeding under subdivision (a), the court may limit participation to the tribe with which the child has the most significant contacts, as determined in accordance with paragraph (2) of subdivision (d) of Section 170 of the Family Code.

(d) This section is intended to assist the court in making decisions that are in the best interest of the child by permitting a tribe in the circumstances set out in subdivision (a) to inform the court and parties to the proceeding about placement options for the child within the child's extended family or the tribal community, services and programs available to the child and the child's parents as Indians, and other unique interests the child or the child's parents may have as Indians. This section shall not be construed to make the Indian Child Welfare Act (25 U.S.C. Sec. 1901 et seq.), or any state law implementing the Indian Child Welfare Act, applicable to the proceedings, or to limit the court's discretion to permit other interested persons to participate in these or any other proceedings.

(e) The court shall, on a case-by-case basis, make a determination if this section is applicable and may request information from the tribe, or the entity claiming to be a tribe, from which the child is descended for the purposes of making this determination, if the child would otherwise be an Indian child pursuant to subdivision (a). *(Added by Stats. 2006, c. 838 (S.B.678), § 45.)*

Commentary

Although this section permits a juvenile court to allow a tribe that is not federally recognized to appear in a dependency proceeding, it does not require the court or a social services agency to give notice of the dependency proceeding to the tribe. *In re A. C., 155 Cal.App.4th 282, 65 Cal.Rptr.3d 767 (2007), review denied.*

Research References

Treatises and Practice Aids

Witkin, California Summary 10th Parent and Child § 527A, (New) Participation Of Unrecognized Tribe.

§ 307. Alternative proceedings; release; notice to appear; taking minor before probation officer

A peace officer or probation officer who takes a minor into temporary custody under the provisions of Section 305 shall thereafter proceed as follows:

(a) The officer may release the minor.

(b) The officer may prepare in duplicate a written notice for the parent or parents of the minor to appear with the minor before the probation officer of the county in which the minor was taken into custody at a time and place specified in the notice. The notice shall also contain a concise statement of the reasons the minor was taken into custody. The officer shall deliver one copy of the notice to the minor and a parent, guardian, or responsible relative of the minor and may require the minor and the parent, guardian, or relative to sign a written promise that he or she shall appear at the time and place designated in the notice. Upon the execution of the promise to appear, the officer shall immediately release the minor. The officer shall, as soon as practicable, file one copy of the notice with the probation officer.

(c) The officer may take the minor without unnecessary delay before the probation officer of the county in which the minor was taken into custody, or in which the minor resides, or in which the acts take place or the circumstances exist which are alleged to bring the minor within the provisions of Section 300, and deliver the minor into the custody of the probation officer.

In determining which disposition of the minor shall be made, the officer shall give preference to the alternative which least interferes with the parents' or guardians' custody of the minor if this alternative is compatible with the safety of the minor. The officer shall also consider the needs of the minor for the least restrictive environment and the protective needs of the community. *(Added by Stats.1976, c. 1068, p. 4760, § 7. Amended by Stats.1982, c. 978, § 5, eff. Sept. 13, 1982, operative July 1, 1982.)*

Research References

Treatises and Practice Aids

Witkin, California Summary 10th Parent and Child § 494, Records Of Dependent Children.

Witkin, California Summary 10th Parent and Child § 503, Petition and Order.

Witkin, California Summary 10th Parent and Child § 553, Disposition by Peace Officer.

§ 307.4. Notice to parent or guardian; written statement of procedural rights and preliminary proceedings; failure to notify

(a) Any peace officer, probation officer, or social worker who takes into temporary custody pursuant to Sections 305 to 307, inclusive, a minor who comes within the description of Section 300 shall immediately inform, through the most efficient means available, the parent, guardian, or responsible relative, that the minor has been taken into protective custody and that a written statement is available which explains the parent's or guardian's procedural rights and the preliminary stages of the dependency investigation and hearing. The Judicial Council shall, in consultation with the County Welfare Directors Association of California, adopt a form for the written statement, which shall be in simple language and shall be printed and distributed by the county. The written statement shall be made available for distribution through all public schools, probation offices, and appropriate welfare offices. It shall include, but is not limited to, the following information:

(1) The conditions under which the minor will be released, hearings which may be required, and the means whereby further specific information about the minor's case and conditions of confinement may be obtained.

(2) The rights to counsel, privileges against self-incrimination, and rights to appeal possessed by the minor, and his or her parents, guardians, or responsible relative.

(b) If a good faith attempt was made at notification, the failure on the part of the peace officer, probation officer, or social worker to notify the parent or guardian that the written information required by subdivision (a) is available shall be considered to be due to circumstances beyond the control of the peace officer, probation officer, or social worker, and shall not be construed to permit a new defense to any juvenile or judicial proceeding or to interfere with any rights, procedures, or investigations accorded under any other law. *(Added by Stats.1986, c. 386, § 1.)*

Research References

Treatises and Practice Aids

Witkin, California Summary 10th Parent and Child § 554, Notice and Telephone Contact.

§ 307.5. Taking minor to community service program for abused or neglected children; employees of program; notice to parent or guardian

Notwithstanding the provisions of Section 307, an officer who takes a minor suspected of being a person described in Section 300 into temporary custody pursuant to subdivision (a) of Section 305 may, in a case where he or she deems that it is in the best interest of the minor and the public, take the minor to a community service program for abused or neglected children. Organizations or programs receiving referrals pursuant to this section shall have a contract or an agreement with the county to provide shelter care or counseling. Employees of a program receiving referrals pursuant to this section are "child care custodians" for the purpose of the requirements of Section 11165.7 of the Penal Code. The receiving organization shall take immediate steps to notify the minor's parent, guardian, or a responsible relative of the place to which the minor was taken. *(Added by Stats.1982, c. 461, § 1. Amended by Stats.1989, c. 913, § 5.)*

Research References

Treatises and Practice Aids

Witkin, California Summary 10th Parent and Child § 494, Records Of Dependent Children.

Witkin, California Summary 10th Parent and Child § 553, Disposition by Peace Officer.

Witkin, California Summary 10th Parent and Child § 561, Investigation by Social Worker.

§ 308. Notice to parent or guardian; right to make telephone calls

(a) When a peace officer or social worker takes a minor into custody pursuant to this article, he or she shall take immediate steps to notify the minor's parent, guardian, or a responsible relative that the minor is in custody and that the child has been placed in a facility authorized by law to care for the child, and shall provide a telephone number at which the minor may be contacted. The confidentiality of the address of any licensed foster family home in which the child has been placed shall be maintained until the dispositional hearing, at which time the judge may authorize, upon a finding of good cause, the disclosure of the address. However, the court may order the release of the address of the licensed foster family home to the minor's parent, guardian, or responsible relative upon notification of the licensed foster family home in cases where a petition to challenge jurisdiction or other motion to delay the dispositional hearing beyond 60 days after the hearing at which the minor was ordered removed or detained, pursuant to subdivision (b) of Section 352, is granted. Moreover, a foster parent may authorize the release of the address of the foster family home at any time during the placement. The county welfare department shall make a diligent and reasonable effort to ensure regular telephone contact between the parent and a child of any age, prior to the detention hearing, unless that contact would be detrimental to the child. The initial telephone contact shall take place as soon as practicable, but no later than five hours after the child is taken into custody.

(b) Immediately after being taken to a place of confinement pursuant to this article and, except where physically impossible, no later than one hour after he or she has been taken into custody, a minor 10 years of age or older shall be advised that he or she has the right to make at least two telephone calls from the place where he or she is being held, one call completed to his or her parent, guardian, or a responsible relative, and another call completed to an attorney. The calls shall be at public expense, if the calls are completed to telephone numbers within the local calling area, and in the presence of a public officer or employee. Any public officer or employee who willfully deprives a minor taken into custody of his or her right to make these telephone calls is guilty of a misdemeanor. *(Added by Stats.1976, c. 1068, p. 4761, § 7. Amended by Stats.1978, c. 1168, p. 3777, § 2; Stats.1980, c. 1092, p. 3505, § 1; Stats.1982, c. 978, § 6, eff. Sept. 13, 1982, operative July 1, 1982; Stats.1984, c. 1370, § 1; Stats.1987, c. 1485, § 14; Stats.1988, c. 1083, § 1; Stats.1990, c. 320 (A.B.4122), § 1; Stats.1996, c. 275 (A.B. 2329), § 1.)*

Research References

Forms

West's California Judicial Council Forms JV-295, De Facto Parent Request.

West's California Judicial Council Forms JV-322, Confidential Information--Prospective Adoptive Parent.

Treatises and Practice Aids

Witkin, California Summary 10th Parent and Child § 554, Notice and Telephone Contact.

§ 309. Investigation; release or detention; temporary placement with relative or nonrelative extended family member; identification of adult relatives; notice of removal

(a) Upon delivery to the social worker of a child who has been taken into temporary custody under this article, the social worker shall immediately investigate the circumstances of the child and the facts surrounding the child's being taken into custody and attempt to maintain the child with the child's family through the provision of services. The social worker shall immediately release the child to the custody of the child's parent, guardian, or * * * relative, regardless of the parent's, guardian's, or relative's immigration status, unless one or more of the following conditions exist:

(1) The child has no parent, guardian, or * * * relative * * * willing to provide care for the child.

(2) Continued detention of the child is a matter of immediate and urgent necessity for the protection of the child and there are no reasonable means by which the child can be protected in his or her home or the home of a * * * relative.

(3) There is substantial evidence that a parent, guardian, or custodian of the child is likely to flee the jurisdiction of the court.

(4) The child has left a placement in which he or she was placed by the juvenile court.

(5) The parent or other person having lawful custody of the child voluntarily surrendered physical custody of the child pursuant to Section 1255.7 of the Health and Safety Code and did not reclaim the child within the 14-day period specified in subdivision (e) of that section.

(b) In any case in which there is reasonable cause for believing that a child who is under the care of a physician and surgeon or a hospital, clinic, or other medical facility * * *, cannot be immediately moved, and is a person described in Section 300, the child shall be deemed to have been taken into temporary custody and delivered to the social worker for the purposes of this chapter while the child is at the office of the physician and surgeon or the medical facility.

(c) If the child is not released to his or her parent or guardian, the child shall be deemed detained for purposes of this chapter.

(d)(1) If * * * a relative, as defined in Section 319, or * * * a nonrelative extended family member, as defined in Section 362.7, is available and requests emergency placement of the child pending the detention hearing, or after the detention hearing and pending the dispositional hearing conducted pursuant to Section 358, the county welfare department shall initiate an assessment of the relative's or nonrelative extended family member's suitability * * * for emergency placement pursuant to Section 361.4.

(2) Upon completion of the assessment pursuant to Section 361.4, the child may be placed in the home on an emergency basis * * *. Following the emergency placement of the child * * *, the county welfare department shall evaluate and approve or deny the home pursuant to Section 16519.5. The county shall require the relative or nonrelative extended family member to submit an application for approval as a resource family and initiate the home environment assessment no later than five business days after the placement.

* * *

(e)(1) If the child is removed, the social worker shall conduct, within 30 days, an investigation in order to identify and locate all grandparents, parents of a sibling of the child, if the parent has legal custody of the sibling, adult siblings, and other adult relatives of the child, as defined in paragraph (2) of subdivision (f) of Section 319, including any other adult relatives suggested by the parents. As used in this section, "sibling" means a person related to the identified child by blood, adoption, or affinity through a common legal or biological parent. The social worker shall provide to all adult relatives who are located, except when that relative's history of family or domestic violence makes notification inappropriate, within 30 days of removal of the child, written notification and shall also, whenever appropriate, provide oral notification, in person or by telephone, of all the following information:

(A) The child has been removed from the custody of his or her parent or parents, or his or her guardians.

(B) An explanation of the various options to participate in the care and placement of the child and support for the child's family, including any options that may be lost by failing to respond. The notice shall provide information about providing care for the child while the family receives reunification services with the goal of returning the child to the parent or guardian, how to become a resource family, and additional services and support that are available in out-of-home placements. The notice shall also include information regarding the Kin-GAP Program (Article 4.5 (commencing with Section 11360) of Chapter 2 of Part 3 of Division 9), the CalWORKs program for approved relative caregivers (Chapter 2 (commencing with Section 11200) of Part 3 of Division 9), adoption, and adoption assistance (Chapter 2.1 (commencing with Section 16115) of Part 4 of Division 9), as well as other options for contact with the child, including, but not limited to, visitation. The State Department of Social Services, in consultation with the County Welfare Directors Association of California and other interested stakeholders, shall develop the written notice.

(2) The social worker shall also provide the adult relatives notified pursuant to paragraph (1) with a relative information form to provide information to the social worker and the court regarding the needs of the child. The form shall include a provision whereby the relative may request the permission of the court to address the court, if the relative so chooses. The Judicial Council, in consultation with the State Department of Social Services and the County Welfare Directors Association of California, shall develop the form.

(3) The social worker shall use due diligence in investigating the names and locations of the relatives pursuant to paragraph (1), including, but not limited to, asking the child in an age-appropriate manner about relatives important to the child, consistent with the child's best interest, and obtaining information regarding the location of the child's adult relatives. Each county welfare department shall create and make public a procedure by which relatives of a child who has been removed from his or her parents or guardians may identify themselves to the county welfare department and be provided with the notices required by paragraphs (1) and (2). *(Added by Stats.1976, c. 1068, p. 4760, § 7. Amended by Stats.1982, c. 978, § 7, eff. Sept. 13, 1982, operative July 1, 1982; Stats.1987, c. 1485, § 15; Stats.1989, c. 913, § 6; Stats.1997, c. 793 (A.B.1544), § 10; Stats.1998, c. 1054 (A.B.1091), § 8; Stats.2000, c. 421 (S.B.2161), § 4, eff. Sept. 13, 2000; Stats.2000, c. 824 (S.B.1368), § 4; Stats.2001, c. 653 (A.B.1695), § 7, eff. Oct. 10, 2001; Stats.2002, c. 918 (A.B.1694), § 3; Stats.2004, c. 373 (A.B.1913), § 1; Stats. 2006, c. 726 (A.B.1774), § 1, eff. Sept. 29, 2006; Stats.2008, c. 701 (A.B.2651), § 11, eff. Sept. 30, 2008; Stats.2009, c. 261 (A.B.938), § 1; Stats.2012, c. 845 (S.B.1064), § 4; Stats.2014, c. 765 (A.B.1761), § 1, eff. Jan. 1, 2015; Stats.2015, c. 425 (S.B.794), § 5, eff. Jan. 1, 2016; Stats.2016, c. 612 (A.B.1997), § 68, eff. Jan. 1, 2017; Stats.2017, c. 732 (A.B.404), § 43, eff. Jan. 1, 2018.)*

Research References

Forms

West's California Judicial Council Forms JV-285, Relative Information.

Treatises and Practice Aids

Witkin, California Summary 10th Parent and Child § 555, Investigation, Detention, and Release.

Witkin, California Summary 10th Parent and Child § 556, Assessment Of Prospective Placement.

Witkin, California Summary 10th Parent and Child § 607, Findings and Orders.

Witkin, California Summary 10th Parent and Child § 638, Preferential Right Of Relatives.

Witkin, California Summary 10th Parent and Child § 750, Segregation Of Minors and Adults.

§ 310. Written promise to appear

As a condition for the release of such minor, the probation officer may require such minor or his parent, guardian, or relative, or both, to sign a written promise that either or both of them will appear before the probation officer at a suitable place designated by the probation officer at a specified time. *(Added by Stats.1976, c. 1068, p. 4760, § 7. Amended by Stats.1978, c. 1168, p. 3777, § 3.)*

Research References

Treatises and Practice Aids

Witkin, California Summary 10th Parent and Child § 555, Investigation, Detention, and Release.

§ 311. Filing petition if minor shall be retained in custody; privilege against self-incrimination and right to confrontation by, and cross-examination

(a) If the probation officer determines that the minor shall be retained in custody, he or she shall immediately file a petition pursuant to Section 332 with the clerk of the juvenile court who shall set the matter for hearing on the detention hearing calendar.

(b) In the hearing, the child, parents, or guardians have a privilege against self-incrimination and have a right to confrontation by, and cross-examination of, any person examined by the court as provided in Section 319. *(Added by Stats.1976, c. 1068, p. 4760, § 7. Amended by Stats.1982, c. 978, § 8, eff. Sept. 13, 1982, operative July 1, 1982; Stats.2002, c. 416 (S.B.1956), § 2.)*

Research References

Treatises and Practice Aids

Witkin, California Summary 10th Parent and Child § 369, Dependency Proceeding Pending.

Witkin, California Summary 10th Parent and Child § 564, in General.

Witkin, California Summary 10th Parent and Child § 567, Statutory Rights.

Witkin, California Summary 10th Parent and Child § 576, in General.

Witkin, California Summary 10th Parent and Child § 578, Confrontation and Cross-Examination.

Witkin, California Summary 10th Parent and Child § 600, Petition and Notice Of Hearing.

Witkin, California Summary 10th Parent and Child § 605, Rights Of Child, Parent, and Guardian.

§ 313. Release within 48 hours; exceptions; written explanation for custody over 6 hours

(a) Whenever a minor is taken into custody by a peace officer or probation officer, except when such minor willfully misrepresents himself as 18 or more years of age, such minor shall be released within 48 hours after having been taken into custody, excluding nonjudicial days, unless within said period of time a petition to declare him a dependent child has been filed pursuant to the provisions of this chapter.

(b) Whenever a minor who has been held in custody for more than six hours by the probation officer is subsequently released and no petition is filed, the probation officer shall prepare a written explanation of why the minor was held in custody for more than six hours. The written explanation shall be prepared within 72 hours after the minor is released from custody and filed in the record of the case. A copy of the written explanation shall be sent to the parents, guardian, or other person having care or custody of the minor. *(Added by Stats.1976, c. 1068, p. 4760, § 7.)*

Research References

Treatises and Practice Aids

Witkin, California Summary 10th Parent and Child § 557, Retention Of Custody.

§ 314. Misrepresentation of age

When a minor willfully misrepresents himself to be 18 or more years of age when taken into custody by a peace officer or probation officer, and this misrepresentation effects a material delay in investigation which prevents the filing of a petition pursuant to the provisions of this chapter, such petition or complaint shall be filed within 48 hours from the time his true age is determined, excluding nonjudicial days. If, in such cases, the petition is not filed within the time prescribed by this section, the minor shall be immediately released from custody. *(Added by Stats.1976, c. 1068, p. 4760, § 7.)*

Research References

Treatises and Practice Aids

Witkin, California Summary 10th Parent and Child § 557, Retention Of Custody.

§ 315. Detention hearing; timeliness; release

If a minor has been taken into custody under this article and not released to a parent or guardian, the juvenile court shall hold a hearing (which shall be referred to as a "detention hearing") to determine whether the minor shall be further detained. This hearing shall be held as soon as possible, but in any event before the expiration of the next judicial day after a petition to declare the minor a dependent child has been filed. If the hearing is not held within the period prescribed by this section, the minor shall be released from custody. *(Added by Stats.1987, c. 1485, § 17.)*

Research References

Treatises and Practice Aids

Witkin, California Summary 10th Parent and Child § 557, Retention Of Custody.

Witkin, California Summary 10th Parent and Child § 598, in General.

Witkin, California Summary 10th Parent and Child § 607, Findings and Orders.

§ 316. Informing parent or guardian and minor as to reasons for custody, nature of proceedings, and right to counsel

Upon his or her appearance before the court at the detention hearing, each parent or guardian and the minor, if present, shall first be informed of the reasons why the minor was taken into custody, the nature of the juvenile court proceedings, and the right of each parent or guardian and any minor to be represented at every stage of the proceedings by counsel. *(Added by Stats.1987, c. 1485, § 19.)*

Research References

Treatises and Practice Aids

Witkin, California Summary 10th Parent and Child § 570, in General.

Witkin, California Summary 10th Parent and Child § 579, in General.

Witkin, California Summary 10th Parent and Child § 602, Explanation and Information.

§ 316.1. Designation of permanent mailing address or electronic service address used for notice purposes

(a) * * * Upon his or her appearance before the court, each parent or guardian shall designate for the court his or her permanent mailing address. The court shall advise each parent or guardian that the designated mailing address will be used by the court and the social services agency for notice purposes unless and until the parent or guardian notifies the court or the social services agency of a new mailing address in writing.

* * * (b) Upon his or her * * * appearance before the court, each party who consents to electronic service * * * pursuant to Section 212.5 shall designate for the court his or her electronic service address. The court shall advise each party that the electronic service address will be used by the court and the social services agency for purposes of providing notice pursuant to Sections * * * 291, 292, 293, 294, * * * 295, 297, and 342, unless and until the party notifies the court or the social services agency of a new electronic service address in writing or unless the party withdraws consent to electronic service.

* * * *(Added by Stats.1992, c. 288 (S.B.1741), § 1. Amended by Stats.2015, c. 219 (A.B.879), § 15, eff. Jan. 1, 2016; Stats.2017, c. 319 (A.B.976), § 127, eff. Jan. 1, 2018.)*

Research References

Forms

West's California Judicial Council Forms JV-140, Notification Of Mailing Address.

West's California Judicial Council Forms JV-141, E-Mail Notice Of Hearing: Consent, Withdrawal Of Consent, Address Change (Juvenile Dependency).

West's California Judicial Council Forms EFS-005, E-Mail Notice Of Hearing: Consent, Withdrawal Of Consent, Address Change (Juvenile Dependency).

Treatises and Practice Aids

Witkin, California Summary 10th Parent and Child § 576, in General.

Witkin, California Summary 10th Parent and Child § 585, in General.

Witkin, California Summary 10th Parent and Child § 712, Notice Of Appeal.

§ 316.2. Presumed or alleged fathers; inquiry by court; notice; termination of rights; jurisdiction

(a) At the detention hearing, or as soon thereafter as practicable, the court shall inquire of the mother and any other appropriate person as to the identity and address of all presumed or alleged fathers. The presence at the hearing of a man claiming to be the father shall not relieve the court of its duty of inquiry. The inquiry shall include at least all of the following, as the court deems appropriate:

(1) Whether a judgment of paternity already exists.

(2) Whether the mother was married or believed she was married at the time of conception of the child or at any time thereafter.

(3) Whether the mother was cohabiting with a man at the time of conception or birth of the child.

(4) Whether the mother has received support payments or promises of support with respect to the child or in connection with her pregnancy.

(5) Whether any man has formally or informally acknowledged or declared his possible paternity of the child, including by signing a voluntary declaration of paternity.

(6) Whether paternity tests have been administered and the results, if any.

(7) Whether any man otherwise qualifies as a presumed father pursuant to Section 7611, or any other provision, of the Family Code.

(b) If, after the court inquiry, one or more men are identified as an alleged father, each alleged father shall be provided notice at his last and usual place of abode by certified mail return receipt requested alleging that he is or could be the father of the child. The notice shall state that the child is the subject of proceedings under Section 300 and that the proceedings could result in the termination of parental rights and adoption of the child. Judicial Council form Paternity–Waiver of Rights (JV–505) shall be included with the notice. Nothing in this section shall preclude a court from terminating a father's parental rights even if an action has been filed under Section 7630 or 7631 of the Family Code.

(c) The court may determine that the failure of an alleged father to return the certified mail receipt is not good cause to continue a hearing pursuant to Section 355, 358, 360, 366.21, or 366.22.

(d) If a man appears in the dependency action and files an action under Section 7630 or 7631 of the Family Code, the court shall determine if he is the father.

(e) After a petition has been filed to declare a child a dependent of the court, and until the time that the petition is dismissed, dependency is terminated, or parental rights are terminated pursuant to Section 366.26 or proceedings are commenced under Part 4 (commencing with Section 7800) of Division 12 of the Family Code, the juvenile court which has jurisdiction of the dependency action shall have exclusive jurisdiction to hear an action filed under Section 7630 or 7631 of the Family Code.

(f) After any inquiry, proceeding, or determination made pursuant to this section, the juvenile court shall note its findings in the minutes of the court. *(Added by Stats.1997, c. 793 (A.B.1544), § 11. Amended by Stats.2000, c. 56 (A.B. 1716), § 1.)*

Commentary

Applying subsection (e), which gives the juvenile court exclusive jurisdiction once a dependency petition has been *filed*, *In re Alexander*

P., 4 Cal.App.5th 475, 209 Cal.Rptr.3d 130 (2016), review denied, held that family court parentage orders entered two weeks after the filing of a dependency petition were void.

Alexander P. also holds that whether a person is a presumed parent must be determined at the detention hearing. A prior determination that a person is a presumed parent cannot be considered because whether a person is currently a presumed parent requires examination of present, not past, circumstances. This holding of *Alexander P.* was rejected by *In re L.L., 13 Cal.App.5th 1302, 220 Cal.Rptr.3d 904 (2017)*, which approves the use of prior judicial determinations of presumed parenthood.

Under subsection (d), when a man alleged to be a child's biological father appears at a detention hearing and requests a parentage determination, a juvenile court *must* make a determination of the dependent child's biological paternity. *In re J.H., 198 Cal.App.4th 635, 130 Cal.Rptr.3d 389 (2011)*.

However, a juvenile court did not abuse its discretion when it terminated parental rights and denied paternity testing for a man who was an alleged but not a presumed father when the child was conceived while the man was in prison, because testing was not required to determine that he was not the child's biological parent. *In re D.P, 240 Cal.App.4th 689, 193 Cal.Rptr.3d 1 (2015), review denied.*

Although notice to an alleged father did not satisfy subsection (b), *In re Kobe A., 146 Cal.App.4th 1113, 53 Cal.Rptr.3d 437 (2007)*, sustained a trial court's termination of an incarcerated alleged father's parental rights and selection of adoption as a permanency plan because deficient notice was harmless error.

Research References

Treatises and Practice Aids

Witkin, California Summary 10th Parent and Child § 451, in General.

Witkin, California Summary 10th Parent and Child § 520, Jurisdiction.

Witkin, California Summary 10th Parent and Child § 583, Alleged Father.

Witkin, California Summary 10th Parent and Child § 603, Identification Of Presumed or Alleged Fathers.

Witkin, California Summary 10th Parent and Child § 635, in General.

§ 317. Appointment of counsel

(a)(1) When it appears to the court that a parent or guardian of the child desires counsel but is presently financially unable to afford and cannot for that reason employ counsel, the court may appoint counsel as provided in this section.

(2) When it appears to the court that a parent or Indian custodian in an Indian child custody proceeding desires counsel but is presently unable to afford and cannot for that reason employ counsel, the provisions of Section 1912(b) of Title 25 of the United States Code and Section 23.13 of Title 25 of the Code of Federal Regulations shall apply.

(b) When it appears to the court that a parent or guardian of the child is presently financially unable to afford and cannot for that reason employ counsel, and the child has been placed in out-of-home care, or the petitioning agency is recommending that the child be placed in out-of-home care, the court shall appoint counsel for the parent or guardian, unless the court finds that the parent or guardian has made a knowing and intelligent waiver of counsel as provided in this section.

(c)(1) If a child or nonminor dependent is not represented by counsel, the court shall appoint counsel for the child or nonminor dependent, unless the court finds that the child or nonminor dependent would not benefit from the appointment of counsel. The court shall state on the record its reasons for that finding.

(2) A primary responsibility of counsel appointed to represent a child or nonminor dependent pursuant to this section shall be to advocate for the protection, safety, and physical and emotional well-being of the child or nonminor dependent.

(3) Counsel may be a district attorney, public defender, or other member of the bar, provided that he or she does not represent another party or county agency whose interests conflict with the child's or nonminor dependent's interests. The fact that the district attorney represents the child or nonminor dependent in a proceeding pursuant to Section 300 as well as conducts a criminal investigation or files a criminal complaint or information arising from the same or reasonably related set of facts as the proceeding pursuant to Section 300 is not in and of itself a conflict of interest.

(4) The court may fix the compensation for the services of appointed counsel.

(5)(A) The appointed counsel shall have a caseload and training that ensures adequate representation of the child or nonminor dependent. The Judicial Council shall promulgate rules of court that establish caseload standards, training requirements, and guidelines for appointed counsel for children and shall adopt rules as required by Section 326.5 no later than July 1, 2001.

(B) The training requirements imposed pursuant to subparagraph (A) shall include instruction on both of the following:

(i) Cultural competency and sensitivity relating to, and best practices for, providing adequate care to lesbian, gay, bisexual, and transgender youth in out-of-home care.

(ii) The information described in subdivision (d) of Section 16501.4.

(d) Counsel shall represent the parent, guardian, child, or nonminor dependent at the detention hearing and at all subsequent proceedings before the juvenile court. Counsel shall continue to represent the parent, guardian, child, or nonminor dependent unless relieved by the court upon the substitution of other counsel or for cause. The representation shall include representing the parent, guardian, or the child in termination proceedings and in those proceedings relating to the institution or setting aside of a legal guardianship. On and after January 1, 2012, in the case of a nonminor dependent, as described in subdivision (v) of Section 11400, no representation by counsel shall be provided for a parent, unless the parent is receiving court-ordered family reunification services.

(e)(1) Counsel shall be charged in general with the representation of the child's interests. To that end, counsel shall make or cause to have made any further investigations that he or she deems in good faith to be reasonably necessary to ascertain the facts, including the interviewing of witnesses, and shall examine and cross-examine witnesses in both the adjudicatory and dispositional hearings. Counsel may also introduce and examine his or her own witnesses, make recommendations to the court concerning the child's welfare, and participate further in the proceedings to the degree necessary to adequately represent the child. When counsel is appointed to represent a nonminor dependent, counsel is charged with representing the wishes of the nonminor dependent except when advocating for those wishes conflicts with the protection or safety of the nonminor dependent. If the court finds that a nonminor dependent is not competent to direct counsel, the court shall appoint a guardian ad litem for the nonminor dependent.

(2) If the child is four years of age or older, counsel shall interview the child to determine the child's wishes and assess the child's well-being, and shall advise the court of the child's wishes. Counsel shall not advocate for the return of the child if, to the best of his or her knowledge, return of the child conflicts with the protection and safety of the child.

(3) Counsel shall investigate the interests of the child beyond the scope of the juvenile proceeding, and report to the court other interests of the child that may need to be protected by the institution of other administrative or judicial proceedings. Counsel representing a child in a dependency proceeding is not required to assume the responsibilities of a social worker, and is not expected to provide nonlegal services to the child.

(4)(A) At least once every year, if the list of educational liaisons is available on the Internet Web site for the State Department of Education, both of the following shall apply:

(i) Counsel shall provide his or her contact information to the educational liaison, as described in subdivision (c) of Section 48853.5 of the Education Code, of each local educational agency serving counsel's foster child clients in the county of jurisdiction.

(ii) If counsel is part of a firm or organization representing foster children, the firm or organization may provide its contact information in lieu of contact information for the individual counsel. The firm or organization may designate a person or persons within the firm or organization to receive communications from educational liaisons.

(B) The child's caregiver or other person holding the right to make educational decisions for the child may provide the contact information of the child's attorney to the child's local educational agency.

(C) Counsel for the child and counsel's agent may, but are not required to, disclose to an individual who is being assessed for the possibility of placement pursuant to Section 361.3 the fact that the child is in custody, the alleged reasons that the child is in custody, and the projected likely date for the child's return home, placement for adoption, or legal guardianship. Nothing in this paragraph shall be construed to prohibit counsel from making other disclosures pursuant to this subdivision, as appropriate.

(5) Nothing in this subdivision shall be construed to permit counsel to violate a child's attorney-client privilege.

(6) The changes made to this subdivision during the 2011–12 Regular Session of the Legislature by the act adding subparagraph (C) of paragraph (4) and paragraph (5) are declaratory of existing law.

(7) The court shall take whatever appropriate action is necessary to fully protect the interests of the child.

(f) Either the child or counsel for the child, with the informed consent of the child if the child is found by the court to be of sufficient age and maturity to consent, which shall be presumed, subject to rebuttal by clear and convincing evidence, if the child is over 12 years of age, may invoke the psychotherapist-client privilege, physician-patient privilege, and clergyman-penitent privilege. If the child invokes the privilege, counsel may not waive it, but if counsel invokes the privilege, the child may waive it. Counsel shall be the holder of these privileges if the child is found by the court not to be of sufficient age and maturity to consent. For the sole purpose of fulfilling his or her obligation to provide legal representation of the child, counsel shall have access to all records with regard to the child maintained by a health care facility, as defined in Section 1545 of the Penal Code, health care providers, as defined in Section 6146 of the Business and Professions Code, a physician and surgeon or other health practitioner, as defined in former Section 11165.8 of the Penal Code, as that section read on January 1, 2000, or a child care custodian, as defined in former Section 11165.7 of the Penal Code, as that section read on January 1, 2000. Notwithstanding any other law, counsel shall be given access to all records relevant to the case that are maintained by state or local public agencies. All information requested from a child protective agency regarding a child who is in protective custody, or from a child's guardian ad litem, shall be provided to the child's counsel within 30 days of the request.

(g) In a county of the third class, if counsel is to be provided to a child at the county's expense other than by counsel for the agency, the court shall first use the services of the public defender before appointing private counsel. Nothing in this subdivision shall be construed to require the appointment of the public defender in any case in which the public defender has a conflict of interest. In the interest of justice, a court may depart from that portion of the procedure requiring appointment of the public defender after making a finding of good cause and stating the reasons therefor on the record.

(h) In a county of the third class, if counsel is to be appointed to provide legal counsel for a parent or guardian at the county's expense, the court shall first use the services of the alternate public defender before appointing private counsel. Nothing in this subdivision shall be construed to require the appointment of the alternate public defender in any case in which the public defender has a conflict of interest. In the interest of justice, a court may depart from that portion of the procedure requiring appointment of the alternate public defender after making a finding of good cause and stating the reasons therefor on the record. *(Added by Stats.1987, c. 1485, § 21, operative Jan. 1, 1989. Amended by Stats.1992, c. 433 (A.B.2448), § 1; Stats.1996, c. 1084 (S.B.1516), § 3; Stats.1998, c. 900 (A.B.2316), § 2; Stats. 2000, c. 450 (S.B.2160), § 1; Stats.2006, c. 385 (A.B.2480), § 1; Stats.2006, c. 838 (S.B.678), § 46.5; Stats.2010, c. 559 (A.B.12), § 8.5; Stats.2011, c. 132 (S.B.926), § 1; Stats.2012, c. 846 (A.B.1712), § 13; Stats.2012, c. 849 (A.B.1909), § 6.5; Stats.2013, c. 300 (A.B.868), § 4; Stats.2015, c. 534 (S.B.238), § 4, eff. Jan. 1, 2016; Stats.2015, c. 554 (A.B.224), § 6.1, eff. Jan. 1, 2016.)*

Commentary

In re Joshua B., 48 Cal.App.4th 1676, 56 Cal.Rptr.2d 556 (1996), says in dictum that a *respondent* indigent parent is not entitled to appointed counsel as a matter of right in a dependency appeal, although appellate courts have discretion to appoint counsel for respondent parents when the parent's custody or control of a child is at stake. See Family Code Sections 7822, 7860, 7863 and 7895, and Commentary.

In re Mary C., 41 Cal.App.4th 71, 48 Cal.Rptr.2d 346 (1995), holds that, in an appeal from an order terminating parental rights, an appellate court is not required to provide separate counsel for the child unless there is a conflict of interest between the child and the local child protection agency, or protection of the child's best interest requires that the child be represented by separate counsel. Interpreting Section 317(c), *In re Shawn B., 51 Cal.App.4th 1257, 59 Cal.Rptr.2d 613 (1996), review denied April 2, 1997,* holds that Dependency Court has discretion to appoint independent counsel (rather than the county attorney) to represent children even when there is no conflict of interest between the children and the county. *In re Jesse C., 71 Cal.App.4th 1481, 84 Cal.Rptr.2d 609 (1999), review denied August 11, 1999,* holds that counsel appointed for a dependent child under subsection (d) may be relieved "for cause" when the court finds that representation no longer benefits the child.

Cf. *M.L.B. v. S.L.J., 117 S.Ct. 555, 136 L.Ed.2d 473 (1996)* (on appeal from judgment terminating indigent appellant's parental rights, state must pay appellant's fees for record preparation).

In re Josiah Z., 36 Cal.4th 664, 115 P.3d 1133, 31 Cal.Rptr.3d 472 (2005), holds that in a child's dependency appeal, appellate counsel may request funds to meet with the child to investigate whether dismissal of the appeal would be in the child's best interests and, after consultation with and authorization by the child or the child's guardian ad litem, appellate counsel has the power to seek dismissal of the appeal on the ground that dismissal would be in the child's best interests.

Research References

Treatises and Practice Aids

Witkin, California Summary 10th Husband and Wife § 181, No Award in Unrelated Proceeding.
Witkin, California Summary 10th Parent and Child § 563, Program Of Supervision.
Witkin, California Summary 10th Parent and Child § 570, in General.
Witkin, California Summary 10th Parent and Child § 571, in General.
Witkin, California Summary 10th Parent and Child § 572, Appointment Of Guardian Ad Litem or Child Advocate.
Witkin, California Summary 10th Parent and Child § 573, Powers and Duties Of Counsel.
Witkin, California Summary 10th Parent and Child § 574, in General.
Witkin, California Summary 10th Parent and Child § 575, Joint Representation as Error.
Witkin, California Summary 10th Parent and Child § 579, in General.
Witkin, California Summary 10th Parent and Child § 580, Right to Competent Counsel.
Witkin, California Summary 10th Parent and Child § 581, Relief Of Counsel.
Witkin, California Summary 10th Parent and Child § 596, Disposition Where Burden Of Proof Not Met.
Witkin, California Summary 10th Parent and Child § 613, Commencement Of Hearing.
Witkin, California Summary 10th Parent and Child § 620, Privileges.
Witkin, California Summary 10th Parent and Child § 635, in General.
Witkin, California Summary 10th Parent and Child § 683, Appointment Of Counsel.
Witkin, California Summary 10th Parent and Child § 684, Testimony and Wishes Of Child.
Witkin, California Summary 10th Parent and Child § 708, Counsel on Appeal.
Witkin, California Summary 10th Parent and Child § 709, in General.
Witkin, California Summary 10th Parent and Child § 521A, (New) Continuation or Termination Of Jurisdiction Over Nonminor or Nonminor Dependent.

§ 317.5. Competent counsel; entitlement; dependency proceedings

(a) All parties who are represented by counsel at dependency proceedings shall be entitled to competent counsel.

(b) Each minor who is the subject of a dependency proceeding is a party to that proceeding. *(Added by Stats. 1994, c. 1073 (S.B.783), § 1.)*

Commentary

A party may obtain judicial review of a claim of ineffective counsel by making a prima facie showing that (i) the counsel failed to perform as would a reasonably competent attorney and (ii) the party was prejudiced by the error. *In re Kristin H., 46 Cal.App.4th 1635, 54 Cal.Rptr.2d 722 (1996).*

See also *In re Jasmine S.,* depublished by the California Supreme Court on November 12, 1997. In *Jasmine S.*, the depublished court of appeal opinion, 58 Cal.App.4th 30, 68 Cal.Rptr.2d 24 (1997), purported to hold that where an incarcerated father whose parental rights were terminated had not received any reunification services and the father's attorney failed to seek timely review of the Juvenile Court's order setting a section 366.26 termination hearing, the father was entitled to a new period of reunification services. To similar effect, see *Mark N. v. Superior Court, 60 Cal.App.4th 996, 70 Cal.Rptr.2d 603 (1998)* (holding that the juvenile court may not terminate parental rights at a permanency plan hearing absent substantial evidence that the parent has been provided with reasonable reunification services, relying on Section 366.26 (c)(2)).

Research References

Treatises and Practice Aids

Witkin, California Summary 10th Parent and Child § 580, Right to Competent Counsel.

§ 317.6. Appointment of competent counsel; dependency proceedings; rules; procedures

(a) On or before January 1, 1996, the Judicial Council shall, after consulting with representatives from the State Bar of California, county counsels, district attorneys, public defenders, county welfare directors, and children's advocacy groups, adopt rules of court regarding the appointment of competent counsel in dependency proceedings, including, but not limited to, the following:

(1) The screening and appointment of competent counsel.

(2) Establishing minimum standards of experience and education necessary to qualify as competent counsel to represent a party in dependency proceedings.

(3) Procedures for handling client complaints regarding attorney performance, including measures to inform clients of the complaint process.

(4) Procedures for informing the court of any interests of the minor that may need to be protected in other proceedings.

(b) On or before July 1, 1996, each superior court shall, after consulting with representatives from the State Bar of California and the local offices of the county counsel, district attorney, public defender, county welfare department, and children's advocacy groups, adopt local rules of court regarding the conduct of dependency proceedings that address items such as procedures and timeframes for the presentation of contested issues and witness lists to eliminate unnecessary delays in dependency hearings. *(Added by Stats.1994, c. 1073 (S.B.783), § 2. Amended by Stats.1995, c. 91 (S.B.975), § 183.)*

Research References

Treatises and Practice Aids

Witkin, California Summary 10th Parent and Child § 580, Right to Competent Counsel.

§ 318. Representation of minor by district attorney in dependency hearings; other proceedings; confidentiality

If a district attorney has represented a minor in a dependency proceeding, that district attorney shall not appear, on behalf of the people of the State of California, in any juvenile court hearing which is based upon a petition that alleges that the same minor is a person within the description of Section 602.

Records kept by the district attorney in the course of representation of a minor described in Section 300 are confidential and shall be held separately, and shall not be inspected by members of the district attorney's office not directly involved in the representation of that minor. A district attorney who represents or who has represented a minor in a proceeding brought pursuant to Section 300 shall not discuss the substance of that case with a district attorney representing the people pursuant to Section 681 in a proceeding brought pursuant to Section 602 in which that same minor is the subject of the petition. *(Added by Stats.1992, c. 1327 (A.B.3663), § 1.)*

Research References

Treatises and Practice Aids

Witkin, California Summary 10th Parent and Child § 788, Duty to Provide Counsel.

§ 318.5. Representation of petitioner by county counsel or district attorney

In a juvenile court hearing, where the parent or guardian is represented by counsel, the county counsel or district attorney shall, at the request of the juvenile court judge, appear and participate in the hearing to represent the petitioner. *(Formerly § 351, added by Stats.1976, c. 1068, § 9. Renumbered § 318 and amended by Stats.1986, c. 1122, § 7. Renumbered § 318.5 and amended by Stats.1987, c. 56, § 181.)*

Research References

Treatises and Practice Aids

Witkin, California Summary 10th Parent and Child § 592, Participation by District Attorney.

§ 319. Initial petition hearing; examination and report; release; grounds for continued detention; judicial findings and order; limitations upon right to make educational or developmental services decisions for the child

(a) At the initial petition hearing, the court shall examine the child's parents, guardians, or other persons having relevant knowledge and hear the relevant evidence as the child, the child's parents or guardians, the petitioner, or their counsel desires to present. The court may examine the child, as provided in Section 350.

(b) The social worker shall report to the court on the reasons why the child has been removed from the parent's physical custody, the need, if any, for continued detention, the available services and the referral methods to those services that could facilitate the return of the child to the custody of the child's parents or guardians, and whether there are any relatives who are able and willing to take temporary physical custody of the child. The court shall order the release of the child from custody unless a prima facie showing has been made that the child comes within Section 300, the court finds that continuance in the parent's or guardian's home is contrary to the child's welfare, and any of the following circumstances exist:

(1) There is a substantial danger to the physical health of the child or the child is suffering severe emotional damage, and there are no reasonable means by which the child's physical or emotional health may be protected without removing the child from the parent's or guardian's physical custody.

(2) There is substantial evidence that a parent, guardian, or custodian of the child is likely to flee the jurisdiction of the court.

(3) The child has left a placement in which he or she was placed by the juvenile court.

(4) The child indicates an unwillingness to return home, if the child has been physically or sexually abused by a person residing in the home.

(c) If the matter is continued pursuant to Section 322 or for any other reason, the court shall find that the continuance of the child in the parent's or guardian's home is contrary to the child's welfare at the initial petition hearing or order the release of the child from custody.

(d)(1) The court shall also make a determination on the record, referencing the social worker's report or other evidence relied upon, as to whether reasonable efforts were made to prevent or eliminate the need for removal of the child from his or her home, pursuant to subdivision (b) of Section 306, and whether there are available services that would prevent the need for further detention. Services to be considered for purposes of making this determination are case management, counseling, emergency shelter care, emergency in-home caretakers, out-of-home respite care, teaching and demonstrating homemakers, parenting training, transportation, and any other child welfare services authorized by the State Department of Social Services pursuant to Chapter 5 (commencing with Section 16500) of Part 4 of Division 9. The court shall also review whether the social worker has considered whether a referral to public assistance services pursuant to Chapter 2 (commencing with Section 11200) and Chapter 7 (commencing with Section 14000) of Part 3, Chapter 1 (commencing with Section 17000) of Part 5, and Chapter 10 (commencing with Section 18900) of Part 6 of Division 9 would have eliminated the need to take temporary custody of the child or would prevent the need for further detention.

(2) If the child can be returned to the custody of his or her parent or guardian through the provision of those services, the court shall place the child with his or her parent or guardian and order that the services shall be provided. If the child cannot be returned to the physical custody of his or her parent or guardian, the court shall determine if there is a relative who is able and willing to care for the child, and has been assessed pursuant to * * * Section 361.4.

(3) In order to preserve the bond between the child and the parent and to facilitate family reunification, the court shall consider whether the child can be returned to the custody of his or her parent who is enrolled in a certified substance abuse treatment facility that allows a dependent child to reside with his or her parent. The fact that the parent is enrolled in a certified substance abuse treatment facility that allows a dependent child to reside with his or her parent shall not be, for that reason alone, prima facie evidence of substantial danger. The court shall specify the factual basis for its conclusion that the return of the child to the custody of his or her parent would pose a substantial danger or would not pose a substantial danger to the physical health, safety, protection, or physical or emotional well-being of the child.

(e) If a court orders a child detained, the court shall state the facts on which the decision is based, specify why the initial removal was necessary, reference the social worker's report or other evidence relied upon to make its determination whether continuance in the home of the parent or legal guardian is contrary to the child's welfare, order temporary placement and care of the child to be vested with the county child welfare department pending the hearing held pursuant to Section 355 or further order of the court, and order services to be provided as soon as possible to reunify the child and his or her family if appropriate.

(f)(1)(A) If the child is not released from custody, the court may order * * * the temporary placement of the child * * * in any of the following for a period not to exceed 15 judicial days:

(i) The home of a relative or a nonrelative extended family member, as defined in Section 362.7, that has been assessed pursuant to Section 361.4.

(ii) The approved home of a resource family, as defined in Section 16519.5.

(iii) An emergency shelter or other suitable licensed place * * *.

(iv) A place exempt from licensure designated by the juvenile court * * *.

(B) A runaway and homeless youth shelter licensed by the State Department of Social Services pursuant to Section 1502.35 of the Health and Safety Code shall not be a placement option pursuant to this section.

(2) * * * Relatives shall be given preferential consideration for placement of the child * * *. As used in this section, "relative" means an adult who is related to the child by blood, adoption, or affinity within the fifth degree of kinship, including stepparents, stepsiblings, and all relatives whose status is preceded by the words "great," "great-great," or "grand," or the spouse of any of these persons, even if the marriage was terminated by death or dissolution.

(3) * * * When placing in the home of a relative or nonrelative extended family member, the court shall consider the recommendations of the social worker based on the assessment pursuant to * * * Section 361.4 of the * * * home of the relative or nonrelative extended family member, including the results of a criminal records check and prior child abuse allegations, if any, prior to ordering that the child be placed with a relative or nonrelative extended family member. The court shall order the parent to disclose to the social worker the names, residences, and any known identifying information of any maternal or paternal relatives of the child. The social worker shall initiate the assessment pursuant to Section 361.3 of any relative to be considered for continuing placement.

(g)(1) At the initial hearing upon the petition filed in accordance with subdivision (c) of Rule 5.520 of the California Rules of Court or anytime thereafter up until the time that the minor is adjudged a dependent child of the court or a finding is made dismissing the petition, the court may temporarily limit the right of the parent or guardian to make educational or developmental services decisions for the child and temporarily appoint a responsible adult to make educational or developmental services decisions for the child if all of the following conditions are found:

(A) The parent or guardian is unavailable, unable, or unwilling to exercise educational or developmental services rights for the child.

(B) The county placing agency has made diligent efforts to locate and secure the participation of the parent or guardian in educational or developmental services decisionmaking.

(C) The child's educational and developmental services needs cannot be met without the temporary appointment of a responsible adult.

(2) If the court limits the parent's educational rights under this subdivision, the court shall determine whether there is a responsible adult who is a relative, nonrelative extended family member, or other adult known to the child and who is available and willing to serve as the child's educational representative before appointing an educational representative or surrogate who is not known to the child.

(3) If the court cannot identify a responsible adult to make educational decisions for the child and the appointment of a surrogate parent, as defined in subdivision (a) of Section 56050 of the Education Code, is not warranted, the court may, with the input of any interested person, make educational decisions for the child. If the child is receiving services from a regional center, the provision of any developmental

services related to the court's decision shall be consistent with the child's individual program plan and pursuant to the provisions of the Lanterman Developmental Disabilities Services Act (Division 4.5 (commencing with Section 4500)). If the court cannot identify a responsible adult to make developmental services decisions for the child, the court may, with the input of any interested person, make developmental services decisions for the child. If the court makes educational or developmental services decisions for the child, the court shall also issue appropriate orders to ensure that every effort is made to identify a responsible adult to make future educational or developmental services decisions for the child.

(4) A temporary appointment of a responsible adult and temporary limitation on the right of the parent or guardian to make educational or developmental services decisions for the child shall be specifically addressed in the court order. An order made under this section shall expire at the conclusion of the hearing held pursuant to Section 361 or upon dismissal of the petition. Upon the entering of disposition orders, additional needed limitation on the parent's or guardian's educational or developmental services rights shall be addressed pursuant to Section 361.

(5) This section does not remove the obligation to appoint surrogate parents for students with disabilities who are without parental representation in special education procedures as required by state and federal law, including Section 1415(b)(2) of Title 20 of the United States Code, Section 56050 of the Education Code, Section 7579.5 of the Government Code, and Rule 5.650 of the California Rules of Court.

(6) If the court appoints a developmental services decisionmaker pursuant to this section, he or she shall have the authority to access the child's information and records pursuant to subdivision (u) of Section 4514 and subdivision (y) of Section 5328, and to act on the child's behalf for the purposes of the individual program plan process pursuant to Sections 4646, 4646.5, and 4648 and the fair hearing process pursuant to Chapter 7 (commencing with Section 4700), and as set forth in the court order. *(Added by Stats.1976, c. 1068, p. 4760, § 7. Amended by Stats.1982, c. 978, § 9, eff. Sept. 13, 1982, operative July 1, 1982; Stats.1983, c. 309, § 4; Stats. 1984, c. 1608, § 2, eff. Sept. 30, 1984; Stats.1985, c. 440, § 1; Stats.1986, c. 1121, § 1; Stats.1986, c. 1122, § 3; Stats.1987, c. 1485, § 24; Stats.1990, c. 1530 (S.B.2232), § 4; Stats.1994, c. 469 (A.B.1579), § 2; Stats.1997, c. 793 (A.B.1544), § 12; Stats.1998, c. 1054 (A.B.1091), § 9; Stats.1998, c. 1056 (A.B.2773), § 10; Stats.1999, c. 83 (S.B.966), § 192; Stats. 2001, c. 653 (A.B.1695), § 9, eff. Oct. 10, 2001; Stats.2004, c. 373 (A.B.1913), § 3; Stats.2005, c. 639 (A.B.1261), § 9; Stats.2006, c. 538 (S.B.1852), § 685; Stats.2007, c. 130 (A.B.299), § 243; Stats.2011, c. 471 (S.B.368), § 1; Stats. 2012, c. 162 (S.B.1171), § 187; Stats.2012, c. 176 (A.B.2060), § 1; Stats.2013, c. 485 (A.B.346), § 3; Stats.2014, c. 219 (S.B.977), § 1, eff. Jan. 1, 2015; Stats.2015, c. 303 (A.B.731), § 567, eff. Jan. 1, 2016; Stats.2017, c. 732 (A.B.404), § 44, eff. Jan. 1, 2018.)*

Research References

Forms

West's California Judicial Council Forms JV-405, Continuance--Dependency Detention Hearing.

West's California Judicial Council Forms JV-410, Findings and Orders After Detention Hearing (Welf. & Inst. Code, S319.

Treatises and Practice Aids

Witkin, California Summary 10th Parent and Child § 12, Parental or Marital Rights Of Prisoners.

Witkin, California Summary 10th Parent and Child § 552, in General.

Witkin, California Summary 10th Parent and Child § 558, Medical Examination.

Witkin, California Summary 10th Parent and Child § 599, Grounds for Detention.

Witkin, California Summary 10th Parent and Child § 601, Continuance Of Hearing.

Witkin, California Summary 10th Parent and Child § 604, in General.

Witkin, California Summary 10th Parent and Child § 605, Rights Of Child, Parent, and Guardian.

Witkin, California Summary 10th Parent and Child § 607, Findings and Orders.

Witkin, California Summary 10th Parent and Child § 631, Procedure.

Witkin, California Summary 10th Parent and Child § 709, in General.

Witkin, California Summary 10th Parent and Child § 607A, (New) Educational and Developmental Services Decisions.

§ 319.1. Minors in need of specialized mental health treatment; notification of county mental health department

When the court finds a minor to be a person described by Section 300, and believes that the minor may need specialized mental health treatment while the minor is unable to reside in his or her natural home, the court shall notify the director of the county mental health department in the county where the minor resides. The county mental health department shall perform the duties required under Section 5694.7 for all those minors.

Nothing in this section shall restrict the provisions of emergency psychiatric services to those minors who are involved in dependency cases and have not yet reached the point of adjudication or disposition, nor shall it operate to restrict evaluations at an earlier stage of the proceedings or to restrict orders removing the minor from a detention facility for psychiatric treatment. *(Added by Stats.1985, c. 1286, § 1.6, eff. Sept. 30, 1985. Amended by Stats.1999, c. 892 (A.B.1672), § 16; Stats.2001, c. 854 (S.B.205), § 70.)*

Research References

Treatises and Practice Aids

Witkin, California Summary 10th Parent and Child § 607, Findings and Orders.

§ 319.2. Children under the age of six years; placement in licensed group home or temporary shelter care facility

Notwithstanding Section 319, when a child under the age of six years is not released from the custody of the court, the child may be placed in a community care facility licensed as a group home for children or in a temporary shelter care facility, as defined in Section 1530.8 of the Health and Safety Code, only when the court finds that placement is necessary to secure a complete and adequate evaluation, including placement planning and transition time. The placement period shall not exceed 60 days unless a case plan has been developed and the need for additional time is documented in the case plan and has been approved by the deputy director or director of the county child welfare department or an assistant chief probation officer or chief probation officer of the county probation department. *(Added by Stats.1993, c. 1088 (A.B.1197), § 3. Amended by Stats.2013, c. 21 (A.B.74), § 7, eff. June 27, 2013.)*

Research References

Treatises and Practice Aids

Witkin, California Summary 10th Parent and Child § 607, Findings and Orders.

Witkin, California Summary 10th Parent and Child § 759, in General.

§ 319.3. Children 6 to 12 years of age; placement in licensed group home, short-term residential therapeutic program, or temporary shelter care facility

Notwithstanding Section 319, a * * * child who is the subject of a petition under Section 300 and who is 6 to 12 years of age, inclusive, may be placed in a community care facility licensed as a group home for children, a short-term residential therapeutic program, or in a temporary shelter care facility, as defined in Section 1530.8 of the Health and Safety Code, only when the court finds that placement is necessary to secure a complete and adequate evaluation, including placement planning and transition time. The placement period in a group home for children or a short-term residential therapeutic program shall not exceed 60 days unless a case plan has been developed and the need for additional time is documented in the case plan and has been approved by a deputy director or director of the county child welfare department or an assistant chief probation officer or chief probation officer of the county probation department. The placement period in a temporary shelter care facility shall not exceed 10 days. *(Added by Stats.2013, c. 21 (A.B.74), § 8, eff. June 27, 2013. Amended by Stats.2015, c. 773 (A.B.403), § 46, eff. Jan. 1, 2016; Stats.2016, c. 612 (A.B.1997), § 69, eff. Jan. 1, 2017; Stats.2017, c. 732 (A.B. 404), § 45, eff. Jan. 1, 2018.)*

Research References

Treatises and Practice Aids

Witkin, California Summary 10th Parent and Child § 607, Findings and Orders.

Witkin, California Summary 10th Parent and Child § 759, in General.

§ 321. Rehearing; continuance

When a hearing is held under the provisions of this article and no parent or guardian of the minor is present and no parent or guardian has had actual notice of the hearing, a parent or guardian of the minor may file an affidavit setting forth the facts with the clerk of the juvenile court and the clerk shall immediately set the matter for rehearing at a time within 24 hours, excluding Sundays and nonjudicial days from the filing of the affidavit. Upon the rehearing, the court shall proceed in the same manner as upon the original hearing.

If the minor, a parent or guardian or the minor's attorney or guardian ad litem, if either one or the other has been appointed by the court, requests evidence of the prima facie case, a rehearing shall be held within three judicial days to consider evidence of the prima facie case. If the prima facie case is not established, the minor shall be released from detention.

In lieu of a requested rehearing, the court may set the matter for trial within 10 days.

When the court ascertains that the rehearing cannot be held within three judicial days because of the unavailability of a witness, a reasonable continuance may be granted for a period not to exceed five judicial days. *(Added by Stats.1976, c. 1068, p. 4760, § 7. Amended by Stats.1982, c. 978, § 11, eff. Sept. 13, 1982, operative July 1, 1982; Stats.1983, c. 309, § 5; Stats.1984, c. 144, § 216.)*

Research References

Treatises and Practice Aids

Witkin, California Summary 10th Parent and Child § 606, Rehearing.

§ 322. Continuance; motion

Upon motion of the minor or a parent or guardian of such minor, the court shall continue any hearing or rehearing held under the provisions of this article for one day, excluding Sundays and nonjudicial days. *(Added by Stats.1976, c. 1068, p. 4760, § 7.)*

Research References

Forms

West's California Judicial Council Forms JV-405, Continuance--Dependency Detention Hearing.

Treatises and Practice Aids

Witkin, California Summary 10th Parent and Child § 601, Continuance Of Hearing.

§ 323. Order requiring reappearance of minor, parent or guardian

Upon any hearing or rehearing under the provisions of this article, the court may order such minor or any parent or guardian of such minor who is present in court to again appear before the court, the probation officer or the county financial evaluation officer at a time and place specified in said order. *(Added by Stats.1976, c. 1068, p. 4760, § 7. Amended by Stats.1985, c. 1485, § 7.)*

Research References

Treatises and Practice Aids

Witkin, California Summary 10th Parent and Child § 607, Findings and Orders.

§ 324. County of custody; petition and warrant of requesting county

Whenever any minor is taken into temporary custody under the provisions of this article in any county other than the county in which the minor is alleged to be within or to come within the jurisdiction of the juvenile court, which county is referred to herein as the requesting county, the officer who has taken the minor into temporary custody may notify the law enforcement agency in the requesting county of the fact that the minor is in custody. When a law enforcement officer, of such requesting county files a petition pursuant to Section 332 with the clerk of the juvenile court of his respective county and secures a warrant therefrom, he shall forward said warrant, or a telegraphic copy thereof to the officer who has the minor in temporary custody as soon as possible within 48 hours, excluding Sundays and nonjudicial days, from the time said juvenile was taken into temporary custody. Thereafter an officer from said requesting county shall take custody of the minor within five days, in the county in which the minor is in temporary custody, and shall take the minor before the juvenile court judge who issued the warrant, or before some other juvenile court of the same county without unnecessary delay. If the minor is not brought before a judge of the juvenile court within the period prescribed by this section, he must be released from custody. *(Added by Stats.1976, c. 1068, p. 4760, § 7.)*

Research References

Treatises and Practice Aids

Witkin, California Summary 10th Parent and Child § 557, Retention Of Custody.

§ 324.5. Medical examination of child in protective custody when child abuse suspected

(a) Whenever allegations of physical or sexual abuse of a child come to the attention of a local law enforcement agency or the local child welfare department and the child is taken into protective custody, the local law enforcement agency, or child welfare department may, as soon as practically possible, consult with a medical practitioner, who has specialized training in detecting and treating child abuse injuries and neglect, to determine whether a physical examination of the child is appropriate. If deemed appropriate, the local law enforcement agency, or the child welfare department, shall cause the child to undergo a physical examination performed by a medical practitioner who has specialized training in detecting and treating child abuse injuries and neglect, and, whenever possible, shall ensure that this examination take place within 72 hours of the time the child was taken into protective custody. In the event the allegations are made while the child is in custody, the physical examination shall be performed within 72 hours of the time the allegations were made.

In the case of a petition filed pursuant to Section 319, the department shall provide the results of the physical examination to the court and to any counsel for the minor, and counsel for the parent or guardian of the minor. Failure to obtain this physical examination shall not be grounds to deny a petition under this section.

(b) The local child welfare agency shall, whenever possible, request that additional medical examinations to determine child abuse injuries or neglect, be performed by the same medical practitioner who performed the examinations described in subdivision (a). If it is not possible to obtain additional medical examinations, the local child welfare agency shall ensure that future medical practitioners to whom the child has been referred for ongoing diagnosis and treatment have specialized training in detecting and treating child abuse injuries and neglect and have access to the child's medical records covering the current and previous incidents of child abuse. *(Added by Stats.1998, c. 949 (S.B.645), § 2.)*

Research References

Treatises and Practice Aids

Witkin, California Summary 10th Parent and Child § 558, Medical Examination.

Witkin, California Summary 10th Parent and Child § 604, in General.

ARTICLE 8. DEPENDENT CHILDREN—COMMENCEMENT OF PROCEEDINGS

§ 325. Filing of petition

A proceeding in the juvenile court to declare a child to be a dependent child of the court is commenced by the filing with the court, by the social worker, of a petition, in conformity with the requirements of this article. *(Added by Stats.1976, c. 1068, p. 4765, § 8. Amended by Stats.1998, c. 1054 (A.B. 1091), § 10.)*

Research References

Treatises and Practice Aids

Witkin, California Summary 10th Parent and Child § 564, in General.

Witkin, California Summary 10th Parent and Child § 567, Statutory Rights.

Witkin, California Summary 10th Parent and Child § 749, Segregation Of Classes Of Minors.

Witkin, California Summary 10th Parent and Child § 899A, (New) Hearing Before Termination Of Jurisdiction.

§ 326.5. Rules of court; appointment of guardian ad litem

The Judicial Council shall adopt a rule of court effective July 1, 2001, that complies with the requirement of the federal Child Abuse Prevention and Treatment Act (Public

Law 93–247) for the appointment of a guardian ad litem, who may be an attorney or a court-appointed special advocate, for a child in cases in which a petition is filed based upon neglect or abuse of the child or in which a prosecution is initiated under the Penal Code arising from neglect or abuse of the child. The rule of court may include guidelines to the courts for determining when an attorney should be appointed rather than a court appointed special advocate, and caseload standards for guardians ad litem. *(Added by Stats.2000, c. 450 (S.B.2160), § 3.)*

Commentary

This section is not retroactive and thus does not require the appointment of a new guardian ad litem in cases filed before its effective date, July 1, 2001. *In re S.D., 102 Cal.App.4th 560, 125 Cal.Rptr.2d 570 (2002).*

Research References

Treatises and Practice Aids

Witkin, California Summary 10th Parent and Child § 572, Appointment Of Guardian Ad Litem or Child Advocate.

Witkin, California Summary 10th Parent and Child § 708, Counsel on Appeal.

§ 326.7. Appointment of guardian ad litem for minor parent

Appointment of a guardian ad litem shall not be required for a minor who is a parent of the child who is the subject of the dependency petition, unless the minor parent is unable to understand the nature of the proceedings or to assist counsel in preparing the case. *(Added by Stats.2008, c. 181 (S.B. 1612), § 3.)*

Research References

Treatises and Practice Aids

Witkin, California Summary 10th Parent and Child § 572, Appointment Of Guardian Ad Litem or Child Advocate.

Witkin, California Summary 10th Parent and Child § 577, Hearing.

§ 327. Venue

Either the juvenile court in the county in which a minor resides or in the county where the minor is found or in the county in which the acts take place or the circumstances exist which are alleged to bring such minor within the provisions of Section 300, is the proper court to commence proceedings under this chapter. *(Added by Stats.1976, c. 1068, p. 4765, § 8.)*

Research References

Treatises and Practice Aids

Witkin, California Summary 10th Parent and Child § 456, Proper Court.

§ 328. Cause for investigation; referral to child welfare services; investigation when allegations are raised in family court dispute

Whenever the social worker has cause to believe that there was or is within the county, or residing therein, a person described in Section 300, the social worker shall immediately make any investigation he or she deems necessary to determine whether child welfare services should be offered to the family and whether proceedings in the juvenile court should be commenced. If the social worker determines that it is appropriate to offer child welfare services to the family, the social worker shall make a referral to these services pursuant to Chapter 5 (commencing with Section 16500) of Part 4 of Division 9. No inference regarding the credibility of the allegations or the need for child welfare services shall be drawn from the mere existence of a child custody or visitation dispute.

However, this section does not require an investigation by the social worker with respect to a child delivered or referred to any agency pursuant to Section 307.5.

The social worker shall interview any child four years of age or older who is a subject of an investigation, and who is in juvenile hall or other custodial facility, or has been removed to a foster home, to ascertain the child's view of the home environment. If proceedings are commenced, the social worker shall include the substance of the interview in any written report submitted at an adjudicatory hearing, or if no report is then received in evidence, the social worker shall include the substance of the interview in the social study required by Section 358. A referral based on allegations of child abuse from the family court pursuant to Section 3027 of the Family Code shall be investigated to the same extent as any other child abuse allegation. *(Added by Stats.1976, c. 1068, p. 4765, § 8. Amended by Stats.1981, c. 875, p. 3362, § 1; Stats.1982, c. 461, § 2; Stats.1982, c. 978, § 12, eff. Sept. 13, 1982, operative July 1, 1982; Stats.1982, c. 1094, § 1.1; Stats.1984, c. 260, § 1; Stats.1987, c. 1485, § 25; Stats.1998, c. 1054 (A.B.1091), § 11; Stats.2010, c. 352 (A.B.939), § 20.)*

Research References

Treatises and Practice Aids

Witkin, California Summary 10th Parent and Child § 283, Sexual Abuse Allegation.

Witkin, California Summary 10th Parent and Child § 561, Investigation by Social Worker.

Witkin, California Summary 10th Parent and Child § 698, Other Procedures.

Witkin, California Summary 10th Wills and Probate § 922, Investigation and Report.

§ 328.3. Taking minor to community service program for abused or neglected children; investigation; initiation of service program; written notification to referring officer

Whenever any officer refers or delivers a minor pursuant to Section 307.5, the agency to which the minor is referred shall immediately make such investigation as it deems necessary to determine what disposition of the referral or delivery should be made. If the referral agency does not initiate a service program on behalf of a minor referred to the agency within 20 calendar days, or initiate a service program on behalf of a minor delivered to the agency within 10 calendar days, that agency shall immediately notify the referring officer of that decision in writing. The referral agency shall retain a copy of that written notification for 30 days. *(Added by Stats.1984, c. 260, § 2.)*

Research References

Treatises and Practice Aids

Witkin, California Summary 10th Parent and Child § 553, Disposition by Peace Officer.

Witkin, California Summary 10th Parent and Child § 561, Investigation by Social Worker.

§ 329. Application to commence proceedings; affidavit; investigation; notification of decision

Whenever any person applies to the social worker to commence proceedings in the juvenile court, the application shall be in the form of an affidavit alleging that there was or is within the county, or residing therein, a child within the provisions of Section 300, and setting forth facts in support thereof. The social worker shall immediately investigate as he or she deems necessary to determine whether proceedings in the juvenile court should be commenced. If the social worker does not take action under Section 301 and does not file a petition in the juvenile court within three weeks after the application, he or she shall endorse upon the affidavit of the applicant his or her decision not to proceed further, including any recommendation made to the applicant, if one is made, to consider commencing a probate guardianship for the child, and his or her reasons therefor and shall immediately notify the applicant of the action taken or the decision rendered by him or her under this section. The social worker shall retain the affidavit and his or her endorsement thereon for a period of 30 days after notifying the applicant. *(Added by Stats.1976, c. 1068, p. 4765, § 8. Amended by Stats.1998, c. 1054 (A.B.1091), § 12; Stats.2012, c. 638 (A.B.1757), § 15.)*

Commentary

In re M.C., 199 Cal.App.4th 784, 131 Cal.Rptr.3d 194 (2011), holds that section 331, read together this section, authorizes a juvenile court to order a social services agency to file a dependency petition over the agency's objection, reasoning that this exercise of judicial power does not violate the separation of powers doctrine.

Research References

Forms

West's California Judicial Council Forms JV-210, Application to Commence Proceedings by Affidavit and Decision by Social Worker.

Treatises and Practice Aids

Witkin, California Summary 10th Parent and Child § 494, Records Of Dependent Children.

Witkin, California Summary 10th Parent and Child § 561, Investigation by Social Worker.

Witkin, California Summary 10th Parent and Child § 562, Application to Social Worker.

Witkin, California Summary 10th Parent and Child § 642, in General.

Witkin, California Summary 10th Parent and Child § 898, Court Supervision Of Child.

Witkin, California Summary 10th Parent and Child § 452E, (New) Termination Of Jurisdiction Over Minor.

Witkin, California Summary 10th Parent and Child § 899A, (New) Hearing Before Termination Of Jurisdiction.

Witkin, California Summary 10th Wills and Probate § 922, Investigation and Report.

§ 331. Failure of social worker to file petition; review of decision

When any person has applied to the social worker, pursuant to Section 329, to commence juvenile court proceedings and the social worker fails to file a petition within three weeks after the application, the person may, within one month after making the application, apply to the juvenile court to review the decision of the social worker, and the court may either affirm the decision of the social worker or order him or her to commence juvenile court proceedings. *(Added by Stats.1976, c. 1068, p. 4765, § 8. Amended by Stats.1998, c. 1054 (A.B.1091), § 13.)*

Commentary

In re M.C., 199 Cal.App.4th 784, 131 Cal.Rptr.3d 194 (2011), holds that this section, read together with section 329, authorizes a juvenile court to order a social services agency to file a dependency petition over the agency's objection, reasoning that this exercise of judicial power does not violate the separation of powers doctrine.

In re Michael H., 229 Cal.App.4th 1366, 178 Cal.Rptr.3d 71 (2014), review denied, held that a juvenile court's order affirming a social worker's decision not to file a dependency petition is not an appealable order, reasoning that neither this section nor section 395 expressly authorizes an appeal.

Research References

Forms

West's California Judicial Council Forms JV-215, Application to Review Decision by Social Worker Not to Commence Proceedings.

Treatises and Practice Aids

Witkin, California Summary 10th Parent and Child § 494, Records Of Dependent Children.

Witkin, California Summary 10th Parent and Child § 562, Application to Social Worker.

Witkin, California Summary 10th Parent and Child § 564, in General.

Witkin, California Summary 10th Parent and Child § 704, Miscellaneous Orders.

Witkin, California Summary 10th Parent and Child § 705, in General.

§ 331.5. Decision not to initiate service program for child delivered or referred; application for review

When any officer has referred or delivered a child to an agency pursuant to Section 307.5, and that agency does not initiate a service program for the child within the time periods required by Section 328.3, the referring agency may, within 10 court days following receipt of the notification from the referral agency, apply to the social worker for a review of that decision. *(Added by Stats.1984, c. 260, § 3. Amended by Stats.1998, c. 1054 (A.B.1091), § 14.)*

Research References

Treatises and Practice Aids

Witkin, California Summary 10th Parent and Child § 553, Disposition by Peace Officer.

§ 332. Petition; verification; contents

A petition to commence proceedings in the juvenile court to declare a child a * * * dependent child of the court shall be verified and shall contain all of the following:

(a) The name of the court to which it is addressed.

(b) The title of the proceeding.

(c) The code section and the subdivision under which the proceedings are instituted. If it is alleged that the child is a person described by subdivision (e) of Section 300, the petition shall include an allegation pursuant to that section.

(d) The name, age, and address, if any, of the child upon whose behalf the petition is brought.

(e) The names and residence addresses, if known to the petitioner, of both parents and any guardian of the child. If there is no parent or guardian residing within the state, or if his or her place of residence is not known to the petitioner, the petition shall also contain the name and residence address, if known, of any adult relative residing within the county, or, if there is none, the adult relative residing nearest to the location of the court. If it is known to the petitioner that one of the parents is a victim of domestic violence and that parent is currently living separately from the batterer-parent, the address of the victim-parent shall remain confidential.

(f) A concise statement of facts, separately stated, to support the conclusion that the child upon whose behalf the petition is being brought is a person within the definition of each of the sections and subdivisions under which the proceedings are being instituted.

(g) The fact that the child upon whose behalf the petition is brought is detained in custody or is not detained in custody, and if he or she is detained in custody, the date and the precise time the child was taken into custody.

(h) A notice to the father, mother, spouse, or other person liable for support of the child, of all of the following: (1) Section 903 makes that person, the estate of that person, and the estate of the child, liable for the cost of the care, support, and maintenance of the child in any county institution or any other place in which the child is placed, detained, or committed pursuant to an order of the juvenile court; (2) Section 903.1 makes that person, the estate of that person, and the estate of the child, liable for the cost to the county of legal services rendered to the child or the parent by a private attorney or a public defender appointed pursuant to the order of the juvenile court; (3) Section 903.2 makes that person, the estate of that person, and the estate of the child, liable for the cost to the county of the supervision of the child by the social worker pursuant to the order of the juvenile court; and (4) the liabilities established by these sections are joint and several. *(Added by Stats.1976, c. 1068, p. 4765, § 8. Amended by Stats.1982, c. 1276, § 3, eff. Sept. 22, 1982; Stats.1984, c. 1246, § 2; Stats.1986, c. 1122, § 5; Stats.1987, c. 1485, § 26; Stats.1989, c. 1151, § 3; Stats.1990, c. 1530 (S.B.2232), § 5; Stats.1996, c. 1139 (A.B.2647), § 7; Stats. 1998, c. 1054 (A.B.1091), § 15; Stats.2017, c. 678 (S.B.190), § 6, eff. Jan. 1, 2018.)*

Research References

Treatises and Practice Aids

Witkin, California Summary 10th Parent and Child § 494, Records Of Dependent Children.

Witkin, California Summary 10th Parent and Child § 546, Severe Physical Abuse.

Witkin, California Summary 10th Parent and Child § 557, Retention Of Custody.

Witkin, California Summary 10th Parent and Child § 563, Program Of Supervision.

Witkin, California Summary 10th Parent and Child § 565, Form and Content.

Witkin, California Summary 10th Parent and Child § 566, Notices, Citations, Warrants, and Subpenas.

Witkin, California Summary 10th Parent and Child § 600, Petition and Notice Of Hearing.

Witkin, California Summary 10th Parent and Child § 627, in General.

Witkin, California Summary 10th Parent and Child § 657, Filing, Setting for Hearing, and Notice.

§ 333. Unverified petition; dismissal without prejudice

Any petition filed in juvenile court to commence proceedings pursuant to this chapter that is not verified may be dismissed without prejudice by such court. *(Added by Stats.1976, c. 1068, p. 4765, § 8.)*

Research References

Treatises and Practice Aids

Witkin, California Summary 10th Parent and Child § 565, Form and Content.

§ 334. Time for hearing

Upon the filing of the petition, the clerk of the juvenile court shall set the same for hearing within 30 days, except that in the case of a minor detained in custody at the time of the filing of the petition, the petition must be set for hearing within 15 judicial days from the date of the order of the court directing such detention. *(Added by Stats.1976, c. 1068, p. 4765, § 8.)*

Research References

Treatises and Practice Aids

Witkin, California Summary 10th Parent and Child § 609, Time for Hearing.

§ 338. Notice; citation; issuance and service

In addition to the notice provided in Sections 290.1 and 290.2 the juvenile court may issue its citation directing any parent or guardian of the person concerning whom a petition has been filed to appear at the time and place set for any hearing or financial evaluation under the provisions of this chapter, including a hearing under the provisions of Section 257, and directing any person having custody or control of the minor concerning whom the petition has been filed to bring such minor with him or her. The notice shall in addition state that a parent or guardian may be required to participate in a counseling program with the minor concerning whom the petition has been filed. Personal service of such citation shall be made at least 24 hours before the time stated therein for that appearance. *(Added by Stats.1976, c. 1068, p. 4768, § 8. Amended by Stats.1985, c. 1485, § 9; Stats.2002, c. 416 (S.B.1956), § 7.)*

Research References

Treatises and Practice Aids

Witkin, California Summary 10th Parent and Child § 566, Notices, Citations, Warrants, and Subpenas.

§ 339. Warrant of arrest against parent or guardian

In case such citation cannot be served, or the person served fails to obey it, or in any case in which it appears to the court that the citation will probably be ineffective, a warrant of arrest may issue on the order of the court either against the parent, or guardian, or the person having the custody of the minor, or with whom the minor is living. *(Added by Stats.1976, c. 1068, p. 4765, § 8.)*

Research References

Treatises and Practice Aids

Witkin, California Summary 10th Parent and Child § 566, Notices, Citations, Warrants, and Subpenas.

§ 340. Protective custody warrant; cause for issuance with or without a petition; investigation

(a) Whenever a petition has been filed in the juvenile court alleging that a minor comes within Section 300 and praying for a hearing * * * on that petition, or whenever any subsequent petition has been filed praying for a hearing in the matter of the minor and it appears to the court that the circumstances of his or her home environment may endanger the health, person, or welfare of the minor, or whenever a dependent minor has run away from his or her court-ordered placement, a protective custody warrant may be issued immediately for the minor.

(b) A protective custody warrant may be issued without filing a petition under Section 300 if the court finds probable cause to support all of the following:

(1) The child is a person described in Section 300.

(2) There is a substantial danger to the safety or to the physical or emotional health of the child.

(3) There are no reasonable means to protect the child's safety or physical health without removal.

(c) Any child taken into protective custody pursuant to this section shall immediately be delivered to the social worker who shall investigate, pursuant to Section 309, the facts and circumstances of the child and the facts surrounding the child being taken into custody and attempt to maintain the child with the child's family through the provision of services.

(d)(1) Nothing in this section is intended to limit any other circumstance that permits a magistrate to issue a warrant for a person.

(2) Nothing in this section is intended to limit a social worker from taking into and maintaining temporary custody of a minor pursuant to paragraph (2) of subdivision (a) of Section 306. *(Added by Stats.1976, c. 1068, p. 4765, § 8. Amended by Stats.1987, c. 1485, § 29; Stats.2017, c. 262 (A.B.1401), § 1, eff. Jan. 1, 2018.)*

Research References

Treatises and Practice Aids

Witkin, California Summary 10th Parent and Child § 566, Notices, Citations, Warrants, and Subpenas.

Witkin, California Summary 10th Parent and Child § 699A, (New) in General.

§ 340.5. Parental threats against assigned social worker; restraining order; good cause; violation

(a) Whenever pursuant to Article 10 (commencing with Section 360) a social worker is assigned to provide child welfare services, family reunification services, or other services to a dependent child of the juvenile court, the juvenile court may, for good cause shown and after an ex parte hearing, issue its order restraining the parents of the dependent child from threatening the social worker, or any member of the social worker's family, with physical harm.

(b) For purposes of this section, "good cause" means at least one threat of physical harm to the social worker, or any member of the social worker's family, made by the person who is to be the subject of the restraining order, with the apparent ability to carry out the threat.

(c) Violation of a restraining order issued pursuant to this section shall be punishable as contempt. *(Added by Stats. 1991, c. 980 (S.B.704), § 1.)*

Commentary

In re Matthew F., 132 Cal.App.4th 883, 33 Cal.Rptr.3d 909 (2005), review denied, holds that a juvenile court may issue a permanent restraining order to protect a social worker even though she is no longer assigned to the case in which a parent threatened her.

Research References

Treatises and Practice Aids

Witkin, California Summary 10th Parent and Child § 642, in General.

§ 341. Subpoenas

Upon request of the social worker, district attorney, the child, or the child's parent, guardian, or custodian, or on the court's own motion, the court or the clerk of the court, or an attorney, pursuant to Section 1985 of the Code of Civil Procedure, shall issue subpoenas requiring attendance and testimony of witnesses and production of papers at any hearing regarding a child who is alleged or determined by the court to be a person described by Section 300. When a person attends a juvenile court hearing as a witness upon a subpoena, in its discretion, the court may by an order on its minutes, direct the county auditor to draw his or her warrant upon the county treasurer in favor of the witness for witness fees in the amount and manner prescribed by Section 68093 of the Government Code. The fees are county charges. *(Added by Stats.1976, c. 1068, p. 4765, § 8. Amended by Stats.1982, c. 978, § 14, eff. Sept. 13, 1982, operative July 1, 1982; Stats.1996, c. 90 (A.B.2007), § 1; Stats.1998, c. 1054 (A.B.1091), § 17.)*

Commentary

In a dependency proceeding, a parent who claims to have been drug-free for six years himself tenders the issue of past drug use and thus forfeits the patient-physician privilege as to past drug use. *In re R.R., 187 Cal.App.4th 1264, 114 Cal.Rptr.3d 765 (2010).*

Research References

Treatises and Practice Aids

Witkin, California Summary 10th Parent and Child § 566, Notices, Citations, Warrants, and Subpenas.

§ 342. Allegations of new facts or circumstances; subsequent petition; applicable procedure

(a) In any case in which a minor has been found to be a person described by Section 300 and the petitioner alleges new facts or circumstances, other than those under which the original petition was sustained, sufficient to state that the minor is a person described in Section 300, the petitioner shall file a subsequent petition. This section does not apply if the jurisdiction of the juvenile court has been terminated prior to the new allegations.

* * * (b) Unless otherwise provided by law, all procedures and hearings required for an original petition are applicable to a subsequent petition filed under this section. *(Added by Stats.1987, c. 1485, § 30. Amended by Stats.1988, c. 1075, § 3; Stats.2017, c. 319 (A.B.976), § 129, eff. Jan. 1, 2018.)*

Research References

Treatises and Practice Aids

Witkin, California Summary 10th Parent and Child § 668, Subsequent Petition.

ARTICLE 9. DEPENDENT CHILDREN—HEARINGS

§ 345. Special or separate session; presence of persons on trial or awaiting trial

All cases under this chapter shall be heard at a special or separate session of the court, and no other matter shall be heard at such a session. No person on trial, awaiting trial, or under accusation of crime, other than a parent, guardian, or relative of the minor, shall be permitted to be present at any such session, except as a witness.

Cases in which the minor is detained and the sole allegation is that the minor is a person described in Section 300 shall be granted precedence on the calendar of the court for the day on which the case is set for hearing. *(Added by Stats.1976, c. 1068, p. 4769, § 9. Amended by Stats.1986, c. 1122, § 6; Stats.1987, c. 1485, § 31.)*

Research References

Forms

West's California Judicial Council Forms JV-245, Request for Restraining Order--Juvenile.

Treatises and Practice Aids

Witkin, California Summary 10th Parent and Child § 586, Hearing is Usually Private.

Witkin, California Summary 10th Parent and Child § 598, in General.

§ 346. Admission of public and persons having interest in case

Unless requested by a parent or guardian and consented to or requested by the minor concerning whom the petition has been filed, the public shall not be admitted to a juvenile court hearing. The judge or referee may nevertheless admit such persons as he deems to have a direct and legitimate interest in the particular case or the work of the court. *(Added by Stats.1976, c. 1068, p. 4769, § 9. Amended by Stats.1982, c. 978, § 15, eff. Sept. 13, 1982, operative July 1, 1982.)*

Research References

Treatises and Practice Aids

Witkin, California Summary 10th Parent and Child § 499, Disclosure to Press.

Witkin, California Summary 10th Parent and Child § 586, Hearing is Usually Private.

Witkin, California Summary 10th Parent and Child § 588, Persons Who May be Admitted.

§ 347. Court reporter; writing out and transcribing notes; costs

At any juvenile court hearing conducted by a juvenile court judge, an official court reporter shall, and at any such hearing conducted by a juvenile court referee, the official reporter, as directed by the court, may take down in shorthand all the testimony and all of the statements and remarks of the judge and all persons appearing at the hearing; and, if directed by the judge, or requested by the person on whose behalf the petition was brought, or by his parent or legal guardian, or the attorneys of such persons, he must, within such reasonable time after the hearing of the petition as the court may designate, write out the same or such specific portions thereof as may be requested in plain and legible longhand or by typewriter or other printing machine and certify to the same as being correctly reported and transcribed, and when directed by the court, file the same with the clerk of the court. Unless otherwise directed by the judge, the costs of writing out and transcribing all or any portion of the reporter's shorthand notes shall be paid in advance at the rates fixed for transcriptions in a civil action by the person requesting the same. *(Added by Stats.1976, c. 1068, p. 4769, § 9.)*

Research References

Treatises and Practice Aids

Witkin, California Summary 10th Parent and Child § 339, Effective Assistance Of Counsel.

Witkin, California Summary 10th Parent and Child § 591, Reporter and Transcript.

§ 348. Variance and amendment of pleadings; applicability of Code of Civil Procedure

The provisions of Chapter 8 (commencing with Section 469) of Title 6 of Part 2 of the Code of Civil Procedure relating to variance and amendment of pleadings in civil actions shall apply to petitions and proceedings under this chapter, to the same extent and with the same effect as if proceedings under this chapter were civil actions. *(Added by Stats.1976, c. 1068, p. 4769, § 9.)*

Research References

Treatises and Practice Aids

Witkin, California Summary 10th Parent and Child § 564, in General.
Witkin, California Summary 10th Parent and Child § 654, Power to Modify or Correct.
Witkin, California Summary 10th Parent and Child § 706, Waiver Of Appellate Review.

§ 349. Minor and any person entitled to notice; right to attend and participate in hearing; right to counsel

(a) A minor who is the subject of a juvenile court hearing, and any person entitled to notice of the hearing under Sections 290.1 and 290.2, is entitled to be present at the hearing.

(b) The minor and any person who is entitled to that notice has the right to be represented at the hearing by counsel of his or her own choice.

(c) If the minor is present at the hearing, the court shall inform the minor that he or she has the right to address the court and participate in the hearing and the court shall allow the minor, if the minor so desires, to address the court and participate in the hearing.

(d) If the minor is 10 years of age or older and he or she is not present at the hearing, the court shall determine whether the minor was properly notified of his or her right to attend the hearing and inquire whether the minor was given an opportunity to attend. If that minor was not properly notified or if he or she wished to be present and was not given an opportunity to be present, the court shall continue the hearing to allow the minor to be present unless the court finds that it is in the best interest of the minor not to continue the hearing. The court shall continue the hearing only for that period of time necessary to provide notice and secure the presence of the child. The court may issue any and all orders reasonably necessary to ensure that the child has an opportunity to attend.

(e) Nothing in this section shall prevent or limit any child's right to attend or participate in the hearing. *(Added by Stats.1976, c. 1068, p. 4769, § 9. Amended by Stats.2003, c. 813 (A.B.408), § 1; Stats.2008, c. 166 (A.B.3051), § 3; Stats.2015, c. 36 (A.B.217), § 1, eff. Jan. 1, 2016.)*

Research References

Treatises and Practice Aids

Witkin, California Summary 10th Parent and Child § 567, Statutory Rights.
Witkin, California Summary 10th Parent and Child § 570, in General.
Witkin, California Summary 10th Parent and Child § 579, in General.
Witkin, California Summary 10th Parent and Child § 587, Persons Entitled to be Present.
Witkin, California Summary 10th Parent and Child § 685, Hearing.

§ 350. Control and conduct of proceedings; dependency mediation program; testimony of minor in chambers; actions of court upon failure of department to meet burden

(a)(1) The judge of the juvenile court shall control all proceedings during the hearings with a view to the expeditious and effective ascertainment of the jurisdictional facts and the ascertainment of all information relative to the present condition and future welfare of the person upon whose behalf the petition is brought. Except where there is a contested issue of fact or law, the proceedings shall be conducted in an informal nonadversary atmosphere with a view to obtaining the maximum cooperation of the minor upon whose behalf the petition is brought and all persons interested in his or her welfare with any provisions that the court may make for the disposition and care of the minor.

(2) Each juvenile court is encouraged to develop a dependency mediation program to provide a problem-solving forum for all interested persons to develop a plan in the best interests of the child, emphasizing family preservation and strengthening. The Legislature finds that mediation of these matters assists the court in resolving conflict, and helps the court to intervene in a constructive manner in those cases where court intervention is necessary. Notwithstanding any other provision of law, no person, except the mediator, who is required to report suspected child abuse pursuant to the Child Abuse and Neglect Reporting Act (Article 2.5 (commencing with Section 11164) of Chapter 2 of Title 1 of Part 4 of the Penal Code), shall be exempted from those requirements under Chapter 2 (commencing with Section 1115) of Division 9 of the Evidence Code because he or she agreed to participate in a dependency mediation program established in the juvenile court.

If a dependency mediation program has been established in a juvenile court, and if mediation is requested by any person who the judge or referee deems to have a direct and legitimate interest in the particular case, or on the court's own motion, the matter may be set for confidential mediation to develop a plan in the best interests of the child, utilizing resources within the family first and within the community if required.

(b) The testimony of a minor may be taken in chambers and outside the presence of the minor's parent or parents, if the minor's parent or parents are represented by counsel, the counsel is present and any of the following circumstances exist:

(1) The court determines that testimony in chambers is necessary to ensure truthful testimony.

(2) The minor is likely to be intimidated by a formal courtroom setting.

(3) The minor is afraid to testify in front of his or her parent or parents.

After testimony in chambers, the parent or parents of the minor may elect to have the court reporter read back the testimony or have the testimony summarized by counsel for the parent or parents.

The testimony of a minor also may be taken in chambers and outside the presence of the guardian or guardians of a minor under the circumstances specified in this subdivision.

(c) At any hearing in which the probation department bears the burden of proof, after the presentation of evidence on behalf of the probation department and the minor has been closed, the court, on motion of the minor, parent, or guardian, or on its own motion, shall order whatever action the law requires of it if the court, upon weighing all of the evidence then before it, finds that the burden of proof has not been met. That action includes, but is not limited to, the dismissal of the petition and release of the minor at a jurisdictional hearing, the return of the minor at an out-of-home review held prior to the permanency planning hearing, or the termination of jurisdiction at an in-home review. If the motion is not granted, the parent or guardian may offer evidence without first having reserved that right. *(Added by Stats.1976, c. 1068, p. 4769, § 9. Amended by Stats.1985, c. 528, § 2; Stats.1986, c. 248, § 245; Stats.1987, c. 1485, § 32; Stats.1992, c. 360 (S.B.1420), § 2, eff. July 27, 1992; Stats. 1994, c. 24 (A.B.875), § 1; Stats.1996, c. 405 (S.B.1675), § 2; Stats.1997, c. 772 (A.B.939), § 12.)*

Law Revision Commission Comments

1997 Amendment

Subdivision (a)(2) of Section 350 is amended to reflect the relocation of former Evidence Code Section 1152.5 and the addition of new Evidence Code provisions governing mediation confidentiality. See Evid. Code §§ 1115–1128 (mediation). [1997–98 Annual Report, 27 Cal.L.Rev.Comm. Reports App. 5 (1997)].

Commentary

Reading subsection (a)(1) together with section 356, *In re Nicholas E., 236 Cal.App.4th 458, 186 Cal.Rptr.3d 656 (2015)*, holds that once children had been declared dependents of the court, a court erred in dismissing the dependency proceeding without conducting an evidentiary hearing on the ground that family court had already awarded custody of the children to the non-offending father. *Nicholas E.* explains that juvenile court, with its ultimate concern about the welfare of a dependent child, has primacy over family court, which merely resolves the best interest of a child as between two parents.

In re Dennis H., 88 Cal.App.4th 94, 105 Cal.Rptr.2d 705 (2001), review denied July 18, 2001, holds that a district attorney may not participate in a juvenile dependency proceeding to represent the state's interests without express statutory authorization, and this section does not provide such authorization.

A divorced mother lacked standing to appeal dismissal of a dependency proceeding alleging child molestation by her former husband because the proceeding did not alter her status as the child's custodian and she was thus not an "aggrieved party." Moreover, a remedy was available in family court. *In re Carissa G., 76 Cal.App.4th 731, 90 Cal.Rptr.2d 561 (1999), review denied February 16, 2000.* But see *In re Lauren P., 44 Cal.App.4th 763, 52 Cal.Rptr.2d 170 (1996).*

Research References

Treatises and Practice Aids

Witkin, California Summary 10th Parent and Child § 578, Confrontation and Cross-Examination.

Witkin, California Summary 10th Parent and Child § 589, Informality and Control by Court.

Witkin, California Summary 10th Parent and Child § 596, Disposition Where Burden Of Proof Not Met.

Witkin, California Summary 10th Parent and Child § 604, in General.

Witkin, California Summary 10th Parent and Child § 608, Nature and Purpose Of Hearing.

Witkin, California Summary 10th Parent and Child § 615, in General.

§ 352. Continuance of hearing under this chapter

(a) Upon request of counsel for the parent, guardian, minor, or petitioner, the court may continue any hearing under this chapter beyond the time limit within which the hearing is otherwise required to be held, provided that no continuance shall be granted that is contrary to the interest of the minor. In considering the minor's interests, the court shall give substantial weight to a minor's need for prompt resolution of his or her custody status, the need to provide children with stable environments, and the damage to a minor of prolonged temporary placements.

Continuances shall be granted only upon a showing of good cause and only for that period of time shown to be necessary by the evidence presented at the hearing on the motion for the continuance. Neither a stipulation between counsel nor the convenience of the parties is in and of itself a good cause. Further, neither a pending criminal prosecution nor family law matter shall be considered in and of itself as good cause. Whenever any continuance is granted, the facts proven which require the continuance shall be entered upon the minutes of the court.

In order to obtain a motion for a continuance of the hearing, written notice shall be filed at least two court days prior to the date set for hearing, together with affidavits or declarations detailing specific facts showing that a continuance is necessary, unless the court for good cause entertains an oral motion for continuance.

(b) Notwithstanding any other provision of law, if a minor has been removed from the parents' or guardians' custody, no continuance shall be granted that would result in the dispositional hearing, held pursuant to Section 361, being completed longer than 60 days after the hearing at which the minor was ordered removed or detained, unless the court finds that there are exceptional circumstances requiring such a continuance. The facts supporting such a continuance shall be entered upon the minutes of the court. In no event shall the court grant continuances that would cause the hearing pursuant to Section 361 to be completed more than six months after the hearing pursuant to Section 319.

(c) In any case in which the parent, guardian, or minor is represented by counsel and no objection is made to an order continuing any such hearing beyond the time limit within which the hearing is otherwise required to be held, the absence of such an objection shall be deemed a consent to the continuance. The consent does not affect the requirements of subdivision (a). *(Added by Stats.1976, c. 1068, p. 4769, § 9. Amended by Stats.1982, c. 978, § 16, eff. Sept. 13, 1982, operative July 1, 1982; Stats.1986, c. 1122, § 8.)*

Validity

For validity of this section, see In re A.R. (App. 4 Dist. 2009) 88 Cal.Rptr.3d 448, 170 Cal.App.4th 733.

Commentary

In re Elizabeth R., 35 Cal.App.4th 1774, 42 Cal.Rptr.2d 200 (1995), holds that the juvenile court has discretion to extend reunification services beyond 18 months in order to foster family preservation. In *Elizabeth R*, the mother had an excellent record of visitation and compliance with the reunification plan; nevertheless, her involuntary hospitalization for mental illness made it impossible to complete reunification within an 18–month period.

In re J.E., 3 Cal.App.5th 557, 207 Cal.Rptr.3d 642 (2016), review denied, held that a juvenile court did not abuse its discretion in continuing an 18-month review hearing and extending family reunification services to 24 months, when county social services did not provide a minor with the specific services required to achieve reunification with her family.

Interpreting subsection (b), *Renee S. v. Superior Court, 76 Cal. App.4th 187, 90 Cal.Rptr.2d 134 (1999)*, holds that the court must conclude the adjudicatory phase of a dependency proceeding promptly, ordinarily within 60 days of the child's detention, unless extraordinary circumstances justify a continuance.

Research References

Forms

West's California Judicial Council Forms JV-406, Continuance--Dependency General.

Treatises and Practice Aids

Witkin, California Summary 10th Parent and Child § 554, Notice and Telephone Contact.

Witkin, California Summary 10th Parent and Child § 594, in General.

Witkin, California Summary 10th Parent and Child § 595, Limitations on Continuances.

Witkin, California Summary 10th Parent and Child § 664, in General.

§ 353. Reading petition; explanation; advising of right to counsel; appointment of counsel; continuance

At the beginning of the hearing on a petition filed pursuant to Article 8 (commencing with Section 325) of this chapter, the judge or clerk shall first read the petition to those present. Upon request of any parent, guardian, or adult relative, counsel for the minor, or the minor, if he or she is present, the judge shall explain any term of allegation contained therein and the nature of the hearing, its procedures, and possible consequences. The judge shall ascertain whether the parent, guardian, or adult relative and, when required by Section 317, the minor have been informed of their right to be represented by counsel, and if not, the judge shall advise those persons, if present, of the right to have counsel present and where applicable, of the right to appointed counsel. If such a person is unable to afford counsel and desires to be represented by counsel, the court shall appoint counsel in accordance with Section 317. The court shall continue the hearing for not to exceed seven days, as necessary to make an appointment of counsel, or to enable counsel to acquaint himself or herself with the case, or to determine whether the parent or guardian or adult relative is unable to afford counsel at his or her own expense, and shall continue the hearing as necessary to provide reasonable opportunity for the minor and the parent or guardian or adult relative to prepare for the hearing. *(Added by Stats.1976, c. 1068, p. 4769, § 9. Amended by Stats.1987, c. 1485, § 33; Stats.1989, c. 913, § 7.)*

Research References

Forms

West's California Judicial Council Forms JV-412, Findings and Orders After Jurisdictional Hearing (Welf. & Inst. Code, S356).

Treatises and Practice Aids

Witkin, California Summary 10th Parent and Child § 567, Statutory Rights.

Witkin, California Summary 10th Parent and Child § 570, in General.

Witkin, California Summary 10th Parent and Child § 611, Continuance Of Hearing.

Witkin, California Summary 10th Parent and Child § 613, Commencement Of Hearing.

§ 353.1. Petitions to change, modify or set aside orders or to terminate jurisdiction; right to petition; notice

(a) At the hearing on a petition filed pursuant to Article 8 (commencing with Section 325) of this chapter, any person adjudged a dependent child of the juvenile court shall be informed, both orally and in writing by the court as provided in subdivision (b), of both of the following:

(1) His or her rights pursuant to Section 388.

(2) The procedure for bringing a petition pursuant to Section 388, including the availability of all appropriate and necessary Judicial Council forms.

(b) Where the dependent child has attained the age of 12 years, the court shall directly inform the child as required by subdivision (a) in clear language appropriate for the child's level of cognitive development. Where the dependent child is under the age of 12 years, the court shall inform the child as required by subdivision (a) through the child's guardian ad litem or legal counsel. *(Added by Stats.1994, c. 159 (A.B. 1013), § 1. Amended by Stats.1995, c. 91 (S.B.975), § 184.)*

Research References

Forms

West's California Judicial Council Forms JV-185, Child's Information Sheet--Request to Change Court Order (Welf. & Inst. Code).

Treatises and Practice Aids

Witkin, California Summary 10th Parent and Child § 567, Statutory Rights.

Witkin, California Summary 10th Parent and Child § 673, Child in Foster Care.

§ 354. Continuance of hearing on petition filed pursuant to article 8 of this chapter

Except where a minor is in custody, any hearing on a petition filed pursuant to Article 8 (commencing with Section 325) of this chapter may be continued by the court for not more than 10 days in addition to any other continuance authorized in this chapter whenever the court is satisfied that an unavailable and necessary witness will be available within such time. *(Added by Stats.1976, c. 1068, p. 4769, § 9.)*

Research References

Treatises and Practice Aids

Witkin, California Summary 10th Parent and Child § 611, Continuance Of Hearing.

§ 355. Jurisdictional hearing; social study; hearsay evidence; timely objection

(a) At the jurisdictional hearing, the court shall first consider only the question whether the minor is a person described by Section 300. Any legally admissible evidence that is relevant to the circumstances or acts that are alleged to bring the minor within the jurisdiction of the juvenile court is admissible and may be received in evidence. Proof by a preponderance of evidence must be adduced to support a finding that the minor is a person described by Section 300. Objections that could have been made to evidence introduced shall be deemed to have been made by a parent or guardian who is present at the hearing and unrepresented by counsel, unless the court finds that the parent or guardian has made a knowing and intelligent waiver of the right to counsel. Objections that could have been made to evidence introduced shall be deemed to have been made by an unrepresented child.

(b) A social study prepared by the petitioning agency, and hearsay evidence contained in it, is admissible and constitutes competent evidence upon which a finding of jurisdiction pursuant to Section 300 may be based, to the extent allowed by subdivisions (c) and (d).

(1) For purposes of this section, "social study" means any written report furnished to the juvenile court and to all parties or their counsel by the county probation or welfare department in any matter involving the custody, status, or welfare of a minor in a dependency proceeding pursuant to Article 6 (commencing with Section 300) to Article 12 (commencing with Section 385), inclusive.

(2) The preparer of the social study shall be made available for cross-examination upon a timely request by a party. The court may deem the preparer available for cross-examination if it determines that the preparer is on telephone standby and can be present in court within a reasonable time of the request.

(3) The court may grant a reasonable continuance not to exceed 10 days upon request by any party if the social study is not provided to the parties or their counsel within a reasonable time before the hearing.

(c)(1) If a party to the jurisdictional hearing raises a timely objection to the admission of specific hearsay evidence contained in a social study, the specific hearsay evidence shall not be sufficient by itself to support a jurisdictional finding or any ultimate fact upon which a jurisdictional finding is based, unless the petitioner establishes one or more of the following exceptions:

(A) The hearsay evidence would be admissible in any civil or criminal proceeding under any statutory or decisional exception to the prohibition against hearsay.

(B) The hearsay declarant is a minor under 12 years of age who is the subject of the jurisdictional hearing. However, the hearsay statement of a minor under 12 years of age shall not be admissible if the objecting party establishes that the statement is unreliable because it was the product of fraud, deceit, or undue influence.

(C) The hearsay declarant is a peace officer as defined by Chapter 4.5 (commencing with Section 830) of Title 3 of Part 2 of the Penal Code, a health practitioner described in paragraphs (21) to (28), inclusive, of subdivision (a) of Section 11165.7 of the Penal Code, a social worker licensed pursuant to Chapter 14 (commencing with Section 4991) of Division 2 of the Business and Professions Code, or a teacher who holds a credential pursuant to Chapter 2 (commencing with Section 44200) of Part 25 of Division 3 of Title 2 of the Education Code. For the purpose of this subdivision, evidence in a declaration is admissible only to the extent that it would otherwise be admissible under this section or if the declarant were present and testifying in court.

(D) The hearsay declarant is available for cross-examination. For purposes of this section, the court may deem a witness available for cross-examination if it determines that the witness is on telephone standby and can be present in court within a reasonable time of a request to examine the witness.

(2) For purposes of this subdivision, an objection is timely if it identifies with reasonable specificity the disputed hearsay evidence and it gives the petitioner a reasonable period of time to meet the objection prior to a contested hearing.

(d) This section shall not be construed to limit the right of a party to the jurisdictional hearing to subpoena a witness whose statement is contained in the social study or to introduce admissible evidence relevant to the weight of the hearsay evidence or the credibility of the hearsay declarant.

(Added by Stats.1976, c. 1068, p. 4769, § 9. Amended by Stats.1987, c. 1485, § 34; Stats.1996, c. 36 (S.B.86), § 1; Stats.1997, c. 793 (A.B.1544), § 13; Stats.2003, c. 468 (S.B. 851), § 31; Stats.2003, c. 365 (A.B.1710), § 8; Stats.2012, c. 518 (S.B.1264), § 3; Stats.2014, c. 71 (S.B.1304), § 181, eff. Jan. 1, 2015.)

Validity

A prior version of this statute was limited on constitutional grounds in the decision of In re Lucero L. (2000) 96 Cal.Rptr.2d 56, 22 Cal.4th 1227, 998 P.2d 1019.

Commentary

In re Lucero L., 22 Cal.4th 1227, 998 P.2d 1019, 96 Cal.Rptr.2d 56 (2000), held that the admission of hearsay statements contained in a social study of an incompetent minor who was the subject of a dependency hearing does not violate the parent's due process rights, but a minor's hearsay statements cannot be the sole basis for a jurisdictional finding unless the court finds that they have special indicia of reliability. In *Lucero L.*, the California Supreme Court concluded that the statements of a three-year-old child indicating that her father had sexually abused her showed sufficient indicia of reliability to be admissible and to constitute the requisite substantial evidence on the issue of dependency jurisdiction.

The rule of *Crawford v. Washington, 541 U.S. 36 (2004)*, that out-of-court testimonial statements (hearsay) must be excluded under the Sixth Amendment confrontation clause unless the witness is unavailable and the defendant has had a prior opportunity to cross-examine the declarant, does not apply to parents in child dependency proceeding. *In re April C., 131 Cal.App.4th 599, 31 Cal.Rptr.3d 804 (2005)*.

Research References

Forms

West's California Judicial Council Forms JV-412, Findings and Orders After Jurisdictional Hearing (Welf. & Inst. Code, S356).

Treatises and Practice Aids

Witkin, California Summary 10th Parent and Child § 12, Parental or Marital Rights Of Prisoners.

Witkin, California Summary 10th Parent and Child § 452, Jurisdiction Retained After Majority.

Witkin, California Summary 10th Parent and Child § 585, in General.

Witkin, California Summary 10th Parent and Child § 608, Nature and Purpose Of Hearing.

Witkin, California Summary 10th Parent and Child § 615, in General.

Witkin, California Summary 10th Parent and Child § 617, in General.

Witkin, California Summary 10th Parent and Child § 618, Admissibility and Weight Of Social Study.

§ 355.1. Injuries or detrimental condition resulting from those who have care or custody as prima facie evidence; presumptions and burden of proof

(a) Where the court finds, based upon competent professional evidence, that an injury, injuries, or detrimental condition sustained by a minor is of a nature as would ordinarily not be sustained except as the result of the unreasonable or neglectful acts or omissions of either parent, the guardian, or other person who has the care or custody of the minor, that finding shall be prima facie evidence that the minor is a person described by subdivision (a), (b), or (d) of Section 300.

(b) Proof that either parent, the guardian, or other person who has the care or custody of a minor who is the subject of a petition filed under Section 300 has physically abused, neglected, or cruelly treated another minor shall be admissible in evidence.

(c) The presumption created by subdivision (a) constitutes a presumption affecting the burden of producing evidence.

(d) Where the court finds that either a parent, a guardian, or any other person who resides with, or has the care or custody of, a minor who is currently the subject of the petition filed under Section 300 (1) has been previously convicted of sexual abuse as defined in Section 11165.1 of the Penal Code, (2) has been previously convicted of an act in another state that would constitute sexual abuse as defined in Section 11165.1 of the Penal Code if committed in this state, (3) has been found in a prior dependency hearing or similar proceeding in the corresponding court of another state to have committed an act of sexual abuse, or (4) is required, as the result of a felony conviction, to register as a sex offender pursuant to Section 290 of the Penal Code, that finding shall be prima facie evidence in any proceeding that the subject minor is a person described by subdivision (a), (b), (c), or (d) of Section 300 and is at substantial risk of abuse or neglect. The prima facie evidence constitutes a presumption affecting the burden of producing evidence.

(e) Where the court believes that a child has suffered criminal abuse or neglect, the court may direct a representative of the child protective agency to take action pursuant to subdivision (i) of Section 11166 of the Penal Code.

(f) Testimony by a parent, guardian, or other person who has the care or custody of the minor made the subject of a proceeding under Section 300 shall not be admissible as evidence in any other action or proceeding. *(Formerly § 701.1, added by Stats.1976, c. 89, p. 146, § 1. Amended by Stats.1977, c. 579, p. 1922, § 197. Renumbered § 355.1 and amended by Stats.1977, c. 910, p. 2783, § 8; Stats.1978, c. 380, p. 1211, § 158. Amended by Stats.1987, c. 1485, § 35; Stats.1999, c. 417 (S.B.208), § 2, eff. Sept. 16, 1999.)*

Commentary

Interpreting and applying subsection (d), *In re John S., 88 Cal.App.4th 1140, 106 Cal.Rptr.2d 476 (2001)* holds that a trial court properly found dependency jurisdiction when the child's father failed to rebut the presumption by presenting evidence that his status as a registered sex offender did not put the child at risk.

In re Ricky T., 214 Cal.App.4th 515, 154 Cal.Rptr.3d 172 (2013), held that the juvenile court properly declared a three-year-old boy dependent because his grandfather's conviction for sexual abuse of a step-granddaughter raised the presumption of this section, which the grandfather failed to rebut.

When a father had been imprisoned for sexually assaulting two young boys and had been civilly committed as a sexually violent predator, the juvenile court's findings that the crimes had occurred 25 years earlier and the father had been unconditionally released from his commitment, were insufficient as a matter of law to overcome the presumption of subsection (d) that the father's two-year-old son was at substantial risk of abuse. *Los Angeles County Dept. of Children and Family Services v. Superior Court, 215 Cal. App.4th 962, 156 Cal.Rptr.3d 502 (2013)*.

Resolving a conflict among the courts of appeal, *In re I.J., 56 Cal.4th 776, 299 P.3d 1254, 156 Cal.Rptr.3d (2013)*, held that a father's severe sexual abuse of one child is sufficient to support dependency jurisdiction over all his children, regardless of gender. Subsequently, the California Supreme Court, *301 P.3d 1175, 157 Cal.Rptr.3d 569 (2013)*, ordered the court of appeal to vacate its decision in *In re David R., 151 Cal.Rptr.3d 253 (2012)*, and to reconsider the cause is light of *In re I.J.* In *David R.*, the vacated decision of the court of appeal had reversed a trial court order that declared a father's two-year-old son a dependent of the court, based upon a single incident in which the father molested the child's six-year-old sister, when there was no other evidence that the son was at substantial risk of being sexually abused by the father. On remand to Division One of the Second Appellate District, the court of appeal, in an unpublished opinion, reversed its initial decision and affirmed the trial's courts order declaring that *David R.* was a dependent of the court because he was at risk of sexual abuse (2013 WL 4630479). Nevertheless, shortly thereafter, the same court reversed a juvenile court order that declared a father's two sons dependents of the court because they were at substantial risk of being molested by the father, solely because the father had sexually molested an unrelated girl while fully clothed. *In re A.A, 164 Cal.Rptr.3d (2013)* (reasoning that sexual molestation of an unrelated girl while fully clothed did not suffice to support a finding that the sons were at substantial risk of sexual abuse). The California Supreme Court denied review and ordered that *A.A.* not be officially published.

Research References

Treatises and Practice Aids

Witkin, California Summary 10th Parent and Child § 3, in General.

Witkin, California Summary 10th Parent and Child § 538, Governing Law.

Witkin, California Summary 10th Parent and Child § 540, in General.

Witkin, California Summary 10th Parent and Child § 551, Sibling Abused or Neglected.

Witkin, California Summary 10th Parent and Child § 594, in General.
Witkin, California Summary 10th Parent and Child § 616, Presumptions from Parental Misconduct.
Witkin, California Summary 10th Parent and Child § 617, in General.

§ 356. Findings and orders

After hearing the evidence, the court shall make a finding, noted in the minutes of the court, whether or not the minor is a person described by Section 300 and the specific subdivisions of Section 300 under which the petition is sustained. If it finds that the minor is not such a person, it shall order that the petition be dismissed and the minor be discharged from any detention or restriction theretofore ordered. If the court finds that the minor is such a person, it shall make and enter its findings and order accordingly. *(Added by Stats.1976, c. 1068, p. 4769, § 9. Amended by Stats.1982, c. 978, § 18, eff. Sept. 13, 1982, operative July 1, 1982; Stats.1984, c. 1246, § 3; Stats.1985, c. 1341, § 1; Stats.1986, c. 1122, § 9.)*

Commentary

Reading this section together with subsection (a)(1) of section 350, *In re Nicholas E., 236 Cal.App.4th 458, 186 Cal.Rptr.3d 656 (2015)*, holds that once children had been declared dependents of the court, a court erred in dismissing the dependency proceeding without conducting an evidentiary hearing on the ground that family court had already awarded custody of the children to the non-offending father. *Nicholas E.* explains that juvenile court, with its ultimate concern about the welfare of a dependent child, has primacy over family court, which merely resolves the best interest of a child as between two parents.

Research References

Forms

West's California Judicial Council Forms JV-412, Findings and Orders After Jurisdictional Hearing (Welf. & Inst. Code, S356).

Treatises and Practice Aids

Witkin, California Summary 10th Parent and Child § 483, Juvenile Court Proceedings.
Witkin, California Summary 10th Parent and Child § 607, Findings and Orders.
Witkin, California Summary 10th Parent and Child § 608, Nature and Purpose Of Hearing.
Witkin, California Summary 10th Parent and Child § 622, Findings and Order.
Witkin, California Summary 10th Parent and Child § 623, Continuance Pending Disposition Hearing.
Witkin, California Summary 10th Parent and Child § 673, Child in Foster Care.

§ 356.5. Child advocates; appointment; duties; training

A child advocate appointed by the court to represent the interests of a dependent child in a proceeding under this chapter shall have the same duties and responsibilities as a guardian ad litem and shall be trained by and function under the auspices of a court appointed special advocate guardian ad litem program, formed and operating under the guidelines established by the National Court Appointed Special Advocate Association. *(Added by Stats.1985, c. 1341, § 2.)*

Research References

Treatises and Practice Aids

Witkin, California Summary 10th Parent and Child § 572, Appointment Of Guardian Ad Litem or Child Advocate.

§ 357. Holding minor in psychopathic ward of county hospital

Whenever the court, before or during the hearing on the petition, is of the opinion that the minor is mentally ill or if the court is in doubt concerning the mental health of any such person, the court may order that such person be held temporarily in the psychopathic ward of the county hospital or hospital whose services have been approved and/or contracted for by the department of health of the county, for observation and recommendation concerning the future care, supervision, and treatment of such person. *(Added by Stats.1976, c. 1068, p. 4769, § 9.)*

Research References

Treatises and Practice Aids

Witkin, California Summary 10th Parent and Child § 567, Statutory Rights.

§ 358. Disposition of child; evidence; continuance; proceeding

(a) After finding that a child is a person described in Section 300, the court shall hear evidence on the question of the proper disposition to be made of the child. Prior to making a finding required by this section, the court may continue the hearing on its own motion, the motion of the parent or guardian, or the motion of the child, as follows:

(1) If the child is detained during the continuance, and the social worker is not alleging that subdivision (b) of Section 361.5 is applicable, the continuance shall not exceed 10 judicial days. The court may make an order for detention of the child or for the child's release from detention, during the period of continuance, as is appropriate.

(2) If the child is not detained during the continuance, the continuance shall not exceed 30 days after the date of the finding pursuant to Section 356. However, the court may, for cause, continue the hearing for an additional 15 days.

(3) If the social worker is alleging that subdivision (b) of Section 361.5 is applicable, the court shall continue the proceedings for a period not to exceed 30 days. The social worker shall notify each parent of the content of subdivision (b) of Section 361.5 and shall inform each parent that if the court does not order reunification a permanency planning hearing will be held, and that his or her parental rights may be terminated within the timeframes specified by law.

(b)(1) Before determining the appropriate disposition, the court shall receive in evidence the social study of the child made by the social worker, any study or evaluation made by a child advocate appointed by the court, and other relevant and material evidence as may be offered, including, but not limited to, the willingness of the caregiver to provide legal permanency for the child if reunification is unsuccessful. In any judgment and order of disposition, the court shall specifically state that the social study made by the social worker and the study or evaluation made by the child advocate appointed by the court, if there be any, has been read and considered by the court in arriving at its judgment and order of disposition. Any social study or report submitted to the court by the social worker shall include the individual child's case plan developed pursuant to Section 16501.1.

(2) Whenever a child is removed from a parent's or guardian's custody, the court shall make a finding as to whether the social worker has exercised due diligence in conducting the investigation, as required pursuant to paragraph (1) of subdivision (e) of Section 309, to identify, locate, and notify the child's relatives, including both maternal and paternal relatives.

(3) When making the determination required pursuant to paragraph (2), the court may consider, among other examples of due diligence, the extent to which the social worker has complied with paragraph (1) of subdivision (e) of Section 309, and has done any of the following:

(A) Asked the child, in an age-appropriate manner and consistent with the child's best interest, about his or her relatives.

(B) Obtained information regarding the location of the child's relatives.

(C) Reviewed the child's case file for any information regarding the child's relatives.

(D) Telephoned, emailed, or visited all identified relatives.

(E) Asked located relatives for the names and locations of other relatives.

(F) Used Internet search tools to locate relatives identified as supports.

(c) If the court finds that a child is described by subdivision (h) of Section 300 or that subdivision (b) of Section 361.5 may be applicable, the court shall conduct the dispositional proceeding pursuant to subdivision (c) of Section 361.5. *(Added by Stats.1987, c. 1485, § 37, operative Jan. 1, 1989. Amended by Stats.1991, c. 1203 (S.B.1125), § 5; Stats.1998, c. 1054 (A.B.1091), § 20; Stats.2003, c. 812 (S.B.591), § 1; Stats.2016, c. 890 (S.B.1336), § 1, eff. Jan. 1, 2017.)*

Research References

Treatises and Practice Aids

Witkin, California Summary 10th Parent and Child § 4, Public Welfare Services.

Witkin, California Summary 10th Parent and Child § 12, Parental or Marital Rights Of Prisoners.

Witkin, California Summary 10th Parent and Child § 483, Juvenile Court Proceedings.

Witkin, California Summary 10th Parent and Child § 556, Assessment Of Prospective Placement.

Witkin, California Summary 10th Parent and Child § 561, Investigation by Social Worker.

Witkin, California Summary 10th Parent and Child § 622, Findings and Order.

Witkin, California Summary 10th Parent and Child § 623, Continuance Pending Disposition Hearing.

Witkin, California Summary 10th Parent and Child § 624, in General.

Witkin, California Summary 10th Parent and Child § 625, Preparation Of Social Study.

Witkin, California Summary 10th Parent and Child § 626, Conduct Of Hearing.

§ 358.1. Social studies or evaluations; contents

Each social study or evaluation made by a social worker or child advocate appointed by the court, required to be received in evidence pursuant to Section 358, shall include, but not be limited to, a factual discussion of each of the following subjects:

(a) Whether the county welfare department or social worker has considered either of the following:

(1) Child protective services, as defined in Chapter 5 (commencing with Section 16500) of Part 4 of Division 9, as a possible solution to the problems at hand, and has offered these services to qualified parents if appropriate under the circumstances.

(2) Whether the child can be returned to the custody of his or her parent who is enrolled in a certified substance abuse treatment facility that allows a dependent child to reside with his or her parent.

(b) What plan, if any, for return of the child to his or her parents and for achieving legal permanence for the child if efforts to reunify fail, is recommended to the court by the county welfare department or probation officer.

(c) Whether the best interests of the child will be served by granting reasonable visitation rights with the child to his or her grandparents, in order to maintain and strengthen the child's family relationships.

(d)(1) Whether the child has siblings under the court's jurisdiction, and, if any siblings exist, all of the following:

(A) The nature of the relationship between the child and his or her siblings.

(B) The appropriateness of developing or maintaining the sibling relationships pursuant to Section 16002.

(C) If the siblings are not placed together in the same home, why the siblings are not placed together and what efforts are being made to place the siblings together, or why those efforts are not appropriate.

(D) If the siblings are not placed together, all of the following:

(i) The frequency and nature of the visits between the siblings.

(ii) If there are visits between the siblings, whether the visits are supervised or unsupervised. If the visits are supervised, a discussion of the reasons why the visits are supervised, and what needs to be accomplished in order for the visits to be unsupervised.

(iii) If there are visits between the siblings, a description of the location and length of the visits.

(iv) Any plan to increase visitation between the siblings.

(E) The impact of the sibling relationships on the child's placement and planning for legal permanence.

(2) The factual discussion shall include a discussion of indicators of the nature of the child's sibling relationships, including, but not limited to, whether the siblings were raised together in the same home, whether the siblings have shared significant common experiences or have existing close and

strong bonds, whether either sibling expresses a desire to visit or live with his or her sibling, as applicable, and whether ongoing contact is in the child's best emotional interest.

(e) If the parent or guardian is unwilling or unable to participate in making an educational decision for his or her child, or if other circumstances exist that compromise the ability of the parent or guardian to make educational decisions for the child, the county welfare department or social worker shall consider whether the right of the parent or guardian to make educational decisions for the child should be limited. If the study or evaluation makes that recommendation, it shall identify whether there is a responsible adult available to make educational decisions for the child pursuant to Section 361.

(f) Whether the child appears to be a person who is eligible to be considered for further court action to free the child from parental custody and control.

(g) Whether the parent has been advised of his or her option to participate in adoption planning, including the option to enter into a postadoption contact agreement as described in Section 8616.5 of the Family Code, and to voluntarily relinquish the child for adoption if an adoption agency is willing to accept the relinquishment.

(h) The appropriateness of any relative placement pursuant to Section 361.3. However, this consideration may not be cause for continuance of the dispositional hearing.

(i) Whether the caregiver desires, and is willing, to provide legal permanency for the child if reunification is unsuccessful.

(j) For an Indian child, in consultation with the Indian child's tribe, whether tribal customary adoption is an appropriate permanent plan for the child if reunification is unsuccessful.

(k) On and after the date that the director executes a declaration pursuant to Section 11217, whether the child has been placed in an approved relative's home under a voluntary placement agreement for a period not to exceed 180 days, the parent or guardian is not interested in additional family maintenance or family reunification services, and the relative desires and is willing to be appointed the child's legal guardian. *(Added by Stats.1980, c. 716, p. 2140, § 1. Amended by Stats.1983, c. 1170, § 1; Stats.1985, c. 1341, § 4; Stats.1989, c. 913, § 8; Stats.1993, c. 892 (S.B.426), § 1; Stats.1997, c. 793 (A.B.1544), § 14; Stats.1998, c. 1054 (A.B.1091), § 21; Stats.2000, c. 909 (A.B.1987), § 1; Stats. 2000, c. 930 (S.B.2157), § 5; Stats.2001, c. 754 (A.B.1697), § 5; Stats.2002, c. 785 (S.B.1677), § 2; Stats.2003, c. 812 (S.B.591), § 2; Stats.2009, c. 287 (A.B.1325), § 4, operative July 1, 2010; Stats.2010, c. 559 (A.B.12), § 9; Stats.2012, c. 35 (S.B.1013), § 45, eff. June 27, 2012; Stats.2014, c. 219 (S.B.977), § 2, eff. Jan. 1, 2015; Stats.2014, c. 773 (S.B.1099), § 1.5, eff. Jan. 1, 2015.)*

Research References

Treatises and Practice Aids

Witkin, California Summary 10th Parent and Child § 483, Juvenile Court Proceedings.

Witkin, California Summary 10th Parent and Child § 625, Preparation Of Social Study.

Witkin, California Summary 10th Parent and Child § 638, Preferential Right Of Relatives.

Witkin, California Summary 10th Parent and Child § 643, Duration Of Services.

Witkin, California Summary 10th Parent and Child § 651, Criminal or Addictive Behavior.

§ 359. Minor using narcotics or restricted dangerous drug; continuance of hearing; 72–hour treatment and evaluation; report; disposition; reimbursement of expenditure

(a) Whenever a minor who appears to be a danger to himself or others as a result of the use of narcotics, as defined in Section 11019 of the Health and Safety Code, or a restricted dangerous drug (as defined in former Section 11901 of the Health and Safety Code), is brought before any judge of the juvenile court, the judge may continue the hearing and proceed pursuant to this section. The court may order the minor taken to a facility designated by the county and approved by the State Department of Health Care Services as a facility for 72–hour treatment and evaluation. Thereupon the provisions of Section 11922 of the Health and Safety Code shall apply, except that the professional person in charge of the facility shall make a written report to the court concerning the results of the evaluation of the minor.

(b) If the professional person in charge of the facility for 72–hour evaluation and treatment reports to the juvenile court that the minor is not a danger to himself or others as a result of the use of narcotics or restricted dangerous drugs or that the minor does not require 14–day intensive treatment, or if the minor has been certified for not more than 14 days of intensive treatment and the certification is terminated, the minor shall be released if the juvenile court proceedings have been dismissed; referred for further care and treatment on a voluntary basis, subject to the disposition of the juvenile court proceedings; or returned to the juvenile court, in which event the court shall proceed with the case pursuant to this chapter.

(c) Any expenditure for the evaluation or intensive treatment of a minor under this section shall be considered an expenditure made under Part 2 (commencing with Section 5600) of Division 5, and shall be reimbursed by the state as are other local expenditures pursuant to that part. *(Added by Stats.1976, c. 1068, p. 4769, § 9. Amended by Stats.1978, c. 380, p. 1206, § 151; Stats.2012, c. 34 (S.B.1009), § 40, eff. June 27, 2012; Stats.2013, c. 23 (A.B.82), § 27, eff. June 27, 2013.)*

Commentary

In re Carmen M., 141 Cal.App.4th 478, 46 Cal.Rptr.3d 117 (2006), holds that Sections 202(a) and 362 (a) suffice to authorize a juvenile court to order random drug tests to help a dependent child remain drug-free even though the child has not been found, under this section, to be a danger to herself or others as a result of drug use.

Research References

Treatises and Practice Aids

Witkin, California Summary 10th Parent and Child § 594, in General.

Witkin, California Summary 10th Parent and Child § 633, in General.

ARTICLE 10. DEPENDENT CHILDREN—JUDGMENTS AND ORDERS

Section

§ 360. Legal guardianship; assessments and appointments; eligibility for aid under Kin–GAP program; supervision by social worker; petition for new hearing; dependent child of court

After receiving and considering the evidence on the proper disposition of the case, the juvenile court may enter judgment as follows:

(a) Notwithstanding any other provision of law, if the court finds that the child is a person described by Section 300 and the parent has advised the court that the parent is not interested in family maintenance or family reunification services, it may, in addition to or in lieu of adjudicating the child a dependent child of the court, order a legal guardianship, appoint a legal guardian, and issue letters of guardianship, if the court determines that a guardianship is in the best interest of the child, provided the parent and the child agree to the guardianship, unless the child's age or physical, emotional, or mental condition prevents the child's meaningful response. The court shall advise the parent and the child that no reunification services will be provided as a result of the establishment of a guardianship. The proceeding for the appointment of a guardian shall be in the juvenile court.

Any application for termination of guardianship shall be filed in juvenile court in a form as may be developed by the Judicial Council pursuant to Section 68511 of the Government Code. Sections 366.4 and 388 shall apply to this order of guardianship.

No person shall be appointed a legal guardian under this section until an assessment as specified in subdivision (g) of Section 361.5 is read and considered by the court and reflected in the minutes of the court.

On and after the date that the director executes a declaration pursuant to Section 11217, if the court appoints an approved relative caregiver as the child's legal guardian, the child has been in the care of that approved relative for a period of six consecutive months under a voluntary placement agreement, and the child otherwise meets the conditions for federal financial participation, the child shall be eligible for aid under the Kin–GAP Program as provided in Article 4.7 (commencing with Section 11385) of Chapter 2. The nonfederally eligible child placed with an approved relative caregiver who is appointed as the child's legal guardian shall be eligible for aid under the state-funded Kin–GAP Program, as provided for in Article 4.5 (commencing with Section 11360) of Chapter 2.

The person responsible for preparing the assessment may be called and examined by any party to the guardianship proceeding.

(b) If the court finds that the child is a person described by Section 300, it may, without adjudicating the child a dependent child of the court, order that services be provided to keep the family together and place the child and the child's parent or guardian under the supervision of the social worker for a time period consistent with Section 301.

(c) If the family subsequently is unable or unwilling to cooperate with the services being provided, the social worker may file a petition with the juvenile court pursuant to Section 332 alleging that a previous petition has been sustained and that disposition pursuant to subdivision (b) has been ineffective in ameliorating the situation requiring the child welfare services. Upon hearing the petition, the court shall order either that the petition shall be dismissed or that a new disposition hearing shall be held pursuant to subdivision (d).

(d) If the court finds that the child is a person described by Section 300, it may order and adjudge the child to be a dependent child of the court. *(Added by Stats.1976, c. 1068, p. 4773, § 10. Amended by Stats.1982, c. 978, § 19, eff. Sept. 13, 1982, operative July 1, 1982; Stats.1984, c. 1608, § 3, eff. Sept. 30, 1984; Stats.1991, c. 1203 (S.B.1125), § 6; Stats.1994, c. 900 (S.B.1407), § 1; Stats.1998, c. 1054 (A.B.1091), § 22; Stats.2002, c. 416 (S.B.1956), § 8; Stats.2010, c. 559 (A.B.12), § 11.)*

Commentary

In re Adam D., 183 Cal.App.4th 1250, 108 Cal.Rptr.3d 611 (2010), holds that a subsection (b) order requiring supervision of the parents of a section 300 child, is a dispositional order and is therefore appealable.

In re Summer H., 139 Cal.App.4th 1315, 43 Cal.Rptr.3d 682 (2006), holds that, in lieu of declaring dependency, a juvenile court may appoint a person with a criminal record as the child's legal guardian under Section 360 even though a criminal records exemption has not been granted under Section 361.4, if the child's parent consents to the guardianship and the juvenile court concludes that the guardianship is in the child's best interests.

Research References

Forms

California Transactions Forms--Family Law § 5:3, Rights Of Nonparents Generally.
California Transactions Forms--Family Law § 5:4, Rights Of De Facto Parents.
California Transactions Forms--Family Law § 6:40, Structuring the Adoption.
California Transactions Forms--Family Law § 6:46, Matters to Consider in Structuring the Adoption.
California Transactions Forms--Family Law § 6:47, Matters to Consider in Drafting Petition for Independent Adoption Of Unmarried Minor.
West's California Judicial Council Forms JV-416, Dispositional Attachment: Dismissal Of Petition With or Without Informal Supervision (Welf. & Inst. Code, S360(B)).
West's California Judicial Council Forms JV-418, Dispositional Attachment: Appointment Of Guardian (Welf. & Inst. Code, 360(a)).
West's California Judicial Council Forms JV-419, Guardianship--Consent and Waiver Of Rights.

West's California Judicial Council Forms JV-419A, Guardianship--Child's Consent and Waiver Of Rights.

Treatises and Practice Aids

Witkin, California Summary 10th Parent and Child § 132, Petition.
Witkin, California Summary 10th Parent and Child § 308, Dependency Proceeding Distinguished.
Witkin, California Summary 10th Parent and Child § 325, Statutory Ground.
Witkin, California Summary 10th Parent and Child § 329, Dependent Child Without Reunification Services.
Witkin, California Summary 10th Parent and Child § 625, Preparation Of Social Study.
Witkin, California Summary 10th Parent and Child § 626, Conduct Of Hearing.
Witkin, California Summary 10th Parent and Child § 627, in General.
Witkin, California Summary 10th Parent and Child § 628, Legal Guardianship.
Witkin, California Summary 10th Parent and Child § 642, in General.
Witkin, California Summary 10th Parent and Child § 661, Hearing After Supplemental Petition is Sustained.
Witkin, California Summary 10th Parent and Child § 668, Subsequent Petition.
Witkin, California Summary 10th Parent and Child § 671, Supplemental Report.
Witkin, California Summary 10th Parent and Child § 673, Child in Foster Care.
Witkin, California Summary 10th Parent and Child § 680, Statutory Procedure is Exclusive.
Witkin, California Summary 10th Parent and Child § 696, Continuing Jurisdiction.
Witkin, California Summary 10th Parent and Child § 697, Status Review Hearings.
Witkin, California Summary 10th Parent and Child § 698, Other Procedures.
Witkin, California Summary 10th Parent and Child § 701, in General.
Witkin, California Summary 10th Parent and Child § 452G, (New) Assumption Of Jurisdiction Over Nonminor.
Witkin, California Summary 10th Parent and Child § 669A, (New) Review Hearings Just Before and After Minor Attains Age 18.

§ 361. Limitations on parental or guardian control; right to make educational or developmental services decisions; appointment of responsible adult; relinquishment of child; grounds for removal of child; placement; findings

(a)(1) In all cases in which a minor is adjudged a dependent child of the court on the ground that the minor is a person described by Section 300, the court may limit the control to be exercised over the dependent child by any parent or guardian and shall by its order clearly and specifically set forth all those limitations. Any limitation on the right of the parent or guardian to make educational or developmental services decisions for the child shall be specifically addressed in the court order. The limitations may not exceed those necessary to protect the child. If the court specifically limits the right of the parent or guardian to make educational or developmental services decisions for the child, or, for the nonminor dependent, if the court finds the appointment of a developmental services decisionmaker to be in the best interests of the nonminor dependent, the court shall at the same time appoint a responsible adult to make educational or developmental services decisions for the child or nonminor dependent until one of the following occurs:

(A) The minor reaches 18 years of age, unless the child or nonminor dependent chooses not to make educational or developmental services decisions for himself or herself, or is deemed by the court to be incompetent.

(B) Another responsible adult is appointed to make educational or developmental services decisions for the minor pursuant to this section.

(C) The right of the parent or guardian to make educational or developmental services decisions for the minor is fully restored.

(D) A successor guardian or conservator is appointed.

(E) The child is placed into a planned permanent living arrangement pursuant to paragraph (5) of subdivision (g) of Section 366.21, Section 366.22, Section 366.26, or subdivision (i) of Section 366.3, at which time, for educational decisionmaking, the foster parent, relative caretaker, or nonrelative extended family member as defined in Section 362.7, has the right to represent the child in educational matters pursuant to Section 56055 of the Education Code, and for decisions relating to developmental services, unless the court specifies otherwise, the foster parent, relative caregiver, or nonrelative extended family member of the planned permanent living arrangement has the right to represent the child or nonminor dependent in matters related to developmental services.

(2) An individual who would have a conflict of interest in representing the child or nonminor dependent shall not be appointed to make educational or developmental services decisions. For purposes of this section, "an individual who would have a conflict of interest" means a person having any interests that might restrict or bias his or her ability to make educational or developmental services decisions, including, but not limited to, those conflicts of interest prohibited by Section 1126 of the Government Code, and the receipt of compensation or attorney's fees for the provision of services pursuant to this section. A foster parent shall not be deemed to have a conflict of interest solely because he or she receives compensation for the provision of services pursuant to this section.

(3) Regardless of the person or persons currently holding the right to make educational decisions for the child, a foster parent, relative caregiver, nonrelated extended family member, or resource family shall retain rights and obligations regarding accessing and maintaining health and education information pursuant to Sections 49069.3 and 49076 of the Education Code and Section 16010 of this code.

(4)(A) If the court limits the parent's educational rights pursuant to this subdivision, the court shall determine whether there is a responsible adult who is a relative, nonrelative extended family member, or other adult known to the child who is available and willing to serve as the child's educational representative before appointing an educational representative or surrogate who is not known to the child.

(B) If the court cannot identify a responsible adult who is known to the child and available to make educational decisions for the child, subparagraphs (A) to (E), inclusive, of paragraph (1) do not apply, and the child has either been referred to the local educational agency for special education and related services, or has a valid individualized education program, the court shall refer the child to the local educational agency for appointment of a surrogate parent pursuant to Section 7579.5 of the Government Code.

(C) If the court cannot identify a responsible adult to make educational decisions for the child, the appointment of a surrogate parent as defined in subdivision (a) of Section 56050 of the Education Code is not warranted, and there is no foster parent to exercise the authority granted by Section 56055 of the Education Code, the court may, with the input of any interested person, make educational decisions for the child.

(5)(A) If the court appoints a developmental services decisionmaker pursuant to this section, he or she shall have the authority to access the child's or nonminor dependent's information and records pursuant to subdivision (u) of Section 4514 and subdivision (y) of Section 5328, and to act on the child's or nonminor dependent's behalf for the purposes of the individual program plan process pursuant to Sections 4646, 4646.5, and 4648 and the fair hearing process pursuant to Chapter 7 (commencing with Section 4700) of Division 4.5, and as set forth in the court order.

(B) If the court cannot identify a responsible adult to make developmental services decisions for the child or nonminor dependent, the court may, with the input of any interested person, make developmental services decisions for the child or nonminor dependent. If the child is receiving services from a regional center, the provision of any developmental services related to the court's decision must be consistent with the child's or nonminor dependent's individual program plan and pursuant to the provisions of the Lanterman Developmental Disabilities Services Act (Division 4.5 (commencing with Section 4500)).

(6) All educational and school placement decisions shall seek to ensure that the child is in the least restrictive educational programs and has access to the academic resources, services, and extracurricular and enrichment activities that are available to all pupils. In all instances, educational and school placement decisions shall be based on the best interests of the child. If an educational representative or surrogate is appointed for the child, the representative or surrogate shall meet with the child, shall investigate the child's educational needs and whether those needs are being met, and shall, prior to each review hearing held under this article, provide information and recommendations concerning the child's educational needs to the child's social worker, make written recommendations to the court, or attend the hearing and participate in those portions of the hearing that concern the child's education.

(7) Nothing in this section in any way removes the obligation to appoint surrogate parents for students with disabilities who are without parental representation in special education procedures as required by state and federal law, including Section 1415(b)(2) of Title 20 of the United States Code, Section 56050 of the Education Code, Section 7579.5 of the Government Code, and Rule 5.650 of the California Rules of Court.

(b)(1) Subdivision (a) does not limit the ability of a parent to voluntarily relinquish his or her child to the State Department of Social Services, to a county adoption agency, or to a licensed private adoption agency at any time while the child is the subject of a petition to declare him or her, or is, a dependent child of the juvenile court, if the department, county adoption agency, or licensed private adoption agency is willing to accept the relinquishment.

(2) When accepting the relinquishment of a child described in paragraph (1), the department or a county adoption agency shall comply with Section 8700 of the Family Code and, within five court days of accepting the relinquishment, shall file written notice of that fact with the court and all parties to the case and their counsel.

(3) When accepting the relinquishment of a child described in paragraph (1), a licensed private adoption agency shall comply with Section 8700 of the Family Code and, within 10 court days of accepting the relinquishment, shall file or allow another party or that party's counsel to file with the court one original and five copies of a request to approve the relinquishment. The clerk of the court shall file the request under seal, subject to examination only by the parties and their counsel or by others upon court approval. If the request is accompanied by the written agreement of all parties, the court may issue an ex parte order approving the relinquishment. Unless approved pursuant to that agreement, the court shall set the matter for hearing no later than 10 court days after filing, and shall provide notice of the hearing to all parties and their counsel, and to the licensed private adoption agency and its counsel. The licensed private adoption agency and any prospective adoptive parent or parents named in the relinquishment shall be permitted to attend the hearing and participate as parties regarding the strictly limited issue of whether the court should approve the relinquishment. The court shall issue an order approving or denying the relinquishment within 10 court days after the hearing.

(c) A dependent child shall not be taken from the physical custody of his or her parents or guardian or guardians with whom the child resides at the time the petition was initiated, unless the juvenile court finds clear and convincing evidence of any of the following circumstances listed in paragraphs (1) to (5), inclusive, and, in an Indian child custody proceeding, paragraph (6):

(1) There is or would be a substantial danger to the physical health, safety, protection, or physical or emotional well-being of the minor if the minor were returned home, and there are no reasonable means by which the minor's physical health can be protected without removing the minor from the minor's parent's or guardian's physical custody. The fact that a minor has been adjudicated a dependent child of the court pursuant to subdivision (e) of Section 300 shall constitute prima facie evidence that the minor cannot be safely left in the physical custody of the parent or guardian with whom the minor resided at the time of injury. The court shall consider, as a reasonable means to protect the minor, each of the following:

(A) The option of removing an offending parent or guardian from the home.

(B) Allowing a nonoffending parent or guardian to retain physical custody as long as that parent or guardian presents a plan acceptable to the court demonstrating that he or she will be able to protect the child from future harm.

(2) The parent or guardian of the minor is unwilling to have physical custody of the minor, and the parent or guardian has been notified that if the minor remains out of their physical custody for the period specified in Section 366.26, the minor may be declared permanently free from their custody and control.

(3) The minor is suffering severe emotional damage, as indicated by extreme anxiety, depression, withdrawal, or untoward aggressive behavior toward himself or herself or others, and there are no reasonable means by which the minor's emotional health may be protected without removing the minor from the physical custody of his or her parent or guardian.

(4) The minor or a sibling of the minor has been sexually abused, or is deemed to be at substantial risk of being sexually abused, by a parent, guardian, or member of his or her household, or other person known to his or her parent, and there are no reasonable means by which the minor can be protected from further sexual abuse or a substantial risk of sexual abuse without removing the minor from his or her parent or guardian, or the minor does not wish to return to his or her parent or guardian.

(5) The minor has been left without any provision for his or her support, or a parent who has been incarcerated or institutionalized cannot arrange for the care of the minor, or a relative or other adult custodian with whom the child has been left by the parent is unwilling or unable to provide care or support for the child and the whereabouts of the parent is unknown and reasonable efforts to locate him or her have been unsuccessful.

(6) In an Indian child custody proceeding, continued custody of the child by the parent or Indian custodian is likely to result in serious emotional or physical damage to the child, and that finding is supported by testimony of a "qualified expert witness" as described in Section 224.6.

(A) * * * For purposes of this paragraph, stipulation by the parent, Indian custodian, or the Indian child's tribe, or failure to object, may waive the requirement of producing evidence of the likelihood of serious damage only if the court is satisfied that the party has been fully advised of the requirements of the federal Indian Child Welfare Act (25 U.S.C. Sec. 1901 et seq.), and has knowingly, intelligently, and voluntarily waived them.

(B) * * * For purposes of this paragraph, failure to meet non-Indian family and child-rearing community standards, or the existence of other behavior or conditions that meet the removal standards of this section, will not support an order for placement in the absence of the finding in this paragraph.

(d) A dependent child shall not be taken from the physical custody of his or her parents with whom the child did not reside at the time the petition was initiated, unless the juvenile court finds clear and convincing evidence that there would be a substantial danger to the physical health, safety, protection, or physical or emotional well-being of the child for the parent to live with the child or otherwise exercise the parent's right to physical custody, and there are no reasonable means by which the child's physical and emotional health can be protected without removing the child from the child's parent's physical custody.

(e) The court shall make a determination as to whether reasonable efforts were made to prevent or to eliminate the need for removal of the minor from his or her home or, if the minor is removed for one of the reasons stated in paragraph (5) of subdivision (c), whether it was reasonable under the circumstances not to make any of those efforts, or, in the case of an Indian child custody proceeding, whether active efforts as required in Section 361.7 were made and that these efforts have proved unsuccessful. The court shall state the facts on which the decision to remove the minor is based.

(f) The court shall make all of the findings required by subdivision (a) of Section 366 in either of the following circumstances:

(1) The minor has been taken from the custody of his or her parent or guardian and has been living in an out-of-home placement pursuant to Section 319.

(2) The minor has been living in a voluntary out-of-home placement pursuant to Section 16507.4. *(Added by Stats. 1976, c. 1068, p. 4773, § 10. Amended by Stats.1982, c. 978, § 20, eff. Sept. 13, 1982, operative July 1, 1982; Stats.1984, c. 867, § 1; Stats.1984, c. 1246, § 4; Stats.1984, c. 1608, § 4, eff. Sept. 30, 1984; Stats.1984, c. 1608, § 12, eff. Sept. 30, 1984, operative Jan. 1, 1985; Stats.1985, c. 440, § 2; Stats.1986, c. 1122, § 11; Stats.1987, c. 1485, § 38; Stats.1990, c. 182 (A.B.1528), § 7; Stats.1992, c. 382 (S.B.1646), § 2; Stats. 1996, c. 1084 (S.B.1516), § 4; Stats.1996, c. 1139 (A.B.2647), § 8.5; Stats.1997, c. 793 (A.B.1544), § 15; Stats.2002, c. 180 (A.B.886), § 2; Stats.2003, c. 862 (A.B.490), § 10; Stats.2005, c. 639 (A.B.1261), § 10; Stats.2006, c. 838 (S.B.678), § 48; Stats.2011, c. 471 (S.B.368), § 2; Stats.2012, c. 35 (S.B.1013), § 47, eff. June 27, 2012; Stats.2012, c. 176 (A.B.2060), § 2; Stats.2012, c. 845 (S.B.1064), § 5; Stats.2012, c. 846 (A.B. 1712), § 14.3; Stats.2014, c. 219 (S.B.977), § 3, eff. Jan. 1, 2015; Stats.2014, c. 763 (A.B.1701), § 16.5, eff. Jan. 1, 2015; Stats.2016, c. 474 (A.B.2882), § 30, eff. Jan. 1, 2017; Stats. 2017, c. 665 (A.B.1332), § 1, eff. Jan. 1, 2018; Stats.2017, c. 829 (S.B.233), § 4.5, eff. Jan. 1, 2018.)*

Commentary

Interpreting subsection (b), *Teresa J. v. Superior Court, 102 Cal.App.4th 366, 125 Cal.Rptr.2d 506 (2002)*, holds that even though a child has already been adjudicated a dependent of the juvenile court under Welfare and Institutions Code § 300, the child's birth mother may relinquish the child for adoption to a private adoption agency, subject to the juvenile court's power to limit the parent's control over the child.

Applying subsection (c), *In re A.E., 228 Cal.App.4th 820, 175 Cal.Rptr.3d 629 (2014)*, reversed a juvenile court order removing a child from her father's custody based on a single episode of physical discipline because the isolated episode did not support a finding of clear and convincing evidence of a substantial danger to the child's safety or well-being were she to remain with her father.

In re Rebecca C., 228 Cal.App.4th 720, 175 Cal.Rptr.3d 264 (2014), reversed an order declaring a teenage daughter a dependent child based on her mother's drug abuse when there was no evidence that the mother's drug abuse endangered the child's health and safety or put her at risk of harm.

For purposes of subsection (c)(1), in the absence of unsanitary conditions or resultant illness, chronic poor housekeeping is not clear and convincing evidence of substantial risk of harm and, therefore, does not justify removal of the child. *In re Paul E., 39 Cal.App.4th 996, 46 Cal.Rptr.2d 289 (1995)*. For discussion of the sufficiency of a petition alleging subsection (b) grounds, see *In re Alysha S., 51*

Cal.App.4th 393, 58 Cal.Rptr.2d 494 (1996), review denied February 19, 1997. Alysha S. allowed the parent to argue for the first time on appeal that the dependency petition failed to state a claim under this section. *In re Shelley J., 68 Cal.App.4th 322, 79 Cal.Rptr.2d 922 (1998), review denied March 9, 1999,* declined to follow *Alysha S.* and held that a challenge to the sufficiency of dependency pleadings may not be raised for the first time on appeal.

Applying subsection (c)(1), *In re Isayah C., 118 Cal.App.4th 684, 13 Cal.Rptr.3d 198 (2004)*, held that a juvenile court erred in declining to grant a *nonoffending* father's request to place a dependent child with paternal relatives during the father's incarceration when there was no clear and convincing evidence that the placement would be a threat to the child's physical health or pose a danger of future harm.

In re J.C., 233 Cal.App.4th 1, 182 Cal.Rptr.3d 215 (2014), held that where dependency jurisdiction and placement of a child in foster care was warranted based on the mother's conduct, it was unnecessary to consider whether it was also warranted based on the father's conduct.

In re H.E., 169 Cal.App.4th 710, 86 Cal.Rptr.3d 820 (2008), review denied, held that a juvenile court, applying subsection (c)(1), properly removed young children from a mother's custody when they were at risk of, and may have already suffered, emotional harm from the mother's incessant unfounded accusations, in front of the children, that their father sexually molested them.

In re Ashly F., 225 Cal.App.4th 803, 170 Cal.Rptr.3d 523 (2014), reversed a dispositional order removing children from the parental home, finding that the evidence did not support the juvenile court's finding that reasonable efforts had been made to prevent the minors' removal and there were no reasonable means to protect the minors other than removing them from their home, as required by subsections (c)(1) and (d). For further treatment of reasonable efforts and means, see Rules of Court, Rule 5.678(c) and Rule 5.690 (a)(1)(B)(i).

Subsection (c)(6) has no application when a juvenile court removes an Indian child from the custody of one parent and places the child in the custody of the other parent, because section 244.1(c) does not include within the definition of an "Indian child custody proceeding" a proceeding in which custody is transferred from one parent to the other parent. *In re J.B., 178 Cal.App.4th 751, 100 Cal.Rptr.3d 679 (2009)*.

In re Damonte A., 57 Cal.App.4th 894, 67 Cal.Rptr.2d 369 (1997), review denied December 10, 1997, holds that the juvenile court may not declare children the dependents of the court, commit them to the custody of DHHS, and then place them "temporarily" in the home of the parent with whom they were living, under DHHS supervision. Instead, the statutes contemplate that removal of a child from the physical custody of a parent will result in physical custody by some person other than that parent. See particularly subsection (d) and § 361.2 (a) and (e). Accord, *In re Andres G., 64 Cal.App.4th 476, 75 Cal.Rptr.2d 285 (1998)*.

Research References

Forms

West's California Judicial Council Forms JV-415, Findings and Orders After Dispositional Hearing (Welf. & Inst. Code, S361 et seq.).

West's California Judicial Council Forms JV-417, Dispositional Attachment: In-Home Placement With Formal Supervision (Welf. & Inst. Code, 361).

West's California Judicial Council Forms JV-420, Dispositional Attachment: Removal from Custodial Parent--Placement With Previously Noncustodial Parent (Welf. & Inst. Code, §§ 361, 361.2).

West's California Judicial Council Forms JV-421, Dispositional Attachment: Removal from Custodial Parent--Placement With Nonparent (Welf. & Inst. Code, §§ 361, 361.2).

West's California Judicial Council Forms JV-535, Order Designating Educational Rights Holder.

West's California Judicial Council Forms JV-535(A), Attachment to Order Designating Educational Rights Holder.

Treatises and Practice Aids

Witkin, California Summary 10th Parent and Child § 12, Parental or Marital Rights Of Prisoners.

Witkin, California Summary 10th Parent and Child § 109, in General.

Witkin, California Summary 10th Parent and Child § 110, Finality and Effect Of Relinquishment.

Witkin, California Summary 10th Parent and Child § 220, Illustrations: Guardianship Cases.

Witkin, California Summary 10th Parent and Child § 226, in General.

Witkin, California Summary 10th Parent and Child § 325, Statutory Ground.

Witkin, California Summary 10th Parent and Child § 334, Offer Of Less Detrimental Alternatives.

Witkin, California Summary 10th Parent and Child § 534, Out-Of-Home Placement or Guardianship.

Witkin, California Summary 10th Parent and Child § 535, Placement Standards and Preferences.

Witkin, California Summary 10th Parent and Child § 615, in General.

Witkin, California Summary 10th Parent and Child § 627, in General.

Witkin, California Summary 10th Parent and Child § 628, Legal Guardianship.

Witkin, California Summary 10th Parent and Child § 629, Limitations on Parental Control.

Witkin, California Summary 10th Parent and Child § 630, Bases for Removal.

Witkin, California Summary 10th Parent and Child § 631, Procedure.

Witkin, California Summary 10th Parent and Child § 632, Standard Of Proof.

Witkin, California Summary 10th Parent and Child § 633, in General.

Witkin, California Summary 10th Parent and Child § 635, in General.

Witkin, California Summary 10th Parent and Child § 637, Priority Right Of Noncustodial Parent.

Witkin, California Summary 10th Parent and Child § 638, Preferential Right Of Relatives.

Witkin, California Summary 10th Parent and Child § 641, Visitation Rights.

Witkin, California Summary 10th Parent and Child § 649, Previous Occurrences.

Witkin, California Summary 10th Parent and Child § 658, Hearing.

Witkin, California Summary 10th Parent and Child § 664, in General.

Witkin, California Summary 10th Parent and Child § 672, Child in Custody Of Parent or Guardian.

Witkin, California Summary 10th Parent and Child § 607A, (New) Educational and Developmental Services Decisions.

§ 361.1. Child removed from physical custody of parent or guardian on ground child may come within jurisdiction of juvenile court pursuant to § 300; release from custody and return of child

(a) If a child is removed from the physical custody of a parent or guardian on the ground that the child may come within the jurisdiction of the juvenile court pursuant to Section 300, the child shall be returned to the physical custody of that parent or guardian immediately after a finding by the juvenile court that the child is not a person described in Section 300, but, in any case, not more than two working days following the date of that finding, unless the parent or guardian and the agency with custody of the child agree to a later date for the child's release. Nothing in this section shall affect a parent or guardian's remedies when a child is not returned immediately, as those remedies existed prior to enactment of this section.

(b) The Judicial Council shall adopt a rule of court to ensure proper notice to a parent or guardian regarding the circumstances and the timeframe in which a child is required to be released from custody pursuant to this section. *(Added by Stats.2003, c. 306 (A.B.524), § 1.)*

Research References

Treatises and Practice Aids

Witkin, California Summary 10th Parent and Child § 622, Findings and Order.

§ 361.2. Determinations prior to order for removal; placement with parent; placement upon removal; placement outside the United States; grandparents' visitation; consideration of siblings

(a) When a court orders removal of a child pursuant to Section 361, the court shall first determine whether there is a parent of the child, with whom the child was not residing at the time that the events or conditions arose that brought the child within the provisions of Section 300, who desires to assume custody of the child. If that parent requests custody, the court shall place the child with the parent unless it finds that placement with that parent would be detrimental to the safety, protection, or physical or emotional well-being of the child. The fact that the parent is enrolled in a certified substance abuse treatment facility that allows a dependent child to reside with his or her parent shall not be, for that reason alone, prima facie evidence that placement with that parent would be detrimental.

(b) If the court places the child with that parent it may do any of the following:

(1) Order that the parent become legal and physical custodian of the child. The court may also provide reasonable visitation by the noncustodial parent. The court shall then terminate its jurisdiction over the child. The custody order shall continue unless modified by a subsequent order of the superior court. The order of the juvenile court shall be filed in any domestic relation proceeding between the parents.

(2) Order that the parent assume custody subject to the jurisdiction of the juvenile court and require that a home visit be conducted within three months. In determining whether to take the action described in this paragraph, the court shall consider any concerns that have been raised by the child's current caregiver regarding the parent. After the social worker conducts the home visit and files his or her report with the court, the court may then take the action described in paragraph (1), (3), or this paragraph. However, nothing in this paragraph shall be interpreted to imply that the court is required to take the action described in this paragraph as a prerequisite to the court taking the action described in either paragraph (1) or (3).

(3) Order that the parent assume custody subject to the supervision of the juvenile court. In that case the court may order that reunification services be provided to the parent or guardian from whom the child is being removed, or the court may order that services be provided solely to the parent who is assuming physical custody in order to allow that parent to retain later custody without court supervision, or that services be provided to both parents, in which case the court shall determine, at review hearings held pursuant to Section 366, which parent, if either, shall have custody of the child.

(c) The court shall make a finding either in writing or on the record of the basis for its determination under subdivisions (a) and (b).

(d) Part 6 (commencing with Section 7950) of Division 12 of the Family Code shall apply to the placement of a child pursuant to paragraphs (1) and (2) of subdivision (e).

(e) When the court orders removal pursuant to Section 361, the court shall order the care, custody, control, and conduct of the child to be under the supervision of the social worker who may place the child in any of the following:

(1) The home of a noncustodial parent as described in subdivision (a), regardless of the parent's immigration status.

(2) The approved home of a relative, or the home of a relative who has been assessed pursuant to Section 361.4 and is pending approval pursuant to Section 16519.5, regardless of the relative's immigration status.

(3) The approved home of a nonrelative extended family member as defined in Section 362.7, or the home of a nonrelative extended family member who has been assessed pursuant to Section 361.4 and is pending approval pursuant to Section 16519.5.

(4) The approved home of a resource family as defined in Section 16519.5, or a home that is pending approval pursuant to paragraph (1) of subdivision (e) of Section 16519.5.

(5) A foster home considering first a foster home in which the child has been placed before an interruption in foster care, if that placement is in the best interest of the child and space is available.

(6) A home or facility in accordance with the federal Indian Child Welfare Act (25 U.S.C. Sec. 1901 et seq.).

(7) A suitable licensed community care facility, except a runaway and homeless youth shelter licensed by the State Department of Social Services pursuant to Section 1502.35 of the Health and Safety Code.

(8) With a foster family agency, as defined in subdivision (g) of Section 11400 and paragraph (4) of subdivision (a) of Section 1502 of the Health and Safety Code, to be placed in a suitable family home certified or approved by the agency, with prior approval of the county placing agency.

(9) A * * * community care facility licensed as a group home for children or a short-term residential therapeutic program, as defined in subdivision (ad) of Section 11400 of this code and paragraph (18) of subdivision (a) of Section 1502 of the Health and Safety Code * * *. A child of any age who is placed in a community care facility licensed as a group home for children or a short-term residential therapeutic program shall have a case plan that indicates that placement is for purposes of providing short-term, specialized, and intensive treatment for the child, the case plan specifies the need for, nature of, and anticipated duration of

this treatment, pursuant to paragraph (2) of subdivision (d) of Section 16501.1, and the case plan includes transitioning the child to a less restrictive environment and the projected timeline by which the child will be transitioned to a less restrictive environment. * * * Any placement * * * longer than six months * * * shall be documented consistent with paragraph (3) of subdivision (a) of Section 16501.1 and, unless subparagraph (A) or (B) applies to the child, shall be approved by the deputy director or director of the county child welfare department no less frequently than every six months.

(A) A child under six years of age shall not be placed in a community care facility licensed as a group home for children, or a short-term residential therapeutic program except under the following circumstances:

(i) When the facility meets the applicable regulations adopted under Section 1530.8 of the Health and Safety Code and standards developed pursuant to Section 11467.1 of this code, and the deputy director or director of the county child welfare department has approved the case plan.

(ii) The short-term, specialized, and intensive treatment period shall not exceed 120 days, unless the county has made progress toward or is actively working toward implementing the case plan that identifies the services or supports necessary to transition the child to a family setting, circumstances beyond the county's control have prevented the county from obtaining those services or supports within the timeline documented in the case plan, and the need for additional time pursuant to the case plan is documented by the caseworker and approved by a deputy director or director of the county child welfare department.

(iii) To the extent that placements pursuant to this paragraph are extended beyond an initial 120 days, the requirements of clauses (i) and (ii) shall apply to each extension. In addition, the deputy director or director of the county child welfare department shall approve the continued placement no less frequently than every 60 days.

(iv) In addition, when a case plan indicates that placement is for purposes of providing family reunification services, the facility shall offer family reunification services that meet the needs of the individual child and his or her family, permit parents to have reasonable access to their children 24 hours a day, encourage extensive parental involvement in meeting the daily needs of their children, and employ staff trained to provide family reunification services. In addition, one of the following conditions exists:

(I) The child's parent is also under the jurisdiction of the court and resides in the facility.

(II) The child's parent is participating in a treatment program affiliated with the facility and the child's placement in the facility facilitates the coordination and provision of reunification services.

(III) Placement in the facility is the only alternative that permits the parent to have daily 24–hour access to the child in accordance with the case plan, to participate fully in meeting all of the daily needs of the child, including feeding and personal hygiene, and to have access to necessary reunification services.

(B) A child who is 6 to 12 years of age, inclusive, may be placed in a community care facility licensed as a group home for children or a short-term residential therapeutic program under the following conditions:

(i) The deputy director of the county welfare department shall approve the case prior to initial placement.

(ii) The short-term, specialized, and intensive treatment period shall not exceed six months, unless the county has made progress or is actively working toward implementing the case plan that identifies the services or supports necessary to transition the child to a family setting, circumstances beyond the county's control have prevented the county from obtaining those services or supports within the timeline documented in the case plan, and the need for additional time pursuant to the case plan is documented by the caseworker and approved by a deputy director or director of the county child welfare department.

(iii) To the extent that placements pursuant to this paragraph are extended beyond an initial six months, the requirements of this subparagraph shall apply to each extension. In addition, the deputy director or director of the county child welfare department shall approve the continued placement no less frequently than every 60 days.

(10) Any child placed in a short-term residential therapeutic program shall be either of the following:

(A) A child who has been assessed as meeting one of the placement requirements set forth in subdivisions (b) and (e) of Section 11462.01.

(B) A child under 6 years of age who is placed with his or her minor parent or for the purpose of reunification pursuant to clause (iv) of subparagraph (A) of paragraph (9).

(11) Nothing in this subdivision shall be construed to allow a social worker to place any dependent child outside the United States, except as specified in subdivision (f).

(f)(1) A child under the supervision of a social worker pursuant to subdivision (e) shall not be placed outside the United States prior to a judicial finding that the placement is in the best interest of the child, except as required by federal law or treaty.

(2) The party or agency requesting placement of the child outside the United States shall carry the burden of proof and shall show, by clear and convincing evidence, that placement outside the United States is in the best interest of the child.

(3) In determining the best interest of the child, the court shall consider, but not be limited to, the following factors:

(A) Placement with a relative.

(B) Placement of siblings in the same home.

(C) Amount and nature of any contact between the child and the potential guardian or caretaker.

(D) Physical and medical needs of the dependent child.

(E) Psychological and emotional needs of the dependent child.

(F) Social, cultural, and educational needs of the dependent child.

(G) Specific desires of any dependent child who is 12 years of age or older.

(4) If the court finds that a placement outside the United States is, by clear and convincing evidence, in the best interest of the child, the court may issue an order authorizing the social worker to make a placement outside the United States. A child subject to this subdivision shall not leave the United States prior to the issuance of the order described in this paragraph.

(5) For purposes of this subdivision, "outside the United States" shall not include the lands of any federally recognized American Indian tribe or Alaskan Natives.

(6) This subdivision shall not apply to the placement of a dependent child with a parent pursuant to subdivision (a).

(g)(1) If the child is taken from the physical custody of the child's parent or guardian and unless the child is placed with relatives, the child shall be placed in foster care in the county of residence of the child's parent or guardian in order to facilitate reunification of the family.

(2) In the event that there are no appropriate placements available in the parent's or guardian's county of residence, a placement may be made in an appropriate place in another county, preferably a county located adjacent to the parent's or guardian's community of residence.

(3) Nothing in this section shall be interpreted as requiring multiple disruptions of the child's placement corresponding to frequent changes of residence by the parent or guardian. In determining whether the child should be moved, the social worker shall take into consideration the potential harmful effects of disrupting the placement of the child and the parent's or guardian's reason for the move.

(4) When it has been determined that it is necessary for a child to be placed in a county other than the child's parent's or guardian's county of residence, the specific reason the out-of-county placement is necessary shall be documented in the child's case plan. If the reason the out-of-county placement is necessary is the lack of resources in the sending county to meet the specific needs of the child, those specific resource needs shall be documented in the case plan.

(5) When it has been determined that a child is to be placed out of county either in a group home or with a foster family agency for subsequent placement in a certified foster family home, and the sending county is to maintain responsibility for supervision and visitation of the child, the sending county shall develop a plan of supervision and visitation that specifies the supervision and visitation activities to be performed and specifies that the sending county is responsible for performing those activities. In addition to the plan of supervision and visitation, the sending county shall document information regarding any known or suspected dangerous behavior of the child that indicates the child may pose a safety concern in the receiving county. Upon implementation of the Child Welfare Services Case Management System, the plan of supervision and visitation, as well as information regarding any known or suspected dangerous behavior of the child, shall be made available to the receiving county upon placement of the child in the receiving county. If placement occurs on a weekend or holiday, the information shall be made available to the receiving county on or before the end of the next business day.

(6) When it has been determined that a child is to be placed out of county and the sending county plans that the receiving county shall be responsible for the supervision and visitation of the child, the sending county shall develop a formal agreement between the sending and receiving counties. The formal agreement shall specify the supervision and visitation to be provided the child, and shall specify that the receiving county is responsible for providing the supervision and visitation. The formal agreement shall be approved and signed by the sending and receiving counties prior to placement of the child in the receiving county. In addition, upon completion of the case plan, the sending county shall provide a copy of the completed case plan to the receiving county. The case plan shall include information regarding any known or suspected dangerous behavior of the child that indicates the child may pose a safety concern to the receiving county.

(h) Whenever the social worker must change the placement of the child and is unable to find a suitable placement within the county and must place the child outside the county, the placement shall not be made until he or she has served written notice on the parent or guardian, the child's attorney, and, if the child is 10 years of age or older, on the child, at least 14 days prior to the placement, unless the child's health or well-being is endangered by delaying the action or would be endangered if prior notice were given. The notice shall state the reasons that require placement outside the county. The child or parent or guardian may object to the placement not later than seven days after receipt of the notice and, upon objection, the court shall hold a hearing not later than five days after the objection and prior to the placement. The court shall order out-of-county placement if it finds that the child's particular needs require placement outside the county.

(i) If the court has ordered removal of the child from the physical custody of his or her parents pursuant to Section 361, the court shall consider whether the family ties and best interest of the child will be served by granting visitation rights to the child's grandparents. The court shall clearly specify those rights to the social worker.

(j) If the court has ordered removal of the child from the physical custody of his or her parents pursuant to Section 361, the court shall consider whether there are any siblings under the court's jurisdiction, or any nondependent siblings in the physical custody of a parent subject to the court's jurisdiction, the nature of the relationship between the child and his or her siblings, the appropriateness of developing or maintaining the sibling relationships pursuant to Section 16002, and the impact of the sibling relationships on the child's placement and planning for legal permanence.

(k)(1) An agency shall ensure placement of a child in a home that, to the fullest extent possible, best meets the day-to-day needs of the child. A home that best meets the day-to-day needs of the child shall satisfy all of the following criteria:

(A) The child's caregiver is able to meet the day-to-day health, safety, and well-being needs of the child.

(B) The child's caregiver is permitted to maintain the least restrictive family setting that promotes normal childhood experiences and that serves the day-to-day needs of the child.

(C) The child is permitted to engage in reasonable, age-appropriate day-to-day activities that promote normal childhood experiences for the foster child.

(2) The foster child's caregiver shall use a reasonable and prudent parent standard, as defined in paragraph (2) of subdivision (a) of Section 362.04, to determine day-to-day activities that are age appropriate to meet the needs of the child. Nothing in this section shall be construed to permit a child's caregiver to permit the child to engage in day-to-day activities that carry an unreasonable risk of harm, or subject the child to abuse or neglect.

* * * *(Added by Stats.2015, c. 773 (A.B.403), § 48, eff. Jan. 1, 2016, operative Jan. 1, 2017. Amended by Stats.2016, c. 605 (A.B.1688), § 1, eff. Jan. 1, 2017; Stats.2016, c. 612 (A.B.1997), § 70.5, eff. Jan. 1, 2017; Stats.2017, c. 561 (A.B.1516), § 264, eff. Jan. 1, 2018; Stats.2017, c. 732 (A.B.404), § 46, eff. Jan. 1, 2018.)*

Commentary

A juvenile court may not award child custody to a noncustodial parent without first removing the child from the custodial parent. *In re Miguel C., 198 Cal.App.4th 965, 129 Cal.Rptr.3d 684 (2011).*

Under subsection (a), if a noncustodial parent requests custody of a dependent child who has been removed from the custody of the other parent, the juvenile court must place the child with the noncustodial parent unless it finds that placement with that parent would be detrimental to the well-being of the child. Requiring that the noncustodial parent prove her fitness would violate the parent's constitutional rights. *In re Z.K., 201 Cal.App.4th 51, 133 Cal.Rptr.3d 597 (2011).* To the same effect, *In re Abram L., 219 Cal.App.4th 452, 161 Cal.Rptr.3d 837 (2013),* holds that the juvenile court erred in denying a noncustodial father physical custody of his two sons when the court failed to consider whether placement with the father would be detrimental to the children.

In re D'Anthony D., 230 Cal.App.4th 292, 178 Cal.Rptr.3d 574 (2014), held that the juvenile court erred when it failed to consider a noncustodial father's request for custody under this section, but concluded that the error was harmless because the court made a finding that placement with the father would be detrimental to the well-being of his children.

In re Patrick S. III, 218 Cal.App.4th 1254, 160 Cal.Rptr.3d 832 (2013), holds that the juvenile court erred in finding that placement with his father would be detrimental to a child because the child wished to remain with his foster parents and was anxious about living with his father, when the father was a caring and competent parent and had consistently paid child support for 11 years while he was searching for his son.

In re Zacharia D., 6 Cal.4th 435, 862 P.2d 751, 24 Cal.Rptr.2d 751 (1993), holds that subsection (a), which requires placement of the child with a noncustodial parent who requests custody unless such placement would be detrimental to the child, applies only when the child is first removed from the home of the custodial parent or guardian and only when the noncustodial parent is a "presumed parent." (For the definition of "presumed parent," see Family Code Section 7611.) *Zacharia D.* additionally holds that a biological father who is not a presumed father is not entitled to reunification services. For further clarification of parental rights of access to the status of presumed parenthood and of the meaning of *Zacharia D.*, see *Adoption of Michael H., 10 Cal.4th 1043, 898 P.2d 891, 43 Cal.Rptr.2d 445 (1995),* and *Adoption of Kelsey S., 1 Cal.4th 816, 4 Cal.Rptr.2d 615 (1992). Michael H.* and *Kelsey S.* are discussed in the Commentary to Family Code Section 7611. Distinguishing *Zacharia D.* on the facts, *In re Julia U., 64 Cal.App.4th 532, 74 Cal.Rptr.2d 920 (1998),* held that when an unwed biological father promptly came forward and demonstrated a full commitment to his parental responsibilities, the juvenile court deprived him of his constitutional rights by refusing him reunification services and terminating his parental rights. See also *Adoption of Baby Boy W., 232 Cal.App.4th 438, 181 Cal.Rptr.3d 130 (2015), review denied.*

Purporting to rely on *Zacharia D., supra, In re Vincent M., 161 Cal.App.4th 943, 74 Cal.Rptr.3d 755 (2008), review denied,* holds that a person who is not a presumed father under Family Code section 7611 and whose paternity was concealed from him by the mother, but who does not come forward in a dependency proceeding until after the reunification period has ended, cannot be treated as a *Kelsey S.* father entitled to reunification services without regard to the best interests of the child, who was placed with prospective adoptive parents when he was four days old and was thriving in their home for nine months before the biological father asserted his *Kelsey S.* claim. *Vincent M.* states, in dictum, that after the reunification period has expired, the biological father's only remedy is a Welfare and Institutions Code section 388 modification petition, which requires changed circumstances or new evidence showing that it is in the child's best interest to grant the biological father custody or reunification services.

Section 7612 (c) now provides that a child may have more than two legal parents, overturning *In re M.C., 195 Cal.App.4th 197, 123 Cal.Rptr.3d 856 (2011),* which held that when a dependent child had more than two presumed parents, the court was required to resolve the conflicting presumptions of parentage by reducing the number of presumed parents to no more than two.

Interpreting the subsection (a) requirement that the child shall be placed with a parent unless "placement with that parent would be detrimental to the minor," *In re Marquis D., 38 Cal.App.4th 1813, 46 Cal.Rptr.2d 198 (1995),* holds that the finding of detriment must be supported by clear and convincing evidence.

The reunification time limits of section 361.5 do not start to run when a child is removed from one parent and placed with the other parent under subsection (a) of this section. Instead they start to run when a child is removed from all parental custody. *In re A.C., 169 Cal.App.4th 636, 88 Cal.Rptr.3d 1 (2008).*

In re Pedro Z., 190 Cal.App.4th 12, 117 Cal.Rptr.3d 605 (2010), holds that a juvenile court is not required, under section 361.5, to provide a former custodial parent with family reunification services when a dependent child is returned to the custody of the other parent at a disposition hearing.

Section 361.5 allows a juvenile court to bypass reunification services to a noncustodial parent who has been denied placement under subsection (a) of this section. *In re Adrianna P., 166 Cal. App.4th 44, 81 Cal.Rptr.3d 918 (2008).*

In re V.F., 157 Cal.App.4th 962, 69 Cal.Rptr.3d 159 (2007), holds that when the noncustodial parent of a dependent child is incarcerated, then, at a disposition hearing, the juvenile court must determine, under subsection (a), whether the incarcerated parent wishes to assume custody of the child and whether placement with that parent would be detrimental to the child's well-being in view of the parent's ability to arrange appropriate care for the child.

Interpreting subsection (b), *In re Austin P., 118 Cal.App.4th 1124, 13 Cal.Rptr.3d 616 (2004), review denied,* holds that a juvenile court properly placed a child with a nonoffending parent without terminating its dependency jurisdiction when there was a need for continuing court supervision because the nonoffending parent and child had previously had only sporadic contact and the court wanted to monitor conflict among the adults to ensure that the child would not be blamed for his dependency.

In re Jaden E., 229 Cal.App.4th 1277, 177 Cal.Rptr.3d 876 (2014), holds that when a dependent minor has been placed with a noncustodial parent under this section and reunification services have been offered, under subsection (b)(3), to the parent from whom the child has been removed, no reasonable services finding need be made when, at a periodic review hearing monitoring the placement, the reunification services are terminated because of the parent's lack of potential to provide the child with a safe, stable or permanent home.

In re Janee W., 140 Cal.App.4th 1444, 45 Cal.Rptr.3d 445 (2006), held that when dependent children are removed from a custodial parent's home and legal and physical custody is awarded to the other parent, once the juvenile court determines that further supervision of the children is no longer necessary, it may terminate its jurisdiction even though the original custodial parent has not been provided reunification services.

In re Damonte A., 57 Cal.App.4th 894, 67 Cal.Rptr.2d 369 (1997), review denied December 10, 1997, holds that the juvenile court may not declare children the dependents of the court, commit them to the custody of DHHS, and then place them "temporarily" in the home of the parent with whom they were living, under DHHS supervision. Instead, the statutes contemplate that removal of a child from the physical custody of a parent will result in physical custody by some person other than that parent. See particularly subsections (a) and (e) and Section 361 (d). Accord, *In re Andres G., 64 Cal.App.4th 476, 75 Cal.Rptr.2d 285 (1998).*

In re Luke H., 221 Cal.App.4th 1082, 165 Cal.Rptr.3d 63 (2013), held that a juvenile court did not have jurisdiction under subsection (j) to grant a dependent child's modification petition for visitation with a sibling who was not a dependent of the court, because the court had no jurisdiction over the sibling. Nor did section 388(a) authorize the court to issue an order affecting a child outside its jurisdiction.

Research References

Forms

West's California Judicial Council Forms JV-200, Custody Order - Juvenile - Final Judgment.
West's California Judicial Council Forms JV-400, Visitation Attachment: Parents, Legal Guardian, Indian Custodian, Other Important Person.
West's California Judicial Council Forms JV-402, Visitation Attachment: Grandparent.
West's California Judicial Council Forms JV-420, Dispositional Attachment: Removal from Custodial Parent--Placement With Previously Noncustodial Parent (Welf. & Inst. Code, §§ 361, 361.2).
West's California Judicial Council Forms JV-421, Dispositional Attachment: Removal from Custodial Parent--Placement With Nonparent (Welf. & Inst. Code, §§ 361, 361.2).

Treatises and Practice Aids

Witkin, California Summary 10th Parent and Child § 226, in General.
Witkin, California Summary 10th Parent and Child § 459, Residence Of Child.
Witkin, California Summary 10th Parent and Child § 577, Hearing.
Witkin, California Summary 10th Parent and Child § 583, Alleged Father.
Witkin, California Summary 10th Parent and Child § 60D, (New) Determination Of Rights Of Biological Mother, Presumed Mother, and Kelsey S. Father.
Witkin, California Summary 10th Parent and Child § 627, in General.
Witkin, California Summary 10th Parent and Child § 630, Bases for Removal.
Witkin, California Summary 10th Parent and Child § 635, in General.
Witkin, California Summary 10th Parent and Child § 637, Priority Right Of Noncustodial Parent.
Witkin, California Summary 10th Parent and Child § 638, Preferential Right Of Relatives.
Witkin, California Summary 10th Parent and Child § 639, Foster Care.
Witkin, California Summary 10th Parent and Child § 640, Change to Out-Of-County Placement.
Witkin, California Summary 10th Parent and Child § 641, Visitation Rights.
Witkin, California Summary 10th Parent and Child § 643, Duration Of Services.
Witkin, California Summary 10th Parent and Child § 644, Persons Entitled to Services.
Witkin, California Summary 10th Parent and Child § 672, Child in Custody Of Parent or Guardian.
Witkin, California Summary 10th Parent and Child § 676, in General.
Witkin, California Summary 10th Parent and Child § 678, Twelve-Month Review.
Witkin, California Summary 10th Parent and Child § 679, Eighteen-Month Review.
Witkin, California Summary 10th Parent and Child § 700, Right to Appeal.
Witkin, California Summary 10th Parent and Child § 759, in General.
Witkin, California Summary 10th Parent and Child § 941, Commitment Of Minor for Status Offense.

§ 361.21. Placement in out-of-state group home; order of placement; required findings; periodic review; funding

(a) The court shall not order the placement of a minor in an out-of-state group home, unless the court finds, in its order of placement, that all of the following conditions have been met:

(1) The out-of-state group home is licensed or certified for the placement of minors by an agency of the state in which the minor will be placed.

(2) The out-of-state group home meets the requirements of Section 7911.1 of the Family Code.

(3) In–state facilities or programs have been determined to be unavailable or inadequate to meet the needs of the minor.

(b) At least every six months, the court shall review each placement made pursuant to subdivision (a) in order to determine compliance with that subdivision.

(c) A county shall not be entitled to receive or expend any public funds for the placement of a minor in an out-of-state group home unless the requirements of subdivisions (a) and (b) are met. *(Added by Stats.1998, c. 311 (S.B.933), § 52, eff. Aug. 19, 1998. Amended by Stats.1999, c. 881 (A.B.1659), § 6, eff. Oct. 10, 1999.)*

Research References

Treatises and Practice Aids

Witkin, California Summary 10th Parent and Child § 635, in General.
Witkin, California Summary 10th Parent and Child § 670, Notice Of Hearing.
Witkin, California Summary 10th Parent and Child § 673, Child in Foster Care.

§ 361.3. Removal of child from custody of parents; preferential consideration of relative's request for placement of child with relative; search for relative and furnishing identifying information

(a) In any case in which a child is removed from the physical custody of his or her parents pursuant to Section 361, preferential consideration shall be given to a request by a relative of the child for placement of the child with the relative, regardless of the relative's immigration status. In determining whether placement with a relative is appropriate, the county social worker and court shall consider, but shall not be limited to, consideration of all the following factors:

(1) The best interest of the child, including special physical, psychological, educational, medical, or emotional needs.

(2) The wishes of the parent, the relative, and child, if appropriate.

(3) The provisions of Part 6 (commencing with Section 7950) of Division 12 of the Family Code regarding relative placement.

(4) Placement of siblings and half siblings in the same home, unless that placement is found to be contrary to the safety and well-being of any of the siblings, as provided in Section 16002.

(5) The good moral character of the relative and any other adult living in the home, including whether any individual residing in the home has a prior history of violent criminal acts or has been responsible for acts of child abuse or neglect.

(6) The nature and duration of the relationship between the child and the relative, and the relative's desire to care for, and to provide legal permanency for, the child if reunification is unsuccessful.

(7) The ability of the relative to do the following:

(A) Provide a safe, secure, and stable environment for the child.

(B) Exercise proper and effective care and control of the child.

(C) Provide a home and the necessities of life for the child.

(D) Protect the child from his or her parents.

(E) Facilitate court-ordered reunification efforts with the parents.

(F) Facilitate visitation with the child's other relatives.

(G) Facilitate implementation of all elements of the case plan.

(H)(i) Provide legal permanence for the child if reunification fails.

(ii) However, any finding made with respect to the factor considered pursuant to this subparagraph and pursuant to subparagraph (G) shall not be the sole basis for precluding preferential placement with a relative.

(I) Arrange for appropriate and safe child care, as necessary.

(8)(A) The safety of the relative's home. For a relative to be considered appropriate to receive placement of a child under this section on an emergency basis, the relative's home shall first be assessed pursuant to the process and standards described in * * * Section <u>361.4</u>.

(B) In this regard, the Legislature declares that a physical disability, such as blindness or deafness, is no bar to the raising of children, and a county social worker's determination as to the ability of a disabled relative to exercise care and control should center upon whether the relative's disability prevents him or her from exercising care and control. The court shall order the parent to disclose to the county social worker the names, residences, and any other known identifying information of any maternal or paternal relatives of the child. This inquiry shall not be construed, however, to guarantee that the child will be placed with any person so identified. The county social worker shall initially contact the relatives given preferential consideration for placement to determine if they desire the child to be placed with them. Those desiring placement shall be assessed according to the factors enumerated in this subdivision. The county social worker shall document these efforts in the social study prepared pursuant to Section 358.1. The court shall authorize the county social worker, while assessing these relatives for the possibility of placement, to disclose to the relative, as appropriate, the fact that the child is in custody, the alleged reasons for the custody, and the projected likely date for the child's return home or placement for adoption or legal guardianship. However, this investigation shall not be construed as good cause for continuance of the dispositional hearing conducted pursuant to Section 358.

(b) In any case in which more than one * * * relative requests preferential consideration pursuant to this section, each relative shall be considered under the factors enumerated in subdivision (a). Consistent with the legislative intent for children to be placed immediately with a * * * relative, this section does not limit the county social worker's ability to place a child in the home of * * * <u>a</u> relative or a nonrelative extended family member pending the consideration of other relatives who have requested preferential consideration.

(c) For purposes of this section:

(1) "Preferential consideration" means that the relative seeking placement shall be the first placement to be considered and investigated.

(2) "Relative" means an adult who is related to the child by blood, adoption, or affinity within the fifth degree of kinship, including stepparents, stepsiblings, and all relatives whose status is preceded by the words "great," "great-great," or "grand," or the spouse of any of these persons even if the marriage was terminated by death or dissolution. * * *

(d) Subsequent to the hearing conducted pursuant to Section 358, whenever a new placement of the child must be made, consideration for placement shall again be given as described in this section to relatives who have not been found to be unsuitable and who will fulfill the child's reunification or permanent plan requirements. In addition to the factors described in subdivision (a), the county social worker shall consider whether the relative has established and maintained a relationship with the child.

(e) If the court does not place the child with a relative who has been considered for placement pursuant to this section, the court shall state for the record the reasons placement with that relative was denied.

(f)(1) With respect to a child who satisfies the criteria set forth in paragraph (2), the department and any licensed adoption agency may search for a relative and furnish identifying information relating to the child to that relative if it is believed the child's welfare will be promoted thereby.

(2) Paragraph (1) shall apply if both of the following conditions are satisfied:

(A) The child was previously a dependent of the court.

(B) The child was previously adopted and the adoption has been disrupted, set aside pursuant to Section 9100 or 9102 of the Family Code, or the child has been released into the custody of the department or a licensed adoption agency by the adoptive parent or parents.

(3) As used in this subdivision, "relative" includes a member of the child's birth family and nonrelative extended family members, regardless of whether the parental rights were terminated, provided that both of the following are true:

(A) No appropriate potential caretaker is known to exist from the child's adoptive family, including nonrelative extended family members of the adoptive family.

(B) The child was not the subject of a voluntary relinquishment by the birth parents pursuant to Section 8700 of the Family Code or Section 1255.7 of the Health and Safety Code. *(Added by Stats.1986, c. 640, § 1. Amended by Stats.1987, c. 56, § 182; Stats.1989, c. 913, § 9; Stats.1992, c. 495 (A.B.3441), § 1; Stats.1993, c. 451 (S.B.270), § 1; Stats. 1993, c. 892 (S.B.426), § 2.5; Stats.1997, c. 268 (A.B.1196), § 1; Stats.1997, c. 793 (A.B.1544), § 16; Stats.1998, c. 949 (S.B.0645), § 3; Stats.1998, c. 1056 (A.B.2773), § 11.1; Stats. 2001, c. 653 (A.B.1695), § 11, eff. Oct. 10, 2001; Stats.2003, c. 812 (S.B.591), § 3; Stats.2007, c. 108 (A.B.714), § 2; Stats. 2012, c. 845 (S.B.1064), § 7; Stats.2014, c. 765 (A.B.1761), § 2, eff. Jan. 1, 2015; Stats.2016, c. 612 (A.B.1997), § 71, eff. Jan. 1, 2017; Stats.2017, c. 732 (A.B.404), § 47, eff. Jan. 1, 2018.)*

Commentary

In re A.K., 12 Cal.App.5th 492, 218 Cal.Rptr.3d 845 (2017), review denied, held that a father whose parental rights had been terminated at a hearing in which the child was freed for adoption, lacked standing to assert on appeal that the trial court erred in not assessing, sua sponte, the child's paternal grandmother for placement when the father had not raised the issue at the hearing.

In re Isabella G., 246 Cal.App.4th 708, 201 Cal.Rptr.3d 64 (2016), reversed an order denying the grandparents' request for a section 366.26(k) hearing because, under this section, the grandparents were entitled to a hearing without having to file a section 388 petition when the grandparents requested placement of the child before the dispositional hearing but the social services agency failed to complete a relative home assessment as required by law.

In re E.T., 217 Cal.App.4th 426, 158 Cal.Rptr.3d 322 (2013), holds that this section does not require that the court give preferential consideration to a child's biological father who was not a presumed father and had no relationship with the child.

Cesar V. v. Superior Court, 91 Cal.App.4th 1023, 111 Cal.Rptr.2d 243 (2001), holds that this section's preference for placement with a relative applies when a new placement for a dependent child becomes necessary after reunification services are terminated but before parental rights are terminated and adoptive placement is at issue. Similarly, *In re K.L., 248 Cal.App.4th 52, 203 Cal.Rptr.3d 159 (2016)*, affirmed the juvenile court's denial of a mother's section 388 petition to modify the placements of her three children and order that they be placed with their maternal grandmother under this section's preference for a relative, because that preference does not apply when the court has already selected adoption as the permanent placement goal.

In re R.T. 232 Cal.App.4th 1284, 182 Cal.Rptr.3d 338 (2015), review denied, reversed a trial court order that failed to apply this section's preference for a qualified relative, when a child's relatives petitioned for modification of an order placing the four-month-old child for adoption by a nonrelative.

In re Vivian F., originally published at *64 Cal.Rptr.2d 152 (1997)*, was depublished by the California Supreme Court when it denied review on August 27, 1997. The depublished opinion held that granting "preferential consideration" to a relative requires that a child be placed with a relative who satisfies the criteria of this section.

In re H.G., 146 Cal.App.4th 1, 52 Cal.Rptr.3d 364 (2006), held that a juvenile court erred in removing a child from the home of her grandparents without considering whether the child's placement with relatives was no longer appropriate under the criteria listed in this section.

In re Antonio G., 159 Cal.App.4th 369, 71 Cal.Rptr.3d 79 (2007), concluded that the removal of dependent children from their grandmother's home after an allegation that she allowed their mother unsupervised visits and left the children unsupervised in the home, was not a finding that the grandmother was unsuitable within the meaning of subsection (d). Therefore, the trial court erred in not applying the subsection (a) criteria to the grandmother when a new placement was required.

In re Lauren R., 148 Cal.App.4th 841, 56 Cal.Rptr.3d 151 (2007), held that, in ordering a child placed for adoption with an aunt, a juvenile court erred in applying the temporary placement factors of subsection (a), instead of the caretaker preference criteria of subsection (k) of section 366.26.

In re Joshua A., 239 Cal.App.4th 208, 190 Cal.Rptr.3d 655 (2015), held that a juvenile court erred as a matter of law when it ruled that a parent is not a *relative* within the meaning of subsection (c)(2) and that the mother's boyfriend therefore did not qualify as a nonrelative extended family member under section 362.7.

Research References

Treatises and Practice Aids

Witkin, California Summary 10th Parent and Child § 535, Placement Standards and Preferences.

Witkin, California Summary 10th Parent and Child § 573, Powers and Duties Of Counsel.

Witkin, California Summary 10th Parent and Child § 607, Findings and Orders.

Witkin, California Summary 10th Parent and Child § 625, Preparation Of Social Study.

Witkin, California Summary 10th Parent and Child § 635, in General.

Witkin, California Summary 10th Parent and Child § 638, Preferential Right Of Relatives.

Witkin, California Summary 10th Parent and Child § 656, Form and Content.

Witkin, California Summary 10th Parent and Child § 659, Sufficiency Of Evidence.

Witkin, California Summary 10th Parent and Child § 682, Preliminary Assessment.

Witkin, California Summary 10th Parent and Child § 694, Adoption Proceeding.

Witkin, California Summary 10th Parent and Child § 700, Right to Appeal.

Witkin, California Summary 10th Parent and Child § 941, Commitment Of Minor for Status Offense.

§ 361.31. Placement of children with Indian ancestry; considerations; priority of placement in adoptions; record of foster care

(a) In any case in which an Indian child is removed from the physical custody of his or her parents or Indian custodian pursuant to Section 361, the child's placement shall comply with this section.

(b) Any foster care or guardianship placement of an Indian child, or any emergency removal of a child who is known to be, or there is reason to know that the child is, an Indian child shall be in the least restrictive setting which most approximates a family situation and in which the child's special needs, if any, may be met. The child shall also be placed within reasonable proximity to the child's home, taking into account any special needs of the child. Preference shall be given to the child's placement with one of the following, in descending priority order:

(1) A member of the child's extended family, as defined in Section 1903 of the Indian Child Welfare Act (25 U.S.C. Sec. 1901 et seq.).

(2) A foster home licensed, approved, or specified by the child's tribe.

(3) An Indian foster home licensed or approved by an authorized non-Indian licensing authority.

(4) An institution for children approved by an Indian tribe or operated by an Indian organization which has a program suitable to meet the Indian child's needs.

(c) In any adoptive placement of an Indian child, preference shall be given to a placement with one of the following, in descending priority order:

(1) A member of the child's extended family, as defined in Section 1903 of the Indian Child Welfare Act (25 U.S.C. Sec. 1901 et seq.).

(2) Other members of the child's tribe.

(3) Another Indian family.

(d) Notwithstanding the placement preferences listed in subdivisions (b) and (c), if a different order of placement preference is established by the child's tribe, the court or agency effecting the placement shall follow the order of preference established by the tribe, so long as the placement is the least restrictive setting appropriate to the particular needs of the child as provided in subdivision (b).

(e) Where appropriate, the placement preference of the Indian child, when of sufficient age, or parent shall be considered. In applying the preferences, a consenting parent's request for anonymity shall also be given weight by the court or agency effecting the placement.

(f) The prevailing social and cultural standards of the Indian community in which the parent or extended family members of an Indian child reside, or with which the parent or extended family members maintain social and cultural ties, or the prevailing social and cultural standards of the Indian child's tribe shall be applied in meeting the placement preferences under this section. A determination of the applicable prevailing social and cultural standards may be confirmed by the Indian child's tribe or by the testimony or other documented support of a qualified expert witness, as defined in subdivision (c) of Section 224.6, who is knowledgeable regarding the social and cultural standards of the Indian child's tribe.

(g) Any person or court involved in the placement of an Indian child shall use the services of the Indian child's tribe, whenever available through the tribe, in seeking to secure placement within the order of placement preference established in this section and in the supervision of the placement.

(h) The court may determine that good cause exists not to follow placement preferences applicable under subdivision (b), (c), or (d) in accordance with subdivision (e).

(i) When no preferred placement under subdivision (b), (c), or (d) is available, active efforts shall be made to place the child with a family committed to enabling the child to have extended family visitation and participation in the cultural and ceremonial events of the child's tribe.

(j) The burden of establishing the existence of good cause not to follow placement preferences applicable under subdivision (b), (c), or (d) shall be on the party requesting that the preferences not be followed.

(k) A record of each foster care placement or adoptive placement of an Indian child shall be maintained in perpetuity by the State Department of Social Services. The record shall document the active efforts to comply with the applicable order of preference specified in this section. *(Added by Stats.2006, c. 838 (S.B.678), § 49.)*

Commentary

Invoking subsection (b), *In re Anthony T., 208 Cal.App.4th 1019, 146 Cal.Rptr.3d 124 (2012)*, reversed an order placing a dependent Indian child in the foster home preferred by his tribe, because the foster home was not within reasonable proximity to his mother's home and interfered with her frequent visitation of the child.

Applying subsection (j), *In re Alexandria P., 228 Cal.App.4th 1322, 176 Cal.Rptr.3d 468 (2014)*, reversed a trial court order removing an Indian toddler who had lived with her non-Indian foster parents for two-and-a-half years, because her foster parents did not prove to a certainty that the child would suffer emotional harm as a result of her transfer to a non-Indian couple related to the child's father, who had failed to reunite with the child. *Alexandria P.* held that the standard of proof for the good cause exception is clear and convincing evidence, not proof to a certainty.

Research References

Forms

California Transactions Forms--Family Law § 3:4, Subject Matter Jurisdiction for Custody Determinations.

California Transactions Forms--Family Law § 5:3, Rights Of Non-parents Generally.

Treatises and Practice Aids

Witkin, California Summary 10th Parent and Child § 113, Consideration Of Relatives and Foster Parents.

Witkin, California Summary 10th Parent and Child § 218, Statutory Rule.

Witkin, California Summary 10th Parent and Child § 524, Jurisdiction.

Witkin, California Summary 10th Parent and Child § 535, Placement Standards and Preferences.

Witkin, California Summary 10th Parent and Child § 537, Proceedings After Termination or Removal.

Witkin, California Summary 10th Parent and Child § 288C, (New) Applicable Law.

§ 361.4. Emergency placement of child; duties of department; criminal records check; fingerprint clearance check

(a) Prior to making the emergency placement of a child pursuant to subdivision (d) of Section 309 or Section 361.45, the county welfare department shall do all of the following:

(1) Conduct an in-home inspection to assess the safety of the home and the ability of the relative or nonrelative extended family member to care for the child's needs.

(2) Cause a state-level criminal records check to be conducted by an appropriate government agency through the California Law Enforcement Telecommunications System (CLETS) pursuant to Section 16504.5 for all of the following:

(A) All persons over 18 years of age living in the home of the relative or nonrelative extended family member seeking emergency placement of the child, excluding any person who is a nonminor dependent, as defined in subdivision (v) of Section 11400.

(B) At the discretion of the county welfare department, any other person over 18 years of age known to the department to be regularly present in the home, other than professionals providing professional services to the child.

(C) At the discretion of the county welfare department, any person over 14 years of age living in the home who the department believes may have a criminal record. This subparagraph shall not apply to a child under the jurisdiction of the juvenile court.

(3) Conduct a check of allegations of prior child abuse or neglect concerning the relative or nonrelative extended family member and other adults in the home.

(b)(1) If CLETS information obtained pursuant to paragraph (2) of subdivision (a) indicates that the person has no criminal record, the child may be placed in the home on an emergency basis.

(2) If the CLETS information obtained pursuant to paragraph (2) of subdivision (a) indicates that the person has been convicted of an offense described in subparagraph (B) or (D) of paragraph (2) of subdivision (g) of Section 1522 of the Health and Safety Code, the child shall not be placed in the home unless a criminal records exemption has been granted using the exemption criteria specified in paragraph (2) of subdivision (g) of Section 1522 of the Health and Safety Code.

(3) Notwithstanding paragraph (2), a child may be placed on an emergency basis who has been convicted of an offense not described in clause (i) of subparagraph (B) of paragraph (2) of subdivision (g) of Section 1522 of the Health and Safety Code, pending a criminal records exemption decision, if the deputy director or director of the county welfare department, or his or her designee, determines that the placement is in the best interests of the child and a party to the case does not object.

(4) If the CLETS information obtained pursuant to paragraph (2) of subdivision (a) indicates that the person has been arrested for any offense described in paragraph (2) of subdivision (e) of Section 1522 of the Health and Safety Code, the child shall not be placed on an emergency basis in the home until the investigation required by paragraph (1) of subdivision (e) of Section 1522 of the Health and Safety Code has been completed and the deputy director or director of the county welfare department, or his or her designee, and the court have considered the investigation results when determining whether the placement is in the best interests of the child.

(5) If the CLETS information obtained pursuant to paragraph (2) of subdivision (a) indicates that the person has been convicted of an offense described in subparagraph (A) of paragraph (2) of subdivision (g) of Section 1522 of the Health and Safety Code, the child shall not be placed in the home on an emergency basis.

(c) Within 10 calendar days following the criminal records check conducted through the CLETS or five business days of making the emergency placement, whichever is sooner, the social worker shall ensure that a fingerprint clearance check of the relative or nonrelative extended family member and any other person whose criminal record was obtained pursuant to this section is initiated through the Department of Justice to ensure the accuracy of the criminal records check conducted through the CLETS and ensure criminal record clearance of the relative or nonrelative extended family member and all adults in the home pursuant to subparagraph (A) of paragraph (2) of subdivision (d) of Section 16519.5 and any associated written directives or regulations.

(d) An identification card from a foreign consulate or foreign passport shall be considered a valid form of identification for conducting a criminal records check pursuant to this section. *(Added by Stats.2017, c. 733 (S.B.213), § 3.2, eff. Jan. 1, 2018.)*

§ 361.45. Temporary placement in home of relative or nonrelative extended family member on an emergency basis; assessment of suitability; AFDC–FC eligibility; nonminor dependents

(a) Notwithstanding any other law, when the sudden unavailability of a foster caregiver requires a change in placement * * * for a child who is under the jurisdiction of the juvenile court pursuant to Section 300, if * * * a relative, as defined in Section 319, or * * * a nonrelative extended family member, as defined in Section 362.7, is available and requests temporary placement of the child * * *, the county welfare department shall initiate an assessment of the relative's or nonrelative extended family member's suitability * * * pursuant to * * * Section * * * 361.4.

(b) Upon completion of the assessment pursuant to Section 361.4, the child may be placed in the home on an emergency basis. Following the emergency placement of the child * * *, the county welfare department shall require the relative or * * * nonrelative extended family member to submit an application for approval as a resource family and initiate the home environment assessment no later than five business days after the placement. Thereafter, the county welfare department shall evaluate and approve or deny the home pursuant to Section 16519.5.

(c)(1) On and after January 1, 2012, if a nonminor dependent, as defined in subdivision (v) of Section 11400, is placed in the home of a relative or nonrelative extended family member, the home shall be approved using the same standards set forth in regulations as described in Section 1502.7 of the Health and Safety Code.

(2) On or before July 1, 2012, the department, in consultation with representatives of the Legislature, the County Welfare Directors Association, the Chief Probation Officers of California, the California Youth Connection, the Judicial Council, former foster youth, child advocacy organizations, dependency counsel for children, juvenile justice advocacy organizations, foster caregiver organizations, labor organizations, and representatives of Indian tribes, shall revise regulations regarding health and safety standards for approving relative homes in which nonminor dependents, as defined in subdivision (v) of Section 11400, of the juvenile court are placed under the responsibility of the county welfare or probation department, or an Indian tribe that entered into an agreement pursuant to Section 10553.1.

(3) Notwithstanding the Administrative Procedure Act (Chapter 3.5 (commencing with Section 11340) of Part 1 of Division 3 of Title 2 of the Government Code), the department, in consultation with the stakeholders listed in paragraph (2), shall prepare for implementation of the applicable provisions of this section by publishing all-county letters or similar instructions from the department by October 1, 2011, to be effective January 1, 2012. Emergency regulations to implement this section may be adopted by the director in accordance with the Administrative Procedure Act. The initial adoption of the emergency regulations and one readoption of the initial regulations shall be deemed to be an emergency and necessary for the immediate preservation of the public peace, health, safety, or general welfare. Initial emergency regulations and the first readoption of those emergency regulations shall be exempt from review by the Office of Administrative Law. The emergency regulations authorized by this section shall be submitted to the Office of Administrative Law for filing with the Secretary of State and shall remain in effect for no more than 180 days. *(Added by Stats.2006, c. 383 (A.B.2195), § 1. Amended by Stats.2010, c. 559 (A.B.12), § 12; Stats.2016, c. 612 (A.B.1997), § 73, eff. Jan. 1, 2017; Stats.2017, c. 732 (A.B.404), § 50, eff. Jan. 1, 2018.)*

Research References

Treatises and Practice Aids

Witkin, California Summary 10th Parent and Child § 636, Criminal Records Check and Fingerprint Clearance.

Witkin, California Summary 10th Parent and Child § 639, Foster Care.

§ 361.49. Date of foster care entry

Regardless of his or her age, a child shall be deemed to have entered foster care on the earlier of the date of the jurisdictional hearing held pursuant to Section 356 or the date that is 60 days after the date on which the child was initially removed from the physical custody of his or her parent or guardian. *(Added by Stats.2009, c. 120 (A.B.706), § 1, eff. Aug. 6, 2009.)*

Research References

Treatises and Practice Aids

Witkin, California Summary 10th Parent and Child § 643, Duration Of Services.

Witkin, California Summary 10th Parent and Child § 673, Child in Foster Care.

Witkin, California Summary 10th Parent and Child § 676, in General.

Witkin, California Summary 10th Parent and Child § 678, Twelve-Month Review.

§ 361.5. Child welfare services; reunification of family; hearing; findings by court; incarcerated parents; adoption assessment

(a) Except as provided in subdivision (b), or when the parent has voluntarily relinquished the child and the relinquishment has been filed with the State Department of Social Services, or upon the establishment of an order of guardianship pursuant to Section 360, or when a court adjudicates a petition under Section 329 to modify the court's jurisdiction from delinquency jurisdiction to dependency jurisdiction pursuant to subparagraph (A) of paragraph (2) of subdivision (b) of Section 607.2 and the parents or guardian of the ward have had reunification services terminated under the delinquency jurisdiction, whenever a child is removed from a parent's or guardian's custody, the juvenile court shall order the social worker to provide child welfare services to the child and the child's mother and statutorily presumed father or guardians. Upon a finding and declaration of paternity by the juvenile court or proof of a prior declaration of paternity by any court of competent jurisdiction, the juvenile court may order services for the child and the biological father, if the court determines that the services will benefit the child.

(1) Family reunification services, when provided, shall be provided as follows:

(A) Except as otherwise provided in subparagraph (C), for a child who, on the date of initial removal from the physical custody of his or her parent or guardian, was three years of age or older, court-ordered services shall be provided beginning with the dispositional hearing and ending 12 months after the date the child entered foster care as provided in Section 361.49, unless the child is returned to the home of the parent or guardian.

(B) For a child who, on the date of initial removal from the physical custody of his or her parent or guardian, was under three years of age, court-ordered services shall be provided for a period of 6 months from the dispositional hearing as provided in subdivision (e) of Section 366.21, but no longer than 12 months from the date the child entered foster care, as provided in Section 361.49, unless the child is returned to the home of the parent or guardian.

(C) For the purpose of placing and maintaining a sibling group together in a permanent home should reunification efforts fail, for a child in a sibling group whose members were removed from parental custody at the same time, and in which one member of the sibling group was under three years of age on the date of initial removal from the physical custody of his or her parent or guardian, court-ordered services for some or all of the sibling group may be limited as set forth in subparagraph (B). For the purposes of this paragraph, "a sibling group" shall mean two or more children who are related to each other as full or half siblings.

(2) Any motion to terminate court-ordered reunification services prior to the hearing set pursuant to subdivision (f) of Section 366.21 for a child described by subparagraph (A) of paragraph (1), or prior to the hearing set pursuant to subdivision (e) of Section 366.21 for a child described by subparagraph (B) or (C) of paragraph (1), shall be made pursuant to the requirements set forth in subdivision (c) of Section 388. A motion to terminate court-ordered reunification services shall not be required at the hearing set pursuant to subdivision (e) of Section 366.21 if the court finds by clear and convincing evidence one of the following:

(A) That the child was removed initially under subdivision (g) of Section 300 and the whereabouts of the parent are still unknown.

(B) That the parent has failed to contact and visit the child.

(C) That the parent has been convicted of a felony indicating parental unfitness.

(3)(A) Notwithstanding subparagraphs (A), (B), and (C) of paragraph (1), court-ordered services may be extended up to a maximum time period not to exceed 18 months after the date the child was originally removed from physical custody of his or her parent or guardian if it can be shown, at the hearing held pursuant to subdivision (f) of Section 366.21, that the permanent plan for the child is that he or she will be returned and safely maintained in the home within the extended time period. The court shall extend the time period only if it finds that there is a substantial probability that the child will be returned to the physical custody of his or her parent or guardian within the extended time period or that reasonable services have not been provided to the parent or guardian. In determining whether court-ordered services may be extended, the court shall consider the special circumstances of an incarcerated or institutionalized parent or parents, parent or parents court-ordered to a residential substance abuse treatment program, or a parent who has been arrested and issued an immigration hold, detained by the United States Department of Homeland Security, or deported to his or her country of origin, including, but not limited to, barriers to the parent's or guardian's access to services and ability to maintain contact with his or her child. The court shall also consider, among other factors, good faith efforts that the parent or guardian has made to maintain contact with the child. If the court extends the time period, the court shall specify the factual basis for its conclusion that there is a substantial probability that the child will be returned to the physical custody of his or her parent or guardian within the extended time period. The court also shall make findings pursuant to subdivision (a) of Section 366 and subdivision (e) of Section 358.1.

(B) When counseling or other treatment services are ordered, the parent or guardian shall be ordered to participate in those services, unless the parent's or guardian's participation is deemed by the court to be inappropriate or potentially detrimental to the child, or unless a parent or guardian is incarcerated or detained by the United States Department of Homeland Security and the corrections facility in which he or she is incarcerated does not provide access to the treatment services ordered by the court, or has been deported to his or her country of origin and services ordered by the court are not accessible in that country. Physical custody of the child by the parents or guardians during the applicable time period under subparagraph (A), (B), or (C) of paragraph (1) shall not serve to interrupt the running of the time period. If at the end of the applicable time period, a child cannot be safely returned to the care and custody of a parent or guardian without court supervision, but the child clearly desires contact with the parent or guardian, the court shall take the child's desire into account in devising a permanency plan.

(C) In cases where the child was under three years of age on the date of the initial removal from the physical custody of his or her parent or guardian or is a member of a sibling group as described in subparagraph (C) of paragraph (1), the court shall inform the parent or guardian that the failure of the parent or guardian to participate regularly in any court-ordered treatment programs or to cooperate or avail himself or herself of services provided as part of the child welfare services case plan may result in a termination of efforts to reunify the family after six months. The court shall inform the parent or guardian of the factors used in subdivision (e) of Section 366.21 to determine whether to limit services to six months for some or all members of a sibling group as described in subparagraph (C) of paragraph (1).

(4)(A) Notwithstanding paragraph (3), court-ordered services may be extended up to a maximum time period not to exceed 24 months after the date the child was originally removed from physical custody of his or her parent or guardian if it is shown, at the hearing held pursuant to subdivision (b) of Section 366.22, that the permanent plan for the child is that he or she will be returned and safely maintained in the home within the extended time period. The court shall extend the time period only if it finds that it is in the child's best interest to have the time period extended and that there is a substantial probability that the child will be returned to the physical custody of his or her parent or guardian who is described in subdivision (b) of Section 366.22 within the extended time period, or that reasonable services have not been provided to the parent or guardian. If the court extends the time period, the court shall specify the factual basis for its conclusion that there is a substantial probability that the child will be returned to the physical custody of his or her parent or guardian within the extended time period. The court also shall make findings pursuant to subdivision (a) of Section 366 and subdivision (e) of Section 358.1.

(B) When counseling or other treatment services are ordered, the parent or guardian shall be ordered to participate in those services, in order for substantial probability to be found. Physical custody of the child by the parents or guardians during the applicable time period under subparagraph (A), (B), or (C) of paragraph (1) shall not serve to interrupt the running of the time period. If at the end of the applicable time period, the child cannot be safely returned to the care and custody of a parent or guardian without court supervision, but the child clearly desires contact with the parent or guardian, the court shall take the child's desire into account in devising a permanency plan.

(C) Except in cases where, pursuant to subdivision (b), the court does not order reunification services, the court shall inform the parent or parents of Section 366.26 and shall specify that the parent's or parents' parental rights may be terminated.

(b) Reunification services need not be provided to a parent or guardian described in this subdivision when the court finds, by clear and convincing evidence, any of the following:

(1) That the whereabouts of the parent or guardian are unknown. A finding pursuant to this paragraph shall be supported by an affidavit or by proof that a reasonably diligent search has failed to locate the parent or guardian. The posting or publication of notices is not required in that search.

(2) That the parent or guardian is suffering from a mental disability that is described in Chapter 2 (commencing with Section 7820) of Part 4 of Division 12 of the Family Code and that renders him or her incapable of utilizing those services.

(3) That the child or a sibling of the child has been previously adjudicated a dependent pursuant to any subdivi-

sion of Section 300 as a result of physical or sexual abuse, that following that adjudication the child had been removed from the custody of his or her parent or guardian pursuant to Section 361, that the child has been returned to the custody of the parent or guardian from whom the child had been taken originally, and that the child is being removed pursuant to Section 361, due to additional physical or sexual abuse.

(4) That the parent or guardian of the child has caused the death of another child through abuse or neglect.

(5) That the child was brought within the jurisdiction of the court under subdivision (e) of Section 300 because of the conduct of that parent or guardian.

(6)(A) That the child has been adjudicated a dependent pursuant to any subdivision of Section 300 as a result of severe sexual abuse or the infliction of severe physical harm to the child, a sibling, or a half sibling by a parent or guardian, as defined in this subdivision, and the court makes a factual finding that it would not benefit the child to pursue reunification services with the offending parent or guardian.

(B) A finding of severe sexual abuse, for the purposes of this subdivision, may be based on, but is not limited to, sexual intercourse, or stimulation involving genital-genital, oral-genital, anal-genital, or oral-anal contact, whether between the parent or guardian and the child or a sibling or half sibling of the child, or between the child or a sibling or half sibling of the child and another person or animal with the actual or implied consent of the parent or guardian; or the penetration or manipulation of the child's, sibling's, or half sibling's genital organs or rectum by any animate or inanimate object for the sexual gratification of the parent or guardian, or for the sexual gratification of another person with the actual or implied consent of the parent or guardian.

(C) A finding of the infliction of severe physical harm, for the purposes of this subdivision, may be based on, but is not limited to, deliberate and serious injury inflicted to or on a child's body or the body of a sibling or half sibling of the child by an act or omission of the parent or guardian, or of another individual or animal with the consent of the parent or guardian; deliberate and torturous confinement of the child, sibling, or half sibling in a closed space; or any other torturous act or omission that would be reasonably understood to cause serious emotional damage.

(7) That the parent is not receiving reunification services for a sibling or a half sibling of the child pursuant to paragraph (3), (5), or (6).

(8) That the child was conceived by means of the commission of an offense listed in Section 288 or 288.5 of the Penal Code, or by an act committed outside of this state that, if committed in this state, would constitute one of those offenses. This paragraph only applies to the parent who committed the offense or act.

(9) That the child has been found to be a child described in subdivision (g) of Section 300; that the parent or guardian of the child willfully abandoned the child, and the court finds that the abandonment itself constituted a serious danger to the child; or that the parent or other person having custody of the child voluntarily surrendered physical custody of the child pursuant to Section 1255.7 of the Health and Safety Code. For the purposes of this paragraph, "serious danger" means that without the intervention of another person or agency, the child would have sustained severe or permanent disability, injury, illness, or death. For purposes of this paragraph, "willful abandonment" shall not be construed as actions taken in good faith by the parent without the intent of placing the child in serious danger.

(10) That the court ordered termination of reunification services for any siblings or half siblings of the child because the parent or guardian failed to reunify with the sibling or half sibling after the sibling or half sibling had been removed from that parent or guardian pursuant to Section 361 and that parent or guardian is the same parent or guardian described in subdivision (a) and that, according to the findings of the court, this parent or guardian has not subsequently made a reasonable effort to treat the problems that led to removal of the sibling or half sibling of that child from that parent or guardian.

(11) That the parental rights of a parent over any sibling or half sibling of the child had been permanently severed, and this parent is the same parent described in subdivision (a), and that, according to the findings of the court, this parent has not subsequently made a reasonable effort to treat the problems that led to removal of the sibling or half sibling of that child from the parent.

(12) That the parent or guardian of the child has been convicted of a violent felony, as defined in subdivision (c) of Section 667.5 of the Penal Code.

(13) That the parent or guardian of the child has a history of extensive, abusive, and chronic use of drugs or alcohol and has resisted prior court-ordered treatment for this problem during a three-year period immediately prior to the filing of the petition that brought that child to the court's attention, or has failed or refused to comply with a program of drug or alcohol treatment described in the case plan required by Section 358.1 on at least two prior occasions, even though the programs identified were available and accessible.

(14)(A) That the parent or guardian of the child has advised the court that he or she is not interested in receiving family maintenance or family reunification services or having the child returned to or placed in his or her custody and does not wish to receive family maintenance or reunification services.

(B) The parent or guardian shall be represented by counsel and shall execute a waiver of services form to be adopted by the Judicial Council. The court shall advise the parent or guardian of any right to services and of the possible consequences of a waiver of services, including the termination of parental rights and placement of the child for adoption. The court shall not accept the waiver of services unless it states on the record its finding that the parent or guardian has knowingly and intelligently waived the right to services.

(15) That the parent or guardian has on one or more occasions willfully abducted the child or child's sibling or half sibling from his or her placement and refused to disclose the child's or child's sibling's or half sibling's whereabouts, refused to return physical custody of the child or child's sibling or half sibling to his or her placement, or refused to return physical custody of the child or child's sibling or half sibling to the social worker.

(16) That the parent or guardian has been required by the court to be registered on a sex offender registry under the federal Adam Walsh Child Protection and Safety Act of 2006 (42 U.S.C. Sec. 16913(a)), as required in Section 106(b)(2)(B)(xvi)(VI) of the federal Child Abuse Prevention and Treatment Act * * * (42 U.S.C. Sec. 5106a(2)(B)(xvi)(VI)).

(17) That the parent or guardian knowingly participated in, or permitted, the sexual exploitation, as described in subdivision (c) or (d) of Section 11165.1 of, or subdivision (c) of Section 236.1 of, the Penal Code, of the child. This shall not include instances in which the parent or guardian demonstrated by a preponderance of the evidence that he or she was coerced into permitting, or participating in, the sexual exploitation of the child.

(c)(1) In deciding whether to order reunification in any case in which this section applies, the court shall hold a dispositional hearing. The social worker shall prepare a report that discusses whether reunification services shall be provided. When it is alleged, pursuant to paragraph (2) of subdivision (b), that the parent is incapable of utilizing services due to mental disability, the court shall order reunification services unless competent evidence from mental health professionals establishes that, even with the provision of services, the parent is unlikely to be capable of adequately caring for the child within the time limits specified in subdivision (a).

(2) The court shall not order reunification for a parent or guardian described in paragraph (3), (4), (6), (7), (8), (9), (10), (11), (12), (13), (14), (15), (16), or (17) of subdivision (b) unless the court finds, by clear and convincing evidence, that reunification is in the best interest of the child.

(3) In addition, the court shall not order reunification in any situation described in paragraph (5) of subdivision (b) unless it finds that, based on competent testimony, those services are likely to prevent reabuse or continued neglect of the child or that failure to try reunification will be detrimental to the child because the child is closely and positively attached to that parent. The social worker shall investigate the circumstances leading to the removal of the child and advise the court whether there are circumstances that indicate that reunification is likely to be successful or unsuccessful and whether failure to order reunification is likely to be detrimental to the child.

(4) The failure of the parent to respond to previous services, the fact that the child was abused while the parent was under the influence of drugs or alcohol, a past history of violent behavior, or testimony by a competent professional that the parent's behavior is unlikely to be changed by services are among the factors indicating that reunification services are unlikely to be successful. The fact that a parent or guardian is no longer living with an individual who severely abused the child may be considered in deciding that reunification services are likely to be successful, provided that the court shall consider any pattern of behavior on the part of the parent that has exposed the child to repeated abuse.

(d) If reunification services are not ordered pursuant to paragraph (1) of subdivision (b) and the whereabouts of a parent become known within six months of the out-of-home placement of the child, the court shall order the social worker to provide family reunification services in accordance with this subdivision.

(e)(1) If the parent or guardian is incarcerated, institutionalized, or detained by the United States Department of Homeland Security, or has been deported to his or her country of origin, the court shall order reasonable services unless the court determines, by clear and convincing evidence, those services would be detrimental to the child. In determining detriment, the court shall consider the age of the child, the degree of parent-child bonding, the length of the sentence, the length and nature of the treatment, the nature of the crime or illness, the degree of detriment to the child if services are not offered and, for children 10 years of age or older, the child's attitude toward the implementation of family reunification services, the likelihood of the parent's discharge from incarceration, institutionalization, or detention within the reunification time limitations described in subdivision (a), and any other appropriate factors. In determining the content of reasonable services, the court shall consider the particular barriers to an incarcerated, institutionalized, detained, or deported parent's access to those court-mandated services and ability to maintain contact with his or her child, and shall document this information in the child's case plan. Reunification services are subject to the applicable time limitations imposed in subdivision (a). Services may include, but shall not be limited to, all of the following:

(A) Maintaining contact between the parent and child through collect telephone calls.

(B) Transportation services, when appropriate.

(C) Visitation services, when appropriate.

(D)(i) Reasonable services to extended family members or foster parents providing care for the child if the services are not detrimental to the child.

(ii) An incarcerated or detained parent may be required to attend counseling, parenting classes, or vocational training programs as part of the reunification service plan if actual access to these services is provided. The social worker shall document in the child's case plan the particular barriers to an incarcerated, institutionalized, or detained parent's access to those court-mandated services and ability to maintain contact with his or her child.

(E) Reasonable efforts to assist parents who have been deported to contact child welfare authorities in their country of origin, to identify any available services that would substantially comply with case plan requirements, to document the parents' participation in those services, and to accept reports from local child welfare authorities as to the parents' living situation, progress, and participation in services.

(2) The presiding judge of the juvenile court of each county may convene representatives of the county welfare department, the sheriff's department, and other appropriate entities for the purpose of developing and entering into protocols for ensuring the notification, transportation, and presence of an incarcerated or institutionalized parent at all court hearings involving proceedings affecting the child pursuant to Section 2625 of the Penal Code. The county welfare department shall utilize the prisoner locator system

developed by the Department of Corrections and Rehabilitation to facilitate timely and effective notice of hearings for incarcerated parents.

(3) Notwithstanding any other law, if the incarcerated parent is a woman seeking to participate in the community treatment program operated by the Department of Corrections and Rehabilitation pursuant to Chapter 4.8 (commencing with Section 1174) of Title 7 of Part 2 of, Chapter 4 (commencing with Section 3410) of Title 2 of Part 3 of, the Penal Code, the court shall determine whether the parent's participation in a program is in the child's best interest and whether it is suitable to meet the needs of the parent and child.

(f) If the court, pursuant to paragraph (2), (3), (4), (5), (6), (7), (8), (9), (10), (11), (12), (13), (14), (15), (16), or (17) of subdivision (b) or paragraph (1) of subdivision (e), does not order reunification services, it shall, at the dispositional hearing, that shall include a permanency hearing, determine if a hearing under Section 366.26 shall be set in order to determine whether adoption, guardianship, placement with a fit and willing relative, or another planned permanent living arrangement, or, in the case of an Indian child, in consultation with the child's tribe, tribal customary adoption, is the most appropriate plan for the child, and shall consider in-state and out-of-state placement options. If the court so determines, it shall conduct the hearing pursuant to Section 366.26 within 120 days after the dispositional hearing. However, the court shall not schedule a hearing so long as the other parent is being provided reunification services pursuant to subdivision (a). The court may continue to permit the parent to visit the child unless it finds that visitation would be detrimental to the child.

(g)(1) Whenever a court orders that a hearing shall be held pursuant to Section 366.26, including, when, in consultation with the child's tribe, tribal customary adoption is recommended, it shall direct the agency supervising the child and the county adoption agency, or the State Department of Social Services when it is acting as an adoption agency, to prepare an assessment that shall include:

(A) Current search efforts for an absent parent or parents and notification of a noncustodial parent in the manner provided for in Section 291.

(B) A review of the amount of and nature of any contact between the child and his or her parents and other members of his or her extended family since the time of placement. Although the extended family of each child shall be reviewed on a case-by-case basis, "extended family" for the purpose of this subparagraph shall include, but not be limited to, the child's siblings, grandparents, aunts, and uncles.

(C)(i) An evaluation of the child's medical, developmental, scholastic, mental, and emotional status.

(ii) The evaluation pursuant to clause (i) shall include, but is not limited to, providing a copy of the complete health and education summary as required under Section 16010, including the name and contact information of the person or persons currently holding the right to make educational decisions for the child.

(iii) In instances where it is determined that disclosure pursuant to clause (ii) of the contact information of the person or persons currently holding the right to make educational decisions for the child poses a threat to the health and safety of that individual or those individuals, that contact information shall be redacted or withheld from the evaluation.

(D) A preliminary assessment of the eligibility and commitment of any identified prospective adoptive parent or guardian, including a prospective tribal customary adoptive parent, particularly the caretaker, to include a social history, including screening for criminal records and prior referrals for child abuse or neglect, the capability to meet the child's needs, and the understanding of the legal and financial rights and responsibilities of adoption and guardianship. If a proposed guardian is a relative of the minor, the assessment shall also consider, but need not be limited to, all of the factors specified in subdivision (a) of Section 361.3 and in Section 361.4. As used in this subparagraph, "relative" means an adult who is related to the minor by blood, adoption, or affinity within the fifth degree of kinship, including stepparents, stepsiblings, and all relatives whose status is preceded by the words "great," "great-great," or "grand," or the spouse of any of those persons even if the marriage was terminated by death or dissolution. If the proposed permanent plan is guardianship with an approved relative caregiver for a minor eligible for aid under the Kin–GAP Program, as provided for in Article 4.7 (commencing with Section 11385) of Chapter 2 of Part 3 of Division 9, "relative" as used in this section has the same meaning as "relative" as defined in subdivision (c) of Section 11391.

(E) The relationship of the child to any identified prospective adoptive parent or guardian, including a prospective tribal customary parent, the duration and character of the relationship, the degree of attachment of the child to the prospective relative guardian or adoptive parent, the relative's or adoptive parent's strong commitment to caring permanently for the child, the motivation for seeking adoption or guardianship, a statement from the child concerning placement and the adoption or guardianship, and whether the child over 12 years of age has been consulted about the proposed relative guardianship arrangements, unless the child's age or physical, emotional, or other condition precludes his or her meaningful response, and if so, a description of the condition.

(F) An analysis of the likelihood that the child will be adopted if parental rights are terminated.

(G) In the case of an Indian child, in addition to subparagraphs (A) to (F), inclusive, an assessment of the likelihood that the child will be adopted, when, in consultation with the child's tribe, a tribal customary adoption, as defined in Section 366.24, is recommended. If tribal customary adoption is recommended, the assessment shall include an analysis of both of the following:

(i) Whether tribal customary adoption would or would not be detrimental to the Indian child and the reasons for reaching that conclusion.

(ii) Whether the Indian child cannot or should not be returned to the home of the Indian parent or Indian custodian and the reasons for reaching that conclusion.

(2)(A) A relative caregiver's preference for legal guardianship over adoption, if it is due to circumstances that do not include an unwillingness to accept legal or financial responsibility for the child, shall not constitute the sole basis for recommending removal of the child from the relative caregiver for purposes of adoptive placement.

(B) Regardless of his or her immigration status, a relative caregiver shall be given information regarding the permanency options of guardianship and adoption, including the long-term benefits and consequences of each option, prior to establishing legal guardianship or pursuing adoption. If the proposed permanent plan is guardianship with an approved relative caregiver for a minor eligible for aid under the Kin–GAP Program, as provided for in Article 4.7 (commencing with Section 11385) of Chapter 2 of Part 3 of Division 9, the relative caregiver shall be informed about the terms and conditions of the negotiated agreement pursuant to Section 11387 and shall agree to its execution prior to the hearing held pursuant to Section 366.26. A copy of the executed negotiated agreement shall be attached to the assessment.

(h) If, at any hearing held pursuant to Section 366.26, a guardianship is established for the minor with an approved relative caregiver and juvenile court dependency is subsequently dismissed, the minor shall be eligible for aid under the Kin–GAP Program as provided for in Article 4.5 (commencing with Section 11360) or Article 4.7 (commencing with Section 11385), as applicable, of Chapter 2 of Part 3 of Division 9.

(i) In determining whether reunification services will benefit the child pursuant to paragraph (6) or (7) of subdivision (b), the court shall consider any information it deems relevant, including the following factors:

(1) The specific act or omission comprising the severe sexual abuse or the severe physical harm inflicted on the child or the child's sibling or half sibling.

(2) The circumstances under which the abuse or harm was inflicted on the child or the child's sibling or half sibling.

(3) The severity of the emotional trauma suffered by the child or the child's sibling or half sibling.

(4) Any history of abuse of other children by the offending parent or guardian.

(5) The likelihood that the child may be safely returned to the care of the offending parent or guardian within 12 months with no continuing supervision.

(6) Whether or not the child desires to be reunified with the offending parent or guardian.

(j) When the court determines that reunification services will not be ordered, it shall order that the child's caregiver receive the child's birth certificate in accordance with Sections 16010.4 and 16010.5. Additionally, when the court determines that reunification services will not be ordered, it shall order, when appropriate, that a child who is 16 years of age or older receive his or her birth certificate.

(k) The court shall read into the record the basis for a finding of severe sexual abuse or the infliction of severe physical harm under paragraph (6) of subdivision (b), and shall also specify the factual findings used to determine that the provision of reunification services to the offending parent or guardian would not benefit the child. *(Added by Stats. 1996, c. 1083 (A.B.1524), § 2.7, operative Jan. 1, 1999. Amended by Stats.1997, c. 793 (A.B.1544), § 18, operative Jan. 1, 1999; Stats.1998, c. 75 (S.B.2091), § 1, operative Jan. 1, 1999; Stats.1998, c. 1054 (A.B.1091), § 25, operative Jan. 1, 1999; Stats.1998, c. 1055 (S.B.1901), § 2; Stats.1998, c. 1056 (A.B.2773), § 12.5; Stats.1999, c. 399 (S.B.1226), § 1; Stats. 1999, c. 805 (A.B.740), § 1.2; Stats.2000, c. 135 (A.B.2539), § 165; Stats.2000, c. 824 (S.B.1368), § 5; Stats.2001, c. 653 (A.B.1695), § 11.3, eff. Oct. 10, 2001; Stats.2002, c. 918 (A.B.1694), § 7; Stats.2003, c. 28 (A.B.353), § 1; Stats.2005, c. 625 (S.B.116), § 5; Stats.2007, c. 565 (A.B.298), § 1; Stats.2007, c. 583 (S.B.703), § 25.5; Stats.2008, c. 457 (A.B. 2341), § 1; Stats.2008, c. 482 (A.B.2070), § 1.7; Stats.2009, c. 120 (A.B.706), § 2, eff. Aug. 6, 2009; Stats.2009, c. 287 (A.B.1325), § 6, operative July 1, 2010; Stats.2010, c. 559 (A.B.12), § 13; Stats.2011, c. 59 (A.B.791), § 1; Stats.2012, c. 35 (S.B.1013), § 48, eff. June 27, 2012; Stats.2012, c. 845 (S.B.1064), § 9; Stats.2012, c. 846 (A.B.1712), § 15; Stats. 2012, c. 847 (S.B.1521), § 1.3; Stats.2016, c. 124 (A.B.1702), § 1, eff. Jan. 1, 2017; Stats.2016, c. 612 (A.B.1997), § 74.5, eff. Jan. 1, 2017; Stats.2017, c. 829 (S.B.233), § 5, eff. Jan. 1, 2018.)*

Commentary

M.C. v. Superior Court of Del Norte County, 3 Cal.App.5th 838, 208 Cal.Rptr.3d 88 (2016), held that a juvenile court erred in terminating a mother's reunification services at the six-month review after determining that the likelihood of reunification was extremely low, because the reunification periods set out in subsection (a)(*l*) are mandatory, subject only to the three exceptions contained in subsection (a)(2) and the procedure setforth in section 388.

In re A.G., 12 Cal.App.5th 994, 219 Cal.Rptr.3d 239 (2017), held that reasonable services had not been provided to a father who had been deported to Mexico after assaulting the children's mother when he had not been provided services and there was no evidence that reasonable reunification services were unavailable in Mexico. That the father was responsible for his own deportation did not excuse the county agency from making reasonable efforts to provide services.

In re J.P., 14 Cal.App.5th 616, 2017 Cal.App. LEXIS 715 (2017), held that a juvenile court abused its discretion when it ordered a reunification plan with which the father was clearly unable to comply because of a language barrier.

In re Jonathan P., 226 Cal.App.4th 1240, 172 Cal.Rptr.3d 846 (2014), held that the juvenile court erred in denying a nonoffending, noncustodial father reunification services on the ground that the child's whereabouts were unknown, because the court should have ordered the county department of children and family services to determine whether there were any services that could be offered to the father in the child's absence.

In re I.G., 226 Cal.App.4th 380, 171 Cal.Rptr.3d 867 (2014), held that a juvenile court erred in terminating dependency jurisdiction with respect to a defiant teenager who habitually ran away from group homes, when it found that the minor would be at risk if returned to the custody of a drug-dependent mother who had made no progress in overcoming the conditions that required the minor's out-of-home placement.

In re Pedro Z., 190 Cal.App.4th 12, 117 Cal.Rptr.3d 605 (2010), holds that a juvenile court is not required, as a matter of law, to provide a former custodial parent with family reunification services when a dependent child is returned to the custody of the other parent at a disposition hearing.

In re A.C., 169 Cal.App.4th 636, 88 Cal.Rptr.3d 1 (2008), holds that the time limits for reunification services start to run when a child is removed from all parental custody at a disposition hearing, not when the child is removed from one parent and placed with the other parent.

Although subsection (a)(1) allows a juvenile court to order reunification services of up to 12 months when a child is three years of age or older, the court, under section 366.21(e), has discretion at a six-month review hearing to terminate those services when a parent is unable or unwilling to benefit from additional reunification services. *In re Derrick S., 156 Cal.App.4th 436, 67 Cal.Rptr.3d 367 (2007).*

See generally *In re Luis G., 37 Cal.App.4th 458, 43 Cal.Rptr.2d 744 (1995)* (Section 361.5 does not require an express finding that reunification services would be detrimental to the child when a court commissioner decides not to order such services for an incarcerated parent; in any event, the commissioner's remarks about the nature of the parent's crime, child molestation, implied a finding of detriment). For further discussion of reunification services, see Commentary to Section 366.26.

Notwithstanding the mandatory language of subsection (a), a predependency or Probate Code guardianship may be terminated before a guardian is offered reunification services. *In re Merrick V., 122 Cal.App.4th 235, 19 Cal.Rptr.3d 490 (2004), review denied.*

Reading subsection (a) and Section 366.21(e) together, *In re Aryanna C., 132 Cal.App.4th 1234, 34 Cal.Rptr.3d 288 (2005), review denied,* held that the juvenile court has discretion to terminate reunification services at any time. In *Aryanna C.*, the juvenile court ended reunification services three months after the children entered foster care because the father missed virtually all scheduled visits with the children, missed scheduled assessments, tested positive for illicit drugs, and at the time of the hearing was in custody pending trial on burglary and other charges.

In re Zacharia D., 6 Cal.4th 435, 862 P.2d 751, 24 Cal.Rptr.2d 751 (1993), holds that a biological father who is not a presumed father is not entitled to reunification services. *Zacharia D.* additionally holds that Section 361.2 (a), which requires placement of the child with a noncustodial parent who requests custody unless such placement would be detrimental to the child, applies only when the child is first removed from the home of the custodial parent or guardian and only when the noncustodial parent is a "presumed parent." (For the definition of "presumed parent," see Family Code Section 7611.) For further clarification of parental rights of access to the status of presumed parenthood and the meaning of *Zacharia D.*, see *Adoption of Michael H., 10 Cal.4th 1043, 898 P.2d 891, 43 Cal.Rptr.2d 445 (1995)*, and *Adoption of Kelsey S., 1 Cal.4th 816, 4 Cal.Rptr.2d 615 (1992)*. *Michael H.* and *Kelsey S.* are discussed in the Commentary to Family Code Section 7611. Distinguishing Zacharia D. on the facts, *In re Julia U., 64 Cal.App.4th 532, 74 Cal.Rptr.2d 920 (1998),* held that when an unwed biological father promptly came forward and demonstrated a full commitment to his parental responsibilities, the juvenile court deprived him of his constitutional rights by refusing him reunification services and terminating his parental rights. See also *Adoption of Baby Boy W., 232 Cal.App.4th 438, 181 Cal.Rptr.3d 130 (2015), review denied.*

Although an unwed father is a father under Family Code section 7636 because he has been judicially determined to be the children's father and has been ordered to pay child support, he is not a section 7611 "presumed father" if he never lived with the children or openly held them out to be his own. Therefore, in a dependency proceeding, a juvenile court could deny him reunification services because only presumed fathers are entitled to reunification services. *In re E.O., 182 Cal.App.4th 722, 107 Cal.Rptr.3d 1 (2010), review denied. E.O.* reasons that the category "presumed father" functions in dependency cases to identify social fathers, even those who may not be biological fathers, while the issue in a paternity proceeding brought against an unwed father is biological paternity.

Purporting to rely on *Zacharia D., supra, In re Vincent M., 161 Cal.App.4th 943, 74 Cal.Rptr.3d 755 (2008), review denied*, holds that a person who is not a presumed father under section 7611 and whose paternity was concealed from him by the mother, but who does not come forward in a dependency proceeding until after the reunification period has ended, cannot be treated as a *Kelsey S.* father entitled to reunification services without regard to the best interests of the child, who was placed with prospective adoptive parents when he was four days old and was thriving in their home for nine months before the biological father asserted his *Kelsey S.* claim. *Vincent M.* states, in dictum, that after the reunification period has expired, the biological father's only remedy is a Welfare and Institutions Code section 388 modification petition, which requires changed circumstances or new evidence showing that it is in the child's best interest to grant the biological father custody or reunification services.

In *In re Nicholas H., 28 Cal.4th 56, 407A, 46 P.3d 932, 120 Cal.Rptr.2d 146 (2002)*, the California Supreme Court interpreted the "in an appropriate action" language of § 7612(a) to limit the rebuttal of presumed fatherhood to cases where rebuttal is appropriate rather than to allow it in all cases. In *Nicholas H.*, a dependency proceeding, a fit presumptive father seeking to assume parental obligations admitted that he was not the child's biological father. In reversing the court of appeal, which had held that his admission and the mother's testimony to the same effect rebutted the presumption that he was the child's father, the supreme court held that when no other man was asserting paternity and a presumed father sought to accept the responsibilities of paternity, an "appropriate action" was lacking. The supreme court opined that an "appropriate action" for rebuttal of a presumption of paternity might be one in which two men seek to establish paternity of a child or one in which a presumed father seeks to avoid the responsibilities of paternity. The court emphasized that it did not reach the question posed by *Steven W.* and *Kiana A.*, discussed in the Commentary to § 7612 and in the next paragraph. Nor did it reach the question addressed by *In re Jerry P.*, to which the California Supreme Court granted review on May 1, 2002 (46 P.3d 331, 119 Cal.Rptr.2d 856), ordered published on June 6, 2002 (47 P.3d 988, 121 Cal.Rptr.2d 106), and dismissed review and remanded on August 28, 2002 (53 P.3d 133, 124 Cal.Rptr.2d 718). The published opinion of the court of appeal in *Jerry P.*, 95 Cal.App.4th 793, 116 Cal.Rptr.2d 123 (2002), held that the status of "presumed father" for purposes of a dependency proceeding (see Welfare and Institutions Code § 361.5(a)) suffices to qualify that person for child welfare services, including reunification services, without any inquiry whether the presumed father is also the biological father. *Jerry P.* reasoned that while the purpose of the paternity presumption (§ 7611) in the paternity provisions of the Family Code (§§ 7500–7952) is evidentiary, that same presumption is used in the Welfare and Institutions Code solely for the purpose of identifying fathers by reference to their familial bonds to a dependent child. *Jerry P.* was followed in *In re Raphael P. III, 97 Cal.App.4th 716, 118 Cal.Rptr.2d 610 (2002), review denied June 19, 2002*, which holds, in a dependency proceeding, that Family Code §§ 7551 and 7554 do not authorize court to order genetic testing of a man who meets the requirements of presumed fatherhood. *Raphael P.* also observes that § 7551 allows a court to order paternity testing only when paternity is a relevant fact, which it arguably is not in a dependency proceeding when a man claims presumptive paternity and no other man asserts paternity.

In re Jovanni B., 221 Cal.App.4th 1482, 165 Cal.Rptr.3d 430 (2013), held that the juvenile court erroneously dismissed a man who had signed a voluntary declaration of paternity from dependency proceedings without determining whether the man was the child's presumed father under section Family Code section 7611(d). However, the California Supreme Court *granted review, 317 P.3d 1182 (2014), superseding In re Brianna M., 163 Cal.Rptr.3d 665 (2013)*, where the juvenile court excused from a dependency proceeding a man who signed a voluntary declaration of paternity, on the basis of DNA tests showing that he was not the father, without considering whether he was a presumed father under section (d). The California Supreme Court later dismissed review for failure of petitioner to file an opening brief, *330 P.3d 327 (2014)*.

In re D.M., 210 Cal.App.4th 541, 148 Cal.Rptr.3d 349 (2012), review denied, held that an alleged father who was not the child's biological father, was not married to the mother, and did not meet the requirements for a statutory father could not, in a dependency proceeding, be a constitutionally presumed father under *Kelsey S.* and

Jerry P. because he did not have an "existing familial bond with the child." Compare *R.M. v. T.A., 233 Cal.App.4th 760, 182 Cal.Rptr.3d 836 (2015)*, affirming a trial court grant of Family Code section 7611(d) presumed parent status to a mother's former partner where a fully developed parent-child relationship had been established between a child and the former partner.

In re T.R., 132 Cal.App.4th 1202, 34 Cal.Rptr.3d 215 (2005), inverts the case law doctrine that, depending on the context, Section 7611 presumptions may not be rebuttable by evidence of non-paternity. Although a child's step-father received the child into his home and openly held the child as his own natural child, *T.R.* concludes, for purposes of a dependency proceeding where biological paternity is immaterial, that the Section 7611(d) presumption of paternity is rebutted under Section 7612 by the step-father's inappropriate conduct and prior convictions for sexually molesting children.

With *Jerry P.* and *Raphael P.*, compare *In re Kiana A., 93 Cal.App.4th 1109, 113 Cal.Rptr.2d 669 (2001)*, where there were two § 7611 presumptive fathers in a dependency proceeding and the juvenile court applied Family Code § 7612(b) to award the presumption to a man who may not have been the biological father. The court of appeal found that the other presumptive father, who may have been the biological father, had waived his right to genetic testing in the juvenile court proceeding by failing to seek testing, although a request for genetic testing, which was denied by the juvenile court, had been made by the other presumptive father and the Department of Social Services. *Kiana A.* additionally states, in dictum, that even if the biological father could have raised the issue of paternity, his challenge would not necessarily have defeated the nonbiological father's § 7611(d) presumption of paternity, which arose from receiving a child into one's home and holding the child out as one's natural child. But see Welfare and Institutions Code § 7630 (b), which provides that "[a]ny interested party may bring an action at any time for the purpose of determining the existence or nonexistence of the father and child relationship presumed under subdivision (d) of Section 7611."

In re Karen C., 101 Cal.App.4th 932, 124 Cal.Rptr.2d 677 (2002), extends to women asserting the status of "presumed mother" the rule of *In re Nicholas H.*, supra. *Nicholas H.* holds that the Family Code § 7611(d) presumption of paternity arising from a man's reception of a child into his home may, according to Family Code § 7612(a), be disputed only "in an appropriate action."

In re Adrianna P., 166 Cal.App.4th 44, 81 Cal.Rptr.3d 918 (2008), holds that this section allows a juvenile court to bypass reunification services to a noncustodial parent who has been denied placement under section 361.2(a).

Robert L. v. Superior Court, 45 Cal.App.4th 619, 53 Cal.Rptr.2d 41 (1996), holds that a noncustodial parent who does not seek custody of his children is not entitled to reunification services. *Clifford S. v. Superior Court, 38 Cal. App.4th 747, 45 Cal.Rptr.2d 333 (1995)*, holds that a de facto parent lacks standing to challenge denial of reunification services because a de facto parent has no right to reunification services, citing *In re Keisha E., 6 Cal.4th 68, 82, 859 P.2d 1290, 23 Cal.Rptr.2d 775 (1993)*. *In re Carlos E., 129 Cal.App.4th 1408, 29 Cal.Rptr.3d 317 (2005), review denied*, holds that a dependent child's court-appointed guardian has no right to reunification services and cannot challenge the adequacy of those services.

In *Sara M. v Superior Court, 36 Cal.4th 998, 116 P.3d 550, 32 Cal.Rptr.3d 89 (2005)*, the California Supreme Court sustained California Rules of Court, Rule 1460(f)(1)(B), which, interpreting subsection (e) of this section, allows the juvenile court to terminate reunification services when a parent has failed to visit or contact a dependent child for six months following the commencement of reunification services.

Daria D. v. Superior Court, 61 Cal.App.4th 606, 71 Cal.Rptr.2d 668 (1998), sustains the constitutionality of subsection (a)(2), which allows termination of parental rights after six months of reunification services when the minor was under the age of three years on the date of initial removal. To the same effect, see *Armando D. v. Superior Court, 71 Cal.App.4th 1011, 99 Cal.Rptr.2d 189 (1999), review denied June 16, 1999* (interpreting a prior version of subsection (a) and concluding that when dependent child was under the age of three on the date of detention, the juvenile court could terminate parent's reunification services after six months upon finding that there was no substantial probability that the child would be reunified with the parent within eighteen months). Compare *Miguel V. v. Superior Court*, depublished by the California Supreme Court when it denied review on September 15, 1999. In *Miguel V.*, the depublished opinion of the Court of Appeal, 85 Cal.Rptr.2d 923 (1999), concluded that under the current version of the statute, at a six-month review hearing for children who were under the age of three at the time of removal, an incarcerated parent's reunification services could not be terminated absent substantial evidence of his noncompliance with the reunification plan because the current statute requires 12 months of reunification services when a parent does comply with the reunification plan, regardless of the likelihood of reunification at the end of the 12-month period. *In re Baby Boy H., 63 Cal.App.4th 470, 73 Cal.Rptr.2d 793 (1998), review denied July 8, 1998*, sustains the constitutionality of subsection (b)(10), which provides that the juvenile court may deny reunification services to a parent who has previously failed to reunify with another child. *Randi R. v. Superior Court, 64 Cal.App.4th 67, 74 Cal.Rptr.2d 770 (1998)* holds that the court may properly deny reunification services to a parent who previously failed to reunify with a single child, even though she completed the prior reunification plan, under which she reunified with other children. *Riverside County Dept. of Social Services v. Superior Court, 71 Cal.App.4th 483, 83 Cal.Rptr.2d 777 (1999)*, holds that the juvenile court may deny reunification services under subsection (b)(10) so long as the failure of reunification or the termination of parental rights with respect to another child occurs before the dispositional hearing for the child who is the subject of this proceeding.

In re C.C., 111 Cal.App.4th 76, 3 Cal.Rptr.3d 354 (2003), review denied, holds that a juvenile court may deny reunification services to a parent who refuses to comply with a valid court order for a psychological evaluation.

In re Arlena M., 121 Cal.App.4th 566, 17 Cal.Rptr.3d 354 (2004), holds that the required subsection (a)(3) warning to a parent, that failure to participate regularly in a court-ordered treatment program may result in termination of reunification services, may be provided in writing so long as the record indicates that the parent read and understood the advice, in which case any error was harmless. The California Supreme Court has held that a juvenile court, as part of a reunification plan, has the power to order a parent to participate in a substance abuse program; however, the court may not use the contempt sanction as punishment solely because a parent has failed to satisfy a reunification condition. *In re Nolan W., 45 Cal.4th 1217, 91 Cal.Rptr.3d 140, 203 P.3d 454 (2009)*.

In re Joel T., 70 Cal.App.4th 263, 1287A, 82 Cal.Rptr.2d 538 (1999), review denied May 26, 1999, holds that the juvenile court erred in denying reunification services to a parent because she had already received eighteen months of "family preservation" services before the children were removed from her home. Although the provision of court-ordered services is limited to eighteen months once a child is removed from a parent's home and family maintenance services may be limited to twelve months when a child remains in the parental home, when children are removed from the home for the first time, the juvenile court must order reunification services in compliance with this section.

Tonya M. v. Superior Court, 42 Cal.4th 836, 69 Cal.Rptr.3d 96, 172 P.3d 402 (2007), held that at a delayed six-month hearing, the juvenile court should consider the likelihood of reunification within the less-than-six months remaining until the 12–month hearing, rather than within the six months following the delayed six-month review hearing.

In re A. M., 217 Cal.App.4th 1067, 159 Cal.Rpt.3d 134 (2013), held that a juvenile court erred in granting a mother reunification services with respect to two children, a toddler and a baby who suffered serious physical abuse, without making the findings of best interests and the likelihood of prevention of further abuse that are required under subsection (b).

For discussion of the (b)(4) exception that reunification services need not be provided for a parent who "has caused the death of another minor through abuse or neglect," see *In re Alexis M., 54 Cal.App.4th 848, 63 Cal.Rptr.2d 356 (1997), review denied June 18, 1997.* See also *In re Salman Y., 69 Cal.App.4th 933, 81 Cal.Rptr.2d 662 (1999),* holding that the juvenile court properly terminated reunification services to a mother upon finding that her neglect enabled a male companion to inflict a fatal injury on the child's sibling and that reunification would not be in the surviving child's best interests. Applying subsection (b)(4), *In re Ethan N., 122 Cal.App.4th 55, 18 Cal.Rptr.3d 504 (2004), review denied,* held that the juvenile court abused its discretion when it granted reunification services to a mother who had been responsible for the death of another child through abuse or neglect. In *Ethan N.*, the mother had, moreover, failed to reunite with three other children and had a long history of drug abuse, family violence, and the abuse and neglect of other children.

Mardardo F. v. Superior Court, 164 Cal.App.4th 481, 78 Cal.Rptr.3d 884 (2008), held that reunification services need not be provided to a man who murdered a teen-age girl before he became a parent, because subsection (b)(4) refers to the parent's status in the current proceeding and to the death of any child.

Subsection (b)(6) allows denial of reunification services to a parent or guardian who has caused serious emotional damage to a child. *Jose O. v. Superior Court, 169 Cal.App.4th 703, 87 Cal.Rptr.3d 1 (2008), review denied* (father stabbing mother to death in front of their child constitutes "a torturous act…that would reasonably be understood to cause serious emotional damage").

In re Amber K., 146 Cal.App.4th 553, 52 Cal.Rptr.3d 701 (2006), held that a juvenile court properly applied subsection (b)(6) to deny a mother reunification services after finding that she was an "offending parent" because, by her actions, she impliedly consented to the father's sexual abuse of their child.

Interpreting subsection (b)(6), *Pablo S. v. Superior Court, 98 Cal.App.4th 292, 119 Cal.Rptr.2d 523 (2002)*, holds that a juvenile court properly denied reunification services when the parent's failure to obtain medical treatment for the son's broken leg inflicted serious injury on the child and could reasonably be understood to cause serious emotional injury. Also, interpreting subsection (b)(6), *In re Tanyann W., 97 Cal.App.4th 675, 118 Cal.Rptr.2d 596 (2002)*, holds that a guardian's ward is not a "sibling or half-sibling" of a guardian's biological child or other ward. Thus the juvenile court may not use subsection (b)(6) to deny a guardian reunification services with a ward or biological child when the guardian is accused of abusing another ward.

Anthony J. v. Superior Court, 132 Cal.App.4th 419, 33 Cal.Rptr.3d 677 (2005), held that a juvenile court properly denied a father reunification services with his son under subsection (b)(6) on the basis of the father's abuse of his son's half-siblings, who were neither the father's children or wards. *Anthony J.* reasoned that "by a parent or guardian" refers to relationship between the person inflicting harm and the child whose reunification is at issue in the current proceeding, not the relationship between that person and the child's siblings.

Applying subsection (b)(10), *In re B.H., 243 Cal.App.4th 729, 196 Cal.Rptr.3d 718 (2016)*, held that a trial court properly denied reunification services to a father who failed to reunify with a sibling of the child, rejecting the father's argument that the sibling had not been "removed" from him because he was not the sibling's custodial parent.

In re T.G., 242 Cal.App.4th 976, 195 Cal.Rptr.3d 649 (2015), held that the juvenile court properly denied a mother reunification services based on orders terminating her parental rights with respect to the child's siblings, even though those orders were on appeal at the time of the dispositional hearing.

Cheryl P. v. Superior Court, 139 Cal.App.4th 87, 42 Cal.Rptr.3d 504 (2006), held that a juvenile court should not have denied reunification services, under subsection (b)(10), to parents who had failed to reunify with a dependent child's sibling when the parents had made reasonable efforts to treat the problems that led to the sibling's removal. *In re Albert T., 144 Cal.App.4th 207, 50 Cal.Rptr.3d 227 (2006)*, held that it was error to deny reunification services to a mother who had previously failed to reunify with a dependent child's sibling when the mother had made reasonable efforts to treat the problem, her propensity to form relationships with violent men, which led to the removal of the sibling.

R.T. v. Superior Court, 202 Cal.App.4th 908, 135 Cal.Rptr.3d 309 (2012), sustained a trial court's denial of reunification services to a parent under subsections (b)(10) and (11), when she had earlier failed to reunify with the child's older sibling and to make meaningful efforts to cure her substance abuse problem.

In re Gabriel K, 203 Cal.App.4th 188, 136 Cal.Rptr.3d 813 (2012), held that subsection (b)(10), which permits denial of reunification services based on a previous termination of reunification services with a dependent child's sibling, should be expansively read to also permit denial of reunification services based on a previous termination of reunification services with respect to the same child. But see *In re B.L., 204 Cal.App.4th 1111, 139 Cal.Rptr.3d 525 (2012)*, which concludes that (b)(10) should be read literally and thus should not permit denial of reunification services because they have previously been terminated with respect to the same child. However, *B.L.* sustained the trial court's denial of reunification services for the parents on the alternative ground that the child's grandparents had custody pursuant to a guardianship order in the first dependency proceeding, and it was therefore the grandparents who were entitled to receive reunification services under this section.

B.L.'s restrictive reading of subsection (b)(10) was followed in *J.A. v. Superior Court, 214 Cal.App.4th 279, 153 Cal.Rptr.3d 774 (2013)* (reunification services for father improperly terminated).

Melissa R. v. Superior Court, 207 Cal.App.4th 816, 144 Cal.Rptr.3d 48 (2012), held that the juvenile court erred in denying reunification services to a parent, based on the parent's previous failure to reunite with the a half-brother of the dependent child, when the half-brother had been removed pursuant to Wisconsin law and not pursuant to section 361. *Melissa R.* reasoned that the law and procedure of the two states with respect to reunification services might be materially different and therefore the California court should not have relied on Wisconsin proceedings in denying reunification services.

Francisco G. v. Superior Court, 91 Cal.App.4th 586, 110 Cal.Rptr.2d 679 (2001), holds that subsection (b)(11) (formerly (b)(10)(B)), which permits the court to deny reunification services to a parent whose rights to a dependent child's sibling or half-sibling were terminated in a previous proceeding, can be applied to a parent whose rights were terminated while his status was that of an alleged or biological father, rather than a presumed father, and to a parent whose rights were terminated when he was not the custodial parent of the sibling or half-sibling.

Rejecting the holding of *Renee J. v. Superior Court, 26 Cal.4th 735, 28 P.3d 876, 110 Cal.Rptr.2d 828 (2001)* (under former subsection (10), the reasonable-efforts proviso applies only to termination of parental rights over siblings or half-siblings, and not to termination of reunification services with siblings or half-siblings), in 2001 the legislature divided former subsection (10) into new subsections (10) and (11) and included the reasonable-efforts proviso in both. 2001 Cal. Stat., ch. 653 (A.B.1695), § 11.3. Subsequently, in *Renee J. v. Superior Court, 96 Cal.App.4th 1450, 118 Cal.Rptr.2d 118 (2002), review denied June 12, 2002*, the court of appeal granted the parent's petition for extraordinary relief from an order terminating her reunification services, and held that the California Supreme Court's restrictive interpretation should not be applied when the legislature amended the statute almost immediately to reject the court's reading of the statute and the legislature intended the amendment as a retroactive clarification applicable to all pending cases.

In re Angelique C., 113 Cal.App.4th 509, 6 Cal.Rptr.3d 395 (2003), review denied, holds that subsection (b)(11) applies, *inter alia,* when a parent's rights with respect to a child's sibling have been permanently severed by the parent's voluntary relinquishment of those rights.

In re Allison J., 190 Cal.App.4th 1106, 118 Cal.Rptr.3d 856 (2010), review denied, holds that subsection (b)(12), which allows a juvenile court to deny reunification services to a parent who has been convicted of a violent felony does not violate the parent's substantive due process fundamental right to parent when subsection (b)(12) is read in light of subsection (c), which allows the court to order reunification services for the parent if it is in the best interest of the child.

In re E.G., 247 Cal.App.4th 1417, 202 Cal.Rptr.3d 765 (2016), held that drug treatment ordered as a deferred-entry-of-judgment program under Penal Code section 1000 is "prior court-ordered treatment" for purposes of subsection (b)(13).

Interpreting subsection (b)(13) (formerly (b)(12)), *Laura B. v. Superior Court, 68 Cal.App.4th 776, 80 Cal.Rptr.2d 472 (1998),* holds that the juvenile court properly denied reunification services when the parent resumed drug use after completion of three substance abuse rehabilitation programs. *In re Joshua M., 66 Cal.App.4th 458, 78 Cal.Rptr.2d 110 (1998), review denied November 24, 1998,* holds that subsections (b)(10), (11), and (13) (formerly (b)(10) and (12)), operative on January 1, 1997, which permit the juvenile court not to order reunification services for a parent who has failed to reunify with a child's sibling or to comply with a substance abuse program, are not unconstitutionally retroactive when applied to events that occurred before the operative date of the provisions.

Applying subsection (b)(13), *In re William B., 163 Cal.App.4th 1220, 78 Cal.Rptr.3d 91 (2008)*, held that a juvenile court abused its discretion when it ordered reunification services for a mother, having found that it would be in the best interests of her children, because the children had been removed from her custody three times for long-standing drug abuse that she had repeatedly failed to overcome despite years of reunification services. The court of appeal observed that the juvenile court had improperly focused on the children's love for their mother, rather than any realistic chance of permanence and stability.

For interpretation of subsection (b)(15), see *A.A. v. Superior Court, 209 Cal.App.4th 237, 146 Cal.Rptr.3d 805 (2012)*, which reversed a trial court order denying a parent reunification services, because her behavior did not constitute willful abduction of her child.

Applying subsection (b)(16), *In re S.B., 222 Cal.App.4th 612, 165 Cal.Rptr.3d 887 (2013)*, affirmed a judgment denying reunification services to a father because he was a registered sex offender and clear and convincing evidence supported the juvenile court's finding that reunification was not in the child's best interests.

Applying the subsection (c) exception to termination "when failure to try reunification will be detrimental to the child because the child is closely and positively attached to that parent," *In re G.L., 222 Cal.App.4th 1153, 166 Cal.Rptr.3d 579 (2014)*, held that a juvenile court acted within its discretion in providing reunification services to a mother even though she had a long history of drug abuse and had previously resisted court-ordered treatment.

In re Taylor J., 223 Cal.App.4th 1446, 168 Cal.Rptr.3d 149 (2014), reversed an order terminating a mother's reunification services for failure to provide reasonable reunification services, when the Department of Children and Family Services ordered the mother to counseling but did not provide appropriate referrals, and did not provide any reunification services between the 12-month and 18-month reviews.

For discussion of the subsection (c) proviso that the court shall not order reunification services with respect to an abused child unless it finds that child welfare services are likely to prevent reabuse, see *Raymond C. v. Superior Court, 55 Cal.App.4th 159, 64 Cal.Rptr.2d 33 (1997)* (once court finds child is a victim of severe physical abuse by a parent, social services agency is not required to prove that reunification services will not prevent reabuse before court withholds services from parents).

For treatment of subsection (e) visitation when parents of dependent children are incarcerated, see *In re Jonathan M., 53 Cal.App.4th 1234, 62 Cal.Rptr.2d 208 (1997)* (disapproving juvenile court establishment of mileage limits beyond which visitation will not be provided for incarcerated parents); and *In re Dylan T., 65 Cal. App.4th 765, 76 Cal.Rptr.2d 684 (1998)* (holding that an order prohibiting visitation of an incarcerated mother with a defendant child during reunification period solely because of child's age, without substantial evidence of detriment to child, was error). *In re Edgar O., 84 Cal.App.4th 13, 100 Cal.Rptr.2d 540 (2000)*, holds that subsection (e) applies to parents who are incarcerated and awaiting trial, even though they are not serving a sentence for a crime.

Cynthia C. v. Superior Court, 72 Cal.App.4th 1196, 85 Cal.Rptr.2d 669 (1999), held that the juvenile court did not abuse its discretion when it refused to permit a parent to withdraw a waiver of reunification services made knowingly and intelligently five months earlier.

In re Christina A., 91 Cal.App.4th 1153, 111 Cal.Rptr.2d 310 (2001), holds that when a dependent child under the age of three has been removed from parental custody and reunification services have been ordered, Welfare and Institutions Code §§ 361.5(a)(2), 366.21(e), and 366(a) require that a status review hearing be set within six months from the date of the jurisdictional hearing, rather than six months from the date of the dispositional hearing.

Research References

Forms

West's California Judicial Council Forms JV-195, Waiver Of Reunification Services.

West's California Judicial Council Forms JV-206, Reasons for No or Supervised Visitation--Juvenile.

West's California Judicial Council Forms JV-421, Dispositional Attachment: Removal from Custodial Parent--Placement With Nonparent (Welf. & Inst. Code, §§ 361, 361.2).

Treatises and Practice Aids

Witkin, California Summary 10th Parent and Child § 329, Dependent Child Without Reunification Services.

Witkin, California Summary 10th Parent and Child § 334, Offer Of Less Detrimental Alternatives.

Witkin, California Summary 10th Parent and Child § 483, Juvenile Court Proceedings.

Witkin, California Summary 10th Parent and Child § 519, Nature Of Dependency Proceedings.

Witkin, California Summary 10th Parent and Child § 534, Out-Of-Home Placement or Guardianship.

Witkin, California Summary 10th Parent and Child § 536, Termination Of Parental Rights.

Witkin, California Summary 10th Parent and Child § 548, Child Left Without Care or Support.

Witkin, California Summary 10th Parent and Child § 577, Hearing.

Witkin, California Summary 10th Parent and Child § 610, Notice Of Hearing.

Witkin, California Summary 10th Parent and Child § 615, in General.

Witkin, California Summary 10th Parent and Child § 623, Continuance Pending Disposition Hearing.

Witkin, California Summary 10th Parent and Child § 624, in General.

Witkin, California Summary 10th Parent and Child § 625, Preparation Of Social Study.

Witkin, California Summary 10th Parent and Child § 628, Legal Guardianship.

Witkin, California Summary 10th Parent and Child § 631, Procedure.
Witkin, California Summary 10th Parent and Child § 637, Priority Right Of Noncustodial Parent.
Witkin, California Summary 10th Parent and Child § 642, in General.
Witkin, California Summary 10th Parent and Child § 643, Duration Of Services.
Witkin, California Summary 10th Parent and Child § 644, Persons Entitled to Services.
Witkin, California Summary 10th Parent and Child § 645, Persons Who Must Participate.
Witkin, California Summary 10th Parent and Child § 646, Incarcerated or Institutionalized Parent or Guardian.
Witkin, California Summary 10th Parent and Child § 647, in General.
Witkin, California Summary 10th Parent and Child § 648, Parent or Guardian Absent, Unwilling, or Incapable.
Witkin, California Summary 10th Parent and Child § 649, Previous Occurrences.
Witkin, California Summary 10th Parent and Child § 650, Abuse, Neglect, or Abduction Of Child.
Witkin, California Summary 10th Parent and Child § 651, Criminal or Addictive Behavior.
Witkin, California Summary 10th Parent and Child § 652, Determination Whether to Order Services.
Witkin, California Summary 10th Parent and Child § 661, Hearing After Supplemental Petition is Sustained.
Witkin, California Summary 10th Parent and Child § 662, Nature and Purpose.
Witkin, California Summary 10th Parent and Child § 663, Form, Content, and Filing.
Witkin, California Summary 10th Parent and Child § 664, in General.
Witkin, California Summary 10th Parent and Child § 671, Supplemental Report.
Witkin, California Summary 10th Parent and Child § 673, Child in Foster Care.
Witkin, California Summary 10th Parent and Child § 676, in General.
Witkin, California Summary 10th Parent and Child § 677, Scheduling Selection and Implementation Hearing.
Witkin, California Summary 10th Parent and Child § 678, Twelve-Month Review.
Witkin, California Summary 10th Parent and Child § 682, Preliminary Assessment.
Witkin, California Summary 10th Parent and Child § 686, Alternative Dispositions.
Witkin, California Summary 10th Parent and Child § 687, Termination Of Parental Rights to Free Child for Adoption.
Witkin, California Summary 10th Parent and Child § 689, in General.
Witkin, California Summary 10th Parent and Child § 691, Constitutionality Of Termination Procedure.
Witkin, California Summary 10th Parent and Child § 695, Legal Guardianship.
Witkin, California Summary 10th Parent and Child § 698, Other Procedures.
Witkin, California Summary 10th Parent and Child § 897, Reunification Services.
Witkin, California Summary 10th Parent and Child § 688A, (New) Tribal Customary Adoption.
Witkin, California Summary 10th Parent and Child § 699A, (New) in General.

§ 361.6. Nonminor dependents; court-ordered family reunification services; continuation; termination

(a) Notwithstanding any other law, the court may order family reunification services to continue for a nonminor dependent, as defined in subdivision (v) of Section 11400, if the nonminor dependent and parent, parents, or legal guardian are in agreement and the court finds that the continued provision of court-ordered family reunification services is in the best interests of the nonminor dependent and there is a substantial probability that the nonminor dependent will be able to safely reside in the home of the parent or guardian by the next review hearing. The continuation of the court-ordered reunification services shall not exceed the timeframes as set forth in Section 361.5. If the nonminor dependent or parent, parents, or legal guardian are not in agreement, or the court finds there is not a substantial probability that the nonminor will be able to safely reside in the home of the parent or guardian, the court shall terminate family reunification services to the parents or guardian. The nonminor dependent's legal status as an adult is, in and of itself, a compelling reason not to hold a hearing pursuant to Section 366.26. The court may order that a nonminor dependent who is otherwise eligible for AFDC–FC benefits pursuant to Section 11403 remain in a planned, permanent living arrangement.

(b) Any motion to terminate court-ordered family reunification services for a nonminor dependent prior to the hearing set pursuant to Section 366.31 shall be made pursuant to subdivision (c) of Section 388.

(c) An order terminating court-ordered family reunification services under this section shall not be considered evidence of a condition required for the filing of a petition to terminate a parent's or legal guardian's court-ordered family reunification services with the nonminor dependent's sibling or half-sibling under subdivision (c) of Section 388.

(d) An order terminating court-ordered family reunification services under this section shall not be used to deny family reunification services to a parent or legal guardian for a nonminor dependent's sibling or half-sibling under subdivision (b) of Section 361.5.

(e) The continuation of court-ordered family reunification services under this section does not affect the nonminor's eligibility for extended foster care benefits as a nonminor dependent as defined in subdivision (v) of Section 11400. The reviews conducted for any nonminor dependent shall be held pursuant to Section 366.31. *(Added by Stats.2012, c. 846 (A.B.1712), § 16.)*

Research References

Treatises and Practice Aids

Witkin, California Summary 10th Parent and Child § 699, Notice.
Witkin, California Summary 10th Parent and Child § 669A, (New) Review Hearings Just Before and After Minor Attains Age 18.
Witkin, California Summary 10th Parent and Child § 699A, (New) in General.

§ 361.7. Termination of parental rights or involuntary placement of a child with Indian ancestry; standards

(a) Notwithstanding Section 361.5, a party seeking an involuntary foster care placement of, or termination of parental rights over, an Indian child shall provide evidence to the court that active efforts have been made to provide remedial services and rehabilitative programs designed to prevent the breakup of the Indian family and that these efforts have proved unsuccessful.

(b) What constitutes active efforts shall be assessed on a case-by-case basis. The active efforts shall be made in a manner that takes into account the prevailing social and cultural values, conditions, and way of life of the Indian child's tribe. Active efforts shall utilize the available resources of the Indian child's extended family, tribe, tribal and other Indian social service agencies, and individual Indian caregiver service providers.

(c) No foster care placement or guardianship may be ordered in the proceeding in the absence of a determination, supported by clear and convincing evidence, including testimony of a qualified expert witness, as defined in Section 224.6, that the continued custody of the child by the parent or Indian custodian is likely to result in serious emotional or physical damage to the child. *(Added by Stats.2006, c. 838 (S.B.678), § 50.)*

Research References

Forms

California Transactions Forms--Family Law § 3:4, Subject Matter Jurisdiction for Custody Determinations.
California Transactions Forms--Family Law § 5:3, Rights Of Nonparents Generally.
West's California Judicial Council Forms JV-320, Orders Under Welfare and Institutions Code Sections 366.26, 727.3, 727.31.

Treatises and Practice Aids

Witkin, California Summary 10th Parent and Child § 218, Statutory Rule.
Witkin, California Summary 10th Parent and Child § 534, Out-Of-Home Placement or Guardianship.
Witkin, California Summary 10th Parent and Child § 536, Termination Of Parental Rights.
Witkin, California Summary 10th Parent and Child § 631, Procedure.
Witkin, California Summary 10th Parent and Child § 635, in General.
Witkin, California Summary 10th Parent and Child § 673, Child in Foster Care.
Witkin, California Summary 10th Parent and Child § 689, in General.
Witkin, California Summary 10th Parent and Child § 288C, (New) Applicable Law.
Witkin, California Summary 10th Parent and Child § 348A, (New) Additional Findings for Indian Child.

§ 361.8. Children of minor or nonminor dependent parents; considerations regarding risk of abuse or neglect; right to legal consultation

(a) The Legislature declares that a child of a minor parent or nonminor dependent parent shall not be considered to be at risk of abuse or neglect solely on the basis of information concerning the parent's or parents' placement history, past behaviors, or health or mental health diagnoses occurring prior to the pregnancy, although that information may be taken into account when considering whether other factors exist that place the child at risk of abuse or neglect.

(b) In the case of a child for whom one or both minor parents have been adjudged to be dependent children of the juvenile court pursuant to Section 300, or adjudged to be wards of the court pursuant to Section 601 or 602, all of the following shall apply:

(1) Paragraphs (10) and (11) of subdivision (b) of Section 361.5 shall not apply, unless one or more of the circumstances described in paragraphs (1) to (9), inclusive, and paragraphs (12) to (17), inclusive, of subdivision (b) of Section 361.5 apply.

(2) A party seeking an involuntary foster care placement of, or termination of parental rights over, a child born to a parent or parents who were minors at the time of the child's birth shall demonstrate to the court that reasonable efforts were made to provide remedial services designed to prevent the removal of the child from the minor parent or parents, and that these efforts have proved unsuccessful.

(3) The efforts made pursuant to paragraph (2) shall utilize the available resources of the child and his or her minor parent's or parents' extended family, social services agencies, caregivers, and other available service providers.

(c) Except as provided in Section 301, prior to a social worker or probation officer arranging any informal or formal custody agreement that includes a temporary or permanent voluntary relinquishment of custody by a parent who is a ward of the juvenile court or a dependent or nonminor dependent parent, or recommending that a nonparent seek legal guardianship of the child of a ward, dependent, or nonminor dependent parent, the parent shall be advised of the right and have the opportunity to consult with his or her legal counsel. The social worker or probation officer shall note in the case file whether the dependent, nonminor dependent, or ward consulted with legal counsel, or if the opportunity for consultation was provided and the consultation did not occur, the reason that the consultation did not occur.

(d) For purposes of this section, "child" and "minor parent" shall have the same definitions as set forth in Section 16002.5. *(Added by Stats.2015, c. 511 (A.B.260), § 1, eff. Jan. 1, 2016. Amended by Stats.2017, c. 666 (A.B.1371), § 2, eff. Jan. 1, 2018.)*

Research References

Treatises and Practice Aids

Witkin, California Summary 10th Parent and Child § 494, Records Of Dependent Children.
Witkin, California Summary 10th Parent and Child § 538, Governing Law.
Witkin, California Summary 10th Parent and Child § 631, Procedure.
Witkin, California Summary 10th Parent and Child § 649, Previous Occurrences.
Witkin, California Summary 10th Parent and Child § 689, in General.

§ 362. Court orders and proceedings; child welfare services; parent counseling or education programs; school attendance

(a) If a child is adjudged a dependent child of the court on the ground that the child is a person described by Section 300, the court may make any and all reasonable orders for the care, supervision, custody, conduct, maintenance, and support of the child, including medical treatment, subject to further order of the court.

(b)(1) To facilitate coordination and cooperation among agencies, the court may, at any time after a petition has been filed, after giving notice and an opportunity to be heard, join in the juvenile court proceedings any agency that the court determines has failed to meet a legal obligation to provide services to a child for whom a petition has been filed under Section 300, to a nonminor, as described in Section 303, or to a nonminor dependent, as defined in subdivision (v) of Section 11400, regardless of the status of the adjudication. In any proceeding in which an agency is joined, the court shall not impose duties upon the agency beyond those mandated by law. Nothing in this section shall prohibit agencies that have received notice of the hearing on joinder from meeting prior to the hearing to coordinate services.

(2) The court has no authority to order services unless it has been determined through the administrative process of an agency that has been joined as a party, that the child, nonminor, or nonminor dependent is eligible for those services. With respect to mental health assessment, treatment, and case management services pursuant to Chapter 26.5 (commencing with Section 7570) of Division 7 of Title 1 of the Government Code, the court's determination shall be limited to whether the agency has complied with that chapter.

(3) For the purposes of this subdivision, "agency" means any governmental agency or any private service provider or individual that receives federal, state, or local governmental funding or reimbursement for providing services directly to a child, nonminor, or nonminor dependent.

(c) If a child is adjudged a dependent child of the court, on the ground that the child is a person described by Section 300, and the court orders that a parent or guardian shall retain custody of the child subject to the supervision of the social worker, the parents or guardians shall be required to participate in child welfare services or services provided by an appropriate agency designated by the court.

(d) The juvenile court may direct any reasonable orders to the parents or guardians of the child who is the subject of any proceedings under this chapter as the court deems necessary and proper to carry out this section, including orders to appear before a county financial evaluation officer. That order may include a direction to participate in a counseling or education program, including, but not limited to, a parent education and parenting program operated by a community college, school district, or other appropriate agency designated by the court. A foster parent or relative with whom the child is placed may be directed to participate in such a program in cases in which the court deems participation is appropriate and in the child's best interest. The program in which a parent or guardian is required to participate shall be designed to eliminate those conditions that led to the court's finding that the child is a person described by Section 300.

(e) If a child is adjudged a dependent child of the court, the juvenile court may direct any reasonable orders to the parents or guardians of the child who is the subject of any proceedings under this chapter to ensure the child's regular school attendance and to make reasonable efforts to obtain educational services necessary to meet the specific needs of the child. *(Added by Stats.1976, c. 1070, p. 4812, § 3.7, eff. Sept. 21, 1976, operative Jan. 1, 1977. Amended by Stats.1977, c. 21, p. 49, § 8, eff. April 6, 1977; Stats.1978, c. 380, p. 1207, § 152; Stats.1978, c. 429, p. 1437, § 176, eff. July 17, 1978, operative July 1, 1978; Stats.1982, c. 978, § 21, eff. Sept. 13, 1982, operative July 1, 1982; Stats.1983, c. 467, § 1; Stats. 1983, c. 1170, § 2.5; Stats.1984, c. 162, § 1; Stats.1984, c. 867, § 3; Stats.1985, c. 1485, § 10; Stats.1986, c. 1120, § 9, eff. Sept. 24, 1986; Stats.1986, c. 1122, § 14; Stats.1992, c. 1307 (A.B.3553), § 1; Stats.1996, c. 1139 (A.B.2647), § 9; Stats.1998, c. 1054 (A.B.1091), § 26; Stats.2000, c. 908 (S.B.1611), § 2; Stats.2000, c. 910 (A.B.2921), § 8.5; Stats. 2000, c. 911 (A.B.686), § 1.5; Stats.2012, c. 130 (S.B.1048), § 1.)*

Commentary

A presumed father was not entitled, under subsection (c), to reunification services when the juvenile court's order did not disrupt the mother's custody and prescribed "family enhancement" services for the presumed father. *In re A.L., 188 Cal.App.4th 138, 115 Cal.Rptr.3d 560 (2010)*.

In re Carmen M., 141 Cal.App.4th 478, 46 Cal.Rptr.3d 117 (2006), holds that subsection (a) of this section and subsection (a) of Section 202 are sufficient to authorize a juvenile court to order random drug tests to help a dependent child remain drug-free even though the child has not been found, under Section 359, to be a danger to herself or others as a result of drug use.

In re Neil D., 155 Cal.App.4th 219, 65 Cal.Rptr.3d 771 (2007), held that a court's subsection (c) authority to direct "all reasonable orders to the parents" allowed a juvenile court to order a parent to complete an inpatient drug rehabilitation program as part of her reunification program. The juvenile court was not required to consider other less restrictive alternatives.

On September 29, 2010, the California Supreme Court denied a petition for review and depublished *In re G.G., 111 Cal.Rptr.3d 356 (2010)*, in which the court of appeal purported to hold that a trial court did not abuse its discretion in requiring, as part of a reunification plan, that a father participate in counseling to address his repeated angry use of racial, ethnic and gender epithets, even though there was no evidence that he used such epithets in the presence of the children, because the court could reasonably have concluded that this behavior was part of the father's broader anger management problem that gave rise to the dependency proceeding.

In re Daniel B., 231 Cal.App.4th 663, 180 Cal.Rptr.3d 26 (2014), reversed an order requiring a mother to participate in a domestic violence victims support group, because the court improperly delegated to the group's counselors sole discretion to determine the length of her participation in the group. Although the duration of participation could be left open, any final determination that the mother had successfully completed that portion of the case plan had to be made by the juvenile court, not the counselors.

In re Jasmin C., 106 Cal.App.4th 177, 130 Cal.Rptr.2d 558 (2003), holds that a juvenile court may not order a non-offending custodial parent to attend a parenting class where there is no substantial evidence that either the parent or the children would benefit from it.

In re Silvia R., 159 Cal.App.4th 337, 71 Cal.Rptr.3d 496 (2008), held that a juvenile court has no authority to order a dependent child's stepfather and brother, who had sexually abused the child, to attend sexual abuse counseling for perpetrators, because the dependent child had not been placed with them.

Research References

Forms

West's California Judicial Council Forms JV-250, Notice Of Hearing and Temporary Restraining Order--Juvenile.

West's California Judicial Council Forms JV-540, Notice Of Hearing on Joinder - Juvenile.

Treatises and Practice Aids

Witkin, California Summary 10th Parent and Child § 334, Offer Of Less Detrimental Alternatives.

Witkin, California Summary 10th Parent and Child § 373, Order Requiring Therapy.
Witkin, California Summary 10th Parent and Child § 442, General Purposes.
Witkin, California Summary 10th Parent and Child § 541, Mental Illness and Substance Abuse.
Witkin, California Summary 10th Parent and Child § 556, Assessment Of Prospective Placement.
Witkin, California Summary 10th Parent and Child § 624, in General.
Witkin, California Summary 10th Parent and Child § 633, in General.
Witkin, California Summary 10th Parent and Child § 643, Duration Of Services.
Witkin, California Summary 10th Parent and Child § 645, Persons Who Must Participate.
Witkin, California Summary 10th Parent and Child § 669, in General.
Witkin, California Summary 10th Parent and Child § 679, Eighteen-Month Review.
Witkin, California Summary 10th Torts § 127, in General.

§ 362.04. Babysitting of foster child

(a) For purposes of this section:

(1) "Caregiver" means any licensed certified foster parent, approved relative caregiver, or approved nonrelative extended family member, or approved resource family.

(2) "Reasonable and prudent parent" or "reasonable and prudent parent standard" has the meaning set forth in subdivision (c) of Section 362.05.

(3) "Short term" means no more than 24 consecutive hours.

(b) Every caregiver may arrange for occasional short-term babysitting of their foster child and allow individuals to supervise the foster child for the purposes set forth in Section 362.05, or on occasions, including, but not limited to, when the foster parent has a medical or other health care appointment, grocery or other shopping, personal grooming appointments, special occasions for the foster parents, foster parent training classes, school-related meetings (such as parent-teacher conferences), business meetings, adult social gatherings, or an occasional evening out by the foster parent.

(c) Caregivers shall use a reasonable and prudent parent standard in determining and selecting appropriate babysitters for occasional short-term use.

(d) The caregiver shall endeavor to provide the babysitter with the following information before leaving the child for purposes of short-term care:

(1) Information about the child's emotional, behavioral, medical, or physical conditions, if any, necessary to provide care for the child during the time the foster child is being supervised by the babysitter.

(2) Any medication that should be administered to the foster child during the time the foster child is being supervised by the babysitter.

(3) Emergency contact information that is valid during the time the foster child is being supervised by the babysitter.

(e) Babysitters selected by the caregiver to provide occasional short-term care to a foster child under the provisions of this section shall be exempt from any department regulation requiring health screening or cardiopulmonary resuscitation certification or training.

(f) Each state and local entity shall ensure that private agencies that provide foster care services to dependent children have policies consistent with this section. Policies that are not consistent with this section include those that are incompatible with, contradictory to, or more restrictive than this section. *(Added by Stats.2005, c. 628 (S.B.358), § 3. Amended by Stats.2014, c. 772 (S.B.1460), § 11, eff. Jan. 1, 2015; Stats.2015, c. 425 (S.B.794), § 6, eff. Jan. 1, 2016.)*

Research References

Treatises and Practice Aids

Witkin, California Summary 10th Parent and Child § 9, Rights and Responsibilities Of Foster Parents.
Witkin, California Summary 10th Parent and Child § 635, in General.

§ 362.05. Extracurricular, enrichment, and social activities for dependent children

(a)(1) Every child adjudged a dependent child of the juvenile court shall be entitled to participate in age-appropriate extracurricular, enrichment, and social activities. No state or local regulation or policy may prevent, or create barriers to, participation in those activities. Each state and local entity shall ensure that private agencies that provide foster care services to dependent children have policies consistent with this section and that those agencies promote and protect the ability of dependent children to participate in age-appropriate extracurricular, enrichment, and social activities. A short-term residential therapeutic program or a group home administrator, * * * facility manager, or his or her responsible designee, and a caregiver, as defined in paragraph (1) of subdivision (a) of Section 362.04, shall use a reasonable and prudent parent standard in determining whether to give permission for a child residing in foster care to participate in extracurricular, enrichment, and social activities. A short-term residential therapeutic program or a group home administrator, * * * facility manager, or his or her responsible designee, and a caregiver shall take reasonable steps to determine the appropriateness of the activity in consideration of the child's age, maturity, and developmental level.

(2) Training for caregivers shall include knowledge and skills relating to the reasonable and prudent parent standard for the participation of the child in age or developmentally appropriate activities, consistent with this section and Section 671(a)(24) of Title 42 of the United States Code.

(b) A short-term residential therapeutic program or a group home administrator * * *, facility manager, or his or her responsible designee, is encouraged to consult with social work or treatment staff members who are most familiar with the child at the group home in applying and using the reasonable and prudent parent standard.

(c)(1) "Reasonable and prudent parent" or "reasonable and prudent parent standard" means the standard characterized by careful and sensible parental decisions that maintain the health, safety, and best interests of a child while at the same time encouraging the emotional and developmental growth of the child, that a caregiver shall use when determining whether to allow a child in foster care under the responsibility of the state to participate in age or developmentally appropriate extracurricular, enrichment, cultural, and social activities.

(2) The term "age or developmentally appropriate" means both of the following:

(A) Activities or items that are generally accepted as suitable for children of the same chronological age or level of maturity or that are determined to be developmentally appropriate for a child, based on the development of cognitive, emotional, physical, and behavioral capacities that are typical for an age or age group.

(B) In the case of a specific child, activities or items that are suitable for the child based on the developmental stages attained by the child with respect to the cognitive, emotional, physical, and behavioral capacities of the child. *(Added by Stats.2003, c. 813 (A.B.408), § 2. Amended by Stats.2005, c. 628 (S.B.358), § 4; Stats.2008, c. 483 (A.B.2096), § 1; Stats. 2015, c. 425 (S.B.794), § 7, eff. Jan. 1, 2016; Stats.2017, c. 732 (A.B.404), § 51, eff. Jan. 1, 2018.)*

Research References

Treatises and Practice Aids

Witkin, California Summary 10th Parent and Child § 9, Rights and Responsibilities Of Foster Parents.

Witkin, California Summary 10th Parent and Child § 567, Statutory Rights.

§ 362.1. Visitation; parents, guardians, and siblings

(a) In order to maintain ties between the parent or guardian and any siblings and the child, and to provide information relevant to deciding if, and when, to return a child to the custody of his or her parent or guardian, or to encourage or suspend sibling interaction, any order placing a child in foster care, and ordering reunification services, shall provide as follows:

(1)(A) Subject to subparagraph (B), for visitation between the parent or guardian and the child. Visitation shall be as frequent as possible, consistent with the well-being of the child.

(B) No visitation order shall jeopardize the safety of the child. To protect the safety of the child, the court may keep the child's address confidential. If the parent of the child has been convicted of murder in the first degree, as defined in Section 189 of the Penal Code, and the victim of the murder was the other parent of the child, the court shall order visitation between the child and the parent only if that order would be consistent with Section 3030 of the Family Code.

(2) Pursuant to subdivision (b) of Section 16002, for visitation between the child and any siblings, unless the court finds by clear and convincing evidence that sibling interaction is contrary to the safety or well-being of either child.

(3) Pursuant to subdivision (c) of Section 16002, for review of the reasons for any suspension of sibling interaction at each periodic review hearing pursuant to Section 366, and for a requirement that, in order for a suspension to continue, the court shall make a renewed finding that sibling interaction is contrary to the safety or well-being of either child.

(4) If the child is a teen parent who has custody of his or her child and that child is not a dependent of the court pursuant to this chapter, for visitation among the teen parent, the child's noncustodial parent, and appropriate family members, unless the court finds by clear and convincing evidence that visitation would be detrimental to the teen parent.

(b) When reunification services are not ordered pursuant to Section 361.5, the child's plan for legal permanency shall include consideration of the existence of and the relationship with any sibling pursuant to Section 16002, including their impact on placement and visitation.

(c) As used in this section, "sibling" means a person related to the identified child by blood, adoption, or affinity through a common legal or biological parent. *(Added by Stats.1986, c. 1122, § 15. Amended by Stats.1994, c. 663 (S.B.17), § 1; Stats.1996, c. 1139 (A.B.2647), § 10; Stats. 1998, c. 704 (A.B.2745), § 2; Stats.1998, c. 705 (A.B.2386), § 2; Stats.2000, c. 909 (A.B.1987), § 3; Stats.2005, c. 630 (S.B.500), § 2; Stats.2010, c. 560 (A.B.743), § 1; Stats.2014, c. 773 (S.B.1099), § 3, eff. Jan. 1, 2015; Stats.2015, c. 425 (S.B.794), § 8, eff. Jan. 1, 2016.)*

Commentary

Despite subsection (a)(1)(A), a juvenile court may not order visitation that would contravene a lawful condition of a parent's parole and the court may properly take into account a parent's parole conditions when fashioning orders in a dependent child's best interests. *Kevin R. v. Superior Court, 191 Cal.App.4th 676, 120 Cal.Rptr.3d 549 (2010)*.

For treatment of parental visitation when a parent is incarcerated, see *In re Jonathan M., 53 Cal.App.4th 1234, 62 Cal.Rptr.2d 208 (1997)* (disapproving juvenile court establishment of mileage limits beyond which visitation would not be provided for incarcerated parents); and *In re Dylan T., 65 Cal.App.4th 765, 76 Cal.Rptr.2d 684 (1998)* (holding that an order prohibiting visitation of an incarcerated mother with a dependent child during reunification period solely because of the child's age, without substantial evidence of detriment to child, was error).

In re Ethan G., 145 Cal.App.4th 692, 51 Cal.Rptr.3d 816 (2006), held that it was error, under subsection (a)(1)(B), to allow a father who sexually abused a child, found dependent under section 300 (b) and (d), to return to the family home so long as his conduct was monitored at all times. The court reasoned that monitored visitation cannot be effective to protect a child when an offending parent enjoys around-the-clock home contact.

In re C.C., 172 Cal.App.4th 1481, 92 Cal.Rptr.3d 168 (2009), held that a juvenile court erred in denying a mother visitation on the ground of overall detriment to the child, rather than jeopardy to the safety of the child, as required by subsection (a)(1)(B).

Research References

Forms

West's California Judicial Council Forms JV-401, Visitation Attachment: Sibling.

Treatises and Practice Aids

Witkin, California Summary 10th Parent and Child § 641, Visitation Rights.

Witkin, California Summary 10th Parent and Child § 652, Determination Whether to Order Services.

Witkin, California Summary 10th Parent and Child § 688, Other Alternatives.

§ 362.2. Out-of-home placement for individualized education program; location

It is the intent of the Legislature that if a placement out-of-home is necessary pursuant to an individualized education program, that this placement be as near the child's home as possible, unless it is not in the best interest of the child. When the court determines that it is the best interest of the child to be placed out-of-state, the court shall read into the record that in-state alternatives have been explored and that they cannot meet the needs of the child, and the court shall state on the record the reasons for the out-of-state placement. *(Added by Stats.1994, c. 1128 (A.B.1892), § 2.)*

Research References

Treatises and Practice Aids

Witkin, California Summary 10th Parent and Child § 635, in General.

§ 362.3. Notice; citation to appear at hearing; issuance, contents, service

In addition to the notice provided in Sections 297 and 332, the juvenile court may issue its citation directing any parent, guardian, or foster parent of the person concerning whom a petition has been filed to appear at the time and place set for any hearing under the provisions of this chapter, and directing any person having custody or control of the child concerning whom the petition has been filed to bring the child with him or her. The citation shall, in addition, state that a parent, guardian, or foster parent may be required to participate in a counseling or education program with the child concerning whom the petition has been filed. Personal service of the citation shall be made at least 24 hours before the time stated therein for the appearance. *(Added by Stats.1984, c. 162, § 2. Amended by Stats.2002, c. 416 (S.B.1956), § 9.)*

Research References

Treatises and Practice Aids

Witkin, California Summary 10th Parent and Child § 566, Notices, Citations, Warrants, and Subpenas.

Witkin, California Summary 10th Parent and Child § 657, Filing, Setting for Hearing, and Notice.

Witkin, California Summary 10th Parent and Child § 664, in General.

Witkin, California Summary 10th Parent and Child § 668, Subsequent Petition.

§ 362.4. Termination of juvenile court jurisdiction; pending proceedings relating to parental marriage or custody order; restraining visitation or custody orders; opening of file relating to custody

* * * (a) If the juvenile court terminates its jurisdiction over a minor who has been adjudged a dependent child of the juvenile court prior to the minor's attainment of the age of 18 years, and proceedings for dissolution of marriage, for nullity of marriage, or for legal separation, of the minor's parents, or proceedings to establish the paternity of the minor child brought under the Uniform Parentage Act, Part 3 (commencing with Section 7600) of Division 12 of the Family Code, are pending in the superior court of any county, or an order has been entered with regard to the custody of that minor, the juvenile court on its own motion, may issue a protective order as provided for in Section 213.5 or as defined in Section 6218 of the Family Code, and an order determining the custody of, or visitation with, the child.

(b) Any order issued pursuant to this section shall continue until modified or terminated by a subsequent order of the superior court. The order of the juvenile court shall be filed in the proceeding for nullity, dissolution, or legal separation, or in the proceeding to establish paternity, at the time the juvenile court terminates its jurisdiction over the minor, and shall become a part thereof.

(c) If no action is filed or pending relating to the custody of the minor in the superior court of any county, the juvenile court order may be used as the sole basis for opening a file in the superior court of the county in which the parent, who has been given custody, resides. The court may direct the parent or the clerk of the juvenile court to transmit the order to the clerk of the superior court of the county in which the order is to be filed. The clerk of the superior court shall, immediately upon receipt, open a file, without a filing fee, and assign a case number.

(d) The clerk of the superior court shall, upon the filing of any juvenile court custody order, send * * * a copy of the order with the case number by first-class mail or by electronic means pursuant to Section 212.5 to the juvenile court and to the parents at the address listed on the order.

(e) The Judicial Council shall adopt forms for any custody or restraining order issued under this section. These form orders shall not be confidential. *(Formerly § 362.3, added by Stats.1984, c. 813, § 1. Renumbered § 362.4 and amended by Stats.1986, c. 248, § 246. Amended by Stats.1989, c. 137, § 2; Stats.1992, c. 163 (A.B.2641), § 137, operative Jan. 1, 1994; Stats.1993, c. 219 (A.B.1500), § 226.5; Stats.1996, c. 1138 (A.B.2154), § 3; Stats.1996, c. 1139 (A.B.2647), § 11; Stats. 2017, c. 319 (A.B.976), § 130, eff. Jan. 1, 2018.)*

Law Revision Commission Comments

1992 Amendment [Revised Comment]

Section 362.4 is amended to substitute the new reference to the Uniform Parentage Act. The reference to Family Code Section 6218 is broader than the former reference. Section 6218 includes an order restraining specific acts, excluding a party from a dwelling, and restraining additional behavior necessary to enforce the first two orders. The former reference did not include the order restraining additional behavior. [23 Cal.L.Rev.Comm. Reports 1 (1993)].

Commentary

A juvenile court's exit order awarding custody has the status of a final, or permanent, custody order when this section is read together with section 301(d), which requires "changed circumstances" to modify the order. *Heidi S. v. David H., 1 Cal App.5th 1150, 205 Cal.Rptr.3d 335 (2016).*

Applying this section and Section 302(d), *In re Marriage of David and Martha M., 140 Cal.App.4th 96, 44 Cal.Rptr.3d 388 (2006),* holds that a family court erred in applying only the "best interests of the child" standard, rather than also applying the "changed circumstances" rule prescribed by Section 302(d) in ordering modification of a juvenile court's exit order regarding child custody and visitation.

In re Chantal, 13 Cal.4th 196, 913 P.2d 1075, 51 Cal.Rptr.2d 866 (1996), holds that a juvenile court, when terminating its dependency jurisdiction, may order as a condition of visitation that a parent receive psychotherapy; a juvenile court is not limited by Family Code Section 3190, which applies only to counseling ordered by a family court. Compare *In re Donnovan J., 58 Cal.App.4th 1474, 68 Cal.Rptr.2d 714 (1997),* holding that the juvenile court unlawfully delegated judicial authority to therapists when it provided that a parent was to have "no visitation rights without permission of minors' therapists," because the court set no criteria to instruct the therapists when to allow visitation.

In re T.H., 190 Cal.App.4th 1119, 119 Cal.Rptr.3d 1 (2010), held that a juvenile court terminating dependency jurisdiction erred when its exit order granting one parent physical custody and the other parent supervised visitation "to be determined by the parents" when the parents did not get along. *T.H.* reasoned that the order granted the custodial parent an effective veto over the other parent's visitation. By contrast, *In re Grace C., 190 Cal.App.4th 1470, 119 Cal.Rptr.3d 474 (2010)*, held that a juvenile court terminating dependency jurisdiction after appointing relatives as legal guardians of dependent children, did not improperly delegate discretion over the mother's visitation to the guardians and children's therapist when it was undisputed that the guardians were providing the mother with regular visitation and the visits were going well and expected to continue indefinitely.

In re J.T., 228 Cal.App.4th 953, 175 Cal.Rptr.3d 744 (2014), held that the juvenile court acted within its authority in granting visitation to a grandparent, over the objection of the child's mother, in a proceeding terminating jurisdiction over the child. Although termination of jurisdiction may have reinstated the mother's presumption of parental fitness, the Family Code section 3104 presumption that visitation with a grandparent over the objection of the custodial parent is not in the child's best interest does not apply in dependency proceedings, where the court has special responsibility to children upon the termination of dependency jurisdiction.

Research References

Forms

West's California Judicial Council Forms JV-200, Custody Order - Juvenile - Final Judgment.
West's California Judicial Council Forms JV-205, Visitation Order--Juvenile.
West's California Judicial Council Forms JV-206, Reasons for No or Supervised Visitation--Juvenile.
West's California Judicial Council Forms JV-245, Request for Restraining Order--Juvenile.
West's California Judicial Council Forms JV-250, Notice Of Hearing and Temporary Restraining Order--Juvenile.
West's California Judicial Council Forms JV-255, Restraining Order - Juvenile Order After Hearing.

Treatises and Practice Aids

Witkin, California Summary 10th Husband and Wife § 387, Electronic Transmission and Recording Of Data.
Witkin, California Summary 10th Parent and Child § 370, in General.
Witkin, California Summary 10th Parent and Child § 371, Modification Of Order.
Witkin, California Summary 10th Parent and Child § 372, Order Splitting Custody.
Witkin, California Summary 10th Parent and Child § 373, Order Requiring Therapy.
Witkin, California Summary 10th Parent and Child § 653, Ex Parte Orders Pending Nullity or Dissolution Proceedings.
Witkin, California Summary 10th Parent and Child § 672, Child in Custody Of Parent or Guardian.
Witkin, California Summary 10th Parent and Child § 703, Appeal After Termination Of Dependency Jurisdiction.
Witkin, California Summary 10th Parent and Child § 712, Notice Of Appeal.

§ 362.5. Nonminor dependents; opening of separate court file; access to file

(a) The clerk of the superior court shall open a separate court file for nonminor dependents under the dependency, delinquency, or transition jurisdiction of the court.

(b) Access to the nonminor dependent court file shall be limited to all of the following:

(1) Court personnel.

(2) The district attorney, if the nonminor dependent is also a delinquent ward.

(3) The nonminor dependent.

(4) The attorney for the nonminor dependent.

(5) Judges, referees, and other hearing officers actively participating in juvenile proceedings involving the nonminor dependent.

(6) The social services agency or probation department.

(7) The State Department of Social Services, to carry out its duties pursuant to Division 9 (commencing with Section 10000), and Part 5 (commencing with Section 7900) of Division 12 of the Family Code, to oversee and monitor county child welfare agencies, children in foster care or receiving foster care assistance; and out-of-state placements, Section 10850.4, and pursuant to Section 2.

(8) The county counsel.

(9) Authorized legal staff or special investigators who are peace officers who are employed by, or who are authorized representatives of, the State Department of Social Services, as necessary for the performance of their duties to inspect, license, and investigate community care facilities, to ensure that the standards of care and services provided in those facilities are adequate and appropriate, and to ascertain compliance with the rules and regulations to which the facilities are subject. The confidential information shall remain confidential except for purposes of inspection, licensing, or investigation pursuant to Chapter 3 (commencing with Section 1500) and Chapter 3.4 (commencing with Section 1596.70) of Division 2 of the Health and Safety Code, or a criminal, civil, or administrative proceeding in relation thereto. The confidential information may be used by the State Department of Social Services in a criminal, civil, or administrative proceeding. The confidential information shall be available only to the judge or hearing officer and to the parties to the case. Names that are confidential shall be listed in attachments separate from the general pleadings. The confidential information shall be sealed after the conclusion of the criminal, civil, or administrative hearings, and may not subsequently be released, except in accordance with this subdivision. If the confidential information does not result in a criminal, civil, or administrative proceeding, it shall be sealed after the State Department of Social Services decides that no further action will be taken in the matter of suspected licensing violations. Except as otherwise provided in this subdivision, confidential information in the possession of the State Department of Social Services may not contain the name of the nonminor dependent.

(c) The nonminor dependent's parent and the parent's attorney may only access the file if the parent is still receiving reunification services.

(d) All other individuals requesting access to the court file must be designated by court order of the judge of the juvenile court upon filing a petition, which shall be determined pursuant to Section 827. *(Added by Stats.2012, c. 846 (A.B.1712), § 17.)*

Research References

Treatises and Practice Aids

Witkin, California Summary 10th Parent and Child § 699A, (New) in General.

§ 362.6. State prison sentence for certain crimes; child victims; visitation; hearing; modification

(a) When a hearing is requested pursuant to Section 1202.05 of the Penal Code, the sentencing court shall forward a copy of the request to the child protective services agency (CPS), or the appropriate entity, in the county in which any related dependency matters as to the affected child victim have been heard or to the county in which the child victim resides. CPS, or the appropriate entity, shall initiate a hearing to determine whether visitation between the child victim and the incarcerated person would be in the best interests of the child victim. If the court determines that visitation with the incarcerated person is in the best interests of the child victim, CPS, or the appropriate entity, shall notify the Department of Corrections to provide for contact or visitation, or both, as ordered by the court.

(b) The court, if visitation is allowed, may impose whatever safeguards or restrictions it deems appropriate to protect the child victim.

(c) The court's order shall be transmitted to all parties and to the Department of Corrections.

(d) Any party may return to the juvenile court at any time prior to the child victim's 18th birthday and request modification of the court's order based on a change of circumstances. For these purposes, the juvenile court shall retain jurisdiction over the matter until the child victim reaches the age of 18 years. *(Added by Stats.1992, c. 1008 (A.B.3560), § 4.)*

Commentary

Robin J. v. Superior Court, 124 Cal.App.4th 414, 21 Cal.Rptr.3d 417 (2004), review denied, holds that, in a petition brought under this section, a juvenile court lacked authority to enjoin the California Department of Corrections from enforcing its regulation prohibiting prisoners incarcerated for certain sexual crimes from participating in visitation with their minor children. This section applies only when a sentencing court has prohibited visitation pursuant to Penal Code § 1202.05.

Research References

Treatises and Practice Aids

Witkin, California Summary 10th Parent and Child § 607, Findings and Orders.

Witkin, California Summary 10th Parent and Child § 641, Visitation Rights.

Witkin, California Summary 10th Parent and Child § 646, Incarcerated or Institutionalized Parent or Guardian.

§ 362.7. Nonrelative extended family member; evaluation of home

When the home of a nonrelative extended family member is being considered for placement of a child, the home shall be evaluated, and approval of that home shall be granted or denied, pursuant to the same standards set forth in the regulations for the licensing of foster family homes that prescribe standards of safety and sanitation for the physical plant and standards for basic personal care, supervision, and services provided by the caregiver.

A "nonrelative extended family member" is defined as an adult caregiver who has an established familial relationship with a relative of the child, as defined in paragraph (2) of subdivision (c) of Section 361.3, or a familial or mentoring relationship with the child. The county welfare department shall verify the existence of a relationship through interviews with the parent and child or with one or more third parties. The parties may include relatives of the child, teachers, medical professionals, clergy, neighbors, and family friends. *(Added by Stats.2001, c. 653 (A.B.1695), § 12, eff. Oct. 10, 2001. Amended by Stats.2013, c. 294 (A.B.545), § 1.)*

Commentary

A 2013 amendment to this section expanded the definition of nonrelative extended family member to include an "adult caregiver who has an established familial relationship with a relative of a child." In view of the undefined term *familial*, it is unclear whether this amendment overrules *In re Samantha T., 197 Cal.App.4th 94, 128 Cal.Rptr.3d 522 (2011)*, which held that a juvenile court erred in determining that a long-time friend of the mother of two dependent children was a nonrelative extended family member when the friend had no existing relationship with the children.

In re Joshua A., 239 Cal.App.4th 208, 190 Cal.Rptr.3d 655 (2015), held that a juvenile court erred as a matter of law when it ruled that a parent is not a *relative* within the meaning of subsection (c)(2) of section 361.3, and that the mother's boyfriend therefore did not qualify as a *nonrelative extended family* member under this section.

Research References

Treatises and Practice Aids

Witkin, California Summary 10th Parent and Child § 556, Assessment Of Prospective Placement.

Witkin, California Summary 10th Parent and Child § 635, in General.

Witkin, California Summary 10th Parent and Child § 941, Commitment Of Minor for Status Offense.

§ 363. Reduction of assistance of person legally responsible for care of minor removed from unfit home

If the parent or person legally responsible for the care of any minor who is found to be a person described in Section 300 receives public assistance or care, any portion of which is attributable to the minor, a copy of the order of the court providing for the removal of the minor from his or her home shall be furnished to the appropriate social services official, who shall reduce the public assistance and care furnished the parent or other person by the amount attributable to the minor. *(Added by Stats.1976, c. 1068, p. 4773, § 10. Amended by Stats.1988, c. 701, § 4, eff. Aug. 29, 1988.)*

Research References

Treatises and Practice Aids

Witkin, California Summary 10th Parent and Child § 633, in General.

§ 364. Retention by parent or guardian of child adjudged a dependent child; continuance; report; determination; subsequent proceedings

(a) Every hearing in which an order is made placing a child under the supervision of the juvenile court pursuant to Section 300 and in which the child is not removed from the physical custody of his or her parent or guardian shall be continued to a specific future date not to exceed six months after the date of the original dispositional hearing. The continued hearing shall be placed on the appearance calendar. The court shall advise all persons present of the date of the future hearings, of their rights to be present, and to be represented by counsel.

(b) At least 10 calendar days prior to the hearing, the social worker shall file a supplemental report with the court describing the services offered to the family and the progress made by the family in eliminating the conditions or factors requiring court supervision. The social worker shall also make a recommendation regarding the necessity of continued supervision. A copy of this report shall be furnished to all parties at least 10 calendar days prior to the hearing.

(c) After hearing any evidence presented by the social worker, the parent, the guardian, or the child, the court shall determine whether continued supervision is necessary. The court shall terminate its jurisdiction unless the social worker or his or her department establishes by a preponderance of evidence that the conditions still exist which would justify initial assumption of jurisdiction under Section 300, or that those conditions are likely to exist if supervision is withdrawn. Failure of the parent or guardian to participate regularly in any court ordered treatment program shall constitute prima facie evidence that the conditions which justified initial assumption of jurisdiction still exist and that continued supervision is necessary.

(d) If the court retains jurisdiction it shall continue the matter to a specified date, not more than six months from the time of the hearing, at which point the court shall again follow the procedure specified in subdivision (c).

(e) In any case in which the court has ordered that a parent or guardian shall retain physical custody of a child subject to supervision by a social worker, and the social worker subsequently receives a report of acts or circumstances which indicate that there is reasonable cause to believe that the child is a person described in subdivision (a), (d), or (e) of Section 300, the social worker shall commence proceedings under this chapter. If, as a result of the proceedings required, the court finds that the child is a person described in subdivision (a), (d), or (e) of Section 300, the court shall remove the child from the care, custody, and control of the child's parent or guardian and shall commit the child to the care, custody, and control of the social worker pursuant to Section 361. *(Added by Stats.1976, c. 1068, p. 4773, § 10. Amended by Stats.1982, c. 978, § 22, eff. Sept. 13, 1982, operative July 1, 1982; Stats.1986, c. 1122, § 16; Stats.1987, c. 1485, § 40, operative Jan. 1, 1989; Stats.1989, c. 913, § 11; Stats.1998, c. 1054 (A.B.1091), § 29.)*

Commentary

In re N.S., 97 Cal.App.4th 167, 118 Cal.Rptr.2d 259 (2002), holds that a juvenile court is required by subsection (c) to terminate its jurisdiction over a dependent child who has been returned to her father's custody, when there is no evidence that the conditions that warranted the court's assumption of jurisdiction continue to exist or would exist if supervision were terminated.

When a social services agency recommended termination of jurisdiction over a child because the circumstances requiring initial assumption of jurisdiction no longer existed, a juvenile court had no authority to continue dependency jurisdiction over the child. *In re D.B., 239 Cal.App.4th 1073, 191 Cal.Rptr.3d 641 (2015).*

When a social services agency recommends termination of dependency jurisdiction and the dependent child opposes the recommendation, the child must establish by a preponderance of the evidence that the conditions requiring the initial assumption of dependency jurisdiction continue to exist or are likely to exist if jurisdiction is terminated. *In re Aurora P., 241 Cal.App.4th 1142, 194 Cal.Rptr.3d 383 (2015).*

When there is no showing of continued risk to the children, under this section the juvenile court must immediately terminate dependency jurisdiction, leaving issues of custody, visitation, and child support to the family court. Thus it was error for the juvenile court, immediately before it terminated dependency jurisdiction, to refuse to accept the divorced parents' settlement agreement regarding child custody and visitation, to order a different custody and visitation schedule, and to terminate child support payments. *In re Alexandria M., 156 Cal.App.4th 1088, 68 Cal.Rptr.3d 10 (2007).*

In re Armando L., 1 Cal.App.5th 606, 204 Cal.Rptr.3d 859 (2016), held that a juvenile court denied a mother her due process right to present evidence when it denied her a contested evidentiary hearing under this section and terminated its jurisdiction over her son, granting physical custody to the child's father. The mother wished to raise the issues of dependency jurisdiction, custody of the minor and further potential services for the minor.

Research References

Forms

West's California Judicial Council Forms JV-425, Findings and Orders After In-Home Status Review Hearing (Welf. & Inst. Code, S364).

West's California Judicial Council Forms JV-426, Findings and Orders After In-Home Status Review Hearing--Child Placed With Previously Noncustodial Parent (Welf. & Inst. Code, §§ 364, 366.21).

Treatises and Practice Aids

Witkin, California Summary 10th Parent and Child § 4, Public Welfare Services.

Witkin, California Summary 10th Parent and Child § 483, Juvenile Court Proceedings.

Witkin, California Summary 10th Parent and Child § 564, in General.

Witkin, California Summary 10th Parent and Child § 630, Bases for Removal.

Witkin, California Summary 10th Parent and Child § 637, Priority Right Of Noncustodial Parent.

Witkin, California Summary 10th Parent and Child § 661, Hearing After Supplemental Petition is Sustained.

Witkin, California Summary 10th Parent and Child § 668, Subsequent Petition.

Witkin, California Summary 10th Parent and Child § 669, in General.

Witkin, California Summary 10th Parent and Child § 670, Notice Of Hearing.

Witkin, California Summary 10th Parent and Child § 671, Supplemental Report.

Witkin, California Summary 10th Parent and Child § 672, Child in Custody Of Parent or Guardian.

Witkin, California Summary 10th Parent and Child § 676, in General.

§ 364.05. Section 364(b) report to be provided all parties before hearing; delivery and time frames; granting of continuance; presumption and burden of proof

Notwithstanding Section 364, in a county of the first class, a copy of the report required pursuant to subdivision (b) of Section 364 shall be provided to all parties at least 10 calendar days * * * before the hearing. This may be accomplished by electronically serving the report pursuant to Section 212.5 or by mailing the report at least 15 calendar days * * * before the hearing to a party whose address is within the State of California, or at least 20 calendar days * * * before the hearing to a party whose address is outside the State of California. The court shall grant a reasonable continuance, not to exceed 10 calendar days, upon request by any party or his or her counsel on the ground that the report was not provided at least 10 calendar days * * * before the hearing as required by this section, unless the party or his or her counsel has expressly waived the requirement that the report be provided within the 10–day period or the court finds that the party's ability to proceed at the hearing is not prejudiced by the lack of timely service of the report. In making this determination, the court shall presume that a party is prejudiced by the lack of timely service of the report, and may find that the party is not prejudiced only by clear and convincing evidence to the contrary. *(Added by Stats. 2003, c. 516 (A.B.1469), § 1. Amended by Stats.2017, c. 319 (A.B.976), § 131, eff. Jan. 1, 2018.)*

Research References

Treatises and Practice Aids

Witkin, California Summary 10th Parent and Child § 671, Supplemental Report.

§ 365. Periodic reports

The court may require the social worker or any other agency to render any periodic reports concerning children committed to its care, custody, and control under the provisions of Section 362 that the court deems necessary or desirable. The court may require that the social worker, or any other public agency organized to provide care for needy or neglected children, shall perform the visitation and make periodic reports to the courts concerning children committed under those provisions that the court deems necessary or desirable. *(Added by Stats.1976, c. 1068, p. 4773, § 10. Amended by Stats.1982, c. 978, § 23, eff. Sept. 13, 1982, operative July 1, 1982; Stats.1998, c. 1054 (A.B.1091), § 30.)*

Research References

Treatises and Practice Aids

Witkin, California Summary 10th Parent and Child § 669, in General.

§ 366. Periodic status review

(a)(1) The status of every dependent child in foster care shall be reviewed periodically as determined by the court but no less frequently than once every six months, as calculated from the date of the original dispositional hearing, until the hearing described in Section 366.26 is completed. The court shall consider the safety of the child and shall determine all of the following:

(A) The continuing necessity for and appropriateness of the placement.

(B) The extent of the agency's compliance with the case plan in making reasonable efforts, or, in the case of a child 16 years of age or older with another planned permanent living arrangement, the ongoing and intensive efforts, or, in the case of an Indian child, active efforts as described in Section 361.7, to return the child to a safe home and to complete any steps necessary to finalize the permanent placement of the child, including efforts to maintain relationships between a child who is 10 years of age or older and who has been in an out-of-home placement for six months or longer, and individuals other than the child's siblings who are important to the child, consistent with the child's best interests.

(C) Whether there should be any limitation on the right of the parent or guardian to make educational decisions or developmental services decisions for the child. That limitation shall be specifically addressed in the court order and may not exceed those necessary to protect the child. Whenever the court specifically limits the right of the parent or guardian to make educational decisions or developmental services decisions for the child, the court shall at the same time appoint a responsible adult to make educational decisions or developmental services decisions for the child pursuant to Section 361.

(D)(i) Whether the child has other siblings under the court's jurisdiction, and, if any siblings exist, all of the following:

(I) The nature of the relationship between the child and his or her siblings.

(II) The appropriateness of developing or maintaining the sibling relationships pursuant to Section 16002.

(III) If the siblings are not placed together in the same home, why the siblings are not placed together and what efforts are being made to place the siblings together, or why those efforts are not appropriate.

(IV) If the siblings are not placed together, all of the following:

(ia) The frequency and nature of the visits between the siblings.

(ib) If there are visits between the siblings, whether the visits are supervised or unsupervised. If the visits are supervised, a discussion of the reasons why the visits are supervised, and what needs to be accomplished in order for the visits to be unsupervised.

(ic) If there are visits between the siblings, a description of the location and length of the visits.

(id) Any plan to increase visitation between the siblings.

(V) The impact of the sibling relationships on the child's placement and planning for legal permanence.

(VI) The continuing need to suspend sibling interaction, if applicable, pursuant to subdivision (c) of Section 16002.

(ii) The factors the court may consider in making a determination regarding the nature of the child's sibling relationships may include, but are not limited to, whether the siblings were raised together in the same home, whether the siblings have shared significant common experiences or have existing close and strong bonds, whether either sibling expresses a desire to visit or live with his or her sibling, as applicable, and whether ongoing contact is in the child's best emotional interests.

(E) The extent of progress that has been made toward alleviating or mitigating the causes necessitating placement in foster care.

(F) If the review hearing is the last review hearing to be held before the child attains 18 years of age, the court shall conduct the hearing pursuant to Section 366.31 or 366.32.

(2) The court shall project a likely date by which the child may be returned to and safely maintained in the home or placed for adoption, tribal customary adoption in the case of an Indian child, legal guardianship, placed with a fit and willing relative, or in another planned permanent living arrangement.

(b) Subsequent to the hearing, periodic reviews of each child in foster care shall be conducted pursuant to the requirements of Sections 366.3 and 16503.

(c) If the child has been placed out of state, each review described in subdivision (a) and any reviews conducted pursuant to Sections 366.3 and 16503 shall also address whether the out-of-state placement continues to be the most appropriate placement selection and in the best interests of the child.

(d)(1) A review described in subdivision (a) and any reviews conducted pursuant to Sections 366.3 and 16503 shall not result in a placement of a child outside the United States prior to a judicial finding that the placement is in the best interest of the child, except as required by federal law or treaty.

(2) The party or agency requesting placement of the child outside the United States shall carry the burden of proof and must show, by clear and convincing evidence, that a placement outside the United States is in the best interest of the child.

(3) In determining the best interest of the child, the court shall consider, but not be limited to, the following factors:

(A) Placement with a relative.

(B) Placement of siblings in the same home.

(C) Amount and nature of any contact between the child and the potential guardian or caretaker.

(D) Physical and medical needs of the dependent child.

(E) Psychological and emotional needs of the dependent child.

(F) Social, cultural, and educational needs of the dependent child.

(G) Specific desires of any dependent child who is 12 years of age or older.

(4) If the court finds that a placement outside the United States is, by clear and convincing evidence, in the best interest of the child, the court may issue an order authorizing the social worker or placing agency to make a placement outside the United States. A child subject to this subdivision shall not leave the United States prior to the issuance of the order described in this paragraph.

(5) For purposes of this subdivision, "outside the United States" shall not include the lands of any federally recognized American Indian tribe or Alaskan Natives.

(6) This section shall not apply to the placement of a dependent child with a parent.

(e) A child may not be placed in an out-of-state group home, or remain in an out-of-state group home, unless the group home is in compliance with Section 7911.1 of the Family Code.

(f) The status review of every nonminor dependent, as defined in subdivision (v) of Section 11400, shall be conducted pursuant to the requirements of Sections 366.3, 366.31, or 366.32, and 16503 until dependency jurisdiction is terminated pursuant to Section 391. *(Added by Stats.1982, c. 978, § 25, eff. Sept. 13, 1982, operative July 1, 1982. Amended by Stats.1984, c. 1246, § 5; Stats.1984, c. 1608, § 5, eff. Sept. 30, 1984; Stats.1984, c. 1608, § 13, eff. Sept. 30, 1984, operative Jan. 1. 1985; Stats.1986, c. 1122, § 17; Stats.1989, c. 913, § 12; Stats.1994, c. 663 (S.B.17), § 2; Stats.1997, c. 793 (A.B.1544), § 19; Stats.1998, c. 311 (S.B.933), § 53, eff. Aug. 19, 1998; Stats.1998, c. 1056 (A.B.2773), § 13; Stats.1999, c. 887 (S.B.1270), § 1; Stats.2000, c. 909 (A.B.1987), § 4; Stats.2001, c. 111 (A.B.429), § 25, eff. July 30, 2001; Stats. 2001, c. 653 (A.B.1695), § 12.3, eff. Oct. 10, 2001; Stats.2002, c. 785 (S.B.1677), § 3; Stats.2003, c. 813 (A.B.408), § 3; Stats.2004, c. 810 (A.B.2807), § 1; Stats.2005, c. 640 (A.B. 1412), § 2; Stats.2006, c. 838 (S.B.678), § 51; Stats.2010, c. 559 (A.B.12), § 15; Stats.2012, c. 144 (A.B.2209), § 2; Stats.2012, c. 846 (A.B.1712), § 18.5; Stats.2014, c. 773 (S.B.1099), § 4, eff. Jan. 1, 2015; Stats.2015, c. 425 (S.B.794), § 9, eff. Jan. 1, 2016.)*

Commentary

In re Christina A., 91 Cal.App.4th 1153, 111 Cal.Rptr.2d 310 (2001), holds that when a dependent child under the age of three has been removed from parental custody and reunification services have been ordered, Welfare and Institutions Code §§ 361.5(a)(2), 366(a), and 366.21(e) require that a status review hearing be set within six months from the date of the jurisdictional hearing, rather than six months from the date of the dispositional hearing.

Research References

Forms

West's California Judicial Council Forms JV-403, Sibling Attachment: Contact and Placement.

West's California Judicial Council Forms JV-460, Attachment: Additional Findings and Orders for Child Approaching Majority--Dependency.

Treatises and Practice Aids

Witkin, California Summary 10th Parent and Child § 4, Public Welfare Services.

Witkin, California Summary 10th Parent and Child § 463, Transfer-In Hearing.

Witkin, California Summary 10th Parent and Child § 483, Juvenile Court Proceedings.

Witkin, California Summary 10th Parent and Child § 627, in General.

Witkin, California Summary 10th Parent and Child § 631, Procedure.

Witkin, California Summary 10th Parent and Child § 637, Priority Right Of Noncustodial Parent.

Witkin, California Summary 10th Parent and Child § 641, Visitation Rights.

Witkin, California Summary 10th Parent and Child § 643, Duration Of Services.

Witkin, California Summary 10th Parent and Child § 669, in General.

Witkin, California Summary 10th Parent and Child § 671, Supplemental Report.

Witkin, California Summary 10th Parent and Child § 673, Child in Foster Care.

Witkin, California Summary 10th Parent and Child § 674, Return Of Child.
Witkin, California Summary 10th Parent and Child § 676, in General.
Witkin, California Summary 10th Parent and Child § 686, Alternative Dispositions.

§ 366.05. Supplemental reports filed in connection with status review hearing; provision to parent or legal guardian and to counsel before hearing; delivery and time frames; granting of continuance; presumptions and burden of proof

Notwithstanding subdivision (c) of Section 366.21, in a county of the first class, any supplemental report filed in connection with a status review hearing held pursuant to subdivision (a) of Section 366 shall be provided to the parent or legal guardian and to counsel for the child at least 10 calendar days * * * before the hearing. This may be accomplished by electronically serving the report pursuant to Section 212.5 or by mailing the report at least 15 calendar days * * * before the hearing to a party whose address is within the State of California, or at least 20 calendar days * * * before the hearing to a party whose address is outside the State of California. The court shall grant a reasonable continuance, not to exceed 10 calendar days, upon request by any party or his or her counsel on the ground that the report was not provided at least 10 calendar days * * * before the hearing as required by this section, unless the party or his or her counsel has expressly waived the requirement that the report be provided within the 10–day period or the court finds that the party's ability to proceed at the hearing is not prejudiced by the lack of timely service of the report. In making this determination, the court shall presume that a party is prejudiced by the lack of timely service of the report, and may find that the party is not prejudiced only by clear and convincing evidence to the contrary. *(Added by Stats. 2003, c. 516 (A.B.1469), § 2. Amended by Stats.2017, c. 319 (A.B.976), § 132, eff. Jan. 1, 2018.)*

§ 366.1. Supplemental report; contents

Each supplemental report required to be filed pursuant to Section 366 shall include, but not be limited to, a factual discussion of each of the following subjects:

(a) Whether the county welfare department social worker has considered either of the following:

(1) Child protective services, as defined in Chapter 5 (commencing with Section 16500) of Part 4 of Division 9, as a possible solution to the problems at hand, and has offered those services to qualified parents, if appropriate under the circumstances.

(2) Whether the child can be returned to the custody of his or her parent who is enrolled in a certified substance abuse treatment facility that allows a dependent child to reside with his or her parent.

(b) What plan, if any, for the return and maintenance of the child in a safe home is recommended to the court by the county welfare department social worker.

(c) Whether the subject child appears to be a person who is eligible to be considered for further court action to free the child from parental custody and control.

(d) What actions, if any, have been taken by the parent to correct the problems that caused the child to be made a dependent child of the court.

(e) If the parent or guardian is unwilling or unable to participate in making an educational decision for his or her child, or if other circumstances exist that compromise the ability of the parent or guardian to make educational decisions for the child, the county welfare department or social worker shall consider whether the right of the parent or guardian to make educational decisions for the child should be limited. If the supplemental report makes that recommendation, the report shall identify whether there is a responsible adult available to make educational decisions for the child pursuant to Section 361.

(f)(1) The health and education of the minor, including a copy of the complete health and education summary as required under Section 16010, including the name and contact information of the person or persons currently holding the right to make educational decisions for the child.

(2) In instances where it is determined that disclosure pursuant to paragraph (1) of the contact information of the person or persons currently holding the right to make educational decisions for the child poses a threat to the health and safety of that individual or those individuals, that contact information shall be redacted or withheld from the health and education summary within the supplemental report described in this section.

(g)(1) Whether the child has any siblings under the court's jurisdiction, and, if any siblings exist, all of the following:

(A) The nature of the relationship between the child and his or her siblings.

(B) The appropriateness of developing or maintaining the sibling relationships pursuant to Section 16002.

(C) If the siblings are not placed together in the same home, why the siblings are not placed together and what efforts are being made to place the siblings together, or why those efforts are not appropriate.

(D) If the siblings are not placed together, all of the following:

(i) The frequency and nature of the visits between the siblings.

(ii) If there are visits between the siblings, whether the visits are supervised or unsupervised. If the visits are supervised, a discussion of the reasons why the visits are supervised, and what needs to be accomplished in order for the visits to be unsupervised.

(iii) If there are visits between the siblings, a description of the location and length of the visits.

(iv) Any plan to increase visitation between the siblings.

(E) The impact of the sibling relationships on the child's placement and planning for legal permanence.

(2) The factual discussion shall include a discussion of indicators of the nature of the child's sibling relationships, including, but not limited to, whether the siblings were raised together in the same home, whether the siblings have shared significant common experiences or have existing close and strong bonds, whether either sibling expresses a desire to visit

or live with his or her sibling, as applicable, and whether ongoing contact is in the child's best emotional interests.

(h) Whether a child who is 10 years of age or older and who has been in an out-of-home placement for six months or longer has relationships with individuals other than the child's siblings that are important to the child, consistent with the child's best interests, and actions taken to maintain those relationships. The social worker shall ask every child who is 10 years of age or older and who has been in an out-of-home placement for six months or longer to identify any individuals other than the child's siblings who are important to the child, consistent with the child's best interest. The social worker may ask any other child to provide that information, as appropriate.

(i) The implementation and operation of the amendments to subdivision (h) enacted at the 2005–06 Regular Session shall be subject to appropriation through the budget process and by phase, as provided in Section 366.35. *(Added by Stats.1980, c. 716, p. 2140, § 2. Amended by Stats.1987, c. 1485, § 41; Stats.1998, c. 1054 (A.B.1091), § 31; Stats.1998, c. 1056 (A.B.2773), § 14; Stats.2000, c. 909 (A.B.1987), § 5; Stats.2001, c. 111 (A.B.429), § 26, eff. July 30, 2001; Stats. 2001, c. 653 (A.B.1695), § 12.6, eff. Oct. 10, 2001; Stats.2002, c. 785 (S.B.1677), § 4; Stats.2003, c. 813 (A.B.408), § 4; Stats.2004, c. 810 (A.B.2807), § 2; Stats.2005, c. 640 (A.B. 1412), § 3; Stats.2014, c. 219 (S.B.977), § 5, eff. Jan. 1, 2015; Stats.2014, c. 773 (S.B.1099), § 5.5, eff. Jan. 1, 2015; Stats. 2017, c. 829 (S.B.233), § 6, eff. Jan. 1, 2018.)*

Research References

Treatises and Practice Aids

Witkin, California Summary 10th Parent and Child § 669, in General.

Witkin, California Summary 10th Parent and Child § 671, Supplemental Report.

Witkin, California Summary 10th Parent and Child § 678, Twelve-Month Review.

Witkin, California Summary 10th Parent and Child § 679, Eighteen-Month Review.

§ 366.21. Status review hearings

(a) Every hearing conducted by the juvenile court reviewing the status of a dependent child shall be placed on the appearance calendar. The court shall advise all persons present at the hearing of the date of the future hearing and of their right to be present and represented by counsel.

(b) Except as provided in Sections 294 and 295, notice of the hearing shall be provided pursuant to Section 293.

(c) At least 10 calendar days * * * before the hearing, the social worker shall file a supplemental report with the court regarding the services provided or offered to the parent or legal guardian to enable him or her to assume custody and the efforts made to achieve legal permanence for the child if efforts to reunify fail, including, but not limited to, efforts to maintain relationships between a child who is 10 years of age or older and has been in out-of-home placement for six months or longer and individuals who are important to the child, consistent with the child's best interests; the progress made; and, where relevant, the prognosis for return of the child to the physical custody of his or her parent or legal guardian; and shall make his or her recommendation for disposition. If the child is a member of a sibling group described in subparagraph (C) of paragraph (1) of subdivision (a) of Section 361.5, the report and recommendation may also take into account those factors described in subdivision (e) relating to the child's sibling group. If the recommendation is not to return the child to a parent or legal guardian, the report shall specify why the return of the child would be detrimental to the child. The social worker shall provide the parent or legal guardian, counsel for the child, and any court-appointed child advocate with a copy of the report, including his or her recommendation for disposition, at least 10 calendar days * * * before the hearing. The report may be served pursuant to Section 212.5. In the case of a child removed from the physical custody of his or her parent or legal guardian, the social worker shall, at least 10 calendar days * * * before the hearing, provide a summary of his or her recommendation for disposition to any foster parents, relative caregivers, and certified foster parents who have been approved for adoption by the State Department of Social Services when it is acting as an adoption agency or by a county adoption agency, community care facility, or foster family agency having the physical custody of the child. The social worker shall include a copy of the Judicial Council Caregiver Information Form (JV–290) with the summary of * * * his or her recommendation to the child's foster parents, relative caregivers, or foster parents approved for adoption, in the caregiver's primary language when available, along with information on how to file the form with the court. The form and summary of the recommendation may be served electronically pursuant to Section 212.5.

(d) Prior to any hearing involving a child in the physical custody of a community care facility or a foster family agency that may result in the return of the child to the physical custody of his or her parent or legal guardian, or in adoption or the creation of a legal guardianship, or in the case of an Indian child, in consultation with the child's tribe, tribal customary adoption, the facility or agency shall file with the court a report, or a Judicial Council Caregiver Information Form (JV–290), containing its recommendation for disposition. Prior to the hearing involving a child in the physical custody of a foster parent, a relative caregiver, or a certified foster parent who has been approved for adoption by the State Department of Social Services when it is acting as an adoption agency or by a county adoption agency, the foster parent, relative caregiver, or the certified foster parent who has been approved for adoption by the State Department of Social Services when it is acting as an adoption agency or by a county adoption agency, may file with the court a report containing his or her recommendation for disposition. The court shall consider the report and recommendation filed pursuant to this subdivision prior to determining any disposition.

(e)(1) At the review hearing held 6 months after the initial dispositional hearing, but no later than 12 months after the date the child entered foster care as determined in Section 361.49, whichever occurs earlier, after considering the admissible and relevant evidence, the court shall order the return of the child to the physical custody of his or her parent or legal guardian unless the court finds, by a preponderance of the evidence, that the return of the child to his or her parent or legal guardian would create a substantial risk of detriment to the safety, protection, or physical or emotional well-being of the child. The social worker shall have the burden of establishing that detriment. At the hearing, the court shall consider the criminal history, obtained pursuant to paragraph (1) of subdivision (f) of Section 16504.5, of the parent or legal guardian subsequent to the child's removal to the extent that the criminal record is substantially related to the welfare of the child or the parent's or guardian's ability to exercise custody and control regarding his or her child, provided the parent or legal guardian agreed to submit fingerprint images to obtain criminal history information as part of the case plan. The court shall also consider whether the child can be returned to the custody of his or her parent who is enrolled in a certified substance abuse treatment facility that allows a dependent child to reside with his or her parent. The fact that the parent is enrolled in a certified substance abuse treatment facility shall not be, for that reason alone, prima facie evidence of detriment. The failure of the parent or legal guardian to participate regularly and make substantive progress in court-ordered treatment programs shall be prima facie evidence that return would be detrimental. In making its determination, the court shall review and consider the social worker's report and recommendations and the report and recommendations of any child advocate appointed pursuant to Section 356.5; and shall consider the efforts or progress, or both, demonstrated by the parent or legal guardian and the extent to which he or she availed himself or herself of services provided, taking into account the particular barriers to a minor parent or a nonminor dependent parent, or an incarcerated, institutionalized, detained, or deported parent's or legal guardian's access to those court-mandated services and ability to maintain contact with his or her child.

(2) Regardless of whether the child is returned to a parent or legal guardian, the court shall specify the factual basis for its conclusion that the return would be detrimental or would not be detrimental. The court also shall make appropriate findings pursuant to subdivision (a) of Section 366; and, when relevant, shall order any additional services reasonably believed to facilitate the return of the child to the custody of his or her parent or legal guardian. The court shall also inform the parent or legal guardian that if the child cannot be returned home by the 12–month permanency hearing, a proceeding pursuant to Section 366.26 may be instituted. This section does not apply in a case in which, pursuant to Section 361.5, the court has ordered that reunification services shall not be provided.

(3) If the child was under three years of age on the date of the initial removal, or is a member of a sibling group described in subparagraph (C) of paragraph (1) of subdivision (a) of Section 361.5, and the court finds by clear and convincing evidence that the parent failed to participate regularly and make substantive progress in a court-ordered treatment plan, the court may schedule a hearing pursuant to Section 366.26 within 120 days. If, however, the court finds there is a substantial probability that the child, who was under three years of age on the date of initial removal or is a member of a sibling group described in subparagraph (C) of paragraph (1) of subdivision (a) of Section 361.5, may be returned to his or her parent or legal guardian within six months or that reasonable services have not been provided, the court shall continue the case to the 12–month permanency hearing.

(4) For the purpose of placing and maintaining a sibling group together in a permanent home, the court, in making its determination to schedule a hearing pursuant to Section 366.26 for some or all members of a sibling group, as described in subparagraph (C) of paragraph (1) of subdivision (a) of Section 361.5, shall review and consider the social worker's report and recommendations. Factors the report shall address, and the court shall consider, may include, but need not be limited to, whether the sibling group was removed from parental care as a group, the closeness and strength of the sibling bond, the ages of the siblings, the appropriateness of maintaining the sibling group together, the detriment to the child if sibling ties are not maintained, the likelihood of finding a permanent home for the sibling group, whether the sibling group is currently placed together in a preadoptive home or has a concurrent plan goal of legal permanency in the same home, the wishes of each child whose age and physical and emotional condition permits a meaningful response, and the best interests of each child in the sibling group. The court shall specify the factual basis for its finding that it is in the best interests of each child to schedule a hearing pursuant to Section 366.26 within 120 days for some or all of the members of the sibling group.

(5) If the child was removed initially under subdivision (g) of Section 300 and the court finds by clear and convincing evidence that the whereabouts of the parent are still unknown, or the parent has failed to contact and visit the child, the court may schedule a hearing pursuant to Section 366.26 within 120 days. The court shall take into account any particular barriers to a parent's ability to maintain contact with his or her child due to the parent's incarceration, institutionalization, detention by the United States Department of Homeland Security, or deportation. If the court finds by clear and convincing evidence that the parent has been convicted of a felony indicating parental unfitness, the court may schedule a hearing pursuant to Section 366.26 within 120 days.

(6) If the child had been placed under court supervision with a previously noncustodial parent pursuant to Section 361.2, the court shall determine whether supervision is still necessary. The court may terminate supervision and transfer permanent custody to that parent, as provided for by paragraph (1) of subdivision (b) of Section 361.2.

(7) In all other cases, the court shall direct that any reunification services previously ordered shall continue to be offered to the parent or legal guardian pursuant to the time periods set forth in subdivision (a) of Section 361.5, provided that the court may modify the terms and conditions of those services.

(8) If the child is not returned to his or her parent or legal guardian, the court shall determine whether reasonable services that were designed to aid the parent or legal guardian in overcoming the problems that led to the initial removal and the continued custody of the child have been provided or offered to the parent or legal guardian. The court shall order that those services be initiated, continued, or terminated.

(f)(1) The permanency hearing shall be held no later than 12 months after the date the child entered foster care, as that date is determined pursuant to Section 361.49. At the permanency hearing, the court shall determine the permanent plan for the child, which shall include a determination of whether the child will be returned to the child's home and, if so, when, within the time limits of subdivision (a) of Section 361.5. After considering the relevant and admissible evidence, the court shall order the return of the child to the physical custody of his or her parent or legal guardian unless the court finds, by a preponderance of the evidence, that the return of the child to his or her parent or legal guardian would create a substantial risk of detriment to the safety, protection, or physical or emotional well-being of the child. The social worker shall have the burden of establishing that detriment.

(A) At the permanency hearing, the court shall consider the criminal history, obtained pursuant to paragraph (1) of subdivision (f) of Section 16504.5, of the parent or legal guardian subsequent to the child's removal to the extent that the criminal record is substantially related to the welfare of the child or the parent's or legal guardian's ability to exercise custody and control regarding his or her child, provided that the parent or legal guardian agreed to submit fingerprint images to obtain criminal history information as part of the case plan. The court shall also determine whether reasonable services that were designed to aid the parent or legal guardian to overcome the problems that led to the initial removal and continued custody of the child have been provided or offered to the parent or legal guardian.

(B) The court shall also consider whether the child can be returned to the custody of his or her parent who is enrolled in a certified substance abuse treatment facility that allows a dependent child to reside with his or her parent. The fact that the parent is enrolled in a certified substance abuse treatment facility shall not be, for that reason alone, prima facie evidence of detriment. The failure of the parent or legal guardian to participate regularly and make substantive progress in court-ordered treatment programs shall be prima facie evidence that return would be detrimental.

(C) In making its determination, the court shall review and consider the social worker's report and recommendations and the report and recommendations of any child advocate appointed pursuant to Section 356.5, shall consider the efforts or progress, or both, demonstrated by the parent or legal guardian and the extent to which he or she availed himself or herself of services provided, taking into account the particular barriers to a minor parent or a nonminor dependent parent, or an incarcerated, institutionalized, detained, or deported parent's or legal guardian's access to those court-mandated services and ability to maintain contact with his or her child, and shall make appropriate findings pursuant to subdivision (a) of Section 366.

(D) For each youth 16 years of age and older, the court shall also determine whether services have been made available to assist him or her in making the transition from foster care to successful adulthood.

(2) Regardless of whether the child is returned to his or her parent or legal guardian, the court shall specify the factual basis for its decision. If the child is not returned to a parent or legal guardian, the court shall specify the factual basis for its conclusion that the return would be detrimental. The court also shall make a finding pursuant to subdivision (a) of Section 366. If the child is not returned to his or her parent or legal guardian, the court shall consider, and state for the record, in-state and out-of-state placement options. If the child is placed out of the state, the court shall make a determination whether the out-of-state placement continues to be appropriate and in the best interests of the child.

(g) If the time period in which the court-ordered services were provided has met or exceeded the time period set forth in subparagraph (A), (B), or (C) of paragraph (1) of subdivision (a) of Section 361.5, as appropriate, and a child is not returned to the custody of a parent or legal guardian at the permanency hearing held pursuant to subdivision (f), the court shall do one of the following:

(1) Continue the case for up to six months for a permanency review hearing, provided that the hearing shall occur within 18 months of the date the child was originally taken from the physical custody of his or her parent or legal guardian. The court shall continue the case only if it finds that there is a substantial probability that the child will be returned to the physical custody of his or her parent or legal guardian and safely maintained in the home within the extended period of time or that reasonable services have not been provided to the parent or legal guardian. For * * * purposes of this section, in order to find a substantial probability that the child will be returned to the physical custody of his or her parent or legal guardian and safely maintained in the home within the extended period of time, the court shall be required to find all of the following:

(A) That the parent or legal guardian has consistently and regularly contacted and visited with the child.

(B) That the parent or legal guardian has made significant progress in resolving problems that led to the child's removal from the home.

(C) The parent or legal guardian has demonstrated the capacity and ability both to complete the objectives of his or her treatment plan and to provide for the child's safety, protection, physical and emotional well-being, and special needs.

(i) For purposes of this subdivision, the court's decision to continue the case based on a finding or substantial probability that the child will be returned to the physical custody of his or her parent or legal guardian is a compelling reason for determining that a hearing held pursuant to Section 366.26 is not in the best interests of the child.

(ii) The court shall inform the parent or legal guardian that if the child cannot be returned home by the next permanency review hearing, a proceeding pursuant to Section 366.26 may be instituted. The court shall not order that a hearing pursuant to Section 366.26 be held unless there is clear and convincing evidence that reasonable services have been provided or offered to the parent or legal guardian.

(2) Continue the case for up to six months for a permanency review hearing, provided that the hearing shall occur within 18 months of the date the child was originally taken from the physical custody of his or her parent or legal guardian, if the parent has been arrested and issued an

immigration hold, detained by the United States Department of Homeland Security, or deported to his or her country of origin, and the court determines either that there is a substantial probability that the child will be returned to the physical custody of his or her parent or legal guardian and safely maintained in the home within the extended period of time or that reasonable services have not been provided to the parent or legal guardian.

(3) For purposes of paragraph (2), in order to find a substantial probability that the child will be returned to the physical custody of his or her parent or legal guardian and safely maintained in the home within the extended period of time, the court shall find all of the following:

(A) The parent or legal guardian has consistently and regularly contacted and visited with the child, taking into account any particular barriers to a parent's ability to maintain contact with his or her child due to the parent's arrest and receipt of an immigration hold, detention by the United States Department of Homeland Security, or deportation.

(B) The parent or legal guardian has made significant progress in resolving the problems that led to the child's removal from the home.

(C) The parent or legal guardian has demonstrated the capacity or ability both to complete the objectives of his or her treatment plan and to provide for the child's safety, protection, physical and emotional well-being, and special needs.

(4) Order that a hearing be held within 120 days, pursuant to Section 366.26, but only if the court does not continue the case to the permanency planning review hearing and there is clear and convincing evidence that reasonable services have been provided or offered to the parents or legal guardians. On and after January 1, 2012, a hearing pursuant to Section 366.26 shall not be ordered if the child is a nonminor dependent, unless the nonminor dependent is an Indian child and tribal customary adoption is recommended as the permanent plan.

(5) Order that the child remain in foster care, but only if the court finds by clear and convincing evidence, based upon the evidence already presented to it, including a recommendation by the State Department of Social Services when it is acting as an adoption agency or by a county adoption agency, that there is a compelling reason for determining that a hearing held pursuant to Section 366.26 is not in the best interests of the child because the child is not a proper subject for adoption and has no one willing to accept legal guardianship as of the hearing date. For purposes of this section, a recommendation by the State Department of Social Services when it is acting as an adoption agency or by a county adoption agency that adoption is not in the best interests of the child shall constitute a compelling reason for the court's determination. That recommendation shall be based on the present circumstances of the child and shall not preclude a different recommendation at a later date if the child's circumstances change. On and after January 1, 2012, the nonminor dependent's legal status as an adult is in and of itself a compelling reason not to hold a hearing pursuant to Section 366.26. The court may order that a nonminor dependent who otherwise is eligible pursuant to Section 11403 remain in a planned, permanent living arrangement.

(A) The court shall make factual findings identifying any barriers to achieving the permanent plan as of the hearing date. When the child is under 16 years of age, the court shall order a permanent plan of return home, adoption, tribal customary adoption in the case of an Indian child, legal guardianship, or placement with a fit and willing relative, as appropriate. When the child is 16 years of age or older, or is a nonminor dependent, and no other permanent plan is appropriate at the time of the hearing, the court may order another planned permanent living arrangement, as described in paragraph (2) of subdivision (i) of Section 16501.

(B) If the court orders that a child who is 10 years of age or older remain in foster care, the court shall determine whether the agency has made reasonable efforts to maintain the child's relationships with individuals other than the child's siblings who are important to the child, consistent with the child's best interests, and may make any appropriate order to ensure that those relationships are maintained.

(C) If the child is not returned to his or her parent or legal guardian, the court shall consider, and state for the record, in-state and out-of-state options for permanent placement. If the child is placed out of the state, the court shall make a determination whether the out-of-state placement continues to be appropriate and in the best interests of the child.

(h) In any case in which the court orders that a hearing pursuant to Section 366.26 shall be held, it shall also order the termination of reunification services to the parent or legal guardian. The court shall continue to permit the parent or legal guardian to visit the child pending the hearing unless it finds that visitation would be detrimental to the child. The court shall make any other appropriate orders to enable the child to maintain relationships with individuals, other than the child's siblings, who are important to the child, consistent with the child's best interests. When the court orders a termination of reunification services to the parent or legal guardian, it shall also order that the child's caregiver receive the child's birth certificate in accordance with Sections 16010.4 and 16010.5. Additionally, when the court orders a termination of reunification services to the parent or legal guardian, it shall order, when appropriate, that a child who is 16 years of age or older receive his or her birth certificate.

(i)(1) Whenever a court orders that a hearing pursuant to Section 366.26, including, when, in consultation with the child's tribe, tribal customary adoption is recommended, shall be held, it shall direct the agency supervising the child and the county adoption agency, or the State Department of Social Services when it is acting as an adoption agency, to prepare an assessment that shall include:

(A) Current search efforts for an absent parent or parents or legal guardians.

(B) A review of the amount of and nature of any contact between the child and his or her parents or legal guardians and other members of his or her extended family since the time of placement. Although the extended family of each child shall be reviewed on a case-by-case basis, "extended family" for the purpose of this subparagraph shall include, but not be limited to, the child's siblings, grandparents, aunts, and uncles.

(C)(i) An evaluation of the child's medical, developmental, scholastic, mental, and emotional status.

(ii) The evaluation pursuant to clause (i) shall include, but is not limited to, providing a copy of the complete health and education summary as required under Section 16010, including the name and contact information of the person or persons currently holding the right to make educational decisions for the child.

(iii) In instances where it is determined that disclosure pursuant to clause (ii) of the contact information of the person or persons currently holding the right to make educational decisions for the child poses a threat to the health and safety of that individual or those individuals, that contact information shall be redacted or withheld from the evaluation.

(D) A preliminary assessment of the eligibility and commitment of any identified prospective adoptive parent or legal guardian, including the prospective tribal customary adoptive parent, particularly the caretaker, to include a social history including screening for criminal records and prior referrals for child abuse or neglect, the capability to meet the child's needs, and the understanding of the legal and financial rights and responsibilities of adoption and guardianship. If a proposed guardian is a relative of the minor, the assessment shall also consider, but need not be limited to, all of the factors specified in subdivision (a) of Section 361.3 and in Section 361.4.

(E) The relationship of the child to any identified prospective adoptive parent or legal guardian, the duration and character of the relationship, the degree of attachment of the child to the prospective relative guardian or adoptive parent, the relative's or adoptive parent's strong commitment to caring permanently for the child, the motivation for seeking adoption or guardianship, a statement from the child concerning placement and the adoption or guardianship, and whether the child, if over 12 years of age, has been consulted about the proposed relative guardianship arrangements, unless the child's age or physical, emotional, or other condition precludes his or her meaningful response, and if so, a description of the condition.

(F) A description of efforts to be made to identify a prospective adoptive parent or legal guardian, including, but not limited to, child-specific recruitment and listing on an adoption exchange within the state or out of the state.

(G) An analysis of the likelihood that the child will be adopted if parental rights are terminated.

(H) In the case of an Indian child, in addition to subparagraphs (A) to (G), inclusive, an assessment of the likelihood that the child will be adopted, when, in consultation with the child's tribe, a tribal customary adoption, as defined in Section 366.24, is recommended. If tribal customary adoption is recommended, the assessment shall include an analysis of both of the following:

(i) Whether tribal customary adoption would or would not be detrimental to the Indian child and the reasons for reaching that conclusion.

(ii) Whether the Indian child cannot or should not be returned to the home of the Indian parent or Indian custodian and the reasons for reaching that conclusion.

(2)(A) A relative caregiver's preference for legal guardianship over adoption, if it is due to circumstances that do not include an unwillingness to accept legal or financial responsibility for the child, shall not constitute the sole basis for recommending removal of the child from the relative caregiver for purposes of adoptive placement.

(B) Regardless of his or her immigration status, a relative caregiver shall be given information regarding the permanency options of guardianship and adoption, including the long-term benefits and consequences of each option, prior to establishing legal guardianship or pursuing adoption. If the proposed permanent plan is guardianship with an approved relative caregiver for a minor eligible for aid under the Kin–GAP Program, as provided for in Article 4.7 (commencing with Section 11385) of Chapter 2 of Part 3 of Division 9, the relative caregiver shall be informed about the terms and conditions of the negotiated agreement pursuant to Section 11387 and shall agree to its execution prior to the hearing held pursuant to Section 366.26. A copy of the executed negotiated agreement shall be attached to the assessment.

(j) If, at any hearing held pursuant to Section 366.26, a guardianship is established for the minor with an approved relative caregiver, and juvenile court dependency is subsequently dismissed, the minor shall be eligible for aid under the Kin–GAP Program, as provided for in Article 4.5 (commencing with Section 11360) or Article 4.7 (commencing with Section 11385), as applicable, of Chapter 2 of Part 3 of Division 9.

(k) As used in this section, "relative" means an adult who is related to the minor by blood, adoption, or affinity within the fifth degree of kinship, including stepparents, stepsiblings, and all relatives whose status is preceded by the words "great," "great-great," or "grand," or the spouse of any of those persons even if the marriage was terminated by death or dissolution. If the proposed permanent plan is guardianship with an approved relative caregiver for a minor eligible for aid under the Kin–GAP Program, as provided for in Article 4.7 (commencing with Section 11385) of Chapter 2 of Part 3 of Division 9, "relative" as used in this section has the same meaning as "relative" as defined in subdivision (c) of Section 11391.

(*l*) For purposes of this section, evidence of any of the following circumstances shall not, in and of itself, be deemed a failure to provide or offer reasonable services:

(1) The child has been placed with a foster family that is eligible to adopt a child, or has been placed in a preadoptive home.

(2) The case plan includes services to make and finalize a permanent placement for the child if efforts to reunify fail.

(3) Services to make and finalize a permanent placement for the child, if efforts to reunify fail, are provided concurrently with services to reunify the family. *(Added by Stats. 1995, c. 540 (A.B.1523), § 3, operative Jan. 1, 1999. Amended by Stats.1996, c. 1028 (A.B.3088), § 2, operative Jan. 1, 1999; Stats.1996, c. 1082 (A.B.2679), § 4, operative Jan. 1, 1999; Stats.1996, c. 1083 (A.B.1524), § 4, operative Jan. 1, 1999; Stats.1996, c. 1084 (S.B.1516), § 7.9, operative Jan. 1, 1999; Stats.1997, c. 17 (S.B.947), § 149, operative Jan. 1, 1999; Stats.1997, c. 793 (A.B.1544), § 21, operative Jan. 1, 1999; Stats.1998, c. 1054 (A.B.1091), § 33, operative Jan. 1, 1999;*

Stats.1998, c. 1055 (S.B.1901), § 3; Stats.1998, c. 1056 (A.B.2773), § 15.1; Stats.1999, c. 399 (S.B.1226), § 2; Stats. 1999, c. 805 (A.B.740), § 2.2; Stats.2000, c. 108 (A.B.2876), § 19, eff. July 10, 2000; Stats.2000, c. 910 (A.B.2921), § 9; Stats.2001, c. 747 (A.B.705), § 2; Stats.2002, c. 416 (S.B. 1956), § 10; Stats.2002, c. 918 (A.B.1694), § 9; Stats.2003, c. 558 (A.B.579), § 8; Stats.2003, c. 813 (A.B.408), § 5.5; Stats.2004, c. 810 (A.B.2807), § 3; Stats.2004, c. 811 (A.B. 3079), § 14.5; Stats.2005, c. 22 (S.B.1108), § 214; Stats.2005, c. 640 (A.B.1412), § 4; Stats.2006, c. 75 (A.B.1808), § 26, eff. July 12, 2006; Stats.2006, c. 389 (S.B.1667), § 2; Stats.2006, c. 726 (A.B.1774), § 3, eff. Sept. 29, 2006; Stats.2006, c. 726 (A.B.1774), § 3.5, eff. Sept. 29, 2006, operative Jan. 1, 2007; Stats.2007, c. 177 (S.B.84), § 14, eff. Aug. 24, 2007; Stats. 2007, c. 565 (A.B.298), § 2; Stats.2007, c. 583 (S.B.703), § 26.5; Stats.2008, c. 482 (A.B.2070), § 2; Stats.2009, c. 120 (A.B.706), § 3, eff. Aug. 6, 2009; Stats.2009, c. 287 (A.B. 1325), § 8, operative July 1, 2010; Stats.2010, c. 559 (A.B.12), § 16; Stats.2011, c. 59 (A.B.791), § 3; Stats.2012, c. 162 (S.B.1171), § 188; Stats.2012, c. 35 (S.B.1013), § 50, eff. June 27, 2012; Stats.2012, c. 208 (A.B.2292), § 1; Stats.2012, c. 845 (S.B.1064), § 10; Stats.2012, c. 846 (A.B.1712), § 19.3; Stats. 2013, c. 76 (A.B.383), § 200; Stats.2014, c. 219 (S.B.977), § 6, eff. Jan. 1, 2015; Stats.2015, c. 284 (S.B.68), § 1, eff. Jan. 1, 2016; Stats.2015, c. 425 (S.B.794), § 10.5, eff. Jan. 1, 2016; Stats.2016, c. 86 (S.B.1171), § 311, eff. Jan. 1, 2017; Stats. 2017, c. 319 (A.B.976), § 133, eff. Jan. 1, 2018; Stats.2017, c. 829 (S.B.233), § 7.5, eff. Jan. 1, 2018.)

Commentary

Although section 361.5(a)(1) allows a juvenile court to order reunification services of up to 12 months when a child is three years of age or older, the court, under subsection (e) of this section, has discretion at a six-month review hearing to terminate those services when a parent is unable or unwilling to benefit from additional reunification services. *In re Derrick S., 156 Cal.App.4th 436, 67 Cal.Rptr.3d 367 (2007)*.

Fabian L. v. Superior Court of Orange County, 214 Cal.App.4th 1018, Cal.Rptr.3d (2013), affirmed an order terminating an incarcerated father's reunification services despite his compliance with his case plan, because the needed reunification services were unavailable and there was no substantial probability that the child would be returned to the father within six months.

In re Jesse W., 157 Cal.App.4th 49, 68 Cal.Rptr.3d 435 (2007), review denied, holds that at a six-month review hearing involving children under the age of three, the juvenile court has discretion under subsection (e) to terminate reunification services for one parent while continuing reunification services for the other parent, even though the court does not set a selection and implementation hearing under section 366.26.

For discussion of subsection (e) failure "to contact and visit the child," see *In re Tameka M., 33 Cal.App.4th 1747, 40 Cal.Rptr.2d 64 (1995)*, (mother's "contact" with child at paternity testing was not sufficient to upset trial court finding, for purposes of termination hearing, that she failed "to contact and visit" child for six months).

In determining, under subsection (e), whether there was a substantial probability that dependent children would be returned to their mother's care by the time of the 12–month review hearing, *Tonya M. v. Superior Court, 42 Cal.4th 836, 69 Cal.Rptr.3d 96, 172 P.3d 402 (2007)*, held that at a delayed six-month hearing, the juvenile court should consider the likelihood of reunification within the less-than-six months remaining until the 12–month hearing, rather than within the six months following the delayed six-month review hearing.

In re Christina A., 91 Cal.App.4th 1153, 111 Cal.Rptr.2d 310 (2001), holds that when a dependent child under the age of three has been removed from parental custody and reunification services have been ordered, Welfare and Institutions Code §§ 361.5(a)(2), 366(a), and 366.21(e) require that a status review hearing be set within six months from the date of the jurisdictional hearing, rather than six months from the date of the dispositional hearing.

Daria D. v. Superior Court, 61 Cal.App.4th 606, 71 Cal.Rptr.2d 668 (1998), sustains the constitutionality of the subsection (e) paragraph allowing termination of parental rights after six months of reunification services when the minor was under the age of three years on the date of initial removal. To the same effect, see *Armando D. v. Superior Court, 71 Cal.App.4th 1011, 99 Cal.Rptr.2d 189 (1999), review denied June 16, 1999* (interpreting a prior version of subsection (a) and concluding that when dependent child was under the age of three on the date of detention, the juvenile court could terminate parent's reunification services after six months upon finding that there is no substantial probability that the child will be reunified with the parent within eighteen months). Compare *Miguel V. v. Superior Court*, depublished by the California Supreme Court when it denied review on September 15, 1999. In *Miguel V.*, the depublished opinion of the Court of Appeal, 85 Cal.Rptr.2d 923 (1999), concluded that under the current version of the statute, at a six-month review hearing for children who were under the age of three at the time of removal, an incarcerated parent's reunification services could not be terminated absent substantial evidence of his noncompliance with the reunification plan because the current statute requires 12 months of reunification services when a parent does comply with the reunification plan, regardless of the likelihood of reunification at the end of the 12–month period.

In re Janee W, 140 Cal.App.4th 1444, 45 Cal.Rptr.3d 445 (2006), held that when dependent children are removed from a custodial parent's home and legal and physical custody is awarded to the other parent, once the juvenile court determines that further supervision of the children is no longer necessary, it may terminate its jurisdiction even though the original custodial parent has not been provided reunification services.

When a child was removed from his mother, who was arrested for child endangerment, and placed with his previously noncustodial father, *In re Maya L. 232 Cal.App.4th 81, 180 Cal.Rptr.3d 426 (2014)*, affirmed a juvenile court order entered at a six-month review hearing, which terminated jurisdiction and gave the father physical and legal custody of the child, holding that subsection (e) does not require that the child be returned to the mother unless the Department of Child and Family Services establishes that doing so would create a substantial risk of harm to the child's physical or emotional well-being.

In *Sara M. v Superior Court, 36 Cal.4th 998, 116 P.3d 550, 32 Cal.Rptr.3d 89 (2005)*, the California Supreme Court sustained California Rules of Court, Rule 1460(f)(1)(B), which, interpreting subsection (e) of this section, allows the juvenile court to terminate reunification services when a parent has failed to visit or contact a dependent child for six months following the commencement of reunification services.

Interpreting subsection (e) and Section 361.5(a) together, *In re Aryanna C., 132 Cal.App.4th 1234, 34 Cal.Rptr.3d 288 (2005), review denied*, held that the juvenile court has discretion to terminate reunification services at any time. In *Aryanna C.*, the juvenile court ended reunification services three months after the children entered foster care because the father missed virtually all scheduled visits with the children, missed scheduled assessments, tested positive for illicit drugs, and at the time of the hearing was in custody pending trial on burglary and other charges.

In re Alanna A, 135 Cal.App.4th 555, 37 Cal.Rptr.3d 579 (2005), holds that a juvenile court has discretion at a 12–month review hearing to terminate one parent's reunification services and continue the other parent's reunification services to an 18–month review hearing. In *Alanna A.*, the parent whose services were terminated did not use those services and did not visit the child for most of the 12–month reunification period, while the parent whose services were continued consistently visited the child and made progress in resolving problems.

Interpreting subsection (g), *Los Angeles County Department of Children and Family Services v. Superior Court, 60 Cal.App.4th 1088, 70 Cal.Rptr.2d 658 (1998),* held that a juvenile court order extending reunification services beyond 18 months exceeded the court's statutory jurisdiction, which limits services to an 18–month period and, additionally, constituted an abuse of discretion because the parent made no showing that he would be able to complete the treatment programs required for the child's return within the extended period.i

Tracy J. v. Superior Court, 202 Cal.App.4th 1415, 136 Cal.Rptr.3d 505 (2012), held that a juvenile court erred in terminating reunification services for developmentally disabled parents when substantial evidence did not support the court's conclusion that reasonable services had been offered, and that services must be tailored to the particular needs of the family.

In re K.C., 212 Cal.App.4th 323, 151 Cal.Rptr.3d 161 (2012), reversed an order terminating a father's reunification services because the Department of Children and Family Services did not obtain a psychotropic medication evaluation recommended by a psychological evaluation, when the psychological evaluation indicated that mental health issues were the cause of father's loss of custody.

Applying subsection (g)(1), *In re Amanda H. v. Superior Court, 166 Cal.App.4th 1340, 83 Cal.Rptr.3d 229 (2008)*, held that the juvenile court erred in terminating reunification services after 12 months when the Department of Children and Family Services did not prove by clear and convincing evidence that reasonable reunification services had been provided to the parent. Specifically, the social worker incorrectly informed the parent that she had enrolled in all court-ordered programs when she was not in fact enrolled in a court-required domestic violence program.

A juvenile court has discretion to continue reunification services for an incarcerated parent even though the three criteria of subsection (g) are not satisfied. *S.T. v. Superior Court, 177 Cal. App.4th 1009, 99 Cal.Rptr.3d 412 (2009)*.

With respect to subsection (h), see *In re Cicely L., 28 Cal.App.4th 1697, 34 Cal.Rptr.2d 345 (1994)* (juvenile court orders terminating an imprisoned father's reunification services were appealable orders that, having become final, could not be challenged on appeal from a subsequent order terminating the father's parental rights). Compare *In re Isaiah W., 1 Cal.5th 1, 373 P.3d 444, 203 Cal.Rptr.3d 633 (2016)*, holding that a mother's failure to appeal from an order in which the court found that the Indian Child Welfare Act was inapplicable, did not preclude her from challenging a subsequent order terminating her parental rights on the ground that the court had reason to know the child was an Indian child but did not order the Department to comply with the Act's notice requirements. Noting that the juvenile court has a continuing duty to inquire about the child's Indian status, the California Supreme Court concluded that the juvenile court had to duty to inquire at the proceeding to terminate parental rights. In *Isaiah W.*, the supreme court explicitly overruled *In re Pedro N., 35 Cal.App.4th 183, 41 Cal.Rptr.2d 819 (1995)*, which did not treat the Act's notice requirements as imposing a continuing duty on courts in legal proceedings.

For discussion of subsection (i)(5) statements "from the minor concerning placement," see *In re Cody S., 56 Cal.App.4th 230, 65 Cal.Rptr.2d 22 (1997)* (adoption assessment explanation that 4–year-old child is too young to make a meaningful statement about adoption is sufficient to satisfy subsection (i)(5)).

Research References

Forms

West's California Judicial Council Forms JV-280, Notice Of Review Hearing.

West's California Judicial Council Forms JV-290, Caregiver Information Form.

West's California Judicial Council Forms JV-426, Findings and Orders After In-Home Status Review Hearing--Child Placed With Previously Noncustodial Parent (Welf. & Inst. Code, §§ 364, 366.21).

West's California Judicial Council Forms JV-430, Findings and Orders After Six-Month Prepermanency Hearing (Welf. & Inst. Code, S361.21(E)).

West's California Judicial Council Forms JV-431, Six-Month Prepermanency Attachment: Child Reunified (Welf. & Inst. Code, S361.21(E)).

West's California Judicial Council Forms JV-432, Six-Month Prepermanency Attachment: Reunification Services Continued (Welf. & Inst. Code, S366.21(E)).

West's California Judicial Council Forms JV-433, Six-Month Prepermanency Attachment: Reunification Services Terminated (Welf. & Inst. Code, S366.21(E)).

West's California Judicial Council Forms JV-435, Findings and Orders After 12-Month Permanency Hearing (Welf. & Inst. Code, S366.21(F)).

West's California Judicial Council Forms JV-436, Twelve-Month Permanency Attachment: Child Reunified (Welf. & Inst. Code, S366.21(F)).

West's California Judicial Council Forms JV-437, Twelve-Month Permanency Attachment: Reunification Services Continued (Welf. & Inst. Code, S366.21(F)).

West's California Judicial Council Forms JV-438, Twelve-Month Permanency Attachment: Reunification Services Terminated (Welf. & Inst. Code, S366.21(F)).

West's California Judicial Council Forms JV-290-INFO, Instruction Sheet for Caregiver Information Form.

Treatises and Practice Aids

Witkin, California Summary 10th Parent and Child § 4, Public Welfare Services.

Witkin, California Summary 10th Parent and Child § 12, Parental or Marital Rights Of Prisoners.

Witkin, California Summary 10th Parent and Child § 483, Juvenile Court Proceedings.

Witkin, California Summary 10th Parent and Child § 576, in General.

Witkin, California Summary 10th Parent and Child § 585, in General.

Witkin, California Summary 10th Parent and Child § 637, Priority Right Of Noncustodial Parent.

Witkin, California Summary 10th Parent and Child § 642, in General.

Witkin, California Summary 10th Parent and Child § 643, Duration Of Services.

Witkin, California Summary 10th Parent and Child § 662, Nature and Purpose.

Witkin, California Summary 10th Parent and Child § 664, in General.

Witkin, California Summary 10th Parent and Child § 669, in General.

Witkin, California Summary 10th Parent and Child § 670, Notice Of Hearing.

Witkin, California Summary 10th Parent and Child § 671, Supplemental Report.

Witkin, California Summary 10th Parent and Child § 673, Child in Foster Care.

Witkin, California Summary 10th Parent and Child § 674, Return Of Child.

Witkin, California Summary 10th Parent and Child § 675, Reunification Services.

Witkin, California Summary 10th Parent and Child § 676, in General.

Witkin, California Summary 10th Parent and Child § 677, Scheduling Selection and Implementation Hearing.

Witkin, California Summary 10th Parent and Child § 678, Twelve-Month Review.
Witkin, California Summary 10th Parent and Child § 679, Eighteen-Month Review.
Witkin, California Summary 10th Parent and Child § 682, Preliminary Assessment.
Witkin, California Summary 10th Parent and Child § 686, Alternative Dispositions.
Witkin, California Summary 10th Parent and Child § 687, Termination Of Parental Rights to Free Child for Adoption.
Witkin, California Summary 10th Parent and Child § 695, Legal Guardianship.
Witkin, California Summary 10th Parent and Child § 696, Continuing Jurisdiction.
Witkin, California Summary 10th Parent and Child § 697, Status Review Hearings.
Witkin, California Summary 10th Parent and Child § 707, Treatment Of Appeal as Writ Petition.
Witkin, California Summary 10th Parent and Child § 712, Notice Of Appeal.
Witkin, California Summary 10th Parent and Child § 897, Reunification Services.
Witkin, California Summary 10th Parent and Child § 452F, (New) Termination Of Jurisdiction Over Nonminor.
Witkin, California Summary 10th Parent and Child § 669A, (New) Review Hearings Just Before and After Minor Attains Age 18.
Witkin, California Summary 10th Parent and Child § 675A, (New) Setting Selection and Implementation Hearing.
Witkin, California Summary 10th Parent and Child § 679A, (New) Twenty-Four Month Review.
Witkin, California Summary 10th Parent and Child § 688A, (New) Tribal Customary Adoption.
Witkin, California Summary 10th Parent and Child § 699A, (New) in General.

§ 366.215. Six month review hearing; consideration of parental incarceration, institutionalization, detention by Department of Homeland Security or deportation

With respect to a hearing held pursuant to subdivision (e) of Section 366.21, if the child in question was under three years of age on the date of the initial removal, or is a member of a sibling group described in subparagraph (C) of paragraph (1) of subdivision (a) of Section 361.5, the court, in determining whether to schedule a hearing pursuant to Section 366.26, shall take into account any particular barriers to a parent's ability to maintain contact with his or her child due to the parent's incarceration, institutionalization, detention by the United States Department of Homeland Security, or deportation. *(Added by Stats.2009, c. 339 (S.B.597), § 3. Amended by Stats.2012, c. 845 (S.B.1064), § 11.)*

Research References

Treatises and Practice Aids

Witkin, California Summary 10th Parent and Child § 677, Scheduling Selection and Implementation Hearing.

§ 366.22. Permanency review hearing; return of child to parent or guardian; decision not to return child; hearing; assessment by agency supervising the child and the adoption agency

(a)(1) When a case has been continued pursuant to paragraph (1) or (2) of subdivision (g) of Section 366.21, the permanency review hearing shall occur within 18 months after the date the child was originally removed from the physical custody of his or her parent or legal guardian. After considering the admissible and relevant evidence, the court shall order the return of the child to the physical custody of his or her parent or legal guardian unless the court finds, by a preponderance of the evidence, that the return of the child to his or her parent or legal guardian would create a substantial risk of detriment to the safety, protection, or physical or emotional well-being of the child. The social worker shall have the burden of establishing that detriment. At the permanency review hearing, the court shall consider the criminal history, obtained pursuant to paragraph (1) of subdivision (f) of Section 16504.5, of the parent or legal guardian subsequent to the child's removal, to the extent that the criminal record is substantially related to the welfare of the child or the parent's or legal guardian's ability to exercise custody and control regarding his or her child, provided that the parent or legal guardian agreed to submit fingerprint images to obtain criminal history information as part of the case plan. The court shall also consider whether the child can be returned to the custody of his or her parent who is enrolled in a certified substance abuse treatment facility that allows a dependent child to reside with his or her parent. The fact that the parent is enrolled in a certified substance abuse treatment facility shall not be, for that reason alone, prima facie evidence of detriment. The failure of the parent or legal guardian to participate regularly and make substantive progress in court-ordered treatment programs shall be prima facie evidence that return would be detrimental. In making its determination, the court shall review and consider the social worker's report and recommendations and the report and recommendations of any child advocate appointed pursuant to Section 356.5; shall consider the efforts or progress, or both, demonstrated by the parent or legal guardian and the extent to which he or she availed himself or herself of services provided, taking into account the particular barriers of a minor parent or a nonminor dependent parent, or an incarcerated or institutionalized parent's or legal guardian's access to those court-mandated services and ability to maintain contact with his or her child; and shall make appropriate findings pursuant to subdivision (a) of Section 366.

(2) Whether or not the child is returned to his or her parent or legal guardian, the court shall specify the factual basis for its decision. If the child is not returned to a parent or legal guardian, the court shall specify the factual basis for its conclusion that return would be detrimental. If the child is not returned to his or her parent or legal guardian, the court shall consider, and state for the record, in-state and out-of-state options for the child's permanent placement. If the child is placed out of the state, the court shall make a determination whether the out-of-state placement continues to be appropriate and in the best interests of the child.

(3) Unless the conditions in subdivision (b) are met and the child is not returned to a parent or legal guardian at the permanency review hearing, the court shall order that a hearing be held pursuant to Section 366.26 in order to determine whether adoption, or, in the case of an Indian child, in consultation with the child's tribe, tribal customary adoption, guardianship, or continued placement in foster care is the most appropriate plan for the child. On and after January 1, 2012, a hearing pursuant to Section 366.26 shall not be ordered if the child is a nonminor dependent, unless

the nonminor dependent is an Indian child, and tribal customary adoption is recommended as the permanent plan. However, if the court finds by clear and convincing evidence, based on the evidence already presented to it, including a recommendation by the State Department of Social Services when it is acting as an adoption agency or by a county adoption agency, that there is a compelling reason, as described in paragraph (5) of subdivision (g) of Section 366.21, for determining that a hearing held under Section 366.26 is not in the best interests of the child because the child is not a proper subject for adoption and has no one willing to accept legal guardianship as of the hearing date, the court may, only under these circumstances, order that the child remain in foster care with a permanent plan of return home, adoption, tribal customary adoption in the case of an Indian child, legal guardianship, or placement with a fit and willing relative, as appropriate. If the child is 16 years of age or older or is a nonminor dependent, and no other permanent plan is appropriate at the time of the hearing, the court may order another planned permanent living arrangement, as described in paragraph (2) of subdivision (i) of Section 16501. The court shall make factual findings identifying any barriers to achieving the permanent plan as of the hearing date. On and after January 1, 2012, the nonminor dependent's legal status as an adult is in and of itself a compelling reason not to hold a hearing pursuant to Section 366.26. The court may order that a nonminor dependent who otherwise is eligible pursuant to Section 11403 remain in a planned, permanent living arrangement. If the court orders that a child who is 10 years of age or older remain in foster care, the court shall determine whether the agency has made reasonable efforts to maintain the child's relationships with individuals other than the child's siblings who are important to the child, consistent with the child's best interests, and may make any appropriate order to ensure that those relationships are maintained. The hearing shall be held no later than 120 days from the date of the permanency review hearing. The court shall also order termination of reunification services to the parent or legal guardian. The court shall continue to permit the parent or legal guardian to visit the child unless it finds that visitation would be detrimental to the child. The court shall determine whether reasonable services have been offered or provided to the parent or legal guardian. For purposes of this subdivision, evidence of any of the following circumstances shall not, in and of themselves, be deemed a failure to provide or offer reasonable services:

(A) The child has been placed with a foster family that is eligible to adopt a child, or has been placed in a preadoptive home.

(B) The case plan includes services to make and finalize a permanent placement for the child if efforts to reunify fail.

(C) Services to make and finalize a permanent placement for the child, if efforts to reunify fail, are provided concurrently with services to reunify the family.

(b) If the child is not returned to a parent or legal guardian at the permanency review hearing and the court determines by clear and convincing evidence that the best interests of the child would be met by the provision of additional reunification services to a parent or legal guardian who is making significant and consistent progress in a court-ordered residential substance abuse treatment program, a parent who was either a minor parent or a nonminor dependent parent at the time of the initial hearing making significant and consistent progress in establishing a safe home for the child's return, or a parent recently discharged from incarceration, institutionalization, or the custody of the United States Department of Homeland Security and making significant and consistent progress in establishing a safe home for the child's return, the court may continue the case for up to six months for a subsequent permanency review hearing, provided that the hearing shall occur within 24 months of the date the child was originally taken from the physical custody of his or her parent or legal guardian. The court shall continue the case only if it finds that there is a substantial probability that the child will be returned to the physical custody of his or her parent or legal guardian and safely maintained in the home within the extended period of time or that reasonable services have not been provided to the parent or legal guardian. For the purposes of this section, in order to find a substantial probability that the child will be returned to the physical custody of his or her parent or legal guardian and safely maintained in the home within the extended period of time, the court shall be required to find all of the following:

(1) That the parent or legal guardian has consistently and regularly contacted and visited with the child.

(2) That the parent or legal guardian has made significant and consistent progress in the prior 18 months in resolving problems that led to the child's removal from the home.

(3)(A) The parent or legal guardian has demonstrated the capacity and ability both to complete the objectives of his or her substance abuse treatment plan as evidenced by reports from a substance abuse provider as applicable, or complete a treatment plan postdischarge from incarceration, institutionalization, or detention, or following deportation to his or her country of origin and his or her return to the United States, and to provide for the child's safety, protection, physical and emotional well-being, and special needs.

(B) For purposes of this subdivision, the court's decision to continue the case based on a finding or substantial probability that the child will be returned to the physical custody of his or her parent or legal guardian is a compelling reason for determining that a hearing held pursuant to Section 366.26 is not in the best interests of the child.

(C) The court shall inform the parent or legal guardian that if the child cannot be returned home by the subsequent permanency review hearing, a proceeding pursuant to Section 366.26 may be instituted. The court shall not order that a hearing pursuant to Section 366.26 be held unless there is clear and convincing evidence that reasonable services have been provided or offered to the parent or legal guardian.

(c)(1) Whenever a court orders that a hearing pursuant to Section 366.26, including when a tribal customary adoption is recommended, shall be held, it shall direct the agency supervising the child and the county adoption agency, or the State Department of Social Services when it is acting as an adoption agency, to prepare an assessment that shall include:

(A) Current search efforts for an absent parent or parents.

(B) A review of the amount of and nature of any contact between the child and his or her parents and other members of his or her extended family since the time of placement. Although the extended family of each child shall be reviewed on a case-by-case basis, "extended family" for the purposes of this subparagraph shall include, but not be limited to, the child's siblings, grandparents, aunts, and uncles.

(C)(i) An evaluation of the child's medical, developmental, scholastic, mental, and emotional status.

(ii) The evaluation pursuant to clause (i) shall include, but is not limited to, providing a copy of the complete health and education summary as required under Section 16010, including the name and contact information of the person or persons currently holding the right to make educational decisions for the child.

(iii) In instances where it is determined that disclosure pursuant to clause (ii) of the contact information of the person or persons currently holding the right to make educational decisions for the child poses a threat to the health and safety of that individual or those individuals, that contact information shall be redacted or withheld from the evaluation.

(D) A preliminary assessment of the eligibility and commitment of any identified prospective adoptive parent or legal guardian, particularly the caretaker, to include a social history including screening for criminal records and prior referrals for child abuse or neglect, the capability to meet the child's needs, and the understanding of the legal and financial rights and responsibilities of adoption and guardianship. If a proposed legal guardian is a relative of the minor, the assessment shall also consider, but need not be limited to, all of the factors specified in subdivision (a) of Section 361.3 and Section 361.4.

(E) The relationship of the child to any identified prospective adoptive parent or legal guardian, the duration and character of the relationship, the degree of attachment of the child to the prospective relative guardian or adoptive parent, the relative's or adoptive parent's strong commitment to caring permanently for the child, the motivation for seeking adoption or legal guardianship, a statement from the child concerning placement and the adoption or legal guardianship, and whether the child, if over 12 years of age, has been consulted about the proposed relative guardianship arrangements, unless the child's age or physical, emotional, or other condition precludes his or her meaningful response, and if so, a description of the condition.

(F) An analysis of the likelihood that the child will be adopted if parental rights are terminated.

(G) In the case of an Indian child, in addition to subparagraphs (A) to (F), inclusive, an assessment of the likelihood that the child will be adopted, when, in consultation with the child's tribe, a tribal customary adoption, as defined in Section 366.24, is recommended. If tribal customary adoption is recommended, the assessment shall include an analysis of both of the following:

(i) Whether tribal customary adoption would or would not be detrimental to the Indian child and the reasons for reaching that conclusion.

(ii) Whether the Indian child cannot or should not be returned to the home of the Indian parent or Indian custodian and the reasons for reaching that conclusion.

(2)(A) A relative caregiver's preference for legal guardianship over adoption, if it is due to circumstances that do not include an unwillingness to accept legal or financial responsibility for the child, shall not constitute the sole basis for recommending removal of the child from the relative caregiver for purposes of adoptive placement.

(B) Regardless of his or her immigration status, a relative caregiver shall be given information regarding the permanency options of guardianship and adoption, including the long-term benefits and consequences of each option, prior to establishing legal guardianship or pursuing adoption. If the proposed permanent plan is guardianship with an approved relative caregiver for a minor eligible for aid under the Kin–GAP Program, as provided for in Article 4.7 (commencing with Section 11385) of Chapter 2 of Part 3 of Division 9, the relative caregiver shall be informed about the terms and conditions of the negotiated agreement pursuant to Section 11387 and shall agree to its execution prior to the hearing held pursuant to Section 366.26. A copy of the executed negotiated agreement shall be attached to the assessment.

(d) This section shall become operative January 1, 1999. If at any hearing held pursuant to Section 366.26, a legal guardianship is established for the minor with an approved relative caregiver, and juvenile court dependency is subsequently dismissed, the minor shall be eligible for aid under the Kin–GAP Program, as provided for in Article 4.5 (commencing with Section 11360) or Article 4.7 (commencing with Section 11385), as applicable, of Chapter 2 of Part 3 of Division 9.

(e) As used in this section, "relative" means an adult who is related to the child by blood, adoption, or affinity within the fifth degree of kinship, including stepparents, stepsiblings, and all relatives whose status is preceded by the words "great," "great-great," or "grand," or the spouse of any of those persons even if the marriage was terminated by death or dissolution. If the proposed permanent plan is guardianship with an approved relative caregiver for a minor eligible for aid under the Kin–GAP Program, as provided for in Article 4.7 (commencing with Section 11385) of Chapter 2 of Part 3 of Division 9, "relative" as used in this section has the same meaning as "relative" as defined in subdivision (c) of Section 11391. *(Added by Stats.1995, c. 540 (A.B.1523), § 5, operative Jan. 1, 1999. Amended by Stats.1996, c. 1028 (A.B.3088), § 4; Stats.1996, c. 1084 (S.B.1516), § 9, operative Jan. 1, 1999; Stats.1997, c. 793 (A.B.1544), § 23, operative Jan. 1, 1999; Stats.1998, c. 1054 (A.B.1091), § 34, operative Jan. 1, 1999; Stats.1998, c. 1055 (S.B.1901), § 4; Stats.1998, c. 1056 (A.B.2773), § 16.1, operative Jan. 1, 1999; Stats.1999, c. 399 (S.B.1226), § 3; Stats.2000, c. 108 (A.B.2876), § 20, eff. July 10, 2000; Stats.2000, c. 910 (A.B.2921), § 10; Stats.2003, c. 813 (A.B.408), § 6; Stats.2004, c. 810 (A.B.2807), § 4; Stats.2005, c. 640 (A.B.1412), § 5; Stats.2006, c. 75 (A.B.1808), § 27, eff. July 12, 2006; Stats.2006, c. 726 (A.B.1774), § 4, eff. Sept. 29, 2006; Stats.2007, c. 177 (S.B.84), § 15, eff. Aug. 24, 2007; Stats.2007, c. 565 (A.B.298), § 3; Stats.2007, c. 583 (S.B.703), § 27.5; Stats.2008, c. 482 (A.B.2070), § 3; Stats.2009, c. 287 (A.B.1325), § 10, operative July 1, 2010; Stats.2010, c. 559 (A.B.12), § 18; Stats.2012, c. 35 (S.B.1013), § 52, eff. June 27, 2012; Stats.2012, c. 208 (A.B.2292), § 2; Stats.2012, c. 845 (S.B.1064), § 12; Stats.2012, c. 846 (A.B.1712), § 20.3; Stats.2013, c. 76 (A.B.383), § 201; Stats.2014, c. 219 (S.B.977), § 7, eff. Jan. 1, 2015; Stats.2015, c. 284 (S.B.68), § 2, eff. Jan. 1, 2016; Stats.2015, c. 425 (S.B.794), § 11.5, eff. Jan. 1, 2016; Stats.2017, c. 829 (S.B.233), § 8, eff. Jan. 1, 2018.)*

Commentary

In re Marilyn A., 148 Cal.App.4th 285, 55 Cal.Rptr.3d 647 (2007), held that a juvenile court may return a dependent child to a parent's home at an 18–month dependency hearing, but also continue services and court supervision to ensure the child's safety. *Marilyn A.* relies on the broad discretion conferred on the court by subsection (a) and consequently approves the explicit authorization granted by Cal. Rules of Ct., Rule 5.710(e)(2).

David B. v. Superior Court, 140 Cal.App.4th 772, 44 Cal.Rptr.3d 799 (2006), holds that the parent of a dependent child has a due process right to an 18–month-review hearing and that hearing may not be conditioned on the parent's offer of proof. *David B.* reasons that a parent has a right to a contested hearing and to cross-examine social workers in order to test adverse evidence.

Interpreting subsection (a), *In re Katie V., 130 Cal.App.4th 586, 30 Cal.Rptr.3d 320 (2005)*, holds that at an 18–month review hearing, the standard of proof for finding that reasonable services were offered to the parent or guardian is "preponderance of the evidence," rather than "clear and convincing evidence."

Interpreting subsection (a), *Constance K. v. Superior Court, 61 Cal.App.4th 689, 71 Cal.Rptr.2d 780 (1998), review denied April 29, 1998,* holds that the juvenile court may terminate reunification services at an 18–month hearing despite the parent's compliance with the reunification plan, when there was substantial evidence that return of the children would pose risk to their well-being because of the parent's inadequacies.

Also interpreting subsection (a) and invoking § 300.2, *Jennifer A. v. Superior Court, 117 Cal.App.4th 1322, 12 Cal.Rptr.3d 572 (2004)*, held that the juvenile court's finding, at an 18–month review hearing, that return to their mother would create a substantial risk of detriment to the physical or emotional well-being of children, who had been removed from their mother's home because she once left them alone while she was working, was not supported by evidence of some drug test failures when there was neither evidence that the mother had a clinically significant substance abuse problem nor that her marijuana and alcohol use affected her parenting judgment and skills.

Interpreting subsection (a), *In re Yvonne W., 165 Cal.App.4th 1394, 81 Cal.Rptr.3d 747 (2008)*, held that a juvenile court erred in concluding, at an 18–month review hearing, that a dependent child would be at substantial risk of detriment if returned to the custody of the mother, who lived in stable and appropriate housing at a long-term shelter, when the finding of detriment was based on the child's expressed fear and anxiety about living in shelter housing.

In re Elizabeth R., 35 Cal.App.4th 1774, 42 Cal.Rptr.2d 200 (1995), holds that the juvenile court has discretion to extend reunification services beyond 18 months in order to foster family preservation. In *Elizabeth R.,* the mother had an excellent record of visitation and compliance with the reunification plan; nevertheless, her involuntary hospitalization for mental illness made it impossible to complete reunification within an 18–month period.

Compare *Los Angeles County Department of Children and Family Services v. Superior Court, 60 Cal.App.4th 1088, 70 Cal.Rptr.2d 658 (1998),* which held that a juvenile court order extending reunification services beyond 18 months exceeded the court's statutory jurisdiction, which limits services to an 18–month period and, additionally, constituted an abuse of discretion because the parent made no showing that he would be able to complete the treatment programs required for the child's return within the extended period. *In re Brequia Y., 57 Cal.App.4th 1060, 67 Cal.Rptr.2d 389 (1997),* held that the juvenile court abused its discretion by ordering six months' additional reunification services for a parent with a continuing alcohol problem.

In re Maria S., 60 Cal.App.4th 1309, 71 Cal.Rptr.2d 30 (1997), holds that a father's inability to appear at a permanent plan hearing because of his incarceration in a federal prison does not unconstitutionally deprive him of his right to participate in such hearing. Additionally, the 18–month period is not tolled by a parent's incarceration. For further discussion of *Maria S.*, see Commentary to Penal Code Section 2625.

In re Genesha S., originally reported at 74 Cal.Rptr.2d 481 (1998), held that under pre–1998 law a biological father had no statutory right to notice of a dependency hearing when his identity was neither known nor ascertainable; due process was not violated when he was neither a "presumed" father nor fell within the rule of *Kelsey S.* (See Family Code Section 7611, Commentary.) However, the Supreme Court depublished *Ganesha S.* on July 8, 1998.

In re Urayna L., 75 Cal.App.4th 883, 89 Cal.Rptr.2d 437 (1999), holds that although subsection (b)(2) requires, prior to a § 366.26 hearing, that the Department of Social Services review the amount and nature of any contact between a child and the child's extended family, a parent waives the issue of adequacy of the adoption assessment by failing to challenge it at the parental rights termination proceeding. The parent may not subsequently appeal termination of parental rights on the ground of an assessment to which no objection was made at the termination hearing.

Research References

Forms

West's California Judicial Council Forms JV-280, Notice Of Review Hearing.

West's California Judicial Council Forms JV-440, Findings and Orders After 18-Month Permanency Hearing (Welf. & Inst. Code, S366.22).

West's California Judicial Council Forms JV-441, Eighteen-Month Permanency Attachment: Child Reunified (Welf. & Inst. Code, S366.22).

West's California Judicial Council Forms JV-442, Eighteen-Month Permanency Attachment: Reunification Services Terminated (Welf. & Inst. Code, S366.22).

West's California Judicial Council Forms JV-443, Eighteen-Month Permanency Attachment: Reunification Services Continued (Welf. & Inst. Code, S366.22).

Treatises and Practice Aids

Witkin, California Summary 10th Parent and Child § 4, Public Welfare Services.

Witkin, California Summary 10th Parent and Child § 12, Parental or Marital Rights Of Prisoners.

Witkin, California Summary 10th Parent and Child § 594, in General.

Witkin, California Summary 10th Parent and Child § 643, Duration Of Services.

Witkin, California Summary 10th Parent and Child § 664, in General.

Witkin, California Summary 10th Parent and Child § 669, in General.

Witkin, California Summary 10th Parent and Child § 670, Notice Of Hearing.

Witkin, California Summary 10th Parent and Child § 671, Supplemental Report.

Witkin, California Summary 10th Parent and Child § 673, Child in Foster Care.

Witkin, California Summary 10th Parent and Child § 674, Return Of Child.

Witkin, California Summary 10th Parent and Child § 675, Reunification Services.

Witkin, California Summary 10th Parent and Child § 677, Scheduling Selection and Implementation Hearing.

Witkin, California Summary 10th Parent and Child § 679, Eighteen-Month Review.

Witkin, California Summary 10th Parent and Child § 682, Preliminary Assessment.

Witkin, California Summary 10th Parent and Child § 686, Alternative Dispositions.

Witkin, California Summary 10th Parent and Child § 687, Termination Of Parental Rights to Free Child for Adoption.

Witkin, California Summary 10th Parent and Child § 695, Legal Guardianship.

Witkin, California Summary 10th Parent and Child § 696, Continuing Jurisdiction.

Witkin, California Summary 10th Parent and Child § 697, Status Review Hearings.

Witkin, California Summary 10th Parent and Child § 698, Other Procedures.

Witkin, California Summary 10th Parent and Child § 701, in General.

Witkin, California Summary 10th Parent and Child § 707, Treatment Of Appeal as Writ Petition.

Witkin, California Summary 10th Parent and Child § 897, Reunification Services.

Witkin, California Summary 10th Parent and Child § 452F, (New) Termination Of Jurisdiction Over Nonminor.

Witkin, California Summary 10th Parent and Child § 669A, (New) Review Hearings Just Before and After Minor Attains Age 18.

Witkin, California Summary 10th Parent and Child § 675A, (New) Setting Selection and Implementation Hearing.

Witkin, California Summary 10th Parent and Child § 679A, (New) Twenty-Four Month Review.

Witkin, California Summary 10th Parent and Child § 688A, (New) Tribal Customary Adoption.

Witkin, California Summary 10th Parent and Child § 699A, (New) in General.

§ 366.23. Noncustodial parent seeking placement or custody; notice of right to provide court with input regarding placement of child

If a noncustodial parent is seeking placement or custody of a child, the social worker shall inform the caretaker that he or she has the right to provide the court with input regarding the placement of the child. The social worker shall provide the "Caregiver Information Form" to the caretaker to complete and request that the caregiver provide any particular information the caregiver might have regarding the noncustodial parent now seeking custody. If a report is required or otherwise due, the completed form shall be attached to the social worker's report to be filed with the court. If not, the social worker shall ensure that, if the foster parent completes the form, the completed form is returned to the court for review and consideration before the child is placed with the noncustodial parent. *(Added by Stats.2005, c. 632 (S.B.726), § 3.)*

Research References

Forms

West's California Judicial Council Forms JV-310, Proof Of Service Under Section 366.26 Of the Welfare and Institutions Code.

Treatises and Practice Aids

Witkin, California Summary 10th Parent and Child § 637, Priority Right Of Noncustodial Parent.

Witkin, California Summary 10th Parent and Child § 681, Notice.

Witkin, California Summary 10th Parent and Child § 899, Termination Of Parental Rights.

§ 366.24. Tribal customary adoptions

(a)(1) For purposes of this section, "tribal customary adoption" means adoption by and through the tribal custom, traditions, or law of an Indian child's tribe. Termination of parental rights is not required to effect the tribal customary adoption.

(2) For purposes of this section, "Indian child" also includes a nonminor dependent as described in subdivision (v) of Section 11400, unless the nonminor dependent has elected not to be considered an Indian child pursuant to subdivision (b) of Section 224.1.

(b) Whenever an assessment is ordered pursuant to Section 361.5, 366.21, 366.22, 366.25, or 366.26 for Indian children, the assessment shall address the option of tribal customary adoption.

(c) For purposes of Section 366.26, in the case of tribal customary adoptions, all of the following apply:

(1) The child's tribe or the tribe's designee shall conduct a tribal customary adoptive home study prior to final approval of the tribal customary adoptive placement.

(A) If a tribal designee is conducting the home study, the designee shall do so in consultation with the Indian child's tribe. The designee may include a county adoption agency, the State Department of Social Services when it is acting as an adoption agency, or a California- licensed adoption agency. Any tribal designee must be an entity that is authorized to request a search of the Child Abuse Central Index and, if necessary, a check of any other state's child abuse and neglect registry, and must be an entity that is authorized to request a search for state and federal level criminal offender records information through the Department of Justice.

(B) The standard for the evaluation of the prospective adoptive parents' home shall be the prevailing social and cultural standard of the child's tribe. The home study shall include an evaluation of the background, safety, and health information of the adoptive home, including the biological, psychological, and social factors of the prospective adoptive parent or parents, and an assessment of the commitment, capability, and suitability of the prospective adoptive parent or parents to meet the child's needs.

(2) In all cases, an in-state check of the Child Abuse Central Index and, if necessary, a check of any other state's child abuse and neglect registry shall be conducted. If the tribe chooses a designee to conduct the home study, the designee shall perform a check of the Child Abuse Central Index pursuant to Section 1522.1 of the Health and Safety Code as it applies to prospective adoptive parents and persons over 18 years of age residing in their household. If the tribe conducts its own home study, the agency that has the placement and care responsibility of the child shall perform the check.

(3)(A) In all cases prior to final approval of the tribal customary adoptive placement, a state and federal criminal background check through the Department of Justice shall be conducted on the prospective tribal customary adoptive parents and on persons over 18 years of age residing in their household.

(B) If the tribe chooses a designee to conduct the home study, the designee shall perform the state and federal criminal background check required pursuant to subparagraph (A) through the Department of Justice prior to final approval of the adoptive placement.

(C) If the tribe conducts its own home study, the public adoption agency that is otherwise authorized to obtain criminal background information for the purpose of adoption shall perform the state and federal criminal background check required pursuant to subparagraph (A) through the Department of Justice prior to final approval of the adoptive placement.

(D) An individual who is the subject of a background check conducted pursuant to this paragraph may be provided by the entity performing the background check with a copy of his or her state or federal level criminal offender record information search response as provided to that entity by the Department of Justice if the entity has denied a criminal background clearance based on this information and the individual makes a written request to the entity for a copy specifying an address to which it is to be sent. The state or federal level criminal offender record information search response shall not be modified or altered from its form or content as provided by the Department of Justice and shall be provided to the address specified by the individual in his or her written request. The entity shall retain a copy of the individual's written request and the response and date provided.

(4) If federal or state law provides that tribes may conduct all required background checks for prospective adoptive parents, the tribally administered background checks shall satisfy the requirements of this section, so long as the standards for the background checks are the same as those applied to all other prospective adoptive parents in the State of California.

(5) Under no circumstances shall final approval be granted for an adoptive placement in any home if the prospective adoptive parent or any adult living in the prospective tribal customary adoptive home has any of the following:

(A) A felony conviction for child abuse or neglect, spousal abuse, crimes against a child, including child pornography, or a crime involving violence, including rape, sexual assault, or homicide, but not including other physical assault and battery. For purposes of this subdivision, crimes involving violence means those violent crimes contained in clause (i) of subparagraph (A) and subparagraph (B), or paragraph (1) of, subdivision (g) of Section 1522 of the Health and Safety Code.

(B) A felony conviction that occurred within the last five years for physical assault, battery, or a drug-related offense.

(6) If the tribe identifies tribal customary adoption as the permanent placement plan for the Indian child, the court may continue the selection and implementation hearing governed by Section 366.26 for a period not to exceed 120 days to permit the tribe to complete the process for tribal customary adoption and file with the court a tribal customary adoption order evidencing that a tribal customary adoption has been completed. The tribe shall file with the court the tribal customary adoption order no less than 20 days prior to the date set by the court for the continued selection and implementation hearing. The department shall file with the court the addendum selection and implementation hearing court report no less than seven days prior to the date set by the court for the continued selection and implementation hearing. The court shall have discretion to grant an additional continuance to the tribe for filing a tribal customary adoption order up to, but not exceeding, 60 days. If the child's tribe does not file the tribal customary adoption order within the designated time period, the court shall make new findings and orders pursuant to subdivision (b) of Section 366.26 and this subdivision to determine the best permanent plan for the child.

(7) The child, birth parents, or Indian custodian and the tribal customary adoptive parents and their counsel, if applicable, may present evidence to the tribe regarding the tribal customary adoption and the child's best interest.

(8) Upon the court affording full faith and credit to the tribal customary adoption order and the tribe's approval of the home study, the child shall be eligible for tribal customary adoptive placement. The agency that has placement and care responsibility of the child shall be authorized to make a tribal customary adoptive placement and sign a tribal customary adoptive placement agreement and, thereafter, shall sign the adoption assistance agreement pursuant to subdivision (g) of Section 16120. The prospective adoptive parent or parents desiring to adopt the child may then file the petition for adoption. The agency shall supervise the adoptive placement for a period of six months unless either of the following circumstances exists:

(A) The child to be adopted is a foster child of the prospective adoptive parents whose foster care placement has been supervised by an agency before the signing of the adoptive placement agreement in which case the supervisory period may be shortened by one month for each full month that the child has been in foster care with the family.

(B) The child to be adopted is placed with a relative with whom he or she has an established relationship.

(9) All licensed public adoption agencies shall cooperate with and assist the department in devising a plan that will effectuate the effective and discreet transmission to tribal customary adoptees or prospective tribal customary adoptive parents of pertinent medical information reported to the department or the licensed public adoption agency, upon the request of the person reporting the medical information.

(A) A licensed public adoption agency may not place a child for tribal customary adoption unless a written report on the child's medical background and, if available, the medical background on the child's biological parents, so far as ascertainable, has been submitted to the prospective tribal customary adoptive parents and they have acknowledged in writing the receipt of the report.

(B) The report on the child's background shall contain all known diagnostic information, including current medical reports on the child, psychological evaluations, and scholastic information, as well as all known information regarding the child's developmental history.

(10) The tribal customary adoption order shall include, but not be limited to, a description of (A) the modification of the legal relationship of the birth parents or Indian custodian and the child, including contact, if any, between the child and the birth parents or Indian custodian, responsibilities of the birth parents or Indian custodian, and the rights of inheritance of the child and (B) the child's legal relationship with the tribe. The order shall not include any child support obligation from the birth parents or Indian custodian. There shall be a conclusive presumption that any parental rights or obligations not specified in the tribal customary adoption order shall vest in the tribal customary adoptive parents.

(11) Prior consent to a permanent plan of tribal customary adoption of an Indian child shall not be required of an Indian parent or Indian custodian whose parental relationship to the child will be modified by the tribal customary adoption.

(12) After the prospective adoptive parent or parents desiring to adopt the child have filed the adoption petition, the agency that has placement, care, and responsibility for the child shall submit to the court, a full and final report of the facts of the proposed tribal customary adoption. The requisite elements of the final court report shall be those specified for court reports in the department's regulations governing agency adoptions.

(13) Notwithstanding any other provision of law, after the tribal customary adoption order has been issued and afforded full faith and credit by the state court, supervision of the adoptive placement has been completed, and the state court has issued a final decree of adoption, the tribal customary adoptive parents shall have all of the rights and privileges afforded to, and are subject to all the duties of, any other adoptive parent or parents pursuant to the laws of this state.

(14) Consistent with Section 366.3, after the tribal customary adoption has been afforded full faith and credit and a final adoption decree has been issued, the court shall terminate its jurisdiction over the Indian child.

(15) Nothing in this section is intended to prevent the transfer of those proceedings to a tribal court where transfer is otherwise permitted under applicable law.

(d) The following disclosure provisions shall apply to tribal customary adoptions:

(1) The petition, agreement, order, report to the court from any investigating agency, and any power of attorney filed in a tribal customary adoption proceeding is not open to inspection by any person other than the parties to the proceeding and their attorneys and the department, except upon the written authority of the judge of the juvenile court. A judge may not authorize anyone to inspect the petition, agreement, order, report to the court from any investigating agency, and any power of attorney except in exceptional circumstances and for good cause approaching the necessitous.

(2) Except as otherwise permitted or required by statute, neither the department, county adoption agency, nor any licensed adoption agency shall release information that would identify persons who receive, or have received, tribal customary adoption services. However, employees of the department, county adoption agencies, and licensed adoption agencies shall release to the State Department of Social Services any requested information, including identifying information, for the purpose of recordkeeping and monitoring, evaluation, and regulation of the provision of tribal customary adoption services.

(3) The department, county adoption agency, or licensed adoption agency may, upon written authorization for the release of specified information by the subject of that information, share information regarding a prospective tribal customary adoptive parent or birth parent with other social service agencies, including the department, county adoption agencies, and other licensed adoption agencies, or providers of health care as defined in Section 56.05 of the Civil Code.

(4) Notwithstanding any other law, the department, county adoption agency, or licensed adoption agency may furnish information relating to a tribal customary adoption petition or to a child in the custody of the department or any public adoption agency to the juvenile court, county welfare department, public welfare agency, private welfare agency licensed by the department, provider of foster care services, potential adoptive parents, or provider of health care as defined in Section 56.05 of the Civil Code, if it is believed the child's welfare will be promoted thereby.

(5) The department, county adoption agency, or licensed adoption agency may make tribal customary adoption case records, including identifying information, available for research purposes, provided that the research will not result in the disclosure of the identity of the child or the parties to the tribal customary adoption to anyone other than the entity conducting the research.

(e) This section shall remain operative only to the extent that compliance with its provisions does not conflict with federal law as a condition of receiving funding under Title IV–E or the federal Social Security Act (42 U.S.C. Sec. 670 et seq.).

(f) The Judicial Council shall adopt rules of court and necessary forms required to implement tribal customary adoption as a permanent plan for dependent Indian children. The Judicial Council shall study California's tribal customary adoption provisions and their effects on children, birth parents, adoptive parents, Indian custodians, tribes, and the court, and shall report all of its findings to the Legislature on or before January 1, 2013. The report shall include, but not be limited to, the following:

(1) The number of families served and the number of completed tribal customary adoptions.

(2) The length of time it takes to complete a tribal customary adoption.

(3) The challenges faced by social workers, court, and tribes in completing tribal customary adoptions.

(4) The benefits or detriments to Indian children from a tribal customary adoption. *(Added by Stats.2009, c. 287 (A.B.1325), § 12, operative July 1, 2010. Amended by Stats. 2010, c. 467 (A.B.2417), § 1; Stats.2011, c. 296 (A.B.1023), § 318; Stats.2012, c. 35 (S.B.1013), § 54, eff. June 27, 2012; Stats.2012, c. 846 (A.B.1712), § 21.)*

Research References

Forms

West's California Judicial Council Forms JV-300, Notice Of Hearing on Selection Of a Permanent Plan.

West's California Judicial Council Forms JV-320, Orders Under Welfare and Institutions Code Sections 366.26, 727.3, 727.31.

West's California Judicial Council Forms JV-321, Request for Prospective Adoptive Parent Designation.

West's California Judicial Council Forms JV-327, Prospective Adoptive Parent Designation Order.

West's California Judicial Council Forms ADOPT-200, Adoption Request.

West's California Judicial Council Forms ADOPT-210, Adoption Agreement.

West's California Judicial Council Forms ADOPT-215, Adoption Order.

Treatises and Practice Aids

Witkin, California Summary 10th Parent and Child § 70, Types Of Adoption.

Witkin, California Summary 10th Parent and Child § 494, Records Of Dependent Children.

Witkin, California Summary 10th Parent and Child § 682, Preliminary Assessment.

Witkin, California Summary 10th Parent and Child § 686, Alternative Dispositions.

Witkin, California Summary 10th Parent and Child § 688, Other Alternatives.

Witkin, California Summary 10th Parent and Child § 689, in General.

Witkin, California Summary 10th Parent and Child § 692, in General.

Witkin, California Summary 10th Parent and Child § 693, Termination Of Parental Rights.

Witkin, California Summary 10th Parent and Child § 694, Adoption Proceeding.

Witkin, California Summary 10th Parent and Child § 898, Court Supervision Of Child.

Witkin, California Summary 10th Parent and Child § 899, Termination Of Parental Rights.

Witkin, California Summary 10th Parent and Child § 688A, (New) Tribal Customary Adoption.

§ 366.25. Subsequent permanency review hearing; assessment; Kin–GAP eligibility

(a)(1) When a case has been continued pursuant to subdivision (b) of Section 366.22, the subsequent permanency review hearing shall occur within 24 months after the date the child was originally removed from the physical custody of his or her parent or legal guardian. After considering the relevant and admissible evidence, the court shall order the return of the child to the physical custody of his or her parent or legal guardian unless the court finds, by a preponderance of the evidence, that the return of the child to his or her parent or legal guardian would create a substantial risk of detriment to the safety, protection, or physical or emotional well-being of the child. The social worker shall have the burden of establishing that detriment. At the subsequent permanency review hearing, the court shall consider the criminal history, obtained pursuant to paragraph (1) of subdivision (f) of Section 16504.5, of the parent or legal guardian subsequent to the child's removal to the extent that the criminal record is substantially related to the welfare of the child or parent's or legal guardian's ability to exercise custody and control regarding his or her child provided that the parent or legal guardian agreed to submit fingerprint images to obtain criminal history information as part of the case plan. The court shall also consider whether the child can be returned to the custody of a parent who is enrolled in a certified substance abuse treatment facility that allows a dependent child to reside with his or her parent. The fact that the parent is enrolled in a certified substance abuse treatment facility shall not be, for that reason alone, prima facie evidence of detriment. The failure of the parent or legal guardian to participate regularly and make substantive progress in court-ordered treatment programs shall be prima facie evidence that return would be detrimental. In making its determination, the court shall review and consider the social worker's report and recommendations and the report and recommendations of any child advocate appointed pursuant to Section 356.5; shall consider the efforts or progress, or both, demonstrated by the parent or legal guardian and the extent to which he or she availed himself or herself of services provided; and shall make appropriate findings pursuant to subdivision (a) of Section 366.

(2) Whether or not the child is returned to his or her parent or legal guardian, the court shall specify the factual basis for its decision. If the child is not returned to a parent or legal guardian, the court shall specify the factual basis for its conclusion that return would be detrimental. If the child is not returned to his or her parent or legal guardian, the court shall consider and state for the record, in-state and out-of-state options for the child's permanent placement. If the child is placed out of the state, the court shall make a determination whether the out-of-state placement continues to be appropriate and in the best interests of the child.

(3) If the child is not returned to a parent or legal guardian at the subsequent permanency review hearing, the court shall order that a hearing be held pursuant to Section 366.26 in order to determine whether adoption, or, in the case of an Indian child, tribal customary adoption, guardianship, or, in the case of a child 16 years of age or older when no other permanent plan is appropriate, another planned permanent living arrangement is the most appropriate plan for the child. On and after January 1, 2012, a hearing pursuant to Section 366.26 shall not be ordered if the child is a nonminor dependent, unless the nonminor dependent is an Indian child and tribal customary adoption is recommended as the permanent plan. However, if the court finds by clear and convincing evidence, based on the evidence already presented to it, including a recommendation by the State Department of Social Services when it is acting as an adoption agency or by a county adoption agency, that there is a compelling reason, as described in paragraph (5) of subdivision (g) of Section 366.21, for determining that a hearing held under Section 366.26 is not in the best interest of the child because the child is not a proper subject for adoption or, in the case of an Indian child, tribal customary adoption, and has no one willing to accept legal guardianship as of the hearing date, then the court may, only under these circumstances, order that the child remain in foster care with a permanent plan of return home, adoption, tribal customary adoption in the case of an Indian child, legal guardianship, or placement with a fit and willing relative, as appropriate. If the child is 16 years of age or older or is a nonminor dependent, and no other permanent plan is appropriate at the time of the hearing, the

court may order another planned permanent living arrangement, as described in paragraph (2) of subdivision (i) of Section 16501. The court shall make factual findings identifying any barriers to achieving the permanent plan as of the hearing date. On and after January 1, 2012, the nonminor dependent's legal status as an adult is in and of itself a compelling reason not to hold a hearing pursuant to Section 366.26. The court may order that a nonminor dependent who otherwise is eligible pursuant to Section 11403 remain in a planned, permanent living arrangement. If the court orders that a child who is 10 years of age or older remain in foster care, the court shall determine whether the agency has made reasonable efforts to maintain the child's relationships with individuals other than the child's siblings who are important to the child, consistent with the child's best interests, and may make any appropriate order to ensure that those relationships are maintained. The hearing shall be held no later than 120 days from the date of the subsequent permanency review hearing. The court shall also order termination of reunification services to the parent or legal guardian. The court shall continue to permit the parent or legal guardian to visit the child unless it finds that visitation would be detrimental to the child. The court shall determine whether reasonable services have been offered or provided to the parent or legal guardian. For purposes of this paragraph, evidence of any of the following circumstances shall not, in and of themselves, be deemed a failure to provide or offer reasonable services:

(A) The child has been placed with a foster family that is eligible to adopt a child, or has been placed in a preadoptive home.

(B) The case plan includes services to make and finalize a permanent placement for the child if efforts to reunify fail.

(C) Services to make and finalize a permanent placement for the child, if efforts to reunify fail, are provided concurrently with services to reunify the family.

(b)(1) Whenever a court orders that a hearing pursuant to Section 366.26 shall be held, it shall direct the agency supervising the child and the county adoption agency, or the State Department of Social Services when it is acting as an adoption agency, to prepare an assessment that shall include:

(A) Current search efforts for an absent parent or parents.

(B) A review of the amount of, and nature of, any contact between the child and his or her parents and other members of his or her extended family since the time of placement. Although the extended family of each child shall be reviewed on a case-by-case basis, "extended family" for the purposes of this paragraph shall include, but not be limited to, the child's siblings, grandparents, aunts, and uncles.

(C) An evaluation of the child's medical, developmental, scholastic, mental, and emotional status.

(D) A preliminary assessment of the eligibility and commitment of any identified prospective adoptive parent or legal guardian, including a prospective tribal customary adoptive parent, particularly the caretaker, to include a social history including screening for criminal records and prior referrals for child abuse or neglect, the capability to meet the child's needs, and the understanding of the legal and financial rights and responsibilities of adoption and guardianship. If a proposed legal guardian is a relative of the minor, the assessment shall also consider, but need not be limited to, all of the factors specified in subdivision (a) of Section 361.3 and in Section 361.4.

(E) The relationship of the child to any identified prospective adoptive parent or legal guardian, including a prospective tribal customary adoptive parent, the duration and character of the relationship, the degree of attachment of the child to the prospective relative guardian or adoptive parent, the relative's or adoptive parent's strong commitment to caring permanently for the child, the motivation for seeking adoption or legal guardianship, a statement from the child concerning placement and the adoption or legal guardianship, and whether the child, if over 12 years of age, has been consulted about the proposed relative guardianship arrangements, unless the child's age or physical, emotional, or other condition precludes his or her meaningful response, and if so, a description of the condition.

(F) An analysis of the likelihood that the child will be adopted if parental rights are terminated.

(G) In the case of an Indian child, in addition to subparagraphs (A) to (F), inclusive, an assessment of the likelihood that the child will be adopted, when, in consultation with the child's tribe, a tribal customary adoption, as defined in Section 366.24, is recommended. If tribal customary adoption is recommended, the assessment shall include an analysis of both of the following:

(i) Whether tribal customary adoption would or would not be detrimental to the Indian child and the reasons for reaching that conclusion.

(ii) Whether the Indian child cannot or should not be returned to the home of the Indian parent or Indian custodian and the reasons for reaching that conclusion.

(2)(A) A relative caregiver's preference for legal guardianship over adoption, if it is due to circumstances that do not include an unwillingness to accept legal or financial responsibility for the child, shall not constitute the sole basis for recommending removal of the child from the relative caregiver for purposes of adoptive placement.

(B) Regardless of his or her immigration status, a relative caregiver shall be given information regarding the permanency options of guardianship and adoption, including the long-term benefits and consequences of each option, prior to establishing legal guardianship or pursuing adoption. If the proposed permanent plan is guardianship with an approved relative caregiver for a minor eligible for aid under the Kin–GAP Program, as provided for in Article 4.7 (commencing with Section 11385) of Chapter 2 of Part 3 of Division 9, the relative caregiver shall be informed about the terms and conditions of the negotiated agreement pursuant to Section 11387 and shall agree to its execution prior to the hearing held pursuant to Section 366.26. A copy of the executed negotiated agreement shall be attached to the assessment.

(c) If, at any hearing held pursuant to Section 366.26, a guardianship is established for the minor with an approved relative caregiver, and juvenile court dependency is subsequently dismissed, the minor shall be eligible for aid under the Kin–GAP Program, as provided for in Article 4.5 (commencing with Section 11360) or Article 4.7 (commencing with Section 11385), as applicable, of Chapter 2 of Part 3 of Division 9.

(d) As used in this section, "relative" means an adult who is related to the minor by blood, adoption, or affinity within the fifth degree of kinship, including stepparents, stepsiblings, and all relatives whose status is preceded by the words "great," "great-great," or "grand," or the spouse of any of those persons even if the marriage was terminated by death or dissolution. If the proposed permanent plan is guardianship with an approved relative caregiver for a minor eligible for aid under the Kin–GAP Program, as provided in Article 4.7 (commencing with Section 11385) of Chapter 2 of Part 3 of Division 9, "relative" as used in this section has the same meaning as "relative" as defined in subdivision (c) of Section 11391. *(Added by Stats.2008, c. 482 (A.B.2070), § 4. Amended by Stats.2009, c. 287 (A.B.1325), § 13, operative July 1, 2010; Stats.2010, c. 559 (A.B.12), § 20; Stats.2012, c. 35 (S.B.1013), § 55, eff. June 27, 2012; Stats.2012, c. 208 (A.B.2292), § 3; Stats.2012, c. 845 (S.B.1064), § 13; Stats. 2012, c. 846 (A.B.1712), § 22.3; Stats.2013, c. 76 (A.B.383), § 202; Stats.2014, c. 219 (S.B.977), § 8, eff. Jan. 1, 2015; Stats.2015, c. 425 (S.B.794), § 12, eff. Jan. 1, 2016.)*

Research References

Forms

West's California Judicial Council Forms JV-455, Findings and Orders After 24-Month Permanency Hearing (Welf. & Inst. Code, S366.25).

West's California Judicial Council Forms JV-456, Twenty-Four-Month Permanency Attachment: Child Reunified (Welf. & Inst. Code, S366.25).

West's California Judicial Council Forms JV-457, Twenty-Four-Month Permanency Attachment: Reunification Services Terminated (Welf. & Inst. Code, S366.25).

Treatises and Practice Aids

Witkin, California Summary 10th Parent and Child § 4, Public Welfare Services.

Witkin, California Summary 10th Parent and Child § 12, Parental or Marital Rights Of Prisoners.

Witkin, California Summary 10th Parent and Child § 79, Adoption Information.

Witkin, California Summary 10th Parent and Child § 669, in General.

Witkin, California Summary 10th Parent and Child § 670, Notice Of Hearing.

Witkin, California Summary 10th Parent and Child § 671, Supplemental Report.

Witkin, California Summary 10th Parent and Child § 673, Child in Foster Care.

Witkin, California Summary 10th Parent and Child § 674, Return Of Child.

Witkin, California Summary 10th Parent and Child § 675, Reunification Services.

Witkin, California Summary 10th Parent and Child § 682, Preliminary Assessment.

Witkin, California Summary 10th Parent and Child § 686, Alternative Dispositions.

Witkin, California Summary 10th Parent and Child § 695, Legal Guardianship.

Witkin, California Summary 10th Parent and Child § 696, Continuing Jurisdiction.

Witkin, California Summary 10th Parent and Child § 697, Status Review Hearings.

Witkin, California Summary 10th Parent and Child § 897, Reunification Services.

Witkin, California Summary 10th Parent and Child § 452F, (New) Termination Of Jurisdiction Over Nonminor.

Witkin, California Summary 10th Parent and Child § 669A, (New) Review Hearings Just Before and After Minor Attains Age 18.

Witkin, California Summary 10th Parent and Child § 675A, (New) Setting Selection and Implementation Hearing.

Witkin, California Summary 10th Parent and Child § 679A, (New) Twenty-Four Month Review.

Witkin, California Summary 10th Parent and Child § 688A, (New) Tribal Customary Adoption.

Witkin, California Summary 10th Parent and Child § 699A, (New) in General.

§ 366.26. Hearings terminating parental rights or establishing guardianship of children adjudged dependent children of court

(a) This section applies to children who are adjudged dependent children of the juvenile court pursuant to subdivision (d) of Section 360. The procedures specified * * * in this section are the exclusive procedures for conducting these hearings * * *. The procedures in Part 2 (commencing with Section 3020) of Division 8 of the Family Code are not applicable to these proceedings. Section 8616.5 of the Family Code is applicable and available to all dependent children meeting the requirements of that section, if the postadoption contact agreement has been entered into voluntarily. For children who are adjudged dependent children of the juvenile court pursuant to subdivision (d) of Section 360, this section, and Sections 8604, 8605, 8606, and 8700 of the Family Code and Chapter 5 (commencing with Section 7660) of Part 3 of Division 12 of the Family Code specify the exclusive procedures for permanently terminating parental rights with regard to, or establishing legal guardianship of, the child while the child is a dependent child of the juvenile court.

(b) At the hearing, which shall be held in juvenile court for all children who are dependents of the juvenile court, the court, in order to provide stable, permanent homes for these children, shall review the report as specified in Section 361.5, 366.21, 366.22, or 366.25, shall indicate that the court has read and considered it, shall receive other evidence that the parties may present, and then shall make findings and orders in the following order of preference:

(1) Terminate the rights of the parent or parents and order that the child be placed for adoption and, upon the filing of a petition for adoption in the juvenile court, order that a hearing be set. The court shall proceed with the adoption after the appellate rights of the natural parents have been exhausted.

(2) Order, without termination of parental rights, the plan of tribal customary adoption, as described in Section 366.24, through tribal custom, traditions, or law of the Indian child's tribe, and upon the court affording the tribal customary adoption order full faith and credit at the continued selection and implementation hearing, order that a hearing be set pursuant to paragraph (2) of subdivision (e).

(3) Appoint a relative or relatives with whom the child is currently residing as legal guardian or guardians for the child, and order that letters of guardianship issue.

(4) On making a finding under paragraph (3) of subdivision (c), identify adoption or tribal customary adoption as the permanent placement goal and order that efforts be made to locate an appropriate adoptive family for the child within a period not to exceed 180 days.

(5) Appoint a nonrelative legal guardian for the child and order that letters of guardianship issue.

(6) Order that the child be permanently placed with a fit and willing relative, subject to the periodic review of the juvenile court under Section 366.3.

(7) Order that the child remain in foster care, subject to the conditions described in paragraph (4) of subdivision (c) and the periodic review of the juvenile court under Section 366.3.

In choosing among the * * * alternatives in this subdivision, the court shall proceed pursuant to subdivision (c).

(c)(1) If the court determines, based on the assessment provided as ordered under subdivision (i) of Section 366.21, subdivision (b) of Section 366.22, or subdivision (b) of Section 366.25, and any other relevant evidence, by a clear and convincing standard, that it is likely the child will be adopted, the court shall terminate parental rights and order the child placed for adoption. The fact that the child is not yet placed in a preadoptive home nor with a relative or foster family who is prepared to adopt the child, shall not constitute a basis for the court to conclude that it is not likely the child will be adopted. A finding under subdivision (b) or paragraph (1) of subdivision (e) of Section 361.5 that reunification services shall not be offered, under subdivision (e) of Section 366.21 that the whereabouts of a parent have been unknown for six months or that the parent has failed to visit or contact the child for six months, or that the parent has been convicted of a felony indicating parental unfitness, or, under Section 366.21 or 366.22, that the court has continued to remove the child from the custody of the parent or guardian and has terminated reunification services, shall constitute a sufficient basis for termination of parental rights. Under these circumstances, the court shall terminate parental rights unless either of the following applies:

(A) The child is living with a relative who is unable or unwilling to adopt the child because of circumstances that do not include an unwillingness to accept legal or financial responsibility for the child, but who is willing and capable of providing the child with a stable and permanent environment through legal guardianship, and the removal of the child from the custody of his or her relative would be detrimental to the emotional well-being of the child. For purposes of an Indian child, "relative" shall include an "extended family member," as defined in the federal Indian Child Welfare Act of 1978 (25 U.S.C. Sec. 1903(2)).

(B) The court finds a compelling reason for determining that termination would be detrimental to the child due to one or more of the following circumstances:

(i) The parents have maintained regular visitation and contact with the child and the child would benefit from continuing the relationship.

(ii) A child 12 years of age or older objects to termination of parental rights.

(iii) The child is placed in a residential treatment facility, adoption is unlikely or undesirable, and continuation of parental rights will not prevent finding the child a permanent family placement if the parents cannot resume custody when residential care is no longer needed.

(iv) The child is living with a foster parent or Indian custodian who is unable or unwilling to adopt the child because of exceptional circumstances, that do not include an unwillingness to accept legal or financial responsibility for the child, but who is willing and capable of providing the child with a stable and permanent environment and the removal of the child from the physical custody of his or her foster parent or Indian custodian would be detrimental to the emotional well-being of the child. This clause does not apply to any child who is either (I) under six years of age or (II) a member of a sibling group where at least one child is under six years of age and the siblings are, or should be, permanently placed together.

(v) There would be substantial interference with a child's sibling relationship, taking into consideration the nature and extent of the relationship, including, but not limited to, whether the child was raised with a sibling in the same home, whether the child shared significant common experiences or has existing close and strong bonds with a sibling, and whether ongoing contact is in the child's best interest, including the child's long-term emotional interest, as compared to the benefit of legal permanence through adoption.

(vi) The child is an Indian child and there is a compelling reason for determining that termination of parental rights would not be in the best interest of the child, including, but not limited to:

(I) Termination of parental rights would substantially interfere with the child's connection to his or her tribal community or the child's tribal membership rights.

(II) The child's tribe has identified guardianship, foster care with a fit and willing relative, tribal customary adoption, or another planned permanent living arrangement for the child.

(III) The child is a nonminor dependent, and the nonminor and the nonminor's tribe have identified tribal customary adoption for the nonminor.

(C) For purposes of subparagraph (B), in the case of tribal customary adoptions, Section 366.24 shall apply.

(D) If the court finds that termination of parental rights would be detrimental to the child pursuant to clause (i), (ii), (iii), (iv), (v), or (vi), it shall state its reasons in writing or on the record.

(2) The court shall not terminate parental rights if:

(A) At each hearing at which the court was required to consider reasonable efforts or services, the court has found that reasonable efforts were not made or that reasonable services were not offered or provided.

(B) In the case of an Indian child:

(i) At the hearing terminating parental rights, the court has found that active efforts were not made as required in Section 361.7.

(ii) The court does not make a determination at the hearing terminating parental rights, supported by evidence beyond a reasonable doubt, including testimony of one or more "qualified expert witnesses" as defined in Section 224.6, that the continued custody of the child by the parent is likely to result in serious emotional or physical damage to the child.

(iii) The court has ordered tribal customary adoption pursuant to Section 366.24.

(3) If the court finds that termination of parental rights would not be detrimental to the child pursuant to paragraph (1) and that the child has a probability for adoption but is difficult to place for adoption and there is no identified or available prospective adoptive parent, the court may identify adoption as the permanent placement goal and, without terminating parental rights, order that efforts be made to locate an appropriate adoptive family for the child, within the state or out of the state, within a period not to exceed 180 days. During this 180–day period, the public agency responsible for seeking adoptive parents for each child shall, to the extent possible, ask each child who is 10 years of age or older to identify any individuals, other than the child's siblings, who are important to the child, in order to identify potential adoptive parents. The public agency may ask any other child to provide that information, as appropriate. During the 180–day period, the public agency shall, to the extent possible, contact other private and public adoption agencies regarding the availability of the child for adoption. During the 180–day period, the public agency shall conduct the search for adoptive parents in the same manner as prescribed for children in Sections 8708 and 8709 of the Family Code. At the expiration of this period, another hearing shall be held and the court shall proceed pursuant to paragraph (1), (2), (3), (5), or (6) of subdivision (b). For purposes of this section, a child may only be found to be difficult to place for adoption if there is no identified or available prospective adoptive parent for the child because of the child's membership in a sibling group, or the presence of a diagnosed medical, physical, or mental handicap, or the child is seven years of age or older.

(4)(A) If the court finds that adoption of the child or termination of parental rights is not in the best interest of the child, because one of the conditions in clause (i), (ii), (iii), (iv), (v), or (vi) of subparagraph (B) of paragraph (1) or in paragraph (2) applies, the court shall order that the present caretakers or other appropriate persons shall become legal guardians of the child, or, in the case of an Indian child, consider a tribal customary adoption pursuant to Section 366.24. Legal guardianship shall be considered before continuing the child in foster care under any other permanent plan, if it is in the best interests of the child and if a suitable guardian can be found. If the child continues in foster care, the court shall make factual findings identifying any barriers to achieving adoption, tribal customary adoption in the case of an Indian child, legal guardianship, or placement with a fit and willing relative as of the date of the hearing. A child who is 10 years of age or older, shall be asked to identify any individuals, other than the child's siblings, who are important to the child, in order to identify potential guardians or, in the case of an Indian child, prospective tribal customary adoptive parents. The agency may ask any other child to provide that information, as appropriate.

(B)(i) If the child is living with an approved relative who is willing and capable of providing a stable and permanent environment, but not willing to become a legal guardian as of the hearing date, the court shall order a permanent plan of placement with a fit and willing relative, and the child shall not be removed from the home if the court finds the removal would be seriously detrimental to the emotional well-being of the child because the child has substantial psychological ties to the relative caretaker.

(ii) If the child is living with a nonrelative caregiver who is willing and capable of providing a stable and permanent environment, but not willing to become a legal guardian as of the hearing date, the court shall order that the child remain in foster care with a permanent plan of return home, adoption, legal guardianship, or placement with a fit and willing relative, as appropriate. If the child is 16 years of age or older, or a nonminor dependent, and no other permanent plan is appropriate at the time of the hearing, the court may order another planned permanent living arrangement, as described in paragraph (2) of subdivision (i) of Section 16501. Regardless of the age of the child, the child shall not be removed from the home if the court finds the removal would be seriously detrimental to the emotional well-being of the child because the child has substantial psychological ties to the caregiver.

(iii) If the child is living in a group home or, on or after January 1, 2017, a short-term residential therapeutic program, the court shall order that the child remain in foster care with a permanent plan of return home, adoption, tribal customary adoption in the case of an Indian child, legal guardianship, or placement with a fit and willing relative, as appropriate. If the child is 16 years of age or older, or a nonminor dependent, and no other permanent plan is appropriate at the time of the hearing, the court may order another planned permanent living arrangement, as described in paragraph (2) of subdivision (i) of Section 16501.

(C) The court shall also make an order for visitation with the parents or guardians unless the court finds by a preponderance of the evidence that the visitation would be detrimental to the physical or emotional well-being of the child.

(5) If the court finds that the child should not be placed for adoption, that legal guardianship shall not be established, that placement with a fit and willing relative is not appropriate as of the hearing date, and that there are no suitable foster parents except certified family homes or resource families of a foster family agency available to provide the child with a stable and permanent environment, the court may order the care, custody, and control of the child transferred from the county welfare department to a licensed foster family agency. The court shall consider the written recommendation of the county welfare director regarding the suitability of the transfer. The transfer shall be subject to further court orders.

The licensed foster family agency shall place the child in a suitable licensed or certified family home that has been certified by the agency as meeting licensing standards or with a resource family approved by the agency. The licensed foster family agency shall be responsible for supporting the child and providing appropriate services to the child, including those services ordered by the court. Responsibility for the support of the child shall not, in and of itself, create liability on the part of the foster family agency to third persons injured by the child. Those children whose care, custody, and control are transferred to a foster family agency shall not be eligible for foster care maintenance payments or child welfare services, except for emergency response services pursuant to Section 16504.

(d) The proceeding for the appointment of a guardian for a child who is a dependent of the juvenile court shall be conducted in the juvenile court. If the court finds pursuant to this section that legal guardianship is the appropriate permanent plan, it shall appoint the legal guardian and issue letters of guardianship. The assessment prepared pursuant to subdivision (g) of Section 361.5, subdivision (i) of Section 366.21, subdivision (c) of Section 366.22, and subdivision (b) of Section 366.25 shall be read and considered by the court prior to the appointment, and this shall be reflected in the minutes of the court. The assessment may also include the naming of a prospective successor guardian, if one is identified. In the event of the incapacity or death of the appointed guardian, the named successor guardian may be assessed and appointed pursuant to this section. The person preparing the assessment may be called and examined by any party to the proceeding.

(e)(1) The proceeding for the adoption of a child who is a dependent of the juvenile court shall be conducted in the juvenile court if the court finds pursuant to this section that adoption is the appropriate permanent plan and the petition for adoption is filed in the juvenile court. Upon the filing of a petition for adoption, the juvenile court shall order that an adoption hearing be set. The court shall proceed with the adoption after the appellate rights of the natural parents have been exhausted. The full report required by Section 8715 of the Family Code shall be read and considered by the court prior to the adoption and this shall be reflected in the minutes of the court. The person preparing the report may be called and examined by any party to the proceeding. It is the intent of the Legislature, pursuant to this subdivision, to give potential adoptive parents the option of filing in the juvenile court the petition for the adoption of a child who is a dependent of the juvenile court. Nothing in this section is intended to prevent the filing of a petition for adoption in any other court as permitted by law, instead of in the juvenile court.

(2) In the case of an Indian child, if the Indian child's tribe has elected a permanent plan of tribal customary adoption, the court, upon receiving the tribal customary adoption order will afford the tribal customary adoption order full faith and credit to the same extent that the court would afford full faith and credit to the public acts, records, judicial proceedings, and judgments of any other entity. Upon a determination that the tribal customary adoption order may be afforded full faith and credit, consistent with Section 224.5, the court shall thereafter order a hearing to finalize the adoption be set upon the filing of the adoption petition. The prospective tribal customary adoptive parents and the child who is the subject of the tribal customary adoption petition shall appear before the court for the finalization hearing. The court shall thereafter issue an order of adoption pursuant to Section 366.24.

(3) If a child who is the subject of a finalized tribal customary adoption shows evidence of a developmental disability or mental illness as a result of conditions existing before the tribal customary adoption to the extent that the child cannot be relinquished to a licensed adoption agency on the grounds that the child is considered unadoptable, and of which condition the tribal customary adoptive parent or parents had no knowledge or notice before the entry of the tribal customary adoption order, a petition setting forth those facts may be filed by the tribal customary adoptive parent or parents with the juvenile court that granted the tribal customary adoption petition. If these facts are proved to the satisfaction of the juvenile court, it may make an order setting aside the tribal customary adoption order. The set-aside petition shall be filed within five years of the issuance of the tribal customary adoption order. The court clerk shall immediately notify the child's tribe and the department in Sacramento of the petition within 60 days after the notice of filing of the petition. The department shall file a full report with the court and shall appear before the court for the purpose of representing the child. Whenever a final decree of tribal customary adoption has been vacated or set aside, the child shall be returned to the custody of the county in which the proceeding for tribal customary adoption was finalized. The biological parent or parents of the child may petition for return of custody. The disposition of the child after the court has entered an order to set aside a tribal customary adoption shall include consultation with the child's tribe.

(f) At the beginning of any proceeding pursuant to this section, if the child or the parents are not being represented by previously retained or appointed counsel, the court shall proceed as follows:

(1) In accordance with subdivision (c) of Section 317, if a child before the court is without counsel, the court shall appoint counsel unless the court finds that the child would not benefit from the appointment of counsel. The court shall state on the record its reasons for that finding.

(2) If a parent appears without counsel and is unable to afford counsel, the court shall appoint counsel for the parent, unless this representation is knowingly and intelligently waived. The same counsel shall not be appointed to represent both the child and his or her parent. The public defender or private counsel may be appointed as counsel for the parent.

(3) Private counsel appointed under this section shall receive a reasonable sum for compensation and expenses, the amount of which shall be determined by the court. The amount shall be paid by the real parties in interest, other than the child, in any proportions the court deems just. However, if the court finds that any of the real parties in interest are unable to afford counsel, the amount shall be paid out of the general fund of the county.

(g) The court may continue the proceeding for a period of time not to exceed 30 days as necessary to appoint counsel, and to enable counsel to become acquainted with the case.

(h)(1) At all proceedings under this section, the court shall consider the wishes of the child and shall act in the best interests of the child.

(2) In accordance with Section 349, the child shall be present in court if the child or the child's counsel so requests or the court so orders. If the child is 10 years of age or older and is not present at a hearing held pursuant to this section,

the court shall determine whether the minor was properly notified of his or her right to attend the hearing and inquire as to the reason why the child is not present.

(3)(A) The testimony of the child may be taken in chambers and outside the presence of the child's parent or parents, if the child's parent or parents are represented by counsel, the counsel is present, and any of the following circumstances exist:

(i) The court determines that testimony in chambers is necessary to ensure truthful testimony.

(ii) The child is likely to be intimidated by a formal courtroom setting.

(iii) The child is afraid to testify in front of his or her parent or parents.

(B) After testimony in chambers, the parent or parents of the child may elect to have the court reporter read back the testimony or have the testimony summarized by counsel for the parent or parents.

(C) The testimony of a child also may be taken in chambers and outside the presence of the guardian or guardians of a child under the circumstances specified in this subdivision.

(i)(1) Any order of the court permanently terminating parental rights under this section shall be conclusive and binding upon the child, upon the parent or parents and, upon all other persons who have been served with citation by publication or otherwise as provided in this chapter. After making the order, the juvenile court shall have no power to set aside, change, or modify it, except as provided in paragraph (2), but nothing in this section shall be construed to limit the right to appeal the order.

(2) A tribal customary adoption order evidencing that the Indian child has been the subject of a tribal customary adoption shall be afforded full faith and credit and shall have the same force and effect as an order of adoption authorized by this section. The rights and obligations of the parties as to the matters determined by the Indian child's tribe shall be binding on all parties. A court shall not order compliance with the order absent a finding that the party seeking the enforcement participated, or attempted to participate, in good faith, in family mediation services of the court or dispute resolution through the tribe regarding the conflict, prior to the filing of the enforcement action.

(3) A child who has not been adopted after the passage of at least three years from the date the court terminated parental rights and for whom the court has determined that adoption is no longer the permanent plan may petition the juvenile court to reinstate parental rights pursuant to the procedure prescribed by Section 388. The child may file the petition prior to the expiration of this three-year period if the State Department of Social Services, county adoption agency, or licensed adoption agency that is responsible for custody and supervision of the child as described in subdivision (j) and the child stipulate that the child is no longer likely to be adopted. A child over 12 years of age shall sign the petition in the absence of a showing of good cause as to why the child could not do so. If it appears that the best interests of the child may be promoted by reinstatement of parental rights, the court shall order that a hearing be held and shall give prior notice, or cause prior notice to be given, to the social worker or probation officer and to the child's attorney of record, or, if there is no attorney of record for the child, to the child, and the child's tribe, if applicable, by means prescribed by subdivision (c) of Section 297. The court shall order the child or the social worker or probation officer to give prior notice of the hearing to the child's former parent or parents whose parental rights were terminated in the manner prescribed by subdivision (f) of Section 294 where the recommendation is adoption. The juvenile court shall grant the petition if it finds by clear and convincing evidence that the child is no longer likely to be adopted and that reinstatement of parental rights is in the child's best interest. If the court reinstates parental rights over a child who is under 12 years of age and for whom the new permanent plan will not be reunification with a parent or legal guardian, the court shall specify the factual basis for its findings that it is in the best interest of the child to reinstate parental rights. This subdivision is intended to be retroactive and applies to any child who is under the jurisdiction of the juvenile court at the time of the hearing regardless of the date parental rights were terminated.

(j) If the court, by order or judgment, declares the child free from the custody and control of both parents, or one parent if the other does not have custody and control, or declares the child eligible for tribal customary adoption, the court shall at the same time order the child referred to the State Department of Social Services, county adoption agency, or licensed adoption agency for adoptive placement by the agency. However, except in the case of a tribal customary adoption where there is no termination of parental rights, a petition for adoption may not be granted until the appellate rights of the natural parents have been exhausted. The State Department of Social Services, county adoption agency, or licensed adoption agency shall be responsible for the custody and supervision of the child and shall be entitled to the exclusive care and control of the child at all times until a petition for adoption or tribal customary adoption is granted, except as specified in subdivision (n). With the consent of the agency, the court may appoint a guardian of the child, who shall serve until the child is adopted.

(k)(1) Notwithstanding any other law, the application of any person who, as a relative caretaker or foster parent, has cared for a dependent child for whom the court has approved a permanent plan for adoption, or who has been freed for adoption, shall be given preference with respect to that child over all other applications for adoptive placement if the agency making the placement determines that the child has substantial emotional ties to the relative caretaker or foster parent and removal from the relative caretaker or foster parent would be seriously detrimental to the child's emotional well-being.

(2) As used in this subdivision, "preference" means that the application shall be processed and, if satisfactory, the family study shall be completed before the processing of the application of any other person for the adoptive placement of the child.

(*l*)(1) An order by the court that a hearing pursuant to this section be held is not appealable at any time unless all of the following apply:

(A) A petition for extraordinary writ review was filed in a timely manner.

(B) The petition substantively addressed the specific issues to be challenged and supported that challenge by an adequate record.

(C) The petition for extraordinary writ review was summarily denied or otherwise not decided on the merits.

(2) Failure to file a petition for extraordinary writ review within the period specified by rule, to substantively address the specific issues challenged, or to support that challenge by an adequate record shall preclude subsequent review by appeal of the findings and orders made pursuant to this section.

(3) The Judicial Council shall adopt rules of court, effective January 1, 1995, to ensure all of the following:

(A) A trial court, after issuance of an order directing a hearing pursuant to this section be held, shall advise all parties of the requirement of filing a petition for extraordinary writ review as set forth in this subdivision in order to preserve any right to appeal in these issues.

* * * (i) If a party is present at the time of the making of the order * * *, the notice shall be made orally to the party.

(ii) If the party is not present at the time of * * * making the order, the notice shall be made by the clerk of the court by first-class mail to the last known address of a party or by electronic service pursuant to Section 212.5. If the notice is for a hearing at which the social worker will recommend the termination of parental rights, the notice may be electronically served pursuant to Section 212.5, but only in addition to service of the notice by first-class mail.

(B) The prompt transmittal of the records from the trial court to the appellate court.

(C) That adequate time requirements for counsel and court personnel exist to implement the objective of this subdivision.

(D) That the parent or guardian, or their trial counsel or other counsel, is charged with the responsibility of filing a petition for extraordinary writ relief pursuant to this subdivision.

(4) The intent of this subdivision is to do both of the following:

(A) Make every reasonable attempt to achieve a substantive and meritorious review by the appellate court within the time specified in Sections 366.21, 366.22, and 366.25 for holding a hearing pursuant to this section.

(B) Encourage the appellate court to determine all writ petitions filed pursuant to this subdivision on their merits.

(5) This subdivision shall only apply to cases in which an order to set a hearing pursuant to this section is issued on or after January 1, 1995.

(m) Except for subdivision (j), this section shall also apply to minors adjudged wards pursuant to Section 727.31.

(n)(1) Notwithstanding Section 8704 of the Family Code or any other law, the court, at a hearing held pursuant to this section or anytime thereafter, may designate a current caretaker as a prospective adoptive parent if the child has lived with the caretaker for at least six months, the caretaker currently expresses a commitment to adopt the child, and the caretaker has taken at least one step to facilitate the adoption process. In determining whether to make that designation, the court may take into consideration whether the caretaker is listed in the preliminary assessment prepared by the county department in accordance with subdivision (i) of Section 366.21 as an appropriate person to be considered as an adoptive parent for the child and the recommendation of the State Department of Social Services, county adoption agency, or licensed adoption agency.

(2) For purposes of this subdivision, steps to facilitate the adoption process include, but are not limited to, the following:

(A) Applying for an adoption homestudy.

(B) Cooperating with an adoption homestudy.

(C) Being designated by the court or the adoption agency as the adoptive family.

(D) Requesting de facto parent status.

(E) Signing an adoptive placement agreement.

(F) Engaging in discussions regarding a postadoption contact agreement.

(G) Working to overcome any impediments that have been identified by the State Department of Social Services, county adoption agency, or licensed adoption agency.

(H) Attending classes required of prospective adoptive parents.

(3) Prior to a change in placement and as soon as possible after a decision is made to remove a child from the home of a designated prospective adoptive parent, the agency shall notify the court, the designated prospective adoptive parent or the current caretaker, if that caretaker would have met the threshold criteria to be designated as a prospective adoptive parent pursuant to paragraph (1) on the date of service of this notice, the child's attorney, and the child, if the child is 10 years of age or older, of the proposal in the manner described in Section 16010.6.

(A) Within five court days or seven calendar days, whichever is longer, of the date of notification, the child, the child's attorney, or the designated prospective adoptive parent may file a petition with the court objecting to the proposal to remove the child, or the court, upon its own motion, may set a hearing regarding the proposal. The court may, for good cause, extend the filing period. A caretaker who would have met the threshold criteria to be designated as a prospective adoptive parent pursuant to paragraph (1) on the date of service of the notice of proposed removal of the child may file, together with the petition under this subparagraph, a petition for an order designating the caretaker as a prospective adoptive parent for purposes of this subdivision.

(B) A hearing ordered pursuant to this paragraph shall be held as soon as possible and not later than five court days after the petition is filed with the court or the court sets a hearing upon its own motion, unless the court for good cause is unable to set the matter for hearing five court days after the petition is filed, in which case the court shall set the matter for hearing as soon as possible. At the hearing, the court shall determine whether the caretaker has met the threshold criteria to be designated as a prospective adoptive parent pursuant to paragraph (1), and whether the proposed removal of the child from the home of the designated prospective adoptive parent is in the child's best interest, and the child may not be removed from the home of the designated prospective adoptive parent unless the court finds that removal is in the child's best interest. If the court determines that the caretaker did not meet the threshold criteria to be designated as a prospective adoptive parent on the date of service of the notice of proposed removal of the child, the petition objecting to the proposed removal filed by the caretaker shall be dismissed. If the caretaker was designated as a prospective adoptive parent prior to this hearing, the court shall inquire into any progress made by the caretaker towards the adoption of the child since the caretaker was designated as a prospective adoptive parent.

(C) A determination by the court that the caretaker is a designated prospective adoptive parent pursuant to paragraph (1) or subparagraph (B) does not make the caretaker a party to the dependency proceeding nor does it confer on the caretaker any standing to object to any other action of the department, county adoption agency, or licensed adoption agency, unless the caretaker has been declared a de facto parent by the court prior to the notice of removal served pursuant to paragraph (3).

(D) If a petition objecting to the proposal to remove the child is not filed, and the court, upon its own motion, does not set a hearing, the child may be removed from the home of the designated prospective adoptive parent without a hearing.

(4) Notwithstanding paragraph (3), if the State Department of Social Services, county adoption agency, or licensed adoption agency determines that the child must be removed from the home of the caretaker who is or may be a designated prospective adoptive parent immediately, due to a risk of physical or emotional harm, the agency may remove the child from that home and is not required to provide notice prior to the removal. However, as soon as possible and not longer than two court days after the removal, the agency shall notify the court, the caretaker who is or may be a designated prospective adoptive parent, the child's attorney, and the child, if the child is 10 years of age or older, of the removal. Within five court days or seven calendar days, whichever is longer, of the date of notification of the removal, the child, the child's attorney, or the caretaker who is or may be a designated prospective adoptive parent may petition for, or the court on its own motion may set, a noticed hearing pursuant to paragraph (3). The court may, for good cause, extend the filing period.

(5) Except as provided in subdivision (b) of Section 366.28, an order by the court issued after a hearing pursuant to this subdivision shall not be appealable.

(6) Nothing in this section shall preclude a county child protective services agency from fully investigating and responding to alleged abuse or neglect of a child pursuant to Section 11165.5 of the Penal Code.

(7) The Judicial Council shall prepare forms to facilitate the filing of the petitions described in this subdivision, which shall become effective on January 1, 2006. *(Added by Stats.1995, c. 540 (A.B.1523), § 7, operative Jan. 1, 1999. Amended by Stats.1996, c. 1082 (A.B.2679), § 6, operative Jan. 1, 1999; Stats.1996, c. 1083 (A.B.1524), § 6.5, operative Jan. 1, 1999; Stats.1997, c. 510 (A.B.329), § 4, operative Jan. 1, 1999; Stats.1997, c. 793 (A.B.1544), § 26, operative Jan. 1, 1999; Stats.1998, c. 572 (A.B.2310), § 1, operative Jan. 1, 1999; Stats.1998, c. 1054 (A.B.1091), § 36, operative Jan. 1, 1999; Stats.1998, c. 1056 (A.B.2773), § 17.1; Stats.1999, c. 83 (S.B.966), § 193; Stats.1999, c. 997 (A.B.575), § 3; Stats. 2000, c. 910 (A.B.2921), § 13; Stats.2001, c. 747 (A.B.705), § 3; Stats.2003, c. 813 (A.B.408), § 7; Stats.2004, c. 810 (A.B.2807), § 5; Stats.2005, c. 626 (S.B.218), § 1; Stats.2005, c. 634 (A.B.519), § 2; Stats.2005, c. 640 (A.B.1412), § 6.5; Stats.2006, c. 838 (S.B.678), § 52; Stats.2007, c. 565 (A.B. 298), § 4; Stats.2007, c. 583 (S.B.703), § 28.5; Stats.2008, c. 482 (A.B.2070), § 5; Stats.2009, c. 287 (A.B.1325), § 15, operative July 1, 2010; Stats.2012, c. 35 (S.B.1013), § 57, eff. June 27, 2012; Stats.2012, c. 846 (A.B.1712), § 23; Stats.2015, c. 425 (S.B.794), § 13, eff. Jan. 1, 2016; Stats.2016, c. 612 (A.B.1997), § 75, eff. Jan. 1, 2017; Stats.2017, c. 307 (S.B. 438), § 1, eff. Jan. 1, 2018; Stats.2017, c. 319 (A.B.976), § 134.5, eff. Jan. 1, 2018.)*

Commentary

Applying subsection (n)(1) and (n)(3) of this section, *In re M.M, 235 Cal.App.4th 54, 184 Cal.Rptr.3d 727 (2015)*, held that failure to provide notice to a de facto parent of a hearing that might result in removal of a child from her home deprived her of the opportunity to request designation as a prospective adoptive parent and to be heard on the issue of removal. A de facto parent's possible knowledge that social services was considering other prospective adoptive parents does not satisfy the written notice required under this section.

In re Hunter W., 200 Cal.App.4th 1454, 135 Cal.Rptr.3d 355 (2011), held that a juvenile court abused its discretion when it denied the request of the parents' counsel for a brief two-hour delay to locate a dependent child's parents, who had already checked in at the court's morning calendar call, and thus deprived them of the opportunity to testify before the court denied their petition under section 388 and terminated their parental rights under this section.

When a section 366.26 hearing has been set but has not yet commenced and the dependent child's birth parents voluntarily relinquish the child to a public adoption agency under Family Code section 8700, the relinquishment obviates any need for the hearing and the juvenile court may not make any order that interferes with the parents' unlimited right to voluntarily relinquish the child. *In re R.S., 179 Cal.App.4th 1137, 101 Cal.Rptr.3d 910 (2009)*.

When a court of appeal reversed a juvenile court order denying a mother's petition under section 388, it also necessarily vacated the juvenile court's subsequent hearing and parental rights termination orders under this section. Thus, on remand from the court of appeal, the juvenile court erred in not reinstating the father's as well as the mother's parental rights. *In re A.L., 188 Cal.App.4th 138, 115 Cal.Rptr.3d 560 (2010)*.

In re Gladys L., 141 Cal.App.4th 845, 46 Cal.Rptr.3d 434 (2006), holds that a presumed parent's rights may not be terminated under this section absent clear and convincing evidence that the parent is unfit. In *Gladys L.*, the parent was neither alleged nor proven unfit. To the same effect, see *In re Frank R., 192 Cal.App.4th 532, 121 Cal.Rptr.3d 348 (2011)*; *In re T.G., 215 Cal.App.4th 1, 155 Cal.Rptr.3d 1 (2013)*.

In re G.S.R., 159 Cal.App.4th 1202, 72 Cal.Rptr.3d 398 (2008), held that a juvenile court should not have terminated a presumed father's parental rights on the basis of the father's poverty without making a finding that the father was otherwise an unfit father. *In re P.C., 165 Cal.App.4th 98, 80 Cal.Rptr.3d 595 (2008)*, held that a mother's homelessness, a result of poverty even though she worked steadily, was not a sufficient reason for terminating her parental rights. Her homelessness was attributable to the social services agency's failure to provide reasonable assistance in finding safe, affordable housing, and thus the juvenile court's finding that the agency had provided or offered all reasonable reunification services was not supported by substantial evidence.

In re Baby Boy V., 140 Cal.App.4th 1108, 45 Cal.Rptr.3d 198 (2006), holds that a juvenile court improperly denied a request for a paternity test by a man who came forward as soon as he learned of the existence of a child of whom he believed he was the father (a *Kelsey S.* father entitled to presumed father status; see commentary to Family Code Section 7611) and terminated the man's parental rights in order to free the child for adoption. Moreover, under California Rule of Court 1413 (h), a court juvenile court must grant permission when a man requests a finding of paternity and, upon request, must determine whether a man is a presumed father.

An order terminating parental rights under this section fully severs the parent-child relationship. Therefore, the juvenile court has no authority to order child support from a parent whose rights have been terminated. *County of Ventura v. Gonzalez, 88 Cal.App.4th 1120, 106 Cal.Rptr.2d 461 (2001)*. See also Family Code § 7803.

Under this section, the trial court must order the adoption of an adoptable child if none of the subsection (c) exceptions apply; the court does not otherwise have discretion to choose between adoption and some less permanent alternative, such as guardianship. *In re Jose V., 50 Cal.App.4th 1792, 58 Cal.Rptr.2d 684 (1996), review denied February 19, 1997.*

Resolving a conflict among the courts of appeal, the California Supreme Court held that subsection (c)(3) orders are appealable under Welfare and Institutions Code section 395. *In re S.B., 46 Cal.4th 529, 207 P.3d 525, 94 Cal.Rptr.3d 24 (2009)*.

In the absence of clear and convincing proof that a dependent child is likely to be adopted, parental rights may not be terminated under this section. *In re Heather B., 9 Cal.App.4th 535, 11 Cal.Rptr.2d 891 (1992)*. *In re Yuridia G., 80 Cal.Rptr.2d 921 (1998),* which was depublished by the Supreme Court on April 14, 1999, held that in the case of two orphaned siblings, one of whom had AIDS, before the "parental rights" of the children's aunt, uncle and grandparents, who were willing to adopt the children or become their guardians, could be terminated, subsection (c)(1) clear and convincing evidence that the children will be adopted could only be satisfied by a showing that prospective adoptive parents had been identified and were waiting to adopt the children. Nevertheless, the "preponderance of the evidence" standard is otherwise applicable in a proceeding to terminate parental rights under Section 366.26; and this lesser standard satisfies constitutional requirements. *Cynthia D. v. Superior Court, 5 Cal.4th 242, 19 Cal.Rptr.2d 698 (1993), cert denied sub nom. Dobles v. San Diego Dept. of Social Services, 114 S.Ct. 1221 (1994)*.

In re G.M., 181 Cal.App.4th 552, 105 Cal.Rptr.3d 32 (2010), stated in dictum that evidence of a legal impediment to adoption is relevant and admissible when a social worker's opinion that a child is adoptable is partly based on a prospective adoptive parent's willingness to adopt.

In re Thomas R., 145 Cal.App.4th 726, 51 Cal.Rptr.3d 864 (2006), held that a parent who is a party to a hearing under this section has a due process right to conduct examination and test the sufficiency of the evidence offered by a social services agency on the issue of adoptability.

In re Brian P., 99 Cal.App.4th 616, 1333F, 121 Cal.Rptr.2d 326 (2002), holds that on appeal a parent may challenge the sufficiency of the evidence supporting a juvenile court's finding that a child is adoptable even though the parent did not raise the issue at the juvenile court hearing. In *Brian P.*, the evidence of adoptability was insufficient because it was based solely on the opinion of a social worker.

In re Brandon T., 164 Cal.App.4th 1400, 80 Cal.Rptr.3d 287 (2008), review denied, held that even though a developmentally disabled child was not generally adoptable, the adoptability requirement of this section was satisfied because he was specifically adoptable by his relative caretakers, who were aware of his delays, committed to adopting him, and able to meet his needs.

In re Josue G., 106 Cal.App.4th 725, 131 Cal.Rptr.2d 92 (2003), holds that the juvenile court erred in concluding that a dependent child was not adoptable because of the advanced age of the child's prospective adoptive parents, who were the child's foster parents. Consequently, the court also erred in selecting a legal guardianship by the foster parents. *Josue G.* reasoned that the issue was not whether the foster parents would succeed in adopting the child, but whether the child was adoptable.

In re Zeth S., 31 Cal.4th 396, 2 Cal.Rptr.3d 683, 73 P.3d 541 (2003), holds that an appellate court may not consider postjudgment evidence in order to reverse and remand a judgment terminating parental rights.

For general discussion of the adequacy of reunification services and the standard applied in appellate review of juvenile court orders, see *Angela S. v. Superior Court, 36 Cal.App.4th 758, 42 Cal.Rptr.2d 755 (1995), review denied 7/26/95*.

To satisfy the subsection (c)(1)(B)(i) parental relationship exception to termination of parental rights, it was not sufficient for a mother to show that her son would benefit from a continued relationship with her. She was additionally required to show a "compelling reason" that termination of the relationship would be detrimental to the child. *In re Logan B., 3 Cal.App.5th 1000, 207 Cal.Rptr.3d 837 (2016), review denied*.

For discussion of the subsection (c)(1)(B) "benefit from continuing the relationship" exception to termination of parental rights, see *In re Autumn H., 27 Cal.App.4th 567, 32 Cal.Rptr.2d 535 (1994), review denied 10/27/94* (interpreting subsection (c)(1)(B) to require that the benefit of continuing the relationship with a natural parent outweigh the benefit the child would gain in a permanent home with adoptive parents). Accord *In re Teneka W., 37 Cal.App.4th 721, 43 Cal.Rptr.2d 666 (1995), review denied 11/2/95*. See also *In re Lorenzo C., 54 Cal.App.4th 1330, 63 Cal.Rptr.2d 562 (1997), review denied August 13, 1997* (when there is clear and convincing proof of a child's adoptability, the court must terminate parental rights unless the parent proves that the child would benefit from continuing the parent-child relationship) and *In re Beatrice M., 29 Cal.App.4th 1411, 35 Cal.Rptr.2d 162 (1994), review denied 1/19/95* (subsection (c)(1)(B) provision that parental rights shall not be terminated when termination would be detrimental to the dependent child because child would benefit from regular and continuing relationship with parent has no application when parent has frequent and loving contact with child but does not occupy a parental role). To the same effect, see *In re Jasmine D., 78 Cal.App.4th 1339, 93 Cal.Rptr.2d 644 (2000)* (mother had a "special," rather than a parent-child, relationship with child; when considering a permanent plan for an adoptable child, subsection (c)(1)(B) applies only when the parental relationship serves the child's well-being sufficiently to outweigh the benefit the child would gain in a permanent adoptive home); *In re Angel B., 97 Cal.App.4th 454, 118 Cal.Rptr.2d 482 (2002)* (the subsection (c)(1)(B) exception to termination of parental rights did not apply to the mother because she failed to present evidence that her relationship with her child was sufficiently significant that its termination would cause detriment to the child); *In re Brittany C., 76 Cal.App.4th 847, 90 Cal.Rptr.2d 737 (1999), review denied February 16, 2000* ((c)(1)(B) exception to termination of parental rights with respect to an adoptable child requires showing of a parent-child relationship, as contrasted with one of mere "friendship"); *In re Derek W., 73 Cal.App.4th 823, 86 Cal.Rptr.2d 739 (1999)* (juvenile court properly terminated the father's parental rights when he visited the child but failed to show that he occupied a parental role in the child's life) and *In re Casey D., 70 Cal.App.4th 38, 82 Cal.Rptr.2d 426 (1999)* (juvenile court properly terminated rights of an adoptable child's parents when child and mother had only a "friendly visitor" relationship).

In re Grace P., 8 Cal.App.5th 605, 213 Cal.Rptr.3d 714 (2017), held that a juvenile court abused its discretion in denying a father a contested hearing on the subsection (c)(1)(B)(i) exception when the father had consistently visited his children and offered testimony about the quality of the parent-child relationship and the detriment that would be caused by its termination.

In re Noah G., 247 Cal.App.4th 1292, 203 Cal.Rptr.3d 91 (2016), review denied, held that a trial court did not err in declining to apply the subsection (c)(1)(B)(i) beneficial parent-child relationship exception to a mother who, even though she remained actively engaged in her children's daily care, failed to comply with court-ordered substance abuse and drug testing, when the children's maternal grandmother was willing to adopt the children.

In determining to terminate parental rights despite the parent's strong (c)(1)(B) relationship with her children, the juvenile court erred in considering the likelihood that the adoptive parents would permit the child's mother to visit the children. *In re C.B., 190 Cal.App.4th 102, 117 Cal.Rptr.3d 846 (2010).*

In re Tamika T., 97 Cal.App.4th 1114, 118 Cal.Rptr.2d 873 (2002), review denied July 10, 2002, holds that the juvenile court did not deny a parent due process when it required that the parent make an offer of proof before conducting a contested hearing on whether the parent could satisfy the requirements of subsection (c)(1)(B).

For a case holding that a juvenile court erred in choosing adoption as a permanent plan when the parent-child exception to termination of parental rights (subsection (c)(1)(B)) applied, see *In re Scott B., 188 Cal.App.4th 452, 115 Cal.Rptr.3d 321 (2010).*

In re Brandon C., 71 Cal.App.4th 1530, 84 Cal.Rptr.2d 505 (1999), held that the juvenile court properly selected guardianship by the grandmother as the permanent plan for two adoptable children after it found that the mother had regularly visited the children and they would benefit from a continuing relationship with her. Compare *In re Jasmine T., 73 Cal.App.4th 209, 86 Cal.Rptr.2d 128 (1999),* which held that the juvenile court properly selected adoption by the grandmother, rather than legal guardianship for the grandmother, which was proposed by the child's mother, on the ground that the fact that a prospective adoptive parent is related to a birth parent is not a ground to prefer guardianship to adoption.

Interpreting subsection (c)(1)(B)(vi)(II), *In re T.S., 175 Cal. App.4th 1031, 96 Cal.Rptr.3d 706 (2009),* held that this Indian child exception to adoption applies only if the described circumstances are present and there is a compelling reason that termination of parental rights would be detrimental to the child.

In re D.M., 205 Cal.App.4th 283, 140 Cal.Rptr.3d 311 (2012), held that a child had standing to challenge a trial court's finding that the subsection (c)(1)(B)(v) sibling relationship exception was inapplicable, but did not have standing to challenge the court's finding that his two younger siblings were adoptable.

For guidance on the application of subsection (c)(1)(D), see *In re Fernando M., 138 Cal.App.4th 529, 41 Cal.Rptr.3d 511 (2006)* (juvenile court erred in choosing adoption instead of legal guardianship as permanent plan when parental rights termination would be detrimental to child living in a stable home with his grandmother and siblings and exceptional circumstances justified selection of legal guardianship because adoption would interfere with sibling relationships and grandmother's remarriage).

Once the juvenile court applied subsection (c)(1)(a) and determined that preserving the child's relationship with the mother through twice-yearly visitation was in the child's best interests and appointed as permanent guardian the child's foster father, who was relocating to Ohio, the court was obligated to maintain dependency jurisdiction and hold periodic review hearing to ascertain whether there was regular visitation. *In re K.D., 124 Cal.App.4th 1013, 21 Cal.Rptr.3d 711 (2004).*

In re Raymond E., 97 Cal.App.4th 613, 118 Cal.Rptr.2d 376 (2002), review denied June 12, 2002, holds that subsection (c)(1)(E), which became effective on January 1, 2002, does not apply retroactively to cases in which parental rights have already been terminated by the trial court. Accord, *In re Daniel H., 99 Cal.App.4th 804, 121 Cal.Rptr.2d 475 (2002), review denied.*

In re Earl L., 121 Cal.App.4th 1050, 18 Cal.Rptr.3d 74 (2004), held that a parent's right to due process is not violated when the juvenile court exercises its discretion to require a parent of dependent children to make an offer of proof to identify contested issues before the court schedules a subsection (c)(1)(E) hearing to determine whether that subsection is applicable.

In re Celine R., 31 Cal.4th 45, 1 Cal.Rptr.3d 432, 71 P.3d 787 (2003), held that a juvenile court may reject adoption as a child's permanent plan under subsection (c)(1)(e) only if the court finds that adoption would be detrimental to the child for whom adoption is being considered. *Celine R.* additionally held that the court may appoint a single attorney to represent siblings unless an actual conflict of interest exists or is reasonably likely to arise.

Carroll v. Superior Court, 101 Cal.App.4th 1423, 124 Cal.Rptr.2d 891 (2002), holds that when, pursuant to subsection (c)(1)(E), counsel representing multiple minors considers and advocates against adoption of some of the minors while simultaneously considering and advocating for adoption of other minors, there may be an actual conflict of interest requiring counsel to discontinue representation of each of the minors.

In re Daisy D., 144 Cal.App.4th 287, 50 Cal.Rptr.3d 242 (2006), held that a juvenile court is not required to make a sua sponte determination whether the current subsection (c)(1)(B)(v) exception to adoption, "substantial interference with a child's sibling relationship," applies to a dependent child. A parent forfeits the exception by failing to raise it.

In re J.S., 10 Cal.App.5th 1071, 217 Cal.Rptr.3d 91 (2017), held that a juvenile court violated a mother's due process rights when it prevented the mother, who sought to establish the subsection (c)(1)(B)(v) sibling relationship exception to termination of parental rights, from testifying about the minor's relationship with a sibling who lived with the mother.

In re D.H., 14 Cal.App.5th 719, 222 Cal.Rptr.3d 305 (2017), held that a father's due process rights were violated when, in the course of a dependency action alleging that the child was neglected by his grandparents, who were his legal guardians, the juvenile court terminated the father's parental rights without finding that he was an unfit parent or that awarding him custody would be detrimental to the child.

In re D.O., 247 Cal.App.4th 166, 201 Cal.Rptr.3d 642 (2016), held that the subsection (c)(1)(B)(v) "substantial interference with sibling relationship" exception to adoption did not apply when the child's caregiver demonstrated that she was committed to facilitating the child's continuing relationship with the sibling and had a demonstrated history of having done so.

Once the court has terminated reunification services because of the parent's failure to comply with the reunification plan, the court may properly deny the parent's request for a "bonding study" to show that the children would benefit from a continued parent-child relationship. *In re Richard C., 68 Cal.App.4th 1191, 80 Cal.Rptr.2d 887 (1998), review denied April 14, 1999. Richard C.* reasons that once that the court has determined that the goal of family preservation cannot be realized and has therefore terminated reunification services, the court need not consider whether the children would benefit from a continuing relationship with the parent at a permanency planning hearing; instead the parent has the burden of showing changed circumstances that would justify resumption of reunification services under Section 388.

A minor who demonstrates a close relationship with a sibling may oppose a permanent plan for adoption of that sibling under the current subsection (c)(1)(B)(v) exception. *In re Hector A., 125 Cal.App.4th 783, 23 Cal.Rptr.3d 104 (2005).*

In re I.R., 226 Cal.App.4th 201, 171 Cal.Rptr.3d 469 (2014), held that the juvenile court erred in holding that the sibling exception applied to block an adoption when the dependent child was a toddler and was therefore not yet capable of forming a deep and significant relationship with her older siblings.

In re Valerie A., 139 Cal.App.4th 1519, 43 Cal.Rptr.3d 734 (2006), review denied, holds that a half-sister of two dependent children remains a "sibling" of two dependent children within the meaning of current subsection (c)(1)(B)(v) even when she is adopted by her maternal grandmother. On remand, however, the trial court found that the children's best interests were served by adoption, which was not precluded by the sibling relationship exception to the termination of parental rights. *In re Valerie A., 152 Cal.App.4th 987, 61 Cal.Rptr.3d 403 (2007).*

A father who failed to appeal a juvenile court's termination of his parental rights did not have standing to appeal an order denying a petition by the child's paternal grandparents for placement of the child with them, because the father was not a person aggrieved by the denial. *In re K.C., 52 Cal.4th 231, 128 Cal.Rptr.3d 276, 255 P.3d 953 (2011).*

In re Devin M., 58 Cal.App.4th 1538, 68 Cal.Rptr.2d 666 (1997), review denied December 23, 1997, held that a parent lacks standing to challenge the termination of parental rights on the ground that freeing the child for adoption would result in the termination of the child's relationship with foster parents to whom the child had bonded. *Devin M* reviews the case law limiting a parent's standing to challenge termination of parental rights on grounds that do not affect the parent's own rights but instead involve the rights of siblings or grandparents. Similarly, *In re Caitlin B., 78 Cal.App.4th 1190, 93 Cal.Rptr.2d 480 (2000), review denied May 24, 2000,* holds that the mother of two dependent children lacks standing to challenge an order terminating parental rights on the ground that the children's alleged fathers were not given notice of the proceeding, because her interest was in the continuation of her parental rights, not those of other persons with whom she had no continuing relationship. *In re Frank L., 81 Cal.App.4th 700, 97 Cal.Rptr.2d 88 (2000),* holds that an incarcerated mother lacked standing to challenge an order separating her son from his siblings, because the son's relationship with his siblings was an issue unrelated to the mother's interests; and that the mother also lacked standing to challenge the adequacy of son's counsel on the ground that counsel had a conflict of interest in representing both the son and his siblings, because the alleged conflict did not affect the mother's interests. But compare *In re L. Y. L., 101 Cal.App.4th 942, 124 Cal.Rptr.2d 688 (2002), review denied November 13, 2002,* holding that a mother had standing to assert the current subsection (c)(1)(B)(v) "sibling relationship" exception to termination of parental rights, but concluding that substantial evidence supported the trial court's finding that the benefits of adoption outweighed the benefits of continuing the child's sibling relationship.

In re J.T., 195 Cal.App.4th 707, 124 Cal.Rptr.3d 716 (2011), review denied, held that a child's sibling lacked standing to appeal, on behalf of the child, a parental rights termination order, because the sibling's legal rights were not affected by an order terminating parental rights.

In the case of *In re S.B., 32 Cal.4th 1287, 13 Cal.Rptr.3d 786, 90 P.3d 746 (2004),* the California Supreme Court held that a juvenile court may delegate to a child's legal guardian the decision whether and when to allow parental visitation. Nevertheless, *In re M.R., 132 Cal.App.4th 269, 33 Cal.Rptr.3d 629 (2005), review denied,* held that a juvenile court's order that parent-child visitation would be "supervised and arranged by the legal guardians at their discretion" was an improper delegation of the court's power and duty to decide whether a mother could visit her children. *M.R.* relied on subdivision (c)(4)(C), effective January 1, 2005, which requires the court to "make an order for visitation with the parents or guardians unless the court finds by a preponderance of the evidence that visitation would be detrimental to the physical or emotional well-being of the child."

In re Cicely L., 28 Cal.App.4th 1697, 34 Cal.Rptr.2d 345 (1994), held that juvenile court orders terminating an imprisoned father's reunification services were appealable orders that, having become final, could not be challenged on appeal from a subsequent order terminating the father's parental rights. *In re Meranda P., 56 Cal.App.4th 1143, 65 Cal.Rptr.2d 913 (1997)* (a parent who fails to raise timely claims of ineffective assistance of counsel during earlier dependency proceedings prior to the Section 366.26 termination proceeding cannot raise those claims on appeal from a Section 366.26 order terminating parental rights); and *In re Joshua M., 56 Cal. App.4th 801, 65 Cal.Rptr.2d 748 (1997)* (parent may not claim ineffective assistance of other incarcerated parent's counsel when other parent has not appealed from termination of parental rights). Compare *In re Jasmine S.,* depublished by the California Supreme Court on November 12, 1997. In *Jasmine S.*, the depublished court of appeal opinion, 58 Cal.App.4th 30, 68 Cal.Rptr.2d 24 (1997), purported to hold that where an incarcerated father whose parental rights were terminated had not received any reunification services and the father's attorney failed to seek timely review of the Juvenile Court's order setting a section 366.26 termination hearing, the father was entitled to a new period of reunification services. To similar effect, see *Mark N. v. Superior Court, 60 Cal.App.4th 996, 70 Cal.Rptr.2d 603 (1998)* (holding that the juvenile court may not terminate parental rights at a permanency plan hearing absent substantial evidence that the parent has been provided with reasonable reunification services, relying on Section 366.26 (c)(2)).

In re Isaiah W., Isaiah W., 1 Cal.5th 1, 373 P.3d 444, 203 Cal.Rptr.3d 633 (2016), held that a mother's failure to appeal from an order in which the court found that the Indian Child Welfare Act was inapplicable, did not preclude her from challenging a subsequent order terminating her parental rights on the ground that the court had reason to know the child was an Indian child but did not order the Department to comply with the Act's notice requirements. Noting that the juvenile court has a continuing duty to inquire about the child's Indian status, the California Supreme Court concluded that the juvenile court had to duty to inquire at the proceeding to terminate parental rights. In *Isaiah W.*, the supreme court explicitly overruled *In re Pedro N., 35 Cal.App.4th 183, 41 Cal.Rptr.2d 819 (1995),* which did not treat the Act's notice requirements as imposing a continuing duty on courts in legal proceedings.

In re Sade C., 13 Cal.4th 952, 920 P.2d 716, 55 Cal.Rptr.2d 771 (1996), holds that the court of appeal is not required to make an independent review of the entire record (a "Wende" review; see *People v. Wende, 25 Cal.3d 436, 600 P.2d 1071, 158 Cal.Rptr. 839 (1979)*) when a parent appeals from a judgment adversely affecting his custody of a child or his status as a parent if the appellate court does not find any arguably meritorious basis for the appeal. Interpreting *Sade C., In re Sara H., 52 Cal.App.4th 198, 60 Cal.Rptr.2d 434 (1997),* holds that the appellate court has no discretionary authority in dependency appeals to conduct an independent "Wende" review of the entire record to discover whether there exists some arguably meritorious basis for appeal from a judgment terminating parental rights.

In re Conservatorship of Ben C., 40 Cal.4th 529, 53 Cal.Rptr.3d 856, 150 P.3d 738 (2007), held that while *Wende* protections are inapplicable in conservatorship proceedings, a conservatee nevertheless has the right to file a supplemental brief in propria persona when his counsel finds no appealable issue.

The court may terminate the parental rights of a parent even though he is in full compliance with a reunification plan. *In re Amanda D., 55 Cal.App.4th 813, 64 Cal.Rptr.2d 108 (1997), review denied July 30, 1997* (affirming termination of the parental rights of an incarcerated parent), and cases cited therein.

Janice J. v. Superior Court, 55 Cal.App.4th 690, 64 Cal.Rptr.2d 227 (1997), holds that a writ petition challenging a court order setting a Section 366.26 hearing should be summarily denied when it has not been authorized by the client-parent. Additionally, an attorney has no duty to pursue a parent who has disappeared or to file a petition absent the parent's authorization. Accordingly, *Janice J.* dismissed a petition signed by an attorney on behalf of a client the attorney could not locate.

A subsection (c)(3) order continuing a permanency hearing for 180 days to allow additional time to find adoptive parents for a dependent child is an unappealable interim order. *In re Cody C., 121 Cal.App.4th 1297, 17 Cal.Rptr.3d 928 (2004), review denied*.

Interpreting subsection (j) together with section 366.3 (a) and Family Code section 8704, *Department of Social Services v. Superior Court, 58 Cal.App.4th 721, 68 Cal.Rptr.2d 239 (1997), review denied January 21, 1998,* holds that absent a showing that an interim adoptive placement made by the Department of Social Services is arbitrary and capricious in light of the child's best interest, the juvenile court may not interfere with or disapprove the placement, because Family Code section 8704 grants the agency "exclusive" custody and control of the child until an order of adoption is granted. Accord, *Los Angeles County Department of Child and Family Services v. Superior Court, 62 Cal.App.4th 1, 72 Cal.Rptr.2d 369 (1998), review denied June 10, 1998.*

Interpreting subsection (j) of this section together with Family Code § 8704, *In re Jacob E., 121 Cal.App.4th 909, 18 Cal.Rptr.3d 15 (2004), review denied*, held that a grandmother was not entitled to a hearing before the department of family services removed a dependent child from her custody for failure to provide adequate parenting, because the grandmother had not been identified as a prospective adoptive parent of the child after his mother's parental rights were terminated.

In re Lauren R., 148 Cal.App.4th 841, 56 Cal.Rptr.3d 151 (2007), held that, in ordering a child placed for adoption with an aunt, a juvenile court erred in applying the temporary placement factors of subsection (a) of section 361.3, instead of the caretaker preference criteria of subsection (k) of this section.

Applying subsection (*l*), *In re Charmice G., 66 Cal.App.4th 659, 78 Cal.Rptr.2d 212 (1998),* ruled that an order setting a Section 366.26 hearing is not an appealable order. Thus an order setting a hearing may be challenged only by special writ as provided in subsection (*l*), or by appeal from the subsequent order entered after the permanency planning hearing. *In re Anthony B., 72 Cal.App.4th 1017, 85 Cal.Rptr.2d 594 (1999),* holds that a party cannot appeal a collateral order (denying the mother supervised visitation) made at a hearing at which an order setting a Section 366.26 hearing is scheduled, unless the party first seeks writ review of the order under subsection (*l*).

Interpreting subsection (*l*)(3) and California Rule of Court 8.450, *In re A.H., 218 Cal.App.4th 337, 159 Cal.Rptr.3d 891 (2013), review denied*, held that parents who became upset and walked out of an 18-month review hearing before the judge could orally advise them of the writ requirement for challenging an order setting a hearing under this section and who also failed to notify the court of a change in their permanent mailing address, did not show good cause for noncompliance with the writ requirement. Thus the trial court properly denied a motion to vacate or modify, under section 388, a default judgment that placed the two dependent children with relatives.

Wayne F. v. Superior Court, 145 Cal.App.4th 1331, 52 Cal.Rptr.3d 519 (2006), held that a person designated a "prospective adoptive parent" under subsection (n), has standing to fully participate in a removal proceeding conducted under this section.

R.H. v. Superior Court, 209 Cal.App.4th 364, 147 Cal.Rptr.3d 8 (2012), review denied, held a child's grandparents, who were designated as her de facto parents and prospective adoptive parents, did not a have a due process right to appointed counsel at a subsection (n) hearing on the removal of the child from their home because of allegations of physical abuse of her siblings.

Glen C. v. Superior Court, 78 Cal.App.4th 570, 93 Cal.Rptr.2d 103 (2000), announces that future petitions for writ review of juvenile court orders denying reunification services or setting implementation hearings will be summarily denied if they fail to comply with the procedural requirements of this section and Welfare and Institutions Code § 366.26. *Glen C.* also threatens to report attorneys who file procedurally inadequate petitions to the State Bar or to initiate sanction proceedings against them.

In a dependency proceeding, the "waiver rule" ordinarily bars an appellate court from examining objections to prior appealable orders in an appeal from a subsequent appealable order. The waiver rule may, however, be relaxed when the defect complained of fundamentally undermined the statutory scheme and prevented the parent from securing the protections of the statutory scheme as a whole. *In re Janee J., 74 Cal.App.4th 198, 87 Cal.Rptr.2d 634 (1999), review denied November 17, 1999. In re S.D., 99 Cal.App.4th 1068, 121 Cal.Rptr.2d 518 (2002)*, held that the juvenile court erred in finding dependency jurisdiction on the ground that no parent was available to care for the child when there was neither allegation nor evidence that the incarcerated parent could not arrange for care of the child during her incarceration. *S.D.* additionally held that the parent could challenge dependency jurisdiction for the first time on appeal of an order terminating her parental rights because the jurisdictional order was the direct result of ineffective assistance of counsel. *In re Darlice C., 105 Cal.App.4th 459, 129 Cal.Rptr.2d 472 (2003)*, holds that habeas corpus may be used to challenge, on the ground of ineffective assistance of counsel, an order terminating parental rights. On November 19, 2003, the California Supreme Court denied review and ordered depublication of *In re Jacqueline P.*, in which the court of appeal, 4 Cal.Rptr.3d 850 (2003), had held that a mother was entitled to habeas corpus relief to deem timely, under the doctrine of constructive filing, a tardy notice of appeal of an order terminating her parental rights, when the mother timely notified her attorney of her desire to appeal, but her attorney did not timely file the notice of appeal. *In re O.S., 102 Cal.App.4th 1402, 126 Cal.Rptr.2d 571 (2002)*, granted a habeas corpus petition to a father whose parental rights were unconstitutionally terminated because the father's counsel was ineffective in failing to (1) communicate with the father, (2) obtain paternity testing, (3) object to the father's lack of notice of the proceeding, and (4) attempt to establish that the father was a presumed father. *In re Urayna L., 75 Cal.App.4th 883, 89 Cal.Rptr.2d 437 (1999)*, holds that although § 366.22 (b)(2) requires, prior to a § 366.26 hearing, that the Department of Social Services review the amount and nature of any contact between a child and the child's extended family, a parent waives the issue of adequacy of the adoption assessment by failing to challenge it at the parental rights termination proceeding. The parent may not subsequently appeal § 366.26 termination of parental rights on the ground of a § 366.22 assessment to which no objection was made at the termination hearing.

In re Andrea R., 75 Cal.App.4th 1093, 89 Cal.Rptr.2d 664 (1999), review denied December 15, 1999, holds that § 366.3(c) allows the court to schedule a new § 366.26 hearing to change the child's permanent plan from legal guardianship to adoption without first holding a separate hearing under § 388 to determine whether changed circumstances support a change in the permanent plan.

Interpreting the Soldiers' and Sailors' Civil Relief Act of 1940 (50 U.S.C.A. App. §§ 501 et seq.), *Christine M. v. Superior Court, 69 Cal.App.4th 1233, 82 Cal.Rptr.2d 220 (1999),* held that a sailor's alleged inability to attend parenting classes while at sea did not entitle him to a stay of dependency proceedings under the SSCRA. The court reasoned that the SSCRA requires a stay only when the military person's rights would otherwise be adversely affected; here the father's conduct indicated a lack of interest and an inability to parent, so the court properly terminated his reunification services and scheduled a proceeding under this section. *Louis J. v. Superior Court, 103 Cal.App.4th 711, 127 Cal.Rptr.2d 26 (2002)*, sustained the trial court's denial of a request for a stay of an 18–month review hearing under the Soldiers' and Sailors' Relief Act to a father whose purpose was not to postpone the hearing until he could attend and participate, but rather to gain time to better his position.

In re Emily R., 80 Cal.App.4th 1344, 96 Cal.Rptr.2d 285 (2000), holds that Code of Civil Procedure § 372 does not require that a juvenile court appoint a guardian ad litem for a minor alleged father who does not appear in a permanency planning proceeding. *Emily R.* reasoned that the minor was not a party to the dependency proceeding because he had not appeared and asserted a position. Until such appearance, he was merely an "interested person" entitled only to notice of the proceedings. *Emily R.* further held when the address of an alleged father is unknown and cannot be determined with due diligence, due process is satisfied by notice by publication.

In re Jesse W., 93 Cal.App.4th 349, 113 Cal.Rptr.2d 184 (2001), review denied January 23, 2002, held that an order under this section appointing grandparents as guardians of dependent children was not void despite the absence of a judge's countersignature, as required by Welfare and Institutions Code § 249, on an earlier referee's dispositional order removing the children from their mother's home.

On July 23, 2002, the court of appeal granted a rehearing to *In re Alexander B., 121 Cal.Rptr.2d 512 (2002)*, which originally held, under Penal Code § 2625, that when a juvenile court has been notified that an incarcerated parent wishes to attend a Welfare and Institutions Code § 366.26 hearing, it must either arrange for the parent's presence at the hearing or obtain the parent's signed waiver of the right to be physically present. Nevertheless, the first judgment of the court of appeal concluded that the juvenile court's failure to comply with the requirements of the section was harmless error because the parent, who was represented by counsel at the hearing that resulted in an order terminating her parental rights, failed to demonstrate that any prejudice resulted from her absence at the hearing.

On September 28, 2005, the California Supreme Court denied review and depublished *In re Michelle C.,* in which the depublished opinion of the court of appeal held that when a parent had not waived her right to be heard or represented by counsel, the juvenile court violated due process by terminating her parental rights at a hearing at which neither she nor her attorney were present, and the error was a structural one requiring automatic reversal.

Research References

Forms

West's California Code Forms, Probate § 1500-1502 Form 1, Nomination Of Guardian.
West's California Code Forms, Probate § 1500-1502 Form 2, Probate Guardianship Pamphlet--Judicial Council Form GC-205.
West's California Judicial Council Forms JV-300, Notice Of Hearing on Selection Of a Permanent Plan.
West's California Judicial Council Forms JV-310, Proof Of Service Under Section 366.26 Of the Welfare and Institutions Code.
West's California Judicial Council Forms JV-320, Orders Under Welfare and Institutions Code Sections 366.26, 727.3, 727.31.
West's California Judicial Council Forms JV-321, Request for Prospective Adoptive Parent Designation.
West's California Judicial Council Forms JV-322, Confidential Information--Prospective Adoptive Parent.
West's California Judicial Council Forms JV-323, Notice Of Intent to Remove Child and Proof Of Notice, Objection to Removal, and Order After Hearing.
West's California Judicial Council Forms JV-324, Notice Of Emergency Removal, Objection to Removal, and Order After Hearing.
West's California Judicial Council Forms JV-325, Objection to Removal.
West's California Judicial Council Forms JV-326, Proof Of Notice.
West's California Judicial Council Forms JV-327, Prospective Adoptive Parent Designation Order.
West's California Judicial Council Forms JV-328, Prospective Adoptive Parent Order After Hearing.
West's California Judicial Council Forms JV-820, Notice Of Intent to File Writ Petition and Request for Record to Review Order Setting a Hearing Under Welfare and Institutions Code Section 366.26.
West's California Judicial Council Forms JV-822. Notice Of Intent to File Writ Petition and Request for Record to Review Order Designating or Denying Specific Placement Of a Dependent Child After Termination Of Parental Rights...
West's California Judicial Council Forms JV-825, Petition for Extraordinary Writ (Cal. Rules Of Court, Rules 8.452, 8.456).
West's California Judicial Council Forms JV-826, Denial Of Petition (California Rules Of Court, Rules 8.452, 8.456).
West's California Judicial Council Forms ADOPT-310, Contact After Adoption Agreement.
West's California Judicial Council Forms ADOPT-315, Request To: Enforce, Change, End Contact After Adoption Agreement.
West's California Judicial Council Forms ADOPT-320, Answer to Request To: Enforce, Change, End Contact After Adoption Agreement.
West's California Judicial Council Forms ADOPT-325, Judge's Order To: Enforce, Change, End Contact After Adoption Agreement.

Treatises and Practice Aids

Witkin, California Summary 10th Constitutional Law § 107, Severability Clause.
Witkin, California Summary 10th Parent and Child § 4, Public Welfare Services.
Witkin, California Summary 10th Parent and Child § 12, Parental or Marital Rights Of Prisoners.
Witkin, California Summary 10th Parent and Child § 46, in General.
Witkin, California Summary 10th Parent and Child § 79, Adoption Information.
Witkin, California Summary 10th Parent and Child § 104, in General.
Witkin, California Summary 10th Parent and Child § 105, Notice is Not Required.
Witkin, California Summary 10th Parent and Child § 110, Finality and Effect Of Relinquishment.
Witkin, California Summary 10th Parent and Child § 118, Petition.
Witkin, California Summary 10th Parent and Child § 308, Dependency Proceeding Distinguished.
Witkin, California Summary 10th Parent and Child § 356, Change in Circumstances Pending Appeal.
Witkin, California Summary 10th Parent and Child § 363, Applicability Of Family Code Custody Provisions.
Witkin, California Summary 10th Parent and Child § 424, Termination on Contingency or Other Event.
Witkin, California Summary 10th Parent and Child § 451, in General.
Witkin, California Summary 10th Parent and Child § 467, Power to Hear Cases.
Witkin, California Summary 10th Parent and Child § 520, Jurisdiction.
Witkin, California Summary 10th Parent and Child § 522, Nature and Scope Of Indian Child Welfare Act.
Witkin, California Summary 10th Parent and Child § 524, Jurisdiction.
Witkin, California Summary 10th Parent and Child § 525, Existing Indian Family Doctrine.
Witkin, California Summary 10th Parent and Child § 528, in General.
Witkin, California Summary 10th Parent and Child § 529, Formal Requisites.
Witkin, California Summary 10th Parent and Child § 530, Waiver Of Notice.
Witkin, California Summary 10th Parent and Child § 531, Determining Adequacy Of Notice.
Witkin, California Summary 10th Parent and Child § 534, Out-Of-Home Placement or Guardianship.
Witkin, California Summary 10th Parent and Child § 536, Termination Of Parental Rights.
Witkin, California Summary 10th Parent and Child § 573, Powers and Duties Of Counsel.
Witkin, California Summary 10th Parent and Child § 575, Joint Representation as Error.
Witkin, California Summary 10th Parent and Child § 576, in General.

Witkin, California Summary 10th Parent and Child § 577, Hearing.
Witkin, California Summary 10th Parent and Child § 580, Right to Competent Counsel.
Witkin, California Summary 10th Parent and Child § 582, De Facto Parents.
Witkin, California Summary 10th Parent and Child § 583, Alleged Father.
Witkin, California Summary 10th Parent and Child § 584, Rights Of Siblings.
Witkin, California Summary 10th Parent and Child § 585, in General.
Witkin, California Summary 10th Parent and Child § 594, in General.
Witkin, California Summary 10th Parent and Child § 603, Identification Of Presumed or Alleged Fathers.
Witkin, California Summary 10th Parent and Child § 630, Bases for Removal.
Witkin, California Summary 10th Parent and Child § 637, Priority Right Of Noncustodial Parent.
Witkin, California Summary 10th Parent and Child § 638, Preferential Right Of Relatives.
Witkin, California Summary 10th Parent and Child § 642, in General.
Witkin, California Summary 10th Parent and Child § 643, Duration Of Services.
Witkin, California Summary 10th Parent and Child § 646, Incarcerated or Institutionalized Parent or Guardian.
Witkin, California Summary 10th Parent and Child § 652, Determination Whether to Order Services.
Witkin, California Summary 10th Parent and Child § 655, Nature and Purpose.
Witkin, California Summary 10th Parent and Child § 659, Sufficiency Of Evidence.
Witkin, California Summary 10th Parent and Child § 661, Hearing After Supplemental Petition is Sustained.
Witkin, California Summary 10th Parent and Child § 662, Nature and Purpose.
Witkin, California Summary 10th Parent and Child § 663, Form, Content, and Filing.
Witkin, California Summary 10th Parent and Child § 664, in General.
Witkin, California Summary 10th Parent and Child § 665, Right to Hearing.
Witkin, California Summary 10th Parent and Child § 667, Due Process Attack on Decree.
Witkin, California Summary 10th Parent and Child § 669, in General.
Witkin, California Summary 10th Parent and Child § 673, Child in Foster Care.
Witkin, California Summary 10th Parent and Child § 675, Reunification Services.
Witkin, California Summary 10th Parent and Child § 676, in General.
Witkin, California Summary 10th Parent and Child § 677, Scheduling Selection and Implementation Hearing.
Witkin, California Summary 10th Parent and Child § 678, Twelve-Month Review.
Witkin, California Summary 10th Parent and Child § 679, Eighteen-Month Review.
Witkin, California Summary 10th Parent and Child § 680, Statutory Procedure is Exclusive.
Witkin, California Summary 10th Parent and Child § 681, Notice.
Witkin, California Summary 10th Parent and Child § 682, Preliminary Assessment.
Witkin, California Summary 10th Parent and Child § 683, Appointment Of Counsel.
Witkin, California Summary 10th Parent and Child § 684, Testimony and Wishes Of Child.
Witkin, California Summary 10th Parent and Child § 685, Hearing.
Witkin, California Summary 10th Parent and Child § 686, Alternative Dispositions.
Witkin, California Summary 10th Parent and Child § 687, Termination Of Parental Rights to Free Child for Adoption.
Witkin, California Summary 10th Parent and Child § 688, Other Alternatives.
Witkin, California Summary 10th Parent and Child § 689, in General.
Witkin, California Summary 10th Parent and Child § 690, Benefit to Child.
Witkin, California Summary 10th Parent and Child § 691, Constitutionality Of Termination Procedure.
Witkin, California Summary 10th Parent and Child § 692, in General.
Witkin, California Summary 10th Parent and Child § 693, Termination Of Parental Rights.
Witkin, California Summary 10th Parent and Child § 694, Adoption Proceeding.
Witkin, California Summary 10th Parent and Child § 695, Legal Guardianship.
Witkin, California Summary 10th Parent and Child § 696, Continuing Jurisdiction.
Witkin, California Summary 10th Parent and Child § 697, Status Review Hearings.
Witkin, California Summary 10th Parent and Child § 698, Other Procedures.
Witkin, California Summary 10th Parent and Child § 699, Notice.
Witkin, California Summary 10th Parent and Child § 700, Right to Appeal.
Witkin, California Summary 10th Parent and Child § 701, in General.
Witkin, California Summary 10th Parent and Child § 704, Miscellaneous Orders.
Witkin, California Summary 10th Parent and Child § 705, in General.
Witkin, California Summary 10th Parent and Child § 707, Treatment Of Appeal as Writ Petition.
Witkin, California Summary 10th Parent and Child § 709, in General.
Witkin, California Summary 10th Parent and Child § 711, Expedited Appeal.
Witkin, California Summary 10th Parent and Child § 712, Notice Of Appeal.
Witkin, California Summary 10th Parent and Child § 716, in General.
Witkin, California Summary 10th Parent and Child § 717, in General.
Witkin, California Summary 10th Parent and Child § 718, Prior Orders.
Witkin, California Summary 10th Parent and Child § 719, Related Orders.
Witkin, California Summary 10th Parent and Child § 720, Notice Of Intent.
Witkin, California Summary 10th Parent and Child § 721, Record.
Witkin, California Summary 10th Parent and Child § 722, Writ Petition and Response.
Witkin, California Summary 10th Parent and Child § 723, Hearing and Decision.
Witkin, California Summary 10th Parent and Child § 727, Hearing and Decision.
Witkin, California Summary 10th Parent and Child § 749, Segregation Of Classes Of Minors.
Witkin, California Summary 10th Parent and Child § 896, General Requirements.
Witkin, California Summary 10th Parent and Child § 898, Court Supervision Of Child.
Witkin, California Summary 10th Parent and Child § 899, Termination Of Parental Rights.

Witkin, California Summary 10th Parent and Child § 914, Notification Of Appeal Rights.

Witkin, California Summary 10th Parent and Child § 452G, (New) Assumption Of Jurisdiction Over Nonminor.

Witkin, California Summary 10th Parent and Child § 675A, (New) Setting Selection and Implementation Hearing.

Witkin, California Summary 10th Parent and Child § 679A, (New) Twenty-Four Month Review.

Witkin, California Summary 10th Parent and Child § 688A, (New) Tribal Customary Adoption.

Witkin, California Summary 10th Parent and Child § 693A, (New) in General.

Witkin, California Summary 10th Parent and Child § 693B, (New) Designation Of Prospective Adoptive Parent.

Witkin, California Summary 10th Parent and Child § 693C, (New) Nonemergency Removal from Prospective Adoptive Parent.

Witkin, California Summary 10th Parent and Child § 693D, (New) Emergency Removal from Prospective Adoptive Parent.

Witkin, California Summary 10th Parent and Child § 693E, (New) Reinstatement Of Parental Rights.

Witkin, California Summary 10th Parent and Child § 699A, (New) in General.

Witkin, California Summary 10th Torts § 1389, Listed Persons Under Current Law.

Witkin, California Summary 10th Torts § 1397, Other Persons.

Witkin, California Summary 10th Wills and Probate § 916, in General.

Witkin, California Summary 10th Wills and Probate § 967, in General.

Witkin, California Summary 10th Wills and Probate § 969, Statewide Registry.

§ 366.27. Consent for medical care by relative providing living arrangement; educational decisions

(a) If a court, pursuant to paragraph (5) of subdivision (g) of Section 366.21, Section 366.22, Section 366.25, or Section 366.26, orders the placement of a minor in a planned permanent living arrangement with a relative, the court may authorize the relative to provide the same legal consent for the minor's medical, surgical, and dental care as the custodial parent of the minor.

(b) If a court orders the placement of a minor in a planned permanent living arrangement with a foster parent, relative caretaker, or nonrelative extended family member as defined in Section 362.7, the court may limit the right of the minor's parent or guardian to make educational decisions on the minor's behalf, so that the foster parent, relative caretaker, or nonrelative extended family member may exercise the educational consent duties pursuant to Section 56055 of the Education Code.

(c) If a court orders the placement of a minor in a planned permanent living arrangement, for purposes of this section, a foster parent shall include a person, relative caretaker, or a nonrelative extended family member as defined in Section 362.7, who has been licensed or approved by the county welfare department, county probation department, or the State Department of Social Services, or has been designated by the court as a specified placement. *(Added by Stats.1993, c. 1089 (A.B.2129), § 6. Amended by Stats.2003, c. 862 (A.B.490), § 11; Stats.2008, c. 482 (A.B.2070), § 6; Stats. 2012, c. 845 (S.B.1064), § 14.)*

Research References

Forms

West's California Judicial Council Forms JV-448, Order Granting Authority to Consent to Medical, Surgical, and Dental Care.

Treatises and Practice Aids

Witkin, California Summary 10th Parent and Child § 673, Child in Foster Care.

Witkin, California Summary 10th Parent and Child § 678, Twelve-Month Review.

Witkin, California Summary 10th Parent and Child § 679, Eighteen-Month Review.

Witkin, California Summary 10th Parent and Child § 686, Alternative Dispositions.

Witkin, California Summary 10th Parent and Child § 679A, (New) Twenty-Four Month Review.

Witkin, California Summary 10th Parent and Child § 699A, (New) in General.

§ 366.28. Appealing decisions involving placement or removal orders following the termination of parental rights

(a) The Legislature finds and declares that delays caused by appeals from court orders designating the specific placement of a dependent child after parental rights have been terminated may cause a substantial detriment to the child. The Legislature recognizes that the juvenile court intervenes in placement decisions after parental rights have been terminated only in exceptional circumstances, and this section is not intended to place additional authority or responsibility on the juvenile court.

(b)(1) After parental rights have been terminated pursuant to Section 366.26, an order by the court that a dependent child is to reside in, be retained in, or be removed from a specific placement, is not appealable at any time unless all of the following apply:

(A) A petition for extraordinary writ review was filed in a timely manner.

(B) The petition substantively addressed the specific issues to be challenged and supported that challenge by an adequate record.

(C) The petition was summarily denied or otherwise not decided on the merits.

(2) Failure to file a petition for extraordinary writ review within the period specified by rule of court, to substantively address the specific placement order that is challenged, or to support that challenge by an adequate record shall preclude subsequent review by appeal of the findings and orders made pursuant to this section.

(c) This section does not affect the right of a parent, a legal guardian, or the child to appeal any order that is otherwise appealable and that is issued at a hearing held pursuant to Section 366.26.

(d) The Judicial Council shall adopt a rule of court on or before January 1, 2005, to implement this section. This section shall become operative after the rule of court is adopted. *(Added by Stats.2003, c. 247 (S.B.59), § 1. Amended by Stats.2004, c. 249 (S.B.749), § 3, eff. Aug. 23, 2004.)*

Operative Effect

For operative effect of this section, see its terms.

Research References

Forms

West's California Judicial Council Forms JV-825, Petition for Extraordinary Writ (Cal. Rules Of Court, Rules 8.452, 8.456).
West's California Judicial Council Forms JV-826, Denial Of Petition (California Rules Of Court, Rules 8.452, 8.456).

Treatises and Practice Aids

Witkin, California Summary 10th Parent and Child § 704, Miscellaneous Orders.
Witkin, California Summary 10th Parent and Child § 705, in General.
Witkin, California Summary 10th Parent and Child § 709, in General.
Witkin, California Summary 10th Parent and Child § 716, in General.
Witkin, California Summary 10th Parent and Child § 724, in General.
Witkin, California Summary 10th Parent and Child § 693A, (New) in General.

§ 366.29. Post-adoptive sibling contact; jurisdiction of juvenile court with respect to dependency proceedings; jurisdiction over the postadoption contract agreement

(a) When a court, pursuant to Section 366.26, orders that a dependent child be placed for adoption, nothing in the adoption laws of this state shall be construed to prevent the prospective adoptive parent or parents of the child from expressing a willingness to facilitate postadoptive sibling contact. With the consent of the adoptive parent or parents, the court may include in the final adoption order provisions for the adoptive parent or parents to facilitate postadoptive sibling contact. In no event shall the continuing validity of the adoption be contingent upon the postadoptive contact, nor shall the ability of the adoptive parent or parents and the child to change residence within or outside the state be impaired by the order for contact.

(b) If, following entry of an order for sibling contact pursuant to subdivision (a), it is determined by the adoptive parent or parents that sibling contact poses a threat to the health, safety, or well-being of the adopted child, the adoptive parent or parents may terminate the sibling contact, provided that the adoptive parent or parents shall submit written notification to the court within 10 days after terminating the contact, which notification shall specify to the court the reasons why the health, safety, or well-being of the adopted child would be threatened by continued sibling contact.

(c) Upon the granting of the adoption petition and the issuing of the order of adoption of a child who is a dependent of the juvenile court, the jurisdiction of the juvenile court with respect to the dependency proceedings of that child shall be terminated. Nonetheless, the court granting the petition of adoption shall maintain jurisdiction over the child for enforcement of the postadoption contact agreement. The court may only order compliance with the postadoption contact agreement upon a finding of both of the following:

(1) The party seeking the enforcement participated, in good faith, in mediation or other appropriate alternative dispute resolution proceedings regarding the conflict, prior to the filing of the enforcement action.

(2) The enforcement is in the best interest of the child. *(Added by Stats.1998, c. 1072 (A.B.2196), § 2. Amended by Stats.2001, c. 747 (A.B.705), § 4.)*

Research References

Treatises and Practice Aids

Witkin, California Summary 10th Parent and Child § 694, Adoption Proceeding.
Witkin, California Summary 10th Parent and Child § 696, Continuing Jurisdiction.

§ 366.3. Order for permanent plan of adoption, tribal customary adoption, adoption of nonminor dependent, or legal guardianship; termination of guardianship; change of circumstances; status review

(a) If a juvenile court orders a permanent plan of adoption, tribal customary adoption, adoption of a nonminor dependent pursuant to subdivision (f) of Section 366.31, or legal guardianship pursuant to Section 360 or 366.26, the court shall retain jurisdiction over the child or nonminor dependent until the child or nonminor dependent is adopted or the legal guardianship is established, except as provided for in Section 366.29 or, on and after January 1, 2012, Section 366.32. The status of the child or nonminor dependent shall be reviewed every six months to ensure that the adoption or legal guardianship is completed as expeditiously as possible. When the adoption of the child or nonminor dependent has been granted, or in the case of a tribal customary adoption, when the tribal customary adoption order has been afforded full faith and credit and the petition for adoption has been granted, the court shall terminate its jurisdiction over the child or nonminor dependent. Following establishment of a legal guardianship, the court may continue jurisdiction over the child as a dependent child of the juvenile court or may terminate its dependency jurisdiction and retain jurisdiction over the child as a ward of the legal guardianship, as authorized by Section 366.4. If, however, a relative of the child is appointed the legal guardian of the child and the child has been placed with the relative for at least six months, the court shall, except if the relative guardian objects, or upon a finding of exceptional circumstances, terminate its dependency jurisdiction and retain jurisdiction over the child as a ward of the guardianship, as authorized by Section 366.4. Following a termination of parental rights, the parent or parents shall not be a party to, or receive notice of, any subsequent proceedings regarding the child.

(b)(1) If the court has dismissed dependency jurisdiction following the establishment of a legal guardianship, or no dependency jurisdiction attached because of the granting of a legal guardianship pursuant to Section 360, and the legal guardianship is subsequently revoked or otherwise terminated, the county department of social services or welfare department shall notify the juvenile court of this fact. The court may vacate its previous order dismissing dependency jurisdiction over the child.

(2) Notwithstanding Section 1601 of the Probate Code, the proceedings to terminate a legal guardianship that has been granted pursuant to Section 360 or 366.26 shall be held either in the juvenile court that retains jurisdiction over the

guardianship as authorized by Section 366.4 or the juvenile court in the county where the guardian and child currently reside, based on the best interests of the child, unless the termination is due to the emancipation or adoption of the child. The juvenile court having jurisdiction over the guardianship shall receive notice from the court in which the petition is filed within five calendar days of the filing. Prior to the hearing on a petition to terminate legal guardianship pursuant to this subdivision, the court shall order the county department of social services or welfare department having jurisdiction or jointly with the county department where the guardian and child currently reside to prepare a report, for the court's consideration, that shall include an evaluation of whether the child could safely remain in, or be returned to, the legal guardian's home, without terminating the legal guardianship, if services were provided to the child or legal guardian. If applicable, the report shall also identify recommended family maintenance or reunification services to maintain the legal guardianship and set forth a plan for providing those services. If the petition to terminate legal guardianship is granted, either juvenile court may resume dependency jurisdiction over the child, and may order the county department of social services or welfare department to develop a new permanent plan, which shall be presented to the court within 60 days of the termination. If no dependency jurisdiction has attached, the social worker shall make any investigation he or she deems necessary to determine whether the child may be within the jurisdiction of the juvenile court, as provided in Section 328.

(3) Unless the parental rights of the child's parent or parents have been terminated, they shall be notified that the legal guardianship has been revoked or terminated and shall be entitled to participate in the new permanency planning hearing. The court shall try to place the child in another permanent placement. At the hearing, the parents may be considered as custodians but the child shall not be returned to the parent or parents unless they prove, by a preponderance of the evidence, that reunification is the best alternative for the child. The court may, if it is in the best interests of the child, order that reunification services again be provided to the parent or parents.

(c) If, following the establishment of a legal guardianship, the county welfare department becomes aware of changed circumstances that indicate adoption or, for an Indian child, tribal customary adoption, may be an appropriate plan for the child, the department shall so notify the court. The court may vacate its previous order dismissing dependency jurisdiction over the child and order that a hearing be held pursuant to Section 366.26 to determine whether adoption or continued legal guardianship is the most appropriate plan for the child. The hearing shall be held no later than 120 days from the date of the order. If the court orders that a hearing shall be held pursuant to Section 366.26, the court shall direct the agency supervising the child and the county adoption agency, or the State Department of Social Services if it is acting as an adoption agency, to prepare an assessment under subdivision (b) of Section 366.22.

(d) If the child or, on and after January 1, 2012, nonminor dependent is in a placement other than the home of a legal guardian and jurisdiction has not been dismissed, the status of the child shall be reviewed at least every six months. The review of the status of a child for whom the court has ordered parental rights terminated and who has been ordered placed for adoption shall be conducted by the court. The review of the status of a child or, on and after January 1, 2012, nonminor dependent for whom the court has not ordered parental rights terminated and who has not been ordered placed for adoption may be conducted by the court or an appropriate local agency. The court shall conduct the review under the following circumstances:

(1) Upon the request of the child's parents or legal guardians.

(2) Upon the request of the child or, on and after January 1, 2012, nonminor dependent.

(3) It has been 12 months since a hearing held pursuant to Section 366.26 or an order that the child remain in foster care pursuant to Section 366.21, 366.22, 366.25, 366.26, or subdivision (h).

(4) It has been 12 months since a review was conducted by the court.

The court shall determine whether or not reasonable efforts to make and finalize a permanent placement for the child have been made.

(e) Except as provided in subdivision (g), at the review held every six months pursuant to subdivision (d), the reviewing body shall inquire about the progress being made to provide a permanent home for the child, shall consider the safety of the child, and shall determine all of the following:

(1) The continuing necessity for, and appropriateness of, the placement.

(2) Identification of individuals other than the child's siblings who are important to a child who is 10 years of age or older and has been in out-of-home placement for six months or longer, and actions necessary to maintain the child's relationship with those individuals, provided that those relationships are in the best interest of the child. The social worker shall ask every child who is 10 years of age or older and who has been in out-of-home placement for six months or longer to identify individuals other than the child's siblings who are important to the child, and may ask any other child to provide that information, as appropriate. The social worker shall make efforts to identify other individuals who are important to the child, consistent with the child's best interests.

(3) The continuing appropriateness and extent of compliance with the permanent plan for the child, including efforts to maintain relationships between a child who is 10 years of age or older and who has been in out-of-home placement for six months or longer and individuals who are important to the child and efforts to identify a prospective adoptive parent or legal guardian, including, but not limited to, child-specific recruitment efforts and listing on an adoption exchange.

(4) The extent of the agency's compliance with the child welfare services case plan in making reasonable efforts either to return the child to the safe home of the parent or to complete whatever steps are necessary to finalize the permanent placement of the child. If the reviewing body determines that a second period of reunification services is in the child's best interests, and that there is a significant likelihood of the child's return to a safe home due to changed

circumstances of the parent, pursuant to subdivision (f), the specific reunification services required to effect the child's return to a safe home shall be described.

(5) Whether there should be any limitation on the right of the parent or guardian to make educational decisions or developmental services decisions for the child. That limitation shall be specifically addressed in the court order and may not exceed what is necessary to protect the child. If the court specifically limits the right of the parent or guardian to make educational decisions or developmental services decisions for the child, the court shall at the same time appoint a responsible adult to make educational decisions or developmental services decisions for the child pursuant to Section 361.

(6) The adequacy of services provided to the child. The court shall consider the progress in providing the information and documents to the child, as described in Section 391. The court shall also consider the need for, and progress in providing, the assistance and services described in Section 391.

(7) The extent of progress the parents or legal guardians have made toward alleviating or mitigating the causes necessitating placement in foster care.

(8) The likely date by which the child may be returned to, and safely maintained in, the home, placed for adoption, legal guardianship, placed with a fit and willing relative, or, for an Indian child, in consultation with the child's tribe, placed for tribal customary adoption, or, if the child is 16 years of age or older, and no other permanent plan is appropriate at the time of the hearing, in another planned permanent living arrangement.

(9) Whether the child has any siblings under the court's jurisdiction, and, if any siblings exist, all of the following:

(A) The nature of the relationship between the child and his or her siblings.

(B) The appropriateness of developing or maintaining the sibling relationships pursuant to Section 16002. At the first review conducted for a child for whom the court has ordered parental rights terminated and who has been ordered placed for adoption, the court shall inquire into the status of the development of a voluntary postadoption sibling contact agreement pursuant to subdivision (e) of Section 16002.

(C) If the siblings are not placed together in the same home, why the siblings are not placed together and what efforts are being made to place the siblings together, or why those efforts are not appropriate.

(D) If the siblings are not placed together, all of the following:

(i) The frequency and nature of the visits between the siblings.

(ii) If there are visits between the siblings, whether the visits are supervised or unsupervised. If the visits are supervised, a discussion of the reasons why the visits are supervised, and what needs to be accomplished in order for the visits to be unsupervised.

(iii) If there are visits between the siblings, a description of the location and length of the visits.

(iv) Any plan to increase visitation between the siblings.

(E) The impact of the sibling relationships on the child's placement and planning for legal permanence.

The factors the court may consider as indicators of the nature of the child's sibling relationships include, but are not limited to, whether the siblings were raised together in the same home, whether the siblings have shared significant common experiences or have existing close and strong bonds, whether either sibling expresses a desire to visit or live with his or her sibling, as applicable, and whether ongoing contact is in the child's best emotional interests.

(10) For a child who is 14 years of age or older, and, effective January 1, 2012, for a nonminor dependent, the services needed to assist the child or nonminor dependent to make the transition from foster care to successful adulthood.

The reviewing body shall determine whether or not reasonable efforts to make and finalize a permanent placement for the child have been made.

Each licensed foster family agency shall submit reports for each child in its care, custody, and control to the court concerning the continuing appropriateness and extent of compliance with the child's permanent plan, the extent of compliance with the case plan, and the type and adequacy of services provided to the child.

(f) Unless their parental rights have been permanently terminated, the parent or parents of the child are entitled to receive notice of, and participate in, those hearings. It shall be presumed that continued care is in the best interests of the child, unless the parent or parents prove, by a preponderance of the evidence, that further efforts at reunification are the best alternative for the child. In those cases, the court may order that further reunification services to return the child to a safe home environment be provided to the parent or parents up to a period of six months, and family maintenance services, as needed for an additional six months in order to return the child to a safe home environment. On and after January 1, 2012, this subdivision shall not apply to the parents of a nonminor dependent.

(g) At the review conducted by the court and held at least every six months, regarding a child for whom the court has ordered parental rights terminated and who has been ordered placed for adoption, or, for an Indian child for whom parental rights are not being terminated and a tribal customary adoption is being considered, the county welfare department shall prepare and present to the court a report describing the following:

(1) The child's present placement.

(2) The child's current physical, mental, emotional, and educational status.

(3) If the child has not been placed with a prospective adoptive parent or guardian, identification of individuals, other than the child's siblings, who are important to the child and actions necessary to maintain the child's relationship with those individuals, provided that those relationships are in the best interest of the child. The agency shall ask every child who is 10 years of age or older to identify any individuals who are important to him or her, consistent with the child's best interest, and may ask any child who is younger than 10 years of age to provide that information as appropriate. The

agency shall make efforts to identify other individuals who are important to the child.

(4) Whether the child has been placed with a prospective adoptive parent or parents.

(5) Whether an adoptive placement agreement has been signed and filed.

(6) If the child has not been placed with a prospective adoptive parent or parents, the efforts made to identify an appropriate prospective adoptive parent or legal guardian, including, but not limited to, child-specific recruitment efforts and listing on an adoption exchange.

(7) Whether the final adoption order should include provisions for postadoptive sibling contact pursuant to Section 366.29.

(8) The progress of the search for an adoptive placement if one has not been identified.

(9) Any impediments to the adoption or the adoptive placement.

(10) The anticipated date by which the child will be adopted or placed in an adoptive home.

(11) The anticipated date by which an adoptive placement agreement will be signed.

(12) Recommendations for court orders that will assist in the placement of the child for adoption or in the finalization of the adoption.

The court shall determine whether or not reasonable efforts to make and finalize a permanent placement for the child have been made.

The court shall make appropriate orders to protect the stability of the child and to facilitate and expedite the permanent placement and adoption of the child.

(h)(1) At the review held pursuant to subdivision (d) for a child in foster care, the court shall consider all permanency planning options for the child including whether the child should be returned to the home of the parent, placed for adoption, or, for an Indian child, in consultation with the child's tribe, placed for tribal customary adoption, or appointed a legal guardian, placed with a fit and willing relative, or, if compelling reasons exist for finding that none of the foregoing options are in the best interest of the child and the child is 16 years of age or older, whether the child should be placed in another planned permanent living arrangement. The court shall order that a hearing be held pursuant to Section 366.26, unless it determines by clear and convincing evidence that there is a compelling reason for determining that a hearing held pursuant to Section 366.26 is not in the best interest of the child because the child is being returned to the home of the parent, the child is not a proper subject for adoption, or no one is willing to accept legal guardianship as of the hearing date. If the county adoption agency, or the department when it is acting as an adoption agency, has determined it is unlikely that the child will be adopted or one of the conditions described in paragraph (1) of subdivision (c) of Section 366.26 applies, that fact shall constitute a compelling reason for purposes of this subdivision. Only upon that determination may the court order that the child remain in foster care, without holding a hearing pursuant to Section 366.26. The court shall make factual findings identifying any barriers to achieving the permanent plan as of the hearing date. On and after January 1, 2012, the nonminor dependent's legal status as an adult is in and of itself a compelling reason not to hold a hearing pursuant to Section 366.26.

(2) When the child is 16 years of age or older and in another planned permanent living arrangement, the court shall do all of the following:

(A) Ask the child about his or her desired permanency outcome.

(B) Make a judicial determination explaining why, as of the hearing date, another planned permanent living arrangement is the best permanency plan for the child.

(C) State for the record the compelling reason or reasons why it continues not to be in the best interest of the child to return home, be placed for adoption, be placed for tribal customary adoption in the case of an Indian child, be placed with a legal guardian, or be placed with a fit and willing relative.

(3) When the child is 16 years of age or older and is in another planned permanent living arrangement, the social study prepared for the hearing shall include a description of all of the following:

(A) The intensive and ongoing efforts to return the child to the home of the parent, place the child for adoption, or establish a legal guardianship, as appropriate.

(B) The steps taken to do both of the following:

(i) Ensure that the child's care provider is following the reasonable and prudent parent standard.

(ii) Determine whether the child has regular, ongoing opportunities to engage in age or developmentally appropriate activities, including consulting with the child about opportunities for the child to participate in those activities.

(4) When the child is under 16 years of age and has a permanent plan of return home, adoption, legal guardianship, or placement with a fit and willing relative, <u>the social study shall include a description of</u> any barriers to achieving the permanent plan and the efforts made by the agency <u>to</u> address those barriers.

(i) If, as authorized by subdivision (h), the court orders a hearing pursuant to Section 366.26, the court shall direct the agency supervising the child and the county adoption agency, or the State Department of Social Services when it is acting as an adoption agency, to prepare an assessment as provided for in subdivision (i) of Section 366.21 or subdivision (b) of Section 366.22. A hearing held pursuant to Section 366.26 shall be held no later than 120 days from the date of the 12–month review at which it is ordered, and at that hearing the court shall determine whether adoption, tribal customary adoption, legal guardianship, placement with a fit and willing relative, or, for a child 16 years of age or older, another planned permanent living arrangement is the most appropriate plan for the child. On and after January 1, 2012, a hearing pursuant to Section 366.26 shall not be ordered if the child is a nonminor dependent, unless the nonminor dependent is an Indian child and tribal customary adoption is recommended as the permanent plan. The court may order that a nonminor dependent who otherwise is eligible pursuant to Section 11403 remain in a planned, permanent living arrangement. At the request of the nonminor dependent who has an established relationship with an adult determined to be the nonminor dependent's permanent connection, the court may order adoption of the nonminor dependent pursuant to subdivision (f) of Section 366.31.

(j) The reviews conducted pursuant to subdivision (a) or (d) may be conducted earlier than every six months if the court determines that an earlier review is in the best interests of the child or as court rules prescribe. *(Added by Stats.1987, c. 1485, § 49, operative Jan. 1, 1989. Amended by Stats.1989, c. 913, § 18; Stats.1990, c. 1530 (S.B.2232), § 8; Stats.1994, c. 900 (S.B.1407), § 3; Stats.1995, c. 540 (A.B.1523), § 9; Stats.1996, c. 1138 (A.B.2154), § 5; Stats.1997, c. 793 (A.B. 1544), § 27; Stats.1998, c. 355 (S.B.1482), § 1; Stats.1998, c. 1054 (A.B.1091), § 37; Stats.1998, c. 1055 (S.B.1901), § 5; Stats.1998, c. 1056 (A.B.2773), § 18.7; Stats.1999, c. 887 (S.B.1270), § 2; Stats.2000, c. 108 (A.B.2876), § 21, eff. July 10, 2000; Stats.2000, c. 909 (A.B.1987), § 6; Stats.2000, c. 910 (A.B.2921), § 14.1; Stats.2000, c. 911 (A.B.686), § 2.3; Stats. 2001, c. 747 (A.B.705), § 5; Stats.2002, c. 785 (S.B.1677), § 5; Stats.2003, c. 813 (A.B.408), § 8; Stats.2004, c. 810 (A.B. 2807), § 6; Stats.2005, c. 640 (A.B.1412), § 7; Stats.2006, c. 567 (A.B.2303), § 26; Stats.2007, c. 565 (A.B.298), § 5; Stats.2008, c. 482 (A.B.2070), § 7; Stats.2009, c. 287 (A.B. 1325), § 17, operative July 1, 2010; Stats.2010, c. 559 (A.B.12), § 22; Stats.2012, c. 35 (S.B.1013), § 59, eff. June 27, 2012; Stats.2012, c. 846 (A.B.1712), § 24; Stats.2014, c. 773 (S.B. 1099), § 6, eff. Jan. 1, 2015; Stats.2015, c. 425 (S.B.794), § 14, eff. Jan. 1, 2016; Stats.2016, c. 719 (S.B.1060), § 2, eff. Jan. 1, 2017; Stats.2017, c. 561 (A.B.1516), § 265, eff. Jan. 1, 2018; Stats.2017, c. 732 (A.B.404), § 52, eff. Jan. 1, 2018.)*

Commentary

For treatment of subsection (a) "exceptional circumstances" that would justify continuing dependency jurisdiction when children have been placed with a relative guardian, see *In re Joshua S., 41 Cal.4th 261, 59 Cal.Rptr.3d 460, 159 P.3d 49 (2007)*.

In re Ethan J., 236 Cal.App.4th 654, 186 Cal.Rptr.3d 740 (2015), held that a juvenile court erred in terminating jurisdiction over a child for which it had ordered legal guardianship with visitation to the mother, when it did not find that continuing visitation would be detrimental to the child but knew that visitation would not occur because the child refused visitation. Effectively, termination of jurisdiction impermissibly delegated authority over visitation to the child.

Applying subsections (a) and (b), *In re Priscilla D., 234 Cal.App.4th 1207, 184 Cal.Rptr.3d 468 (2015)*, held that a legal guardianship can be terminated by a parent under this section, and the parent does not have to show that the guardianship is detrimental to the children, but only that due to changed circumstances termination is in their best interests.

Interpreting subsection (a) together with section 366.26 (j) and Family Code section 8704, *Department of Social Services v. Superior Court, 58 Cal.App.4th 721, 68 Cal.Rptr.2d 239 (1997), review denied January 21, 1998,* holds that absent a showing that an interim adoptive placement made by the Department of Social Services is arbitrary and capricious in light of the child's best interests, the juvenile court may not interfere with or disapprove the placement, because Family Code section 8704 grants the agency "exclusive" custody and control of the child until an order of adoption is granted. Accord, *Los Angeles County Department of Child and Family Services v. Superior Court, 62 Cal.App.4th 1, 72 Cal.Rptr.2d 369 (1998), review denied June 10, 1998.*

Invoking subsection (b), *In re Jessica C., 151 Cal.App.4th 474, 59 Cal.Rptr.3d 855 (2007)*, held that a juvenile court erred by failing to consider whether provision to a grandfather of maintenance services, as described in Welfare and Institutions Code section 301, could have been provided to preserve the guardianship of grandparents, with whom the children had lived for many years and with whom the children desired to continue to live.

In re Andrea R., 75 Cal.App.4th 1093, 89 Cal.Rptr.2d 664 (1999), review denied December 15, 1999, holds that subsection (c) allows the court to schedule a new § 366.26 hearing to change the child's permanent plan from legal guardianship to adoption without first holding a separate hearing under § 388 to determine whether changed circumstances support a change in the permanent plan.

For discussion of the subsection (e) presumption that continued care "is in the interests of the minor," see *Nahid H. v. Superior Court, 53 Cal.App.4th 1051, 62 Cal.Rptr.2d 281 (1997)* (holding juvenile court should develop a reunification plan for Iranian refugee mother despite daughters' resistance founded on fears based on mother's supposed political beliefs).

In re Josiah S., 102 Cal.App.4th 403, 125 Cal.Rptr.2d 413 (2002), held that the juvenile court erred in denying a mother's request to contest the continued long-term placement of her son, reasoning that the last paragraph of subsection (e) allows a parent whose parental rights have not been terminated to participate in a status review under this section.

Amber R. v. Superior Court, 139 Cal.App.4th 897, 43 Cal.Rptr.3d 297 (2006), review denied, holds that a parent whose rights have been terminated lacks standing to file a petition under Section 388 to be declared a subsection (e)(2) individual who is important to a dependent child and allowed continued contact with the child.

Interpreting subsection (f), *In re J.F., 196 Cal.App.4th 321, 126 Cal.Rptr.3d 108 (2011)*, holds that a parent is not required to submit an offer of proof in order to participate in a post-permanency review hearing.

Research References

Forms

West's California Judicial Council Forms JV-280, Notice Of Review Hearing.

West's California Judicial Council Forms JV-281, Notice Of Hearing--Nonminor Dependent Review Hearing / Other.

West's California Judicial Council Forms JV-403, Sibling Attachment: Contact and Placement.

West's California Judicial Council Forms JV-445, Findings and Orders After Postpermanency Hearing--Parental Rights Terminated; Permanent Plan Of Adoption (Welf. & Inst. Code, S366.3).

West's California Judicial Council Forms JV-446, Findings and Orders After Postpermanency Hearing--Permanent Plan Other Than Adoption (Welf. & Inst. Code, S366.3).

West's California Judicial Council Forms JV-460, Attachment: Additional Findings and Orders for Child Approaching Majority--Dependency.

Treatises and Practice Aids

Witkin, California Summary 10th Parent and Child § 4, Public Welfare Services.

Witkin, California Summary 10th Parent and Child § 643, Duration Of Services.

Witkin, California Summary 10th Parent and Child § 665, Right to Hearing.

Witkin, California Summary 10th Parent and Child § 673, Child in Foster Care.

Witkin, California Summary 10th Parent and Child § 679, Eighteen-Month Review.

Witkin, California Summary 10th Parent and Child § 686, Alternative Dispositions.

Witkin, California Summary 10th Parent and Child § 692, in General.
Witkin, California Summary 10th Parent and Child § 696, Continuing Jurisdiction.
Witkin, California Summary 10th Parent and Child § 697, Status Review Hearings.
Witkin, California Summary 10th Parent and Child § 698, Other Procedures.
Witkin, California Summary 10th Parent and Child § 699, Notice.
Witkin, California Summary 10th Parent and Child § 701, in General.
Witkin, California Summary 10th Parent and Child § 452F, (New) Termination Of Jurisdiction Over Nonminor.
Witkin, California Summary 10th Parent and Child § 669A, (New) Review Hearings Just Before and After Minor Attains Age 18.
Witkin, California Summary 10th Parent and Child § 688A, (New) Tribal Customary Adoption.

§ 366.31. Last review hearing held before minor attains 18 years of age; review hearings occurring in six-month period before minor attains 18 years of age; review hearings for nonminor dependents; hearing to consider permanent plan of adoption for nonminor dependent; submission of reports regarding nonminor dependents by licensed foster family agencies

(a) If a review hearing is the last review hearing to be held before the minor attains 18 years of age, the court shall ensure all of the following:

(1) The minor's case plan includes a plan for the minor to satisfy one or more of the participation conditions described in paragraphs (1) to (5), inclusive, of subdivision (b) of Section 11403, so that the minor is eligible to remain in foster care as a nonminor dependent.

(2) The minor has been informed of his or her right to seek termination of dependency jurisdiction pursuant to Section 391, and understands the potential benefits of continued dependency.

(3) The minor is informed of his or her right to have dependency reinstated pursuant to subdivision (e) of Section 388, and understands the potential benefits of continued dependency.

(b) At the review hearing that occurs in the six-month period prior to the minor's attaining 18 years of age, and at every subsequent review hearing for the nonminor dependent, as described in subdivision (v) of Section 11400, the report shall describe all of the following:

(1) The minor's and nonminor's plans to remain in foster care and plans to meet one or more of the participation conditions as described in paragraphs (1) to (5), inclusive, of subdivision (b) of Section 11403 to continue to receive AFDC–FC benefits as a nonminor dependent.

(2) The efforts made and assistance provided to the minor and nonminor by the social worker or the probation officer so that the minor and nonminor will be able to meet the participation conditions.

(3) Efforts toward completing the items described in paragraph (2) of subdivision (e) of Section 391.

(c) The reviews conducted pursuant to this section for a nonminor dependent shall be conducted in a manner that respects the nonminor's status as a legal adult, focused on the goals and services described in the youth's transitional independent living case plan, as described in subdivision (y) of Section 11400, including efforts made to maintain connections with caring and permanently committed adults, and attended, as appropriate, by additional participants invited by the nonminor dependent.

(d) For a nonminor dependent whose case plan is continued court-ordered family reunification services pursuant to Section 361.6, the court shall consider whether the nonminor dependent may safely reside in the home of the parent or guardian. If the nonminor cannot reside safely in the home of the parent or guardian or if it is not in the nonminor dependent's best interest to reside in the home of the parent or guardian, the court must consider whether to continue or terminate reunification services for the parent or legal guardian.

(1) The review report shall include a discussion of all of the following:

(A) Whether foster care placement continues to be necessary and appropriate.

(B) The likely date by which the nonminor dependent may reside safely in the home of the parent or guardian or will achieve independence.

(C) Whether the parent or guardian and nonminor dependent were actively involved in the development of the case plan.

(D) Whether the social worker or probation officer has provided reasonable services designed to aid the parent or guardian to overcome the problems that led to the initial removal of the nonminor dependent.

(E) The extent of progress the parents or guardian have made toward alleviating or mitigating the causes necessitating placement in foster care.

(F) Whether the nonminor dependent and parent, parents, or guardian are in agreement with the continuation of reunification services.

(G) Whether continued reunification services are in the best interest of the nonminor dependent.

(H) Whether there is a substantial probability that the nonminor dependent will be able to safely reside in the home of the parent or guardian by the next review hearing date.

(I) The efforts to maintain the nonminor's connections with caring and permanently committed adults.

(J) The agency's compliance with the nonminor dependent's transitional independent living case plan, including efforts to finalize the nonminor's permanent plan and prepare the nonminor dependent for independence.

(K) The progress in providing the information and documents to the nonminor dependent as described in Section 391.

(2) The court shall inquire about the progress being made to provide a permanent home for the nonminor, shall consider the safety of the nonminor dependent, and shall determine all of the following:

(A) The continuing necessity for, and appropriateness of, the placement.

(B) Whether the agency has made reasonable efforts to maintain relationships between the nonminor dependent and individuals who are important to the nonminor dependent.

(C) The extent of the agency's compliance with the case plan in making reasonable efforts or, in the case of an Indian child, active efforts, as described in Section 361.7, to create a safe home of the parent or guardian for the nonminor to reside in or to complete whatever steps are necessary to finalize the permanent placement of the nonminor dependent.

(D) The extent of the agency's compliance with the nonminor dependent's transitional independent living case plan, including efforts to finalize the youth's permanent plan and prepare the nonminor dependent for independence.

(E) The adequacy of services provided to the parent or guardian and to the nonminor dependent. The court shall consider the progress in providing the information and documents to the nonminor dependent as described in Section 391. The court shall also consider the need for, and progress in providing, the assistance and services described in Section 391.

(F) The extent of progress the parents or legal guardians have made toward alleviating or mitigating the causes necessitating placement in foster care.

(G) The likely date by which the nonminor dependent may safely reside in the home of the parent or guardian or, if the court is terminating reunification services, the likely date by which it is anticipated the nonminor dependent will achieve independence, or, for an Indian child, in consultation with the child's tribe, placed for tribal customary adoption.

(H) Whether the agency has made reasonable efforts as required in subparagraph (D) of paragraph (1) of subdivision (a) of Section 366 to establish or maintain the nonminor dependent's relationship with his or her siblings who are under the juvenile court's jurisdiction.

(I) The services needed to assist the nonminor dependent to make the transition from foster care to successful adulthood.

(J) Whether or not reasonable efforts to make and finalize a permanent placement for the nonminor have been made.

(3) If the court determines that a nonminor dependent may safely reside in the home of the parent or former guardian, the court may order the nonminor dependent to return to the family home. After the nonminor dependent returns to the family home, the court may terminate jurisdiction and proceed under applicable provisions of Section 391 or continue jurisdiction as a nonminor under subdivision (a) of Section 303 and hold hearings as follows:

(A) At every hearing for a nonminor dependent residing in the home of the parent or guardian, the court shall set a hearing within six months of the previous hearing. The court shall advise the parties of their right to be present. At least 10 calendar days before the hearing, the social worker or probation officer shall file a report with the court describing the services offered to the family and the progress made by the family in eliminating the conditions or factors requiring court supervision. The report shall address all of the following:

(i) Whether the parent or guardian and the nonminor dependent were actively involved in the development of the case plan.

(ii) Whether the social worker or probation officer has provided reasonable services to eliminate the need for court supervision.

(iii) The progress of providing information and documents to the nonminor dependent as described in Section 391.

(B) The court shall inquire about progress being made, shall consider the safety of the nonminor dependent, and shall determine all of the following:

(i) The continuing need for court supervision.

(ii) The extent of the agency's compliance with the case plan in making reasonable efforts to maintain a safe family home for the nonminor dependent.

(C) If the court finds that court supervision is no longer necessary, the court shall terminate jurisdiction under applicable provisions of Section 391.

(e) For a nonminor dependent who is no longer receiving court-ordered family reunification services and is in a permanent plan of another planned permanent living arrangement, at the review hearing held every six months pursuant to subdivision (d) of Section 366.3, the reviewing body shall inquire about the progress being made to provide permanent connections with caring, committed adults for the nonminor dependent, shall consider the safety of the nonminor, shall consider the transitional independent living case plan, and shall determine all of the following:

(1) The continuing necessity for, and appropriateness of, the placement.

(2) The continuing appropriateness and extent of compliance with the permanent plan for the nonminor dependent, including efforts to identify and maintain relationships with individuals who are important to the nonminor dependent.

(3) The extent of the agency's compliance with the nonminor dependent's transitional independent living case plan, including whether or not reasonable efforts have been made to make and finalize the youth's permanent plan and prepare the nonminor dependent for independence.

(4) Whether a prospective adoptive parent has been identified and assessed as appropriate for the nonminor dependent's adoption under this section, whether the prospective adoptive parent has been informed about the terms of the written negotiated adoption assistance agreement pursuant to Section 16120, and whether adoption should be ordered as the nonminor dependent's permanent plan. If nonminor dependent adoption is ordered as the nonminor dependent's permanent plan, a hearing pursuant to subdivision (f) shall be held within 60 days. When the court orders a hearing pursuant to subdivision (f), it shall direct the agency to prepare a report that shall include the provisions of paragraph (5) of subdivision (f).

(5) For the nonminor dependent who is an Indian child, whether, in consultation with the nonminor's tribe, the nonminor should be placed for tribal customary adoption.

(6) The adequacy of services provided to the nonminor dependent. The court shall consider the progress in providing the information and documents to the nonminor depen-

dent as described in Section 391. The court shall also consider the need for, and progress in providing, the assistance and services described in Section 391.

(7) The likely date by which it is anticipated the nonminor dependent will achieve adoption or independence.

(8) Whether the agency has made reasonable efforts as required in subparagraph (D) of paragraph (1) of subdivision (a) of Section 366 to establish or maintain the nonminor dependent's relationship with his or her siblings who are under the juvenile court's jurisdiction.

(9) The services needed to assist the nonminor dependent to make the transition from foster care to successful adulthood.

(10) When the hearing described in this subdivision is held pursuant to paragraph (3) or (4) of subdivision (d) of Section 366.3, and the nonminor dependent has a permanent plan of another planned permanent living arrangement, the court shall do all of the following:

(A) Ask the nonminor dependent about his or her desired permanency outcome.

(B) Make a judicial determination explaining why, as of the hearing date, another planned permanent living arrangement is the best permanency plan for the nonminor dependent.

(C) State for the record the compelling reason or reasons why it continues not to be in the best interest of the nonminor dependent to return home, be placed for adoption, be placed for tribal customary adoption in the case of an Indian child, be placed with a legal guardian, or be placed with a fit and willing relative.

(f)(1) At a hearing to consider a permanent plan of adoption for a nonminor dependent, the court shall read and consider the report in paragraph (5) and receive other evidence that the parties may present. A copy of the executed negotiated agreement shall be attached to the report. If the court finds pursuant to this section that nonminor dependent adoption is the appropriate permanent plan, it shall make findings and orders to do the following:

(A) Approve the adoption agreement and declare the nonminor dependent is the adopted child of the adoptive parent, and that the nonminor dependent and adoptive parents agree to assume toward each other the legal relationship of parents and child and to have all of the rights and be subject to all of the duties and responsibilities of that relationship.

(B) Declare that the birth parents of the nonminor dependent are, from the time of the adoption, relieved of all parental duties toward, and responsibility for, the adopted nonminor dependent and have no rights over the adopted nonminor dependent.

(2) If the court finds that the nonminor dependent and the prospective adoptive parent have mutually consented to the adoption, the court may enter the adoption order after it determines all of the following:

(A) Whether the notice was given as required by law.

(B) Whether the nonminor dependent and prospective adoptive parent are present for the hearing.

(C) Whether the court has read and considered the assessment prepared by the social worker or probation officer.

(D) Whether the court considered the wishes of the nonminor dependent.

(E) If the nonminor dependent is eligible, the prospective adoptive parent has signed the negotiated adoption assistance agreement pursuant to subdivision (g) of Section 16120, and whether a copy of the executed negotiated agreement is attached to the report.

(F) Whether the adoption is in the best interest of the nonminor dependent.

(3) If the court orders the establishment of the nonminor dependent adoption, it shall dismiss dependency or transitional jurisdiction.

(4) If the court does not order the establishment of the nonminor dependent adoption, the nonminor dependent shall remain in a planned permanent living arrangement subject to periodic review of the juvenile court pursuant to this section.

(5) At least 10 calendar days before the hearing, the social worker or probation officer shall file a report with the court and provide a copy of the report to all parties. The report shall describe the following:

(A) Whether or not the nonminor dependent has any developmental disability and whether the proposed adoptive parent is suitable to meet the needs of the nonminor dependent.

(B) The length and nature of the relationship between the prospective adoptive parent and the nonminor dependent, including whether the prospective adoptive parent has been determined to have been established as the nonminor's permanent connection.

(C) Whether the nonminor dependent has been determined to be eligible for the adoption assistance program and, if so, whether the prospective adoptive parent has signed the negotiated adoption assistance agreement pursuant to subdivision (g) of Section 16120.

(D) Whether a copy of the executed negotiated agreement is attached to the report.

(E) Whether criminal background clearances were completed for the prospective adoptive parent as required by Section 671(a)(20)(A) and (a)(20)(C) of Title 42 of the United States Code.

(F) Whether the prospective adoptive parent who is married and not legally separated from that spouse has the consent of the spouse, provided that the spouse is capable of giving that consent.

(G) Whether the adoption of the nonminor dependent is in the best interests of the nonminor dependent and the prospective adoptive parent.

(H) Whether the nonminor dependent and the prospective adoptive parent have mutually consented to the adoption.

(6) The social worker or probation officer shall serve written notice of the hearing in the manner and to the persons set forth in Section 295, including the prospective

adoptive parent or parents, except that notice to the nonminor's birth parents is not required.

(7) Nothing in this section shall prevent a nonminor dependent from filing an adoption petition pursuant to Section 9300 of the Family Code.

(g) Each licensed foster family agency shall submit reports for each nonminor dependent in its care to the court concerning the continuing appropriateness and extent of compliance with the nonminor dependent's permanent plan, the extent of compliance with the transitional independent living case plan, and the type and adequacy of services provided to the nonminor dependent. The report shall document that the nonminor has received all the information and documentation described in paragraph (2) of subdivision (e) of Section 391. If the court is considering terminating dependency jurisdiction for a nonminor dependent it shall first hold a hearing pursuant to Section 391.

(h) When the nonminor dependent is in another planned permanent living arrangement, the social study prepared for the hearing held under subdivision (e) shall include a description of all of the following:

(1) The intensive and ongoing efforts to return the nonminor dependent to the home of the parent, place the nonminor dependent for adoption, or place the nonminor dependent with a fit and willing relative, as appropriate.

(2) The steps taken to do both of the following:

(A) Ensure that the nonminor dependent's care provider is following the reasonable and prudent parent standard.

(B) Determine whether the nonminor dependent has regular, ongoing opportunities to engage in age or developmentally appropriate activities, including consulting with the nonminor dependent about opportunities for the nonminor dependent to participate in those activities. *(Added by Stats.2012, c. 846 (A.B.1712), § 26. Amended by Stats.2013, c. 487 (A.B.787), § 1; Stats.2014, c. 71 (S.B.1304), § 182, eff. Jan. 1, 2015; Stats.2015, c. 425 (S.B.794), § 15, eff. Jan. 1, 2016.)*

Research References

Forms

West's California Judicial Council Forms JV-475, Agreement Of Adoption Of Nonminor Dependent.
West's California Judicial Council Forms JV-477, Consent Of Spouse or Registered Partner to Adoption Of Nonminor Dependent.
West's California Judicial Council Forms JV-479, Order Of Adoption Of Nonminor Dependent.

Treatises and Practice Aids

Witkin, California Summary 10th Parent and Child § 4, Public Welfare Services.
Witkin, California Summary 10th Parent and Child § 662, Nature and Purpose.
Witkin, California Summary 10th Parent and Child § 671, Supplemental Report.
Witkin, California Summary 10th Parent and Child § 673, Child in Foster Care.
Witkin, California Summary 10th Parent and Child § 696, Continuing Jurisdiction.
Witkin, California Summary 10th Parent and Child § 698, Other Procedures.
Witkin, California Summary 10th Parent and Child § 897, Reunification Services.
Witkin, California Summary 10th Parent and Child § 452G, (New) Assumption Of Jurisdiction Over Nonminor.
Witkin, California Summary 10th Parent and Child § 669A, (New) Review Hearings Just Before and After Minor Attains Age 18.
Witkin, California Summary 10th Parent and Child § 699A, (New) in General.

§ 366.32. Nonminor dependents having permanent plan of long-term foster care; continuing jurisdiction

(a) With respect to a nonminor dependent, as defined in subdivision (v) of Section 11400, who has a permanent plan of long-term foster care that was ordered pursuant to Section 366.21, 366.22, 366.25, or 366.26, the court may continue jurisdiction of the nonminor as a nonminor dependent of the juvenile court or may dismiss dependency jurisdiction pursuant to Section 391.

(b) If the court continues dependency jurisdiction of the nonminor as a nonminor dependent of the juvenile court, the court shall order the development of a planned permanent living arrangement under a mutual agreement, as described in subdivision (u) of Section 11400, which may include continued placement with the current caregiver or another licensed or approved caregiver or in a supervised independent living placement, as defined in subdivision (w) of Section 11400, consistent with the youth's Transitional Independent Living Case Plan. At the request of the nonminor dependent who has an established relationship with an adult determined to be the nonminor dependent's permanent connection, the court may order nonminor dependent adoption pursuant to subdivision (f) of Section 366.31 as the nonminor dependent's permanent plan.

(c) If the court terminates its dependency jurisdiction over a nonminor dependent pursuant to subdivision (a), it shall retain general jurisdiction over the youth pursuant to Section 303. If the court has dismissed dependency jurisdiction pursuant to subdivision (d) of Section 391, the nonminor, who has not attained 21 years of age, may subsequently file a petition pursuant to subdivision (e) of Section 388 to have dependency jurisdiction resumed and the court may vacate its previous order dismissing dependency jurisdiction over the nonminor dependent. *(Added by Stats.2012, c. 846 (A.B. 1712), § 27.)*

Research References

Treatises and Practice Aids

Witkin, California Summary 10th Parent and Child § 673, Child in Foster Care.
Witkin, California Summary 10th Parent and Child § 696, Continuing Jurisdiction.
Witkin, California Summary 10th Parent and Child § 699A, (New) in General.

§ 366.35. Implementation and operation of enumerated provisions subject to appropriations; county's nonfederal share of costs

(a) The implementation and operation of the amendments to subparagraph (B) of paragraph (1) of subdivision (a) of Section 366, subdivision (g) of Section 366.1, subdivisions (c) and (g) of Section 366.21, subdivision (a) of Section 366.22, subdivision (a) of Section 366.25, paragraph (3) of, and subparagraph (A) of paragraph (4) of, subdivision (c) of Section 366.26, paragraphs (2) and (3) of subdivision (e) of Section 366.3, and subdivision (i) of Section 16501.1 enacted at the 2005–06 Regular Session shall be phased in, consistent with the child's best interests, as follows:

(1) The first phase of expansion shall apply to a child who is 10 years of age or older and placed with a nonrelative for six months or longer.

(2) The second phase of expansion shall apply to a child who is 10 years of age or older and placed with a nonrelative or in permanent placement relative care for six months or longer.

(3) The final phase of expansion shall apply to a child who is 10 years of age or older and who has been in out-of-home placement for six months or longer.

(b) All phases of subdivision (a) shall be subject to appropriation through the budget process. Those appropriations shall apply only to the state's share of costs. Counties shall remain responsible for their nonfederal share of costs. *(Added by Stats.2005, c. 640 (A.B.1412), § 8. Amended by Stats.2008, c. 482 (A.B.2070), § 8.)*

Research References

Treatises and Practice Aids

Witkin, California Summary 10th Parent and Child § 671, Supplemental Report.

Witkin, California Summary 10th Parent and Child § 673, Child in Foster Care.

Witkin, California Summary 10th Parent and Child § 678, Twelve-Month Review.

Witkin, California Summary 10th Parent and Child § 679, Eighteen-Month Review.

Witkin, California Summary 10th Parent and Child § 688, Other Alternatives.

Witkin, California Summary 10th Parent and Child § 679A, (New) Twenty-Four Month Review.

§ 366.4. Guardianships resulting from selection or implementation of a permanency plan; jurisdiction; law governing; exemption applicable to nonrelated legal guardians

(a) Any minor for whom a guardianship has been established resulting from the selection or implementation of a permanency plan pursuant to Section 366.26, or for whom a related guardianship has been established pursuant to Section 360, or, on and after the date that the director executes a declaration pursuant to Section 11217, a nonminor who is receiving Kin–GAP payments pursuant to Section 11363 or 11386, or, on or after January 1, 2012, a nonminor former dependent child of the juvenile court who is receiving AFDC–FC benefits pursuant to Section 11405, is within the jurisdiction of the juvenile court. For those minors, Part 2 (commencing with Section 1500) of Division 4 of the Probate Code, relating to guardianship, shall not apply. If no specific provision of this code or the California Rules of Court is applicable, the provisions applicable to the administration of estates under Part 4 (commencing with Section 2100) of Division 4 of the Probate Code govern so far as they are applicable to like situations.

(b) Nonrelated legal guardians of the person of a guardianship pursuant to Section 360 or 366.26 shall be exempt from the provisions of Sections 2850 and 2851 of the Probate Code. *(Added by Stats.1990, c. 1530 (S.B.2232), § 9. Amended by Stats.1998, c. 1056 (A.B.2773), § 19; Stats.2002, c. 1115 (A.B.3036), § 5; Stats.2003, c. 62 (S.B.600), § 320; Stats.2010, c. 559 (A.B.12), § 25; Stats.2011, c. 459 (A.B.212), § 9, eff. Oct. 4, 2011.)*

Research References

Treatises and Practice Aids

Witkin, California Summary 10th Parent and Child § 521, Termination Of Jurisdiction.

Witkin, California Summary 10th Parent and Child § 628, Legal Guardianship.

Witkin, California Summary 10th Parent and Child § 696, Continuing Jurisdiction.

Witkin, California Summary 10th Parent and Child § 698, Other Procedures.

§ 366.5. Suspension of dependency jurisdiction for dual status children

The dependency jurisdiction shall be suspended for a child whom the juvenile court declares to be a dual status child based on the joint assessment and recommendation of the county probation department and the child welfare services department pursuant to subparagraph (A) of paragraph (5) of subdivision (e) of Section 241.1. The suspension shall be in effect while the child is a ward of the court. If the jurisdiction established pursuant to Section 601 or 602 is terminated without the need for continued dependency proceedings concerning the child, the juvenile court shall terminate the child's dual status. If the termination of the Section 601 or 602 jurisdiction is likely and reunification of the child with his or her parent or guardian would be detrimental to the child, the county probation department and child welfare services department shall jointly assess and produce a recommendation regarding whether the court's dependency jurisdiction shall be resumed. *(Added by Stats. 2004, c. 468 (A.B.129), § 3.)*

Research References

Treatises and Practice Aids

Witkin, California Summary 10th Parent and Child § 450, Dual Bases Of Jurisdiction.

Witkin, California Summary 10th Parent and Child § 655, Nature and Purpose.

§ 367. Detention until execution of commitment order; review of detention of minor

(a) Whenever a person has been adjudged a dependent child of the juvenile court and has been committed or otherwise disposed of as provided in this chapter for the care of dependent children of the juvenile court, the court may order that the dependent child be detained in a suitable place designated as the court deems fit until the execution of the order of commitment or of other disposition.

(b) In any case in which a child is detained for more than 15 days pending the execution of the order of commitment or of any other disposition, the court shall periodically review the case to determine whether the delay is reasonable. These periodic reviews shall be held at least every 15 days, commencing from the time the child was initially detained pending the execution of the order of commitment or of any other disposition, and during the course of each review the court shall inquire regarding the action taken by the social worker to carry out its order, the reasons for the delay, and the effect of the delay upon the child. *(Added by Stats.1976, c. 1068, p. 4773, § 10. Amended by Stats.1978, c. 1168, p. 3777, § 5; Stats.1998, c. 1054 (A.B.1091), § 38; Stats.2001, c. 854 (S.B.205), § 71.)*

Research References

Treatises and Practice Aids

Witkin, California Summary 10th Parent and Child § 633, in General.

§ 368. Nonresident dependent children of court

In a case where the residence of a dependent child of the juvenile court is out of the state and in another state or foreign country, or in a case where that child is a resident of this state but his or her parents, relatives, guardian, or person charged with his or her custody is in another state, the court may order that child sent to his or her parents, relatives, or guardian, or to the person charged with his or her custody, or, if the child is a resident of a foreign country, to an official of a juvenile court of that foreign country or an agency of a country authorized to accept the child, and in that case may order transportation and accommodation furnished, with or without an attendant, as the court deems necessary. If the court deems an attendant necessary, the court may order the social worker or other suitable person to serve as the attendant. The social worker shall authorize the necessary expenses of the child and of the attendant and claims therefor shall be audited, allowed and paid in the same manner as other county claims. *(Added by Stats.1976, c. 1068, p. 4773, § 10. Amended by Stats.1998, c. 1054 (A.B.1091), § 39.)*

Research References

Treatises and Practice Aids

Witkin, California Summary 10th Parent and Child § 627, in General.

§ 369. Medical, surgical or dental care; recommendation of physician and surgeon; court order; release of information; construction of section

(a) Whenever a person is taken into temporary custody under Article 7 (commencing with Section 305) and is in need of medical, surgical, dental, or other remedial care, the social worker may, upon the recommendation of the attending physician and surgeon or, if the person needs dental care and there is an attending dentist, the attending dentist, authorize the performance of the medical, surgical, dental, or other remedial care. The social worker shall notify the parent, guardian, or person standing in loco parentis of the person, if any, of the care found to be needed before that care is provided, and if the parent, guardian, or person standing in loco parentis objects, that care shall be given only upon order of the court in the exercise of its discretion.

(b) Whenever it appears to the juvenile court that a person concerning whom a petition has been filed with the court is in need of medical, surgical, dental, or other remedial care, and that there is no parent, guardian, or person standing in loco parentis capable of authorizing or willing to authorize the remedial care or treatment for that person, the court, upon the written recommendation of a licensed physician and surgeon or, if the person needs dental care, a licensed dentist, and after due notice to the parent, guardian, or person standing in loco parentis, if any, may make an order authorizing the performance of the necessary medical, surgical, dental, or other remedial care for that person.

(c) Whenever a dependent child of the juvenile court is placed by order of the court within the care and custody or under the supervision of a social worker of the county where the dependent child resides and it appears to the court that there is no parent, guardian, or person standing in loco parentis capable of authorizing or willing to authorize medical, surgical, dental, or other remedial care or treatment for the dependent child, the court may, after due notice to the parent, guardian, or person standing in loco parentis, if any, order that the social worker may authorize the medical, surgical, dental, or other remedial care for the dependent child, by licensed practitioners, as necessary.

(d) Whenever it appears that a child otherwise within subdivision (a), (b), or (c) requires immediate emergency medical, surgical, or other remedial care in an emergency situation, that care may be provided by a licensed physician and surgeon or, if the child needs dental care in an emergency situation, by a licensed dentist, without a court order and upon authorization of a social worker. The social worker shall make reasonable efforts to obtain the consent of, or to notify, the parent, guardian, or person standing in loco parentis prior to authorizing emergency medical, surgical, dental, or other remedial care. "Emergency situation," for the purposes of this subdivision means a child requires immediate treatment for the alleviation of severe pain or an immediate diagnosis and treatment of an unforeseeable medical, surgical, dental, or other remedial condition or contagious disease which if not immediately diagnosed and treated, would lead to serious disability or death.

(e) In any case in which the court orders the performance of any medical, surgical, dental, or other remedial care pursuant to this section, the court may also make an order authorizing the release of information concerning that care to social workers, parole officers, or any other qualified individuals or agencies caring for or acting in the interest and welfare of the child under order, commitment, or approval of the court.

(f) Nothing in this section shall be construed as limiting the right of a parent, guardian, or person standing in loco parentis, who has not been deprived of the custody or control of the child by order of the court, in providing any medical, surgical, dental, or other remedial treatment recognized or permitted under the laws of this state.

(g) The parent of a person described in this section may authorize the performance of medical, surgical, dental, or other remedial care provided for in this section notwithstanding his or her age or marital status. In nonemergency situations, the parent authorizing the care shall notify the other parent prior to the administration of that care.

(h) Nothing in this section shall be construed as limiting the rights of dependent children, pursuant to Chapter 3 (commencing with Section 6920) of Part 4 of Division 11 of the Family Code, to consent to, among other things, the diagnosis and treatment of sexual assault, medical care relating to the prevention or treatment of pregnancy, including contraception, abortion, and prenatal care, treatment of infectious, contagious, or communicable diseases, mental health treatment, and treatment for alcohol and drug abuse. If a dependent child is 12 years of age or older, his or her social worker is authorized to inform the child of his or her right as a minor to consent to and receive those health services, as necessary. Social workers are authorized to provide dependent children access to age-appropriate, medically accurate information about sexual development, reproductive health, and prevention of unplanned pregnancies and sexually transmitted infections. *(Added by Stats.1976, c. 1068, p. 4773, § 10. Amended by Stats.1990, c. 566 (A.B. 2193), § 1; Stats.1998, c. 1054 (A.B.1091), § 40; Stats.2013, c. 338 (S.B.528), § 1.)*

Commentary

A juvenile court lacked jurisdiction to order a minor to undergo blood transfusions against his will and over the objection of his parents when the state agency failed to file a juvenile dependency petition pursuant to section 300(b), asserting that the minor was at substantial risk of suffering serious physical harm because of his parent's religiously-based refusal to provide him with necessary medical treatment. The minor also had not been taken in custody pursuant to section 305 and had not been adjudicated a dependent child. The court could not dispense with the statutory requirements in order to avoid stigma to the parents. *San Joaquin County Human Services Agency v. Marcus W., 185 Cal.App.4th 182, 110 Cal.Rptr.3d 232 (2010).*

Research References

Treatises and Practice Aids

Witkin, California Summary 10th Parent and Child § 559, Medical Care.

§ 369.5. Psychotropic medications; authorization based on physician request; adoption of rules and forms for implementation of section; agency completion of request; time for decision on request

(a)(1) If a child is adjudged a dependent child of the court under Section 300 and the child has been removed from the physical custody of the parent under Section 361, only a juvenile court judicial officer shall have authority to make orders regarding the administration of psychotropic medications for that child. The juvenile court may issue a specific order delegating this authority to a parent upon making findings on the record that the parent poses no danger to the child and has the capacity to authorize psychotropic medications. Court authorization for the administration of psychotropic medication shall be based on a request from a physician, indicating the reasons for the request, a description of the child's diagnosis and behavior, the expected results of the medication, and a description of any side effects of the medication.

(2)(A) On or before July 1, 2016, the Judicial Council shall amend and adopt rules of court and develop appropriate forms for the implementation of this section, in consultation with the State Department of Social Services, the State Department of Health Care Services, and stakeholders, including, but not limited to, the County Welfare Directors Association of California, the County Behavioral Health Directors Association of California, the Chief Probation Officers of California, associations representing current and former foster children, caregivers, and children's attorneys. This effort shall be undertaken in coordination with the updates required under paragraph (2) of subdivision (a) of Section 739.5.

(B) The rules of court and forms developed pursuant to subparagraph (A) shall address all of the following:

(i) The child and his or her caregiver and court-appointed special advocate, if any, have an opportunity to provide input on the medications being prescribed.

(ii) Information regarding the child's overall mental health assessment and treatment plan is provided to the court.

(iii) Information regarding the rationale for the proposed medication, provided in the context of past and current treatment efforts, is provided to the court. This information shall include, but not be limited to, information on other pharmacological and nonpharmacological treatments that have been utilized and the child's response to those treatments, a discussion of symptoms not alleviated or ameliorated by other current or past treatment efforts, and an explanation of how the psychotropic medication being prescribed is expected to improve the child's symptoms.

(iv) Guidance is provided to the court on how to evaluate the request for authorization, including how to proceed if information, otherwise required to be included in a request for authorization under this section, is not included in a request for authorization submitted to the court.

(C) The rules of court and forms developed pursuant to subparagraph (A) shall include a process for periodic oversight by the court of orders regarding the administration of psychotropic medications that includes the caregiver's and child's observations regarding the effectiveness of the medication and side effects, information on medication management appointments and other followup appointments with medical practitioners, and information on the delivery of other mental health treatments that are a part of the child's overall treatment plan. The periodic oversight shall be facilitated by the county social worker, public health nurse, or other appropriate county staff. This oversight process shall be conducted in conjunction with other regularly scheduled court hearings and reports provided to the court by the county child welfare agency.

(b)(1) In counties in which the county child welfare agency completes the request for authorization for the administration of psychotropic medication, the agency is encouraged to complete the request within three business days of receipt from the physician of the information necessary to fully complete the request.

(2) Nothing in this subdivision is intended to change current local practice or local court rules with respect to the preparation and submission of requests for authorization for the administration of psychotropic medication.

(c)(1) Within seven court days from receipt by the court of a completed request, the juvenile court judicial officer shall either approve or deny in writing a request for authorization for the administration of psychotropic medication to the child, or shall, upon a request by the parent, the legal guardian, or the child's attorney, or upon its own motion, set the matter for hearing.

(2) Notwithstanding Section 827 or any other law, upon the approval or denial by the juvenile court judicial officer of a request for authorization for the administration of psychotropic medication, the county child welfare agency or other person or entity who submitted the request shall provide a copy of the court order approving or denying the request to the child's caregiver.

(d) Psychotropic medication or psychotropic drugs are those medications administered for the purpose of affecting the central nervous system to treat psychiatric disorders or illnesses. These medications include, but are not limited to, anxiolytic agents, antidepressants, mood stabilizers, antipsychotic medications, anti-Parkinson agents, hypnotics, medications for dementia, and psychostimulants.

(e) Nothing in this section is intended to supersede local court rules regarding a minor's right to participate in mental health decisions.

(f) This section does not apply to nonminor dependents, as defined in subdivision (v) of Section 11400. *(Added by Stats.1999, c. 552 (S.B.543), § 1. Amended by Stats.2004, c. 329 (A.B.2502), § 1; Stats.2012, c. 846 (A.B.1712), § 28; Stats.2015, c. 534 (S.B.238), § 5, eff. Jan. 1, 2016.)*

Research References

Forms

West's California Judicial Council Forms JV-218, Child's Opinion About the Medicine.
West's California Judicial Council Forms JV-219, Statement About Medicine Prescribed.
West's California Judicial Council Forms JV-220, Application and Order for Authorization to Administer Psychotropic Medication.
West's California Judicial Council Forms JV-221, Proof Of Notice: Application Regarding Psychotropic Medication.
West's California Judicial Council Forms JV-222, Opposition to Application Regarding Psychotropic Medication.
West's California Judicial Council Forms JV-223, Order Regarding Application for Psychotropic Medication.
West's California Judicial Council Forms JV-224, Order Regarding Eligibility for Special Immigrant Juvenile Status.
West's California Judicial Council Forms JV-220(A), Prescribing Physician's Statement--Attachment.
West's California Judicial Council Forms JV-220(B), Physician's Request to Continue Medication--Attachment.
West's California Judicial Council Forms JV-217-INFO, Guide to Psychotropic Medication Forms.
West's California Judicial Council Forms JV-219-INFO, Information About Psychotropic Medication Forms.

Treatises and Practice Aids

Witkin, California Summary 10th Parent and Child § 629, Limitations on Parental Control.
Witkin, California Summary 10th Parent and Child § 699A, (New) in General.

§ 369.6. Record review for authorization requests for psychotropic medications

(a)(1) The State Department of Social Services, in consultation with the State Department of Health Care Services, shall contract for child psychiatry services to complete a record review for all authorization requests for psychotropic medications for which a second opinion review is requested by a county. To the extent feasible, the second opinion review shall occur within three business days of the county request and shall include discussion of the psychosocial interventions that have been or will be offered to the child and caretaker, if appropriate, to address the behavioral health needs of the child.

(2)(A) Recommended indicators for identifying those requests for authorizations of psychotropic medications for which a county may request a second opinion record review may include, but are not limited to, prescriptions for concurrent psychotropic medications, dosages that exceed recommended guidelines for use in children, off-label prescribing, and requests for psychotropic medication usage without any other concurrent psychosocial services.

(B) The State Department of Social Services shall, by July 1, 2018, issue guidance regarding the second opinion review process and may periodically revise that guidance following consultation with counties, other state departments, advocates for children and youth, and other stakeholders.

(3) The child psychiatry services contracted for by the State Department of Social Services shall be available to provide second opinion reviews to those counties that do not have a second opinion review program. This section does not prohibit a county from operating its own second opinion review program and does not supersede any county-operated second opinion review program.

(4) This section does not prevent the administration of medication in an emergency, as otherwise authorized or required by law or regulation.

(b) The State Department of Health Care Services shall seek any necessary federal approvals to obtain federal financial participation for the second opinion review service pursuant to this section, including any approvals necessary to obtain enhanced federal financial participation as applicable. Notwithstanding any other law, this section shall be implemented only if, and to the extent that, any necessary federal approvals are obtained by the department and federal financial participation is available and is not otherwise jeopardized. *(Added by Stats.2017, c. 24 (S.B.89), § 11, eff. June 27, 2017.)*

§ 370. Services of psychiatrists, psychologists and clinical experts; payment

The juvenile court may, in any case before it in which a petition has been filed as provided in Article 7 (commencing with Section 305), order that the social worker obtain the services of those psychiatrists, psychologists, or other clinical experts as may be required to assist in determining the appropriate treatment of the child and as may be required in the conduct or implementation of that treatment. Payment for those services shall be a charge against the county. *(Added by Stats.1976, c. 1068, p. 4773, § 10. Amended by Stats.1998, c. 1054 (A.B.1091), § 41.)*

Research References

Treatises and Practice Aids

Witkin, California Summary 10th Parent and Child § 490, Psychiatric and Other Clinical Experts.

Witkin, California Summary 10th Parent and Child § 577, Hearing.

§ 371. Information to be provided regarding working with mental health providers

When the court has ordered a dependent child or a ward of the juvenile court placed for adoption or has appointed a relative or nonrelative legal guardian, the social worker or probation officer shall provide the prospective adoptive family or the guardian or guardians information, in writing, regarding the importance of working with mental health providers that have specialized adoption or permanency clinical training and experience if the family needs clinical support, and a description of the desirable clinical expertise the family should look for when choosing an adoption- or permanency-competent mental health professional. *(Added by Stats.2017, c. 714 (A.B.1006), § 1, eff. Jan. 1, 2018.)*

ARTICLE 11. DEPENDENT CHILDREN—TRANSFER OF CASES BETWEEN COUNTIES

§ 375. Petition; conditions for transfer; change of residence of nonminor dependent

(a) Whenever a petition is filed in the juvenile court of a county other than the residence of the person named in the petition, or whenever, subsequent to the filing of a petition in the juvenile court of the county where that minor resides, the residence of the person who would be legally entitled to the custody of the minor were it not for the existence of a court order issued pursuant to this chapter is changed to another county, the entire case may be transferred to the juvenile court of the county where that person then resides at any time after the court has made a finding of the facts upon which it has exercised its jurisdiction over the minor, and the juvenile court of the county where that person then resides shall take jurisdiction of the case upon the receipt and filing of the finding of the facts upon which the court exercised its jurisdiction and an order transferring the case.

(b)(1) Whenever a minor under the dependency jurisdiction or transition jurisdiction of the juvenile court attains 18 years of age and remains under the court's jurisdiction as a nonminor dependent, as defined in subdivision (v) of Section 11400, the residence of the nonminor dependent may be changed to another county if the court finds that the nonminor dependent meets the conditions of subdivision (f) of Section 17.1. The entire case may be transferred to the juvenile court of the county where the nonminor dependent then resides at any time after the court has made a finding of the facts upon which the court has exercised its jurisdiction over the nonminor. The juvenile court of the county where a nonminor then resides shall take jurisdiction of the case upon the receipt and filing of that finding and an order transferring the case.

(2) Whenever a petition pursuant to subdivision (e) of Section 388 is submitted in the juvenile court of a county other than the county that retained general jurisdiction under subdivision (b) of Section 303 of the nonminor dependent, as defined in subdivision (v) of Section 11400, the residence of the nonminor dependent may be changed to another county if the nonminor dependent meets the conditions of subdivision (g) of Section 17.1. The entire case may be transferred to the juvenile court of the county where the nonminor dependent then resides at any time after the county that retained general jurisdiction has granted the petition and resumed dependency jurisdiction, or has assumed or resumed transition jurisdiction. The juvenile court of the county where the nonminor then resides shall take jurisdiction of the case upon the receipt and filing of the finding of the facts upon which the court exercised its jurisdiction over the nonminor and an order transferring the case. *(Added by Stats.1976, c. 1068, p. 4777, § 11. Amended by Stats.2012, c. 846 (A.B.1712), § 29.)*

Commentary

In re Christopher T., 60 Cal.App.4th 1282, 71 Cal.Rptr.2d 116 (1998), review denied April 15, 1998, holds that, reading this section together with Cal. Rules of Ct., Rule 1425, a juvenile court may transfer a dependency proceeding from the country where a parent resides to a county where the dependent child has relocated with his guardians.

Research References

Forms

West's California Judicial Council Forms JV-550, Juvenile Court Transfer Orders.

Treatises and Practice Aids

Witkin, California Summary 10th Parent and Child § 457, in General.
Witkin, California Summary 10th Parent and Child § 458, Conditions for Transfer.
Witkin, California Summary 10th Parent and Child § 461, Transfer-Out Hearing and Order.
Witkin, California Summary 10th Parent and Child § 463, Transfer-In Hearing.
Witkin, California Summary 10th Parent and Child § 704, Miscellaneous Orders.

§ 376. Expenses

The expense of the transfer and all expenses in connection with the transfer and for the support and maintenance of such person shall be paid from the county treasury of the court ordering the transfer until the receipt and filing of the finding and order of transfer in the juvenile court of the transferee county.

The judge shall inquire into the financial condition of such person and of the parent, parents, guardian, or other person charged with his support and maintenance, and if he finds such person, parent, parents, guardian, or other person able, in whole or in part, to pay the expense of such transfer, he shall make a further order requiring such person, parent, parents, guardian, or other person to repay to the county such part, or all, of such expense of transfer as, in the opinion of the court, is proper. Such repayment shall be made to the probation officer who shall keep suitable accounts of such expenses and repayments and shall deposit all such collections in the county treasury. *(Added by Stats.1976, c. 1068, p. 4777, § 11.)*

Research References

Treatises and Practice Aids

Witkin, California Summary 10th Parent and Child § 457, in General.

§ 377. Order for transfer; accompanying documents

Whenever a case is transferred as provided in Section 375, the order of transfer shall recite each and all of the findings, orders, or modification of orders that have been made in the case, and shall include the name and address of the legal residence of the parent or guardian of the minor. All papers contained in the file shall be transferred to the county where such person resides. A copy of the order of transfer and of the findings of fact as required in Section 375 shall be kept in the file of the transferring county. *(Added by Stats.1976, c. 1068, p. 4777, § 11.)*

Research References

Treatises and Practice Aids

Witkin, California Summary 10th Parent and Child § 461, Transfer-Out Hearing and Order.

§ 378. Procedure on transfer

Whenever an order of transfer from another county is filed with the clerk of any juvenile court, the clerk shall place the transfer order on the calendar of the court, and it shall have precedence over all actions and civil proceedings not specifically given precedence by other provisions of law and shall be heard by the court at the earliest possible moment following the filing of the order. *(Added by Stats.1976, c. 1068, p. 4777, § 11.)*

Research References

Treatises and Practice Aids

Witkin, California Summary 10th Parent and Child § 463, Transfer-In Hearing.

Witkin, California Summary 10th Parent and Child § 464A, (New) Transfer to Indian Tribe.

§ 379. County appeal from residence order

In any action under the provisions of this article in which the residence of a minor person is determined, both the county in which the court is situated and any other county which, as a result of the determination of residence, might be determined to be the county of residence of the minor person, shall be considered to be parties in the action and shall have the right to appeal any order by which residence of the minor person is determined. *(Added by Stats.1976, c. 1068, p. 4777, § 11.)*

Research References

Treatises and Practice Aids

Witkin, California Summary 10th Parent and Child § 460, Appeal from Determination Of Residence.

Witkin, California Summary 10th Parent and Child § 704, Miscellaneous Orders.

§ 380. Order permitting residence in different county

Any person adjudged to be a dependent child of the juvenile court may be permitted by order of the court to reside in a county other than the county of his or her legal residence, and the court shall retain jurisdiction over that person.

Whenever a dependent child of the juvenile court is permitted to reside in a county other than the county of his or her legal residence, he or she may be placed under the supervision of the social worker of the county of actual residence, with the consent of the social worker. The dependent child shall comply with the instructions of the social worker and upon failure to do so shall be returned to the county of his or her legal residence for further hearing and order of the court. *(Added by Stats.1976, c. 1068, p. 4777, § 11. Amended by Stats.1998, c. 1054 (A.B.1091), § 42.)*

Research References

Treatises and Practice Aids

Witkin, California Summary 10th Parent and Child § 464, Continuing Jurisdiction Outside County.

Witkin, California Summary 10th Parent and Child § 627, in General.

§ 381. Transfer from juvenile court of a county to a tribe; order of transfer; prioritization with other matters on court calendar

(a) If a transfer is made from a juvenile court of a county to a tribe pursuant to Section 305.5, the case shall be transferred to the tribe after the court has made a determination that the transfer is required pursuant to subdivision (a), (b), or (f) of Section 305.5. The Juvenile court and the tribe shall each document the finding of the facts supporting jurisdiction over the minor.

(b) The juvenile court shall issue an order of transfer of the case that states all of the findings, orders, or modification of orders that have been made in the case, and the name and address of the tribe having jurisdiction. All papers contained in the file shall be transferred to the tribe having jurisdiction. The transferring county shall maintain a copy of the order of transfer and the findings of fact.

(c) If an order of transfer from a county to a tribe is filed with the clerk of a juvenile court, the clerk shall place the transfer order on the calendar of the court, and, notwithstanding Section 378, that matter shall have precedence over all actions and civil proceedings not specifically given precedence by any other law and shall be heard by the court at the earliest possible moment after the order is filed. *(Added by Stats.2014, c. 772 (S.B.1460), § 12, eff. Jan. 1, 2015.)*

Research References

Treatises and Practice Aids

Witkin, California Summary 10th Parent and Child § 464A, (New) Transfer to Indian Tribe.

ARTICLE 12. DEPENDENT CHILDREN—MODIFICATION OF JUVENILE COURT JUDGMENTS AND ORDERS

§ 385. Changing, modifying or setting aside orders; procedural requirements

Any order made by the court in the case of any person subject to its jurisdiction may at any time be changed, modified, or set aside, as the judge deems meet and proper, subject to such procedural requirements as are imposed by this article. *(Added by Stats.1976, c. 1068, p. 4778, § 12.)*

Research References

Treatises and Practice Aids

Witkin, California Summary 10th Parent and Child § 654, Power to Modify or Correct.

Witkin, California Summary 10th Parent and Child § 665, Right to Hearing.

§ 386. Notice of application

No order changing, modifying, or setting aside a previous order of the juvenile court shall be made either in chambers, or otherwise, unless prior notice of the application therefor has been given by the judge or the clerk of the court to the social worker and to the child's counsel of record, or, if there is no counsel of record, to the child and his or her parent or guardian. *(Added by Stats.1976, c. 1068, p. 4778, § 12. Amended by Stats.1998, c. 1054 (A.B.1091), § 43.)*

Research References

Treatises and Practice Aids

Witkin, California Summary 10th Parent and Child § 584, Rights Of Siblings.

Witkin, California Summary 10th Parent and Child § 654, Power to Modify or Correct.

Witkin, California Summary 10th Parent and Child § 664, in General.

§ 387. Order for removal from custody and placement in foster home or institution; hearing upon supplemental petition; dependency jurisdiction for dual status children

(a) An order changing or modifying a previous order by removing a child from the physical custody of a parent, guardian, relative, or friend and directing placement in a foster home, or commitment to a private or county institution, shall be made only after noticed hearing upon a supplemental petition.

(b) The supplemental petition shall be filed by the social worker in the original matter and shall contain a concise statement of facts sufficient to support the conclusion that the previous disposition has not been effective in the rehabilitation or protection of the child or, in the case of a placement with a relative, sufficient to show that the placement is not appropriate in view of the criteria in Section 361.3.

(c) Notwithstanding subdivision (a), dependency jurisdiction shall be resumed for a child as to whom dependency jurisdiction has been suspended pursuant to Section 366.5 if the jurisdiction established pursuant to Section 601 or 602 is terminated and if, after the issuance of a joint assessment pursuant to Section 366.5, the court determines that the court's dependency jurisdiction should be resumed.

(d) Upon the filing of the supplemental petition, the clerk of the juvenile court shall immediately set the same for hearing within 30 days, and the social worker shall cause notice thereof to be served upon the persons and in the manner prescribed by Sections 290.1 and 291, except that service under this subdivision may be delivered by electronic service pursuant to Section 212.5.

(e) An order for the detention of the child pending adjudication of the petition may be made only after a hearing is conducted pursuant to Article 7 (commencing with Section 305). *(Added by Stats.1976, c. 1068, p. 4778, § 12. Amended by Stats.1984, c. 1227, § 2; Stats.1997, c. 268 (A.B.1196), § 2; Stats.1997, c. 793 (A.B.1544), § 28; Stats.1998, c. 1054 (A.B.1091), § 44; Stats.2002, c. 416 (S.B.1956), § 12; Stats. 2003, c. 468 (S.B.851), § 32; Stats.2004, c. 468 (A.B.129), § 4; Stats.2005, c. 22 (S.B.1108), § 215; Stats.2017, c. 319 (A.B. 976), § 135, eff. Jan. 1, 2018.)*

Commentary

A petition under section 388, which requires less demanding findings than a petition under this section, is the appropriate petition for an agency wanting to move a dependent child who has already been freed for adoption to a new placement, such as from a temporary foster home to a group home. *In re A.C., 186 Cal.App.4th 976, 112 Cal.Rptr.3d 593 (2010).*

Kimberly R. v. Superior Court, 96 Cal.App.4th 1067, 117 Cal.Rptr.2d 670 (2002), holds that a removal petition alleging only a parent's single instance of tardiness in picking the child up from day care, is inadequate to support a petition to remove a child. *Kimberly R.* also states, in dictum, that a county social services agency may not unilaterally dismiss a proceeding under this section over the objection of a dependent child's counsel. Once the child's counsel objects, the agency must show that dismissal would serve the welfare of the child.

When a juvenile court sustains the allegations of a supplemental petition under this section, Rule 5.565(f) of California Rules of Court requires the court to proceed directly to a section 366.26 selection and implementation hearing and to comply with section 361.4, which prohibits placement of a dependent child with a person with a criminal record unless an exemption is obtained. *In re G. W., 173 Cal.App.4th 1428, 94 Cal.Rptr.3d 53 (2009), review denied.*

In re M.L., 205 Cal.App.4th 210, 139 Cal.Rptr.3d 911 (2012), held that a trial court erred when it denied an agency's petition to remove a child from her grandparents' custody because of her grandfather's criminal history, when the agency had denied a criminal history exemption under section 361.4(d)(2).

Research References

Forms

West's California Judicial Council Forms JV-150, Supplemental Petition for More Restrictive Placement (Attachment)(Welfare and Institutions Code, S387).

Treatises and Practice Aids

Witkin, California Summary 10th Parent and Child § 582, De Facto Parents.
Witkin, California Summary 10th Parent and Child § 636, Criminal Records Check and Fingerprint Clearance.
Witkin, California Summary 10th Parent and Child § 638, Preferential Right Of Relatives.
Witkin, California Summary 10th Parent and Child § 643, Duration Of Services.
Witkin, California Summary 10th Parent and Child § 655, Nature and Purpose.
Witkin, California Summary 10th Parent and Child § 656, Form and Content.
Witkin, California Summary 10th Parent and Child § 657, Filing, Setting for Hearing, and Notice.
Witkin, California Summary 10th Parent and Child § 658, Hearing.
Witkin, California Summary 10th Parent and Child § 659, Sufficiency Of Evidence.
Witkin, California Summary 10th Parent and Child § 660, Appeal.
Witkin, California Summary 10th Parent and Child § 661, Hearing After Supplemental Petition is Sustained.
Witkin, California Summary 10th Parent and Child § 662, Nature and Purpose.
Witkin, California Summary 10th Parent and Child § 663, Form, Content, and Filing.
Witkin, California Summary 10th Parent and Child § 691, Constitutionality Of Termination Procedure.
Witkin, California Summary 10th Parent and Child § 698, Other Procedures.
Witkin, California Summary 10th Parent and Child § 700, Right to Appeal.
Witkin, California Summary 10th Parent and Child § 705, in General.

§ 388. Petitions; modification of order; termination of jurisdiction; siblings; court hearing and notice; nonminor dependents

(a)(1) Any parent or other person having an interest in a child who is a dependent child of the juvenile court or a nonminor dependent as defined in subdivision (v) of Section 11400, or the child himself or herself or the nonminor dependent through a properly appointed guardian may, upon grounds of change of circumstance or new evidence, petition the court in the same action in which the child was found to be a dependent child of the juvenile court or in which a guardianship was ordered pursuant to Section 360 for a hearing to change, modify, or set aside any order of court previously made or to terminate the jurisdiction of the court. The petition shall be verified and, if made by a person other than the child or the nonminor dependent shall state the petitioner's relationship to or interest in the child or the nonminor dependent and shall set forth in concise language any change of circumstance or new evidence that is alleged to require the change of order or termination of jurisdiction.

(2) When any party, including a child who is a dependent of the juvenile court, petitions the court prior to an order terminating parental rights, to modify the order that reunification services were not needed pursuant to paragraphs (4), (5), and (6) of subdivision (b) of Section 361.5, or to modify any orders related to custody or visitation of the subject child, and the court orders a hearing pursuant to subdivision (d), the court shall modify the order that reunification services were not needed pursuant to paragraphs (4), (5), and (6) of subdivision (b) of Section 361.5, or any orders related to the custody or visitation of the child for whom reunification services were not ordered pursuant to paragraphs (4), (5), and (6) of subdivision (b) of Section 361.5, only if the court finds by clear and convincing evidence that the proposed change is in the best interests of the child.

(b)(1) Any person, including a child or a nonminor dependent who is a dependent of the juvenile court, may petition the court to assert a relationship as a sibling related by blood, adoption, or affinity through a common legal or biological parent to a child who is, or is the subject of a petition for adjudication as, a dependent of the juvenile court, and may request visitation with the dependent child, placement with or near the dependent child, or consideration when determining or implementing a case plan or permanent plan for the dependent child or make any other request for an order which may be shown to be in the best interest of the dependent child.

(2) A child or nonminor dependent who is a dependent of the juvenile court may petition the court to assert a relationship as a sibling related by blood, adoption, or affinity through a common legal or biological parent to a child who is in the physical custody of a common legal or biological parent, and may request visitation with the nondependent sibling in parental custody.

(3) Pursuant to subdivision (b) of Section 16002, a request for sibling visitation may be granted unless it is determined by the court that sibling visitation is contrary to the safety and well-being of any of the siblings.

(4) The court may appoint a guardian ad litem to file the petition for a dependent child asserting a sibling relationship pursuant to this subdivision if the court determines that the appointment is necessary for the best interests of the dependent child. The petition shall be verified and shall set forth the following:

(A) Through which parent he or she is related to the sibling.

(B) Whether he or she is related to the sibling by blood, adoption, or affinity.

(C) The request or order that the petitioner is seeking.

(D) Why that request or order is in the best interest of the dependent child.

(c)(1) Any party, including a child who is a dependent of the juvenile court, may petition the court, prior to the hearing set pursuant to subdivision (f) of Section 366.21 for a child described by subparagraph (A) of paragraph (1) of subdivision (a) of Section 361.5, or prior to the hearing set pursuant to subdivision (e) of Section 366.21 for a child described by subparagraph (B) or (C) of paragraph (1) of subdivision (a) of Section 361.5, to terminate court-ordered reunification services provided under subdivision (a) of Section 361.5 only if one of the following conditions exists:

(A) It appears that a change of circumstance or new evidence exists that satisfies a condition set forth in subdivision (b) or (e) of Section 361.5 justifying termination of court-ordered reunification services.

(B) The action or inaction of the parent or guardian creates a substantial likelihood that reunification will not occur, including, but not limited to, the parent's or guardian's failure to visit the child, or the failure of the parent or guardian to participate regularly and make substantive progress in a court-ordered treatment plan.

(2) In determining whether the parent or guardian has failed to visit the child or participate regularly or make progress in the treatment plan, the court shall consider factors that include but are not limited to, the parent's or guardian's incarceration, institutionalization, detention by the United States Department of Homeland Security, deportation, or participation in a court-ordered residential substance abuse treatment program.

(3) The court shall terminate reunification services during the above-described time periods only upon a finding by a preponderance of evidence that reasonable services have been offered or provided, and upon a finding of clear and convincing evidence that one of the conditions in subparagraph (A) or (B) of paragraph (1) exists.

(4) Any party, including a nonminor dependent, as defined in subdivision (v) of Section 11400, may petition the court prior to the review hearing set pursuant to subdivision (d) of Section 366.31 to terminate the continuation of court-ordered family reunification services for a nonminor dependent who has attained 18 years of age. The court shall terminate family reunification services to the parent or guardian if the nonminor dependent or parent or guardian are not in agreement that the continued provision of court-ordered family reunification services is in the best interests of the nonminor dependent.

(5) If the court terminates reunification services, it shall order that a hearing pursuant to Section 366.26 be held within 120 days. On and after January 1, 2012, a hearing pursuant to Section 366.26 shall not be ordered if the child is a nonminor dependent. The court may order a nonminor dependent who is otherwise eligible to AFDC–FC benefits pursuant to Section 11403 to remain in a planned, permanent living arrangement.

(d) If it appears that the best interests of the child or the nonminor dependent may be promoted by the proposed change of order, modification of reunification services, custody, or visitation orders concerning a child for whom reunification services were not ordered pursuant to paragraphs (4), (5), and (6) of subdivision (b) of Section 361.5, recognition of a sibling relationship, termination of jurisdiction, or clear and convincing evidence supports revocation or termination of court-ordered reunification services, the court shall order that a hearing be held and shall give prior notice, or cause prior notice to be given, to the persons and in the manner prescribed by Section 386, and, in those instances in which the manner of giving notice is not prescribed by those sections, then in the manner the court prescribes.

(e)(1) * * * (A) A nonminor who attained 18 years of age while subject to an order for foster care placement and * * * who has not attained * * * 21 years of age, or as described in Section 10103.5, for whom the court has dismissed dependency jurisdiction pursuant to Section 391, or delinquency jurisdiction pursuant to Section 607.2, or transition jurisdiction pursuant to Section 452, but has retained general jurisdiction under subdivision (b) of Section 303, or the county child welfare services, probation department, or tribal placing agency on behalf of the nonminor, may petition the court in the same action in which the child was found to be a dependent or delinquent child of the juvenile court, for a hearing to resume the dependency jurisdiction over a former dependent or to assume or resume transition jurisdiction over a former delinquent ward pursuant to Section 450. The petition shall be filed within the period that the nonminor is of the age described in this paragraph. If the nonminor has completed the voluntary reentry agreement, as described in subdivision (z) of Section 11400, with the placing agency, the agency shall file the petition on behalf of the nonminor within 15 judicial days of the date the agreement was signed unless the nonminor elects to file the petition at an earlier date.

(B) The petition may be brought notwithstanding a court order vacating the underlying adjudication pursuant to Section 236.14 of the Penal Code.

(2)(A) The petition to resume jurisdiction may be filed in the juvenile court that retains general jurisdiction under subdivision (b) of Section 303, or the petition may be submitted to the juvenile court in the county where the youth resides and forwarded to the juvenile court that retained general jurisdiction and filed with that court. The juvenile court having general jurisdiction under Section 303 shall receive the petition from the court where the petition was submitted within five court days of its submission, if the petition is filed in the county of residence. The juvenile court that retained general jurisdiction shall order that a hearing be held within 15 judicial days of the date the petition was filed if there is a prima facie showing that the nonminor satisfies the following criteria:

(i) He or she was previously under juvenile court jurisdiction, subject to an order for foster care placement when he or she attained 18 years of age, and has not attained * * * 21 years of age.

(ii) He or she intends to satisfy at least one of the conditions set forth in paragraphs (1) to (5), inclusive, of subdivision (b) of Section 11403.

(iii) He or she wants assistance either in maintaining or securing appropriate supervised placement, or is in need of immediate placement and agrees to supervised placement pursuant to the voluntary reentry agreement as described in subdivision (z) of Section 11400.

(B) Upon ordering a hearing, the court shall give prior notice, or cause prior notice to be given, to the persons and by the means prescribed by Section 386, except that notice to parents or former guardians shall not be provided unless the nonminor requests, in writing on the face of the petition, notice to the parents or former guardians.

(3) The Judicial Council, by January 1, 2012, shall adopt rules of court to allow for telephonic appearances by nonminor former dependents or delinquents in these proceedings, and for telephonic appearances by nonminor dependents in any proceeding in which the nonminor dependent is a party, and he or she declines to appear and elects a telephonic appearance.

(4) Prior to the hearing on a petition to resume dependency jurisdiction or to assume or resume transition jurisdiction, the court shall order the county child welfare or probation department to prepare a report for the court addressing whether the nonminor intends to satisfy at least one of the criteria set forth in subdivision (b) of Section 11403. When the recommendation is for the nonminor dependent to be placed in a setting where minor dependents also reside, the results of a background check of the petitioning nonminor conducted pursuant to Section 16504.5, may be used by the placing agency to determine appropriate placement options for the nonminor. The existence of a criminal conviction is not a bar to eligibility for reentry or resumption of dependency jurisdiction or the assumption or resumption of transition jurisdiction over a nonminor.

(5)(A) The court shall resume dependency jurisdiction over a former dependent or assume or resume transition jurisdiction over a former delinquent ward pursuant to Section 450, and order that the nonminor's placement and care be under the responsibility of the county child welfare services department, the probation department, tribe, consortium of tribes, or tribal organization, if the court finds all of the following:

(i) The nonminor was previously under juvenile court jurisdiction, subject to an order for foster care placement when he or she attained 18 years of age.

(ii) The nonminor has not attained * * * 21 years of age.

(iii) Reentry and remaining in foster care are in the nonminor's best interests.

(iv) The nonminor intends to satisfy, and agrees to satisfy, at least one of the criteria set forth in paragraphs (1) to (5), inclusive, of subdivision (b) of Section 11403, and demonstrates his or her agreement to placement in a supervised setting under the placement and care responsibility of the placing agency and to satisfy the criteria by signing the voluntary reentry agreement as described in subdivision (z) of Section 11400.

(B) In no event shall the court grant a continuance that would cause the hearing to resume dependency jurisdiction or to assume or resume transition jurisdiction to be completed more than 120 days after the date the petition was filed.

(C) The agency made responsible for the nonminor's placement and care pursuant to subparagraph (A) shall prepare a new transitional independent living case plan within 60 calendar days from the date the nonminor signed the voluntary reentry agreement as described in subdivision (z) of Section 11400 and submit it to the court for the review hearing under Section 366.31, to be held within 70 days of the resumption of dependency jurisdiction or assumption or resumption of transition jurisdiction. In no event shall the review hearing under Section 366.3 be held more than 170 calendar days from the date the nonminor signed the voluntary reentry agreement. *(Added by Stats.1976, c. 1068, p. 4778, § 12. Amended by Stats.1994, c. 900 (S.B.1407), § 4; Stats.2000, c. 909 (A.B.1987), § 7; Stats.2008, c. 457 (A.B. 2341), § 2; Stats.2009, c. 120 (A.B.706), § 4, eff. Aug. 6, 2009; Stats.2010, c. 559 (A.B.12), § 26; Stats.2011, c. 459 (A.B.212), § 10, eff. Oct. 4, 2011; Stats.2012, c. 179 (S.B.1425), § 1, eff. Aug. 17, 2012; Stats.2012, c. 845 (S.B.1064), § 15; Stats.2012, c. 846 (A.B.1712), § 30.5; Stats.2014, c. 773 (S.B.1099), § 7, eff. Jan. 1, 2015; Stats.2017, c. 707 (A.B.604), § 2, eff. Jan. 1, 2018.)*

Commentary

In re Alayah J., 9 Cal.App.5th 469, 215 Cal.Rptr.3d 140 (2017), held that a juvenile court erred when it granted an evidentiary hearing under this section on a mother's modification petition, but conditioned the grant on nontermination of her parental rights in a termination proceeding. However, the error was harmless because, on the facts, a section 388 hearing would not have prevented termination of the mother's parental rights.

When a social service agency had mistakenly removed a baby from its first foster home and placed it in a second foster home, the agency sought to remove the child from the second home and return it to the first home. Both sets of foster parents filed section 388 petitions. *In re F.A., 241 Cal.App.4th 107, 193 Cal.Rptr.3d (2015)*, held that the juvenile court did not abuse its discretion in ordering the social services agency not to remove a baby from the second foster home pending resolution of the competing petitions.

In re Xavier R., 201 Cal.App.4th 1398, 134 Cal.Rptr.3d 410 (2011), held that a juvenile court may terminate a Probate Code guardianship pursuant to Welfare and Institutions Code section 728 after reunification services have been offered without first granting a petition to terminate reunification services under this section, because section 728 gives the court authority to terminate Probate Code guardianships at any point in a dependency proceeding. Moreover, California Rules of Court, Rule 5.620(e) does not require a petition under this section before hearing a motion to terminate a guardianship.

Reading this section as a whole, *In re Katelynn Y., 209 Cal.App.4th 871, 147 Cal.Rptr.3d 423 (2012), review denied*, held that a juvenile court properly terminated reunification services for a mother under subsection (c)(1)(B), while not setting a section 366.26 hearing under subsection (c)(4) because the other parent was still receiving reunification services.

A belated submission of an expert opinion based on evidence available at a prior jurisdictional hearing is not "new evidence" that would support a subsection (a) motion to modify or set aside a juvenile court's orders. The term "new evidence" means material evidence that, with due diligence, the party could not have presented at the prior hearing. *In re H.S., 188 Cal.App.4th 103, 114 Cal.Rptr.3d 898 (2010), review denied*.

A petition under this section, which requires less demanding findings than a section 387 petition, is the appropriate petition for an agency wanting to move a dependent child who has already been freed for adoption to a new placement, such as from a temporary foster home to a group home. *In re A.C., 186 Cal.App.4th 976, 112 Cal.Rptr.3d 593 (2010)*.

When a court of appeal reversed a juvenile court order denying a mother's petition under this section, it also necessarily vacated the juvenile court's subsequent section 366.26 hearing and parental rights termination orders. Thus, on remand from the court of appeal, the juvenile court erred in not reinstating the father's as well as the mother's parental rights. *In re A.L., 188 Cal.App.4th 138, 115 Cal.Rptr.3d 560 (2010)*.

Purporting to rely on *Zacharia D., supra, In re Vincent M., 161 Cal.App.4th 943, 74 Cal.Rptr.3d 755 (2008), review denied*, held that a biological father who is not a presumed father under Family Code section 7611 and whose paternity was concealed from him by the mother, but who does not come forward in a dependency proceeding until after the reunification period has ended, cannot be treated as a *Kelsey S.* father entitled to reunification services without regard to the best interests of the child, who was placed with prospective adoptive parents when he was four days old and was thriving in their home for nine months before the biological father asserted his *Kelsey S.* claim. *Vincent M.* states, in dictum, that after the reunification period has expired, the biological father's only remedy is a modification petition under this section, which requires changed circumstances or new evidence showing that it is in the child's best interest to grant the biological father custody or reunification services.

The termination of parental rights in a dependency proceeding does not sever the sibling relationship between a dependent child and his biological siblings because, under subsection (b), a dependent child may establish a sibling relationship by blood, adoption or affinity through a common legal or biological parent. *In re Miguel A., 156 Cal.App.4th 389, 67 Cal.Rptr.3d 307 (2007)* (dictum).

In re Terrance B., 144 Cal.App.4th 965, 50 Cal.Rptr.3d 815 (2006), review denied Feb. 7, 2007, held that a juvenile court lacked jurisdiction to consider a mother's petition for modification under this section when the court of appeal remanded the juvenile court's judgment terminating her parental rights for the sole purpose of ensuring compliance with the notice requirements of the Indian Child Welfare Act (25 U.S.C. § 1901 et seq.).

Once the court has terminated reunification services because of the parent's failure to comply with the reunification plan, the court may properly deny the parent's request for a Section 366.26 (c)(1)(A) "bonding study" to show that the children would benefit from a continued parent-child relationship. *In re Richard C., 68 Cal.App.4th 1191, 80 Cal.Rptr.2d 887 (1998), review denied April 14, 1999. Richard C.* reasons that once that the court has determined that the goal of family preservation cannot be realized and has therefore terminated reunification services, the court need not consider whether the children would benefit from a continuing relationship with the parent at a permanency planning hearing; instead the parent has the burden of showing changed circumstances that would justify resumption of reunification services under Section 388.

In re Hashem H., 45 Cal.App.4th 1791, 53 Cal.Rptr.2d 294 (1996), holds that a parent need only make a prima facie showing of changed circumstances to obtain a hearing under this section. Thus, when a mother alleged she was making progress in psychotherapy, it was error for the trial court to dismiss her petition without hearing on the ground she did not plead that she had successfully completed psychotherapy. To similar effect, see *In re Aljamie D., 84 Cal.App.4th 424,100 Cal.Rptr.2d 811 (2000)* (trial court abused its discretion when it denied appellant full hearing under this section when she established a prima facie case of changed circumstances, having completed numerous parent education classes, repeatedly tested clean in drug tests, visited consistently with her children, and continued to have a strong relationship with them). Compare *In re Jamika W., 54 Cal.App.4th 1446, 63 Cal.Rptr.2d 513 (1997),* holding that the trial court properly denied a modification hearing sought by the child's mother to set aside a guardianship when the petition, although alleging changed circumstances, failed to allege any circumstance that "might require a change of order." *In re Angel B., 97 Cal.App.4th 454, 118 Cal.Rptr.2d 482 (2002),* holds that the juvenile court did not abuse its discretion in denying a mother's petition under this section without hearing when the mother demonstrated that she was doing well after enrolling in a drug rehabilitation program but failed to show that modification would serve her child's best interests. *Angel B.* also holds that the § 366.26(c)(1)(A) exception to termination of parental rights did not apply to the mother because she failed to present evidence that her relationship with her child was sufficiently significant that its termination would cause detriment to the child. Similarly, *In re Sylvia R., 55 Cal.App.4th 559, 64 Cal.Rptr.2d 93 (1997),* holds that a prosecutor's dismissal of spousal abuse charges against a father is not a "changed circumstance" requiring reconsideration of a Section 388 order terminating the father's reunification services and scheduling a permanency planning hearing for the children. Section 388 requires a hearing only when the child's best interests "may be promoted by the proposed change of order." Similarly, *In re Zachary G., 77 Cal.App.4th 799, 92 Cal.Rptr.2d 20 (2000),* holds that it was not error for the juvenile court to deny a hearing under this section when the mother's petition alleged changed circumstances, but failed to make a prima facie showing that the proposed modification would promote the child's best interests. See also *In re Anthony W., 87 Cal.App.4th 246, 104 Cal.Rptr.2d 422 (2001)* (affirming trial court's summary denial of mother's petition under this section when petition contained only conclusory statements unsupported by any evidence, and failed to make a showing of changed circumstances and how modification would be in the children's best interests).

In re Jessica K., 79 Cal.App.4th 1313, 94 Cal.Rptr.2d 798 (2000), held that it had no jurisdiction to hear a parent's appeal from an order denying a § 388 modification petition because the parent failed to appeal from a subsequent order terminating parental rights.

To modify a dependent child's placement, a parent must show by a preponderance of the evidence that circumstances have changed and modification would serve the child's interests. The parent need not allege or prove that the child suffers detriment in the current placement with a nonparent. *In re Michael D., 51 Cal.App.4th 1074, 59 Cal.Rptr.2d 575 (1996), review denied March 12, 1997.*

When a mother who lost custody of her children because her home was dirty and unsanitary later demonstrated that she was able to maintain a sanitary home, her request for modification under this section should have been granted and her rights as a parent should not have been terminated pursuant to Section 366.26 on the basis of "the mother's psychological disorder, her narcissistic personality." *In re Kimberly F., 56 Cal.App.4th 519, 65 Cal.Rptr.2d 495 (1997).*

In re Andrea R., 75 Cal.App.4th 1093, 89 Cal.Rptr.2d 664 (1999), review denied December 15, 1999, holds that § 366.3(c) allows the court to schedule a new § 366.26 hearing to change the child's permanent plan from legal guardianship to adoption without first holding a separate hearing under this section to determine whether changed circumstances support a change in the permanent plan.

In re Matthew P., 71 Cal.App.4th 841, 84 Cal.Rptr.2d 269 (1999), holds that the juvenile court violated the de facto parents' due process rights by admitting the reports of social workers in a modification hearing without allowing the de facto parents to cross examine the social workers.

In re Lance V., 90 Cal.App.4th 668, 108 Cal.Rptr.2d 847 (2001), holds that having granted a mother's request for mediation of the implementation of visitation orders, the trial court erred when, after the parties failed to reach a mediated agreement, it reduced the mother's visitation without holding a noticed hearing under this section.

Having established a guardianship for two dependent children, a juvenile court lacked authority to terminate its jurisdiction without an evidentiary hearing and refer the case to family court for modification of prior visitation orders. *In re Kenneth S., Jr., 169 Cal.App.4th 1353, 87 Cal.Rptr.3d 715 (2008), review denied.*

In re Hunter W., 200 Cal.App.4th 1454, 135 Cal.Rptr.3d 355 (2011), held that a juvenile court abused its discretion when it denied the request of the parents' counsel for a brief two-hour delay to locate a dependent child's parents, who had already checked in at the court's morning calendar call, and thus deprived them of the opportunity to testify before the court denied their petition under this section and terminated their parental rights under section 366.26.

In re Y.M., 207 Cal.App.4th 892, 144 Cal.Rptr.3d 54 (2012), held that the juvenile court erred when it terminated dependency jurisdiction over a special-needs child victim of human sexual trafficking abducted from Guatemala and brought to the United States. A Guatemalan Protocol concerning human trafficking was not an international treaty and thus did not deprive the California court of jurisdiction.

In re Luke H., 221 Cal.App.4th 1082, 165 Cal.Rptr.3d 63 (2013), held that a juvenile court did not have jurisdiction under section 361.2(j) to grant a dependent child's modification petition for visitation with a sibling who was not a dependent of the court, because the court had no jurisdiction over the sibling. Nor did subsection (a) of this section authorize the court to issue an order affecting a child outside its jurisdiction.

In re Ernesto R., 230 Cal.App.4th 219, 178 Cal.Rptr.3d 451 (2014), held that an attorney's decision not to file a section 388 petition to modify an order in a dependency case did not constitute ineffective assistance of counsel when filing such a petition would have been futile.

Research References

Forms

West's California Judicial Council Forms JV-182, Confidential Information (Request to Change Court Order).
West's California Judicial Council Forms JV-183, Court Order on Form Jv-180, Request to Change Court Order.
West's California Judicial Council Forms JV-184, Order After Hearing on Form Jv-180, Request to Change Court Order.
West's California Judicial Council Forms JV-185, Child's Information Sheet--Request to Change Court Order (Welf. & Inst. Code).
West's California Judicial Council Forms JV-466, Request to Return to Juvenile Court Jurisdiction and Foster Care.
West's California Judicial Council Forms JV-468, Confidential Information--Request to Return to Juvenile Court Jurisdiction and Foster Care.
West's California Judicial Council Forms JV-470, Findings and Orders Regarding Prima Facie Showing on Nonminor's Request to Reenter Foster Care.
West's California Judicial Council Forms JV-472, Findings and Orders After Hearing to Consider Nonminor's Request to Reenter Foster Care.
West's California Judicial Council Forms JV-464-INFO, How to Ask to Return to Juvenile Court Jurisdiction and Foster Care.

Treatises and Practice Aids

Witkin, California Summary 10th Parent and Child § 359, Dissolution Proceedings.
Witkin, California Summary 10th Parent and Child § 458, Conditions for Transfer.
Witkin, California Summary 10th Parent and Child § 463, Transfer-In Hearing.
Witkin, California Summary 10th Parent and Child § 501, Nature and Use Of Records.
Witkin, California Summary 10th Parent and Child § 521, Termination Of Jurisdiction.
Witkin, California Summary 10th Parent and Child § 529, Formal Requisites.
Witkin, California Summary 10th Parent and Child § 531, Determining Adequacy Of Notice.
Witkin, California Summary 10th Parent and Child § 536, Termination Of Parental Rights.
Witkin, California Summary 10th Parent and Child § 567, Statutory Rights.
Witkin, California Summary 10th Parent and Child § 577, Hearing.
Witkin, California Summary 10th Parent and Child § 580, Right to Competent Counsel.
Witkin, California Summary 10th Parent and Child § 582, De Facto Parents.
Witkin, California Summary 10th Parent and Child § 584, Rights Of Siblings.
Witkin, California Summary 10th Parent and Child § 603, Identification Of Presumed or Alleged Fathers.
Witkin, California Summary 10th Parent and Child § 627, in General.
Witkin, California Summary 10th Parent and Child § 628, Legal Guardianship.
Witkin, California Summary 10th Parent and Child § 636, Criminal Records Check and Fingerprint Clearance.
Witkin, California Summary 10th Parent and Child § 637, Priority Right Of Noncustodial Parent.
Witkin, California Summary 10th Parent and Child § 641, Visitation Rights.
Witkin, California Summary 10th Parent and Child § 642, in General.
Witkin, California Summary 10th Parent and Child § 643, Duration Of Services.
Witkin, California Summary 10th Parent and Child § 644, Persons Entitled to Services.
Witkin, California Summary 10th Parent and Child § 648, Parent or Guardian Absent, Unwilling, or Incapable.
Witkin, California Summary 10th Parent and Child § 650, Abuse, Neglect, or Abduction Of Child.
Witkin, California Summary 10th Parent and Child § 652, Determination Whether to Order Services.
Witkin, California Summary 10th Parent and Child § 654, Power to Modify or Correct.
Witkin, California Summary 10th Parent and Child § 655, Nature and Purpose.
Witkin, California Summary 10th Parent and Child § 662, Nature and Purpose.
Witkin, California Summary 10th Parent and Child § 663, Form, Content, and Filing.
Witkin, California Summary 10th Parent and Child § 664, in General.
Witkin, California Summary 10th Parent and Child § 665, Right to Hearing.
Witkin, California Summary 10th Parent and Child § 666, Scope Of Hearing.
Witkin, California Summary 10th Parent and Child § 667, Due Process Attack on Decree.
Witkin, California Summary 10th Parent and Child § 672, Child in Custody Of Parent or Guardian.
Witkin, California Summary 10th Parent and Child § 676, in General.
Witkin, California Summary 10th Parent and Child § 685, Hearing.
Witkin, California Summary 10th Parent and Child § 686, Alternative Dispositions.
Witkin, California Summary 10th Parent and Child § 691, Constitutionality Of Termination Procedure.
Witkin, California Summary 10th Parent and Child § 692, in General.
Witkin, California Summary 10th Parent and Child § 693, Termination Of Parental Rights.
Witkin, California Summary 10th Parent and Child § 694, Adoption Proceeding.
Witkin, California Summary 10th Parent and Child § 696, Continuing Jurisdiction.
Witkin, California Summary 10th Parent and Child § 697, Status Review Hearings.
Witkin, California Summary 10th Parent and Child § 698, Other Procedures.
Witkin, California Summary 10th Parent and Child § 700, Right to Appeal.
Witkin, California Summary 10th Parent and Child § 701, in General.
Witkin, California Summary 10th Parent and Child § 704, Miscellaneous Orders.
Witkin, California Summary 10th Parent and Child § 709, in General.
Witkin, California Summary 10th Parent and Child § 712, Notice Of Appeal.
Witkin, California Summary 10th Parent and Child § 719, Related Orders.
Witkin, California Summary 10th Parent and Child § 910, in General.
Witkin, California Summary 10th Parent and Child § 452C, (New) Termination Of Jurisdiction.

Witkin, California Summary 10th Parent and Child § 521A, (New) Continuation or Termination Of Jurisdiction Over Nonminor or Nonminor Dependent.
Witkin, California Summary 10th Parent and Child § 667A, (New) Appeal.
Witkin, California Summary 10th Parent and Child § 669A, (New) Review Hearings Just Before and After Minor Attains Age 18.
Witkin, California Summary 10th Parent and Child § 693B, (New) Designation Of Prospective Adoptive Parent.
Witkin, California Summary 10th Parent and Child § 693E, (New) Reinstatement Of Parental Rights.
Witkin, California Summary 10th Parent and Child § 699A, (New) in General.
Witkin, California Summary 10th Parent and Child § 899A, (New) Hearing Before Termination Of Jurisdiction.

§ 388.1. Nonminor under 21 years of age; petition to assume dependency jurisdiction; conditions; hearing; order for placement and care; voluntary reentry agreement

(a) On and after January 1, 2014, a nonminor who has not attained 21 years of age may petition the court in which he or she was previously found to be a dependent or delinquent child of the juvenile court for a hearing to determine whether to assume dependency jurisdiction over the nonminor, if he or she meets any of the following descriptions:

(1) He or she is a nonminor former dependent, as defined in subdivision (aa) of Section 11400, who received aid after attaining 18 years of age under Kin–GAP pursuant to Article 4.5 (commencing with Section 11360) or Article 4.7 (commencing with Section 11385) of Chapter 2 of Part 3 of Division 9, or pursuant to subdivision (e) of Section 11405, and whose former guardian or guardians died after the nonminor attained 18 years of age, but before he or she attains 21 years of age.

(2) He or she is a nonminor former dependent, as defined in subdivision (aa) of Section 11400, who received aid after attaining 18 years of age under Kin–GAP pursuant to Article 4.5 (commencing with Section 11360) or Article 4.7 (commencing with Section 11385) of Chapter 2 of Part 3 of Division 9, or pursuant to subdivision (e) of Section 11405, and whose former guardian or guardians no longer provide ongoing support to, and no longer receive aid on behalf of, the nonminor after the nonminor attained 18 years of age, but before he or she attains 21 years of age.

(3) He or she is a nonminor who received adoption assistance payments after attaining 18 years of age pursuant to Chapter 2.1 (commencing with Section 16115) of Part 4 of Division 9 and his or her adoptive parent or parents died after the nonminor attained 18 years of age, but before he or she attains 21 years of age.

(4) He or she is a nonminor who received adoption assistance payments after attaining 18 years of age pursuant to Chapter 2.1 (commencing with Section 16115) of Part 4 of Division 9 and his or her adoptive parent or parents no longer provide ongoing support to, and no longer receive benefits on behalf of, the nonminor after the nonminor attained 18 years of age, but before he or she attains 21 years of age.

(b)(1) The petition to assume jurisdiction may be filed in either of the following:

(A) The juvenile court that established the guardianship pursuant to Section 360, Section 366.26, or subdivision (d) of Section 728.

(B) The juvenile court that had jurisdiction over the minor or nonminor dependent when his or her adoption was finalized.

(2) A nonminor described in subdivision (a) may submit a petition to assume dependency jurisdiction to the juvenile court in the county where he or she resides. A petition submitted pursuant to this paragraph shall, within five days of submission, be forwarded to the court that had jurisdiction over the child at the time of the guardianship or adoption. The clerk of the court that had jurisdiction over the child at the time of the guardianship or adoption shall file the petition within one judicial day of receipt.

(c)(1) The juvenile court in which the petition was filed shall order a hearing to be held within 15 judicial days of the date the petition was filed if there is a prima facie showing that the nonminor satisfies all of the following criteria:

(A) He or she was a minor under juvenile court jurisdiction at the time of the establishment of a guardianship pursuant to Section 360, Section 366.26, or subdivision (d) of Section 728, or he or she was a minor or nonminor dependent when his or her adoption was finalized.

(B)(i) His or her guardian or guardians, or adoptive parent or parents, as applicable, died after the nonminor attained 18 years of age, but before he or she attained 21 years of age.

(ii) His or her guardian or guardians, or adoptive parent or parents, as applicable, no longer provide ongoing support to, and no longer receive payment on behalf of, the nonminor after the nonminor attained 18 years of age, but before he or she attained 21 years of age, and it may be in the nonminor's best interest for the court to assume dependency jurisdiction.

(C) He or she intends to satisfy at least one of the conditions set forth in paragraphs (1) to (5), inclusive, of subdivision (b) of Section 11403.

(D) He or she is requesting assistance in maintaining or securing appropriate supervised placement, or needs immediate placement and agrees to supervised placement pursuant to the voluntary reentry agreement described in subdivision (z) of Section 11400.

(2) Upon ordering a hearing, the court shall give prior notice, or cause prior notice to be given, to the nonminor, the appropriate child welfare agency or probation department, and any other person requested by the nonminor in the petition.

(3) Pursuant to applicable rules of court, the juvenile court shall allow for telephonic appearances by the nonminor in these proceedings and in any proceeding in which the nonminor dependent is a party.

(4) Prior to the hearing, the court shall order the county child welfare or probation department to prepare a report for the court that addresses both of the following:

(A) The nonminor's plans to satisfy at least one of the criteria set forth in paragraphs (1) to (5), inclusive, of subdivision (b) of Section 11403.

(B) The appropriate placement setting for the nonminor. When the recommendation is for the nonminor to be placed in a setting where minor dependents also reside, the results of a background check of the petitioning nonminor conducted pursuant to Section 16504.5 may be used by the placing agency to determine appropriate placement options for him or her.

(5) The court shall assume dependency jurisdiction over a former dependent or ward, and order his or her placement and care be under the responsibility of the county child welfare services department, the probation department, tribe, consortium of tribes, or tribal organization, if the court finds all of the following:

(A) The nonminor was a minor under juvenile court jurisdiction at the time of the establishment of a guardianship pursuant to Section 360, Section 366.26, or subdivision (d) of Section 728, or he or she was a dependent at the time his or her adoption was finalized.

(B) The nonminor's guardian or guardians, or adoptive parent or parents, as applicable, have died, or no longer provide ongoing support to, and no longer receive payment on behalf of, the nonminor, and it is in the nonminor's best interests for the court to assume dependency jurisdiction.

(C) The nonminor has not attained 21 years of age.

(D) Reentry and remaining in foster care are in the nonminor's best interests.

(E) The nonminor intends to satisfy, and agrees to satisfy, at least one of the criteria set forth in paragraphs (1) to (5), inclusive, of subdivision (b) of Section 11403, and demonstrates his or her agreement to placement in a supervised setting under the placement and care responsibility of the placing agency by signing the voluntary reentry agreement described in subdivision (z) of Section 11400.

(6) The existence of a criminal conviction is not a bar to eligibility for reentry to foster care or assumption of dependency jurisdiction over a nonminor.

(7) The court shall not grant a continuance that would cause the hearing to be completed more than 120 days after the date the petition is filed.

(d) The agency made responsible for the nonminor's placement and care pursuant to paragraph (5) of subdivision (c) shall prepare a new transitional independent living case plan within 60 calendar days of the date the nonminor signs the voluntary reentry agreement and shall submit the plan to the court for the review hearing specified in Section 366.31, to be held within 70 days of the assumption of dependency jurisdiction. The review hearing under Section 366.31 shall not be held more than 170 calendar days from the date the nonminor signs the voluntary reentry agreement.

(e)(1) A nonminor described in subdivision (a) may enter into a voluntary reentry agreement as defined in subdivision (z) of Section 11400 in order to establish eligibility for foster care benefits under subdivision (e) of Section 11401 before or after filing a petition to assume dependency jurisdiction. If the nonminor enters into a voluntary reentry agreement prior to filing the petition, the nonminor is entitled to placement and supervision pending the court's assumption of jurisdiction.

(2) If the nonminor completes a voluntary reentry agreement with a placing agency, the placing agency shall file the petition to assume dependency jurisdiction on behalf of the nonminor within 15 judicial days of the date the agreement is signed, unless the nonminor elects to file the petition at an earlier date. *(Added by Stats.2013, c. 487 (A.B.787), § 2. Amended by Stats.2014, c. 769 (A.B.2454), § 1, eff. Jan. 1, 2015.)*

Commentary

In re Jesse S., 12 Cal.App.5th 611, 219 Cal.Rptr.3d 149 (2017), reluctantly affirmed a juvenile court's denial of a 19-year-old's request to return to juvenile court jurisdiction and the foster care system, because although his adoptive parents were no longer supporting him, he could not satisfy the literal requirements of subsection (a)(4) since they continued to receive payments on his behalf from the Adoptive Assistance Program.

Research References

Forms

West's California Judicial Council Forms JV-466, Request to Return to Juvenile Court Jurisdiction and Foster Care.

West's California Judicial Council Forms JV-470, Findings and Orders Regarding Prima Facie Showing on Nonminor's Request to Reenter Foster Care.

West's California Judicial Council Forms JV-472, Findings and Orders After Hearing to Consider Nonminor's Request to Reenter Foster Care.

West's California Judicial Council Forms JV-464-INFO, How to Ask to Return to Juvenile Court Jurisdiction and Foster Care.

Treatises and Practice Aids

Witkin, California Summary 10th Parent and Child § 452G, (New) Assumption Of Jurisdiction Over Nonminor.

Witkin, California Summary 10th Parent and Child § 699C, (New) Request for Resumption Of Jurisdiction.

§ 389. Petition for sealing records; notice; hearing; grounds for and effect of order; inspection and destruction of records

(a) In any case in which a petition has been filed with a juvenile court to commence proceedings to adjudge a person a dependent child of the court, in any case in which a person is cited to appear before a probation officer or is taken before a probation officer pursuant to Section 307, or in any case in which a minor is taken before any officer of a law enforcement agency, the person or the county probation officer may, five years or more after the jurisdiction of the juvenile court has terminated as to the person, or, in a case in which no petition is filed, five years or more after the person was cited to appear before a probation officer or was taken before a probation officer pursuant to Section 307 or was taken before any officer of a law enforcement agency, or, in any case, at any time after the person has reached the age of 18 years, petition the court for sealing of the records, including records of arrest, relating to the person's case, in the custody of the juvenile court and probation officer and any other agencies, including law enforcement agencies, and public officials as petitioner alleges, in his petition, to have custody of such records. The court shall notify the district attorney of the county and the county probation officer, if he is not the petitioner of the petition, and such district attorney or probation officer or any of their deputies or any other person having relevant evidence may testify at the hearing on the petition. If, after hearing, the court finds that since such termination of jurisdiction or action pursuant to Section 307, as the case may be, he has not been convicted of a felony or of any misdemeanor involving moral turpitude and that rehabilitation has been attained to the satisfaction of the court, it shall order sealed all records, papers, and exhibits in the person's case in the custody of the juvenile court, including the juvenile court record, minute book entries, and entries on dockets, and other records relating to the case in the custody of such other agencies and officials as are named in the order. Thereafter, the proceedings in such case shall be deemed never to have occurred, and the person may properly reply accordingly to any inquiry about the events, records of which are ordered sealed. The court shall send a copy of the order to each agency and official named therein directing the agency to seal its records and five years thereafter to destroy the sealed records. Each such agency and official shall seal records in its custody as directed by the order, shall advise the court of its compliance, and thereupon shall seal the copy of the court's order for sealing of records that it or he received. The person who is the subject of records sealed pursuant to this section may petition the superior court to permit inspection of the records by persons named in the petition, and the superior court may so order. Otherwise, except as provided in subdivision (b), such records shall not be open to inspection.

(b) In any action or proceeding based upon defamation, a court, upon a showing of good cause, may order any records sealed under this section to be opened and admitted into evidence. The records shall be confidential and shall be available for inspection only by the court, jury, parties, counsel for the parties, and any other person who is authorized by the court to inspect them. Upon the judgment in the action or proceeding becoming final, the court shall order the records sealed.

(c) Five years after a juvenile court record has been sealed, the court shall order the destruction of the sealed juvenile court record unless for good cause the court determines that the juvenile court record shall be retained. Any other agency in possession of sealed records shall destroy their records five years after the records were ordered sealed. *(Added by Stats.1976, c. 1068, p. 4778, § 12. Amended by Stats.1980, c. 1104, p. 3552, § 1.)*

Research References

Forms

West's California Judicial Council Forms JV-710, Juvenile Fitness Hearing Order.

Treatises and Practice Aids

Witkin, California Summary 10th Parent and Child § 501, Nature and Use Of Records.

Witkin, California Summary 10th Parent and Child § 503, Petition and Order.

Witkin, California Summary 10th Parent and Child § 507, Sealed Records.

§ 390. Dismissal of petition; grounds

A judge of the juvenile court in which a petition was filed, at any time before the minor reaches the age of 21 years, may dismiss the petition or may set aside the findings and dismiss the petition if the court finds that the interests of justice and the welfare of the minor require the dismissal, and that the parent or guardian of the minor is not in need of treatment or rehabilitation. *(Added by Stats.1976, c. 1068, p. 4778, § 12. Amended by Stats.1987, c. 1485, § 50.)*

Research References

Treatises and Practice Aids

Witkin, California Summary 10th Parent and Child § 607, Findings and Orders.

Witkin, California Summary 10th Parent and Child § 627, in General.

Witkin, California Summary 10th Parent and Child § 654, Power to Modify or Correct.

§ 391. Termination of jurisdiction over nonminor; hearing; duties of county welfare department; continued jurisdiction

(a) The dependency court shall not terminate jurisdiction over a nonminor unless a hearing is conducted pursuant to this section.

(b) At any hearing for a nonminor at which the court is considering termination of the jurisdiction of the juvenile court, the county welfare department shall do all of the following:

(1) Ensure that the dependent nonminor is present in court, unless the nonminor does not wish to appear in court, and elects a telephonic appearance, or document reasonable efforts made by the county welfare department to locate the nonminor when the nonminor is not available.

(2) Submit a report describing whether it is in the nonminor's best interests to remain under the court's dependency jurisdiction, which includes a recommended transitional independent living case plan for the nonminor when the report describes continuing dependency jurisdiction as being in the nonminor's best interest.

(3) If the county welfare department recommends termination of the court's dependency jurisdiction, submit documentation of the reasonable efforts made by the department to provide the nonminor with the assistance needed to meet or maintain eligibility as a nonminor dependent, as defined in paragraphs (1) to (5), inclusive, of subdivision (b) of Section 11403.

(4) If the nonminor has indicated that he or she does not want dependency jurisdiction to continue, the report shall address the manner in which the nonminor was advised of his or her options, including the benefits of remaining in foster care, and of his or her right to reenter foster care and to file a petition pursuant to subdivision (e) of Section 388 to resume dependency jurisdiction prior to attaining 21 years of age.

(c)(1) The court shall continue dependency jurisdiction over a nonminor who meets the definition of a nonminor dependent as described in subdivision (v) of Section 11400 unless the court finds either of the following:

(A) That the nonminor does not wish to remain subject to dependency jurisdiction.

(B) That the nonminor is not participating in a reasonable and appropriate transitional independent living case plan.

(2) In making the findings pursuant to paragraph (1), the court shall also find that the nonminor has been informed of his or her options including the benefits of remaining in foster care and the right to reenter foster care by filing a

petition pursuant to subdivision (e) of Section 388 to resume dependency jurisdiction and by completing a voluntary reentry agreement pursuant to subdivision (z) of Section 11400, and has had an opportunity to confer with his or her counsel if counsel has been appointed pursuant to Section 317.

(d)(1) The court may terminate its jurisdiction over a nonminor if the court finds after reasonable and documented efforts the nonminor cannot be located.

(2) When terminating dependency jurisdiction, the court shall maintain general jurisdiction over the nonminor to allow for the filing of a petition to resume dependency jurisdiction under subdivision (e) of Section 388 until the nonminor attains 21 years of age, although no review proceedings shall be required. A nonminor may petition the court pursuant to subdivision (e) of Section 388 to resume dependency jurisdiction at any time before attaining 21 years of age.

(e) The court shall not terminate dependency jurisdiction over a nonminor who has attained 18 years of age until a hearing is conducted pursuant to this section and the department has submitted a report verifying that the following information, documents, and services have been provided to the nonminor, or in the case of a nonminor who, after reasonable efforts by the county welfare department, cannot be located, verifying the efforts made to make the following available to the nonminor:

(1) Written information concerning the nonminor's case, including any known information regarding the nonminor's Indian heritage or tribal connections, if applicable, his or her family history and placement history, any photographs of the nonminor or his or her family in the possession of the county welfare department, other than forensic photographs, the whereabouts of any siblings under the jurisdiction of the juvenile court, unless the court determines that sibling contact would jeopardize the safety or welfare of the sibling, directions on how to access the documents the nonminor is entitled to inspect under Section 827, and the date on which the jurisdiction of the juvenile court would be terminated.

(2) The following documents:

(A) Social security card.

(B) Certified copy of his or her birth certificate.

(C) Health and education summary, as described in subdivision (a) of Section 16010.

(D) Driver's license, as described in Section 12500 of the Vehicle Code, or identification card, as described in Section 13000 of the Vehicle Code.

(E) A letter prepared by the county welfare department that includes the following information:

(i) The nonminor's name and date of birth.

(ii) The dates during which the nonminor was within the jurisdiction of the juvenile court.

(iii) A statement that the nonminor was a foster youth in compliance with state and federal financial aid documentation requirements.

(F) If applicable, the death certificate of the parent or parents.

(G) If applicable, proof of the nonminor's citizenship or legal residence.

(H) An advance health care directive form.

(I) The Judicial Council form that the nonminor would use to file a petition pursuant to subdivision (e) of Section 388 to resume dependency jurisdiction.

(J) The written 90–day transition plan prepared pursuant to Section 16501.1.

(K) Written verification that the eligible nonminor is enrolled in Medi–Cal and the nonminor's Medi–Cal Benefits Identification Card.

(3) Continued and uninterrupted enrollment in Medi–Cal for eligible nonminors pursuant to Section 14005.28 or 14005.285.

(4) Referrals to transitional housing, if available, or assistance in securing other housing.

(5) Assistance in obtaining employment or other financial support.

(6) Assistance in applying for admission to college or to a vocational training program or other educational institution and in obtaining financial aid, where appropriate.

(7) Assistance in maintaining relationships with individuals who are important to a nonminor who has been in out-of-home placement for six months or longer from the date the nonminor entered foster care, based on the nonminor's best interests.

(8) For nonminors between 18 and 21 years of age, assistance in accessing the Independent Living Aftercare Program in the nonminor's county of residence, and, upon the nonminor's request, assistance in completing a voluntary reentry agreement for care and placement pursuant to subdivision (z) of Section 11400 and in filing a petition pursuant to subdivision (e) of Section 388 to resume dependency jurisdiction.

(9) Written information notifying the child that current or former dependent children who are or have been in foster care are granted a preference for student assistant or internship positions with state agencies pursuant to Section 18220 of the Government Code. The preference shall be granted to applicants up to 26 years of age.

(f) At the hearing closest to and before a dependent minor's 18th birthday and every review hearing thereafter for nonminors, the department shall submit a report describing efforts toward completing the items described in paragraph (2) of subdivision (e).

(g) The Judicial Council shall develop and implement standards, and develop and adopt appropriate forms necessary to implement this provision. *(Added by Stats.2010, c. 559 (A.B.12), § 28, operative Jan. 1, 2012. Amended by Stats. 2011, c. 459 (A.B.212), § 11, eff. Oct. 4, 2011, operative Jan. 1, 2012; Stats.2011, c. 464 (A.B.735), § 2.5; Stats.2012, c. 162 (S.B.1171), § 190; Stats.2013, c. 487 (A.B.787), § 3; Stats. 2015, c. 303 (A.B.731), § 569, eff. Jan. 1, 2016; Stats.2016, c. 609 (A.B.1849), § 1, eff. Jan. 1, 2017.)*

Commentary

In re Shannon M., 221 Cal.App.4th 282, 164 Cal.Rptr.3d 199 (2013), held that this section applies to all nonminor dependents subject to a court's dependency jurisdiction, and not solely to those nonminor dependents eligible for extended foster care benefits.

Research References

Forms

West's California Judicial Council Forms JV-365, Termination Of Juvenile Court Jurisdiction--Nonminor.
West's California Judicial Council Forms JV-367, Findings and Orders After Hearing to Consider Termination Of Juvenile Court Jurisdiction Over a Nonminor.

Treatises and Practice Aids

Witkin, California Summary 10th Parent and Child § 492, in General.
Witkin, California Summary 10th Parent and Child § 521, Termination Of Jurisdiction.
Witkin, California Summary 10th Parent and Child § 662, Nature and Purpose.
Witkin, California Summary 10th Parent and Child § 673, Child in Foster Care.
Witkin, California Summary 10th Parent and Child § 696, Continuing Jurisdiction.
Witkin, California Summary 10th Parent and Child § 452C, (New) Termination Of Jurisdiction.
Witkin, California Summary 10th Parent and Child § 521A, (New) Continuation or Termination Of Jurisdiction Over Nonminor or Nonminor Dependent.
Witkin, California Summary 10th Parent and Child § 669A, (New) Review Hearings Just Before and After Minor Attains Age 18.
Witkin, California Summary 10th Parent and Child § 699A, (New) in General.
Witkin, California Summary 10th Parent and Child § 899A, (New) Hearing Before Termination Of Jurisdiction.
Witkin, California Summary 10th Wills and Probate § 916, in General.

ARTICLE 13. DEPENDENT CHILDREN—APPEALS

§ 395. Appealable orders and judgments; stay; precedence; transcript; appellate proceedings in which a child is the appellant

(a)(1) A judgment in a proceeding under Section 300 may be appealed in the same manner as any final judgment, and any subsequent order may be appealed as an order after judgment. However, that order or judgment shall not be stayed by the appeal, unless, pending the appeal, suitable provision is made for the maintenance, care, and custody of the person alleged or found to come within the provisions of Section 300, and unless the provision is approved by an order of the juvenile court. The appeal shall have precedence over all other cases in the court to which the appeal is taken.

(2) A judgment or subsequent order entered by a referee shall become appealable whenever proceedings pursuant to Section 252, 253, or 254 have become completed or, if proceedings pursuant to Section 252, 253, or 254 are not initiated, when the time for initiating the proceedings has expired.

(3) An appellant unable to afford counsel, shall be provided a free copy of the transcript in any appeal.

(4) The record shall be prepared and transmitted immediately after filing of the notice of appeal, without advance payment of fees. If the appellant is able to afford counsel, the county may seek reimbursement for the cost of the transcripts under subdivision (d) of Section 68511.3 of the Government Code as though the appellant had been granted permission to proceed in forma pauperis.

(b)(1) In any appellate proceeding in which the child is an appellant, the court of appeal shall appoint separate counsel for the child. If the child is not an appellant, the court of appeal shall appoint separate counsel for the child if the court of appeal determines, after considering the recommendation of the trial counsel or guardian ad litem appointed for the child pursuant to subdivision (e) of Section 317, Section 326.5, and California Rule of Court 1448, that appointment of counsel would benefit the child. In order to assist the court of appeal in making its determination under this subdivision, the trial counsel or guardian ad litem shall make a recommendation to the court of appeal that separate counsel be appointed in any case in which the trial counsel or guardian ad litem determines that, for the purposes of the appeal, the child's best interests cannot be protected without the appointment of separate counsel, and shall set forth the reasons why the appointment is in the child's best interests. The court of appeal shall consider that recommendation when determining whether the child would benefit from the appointment of counsel. The Judicial Council shall implement this provision by adopting a rule of court on or before July 1, 2007, to set forth the procedures by which the trial counsel or guardian ad litem may participate in an appeal, as well as the factors to be considered by the trial counsel or guardian ad litem in making a recommendation to the court of appeal, including, but not limited to, the extent to which there exists a potential conflict between the interests of the child and the interests of any respondent.

(2) The Judicial Council shall report to the Legislature on or before July 1, 2008, information regarding the status of appellate representation of dependent children, the results of implementing this subdivision, any recommendations regarding the representation of dependent children in appellate proceedings made by the California Judicial Council's Blue Ribbon Commission on Children in Foster Care, any actions taken, including rules of court proposed or adopted, in response to those recommendations or taken in order to comply with the Child Abuse Prevention and Treatment Act, as well as any recommendations for legislative change that are deemed necessary to protect the best interests of dependent children in appellate proceedings or ensure compliance with the Child Abuse Prevention and Treatment Act. *(Added by Stats.1976, c. 1068, p. 4781, § 13. Amended by Stats.1980, c. 1095, p. 3511, § 1; Stats.1986, c. 823, § 4; Stats.2006, c. 385 (A.B.2480), § 2; Stats.2007, c. 738 (A.B. 1248), § 55.)*

Commentary

In re Michael H., 229 Cal.App.4th 1366, 178 Cal.Rptr.3d 71 (2014), *review denied*, held that a juvenile court's order affirming a social worker's decision not to file a dependency petition is not an appealable order, reasoning that neither this section nor section 331 expressly authorizes an appeal.

Research References

Forms

West's California Judicial Council Forms JV-810, Recommendation for Appointment Of Appellate Attorney for Child (California Rules Of Court, Rule 5.661).

Treatises and Practice Aids

Witkin, California Summary 10th Parent and Child § 476, Appeal.
Witkin, California Summary 10th Parent and Child § 700, Right to Appeal.
Witkin, California Summary 10th Parent and Child § 701, in General.
Witkin, California Summary 10th Parent and Child § 704, Miscellaneous Orders.
Witkin, California Summary 10th Parent and Child § 705, in General.
Witkin, California Summary 10th Parent and Child § 708, Counsel on Appeal.
Witkin, California Summary 10th Parent and Child § 709, in General.
Witkin, California Summary 10th Parent and Child § 713, in General.
Witkin, California Summary 10th Parent and Child § 716, in General.
Witkin, California Summary 10th Parent and Child § 718, Prior Orders.

ARTICLE 14. WARDS—JURISDICTION

§ 601. Minors habitually disobedient or truant; contact with minor in truancy program; notice to appear

(a) Any person under 18 years of age who persistently or habitually refuses to obey the reasonable and proper orders or directions of his or her parents, guardian, or custodian, or who is beyond the control of that person, or who is under the age of 18 years when he or she violated any ordinance of any city or county of this state establishing a curfew based solely on age is within the jurisdiction of the juvenile court which may adjudge the minor to be a ward of the court.

(b) If a minor has four or more truancies within one school year as defined in Section 48260 of the Education Code or a school attendance review board or probation officer determines that the available public and private services are insufficient or inappropriate to correct the habitual truancy of the minor, or to correct the minor's persistent or habitual refusal to obey the reasonable and proper orders or directions of school authorities, or if the minor fails to respond to directives of a school attendance review board or probation officer or to services provided, the minor is then within the jurisdiction of the juvenile court which may adjudge the minor to be a ward of the court. However, it is the intent of the Legislature that a minor who is described in this subdivision, adjudged a ward of the court pursuant solely to this subdivision, or found in contempt of court for failure to comply with a court order pursuant to this subdivision, shall not be held in a secure facility and shall not be removed from the custody of the parent or guardian except for the purposes of school attendance.

(c) To the extent practically feasible, a minor who is adjudged a ward of the court pursuant to this section shall not be permitted to come into or remain in contact with any minor ordered to participate in a truancy program, or the equivalent thereof, pursuant to Section 602.

(d) Any peace officer or school administrator may issue a notice to appear to a minor who is within the jurisdiction of the juvenile court pursuant to this section. *(Added by Stats.1961, c. 1616, p. 3471, § 2. Amended by Stats.1971, c. 1748, p. 3766, § 65; Stats.1974, c. 1215, p. 2629, § 8; Stats.1975, c. 192, p. 550, § 1; Stats.1975, c. 1183, p. 2917, § 2, eff. Sept. 30, 1975; Stats.1976, c. 1071, p. 4818, § 11; Stats.1994, c. 1023 (S.B.1728), § 6; Stats.1994, c. 1024 (A.B.2658), § 4.2; Stats.2014, c. 70 (S.B.1296), § 4, eff. Jan. 1, 2015.)*

Research References

Forms

West's California Judicial Council Forms JV-550, Juvenile Court Transfer Orders.
West's California Judicial Council Forms JV-610, Child Habitually Disobedient S601(a).
West's California Judicial Council Forms JV-611, Child Habitually Truant S601(B).

Treatises and Practice Aids

Witkin, California Summary 10th Parent and Child § 300, Family Relationships.
Witkin, California Summary 10th Parent and Child § 449, Nature and Scope Of Jurisdiction: Three Classes Of Minors.
Witkin, California Summary 10th Parent and Child § 450, Dual Bases Of Jurisdiction.

Witkin, California Summary 10th Parent and Child § 451, in General.
Witkin, California Summary 10th Parent and Child § 456, Proper Court.
Witkin, California Summary 10th Parent and Child § 464, Continuing Jurisdiction Outside County.
Witkin, California Summary 10th Parent and Child § 479, Jurisdiction.
Witkin, California Summary 10th Parent and Child § 480, Hearings and Orders.
Witkin, California Summary 10th Parent and Child § 485, Reports.
Witkin, California Summary 10th Parent and Child § 491, Other Agencies.
Witkin, California Summary 10th Parent and Child § 494, Records Of Dependent Children.
Witkin, California Summary 10th Parent and Child § 500, Disclosure on Petition.
Witkin, California Summary 10th Parent and Child § 507, Sealed Records.
Witkin, California Summary 10th Parent and Child § 508, Unsealed Records.
Witkin, California Summary 10th Parent and Child § 513, Legal Services.
Witkin, California Summary 10th Parent and Child § 517, Collection Procedure.
Witkin, California Summary 10th Parent and Child § 522, Nature and Scope Of Indian Child Welfare Act.
Witkin, California Summary 10th Parent and Child § 526, Determination Of Indian Status.
Witkin, California Summary 10th Parent and Child § 529, Formal Requisites.
Witkin, California Summary 10th Parent and Child § 567, Statutory Rights.
Witkin, California Summary 10th Parent and Child § 635, in General.
Witkin, California Summary 10th Parent and Child § 655, Nature and Purpose.
Witkin, California Summary 10th Parent and Child § 728, Statutory Framework.
Witkin, California Summary 10th Parent and Child § 729, Statutory Grounds.
Witkin, California Summary 10th Parent and Child § 730, Truancy.
Witkin, California Summary 10th Parent and Child § 731, in General.
Witkin, California Summary 10th Parent and Child § 732, Criminal Intent and Capacity.
Witkin, California Summary 10th Parent and Child § 743, in General.
Witkin, California Summary 10th Parent and Child § 744, Conditions.
Witkin, California Summary 10th Parent and Child § 749, Segregation Of Classes Of Minors.
Witkin, California Summary 10th Parent and Child § 755, Secure Detention Of Status Offender.
Witkin, California Summary 10th Parent and Child § 756, Inspection Of Facilities.
Witkin, California Summary 10th Parent and Child § 757, in General.
Witkin, California Summary 10th Parent and Child § 759, in General.
Witkin, California Summary 10th Parent and Child § 761, Rights Of Minor.
Witkin, California Summary 10th Parent and Child § 765, Intake Program.
Witkin, California Summary 10th Parent and Child § 766, Investigation by Probation Officer.
Witkin, California Summary 10th Parent and Child § 767, in General.
Witkin, California Summary 10th Parent and Child § 771, in General.
Witkin, California Summary 10th Parent and Child § 772, Discretion Of Probation Officer and Prosecutor.
Witkin, California Summary 10th Parent and Child § 773, Form and Content.
Witkin, California Summary 10th Parent and Child § 779, Citation.
Witkin, California Summary 10th Parent and Child § 780, Arrest Warrant.
Witkin, California Summary 10th Parent and Child § 781, Subpenas to Witnesses.
Witkin, California Summary 10th Parent and Child § 782, Statutory Rights.
Witkin, California Summary 10th Parent and Child § 788, Duty to Provide Counsel.
Witkin, California Summary 10th Parent and Child § 799, Competency to Stand Trial.
Witkin, California Summary 10th Parent and Child § 804, Admission Of Guilt.
Witkin, California Summary 10th Parent and Child § 807, in General.
Witkin, California Summary 10th Parent and Child § 808, in General.
Witkin, California Summary 10th Parent and Child § 815, Participation by District Attorney.
Witkin, California Summary 10th Parent and Child § 816, Impartial Judge or Referee.
Witkin, California Summary 10th Parent and Child § 817, Discretionary Continuance.
Witkin, California Summary 10th Parent and Child § 820, Petition and Setting for Hearing.
Witkin, California Summary 10th Parent and Child § 827, in General.
Witkin, California Summary 10th Parent and Child § 855, in General.
Witkin, California Summary 10th Parent and Child § 867, Findings.
Witkin, California Summary 10th Parent and Child § 870, in General.
Witkin, California Summary 10th Parent and Child § 871, Time for Consideration Of Probation Report and Social Study.
Witkin, California Summary 10th Parent and Child § 872, in General.
Witkin, California Summary 10th Parent and Child § 878, Sufficiency Of Evidence.
Witkin, California Summary 10th Parent and Child § 880, Immunity in Welf.C. 601 Proceeding.
Witkin, California Summary 10th Parent and Child § 882, Findings.
Witkin, California Summary 10th Parent and Child § 883, Continuance Pending Disposition Hearing.
Witkin, California Summary 10th Parent and Child § 886, Conduct Of Hearing.
Witkin, California Summary 10th Parent and Child § 887, in General.
Witkin, California Summary 10th Parent and Child § 889, Dismissal in Interests Of Justice.
Witkin, California Summary 10th Parent and Child § 890, Probation Without Wardship.
Witkin, California Summary 10th Parent and Child § 892, in General.
Witkin, California Summary 10th Parent and Child § 896, General Requirements.
Witkin, California Summary 10th Parent and Child § 898, Court Supervision Of Child.
Witkin, California Summary 10th Parent and Child § 908, Notice and Setting for Hearing.
Witkin, California Summary 10th Parent and Child § 913, Minor's Right to Appeal.
Witkin, California Summary 10th Parent and Child § 914, Notification Of Appeal Rights.

Witkin, California Summary 10th Parent and Child § 915, in General.
Witkin, California Summary 10th Parent and Child § 930, Alcohol or Drug Testing.
Witkin, California Summary 10th Parent and Child § 941, Commitment Of Minor for Status Offense.
Witkin, California Summary 10th Parent and Child § 480A, (New) Hearings and Orders for Truants.
Witkin, California Summary 10th Parent and Child § 699A, (New) in General.
Witkin, California Summary 10th Parent and Child § 936A, (New) Gps Monitoring.

§ 601.2. Failure of parent, guardian, or person in charge of minor to respond to directives of school attendance review board; disposition of minor

In the event that a parent or guardian or person in charge of a minor described in Section 48264.5 of the Education Code fails to respond to directives of the school attendance review board or to services offered on behalf of the minor, the school attendance review board shall direct that the minor be referred to the probation department or to the county welfare department under Section 300, and the school attendance review board may require the school district to file a complaint against the parent, guardian, or other person in charge of such minor as provided in Section 48291 or Section 48454 of the Education Code. *(Added by Stats.1974, c. 1215, p. 2629, § 10. Amended by Stats.1976, c. 1068, p. 4782, § 21; Stats.1978, c. 380, p. 1208, § 154; Stats.1994, c. 1023 (S.B.1728), § 8.)*

Research References

Treatises and Practice Aids

Witkin, California Summary 10th Parent and Child § 451, in General.
Witkin, California Summary 10th Parent and Child § 730, Truancy.

§ 601.3. Truancy mediation program

(a) If the district attorney or the probation officer receives notice from the school district pursuant to subdivision (b) of Section 48260.6 of the Education Code that a minor continues to be classified as a truant after the parents or guardians have been notified pursuant to subdivision (a) of Section 48260.5 of the Education Code, or if the district attorney or the probation officer receives notice from the school attendance review board, or the district attorney receives notice from the probation officer, pursuant to subdivision (a) of Section 48263.5 of the Education Code that a minor continues to be classified as a truant after review and counseling by the school attendance review board or probation officer, the district attorney or the probation officer, or both, may request the parents or guardians and the child to attend a meeting in the district attorney's office or at the probation department to discuss the possible legal consequences of the minor's truancy.

(b) Notice of a meeting to be held pursuant to this section shall contain all of the following:

(1) The name and address of the person to whom the notice is directed.

(2) The date, time, and place of the meeting.

(3) The name of the minor classified as a truant.

(4) The section pursuant to which the meeting is requested.

(5) Notice that the district attorney may file a criminal complaint against the parents or guardians pursuant to Section 48293 of the Education Code for failure to compel the attendance of the minor at school.

(c) Notice of a meeting to be held pursuant to this section shall be served at least five days prior to the meeting on each person required to attend the meeting. Service shall be made personally or by certified mail with return receipt requested.

(d) At the commencement of the meeting authorized by this section, the district attorney or the probation officer shall advise the parents or guardians and the child that any statements they make could be used against them in subsequent court proceedings.

(e) Upon completion of the meeting authorized by this section, the probation officer or the district attorney, after consultation with the probation officer, may file a petition pursuant to Section 601 if the district attorney or the probation officer determines that available community resources cannot resolve the truancy problem, or if the pupil or the parents or guardians of the pupil, or both, have failed to respond to services provided or to the directives of the school, the school attendance review board, the probation officer, or the district attorney.

(f) The truancy mediation program authorized by this section may be established by the district attorney or by the probation officer. The district attorney and the probation officer shall coordinate their efforts and shall cooperate in determining which office is best able to operate a truancy mediation program in their county pursuant to this section. *(Added by Stats.1984, c. 754, § 5. Amended by Stats.1991, c. 1202 (S.B.377), § 14; Stats.1992, c. 427 (A.B.3355), § 175; Stats.1994, c. 1024 (A.B.2658), § 6.)*

Research References

Forms

West's California Code Forms, Education § 48980 Form 1, Notice to Parents and Guardians Regarding Statutory Rights.

Treatises and Practice Aids

Witkin, California Summary 10th Parent and Child § 730, Truancy.
Witkin, California Summary 10th Parent and Child § 766, Investigation by Probation Officer.
Witkin, California Summary 10th Parent and Child § 771, in General.

§ 601.4. Compulsory education violations; jurisdiction; prosecution; coordinating actions

(a) The juvenile court judge may be assigned to sit as a superior court judge to hear any complaint alleging that a parent, guardian, or other person having control or charge of a minor has violated Section 48293 of the Education Code. The jurisdiction of the juvenile court granted by this section shall not be exclusive and the charge may be prosecuted instead in a superior court. However, upon motion, that action shall be transferred to the juvenile court.

(b) Notwithstanding Section 737 of the Penal Code, a violation of Section 48293 of the Education Code may be prosecuted pursuant to subdivision (a), by written complaint filed in the same manner as an infraction may be prosecuted. The juvenile court judge, sitting as a superior court judge, may coordinate the action involving the minor with any action involving the parent, guardian, or other person having control or charge of the minor. Both matters may be heard and decided at the same time unless the parent, guardian, other person having control or charge of the minor, or any member of the press or public objects to a closed hearing of the proceedings charging violation of Section 48293 of the Education Code. *(Added by Stats.1985, c. 120, § 2. Amended by Stats.1989, c. 1117, § 5; Stats.1998, c. 931 (S.B.2139), § 470, eff. Sept. 28, 1998; Stats.2002, c. 784 (S.B.1316), § 612.)*

Law Revision Commission Comments

1998 Amendment

Section 601.4 is amended to accommodate unification of the municipal and superior courts in a county. Cal. Const. art. VI, § 5(e). The jurisdictional and procedural distinctions between a judge sitting as a juvenile court judge and sitting as a superior court judge are significant and are preserved in this amendment. The section is also amended to reflect elimination of the justice court. Cal. Const. art. VI, §§ 1, 5(b). [28 Cal.L.Rev.Comm. Reports 51 (1998)].

2002 Amendment

Section 601.4 is amended to reflect unification of the municipal and superior courts pursuant to Article VI, Section 5(e), of the California Constitution. [32 Cal.L.Rev.Comm. Reports 553 (2002)].

Research References

Treatises and Practice Aids

Witkin, California Summary 10th Parent and Child § 453, Jurisdiction Over Adults.

Witkin, California Summary 10th Parent and Child § 730, Truancy.

§ 601.5. At–Risk Youth Early Intervention Program; establishment; Youth Referral Centers

(a) Any county may, upon adoption of a resolution by the board of supervisors, establish an At–Risk Youth Early Intervention Program designed to assess and serve families with children who have chronic behavioral problems that place the child at risk of becoming a ward of the juvenile court under Section 601 or 602. The purpose of the program is to provide a swift and local service response to youth behavior problems so that future involvement with the justice system may be avoided.

(b) The At–Risk Youth Early Intervention Program shall be designed and developed by a collaborative group which shall include representatives of the juvenile court, the probation department, the district attorney, the public defender, the county department of social services, the county education department, county health and mental health agencies, and local and community-based youth and family service providers.

(c) The At–Risk Youth Early Intervention Program shall include one or more neighborhood-based Youth Referral Centers for at-risk youth and their families. These Youth Referral Centers shall be flexibly designed by each participating county to serve the local at-risk youth population with family assessments, onsite services, and referrals to offsite services. The operator of a Youth Referral Center may be a private nonprofit community-based agency or a public agency, or both. A center shall be staffed by youth and family service counselors who may be public or private employees and who shall be experienced in dealing with at-risk youth who are eligible for the program, as described in subdivision (d). The center may also be staffed as a collaborative service model involving onsite youth and family counselors, probation officers, school representatives, health and mental health practitioners, or other service providers. A center shall be located at one or more community sites that are generally accessible to at-risk youth and families and shall be open during daytime, evening, and weekend hours, as appropriate, based upon local service demand and resources available to the program.

(d) A minor may be referred to a Youth Referral Center by a parent or guardian, a law enforcement officer, a probation officer, a child welfare agency, or a school, or a minor may self-refer. A minor may be referred to the program if the minor is at least 10 years of age and is believed by the referring source to be at risk of justice system involvement due to chronic disobedience to parents, curfew violations, repeat truancy, incidents of running away from home, experimentation with drugs or alcohol, or other serious behavior problems. Whenever a minor is referred to the program, the Youth Referral Center shall make an initial determination as to whether the minor is engaged in a pattern of at-risk behavior likely to result in future justice system involvement, and, if satisfied that the minor is significantly at risk, the center shall initiate a family assessment. The family assessment shall identify the minor's behavioral problem, the family's circumstances and relationship to the problem, and the needs of the minor or the family in relation to the behavioral problem. The assessment shall be performed using a risk and needs assessment instrument, based on national models of successful youth risk and needs assessment instruments and utilizing objective assessment criteria, as appropriate for the clientele served by the program. At a minimum, the assessment shall include information drawn from interviews with the minor and with the parents or other adults having custody of the minor, and it shall include information on the minor's probation, school, health, and mental health status to the extent such information may be available and accessible.

(e) If the Youth Referral Center confirms upon assessment that the minor is at significant risk of future justice system involvement and that the minor may benefit from referral to services, the Youth Referral Center staff shall work with the minor and the parents to produce a written service plan to be implemented over a period of up to six months. The plan shall identify specific programs or services that are recommended by the center and are locally available to the minor and the family as a means of addressing the behavior problems that led to the referral. The plan may include a requirement that the minor obey reasonable rules of conduct at home or in school including reasonable home curfew and school attendance rules, while the service plan is being implemented. The plan may also require, as a condition of further participation in the program, that a parent or other family member engage in counseling, parenting classes, or other relevant activities. To the extent possible given available resources, the staff at the Youth

Referral Center shall facilitate compliance with the service plan by assisting the minor and the family in making appointments with service providers, by responding to requests for help by the minor or the parent as they seek to comply with the plan, and by monitoring compliance until the plan is completed.

(f)(1) The caseworker at the Youth Referral Center shall explain the service plan to the minor and the parents and, prior to any referral to services, the minor and the parents shall agree to the plan. The minor and the parents shall be informed that the minor's failure to accept or to cooperate with the service plan may result in the filing of a petition and a finding of wardship under Section 601.

(2) With the cooperation of the collaborative group described in subdivision (b), the Youth Referral Center shall review youth and family services offered within its local service area and shall identify providers, programs, and services that are available for referral of minors and parents under this section. Providers to which minors and parents may be referred under this section may be public or private agencies or individuals offering counseling, health, educational, parenting, mentoring, community service, skill-building, and other relevant services that are considered likely to resolve the behavioral problems that are referred to the center.

(g)(1) Unless the probation department is directly operating and staffing the Youth Referral Center, the probation department shall designate one or more probation officers to serve as liaison to a Youth Referral Center for the purpose of facilitating and monitoring compliance with service plans established in individual cases by the center.

(2) If, upon consultation with the minor's parents and with providers designated in the service plan, the supervising caseworker at the center and the liaison probation officer agree that the minor has willfully, significantly, and repeatedly failed to cooperate with the service plan, the minor shall be referred to the probation department which shall verify the failure and, upon verification, shall file a petition seeking to declare the minor a ward of the juvenile court under subdivision (a) of Section 601. No minor shall be referred to the probation department for the filing of a petition under this subdivision until at least 90 days have elapsed after the first attempt to implement the service plan. No minor shall be subject to filing of a petition under this subdivision for a failure to complete the service plan which is due principally to an inability of the minor or the family to pay for services listed in the service plan.

(3) If, within 180 days of the start of the service plan, the minor and the family have substantially completed the service plan and the minor's behavior problem appears to have been resolved, the center shall notify the probation department that the plan has been successfully completed.

(h) If a petition to declare the minor a ward of the juvenile court under subdivision (a) of Section 601 has been filed by the probation officer under this section, the court shall review the petition and any other facts which the court deems appropriate in relation to the minor's alleged failure to comply with the service plan described in subdivision (e). Based upon this review, the court may continue any hearing on the petition for up to six months so that the minor and the minor's parents may renew their efforts to comply with the service plan under court supervision. During the period in which the hearing is continued, the court may order that the minor and the parent cooperate with the service plan designed by the Youth Referral Center, or the court may modify the service plan or may impose additional conditions upon the minor or the parents as may be appropriate to encourage resolution of the behavior problems that led to the filing of the petition. The court shall, during the period of continuance, periodically review compliance with the extended service plan through reports from the probation officer or by calling the parties back into court, based upon a review schedule deemed appropriate by the court.

(i) The juvenile court of any county participating in the At–Risk Youth Early Intervention Program shall designate a judicial officer to serve as a liaison to the program in order to participate in the development of the program and to coordinate program operations with the juvenile court. The liaison judicial officer may be designated by the juvenile court as the principal judicial officer assigned to review and hear petitions filed under this section, or if the court does not elect to designate a principal judicial officer to hear these cases, the juvenile court shall take steps to train or familiarize other judicial officers reviewing or hearing these cases as to the operations, procedures, and services of the At–Risk Youth Early Intervention Program. *(Added by Stats.1997, c. 909 (S.B.1050), § 1.)*

Research References

Treatises and Practice Aids

Witkin, California Summary 10th Parent and Child § 731, in General.

§ 602. Minors violating laws defining crime; ward of court

Except as provided in Section 707, any person who is under 18 years of age when he or she violates any law of this state or of the United States or any ordinance of any city or county of this state defining crime other than an ordinance establishing a curfew based solely on age, is within the jurisdiction of the juvenile court, which may adjudge such person to be a ward of the court. *(Added by Stats.1961, c. 1616, p. 3472, § 2. Amended by Stats.1971, c. 1748, p. 3766, § 66; Stats.1972, c. 84, p. 109, § 1, eff. May 19, 1972; Stats.1976, c. 1071, p. 4819, § 12; Stats.1999, c. 996 (S.B.334), § 12.2; Initiative Measure (Prop. 21, § 18, approved March 7, 2000, eff. March 8, 2000); Stats.2001, c. 854 (S.B.205), § 72; Stats.2014, c. 54 (S.B.1461), § 18, eff. Jan. 1, 2015; Initiative Measure (Prop. 57, § 4.1, approved Nov. 8, 2016, eff. Nov. 9, 2016).)*

Research References

Forms

West's California Judicial Council Forms JV-550, Juvenile Court Transfer Orders.

Treatises and Practice Aids

Witkin, California Summary 10th Parent and Child § 300, Family Relationships.

Witkin, California Summary 10th Parent and Child § 446, in General.

Witkin, California Summary 10th Parent and Child § 449, Nature and Scope Of Jurisdiction: Three Classes Of Minors.

Witkin, California Summary 10th Parent and Child § 450, Dual Bases Of Jurisdiction.
Witkin, California Summary 10th Parent and Child § 451, in General.
Witkin, California Summary 10th Parent and Child § 452, Jurisdiction Retained After Majority.
Witkin, California Summary 10th Parent and Child § 454, Jurisdiction Improperly Invoked.
Witkin, California Summary 10th Parent and Child § 456, Proper Court.
Witkin, California Summary 10th Parent and Child § 458, Conditions for Transfer.
Witkin, California Summary 10th Parent and Child § 467, Power to Hear Cases.
Witkin, California Summary 10th Parent and Child § 483, Juvenile Court Proceedings.
Witkin, California Summary 10th Parent and Child § 491, Other Agencies.
Witkin, California Summary 10th Parent and Child § 492, in General.
Witkin, California Summary 10th Parent and Child § 494, Records Of Dependent Children.
Witkin, California Summary 10th Parent and Child § 497, Authorized Disclosure to Law Enforcement Agencies.
Witkin, California Summary 10th Parent and Child § 498, Authorized Disclosure About Specified Crimes.
Witkin, California Summary 10th Parent and Child § 500, Disclosure on Petition.
Witkin, California Summary 10th Parent and Child § 501, Nature and Use Of Records.
Witkin, California Summary 10th Parent and Child § 507, Sealed Records.
Witkin, California Summary 10th Parent and Child § 508, Unsealed Records.
Witkin, California Summary 10th Parent and Child § 512, Illustrations.
Witkin, California Summary 10th Parent and Child § 513, Legal Services.
Witkin, California Summary 10th Parent and Child § 517, Collection Procedure.
Witkin, California Summary 10th Parent and Child § 522, Nature and Scope Of Indian Child Welfare Act.
Witkin, California Summary 10th Parent and Child § 526, Determination Of Indian Status.
Witkin, California Summary 10th Parent and Child § 529, Formal Requisites.
Witkin, California Summary 10th Parent and Child § 567, Statutory Rights.
Witkin, California Summary 10th Parent and Child § 570, in General.
Witkin, California Summary 10th Parent and Child § 655, Nature and Purpose.
Witkin, California Summary 10th Parent and Child § 729, Statutory Grounds.
Witkin, California Summary 10th Parent and Child § 731, in General.
Witkin, California Summary 10th Parent and Child § 732, Criminal Intent and Capacity.
Witkin, California Summary 10th Parent and Child § 734, Procedure on Insanity Plea.
Witkin, California Summary 10th Parent and Child § 735, Defense Of Statute Of Limitations.
Witkin, California Summary 10th Parent and Child § 736, Mandatory Prosecution.
Witkin, California Summary 10th Parent and Child § 737, Discretionary Prosecution.
Witkin, California Summary 10th Parent and Child § 738, Prosecution by Indictment.
Witkin, California Summary 10th Parent and Child § 739, Sentencing.
Witkin, California Summary 10th Parent and Child § 743, in General.
Witkin, California Summary 10th Parent and Child § 744, Conditions.
Witkin, California Summary 10th Parent and Child § 745, Limitations.
Witkin, California Summary 10th Parent and Child § 747, Juvenile Ranches and Camps.
Witkin, California Summary 10th Parent and Child § 748, Regional Youth Educational Facilities.
Witkin, California Summary 10th Parent and Child § 749, Segregation Of Classes Of Minors.
Witkin, California Summary 10th Parent and Child § 753, Minor in Temporary Custody.
Witkin, California Summary 10th Parent and Child § 754, Administration Of Evaluation or Test.
Witkin, California Summary 10th Parent and Child § 756, Inspection Of Facilities.
Witkin, California Summary 10th Parent and Child § 757, in General.
Witkin, California Summary 10th Parent and Child § 759, in General.
Witkin, California Summary 10th Parent and Child § 761, Rights Of Minor.
Witkin, California Summary 10th Parent and Child § 763, Investigation, Release, and Conditions.
Witkin, California Summary 10th Parent and Child § 764, Retention Of Custody.
Witkin, California Summary 10th Parent and Child § 765, Intake Program.
Witkin, California Summary 10th Parent and Child § 766, Investigation by Probation Officer.
Witkin, California Summary 10th Parent and Child § 767, in General.
Witkin, California Summary 10th Parent and Child § 768, Eligibility.
Witkin, California Summary 10th Parent and Child § 770, Time for Filing Welf.C. 602 Petition.
Witkin, California Summary 10th Parent and Child § 771, in General.
Witkin, California Summary 10th Parent and Child § 772, Discretion Of Probation Officer and Prosecutor.
Witkin, California Summary 10th Parent and Child § 773, Form and Content.
Witkin, California Summary 10th Parent and Child § 774, Variance and Amendment.
Witkin, California Summary 10th Parent and Child § 776, Persons Entitled to Notice.
Witkin, California Summary 10th Parent and Child § 780, Arrest Warrant.
Witkin, California Summary 10th Parent and Child § 781, Subpenas to Witnesses.
Witkin, California Summary 10th Parent and Child § 782, Statutory Rights.
Witkin, California Summary 10th Parent and Child § 785, No Right to Jury.
Witkin, California Summary 10th Parent and Child § 788, Duty to Provide Counsel.
Witkin, California Summary 10th Parent and Child § 789, Counsel's Right to Argue.
Witkin, California Summary 10th Parent and Child § 791, Right to Interpreter.
Witkin, California Summary 10th Parent and Child § 795, Doctrine Applies in Juvenile Court.
Witkin, California Summary 10th Parent and Child § 796, Successive Juvenile Court Proceedings.
Witkin, California Summary 10th Parent and Child § 797, Juvenile Court Proceedings and Criminal Prosecution.

Witkin, California Summary 10th Parent and Child § 798, Multiple Prosecutions Prohibited.
Witkin, California Summary 10th Parent and Child § 799, Competency to Stand Trial.
Witkin, California Summary 10th Parent and Child § 800, Crime Not Charged in Petition.
Witkin, California Summary 10th Parent and Child § 804, Admission Of Guilt.
Witkin, California Summary 10th Parent and Child § 805, Presence at Trial.
Witkin, California Summary 10th Parent and Child § 806, Rights Of Victims.
Witkin, California Summary 10th Parent and Child § 807, in General.
Witkin, California Summary 10th Parent and Child § 808, in General.
Witkin, California Summary 10th Parent and Child § 809, Victims and Support Persons.
Witkin, California Summary 10th Parent and Child § 810, Interested Persons.
Witkin, California Summary 10th Parent and Child § 811, Members Of the Public.
Witkin, California Summary 10th Parent and Child § 815, Participation by District Attorney.
Witkin, California Summary 10th Parent and Child § 817, Discretionary Continuance.
Witkin, California Summary 10th Parent and Child § 819, Time Of Hearing.
Witkin, California Summary 10th Parent and Child § 820, Petition and Setting for Hearing.
Witkin, California Summary 10th Parent and Child § 827, in General.
Witkin, California Summary 10th Parent and Child § 834, Orders.
Witkin, California Summary 10th Parent and Child § 835, Nature and Scope Of Hearing.
Witkin, California Summary 10th Parent and Child § 837, Designated Crimes.
Witkin, California Summary 10th Parent and Child § 838, Accused Who Has Reached Adulthood.
Witkin, California Summary 10th Parent and Child § 840, in General.
Witkin, California Summary 10th Parent and Child § 847, Effect Of Finding on Later Petition.
Witkin, California Summary 10th Parent and Child § 855, in General.
Witkin, California Summary 10th Parent and Child § 857, Dismissal for Delay in Commencement.
Witkin, California Summary 10th Parent and Child § 858, Refiling After Dismissal.
Witkin, California Summary 10th Parent and Child § 859, Continuance.
Witkin, California Summary 10th Parent and Child § 860, Nature and Purpose Of Rule.
Witkin, California Summary 10th Parent and Child § 863, Motion to Compel Disclosure.
Witkin, California Summary 10th Parent and Child § 867, Findings.
Witkin, California Summary 10th Parent and Child § 868, Admissions Based on Agreement.
Witkin, California Summary 10th Parent and Child § 869, No Contest in Lieu Of Admission.
Witkin, California Summary 10th Parent and Child § 870, in General.
Witkin, California Summary 10th Parent and Child § 871, Time for Consideration Of Probation Report and Social Study.
Witkin, California Summary 10th Parent and Child § 872, in General.
Witkin, California Summary 10th Parent and Child § 875, Exclusion Of Illegally Obtained Evidence.
Witkin, California Summary 10th Parent and Child § 876, Consent to Search.
Witkin, California Summary 10th Parent and Child § 878, Sufficiency Of Evidence.
Witkin, California Summary 10th Parent and Child § 879, in General.
Witkin, California Summary 10th Parent and Child § 881, Immunity in Welf.C. 602 Proceeding.
Witkin, California Summary 10th Parent and Child § 882, Findings.
Witkin, California Summary 10th Parent and Child § 883, Continuance Pending Disposition Hearing.
Witkin, California Summary 10th Parent and Child § 886, Conduct Of Hearing.
Witkin, California Summary 10th Parent and Child § 887, in General.
Witkin, California Summary 10th Parent and Child § 889, Dismissal in Interests Of Justice.
Witkin, California Summary 10th Parent and Child § 890, Probation Without Wardship.
Witkin, California Summary 10th Parent and Child § 891, Deferred Entry Of Judgment.
Witkin, California Summary 10th Parent and Child § 892, in General.
Witkin, California Summary 10th Parent and Child § 896, General Requirements.
Witkin, California Summary 10th Parent and Child § 898, Court Supervision Of Child.
Witkin, California Summary 10th Parent and Child § 900, in General.
Witkin, California Summary 10th Parent and Child § 901, Restitution Fine.
Witkin, California Summary 10th Parent and Child § 902, Restitution to Victim.
Witkin, California Summary 10th Parent and Child § 903, Liability Of Parent or Guardian for Restitution.
Witkin, California Summary 10th Parent and Child § 907, Nature and Purpose.
Witkin, California Summary 10th Parent and Child § 908, Notice and Setting for Hearing.
Witkin, California Summary 10th Parent and Child § 913, Minor's Right to Appeal.
Witkin, California Summary 10th Parent and Child § 914, Notification Of Appeal Rights.
Witkin, California Summary 10th Parent and Child § 915, in General.
Witkin, California Summary 10th Parent and Child § 916, Appeal by Prosecution.
Witkin, California Summary 10th Parent and Child § 922, Conditions Of Supervised Probation.
Witkin, California Summary 10th Parent and Child § 928, Restitution.
Witkin, California Summary 10th Parent and Child § 930, Alcohol or Drug Testing.
Witkin, California Summary 10th Parent and Child § 933, School Performance.
Witkin, California Summary 10th Parent and Child § 938, Driving Restrictions.
Witkin, California Summary 10th Parent and Child § 939, Other Conditions.
Witkin, California Summary 10th Parent and Child § 942, Types Of Sanctions.
Witkin, California Summary 10th Parent and Child § 943, Invalid Commitment.
Witkin, California Summary 10th Parent and Child § 944, in General.
Witkin, California Summary 10th Parent and Child § 949, Mentally Ill Ward.
Witkin, California Summary 10th Parent and Child § 951, in General.

Witkin, California Summary 10th Parent and Child § 964, Procedure in Aggregating Prior Offenses.
Witkin, California Summary 10th Parent and Child § 971, Notice and Hearing.
Witkin, California Summary 10th Parent and Child § 693D, (New) Emergency Removal from Prospective Adoptive Parent.
Witkin, California Summary 10th Parent and Child § 699A, (New) in General.
Witkin, California Summary 10th Parent and Child § 793A, (New) Recordation Of Interrogation Of Minor Suspected Of Murder.
Witkin, California Summary 10th Parent and Child § 885A, (New) Minor With Mental or Emotional Disorder or Developmental Disability.
Witkin, California Summary 10th Parent and Child § 940A, (New) Successful Completion Of Probation.

§ 602.3. Personal use of firearm in the commission of a violent felony; placement order

(a) Notwithstanding any other law and pursuant to the provisions of this section, the juvenile court shall commit any minor adjudicated to be a ward of the court for the personal use of a firearm in the commission of a violent felony, as defined in subdivision (c) of Section 667.5 of the Penal Code, to placement in a juvenile hall, ranch, camp, or with the Department of the Youth Authority.

(b) A court may impose a treatment-based alternative placement order on any minor subject to this section if the court finds the minor has a mental disorder requiring intensive treatment. Any alternative placement order under this subdivision shall be made on the record, in writing, and in accordance with Article 3 (commencing with Section 6550) of Chapter 2 of Part 2 of Division 6. *(Formerly § 602.5, added by Stats.1999, c. 996 (S.B.334), § 13. Renumbered § 602.3 and amended by Stats.2001, c. 854 (S.B.205), § 73.)*

Research References

Treatises and Practice Aids

Witkin, California Summary 10th Parent and Child § 739, Sentencing.
Witkin, California Summary 10th Parent and Child § 942, Types Of Sanctions.
Witkin, California Summary 10th Parent and Child § 949, Mentally Ill Ward.

§ 602.5. Minor's criminal history; report

The juvenile court shall report the complete criminal history of any minor found to be a person adjudged to be a ward of the court under Section 602 because of the commission of any felony offense to the Department of Justice. The Department of Justice shall retain this information and make it available in the same manner as information gathered pursuant to Chapter 2 (commencing with Section 13100) of Title 3 of Part 4 of the Penal Code. *(Added by Initiative Measure (Prop. 21, § 19, approved March 7, 2000, eff. March 8, 2000).)*

Research References

Treatises and Practice Aids

Witkin, California Summary 10th Parent and Child § 498, Authorized Disclosure About Specified Crimes.

Witkin, California Summary 10th Parent and Child § 891, Deferred Entry Of Judgment.

§ 603. Preliminary examination; trying case upon accusatory pleading

(a) No court shall have jurisdiction to conduct a preliminary examination or to try the case of any person upon an accusatory pleading charging that person with the commission of a public offense or crime when the person was under the age of 18 years at the time of the alleged commission thereof unless the matter has first been submitted to the juvenile court by petition as provided in Article 7 (commencing with Section 650), and the juvenile court has made an order directing that the person be prosecuted under the general law.

(b) This section shall not apply in any case involving a minor against whom a complaint may be filed directly in a court of criminal jurisdiction pursuant to Section 707.01. *(Added by Stats.1961, c. 1616, p. 3472, § 2. Amended by Stats.1996, c. 481 (S.B.1377), § 1.)*

Research References

Treatises and Practice Aids

Witkin, California Summary 10th Parent and Child § 740, Limitation on Jurisdiction Of Criminal Court.

§ 603.5. Vehicle Code infractions or violations of local ordinances involving motor vehicles; jurisdiction; referral to juvenile court; application of section

(a) Notwithstanding any other provision of law, in a county that adopts the provisions of this section, jurisdiction over the case of a minor alleged to have committed only a violation of the Vehicle Code classified as an infraction or a violation of a local ordinance involving the driving, parking, or operation of a motor vehicle, is with the superior court, except that the court may refer to the juvenile court for adjudication, cases involving a minor who has been adjudicated a ward of the juvenile court, or who has other matters pending in the juvenile court.

(b) The cases specified in subdivision (a) shall not be governed by the procedures set forth in the juvenile court law.

(c) Any provisions of juvenile court law requiring that confidentiality be observed as to cases and proceedings, prohibiting or restricting the disclosure of juvenile court records, or restricting attendance by the public at juvenile court proceedings shall not apply. The procedures for bail specified in Chapter 1 (commencing with Section 1268) of Title 10 of Part 2 of the Penal Code shall apply.

(d) The provisions of this section shall apply in a county in which the trial courts make the section applicable as to any matters to be heard and the court has determined that there is available funding for any increased costs. *(Added by Stats.1980, c. 1299, p. 4390, § 4. Amended by Stats.1993, c. 1151 (A.B.1436), § 1; Stats.1994, c. 478 (A.B.3115), § 1, eff. Sept. 12, 1994; Stats.1996, c. 93 (A.B.2686), § 1; Stats.1998, c. 931 (S.B.2139), § 471, eff. Sept. 28, 1998; Stats.2001, c. 824 (A.B.1700), § 38; Stats.2008, c. 56 (S.B.1182), § 11.)*

Law Revision Commission Comments

1998 Amendment

Section 603.5 is amended to accommodate unification of the municipal and superior courts in a county. Cal. Const. art. VI, § 5(e). [28 Cal.L.Rev.Comm. Reports 51 (1998)].

2008 Amendment

Subdivision (a) of Section 603.5 is amended to reflect unification of the municipal and superior courts pursuant to former Section 5(e) of Article VI of the California Constitution.

Subdivision (a) is further amended to make stylistic revisions. [37 Cal.L.Rev.Comm. Reports 171 (2007)].

Research References

Treatises and Practice Aids

Witkin, California Summary 10th Parent and Child § 478, in General.

Witkin, California Summary 10th Parent and Child § 479, Jurisdiction.

Witkin, California Summary 10th Parent and Child § 480, Hearings and Orders.

§ 604. Proceedings; suspension, resumption, new proceedings; certification to juvenile court; pleadings

(a) Whenever a case is before any court upon an accusatory pleading and it is suggested or appears to the judge before whom the person is brought that the person charged was, at the date the offense is alleged to have been committed, under the age of 18 years, the judge shall immediately suspend all proceedings against the person on the charge. The judge shall examine into the age of the person, and if, from the examination, it appears to his or her satisfaction that the person was at the date the offense is alleged to have been committed under the age of 18 years, he or she shall immediately certify all of the following to the juvenile court of the county:

(1) That the person (naming him or her) is charged with a crime (briefly stating its nature).

(2) That the person appears to have been under the age of 18 years at the date the offense is alleged to have been committed, giving the date of birth of the person when known.

(3) That proceedings have been suspended against the person on the charge by reason of his or her age, with the date of the suspension.

The judge shall attach a copy of the accusatory pleading to the certification.

(b) When a court certifies a case to the juvenile court pursuant to subdivision (a), it shall be deemed that jeopardy has not attached by reason of the proceedings prior to certification, but the court may not resume proceedings in the case, nor may a new proceeding under the general law be commenced in any court with respect to the same matter unless the juvenile court has found that the minor is not a fit subject for consideration under the juvenile court law and has ordered that proceedings under the general law resume or be commenced.

(c) The certification and accusatory pleading shall be promptly transmitted to the clerk of the juvenile court. Upon receipt thereof, the clerk of the juvenile court shall immediately notify the probation officer who shall immediately proceed in accordance with Article 16 (commencing with Section 650).

(d) This section does not apply to any minor who may have a complaint filed directly against him or her in a court of criminal jurisdiction pursuant to Section 707.01. *(Added by Stats.1982, c. 1088, § 3. Amended by Stats.1984, c. 1412, § 1; Stats.1996, c. 481 (S.B.1377), § 2.)*

Research References

Treatises and Practice Aids

Witkin, California Summary 10th Parent and Child § 451, in General.

Witkin, California Summary 10th Parent and Child § 741, Duty to Suspend Proceedings and Certify to Juvenile Court.

Witkin, California Summary 10th Parent and Child § 742, Effect Of Certification.

Witkin, California Summary 10th Parent and Child § 764, Retention Of Custody.

Witkin, California Summary 10th Parent and Child § 772, Discretion Of Probation Officer and Prosecutor.

§ 605. Statute of limitations; suspension

Whenever a petition is filed in a juvenile court alleging that a minor is a person within the description of Section 602, and while the case is before the juvenile court, the statute of limitations applicable under the general law to the offense alleged to bring the minor within such description is suspended. *(Added by Stats.1961, c. 1616, p. 3473, § 2.)*

Research References

Treatises and Practice Aids

Witkin, California Summary 10th Parent and Child § 731, in General.

§ 606. Subjecting minor to criminal prosecution

When a petition has been filed in a juvenile court, the minor who is the subject of the petition shall not thereafter be subject to criminal prosecution based on the facts giving rise to the petition unless the juvenile court finds that the minor is not a fit and proper subject to be dealt with under this chapter and orders that criminal proceedings be resumed or instituted against him, or the petition is transferred to a court of criminal jurisdiction pursuant to subdivision (b) of Section 707.01. *(Added by Stats.1961, c. 1616, p. 3473, § 2. Amended by Stats.1999, c. 996 (S.B.334), § 14.)*

Research References

Treatises and Practice Aids

Witkin, California Summary 10th Parent and Child § 797, Juvenile Court Proceedings and Criminal Prosecution.

Witkin, California Summary 10th Parent and Child § 846, Effect Of Finding on Earlier Petition.

§ 607. Retention of, and discharge from, jurisdiction

(a) The court may retain jurisdiction over any person who is found to be a ward or dependent child of the juvenile court until the ward or dependent child attains 21 years of age, except as provided in subdivisions (b), (c), and (d).

(b) The court may retain jurisdiction over any person who is found to be a person described in Section 602 by reason of the commission of any of the offenses listed in subdivision (b) or paragraph (2) of subdivision (d) of Section 707, until that person attains 25 years of age if the person was committed to the Department of Corrections and Rehabilitation, Division of Juvenile Facilities.

(c) The court shall not discharge any person from its jurisdiction who has been committed to the Department of Corrections and Rehabilitation, Division of Juvenile Facilities so long as the person remains under the jurisdiction of the Department of Corrections and Rehabilitation, Division of Juvenile Facilities, including periods of extended control ordered pursuant to Section 1800.

(d) The court may retain jurisdiction over any person described in Section 602 by reason of the commission of any of the offenses listed in subdivision (b) or paragraph (2) of subdivision (d) of Section 707, who has been confined in a state hospital or other appropriate public or private mental health facility pursuant to Section 702.3 until that person attains 25 years of age, unless the court that committed the person finds, after notice and hearing, that the person's sanity has been restored.

(e) The court may retain jurisdiction over any person while that person is the subject of a warrant for arrest issued pursuant to Section 663.

(f) Notwithstanding subdivisions (b) and (d), on and after July 1, 2012, every person committed by the juvenile court to the Department of Corrections and Rehabilitation, Division of Juvenile Facilities, who is found to be a person described in Section 602 by reason of the violation of any of the offenses listed in subdivision (b) or paragraph (2) of subdivision (d) of Section 707 shall be discharged upon the expiration of a two-year period of control, or when the person attains 23 years of age, whichever occurs later, unless an order for further detention has been made by the committing court pursuant to Article 6 (commencing with Section 1800) of Chapter 1 of Division 2.5. This section shall not apply to persons committed to the Department of Corrections and Rehabilitation, Division of Juvenile Facilities, or persons confined in a state hospital or other appropriate public or private mental health facility, by a court prior to July 1, 2012, pursuant to subdivisions (b) and (d).

(g) The amendments to this section made by the act [1] adding this subdivision shall apply retroactively. *(Added by Stats.1961, c. 1616, p. 3473, § 2. Amended by Stats.1971, c. 1748, p. 3767, § 68; Stats.1976, c. 1068, p. 4782, § 22; Stats.1976, c. 1071, p. 4819, § 13; Stats.1982, c. 1102, § 1; Stats.1983, c. 936, § 1; Stats.1988, c. 713, § 1; Stats.1994, c. 453 (A.B.560), § 3; Stats.2010, c. 729 (A.B.1628), § 9, eff. Oct. 19, 2010; Stats.2012, c. 41 (S.B.1021), § 87, eff. June 27, 2012; Stats.2012, c. 342 (A.B.1481), § 3, eff. Sept. 17, 2012.)*

[1] Stats.2012, c. 342 (A.B.1481).

Research References

Treatises and Practice Aids

Witkin, California Summary 10th Parent and Child § 452, Jurisdiction Retained After Majority.

Witkin, California Summary 10th Parent and Child § 734, Procedure on Insanity Plea.

Witkin, California Summary 10th Parent and Child § 837, Designated Crimes.

Witkin, California Summary 10th Parent and Child § 944, in General.

Witkin, California Summary 10th Parent and Child § 899A, (New) Hearing Before Termination Of Jurisdiction.

§ 607.1. Retention of jurisdiction; criteria

(a) This section shall become operative on the 90th day after the enactment of the act adding this section.[1]

(b)(1) Notwithstanding Section 607, the court shall retain jurisdiction as described in paragraph (2) over any person who meets both of the following criteria:

(A) The person has been discharged from the physical custody of a facility of the Department of Corrections and Rehabilitation, Division of Juvenile Facilities.

(B) The person is subject to subdivision (b) of Section 1766 or subdivision (c) of Section 1766.01.

(2) The court shall retain jurisdiction over a person who is described in paragraph (1) until one of the following applies:

(A) The person attains the age of 25 years.

(B) The court terminates jurisdiction pursuant to Section 778 or 779, or any other applicable law.

(C) Jurisdiction is terminated by operation of any other applicable law. *(Added by Stats.2010, c. 729 (A.B.1628), § 10, eff. Oct. 19, 2010, operative Jan. 17, 2011.)*

[1] Stats.2010, c. 729 (A.B.1628), eff. Oct. 19, 2010.

Research References

Treatises and Practice Aids

Witkin, California Summary 10th Parent and Child § 452, Jurisdiction Retained After Majority.

§ 607.2. Termination of jurisdiction over ward satisfying specified criteria; hearing

(a)(1) On and after January 1, 2012, the court shall hold a hearing prior to terminating jurisdiction over a ward who satisfies any of the following criteria:

(A) Is a minor subject to an order for foster care placement described in Section 11402 as a ward who has not previously been subject to the jurisdiction of the court as a result of a petition filed pursuant to Section 325.

(B) Is a nonminor who was subject to an order for foster care placement described in Section 11402 as a ward on the day he or she attained 18 years of age.

(C) Is a ward who was subject to an order for foster care placement described in Section 11402 as a dependent of the court at the time the court adjudged the child to be a ward of the court under Section 725.

(2) The notice of hearing under this subdivision may be served electronically pursuant to Section 212.5.

(b) At a hearing during which termination of jurisdiction over a ward described in subdivision (a) is being considered, the court shall take one of the following actions:

(1) Modify its jurisdiction from delinquency jurisdiction to transition jurisdiction, if the court finds the ward is a person described in Section 450.

(2)(A) For a ward who was not previously subject to the jurisdiction of the court as a result of a petition filed pursuant to Section 325, order the probation department or the ward's attorney to submit an application to the child welfare services department pursuant to Section 329 to declare the minor a dependent of the court and modify the court's jurisdiction from delinquency jurisdiction to dependency jurisdiction, if the court finds all of the following:

(i) The ward is a minor.

(ii) The ward does not come within the description in Section 450, but jurisdiction as a ward may no longer be required.

(iii) The ward appears to come within the description of Section 300 and cannot be returned home safely.

(B) The court shall set a hearing within 20 judicial days of the date of the order described in subparagraph (A) to review the child welfare services department's decision and may either affirm its decision not to file a petition pursuant to Section 300 or order the child welfare services department to file a petition pursuant to Section 300. The notice of hearing under this subparagraph may be served electronically pursuant to Section 212.5.

(3) Vacate the order terminating jurisdiction over the minor as a dependent of the court, resume jurisdiction pursuant to Section 300 based on the prior petition filed pursuant to Section 325, and terminate the court's jurisdiction over the minor as a ward, if the minor was subject to an order for foster care placement described in Section 11402 as a dependent of the court at the time the court adjudged the minor to be a ward and assumed jurisdiction over the minor under Section 725.

(4) Continue its delinquency jurisdiction over a ward pursuant to Section 303 as a nonminor dependent, as defined in subdivision (v) of Section 11400, who is eligible to remain in foster care pursuant to Section 11403, if the ward is a nonminor and the court did not modify its jurisdiction as described in Section 450, unless the court finds that after reasonable and documented efforts, the ward cannot be located or does not wish to become a nonminor dependent. In making this finding and prior to entering an order terminating its delinquency jurisdiction, the court shall ensure that the ward has had an opportunity to confer with his or her counsel and has been informed of his or her options, including the right to reenter foster care placement by completing a voluntary reentry agreement as described in subdivision (z) of Section 11400 and to file a petition pursuant to subdivision (e) of Section 388 for the court to assume or resume transition jurisdiction over him or her pursuant to Section 450. The fact that a ward declines to be a nonminor dependent does not restrict the authority of the court to maintain delinquency jurisdiction pursuant to Section 607.

(5) Continue its delinquency jurisdiction.

(6) Terminate its delinquency jurisdiction if the ward does not come within the provisions of paragraphs (1) to (4), inclusive.

(c) If the court modifies jurisdiction, its order shall comply with the requirements of subdivision (f) of Section 241.1.

(d) This section shall not be construed as changing the requirements of Section 727.2 or 727.3 with respect to reunification of minors with their families or the establishment of an alternative permanent plan for minors for whom reunification is not pursued. *(Added by Stats.2011, c. 459 (A.B.212), § 15, eff. Oct. 4, 2011. Amended by Stats.2017, c. 319 (A.B.976), § 136, eff. Jan. 1, 2018.)*

Research References

Forms

West's California Judicial Council Forms JV-680, Findings and Orders for Child Approaching Majority--Delinquency.

West's California Judicial Council Forms JV-681, Attachment: Hearing for Dismissal--Additional Findings and Orders--Foster Care Placement--Delinquency.

Treatises and Practice Aids

Witkin, California Summary 10th Parent and Child § 450, Dual Bases Of Jurisdiction.

Witkin, California Summary 10th Parent and Child § 642, in General.

Witkin, California Summary 10th Parent and Child § 662, Nature and Purpose.

Witkin, California Summary 10th Parent and Child § 898, Court Supervision Of Child.

Witkin, California Summary 10th Parent and Child § 452D, (New) Modification Of Jurisdiction.

Witkin, California Summary 10th Parent and Child § 452E, (New) Termination Of Jurisdiction Over Minor.

Witkin, California Summary 10th Parent and Child § 899A, (New) Hearing Before Termination Of Jurisdiction.

§ 607.3. Hearing for termination of jurisdiction over ward satisfying specified criteria; duties of probation department

On and after January 1, 2012, at the hearing required under Section 607.2 for a ward who is 18 years of age or older and subject to an order for foster care placement as described in Section 11402, the probation department shall complete all of the following actions:

(a) Ensure that the nonminor has been informed of his or her options, including the right to reenter foster care placement by completing a voluntary reentry agreement as described in subdivision (z) of Section 11400 and the right to file a petition pursuant to subdivision (e) of Section 388 for the court to resume transition jurisdiction pursuant to Section 450.

(b) Ensure that the ward has had an opportunity to confer with his or her counsel.

(c) Ensure that the ward is present in court for the hearing, unless the ward has waived his or her right to appear in court and elects to appear by a telephone instead, or document the efforts it made to locate the ward when the ward is not available to appear at the hearing.

(d) Submit a report to the court describing all of the following:

(1) Whether it is in the ward's best interest for a court to assume or continue transition jurisdiction over the ward as a nonminor dependent pursuant to Section 450.

(2) Whether the ward has indicated that he or she does not want juvenile court jurisdiction to continue.

(3) Whether the ward has been informed of his or her right to reenter foster care by completing the voluntary reentry agreement as described in subdivision (z) of Section 11400.

(e) Submit to the court the completed 90–day transition plan.

(f) Submit to the court written verification that the information, documents, and services set forth in paragraphs (1) to (8), inclusive, of subdivision (e) of Section 391 have been provided to the ward.

(g) Submit to the court written verification that the requirements set forth in Section 607.5 have been completed. *(Added by Stats.2011, c. 459 (A.B.212), § 16, eff. Oct. 4, 2011.)*

Research References

Forms

West's California Judicial Council Forms JV-367, Findings and Orders After Hearing to Consider Termination Of Juvenile Court Jurisdiction Over a Nonminor.

Treatises and Practice Aids

Witkin, California Summary 10th Parent and Child § 452E, (New) Termination Of Jurisdiction Over Minor.

Witkin, California Summary 10th Parent and Child § 899A, (New) Hearing Before Termination Of Jurisdiction.

§ 607.5. Termination of jurisdiction over ward designated dependent of court, or release of ward from facility that is not a foster care facility; information to be provided to person

(a) Notwithstanding any other provision of law, whenever the juvenile court terminates jurisdiction over a ward who has also been designated a dependent of the court, or upon release of a ward from a facility that is not a foster care facility, a probation officer or parole officer shall provide the person with, at a minimum, all of the following:

(1) A written notice stating that the person is a former foster child and may be eligible for the services and benefits that are available to a former foster child through public and private programs, including, but not limited to, any independent living program for former foster children. Providing the proof of dependency and wardship document described in All–County Letter 07–33 and Section 31–525.6 of Chapter 31–500 of Division 31 of the State Department of Social Services Manual of Policies and Procedures, as it existed on January 1, 2010, shall satisfy this requirement.

(2) Existing information described in Section 31–525.61 of Chapter 31–500 of Division 31 of the State Department of Social Services Manual of Policies and Procedures, as it existed on January 1, 2010, that informs the person of the availability of assistance to enable the person to apply for, and gain acceptance into, federal and state programs that provide benefits to former foster children, including, but not limited to, financial assistance, housing, and educational resources for which he or she may be eligible.

(3) Existing information described in Section 31–525.61 of Chapter 31–500 of Division 31 of the State Department of Social Services Manual of Policies and Procedures, as it existed on January 1, 2010, that informs the person of the availability of assistance to enable the person to apply for, and gain acceptance into, federal and state programs that provide independent living services to youth 16 years of age and over who may be eligible for services.

(b) This section shall apply to any ward who was previously adjudged a dependent child of the court pursuant to Section 300 or a child who at any time has been placed in foster care pursuant to Section 727.

(c) Nothing in this section shall be interpreted to alter or amend the obligations of probation officers under current law. *(Added by Stats.2010, c. 631 (S.B.945), § 2.)*

Research References

Treatises and Practice Aids

Witkin, California Summary 10th Parent and Child § 451, in General.

Witkin, California Summary 10th Parent and Child § 452C, (New) Termination Of Jurisdiction.

Witkin, California Summary 10th Parent and Child § 452E, (New) Termination Of Jurisdiction Over Minor.

Witkin, California Summary 10th Parent and Child § 899A, (New) Hearing Before Termination Of Jurisdiction.

§ 608. Age of person at issue; method of examination to determine by scientific or medical test

In any case in which a person is alleged to be a person described in Section 601 or 602, or subdivision (a) of Section 604, and the age of the person is at issue and the court finds that a scientific or medical test would be of assistance in determining the age of the person, the court may consider ordering an examination of the minor using the method described in "The Permanent Mandibular Third Molar" from the Journal of Forensic Odonto-Stomatology, Vol. 1: No. 1: January–June 1983. *(Added by Stats.1990, c. 749 (A.B.3877), § 1.)*

Research References

Treatises and Practice Aids

Witkin, California Summary 10th Parent and Child § 451, in General.

Division 9

PUBLIC SOCIAL SERVICES

Part 3

AID AND MEDICAL ASSISTANCE

CHAPTER 2. CALIFORNIA WORK OPPORTUNITY AND RESPONSIBILITY TO KIDS ACT

ARTICLE 4. RELATIVES' RESPONSIBILITY

§ 11351.5. Contribution of unrelated adult male residing with family applying for or receiving aid

Whenever an unrelated adult male resides with a family applying for or receiving aid under this chapter, he shall be required to make a financial contribution to the family which shall not be less than it would cost him to provide himself with an independent living arrangement.

The minimum financial contribution to the family shall be determined in accordance with standards established by the department which takes into account such adult male person's income and expenses. The regulations formulated by the department shall require the mother of the children and the unrelated male to present all of the facts in connection with the sharing of expenses which comprise the agreement whereby said adult male resides with the family. The conditions of the agreement and the facts related to the sharing of the family expenses shall be signed under penalty of perjury by both the mother of the child and the unrelated male. In the event that either the mother or the adult male person willfully and knowingly fails to cooperate during the period such joint sharing of expenses arrangement exists in setting forth all of the facts in accordance with provisions of this section, aid to the family may be discontinued.

The provisions of this section do not apply to a bona fide paying lodger, roomer or boarder living in the home of a family applying for or receiving aid under this chapter. *(Added by Stats.1969, c. 1417, p. 2904, § 2.)*

§ 11353. Statement of parents' current monthly income and expenses; penalty

Any parent whose absence is the basis upon which an application is filed for aid in behalf of a child shall complete and return to the county within 15 days after service pursuant to Section 11476 a written statement of his current monthly income, his total income over the past 12 months, a description of all real and personal property owned by him, together with an estimate of its value, the number of dependents for whom he is providing support, the amount he is contributing regularly, toward the support of all children for whom application for aid is made under this chapter, his social security number, his current monthly living expenses and such other information as is pertinent to determining his ability to support his children.

A violation of this section constitutes a misdemeanor. *(Added by Stats.1965, c. 1784, p. 4012, § 5. Amended by Stats.1971, c. 578, p. 1158, § 27, eff. Aug. 13, 1971.)*

ARTICLE 5. AID TO FAMILIES WITH DEPENDENT CHILDREN—FOSTER CARE

§ 11410. Federal matching funds used to subsidize child care for foster parents; guidelines; matching county funds

(a) The department shall amend the foster care state plan required under Subtitle IV–E (commencing with Section 470) of the federal Social Security Act (42 U.S.C. Sec. 670 et seq.), to authorize counties that elect to subsidize child care for foster parents to use federal matching funds under Subtitle IV–E for that purpose.

(b) When approved by the federal government, counties electing to administer the Foster Parent Child Care Program shall follow the guidelines developed by the State Department of Social Services.

(c) Federal funds used by a county pursuant to this section shall be matched only by county funds pursuant to Section 15200.5. *(Added by Stats.2004, c. 845 (S.B.1612), § 1, eff. Sept. 28, 2004.)*

ARTICLE 7. ENFORCEMENT

§ 11476.6. Data revealing range and median time periods for notification of receipt of support payments to local welfare department; submission to department

Each local child support agency shall submit to the department data revealing the range and median time periods by which notification of the receipt of child support payments collected on behalf of a family receiving aid under this chapter is made to the local welfare department. The data shall contain the number and percentage of cases in which the payments described herein are conveyed within the time period prescribed by federal law. *(Added by Stats.1986, c. 1402, § 9.5. Amended by Stats.1999, c. 478 (A.B.196), § 34; Stats.2004, c. 193 (S.B.111), § 235.)*

Law Revision Commission Comments

2004 Amendment

Section 11476.6 is amended to delete reference to an obsolete reporting requirement. The required report was to be completed by April 1, 1987. [33 Cal.L.Rev.Comm. Reports 542 (2003)].

§ 11477. Conditions of aid eligibility; assignment of support rights; cooperation

As a condition of eligibility for aid paid under this chapter, each applicant or recipient shall do all of the following:

(a)(1) Do either of the following:

(A) For applications received before October 1, 2009, assign to the county any rights to support from any other person the applicant or recipient may have on his or her own behalf or on behalf of any other family member for whom the applicant or recipient is applying for or receiving aid, not exceeding the total amount of cash assistance provided to the family under this chapter. Receipt of public assistance under this chapter operates as an assignment by operation of law. An assignment of support rights to the county shall also constitute an assignment to the state. If support rights are assigned pursuant to this subdivision, the assignee may become an assignee of record by the local child support agency or other public official filing with the court clerk an affidavit showing that an assignment has been made or that there has been an assignment by operation of law. This procedure does not limit any other means by which the assignee may become an assignee of record.

(B) For applications received on or after October 1, 2009, assign to the county any rights to support from any other person the applicant or recipient may have on his or her own behalf, or on behalf of any other family member for whom the applicant or recipient is applying for or receiving aid. The assignment shall apply only to support that accrues during the period of time that the applicant is receiving assistance under this chapter, and shall not exceed the total amount of cash assistance provided to the family under this chapter. Receipt of public assistance under this chapter shall operate as an assignment by operation of law. An assignment of support rights to the county shall also constitute an assignment to the state. If support rights are assigned pursuant to this subdivision, the assignee may become an assignee of record by the local child support agency or other public official filing with the court clerk an affidavit showing that an assignment has been made or that there has been an assignment by operation of law. This procedure does not limit any other means by which the assignee may become an assignee of record.

(2) Support that has been assigned pursuant to paragraph (1) and that accrues while the family is receiving aid under this chapter shall be permanently assigned until the entire amount of aid paid has been reimbursed.

(3) If the federal government does not permit states to adopt the same order of distribution for preassistance and postassistance child support arrears that are assigned on or after October 1, 1998, support arrears that accrue before the family receives aid under this chapter that are assigned pursuant to this subdivision shall be assigned as follows:

(A) Child support assigned prior to January 1, 1998, shall be permanently assigned until aid is no longer received and the entire amount of aid has been reimbursed.

(B) Child support assigned on or after January 1, 1998, but prior to October 1, 2000, shall be temporarily assigned until aid under this chapter is no longer received and the entire amount of aid paid has been reimbursed or until October 1, 2000, whichever comes first.

(C) On or after October 1, 2000, support assigned pursuant to this subdivision that was not otherwise permanently assigned shall be temporarily assigned to the county until aid is no longer received.

(D) On or after October 1, 2000, support that was temporarily assigned pursuant to this subdivision shall, when a payment is received from the federal tax intercept program, be temporarily assigned until the entire amount of aid paid has been reimbursed.

(4) If the federal government permits states to adopt the same order of distribution for preassistance and postassistance child support arrears, child support arrears shall be assigned, as follows:

(A) Child support assigned pursuant to this subdivision prior to October 1, 1998, shall be assigned until aid under this chapter is no longer received and the entire amount has been reimbursed.

(B) On or after October 1, 1998, child support assigned pursuant to this subdivision that accrued before the family receives aid under this chapter and that was not otherwise permanently assigned shall be temporarily assigned until aid under this chapter is no longer received.

(C) On or after October 1, 1998, support that was temporarily assigned pursuant to this subdivision shall, when a payment is received from the federal tax intercept program, be temporarily assigned until the entire amount of aid paid has been reimbursed.

(b)(1) Cooperate with the county welfare department and local child support agency in establishing the paternity of a child of the applicant or recipient born out of wedlock with respect to whom aid is claimed, and in establishing, modifying, or enforcing a support order with respect to a child of the individual for whom aid is requested or obtained, unless the applicant or recipient qualifies for a good cause exception pursuant to Section 11477.04. The granting of aid shall not be delayed or denied if the applicant is otherwise eligible, completes the necessary forms, and agrees to cooperate with the local child support agency in securing support and determining paternity, if applicable. The local child support agency shall have staff available, in person or by telephone, at all county welfare offices and shall conduct an interview with each applicant to obtain information necessary to establish paternity and establish, modify, or enforce a support order at the time of the initial interview with the welfare office. The local child support agency shall make the determination of cooperation. If the applicant or recipient attests under penalty of perjury that he or she cannot provide the information required by this subdivision, the local child support agency shall make a finding regarding whether the individual could reasonably be expected to provide the information before the local child support agency determines whether the individual is cooperating. In making the finding, the local child support agency shall consider all of the following:

(A) The age of the child for whom support is sought.

(B) The circumstances surrounding the conception of the child.

(C) The age or mental capacity of the parent or caretaker of the child for whom aid is being sought.

(D) The time that has elapsed since the parent or caretaker last had contact with the alleged father or obligor.

(2) Cooperation includes all of the following:

(A) Providing the name of the alleged parent or obligor and other information about that person if known to the applicant or recipient, such as address, social security number, telephone number, place of employment or school, and the names and addresses of relatives or associates.

(B) Appearing at interviews, hearings, and legal proceedings, provided the applicant or recipient is provided with reasonable advance notice of the interview, hearing, or legal proceeding and does not have good cause not to appear.

(C) If paternity is at issue, submitting to genetic tests, including genetic testing of the child, if necessary.

(D) Providing any additional information known to, or reasonably obtainable by, the applicant or recipient necessary to establish paternity or to establish, modify, or enforce a child support order.

(3) A recipient or applicant shall not be required to sign a voluntary declaration of paternity, as set forth in Chapter 3 (commencing with Section 7570) of Part 2 of Division 12 of the Family Code, as a condition of cooperation.

(c)(1) This section does not apply if all of the adults are excluded from the assistance unit pursuant to Section 11251.3, 11454, or 11486.5, or if all eligible adults have been subject to Section 11327.5 for at least 12 consecutive months.

(2) It is the intent of the Legislature that the regular receipt of child support in the preceding reporting period be considered in determining reasonably anticipated income for the following reporting period.

(3) In accordance with Sections 11265.2 and 11265.46, if the income of an assistance unit described in paragraph (1) includes reasonably anticipated income derived from child support, the amount established in Section 17504 of the Family Code and Section 11475.3 of the Welfare and Institutions Code of any amount of child support received each month shall not be considered income or resources and shall not be deducted from the amount of aid to which the assistance unit otherwise would be eligible. *(Added by Stats.1975, c. 924, p. 2037, § 15, eff. Sept. 20, 1975. Amended by Stats.1976, c. 1298, p. 5811, § 1; Stats.1977, c. 1252, p. 4659, § 808, operative July 1, 1978; Stats.1979, c. 1030, § 13; Stats.1981–82, 1st Ex.Sess., c. 3, p. 6909, § 37, eff. Feb. 17, 1982; Stats.1982, c. 497, § 182.5, operative July 1, 1983; Stats.1997, c. 270 (A.B.1542), § 149, eff. Aug. 11, 1997, operative Jan. 1, 1998; Stats.1998, c. 902 (A.B.2772), § 52; Stats.1999, c. 478 (A.B.196), § 35; Stats.2000, c. 808 (A.B. 1358), § 125, eff. Sept. 28, 2000; Stats.2007, c. 488 (A.B.176), § 2; Stats.2014, c. 29 (S.B.855), § 75, eff. June 20, 2014; Stats.2014, c. 685 (S.B.873), § 10, eff. Sept. 27, 2014; Stats. 2015, c. 303 (A.B.731), § 595, eff. Jan. 1, 2016; Stats.2015, c. 20 (S.B.79), § 21, eff. June 24, 2015; Stats.2016, c. 86 (S.B.1171), § 316, eff. Jan. 1, 2017.)*

Research References

Forms

California Practice Guide: Rutter Family Law Forms Form 9:3, Marital Settlement Agreement.

California Transactions Forms--Family Law § 2:64, Amount Of Support.

California Transactions Forms--Family Law § 2:88, Marital Settlement Agreement.

California Transactions Forms--Family Law § 2:91, Add-On Expenses in Conjunction With Family Support.

California Transactions Forms--Family Law § 2:93.5, Child Support Provision Regarding Electronic Transfer Of Funds.

West's California Code Forms, Family § 4050, Comment Overview--Statewide Uniform Guideline.

West's California Code Forms, Family § 2338 Form 8, Marital Agreement.

West's California Code Forms, Family § 2338 Form 9, Marital Agreement--Both Spouses Employed.

West's California Code Forms, Family § 3585 Form 2, Child Support Provisions.

West's California Code Forms, Family § 3585 Form 3, Child Support Provisions--Short Form.

Treatises and Practice Aids

Witkin, California Summary 10th Husband and Wife § 311, Duties Of Public Assistance Recipient.
Witkin, California Summary 10th Husband and Wife § 312, Referral to Agency by County Welfare Department.
Witkin, California Summary 10th Husband and Wife § 313, Payment to County by Court and Referral.
Witkin, California Summary 10th Husband and Wife § 319, Venue.
Witkin, California Summary 10th Parent and Child § 350, Vacating Order for Fraud.
Witkin, California Summary 10th Parent and Child § 410, Uninsured Health Care Costs.
Witkin, California Summary 10th Parent and Child § 414, Stipulated Support Agreements.
Witkin, California Summary 10th Workers' Compensation § 406, Permissible Liens.

§ 11477.02. Good cause for noncooperation with child support enforcement

Prior to referral of any individual or recipient, or that person's case, to the local child support agency for child support services under Section 17400 or 17404 of the Family Code, the county welfare department shall determine if an applicant or recipient has good cause for noncooperation, as set forth in Section 11477.04. If the applicant or recipient claims a good cause exception at any subsequent time to the county welfare department or the local child support agency, the local child support agency shall suspend child support services until the county welfare department determines the good cause claim, as set forth in Section 11477.04. If good cause is determined to exist, the local child support agency shall suspend child support services until the applicant or recipient requests their resumption, and shall take such other measures as are necessary to protect the applicant or recipient and the children. If the applicant or recipient is the parent of the child for whom aid is sought and the parent is found to have not coöperated without good cause as provided in Section 11477.04, the applicant's or recipient's family grant shall be reduced by 25 percent for such time as the failure to cooperate lasts. *(Added by Stats.1997, c. 270 (A.B.1542), § 150, eff. Aug. 11, 1997, operative Jan. 1, 1998. Amended by Stats.1999, c. 478 (A.B.196), § 36; Stats.2000, c. 808 (A.B. 1358), § 126, eff. Sept. 28, 2000.)*

§ 11477.04. Eligibility for aid; cooperation or good cause for noncooperation; conditions; evidence; abuse

(a) An applicant or a recipient shall be considered to be cooperating in good faith with the county welfare department or the local child support agency for purposes of Section 11477 and shall be eligible for aid, if otherwise eligible, if he or she cooperates or has good cause for noncooperation. The county welfare department shall make the good cause determination.

(b) Good cause shall be found if any of the following conditions exist:

(1) Efforts to establish paternity or establish, modify, or enforce a support obligation would increase the risk of physical, sexual, or emotional harm to the child for whom support is being sought.

(2) Efforts to establish paternity or establish, modify, or enforce a support obligation would increase the risk of abuse, as defined in Section 11495.1, to the parent or caretaker with whom the child is living.

(3) The child for whom support is sought was conceived as a result of incest or rape. A conviction for incest or rape is not necessary for this paragraph to apply.

(4) Legal proceedings for the adoption of the child are pending before a court of competent jurisdiction.

(5) The applicant or recipient is currently being assisted by a public or licensed private adoption agency to resolve the issue of whether to keep the child or relinquish the child for adoption.

(6) The applicant or recipient is cooperating in good faith but is unable to identify or assist in locating the alleged father or obligor.

(7) Any other reason that would make efforts to establish paternity or establish, modify, or enforce a support obligation contrary to the best interests of the child.

(c) Evidence supporting a claim for good cause includes, but is not limited to, the following:

(1) Police, governmental agency, or court records, documentation from a domestic violence program or a legal, clerical, medical, mental health, or other professional from whom the applicant or recipient has sought assistance in dealing with abuse, physical evidence of abuse, or any other evidence that supports the claim of good cause.

(2) Statements under penalty of perjury from individuals, including the applicant or recipient, with knowledge of the circumstances that provide the basis for the good cause claim.

(3) Birth certificates or medical, mental health, rape crisis, domestic violence program, or law enforcement records that indicate that the child was conceived as the result of incest or rape.

(4) Court documents or other records that indicate that legal proceedings for adoption are pending before a court of competent jurisdiction.

(5) A written statement from a public or licensed private adoption agency that the applicant or recipient is being assisted by the agency to resolve the issue of whether to keep the child or relinquish the child for adoption.

(d) A sworn statement by a victim shall be sufficient to establish abuse unless the agency documents in writing an independent, reasonable basis to find the recipient not credible.

(e) Applicants or recipients who inquire about or claim good cause, or otherwise indicate that they or their children are at risk of abuse, shall be given referrals by the county welfare department to appropriate community, legal, medical, and support services. Followup by the applicant or recipient on those referrals shall not affect eligibility for assistance under this chapter or the determination of cooperation. *(Added by Stats.1997, c. 270 (A.B.1542), § 151, eff. Aug. 11, 1997, operative Jan. 1, 1998. Amended by Stats.1999, c. 478 (A.B.196), § 37.)*

Research References

Treatises and Practice Aids

Witkin, California Summary 10th Husband and Wife § 311, Duties Of Public Assistance Recipient.

Witkin, California Summary 10th Husband and Wife § 312, Referral to Agency by County Welfare Department.

§ 11477.1. Polygraph tests; written notice and consent required

No polygraph tests shall be administered to any applicant or recipient of aid under this chapter for the purposes of enforcement of Title IV–D of the Social Security Act,[1] without written notice to applicant or recipient that such test is not required and without written consent thereto by such applicant or recipient. *(Added by Stats.1975, c. 924, p. 2038, § 15.5, eff. Sept. 20, 1975.)*

[1] 42 U.S.C.A. § 651 et seq.

§ 11478.1. Confidential information; support enforcement and child abduction records; authorized disclosure of information; definitions; violations

(a) It is the intent of the Legislature to protect individual rights of privacy, and to facilitate and enhance the effectiveness of the child and spousal support enforcement program, by ensuring the confidentiality of support enforcement and child abduction records, and to thereby encourage the full and frank disclosure of information relevant to all of the following:

(1) The establishment or maintenance of parent and child relationships and support obligations.

(2) The enforcement of the child support liability of absent parents.

(3) The enforcement of spousal support liability of the spouse or former spouse to the extent required by the state plan under Section 11475.2 of this code and Part 6 (commencing with Section 5700.101) of Division 9 of the Family Code.

(4) The location of absent parents.

(5) The location of parents and children abducted, concealed, or detained by them.

(b)(1) Except as provided in subdivision (c), all files, applications, papers, documents, and records established or maintained by any public entity pursuant to the administration and implementation of the child and spousal support enforcement program established pursuant to Part D (commencing with Section 651) of Subchapter IV of Chapter 7 of Title 42 of the United States Code and this article, shall be confidential, and shall not be open to examination or released for disclosure for any purpose not directly connected with the administration of the child and spousal support enforcement program. No public entity shall disclose any file, application, paper, document, or record, or the information contained therein, except as expressly authorized by this section.

(2) In no case shall information be released or the whereabouts of one party or the child disclosed to another party, or to the attorney of any other party, if a protective order has been issued by a court or administrative agency with respect to the former party, a good cause claim under Section 11477.04 has been approved or is pending, or the public agency responsible for establishing paternity or enforcing support has reason to believe that the release of the information may result in physical or emotional harm to the former party or the child.

(3) Notwithstanding any other provision of law, a proof of service filed by the district attorney shall not disclose the address where service of process was accomplished. Instead, the district attorney shall keep the address in his or her own records. The proof of service shall specify that the address is on record at the district attorney's office and that the address may be released only upon an order from the court pursuant to paragraph (6) of subdivision (c). The district attorney shall, upon request by a party served, release to that person the address where service was effected.

(c) Disclosure of the information described in subdivision (b) is authorized as follows:

(1) All files, applications, papers, documents, and records as described in subdivision (b) shall be available and may be used by a public entity for all administrative, civil, or criminal investigations, actions, proceedings, or prosecutions conducted in connection with the administration of the child and spousal support enforcement program approved under Part D (commencing with Section 651) of Subchapter IV of Chapter 7 of Title 42 of the United States Code, and any other plan or program described in Section 303.21 of Title 45 of the Code of Federal Regulations and to the county welfare department responsible for administering a program operated under a state plan pursuant to Subpart 1 or 2 of Part B or Part E of Subchapter IV of Chapter 7 of Title 42 of the United States Code.

(2) A document requested by a person who wrote, prepared, or furnished the document may be examined by or disclosed to that person or his or her designee.

(3) The payment history of an obligor pursuant to a support order may be examined by or released to the court, the obligor, or the person on whose behalf enforcement actions are being taken or that person's designee.

(4) Income and expense information of either parent may be released to the other parent for the purpose of establishing or modifying a support order.

(5) Public records subject to disclosure under the California Public Records Act (Chapter 3.5 (commencing with Section 6250) of Division 7 of Title 1 of the Government Code) may be released.

(6) After a noticed motion and a finding by the court, in a case in which establishment or enforcement actions are being taken, that release or disclosure to the obligor or obligee is required by due process of law, the court may order a public entity that possesses an application, paper, document, or record as described in subdivision (b) to make that item available to the obligor or obligee for examination or copying, or to disclose to the obligor or obligee the contents of that item. Article 9 (commencing with Section 1040) of Chapter 4 of Division 8 of the Evidence Code shall not be applicable to proceedings under this part. At any hearing of a motion filed pursuant to this section, the court shall inquire of the district attorney and the parties appearing at the hearing if there is reason to believe that release of the requested information may result in physical or emotional harm to a

party. If the court determines that harm may occur, the court shall issue any protective orders or injunctive orders restricting the use and disclosure of the information as are necessary to protect the individuals.

(7) To the extent not prohibited by federal law or regulation, information indicating the existence or imminent threat of a crime against a child; location of a concealed, detained, or abducted child; or the location of the concealing, detaining, or abducting person, may be disclosed to any district attorney, any appropriate law enforcement agency, or to any state or county child protective agency, or may be used in any judicial proceedings to prosecute that crime or to protect the child.

(8)(A) The social security number, most recent address, and the place of employment of the absent parent may be released to an authorized person as defined in Section 653(c) of Title 42 of the United States Code, only if the authorized person has filed a request for the information, and only if the information has been provided to the California Parent Locator Service by the federal Parent Locator Service pursuant to Section 653 of Title 42 of the United States Code.

(B) The information described in subparagraph (A) may be disclosed to the county child welfare agency and the county probation department responsible for administering a program operated under a state plan pursuant to Subpart 1 (commencing with Section 621) or 2 (commencing with Section 629) of Part B of, or pursuant to Part E (commencing with Section 670) of, Subchapter IV of Chapter 7 of Title 42 of the United States Code. Information exchanged between the California Parent Locator Service or the California Child Support Automation System, or its replacement, and the county welfare agency shall be through automated processes to the maximum extent feasible.

(C) On or before July 1, 2013, the State Department of Social Services and the Department of Child Support Services shall issue an all-county letter or similar instruction explaining that county child welfare and probation agencies are entitled to the information described in paragraph (9) of subdivision (c) of Section 17212 and subdivision (c) of Section 17506 of the Family Code.

(d)(1) "Administration and implementation of the child and spousal support enforcement program," as used in this section, means the carrying out of the state and local plans for establishing, modifying, and enforcing child support obligations, enforcing spousal support orders, and determining paternity pursuant to Part D (commencing with Section 651) of Subchapter IV of Chapter 7 of Title 42 of the United States Code and this article.

(2) For purposes of this section, "obligor" means any person owing a duty of support.

(3) As used in this chapter, "putative parent" shall refer to any person reasonably believed to be the parent of a child for whom the local child support agency is attempting to establish paternity or establish, modify, or enforce support pursuant to Section 17400 of the Family Code.

(e) Any person who willfully, knowingly, and intentionally violates this section is guilty of a misdemeanor.

(f) Nothing in this section shall be construed to compel the disclosure of information relating to a deserting parent who is a recipient of aid under a public assistance program for which federal aid is paid to this state, if that information is required to be kept confidential by the federal law or regulations relating to the program. *(Added by Stats.1991, c. 943 (A.B.1524), § 2. Amended by Stats.1992, c. 163 (A.B.2641), § 147; Stats.1992, c. 1192 (A.B.973), § 2, eff. Sept. 30, 1992; Stats.1993, c. 219 (A.B.1500), § 231; Stats.1997, c. 599 (A.B.573), § 56; Stats.1998, c. 858 (A.B.2169), § 10; Stats. 1998, c. 1056 (A.B.2773), § 24.5; Stats.2012, c. 637 (A.B. 1751), § 5; Stats.2015, c. 493 (S.B.646), § 15, eff. Jan. 1, 2016.)*

Law Revision Commission Comments

1993 Amendment

Subdivision (a) of Section 11478.1 is amended to substitute references to the provisions of the Family Code that replaced former Section 1650 of the Code of Civil Procedure. A reference to the Uniform Reciprocal Enforcement of Support Act, now in the Family Code, has been substituted for the reference to former Code of Civil Procedure Section 1650, which merely provided the short title for the uniform act. The substituted reference in Section 11478.1 includes the entire uniform act. [23 Cal.L.Rev.Comm. Reports 1 (1993)].

Research References

Treatises and Practice Aids

Witkin, California Summary 10th Husband and Wife § 314, Acquisition and Confidentiality Of Information.

§ 11479. Paternity not established; adoption being considered; investigation and action

In all cases in which the paternity of the child has not been established to the satisfaction of the county department, the county department shall refer the applicant to local child support agency at the time the application is signed. Upon the advice of a county department that a child is being considered for adoption, and regardless of whether or not the whereabouts of the parent is known, the local child support agency shall delay the investigation and other action with respect to the case until advised that the adoption is no longer under consideration. The local child support agency shall conduct such investigation as the agency considers necessary, and where he or she deems it appropriate, the agency may bring an action under Chapter 4 (commencing with Section 7630) of Part 3 of Division 12 of the Family Code. When the cause is at issue, it shall be set for trial at the earliest possible date and shall take precedence over all other cases except older matters of the same character and matters to which precedence may be given by law. *(Added by Stats.1965, c. 1784, p. 4018, § 5. Amended by Stats.1980, c. 676, p. 2047, § 351; Stats.1994, c. 1269 (A.B.2208), § 64.5; Stats.1999, c. 478 (A.B.196), § 46.)*

Law Revision Commission Comments

1994 Amendment

Section 11479 is amended to correct a cross-reference to former Civil Code Section 231 which was repealed in 1975 and superseded by Civil Code Sections 7006 and 7015. These sections, in turn, have been superseded by the Family Code sections. These are technical, nonsubstantive changes. [24 Cal.L.Rev.Comm.Reports 547 (1994), Annual Report for 1994, App. 5].

§ 11480. Receipt or use of aid for purpose other than support

Any person other than a needy child, who willfully and knowingly receives or uses any part of an aid grant paid pursuant to this chapter for a purpose other than support of the needy children and the caretaker involved, is guilty of a misdemeanor. *(Added by Stats.1965, c. 1784, p. 4018, § 5.)*

§ 11481. Prosecution for contributing to delinquency of minor

If the district attorney, during the course of any investigation made by him pursuant to this article, determines that any person has committed any act or has omitted the performance of any duty, which act or omission causes or tends to cause or encourage any child receiving aid under this chapter to come within the provisions of Sections 300, 601, or 602 of this code, the district attorney shall prosecute such person under the provisions of Section 272 of the Penal Code. *(Added by Stats.1965, c. 1784, p. 4018, § 5. Amended by Stats.1979, c. 373, § 379.)*

§ 11481.5. Welfare fraud hotline pilot project; effectiveness evaluation

The department shall evaluate the effectiveness of a 24-hour welfare fraud hotline pilot project, to assess greater public involvement and assistance in welfare fraud detection. *(Added by Stats.1984, c. 1448, § 3.5.)*

§ 11482. False representation to obtain aid; unlawfully receiving or attempting to receive aid

Any person other than a needy child, who willfully and knowingly, with the intent to deceive, makes a false statement or representation or knowingly fails to disclose a material fact to obtain aid, or who, knowing he or she is not entitled thereto, attempts to obtain aid or to continue to receive aid to which he or she is not entitled, or a larger amount than that to which he or she is legally entitled, is guilty of a misdemeanor, except as specified in Section 11482.5 and shall be subject to prosecution under the provisions of Chapter 9 (commencing with Section 10980) of Part 2. *(Added by Stats.1965, c. 1784, p. 4018, § 5. Amended by Stats.1983, c. 1235, § 1; Stats.1984, c. 1448, § 4.)*

§ 11482.5. Applications claiming multiple entitlements, false identity, or for fictitious or nonexistent persons; punishment

Any person who knowingly makes more than one application for aid with the intent of establishing multiple entitlements for any person for the same period, or who makes an application for aid by claiming a false identity for any person or by making an application for a fictitious or nonexistent person, is guilty of a felony and shall be subject to prosecution under the provisions of Chapter 9 (commencing with Section 10980) of Part 2. *(Added by Stats.1983, c. 1235, § 2. Amended by Stats.1984, c. 1448, § 5.)*

§ 11483. Fraud in obtaining aid; punishment; restitution

Except as specified in Section 11483.5, whenever any person has, by means of false statement or representation or by impersonation or other fraudulent device, obtained aid for a child not in fact entitled thereto, the person obtaining such aid shall be subject to prosecution under the provisions of Chapter 9 (commencing with Section 10980) of Part 2.

When the allegation is limited to failure to report not more than two thousand dollars ($2,000) of income or resources, or the failure to report the presence of an additional person or persons in the household, all actions necessary to secure restitution shall be brought against persons in violation of Section 10980. The action for restitution may be satisfied by sending a registered letter requesting restitution to the last address at which the person was receiving public assistance. *(Added by Stats.1965, c. 1784, p. 4018, § 5. Amended by Stats.1970, c. 693, p. 1322, § 1; Stats.1977, c. 165, p. 679, § 95, eff. June 29, 1977, operative July 1, 1977; Stats.1979, c. 373, § 380; Stats.1979, c. 1170, § 12; Stats.1979, c. 1171, § 1; Stats.1983, c. 1092, § 422, eff. Sept. 27, 1983, operative Jan. 1, 1984; Stats.1983, c. 711, § 4; Stats.1984, c. 1448, § 6.)*

§ 11483.5. Obtaining aid by applications claiming multiple entitlements, false identity, or for fictitious or nonexistent persons; punishment

Any person who obtains more than one aid payment for any person as a result of knowingly making more than one application for aid with the intent of establishing multiple entitlements for that person during the same period, or who obtains aid for any person by making an application claiming a false identity or by making an application for a fictitious or nonexistent person, is guilty of a felony, and shall be subject to prosecution under the provisions of Chapter 9 (commencing with Section 10980) of Part 2. *(Added by Stats.1983, c. 1235, § 3. Amended by Stats.1984, c. 1448, § 7.)*

§ 11484. Public assistance fraud; cooperation of agencies to assist in investigation and prevention

On request, all state, county, and local agencies shall cooperate with an investigator of an agency whose primary function is to detect, prevent, or prosecute public assistance fraud, by providing all information on hand relative to the location and prosecution of any person who has, by means of false statement or representation or by impersonation or other fraudulent device, obtained aid, or attempted to obtain aid for an individual under this chapter. That information is subject to confidentiality requirements under Chapter 5 (commencing with Section 10850) of Part 2. For purposes of this section, "information" shall not include taxpayer return information as defined in Section 19549 of the Revenue and Taxation Code, unless disclosure of this information is expressly authorized pursuant to Article 2 (commencing with Section 19501) of Chapter 7 of Part 10.2 of the Revenue and Taxation Code. *(Added by Stats.2000, c. 808 (A.B.1358), § 128, eff. Sept. 28, 2000.)*

§ 11485. Divorce or separation; children receiving or likely to receive aid; notices; non-exclusive remedies

If, to the knowledge of the court, aid has been applied for or granted to a child of parents who are engaged in a divorce or separate maintenance action which is pending, or if the court at any stage of the litigation believes that within the near future there is a likelihood that aid will be applied for on behalf of the child, the court shall direct the clerk to notify the local child support agency and the county department of the pending action.

In any case in which aid has been applied for on behalf of the child, and the county department has knowledge that an action for divorce or separate maintenance has been filed, it shall be the duty of the county director to notify the court that aid is being paid or has been applied for, and to furnish to it such information as is available to the county department as to the financial resources of the parents which might be applied to child support.

The enforcement remedies provided the local child support agency under this article shall not preclude the use of any other remedy which he has under the law to enforce this article. *(Added by Stats.1965, c. 1784, p. 4019, § 5. Amended by Stats.1999, c. 478 (A.B.196), § 49.)*

§ 11486. Fraudulent or misleading statements relating to eligibility for or amount of aid; sanctions

(a) The needs of any individual who is a member of a family applying for, or receiving, aid under this chapter shall not be taken into account in making the determination under Section 11450 with respect to his or her family beginning on the date, or at any time thereafter, the individual is found in state or federal court or pursuant to an administrative hearing decision, including any determination made on the basis of a plea of guilty or nolo contendere, to have committed any of the following acts:

(1) Making a fraudulent statement or representation with respect to the place of residence of the individual in order to receive assistance simultaneously from two or more states or counties.

(2) Submitting documents for nonexistent children, or submitting false documents for the purpose of showing ineligible children to be eligible for aid.

(3) When there has been a receipt of cash benefits that exceeds ten thousand dollars ($10,000) as a result of intentionally and willfully doing any of the following acts for the purpose of establishing or maintaining the family's eligibility for aid or increasing or preventing a reduction in the amount of aid:

(A) Making a false or misleading statement or misrepresenting, concealing, or withholding facts.

(B) Committing any act intended to mislead, misrepresent, conceal, or withhold facts or propound a falsity.

(b) The needs of any individual who is a member of a family applying for, or receiving, aid under this chapter shall not be taken into account in making the determination under Section 11450 with respect to his or her family for the following periods beginning on the date or any time thereafter the individual is convicted of a felony in state or federal court, including any determination made on the basis of a plea of guilty or nolo contendere, for committing fraud in the receipt or attempted receipt of aid:

(1) For two years, if the amount of aid is less than two thousand dollars ($2,000).

(2) For five years, if the amount of aid is two thousand dollars ($2,000) or more but is less than five thousand dollars ($5,000).

(3) Permanently, if the amount of aid is five thousand dollars ($5,000) or more.

(c)(1) Except as provided in subdivisions (a) and (b), the needs of any individual who is a member of a family applying for, or receiving, aid under this chapter to whom paragraph (2) applies shall not be taken into account in making the determination under Section 11450 with respect to his or her family for the following periods:

(A) For a period of six months upon the first occasion of any offense referred to in paragraph (2).

(B) For a period of 12 months upon the second occasion of any of those offenses referred to in paragraph (2).

(C) Permanently, upon the third occasion of any offense referred to in subdivision (b) and paragraph (2).

(2) Except as provided in subdivisions (a), (b), and (d), paragraph (1) shall apply to any individual who is found by a federal or state court, or pursuant to a special administrative hearing meeting the requirements of regulations adopted by the United States Secretary of Health and Human Services, including any determination made on the basis of a plea of guilty or nolo contendere, to have done any of the following acts for the purpose of establishing or maintaining the family's eligibility for aid or increasing, or preventing a reduction in, the amount of that aid:

(A) Making a false or misleading statement or misrepresenting, concealing, or withholding facts.

(B) Committing any act intended to mislead, misrepresent, conceal, or withhold facts or propound a falsity.

(d)(1) Except as provided in subdivisions (a) and (b), and notwithstanding subdivision (c), the needs of any individual who is a member of a family applying for, or receiving, aid under this chapter to whom paragraph (2) applies shall not be taken into account in making the determination under Section 11450 with respect to his or her family for the following periods:

(A) For a period of two years upon the first occasion of any offense referred to in paragraph (2).

(B) For a period of four years upon the second occasion of any offense referred to in paragraph (2).

(C) Permanently, upon the third occasion of any offense referred to in subdivision (b) and paragraph (2).

(2) Paragraph (1) shall apply to any individual who is found by a federal or state court, or pursuant to a special administrative hearing meeting the requirements of regulations adopted by the United States Secretary of Health and Human Services, including any determination made on the basis of a plea of guilty or nolo contendere, to have submitted more than one application for the same type of aid for the same period of time, for the purpose of receiving more than one grant of aid in order to establish or maintain the family's eligibility for aid or increasing, or preventing a reduction in, the amount of that aid.

(e) Proceedings against any individual alleged to have committed an offense described in subdivision (c) or (d) may be held either by hearing, pursuant to Section 10950 and in conformity with the regulations of the United States Secretary of Health and Human Services, if appropriate, or by referring the matter to the appropriate authorities for civil or criminal action in court.

(f) The department shall coordinate any action taken under this section with any corresponding actions being taken under CalFresh in any case where the factual issues involved arise from the same or related circumstances.

(g) Any period for which sanctions are imposed under this section shall remain in effect, without possibility of administrative stay, unless and until the findings upon which the sanctions were imposed are subsequently reversed by a court of appropriate jurisdiction, but in no event shall the duration of the period for which the sanctions are imposed be subject to review.

(h) Sanctions imposed under this section shall be in addition to, and not in substitution for, any other sanctions which may be provided for by law with respect to the offenses for which the sanctions are imposed.

(i) The department shall adopt regulations to ensure that any investigations made under this chapter are conducted throughout the state in such a manner as to protect the confidentiality of the current or former working recipient.

(j) Each county shall receive an amount equal to 12.5 percent of the actual amount of aid under this chapter repaid or recovered by a county, as determined by the Director of the Department of Finance resulting from the detection of fraud. *(Added by Stats.1997, c. 270 (A.B.1542), § 153, eff. Aug. 11, 1997, operative Jan. 1, 1998. Amended by Stats.2002, c. 1022 (A.B.444), § 45, eff. Sept. 28, 2002; Stats.2011, c. 227 (A.B.1400), § 57.)*

§ 11486.3. Examination of CalWORKs sanction policy; scope of examination; development of recommendations; report

(a) The department, in consultation with system stakeholders, including county welfare departments, shall examine the CalWORKs sanction policy, its implementation, and effect on work participation, including but not limited to all of the following:

(1) The characteristics of the persons being sanctioned.

(2) The reason participants are being sanctioned.

(3) The length of time in sanctioned status.

(4) Positive and negative sanction outcomes.

(5) County variances in sanction policies, rates, and outcomes.

(6) The relationship between sanction rates and work participation.

(7) The impact of sanctions on families and their ability to become self-sufficient.

(8) Adequacy of procedures to resolve noncompliance prior to the implementation of sanctions.

(b) The department shall develop recommendations to improve the effectiveness of sanctions in achieving participant compliance, assisting families in becoming self-sufficient, and other desired program outcomes.

(c) The department shall report its findings and recommendations to the appropriate fiscal and policy committees of the Legislature by April 1, 2005. *(Added by Stats.2004, c. 229 (S.B.1104), § 38, eff. Aug. 16, 2004.)*

§ 11486.5. Eligibility for aid; fleeing prosecution or custody or confinement; violation of condition of probation or parole

(a) An individual shall not be eligible for aid under this chapter if he or she is either:

(1) Fleeing to avoid prosecution, or custody and confinement after conviction, under the laws of the place from which the individual is fleeing, for a crime or an attempt to commit a crime that is a felony under the laws of the place from which the individual is fleeing, or which, in the case of the State of New Jersey, is a high misdemeanor under the laws of that state.

(2) Violating a condition of probation or parole imposed under federal law or the law of any state.

(b) Subdivision (a) shall not apply with respect to conduct of an individual for any month beginning after the President of the United States grants a pardon with respect to the conduct. *(Added by Stats.1997, c. 270 (A.B.1542), § 154, eff. Aug. 11, 1997, operative Jan. 1, 1998.)*

§ 11487. Aid repaid to the state by means of child support collections; state, federal, and county shares

(a) Whenever any aid under this chapter is repaid to the state by means of child support collections, the state shall be entitled to the amount received or recovered, except to the extent that county and federal funds were expended. If funds advanced by the federal government were paid, the federal government shall be entitled to a share of the amount received or recovered, proportionate to the amount of federal funds paid. Except as provided in subdivision (b), if funds were paid by a county, the county shall be entitled to a share of the amount received or recovered, proportionate to the amount of county funds paid.

(b) For the 2011–12 and 2012–13 fiscal years, the county share of funds received or recovered pursuant to subdivision (a) shall instead be suspended and these funds shall be retained by the state. *(Added by Stats.1965, c. 1784, p. 4019, § 5. Amended by Stats.1971, c. 578, p. 1165, § 31, eff. Aug. 13, 1971, operative Oct. 1, 1971; Stats.1975, c. 924, p. 2039, § 17, eff. Sept. 20, 1975; Stats.2011, c. 8 (S.B.72), § 30, eff. March 24, 2011; Stats.2011, c. 32 (A.B.106), § 57, eff. June 29, 2011; Stats.2012, c. 47 (S.B.1041), § 31, eff. June 27, 2012.)*

§ 11487.1. Aid recovered by or repaid to county; state and federal government shares

Except as provided in Sections 11457 and 11487, whenever any aid under this chapter is repaid to a county or recovered by a county, the state shall be entitled to a share of the amount received or recovered, proportionate to the amount of state funds paid, and, if funds advanced by the federal government were paid, the federal government shall be entitled to a share of the amount received or recovered, proportionate to the amount of federal funds paid. *(Added by Stats.2011, c. 32 (A.B.106), § 58, eff. June 29, 2011.)*

§ 11487.5. Reimbursements for overpayment recoveries under § 11004; programs

(a) Notwithstanding any other provision of law, including Sections 11487 and 15204.5, the department shall implement a program in any participating county whereby the county shall be reimbursed for overpayment recoveries under Section 11004 as follows:

(1) Reimbursement shall be made to a participating county based on a plan of operations for a program of overpayment recoveries that is approved by the department. No operating plan shall be approved by the department unless the plan contains assurances that the participating county will maintain a centralized unit or designate a person or persons to perform the overpayment recovery activities.

(2) Reimbursement shall be made for all allowable administrative costs incurred, as defined by the department, to make a recovery of overpayments under Section 11004, not to exceed the state's share of the overpayments recovered by the county.

(b) For purposes of this section, "participating county" means any county in which the welfare director applies to the department for participation in the program prescribed by this section.

(c) This section shall be implemented when both of the following have occurred:

(1) The federal government has made funding available for the activities described in this section.

(2) The Department of Finance has examined the annual projection of costs and savings for these activities certified by the director, and has determined that during each fiscal year in which the director proposes to implement these provisions the savings to the General Fund from increased overpayment recoveries equals or exceeds the additional costs to the state. *(Added by Stats.1996, c. 206 (S.B.1780), § 13, eff. July 22, 1996. Amended by Stats.2001, c. 745 (S.B.1191), § 246, eff. Oct. 12, 2001.)*

Implementation

Implementation of this section, by its own terms, is contingent.

CHAPTER 11. ELDER ABUSE AND DEPENDENT ADULT CIVIL PROTECTION ACT

ARTICLE 3. MANDATORY AND NONMANDATORY REPORTS OF ABUSE

§ 15630.1. Mandated reporter of suspected financial abuse of an elder or dependent adult; definitions and reporting requirements; power of attorney

(a) As used in this section, "mandated reporter of suspected financial abuse of an elder or dependent adult" means all officers and employees of financial institutions.

(b) As used in this section, the term "financial institution" means any of the following:

(1) A depository institution, as defined in Section 3(c) of the Federal Deposit Insurance Act (12 U.S.C. Sec. 1813(c)).

(2) An institution-affiliated party, as defined in Section 3(u) of the Federal Deposit Insurance Act (12 U.S.C. Sec. 1813(u)).

(3) A federal credit union or state credit union, as defined in Section 101 of the Federal Credit Union Act (12 U.S.C. Sec. 1752), including, but not limited to, an institution-affiliated party of a credit union, as defined in Section 206(r) of the Federal Credit Union Act (12 U.S.C. Sec. 1786(r)).

(c) As used in this section, "financial abuse" has the same meaning as in Section 15610.30.

(d)(1) Any mandated reporter of suspected financial abuse of an elder or dependent adult who has direct contact with the elder or dependent adult or who reviews or approves the elder or dependent adult's financial documents, records, or transactions, in connection with providing financial services with respect to an elder or dependent adult, and who, within the scope of his or her employment or professional practice, has observed or has knowledge of an incident, that is directly related to the transaction or matter that is within that scope of employment or professional practice, that reasonably appears to be financial abuse, or who reasonably suspects that abuse, based solely on the information before him or her at the time of reviewing or approving the document, record, or transaction in the case of mandated reporters who do not have direct contact with the elder or dependent adult, shall report the known or suspected instance of financial abuse by telephone or through a confidential Internet reporting tool, as authorized pursuant to Section 15658, immediately, or as soon as practicably possible. If reported by telephone, a written report shall be sent, or an Internet report shall be made through the confidential Internet reporting tool established in Section 15658, within two working days to the local adult protective services agency or the local law enforcement agency.

(2) When two or more mandated reporters jointly have knowledge or reasonably suspect that financial abuse of an elder or a dependent adult for which the report is mandated has occurred, and when there is an agreement among them, the telephone report or Internet report, as authorized by Section 15658, may be made by a member of the reporting team who is selected by mutual agreement. A single report may be made and signed by the selected member of the reporting team. Any member of the team who has knowledge that the member designated to report has failed to do so shall thereafter make that report.

(3) If the mandated reporter knows that the elder or dependent adult resides in a long-term care facility, as defined in Section 15610.47, the report shall be made to the local ombudsman or local law enforcement agency.

(e) An allegation by the elder or dependent adult, or any other person, that financial abuse has occurred is not sufficient to trigger the reporting requirement under this section if both of the following conditions are met:

(1) The mandated reporter of suspected financial abuse of an elder or dependent adult is aware of no other corroborating or independent evidence of the alleged financial abuse of an elder or dependent adult. The mandated reporter of suspected financial abuse of an elder or dependent adult is not required to investigate any accusations.

(2) In the exercise of his or her professional judgment, the mandated reporter of suspected financial abuse of an elder or dependent adult reasonably believes that financial abuse of an elder or dependent adult did not occur.

(f) Failure to report financial abuse under this section shall be subject to a civil penalty not exceeding one thousand dollars ($1,000) or if the failure to report is willful, a civil penalty not exceeding five thousand dollars ($5,000), which shall be paid by the financial institution that is the employer of the mandated reporter to the party bringing the action. Subdivision (h) of Section 15630 shall not apply to violations of this section.

(g)(1) The civil penalty provided for in subdivision (f) shall be recovered only in a civil action brought against the financial institution by the Attorney General, district attorney, or county counsel. No action shall be brought under this section by any person other than the Attorney General, district attorney, or county counsel. Multiple actions for the civil penalty may not be brought for the same violation.

(2) Nothing in the Financial Elder Abuse Reporting Act of 2005 shall be construed to limit, expand, or otherwise modify any civil liability or remedy that may exist under this or any other law.

(h) As used in this section, "suspected financial abuse of an elder or dependent adult" occurs when a person who is required to report under subdivision (a) observes or has knowledge of behavior or unusual circumstances or transactions, or a pattern of behavior or unusual circumstances or transactions, that would lead an individual with like training or experience, based on the same facts, to form a reasonable belief that an elder or dependent adult is the victim of financial abuse as defined in Section 15610.30.

(i) Reports of suspected financial abuse of an elder or dependent adult made by an employee or officer of a financial institution pursuant to this section are covered under subdivision (b) of Section 47 of the Civil Code.

(j)(1) A mandated reporter of suspected financial abuse of an elder or dependent adult is authorized to not honor a power of attorney described in Division 4.5 (commencing with Section 4000) of the Probate Code as to an attorney-in-fact, if the mandated reporter of suspected financial abuse of an elder or dependent adult makes a report to an adult protective services agency or a local law enforcement agency of any state that the principal may be subject to financial abuse, as described in this chapter or as defined in similar laws of another state, by that attorney-in-fact or person acting for or with that attorney-in-fact.

(2) If a mandated reporter of suspected financial abuse of an elder or dependent adult does not honor a power of attorney as to an attorney-in-fact pursuant to paragraph (1), the power of attorney shall remain enforceable as to every other attorney-in-fact also designated in the power of attorney about whom a report has not been made.

(3) For purposes of this subdivision, the terms "principal" and "attorney-in-fact" shall have the same meanings as those terms are used in Division 4.5 (commencing with Section 4000) of the Probate Code. *(Added by Stats.2005, c. 140 (S.B.1018), § 4, operative Jan. 1, 2007. Amended by Stats. 2011, c. 372 (S.B.33), § 1; Stats.2011, c. 373 (S.B.718), § 2.5; Stats.2017, c. 408 (A.B.611), § 1, eff. Jan. 1, 2018.)*

Research References

Treatises and Practice Aids

Witkin, California Summary 10th Torts § 148A, (New) Reporting by Financial Institutions.

ARTICLE 4. CONFIDENTIALITY

§ 15633. Confidentiality of reports; disclosure

(a) The reports made pursuant to Sections 15630, 15630.1, and 15631 shall be confidential and may be disclosed only as provided in subdivision (b). Any violation of the confidentiality required by this chapter is a misdemeanor punishable by not more than six months in the county jail, by a fine of five hundred dollars ($500), or by both that fine and imprisonment.

(b) Reports of suspected abuse of an elder or dependent adult and information contained therein may be disclosed only to the following:

(1) Persons or agencies to whom disclosure of information or the identity of the reporting party is permitted under Section 15633.5.

(2)(A) Persons who are trained and qualified to serve on multidisciplinary personnel teams may disclose to one another information and records that are relevant to the prevention, identification, or treatment of abuse of elderly or dependent persons.

(B) Except as provided in subparagraph (A), any personnel of the multidisciplinary team or agency that receives information pursuant to this chapter, shall be under the same obligations and subject to the same confidentiality penalties as the person disclosing or providing that information. The information obtained shall be maintained in a manner that ensures the maximum protection of privacy and confidentiality rights.

(c) This section shall not be construed to allow disclosure of any reports or records relevant to the reports of abuse of an elder or dependent adult if the disclosure would be prohibited by any other provisions of state or federal law applicable to the reports or records relevant to the reports of the abuse, nor shall it be construed to prohibit the disclosure by a financial institution of any reports or records relevant to the reports of abuse of an elder or dependent adult if the disclosure would be required of a financial institution by otherwise applicable state or federal law or court order. *(Added by Stats.1994, c. 594 (S.B.1681), § 14. Amended by Stats.1998, c. 946 (S.B.2199) § 9; Stats.1998, c. 980 (A.B. 1780), § 2; Stats.2005, c. 140 (S.B.1018), § 5, operative Jan. 1, 2007; Stats.2011, c. 372 (S.B.33), § 2.)*

Research References

Treatises and Practice Aids

Witkin, California Summary 10th Torts § 149, Confidentiality and Disclosure.

§ 15633.5. Information given to investigator; reporting person's identity; confidentiality

(a) Information relevant to the incident of elder or dependent adult abuse may be given to an investigator from an adult protective services agency, a local law enforcement agency, the office of the district attorney, the office of the public guardian, the probate court, the bureau, or an investigator of the Department of Consumer Affairs, Division of Investigation who is investigating a known or suspected case of elder or dependent adult abuse.

(b) The identity of any person who reports under this chapter shall be confidential and disclosed only among the following agencies or persons representing an agency:

(1) An adult protective services agency.

(2) A long-term care ombudsperson program.

(3) A licensing agency.

(4) A local law enforcement agency.

(5) The office of the district attorney.

(6) The office of the public guardian.

(7) The probate court.

(8) The bureau.

(9) The Department of Consumer Affairs, Division of Investigation.

(10) Counsel representing an adult protective services agency.

(c) The identity of a person who reports under this chapter may also be disclosed under the following circumstances:

(1) To the district attorney in a criminal prosecution.

(2) When a person reporting waives confidentiality.

(3) By court order.

(d) Notwithstanding subdivisions (a), (b), and (c), any person reporting pursuant to Section 15631 shall not be required to include his or her name in the report. *(Added by Stats.1994, c. 594 (S.B.1681), § 16. Amended by Stats.1998, c. 970 (A.B.2802), § 211; Stats.2002, c. 54 (A.B.255), § 10; Stats.2002, c. 552 (A.B.2735), § 2.)*

Research References

Treatises and Practice Aids

Witkin, California Summary 10th Torts § 149, Confidentiality and Disclosure.

§ 15634. Civil or criminal liability of reporter

(a) No care custodian, clergy member, health practitioner, mandated reporter of suspected financial abuse of an elder or dependent adult, or employee of an adult protective services agency or a local law enforcement agency who reports a known or suspected instance of abuse of an elder or dependent adult shall be civilly or criminally liable for any report required or authorized by this article. Any other person reporting a known or suspected instance of abuse of an elder or dependent adult shall not incur civil or criminal liability as a result of any report authorized by this article, unless it can be proven that a false report was made and the person knew that the report was false. No person required to make a report pursuant to this article, or any person taking photographs at his or her discretion, shall incur any civil or criminal liability for taking photographs of a suspected victim of abuse of an elder or dependent adult or causing photographs to be taken of such a suspected victim or for disseminating the photographs with the reports required by this article. However, this section shall not be construed to grant immunity from this liability with respect to any other use of the photographs.

(b) No care custodian, clergy member, health practitioner, mandated reporter of suspected financial abuse of an elder or dependent adult, or employee of an adult protective services agency or a local law enforcement agency who, pursuant to a request from an adult protective services agency or a local law enforcement agency investigating a report of known or suspected abuse of an elder or dependent adult, provides the requesting agency with access to the victim of a known or suspected instance of abuse of an elder or dependent adult, shall incur civil or criminal liability as a result of providing that access.

(c) The Legislature finds that, even though it has provided immunity from liability to persons required to report abuse of an elder or dependent adult, immunity does not eliminate the possibility that actions may be brought against those persons based upon required reports of abuse. In order to further limit the financial hardship that those persons may incur as a result of fulfilling their legal responsibilities, it is necessary that they not be unfairly burdened by legal fees incurred in defending those actions. Therefore, a care custodian, clergy member, health practitioner, or an employee of an adult protective services agency or a local law enforcement agency may present to the Department of General Services a claim for reasonable attorneys' fees incurred in any action against that person on the basis of making a report required or authorized by this article if the court has dismissed the action upon a demurrer or motion for summary judgment made by that person, or if he or she prevails in the action. The Department of General Services shall allow that claim if the requirements of this subdivision are met, and the claim shall be paid from an appropriation to be made for that purpose. Attorneys' fees awarded pursuant to this section shall not exceed an hourly rate greater than the rate charged by the Attorney General at the time the award is made and shall not exceed an aggregate amount of fifty thousand dollars ($50,-000). This subdivision shall not apply if a public entity has provided for the defense of the action pursuant to Section 995 of the Government Code. *(Added by Stats.1985, c. 1164, § 11, eff. Sept. 28, 1985. Amended by Stats.1986, c. 769, § 14, eff. Sept. 15, 1986; Stats.1990, c. 241 (S.B.1911), § 2; Stats. 2002, c. 54 (A.B.255), § 11; Stats.2005, c. 140 (S.B.1018), § 7, operative Jan. 1, 2007; Stats.2011, c. 372 (S.B.33), § 4; Stats.2016, c. 31 (S.B.836), § 285, eff. June 27, 2016.)*

Research References

Treatises and Practice Aids

Witkin, California Summary 10th Torts § 150, Immunity for Reporting.

ARTICLE 5. LOCAL AGENCY CROSS–REPORTING

§ 15640. Criminal activity and abuse instances requiring reports; referring agencies; abuse by licensed health practitioners; abuse at long-term care facilities; consent of victim for reporting; neglect or abandonment

(a)(1) An adult protective services agency shall immediately, or as soon as practically possible, report by telephone to the law enforcement agency having jurisdiction over the case any known or suspected instance of criminal activity, and to any public agency given responsibility for investigation in that jurisdiction of cases of elder and dependent adult abuse, every known or suspected instance of abuse pursuant to Section 15630 or 15630.1 of an elder or dependent adult. A county adult protective services agency shall also send a written report thereof within two working days of receiving the information concerning the incident to each agency to which it is required to make a telephone report under this subdivision. Prior to making any cross-report of allegations of financial abuse to law enforcement agencies, an adult protective services agency shall first determine whether there is reasonable suspicion of any criminal activity.

(2) If an adult protective services agency receives a report of abuse alleged to have occurred in a long-term care facility, that adult protective services agency shall immediately inform the person making the report that he or she is required to make the report to the long-term care ombudsman program or to a local law enforcement agency. The adult protective services agency shall not accept the report by telephone but shall forward any written report received to the long-term care ombudsman.

(b) If an adult protective services agency or local law enforcement agency or ombudsman program receiving a report of known or suspected elder or dependent adult abuse determines, pursuant to its investigation, that the abuse is being committed by a health practitioner licensed under Division 2 (commencing with Section 500) of the Business and Professions Code, or any related initiative act, or by a person purporting to be a licensee, the adult protective services agency or local law enforcement agency or ombudsman program shall immediately, or as soon as practically possible, report this information to the appropriate licensing agency. The licensing agency shall investigate the report in light of the potential for physical harm. The transmittal of information to the appropriate licensing agency shall not relieve the adult protective services agency or local law enforcement agency or ombudsman program of the responsibility to continue its own investigation as required under applicable provisions of law. The information reported pursuant to this paragraph shall remain confidential and shall not be disclosed.

(c) A local law enforcement agency shall immediately, or as soon as practically possible, report by telephone to the long-term care ombudsman program when the abuse is alleged to have occurred in a long-term care facility or to the county adult protective services agency when it is alleged to have occurred anywhere else, and to the agency given responsibility for the investigation of cases of elder and dependent adult abuse every known or suspected instance of abuse of an elder or dependent adult. A local law enforcement agency shall also send a written report thereof within two working days of receiving the information concerning the incident to any agency to which it is required to make a telephone report under this subdivision.

(d) A long-term care ombudsman coordinator may report the instance of abuse to the county adult protective services agency or to the local law enforcement agency for assistance in the investigation of the abuse if the victim gives his or her consent. A long-term care ombudsman program and the Licensing and Certification Division of the State Department of Public Health shall immediately report by telephone and in writing within two working days to the bureau any instance of neglect occurring in a health care facility, that has seriously harmed any patient or reasonably appears to present a serious threat to the health or physical well-being of a patient in that facility. If a victim or potential victim of the neglect withholds consent to being identified in that report, the report shall contain circumstantial information about the neglect but shall not identify that victim or potential victim and the bureau and the reporting agency shall maintain the confidentiality of the report until the report becomes a matter of public record.

(e) When a county adult protective services agency, a long-term care ombudsman program, or a local law enforcement agency receives a report of abuse, neglect, or abandonment of an elder or dependent adult alleged to have occurred in a long-term care facility, that county adult protective services agency, long-term care ombudsman coordinator, or local law enforcement agency shall report the incident to the licensing agency by telephone as soon as possible.

(f) County adult protective services agencies, long-term care ombudsman programs, and local law enforcement agencies shall report the results of their investigations of referrals or reports of abuse to the respective referring or reporting agencies. *(Added by Stats.1994, c. 594 (S.B.1681), § 20. Amended by Stats.1995, c. 91 (S.B.975), § 188; Stats.1998, c. 946 (S.B.2199), § 9.5; Stats.2005, c. 140 (S.B.1018), § 9, operative Jan. 1, 2007; Stats.2011, c. 372 (S.B.33), § 6.)*

Research References

Treatises and Practice Aids

Witkin, California Summary 10th Torts § 148, Required or Authorized Reporting.

ARTICLE 7. INTERAGENCY COORDINATION

Section

§ 15655.5. Provision of instructional materials regarding elder and dependent adult abuse and neglect and reporting requirements to specified organizations and mandated reporters; contents

A county adult protective services agency shall provide the organizations listed in paragraphs (v), (w), and (x) of Section 15610.17, and mandated reporters of suspected financial abuse of an elder or dependent adult pursuant to Section 15630.1, with instructional materials regarding abuse and neglect of an elder or dependent adult and their obligation to report under this chapter. At a minimum, the instructional materials shall include the following:

(a) An explanation of abuse and neglect of an elder or dependent adult, as defined in this chapter.

(b) Information on how to recognize potential abuse and neglect of an elder or dependent adult.

(c) Information on how the county adult protective services agency investigates reports of known or suspected abuse and neglect.

(d) Instructions on how to report known or suspected incidents of abuse and neglect, including the appropriate telephone numbers to call and what types of information would assist the county adult protective services agency with its investigation of the report. *(Added by Stats.2002, c. 54 (A.B.255), § 12.5. Amended by Stats.2005, c. 140 (S.B.1018), § 11, operative Jan. 1, 2007; Stats.2011, c. 372 (S.B.33), § 8.)*

ARTICLE 8.5. CIVIL ACTIONS FOR ABUSE OF ELDERLY OR DEPENDENT ADULTS

§ 15657.04. Addresses or locations of persons protected under court order; prohibition upon certain enjoined parties from acting to obtain such information

(a) The court shall order that any party enjoined pursuant to Section 15657.03 be prohibited from taking any action to obtain the address or location of any protected person, unless there is good cause not to make that order.

(b) The Judicial Council shall develop forms necessary to effectuate this section. *(Added by Stats.2005, c. 472 (A.B. 978), § 7. Amended by Stats.2010, c. 572 (A.B.1596), § 27, operative Jan. 1, 2012.)*

Part 4

SERVICES FOR THE CARE OF CHILDREN

CHAPTER 1. FOSTER CARE PLACEMENT

§ 16000. Legislative intent

(a) It is the intent of the Legislature to preserve and strengthen a child's family ties whenever possible, removing the child from the custody of his or her parents only when necessary for his or her welfare or for the safety and protection of the public. If a child is removed from the physical custody of his or her parents, preferential consideration shall be given whenever possible to the placement of the child with the relative as required by Section 7950 of the Family Code. If the child is removed from his or her own family, it is the purpose of this chapter to secure as nearly as possible for the child the custody, care, and discipline equivalent to that which should have been given to the child by his or her parents. It is further the intent of the Legislature to reaffirm its commitment to children who are in out-of-home placement to live in the least restrictive family setting promoting normal childhood experiences that is suited to meet the child's or youth's individual needs, and to live as close to the child's family as possible pursuant to subdivision (c) of Section 16501.1. Family reunification services shall be provided for expeditious reunification of the child with his or her family, as required by law. If reunification is not possible or likely, a permanent alternative shall be developed.

(b) It is further the intent of the Legislature that all children live with a committed, permanent, and nurturing family. Services and supports should be tailored to meet the needs of the individual child and family being served, with the ultimate goal of maintaining the family, or when this is not possible, transitioning the child or youth to a permanent family or preparing the child or youth for a successful transition into adulthood. When needed, short-term residential therapeutic program services are a short-term, specialized, and intensive intervention that is just one part of a continuum of care available for children, youth, young adults, and their families.

(c) It is further the intent of the Legislature to ensure that all pupils in foster care and those who are homeless as defined by the federal McKinney–Vento Homeless Assistance Act (42 U.S.C. Sec. 11301 et seq.) have the opportunity to meet the challenging state pupil academic achievement standards to which all pupils are held. In fulfilling their responsibilities to pupils in foster care, educators, county placing agencies, care providers, advocates, and the juvenile courts shall work together to maintain stable school placements and to ensure that each pupil is placed in the least restrictive educational programs, and has access to the academic resources, services, and extracurricular and enrichment activities that are available to all pupils. In all instances, educational and school placement decisions shall be based on the best interests of the child. *(Added by Stats.1990, c. 1370 (S.B.615), § 1. Amended by Stats.1993, c. 1089 (A.B.2129), § 30; Stats.2000, c. 745 (A.B.2307), § 3; Stats.2003, c. 862 (A.B.490), § 15; Stats.2015, c. 773 (A.B. 403), § 105, eff. Jan. 1, 2016; Stats.2016, c. 612 (A.B.1997), § 113, eff. Jan. 1, 2017.)*

Research References

Treatises and Practice Aids

Witkin, California Summary 10th Parent and Child § 10, Rights Of Foster Children.

Witkin, California Summary 10th Parent and Child § 519, Nature Of Dependency Proceedings.

Witkin, California Summary 10th Parent and Child § 638, Preferential Right Of Relatives.

Witkin, California Summary 10th Wills and Probate § 985, Amount Of Bond.

§ 16000.1. Legislative findings and declarations; intent; duty to care for and protect children in foster care

(a) The Legislature finds and declares all of the following:

(1) The state has a duty to care for and protect the children that the state places into foster care, and as a matter of public policy, the state assumes an obligation of the highest order to ensure the safety of children in foster care.

(2) A judicial order establishing jurisdiction over a child placed into foster care supplants or limits parental or previous adult authority.

(3) Nothing in this section is intended to change the balance of liability between the state and the counties as it existed prior to the decision of the California Court of Appeal in County of Los Angeles v. Superior Court of Los Angeles: Real Party in Interest Terrell R. (2002) 102 Cal.App.4th 627,[1] as established by the decision of the California Court of Appeal in Scott v. County of Los Angeles (1994) 27 Cal.App.4th 125.[2] Furthermore, nothing in this section is intended to increase or decrease the liability of the state as it existed prior to the Terrell R. case.

(b)(1) It is the intent of the Legislature that nothing in the decision of the California Court of Appeal in County of Los Angeles v. Superior Court of Los Angeles: Real Party in Interest Terrell R. (2002) 102 Cal.App.4th 627,[1] shall be held to change the standards of liability and immunity for injuries to children in protective custody that existed prior to that decision.

(2) It is the intent of the Legislature to confirm the state's duty to comply with all requirements under Part B of Title IV of the Social Security Act (42 U.S.C. Sec. 620 et seq.) and Part E of Title IV of the Social Security Act (42 U.S.C. Sec. 670 et seq.) that are relevant to the protection and welfare of children in foster care. *(Added by Stats.2003, c. 847 (A.B. 1151), § 5.)*

[1] County of Los Angeles v. Superior Court: Real Party in Interest Terrell R. (App. 2 Dist. 2002) 125 Cal.Rptr.2d 637.

[2] Scott v. County of Los Angeles (App. 3 Dist. 1994) 32 Cal. Rptr.2d 643.

§ 16000.5. Legislative findings and declarations; Indian tribes operating foster care, adoption assistance or kinship guardianship assistance programs; maximization of opportunities to operate foster care programs

The Legislature finds and declares all of the following:

(a) The Fostering Connections to Success and Increasing Adoptions Act of 2008 (Public Law 110–351)[1] provides Indian tribes with the option, effective October 1, 2009, to operate a foster care, adoption assistance, and, at tribal option, a kinship guardianship assistance program under Title IV–E of the Social Security Act (42 U.S.C. Sec. 671 et seq.). The federal government will share the costs of a tribe operating an approved Title IV–E program.

(b) It shall be the policy of the state to maximize the opportunities for Indian tribes to operate foster care programs for Indian children pursuant to the federal Fostering Connections to Success and Increasing Adoptions Act of 2008. *(Added by Stats.2009, c. 124 (A.B.770), § 1.)*

[1] See 42 U.S.C.A. § 679C.

Research References

Treatises and Practice Aids

Witkin, California Summary 10th Parent and Child § 11, Programs for Foster Children.

Witkin, California Summary 10th Parent and Child § 86, Programs to Facilitate Adoption.

§ 16000.6. Negotiation of agreements in good faith on behalf of Indian children

The State Department of Social Services shall negotiate in good faith with the Indian tribe, organization, or consortium in the state that requests development of an agreement with the state to administer all or part of the programs under Title IV–E of the Social Security Act (42 U.S.C. Sec. 671 et seq.) on behalf of the Indian children who are under the authority of the tribe, organization, or consortium. *(Added by Stats. 2009, c. 124 (A.B.770), § 2.)*

§ 16001. Technical assistance; placement needs, resources and programs; out-of-county and out-of-state placements

(a) The State Department of Social Services shall provide technical assistance to encourage and facilitate the county placement agency's evaluation of placement needs and the development of needed placement resources and programs. County placement agencies shall, on a regular basis, conduct an evaluation of the county's placement resources and programs in relation to the needs of children placed in out-of-home care. County placement agencies shall examine the adequacy of existing placement resources and programs and identify the type of additional placement resources and programs needed. The county placement agency shall specifically examine placements which are out of county and shall determine the reason the placement was necessary, and identify the additional placement resources and programs which need to be developed and available to allow a child to remain within the county and as close as possible to his or her home. The department shall also support the development and operation of a consortia of county placement agencies on a regional basis for the purpose of developing specialized programs serving a multicounty area.

(b) It is the intent of the Legislature that the reason for each out-of-county and out-of-state placement be included in the Child Welfare Services Case Management System, and that the State Department of Social Services utilize that data to evaluate out-of-county and out-of-state placements and to assist in the identification of resource and placement needs.

(c) It is the intent of the Legislature that the State Department of Social Services review the out-of-state placement of children to determine the reason for out-of-state placement. The department shall make the information available to the Legislature upon request. *(Added by Stats. 1993, c. 1089 (A.B.2129), § 31.)*

§ 16001.5. Promotion of self-esteem in foster children; distribution of information

The State Department of Social Services shall annually distribute information declaring the importance of promoting self-esteem with respect to foster children to all of the following:

(a) Each county independent living program administrator.

(b) Each licensed foster family agency, group home, and small family home.

(c) Each county welfare department.

(d) Each county director of child protective services.

(e) Each county director of social services.

(f) Each county foster home services director.

(g) The Director of the Community Care Licensing Division of the State Department of Social Services.

(h) The Director of State Adoptions Branch of the State Department of Social Services. *(Added by Stats.1997, c. 542 (S.B.916), § 3.)*

§ 16001.7. Participation of current and former foster youth in development of state foster care and child welfare policy; contract for technical assistance and outreach

(a) The department shall promote the participation of current and former foster youth in the development of state foster care and child welfare policy. Subject to the availability of funds, the department shall contract with the California Youth Connection to provide technical assistance and outreach to current and former foster youth. In executing this contract, the responsibilities of the California Youth Connection shall include, but are not limited to, all of the following:

(1) Providing leadership training to current and former foster youth between the ages of 14 and 21 years.

(2) Providing outreach and technical assistance to current and former foster youth to form and maintain California Youth Connection chapters, including recruiting and training adult volunteer supporters.

(3) Enabling foster youth to be represented in policy discussions pertinent to foster care and child welfare issues.

(4) Enhancing the well-being of foster youth and increasing public understanding of foster care and child welfare issues.

(5) Developing educational materials and forums related to foster care.

(b) Funds provided to the California Youth Connection pursuant to the contract shall not be used for activities not allowed under federal law relating to the receipt of federal financial participation for independent living services, including, but not limited to, lobbying and litigation. *(Added by Stats.2000, c. 108 (A.B.2876), § 50, eff. July 10, 2000.)*

§ 16001.8. Working group on rights of minors and nonminors in foster care

(a) The State Department of Social Services shall convene a working group regarding the rights of all minors and nonminors in foster care, as specified in Section 16001.9, in order to educate foster youth, foster care providers, and others. Responsibilities of the working group shall include all of the following:

(1) By January 1, 2018, make recommendations to the Legislature for revising the rights based on a review of state law.

(2) By July 1, 2018, develop standardized information regarding the revised rights in an age-appropriate manner and reflective of any relevant licensing requirements with respect to the foster care providers' responsibilities to adequately supervise children in care.

(3) By July 1, 2018, develop recommendations regarding methods for disseminating the standardized information specified in paragraph (2), including whether to require the signature of a foster child verifying that he or she has received and understands his or her rights.

(4) By July 1, 2018, develop recommendations for measuring and improving, if necessary, the degree to which foster youth are adequately informed of their rights.

(b) The working group shall be composed of all of the following:

(1) The Office of the State Foster Care Ombudsperson.

(2) The bureau at the Department of Justice whose mission is to protect the rights of children.

(3) The County Welfare Directors Association of California.

(4) The Chief Probation Officers of California.

(5) The County Behavioral Health Directors Association of California.

(6) Current and former foster youth.

(7) Foster parents and caregivers.

(8) Foster children advocacy groups.

(9) Foster care provider associations.

(10) Any other interested parties. *(Added by Stats.2016, c. 851 (A.B.1067), § 1, eff. Jan. 1, 2017.)*

§ 16001.9. Rights of minors and nonminors in foster care

(a) It is the policy of the state that all minors and nonminors in foster care shall have the following rights:

(1) To live in a safe, healthy, and comfortable home where he or she is treated with respect.

(2) To be free from physical, sexual, emotional, or other abuse, or corporal punishment.

(3) To receive adequate and healthy food, adequate clothing, and, for youth in group homes, an allowance.

(4) To receive medical, dental, vision, and mental health services.

(5) To be free of the administration of medication or chemical substances, unless authorized by a physician.

(6) To contact family members, unless prohibited by court order, and social workers, attorneys, foster youth advocates and supporters, Court Appointed Special Advocates (CASAs), and probation officers.

(7) To visit and contact brothers and sisters, unless prohibited by court order.

(8) To contact the Community Care Licensing Division of the State Department of Social Services or the State Foster Care Ombudsperson regarding violations of rights, to speak to representatives of these offices confidentially, and to be free from threats or punishment for making complaints.

(9) To make and receive confidential telephone calls and send and receive unopened mail, unless prohibited by court order.

(10) To attend religious services and activities of his or her choice.

(11) To maintain an emancipation bank account and manage personal income, consistent with the child's age and developmental level, unless prohibited by the case plan.

(12) To not be locked in a room, building, or facility premises, unless placed in a community treatment facility.

(13) To attend school and participate in extracurricular, cultural, and personal enrichment activities, consistent with the child's age and developmental level, with minimal disruptions to school attendance and educational stability.

(14) To work and develop job skills at an age-appropriate level, consistent with state law.

(15) To have social contacts with people outside of the foster care system, including teachers, church members, mentors, and friends.

(16) To attend Independent Living Program classes and activities if he or she meets age requirements.

(17) To attend court hearings and speak to the judge.

(18) To have storage space for private use.

(19) To be involved in the development of his or her own case plan and plan for permanent placement.

(20) To review his or her own case plan and plan for permanent placement, if he or she is 12 years of age or older and in a permanent placement, and to receive information about his or her out-of-home placement and case plan, including being told of changes to the plan.

(21) To be free from unreasonable searches of personal belongings.

(22) To the confidentiality of all juvenile court records consistent with existing law.

(23) To have fair and equal access to all available services, placement, care, treatment, and benefits, and to not be subjected to discrimination or harassment on the basis of actual or perceived race, ethnic group identification, ancestry, national origin, color, religion, sex, sexual orientation, gender identity, mental or physical disability, or HIV status.

(24) To be placed in out-of-home care according to their gender identity, regardless of the gender or sex listed in their court or child welfare records.

(25) To have caregivers and child welfare personnel who have received instruction on cultural competency and sensitivity relating to, and best practices for, providing adequate care to lesbian, gay, bisexual, and transgender youth in out-of-home care.

(26) At 16 years of age or older, to have access to existing information regarding the educational options available, including, but not limited to, the coursework necessary for vocational and postsecondary educational programs, and information regarding financial aid for postsecondary education.

(27) To have access to age-appropriate, medically accurate information about reproductive health care, the prevention of unplanned pregnancy, and the prevention and treatment of sexually transmitted infections at 12 years of age or older.

(b) Nothing in this section shall be interpreted to require a foster care provider to take any action that would impair the health and safety of children in out-of-home placement.

(c) The State Department of Social Services and each county welfare department are encouraged to work with the Student Aid Commission, the University of California, the California State University, and the California Community Colleges to receive information pursuant to paragraph (26) of subdivision (a). *(Added by Stats.2001, c. 683 (A.B.899), § 3. Amended by Stats.2003, c. 331 (A.B.458), § 5; Stats.2004, c. 668 (S.B.1639), § 5; Stats.2005, c. 640 (A.B.1412), § 9; Stats.2008, c. 557 (A.B.3015), § 3; Stats.2010, c. 557 (S.B. 1353), § 3; Stats.2012, c. 639 (A.B.1856), § 3; Stats.2013, c.*

338 (S.B.528), § 2; Stats.2015, c. 805 (S.B.731), § 2, eff. Jan. 1, 2016.)

Research References

Treatises and Practice Aids

Witkin, California Summary 10th Parent and Child § 10, Rights Of Foster Children.

Witkin, California Summary 10th Parent and Child § 626, Conduct Of Hearing.

§ 16002. Sibling group placement; sibling interaction; suspension; modification of forms

(a)(1) It is the intent of the Legislature to maintain the continuity of the family unit, and ensure the preservation and strengthening of the child's family ties by ensuring that when siblings have been removed from their home, either as a group on one occurrence or individually on separate occurrences, the siblings will be placed in foster care together, unless it has been determined that placement together is contrary to the safety or well-being of any sibling. The Legislature recognizes that in order to ensure the placement of a sibling group in the same foster care placement, placement resources need to be expanded.

(2) It is also the intent of the Legislature to preserve and strengthen a child's sibling relationship so that when a child has been removed from his or her home and he or she has a sibling or siblings who remain in the custody of a mutual parent subject to the court's jurisdiction, the court has the authority to develop a visitation plan for the siblings, unless it has been determined that visitation is contrary to the safety or well-being of any sibling.

(b) The responsible local agency shall make a diligent effort in all out-of-home placements of dependent children and wards in foster care, including those with relatives, to place siblings together in the same placement, and to develop and maintain sibling relationships. If siblings are not placed together in the same home, the social worker or probation officer shall explain why the siblings are not placed together and what efforts he or she is making to place the siblings together or why making those efforts would be contrary to the safety and well-being of any of the siblings. When placement of siblings together in the same home is not possible, a diligent effort shall be made, and a case plan prepared, to provide for ongoing and frequent interaction among siblings until family reunification is achieved, or, if parental rights are terminated, as part of developing the permanent plan for the child. If the court determines by clear and convincing evidence that sibling interaction is contrary to the safety and well-being of any of the siblings, the reasons for the determination shall be noted in the court order, and interaction shall be suspended.

(c) When there has been a judicial suspension of sibling interaction, the reasons for the suspension shall be reviewed at each periodic review hearing pursuant to Section 366 or 727.3. In order for the suspension to continue, the court shall make a renewed finding that sibling interaction is contrary to the safety or well-being of either child. When the court determines that sibling interaction can be safely resumed, that determination shall be noted in the court order and the case plan shall be revised to provide for sibling interaction.

(d) If the case plan for the child has provisions for sibling interaction, the child, or his or her parent or legal guardian, shall have the right to comment on those provisions. If a person wishes to assert a sibling relationship with a dependent child or ward, he or she may file a petition in the juvenile court having jurisdiction over the dependent child pursuant to subdivision (b) of Section 388 or the ward in foster care pursuant to Section 778.

(e) If parental rights are terminated and the court orders a dependent child or ward to be placed for adoption, the county adoption agency or the State Department of Social Services shall take all of the following steps to facilitate ongoing sibling contact, except in those cases provided in subdivision (b) where the court determines by clear and convincing evidence that sibling interaction is contrary to the safety or well-being of the child:

(1) Include in training provided to prospective adoptive parents information about the importance of sibling relationships to the adopted child and counseling on methods for maintaining sibling relationships.

(2) Provide prospective adoptive parents with information about siblings of the child, except the address where the siblings of the children reside. However, this address may be disclosed by court order for good cause shown.

(3) (A) To the extent practicable, the county placing agency shall convene a meeting with the child, the sibling or siblings of the child, the prospective adoptive parent or parents, and a facilitator for the purpose of deciding whether to voluntarily execute a postadoption sibling contact agreement pursuant to Section 8616.5 of the Family Code on a date after termination of parental rights and prior to finalization of the adoption. The county placing agency may comply with the requirements of this paragraph by allowing a nonprofit organization authorized to provide permanency placement and postadoption mediation for adoptive and birth families to facilitate the meeting and develop the agreement.

(B) The county placing agency is not required to convene a meeting to decide whether to voluntarily execute a postadoption sibling contact agreement pursuant to Section 8616.5 of the Family Code in either of the following circumstances:

(i) The county placing agency determines that such a meeting or postadoption sibling contact agreement would be contrary to the safety and well-being of the child.

(ii) The child requests that a meeting shall not occur.

(C) The child may petition the court for an order requiring the county placing agency to convene a meeting to decide whether to voluntarily execute a postadoption sibling contact agreement pursuant to Section 8616.5 of the Family Code. If the court determines by a preponderance of the evidence that a postadoption sibling contact agreement or a meeting for the purpose of deciding whether to voluntarily execute such an agreement is contrary to the safety and well-being of the child, the reasons for the determination shall be noted in the court order, and the meeting is not required to occur.

(D) Counsel to the child and counsel to the siblings who are dependents of the court shall be notified of, and may attend, both the meeting and the hearing described in this paragraph.

(E) This paragraph shall not require attendance by a child, sibling, or other party at a meeting to decide whether to voluntarily execute a postadoption sibling contact agreement pursuant to Section 8616.5 of the Family Code if the child, sibling, or other party cannot be located or does not wish to attend the meeting. This paragraph shall not prohibit a county placing agency from convening a meeting if not all of the parties are secured to attend.

(f) Information regarding sibling interaction, contact, or visitation that has been authorized or ordered by the court shall be provided to the foster parent, relative caretaker, or legal guardian of the child as soon as possible after the court order is made, in order to facilitate the interaction, contact, or visitation.

(g) As used in this section, "sibling" means a person related to the identified child by blood, adoption, or affinity through a common legal or biological parent.

(h) The court documentation on sibling placements required under this section shall not require the modification of existing court order forms until the Child Welfare Services/Case Management System (CWS/CMS) is implemented on a statewide basis. *(Added by Stats.1993, c. 1089 (A.B. 2129), § 32. Amended by Stats.1994, c. 663 (S.B.17), § 4; Stats.1998, c. 1072 (A.B.2196), § 3; Stats.2000, c. 909 (A.B. 1987), § 8; Stats.2003, c. 812 (S.B.591), § 4; Stats.2010, c. 560 (A.B.743), § 2; Stats.2012, c. 35 (S.B.1013), § 102, eff. June 27, 2012; Stats.2014, c. 772 (S.B.1460), § 17, eff. Jan. 1, 2015; Stats.2014, c. 773 (S.B.1099), § 10.5, eff. Jan. 1, 2015; Stats.2015, c. 425 (S.B.794), § 22, eff. Jan. 1, 2016; Stats.2016, c. 719 (S.B.1060), § 4, eff. Jan. 1, 2017.)*

Commentary

When, under this section, an agency made a diligent but unsuccessful effort to place siblings in the same foster home, the juvenile court properly permitted the siblings to be separated and placed in long-term foster care when they had been living in an emergency group shelter home for over a year and had a better chance of long-term foster care if they were placed separately. *In re A.S., 205 Cal.4th 1332, 141 Cal.Rptr.3d 255 (2012), review denied.*

Research References

Treatises and Practice Aids

Witkin, California Summary 10th Parent and Child § 10, Rights Of Foster Children.

Witkin, California Summary 10th Parent and Child § 119, Investigation, Report, and Recommendation.

Witkin, California Summary 10th Parent and Child § 671, Supplemental Report.

Witkin, California Summary 10th Parent and Child § 673, Child in Foster Care.

Witkin, California Summary 10th Parent and Child § 678, Twelve-Month Review.

Witkin, California Summary 10th Parent and Child § 679, Eighteen-Month Review.

Witkin, California Summary 10th Parent and Child § 689, in General.

Witkin, California Summary 10th Parent and Child § 692, in General.

Witkin, California Summary 10th Parent and Child § 896, General Requirements.

§ 16002.5. Dependent minor and nonminor parents and their children; placement together; access to services; access to social workers; school attendance and appropriate activities; support and assistance; contact with child

It is the intent of the Legislature to maintain the continuity of the family unit and to support and preserve families headed by minor parents and nonminor dependent parents who are themselves under the jurisdiction of the juvenile court by ensuring that minor parents and nonminor dependent parents and their children are placed together in as family-like a setting as possible, unless it has been determined that placement together poses a risk to the child. It is also the intent of the Legislature to ensure that complete and accurate data on parenting minor and nonminor dependents is collected, and that the State Department of Social Services shall ensure that the following information is publicly available on a quarterly basis by county about parenting minor and nonminor dependents: total number of parenting minor and nonminor dependents in each county, their age, their ethnic group, their placement type, their time in care, the number of children they have, and whether their children are court dependents.

(a) To the greatest extent possible, minor parents and nonminor dependent parents and their children shall be provided with access to existing services for which they may be eligible, that are specifically targeted at supporting, maintaining, and developing both the parent-child bond and the dependent parent's ability to provide a permanent and safe home for the child. Examples of these services may include, but are not limited to, child care, parenting classes, child development classes, and frequent visitation.

(b) Child welfare agencies may provide minor parents and nonminor dependent parents with access to social workers or resource specialists who have received training on the needs of teenage parents and available resources, including, but not limited to, maternal and child health programs, child care, and child development classes. Child welfare agencies are encouraged to update the case plans for pregnant and parenting dependents within 60 calendar days of the date the agency is informed of a pregnancy. When updating the case plan, child welfare agencies may hold a specialized conference to assist pregnant or parenting foster youth and nonminor dependents with planning for healthy parenting and identifying appropriate resources and services, and to inform the case plan. The specialized conference shall include the pregnant or parenting minor or nonminor dependent, family members, and other supportive adults, and the specially trained social worker or resource specialist. The specialized conference may include other individuals, including, but not limited to, a public health nurse, a community health worker, or other personnel with a comprehensive knowledge of available maternal and child resources, including public benefit programs. Participation in the specialized conference shall be voluntary on the part of the foster youth or nonminor dependent and assistance in identifying and accessing resources shall not be dependent on participation in the conference.

(c) The minor parents and nonminor dependent parents shall be given the ability to attend school, complete homework, and participate in age and developmentally appropriate activities unrelated to and separate from parenting.

(d) Child welfare agencies, local educational agencies, and child care resource and referral agencies may make reasonable and coordinated efforts to ensure that minor parents and nonminor dependent parents who have not completed high school have access to school programs that provide onsite or coordinated child care.

(e) Foster care placements for minor parents and nonminor dependent parents and their children shall demonstrate a willingness and ability to provide support and assistance to minor parents and nonminor dependent parents and their children, shall support the preservation of the family unit, and shall refer a minor parent or nonminor dependent parent to preventive services to address any concerns regarding the safety, health, or well-being of the child, and to help prevent, whenever possible, the filing of a petition to declare the child a dependent of the juvenile court pursuant to Section 300.

(f) Contact between the child, the custodial parent, and the noncustodial parent shall be facilitated if that contact is found to be in the best interest of the child.

(g) For the purpose of this section, "child" refers to the child born to the minor parent.

(h) For the purpose of this section, "minor parent" refers to a dependent child who is also a parent.

(i) For the purpose of this section, "nonminor dependent parent" refers to a nonminor dependent, as described in subdivision (v) of Section 11400, who also is a parent. *(Added by Stats.2004, c. 841 (S.B.1178), § 3. Amended by Stats.2012, c. 846 (A.B.1712), § 46; Stats.2013, c. 338 (S.B. 528), § 3; Stats.2015, c. 511 (A.B.260), § 3, eff. Jan. 1, 2016.)*

Research References

Treatises and Practice Aids

Witkin, California Summary 10th Parent and Child § 10, Rights Of Foster Children.

Witkin, California Summary 10th Parent and Child § 692, in General.

§ 16003.5. State funding allocated to counties for purpose of recruiting, retaining, and supporting foster parents, relative caregivers, and resource families; allowable expenditures; provision of funding based on approval of plans; required report

(a) Any state funding allocated to counties for the purpose of recruiting, retaining, and supporting foster parents, relative caregivers, and resource families shall be used to increase the capacity and use of home-based family care and the provision of services and supports to such caregivers. Allowable expenditures of those funds shall include, but not be limited to, and shall be used to supplement and not supplant, resources used by a county for any of the following purposes:

(1) Staffing to provide and improve direct services and supports to licensed foster family homes, approved resource families, and relative caregivers, and to remove any barriers in those areas defined as priorities in the county implementation plan and subsequent reports on outcomes.

(2) Exceptional child needs not covered by the caregiver-specific rate that would normalize the child's experience, stabilize the placement, or enhance the child's well-being.

(3) Child care for licensed foster parents, approved resource families, and relative caregivers.

(4) Intensive relative finding, engagement, and navigation efforts.

(5) Emerging technological, evidence-informed, or other nontraditional approaches to outreach to potential foster family homes, resource families, and relatives.

(b)(1) The department shall provide available funding to counties based upon its approval of plans submitted by each county that requests funding described in subdivision (a). Each county plan shall be submitted by September 1 of any year in which funding is available. Each county plan shall include all of the following:

(A) A definition of the specific goal or goals related to increasing the capacity and use of home-based family care and the provision of services and supports to such caregivers that the county intends to achieve.

(B) A description of the strategy or strategies the county proposes to pursue to address the goal or goals identified in subparagraph (A).

(C) An explanation or rationale for the proposed strategy or strategies relative to the goal or goals identified in subparagraph (A).

(D) A list or description of the outcomes that shall be reported pursuant to subdivision (c), including baseline data for those outcomes.

(2) The department shall develop, following consultation with the County Welfare Directors Association of California and the Chief Probation Officers of California, criteria for the approval of county plans submitted pursuant to paragraph (1).

(c) As a condition of accepting state funding described in subdivision (a), counties receiving that funding shall, by September 30 of the year following the end of the fiscal year in which the funding was available, report to the department the outcomes achieved through the use of that funding and the activities that contributed to those outcomes. This report from each receiving county shall be made in a manner prescribed by the department, following consultation with the County Welfare Directors Association of California and the Chief Probation Officers of California. Using these reports, the department shall share best practices among counties and shall periodically update the Legislature.

(d) Funding for the purposes of this section shall be subject to an appropriation by the Legislature. *(Added by Stats.2015, c. 773 (A.B.403), § 107, eff. Jan. 1, 2016.)*

§ 16004. Sibling placement resources

(a) The Legislature finds and declares that there is an urgent need to develop placement resources to permit sibling groups to remain together in out-of-home care when removed from the custody of their parents due to child abuse or neglect. Multiple barriers exist, including local ordinances and community care licensing standards, that limit or prevent the county placement agency from fulfilling its obligation pursuant to subdivision (b) of Section 16002 to place siblings together.

Therefore, the Legislature declares its intent to develop specific placement resources to accommodate sibling groups.

(b) The State Department of Social Services shall, in consultation with the County Welfare Directors Association, the Judicial Council, organizations representing foster youth, and other similar, interested organizations, make recommendations to increase the available sibling placement resources. The possible policy changes to be addressed shall include, but shall not be limited to, the following:

(1) The creation of a special licensing category for sibling care, including sibling group foster homes.

(2) Development of children's villages with separate cottages to provide a home for each sibling group.

(3) Funding for targeted recruitment of foster parents for large sibling groups.

(4) Establishment of a higher foster care payment rate for caretakers who accept sibling groups.

(5) Funding for one-time capital improvement costs to remodel homes to accommodate placement of siblings and provide for other up-front costs, such as vans, car seats, and other items.

(6) Establishment of guidelines for placing siblings, who cannot be placed in the same home, within geographic proximity to each other and exploration of the possibility of permitting these siblings to have the option of enrolling in the same school district even when the siblings reside in different school districts.

(c) The department shall develop recommendations for the Legislature, in consultation with the Chief Probation Officers Association and the County Welfare Directors Association, regarding procedures for doing both of the following:

(1) Placing siblings together when one or more siblings are in the juvenile dependency system and one or more siblings are in the juvenile delinquency systems, when such placements are appropriate.

(2) Maintaining contact and sharing information between siblings who are placed separately in out-of-home care under the juvenile dependency and the juvenile delinquency systems.

(d) The department shall submit the recommendations described in subdivisions (b) and (c) to the Legislature by November 1, 2001. *(Added by Stats.2000, c. 909 (A.B.1987), § 9.)*

Research References

Treatises and Practice Aids

Witkin, California Summary 10th Parent and Child § 10, Rights Of Foster Children.

Witkin, California Summary 10th Parent and Child § 584, Rights Of Siblings.

§ 16004.5. Dependent minor parents and their children; placement resources

(a) The Legislature finds and declares that there is an urgent need to develop placement resources to permit minor parents and their children to remain together in out-of-home care when the minor parent is removed from the custody of his or her parents due to abuse or neglect.

(b) To the greatest extent possible, child welfare agencies, in conjunction with providers and the state, and in conjunction with ongoing development of placements and the allocation of existing placement resources, shall identify and utilize whole family placements and other placement models that provide supportive family focused care for dependent teens and their children. In identifying these placements, child welfare agencies shall work with providers and stakeholders to identify and develop programs and program models designed to meet these goals.

(c) In order to effectively plan, identify, and develop needed resources, and effectively address the needs of this population, the department and local child welfare agencies are encouraged to collect data on the number of minors in foster care who give birth and the number of minor parents who remain in placement with their minor children. The department shall aggregate the data annually.

(d) In order to recruit, train, and retain qualified and supportive foster care providers for this population, the department and local child welfare agencies, in consultation with other interested stakeholders, are encouraged to collect information to be used to develop a more cost-effective infant supplemental payment rate structure that more adequately reimburses caregivers for the costs of infant care and teen parent mentoring. *(Added by Stats.2004, c. 841 (S.B.1178), § 4.)*

Research References

Treatises and Practice Aids

Witkin, California Summary 10th Parent and Child § 10, Rights Of Foster Children.

§ 16005. Sibling group case worker assignment

Siblings shall be assigned to the same social worker when there is a prospective adoptive family that intends to adopt the children as a sibling group, unless the responsible local agency finds that assigning the siblings to the same social worker would not be in the best interest of the child or the siblings or the operation of the county office. *(Added by Stats.2001, c. 353 (A.B.538), § 4.)*

Research References

Treatises and Practice Aids

Witkin, California Summary 10th Parent and Child § 686, Alternative Dispositions.

§ 16006. Placement according to gender identity

Children and nonminor dependents in out-of-home care shall be placed according to their gender identity, regardless of the gender or sex listed in their court or child welfare records. *(Added by Stats.2015, c. 805 (S.B.731), § 3, eff. Jan. 1, 2016.)*

§ 16010. Health and education records of minors and nonminor dependents; inclusion in case plan on placement; disclosure of information to prospective caretakers; review and update

(a)(1) When a child is placed in foster care, the case plan for each child recommended pursuant to Section 358.1 shall include a summary of the health and education information or records, including mental health information or records, of the child. The summary may be maintained in the form of a health and education passport, or a comparable format designed by the child protective agency. The health and education summary shall include, but not be limited to, the names and addresses of the child's health, dental, and education providers; the child's grade level performance; the child's school record; assurances that the child's placement in foster care takes into account proximity to the school in which the child is enrolled at the time of placement; the number of school transfers the child has already experienced; the child's educational progress, as demonstrated by factors, including, but not limited to, academic proficiency scores; credits earned toward graduation; a record of the child's immunizations and allergies; the child's known medical problems; the child's current medications, past health problems, and hospitalizations; a record of the child's relevant mental health history; the child's known mental health condition and medications; and any other relevant mental health, dental, health, and education information concerning the child determined to be appropriate by the Director of Social Services. The health and education summary may also include the name and contact information of the person or persons currently holding the right to make educational decisions for the child; the name and contact information for the educational liaison, as described in subdivision (c) of Section 48853.5 of the Education Code, of the child's local educational agency; and the contact information for the nearest foster youth services coordinating program. If any other law imposes more stringent information requirements, then that section shall prevail.

(2) In instances where it is determined that disclosure pursuant to paragraph (1) of the contact information of the person or persons currently holding the right to make educational decisions for the child poses a threat to the health and safety of that individual or those individuals, that contact information shall be redacted or withheld from the evaluation.

(b) Additionally, a court report or assessment required pursuant to subdivision (g) of Section 361.5, Section 366.1, subdivision (d) of Section 366.21, or subdivision (c) of Section 366.22 shall include a copy of the current health and education summary described in subdivision (a), including the name and contact information of the person or persons currently holding the right to make educational decisions for the child. With respect to a nonminor dependent, as described in subdivision (v) of Section 11400, a copy of the current health and education summary shall be included in the court report only if and when the nonminor dependent consents in writing to its inclusion.

(c) As soon as possible, but not later than 30 days after initial placement of a child into foster care, the child protective agency shall provide the caregiver with the child's current health and education summary as described in subdivision (a). For each subsequent placement of a child or nonminor dependent, the child protective agency shall provide the caregiver with a current summary as described in subdivision (a) within 48 hours of the placement. With respect to a nonminor dependent, as described in subdivision (v) of Section 11400, the social worker or probation officer shall advise the young adult of the social worker's or probation officer's obligation to provide the health and education summary to the new caregiver and the court, and shall discuss with the youth the benefits and liabilities of sharing that information.

(d)(1) Notwithstanding Section 827 or any other law, the child protective agency may disclose any information described in this section to a prospective caregiver or caregivers prior to placement of a child if all of the following requirements are met:

(A) The child protective agency intends to place the child with the prospective caregiver or caregivers.

(B) The prospective caregiver or caregivers are willing to become the adoptive parent or parents of the child.

(C) The prospective caregiver or caregivers have an approved adoption assessment or home study, a foster family home license, certification by a licensed foster family agency, or approval pursuant to the requirements in Sections 361.3 and 361.4.

(2) In addition to the information required to be provided under this section, the child protective agency may disclose to the prospective caregiver specified in paragraph (1), placement history or underlying source documents that are provided to adoptive parents pursuant to subdivisions (a) and (b) of Section 8706 of the Family Code.

(e) The child's caregiver shall be responsible for reviewing and receiving pupil records pursuant to subdivision (a) of Section 49069.3 of the Education Code for the purposes specified in subdivision (b) of Section 49069.3 of the Education Code. The child's caregiver shall be responsible for obtaining and maintaining accurate and thorough information from physicians and educators for the child's summary as described in subdivision (a) during the time that the child is in the care of the caregiver. On each required visit, the child protective agency or its designee * * * foster family agency shall inquire of the caregiver whether there is any new information that should be added to the child's summary as described in subdivision (a). The child protective agency shall update the summary with the information as appropriate, but not later than the next court date or within 48 hours of a change in placement. The child protective agency or its designee * * * foster family agency shall take all necessary steps to assist the caregiver in obtaining relevant health and education information for the child's health and education summary as described in subdivision (a). These steps shall include, but are not limited to, obtaining educational information to share with caregivers, providing appropriate notation on documentation caregivers receive that confirms their status as approved caregivers and their right to access information, and explaining caregiver rights and responsibilities with regard to accessing educational information under Sections 49069.3 and 56055 of the Education Code. The caregiver of a nonminor dependent, as described in subdivision (v) of Section 11400, is not responsible for obtaining and maintaining the nonminor dependent's health and educational information, but may assist the nonminor dependent with any recordkeeping that the nonminor requests of the caregiver.

(f) At the initial hearing, the court shall direct each parent to provide to the child protective agency complete medical, dental, mental health, and educational information, and medical background, of the child and of the child's mother and the child's biological father if known. The Judicial Council shall create a form for the purpose of obtaining health and education information from the child's parents or guardians at the initial hearing. The court shall determine at the hearing held pursuant to Section 358 whether the medical, dental, mental health, and educational information has been provided to the child protective agency. *(Added by Stats.1990, c. 1370 (S.B.615), § 1. Amended by Stats.1999, c.*

552 (S.B.543), § 2; Stats.2001, c. 353 (A.B.538), § 5; Stats. 2010, c. 557 (S.B.1353), § 4; Stats.2012, c. 846 (A.B.1712), § 47; Stats.2012, c. 849 (A.B.1909), § 7.5; Stats.2015, c. 554 (A.B.224), § 7, eff. Jan. 1, 2016; Stats.2017, c. 829 (S.B.233), § 9, eff. Jan. 1, 2018.)

Research References

Forms

West's California Judicial Council Forms JV-225, Your Child's Health and Education.

Treatises and Practice Aids

Witkin, California Summary 10th Parent and Child § 4, Public Welfare Services.

Witkin, California Summary 10th Parent and Child § 9, Rights and Responsibilities Of Foster Parents.

Witkin, California Summary 10th Parent and Child § 602, Explanation and Information.

Witkin, California Summary 10th Parent and Child § 625, Preparation Of Social Study.

Witkin, California Summary 10th Parent and Child § 626, Conduct Of Hearing.

Witkin, California Summary 10th Parent and Child § 639, Foster Care.

Witkin, California Summary 10th Parent and Child § 671, Supplemental Report.

Witkin, California Summary 10th Parent and Child § 682, Preliminary Assessment.

§ 16010.2. Plan for ongoing oversight and coordination of health care services

The department, in consultation with pediatricians, other health care experts, including public health nurses, and experts in and recipients of child welfare services, including parents, shall develop a plan for the ongoing oversight and coordination of health care services for a child in a foster care placement. The plan shall ensure a coordinated strategy to identify and respond to the health care needs of foster children, including mental health and dental needs, consistent with Section 205 of the federal Fostering Connections to Success and Increasing Adoptions Act of 2008 (Public Law 110–351).[1] *(Added by Stats.2009, c. 339 (S.B.597), § 6.)*

[1] For public law sections classified to the U.S.C.A., see USCA–Tables.

Research References

Treatises and Practice Aids

Witkin, California Summary 10th Parent and Child § 11, Programs for Foster Children.

§ 16010.4. Legislative findings and declarations; information to foster parents and other caregivers; caretaker interest in providing legal permanency

The Legislature finds and declares all of the following:

(a) Foster parents are one of the most important sources of information about the children in their care. Courts, lawyers, and social workers should have the benefit of caregivers' perceptions. Both federal and state law recognize the importance of foster parents' participation in juvenile court proceedings. Federal law requires that foster parents and other caregivers receive expanded opportunities for notice, the right to participate in dependency court review and permanency hearings, and the right to communicate concerns to the courts. State law similarly provides that caregivers may submit their concerns to courts in writing.

(b) It is in the children's best interests that their caregivers are privy to important information about them. This information is necessary to obtain social and health services for children, enroll children in school and extracurricular activities, and update social workers and court personnel about important developments affecting foster children.

(c) Most school districts and extracurricular organizations require proof of age before enrolling a child in their programs. Moreover, caregivers are required to obtain a medical appointment for their foster children within the first month of receiving the children into their homes. It would therefore be in both the children's and the caregivers' best interests to be provided with any available medical information, medications and instructions for use, and identifying information about the children upon receiving the children into their homes.

(d) Caregivers should have certain basic information in order to provide for the needs of children placed in their care, including all of the following:

(1) The name, mailing address, telephone number, facsimile number, and email address of the child's social worker and the social worker's supervisor.

(2) The name, mailing address, telephone number, facsimile number, and email address of the child's attorney and court-appointed special advocate (CASA), if any.

(3) The name, address, and department number of the juvenile court in which the child's juvenile court case is pending.

(4) The case number assigned to the child's juvenile court case.

(5) A copy of the child's birth certificate, passport, or other identifying documentation of age as may be required for enrollment in school and extracurricular activities.

(6) The child's State Department of Social Services identification number.

(7) The child's Medi–Cal identification number or group health insurance plan number.

(8) Medications or treatments in effect for the child at the time of placement, and instructions for their use.

(9) A plan outlining the child's needs and services, including information on family and sibling visitation.

(10) A copy of the health and education summary as required under Section 16010, with the name and current contact information of the person or persons currently holding the right to make educational decisions for the child.

(e) Caregivers should have knowledge of all of the following:

(1) Their right to receive notice of all review and permanency hearings concerning the child during the placement.

(2) Their right to attend those hearings or submit information they deem relevant to the court in writing.

(3) The "Caregiver Information Form" (Judicial Council Form JV–290), which allows the caregiver to provide information directly to the court.

(4) Information about and referrals to any existing services, including transportation, translation, training, forms, and other available services.

(5) The caregiver's obligation to cooperate with any reunification, concurrent, or permanent planning for the child.

(6) Any known siblings or half-siblings of the child, whether the child has, expects, or desires to have contact or visitation with any or all siblings, and how and when caregivers facilitate the contact or visitation.

(7) The importance of the caregiver's role in education, educational protections specific to foster youth under state and federal law, and the rights and obligations of caregivers to access and maintain educational and health information, including the requirements under Sections 49069.3, 49076, and 56055 of the Education Code and Section 16010 of this code.

(f) Courts should know, at the earliest possible date, the interest of the caretaker in providing legal permanency for the child. *(Added by Stats.2003, c. 812 (S.B.591), § 5. Amended by Stats.2016, c. 619 (A.B.2767), § 1, eff. Jan. 1, 2017; Stats.2017, c. 829 (S.B.233), § 10, eff. Jan. 1, 2018.)*

Research References

Treatises and Practice Aids

Witkin, California Summary 10th Parent and Child § 4, Public Welfare Services.

§ 16010.5. Medication, information, and documentation to be provided to foster parents and other caregivers

(a) When initially placing a child into foster care or kinship care, and within 48 hours of any subsequent placement of that child, the placing agency shall provide to the child's caretaker both of the following:

(1) Prescribed medications for the child that are in the possession of the placing agency, with instructions for the use of the medication.

(2) Information regarding any treatments that are known to the placing agency and that are in effect for the child at the time of the placement.

(b) As soon as possible after placing a child into foster care or kinship care, and no later than 30 days after placing the child, the placing agency shall provide to the child's caregiver any available documentation or proof of the child's age that may be required for enrollment in school or activities that require proof of age.

(c) Within 30 days of receiving a copy of a child's birth certificate or passport, a placing agency shall provide a copy of that document to the child's caregiver.

(d) Nothing shall preclude the placing agency from providing the name, mailing address, telephone number, and facsimile number of the child's attorney and the child's court-appointed special advocate, if any, to the child or the child's caregiver upon their request. *(Added by Stats.2003, c. 812 (S.B.591), § 6.)*

Research References

Treatises and Practice Aids

Witkin, California Summary 10th Parent and Child § 4, Public Welfare Services.

§ 16010.6. Notification of decision to make or change placement of dependent; placement of child outside of United States; notification and investigation of proposed sibling separation; contact and caregiver information; information provided to child

(a) As soon as a placing agency makes a decision with respect to a placement or a change in placement of a dependent child, but not later than the close of the following business day, the placing agency shall notify the child's attorney and provide to the child's attorney information regarding the child's address, telephone number, and caregiver.

(b)(1) A placing agency shall not make a placement or a change in placement of a child outside the United States prior to a judicial finding that the placement is in the best interest of the child, except as required by federal law or treaty.

(2) The placing agency shall carry the burden of proof and show, by clear and convincing evidence, that placement outside the United States is in the best interest of the child.

(3) In determining the best interest of the child, the court shall consider, but not be limited to, the following factors:

(A) Placement with a relative.

(B) Placement of siblings in the same home.

(C) Amount and nature of any contact between the child and the potential guardian or caretaker.

(D) Physical and medical needs of the dependent child.

(E) Psychological and emotional needs of the dependent child.

(F) Social, cultural, and educational needs of the dependent child.

(G) Specific desires of any dependent child who is 12 years of age or older.

(4) If the court finds that a placement outside the United States is, by clear and convincing evidence, in the best interest of the child, the court may issue an order authorizing the placing agency to make a placement outside the United States. A child subject to this subdivision shall not leave the United States prior to the issuance of the order described in this paragraph.

(5) For purposes of this subdivision, "outside the United States" shall not include the lands of any federally recognized American Indian tribe or Alaskan Natives.

(6) This section shall not apply to the placement of a dependent child with a parent.

(c) Absent exigent circumstances, as soon as a placing agency becomes aware of the need for a change in placement of a dependent child or ward that will result in the separation of siblings currently placed together, the placing agency shall notify the child's attorney and the child's siblings' attorney of this proposed separation no less than 10 calendar days prior to the planned change of placement so that the attorneys may investigate the circumstances of the proposed separation. If the placing agency first becomes aware, by written notification from a foster family agency, group home, or other foster care provider, of the need for a change in placement for a dependent child or ward that will result in the separation of siblings currently placed together, and that the child or children shall be removed within seven days, then notice shall be provided to the attorneys by the end of the next business day after the receipt of notice from the provider. In an emergency, the placing agency shall provide notice as soon as possible, but no later than the close of the first business day following the change of placement. This notification shall be deemed sufficient notice for the purposes of subdivision (a).

(d) When the required notice is given prior to a change in placement, the notice shall include information regarding the child's address, telephone number, and caregiver or any one or more of these items of information to the extent that this information is known at the time that the placing agency provides notice to the child's attorney. When the required notice is given after the change in placement, notice shall include information regarding the child's address, telephone number, and caregiver.

(e) The Judicial Council shall adopt a rule of court directing the attorney for a child for whom a dependency petition has been filed, upon receipt from the agency responsible for placing the child of the name, address, and telephone number of the child's caregiver, to timely provide the attorney's contact information to the caregiver and, if the child is 10 years of age or older, to the child. This rule does not preclude an attorney from giving contact information to a child who is younger than 10 years of age. *(Added by Stats.2010, c. 560 (A.B.743), § 4. Amended by Stats.2012, c. 144 (A.B.2209), § 3; Stats.2014, c. 772 (S.B.1460), § 18, eff. Jan. 1, 2015.)*

Research References

Treatises and Practice Aids

Witkin, California Summary 10th Parent and Child § 573, Powers and Duties Of Counsel.

Witkin, California Summary 10th Parent and Child § 639, Foster Care.

Witkin, California Summary 10th Parent and Child § 896, General Requirements.

Witkin, California Summary 10th Parent and Child § 693C, (New) Nonemergency Removal from Prospective Adoptive Parent.

§ 16010.8. Legislative intent regarding duration of foster care or group care; provision of updates to Legislature

It is the intent of the Legislature that no child or youth in foster care reside in group care for longer than one year. The State Department of Social Services shall provide updates to the Legislature, commencing no later than January 1, 2014, regarding the outcomes of assessments of children and youth who have been in group homes for longer than one year and the corresponding outcomes of transitions, or plans to transition, them into family settings. *(Added by Stats.2013, c. 21 (A.B.74), § 41, eff. June 27, 2013.)*

§ 16011. Pilot Internet-based health and education passport system for Los Angeles County

(a) Subject to the conditions prescribed by this section, Los Angeles County may pursue the development and evaluation of a pilot Internet-based health and education passport system. The system shall be known as the Passport System. The Passport System shall collect and maintain health and education records for foster children under the supervision of the county social services or probation department, as required by Section 16010. The Passport System shall initially be conducted as a limited pilot project in a subset of Los Angeles County, and upon successful evaluation, may be expanded statewide.

(1) Los Angeles County shall be responsible for the planning, development, and implementation of the Passport System. Los Angeles County is responsible for the development of the advance planning document (APD) as prescribed by federal regulations, requesting funding consistent with the child welfare services program. The APD shall include, but not be limited to, the design of an interface between the web-based Passport System and the Child Welfare Services/Case Management System (CWS/CMS) so that information entered into the Passport System shall automatically and permanently reside in the CWS/CMS. In addition, the APD shall include the scope of the pilot project, the evaluation plan pursuant to subdivisions (b) and (d), and the county shall address a plan for compliance with pertinent provisions in state and federal law requiring that privacy of confidential information be maintained.

(2) The department shall review and, upon approval by the appropriate state agencies, shall transmit the APD to the federal Department of Health and Human Services. The department shall facilitate assistance as appropriate to gain federal approval of the APD. Implementation of the pilot system shall be contingent upon federal approval of the APD and of the request for federal funding consistent with the child welfare services program. It shall also be contingent upon assurance by the United States Secretary of Health and Human Services that the federal funding for the CWS/CMS shall not be adversely impacted by the development and implementation of the Passport System. If the department is unable to gain federal approval of the pilot project by January 1, 2004, authorization for the pilot project established by this section shall cease.

(3) The Passport System shall provide real-time access to health, mental health, and educational information by health and mental health care providers, educators, licensed or approved foster care givers, and local agency staff in order to improve the accuracy and reliability of information necessary to ensure receipt of appropriate services for children in foster care, to improve health and educational outcomes, and to reduce and eliminate the risk of inadequate treatment by service providers, multiple immunizations, other severe health and education problems, and death.

(4) The Passport System shall meet all the operational and administrative needs of local participating agencies; be scalable and flexible to interface with and integrate data from multiple Los Angeles County and other county departments and state agencies that provide services to children, using data matching algorithms that provide a high level of confidence and reliability; maximize the use and availability of information in a secured and reliable environment; allow relevant county staff, health, mental health, education providers, and licensed or approved foster care givers to update or view appropriate data through a web-enabled application via

the Internet; contain fire walls and safeguards to ensure that only authorized persons inquire and update only those cases which they have been authorized to access; and to ensure the integrity and confidentiality of the system.

(b) Prior to commencement of the pilot project, Los Angeles County, in consultation with the department, shall develop a pilot evaluation plan subject to approval by the department and the United States Secretary of Health and Human Services. The plan shall include, but is not limited to, identification of measurable objectives, and benefits that the pilot project is expected to achieve, the methodology, and plan criteria for evaluating the pilot project.

(c) The pilot plan shall include a strategy to incentivize health, mental health, and educational providers servicing foster children to utilize and update the Internet-based system.

(d) Implementation of the interface between the Internet-based Passport System and the CWS/CMS shall be contingent upon approval of federal reimbursement consistent with the child welfare services program. Funding shall be subject to the sharing ratios that apply to the administration of child welfare services programs. Any funds appropriated for this purpose not expended in the 2001–02 fiscal year shall be available for the purposes of this section as expenditure in subsequent years. After one year of operation of the pilot project, Los Angeles County shall complete a pilot evaluation as described in the pilot evaluation plan. The results of the evaluation shall be provided to the chairpersons of the fiscal and policy committees of each house of the Legislature, the Chairperson of the Joint Legislative Budget Committee, and the Department of Finance. *(Added by Stats.2001, c. 125 (A.B.427), § 8. Amended by Stats.2002, c. 1022 (A.B.444), § 52, eff. Sept. 28, 2002.)*

§ 16013. State policy with respect to persons engaged in providing care and services to foster children; fair and equal access; discrimination or harassment

(a) It is the policy of this state that all persons engaged in providing care and services to foster children, including, but not limited to, foster parents, adoptive parents, relative caregivers, and other caregivers contracting with a county welfare department, shall have fair and equal access to all available programs, services, benefits, and licensing processes, and shall not be subjected to discrimination or harassment on the basis of their clients' or their own actual or perceived race, ethnic group identification, ancestry, national origin, color, religion, sex, sexual orientation, gender identity, mental or physical disability, or HIV status.

(b) Nothing in this section shall be interpreted to create or modify existing preferences for foster placements or to limit the local placement agency's ability to make placement decisions for a child based on the child's best interests. *(Added by Stats.2003, c. 331 (A.B.458), § 7. Amended by Stats.2008, c. 557 (A.B.3015), § 5.)*

§ 16014. Maximization of federal funding for foster youth services; responsibility for nonfederal share of payments

(a) It is the intent of the Legislature to maximize federal funding for foster youth services provided by local educational agencies.

(b) The State Department of Education and the State Department of Social Services shall collaborate with the County Welfare Directors Association, representatives from local educational agencies, and representatives of private, nonprofit foster care providers to establish roles and responsibilities, claiming requirements, and sharing of eligibility information eligible for funding under Part E (commencing with Section 470) of Title IV of the federal Social Security Act (42 U.S.C. Sec. 301 et seq.). These state agencies shall also assist counties and local educational agencies in drafting memorandums of understanding between agencies to access funding for case management activities associated with providing foster youth services for eligible children. That federal funding shall be an augmentation to the current program and shall not supplant existing state general funds allocated to this program.

(c) School districts shall be responsible for 100 percent of the nonfederal share of payments received under that act. *(Added by Stats.2004, c. 914 (A.B.1858), § 16.)*

CHAPTER 2. COUNTY ADOPTION AGENCIES

§ 16100. Authorized activities; contracts for services

(a) Any county may perform the home-finding and placement functions, to investigate, examine, and make reports upon petitions for adoption filed in the superior court, to act as a placement agency in the placement of children for adoption, to accept relinquishments for adoption, and to perform such other functions in connection with adoption as the department deems necessary, or to do any of them. Nothing in this section shall be construed to authorize a county adoption agency, as provided in subdivision (d), to provide intercountry adoption services.

(b) Notwithstanding any other law, a county adoption agency performing the functions specified in subdivision (a) may contract for services described in subdivision (a) from any licensed private adoption agency that the private adoption agency is licensed to provide pursuant to Chapter 3 (commencing with Section 1500) of Division 2 of the Health and Safety Code. A licensed county adoption agency may also contract for services described in subdivision (a) from any out-of-state licensed public or private adoption agency that is licensed pursuant to the laws of that state. Any services contracted for shall substantially meet the standards and criteria established in California adoption regulations as determined by the licensed county adoption agency. These services shall be contracted for in order to facilitate adoptive placement of a specified category of children for whom the licensed county adoption agency has determined it cannot provide adequate services.

(c) Counties that elect not to provide the adoption services specified in subdivision (a) may contract with the department or another county adoption agency to provide those services. *(Added by Stats.1965, c. 1784, p. 4078, § 5. Amended by*

Stats.1972, c. 1148, p. 2241, § 14, operative July 1, 1973; Stats.1973, c. 1203, p. 2593, § 8; Stats.1977, c. 1252, p. 4686, § 878, operative July 1, 1978; Stats.1984, c. 1116, § 9, eff. Sept. 13, 1984; Stats.1992, c. 163 (A.B.2641), § 155, operative Jan. 1, 1994; Stats.1996, c. 1083 (A.B.1524), § 7; Stats.1998, c. 1056 (A.B.2773), § 25; Stats.2012, c. 35 (S.B.1013), § 103, eff. June 27, 2012.)

Law Revision Commission Comments

1992 Amendment

Section 16100 is amended to substitute references to the Family Code provisions that replaced the former Civil Code provisions. [22 Cal.L.Rev.Comm.Reports 1 (1992)].

Research References

Treatises and Practice Aids

Witkin, California Summary 10th Parent and Child § 88, County Adoption Agencies.

§ 16101. Cost of administration

(a) Prior to the 2011–12 fiscal year, the cost of administering the adoption programs undertaken by a county under license issued pursuant to Section 16100 of this code shall be borne by the state in the amount found necessary by the department for proper and efficient administration. The state shall reimburse the county for all such necessary administrative costs, after deducting therefrom the amount of fees collected by the county agency pursuant to Section 8716 of the Family Code.

(b) Beginning in the 2011–12 fiscal year, and each fiscal year thereafter, funding and expenditures for programs and activities under the section for the purposes of administering the adoption programs shall be in accordance with the requirements provided in Sections 30025 and 30026.5 of the Government Code. *(Added by Stats.1965, c. 1784, p. 4078, § 5. Amended by Stats.1968, c. 879, p. 1669, § 2; Stats.1990, c. 1363 (A.B.3532), § 17, operative July 1, 1991; Stats.1992, c. 163 (A.B.2641), § 156, operative Jan. 1, 1994; Stats.2012, c. 35 (S.B.1013), § 104, eff. June 27, 2012.)*

Law Revision Commission Comments

1992 Amendment

Section 16101 is amended to substitute a reference to the Family Code provision that replaced former Civil Code Section 222.72. [22 Cal.L.Rev.Comm.Reports 1 (1992)].

§ 16105. Application of federal grant amounts to defer cost of administration or care

If any grants-in-aid are made by the federal government for the cost of administering an adoption program, or for the cost of care of children relinquished for adoption, the amount of the federal grant shall be applied to defer the cost of administration or of care. *(Added by Stats.1965, c. 1784, p. 4079, § 5. Amended by Stats.2012, c. 35 (S.B.1013), § 105, eff. June 27, 2012.)*

§ 16106. Reimbursement of counties; adjustments

The state shall reimburse each county for the cost of care of any child placed under the custody of a county department pursuant to Section 8805 or 8918 of the Family Code. County claims for reimbursement of expenses incurred pursuant to Section 8805 or 8918 of the Family Code shall be filed with the department at the time and in the manner specified by the department, and the claims shall be subject to audit by the department. Whenever a claim covering a prior fiscal year is found to have been in error, adjustment may be made on a current claim without the necessity of applying adjustment to the appropriation for the prior fiscal year. *(Added by Stats.1965, c. 1784, § 5. Amended by Stats.1990, c. 1363 (A.B.3532), § 18, operative July 1, 1991; Stats.1992, c. 163 (A.B.2641), § 157, operative Jan. 1, 1994.)*

Law Revision Commission Comments

1992 Amendment

Section 16106 is amended to substitute references to the Family Code provisions that replaced the former Civil Code provisions. [22 Cal.L.Rev.Comm.Reports 1 (1992)].

CHAPTER 2.1. AID FOR ADOPTION OF CHILDREN

§ 16115. Designation

Aid under this chapter shall be known as the Adoption Assistance Program. *(Added by Stats.1968, c. 1322, p. 2498, § 1, operative Jan. 1, 1969. Amended by Stats.1982, c. 977, p. 3519, § 18, eff. Sept. 13, 1982, operative Oct. 1, 1982.)*

Research References

Treatises and Practice Aids

Witkin, California Summary 10th Parent and Child § 86, Programs to Facilitate Adoption.

§ 16115.5. Legislative intent

It is the intent of the Legislature in enacting this chapter to benefit children residing in foster homes by providing the stability and security of permanent homes, and in so doing, achieve a reduction in foster home care. It is not the intent of this chapter to increase expenditures but to provide for payments to adoptive parents to enable them to meet the needs of children who meet the criteria established in Sections 16116, 16120, and 16121. *(Added by Stats.1976, c. 504, p. 1253, § 21, eff. Aug. 20, 1976. Amended by Stats.1978, c. 380, § 184; Stats.1982, c. 977, p. 3519, § 19, eff. Sept. 13, 1982, operative Oct. 1, 1982; Stats.1986, c. 767, § 3; Stats. 1986, c. 1517, § 1, eff. Sept. 30, 1986; Stats.1993, c. 1087 (A.B.930), § 1, eff. Oct. 11, 1993.)*

Research References

Treatises and Practice Aids

Witkin, California Summary 10th Parent and Child § 86, Programs to Facilitate Adoption.

§ 16118. Establishment and administration of program; records; certification that child meets eligibility criteria; financial assistance

(a) The department shall establish and administer the program to be carried out by the department or the county pursuant to this chapter. The department shall adopt any regulations necessary to carry out the provisions of this chapter.

(b) The department shall keep the records necessary to evaluate the program's effectiveness in encouraging and promoting the adoption of children eligible for the Adoption Assistance Program.

(c) The department or the county responsible for providing financial aid in the amount determined in Section 16120 shall have responsibility for certifying that the child meets the eligibility criteria and for determining the amount of financial assistance needed by the child and the adopting family.

(d) The department shall actively seek and make maximum use of federal funds that may be available for the purposes of this chapter. In accordance with federal law, any savings realized from the change in federal funding for adoption assistance resulting from the enactment of the federal Fostering Connections to Success and Increasing Adoptions Act of 2008 (Public Law 110–351) [1] shall be spent for the provision of foster care and adoption services, and the counties shall annually report to the department how these savings are spent, including any expenditures for postadoption services. Not less than 30 percent of these savings shall be spent on postadoption services, postguardianship services, and services to support and sustain positive permanent outcomes for children who otherwise might enter into foster care. Of that 30–percent amount, at least two-thirds shall be spent on postadoption and postguardianship services. The process for submitting this information shall be developed by the department, in consultation with counties. All gifts or grants received from private sources for the purpose of this chapter shall be used to offset public costs incurred under the program established by this chapter.

(e) For purposes of this chapter, the county responsible for determining the child's Adoption Assistance Program eligibility status and for providing financial aid in the amount determined in Sections 16120 and 16120.1 shall be the county that, at the time of the adoptive placement, would otherwise be responsible for making a payment pursuant to Section 11450 under the CalWORKs program or Section 11461 under the Aid to Families with Dependent Children–Foster Care program if the child were not adopted. When the child has been voluntarily relinquished for adoption prior to a determination of eligibility for this payment, the responsible county shall be the county in which the relinquishing parent resides. The responsible county for all other eligible children shall be the county where the child is physically residing prior to placement with the adoptive family. The responsible county shall certify eligibility on a form prescribed by the department.

(f) Beginning in the 2011–12 fiscal year, and for each fiscal year thereafter, funding and expenditures for programs and activities under this section shall be in accordance with the requirements provided in Sections 30025 and 30026.5 of the Government Code. *(Added by Stats.1968, c. 1322, p. 2498, § 1, operative Jan. 1, 1969. Amended by Stats.1969, c. 261, p. 613, § 2; Stats.1971, c. 123, p. 167, § 3; Stats.1971, c. 1724, p. 3670, § 3, eff. Dec. 14, 1971; Stats.1982, c. 977, p. 3519, § 22, eff. Sept. 13, 1982, operative Oct. 1, 1982; Stats.1986, c. 767, § 5; Stats.1986, c. 1517, § 3, eff. Sept. 30, 1986; Stats.1992, c. 722 (S.B.485), § 130, eff. Sept. 15, 1992, operative Oct. 1, 1992; Stats.1993, c. 1087 (A.B.930), § 3, eff. Oct. 11, 1993; Stats. 1999, c. 83 (S.B.966), § 207; Stats.1999, c. 547 (A.B.390), § 1; Stats.2009, c. 222 (A.B.154), § 1; Stats.2012, c. 35 (S.B.1013), § 106, eff. June 27, 2012; Stats.2015, c. 425 (S.B.794), § 24, eff. Jan. 1, 2016.)*

[1] For public law sections classified to the U.S.C.A., see USCA–Tables.

Research References

Treatises and Practice Aids

Witkin, California Summary 10th Parent and Child § 86, Programs to Facilitate Adoption.

§ 16119. Information; financial aid to adoptive family

(a) At the time application for adoption of a child who is potentially eligible for Adoption Assistance Program benefits is made, and at the time immediately prior to the finalization of the adoption decree, the department, county adoption agency, or the licensed adoption agency, whichever is appropriate, shall provide the prospective adoptive family with information, in writing, on the availability of Adoption Assistance Program benefits, with an explanation of the difference between these benefits and foster care payments. The department, county adoption agency, or the licensed adoption agency shall also provide the prospective adoptive family with information, in writing, on the availability of reimbursement for the nonrecurring expenses incurred in the adoption of the Adoption Assistance Program eligible child. The department, county adoption agency, or licensed adoption agency shall also provide the prospective adoptive family with information on the availability of mental health services through the Medi–Cal program or other programs, including information, in writing, regarding the importance of working with mental health providers that have specialized adoption or permanency clinical training and experience if the family needs clinical support, and a description of the desirable clinical expertise the family should look for when choosing an adoption- or permanency-competent mental health professional. The department, county adoption agency, or licensed adoption agency shall also provide information regarding the federal adoption tax credit for any individual who is adopting or considering adopting a child in foster care, in accordance with Section 403 of the federal Fostering Connections to Success and Increasing Adoptions Act of 2008 (Public Law 110–351).[1]

(b) The department, county adoption agency, or licensed adoption agency shall encourage families that elect not to sign an adoption assistance agreement to sign a deferred adoption assistance agreement.

(c) The department or the county, whichever is responsible for determining the child's eligibility for the Adoption Assistance Program, shall assess the needs of the child and the circumstances of the family.

(d)(1) The amount of an adoption assistance cash benefit, if any, shall be a negotiated amount based upon the needs of the child and the circumstances of the family. There shall be no means test used to determine an adoptive family's eligibility for the Adoption Assistance Program, or the amount of adoption assistance payments. In those instances where an otherwise eligible child does not require a cash benefit, Medi–Cal eligibility may be established for the child, as needed.

(2) For purposes of paragraph (1), "circumstances of the family" includes the family's ability to incorporate the child into the household in relation to the lifestyle, standard of living, and future plans and to the overall capacity to meet the immediate and future plans and needs, including education, of the child.

(e) The department, county adoption agency, or licensed adoption agency shall inform the prospective adoptive family regarding the county responsible for providing financial aid to the adoptive family in an amount determined pursuant to Sections 16120 and 16120.1.

(f) The department, county adoption agency, or licensed adoption agency shall inform the prospective adoptive family that the adoptive parents will continue to receive benefits in the agreed upon amount unless one of the following occurs:

(1) The department or county adoption agency determines that the adoptive parents are no longer legally responsible for the support of the child.

(2) The department or county adoption agency determines that the child is no longer receiving support from the adoptive family.

(3) The adoption assistance payment exceeds the amount that the child would have been eligible for in a licensed foster home, or a resource family at the basic rate, inclusive of any level of care rate determination.

(4) The adoptive parents demonstrate a need for an increased payment.

(5) The adoptive parents voluntarily reduce or terminate payments.

(6) The adopted child has an extraordinary need that was not anticipated at the time the amount of the adoption assistance was originally negotiated.

(g) The department, county adoption agency, or licensed adoption agency shall inform the prospective adoptive family of their potential eligibility for a federal tax credit under Section 23 of the Internal Revenue Code of 1986 (26 U.S.C. Sec. 23) and a state tax credit under Section 17052.25 of the Revenue and Taxation Code. *(Added by Stats.1968, c. 1322, p. 2498, § 1, operative Jan. 1, 1969. Amended by Stats.1971, c. 123, p. 167, § 4; Stats.1971, c. 1724, p. 3670, § 4, eff. Dec. 14, 1971; Stats.1986, c. 767, § 6; Stats.1987, c. 978, § 1; Stats. 1989, c. 1376, § 1; Stats.1992, c. 722 (S.B.485), § 131, eff. Sept. 15, 1992, operative Oct. 1, 1992; Stats.1993, c. 1087 (A.B.930), § 4, eff. Oct. 11, 1993; Stats.1999, c. 547 (A.B.390), § 2; Stats.1999, c. 905 (A.B.1225), § 1, eff. Oct. 10, 1999; Stats.1999, c. 905 (A.B.1225), § 2, eff. Oct. 10, 1999, operative Jan. 1, 2000; Stats.2009, c. 222 (A.B.154), § 2; Stats.2009, c. 339 (S.B.597), § 7.5; Stats.2012, c. 35 (S.B.1013), § 107, eff. June 27, 2012; Stats.2017, c. 714 (A.B.1006), § 2, eff. Jan. 1, 2018; Stats.2017, c. 732 (A.B.404), § 95.5, eff. Jan. 1, 2018.)*

[1] For public law sections classified to the U.S.C.A., see USCA–Tables.

Research References

Forms

West's California Judicial Council Forms ADOPT-200, Adoption Request.

Treatises and Practice Aids

Witkin, California Summary 10th Parent and Child § 86, Programs to Facilitate Adoption.

§ 16120. Adoption Assistance Program benefits; eligibility

A child is eligible for Adoption Assistance Program benefits if all of the conditions specified in subdivisions (a) to (*l*), inclusive, are met or if the conditions specified in subdivision (m) are met.

(a) It has been determined that the child cannot or should not be returned to the home of his or her parents as evidenced by a petition for termination of parental rights, a court order terminating parental rights, or a signed relinquishment, or, in the case of a tribal customary adoption, if the court has given full faith and credit to a tribal customary adoption order as provided for pursuant to paragraph (2) of subdivision (e) of Section 366.26, or, in the case of a nonminor dependent the court has dismissed dependency or transitional jurisdiction subsequent to the approval of the nonminor dependent, adoption petition pursuant to subdivision (f) of Section 366.31.

(b) The child has at least one of the following characteristics that are barriers to his or her adoption:

(1) Adoptive placement without financial assistance is unlikely because of membership in a sibling group that should remain intact or by virtue of race, ethnicity, color, language, age of three years or older, or parental background of a medical or behavioral nature that can be determined to adversely affect the development of the child.

(2) Adoptive placement without financial assistance is unlikely because the child has a mental, physical, emotional, or medical disability that has been certified by a licensed professional competent to make an assessment and operating within the scope of his or her profession. This paragraph shall also apply to children with a developmental disability, as defined in subdivision (a) of Section 4512, including those determined to require out-of-home nonmedical care, as described in Section 11464.

(c) The need for an adoption subsidy is evidenced by an unsuccessful search for an adoptive home to take the child without financial assistance, as documented in the case file of the prospective adoptive child. The requirement for this search shall be waived when it would be against the best interest of the child because of the existence of significant emotional ties with prospective adoptive parents while in the care of these persons as a foster child.

(d) The child satisfies any of the following criteria:

(1) He or she is under 18 years of age.

(2) He or she is under 21 years of age and has a mental or physical handicap that warrants the continuation of assistance.

(3) Effective January 1, 2012, he or she is under 19 years of age, effective January 1, 2013, he or she is under 20 years of age, and effective January 1, 2014, he or she is under 21 years of age and as described in Section 10103.5, and has attained 16 years of age before the adoption assistance agreement became effective, and one or more of the conditions specified in paragraphs (1) to (5), inclusive, of subdivision (b) of Section 11403 applies.

(e) The adoptive family is responsible for the child pursuant to the terms of an adoptive placement agreement or a final decree of adoption and has signed an adoption assistance agreement.

(f) The adoptive family is legally responsible for the support of the child and the child is receiving support from the adoptive parent.

(g) The department or the county responsible for determining the child's Adoption Assistance Program eligibility status and for providing financial aid, and the prospective adoptive parent, prior to or at the time the adoption decree is issued by the court, have signed an adoption assistance agreement that stipulates the need for, and the amount of, Adoption Assistance Program benefits.

(h) The prospective adoptive parent or any adult living in the prospective adoptive home has completed the criminal background check requirements pursuant to Section 671(a)(20)(A) and (C) of Title 42 of the United States Code.

(i) To be eligible for state funding, the child is the subject of an agency adoption, as defined in Section 8506 of the Family Code, and was any of the following:

(1) Under the supervision of a county welfare department as the subject of a legal guardianship or juvenile court dependency.

(2) Relinquished for adoption to a licensed California private or public adoption agency, or another public agency operating a Title IV–E program on behalf of the state, and would have otherwise been at risk of dependency as certified by the responsible public child welfare agency.

(3) Committed to the care of the department pursuant to Section 8805 or 8918 of the Family Code.

(4) The child is an Indian child and the subject of an order of adoption based on tribal customary adoption of an Indian child, as described in Section 366.24. Notwithstanding Section 8600.5 of the Family Code, for purposes of this subdivision a tribal customary adoption shall be considered an agency adoption.

(j) To be eligible for federal funding, in the case of a child who is not an applicable child for the federal fiscal year as defined in subdivision (n), the child satisfies any of the following criteria:

(1) Prior to the finalization of an agency adoption, as defined in Section 8506 of the Family Code, or an independent adoption, as defined in Section 8524 of the Family Code, is filed, the child has met the requirements to receive federal supplemental security income benefits pursuant to Subchapter 16 (commencing with Section 1381) of Chapter 7 of Title 42 of the United States Code, as determined and documented by the federal Social Security Administration.

(2) The child was removed from the home of a specified relative and the child would have been AFDC eligible in the home of removal according to Section 606(a) or 607 of Title 42 of the United States Code, as those sections were in effect on July 16, 1996, in the month of the voluntary placement agreement or in the month court proceedings are initiated to remove the child, resulting in a judicial determination that continuation in the home would be contrary to the child's welfare. The child must have been living with the specified relative from whom he or she was removed within six months of the month the voluntary placement agreement was signed or the petition to remove was filed.

(3) The child was voluntarily relinquished to a licensed public or private adoption agency, or another public agency operating a Title IV–E program on behalf of the state, and there is a petition to the court to remove the child from the home within six months of the time the child lived with a specified relative and a subsequent judicial determination that remaining in the home would be contrary to the child's welfare.

(4) Title IV–E foster care maintenance was paid on behalf of the child's minor parent and covered the cost of the minor parent's child while the child was in the foster family home or child care institution with the minor parent.

(5) The child is an Indian child and the subject of an order of adoption based on tribal customary adoption of an Indian child, as described in Section 366.24.

(k) To be eligible for federal funding, in the case of a child who is an applicable child for the federal fiscal year, as defined in subdivision (n), the child meets any of the following criteria:

(1) At the time of initiation of adoptive proceedings was in the care of a public or licensed private child placement agency or Indian tribal organization pursuant to either of the following:

(A) An involuntary removal of the child from the home in accordance with a judicial determination to the effect that continuation in the home would be contrary to the welfare of the child.

(B) A voluntary placement agreement or a voluntary relinquishment.

(2) He or she meets all medical or disability requirements of Title XVI with respect to eligibility for supplemental security income benefits.

(3) He or she was residing in a foster family home or a child care institution with the child's minor parent, and the

child's minor parent was in the foster family home or child care institution pursuant to either of the following:

(A) An involuntary removal of the child from the home in accordance with a judicial determination to the effect that continuation in the home would be contrary to the welfare of the child.

(B) A voluntary placement agreement or voluntary relinquishment.

(4) The child is an Indian child and the subject of an order of adoption based on tribal customary adoption of an Indian child, as described in Section 366.24.

(5) The nonminor dependent, as described in subdivision (v) of Section 11400, is the subject of an adoption pursuant to subdivision (f) of Section 366.31.

(*l*) The child is a citizen of the United States or a qualified alien as defined in Section 1641 of Title 8 of the United States Code. If the child is a qualified alien who entered the United States on or after August 22, 1996, and is placed with an unqualified alien, the child must meet the five-year residency requirement pursuant to Section 673(a)(2)(B) of Title 42 of the United States Code, unless the child is a member of one of the excepted groups pursuant to Section 1612(b) of Title 8 of the United States Code.

(m) A child or nonminor shall be eligible for Adoption Assistance Program benefits if the following conditions are met:

(1) The child or nonminor received Adoption Assistance Program benefits with respect to a prior adoption and the child or nonminor is again available for adoption because the prior adoption was dissolved and the parental rights of the adoptive parents were terminated or because the child's or nonminor's adoptive parents died and the child or nonminor meets the special needs criteria described in subdivisions (a) to (c), inclusive. When a nonminor is receiving Adoption Assistance Program benefits after 18 years of age and the nonminor's adoptive parents die, the juvenile court may resume dependency jurisdiction over the nonminor pursuant to Section 388.1.

(2) To receive federal funding, the citizenship requirements in subdivision (*l*).

(n)(1) Except as provided in this subdivision, "applicable child" means a child for whom an adoption assistance agreement is entered into under this section during any federal fiscal year described in this subdivision if the child attained the applicable age for that federal fiscal year before the end of that federal fiscal year.

(A) For federal fiscal year 2010, the applicable age is 16 years.

(B) For federal fiscal year 2011, the applicable age is 14 years.

(C) For federal fiscal year 2012, the applicable age is 12 years.

(D) For federal fiscal year 2013, the applicable age is 10 years.

(E) For federal fiscal year 2014, the applicable age is eight years.

(F) For federal fiscal year 2015, the applicable age is six years.

(G) For federal fiscal year 2016, the applicable age is four years.

(H) For federal fiscal year 2017, the applicable age is two years.

(I) For federal fiscal year 2018 and thereafter, any age.

(2) Beginning with the 2010 federal fiscal year, the term "applicable child" shall include a child of any age on the date on which an adoption assistance agreement is entered into on behalf of the child under this section if the child meets both of the following criteria:

(A) He or she has been in foster care under the responsibility of the state for at least 60 consecutive months.

(B) He or she meets the requirements of subdivision (k).

(3) Beginning with the 2010 federal fiscal year, an applicable child shall include a child of any age on the date that an adoption assistance agreement is entered into on behalf of the child under this section, without regard to whether the child is described in paragraph (2), if the child meets all of the following criteria:

(A) He or she is a sibling of a child who is an applicable child for the federal fiscal year, under subdivision (n) or paragraph (2).

(B) He or she is to be placed in the same adoption placement as an "applicable child" for the federal fiscal year who is their sibling.

(C) He or she meets the requirements of subdivision (k). *(Added by Stats.2009–2010, 4th Ex. Sess., c. 4 (A.B.4), § 35, eff. July 28, 2009. Amended by Stats.2009, c. 287 (A.B.1325), § 19, operative July 1, 2010; Stats.2010, c. 559 (A.B.12), § 58; Stats.2011, c. 459 (A.B.212), § 39, eff. Oct. 4, 2011; Stats.2012, c. 35 (S.B.1013), § 108, eff. June 27, 2012; Stats.2012, c. 846 (A.B.1712), § 48; Stats.2013, c. 487 (A.B.787), § 8; Stats. 2015, c. 303 (A.B.731), § 628, eff. Jan. 1, 2016.)*

Research References

Treatises and Practice Aids

Witkin, California Summary 10th Parent and Child § 86, Programs to Facilitate Adoption.

§ 16120.05. Adoption assistance agreement; contents

The adoption assistance agreement shall, at a minimum, specify the amount and duration of assistance, and that the amount is subject to any applicable increases pursuant to the cost-of-living adjustments established by statute. The date for reassessment of the child's needs shall be set at the time of the initial negotiation of the adoption assistance agreement, and shall, thereafter be set at each subsequent reassessment. The interval between any reassessments may not exceed two years.

The adoption assistance agreement shall also specify the responsibility of the adopting family for reporting changes in circumstances that might negatively affect their ability to provide for the identified needs of the child. *(Added by Stats.1993, c. 1087 (A.B.930), § 7, eff. Oct. 11, 1993. Amended by Stats.1999, c. 547 (A.B.390), § 3; Stats.2011, c. 32 (A.B.106), § 66, eff. June 29, 2011.)*

§ 16120.1. Reimbursement for reasonable nonrecurring expenses incurred as result of adoption of special needs child

Upon the authorization of the department or, where appropriate, the county responsible for determining the child's or nonminor dependent's Adoption Assistance Program eligibility status and for providing financial aid, the responsible county shall directly reimburse eligible individuals for reasonable nonrecurring expenses, as defined by the department, incurred as a result of the adoption of a special needs child, as defined in subdivisions (a) to (c), inclusive, and subdivision (*l*), of Section 16120. Reimbursements shall conform to the eligibility criteria and claiming procedures established by the department and shall be subject to the following conditions:

(a) The amount of the payment shall be determined through agreement between the adopting parent or parents and the department or the county responsible for determining the child's Adoption Assistance Program eligibility status and for providing financial aid. The agreement shall indicate the nature and the amount of the nonrecurring expenses to be paid. Payments shall be limited to an amount not to exceed four hundred dollars ($400) for each placement eligible for the Adoption Assistance Program.

(b) There shall be no income eligibility requirement for an adoptive parent or adoptive parents in determining whether payments for nonrecurring expenses shall be made.

(c) Reimbursement for nonrecurring expenses shall be limited to costs incurred by or on behalf of an adoptive parent or adoptive parents that are not reimbursed from other sources. No payments shall be made under this section if the federal program for reimbursement of nonrecurring expenses for the adoption of children eligible for the Adoption Assistance Program pursuant to Section 673 of Title 42 of the United States Code is terminated.

(d) Reimbursement for nonrecurring expenses shall be in addition to any adoption expenses paid pursuant to Section 16121 and shall not be included in the computation of maximum benefits for which the adoptive family is eligible pursuant to Section 16121. *(Added by Stats.1989, c. 1376, § 2. Amended by Stats.1991, c. 987 (S.B.700), § 1; Stats. 1992, c. 722 (S.B.485), § 133, eff. Sept. 15, 1992, operative Oct. 1, 1992; Stats.1993, c. 1087 (A.B.930), § 8, eff. Oct. 11, 1993; Stats.1993, c. 1089 (A.B.2129), § 33; Stats.2009, c. 339 (S.B.597), § 8; Stats.2012, c. 35 (S.B.1013), § 110, eff. June 27, 2012; Stats.2012, c. 846 (A.B.1712), § 49.)*

§ 16121. Adoption assistance; amount; out-of-home placements; maximum time; application; adjustment to adoption assistance payment rate structure

(a)(1) For initial adoption assistance agreements executed on October 1, 1992, to December 31, 2007, inclusive, the adoptive family shall be paid an amount of aid based on the child's needs otherwise covered in AFDC–FC payments and the circumstances of the adopting parents, but that shall not exceed the basic foster care maintenance payment rate structure in effect on December 31, 2007, that would have been paid based on the age-related state-approved foster family home rate, and any applicable specialized care increment, for a child placed in a licensed or approved family home.

(2) For initial adoption assistance agreements executed from January 1, 2008, to December 31, 2009, inclusive, the adoptive family shall be paid an amount of aid based on the child's needs otherwise covered in AFDC–FC payments and the circumstances of the adopting parents, but that shall not exceed the basic foster care maintenance payment rate structure in effect on December 31, 2009, that would have been paid based on the age-related state-approved foster family home rate, and any applicable specialized care increment, for a child placed in a licensed or approved family home.

(3) Notwithstanding any other provision of this section, for initial adoption assistance agreements executed on January 1, 2010, to June 30, 2011, inclusive, or the effective date specified in a final order, for which the time to appeal has passed, issued by a court of competent jurisdiction in California State Foster Parent Association, et al. v. William Lightbourne, et al., (U.S. Dist. Ct. No. C 07–08056 WHA), whichever is earlier, where the adoption is finalized on or before June 30, 2011, or the date specified in that order, whichever is earlier, the adoptive family shall be paid an amount of aid based on the child's needs otherwise covered in AFDC–FC payments and the circumstance of the adopting parents, but that amount shall not exceed the basic foster care maintenance payment rate structure in effect on June 30, 2011, or the date immediately prior to the date specified in the order described in this paragraph, whichever is earlier, and any applicable specialized care increment, that the child would have received while placed in a licensed or approved family home. Adoption assistance benefit payments shall not be increased based solely on age. This paragraph shall not preclude any reassessments of the child's needs, consistent with other provisions of this chapter.

(4) Notwithstanding any other provision of this section, for initial adoption assistance agreements executed on or after July 1, 2011, or the effective date specified in a final order, for which the time to appeal has passed, issued by a court of competent jurisdiction in California State Foster Parent Association, et al. v. William Lightbourne, et al. (U.S. Dist. Ct. No. C 07–05086 WHA), whichever is earlier, where the adoption is finalized on or after July 1, 2011, or the effective date of that order, whichever is earlier, and for initial adoption assistance agreements executed before July 1, 2011, or the date specified in that order, whichever is earlier, where the adoption is finalized on or after the earlier of July 1, 2011, or that specified date, the adoptive family shall be paid an amount of aid based on the child's needs otherwise covered in AFDC–FC payments and the circumstances of the adopting parents, but that amount shall not exceed the basic foster family home or resource family rate as set forth in * * * subdivision (g) of Section 11461, inclusive of any level of care determination, plus any applicable specialized care increment. These adoption assistance benefit payments shall not be increased based solely on age. This paragraph shall not preclude any reassessments of the child's needs, consistent with other provisions of this chapter.

(b) Payment may be made on behalf of an otherwise eligible child in a state-approved group home, short-term residential therapeutic program, or residential care treatment facility if the department or county responsible for determining payment has confirmed that the placement is necessary for the temporary resolution of mental or emotional problems related to a condition that existed prior to the adoptive placement. Out–of–home placements shall be in accordance with the applicable provisions of Chapter 3 (commencing with Section 1500) of Division 2 of the Health and Safety Code and other applicable statutes and regulations governing eligibility for AFDC–FC payments for placements in in-state and out-of-state facilities. The designation of the placement facility shall be made after consultation with the family by the department or county welfare agency responsible for determining the Adoption Assistance Program (AAP) eligibility and authorizing financial aid. Group home, short-term residential therapeutic program, or residential placement shall only be made as part of a plan for return of the child to the adoptive family, that shall actively participate in the plan. Adoption Assistance Program benefits may be authorized for payment for an eligible child's group home, short-term residential therapeutic program, or residential treatment facility placement if the placement is justified by a specific episode or condition and does not exceed an 18–month cumulative period of time. After an initial authorized group home, short-term residential therapeutic program, or residential treatment facility placement, subsequent authorizations for payment for a group home, short-term residential therapeutic program, or residential treatment facility placement may be based on an eligible child's subsequent specific episodes or conditions.

(c)(1) Payments on behalf of a child who is a recipient of AAP benefits who is also a consumer of regional center services shall be based on the rates established by the State Department of Social Services pursuant to Section 11464 and subject to the process described in paragraph (1) of subdivision (d) of Section 16119.

(2)(A) Except as provided for in subparagraph (B), this subdivision shall apply to adoption assistance agreements signed on or after July 1, 2007.

(B) Rates paid on behalf of regional center consumers who are recipients of AAP benefits and for whom an adoption assistance agreement was executed before July 1, 2007, shall remain in effect, and may only be changed in accordance with Section 16119.

(i) If the rates paid pursuant to adoption assistance agreements executed before July 1, 2007, are lower than the rates specified in paragraph (1) of subdivision (c) or paragraph (1) of subdivision (d) of Section 11464, respectively, those rates shall be increased, as appropriate and in accordance with Section 16119, to the amount set forth in paragraph (1) of subdivision (c) or paragraph (1) of subdivision (d) of Section 11464, effective July 1, 2007. Once set, the rates shall remain in effect and may only be changed in accordance with Section 16119.

(ii) For purposes of this clause, for a child who is a recipient of AAP benefits or for whom the execution of an AAP agreement is pending, and who has been deemed eligible for or has sought an eligibility determination for regional center services pursuant to subdivision (a) of Section 4512, and for whom a determination of eligibility for those regional center services has been made, and for whom, prior to July 1, 2007, a maximum rate determination has been requested and is pending, the rate shall be determined through an individualized assessment and pursuant to subparagraph (C) of paragraph (1) of subdivision (c) of Section 35333 of Title 22 of the California Code of Regulations as in effect on January 1, 2007, or the rate established in subdivision (b) of Section 11464, whichever is greater. Once the rate has been set, it shall remain in effect and may only be changed in accordance with Section 16119. Other than the circumstances described in this clause, regional centers shall not make maximum rate benefit determinations for the AAP.

(3) Regional centers shall separately purchase or secure the services contained in the child's IFSP or IPP, pursuant to Section 4684.

(4) Regulations adopted by the department pursuant to this subdivision shall be adopted as emergency regulations in accordance with Chapter 3.5 (commencing with Section 11340) of Part 1 of Division 3 of Title 2 of the Government Code, and for the purposes of that chapter, including Section 11349.6 of the Government Code, the adoption of these regulations is an emergency and shall be considered by the Office of Administrative Law as necessary for the immediate preservation of the public peace, health, safety, and general welfare. The regulations authorized by this paragraph shall remain in effect for no more than 180 days, by which time final regulations shall be adopted.

(d)(1) In the event that a family signs an adoption assistance agreement where a cash benefit is not awarded, the adopting family shall be otherwise eligible to receive Medi–Cal benefits for the child if it is determined that the benefits are needed pursuant to this chapter.

(2) Regional centers shall separately purchase or secure the services that are contained in the child's Individualized Family Service Plan (IFSP) or Individual Program Plan (IPP) pursuant to Section 4684.

(e) Subdivisions (a), (b), and (d) shall apply only to adoption assistance agreements signed on or after October 1, 1992. An adoption assistance agreement executed prior to October 1, 1992, shall continue to be paid in accordance with the terms of that agreement, and shall not be eligible for any increase in the basic foster care maintenance rate structure that occurred after December 31, 2007.

(f) This section shall supersede the requirements of subparagraph (C) of paragraph (1) of Section 35333 of Title 22 of the California Code of Regulations.

(g) The adoption assistance payment rate structure identified in subdivisions (a) and (e) shall be adjusted by the percentage changes in the California Necessities Index, beginning with the 2011–12 fiscal year, and shall not require a reassessment. *(Added by Stats.1982, c. 977, p. 3520, § 28, eff. Sept. 13, 1982, operative Oct. 1, 1982. Amended by Stats.1987, c. 360, § 3; Stats.1988, c. 160, § 194; Stats.1992, c. 722 (S.B.485), § 135, eff. Sept. 15, 1992, operative Oct. 1, 1992; Stats.1993, c. 1087 (A.B.930), § 10, eff. Oct. 11, 1993; Stats.1995, c. 540 (A.B.1523), § 11; Stats.2007, c. 177 (S.B.84), § 36.5, eff. Aug. 24, 2007; Stats.2009–2010, 4th Ex.Sess., c. 4 (A.B.4), § 36, eff. July 28, 2009; Stats.2009, c. 339 (S.B.597), § 9; Stats.2011, c. 32 (A.B.106), § 67, eff. June 29, 2011; Stats.2017, c. 732 (A.B.404), § 96, eff. Jan. 1, 2018.)*

§ 16121.05. Adoption assistance and receipt of benefits; recovery of overpayments; regulations

(a) The department or county adoption agency may recover any overpayments of financial assistance under the Adoption Assistance Program, and shall develop regulations that establish the means to recoup them, including an appropriate notice of action and appeal rights, when the department determines either of the following applies:

(1) The adoptive parents are no longer legally responsible for the support of the child.

(2) The child is no longer receiving support from the adoptive family.

(3) The adoptive family has committed fraud in its application for, or reassessment of, the adoption assistance.

(b) Children on whose behalf an adoption assistance agreement had been executed prior to October 1, 1992, shall continue to receive adoption assistance in accordance with the terms of that agreement.

(c) Payment shall begin on or after the effective date of an adoption assistance agreement, or a deferred adoption assistance agreement, or a final decree of adoption, provided that the adoption assistance agreement has been signed by all required parties prior to or at the time the adoption decree is issued by the court. The amount and duration of assistance shall not be changed without the concurrence of the adoptive parents, unless any of the following has occurred:

(1) The child has attained 18 years of age, or 21 years of age where the child has a mental or physical disability that warrants the continuation of assistance.

(2) The adoptive parents are no longer legally responsible for the support of the child.

(3) The child is no longer receiving any support from adoptive parents. *(Added by Stats.1993, c. 1087 (A.B.930), § 11, eff. Oct. 11, 1993. Amended by Stats.1999, c. 547 (A.B.390), § 4; Stats.2004, c. 183 (A.B.3082), § 392; Stats. 2009, c. 339 (S.B.597), § 10; Stats.2012, c. 35 (S.B.1013), § 111, eff. June 27, 2012.)*

§ 16121.1. Residence of adoptive parents; effect on eligibility

Notwithstanding the provisions of Section 11105, the residence of the adoptive parents at the time of or subsequent to adoptive placement shall not terminate the eligibility of a child who is otherwise eligible for adoptive assistance payments. *(Added by Stats.1982, c. 977, p. 3521, § 28.5, eff. Sept. 13, 1982, operative Oct. 1, 1982.)*

§ 16121.2. Interstate agreements

The Director of Social Services and the Director of Health Services may enter into interstate agreements pursuant to Chapter 2.6 (commencing with Section 16170) that provide for medical and other necessary services for special needs children, establish procedures for interstate delivery of adoption assistance and related services and benefits, and provide for the adoption of related regulations. *(Added by Stats.1999, c. 887 (S.B.1270), § 8.)*

Research References

Treatises and Practice Aids

Witkin, California Summary 10th Parent and Child § 86, Programs to Facilitate Adoption.

§ 16122. Legislative intent of chapter; private adoption agencies; reimbursement

(a) It is the intent of the Legislature in enacting this chapter to provide children or nonminor dependents who would otherwise remain in long-term foster care with permanent adoptive homes. It is also the intent of this Legislature to encourage private adoption agencies to continue placing these children, and in so doing, to achieve a substantial savings to the state in foster care costs.

(b) From any funds appropriated for this purpose, the state shall compensate private adoption agencies licensed pursuant to Chapter 3 (commencing with Section 1500) of Division 2 of the Health and Safety Code for costs of placing for adoption children or nonminor dependents eligible for Adoption Assistance Program benefits pursuant to Section 16120.

These agencies shall be compensated for otherwise unreimbursed costs for the placement of these children in an amount not to exceed a total of three thousand five hundred dollars ($3,500) per child adopted. Half of the compensation shall be paid at the time the adoptive placement agreement is signed. The remainder shall be paid at the time the adoption petition is granted by the court. Requests for compensation shall conform to claims procedures established by the department. This section shall not be construed to authorize reimbursement to private agencies for intercountry adoption services.

(c) Effective July 1, 1999, the maximum amount of reimbursement pursuant to subdivision (b) shall be five thousand dollars ($5,000).

(d) Effective February 1, 2008, the maximum amount of reimbursement pursuant to subdivision (b) shall be ten thousand dollars ($10,000). This rate increase shall apply only to those cases for which the adoptive home study approval occurred on or after July 1, 2007. *(Added by Stats.1982, c. 977, p. 3521, § 30, eff. Sept. 13, 1982, operative Oct. 1, 1982. Amended by Stats.1984, c. 1116, § 10, eff. Sept. 13, 1984; Stats.1986, c. 767, § 8; Stats.1986, c. 1517, § 5, eff. Sept. 30, 1986; Stats.1988, c. 160, § 195; Stats.1996, c. 1083 (A.B.1524), § 8; Stats.1999, c. 905 (A.B.1225), § 3, eff. Oct. 10, 1999; Stats.2007, c. 177 (S.B.84), § 38, eff. Aug. 24, 2007; Stats.2012, c. 35 (S.B.1013), § 112, eff. June 27, 2012; Stats.2012, c. 846 (A.B.1712), § 50.)*

Research References

Treatises and Practice Aids

Witkin, California Summary 10th Parent and Child § 86, Programs to Facilitate Adoption.

§ 16123. Adoption assistance; children with mental and physical handicaps; availability of funds

The provisions of Section 16120, permitting the payment of adoption assistance until a child attains 18 or 21 years of age if the child has mental or physical handicaps, or effective January 1, 2012, up to 21 years of age, if the child or nonminor meets the criteria specified in paragraph (3) of subdivision (d) of Section 16120, shall be effective as long as federal funds are available under Title IV–E of the federal Social Security Act (Part E (commencing with Section 670) of Subchapter 4 of Chapter 7 of Title 42 of the United States Code), and the state continues to exercise its option to extend payments up to 21 years of age, pursuant to Section 473(a)(4) of the federal Social Security Act (42 U.S.C. Sec. 673(a) (4)). When those funds cease to be available, the maximum length for payment of the Adoption Assistance Program shall be five years except in instances in which there is a continuing need, related to a chronic health condition of the child which necessitated the initial financial assistance. On and after October 1, 1992, the parent may petition the department or the responsible county to continue financial assistance up to the age of majority. *(Added by Stats.1982, c. 977, p. 3521, § 31, eff. Sept. 13, 1982, operative Oct. 1, 1982. Amended by Stats.1992, c. 722 (S.B.485), § 136, eff. Sept. 15, 1992; Stats.2010, c. 559 (A.B.12), § 60; Stats.2012, c. 35 (S.B.1013), § 113, eff. June 27, 2012; Stats.2012, c. 846 (A.B.1712), § 51.)*

§ 16124. Project to provide preadoption and postadoption services; establishment criteria; funding; allocation of funds; federal matching funds; implementation; development of project requirements; analysis of effects and report to Legislature; public-private partnerships

(a)(1) Upon the appropriation of funds by the Legislature for the purposes set forth in this section, the State Department of Social Services shall establish a project in four counties and one state district office of the department to provide preadoption and postadoption services to ensure the successful adoption of children and youth who have been in foster care 18 months or more, are at least nine years of age, and are placed in an unrelated foster home or in a group home.

(2) The participating entities shall include the following:

(A) City and County of San Francisco.

(B) County of Los Angeles.

(C) Two additional counties and one state district office, based on criteria developed by the department in consultation with the County Welfare Directors Association, which shall demonstrate geographic diversity.

(3) A county that elects to apply for funding pursuant to this section shall submit an application to the department no later than a date determined by the department to ensure timely allocation of funds. The department shall review the applications received, and select the eligible counties in accordance with this section.

(b) Each entity identified pursuant to paragraph (2) of subdivision (a) shall receive funding to provide preadoption and postadoption services to the adoptive parents and the targeted population identified in paragraph (1) of subdivision (a).

(1) Preadoption and postadoption services for the child and each family may include, but shall not be limited to, all of the following:

(A) Individualized or other recruitment efforts.

(B) Postadoption services, including respite care.

(C) Behavioral health services.

(D) Peer support groups.

(E) Information and referral services.

(F) Other locally designed services, as appropriate.

(G) Relative search efforts.

(H) Training of adoptive parents, foster youth, or mentoring families.

(I) Mediation services.

(J) Facilitation of siblings in the same placement.

(K) Facilitation of postadoption contact.

(L) Engaging youth in permanency decisionmaking.

(M) Any service or support necessary to resolve any identified barrier to adoption.

(2) The services specified in paragraph (1) may be provided directly by the county, contracted for by the county, or provided through reimbursement to the family, as approved by the county.

(c) The amount of funding provided in the appropriation of funds provided by the annual Budget Act to each county participating in the project shall be allocated as follows:

(1) Seven hundred fifty thousand dollars ($750,000) to the City and County of San Francisco.

(2) One million two hundred fifty thousand dollars ($1,250,000) to the County of Los Angeles.

(3) A total of two million dollars ($2,000,000), to be awarded to the two additional counties and the district office selected pursuant to subparagraph (C) of paragraph (2) of subdivision (a), minus any funds subtracted by the department for the purpose of administering the project. The amount of funds provided to the department for administration of the project, including the costs of collecting and analyzing data pursuant to subdivision (h) and developing the information pursuant to subdivision (i), shall not exceed three hundred thousand dollars ($300,000).

(4) If the appropriated amount in the annual Budget Act differs from the total amount specified above, then the funds shall be distributed in the same proportion as the amounts listed in paragraphs (1) to (3), inclusive.

(d) Funds shall be allocated to the counties pursuant to subdivision (c) no later than January 1 of each year, and shall remain available for expenditure until June 30, 2010.

(e)(1) The department shall seek approval for any federal matching funds that may be available to supplement the project.

(2) The implementation of the project shall not be dependent upon the receipt of federal funding.

(3) Project funds shall supplement, and not supplant, existing federal, state, and local funds, and shall be used only in accordance with the terms and conditions of the project.

(4) No expenditure made for services specified in subdivision (b) may be made to the extent that it renders the family ineligible for federal adoption assistance.

(f) The project shall be implemented only upon the adoption of a resolution adopted by each county board of supervisors.

(g) The department shall work with the counties to develop the requirements for the project, including the number of families that may participate in the project, given the available resources, and guidelines for data collection, as required by subdivision (h).

(h)(1) The department shall work with the participating county and the state district office to analyze the effects of the project.

(2) Measures assessed by the state and counties shall include, but shall not be limited to, the following:

(A) The extent to which the adoptions of the targeted population identified in paragraph (1) of subdivision (a) increased as a result of the project.

(B) The number of families and children served by the project.

(C) The type and amount of preadoption and postadoption services that were provided to children and families under the project.

(i) The department shall provide information to the Legislature on the results of the project by May 31, 2011.

(j) Adoption programs in the project counties shall be encouraged to create public-private partnerships with private adoption agencies to maximize their success in improving permanent outcomes for older foster youth. *(Added by Stats.2006, c. 75 (A.B.1808), § 37.1, eff. July 12, 2006. Amended by Stats.2009, c. 427 (A.B.295), § 1; Stats.2010, c. 328 (S.B.1330), § 257.)*

§ 16125. Foster child whose adoption becomes final who is receiving Adoption Assistance Program assistance; providing mental health services; identification of barriers to receiving care

A foster child whose adoption has become final, who is receiving or is eligible to receive Adoption Assistance Program assistance, including Medi–Cal, and whose foster care court supervision has been terminated, shall be provided medically necessary specialty mental health services by the local mental health plan in the county of residence of his or her adoptive parents, pursuant to all of the following:

(a) The host county mental health plan shall be responsible for submitting the treatment authorization request (TAR) to the mental health plan in the county of origin.

(b) The requesting public or private service provider shall prepare the TAR.

(c) The county of origin shall retain responsibility for authorization and reauthorization of services utilizing an expedited TAR process.

(d)(1) The State Department of Social Services shall convene a stakeholder group to identify barriers to the provision of mental health services by mental health professionals with specialized clinical training in adoption or permanency issues to children who are receiving services pursuant to this section. The stakeholder group shall include, but is not limited to, all of the following persons:

(A) Adoptive parents.

(B) Former foster youth.

(C) Representatives from the mental health and child welfare fields, including associations representing county mental health departments and private organizations providing specialty mental health services.

(D) Representatives from mental health and social work graduate degree-granting postsecondary education institutions.

(E) Representatives from relevant state and local agencies.

(2) The stakeholder group shall, on or before January 31, 2016, make specific recommendations for voluntary measures available to state and local government agencies and private entities, as appropriate, to address those barriers. The department shall collect existing research and professional literature pertinent to the need for specialized clinical training in adoption and permanency issues, and shall distribute the information to the stakeholder group for consideration and use in making its recommendations. The stakeholder group shall coordinate with, and endeavor not to duplicate, existing local, state, or national initiatives.

(3) A recommendation made pursuant to paragraph (2) shall not be construed to be binding on any state or local government agency or private entity. *(Added by Stats.2007, c. 469 (S.B.785), § 3. Amended by Stats.2014, c. 766 (A.B. 1790), § 1, eff. Jan. 1, 2015.)*

CHAPTER 2.2. STATE ADOPTION SERVICES

§ 16130. Establishment of services

In any county which does not have a county adoption agency established pursuant to Section 16100, the department may establish services incident to the relinquishment of children for adoption. The services shall be provided in such manner as may be deemed advisable by the department. *(Added by Stats.1968, c. 879, p. 1669, § 6.)*

Research References

Treatises and Practice Aids

Witkin, California Summary 10th Parent and Child § 88, County Adoption Agencies.

§ 16131. Conformity of state statutes to federal legislation

It is the intent of the Legislature to conform state statutes to federal legislation, including the Preventing Sex Trafficking and Strengthening Families Act (Public Law 113–183) and the Adoption and Safe Families Act of 1997 (Public Law 105–89),[1] and to reinvest any incentive payments received through implementation of the federal act into the child welfare system in order to provide adoption services and other legal permanency options for children. *(Added by Stats.1998, c. 1056 (A.B.2773), § 27. Amended by Stats.2002, c. 1022 (A.B.444), § 53, eff. Sept. 28, 2002; Stats.2015, c. 425 (S.B.794), § 25, eff. Jan. 1, 2016.)*

[1] For public law sections classified to the U.S.C.A., see USCA–Tables.

§ 16131.5. Older children; funds; federal incentive payments

(a) The state shall reinvest adoption and guardianship incentive payments received through the implementation of the federal Fostering Connections to Success and Increasing Adoptions Act of 2008 (Public Law 110–351) [1] and the Preventing Sex Trafficking and Strengthening Families Act (Public Law 113–183) into the child welfare system, in order to provide legal permanency outcomes for older children, including, but not limited to, adoption, guardianship, and reunification of children whose reunification services were previously terminated.

(b) The incentive payments received pursuant to subdivision (a), upon appropriation by the Legislature in the annual Budget Act or another statute, shall be allocated by the State Department of Social Services to the counties, and the department for a county in which the department serves as an adoption agency, based on documented increases in legal permanency outcomes for older children achieved by each county, as determined by the department, in consultation with counties, for the purposes specified in this section.

(c) A county, or the department when it acts as the adoption agency for a county, shall use adoption and guardianship incentive payment funds to improve or sustain legal permanency outcomes for older children.

(d) Nothing in this section shall be construed to supplant funds currently being spent on programs to provide legal permanency outcomes. *(Added by Stats.2004, c. 810 (A.B. 2807), § 9. Amended by Stats.2009, c. 250 (A.B.665), § 1; Stats.2015, c. 425 (S.B.794), § 26, eff. Jan. 1, 2016.)*

[1] For public law sections classified to the U.S.C.A., see USCA–Tables.

§ 16132. Federal Fostering Connections to Success and Increasing Adoptions Act; conformity of state statutes; use of funds

It is the intent of the Legislature to conform state statutes to recently enacted federal legislation, the Fostering Connections to Success and Increasing Adoptions Act of 2008 (Public Law 110–351)[1] and to expend savings resulting from changes in eligibility for adoption assistance on services, including, but not limited to, postadoption assistance, that may be provided under Title IV–B and IV–E of the federal Social Security Act. *(Added by Stats.2009, c. 222 (A.B.154), § 3.)*

[1] For public law sections classified to the U.S.C.A., see USCA–Tables.

§ 16133. Former employees of the State Department of Social Services; employee benefits

On and after July 1, 2011, when a person has been an employee of the State Department of Social Services within the 12–month period prior to his or her employment by a county, the board of supervisors, to the extent feasible, may allow that person to retain, as a county employee, those employee benefits to which that person was entitled or had accumulated as an employee of the State Department of Social Services, or provide that employee with comparable benefits provided for other county employees whose services as county employees is equal to the state service of the former employee of the State Department of Social Services. These benefits include, but are not limited to, retirement benefits, seniority rights under civil service, accumulated vacation, and sick leave. *(Added by Stats.2012, c. 35 (S.B.1013), § 114, eff. June 27, 2012.)*

CHAPTER 2.3. ADOPTION OF ALCOHOL– AND DRUG–EXPOSED AND HIV POSITIVE CHILDREN

Section

§ 16135. Purpose of chapter

The purpose of this chapter is to establish a program for special training and services to facilitate the adoption of children who are HIV positive, or born to a substance-abusing mother. This program shall be available to any county that elects to participate pursuant to procedures established by the department. *(Added by Stats.1998, c. 1014 (A.B.2198), § 2. Amended by Stats.2012, c. 35 (S.B.1013), § 116, eff. June 27, 2012.)*

Research References

Treatises and Practice Aids

Witkin, California Summary 10th Parent and Child § 86, Programs to Facilitate Adoption.

§ 16135.1. Definitions

(a) "Eligible child" means any child who meets the requirements of paragraph (1) or (2), and paragraph (3).

(1) Any child who has a condition or symptoms resulting from, or are suspected as resulting from, alcohol or substance abuse by the mother.

(2) Any child who is HIV positive.

(3) Any child who meets the requirements of either paragraph (1) or (2) and who meets all of the following requirements:

(A) The child is a dependent child of the court.

(B) The child has an adoption case plan and resides with a preadoptive or adoptive caregiver, or the plan is to transition and move the child to a preadoptive or adoptive caregiver.

(b) "TIES for Adoption" means Training, Intervention, Education, and Services for Adoption, a training project developed and implemented by the Adoptions Division of the Los Angeles County Department of Children's Services, the

UCLA Center for Healthier Children, Families, and Communities, and the UCLA Psychology Department, a demonstration project funded by the Federal Adoption Opportunities Program from September 30, 1995, to December 31, 1997, inclusive.

(c) "HIV positive" means having a human immunodeficiency virus infection.

(d) "Specialized in-home health care" means, but is not limited to, those services identified by the child's primary physician as appropriately administered by a prospective adoptive parent who has been trained by mental health or health care professionals. *(Added by Stats.1998, c. 1014 (A.B.2198), § 2.)*

§ 16135.10. Training and supportive services for families

(a) In order to promote successful adoptions of substance and alcohol exposed court dependent children, participating counties shall maintain a program of specialized training and supportive services to families adopting court dependent children who are either HIV positive or assessed as being prenatally exposed to alcohol or a controlled substance.

(b) The program shall include respite services. Notwithstanding any other provision of law, respite services shall be funded with a 30 percent nonfederal county share consistent with the normal sharing ratio for child welfare services. This county share may be provided with county general funds, in-kind contributions, or other funds. The source of the county share shall meet all applicable state and federal requirements and provide counties with maximum flexibility.

(c) Notwithstanding subdivision (b), beginning in the 2011–12 fiscal year, and each fiscal year thereafter, funding and expenditures for programs and activities under this section shall be in accordance with the requirements provided in Sections 30025 and 30026.5 of the Government Code. *(Added by Stats.1998, c. 1014 (A.B.2198), § 2. Amended by Stats.2012, c. 35 (S.B.1013), § 117, eff. June 27, 2012.)*

§ 16135.13. Recruited adoptive parents; special training

(a) A participating county shall provide special training to recruited adoptive parents to care for eligible children. The training curriculum shall include, but is not limited to, all of the following:

(1) Orientation.

(2) Effect of alcohol and controlled substances on the fetus and children.

(3) Normal and abnormal infant and early childhood development.

(4) Special medical needs and disabilities.

(5) Recovery from addiction to alcohol and controlled substances.

(6) Self-care for the caregiver.

(7) HIV/AIDS in children.

(8) Issues in parenting and providing lifelong permanency and substance abuse prevention to, children with prenatal alcohol and other controlled substances exposure.

(9) Issues specific to caring for a child who tests HIV positive.

(b) Participating counties may provide the same special training to relative caretakers in the process of adopting program-eligible children. *(Added by Stats.1998, c. 1014 (A.B.2198), § 2.)*

§ 16135.14. Specialized prospective adoptive homes

(a) The county shall determine whether a child is eligible for services pursuant to this section.

(b) A participating county shall select a specialized prospective adoptive home for the child.

(c) If an eligible child's adoptive placement changes from one participating county to another participating county, the child shall remain eligible for services. *(Added by Stats.1998, c. 1014 (A.B.2198), § 2.)*

§ 16135.16. Implementation of TIES for Adoption program; effect

The requirements of this section may be met by the implementation of the TIES for Adoption program as defined in Subdivision (b) of Section 16135.1. *(Added by Stats.1998, c. 1014 (A.B.2198), § 2. Amended by Stats.2012, c. 35 (S.B.1013), § 118, eff. June 27, 2012.)*

§ 16135.17. Adoption services case plan; nonmedical support services

Participating counties shall prepare an adoption services case plan pursuant to regulations adopted by the department and arrange for nonmedical support services. Nonmedical support services shall include respite care for specially trained prospective adoptive parents, including relative caretakers, pursuant to regulations adopted by the department. Nonmedical support services may also include, but are not limited to, temperament and behavior management training, consultation regarding medical and psychological issues and services, and educational advocacy. *(Added by Stats.1998, c. 1014 (A.B.2198), § 2.)*

§ 16135.25. Duties of department

The department shall do all of the following:

(a) Develop necessary procedures and standardized programs for a specialized adoptive home training project.

(b) Assist counties in coordinating sources of funding and services available to eligible children in order to maximize the social services provided to these children and avoid duplication of program funding.

(c) Require that participating counties coordinate available services for this population and their adoptive families.

(d) Provide to a requesting county information necessary to establish a program. *(Added by Stats.1998, c. 1014 (A.B.2198), § 2.)*

§ 16135.30. Placement of children in prospective adoptive homes

(a) Notwithstanding any other provision of law, subdivisions (b) and (c) shall control the placement of a child pursuant to this chapter.

(b) A county may place children who are alcohol or controlled substance exposed or HIV positive in prospective adoptive homes pursuant to Chapter 3 (commencing with Section 1500) of Division 2 of the Health and Safety Code.

(c) If a county makes a placement pursuant to subdivision (b), a preadoptive parent trained by health care professionals may provide specialized in-home health care to that child who was placed in their home for the purpose of adoption. *(Added by Stats.1998, c. 1014 (A.B.2198), § 2.)*

CHAPTER 2.5. FOSTER CHILD OMBUDSMAN PROGRAM

§ 16160. Legislative findings, declarations and intent

The Legislature finds and declares that the people of California have benefited from the establishment of a long-term care ombudsperson pursuant to Section 9710 of the Welfare and Institutions Code and a child care ombudsperson program pursuant to Section 1596.872a of the Health and Safety Code. It is the intent of the Legislature to provide similar protections for foster children by establishing a foster care ombudsperson program within the State Department of Social Services. *(Added by Stats.1998, c. 311 (S.B.933), § 66, eff. Aug. 19, 1998.)*

Research References

Treatises and Practice Aids

Witkin, California Summary 10th Parent and Child § 11, Programs for Foster Children.

§ 16161. Establishment

The Office of the State Foster Care Ombudsperson shall be established as an autonomous entity within the department for the purpose of providing children who are placed in foster care, either voluntarily or pursuant to Section 300 and Sections 600 and following, with a means to resolve issues related to their care, placement, or services. *(Added by Stats.1998, c. 311 (S.B.933), § 66, eff. Aug. 19, 1998.)*

Research References

Treatises and Practice Aids

Witkin, California Summary 10th Parent and Child § 11, Programs for Foster Children.

§ 16162. Appointment

The director, in consultation with a committee of interested individuals, shall appoint an ombudsperson qualified by training and experience to perform the duties of the office for a term of four years. The director may reappoint the ombudsperson for consecutive terms. The director shall select the committee members, the majority of whom shall be representatives of children's advocacy organizations and current or former foster youth. *(Added by Stats.1998, c. 311 (S.B.933), § 66, eff. Aug. 19, 1998. Amended by Stats.2002, c. 1160 (A.B.2294), § 2.)*

§ 16163. Personnel; priority

The department shall hire the necessary personnel to perform the functions of the office. Priority shall be given to former foster youth in hiring decisions. *(Added by Stats.1998, c. 311 (S.B.933), § 66, eff. Aug. 19, 1998.)*

§ 16164. Functions; regional or local office; standardized information explaining rights

(a) The Office of the State Foster Care Ombudsperson shall do all of the following:

(1) Disseminate information on the rights of children and youth in foster care and the services provided by the office. The rights of children and youths in foster care are listed in Section 16001.9. The information shall include notification that conversations with the office may not be confidential.

(2) Investigate and attempt to resolve complaints made by or on behalf of children placed in foster care, related to their care, placement, or services.

(3) Decide, in its discretion, whether to investigate a complaint, or refer complaints to another agency for investigation.

(4) Upon rendering a decision to investigate a complaint from a complainant, notify the complainant of the intention to investigate. If the office declines to investigate a complaint or continue an investigation, the office shall notify the complainant of the reason for the action of the office.

(5) Update the complainant on the progress of the investigation and notify the complainant of the final outcome.

(6) Document the number, source, origin, location, and nature of complaints.

(7)(A) Compile and make available to the Legislature all data collected over the course of the year including, but not limited to, the number of contacts to the toll-free telephone number, the number of complaints made, including the type and source of those complaints, the number of investigations performed by the office, the trends and issues that arose in the course of investigating complaints, the number of referrals made, and the number of pending complaints.

(B) Present this compiled data, on an annual basis, at appropriate child welfare conferences, forums, and other events, as determined by the department, that may include presentations to, but are not limited to, representatives of the Legislature, the County Welfare Directors Association, child welfare organizations, children's advocacy groups, consumer and service provider organizations, and other interested parties.

(C) It is the intent of the Legislature that representatives of the organizations described in subparagraph (B) consider this data in the development of any recommendations offered toward improving the child welfare system.

(D) The compiled data shall be posted so that it is available to the public on the existing Web site of the State Foster Care Ombudsperson.

(8) Have access to any record of a state or local agency that is necessary to carry out his or her responsibilities, and may meet or communicate with any foster child in his or her placement or elsewhere.

(b) The office may establish, in consultation with a committee of interested individuals, regional or local foster care ombudsperson offices for the purposes of expediting investigations and resolving complaints, subject to appropriations in the annual Budget Act.

(c)(1) The office, in consultation with the California Welfare Directors Association, Chief Probation Officers of California, foster youth advocate and support groups, groups representing children, families, foster parents, children's facilities, and other interested parties, shall develop, no later than July 1, 2002, standardized information explaining the rights specified in Section 16001.9. The information shall be developed in an age-appropriate manner, and shall reflect any relevant licensing requirements with respect to foster care providers' responsibilities to adequately supervise children in care.

(2) The office, counties, foster care providers, and others may use the information developed in paragraph (1) in carrying out their responsibilities to inform foster children and youth of their rights pursuant to Section 1530.91 of the Health and Safety Code, Sections 27 and 16501.1, and this section. *(Added by Stats.1998, c. 311 (S.B.933), § 66, eff. Aug. 19, 1998. Amended by Stats.1999, c. 147 (A.B.1111), § 37, eff. July 22, 1999; Stats.2001, c. 683 (A.B.899), § 4; Stats.2002, c. 1160 (A.B.2294), § 3.)*

Research References

Treatises and Practice Aids

Witkin, California Summary 10th Parent and Child § 10, Rights Of Foster Children.

§ 16165. Complaints related to foster care; authority

In his or her efforts to resolve complaints related to foster care, the ombudsperson may do all of the following:

(a) Conduct whatever investigation he or she deems necessary.

(b) Attempt to resolve the complaint informally.

(c) Submit a written plan to the relevant state or county agency recommending a course of action to resolve the complaint. If the ombudsperson makes a written recommendation, the state or county agency shall submit a written response to the ombudsperson within 30 business days. *(Added by Stats.1998, c. 311 (S.B.933), § 66, eff. Aug. 19, 1998.)*

§ 16167. Toll-free number

(a) A toll-free number shall be established for the office.

(b) Social workers shall provide foster children with the toll-free number for the office and verbal or written information regarding the existence and purpose of the office. *(Added by Stats.1998, c. 311 (S.B.933), § 66, eff. Aug. 19, 1998.)*

CHAPTER 2.6. INTERSTATE ADOPTION ASSISTANCE AGREEMENTS

§ 16170. Legislative findings and declarations

The Legislature finds and declares all of the following:

(a) Finding adoptive families for children, for whom state assistance is desirable pursuant to Chapter 2.1 (commencing with Section 16115), and assuring the protection of the interests of the children affected during the entire assistance period, require special measures when the adoptive parents move to other states or are residents of another state.

(b) Provision of medical and other necessary services for children, with state assistance, encounters special difficulties when the provision of services takes place in other states. *(Added by Stats.1999, c. 887 (S.B.1270), § 9.)*

Research References

Treatises and Practice Aids

Witkin, California Summary 10th Parent and Child § 86, Programs to Facilitate Adoption.

§ 16171. Purpose

The purposes of this chapter are to:

(a) Authorize the State Department of Social Services and the State Department of Health Services to enter into interstate agreements with agencies of other states for the protection of children on behalf of whom adoption assistance is being provided by the State Department of Social Services.

(b) Provide procedures for interstate children's adoption assistance payments, including medical payments. *(Added by Stats.1999, c. 887 (S.B.1270), § 9.)*

§ 16172. Definitions

As used in this chapter, the following definitions apply, unless the context clearly indicates otherwise:

(a) "Adoption assistance state" means the state that is signatory to an adoption assistance agreement in a particular case.

(b) "Residence state" means the state where the child is living.

(c) "State" means a state of the United States, the District of Columbia, the Commonwealth of Puerto Rico, the Virgin Islands, Guam, the Commonwealth of the Northern Mariana Islands, or a territory or possession of or administered by the United States. *(Added by Stats.1999, c. 887 (S.B.1270), § 9.)*

§ 16173. Authorization

The State Department of Social Services and the State Department of Health Services are authorized to develop, participate in the development of, negotiate, or enter into one or more interstate compacts on behalf of this state with other states to implement one or more of the purposes set forth in this chapter. When entered into, and for so long as it shall remain in force, a compact shall have the force and effect of law. *(Added by Stats.1999, c. 887 (S.B.1270), § 9.)*

§ 16174. Required contents

A compact entered into pursuant to the authority conferred by this chapter shall contain all of the following:

(a) A provision making it available for joinder by all states.

(b) A provision for withdrawal from the compact upon written notice to the parties, with a period of one year between the date of the notice and the effective date of the withdrawal.

(c) A requirement that the protections afforded by the compact continue in force for the duration of the adoption assistance and be applicable to all children and their adoptive parents who on the effective date of the withdrawal are receiving adoption assistance from a party state other than the one in which they are resident and have their principal place of abode.

(d) A requirement that each instance of adoption assistance to which the compact applies be covered by an adoption assistance agreement in writing between the adoptive parents and the state child welfare agency of the state which undertakes to provide the adoption assistance, and further, that any such agreement be expressly for the benefit of the adopted child and enforceable by the adoptive parents, and the state agency providing the adoption assistance.

(e) Any other provision as may be appropriate to implement the proper administration of the compact. *(Added by Stats.1999, c. 887 (S.B.1270), § 9.)*

§ 16175. Additional contents

A compact entered into pursuant to the authority conferred by this chapter may contain provisions in addition to those required pursuant to Section 16174, as follows:

(a) Provisions establishing procedures and entitlement to medical and other necessary social services for the child in accordance with applicable laws, even though the child and the adoptive parents are in a state other than the one responsible for or providing the services or the funds to defray part or all of the costs thereof.

(b) Any other provision as may be appropriate or incidental to the proper administration of the compact. *(Added by Stats.1999, c. 887 (S.B.1270), § 9.)*

§ 16176. Benefits eligibility

(a)(1) Any child who is a resident of California and who is the subject of a state-only adoption assistance agreement with another state, shall be eligible to receive Medi–Cal benefits whether or not there is a cash benefit.

(2) Any child with special needs who is the subject of a state-only adoption assistance agreement with California shall continue to be eligible for Medi–Cal benefits if the child is placed out-of-state or with his or her adoptive family, moves out-of-state, and the receiving state does not provide Medicaid benefits to the child.

(b) The departments shall adopt regulations to implement the provisions of this chapter. *(Added by Stats.1999, c. 887 (S.B.1270), § 9.)*

§ 16177. Federal assistance

Consistent with federal law, the State Department of Social Services and the State Department of Health Services, in connection with the administration of this chapter and any compact pursuant thereto, shall include in any state plan made pursuant to the Adoption Assistance and Child Welfare of 1980 (Public Law 96–272), [1] Titles IV (e) and XIX of the Social Security Act, or any other applicable federal laws, the provision of adoption assistance and medical assistance for which the federal government pays some or all the cost. The departments shall apply for and administer all relevant federal aid in accordance with law. *(Added by Stats.1999, c. 887 (S.B.1270), § 9.)*

[1] 42 U.S.C.A. § 670 et seq.

UNITED STATES CODE

TITLE 1

GENERAL PROVISIONS

CHAPTER 1—RULES OF CONSTRUCTION

§ 7. Definition of "marriage" and "spouse"

In determining the meaning of any Act of Congress, or of any ruling, regulation, or interpretation of the various administrative bureaus and agencies of the United States, the word "marriage" means only a legal union between one man and one woman as husband and wife, and the word "spouse" refers only to a person of the opposite sex who is a husband or a wife. *(Added Pub.L. 104–199, § 3(a), Sept. 21, 1996, 110 Stat. 2419.)*

Validity

The United States Supreme Court has held section 3(a) of Pub.L. 104–199, which added this section, unconstitutional. U.S. v. Windsor, U.S.2013, 133 S.Ct. 2675, 186 L.Ed.2d 808.

Commentary

In *United States v. Windsor, 133 S.Ct. 2675 (2013)*, the United States Supreme Court held that this section violates the Fifth Amendment guarantees of personal liberty and equal protection insofar as it declines to recognize same-sex marriages lawfully entered under state law. Thus the section is entirely inoperative and the federal government must recognize same-sex marriages lawfully contracted under state law. The court's rationale in *Windsor* may in future cases extend, under the Fourteenth Amendment, equally to those states that decline to recognize same-sex marriages lawfully contracted elsewhere and, ultimately, to those states that decline to allow same-sex couples to marry.

In Matter of Fonberg, 736 F.3d 901 (Judicial Council of the 9th Cir. 2013), an administrative proceeding of the Judicial Council of the United States, a three-judge panel of the Ninth Circuit held that the Office of Personnel Management discriminated against an Oregon federal district court employee on the basis of sex and sexual orientation when it denied her request to enroll her Oregon registered same-sex domestic partner in the employer-sponsored family health plan, even though registered domestic partners were entitled, under Oregon law, to all the state law rights and benefits of marriage, and marriage was then unavailable in Oregon to same-sex couples. Effectively, the Ninth Circuit extended the holding and rationale of *Windsor* to same-sex domestic partners of federal employees who lived in states that authorized domestic partnerships or civil unions, but did not authorize same-sex marriage.

TITLE 5

GOVERNMENT ORGANIZATION AND EMPLOYEES

PART III—EMPLOYEES

SUBPART G—INSURANCE AND ANNUITIES

CHAPTER 83—RETIREMENT

SUBCHAPTER III—CIVIL SERVICE RETIREMENT

§ 8339. Computation of annuity

(a) Except as otherwise provided by this section, the annuity of an employee retiring under this subchapter is—

(1) 1½ percent of his average pay multiplied by so much of his total service as does not exceed 5 years; plus

(2) 1¾ percent of his average pay multiplied by so much of his total service as exceeds 5 years but does not exceed 10 years; plus

(3) 2 percent of his average pay multiplied by so much of his total service as exceeds 10 years.

However, when it results in a larger annuity, 1 percent of his average pay plus $25 is substituted for the percentage specified by paragraph (1), (2), or (3) of this subsection, or any combination thereof.

(b) The annuity of a Congressional employee, or former Congressional employee, retiring under this subchapter is computed under subsection (a) of this section, except, if he has had—

(1) at least 5 years' service as a Congressional employee or Member or any combination thereof; and

(2) deductions withheld from his pay or has made deposit covering his last 5 years of civilian service;

his annuity is computed, with respect to his service as a Congressional employee, his military service not exceeding 5 years, and any Member service, by multiplying 2½ percent of his average pay by the years of that service.

(c) The annuity of a Member, or former Member with title to Member annuity, retiring under this subchapter is computed under subsection (a) of this section, except, if he has had at least 5 years' service as a Member or Congressional employee or any combination thereof, his annuity is computed with respect to—

(1) his service as a Member and so much of his military service as is creditable for the purpose of this paragraph; and

(2) his Congressional employee service;

by multiplying 2½ percent of his average pay by the years of that service.

(d)(1) The annuity of an employee retiring under section 8335(b) or 8336(c) of this title is—

(A) 2½ percent of his average pay multiplied by so much of his total service as does not exceed 20 years; plus

(B) 2 percent of his average pay multiplied by so much of his total service as exceeds 20 years.

(2) The annuity of an employee retiring under this subchapter who was employed by the Panama Canal Company or Canal Zone Government on September 30, 1979, is computed with respect to the period of continuous Panama Canal service from that date, disregarding any break in service of not more than 3 days, by adding—

(A) 2½ percent of the employee's average pay multiplied by so much of that service as does not exceed 20 years; plus

(B) 2 percent of the employee's average pay multiplied by so much of that service as exceeds 20 years.

(3) The annuity of an employee retiring under this subchapter who is employed by the Panama Canal Commission at any time during the period beginning October 1, 1990, and ending December 31, 1999, is computed, with respect to any period of service with the Panama Canal Commission, by adding—

(A) 2½ percent of the employee's average pay multiplied by so much of that service as does not exceed 20 years; plus

(B) 2 percent of the employee's average pay multiplied by so much of that service as exceeds 20 years.

(4)(A) In the case of an employee who has service as a law enforcement officer or firefighter to which paragraph (2) of this subsection applies, the annuity of that employee is increased by $8 for each full month of that service which is performed in the Republic of Panama.

(B) In the case of an employee retiring under this subchapter who—

(i) was employed as a law enforcement officer or firefighter by the Panama Canal Company or Canal Zone Government at any time during the period beginning March 31, 1979, and ending September 30, 1979; and

(ii) does not meet the age and service requirements of section 8336(c) of this title;

the annuity of that employee is increased by $12 for each full month of that service which occurred before October 1, 1979.

(C) An annuity increase under this paragraph does not apply with respect to service performed after completion of 20 years of service (or any combination of service) as a law enforcement officer or firefighter.

(5) For the purpose of this subsection—

(A) "Panama Canal service" means—

(i) service as an employee of the Panama Canal Commission; or

(ii) service at a permanent duty station in the Canal Zone or Republic of Panama as an employee of an Executive agency conducting operations in the Canal Zone or Republic of Panama; and

(B) "Executive agency" includes the Smithsonian Institution.

(6) The annuity of an employee retiring under section 8336(j) of this title is computed under subsection (a) of this section, except that with respect to service on or after December 21, 1972, the employee's annuity is—

(A) 2½ percent of the employee's average pay multiplied by so much of the employee's service on or after that date as does not exceed 20 years; plus

(B) 2 percent of the employee's average pay multiplied by so much of the employee's service on or after that date as exceeds 20 years.

(7) The annuity of an employee who is a judge of the United States Court of Appeals for the Armed Forces, or a former judge of such court, retiring under this subchapter is computed under subsection (a) of this section, except, with respect to his service as a judge of such court, his service as a Member, his congressional employee service, and his military service (not exceeding 5 years) creditable under section 8332 of this title, his annuity is computed by multiplying 2½ percent of his average pay by the years of that service.

(e) The annuity of an employee retiring under section 8336(e) of this title is computed under subsection (a) of this section. That annuity may not be less than 50 percent of the average pay of the employee unless such employee has received, pursuant to section 8342 of this title, payment of the lump-sum credit attributable to deductions under section 8334(a) of this title during any period of employment as an air traffic controller and such employee has not deposited in the Fund the amount received, with interest, pursuant to section 8334(d)(1) of this title.

(f) The annuity computed under subsections (a) through (e), (n), (q), (r), and (s) may not exceed 80 percent of—

(1) the average pay of the employee; or

(2) the greatest of—

(A) the final basic pay of the Member;

(B) the average pay of the Member; or

(C) the final basic pay of the appointive position of a former Member who elects to have his annuity computed or recomputed under section 8344(d)(1) of this title.

(g) The annuity of an employee or Member retiring under section 8337 of this title is at least the smaller of—

(1) 40 percent of his average pay; or

(2) the sum obtained under subsections (a) through (c), (n), (q), (r), or (s) after increasing his service of the type last performed by the period elapsing between the date of separation and the date he becomes 60 years of age.

However, if an employee or Member retiring under section 8337 of this title is receiving retired pay or retainer pay for military service (except that specified in section 8332(c)(1) or (2) of this title) or pension or compensation from the Department of Veterans Affairs in lieu of such retired or retainer pay, the annuity of that employee or Member shall be computed under subsection (a), (b), (c), (n), (q), (r), or (s), as appropriate, excluding credit for military service from that computation. If the amount of the annuity so computed, plus the retired or retainer pay which is received, or which would be received but for the pension or compensation from the Department of Veterans Affairs in lieu of such retired or retainer pay, is less than the smaller of the annuity otherwise payable under paragraph (1) or (2) of this subsection, an amount equal to the difference shall be added to the annuity payable under subsection (a), (b), (c), (n), (q), (r), or (s), as appropriate.

(h) The annuity computed under subsections (a), (b), (d)(5), and (f) of this section for an employee retiring under section 8336(d), (h), (j), or (*o*) of this title is reduced by ⅙ of 1 percent for each full month the employee is under 55 years of age at the date of separation. The annuity computed under subsections (c) and (f) of this section for a Member retiring under the second or third sentence of section 8336(g) of this title or the third sentence of section 8338(b) of this title is reduced by 1/12 of 1 percent for each full month not in excess of 60 months, and ⅙ of 1 percent for each full month in excess of 60 months, the Member is under 60 years of age at the date of separation. The annuity computed under subsections (a), (d)(6), and (f) of this section for a judge of the United States Court of Appeals for the Armed Forces retiring under the second sentence of section 8336(k) of this title or the third sentence of section 8338(c) of this title is reduced by 1/12 of 1 percent for each full month not in excess of 60 months, and ⅙ of 1 percent for each full month in excess of 60 months, the judge is under 60 years of age at the date of separation.

(i) For the purposes of subsections (a)–(h), (n), (q), (r), or (s), the total service of any employee or Member shall not include any period of civilian service after July 31, 1920, for which retirement deductions or deposits have not been made under section 8334(a) of this title unless—

(1) the employee or Member makes a deposit for such period as provided in section 8334(c) or (d)(1) of this title; or

(2) no deposit is required for such service, as provided under section 8334(g) of this title or under any statute.

(j)(1) The annuity computed under subsections (a)–(i), (n), (q), (r), and (s) (or a portion of the annuity, if jointly designated for this purpose by the employee or Member and the spouse of the employee or Member under procedures prescribed by the Office of Personnel Management) for an employee or Member who is married at the time of retiring under this subchapter is reduced as provided in paragraph

(4) of this subsection in order to provide a survivor annuity for the spouse under section 8341(b) of this title, unless the employee or Member and the spouse jointly waive the spouse's right to a survivor annuity in a written election filed with the Office at the time that the employee or Member retires. Each such election shall be made in accordance with such requirements as the Office shall, by regulation, prescribe, and shall be irrevocable. The Office shall provide, by regulation, that an employee or Member may waive the survivor annuity without the spouse's consent if the employee or Member establishes to the satisfaction of the Office—

(A) that the spouse's whereabouts cannot be determined, or

(B) that, due to exceptional circumstances, requiring the employee or Member to seek the spouse's consent would otherwise be inappropriate.

(2) If an employee or Member has a former spouse who is entitled to a survivor annuity as provided in section 8341(h) of this title, the annuity of the employee or Member computed under subsections (a)–(i), (n), (q), (r), and (s) (or any designated portion of the annuity, in the event that the former spouse is entitled to less than 55 percent of the employee or Member's annuity) is reduced as provided in paragraph (4) of this subsection.

(3) An employee or Member who has a former spouse may elect, under procedures prescribed by the Office, to have the annuity computed under subsections (a)–(i), (n), (q), (r), and (s) or a portion thereof reduced as provided in paragraph (4) of this subsection in order to provide a survivor annuity for such former spouse under section 8341(h) of this title, unless all rights to survivor benefits for such former spouse under this subchapter based on marriage to such employee or Member were waived under paragraph (1) of this subsection. An election under this paragraph shall be made at the time of retirement or, if later, within 2 years after the date on which the marriage of the former spouse to the employee or Member is dissolved, subject to a deposit in the Fund by the retired employee or Member of an amount determined by the Office, as nearly as may be administratively feasible, to reflect the amount by which the annuity of such employee or Member would have been reduced if the election had been continuously in effect since the date the annuity commenced, plus interest. For the purposes of the preceding sentence, the annual rate of interest for each year during which the annuity would have been reduced if the election had been in effect since the date the annuity commenced shall be 6 percent. The Office shall, by regulation, provide for payment of the deposit required under this paragraph by a reduction in the annuity of the employee or Member. The reduction shall, to the extent practicable, be designed so that the present value of the future reduction is actuarially equivalent to the deposit required under this paragraph, except that the total reductions in the annuity of an employee or Member to pay deposits required by the provisions of this paragraph, paragraph (5), or subsection (k)(2) shall not exceed 25 percent of the annuity computed under subsections (a) through (i), (n), (q), and (r), including adjustments under section 8340. The reduction, which shall be effective on the same date as the election under this paragraph, shall be permanent and unaffected by any future termination of the entitlement of the former spouse. Such reduction shall be independent of and in addition to the reduction required under the first sentence of this paragraph. An election under this paragraph—

(A) shall not be effective to the extent that it—

(i) conflicts with—

(I) any court order or decree referred to in subsection (h)(1) of section 8341 of this title, which was issued before the date of such election; or

(II) any agreement referred to in such subsection which was entered into before such date; or

(ii) would cause the total of survivor annuities payable under subsections (b), (d), (f), and (h) of section 8341 of this title based on the service of the employee or Member to exceed 55 percent of the annuity to which the employee or Member is entitled under subsections (a)–(i), (n), (q), (r), and (s); and

(B) shall not be effective, in the case of an employee or Member who is then married, unless it is made with the spouse's written consent.

The Office shall provide by regulation that subparagraph (B) of this paragraph may be waived for either of the reasons set forth in the last sentence of paragraph (1) of this subsection. In the case of a retired employee or Member whose annuity is being reduced in order to provide a survivor annuity for a former spouse, an election to provide or increase a survivor annuity for any other former spouse (and to continue an appropriate reduction) may be made within the same period that, and subject to the same conditions under which, an election could be made under paragraph (5)(B) of this subsection for a current spouse (subject to the provisions of this paragraph relating to consent of a current spouse, if the retired employee or Member is then married). The opportunity to make an election under the preceding sentence is in addition to any opportunity otherwise afforded under this paragraph.

(4) In order to provide a survivor annuity or combination of survivor annuities under subsections (b), (d), (f), and (h) of section 8341 of this title, the annuity of an employee or Member (or any designated portion or portions thereof) is reduced by 2½ percent of the first $3,600 thereof plus 10 percent of so much thereof as exceeds $3,600.

(5)(A) Any reduction in an annuity for the purpose of providing a survivor annuity for the current spouse of a retired employee or Member shall be terminated for each full month—

(i) after the death of the spouse, or

(ii) after the dissolution of the spouse's marriage to the employee or Member, except that an appropriate reduction shall be made thereafter if the spouse is entitled, as a former spouse, to a survivor annuity under section 8341(h) of this title.

(B) Any reduction in an annuity for the purpose of providing a survivor annuity for a former spouse of a retired employee or Member shall be terminated for each full month after the former spouse remarries before reaching age 55 or dies. This reduction shall be replaced by an appropriate reduction or reductions under paragraph (4) of this subsection if the retired employee or Member has (i) another former spouse who is entitled to a survivor annuity under section 8341(h) of this title, (ii) a current spouse to whom the employee or Member was married at the time of retirement and with respect to whom a survivor annuity was not jointly waived under paragraph (1) of this subsection, or (iii) a current spouse whom the employee or Member married after retirement and with respect to whom an election has been made under subparagraph (C) of this paragraph or subsection (k)(2) of this section.

(C)(i) Upon remarriage, a retired employee or Member who was married at the time of retirement (including an employee or Member whose annuity was not reduced to provide a survivor annuity for the employee or Member's spouse or former spouse as of the time of retirement) may irrevocably elect during such marriage, in a signed writing received by the Office within 2 years after such remarriage or, if later, within 2 years after the death or remarriage of any former spouse of such employee or Member who was entitled to a survivor annuity under section 8341(h) of this title (or of the last such surviving former spouse, if there was more than one), a reduction in the employee or Member's annuity under paragraph (4) of this subsection for the purpose of providing an annuity for such employee or Member's spouse in the event such spouse survives the employee or Member.

(ii) Such election and reduction shall be effective the first day of the second month after the election is received by the Office, but not less than 9 months after the date of the remarriage, and the retired employee or Member shall deposit in the Fund an amount determined by the Office of Personnel Management, as nearly as may be administratively feasible, to reflect the amount by which the annuity of such retired employee or Member would have been reduced if the election had been in effect since the date of retirement or, if later, the date the previous reduction in such retired employee or Member's annuity was terminated under subparagraph (A) or (B) of this paragraph, plus interest. For the purposes of the preceding sentence, the annual rate of interest for each year during which an annuity would have been reduced if the election had been in effect on and after the applicable date referred to in such sentence shall be 6 percent.

(iii) The Office shall, by regulation, provide for payment of the deposit required under clause (ii) by a reduction in the annuity of the employee or Member. The reduction shall, to the extent practicable, be designed so that the present value of the future reduction is actuarially equivalent to the deposit required under clause (ii), except that total reductions in the annuity of an employee or Member to pay deposits required by the provisions of this paragraph or paragraph (3) shall not exceed 25 percent of the annuity computed under subsections (a) through (i), (n), (q), and (r), including adjustments under section 8340. The reduction required by this clause, which shall be effective on the same date as the election under clause (i), shall be permanent and unaffected by any future termination of the marriage. Such reduction shall be independent of and in addition to the reduction required under clause (i).

(iv) Notwithstanding any other provision of this subparagraph, an election under this subparagraph may not be made for the purpose of providing an annuity in the case of a spouse by remarriage if such spouse was married to the employee or Member at the time of such employee or Member's retirement, and all rights to survivor benefits for such spouse under this subchapter based on marriage to such employee or Member were then waived under paragraph (1) of this subsection or a similar prior provision of law.

(v) An election to provide a survivor annuity to a person under this subparagraph—

(I) shall prospectively void any election made by the employee or Member under subsection (k)(1) of this section with respect to such person; or

(II) shall, if an election was made by the employee or Member under such subsection (k)(1) with respect to a different person, prospectively void such election if appropriate written application is made by such employee or Member at the time of making the election under this subparagraph.

(vi) The deposit provisions of clauses (ii) and (iii) of this subparagraph shall not apply if—

(I) the employee or Member makes an election under this subparagraph after having made an election under subsection (k)(1) of this section; and

(II) the election under such subsection (k)(1) becomes void under clause (v) of this subparagraph.

(k)(1) At the time of retiring under section 8336 or 8338 of this title, an employee or Member who is found to be in good health by the Office may elect a reduced annuity instead of an annuity computed under subsections (a)–(i), (n), (q), (r), and (s) and name in writing an individual having an insurable interest in the employee or Member to receive an annuity under section 8341(c) of this title after the death of the retired employee or Member. The annuity of the employee or Member making the election is reduced by 10 percent, and by 5 percent for each full 5 years the individual named is younger than the retiring employee or Member. However, the total reduction may not exceed 40 percent. An annuity which is reduced under this paragraph or any similar prior provision of law shall, effective the first day of the month following the death of the individual named under this paragraph, be recomputed and paid as if the annuity had not been so reduced. In the case of a married employee or Member, an election under this paragraph on behalf of the spouse may be made only if any right of such spouse to a survivor annuity based on the service of such employee or Member is waived in accordance with subsection (j)(1) of this section.

(2)(A) An employee or Member, who is unmarried at the time of retiring under a provision of law which permits election of a reduced annuity with a survivor annuity payable to such employee or Member's spouse and who later marries, may irrevocably elect, in a signed writing received in the Office within 2 years after such employee or Member marries or, if later, within 2 years after the death or remarriage of any former spouse of such employee or Member who was entitled to a survivor annuity under section 8341(h) of this title (or of the last such surviving former spouse, if there was more than one), a reduction in the retired employee or Member's current annuity as provided in subsection (j) of this section.

(B)(i) The election and reduction shall take effect on the first day of the first month beginning after the expiration of the 9-month period beginning on the date of marriage. Any such election to provide a survivor annuity for a person—

(I) shall prospectively void any election made by the employee or Member under paragraph (1) of this subsection with respect to such person; or

(II) shall, if an election was made by the employee or Member under such paragraph with respect to a different person, prospectively void such election if appropriate written application is made by such employee or Member at the time of making the election under this paragraph.

(ii) The retired employee or Member shall deposit in the Fund an amount determined by the Office of Personnel Management, as nearly as may be administratively feasible, to reflect the amount by which the retired employee or Member's annuity would have been reduced under subsection (j)(4) of this section since the commencing date of the annuity, if the employee or Member had been married at the time of retirement and had elected to provide a survivor annuity at that time, plus interest. For the purposes of the preceding sentence, the annual rate of interest for each year during which the annuity would have been reduced if the election had been in effect since the date of the annuity commenced shall be 6 percent.

(C) The Office shall, by regulation, provide for payment of the deposit required under subparagraph (B)(ii) by a reduction in the annuity of the employee or Member. The reduction shall, to the extent practicable, be designed so that the present value of the future reduction is actuarially equivalent to the deposit required under subparagraph (B)(ii), except that total reductions in the annuity of an employee or Member to pay deposits required by this subsection or subsection (j)(3) shall not exceed 25 percent of the annuity computed under subsections (a) through (i), (n), (q), and (r), including adjustments under section 8340. The reduction required by this subparagraph, which shall be effective on the same date as the election under subparagraph (A), shall be permanent and unaffected by any future termination of the marriage. Such reduction shall be independent of and in addition to the reduction required under subparagraph (A).

(D) Subparagraphs (B)(ii) and (C) of this paragraph shall not apply if—

(i) the employee or Member makes an election under this paragraph after having made an election under paragraph (1) of this subsection; and

(ii) the election under such paragraph (1) becomes void under subparagraph (B)(i) of this paragraph.

(l) The annuity computed under subsections (a)–(k), (n), (q), (r), and (s) for an employee who is a citizen of the United States is increased by $36 for each year of service in the employ of—

(1) the Alaska Engineering Commission, or The Alaska Railroad, in Alaska between March 12, 1914, and July 1, 1923; or

(2) the Isthmian Canal Commission, or the Panama Railroad Company, on the Isthmus of Panama between May 4, 1904, and April 1, 1914.

(m) In computing any annuity under subsections (a) through (e), (n), (q), (r), and (s), the total service of an employee who retires on an immediate annuity or dies leaving a survivor or survivors entitled to annuity includes, without regard to the limitations imposed by subsection (f) of this section, the days of unused sick leave to his credit under a formal leave system, except that these days will not be counted in determining average pay or annuity eligibility under this subchapter. For the purpose of this subsection, in the case of any such employee who is excepted from subchapter I of chapter 63 of this title under section 6301(2)(x)–(xiii) of this title, the days of unused sick leave to his credit include any unused sick leave standing to his credit when he was excepted from such subchapter.

(n) The annuity of an employee who is a Court of Federal Claims judge, bankruptcy judge, or United States magistrate judge is computed, with respect to service as a Court of Federal Claims judge, as a commissioner of the Court of Claims, as a referee in bankruptcy, as a bankruptcy judge, as a United States magistrate judge, and as a United States commissioner, and with respect to the military service of any such individual (not exceeding 5 years) creditable under section 8332 of this title, by multiplying 2½ percent of the individual's average pay by the years of that service.

***(o)*(1)(A)** An employee or Member—

(i) who, at the time of retirement, is married, and

(ii) who notifies the Office at such time (in accordance with subsection (j)) that a survivor annuity under section 8341(b) of this title is not desired,

may, during the 18–month period beginning on the date of the retirement of such employee or Member, elect to have a reduction under subsection (j) made in the annuity of the employee or Member (or in such portion thereof as the employee or Member may designate) in order to provide a survivor annuity for the spouse of such employee or Member.

(B) An employee or Member—

(i) who, at the time of retirement, is married, and

(ii) who at such time designates (in accordance with subsection (j)) that a limited portion of the annuity of such employee or Member is to be used as the base for a survivor annuity under section 8341(b) of this title,

may, during the 18–month period beginning on the date of the retirement of such employee or Member, elect to have a greater portion of the annuity of such employee or Member so used.

(2)(A) An election under subparagraph (A) or (B) of paragraph (1) of this subsection shall not be considered effective unless the amount specified in subparagraph (B) of this paragraph is deposited into the Fund before the expiration of the applicable 18–month period under paragraph (1).

(B) The amount to be deposited with respect to an election under this subsection is an amount equal to the sum of—

(i) the additional cost to the System which is associated with providing a survivor annuity under subsection (b)(2) of this section and results from such election taking into account (I) the difference (for the period between the date on which the annuity of the participant or former participant commences and the date of the election) between the amount paid to such participant or former participant under this subchapter and the amount which would have been paid if such election had been made at the time the participant or former participant applied for the annuity, and (II) the costs associated with providing for the later election; and

(ii) interest on the additional cost determined under clause (i) of this subparagraph computed using the interest rate specified or determined under section 8334(e) of this title for the calendar year in which the amount to be deposited is determined.

(3) An election by an employee or Member under this subsection voids prospectively any election previously made in the case of such employee or Member under subsection (j).

(4) An annuity which is reduced in connection with an election under this subsection shall be reduced by the same percentage reductions as were in effect at the time of the retirement of the employee or Member whose annuity is so reduced.

(5) Rights and obligations resulting from the election of a reduced annuity under this subsection shall be the same as the rights and obligations which would have resulted had the employee or Member involved elected such annuity at the time of retiring.

(6) The Office shall, on an annual basis, inform each employee or Member who is eligible to make an election under this subsection of the right to make such election and the procedures and deadlines applicable to such election.

(p)(1) In computing an annuity under this subchapter for an employee whose service includes service that was performed on a part-time basis—

(A) the average pay of the employee, to the extent that it includes pay for service performed in any position on a part-time basis, shall be determined by using the annual rate of basic pay that would be payable for full-time service in the position; and

(B) the benefit so computed shall then be multiplied by a fraction equal to the ratio which the employee's actual service, as determined by prorating an employee's total service to reflect the service that was performed on a part-time basis, bears to the total service that would be creditable for the employee if all of the service had been performed on a full-time basis.

(2) For the purpose of this subsection, employment on a part-time basis shall not be considered to include employment on a temporary or intermittent basis.

(3) In the administration of paragraph (1)—

(A) subparagraph (A) of such paragraph shall apply with respect to service performed before, on, or after April 7, 1986; and

(B) subparagraph (B) of such paragraph—

(i) shall apply with respect to that portion of any annuity which is attributable to service performed on or after April 7, 1986; and

(ii) shall not apply with respect to that portion of any annuity which is attributable to service performed before April 7, 1986.

(q) The annuity of a member of the Capitol Police, or former member of the Capitol Police, retiring under this subchapter is computed in accordance with subsection (b), except that, in the case of a member who retires under section 8335(c) or 8336(m), and who meets the requirements of subsection (b)(2), the annuity of such member is—

(1) 2½ percent of the member's average pay multiplied by so much of such member's total service as does not exceed 20 years; plus

(2) 2 percent of the member's average pay multiplied by so much of such member's total service as exceeds 20 years.

(r) The annuity of a member of the Supreme Court Police, or former member of the Supreme Court Police, retiring under this subchapter is computed in accordance with subsection (d).

(s) [1] The annuity of a Member who has served in a position in the executive branch for which the rate of basic pay was reduced for the duration of the service of the Member in that position to remove the impediment to the appointment of the Member imposed by article I, section 6, clause 2 of the Constitution, shall, subject to a deposit in the Fund as provided under section 8334(m), be computed as though the rate of basic pay which would otherwise have been in effect during that period of service had been in effect.

(s)(1) [1] For purposes of this subsection, the term "physicians comparability allowance" refers to an amount described in section 8331(3)(H).

(2) Except as otherwise provided in this subsection, no part of a physicians comparability allowance shall be treated as basic pay for purposes of any computation under this section unless, before the date of the separation on which entitlement to annuity is based, the separating individual has completed at least 15 years of service as a Government physician (whether performed before, on, or after the date of the enactment of this subsection).

(3) If the condition under paragraph (2) is met, then, any amounts received by the individual in the form of a physicians comparability allowance shall (for the purposes referred to in paragraph (2)) be treated as basic pay, but only to the extent that such amounts are attributable to service performed on or after the date of the enactment of this subsection, and only to the extent of the percentage allowable, which shall be determined as follows:

If the total amount of service performed, on or after the date of the enactment of this subsection, as a Government physician is:	Then, the percentage allowable is:
Less than 2 years	0
At least 2 but less than 4 years	25
At least 4 but less than 6 years	50
At least 6 but less than 8 years	75
At least 8 years	100.

(4) Notwithstanding any other provision of this subsection, 100 percent of all amounts received as a physicians comparability allowance shall, to the extent attributable to service performed on or after the date of the enactment of this subsection, be treated as basic pay (without regard to any of the preceding provisions of this subsection) for purposes of computing—

(A) an annuity under subsection (g); and

(B) a survivor annuity under section 8341, if based on the service of an individual who dies before separating from service.

(u) [2] The annuity of an employee retiring under this subchapter with service credited under section 8332(b)(17) shall be reduced by the amount necessary to ensure that the present value of the annuity payable to the employee is actuarially equivalent to the present value of the annuity that would be payable to the employee under this subchapter if it were computed—

(1) on the basis of service that does not include service credited under section 8332(b)(17); and

(2) assuming the employee separated from service on the actual date of the separation of the employee.

The amount of the reduction shall be computed under regulations prescribed by the Office of Personnel Management for the administration of this subsection. *(Pub.L. 89–554, Sept. 6, 1966, 80 Stat. 574; Pub.L. 90–83, § 1(78), Sept. 11, 1967, 81 Stat. 214; Pub.L. 90–206, Title II, § 224(b), Dec. 16, 1967, 81 Stat. 642; Pub.L. 90–486, § 5(c), Aug. 13, 1968, 82 Stat. 757; Pub.L. 91–93, Title II, § 203, Oct. 20, 1969, 83 Stat. 139; Pub.L. 91–658, § 2, Jan. 8, 1971, 84 Stat. 1961; Pub.L. 92–297, §§ 6, 7(3), May 16, 1972, 86 Stat. 144; Pub.L. 93–260, § 2(a), Apr. 9, 1974, 88 Stat. 76; Pub.L. 93–350, § 6, July 12, 1974, 88 Stat. 356; Pub.L. 93–474, § 1, Oct. 26, 1974, 88 Stat. 1438; Pub.L. 94–126, § 1(b), Nov. 12, 1975, 89 Stat. 679; Pub.L. 94–397, § 1(d), Sept. 3, 1976, 90 Stat. 1203; Pub.L. 95–256, § 5(d), Apr. 6, 1978, 92 Stat. 191; Pub.L. 95–317, §§ 1(a), (c), 2, July 10, 1978, 92 Stat. 382; Pub.L. 95–454, Title IV, § 412(b), Title IX, § 906(a)(2), (3), Oct. 13, 1978, 92 Stat. 1175, 1224; Pub.L. 95–519, § 3, Oct. 25, 1978, 92 Stat. 1819; Pub.L. 95–598, Title III, § 338(a), Nov. 6, 1978, 92 Stat. 2681; Pub.L. 96–54, § 2(a)(49), Aug. 14, 1979, 93 Stat. 384; Pub.L. 96–70, Title I, § 1242(a), Sept. 27, 1979, 93 Stat. 472; Pub.L. 96–135, § 1(b), (c), Dec. 5, 1979, 93 Stat. 1057; Pub.L. 96–391, § 1, Oct. 7, 1980, 94 Stat. 1557; Pub.L. 96–499, Title IV, § 404(a), Dec. 5, 1980, 94 Stat. 2606; Pub.L. 97–253, Title III, § 303(b), Sept. 8, 1982, 96 Stat. 794; Pub.L. 97–276, § 151(f), Oct. 2, 1982, 96 Stat. 1202; Pub.L. 98–94, Title XII, § 1256(e), Sept. 24, 1983, 97 Stat. 702; Pub.L. 98–249, § 3(a), Mar. 31, 1984, 98 Stat. 117; Pub.L. 98–271, § 3(a), Apr. 30, 1984, 98 Stat. 163; Pub.L. 98–299, § 3(a), May 25, 1984, 98 Stat. 214; Pub.L. 98–325, § 3(a), June 20, 1984, 98 Stat. 268; Pub.L. 98–353, Title I, §§ 112, 116(d), 121(f), July 10, 1984, 98 Stat. 343, 344, 346; Pub.L. 98–531, § 2(c), Oct. 19, 1984, 98 Stat. 2704; Pub.L. 98–615, § 2(3), Nov. 8, 1984, 98 Stat. 3195; Pub.L. 99–251, Title II, § 203(a) to (c), Title III, § 307(a), Feb. 27, 1986, 100 Stat. 23, 24, 28; Pub.L. 99–272, Title XV, § 15204(a)(1), Apr. 7, 1986, 100 Stat. 334; Pub.L. 100–53, § 2(d), June 18, 1987, 101 Stat. 368; Pub.L. 101–194, Title V, § 506(b)(8), Nov. 30, 1989, 103 Stat. 1759; Pub.L. 101–428, § 2(c)(1), (d)(2) to (6), Oct. 15, 1990, 104 Stat. 928, 929; Pub.L. 101–508, Title VII, § 7001(b)(2)(B), (C), Nov. 5, 1990, 104 Stat. 1388–329; Pub.L. 101–510, Div. C, Title XXXV, § 3506(b), Nov. 5, 1990, 104 Stat. 1847; Pub.L. 101–650, Title III, §§ 306(c)(4), 321, Dec. 1, 1990, 104 Stat. 5110, 5117; Pub.L. 102–54, § 13(b)(4), June 13, 1991, 105 Stat. 274; Pub.L. 102–198, § 7(b), Dec. 9, 1991, 105 Stat. 1624; Pub.L. 102–378, § 2(62), Oct. 2, 1992, 106 Stat. 1354; Pub.L. 102–572, Title IX, § 902(b)(2), Oct. 29, 1992, 106 Stat. 4516; Pub.L. 103–66, Title XI, § 11004(a)(1), (2), Aug. 10, 1993, 107 Stat. 410, 411; Pub.L. 103–337, Div. A, Title IX, § 924(d)(1)(A), Oct. 5, 1994, 108 Stat. 2832; Pub.L. 104–106, Div. A, Title XV, § 1505(b)(3), Feb. 10, 1996, 110 Stat. 514; Pub.L. 105–61, Title V, § 516(a)(3), Oct. 10, 1997, 111 Stat. 1306; Pub.L. 105–261, Div. A, Title XI, § 1109(c)(1), Oct. 17, 1998, 112 Stat. 2145; Pub.L. 106–58, Title VI, § 651(b), Sept. 29, 1999, 113 Stat. 480; Pub.L. 106–398, § 1 [Div. A, Title X, § 1087(f)(4), Title XI, § 1152(c)(1)], Oct. 30, 2000, 114 Stat. 1654, 1654A–293, 1654A–322; Pub.L. 106–553, § 1(a)(2) [Title III, § 308(b)(4), (h)(2) to (6)], Dec. 21, 2000, 114 Stat. 2762, 2762A–87, 2762A–88, 2762A–89; Pub.L. 106–554, § 1(a)(4) [Div. B, Title I, § 141(b)], Dec. 21, 2000, 114 Stat. 2763, 2763A–235; Pub.L. 106–571, § 3(b)(1), Dec. 28, 2000, 114 Stat. 3055; Pub.L. 107–107, Div. A, Title XI, § 1132(a)(3), Dec. 28, 2001, 115 Stat. 1243; Pub.L. 107–296, Title XIII, § 1321(a)(4)(B), Nov. 25, 2002, 116 Stat. 2297; Pub.L. 111–84, Div. A, Title XIX, § 1903(a), Oct. 28, 2009, 123 Stat. 2616.)*

[1] So in original. Two subsecs. (s) were enacted.

[2] So in original. No subsec. (t) was enacted.

Commentary

Applying subsection (j)(3) of this section and section 8341(h)(1), *Downing v. Office of Personnel Management, 619 F.3d 1374 (D.C. Cir. 2010)*, held that a former wife was not entitled to a former spouse survivor annuity under the Civil Service Retirement System when her former husband failed to re-elect former spouse survivor benefits within two years of their divorce and the divorce decree did not mention survivor benefits, even though the benefit her husband received after divorce continued to be reduced to reflect his pre-divorce election of a survivor benefit for his wife. This result would not occur with an ERISA-regulated private sector pension. See *Carmona v. Carmona, 544 F.3d 988 (9th Cir. 2008)*, discussed in Commentary to 29 USC §§ 1055 and 1056.

§ 8341. Survivor annuities

(a) For the purpose of this section—

(1) "widow" means the surviving wife of an employee or Member who—

(A) was married to him for at least 9 months immediately before his death; or

(B) is the mother of issue by that marriage;

(2) "widower" means the surviving husband of an employee or Member who—

(A) was married to her for at least 9 months immediately before her death; or

(B) is the father of issue by that marriage;

(3) "dependent", in the case of any child, means that the employee or Member involved was, at the time of the employee or Member's death, either living with or contributing to the support of such child, as determined in accordance with such regulations as the Office of Personnel Management shall prescribe; and

(4) "child" means—

(A) an unmarried dependent child under 18 years of age, including (i) an adopted child, and (ii) a stepchild but only if the stepchild lived with the employee or Member in a regular parent-child relationship, and (iii) a recognized natural child, and (iv) a child who lived with and for whom a petition of adoption was filed by an employee or Member, and who is adopted by the surviving spouse of the employee or Member after his death;

(B) such unmarried dependent child regardless of age who is incapable of self-support because of mental or physical disability incurred before age 18; or

(C) such unmarried dependent child between 18 and 22 years of age who is a student regularly pursuing a full-time course of study or training in residence in a high school, trade school, technical or vocational institute, junior college, college, university, or comparable recognized educational institution.

For the purpose of this paragraph and subsection (e) of this section, a child whose 22nd birthday occurs before July 1 or after August 31 of a calendar year, and while he is regularly pursuing such a course of study or training, is deemed to have become 22 years of age on the first day of July after that birthday. A child who is a student is deemed not to have ceased to be a student during an interim between school years if the interim is not more than 5 months and if he shows to the satisfaction of the Office of Personnel Management that he has a bona fide intention of continuing to pursue a course of study or training in the same or different school during the school semester (or other period into which the school year is divided) immediately after the interim.

(b)(1) Except as provided in paragraph (2) of this subsection, if an employee or Member dies after having retired under this subchapter and is survived by a widow or widower, the widow or widower is entitled to an annuity equal to 55 percent (or 50 percent if retired before October 11, 1962) of an annuity computed under section 8339(a)–(i), (n), (p), (q), (r), and (s) as may apply with respect to the annuitant, or of such portion thereof as may have been designated for this purpose under section 8339(j)(1) of this title, unless the right to a survivor annuity was waived under such section 8339(j)(1) or, in the case of remarriage, the employee or Member did not file an election under section 8339(j)(5)(C) or section 8339(k)(2) of this title, as the case may be.

(2) If an annuitant—

(A) who retired before April 1, 1948; or

(B) who elected a reduced annuity provided in paragraph (2) of section 8339(k) of this title;

dies and is survived by a widow or widower, the widow or widower is entitled to an annuity in an amount which would have been paid had the annuitant been married to the widow or widower at the time of retirement.

(3) A spouse acquired after retirement is entitled to a survivor annuity under this subsection only upon electing this annuity instead of any other survivor benefit to which he may be entitled under this subchapter or another retirement system for Government employees. The annuity of the widow or widower under this subsection commences on the day after the annuitant dies. This annuity and the right thereto terminate on the last day of the month before the widow or widower—

(A) dies; or

(B) except as provided in subsection (k), remarries before becoming 55 years of age.

(4) Notwithstanding the preceding provisions of this subsection, the annuity payable under this subsection to the widow or widower of a retired employee or Member may not exceed the difference between—

(A) the amount which would otherwise be payable to such widow or widower under this subsection (determined without regard to any waiver or designation under section 8339(j)(1) of this title or a prior similar provision of law), and

(B) the amount of the survivor annuity payable to any former spouse of such employee or Member under subsection (h) of this section.

(c) The annuity of a survivor named under section 8339(k)(1) of this title is 55 percent of the reduced annuity of the retired employee or Member. The annuity of the survivor commences on the day after the retired employee or Member dies. This annuity and the right thereto terminate on the last day of the month before the survivor dies.

(d) If an employee or Member dies after completing at least 18 months of civilian service, his widow or widower is entitled to an annuity equal to 55 percent of an annuity computed under section 8339(a)–(f), (i), (n), (p), (q), (r), and (s) as may apply with respect to the employee or Member, except that, in the computation of the annuity under such section, the annuity of the employee or Member shall be at least the smaller of—

(1) 40 percent of his average pay; or

(2) the sum obtained under such section after increasing his service of the type last performed by the period elapsing between the date of death and the date he would have become 60 years of age.

Notwithstanding the preceding sentence, the annuity payable under this subsection to the widow or widower of an employee or Member may not exceed the difference between—

(A) the amount which would otherwise be payable to such widow or widower under this subsection, and

(B) the amount of the survivor annuity payable to any former spouse of such employee or Member under subsection (h) of this section.

The annuity of the widow or widower commences on the day after the employee or Member dies. This annuity and the right thereto terminate on the last day of the month before the widow or widower—

(i) dies; or

(ii) except as provided in subsection (k), remarries before becoming 55 years of age.

(e)(1) For the purposes of this subsection, "former spouse" includes a former spouse who was married to an employee or Member for less than 9 months and a former spouse of an employee or Member who completed less than 18 months of service covered by this subchapter.

(2) If an employee or Member dies after completing at least 18 months of civilian service, or an employee or Member dies after retiring under this subchapter, and is survived by a spouse or a former spouse who is the natural or adoptive parent of a surviving child of the employee or Member, that surviving child is entitled to an annuity equal to the smallest of—

(A) 60 percent of the average pay of the employee or Member divided by the number of children;

(B) $900; or

(C) $2,700 divided by the number of children;

subject to section 8340 of this title. If the employee or Member is not survived by a spouse or a former spouse who is the natural or adoptive parent of a surviving child of the employee or Member, that surviving child is entitled to an annuity equal to the smallest of—

(i) 75 percent of the average pay of the employee or Member divided by the number of children;

(ii) $1,080; or

(iii) $3,240 divided by the number of children;

subject to section 8340 of this title.

(3) The annuity of a child under this subchapter or under the Act of May 29, 1930, as amended from and after February 28, 1948, commences on the day after the employee or Member dies, or commences or resumes on the first day of the month in which the child later becomes or again becomes a student as described by subsection (a)(3) of this section, if any lump sum paid is returned to the Fund. This annuity and the right thereto terminate on the last day of the month before the child—

(A) becomes 18 years of age unless he is then a student as described or incapable of self-support;

(B) becomes capable of self-support after becoming 18 years of age unless he is then such a student;

(C) becomes 22 years of age if he is then such a student and capable of self-support;

(D) ceases to be such a student after becoming 18 years of age unless he is then incapable of self-support; or

(E) dies or marries;

whichever first occurs. On the death of the surviving spouse or former spouse or termination of the annuity of a child, the annuity of any other child or children shall be recomputed and paid as though the spouse, former spouse, or child had not survived the employee or Member.

(4) If the annuity of a child under this subchapter terminates under paragraph (3)(E) because of marriage, then, if such marriage ends, such annuity shall resume on the first day of the month in which it ends, but only if—

(A) any lump sum paid is returned to the Fund; and

(B) that individual is not otherwise ineligible for such annuity.

(f) If a Member heretofore or hereafter separated from the service with title to deferred annuity from the Fund hereafter dies before having established a valid claim for annuity and is survived by a spouse to whom married at the date of separation, the surviving spouse—

(1) is entitled to an annuity equal to 55 percent of the deferred annuity of the Member commencing on the day after the Member dies and terminating on the last day of the month before the surviving spouse dies or remarries; or

(2) may elect to receive the lump-sum credit instead of annuity if the spouse is the individual who would be entitled to the lump-sum credit and files application therefor with the Office before the award of the annuity.

Notwithstanding the preceding sentence, an annuity payable under this subsection to the surviving spouse of a Member may not exceed the difference between—

(A) the annuity which would otherwise be payable to such surviving spouse under this subsection, and

(B) the amount of the survivor annuity payable to any former spouse of such Member under subsection (h) of this section.

(g) In the case of a surviving spouse whose annuity under this section is terminated because of remarriage before becoming 55 years of age, annuity at the same rate shall be restored commencing on the day the remarriage is dissolved by death, annulment, or divorce, if—

(1) the surviving spouse elects to receive this annuity instead of a survivor benefit to which he may be entitled, under this subchapter or another retirement system for Government employees, by reason of the remarriage; and

(2) any lump sum paid on termination of the annuity is returned to the Fund.

(h)(1) Subject to paragraphs (2) through (5) of this subsection, a former spouse of a deceased employee, Member, annuitant, or former Member who was separated from the service with title to a deferred annuity under section 8338(b) of this title is entitled to a survivor annuity under this subsection, if and to the extent expressly provided for in an election under section 8339(j)(3) of this title, or in the terms of any decree of divorce or annulment or any court order or court-approved property settlement agreement incident to such decree.

(2)(A) The annuity payable to a former spouse under this subsection may not exceed the difference between—

(i) the amount applicable in the case of such former spouse, as determined under subparagraph (B) of this paragraph, and

(ii) the amount of any annuity payable under this subsection to any other former spouse of the employee, Member, or annuitant, based on an election previously made under section 8339(j)(3) of this title, or a court order previously issued.

(B) The applicable amount, for purposes of subparagraph (A)(i) of this paragraph in the case of a former spouse, is the amount which would be applicable—

(i) under subsection (b)(4)(A) of this section in the case of a widow or widower, if the deceased was an employee or Member who died after retirement;

(ii) under subparagraph (A) of subsection (d) of this section in the case of a widow or widower, if the deceased was an employee or Member described in the first sentence of such subsection; or

(iii) under subparagraph (A) of subsection (f) of this section in the case of a surviving spouse, if the deceased was a Member described in the first sentence of such subsection.

(3) The commencement and termination of an annuity payable under this subsection shall be governed by the terms of the applicable order, decree, agreement, or election, as the case may be, except that any such annuity—

(A) shall not commence before—

(i) the day after the employee, Member, or annuitant dies, or

(ii) the first day of the second month beginning after the date on which the Office receives written notice of the order, decree, agreement, or election, as the case may be, together with such additional information or documentation as the Office may prescribe,

whichever is later, and

(B) shall terminate—

(i) except as provided in subsection (k), in the case of an annuity computed by reference to clause (i) or (ii) of paragraph (2)(B) of this subsection, no later than the last day of the month before the former spouse remarries before becoming 55 years of age or dies; or

(ii) in the case of an annuity computed by reference to clause (iii) of such paragraph, no later than the last day of the month before the former spouse remarries or dies.

(4) For purposes of this subchapter, a modification in a decree, order, agreement, or election referred to in paragraph (1) of this subsection shall not be effective—

(A) if such modification is made after the retirement or death of the employee or Member concerned, and

(B) to the extent that such modification involves an annuity under this subsection.

(5) For purposes of this subchapter, a decree, order, agreement, or election referred to in paragraph (1) of this subsection shall not be effective, in the case of a former spouse, to the extent that it is inconsistent with any joint designation or waiver previously executed with respect to such former spouse under section 8339(j)(1) of this title or a similar prior provision of law.

(6) Any payment under this subsection to a person bars recovery by any other person.

(7) As used in this subsection, "court" means any court of any State, the District of Columbia, the Commonwealth of Puerto Rico, Guam, the Northern Mariana Islands, or the Virgin Islands, and any Indian court.

(i) The requirement in subsections (a)(1)(A) and (a)(2)(A) of this section that the surviving spouse of an employee or Member have been married to such employee or Member for at least 9 months immediately before the employee or Member's death in order to qualify as the widow or widower of such employee or Member shall be deemed satisfied in any case in which the employee or Member dies within the applicable 9–month period, if—

(1) the death of the employee or Member was accidental; or

(2) the surviving spouse of such individual had been previously married to the individual and subsequently divorced, and the aggregate time married is at least 9 months.

(k)(1) [1] Subsections (b)(3)(B), (d)(ii), and (h)(3)(B)(i) (to the extent that they provide for termination of a survivor annuity because of a remarriage before age 55) shall not apply if the widow, widower, or former spouse was married for at least 30 years to the individual on whose service the survivor annuity is based.

(2) A remarriage described in paragraph (1) shall not be taken into account for purposes of section 8339(j)(5)(B) or (C) or any other provision of this chapter which the Office may by regulation identify in order to carry out the purposes of this subsection. *(Pub.L. 89–554, Sept. 6, 1966, 80 Stat. 577; Pub.L. 90–83, § 1(80), Sept. 11, 1967, 81 Stat. 216; Pub.L. 91–93, Title II, § 206, Oct. 20, 1969, 83 Stat. 140; Pub.L. 91–658, § 3, Jan. 8, 1971, 84 Stat. 1961; Pub.L. 92–243, § 1, Mar. 9, 1972, 86 Stat. 56; Pub.L. 92–297, § 7(4), May 16, 1972, 86 Stat. 145; Pub.L. 93–260, § 1(a), Apr. 9, 1974, 88 Stat. 76; Pub.L. 94–183, § 2(36), Dec. 31, 1975, 89 Stat. 1058; Pub.L. 95–317, § 1(b), July 10, 1978, 92 Stat. 382; Pub.L. 95–318, § 2, July 10, 1978, 92 Stat. 384; Pub.L. 95–454, Title IX, § 906(a)(2), (3), Oct. 13, 1978, 92 Stat. 1224; Pub.L. 95–598, Title III, § 338(c), Nov. 6, 1978, 92 Stat. 2681; Pub.L. 96–179, § 1, Jan. 2, 1980, 93 Stat. 1299; Pub.L. 98–353, Title I, § 112, July 10, 1984, 98 Stat. 343; Pub.L. 98–615, § 2(4), Nov. 8, 1984, 98 Stat. 3199; Pub.L. 99–251, Title II, §§ 205 to 207, Feb. 27, 1986, 100 Stat. 25; Pub.L. 99–272, Title XV, § 15204(a)(2), Apr. 7, 1986, 100 Stat. 335; Pub.L. 101–428, § 2(d)(7), Oct. 15, 1990, 104 Stat. 929; Pub.L. 102–378, § 2(63), Oct. 2, 1992, 106 Stat. 1354; Pub.L. 104–208, Div. A, Title I, § 101(f) [Title VI, § 633(a)(1)], Sept. 30, 1996, 110 Stat. 3009–362; Pub.L.*

105–61, Title V, §§ 516(a)(4), 518(a), Oct. 10, 1997, 111 Stat. 1306, 1307; Pub.L. 106–553, § 1(a)(2) [Title III, § 308(h)(7)], Dec. 21, 2000, 114 Stat. 2762, 2762A–89.)

[1] So in original. No subsec. (j) was enacted.

Commentary

Applying section 8339(j)(3) and subsection (h)(1) of this section, *Downing v. Office of Personnel Management, 619 F.3d 1374 (D.C. Cir. 2010)*, held that a former wife was not entitled to a former spouse survivor annuity under the Civil Service Retirement System when her former husband failed to re-elect former spouse survivor benefits within two years of their divorce and the divorce decree did not mention survivor benefits, even though the benefit her husband received after divorce continued to be reduced to reflect his pre-divorce election of a survivor benefit for his wife. This result would not occur with an ERISA-regulated private sector pension. See *Carmona v. Carmona, 544 F.3d 988 (9th Cir. 2008)*, discussed in Commentary to 29 USC §§ 1055 and 1056.

§ 8345. Payment of benefits; commencement, termination, and waiver of annuity

(a) Each annuity is stated as an annual amount, one-twelfth of which, rounded to the next lowest dollar, constitutes the monthly rate payable on the first business day of the month after the month or other period for which it has accrued.

(b)(1) Except as otherwise provided—

(A) an annuity of an employee or Member commences on the first day of the month after—

(i) separation from the service; or

(ii) pay ceases and the service and age requirements for title to annuity are met; and

(B) any other annuity payable from the Fund commences on the first day of the month after the occurrence of the event on which payment thereof is based.

(2) The annuity of—

(A) an employee involuntarily separated from service, except by removal for cause on charges of misconduct or delinquency; and

(B) an employee or Member retiring under section 8337 of this title due to a disability;

shall commence on the day after separation from the service or the day after pay ceases and the service and age or disability requirements for title to annuity are met.

(c) The annuity of a retired employee or Member terminates on the day death or other terminating event provided by this subchapter occurs. The annuity of a survivor terminates on the last day of the month before death or other terminating event occurs.

(d) An individual entitled to annuity from the Fund may decline to accept all or any part of the annuity by a waiver signed and filed with the Office of Personnel Management. The waiver may be revoked in writing at any time. Payment of the annuity waived may not be made for the period during which the waiver was in effect.

(e) Payment due a minor, or an individual mentally incompetent or under other legal disability, may be made to the person who is constituted guardian or other fiduciary by the law of the State of residence of the claimant or is otherwise legally vested with the care of the claimant or his estate. If a guardian or other fiduciary of the individual under legal disability has not been appointed under the law of the State of residence of the claimant, payment may be made to any person who, in the judgment of the Office, is responsible for the care of the claimant, and the payment bars recovery by any other person.

[**(f)** Repealed. Pub.L. 99–251, Title III, § 305(a), Feb. 27, 1986, 100 Stat. 26]

(g) The Office shall prescribe regulations to provide that the amount of any monthly annuity payable under this section accruing for any month and which is computed with regard to service that includes any service referred to in section 8332(b)(6) performed by an individual prior to January 1, 1969, shall be reduced by the portion of any benefits under any State retirement system to which such individual is entitled (or on proper application would be entitled) for such month which is attributable to such service performed by such individual before such date.

(h) An individual entitled to an annuity from the Fund may make allotments or assignments of amounts from his annuity for such purposes as the Office of Personnel Management in its sole discretion considers appropriate.

(i)(1) No payment shall be made from the Fund unless an application for benefits based on the service of an employee or Member is received in the Office of Personnel Management before the one hundred and fifteenth anniversary of his birth.

(2) Notwithstanding paragraph (1) of this subsection, after the death of an employee, Member, or annuitant, no benefit based on his service shall be paid from the Fund unless an application therefor is received in the Office of Personnel Management within 30 years after the death or other event which gives rise to title to the benefit.

(j)(1) Payments under this subchapter which would otherwise be made to an employee, Member, or annuitant based on service of that individual shall be paid (in whole or in part) by the Office to another person if and to the extent expressly provided for in the terms of—

(A) any court decree of divorce, annulment, or legal separation, or the terms of any court order or court-approved property settlement agreement incident to any court decree of divorce, annulment, or legal separation; or

(B) any court order or other similar process in the nature of garnishment for the enforcement of a judgment rendered against such employee, Member, or annuitant, for physically, sexually, or emotionally abusing a child.

In the event that the Office is served with more than 1 decree, order, or other legal process with respect to the same moneys due or payable to any individual, such moneys shall be available to satisfy such processes on a first-come, first-served basis, with any such process being satisfied out of such moneys as remain after the satisfaction of all such processes which have been previously served.

(2) Paragraph (1) shall only apply to payments made by the Office under this subchapter after the date of receipt in the Office of written notice of such decree, order, other legal process, or agreement, and such additional information and documentation as the Office may prescribe.

(3) For the purpose of this subsection—

(A) the term "court" means any court of any State, the District of Columbia, the Commonwealth of Puerto Rico, Guam, the Northern Mariana Islands, or the Virgin Islands, and any Indian court;

(B) the term "judgment rendered for physically, sexually, or emotionally abusing a child" means any legal claim perfected through a final enforceable judgment, which claim is based in whole or in part upon the physical, sexual, or emotional abuse of a child, whether or not that abuse is accompanied by other actionable wrongdoing, such as sexual exploitation or gross negligence; and

(C) the term "child" means an individual under 18 years of age.

(k)(1) The Office shall, in accordance with this subsection, enter into an agreement with any State within 120 days of a request for agreement from the proper State official. The agreement shall provide that the Office shall withhold State income tax in the case of the monthly annuity of any annuitant who voluntarily requests, in writing, such withholding. The amounts withheld during any calendar quarter shall be held in the Fund and disbursed to the States during the month following that calendar quarter.

(2) An annuitant may have in effect at any time only one request for withholding under this subsection, and an annuitant may not have more than two such requests in effect during any one calendar year.

(3) Subject to paragraph (2) of this subsection, an annuitant may change the State designated by that annuitant for purposes of having withholdings made, and may request that the withholdings be remitted in accordance with such change. An annuitant also may revoke any request of that annuitant for withholding. Any change in the State designated or revocation is effective on the first day of the month after the month in which the request or the revocation is processed by the Office, but in no event later than on the first day of the second month beginning after the day on which such request or revocation is received by the Office.

(4) This subsection does not give the consent of the United States to the application of a statute which imposes more burdensome requirements on the United States than on employers generally, or which subjects the United States or any annuitant to a penalty or liability because of this subsection. The Office may not accept pay from a State for services performed in withholding State income taxes from annuities. Any amount erroneously withheld from an annuity and paid to a State by the Office shall be repaid by the State in accordance with regulations issued by the Office.

(5) For the purpose of this subsection, "State" means a State, the District of Columbia, or any territory or possession of the United States.

(*l*) Transfers of contributions and deposits authorized by section 408(a)(3) of the Foreign Service Act of 1980 shall be deemed to be a complete and final payment of benefits under this chapter. *(Pub.L. 89–554, Sept. 6, 1966, 80 Stat. 582; Pub.L. 93–273, § 1, Apr. 26, 1974, 88 Stat. 93; Pub.L. 94–126, § 1(c), Nov. 12, 1975, 89 Stat. 679; Pub.L. 94–166, § 1, Dec. 23, 1975, 89 Stat. 1002; Pub.L. 94–183, § 1, Dec. 31, 1975, 89 Stat. 1057; Pub.L. 95–366, § 1(a), Sept. 15, 1978, 92 Stat. 600; Pub.L. 95–454, Title IX, § 906(a)(2), (3), Oct. 13, 1978, 92 Stat. 1224; Pub.L. 97–35, Title XVII, § 1705(a), Aug. 13, 1981, 95 Stat. 758; Pub.L. 97–253, Title III, §§ 304(b), 305(a), Sept. 8, 1982, 96 Stat. 795; Pub.L. 98–615, § 2(6), Nov. 8, 1984, 98 Stat. 3202; Pub.L. 99–251, Title III, § 305(a), Feb. 27, 1986, 100 Stat. 26; Pub.L. 101–246, Title I, § 141(b), Feb. 16, 1990, 104 Stat. 35; Pub.L. 103–358, § 2(a), Oct. 14, 1994, 108 Stat. 3420.)*

CHAPTER 89—HEALTH INSURANCE

§ 8901. Definitions

For the purpose of this chapter—

(1) "employee" means—

(A) an employee as defined by section 2105 of this title;

(B) a Member of Congress as defined by section 2106 of this title;

(C) a Congressional employee as defined by section 2107 of this title;

(D) the President;

(E) an individual first employed by the government of the District of Columbia before October 1, 1987;

(F) an individual employed by Gallaudet College;

(G) an individual employed by a county committee established under section 590h(b) of title 16;

(H) an individual appointed to a position on the office staff of a former President under section 1(b) of the Act of August 25, 1958 (72 Stat. 838);

(I) an individual appointed to a position on the office staff of a former President, or a former Vice President under section 5 of the Presidential Transition Act of 1963, as amended (78 Stat. 153), who immediately before the date of such appointment was an employee as defined under any other subparagraph of this paragraph; and

(J) an individual who is employed by the Roosevelt Campobello International Park Commission and is a citizen of the United States,

but does not include—

(i) an employee of a corporation supervised by the Farm Credit Administration if private interests elect or appoint a member of the board of directors;

(ii) an individual who is not a citizen or national of the United States and whose permanent duty station is outside the United States, unless the individual was an employee for the purpose of this chapter on September 30, 1979, by reason of service in an Executive agency, the United States Postal Service, or the Smithsonian Institution in the area which was then known as the Canal Zone;

(iii) an employee of the Tennessee Valley Authority; or

(iv) an employee excluded by regulation of the Office of Personnel Management under section 8913(b) of this title;

(2) "Government" means the Government of the United States and the government of the District of Columbia;

(3) "annuitant" means—

(A) an employee who retires—

(i) on an immediate annuity under subchapter III of chapter 83 of this title, or another retirement system for employees of the Government, after 5 or more years of service;

(ii) under section 8412 or 8414 of this title;

(iii) for disability under subchapter III of chapter 83 of this title, chapter 84 of this title, or another retirement system for employees of the Government; or

(iv) on an immediate annuity under a retirement system established for employees described in section 2105(c), in the case of an individual who elected under section 8347(q)(2) or 8461(n)(2) to remain subject to such a system;

(B) a member of a family who receives an immediate annuity as the survivor of an employee (including a family member entitled to an amount under section 8442(b)(1)(A), whether or not such family member is entitled to an annuity under section 8442(b)(1)(B)) or of a retired employee described by subparagraph (A) of this paragraph;

(C) an employee who receives monthly compensation under subchapter I of chapter 81 of this title and who is determined by the Secretary of Labor to be unable to return to duty; and

(D) a member of a family who receives monthly compensation under subchapter I of chapter 81 of this title as the surviving beneficiary of—

(i) an employee who dies as a result of injury or illness compensable under that subchapter; or

(ii) a former employee who is separated after having completed 5 or more years of service and who dies while receiving monthly compensation under that subchapter and who has been held by the Secretary to have been unable to return to duty;

(4) "service", as used by paragraph (3) of this section, means service which is creditable under subchapter III of chapter 83 or chapter 84 of this title;

(5) "member of family" means the spouse of an employee or annuitant and an unmarried dependent child under 22 years of age, including—

(A) an adopted child or recognized natural child; and

(B) a stepchild or foster child but only if the child lives with the employee or annuitant in a regular parent-child relationship;

or such an unmarried dependent child regardless of age who is incapable of self-support because of mental or physical disability which existed before age 22;

(6) "health benefits plan" means a group insurance policy or contract, medical or hospital service agreement, membership or subscription contract, or similar group arrangement provided by a carrier for the purpose of providing, paying for, or reimbursing expenses for health services;

(7) "carrier" means a voluntary association, corporation, partnership, or other nongovernmental organization which is lawfully engaged in providing, paying for, or reimbursing the cost of, health services under group insurance policies or contracts, medical or hospital service agreements, membership or subscription contracts, or similar group arrangements, in consideration of premiums or other periodic charges payable to the carrier, including a health benefits plan duly sponsored or underwritten by an employee organization and an association of organizations or other entities described in this paragraph sponsoring a health benefits plan;

(8) "employee organization" means—

(A) an association or other organization of employees which is national in scope, or in which membership is open to all employees of a Government agency who are eligible to enroll in a health benefits plan under this chapter and which, after December 31, 1978, and before January 1, 1980, applied to the Office for approval of a plan provided under section 8903(3) of this title; and

(B) an association or other organization which is national in scope, in which membership is open only to employees, annuitants, or former spouses, or any combination thereof, and which, during the 90-day period beginning on the date of enactment of section 8903a of this title, applied to the Office for approval of a plan provided under such section;

(9) "dependent", in the case of any child, means that the employee or annuitant involved is either living with or contributing to the support of such child, as determined in accordance with such regulations as the Office shall prescribe;

(10) "former spouse" means a former spouse of an employee, former employee, or annuitant—

(A) who has not remarried before age 55 after the marriage to the employee, former employee, or annuitant was dissolved,

(B) who was enrolled in an approved health benefits plan under this chapter as a family member at any time during the 18-month period before the date of the dissolution of the marriage to the employee, former employee, or annuitant, and

(C)(i) who is receiving any portion of an annuity under section 8345(j) or 8467 of this title or a survivor annuity under section 8341(h) or 8445 of this title (or benefits similar to either of the aforementioned annuity benefits under a retirement system for Government employees other than the Civil Service Retirement System or the Federal Employees' Retirement System),

(ii) as to whom a court order or decree referred to in section 8341(h), 8345(j), 8445, or 8467 of this title (or similar provision of law under any such retirement system other than the Civil Service Retirement System or the Federal Employees' Retirement System) has been issued, or for whom an election has been made under section 8339(j)(3) or 8417(b) of this title (or similar provision of law), or

(iii) who is otherwise entitled to an annuity or any portion of an annuity as a former spouse under a retirement system for Government employees,

except that such term shall not include any such unremarried former spouse of a former employee whose marriage was dissolved after the former employee's separation from the service (other than by retirement); and

(11) "qualified clinical social worker" means an individual—

(A) who is licensed or certified as a clinical social worker by the State in which such individual practices; or

(B) who, if such State does not provide for the licensing or certification of clinical social workers—

(i) is certified by a national professional organization offering certification of clinical social workers; or

(ii) meets equivalent requirements (as prescribed by the Office).

(Pub.L. 89–554, Sept. 6, 1966, 80 Stat. 600; Pub.L. 90–83, § 1(95), Sept. 11, 1967, 81 Stat. 219; Pub.L. 91–418, §§ 2, 3(b), Sept. 25, 1970, 84 Stat. 869; Pub.L. 93–160, § 1(b), Nov. 27, 1973, 87 Stat. 635; Pub.L. 95–368, § 2, Sept. 17, 1978, 92 Stat. 606; Pub.L. 95–454, Title IX, § 906(a)(2), (3), Oct. 13, 1978, 92 Stat. 1224; Pub.L. 95–583, § 2, Nov. 2, 1978, 92 Stat. 2482; Pub.L. 96–54, § 2(a)(52), Aug. 14, 1979, 93 Stat. 384; Pub.L. 96–70, Title I, § 1209(c), Sept. 27, 1979, 93 Stat. 463; Pub.L. 96–179, § 2, Jan. 2, 1980, 93 Stat. 1299; Pub.L. 98–615, § 3(1), Nov. 8, 1984, 98 Stat. 3202; Pub.L. 99–53, § 1(a), June 17, 1985, 99 Stat. 93; Pub.L. 99–251, Title I, § 105(a), Feb. 27, 1986, 100 Stat. 15; Pub.L. 99–335, Title II, § 207(l), June 6, 1986, 100 Stat. 598; Pub.L. 99–556, Title V, § 503, Oct. 27, 1986, 100 Stat. 3141; Pub.L. 100–679, § 13(c), Nov. 17, 1988, 102 Stat. 4071; Pub.L. 101–508, Title VII, § 7202(l), Nov. 5, 1990, 104 Stat. 1388–339; Pub.L. 102–378, § 2(75), Oct. 2, 1992, 106 Stat. 1355; Pub.L. 105–266, § 3(a), Oct. 19, 1998, 112 Stat. 2366; Pub.L. 110–74, § 1, Aug. 9, 2007, 121 Stat. 723; Pub.L. 114–136, § 2(c)(5), Mar. 18, 2016, 130 Stat. 305.)

§ 8905. Election of coverage

(a) An employee may enroll in an approved health benefits plan described in section 8903 or 8903a—

(1) as an individual;

(2) for self plus one; or

(3) for self and family.

(b) An annuitant who at the time he becomes an annuitant was enrolled in a health benefits plan under this chapter—

(1) as an employee for a period of not less than—

(A) the 5 years of service immediately before retirement;

(B) the full period or periods of service between the last day of the first period, as prescribed by regulations of the Office of Personnel Management, in which he is eligible to enroll in the plan and the date on which he becomes an annuitant; or

(C) the full period or periods of service beginning with the enrollment which became effective before January 1, 1965, and ending with the date on which he becomes an annuitant;

whichever is shortest; or

(2) as a member of the family of an employee or annuitant;

may continue his enrollment under the conditions of eligibility prescribed by regulations of the Office. The Office may, in its sole discretion, waive the requirements of this subsection in the case of an individual who fails to satisfy such requirements if the Office determines that, due to exceptional circumstances, it would be against equity and good conscience not to allow such individual to be enrolled as an annuitant in a health benefits plan under this chapter [1]

(c)(1) A former spouse may—

(A) within 60 days after the dissolution of the marriage, or

(B) in the case of a former spouse of a former employee whose marriage was dissolved after the employee's retirement, within 60 days after the dissolution of the marriage or, if later, within 60 days after an election is made under section 8339(j)(3) or 8417(b) of this title for such former spouse by the retired employee,

enroll in an approved health benefits plan described by section 8903 or 8903a of this title as an individual or for [2] for self plus one or self and family as provided in paragraph (2) of this subsection, subject to agreement to pay the full subscription charge of the enrollment, including the amounts determined by the Office to be necessary for administration and reserves pursuant to section 8909(b) of this title. The former spouse shall submit an enrollment application and make premium payments to the agency which, at the time of divorce or annulment, employed the employee to whom the former spouse was married or, in the case of a former spouse who is receiving annuity payments under section 8341(h), 8345(j), 8445, or 8467 of this title, to the Office of Personnel Management.

(2) Coverage for self plus one or for self and family under this subsection shall be limited to—

(A) the former spouse; and

(B) unmarried dependent natural or adopted children (or, in the case of self plus one coverage, not more than 1 such child) of the former spouse and the employee who are—

(i) under 22 years of age; or

(ii) incapable of self-support because of mental or physical disability which existed before age 22.

(d) An individual whom the Secretary of Defense determines is an eligible beneficiary under subsection (b) of section 1108 of title 10 may enroll, as part of the demonstration project under such section, in a health benefits plan under this chapter in accordance with the agreement under subsection (a) of such section between the Secretary and the Office and applicable regulations under this chapter.

(e) If an employee, annuitant, or other individual eligible to enroll in a health benefits plan under this chapter has a spouse who is also eligible to enroll, either spouse, but not both, may enroll for self and family, or for a self plus one enrollment that covers the spouse, or each spouse may enroll as an individual or for a self plus one enrollment that does not cover the other spouse or a child who is covered under the enrollment of the other spouse. However, an individual may not be enrolled both as an employee, annuitant, or other individual eligible to enroll and as a member of the family.

(f) An employee, annuitant, former spouse, or person having continued coverage under section 8905a of this title enrolled in a health benefits plan under this chapter may change his coverage or that of himself and members of his family by an application filed within 60 days after a change in family status or at other times and under conditions prescribed by regulations of the Office.

(g)(1) Under regulations prescribed by the Office, the Office shall, before the start of any contract term in which—

(A) an adjustment is made in any of the rates charged or benefits provided under a health benefits plan described by section 8903 or 8903a of this title,

(B) a newly approved health benefits plan is offered, or

(C) an existing plan is terminated,

provide a period of not less than 3 weeks during which any employee, annuitant, former spouse, or person having continued coverage under section 8905a of this title enrolled in a health benefits plan described by such section shall be permitted to transfer that individual's enrollment to another such plan or to cancel such enrollment.

(2) In addition to any opportunity afforded under paragraph (1) of this subsection, an employee, annuitant, former spouse, or person having continued coverage under section 8905a of this title enrolled in a health benefits plan under this chapter shall be permitted to transfer that individual's enrollment to another such plan, or to cancel such enrollment, at such other times and subject to such conditions as the Office may prescribe in regulations.

(3)(A) In addition to any informational requirements otherwise applicable under this chapter, the regulations shall include provisions to ensure that each employee eligible to enroll in a health benefits plan under this chapter (whether actually enrolled or not) is notified in writing as to the rights afforded under section 8905a of this title.

(B) Notification under this paragraph shall be provided by employing agencies at an appropriate point in time before each period under paragraph (1) so that employees may be aware of their rights under section 8905a of this title when making enrollment decisions during such period.

(h)(1) An unenrolled employee who is required by a court or administrative order to provide health insurance coverage for 1 or more children who meets the requirements of section 8901(5) may enroll for self plus one or self and family coverage, as necessary to provide health insurance coverage for each child who is covered under the order, in a health benefits plan under this chapter. If such employee fails to enroll for self plus one or self and family coverage, as necessary to provide health insurance coverage for each child who is covered under the order, in a health benefits plan that provides full benefits and services in the location in which the child or children reside, and the employee does not provide documentation showing that such coverage has been provided through other health insurance, the employing agency shall enroll the employee in a self plus one or self and family enrollment, as necessary to provide health insurance coverage for each child who is covered under the order, in the option which provides the lower level of coverage under the Service Benefit Plan.

(2) An employee who is enrolled as an individual in a health benefits plan under this chapter and who is required by a court or administrative order to provide health insurance coverage for 1 or more children who meets the requirements of section 8901(5) may change to a self plus one or self and family enrollment, as necessary to provide health insurance coverage for each child who is covered under the order, in the same or another health benefits plan under this chapter. If such employee fails to change to a self plus one or self and family enrollment, as necessary to provide health insurance coverage for each child who is covered under the order, and the employee does not provide documentation showing that such coverage has been provided through other health insurance, the employing agency shall change the enrollment of the employee to a self plus one or self and family enrollment, as necessary to provide health insurance coverage for each child who is covered under the order, in the plan in which the employee is enrolled if that plan provides full benefits and services in the location where the child or children reside. If the plan in which the employee is enrolled does not provide full benefits and services in the location in which the child or children reside, or, if the employee fails to change to a self plus one or self and family enrollment, as necessary to provide health insurance coverage for each child who is covered under the order, in a plan that provides full benefits and services in the location where the child or children reside, the employing agency shall change the coverage of the employee to a self plus one or self and family enrollment, as necessary to provide health insurance coverage for each child who is covered under the order, in the option which provides the lower level of coverage under the Service Benefits Plan.

(3) The employee may not discontinue the self plus one or self and family enrollment, as necessary to provide health insurance coverage for each child who is covered under the order, in a plan that provides full benefits and services in the

location in which the child or children reside for so long as the court or administrative order remains in effect and the child or children continue to meet the requirements of section 8901(5), unless the employee provides documentation showing that such coverage has been provided through other health insurance. *(Pub.L. 89–554, Sept. 6, 1966, 80 Stat. 603; Pub.L. 95–454, Title IX, § 906(a)(2), (3), Oct. 13, 1978, 92 Stat. 1224; Pub.L. 98–615, § 3(4), Nov. 8, 1984, 98 Stat. 3203; Pub.L. 99–53, § 2(a), (c), June 17, 1985, 99 Stat. 94; Pub.L. 99–251, Title I, §§ 103, 104(a), Feb. 27, 1986, 100 Stat. 14; Pub.L. 99–335, Title II, § 207(m), June 6, 1986, 100 Stat. 598; Pub.L. 100–654, Title II, §§ 201(c), (d), 202(c), Nov. 14, 1988, 102 Stat. 3845; Pub.L. 102–378, § 2(77), Oct. 2, 1992, 106 Stat. 1355; Pub.L. 105–261, Div. A, Title VI, § 721(b)(1), Oct. 17, 1998, 112 Stat. 2065; Pub.L. 106–394, § 2, Oct. 30, 2000, 114 Stat. 1629; Pub.L. 113–67, Div. A, Title VII, § 706(a), Dec. 26, 2013, 127 Stat. 1193.)*

[1] So in original. Probably should be followed by a period.

[2] So in original. The word "for" probably should precede "self and family".

§ 8905a. Continued coverage

(a) Any individual described in subsection (b) may elect to continue coverage under this chapter in accordance with the provisions of this section.

(b) This section applies with respect to—

(1) any employee who—

(A) is separated from service, whether voluntarily or involuntarily, except that if the separation is involuntary, this section shall not apply if the separation is for gross misconduct (as defined under regulations which the Office of Personnel Management shall prescribe); and

(B) would not otherwise be eligible for any benefits under this chapter (determined without regard to any temporary extension of coverage and without regard to any benefits available under a nongroup contract);

(2) any individual who—

(A) ceases to meet the requirements for being considered an unmarried dependent child under this chapter;

(B) on the day before so ceasing to meet the requirements referred to in subparagraph (A), was covered under a health benefits plan under this chapter as a member of the family of an employee or annuitant; and

(C) would not otherwise be eligible for any benefits under this chapter (determined without regard to any temporary extension of coverage and without regard to any benefits available under a nongroup contract); and

(3) any employee who—

(A) is enrolled in a health benefits plan under this chapter;

(B) is a member of a reserve component of the armed forces;

(C) is called or ordered to active duty in support of a contingency operation (as defined in section 101(a)(13) of title 10);

(D) is placed on leave without pay or separated from service to perform active duty; and

(E) serves on active duty for a period of more than 30 consecutive days.

(c)(1) The Office shall prescribe regulations and provide for the inclusion of appropriate terms in contracts with carriers to provide that—

(A) with respect to an employee who becomes (or will become) eligible for continued coverage under this section as a result of separation from service, the separating agency shall, before the end of the 30–day period beginning on the date as of which coverage (including any temporary extensions of coverage) would otherwise end, notify the individual of such individual's rights under this section; and

(B) with respect to a child of an employee or annuitant who becomes eligible for continued coverage under this section as a result of ceasing to meet the requirements for being considered a member of the employee's or annuitant's family—

(i) the employee or annuitant may provide written notice of the child's change in status (complete with the child's name, address, and such other information as the Office may by regulation require)—

(I) to the employee's employing agency; or

(II) in the case of an annuitant, to the Office; and

(ii) if the notice referred to in clause (i) is received within 60 days after the date as of which the child involved first ceases to meet the requirements involved, the employing agency or the Office (as the case may be) must, within 14 days after receiving such notice, notify the child of such child's rights under this section.

(2) In order to obtain continued coverage under this section, an appropriate written election (submitted in such manner as the Office by regulation prescribes) must be made—

(A) in the case of an individual seeking continued coverage based on a separation from service, before the end of the 60–day period beginning on the later of—

(i) the effective date of the separation; or

(ii) the date the separated individual receives the notice required under paragraph (1)(A); or

(B) in the case of an individual seeking continued coverage based on a change in circumstances making such individual ineligible for coverage as an unmarried dependent child, before the end of the 60–day period beginning on the later of—

(i) the date as of which such individual first ceases to meet the requirements for being considered an unmarried dependent child; or

(ii) the date such individual receives notice under paragraph (1)(B)(ii);

except that if a parent fails to provide the notice required under paragraph (1)(B)(i) in timely fashion, the 60–day period under this subparagraph shall be based on the date under clause (i), irrespective of whether or not any notice under paragraph (1)(B)(ii) is provided.

(d)(1)(A) Except as provided in paragraphs (4), (5), and (6), an individual receiving continued coverage under this section shall be required to pay currently into the Employees Health Benefits Fund, under arrangements satisfactory to the Office, an amount equal to the sum of—

(i) the employee and agency contributions which would be required in the case of an employee enrolled in the same health benefits plan and level of benefits; and

(ii) an amount, determined under regulations prescribed by the Office, necessary for administrative expenses, but not to exceed 2 percent of the total amount under clause (i).

(B) Payments under this section to the Fund shall—

(i) in the case of an individual whose continued coverage is based on such individual's separation, be made through the agency which last employed such individual; or

(ii) in the case of an individual whose continued coverage is based on a change in circumstances referred to in subsection (c)(2)(B), be made through—

(I) the Office, if, at the time coverage would (but for this section) otherwise have been discontinued, the individual was covered as the child of an annuitant; or

(II) if, at the time referred to in subclause (I), the individual was covered as the child of an employee, the employee's employing agency as of such time.

(2) If an individual elects to continue coverage under this section before the end of the applicable period under subsection (c)(2), but after such individual's coverage under this chapter (including any temporary extensions of coverage) expires, coverage shall be restored retroactively, with appropriate contributions (determined in accordance with paragraph (1), (4), or (5), as the case may be) and claims (if any), to the same extent and effect as though no break in coverage had occurred.

(3)(A) An individual making an election under subsection (c)(2)(B) may, at such individual's option, elect coverage either as an individual or, if appropriate, for self plus one or for self and family.

(B) For the purpose of this paragraph, members of an individual's family shall be determined in the same way as would apply under this chapter in the case of an enrolled employee.

(C) Nothing in this paragraph shall be considered to limit an individual making an election under subsection (c)(2)(A) to coverage for self alone.

(4)(A) If the basis for continued coverage under this section is an involuntary separation from a position, or a voluntary separation from a surplus position, in or under the Department of Defense due to a reduction in force, or the Department of Energy due to a reduction in force resulting from the establishment of the National Nuclear Security Administration—

(i) the individual shall be liable for not more than the employee contributions referred to in paragraph (1)(A)(i); and

(ii) the agency which last employed the individual shall pay the remaining portion of the amount required under paragraph (1)(A).

(B) This paragraph shall apply with respect to any individual whose continued coverage is based on a separation occurring on or after the date of enactment of this paragraph and before—

(i) December 31, 2016; or

(ii) February 1, 2017, if specific notice of such separation was given to such individual before December 31, 2016.

(C) For the purpose of this paragraph, "surplus position" means a position which is identified in pre-reduction-in-force planning as no longer required, and which is expected to be eliminated under formal reduction-in-force procedures.

(5)(A) If the basis for continued coverage under this section is an involuntary separation from a position in or under the Department of Veterans Affairs due to a reduction in force or a title 38 staffing readjustment, or a voluntary or involuntary separation from a Department of Energy position at a Department of Energy facility at which the Secretary is carrying out a closure project selected under section 4421 of the Atomic Energy Defense Act—

(i) the individual shall be liable for not more than the employee contributions referred to in paragraph (1)(A)(i); and

(ii) the agency which last employed the individual shall pay the remaining portion of the amount required under paragraph (1)(A).

(B) This paragraph shall only apply with respect to individuals whose continued coverage is based on a separation occurring on or after the date of the enactment of this paragraph.

(6)(A) If the basis for continued coverage under this section is, as a result of the termination of the Space Shuttle Program, an involuntary separation from a position due to a reduction–in–force or declination of a directed reassignment or transfer of function, or a voluntary separation from a surplus position in the National Aeronautics and Space Administration —

(i) the individual shall be liable for not more than the employee contributions referred to in paragraph (1)(A)(i); and

(ii) the National Aeronautics and Space Administration shall pay the remaining portion of the amount required under paragraph (1)(A).

(B) This paragraph shall only apply with respect to individuals whose continued coverage is based on a separation occurring on or after the date of enactment of this paragraph and before December 31, 2010.

(C) For purposes of this paragraph, "surplus position" means a position which is—

(i) identified in pre-reduction-in-force planning as no longer required, and which is expected to be eliminated under formal reduction-in-force procedures as a result of the termination of the Space Shuttle Program; or

(ii) encumbered by an employee who has received official certification from the National Aeronautics and Space Administration consistent with the Administration's career transition assistance program regulations that the position is being abolished as a result of the termination of the Space Shuttle Program.

(e)(1) Continued coverage under this section may not extend beyond—

(A) in the case of an individual whose continued coverage is based on separation from service, the date which is 18 months after the effective date of the separation;

(B) in the case of an individual whose continued coverage is based on ceasing to meet the requirements for being considered an unmarried dependent child, the date which is 36 months after the date on which the individual first ceases to meet those requirements, subject to paragraph (2); or

(C) in the case of an employee described in subsection (b)(3), the date which is 24 months after the employee is placed on leave without pay or separated from service to perform active duty.

(2) In the case of an individual who—

(A) ceases to meet the requirements for being considered an unmarried dependent child;

(B) as of the day before so ceasing to meet the requirements referred to in subparagraph (A), was covered as the child of a former employee receiving continued coverage under this section based on the former employee's separation from service; and

(C) so ceases to meet the requirements referred to in subparagraph (A) before the end of the 18–month period beginning on the date of the former employee's separation from service,

extended coverage under this section may not extend beyond the date which is 36 months after the separation date referred to in subparagraph (C).

(f)(1) The Office shall prescribe regulations under which, in addition to any individual otherwise eligible for continued coverage under this section, and to the extent practicable, continued coverage may also, upon appropriate written application, be afforded under this section—

(A) to any individual who—

(i) if subparagraphs (A) and (C) of paragraph (10) of section 8901 were disregarded, would be eligible to be considered a former spouse within the meaning of such paragraph; but

(ii) would not, but for this subsection, be eligible to be so considered; and

(B) to any individual whose coverage as a family member would otherwise terminate as a result of a legal separation.

(2) The terms and conditions for coverage under the regulations shall include—

(A) consistent with subsection (c), any necessary notification provisions, and provisions under which an election period of at least 60 days' duration is afforded;

(B) terms and conditions identical to those under subsection (d), except that contributions to the Employees Health Benefits Fund shall be made through such agency as the Office by regulation prescribes;

(C) provisions relating to the termination of continued coverage, except that continued coverage under this section may not (subject to paragraph (3)) extend beyond the date which is 36 months after the date on which the qualifying event under this subsection (the date of divorce, annulment, or legal separation, as the case may be) occurs; and

(D) provisions designed to ensure that any coverage pursuant to this subsection does not adversely affect any eligibility for coverage which the individual involved might otherwise have under this chapter (including as a result of any change in personal circumstances) if this subsection had not been enacted.

(3) In the case of an individual—

(A) who becomes eligible for continued coverage under this subsection based on a divorce, annulment, or legal separation from a person who, as of the day before the date of the divorce, annulment, or legal separation (as the case may be) was receiving continued coverage under this section based on such person's separation from service under a self plus one enrollment that covered the individual or under a self and family enrollment; and

(B) whose divorce, annulment, or legal separation (as the case may be) occurs before the end of the 18–month period beginning on the date of the separation from service referred to in subparagraph (A),

extended coverage under this section may not extend beyond the date which is 36 months after the date of the separation from service, as referred to in subparagraph (A). *(Added Pub.L. 100–654, Title II, § 201(a)(1), Nov. 14, 1988, 102 Stat. 3841; amended Pub.L. 102–484, Div. D, Title XLIV, § 4438(a), Oct. 23, 1992, 106 Stat. 2725; Pub.L. 103–337, Div. A, Title III, § 341(d), Oct. 5, 1994, 108 Stat. 2720; Pub.L. 104–106, Div. A, Title X, § 1036, Feb. 10, 1996, 110 Stat. 431; Pub.L. 106–65, Div. A, Title XI, § 1104(c), Div. C, Title XXXII, § 3244, Oct. 5, 1999, 113 Stat. 777, 965; Pub.L. 106–117, Title XI, § 1106, Nov. 30, 1999, 113 Stat. 1598; Pub.L. 107–314, Div. A, Title XI, § 1103, Dec. 2, 2002, 116 Stat. 2661; Pub.L. 107–314, Div. D, Title XLVI, § 4603(h), formerly Pub.L. 106-398, § 1 [Div. C, Title XXXI, § 3136(h)], Oct. 30, 2000, 114 Stat. 1654, 1654A–459, renumbered § 4603(h) of Pub.L. 107–314 by Pub.L. 108–136, Div. C, Title XXXI, § 3141(i)(4)(A) to (C), Nov. 24, 2003, 117 Stat. 1777; Pub.L. 108–136, Div. C, Title XXXI, § 3141(m)(3), Nov. 24, 2003, 117 Stat. 1787; Pub.L. 108–375, Div. A, Title XI, § 1101(a), Oct. 28, 2004, 118 Stat. 2072; Pub.L. 109–163, Div. A, Title XI, § 1101, Jan. 6, 2006, 119 Stat. 3447; Pub.L. 110–422, Title VI, § 615, Oct. 15, 2008, 122 Stat. 4800; Pub.L. 111–242, § 151, as added Pub.L. 111–322, Title I, § 1(a)(2), Dec. 22, 2010, 124 Stat. 3519; Pub.L. 112–81, Div.*

A, Title XI, § 1123, Dec. 31, 2011, 125 Stat. 1617; Pub.L. 113–67, Div. A, Title VII, § 706(b), Dec. 26, 2013, 127 Stat. 1194.)

TITLE 10

ARMED FORCES

SUBTITLE A—GENERAL MILITARY LAW

PART II—PERSONNEL

CHAPTER 53—MISCELLANEOUS RIGHTS AND BENEFITS

§ 1044d. Military testamentary instruments: requirement for recognition by States

(a) Testamentary instruments to be given legal effect.—A military testamentary instrument—

(1) is exempt from any requirement of form, formality, or recording before probate that is provided for testamentary instruments under the laws of a State; and

(2) has the same legal effect as a testamentary instrument prepared and executed in accordance with the laws of the State in which it is presented for probate.

(b) Military testamentary instruments.—For purposes of this section, a military testamentary instrument is an instrument that is prepared with testamentary intent in accordance with regulations prescribed under this section and that—

(1) is executed in accordance with subsection (c) by (or on behalf of) a person, as a testator, who is eligible for military legal assistance;

(2) makes a disposition of property of the testator; and

(3) takes effect upon the death of the testator.

(c) Requirements for execution of military testamentary instruments.—An instrument is valid as a military testamentary instrument only if—

(1) the instrument is executed by the testator (or, if the testator is unable to execute the instrument personally, the instrument is executed in the presence of, by the direction of, and on behalf of the testator);

(2) the execution of the instrument is notarized by—

(A) a military legal assistance counsel;

(B) a person who is authorized to act as a notary under section 1044a of this title who—

(i) is not an attorney; and

(ii) is supervised by a military legal assistance counsel; or

(C) a State-licensed notary employed by a military department or the Coast Guard who is supervised by a military legal assistance counsel;

(3) the instrument is executed in the presence of at least two disinterested witnesses (in addition to the person notarizing the instrument in accordance with paragraph (2)), each of whom attests to witnessing the testator's execution of the instrument by signing it; and

(4) the instrument is executed in accordance with such additional requirements as may be provided in regulations prescribed under this section.

(d) Self-proving military testamentary instruments.—**(1)** If the document setting forth a military testamentary instrument meets the requirements of paragraph (2), then the signature of a person on the document as the testator, an attesting witness, a notary, or the presiding attorney, together with a written representation of the person's status as such and the person's military grade (if any) or other title, is prima facie evidence of the following:

(A) That the signature is genuine.

(B) That the signatory had the represented status and title at the time of the execution of the will.

(C) That the signature was executed in compliance with the procedures required under the regulations prescribed under subsection (f).

(2) A document setting forth a military testamentary instrument meets the requirements of this paragraph if it includes (or has attached to it), in a form and content required under the regulations prescribed under subsection (f), each of the following:

(A) A certificate, executed by the testator, that includes the testator's acknowledgment of the testamentary instrument.

(B) An affidavit, executed by each witness signing the testamentary instrument, that attests to the circumstances under which the testamentary instrument was executed.

(C) A notarization, including a certificate of any administration of an oath required under the regulations, that is signed by the notary or other official administering the oath.

(e) Statement to be included.—**(1)** Under regulations prescribed under this section, each military testamentary instrument shall contain a statement that sets forth the provisions of subsection (a).

(2) Paragraph (1) shall not be construed to make inapplicable the provisions of subsection (a) to a testamentary instrument that does not include a statement described in that paragraph.

(f) Regulations.—Regulations for the purposes of this section shall be prescribed jointly by the Secretary of Defense and by the Secretary of Homeland Security with respect to the Coast Guard when it is not operating as a service in the Department of the Navy.

(g) Definitions.—In this section:

(1) The term "person eligible for military legal assistance" means a person who is eligible for legal assistance under section 1044 of this title.

(2) The term "military legal assistance counsel" means—

(A) a judge advocate (as defined in section 801(13) of this title); or

(B) a civilian attorney serving as a legal assistance officer under the provisions of section 1044 of this title.

(3) The term "State" includes the District of Columbia, the Commonwealth of Puerto Rico, the Commonwealth of the Northern Mariana Islands, and each possession of the United States.

(Added Pub.L. 106–398, § 1 [Div. A, Title V, § 551(a)], Oct. 30, 2000, 114 Stat. 1654, 1654A–123; amended Pub.L. 107–296, Title XVII, § 1704(b)(1), Nov. 25, 2002, 116 Stat. 2314; Pub.L. 114–328, Div. A, Title V, § 523(a), Dec. 23, 2016, 130 Stat. 2116.)

CHAPTER 55—MEDICAL AND DENTAL CARE

§ 1072. Definitions

In this chapter:

(1) The term "uniformed services" means the armed forces and the Commissioned Corps of the National Oceanic and Atmospheric Administration and of the Public Health Service.

(2) The term "dependent," with respect to a member or former member of a uniformed service, means—

(A) the spouse;

(B) the unremarried widow;

(C) the unremarried widower;

(D) a child who—

(i) has not attained the age of 21;

(ii) has not attained the age of 23, is enrolled in a full-time course of study at an institution of higher learning approved by the administering Secretary and is, or was at the time of the member's or former member's death, in fact dependent on the member or former member for over one-half of the child's support; or

(iii) is incapable of self-support because of a mental or physical incapacity that occurs while a dependent of a member or former member under clause (i) or (ii) and is, or was at the time of the member's or former member's death, in fact dependent on the member or former member for over one-half of the child's support;

(E) a parent or parent-in-law who is, or was at the time of the member's or former member's death, in fact dependent on him for over one-half of his support and residing in his household;

(F) the unremarried former spouse of a member or former member who (i) on the date of the final decree of divorce, dissolution, or annulment, had been married to the member or former member for a period of at least 20 years during which period the member or former member performed at least 20 years of service which is creditable in determining that member's or former member's eligibility for retired or retainer pay, or equivalent pay, and (ii) does not have medical coverage under an employer-sponsored health plan;

(G) a person who (i) is the unremarried former spouse of a member or former member who performed at least 20 years of service which is creditable in determining the member or former member's eligibility for retired or retainer pay, or equivalent pay, and on the date of the final decree of divorce, dissolution, or annulment before April 1, 1985, had been married to the member or former member for a period of at least 20 years, at least 15 of which, but less than 20 of which, were during the period the member or former member performed service creditable in determining the member or former member's eligibility for retired or retainer pay, and (ii) does not have medical coverage under an employer-sponsored health plan;

(H) a person who would qualify as a dependent under clause (G) but for the fact that the date of the final decree of divorce, dissolution, or annulment of the person is on or after April 1, 1985, except that the term does not include the person after the end of the one-year period beginning on the date of that final decree; and

(I) an unmarried person who—

(i) is placed in the legal custody of the member or former member as a result of an order of a court of competent jurisdiction in the United States (or possession of the United States) for a period of at least 12 consecutive months;

(ii) either—

(I) has not attained the age of 21;

(II) has not attained the age of 23 and is enrolled in a full time course of study at an institution of higher learning approved by the administering Secretary; or

(III) is incapable of self support because of a mental or physical incapacity that occurred while the person was considered a dependent of the member or former member under this subparagraph pursuant to subclause (I) or (II);

(iii) is dependent on the member or former member for over one-half of the person's support;

(iv) resides with the member or former member unless separated by the necessity of military service or to receive institutional care as a result of disability or incapacitation or under such other circumstances as the administering Secretary may by regulation prescribe; and

(v) is not a dependent of a member or a former member under any other subparagraph.

(3) The term "administering Secretaries" means the Secretaries of executive departments specified in section 1073 of this title as having responsibility for administering this chapter.

(4) The term "Civilian Health and Medical Program of the Uniformed Services" means the program authorized under sections 1079 and 1086 of this title and includes contracts entered into under section 1091 or 1097 of this title and demonstration projects under section 1092 of this title.

(5) The term "covered beneficiary" means a beneficiary under this chapter other than a beneficiary under section 1074(a) of this title.

(6) The term "child", with respect to a member or former member of a uniformed service, means the following:

(A) An unmarried legitimate child.

(B) An unmarried adopted child.

(C) An unmarried stepchild.

(D) An unmarried person—

(i) who is placed in the home of the member or former member by a placement agency (recognized by the Secretary of Defense), or by any other source authorized by State or local law to provide adoption placement, in anticipation of the legal adoption of the person by the member or former member; and

(ii) who otherwise meets the requirements specified in paragraph (2)(D).

(7) The term "TRICARE program" means the various programs carried out by the Secretary of Defense under this chapter and any other provision of law providing for the furnishing of medical and dental care and health benefits to members and former members of the uniformed services and their dependents, including the following health plan options:

(A) TRICARE Prime.

(B) TRICARE Select.

(C) TRICARE for Life.

(8) The term "custodial care" means treatment or services, regardless of who recommends such treatment or services or where such treatment or services are provided, that—

(A) can be rendered safely and reasonably by a person who is not medically skilled; or

(B) is or are designed mainly to help the patient with the activities of daily living.

(9) The term "domiciliary care" means care provided to a patient in an institution or homelike environment because—

(A) providing support for the activities of daily living in the home is not available or is unsuitable; or

(B) members of the patient's family are unwilling to provide the care.

(10) The term "health care" includes mental health care.

(11) The term "TRICARE Extra" means the preferred-provider option of the TRICARE program made available prior to January 1, 2018, under which TRICARE Standard beneficiaries may obtain discounts on cost sharing as a result of using TRICARE network providers.

(12) The term "TRICARE Select" means the self-managed, preferred-provider network option under the TRICARE program established by section 1075 of this title.

(13) The term "TRICARE for Life" means the Medicare wraparound coverage option of the TRICARE program made available to the beneficiary by reason of section 1086(d) of this title.

(14) The term "TRICARE Prime" means the managed care option of the TRICARE program.

(15) The term "TRICARE Standard" means the TRICARE program made available prior to January 1, 2018, covering—

(A) medical care to which a dependent described in section 1076(a)(2) of this title is entitled; and

(B) health benefits contracted for under the authority of section 1079(a) of this title and subject to the same rates and conditions as apply to persons covered under that section.

(Added Pub.L. 85–861, § 1(25)(B), Sept. 2, 1958, 72 Stat. 1446; amended Pub.L. 89–614, § 2(1), Sept. 30, 1966, 80 Stat. 862; Pub.L. 89–718, § 8(a), Nov. 2, 1966, 80 Stat. 1117; Pub.L. 96–513, Title I, § 115(b), Title V, § 511(34)(A), (35), (36), Dec. 12, 1980, 94 Stat. 2877, 2922, 2923; Pub.L. 97–252, Title X, § 1004(a), Sept. 8, 1982, 96 Stat. 737; Pub.L. 98–525, Title VI, § 645(a), Oct. 19, 1984, 98 Stat. 2548; Pub.L. 98–557, § 19(1), Oct. 30, 1984, 98 Stat. 2869; Pub.L. 99–661, Div. A, Title VII, § 701(b), Nov. 14, 1986, 100 Stat. 3898; Pub.L. 101–189, Div. A, Title VII, § 731(a), Nov. 29, 1989, 103 Stat. 1481; Pub.L. 102–484, Div. A, Title VII, § 706, Oct. 23, 1992, 106 Stat. 2433; Pub.L. 103–160, Div. A, Title VII, § 702(a), Nov. 30, 1993, 107 Stat. 1686; Pub.L. 103–337, Div. A, Title VII, § 701(a), Oct. 5, 1994, 108 Stat. 2797; Pub.L. 105–85, Div. A, Title VII, § 711, Nov. 18, 1997, 111 Stat. 1808; Pub.L. 107–107, Div. A, Title VII, § 701(c), Dec. 28, 2001, 115 Stat. 1160; Pub.L. 109–163, Div. A, Title V, § 592(b), Title X, § 1057(a)(2), Jan. 6, 2006, 119 Stat. 3280, 3440; Pub.L. 110–181, Div. A, Title VII, § 708(a), Jan. 28, 2008, 122 Stat. 190; Pub.L. 114–328, Div. A, Title VII, § 701(j)(1)(A), Dec. 23, 2016, 130 Stat. 2191.)

§ 1076. Medical and dental care for dependents: general rule

(a)(1) A dependent described in paragraph (2) is entitled, upon request, to the medical and dental care prescribed by section 1077 of this title in facilities of the uniformed services, subject to the availability of space and facilities and the capabilities of the medical and dental staff.

(2) A dependent referred to in paragraph (1) is a dependent of a member of a uniformed service described in one of the following subparagraphs:

(A) A member who is on active duty for a period of more than 30 days or died while on that duty.

(B) A member who died from an injury, illness, or disease incurred or aggravated—

(i) while the member was on active duty under a call or order to active duty of 30 days or less, on active duty for training, or on inactive-duty training; or

(ii) while the member was traveling to or from the place at which the member was to perform, or had performed, such active duty, active duty for training, or inactive-duty training.

(C) A member who died from an injury, illness, or disease incurred or aggravated in the line of duty while the member remained overnight immediately before the commencement of inactive-duty training, or while the member remained overnight between successive periods of inactive-duty training, at or in the vicinity of the site of the inactive-duty training.

(D) A member on active duty who is entitled to benefits under subsection (e) of section 1074a of this title by reason of paragraph (1), (2), or (3) of subsection (a) of such section.

(E) A member who died from an injury, illness, or disease incurred or aggravated while the member—

(i) was serving on funeral honors duty under section 12503 of this title or section 115 of title 32;

(ii) was traveling to or from the place at which the member was to so serve; or

(iii) remained overnight at or in the vicinity of that place immediately before so serving, if the place is outside reasonable commuting distance from the member's residence.

(b) Under regulations to be prescribed jointly by the administering Secretaries, a dependent of a member or former member—

(1) who is, or (if deceased) was at the time of his death, entitled to retired or retainer pay or equivalent pay; or

(2) who died before attaining age 60 and at the time of his death would have been eligible for retired pay under chapter 1223 of this title (or under chapter 67 of this title as in effect before December 1, 1994) but for the fact that he was under 60 years of age;

may, upon request, be given the medical and dental care prescribed by section 1077 of this title in facilities of the uniformed services, subject to the availability of space and facilities and the capabilities of the medical and dental staff, except that a dependent of a member or former member described in paragraph (2) may not be given such medical or dental care until the date on which such member or former member would have attained age 60.

(c) A determination by the medical or dental officer in charge, or the contract surgeon in charge, or his designee, as to the availability of space and facilities and to the capabilities of the medical and dental staff is conclusive. Care under this section may not be permitted to interfere with the primary mission of those facilities.

(d) To utilize more effectively the medical and dental facilities of the uniformed services, the administering Secretaries shall prescribe joint regulations to assure that dependents entitled to medical or dental care under this section will not be denied equal opportunity for that care because the facility concerned is that of a uniformed service other than that of the member.

(e)(1) Subject to paragraph (3), the administering Secretary shall furnish an abused dependent of a former member of a uniformed service described in paragraph (4), during that period that the abused dependent is in receipt of transitional compensation under section 1059 of this title, with medical and dental care, including mental health services, in facilities of the uniformed services in accordance with the same eligibility and benefits as were applicable for that abused dependent during the period of active service of the former member.

(2) Subject to paragraph (3), upon request of any dependent of a former member of a uniformed service punished for an abuse described in paragraph (4), the administering Secretary for such uniformed service may furnish medical care in facilities of the uniformed services to the dependent for the treatment of any adverse health condition resulting from such dependent's knowledge of (A) the abuse, or (B) any injury or illness suffered by the abused person as a result of such abuse.

(3) Medical and dental care furnished to a dependent of a former member of the uniformed services in facilities of the uniformed services under paragraph (1) or (2)—

(A) shall be limited to the health care prescribed by section 1077 of this title; and

(B) shall be subject to the availability of space and facilities and the capabilities of the medical and dental staff.

(4)(A) A former member of a uniformed service referred to in paragraph (1) is a member who—

(i) received a dishonorable or bad-conduct discharge or was dismissed from a uniformed service as a result of a court-martial conviction for an offense, under either military or civil law, involving abuse of a dependent of the member; or

(ii) was administratively discharged from a uniformed service as a result of such an offense.

(B) A determination of whether an offense involved abuse of a dependent of the member shall be made in accordance with regulations prescribed by the administering Secretary for such uniformed service.

(f)(1) The administering Secretaries shall furnish an eligible dependent a physical examination that is required by a school in connection with the enrollment of the dependent as a student in that school.

(2) A dependent is eligible for a physical examination under paragraph (1) if the dependent—

(A) is entitled to receive medical care under subsection (a) or is authorized to receive medical care under subsection (b); and

(B) is at least 5 years of age and less than 12 years of age.

(3) Nothing in paragraph (2) may be construed to prohibit the furnishing of a school-required physical examination to any dependent who, except for not satisfying the age requirement under that paragraph, would otherwise be eligible for a physical examination required to be furnished under this subsection. *(Added Pub.L. 85–861, § 1(25)(B), Sept. 2, 1958, 72 Stat. 1447; amended Pub.L. 89–614, § 2(3), Sept. 30, 1966, 80 Stat. 862; Pub.L. 95–397, Title III, § 301, Sept. 30, 1978, 92 Stat. 849; Pub.L. 96–513, Title V, § 511(36), Dec. 12, 1980, 94 Stat. 2923; Pub.L. 97–252, Title X, § 1004(b), Sept. 8, 1982, 96 Stat. 737; Pub.L. 98–557, § 19(5), Oct. 30, 1984, 98 Stat. 2869; Pub.L. 99–145, Title VI, § 652(a), Nov. 8, 1985, 99 Stat. 656; Pub.L. 99–661, Div. A, Title VI, §§ 604(f)(1)(C), 652(c), Nov. 14, 1986, 100 Stat. 3877, 3889; Pub.L. 100–456, Div. A, Title VI, § 651(a), Sept. 29, 1988, 102 Stat. 1990; Pub.L. 101–189, Div. A, Title VI, § 653(a)(4), Title VII, § 731(c)(1), Nov. 29, 1989, 103 Stat. 1462, 1482; Pub.L. 103–337, Div. A, Title VII, § 704(a), (b), Title XVI, § 1671(c)(7)(A), Oct. 5, 1994, 108 Stat. 2798, 3014; Pub.L. 104–106, Div. A, Title VII, § 703, Title XV, § 1501(c)(11), Feb. 10, 1996, 110 Stat. 372, 499; Pub.L. 105–85, Div. A, Title V, § 513(b), Title X, § 1073(d)(1)(D), Nov. 18, 1997, 111 Stat. 1730, 1905; Pub.L. 105–261, Div. A, Title VII, § 732, Oct. 17, 1998, 12 Stat. 2071; Pub.L. 106–65, Div. A, Title V, § 578(i)(2), Title VII, § 705(c), Oct. 5, 1999, 113 Stat. 629, 684; Pub.L. 106–398, § 1 [Div. A, Title VII, § 703], Oct. 30, 2000, 114 Stat. 1654, 1654A–174; Pub.L. 107–107, Div. A, Title V, § 513(a), Dec. 28, 2001, 115 Stat. 1093.)*

CHAPTER 71—COMPUTATION OF RETIRED PAY

§ 1408. Payment of retired or retainer pay in compliance with court orders

(a) Definitions.—In this section:

(1) The term "court" means—

(A) any court of competent jurisdiction of any State, the District of Columbia, the Commonwealth of Puerto Rico, Guam, American Samoa, the Virgin Islands, the Northern Mariana Islands, and the Trust Territory of the Pacific Islands;

(B) any court of the United States (as defined in section 451 of title 28) having competent jurisdiction;

(C) any court of competent jurisdiction of a foreign country with which the United States has an agreement requiring the United States to honor any court order of such country; and

(D) any administrative or judicial tribunal of a State competent to enter orders for support or maintenance (including a State agency administering a program under a State plan approved under part D of title IV of the Social Security Act), and, for purposes of this subparagraph, the term "State" includes the District of Columbia, the Commonwealth of Puerto Rico, the Virgin Islands, Guam, and American Samoa.

(2) The term "court order" means a final decree of divorce, dissolution, annulment, or legal separation issued by a court, or a court ordered, ratified, or approved property settlement incident to such a decree (including a final decree modifying the terms of a previously issued decree of divorce, dissolution, annulment, or legal separation, or a court ordered, ratified, or approved property settlement incident to such previously issued decree), or a support order, as defined in section 453(p) of the Social Security Act (42 U.S.C. 653(p)), which—

(A) is issued in accordance with the laws of the jurisdiction of that court;

(B) provides for—

(i) payment of child support (as defined in section 459(i)(2) of the Social Security Act (42 U.S.C. 659(i)(2)));

(ii) payment of alimony (as defined in section 459(i)(3) of the Social Security Act (42 U.S.C. 659(i)(3))); or

(iii) division of property (including a division of community property); and

(C) in the case of a division of property, specifically provides for the payment of an amount, expressed in dollars or as a percentage of disposable retired pay, from the disposable retired pay of a member to the spouse or former spouse of that member.

(3) The term "final decree" means a decree from which no appeal may be taken or from which no appeal has been taken within the time allowed for taking such appeals under the laws applicable to such appeals, or a decree from which timely appeal has been taken and such appeal has been finally decided under the laws applicable to such appeals.

(4)(A) The term "disposable retired pay" means the total monthly retired pay to which a member is entitled (as determined pursuant to subparagraph (B)[1] less amounts which—

(i) are owed by that member to the United States for previous overpayments of retired pay and for recoupments required by law resulting from entitlement to retired pay;

(ii) are deducted from the retired pay of such member as a result of forfeitures of retired pay ordered by a court-marital or as a result of a waiver of retired pay required by law in order to receive compensation under title 5 or title 38;

(iii) in the case of a member entitled to retired pay under chapter 61 of this title, are equal to the amount of retired pay of the member under that chapter computed using the percentage of the member's disability on the date when the member was retired (or the date on which the member's name was placed on the temporary disability retired list); or

(iv) are deducted because of an election under chapter 73 of this title to provide an annuity to a spouse or former spouse to whom payment of a portion of such member's retired pay is being made pursuant to a court order under this section.

(B) For purposes of subparagraph (A), the total monthly retired pay to which a member is entitled shall be—

(i) the amount of basic pay payable to the member for the member's pay grade and years of service at the time of the court order, as increased by

(ii) each cost-of-living adjustment that occurs under section 1401a(b) of this title between the time of the court order and the time of the member's retirement using the adjustment provisions under that section applicable to the member upon retirement.

(5) The term "member" includes a former member entitled to retired pay under section 12731 of this title.

(6) The term "spouse or former spouse" means the husband or wife, or former husband or wife, respectively, of a member who, on or before the date of a court order, was married to that member.

(7) The term "retired pay" includes retainer pay.

(b) Effective service of process.—For the purposes of this section—

(1) service of a court order is effective if—

(A) an appropriate agent of the Secretary concerned designated for receipt of service of court orders under regulations prescribed pursuant to subsection (i) or, if no agent has been so designated, the Secretary concerned, is personally served or is served by facsimile or electronic transmission or by mail;

(B) the court order is regular on its face;

(C) the court order or other documents served with the court order identify the member concerned and include, if possible, the social security number of such member; and

(D) the court order or other documents served with the court order certify that the rights of the member under the Servicemembers Civil Relief Act (50 U.S.C. 3901 et seq.) were observed; and

(2) a court order is regular on its face if the order—

(A) is issued by a court of competent jurisdiction;

(B) is legal in form; and

(C) includes nothing on its face that provides reasonable notice that it is issued without authority of law.

(c) Authority for court to treat retired pay as property of the member and spouse.—(1) Subject to the limitations of this section, a court may treat disposable retired pay payable to a member for pay periods beginning after June 25, 1981, either as property solely of the member or as property of the member and his spouse in accordance with the law of the jurisdiction of such court. A court may not treat retired pay as property in any proceeding to divide or partition any amount of retired pay of a member as the property of the member and the member's spouse or former spouse if a final decree of divorce, dissolution, annulment, or legal separation (including a court ordered, ratified, or approved property settlement incident to such decree) affecting the member and the member's spouse or former spouse (A) was issued before June 25, 1981, and (B) did not treat (or reserve jurisdiction to treat) any amount of retired pay of the member as property of the member and the member's spouse or former spouse.

(2) Notwithstanding any other provision of law, this section does not create any right, title, or interest which can be sold, assigned, transferred, or otherwise disposed of (including by inheritance) by a spouse or former spouse. Payments by the Secretary concerned under subsection (d) to a spouse or former spouse with respect to a division of retired pay as the property of a member and the member's spouse under this subsection may not be treated as amounts received as retired pay for service in the uniformed services.

(3) This section does not authorize any court to order a member to apply for retirement or retire at a particular time in order to effectuate any payment under this section.

(4) A court may not treat the disposable retired pay of a member in the manner described in paragraph (1) unless the court has jurisdiction over the member by reason of (A) his residence, other than because of military assignment, in the territorial jurisdiction of the court, (B) his domicile in the territorial jurisdiction of the court, or (C) his consent to the jurisdiction of the court.

(d) Payments by Secretary concerned to (or for benefit of) spouse or former spouse.—(1) After effective service on the Secretary concerned of a court order providing for the payment of child support or alimony or, with respect to a division of property, specifically providing for the payment of an amount of the disposable retired pay from a member to the spouse or a former spouse of the member, the Secretary shall make payments (subject to the limitations of this section) from the disposable retired pay of the member to the spouse or former spouse (or for the benefit of such spouse or former spouse to a State disbursement unit established pursuant to section 454B of the Social Security Act or other public payee designated by a State, in accordance with part D of title IV of the Social Security Act, as directed by court order, or as otherwise directed in accordance with such part D) in an amount sufficient to satisfy the amount of child support and alimony set forth in the court order and, with respect to a division of property, in the amount of disposable retired pay specifically provided for in the court order. In the case of a spouse or former spouse who, pursuant to section 408(a)(3) of the Social Security Act (42 U.S.C. 608(a)(4)), assigns to a State the rights of the spouse or former spouse to receive support, the Secretary concerned may make the child support payments referred to in the preceding sentence to that State in amounts consistent with that assignment of rights. In the case of a member entitled to receive retired pay on the date of the effective service of the court order, such payments shall begin not later than 90 days after the date of effective service. In the case of a member not entitled to receive retired pay on the date of the effective service of the court order, such payments shall begin not later than 90 days after the date on which the member first becomes entitled to receive retired pay.

(2) If the spouse or former spouse to whom payments are to be made under this section was not married to the member for a period of 10 years or more during which the member performed at least 10 years of service creditable in determining the member's eligibility for retired pay, payments may not be made under this section to the extent that they include an amount resulting from the treatment by the court under subsection (c) of disposable retired pay of the member as property of the member or property of the member and his spouse.

(3) Payments under this section shall not be made more frequently than once each month, and the Secretary concerned shall not be required to vary normal pay and disbursement cycles for retired pay in order to comply with a court order.

(4) Payments from the disposable retired pay of a member pursuant to this section shall terminate in accordance with the terms of the applicable court order, but not later than the date of the death of the member or the date of the death of the spouse or former spouse to whom payments are being made, whichever occurs first.

(5) If a court order described in paragraph (1) provides for a division of property (including a division of community property) in addition to an amount of child support or alimony or the payment of an amount of disposable retired pay as the result of the court's treatment of such pay under subsection (c) as property of the member and his spouse, the Secretary concerned shall pay (subject to the limitations of this section) from the disposable retired pay of the member to the spouse or former spouse of the member, any part of the amount payable to the spouse or former spouse under the division of property upon effective service of a final court order of garnishment of such amount from such retired pay.

(6) In the case of a court order for which effective service is made on the Secretary concerned on or after August 22, 1996, and which provides for payments from the disposable retired pay of a member to satisfy the amount of child support set forth in the order, the authority provided in paragraph (1) to make payments from the disposable retired pay of a member to satisfy the amount of child support set forth in a court order shall apply to payment of any amount of child support arrearages set forth in that order as well as to amounts of child support that currently become due.

(7)(A) The Secretary concerned may not accept service of a court order that is an out-of-State modification, or comply with the provisions of such a court order, unless the court issuing that order has jurisdiction in the manner specified in subsection (c)(4) over both the member and the spouse or former spouse involved.

(B) A court order shall be considered to be an out-of-State modification for purposes of this paragraph if the order—

(i) modifies a previous court order under this section upon which payments under this subsection are based; and

(ii) is issued by a court of a State other than the State of the court that issued the previous court order.

(e) Limitations.—(1) The total amount of the disposable retired pay of a member payable under all court orders pursuant to subsection (c) may not exceed 50 percent of such disposable retired pay.

(2) In the event of effective service of more than one court order which provide for payment to a spouse and one or more former spouses or to more than one former spouse, the disposable retired pay of the member shall be used to satisfy (subject to the limitations of paragraph (1)) such court orders on a first-come, first-served basis. Such court orders shall be satisfied (subject to the limitations of paragraph (1)) out of that amount of disposable retired pay which remains after the satisfaction of all court orders which have been previously served.

(3)(A) In the event of effective service of conflicting court orders under this section which assert to direct that different amounts be paid during a month to the same spouse or former spouse of the same member, the Secretary concerned shall—

(i) pay to that spouse from the member's disposable retired pay the least amount directed to be paid during that month by any such conflicting court order, but not more than the amount of disposable retired pay which remains available for payment of such court orders based on when such court orders were effectively served and the limitations of paragraph (1) and subparagraph (B) of paragraph (4);

(ii) retain an amount of disposable retired pay that is equal to the lesser of—

(I) the difference between the largest amount required by any conflicting court order to be paid to the spouse or former spouse and the amount payable to the spouse or former spouse under clause (i); and

(II) the amount of disposable retired pay which remains available for payment of any conflicting court order based on when such court order was effectively served and the limitations of paragraph (1) and subparagraph (B) of paragraph (4); and

(iii) pay to that member the amount which is equal to the amount of that member's disposable retired pay (less any amount paid during such month pursuant to legal process served under section 459 of the Social Security Act (42 U.S.C. 659) and any amount paid during such month pursuant to court orders effectively served under this section, other than such conflicting court orders) minus—

(I) the amount of disposable retired pay paid under clause (i); and

(II) the amount of disposable retired pay retained under clause (ii).

(B) The Secretary concerned shall hold the amount retained under clause (ii) of subparagraph (A) until such time as that Secretary is provided with a court order which has been certified by the member and the spouse or former spouse to be valid and applicable to the retained amount. Upon being provided with such an order, the Secretary shall pay the retained amount in accordance with the order.

(4)(A) In the event of effective service of a court order under this section and the service of legal process pursuant to section 459 of the Social Security Act (42 U.S.C. 659), both of which provide for payments during a month from the same member, satisfaction of such court orders and legal process from the retired pay of the member shall be on a first-come, first-served basis. Such court orders and legal process shall be satisfied out of moneys which are subject to such orders and legal process and which remain available in accordance with the limitations of paragraph (1) and subparagraph (B) of this paragraph during such month after the satisfaction of all court orders or legal process which have been previously served.

(B) Notwithstanding any other provision of law, the total amount of the disposable retired pay of a member payable by the Secretary concerned under all court orders pursuant to this section and all legal processes pursuant to section 459 of the Social Security Act (42 U.S.C. 659) with respect to a member may not exceed 65 percent of the amount of the retired pay payable to such member that is considered under section 462 of the Social Security Act (42 U.S.C. 662) to be remuneration for employment that is payable by the United States.

(5) A court order which itself or because of previously served court orders provides for the payment of an amount which exceeds the amount of disposable retired pay available for payment because of the limit set forth in paragraph (1), or which, because of previously served court orders or legal process previously served under section 459 of the Social Security Act (42 U.S.C. 659), provides for payment of an amount that exceeds the maximum amount permitted under paragraph (1) or subparagraph (B) of paragraph (4), shall not be considered to be irregular on its face solely for that reason. However, such order shall be considered to be fully satisfied for purposes of this section by the payment to the spouse or former spouse of the maximum amount of disposable retired pay permitted under paragraph (1) and subparagraph (B) of paragraph (4).

(6) Nothing in this section shall be construed to relieve a member of liability for the payment of alimony, child support, or other payments required by a court order on the grounds that payments made out of disposable retired pay under this section have been made in the maximum amount permitted under paragraph (1) or subparagraph (B) of paragraph (4). Any such unsatisfied obligation of a member may be enforced by any means available under law other than the means provided under this section in any case in which the maximum amount permitted under paragraph (1) has been paid and under section 459 of the Social Security Act (42 U.S.C. 659) in any case in which the maximum amount permitted under subparagraph (B) of paragraph (4) has been paid.

(f) Immunity of officers and employees of United States.—(1) The United States and any officer or employee of the United States shall not be liable with respect to any payment made from retired pay to any member, spouse, or former spouse pursuant to a court order that is regular on its face if such payment is made in accordance with this section and the regulations prescribed pursuant to subsection (i).

(2) An officer or employee of the United States who, under regulations prescribed pursuant to subsection (i), has the duty to respond to interrogatories shall not be subject under any law to any disciplinary action or civil or criminal liability or penalty for, or because of, any disclosure of information made by him in carrying out any of his duties which directly or indirectly pertain to answering such interrogatories.

(g) Notice to member of service of court order on Secretary concerned.—A person receiving effective service of a court order under this section shall, as soon as possible, but not later than 30 days after the date on which effective service is made, send a written notice of such court order (together with a copy of such order) to the member affected by the court order at his last known address.

(h) Benefits for dependents who are victims of abuse by members losing right to retired pay.—(1)(A) If, in the case of a member or former member of the armed forces referred to in paragraph (2)(A), a court order provides (in the manner applicable to a division of property) for the payment of an amount from the disposable retired pay of that member or former member (as certified under paragraph (4)) to an eligible spouse or former spouse of that member or former member, the Secretary concerned, beginning upon effective service of such court order, shall pay that amount in accordance with this subsection to such spouse or former spouse.

(B) If, in the case of a member or former member of the armed forces referred to in paragraph (2)(A), a court order provides for the payment as child support of an amount from the disposable retired pay of that member or former member (as certified under paragraph (4)) to an eligible dependent child of the member or former member, the Secretary concerned, beginning upon effective service of such court order, shall pay that amount in accordance with this subsection to such dependent child.

(2) A spouse or former spouse, or a dependent child, of a member or former member of the armed forces is eligible to receive payment under this subsection if—

(A) the member or former member, while a member of the armed forces and after becoming eligible to be retired from the armed forces on the basis of years of service, has eligibility to receive retired pay terminated as a result of misconduct while a member involving abuse of a spouse or dependent child (as defined in regulations prescribed by the Secretary of Defense or, for the Coast Guard when it is not operating as a service in the Navy, by the Secretary of Homeland Security);

(B) in the case of eligibility of a spouse or former spouse under paragraph (1)(A), the spouse or former spouse—

(i) was the victim of the abuse and was married to the member or former member at the time of that abuse; or

(ii) is a natural or adopted parent of a dependent child of the member or former member who was the victim of the abuse; and

(C) in the case of eligibility of a dependent child under paragraph (1) (B), the other parent of the child died as a result of the misconduct that resulted in the termination of retired pay.

(3) The amount certified by the Secretary concerned under paragraph (4) with respect to a member or former member of the armed forces referred to in paragraph (2)(A) shall be deemed to be the disposable retired pay of that member or former member for the purposes of this subsection.

(4) Upon the request of a court or an eligible spouse or former spouse, or an eligible dependent child, of a member or former member of the armed forces referred to in paragraph (2)(A) in connection with a civil action for the issuance of a court order in the case of that member or former member, the Secretary concerned shall determine and certify the amount of the monthly retired pay that the member or former member would have been entitled to receive as of the date of the certification—

(A) if the member or former member's eligibility for retired pay had not been terminated as described in paragraph (2)(A); and

(B) if, in the case of a member or former member not in receipt of retired pay immediately before that termination of eligibility for retired pay, the member or former member had retired on the effective date of that termination of eligibility.

(5) A court order under this subsection may provide that whenever retired pay is increased under section 1401a of this title (or any other provision of law), the amount payable under the court order to the spouse or former spouse, or the dependent child, of a member or former member described in paragraph (2)(A) shall be increased at the same time by the percent by which the retired pay of the member or former member would have been increased if the member or former member were receiving retired pay.

(6) Notwithstanding any other provision of law, a member or former member of the armed forces referred to in paragraph (2)(A) shall have no ownership interest in, or claim against, any amount payable under this section to a spouse or former spouse, or to a dependent child, of the member or former member.

(7)(A) If a former spouse receiving payments under this subsection with respect to a member or former member referred to in paragraph (2)(A) marries again after such payments begin, the eligibility of the former spouse to receive further payments under this subsection shall terminate on the date of such marriage.

(B) A person's eligibility to receive payments under this subsection that is terminated under subparagraph (A) by reason of remarriage shall be resumed in the event of the termination of that marriage by the death of that person's spouse or by annulment or divorce. The resumption of payments shall begin as of the first day of the month in which that marriage is so terminated. The monthly amount of the payments shall be the amount that would have been paid if the continuity of the payments had not been interrupted by the marriage.

(8) Payments in accordance with this subsection shall be made out of funds in the Department of Defense Military Retirement Fund established by section 1461 of this title or, in the case of the Coast Guard, out of funds appropriated to the Department of Homeland Security for payment of retired pay for the Coast Guard.

(9)(A) A spouse or former spouse of a member or former member of the armed forces referred to in paragraph (2)(A), while receiving payments in accordance with this subsection, shall be entitled to receive medical and dental care, to use commissary and exchange stores, and to receive any other benefit that a spouse or a former spouse of a retired member of the armed forces is entitled to receive on the basis of being a spouse or former spouse, as the case may be, of a retired member of the armed forces in the same manner as if the member or former member referred to in paragraph (2)(A) was entitled to retired pay.

(B) A dependent child of a member or former member referred to in paragraph (2)(A) who was a member of the household of the member or former member at the time of the misconduct described in paragraph (2)(A) shall be entitled to receive medical and dental care, to use commissary and exchange stores, and to have other benefits provided to dependents of retired members of the armed forces in the same manner as if the member or former member referred to in paragraph (2)(A) was entitled to retired pay.

(C) If a spouse or former spouse or a dependent child eligible or entitled to receive a particular benefit under this paragraph is eligible or entitled to receive that benefit under another provision of law, the eligibility or entitlement of that spouse or former spouse or dependent child to such benefit shall be determined under such other provision of law instead of this paragraph.

(10)(A) For purposes of this subsection, in the case of a member of the armed forces who has been sentenced by a court-martial to receive a punishment that will terminate the eligibility of that member to receive retired pay if executed, the eligibility of that member to receive retired pay may, as determined by the Secretary concerned, be considered terminated effective upon the approval of that sentence by the person acting under section 860(c) of this title (article 60(c) of the Uniform Code of Military Justice).

(B) If each form of the punishment that would result in the termination of eligibility to receive retired pay is later remitted, set aside, or mitigated to a punishment that does not result in the termination of that eligibility, a payment of benefits to the eligible recipient under this subsection that is based on the punishment so vacated, set aside, or mitigated shall cease. The cessation of payments shall be effective as of the first day of the first month following the month in which the Secretary concerned notifies the recipient of such benefits in writing that payment of the benefits will cease. The recipient may not be required to repay the benefits received before that effective date (except to the extent necessary to recoup any amount that was erroneous when paid).

(11) In this subsection, the term "dependent child", with respect to a member or former member of the armed forces referred to in paragraph (2)(A), means an unmarried legitimate child, including an adopted child or a stepchild of the member or former member, who—

(A) is under 18 years of age;

(B) is incapable of self-support because of a mental or physical incapacity that existed before becoming 18 years of age and is dependent on the member or former member for over one-half of the child's support; or

(C) if enrolled in a full-time course of study in an institution of higher education recognized by the Secretary of Defense for the purposes of this subparagraph, is under 23 years of age and is dependent on the member or former member for over one-half of the child's support.

(i) Certification date.—It is not necessary that the date of a certification of the authenticity or completeness of a copy of a court order for child support received by the Secretary concerned for the purposes of this section be recent in relation to the date of receipt by the Secretary.

(j) Regulations.—The Secretaries concerned shall prescribe uniform regulations for the administration of this section.

(k) Relationship to other laws.—In any case involving an order providing for payment of child support (as defined in section 459(i)(2) of the Social Security Act) by a member who has never been married to the other parent of the child, the provisions of this section shall not apply, and the case shall be subject to the provisions of section 459 of such Act.

(Added Pub.L. 97–252, Title X, § 1002(a), Sept. 8, 1982, 96 Stat. 730; amended Pub.L. 98–525, Title VI, § 643(a) to (d), Oct. 19, 1984, 98 Stat. 2547; Pub.L. 99–661, Div. A, Title VI, § 644(a), Nov. 14, 1986, 100 Stat. 3887; Pub.L. 100–26, §§ 3(3), 7(h)(1), Apr. 21, 1987, 101 Stat. 273, 282; Pub.L. 101–189, Div. A, Title VI, § 653(a)(5), Title XVI, § 1622(e)(6), Nov. 29, 1989, 103 Stat. 1462, 1605; Pub.L. 101–510, Div. A, Title V, § 555(a) to (d), (f), (g), Nov. 5, 1990, 104 Stat. 1569, 1570; Pub.L. 102–190, Div. A, Title X, § 1061(a)(7), Dec. 5, 1991, 105 Stat. 1472; Pub.L. 102–484, Div. A, Title VI, § 653(a), Oct. 23, 1992, 106 Stat. 2426; Pub.L. 103–160, Div. A, Title V, § 555(a), (b), Title XI, § 1182(a)(2), Nov. 30, 1993, 107 Stat. 1666, 1771; Pub.L. 104–106, Div. A, Title XV, § 1501(c)(16), Feb. 10, 1996, 110 Stat. 499; Pub.L. 104–193, Title III, §§ 362(c), 363(c)(1) to (3), Aug. 22, 1996, 110 Stat. 2246, 2249; Pub.L. 104–201, Div. A, Title VI, § 636, Sept. 23, 1996, 110 Stat. 2579; Pub.L. 105–85, Div. A, Title X, § 1073(a)(24), (25), Nov. 18, 1997, 111 Stat. 1901; Pub.L. 107–107, Div. A, Title X, § 1048(c)(9), Dec. 28, 2001, 115 Stat. 1226; Pub.L. 107–296, Title XVII, § 1704(b)(1), Nov. 25, 2002, 116 Stat. 2314; Pub.L. 108–189, § 2(c), Dec. 19, 2003, 117 Stat. 2866; Pub.L. 109–163, Div. A, Title VI, § 665(a), Jan. 6, 2006, 119 Stat. 3317; Pub.L. 111–84, Div. A, Title X, § 1073(a)(15), Oct. 28, 2009, 123 Stat. 2473; Pub.L. 114–328, Div. A, Title VI, § 641(a), Title X, § 1081(b)(2)(B), Dec. 23, 2016, 130 Stat. 2164, 2418.)

[1] So in original. Probably should read "subparagraph (B))".

Commentary

Mansell v. Mansell, 490 U.S. 581 (1989), holds that subsection (c) restricts state marital property distribution of armed services benefits to "disposable retired or retainer pay" and hence does not authorize state law distribution of disability pay. Despite the holding of *Mansell, In re Marriage of Babauta, 66 Cal.App.4th 784, 78 Cal.Rptr.2d 281 (1998),* held that Marine Corps voluntary separation pay is subject to state law distribution at divorce.

However, *In re Marriage of Smith, 148 Cal.App.4th 1115, 56 Cal.Rptr.3d 341 (2007), review denied April 19, 2007,* approved a trial court judgment stipulated by the parties, which divided the community property portion of a husband's future retirement pay, required that the husband name the wife the beneficiary of a survivor's benefit so that she would not lose her interest in the retirement pay if he were to predecease her, and provided that if the husband elected in the future to receive disability in lieu of retirement pay, he would indemnify his former wife for his unilateral reduction of the value of the retirement benefits. The final provision was intended to insure that the wife received the value of the bargain she made at dissolution. *Smith* distinguished *Mansell* on the ground that *Mansell* held that federal law does not give state divorce courts the power to distribute military retirement pay that has been waived to receive disability benefits. In *Smith*, the judgment distributed an existing asset, the community property portion of future retirement pay.

The holding of *In re Marriage of Smith, supra,* may be called into question by *Howell v.Howell, 137 S.Ct. 1400, 197 L.Ed.2d 781 (2017),* in which the United States Supreme Court held that a state court may not order a veteran to reimburse a former spouse for military retirement benefits that were awarded to the nonmilitary spouse in a divorce, but which the veteran later waived in order to receive military disability benefits. Alternatively, *Smith* may be distinguished from *Howell* in that the former spouse's entitlement in *Smith* was based on the parties' contract, rather than upon a state court order.

Subsection (a) 4B, added by a 2016 amendment, prohibits a California court from applying the California time rule to "disposable retired or retainer pay." Instead, the value of the pension of a service member who has not yet retired is frozen at the time of the court order dividing the pension.

CHAPTER 73—ANNUITIES BASED ON RETIRED OR RETAINER PAY

SUBCHAPTER II—SURVIVOR BENEFIT PLAN

Sec.

§ 1447. Definitions

In this subchapter:

(1) Plan.—The term "Plan" means the Survivor Benefit Plan established by this subchapter.

(2) Standard annuity.—The term "standard annuity" means an annuity provided by virtue of eligibility under section 1448(a)(1)(A) of this title.

(3) Reserve-component annuity.—The term "reserve-component annuity" means an annuity provided by virtue of eligibility under section 1448(a)(1)(B) of this title.

(4) Retired pay.—The term "retired pay" includes retainer pay paid under section 6330 of this title.

(5) Reserve-component retired pay.—The term "reserve-component retired pay" means retired pay under chapter 1223 of this title (or under chapter 67 of this title as in effect before the effective date of the Reserve Officer Personnel Management Act).

(6) Base amount.—The term "base amount" means the following:

(A) Full amount under standard annuity.—In the case of a person who dies after becoming entitled to retired pay, such term means the amount of monthly retired pay (determined without regard to any reduction under section 1409(b)(2) of this title) to which the person—

(i) was entitled when he became eligible for that pay; or

(ii) later became entitled by being advanced on the retired list, performing active duty, or being transferred from the temporary disability retired list to the permanent disability retired list.

(B) Full amount under reserve-component annuity.—In the case of a person who would have become eligible for reserve-component retired pay but for the fact that he died before becoming 60 years of age, such term means the amount of monthly retired pay for which the person would have been eligible—

(i) if he had been 60 years of age on the date of his death, for purposes of an annuity to become effective on the day after his death in accordance with a designation made under section 1448(e) of this title; or

(ii) upon becoming 60 years of age (if he had lived to that age), for purposes of an annuity to become effective on the 60th anniversary of his birth in accordance with a designation made under section 1448(e) of this title.

(C) Reduced amount.—Such term means any amount less than the amount otherwise applicable under subparagraph (A) or (B) with respect to an annuity provided under the Plan but which is not less than $300 and which is designated by the person (with the concurrence of the person's spouse, if required under section 1448(a)(3) of this title) providing the annuity on or before—

(i) the first day for which he becomes eligible for retired pay, in the case of a person providing a standard annuity, or

(ii) the end of the 90–day period beginning on the date on which he receives the notification required by section 12731(d) of this title that he has completed the years of service required for eligibility for reserve-component retired pay, in the case of a person providing a reserve-component annuity.

(7) Widow.—The term "widow" means the surviving wife of a person who, if not married to the person at the time he became eligible for retired pay—

(A) was married to him for at least one year immediately before his death; or

(B) is the mother of issue by that marriage.

(8) Widower.—The term "widower" means the surviving husband of a person who, if not married to the person at the time she became eligible for retired pay—

(A) was married to her for at least one year immediately before her death; or

(B) is the father of issue by that marriage.

(9) Surviving spouse.—The term "surviving spouse" means a widow or widower.

(10) Former spouse.—The term "former spouse" means the surviving former husband or wife of a person who is eligible to participate in the Plan.

(11) Dependent child.—

(A) In general.—The term "dependent child" means a person who—

(i) is unmarried;

(ii) is (I) under 18 years of age, (II) at least 18, but under 22, years of age and pursuing a full-time course of study or training in a high school, trade school, technical or vocational institute, junior college, college, university, or comparable recognized educational institution, or (III) incapable of self support because of a mental or physical incapacity existing before the person's eighteenth birthday or incurred on or after that birthday, but before the person's twenty-second birthday, while pursuing such a full-time course of study or training; and

(iii) is the child of a person to whom the Plan applies, including (I) an adopted child, and (II) a stepchild, foster child, or recognized natural child who lived with that person in a regular parent-child relationship.

(B) Special rules for college students.—For the purpose of subparagraph (A), a child whose twenty-second birthday occurs before July 1 or after August 31 of a calendar year, and while regularly pursuing such a course of study or training, is considered to have become 22 years of age on the first day of July after that birthday. A child who is a student is considered not to have ceased to be a student during an interim between school years if the interim is not more than 150 days and if the child shows to the satisfaction of the Secretary of Defense that the child has a bona fide intention of continuing to pursue a course of study or training in the same or a different school during the school semester (or other period into which the school year is divided) immediately after the interim.

(C) Foster children.—A foster child, to qualify under this paragraph as the dependent child of a person to whom the Plan applies, must, at the time of the death of that person, also reside with, and receive over one-half of his support from, that person, and not be cared for under a social agency contract. The temporary absence of a foster child from the residence of that person, while a student as described in this paragraph, shall not be considered to affect the residence of such a foster child.

(12) Court.—The term "court" has the meaning given that term by section 1408(a)(1) of this title.

(13) Court order.—

(A) In general.—The term "court order" means a court's final decree of divorce, dissolution, or annulment or a court ordered, ratified, or approved property settlement incident to such a decree (including a final decree modifying the terms of a previously issued decree of divorce, dissolution, annulment, or legal separation, or of a court ordered, ratified, or approved property settlement agreement incident to such previously issued decree).

(B) Final decree.—The term "final decree" means a decree from which no appeal may be taken or from which no appeal has been taken within the time allowed for the taking of such appeals under the laws applicable to such appeals, or a decree from which timely appeal has been taken and such appeal has been finally decided under the laws applicable to such appeals.

(C) Regular on its face.—The term "regular on its face", when used in connection with a court order, means a court order that meets the conditions prescribed in section 1408(b)(2) of this title.

(Added Pub.L. 92–425, § 1(3), Sept. 21, 1972, 86 Stat. 706; amended Pub.L. 94–496, § 1(1), Oct. 14, 1976, 90 Stat. 2375; Pub.L. 95–397, Title II, § 201, Sept. 30, 1978, 92 Stat. 843; Pub.L. 96–402, § 2, Oct. 9, 1980, 94 Stat. 1705; Pub.L. 97–252, Title X, § 1003(a), Sept. 8, 1982, 96 Stat. 735; Pub.L. 98–94, Title IX, § 941(c)(1), Sept. 24, 1983, 97 Stat. 653; Pub.L. 99–145, Title VII, §§ 719(1), (2), 721(b), Nov. 8, 1985, 99 Stat. 675, 676; Pub.L. 99–348, Title III, § 301(a)(1), July 1, 1986, 100 Stat. 702; Pub.L. 99–661, Div. A, Title XIII, § 1343(a)(8)(A), Nov. 14, 1986, 100 Stat. 3992; Pub.L. 100–180, Div. A, Title XII, § 1231(17), Dec. 4, 1987, 101 Stat. 1161; Pub.L. 101–189, Div. A, Title XIV, § 1407(a)(1) to (3), Nov. 29, 1989, 103 Stat. 1588; Pub.L. 101–510, Div. A, Title XIV, § 1484(l)(4)(C)(i), Nov. 5, 1990, 104 Stat. 1720; Pub.L. 103–337, Div. A, Title XVI, § 1671(d), Oct. 5, 1994, 108 Stat. 3014; Pub.L. 104–201, Div. A, Title VI, § 634, Sept. 23, 1996, 110 Stat. 2551.)

§ 1448. Application of Plan

(a) General rules for participation in the Plan.—

(1) Name of Plan; eligible participants.—The program established by this subchapter shall be known as the Survivor Benefit Plan. The following persons are eligible to participate in the Plan:

(A) Persons entitled to retired pay.

(B) Persons who would be eligible for reserve-component retired pay but for the fact that they are under 60 years of age.

(2) Participants in the Plan.—The Plan applies to the following persons, who shall be participants in the Plan:

(A) Standard annuity participants.—A person who is eligible to participate in the Plan under paragraph (1)(A) and who is married or has a dependent child when he becomes entitled to retired pay, unless he elects (with his spouse's concurrence, if required under paragraph (3)) not to participate in the Plan before the first day for which he is eligible for that pay.

(B) Reserve-component annuity participants.—A person who (i) is eligible to participate in the Plan under paragraph (1)(B), and (ii) is married or has a dependent child when he is notified under section 12731(d) of this title that he has completed the years of service required for eligibility for reserve-component retired pay, unless the person elects (with his spouse's concurrence, if required under paragraph (3)) not to participate in the Plan before the end of the 90–day period beginning on the date on which he receives that notification.

A person who elects under subparagraph (B) not to participate in the Plan remains eligible, upon reaching 60 years of age and otherwise becoming entitled to retired pay, to participate in the Plan in accordance with eligibility under paragraph (1)(A).

(3) Elections.—

(A) Spousal consent for certain elections respecting standard annuity.—A married person who is eligible to provide a standard annuity may not without the concurrence of the person's spouse elect—

(i) not to participate in the Plan;

(ii) to provide an annuity for the person's spouse at less than the maximum level; or

(iii) to provide an annuity for a dependent child but not for the person's spouse.

(B) Spousal consent for certain elections respecting reserve-component annuity.—A married person who is eligible to provide a reserve-component annuity may not without the concurrence of the person's spouse elect—

(i) not to participate in the Plan;

(ii) to designate under subsection (e)(2) the effective date for commencement of annuity payments under the Plan in the event that the member dies before becoming 60 years of age to be the 60th anniversary of the member's birth (rather than the day after the date of the member's death);

(iii) to provide an annuity for the person's spouse at less than the maximum level; or

(iv) to provide an annuity for a dependent child but not for the person's spouse.

(C) Exception when spouse unavailable.—A person may make an election described in subparagraph (A) or (B) without the concurrence of the person's spouse if the person establishes to the satisfaction of the Secretary concerned—

(i) that the spouse's whereabouts cannot be determined; or

(ii) that, due to exceptional circumstances, requiring the person to seek the spouse's consent would otherwise be inappropriate.

(D) Construction with former spouse election provisions.—This paragraph does not affect any right or obligation to elect to provide an annuity for a former spouse (or for a former spouse and dependent child) under subsection (b)(2).

(E) Notice to spouse of election to provide former spouse annuity.—If a married person who is eligible to provide a standard annuity elects to provide an annuity for a former spouse (or for a former spouse and dependent child) under subsection (b)(2), that person's spouse shall be notified of that election.

(4) Irrevocability of elections.—

(A) Standard annuity.—An election under paragraph (2)(A) is irrevocable if not revoked before the date on which the person first becomes entitled to retired pay.

(B) Reserve-component annuity.—An election under paragraph (2)(B) is irrevocable if not revoked before the end of the 90–day period referred to in that paragraph.

(5) Participation by person marrying after retirement, etc.—

(A) Election to participate in Plan.—A person who is not married and has no dependent child upon becoming eligible to participate in the Plan but who later marries or acquires a dependent child may elect to participate in the Plan.

(B) Manner and time of election.—Such an election must be written, signed by the person making the election, and received by the Secretary concerned within one year after the date on which that person marries or acquires that dependent child.

(C) Limitation on revocation of election.—Such an election may not be revoked except in accordance with subsection (b)(3).

(D) Effective date of election.—The election is effective as of the first day of the first calendar month following the month in which the election is received by the Secretary concerned.

(E) Designation if RCSBP election.—In the case of a person providing a reserve-component annuity, such an election shall include a designation under subsection (e).

(6) Election out of Plan by person with spouse coverage who remarries.—

(A) General rule.—A person—

(i) who is a participant in the Plan and is providing coverage under the Plan for a spouse (or a spouse and child);

(ii) who does not have an eligible spouse beneficiary under the Plan; and

(iii) who remarries,

may elect not to provide coverage under the Plan for the person's spouse.

(B) Effect of election on retired pay.—If such an election is made, reductions in the retired pay of that person under section 1452 of this title shall not be made.

(C) Terms and conditions of election.—An election under this paragraph—

(i) is irrevocable;

(ii) shall be made within one year after the person's remarriage; and

(iii) shall be made in such form and manner as may be prescribed in regulations under section 1455 of this title.

(D) Notice to spouse.—If a person makes an election under this paragraph—

(i) not to participate in the Plan;

(ii) to provide an annuity for the person's spouse at less than the maximum level; or

(iii) to provide an annuity for a dependent child but not for the person's spouse,

the person's spouse shall be notified of that election.

(E) Construction with former spouse election provisions.—This paragraph does not affect any right or obligation to elect to provide an annuity to a former spouse under subsection (b).

(b) Insurable interest and former spouse coverage.—

(1) Coverage for person with insurable interest.—

(A) General rule.—A person who is not married and does not have a dependent child upon becoming eligible to participate in the Plan may elect to provide an annuity under the Plan to a natural person with an insurable interest in that person. In the case of a person providing a reserve-component annuity, such an election shall include a designation under subsection (e).

(B) Termination of coverage.—An election under subparagraph (A) for a beneficiary who is not the former spouse of the person providing the annuity may be terminated. Any such termination shall be made by a participant by the submission to the Secretary concerned of a request to discontinue participation in the Plan, and such participation in the Plan shall be discontinued effective on the first day of the first month following the month in which the request is received by the Secretary concerned. Effective on such date, the Secretary concerned shall discontinue the reduction being made in such person's retired pay on account of participation in the Plan or, in the case of a person who has been required to make deposits in the Treasury on account of participation in the Plan, such person may discontinue making such deposits effective on such date.

(C) Form for discontinuation.—A request under subparagraph (B) to discontinue participation in the Plan shall be in such form and shall contain such information as may be required under regulations prescribed by the Secretary of Defense.

(D) Withdrawal of request for discontinuation.—The Secretary concerned shall furnish promptly to each person who submits a request under subparagraph (B) to discontinue participation in the Plan a written statement of the advantages and disadvantages of participating in the Plan and the possible disadvantages of discontinuing participation. A person may withdraw the request to discontinue participation if withdrawn within 30 days after having been submitted to the Secretary concerned.

(E) Consequences of discontinuation.—Once participation is discontinued, benefits may not be paid in conjunction with the earlier participation in the Plan and premiums paid may not be refunded. Participation in the Plan may not later be resumed except through a qualified election under paragraph (5) of subsection (a) or under subparagraph (G) of this paragraph.

(F) Vitiation of election by disability retiree who dies of disability-related cause.—If a member retired after November 23, 2003, under chapter 61 of this title dies within one year after the date on which the member is so retired and the cause of death is related to a disability for which the member was retired under that chapter (as determined under regulations prescribed by the Secretary of Defense)—

(i) an election made by the member under paragraph (1) to provide an annuity under the Plan to any person other than a dependent of that member (as defined in section 1072(2) of this title) is vitiated; and

(ii) the amounts by which the member's retired pay was reduced under section 1452 of this title shall be refunded and paid to the person to whom the annuity under the Plan would have been paid pursuant to such election.

(G) Election of new beneficiary upon death of previous beneficiary.—

(i) Authority for election.—If the reason for discontinuation in the Plan is the death of the beneficiary, the participant in the Plan may elect a new beneficiary. Any such beneficiary must be a natural person with an insurable interest in the participant. Such an election may be made only during the 180-day period beginning on the date of the death of the previous beneficiary.

(ii) Procedures.—Such an election shall be in writing, signed by the participant, and made in such form and manner as the Secretary concerned may prescribe. Such an election shall be effective the first day of the first month following the month in which the election is received by the Secretary.

(iii) Vitiation of election by participant who dies within two years of election.—If a person providing an annuity under a election under clause (i) dies before the end of the two-year period beginning on the effective date of the election—

(I) the election is vitiated; and

(II) the amount by which the person's retired pay was reduced under section 1452 of this title that is attributable to the election shall be paid in a lump sum to the person who would have been the deceased person's beneficiary under the vitiated election if the deceased person had died after the end of such two-year period.

(2) Former spouse coverage upon becoming a participant in the Plan.—

(A) General rule.—A person who has a former spouse upon becoming eligible to participate in the Plan may elect to provide an annuity to that former spouse.

(B) Effect of former spouse election on spouse or dependent child.—In the case of a person with a spouse or a dependent child, such an election prevents payment of an annuity to that spouse or child (other than a child who is a beneficiary under an election under paragraph (4)), including payment under subsection (d).

(C) Designation if more than one former spouse.—If there is more than one former spouse, the person shall designate which former spouse is to be provided the annuity.

(D) Designation if RCSBP election.—In the case of a person providing a reserve-component annuity, such an election shall include a designation under subsection (e).

(3) Former spouse coverage by persons already participating in Plan.—

(A) Election of coverage.—

(i) Authority for election.—A person—

(I) who is a participant in the Plan and is providing coverage for a spouse or a spouse and child (even though there is no beneficiary currently eligible for such coverage), and

(II) who has a former spouse who was not that person's former spouse when that person became eligible to participate in the Plan,

may (subject to subparagraph (B)) elect to provide an annuity to that former spouse.

(ii) **Termination of previous coverage.**—Any such election terminates any previous coverage under the Plan.

(iii) **Manner and time of election.**—Any such election must be written, signed by the person making the election, and received by the Secretary concerned within one year after the date of the decree of divorce, dissolution, or annulment.

(B) **Limitation on election.**—A person may not make an election under subparagraph (A) to provide an annuity to a former spouse who that person married after becoming eligible for retired pay unless—

(i) the person was married to that former spouse for at least one year, or

(ii) that former spouse is the parent of issue by that marriage.

(C) **Irrevocability, etc.**—An election under this paragraph may not be revoked except in accordance with section 1450(f) of this title. This paragraph does not provide the authority to change a designation previously made under subsection (e).

(D) **Notice to spouse.**—If a person who is married makes an election to provide an annuity to a former spouse under this paragraph, that person's spouse shall be notified of the election.

(E) **Effective date of election.**—An election under this paragraph is effective as of—

(i) the first day of the first month following the month in which the election is received by the Secretary concerned; or

(ii) in the case of a person required (as described in section 1450(f)(3)(B) of this title) to make the election by reason of a court order or filing the date of which is after October 16, 1998, the first day of the first month which begins after the date of that court order or filing.

(4) **Former spouse and child coverage.**—A person who elects to provide an annuity for a former spouse under paragraph (2) or (3) may, at the time of the election, elect to provide coverage under that annuity for both the former spouse and a dependent child, if the child resulted from the person's marriage to that former spouse.

(5) **Disclosure of whether election of former spouse coverage is required.**—A person who elects to provide an annuity to a former spouse under paragraph (2) or (3) shall, at the time of making the election, provide the Secretary concerned with a written statement (in a form to be prescribed by that Secretary and signed by such person and the former spouse) setting forth—

(A) whether the election is being made pursuant to the requirements of a court order; or

(B) whether the election is being made pursuant to a written agreement previously entered into voluntarily by such person as a part of, or incident to, a proceeding of divorce, dissolution, or annulment and (if so) whether such voluntary written agreement has been incorporated in, or ratified or approved by, a court order.

(6) **Special needs trusts for sole benefit of certain dependent children.**—A person who has established a supplemental or special needs trust under subparagraph (A) or (C) of section 1917(d)(4) of the Social Security Act (42 U.S.C. 1396p(d)(4)) for the sole benefit of a dependent child considered disabled under section 1614(a)(3) of that Act (42 U.S.C. 1382c(a)(3)) who is incapable of self-support because of mental or physical incapacity may elect to provide an annuity to that supplemental or special needs trust.

(7) **Effect of death of former spouse beneficiary.**—

(A) **Termination of participation in Plan.**—A person who elects to provide an annuity to a former spouse under paragraph (2) or (3) and whose former spouse subsequently dies is no longer a participant in the Plan, effective on the date of death of the former spouse.

(B) **Authority for election of new spouse beneficiary.**—If a person's participation in the Plan is discontinued by reason of the death of a former spouse beneficiary, the person may elect to resume participation in the Plan and to elect a new spouse beneficiary as follows:

(i) **Married on the date of death of former spouse.**—A person who is married at the time of the death of the former spouse beneficiary may elect to provide coverage to that person's spouse. Such an election must be received by the Secretary concerned within one year after the date of death of the former spouse beneficiary.

(ii) **Marriage after death of former spouse beneficiary.**—A person who is not married at the time of the death of the former spouse beneficiary and who later marries may elect to provide spouse coverage. Such an election must be received by the Secretary concerned within one year after the date on which that person marries.

(C) **Effective date of election.**—The effective date of election under this paragraph shall be as follows:

(i) An election under subparagraph (B)(i) is effective as of the first day of the first calendar month following the death of the former spouse beneficiary.

(ii) An election under subparagraph (B)(ii) is effective as of the first day of the first calendar month following the month in which the election is received by the Secretary concerned.

(D) **Level of coverage.**—A person making an election under subparagraph (B) may not reduce the base amount previously elected.

(E) **Procedures.**—An election under this paragraph shall be in writing, signed by the participant, and made in such form and manner as the Secretary concerned may prescribe.

(F) Irrevocability.—An election under this paragraph is irrevocable.

(c) Persons on temporary disability retired list.—The application of the Plan to a person whose name is on the temporary disability retired list terminates when his name is removed from that list and he is no longer entitled to disability retired pay.

(d) Coverage for survivors of members who die on active duty.—

(1) Surviving spouse annuity.—Except as provided in paragraph (2)(B), the Secretary concerned shall pay an annuity under this subchapter to the surviving spouse of—

(A) a member who dies while on active duty after—

(i) becoming eligible to receive retired pay;

(ii) qualifying for retired pay except that the member has not applied for or been granted that pay; or

(iii) completing 20 years of active service but before the member is eligible to retire as a commissioned officer because the member has not completed 10 years of active commissioned service; or

(B) a member not described in subparagraph (A) who dies in line of duty while on active duty.

(2) Dependent children.—

(A) Annuity when no eligible surviving spouse.—In the case of a member described in paragraph (1), the Secretary concerned shall pay an annuity under this subchapter to the member's dependent children under subsection (a)(2) or (a)(4) of section 1450 of this title as applicable.

(B) Optional annuity when there is an eligible surviving spouse.—In the case of a member described in paragraph (1) who dies after October 7, 2001, and for whom there is a surviving spouse eligible for an annuity under paragraph (1), the Secretary may pay an annuity under this subchapter to the member's dependent children under subsection (a)(3) or (a)(4) of section 1450 of this title, if applicable, instead of paying an annuity to the surviving spouse under paragraph (1), if the Secretary concerned, in consultation with the surviving spouse, determines it appropriate to provide an annuity for the dependent children under this paragraph instead of an annuity for the surviving spouse under paragraph (1).

(3) Mandatory former spouse annuity.—If a member described in paragraph (1) is required under a court order or spousal agreement to provide an annuity to a former spouse upon becoming eligible to be a participant in the Plan or has made an election under subsection (b) to provide an annuity to a former spouse, the Secretary—

(A) may not pay an annuity under paragraph (1) or (2); but

(B) shall pay an annuity to that former spouse as if the member had been a participant in the Plan and had made an election under subsection (b) to provide an annuity to the former spouse, or in accordance with that election, as the case may be, if the Secretary receives a written request from the former spouse concerned that the election be deemed to have been made in the same manner as provided in section 1450(f)(3) of this title.

(4) Priority.—An annuity that may be provided under this subsection shall be provided in preference to an annuity that may be provided under any other provision of this subchapter on account of service of the same member.

(5) Computation.—The amount of an annuity under this subsection is computed under section 1451(c) of this title.

(6) Deemed election.—

(A) Annuity for dependent.—In the case of a member described in paragraph (1) who dies after November 23, 2003, the Secretary concerned may, if no other annuity is payable on behalf of the member under this subchapter, pay an annuity to a natural person who has an insurable interest in such member as if the annuity were elected by the member under subsection (b)(1). The Secretary concerned may pay such an annuity under this paragraph only in the case of a person who is a dependent of that member (as defined in section 1072(2) of this title).

(B) Computation of annuity.—An annuity under this subparagraph shall be computed under section 1451(b) of this title as if the member had retired for total disability on the date of death with reductions as specified under section 1452(c) of this title, as applicable to the ages of the member and the natural person with an insurable interest.

(e) Designation for commencement of reserve-component annuity.—In any case in which a person is required to make a designation under this subsection, the person shall designate whether, in the event he dies before becoming 60 years of age, the annuity provided shall become effective on—

(1) the day after the date of his death; or

(2) the 60th anniversary of his birth.

(f) Coverage of survivors of persons dying when or before eligible to elect reserve-component annuity.—

(1) Surviving spouse annuity.—The Secretary concerned shall pay an annuity under this subchapter to the surviving spouse of a person who—

(A) is eligible to provide a reserve-component annuity and dies—

(i) before being notified under section 12731(d) of this title that he has completed the years of service required for eligibility for reserve-component retired pay; or

(ii) during the 90–day period beginning on the date he receives notification under section 12731(d) of this title that he has completed the years of service required for eligibility for reserve-component retired pay if he had not made an election under subsection (a)(2)(B) to participate in the Plan; or

(B) is a member of a reserve component not described in subparagraph (A) and dies from an injury or illness incurred or aggravated in the line of duty during inactive-duty training.

(2) Dependent children annuity.—

(A) Annuity when no eligible surviving spouse.—In the case of a person described in paragraph (1), the Secretary concerned shall pay an annuity under this subchapter to the dependent children of that person under section 1450(a)(2) of this title as applicable.

(B) Optional annuity when there is an eligible surviving spouse.—The Secretary may pay an annuity under this subchapter to the dependent children of a person described in paragraph (1) under section 1450(a)(3) of this title, if applicable, instead of paying an annuity to the surviving spouse under paragraph (1), if the Secretary concerned, in consultation with the surviving spouse, determines it appropriate to provide an annuity for the dependent children under this paragraph instead of an annuity for the surviving spouse under paragraph (1).

(3) Mandatory former spouse annuity.—If a person described in paragraph (1) is required under a court order or spousal agreement to provide an annuity to a former spouse upon becoming eligible to be a participant in the Plan or has made an election under subsection (b) to provide an annuity to a former spouse, the Secretary—

(A) may not pay an annuity under paragraph (1) or (2); but

(B) shall pay an annuity to that former spouse as if the person had been a participant in the Plan and had made an election under subsection (b) to provide an annuity to the former spouse, or in accordance with that election, as the case may be, if the Secretary receives a written request from the former spouse concerned that the election be deemed to have been made in the same manner as provided in section 1450(f)(3) of this title.

(4) Computation.—The amount of an annuity under this subsection is computed under section 1451(c) of this title.

(5) Deemed election to provide an annuity for dependent.—Paragraph (6) of subsection (d) shall apply in the case of a member described in paragraph (1) who dies after November 23, 2003, when no other annuity is payable on behalf of the member under this subchapter.

(g) Election to increase coverage upon remarriage.—

(1) Election.—A person—

(A) who is a participant in the Plan and is providing coverage under subsection (a) for a spouse or a spouse and child, but at less than the maximum level; and

(B) who remarries,

may elect, within one year of such remarriage, to increase the level of coverage provided under the Plan to a level not in excess of the current retired pay of that person.

(2) Payment required.—Such an election shall be contingent on the person paying to the United States the amount determined under paragraph (3) plus interest on such amount at a rate determined under regulations prescribed by the Secretary of Defense.

(3) Amount to be paid.—The amount referred to in paragraph (2) is the amount equal to the difference between—

(A) the amount that would have been withheld from such person's retired pay under section 1452 of this title if the higher level of coverage had been in effect from the time the person became a participant in the Plan; and

(B) the amount of such person's retired pay actually withheld.

(4) Manner of making election.—An election under paragraph (1) shall be made in such manner as the Secretary shall prescribe and shall become effective upon receipt of the payment required by paragraph (2).

(5) Disposition of payments.—A payment received under this subsection by the Secretary of Defense shall be deposited into the Department of Defense Military Retirement Fund. Any other payment received under this subsection shall be deposited in the Treasury as miscellaneous receipts.

(Added Pub.L. 92–425, § 1(3), Sept. 21, 1972, 86 Stat. 707; amended Pub.L. 94–496, § 1(2), Oct. 14, 1976, 90 Stat. 2375; Pub.L. 95–397, Title II, § 202, Sept. 30, 1978, 92 Stat. 844; Pub.L. 97–252, Title X, § 1003(b), Sept. 8, 1982, 96 Stat. 735; Pub.L. 97–295, § 1(18), Oct. 12, 1982, 96 Stat. 1290; Pub.L. 98–94, Title IX, § 941 (a)(1), (2), (c)(2), Sept. 24, 1983, 97 Stat. 652, 653; Pub.L. 99–145, Title V, § 513(b), Title VII, §§ 712(a), 713(a), 715, 716(a), 719(3), (8)(A), 721(a), Nov. 8, 1985, 99 Stat. 628, 670, 671, 673 to 676; Pub.L. 99–661, Div. A, Title VI, §§ 641(b)(1), 642(a), Title XIII, § 1343(a)(8)(B), Nov. 14, 1986, 100 Stat. 3885, 3886, 3992; Pub.L. 101–189, Div. A, Title XIV, § 1407(a)(2), (3), Nov. 29, 1989, 103 Stat. 1588; Pub.L. 103–337, Div. A, Title VI, § 638, Title XVI, § 1671(d)(2), Oct. 5, 1994, 108 Stat. 2791, 3015; Pub.L. 104–201, Div. A, Title VI, § 634, Sept. 23, 1996, 110 Stat. 2553; Pub.L. 105–85, Div. A, Title X, § 1073(a)(27), Nov. 18, 1997, 111 Stat. 1901; Pub.L. 105–261, Div. A, Title VI, § 643(a), Oct. 17, 1998, 112 Stat. 2047; Pub.L. 106–65, Div. A, Title X, § 1066(a)(12), Oct. 5, 1999, 113 Stat. 771; Pub.L. 106–398, § 1 [Div. A, Title VI, § 655(a) to (c)(3), Title X, § 1087(a)(10)], Oct. 30, 2000, 114 Stat. 1654, 1654A–165, 1654A–166, 1654A–290; Pub.L. 107–107, Div. A, Title VI, § 642(a), (c)(1), Dec. 28, 2001, 115 Stat. 1151, 1152; Pub.L. 108–136, Div. A, Title VI, §§ 644(a), (b), 645(a), (b)(1), (c), Nov. 24, 2003, 117 Stat. 1517; Pub.L. 108–375,

Div. A, Title X, § 1084(d)(10), Oct. 28, 2004, 118 Stat. 2061; Pub.L. 109–364, Div. A, Title VI, §§ 643(a), 644(a), Title X, § 1071(a)(8), Oct. 17, 2006, 120 Stat. 2260, 2261, 2398; Pub.L. 113–291, Div. A, Title VI, § 624(a)(2)(B), Dec. 19, 2014, 128 Stat. 3403; Pub.L. 114–92, Div. A, Title VI, § 641(a), Nov. 25, 2015, 129 Stat. 852; Pub.L. 114–328, Div. A, Title VI, § 642(b), (c), Dec. 23, 2016, 130 Stat. 2165.)

§ 1448a. Election to discontinue participation: one-year opportunity after second anniversary of commencement of payment of retired pay

(a) Authority.—A participant in the Plan may, subject to the provisions of this section, elect to discontinue participation in the Plan at any time during the one-year period beginning on the second anniversary of the date on which payment of retired pay to the participant commences.

(b) Concurrence of spouse.—

(1) Concurrence required.—A married participant may not (except as provided in paragraph (2)) make an election under subsection (a) without the concurrence of the participant's spouse.

(2) Exceptions.—A participant may make such an election without the concurrence of the participant's spouse by establishing to the satisfaction of the Secretary concerned that one of the conditions specified in section 1448(a)(3)(C) of this title exists.

(3) Form of concurrence.—The concurrence of a spouse under paragraph (1) shall be made in such written form and shall contain such information as may be required under regulations prescribed by the Secretary of Defense.

(c) Limitation on election when former spouse coverage in effect.—The limitation set forth in section 1450(f)(2) of this title applies to an election to discontinue participation in the Plan under subsection (a).

(d) Withdrawal of election to discontinue.—Section 1448(b)(1)(D) of this title applies to an election under subsection (a).

(e) Consequences of discontinuation.—Section 1448(b)(1)(E) of this title applies to an election under subsection (a).

(f) Notice to affected beneficiaries.—The Secretary concerned shall notify any former spouse or other natural person previously designated under section 1448(b) of this title of an election to discontinue participation under subsection (a).

(g) Effective date of election.—An election under subsection (a) is effective as of the first day of the first calendar month following the month in which the election is received by the Secretary concerned.

(h) Inapplicability of irrevocability provisions.—Paragraphs (4)(B) and (5)(C) of section 1448(a) of this title do not apply to prevent an election under subsection (a). *(Added Pub.L. 105–85, Div. A, Title VI, § 641(a)(1), Nov. 18, 1997, 111 Stat. 1797.)*

§ 1450. Payment of annuity: beneficiaries

(a) In general.—Effective as of the first day after the death of a person to whom section 1448 of this title applies (or on such other day as that person may provide under subsection (j)), a monthly annuity under section 1451 of this title shall be paid to the person's beneficiaries under the Plan, as follows:

(1) Surviving spouse or former spouse.—The eligible surviving spouse or the eligible former spouse.

(2) Surviving children.—The surviving dependent children in equal shares, if the eligible surviving spouse or the eligible former spouse is dead, dies, or otherwise becomes ineligible under this section.

(3) Dependent children.—The dependent children in equal shares if the person to whom section 1448 of this title applies (with the concurrence of the person's spouse, if required under section 1448(a)(3) of this title) elected to provide an annuity for dependent children but not for the spouse or former spouse.

(4) Special needs trusts for sole benefit of certain dependent children.—Notwithstanding subsection (i), a supplemental or special needs trust established under subparagraph (A) or (C) of section 1917(d)(4) of the Social Security Act (42 U.S.C. 1396p(d)(4)) for the sole benefit of a dependent child considered disabled under section 1614(a)(3) of that Act (42 U.S.C. 1382c(a)(3)) who is incapable of self-support because of mental or physical incapacity.

(5) Natural person designated under "insurable interest" coverage.—The natural person designated under section 1448(b)(1) of this title, unless the election to provide an annuity to the natural person has been changed as provided in subsection (f).

(b) Termination of annuity for death, remarriage before age 55, etc.—

(1) General rule.—An annuity payable to the beneficiary terminates effective as of the first day of the month in which eligibility is lost.

(2) Termination of spouse annuity upon death or remarriage before age 55.—An annuity for a surviving spouse or former spouse shall be paid to the surviving spouse or former spouse while the surviving spouse or former spouse is living or, if the surviving spouse or former spouse remarries before reaching age 55, until the surviving spouse or former spouse remarries.

(3) Effect of termination of subsequent marriage before age 55.—If the surviving spouse or former spouse remarries before reaching age 55 and that marriage is terminated by death, annulment, or divorce, payment of the annuity shall be resumed effective as of the first day of the month in which the marriage is so terminated. However, if the surviving spouse or former spouse is also entitled to an annuity under the Plan based upon the marriage so terminated, the surviving spouse or former spouse may not receive both annuities but must elect which to receive.

(c) Offset for amount of dependency and indemnity compensation.—

(1) Required offset.—If, upon the death of a person to whom section 1448 of this title applies, the surviving spouse or former spouse of that person is also entitled to dependency and indemnity compensation under section 1311(a) of title 38, the surviving spouse or former spouse may be paid an annuity under this section, but only in the amount that the annuity otherwise payable under this section would exceed that compensation.

(2) Effective date of offset.—A reduction in an annuity under this section required by paragraph (1) shall be effective on the date of the commencement of the period of payment of such dependency and indemnity compensation under title 38.

(3) Limitation on recoupment of offset amount.—Any amount subject to offset under this subsection that was previously paid to the surviving spouse or former spouse shall be recouped only to the extent that the amount paid exceeds any amount to be refunded under subsection (e). In notifying a surviving spouse or former spouse of the recoupment requirement, the Secretary shall provide the spouse or former spouse—

(A) a single notice of the net amount to be recouped or the net amount to be refunded, as applicable, under this subsection or subsection (e);

(B) a written explanation of the statutory requirements for recoupment of the offset amount and for refund of any applicable amount deducted from retired pay;

(C) a detailed accounting of how the offset amount being recouped and retired pay deduction amount being refunded were calculated; and

(D) contact information for a person who can provide information about the offset recoupment and retired pay deduction refund processes and answer questions the surviving spouse or former spouse may have about the requirements, processes, or amounts.

(d) Limitation on payment of annuities when coverage under civil service retirement elected.—If, upon the death of a person to whom section 1448 of this title applies, that person had in effect a waiver of that person's retired pay for the purposes of subchapter III of chapter 83 of title 5 or chapter 84 of such title, an annuity under this section shall not be payable unless, in accordance with section 8339(j) or 8416(a) of title 5, that person notified the Office of Personnel Management that he did not desire any spouse surviving him to receive an annuity under section 8341(b) or 8442(a) of that title.

(e) Refund of amounts deducted from retired pay or CRSC when DIC offset is applicable.—

(1) Full refund when DIC greater than SBP annuity.—If an annuity under this section is not payable because of subsection (c), any amount deducted from the retired pay or combat-related special compensation of the deceased under section 1452 of this title shall be refunded to the surviving spouse or former spouse.

(2) Partial refund when SBP annuity reduced by DIC.—If, because of subsection (c), the annuity payable is less than the amount established under section 1451 of this title, the annuity payable shall be recalculated under that section. The amount of the reduction in the retired pay required to provide that recalculated annuity shall be computed under section 1452 of this title, and the difference between the amount deducted before the computation of that recalculated annuity and the amount that would have been deducted on the basis of that recalculated annuity shall be refunded to the surviving spouse or former spouse.

(f) Change in election of insurable interest or former spouse beneficiary.—

(1) Authorized changes.—

(A) Election in favor of spouse or child.—A person who elects to provide an annuity to a person designated by him under section 1448(b) of this title may, subject to paragraph (2), change that election and provide an annuity to his spouse or dependent child.

(B) Notice.—The Secretary concerned shall notify the former spouse or other natural person previously designated under section 1448(b) of this title of any change of election under subparagraph (A).

(C) Procedures, effective date, etc.—Any such change of election is subject to the same rules with respect to execution, revocation, and effectiveness as are set forth in section 1448(a)(5) of this title (without regard to the eligibility of the person making the change of election to make such an election under that section). Notwithstanding the preceding sentence, a change of election under this subsection to provide an annuity to a spouse instead of a former spouse may (subject to paragraph (2)) be made at any time after the person providing the annuity remarries without regard to the time limitation in section 1448(a)(5)(B) of this title.

(2) Limitation on change in beneficiary when former spouse coverage in effect.—A person who, incident to a proceeding of divorce, dissolution, or annulment, is required by a court order to elect under section 1448(b) of this title to provide an annuity to a former spouse (or to both a former spouse and child), or who enters into a written agreement (whether voluntary or required by a court order) to make such an election, and who makes an election pursuant to such order or agreement, may not change that election under paragraph (1) unless, of the following requirements, whichever are applicable in a particular case are satisfied:

(A) In a case in which the election is required by a court order, or in which an agreement to make the election has been incorporated in or ratified or approved by a court order, the person—

(i) furnishes to the Secretary concerned a certified copy of a court order which is regular on its face and which modifies the provisions of all previous court orders relating to such election, or the agreement to make such election, so as to permit the person to change the election; and

(ii) certifies to the Secretary concerned that the court order is valid and in effect.

(B) In a case of a written agreement that has not been incorporated in or ratified or approved by a court order, the person—

(i) furnishes to the Secretary concerned a statement, in such form as the Secretary concerned may prescribe, signed by the former spouse and evidencing the former spouse's agreement to a change in the election under paragraph (1); and

(ii) certifies to the Secretary concerned that the statement is current and in effect.

(3) Required former spouse election to be deemed to have been made.—

(A) Deemed election upon request by former spouse.—If a person described in paragraph (2) or (3) of section 1448(b) of this title is required (as described in subparagraph (B)) to elect under section 1448(b) of this title to provide an annuity to a former spouse and such person then fails or refuses to make such an election, such person shall be deemed to have made such an election if the Secretary concerned receives the following:

(i) Request from former spouse.—A written request, in such manner as the Secretary shall prescribe, from the former spouse concerned requesting that such an election be deemed to have been made.

(ii) Copy of court order or other official statement.—Either—

(I) a copy of the court order, regular on its face, which requires such election or incorporates, ratifies, or approves the written agreement of such person; or

(II) a statement from the clerk of the court (or other appropriate official) that such agreement has been filed with the court in accordance with applicable State law.

(B) Persons required to make election.—A person shall be considered for purposes of subparagraph (A) to be required to elect under section 1448(b) of this title to provide an annuity to a former spouse if—

(i) the person enters, incident to a proceeding of divorce, dissolution, or annulment, into a written agreement to make such an election and the agreement (I) has been incorporated in or ratified or approved by a court order, or (II) has been filed with the court of appropriate jurisdiction in accordance with applicable State law; or

(ii) the person is required by a court order to make such an election.

(C) Time limit for request by former spouse.—An election may not be deemed to have been made under subparagraph (A) in the case of any person unless the Secretary concerned receives a request from the former spouse of the person within one year of the date of the court order or filing involved.

(D) Effective date of deemed election.—An election deemed to have been made under subparagraph (A) shall become effective on the day referred to in section 1448(b)(3)(E)(ii) of this title.

(4) Former spouse coverage may be required by court order.—A court order may require a person to elect (or to enter into an agreement to elect) under section 1448(b) of this title to provide an annuity to a former spouse (or to both a former spouse and child).

(g) Limitation on changing or revoking elections.—

(1) In general.—An election under this section may not be changed or revoked.

(2) Exceptions.—Paragraph (1) does not apply to—

(A) a revocation of an election under section 1449(b) of this title; or

(B) a change in an election under subsection (f).

(h) Treatment of annuities under other laws.—Except as provided in section 1451 of this title, an annuity under this section is in addition to any other payment to which a person is entitled under any other provision of law. Such annuity shall be considered as income under laws administered by the Secretary of Veterans Affairs.

(i) Annuities exempt from certain legal process.—Except as provided in subsection (a)(4) or (*l*)(3)(B), an annuity under this section is not assignable or subject to execution, levy, attachment, garnishment, or other legal process.

(j) Effective date of reserve-component annuities.—

(1) Persons making section 1448(e) designation.—A reserve-component annuity shall be effective in accordance with the designation made under section 1448(e) of this title by the person providing the annuity.

(2) Persons dying before making section 1448(e) designation.—An annuity payable under section 1448(f) of this title shall be effective on the day after the date of the death of the person upon whose service the right to the annuity is based.

(k) Adjustment of spouse or former spouse annuity upon loss of dependency and indemnity compensation.—

(1) Readjustment if beneficiary 55 years of age or more.—If a surviving spouse or former spouse whose annuity has been adjusted under subsection (c) subsequently loses entitlement to dependency and indemnity compensation under section 1311(a) of title 38 because of the remarriage of the surviving spouse, or former spouse, and if at the time of such remarriage the surviving spouse or former spouse is 55 years of age or more, the amount of the annuity of the surviving spouse or former spouse shall be readjusted, effective on the effective date of such loss of dependency and indemnity compensation, to the amount of the annuity which would be in effect with respect to the surviving spouse or former spouse if the adjustment under subsection (c) had never been made.

(2) Repayment of amounts previously refunded.—

(A) **General rule.**—A surviving spouse or former spouse whose annuity is readjusted under paragraph (1) shall repay any amount refunded under subsection (e) by reason of the adjustment under subsection (c).

(B) **Interest required if repayment not a lump sum.**—If the repayment is not made in a lump sum, the surviving spouse or former spouse shall pay interest on the amount to be repaid. Such interest shall commence on the date on which the first such payment is due and shall be applied over the period during which any part of the repayment remains to be paid.

(C) **Manner of repayment; rate of interest.**—The manner in which such repayment shall be made, and the rate of any such interest, shall be prescribed in regulations under section 1455 of this title.

(D) **Deposit of amounts repaid.**—An amount repaid under this paragraph (including any such interest) received by the Secretary of Defense shall be deposited into the Department of Defense Military Retirement Fund. Any other amount repaid under this paragraph shall be deposited into the Treasury as miscellaneous receipts.

(*l*) **Participants in the plan who are missing.**—

(1) **Authority to presume death of missing participant.**—

(A) **In general.**—Upon application of the beneficiary of a participant in the Plan who is missing, the Secretary concerned may determine for purposes of this subchapter that the participant is presumed dead.

(B) **Participant who is missing.**—A participant in the Plan is considered to be missing for purposes of this subsection if—

(i) the retired pay of the participant has been suspended on the basis that the participant is missing; or

(ii) in the case of a participant in the Plan who would be eligible for reserve-component retired pay but for the fact that he is under 60 years of age, his retired pay, if he were entitled to retired pay, would be suspended on the basis that he is missing.

(C) **Requirements applicable to presumption of death.**—Any such determination shall be made in accordance with regulations prescribed under section 1455 of this title. The Secretary concerned may not make a determination for purposes of this subchapter that a participant who is missing is presumed dead unless the Secretary finds that—

(i) the participant has been missing for at least 30 days; and

(ii) the circumstances under which the participant is missing would lead a reasonably prudent person to conclude that the participant is dead.

(2) **Commencement of annuity.**—Upon a determination under paragraph (1) with respect to a participant in the Plan, an annuity otherwise payable under this subchapter shall be paid as if the participant died on the date as of which the retired pay of the participant was suspended.

(3) **Effect of person not being dead.**—

(A) **Termination of annuity.**—If, after a determination under paragraph (1), the Secretary concerned determines that the participant is alive—

(i) any annuity being paid under this subchapter by reason of this subsection shall be terminated; and

(ii) the total amount of any annuity payments made by reason of this subsection shall constitute a debt to the United States.

(B) **Collection from participant of annuity amounts erroneously paid.**—A debt under subparagraph (A)(ii) may be collected or offset—

(i) from any retired pay otherwise payable to the participant;

(ii) if the participant is entitled to compensation under chapter 11 of title 38, from that compensation; or

(iii) if the participant is entitled to any other payment from the United States, from that payment.

(C) **Collection from beneficiary.**—If the participant dies before the full recovery of the amount of annuity payments described in subparagraph (A)(ii) has been made by the United States, the remaining amount of such annuity payments may be collected from the participant's beneficiary under the Plan if that beneficiary was the recipient of the annuity payments made by reason of this subsection.

(m) **Special survivor indemnity allowance.**—

(1) **Provision of allowance.**—The Secretary concerned shall pay a monthly special survivor indemnity allowance under this subsection to the surviving spouse or former spouse of a member of the uniformed services to whom section 1448 of this title applies if—

(A) the surviving spouse or former spouse is entitled to dependency and indemnity compensation under section 1311(a) of title 38;

(B) except for subsection (c) of this section, the surviving spouse or former spouse is eligible for an annuity by reason of a participant in the Plan under subsection (a)(1) of section 1448 of this title or by reason of coverage under subsection (d) or (f) of such section; and

(C) the eligibility of the surviving spouse or former spouse for an annuity as described in subparagraph (B) is affected by subsection (c) of this section.

(2) **Amount of payment.**—Subject to paragraph (3), the amount of the allowance paid to an eligible survivor under paragraph (1) for a month shall be equal to—

(A) for months during fiscal year 2009, $50;

(B) for months during fiscal year 2010, $60;

(C) for months during fiscal year 2011, $70;

(D) for months during fiscal year 2012, $80;

(E) for months during fiscal year 2013, $90;

(F) for months during fiscal year 2014, $150;

(G) for months during fiscal year 2015, $200;

(H) for months during fiscal year 2016, $275; and

(I) for months during each of fiscal years 2017 and 2018, $310.

(3) Limitation.—The amount of the allowance paid to an eligible survivor under paragraph (1) for any month may not exceed the amount of the annuity for that month that is subject to offset under subsection (c).

(4) Status of payments.—An allowance paid under this subsection does not constitute an annuity, and amounts so paid are not subject to adjustment under any other provision of law.

(5) Source of funds.—The special survivor indemnity allowance shall be paid from amounts in the Department of Defense Military Retirement Fund established under section 1461 of this title.

(6) Effective date and duration.—This subsection shall only apply with respect to the month beginning on October 1, 2008, and subsequent months through the month ending on May 31, 2018. Effective on June 1, 2018, the authority provided by this subsection shall terminate. No special survivor indemnity allowance may be paid to any person by reason of this subsection for any period before October 1, 2008, or beginning on or after June 1, 2018.

(Added Pub.L. 92–425, § 1(3), Sept. 21, 1972, 86 Stat. 708; amended Pub.L. 94–496, § 1(3), (4), Oct. 14, 1976, 90 Stat. 2375; Pub.L. 95–397, Title II, §§ 203, 207(b), (c), Sept. 30, 1978, 92 Stat. 845, 848; Pub.L. 97–22, § 11(a)(3), July 10, 1981, 95 Stat. 137; Pub.L. 97–252, Title X, § 1003(c), (d), Sept. 8, 1982, 96 Stat. 736; Pub.L. 98–94, Title IX, § 941(a)(3), (c)(3), Sept. 24, 1983, 97 Stat. 653; Pub.L. 98–525, Title VI, §§ 642(b), 644, Oct. 19, 1984, 98 Stat. 2546, 2548; Pub.L. 99–145, Title VII, §§ 713(b), 717, 718, 719(4) to (6), (8)(A), 722, 723(a), (b)(1), Title XIII, § 1303(a)(11), Nov. 8, 1985, 99 Stat. 672, 674 to 677, 739; Pub.L. 99–661, Div. A, Title VI, §§ 641(a), (b)(2), (3), 643(a), Title XIII § 1343(a)(8)(C), Nov. 14, 1986, 100 Stat. 3885, 3886, 3992; Pub.L. 100–26, § 3(3), Apr. 21, 1987, 101 Stat. 273; Pub.L. 100–180, Div. A, Title VI, § 636(a), Dec. 4, 1987, 101 Stat. 1106; Pub.L. 100–224, § 5(b)(1), Dec. 30, 1987, 101 Stat. 1538; Pub.L. 101–189, Div. A, Title XIV, § 1407(a)(2) to (4), Title XVI, § 1621(a)(1), Nov. 29, 1989, 103 Stat. 1588, 1602; Pub.L. 103–337, Div. A, Title X, § 1070(e)(3), Oct. 5, 1994, 108 Stat. 2859; Pub.L. 104–201, Div. A, Title VI, § 634, Sept. 23, 1996, 110 Stat. 2561; Pub.L. 105–85, Div. A, Title VI, § 642(a), Nov. 18, 1997, 111 Stat. 1799; Pub.L. 105–261, Div. A, Title VI, § 643(b), Oct. 17, 1998, 112 Stat. 2048; Pub.L. 106–398, § 1 [Div. A, Title VI, § 655(c)(4)], Oct. 30, 2000, 114 Stat. 1654, 1654A–166; Pub.L. 110–181, Div. A, Title VI, §§ 643(a), 644, Jan. 28, 2008, 122 Stat. 157, 158; Pub.L. 110–417, Div. A, Title VI, § 631(a), Oct. 14, 2008, 122 Stat. 4492; Pub.L. 111–31, Div. B, Title II, § 201, June 22, 2009, 123 Stat. 1857; Pub.L. 112–239, Div. A, Title VI, § 641(b), Jan. 2, 2013, 126 Stat. 1783; Pub.L. 113–291, Div. A, Title VI, § 624(a)(1), (2)(A), Dec. 19, 2014, 128 Stat. 3403; Pub.L. 114–328, Div. A, Title VI, §§ 642(d), 643(c)(2), 646, Dec. 23, 2016, 130 Stat. 2165, 2166, 2168.)

TITLE 11

BANKRUPTCY

CHAPTER 3—CASE ADMINISTRATION

SUBCHAPTER I—COMMENCEMENT OF A CASE

§ 302. Joint cases

(a) A joint case under a chapter of this title is commenced by the filing with the bankruptcy court of a single petition under such chapter by an individual that may be a debtor under such chapter and such individual's spouse. The commencement of a joint case under a chapter of this title constitutes an order for relief under such chapter.

(b) After the commencement of a joint case, the court shall determine the extent, if any, to which the debtors' estates shall be consolidated. *(Pub.L. 95–598, Nov. 6, 1978, 92 Stat. 2558.)*

Commentary

In re Villaverde and Hight, 540 B.R. 431 (U.S. Bankruptcy Court, C.D. California, 2015), held that same-sex California registered domestic partners are ineligible to file a joint petition for bankruptcy under this section, because they could marry, but did not do so.

SUBCHAPTER IV—ADMINISTRATIVE POWERS

§ 362. Automatic stay

(a) Except as provided in subsection (b) of this section, a petition filed under section 301, 302, or 303 of this title, or an application filed under section 5(a)(3) of the Securities Investor Protection Act of 1970, operates as a stay, applicable to all entities, of—

(1) the commencement or continuation, including the issuance or employment of process, of a judicial, administrative, or other action or proceeding against the debtor that was or could have been commenced before the commencement of the case under this title, or to recover a claim against the debtor that arose before the commencement of the case under this title;

(2) the enforcement, against the debtor or against property of the estate, of a judgment obtained before the commencement of the case under this title;

(3) any act to obtain possession of property of the estate or of property from the estate or to exercise control over property of the estate;

(4) any act to create, perfect, or enforce any lien against property of the estate;

(5) any act to create, perfect, or enforce against property of the debtor any lien to the extent that such lien secures a claim that arose before the commencement of the case under this title;

(6) any act to collect, assess, or recover a claim against the debtor that arose before the commencement of the case under this title;

(7) the setoff of any debt owing to the debtor that arose before the commencement of the case under this title against any claim against the debtor; and

(8) the commencement or continuation of a proceeding before the United States Tax Court concerning a tax liability of a debtor that is a corporation for a taxable period the bankruptcy court may determine or concerning the tax liability of a debtor who is an individual for a taxable period ending before the date of the order for relief under this title.

(b) The filing of a petition under section 301, 302, or 303 of this title, or of an application under section 5(a)(3) of the Securities Investor Protection Act of 1970, does not operate as a stay—

(1) under subsection (a) of this section, of the commencement or continuation of a criminal action or proceeding against the debtor;

(2) under subsection (a)—

(A) of the commencement or continuation of a civil action or proceeding—

(i) for the establishment of paternity;

(ii) for the establishment or modification of an order for domestic support obligations;

(iii) concerning child custody or visitation;

(iv) for the dissolution of a marriage, except to the extent that such proceeding seeks to determine the division of property that is property of the estate; or

(v) regarding domestic violence;

(B) of the collection of a domestic support obligation from property that is not property of the estate;

(C) with respect to the withholding of income that is property of the estate or property of the debtor for payment of a domestic support obligation under a judicial or administrative order or a statute;

(D) of the withholding, suspension, or restriction of a driver's license, a professional or occupational license, or a recreational license, under State law, as specified in section 466(a)(16) of the Social Security Act;

(E) of the reporting of overdue support owed by a parent to any consumer reporting agency as specified in section 466(a)(7) of the Social Security Act;

(F) of the interception of a tax refund, as specified in sections 464 and 466(a)(3) of the Social Security Act or under an analogous State law; or

(G) of the enforcement of a medical obligation, as specified under title IV of the Social Security Act;

(3) under subsection (a) of this section, of any act to perfect, or to maintain or continue the perfection of, an interest in property to the extent that the trustee's rights and powers are subject to such perfection under section 546(b) of this title or to the extent that such act is accomplished within the period provided under section 547(e)(2)(A) of this title;

(4) under paragraph (1), (2), (3), or (6) of subsection (a) of this section, of the commencement or continuation of an action or proceeding by a governmental unit or any organization exercising authority under the Convention on the Prohibition of the Development, Production, Stockpiling and Use of Chemical Weapons and on Their Destruction, opened for signature on January 13, 1993, to enforce such governmental unit's or organization's police and regulatory power, including the enforcement of a judgment other than a money judgment, obtained in an action or proceeding by the governmental unit to enforce such governmental unit's or organization's police or regulatory power;

[**(5) Repealed.** Pub.L. 105–277, Div. I, Title VI, § 603(1), Oct. 21, 1998, 112 Stat. 2681–886]

(6) under subsection (a) of this section, of the exercise by a commodity broker, forward contract merchant, stockbroker, financial institution, financial participant, or securities clearing agency of any contractual right (as defined in section 555 or 556) under any security agreement or arrangement or other credit enhancement forming a part of or related to any commodity contract, forward contract or securities contract, or of any contractual right (as defined in section 555 or 556) to offset or net out any termination value, payment amount, or other transfer obligation arising under or in connection with 1 or more such contracts, including any master agreement for such contracts;

(7) under subsection (a) of this section, of the exercise by a repo participant or financial participant of any contractual right (as defined in section 559) under any security agreement or arrangement or other credit enhancement forming a part of or related to any repurchase agreement, or of any contractual right (as defined in section 559) to offset or net out any termination value, payment amount, or other transfer obligation arising under or in connection with 1 or more such agreements, including any master agreement for such agreements;

(8) under subsection (a) of this section, of the commencement of any action by the Secretary of Housing and Urban Development to foreclose a mortgage or deed of trust in any case in which the mortgage or deed of trust held by the Secretary is insured or was formerly insured under the National Housing Act and covers property, or combinations of property, consisting of five or more living units;

(9) under subsection (a), of—

(A) an audit by a governmental unit to determine tax liability;

(B) the issuance to the debtor by a governmental unit of a notice of tax deficiency;

(C) a demand for tax returns; or

(D) the making of an assessment for any tax and issuance of a notice and demand for payment of such an assessment (but any tax lien that would otherwise attach to property of the estate by reason of such an assessment shall not take effect unless such tax is a debt of the debtor that will not be discharged in the case and such property or its proceeds are transferred out of the estate to, or otherwise revested in, the debtor).

(10) under subsection (a) of this section, of any act by a lessor to the debtor under a lease of nonresidential real property that has terminated by the expiration of the stated term of the lease before the commencement of or during a case under this title to obtain possession of such property;

(11) under subsection (a) of this section, of the presentment of a negotiable instrument and the giving of notice of and protesting dishonor of such an instrument;

(12) under subsection (a) of this section, after the date which is 90 days after the filing of such petition, of the commencement or continuation, and conclusion to the entry of final judgment, of an action which involves a debtor subject to reorganization pursuant to chapter 11 of this title and which was brought by the Secretary of Transportation under section 31325 of title 46 (including distribution of any proceeds of sale) to foreclose a preferred ship or fleet mortgage, or a security interest in or relating to a vessel or vessel under construction, held by the Secretary of Transportation under chapter 537 of title 46 or section 109(h) of title 49, or under applicable State law;

(13) under subsection (a) of this section, after the date which is 90 days after the filing of such petition, of the commencement or continuation, and conclusion to the entry of final judgment, of an action which involves a debtor subject to reorganization pursuant to chapter 11 of this title and which was brought by the Secretary of Commerce under section 31325 of title 46 (including distribution of any proceeds of sale) to foreclose a preferred ship or fleet mortgage in a vessel or a mortgage, deed of trust, or other security interest in a fishing facility held by the Secretary of Commerce under chapter 537 of title 46;

(14) under subsection (a) of this section, of any action by an accrediting agency regarding the accreditation status of the debtor as an educational institution;

(15) under subsection (a) of this section, of any action by a State licensing body regarding the licensure of the debtor as an educational institution;

(16) under subsection (a) of this section, of any action by a guaranty agency, as defined in section 435(j) of the Higher Education Act of 1965 or the Secretary of Education regarding the eligibility of the debtor to participate in programs authorized under such Act;

(17) under subsection (a) of this section, of the exercise by a swap participant or financial participant of any contractual right (as defined in section 560) under any security agreement or arrangement or other credit enhancement forming a part of or related to any swap agreement, or of any contractual right (as defined in section 560) to offset or net out any termination value, payment amount, or other transfer obligation arising under or in connection with 1 or more such agreements, including any master agreement for such agreements;

(18) under subsection (a) of the creation or perfection of a statutory lien for an ad valorem property tax, or a special tax or special assessment on real property whether or not ad valorem, imposed by a governmental unit, if such tax or assessment comes due after the date of the filing of the petition;

(19) under subsection (a), of withholding of income from a debtor's wages and collection of amounts withheld, under the debtor's agreement authorizing that withholding and collection for the benefit of a pension, profit-sharing, stock bonus, or other plan established under section 401, 403, 408, 408A, 414, 457, or 501(c) of the Internal Revenue Code of 1986, that is sponsored by the employer of the debtor, or an affiliate, successor, or predecessor of such employer—

(A) to the extent that the amounts withheld and collected are used solely for payments relating to a loan from a plan under section 408(b)(1) of the Employee Retirement Income Security Act of 1974 or is subject to section 72(p) of the Internal Revenue Code of 1986; or

(B) a loan from a thrift savings plan permitted under subchapter III of chapter 84 of title 5, that satisfies the requirements of section 8433(g) of such title;

but nothing in this paragraph may be construed to provide that any loan made under a governmental plan under section 414(d), or a contract or account under section 403(b), of the Internal Revenue Code of 1986 constitutes a claim or a debt under this title;

(20) under subsection (a), of any act to enforce any lien against or security interest in real property following entry of the order under subsection (d)(4) as to such real property in any prior case under this title, for a period of 2 years after the date of the entry of such an order, except that the debtor, in a subsequent case under this title, may move for relief from such order based upon changed circumstances or for other good cause shown, after notice and a hearing;

(21) under subsection (a), of any act to enforce any lien against or security interest in real property—

(A) if the debtor is ineligible under section 109(g) to be a debtor in a case under this title; or

(B) if the case under this title was filed in violation of a bankruptcy court order in a prior case under this title prohibiting the debtor from being a debtor in another case under this title;

(22) subject to subsection (*l*), under subsection (a)(3), of the continuation of any eviction, unlawful detainer action, or similar proceeding by a lessor against a debtor involving residential property in which the debtor resides as a tenant under a lease or rental agreement and with respect to which the lessor has obtained before the date of the filing of the bankruptcy petition, a judgment for possession of such property against the debtor;

(23) subject to subsection (m), under subsection (a)(3), of an eviction action that seeks possession of the residential property in which the debtor resides as a tenant under a lease or rental agreement based on endangerment of such property or the illegal use of controlled substances on such property, but only if the lessor files with the court, and serves upon the debtor, a certification under penalty of perjury that such an eviction action has been filed, or that the debtor, during the 30–day period preceding the date of the filing of the certification, has endangered property or illegally used or allowed to be used a controlled substance on the property;

(24) under subsection (a), of any transfer that is not avoidable under section 544 and that is not avoidable under section 549;

(25) under subsection (a), of—

(A) the commencement or continuation of an investigation or action by a securities self regulatory organization to enforce such organization's regulatory power;

(B) the enforcement of an order or decision, other than for monetary sanctions, obtained in an action by such securities self regulatory organization to enforce such organization's regulatory power; or

(C) any act taken by such securities self regulatory organization to delist, delete, or refuse to permit quotation of any stock that does not meet applicable regulatory requirements;

(26) under subsection (a), of the setoff under applicable nonbankruptcy law of an income tax refund, by a governmental unit, with respect to a taxable period that ended before the date of the order for relief against an income tax liability for a taxable period that also ended before the date of the order for relief, except that in any case in which the setoff of an income tax refund is not permitted under applicable nonbankruptcy law because of a pending action to determine the amount or legality of a tax liability, the governmental unit may hold the refund pending the resolution of the action, unless the court, on the motion of the trustee and after notice and a hearing, grants the taxing authority adequate protection (within the meaning of section 361) for the secured claim of such authority in the setoff under section 506(a);

(27) under subsection (a) of this section, of the exercise by a master netting agreement participant of any contractual right (as defined in section 555, 556, 559, or 560) under any security agreement or arrangement or other credit enhancement forming a part of or related to any master netting agreement, or of any contractual right (as defined in section 555, 556, 559, or 560) to offset or net out any termination value, payment amount, or other transfer obligation arising under or in connection with 1 or more such master netting agreements to the extent that such participant is eligible to exercise such rights under paragraph (6), (7), or (17) for each individual contract covered by the master netting agreement in issue; and

(28) under subsection (a), of the exclusion by the Secretary of Health and Human Services of the debtor from participation in the medicare program or any other Federal health care program (as defined in section 1128B(f) of the Social Security Act pursuant to title XI or XVIII of such Act).

The provisions of paragraphs (12) and (13) of this subsection shall apply with respect to any such petition filed on or before December 31, 1989.

(c) Except as provided in subsections (d), (e), (f), and (h) of this section—

(1) the stay of an act against property of the estate under subsection (a) of this section continues until such property is no longer property of the estate;

(2) the stay of any other act under subsection (a) of this section continues until the earliest of—

(A) the time the case is closed;

(B) the time the case is dismissed; or

(C) if the case is a case under chapter 7 of this title concerning an individual or a case under chapter 9, 11, 12, or 13 of this title, the time a discharge is granted or denied;

(3) if a single or joint case is filed by or against a debtor who is an individual in a case under chapter 7, 11, or 13, and if a single or joint case of the debtor was pending within the preceding 1–year period but was dismissed, other than a case refiled under a chapter other than chapter 7 after dismissal under section 707(b)—

(A) the stay under subsection (a) with respect to any action taken with respect to a debt or property securing such debt or with respect to any lease shall terminate with respect to the debtor on the 30th day after the filing of the later case;

(B) on the motion of a party in interest for continuation of the automatic stay and upon notice and a hearing, the court may extend the stay in particular cases as to any or all creditors (subject to such conditions or limitations as the court may then impose) after notice and a hearing completed before the expiration of the 30–day period only if the party in interest demonstrates that the filing of the later case is in good faith as to the creditors to be stayed; and

(C) for purposes of subparagraph (B), a case is presumptively filed not in good faith (but such presumption may be rebutted by clear and convincing evidence to the contrary)—

(i) as to all creditors, if—

(I) more than 1 previous case under any of chapters 7, 11, and 13 in which the individual was a debtor was pending within the preceding 1–year period;

(II) a previous case under any of chapters 7, 11, and 13 in which the individual was a debtor was dismissed within such 1–year period, after the debtor failed to—

(aa) file or amend the petition or other documents as required by this title or the court without substantial excuse (but mere inadvertence or negligence shall not be a substantial excuse unless the dismissal was caused by the negligence of the debtor's attorney);

(bb) provide adequate protection as ordered by the court; or

(cc) perform the terms of a plan confirmed by the court; or

(III) there has not been a substantial change in the financial or personal affairs of the debtor since the dismissal of the next most previous case under chapter 7, 11, or 13 or any other reason to conclude that the later case will be concluded—

(aa) if a case under chapter 7, with a discharge; or

(bb) if a case under chapter 11 or 13, with a confirmed plan that will be fully performed; and

(ii) as to any creditor that commenced an action under subsection (d) in a previous case in which the individual was a debtor if, as of the date of dismissal of such case, that action was still pending or had been resolved by terminating, conditioning, or limiting the stay as to actions of such creditor; and

(4)(A)(i) if a single or joint case is filed by or against a debtor who is an individual under this title, and if 2 or more single or joint cases of the debtor were pending within the previous year but were dismissed, other than a case refiled under a chapter other than chapter 7 after dismissal under section 707(b), the stay under subsection (a) shall not go into effect upon the filing of the later case; and

(ii) on request of a party in interest, the court shall promptly enter an order confirming that no stay is in effect;

(B) if, within 30 days after the filing of the later case, a party in interest requests the court may order the stay to take effect in the case as to any or all creditors (subject to such conditions or limitations as the court may impose), after notice and a hearing, only if the party in interest demonstrates that the filing of the later case is in good faith as to the creditors to be stayed;

(C) a stay imposed under subparagraph (B) shall be effective on the date of the entry of the order allowing the stay to go into effect; and

(D) for purposes of subparagraph (B), a case is presumptively filed not in good faith (but such presumption may be rebutted by clear and convincing evidence to the contrary)—

(i) as to all creditors if—

(I) 2 or more previous cases under this title in which the individual was a debtor were pending within the 1–year period;

(II) a previous case under this title in which the individual was a debtor was dismissed within the time period stated in this paragraph after the debtor failed to file or amend the petition or other documents as required by this title or the court without substantial excuse (but mere inadvertence or negligence shall not be substantial excuse unless the dismissal was caused by the negligence of the debtor's attorney), failed to provide adequate protection as ordered by the court, or failed to perform the terms of a plan confirmed by the court; or

(III) there has not been a substantial change in the financial or personal affairs of the debtor since the dismissal of the next most previous case under this title, or any other reason to conclude that the later case will not be concluded, if a case under chapter 7, with a discharge, and if a case under chapter 11 or 13, with a confirmed plan that will be fully performed; or

(ii) as to any creditor that commenced an action under subsection (d) in a previous case in which the individual was a debtor if, as of the date of dismissal of such case, such action was still pending or had been resolved by terminating, conditioning, or limiting the stay as to such action of such creditor.

(d) On request of a party in interest and after notice and a hearing, the court shall grant relief from the stay provided under subsection (a) of this section, such as by terminating, annulling, modifying, or conditioning such stay—

(1) for cause, including the lack of adequate protection of an interest in property of such party in interest;

(2) with respect to a stay of an act against property under subsection (a) of this section, if—

(A) the debtor does not have an equity in such property; and

(B) such property is not necessary to an effective reorganization;

(3) with respect to a stay of an act against single asset real estate under subsection (a), by a creditor whose claim is secured by an interest in such real estate, unless, not later than the date that is 90 days after the entry of the order for relief (or such later date as the court may determine for cause by order entered within that 90–day period) or 30 days after the court determines that the debtor is subject to this paragraph, whichever is later—

(A) the debtor has filed a plan of reorganization that has a reasonable possibility of being confirmed within a reasonable time; or

(B) the debtor has commenced monthly payments that—

(i) may, in the debtor's sole discretion, notwithstanding section 363(c)(2), be made from rents or other income generated before, on, or after the date of the commencement of the case by or from the property to each creditor whose claim is secured by such real estate (other than a claim secured by a judgment lien or by an unmatured statutory lien); and

(ii) are in an amount equal to interest at the then applicable nondefault contract rate of interest on the value of the creditor's interest in the real estate; or

(4) with respect to a stay of an act against real property under subsection (a), by a creditor whose claim is secured by an interest in such real property, if the court finds that the filing of the petition was part of a scheme to delay, hinder, or defraud creditors that involved either—

(A) transfer of all or part ownership of, or other interest in, such real property without the consent of the secured creditor or court approval; or

(B) multiple bankruptcy filings affecting such real property.

If recorded in compliance with applicable State laws governing notices of interests or liens in real property, an order entered under paragraph (4) shall be binding in any other case under this title purporting to affect such real property filed not later than 2 years after the date of the entry of such order by the court, except that a debtor in a subsequent case under this title may move for relief from such order based upon changed circumstances or for good cause shown, after notice and a hearing. Any Federal, State, or local governmental unit that accepts notices of interests or liens in real property shall accept any certified copy of an order described in this subsection for indexing and recording.

(e)(1) Thirty days after a request under subsection (d) of this section for relief from the stay of any act against property of the estate under subsection (a) of this section, such stay is terminated with respect to the party in interest making such request, unless the court, after notice and a hearing, orders such stay continued in effect pending the conclusion of, or as a result of, a final hearing and determination under subsection (d) of this section. A hearing under this subsection may be a preliminary hearing, or may be consolidated with the final hearing under subsection (d) of this section. The court shall order such stay continued in effect pending the conclusion of the final hearing under subsection (d) of this section if there is a reasonable likelihood that the party opposing relief from such stay will prevail at the conclusion of such final hearing. If the hearing under this subsection is a preliminary hearing, then such final hearing shall be concluded not later than thirty days after the conclusion of such preliminary hearing, unless the 30–day period is extended with the consent of the parties in interest or for a specific time which the court finds is required by compelling circumstances.

(2) Notwithstanding paragraph (1), in a case under chapter 7, 11, or 13 in which the debtor is an individual, the stay under subsection (a) shall terminate on the date that is 60 days after a request is made by a party in interest under subsection (d), unless—

(A) a final decision is rendered by the court during the 60–day period beginning on the date of the request; or

(B) such 60–day period is extended—

(i) by agreement of all parties in interest; or

(ii) by the court for such specific period of time as the court finds is required for good cause, as described in findings made by the court.

(f) Upon request of a party in interest, the court, with or without a hearing, shall grant such relief from the stay provided under subsection (a) of this section as is necessary to prevent irreparable damage to the interest of an entity in property, if such interest will suffer such damage before there is an opportunity for notice and a hearing under subsection (d) or (e) of this section.

(g) In any hearing under subsection (d) or (e) of this section concerning relief from the stay of any act under subsection (a) of this section—

(1) the party requesting such relief has the burden of proof on the issue of the debtor's equity in property; and

(2) the party opposing such relief has the burden of proof on all other issues.

(h)(1) In a case in which the debtor is an individual, the stay provided by subsection (a) is terminated with respect to personal property of the estate or of the debtor securing in whole or in part a claim, or subject to an unexpired lease, and such personal property shall no longer be property of the estate if the debtor fails within the applicable time set by section 521(a)(2)—

(A) to file timely any statement of intention required under section 521(a)(2) with respect to such personal property or to indicate in such statement that the debtor will either surrender such personal property or retain it and, if retaining such personal property, either redeem such personal property pursuant to section 722, enter into an agreement of the kind specified in section 524(c) applicable to the debt secured by such personal property, or assume such unexpired lease pursuant to section 365(p) if the trustee does not do so, as applicable; and

(B) to take timely the action specified in such statement, as it may be amended before expiration of the period for taking action, unless such statement specifies the debtor's intention to reaffirm such debt on the original contract terms and the creditor refuses to agree to the reaffirmation on such terms.

(2) Paragraph (1) does not apply if the court determines, on the motion of the trustee filed before the expiration of the applicable time set by section 521(a)(2), after notice and a hearing, that such personal property is of consequential value or benefit to the estate, and orders appropriate adequate protection of the creditor's interest, and orders the debtor to deliver any collateral in the debtor's possession to the trustee. If the court does not so determine, the stay provided by subsection (a) shall terminate upon the conclusion of the hearing on the motion.

(i) If a case commenced under chapter 7, 11, or 13 is dismissed due to the creation of a debt repayment plan, for purposes of subsection (c)(3), any subsequent case commenced by the debtor under any such chapter shall not be presumed to be filed not in good faith.

(j) On request of a party in interest, the court shall issue an order under subsection (c) confirming that the automatic stay has been terminated.

(k)(1) Except as provided in paragraph (2), an individual injured by any willful violation of a stay provided by this section shall recover actual damages, including costs and attorneys' fees, and, in appropriate circumstances, may recover punitive damages.

(2) If such violation is based on an action taken by an entity in the good faith belief that subsection (h) applies to the debtor, the recovery under paragraph (1) of this subsection against such entity shall be limited to actual damages.

(*l*)(1) Except as otherwise provided in this subsection, subsection (b) (22) shall apply on the date that is 30 days after the date on which the bankruptcy petition is filed, if the debtor files with the petition and serves upon the lessor a certification under penalty of perjury that—

(A) under nonbankruptcy law applicable in the jurisdiction, there are circumstances under which the debtor would be permitted to cure the entire monetary default that gave rise to the judgment for possession, after that judgment for possession was entered; and

(B) the debtor (or an adult dependent of the debtor) has deposited with the clerk of the court, any rent that would become due during the 30–day period after the filing of the bankruptcy petition.

(2) If, within the 30–day period after the filing of the bankruptcy petition, the debtor (or an adult dependent of the debtor) complies with paragraph (1) and files with the court and serves upon the lessor a further certification under penalty of perjury that the debtor (or an adult dependent of the debtor) has cured, under nonbankruptcy law applicable in the jurisdiction, the entire monetary default that gave rise to the judgment under which possession is sought by the lessor, subsection (b)(22) shall not apply, unless ordered to apply by the court under paragraph (3).

(3)(A) If the lessor files an objection to any certification filed by the debtor under paragraph (1) or (2), and serves such objection upon the debtor, the court shall hold a hearing within 10 days after the filing and service of such objection to determine if the certification filed by the debtor under paragraph (1) or (2) is true.

(B) If the court upholds the objection of the lessor filed under subparagraph (A)—

(i) subsection (b)(22) shall apply immediately and relief from the stay provided under subsection (a)(3) shall not be required to enable the lessor to complete the process to recover full possession of the property; and

(ii) the clerk of the court shall immediately serve upon the lessor and the debtor a certified copy of the court's order upholding the lessor's objection.

(4) If a debtor, in accordance with paragraph (5), indicates on the petition that there was a judgment for possession of the residential rental property in which the debtor resides and does not file a certification under paragraph (1) or (2)—

(A) subsection (b)(22) shall apply immediately upon failure to file such certification, and relief from the stay provided under subsection (a)(3) shall not be required to enable the lessor to complete the process to recover full possession of the property; and

(B) the clerk of the court shall immediately serve upon the lessor and the debtor a certified copy of the docket indicating the absence of a filed certification and the applicability of the exception to the stay under subsection (b)(22).

(5)(A) Where a judgment for possession of residential property in which the debtor resides as a tenant under a lease or rental agreement has been obtained by the lessor, the debtor shall so indicate on the bankruptcy petition and shall provide the name and address of the lessor that obtained that pre-petition judgment on the petition and on any certification filed under this subsection.

(B) The form of certification filed with the petition, as specified in this subsection, shall provide for the debtor to certify, and the debtor shall certify—

(i) whether a judgment for possession of residential rental housing in which the debtor resides has been obtained against the debtor before the date of the filing of the petition; and

(ii) whether the debtor is claiming under paragraph (1) that under nonbankruptcy law applicable in the jurisdiction, there are circumstances under which the debtor would be permitted to cure the entire monetary default that gave rise to the judgment for possession, after that judgment of possession was entered, and has made the appropriate deposit with the court.

(C) The standard forms (electronic and otherwise) used in a bankruptcy proceeding shall be amended to reflect the requirements of this subsection.

(D) The clerk of the court shall arrange for the prompt transmittal of the rent deposited in accordance with paragraph (1)(B) to the lessor.

(m)(1) Except as otherwise provided in this subsection, subsection (b) (23) shall apply on the date that is 15 days after the date on which the lessor files and serves a certification described in subsection (b)(23).

(2)(A) If the debtor files with the court an objection to the truth or legal sufficiency of the certification described in subsection (b)(23) and serves such objection upon the lessor, subsection (b)(23) shall not apply, unless ordered to apply by the court under this subsection.

(B) If the debtor files and serves the objection under subparagraph (A), the court shall hold a hearing within 10 days after the filing and service of such objection to determine if the situation giving rise to the lessor's certification under paragraph (1) existed or has been remedied.

(C) If the debtor can demonstrate to the satisfaction of the court that the situation giving rise to the lessor's certification under paragraph (1) did not exist or has been remedied, the stay provided under subsection (a)(3) shall remain in effect until the termination of the stay under this section.

(D) If the debtor cannot demonstrate to the satisfaction of the court that the situation giving rise to the lessor's certification under paragraph (1) did not exist or has been remedied—

(i) relief from the stay provided under subsection (a)(3) shall not be required to enable the lessor to proceed with the eviction; and

(ii) the clerk of the court shall immediately serve upon the lessor and the debtor a certified copy of the court's order upholding the lessor's certification.

(3) If the debtor fails to file, within 15 days, an objection under paragraph (2)(A)—

(A) subsection (b)(23) shall apply immediately upon such failure and relief from the stay provided under subsection (a)(3) shall not be required to enable the lessor to complete the process to recover full possession of the property; and

(B) the clerk of the court shall immediately serve upon the lessor and the debtor a certified copy of the docket indicating such failure.

(n)(1) Except as provided in paragraph (2), subsection (a) does not apply in a case in which the debtor—

(A) is a debtor in a small business case pending at the time the petition is filed;

(B) was a debtor in a small business case that was dismissed for any reason by an order that became final in the 2–year period ending on the date of the order for relief entered with respect to the petition;

(C) was a debtor in a small business case in which a plan was confirmed in the 2–year period ending on the date of the order for relief entered with respect to the petition; or

(D) is an entity that has acquired substantially all of the assets or business of a small business debtor described in subparagraph (A), (B), or (C), unless such entity establishes by a preponderance of the evidence that such entity acquired substantially all of the assets or business of such small business debtor in good faith and not for the purpose of evading this paragraph.

(2) Paragraph (1) does not apply—

(A) to an involuntary case involving no collusion by the debtor with creditors; or

(B) to the filing of a petition if—

(i) the debtor proves by a preponderance of the evidence that the filing of the petition resulted from circumstances beyond the control of the debtor not foreseeable at the time the case then pending was filed; and

(ii) it is more likely than not that the court will confirm a feasible plan, but not a liquidating plan, within a reasonable period of time.

(*o*) The exercise of rights not subject to the stay arising under subsection (a) pursuant to paragraph (6), (7), (17), or (27) of subsection (b) shall not be stayed by any order of a court or administrative agency in any proceeding under this title. *(Pub.L. 95–598, Nov. 6, 1978, 92 Stat. 2570; Pub.L. 97–222, § 3, July 27, 1982, 96 Stat. 235; Pub.L. 98–353, Title III, §§ 304, 363(b), 392, 441, July 10, 1984, 98 Stat. 352, 363, 365, 371; Pub.L. 99–509, Title V, § 5001(a), Oct. 21, 1986, 100 Stat. 1911; Pub.L. 99–554, Title II, §§ 257(j), 283(d), Oct. 27, 1986, 100 Stat. 3115, 3116; Pub.L. 101–311, Title I, § 102, Title II, § 202, June 25, 1990, 104 Stat. 267, 269; Pub.L. 101–508, Title III, § 3007(a)(1), Nov. 5, 1990, 104 Stat. 1388–28; Pub.L. 103–394, Title I, §§ 101, 116, Title II, §§ 204(a), 218(b), Title III, § 304(b), Title IV, § 401, Title V, § 501(b)(2), (d)(7), Oct. 22, 1994, 108 Stat. 4107, 4119, 4122, 4128, 4132, 4141, 4142, 4144; Pub.L. 105–277, Div. I, Title VI, § 603, Oct. 21, 1998, 112 Stat. 2681–886; Pub.L. 109–8, Title I, § 106(f), Title II, §§ 214, 224(b), Title III, §§ 302, 303, 305(1), 311, 320, Title IV, §§ 401(b), 441, 444, Title VII, §§ 709, 718, Title IX, § 907(d), (o)(1), (2), Title XI, § 1106, Title XII, § 1225, Apr. 20, 2005, 119 Stat. 41, 54, 64, 75, 77, 79, 84, 94, 104, 114, 117, 127, 131, 176, 181, 182, 192, 199; Pub.L. 109–304, § 17(b)(1), Oct. 6, 2006, 120 Stat. 1706; Pub.L. 109–390, § 5(a)(2), Dec. 12, 2006, 120 Stat. 2696; Pub.L. 111–327, § 2(a)(12), Dec. 22, 2010, 124 Stat. 3558.)*

Commentary

In re Gruntz, 202 F.3d 1074 (9th Cir. en banc 2000), holds that an automatic stay in bankruptcy does not enjoin a state criminal prosecution for willful failure to pay child support. *Gruntz* also holds that a state court modification of an automatic stay is not binding on a federal court.

A Bankruptcy Court properly permitted a former wife to seek a Qualified Domestic Relations Order (QDRO) in state court to determine whether former husband's pension was ERISA-qualified and hence exempt from his bankruptcy estate, but the Bankruptcy Court erred in concluding that the Pennsylvania state court's distribution to wife of a 38.7 percent interest in husband's pension was a dischargeable money judgment rather than a nondischargeable ownership interest in the plan assets. *In re Lowenschuss, 170 F.3d 923 (9th Cir. 1999).* See also *In re Gendreau, 122 F.3d 815 (9th Cir. 1997)* (former spouse's ownership interest in pension not a debt and hence not dischargeable in debtor's bankruptcy). *In re Carbaugh, 278 B.R. 512 (10th Cir. BAP 2002)* holds that the bankruptcy court properly acted within its discretion in lifting an automatic stay in order to allow a former wife to pursue state court litigation to determine her prebankruptcy property rights in her former husband's ERISA-qualified pension plan under the former spouses' settlement agreement, even though the former wife had not yet obtained a QDRO, reasoning that a QDRO does not create an interest, but merely allows enforcement of an already existing interest. Interpreting 11 U.S.C. § 541(c)(2), *Carbaugh* additionally holds that a debtor's interest in an ERISA-qualified pension plan is excluded from the property of the estate because ERISA's anti-alienation clause makes it a "trust that is enforceable under applicable nonbankruptcy law," but that monies distributed from ERISA pension plans are not excluded if they are not rolled over into another ERISA-qualified plan.

A Bankruptcy Court properly permitted a former wife to seek a Qualified Domestic Relations Order (QDRO) in state court to determine whether former husband's pension was ERISA-qualified and hence exempt from his bankruptcy estate, but the Bankruptcy Court erred in concluding that the Pennsylvania state court's distribution to wife of a 38.7 percent interest in husband's pension was a dischargeable money judgment rather than a nondischargeable ownership interest in the plan assets. *In re Lowenschuss, 170 F.3d 923 (9th Cir. 1999).* See also *In re Gendreau, 122 F.3d 815 (9th Cir. 1997)* (former spouse's ownership interest in pension not a debt and hence not dischargeable in debtor's bankruptcy).

Allen v. Allen, 275 F.3d 1160 (9th Cir. 2002), holds that a former wife's state court proceeding to modify spousal support is wholly exempt under subsection (b)(2)(A)(ii) from the automatic stay imposed by her former husband's bankruptcy proceeding.

In re Marriage of Sprague & Spiegel–Sprague, 105 Cal.App.4th 215, 129 Cal.Rptr.2d 261 (2002), holds that a creditor must obtain relief from the automatic bankruptcy stay in bankruptcy court in order to pursue a family law matter in state court if the family law matter is a core bankruptcy matter. Whether a family law order to pay attorney's fees is excepted, under subsection (b)(2)(B), from the automatic stay is a matter of bankruptcy law that must be determined by bankruptcy court, and may not be determined by a state court.

CHAPTER 5—CREDITORS, THE DEBTOR, AND THE ESTATE

SUBCHAPTER I—CREDITORS AND CLAIMS

SUBCHAPTER II—DEBTOR'S DUTIES AND BENEFITS

SUBCHAPTER III—THE ESTATE

SUBCHAPTER I—CREDITORS AND CLAIMS

§ 502. Allowance of claims or interests

(a) A claim or interest, proof of which is filed under section 501 of this title, is deemed allowed, unless a party in interest, including a creditor of a general partner in a partnership that is a debtor in a case under chapter 7 of this title, objects.

(b) Except as provided in subsections (e)(2), (f), (g), (h) and (i) of this section, if such objection to a claim is made, the court, after notice and a hearing, shall determine the amount of such claim in lawful currency of the United States as of the date of the filing of the petition, and shall allow such claim in such amount, except to the extent that—

(1) such claim is unenforceable against the debtor and property of the debtor, under any agreement or applicable law for a reason other than because such claim is contingent or unmatured;

(2) such claim is for unmatured interest;

(3) if such claim is for a tax assessed against property of the estate, such claim exceeds the value of the interest of the estate in such property;

(4) if such claim is for services of an insider or attorney of the debtor, such claim exceeds the reasonable value of such services;

(5) such claim is for a debt that is unmatured on the date of the filing of the petition and that is excepted from discharge under section 523(a)(5) of this title;

(6) if such claim is the claim of a lessor for damages resulting from the termination of a lease of real property, such claim exceeds—

(A) the rent reserved by such lease, without acceleration, for the greater of one year, or 15 percent, not to exceed three years, of the remaining term of such lease, following the earlier of—

(i) the date of the filing of the petition; and

(ii) the date on which such lessor repossessed, or the lessee surrendered, the leased property; plus

(B) any unpaid rent due under such lease, without acceleration, on the earlier of such dates;

(7) if such claim is the claim of an employee for damages resulting from the termination of an employment contract, such claim exceeds—

(A) the compensation provided by such contract, without acceleration, for one year following the earlier of—

(i) the date of the filing of the petition; or

(ii) the date on which the employer directed the employee to terminate, or such employee terminated, performance under such contract; plus

(B) any unpaid compensation due under such contract, without acceleration, on the earlier of such dates;

(8) such claim results from a reduction, due to late payment, in the amount of an otherwise applicable credit available to the debtor in connection with an employment tax on wages, salaries, or commissions earned from the debtor; or

(9) proof of such claim is not timely filed, except to the extent tardily filed as permitted under paragraph (1), (2), or (3) of section 726(a) of this title or under the Federal Rules of Bankruptcy Procedure, except that a claim of a governmental unit shall be timely filed if it is filed before 180 days after the date of the order for relief or such later time as the Federal Rules of Bankruptcy Procedure may provide, and except that in a case under chapter 13, a claim of a governmental unit for a tax with respect to a return filed under section 1308 shall be timely if the claim is filed on or before the date that is 60 days after the date on which such return was filed as required.

(c) There shall be estimated for purpose of allowance under this section—

(1) any contingent or unliquidated claim, the fixing or liquidation of which, as the case may be, would unduly delay the administration of the case; or

(2) any right to payment arising from a right to an equitable remedy for breach of performance.

(d) Notwithstanding subsections (a) and (b) of this section, the court shall disallow any claim of any entity from which property is recoverable under section 542, 543, 550, or 553 of this title or that is a transferee of a transfer avoidable under section 522(f), 522(h), 544, 545, 547, 548, 549, or 724(a) of this title, unless such entity or transferee has paid the amount, or turned over any such property, for which such entity or transferee is liable under section 522(i), 542, 543, 550, or 553 of this title.

(e)(1) Notwithstanding subsections (a), (b), and (c) of this section and paragraph (2) of this subsection, the court shall disallow any claim for reimbursement or contribution of an entity that is liable with the debtor on or has secured the claim of a creditor, to the extent that—

(A) such creditor's claim against the estate is disallowed;

(B) such claim for reimbursement or contribution is contingent as of the time of allowance or disallowance of such claim for reimbursement or contribution; or

(C) such entity asserts a right of subrogation to the rights of such creditor under section 509 of this title.

(2) A claim for reimbursement or contribution of such an entity that becomes fixed after the commencement of the case shall be determined, and shall be allowed under subsection (a), (b), or (c) of this section, or disallowed under subsection (d) of this section, the same as if such claim had become fixed before the date of the filing of the petition.

(f) In an involuntary case, a claim arising in the ordinary course of the debtor's business or financial affairs after the commencement of the case but before the earlier of the appointment of a trustee and the order for relief shall be determined as of the date such claim arises, and shall be allowed under subsection (a), (b), or (c) of this section or disallowed under subsection (d) or (e) of this section, the same as if such claim had arisen before the date of the filing of the petition.

(g)(1) A claim arising from the rejection, under section 365 of this title or under a plan under chapter 9, 11, 12, or 13 of this title, of an executory contract or unexpired lease of the debtor that has not been assumed shall be determined, and shall be allowed under subsection (a), (b), or (c) of this section or disallowed under subsection (d) or (e) of this section, the same as if such claim had arisen before the date of the filing of the petition.

(2) A claim for damages calculated in accordance with section 562 shall be allowed under subsection (a), (b), or (c), or disallowed under subsection (d) or (e), as if such claim had arisen before the date of the filing of the petition.

(h) A claim arising from the recovery of property under section 522, 550, or 553 of this title shall be determined, and shall be allowed under subsection (a), (b), or (c) of this section, or disallowed under subsection (d) or (e) of this section, the same as if such claim had arisen before the date of the filing of the petition.

(i) A claim that does not arise until after the commencement of the case for a tax entitled to priority under section 507(a)(8) of this title shall be determined, and shall be allowed under subsection (a), (b), or (c) of this section, or disallowed under subsection (d) or (e) of this section, the same as if such claim had arisen before the date of the filing of the petition.

(j) A claim that has been allowed or disallowed may be reconsidered for cause. A reconsidered claim may be allowed or disallowed according to the equities of the case. Reconsideration of a claim under this subsection does not affect the validity of any payment or transfer from the estate made to a holder of an allowed claim on account of such allowed claim that is not reconsidered, but if a reconsidered claim is allowed and is of the same class as such holder's claim, such holder may not receive any additional payment or transfer from the estate on account of such holder's allowed claim until the holder of such reconsidered and allowed claim receives payment on account of such claim proportionate in value to that already received by such other holder. This subsection does not alter or modify the trustee's right to recover from a creditor any excess payment or transfer made to such creditor.

(k)(1) The court, on the motion of the debtor and after a hearing, may reduce a claim filed under this section based in whole on an unsecured consumer debt by not more than 20 percent of the claim, if—

(A) the claim was filed by a creditor who unreasonably refused to negotiate a reasonable alternative repayment schedule proposed on behalf of the debtor by an approved nonprofit budget and credit counseling agency described in section 111;

(B) the offer of the debtor under subparagraph (A)—

(i) was made at least 60 days before the date of the filing of the petition; and

(ii) provided for payment of at least 60 percent of the amount of the debt over a period not to exceed the repayment period of the loan, or a reasonable extension thereof; and

(C) no part of the debt under the alternative repayment schedule is nondischargeable.

(2) The debtor shall have the burden of proving, by clear and convincing evidence, that—

(A) the creditor unreasonably refused to consider the debtor's proposal; and

(B) the proposed alternative repayment schedule was made prior to expiration of the 60–day period specified in paragraph (1)(B)(i).

(Pub.L. 95–598, Nov. 6, 1978, 92 Stat. 2579; Pub.L. 98–353, Title III, § 445, July 10, 1984, 98 Stat. 373; Pub.L. 99–554, Title II, §§ 257(j), 283(f), Oct. 27, 1986, 100 Stat. 3115, 3117; Pub.L. 103–394, Title II, § 213(a), Title III, § 304(h)(1), Oct. 22, 1994, 108 Stat. 4125, 4134; Pub.L. 109–8, Title II, § 201(a), Title VII, § 716(d), Title IX, § 910(b), Apr. 20, 2005, 119 Stat. 42, 130, 184.)

Commentary

In re Foster, 319 F.3d 495 (9th Cir. 2003), holds that the interest on a nondischargeable child support obligation continues to accrue after filing of a bankruptcy petition, is not dischargeable, and may be collected after discharge of the underlying child support debt.

SUBCHAPTER II—DEBTOR'S DUTIES AND BENEFITS

§ 522. Exemptions

(a) In this section—

(1) "dependent" includes spouse, whether or not actually dependent; and

(2) "value" means fair market value as of the date of the filing of the petition or, with respect to property that becomes property of the estate after such date, as of the date such property becomes property of the estate.

(b)(1) Notwithstanding section 541 of this title, an individual debtor may exempt from property of the estate the property listed in either paragraph (2) or, in the alternative, paragraph (3) of this subsection. In joint cases filed under section 302 of this title and individual cases filed under section 301 or 303 of this title by or against debtors who are husband and wife, and whose estates are ordered to be jointly administered under Rule 1015(b) of the Federal Rules of Bankruptcy Procedure, one debtor may not elect to exempt property listed in paragraph (2) and the other debtor elect to exempt property listed in paragraph (3) of this subsection. If the parties cannot agree on the alternative to be elected, they shall be deemed to elect paragraph (2), where such election is permitted under the law of the jurisdiction where the case is filed.

(2) Property listed in this paragraph is property that is specified under subsection (d), unless the State law that is applicable to the debtor under paragraph (3)(A) specifically does not so authorize.

(3) Property listed in this paragraph is—

(A) subject to subsections (*o*) and (p), any property that is exempt under Federal law, other than subsection (d) of this section, or State or local law that is applicable on the date of the filing of the petition to the place in which the debtor's domicile has been located for the 730 days immediately preceding the date of the filing of the petition or if the debtor's domicile has not been located in a single State for such 730–day period, the place in which the debtor's domicile was located for 180 days immediately preceding the 730–day period or for a longer portion of such 180–day period than in any other place;

(B) any interest in property in which the debtor had, immediately before the commencement of the case, an interest as a tenant by the entirety or joint tenant to the extent that such interest as a tenant by the entirety or joint tenant is exempt from process under applicable nonbankruptcy law; and

(C) retirement funds to the extent that those funds are in a fund or account that is exempt from taxation under section 401, 403, 408, 408A, 414, 457, or 501(a) of the Internal Revenue Code of 1986.

If the effect of the domiciliary requirement under subparagraph (A) is to render the debtor ineligible for any exemption, the debtor may elect to exempt property that is specified under subsection (d).

(4) For purposes of paragraph (3)(C) and subsection (d)(12), the following shall apply:

(A) If the retirement funds are in a retirement fund that has received a favorable determination under section 7805 of the Internal Revenue Code of 1986, and that determination is in effect as of the date of the filing of the petition in a case under this title, those funds shall be presumed to be exempt from the estate.

(B) If the retirement funds are in a retirement fund that has not received a favorable determination under such section 7805, those funds are exempt from the estate if the debtor demonstrates that—

(i) no prior determination to the contrary has been made by a court or the Internal Revenue Service; and

(ii)(I) the retirement fund is in substantial compliance with the applicable requirements of the Internal Revenue Code of 1986; or

(II) the retirement fund fails to be in substantial compliance with the applicable requirements of the Internal Revenue Code of 1986 and the debtor is not materially responsible for that failure.

(C) A direct transfer of retirement funds from 1 fund or account that is exempt from taxation under section 401, 403, 408, 408A, 414, 457, or 501(a) of the Internal Revenue Code of 1986, under section 401(a)(31) of the Internal Revenue Code of 1986, or otherwise, shall not cease to qualify for exemption under paragraph (3)(C) or subsection (d)(12) by reason of such direct transfer.

(D)(i) Any distribution that qualifies as an eligible rollover distribution within the meaning of section 402(c) of the Internal Revenue Code of 1986 or that is described in clause (ii) shall not cease to qualify for exemption under paragraph (3)(C) or subsection (d)(12) by reason of such distribution.

(ii) A distribution described in this clause is an amount that—

(I) has been distributed from a fund or account that is exempt from taxation under section 401, 403, 408, 408A, 414, 457, or 501(a) of the Internal Revenue Code of 1986; and

(II) to the extent allowed by law, is deposited in such a fund or account not later than 60 days after the distribution of such amount.

(c) Unless the case is dismissed, property exempted under this section is not liable during or after the case for any debt of the debtor that arose, or that is determined under section 502 of this title as if such debt had arisen, before the commencement of the case, except—

(1) a debt of a kind specified in paragraph (1) or (5) of section 523(a) (in which case, notwithstanding any provision of applicable nonbankruptcy law to the contrary, such property shall be liable for a debt of a kind specified in such paragraph);

(2) a debt secured by a lien that is—

(A)(i) not avoided under subsection (f) or (g) of this section or under section 544, 545, 547, 548, 549, or 724(a) of this title; and

(ii) not void under section 506(d) of this title; or

(B) a tax lien, notice of which is properly filed;

(3) a debt of a kind specified in section 523(a)(4) or 523(a)(6) of this title owed by an institution-affiliated party of an insured depository institution to a Federal depository institutions regulatory agency acting in its capacity as conservator, receiver, or liquidating agent for such institution; or

(4) a debt in connection with fraud in the obtaining or providing of any scholarship, grant, loan, tuition, discount, award, or other financial assistance for purposes of financing an education at an institution of higher education (as that term is defined in section 101 of the Higher Education Act of 1965 (20 U.S.C. 1001)).

(d) The following property may be exempted under subsection (b)(2) of this section:

(1) The debtor's aggregate interest, not to exceed $23,675 [1] in value, in real property or personal property that the debtor or a dependent of the debtor uses as a residence, in a cooperative that owns property that the debtor or a dependent of the debtor uses as a residence, or in a burial plot for the debtor or a dependent of the debtor.

(2) The debtor's interest, not to exceed $3,775 [1] in value, in one motor vehicle.

(3) The debtor's interest, not to exceed $600 [1] in value in any particular item or $12,625 [1] in aggregate value, in household furnishings, household goods, wearing apparel, appliances, books, animals, crops, or musical instruments, that are held primarily for the personal, family, or household use of the debtor or a dependent of the debtor.

(4) The debtor's aggregate interest, not to exceed $1,600 [1] in value, in jewelry held primarily for the personal, family, or household use of the debtor or a dependent of the debtor.

(5) The debtor's aggregate interest in any property, not to exceed in value $1,250 [1] plus up to $11,850 [1] of any unused amount of the exemption provided under paragraph (1) of this subsection.

(6) The debtor's aggregate interest, not to exceed $2,375 [1] in value, in any implements, professional books, or tools, of the trade of the debtor or the trade of a dependent of the debtor.

(7) Any unmatured life insurance contract owned by the debtor, other than a credit life insurance contract.

(8) The debtor's aggregate interest, not to exceed in value $12,625 [1] less any amount of property of the estate transferred in the manner specified in section 542(d) of this title, in any accrued dividend or interest under, or loan value of, any unmatured life insurance contract owned by the debtor under which the insured is the debtor or an individual of whom the debtor is a dependent.

(9) Professionally prescribed health aids for the debtor or a dependent of the debtor.

(10) The debtor's right to receive—

(A) a social security benefit, unemployment compensation, or a local public assistance benefit;

(B) a veterans' benefit;

(C) a disability, illness, or unemployment benefit;

(D) alimony, support, or separate maintenance, to the extent reasonably necessary for the support of the debtor and any dependent of the debtor;

(E) a payment under a stock bonus, pension, profitsharing, annuity, or similar plan or contract on account of illness, disability, death, age, or length of service, to the extent reasonably necessary for the support of the debtor and any dependent of the debtor, unless—

(i) such plan or contract was established by or under the auspices of an insider that employed the debtor at the time the debtor's rights under such plan or contract arose;

(ii) such payment is on account of age or length of service; and

(iii) such plan or contract does not qualify under section 401(a), 403(a), 403(b), or 408 of the Internal Revenue Code of 1986.

(11) The debtor's right to receive, or property that is traceable to—

(A) an award under a crime victim's reparation law;

(B) a payment on account of the wrongful death of an individual of whom the debtor was a dependent, to the extent reasonably necessary for the support of the debtor and any dependent of the debtor;

(C) a payment under a life insurance contract that insured the life of an individual of whom the debtor was a dependent on the date of such individual's death, to the extent reasonably necessary for the support of the debtor and any dependent of the debtor;

(D) a payment, not to exceed $23,675,[1] on account of personal bodily injury, not including pain and suffering or compensation for actual pecuniary loss, of the debtor or an individual of whom the debtor is a dependent; or

(E) a payment in compensation of loss of future earnings of the debtor or an individual of whom the debtor is or was a dependent, to the extent reasonably necessary for the support of the debtor and any dependent of the debtor.

(12) Retirement funds to the extent that those funds are in a fund or account that is exempt from taxation under section 401, 403, 408, 408A, 414, 457, or 501(a) of the Internal Revenue Code of 1986.

(e) A waiver of an exemption executed in favor of a creditor that holds an unsecured claim against the debtor is unenforceable in a case under this title with respect to such claim against property that the debtor may exempt under subsection (b) of this section. A waiver by the debtor of a power under subsection (f) or (h) of this section to avoid a transfer, under subsection (g) or (i) of this section to exempt property, or under subsection (i) of this section to recover property or to preserve a transfer, is unenforceable in a case under this title.

(f)(1) Notwithstanding any waiver of exemptions but subject to paragraph (3), the debtor may avoid the fixing of a lien on an interest of the debtor in property to the extent that such lien impairs an exemption to which the debtor would have been entitled under subsection (b) of this section, if such lien is—

(A) a judicial lien, other than a judicial lien that secures a debt of a kind that is specified in section 523(a)(5); or

(B) a nonpossessory, nonpurchase-money security interest in any—

(i) household furnishings, household goods, wearing apparel, appliances, books, animals, crops, musical instruments, or jewelry that are held primarily for the personal, family, or household use of the debtor or a dependent of the debtor;

(ii) implements, professional books, or tools, of the trade of the debtor or the trade of a dependent of the debtor; or

(iii) professionally prescribed health aids for the debtor or a dependent of the debtor.

(2)(A) For the purposes of this subsection, a lien shall be considered to impair an exemption to the extent that the sum of—

(i) the lien;

(ii) all other liens on the property; and

(iii) the amount of the exemption that the debtor could claim if there were no liens on the property;

exceeds the value that the debtor's interest in the property would have in the absence of any liens.

(B) In the case of a property subject to more than 1 lien, a lien that has been avoided shall not be considered in making the calculation under subparagraph (A) with respect to other liens.

(C) This paragraph shall not apply with respect to a judgment arising out of a mortgage foreclosure.

(3) In a case in which State law that is applicable to the debtor—

(A) permits a person to voluntarily waive a right to claim exemptions under subsection (d) or prohibits a debtor from claiming exemptions under subsection (d); and

(B) either permits the debtor to claim exemptions under State law without limitation in amount, except to the extent that the debtor has permitted the fixing of a consensual lien on any property or prohibits avoidance of a consensual lien on property otherwise eligible to be claimed as exempt property;

the debtor may not avoid the fixing of a lien on an interest of the debtor or a dependent of the debtor in property if the lien is a nonpossessory, nonpurchase-money security interest in implements, professional books, or tools of the trade of the debtor or a dependent of the debtor or farm animals or crops of the debtor or a dependent of the debtor to the extent the value of such implements, professional books, tools of the trade, animals, and crops exceeds $6,425 [1].

(4)(A) Subject to subparagraph (B), for purposes of paragraph (1)(B), the term "household goods" means—

(i) clothing;

(ii) furniture;

(iii) appliances;

(iv) 1 radio;

(v) 1 television;

(vi) 1 VCR;

(vii) linens;

(viii) china;

(ix) crockery;

(x) kitchenware;

(xi) educational materials and educational equipment primarily for the use of minor dependent children of the debtor;

(xii) medical equipment and supplies;

(xiii) furniture exclusively for the use of minor children, or elderly or disabled dependents of the debtor;

(xiv) personal effects (including the toys and hobby equipment of minor dependent children and wedding rings) of the debtor and the dependents of the debtor; and

(xv) 1 personal computer and related equipment.

(B) The term "household goods" does not include—

(i) works of art (unless by or of the debtor, or any relative of the debtor);

(ii) electronic entertainment equipment with a fair market value of more than $675 [1] in the aggregate (except 1 television, 1 radio, and 1 VCR);

(iii) items acquired as antiques with a fair market value of more than $675 [1] in the aggregate;

(iv) jewelry with a fair market value of more than $675 [1] in the aggregate (except wedding rings); and

(v) a computer (except as otherwise provided for in this section), motor vehicle (including a tractor or lawn tractor), boat, or a motorized recreational device, conveyance, vehicle, watercraft, or aircraft.

(g) Notwithstanding sections 550 and 551 of this title, the debtor may exempt under subsection (b) of this section property that the trustee recovers under section 510(c)(2), 542, 543, 550, 551, or 553 of this title, to the extent that the debtor could have exempted such property under subsection (b) of this section if such property had not been transferred, if—

(1)(A) such transfer was not a voluntary transfer of such property by the debtor; and

(B) the debtor did not conceal such property; or

(2) the debtor could have avoided such transfer under subsection (f)(1)(B) of this section.

(h) The debtor may avoid a transfer of property of the debtor or recover a setoff to the extent that the debtor could have exempted such property under subsection (g)(1) of this section if the trustee had avoided such transfer, if—

(1) such transfer is avoidable by the trustee under section 544, 545, 547, 548, 549, or 724(a) of this title or recoverable by the trustee under section 553 of this title; and

(2) the trustee does not attempt to avoid such transfer.

(i)(1) If the debtor avoids a transfer or recovers a setoff under subsection (f) or (h) of this section, the debtor may recover in the manner prescribed by, and subject to the limitations of, section 550 of this title, the same as if the trustee had avoided such transfer, and may exempt any property so recovered under subsection (b) of this section.

(2) Notwithstanding section 551 of this title, a transfer avoided under section 544, 545, 547, 548, 549, or 724(a) of this title, under subsection (f) or (h) of this section, or property recovered under section 553 of this title, may be preserved for the benefit of the debtor to the extent that the debtor may exempt such property under subsection (g) of this section or paragraph (1) of this subsection.

(j) Notwithstanding subsections (g) and (i) of this section, the debtor may exempt a particular kind of property under subsections (g) and (i) of this section only to the extent that the debtor has exempted less property in value of such kind than that to which the debtor is entitled under subsection (b) of this section.

(k) Property that the debtor exempts under this section is not liable for payment of any administrative expense except—

(1) the aliquot share of the costs and expenses of avoiding a transfer of property that the debtor exempts under subsection (g) of this section, or of recovery of such property, that is attributable to the value of the portion of such property exempted in relation to the value of the property recovered; and

(2) any costs and expenses of avoiding a transfer under subsection (f) or (h) of this section, or of recovery of property under subsection (i)(1) of this section, that the debtor has not paid.

(*l*) The debtor shall file a list of property that the debtor claims as exempt under subsection (b) of this section. If the debtor does not file such a list, a dependent of the debtor may file such a list, or may claim property as exempt from property of the estate on behalf of the debtor. Unless a party in interest objects, the property claimed as exempt on such list is exempt.

(m) Subject to the limitation in subsection (b), this section shall apply separately with respect to each debtor in a joint case.

(n) For assets in individual retirement accounts described in section 408 or 408A of the Internal Revenue Code of 1986, other than a simplified employee pension under section 408(k) of such Code or a simple retirement account under section 408(p) of such Code, the aggregate value of such assets exempted under this section, without regard to amounts attributable to rollover contributions under section 402(c), 402(e)(6), 403(a)(4), 403(a)(5), and 403(b)(8) of the

Internal Revenue Code of 1986, and earnings thereon, shall not exceed $1,283,025 [1] in a case filed by a debtor who is an individual, except that such amount may be increased if the interests of justice so require.

(*o*) For purposes of subsection (b)(3)(A), and notwithstanding subsection (a), the value of an interest in—

(1) real or personal property that the debtor or a dependent of the debtor uses as a residence;

(2) a cooperative that owns property that the debtor or a dependent of the debtor uses as a residence;

(3) a burial plot for the debtor or a dependent of the debtor; or

(4) real or personal property that the debtor or a dependent of the debtor claims as a homestead;

shall be reduced to the extent that such value is attributable to any portion of any property that the debtor disposed of in the 10–year period ending on the date of the filing of the petition with the intent to hinder, delay, or defraud a creditor and that the debtor could not exempt, or that portion that the debtor could not exempt, under subsection (b), if on such date the debtor had held the property so disposed of.

(p)(1) Except as provided in paragraph (2) of this subsection and sections 544 and 548, as a result of electing under subsection (b)(3)(A) to exempt property under State or local law, a debtor may not exempt any amount of interest that was acquired by the debtor during the 1215–day period preceding the date of the filing of the petition that exceeds in the aggregate $160,375 [1] in value in—

(A) real or personal property that the debtor or a dependent of the debtor uses as a residence;

(B) a cooperative that owns property that the debtor or a dependent of the debtor uses as a residence;

(C) a burial plot for the debtor or a dependent of the debtor; or

(D) real or personal property that the debtor or dependent of the debtor claims as a homestead.

(2)(A) The limitation under paragraph (1) shall not apply to an exemption claimed under subsection (b)(3)(A) by a family farmer for the principal residence of such farmer.

(B) For purposes of paragraph (1), any amount of such interest does not include any interest transferred from a debtor's previous principal residence (which was acquired prior to the beginning of such 1215–day period) into the debtor's current principal residence, if the debtor's previous and current residences are located in the same State.

(q)(1) As a result of electing under subsection (b)(3)(A) to exempt property under State or local law, a debtor may not exempt any amount of an interest in property described in subparagraphs (A), (B), (C), and (D) of subsection (p)(1) which exceeds in the aggregate $160,375 [1] if—

(A) the court determines, after notice and a hearing, that the debtor has been convicted of a felony (as defined in section 3156 of title 18), which under the circumstances, demonstrates that the filing of the case was an abuse of the provisions of this title; or

(B) the debtor owes a debt arising from—

(i) any violation of the Federal securities laws (as defined in section 3(a)(47) of the Securities Exchange Act of 1934), any State securities laws, or any regulation or order issued under Federal securities laws or State securities laws;

(ii) fraud, deceit, or manipulation in a fiduciary capacity or in connection with the purchase or sale of any security registered under section 12 or 15(d) of the Securities Exchange Act of 1934 or under section 6 of the Securities Act of 1933;

(iii) any civil remedy under section 1964 of title 18; or

(iv) any criminal act, intentional tort, or willful or reckless misconduct that caused serious physical injury or death to another individual in the preceding 5 years.

(2) Paragraph (1) shall not apply to the extent the amount of an interest in property described in subparagraphs (A), (B), (C), and (D) of subsection (p)(1) is reasonably necessary for the support of the debtor and any dependent of the debtor. *(Pub.L. 95–598, Nov. 6, 1978, 92 Stat. 2586; Pub.L. 98–353, Title III, §§ 306, 453, July 10, 1984, 98 Stat. 353, 375; Pub.L. 99–554, Title II, § 283(i), Oct. 27, 1986, 100 Stat. 3117; Pub.L. 101–647, Title XXV, § 2522(b), Nov. 29, 1990, 104 Stat. 4866; Pub.L. 103–394, Title I, § 108(d), Title III, §§ 303, 304(d), 310, Title V, § 501(d)(12), Oct. 22, 1994, 108 Stat. 4112, 4132, 4133, 4137, 4145; Pub.L. 106–420, § 4, Nov. 1, 2000, 114 Stat. 1868; Pub.L. 109–8, Title II, §§ 216, 224(a), (e)(1), Title III, §§ 307, 308, 313(a), 322(a), Apr. 20, 2005, 119 Stat. 55, 62, 65, 81, 87, 96; Pub.L. 111–327, § 2(a)(17), Dec. 22, 2010, 124 Stat. 3559.)*

[1] Dollar amount as adjusted by the Judicial Conference of the United States. See Adjustment of Dollar Amounts notes set out under this section and 11 U.S.C.A. § 104.

Commentary

Divorced spouses who elect mutually exclusive exemption options in their individual bankruptcy filings are presumed to elect state exemptions, including California's $50,000 homestead exemption, when their cases are subsequently consolidated. *In re Steward, 227 B.R. 895 (9th Cir. Bankruptcy Appellate Panel 1998).*

§ 523. Exceptions to discharge

(a) A discharge under section 727, 1141, 1228(a), 1228(b), or 1328(b) of this title does not discharge an individual debtor from any debt—

(1) for a tax or a customs duty—

(A) of the kind and for the periods specified in section 507(a)(3) or 507(a)(8) of this title, whether or not a claim for such tax was filed or allowed;

(B) with respect to which a return, or equivalent report or notice, if required—

(i) was not filed or given; or

(ii) was filed or given after the date on which such return, report, or notice was last due, under applicable law or under any extension, and after two years before the date of the filing of the petition; or

(C) with respect to which the debtor made a fraudulent return or willfully attempted in any manner to evade or defeat such tax;

(2) for money, property, services, or an extension, renewal, or refinancing of credit, to the extent obtained by—

(A) false pretenses, a false representation, or actual fraud, other than a statement respecting the debtor's or an insider's financial condition;

(B) use of a statement in writing—

(i) that is materially false;

(ii) respecting the debtor's or an insider's financial condition;

(iii) on which the creditor to whom the debtor is liable for such money, property, services, or credit reasonably relied; and

(iv) that the debtor caused to be made or published with intent to deceive; or

(C)(i) for purposes of subparagraph (A)—

(I) consumer debts owed to a single creditor and aggregating more than $675 [1] for luxury goods or services incurred by an individual debtor on or within 90 days before the order for relief under this title are presumed to be nondischargeable; and

(II) cash advances aggregating more than $950 [1] that are extensions of consumer credit under an open end credit plan obtained by an individual debtor on or within 70 days before the order for relief under this title, are presumed to be nondischargeable; and

(ii) for purposes of this subparagraph—

(I) the terms "consumer", "credit", and "open end credit plan" have the same meanings as in section 103 of the Truth in Lending Act; and

(II) the term "luxury goods or services" does not include goods or services reasonably necessary for the support or maintenance of the debtor or a dependent of the debtor;

(3) neither listed nor scheduled under section 521(a)(1) of this title, with the name, if known to the debtor, of the creditor to whom such debt is owed, in time to permit—

(A) if such debt is not of a kind specified in paragraph (2), (4), or (6) of this subsection, timely filing of a proof of claim, unless such creditor had notice or actual knowledge of the case in time for such timely filing; or

(B) if such debt is of a kind specified in paragraph (2), (4), or (6) of this subsection, timely filing of a proof of claim and timely request for a determination of dischargeability of such debt under one of such paragraphs, unless such creditor had notice or actual knowledge of the case in time for such timely filing and request;

(4) for fraud or defalcation while acting in a fiduciary capacity, embezzlement, or larceny;

(5) for a domestic support obligation;

(6) for willful and malicious injury by the debtor to another entity or to the property of another entity;

(7) to the extent such debt is for a fine, penalty, or forfeiture payable to and for the benefit of a governmental unit, and is not compensation for actual pecuniary loss, other than a tax penalty—

(A) relating to a tax of a kind not specified in paragraph (1) of this subsection; or

(B) imposed with respect to a transaction or event that occurred before three years before the date of the filing of the petition;

(8) unless excepting such debt from discharge under this paragraph would impose an undue hardship on the debtor and the debtor's dependents, for—

(A)(i) an educational benefit overpayment or loan made, insured, or guaranteed by a governmental unit, or made under any program funded in whole or in part by a governmental unit or nonprofit institution; or

(ii) an obligation to repay funds received as an educational benefit, scholarship, or stipend; or

(B) any other educational loan that is a qualified education loan, as defined in section 221(d)(1) of the Internal Revenue Code of 1986, incurred by a debtor who is an individual;

(9) for death or personal injury caused by the debtor's operation of a motor vehicle, vessel, or aircraft if such operation was unlawful because the debtor was intoxicated from using alcohol, a drug, or another substance;

(10) that was or could have been listed or scheduled by the debtor in a prior case concerning the debtor under this title or under the Bankruptcy Act in which the debtor waived discharge, or was denied a discharge under section 727(a)(2), (3), (4), (5), (6), or (7) of this title, or under section 14c(1), (2), (3), (4), (6), or (7) of such Act;

(11) provided in any final judgment, unreviewable order, or consent order or decree entered in any court of the United States or of any State, issued by a Federal depository institutions regulatory agency, or contained in any settlement agreement entered into by the debtor, arising from any act of fraud or defalcation while acting in a fiduciary capacity committed with respect to any depository institution or insured credit union;

(12) for malicious or reckless failure to fulfill any commitment by the debtor to a Federal depository institutions regulatory agency to maintain the capital of an insured depository institution, except that this paragraph shall not extend any such commitment which would otherwise be terminated due to any act of such agency;

(13) for any payment of an order of restitution issued under title 18, United States Code;

(14) incurred to pay a tax to the United States that would be nondischargeable pursuant to paragraph (1);

(14A) incurred to pay a tax to a governmental unit, other than the United States, that would be nondischargeable under paragraph (1);

(14B) incurred to pay fines or penalties imposed under Federal election law;

(15) to a spouse, former spouse, or child of the debtor and not of the kind described in paragraph (5) that is incurred by the debtor in the course of a divorce or separation or in connection with a separation agreement, divorce decree or other order of a court of record, or a determination made in accordance with State or territorial law by a governmental unit;

(16) for a fee or assessment that becomes due and payable after the order for relief to a membership association with respect to the debtor's interest in a unit that has condominium ownership, in a share of a cooperative corporation, or a lot in a homeowners association, for as long as the debtor or the trustee has a legal, equitable, or possessory ownership interest in such unit, such corporation, or such lot, but nothing in this paragraph shall except from discharge the debt of a debtor for a membership association fee or assessment for a period arising before entry of the order for relief in a pending or subsequent bankruptcy case;

(17) for a fee imposed on a prisoner by any court for the filing of a case, motion, complaint, or appeal, or for other costs and expenses assessed with respect to such filing, regardless of an assertion of poverty by the debtor under subsection (b) or (f)(2) of section 1915 of title 28 (or a similar non–Federal law), or the debtor's status as a prisoner, as defined in section 1915(h) of title 28 (or a similar non–Federal law);

(18) owed to a pension, profit-sharing, stock bonus, or other plan established under section 401, 403, 408, 408A, 414, 457, or 501(c) of the Internal Revenue Code of 1986, under—

(A) a loan permitted under section 408(b)(1) of the Employee Retirement Income Security Act of 1974, or subject to section 72(p) of the Internal Revenue Code of 1986; or

(B) a loan from a thrift savings plan permitted under subchapter III of chapter 84 of title 5, that satisfies the requirements of section 8433(g) of such title;

but nothing in this paragraph may be construed to provide that any loan made under a governmental plan under section 414(d), or a contract or account under section 403(b), of the Internal Revenue Code of 1986 constitutes a claim or a debt under this title; or

(19) that—

(A) is for—

(i) the violation of any of the Federal securities laws (as that term is defined in section 3(a)(47) of the Securities Exchange Act of 1934), any of the State securities laws, or any regulation or order issued under such Federal or State securities laws; or

(ii) common law fraud, deceit, or manipulation in connection with the purchase or sale of any security; and

(B) results, before, on, or after the date on which the petition was filed, from—

(i) any judgment, order, consent order, or decree entered in any Federal or State judicial or administrative proceeding;

(ii) any settlement agreement entered into by the debtor; or

(iii) any court or administrative order for any damages, fine, penalty, citation, restitutionary payment, disgorgement payment, attorney fee, cost, or other payment owed by the debtor.

For purposes of this subsection, the term "return" means a return that satisfies the requirements of applicable nonbankruptcy law (including applicable filing requirements). Such term includes a return prepared pursuant to section 6020(a) of the Internal Revenue Code of 1986, or similar State or local law, or a written stipulation to a judgment or a final order entered by a nonbankruptcy tribunal, but does not include a return made pursuant to section 6020(b) of the Internal Revenue Code of 1986, or a similar State or local law.

(b) Notwithstanding subsection (a) of this section, a debt that was excepted from discharge under subsection (a)(1), (a)(3), or (a)(8) of this section, under section 17a(1), 17a(3), or 17a(5) of the Bankruptcy Act, under section 439A of the Higher Education Act of 1965, or under section 733(g) of the Public Health Service Act in a prior case concerning the debtor under this title, or under the Bankruptcy Act, is dischargeable in a case under this title unless, by the terms of subsection (a) of this section, such debt is not dischargeable in the case under this title.

(c)(1) Except as provided in subsection (a)(3)(B) of this section, the debtor shall be discharged from a debt of a kind specified in paragraph (2), (4), or (6) of subsection (a) of this section, unless, on request of the creditor to whom such debt is owed, and after notice and a hearing, the court determines such debt to be excepted from discharge under paragraph (2), (4), or (6), as the case may be, of subsection (a) of this section.

(2) Paragraph (1) shall not apply in the case of a Federal depository institutions regulatory agency seeking, in its capacity as conservator, receiver, or liquidating agent for an insured depository institution, to recover a debt described in subsection (a)(2), (a)(4), (a)(6), or (a)(11) owed to such institution by an institution-affiliated party unless the receiver, conservator, or liquidating agent was appointed in time to reasonably comply, or for a Federal depository institutions regulatory agency acting in its corporate capacity as a successor to such receiver, conservator, or liquidating agent to reasonably comply, with subsection (a)(3)(B) as a creditor of such institution-affiliated party with respect to such debt.

(d) If a creditor requests a determination of dischargeability of a consumer debt under subsection (a)(2) of this section, and such debt is discharged, the court shall grant judgment in favor of the debtor for the costs of, and a reasonable attorney's fee for, the proceeding if the court finds that the position of the creditor was not substantially justified, except that the court shall not award such costs and fees if special circumstances would make the award unjust.

(e) Any institution-affiliated party of an insured depository institution shall be considered to be acting in a fiduciary capacity with respect to the purposes of subsection (a)(4) or (11). *(Pub.L. 95–598, Nov. 6, 1978, 92 Stat. 2590; Pub.L. 96–56, § 3, Aug. 14, 1979, 93 Stat. 387; Pub.L. 97–35, Title XXIII, § 2334(b), Aug. 13, 1981, 95 Stat. 863; Pub.L. 98–353, Title III, §§ 307, 371, 454, July 10, 1984, 98 Stat. 353, 364, 375; Pub.L. 99–554, Title II, §§ 257(n), 281, 283(j), Oct. 27, 1986, 100 Stat. 3115 to 3117; Pub.L. 101–581, § 2(a), Nov. 15, 1990, 104 Stat. 2865; Pub.L. 101–647, Title XXV, § 2522(a), Title XXXI, § 3102(a), Title XXXVI, § 3621, Nov. 29, 1990, 104 Stat. 4865, 4916, 4964; Pub.L. 103–322, Title XXXII, § 320934, Sept. 13, 1994, 108 Stat. 2135; Pub.L. 103–394, Title II, § 221, Title III, §§ 304(e), (h)(3), 306, 309, Title V, § 501(d)(13), Oct. 22, 1994, 108 Stat. 4129, 4133 to 4135, 4137, 4145; Pub.L. 104–134, Title I, § 101[(a)] [Title VIII, § 804(b)], Apr. 26, 1996, 110 Stat. 1321, 1321–74; renumbered Title I Pub.L. 104–140, § 1(a), May 2, 1996, 110 Stat. 1327; amended Pub.L. 104–193, Title III, § 374(a), Aug. 22, 1996, 110 Stat. 2255; Pub.L. 105–244, Title IX, § 971(a), Oct. 7, 1998, 112 Stat. 1837; Pub.L. 107–204, Title VIII, § 803, July 30, 2002, 116 Stat. 801; Pub.L. 109–8, Title II, §§ 215, 220, 224(c), Title III, §§ 301, 310, 314(a), Title IV, § 412, Title VII, § 714, Title XII, §§ 1209, 1235, Title XIV, § 1404(a), Title XV, § 1502(a)(2), Apr. 20, 2005, 119 Stat. 54, 59, 64, 75, 84, 88, 107, 128, 194, 204, 215, 216; Pub.L. 111–327, § 2(a)(18), Dec. 22, 2010, 124 Stat. 3559.)*

[1] Dollar amount as adjusted by the Judicial Conference of the United States. See Adjustment of Dollar Amounts notes set out under this section and 11 U.S.C.A. § 104.

Commentary

Interpreting subsection (a)(2)(A), *In re Tsurukawa, 258 B.R. 192 (9th Cir. BAP, 2001)*, holds that fraud cannot be imputed from one spouse to the other on the basis of the marriage relationship alone, but instead requires a finding of fraudulent intent or an agency relationship between the spouses. *In re Tsurukawa, 287 Bankr. 515 (9th Circ. BAP 2002)*, holds that one spouse's fraud may be imputed to the other spouse under agency principles when the spouses are business partners.

Interpreting subsection (a)(4), the Ninth Circuit Bankruptcy Appellate Panel held that a former husband's debt to his wife for pension benefits, which were received by him prior to the decree dividing the parties' community property, was nondischargeable in bankruptcy because California law imposes a fiduciary duty on each spouse with respect to community property. *In re Stanifer, 236 B.R. 709 (1999)*. *Stanifer* distinguished on two grounds *In re Teichman, 774 F.2d 1395 (9th Cir. 1985)*, in which the Court of Appeals held that the subsection (a)(4) exception to discharge did not apply to obligations created by a dissolution decree with respect to post-decretal pension benefits. First, the property in *Stanifer* was still community property when it was received; the property in *Teichman* was not for the marriage had already been dissolved and the community property distributed. Second, since *Teichman*, the California legislature has upgraded the "good faith" duty between spouses to a "fiduciary duty." See Family Code §§ 721, 1100, 1101, and 2102.

In re Chang, 163 F.3d 1138 (9th Cir. 1998), cert. denied sub nom. Chang v. Beaupied, 119 S.Ct. 2029, 143 L.Ed.2d 1039 (1999), holds that debts for fees for experts and guardians ad litem incurred in a child custody proceeding are in the nature of child support and are nondischargeable in bankruptcy. Reversing a decision of the Bankruptcy Panel, which reasoned that the debts did not satisfy subsection (a)(5) because they were not debts "to a spouse, former spouse, or child of the debtor . . . for alimony . . . or support," the Ninth Circuit Court of Appeals concluded that the nature of the debt, rather than the identity of the payee, is controlling.

Even though the California child support obligation does not extend to a child's postmajority education, a parent's obligation, pursuant to a marital settlement agreement, to pay one-half his children's college education expenses was a child support obligation that was nondischargeable in bankruptcy. *In re Seixas, 239 B.R. 398 (B.A.P. 1st Cir. 1999)*.

Interest on a nondischargeable child support obligation accruing before or after filing of a bankruptcy petition is also nondischargeable in bankruptcy. *In re Foross, 242 B.R.692 (B.A.P. 9th Cir. 1999)*.

Interpreting subsection (a)(6), the Ninth Circuit Bankruptcy Panel held that statutory attorney fees and costs awarded in a state court civil contempt proceeding to a creditor injured by a debtor's willful and malicious conduct are nondischargeable in bankruptcy, despite the absence of an underlying judgment debt for contempt. *In re Suarez, 400 Bankr. 732 (U.S. Bankr. App. Pan., 9th Cir. 2009)*.

Subsections (a)(5) and (a)(15) provide that support obligations and property distribution obligations are nondischargeable in Chapter 7 bankruptcy proceedings. However, property distribution obligations may be dischargeable in Chapter 13 reorganization. After an individual has successfully completed a confirmed Chapter 13 plan, the court's entry of a Chapter 13 bankruptcy discharge has the effect of discharging any debts relating to property division. 11 U.S.C. § 1328(a)(2) (by omission).

In re Taylor, 737 F.3d 670 (10th Cir. 2013), held that a former wife who caused her former husband's overpayment of spousal support and who attempted, by declaring bankruptcy, to avoid her obligation to reimburse him, was not entitled to discharge the obligation under subsections (a) (5) and (15).

In re Francis, 505 B.R. 914 (U.S. Bankr. App. Pan. 9th Cir. 2014), affirmed a bankruptcy court's decision that a debtor's obligation to pay his wife's credit card debts and hold her harmless from the debts, as agreed in the parties' marital settlement agreement, was undischargeable under subsection (a)(15).

In re Leibowitz, 217 F.3d 799 (9th Cir. 2000), holds that a parent owing money to a county for reimbursement of child support payments is not entitled to discharge any portion of the debt, including any amount that accumulated before entry of the child support order, even though the debt would have been dischargeable under prior law, in light of enactment of the Personal Responsibility and Work Opportunity Reconciliation Act of 1996 (PRWORA), which provides that a debt "in the nature of support" owed under state law to a state or municipality is not released by a discharge in bankruptcy, 11 U.S.C. Section 523 (a)(18); 42 U.S.C. Section 656 (b). *In re Cervantes, 219 F.3d 955 (9th Cir. 2000)*, holds that *Leibowitz* applies to all bankruptcy filings under Title 11, that is, to filings under both Chapter 7 and Chapter 13.

SUBCHAPTER III—THE ESTATE

§ 541. Property of the estate

(a) The commencement of a case under section 301, 302, or 303 of this title creates an estate. Such estate is comprised of all the following property, wherever located and by whomever held:

(1) Except as provided in subsections (b) and (c)(2) of this section, all legal or equitable interests of the debtor in property as of the commencement of the case.

(2) All interests of the debtor and the debtor's spouse in community property as of the commencement of the case that is—

(A) under the sole, equal, or joint management and control of the debtor; or

(B) liable for an allowable claim against the debtor, or for both an allowable claim against the debtor and an allowable claim against the debtor's spouse, to the extent that such interest is so liable.

(3) Any interest in property that the trustee recovers under section 329(b), 363(n), 543, 550, 553, or 723 of this title.

(4) Any interest in property preserved for the benefit of or ordered transferred to the estate under section 510(c) or 551 of this title.

(5) Any interest in property that would have been property of the estate if such interest had been an interest of the debtor on the date of the filing of the petition, and that the debtor acquires or becomes entitled to acquire within 180 days after such date—

(A) by bequest, devise, or inheritance;

(B) as a result of a property settlement agreement with the debtor's spouse, or of an interlocutory or final divorce decree; or

(C) as a beneficiary of a life insurance policy or of a death benefit plan.

(6) Proceeds, product, offspring, rents, or profits of or from property of the estate, except such as are earnings from services performed by an individual debtor after the commencement of the case.

(7) Any interest in property that the estate acquires after the commencement of the case.

(b) Property of the estate does not include—

(1) any power that the debtor may exercise solely for the benefit of an entity other than the debtor;

(2) any interest of the debtor as a lessee under a lease of nonresidential real property that has terminated at the expiration of the stated term of such lease before the commencement of the case under this title, and ceases to include any interest of the debtor as a lessee under a lease of nonresidential real property that has terminated at the expiration of the stated term of such lease during the case;

(3) any eligibility of the debtor to participate in programs authorized under the Higher Education Act of 1965 (20 U.S.C. 1001 et seq.; 42 U.S.C. 2751 et seq.), or any accreditation status or State licensure of the debtor as an educational institution;

(4) any interest of the debtor in liquid or gaseous hydrocarbons to the extent that—

(A)(i) the debtor has transferred or has agreed to transfer such interest pursuant to a farmout agreement or any written agreement directly related to a farmout agreement; and

(ii) but for the operation of this paragraph, the estate could include the interest referred to in clause (i) only by virtue of section 365 or 544(a)(3) of this title; or

(B)(i) the debtor has transferred such interest pursuant to a written conveyance of a production payment to an entity that does not participate in the operation of the property from which such production payment is transferred; and

(ii) but for the operation of this paragraph, the estate could include the interest referred to in clause (i) only by virtue of section 365 or 542 of this title;

(5) funds placed in an education individual retirement account (as defined in section 530(b)(1) of the Internal Revenue Code of 1986) not later than 365 days before the date of the filing of the petition in a case under this title, but—

(A) only if the designated beneficiary of such account was a child, stepchild, grandchild, or stepgrandchild of the debtor for the taxable year for which funds were placed in such account;

(B) only to the extent that such funds—

(i) are not pledged or promised to any entity in connection with any extension of credit; and

(ii) are not excess contributions (as described in section 4973(e) of the Internal Revenue Code of 1986); and

(C) in the case of funds placed in all such accounts having the same designated beneficiary not earlier than 720 days nor later than 365 days before such date, only so much of such funds as does not exceed $6,425 [1];

(6) funds used to purchase a tuition credit or certificate or contributed to an account in accordance with section 529(b)(1)(A) of the Internal Revenue Code of 1986 under a qualified State tuition program (as defined in section 529(b)(1) of such Code) not later than 365 days before the date of the filing of the petition in a case under this title, but—

(A) only if the designated beneficiary of the amounts paid or contributed to such tuition program was a child, stepchild, grandchild, or stepgrandchild of the debtor for the taxable year for which funds were paid or contributed;

(B) with respect to the aggregate amount paid or contributed to such program having the same designated beneficiary, only so much of such amount as does not exceed the total contributions permitted under section 529(b)(6) of such Code with respect to such beneficiary, as adjusted beginning on the date of the filing of the petition in a case under this title by the annual increase or decrease (rounded to the nearest tenth of 1 percent) in the education expenditure category of the Consumer Price Index prepared by the Department of Labor; and

(C) in the case of funds paid or contributed to such program having the same designated beneficiary not earlier than 720 days nor later than 365 days before such date, only so much of such funds as does not exceed $6,425 [1];

(7) any amount—

(A) withheld by an employer from the wages of employees for payment as contributions—

(i) to—

(I) an employee benefit plan that is subject to title I of the Employee Retirement Income Security Act of 1974 or under an employee benefit plan which is a governmental plan under section 414(d) of the Internal Revenue Code of 1986;

(II) a deferred compensation plan under section 457 of the Internal Revenue Code of 1986; or

(III) a tax-deferred annuity under section 403(b) of the Internal Revenue Code of 1986;

except that such amount under this subparagraph shall not constitute disposable income as defined in section 1325(b)(2); or

(ii) to a health insurance plan regulated by State law whether or not subject to such title; or

(B) received by an employer from employees for payment as contributions—

(i) to—

(I) an employee benefit plan that is subject to title I of the Employee Retirement Income Security Act of 1974 or under an employee benefit plan which is a governmental plan under section 414(d) of the Internal Revenue Code of 1986;

(II) a deferred compensation plan under section 457 of the Internal Revenue Code of 1986; or

(III) a tax-deferred annuity under section 403(b) of the Internal Revenue Code of 1986;

except that such amount under this subparagraph shall not constitute disposable income, as defined in section 1325(b)(2); or

(ii) to a health insurance plan regulated by State law whether or not subject to such title;

(8) subject to subchapter III of chapter 5, any interest of the debtor in property where the debtor pledged or sold tangible personal property (other than securities or written or printed evidences of indebtedness or title) as collateral for a loan or advance of money given by a person licensed under law to make such loans or advances, where—

(A) the tangible personal property is in the possession of the pledgee or transferee;

(B) the debtor has no obligation to repay the money, redeem the collateral, or buy back the property at a stipulated price; and

(C) neither the debtor nor the trustee have exercised any right to redeem provided under the contract or State law, in a timely manner as provided under State law and section 108(b);

(9) any interest in cash or cash equivalents that constitute proceeds of a sale by the debtor of a money order that is made—

(A) on or after the date that is 14 days prior to the date on which the petition is filed; and

(B) under an agreement with a money order issuer that prohibits the commingling of such proceeds with property of the debtor (notwithstanding that, contrary to the agreement, the proceeds may have been commingled with property of the debtor),

unless the money order issuer had not taken action, prior to the filing of the petition, to require compliance with the prohibition; or

(10) funds placed in an account of a qualified ABLE program (as defined in section 529A(b) of the Internal Revenue Code of 1986) not later than 365 days before the date of the filing of the petition in a case under this title, but—

(A) only if the designated beneficiary of such account was a child, stepchild, grandchild, or stepgrandchild of the debtor for the taxable year for which funds were placed in such account;

(B) only to the extent that such funds—

(i) are not pledged or promised to any entity in connection with any extension of credit; and

(ii) are not excess contributions (as described in section 4973(h) of the Internal Revenue Code of 1986); and

(C) in the case of funds placed in all such accounts having the same designated beneficiary not earlier than 720 days nor later than 365 days before such date, only so much of such funds as does not exceed $6,225.

Paragraph (4) shall not be construed to exclude from the estate any consideration the debtor retains, receives, or is entitled to receive for transferring an interest in liquid or gaseous hydrocarbons pursuant to a farmout agreement.

(c)(1) Except as provided in paragraph (2) of this subsection, an interest of the debtor in property becomes property of the estate under subsection (a)(1), (a)(2), or (a)(5) of this section notwithstanding any provision in an agreement, transfer instrument, or applicable nonbankruptcy law—

(A) that restricts or conditions transfer of such interest by the debtor; or

(B) that is conditioned on the insolvency or financial condition of the debtor, on the commencement of a case under this title, or on the appointment of or taking possession by a trustee in a case under this title or a custodian before such commencement, and that effects or gives an option to effect a forfeiture, modification, or termination of the debtor's interest in property.

(2) A restriction on the transfer of a beneficial interest of the debtor in a trust that is enforceable under applicable nonbankruptcy law is enforceable in a case under this title.

(d) Property in which the debtor holds, as of the commencement of the case, only legal title and not an equitable interest, such as a mortgage secured by real property, or an interest in such a mortgage, sold by the debtor but as to which the debtor retains legal title to service or supervise the servicing of such mortgage or interest, becomes property of the estate under subsection (a)(1) or (2) of this section only to the extent of the debtor's legal title to such property, but not to the extent of any equitable interest in such property that the debtor does not hold.

(e) In determining whether any of the relationships specified in paragraph (5)(A) or (6)(A) of subsection (b) exists, a legally adopted child of an individual (and a child who is a member of an individual's household, if placed with such individual by an authorized placement agency for legal adoption by such individual), or a foster child of an individual (if such child has as the child's principal place of abode the home of the debtor and is a member of the debtor's household) shall be treated as a child of such individual by blood.

(f) Notwithstanding any other provision of this title, property that is held by a debtor that is a corporation described in section 501(c)(3) of the Internal Revenue Code of 1986 and exempt from tax under section 501(a) of such Code may be transferred to an entity that is not such a corporation, but only under the same conditions as would apply if the debtor had not filed a case under this title. *(Pub.L. 95–598, Nov. 6, 1978, 92 Stat. 2594; Pub.L. 98–353, Title III, §§ 363(a), 456, July 10, 1984, 98 Stat. 363, 376; Pub.L. 101–508, Title III, § 3007(a)(2), Nov. 5, 1990, 104 Stat. 1388–28; Pub.L. 102–486, Title XXX, § 3017(b), Oct. 24, 1992, 106 Stat. 3130; Pub.L. 103–394, Title II, §§ 208(b), 223, Oct. 22, 1994, 108 Stat. 4124, 4129; Pub.L. 109–8, Title II, § 225(a), Title III, § 323, Title XII, §§ 1212, 1221(c), 1230, Apr. 20, 2005, 119 Stat. 65, 97, 194, 196, 201; Pub.L. 111–327, § 2(a)(22), Dec. 22, 2010, 124 Stat. 3560; Pub.L. 113–295, Div. B, Title I, § 104(a), Dec. 19, 2014, 128 Stat. 4063.)*

[1] Dollar amount as adjusted by the Judicial Conference of the United States. See Adjustment of Dollar Amounts notes set out under this section and 11 U.S.C.A. § 104.

Commentary

Even though a petition of dissolution has been filed, when one spouse files a bankruptcy petition *before* the community property has been distributed to the parties in the dissolution action, subsection (a)(2) includes in the bankruptcy estate the entire equity in the couple's community property home despite the other spouse's Family Code Section 2640 right of reimbursement for separate funds contributed to the purchase price of the home. *In re Mantle, 153 F.3d 1082 (9th Cir. 1998), cert. denied 119 S.Ct. 1146, 143 L.Ed.2d 547 (1999).*

In re Carbaugh, 278 B.R. 512 (10th Cir. BAP 2002) holds that a debtor's interest in an ERISA-qualified pension plan is excluded from the property of the estate because ERISA's anti-alienation clause makes it a "trust enforceable under applicable nonbankruptcy law within the meaning of subsection (c)(2). *Carbaugh* also holds that monies distributed from ERISA pension plans are not excluded if they are not rolled over into another ERISA-qualified plan. A Nevada self-employed debtor's profit-sharing plan in which he is the sole shareholder cannot be excluded from the bankruptcy estate under subsection (c)(2) because the debtor-owner is not an "employee" and hence the plan is not an "employee benefit plan" under ERISA (29 U.S.C. Section 10001 et seq.). *In re Watson, 161 F.3d. 593 (9th Cir. 1998).*

Interpreting subsection (c)(2), the Eighth Circuit Court of Appeals held in *In re Nelson, 322 F.3d 541 (8th Cir. 2003)*, that a debtor's alternate-payee interest in an ERISA plan, which is derived from a qualified domestic relations order (QDRO), is properly excluded from the debtor's bankruptcy estate even though the pension plan is simultaneously determining whether the domestic relations order awarding the debtor an interest in the plan qualifies as a QDRO. *Nelson* relies, in part, on the reasoning of *In re Gendreau, 122 F.3d 815 (9th Cir. 1997)*, which concluded that the existence of an alternate-payee interest does not depend on an enforceable QDRO. A QDRO is merely necessary to enforce that interest.

A Bankruptcy Court properly permitted a former wife to seek a Qualified Domestic Relations Order (QDRO) in state court to determine whether former husband's pension was ERISA-qualified and hence exempt from his bankruptcy estate, but the Bankruptcy Court erred in concluding that the Pennsylvania state court's distribution to wife of a 38.7 percent interest in husband's pension was a dischargeable money judgment rather than a nondischargeable ownership interest in the plan assets. *In re Lowenschuss, 170 F.3d 923 (9th Cir. 1999).* See also *In re Gendreau, 122 F.3d 815 (9th Cir. 1997)* (former spouse's ownership interest in pension not a debt and hence not dischargeable in debtor's bankruptcy).

TITLE 18

CRIMES AND CRIMINAL PROCEDURE

PART I—CRIMES

CHAPTER 11A—CHILD SUPPORT

§ 228. Failure to pay legal child support obligations

(a) Offense.—Any person who—

(1) willfully fails to pay a support obligation with respect to a child who resides in another State, if such obligation has remained unpaid for a period longer than 1 year, or is greater than $5,000;

(2) travels in interstate or foreign commerce with the intent to evade a support obligation, if such obligation has remained unpaid for a period longer than 1 year, or is greater than $5,000; or

(3) willfully fails to pay a support obligation with respect to a child who resides in another State, if such obligation has remained unpaid for a period longer than 2 years, or is greater than $10,000;

shall be punished as provided in subsection (c).

(b) Presumption.—The existence of a support obligation that was in effect for the time period charged in the indictment or information creates a rebuttable presumption that the obligor has the ability to pay the support obligation for that time period.

(c) Punishment.—The punishment for an offense under this section is—

(1) in the case of a first offense under subsection (a)(1), a fine under this title, imprisonment for not more than 6 months, or both; and

(2) in the case of an offense under paragraph (2) or (3) of subsection (a), or a second or subsequent offense under subsection (a)(1), a fine under this title, imprisonment for not more than 2 years, or both.

(d) Mandatory restitution.—Upon a conviction under this section, the court shall order restitution under section 3663A in an amount equal to the total unpaid support obligation as it exists at the time of sentencing.

(e) Venue.—With respect to an offense under this section, an action may be inquired of and prosecuted in a district court of the United States for—

(1) the district in which the child who is the subject of the support obligation involved resided during a period during which a person described in subsection (a) (referred to in this subsection as an "obliger") failed to meet that support obligation;

(2) the district in which the obliger resided during a period described in paragraph (1); or

(3) any other district with jurisdiction otherwise provided for by law.

(f) Definitions.—As used in this section—

(1) the term "Indian tribe" has the meaning given that term in section 102 of the Federally Recognized Indian Tribe List Act of 1994 (25 U.S.C. 479a);

(2) the term "State" includes any State of the United States, the District of Columbia, and any commonwealth, territory, or possession of the United States; and

(3) the term "support obligation" means any amount determined under a court order or an order of an administrative process pursuant to the law of a State or of an Indian tribe to be due from a person for the support and maintenance of a child or of a child and the parent with whom the child is living.

(Added Pub.L. 102–521, § 2(a), Oct. 25, 1992, 106 Stat. 3403; amended Pub.L. 104–294, Title VI, § 607(l), Oct. 11, 1996, 110 Stat. 3512; Pub.L. 105–187, § 2, June 24, 1998, 112 Stat. 618.)

Commentary

United States v. Kukafka, 478 F.3d 531 (3d Cir. 2007), cert den., 128 S.Ct. 158, 169 L.Ed.2d 108 (2007), held that this section's treatment of willful failure to pay out-of-state child support as a federal crime is a valid exercise of Congressional power under the Commerce Clause of the U.S. Constitution.

United States v. Edelkind, 525 F.3d 388 (5th Cir. 2008), interpreting subsection (a)(3), holds that failure to pay child support is a continuing offense for purposes of the statute of limitations.

United States v. Mussari, 152 F.3d 1156 (9th Cir. 1998), holds that retroactive application of the CSRA, which was enacted in 1992, is unconstitutional insofar as it would subject the defendant to federal *criminal* penalties for nonpayment alleged to have occurred before the CSRA's date of enactment.

United States v. Ballek, 170 F.3d 871 (9th Cir. 1999), holds that a noncustodial parent may be imprisoned under the CSRA for "willful failure" to pay court-ordered support when he left his regular employment as a general contractor after divorce and for nine years took only low-paying jobs. *Ballek* also holds that imprisonment under the CSRA does not violate the constitutional prohibition against slavery or imprisonment for debt, and that imposition of an order to pay more than $50,000 in past due child support does not entitle the debtor to a jury trial because the payment is in the nature of restitution, which does not constitute an additional obligation but merely represents a debt already owed to the victim. *Ballek* rejects the dictum of *Mussari,* supra, that in ordering restitution the federal court should consider the financial resources of defendant. *Ballek* reasons that the proper venue for the defense of inability to pay is the state court proceeding that was or should have been brought to reduce the child support obligation. *United States v. Gill, 264 F.3d 929 (9th Cir. 2001)*, holds that a district court's order of restitution for willful failure to pay child support under this section may include accrued interest as part of defendant's unpaid child support obligation when state law requires that interest be imposed at a statutory rate on each delinquent payment as it becomes due.

United States v. Craig, 181 F.3d 1124 (9th Cir. 1999), holds that, under this Act, *restitution* includes the defendant's entire past due support obligation whenever incurred, and the federal trial court should not inquire into the defendant's ability to pay before ordering restitution.

United States v. Stephens, 374 F.3d 867 (9th Cir. 2004), held that a district court properly required an Arizona resident, who failed to pay a Georgia child support obligation in violation of this section, to pay interest on past-due child support payments in accordance with Georgia law and, under the Mandatory Victims Restitution Act of 1996, 18 U.S.C. § 3663A, to pay a portion of the support restitution award to the state of Georgia after it paid restitution due to the mother.

United States v. Hill, 279 F.3d 731 (9th Cir. 2002), holds that when a husband violated this section by failing to pay more than $100,000 of past-due child support, his wife could constitutionally be prosecuted for harboring her fugitive husband and being an accessory after the fact to her husband's violation of § 228. *Hill* sustained the wife's conviction for harboring her husband, but reversed her conviction for being an accessory because the indictment was insufficient in failing to state the principal's crime.

CHAPTER 55—KIDNAPPING

§ 1204. International parental kidnapping

(a) Whoever removes a child from the United States, or attempts to do so, or retains a child (who has been in the United States) outside the United States with intent to obstruct the lawful exercise of parental rights shall be fined under this title or imprisoned not more than 3 years, or both.

(b) As used in this section—

(1) the term "child" means a person who has not attained the age of 16 years; and

(2) the term "parental rights", with respect to a child, means the right to physical custody of the child—

(A) whether joint or sole (and includes visiting rights); and

(B) whether arising by operation of law, court order, or legally binding agreement of the parties.

(c) It shall be an affirmative defense under this section that—

(1) the defendant acted within the provisions of a valid court order granting the defendant legal custody or visitation rights and that order was obtained pursuant to the Uniform Child Custody Jurisdiction Act or the Uniform Child Custody Jurisdiction and Enforcement Act and was in effect at the time of the offense;

(2) the defendant was fleeing an incidence or pattern of domestic violence; or

(3) the defendant had physical custody of the child pursuant to a court order granting legal custody or visitation rights and failed to return the child as a result of circumstances beyond the defendant's control, and the defendant notified or made reasonable attempts to notify the other parent or lawful custodian of the child of such circumstances within 24 hours after the visitation period had expired and returned the child as soon as possible.

(d) This section does not detract from The Hague Convention on the Civil Aspects of International Parental Child Abduction, done at The Hague on October 25, 1980. *(Added Pub.L. 103–173, § 2(a), Dec. 2, 1993, 107 Stat. 1998; amended Pub.L. 108–21, Title I, § 107, Apr. 30, 2003, 117 Stat. 655.)*

Commentary

United States v. Cummings, 281 F.3d 1046 (9th Cir. 2002), sustains the constitutionality of this section as a valid exercise of Congressional authority under the Commerce Clause.

United States v. Ventre, 338 F.3 1047 (9th Cir. 2003), cert. denied, Ventre v. U.S., 124 S.Ct. 951, 157 L.Ed.2d 763 (2003), holds that the return of a child to the United States as a result of a civil proceeding under the Hague Convention (42 U.S.C. §§ 11601–11611) does not bar criminal prosecution under this section.

As to appeals and stay of proceedings as to judgment or order affecting custody generally, see Code of Civil Procedure § 917.7.

CHAPTER 110A—DOMESTIC VIOLENCE AND STALKING

§ 2261. Interstate domestic violence

(a) Offenses.—

(1) Travel or conduct of offender.—A person who travels in interstate or foreign commerce or enters or leaves Indian country or is present within the special maritime and territorial jurisdiction of the United States with the intent to kill, injure, harass, or intimidate a spouse, intimate partner, or dating partner, and who, in the course of or as a result of such travel or presence, commits or attempts to commit a crime of violence against that spouse, intimate partner, or dating partner, shall be punished as provided in subsection (b).

(2) Causing travel of victim.—A person who causes a spouse, intimate partner, or dating partner to travel in interstate or foreign commerce or to enter or leave Indian country by force, coercion, duress, or fraud, and who, in the course of, as a result of, or to facilitate such conduct or travel, commits or attempts to commit a crime of violence against that spouse, intimate partner, or dating partner, shall be punished as provided in subsection (b).

(b) Penalties.—A person who violates this section or section 2261A shall be fined under this title, imprisoned—

(1) for life or any term of years, if death of the victim results;

(2) for not more than 20 years if permanent disfigurement or life threatening bodily injury to the victim results;

(3) for not more than 10 years, if serious bodily injury to the victim results or if the offender uses a dangerous weapon during the offense;

(4) as provided for the applicable conduct under chapter 109A if the offense would constitute an offense under chapter 109A (without regard to whether the offense was committed in the special maritime and territorial jurisdiction of the United States or in a Federal prison); and

(5) for not more than 5 years, in any other case,

or both fined and imprisoned.

(6) Whoever commits the crime of stalking in violation of a temporary or permanent civil or criminal injunction, restraining order, no-contact order, or other order described in section 2266 of title 18, United States Code, shall be punished by imprisonment for not less than 1 year.

(Added Pub.L. 103–322, Title IV, § 40221(a), Sept. 13, 1994, 108 Stat. 1926; amended Pub.L. 104–201, Div. A, Title X, § 1069(b)(1), (2), Sept. 23, 1996, 110 Stat. 2656; Pub.L. 106–386, Div. B, Title I, § 1107(a), Oct. 28, 2000, 114 Stat. 1497; Pub.L. 109–162, Title I, §§ 114(b), 116(a), 117(a), Jan. 5, 2006, 119 Stat. 2988, 2989; Pub.L. 113–4, Title I, § 107(a), Mar. 7, 2013, 127 Stat. 77.)

Commentary

In *United States v. Larsen, 615 F.3d 780 (2010), cert. denied*, the Seventh Circuit Court of Appeals held that this section is constitutional in that it does not exceed the legislative power of Congress under the Commerce Clause.

§ 2261A. Stalking [1]

Whoever—

(1) travels in interstate or foreign commerce or is present within the special maritime and territorial jurisdiction of the United States, or enters or leaves Indian country, with the intent to kill, injure, harass, intimidate, or place under surveillance with intent to kill, injure, harass, or intimidate another person, and in the course of, or as a result of, such travel or presence engages in conduct that—

(A) places that person in reasonable fear of the death of, or serious bodily injury to—

(i) that person;

(ii) an immediate family member (as defined in section 115) of that person; or

(iii) a spouse or intimate partner of that person; or

(B) causes, attempts to cause, or would be reasonably expected to cause substantial emotional distress to a person described in clause (i), (ii), or (iii) of subparagraph (A); or

(2) with the intent to kill, injure, harass, intimidate, or place under surveillance with intent to kill, injure, harass, or intimidate another person, uses the mail, any interactive computer service or electronic communication service or electronic communication system of interstate commerce, or any other facility of interstate or foreign commerce to engage in a course of conduct that—

(A) places that person in reasonable fear of the death of or serious bodily injury to a person described in clause (i), (ii), or (iii) of paragraph (1)(A); or

(B) causes, attempts to cause, or would be reasonably expected to cause substantial emotional distress to a person described in clause (i), (ii), or (iii) of paragraph (1)(A),

shall be punished as provided in section 2261(b) of this title.

(Added Pub.L. 104–201, Div. A, Title X, § 1069(a), Sept. 23, 1996, 110 Stat. 2655; amended Pub.L. 106–386, Div. B, Title I, § 1107(b)(1), Oct. 28, 2000, 114 Stat. 1498; Pub.L. 109–162, Title I, § 114(a), Jan. 5, 2006, 119 Stat. 2987; Pub.L. 113–4, Title I, § 107(b), Mar. 7, 2013, 127 Stat. 77.)

[1] Section was amended without corresponding amendment to analysis.

§ 2262. Interstate violation of protection order

(a) Offenses.—

(1) Travel or conduct of offender.—A person who travels in interstate or foreign commerce, or enters or leaves Indian country or is present within the special maritime and territorial jurisdiction of the United States, with the intent to engage in conduct that violates the portion of a protection order that prohibits or provides protection against violence, threats, or harassment against, contact or communication with, or physical proximity to, another person, or that would violate such a portion of a protection order in the jurisdiction in which the order was issued, and subsequently engages in such conduct, shall be punished as provided in subsection (b).

(2) Causing travel of victim.—A person who causes another person to travel in interstate or foreign commerce or to enter or leave Indian country by force, coercion, duress, or fraud, and in the course of, as a result of, or to facilitate such conduct or travel engages in conduct that violates the portion of a protection order that prohibits or provides protection against violence, threats, or harassment against, contact or communication with, or physical proximity to, another person, or that would violate such a portion of a protection order in the jurisdiction in which the order was issued, shall be punished as provided in subsection (b).

(b) Penalties.—A person who violates this section shall be fined under this title, imprisoned—

(1) for life or any term of years, if death of the victim results;

(2) for not more than 20 years if permanent disfigurement or life threatening bodily injury to the victim results;

(3) for not more than 10 years, if serious bodily injury to the victim results or if the offender uses a dangerous weapon during the offense;

(4) as provided for the applicable conduct under chapter 109A if the offense would constitute an offense under chapter 109A (without regard to whether the offense was committed in the special maritime and territorial jurisdiction of the United States or in a Federal prison); and

(5) for not more than 5 years, in any other case,

or both fined and imprisoned. *(Added Pub.L. 103–322, Title IV, § 40221(a), Sept. 13, 1994, 108 Stat. 1927; amended Pub.L. 104–201, Div. A, Title X, § 1069(b)(2), Sept. 23, 1996, 110 Stat. 2656; Pub.L. 104–294, Title VI, § 605(d), Oct. 11, 1996, 110 Stat. 3509; Pub.L. 106–386, Div. B, Title I, § 1107(c), Oct. 28, 2000, 114 Stat. 1498; Pub.L. 109–162, Title I, § 117(b), Jan. 5, 2006, 119 Stat. 2989; Pub.L. 113–4, Title I, § 107(c), Mar. 7, 2013, 127 Stat. 78.)*

§ 2263. Pretrial release of defendant

In any proceeding pursuant to section 3142 for the purpose of determining whether a defendant charged under this chapter shall be released pending trial, or for the purpose of determining conditions of such release, the alleged victim shall be given an opportunity to be heard regarding the danger posed by the defendant. *(Added Pub.L. 103–322, Title IV, § 40221(a), Sept. 13, 1994, 108 Stat. 1928.)*

§ 2264. Restitution

(a) In general.—Notwithstanding section 3663 or 3663A, and in addition to any other civil or criminal penalty authorized by law, the court shall order restitution for any offense under this chapter.

(b) Scope and nature of order.—

(1) Directions.—The order of restitution under this section shall direct the defendant to pay the victim (through the appropriate court mechanism) the full amount of the victim's losses as determined by the court pursuant to paragraph (2).

(2) Enforcement.—An order of restitution under this section shall be issued and enforced in accordance with section 3664 in the same manner as an order under section 3663A.

(3) Definition.—For purposes of this subsection, the term "full amount of the victim's losses" includes any costs incurred by the victim for—

(A) medical services relating to physical, psychiatric, or psychological care;

(B) physical and occupational therapy or rehabilitation;

(C) necessary transportation, temporary housing, and child care expenses;

(D) lost income;

(E) attorneys' fees, plus any costs incurred in obtaining a civil protection order; and

(F) any other losses suffered by the victim as a proximate result of the offense.

(4) Order mandatory.—(A) The issuance of a restitution order under this section is mandatory.

(B) A court may not decline to issue an order under this section because of—

(i) the economic circumstances of the defendant; or

(ii) the fact that a victim has, or is entitled to, receive compensation for his or her injuries from the proceeds of insurance or any other source.

(c) Victim defined.—For purposes of this section, the term "victim" means the individual harmed as a result of a commission of a crime under this chapter, including, in the case of a victim who is under 18 years of age, incompetent, incapacitated, or deceased, the legal guardian of the victim or representative of the victim's estate, another family member, or any other person appointed as suitable by the court, but in no event shall the defendant be named as such representative or guardian. *(Added Pub.L. 103–322, Title IV, § 40221(a), Sept. 13, 1994, 108 Stat. 1928; amended Pub.L. 104–132, Title II, § 205(d), Apr. 24, 1996, 110 Stat. 1231.)*

§ 2265. Full faith and credit given to protection orders

(a) Full Faith and Credit.—Any protection order issued that is consistent with subsection (b) of this section by the court of one State, Indian tribe, or territory (the issuing State, Indian tribe, or territory) shall be accorded full faith and credit by the court of another State, Indian tribe, or territory (the enforcing State, Indian tribe, or territory) and enforced by the court and law enforcement personnel of the other State, Indian tribal government or Territory [1] as if it were the order of the enforcing State or tribe.

(b) Protection order.—A protection order issued by a State, tribal, or territorial court is consistent with this subsection if—

(1) such court has jurisdiction over the parties and matter under the law of such State, Indian tribe, or territory; and

(2) reasonable notice and opportunity to be heard is given to the person against whom the order is sought sufficient to protect that person's right to due process. In the case of ex parte orders, notice and opportunity to be heard must be provided within the time required by State, tribal, or territorial law, and in any event within a reasonable time after the order is issued, sufficient to protect the respondent's due process rights.

(c) Cross or counter petition.—A protection order issued by a State, tribal, or territorial court against one who has petitioned, filed a complaint, or otherwise filed a written pleading for protection against abuse by a spouse or intimate partner is not entitled to full faith and credit if—

(1) no cross or counter petition, complaint, or other written pleading was filed seeking such a protection order; or

(2) a cross or counter petition has been filed and the court did not make specific findings that each party was entitled to such an order.

(d) Notification and registration.—

(1) Notification.—A State, Indian tribe, or territory according full faith and credit to an order by a court of another State, Indian tribe, or territory shall not notify or require notification of the party against whom a protection order has been issued that the protection order has been registered or filed in that enforcing State, tribal, or territorial jurisdiction unless requested to do so by the party protected under such order.

(2) No prior registration or filing as prerequisite for enforcement.—Any protection order that is otherwise consistent with this section shall be accorded full faith and credit, notwithstanding failure to comply with any requirement that the order be registered or filed in the enforcing State, tribal, or territorial jurisdiction.

(3) Limits on Internet publication of registration information.—A State, Indian tribe, or territory shall not make available publicly on the Internet any information regarding the registration, filing of a petition for, or issuance of a protection order, restraining order or injunction, restraining order, or injunction [2] in either the issuing or enforcing State, tribal or territorial jurisdiction, if such publication would be likely to publicly reveal the identity or location of the party protected under such order. A State, Indian tribe, or territory may share court-generated and law enforcement-generated information contained in secure, governmental registries for protection order enforcement purposes.

(e) Tribal court jurisdiction.—For purposes of this section, a court of an Indian tribe shall have full civil jurisdiction to issue and enforce protection orders involving any person, including the authority to enforce any orders through civil contempt proceedings, to exclude violators from Indian land, and to use other appropriate mechanisms, in matters arising anywhere in the Indian country of the Indian tribe (as defined in section 1151) or otherwise within the authority of the Indian tribe. *(Added Pub.L. 103–322, Title IV, § 40221(a), Sept. 13, 1994, 108 Stat. 1930; amended Pub.L. 106–386, Div. B, Title I, § 1101(b)(4), Oct. 28, 2000, 114 Stat. 1493; Pub.L. 109–162, Title I, § 106(a) to (c), Jan. 5, 2006, 119 Stat. 2981, 2982; Pub.L. 109–271, § 2(n), Aug. 12, 2006, 120 Stat. 754; Pub.L. 113–4, Title IX, § 905, Mar. 7, 2013, 127 Stat. 124.)*

[1] So in original. Probably should not be capitalized.

[2] So in original.

§ 2265A. Repeat offenders[1]

(a) Maximum term of imprisonment.—The maximum term of imprisonment for a violation of this chapter after a prior domestic violence or stalking offense shall be twice the term otherwise provided under this chapter.

(b) Definition.—For purposes of this section—

(1) the term "prior domestic violence or stalking offense" means a conviction for an offense—

(A) under section 2261, 2261A, or 2262 of this chapter; or

(B) under State or tribal law for an offense consisting of conduct that would have been an offense under a section referred to in subparagraph (A) if the conduct had occurred within the special maritime and territorial jurisdiction of the United States, or in interstate or foreign commerce; and

(2) the term "State" means a State of the United States, the District of Columbia, or any commonwealth, territory, or possession of the United States.

(Added Pub.L. 109–162, Title I, § 115, Jan. 5, 2006, 119 Stat. 2988; amended Pub.L. 113–4, Title IX, § 906(c), Mar. 7, 2013, 127 Stat. 125.)

[1] Section was enacted without corresponding amendment to analysis.

§ 2266. Definitions

In this chapter:

(1) Bodily injury.—The term "bodily injury" means any act, except one done in self-defense, that results in physical injury or sexual abuse.

(2) Course of conduct.—The term "course of conduct" means a pattern of conduct composed of 2 or more acts, evidencing a continuity of purpose.

(3) Enter or leave Indian country.—The term "enter or leave Indian country" includes leaving the jurisdiction of 1 tribal government and entering the jurisdiction of another tribal government.

(4) Indian country.—The term "Indian country" has the meaning stated in section 1151 of this title.

(5) Protection order.—The term "protection order" includes—

(A) any injunction, restraining order, or any other order issued by a civil or criminal court for the purpose of preventing violent or threatening acts or harassment against, sexual violence, or contact or communication with or physical proximity to, another person, including any temporary or final order issued by a civil or criminal court whether obtained by filing an independent action or as a pendente lite order in another proceeding so long as any civil or criminal order was issued in response to a complaint, petition, or motion filed by or on behalf of a person seeking protection; and

(B) any support, child custody or visitation provisions, orders, remedies or relief issued as part of a protection order, restraining order, or injunction pursuant to State, tribal, territorial, or local law authorizing the issuance of protection orders, restraining orders, or injunctions for the protection of victims of domestic violence, sexual assault, dating violence, or stalking.

(6) Serious bodily injury.—The term "serious bodily injury" has the meaning stated in section 2119(2).

(7) Spouse or intimate partner.—The term "spouse or intimate partner" includes—

(A) for purposes of—

(i) sections other than 2261A—

(I) a spouse or former spouse of the abuser, a person who shares a child in common with the abuser, and a person who cohabits or has cohabited as a spouse with the abuser; or

(II) a person who is or has been in a social relationship of a romantic or intimate nature with the abuser, as determined by the length of the relationship, the type of relationship, and the frequency of interaction between the persons involved in the relationship; and

(ii) section 2261A—

(I) a spouse or former spouse of the target of the stalking, a person who shares a child in common with the target of the stalking, and a person who cohabits or has cohabited as a spouse with the target of the stalking; or

(II) a person who is or has been in a social relationship of a romantic or intimate nature with the target of the stalking, as determined by the length of the relationship, the type of the relationship, and the frequency of interaction between the persons involved in the relationship.[1]

(B) any other person similarly situated to a spouse who is protected by the domestic or family violence laws of the State or tribal jurisdiction in which the injury occurred or where the victim resides.

(8) **State.**—The term "State" includes a State of the United States, the District of Columbia, and a commonwealth, territory, or possession of the United States.

(9) **Travel in interstate or foreign commerce.**—The term "travel in interstate or foreign commerce" does not include travel from 1 State to another by an individual who is a member of an Indian tribe and who remains at all times in the territory of the Indian tribe of which the individual is a member.

(10) **Dating partner.**—The term "dating partner" refers to a person who is or has been in a social relationship of a romantic or intimate nature with the abuser. The existence of such a relationship is based on a consideration of—

(A) the length of the relationship; and

(B) the type of relationship; and

(C) the frequency of interaction between the persons involved in the relationship.

(Added Pub.L. 103–322, Title IV, § 40221(a), Sept. 13, 1994, 108 Stat. 1931; amended Pub.L. 106–386, Div. B, Title I, § 1107(d), Oct. 28, 2000, 114 Stat. 1499; Pub.L. 109–162, Title I, §§ 106(d), 116(b), Jan. 5, 2006, 119 Stat. 2982, 2988; Pub.L. 109–271, § 2(c), (i), Aug. 12, 2006, 120 Stat. 752.)

[1] So in original. The period probably should be "; and".

TITLE 22

FOREIGN RELATIONS AND INTERCOURSE

CHAPTER 52—FOREIGN SERVICE

SUBCHAPTER VIII—FOREIGN SERVICE RETIREMENT AND DISABILITY

PART I—FOREIGN SERVICE RETIREMENT AND DISABILITY SYSTEM

SUBCHAPTER VIII—FOREIGN SERVICE RETIREMENT AND DISABILITY

PART I—FOREIGN SERVICE RETIREMENT AND DISABILITY SYSTEM

§ 4054. Former spouses

(a) Living Service members

(1) Unless otherwise expressly provided by any spousal agreement or court order under section 4060(b)(1) of this title, a former spouse of a participant or former participant is entitled to an annuity if such former spouse was married to the participant for at least 10 years during service of the participant which is creditable under this subchapter with at least 5 of such years occurring while the participant was a member of the Foreign Service and—

(A) if married to the participant throughout the creditable service of the participant, equal to 50 percent of the annuity of the participant; or

(B) if not married to the participant throughout such creditable service, equal to that former spouse's pro rata share of 50 percent of such annuity.

For the purposes of this paragraph, the term "creditable service" means service which is creditable under part I or II of this subchapter.

(2) A former spouse shall not be qualified for an annuity under this subsection if before the commencement of that annuity the former spouse remarries before becoming 60 years of age.

(3) The annuity of a former spouse under this subsection commences on the later of the day the participant upon whose service the annuity is based becomes entitled to an annuity under this part or the first day of the month in which the divorce or annulment involved becomes final. The annuity of such former spouse and the right thereto terminate on—

(A) the last day of the month before the former spouse dies or remarries before 60 years of age; or

(B) the date the annuity of the participant terminates (except in the case of an annuity subject to paragraph (5)(B)).

(4) No spousal agreement or court order under section 4060(b)(1) of this title involving any participant may provide for an annuity or any combination of annuities under this subsection which exceeds the annuity of the participant, nor may any such court order relating to an annuity under this subsection be given effect if it is issued more than 24 months after the date the divorce or annulment involved becomes final.

(5)(A) The annuity payable to any participant shall be reduced by the amount of an annuity under this subsection paid to any former spouse based upon the service of that participant. Such reduction shall be disregarded in calculating the survivor annuity for any spouse, former spouse, or other survivor under this part, and in calculating any reduction in the annuity of the participant to provide survivor benefits under subsection (b) of this section or section 4046(b)(3) of this title.

(B) If any annuitant whose annuity is reduced under subparagraph (A) is recalled to service under section 3948 of this title, or reinstated or reappointed in the Service in the case of a recovered disability annuitant or if any annuitant is reemployed as provided for under section 4064 of this title, the salary of that annuitant shall be reduced by the same amount as the annuity would have been reduced if it had continued. Amounts equal to the reductions under this subparagraph shall be deposited in the Treasury of the United States to the credit of the Fund.

(6) Notwithstanding paragraph (3), in the case of any former spouse of a disability annuitant—

(A) the annuity of that former spouse shall commence on the date the participant would qualify on the basis of his or her creditable service for an annuity under this part (other than a disability annuity) or the date the disability annuity begins, whichever is later, and

(B) the amount of the annuity of the former spouse shall be calculated on the basis of the annuity for which the participant would otherwise so qualify.

(7) An annuity under this subsection shall be treated the same as a survivor annuity under subsection (b) of this section for purposes of section 4046(h) of this title or any comparable provision of law.

(b) Deceased Service members

(1) Subject to any election under section 4046(b)(1)(C) of this title and unless otherwise expressly provided by any spousal agreement or court order under section 4060(b)(1) of this title, if a former participant who is entitled to receive an annuity is survived by a former spouse, the former spouse shall be entitled to a survivor annuity—

(A) if married to the participant throughout the creditable service of the participant, equal to 55 percent of the full amount of the participant's annuity, as computed under section 4046(a) of this title; or

(B) if not married to the participant throughout such creditable service, equal to that former spouse's pro rata share of 55 percent of the full amount of such annuity.

For the purposes of this paragraph, the term "creditable service" means service which is creditable under part I or II of this subchapter.

(2) A former spouse shall not be qualified for an annuity under this subsection if before the commencement of that annuity the former spouse remarries before becoming 60 years of age.

(3) An annuity payable from the Fund under this part to a surviving former spouse under this subsection shall commence on the day after the annuitant dies and shall terminate on the last day of the month before the former spouse's death or remarriage before attaining age 60. If such a survivor annuity is terminated because of remarriage, it shall be restored at the same rate commencing on the date such remarriage is terminated if any lump sum paid upon termination of the annuity is returned to the Fund.

(4)(A) The maximum survivor annuity or combination of survivor annuities under this section (and section 4046(b)(3) of this title) with respect to any participant or former participant may not exceed 55 percent of the full amount of the participant's annuity, as calculated under section 4046(a) of this title.

(B) Once a survivor annuity has been provided for under this subsection for any former spouse, a survivor annuity may thereafter be provided for under this subsection (or section 4046(b)(3) of this title) with respect to a participant or former participant only for that portion (if any) of the maximum available which is not committed for survivor benefits for any former spouse whose prospective right to such annuity has not terminated by reason of death or remarriage.

(C) After the death of a participant or former participant, a court order under section 4060(b)(1) of this title may not adjust the amount of the annuity of any former spouse under this section.

(5)(A) For each full month after a former spouse of a participant or former participant dies or remarries before attaining age 60, the annuity of the participant, if reduced to provide a survivor annuity for that former spouse, shall be recomputed and paid as if the annuity had not been so reduced, unless an election is in effect under subparagraph (B).

(B) Subject to paragraph (4)(B), the participant may elect in writing within one year after receipt of notice of the death or remarriage of the former spouse to continue the reduction in order to provide a higher survivor annuity under section 4046(b)(3) of this title for any spouse of the participant.

(c) Additional survivor annuity

(1) In the case of any participant or former participant providing a survivor annuity benefit under subsection (b) of this section for a former spouse—

(A) such participant may elect, or

(B) a spousal agreement or court order under section 4060(b)(1) of this title may provide for,

an additional survivor annuity under this subsection for any other former spouse or spouse surviving the participant, if the participant satisfactorily passes a physical examination as prescribed by the Secretary of State.

(2) Neither the total amount of survivor annuity or annuities under this subsection with respect to any participant or former participant, nor the survivor annuity or annuities for any one surviving spouse or former spouse of such participant under this section and section 4046 of this title, shall exceed 55 percent of the full amount of the participant's annuity, as computed under section 4046(a) of this title.

(3)(A) In accordance with regulations which the Secretary of State shall prescribe, the participant involved may provide for any annuity under this subsection—

(i) by a reduction in the annuity or an allotment from the salary of the participant,

(ii) by a lump sum payment or installment payments to the Fund, or

(iii) by any combination thereof.

(B) The present value of the total amount to accrue to the Fund under subparagraph (A) to provide any annuity under this subsection shall be actuarially equivalent in value to such annuity, as calculated upon such tables of mortality as may from time to time be prescribed for this purpose by the Secretary of State.

(C) If a former spouse predeceases the participant or remarries before attaining age 60 (or, in the case of a spouse, the spouse does not qualify as a former spouse upon dissolution of the marriage)—

(i) if an annuity reduction or salary allotment under subparagraph (A) is in effect for that spouse or former spouse, the annuity shall be recomputed and paid as if it had not been reduced or the salary allotment terminated, as the case may be, and

(ii) any amount accruing to the Fund under subparagraph (A) shall be refunded, but only to the extent that such amount may have exceeded the actuarial cost of providing benefits under this subsection for the period such benefits were provided, as determined under regulations prescribed by the Secretary of State.

(D) Under regulations prescribed by the Secretary of State, an annuity shall be recomputed (or salary allotment terminated or adjusted), and a refund provided (if appropriate), in a manner comparable to that provided under subparagraph (C), in order to reflect a termination or reduction of future benefits under this subsection for a spouse in the event a former spouse of the participant dies or remarries before attaining age 60 and an increased annuity is provided for that spouse in accordance with this part.

(4) An annuity payable under this subsection to a spouse or former spouse shall commence on the day after the participant dies and shall terminate on the last day of the month before the former spouse's death or remarriage before attaining age 60.

(5) Section 4066 of this title shall not apply to any annuity under this subsection, unless authorized under regulations prescribed by the Secretary of State. *(Pub. L. 96–465, Title I, § 814, Oct. 17, 1980, 94 Stat. 2113; Pub. L. 97–241, Title I, § 125(2), Aug. 24, 1982, 96 Stat. 282; Pub.L. 99–335, Title IV, §§ 402(a)(2), (3), 404(b), June 6, 1986, 100 Stat. 609, 610; Pub.L. 100–238, Title II, § 217(a), (b), (c)(2), Jan. 8, 1988, 101 Stat. 1775.)*

CHAPTER 97—INTERNATIONAL CHILD ABDUCTION REMEDIES

§ 9001. Findings and declarations

(a) Findings

The Congress makes the following findings:

(1) The international abduction or wrongful retention of children is harmful to their well-being.

(2) Persons should not be permitted to obtain custody of children by virtue of their wrongful removal or retention.

(3) International abductions and retentions of children are increasing, and only concerted cooperation pursuant to an international agreement can effectively combat this problem.

(4) The Convention on the Civil Aspects of International Child Abduction, done at The Hague on October 25, 1980, establishes legal rights and procedures for the prompt return of children who have been wrongfully removed or retained, as well as for securing the exercise of visitation rights. Children who are wrongfully removed or retained within the meaning of the Convention are to be promptly returned unless one of the narrow exceptions set forth in the Convention applies. The Convention provides a sound treaty framework to help resolve the problem of international abduction and retention of children and will deter such wrongful removals and retentions.

(b) Declarations

The Congress makes the following declarations:

(1) It is the purpose of this chapter to establish procedures for the implementation of the Convention in the United States.

(2) The provisions of this chapter are in addition to and not in lieu of the provisions of the Convention.

(3) In enacting this chapter the Congress recognizes—

(A) the international character of the Convention; and

(B) the need for uniform international interpretation of the Convention.

(4) The Convention and this chapter empower courts in the United States to determine only rights under the Convention and not the merits of any underlying child custody claims.

(Pub.L. 100–300, § 2, Apr. 29, 1988, 102 Stat. 437.)

Commentary

Gaudin v. Remis, 282 F.3d 1178 (9th Cir. 2002), holds that a parent who properly filed a suit under the Hague Convention (42 U.S.C.A. §§ 11601 et seq.) while residing abroad, may not maintain the suit after permanently moving back to the United States, where the children are located. The court reasoned that when all the parties and the children reside in the same country, the Convention is inapplicable. *Gaudin* remanded the case to the district court to determine whether the mother intended to move permanently back to the United States. On remand, the district court found that she did so intend. On the mother's appeal from that decision, *Gaudin v. Remis, 379 F.3d 631 (9th Cir. 2004)*, the court of appeal reversed the district court's decision, holding that the mother was barred from establishing a domicile in the United States under 8 U.S.C. § 1101(a)(15)(B) and was therefore barred by law from possessing the requisite intent to establish domicile in Hawaii. For further discussion of *Gaudin*, see Commentary to the Hague Convention.

Holder v. Holder, 305 F.3d 854 (9th Cir. 2002), holds that a Washington federal district court erred in staying a Hague Convention petition brought by a U.S. serviceman stationed in Germany for the return of his children from Washington state to Germany, until California state custody proceedings also initiated by the serviceman were resolved. *Holder* reasoned that neither action precluded the other, because the Hague Convention issue was not raised in the state custody proceeding and the Hague Convention is intended to provide a speedy means of seeking return of an abducted child and prevent the abducting parent from using local law to obtain custody of the child. Moreover, a parent invoking the Hague Convention may also seek remedies available under local law. Nevertheless, the Ninth Circuit subsequently affirmed a district court holding that a family's short-term residence on an American military base in Germany did not establish Germany as the children's habitual residence under the Hague Convention. *Holder v. Holder, 392 F.3d 1009 (2004)*.

United States v. Ventre, 338 F.3 1047 (9th Cir. 2003), cert. denied, Ventre v. U.S., 124 S.Ct. 951, 157 L.Ed.2d 763 (2003), holds that the return of a child to the United States as a result of a civil proceeding under the Hague Convention (42 U.S.C. §§ 11601–11611) does not bar criminal prosecution under the International Parental Kidnapping Crime Act, 18 U.S.C. § 1204.

Relying on Article 16 of the Hague Convention, which requires that state custody proceedings be stayed pending resolution of a Hague Convention wrongful removal or retention claim, *Barzilay v. Barzilay, 536 F.3d 844 (8th Cir. 2008)*, held that a federal district court abused its discretion in abstaining, under the *Younger* doctrine, from hearing a Hague Convention claim while a state court custody proceeding was pending.

§ 9002. Definitions

For the purposes of this chapter—

(1) the term "applicant" means any person who, pursuant to the Convention, files an application with the United States Central Authority or a Central Authority of any other party to the Convention for the

return of a child alleged to have been wrongfully removed or retained or for arrangements for organizing or securing the effective exercise of rights of access pursuant to the Convention;

(2) the term "Convention" means the Convention on the Civil Aspects of International Child Abduction, done at The Hague on October 25, 1980;

(3) the term "Parent Locator Service" means the service established by the Secretary of Health and Human Services under section 653 of Title 42;

(4) the term "petitioner" means any person who, in accordance with this chapter, files a petition in court seeking relief under the Convention;

(5) the term "person" includes any individual, institution, or other legal entity or body;

(6) the term "respondent" means any person against whose interests a petition is filed in court, in accordance with this chapter, which seeks relief under the Convention;

(7) the term "rights of access" means visitation rights;

(8) the term "State" means any of the several States, the District of Columbia, and any commonwealth, territory, or possession of the United States; and

(9) the term "United States Central Authority" means the agency of the Federal Government designated by the President under section 9006(a) of this title.

(Pub.L. 100–300, § 3, Apr. 29, 1988, 102 Stat. 437.)

§ 9003. Judicial remedies

(a) Jurisdiction of courts

The courts of the States and the United States district courts shall have concurrent original jurisdiction of actions arising under the Convention.

(b) Petitions

Any person seeking to initiate judicial proceedings under the Convention for the return of a child or for arrangements for organizing or securing the effective exercise of rights of access to a child may do so by commencing a civil action by filing a petition for the relief sought in any court which has jurisdiction of such action and which is authorized to exercise its jurisdiction in the place where the child is located at the time the petition is filed.

(c) Notice

Notice of an action brought under subsection (b) of this section shall be given in accordance with the applicable law governing notice in interstate child custody proceedings.

(d) Determination of case

The court in which an action is brought under subsection (b) of this section shall decide the case in accordance with the Convention.

(e) Burdens of proof

(1) A petitioner in an action brought under subsection (b) of this section shall establish by a preponderance of the evidence—

(A) in the case of an action for the return of a child, that the child has been wrongfully removed or retained within the meaning of the Convention; and

(B) in the case of an action for arrangements for organizing or securing the effective exercise of rights of access, that the petitioner has such rights.

(2) In the case of an action for the return of a child, a respondent who opposes the return of the child has the burden of establishing—

(A) by clear and convincing evidence that one of the exceptions set forth in article 13b or 20 of the Convention applies; and

(B) by a preponderance of the evidence that any other exception set forth in article 12 or 13 of the Convention applies.

(f) Application of Convention

For purposes of any action brought under this chapter—

(1) the term "authorities", as used in article 15 of the Convention to refer to the authorities of the state of the habitual residence of a child, includes courts and appropriate government agencies;

(2) the terms "wrongful removal or retention" and "wrongfully removed or retained", as used in the Convention, include a removal or retention of a child before the entry of a custody order regarding that child; and

(3) the term "commencement of proceedings", as used in article 12 of the Convention, means, with respect to the return of a child located in the United States, the filing of a petition in accordance with subsection (b) of this section.

(g) Full faith and credit

Full faith and credit shall be accorded by the courts of the States and the courts of the United States to the judgment of any other such court ordering or denying the return of a child, pursuant to the Convention, in an action brought under this chapter.

(h) Remedies under Convention not exclusive

The remedies established by the Convention and this chapter shall be in addition to remedies available under other laws or international agreements. *(Pub.L. 100–300, § 4, Apr. 29, 1988, 102 Stat. 438.)*

Commentary

Invoking subsection (b), *Ozaltin v. Ozaltin, 708 F.3d 355 (2d Cir. 2013)*, held that there is a federal right of action to enforce rights of access protected by the Hague Convention. But see *Cantor v. Cohen, 442 F.3d 196 (4th Cir. 2006)*, holding that there is no federal right of action to enforce rights of access under the Hague Convention, reasoning that Article 21 requires that application must be made to the "Central Authorities of the Contracting State."

Gaudin v. Remis, 282 F.3d 1178 (9th Cir. 2002), holds that a parent who properly filed a suit under the Hague Convention (42 U.S.C.A. §§ 11601 et seq.) while residing abroad, may not maintain the suit after permanently moving back to the United States, where the children are located. The court reasoned that when all the parties and the children reside in the same country, the Convention is inapplicable. *Gaudin* remanded the case to the district court to determine whether the mother intended to move permanently back to the United States. On remand, the district court found that she did so intend. On the mother's appeal from that decision, *Gaudin v. Remis, 379 F.3d 631 (9th Cir. 2004)*, the court of appeal reversed the district court's decision, holding that the mother was barred from establishing a domicile in the United States under 8 U.S.C. § 1101(a)(15)(B) and was therefore barred by law from possessing the requisite intent to establish domicile in Hawaii. For further discussion of *Gaudin*, see Commentary to the Hague Convention.

Holder v. Holder, 305 F.3d 854 (9th Cir. 2002), holds that a Washington federal district court erred in staying a Hague Convention petition brought by a U.S. serviceman stationed in Germany for the return of his children from Washington state to Germany, until California state custody proceedings also initiated by the serviceman were resolved. *Holder* reasoned that neither action precluded the other, because the Hague Convention issue was not raised in the state custody proceeding and the Hague Convention is intended to provide a speedy means of seeking return of an abducted child and prevent the abducting parent from using local law to obtain custody of the child. Moreover, a parent invoking the Hague Convention may also seek remedies available under local law. Nevertheless, the Ninth Circuit subsequently affirmed a district court holding that a family's short-term residence on an American military base in Germany did not establish Germany as the children's habitual residence under the Hague Convention. *Holder v. Holder, 392 F.3d 1009 (2004)*.

Relying on subsection (h), *Ariana K., 120Cal.App.4th 690, 15 Cal.Rptr.3d 817 (2004)*, concludes that nothing in the Hague Convention or this implementing act deprives a California court of continuing subject matter jurisdiction to adjudicate a guardianship dispute when the court properly acquired subject matter jurisdiction in an earlier guardianship proceeding. Interpreting Family Code §§ 3402(g) and 3421(a)(1), *Ariana K.* also holds that the UCCJEA does not deprive a California trial court of continuing subject matter jurisdiction because, under the doctrine of continuing jurisdiction, once custody jurisdiction in California is initially established, it continues so long as the child or a parent or guardian of the child continues to reside in California.

United States v. Ventre, 338 F.3 1047 (9th Cir. 2003), cert. denied, Ventre v. U.S., 124 S.Ct. 951, 157 L.Ed.2d 763 (2003), holds that the return of a child to the United States as a result of a civil proceeding under the Hague Convention (42 U.S.C. §§ 11601–11611) does not bar criminal prosecution under the International Parental Kidnapping Crime Act, 18 U.S.C. § 1204.

Applying subsection (e)(2)(B), *Gonzalez-Caballero v. Mena, 251 F.3d 789 (9th Cir. 2001)*, holds that a Panamanian mother's petition to return her daughter to Panama was properly denied on the ground that a preponderance of the evidence supported the trial court's finding that the mother consented to the removal of the child to the United States.

Shalit v. Coppe, 182 F.3d 1124 (9th Cir. 1999), as amended 1999 WL 710394, holds that the mother's retention of a child in Alaska was not "wrongful" for purposes of the Hague Convention when there was no showing that her retention violated the custody rights of the child's father under the law of the child's place of habitual residence. *Shalit* explains that the law of the child's place of habitual residence includes both it local law and its choice of law rules.

Interpreting Article 3 of the Hague Convention, *Gonzalez v. Gutierrez, 311 F.3d 942 (9th Cir. 2002)*, holds that a *ne exeat* clause prohibiting the custodial mother from leaving the jurisdiction without the father's permission did not give the father "rights of custody" that would enable him to invoke the protection of the Hague Convention.

In re Marriage of Witherspoon, 155 Cal. App. 4th 963, 66 Cal. Rptr.3d 586 (2007), held that a trial court properly found that a mother had made a prima facie case for return of her children to Germany on the ground that it was their habitual residence, but that the court erred in failing to make factual findings on whether various Hague Convention exceptions to return, which were raised by the father, were applicable.

§ 9004. Provisional remedies

(a) Authority of courts

In furtherance of the objectives of article 7(b) and other provisions of the Convention, and subject to the provisions of subsection (b) of this section, any court exercising jurisdiction of an action brought under section section 9003(b) of this title may take or cause to be taken measures under Federal or State law, as appropriate, to protect the well-being of the child involved or to prevent the child's further removal or concealment before the final disposition of the petition.

(b) Limitation on authority

No court exercising jurisdiction of an action brought under section 9003(b) of this title may, under subsection (a) of this section, order a child removed from a person having physical control of the child unless the applicable requirements of State law are satisfied. *(Pub.L. 100–300, § 5, Apr. 29, 1988, 102 Stat. 439.)*

§ 9005. Admissibility of documents

With respect to any application to the United States Central Authority, or any petition to a court under section 9003 of this title, which seeks relief under the Convention, or any other documents or information included with such application or petition or provided after such submission which relates to the application or petition, as the case may be, no authentication of such application, petition, document, or information shall be required in order for the application, petition, document, or information to be admissible in court. *(Pub.L. 100–300, § 6, Apr. 29, 1988, 102 Stat. 439.)*

§ 9006. United States Central Authority

(a) Designation

The President shall designate a Federal agency to serve as the Central Authority for the United States under the Convention.

(b) Functions

The functions of the United States Central Authority are those ascribed to the Central Authority by the Convention and this chapter.

(c) Regulatory authority

The United States Central Authority is authorized to issue such regulations as may be necessary to carry out its functions under the Convention and this chapter.

(d) Obtaining information from Parent Locator Service

The United States Central Authority may, to the extent authorized by the Social Security Act, obtain information from the Parent Locator Service.

(e) Grant authority

The United States Central Authority is authorized to make grants to, or enter into contracts or agreements with, any individual, corporation, other Federal, State, or local agency, or private entity or organization in the United States for purposes of accomplishing its responsibilities under the Convention and this chapter.

(f) Limited liability of private entities acting under the direction of the United States Central Authority

(1) Limitation on liability

Except as provided in paragraphs (2) and (3), a private entity or organization that receives a grant from or enters into a contract or agreement with the United States Central Authority under subsection (e) of this section for purposes of assisting the United States Central Authority in carrying out its responsibilities and functions under the Convention and this chapter, including any director, officer, employee, or agent of such entity or organization, shall not be liable in any civil action sounding in tort for damages directly related to the performance of such responsibilities and functions as defined by the regulations issued under subsection (c) of this section that are in effect on October 1, 2004.

(2) Exception for intentional, reckless, or other misconduct

The limitation on liability under paragraph (1) shall not apply in any action in which the plaintiff proves that the private entity, organization, officer, employee, or agent described in paragraph (1), as the case may be, engaged in intentional misconduct or acted, or failed to act, with actual malice, with reckless disregard to a substantial risk of causing injury without legal justification, or for a purpose unrelated to the performance of responsibilities or functions under this chapter.

(3) Exception for ordinary business activities

The limitation on liability under paragraph (1) shall not apply to any alleged act or omission related to an ordinary business activity, such as an activity involving general administration or operations, the use of motor vehicles, or personnel management.

(Pub.L. 100–300, § 7, Apr. 29, 1988, 102 Stat. 439; Pub.L. 105–277, Div. G, Title XXII, § 2213, 112 Stat. 2681–812; Pub.L. 108–370, § 2, Oct. 25, 2004, 118 Stat. 1750.)

Commentary

Ex. Ord. No. 12648, Aug. 11, 1988, 53 F.R. 30637, designated the Department of State as the Central Authority of the United States for purposes of the Hague Convention on the Civil Aspects of International Child Abduction

§ 9007. Costs and fees

(a) Administrative costs

No department, agency, or instrumentality of the Federal Government or of any State or local government may impose on an applicant any fee in relation to the administrative processing of applications submitted under the Convention.

(b) Costs incurred in civil actions

(1) Petitioners may be required to bear the costs of legal counsel or advisors, court costs incurred in connection with their petitions, and travel costs for the return of the child involved and any accompanying persons, except as provided in paragraphs (2) and (3).

(2) Subject to paragraph (3), legal fees or court costs incurred in connection with an action brought under section 9003 of this title shall be borne by the petitioner unless they are covered by payments from Federal, State, or local legal assistance or other programs.

(3) Any court ordering the return of a child pursuant to an action brought under section 9003 of this title shall order the respondent to pay necessary expenses incurred by or on behalf of the petitioner, including court costs, legal fees, foster home or other care during the course of proceedings in the action, and transportation costs related to the return of the child, unless the respondent establishes that such order would be clearly inappropriate. *(Pub.L. 100–300, § 8, Apr. 29, 1988, 102 Stat. 440.)*

Commentary

West v. Dobrev, 735 F.3d 921 (10th Cir. 2013), after sustaining a trial court's order of return, declined to order the abducting father to pay, under subsection (b)(3), fees and costs incurred by the mother to defend against his unsuccessful appeal of the district court order. The Court of Appeals questioned whether it was a "court ordering the return of a child" within the meaning of subsection (b)(3).

Salazar v. Maimon, 750 F.3d 514 (5th Cir. 2014), affirmed a district court award of fees to the mother in a proceeding under subsection (b)(3), where the parties' voluntary agreement to return the child to the mother was incorporated into a court order, even though the district court did not grant the father an evidentiary hearing on the issue of fees, when the husband contested the merits of making any award but did not contest the reasonableness of mother's expenses because, under subsection (b)(3), the court may award fees when it is not "clearly inappropriate."

§ 9008. Collection, maintenance, and dissemination of information

(a) In general

In performing its functions under the Convention, the United States Central Authority may, under such conditions as the Central Authority prescribes by regulation, but subject to subsection (c) of this section, receive from or transmit to any department, agency, or instrumentality of the Federal Government or of any State or foreign government, and receive from or transmit to any applicant, petitioner, or respondent, information necessary to locate a child or for the purpose of otherwise implementing the Convention with respect to a child, except that the United States Central Authority—

(1) may receive such information from a Federal or State department, agency, or instrumentality only pursuant to applicable Federal and State statutes; and

(2) may transmit any information received under this subsection notwithstanding any provision of law other than this chapter.

(b) Requests for information

Requests for information under this section shall be submitted in such manner and form as the United States Central Authority may prescribe by regulation and shall be accompanied or supported by such documents as the United States Central Authority may require.

(c) Responsibility of government entities

Whenever any department, agency, or instrumentality of the United States or of any State receives a request from the United States Central Authority for information authorized to be provided to such Central Authority under subsection (a) of this section, the head of such department, agency, or instrumentality shall promptly cause a search to be made of the files and records maintained by such department, agency, or instrumentality in order to determine whether the information requested is contained in any such files or records. If such search discloses the information requested, the head of such department, agency, or instrumentality shall immediately transmit such information to the United States Central Authority, except that any such information the disclosure of which—

(1) would adversely affect the national security interests of the United States or the law enforcement interests of the United States or of any State; or

(2) would be prohibited by section 9 of Title 13;

shall not be transmitted to the Central Authority. The head of such department, agency, or instrumentality shall, immediately upon completion of the requested search, notify the Central Authority of the results of the search, and whether an exception set forth in paragraph (1) or (2) applies. In the event that the United States Central Authority receives information and the appropriate Federal or State department, agency, or instrumentality thereafter notifies the Central Authority that an exception set forth in paragraph (1) or (2) applies to that information, the Central Authority may not disclose that information under subsection (a) of this section.

(d) Information available from Parent Locator Service

To the extent that information which the United States Central Authority is authorized to obtain under the provisions of subsection (c) of this section can be obtained through the Parent Locator Service, the United States Central Authority shall first seek to obtain such information from the Parent Locator Service, before requesting such information directly under the provisions of subsection (c) of this section.

(e) Recordkeeping

The United States Central Authority shall maintain appropriate records concerning its activities and the disposition of cases brought to its attention. *(Pub.L. 100–300, § 9, Apr. 29, 1988, 102 Stat. 440.)*

§ 9009. Office of Children's Issues

(a) Director requirements

The Secretary of State shall fill the position of Director of the Office of Children's Issues of the Department of State (in this section referred to as the "Office") with an individual of senior rank who can ensure long-term continuity in the management and policy matters of the Office and has a strong background in consular affairs.

(b) Case officer staffing

Effective April 1, 2000, there shall be assigned to the Office of Children's Issues of the Department of State a sufficient number of case officers to ensure that the average caseload for each officer does not exceed 75.

(c) Embassy contact

The Secretary of State shall designate in each United States diplomatic mission an employee who shall serve as the point of contact for matters relating to international abductions of children by parents. The Director of the Office shall regularly inform the designated employee of children of United States citizens abducted by parents to that country.

(d) Reports to parents

(1) In general

Except as provided in paragraph (2), beginning 6 months after November 29, 1999, and at least once every 6 months thereafter, the Secretary of State shall report to each parent who has requested assistance regarding an abducted child overseas. Each such report shall include information on the current status of the abducted child's case and the efforts by the Department of State to resolve the case.

(2) Exception

The requirement in paragraph (1) shall not apply in a case of an abducted child if—

(A) the case has been closed and the Secretary of State has reported the reason the case was closed to the parent who requested assistance; or

(B) the parent seeking assistance requests that such reports not be provided.

(Pub.L. 106–113, Div. B, § 1000(a)(7) [Div. A, Title II, § 201], Nov. 29, 1999, 113 Stat. 1536, 1501A–419.)

§ 9010. Interagency coordinating group

The Secretary of State, the Secretary of Health and Human Services, and the Attorney General shall designate Federal employees and may, from time to time, designate private citizens to serve on an interagency coordinating group to monitor the operation of the Convention and to provide advice on its implementation to the United States Central Authority and other Federal agencies. This group shall meet from time to time at the request of the United States Central Authority. The agency in which the United

States Central Authority is located is authorized to reimburse such private citizens for travel and other expenses incurred in participating at meetings of the interagency coordinating group at rates not to exceed those authorized under subchapter I of chapter 57 of Title 5 for employees of agencies. *(Pub.L. 100–300, § 10, Apr. 29, 1988, 102 Stat. 441.)*

§ 9011. Authorization of appropriations

There are authorized to be appropriated for each fiscal year such sums as may be necessary to carry out the purposes of the Convention and this chapter. *(Pub.L. 100–300, § 12, Apr. 29, 1988, 102 Stat. 442.)*

TITLE 25

INDIANS

CHAPTER 21—INDIAN CHILD WELFARE

§ 1901. Congressional findings

Recognizing the special relationship between the United States and the Indian tribes and their members and the Federal responsibility to Indian people, the Congress finds—

(1) that clause 3, section 8, article I of the United States Constitution provides that "The Congress shall have Power * * * To regulate Commerce * * * with Indian tribes [1]" and, through this and other constitutional authority, Congress has plenary power over Indian affairs;

(2) that Congress, through statutes, treaties, and the general course of dealing with Indian tribes, has assumed the responsibility for the protection and preservation of Indian tribes and their resources;

(3) that there is no resource that is more vital to the continued existence and integrity of Indian tribes than their children and that the United States has a direct interest, as trustee, in protecting Indian children who are members of or are eligible for membership in an Indian tribe;

(4) that an alarmingly high percentage of Indian families are broken up by the removal, often unwarranted, of their children from them by nontribal public and private agencies and that an alarmingly high percentage of such children are placed in non-Indian foster and adoptive homes and institutions; and

(5) that the States, exercising their recognized jurisdiction over Indian child custody proceedings through administrative and judicial bodies, have often failed to recognize the essential tribal relations of Indian people and the cultural and social standards prevailing in Indian communities and families.

(Pub.L. 95–608, § 2, Nov. 8, 1978, 92 Stat. 3069.)

[1] So in original. Probably should be capitalized.

§ 1902. Congressional declaration of policy

The Congress hereby declares that it is the policy of this Nation to protect the best interests of Indian children and to promote the stability and security of Indian tribes and families by the establishment of minimum Federal standards for the removal of Indian children from their families and the placement of such children in foster or adoptive homes which will reflect the unique values of Indian culture, and by providing for assistance to Indian tribes in the operation of child and family service programs. *(Pub.L. 95–608, § 3, Nov. 8, 1978, 92 Stat. 3069.)*

§ 1903. Definitions

For the purposes of this chapter, except as may be specifically provided otherwise, the term—

(1) "child custody proceeding" shall mean and include—

(i) "foster care placement" which shall mean any action removing an Indian child from its parent or Indian custodian for temporary placement in a foster home or institution or the home of a guardian or conservator where the parent or Indian custodian cannot have the child returned upon demand, but where parental rights have not been terminated;

(ii) "termination of parental rights" which shall mean any action resulting in the termination of the parent-child relationship;

(iii) "preadoptive placement" which shall mean the temporary placement of an Indian child in a foster home or institution after the termination of parental rights, but prior to or in lieu of adoptive placement; and

(iv) "adoptive placement" which shall mean the permanent placement of an Indian child for adoption, including any action resulting in a final decree of adoption.

Such term or terms shall not include a placement based upon an act which, if committed by an adult, would be deemed a crime or upon an award, in a divorce proceeding, of custody to one of the parents.

(2) "extended family member" shall be as defined by the law or custom of the Indian child's tribe or, in the absence of such law or custom, shall be a person who has reached the age of eighteen and who is the Indian child's grandparent, aunt or uncle, brother or sister, brother-in-law or sister-in-law, niece or nephew, first or second cousin, or stepparent;

(3) "Indian" means any person who is a member of an Indian tribe, or who is an Alaska Native and a member of a Regional Corporation as defined in section 1606 of Title 43;

(4) "Indian child" means any unmarried person who is under age eighteen and is either (a) a member of an Indian tribe or (b) is eligible for membership in an Indian tribe and is the biological child of a member of an Indian tribe;

(5) "Indian child's tribe" means (a) the Indian tribe in which an Indian child is a member or eligible for membership or (b), in the case of an Indian child who is a member of or eligible for membership in more than one tribe, the Indian tribe with which the Indian child has the more significant contacts;

(6) "Indian custodian" means any Indian person who has legal custody of an Indian child under tribal law or custom or under State law or to whom temporary physical care, custody, and control has been transferred by the parent of such child;

(7) "Indian organization" means any group, association, partnership, corporation, or other legal entity owned or controlled by Indians, or a majority of whose members are Indians;

(8) "Indian tribe" means any Indian tribe, band, nation, or other organized group or community of Indians recognized as eligible for the services provided to Indians by the Secretary because of their status as Indians, including any Alaska Native village as defined in section 1602(c) of Title 43;

(9) "parent" means any biological parent or parents of an Indian child or any Indian person who has lawfully adopted an Indian child, including adoptions under tribal law or custom. It does not include the unwed father where paternity has not been acknowledged or established;

(10) "reservation" means Indian country as defined in section 1151 of Title 18 and any lands, not covered under such section, title to which is either held by the United States in trust for the benefit of any Indian tribe or individual or held by any Indian tribe or individual subject to a restriction by the United States against alienation;

(11) "Secretary" means the Secretary of the Interior; and

(12) "tribal court" means a court with jurisdiction over child custody proceedings and which is either a Court of Indian Offenses, a court established and operated under the code or custom of an Indian tribe, or any other administrative body of a tribe which is vested with authority over child custody proceedings.

(Pub.L. 95–608, § 4, Nov. 8, 1978, 92 Stat. 3069.)

Commentary

Applying the concluding proviso of subsection (1), *In re Enrique O., 137 Cal.App.4th 728, 40 Cal.Rptr.3d 570 (2006), review denied,* holds that in a wardship proceeding, a juvenile court properly failed to send notices under this Act because the proceeding was based on offenses committed by the ward, which if committed by an adult would have been a crime.

To the same effect, see *In re W.B., Jr., 55 Cal.4th 30, 281 P.3d 906, 144 Cal.Rptr.3d 843 (2012)*. With respect to ICWA notice requirements, *W.B.* distinguishes between dependency and delinquency proceedings. In all juvenile court proceedings, both dependency and delinquency, the court, social worker, or probation officer must inquire about the child's Indian status whenever the child is in foster care or conditions in the child's family may potentially require a foster care placement (subsection (a)). Notice to the tribes and other ICWA procedures must be provided only if the case is a "child custody proceeding," as defined by this section. A case is a "child custody proceeding" if it will involve action taken to terminate parental rights or to place an Indian child in foster care or in an adoptive or preadoptive home or institution. Any case involving placement of a child outside the home based upon an act that would be criminal if committed by an adult is not a "child custody proceeding" and is thus exempt from ICWA requirements under subsection (1) of this section.

In re Jennifer A., 103 Cal.App.4th 692, 127 Cal.Rptr.2d 54 (2002), holds that the notice provisions of the Indian Child Welfare Act were applicable when, in a dependency proceeding, a child of possible Indian heritage was removed from her mother, temporarily placed in a foster home, and ultimately placed with her father. *Jennifer A.* reasoned that an involuntary proceeding that may result in a temporary foster home placement falls under the Act (subsection (1)(i)), and the subsection (1) exception for divorce proceedings is inapplicable in a proceeding between unmarried parents that does not arise out of the dissolution of the parties' relationship, but instead out of concern for the child's safety.

In re Alexis H., 132 Cal.App.4th 11, 33 Cal.Rptr.3d 242 (2005), holds that the failure of a social services department to comply with the notice provisions of this section in a dependency proceeding was harmless error because the department was seeking only in-home family reunification services for Indian children, and not foster care or adoption.

In re Brandon M., 54 Cal.App.4th 1387, 63 Cal.Rptr.2d 671 (1997), review denied August 20, 1997, includes a non-Indian former stepparent within the subsection (2) class of "extended family members."

On January 24, 2001, the California Supreme Court denied a petition for review and depublished *In re Adam N., 101 Cal.Rptr.2d 181 (2000)*. Relying on § 1903 (4), the depublished opinion of the court of appeal purported to hold that a parent's nonspecific expression of belief that he had Indian heritage on his mother's side did not trigger the notice provisions of § 1912, reasoning that the parent's statement was insufficient to enable the trial court to know or have reason to know that an Indian child is involved in view of this section's definition of an "Indian child" as one who is either a member of an Indian tribe, or is eligible to be a member of an Indian tribe *and* is the biological child of a member.

Relying on the subsection (4) definition of "Indian child" as "either (a) member of an Indian tribe or (b) . . . eligible for membership in an Indian tribe and . . . the biological child of a member of an Indian tribe," *In re Jose C., 155 Cal.App.4th 844, 66 Cal.Rptr.3d 355 (2007), review denied*, held that the Indian Child Welfare Act does not apply to dependent children when the children and their mother were not enrolled members of an Indian tribe, but were only eligible to be enrolled as members of the tribe.

The California Supreme Court has granted review to and superseded *In re Abbigail A., 173 Cal.Rptr.3d 191 (2014)*, which held that California Rules of Court 5.482(c) and 5.484(c)(2), which require an agency to take active steps to secure tribal membership for a child who is eligible for membership, are inconsistent with state law to the extent that they require application of the Indian Child Welfare Act (25 U.S.C. § 1901 et. seq.) to children who do not fall with the subsection (3) definition of Indian children, which is limited to children who are either enrolled members of a tribe or the biological children of an enrolled member.

Reading subsection (6) of this section together with section 1914, *In re Michael A., 209 Cal.App.4th 661, 147 Cal.Rptr.3d 169 (2012)*, held that a grandmother with de facto parent status did not have standing to raise an Indian Child Welfare Act (ICWA) notice challenge to an order removing her grandchildren from her custody. See also Commentary to California Welfare and Institutions Code §§ 224 and 224.1.

Relying on subsection (8), *In re K.P., 175 Cal.App.4th 1, 95 Cal.Rptr.3d 524 (2009)*, held that compliance with the notice provisions of the Indian Child Welfare Act is not required when a child's parent asserts membership in a tribe that is not recognized by the federal government.

In re O.K., 106 Cal.App.4th 152, 130 Cal.Rptr.2d 276 (2003), review denied May 14, 2003, holds that a paternal grandmother's statement to a juvenile court that the father of dependent children "may have Indian in him" was too vague and speculative to give the court any reason to believe that the dependent children might be Indian children. Therefore, the statement did not trigger the notice requirements of § 1912.

Invoking subsection (9), *In re Daniel M., 110 Cal.App.4th 703, 1 Cal.Rptr.3d 897 (2003)*, holds that an alleged father who has not acknowledged or established his paternity lacks standing to challenge a violation of the notice provisions of the Indian Child Welfare Act. To the same effect, see *In re E.G., 170 Cal.App.4th 1530, 88 Cal.Rptr.3d 871 (2009)*.

SUBCHAPTER I—CHILD CUSTODY PROCEEDINGS

§ 1911. Indian tribe jurisdiction over Indian child custody proceedings

(a) Exclusive jurisdiction

An Indian tribe shall have jurisdiction exclusive as to any State over any child custody proceeding involving an Indian child who resides or is domiciled within the reservation of such tribe, except where such jurisdiction is otherwise vested in the State by existing Federal law. Where an Indian child is a ward of a tribal court, the Indian tribe shall retain exclusive jurisdiction, notwithstanding the residence or domicile of the child.

(b) Transfer of proceedings; declination by tribal court

In any State court proceeding for the foster care placement of, or termination of parental rights to, an Indian child not domiciled or residing within the reservation of the Indian child's tribe, the court, in the absence of good cause to the contrary, shall transfer such proceeding to the jurisdiction of the tribe, absent objection by either parent, upon the petition of either parent or the Indian custodian or the Indian child's tribe: *Provided*, That such transfer shall be subject to declination by the tribal court of such tribe.

(c) State court proceedings; intervention

In any State court proceeding for the foster care placement of, or termination of parental rights to, an Indian child, the Indian custodian of the child and the Indian child's tribe shall have a right to intervene at any point in the proceeding.

(d) Full faith and credit to public acts, records, and judicial proceedings of Indian tribes

The United States, every State, every territory or possession of the United States, and every Indian tribe shall give full faith and credit to the public acts, records, and judicial proceedings of any Indian tribe applicable to Indian child custody proceedings to the same extent that such entities give full faith and credit to the public acts, records, and judicial proceedings of any other entity. *(Pub.L. 95–608, Title I, § 101, Nov. 8, 1978, 92 Stat. 3071.)*

Commentary

California is a "mandatory Public Law 280" state. Public Law 280, codified at 18 U.S.C. § 1162(a) (criminal offenses) and 28 U.S.C. § 1360(a) (civil actions), gives California broad criminal jurisdiction and limited civil jurisdiction in Indian country. *Doe v. Mann, 415 F.3d 1038 (9th Cir., 2005)*, addressed the question whether Public Law 280 gives California jurisdiction to terminate an Indian mother's parental rights and order the adoption of an Indian child domiciled on a reservation. *Doe v. Mann* held that, under the limited civil jurisdiction granted under Public Law 280, in California the Indian Child Welfare Act does not provide an Indian tribe with exclusive jurisdiction over a child custody proceeding involving an Indian child domiciled on a reservation unless the tribe has reassumed jurisdiction over child custody proceedings after following the procedures prescribed in Section 1918. Thus, the court concluded, California has properly been exercising concurrent jurisdiction over dependency proceedings and properly transferring a proceeding to a tribe only when the tribe has reassumed exclusive jurisdiction over an Indian child custody proceeding under Section 1918 of the Indian Child Welfare Act.

In re M.A., 137 Cal.App.4th 567, 40 Cal.Rptr.3d 439 (2006), review denied, holds that, in a juvenile dependency proceeding, the trial court properly granted a tribal petition to transfer the matter to the tribal court even though the tribal court was not approved by the Secretary of the U.S. Department of the Interior to exercise transfer jurisdiction over child custody matters.

In re M. M., 154 Cal.App.4th 897, 65 Cal.Rptr.3d 273 (2007), review denied, held that the completed transfer of a juvenile dependency case from state court to tribal court, under subsection (b), precludes any appeal from the transfer order because the transfer order deprives a California court of jurisdiction over the case.

In re Sadie S., 241 Cal.App.4th 1289, 194 Cal.Rptr.3d 596 (2015), review denied, held that a juvenile court, having found that children were Indian children within the meaning of this act and having entered a California Welfare and Institutions Code section 366.26 judgment selecting tribal customary adoption, properly accorded full faith and credit to the tribal customary adoption order, reasoning that the tribe was not required to exercise subject matter jurisdiction before the initiation of dependency proceedings or transfer to a tribe for custody determination.

In re Isaiah W., 1 Cal.5th 1, 373 P.3d 444, 203 Cal.Rptr.3d 633 (2016), held that a mother's failure to appeal from an order in which the court found that the Indian Child Welfare Act was inapplicable, did not preclude her from challenging a subsequent order terminating her parental rights on the ground that the court had reason to know the child was an Indian child but did not order the Department to comply with the Act's notice requirements. Noting that the juvenile court has a continuing duty to inquire about the child's Indian status, the California Supreme Court concluded that the juvenile court had to duty to inquire at the proceeding to terminate parental rights. In Isaiah W., the supreme court explicitly overruled *In re Pedro N., 35 Cal.App.4th 183, 41 Cal.Rptr.2d 819 (1995)*, which did not treat the Act's notice requirements as imposing a continuing duty on courts in legal proceedings.

In *Boozer v. Wilder, 381 F.3d 931 (9th Cir. 2004)*, the Ninth Circuit held that the district court properly dismissed, for failure to exhaust tribal court remedies, a father's complaint challenging a tribal court's custody jurisdiction. Although 28 USC § 1331 authorized a non-Indian to challenge tribal court jurisdiction in a federal common law action, the federal court must accord the tribal court full opportunity to determine its own jurisdiction, including exhaustion of opportunities for appellate review, before the federal court may entertain a claim that the tribal court has exceeded its jurisdiction. However, *Boozer* explains that exhaustion is not required where a tribal court's action patently violates express jurisdictional prohibitions, the tribal court clearly lacks jurisdiction, the tribal court action is intended to harass or is conducted in bad faith, or exhaustion would be futile because there is no adequate opportunity to challenge the tribal court's jurisdiction.

Interpreting Section 1911(b), *In re Larissa G., 43 Cal.App.4th 505, 51 Cal.Rptr.2d 16 (1996)*, holds that a parent of an Indian child who is not domiciled or residing on a reservation has power to veto transfer of jurisdiction from state court to tribal court.

§ 1912. Pending court proceedings

(a) Notice; time for commencement of proceedings; additional time for preparation

In any involuntary proceeding in a State court, where the court knows or has reason to know that an Indian child is involved, the party seeking the foster care placement of, or termination of parental rights to, an Indian child shall notify the parent or Indian custodian and the Indian child's tribe, by registered mail with return receipt requested, of the pending proceedings and of their right of intervention. If the identity or location of the parent or Indian custodian and the tribe cannot be determined, such notice shall be given to the Secretary in like manner, who shall have fifteen days after receipt to provide the requisite notice to the parent or Indian custodian and the tribe. No foster care placement or termination of parental rights proceeding shall be held until at least ten days after receipt of notice by the parent or Indian custodian and the tribe or the Secretary: *Provided*, That the parent or Indian custodian or the tribe shall, upon request, be granted up to twenty additional days to prepare for such proceeding.

(b) Appointment of counsel

In any case in which the court determines indigency, the parent or Indian custodian shall have the right to court-appointed counsel in any removal, placement, or termination proceeding. The court may, in its discretion, appoint counsel for the child upon a finding that such appointment is in the best interest of the child. Where State law makes no provision for appointment of counsel in such proceedings, the court shall promptly notify the Secretary upon appointment of counsel, and the Secretary, upon certification of the presiding judge, shall pay reasonable fees and expenses out of funds which may be appropriated pursuant to section 13 of this title.

(c) Examination of reports or other documents

Each party to a foster care placement or termination of parental rights proceeding under State law involving an Indian child shall have the right to examine all reports or other documents filed with the court upon which any decision with respect to such action may be based.

(d) Remedial services and rehabilitative programs; preventive measures

Any party seeking to effect a foster care placement of, or termination of parental rights to, an Indian child under State law shall satisfy the court that active efforts have been made to provide remedial services and rehabilitative programs designed to prevent the breakup of the Indian family and that these efforts have proved unsuccessful.

(e) Foster care placement orders; evidence; determination of damage to child

No foster care placement may be ordered in such proceeding in the absence of a determination, supported by clear and convincing evidence, including testimony of qualified expert witnesses, that the continued custody of the child by the parent or Indian custodian is likely to result in serious emotional or physical damage to the child.

(f) Parental rights termination orders; evidence; determination of damage to child

No termination of parental rights may be ordered in such proceeding in the absence of a determination, supported by evidence beyond a reasonable doubt, including testimony of qualified expert witnesses, that the continued custody of the child by the parent or Indian custodian is likely to result in serious emotional or physical damage to the child. *(Pub.L. 95–608, Title I, § 102, Nov. 8, 1978, 92 Stat. 3071.)*

Commentary

For discussion and strict application of this section, see *In re Desiree F., 83 Cal.App.4th 460, 99 Cal.Rptr.2d 688 (2000)* (vacating and remanding appealed portions of trial court order made after proceeding that did not satisfy requirements of this section).

In re Jonathon S., 129 Cal.App.4th 324, 28 Cal.Rptr.3d 495 (2005), holds that a non-Indian parent has standing to claim that the notice provision of this section has not been satisfied.

In re Breanna S., 8 Cal.App.5th 636, 214 Cal.Rptr.3d 98 (2017), remanded a proceeding to terminate parental rights in order to provide proper notice, because the county department failed to provide the required information on the ICWA notice forms. That the children could not meet the blood percentage required for tribal membership did not render the error harmless because only the tribe could make membership determinations.

In re Brooke C., 127 Cal.App.4th 377, 25 Cal.Rptr.3d 590 (2005), holds that a social service agency's failure to comply with the notice requirements of the Indian Child Welfare Act (ICWA) does not constitute jurisdictional error in a dependency proceeding involving orders other than those terminating parental rights; thus the juvenile court's jurisdictional and dispositional orders remain in effect until proper notice is given and the juvenile court determines whether the ICWA applies to the proceeding. *In re Rayna N., 163 Cal.App.4th 262, 77 Cal.Rptr.3d 628 (2008), review denied*, held that when a juvenile court fails to comply with the notice requirements of the Indian Child Welfare Act (25 USC § 1901 et seq.) or with the 2006 amendments, effective January 1, 2007, of the California statutes governing Indian child custody proceedings, California Welfare and Institutions Code 224.2(d) does not alter the established practice of limited reversal and remand for the purpose of complying with notice requirements.

When a juvenile court issued an order terminating a mother's parental rights after directing the social service agency to comply with the notice requirements of this section, but the agency subsequently failed to fully comply with those requirements, *In re B.H., 241 Cal.App.4th 603, 194 Cal.Rptr.3d 226 (2015)*, reversed the juvenile court's order.

In re Nicole K., 146 Cal.App.4th 779, 53 Cal.Rptr.3d 251 (2007), explicitly declined to follow the *Brooke C.* holding that ICWA notice error in a proceeding in which a juvenile court terminated reunification plans and scheduled a permanency planning hearing requires only limited remand, without reversal of judgment. *Nicole K.* reasoned that the juvenile court's order must be vacated, because the standards applied in determinations involving an Indian child are different from those otherwise applied. *Nicole K.* would, however, allow reinstatement of the original order if the court subsequently determines that the child is not an Indian child.

In re Alexis H., 132 Cal.App.4th 11, 33 Cal.Rptr.3d 242 (2005), holds that the failure of a social services department to comply with the notice provisions of this section in a dependency proceeding was harmless error because the department was seeking only in-home family reunification services for Indian children, and not foster care or adoption.

In re Francisco W., 139 Cal.App.4th 695, 43 Cal.Rptr.3d 171 (2006), review denied, holds that when a termination of parental rights is appealed because of noncompliance with this section, the practice of issuing limited reversals in which the judgment of the juvenile court will be reinstated if no Indian tribe intervenes after proper notice is consistent with the best interests of children and fundamental principles of appellate practice.

In re Levi U., 78 Cal.App.4th 191, 92 Cal.Rptr.2d 648 (2000), holds that the Department of Social Services and the juvenile court satisfied the notice requirements of subsection (a) by notifying the Bureau of Indian Affairs about a foster care placement of a child possibly of Indian heritage but of unknown tribal identity.

On January 24, 2001, the California Supreme Court denied a petition for review and depublished *In re Adam N., 101 Cal.Rptr.2d 181 (2000)*. Relying on § 1903 (4), the depublished opinion of the court of appeal purported to hold that a parent's nonspecific expression of belief that he had Indian heritage on his mother's side did not trigger the notice provisions of § 1912, reasoning that the parent's statement was insufficient to enable the trial court to know or have reason to know that an Indian child is involved in view of the definition of an "Indian child," under § 1903 (4), as one who is either a member of an Indian tribe, or is eligible to be a member of an Indian tribe *and* is the biological child of a member.

In re O.K., 106 Cal.App.4th 152, 130 Cal.Rptr.2d 276 (2003), review denied May 14, 2003, holds that a paternal grandmother's statement to a juvenile court that the father of dependent children "may have Indian in him" was too vague and speculative to give the court any reason to believe that the dependent children might be Indian children. Therefore, the statement did not trigger the notice requirements of this section.

In re J.L., 10 Cal.App.5th 913, 217 Cal.Rptr.3d 201 (2017), held that a mother's statement that she was not sure whether she had any Indian ancestry was insufficient to trigger the inquiry and notice provisions of the ICWA and the corresponding California Welfare and Institutions Code sections.

On December 1, 1999, the California Supreme Court denied review and depublished *In re Carlos G., 88 Cal.Rptr.2d 623 (1999)*, in which the court of appeal purported to hold that the juvenile court was not required to apply this Act when notices sent to various Indian tribe failed to generate any response establishing that the dependent child was covered by the Act.

In re Isaiah W., 1 Cal.5th 1, 373 P.3d 444, 203 Cal.Rptr.3d 633 (2016), held that a mother's failure to appeal from an order in which the court found that the Indian Child Welfare Act was inapplicable, did not preclude her from challenging a subsequent order terminating her parental rights on the ground that the court had reason to know the child was an Indian child but did not order the Department to comply with the Act's notice requirements. Noting that the juvenile court has a continuing duty to inquire about the child's Indian status, the California Supreme Court concluded that the juvenile court had to duty to inquire at the proceeding to terminate parental rights. In Isaiah W., the supreme court explicitly overruled *In re Pedro N., 35 Cal.App.4th 183, 41 Cal.Rptr.2d 819 (1995)*, which did not treat the Act's notice requirements as imposing a continuing duty on courts in legal proceedings.

Acknowledging that a parent may ordinarily raise a notice defect on appeal even though it was not raised below, *In re Amber F., 150 Cal.App.4th 1152, 58 Cal.Rptr.3d 874 (2007)*, held that a parent may not appeal a second defective notice without having, on remand, raised the issue at the notice review hearing. In *Amber F.*, the parent and her attorney were asked at the notice review hearing whether they had any argument whether lawful notice had been provided, and they responded that they did not.

In *In re Michael G., 63 Cal.App.4th 700, 74 Cal.Rptr.2d 642 (1998)*, applying subsection (d) and holding that the parents had been provided insufficient remedial services, the court of appeal stated in dictum that clear and convincing proof, but not proof beyond a reasonable doubt, is required to satisfy the court that "active efforts have been made to provide remedial services and rehabilitative programs designed to prevent the breakup of the Indian family and that these efforts have proved unsuccessful." Compare subsection (f), which does require proof beyond a reasonable doubt.

When a dependent child's parent was adopted, the agency does not have a duty to investigate the parent's adoption records to determine whether the parent had Indian ancestry. *In re C.Y., 208 Cal.App.4th 34, 144 Cal.Rptr.3d 516 (2012)*.

In *Adoptive Couple v. Baby Girl, 133 S.Ct. 2552 (2013)*, the United States Supreme Court held that subsection (f) does not apply to a biological father who never had custody of the child. Nor does subsection (d) require the provision of remedial services and rehabilitation programs to a parent who abandoned an Indian child before the child's birth and never had custody prior to the termination of his parental rights.

§ 1913. Parental rights; voluntary termination

(a) Consent; record; certification matters; invalid consents

Where any parent or Indian custodian voluntarily consents to a foster care placement or to termination of parental rights, such consent shall not be valid unless executed in writing and recorded before a judge of a court of competent jurisdiction and accompanied by the presiding judge's certificate that the terms and consequences of the consent were fully explained in detail and were fully understood by the parent or Indian custodian. The court shall also certify that either the parent or Indian custodian fully understood the explanation in English or that it was interpreted into a language that the parent or Indian custodian understood. Any consent given prior to, or within ten days after, birth of the Indian child shall not be valid.

(b) Foster care placement; withdrawal of consent

Any parent or Indian custodian may withdraw consent to a foster care placement under State law at any time and, upon such withdrawal, the child shall be returned to the parent or Indian custodian.

(c) Voluntary termination of parental rights or adoptive placement; withdrawal of consent; return of custody

In any voluntary proceeding for termination of parental rights to, or adoptive placement of, an Indian child, the consent of the parent may be withdrawn for any reason at any time prior to the entry of a final decree of termination or adoption, as the case may be, and the child shall be returned to the parent.

(d) Collateral attack; vacation of decree and return of custody; limitations

After the entry of a final decree of adoption of an Indian child in any State court, the parent may withdraw consent thereto upon the grounds that consent was obtained through fraud or duress and may petition the court to vacate such decree. Upon a finding that such consent was obtained through fraud or duress, the court shall vacate such decree and return the child to the parent. No adoption which has been effective for at least two years may be invalidated under the provisions of this subsection unless otherwise permitted under State law. *(Pub.L. 95–608, Title I, § 103, Nov. 8, 1978, 92 Stat. 3072.)*

Commentary

See generally *Mississippi Band of Choctaw Indians v. Holyfield, 490 U.S. 30, 109 S.Ct. 1597, 104 L.Ed.2d 29 (1989)* (Indian Child Welfare Act's goal of fostering tribal self-governance requires strict adherence to provisions granting tribal courts exclusive jurisdiction over foster care and adoptive placement of reservation domiciliaries).

Reversing a trial court order which, under Sections 1913 and 1914, invalidated parental relinquishment of a child for adoption at birth, *In re Bridget R., 41 Cal.App.4th 1483, 49 Cal.Rptr.2d 507 (1996), review denied May 15, 1996*, held that the Indian Child Welfare Act cannot constitutionally apply to invalidate a voluntary termination of parental rights when the child is not domiciled on a reservation unless the biological parents are both American Indian and maintain a significant social, cultural, or political relationship with their tribe. The constitutional rights identified by *Bridget R.* are the due process and equal protection rights of the child settled from birth in an adoptive home. For further discussion of *Bridget R.*, see *In re Alexandria Y., 45 Cal.App.4th 1483, 53 Cal.Rptr.2d 679 (1996), review denied September 18, 1996*; and *Crystal R. v. Superior Court, 59 Cal.App.4th 703, 69 Cal.Rptr.2d 414 (1997), review denied February 18, 1998* (Indian Child Welfare Act does not apply in dependency proceeding unless there is an existing Indian family to protect; reviewing federal and state authority). But see *In re Alicia S., 65 Cal.App.4th 79, 76 Cal.Rptr.2d 121 (1998)* (rejecting "existing Indian family doctrine" as violative of Indian Child Welfare Act; reviewing case law holding otherwise).

As of 2007, the California Courts of Appeal are split on the legitimacy of the "existing Indian family" doctrine. The doctrine has been adopted by divisions of the Second, Fourth, and Sixth District Courts of Appeal. See *Bridget R., Alexandria Y.*, and *Crystal R.*, supra. It has been rejected by divisions of the First, Third, Fifth, and Sixth District Courts of Appeal. See *Adoption of Lindsay C., 229 Cal.App.3d 404, 280 Cal.Rptr. 194 (1991), review denied July 11, 1991; Adoption of Hannah S., 142 Cal.App.4th 998, 48 Cal.Rptr.3d 605 (2006); Alicia S.*, supra; and *In re Vincent M., 150 Cal.App.4th 1247, 59 Cal.Rptr.3d 321 (2007), review denied Sept. 12, 2007.*

§ 1914. Petition to court of competent jurisdiction to invalidate action upon showing of certain violations

Any Indian child who is the subject of any action for foster care placement or termination of parental rights under State law, any parent or Indian custodian from whose custody such child was removed, and the Indian child's tribe may petition any court of competent jurisdiction to invalidate such action upon a showing that such action violated any provision of sections 1911, 1912, and 1913 of this title. *(Pub.L. 95–608, Title I, § 104, Nov. 8, 1978, 92 Stat. 3072.)*

Commentary

See generally *Mississippi Band of Choctaw Indians v. Holyfield, 490 U.S. 30, 109 S.Ct. 1597, 104 L.Ed.2d 29 (1989)* (Indian Child Welfare Act's goal of fostering tribal self-governance requires strict adherence to provisions granting tribal courts exclusive jurisdiction over foster care and adoptive placement of reservation domiciliaries).

Reading this section together with subsection (6) of section 1903, *In re Michael A., 209 Cal.App.4th 661, 147 Cal.Rptr.3d 169 (2012)*, held that a grandmother with de facto parent status did not have standing to raise an Indian Child Welfare Act (ICWA) notice challenge to an order removing her grandchildren from her custody. See also Commentary to California Welfare and Institutions Code §§ 224 and 224.1.

Reversing a trial court order which, under Sections 1913 and 1914, invalidated parental relinquishment of a child for adoption at birth, *In re Bridget R., 41 Cal.App.4th 1483, 49 Cal.Rptr.2d 507 (1996), review denied May 15, 1996, cert. denied by Cindy R. v. James R., 519 U.S.1060 (1997), cert. denied by Dry Creek Rancheria v. Bridget and Lucy R, 520 U.S. 1181 (1997)*, held that the Indian Child Welfare Act cannot constitutionally apply to invalidate a voluntary termination of parental rights when the child is not domiciled on a reservation unless the biological parents are both American Indian and maintain a significant social, cultural, or political relationship with their tribe. The constitutional rights identified by *Bridget R.* are the due process and equal protection rights of the child settled from birth in an adoptive home. For further discussion of *Bridget R.*, see *In re Alexandria Y., 45 Cal.App.4th 1483, 53 Cal.Rptr.2d 679 (1996), review denied September 18, 1996*; *Crystal R. v. Superior Court, 59 Cal.App.4th 703, 69 Cal.Rptr.2d 414 (1997), review denied February 18, 1998* (Indian Child Welfare Act does not apply in dependency proceeding unless there is an existing Indian family to protect; reviewing federal and state authority); and *In re Santos Y., 92 Cal.App.4th 1274, 112 Cal.Rptr.2d 692 (2001), review denied February 13, 2002* (applying "existing Indian family" doctrine and discussing its legal history and constitutional rationale). But see *In re Alicia S., 65 Cal.App.4th 79, 76 Cal.Rptr.2d 121* (rejecting "existing Indian family doctrine" as violative of Indian Child Welfare Act; reviewing case law holding otherwise).

§ 1915. Placement of Indian children

(a) Adoptive placements; preferences

In any adoptive placement of an Indian child under State law, a preference shall be given, in the absence of good cause to the contrary, to a placement with (1) a member of the child's extended family; (2) other members of the Indian child's tribe; or (3) other Indian families.

(b) Foster care or preadoptive placements; criteria; preferences

Any child accepted for foster care or preadoptive placement shall be placed in the least restrictive setting which most approximates a family and in which his special needs, if any, may be met. The child shall also be placed within reasonable proximity to his or her home, taking into account any special needs of the child. In any foster care or preadoptive placement, a preference shall be given, in the absence of good cause to the contrary, to a placement with—

(i) a member of the Indian child's extended family;

(ii) a foster home licensed, approved, or specified by the Indian child's tribe;

(iii) an Indian foster home licensed or approved by an authorized non-Indian licensing authority; or

(iv) an institution for children approved by an Indian tribe or operated by an Indian organization which has a program suitable to meet the Indian child's needs.

(c) Tribal resolution for different order of preference; personal preference considered; anonymity in application of preferences

In the case of a placement under subsection (a) or (b) of this section, if the Indian child's tribe shall establish a different order of preference by resolution, the agency or court effecting the placement shall follow such order so long as the placement is the least restrictive setting appropriate to the particular needs of the child, as provided in subsection (b) of this section. Where appropriate, the preference of the Indian child or parent shall be considered: *Provided*, That where a consenting parent evidences a desire for anonymity, the court or agency shall give weight to such desire in applying the preferences.

(d) Social and cultural standards applicable

The standards to be applied in meeting the preference requirements of this section shall be the prevailing social and cultural standards of the Indian community in which the parent or extended family resides or with which the parent or extended family members maintain social and cultural ties.

(e) Record of placement; availability

A record of each such placement, under State law, of an Indian child shall be maintained by the State in which the placement was made, evidencing the efforts to comply with the order of preference specified in this section. Such record shall be made available at any time upon the request of the Secretary or the Indian child's tribe. *(Pub.L. 95–608, Title I, § 105, Nov. 8, 1978, 92 Stat. 3073.)*

Commentary

In re Alexandria P., 228 Cal.App.4th 1322, 176 Cal.Rptr.3d 468 (2016), review denied, affirmed a trial court order placing an Indian child with her extended family in Utah after concluding that the young child's strong bond with her foster family, with whom she had lived for more than four years, was insufficient to establish subsection (a) good cause to depart from the adoptive preferences set forth by this section, when the foster parents were reluctant to foster the child's relationship with her extended Indian family or encourage her to explore her cultural identity and expose her to her Choctaw cultural identity.

In re Jullian B., 82 Cal.App.4th 1337, 99 Cal.Rptr.2d 241 (2000), reversed a Superior Court order placing an infant tribe member with a non-Indian adoptive family on the ground that the court erred in declining to place the child in an Indian prospective adoptive home (subsection (a)) without assessing the prevailing social and cultural standards of the Indian community in which the parent or extended family resides or maintains cultural ties, as required by subsection (d).

Invoking subsection (b), *In re Anthony T., 208 Cal.App.4th 1019, 146 Cal.Rptr.3d 124 (2012)*, reversed an order placing a dependent Indian child in the foster home preferred by his tribe, because the foster home was not within reasonable proximity to his mother's home and interfered with her frequent visitation of the child.

Applying Family Code section 361.31(j), enacted to effectuate this section, *In re Alexandria P., 228 Cal.App.4th 1322, 176 Cal.Rptr.3d 468 (2014)*, reversed a trial court order removing an Indian toddler who had lived with her non-Indian foster parents for two-and-a-half years because her foster parents did not prove to a certainty that the child would suffer emotional harm as a result of her transfer to a non-Indian couple related to the child's father, who had failed to reunite with the child. *Alexandria P.* held that the standard of proof for the good cause exception is clear and convincing evidence, not proof to a certainty.

§ 1916. Return of custody

(a) Petition; best interests of child

Notwithstanding State law to the contrary, whenever a final decree of adoption of an Indian child has been vacated or set aside or the adoptive parents voluntarily consent to the termination of their parental rights to the child, a biological parent or prior Indian custodian may petition for return of custody and the court shall grant such petition unless there is a showing, in a proceeding subject to the provisions of section 1912 of this title, that such return of custody is not in the best interests of the child.

(b) Removal from foster care home; placement procedure

Whenever an Indian child is removed from a foster care home or institution for the purpose of further foster care, preadoptive, or adoptive placement, such placement shall be in accordance with the provisions of this chapter, except in the case where an Indian child is being returned to the parent or Indian custodian from whose custody the child was originally removed. *(Pub.L. 95–608, Title I, § 106, Nov. 8, 1978, 92 Stat. 3073.)*

§ 1917. Tribal affiliation information and other information for protection of rights from tribal relationship; application of subject of adoptive placement; disclosure by court

Upon application by an Indian individual who has reached the age of eighteen and who was the subject of an adoptive placement, the court which entered the final decree shall inform such individual of the tribal affiliation, if any, of the individual's biological parents and provide such other information as may be necessary to protect any rights flowing from the individual's tribal relationship. *(Pub.L. 95–608, Title I, § 107, Nov. 8, 1978, 92 Stat. 3073.)*

§ 1918. Reassumption of jurisdiction over child custody proceedings

(a) Petition; suitable plan; approval by Secretary

Any Indian tribe which became subject to State jurisdiction pursuant to the provisions of the Act of August 15, 1953 (67 Stat. 588), as amended by Title IV of the Act of April 11, 1968 (82 Stat. 73, 78), or pursuant to any other Federal law, may reassume jurisdiction over child custody proceedings. Before any Indian tribe may reassume jurisdiction over Indian child custody proceedings, such tribe shall present to the Secretary for approval a petition to reassume such jurisdiction which includes a suitable plan to exercise such jurisdiction.

(b) Criteria applicable to consideration by Secretary; partial retrocession

(1) In considering the petition and feasibility of the plan of a tribe under subsection (a), the Secretary may consider, among other things:

(i) whether or not the tribe maintains a membership roll or alternative provision for clearly identifying the persons who will be affected by the reassumption of jurisdiction by the tribe;

(ii) the size of the reservation or former reservation area which will be affected by retrocession and reassumption of jurisdiction by the tribe;

(iii) the population base of the tribe, or distribution of the population in homogeneous communities or geographic areas; and

(iv) the feasibility of the plan in cases of multitribal occupation of a single reservation or geographic area.

(2) In those cases where the Secretary determines that the jurisdictional provisions of section 1911(a) of this title are not feasible, he is authorized to accept partial retrocession which will enable tribes to exercise referral jurisdiction as provided in section 1911(b) of this title, or, where appropriate, will allow them to exercise exclusive jurisdiction as provided in section 1911(a) of this title over limited community or geographic areas without regard for the reservation status of the area affected.

(c) Approval of petition; publication in Federal Register; notice; reassumption period; correction of causes for disapproval

If the Secretary approves any petition under subsection (a), the Secretary shall publish notice of such approval in the Federal Register and shall notify the affected State or States of such approval. The Indian tribe concerned shall reassume jurisdiction sixty days after publication in the Federal Register of notice of approval. If the Secretary disapproves any petition under subsection (a), the Secretary shall provide such technical assistance as may be necessary to enable the tribe to correct any deficiency which the Secretary identified as a cause for disapproval.

(d) Pending actions or proceedings unaffected

Assumption of jurisdiction under this section shall not affect any action or proceeding over which a court has already assumed jurisdiction, except as may be provided pursuant to any agreement under section 1919 of this title. *(Pub.L. 95–608, Title I, § 108, Nov. 8, 1978, 92 Stat. 3074.)*

Commentary

California is a "mandatory Public Law 280" state. Public Law 280, codified at 18 U.S.C. § 1162(a) (criminal offenses) and 28 U.S.C. § 1360(a) (civil actions), gives California broad criminal jurisdiction and limited civil jurisdiction in Indian country. *Doe v. Mann, 415 F.3d 1038 (9th Cir., 2005)*, addressed the question whether Public Law 280 gives California jurisdiction to terminate an Indian mother's parental rights and order the adoption of an Indian child domiciled on a reservation. *Doe v. Mann* held that, under the limited civil jurisdiction granted under Public Law 280, in California Section 1911 of the Indian Child Welfare Act does not provide an Indian tribe with exclusive jurisdiction over a child custody proceeding involving an Indian child domiciled on a reservation unless the tribe has reassumed jurisdiction over child custody proceedings after following the procedures prescribed in Section 1918. Thus, the court concluded, California has properly been exercising concurrent jurisdiction over dependency proceedings and properly transferring a proceeding to a tribe only when the tribe has reassumed exclusive jurisdiction over an Indian child custody proceeding under this section.

§ 1919. Agreements between States and Indian tribes

(a) Subject coverage

States and Indian tribes are authorized to enter into agreements with each other respecting care and custody of Indian children and jurisdiction over child custody proceedings, including agreements which may provide for orderly transfer of jurisdiction on a case-by-case basis and agreements which provide for concurrent jurisdiction between States and Indian tribes.

(b) Revocation; notice; actions or proceedings unaffected

Such agreements may be revoked by either party upon one hundred and eighty days' written notice to the other party. Such revocation shall not affect any action or proceeding over which a court has already assumed jurisdiction, unless the agreement provides otherwise. *(Pub.L. 95–608, Title I, § 109, Nov. 8, 1978, 92 Stat. 3074.)*

§ 1920. Improper removal of child from custody; declination of jurisdiction; forthwith return of child: danger exception

Where any petitioner in an Indian child custody proceeding before a State court has improperly removed the child from custody of the parent or Indian custodian or has improperly retained custody after a visit or other temporary relinquishment of custody, the court shall decline jurisdiction over such petition and shall forthwith return the child to his parent or Indian custodian unless returning the child to his parent or custodian would subject the child to a substantial and immediate danger or threat of such danger. *(Pub.L. 95–608, Title I, § 110, Nov. 8, 1978, 92 Stat. 3075.)*

§ 1921. Higher State or Federal standard applicable to protect rights of parent or Indian custodian of Indian child

In any case where State or Federal law applicable to a child custody proceeding under State or Federal law provides a higher standard of protection to the rights of the parent or Indian custodian of an Indian child than the rights provided under this subchapter, the State or Federal court shall apply the State or Federal standard. *(Pub.L. 95–608, Title I, § 111, Nov. 8, 1978, 92 Stat. 3075.)*

§ 1922. Emergency removal or placement of child; termination; appropriate action

Nothing in this subchapter shall be construed to prevent the emergency removal of an Indian child who is a resident of or is domiciled on a reservation, but temporarily located off the reservation, from his parent or Indian custodian or the emergency placement of such child in a foster home or institution, under applicable State law, in order to prevent imminent physical damage or harm to the child. The State authority, official, or agency involved shall insure that the emergency removal or placement terminates immediately when such removal or placement is no longer necessary to prevent imminent physical damage or harm to the child and shall expeditiously initiate a child custody proceeding subject to the provisions of this subchapter, transfer the child to the jurisdiction of the appropriate Indian tribe, or restore the child to the parent or Indian custodian, as may be appropriate. *(Pub.L. 95–608, Title I, § 112, Nov. 8, 1978, 92 Stat. 3075.)*

§ 1923. Effective date

None of the provisions of this subchapter, except sections 1911(a), 1918, and 1919 of this title, shall affect a proceeding under State law for foster care placement, termination of parental rights, preadoptive placement, or adoptive placement which was initiated or completed prior to one hundred and eighty days after November 8, 1978, but shall apply to any subsequent proceeding in the same matter or subsequent proceedings affecting the custody or placement of the same child. *(Pub.L. 95–608, Title I, § 113, Nov. 8, 1978, 92 Stat. 3075.)*

SUBCHAPTER II—INDIAN CHILD AND FAMILY PROGRAMS

§ 1931. Grants for on or near reservation programs and child welfare codes

(a) Statement of purpose; scope of programs

The Secretary is authorized to make grants to Indian tribes and organizations in the establishment and operation of Indian child and family service programs on or near reservations and in the preparation and implementation of child welfare codes. The objective of every Indian child and family service program shall be to prevent the breakup of Indian families and, in particular, to insure that the permanent removal of an Indian child from the custody of his parent or Indian custodian shall be a last resort. Such child and family service programs may include, but are not limited to—

(1) a system for licensing or otherwise regulating Indian foster and adoptive homes;

(2) the operation and maintenance of facilities for the counseling and treatment of Indian families and for the temporary custody of Indian children;

(3) family assistance, including homemaker and home counselors, day care, afterschool care, and employment, recreational activities, and respite care;

(4) home improvement programs;

(5) the employment of professional and other trained personnel to assist the tribal court in the disposition of domestic relations and child welfare matters;

(6) education and training of Indians, including tribal court judges and staff, in skills relating to child and family assistance and service programs;

(7) a subsidy program under which Indian adoptive children may be provided support comparable to that for which they would be eligible as foster children, taking into account the appropriate State standards of support for maintenance and medical needs; and

(8) guidance, legal representation, and advice to Indian families involved in tribal, State, or Federal child custody proceedings.

(b) Non-Federal matching funds for related Social Security or other Federal financial assistance programs; assistance for such programs unaffected; State licensing or approval for qualification for assistance under federally assisted program

Funds appropriated for use by the Secretary in accordance with this section may be utilized as non-Federal matching share in connection with funds provided under Titles IV–B and XX of the Social Security Act or under any other Federal financial assistance programs which contribute to the purpose for which such funds are authorized to be appropriated for use under this chapter. The provision or possibility of assistance under this chapter shall not be a basis for the denial or reduction of any assistance otherwise authorized under Titles IV–B and XX of the Social Security Act or any other federally assisted program. For purposes of qualifying for assistance under a federally assisted program, licensing or approval of foster or adoptive homes or institutions by an Indian tribe shall be deemed equivalent to licensing or approval by a State. *(Pub.L. 95–608, Title II, § 201, Nov. 8, 1978, 92 Stat. 3075.)*

§ 1932. Grants for off-reservation programs for additional services

The Secretary is also authorized to make grants to Indian organizations to establish and operate off-reservation Indian child and family service programs which may include, but are not limited to—

(1) a system for regulating, maintaining, and supporting Indian foster and adoptive homes, including a subsidy program under which Indian adoptive children may be provided support comparable to that for which they would be eligible as Indian foster children, taking into account the appropriate State standards of support for maintenance and medical needs;

(2) the operation and maintenance of facilities and services for counseling and treatment of Indian families and Indian foster and adoptive children;

(3) family assistance, including homemaker and home counselors, day care, afterschool care, and employment, recreational activities, and respite care; and

(4) guidance, legal representation, and advice to Indian families involved in child custody proceedings.

(Pub.L. 95–608, Title II, § 202, Nov. 8, 1978, 92 Stat. 3076.)

§ 1933. Funds for on and off reservation programs

(a) Appropriated funds for similar programs of Department of Health and Human Services; appropriation in advance for payments

In the establishment, operation, and funding of Indian child and family service programs, both on and off reservation, the Secretary may enter into agreements with the Secretary of Health and Human Services, and the latter Secretary is hereby authorized for such purposes to use funds appropriated for similar programs of the Department of Health and Human Services: *Provided*, That authority to make payments pursuant to such agreements shall be effective only to the extent and in such amounts as may be provided in advance by appropriation Acts.

(b) Appropriation authorization under section 13 of this title

Funds for the purposes of this chapter may be appropriated pursuant to the provisions of section 13 of this title. *(Pub.L. 95–608, Title II, § 203, Nov. 8, 1978, 92 Stat. 3076; Pub.L. 96–88, Title V, § 509(b), Oct. 17, 1979, 93 Stat. 695.)*

§ 1934. "Indian" defined for certain purposes

For the purposes of sections 1932 and 1933 of this title, the term "Indian" shall include persons defined in section 1603(c) of this title. *(Pub.L. 95–608, Title II, § 204, Nov. 8, 1978, 92 Stat. 3077.)*

SUBCHAPTER III—RECORDKEEPING, INFORMATION AVAILABILITY, AND TIMETABLES

§ 1951. Information availability to and disclosure by Secretary

(a) Copy of final decree or order; other information; anonymity affidavit; exemption from Freedom of Information Act

Any State court entering a final decree or order in any Indian child adoptive placement after November 8, 1978, shall provide the Secretary with a copy of such decree or order together with such other information as may be necessary to show—

(1) the name and tribal affiliation of the child;

(2) the names and addresses of the biological parents;

(3) the names and addresses of the adoptive parents; and

(4) the identity of any agency having files or information relating to such adoptive placement.

Where the court records contain an affidavit of the biological parent or parents that their identity remain confidential, the court shall include such affidavit with the other information. The Secretary shall insure that the confidentiality of such information is maintained and such information shall not be subject to the Freedom of Information Act (5 U.S.C. 552), as amended.

(b) Disclosure of information for enrollment of Indian child in tribe or for determination of member rights or benefits; certification of entitlement to enrollment

Upon the request of the adopted Indian child over the age of eighteen, the adoptive or foster parents of an Indian child, or an Indian tribe, the Secretary shall disclose such information as may be necessary for the enrollment of an Indian child in the tribe in which the child may be eligible for enrollment or for determining any rights or benefits associated with that membership. Where the documents relating to such child contain an affidavit from the biological parent or parents requesting anonymity, the Secretary shall certify to the Indian child's tribe, where the information warrants, that the child's parentage and other circumstances of birth entitle the child to enrollment under the criteria established by such tribe. *(Pub.L. 95–608, Title III, § 301, Nov. 8, 1978, 92 Stat. 3077.)*

§ 1952. Rules and regulations

Within one hundred and eighty days after November 8, 1978, the Secretary shall promulgate such rules and regulations as may be necessary to carry out the provisions of this chapter. *(Pub.L. 95–608, Title III, § 302, Nov. 8, 1978, 92 Stat. 3077.)*

SUBCHAPTER IV—MISCELLANEOUS PROVISIONS

§ 1961. Locally convenient day schools

(a) Sense of Congress

It is the sense of Congress that the absence of locally convenient day schools may contribute to the breakup of Indian families.

(b) Report to Congress; contents, etc.

The Secretary is authorized and directed to prepare, in consultation with appropriate agencies in the Department of Health and Human Services, a report on the feasibility of providing Indian children with schools located near their homes, and to submit such report to the Select Committee on Indian Affairs of the United States Senate and the Committee on Interior and Insular Affairs of the United States House of Representatives within two years from November 8, 1978. In developing this report the Secretary shall give particular consideration to the provision of educational facilities for children in the elementary grades. *(Pub.L. 95–608, Title IV, § 401, Nov. 8, 1978, 92 Stat. 3078; Pub.L. 96–88, Title V, § 509(b), Oct. 17, 1979, 93 Stat. 695.)*

§ 1962. Copies to the States

Within sixty days after November 8, 1978, the Secretary shall send to the Governor, chief justice of the highest court of appeal, and the attorney general of each State a copy of this chapter, together with committee reports and an explanation of the provisions of this chapter. *(Pub.L. 95–608, Title IV, § 402, Nov. 8, 1978, 92 Stat. 3078.)*

§ 1963. Severability

If any provision of this chapter or the applicability thereof is held invalid, the remaining provisions of this chapter shall not be affected thereby. *(Pub.L. 95–608, Title IV, § 403, Nov. 8, 1978, 92 Stat. 3078.)*

TITLE 26

INTERNAL REVENUE CODE

SUBTITLE A—INCOME TAXES

CHAPTER 1—NORMAL TAXES AND SURTAXES

SUBCHAPTER A—DETERMINATION OF TAX LIABILITY

PART IV—CREDITS AGAINST TAX

Subpart A—Nonrefundable Personal Credits

§ 23. Adoption expenses

(a) Allowance of credit.—

(1) In general.—In the case of an individual, there shall be allowed as a credit against the tax imposed by this chapter the amount of the qualified adoption expenses paid or incurred by the taxpayer.

(2) Year credit allowed.—The credit under paragraph (1) with respect to any expense shall be allowed—

(A) in the case of any expense paid or incurred before the taxable year in which such adoption becomes final, for the taxable year following the taxable year during which such expense is paid or incurred, and

(B) in the case of an expense paid or incurred during or after the taxable year in which such adoption becomes final, for the taxable year in which such expense is paid or incurred.

(3) $10,000 credit for adoption of child with special needs regardless of expenses.—In the case of an adoption of a child with special needs which becomes final during a taxable year, the taxpayer shall be treated as having paid during such year qualified adoption expenses with respect to such adoption in an amount equal to the excess (if any) of $10,000 over the aggregate qualified adoption expenses actually paid or incurred by the taxpayer with respect to such adoption during such taxable year and all prior taxable years.

(b) Limitations.—

(1) Dollar limitation.—The aggregate amount of qualified adoption expenses which may be taken into account under subsection (a) for all taxable years with respect to the adoption of a child by the taxpayer shall not exceed $10,000.

(2) Income limitation.—

(A) In general.—The amount allowable as a credit under subsection (a) for any taxable year (determined without regard to subsection (c)) shall be reduced (but not below zero) by an amount which bears the same ratio to the amount so allowable (determined without regard to this paragraph but with regard to paragraph (1)) as—

(i) the amount (if any) by which the taxpayer's adjusted gross income exceeds $150,000, bears to

(ii) $40,000.

(B) Determination of adjusted gross income.—For purposes of subparagraph (A), adjusted gross income shall be determined without regard to sections 911, 931, and 933.

(3) Denial of double benefit.—

(A) In general.—No credit shall be allowed under subsection (a) for any expense for which a deduction or credit is allowed under any other provision of this chapter.

(B) Grants.—No credit shall be allowed under subsection (a) for any expense to the extent that funds for such expense are received under any Federal, State, or local program.

[(4) Repealed. Pub.L. 112–240, Title I, § 104(c)(A)(i), Jan. 2, 2013, 126 Stat. 2321]

(c) Carryforwards of unused credit.—

(1) In general.—If the credit allowable under subsection (a) for any taxable year exceeds the limitation imposed by section 26(a) for such taxable year reduced by the sum of the credits allowable under this subpart (other than this section and sections 25D and 1400C), such excess shall be carried to the succeeding taxable year and added to the credit allowable under subsection (a) for such taxable year.

(2) Limitation.—No credit may be carried forward under this subsection to any taxable year following the fifth taxable year after the taxable year in which the credit arose. For purposes of the preceding sentence, credits shall be treated as used on a first-in first-out basis.

[(3) Redesignated (2)]

(d) Definitions.—For purposes of this section—

(1) Qualified adoption expenses.—The term "qualified adoption expenses" means reasonable and necessary adoption fees, court costs, attorney fees, and other expenses—

(A) which are directly related to, and the principal purpose of which is for, the legal adoption of an eligible child by the taxpayer,

(B) which are not incurred in violation of State or Federal law or in carrying out any surrogate parenting arrangement,

(C) which are not expenses in connection with the adoption by an individual of a child who is the child of such individual's spouse, and

(D) which are not reimbursed under an employer program or otherwise.

(2) Eligible child.—The term "eligible child" means any individual who—

(A) has not attained age 18, or

(B) is physically or mentally incapable of caring for himself.

(3) Child with special needs.—The term "child with special needs" means any child if—

(A) a State has determined that the child cannot or should not be returned to the home of his parents,

(B) such State has determined that there exists with respect to the child a specific factor or condition (such as his ethnic background, age, or membership in a minority or sibling group, or the presence of factors such as medical conditions or physical, mental, or emotional handicaps) because of which it is reasonable to conclude that such child cannot be placed with adoptive parents without providing adoption assistance, and

(C) such child is a citizen or resident of the United States (as defined in section 217(h)(3)).

(e) Special rules for foreign adoptions.—In the case of an adoption of a child who is not a citizen or resident of the United States (as defined in section 217(h)(3))—

(1) subsection (a) shall not apply to any qualified adoption expense with respect to such adoption unless such adoption becomes final, and

(2) any such expense which is paid or incurred before the taxable year in which such adoption becomes final shall be taken into account under this section as if such expense were paid or incurred during such year.

(f) Filing requirements.—

(1) Married couples must file joint returns.—Rules similar to the rules of paragraphs (2), (3), and (4) of section 21(e) shall apply for purposes of this section.

(2) Taxpayer must include TIN.—

(A) In general.—No credit shall be allowed under this section with respect to any eligible child unless the taxpayer includes (if known) the name, age, and TIN of such child on the return of tax for the taxable year.

(B) Other methods.—The Secretary may, in lieu of the information referred to in subparagraph (A), require other information meeting the purposes of subparagraph (A), including identification of an agent assisting with the adoption.

(g) Basis adjustments.—For purposes of this subtitle, if a credit is allowed under this section for any expenditure with respect to any property, the increase in the basis of such property which would (but for this subsection) result from such expenditure shall be reduced by the amount of the credit so allowed.

(h) Adjustments for inflation.—In the case of a taxable year beginning after December 31, 2002, each of the dollar amounts in subsection (a)(3) and paragraphs (1) and (2)(A)(i) of subsection (b) shall be increased by an amount equal to—

(1) such dollar amount, multiplied by

(2) the cost-of-living adjustment determined under section 1(f)(3) for the calendar year in which the taxable year begins, determined by substituting "calendar year 2001" for "calendar year 1992" in subparagraph (B) thereof.

If any amount as increased under the preceding sentence is not a multiple of $10, such amount shall be rounded to the nearest multiple of $10.

(i) Regulations.—The Secretary shall prescribe such regulations as may be appropriate to carry out this section and section 137, including regulations which treat unmarried individuals who pay or incur qualified adoption expenses with respect to the same child as 1 taxpayer for purposes of applying the dollar amounts in subsections (a)(3) and (b)(1) of this section and in section 137(b)(1). *(Added Pub.L. 104–188, Title I, § 1807(a), Aug. 20, 1996, 110 Stat. 1899, § 23; amended Pub.L. 105–34, Title XVI, § 1601(h)(2)(A), (B), Aug. 5, 1997, 111 Stat. 1092; Pub.L. 105–206, Title VI, §§ 6008(d)(6), 6018(f)(1), July 22, 1998, 112 Stat. 812, 823; Pub.L. 107–16, Title II, §§ 201(b)(2)(E), 202(a)(1), (b)(1)(A), (b)(2)(A), (c), (d)(1), (e)(1), (f)(1), (f)(2)(A), June 7, 2001, 115 Stat. 46–49; Pub.L. 107–147, Title IV, §§ 411(c)(1)(A) to (E), 418(a)(1), Mar. 9, 2002, 116 Stat. 45, 57; Pub.L. 109–58, Title XIII, § 1335(b)(1), Aug. 8, 2005, 119 Stat. 1036; Pub.L. 109–135, Title IV, § 402(i)(3)(A), (4), Dec. 21, 2005, 119 Stat. 2612, 2615; Pub.L. 110–343, Div. B, Title I, § 106(e)(2)(A), Oct. 3, 2008, 122 Stat. 3817; renumbered § 36C, renumbered § 23 and amended Pub.L. 111–148, Title X, § 10909(a)(1), (b)(1), (2)(I), Mar. 23, 2010, 124 Stat. 1021, 1023; Pub.L. 111–312, Title I, § 101(b)(1), Dec. 17, 2010, 124 Stat. 3298; Pub.L. 112–240, Title I, § 104(c)(2)(A), Jan. 2, 2013, 126 Stat. 2321.)*

§ 24. Child tax credit

(a) Allowance of credit.—There shall be allowed as a credit against the tax imposed by this chapter for the taxable year with respect to each qualifying child of the taxpayer for which the taxpayer is allowed a deduction under section 151 an amount equal to $1,000.

(b) Limitations.—

(1) Limitation based on adjusted gross income.—The amount of the credit allowable under subsection (a) shall be reduced (but not below zero) by $50 for each $1,000 (or fraction thereof) by which the taxpayer's modified adjusted gross income exceeds the threshold amount. For purposes of the preceding sentence, the term "modified adjusted gross income" means adjusted gross income increased by any amount excluded from gross income under section 911, 931, or 933.

(2) Threshold amount.—For purposes of paragraph (1), the term "threshold amount" means—

(A) $110,000 in the case of a joint return,

(B) $75,000 in the case of an individual who is not married, and

(C) $55,000 in the case of a married individual filing a separate return.

For purposes of this paragraph, marital status shall be determined under section 7703.

[(3) **Repealed.** Pub.L. 112–240, Title I, § 104(c)(2)(B)(i), Jan. 2, 2013, 126 Stat. 2321]

(c) Qualifying child.—For purposes of this section—

(1) In general.—The term "qualifying child" means a qualifying child of the taxpayer (as defined in section 152(c)) who has not attained age 17.

(2) Exception for certain noncitizens.—The term "qualifying child" shall not include any individual who would not be a dependent if subparagraph (A) of section 152(b)(3) were applied without regard to all that follows "resident of the United States".

(d) Portion of credit refundable.—

(1) In general.—The aggregate credits allowed to a taxpayer under subpart C shall be increased by the lesser of—

(A) the credit which would be allowed under this section without regard to this subsection and the limitation under section 26(a) or

(B) the amount by which the aggregate amount of credits allowed by this subpart (determined without regard to this subsection) would increase if the limitation imposed by section 26(a) were increased by the greater of—

(i) 15 percent of so much of the taxpayer's earned income (within the meaning of section 32) which is taken into account in computing taxable income for the taxable year as exceeds $3,000, or

(ii) in the case of a taxpayer with 3 or more qualifying children, the excess (if any) of—

(I) the taxpayer's social security taxes for the taxable year, over

(II) the credit allowed under section 32 for the taxable year.

The amount of the credit allowed under this subsection shall not be treated as a credit allowed under this subpart and shall reduce the amount of credit otherwise allowable under subsection (a) without regard to section 26(a). For purposes of subparagraph (B), any amount excluded from gross income by reason of section 112 shall be treated as earned income which is taken into account in computing taxable income for the taxable year.

(2) Social security taxes.—For purposes of paragraph (1)—

(A) In general.—The term "social security taxes" means, with respect to any taxpayer for any taxable year—

(i) the amount of the taxes imposed by sections 3101 and 3201(a) on amounts received by the taxpayer during the calendar year in which the taxable year begins,

(ii) 50 percent of the taxes imposed by section 1401 on the self-employment income of the taxpayer for the taxable year, and

(iii) 50 percent of the taxes imposed by section 3211(a) on amounts received by the taxpayer during the calendar year in which the taxable year begins.

(B) Coordination with special refund of social security taxes.—The term "social security taxes" shall not include any taxes to the extent the taxpayer is entitled to a special refund of such taxes under section 6413(c).

(C) Special rule.—Any amounts paid pursuant to an agreement under section 3121(*l*) (relating to agreements entered into by American employers with respect to foreign affiliates) which are equivalent to the taxes referred to in subparagraph (A)(i) shall be treated as taxes referred to in such subparagraph.

[(3) **Repealed.** Pub.L. 114–113, Div. Q, Title I, § 101(b), Dec. 18, 2015, 129 Stat. 3044]

[(4) **Repealed.** Pub.L. 114–113, Div. Q, Title I, § 101(b), Dec. 18, 2015, 129 Stat. 3044]

(5) Exception for taxpayers excluding foreign earned income.—Paragraph (1) shall not apply to any taxpayer for any taxable year if such taxpayer elects to exclude any amount from gross income under section 911 for such taxable year.

(e) Identification requirements.—

(1) Qualifying child identification requirement.—No credit shall be allowed under this section to a taxpayer with respect to any qualifying child unless the taxpayer includes the name and taxpayer identification number of such qualifying child on the return of tax for the taxable year and such taxpayer identification number was issued on or before the due date for filing such return.

(2) Taxpayer identification requirement.—No credit shall be allowed under this section if the identifying number of the taxpayer was issued after the due date for filing the return for the taxable year.

(f) Taxable year must be full taxable year.—Except in the case of a taxable year closed by reason of the death of the taxpayer, no credit shall be allowable under this section in the case of a taxable year covering a period of less than 12 months.

(g) Restrictions on taxpayers who improperly claimed credit in prior year.—

(1) Taxpayers making prior fraudulent or reckless claims.—

(A) In general.—No credit shall be allowed under this section for any taxable year in the disallowance period.

(B) Disallowance period.—For purposes of subparagraph (A), the disallowance period is—

(i) the period of 10 taxable years after the most recent taxable year for which there was a final determination that the taxpayer's claim of credit under this section was due to fraud, and

(ii) the period of 2 taxable years after the most recent taxable year for which there was a final determination that the taxpayer's claim of credit under this section was due to reckless or intentional disregard of rules and regulations (but not due to fraud).

(2) Taxpayers making improper prior claims.—In the case of a taxpayer who is denied credit under this section for any taxable year as a result of the deficiency procedures under subchapter B of chapter 63, no credit shall be allowed under this section for any subsequent taxable year unless the taxpayer provides such information as the Secretary may require to demonstrate eligibility for such credit.

(Added Pub.L. 105–34, Title I, § 101(a), Aug. 5, 1997, 111 Stat. 796; amended Pub.L. 105–206, Title VI, § 6003(a), July 22, 1998, 112 Stat. 790; Pub.L. 105–277, Div. J, Title II, § 2001(b), Oct. 21, 1998, 112 Stat. 2681–901; Pub.L. 106–170, Title V, § 501(b)(1), Dec. 17, 1999, 113 Stat. 1919; Pub.L. 107–16, Title II, §§ 201(a) to (b)(2)(C), (c)(1), (2), (d), 202(f)(2)(B), Title VI, § 618(b)(2)(A), June 7, 2001, 115 Stat. 45 to 47, 49, 108; Pub.L. 107–90, Title II, § 204(e)(1), Dec. 21, 2001, 115 Stat. 893; Pub.L. 107–147, Title IV, §§ 411(b), 417(23)(A), Mar. 9, 2002, 116 Stat. 45, 57; Pub.L. 108–27, Title I, § 101(a), May 28, 2003, 117 Stat. 753; Pub.L. 108–311, Title I, §§ 101(a), 102(a), 104(a), Title II, § 204, Title IV, § 408(b)(4), Oct. 4, 2004, 118 Stat. 1167, 1168, 1176, 1192; Pub.L. 109–135, Title IV, § 402(i)(3)(B), Dec. 21, 2005, 119 Stat. 2613; Pub.L. 110–172, § 11(c)(1), Dec. 29, 2007, 121 Stat. 2488; Pub.L. 110–343, Div. B, Title I, § 106(e)(2)(B), Title II, § 205(d)(1)(A), Div. C, Title V, § 501(a), Oct. 3, 2008, 122 Stat. 3817, 3838, 3876; Pub.L. 110–351, Title V, § 501(c)(1), Oct. 7, 2008, 122 Stat. 3979; Pub.L. 111–5, Div. B, Title I, §§ 1003(a), 1004(b)(1), 1142(b)(1)(A), 1144(b)(1)(A), Feb. 17, 2009, 123 Stat. 313, 314, 330, 332; Pub.L. 111–148, Title X, § 10909(b)(2)(A), Mar. 23, 2010, 124 Stat. 1023; Pub.L. 111–312, Title I, §§ 101(b)(1), 103(b), Dec. 17, 2010, 124 Stat. 3298, 3299; Pub.L. 112–240, Title I, §§ 103(b), 104(c)(2)(B), Jan. 2, 2013, 126 Stat. 2319, 2321; Pub.L. 113–295, Div. A, Title II, § 209(a), Dec. 19, 2014, 128 Stat. 4028; Pub.L. 114–27, Title VIII, § 807(a), June 29, 2015, 129 Stat. 418; Pub.L. 114–113, Div. Q, Title I, § 101(a), (b), Title II, §§ 205(a), (b), 208(a)(1), Dec. 18, 2015, 129 Stat. 3044, 3081, 3083.)

Sunset Provisions

Notwithstanding Pub.L. 107–16, § 901 [now repealed by Pub.L. 112–240, Title I, § 101(a)(1), Jan. 2, 2013, 126 Stat. 2315], such section shall apply to the amendments made by Pub.L. 111–148, § 10909, and the amendments made by Pub.L. 107–16, § 202, by substituting "Dec. 31, 2011" for "Dec. 31, 2010" in Pub.L. 107–16, § 901(a), see Pub.L. 111–148, § 10909(c), set out as a Sunset Provisions note under 26 U.S.C.A. § 1.

Pub.L. 111–5, Div. B, Title I, § 1004(e), Feb. 17, 2009, 123 Stat. 315, provided that: "The amendment made by subsection (b)(1) [amending subsec. (b)(3)(B) of this section] shall be subject to title IX of the Economic Growth and Tax Relief Reconciliation Act of 2001 [Pub.L. 107–16, Title IX, § 901 et seq., June 7, 2001, 115 Stat. 40, set out as a Sunset Provisions note under 26 U.S.C.A. § 1; now repealed by Pub.L. 112–240, Title I, § 101(a)(1), Jan. 2, 2013, 126 Stat. 2315] in the same manner as the provision of such Act to which such amendment relates."

Pub.L. 111–5, Div. B, Title I, § 1142(e), Feb. 17, 2009, 123 Stat. 331, provided that:

"**(e) Application of EGTRRA Sunset.**—The amendment made by subsection (b)(1)(A) [amending subsec. (b)(3)(B) of this section] shall be subject to title IX of the Economic Growth and Tax Relief Reconciliation Act of 2001 [Pub.L. 107–16, Title IX, § 901 et seq., June 7, 2001, 115 Stat. 40, set out as a Sunset Provisions note under 26 U.S.C.A. § 1; now repealed by Pub.L. 112–240, Title I, § 101(a)(1), Jan. 2, 2013, 126 Stat. 2315] in the same manner as the provision of such Act to which such amendment relates."

Pub.L. 111–5, Div. B, Title I, § 1144(d), Feb. 17, 2009, 123 Stat. 333, provided that:

"**(d) Application of EGTRRA Sunset.**—The amendment made by subsection (b)(1)(A) [amending subsec. (b)(3)(B) of this section] shall be subject to title IX of the Economic Growth and Tax Relief Reconciliation Act of 2001 [Pub.L. 107–16, Title IX, § 901 et seq., June 7, 2001, 115 Stat. 40, set out as a Sunset Provisions note under 26 U.S.C.A. § 1; now repealed by Pub.L. 112–240, Title I, § 101(a)(1), Jan. 2, 2013, 126 Stat. 2315] in the same manner as the provision of such Act to which such amendment relates."

Amendment by Pub.L. 110–343, Div. B, § 205(d)(1)(A), subject to Title IX of Pub.L. 107–16, Title IX, § 901, June 7, 2001, 115 Stat. 150 [now repealed by Pub.L. 112–240, Title I, § 101(a)(1), Jan. 2, 2013, 126 Stat. 2315], see Pub.L. 110–343, Div. B, § 205(f), set out in an Effective and Applicability Provisions note under this section.

Amendment by Pub.L. 110–343, Div. B, § 106(e)(2)(B), subject to Title IX of the Economic Growth and Tax Relief Reconciliation Act of 2001, Pub.L. 107–16, Title IX, § 901, June 7, 2001, 115 Stat. 150 [now repealed by Pub.L. 112–240, Title I, § 101(a)(1), Jan. 2, 2013, 126 Stat. 2315], see Pub.L. 110–343, Div. B, § 106(f)(3), set out in an Effective and Applicability Provisions note under 26 U.S.C.A. § 23.

The inapplicability, after December 31, 2012, of all provisions of, and amendments made by, the Economic Growth and Tax Relief Reconciliation Act of 2001, Pub.L. 107–16, provided for by Pub.L. 107–16, § 901 [now repealed by Pub.L. 112–240, Title I, § 101(a)(1), Jan. 2, 2013, 126 Stat. 2315], was itself made inapplicable to the provisions of, and amendments made by, subtitles A through F of Title VI of such Act [Pub.L. 107–16, Title VI, § 601 to 666], by Pub.L. 109-280, § 811, set out as a note under 26 U.S.C.A. § 1.

Amendments by Pub.L. 109–135, § 402(i)(3), subject to Title IX of the Economic Growth and Tax Relief Reconciliation Act of 2001 [Pub.L. 107–16, Title IX, § 901 et seq., June 7, 2001, 115 Stat. 40; now repealed by Pub.L. 112–240, Title I, § 101(a)(1), Jan. 2, 2013, 126 Stat. 2315], in the same manner as the provisions of that Act to which such amendment relates, see Pub.L. 109–135, § 402(i)(3)(H), set out as a note under 26 U.S.C.A. § 23.

Amendments made by Pub.L. 108–311, Title I, shall be subject to Title IX of the Economic Growth and Tax Relief Reconciliation Act of 2001, Pub.L. 107–16, Title IX, June 7, 2001, 115 Stat. 150 [now repealed by Pub.L. 112–240, Title I, § 101(a)(1), Jan. 2, 2013, 126 Stat. 2315], to the same extent and in the same manner as the provision of such Act to which such amendment relates, see Pub.L. 108–311, § 105, set out as a note under 26 U.S.C.A. § 1.

Amendment to this section by Title I of Pub.L. 108–27 subject to Title IX of the Economic Growth and Tax Relief Reconciliation Act of 2001 [now repealed by Pub.L. 112–240, Title I, § 101(a)(1), Jan. 2, 2013, 126 Stat. 2315], set out as a Sunset Provision under 26 U.S.C.A. § 1, to the same extent and in the same manner as the provision of such Act to which such amendment relates, see Pub.L. 108–27, § 107, set out as a note under 26 U.S.C.A. § 1.

Pub.L. 107–16, § 901, which provided for sunset of amendments by the Economic Growth and Tax Relief Reconciliation Act of

2001, Pub.L. 107–16, June 7, 2001, 115 Stat. 38, was repealed by Pub.L. 112–240, Title I, § 101(a)(1), Jan. 2, 2013, 126 Stat. 2315; see Pub. L. 107–16, § 901, as amended and repealed, set out as a Sunset Provisions note under 26 U.S.C.A. § 1.

Commentary

Gentry (LaTashia) v. Commissioner, T.C. Memo. 2013-16, held that minor cousins of a taxpayer who qualified for a section 152(d) dependency exemption did not qualify for this section's child tax credit because the requirements of this section are more restrictive.

Applying sections 151 and 152 (e)(2), *Armstrong v. Commissioner of Internal Revenue, 745 F.3d 890 (8th Cir. 2014)*, held that the Tax Court properly denied dependency exemption deductions to noncustodial parents when the custodial parents failed to sign the necessary written declaration even though they had agreed to do so. Because dependency deductions were not available, under subsection (c) of this section, the noncustodial parents were not entitled to subsection (a) child tax credits for the children.

§ 25A. Hope and Lifetime Learning Credits

(a) Allowance of credit.—In the case of an individual, there shall be allowed as a credit against the tax imposed by this chapter for the taxable year the amount equal to the sum of—

(1) the Hope Scholarship Credit, plus

(2) the Lifetime Learning Credit.

(b) Hope Scholarship Credit.—

(1) Per student credit.—In the case of any eligible student for whom an election is in effect under this section for any taxable year, the Hope Scholarship Credit is an amount equal to the sum of—

(A) 100 percent of so much of the qualified tuition and related expenses paid by the taxpayer during the taxable year (for education furnished to the eligible student during any academic period beginning in such taxable year) as does not exceed $1,000, plus

(B) 50 percent of such expenses so paid as exceeds $1,000 but does not exceed the applicable limit.

(2) Limitations applicable to Hope Scholarship Credit.—

(A) Credit allowed only for 2 taxable years.—An election to have this section apply with respect to any eligible student for purposes of the Hope Scholarship Credit under subsection (a)(1) may not be made for any taxable year if such an election (by the taxpayer or any other individual) is in effect with respect to such student for any 2 prior taxable years.

(B) Credit allowed for year only if individual is at least ½ time student for portion of year.—The Hope Scholarship Credit under subsection (a)(1) shall not be allowed for a taxable year with respect to the qualified tuition and related expenses of an individual unless such individual is an eligible student for at least one academic period which begins during such year.

(C) Credit allowed only for first 2 years of postsecondary education.—The Hope Scholarship Credit under subsection (a)(1) shall not be allowed for a taxable year with respect to the qualified tuition and related expenses of an eligible student if the student has completed (before the beginning of such taxable year) the first 2 years of postsecondary education at an eligible educational institution.

(D) Denial of credit if student convicted of a felony drug offense.—The Hope Scholarship Credit under subsection (a)(1) shall not be allowed for qualified tuition and related expenses for the enrollment or attendance of a student for any academic period if such student has been convicted of a Federal or State felony offense consisting of the possession or distribution of a controlled substance before the end of the taxable year with or within which such period ends.

(3) Eligible student.—For purposes of this subsection, the term "eligible student" means, with respect to any academic period, a student who—

(A) meets the requirements of section 484(a)(1) of the Higher Education Act of 1965 (20 U.S.C. 1091(a)(1)), as in effect on the date of the enactment of this section, and

(B) is carrying at least ½ the normal full-time work load for the course of study the student is pursuing.

(4) Applicable limit.—For purposes of paragraph (1)(B), the applicable limit for any taxable year is an amount equal to 2 times the dollar amount in effect under paragraph (1)(A) for such taxable year.

(c) Lifetime Learning Credit.—

(1) Per taxpayer credit.—The Lifetime Learning Credit for any taxpayer for any taxable year is an amount equal to 20 percent of so much of the qualified tuition and related expenses paid by the taxpayer during the taxable year (for education furnished during any academic period beginning in such taxable year) as does not exceed $10,000 ($5,000 in the case of taxable years beginning before January 1, 2003).

(2) Special rules for determining expenses.—

(A) Coordination with Hope Scholarship.—The qualified tuition and related expenses with respect to an individual who is an eligible student for whom a Hope Scholarship Credit under subsection (a)(1) is allowed for the taxable year shall not be taken into account under this subsection.

(B) Expenses eligible for Lifetime Learning Credit.—For purposes of paragraph (1), qualified tuition and related expenses shall include expenses described in subsection (f)(1) with respect to any course of instruction at an eligible educational institution to acquire or improve job skills of the individual.

(d) Limitation based on modified adjusted gross income.—

(1) In general.—The amount which would (but for this subsection) be taken into account under subsection (a) for the taxable year shall be reduced (but not below zero) by the amount determined under paragraph (2).

(2) Amount of reduction.—The amount determined under this paragraph is the amount which bears the same ratio to the amount which would be so taken into account as—

(A) the excess of—

(i) the taxpayer's modified adjusted gross income for such taxable year, over

(ii) $40,000 ($80,000 in the case of a joint return), bears to

(B) $10,000 ($20,000 in the case of a joint return).

(3) Modified adjusted gross income.—The term "modified adjusted gross income" means the adjusted gross income of the taxpayer for the taxable year increased by any amount excluded from gross income under section 911, 931, or 933.

(e) Election not to have section apply.—A taxpayer may elect not to have this section apply with respect to the qualified tuition and related expenses of an individual for any taxable year.

(f) Definitions.—For purposes of this section—

(1) Qualified tuition and related expenses.—

(A) In general.—The term "qualified tuition and related expenses" means tuition and fees required for the enrollment or attendance of—

(i) the taxpayer,

(ii) the taxpayer's spouse, or

(iii) any dependent of the taxpayer with respect to whom the taxpayer is allowed a deduction under section 151,

at an eligible educational institution for courses of instruction of such individual at such institution.

(B) Exception for education involving sports, etc.—Such term does not include expenses with respect to any course or other education involving sports, games, or hobbies, unless such course or other education is part of the individual's degree program.

(C) Exception for nonacademic fees.—Such term does not include student activity fees, athletic fees, insurance expenses, or other expenses unrelated to an individual's academic course of instruction.

(2) Eligible educational institution.—The term "eligible educational institution" means an institution—

(A) which is described in section 481 of the Higher Education Act of 1965 (20 U.S.C. 1088), as in effect on the date of the enactment of this section, and

(B) which is eligible to participate in a program under title IV of such Act.

(g) Special rules.—

(1) Identification requirement.—No credit shall be allowed under subsection (a) to a taxpayer with respect to the qualified tuition and related expenses of an individual unless the taxpayer includes the name and taxpayer identification number of such individual on the return of tax for the taxable year.

(2) Adjustment for certain scholarships, etc.—The amount of qualified tuition and related expenses otherwise taken into account under subsection (a) with respect to an individual for an academic period shall be reduced (before the application of subsections (b), (c), and (d)) by the sum of any amounts paid for the benefit of such individual which are allocable to such period as—

(A) a qualified scholarship which is excludable from gross income under section 117,

(B) an educational assistance allowance under chapter 30, 31, 32, 34, or 35 of title 38, United States Code, or under chapter 1606 of title 10, United States Code, and

(C) a payment (other than a gift, bequest, devise, or inheritance within the meaning of section 102(a)) for such individual's educational expenses, or attributable to such individual's enrollment at an eligible educational institution, which is excludable from gross income under any law of the United States.

(3) Treatment of expenses paid by dependent.—If a deduction under section 151 with respect to an individual is allowed to another taxpayer for a taxable year beginning in the calendar year in which such individual's taxable year begins—

(A) no credit shall be allowed under subsection (a) to such individual for such individual's taxable year,

(B) qualified tuition and related expenses paid by such individual during such individual's taxable year shall be treated for purposes of this section as paid by such other taxpayer, and

(C) a statement described in paragraph (8) and received by such individual shall be treated as received by the taxpayer.

(4) Treatment of certain prepayments.—If qualified tuition and related expenses are paid by the taxpayer during a taxable year for an academic period which begins during the first 3 months following such taxable year, such academic period shall be treated for purposes of this section as beginning during such taxable year.

(5) Denial of double benefit.—No credit shall be allowed under this section for any expense for which a deduction is allowed under any other provision of this chapter.

(6) No credit for married individuals filing separate returns.—If the taxpayer is a married individual (within the meaning of section 7703), this section shall apply only if the taxpayer and the taxpayer's spouse file a joint return for the taxable year.

(7) Nonresident aliens.—If the taxpayer is a nonresident alien individual for any portion of the taxable year, this section shall apply only if such individual is treated as a resident alien of the United States for purposes of this chapter by reason of an election under subsection (g) or (h) of section 6013.

(8) Payee statement requirement.—Except as otherwise provided by the Secretary, no credit shall be allowed under this section unless the taxpayer receives a statement furnished under section 6050S(d) which contains all of the information required by paragraph (2) thereof.

(h) Inflation adjustments.—

(1) Dollar limitation on amount of credit.—

(A) In general.—In the case of a taxable year beginning after 2001, each of the $1,000 amounts under subsection (b)(1) shall be increased by an amount equal to—

(i) such dollar amount, multiplied by

(ii) the cost-of-living adjustment determined under section 1(f)(3) for the calendar year in which the taxable year begins, determined by substituting "calendar year 2000" for "calendar year 1992" in subparagraph (B) thereof.

(B) Rounding.—If any amount as adjusted under subparagraph (A) is not a multiple of $100, such amount shall be rounded to the next lowest multiple of $100.

(2) Income limits.—

(A) In general.—In the case of a taxable year beginning after 2001, the $40,000 and $80,000 amounts in subsection (d)(2) shall each be increased by an amount equal to—

(i) such dollar amount, multiplied by

(ii) the cost-of-living adjustment determined under section 1(f)(3) for the calendar year in which the taxable year begins, determined by substituting "calendar year 2000" for "calendar year 1992" in subparagraph (B) thereof.

(B) Rounding.—If any amount as adjusted under subparagraph (A) is not a multiple of $1,000, such amount shall be rounded to the next lowest multiple of $1,000.

(i) American Opportunity Tax Credit.—In the case of any taxable year beginning after 2008—

(1) Increase in credit.—The Hope Scholarship Credit shall be an amount equal to the sum of—

(A) 100 percent of so much of the qualified tuition and related expenses paid by the taxpayer during the taxable year (for education furnished to the eligible student during any academic period beginning in such taxable year) as does not exceed $2,000, plus

(B) 25 percent of such expenses so paid as exceeds $2,000 but does not exceed $4,000.

(2) Credit allowed for first 4 years of post-secondary education.—Subparagraphs (A) and (C) of subsection (b)(2) shall be applied by substituting "4" for "2".

(3) Qualified tuition and related expenses to include required course materials.—For purposes of determining the Hope Scholarship Credit, subsection (f)(1)(A) shall be applied by substituting "tuition, fees, and course materials" for "tuition and fees".

(4) Increase in AGI limits for Hope Scholarship Credit.—In lieu of applying subsection (d) with respect to the Hope Scholarship Credit, such credit (determined without regard to this paragraph) shall be reduced (but not below zero) by the amount which bears the same ratio to such credit (as so determined) as—

(A) the excess of—

(i) the taxpayer's modified adjusted gross income (as defined in subsection (d)(3)) for such taxable year, over

(ii) $80,000 ($160,000 in the case of a joint return), bears to

(B) $10,000 ($20,000 in the case of a joint return).

(5) Portion of credit made refundable.—40 percent of so much of the credit allowed under subsection (a) as is attributable to the Hope Scholarship Credit (determined after application of paragraph (4) and without regard to this paragraph and section 26(a)) shall be treated as a credit allowable under subpart C (and not allowed under subsection (a)). The preceding sentence shall not apply to any taxpayer for any taxable year if such taxpayer is a child to whom subsection (g) of section 1 applies for such taxable year.

(6) Identification numbers.—

(A) Student.—The requirements of subsection (g)(1) shall not be treated as met with respect to the Hope Scholarship Credit unless the individual's taxpayer identification number was issued on or before the due date for filing the return of tax for the taxable year.

(B) Taxpayer.—No Hope Scholarship Credit shall be allowed under this section if the identifying number of the taxpayer was issued after the due date for filing the return for the taxable year.

(C) Institution.—No Hope Scholarship Credit shall be allowed under this section unless the taxpayer includes the employer identification number of any institution to which qualified tuition and related expenses were paid with respect to the individual.

(7) Restrictions on taxpayers who improperly claimed credit in prior year.—

(A) Taxpayers making prior fraudulent or reckless claims.—

(i) In general.—No credit shall be allowed under this section for any taxable year in the disallowance period.

(ii) Disallowance period.—For purposes of clause (i), the disallowance period is—

(I) the period of 10 taxable years after the most recent taxable year for which there was a final determination that the taxpayer's claim of credit under this section was due to fraud, and

(II) the period of 2 taxable years after the most recent taxable year for which there was a final determination that the taxpayer's claim of credit under this section was due to reckless or intentional disregard of rules and regulations (but not due to fraud).

(B) Taxpayers making improper prior claims.—In the case of a taxpayer who is denied credit under this section for any taxable year as a result of the deficiency procedures under subchapter B of chapter 63, no credit shall be allowed under this section for any subsequent taxable year unless the taxpayer provides such information as the Secretary may require to demonstrate eligibility for such credit.

(j) Regulations.—The Secretary may prescribe such regulations as may be necessary or appropriate to carry out this section, including regulations providing for a recapture of the credit allowed under this section in cases where there is a refund in a subsequent taxable year of any amount which was taken into account in determining the amount of such credit. *(Added Pub.L. 105–34, Title II, § 201(a), Aug. 5, 1997, 111 Stat. 799; amended Pub.L. 107–16, Title IV, § 401(g)(2)(A), June 7, 2001, 115 Stat. 60; Pub.L. 111–5, Div. B, Title I, § 1004(a), Feb. 17, 2009, 123 Stat. 313; Pub.L. 111–148, Title X, § 10909(b)(2)(C), Mar. 23, 2010, 124 Stat. 1023; Pub.L. 111–312, Title I, §§ 101(b)(1), 103(a)(1), Dec. 17, 2010, 124 Stat. 3298, 3299; Pub.L. 112–240, Title I, §§ 103(a)(1), 104(c)(2)(D), Jan. 2, 2013, 126 Stat. 2319, 2322; Pub.L. 113–295, Div. A, Title II, § 209(b), Dec. 19, 2014, 128 Stat. 4028; Pub.L. 114–27, Title VIII, § 804(a), June 29, 2015, 129 Stat. 415; Pub.L. 114–113, Div. Q, Title I, § 102(a), Title II, §§ 206(a), 208(a)(2), 211(a), Dec. 18, 2015, 129 Stat. 3044, 3082, 3083, 3085.)*

Sunset Provisions

Notwithstanding Pub.L. 107–16, § 901 [now repealed by Pub.L. 112–240, Title I, § 101(a)(1), Jan. 2, 2013, 126 Stat. 2315], such section shall apply to the amendments made by Pub.L. 111–148, § 10909, and the amendments made by Pub.L. 107–16, § 202, by substituting "Dec. 31, 2011" for "Dec. 31, 2010" in Pub.L. 107–16, —901(a), see Pub.L. 111–148, § 10909(c), set out as a Sunset Provisions note under 26 U.S.C.A. § 1.

Pub.L. 107–16, § 901, which provided for sunset of amendments by the Economic Growth and Tax Relief Reconciliation Act of 2001, Pub.L. 107–16, June 7, 2001, 115 Stat. 38, was repealed by Pub.L. 112–240, Title I, § 101(a)(1), Jan. 2, 2013, 126 Stat. 2315; see Pub.L. 107–16, § 901, as amended and repealed, set out as a Sunset Provisions note under 26 U.S.C.A. § 1.

Commentary

Guidelines pertaining to this section are published at I.R.S. Notice 97–60 and I.R.B. 1997–46 (10/27/97).

Subpart C—Refundable Credits

§ 32. Earned income

(a) Allowance of credit.—

(1) In general.—In the case of an eligible individual, there shall be allowed as a credit against the tax imposed by this subtitle for the taxable year an amount equal to the credit percentage of so much of the taxpayer's earned income for the taxable year as does not exceed the earned income amount.

(2) Limitation.—The amount of the credit allowable to a taxpayer under paragraph (1) for any taxable year shall not exceed the excess (if any) of—

(A) the credit percentage of the earned income amount, over

(B) the phaseout percentage of so much of the adjusted gross income (or, if greater, the earned income) of the taxpayer for the taxable year as exceeds the phaseout amount.

(b) Percentages and amounts.—For purposes of subsection (a)—

(1) Percentages.—The credit percentage and the phaseout percentage shall be determined as follows:

In the case of an eligible individual with:	The credit percentage is:	The phaseout percentage is:
1 qualifying child	34	15.98
2 qualifying children	40	21.06
3 or more qualifying children	45	21.06
No qualifying children	7.65	7.65

(2) Amounts.—

(A) In general.—Subject to subparagraph (B), the earned income amount and the phaseout amount shall be determined as follows:

In the case of an eligible individual with:	The earned income amount is:	The phaseout amount is:
1 qualifying child	$6,330	$11,610
2 or more qualifying children	$8,890	$11,610
No qualifying children	$4,220	$ 5,280

(B) Joint returns.—

(i) In general.—In the case of a joint return filed by an eligible individual and such individual's spouse, the phaseout amount determined under subparagraph (A) shall be increased by $5,000.

(ii) Inflation adjustment.—In the case of any taxable year beginning after 2015, the $5,000 amount in clause (i) shall be increased by an amount equal to—

(I) such dollar amount, multiplied by

(II) the cost of living adjustment determined under section 1(f)(3) for the calendar year in which the taxable year begins determined by substituting "calendar year 2008" for "calendar year 1992" in subparagraph (B) thereof.

(iii) Rounding.—Subparagraph (A) of subsection (j)(2) shall apply after taking into account any increase under clause (ii).

[**(3) Repealed.** Pub.L. 114–113, Div. Q, Title I, § 103(c), Dec. 18, 2015, 129 Stat. 3045]

(c) Definitions and special rules.—For purposes of this section—

(1) Eligible individual.—

(A) In general.—The term "eligible individual" means—

(i) any individual who has a qualifying child for the taxable year, or

(ii) any other individual who does not have a qualifying child for the taxable year, if—

(I) such individual's principal place of abode is in the United States for more than one-half of such taxable year,

(II) such individual (or, if the individual is married, either the individual or the individual's spouse) has attained age 25 but not attained age 65 before the close of the taxable year, and

(III) such individual is not a dependent for whom a deduction is allowable under section 151 to another taxpayer for any taxable year beginning in the same calendar year as such taxable year.

For purposes of the preceding sentence, marital status shall be determined under section 7703.

(B) Qualifying child ineligible.—If an individual is the qualifying child of a taxpayer for any taxable year of such taxpayer beginning in a calendar year, such individual shall not be treated as an eligible individual for any taxable year of such individual beginning in such calendar year.

(C) Exception for individual claiming benefits under section 911.—The term "eligible individual" does not include any individual who claims the benefits of section 911 (relating to citizens or residents living abroad) for the taxable year.

(D) Limitation on eligibility of nonresident aliens.—The term "eligible individual" shall not include any individual who is a nonresident alien individual for any portion of the taxable year unless such individual is treated for such taxable year as a resident of the United States for purposes of this chapter by reason of an election under subsection (g) or (h) of section 6013.

(E) Identification number requirement.—No credit shall be allowed under this section to an eligible individual who does not include on the return of tax for the taxable year—

(i) such individual's taxpayer identification number, and

(ii) if the individual is married (within the meaning of section 7703), the taxpayer identification number of such individual's spouse.

(F) Individuals who do not include TIN, etc., of any qualifying child.—No credit shall be allowed under this section to any eligible individual who has one or more qualifying children if no qualifying child of such individual is taken into account under subsection (b) by reason of paragraph (3)(D).

(2) Earned income.—

(A) The term "earned income" means—

(i) wages, salaries, tips, and other employee compensation, but only if such amounts are includible in gross income for the taxable year, plus

(ii) the amount of the taxpayer's net earnings from self-employment for the taxable year (within the meaning of section 1402(a)), but such net earnings shall be determined with regard to the deduction allowed to the taxpayer by section 164(f).

(B) For purposes of subparagraph (A)—

(i) the earned income of an individual shall be computed without regard to any community property laws,

(ii) no amount received as a pension or annuity shall be taken into account,

(iii) no amount to which section 871(a) applies (relating to income of nonresident alien individuals not connected with United States business) shall be taken into account,

(iv) no amount received for services provided by an individual while the individual is an inmate at a penal institution shall be taken into account,

(v) no amount described in subparagraph (A) received for service performed in work activities as defined in paragraph (4) or (7) of section 407(d) of the Social Security Act to which the taxpayer is assigned under any State program under part A of title IV of such Act shall be taken into account, but only to the extent such amount is subsidized under such State program, and

(vi) a taxpayer may elect to treat amounts excluded from gross income by reason of section 112 as earned income.

(3) Qualifying child.—

(A) In general.—The term "qualifying child" means a qualifying child of the taxpayer (as defined in section 152(c), determined without regard to paragraph (1)(D) thereof and section 152(e)).

(B) Married individual.—The term "qualifying child" shall not include an individual who is married as of the close of the taxpayer's taxable year unless the taxpayer is entitled to a deduction under section 151 for such taxable year with respect to such individual (or would be so entitled but for section 152(e)).

(C) Place of abode.—For purposes of subparagraph (A), the requirements of section 152(c)(1)(B) shall be met only if the principal place of abode is in the United States.

(D) Identification requirements.—

(i) In general.—A qualifying child shall not be taken into account under subsection (b) unless the taxpayer includes the name, age, and TIN of the qualifying child on the return of tax for the taxable year.

(ii) Other methods.—The Secretary may prescribe other methods for providing the information described in clause (i).

(4) Treatment of military personnel stationed outside the United States.—For purposes of paragraphs (1)(A)(ii)(I) and (3)(C), the principal place of abode of a member of the Armed Forces of the United States shall be treated as in the United States during any period during which such member is stationed outside the United States while serving on extended active duty with the Armed Forces of the United States. For purposes of the preceding sentence, the term "extended active duty" means any period of active duty pursuant to a call or order to such duty for a period in excess of 90 days or for an indefinite period.

(d) Married individuals.—In the case of an individual who is married (within the meaning of section 7703), this section shall apply only if a joint return is filed for the taxable year under section 6013.

(e) Taxable year must be full taxable year.—Except in the case of a taxable year closed by reason of the death of the taxpayer, no credit shall be allowable under this section in the case of a taxable year covering a period of less than 12 months.

(f) Amount of credit to be determined under tables.—

(1) In general.—The amount of the credit allowed by this section shall be determined under tables prescribed by the Secretary.

(2) Requirements for tables.—The tables prescribed under paragraph (1) shall reflect the provisions of subsections (a) and (b) and shall have income brackets of not greater than $50 each—

(A) for earned income between $0 and the amount of earned income at which the credit is phased out under subsection (b), and

(B) for adjusted gross income between the dollar amount at which the phaseout begins under subsection (b) and the amount of adjusted gross income at which the credit is phased out under subsection (b).

[(g) Repealed. Pub.L 111–226, Title II, § 219(a)(2), Aug. 10, 2010, 124 Stat. 2403]

[(h) Repealed. Pub.L 107–16, Title III, § 303(c), June 7, 2001, 115 Stat. 55]

(i) Denial of credit for individuals having excessive investment income.—

(1) In general.—No credit shall be allowed under subsection (a) for the taxable year if the aggregate amount of disqualified income of the taxpayer for the taxable year exceeds $2,200.

(2) Disqualified income.—For purposes of paragraph (1), the term "disqualified income" means—

(A) interest or dividends to the extent includible in gross income for the taxable year,

(B) interest received or accrued during the taxable year which is exempt from tax imposed by this chapter,

(C) the excess (if any) of—

(i) gross income from rents or royalties not derived in the ordinary course of a trade or business, over

(ii) the sum of—

(I) the deductions (other than interest) which are clearly and directly allocable to such gross income, plus

(II) interest deductions properly allocable to such gross income,

(D) the capital gain net income (as defined in section 1222) of the taxpayer for such taxable year, and

(E) the excess (if any) of—

(i) the aggregate income from all passive activities for the taxable year (determined without regard to any amount included in earned income under subsection (c)(2) or described in a preceding subparagraph), over

(ii) the aggregate losses from all passive activities for the taxable year (as so determined).

For purposes of subparagraph (E), the term "passive activity" has the meaning given such term by section 469.

(j) Inflation adjustments.—

(1) In general.—In the case of any taxable year beginning after 1996, each of the dollar amounts in subsections (b)(2) and (i)(1) shall be increased by an amount equal to—

(A) such dollar amount, multiplied by

(B) the cost-of-living adjustment determined under section 1(f)(3) for the calendar year in which the taxable year begins, determined—

(i) in the case of amounts in subsections (b)(2)(A) and (i)(1), by substituting "calendar year 1995" for "calendar year 1992" in subparagraph (B) thereof, and

(ii) in the case of the $3,000 amount in subsection (b)(2)(B)(iii), by substituting "calendar year 2007" for "calendar year 1992" in subparagraph (B) of such section 1.

(2) Rounding.—

(A) In general.—If any dollar amount in subsection (b)(2)(A) (after being increased under subparagraph (B) thereof), after being increased under paragraph (1), is not a multiple of $10, such dollar amount shall be rounded to the nearest multiple of $10.

(B) Disqualified income threshold amount.—If the dollar amount in subsection (i)(1), after being increased under paragraph (1), is not a multiple of $50, such amount shall be rounded to the next lowest multiple of $50.

(k) Restrictions on taxpayers who improperly claimed credit in prior year

(1) Taxpayers making prior fraudulent or reckless claims

(A) In general.—No credit shall be allowed under this section for any taxable year in the disallowance period.

(B) Disallowance period.—For purposes of paragraph (1), the disallowance period is—

(i) the period of 10 taxable years after the most recent taxable year for which there was a final determination that the taxpayer's claim of credit under this section was due to fraud, and

(ii) the period of 2 taxable years after the most recent taxable year for which there was a final determination that the taxpayer's claim of credit under this section was due to reckless or intentional disregard of rules and regulations (but not due to fraud).

(2) Taxpayers making improper prior claims.—In the case of a taxpayer who is denied credit under this section for any taxable year as a result of the deficiency procedures under subchapter B of chapter 63, no credit shall be allowed under this section for any subsequent taxable year unless the taxpayer provides such information as the Secretary may require to demonstrate eligibility for such credit.

(*l*) Coordination with certain means-tested programs.—For purposes of—

(1) the United States Housing Act of 1937,

(2) title V of the Housing Act of 1949,

(3) section 101 of the Housing and Urban Development Act of 1965,

(4) sections 221(d)(3), 235, and 236 of the National Housing Act, and

(5) the Food and Nutrition Act of 2008,

any refund made to an individual (or the spouse of an individual) by reason of this section, and any payment made to such individual (or such spouse) by an employer under section 3507, shall not be treated as income (and shall not be taken into account in determining resources for the month of its receipt and the following month).

(m) Identification numbers.—Solely for purposes of subsections (c)(1)(E) and (c)(3)(D), a taxpayer identification number means a social security number issued to an individual by the Social Security Administration (other than a social security number issued pursuant to clause (II) (or that portion of clause (III) that relates to clause (II)) of section 205(c)(2)(B)(i) of the Social Security Act) on or before the due date for filing the return for the taxable year. *(Added Pub.L. 94–12, Title II, § 204(a), Mar. 29, 1975, 89 Stat. 30, § 43; amended Pub.L. 94–164, § 2(c), Dec. 23, 1975, 89 Stat. 971; Pub.L. 94–455, Title IV, § 401(c)(1)(B), (2), Oct. 4, 1976, 90 Stat. 1557; Pub.L. 95–600, Title I, §§ 104(a) to (e), 105(a), Nov. 6, 1978, 92 Stat. 2772, 2773; Pub.L. 95–615, § 202(g)(5), formerly § 202(f)(5), Nov. 8, 1978, 92 Stat. 3100; renumbered § 202(g)(5) and amended Pub.L. 96–222, Title I, §§ 101(a)(1), (2)(E), 108(a)(1)(A) Apr. 1, 1980, 94 Stat. 194, 195, 223; Pub.L. 97–34, Title I, §§ 111(b)(2), 112(b)(3), Aug. 13, 1981, 95 Stat. 194, 195; Pub.L. 98–21, Title I, § 124(c)(4)(B), Apr. 20, 1983, 97 Stat. 91; renumbered § 32 and amended Pub.L. 98–369, Title IV, §§ 423(c)(3), 471(c), Title X, § 1042(a) to (d)(2), July 18, 1984, 98 Stat. 801, 826, 1043; Pub.L. 99–514, Title I, §§ 104(b)(1)(B), 111(a) to (d)(1), Title XII, § 1272(d)(4), Title XIII, § 1301(j)(8), Oct. 22, 1986, 100 Stat. 2103, 2107, 2108, 2594, 2658; Pub.L. 100–647, Title I, §§ 1001(c), 1007(g)(12), Nov. 10, 1988, 102 Stat. 3350, 3436; Pub.L. 101–508, Title XI, §§ 11101(d)(1)(B), 11111(a), (b), (e), Nov. 5, 1990, 104 Stat. 1388–405, 1388–408, 1388–412, 1388–413; Pub.L. 103–66, Title XIII, § 13131(a) to (d)(1), Aug. 10, 1993, 107 Stat. 433 to 435; Pub.L. 103–465, Title VII, §§ 721(a), 722(a), 723(a), 742(a), Dec. 8, 1994, 108 Stat. 5002, 5003, 5010; Pub.L. 104–7, § 4(a), Apr. 11, 1995, 109 Stat. 95; Pub.L. 104–193, Title IV, § 451(a), (b), Title IX, §§ 909(a), (b), 910(a), (b), Aug. 22, 1996, 110 Stat. 2276, 2277, 2351, 2352; Pub.L. 105–34, Title I, § 101(b), Title III, § 312(d)(2), Title X, § 1085(a)(1), (b) to (d), Aug. 5, 1997, 111 Stat. 798, 840, 955 to 957; Pub.L. 105–206, Title VI, §§ 6003(b)(1), 6010(p)(1), (2), 6021(a), (b), July 22, 1998, 112 Stat. 791, 816, 817, 823, 824; Pub.L. 106–170, Title IV, § 412(a), Dec. 17, 1999, 113 Stat. 1917; Pub.L. 107–16, Title II, § 201(c)(3), Title III, § 303(a) to (f), (h), June 7, 2001, 115 Stat. 47, 55–57; Pub.L. 107–147, Title IV, § 416(a)(1), Mar. 9, 2002, 116 Stat. 55; Pub.L. 108–311, Title I, § 104(b), Title II, § 205, Oct. 4, 2004, 118 Stat. 1169, 1176; Pub.L. 109–135, Title III, § 302(a), Dec. 21, 2005, 119 Stat. 2608; Pub.L. 109–432, Div. A, Title I, § 106(a), Dec. 20, 2006, 120 Stat. 2938; Pub.L. 110–234, Title IV, § 4002(b)(1)(B), (2)(O), May 22, 2008, 122 Stat. 1096, 1097; Pub.L. 110–245, Title I, § 102(a), June 17, 2008, 122 Stat. 1625; Pub.L. 110–246, § 4(a), Title IV, § 4002(b)(1)(B), (2)(O), June 18, 2008, 122 Stat. 1664, 1857, 1858; Pub.L. 111–5, Div. B, Title I, § 1002(a), Feb. 17, 2009, 123 Stat. 312; Pub.L. 111–226, Title II, § 219(a)(2), Aug. 10, 2010, 124 Stat. 2403; Pub.L. 111–312, Title I, § 103(c), Dec. 17, 2010, Stat. 3299; Pub.L. 112–240, Title I, § 103(c), Jan. 2, 2013, 126 Stat. 2319; Pub.L. 113–295, Div. A, Title II, §§ 206(a), 221(a)(3), Dec. 19, 2014, 128 Stat. 4027, 4037; Pub.L. 114–113, Div. Q, Title I, § 103(a) to (c), Title II, § 204(a), Dec. 18, 2015, 129 Stat. 3044, 3081.)*

Commentary

Skaggs (Kevin Dewitt) v. Commissioner, 148 T.C. No. 15 (2017), held that income earned by a convicted felon employed in a state hospital during the period of his sentence was, under subsection (c)(2)(B)(iv), not included as income for the purpose of obtaining an earned income tax credit.

In *Rasco (Samuel K.) v. Commissioner, T.C. Memo. 1999–169, 1999 WL 311796 (U.S. Tax Ct. 1999),* the Tax Court held that an unmarried taxpayer could take dependency exemptions for his girlfriend and her two children from a previous marriage when all three lived in the taxpayer's home and received more than half their support from him; consequently, the taxpayer also qualified for head-of-household filing status and the earned income credit, using the two children as "qualifying children" for purposes of the credit.

Jeter (John) v. Commissioner, T.C. Memo 2001–223, 82 T.C.M. (CCH) 445 (U.S. Tax Ct. 2001), aff'd 26 Fed.Appx. 321, 2002 WL 185470 (4th Cir. 2002), holds that, for purposes of the earned income credit, hours spent by children before and after school in the home of a separated parent are not to be considered in determining the children's "principal place of abode" (subsection (c)(3)) for purposes of the earned income credit or in determining whether a parent had "custody for a greater portion of the calendar year" for purposes of the § 152 dependency deduction.

Abdi (Mahamud) v. Commissioner, T.C. Memo 2015-41, interpreting subsection (c)(3)(A) and section 152(c), held that a family member living in an apartment adjacent to the taxpayer's apartment is not a "qualifying child" for purposes of the Earned Income Tax Credit.

Rowe (Cynthia L.) v. Commissioner, 128 T.C. 13, Tax Ct. Rep.(CCH) 56,844 (U.S. Tax Ct. 2007), held that pre-conviction jail time should be disregarded as a "temporary absence" in determining whether a parent shared a residence with her children for purposes of the earned income credit.

SUBCHAPTER B—COMPUTATION OF TAXABLE INCOME

PART I—DEFINITION OF GROSS INCOME, ADJUSTED GROSS INCOME, TAXABLE INCOME, ETC.

§ 61. Gross income defined

(a) General definition.—Except as otherwise provided in this subtitle, gross income means all income from whatever source derived, including (but not limited to) the following items:

(1) Compensation for services, including fees, commissions, fringe benefits, and similar items;

(2) Gross income derived from business;

(3) Gains derived from dealings in property;

(4) Interest;

(5) Rents;

(6) Royalties;

(7) Dividends;

(8) Alimony and separate maintenance payments;

(9) Annuities;

(10) Income from life insurance and endowment contracts;

(11) Pensions;

(12) Income from discharge of indebtedness;

(13) Distributive share of partnership gross income;

(14) Income in respect of a decedent; and

(15) Income from an interest in an estate or trust.

(b) Cross references.—

For items specifically included in gross income, see part II (sec. 71 and following). For items specifically excluded from gross income, see part III (sec. 101 and following).

(Aug. 16, 1954, c. 736, 68A Stat. 17; Pub.L. 98–369, Title V, § 531(c), July 18, 1984, 98 Stat. 884.)

Commentary

Although alimony may be deducted from the income of the payor under § 215, wages from which alimony is ultimately paid are treated as income under this section. In *Chambers (Horace M.) v. Commissioner, T.C. Memo. 2000–218, 80 T.C.M. (CCH) 73 (U.S. Tax Ct. 2000)*, taxpayer claimed that amounts garnished from his wages to pay child support and alimony should not be included in income under this section. The Tax Court rejected the argument, holding that taxpayer must include his ungarnished wages as income, but could take a deduction for the amounts garnished for alimony.

Note that distributions to a spouse or former spouse who is an alternate payee under a QDRO (see 29 U.S.C.A. § 1056) are taxable to that spouse or former spouse under § 402(e)(1)(A). However, a distribution from a qualified retirement plan to a participant's daughter to satisfy a child support obligation is taxable to the participant. *Stahl (Robert L.) v. Commissioner, T.C. Memo. 2001–22, 81 T.C.M. (CCH) 1087 (U.S. Tax Ct. 2001)*.

A court order requiring an ex-husband to liquidate a profit-sharing plan to pay child support and spousal support arrearages to his ex-wife was not a QDRO. Thus the distribution was taxable to him and not to her. He could, of course, take an alimony deduction under sections 71 and 215 for the amount attributable to spousal support. *Amarasinghe (Jeanne E.) v. Commissioner, T.C. Memo 2007–333, 94 T.C.M. (CCH) 447 (U.S. Tax Ct. 2007)*.

§ 66. Treatment of community income

(a) Treatment of community income where spouses live apart.—If—

(1) 2 individuals are married to each other at any time during a calendar year;

(2) such individuals—

(A) live apart at all times during the calendar year, and

(B) do not file a joint return under section 6013 with each other for a taxable year beginning or ending in the calendar year;

(3) one or both of such individuals have earned income for the calendar year which is community income; and

(4) no portion of such earned income is transferred (directly or indirectly) between such individuals before the close of the calendar year,

then, for purposes of this title, any community income of such individuals for the calendar year shall be treated in accordance with the rules provided by section 879(a).

(b) Secretary may disregard community property laws where spouse not notified of community income.—The Secretary may disallow the benefits of any community property law to any taxpayer with respect to any income if such taxpayer acted as if solely entitled to such income and failed to notify the taxpayer's spouse before the due date (including extensions) for filing the return for the taxable year in which the income was derived of the nature and amount of such income.

(c) Spouse relieved of liability in certain other cases.—Under regulations prescribed by the Secretary, if—

(1) an individual does not file a joint return for any taxable year,

(2) such individual does not include in gross income for such taxable year an item of community income properly includible therein which, in accordance with the rules contained in section 879(a), would be treated as the income of the other spouse,

(3) the individual establishes that he or she did not know of, and had no reason to know of, such item of community income, and

(4) taking into account all facts and circumstances, it is inequitable to include such item of community income in such individual's gross income,

then, for purposes of this title, such item of community income shall be included in the gross income of the other spouse (and not in the gross income of the individual). Under procedures prescribed by the Secretary, if, taking into account all the facts and circumstances, it is inequitable to hold the individual liable for any unpaid tax or any deficiency (or any portion of either) attributable to any item for which relief is not available under the preceding sentence, the Secretary may relieve such individual of such liability.

(d) Definitions.—For purposes of this section—

(1) Earned income.—The term "earned income" has the meaning given to such term by section 911(d)(2).

(2) Community income.—The term "community income" means income which, under applicable community property laws, is treated as community income.

(3) Community property laws.—The term "community property laws" means the community property laws of a State, a foreign country, or a possession of the United States.

(Added Pub.L. 96–605, Title I, § 101(a), Dec. 28, 1980, 94 Stat. 3521; amended Pub.L. 98–369, Div. A, Title IV, § 424(b)(1), (2)(A), (B), July 18, 1984, 98 Stat. 802, 803; Pub.L. 101–239, Title VII, § 7841(d)(8), Dec. 19, 1989, 103 Stat. 2428; Pub.L. 105–206, Title III, § 3201(b), July 22, 1998, 112 Stat. 739.)

Commentary

A husband's placement of community property business income in a business bank account does not entitle his wife to subsection (b) treatment of that income. *Shea (John D.) v. Commissioner, 112 T.C. No. 14, Tax Ct. Rep. (CCH) 55318 (U.S. Tax Ct. 1999).*

Whether property is community property or separate property is a matter of governing state law. *Hardy (Cathy Miller) v. Commissioner, 181 F.3d 1002 (9th Cir. 1999).* Although the parties testified that they had an oral agreement that each spouse's earnings during marriage would be that party's separate property, under governing Nevada law this result may only be accomplished by written agreement or court order. Therefore, the husband's earnings during marriage were community property, half of which were taxable to the wife, who filed separate returns from 1981–1986. Nor was the wife eligible for relief under subsection (c), because she was aware of her husband's income.

In *Layman, II (Daniel F.) v. Commissioner, T.C. Memo. 1999–218, 78 T.C.M. (CCH) 11 (U.S. Tax Ct. 1999)*, the husband was domiciled in a community property state (Arizona) that considered his earnings community property despite his separation from his wife, who was domiciled in a separate property state. Although there was no written separation agreement, the husband regularly sent the wife funds to support herself and the children. The husband, under this section, reported only half his income on his tax return, reasoning that the other half was reportable by his wife. The Tax Court agreed, holding that income earned by the husband was divisible between the spouses for tax purposes, despite the wife's domicile in a separate property jurisdiction.

In *Bernal (Kathryn) v. Commissioner, 20 T.C. 102 (U.S. Tax Court 2003)*, the Tax Court declined to review an Internal Revenue Service denial of relief under this section when the court otherwise lacked general jurisdiction to hear the case because the petition for review had been filed too late to be treated as a general petition to review a tax deficiency. This section contains no special authorization for judicial review. Compare § 6015(e), which does contain special authorization to review denial of innocent spouse relief.

PART II—ITEMS SPECIFICALLY INCLUDED IN GROSS INCOME

§ 71. Alimony and separate maintenance payments

(a) General rule.—Gross income includes amounts received as alimony or separate maintenance payments.

(b) Alimony or separate maintenance payments defined.—For purposes of this section—

(1) In general.—The term "alimony or separate maintenance payment" means any payment in cash if—

(A) such payment is received by (or on behalf of) a spouse under a divorce or separation instrument,

(B) the divorce or separation instrument does not designate such payment as a payment which is not includible in gross income under this section and not allowable as a deduction under section 215,

(C) in the case of an individual legally separated from his spouse under a decree of divorce or of separate maintenance, the payee spouse and the payor spouse are not members of the same household at the time such payment is made, and

(D) there is no liability to make any such payment for any period after the death of the payee spouse and there is no liability to make any payment (in cash or property) as a substitute for such payments after the death of the payee spouse.

(2) Divorce or separation instrument.—The term "divorce or separation instrument" means—

(A) a decree of divorce or separate maintenance or a written instrument incident to such a decree,

(B) a written separation agreement, or

(C) a decree (not described in subparagraph (A)) requiring a spouse to make payments for the support or maintenance of the other spouse.

(c) Payments to support children.—

(1) In general.—Subsection (a) shall not apply to that part of any payment which the terms of the divorce or separation instrument fix (in terms of an amount of money or a part of the payment) as a sum which is payable for the support of children of the payor spouse.

(2) Treatment of certain reductions related to contingencies involving child.—For purposes of paragraph (1), if any amount specified in the instrument will be reduced—

(A) on the happening of a contingency specified in the instrument relating to a child (such as attaining a specified age, marrying, dying, leaving school, or a similar contingency), or

(B) at a time which can clearly be associated with a contingency of a kind specified in subparagraph (A),

an amount equal to the amount of such reduction will be treated as an amount fixed as payable for the support of children of the payor spouse.

(3) Special rule where payment is less than amount specified in instrument.—For purposes of this subsection, if any payment is less than the amount specified in the instrument, then so much of such payment as does not exceed the sum payable for support shall be considered a payment for such support.

(d) Spouse.—For purposes of this section, the term "spouse" includes a former spouse.

(e) Exception for joint returns.—This section and section 215 shall not apply if the spouses make a joint return with each other.

(f) Recomputation where excess front-loading of alimony payments.—

(1) In general.—If there are excess alimony payments—

(A) the payor spouse shall include the amount of such excess payments in gross income for the payor spouse's taxable year beginning in the 3rd post-separation year, and

(B) the payee spouse shall be allowed a deduction in computing adjusted gross income for the amount of such excess payments for the payee's taxable year beginning in the 3rd post-separation year.

(2) Excess alimony payments.—For purposes of this subsection, the term "excess alimony payments" mean the sum of—

(A) the excess payments for the 1st post-separation year, and

(B) the excess payments for the 2nd post-separation year.

(3) Excess payments for 1st post-separation year.— For purposes of this subsection, the amount of the excess payments for the 1st post-separation year is the excess (if any) of—

(A) the amount of the alimony or separate maintenance payments paid by the payor spouse during the 1st post-separation year, over

(B) the sum of—

(i) the average of—

(I) the alimony or separate maintenance payments paid by the payor spouse during the 2nd post-separation year, reduced by the excess payments for the 2nd post-separation year, and

(II) the alimony or separate maintenance payments paid by the payor spouse during the 3rd post-separation year, plus

(ii) $15,000.

(4) Excess payments for 2nd post-separation year.— For purposes of this subsection, the amount of the excess payments for the 2nd post-separation year is the excess (if any) of—

(A) the amount of the alimony or separate maintenance payments paid by the payor spouse during the 2nd post-separation year, over

(B) the sum of—

(i) the amount of the alimony or separate maintenance payments paid by the payor spouse during the 3rd post-separation year, plus

(ii) $15,000.

(5) Exceptions.—

(A) Where payment ceases by reason of death or remarriage.—Paragraph (1) shall not apply if—

(i) either spouse dies before the close of the 3rd post-separation year, or the payee spouse remarries before the close of the 3rd post-separation year, and

(ii) the alimony or separate maintenance payments cease by reason of such death or remarriage.

(B) Support payments.—For purposes of this subsection, the term "alimony or separate maintenance payment" shall not include any payment received under a decree described in subsection (b)(2)(C).

(C) Fluctuating payments not within control of payor spouse.—For purposes of this subsection, the term "alimony or separate maintenance payment" shall not include any payment to the extent it is made pursuant to a continuing liability (over a period of not less than 3 years) to pay a fixed portion or portions of the income from a business or property or from compensation for employment or self-employment.

(6) Post-separation years.—For purposes of this subsection, the term "1st post-separation years" means the 1st calendar year in which the payor spouse paid to the payee spouse alimony or separate maintenance payments to which this section applies. The 2nd and 3rd post-separation years shall be the 1st and 2nd succeeding calendar years, respectively.

(g) Cross references.—

(1) For deduction of alimony or separate maintenance payments, see section 215.

(2) For taxable status of income of an estate or trust in the case of divorce, etc., see section 682.

(Aug. 16, 1954, c. 736, 68A Stat. 19; Pub.L. 98–369, Div. A, Title IV, § 422(a), July 18, 1984, 98 Stat. 795; Pub.L. 99–514, Title XVIII, § 1843(a)–(c)(1), (d), Oct. 22, 1986, 100 Stat. 2853, 2855.)

Commentary

Support payments voluntarily made by a taxpayer to his mentally ill former wife did not qualify as alimony because he was under no written obligation to make the payments. *Anderson (Curtis L.) v. Commissioner, T.C. Memo 1999–53, 77 T.C.M. (CCH) 1447 (U.S. Tax Ct. 1999).* In *Leventhal (Hermine) v. Commissioner, T.C. Memo. 2000–92, 79 T.C.M. (CCH) 1670 (U.S. Tax Ct. 2000)*, the Tax Court held that the written agreement requirement of subsection (b) was not satisfied by a letter from the husband specifying a payment arrangement and the wife's subsequent acceptance of those payments, because it was not clear whether the wife agreed to those terms or even whether the terms had been submitted to her for approval. By contrast, a letter from the wife's attorney proposing additional payments, which was signed and returned as an acceptance by the husband's attorney, did constitute a written agreement and hence qualified those payments for tax treatment as alimony.

Dato-Nodurft (Antoinette J.) v. Commissioner, T.C. Memo. 2004–119, 87 T.C.M. (CCH) 1338 (U.S. Tax Ct. 2004), holds that payments made pursuant to a written separation agreement may be subject to this section even though the agreement is not enforceable under state law. All this section requires is a written agreement, made by mutual consent, defining the terms of support.

Mumtaz Ali v. Commissioner, T.C. Memo 2004–284, 88 T.C.M. (CCH) 662 (U.S. Tax Ct. 2004), holds that a retroactive divorce court order for family support is ineffective for purposes of subsection (b) of this section, and therefore family support payments made before entry of the order are not alimony for purposes of this section and Section 215.

Under subsection (b)(1)(D), payments must terminate at the death of the payee. Payments made with respect to obligations that under state law do not terminate on the payee's death do not qualify as alimony. *Preston (Forest R.) v. Commissioner, T.C. Memo. 1999–49, 77 T.C.M. (CCH) 1437 (U.S. Tax Ct. 1999).*

California Family Code section 4337 provides: "Except as otherwise agreed by the parties in writing, the obligation of a party under an order for the support of the other party terminates on the death of either party." In view of this provision, *Johanson v. Commissioner, 541 F.3d. 973 (9th Cir. 2008),* held that payments made pursuant to a California marital settlement agreement satisfied subsection (b)(1)(D) when the marital settlement agreement did not expressly state that spousal support payments would survive the payee's death and the payee failed to clearly and convincingly establish by extrinsic evidence that the parties had some other written agreement to continue payments after the payee's death. Compare *Stedman (Jack R.) v. Commissioner, T.C. Memo 2008–239 (U.S. Tax Court 2008),* where the Tax Court held that an ex-husband's California court-ordered payments of attorney's fees to his ex-wife's attorney were *not* deductible by him as alimony because the court order did not state that the payments would end at his ex-wife's death and, under California law, a court order to pay attorney's fees does not terminate at the death of an ex-wife, as does ordinary spousal support.

Le (Steven and Van) v. Commissioner, T.C. Memo 2008–183, 96 T.C.M. (CCH) 59 (U.S. Tax Ct. 2008), held that the payment of temporary spousal support arrearages qualified for alimony treatment where the obligation to make temporary support payments would have ended on the death of the payee spouse, even though the obligation to pay spousal support arrearages would not have terminated on the death of the payee spouse.

Dennis E. and Paula W. Lofstrom v. Commissioner, 125 T.C. 271 (U.S. Tax Ct. 2005), holds that a third-party installment note, transferred from an ex-husband to his ex-wife in settlement of support obligations, did not qualify as alimony because (1) it was not "cash" or a cash equivalent and (2) payments under the note would not terminate at the death of the ex-wife.

Interpreting subsection (b)(2), *Keegan v. Commissioner, T.C. Memo. 1997–359, 74 T.C.M. (CCH) 284 (1997),* holds that a letter proposing an amount of spousal support is not an "agreement," even though the proposal was ultimately accepted in a stipulated court order. Thus, payments made before entry of the order did not qualify as "alimony or separate maintenance" under this section. Compare *Richardson v. Commissioner, 125 F.3d 551 (7th Cir. 1997),* which, upholding the Tax Court, held that payments made pursuant to a written agreement qualified as alimony even though the agreement was voidable under state law and was subsequently found "procedurally and substantively unconscionable" on appeal to a state court.

Burkes v. Commissioner, T.C. Memo. 1998–61, 75 T.C.M. (CCH) 1772 (1998), held that a divorce decree provision requiring the husband to pay the wife $60,000 "additional alimony towards attorney fees," which obligation would terminate under state law at the wife's death, was sufficient to qualify the payments as "alimony" for purposes of I.R.C. §§ 71 and 215. Compare *Berry (Thomas D.) v. Commissioner, T.C. Memo. 2000–373, 80 T.C.M. (CCH) 825 (U.S. Tax Ct. 2000)* (husband who paid his wife's attorney fees under a court order in divorce action could not deduct the payment as alimony because, under state law, the obligation to pay would survive the wife's death); and *Human v. Commissioner, T.C. Memo. 1998–106, 75 T.C.M. (CCH) 1990 (1998),* holding that "lump-sum alimony" ordered by court does not qualify as "alimony" for tax purposes because under Georgia law the obligation to pay "lump-sum alimony" does not terminate at the obligee's death.

Nye (John D.) v Commissioner, T.C. Memo. 2103-166, held that a husband who paid a lump sum to satisfy all future support obligations could not deduct the amount as alimony, because the obligation to make the payment would not have expired had the wife died before it was approved by a court order.

For treatment of indirect alimony payments, see generally *Medlin (Alexandra M.) v. Commissioner, T.C. Memo. 1998–378, 76 T.C.M. (CCH) 707 (U.S. Tax Ct. 1998),* holding that medical insurance premiums and car expenses paid directly to the vendor by the support obligor for the benefit of a former spouse qualify as alimony. See also *Hopkinson (Helen C.) v. Commissioner, T.C. Memo. 1999–154, 77 T.C.M. (CCH) 1968 (U.S. Tax Ct. 1999)* (education expenses paid by former husband on behalf of former wife directly to college or as reimbursement to the wife, pursuant to the their settlement agreement that he would pay all her expenses in obtaining a college degree, are taxable to the wife as alimony and deductible by the husband); and *Baxter (Linda J.) v. Commissioner, T.C. Memo. 1999–190, 77 T.C.M. (CCH) 2137 (U.S. Tax Ct. 1999)* (mortgage payments made on residence as a form of support to a former wife, which met all statutory requirements, qualified as alimony taxable to the wife and deductible by the husband).But compare *Zinsmeister (Alan Robert) v. Commissioner, T.C. Memo. 2000–364, 80 T.C.M. (CCH) 774 (U.S. Tax Ct. 2000)* (divorced husband not allowed alimony deduction for mortgage payments he made on home owned and occupied by former wife because only husband was liable on the note).

Marten (Virginia M.) v. Commissioner, T.C. Memo. 1999–340 (U.S. Tax Ct. 1999), held that life insurance premiums on a policy insuring the taxpayer's life were taxable alimony to the wife even though the policy proceeds were intended for the support of their disabled child, because the policy was owned by the wife, and the decree did not specify that the premiums were for child support.

(Joshua H.) v. Commissioner, T.C. Summary Opinion 2015-25, allowed an ex-husband to treat homeschooling payments to his ex-wife as deductible alimony, because they were terminable not on a contingency related to the child, but rather one related to the ex-wife's decision to continue home schooling.

In *Jaffe (Irv C.) v. Commissioner, T.C. Memo. 1999–196, 77 T.C.M. (CCH) 2167 (U.S. Tax Ct. 1999),* the divorce court order authorized the wife to withdraw, from an account owned jointly and equally by the spouses, $500 a week as pendente lite alimony, with the proviso that the amount would "be credited against [the husband's] share at equitable distribution." The Tax Court held that only half the amount of the payments was properly treated as alimony taxable to the wife under this section (and deductible by the husband under § 215), for she owned the other half by virtue of her interest in the account.

"Unallocated child support and maintenance" payments made pendente lite pursuant to a Colorado State court decree were not deductible to the payor under § 215 or includable within the income of the payee spouse under this section, because they failed to satisfy subsection (b)(1)(D) in that, under Colorado law, they would not terminate on the death of the obligor but instead could only be terminated by court order. *Miller v. Commissioner, T.C. Memo. 1999–273, 78 T.C.M. (CCH) 307 (U.S. Tax Ct. 1999).* To the same effect, see *Gonzales (Marie A.) v. Commissioner, T.C. Memo. 1999–332, 78 T.C.M. (CCH) 527 (U.S. Tax Ct. 1999),* finding that under New Jersey law unallocated support payments would not necessarily terminate at the death of the payee spouse.

DeLong (Brendon) v. Commissioner, T.C. Memo. 2013-70, allowed a California father an alimony deduction for unallocated family support because California law requires termination of family support upon the death of the payee parent.

John R. Okerson v. Commissioner, 123 T.C. 258 (U.S. Tax Ct. 2004), holds that payments to be made in 113 installments to a

Tennessee ex-wife did not qualify as alimony where they would continue to be paid to the couple's children should the ex-wife die before full satisfaction of the obligation. Compare *Michael K. Berry v. Commissioner, T.C. Memo 2005–91, 89 T.C.M. (CCH) 1090 (U.S. Tax Ct. 2005)*, holding that despite the absence of an explicit provision in the divorce instrument for termination at the death of the payee spouse, unallocated family support payments qualified as alimony because, under California law, support payments to a spouse terminate at her death and the possibility, upon her death, that the children would not be in obligor's custody and he would continue to be required to pay child support is insufficient to prevent treatment of the family support payments as alimony. *Okerson* and *Berry* are reconcilable in terms of state law. In *Okerson*, the law of Tennessee conducts an open-ended inquiry into the intent of the parties to determine whether spousal support ends at the payee's death, while California Family Code § 4337 provides: "Except as otherwise agreed by the parties in writing, the obligation of a party under an order for the support of the other party terminates upon the death of either party."

Interpreting subsection (b), *Benham (Thomas B.) v. Commissioner, T.C. Memo. 2000–165, 79 T.C.M. (CCH) 2054 (U.S. Tax Ct. 2000)*, held that alimony payments were taxable to the payee under this section, and deductible by the payor under § 215, even though the parties continued to reside together in the marital residence, because the payments were made pursuant to a subsection (b)(2)(B) written separation agreement and the parties were not legally separated or divorced (see subsection (b)(1)(C) and Treasury Regs § 1.71–1T (b), Q & A 9).

Interpreting subsection (b)(1)(B), *Tucker (James Alton) v. Commissioner, T.C. Summary Opinion 2013-94*, holds that a state divorce decree that stated, over the support obligor's objection, that certain spousal support payments were nondeductible for income tax purposes was effective to deny alimony tax treatment and that the court would not look beyond the four corners of the agreement to consider whether the provision was voluntary.

When a support obligor pays child support and alimony arrearages, the arrearage payments are not applied to deductible alimony until the child support arrearages have been fully paid. *Farahani (Sam) v. Commissioner, T.C. Memo. 2014-111 (U.S. Tax Ct. 2014)*.

Interpreting subsection (c), Treasury Regs § 1.71–1T (c), Q & A 18, establish a presumption that a payment is child support when payments are to be reduced not more than six months before or after a child will reach the age of 18, 21, or the local age of majority. In *Shepherd (Cathleen C.) v. Commissioner, T.C. Memo. 2000–174, 79 T.C.M. (CCH) 2078 (U.S. Tax Ct. 2000)*, the Tax Court concluded that where the parties' agreement provided both for alimony and child support payments, and the alimony payments would terminate within six months of a child's eighteenth birthday, the presumption that the alimony payments were child support was overcome by evidence that neither party ever considered that the alimony payments would terminate at or about the time the child turned 18, in other words, that the timing was entirely coincidental.

Under subsection (c)(3), support payments that fail to cover child support, whether current obligation or arrearage, are not deductible as alimony. *Haubrich (Gregory A.) v. Commissioner, T.C. Memo 2008–299, 96 T.C.M. (CCH) 509 (U.S. Tax Court 2008)*.

Pettid (Fred J.) v. Commissioner, T.C.Memo 1999–126, 77 T.C.M. (CCH) 1816 (U.S. Tax Ct. 1999), holds that support payments made under annulment settlement qualify as alimony when, according to state law, annulments and divorces are subject to the same alimony statute.

Note that distributions to a spouse or former spouse who is an alternate payee under a QDRO (see 29 U.S.C.A. § 1056) are taxable to that spouse or former spouse under § 402(e)(1)(A). However, a distribution from a qualified retirement plan to a participant's daughter to satisfy a child support obligation is taxable to the participant. *Stahl (Robert L.) v. Commissioner, T.C. Memo. 2001–22, 81 T.C.M. (CCH) 1087 (U.S. Tax Ct. 2001)*.

A court order requiring an ex-husband to liquidate a profit-sharing plan to pay child support and spousal support arrearages to his ex-wife was not a QDRO. Thus the distribution was taxable to him and not to her. He could, of course, take an alimony deduction under sections 71 and 215 for the amount attributable to spousal support. *Amarasinghe (Jeanne E.) v. Commissioner, T.C. Memo 2007–333, 94 T.C.M. (CCH) 447 (U.S. Tax Ct. 2007)*.

With respect to California public employees, unless their pension plans include an ERISA-style bifurcation provision, an employee who continues to work after the first date on which he becomes eligible to retire, may be required to pay his former spouse her community property share of the pension benefits that he would have received had he retired. (See Commentary to Family Code § 2610 discussion of *In re Marriage of Gillmore*.) In *Commissioner v. Dunkin, 500 F.3d 1065 (9th Cir. 2007)*, a Los Angeles policeman who remained on the job although his pension rights were fully vested and matured, was required to make such payments to his former wife. The Ninth Circuit Court of Appeals held that the earnings Dunkin used to satisfy his wife's entitlement were taxable to him, not to her. (Compare payments made directly to a former spouse under an ERISA bifurcated pension; they are taxable to the recipient, not to the pension earner.)

PART III—ITEMS SPECIFICALLY EXCLUDED FROM GROSS INCOME

§ 121. Exclusion of gain from sale of principal residence

(a) Exclusion.—Gross income shall not include gain from the sale or exchange of property if, during the 5–year period ending on the date of the sale or exchange, such property has been owned and used by the taxpayer as the taxpayer's principal residence for periods aggregating 2 years or more.

(b) Limitations.—

(1) In general.—The amount of gain excluded from gross income under subsection (a) with respect to any sale or exchange shall not exceed $250,000.

(2) Special rules for joint returns.—In the case of a husband and wife who make a joint return for the taxable year of the sale or exchange of the property—

(A) $500,000 limitation for certain joint returns.—Paragraph (1) shall be applied by substituting "$500,000" for "$250,000" if.—

(i) either spouse meets the ownership requirements of subsection (a) with respect to such property;

(ii) both spouses meet the use requirements of subsection (a) with respect to such property; and

(iii) neither spouse is ineligible for the benefits of subsection (a) with respect to such property by reason of paragraph (3).

(B) Other joint returns.—If such spouses do not meet the requirements of subparagraph (A), the limitation under paragraph (1) shall be the sum of the limitations under paragraph (1) to which each spouse would be entitled if such spouses had not been married. For purposes of the preceding sentence, each spouse shall be treated as owning the property during the period that either spouse owned the property.

(3) Application to only 1 sale or exchange every 2 years.—Subsection (a) shall not apply to any sale or exchange by the taxpayer if, during the 2-year period ending on the date of such sale or exchange, there was any other sale or exchange by the taxpayer to which subsection (a) applied.

(4) Special rule for certain sales by surviving spouses.—In the case of a sale or exchange of property by an unmarried individual whose spouse is deceased on the date of such sale, paragraph (1) shall be applied by substituting "$500,000" for "$250,000" if such sale occurs not later than 2 years after the date of death of such spouse and the requirements of paragraph (2)(A) were met immediately before such date of death.

(5) Exclusion of gain allocated to nonqualified use.—

(A) In general.—Subsection (a) shall not apply to so much of the gain from the sale or exchange of property as is allocated to periods of nonqualified use.

(B) Gain allocated to periods of nonqualified use.—For purposes of subparagraph (A), gain shall be allocated to periods of nonqualified use based on the ratio which—

(i) the aggregate periods of nonqualified use during the period such property was owned by the taxpayer, bears to

(ii) the period such property was owned by the taxpayer.

(C) Period of nonqualified use.—For purposes of this paragraph—

(i) In general.—The term "period of nonqualified use" means any period (other than the portion of any period preceding January 1, 2009) during which the property is not used as the principal residence of the taxpayer or the taxpayer's spouse or former spouse.

(ii) Exceptions.—The term "period of nonqualified use" does not include—

(I) any portion of the 5-year period described in subsection (a) which is after the last date that such property is used as the principal residence of the taxpayer or the taxpayer's spouse,

(II) any period (not to exceed an aggregate period of 10 years) during which the taxpayer or the taxpayer's spouse is serving on qualified official extended duty (as defined in subsection (d)(9)(C)) described in clause (i), (ii), or (iii) of subsection (d)(9)(A), and

(III) any other period of temporary absence (not to exceed an aggregate period of 2 years) due to change of employment, health conditions, or such other unforeseen circumstances as may be specified by the Secretary.

(D) Coordination with recognition of gain attributable to depreciation.—For purposes of this paragraph—

(i) subparagraph (A) shall be applied after the application of subsection (d)(6), and

(ii) subparagraph (B) shall be applied without regard to any gain to which subsection (d)(6) applies.

(c) Exclusion for taxpayers failing to meet certain requirements.—

(1) In general.—In the case of a sale or exchange to which this subsection applies, the ownership and use requirements of subsection (a), and subsection (b)(3), shall not apply; but the dollar limitation under paragraph (1) or (2) of subsection (b), whichever is applicable, shall be equal to—

(A) the amount which bears the same ratio to such limitation (determined without regard to this paragraph) as

(B)(i) the shorter of—

(I) the aggregate periods, during the 5-year period ending on the date of such sale or exchange, such property has been owned and used by the taxpayer as the taxpayer's principal residence; or

(II) the period after the date of the most recent prior sale or exchange by the taxpayer to which subsection (a) applied and before the date of such sale or exchange, bears to

(ii) 2 years.

(2) Sales and exchanges to which subsection applies.—This subsection shall apply to any sale or exchange if—

(A) subsection (a) would not (but for this subsection) apply to such sale or exchange by reason of—

(i) a failure to meet the ownership and use requirements of subsection (a), or

(ii) subsection (b)(3), and

(B) such sale or exchange is by reason of a change in place of employment, health, or, to the extent provided in regulations, unforeseen circumstances.

(d) Special rules.—

(1) Joint returns.—If a husband and wife make a joint return for the taxable year of the sale or exchange of the property, subsections (a) and (c) shall apply if either spouse meets the ownership and use requirements of subsection (a) with respect to such property.

(2) Property of deceased spouse.—For purposes of this section, in the case of an unmarried individual whose spouse is deceased on the date of the sale or exchange of property, the period such unmarried individual owned and used such property shall include the period such deceased spouse owned and used such property before death.

(3) Property owned by spouse or former spouse.—For purposes of this section—

(A) Property transferred to individual from spouse or former spouse.—In the case of an individual holding property transferred to such individual in a transaction described in section 1041(a), the period such individual owns such property shall include the period the transferor owned the property.

(B) Property used by former spouse pursuant to divorce decree, etc.—Solely for purposes of this section, an individual shall be treated as using property as such individual's principal residence during any period of ownership while such individual's spouse or former spouse is granted use of the property under a divorce or separation instrument (as defined in section 71(b)(2)).

(4) Tenant-stockholder in cooperative housing corporation.—For purposes of this section, if the taxpayer holds stock as a tenant-stockholder (as defined in section 216) in a cooperative housing corporation (as defined in such section), then—

(A) the holding requirements of subsection (a) shall be applied to the holding of such stock, and

(B) the use requirements of subsection (a) shall be applied to the house or apartment which the taxpayer was entitled to occupy as such stockholder.

(5) Involuntary conversions.—

(A) In general.—For purposes of this section, the destruction, theft, seizure, requisition, or condemnation of property shall be treated as the sale of such property.

(B) Application of section 1033.—In applying section 1033 (relating to involuntary conversions), the amount realized from the sale or exchange of property shall be treated as being the amount determined without regard to this section, reduced by the amount of gain not included in gross income pursuant to this section.

(C) Property acquired after involuntary conversion.—If the basis of the property sold or exchanged is determined (in whole or in part) under section 1033(b) (relating to basis of property acquired through involuntary conversion), then the holding and use by the taxpayer of the converted property shall be treated as holding and use by the taxpayer of the property sold or exchanged.

(6) Recognition of gain attributable to depreciation.—Subsection (a) shall not apply to so much of the gain from the sale of any property as does not exceed the portion of the depreciation adjustments (as defined in section 1250(b)(3)) attributable to periods after May 6, 1997, in respect of such property.

(7) Determination of use during periods of out-of-residence care.—In the case of a taxpayer who—

(A) becomes physically or mentally incapable of selfcare, and

(B) owns property and uses such property as the taxpayer's principal residence during the 5-year period described in subsection (a) for periods aggregating at least 1 year,

then the taxpayer shall be treated as using such property as the taxpayer's principal residence during any time during such 5-year period in which the taxpayer owns the property and resides in any facility (including a nursing home) licensed by a State or political subdivision to care for an individual in the taxpayer's condition.

(8) Sales of remainder interests.—For purposes of this section—

(A) In general.—At the election of the taxpayer, this section shall not fail to apply to the sale or exchange of an interest in a principal residence by reason of such interest being a remainder interest in such residence, but this section shall not apply to any other interest in such residence which is sold or exchanged separately.

(B) Exception for sales to related parties.—Subparagraph (A) shall not apply to any sale to, or exchange with, any person who bears a relationship to the taxpayer which is described in section 267(b) or 707(b).

(9) Uniformed services, Foreign Service, and intelligence community.—

(A) In general.—At the election of an individual with respect to a property, the running of the 5-year period described in subsections (a) and (c)(1)(B) and paragraph (7) of this subsection with respect to such property shall be suspended during any period that such individual or such individual's spouse is serving on qualified official extended duty—

(i) as a member of the uniformed services,

(ii) as a member of the Foreign Service of the United States, or

(iii) as an employee of the intelligence community.

(B) Maximum period of suspension.—The 5-year period described in subsection (a) shall not be extended more than 10 years by reason of subparagraph (A).

(C) Qualified official extended duty.—For purposes of this paragraph—

(i) In general.—The term "qualified official extended duty" means any extended duty while serving at a duty station which is at least 50 miles from such property or while residing under Government orders in Government quarters.

(ii) Uniformed services.—The term "uniformed services" has the meaning given such term by section 101(a)(5) of title 10, United States Code, as in effect on the date of the enactment of this paragraph.

(iii) Foreign Service of the United States.—The term "member of the Foreign Service of the United States" has the meaning given the term "member of the Service" by paragraph

(1), (2), (3), (4), or (5) of section 103 of the Foreign Service Act of 1980, as in effect on the date of the enactment of this paragraph.

(iv) Employee of intelligence community.—The term "employee of the intelligence community" means an employee (as defined by section 2105 of title 5, United States Code) of—

(I) the Office of the Director of National Intelligence,

(II) the Central Intelligence Agency,

(III) the National Security Agency,

(IV) the Defense Intelligence Agency,

(V) the National Geospatial-Intelligence Agency,

(VI) the National Reconnaissance Office,

(VII) any other office within the Department of Defense for the collection of specialized national intelligence through reconnaissance programs,

(VIII) any of the intelligence elements of the Army, the Navy, the Air Force, the Marine Corps, the Federal Bureau of Investigation, the Department of Treasury, the Department of Energy, and the Coast Guard,

(IX) the Bureau of Intelligence and Research of the Department of State, or

(X) any of the elements of the Department of Homeland Security concerned with the analyses of foreign intelligence information.

(v) Extended duty.—The term "extended duty" means any period of active duty pursuant to a call or order to such duty for a period in excess of 90 days or for an indefinite period.

(D) Special rules relating to election.—

(i) Election limited to 1 property at a time.—An election under subparagraph (A) with respect to any property may not be made if such an election is in effect with respect to any other property.

(ii) Revocation of election.—An election under subparagraph (A) may be revoked at any time.

(10) Property acquired in like-kind exchange.—If a taxpayer acquires property in an exchange with respect to which gain is not recognized (in whole or in part) to the taxpayer under subsection (a) or (b) of section 1031, subsection (a) shall not apply to the sale or exchange of such property by such taxpayer (or by any person whose basis in such property is determined, in whole or in part, by reference to the basis in the hands of such taxpayer) during the 5-year period beginning with the date of such acquisition.

(11) [Repealed. Pub.L. 111–312, Title III, § 301(a), Dec. 17, 2010, 124 Stat. 3300]

(12) Peace Corps.—

(A) In general.—At the election of an individual with respect to a property, the running of the 5-year period described in subsections (a) and (c)(1)(B) and paragraph (7) of this subsection with respect to such property shall be suspended during any period that such individual or such individual's spouse is serving outside the United States—

(i) on qualified official extended duty (as defined in paragraph (9)(C)) as an employee of the Peace Corps, or

(ii) as an enrolled volunteer or volunteer leader under section 5 or 6 (as the case may be) of the Peace Corps Act (22 U.S.C. 2504, 2505).

(B) Applicable rules.—For purposes of subparagraph (A), rules similar to the rules of subparagraphs (B) and (D) of paragraph (9) shall apply.

(e) Denial of exclusion for expatriates.—This section shall not apply to any sale or exchange by an individual if the treatment provided by section 877(a)(1) applies to such individual.

(f) Election to have section not apply.—This section shall not apply to any sale or exchange with respect to which the taxpayer elects not to have this section apply.

(g) Residences acquired in rollovers under section 1034.—For purposes of this section, in the case of property the acquisition of which by the taxpayer resulted under section 1034 (as in effect on the day before the date of the enactment of this section) in the nonrecognition of any part of the gain realized on the sale or exchange of another residence, in determining the period for which the taxpayer has owned and used such property as the taxpayer's principal residence, there shall be included the aggregate periods for which such other residence (and each prior residence taken into account under section 1223(6) in determining the holding period of such property) had been so owned and used.

(Added Pub.L. 88–272, Title II, § 206(a), Feb. 26, 1964, 78 Stat. 38; amended Pub.L. 94–455, Title XIV, § 1404(a), Title XIX, § 1906(b)(13)(A), Oct. 4, 1976, 90 Stat. 1733, 1834; Pub.L. 95–600, Title IV, § 404(a) to (c) (2), Nov. 6, 1978, 92 Stat. 2869, 2870; Pub.L. 97–34, Title I, § 123(a), Aug. 13, 1981, 95 Stat. 197; Pub.L. 100–647, Title VI, § 6011(a), Nov. 10, 1988, 102 Stat. 3691; Pub.L. 105–34, Title III, § 312(a), Aug. 5, 1997, 111 Stat. 836; Pub.L. 105–206, Title VI, § 6005(e)(1), (2), July 22, 1998, 112 Stat. 805; Pub.L. 107–16, Title V, § 542(c), June 7, 2001, 115 Stat. 84; Pub.L. 108–121, Title I, § 101(a), Nov. 11, 2003, 117 Stat. 1336; Pub.L. 108–357, Title VIII, § 840(a), Oct. 22, 2004, 118 Stat. 1597; Pub.L. 109–135, Title IV, §§ 402(a)(3), 403(ee)(1), (2), Dec. 21, 2005, 119 Stat. 2610, 2631; Pub.L. 109–432, Div. A, Title IV, § 417(a) to (d), Dec. 20, 2006, 120 Stat. 2965; Pub.L. 110–142, § 7(a), Dec. 20, 2007, 121 Stat. 1806; Pub.L. 110–172, § 11(a)(11)(A), Dec. 29, 2007, 121 Stat. 2485; Pub.L. 110–245, Title I, §§ 110(a), 113(a), (b), June 17, 2008, 122 Stat. 1633, 1635; Pub.L. 110–289, Div. C, Title III, § 3092(a), July 30, 2008, 122 Stat. 2911; Pub.L. 111–312, Title III, § 301(a), Dec. 17, 2010, 124 Stat. 3300; Pub.L. 113–295, Div. A, Title II, §§ 212(c), 213(c)(1), 221(a)(20), Dec. 19, 2014, 128 Stat. 4033, 4040.)

Sunset Provisions

All provisions of, and amendments made by, the Economic Growth and Tax Relief Reconciliation Act of 2001, Pub.L. 107–16, June 7, 2001, 115 Stat. 38, not applicable to taxable, plan, or limitation years beginning after December 31, 2010, or to estates of decedents dying, gifts made, or generation skipping transfers, after December 31, 2010, and the Internal Revenue Code of 1986 and the Employee Retirement Income Security Act of 1974 to be applied and administered to those years, estates, gifts, and transfers as if the provisions and amendments of that Act had never been enacted, see section 901 of Pub.L. 107–16, set out as a note under 26 U.S.C.A. § 1.

Commentary

Under the rollover provision referenced in subsection (g) (section 1034, repealed by 1997 legislation), *Snowa v. Commissioner, 123 F.3d 190 (4th Cir. 1997),* held that a taxpayer may include her new spouse's share of investment in a new home as her own for rollover purposes even though she sold her prior residence with a different spouse.

PART V—DEDUCTIONS FOR PERSONAL EXEMPTIONS

§ 151. Allowance of deductions for personal exemptions

(a) Allowance of deductions.—In the case of an individual, the exemptions provided by this section shall be allowed as deductions in computing taxable income.

(b) Taxpayer and spouse.—An exemption of the exemption amount for the taxpayer; and an additional exemption of the exemption amount for the spouse of the taxpayer if a joint return is not made by the taxpayer and his spouse, and if the spouse, for the calendar year in which the taxable year of the taxpayer begins, has no gross income and is not the dependent of another taxpayer.

(c) Additional exemption for dependents.—An exemption of the exemption amount for each individual who is a dependent (as defined in section 152) of the taxpayer for the taxable year.

(d) Exemption amount.—For purposes of this section—

(1) In general.—Except as otherwise provided in this subsection, the term "exemption amount" means $2,000.

(2) Exemption amount disallowed in case of certain dependents.—In the case of an individual with respect to whom a deduction under this section is allowable to another taxpayer for a taxable year beginning in the calendar year in which the individual's taxable year begins, the exemption amount applicable to such individual for such individual's taxable year shall be zero.

(3) Phaseout.—

(A) In general.—In the case of any taxpayer whose adjusted gross income for the taxable year exceeds the applicable amount in effect under section 68(b), the exemption amount shall be reduced by the applicable percentage.

(B) Applicable percentage.—For purposes of subparagraph (A), the term "applicable percentage" means 2 percentage points for each $2,500 (or fraction thereof) by which the taxpayer's adjusted gross income for the taxable year exceeds the applicable amount in effect under section 68(b). In the case of a married individual filing a separate return, the preceding sentence shall be applied by substituting "$1,250" for "$2,500". In no event shall the applicable percentage exceed 100 percent.

(C) Coordination with other provisions.—The provisions of this paragraph shall not apply for purposes of determining whether a deduction under this section with respect to any individual is allowable to another taxpayer for any taxable year.

[(D) Redesignated (C)]

[(E) Repealed. Pub.L. 112–240, Title I, § 101(b)(2)(B)(i)(III), Jan. 2, 2013, 126 Stat. 2317]

[(F) Repealed. Pub.L. 112–240, Title I, § 101(b)(2)(B)(i)(III), Jan. 2, 2013, 126 Stat. 2317]

(4) Inflation adjustment.—In the case of any taxable year beginning in a calendar year after 1989, the dollar amount contained in paragraph (1) shall be increased by an amount equal to—

(A) such dollar amount, multiplied by

(B) the cost-of-living adjustment determined under section 1(f)(3) for the calendar year in which the taxable year begins, by substituting "calendar year 1988" for "calendar year 1992" in subparagraph (B) thereof.

(e) Identifying information required.—No exemption shall be allowed under this section with respect to any individual unless the TIN of such individual is included on the return claiming the exemption. *(Aug. 16, 1954, c. 736, 68A Stat. 42; Pub.L. 91–172, Title VIII, § 801(a)(1), (b)(1), (c)(1), (d)(1), Title IX, § 941(b), Dec. 30, 1969, 83 Stat. 675, 726; Pub.L. 92–178, Title II, § 201(a)(1), (b)(1), (c), Dec. 10, 1971, 85 Stat. 510, 511; Pub.L. 94–455, Title XIX, § 1901(a)(23), Oct. 4, 1976, 90 Stat. 1767; Pub.L. 95–600, Title I, § 102(a), Nov. 6, 1978, 92 Stat. 2771; Pub.L. 97–34, Title I, § 104(c), Aug. 13, 1981, 95 Stat. 189; Pub.L. 98–369, Title IV, § 426(a), July 18, 1984, 98 Stat. 804; Pub.L. 99–514, Title I, § 103, Title XVIII, § 1847(b)(3), Oct. 22, 1986, 100 Stat. 2102, 2856; Pub.L. 100–647, Title VI, § 6010(a), Nov. 10, 1988, 102 Stat. 3691; Pub.L. 101–508, Title XI, §§ 11101(d)(1)(F), 11104(a), Nov. 5, 1990, 104 Stat. 1388–405, 1388–407; Pub.L. 102–318, Title V, § 511, July 3, 1992, 106 Stat. 300; Pub.L. 103–66, Title XIII, §§ 13201(b)(3)(G), 13205, Aug. 10, 1993, 107 Stat. 459, 462; Pub.L. 104–188, Title I, §§ 1615(a)(1), 1702(a)(2), Aug. 20, 1996, 110 Stat. 1853, 1868; Pub.L. 106–554, § 1(a)(7) [Title III, § 306(a)], Dec. 21, 2000, 114 Stat. 2763, 2763A–634; Pub.L. 107–16, Title I, § 102(a), June 7, 2001, 115 Stat. 44; Pub.L. 107–147, Title IV, §§ 412(b), 417(6), Mar. 9, 2002, 116 Stat. 53, 56; Pub.L. 108–311, Title II, § 206, Oct. 4, 2004, 118 Stat. 1176; Pub.L. 112–240, Title I, § 101(b)(2)(B), Jan. 2, 2013, 126 Stat. 2317.)*

Sunset Provisions

All provisions of, and amendments made by, the Economic Growth and Tax Relief Reconciliation Act of 2001, Pub.L. 107–16, June 7, 2001, 115 Stat. 38 [now repealed by Pub.L. 112–240, Title I, § 101(a)(1), Jan. 2, 2013, 126 Stat. 2315; see Sunset Provisions note under 26 U.S.C.A. § 1.], not applicable to taxable, plan, or limitation years beginning after December 31, 2010, or to estates of decedents dying, gifts made, or generation skipping transfers, after December 31, 2010, and the Internal Revenue Code of 1986 and the Employee Retirement Income Security Act of 1974 to be applied and administered to those years, estates, gifts, and transfers as if the provisions and amendments of that Act had never been enacted, see section 901 of Pub.L. 107–16, set out as a note under 26 U.S.C.A. § 1.

Commentary

Davis (Patrick A.) v. Commissioner, T.C. Memo 2014-147 (U.S. Tax Court 2014), holds that a custodial parent for purposes of this section is the parent with whom a child resides most of the year, even if the other parent was awarded legal custody of the child, without any need for a waiver from the parent who was awarded legal custody.

Applying subsection (e), *Kocher (J. Eric) v. Commissioner, T.C. Memo. 2000–238, 80 T.C.M. (CCH) 147 (U.S. Tax Ct. 2000)*, held that dependency exemptions were properly disallowed when parent refused to obtain and provide social security numbers for their children.

In *Rasco (Samuel K.) v. Commissioner, T.C. Memo. 1999–169, 1999 WL 311796 (U.S. Tax Ct. 1999)*, the Tax Court held that an unmarried taxpayer could take dependency exemptions for his girlfriend and her two children from a previous marriage when all three lived in the taxpayer's home and received more than half their support from him; consequently, the taxpayer also qualified for head-of-household filing status and the earned income credit, using the two children as "qualifying children" for purposes of the credit.

Applying this section and subsection (e)(2) of section 152, *Armstrong v. Commissioner of Internal Revenue, 745 F.3d 890 (8th Cir. 2014)*, held that the Tax Court properly denied dependency exemption deductions to noncustodial parents when the custodial parents failed to sign the necessary written declaration even though they had agreed to do so. Because dependency deductions were not available under this section, the noncustodial parents were not entitled to section 24(a) child tax credits for the children.

§ 152. Dependent defined

(a) In general.—For purposes of this subtitle, the term "dependent" means—

(1) a qualifying child, or

(2) a qualifying relative.

(b) Exceptions.—For purposes of this section—

(1) Dependents ineligible.—If an individual is a dependent of a taxpayer for any taxable year of such taxpayer beginning in a calendar year, such individual shall be treated as having no dependents for any taxable year of such individual beginning in such calendar year.

(2) Married dependents.—An individual shall not be treated as a dependent of a taxpayer under subsection (a) if such individual has made a joint return with the individual's spouse under section 6013 for the taxable year beginning in the calendar year in which the taxable year of the taxpayer begins.

(3) Citizens or nationals of other countries.—

(A) In general.—The term "dependent" does not include an individual who is not a citizen or national of the United States unless such individual is a resident of the United States or a country contiguous to the United States.

(B) Exception for adopted child.—Subparagraph (A) shall not exclude any child of a taxpayer (within the meaning of subsection (f)(1)(B)) from the definition of "dependent" if—

(i) for the taxable year of the taxpayer, the child has the same principal place of abode as the taxpayer and is a member of the taxpayer's household, and

(ii) the taxpayer is a citizen or national of the United States.

(c) Qualifying child.—For purposes of this section—

(1) In general.—The term "qualifying child" means, with respect to any taxpayer for any taxable year, an individual—

(A) who bears a relationship to the taxpayer described in paragraph (2),

(B) who has the same principal place of abode as the taxpayer for more than one-half of such taxable year,

(C) who meets the age requirements of paragraph (3),

(D) who has not provided over one-half of such individual's own support for the calendar year in which the taxable year of the taxpayer begins, and

(E) who has not filed a joint return (other than only for a claim of refund) with the individual's spouse under section 6013 for the taxable year beginning in the calendar year in which the taxable year of the taxpayer begins.

(2) Relationship.—For purposes of paragraph (1)(A), an individual bears a relationship to the taxpayer described in this paragraph if such individual is—

(A) a child of the taxpayer or a descendant of such a child, or

(B) a brother, sister, stepbrother, or stepsister of the taxpayer or a descendant of any such relative.

(3) Age requirements.—

(A) In general.—For purposes of paragraph (1)(C), an individual meets the requirements of this paragraph if such individual is younger than the taxpayer claiming such individual as a qualifying child and—

(i) has not attained the age of 19 as of the close of the calendar year in which the taxable year of the taxpayer begins, or

(ii) is a student who has not attained the age of 24 as of the close of such calendar year.

(B) Special rule for disabled.—In the case of an individual who is permanently and totally disabled (as defined in section 22(e)(3)) at any time during such calendar year, the requirements of subparagraph (A) shall be treated as met with respect to such individual.

(4) Special rule relating to 2 or more who can claim the same qualifying child.—

(A) In general.—Except as provided in subparagraphs (B) and (C), if (but for this paragraph) an individual may be claimed as a qualifying child by 2 or more taxpayers for a taxable year beginning in the same calendar year, such individual shall be treated as the qualifying child of the taxpayer who is—

(i) a parent of the individual, or

(ii) if clause (i) does not apply, the taxpayer with the highest adjusted gross income for such taxable year.

(B) More than 1 parent claiming qualifying child.—If the parents claiming any qualifying child do not file a joint return together, such child shall be treated as the qualifying child of—

(i) the parent with whom the child resided for the longest period of time during the taxable year, or

(ii) if the child resides with both parents for the same amount of time during such taxable year, the parent with the highest adjusted gross income.

(C) No parent claiming qualifying child.—If the parents of an individual may claim such individual as a qualifying child but no parent so claims the individual, such individual may be claimed as the qualifying child of another taxpayer but only if the adjusted gross income of such taxpayer is higher than the highest adjusted gross income of any parent of the individual.

(d) Qualifying relative.—For purposes of this section—

(1) In general.—The term "qualifying relative" means, with respect to any taxpayer for any taxable year, an individual—

(A) who bears a relationship to the taxpayer described in paragraph (2),

(B) whose gross income for the calendar year in which such taxable year begins is less than the exemption amount (as defined in section 151(d)),

(C) with respect to whom the taxpayer provides over one-half of the individual's support for the calendar year in which such taxable year begins, and

(D) who is not a qualifying child of such taxpayer or of any other taxpayer for any taxable year beginning in the calendar year in which such taxable year begins.

(2) Relationship.—For purposes of paragraph (1)(A), an individual bears a relationship to the taxpayer described in this paragraph if the individual is any of the following with respect to the taxpayer:

(A) A child or a descendant of a child.

(B) A brother, sister, stepbrother, or stepsister.

(C) The father or mother, or an ancestor of either.

(D) A stepfather or stepmother.

(E) A son or daughter of a brother or sister of the taxpayer.

(F) A brother or sister of the father or mother of the taxpayer.

(G) A son-in-law, daughter-in-law, father-in-law, mother-in-law, brother-in-law, or sister-in-law.

(H) An individual (other than an individual who at any time during the taxable year was the spouse, determined without regard to section 7703, of the taxpayer) who, for the taxable year of the taxpayer, has the same principal place of abode as the taxpayer and is a member of the taxpayer's household.

(3) Special rule relating to multiple support agreements.—For purposes of paragraph (1)(C), over one-half of the support of an individual for a calendar year shall be treated as received from the taxpayer if—

(A) no one person contributed over one-half of such support,

(B) over one-half of such support was received from 2 or more persons each of whom, but for the fact that any such person alone did not contribute over one-half of such support, would have been entitled to claim such individual as a dependent for a taxable year beginning in such calendar year,

(C) the taxpayer contributed over 10 percent of such support, and

(D) each person described in subparagraph (B) (other than the taxpayer) who contributed over 10 percent of such support files a written declaration (in such manner and form as the Secretary may by regulations prescribe) that such person will not claim such individual as a dependent for any taxable year beginning in such calendar year.

(4) Special rule relating to income of handicapped dependents.—

(A) In general.—For purposes of paragraph (1)(B), the gross income of an individual who is permanently and totally disabled (as defined in section 22(e)(3)) at any time during the taxable year shall not include income attributable to services performed by the individual at a sheltered workshop if—

(i) the availability of medical care at such workshop is the principal reason for the individual's presence there, and

(ii) the income arises solely from activities at such workshop which are incident to such medical care.

(B) Sheltered workshop defined.—For purposes of subparagraph (A), the term "sheltered workshop" means a school—

(i) which provides special instruction or training designed to alleviate the disability of the individual, and

(ii) which is operated by an organization described in section 501(c)(3) and exempt from tax under section 501(a), or by a State, a possession of the United States, any political subdivision of any of the foregoing, the United States, or the District of Columbia.

(5) Special rules for support.—For purposes of this subsection—

(A) payments to a spouse which are includible in the gross income of such spouse under section 71 or 682 shall not be treated as a payment by the payor spouse for the support of any dependent, and

(B) in the case of the remarriage of a parent, support of a child received from the parent's spouse shall be treated as received from the parent.

(e) Special rule for divorced parents, etc.—

(1) In general.—Notwithstanding subsection (c)(1)(B), (c)(4), or (d)(1)(C), if—

(A) a child receives over one-half of the child's support during the calendar year from the child's parents—

(i) who are divorced or legally separated under a decree of divorce or separate maintenance,

(ii) who are separated under a written separation agreement, or

(iii) who live apart at all times during the last 6 months of the calendar year, and—

(B) such child is in the custody of 1 or both of the child's parents for more than one-half of the calendar year, such child shall be treated as being the qualifying child or qualifying relative of the noncustodial parent for a calendar year if the requirements described in paragraph (2) or (3) are met.

(2) Exception where custodial parent releases claim to exemption for the year.—For purposes of paragraph (1), the requirements described in this paragraph are met with respect to any calendar year if—

(A) the custodial parent signs a written declaration (in such manner and form as the Secretary may by regulations prescribe) that such custodial parent will not claim such child as a dependent for any taxable year beginning in such calendar year, and

(B) the noncustodial parent attaches such written declaration to the noncustodial parent's return for the taxable year beginning during such calendar year.

(3) Exception for certain pre-1985 instruments.—

(A) In general.—For purposes of paragraph (1), the requirements described in this paragraph are met with respect to any calendar year if—

(i) a qualified pre–1985 instrument between the parents applicable to the taxable year beginning in such calendar year provides that the noncustodial parent shall be entitled to any deduction allowable under section 151 for such child, and

(ii) the noncustodial parent provides at least $600 for the support of such child during such calendar year.

For purposes of this subparagraph, amounts expended for the support of a child or children shall be treated as received from the noncustodial parent to the extent that such parent provided amounts for such support.

(B) Qualified pre-1985 instrument.—For purposes of this paragraph, the term "qualified pre–1985 instrument" means any decree of divorce or separate maintenance or written agreement—

(i) which is executed before January 1, 1985,

(ii) which on such date contains the provision described in subparagraph (A)(i), and

(iii) which is not modified on or after such date in a modification which expressly provides that this paragraph shall not apply to such decree or agreement.

(4) Custodial parent and noncustodial parent.—For purposes of this subsection—

(A) Custodial parent.—The term "custodial parent" means the parent having custody for the greater portion of the calendar year.

(B) Noncustodial parent.—The term "noncustodial parent" means the parent who is not the custodial parent.

(5) Exception for multiple-support agreement.—This subsection shall not apply in any case where over one-half of the support of the child is treated as having been received from a taxpayer under the provision of subsection (d)(3).

(6) Special rule for support received from new spouse of parent.—For purposes of this subsection, in the case of the remarriage of a parent, support of a child received from the parent's spouse shall be treated as received from the parent.

(f) Other definitions and rules.—For purposes of this section—

(1) Child defined.—

(A) In general.—The term "child" means an individual who is—

(i) a son, daughter, stepson, or stepdaughter of the taxpayer, or

(ii) an eligible foster child of the taxpayer.

(B) Adopted child.—In determining whether any of the relationships specified in subparagraph (A)(i) or paragraph (4) exists, a legally adopted individual of the taxpayer, or an individual who is lawfully placed with the taxpayer for legal adoption by the taxpayer, shall be treated as a child of such individual by blood.

(C) Eligible foster child.—For purposes of subparagraph (A)(ii), the term "eligible foster child" means an individual who is placed with the taxpayer by an authorized placement agency or by judgment, decree, or other order of any court of competent jurisdiction.

(2) Student defined.—The term "student" means an individual who during each of 5 calendar months during the calendar year in which the taxable year of the taxpayer begins—

(A) is a full-time student at an educational organization described in section 170(b)(1)(A)(ii), or

(B) is pursuing a full-time course of institutional on-farm training under the supervision of an accredited agent of an educational organization described in section 170(b)(1)(A)(ii) or of a State or political subdivision of a State.

(3) Determination of household status.—An individual shall not be treated as a member of the taxpayer's household if at any time during the taxable year of the taxpayer the relationship between such individual and the taxpayer is in violation of local law.

(4) Brother and sister.—The terms "brother" and "sister" include a brother or sister by the half blood.

(5) Special support test in case of students.—For purposes of subsections (c)(1)(D) and (d)(1)(C), in the case of an individual who is—

(A) a child of the taxpayer, and

(B) a student,

amounts received as scholarships for study at an educational organization described in section 170(b)(1)(A)(ii) shall not be taken into account.

(6) Treatment of missing children.—

(A) In general.—Solely for the purposes referred to in subparagraph (B), a child of the taxpayer—

(i) who is presumed by law enforcement authorities to have been kidnapped by someone who is not a member of the family of such child or the taxpayer, and

(ii) who had, for the taxable year in which the kidnapping occurred, the same principal place of abode as the taxpayer for more than one-half of the portion of such year before the date of the kidnapping,

shall be treated as meeting the requirement of subsection (c)(1)(B) with respect to a taxpayer for all taxable years ending during the period that the child is kidnapped.

(B) Purposes.—Subparagraph (A) shall apply solely for purposes of determining—

(i) the deduction under section 151(c),

(ii) the credit under section 24 (relating to child tax credit),

(iii) whether an individual is a surviving spouse or a head of a household (as such terms are defined in section 2), and

(iv) the earned income credit under section 32.

(C) Comparable treatment of certain qualifying relatives.—For purposes of this section, a child of the taxpayer—

(i) who is presumed by law enforcement authorities to have been kidnapped by someone who is not a member of the family of such child or the taxpayer, and

(ii) who was (without regard to this paragraph) a qualifying relative of the taxpayer for the portion of the taxable year before the date of the kidnapping,

shall be treated as a qualifying relative of the taxpayer for all taxable years ending during the period that the child is kidnapped.

(D) Termination of treatment.—Subparagraphs (A) and (C) shall cease to apply as of the first taxable year of the taxpayer beginning after the calendar year in which there is a determination that the child is dead (or, if earlier, in which the child would have attained age 18).

(7) Cross references.—

For provision treating child as dependent of both parents for purposes of certain provisions, see sections 105(b), 132(h)(2)(B), and 213(d)(5).

(Aug. 16, 1954, c. 736, 68A Stat. 43; Aug. 9, 1955, c. 693, § 2, 69 Stat. 626; Pub.L. 85–866, Title I, § 4(a) to (c), Sept. 2, 1958, 72 Stat. 1607; Pub.L. 86–376, § 1(a), Sept. 23, 1959, 73 Stat. 699; Pub.L. 90–78, § 1, Aug. 31, 1967, 81 Stat. 191; Pub.L. 91–172, Title IX, § 912(a), Dec. 30, 1969, 83 Stat. 722; Pub.L. 92–580, § 1(a), Oct. 27, 1972, 86 Stat. 1276; Pub.L. 94–455, Title XIX, §§ 1901(a)(24), (b)(7)(B), (8)(A), 1906(b)(13)(A), Title XXI, § 2139(a), Oct. 4, 1976, 90 Stat. 1767, 1794, 1834, 1932; Pub.L. 98–369, Div. A, Title IV, §§ 423(a), 482(b)(2), July 18, 1984, 98 Stat. 799, 848; Pub.L. 99–514, Title I, § 104(b)(1)(B), (3), Title XIII, § 1301(j)(8), Oct. 22, 1986, 100 Stat. 2104, 2105, 2658; Pub.L. 108–311, Title II, § 201, Oct. 4, 2004, 118 Stat. 1169; Pub.L. 109–135, Title IV, § 404(a), Dec. 21, 2005, 119 Stat. 2632; Pub.L. 110–351, Title V, § 501(a), (b), (c)(2), Oct. 7, 2008, 122 Stat. 3979, 3980.)

Commentary

In *Rasco (Samuel K.) v. Commissioner, T.C. Memo. 1999–169, 1999 WL 311796 (U.S. Tax Ct. 1999)*, the Tax Court held that an unmarried taxpayer could take dependency exemptions for his girlfriend and her two children from a previous marriage when all three lived in the taxpayer's home and received more than half their support from him; consequently, the taxpayer also qualified for head-of-household filing status and the earned income credit, using the two children as "qualifying children" for purposes of the credit.

Interpreting subsection (b)(3)(a), *Carlebach (Leah M.) v. Commissioner, 139 T.C., No. 1 (2012)*, held that an American mother could not claim her six children, all born in Israel and Israeli citizens, as tax dependents while they were resident in Israel. Although the children were eligible for American citizenship because of their mother's nationality, they had not yet applied for and received their certificates of citizenship. Thus, for tax purposes, American parents should not delay in applying for certificates of American citizenship for their foreign born children.

Smith (Charles F.) v. Commissioner, T.C. Memo 2006–163, 92 T.C.M. (CCH) 105 (U.S. Tax Ct. 2006), held that although subsection (e) applies equally to never-married parents of a child, a father was properly denied an exemption when the custodial mother had not waived the exemption and the father did not present adequate evidence that he had custody for the greater portion of the year.

Jeter (John) v. Commissioner, T.C. Memo 2001–223, 82 T.C.M. (CCH) 445 (U.S. Tax Ct. 2001), aff'd 26 Fed.Appx. 321, 2002 WL 185470 (4th Cir. 2002), holds that hours spent by children before and after school in the home of a separated parent are not to be considered in determining the children's "principal place of abode" for purposes of the earned income credit (§ 32(c)(3)) or in determining whether a parent had "custody for a greater portion of the calendar year" for purposes of the § 152 dependency deduction.

Abdi (Mahamud) v. Commissioner, T.C. Memo 2015-41, interpreting subsection (c) of this section and subsection (c)(3)(A) of section 32, held that a family member living in an apartment adjacent to the taxpayer's apartment is not a "qualifying child" for purposes of the Earned Income Tax Credit.

Interpreting subsection (e)(2), *Loffer (Michael R.) v. Commissioner, T.C. Memo. 2002–298, 84 T.C.M. (CCH) 618 (U.S. Tax Ct. 2002)*, holds that inadequately specified provisions of a divorce decree do not satisfy the requirement of a waiver by the other spouse. A noncustodial parent claiming an exemption for a dependent child must attach to the tax return a written declaration made by the custodial parent that the custodial parent will not claim the same child as a dependent for the specified year, the substance of Internal Revenue Service Form 8332. Compare *Boltinghouse (Michael K.) v. Commissioner, T.C. Memo. 2003–134, 85 T.C.M. (CCH) 1277 (U.S. Tax Court 2003)*, which held that a separation agreement substantially providing information required by Form 8332 was sufficient and that it was immaterial that the agreement had not been incorporated in the final decree.

Interpreting subsection (e)(2), *Miller (Cheryl J.) v. Commissioner, 114 T.C. 184 (U.S. Tax Ct. 2000)*, holds that a state court order providing that the noncustodial parent "shall claim ... [the] children on his tax returns as exemptions" does not satisfy subsection (e)(2), which requires that the custodial parent sign a written declaration that such custodial parent will not claim such child as a dependent. Thus the noncustodial parent was not entitled to claim the dependency exemptions for his minor children.

Applying § 151 (e), *Kocher (J. Eric) v. Commissioner, T.C. Memo. 2000–238, 80 T.C.M. (CCH) 147 (U.S. Tax Ct. 2000)*, held that dependency exemptions were properly disallowed when parents refused to obtain and provide social security numbers for their children.

Cowan (Jean) v. Commissioner, T.C. Memo 2015-25, held that the child of taxpayer's former ward was not a qualifying *child*, because the former ward was no longer an eligible foster child under subsection (f)(1)(C). Although the former ward was, under subsection (d)(2)(H), taxpayer's qualifying dependent *relative* because he lived in her home for the entire year, his child was not a qualifying dependent *relative* because she lived in the home for only 11 months of the year.

Gentry (LaTashia) v. Commissioner, T.C. Memo. 2013-16, held that minor cousins of a taxpayer who qualified as subsection (d) dependents did not qualify for section 24 child tax credits because the requirements of section 24 are more restrictive.

Applying subsection (e)(2) and section 151, *Armstrong v. Commissioner of Internal Revenue, 745 F.3d 890 (8th Cir. 2014)*, held that the Tax Court properly denied dependency exemption deductions to noncustodial parents when the custodial parents failed to sign the necessary written declaration even though they had agreed to do so. Because dependency deductions were not available under this section, the noncustodial parents were not entitled to section 24(a) child tax credits for the children.

Kososki (David. M.) v. Commissioner, T.C. Summary Opinion 2014-28 (U.S. Tax. Ct. 2014), held that a timely filed separate income tax return supersedes a prior filed joint return (Treas. Regs. § 1.6013-1(a)(1)). When children resided with both parents for the same amount of time, under subsection (c)(4)(B), the parent with the higher adjusted gross income is entitled to the entire dependency deduction. To the same effect, see *Bruce (Jason Alan) v. Commissioner, T.C. Summary Opinion 2014-46 (U.S. Tax Court 2014)*.

PART VII—ADDITIONAL ITEMIZED DEDUCTIONS FOR INDIVIDUALS

§ 215. Alimony, etc., payments

(a) General rule.—In the case of an individual, there shall be allowed as a deduction an amount equal to the alimony or separate maintenance payments paid during such individual's taxable year.

(b) Alimony or separate maintenance payments defined.—For purposes of this section, the term "alimony or separate maintenance payment" means any alimony or separate maintenance payment (as defined in section 71(b)) which is includible in the gross income of the recipient under section 71.

(c) Requirement of identification number.—The Secretary may prescribe regulations under which—

(1) any individual receiving alimony or separate maintenance payments is required to furnish such individual's taxpayer identification number to the individual making such payments, and

(2) the individual making such payments is required to include such taxpayer identification number on such individual's return for the taxable year in which such payments are made.

(d) Coordination with section 682.—No deduction shall be allowed under this section with respect to any payment if, by reason of section 682 (relating to income of alimony trusts), the amount thereof is not includible in such individual's gross income. *(Aug. 16, 1954, c. 736, 68A Stat. 71; Pub.L. 98–369, Div. A, Title IV, § 422(b), July 18, 1984, 98 Stat. 797.)*

Commentary

When a support obligor pays child support and alimony arrearages, the arrearage payments are not applied to deductible alimony until the child support arrearages have been fully paid. *Farahani (Sam) v. Commissioner, T.C. Memo. 2014-111 (U.S. Tax Ct. 2014)*.

Although alimony may be deducted from the income of the payor under this section, wages from which alimony is ultimately paid are treated as income under § 61. In *Chambers (Horace M.) v. Commissioner, T.C. Memo. 2000–218, 80 T.C.M. (CCH) 73 (U.S. Tax Ct. 2000)*, taxpayer claimed that amounts garnished from his wages to pay child support and alimony should not be included as income under § 61. The Tax Court rejected the argument, holding that taxpayer must include his ungarnished wages as income, but could take a deduction under this section for the amounts garnished for alimony.

Support payments voluntarily made by a taxpayer to his mentally ill former wife did not qualify as alimony under Section 71 because he was under no written obligation to make the payments. *Anderson (Curtis L.) v. Commissioner, T.C. Memo 1999–53, 77 T.C.M. (CCH) 1447 (U.S. Tax Ct. 1999)*. In *Leventhal (Hermine) v. Commissioner, T.C. Memo. 2000–92, 79 T.C.M. (CCH) 1670 (U.S. Tax Ct. 2000)*, the Tax Court held that the written agreement requirement of § 71 (b) was not satisfied by a letter from the husband specifying a payment arrangement and the wife's subsequent acceptance of those payments, because it was not clear whether the wife agreed to those terms or even whether the terms had been submitted to her for approval. By contrast, a letter from the wife's attorney proposing additional payments, which was signed and returned as an acceptance by the husband's attorney, did constitute a written agreement and hence qualified those payments for tax treatment as alimony.

Mumtaz Ali v. Commissioner, T.C. Memo 2004–284, 88 T.C.M. (CCH) 662 (U.S. Tax Ct. 2004), holds that a retroactive divorce court order for family support is ineffective for purposes of subsection (b) of Section 71, and therefore family support payments made before entry of the order are not alimony for purposes of this section and Section 71.

Under section 71(b)(1)(D), payments must terminate at the death of the payee. Payments made with respect to obligations that under state law do not terminate on the payee's death do not qualify as alimony. *Preston (Forest R.) v. Commissioner, T.C. Memo. 1999–49, 77 T.C.M. (CCH) 1437 (U.S. Tax Ct. 1999).*

California Family Code section 4337 provides: "Except as otherwise agreed by the parties in writing, the obligation of a party under an order for the support of the other party terminates on the death of either party." In view of this provision, *Johanson v. Commissioner, 541 F.3d. 973 (9th Cir. 2008)*, held that payments made pursuant to a California marital settlement agreement satisfied section 71(b)(1)(D) when the marital settlement agreement did not expressly state that spousal support payments would survive the payee's death and the payee failed to clearly and convincingly establish by extrinsic evidence that the parties had some other written agreement to continue payments after the payee's death. Compare *Stedman (Jack R.) v. Commissioner, T.C. Memo 2008–239 (U.S. Tax Court 2008)*, where the Tax Court held that an ex-husband's California court-ordered payments of attorney's fees to his ex-wife's attorney were *not* deductible by him as alimony because the court order did not state that the payments would end at his ex-wife's death and, under California law, a court order to pay attorney's fees does not terminate at the death of an ex-wife, as does ordinary spousal support.

Dennis E. and Paula W. Lofstrom v. Commissioner, 125 T.C. 271 (U.S. Tax Ct. 2005), holds that a third-party installment note, transferred from an ex-husband to his ex-wife in settlement of support obligations, did not qualify as alimony because (1) it was not "cash" or a cash equivalent and (2) payments under the note would not terminate at the death of the ex-wife.

Interpreting section 71 (b)(2), *Keegan v. Commissioner, T.C. Memo. 1997–359, 74 T.C.M. (CCH) 284 (1997)*, holds that a letter proposing an amount of spousal support is not an "agreement," even though the proposal was ultimately accepted in a stipulated court order. Thus, payments made before entry of the order did not qualify as "alimony or separate maintenance" under this section. Compare *Richardson v. Commissioner, 125 F.3d 551 (1997)*, which, upholding the Tax Court, held that payments made pursuant to a written agreement qualified as alimony even though the agreement was voidable under state law and was subsequently found "procedurally and substantively unconscionable" on appeal to a state court.

Burkes v. Commissioner, T.C. Memo. 1998–61, 75 T.C.M. (CCH) 1772 (1998), held that a divorce decree provision requiring the husband to pay the wife $60,000 "additional alimony towards attorney fees," which obligation would terminate under state law at the wife's death, was sufficient to qualify the payments as "alimony" for purposes of I.R.C. §§ 71 and 215.

For treatment of indirect alimony payments, see generally *Medlin (Alexandra M.) v. Commissioner, T.C. Memo. 1998–378, 76 T.C.M. (CCH) 707 (U.S. Tax Ct. 1998)*, holding that medical insurance premiums and car expenses paid directly to the vendor by the support obligor for the benefit of a former spouse qualify as alimony. See also *Hopkinson (Helen C.) v. Commissioner, T.C. Memo. 1999–154, 77 T.C.M. (CCH) 1968 (U.S. Tax Ct. 1999)* (education expenses paid by former husband on behalf of former wife directly to college or as reimbursement to the wife, pursuant to the their settlement agreement that he would pay all her expenses in obtaining a college degree, are taxable to the wife as alimony and deductible by the husband); and *Baxter (Linda J.) v. Commissioner, T.C. Memo. 1999–190, 77 T.C.M. (CCH) 2137 (U.S. Tax Ct. 1999)* (mortgage payments made on residence as a form of support to a former wife, which met all statutory requirements, qualified as alimony taxable to the wife and deductible by the husband).

Marten (Virginia M.) v. Commissioner, T.C. Memo. 1999–340, 78 T.C.M. (CCH) 584 (U.S. Tax Ct. 1999), held that life insurance premiums on a policy insuring the taxpayer's life were taxable alimony to the wife even though the policy proceeds were intended for the support of their disabled child, because the policy was owned by the wife, and the decree did not specify that the premiums were for child support.

(Joshua H.) v. Commissioner, T.C. Summary Opinion 2015-25, allowed an ex-husband to treat homeschooling payments to his ex-wife as deductible alimony, because they were terminable not on a contingency related to the child, but rather one related to the ex-wife's decision to continue home schooling.

In *Jaffe (Irv C.) v. Commissioner, T.C. Memo. 1999–196, 77 T.C.M. (CCH) 2167 (U.S. Tax Ct. 1999)*, the divorce court order authorized the wife to withdraw, from an account owned jointly and equally by the spouses, $500 a week as pendente lite alimony, with the proviso that the amount would "be credited against [the husband's] share at equitable distribution." The Tax Court held that only half the amount of the payments was properly treated as alimony taxable to the wife under § 71 (and deductible by the husband under this section), for she owned the other half by virtue of her interest in the account.

"Unallocated child support and maintenance" payments made pendente lite pursuant to a Colorado State court decree were not deductible to the payor under this section or includable within the income of the payee spouse under § 71, because they failed to satisfy § 71 (b)(1)(D) in that, under Colorado law, they would not terminate on the death of the obligor but instead could only be terminated by court order. *Miller v. Commissioner, T.C. Memo. 1999–273, 78 T.C.M. (CCH) 307 (U.S. Tax Ct. 1999)*. To the same effect, see *Gonzales (Marie A.) v. Commissioner, T.C. Memo. 1999–332, 78 T.C.M. (CCH) 527 (U.S. Tax Ct. 1999)*, finding that under New Jersey law unallocated support payments would not necessarily terminate at the death of the payee spouse.

DeLong (Brendon) v. Commissioner, T.C. Memo. 2013-70, allowed a California father an alimony deduction for unallocated family support because California law requires termination of family support upon the death of the payee parent.

John R. Okerson v. Commissioner, 123 T.C. Memo 258 (U.S. Tax Ct. 2004), holds that payments to be made in 113 installments to a Tennessee ex-wife did not qualify as alimony where they would continue to be paid to the couple's children should the ex-wife die before full satisfaction of the obligation. Compare *Michael K. Berry v. Commissioner, T.C. Memo 2005–91, 89 T.C.M. (CCH) 1089 (U.S. Tax Ct. 2004)*, holding that despite the absence of an explicit provision in the divorce instrument for termination at the death of the payee spouse, unallocated family support payments qualified as alimony because, under California law, support payments to a spouse terminate at her death and the possibility, upon her death, that the children would not be in obligor's custody and he would continue to be required to pay child support is insufficient to prevent treatment of the family support payments as alimony. *Okerson* and *Berry* are reconcilable in terms of state law. In *Okerson*, the law of Tennessee conducts an open-ended inquiry into the intent of the parties to determine whether spousal support ends at the payee's death, while California Family Code § 4337 provides: "Except as otherwise agreed by the parties in writing, the obligation of a party under an order for the support of the other party terminates upon the death of either party."

Similarly, Johanson (Carol A.) v. Commissioner, T.C. Memo. 2006–105, 91 T.C.M. (CCH) 1184 (U.S. Tax Ct. 2006), held that support payments made to an ex-spouse under a California settlement agreement qualified as alimony within the meaning of this section even though the agreement failed to provide for termination upon the supported spouse's death, because California law provides for automatic termination absent a contrary agreement.

Interpreting § 71 (b), *Benham (Thomas B.) v. Commissioner, T.C. Memo. 2000–165, 79 T.C.M. (CCH) 2054 (U.S. Tax Ct. 2000)*, held that alimony payments were taxable to the payee under that section, and deductible by the payor under this section, even though the parties continued to reside together in the marital residence, because the payments were made pursuant to a § 71 (b)(2)(B) written separation agreement and the parties were not legally separated or divorced (see § 71 (b)(1)(C) and Treasury Regs § 1.71–1T (b), Q & A 9).

Interpreting § 71 (c), Treasury Regs § 1.71–1T (c), Q & A 18, establish a presumption that a payment is child support when payments are to be reduced not more than six months before or after a child will reach the age of 18, 21, or the local age of majority. In *Shepherd (Cathleen C.) v. Commissioner, T.C. Memo. 2000–174, 79 T.C.M. (CCH) 2078 (U.S. Tax Ct. 2000)*, the Tax Court concluded that where the parties' agreement provided both for alimony and child support payments, and the alimony payments would terminate within six months of a child's eighteenth birthday, the presumption that the alimony payments were child support was overcome by evidence that neither party ever considered that the alimony payments would terminate at or about the time the child turned 18, in other words, that the timing was merely coincidental.

Pettid (Fred J.) v. Commissioner, T.C.Memo 1999–126, 77 T.C.M. (CCH) 1816 (U.S. Tax Ct. 1999), holds that support payments made under annulment settlement qualify as alimony when, according to state law, annulments and divorces are subject to the same alimony statute.

Note that distributions to a spouse or former spouse who is an alternate payee under a QDRO (see 29 U.S.C.A. § 1056) are taxable to that spouse or former spouse under § 402(e)(1)(A). However, a distribution from a qualified retirement plan to a participant's daughter to satisfy a child support obligation is taxable to the participant. *Stahl (Robert L.) v. Commissioner, T.C. Memo. 2001–22, 81 T.C.M. (CCH) 1087 (U.S. Tax Ct. 2001)*.

A court order requiring an ex-husband to liquidate a profit-sharing plan to pay child support and spousal support arrearages to his ex-wife was not a QDRO. Thus the distribution was taxable to him and not to her. He could, of course, take an alimony deduction under sections 71 and 215 for the amount attributable to spousal support. *Amarasinghe (Jeanne E.) v. Commissioner, T.C. Memo 2007–333, 94 T.C.M. (CCH) 447 (U.S. Tax Ct. 2007)*.

SUBCHAPTER D—DEFERRED COMPENSATION, ETC.

PART I—PENSION, PROFIT-SHARING, STOCK BONUS PLANS, ETC.

Subpart A—General Rule

§ 401. Qualified pension, profit-sharing, and stock bonus plans

(a) Requirements for qualification.—A trust created or organized in the United States and forming part of a stock bonus, pension, or profit-sharing plan of an employer for the exclusive benefit of his employees or their beneficiaries shall constitute a qualified trust under this section—

[Editor's note: Subsections (a)(1)–(12) omitted by author.]

(13) Assignment and alienation.—

(A) In general.—A trust shall not constitute a qualified trust under this section unless the plan of which such trust is a part provides that benefits provided under the plan may not be assigned or alienated. For purposes of the preceding sentence, there shall not be taken into account any voluntary and revocable assignment of not to exceed 10 percent of any benefit payment made by any participant who is receiving benefits under the plan unless the assignment or alienation is made for purposes of defraying plan administration costs. For purposes of this paragraph a loan made to a participant or beneficiary shall not be treated as an assignment or alienation if such loan is secured by the participant's accrued nonforfeitable benefit and is exempt from the tax imposed by section 4975 (relating to tax on prohibited transactions) by reason of section 4975(d)(1). This paragraph shall take effect on January 1, 1976 and shall not apply to assignments which were irrevocable on September 2, 1974.

(B) Special rules for domestic relations orders.—Subparagraph (A) shall apply to the creation, assignment, or recognition of a right to any benefit payable with respect to a participant pursuant to a domestic relations order, except that subparagraph (A) shall not apply if the order is determined to be a qualified domestic relations order.

[Editor's note: The remainder of subsection (a) through subsection (*o*) omitted by author.] *(Aug. 16, 1954, c. 736, 68A Stat. 134; Pub.L. 87–792, § 2, Oct. 10, 1962, 76 Stat. 809; Pub.L. 87–863, § 2(a), Oct. 23, 1962, 76 Stat. 1141; Pub.L. 88–272, Title II, § 219(a), Feb. 26, 1964, 78 Stat. 57; Pub.L. 89–97, Title I, § 106(d)(4), July 30, 1965, 79 Stat. 337; Pub.L. 89–809, Title II, §§ 204(b)(1), (c), 205(a), Nov. 13, 1966, 80 Stat. 1577, 1578; Pub.L. 91–691, § 1(a), Jan. 12, 1971, 84 Stat. 2074; Pub.L. 93–406, Title II, §§ 1012(b), 1016(a)(2), 1021, 1022(a) to (d), (f), 1023, 2001(c) to (e)(4), (h)(1), 2004(a)(1), Sept. 2, 1974, 88 Stat. 913, 929, 935, 938 to 940, 943, 952 to 955, 957, 979; Pub.L. 94–267, § 1(c)(1), (2), Apr. 15, 1976, 90 Stat. 367; Pub.L. 94–455, Title VIII, § 803(b)(2), Title XV, § 1505(b), Title XIX, §§ 1901(a)(56), 1906(b)(13)(A), Oct. 4, 1976, 90 Stat. 1584, 1738, 1773, 1834; Pub.L. 95–600, Title I, §§ 135(a), 141(f)(3), 143(a), 152(e), Nov. 6, 1978, 92 Stat. 2785, 2795, 2796, 2799; Pub.L. 96–222, Title I, § 101(a)(7)(L)(i)(V), (9), (14)(E)(iii), Apr. 1, 1980, 94 Stat. 199, 201, 205; Pub.L. 96–364, Title II, § 208(a), (e), Title IV, § 410(b), Sept. 26, 1980, 94 Stat. 1289, 1290, 1308; Pub.L. 96–605, Title II, §§ 221(a), 225(b)(1), (2), Dec. 28, 1980, 94 Stat. 3528, 3529; Pub.L. 97–34, Title III, §§ 312(b)(1), (c)(2) to (4), (e)(2), 314(a)(1), 335, 338(a), Aug. 13, 1981, 95 Stat. 283 to 286, 297, 298; Pub.L. 97–248, Title II, §§ 237(a), (b), (e)(1), 238(b), (d)(1), (2), 240(b), 242(a), 249(a), 254(a), Sept. 3, 1982, 96 Stat. 511 to 513, 520, 521, 527, 533; Pub.L. 97–448, Title I, § 103(c)(10)(A), (d)(2), (g)(2)(A), Title III, § 306(a)(12), Jan. 12, 1983, 96 Stat. 2377 to 2379, 2405; Pub.L. 98–21, Title I, § 124(c)(4)(A), Apr. 20, 1983, 97 Stat. 91; Pub.L. 98–369, Div. A, Title II, § 211(b)(5), Title IV, §§ 474(r)(13), 491(e)(4), (5), Title V, §§ 521(a), 524(d)(1), 527(a), (b), 528(b), Title VII, § 713(c)(2)(A), (d)(3), July 18, 1984, 98 Stat. 754, 842, 853, 865, 872, 875, 876, 877, 957, 958; Pub.L. 98–397, Title II, §§ 203(a), 204(a), Title III, § 301(b), Aug. 23, 1984, 98 Stat. 1440, 1445, 1451; Pub.L. 99–514, Title XI, §§ 1106(d)(1), 1111(a), (b), 1112(b), (d)(1), 1114(b)(7),*

1116(a) to (e), 1117(a), 1119(a), 1121(b), 1136(a), 1143(a), 1145(a), 1171(b)(5), 1174(c)(2)(A), 1175(a)(1), 1176(a), Title XVIII, §§ 1848(b), 1852(a)(4)(A), (6), (b)(8), (g), (h)(1), 1879(g)(1), (2), 1898(b)(2)(A), (3)(A), (7)(A), (13)(A), (14)(A), (c)(3), 1899A(10), Oct. 22, 1986, 100 Stat. 2423, 2435, 2439, 2444, 2445, 2451, 2454 to 2456, 2459, 2463, 2465, 2485, 2490, 2513, 2518, 2519, 2857, 2865 to 2869, 2906, 2907, 2945, 2948, 2950, 2953, 2958; Pub.L. 100–203, Title IX, § 9341(a), Dec. 22, 1987, 101 Stat. 1330–369; Pub.L. 100–647, Title I, §§ 1011(c)(7)(A), (d)(4), (e)(3), (g)(1) to (3), (h)(3), (k)(1)(A), (B), (2) to (7), (9), (l)(1) to (5)(A), (6), (7), 1011A(j), (l), 1011B(j)(1), (2), (6), (k)(1), (2), Title VI, §§ 6053(a), 6055(a), 6071(a), (b), Nov. 10, 1988, 102 Stat. 3458, 3459, 3460, 3463, 3464, 3468, 3469, 3470, 3483, 3492, 3493, 3696, 3697, 3705; Pub.L. 101–140, Title II, § 203(a)(5), Nov. 8, 1989, 103 Stat. 830; Pub.L. 101–239, Title VII, §§ 7311(a), 7811(g)(1), (h)(3), 7816(l), 7881(i)(1)(A), (4)(A), Dec. 19, 1989, 103 Stat. 2354, 2409, 2421, 2442; Pub.L. 101–508, Title XII, § 12011(b), Nov. 5, 1990, 104 Stat. 1388–571; Pub.L. 102–318, Title V, §§ 521(b)(5) to (8), 522(a)(1), July 3, 1992, 106 Stat. 310, 313; Pub.L. 103–66, Title XIII, § 13212(a), Aug. 10, 1993, 107 Stat. 471; Pub.L. 103–465, Title VII, §§ 732(a), 751(a)(9)(C), 766(b), 776(d), Dec. 8, 1994, 108 Stat. 5004, 5021, 5037, 5048; Pub.L. 104–188, Title I, §§ 1401(b)(5), (6), 1404(a), 1422(a), (b), 1426(a), 1431(b)(2), (c)(1)(B), 1432(a), (b), 1433(a) to (e), 1441(a), 1443(a), (b), 1445(a), 1459(a), (b), 1704(a), (t)(67), Aug. 20, 1996, 110 Stat. 1789, 1791, 1800, 1801, 1803 to 1809, 1811, 1820, 1878, 1890; Pub.L. 105–34, Title XV, §§ 1502(b), 1505(a)(1), (2), (b), 1525(a), 1530(c)(1), Title XVI, § 1601(d)(2)(A), (B), (D), (3), Aug. 5, 1997, 111 Stat. 1060, 1063, 1072, 1078, 1088, 1089; Pub.L. 106–554, § 1(a)(7) [Title III, § 316(c)], Dec. 21, 2000, 114 Stat. 2763, 2763A–644; Pub.L. 107–16, Title VI, §§ 611(c), (f)(3), (g)(1), 641(e)(3), 643(b), 646(a)(1), 657(a), 666(a), June 7, 2001, 115 Stat. 97, 99, 120, 122, 126, 135, 143; Pub.L. 107–147, Title IV, § 411(o)(2), (q)(1), Mar. 9, 2002, 116 Stat. 48, 51; Pub.L. 108–311, Title IV, § 407(b), Oct. 4, 2004, 118 Stat. 1190; Pub.L. 109–280, Title I, § 114(a), Title VIII, §§ 827(b)(1), 861(a), (b), Title IX, §§ 901(a)(1), (2)(A), 902(a), (b), (d)(2)(C), (D), (e)(3)(B), 905(b), Aug. 17, 2006, 120 Stat. 853, 1000, 1021, 1026, 1029, 1033, 1035, 1038, 1050; Pub.L. 110–245, Title I, § 104(a), June 17, 2008, 122 Stat. 1626; Pub.L. 110–458, Title I, §§ 101(d)(2)(A) to (C), 109(a) to (b)(2), Title II, § 201(a), Dec. 23, 2008, 122 Stat. 5099, 5111, 5116; Pub.L. 111–152, Title I, § 1004(d)(5), Mar. 30, 2010, 124 Stat. 1036; Pub.L. 113–97, Title II, § 202(c)(3)(A), (4), (5), Apr. 7, 2014, 128 Stat. 1136; Pub.L. 113–295, Div. A, Title II, § 221(a)(52), Dec. 19, 2014, 128 Stat. 4045.)

§ 408. Individual retirement accounts

[Editor's note: Subsections (a) to (c), (d)(1) to (5) omitted by author.]

(d) Tax treatment of distributions.—

(6) Transfer of account incident to divorce.—The transfer of an individual's interest in an individual retirement account or an individual retirement annuity to his spouse or former spouse under a divorce or separation instrument described in subparagraph (A) of section 71(b)(2) is not to be considered a taxable transfer made by such individual notwithstanding any other provision of this subtitle, and such interest at the time of the transfer is to be treated as an individual retirement account of such spouse, and not of such individual. Thereafter such account or annuity for purposes of this subtitle is to be treated as maintained for the benefit of such spouse.

[Editor's note: Subsections (d)(7), (e) to (r) omitted by author.] *(Added Pub.L. 93–406, Title II, § 2002(b), Sept. 2, 1974, 88 Stat. 959; amended Pub.L. 94–455, Title XV, § 1501(b)(2), (5), (10), Title XIX, § 1906(b)(13)(A), Oct. 4, 1976, 90 Stat. 1735 to 1737, 1834; Pub.L. 95–600, Title I, §§ 152(a), (b), 156(c)(1), (3), 157(c)(1), (d)(1), (e)(1)(A), (g)(3)(h)(2), Title VII, § 2684, 2685, 703(c)(4), Nov. 6, 1978, 92 Stat. 2797, 2802, 2803, 2805, 2806, 2808, 2939; Pub.L. 96–222, Title I, § 101(a)(10)(A), (C), (F), (G), (J)(i), (14)(B), (E)(ii), Apr. 1, 1980, 94 Stat. 201 to 205; Pub.L. 96–605, Title II, § 225(b)(3), (4), Dec. 28, 1980, 94 Stat. 3529; Pub.L. 97–34, Title III, §§ 311(g)(1)(A) to (C), (2), (h)(2), 312(b)(2), (c)(5), 313(b)(2), 314(b)(1), Aug. 13, 1981, 95 Stat. 281 to 284, 286; Pub.L 97–248, Title II, §§ 237(e)(3), 238(d)(3), (4), 243(a), (b)(1)(A), Title III, § 335(a)(1), Sept. 3, 1982, 96 Stat. 512, 513, 521, 522, 628; Pub.L. 97–448, Title I, § 103(d)(1), (e), Jan. 12, 1983, 96 Stat. 2378; Pub.L. 98–369, Div. A, Title I, § 147(a), Title IV, § 491(d)(19) to (24), Title V, §§ 521(b), 522(d)(12), Title VII, § 713(c)(2)(B), (f)(2), (5)(B), (g)(2), (j), July 18, 1984, 98 Stat. 687, 850, 867, 871, 957, 959, 960; Pub.L. 99–514, Title XI, §§ 1102(a), (b)(2), (c), (e)(2), 1108(a), (d) to (g)(1), (4), (6), 1121(c)(2), 1122(e)(2)(B), 1123(d)(2), 1144(a), Title XVIII, §§ 1852(a)(1), (5)(C), (7)(A), 1875(c)(6)(A), (8), 1898(a)(5), Oct. 22, 1986, 100 Stat. 2414, 2415, 2416, 2417, 2431, 2433, 2434, 2465, 2470, 2475, 2490, 2684, 2685, 2866, 2895, 2944; Pub.L. 100–647, Title I, §§ 1011(b)(1) to (3), (c)(7)(C), (f)(1) to (5), (10), (i)(5), 1011A(a)(2)(A), 1018(t)(3)(D), Title VI, § 6057(a), Nov. 10, 1988, 102 Stat. 3456, 3458, 3461 to 3463, 3468, 3472, 3588, 3698; Pub.L. 101–239, Title VII, §§ 7811(m)(7), 7841(a)(1), Dec. 19, 1989, 103 Stat. 2412, 2427; Pub.L. 102–318, Title V, § 521(b)(16) to (19), July 3, 1992, 106 Stat. 311; Pub.L. 103–66, Title XIII, § 13212(b), Aug. 10, 1993, 107 Stat. 472; Pub.L. 103–465, Title VII, § 732(d), Dec. 8, 1994, 108 Stat. 5005; Pub.L. 104–188, Title I, §§ 1421(a), (b)(3)(B), (5), (6), (c), 1427(b)(3), 1431(c)(1)(B), 1455(b)(1), Aug. 20, 1996, 110 Stat. 1792, 1796, 1797, 1798, 1802, 1803, 1817; Pub.L. 105–34, Title III, §§ 302(d), 304(a), Title XV, § 1501(b), Title XVI, § 1601(d)(1)(A) to (C)(i), (D) to (G), Aug. 5, 1997, 111 Stat. 829, 831, 1058, 1087, 1088; Pub.L. 105–206, Title VI, §§ 6015(a), 6016(a)(1), 6018(b), July 22, 1998, 112 Stat. 820, 821, 822; Pub.L. 106–554, § 1(a)(7) [Title III, § 319(3)], Dec. 21, 2000, 114 Stat. 2763, 2763A–646; Pub.L. 107–16, Title VI, §§ 601(b), 602(a), 611(c)(1), (f)(1), (2), (g)(2), 641(e)(8), 642(a), (b)(2), (3), 643(c), 644(b), June 7, 2001, 115 Stat. 95, 97, 99, 121 to 123; Pub.L. 107–147, Title IV, § 411(i)(1), (j)(1), Mar. 9, 2002, 116 Stat. 46, 47; Pub.L. 108–311, Title IV, §§ 404(d), 408(a)(12), (13), Oct. 4, 2004, 118 Stat. 1188, 1191; Pub.L. 109–280, Title XII, § 1201(a), Aug. 17, 2006, 120 Stat. 1063; Pub.L. 109–432, Div. A, Title III, § 307(a), Dec. 20, 2006, 120 Stat. 2951; Pub.L. 110–172, § 3(a), Dec. 29, 2007, 121 Stat. 2474; Pub.L. 110–343, Div. C, Title II, § 205(a), Oct. 3, 2008, 122 Stat. 3865; Pub.L.*

111–312, Title VII, § 725(a), Dec. 17, 2010, 124 Stat. 3316; Pub.L. 112–240, Title II, § 208(a), Jan. 2, 2013, 126 Stat. 2324; Pub.L. 113–295, Div. A, Title I, § 108(a), Title II, § 221(a)(53), Dec. 19, 2014, 128 Stat. 4013, 4045; Pub.L. 114–113, Div. Q, Title I, § 112(a), Title III, § 306(a), Dec. 18, 2015, 129 Stat. 3047, 3089.)

Commentary

ERISA surviving spouse provisions (29 USC § 1055) apply only to employee benefit plans established or maintained by an employer. They have no application to an Individual Retirement Account (IRA) after an employee rolls over distributions from an ERISA-regulated plan into an IRA. *Charles Schwab & Co. v. Debickero, 593 F.3d 916 (9th Cir. 2010).*

Subpart B—Special Rules

§ 414. Definitions and special rules

(1) In general.—Except as provided in paragraph (2), for purposes of sections 401, 408(k), 408(p), 410, 411, 415, and 416, under regulations prescribed by the Secretary, all employees of trades or businesses (whether or not incorporated) which are under common control shall be treated as employed by a single employer. The regulations prescribed under this subsection shall be based on principles similar to the principles which apply in the case of subsection (b).

(2) Special rules relating to church plans.—

(A) General rule.—Except as provided in subparagraphs (B) and (C), for purposes of this subsection and subsection (m), an organization that is otherwise eligible to participate in a church plan shall not be aggregated with another such organization and treated as a single employer with such other organization for a plan year beginning in a taxable year unless—

(i) one such organization provides (directly or indirectly) at least 80 percent of the operating funds for the other organization during the preceding taxable year of the recipient organization, and

(ii) there is a degree of common management or supervision between the organizations such that the organization providing the operating funds is directly involved in the day-to-day operations of the other organization.

(B) Nonqualified church-controlled organizations.—Notwithstanding subparagraph (A), for purposes of this subsection and subsection (m), an organization that is a nonqualified church-controlled organization shall be aggregated with 1 or more other nonqualified church-controlled organizations, or with an organization that is not exempt from tax under section 501, and treated as a single employer with such other organization, if at least 80 percent of the directors or trustees of such other organization are either representatives of, or directly or indirectly controlled by, such nonqualified church-controlled organization. For purposes of this subparagraph, the term "nonqualified church-controlled organization" means a church-controlled tax-exempt organization described in section 501(c)(3) that is not a qualified church-controlled organization (as defined in section 3121(w)(3)(B)).

(C) Permissive aggregation among church-related organizations.—The church or convention or association of churches with which an organization described in subparagraph (A) is associated (within the meaning of subsection (e)(3)(D)), or an organization designated by such church or convention or association of churches, may elect to treat such organizations as a single employer for a plan year. Such election, once made, shall apply to all succeeding plan years unless revoked with notice provided to the Secretary in such manner as the Secretary shall prescribe.

(D) Permissive disaggregation of church-related organizations.—For purposes of subparagraph (A), in the case of a church plan, an employer may elect to treat churches (as defined in section 403(b)(12)(B)) separately from entities that are not churches (as so defined), without regard to whether such entities maintain separate church plans. Such election, once made, shall apply to all succeeding plan years unless revoked with notice provided to the Secretary in such manner as the Secretary shall prescribe.

[Editor's note: Subsections (a)-(*o*) omitted by author.]

(p) Qualified domestic relations order defined.—For purposes of this subsection and section 401(a)(13)—

(1) In general.—

(A) Qualified domestic relations order.—The term "qualified domestic relations order" means a domestic relations order—

(i) which creates or recognizes the existence of an alternate payee's right to, or assigns to an alternate payee the right to, receive all or a portion of the benefits payable with respect to a participant under a plan, and

(ii) with respect to which the requirements of paragraphs (2) and (3) are met.

(B) Domestic relations order.—The term "domestic relations order" means any judgment, decree, or order (including approval of a property settlement agreement) which—

(i) relates to the provision of child support, alimony payments, or marital property rights to a spouse, former spouse, child, or other dependent of a participant, and

(ii) is made pursuant to a State domestic relations law (including a community property law).

(2) Order must clearly specify certain facts.—A domestic relations order meets the requirements of this paragraph only if such order clearly specifies—

(A) the name and the last known mailing address (if any) of the participant and the name and mailing address of each alternate payee covered by the order,

(B) the amount or percentage of the participant's benefits to be paid by the plan to each such alternate payee, or the manner in which such amount or percentage is to be determined,

(C) the number of payments or period to which such order applies, and

(D) each plan to which such order applies.

(3) Order may not alter amount, form, etc., of benefits.—A domestic relations order meets the requirements of this paragraph only if such order—

(A) does not require a plan to provide any type or form of benefit, or any option, not otherwise provided under the plan,

(B) does not require the plan to provide increased benefits (determined on the basis of actuarial value), and

(C) does not require the payment of benefits to an alternate payee which are required to be paid to another alternate payee under another order previously determined to be a qualified domestic relations order.

(4) Exception for certain payments made after earliest retirement age.—

(A) In general.—A domestic relations order shall not be treated as failing to meet the requirements of subparagraph (A) of paragraph (3) solely because such order requires that payment of benefits be made to an alternate payee—

(i) in the case of any payment before a participant has separated from service, on or after the date on which the participant attains (or would have attained) the earliest retirement age,

(ii) as if the participant had retired on the date on which such payment is to begin under such order (but taking into account only the present value of the benefits actually accrued and not taking into account the present value of any employer subsidy for early retirement), and

(iii) in any form in which such benefits may be paid under the plan to the participant (other than in the form of a joint and survivor annuity with respect to the alternate payee and his or her subsequent spouse).

For purposes of clause (ii), the interest rate assumption used in determining the present value shall be the interest rate specified in the plan or, if no rate is specified, 5 percent.

(B) Earliest retirement age.—For purposes of this paragraph, the term "earliest retirement age" means the earlier of—

(i) the date on which the participant is entitled to a distribution under the plan, or

(ii) the later of—

(I) the date the participant attains age 50, or

(II) the earliest date on which the participant could begin receiving benefits under the plan if the participant separated from service.

(5) Treatment of former spouse as surviving spouse for purposes of determining survivor benefits.—To the extent provided in any qualified domestic relations order—

(A) the former spouse of a participant shall be treated as a surviving spouse of such participant for purposes of sections 401(a)(11) and 417 (and any spouse of the participant shall not be treated as a spouse of the participant for such purposes), and

(B) if married for at least 1 year, the surviving former spouse shall be treated as meeting the requirements of section 417(d).

(6) Plan procedures with respect to orders.—

(A) Notice and determination by administrator.—In the case of any domestic relations order received by a plan—

(i) the plan administrator shall promptly notify the participant and each alternate payee of the receipt of such order and the plan's procedures for determining the qualified status of domestic relations orders, and

(ii) within a reasonable period after receipt of such order, the plan administrator shall determine whether such order is a qualified domestic relations order and notify the participant and each alternate payee of such determination.

(B) Plan to establish reasonable procedures.—Each plan shall establish reasonable procedures to determine the qualified status of domestic relations orders and to administer distributions under such qualified orders.

(7) Procedures for period during which determination is being made.—

(A) In general.—During any period in which the issue of whether a domestic relations order is a qualified domestic relations order is being determined (by the plan administrator, by a court of competent jurisdiction, or otherwise), the plan administrator shall separately account for the amounts (hereinafter in this paragraph referred to as the "segregated amounts") which would have been payable to the alternate payee during such period if the order had been determined to be a qualified domestic relations order.

(B) Payment to alternate payee if order determined to be qualified domestic relations order.—If within the 18-month period described in subparagraph (E) the order (or modification thereof) is determined to be a qualified domestic relations order, the plan administrator shall pay the segregated amounts (including any interest thereon) to the person or persons entitled thereto.

(C) Payment to plan participant in certain cases.—If within the 18-month period described in subparagraph (E)—

(i) it is determined that the order is not a qualified domestic relations order, or

(ii) the issue as to whether such order is a qualified domestic relations order is not resolved,

then the plan administrator shall pay the segregated amounts (including any interest thereon) to the person or persons who would have been entitled to such amounts if there had been no order.

(D) Subsequent determination or order to be applied prospectively only.—Any determination that an order is a qualified domestic relations order which is made after the close of the 18-month period described in subparagraph (E) shall be applied prospectively only.

(E) Determination of 18–month period.—For purposes of this paragraph, the 18–month period described in this subparagraph is the 18–month period beginning with the date on which the first payment would be required to be made under the domestic relations order.

(8) Alternate payee defined.—The term "alternate payee" means any spouse, former spouse, child or other dependent of a participant who is recognized by a domestic relations order as having a right to receive all, or a portion of, the benefits payable under a plan with respect to such participant.

(9) Subsection not to apply to plans to which section 401(a)(13) does not apply.—This subsection shall not apply to any plan to which section 401(a)(13) does not apply. For purposes of this title, except as provided in regulations, any distribution from an annuity contract under section 403(b) pursuant to a qualified domestic relations order shall be treated in the same manner as a distribution from a plan to which section 401(a)(13) applies.

(10) Waiver of certain distribution requirements.—With respect to the requirements of subsections (a) and (k) of section 401, section 403(b), section 409(d), and section 457(d), a plan shall not be treated as failing to meet such requirements solely by reason of payments to an alternative payee pursuant to a qualified domestic relations order.

(11) Application of rules to certain other plans.—For purposes of this title, a distribution or payment from a governmental plan (as defined in subsection (d)) or a church plan (as described in subsection (e)) or an eligible deferred compensation plan (within the meaning of section 457(b)) shall be treated as made pursuant to a qualified domestic relations order if it is made pursuant to a domestic relations order which meets the requirement of clause (i) of paragraph (1)(A).

(12) Tax treatment of payments from a section 457 plan.—If a distribution or payment from an eligible deferred compensation plan described in section 457(b) is made pursuant to a qualified domestic relations order, rules similar to the rules of section 402(e)(1)(A) shall apply to such distribution or payment.

(13) Consultation with the Secretary.—In prescribing regulations under this subsection and section 401(a)(13), the Secretary of Labor shall consult with the Secretary.

[Editor's note: Subsections (q)-(y) omitted by author.]

(z) Certain plan transfers and mergers.—

(1) In general.—Under rules prescribed by the Secretary, except as provided in paragraph (2), no amount shall be includible in gross income by reason of—

(A) a transfer of all or a portion of the accrued benefit of a participant or beneficiary, whether or not vested, from a church plan that is a plan described in section 401(a) or an annuity contract described in section 403(b) to an annuity contract described in section 403(b), if such plan and annuity contract are both maintained by the same church or convention or association of churches,

(B) a transfer of all or a portion of the accrued benefit of a participant or beneficiary, whether or not vested, from an annuity contract described in section 403(b) to a church plan that is a plan described in section 401(a), if such plan and annuity contract are both maintained by the same church or convention or association of churches, or

(C) a merger of a church plan that is a plan described in section 401(a), or an annuity contract described in section 403(b), with an annuity contract described in section 403(b), if such plan and annuity contract are both maintained by the same church or convention or association of churches.

(2) Limitation.—Paragraph (1) shall not apply to a transfer or merger unless the participant's or beneficiary's total accrued benefit immediately after the transfer or merger is equal to or greater than the participant's or beneficiary's total accrued benefit immediately before the transfer or merger, and such total accrued benefit is nonforfeitable after the transfer or merger.

(3) Qualification.—A plan or annuity contract shall not fail to be considered to be described in section 401(a) or 403(b) merely because such plan or annuity contract engages in a transfer or merger described in this subsection.

(4) Definitions.—For purposes of this subsection—

(A) Church or convention or association of churches.—The term "church or convention or association of churches" includes an organization described in subparagraph (A) or (B)(ii) of subsection (e)(3).

(B) Annuity contract.—The term "annuity contract" includes a custodial account described in section 403(b)(7) and a retirement income account described in section 403(b)(9).

(C) Accrued benefit.—The term "accrued benefit" means—

(i) in the case of a defined benefit plan, the employee's accrued benefit determined under the plan, and

(ii) in the case of a plan other than a defined benefit plan, the balance of the employee's account under the plan.

(Added Pub.L. 93–406, Title II, § 1015, Sept. 2, 1974, 88 Stat. 925; amended Pub.L. 94–455, Title XIX, §§ 1901(a)(64), 1906(b)(13)(A), Oct. 4, 1976, 90 Stat. 1775, 1834; Pub.L. 95–600, Title I, § 152(d), Nov. 6, 1978, 92 Stat. 2799; Pub.L. 96–364, Title II, §§ 207, 208(a), Title IV, § 407(b), Sept. 26, 1980, 94 Stat. 1288, 1289, 1305; Pub.L. 96–605, Title II, § 201(a), Dec. 28, 1980, 94 Stat. 3526; Pub.L. 96–613, § 5(a), Dec. 28, 1980, 94 Stat. 3580; Pub.L. 97–248, Title II, §§ 240(c), 246(a), 248(a), Sept. 3, 1982, 96 Stat. 520, 525, 526; Pub.L. 98–369, Div. A, Title IV, § 491(d)(26), (27), Title V, § 526(a)(1), (b)(1), (d)(1), (2), Title VII, § 713(i), July 18, 1984, 98 Stat. 850, 874, 875, 960; Pub.L. 98–397, Title II, § 204(b), Aug. 23, 1984, 98 Stat. 1445; Pub.L. 99–514, Title XI, §§ 1114(a), (b)(11), 1115(a), 1117(c), 1146(a), (b), 1151(e)(1), (i), Title XIII, § 1301(j)(4), Title XVIII, §§ 1852(f), 1898(c)(2)(A), (4)(A), (6)(A), (7)(A)(ii) to (vii), 1899A(12), Oct. 22, 1986, 100 Stat. 2448, 2451, 2452, 2462, 2491, 2506, 2507, 2657, 2868, 2951, 2953, 2954, 2958; Pub.L. 100–203, Title IX, § 9305(c), Dec. 22, 1987, 101 Stat. 1330–352; Pub.L. 100–647, Title I, §§ 1011(d)(8), (e)(4), (h)(5), (i)(1) to (3), (4)(A), (j)(1), (2), 1011A(b)(3), 1011B(a)(16), (17), (19), (20), 1018(t)(8)(E) to (G), Title II, § 2005(c)(1), (2), Title III, §§ 3011(b)(4), (5), 3021(b)(1), (2)(A), Title VI, § 6067(a), Nov. 10, 1988, 102 Stat. 3460, 3461, 3465, 3467, 3468, 3473, 3485, 3589, 3611, 3612, 3625, 3631, 3632, 3703; Pub.L. 101–140, Title II, §§ 203(a)(6), 204(b)(2), Nov. 8, 1989, 103 Stat. 831, 833; Pub.L. 101–239, Title VII, §§ 7811(m)(5), 7813(b), 7841(a)(2), Dec. 19, 1989, 103 Stat. 2412, 2413, 2427; Pub.L. 101–508, Title XI, § 11703(b)(1), Nov. 5, 1990, 104 Stat. 1388–517; Pub.L. 102–318, Title V, § 521(b)(20) to (22), July 3, 1992, 106 Stat. 311; Pub.L. 104–188, Title I, §§ 1421(b)(9)(C), 1431(a), (b)(1), (c)(1)(A), (D), (E), 1434(b), 1454(a), 1461(a), 1462(a), 1704(n)(1), Aug. 20, 1996, 110 Stat. 1798, 1802, 1803, 1807, 1817, 1822, 1824, 1883; Pub.L. 105–34, Title XV, § 1522(a), Title XVI, § 1601(d)(6)(A), (7), (h)(2)(D)(i), (ii), Aug. 5, 1997, 111 Stat. 1070, 1089, 1090, 1092; Pub.L. 105–206, Title VI, § 6018(c), July 22, 1998, 112 Stat. 822; Pub.L. 106–554, § 1(a)(7) [Title III, § 314(e)(2)], Dec. 21, 2000, 114 Stat. 2763, 2763A–643; Pub.L. 107–16, Title VI, §§ 631(a), 635(a) to (c), June 7, 2001, 115 Stat. 111, 117; Pub.L. 107–147, Title IV, § 411(o)(3) to (8), Mar. 9, 2002, 116 Stat. 48, 49; Pub.L. 108–311, Title IV, § 408(a)(15), Oct. 4, 2004, 118 Stat. 1192; Pub.L. 109–280, Title I, § 114(c), Title IX, §§ 902(d)(1), 903(a), 906(a)(1), (b)(1)(C), Title XI, 1106(b), Aug. 17, 2006, 120 Stat. 853, 1036, 1040, 1051, 1052, 1062; Pub.L. 110–28, Title VI, § 6611(a)(2), (b)(2), May 25, 2007, 121 Stat. 180, 181; Pub.L. 110–245, Title I, §§ 104(b), 105(b)(1), June 17, 2008, 122 Stat. 1626, 1628; Pub.L. 110–289, Div. A, Title VI, § 1604(b)(4), July 30, 2008, 122 Stat. 2829; Pub.L. 110–458, Title I, §§ 101(d)(2)(E), 109(b)(4) to (6), (c)(1), Dec. 23, 2008, 122 Stat. 5099, 5111; Pub.L. 113–97, Title II, §§ 201, 203(a), Apr. 7, 2014, 128 Stat. 1121, 1138; Pub.L. 113–235, Div. P, § 3(b), Dec. 16, 2014, 128 Stat. 2829; Pub.L. 113–295, Div. A, Title II, § 221(a)(19)(B)(i), (ii), (55), Dec. 19, 2014, 128 Stat. 4039, 4045; Pub.L. 114–113, Div. Q, Title III, § 336(a)(1), (d)(1), Dec. 18, 2015, 129 Stat. 3109, 3112.)

SUBCHAPTER O—GAIN OR LOSS ON DISPOSITION OF PROPERTY

PART III—COMMON NONTAXABLE EXCHANGES

§ 1041. Transfers of property between spouses or incident to divorce

(a) General rule.—No gain or loss shall be recognized on a transfer of property from an individual to (or in trust for the benefit of)—

(1) a spouse, or

(2) a former spouse, but only if the transfer is incident to the divorce.

(b) Transfer treated as gift; transferee has transferor's basis.—In the case of any transfer of property described in subsection (a)—

(1) for purposes of this subtitle, the property shall be treated as acquired by the transferee by gift, and

(2) the basis of the transferee in the property shall be the adjusted basis of the transferor.

(c) Incident to divorce.—For purposes of subsection (a)(2), a transfer of property is incident to the divorce if such transfer—

(1) occurs within 1 year after the date on which the marriage ceases, or

(2) is related to the cessation of the marriage.

(d) Special rule where spouse is nonresident alien.—Subsection (a) shall not apply if the spouse (or former spouse) of the individual making the transfer is a nonresident alien.

(e) Transfers in trust where liability exceeds basis.—Subsection (a) shall not apply to the transfer of property in trust to the extent that—

(1) the sum of the amount of the liabilities assumed, plus the amount of the liabilities to which the property is subject, exceeds

(2) the total of the adjusted basis of the property transferred.

Proper adjustment shall be made under subsection (b) in the basis of the transferee in such property to take into account gain recognized by reason of the preceding sentence. *(Added Pub.L. 98–369, Div. A, Title IV, § 421(a), July 18, 1984, 98 Stat. 793; amended Pub.L. 99–514, Title XVIII, § 1842(b), Oct. 22, 1986, 100 Stat. 2853; Pub.L. 100–647, Title I, § 1018(l)(3), Nov. 10, 1988, 102 Stat. 3584.)*

Commentary

A husband's preretirement withdrawals from an IRA to satisfy marital property obligations imposed by a divorce decree did not qualify for § 1041 treatment. Instead, they were taxable to the husband under § 408 (d)(1), and he was also subject to the 10 percent penalty for early IRA withdrawals under § 72 (t)(1). *Czepiel*

(Richard David) v. Commissioner, T.C. Memo. 1999–289, 78 T.C.M. (CCH) 378 (U.S. Tax Ct. 1999). The transaction would have been nontaxable under this section if he had transferred to his wife an interest in the IRAs themselves and such transfers were made under a marital settlement agreement. Compare, for example, *Young (John B.) v. Commissioner, 113 T.C. 152 (U.S. Tax Ct. 1999)* (when husband transferred appreciated property to wife pursuant to marital property settlement, he was not taxable on the appreciation, which would be subject to taxation only when the property was later sold to a third party).

Note that distributions to a spouse or former spouse who is an alternate payee under a QDRO (see 29 U.S.C.A. § 1056) are taxable to that spouse or former spouse under § 402(e)(1)(A). However, a distribution from a qualified retirement plan to a participant's daughter to satisfy a child support obligation is taxable to the participant. *Stahl (Robert L.) v. Commissioner, T.C. Memo. 2001–22, 81 T.C.M. (CCH) 1087 (U.S. Tax Ct. 2001)*.

A court order requiring an ex-husband to liquidate a profit-sharing plan to pay child support and spousal support arrearages to his ex-wife was not a QDRO. Thus the distribution was taxable to him and not to her. He could, of course, take an alimony deduction under sections 71 and 215 for the amount attributable to spousal support. *Amarasinghe (Jeanne E.) v. Commissioner, T.C. Memo 2007–333, 94 T.C.M. (CCH) 447 (U.S. Tax Ct. 2007)*.

Arnes v. U.S., 981 F.2d 456 (9th Cir. 1992), held that a former wife realized no gain on her half of the community property family corporation stock when, pursuant to the divorce settlement, the stock was redeemed by the corporation on behalf of the husband. The gain was treated instead as income taxable to the husband. The Commissioner has declined to follow *Arnes*. See *Blatt v. Commissioner, 102 T.C. 77, Tax Ct. Rep. (CCH) 49,641 (1994)*. However, in *Read (Carol M.) v. Commissioner, 114 T.C. 14, (U.S. Tax Ct. 2000)*, the Tax Court held that a former wife's redemption of shares in a corporation that she owned jointly with her former husband produced a taxable constructive dividend to the former husband when, pursuant to their divorce settlement and his election under it, she redeemed her shares in exchange for a down payment and installment obligation from the corporation. The Tax Court held that the redemption was "on behalf of" the husband because he had elected it under the settlement. Had he taken his alternative option under the settlement, to simply buy his wife's shares directly with his own money, there would have been no taxable event under this section.

Belot v. Commissioner, T.C. Memo 2016-113 (U.S. Tax Ct.) held that an ex-husband's sale of his shares in a jointly-owned business to his ex-wife a year after their original property settlement qualified for nonrecognition of taxable gain under this section. It was not material that the transfer was in settlement of a civil action rather than a divorce proceeding, because the transfer was made incident to the parties' divorce.

Despite subsection (b), which treats divorce transfers as gifts, in *Seymour v. Commissioner, 109 T.C. No. 14 (1997)*, the Tax Court held that interest payable by one spouse to another on a marital property promissory note may be deductible as investment interest, passive activity interest, or qualified residence interest, as the case may be. The Tax Court rejected the I.R.S. position that Section 1041 gift characterization of such transfers precluded the possibility of any interest deduction. See also *Armacost (Ronald) v. Commissioner, T.C. Memo 1998–150, 75 T.C.M. (CCH) 2177 (1998)* (holding that interest paid by ex-husband to ex-wife on promissory note was deductible as investment interest because it was fully allocable to investment property). Cf. *Liberty Vending, Inc. v. Commissioner, T.C. Memo 1998–177, 75 T.C.M. (CCH) 2285 (1998)* (attorney's fees payable in divorce action were deductible to extent incurred to recover income-producing assets wrongfully seized and dismantled by the other spouse).

A former wife's postdivorce sale of community property to a third party for the purpose of making an equalizing payment required by the divorce decree to her former husband did not satisfy subsection (a)(2) when the sale did not relieve the husband of any debt owed by him to his wife or to a third party. *Ingham v. U. S., 167 F.3d 1240 (9th Cir. 1999)*. Compare *Arnes v. U.S., 981 F.2d 456 (9th Cir. 1992)*, (transfer is considered "on behalf of" a former spouse if it satisfies an obligation or liability of that person).

SUBTITLE B—ESTATE AND GIFT TAXES

CHAPTER 12—GIFT TAX

SUBCHAPTER B—TRANSFERS

§ 2516. Certain property settlements

Where a husband and wife enter into a written agreement relative to their marital and property rights and divorce occurs within the 3-year period beginning on the date 1 year before such agreement is entered into (whether or not such agreement is approved by the divorce decree), any transfers of property or interests in property made pursuant to such agreement—

(1) to either spouse in settlement of his or her marital or property rights, or

(2) to provide a reasonable allowance for the support of issue of the marriage during minority,

shall be deemed to be transfers made for a full and adequate consideration in money or money's worth. *(Aug. 16, 1954, c. 736, 68A Stat. 409; Pub.L. 98–369, Div. A, Title IV, § 425(b), July 18, 1984, 98 Stat. 804.)*

SUBTITLE F—PROCEDURE AND ADMINISTRATION

CHAPTER 61—INFORMATION AND RETURNS

SUBCHAPTER A—RETURNS AND RECORDS

PART II—TAX RETURNS OR STATEMENTS

Subpart B—Income Tax Returns

§ 6013. Joint returns of income tax by husband and wife

(a) Joint returns.—A husband and wife may make a single return jointly of income taxes under subtitle A, even though one of the spouses has neither gross income nor deductions, except as provided below:

(1) no joint return shall be made if either the husband or wife at any time during the taxable year is a nonresident alien;

(2) no joint return shall be made if the husband and wife have different taxable years; except that if such taxable years begin on the same day and end on different days because of the death of either or both, then the joint return may be made with respect to the taxable year of each. The above exception shall not apply if the surviving spouse remarries before the close of his taxable year, nor if the taxable year of either spouse is a fractional part of a year under section 443(a)(1);

(3) in the case of death of one spouse or both spouses the joint return with respect to the decedent may be made only by his executor or administrator; except that in the case of the death of one spouse the joint return may be made by the surviving spouse with respect to both himself and the decedent if no return for the taxable year has been made by the decedent, no executor or administrator has been appointed, and no executor or administrator is appointed before the last day prescribed by law for filing the return of the surviving spouse. If an executor or administrator of the decedent is appointed after the making of the joint return by the surviving spouse, the executor or administrator may disaffirm such joint return by making, within 1 year after the last day prescribed by law for filing the return of the surviving spouse, a separate return for the taxable year of the decedent with respect to which the joint return was made, in which case the return made by the survivor shall constitute his separate return.

(b) Joint return after filing separate return.—

(1) In general.—Except as provided in paragraph (2), if an individual has filed a separate return for a taxable year for which a joint return could have been made by him and his spouse under subsection (a) and the time prescribed by law for filing the return for such taxable year has expired, such individual and his spouse may nevertheless make a joint return for such taxable year. A joint return filed by the husband and wife under this subsection shall constitute the return of the husband and wife for such taxable year, and all payments, credits, refunds, or other repayments made or allowed with respect to the separate return of either spouse for such taxable year shall be taken into account in determining the extent to which the tax based upon the joint return has been paid. If a joint return is made under this subsection, any election (other than the election to file a separate return) made by either spouse in his separate return for such taxable year with respect to the treatment of any income, deduction, or credit of such spouse shall not be changed in the making of the joint return where such election would have been irrevocable if the joint return had not been made. If a joint return is made under this subsection after the death of either spouse, such return with respect to the decedent can be made only by his executor or administrator.

(2) Limitations for making of election.—The election provided for in paragraph (1) may not be made—

(A) after the expiration of 3 years from the last date prescribed by law for filing the return for such taxable year (determined without regard to any extension of time granted to either spouse); or

(B) after there has been mailed to either spouse, with respect to such taxable year, a notice of deficiency under section 6212, if the spouse, as to such notice, files a petition with the Tax Court within the time prescribed in section 6213; or

(C) after either spouse has commenced a suit in any court for the recovery of any part of the tax for such taxable year; or

(D) after either spouse has entered into a closing agreement under section 7121 with respect to such taxable year, or after any civil or criminal case arising against either spouse with respect to such taxable year has been compromised under section 7122.

(3) When return deemed filed.—

(A) Assessment and collection.—For purposes of section 6501 (relating to periods of limitations on assessment and collection), and for purposes of section 6651 (relating to delinquent returns), a joint return made under this subsection shall be deemed to have been filed—

(i) Where both spouses filed separate returns prior to making the joint return—on the date the last separate return was filed (but not earlier than the last date prescribed by law for filing the return of either spouse);

(ii) Where only one spouse filed a separate return prior to the making of the joint return, and the other spouse had less than the exemption amount of gross income for such taxable year—on the date of the filing of such separate return (but not earlier than the last date prescribed by law for the filing of such separate return); or

(iii) Where only one spouse filed a separate return prior to the making of the joint return, and the other spouse had gross income of the exemption amount or more for such taxable year—on the date of the filing of such joint return.

For purposes of this subparagraph, the term "exemption amount" has the meaning given to such term by section 151(d). For purposes of clauses (ii) and (iii), if the spouse whose gross income is being compared to the exemption amount is 65 or over, such clauses shall be applied by substituting "the sum of the exemption amount and the additional standard deduction under section 63(c)(2) by reason of section 63(f)(1)(A)" for "the exemption amount".

(B) Credit or refund.—For purposes of section 6511, a joint return made under this subsection shall be deemed to have been filed on the last date prescribed by law for filing the return for such taxable year (determined without regard to any extension of time granted to either spouse).

(4) **Additional time for assessment.**—If a joint return is made under this subsection, the periods of limitations provided in sections 6501 and 6502 on the making of assessments and the beginning of levy or a proceeding in court for collection shall with respect to such return include one year immediately after the date of the filing of such joint return (computed without regard to the provisions of paragraph (3)).

(5) **Additions to the tax and penalties.**—

(A) **Coordination with part II of subchapter A of chapter 68.**—For purposes of part II of subchapter A of chapter 68, where the sum of the amounts shown as tax on the separate returns of each spouse is less than the amount shown as tax on the joint return made under this subsection—

(i) such sum shall be treated as the amount shown on the joint return,

(ii) any negligence (or disregard of rules or regulations) on either separate return shall be treated as negligence (or such disregard) on the joint return, and

(iii) any fraud on either separate return shall be treated as fraud on the joint return.

(B) **Criminal penalty.**—For purposes of section 7206(1) and (2) and section 7207 (relating to criminal penalties in the case of fraudulent returns) the term "return" includes a separate return filed by a spouse with respect to a taxable year for which a joint return is made under this subsection after the filing of such separate return.

(c) **Treatment of joint return after death of either spouse.**—For purposes of sections 15, 443, and 7851(a)(1)(A), where the husband and wife have different taxable years because of the death of either spouse, the joint return shall be treated as if the taxable years of both spouses ended on the date of the closing of the surviving spouse's taxable year.

(d) **Special rules.**—For purposes of this section—

(1) the status as husband and wife of two individuals having taxable years beginning on the same day shall be determined—

(A) if both have the same taxable year—as of the close of such year; or

(B) if one dies before the close of the taxable year of the other—as of the time of such death;

(2) an individual who is legally separated from his spouse under a decree of divorce or of separate maintenance shall not be considered as married; and

(3) if a joint return is made, the tax shall be computed on the aggregate income and the liability with respect to the tax shall be joint and several.

[(e) **Repealed.** Pub.L. 105–206, Title III, § 3201(e)(1), July 22, 1998, 112 Stat. 740]

(f) **Joint return where individual is in missing status.**—For purposes of this section and subtitle A—

(1) **Election by spouse.**—If—

(A) an individual is in a missing status (within the meaning of paragraph (3)) as a result of service in a combat zone (as determined for purposes of section 112), and

(B) the spouse of such individual is otherwise entitled to file a joint return for any taxable year which begins on or before the day which is 2 years after the date designated under section 112 as the date of termination of combatant activities in such zone,

then such spouse may elect under subsection (a) to file a joint return for such taxable year. With respect to service in the combat zone designated for purposes of the Vietnam conflict, such election may be made for any taxable year while an individual is in missing status.

(2) **Effect of election.**—If the spouse of an individual described in paragraph (1)(A) elects to file a joint return under subsection (a) for a taxable year, then, until such election is revoked—

(A) such election shall be valid even if such individual died before the beginning of such year, and

(B) except for purposes of section 692 (relating to income taxes of members of the Armed Forces, astronauts, and victims of certain terrorist attacks on death), the income tax liability of such individual, his spouse, and his estate shall be determined as if he were alive throughout the taxable year.

(3) **Missing status.**—For purposes of this subsection—

(A) **Uniformed services.**—A member of a uniformed service (within the meaning of section 101(3) of title 37 of the United States Code) is in a missing status for any period for which he is entitled to pay and allowances under section 552 of such title 37.

(B) **Civilian employees.**—An employee (within the meaning of section 5561(2) of title 5 of the United States Code) is in a missing status for any period for which he is entitled to pay and allowances under section 5562 of such title 5.

(4) **Making of election; revocation.**—An election described in this subsection with respect to any taxable year may be made by filing a joint return in accordance with subsection (a) and under such regulations as may be prescribed by the Secretary. Such an election may be revoked by either spouse on or before the due date (including extensions) for such taxable year, and, in the case of an executor or administrator, may be revoked by disaffirming as provided in the last sentence of subsection (a)(3).

(g) **Election to treat nonresident alien individual as resident of the United States.**—

(1) **In general.**—A nonresident alien individual with respect to whom this subsection is in effect for the taxable year shall be treated as a resident of the United States—

(A) for purposes of chapter 1 for all of such taxable year, and

(B) for purposes of chapter 24 (relating to wage withholding) for payments of wages made during such taxable year.

(2) Individuals with respect to whom this subsection is in effect.—This subsection shall be in effect with respect to any individual who, at the close of the taxable year for which an election under this subsection was made, was a nonresident alien individual married to a citizen or resident of the United States, if both of them made such election to have the benefits of this subsection apply to them.

(3) Duration of election.—An election under this subsection shall apply to the taxable year for which made and to all subsequent taxable years until terminated under paragraph (4) or (5); except that any such election shall not apply for any taxable year if neither spouse is a citizen or resident of the United States at any time during such year.

(4) Termination of election.—An election under this subsection shall terminate at the earliest of the following times:

(A) Revocation by taxpayers.—If either taxpayer revokes the election, as of the first taxable year for which the last day prescribed by law for filing the return of tax under chapter 1 has not yet occurred.

(B) Death.—In the case of the death of either spouse, as of the beginning of the first taxable year of the spouse who survives following the taxable year in which such death occurred; except that if the spouse who survives is a citizen or resident of the United States who is a surviving spouse entitled to the benefits of section 2, the time provided by this subparagraph shall be as of the close of the last taxable year for which such individual is entitled to the benefits of section 2.

(C) Legal separation.—In the case of the legal separation of the couple under a decree of divorce or of separate maintenance, as of the beginning of the taxable year in which such legal separation occurs.

(D) Termination by Secretary.—At the time provided in paragraph (5).

(5) Termination by Secretary.—The Secretary may terminate any election under this subsection for any taxable year if he determines that either spouse has failed—

(A) to keep such books and records,

(B) to grant such access to such books and records, or

(C) to supply such other information,

as may be reasonably necessary to ascertain the amount of liability for taxes under chapter 1 of either spouse for such taxable year.

(6) Only one election.—If any election under this subsection for any two individuals is terminated under paragraph (4) or (5) for any taxable year, such two individuals shall be ineligible to make an election under this subsection for any subsequent taxable year.

(h) Joint return, etc., for year in which nonresident alien becomes resident of United States.—

(1) In general.—If—

(A) any individual is a nonresident alien individual at the beginning of any taxable year but is a resident of the United States at the close of such taxable year,

(B) at the close of such taxable year, such individual is married to a citizen or resident of the United States, and

(C) both individuals elect the benefits of this subsection at the time and in the manner prescribed by the Secretary by regulation,

then the individual referred to in subparagraph (A) shall be treated as a resident of the United States for purposes of chapter 1 for all of such taxable year, and for purposes of chapter 24 (relating to wage withholding) for payments of wages made during such taxable year.

(2) Only one election.—If any election under this subsection applies for any 2 individuals for any taxable year, such 2 individuals shall be ineligible to make an election under this subsection for any subsequent taxable year.

(Aug. 16, 1954, c. 736, 68A Stat. 733; Pub.L. 85–866, Title I, § 73, Sept. 2, 1958, 72 Stat. 1660; Pub.L. 91–172, Title VIII, § 801(a)(2), (b)(2), (c)(2), (d)(2), Dec. 30, 1969, 83 Stat. 675, 676; Pub.L. 91–679, § 1, Jan. 12, 1971, 84 Stat. 2063; Pub.L. 92–178, Title II, § 201(a)(2), (b)(2), Dec. 10, 1971, 85 Stat. 510; Pub.L. 93–597, § 3(a), Jan. 2, 1975, 88 Stat. 1950; Pub.L. 94–455, Title X, § 1012(a)(1), Title XIX, § 1906(a)(1), (b)(13)(A), Oct. 4, 1976, 90 Stat. 1612, 1824, 1834; Pub.L. 94–569, § 3(d), Oct. 20, 1976, 90 Stat. 2699; Pub.L. 95–600, Title I, § 102(b)(2), Title VII, § 701(u)(15)(A) to (C), (16)(A), Nov. 6, 1978, 92 Stat. 2771, 2919, 2920; Pub.L. 97–34, Title I, § 104(d)(2), Aug. 13, 1981, 95 Stat. 189; Pub.L. 97–248, Title III, §§ 307(a)(4), (5), 308(a), Sept. 3, 1982, 96 Stat. 589, 591; Pub.L. 97–448, Title III, § 307(c), Jan. 12, 1983, 96 Stat. 2407; Pub.L. 98–67, Title I, § 102(a), Aug. 5, 1983, 97 Stat. 369; Pub.L. 98–369, Div. A, Title IV, §§ 424(a), 474(b)(2), July 18, 1984, 98 Stat. 801, 830; Pub.L. 99–514, Title I, § 104(a)(2), Title XVII, § 1708(a)(3), Oct. 22, 1986, 100 Stat. 2104, 2782; Pub.L. 100–647, Title I, § 1015(b)(1), Nov. 10, 1988, 102 Stat. 3568; Pub.L. 101–239, Title VII, § 7721(c)(6), Dec. 19, 1989, 103 Stat. 2399; Pub.L. 101–508, Title XI, § 11704(a)(22), Nov. 5, 1990, 104 Stat. 1388-519; Pub.L. 104–168, Title IV, § 402(a), July 30, 1996, 110 Stat. 1459; Pub.L. 105–206, Title III, § 3201(e)(1), Title VI, § 6011(e)(2), July 22, 1998, 112 Stat. 740, 818; Pub.L. 107–134, Title I, § 101(b)(2), Jan. 23, 2002, 115 Stat. 2428; Pub.L. 108–121, Title I, § 110(a)(2)(B), Nov. 11, 2003, 117 Stat. 1342.)

Commentary

Even before the United States Supreme Court constitutionally extended the right to marry to same-sex couples (Obergefell v. Hodges, 135 S.Ct. 2584 (2015)), the Treasury Department granted California same-sex married couples and registered domestic partners (RDPs) the tax benefits of income splitting enjoyed by opposite-sex married couples, reasoning that under California community property law each same-sex spouse or RDP owns a one-half interest in the earnings of the other spouse or RDP. IRS Priv. Ltr. Rul. 201021048 (May 5, 2010), relying on *Poe v. Seaborn, 282 U.S. 1010 (1930)*. In the ruling, the Treasury Department announced that it would tax each same-sex spouse or RDP according to the relatively favorable rate schedule applied to individual tax payers. The constitutionally required equal treatment of same-sex and opposite-sex couples, should result in equal treatment of same-sex and opposite-sex married couples, with the consequence of subjecting same-sex married persons to the relatively unfavorable rate schedules for married persons, which give rise to the "marriage penalty." However, RDPS should retain their more favorable schedule because they are not married persons.

When a tax protestor failed to file a tax return, even though income tax had been fully withheld from his wages at the joint-filing rate, the Tax Court denied him joint filing status because he failed to file a return, reasoning that joint filing status must be elected by actually filing a return. Consequently, the taxpayer was taxed at the higher "married filing separately" schedule. *Salzer (Donald T.) v. Commissioner, T.C. Memo 2014-188.*

§ 6015. Relief from joint and several liability on joint return

(a) In general.—Notwithstanding section 6013(d)(3)—

(1) an individual who has made a joint return may elect to seek relief under the procedures prescribed under subsection (b); and

(2) if such individual is eligible to elect the application of subsection (c), such individual may, in addition to any election under paragraph (1), elect to limit such individual's liability for any deficiency with respect to such joint return in the manner prescribed under subsection (c).

Any determination under this section shall be made without regard to community property laws.

(b) Procedures for relief from liability applicable to all joint filers.—

(1) In general.—Under procedures prescribed by the Secretary, if—

(A) a joint return has been made for a taxable year;

(B) on such return there is an understatement of tax attributable to erroneous items of one individual filing the joint return;

(C) the other individual filing the joint return establishes that in signing the return he or she did not know, and had no reason to know, that there was such understatement;

(D) taking into account all the facts and circumstances, it is inequitable to hold the other individual liable for the deficiency in tax for such taxable year attributable to such understatement; and

(E) the other individual elects (in such form as the Secretary may prescribe) the benefits of this subsection not later than the date which is 2 years after the date the Secretary has begun collection activities with respect to the individual making the election,

then the other individual shall be relieved of liability for tax (including interest, penalties, and other amounts) for such taxable year to the extent such liability is attributable to such understatement.

(2) Apportionment of relief.—If an individual who, but for paragraph (1)(C), would be relieved of liability under paragraph (1), establishes that in signing the return such individual did not know, and had no reason to know, the extent of such understatement, then such individual shall be relieved of liability for tax (including interest, penalties, and other amounts) for such taxable year to the extent that such liability is attributable to the portion of such understatement of which such individual did not know and had no reason to know.

(3) Understatement.—For purposes of this subsection, the term "understatement" has the meaning given to such term by section 6662(d)(2)(A).

(c) Procedures to limit liability for taxpayers no longer married or taxpayers legally separated or not living together.—

(1) In general.—Except as provided in this subsection, if an individual who has made a joint return for any taxable year elects the application of this subsection, the individual's liability for any deficiency which is assessed with respect to the return shall not exceed the portion of such deficiency properly allocable to the individual under subsection (d).

(2) Burden of proof.—Except as provided in subparagraph (A)(ii) or (C) of paragraph (3), each individual who elects the application of this subsection shall have the burden of proof with respect to establishing the portion of any deficiency allocable to such individual.

(3) Election.—

(A) Individuals eligible to make election.—

(i) In general.—An individual shall only be eligible to elect the application of this subsection if—

(I) at the time such election is filed, such individual is no longer married to, or is legally separated from, the individual with whom such individual filed the joint return to which the election relates; or

(II) such individual was not a member of the same household as the individual with whom such joint return was filed at any time during the 12–month period ending on the date such election is filed.

(ii) Certain taxpayers ineligible to elect.—If the Secretary demonstrates that assets were transferred between individuals filing a joint return as part of a fraudulent scheme by such individuals, an election under this subsection by either individual shall be invalid (and section 6013(d)(3) shall apply to the joint return).

(B) Time for election.—An election under this subsection for any taxable year may be made at any time after a deficiency for such year is asserted but not later than 2 years after the date on which the Secretary has begun collection activities with respect to the individual making the election.

(C) Election not valid with respect to certain deficiencies.—If the Secretary demonstrates that an individual making an election under this subsection had actual knowledge, at the time such individual signed the return, of any item giving rise to a deficiency (or portion thereof) which is not allocable to such individual under subsection (d), such election shall not apply to such deficiency (or portion). This subparagraph shall not apply where the individual with actual knowledge establishes that such individual signed the return under duress.

(4) Liability increased by reason of transfers of property to avoid tax—

(A) In general.—Notwithstanding any other provision of this subsection, the portion of the deficiency for which the individual electing the application of this subsection is liable (without regard to this paragraph) shall be increased by the value of any disqualified asset transferred to the individual.

(B) Disqualified asset.—For purposes of this paragraph—

(i) In general.—The term "disqualified asset" means any property or right to property transferred to an individual making the election under this subsection with respect to a joint return by the other individual filing such joint return if the principal purpose of the transfer was the avoidance of tax or payment of tax.

(ii) Presumption.—

(I) In general.—For purposes of clause (i), except as provided in subclause (II), any transfer which is made after the date which is 1 year before the date on which the first letter of proposed deficiency which allows the taxpayer an opportunity for administrative review in the Internal Revenue Service Office of Appeals is sent shall be presumed to have as its principal purpose the avoidance of tax or payment of tax.

(II) Exceptions.—Subclause (I) shall not apply to any transfer pursuant to a decree of divorce or separate maintenance or a written instrument incident to such a decree or to any transfer which an individual establishes did not have as its principal purpose the avoidance of tax or payment of tax.

(d) Allocation of deficiency.—For purposes of subsection (c).—

(1) In general.—The portion of any deficiency on a joint return allocated to an individual shall be the amount which bears the same ratio to such deficiency as the net amount of items taken into account in computing the deficiency and allocable to the individual under paragraph (3) bears to the net amount of all items taken into account in computing the deficiency.

(2) Separate treatment of certain items.—If a deficiency (or portion thereof) is attributable to—

(A) the disallowance of a credit; or

(B) any tax (other than tax imposed by section 1 or 55) required to be included with the joint return;

and such item is allocated to one individual under paragraph (3), such deficiency (or portion) shall be allocated to such individual. Any such item shall not be taken into account under paragraph (1).

(3) Allocation of items giving rise to the deficiency.—For purposes of this subsection—

(A) In general.—Except as provided in paragraphs (4) and (5), any item giving rise to a deficiency on a joint return shall be allocated to individuals filing the return in the same manner as it would have been allocated if the individuals had filed separate returns for the taxable year.

(B) Exception where other spouse benefits.—Under rules prescribed by the Secretary, an item otherwise allocable to an individual under subparagraph (A) shall be allocated to the other individual filing the joint return to the extent the item gave rise to a tax benefit on the joint return to the other individual.

(C) Exception for fraud.—The Secretary may provide for an allocation of any item in a manner not prescribed by subparagraph (A) if the Secretary establishes that such allocation is appropriate due to fraud of one or both individuals.

(4) Limitations on separate returns disregarded.—If an item of deduction or credit is disallowed in its entirety solely because a separate return is filed, such disallowance shall be disregarded and the item shall be computed as if a joint return had been filed and then allocated between the spouses appropriately. A similar rule shall apply for purposes of section 86.

(5) Child's liability.—If the liability of a child of a taxpayer is included on a joint return, such liability shall be disregarded in computing the separate liability of either spouse and such liability shall be allocated appropriately between the spouses.

(e) Petition for review by Tax Court.—

(1) In general.—In the case of an individual against whom a deficiency has been asserted and who elects to have subsection (b) or (c) apply, or in the case of an individual who requests equitable relief under subsection (f)—

(A) In general.—In addition to any other remedy provided by law, the individual may petition the Tax Court (and the Tax Court shall have jurisdiction) to determine the appropriate relief available to the individual under this section if such petition is filed—

(i) at any time after the earlier of—

(I) the date the Secretary mails, by certified or registered mail to the taxpayer's last known address, notice of the Secretary's final determination of relief available to the individual, or

(II) the date which is 6 months after the date such election is filed or request is made with the Secretary, and

(ii) not later than the close of the 90th day after the date described in clause (i)(I).

(B) Restrictions applicable to collection of assessment.—

(i) In general.—Except as otherwise provided in section 6851 or 6861, no levy or proceeding in court shall be made, begun, or prosecuted against the individual making an election under subsection (b) or (c) or requesting equitable relief under subsection (f) for collection of any assessment to which such election or request relates until the close of the 90th day referred to in subparagraph (A)(ii), or, if a petition has been filed with the Tax Court under subparagraph (A), until the decision of the Tax Court has become final. Rules similar to the rules of section 7485 shall apply with respect to the collection of such assessment.

(ii) Authority to enjoin collection actions.—Notwithstanding the provisions of section 7421(a), the beginning of such levy or proceeding during the time the prohibition under clause (i) is in force may be enjoined by a proceeding in the proper court, including the Tax Court. The Tax Court shall have no jurisdiction under this subparagraph to enjoin any action or proceeding unless a timely petition has been filed under subparagraph (A) and then only in respect of the amount of the assessment to which the election under subsection (b) or (c) relates or to which the request under subsection (f) relates.

(2) Suspension of running of period of limitations.—The running of the period of limitations in section 6502 on the collection of the assessment to which the petition under paragraph (1)(A) relates shall be suspended—

(A) for the period during which the Secretary is prohibited by paragraph (1)(B) from collecting by levy or a proceeding in court and for 60 days thereafter, and

(B) if a waiver under paragraph (5) is made, from the date the claim for relief was filed until 60 days after the waiver is filed with the Secretary.

(3) Limitation on Tax Court jurisdiction.—If a suit for refund is begun by either individual filing the joint return pursuant to section 6532—

(A) the Tax Court shall lose jurisdiction of the individual's action under this section to whatever extent jurisdiction is acquired by the district court or the United States Court of Federal Claims over the taxable years that are the subject of the suit for refund, and

(B) the court acquiring jurisdiction shall have jurisdiction over the petition filed under this subsection.

(4) Notice to other spouse.—The Tax Court shall establish rules which provide the individual filing a joint return but not making the election under subsection (b) or (c) or the request for equitable relief under subsection (f) with adequate notice and an opportunity to become a party to a proceeding under either such subsection.

(5) Waiver.—An individual who elects the application of subsection (b) or (c) or who requests equitable relief under subsection (f) (and who agrees with the Secretary's determination of relief) may waive in writing at any time the restrictions in paragraph (1)(B) with respect to collection of the outstanding assessment (whether or not a notice of the Secretary's final determination of relief has been mailed).

(6) Suspension of running of period for filing petition in title 11 cases.—In the case of a person who is prohibited by reason of a case under title 11, United States Code, from filing a petition under paragraph (1)(A) with respect to a final determination of relief under this section, the running of the period prescribed by such paragraph for filing such a petition with respect to such final determination shall be suspended for the period during which the person is so prohibited from filing such a petition, and for 60 days thereafter.

(f) Equitable relief.—Under procedures prescribed by the Secretary, if—

(1) taking into account all the facts and circumstances, it is inequitable to hold the individual liable for any unpaid tax or any deficiency (or any portion of either); and

(2) relief is not available to such individual under subsection (b) or (c),

the Secretary may relieve such individual of such liability.

(g) Credits and refunds.—

(1) In general.—Except as provided in paragraphs (2) and (3), notwithstanding any other law or rule of law (other than section 6511, 6512(b), 7121, or 7122), credit or refund shall be allowed or made to the extent attributable to the application of this section.

(2) Res judicata.—In the case of any election under subsection (b) or (c) or of any request for equitable relief under subsection (f), if a decision of a court in any prior proceeding for the same taxable year has become final, such decision shall be conclusive except with respect to the qualification of the individual for relief which was not an issue in such proceeding. The exception contained in the preceding sentence shall not apply if the court determines that the individual participated meaningfully in such prior proceeding.

(3) Credit and refund not allowed under subsection (c).—No credit or refund shall be allowed as a result of an election under subsection (c).

(h) Regulations.—The Secretary shall prescribe such regulations as are necessary to carry out the provisions of this section, including—

(1) regulations providing methods for allocation of items other than the methods under subsection (d)(3); and

(2) regulations providing the opportunity for an individual to have notice of, and an opportunity to participate in, any administrative proceeding with respect to an election made under subsection (b) or (c) or a request for equitable relief made under subsection (f) by the other individual filing the joint return.

(Added Pub.L. 105–206, Title III, § 3201(a), July 22, 1998, 112 Stat. 734; amended Pub.L. 105–277, Div. J, Title IV, § 4002(c)(2), Oct. 21, 1998, 112 Stat. 2681–906; Pub.L. 106–554, § 1(a)(7) [Title III, § 313(a)], Dec. 21, 2000, 114 Stat. 2763, 2763A–640; Pub.L. 109–432, Div. C, Title IV, § 408(a), (b), Dec. 20, 2006, 120 Stat. 3061, 3062; Pub.L. 114–113, Div. Q, Title IV, § 424(a)(1), Dec. 18, 2015, 129 Stat. 3124.)

Commentary

Although subsection (a) provides that any determination concerning innocent spouse relief shall be made without regard to community property laws, *Ordlock (Lois E.) v. Commissioner, 533 F.3d 1136 (9th Cir. 2008)*, holds that state community property law governs the availability of *refunds* pursuant to innocent spouse relief. Thus, a California wife granted innocent spouse relief was not entitled to a refund of any of tax payments already made from community property. *Ordlock* reasons that the purpose of the subsection (a) disregard and of relief under this section generally, is to prevent a spouse or ex-spouse from being unfairly burdened by an obligation to pay taxes on the unreported income of the other spouse. Moreover, under California law, all the community property is liable for the debts of either spouse. Therefore, the community property was fully available to pay the husband's tax debt without regard to the wife's innocent spouse status.

In 2002, the Internal Revenue Service issued final regulations governing relief for innocent spouses. T.D. 9003, 2002–32 I.R.B. 249 (August 12, 2002). The regulations adopt the view that a spouse may be relieved of liability only if he or she lacked factual knowledge upon which to base an inquiry, that is, knowledge of the financial facts giving rise to the liability.

Timothy R. Becherer v. Commissioner, T.C. Memo 2004–282, 88 T.C.M. (CCH) 617 (U.S. Tax Ct. 2004), denied innocent spouse to an ex-husband with respect to unreported income of his ex-wife because he was aware of her employment and had adequate opportunity to review their joint tax return before it was filed to determine whether her income was properly reported.

Compare *Alvarado (Erica L.) v. Commissioner, T.C. Summary Opinion 2013-41*, where the court granted an ex-wife innocent spouse relief when she knew that her husband had omitted certain income at the time she signed the joint return where she derived no benefit from the income, she was divorced from her husband and she complied with all other income tax laws in subsequent years. Although Tax Court Summary Opinions may not be cited as precedent, the court's willingness to grant innocent spouse relief to a wife who knew of the omitted income is noteworthy.

In *Friedman v. Commissioner, 159 F.3d 1346, 1998 WL 613555 (2d Cir. 1998)*, an unpublished opinion, the issue was whether a wife who had not yet paid a tax deficiency for which she had previously been denied relief should be allowed such relief according to the subsequent 1998 liberalization of the innocent spouse statute. After oral argument, the attorney for the Internal Revenue Service agreed that the new statute should be applied "to any liability for tax arising after the date of the enactment of this Act and any liability for tax arising on or before such date but remaining unpaid as of such date," and the case was therefore remanded to the Tax Court for appropriate proceedings.

Taxpayers who are divorced, legally separated, or not living together may, under subsection (c), claim innocent spouse relief if they lacked actual knowledge of the deficiency. Otherwise, a married taxpayer must show, under § 6015(b), that he or she did not know and had no reason to know of the deficiency. See *Charlton (Fredie Lynn) v. Commissioner, 114 T.C. No. 22 (U.S. Tax Ct. 2000)*; and *Von Kalinowski (Julian O.) v. Commissioner, T.C. Memo 2001–21, 81 T.C.M. (CCH) 1081 (U.S. Tax Ct. 2001)*. *Jonson (David C.) v. Commissioner, 118 T.C. 106, Tax Ct. Rep. (CCH) 54, 641 (U.S. Tax Ct. 2002)*, holds that the marital status of a deceased taxpayer must be determined at the time of her death for purposes of innocent spouse relief sought by her estate. Therefore, a spouse married at the time of her death must be treated as married and subject to the more stringent requirements of subsection (b).

An ex-husband was permitted to advance a specific claim for innocent spouse relief even though his general claim for relief had earlier been dismissed for failure to appear at trial. When his general claim was dismissed, he was not yet separated or divorced and thus had no opportunity to be heard on his more specific and less demanding subsection (c) claim, which applies only to divorced spouses. *Santa (Dale H.) v. Commissioner, T.C. Memo 2013-178 (U.S. Tax Court 2013)*.

Raschke (Ronald Arthur) v. Commissioner, T.C. Summary Opinion 2014-32 (U.S. Tax Court 2014), held that an ex-husband had tacitly consented to a joint return electronically filed without his signature by his then-wife, when he had not filed a separate tax return even though he knew he had taxable income to report. However, the court nevertheless granted him equitable innocent spouse relief under subsection (f), with respect to unreported income earned by his wife in light of his financial hardship, serious medical condition, and the fact that the entire tax refund was paid directly to his wife.

In *Kollar (Mary Ann) v. Commissioner, 131 T.C. No.12, Tax Ct. Rep. (CCH) 57–593 (2008)*, the Tax Court held that it has jurisdiction to review an Internal Revenue Service denial of innocent spouse relief when it solely concerns accrued interest on a tax liability that was paid late.

A provision in a separation agreement or divorce decree allocating all joint tax liabilities to one spouse does not affect the government's right to collect from both spouses. In *Barriga (Angela) v. Commissioner, T.C. Memo 2004–102, 87 T.C.M. (CCH) 1236 (U.S. Tax Ct. 2004)*, the Tax Court held that the failure of the I.R.S. to grant equitable relief to a wife whose divorce decree allocated all joint tax liabilities to her former husband was not an abuse of discretion when she knew of the liabilities and would not suffer economic hardship if required to pay them.

Applying subsection (b) to a wife who was living with her husband, *Barranco (Patricia) v. Commissioner, T.C. Memo. 2003–18, 85 T.C.M. (CCH) 778 (U.S. Tax Ct. 2003)*, held that the wife had "reason to know" that her husband was underreporting taxable income when the taxable income reported by the husband was far less than the amount spent by the family. Consequently, before the wife signed the joint returns, she had a duty to inquire about the obvious discrepancy. *Alt (Rosalinda) v. Commissioner, 119 T.C. 306 (U.S. Tax Ct. 2002)*, denied innocent spouse relief to a spouse who remained married to the other spouse on the ground that she benefited from the tax savings that resulted from the other spouse's unlawful underreporting of income. *Nancy A. Sjodin v. Commissioner, T.C. Memo 2004–205, 88 T.C.M. (CCH) 221 (U.S. Tax Ct. 2004)*, denied innocent spouse relief for tax liabilities, which were reported on joint returns but never paid by the husband, to a wife who never separated from her husband on the ground that she should have known that he was unlikely to pay the tax liabilities when she signed the returns.

Begic (Belma) v. Commissioner, T.C. Memo 2007–74, 93 T.C.M. (CCH) 1242 (U.S. Tax Ct. 2007), granted innocent spouse relief to a divorced spouse who did not know about the income giving rise to the deficiency, did not participate in the daily operation of the business, and did not see or sign the joint tax return that gave rise to the deficiency.

Wiskell (David L.) v. Commissioner, T.C. Memo 1999–32, 77 T.C.M. (CCH) 1336 (U.S. Tax Ct. 1999), holds that an ex-spouse who had actual knowledge of the existence of the unreported amount is not entitled to innocent spouse relief under the new version of the statute. To the same effect, see *Amankwah (Andrews) v. Commissioner, T.C. Memo. 1999–382, 78 T.C.M. (CCH) 823 (U.S. Tax Ct. 1999)*, and *Mitchell (Herbert L.) v. Commissioner, T.C. Memo 2000–332, 80 T.C.M. (CCH) 590 (U.S. Tax Ct. 2000).* Similarly, *Cheshire (Kathryn) v. Commissioner, 115 T.C. No. 15 (U.S. Tax Ct. 2000),* holds that a spouse who knows of income but does not know that her spouse failed to include it on their joint return, is ineligible for innocent spouse relief. *Wiest (Michael S.) v. Commissioner, T.C. Memo. 2003–91, 85 T.C.M. (CCH) 1082 (U.S. Tax Ct. 2003),* held that the Internal Revenue Service abused its discretion when it declined to grant equitable relief, under subsection (f), to a taxpayer who knew of the tax liability but was not aware that his divorced spouse, who assumed responsibility for filing their joint returns, failed to file the returns or pay the tax due. *Washington (Connie A.) v. Commissioner, 120 T.C. 137 (U.S. Tax Ct. 2003),* held that the Internal Revenue Service abused its discretion in declining to grant equitable innocent spouse relief to an ex-wife whose ex-husband failed to pay income tax attributable to his own income on the couple's joint return. *Mora (Patricia) v. Commissioner, 117 T.C. 279 (2001), Tax Ct. Rep. (CCH) 54,565 (U.S. Tax Ct. 2001),* holds that under subsection (c), a former spouse may be granted relief if she knew of the investments and their corresponding tax shelter deductions, but not of the facts that made those deductions unlawful. She is relieved of joint and several liability only to the extent that she does not receive a tax benefit on her share of the joint income. Thus, if the deductions are greater than her former husband's share of the income can absorb, the remainder shall be treated as a tax benefit to the former wife and she shall remain liable for that portion of the deficiency. See also *Martin (Evelyn M.) v. Commissioner, T.C. Memo. 2000–346, 80 T.C.M. (CCH) 665 (U.S. Tax Ct. 2000),* where the Tax Court granted innocent spouse relief to a wife who had only general knowledge about the husband's complex business transactions that generated the tax deficiency and his subsequent criminal conviction and incarceration, and *Culver (Michael G.) v. Commissioner, 116 T.C. No. 15 (U.S. Tax Ct. 2001),* which granted innocent spouse relief to a divorced husband who was ignorant of his wife's embezzlement, even though a reasonably prudent person would have entertained suspicions. *Culver* interprets this section to place the burden of proof on the I.R.S. to demonstrate actual knowledge by a preponderance of the evidence. Applying the subsection (c) standard of "actual knowledge of the deficiency," *Charma Gatlin Cook v. Commissioner, T.C. Memo 2005–22 (U.S. Tax Ct. 2005),* granted innocent spouse relief to an ex-wife who prepared her husband's billing invoices, because the Internal Revenue Service failed to prove that the ex-wife knew that payment had actually been received by her former husband. With respect to disallowed deductions, *King (Kathy A.) v. Commissioner, 116 T.C. No.16 (U.S. Tax Ct. 2001)* holds that "actual knowledge" requires knowledge of the factual circumstances that make an item nondeductible. For extensive discussion of the current innocent spouse provision, see *Grossman v. Commissioner, 182 F.3d 275 (4th Cir. 1999).*

Davis and Lois Etkin v. Commissioner, T.C. Memo. 2005–245, 90 T.C.M. (CCH) 417 (U.S. Tax Ct. 2005), held that the Internal Revenue Service properly denied a wife equitable innocent spouse relief under subsection (f) when her husband had transferred substantial property to her and she was unable to demonstrate that the purpose of the transfers was not tax avoidance.

Campbell (Phyllis E.) v. Commissioner, T.C. Memo. 2006–24, 91 T.C.M. (CCH) 735 (U.S. Tax Ct. 2006), awarded innocent spouse relief to a still-married wife for an extremely large disallowed deduction reported by her husband on their joint return because she had no actual or constructive knowledge of the deduction. In light of the large amounts of money handled by the husband and wife's lack of knowledge of his business affairs, the tax court concluded that she did not have a duty of inquiry.

Motsko (Michael R.) v. Commissioner, T.C. Memo. 2006–17, 91 T.C.M. (CCH) 711 (U.S. Tax Ct. 2006), denied equitable innocent spouse relief to a husband who failed to confirm that his wife, who had already been indicted on criminal tax charges, had paid their joint income tax liability. Given her history, he was charged with a duty of inquiry.

Stanley K. and Tomi L. Baumann, T.C. Memo 2005–31, 89 T.C.M. (CCH) 790 (U.S. Tax Ct. 2005), held that the Internal Revenue Service did not abuse its subsection (f) discretion in granting innocent spouse relief to an abused ex-wife who had actual knowledge of the gambling earnings of her husband, which gave rise to the tax deficiency, on the ground that a documented history of physical abuse is sufficient to overcome actual knowledge.

For Internal Revenue Service guidance on the application of equitable relief when the terms of the statute are not satisfied, see Rev. Proc. 2000–15 2000–1 C.B. 447, 2000 WL 42026. §§ 1.6015–0 to 1.6015–9 (REG–106446–98, Fed. Reg. January 17, 2001). When liability is reported on a return but the liability has not been satisfied, the Internal Revenue Service requires that the spouse seeking relief no longer be married to the other spouse, have had no knowledge or reason to know that the tax would not be paid, and demonstrate that she would suffer economic hardship if no relief were allowed. Cases applying this standard and denying relief include *Castle (Susan L.) v. Commissioner, T.C. Memo 2002–142, 83 T.C.M. (CCH) 1788 (U.S. Tax Ct. 2002)*, and *Collier (Sandrus L.) v. Commissioner, T.C. Memo 2002–144, 83 T.C.M. (CCH) 1799 (U.S. Tax Ct. 2002).* But see *Floor (Jeanine T.) v. Commissioner, T.C. Memo. 2004–54, 87 T.C.M. (CCH) 1046 (U.S. Tax Ct. 2004),* which granted subsection (f) equitable relief to a spouse who knew that her husband was not likely to pay the income tax reported on their joint returns on the ground that other factors were strong enough to overcome the knowledge factor. The other factors were: the innocent spouse was divorced at the time she requested relief, would suffer economic hardship if relief were not granted, did not benefit from the unpaid tax liabilities, and had made a good faith effort to comply with the tax laws. Additionally, there were no asset transfers between the spouses.

Applying Treasury Regulation section 1.6015–1(d), *Chen (Paul) v. Commissioner, T.C. Memo 2006–160, 92 T.C.M. (CCH) 95 (U.S. Tax Ct. 2006),* concluded that although the husband was the actual architect of insurance and tax fraud, the wife could not qualify for innocent spouse relief because she "transferred assets to the other spouse as part of a fraudulent scheme."

Corson (Thomas) v. Commissioner, 114 T.C. No. 24 (U.S. Tax Ct. 2000), holds that a person whose former spouse was granted innocent spouse relief by the Internal Revenue Service has standing to contest the action in Tax Court, because a decision to grant one spouse tax relief is also a decision to impose the entire tax burden on the other spouse. For a case in which the Service refused innocent spouse relief but the Tax Court granted it under subsection (b) despite the opposition of a separated spouse, see *Eugene and Ione McClelland v. Commissioner, T.C. Memo 2005–121, 89 T.C.M. (CCH) 1329 (U.S. Tax Ct. 2005). Hale Exemption Trust v. Commissioner, T.C. Memo. 2001–89, 81 T.C.M. (CCH) 1507 (U.S. Tax Ct. 2001),* holds that a trust representing a deceased husband's estate may contest innocent spouse relief granted to the widow. *King (Kathy A.) v. Commissioner, 115 T.C. No. 8 (U.S. Tax Ct. 2000),* holds that when a spouse or former spouse seeks innocent spouse relief, the Internal Revenue Service must provide the other spouse with notice and opportunity to be heard. Compare pre–1998 law, which does not allow a taxpayer to challenge innocent spouse relief granted to the other spouse under pre–1998 law. *Miller (Clifford W.) v. Commissioner, 115 T.C. No. 40 (U.S. Tax Ct. 2000).*

However, in *Baranowicz (Isaac) v. Commissioner, 432 F.3d 972 (2005),* the Ninth Circuit Court of Appeals held that a spouse or ex-spouse who intervened in a Tax Court proceeding concerning innocent spouse relief for the other spouse has no standing to appeal an award of relief to a federal Court of Appeals.

Note that subsection (e) was amended in 2000 to deny Tax Court review to cases in which the Internal Revenue Service has not asserted a tax deficiency, that is, in cases in which tax due was properly reported but not paid. Commissioner v. Ewing, 439 F.3d 1009 (9th Cir. 2006); Billings (David Bruce) v. Commissioner, 127 T.C. No.2 (2006). However, on December 20, 2006, Congress amended this section to allow the Tax Court jurisdiction in such cases. The 2006 amendment applies only to taxes unpaid as of the date of the amendment. *Bock (Debra) v. Commissioner, T.C. Memo 2007–41, 93 T.C.M. (CCH) 927 (U.S. Tax Ct. 2007),* held that the Tax Court lacks jurisdiction to review cases involving reported but unpaid taxes when the taxes were ultimately paid prior to the effective date of the 2006 amendment.

Exercising jurisdiction under the 2006 amendment, in *Farmer (Linda D.) v. Commissioner, T.C. Memo 2007–74, T.C.M. (RIA) 2007–074 (U.S. Tax Ct. 2007),* the Tax Court granted an ex-wife innocent spouse relief even though she was aware that her husband did not intend to pay the taxes reported on their joint return, because she lacked access to business income that might have been used to pay the taxes and the payment of taxes under her current circumstances would cause considerable hardship.

Fain (Suzanne Vance) v. Commissioner, 129 T.C. 89 (U.S. Tax Ct 2007), holds that the subsection (e)(4) right of the other spouse to intervene in an innocent spouse proceeding survives the death of the other spouse and passes to his estate or heirs.

Van Arsdalen (Diana) v. Commissioner, 123 T. C. No. 7, Tax Ct. Rep. (CCH) 55,702 (U.S. Tax Ct. 2004), holds that, under subsection (e)(4), a spouse may intervene in a Tax Court proceeding in order to *support* the innocent spouse claim of his former spouse.

However, in *Maier (John, III) v. Commissioner, 119 T.C. 267 (U.S. Tax Ct. 2002),* the Tax Court held that it is without jurisdiction to review, on the petition of a spouse, innocent spouse relief granted to the other spouse by the Internal Revenue Service.

Although a taxpayer seeking review of an Internal Revenue Service denial could not directly plead of the expiration of the statute of limitations on the tax assessment, which can be pleaded only in defense against an action to collect taxes, still the expiration of the statute of limitations may be pleaded as a factor to be considered in weighing the equities of innocent spouse relief. *Block (Evelyn B.) v. Commissioner, 120 T.C. 62 (U.S. Tax Ct. 2003).*

Innocent spouse relief is available under subsection (f) only to taxpayers who filed a joint income tax return. *Raymond (Ranie M.) v. Commissioner, 119 T.C. 191 (U.S. Tax Ct. 2002).* Compare § 66, which applies to a taxpayer who files a separate return and seeks relief from tax on community income earned by the other spouse.

The Internal Revenue Service's application of overpayments to satisfy underpayment in a prior year is a "collection activity," which requires the Service to notify the taxpayer of the possibility of innocent spouse relief. *McGee v. Commissioner, 123 T.C. 314 (2004).* Where an ex-spouse was not so notified, *Kirsten Nelson v. Commissioner, T.C. Memo 2005–9, 89 T.C.M. (CCH) 685 (U.S. Tax Ct. 2004),* held that the Service abused its subsection (f) discretion in denying her claim for relief solely because she requested relief more than two years after collection activities began.

Helen Foy v. Commissioner, T.C. Memo 2005–116, 89 T.C.M. (CCH) 1299 (U.S. Tax Ct. 2005), holds that the Internal Revenue Service took an unreasonable litigation position with respect to a widow to whom the Service ultimately granted innocent spouse status, and therefore, under Section 7430, was required to pay her litigation costs.

A spouse who was her husband's bookkeeper was not entitled to innocent spouse relief under subsection under subsection (f), because the likelihood that she had actual knowledge of his unreported income outweighed all countervailing factors. *Armour (Bonnie M.) v. Commissioner, T.C. Memo 2016-129, 112 TCM (CCH) 7 (U.S. Tax Court 2016).*

CHAPTER 79—DEFINITIONS

§ 7703. Determination of marital status

(a) General rule.—For purposes of part V of subchapter B of chapter 1 and those provisions of this title which refer to this subsection—

(1) the determination of whether an individual is married shall be made as of the close of his taxable year; except that if his spouse dies during his taxable year such determination shall be made as of the time of such death; and

(2) an individual legally separated from his spouse under a decree of divorce or of separate maintenance shall not be considered as married.

(b) Certain married individuals living apart.—For purposes of those provisions of this title which refer to this subsection, if—

(1) an individual who is married (within the meaning of subsection (a)) and who files a separate return maintains as his home a household which constitutes for more than one-half of the taxable year the principal place of abode of a child (within the meaning of section 152(f)(1)) with respect to whom such individual is entitled to a deduction for the taxable year under section 151 (or would be so entitled but for section 152(e)),

(2) such individual furnishes over one-half of the cost of maintaining such household during the taxable year, and

(3) during the last 6 months of the taxable year, such individual's spouse is not a member of such household,

such individual shall not be considered as married. *(Added Pub.L. 99–514, Title XIII, § 1301(j)(2)(A), Oct. 22, 1986, 100 Stat. 2657; amended Pub.L. 100–647, Title I, § 1018(u)(41), Nov. 10, 1988, 102 Stat. 3592; Pub.L. 108–311, Title II, § 207(26), Oct. 4, 2004, 118 Stat. 1178.)*

Commentary

Chiosie (Keith) v. Commissioner, T.C. Memo. 2000–117, 79 T.C.M. (CCH) 1812 (U.S. Tax Ct. 2000), holds that an "emotionally estranged" couple who did not share the same bedroom could not be considered "unmarried" for tax purposes under subsection (b) because they shared the same residence. Thus the husband could not qualify for "head of household" status. His proper filing status was "married filing separately."

CODE OF FEDERAL REGULATIONS

TITLE 26—INTERNAL REVENUE

CHAPTER I—INTERNAL REVENUE SERVICE, DEPARTMENT OF THE TREASURY

SUBCHAPTER A—INCOME TAX

PART 1—INCOME TAXES

NORMAL TAXES AND SURTAXES

COMPUTATION OF TAXABLE INCOME

Items Specifically Included in Gross Income

NORMAL TAXES AND SURTAXES

COMPUTATION OF TAXABLE INCOME

Items Specifically Included in Gross Income

§ 1.71–1 Alimony and separate maintenance payments; income to wife or former wife.

(a) In general. Section 71 provides rules for treatment in certain cases of payments in the nature of or in lieu of alimony or an allowance for support as between spouses who are divorced or separated. For convenience, the payee spouse will hereafter in this section be referred to as the "wife" and the spouse from whom she is divorced or separated as the "husband." See section 7701(a)(17). For rules relative to the deduction by the husband of periodic payments not attributable to transferred property, see section 215 and the regulations thereunder. For rules relative to the taxable status of income of an estate or trust in case of divorce, etc., see section 682 and the regulations thereunder.

(b) Alimony or separate maintenance payments received from the husband—(1) Decree of divorce or separate maintenance. (i) In the case of divorce or legal separation, paragraph (1) of section 71(a) requires the inclusion in the gross income of the wife of periodic payments (whether or not made at regular intervals) received by her after a decree of divorce or of separate maintenance. Such periodic payments must be made in discharge of a legal obligation imposed upon or incurred by the husband because of the marital or family relationship under a court order or decree divorcing or legally separating the husband and wife or a written instrument incident to the divorce status or legal separation status.

(ii) For treatment of payments attributable to property transferred (in trust or otherwise), see paragraph (c) of this section.

(2) Written separation agreement. (i) Where the husband and wife are separated and living apart and do not file a joint income tax return for the taxable year, paragraph (2) of section 71(a) requires the inclusion in the gross income of the wife of periodic payments (whether or not made at regular intervals) received by her pursuant to a written separation agreement executed after August 16, 1954. The periodic payments must be made under the terms of the written separation agreement after its execution and because of the marital or family relationship. Such payments are includable in the wife's gross income whether or not the agreement is a legally enforceable instrument. Moreover, if the wife is divorced or legally separated subsequent to the written separation agreement, payments made under such agreement continue to fall within the provisions of section 71(a)(2).

(ii) For purposes of section 71(a)(2) any written separation agreement executed on or before August 16, 1954, which is altered or modified in writing by the parties in any material respect after that date will be treated as an agreement executed after August 16, 1954, with respect to payments made after the date of alteration or modification.

(iii) For treatment of payments attributable to property transferred (in trust or otherwise), see paragraph (c) of this section.

(3) Decree for support. (i) Where the husband and wife are separated and living apart and do not file a joint income tax return for the taxable year, paragraph (3) of section 71(a) requires the inclusion in the gross income of the wife of periodic payments (whether or not made at regular intervals) received by her after August 16, 1954, from her husband under any type of court order or decree (including an interlocutory decree of divorce or a decree of alimony pendente lite) entered after March 1, 1954, requiring the husband to make the payments for her support or maintenance. It is not necessary for the wife to be legally separated or divorced from her husband under a court order or decree; nor is it necessary for the order or decree for support to be for the purpose of enforcing a written separation agreement.

(ii) For purposes of section 71(a)(3), any decree which is altered or modified by a court order entered after March 1, 1954, will be treated as a decree entered after such date.

(4) Scope of section 71(a). Section 71(a) applies only to payments made because of the family or marital relationship in recognition of the general obligation to support which is made specific by the decree, instrument, or agreement. Thus, section 71(a) does not apply to that part of any periodic payment which is attributable to the repayment by the husband of, for example, a bona fide loan previously made to him by the wife, the satisfaction of which is specified in the decree, instrument, or agreement as a part of the general settlement between the husband and wife.

(5) Year of inclusion. Periodic payments are includible in the wife's income under section 71(a) only for the taxable year in which received by her. As to such amounts, the wife is to be treated as if she makes her income tax returns on the cash receipts and disbursements method, regardless of whether she normally makes such returns on the accrual method. However, if the periodic payments described in section 71(a) are to be made by an estate or trust, such periodic payments are to be included in the wife's taxable year in which they are includible according to the rules as to income of estates and trusts provided in sections 652, 662, and 682, whether or not such payments are made out of the income of such estates or trusts.

(6) Examples. The foregoing rules are illustrated by the following examples in which it is assumed that the husband and wife file separate income tax returns on the calendar year basis:

Example 1. W files suit for divorce from H in 1953. In consideration of W's promise to relinquish all marital rights and not to make public H's financial affairs, H agrees in writing to pay $200 a month to W during her lifetime if a final decree of divorce is granted without any provision for alimony. Accordingly, W does not request alimony and no provision for alimony is made under a final decree of divorce entered December 31, 1953. During 1954, H pays W $200 a month, pursuant to the promise. The $2,400 thus received by W is includible in her gross income under the provisions of section 71(a)(1). Under section 215, H is entitled to a deduction of $2,400 from his gross income.

Example 2. During 1945, H and W enter into an antenuptial agreement, under which, in consideration of W's relinquishment of all marital rights (including dower) in H's property, and, in order to provide for W's support and household expenses, H promises to pay W $200 a month during her lifetime. Ten years after their marriage, W sues H for divorce but does not ask for or obtain alimony because of the provision already made for her support in the antenuptial agreement. Likewise, the divorce decree is silent as to such agreement and H's obligation to support W. Section 71(a) does not apply to such a case. If, however, the decree were modified so as to refer to the antenuptial agreement, or if reference had been made to the antenuptial agreement in the court's decree or in a written instrument incident to the divorce status, section 71(a)(1) would require the inclusion in W's gross income of the payments received by her after the decree. Similarly, if a written separation agreement were executed after August 16, 1954, and incorporated the payment provisions of the antenuptial agreement, section 71(a)(2) would require the inclusion in W's income of payments received by W after W begins living apart from H, whether or not the divorce decree was subsequently entered and whether or not W was living apart from H when the separation agreement was executed, provided that such payments were made after such agreement was executed and pursuant to its terms. As to including such payments in W's income, if made by a trust created under the antenuptial agreement, regardless of whether referred to in the decree or a later instrument, or created pursuant to the written separation agreement, see section 682 and the regulations thereunder.

Example 3. H and W are separated and living apart during 1954. W sues H for support and on February 1, 1954, the court enters a decree requiring H to pay $200 a month to W for her support and maintenance. No part of the $200 a month support payments is includible in W's income under section 71(a)(3) or deductible by H under section 215. If, however, the decree had been entered after March 1, 1954, or had been altered or modified by a court order entered after March 1, 1954, the payments received by W after August 16, 1954, under the decree as altered or modified would be includible in her income under section 71(a)(3) and deductible by H under section 215.

Example 4. W sues H for divorce in 1954. On January 15, 1954, the court awards W temporary alimony of $25 a week pending the final decree. On September 1, 1954, the court grants W a divorce and awards her $200 a month permanent alimony. No part of the $25 a week temporary alimony received prior to the decree is includible in W's income under section 71(a), but the $200 a month received during the remainder of 1954 by W is includible in her income for 1954. Under section 215, H is entitled to deduct such $200 payments from his income. If, however, the decree awarding W temporary alimony had been entered after March 1, 1954, or had been altered or modified by a court order entered after March 1, 1954, temporary alimony received by her after August 16, 1954, would be includible in her income under section 71(a)(3) and deductible by H under section 215.

(c) Alimony and separate maintenance payments attributable to property. (1)(i) In the case of divorce or legal separation, paragraph (1) of section 71(a) requires the inclusion in the gross income of the wife of periodic payments (whether or not made at regular intervals) attributable to property transferred, in trust or otherwise, and received by her after a decree of divorce or of separate maintenance. Such property must have been transferred in discharge of a legal obligation imposed upon or incurred by the husband because of the marital or family relationship under a decree of divorce or separate maintenance or under a written instrument incident to such divorce status or legal separation status.

(ii) Where the husband and wife are separated and living apart and do not file a joint income tax return for the taxable year, paragraph (2) of section 71(a) requires the inclusion in the gross income of the wife of periodic payments (whether or not made at regular intervals) received by her which are attributable to property transferred, in trust or otherwise, under a written separation agreement executed after August 16, 1954. The property must be transferred because of the marital or family relationship. The periodic payments attributable to the property must be received by the wife after the written separation agreement is executed.

(iii) The periodic payments received by the wife attributable to property transferred under subdivisions (i) and (ii) of this subparagraph and includible in her gross income are not to be included in the gross income of the husband.

(2) The full amount of periodic payments received under the circumstances described in section 71(a)(1), (2), and (3) is required to be included in the gross income of the wife regardless of the source of such payments. Thus, it matters not that such payments are attributable to property in trust, to life insurance, endowment, or annuity contracts, or to any other interest in property, or are paid directly or indirectly by the husband from his income or capital. For example, if in order to meet an alimony or separate maintenance obligation of $500 a month the husband purchases or assigns for the benefit of his wife a commercial annuity contract paying such amount, the full $500 a month received by the wife is includible in her income, and no part of such amount is includible in the husband's income or deductible by him. See section 72(k) and the regulations thereunder. Likewise, if property is transferred by the husband, subject to an annual charge of $5,000, payable to his wife in discharge of his alimony or separate maintenance obligation under the divorce or separation decree or written instrument incident to the divorce status or legal separation status or if such property is transferred pursuant to a written separation agreement and subject to a similar annual charge, the $5,000 received annually is, under section 71(a)(1) or (2), includible in the wife's income, regardless of whether such amount is paid out of income or principal of the property.

(3) The same rule applies to periodic payments attributable to property in trust. The full amount of periodic payments to which section 71(a)(1) and (2) applies is includible in the wife's income regardless of whether such payments are made out of trust income. Such periodic payments are to be included in the wife's income under section 71(a)(1) or (2) and are to be excluded from the husband's income even though the income of the trust would otherwise be includible in his income under Subpart E, Part I, Subchapter J, Chapter 1 of the Code, relating to trust income attributable to grantors and others as substantial owners. As to periodic payments received by a wife attributable to property in trust in cases to which section 71(a)(1) or (2) does not apply because the husband's obligation is not specified in the decree or an instrument incident to the divorce status or legal separation status or the property was not transferred under a written separation agreement, see section 682 and the regulations thereunder.

(4) Section 71(a)(1) or (2) does not apply to that part of any periodic payment attributable to that portion of any interest in property transferred in discharge of the husband's obligation under the decree or instrument incident to the divorce status or legal separation status, or transferred pursuant to the written separation agreement, which interest originally belonged to the wife. It will apply, however, if she received such interest from her husband in contemplation of or as an incident to the divorce or separation without adequate and full consideration in money or money's worth, other than the release of the husband or his property from marital obligations. An example of the first rule is a case where the husband and wife transfer securities, which were owned by them jointly, in trust to pay an annuity to the wife. In this case, the full amount of that part of the annuity received by the wife attributable to the husband's interest in the securities transferred in discharge of his obligation under the decree, or instrument incident to the divorce status or legal separation status, or transferred under the written separation agreement, is taxable to her under section 71(a)(1) or (2), while that portion of the annuity attributable to the wife's interest in the securities so transferred is taxable to her only to the extent it is out of trust income as provided in Part I (sections 641 and following), Subchapter J, Chapter 1 of the Code. If, however, the husband's transfer to his wife is made before such property is transferred in discharge of his obligation under the decree or written instrument, or pursuant to the separation agreement in an attempt to avoid the application of section 71(a)(1) or (2) to part of such payments received by his wife, such transfers will be considered as a part of the same transfer by the husband of his property in discharge of his obligation or pursuant to such agreement. In such a case, section 71(a)(1) or (2) will be applied to the full amount received by the wife. As to periodic payments received under a joint purchase of a commercial annuity contract, see section 72 and the regulations thereunder.

(d) Periodic and installment payments. (1) In general, installment payments discharging a part of an obligation the principal sum of which is, in terms of money or property, specified in the decree, instrument, or agreement are not considered "periodic payments" and therefore are not to be included under section 71(a) in the wife's income.

(2) An exception to the general rule stated in subparagraph (1) of this paragraph is provided, however, in cases where such principal sum, by the terms of the decree, instrument, or agreement, may be or is to be paid over a period ending more than 10 years from the date of such decree, instrument, or agreement. In such cases, the installment payment is considered a periodic payment for the purposes of section 71(a) but only to the extent that the installment payment, or sum of the installment payments, received during the wife's taxable year does not exceed 10 percent of the principal sum. This 10–percent limitation applies to installment payments made in advance but does not apply to delinquent installment payments for a prior taxable year of the wife made during her taxable year.

(3)(i) Where payments under a decree, instrument, or agreement are to be paid over a period ending 10 years or less from the date of such decree, instrument, or agreement, such payments are not installment payments discharging a part of an obligation the principal sum of which is, in terms of money or property, specified in the decree, instrument, or agreement (and are considered periodic payments for the purposes of section 71(a)) only if such payments meet the following two conditions:

(a) Such payments are subject to any one or more of the contingencies of death of either spouse, remarriage of the wife, or change in the economic status of either spouse, and

(b) Such payments are in the nature of alimony or an allowance for support.

(ii) Payments meeting the requirements of subdivision (i) are considered periodic payments for the purposes of section 71(a) regardless of whether—

(a) The contingencies described in subdivision (i)(a) of this subparagraph are set forth in the terms of the decree, instrument, or agreement, or are imposed by local law, or

(b) The aggregate amount of the payments to be made in the absence of the occurrence of the contingencies described in subdivision (i)(a) of this subparagraph is explicitly stated in the decree, instrument, or agreement or may be calculated from the face of the decree, instrument, or agreement, or

(c) The total amount which will be paid may be calculated actuarially.

(4) Where payments under a decree, instrument, or agreement are to be paid over a period ending more than ten years from the date of such decree, instrument, or agreement, but where such payments meet the conditions set forth in subparagraph (3)(i) of this paragraph, such payments are considered to be periodic payments for the purpose of section 71 without regard to the rule set forth in subparagraph (2) of this paragraph. Accordingly, the rules set forth in subparagraph (2) of this paragraph are not applicable to such payments.

(5) The rules as to periodic and installment payments are illustrated by the following examples:

Example 1. Under the terms of a written instrument, H is required to make payments to W which are in the nature of alimony, in the amount of $100 a month for nine years. The instrument provides that if H or W dies the payments are to cease. The payments are periodic.

Example 2. The facts are the same as in example (1) except that the written instrument explicitly provides that H is to pay W the sum of $10,800 in monthly payments of $100 over a period of nine years. The payments are periodic.

Example 3. Under the terms of a written instrument, H is to pay W $100 a month over a period of nine years. The monthly payments are not subject to any of the contingencies of death of H or W, remarriage of W, or change in the economic status of H or W under the terms of the written instrument or by reason of local law. The payments are not periodic.

Example 4. A divorce decree in 1954 provides that H is to pay W $20,000 each year for the next five years, beginning with the date of the decree, and then $5,000 each year for the next ten years. Assuming the wife makes her returns on the calendar year basis, each payment received in the years 1954 to 1958, inclusive, is treated as a periodic payment under section 71(a)(1), but only to the extent of 10 percent of the principal sum of $150,000. Thus, for such taxable years, only $15,000 of the $20,000 received is includible under section 71(a)(1) in the wife's income and is deductible by the husband under section 215. For the years 1959 to 1968, inclusive, the full $5,000 received each year by the wife is includible in her income and is deductible from the husband's income.

(e) **Payments for support of minor children.** Section 71(a) does not apply to that part of any periodic payment which, by the terms of the decree, instrument, or agreement under section 71(a), is specifically designated as a sum payable for the support of minor children of the husband. The statute prescribes the treatment in cases where an amount or portion is so fixed but the amount of any periodic payment is less than the amount of the periodic payment specified to be made. In such cases, to the extent of the amount which would be payable for the support of such children out of the originally specified periodic payment, such periodic payment is considered a payment for such support. For example, if the husband is by terms of the decree, instrument, or agreement required to pay $200 a month to his divorced wife, $100 of which is designated by the decree, instrument, or agreement to be for the support of their minor children, and the husband pays only $150 to his wife, $100 is nevertheless considered to be a payment by the husband for the support of the children. If, however, the periodic payments are received by the wife for the support and maintenance of herself and of minor children of the husband without such specific designation of the portion for the support of such children, then the whole of such amounts is includible in the income of the wife as provided in section 71(a). Except in cases of a designated amount or portion for the support of the husband's minor children, periodic payments described in section 71(a) received by the wife for herself and any other person or persons are includible in whole in the wife's income, whether or not the amount or portion for such other person or persons is designated. *[T.D. 6500, 25 FR 11402, Nov. 26, 1960]*

§ 1.71–1T Alimony and separate maintenance payments (temporary).

(a) In general.

Q–1 What is the income tax treatment of alimony or separate maintenance payments?

A–1 Alimony or separate maintenance payments are, under section 71, included in the gross income of the payee spouse and, under section 215, allowed as a deduction from the gross income of the payor spouse.

Q–2 What is an alimony or separate maintenance payment?

A–2 An alimony or separate maintenance payment is any payment received by or on behalf of a spouse (which for this purpose includes a former spouse) of the payor under a divorce or separation instrument that meets all of the following requirements:

(a) The payment is in cash (see A–5).

(b) The payment is not designated as a payment which is excludible from the gross income of the payee and nondeductible by the payor (see A–8).

(c) In the case of spouses legally separated under a decree of divorce or separate maintenance, the spouses are not members of the same household at the time the payment is made (see A–9).

(d) The payor has no liability to continue to make any payment after the death of the payee (or to make any payment as a substitute for such payment) and the divorce or separation instrument states that there is no such liability (see A–10).

(e) The payment is not treated as child support (see A–15).

(f) To the extent that one or more annual payments exceed $10,000 during any of the 6–post-separation years, the payor is obligated to make annual payments in each of the 6–post-separation years (see A–19).

Q–3 In order to be treated as alimony or separate maintenance payments, must the payments be "periodic" as that term was defined prior to enactment of the Tax Reform Act of 1984 or be made in discharge of a legal obligation of the payor to support the payee arising out of a marital or family relationship?

A–3 No. The Tax Reform Act of 1984 replaces the old requirements with the requirements described in A–2 above.

Thus, the requirements that alimony or separate maintenance payments be "periodic" and be made in discharge of a legal obligation to support arising out of a marital or family relationship have been eliminated.

Q–4 Are the instruments described in section 71(a) of prior law the same as divorce or separation instruments described in section 71, as amended by the Tax Reform Act of 1984?

A–4 Yes.

(b) Specific requirements.

Q–5. May alimony or separate maintenance payments be made in a form other than cash?

A–5 No. Only cash payments (including checks and money orders payable on demand) qualify as alimony or separate maintenance payments. Transfers of services or property (including a debt instrument of a third party or an annuity contract), execution of a debt instrument by the payor, or the use of property of the payor do not qualify as alimony or separate maintenance payments.

Q–6 May payments of cash to a third party on behalf of a spouse qualify as alimony or separate maintenance payments if the payments are pursuant to the terms of a divorce or separation instrument?

A–6 Yes. Assuming all other requirements are satisfied, a payment of cash by the payor spouse to a third party under the terms of the divorce or separation instrument will qualify as a payment of cash which is received "on behalf of a spouse". For example, cash payments of rent, mortgage, tax, or tuition liabilities of the payee spouse made under the terms of the divorce or separation instrument will qualify as alimony or separate maintenance payments. Any payments to maintain property owned by the payor spouse and used by the payee spouse (including mortgage payments, real estate taxes and insurance premiums) are not payments on behalf of a spouse even if those payments are made pursuant to the terms of the divorce or separation instrument. Premiums paid by the payor spouse for term or whole life insurance on the payor's life made under the terms of the divorce or separation instrument will qualify as payments on behalf of the payee spouse to the extent that the payee spouse is the owner of the policy.

Q–7 May payments of cash to a third party on behalf of a spouse qualify as alimony or separate maintenance payments if the payments are made to the third party at the written request of the payee spouse?

A–7 Yes. For example, instead of making an alimony or separate maintenance payment directly to the payee, the payor spouse may make a cash payment to a charitable organization if such payment is pursuant to the written request, consent or ratification of the payee spouse. Such request, consent or ratification must state that the parties intend the payment to be treated as an alimony or separate maintenance payment to the payee spouse subject to the rules of section 71, and must be received by the payor spouse prior to the date of filing of the payor's first return of tax for the taxable year in which the payment was made.

Q–8 How may spouses designate that payments otherwise qualifying as alimony or separate maintenance payments shall be excludible from the gross income of the payee and nondeductible by the payor?

A–8 The spouses may designate that payments otherwise qualifying as alimony or separate maintenance payments shall be nondeductible by the payor and excludible from gross income by the payee by so providing in a divorce or separation instrument (as defined in section 71(b)(2)). If the spouses have executed a written separation agreement (as described in section 71(b)(2)(B)), any writing signed by both spouses which designates otherwise qualifying alimony or separate maintenance payments as nondeductible and excludible and which refers to the written separation agreement will be treated as a written separation agreement (and thus a divorce or separation instrument) for purposes of the preceding sentence. If the spouses are subject to temporary support orders (as described in section 71(b)(2)(C)), the designation of otherwise qualifying alimony or separate payments as nondeductible and excludible must be made in the original or a subsequent temporary support order. A copy of the instrument containing the designation of payments as not alimony or separate maintenance payments must be attached to the payee's first filed return of tax (Form 1040) for each year in which the designation applies.

Q–9 What are the consequences if, at the time a payment is made, the payor and payee spouses are members of the same household?

A–9 Generally, a payment made at the time when the payor and payee spouses are members of the same household cannot qualify as an alimony or separate maintenance payment if the spouses are legally separated under a decree of divorce or of separate maintenance. For purposes of the preceding sentence, a dwelling unit formerly shared by both spouses shall not be considered two separate households even if the spouses physically separate themselves within the dwelling unit. The spouses will not be treated as members of the same household if one spouse is preparing to depart from the household of the other spouse, and does depart not more than one month after the date the payment is made. If the spouses are not legally separated under a decree of divorce or separate maintenance, a payment under a written separation agreement or a decree described in section 71(b)(2)(C) may qualify as an alimony or separate maintenance payment notwithstanding that the payor and payee are members of the same household at the time the payment is made.

Q–10 Assuming all other requirements relating to the qualification of certain payments as alimony or separate maintenance payments are met, what are the consequences if the payor spouse is required to continue to make the payments after the death of the payee spouse?

A–10 None of the payments before (or after) the death of the payee spouse qualify as alimony or separate maintenance payments.

Q–11 What are the consequences if the divorce or separation instrument fails to state that there is no liability for any period after the death of the payee spouse to continue to make any payments which would otherwise qualify as alimony or separate maintenance payments?

A–11 If the instrument fails to include such a statement, none of the payments, whether made before or after the death of the payee spouse, will qualify as alimony or separate maintenance payments.

Example 1. A is to pay B $10,000 in cash each year for a period of 10 years under a divorce or separation instrument which does not state that the payments will terminate upon the death of B. None of the payments will qualify as alimony or separate maintenance payments.

Example 2. A is to pay B $10,000 in cash each year for a period of 10 years under a divorce or separation instrument which states that the payments will terminate upon the death of B. In addition, under the instrument, A is to pay B or B's estate $20,000 in cash each year for a period of 10 years. Because the $20,000 annual payments will not terminate upon the death of B, these payments will not qualify as alimony or separate maintenance payments. However, the separate $10,000 annual payments will qualify as alimony or separate maintenance payments.

Q–12 Will a divorce or separation instrument be treated as stating that there is no liability to make payments after the death of the payee spouse if the liability to make such payments terminates pursuant to applicable local law or oral agreement?

A–12 No. Termination of the liability to make payments must be stated in the terms of the divorce or separation instrument.

Q–13 What are the consequences if the payor spouse is required to make one or more payments (in cash or property) after the death of the payee spouse as a substitute for the continuation of pre-death payments which would otherwise qualify as alimony or separate maintenance payments?

A–13 If the payor spouse is required to make any such substitute payments, none of the otherwise qualifying payments will qualify as alimony or separate maintenance payments. The divorce or separation instrument need not state, however, that there is no liability to make any such substitute payment.

Q–14 Under what circumstances will one or more payments (in cash or property) which are to occur after the death of the payee spouse be treated as a substitute for the continuation of payments which would otherwise qualify as alimony or separate maintenance payments?

A–14 To the extent that one or more payments are to begin to be made, increase in amount, or become accelerated in time as a result of the death of the payee spouse, such payments may be treated as a substitute for the continuation of payments terminating on the death of the payee spouse which would otherwise qualify as alimony or separate maintenance payments. The determination of whether or not such payments are a substitute for the continuation of payments which would otherwise qualify as alimony or separate maintenance payments, and of the amount of the otherwise qualifying alimony or separate maintenance payments for which any such payments are a substitute, will depend on all of the facts and circumstances.

Example 1. Under the terms of a divorce decree, A is obligated to make annual alimony payments to B of $30,000, terminating on the earlier of the expiration of 6 years or the death of B. B maintains custody of the minor children of A and B. The decree provides that at the death of B, if there are minor children of A and B remaining, A will be obligated to make annual payments of $10,000 to a trust, the income and corpus of which are to be used for the benefit of the children until the youngest child attains the age of majority. These facts indicate that A's liability to make annual $10,000 payments in trust for the benefit of his minor children upon the death of B is a substitute for $10,000 of the $30,000 annual payments to B. Accordingly, $10,000 of each of the $30,000 annual payments to B will not qualify as alimony or separate maintenance payments.

Example 2. Under the terms of a divorce decree, A is obligated to make annual alimony payments to B of $30,000, terminating on the earlier of the expiration of 15 years or the death of B. The divorce decree provides that if B dies before the expiration of the 15 year period, A will pay to B's estate the difference between the total amount that A would have paid had B survived, minus the amount actually paid. For example, if B dies at the end of the 10th year in which payments are made, A will pay to B's estate $150,000 ($450,000–$300,000). These facts indicate that A's liability to make a lump sum payment to B's estate upon the death of B is a substitute for the full amount of each of the annual $30,000 payments to B. Accordingly, none of the annual $30,000 payments to B will qualify as alimony or separate maintenance payments. The result would be the same if the lump sum payable at B's death were discounted by an appropriate interest factor to account for the prepayment.

(c) Child support payments.

Q–15 What are the consequences of a payment which the terms of the divorce or separation instrument fix as payable for the support of a child of the payor spouse?

A–15 A payment which under the terms of the divorce or separation instrument is fixed (or treated as fixed) as payable for the support of a child of the payor spouse does not qualify as an alimony or separate maintenance payment. Thus, such a payment is not deductible by the payor spouse or includible in the income of the payee spouse.

Q–16 When is a payment fixed (or treated as fixed) as payable for the support of a child of the payor spouse?

A–16 A payment is fixed as payable for the support of a child of the payor spouse if the divorce or separation instrument specifically designates some sum or portion (which sum or portion may fluctuate) as payable for the support of a child of the payor spouse. A payment will be treated as fixed as payable for the support of a child of the payor spouse if the payment is reduced (a) on the happening of a contingency relating to a child of the payor, or (b) at a time which can clearly be associated with such a contingency. A payment may be treated as fixed as payable for the support of a child of the payor spouse even if other separate payments specifically are designated as payable for the support of a child of the payor spouse.

Q–17 When does a contingency relate to a child of the payor?

A–17 For this purpose, a contingency relates to a child of the payor if it depends on any event relating to that child, regardless of whether such event is certain or likely to occur. Events that relate to a child of the payor include the following: the child's attaining a specified age or income level, dying, marrying, leaving school, leaving the spouse's household, or gaining employment.

Q–18 When will a payment be treated as to be reduced at a time which can clearly be associated with the happening of a contingency relating to a child of the payor?

A–18 There are two situations, described below, in which payments which would otherwise qualify as alimony or separate maintenance payments will be presumed to be reduced at a time clearly associated with the happening of a contingency relating to a child of the payor. In all other situations, reductions in payments will not be treated as clearly associated with the happening of a contingency relating to a child of the payor.

The first situation referred to above is where the payments are to be reduced not more than 6 months before or after the date the child is to attain the age of 18, 21, or local age of majority. The second situation is where the payments are to be reduced on two or more occasions which occur not more than one year before or after a different child of the payor spouse attains a certain age between the ages of 18 and 24, inclusive. The certain age referred to in the preceding sentence must be the same for each such child, but need not be a whole number of years.

The presumption in the two situations described above that payments are to be reduced at a time clearly associated with the happening of a contingency relating to a child of the payor may be rebutted (either by the Service or by taxpayers) by showing that the time at which the payments are to be reduced was determined independently of any contingencies relating to the children of the payor. The presumption in the first situation will be rebutted conclusively if the reduction is a complete cessation of alimony or separate maintenance payments during the sixth post-separation year (described in A–21) or upon the expiration of a 72–month period. The presumption may also be rebutted in other circumstances, for example, by showing that alimony payments are to be made for a period customarily provided in the local jurisdiction, such as a period equal to one-half the duration of the marriage.

Example: A and B are divorced on July 1, 1985, when their children, C (born July 15, 1970) and D (born September 23, 1972), are 14 and 12, respectively. Under the divorce decree, A is to make alimony payments to B of $2,000 per month. Such payments are to be reduced to $1,500 per month on January 1, 1991 and to $1,000 per month on January 1, 1995. On January 1, 1991, the date of the first reduction in payments, C will be 20 years 5 months and 17 days old. On January 1, 1995, the date of the second reduction in payments, D will be 22 years 3 months and 9 days old. Each of the reductions in payments is to occur not more than one year before or after a different child of A attains the age of 21 years and 4 months. (Actually, the reductions are to occur not more than one year before or after C and D attain any of the ages 21 years 3 months and 9 days through 21 years 5 months and 17 days.) Accordingly, the reductions will be presumed to clearly be associated with the happening of a contingency relating to C and D. Unless this presumption is rebutted, payments under the divorce decree equal to the sum of the reduction ($1,000 per month) will be treated as fixed for the support of the children of A and therefore will not qualify as alimony or separate maintenance payments.

(d) Excess front-loading rules.

Q–19 What are the excess front-loading rules?

A–19 The excess front-loading rules are two special rules which may apply to the extent that payments in any calendar year exceed $10,000. The first rule is a minimum term rule, which must be met in order for any annual payment, to the extent in excess of $10,000, to qualify as an alimony or separate maintenance payment (see A–2(f)). This rule requires that alimony or separate maintenance payments be called for, at a minimum, during the 6 "post-separation years". The second rule is a recapture rule which characterizes payments retrospectively by requiring a recalculation and inclusion in income by the payor and deduction by the payee of previously paid alimony or separate maintenance payment to the extent that the amount of such payments during any of the 6 "post-separation years" falls short of the amount of payments during a prior year by more than $10,000.

Q–20 Do the excess front-loading rules apply to payments to the extent that annual payments never exceed $10,000?

A–20 No. For example, A is to make a single $10,000 payment to B. Provided that the other requirements of section 71 are met, the payment will qualify as an alimony or separate maintenance payment. If A were to make a single $15,000 payment to B, $10,000 of the payment would qualify as an alimony or separate maintenance payment and $5,000 of the payment would be disqualified under the minimum term rule because payments were not to be made for the minimum period.

Q–21 Do the excess front-loading rules apply to payments received under a decree described in section 71(b)(2)(C)?

A–21 No. Payments under decrees described in section 71(b)(2)(C) are to be disregarded entirely for purposes of applying the excess front-loading rules.

Q–22 Both the minimum term rule and the recapture rule refer to 6 "post-separation years". What are the 6 "post-separation years"?

A–22 The 6 "post-separation years" are the 6 consecutive calendar years beginning with the first calendar year in which the payor pays to the payee an alimony or separate maintenance payment (except a payment made under a decree described in section 71(b)(2)(C)). Each year within this period is referred to as a "post-separation year". The 6–year period need not commence with the year in which the spouses separate or divorce, or with the year in which payments under the divorce or separation instrument are made, if no payments during such year qualify as alimony or separate maintenance payments. For example, a decree for the divorce of A and B is entered in October, 1985. The decree requires A to make monthly payments to B commencing November 1, 1985, but A and B are members of the same household until February 15, 1986 (and as a result, the payments prior to January 16, 1986, do not qualify as alimony payments). For purposes of applying the excess front-loading rules to payments from A to B, the 6 calendar years 1986 through 1991 are post-separation years. If a spouse has been making payments pursuant to a divorce or separation instrument described in section 71(b)(2)(A) or (B), a modification of the instrument or the substitution of a new instrument (for example, the substitution of a divorce decree for a written separation agreement) will not result in the creation of additional post-separation years. However, if a spouse has been making payments pursuant to a divorce or separation instrument described in section 71(b)(2)(C), the 6–year period does not begin until the first calendar year in which alimony or separate maintenance payments are made under a divorce or separation instrument described in section 71(b)(2)(A) or (B).

Q–23 How does the minimum term rule operate?

A–23 The minimum term rule operates in the following manner. To the extent payments are made in excess of $10,000, a payment will qualify as an alimony or separate maintenance payment only if alimony or separate maintenance payments are to be made in each of the 6 post-separation years. For example, pursuant to a divorce decree, A is to make alimony payments to B of $20,000 in each of the 5 calendar years 1985 through 1989. A is to make no payment in 1990. Under the minimum term rule, only $10,000 will qualify as an alimony payment in each of the calendar years 1985 through 1989. If the divorce decree also required A to make a $1 payment in 1990, the minimum term rule would be satisfied and $20,000 would be treated as an alimony payment in each of the calendar years 1985 through 1989. The recapture rule would, however, apply for 1990. For purposes of determining whether alimony or separate maintenance payments are to be made in any year, the possible termination of such payments upon the happening of a contingency (other than the passage of time) which has not yet occurred is ignored (unless such contingency may cause all or a portion of the payment to be treated as a child support payment).

Q–24 How does the recapture rule operate?

A–24 The recapture rule operates in the following manner. If the amount of alimony or separate maintenance payments paid in any post-separation year (referred to as the "computation year") falls short of the amount of alimony or separate maintenance payments paid in any prior post-separation year by more than $10,000, the payor must compute an "excess amount" for the computation year. The excess amount for any computation year is the sum of excess amounts determined with respect to each prior post-separation year. The excess amount determined with respect to a prior post-separation year is the excess of (1) the amount of alimony or separate maintenance payments paid by the payor spouse during such prior post-separation year, over (2) the amount of the alimony or separate maintenance payments paid by the payor spouse during the computation year plus $10,000. For purposes of this calculation, the amount of alimony or separate maintenance payments made by the payor spouse during any post-separation year preceding the computation year is reduced by any excess amount previously determined with respect to such year. The rules set forth above may be illustrated by the following example. A makes alimony payments to B of $25,000 in 1985 and $12,000 in 1986. The excess amount with respect to 1985 that is recaptured in 1986 is $3,000 ($25,000–($12,000+$10,000)). For purposes of subsequent computation years, the amount deemed paid in 1985 is $22,000. If A makes alimony payments to B of $1,000 in 1987, the excess amount that is recaptured in 1987 will be $12,000. This is the sum of an $11,000 excess amount with respect to 1985 ($22,000–($1,000+$10,000)) and a $1,000 excess amount with respect to 1986 ($12,000–($1,000+$10,000)). If, prior to the end of 1990, payments decline further, additional recapture will occur. The payor spouse must include the excess amount in gross income for his/her taxable year beginning with or in the computation year. The payee spouse is allowed a deduction for the excess amount in computing adjusted gross income for his/her taxable year beginning with or in the computation year. However, the payee spouse must compute the excess amount by reference to the date when payments were made and not when payments were received.

Q–25 What are the exceptions to the recapture rule?

A–25 Apart from the $10,000 threshold for application of the recapture rule, there are three exceptions to the recapture rule. The first exception is for payments received under temporary support orders described in section 71(b)(2)(C) (see A–21). The second exception is for any payment made pursuant to a continuing liability over the period of the post-separation years to pay a fixed portion of the payor's income from a business or property or from compensation for employment or self-employment. The third exception is where the alimony or separate maintenance payments in any post-separation year cease by reason of the death of the payor or payee or the remarriage (as defined under applicable local law) of the payee before the close of the computation year. For example, pursuant to a divorce decree, A is to make cash payments to B of $30,000 in each of the calendar years 1985 through 1990. A makes cash payments of $30,000 in 1985 and $15,000 in 1986, in which year B remarries and A's alimony payments cease. The recapture rule does not apply for 1986 or any subsequent year. If alimony or separate maintenance payments made by A decline or cease during a post-separation year for any other reason (including a failure by the payor to make timely payments, a modification of the divorce or separation instrument, a reduction in the support needs of the payee, or a reduction in the ability of the payor to provide support) excess amounts with respect to prior post-separation years will be subject to recapture.

(e) Effective dates.

Q–26 When does section 71, as amended by the Tax Reform Act of 1984, become effective?

A–26 Generally, section 71, as amended, is effective with respect to divorce or separation instruments (as defined in section 71(b)(2)) executed after December 31, 1984. If a decree of divorce or separate maintenance executed after December 31, 1984, incorporates or adopts without change the terms of the alimony or separate maintenance payments under a divorce or separation instrument executed before January 1, 1985, such decree will be treated as executed before January 1, 1985. A change in the amount of alimony or separate maintenance payments or the time period over which such payments are to continue, or the addition or deletion of any contingencies or conditions relating to such payments is a change in the terms of the alimony or separate maintenance payments. For example, in November 1984, A and B executed a written separation agreement. In February 1985, a decree of divorce is entered in substitution for the written separation agreement. The decree of divorce does not change the terms of the alimony A pays to B. The decree of divorce will be treated as executed before January 1, 1985 and hence alimony payments under the decree will be subject to the rules of section 71 prior to amendment by the Tax Reform Act of 1984. If the amount or time period of the alimony or separate maintenance payments are not specified in the pre–1985 separation agreement or if the decree of divorce changes the amount or term of such payments, the decree of divorce will not be treated as executed before January 1, 1985, and alimony payments under the decree will be subject to the rules of section 71, as amended by the Tax Reform Act of 1984.

Section 71, as amended, also applies to any divorce or separation instrument executed (or treated as executed) before January 1, 1985 that has been modified on or after January 1, 1985, if such modification expressly provides that section 71, as amended by the Tax Reform Act of 1984, shall apply to the instrument as modified. In this case, section 71, as amended, is effective with respect to payments made after the date the instrument is modified.

(Authority: Secs. 1041(d)(4) (98 Stat. 798, 26 U.S.C. 1041(d)(4), 152(e)(2)(A) (98 Stat. 802, 26 U.S.C. 152(e)(2)(A), 215(c) (98 Stat. 800, 26 U.S.C. 215(c)) and 7805 (68A Stat. 917, 26 U.S.C. 7805) of the Internal Revenue Code of 1954.

[T.D. 7973, 49 FR 34455, Aug. 31, 1984; 49 FR 36645, Sept. 19, 1984]

Additional Itemized Deductions for Individuals

§ 1.215–1 Periodic alimony, etc., payments.

(a) A deduction is allowable under section 215 with respect to periodic payments in the nature of, or in lieu of, alimony or an allowance for support actually paid by the taxpayer during his taxable year and required to be included in the income of the payee wife or former wife, as the case may be, under section 71. As to the amounts required to be included in the income of such wife or former wife, see section 71 and the regulations thereunder. For definition of husband and wife see section 7701(a)(17).

(b) The deduction under section 215 is allowed only to the obligor spouse. It is not allowed to an estate, trust, corporation, or any other person who may pay the alimony obligation of such obligor spouse. The obligor spouse, however, is not allowed a deduction for any periodic payment includible under section 71 in the income of the wife or former wife, which payment is attributable to property transferred in discharge of his obligation and which, under section 71(d) or section 682, is not includible in his gross income.

(c) The following examples, in which both H and W file their income tax returns on the basis of a calendar year, illustrate cases in which a deduction is or is not allowed under section 215:

Example 1. Pursuant to the terms of a decree of divorce, H, in 1956, transferred securities valued at $100,000 in trust for the benefit of W, which fully discharged all his obligations to W. The periodic payments made by the trust to W are required to be included in W's income under section 71. Such payments are stated in section 71(d) not to be includible in H's income and, therefore, under section 215 are not deductible from his income.

Example 2. A decree of divorce obtained by W from H incorporated a previous agreement of H to establish a trust, the trustees of which were instructed to pay W $5,000 a year for the remainder of her life. The court retained jurisdiction to order H to provide further payments if necessary for the support of W. In 1956 the trustee paid to W $4,000 from the income of the trust and $1,000 from the corpus of the trust. Under the provisions of sections 71 and 682(b), W would include $5,000 in her income for 1956. H would not include any part of the $5,000 in his income nor take a deduction therefor. If H had paid the $1,000 to W pursuant to court order rather than allowing the trustees to pay it out of corpus, he would have been entitled to a deduction of $1,000 under the provisions of section 215.

(d) For other examples, see sections 71 and 682 and the regulations thereunder. *[T.D. 6500, 25 FR 11402, Nov. 26, 1960]*

§ 1.215–1T Alimony, etc., payments (temporary).

Q–1 What information is required by the Internal Revenue Service when an alimony or separate maintenance payment is claimed as a deduction by a payor?

A–1 The payor spouse must include on his/her first filed return of tax (Form 1040) for the taxable year in which the payment is made the payee's social security number, which the payee is required to furnish to the payor. For penalties applicable to a payor spouse who fails to include such information on his/her return of tax or to a payee spouse who fails to furnish his/her social security number to the payor spouse, see section 6676.

(Authority: 98 Stat. 798, 26 U.S.C. 1041(d)(4); 98 Stat. 802, 26 U.S.C. 152(e)(2)(A); 98 Stat. 800, 26 U.S.C. 215(c); 68A Stat. 917, 26 U.S.C. 7805)

[T.D. 7973, 49 FR 34458, Aug. 31, 1984]

GAIN OR LOSS ON DISPOSITION OF PROPERTY

Common Nontaxable Exchanges

§ 1.1041–1T Treatment of transfer of property between spouses or incident to divorce (temporary).

Q–1: How is the transfer of property between spouses treated under section 1041?

A–1: Generally, no gain or loss is recognized on a transfer of property from an individual to (or in trust for the benefit of) a spouse or, if the transfer is incident to a divorce, a former spouse. The following questions and answers describe more fully the scope, tax consequences and other rules which apply to transfers of property under section 1041.

(a) Scope of section 1041 in general.

Q–2: Does section 1041 apply only to transfers of property incident to divorce?

A–2: No. Section 1041 is not limited to transfers of property incident to divorce. Section 1041 applies to any transfer of property between spouses regardless of whether the transfer is a gift or is a sale or exchange between spouses acting at arm's length (including a transfer in exchange for the relinquishment of property or marital rights or an exchange otherwise governed by another nonrecognition provision of the Code). A divorce or legal separation need not be contemplated between the spouses at the time of the transfer nor must a divorce or legal separation ever occur.

Example 1. A and B are married and file a joint return. A is the sole owner of a condominium unit. A sale or gift of the condominium from A to B is a transfer which is subject to the rules of section 1041.

Example 2. A and B are married and file separate returns. A is the owner of an independent sole proprietorship, X Company. In the ordinary course of business, X Company makes a sale of property to B. This sale is a transfer of property between spouses and is subject to the rules of section 1041.

Example 3. Assume the same facts as in example (2), except that X Company is a corporation wholly owned by A. This sale is not a sale between spouses subject to the rules of section 1041. However, in appropriate circumstances, general tax principles, including the step-transaction doctrine, may be applicable in recharacterizing the transaction.

Q–3: Do the rules of section 1041 apply to a transfer between spouses if the transferee spouse is a nonresident alien?

A–3: No. Gain or loss (if any) is recognized (assuming no other nonrecognition provision applies) at the time of a transfer of property if the property is transferred to a spouse who is a nonresident alien.

Q–4: What kinds of transfers are governed by section 1041?

A–4: Only transfers of property (whether real or personal, tangible or intangible) are governed by section 1041. Transfers of services are not subject to the rules of section 1041.

Q–5: Must the property transferred to a former spouse have been owned by the transferor spouse during the marriage?

A–5: No. A transfer of property acquired after the marriage ceases may be governed by section 1041.

(b) Transfer incident to the divorce.

Q–6: When is a transfer of property incident to the divorce?

A–6: A transfer of property is incident to the divorce in either of the following 2 circumstances—

(1) The transfer occurs not more than one year after the date on which the marriage ceases, or

(2) The transfer is related to the cessation of the marriage.

Thus, a transfer of property occurring not more than one year after the date on which the marriage ceases need not be related to the cessation of the marriage to qualify for section 1041 treatment. (See A–7 for transfers occurring more than one year after the cessation of the marriage.)

Q–7: When is a transfer of property related to the cessation of the marriage?

A–7: A transfer of property is treated as related to the cessation of the marriage if the transfer is pursuant to a divorce or separation instrument, as defined in section 71(b)(2), and the transfer occurs not more than 6 years after the date on which the marriage ceases. A divorce or separation instrument includes a modification or amendment to such decree or instrument. Any transfer not pursuant to a divorce or separation instrument and any transfer occurring more than 6 years after the cessation of the marriage is presumed to be not related to the cessation of the marriage. This presumption may be rebutted only by showing that the transfer was made to effect the division of property owned by the former spouses at the time of the cessation of the marriage. For example, the presumption may be rebutted by showing that (a) the transfer was not made within the one- and six-year periods described above because of factors which hampered an earlier transfer of the property, such as legal or business impediments to transfer or disputes concerning the value of the property owned at the time of the cessation of the marriage, and (b) the transfer is effected promptly after the impediment to transfer is removed.

Q–8: Do annulments and the cessations of marriages that are void *ab initio* due to violations of state law constitute divorces for purposes of section 1041?

A–8: Yes.

(c) Transfers on behalf of a spouse.

Q–9: May transfers of property to third parties on behalf of a spouse (or former spouse) qualify under section 1041?

A–9: Yes. There are three situations in which a transfer of property to a third party on behalf of a spouse (or former spouse) will qualify under section 1041, provided all other requirements of the section are satisfied. The first situation is where the transfer to the third party is required by a divorce or separation instrument. The second situation is where the transfer to the third party is pursuant to the written request of the other spouse (or former spouse). The third situation is where the transferor receives from the other spouse (or former spouse) a written consent or ratification of the transfer to the third party. Such consent or ratification must state that the parties intend the transfer to be treated as a transfer to the nontransferring spouse (or former spouse) subject to the rules of section 1041 and must be received by the transferor prior to the date of filing of the transferor's first return of tax for the taxable year in which the transfer was made. In the three situations described above, the transfer of property will be treated as made directly to the nontransferring spouse (or former spouse) and the nontransferring spouse will be treated as immediately transferring the property to the third party. The deemed transfer from the nontransferring spouse (or former spouse) to the third party is not a transaction that qualifies for nonrecognition of gain under section 1041. This A–9 shall not apply to transfers to which § 1.1041–2 applies.

(d) Tax consequences of transfers subject to section 1041.

Q–10: How is the transferor of property under section 1041 treated for income tax purposes?

A–10: The transferor of property under section 1041 recognizes no gain or loss on the transfer even if the transfer was in exchange for the release of marital rights or other consideration. This rule applies regardless of whether the transfer is of property separately owned by the transferor or is a division (equal or unequal) of community property.

Thus, the result under section 1041 differs from the result in *United States* v. Davis, 370 U.S. 65 (1962).

Q–11: How is the transferee of property under section 1041 treated for income tax purposes?

A–11: The transferee of property under section 1041 recognizes no gain or loss upon receipt of the transferred property. In all cases, the basis of the transferred property in the hands of the transferee is the adjusted basis of such property in the hands of the transferor immediately before the transfer. Even if the transfer is a bona fide sale, the transferee does not acquire a basis in the transferred property equal to the transferee's cost (the fair market value). This carryover basis rule applies whether the adjusted basis of the transferred property is less than, equal to, or greater than its fair market value at the time of transfer (or the value of any consideration provided by the transferee) and applies for purposes of determining loss as well as gain upon the subsequent disposition of the property by the transferee. Thus, this rule is different from the rule applied in section 1015(a) for determining the basis of property acquired by gift.

Q–12: Do the rules described in A–10 and A–11 apply even if the transferred property is subject to liabilities which exceed the adjusted basis of the property?

A–12: Yes. For example, assume A owns property having a fair market value of $10,000 and an adjusted basis of $1,000. In contemplation of making a transfer of this property incident to a divorce from B, A borrows $5,000 from a bank, using the property as security for the borrowing. A then transfers the property to B and B assumes, or takes the property subject to, the liability to pay the $5,000 debt. Under section 1041, A recognizes no gain or loss upon the transfer of the property, and the adjusted basis of the property in the hands of B is $1,000.

Q–13: Will a transfer under section 1041 result in a recapture of investment tax credits with respect to the property transferred?

A–13: In general, no. Property transferred under section 1041 will not be treated as being disposed of by, or ceasing to be section 38 property with respect to, the transferor. However, the transferee will be subject to investment tax credit recapture if, upon or after the transfer, the property is disposed of by, or ceases to be section 38 property with respect to, the transferee. For example, as part of a divorce property settlement, B receives a car from A that has been used in A's business for two years and for which an investment tax credit was taken by A. No part of A's business is transferred to B and B's use of the car is solely personal. B is subject to recapture of the investment tax credit previously taken by A.

(e) Notice and recordkeeping requirement with respect to transactions under section 1041.

Q–14: Does the transferor of property in a transaction described in section 1041 have to supply, at the time of the transfer, the transferee with records sufficient to determine the adjusted basis and holding period of the property at the time of the transfer and (if applicable) with notice that the property transferred under section 1041 is potentially subject to recapture of the investment tax credit?

A–14: Yes. A transferor of property under section 1041 must, at the time of the transfer, supply the transferee with records sufficient to determine the adjusted basis and holding period of the property as of the date of the transfer. In addition, in the case of a transfer of property which carries with it a potential liability for investment tax credit recapture, the transferor must, at the time of the transfer, supply the transferee with records sufficient to determine the amount and period of such potential liability. Such records must be preserved and kept accessible by the transferee.

(f) Property settlements—effective dates, transitional periods and elections.

Q–15: When does section 1041 become effective?

A–15: Generally, section 1041 applies to all transfers after July 18, 1984. However, it does not apply to transfers after July 18, 1984 pursuant to instruments in effect on or before July 18, 1984. (See A–16 with respect to exceptions to the general rule.)

Q–16: Are there any exceptions to the general rule stated in A–15 above?

A–16: Yes. Two transitional rules provide exceptions to the general rule stated in A–15. First, section 1041 will apply to transfers after July 18, 1984 under instruments that were in effect on or before July 18, 1984 if both spouses (or former spouses) elect to have section 1041 apply to such transfers. Second, section 1041 will apply to all transfers after December 31, 1983 (including transfers under instruments in effect on or before July 18, 1984) if both spouses (or former spouses) elect to have section 1041 apply. (See A–18 relating to the time and manner of making the elections under the first or second transitional rule.)

Q–17: Can an election be made to have section 1041 apply to some, but not all, transfers made after December 31, 1983, or some but not all, transfers made after July 18, 1984 under instruments in effect on or before July 18, 1984?

A–17: No. Partial elections are not allowed. An election under either of the two elective transitional rules applies to all transfers governed by that election whether before or after the election is made, and is irrevocable.

(g) Property settlements—time and manner of making the elections under section 1041.

Q–18: How do spouses (or former spouses) elect to have section 1041 apply to transfers after December 31, 1983, or to transfers after July 18, 1984 under instruments in effect on or before July 18, 1984?

A–18: In order to make an election under section 1041 for property transfers after December 31, 1983, or property transfers under instruments that were in effect on or before July 18, 1984, both spouses (or former spouses) must elect the application of the rules of section 1041 by attaching to the transferor's first filed income tax return for the taxable year in which the first transfer occurs, a statement signed by both spouses (or former spouses) which includes each spouse's social security number and is in substantially the form set forth at the end of this answer.

In addition, the transferor must attach a copy of such statement to his or her return for each subsequent taxable year in which a transfer is made that is governed by the transitional election. A copy of the signed statement must be kept by both parties.

The election statements shall be in substantially the following form:

In the case of an election regarding transfers after 1983:

Section 1041 Election

The undersigned hereby elect to have the provisions of section 1041 of the Internal Revenue Code apply to all qualifying transfers of property after December 31, 1983. The undersigned understand that section 1041 applies to all property transferred between spouses, or former spouses incident to divorce. The parties further understand that the effects for Federal income tax purposes of having section 1041 apply are that (1) no gain or loss is recognized by the transferor spouse or former spouse as a result of this transfer; and (2) the basis of the transferred property in the hands of the transferee is the adjusted basis of the property in the hands of the transferor immediately before the transfer, whether or not the adjusted basis of the transferred property is less than, equal to, or greater than its fair market value at the time of the transfer. The undersigned understand that if the transferee spouse or former spouse disposes of the property in a transaction in which gain is recognized, the amount of gain which is taxable may be larger than it would have been if this election had not been made.

In the case of an election regarding preexisting decrees:

Section 1041 Election

The undersigned hereby elect to have the provisions of section 1041 of the Internal Revenue Code apply to all qualifying transfers of property after July 18, 1984 under any instrument in effect on or before July 18, 1984. The undersigned understand that section 1041 applies to all property transferred between spouses, or former spouses incident to the divorce. The parties further understand that the effects for Federal income tax purposes of having section 1041 apply are that (1) no gain or loss is recognized by the transferor spouse or former spouse as a result of this transfer; and (2) the basis of the transferred property in the hands of the transferee is the adjusted basis of the property in the hands of the transferor immediately before the transfer, whether or not the adjusted basis of the transferred property is less than, equal to, or greater than its fair market value at the time of the transfer. The undersigned understand that if the transferee spouse or former spouse disposes of the property in a transaction in which gain is recognized, the amount of gain which is taxable may be larger than it would have been if this election had not been made.

(Authority: Secs. 1041(d)(4), (98 Stat. 798, 26 U.S.C. 1041(d)(4)), 152(e)(2)(A) (98 Stat. 802, 26 U.S.C. 152(e)(2)(A)), 215(c) (98 Stat. 800, 26 U.S.C. 215(c)) and 7805 (68A Stat. 917, 26 U.S.C. 7805) of the Internal Revenue Code of 1954))

[T.D. 7973, 49 FR 34452, Aug. 31, 1984; T.D. 9035, 68 FR 1536, Jan. 13, 2003]

PROCEDURE AND ADMINISTRATION

THE TAX COURT

Declaratory Judgments Relating to Qualification of Certain Retirement Plans

General Actuarial Valuations

§ 1.7703–1 Determination of marital status.

(a) General rule. The determination of whether an individual is married shall be made as of the close of his taxable year unless his spouse dies during his taxable year, in which case such determination shall be made as of the time of such death; and, except as provided in paragraph (b) of this section, an individual shall be considered as married even though living apart from his spouse unless legally separated under a decree of divorce or separate maintenance. The provisions of this paragraph may be illustrated by the following examples:

Example 1. Taxpayer A and his wife B both make their returns on a calendar year basis. In July 1954, they enter into a separation agreement and thereafter live apart, but no decree of divorce or separate maintenance is issued until March 1955. If A itemizes and claims his actual deductions on his return for the calendar year 1954, B may not elect the standard deduction on her return since B is considered as married to A (although permanently separated by agreement) on the last day of 1954.

Example 2. Taxpayer A makes his returns on the basis of a fiscal year ending June 30. His wife B makes her returns on the calendar year basis. A died in October 1954. In such case, since A and B were married as of the date of death, B may not elect the standard deduction for the calendar year 1954 if the income of A for the short taxable year ending with the date of his death is determined without regard to the standard deduction.

(b) Certain married individuals living apart. (1) For purposes of Part IV of Subchapter B of Chapter 1 of the Code, an individual is not considered as married for taxable years beginning after December 31, 1969, if (i) such individual is married (within the meaning of paragraph (a) of this section) but files a separate return; (ii) such individual maintains as his home a household which constitutes for more than one-half of the taxable year the principal place of abode of a dependent (a) who (within the meaning of section 152 and the regulations thereunder) is a son, stepson, daughter, or stepdaughter of the individual, and (b) with respect to whom such individual is entitled to a deduction for the taxable year under section 151; (iii) such individual furnishes over half of the cost of maintaining such household during the taxable year; and (iv) during the entire taxable year such individual's spouse is not a member of such household.

(2) For purposes of subparagraph (1)(ii)(a) of this paragraph, a legally adopted son or daughter of an individual, a child (described in paragraph (c)(2) of § 1.152–2) who is a member of an individual's household if placed with such individual by an authorized placement agency (as defined in paragraph (c)(2) of § 1.152–2) for legal adoption by such individual, or a foster child (described in paragraph (c)(4) of § 1.152–2) of an individual if such child satisfies the requirements of section 152(a)(9) of the Code and paragraph (b) of § 1.152–1 with respect to such individual, shall be treated as a son or daughter of such individual by blood.

(3) For purposes of subparagraph (1)(ii) of this paragraph, the household must actually constitute the home of the individual for his taxable year. However, a physical change in the location of such home will not prevent an individual from qualifying for the treatment provided in subparagraph (1) of this paragraph. It is not sufficient that the individual maintain the household without being its occupant. The individual and the dependent described in subparagraph (1)(ii)(a) of this paragraph must occupy the household for more than one-half of the taxable year of the individual. However, the fact that such dependent is born or dies within the taxable year will not prevent an individual from qualifying for such treatment if the household constitutes the principal place of abode of such dependent for the remaining or preceding part of such taxable year. The individual and such dependent will be considered as occupying the household during temporary absences from the household due to special circumstances. A nonpermanent failure to occupy the common abode by reason of illness, education, business, vacation, military service, or a custody agreement under which a child or stepchild is absent for less than 6 months in the taxable year of the taxpayer, shall be considered a temporary absence due to special circumstances. Such absence will not prevent an individual from qualifying for the treatment provided in subparagraph (1) of this paragraph if (i) it is reasonable to assume that such individual or the dependent will return to the household and (ii) such individual continues to maintain such household or a substantially equivalent household in anticipation of such return.

(4) An individual shall be considered as maintaining a household only if he pays more than one-half of the cost thereof for his taxable year. The cost of maintaining a household shall be the expenses incurred for the mutual benefit of the occupants thereof by reason of its operation as the principal place of abode of such occupants for such taxable year. The cost of maintaining a household shall not include expenses otherwise incurred. The expenses of maintaining a household include property taxes, mortgage interest, rent, utility charges, upkeep and repairs, property insurance, and food consumed on the premises. Such expenses do not include the cost of clothing, education, medical treatment, vacations, life insurance, and transportation. In addition, the cost of maintaining a household shall not include any amount which represents the value of services rendered in the household by the taxpayer or by a dependent described in subparagraph (1)(ii)(a) of this paragraph.

(5) For purposes of subparagraph (1)(iv) of this paragraph, an individual's spouse is not a member of the household during a taxable year if such household does not constitute such spouse's place of abode at any time during such year. An individual's spouse will be considered to be a member of the household during temporary absences from the household due to special circumstances. A nonpermanent failure to occupy such household as his abode by reason of illness, education, business, vacation, or military service shall be considered a mere temporary absence due to special circumstances.

(6) The provisions of this paragraph may be illustrated by the following example:

Example. Taxpayer A, married to B at the close of the calendar year 1971, his taxable year, is living apart from B, but A is not legally separated from B under a decree of divorce or separate maintenance. A maintains a household as his home which is for 7 months of 1971 the principal place of abode of C, his son, with respect to whom A is entitled to a deduction under section 151. A pays for more than one-half the cost of maintaining that household. At no time during 1971 was B a member of the household occupied by A and C. A files a separate return for 1971. Under these circumstances, A is considered as not married under section 143(b) for purposes of the standard deduction. Even though A is married and files a separate return A may claim for 1971 as his standard deduction the larger of the low income allowance up to a maximum of $1,050 consisting of both the basic allowance and additional allowance (rather than the basic allowance only subject to the $500 limitation applicable to a separate return of a married individual) or the percentage standard deduction subject to the $1,500 limitation (rather than the $750 limitation applicable to a separate return of a married individual). See § 1.141–1. For purposes of the provisions of part IV of subchapter B of chapter 1 of the Code and the regulations thereunder, A is treated as unmarried.

[T.D. 7123, 36 FR 11086, June 9, 1971; T.D. 8712, 62 FR 2283, Jan. 16, 1997]

UNITED STATES CODE

TITLE 28

JUDICIARY AND JUDICIAL PROCEDURE

PART V—PROCEDURE

CHAPTER 115—EVIDENCE; DOCUMENTARY

§ 1738A. Full faith and credit given to child custody determinations

(a) The appropriate authorities of every State shall enforce according to its terms, and shall not modify except as provided in subsections (f), (g), and (h) of this section, any custody determination or visitation determination made consistently with the provisions of this section by a court of another State.

(b) As used in this section, the term—

(1) "child" means a person under the age of eighteen;

(2) "contestant" means a person, including a parent or grandparent, who claims a right to custody or visitation of a child;

(3) "custody determination" means a judgment, decree, or other order of a court providing for the custody of a child, and includes permanent and temporary orders, and initial orders and modifications;

(4) "home State" means the State in which, immediately preceding the time involved, the child lived with his parents, a parent, or a person acting as parent, for at least six consecutive months, and in the case of a child less than six months old, the State in which the child lived from birth with any of such persons. Periods of temporary absence of any of such persons are counted as part of the six-month or other period;

(5) "modification" and "modify" refer to a custody or visitation determination which modifies, replaces, supersedes, or otherwise is made subsequent to, a prior custody or visitation determination concerning the same child, whether made by the same court or not;

(6) "person acting as a parent" means a person, other than a parent, who has physical custody of a child and who has either been awarded custody by a court or claims a right to custody;

(7) "physical custody" means actual possession and control of a child;

(8) "State" means a State of the United States, the District of Columbia, the Commonwealth of Puerto Rico, or a territory or possession of the United States; and

(9) "visitation determination" means a judgment, decree, or other order of a court providing for the visitation of a child and includes permanent and temporary orders and initial orders and modifications.

(c) A child custody or visitation determination made by a court of a State is consistent with the provisions of this section only if—

(1) such court has jurisdiction under the law of such State; and

(2) one of the following conditions is met:

(A) such State (i) is the home State of the child on the date of the commencement of the proceeding, or (ii) had been the child's home State within six months before the date of the commencement of the proceeding and the child is absent from such State because of his removal or retention by a contestant or for other reasons, and a contestant continues to live in such State;

(B) (i) it appears that no other State would have jurisdiction under subparagraph (A), and (ii) it is in the best interest of the child that a court of such State assume jurisdiction because (I) the child and his parents, or the child and at least one contestant, have a significant connection with such State other than mere physical presence in such State, and (II) there is available in such State substantial evidence concerning the child's present or future care, protection, training, and personal relationships;

(C) the child is physically present in such State and (i) the child has been abandoned, or (ii) it is necessary in an emergency to protect the child because the child, a sibling, or parent of the child has been subjected to or threatened with mistreatment or abuse;

(D) (i) it appears that no other State would have jurisdiction under subparagraph (A), (B), (C), or (E), or another State has declined to exercise jurisdiction on the ground that the State whose jurisdiction is in issue is the more appropriate forum to determine the custody or visitation of the child, and (ii) it is in the best interest of the child that such court assume jurisdiction; or

(E) the court has continuing jurisdiction pursuant to subsection (d) of this section.

(d) The jurisdiction of a court of a State which has made a child custody or visitation determination consistently with the provisions of this section continues as long as the requirement of subsection (c)(1) of this section continues to be met and such State remains the residence of the child or of any contestant.

(e) Before a child custody or visitation determination is made, reasonable notice and opportunity to be heard shall be given to the contestants, any parent whose parental rights have not been previously terminated and any person who has physical custody of a child.

(f) A court of a State may modify a determination of the custody of the same child made by a court of another State, if—

(1) it has jurisdiction to make such a child custody determination; and

(2) the court of the other State no longer has jurisdiction, or it has declined to exercise such jurisdiction to modify such determination.

(g) A court of a State shall not exercise jurisdiction in any proceeding for a custody or visitation determination commenced during the pendency of a proceeding in a court of another State where such court of that other State is exercising jurisdiction consistently with the provisions of this section to make a custody or visitation determination.

(h) A court of a State may not modify a visitation determination made by a court of another State unless the court of the other State no longer has jurisdiction to modify such determination or has declined to exercise jurisdiction to modify such determination. *(Added Pub.L. 96–611, § 8(a), Dec. 28, 1980, 94 Stat. 3569; amended Pub.L. 105–374, § 1, Nov. 12, 1998, 112 Stat. 3383; Pub.L. 106–386, Div. B, Title III, § 1303(d), Oct. 28, 2000, 114 Stat. 1512.)*

Commentary

See *In re Marriage of Torres, 62 Cal.App.4th 1357, 73 Cal.Rptr.2d 344 (1998)* (six months provision of Family Code § 3403(a)(1) satisfied, making California the "home state," when children lived in California from birth until removal from state by mother, and father filed divorce proceedings within six months of removal; 28 U.S.C.A. § 1738A (c)(2)(A) also satisfied).

§ 1738B. Full faith and credit for child support orders

(a) General rule.—The appropriate authorities of each State—

(1) shall enforce according to its terms a child support order made consistently with this section by a court of another State; and

(2) shall not seek or make a modification of such an order except in accordance with subsections (e), (f), and (i).

(b) Definitions.—In this section:

(1) The term "child" means—

(A) a person under 18 years of age; and

(B) a person 18 or more years of age with respect to whom a child support order has been issued pursuant to the laws of a State.

(2) The term "child's State" means the State in which a child resides.

(3) The term "child's home State" means the State in which a child lived with a parent or a person acting as parent for at least 6 consecutive months immediately preceding the time of filing of a petition or comparable pleading for support and, if a child is less than 6 months old, the State in which the child lived from birth with any of them. A period of temporary absence of any of them is counted as part of the 6–month period.

(4) The term "child support" means a payment of money, continuing support, or arrearages or the provision of a benefit (including payment of health insurance, child care, and educational expenses) for the support of a child.

(5) The term "child support order"—

(A) means a judgment, decree, or order of a court requiring the payment of child support in periodic amounts or in a lump sum; and

(B) includes—

(i) a permanent or temporary order; and

(ii) an initial order or a modification of an order.

(6) The term "contestant" means—

(A) a person (including a parent) who—

(i) claims a right to receive child support;

(ii) is a party to a proceeding that may result in the issuance of a child support order; or

(iii) is under a child support order; and

(B) a State or political subdivision of a State to which the right to obtain child support has been assigned.

(7) The term "court" means a court or administrative agency of a State that is authorized by State law to establish the amount of child support payable by a contestant or make a modification of a child support order.

(8) The term "modification" means a change in a child support order that affects the amount, scope, or duration of the order and modifies, replaces, supersedes, or otherwise is made subsequent to the child support order.

(9) The term "State" means a State of the United States, the District of Columbia, the Commonwealth of Puerto Rico, the territories and possessions of the United States, and Indian country (as defined in section 1151 of title 18).

(c) Requirements of child support orders.—A child support order made by a court of a State is made consistently with this section if—

(1) a court that makes the order, pursuant to the laws of the State in which the court is located and subsections (e), (f), and (g)—

(A) has subject matter jurisdiction to hear the matter and enter such an order; and

(B) has personal jurisdiction over the contestants; and

(2) reasonable notice and opportunity to be heard is given to the contestants.

(d) Continuing jurisdiction.—A court of a State that has made a child support order consistently with this section has continuing, exclusive jurisdiction over the order if the State is the child's State or the residence of any individual contestant or the parties have consented in a record or open court that the tribunal of the State may continue to exercise jurisdiction to modify its order, unless the court of another State, acting in accordance with subsections (e) and (f), has made a modification of the order.

(e) Authority to modify orders.—A court of a State may modify a child support order issued by a court of another State if—

(1) the court has jurisdiction to make such a child support order pursuant to subsection (i); and

(2)(A) the court of the other State no longer has continuing, exclusive jurisdiction of the child support order because that State no longer is the child's State or the residence of any individual contestant and the parties have not consented in a record or open court that the tribunal of the other State may continue to exercise jurisdiction to modify its order; or

(B) each individual contestant has filed written consent with the State of continuing, exclusive jurisdiction for a court of another State to modify the order and assume continuing, exclusive jurisdiction over the order.

(f) Recognition of child support orders.—If 1 or more child support orders have been issued with regard to an obligor and a child, a court shall apply the following rules in determining which order to recognize for purposes of continuing, exclusive jurisdiction and enforcement:

(1) If only 1 court has issued a child support order, the order of that court must be recognized.

(2) If 2 or more courts have issued child support orders for the same obligor and child, and only 1 of the courts would have continuing, exclusive jurisdiction under this section, the order of that court must be recognized.

(3) If 2 or more courts have issued child support orders for the same obligor and child, and more than 1 of the courts would have continuing, exclusive jurisdiction under this section, an order issued by a court in the current home State of the child must be recognized, but if an order has not been issued in the current home State of the child, the order most recently issued must be recognized.

(4) If 2 or more courts have issued child support orders for the same obligor and child, and none of the courts would have continuing, exclusive jurisdiction under this section, a court having jurisdiction over the parties shall issue a child support order, which must be recognized.

(5) The court that has issued an order recognized under this subsection is the court having continuing, exclusive jurisdiction under subsection (d).

(g) Enforcement of modified orders.—A court of a State that no longer has continuing, exclusive jurisdiction of a child support order may enforce the order with respect to nonmodifiable obligations and unsatisfied obligations that accrued before the date on which a modification of the order is made under subsections (e) and (f).

(h) Choice of law.—

(1) In general.—In a proceeding to establish, modify, or enforce a child support order, the forum State's law shall apply except as provided in paragraphs (2) and (3).

(2) Law of State of issuance of order.—In interpreting a child support order including the duration of current payments and other obligations of support, a court shall apply the law of the State of the court that issued the order.

(3) Period of limitation.—In an action to enforce arrears under a child support order, a court shall apply the statute of limitation of the forum State or the State of the court that issued the order, whichever statute provides the longer period of limitation.

(i) Registration for modification.—If there is no individual contestant or child residing in the issuing State, the party or support enforcement agency seeking to modify, or to modify and enforce, a child support order issued in another State shall register that order in a State with jurisdiction over the nonmovant for the purpose of modification. *(Added Pub.L. 103–383, § 3(a), Oct. 20, 1994, 108 Stat. 4064; amended Pub.L. 104–193, Title III, § 322, Aug. 22, 1996, 110 Stat. 2221; Pub.L. 105–33, Title V, § 5554, Aug. 5, 1997, 111 Stat. 636; Pub.L. 113–183, Title III, § 301(f)(2), Sept. 29, 2014, 128 Stat. 1944.)*

Commentary

See generally *In re Marriage of Lurie, 33 Cal.App.4th 658, 39 Cal.Rptr.2d 835 (1995)* (in enforcing a New York support order under URESA, trial court properly applied California's age of majority rather than New York's age of majority). For further discussion, see *FFCCSOA* and *Marriage of Lurie*, 1995 California Family Law Monthly 108–109 (May 1995). But see *In re Marriage of Chester, 37 Cal.App.4th 1624, 44 Cal.Rptr.2d 717 (1995)* (explicitly rejecting the result in *Lurie* and holding that Oregon order requiring child support until age 21 is enforceable in California) and *Kilroy v. Superior Court, 54 Cal.App.4th 793, 63 Cal.Rptr.2d 390 (1997)* (holding that this section deprives a California trial court of URESA jurisdiction to modify a Georgia child support order against a California support obligor when, pursuant to this section, the Georgia court retains continuing exclusive jurisdiction because the custodial parent and child continue to reside Georgia).

Interpreting subsection (h)(3) together with California tolling rules (Code Civ. Proc. § 351, tolling the statute of limitations when a defendant is out of the state), *Trend v. Bell, 57 Cal.App.4th 1092, 68 Cal.Rptr.2d 54 (1997), review denied December 23, 1997,* held that a Montana child support judgment against a California defendant, which was no longer enforceable under Montana law, was nevertheless enforceable under California law.

Where custody has shifted from one parent to the other, *Keith G. v. Susan H., 62 Cal.App.4th 853, 72 Cal.Rptr.2d 525 (1998), review denied June 24, 1998,* holds that a California court may set off a father's unpaid child support arrearages under a California judgment against the mother's current child support obligation under a Missouri judgment.

Interpreting subsections (e), (i), (d), and (f), *Harding v. Harding, 99 Cal.App.4th 626, 121 Cal.Rptr.2d 450 (2002)*, held that the trial court properly concluded that it lacked subject matter jurisdiction to modify a child support order of another state when the support obligor remained a resident of that state. *Harding* also upheld the constitutionality of the California Uniform Interstate Family Support Act (Family Code §§ 4900–5005) and the federal Full Faith and Credit for Child Support Orders Act (28 U.S.C.A. § 1738B).

§ 1738C. Certain acts, records, and proceedings and the effect thereof

No State, territory, or possession of the United States, or Indian tribe, shall be required to give effect to any public act, record, or judicial proceeding of any other State, territory, possession, or tribe respecting a relationship between persons of the same sex that is treated as a marriage under the laws of such other State, territory, possession, or tribe, or a right or claim arising from such relationship. *(Added Pub.L. 104–199, § 2(a), Sept. 21, 1996, 110 Stat. 2419.)*

Validity

This provision does not survive United States v. Windsor, 133 S.Ct. 2675 (2013), which requires the federal government to recognize same-sex marriages lawfully contracted in a state authorizing such marriages and holds that the first section of the Defense of Marriage Act (1 USC 7), which declined to do so, violates the Fifth and Fourteenth Amendments. See also Obergefell v. Hodges, 135 S.Ct. 2584 (2015), which establishes a federal constitutional right to same-sex marriage and requires that states recognize such marriages lawfully contracted elsewhere.

Commentary

In *V.L. v. E.L., 136 S.Ct. 1017, 194 L. Ed 2d 92 (2016)*, the United States Supreme Court held that the Full Faith and Credit Clause of the United States Constitution compelled Alabama to recognize a Georgia final judgment of adoption that recognized a mother's female partner as a second parent of the mother's children.

TITLE 29

LABOR

CHAPTER 18—EMPLOYEE RETIREMENT INCOME SECURITY PROGRAM

SUBCHAPTER I—PROTECTION OF EMPLOYEE BENEFIT RIGHTS

SUBTITLE B—REGULATORY PROVISIONS

Part 2—Participation and Vesting

SUBCHAPTER I—PROTECTION OF EMPLOYEE BENEFIT RIGHTS

SUBTITLE B—REGULATORY PROVISIONS

Part 2—Participation and Vesting

§ 1055. Requirement of joint and survivor annuity and preretirement survivor annuity

(a) Required contents for applicable plans

Each pension plan to which this section applies shall provide that—

(1) in the case of a vested participant who does not die before the annuity starting date, the accrued benefit payable to such participant shall be provided in the form of a qualified joint and survivor annuity, and

(2) in the case of a vested participant who dies before the annuity starting date and who has a surviving spouse, a qualified preretirement survivor annuity shall be provided to the surviving spouse of such participant.

(b) Applicable plans

(1) This section shall apply to—

(A) any defined benefit plan,

(B) any individual account plan which is subject to the funding standards of section 1082 of this title, and

(C) any participant under any other individual account plan unless—

(i) such plan provides that the participant's nonforfeitable accrued benefit (reduced by any security interest held by the plan by reason of a loan outstanding to such participant) is payable in full, on the death of the participant, to the participant's surviving spouse (or, if there is no surviving spouse or the surviving spouse consents in the manner required under subsection (c)(2), to a designated beneficiary),

(ii) such participant does not elect the payment of benefits in the form of a life annuity, and

(iii) with respect to such participant, such plan is not a direct or indirect transferee (in a transfer after December 31, 1984) of a plan which is described in subparagraph (A) or (B) or to which this clause applied with respect to the participant.

Clause (iii) of subparagraph (C) shall apply only with respect to the transferred assets (and income therefrom) if the plan separately accounts for such assets and any income therefrom.

(2)(A) In the case of—

(i) a tax credit employee stock ownership plan (as defined in section 409(a) of Title 26), or

(ii) an employee stock ownership plan (as defined in section 4975(e)(7) of Title 26),

subsection (a) shall not apply to that portion of the employee's accrued benefit to which the requirements of section 409(h) of Title 26 apply.

(B) Subparagraph (A) shall not apply with respect to any participant unless the requirements of clause [1] (i), (ii), and (iii) of paragraph (1)(C) are met with respect to such participant.

(4) [2] This section shall not apply to a plan which the Secretary of the Treasury or his delegate has determined is a plan described in section 404(c) of Title 26 (or a continuation thereof) in which participation is substantially limited to individuals who, before January 1, 1976, ceased employment covered by the plan.

(4) [2] A plan shall not be treated as failing to meet the requirements of paragraph (1)(C) or (2) merely because the plan provides that benefits will not be payable to the surviving spouse of the participant unless the participant and such spouse had been married throughout the 1-year period ending on the earlier of the participant's annuity starting date or the date of the participant's death.

(c) Plans meeting requirements of section

(1) A plan meets the requirements of this section only if—

(A) under the plan, each participant—

(i) may elect at any time during the applicable election period to waive the qualified joint and survivor annuity form of benefit or the qualified preretirement survivor annuity form of benefit (or both),

(ii) if the participant elects a waiver under clause (i), may elect the qualified optional survivor annuity at any time during the applicable election period, and

(iii) may revoke any such election at any time during the applicable election period, and

(B) the plan meets the requirements of paragraphs (2), (3), and (4).

(2) Each plan shall provide that an election under paragraph (1)(A)(i) shall not take effect unless—

(A) (i) the spouse of the participant consents in writing to such election, (ii) such election designates a beneficiary (or a form of benefits) which may not be changed without spousal consent (or the consent of the spouse expressly permits designations by the participant without any requirement of further consent by the spouse), and (iii) the spouse's consent acknowledges the effect of such election and is witnessed by a plan representative or a notary public, or

(B) it is established to the satisfaction of a plan representative that the consent required under subparagraph (A) may not be obtained because there is no spouse, because the spouse cannot be located, or because of such other circumstances as the Secretary of the Treasury may by regulations prescribe.

Any consent by a spouse (or establishment that the consent of a spouse may not be obtained) under the preceding sentence shall be effective only with respect to such spouse.

(3)(A) Each plan shall provide to each participant, within a reasonable period of time before the annuity starting date (and consistent with such regulations as the Secretary of the Treasury may prescribe) a written explanation of—

(i) the terms and conditions of the qualified joint and survivor annuity and of the qualified optional survivor annuity,

(ii) the participant's right to make, and the effect of, an election under paragraph (1) to waive the joint and survivor annuity form of benefit,

(iii) the rights of the participant's spouse under paragraph (2), and

(iv) the right to make, and the effect of, a revocation of an election under paragraph (1).

(B)(i) Each plan shall provide to each participant, within the applicable period with respect to such participant (and consistent with such regulations as the Secretary may prescribe), a written explanation with respect to the qualified preretirement survivor annuity comparable to that required under subparagraph (A).

(ii) For purposes of clause (i), the term "applicable period" means, with respect to a participant, whichever of the following periods ends last:

(I) The period beginning with the first day of the plan year in which the participant attains age 32 and ending with the close of the plan year preceding the plan year in which the participant attains age 35.

(II) A reasonable period after the individual becomes a participant.

(III) A reasonable period ending after paragraph (5) ceases to apply to the participant.

(IV) A reasonable period ending after this section applies to the participant.

In the case of a participant who separates from service before attaining age 35, the applicable period shall be a reasonable period after separation.

(4) Each plan shall provide that, if this section applies to a participant when part or all of the participant's accrued benefit is to be used as security for a loan, no portion of the participant's accrued benefit may be used as security for such loan unless—

(A) the spouse of the participant (if any) consents in writing to such use during the 90–day period ending on the date on which the loan is to be so secured, and

(B) requirements comparable to the requirements of paragraph (2) are met with respect to such consent.

(5)(A) The requirements of this subsection shall not apply with respect to the qualified joint and survivor annuity form of benefit or the qualified preretirement survivor annuity form of benefit, as the case may be, if such benefit may not be waived (or another beneficiary selected) and if the plan fully subsidizes the costs of such benefit.

(B) For purposes of subparagraph (A), a plan fully subsidizes the costs of a benefit if under the plan the failure to waive such benefit by a participant would not result in a decrease in any plan benefits with respect to such participant and would not result in increased contributions from such participant.

(6) If a plan fiduciary acts in accordance with part 4 of this subtitle in—

(A) relying on a consent or revocation referred to in paragraph (1)(A), or

(B) making a determination under paragraph (2),

then such consent, revocation, or determination shall be treated as valid for purposes of discharging the plan from liability to the extent of payments made pursuant to such Act.

(7) For purposes of this subsection, the term "applicable election period" means—

(A) in the case of an election to waive the qualified joint and survivor annuity form of benefit, the 180–day period ending on the annuity starting date, or

(B) in the case of an election to waive the qualified preretirement survivor annuity, the period which begins on the first day of the plan year in which the participant attains age 35 and ends on the date of the participant's death.

In the case of a participant who is separated from service, the applicable election period under subparagraph (B) with respect to benefits accrued before the date of such separation from service shall not begin later than such date.

(8) Notwithstanding any other provision of this subsection—

(A)(i) A plan may provide the written explanation described in paragraph (3)(A) after the annuity starting date. In any case to which this subparagraph applies, the applicable election period under paragraph (7) shall not end before the 30th day after the date on which such explanation is provided.

(ii) The Secretary of the Treasury may by regulations limit the application of clause (i), except that such regulations may not limit the period of time by which the annuity starting date precedes the provision of the written explanation other than by providing that the annuity starting date may not be earlier than termination of employment.

(B) A plan may permit a participant to elect (with any applicable spousal consent) to waive any requirement that the written explanation be provided at least 30 days before the annuity starting date (or to waive the 30–day requirement under subparagraph (A)) if the distribution commences more than 7 days after such explanation is provided.

(d)(1) "Qualified joint and survivor annuity" defined

For purposes of this section, the term "qualified joint and survivor annuity" means an annuity—

(A) for the life of the participant with a survivor annuity for the life of the spouse which is not less than 50 percent of (and is not greater than 100 percent of) the amount of the annuity which is payable during the joint lives of the participant and the spouse, and

(B) which is the actuarial equivalent of a single annuity for the life of the participant.

Such term also includes any annuity in a form having the effect of an annuity described in the preceding sentence.

(2)(A) For purposes of this section, the term "qualified optional survivor annuity" means an annuity—

(i) for the life of the participant with a survivor annuity for the life of the spouse which is equal to the applicable percentage of the amount of the annuity which is payable during the joint lives of the participant and the spouse, and

(ii) which is the actuarial equivalent of a single annuity for the life of the participant.

Such term also includes any annuity in a form having the effect of an annuity described in the preceding sentence.

(B)(i) For purposes of subparagraph (A), if the survivor annuity percentage—

(I) is less than 75 percent, the applicable percentage is 75 percent, and

(II) is greater than or equal to 75 percent, the applicable percentage is 50 percent.

(ii) For purposes of clause (i), the term "survivor annuity percentage" means the percentage which the survivor annuity under the plan's qualified joint and survivor annuity bears to the annuity payable during the joint lives of the participant and the spouse.

(e) "Qualified preretirement survivor annuity" defined

For purposes of this section—

(1) Except as provided in paragraph (2), the term "qualified preretirement survivor annuity" means a survivor annuity for the life of the surviving spouse of the participant if—

(A) the payments to the surviving spouse under such annuity are not less than the amounts which would be payable as a survivor annuity under the qualified joint and survivor annuity under the plan (or the actuarial equivalent thereof) if—

(i) in the case of a participant who dies after the date on which the participant attained the earliest retirement age, such participant had retired with an immediate qualified joint and survivor annuity on the day before the participant's date of death, or

(ii) in the case of a participant who dies on or before the date on which the participant would have attained the earliest retirement age, such participant had—

(I) separated from service on the date of death,

(II) survived to the earliest retirement age,

(III) retired with an immediate qualified joint and survivor annuity at the earliest retirement age, and

(IV) died on the day after the day on which such participant would have attained the earliest retirement age, and

(B) under the plan, the earliest period for which the surviving spouse may receive a payment under such annuity is not later than the month in which the participant would have attained the earliest retirement age under the plan.

In the case of an individual who separated from service before the date of such individual's death, subparagraph (A)(ii)(I) shall not apply.

(2) In the case of any individual account plan or participant described in subparagraph (B) or (C) of subsection (b)(1), the term "qualified preretirement survivor annuity" means an annuity for the life of the surviving spouse the actuarial equivalent of which is not less than 50 percent of the portion of the account balance of the participant (as of the date of death) to which the participant had a nonforfeitable right (within the meaning of section 1053 of this title).

(3) For purposes of paragraphs (1) and (2), any security interest held by the plan by reason of a loan outstanding to the participant shall be taken into account in determining the amount of the qualified preretirement survivor annuity.

(f) Marriage requirements for plan

(1) Except as provided in paragraph (2), a plan may provide that a qualified joint and survivor annuity (or a qualified preretirement survivor annuity) will not be provided unless the participant and spouse had been married throughout the 1–year period ending on the earlier of—

(A) the participant's annuity starting date, or

(B) the date of the participant's death.

(2) For purposes of paragraph (1), if—

(A) a participant marries within 1 year before the annuity starting date, and

(B) the participant and the participant's spouse in such marriage have been married for at least a 1–year period ending on or before the date of the participant's death,

such participant and such spouse shall be treated as having been married throughout the 1–year period ending on the participant's annuity starting date.

(g) Distribution of present value of annuity; written consent; determination of present value

(1) A plan may provide that the present value of a qualified joint and survivor annuity or a qualified preretirement survivor annuity will be immediately distributed if such value does not exceed the amount that can be distributed without the participant's consent under section 1053(e) of this title. No distribution may be made under the preceding sentence after the annuity starting date unless the participant and the spouse of the participant (or where the participant has died, the surviving spouse) consent in writing to such distribution.

(2) If—

(A) the present value of the qualified joint and survivor annuity or the qualified preretirement survivor annuity exceeds the amount that can be distributed without the participant's consent under section 1053(e) of this title, and

(B) the participant and the spouse of the participant (or where the participant has died, the surviving spouse) consent in writing to the distribution,

the plan may immediately distribute the present value of such annuity.

(3)(A) For purposes of paragraphs (1) and (2), the present value shall not be less than the present value calculated by using the applicable mortality table and the applicable interest rate.

(B) For purposes of subparagraph (A)—

(i) The term "applicable mortality table" means a mortality table, modified as appropriate by the Secretary of the Treasury, based on the mortality table specified for the plan year under subparagraph (A) of section 1083(h)(3) of this title (without regard to subparagraph (C) or (D) of such section).

(ii) The term "applicable interest rate" means the adjusted first, second, and third segment rates applied under rules similar to the rules of section 1083(h)(2)(C) of this title (determined by not taking into account any adjustment under clause (iv) thereof) for the month before the date of the distribution or such other time as the Secretary of the Treasury may by regulations prescribe.

(iii) For purposes of clause (ii), the adjusted first, second, and third segment rates are the first, second, and third segment rates which would be determined under section 1083(h)(2)(C) of this title (determined by not taking into account any adjustment under clause (iv) thereof) if section 1083(h)(2)(D) of this title were applied by substituting the average yields for the month described in clause (ii) for the average yields for the 24–month period described in such section.

(h) Definitions

For purposes of this section—

(1) The term "vested participant" means any participant who has a nonforfeitable right (within the meaning of section 1002(19) of this title) to any portion of such participant's accrued benefit.

(2)(A) The term "annuity starting date" means—

(i) the first day of the first period for which an amount is payable as an annuity, or

(ii) in the case of a benefit not payable in the form of an annuity, the first day on which all events have occurred which entitle the participant to such benefit.

(B) For purposes of subparagraph (A), the first day of the first period for which a benefit is to be received by reason of disability shall be treated as the annuity starting date only if such benefit is not an auxiliary benefit.

(3) The term "earliest retirement age" means the earliest date on which, under the plan, the participant could elect to receive retirement benefits.

(i) Increased costs from providing annuity

A plan may take into account in any equitable manner (as determined by the Secretary of the Treasury) any increased costs resulting from providing a qualified joint or survivor annuity or a qualified preretirement survivor annuity.

(j) Use of participant's accrued benefit as security for loan as not preventing distribution

If the use of any participant's accrued benefit (or any portion thereof) as security for a loan meets the requirements of subsection (c)(4), nothing in this section shall prevent any distribution required by reason of a failure to comply with the terms of such loan.

(k) Spousal consent

No consent of a spouse shall be effective for purposes of subsection (g)(1) or (g)(2) (as the case may be) unless requirements comparable to the requirements for spousal consent to an election under subsection (c)(1)(A) are met.

(*l*) Regulations; consultation of Secretary of the Treasury with Secretary of Labor

In prescribing regulations under this section, the Secretary of the Treasury shall consult with the Secretary of Labor.

(Pub.L. 93–406, Title I, § 205, Sept. 2, 1974, 88 Stat. 862; Pub.L. 98–397, Title I, § 103(a), Aug. 23, 1984, 98 Stat. 1429; Pub.L. 99–514, Title XI, §§ 1139(c)(2), 1145(b), Title XVIII, § 1898(b)(1)(B), (2)(B), (3)(B), (4)(B), (5)(B), (6)(B), (7)(B), (8)(B), (9)(B), (10)(B), (11)(B), (12)(B), (13)(B), (14)(B), Oct. 22, 1986, 100 Stat. 2488, 2491, 2945 to 2951; Pub.L. 101–239, Title VII, §§ 7861(d)(2), 7862(d)(1)(B), (3), (6) to (9), 7891(a)(1), (b)(3), (c), (e), 7894(c)(7)(A), Dec. 19, 1989, 103 Stat. 2431, 2434, 2445, 2447, 2449; Pub.L. 103–465, Title VII, § 767(c)(2), Dec. 8, 1994, 108 Stat. 5039; Pub.L. 104–188, Title I, § 1451(b), Aug. 20, 1996, 110 Stat. 1815; Pub.L. 105–34, Title X, § 1071(b)(2), Title XVI, § 1601(d)(5), Aug. 5, 1997, 111 Stat. 948, 1089; Pub.L. 107–147, Title IV, § 411(r)(2), Mar. 9, 2002, 116 Stat. 51; Pub.L. 109–280, Title III, § 302(a), Title X, § 1004(b), Title XI, § 1102(a)(2)(A), Aug. 17, 2006, 120 Stat. 920, 1054, 1056; Pub.L. 110–458, Title I, § 103(b)(1), Dec. 23, 2008, 122 Stat. 5103; Pub.L. 112–141, Div. D, Title II, § 40211(b)(3)(B), July 6, 2012, 126 Stat. 849; Pub.L. 113–295, Div. A, Title II, § 221(a)(57)(B)(ii), Dec. 19, 2014, 128 Stat. 4046.)

[1]So in original. Probably should be "clauses".

[2] So in original. Two subsecs. (b)(4), and no (b)(3), have been enacted.

Commentary

In *Mid-American Pension and Employee Benefits Plan v. Cox, 720 F.3d 715 (2013)*, the Eighth Circuit Court of Appeals held that, under subsection (c)(2)(A)(iii), a premarital agreement was ineffective as a waiver of a wife's right to funds in deceased husband's 401(k) plan.

The surviving spouse provisions of this section apply only to employee benefit plans established or maintained by an employer. They have no application to an Individual Retirement Account (IRA) after an employee rolls over distributions from an ERISA-regulated plan into an IRA. *Charles Schwab & Co. v. Debickero, 593 F.3d 916 (9th Cir. 2010)*.

See generally discussion of ERISA preemption of California law in Family Code Section 2610 Commentary.

Subsection (c)(6) does not absolve the plan of all liability to a surviving widow when her husband has waived her right to a survivor's benefit without her consent. Balancing the equities, *Hearn v. Western Conference of Teamsters Pension Trust Fund, 68 F.3d 301 (9th Cir. 1995)*, holds that her survivor's benefits may be reduced only by the amount that the plan overpaid her deceased husband due to his unauthorized election of benefits for his life only.

Relying on subsection (a)(2) and subsection (d)(3)(F) of Section 1056, *Hamilton v. Washington State Plumbing and Pipefitting Industry Pension Plan, 433 F.3d 1091 (9th Cir. 2006)*, concludes that a surviving spouse's Qualified Preretirement Survivor Annuity can be diverted only to a former surviving spouse. Thus, a dissolution decree requiring decedent ex-husband to name the parties' two children as the beneficiaries of his pension in lieu of life insurance that he was unable to obtain, was insufficient to divest decedent's surviving second wife of her Preretirement Survivor Annuity benefits.

Relying in part on subsection (d)(1), which calculates benefits on the basis of the life of the spouses at the time benefits become payable, *Carmona v. Carmona, 544 F.3d 988 (9th Cir. 2008)*, held that a participant in an ERISA-regulated Qualified Joint and Survivor Annuity (QJSA) may not change his surviving spouse beneficiary after he has retired and the annuity has started to pay out. The QJSA surviving spouse's benefit irrevocably vests in the participant's spouse at the time of the annuity start date and may not be reassigned to a subsequent spouse. Accord, *Hopkins v. AT & T Global Solutions Co., 105 F.3d 153 (4th Cir. 1997)*.

§ 1056. Form and payment of benefits

(a) Commencement date for payment of benefits

Each pension plan shall provide that unless the participant otherwise elects, the payment of benefits under the plan to the participant shall begin not later than the 60th day after the latest of the close of the plan year in which—

(1) occurs the date on which the participant attains the earlier of age 65 or the normal retirement age specified under the plan,

(2) occurs the 10th anniversary of the year in which the participant commenced participation in the plan, or

(3) the participant terminates his service with the employer.

In the case of a plan which provides for the payment of an early retirement benefit, such plan shall provide that a participant who satisfied the service requirements for such early retirement benefit, but separated from the service (with any nonforfeitable right to an accrued benefit) before satisfying the age requirement for such early retirement benefit, is entitled upon satisfaction of such age requirement to receive a benefit not less than the benefit to which he would be entitled at the normal retirement age, actuarially reduced under regulations prescribed by the Secretary of the Treasury.

(b) Decrease in plan benefits by reason of increases in benefit levels under Social Security Act or Railroad Retirement Act of 1937

If—

(1) a participant or beneficiary is receiving benefits under a pension plan, or

(2) a participant is separated from the service and has non-forfeitable rights to benefits,

a plan may not decrease benefits of such a participant by reason of any increase in the benefit levels payable under title II of the Social Security Act or the Railroad Retirement Act of 1937 or any increase in the wage base under such title II, if such increase takes place after September 2, 1974, or (if later) the earlier of the date of first entitlement of such benefits or the date of such separation.

(c) Forfeiture of accrued benefits derived from employer contributions

No pension plan may provide that any part of a participant's accrued benefit derived from employer contributions (whether or not otherwise nonforfeitable) is forfeitable solely because of withdrawal by such participant of any amount attributable to the benefit derived from contributions made by such participant. The preceding sentence shall not apply (1) to the accrued benefit of any participant unless, at the time of such withdrawal, such participant has a nonforfeitable right to at least 50 percent of such accrued benefit, or (2) to the extent that an accrued benefit is permitted to be forfeited in accordance with section 1053(a)(3)(D)(iii) of this title.

(d) Assignment or alienation of plan benefits

(1) Each pension plan shall provide that benefits provided under the plan may not be assigned or alienated.

(2) For the purposes of paragraph (1) of this subsection, there shall not be taken into account any voluntary and revocable assignment of not to exceed 10 percent of any benefit payment, or of any irrevocable assignment or alienation of benefits executed before September 2, 1974. The preceding sentence shall not apply to any assignment or alienation made for the purposes of defraying plan administration costs. For purposes of this paragraph a loan made to a participant or beneficiary shall not be treated as an assignment or alienation if such loan is secured by the participant's accrued non-forfeitable benefit and is exempt from the tax imposed by section 4975 of Title 26 (relating to tax on prohibited transactions) by reason of section 4975(d)(1) of Title 26.

(3)(A) Paragraph (1) shall apply to the creation, assignment, or recognition of a right to any benefit payable with respect to a participant pursuant to a domestic relations order, except that paragraph (1) shall not apply if the order is determined to be a qualified domestic relations order. Each pension plan shall provide for the payment of benefits in accordance with the applicable requirements of any qualified domestic relations order.

(B) For purposes of this paragraph—

(i) the term "qualified domestic relations order" means a domestic relations order—

(I) which creates or recognizes the existence of an alternate payee's right to, or assigns to an alternate payee the right to, receive all or a portion of the benefits payable with respect to a participant under a plan, and

(II) with respect to which the requirements of subparagraphs (C) and (D) are met, and

(ii) the term "domestic relations order" means any judgment, decree, or order (including approval of a property settlement agreement) which—

(I) relates to the provision of child support, alimony payments, or marital property rights to a spouse, former spouse, child, or other dependent of a participant, and

(II) is made pursuant to a State domestic relations law (including a community property law).

(C) A domestic relations order meets the requirements of this subparagraph only if such order clearly specifies—

(i) the name and the last known mailing address (if any) of the participant and the name and mailing address of each alternate payee covered by the order,

(ii) the amount or percentage of the participant's benefits to be paid by the plan to each such alternate payee, or the manner in which such amount or percentage is to be determined,

(iii) the number of payments or period to which such order applies, and

(iv) each plan to which such order applies.

(D) A domestic relations order meets the requirements of this subparagraph only if such order—

(i) does not require a plan to provide any type or form of benefit, or any option, not otherwise provided under the plan,

(ii) does not require the plan to provide increased benefits (determined on the basis of actuarial value), and

(iii) does not require the payment of benefits to an alternate payee which are required to be paid to another alternate payee under another order previously determined to be a qualified domestic relations order.

(E)(i) A domestic relations order shall not be treated as failing to meet the requirements of clause (i) of subparagraph (D) solely because such order requires that payment of benefits be made to an alternate payee—

(I) in the case of any payment before a participant has separated from service, on or after the date on which the participant attains (or would have attained) the earliest retirement age,

(II) as if the participant had retired on the date on which such payment is to begin under such order (but taking into account only the present value of benefits actually accrued and not taking into account the present value of any employer subsidy for early retirement), and

(III) in any form in which such benefits may be paid under the plan to the participant (other than in the form of a joint and survivor annuity with respect to the alternate payee and his or her subsequent spouse).

For purposes of subclause (II), the interest rate assumption used in determining the present value shall be the interest rate specified in the plan or, if no rate is specified, 5 percent.

(ii) For purposes of this subparagraph, the term "earliest retirement age" means the earlier of—

(I) the date on which the participant is entitled to a distribution under the plan, or

(II) the later of the date of [1] the participant attains age 50 or the earliest date on which the participant could begin receiving benefits under the plan if the participant separated from service.

(F) To the extent provided in any qualified domestic relations order—

(i) the former spouse of a participant shall be treated as a surviving spouse of such participant for purposes of section 1055 of this title (and any spouse of the participant shall not be treated as a spouse of the participant for such purposes), and

(ii) if married for at least 1 year, the surviving former spouse shall be treated as meeting the requirements of section 1055(f) of this title.

(G)(i) In the case of any domestic relations order received by a plan—

(I) the plan administrator shall promptly notify the participant and each alternate payee of the receipt of such order and the plan's procedures for determining the qualified status of domestic relations orders, and

(II) within a reasonable period after receipt of such order, the plan administrator shall determine whether such order is a qualified domestic relations order and notify the participant and each alternate payee of such determination.

(ii) Each plan shall establish reasonable procedures to determine the qualified status of domestic relations orders and to administer distributions under such qualified orders. Such procedures—

(I) shall be in writing,

(II) shall provide for the notification of each person specified in a domestic relations order as entitled to payment of benefits under the plan (at the address included in the domestic relations order) of such procedures promptly upon receipt by the plan of the domestic relations order, and

(III) shall permit an alternate payee to designate a representative for receipt of copies of notices that are sent to the alternate payee with respect to a domestic relations order.

(H)(i) During any period in which the issue of whether a domestic relations order is a qualified domestic relations order is being determined (by the plan administrator, by a court of competent jurisdiction, or otherwise), the plan administrator shall separately account for the amounts (hereinafter in this subparagraph referred to as the "segregated amounts") which would have been payable to the alternate payee during such period if the order had been determined to be a qualified domestic relations order.

(ii) If within the 18–month period described in clause (v) the order (or modification thereof) is determined to be a qualified domestic relations order, the plan administrator shall pay the segregated amounts (including any interest thereon) to the person or persons entitled thereto.

(iii) If within the 18–month period described in clause (v)—

(I) it is determined that the order is not a qualified domestic relations order, or

(II) the issue as to whether such order is a qualified domestic relations order is not resolved,

then the plan administrator shall pay the segregated amounts (including any interest thereon) to the person or persons who would have been entitled to such amounts if there had been no order.

(iv) Any determination that an order is a qualified domestic relations order which is made after the close of the 18–month period described in clause (v) shall be applied prospectively only.

(v) For purposes of this subparagraph, the 18–month period described in this clause is the 18–month period beginning with the date on which the first payment would be required to be made under the domestic relations order.

(I) If a plan fiduciary acts in accordance with part 4 of this subtitle in—

(i) treating a domestic relations order as being (or not being) a qualified domestic relations order, or

(ii) taking action under subparagraph (H),

then the plan's obligation to the participant and each alternate payee shall be discharged to the extent of any payment made pursuant to such Act.

(J) A person who is an alternate payee under a qualified domestic relations order shall be considered for purposes of any provision of this chapter a beneficiary under the plan. Nothing in the preceding sentence shall permit a requirement under section 1301 of this title of the payment of more than 1 premium with respect to a participant for any period.

(K) The term "alternate payee" means any spouse, former spouse, child, or other dependent of a participant who is recognized by a domestic relations order as having a right to receive all, or a portion of, the benefits payable under a plan with respect to such participant.

(L) This paragraph shall not apply to any plan to which paragraph (1) does not apply.

(M) Payment of benefits by a pension plan in accordance with the applicable requirements of a qualified domestic relations order shall not be treated as garnishment for purposes of section 1673(a) of Title 15.

(N) In prescribing regulations under this paragraph, the Secretary shall consult with the Secretary of the Treasury.

(4) Paragraph (1) shall not apply to any offset of a participant's benefits provided under an employee pension benefit plan against an amount that the participant is ordered or required to pay to the plan if—

(A) the order or requirement to pay arises—

(i) under a judgment of conviction for a crime involving such plan,

(ii) under a civil judgment (including a consent order or decree) entered by a court in an action brought in connection with a violation (or alleged violation) of part 4 of this subtitle, or

(iii) pursuant to a settlement agreement between the Secretary and the participant, or a settlement agreement between the Pension Benefit Guaranty Corporation and the participant, in connection with a violation (or alleged violation) of part 4 of this subtitle by a fiduciary or any other person,

(B) the judgment, order, decree, or settlement agreement expressly provides for the offset of all or part of the amount ordered or required to be paid to the plan against the participant's benefits provided under the plan, and

(C) in a case in which the survivor annuity requirements of section 1055 of this title apply with respect to distributions from the plan to the participant, if the participant has a spouse at the time at which the offset is to be made—

(i) either—

(I) such spouse has consented in writing to such offset and such consent is witnessed by a notary public or representative of the plan (or it is established to the satisfaction of a plan representative that such consent may not be obtained by reason of circumstances described in section 1055(c)(2)(B) of this title), or

(II) an election to waive the right of the spouse to a qualified joint and survivor annuity or a qualified preretirement survivor annuity is in effect in accordance with the requirements of section 1055(c) of this title,

(ii) such spouse is ordered or required in such judgment, order, decree, or settlement to pay an amount to the plan in connection with a violation of part 4 of this subtitle, or

(iii) in such judgment, order, decree, or settlement, such spouse retains the right to receive the survivor annuity under a qualified joint and survivor annuity provided pursuant to section 1055(a)(1) of this title and under a qualified preretirement survivor annuity provided pursuant to section 1055(a)(2) of this title, determined in accordance with paragraph (5).

A plan shall not be treated as failing to meet the requirements of section 1055 of this title solely by reason of an offset under this paragraph.

(5)(A) The survivor annuity described in paragraph (4)(C)(iii) shall be determined as if—

(i) the participant terminated employment on the date of the offset,

(ii) there was no offset,

(iii) the plan permitted commencement of benefits only on or after normal retirement age,

(iv) the plan provided only the minimum-required qualified joint and survivor annuity, and

(v) the amount of the qualified preretirement survivor annuity under the plan is equal to the amount of the survivor annuity payable under the minimum-required qualified joint and survivor annuity.

(B) For purposes of this paragraph, the term "minimum-required qualified joint and survivor annuity" means the qualified joint and survivor annuity which is the actuarial equivalent of the participant's accrued benefit (within the meaning of section 1002(23) of this title) and under which the survivor annuity is 50 percent of the amount of the annuity which is payable during the joint lives of the participant and the spouse.

(e) Limitation on distributions other than life annuities paid by plan

(1) In general

Notwithstanding any other provision of this part, the fiduciary of a pension plan that is subject to the additional funding requirements of section 1083(j)(4) of this title shall not permit a prohibited payment to be made from a plan during a period in which such plan has a liquidity shortfall (as defined in section 1083(j)(4)(E)(i) of this title).

(2) Prohibited payment

For purposes of paragraph (1), the term "prohibited payment" means—

(A) any payment, in excess of the monthly amount paid under a single life annuity (plus any social security supplements described in the last sentence of section 1054(b)(1)(G) of this title), to a participant or beneficiary whose annuity starting date (as defined in section 1055(h)(2) of this title), that occurs during the period referred to in paragraph (1),

(B) any payment for the purchase of an irrevocable commitment from an insurer to pay benefits, and

(C) any other payment specified by the Secretary of the Treasury by regulations.

(3) Period of shortfall

For purposes of this subsection, a plan has a liquidity shortfall during the period that there is an underpayment of an installment under section 1083(j)(3) of this title by reason of section 1083(j)(4)(A) of this title.

(4) Coordination with other provisions

Compliance with this subsection shall not constitute a violation of any other provision of this chapter.

(f) Missing participants in terminated plans

In the case of a plan covered by section 1350 of this title, upon termination of the plan, benefits of missing participants shall be treated in accordance with section 1350 of this title.

(g) Funding-based limits on benefits and benefit accruals under single-employer plans

(1) Funding-based limitation on shutdown benefits and other unpredictable contingent event benefits under single-employer plans

(A) In general

If a participant of a defined benefit plan which is a single-employer plan is entitled to an unpredictable contingent event benefit payable with respect to any event occurring during any plan year, the plan shall provide that such benefit may not be provided if the adjusted funding target attainment percentage for such plan year—

(i) is less than 60 percent, or

(ii) would be less than 60 percent taking into account such occurrence.

(B) Exemption

Subparagraph (A) shall cease to apply with respect to any plan year, effective as of the first day of the plan year, upon payment by the plan sponsor of a contribution (in addition to any minimum required contribution under section 1083 of this title) equal to—

(i) in the case of subparagraph (A)(i), the amount of the increase in the funding target of the plan (under section 1083 of this title) for the plan year attributable to the occurrence referred to in subparagraph (A), and

(ii) in the case of subparagraph (A)(ii), the amount sufficient to result in an adjusted funding target attainment percentage of 60 percent.

(C) Unpredictable contingent event benefit

For purposes of this paragraph, the term "unpredictable contingent event benefit" means any benefit payable solely by reason of—

(i) a plant shutdown (or similar event, as determined by the Secretary of the Treasury), or

(ii) an event other than the attainment of any age, performance of any service, receipt or derivation of any compensation, or occurrence of death or disability.

(2) Limitations on plan amendments increasing liability for benefits

(A) In general

No amendment to a defined benefit plan which is a single-employer plan which has the effect of increasing liabilities of the plan by reason of increases in benefits, establishment of new benefits, changing the rate of benefit accrual, or changing the rate at which benefits become nonforfeitable may take effect during any plan year if the adjusted funding target attainment percentage for such plan year is—

(i) less than 80 percent, or

(ii) would be less than 80 percent taking into account such amendment.

(B) Exemption

Subparagraph (A) shall cease to apply with respect to any plan year, effective as of the first day of the plan year (or if later, the effective date of the amendment), upon payment by the plan sponsor of a contribution (in addition to any minimum required contribution under section 1083 of this title) equal to—

(i) in the case of subparagraph (A)(i), the amount of the increase in the funding target of the plan (under section 1083 of this title) for the plan year attributable to the amendment, and

(ii) in the case of subparagraph (A)(ii), the amount sufficient to result in an adjusted funding target attainment percentage of 80 percent.

(C) Exception for certain benefit increases

Subparagraph (A) shall not apply to any amendment which provides for an increase in benefits under a formula which is not based on a participant's compensation, but only if the rate of such increase is not in excess of the contemporaneous rate of increase in average wages of participants covered by the amendment.

(3) Limitations on accelerated benefit distributions

(A) Funding percentage less than 60 percent

A defined benefit plan which is a single-employer plan shall provide that, in any case in which the plan's adjusted funding target attainment percentage for a plan year is less than 60 percent, the plan may not pay any prohibited payment after the valuation date for the plan year.

(B) Bankruptcy

A defined benefit plan which is a single-employer plan shall provide that, during any period in which the plan sponsor is a debtor in a case under Title 11, or similar Federal or State law, the plan may not pay any prohibited payment. The preceding sentence shall not apply on or after the date on which the enrolled actuary of the plan certifies that the adjusted funding target attainment percentage of such plan (determined by not taking into account any adjustment of segment rates under section 1083(h)(2)(C)(iv) of this title) is not less than 100 percent.

(C) Limited payment if percentage at least 60 percent but less than 80 percent

(i) In general

A defined benefit plan which is a single-employer plan shall provide that, in any case in which the plan's adjusted funding target attainment percentage for a plan year is 60 percent or greater but less than 80 percent, the plan may not pay any prohibited payment after the valuation date for the plan year to the extent the amount of the payment exceeds the lesser of—

(I) 50 percent of the amount of the payment which could be made without regard to this subsection, or

(II) the present value (determined under guidance prescribed by the Pension Benefit Guaranty Corporation, using the interest and mortality assumptions under section 1055(g) of this title) of the maximum guarantee with respect to the participant under section 1322 of this title.

(ii) One-time application

(I) In general

The plan shall also provide that only 1 prohibited payment meeting the requirements of clause (i) may be made with respect to any participant during any period of consecutive plan years to which the limitations under either subparagraph (A) or (B) or this subparagraph applies.

(II) Treatment of beneficiaries

For purposes of this clause, a participant and any beneficiary on his behalf (including an alternate payee, as defined in subsection (d)(3)(K)) shall be treated as 1 participant. If the accrued benefit of a participant is allocated to such an alternate payee and 1 or more other persons, the amount under clause (i) shall be allocated among such persons in the same manner as the accrued benefit is allocated unless the qualified domestic relations order (as defined in subsection (d)(3)(B)(i)) provides otherwise.

(D) Exception

This paragraph shall not apply to any plan for any plan year if the terms of such plan (as in effect for the period beginning on September 1, 2005, and ending with such plan year) provide for no benefit accruals with respect to any participant during such period.

(E) **Prohibited payment**

For purpose [2] of this paragraph, the term "prohibited payment" means—

(i) any payment, in excess of the monthly amount paid under a single life annuity (plus any social security supplements described in the last sentence of section 1054(b)(1)(G) of this title), to a participant or beneficiary whose annuity starting date (as defined in section 1055(h)(2) of this title) occurs during any period a limitation under subparagraph (A) or (B) is in effect,

(ii) any payment for the purchase of an irrevocable commitment from an insurer to pay benefits, and

(iii) any other payment specified by the Secretary of the Treasury by regulations.

Such term shall not include the payment of a benefit which under section 1053(e) of this title may be immediately distributed without the consent of the participant.

(4) **Limitation on benefit accruals for plans with severe funding shortfalls**

(A) **In general**

A defined benefit plan which is a single-employer plan shall provide that, in any case in which the plan's adjusted funding target attainment percentage for a plan year is less than 60 percent, benefit accruals under the plan shall cease as of the valuation date for the plan year.

(B) **Exemption**

Subparagraph (A) shall cease to apply with respect to any plan year, effective as of the first day of the plan year, upon payment by the plan sponsor of a contribution (in addition to any minimum required contribution under section 1083 of this title) equal to the amount sufficient to result in an adjusted funding target attainment percentage of 60 percent.

(5) **Rules relating to contributions required to avoid benefit limitations**

(A) **Security may be provided**

(i) **In general**

For purposes of this subsection, the adjusted funding target attainment percentage shall be determined by treating as an asset of the plan any security provided by a plan sponsor in a form meeting the requirements of clause (ii).

(ii) **Form of security**

The security required under clause (i) shall consist of—

(I) a bond issued by a corporate surety company that is an acceptable surety for purposes of section 1112 of this title,

(II) cash, or United States obligations which mature in 3 years or less, held in escrow by a bank or similar financial institution, or

(III) such other form of security as is satisfactory to the Secretary of the Treasury and the parties involved.

(iii) **Enforcement**

Any security provided under clause (i) may be perfected and enforced at any time after the earlier of—

(I) the date on which the plan terminates,

(II) if there is a failure to make a payment of the minimum required contribution for any plan year beginning after the security is provided, the due date for the payment under section 1083(j) of this title, or

(III) if the adjusted funding target attainment percentage is less than 60 percent for a consecutive period of 7 years, the valuation date for the last year in the period.

(iv) **Release of security**

The security shall be released (and any amounts thereunder shall be refunded together with any interest accrued thereon) at such time as the Secretary of the Treasury may prescribe in regulations, including regulations for partial releases of the security by reason of increases in the adjusted funding target attainment percentage.

(B) **Prefunding balance or funding standard carryover balance may not be used**

No prefunding balance or funding standard carryover balance under section 1083(f) of this title may be used under paragraph (1), (2), or (4) to satisfy any payment an employer may make under any such paragraph to avoid or terminate the application of any limitation under such paragraph.

(C) **Deemed reduction of funding balances**

(i) **In general**

Subject to clause (iii), in any case in which a benefit limitation under paragraph (1), (2), (3), or (4) would (but for this subparagraph and determined without regard to paragraph (1)(B), (2)(B), or (4)(B)) apply to such plan for the plan year, the plan sponsor of such plan shall be treated for purposes of this chapter as having made an election under section 1083(f) of this title to reduce the prefunding balance or funding standard carryover balance by such amount as is necessary for such benefit limitation to not apply to the plan for such plan year.

(ii) Exception for insufficient funding balances

Clause (i) shall not apply with respect to a benefit limitation for any plan year if the application of clause (i) would not result in the benefit limitation not applying for such plan year.

(iii) Restrictions of certain rules to collectively bargained plans

With respect to any benefit limitation under paragraph (1), (2), or (4), clause (i) shall only apply in the case of a plan maintained pursuant to 1 or more collective bargaining agreements between employee representatives and 1 or more employers.

(6) New plans

Paragraphs (1), (2), and (4) shall not apply to a plan for the first 5 plan years of the plan. For purposes of this paragraph, the reference in this paragraph to a plan shall include a reference to any predecessor plan.

(7) Presumed underfunding for purposes of benefit limitations

(A) Presumption of continued underfunding

In any case in which a benefit limitation under paragraph (1), (2), (3), or (4) has been applied to a plan with respect to the plan year preceding the current plan year, the adjusted funding target attainment percentage of the plan for the current plan year shall be presumed to be equal to the adjusted funding target attainment percentage of the plan for the preceding plan year until the enrolled actuary of the plan certifies the actual adjusted funding target attainment percentage of the plan for the current plan year.

(B) Presumption of underfunding after 10th month

In any case in which no certification of the adjusted funding target attainment percentage for the current plan year is made with respect to the plan before the first day of the 10th month of such year, for purposes of paragraphs (1), (2), (3), and (4), such first day shall be deemed, for purposes of such paragraph, to be the valuation date of the plan for the current plan year and the plan's adjusted funding target attainment percentage shall be conclusively presumed to be less than 60 percent as of such first day.

(C) Presumption of underfunding after 4th month for nearly underfunded plans

In any case in which—

(i) a benefit limitation under paragraph (1), (2), (3), or (4) did not apply to a plan with respect to the plan year preceding the current plan year, but the adjusted funding target attainment percentage of the plan for such preceding plan year was not more than 10 percentage points greater than the percentage which would have caused such paragraph to apply to the plan with respect to such preceding plan year, and

(ii) as of the first day of the 4th month of the current plan year, the enrolled actuary of the plan has not certified the actual adjusted funding target attainment percentage of the plan for the current plan year,

until the enrolled actuary so certifies, such first day shall be deemed, for purposes of such paragraph, to be the valuation date of the plan for the current plan year and the adjusted funding target attainment percentage of the plan as of such first day shall, for purposes of such paragraph, be presumed to be equal to 10 percentage points less than the adjusted funding target attainment percentage of the plan for such preceding plan year.

(8) Treatment of plan as of close of prohibited or cessation period

For purposes of applying this part—

(A) Operation of plan after period

Unless the plan provides otherwise, payments and accruals will resume effective as of the day following the close of the period for which any limitation of payment or accrual of benefits under paragraph (3) or (4) applies.

(B) Treatment of affected benefits

Nothing in this paragraph shall be construed as affecting the plan's treatment of benefits which would have been paid or accrued but for this subsection.

(9) Terms relating to funding target attainment percentage

For purposes of this subsection—

(A) In general

The term "funding target attainment percentage" has the same meaning given such term by section 1083(d)(2) of this title.

(B) Adjusted funding target attainment percentage

The term "adjusted funding target attainment percentage" means the funding target attainment percentage which is determined under subparagraph (A) by increasing each of the amounts under subparagraphs (A) and (B) of section 1083(d)(2) of this title by the aggregate amount of purchases of annuities for employees other than highly compensated employees (as defined in section 414(q) of

Title 26) which were made by the plan during the preceding 2 plan years.

(C) Application to plans which are fully funded without regard to reductions for funding balances

In the case of a plan for any plan year, if the funding target attainment percentage is 100 percent or more (determined without regard to the reduction in the value of assets under section 1083(f)(4) of this title), the funding target attainment percentage for purposes of subparagraphs (A) and (B) shall be determined without regard to such reduction.

(D) Repealed. Pub.L. 113–295, Div. A, Title II, § 221(a)(57)(F)(ii), Dec. 19, 2014, 128 Stat. 4046

(10) Secretarial authority for plans with alternate valuation date

In the case of a plan which has designated a valuation date other than the first day of the plan year, the Secretary of the Treasury may prescribe rules for the application of this subsection which are necessary to reflect the alternate valuation date.

(11) Repealed. Pub.L. 113–295, Div. A, Title II, § 221(a)(57)(G)(ii), Dec. 19, 2014, 128 Stat. 4047

(12) CSEC plans

This subsection shall not apply to a CSEC plan (as defined in section 1060(f) of this title).

(Pub.L. 93–406, Title I, § 206, Sept. 2, 1974, 88 Stat. 864; Pub.L. 98–397, Title I, § 104(a), Aug. 23, 1984, 98 Stat. 1433; Pub.L. 99–514, Title XVIII, § 1898(c)(2)(B), (4)(B), (5), (6)(B), (7)(B), Oct. 22. 1986, 100 Stat. 2952 to 2954; Pub.L. 101–239, Title VII, §§ 7891(a)(1), 7894(c)(8), (9)(A), Dec. 19, 1989, 103 Stat. 2445, 2449; Pub.L. 103–465, Title VII, §§ 761(a)(9)(B)(i), 776(c)(2), Dec. 8, 1994, 108 Stat. 5033, 5048; Pub.L. 105–34, Title XV, § 1502(a), Aug. 5, 1997, 111 Stat. 1058; Pub.L. 109–280, Title I, §§ 103(a), 108(a)(9),(10), formerly § 107(a)(9), (10), Title IV, § 410(b), Aug. 17, 2006, 120 Stat. 809, 819, 935, renumbered § 108(a)(9), (10), Pub.L. 111–192, Title II, § 202(a), June 25, 2010, 124 Stat. 1297; Pub.L. 110–458, Title I, § 101(c)(1)(B) to (G), Dec. 23, 2008, 122 Stat. 5097; Pub.L. 111–192, Title II, § 203(a)(1), June 25, 2010, 124 Stat. 1299; Pub.L. 113–97, Title I, § 102(b)(3), Apr. 7, 2014, 128 Stat. 1116; Pub.L. 113–159, Title II, § 2003(c)(2), Aug. 8, 2014, 128 Stat. 1850; Pub.L. 113–295, Div. A, Title II, § 221(a)(57)(E)(ii), (F)(ii), (G)(ii), Dec. 19, 2014, 128 Stat. 4046, 4047.)

[1] So in original. The word "of" probably should not appear.

[2] So in original. Probably should be "purposes".

Commentary

See generally discussion of ERISA preemption cases in Family Code Section 2610 Commentary.

Relying on subsection (a)(2) of Section 1055 and subsection (d)(3)(F) of this section, *Hamilton v. Washington State Plumbing and Pipefitting Industry Pension Plan, 433 F.3d 1091 (9th Cir. 2006),* concludes that a surviving spouse's Qualified Preretirement Survivor Annuity can be diverted only to a former surviving spouse. Thus, a dissolution decree requiring decedent ex-husband to name the parties' two children as the beneficiaries of his pension in lieu of life insurance that he was unable to obtain, was insufficient to divest decedent's surviving second wife of her Preretirement Survivor Annuity benefits.

Reading subsection (d) together with 29 USC § 1144 (d) and Family Code § 910 (a), *McIntyre v. United States, 222 F.3d 655 (9th Cir. 2000),* holds that the Internal Revenue Service may levy, under 26 USC § 6331 (a), on the entire contents of a spouse's ERISA-regulated pension plan, including the other spouse's California community property interest, in order to satisfy the spouse's tax debt. See also *Babb v. Schmidt, 496 F.2d 957, 959 (9th Cir. 1974)* (relying on Family Code § 910(a) to conclude that a tax debtor has a "right to property" sufficient to allow the Internal Revenue Service to levy, under 26 USC § 6331(a), on all the community property to satisfy that spouse's delinquent tax obligations).

Stewart v. Thorpe Holding Co. Profit Sharing Plan, 207 F.3d 1143 (9th Cir. 2000), held that even if an order did not qualify as a QDRO, a wife had standing to sue the plan when the trustees failed to perform their ERISA fiduciary duties, thereby denying the spouse the opportunity to assert her rights as a alternate payee under subsections (d)(3)(G) and (H). Alternatively, *Stewart* found that the order qualified as a QDRO despite various defects.

In *Owens v. Automotive Machinists Pension Trust, 551 F.3d 1138 (9th Cir. 2009),* a Ninth Circuit panel held that a Washington state court order obtained by a cohabitant who maintained a "quasi-marital" relationship with a plan participant was a valid ERISA Qualified Domestic Relations Order. (Washington treats long-term stable cohabitation as equivalent to marriage for purposes of its community property law.)

Interpreting subsection (d)(3), *Trustees of the Directors Guild of America–Producer Pension Plans v. Tise, 234 F.3d 415, 255 F.3d 661 (9th Cir. 2000),* holds that an alternate payee who has obtained a state law domestic relations order before a participant's retirement, death or other benefit-triggering event, may perfect that order into a QDRO after the benefit-triggering event, subject to the 18–month statutory period following which any accrued benefits are payable to the plan's original beneficiary.

29 C.F.R. § 2530.206, operative August 9, 2010, provides that a state domestic relations order that meets ERISA's QDRO requirements "shall not fail to be treated as a [QDRO] solely because of the time it is issued." Accordingly, such an order issued after the death or divorce of the participant is not defective solely because of the date of issuance.

Also interpreting subsection (d)(3), *Patton v. Denver Post Corp., 326 F.3d 1148 (10th Cir. 2003),* affirmed a trial court order declaring that a state domestic relations order entered nunc pro tunc after a former husband's death, which gave the surviving former wife rights in her former husband's pension, was a QDRO. But see *Samaroo v. Samaroo, 193 F.3d 185 (3d Cir. 1999), cert. denied 529 U.S. 1062 (2000),* which held that a nunc pro tunc order back-dated to a date prior to a plan participant's death cannot qualify as a QDRO because it violates the subsection (d)(3)(D)(ii) requirement that the domestic relations order must not "require the plan to provide increased benefits (determined on the basis of actuarial value)."

In light of the nunc pro tunc cases cited in the last two paragraphs, *In re Marriage of Padgett, 172 Cal.App.4th 830, 91 Cal.Rptr.3d 475 (2009),* held that after the occurrence of the triggering event, which was participant-husband's death, a trial court could not enter a domestic relations order or a qualified domestic relations order nunc pro tunc when the original domestic relations order, the judgment of dissolution issued 20 years earlier, merely reserved jurisdiction over the husband's pension, but did award the wife any interest in the pension.

In re Marriage of Oddino, 16 Cal.4th 67, 939 P.2d 1266, 65 Cal.Rptr.2d 566 (1997), holds that "Rule of 75" early retirement benefits are an "employer subsidy for early retirement" within the meaning of § 1056(d)(3)(E)(i)(II) and hence a QDRO may not require a pension plan to pay such supplementary benefits to an alternate payee *before* the participant's actual retirement. *Oddino* does not preclude recalculation and inclusion of such benefits after the participant's retirement. *Id.* at 16 Cal.4th 88.

Relying in part on subsection (d)(3)(F), *Carmona v. Carmona, 544 F.3d 988 (9th Cir. 2008)*, held that a participant in an ERISA-regulated Qualified Joint and Survivor Annuity (QJSA) may not change his surviving spouse beneficiary after he has retired and the annuity has started to pay out. The QJSA surviving spouse's benefit irrevocably vests in the participant's spouse at the time of the annuity start date and may not be reassigned to a subsequent spouse. Accord, *Hopkins v. AT & T Global Solutions Co., 105 F.3d 153 (4th Cir.1997).*

Part 5—Administration and Enforcement

§ 1144. Other laws

(a) Supersedure; effective date

Except as provided in subsection (b) of this section, the provisions of this subchapter and subchapter III shall supersede any and all State laws insofar as they may now or hereafter relate to any employee benefit plan described in section 1003(a) of this title and not exempt under section 1003(b) of this title. This section shall take effect on January 1, 1975.

(b) Construction and application

(1) This section shall not apply with respect to any cause of action which arose, or any act or omission which occurred, before January 1, 1975.

(2)(A) Except as provided in subparagraph (B), nothing in this subchapter shall be construed to exempt or relieve any person from any law of any State which regulates insurance, banking, or securities.

(B) Neither an employee benefit plan described in section 1003(a) of this title, which is not exempt under section 1003(b) of this title (other than a plan established primarily for the purpose of providing death benefits), nor any trust established under such a plan, shall be deemed to be an insurance company or other insurer, bank, trust company, or investment company or to be engaged in the business of insurance or banking for purposes of any law of any State purporting to regulate insurance companies, insurance contracts, banks, trust companies, or investment companies.

(3) Nothing in this section shall be construed to prohibit use by the Secretary of services or facilities of a State agency as permitted under section 1136 of this title.

(4) Subsection (a) shall not apply to any generally applicable criminal law of a State.

(5)(A) Except as provided in subparagraph (B), subsection (a) shall not apply to the Hawaii Prepaid Health Care Act (Haw.Rev.Stat. §§ 393–1 through 393–51).

(B) Nothing in subparagraph (A) shall be construed to exempt from subsection (a)—

(i) any State tax law relating to employee benefit plans, or

(ii) any amendment of the Hawaii Prepaid Health Care Act enacted after September 2, 1974, to the extent it provides for more than the effective administration of such Act as in effect on such date.

(C) Notwithstanding subparagraph (A), parts 1 and 4 of this subtitle, and the preceding sections of this part to the extent they govern matters which are governed by the provisions of such parts 1 and 4, shall supersede the Hawaii Prepaid Health Care Act (as in effect on or after January 14, 1983), but the Secretary may enter into cooperative arrangements under this paragraph and section 1136 of this title with officials of the State of Hawaii to assist them in effectuating the policies of provisions of such Act which are superseded by such parts 1 and 4 and the preceding sections of this part.

(6)(A) Notwithstanding any other provision of this section—

(i) in the case of an employee welfare benefit plan which is a multiple employer welfare arrangement and is fully insured (or which is a multiple employer welfare arrangement subject to an exemption under subparagraph (B)), any law of any State which regulates insurance may apply to such arrangement to the extent that such law provides—

(I) standards, requiring the maintenance of specified levels of reserves and specified levels of contributions, which any such plan, or any trust established under such a plan, must meet in order to be considered under such law able to pay benefits in full when due, and

(II) provisions to enforce such standards, and

(ii) in the case of any other employee welfare benefit plan which is a multiple employer welfare arrangement, in addition to this subchapter, any law of any State which regulates insurance may apply to the extent not inconsistent with the preceding sections of this subchapter.

(B) The Secretary may, under regulations which may be prescribed by the Secretary, exempt from subparagraph (A)(ii), individually or by class, multiple employer welfare arrangements which are not fully insured. Any such exemption may be granted with respect to any arrangement or class of arrangements only if such arrangement or each arrangement which is a member of such class meets the requirements of section 1002(1) and section 1003 of this title necessary to be considered an employee welfare benefit plan to which this subchapter applies.

(C) Nothing in subparagraph (A) shall affect the manner or extent to which the provisions of this subchapter apply to an employee welfare benefit plan which is not a multiple employer welfare arrangement and which is a plan, fund, or program participating in, subscribing to, or otherwise using a multiple employer welfare arrangement to fund or administer benefits to such plan's participants and beneficiaries.

(D) For purposes of this paragraph, a multiple employer welfare arrangement shall be considered fully insured only if the terms of the arrangement provide for benefits the amount of all of which the Secretary determines are guaranteed under a contract, or policy of insurance, issued by an insurance company, insurance service, or insurance organization, qualified to conduct business in a State.

(7) Subsection (a) shall not apply to qualified domestic relations orders (within the meaning of section 1056(d)(3)(B)(i) of this title), qualified medical child support orders (within the meaning of section 1169(a)(2)(A) of this title), and the provisions of law referred to in section 1169(a)(2)(B)(ii) of this title to the extent they apply to qualified medical child support orders.

(8) Subsection (a) of this section shall not be construed to preclude any State cause of action—

(A) with respect to which the State exercises its acquired rights under section 1169(b)(3) of this title with respect to a group health plan (as defined in section 1167(1) of this title), or

(B) for recoupment of payment with respect to items or services pursuant to a State plan for medical assistance approved under title XIX of the Social Security Act which would not have been payable if such acquired rights had been executed before payment with respect to such items or services by the group health plan.

(9) For additional provisions relating to group health plans, see section 1191 of this title.

(c) Definitions

For purposes of this section:

(1) The term "State law" includes all laws, decisions, rules, regulations, or other State action having the effect of law, of any State. A law of the United States applicable only to the District of Columbia shall be treated as a State law rather than a law of the United States.

(2) The term "State" includes a State, any political subdivisions thereof, or any agency or instrumentality of either, which purports to regulate, directly or indirectly, the terms and conditions of employee benefit plans covered by this subchapter.

(d) Alteration, amendment, modification, invalidation, impairment, or supersedure of any law of the United States prohibited

Nothing in this subchapter shall be construed to alter, amend, modify, invalidate, impair, or supersede any law of the United States (except as provided in sections 1031 and 1137(b) of this title) or any rule or regulation issued under any such law.

(e) Automatic contribution arrangements

(1) Notwithstanding any other provision of this section, this subchapter shall supersede any law of a State which would directly or indirectly prohibit or restrict the inclusion in any plan of an automatic contribution arrangement. The Secretary may prescribe regulations which would establish minimum standards that such an arrangement would be required to satisfy in order for this subsection to apply in the case of such arrangement.

(2) For purposes of this subsection, the term "automatic contribution arrangement" means an arrangement—

(A) under which a participant may elect to have the plan sponsor make payments as contributions under the plan on behalf of the participant, or to the participant directly in cash,

(B) under which a participant is treated as having elected to have the plan sponsor make such contributions in an amount equal to a uniform percentage of compensation provided under the plan until the participant specifically elects not to have such contributions made (or specifically elects to have such contributions made at a different percentage), and

(C) under which such contributions are invested in accordance with regulations prescribed by the Secretary under section 1104(c)(5) of this title.

(3)(A) The plan administrator of an automatic contribution arrangement shall, within a reasonable period before such plan year, provide to each participant to whom the arrangement applies for such plan year notice of the participant's rights and obligations under the arrangement which—

(i) is sufficiently accurate and comprehensive to apprise the participant of such rights and obligations, and

(ii) is written in a manner calculated to be understood by the average participant to whom the arrangement applies.

(B) A notice shall not be treated as meeting the requirements of subparagraph (A) with respect to a participant unless—

(i) the notice includes an explanation of the participant's right under the arrangement not to have elective contributions made on the participant's behalf (or to elect to have such contributions made at a different percentage),

(ii) the participant has a reasonable period of time, after receipt of the notice described in clause (i) and before the first elective contribution is made, to make such election, and

(iii) the notice explains how contributions made under the arrangement will be invested in the absence of any investment election by the participant.

(Pub.L. 93–406, Title I, § 514, Sept. 2, 1974, 88 Stat. 897; Pub.L. 97–473, Title III, §§ 301(a), 302(b), Jan. 14, 1983, 96 Stat. 2611, 2613; Pub.L. 98–397, Title I, § 104(b), Aug. 23, 1984, 98 Stat. 1436; Pub.L. 99–272, Title IX, § 9503(d)(1), Apr. 7, 1986, 100 Stat. 207; Pub.L. 101–239, Title VII, § 7894(f)(2)(A), (3)(A), Dec. 19, 1989, 103 Stat. 2450, 2451; Pub.L. 103–66, Title IV, § 4301(c)(4), Aug. 10, 1993, 107 Stat. 377; Pub.L. 104–191, Title I, § 101(f)(1), Aug. 21, 1996, 110 Stat. 1953; Pub.L. 104–204, Title VI, § 603(b)(3)(G), Sept. 26, 1996, 110 Stat. 2938; Pub.L. 105–200, Title IV, § 401(h)(2)(A)(i), (ii), July 16, 1998, 112 Stat. 668; Pub.L. 109–280, Title IX, § 902(f)(1), Aug. 17, 2006, 120 Stat. 1039.)

Commentary

See generally discussion of ERISA preemption cases in Family Code Section 2610 Commentary.

Reading subsection (d) together with 29 USC § 1056 (d) and Family Code § 910 (a), *McIntyre v. United States, 222 F.3d 655 (9th Cir. 2000)*, holds that the Internal Revenue Service may levy, under 26 USC § 6331 (a), on the entire contents of a spouse's ERISA-regulated pension plan, including the other spouse's California community property interest, in order to satisfy the spouse's tax debt. See also *Babb v. Schmidt, 496 F.2d 957, 959 (9th Cir. 1974)* (relying on Family Code § 910(a) to conclude that a tax debtor has a "right to property" sufficient to allow the Internal Revenue Service to levy, under 26 USC § 6331(a), on all the community property to satisfy that spouse's delinquent tax obligations).

Part 6—Continuation Coverage and Additional Standards For Group Health Plans

§ 1161. Plans must provide continuation coverage to certain individuals

(a) In general

The plan sponsor of each group health plan shall provide, in accordance with this part, that each qualified beneficiary who would lose coverage under the plan as a result of a qualifying event is entitled, under the plan, to elect, within the election period, continuation coverage under the plan.

(b) Exception for certain plans

Subsection (a) shall not apply to any group health plan for any calendar year if all employers maintaining such plan normally employed fewer than 20 employees on a typical business day during the preceding calendar year. *(Pub.L. 93–406, Title I, § 601, as added Pub.L. 99–272, Title X, § 10002(a), Apr. 7, 1986, 100 Stat. 227; amended Pub.L. 101–239, Title VII, §§ 7862(c)(1)(B), 7891(a)(1), Dec. 19, 1989, 103 Stat. 2432, 2445.)*

§ 1162. Continuation coverage

For purposes of section 1161 of this title, the term "continuation coverage" means coverage under the plan which meets the following requirements:

(1) Type of benefit coverage

The coverage must consist of coverage which, as of the time the coverage is being provided, is identical to the coverage provided under the plan to similarly situated beneficiaries under the plan with respect to whom a qualifying event has not occurred. If coverage is modified under the plan for any group of similarly situated beneficiaries, such coverage shall also be modified in the same manner for all individuals who are qualified beneficiaries under the plan pursuant to this part in connection with such group.

(2) Period of coverage

The coverage must extend for at least the period beginning on the date of the qualifying event and ending not earlier than the earliest of the following:

(A) Maximum required period

(i) General rule for terminations and reduced hours

In the case of a qualifying event described in section 1163(2) of this title, except as provided in clause (ii), the date which is 18 months after the date of the qualifying event.

(ii) Special rule for multiple qualifying events

If a qualifying event (other than a qualifying event described in section 1163(6) of this title) occurs during the 18 months after the date of a qualifying event described in section 1163(2) of this title, the date which is 36 months after the date of the qualifying event described in section 1163(2) of this title.

(iii) Special rule for certain bankruptcy proceedings

In the case of a qualifying event described in section 1163(6) of this title (relating to bankruptcy proceedings), the date of the death of the covered employee or qualified beneficiary (described in section 1167(3)(C)(iii) of this title), or in the case of the surviving spouse or dependent children of the covered employee, 36 months after the date of the death of the covered employee.

(iv) General rule for other qualifying events

In the case of a qualifying event not described in section 1163(2) or 1163(6) of this title, the date which is 36 months after the date of the qualifying event.

(v) Special rule for PBGC recipients

In the case of a qualifying event described in section 1163(2) of this title with respect to a covered employee who (as of such qualifying event) has a nonforfeitable right to a benefit any portion of which is to be paid by the Pension Benefit Guaranty Corporation under subchapter III, notwithstanding clause (i) or (ii), the date of the death of the covered employee, or in the case of the surviving spouse or dependent children of the covered employee, 24 months after the date of the death of the covered employee. The preceding sentence shall not require any period of coverage to extend beyond January 1, 2014.

(vi) Special rule for TAA-eligible individuals

In the case of a qualifying event described in section 1163(2) of this title with respect to a covered employee who is (as of the date that the period of coverage would, but for this clause or clause (vii), otherwise terminate under clause (i) or (ii)) a TAA-eligible individual (as defined in section 1165(b)(4)(B) of this title), the period of coverage shall not terminate by reason of clause (i) or (ii), as the case may be, before the later of the date specified in such clause or the date on which such individual ceases to be such a TAA-eligible individual. The preceding sentence shall not require any period of coverage to extend beyond January 1, 2014.

(vii) Medicare entitlement followed by qualifying event

In the case of a qualifying event described in section 1163(2) of this title that occurs less than 18 months after the date the covered employee became entitled to benefits under Title XVIII of the Social Security Act, the period of coverage for qualified beneficiaries other than the covered employee shall not terminate under this subparagraph before the close of the 36–month period beginning on the date the covered employee became so entitled.

(viii) Special rule for disability

In the case of a qualified beneficiary who is determined, under Title II or XVI of the Social Security Act, to have been disabled at any time during the first 60 days of continuation coverage under this part, any reference in clause (i) or (ii) to 18 months is deemed a reference to 29 months (with respect to all qualified beneficiaries), but only if the qualified beneficiary has provided notice of such determination under section 1166(3) of this title before the end of such 18 months.

(B) End of plan

The date on which the employer ceases to provide any group health plan to any employee.

(C) Failure to pay premium

The date on which coverage ceases under the plan by reason of a failure to make timely payment of any premium required under the plan with respect to the qualified beneficiary. The payment of any premium (other than any payment referred to in the last sentence of paragraph (3)) shall be considered to be timely if made within 30 days after the date due or within such longer period as applies to or under the plan.

(D) Group health plan coverage or medicare entitlement

The date on which the qualified beneficiary first becomes, after the date of the election—

(i) covered under any other group health plan (as an employee or otherwise) which does not contain any exclusion or limitation with respect to any preexisting condition of such beneficiary (other than such an exclusion or limitation which does not apply to (or is satisfied by) such beneficiary by reason of chapter 100 of Title 26, part 7 of this subtitle, or title XXVII of the Public Health Service Act), or

(ii) in the case of a qualified beneficiary other than a qualified beneficiary described in section 1167(3)(C) of this title, entitled to benefits under title XVIII of the Social Security Act.

(E) Termination of extended coverage for disability

In the case of a qualified beneficiary who is disabled at any time during the first 60 days of continuation coverage under this part, the month that begins more than 30 days after the date of the final determination under title II or XVI of the Social Security Act that the qualified beneficiary is no longer disabled.

(3) Premium requirements

The plan may require payment of a premium for any period of continuation coverage, except that such premium—

(A) shall not exceed 102 percent of the applicable premium for such period, and

(B) may, at the election of the payor, be made in monthly installments.

In no event may the plan require the payment of any premium before the day which is 45 days after the day on which the qualified beneficiary made the initial election for continuation coverage. In the case of an individual described in the last sentence of paragraph (2)(A), any reference in subparagraph (A) of this paragraph to "102 percent" is deemed a reference to "150 percent" for any month after the 18th month of continuation coverage described in clause (i) or (ii) of paragraph (2)(A).

(4) No requirement of insurability

The coverage may not be conditioned upon, or discriminate on the basis of lack of, evidence of insurability.

(5) Conversion option

In the case of a qualified beneficiary whose period of continuation coverage expires under paragraph (2)(A), the plan must, during the 180–day period ending on such expiration date, provide to the qualified beneficiary the option of enrollment under a conversion health plan otherwise generally available under the plan.

(Pub.L. 93–406, Title I, § 602, as added Pub.L. 99–272, Title X, § 10002(a), Apr. 7, 1986, 100 Stat. 228; amended Pub.L. 99–509, Title IX, § 9501(b)(1)(B), (2)(B), Oct. 21, 1986, 100 Stat. 2076, 2077; Pub.L. 99–514, Title XVIII, § 1895(d)(1)(B), (2)(B), (3)(B), (4)(B), Oct. 22, 1986, 100 Stat. 2936 to 2938; Pub.L. 101–239, Title VI, § 6703(a), (b), Title VII, §§ 7862(c)(3)(B), (4)(A), (5)(B), 7871(c), Dec. 19, 1989, 103 Stat. 2296, 2432, 2433, 2435; Pub.L. 104–188, Title I, § 1704(g)(1)(B), Aug. 20, 1996, 110 Stat. 1880; Pub.L. 104–191, Title IV, § 421(b)(1), Aug. 21, 1996, 110 Stat. 2088; Pub.L. 111–5, Div. B, Title I, § 1899F(a), Feb. 17, 2009, 123 Stat. 428; Pub.L. 111–344, Title I, § 116(a), Dec. 29, 2010, 124 Stat. 3615; Pub.L. 112–40, Title II, § 243(a)(1), (2), Oct. 21, 2011, 125 Stat. 420.)

§ 1163. Qualifying event

For purposes of this part, the term "qualifying event" means, with respect to any covered employee, any of the following events which, but for the continuation coverage required under this part, would result in the loss of coverage of a qualified beneficiary:

(1) The death of the covered employee.

(2) The termination (other than by reason of such employee's gross misconduct), or reduction of hours, of the covered employee's employment.

(3) The divorce or legal separation of the covered employee from the employee's spouse.

(4) The covered employee becoming entitled to benefits under title XVIII of the Social Security Act.

(5) A dependent child ceasing to be a dependent child under the generally applicable requirements of the plan.

(6) A proceeding in a case under Title 11, commencing on or after July 1, 1986, with respect to the employer from whose employment the covered employee retired at any time.

In the case of an event described in paragraph (6), a loss of coverage includes a substantial elimination of coverage with respect to a qualified beneficiary described in section 1167(3)(C) of this title within one year before or after the date of commencement of the proceeding. *(Pub.L. 93–406, Title I, § 603, as added Pub.L. 99–272, Title X, § 10002(a), Apr. 7, 1986, 100 Stat. 229; amended Pub.L. 99–509, Title IX, § 9501(a)(2), Oct. 21, 1986, 100 Stat. 2076.)*

§ 1164. Applicable premium

For purposes of this part—

(1) In general

The term "applicable premium" means, with respect to any period of continuation coverage of qualified beneficiaries, the cost to the plan for such period of the coverage for similarly situated beneficiaries with respect to whom a qualifying event has not occurred (without regard to whether such cost is paid by the employer or employee).

(2) Special rule for self-insured plans

To the extent that a plan is a self-insured plan—

(A) In general

Except as provided in subparagraph (B), the applicable premium for any period of continuation coverage of qualified beneficiaries shall be equal to a reasonable estimate of the cost of providing coverage for such period for similarly situated beneficiaries which—

(i) is determined on an actuarial basis, and

(ii) takes into account such factors as the Secretary may prescribe in regulations.

(B) Determination on basis of past cost

If an administrator elects to have this subparagraph apply, the applicable premium for any period of continuation coverage of qualified beneficiaries shall be equal to—

(i) the cost to the plan for similarly situated beneficiaries for the same period occurring during the preceding determination period under paragraph (3), adjusted by

(ii) the percentage increase or decrease in the implicit price deflator of the gross national product (calculated by the Department of Commerce and published in the Survey of Current Business) for the 12-month period ending on the last day of the sixth month of such preceding determination period.

(C) Subparagraph (B) not to apply where significant change

An administrator may not elect to have subparagraph (B) apply in any case in which there is any significant difference, between the determination period and the preceding determination period, in coverage under, or in employees covered by, the plan. The determination under the preceding sentence for any determination period shall be made at the same time as the determination under paragraph (3).

(3) Determination period

The determination of any applicable premium shall be made for a period of 12 months and shall be made before the beginning of such period.

(Pub.L. 93–406, Title I, § 604, as added Pub.L. 99–272, Title X, § 10002(a), Apr. 7, 1986, 100 Stat. 229.)

§ 1165. Election

(a) In general

For purposes of this part—

(1) Election period

The term "election period" means the period which—

(A) begins not later than the date on which coverage terminates under the plan by reason of a qualifying event,

(B) is of at least 60 days' duration, and

(C) ends not earlier than 60 days after the later of—

(i) the date described in subparagraph (A), or

(ii) in the case of any qualified beneficiary who receives notice under section 1166(4) [1] of this title, the date of such notice.

(2) Effect of election on other beneficiaries

Except as otherwise specified in an election, any election of continuation coverage by a qualified beneficiary described in subparagraph (A)(i) or (B) of section 1167(3) of this title shall be deemed to include an election of continuation coverage on behalf of any other qualified beneficiary who would lose coverage under the plan by reason of the qualifying event. If there is a choice among types of coverage under the plan, each qualified beneficiary is entitled to make a separate selection among such types of coverage.

(b) Temporary extension of COBRA election period for certain individuals

(1) In general

In the case of a nonelecting TAA-eligible individual and notwithstanding subsection (a), such individual may elect continuation coverage under this part during the 60–day period that begins on the first day of the month in which the individual becomes a TAA-eligible individual, but only if such election is made not later than 6 months after the date of the TAA-related loss of coverage.

(2) Commencement of coverage; no reach-back

Any continuation coverage elected by a TAA-eligible individual under paragraph (1) shall commence at the beginning of the 60–day election period described in such paragraph and shall not include any period prior to such 60–day election period.

(3) Preexisting conditions

With respect to an individual who elects continuation coverage pursuant to paragraph (1), the period—

(A) beginning on the date of the TAA-related loss of coverage, and

(B) ending on the first day of the 60–day election period described in paragraph (1), shall be disregarded for purposes of determining the 63–day periods referred to in section 1181(c)(2) of this title, section 2701(c)(2) of the Public Health Service Act, and section 9801(c)(2) of Title 26.

(4) Definitions

For purposes of this subsection:

(A) Nonelecting TAA-eligible individual

The term "nonelecting TAA-eligible individual" means a TAA-eligible individual who—

(i) has a TAA-related loss of coverage; and

(ii) did not elect continuation coverage under this part during the TAA-related election period.

(B) TAA-eligible individual

The term "TAA-eligible individual" means—

(i) an eligible TAA recipient (as defined in paragraph (2) of section 35(c) of Title 26), and

(ii) an eligible alternative TAA recipient (as defined in paragraph (3) of such section).

(C) TAA-related election period

The term "TAA-related election period" means, with respect to a TAA-related loss of coverage, the 60–day election period under this part which is a direct consequence of such loss.

(D) TAA-related loss of coverage

The term "TAA-related loss of coverage" means, with respect to an individual whose separation from employment gives rise to being an TAA-eligible individual, the loss of health benefits coverage associated with such separation.

(Pub.L. 93–406, Title I, § 605, as added Pub.L. 99–272, Title X, § 10002(a), Apr. 7, 1986, 100 Stat. 230; amended Pub.L. 99–514, Title XVIII, § 1895(d)(5)(B), Oct. 22, 1986, 100 Stat. 2939; Pub.L. 107–210, Div. A, Title II, § 203(e)(1), Aug. 6, 2002, 116 Stat. 970.)

[1] So in original. Probably should be "1166(a)(4)".

§ 1166. Notice requirements

(a) In general

In accordance with regulations prescribed by the Secretary—

(1) the group health plan shall provide, at the time of commencement of coverage under the plan, written notice to each covered employee and spouse of the employee (if any) of the rights provided under this subsection,

(2) the employer of an employee under a plan must notify the administrator of a qualifying event described in paragraph (1), (2), (4), or (6) of section 1163 of this title within 30 days (or, in the case of a group health plan which is a multiemployer plan, such longer period of time as may be provided in the terms of the plan) of the date of the qualifying event,

(3) each covered employee or qualified beneficiary is responsible for notifying the administrator of the occurrence of any qualifying event described in paragraph (3) or (5) of section 1163 of this title within 60 days after the date of the qualifying event and each qualified beneficiary who is determined, under title II or XVI of the Social Security Act, to have been disabled at any time during the first 60 days of continuation coverage under this part is responsible for notifying the plan administrator of such determination within 60 days after the date of the determination and for notifying the plan administrator within 30 days after the date of any final determination under such title or titles that the qualified beneficiary is no longer disabled, and

(4) the administrator shall notify—

(A) in the case of a qualifying event described in paragraph (1), (2), (4), or (6) of section 1163 of this title, any qualified beneficiary with respect to such event, and

(B) in the case of a qualifying event described in paragraph (3) or (5) of section 1163 of this title where the covered employee notifies the administrator under paragraph (3), any qualified beneficiary with respect to such event,

of such beneficiary's rights under this subsection.

(b) Alternative means of compliance with requirements for notification of multiemployer plans by employers

The requirements of subsection (a)(2) shall be considered satisfied in the case of a multiemployer plan in connection with a qualifying event described in paragraph (2) of section 1163 of this title if the plan provides that the determination of the occurrence of such qualifying event will be made by the plan administrator.

(c) Rules relating to notification of qualified beneficiaries by plan administrator

For purposes of subsection (a)(4), any notification shall be made within 14 days (or, in the case of a group health plan which is a multiemployer plan, such longer period of time as may be provided in the terms of the plan) of the date on which the administrator is notified under paragraph (2) or (3), whichever is applicable, and any such notification to an individual who is a qualified beneficiary as the spouse of the covered employee shall be treated as notification to all other qualified beneficiaries residing with such spouse at the time such notification is made. *(Pub.L. 93–406, Title I, § 606, as added Pub.L. 99–272, Title X, § 10002(a), Apr. 7, 1986, 100 Stat. 230; amended Pub.L. 99–509, Title IX, § 9501(d)(2), Oct. 21, 1986, 100 Stat. 2077; Pub.L. 99–514, Title XVIII, § 1895(d)(6)(B), Oct. 22, 1986, 100 Stat. 2939; Pub.L. 101–239, Title VI, § 6703(c), Title VII, § 7891(d)(1)(A), Dec. 19, 1989, 103 Stat. 2296, 2445; Pub.L. 104–191, Title IV, § 421(b)(2), Aug. 21, 1996, 110 Stat. 2088.)*

§ 1167. Definitions and special rules

For purposes of this part—

(1) Group health plan

The term "group health plan" means an employee welfare benefit plan providing medical care (as defined in section 213(d) of Title 26) to participants or beneficiaries directly or through insurance, reimbursement, or otherwise. Such term shall not include any plan substantially all of the coverage under which is for qualified long-term care services (as defined in section 7702B(c) of Title 26). Such term shall not include any qualified small employer health reimbursement arrangement (as defined in section 9831(d)(2) of Title 26).

(2) Covered employee

The term "covered employee" means an individual who is (or was) provided coverage under a group health plan by virtue of the performance of services by the individual for 1 or more persons maintaining the plan (including as an employee defined in section 401(c)(1) of Title 26).

(3) Qualified beneficiary

(A) In general

The term "qualified beneficiary" means, with respect to a covered employee under a group health plan, any other individual who, on the day before the qualifying event for that employee, is a beneficiary under the plan—

(i) as the spouse of the covered employee, or

(ii) as the dependent child of the employee.

Such term shall also include a child who is born to or placed for adoption with the covered employee during the period of continuation coverage under this part.

(B) Special rule for terminations and reduced employment

In the case of a qualifying event described in section 1163(2) of this title, the term "qualified beneficiary" includes the covered employee.

(C) Special rule for retirees and widows

In the case of a qualifying event described in section 1163(6) of this title, the term "qualified beneficiary" includes a covered employee who had retired on or before the date of substantial elimination of coverage and any other individual who, on the day before such qualifying event, is a beneficiary under the plan—

(i) as the spouse of the covered employee,

(ii) as the dependent child of the employee, or

(iii) as the surviving spouse of the covered employee.

(4) Employer

Subsection (n) (relating to leased employees) and subsection (t) (relating to application of controlled group rules to certain employee benefits) of section 414 of Title 26 shall apply for purposes of this part in the same manner and to the same extent as such subsections apply for purposes of section 106 of Title 26. Any regulations prescribed by the Secretary pursuant to the preceding sentence shall be consistent and coextensive with any regulations prescribed for similar purposes by the Secretary of the Treasury (or such Secretary's delegate) under such subsections.

(5) Optional extension of required periods

A group health plan shall not be treated as failing to meet the requirements of this part solely because the plan provides both—

(A) that the period of extended coverage referred to in section 1162(2) of this title commences with the date of the loss of coverage, and

(B) that the applicable notice period provided under section 1166(a)(2) of this title commences with the date of the loss of coverage.

(Pub.L. 93–406, Title I, § 607, as added Pub.L. 99–272, Title X, § 10002(a), Apr. 7, 1986, 100 Stat. 231; amended Pub.L. 99–509, Title IX, § 9501(c)(2), Oct. 21, 1986, 100 Stat. 2077; Pub.L. 99–514, Title XVIII, § 1895(d)(8), (9)(A), Oct. 22, 1986, 100 Stat. 2940; Pub.L. 100–647, Title III, § 3011(b)(6), Nov. 10, 1988, 102 Stat. 3625; Pub.L. 101–239, Title VII, §§ 7862(c)(2)(A), (6)(A), 7891(a)(1), (d)(2)(B)(i), Dec. 19, 1989, 103 Stat. 2432, 2433, 2445, 2446; Pub.L. 104–191, Title

III, § 321(d)(2), Title IV, § 421(b)(3), Aug. 21, 1996, 110 Stat. 2058, 2088; Pub.L. 114–255, Div. C, Title XVIII, § 18001(b)(2), Dec. 13, 2016, 130 Stat. 1344.)

§ 1168. Regulations

The Secretary may prescribe regulations to carry out the provisions of this part. *(Pub.L. 93–406, Title I, § 608, as added Pub.L. 99–272, Title X, § 10002(a), Apr. 7, 1986, 100 Stat. 231.)*

§ 1169. Additional standards for group health plans

(a) Group health plan coverage pursuant to medical child support orders

(1) In general

Each group health plan shall provide benefits in accordance with the applicable requirements of any qualified medical child support order. A qualified medical child support order with respect to any participant or beneficiary shall be deemed to apply to each group health plan which has received such order, from which the participant or beneficiary is eligible to receive benefits, and with respect to which the requirements of paragraph (4) are met.

(2) Definitions

For purposes of this subsection—

(A) Qualified medical child support order

The term "qualified medical child support order" means a medical child support order—

(i) which creates or recognizes the existence of an alternate recipient's right to, or assigns to an alternate recipient the right to, receive benefits for which a participant or beneficiary is eligible under a group health plan, and

(ii) with respect to which the requirements of paragraphs (3) and (4) are met.

(B) Medical child support order

The term "medical child support order" means any judgment, decree, or order (including approval of a settlement agreement) which—

(i) provides for child support with respect to a child of a participant under a group health plan or provides for health benefit coverage to such a child, is made pursuant to a State domestic relations law (including a community property law), and relates to benefits under such plan, or

(ii) is made pursuant to a law relating to medical child support described in section 1908 of the Social Security Act (as added by section 13822[1] of the Omnibus Budget Reconciliation Act of 1993) with respect to a group health plan,

if such judgment, decree, or order (I) is issued by a court of competent jurisdiction or (II) is issued through an administrative process established under State law and has the force and effect of law under applicable State law. For purposes of this subparagraph, an administrative notice which is issued pursuant to an administrative process referred to in subclause (II) of the preceding sentence and which has the effect of an order described in clause (i) or (ii) of the preceding sentence shall be treated as such an order.

(C) Alternate recipient

The term "alternate recipient" means any child of a participant who is recognized under a medical child support order as having a right to enrollment under a group health plan with respect to such participant.

(D) Child

The term "child" includes any child adopted by, or placed for adoption with, a participant of a group health plan.

(3) Information to be included in qualified order

A medical child support order meets the requirements of this paragraph only if such order clearly specifies—

(A) the name and the last known mailing address (if any) of the participant and the name and mailing address of each alternate recipient covered by the order, except that, to the extent provided in the order, the name and mailing address of an official of a State or a political subdivision thereof may be substituted for the mailing address of any such alternate recipient,

(B) a reasonable description of the type of coverage to be provided to each such alternate recipient, or the manner in which such type of coverage is to be determined, and

(C) the period to which such order applies.

(4) Restriction on new types or forms of benefits

A medical child support order meets the requirements of this paragraph only if such order does not require a plan to provide any type or form of benefit, or any option, not otherwise provided under the plan, except to the extent necessary to meet the requirements of a law relating to medical child support described in section 1908 of the Social Security Act (as added by section 13822[1] of the Omnibus Budget Reconciliation Act of 1993).

(5) Procedural requirements

(A) Timely notifications and determinations

In the case of any medical child support order received by a group health plan—

(i) the plan administrator shall promptly notify the participant and each alternate recipient of the receipt of such order and the plan's procedures for determining whether medical child support orders are qualified medical child support orders, and

(ii) within a reasonable period after receipt of such order, the plan administrator shall determine whether such order is a qualified medical child support order and notify the participant and each alternate recipient of such determination.

(B) Establishment of procedures for determining qualified status of orders

Each group health plan shall establish reasonable procedures to determine whether medical child support orders are qualified medical child support orders and to administer the provision of benefits under such qualified orders. Such procedures—

(i) shall be in writing,

(ii) shall provide for the notification of each person specified in a medical child support order as eligible to receive benefits under the plan (at the address included in the medical child support order) of such procedures promptly upon receipt by the plan of the medical child support order, and

(iii) shall permit an alternate recipient to designate a representative for receipt of copies of notices that are sent to the alternate recipient with respect to a medical child support order.

(C) National Medical Support Notice deemed to be a qualified medical child support order

(i) In general

If the plan administrator of a group health plan which is maintained by the employer of a noncustodial parent of a child or to which such an employer contributes receives an appropriately completed National Medical Support Notice promulgated pursuant to section 401(b) of the Child Support Performance and Incentive Act of 1998 in the case of such child, and the Notice meets the requirements of paragraphs (3) and (4), the Notice shall be deemed to be a qualified medical child support order in the case of such child.

(ii) Enrollment of child in plan

In any case in which an appropriately completed National Medical Support Notice is issued in the case of a child of a participant under a group health plan who is a noncustodial parent of the child, and the Notice is deemed under clause (i) to be a qualified medical child support order, the plan administrator, within 40 business days after the date of the Notice, shall—

(I) notify the State agency issuing the Notice with respect to such child whether coverage of the child is available under the terms of the plan and, if so, whether such child is covered under the plan and either the effective date of the coverage or, if necessary, any steps to be taken by the custodial parent (or by the official of a State or political subdivision thereof substituted for the name of such child pursuant to paragraph (3)(A)) to effectuate the coverage; and

(II) provide to the custodial parent (or such substituted official) a description of the coverage available and any forms or documents necessary to effectuate such coverage.

(iii) Rule of construction

Nothing in this subparagraph shall be construed as requiring a group health plan, upon receipt of a National Medical Support Notice, to provide benefits under the plan (or eligibility for such benefits) in addition to benefits (or eligibility for benefits) provided under the terms of the plan as of immediately before receipt of such Notice.

(6) Actions taken by fiduciaries

If a plan fiduciary acts in accordance with part 4 of this subtitle in treating a medical child support order as being (or not being) a qualified medical child support order, then the plan's obligation to the participant and each alternate recipient shall be discharged to the extent of any payment made pursuant to such act of the fiduciary.

(7) Treatment of alternate recipients

(A) Treatment as beneficiary generally

A person who is an alternate recipient under a qualified medical child support order shall be considered a beneficiary under the plan for purposes of any provision of this chapter.

(B) Treatment as participant for purposes of reporting and disclosure requirements

A person who is an alternate recipient under any medical child support order shall be considered a participant under the plan for purposes of the reporting and disclosure requirements of part 1 of this subtitle.

(8) Direct provision of benefits provided to alternate recipients

Any payment for benefits made by a group health plan pursuant to a medical child support order in reimbursement for expenses paid by an alternate recipient or an alternate recipient's custodial parent or legal guardian shall be made to the alternate recipient or the alternate recipient's custodial parent or legal guardian.

(9) Payment to State official treated as satisfaction of plan's obligation to make payment to alternate recipient

Payment of benefits by a group health plan to an official of a State or a political subdivision thereof whose name and address have been substituted for the address of an alternate recipient in a qualified medical child support order, pursuant to paragraph (3)(A), shall be treated, for purposes of this subchapter, as payment of benefits to the alternate recipient.

(b) Rights of States with respect to group health plans where participants or beneficiaries thereunder are eligible for medicaid benefits

(1) Compliance by plans with assignment of rights

A group health plan shall provide that payment for benefits with respect to a participant under the plan will be made in accordance with any assignment of rights made by or on behalf of such participant or a beneficiary of the participant as required by a State plan for medical assistance approved under title XIX of the Social Security Act pursuant to section 1912(a)(1)(A) of such Act (as in effect on August 10, 1993).

(2) Enrollment and provision of benefits without regard to medicaid eligibility

A group health plan shall provide that, in enrolling an individual as a participant or beneficiary or in determining or making any payments for benefits of an individual as a participant or beneficiary, the fact that the individual is eligible for or is provided medical assistance under a State plan for medical assistance approved under title XIX of the Social Security Act will not be taken into account.

(3) Acquisition by States of rights of third parties

A group health plan shall provide that, to the extent that payment has been made under a State plan for medical assistance approved under title XIX of the Social Security Act in any case in which a group health plan has a legal liability to make payment for items or services constituting such assistance, payment for benefits under the plan will be made in accordance with any State law which provides that the State has acquired the rights with respect to a participant to such payment for such items or services.

(c) Group health plan coverage of dependent children in cases of adoption

(1) Coverage effective upon placement for adoption

In any case in which a group health plan provides coverage for dependent children of participants or beneficiaries, such plan shall provide benefits to dependent children placed with participants or beneficiaries for adoption under the same terms and conditions as apply in the case of dependent children who are natural children of participants or beneficiaries under the plan, irrespective of whether the adoption has become final.

(2) Restrictions based on preexisting conditions at time of placement for adoption prohibited

A group health plan may not restrict coverage under the plan of any dependent child adopted by a participant or beneficiary, or placed with a participant or beneficiary for adoption, solely on the basis of a preexisting condition of such child at the time that such child would otherwise become eligible for coverage under the plan, if the adoption or placement for adoption occurs while the participant or beneficiary is eligible for coverage under the plan.

(3) Definitions

For purposes of this subsection—

(A) Child

The term "child" means, in connection with any adoption, or placement for adoption, of the child, an individual who has not attained age 18 as of the date of such adoption or placement for adoption.

(B) Placement for adoption

The term "placement", or being "placed", for adoption, in connection with any placement for adoption of a child with any person, means the assumption and retention by such person of a legal obligation for total or partial support of such child in anticipation of adoption of such child. The child's placement with such person terminates upon the termination of such legal obligation.

(d) Continued coverage of costs of a pediatric vaccine under group health plans

A group health plan may not reduce its coverage of the costs of pediatric vaccines (as defined under section 1928(h)(6) of the Social Security Act as amended by section 13830[2] of the Omnibus Budget Reconciliation Act of 1993) below the coverage it provided as of May 1, 1993.

(e) Regulations

Any regulations prescribed under this section shall be prescribed by the Secretary of Labor, in consultation with the Secretary of Health and Human Services. *(Pub.L. 93–406, Title I, § 609, as added Pub.L. 103–66, Title IV, § 4301(a), Aug. 10, 1993, 107 Stat. 371; amended Pub.L. 104–193, Title III, § 381(a), Aug. 22, 1996, 110 Stat. 2257; Pub.L. 105–33, Title V, §§ 5611(a), (b), 5612(a), 5613(a), (b), Aug. 5, 1997, 111 Stat. 647, 648; Pub.L. 105–200, Title IV, §§ 401(d), (h)(2)(A)(iii), (h)(2)(B), (3)(A), July 16, 1998, 112 Stat. 662, 668.)*

[1] So in original. Probably should be section "13623".

[2] So in original. Probably should be section "13631".

Commentary

In *United States v. Morrison, 120 S.Ct. 1740, 146 L.Ed.2d 658 (2000)*, the United States Supreme Court held that this section is unconstitutional because neither the Commerce Clause nor the 14th Amendment gives Congress authority to enact it.

TITLE 34

CRIME CONTROL AND LAW ENFORCEMENT

SUBTITLE I—COMPREHENSIVE ACTS

SUBCHAPTER III—VIOLENCE AGAINST WOMEN

PART C—CIVIL RIGHTS FOR WOMEN

§ 12361. Civil rights

(a) Purpose

Pursuant to the affirmative power of Congress to enact this part under section 5 of the Fourteenth Amendment to the Constitution, as well as under section 8 of Article I of the Constitution, it is the purpose of this part to protect the civil rights of victims of gender motivated violence and to promote public safety, health, and activities affecting interstate commerce by establishing a Federal civil rights cause of action for victims of crimes of violence motivated by gender.

(b) Right to be free from crimes of violence

All persons within the United States shall have the right to be free from crimes of violence motivated by gender (as defined in subsection (d)).

(c) Cause of action

A person (including a person who acts under color of any statute, ordinance, regulation, custom, or usage of any State) who commits a crime of violence motivated by gender and thus deprives another of the right declared in subsection (b) shall be liable to the party injured, in an action for the recovery of compensatory and punitive damages, injunctive and declaratory relief, and such other relief as a court may deem appropriate.

(d) Definitions

For purposes of this section—

(1) the term "crime of violence motivated by gender" means a crime of violence committed because of gender or on the basis of gender, and due, at least in part, to an animus based on the victim's gender; and

(2) the term "crime of violence" means—[1]

(A) an act or series of acts that would constitute a felony against the person or that would constitute a felony against property if the conduct presents a serious risk of physical injury to another, and that would come within the meaning of State or Federal offenses described in section 16 of Title 18, whether or not those acts have actually resulted in criminal charges, prosecution, or conviction and whether or not those acts were committed in the special maritime, territorial, or prison jurisdiction of the United States; and

(B) includes an act or series of acts that would constitute a felony described in subparagraph (A) but for the relationship between the person who takes such action and the individual against whom such action is taken.

(e) Limitation and procedures

(1) Limitation

Nothing in this section entitles a person to a cause of action under subsection (c) for random acts of violence unrelated to gender or for acts that cannot be demonstrated, by a preponderance of the evidence, to be motivated by gender (within the meaning of subsection (d)).

(2) No prior criminal action

Nothing in this section requires a prior criminal complaint, prosecution, or conviction to establish the elements of a cause of action under subsection (c).

(3) Concurrent jurisdiction

The Federal and State courts shall have concurrent jurisdiction over actions brought pursuant to this part.

(4) Supplemental jurisdiction

Neither section 1367 of Title 28 nor subsection (c) of this section shall be construed, by reason of a claim arising under such subsection, to confer on the courts of the United States jurisdiction over any State law claim seeking the establishment of a divorce, alimony, equitable distribution of marital property, or child custody decree.

(Pub.L. 103–322, Title IV, § 40302, Sept. 13, 1994, 108 Stat. 1941.)

[1] So in original. The word "means" probably should appear after "(A)" below.

Validity

The United States Supreme Court, in United States v. Morrison, U.S.Va.2000, 529 U.S. 598, 120 S.Ct. 1740, 146 L.Ed.2d 658, found Congress lacked constitutional authority under both the Commerce Clause and the Fourteenth Amendment to enact this section (Pub.L. 103–322, Title IV, § 40302, Sept. 13, 1994, 108 Stat. 1941, formerly classified as 42 U.S.C.A. § 13981, prior to reclassification as this section), which was part of the Violence Against Women Act of 1994.

Commentary

In *United States v. Morrison, 120 S.Ct. 1740, 146 L.Ed.2d 658 (2000)*, the United States Supreme Court held that this section is unconstitutional because neither the Commerce Clause nor the 14th Amendment gives Congress authority to enact it.

TITLE 42

THE PUBLIC HEALTH AND WELFARE

CHAPTER 7—SOCIAL SECURITY

SUBCHAPTER II—FEDERAL OLD–AGE, SURVIVORS, AND DISABILITY INSURANCE BENEFITS

SUBCHAPTER II—FEDERAL OLD–AGE, SURVIVORS, AND DISABILITY INSURANCE BENEFITS

§ 402. Old-age and survivors insurance benefit payments

(a) Old-age insurance benefits

Every individual who—

(1) is a fully insured individual (as defined in section 414(a) of this title),

(2) has attained age 62, and

(3) has filed application for old-age insurance benefits or was entitled to disability insurance benefits for the month preceding the month in which he attained retirement age (as defined in section 416(*l*) of this title),

shall be entitled to an old-age insurance benefit for each month, beginning with—

(A) in the case of an individual who has attained retirement age (as defined in section 416(*l*) of this title), the first month in which such individual meets the criteria specified in paragraphs (1), (2), and (3), or

(B) in the case of an individual who has attained age 62, but has not attained retirement age (as defined in section 416(*l*) of this title), the first month throughout which such individual meets the criteria specified in paragraphs (1) and (2) (if in that month he meets the criterion specified in paragraph (3)),

and ending with the month preceding the month in which he dies. Except as provided in subsection (q) and subsection (w) of this section, such individual's old-age insurance benefit for any month shall be equal to his primary insurance amount (as defined in section 415(a) of this title) for such month.

(b) Wife's insurance benefits

(1) The wife (as defined in section 416(b) of this title) and every divorced wife (as defined in section 416(d) of this title) of an individual entitled to old-age or disability insurance benefits, if such wife or such divorced wife—

(A) has filed application for wife's insurance benefits,

(B)(i) has attained age 62, or

(ii) in the case of a wife, has in her care (individually or jointly with such individual) at the time of filing such application a child entitled to a child's insurance benefit on the basis of the wages and self-employment income of such individual,

(C) in the case of a divorced wife, is not married, and

(D) is not entitled to old-age or disability insurance benefits, or is entitled to old-age or disability insurance benefits based on a primary insurance amount which is less than one-half of the primary insurance amount of such individual,

shall (subject to subsection (s) of this section) be entitled to a wife's insurance benefit for each month, beginning with—

(i) in the case of a wife or divorced wife (as so defined) of an individual entitled to old-age benefits, if such wife or divorced wife has attained retirement age (as defined in section 416(*l*) of this title), the first month in which she meets the criteria specified in subparagraphs (A), (B), (C), and (D), or

(ii) in the case of a wife or divorced wife (as so defined) of—

(I) an individual entitled to old-age insurance benefits, if such wife or divorced wife has not attained retirement age (as defined in section 416(*l*) of this title), or

(II) an individual entitled to disability insurance benefits,

the first month throughout which she is such a wife or divorced wife and meets the criteria specified in subparagraphs (B), (C), and (D) (if in such month she meets the criterion specified in subparagraph (A)),

whichever is earlier, and ending with the month preceding the month in which any of the following occurs—

(E) she dies,

(F) such individual dies,

(G) in the case of a wife, they are divorced and either (i) she has not attained age 62, or (ii) she has attained age 62 but has not been married to such individual for a period of 10 years immediately before the date the divorce became effective,

(H) in the case of a divorced wife, she marries a person other than such individual,

(I) in the case of a wife who has not attained age 62, no child of such individual is entitled to a child's insurance benefit,

(J) she becomes entitled to an old-age or disability insurance benefit based on a primary insurance amount which is equal to or exceeds one-half of the primary insurance amount of such individual, or

(K) such individual is not entitled to disability insurance benefits and is not entitled to old-age insurance benefits.

(2) Except as provided in subsections (k)(5) and (q) of this section, such wife's insurance benefit for each month shall be equal to one-half of the primary insurance amount of her husband (or, in the case of a divorced wife, her former husband) for such month.

(3) In the case of any divorced wife who marries—

(A) an individual entitled to benefits under subsection (c), (f), (g), or (h) of this section, or

(B) an individual who has attained the age of 18 and is entitled to benefits under subsection (d) of this section,

such divorced wife's entitlement to benefits under this subsection shall, notwithstanding the provisions of paragraph (1) (but subject to subsection (s) of this section), not be terminated by reason of such marriage.

(4)(A) Notwithstanding the preceding provisions of this subsection, except as provided in subparagraph (B), the divorced wife of an individual who is not entitled to old-age or disability insurance benefits, but who has attained age 62 and is a fully insured individual (as defined in section 414 of this title), if such divorced wife—

(i) meets the requirements of subparagraphs (A) through (D) of paragraph (1), and

(ii) has been divorced from such insured individual for not less than 2 years,

shall be entitled to a wife's insurance benefit under this subsection for each month, in such amount, and beginning and ending with such months, as determined (under regulations of the Commissioner of Social Security) in the manner otherwise provided for wife's insurance benefits under this subsection, as if such insured individual had become entitled to old-age insurance benefits on the date on which the divorced wife first meets the criteria for entitlement set forth in clauses (i) and (ii).

(B) A wife's insurance benefit provided under this paragraph which has not otherwise terminated in accordance with subparagraph (E), (F), (H), or (J) of paragraph (1) shall terminate with the month preceding the first month in which the insured individual is no longer a fully insured individual.

(c) Husband's insurance benefits

(1) The husband (as defined in section 416(f) of this title) and every divorced husband (as defined in section 416(d) of this title) of an individual entitled to old-age or disability insurance benefits, if such husband or such divorced husband—

(A) has filed application for husband's insurance benefits,

(B)(i) has attained age 62, or

(ii) in the case of a husband, has in his care (individually or jointly with such individual) at the time of filing such application a child entitled to a child's insurance benefit on the basis of the wages and self-employment income of such individual,

(C) in the case of a divorced husband, is not married, and

(D) is not entitled to old-age or disability insurance benefits, or is entitled to old-age or disability insurance benefits based on a primary insurance amount which is less than one-half of the primary insurance amount of such individual,

shall (subject to subsection (s) of this section) be entitled to a husband's insurance benefit for each month, beginning with—

(i) in the case of a husband or divorced husband (as so defined) of an individual who is entitled to an old-age insurance benefit, if such husband or divorced husband has attained retirement age (as defined in section 416(*l*) of this title), the first month in which he meets the criteria specified in subparagraphs (A), (B), (C), and (D), or

(ii) in the case of a husband or divorced husband (as so defined) of—

(I) an individual entitled to old-age insurance benefits, if such husband or divorced husband has not attained retirement age (as defined in section 416(*l*) of this title), or

(II) an individual entitled to disability insurance benefits,

the first month throughout which he is such a husband or divorced husband and meets the criteria specified in subparagraphs (B), (C), and (D) (if in such month he meets the criterion specified in subparagraph (A)),

whichever is earlier, and ending with the month preceding the month in which any of the following occurs:

(E) he dies,

(F) such individual dies,

(G) in the case of a husband, they are divorced and either (i) he has not attained age 62, or (ii) he has attained age 62 but has not been married to such individual for a period of 10 years immediately before the divorce became effective,

(H) in the case of a divorced husband, he marries a person other than such individual,

(I) in the case of a husband who has not attained age 62, no child of such individual is entitled to a child's insurance benefit,

(J) he becomes entitled to an old-age or disability insurance benefit based on a primary insurance amount which is equal to or exceeds one-half of the primary insurance amount of such individual, or

(K) such individual is not entitled to disability insurance benefits and is not entitled to old-age insurance benefits.

(2) Except as provided in subsections (k)(5) and (q) of this section, such husband's insurance benefit for each month shall be equal to one-half of the primary insurance amount of his wife (or, in the case of a divorced husband, his former wife) for such month.

(3) In the case of any divorced husband who marries—

(A) an individual entitled to benefits under subsection (b), (e), (g), or (h) of this section, or

(B) an individual who has attained the age of 18 and is entitled to benefits under subsection (d) of this section, by reason of paragraph (1)(B)(ii) thereof,

such divorced husband's entitlement to benefits under this subsection, notwithstanding the provisions of paragraph (1) (but subject to subsection (s) of this section), shall not be terminated by reason of such marriage.

(4)(A) Notwithstanding the preceding provisions of this subsection, except as provided in subparagraph (B), the divorced husband of an individual who is not entitled to old-age or disability insurance benefits, but who has attained age 62 and is a fully insured individual (as defined in section 414 of this title), if such divorced husband—

(i) meets the requirements of subparagraphs (A) through (D) of paragraph (1), and

(ii) has been divorced from such insured individual for not less than 2 years,

shall be entitled to a husband's insurance benefit under this subsection for each month, in such amount, and beginning and ending with such months, as determined (under regulations of the Commissioner of Social Security) in the manner otherwise provided for husband's insurance benefits under this subsection, as if such insured individual had become entitled to old-age insurance benefits on the date on which the divorced husband first meets the criteria for entitlement set forth in clauses (i) and (ii).

(B) A husband's insurance benefit provided under this paragraph which has not otherwise terminated in accordance with subparagraph (E), (F), (H), or (J) of paragraph (1) shall terminate with the month preceding the first month in which the insured individual is no longer a fully insured individual.

(d) Child's insurance benefits

(1) Every child (as defined in section 416(e) of this title) of an individual entitled to old-age or disability insurance benefits, or of an individual who dies a fully or currently insured individual, if such child—

(A) has filed application for child's insurance benefits,

(B) at the time such application was filed was unmarried and (i) either had not attained the age of 18 or was a full-time elementary or secondary school student and had not attained the age of 19, or (ii) is under a disability (as defined in section 423(d) of this title) which began before he attained the age of 22, and

(C) was dependent upon such individual—

(i) if such individual is living, at the time such application was filed,

(ii) if such individual has died, at the time of such death, or

(iii) if such individual had a period of disability which continued until he became entitled to old-age or disability insurance benefits, or (if he has died) until the month of his death, at the beginning of such period of disability or at the time he became entitled to such benefits,

shall be entitled to a child's insurance benefit for each month, beginning with—

(i) in the case of a child (as so defined) of such an individual who has died, the first month in which such child meets the criteria specified in subparagraphs (A), (B), and (C), or

(ii) in the case of a child (as so defined) of an individual entitled to an old-age insurance benefit or to a disability insurance benefit, the first month throughout which such child is a child (as so defined) and meets the criteria specified in subparagraphs (B) and (C) (if in such month he meets the criterion specified in subparagraph (A)),

whichever is earlier, and ending with the month preceding whichever of the following first occurs—

(D) the month in which such child dies or marries,

(E) the month in which such child attains the age of 18, but only if he (i) is not under a disability (as so defined) at the time he attains such age, and (ii) is not a full-time elementary or secondary school student during any part of such month,

(F) if such child was not under a disability (as so defined) at the time he attained the age of 18, the earlier of—

(i) the first month during no part of which he is a full-time elementary or secondary school student, or

(ii) the month in which he attains the age of 19,

but only if he was not under a disability (as so defined) in such earlier month;

(G) if such child was under a disability (as so defined) at the time he attained the age of 18 or if he was not under a disability (as so defined) at such time but was under a disability (as so defined) at or prior to the time he attained (or would attain) the age of 22—

(i) the termination month, subject to section 423(e) of this title (and for purposes of this subparagraph, the termination month for any individual shall be the third month following the month in which his disability ceases; except that, in the case of an individual who has a period of trial work which ends as determined by application of section 422(c)(4)(A) of this title, the termination month shall be the earlier of (I) the third month following the earliest month after the end of such period of trial work with respect to which such individual is determined to no longer be suffering from a disabling physical or mental impairment, or (II) the third month following the earliest month in which such individual engages or is determined able to engage in substantial gainful activity, but in no event earlier than the first month occurring after the 36 months following such period of trial work in which he engages or is determined able to engage in substantial gainful activity),

or (if later) the earlier of—

(ii) the first month during no part of which he is a full-time elementary or secondary school student, or

(iii) the month in which he attains the age of 19,

but only if he was not under a disability (as so defined) in such earlier month; or

(H) if the benefits under this subsection are based on the wages and self-employment income of a stepparent who is subsequently divorced from such child's natural parent, the month after the month in which such divorce becomes final.

Entitlement of any child to benefits under this subsection on the basis of the wages and self-employment income of an individual entitled to disability insurance benefits shall also end with the month before the first month for which such individual is not entitled to such benefits unless such individual is, for such later month, entitled to old-age insurance benefits or unless he dies in such month. No payment under this paragraph may be made to a child who would not meet the definition of disability in section 423(d) of this title except for paragraph (1)(B) thereof for any month in which he engages in substantial gainful activity.

(2) Such child's insurance benefit for each month shall, if the individual on the basis of whose wages and self-employment income the child is entitled to such benefit has not died prior to the end of such month, be equal to one-half of the primary insurance amount of such individual for such month. Such child's insurance benefit for each month shall, if such individual has died in or prior to such month, be equal to three-fourths of the primary insurance amount of such individual.

(3) A child shall be deemed dependent upon his father or adopting father or his mother or adopting mother at the time specified in paragraph (1)(C) of this subsection unless, at such time, such individual was not living with or contributing to the support of such child and—

(A) such child is neither the legitimate nor adopted child of such individual, or

(B) such child has been adopted by some other individual.

For purposes of this paragraph, a child deemed to be a child of a fully or currently insured individual pursuant to section 416(h)(2)(B) or section 416(h)(3) of this title shall be deemed to be the legitimate child of such individual.

(4) A child shall be deemed dependent upon his stepfather or stepmother at the time specified in paragraph (1)(C) of this subsection if, at such time, the child was receiving at least one-half of his support from such stepfather or stepmother.

(5) In the case of a child who has attained the age of eighteen and who marries—

(A) an individual entitled to benefits under subsection (a), (b), (c), (e), (f), (g), or (h) of this section or under section 423(a) of this title, or

(B) another individual who has attained the age of eighteen and is entitled to benefits under this subsection,

such child's entitlement to benefits under this subsection shall, notwithstanding the provisions of paragraph (1) of this subsection but subject to subsection (s) of this section, not be terminated by reason of such marriage.

(6) A child whose entitlement to child's insurance benefits on the basis of the wages and self-employment income of an insured individual terminated with the month preceding the month in which such child attained the age of 18, or with a subsequent month, may again become entitled to such benefits (provided no event specified in paragraph (1)(D) has occurred) beginning with the first month thereafter in which he—

(A) (i) is a full-time elementary or secondary school student and has not attained the age of 19, or (ii) is under a disability (as defined in section 423(d) of this title) and has not attained the age of 22, or

(B) is under a disability (as so defined) which began (i) before the close of the 84th month following the month in which his most recent entitlement to child's insurance benefits terminated because he ceased to be under such disability, or (ii) after the close of the 84th month following the month in which his most recent entitlement to child's insurance benefits terminated because he ceased to be under such disability due to performance of substantial gainful activity,

but only if he has filed application for such reentitlement. Such reentitlement shall end with the month preceding whichever of the following first occurs:

(C) the first month in which an event specified in paragraph (1)(D) occurs;

(D) the earlier of (i) the first month during no part of which he is a full-time elementary or secondary school student or (ii) the month in which he attains the age of 19, but only if he is not under a disability (as so defined) in such earlier month; or

(E) if he was under a disability (as so defined), the termination month (as defined in paragraph (1)(G)(i)), subject to section 423(e) of this title, or (if later) the earlier of—

(i) the first month during no part of which he is a full-time elementary or secondary school student, or

(ii) the month in which he attains the age of 19.

(7) For the purposes of this subsection—

(A) A "full-time elementary or secondary school student" is an individual who is in full-time attendance as a student at an elementary or secondary school, as determined by the Commissioner of Social Security (in accordance with regulations prescribed by the Commissioner) in the light of the standards and practices of the schools involved, except that no individual shall be considered a "full-time elementary or secondary school student" if he is paid by his employer while attending an elementary or secondary school at the request, or pursuant to a requirement, of his employer. An individual shall not be considered a "full-time elementary or secondary school student" for the purpose of this section while that individual is confined in a jail, prison, or other penal institution or correctional facility, pursuant to his conviction of an offense (committed after the effective date of this sentence) which constituted a felony under applicable law. An individual who is determined to be a full-time elementary or secondary school student shall be deemed to be such a student throughout the month with respect to which such determination is made.

(B) Except to the extent provided in such regulations, an individual shall be deemed to be a full-time elementary or secondary school student during any period of nonattendance at an elementary or secondary school at which he has been in full-time attendance if (i) such period is 4 calendar months or less, and (ii) he shows to the satisfaction of the Commissioner of Social Security that he intends to continue to be in full-time attendance at an elementary or secondary school immediately following such period. An individual who does not meet the requirement of clause (ii) with respect to such period of nonattendance shall be deemed to have met such requirement (as of the beginning of such period) if he is in full-time attendance at an elementary or secondary school immediately following such period.

(C)(i) An "elementary or secondary school" is a school which provides elementary or secondary education, respectively, as determined under the law of the State or other jurisdiction in which it is located.

(ii) For the purpose of determining whether a child is a "full-time elementary or secondary school student" or "intends to continue to be in full-time attendance at an elementary or secondary school", within the meaning of this subsection, there shall be disregarded any education provided, or to be provided, beyond grade 12.

(D) A child who attains age 19 at a time when he is a full-time elementary or secondary school student (as defined in subparagraph (A) of this paragraph and without application of subparagraph (B) of such paragraph) but has not (at such time) completed the requirements for, or received, a diploma or equivalent certificate from a secondary school (as defined in subparagraph (C)(i)) shall be deemed (for purposes of determining whether his entitlement to benefits under this subsection has terminated under paragraph (1)(F) and for purposes of determining his initial entitlement to such benefits under clause (i) of paragraph (1)(B)) not to have attained such age until the first day of the first month following the end of the quarter or semester in which he is enrolled at such time (or, if the elementary or secondary school (as defined in this paragraph) in which he is enrolled is not operated on a quarter or semester system, until the first day of the first month following the completion of the course in which he is so enrolled or until the first day of the third month beginning after such time, whichever first occurs).

(8) In the case of—

(A) an individual entitled to old-age insurance benefits (other than an individual referred to in subparagraph (B)), or

(B) an individual entitled to disability insurance benefits, or an individual entitled to old-age insurance benefits who was entitled to disability insurance benefits for the month preceding the first month for which he was entitled to old-age insurance benefits,

a child of such individual adopted after such individual became entitled to such old-age or disability insurance benefits shall be deemed not to meet the requirements of clause (i) or (iii) of paragraph (1)(C) unless such child—

(C) is the natural child or stepchild of such individual (including such a child who was legally adopted by such individual), or

(D)(i) was legally adopted by such individual in an adoption decreed by a court of competent jurisdiction within the United States, and

(ii) in the case of a child who attained the age of 18 prior to the commencement of proceedings for adoption, the child was living with or receiving at least one-half of the child's support from such individual for the year immediately preceding the month in which the adoption is decreed.

(9)(A) A child who is a child of an individual under clause (3) of the first sentence of section 416(e) of this title and is not a child of such individual under clause (1) or (2) of such first sentence shall be deemed not to be dependent on such individual at the time specified in subparagraph (1)(C) of this subsection unless (i) such child was living with such individual in the United States and receiving at least one-half of his support from such individual (I) for the year immediately before the month in which such individual became entitled to old-age insurance benefits or disability insurance benefits or died, or (II) if such individual had a period of disability which continued until he had become entitled to old-age insurance benefits, or disability insurance benefits, or died, for the year immediately before the month in which such period of disability began, and (ii) the period during which such child was living with such individual began before the child attained age 18.

(B) In the case of a child who was born in the one-year period during which such child must have been living with and receiving at least one-half of his support from such individual, such child shall be deemed to meet such requirements for such period if, as of the close of such period, such child has lived with such individual in the United States and received at least one-half of his support from such individual for substantially all of the period which begins on the date of such child's birth.

(10) For purposes of paragraph (1)(H)—

(A) each stepparent shall notify the Commissioner of Social Security of any divorce upon such divorce becoming final; and

(B) the Commissioner shall annually notify any stepparent of the rule for termination described in paragraph (1)(H) and of the requirement described in subparagraph (A).

(e) Widow's insurance benefits

(1) The widow (as defined in section 416(c) of this title) and every surviving divorced wife (as defined in section 416(d) of this title) of an individual who died a fully insured individual, if such widow or such surviving divorced wife—

(A) is not married,

(B) (i) has attained age 60, or (ii) has attained age 50 but has not attained age 60 and is under a disability (as defined in section 423(d) of this title) which began before the end of the period specified in paragraph (4),

(C)(i) has filed application for widow's insurance benefits,

(ii) was entitled to wife's insurance benefits, on the basis of the wages and self-employment income of such individual, for the month preceding the month in which such individual died, and—

(I) has attained retirement age (as defined in section 416(l) of this title),

(II) is not entitled to benefits under subsection (a) of this section or section 423 of this title, or

(III) has in effect a certificate (described in paragraph (8)) filed by her with the Commissioner of Social Security, in accordance with regulations prescribed by the Commissioner of Social Security, in which she elects to receive widow's insurance benefits (subject to reduction as provided in subsection (q) of this section), or

(iii) was entitled, on the basis of such wages and self-employment income, to mother's insurance benefits for the month preceding the month in which she attained retirement age (as defined in section 416(l) of this title), and

(D) is not entitled to old-age insurance benefits or is entitled to old-age insurance benefits each of which is less than the primary insurance amount (as determined after application of subparagraphs (B) and (C) of paragraph (2)) of such deceased individual,

shall be entitled to a widow's insurance benefit for each month, beginning with—

(E) if she satisfies subparagraph (B) by reason of clause (i) thereof, the first month in which she becomes so entitled to such insurance benefits, or

(F) if she satisfies subparagraph (B) by reason of clause (ii) thereof—

(i) the first month after her waiting period (as defined in paragraph (5)) in which she becomes so entitled to such insurance benefits, or

(ii) the first month during all of which she is under a disability and in which she becomes so entitled to such insurance benefits, but only if she was previously entitled to insurance benefits under this subsection on the basis of being under a disability and such first month occurs (I) in the period specified in paragraph (4) and (II) after the month in which a previous entitlement to such benefits on such basis terminated,

and ending with the month preceding the first month in which any of the following occurs: she remarries, dies, becomes entitled to an old-age insurance benefit equal to or exceeding the primary insurance amount (as determined after application of subparagraphs (B) and (C) of paragraph (2)) of such deceased individual, or, if she became entitled to such benefits before she attained age 60, subject to section 423(e) of this title, the termination month (unless she attains retirement age (as defined in section 416(l) of this title) on or before the last day of such termination month). For purposes of the preceding sentence, the termination month for any individual shall be the third month following the month in which her disability ceases; except that, in the case of an individual who has a period of trial work which ends as determined by application of section 422(c)(4)(A) of this title, the termination month shall be the earlier of (I) the third month following the earliest month after the end of such period of trial work with respect to which such individual is determined to no longer be suffering from a disabling physical or mental impairment, or (II) the third month following the earliest month in which such individual engages or is determined able to engage in substantial gainful activity, but in no event earlier than the first month occurring after the 36 months following such period of trial work in which she engages or is determined able to engage in substantial gainful activity.

(2)(A) Except as provided in subsection (k)(5) of this section, subsection (q) of this section, and subparagraph (D) of this paragraph, such widow's insurance benefit for each month shall be equal to the primary insurance amount (as determined for purposes of this subsection after application of subparagraphs (B) and (C)) of such deceased individual.

(B)(i) For purposes of this subsection, in any case in which such deceased individual dies before attaining age 62 and section 415(a)(1) of this title (as in effect after December 1978) is applicable in determining such individual's primary insurance amount—

(I) such primary insurance amount shall be determined under the formula set forth in section 415(a)(1)(B)(i) and (ii) of this title which is applicable to individuals who initially become eligible for old-age insurance benefits in the second year after the year specified in clause (ii),

(II) the year specified in clause (ii) shall be substituted for the second calendar year specified in section 415(b)(3)(A)(ii)(I) of this title, and

(III) such primary insurance amount shall be increased under section 415(i) of this title as if it were the primary insurance amount referred to in section 415(i)(2)(A)(ii)(II) of this title, except that it shall be increased only for years beginning after the first year after the year specified in clause (ii).

(ii) The year specified in this clause is the earlier of—

(I) the year in which the deceased individual attained age 60, or would have attained age 60 had he lived to that age, or

(II) the second year preceding the year in which the widow or surviving divorced wife first meets the requirements of paragraph (1)(B) or the second year preceding the year in which the deceased individual died, whichever is later.

(iii) This subparagraph shall apply with respect to any benefit under this subsection only to the extent its application does not result in a primary insurance amount for purposes of this subsection which is less than the primary insurance amount otherwise determined for such deceased individual under section 415 of this title.

(C) If such deceased individual was (or upon application would have been) entitled to an old-age insurance benefit which was increased (or subject to being increased) on account of delayed retirement under the provisions of subsection (w) of this section, then, for purposes of this subsection, such individual's primary insurance amount, if less than the old-age insurance benefit (increased, where applicable, under section 415(f)(5), 415(f)(6), or 415(f)(9)(B) of this title and under section 415(i) of this title as if such individual were still alive in the case of an individual who has died) which he was receiving (or would upon application have received) for the month prior to the month in which he died, shall be deemed to be equal to such old-age insurance benefit, and (notwithstanding the provisions of paragraph (3) of subsection (w) of this section) the number of increment months shall include any month in the months of the calendar year in which he died, prior to the month in which he died, which satisfy the conditions in paragraph (2) of subsection (w) of this section.

(D) If the deceased individual (on the basis of whose wages and self-employment income a widow or surviving divorced wife is entitled to widow's insurance benefits under this subsection) was, at any time, entitled to an old-age insurance benefit which was reduced by reason of the application of subsection (q) of this section, the widow's insurance benefit of such widow or surviving divorced wife for any month shall, if the amount of the widow's insurance benefit of such widow or surviving divorced wife (as determined under subparagraph (A) and after application of subsection (q) of this section) is greater than—

(i) the amount of the old-age insurance benefit to which such deceased individual would have been entitled (after application of subsection (q) of this section) for such month if such individual were still living and section 415(f)(5), 415(f)(6), or 415(f)(9)(B) of this title were applied, where applicable, and

(ii) 82½ percent of the primary insurance amount (as determined without regard to subparagraph (C)) of such deceased individual,

be reduced to the amount referred to in clause (i), or (if greater) the amount referred to in clause (ii).

(3) For purposes of paragraph (1), if—

(A) a widow or surviving divorced wife marries after attaining age 60 (or after attaining age 50 if she was entitled before such marriage occurred to benefits based on disability under this subsection), or

(B) a disabled widow or disabled surviving divorced wife described in paragraph (1)(B)(ii) marries after attaining age 50,

such marriage shall be deemed not to have occurred.

(4) The period referred to in paragraph (1)(B)(ii), in the case of any widow or surviving divorced wife, is the period beginning with whichever of the following is the latest:

(A) the month in which occurred the death of the fully insured individual referred to in paragraph (1) on whose wages and self-employment income her benefits are or would be based, or

(B) the last month for which she was entitled to mother's insurance benefits on the basis of the wages and self-employment income of such individual, or

(C) the month in which a previous entitlement to widow's insurance benefits on the basis of such wages and self-employment income terminated because her disability had ceased,

and ending with the month before the month in which she attains age 60, or, if earlier, with the close of the eighty-fourth month following the month with which such period began.

(5)(A) The waiting period referred to in paragraph (1)(F), in the case of any widow or surviving divorced wife, is the earliest period of five consecutive calendar months—

(i) throughout which she has been under a disability, and

(ii) which begins not earlier than with whichever of the following is the later: (I) the first day of the seventeenth month before the month in which her application is filed, or (II) the first day of the fifth month before the month in which the period specified in paragraph (4) begins.

(B) For purposes of paragraph (1)(F)(i), each month in the period commencing with the first month for which such widow or surviving divorced wife is first eligible for supplemental security income benefits under subchapter XVI of this chapter, or State supplementary payments of the type referred to in section 1382e(a) of this title (or payments of the type described in section 212(a) of Public Law 93–66) which are paid by the Commissioner of Social Security under an agreement referred to in section 1382e(a) of this title (or in section 212(b) of Public Law 93–66), shall be included as one of the months of such waiting period for which the requirements of subparagraph (A) have been met.

(6) In the case of an individual entitled to monthly insurance benefits payable under this section for any month prior to January 1973 whose benefits were not redetermined under section 102(g) of the Social Security Amendments of 1972, such benefits shall not be redetermined pursuant to such section, but shall be increased pursuant to any general benefit increase (as defined in section 415(i)(3) of this title) or any increase in benefits made under or pursuant to section 415(i) of this title, including for this purpose the increase provided effective for March 1974, as though such redetermination had been made.

(7) Any certificate filed pursuant to paragraph (1)(C)(ii)(III) shall be effective for purposes of this subsection—

(A) for the month in which it is filed and for any month thereafter, and

(B) for months, in the period designated by the individual filing such certificate, of one or more consecutive months (not exceeding 12) immediately preceding the month in which such certificate is filed;

except that such certificate shall not be effective for any month before the month in which she attains age 62.

(8) An individual shall be deemed to be under a disability for purposes of paragraph (1)(B)(ii) if such individual is eligible for supplemental security income benefits under subchapter XVI of this chapter, or State supplementary payments of the type referred to in section 1382e(a) of this title (or payments of the type described in section 212(a) of Public Law 93–66) which are paid by the Commissioner of Social Security under an agreement referred to in section 1382e(a) of this title (or in section 212(b) of Public Law 93–66), for the month for which all requirements of paragraph (1) for entitlement to benefits under this subsection (other than being under a disability) are met.

(f) Widower's insurance benefits

(1) The widower (as defined in section 416(g) of this title) and every surviving divorced husband (as defined in section 416(d) of this title) of an individual who died a fully insured individual, if such widower or such surviving divorced husband—

(A) is not married,

(B) (i) has attained age 60, or (ii) has attained age 50 but has not attained age 60 and is under a disability (as defined in section 423(d) of this title) which began before the end of the period specified in paragraph (4),

(C)(i) has filed application for widower's insurance benefits,

(ii) was entitled to husband's insurance benefits, on the basis of the wages and self-employment income of such individual, for the month preceding the month in which such individual died, and—

(I) has attained retirement age (as defined in section 416(*l*) of this title),

(II) is not entitled to benefits under subsection (a) of this section or section 423 of this title, or

(III) has in effect a certificate (described in paragraph (8)) filed by him with the Commissioner of Social Security, in accordance with regulations prescribed by the Commissioner of Social Security, in which he elects to receive widower's insurance benefits (subject to reduction as provided in subsection (q) of this section), or

(iii) was entitled, on the basis of such wages and self-employment income, to father's insurance benefits for the month preceding the month in which he attained retirement age (as defined in section 416(*l*) of this title), and

(D) is not entitled to old-age insurance benefits, or is entitled to old-age insurance benefits each of which is less than the primary insurance amount (as determined after application of subparagraphs (B) and (C) of paragraph (3)) of such deceased individual,

shall be entitled to a widower's insurance benefit for each month, beginning with—

(E) if he satisfies subparagraph (B) by reason of clause (i) thereof, the first month in which he becomes so entitled to such insurance benefits, or

(F) if he satisfies subparagraph (B) by reason of clause (ii) thereof—

(i) the first month after his waiting period (as defined in paragraph (5)) in which he becomes so entitled to such insurance benefits, or

(ii) the first month during all of which he is under a disability and in which he becomes so entitled to such insurance benefits, but only if he was previously entitled to insurance benefits under this subsection on the basis of being under a disability and such first month occurs (I) in the period specified in paragraph (4) and (II) after the month in which a previous entitlement to such benefits on such basis terminated,

and ending with the month preceding the first month in which any of the following occurs: he remarries, dies, or becomes entitled to an old-age insurance benefit equal to or exceeding the primary insurance amount (as determined after application of subparagraphs (B) and (C) of paragraph (3)) of such deceased individual, or, if he became entitled to such benefits before he attained age 60, subject to section 423(e) of this title, the termination month (unless he attains retirement age (as defined in section 416(*l*) of this title) on or before the last day of such termination month). For purposes of the preceding sentence, the termination month for any individual shall be the third month following the month in which his disability ceases; except that, in the case of an individual who has a period of trial work which ends as determined by application of section 422(c)(4)(A) of this title, the termination month shall be the earlier of (I) the third month following the earliest month after the end of such period of trial work with respect to which such individual is determined to no longer be suffering from a disabling physical or mental impairment, or (II) the third month following the earliest month in which such individual engages or is determined able to engage in substantial gainful activity, but in no event earlier than the first month occurring after the 36 months following such period of trial work in which he engages or is determined able to engage in substantial gainful activity.

(2)(A) Except as provided in subsection (k)(5) of this section, subsection (q) of this section, and subparagraph (D) of this paragraph, such widower's insurance benefit for each month shall be equal to the primary insurance amount (as determined for purposes of this subsection after application of subparagraphs (B) and (C)) of such deceased individual.

(B)(i) For purposes of this subsection, in any case in which such deceased individual dies before attaining age 62 and section 415(a)(1) of this title (as in effect after December 1978) is applicable in determining such individual's primary insurance amount—

(I) such primary insurance amount shall be determined under the formula set forth in section 415(a)(1)(B)(i) and (ii) of this title which is applicable to individuals who initially become eligible for old-age insurance benefits in the second year after the year specified in clause (ii),

(II) the year specified in clause (ii) shall be substituted for the second calendar year specified in section 415(b)(3)(A)(ii)(I) of this title, and

(III) such primary insurance amount shall be increased under section 415(i) of this title as if it were the primary insurance amount referred to in section 415(i)(2)(A)(ii)(II) of this title, except that it shall be increased only for years beginning after the first year after the year specified in clause (ii).

(ii) The year specified in this clause is the earlier of—

(I) the year in which the deceased individual attained age 60, or would have attained age 60 had she lived to that age, or

(II) the second year preceding the year in which the widower or surviving divorced husband first meets the requirements of paragraph (1)(B) or the second year preceding the year in which the deceased individual died, whichever is later.

(iii) This subparagraph shall apply with respect to any benefit under this subsection only to the extent its application does not result in a primary insurance amount for purposes of this subsection which is less than the primary insurance amount otherwise determined for such deceased individual under section 415 of this title.

(C) If such deceased individual was (or upon application would have been) entitled to an old-age insurance benefit which was increased (or subject to being increased) on account of delayed retirement under the provisions of subsection (w) of this section, then, for purposes of this subsection, such individual's primary insurance amount, if less than the old-age insurance benefit (increased, where applicable, under section 415(f)(5), 415(f)(6), or 415(f)(9)(B) of this title and under section 415(i) of this title as if such individual were still alive in the case of an individual who has died) which she was receiving (or would upon application have received) for the month prior to the month in which she died, shall be deemed to be equal to such old-age insurance benefit, and (notwithstanding the provisions of paragraph (3) of subsection (w) of this section) the number of increment months shall include any month in the months of the calendar year in which she died, prior to the month in which she died, which satisfy the conditions in paragraph (2) of subsection (w) of this section.

(D) If the deceased individual (on the basis of whose wages and self-employment income a widower or surviving divorced husband is entitled to widower's insurance benefits under this subsection) was, at any time, entitled to an old-age insurance benefit which was reduced by reason of the application of subsection (q) of this section, the widower's insurance benefit of such widower or surviving divorced husband for any month shall, if the amount of the widower's insurance benefit of such widower or surviving divorced husband (as determined under subparagraph (A) and after application of subsection (q) of this section) is greater than—

(i) the amount of the old-age insurance benefit to which such deceased individual would have been entitled (after application of subsection (q) of this section) for such month if such individual were still living and section 415(f)(5), 415(f)(6), or 415(f)(9)(B) of this title were applied, where applicable, and

(ii) 82½ percent of the primary insurance amount (as determined without regard to subparagraph (C)) of such deceased individual;

be reduced to the amount referred to in clause (i), or (if greater) the amount referred to in clause (ii).

(3) For purposes of paragraph (1), if—

(A) a widower or surviving divorced husband marries after attaining age 60 (or after attaining age 50 if he was entitled before such marriage occurred to benefits based on disability under this subsection), or

(B) a disabled widower or surviving divorced husband described in paragraph (1)(B)(ii) marries after attaining age 50,

such marriage shall be deemed not to have occurred.

(4) The period referred to in paragraph (1)(B)(ii), in the case of any widower or surviving divorced husband, is the period beginning with whichever of the following is the latest:

(A) the month in which occurred the death of the fully insured individual referred to in paragraph (1) on whose wages and self-employment income his benefits are or would be based,

(B) the last month for which he was entitled to father's insurance benefits on the basis of the wages and self-employment income of such individual, or

(C) the month in which a previous entitlement to widower's insurance benefits on the basis of such wages and self-employment income terminated because his disability had ceased,

and ending with the month before the month in which he attains age 60, or, if earlier, with the close of the eighty-fourth month following the month with which such period began.

(5)(A) The waiting period referred to in paragraph (1)(F), in the case of any widower or surviving divorced husband, is the earliest period of five consecutive calendar months—

(i) throughout which he has been under a disability, and

(ii) which begins not earlier than with whichever of the following is the later: (I) the first day of the seventeenth month before the month in which his application is filed, or (II) the first day of the fifth month before the month in which the period specified in paragraph (4) begins.

(B) For purposes of paragraph (1)(F)(i), each month in the period commencing with the first month for which such widower or surviving divorced husband is first eligible for supplemental security income benefits under subchapter XVI of this chapter, or State supplementary payments of the type referred to in section 1382e(a) of this title (or payments of the type described in section 212(a) of Public Law 93–66) which are paid by the Commissioner of Social Security under an agreement referred to in section 1382e(a) of this title (or in section 212(b) of Public Law 93–66), shall be included as one of the months of such waiting period for which the requirements of subparagraph (A) have been met.

(6) In the case of an individual entitled to monthly insurance benefits payable under this section for any month prior to January 1973 whose benefits were not redetermined under section 102(g) of the Social Security Amendments of 1972, such benefits shall not be redetermined pursuant to such section, but shall be increased pursuant to any general benefit increase (as defined in section 415(i)(3) of this title) or any increase in benefits made under or pursuant to section 415(i) of this title, including for this purpose the increase provided effective for March 1974, as though such redetermination had been made.

(7) Any certificate filed pursuant to paragraph (1)(C)(ii)(III) shall be effective for purposes of this subsection—

(A) for the month in which it is filed and for any month thereafter, and

(B) for months, in the period designated by the individual filing such certificate, of one or more consecutive months (not exceeding 12) immediately preceding the month in which such certificate is filed;

except that such certificate shall not be effective for any month before the month in which he attains age 62.

(8) An individual shall be deemed to be under a disability for purposes of paragraph (1)(B)(ii) if such individual is eligible for supplemental security income benefits under subchapter XVI of this chapter, or State supplementary payments of the type referred to in section 1382e(a) of this title (or payments of the type described in section 212(a) of Public Law 93–66) which are paid by the Commissioner of Social Security under an agreement referred to in such section 1382e(a) of this title (or in section 212(b) of Public Law 93–66), for the month for which all requirements of paragraph (1) for entitlement to benefits under this subsection (other than being under a disability) are met.

(g) Mother's and father's insurance benefits

(1) The surviving spouse and every surviving divorced parent (as defined in section 416(d) of this title) of an individual who died a fully or currently insured individual, if such surviving spouse or surviving divorced parent—

(A) is not married,

(B) is not entitled to a surviving spouse's insurance benefit,

(C) is not entitled to old-age insurance benefits, or is entitled to old-age insurance benefits each of which is less than three-fourths of the primary insurance amount of such individual,

(D) has filed application for mother's or father's insurance benefits, or was entitled to a spouse's insurance benefit on the basis of the wages and self-employment income of such individual for the month preceding the month in which such individual died,

(E) at the time of filing such application has in his or her care a child of such individual entitled to a child's insurance benefit, and

(F) in the case of a surviving divorced parent—

(i) the child referred to in subparagraph (E) is his or her son, daughter, or legally adopted child, and

(ii) the benefits referred to in such subparagraph are payable on the basis of such individual's wages and self-employment income,

shall (subject to subsection (s) of this section) be entitled to a mother's or father's insurance benefit for each month, beginning with the first month in which he or she becomes so entitled to such insurance benefits and ending with the month preceding the first month in which any of the following occurs: no child of such deceased individual is entitled to a child's insurance benefit, such surviving spouse or surviving divorced parent becomes entitled to an old-age insurance benefit equal to or exceeding three-fourths of the primary insurance amount of such deceased individual, he or she becomes entitled to a surviving spouse's insurance benefit, he or she remarries, or he or she dies. Entitlement to such benefits shall also end, in the case of a surviving divorced parent, with the month immediately preceding the first month in which no son, daughter, or legally adopted child of such surviving divorced parent is entitled to a child's insurance benefit on the basis of the wages and self-employment income of such deceased individual.

(2) Such mother's or father's insurance benefit for each month shall be equal to three-fourths of the primary insurance amount of such deceased individual.

(3) In the case of a surviving spouse or surviving divorced parent who marries—

(A) an individual entitled to benefits under this subsection or subsection (a), (b), (c), (e), (f), or (h) of this section, or under section 423(a) of this title, or

(B) an individual who has attained the age of eighteen and is entitled to benefits under subsection (d) of this section,

the entitlement of such surviving spouse or surviving divorced parent to benefits under this subsection shall, notwithstanding the provisions of paragraph (1) of this subsection but subject to subsection (s) of this section, not be terminated by reason of such marriage.

(h) Parent's insurance benefits

(1) Every parent (as defined in this subsection) of an individual who died a fully insured individual, if such parent—

(A) has attained age 62,

(B) (i) was receiving at least one-half of his support from such individual at the time of such individual's death or, if such individual had a period of disability which did not end prior to the month in which he died, at the time such period began or at the time of such death, and (ii) filed proof of such support within two years after the date of such death, or, if such individual had such a period of disability, within two years after the month in which such individual filed application with respect to such period of disability or two years after the date of such death, as the case may be,

(C) has not married since such individual's death,

(D) is not entitled to old-age insurance benefits, or is entitled to old-age insurance benefits each of which is less than 82½ percent of the primary insurance amount of such deceased individual if the amount of the parent's insurance benefit for such month is determinable under paragraph (2)(A) (or 75 percent of such primary insurance amount in any other case), and

(E) has filed application for parent's insurance benefits,

shall be entitled to a parent's insurance benefit for each month beginning with the first month after August 1950 in which such parent becomes so entitled to such parent's insurance benefits and ending with the month preceding the first month in which any of the following occurs: such parent dies, marries, or becomes entitled to an old-age insurance benefit equal to or exceeding 82½ percent of the primary insurance amount of such deceased individual if the amount of the parent's insurance benefit for such month is determinable under paragraph (2)(A) (or 75 percent of such primary insurance amount in any other case).

(2)(A) Except as provided in subparagraphs (B) and (C), such parent's insurance benefit for each month shall be equal to 82½ percent of the primary insurance amount of such deceased individual.

(B) For any month for which more than one parent is entitled to parent's insurance benefits on the basis of such deceased individual's wages and self-employment income, such benefit for each such parent for such month shall (except as provided in subparagraph (C)) be equal to 75 percent of the primary insurance amount of such deceased individual.

(C) In any case in which—

(i) any parent is entitled to a parent's insurance benefit for a month on the basis of a deceased individual's wages and self-employment income, and

(ii) another parent of such deceased individual is entitled to a parent's insurance benefit for such month on the basis of such wages and self-employment income, and on the basis of an application filed after such month and after the month in which the application for the parent's benefits referred to in clause (i) was filed,

the amount of the parent's insurance benefit of the parent referred to in clause (i) for the month referred to in such clause shall be determined under subparagraph (A) instead of subparagraph (B) and the amount of the parent's insurance benefit of a parent referred to in clause (ii) for such month shall be equal to 150 percent of the primary insurance amount of the deceased individual minus the amount (before the application of section 403(a) of this title) of the benefit for such month of the parent referred to in clause (i).

(3) As used in this subsection, the term "parent" means the mother or father of an individual, a stepparent of an individual by a marriage contracted before such individual attained the age of sixteen, or an adopting parent by whom an individual was adopted before he attained the age of sixteen.

(4) In the case of a parent who marries—

(A) an individual entitled to benefits under this subsection or subsection (b), (c), (e), (f), or (g) of this section, or

(B) an individual who has attained the age of eighteen and is entitled to benefits under subsection (d) of this section,

such parent's entitlement to benefits under this subsection shall, notwithstanding the provisions of paragraph (1) of this subsection but subject to subsection (s) of this section, not be terminated by reason of such marriage.

(i) Lump-sum death payments

Upon the death, after August 1950, of an individual who died a fully or currently insured individual, an amount equal to three times such individual's primary insurance amount (as determined without regard to the amendments made by section 2201 of the Omnibus Budget Reconciliation Act of 1981, relating to the repeal of the minimum benefit provisions), or an amount equal to $255, whichever is the smaller, shall be paid in a lump sum to the person, if any, determined by the Commissioner of Social Security to be the widow or widower of the deceased and to have been living in the same household with the deceased at the time of death. If there is no such person, or if such person dies before receiving payment, then such amount shall be paid—

(1) to a widow (as defined in section 416(c) of this title) or widower (as defined in section 416(g) of this title) who is entitled (or would have been so entitled had a timely application been filed), on the basis of the wages and self-employment income of such insured individual, to benefits under subsection (e), (f), or (g) of this section for the month in which occurred such individual's death; or

(2) if no person qualifies for payment under paragraph (1), or if such person dies before receiving payment, in equal shares to each person who is entitled (or would have been so entitled had a timely application been filed), on the basis of the wages and self-employment income of such insured individual, to benefits under subsection (d) of this section for the month in which occurred such individual's death.

No payment shall be made to any person under this subsection unless application therefor shall have been filed, by or on behalf of such person (whether or not legally competent), prior to the expiration of two years after the date of death of such insured individual, or unless such person was entitled to wife's or husband's insurance benefits, on the basis of the wages and self-employment income of such insured individual, for the month preceding the month in which such individual died. In the case of any individual who died outside the forty-eight States and the District of Columbia after December 1953 and before January 1, 1957, whose death occurred while he was in the active military or naval service of the United States, and who is returned to any of such States, the District of Columbia, Alaska, Hawaii, the Commonwealth of Puerto Rico, the Virgin Islands, Guam, or American Samoa for interment or reinterment, the provisions of the preceding sentence shall not prevent payment to any person under the second sentence of this subsection if application for a lump-sum death payment with respect to such deceased individual is filed by or on behalf of such person (whether or not legally competent) prior to the expiration of two years after the date of such interment or reinterment. In the case of any individual who died outside the fifty States and the District of Columbia after December 1956 while he was performing service, as a member of a uniformed service, to which the provisions of section 410(*l*)(1) of this title are applicable, and who is returned to any State, or to any Territory or possession of the United States, for interment or reinterment, the provisions of the third sentence of this subsection shall not prevent payment to any person under the second sentence of this subsection if application for a lump-sum death payment with respect to such deceased individual is filed by or on behalf of such person (whether or not legally competent) prior to the expiration of two years after the date of such interment or reinterment.

(j) Application for monthly insurance benefits

(1) Subject to the limitations contained in paragraph (4), an individual who would have been entitled to a benefit under subsection (a), (b), (c), (d), (e), (f), (g), or (h) of this section for any month after August 1950 had he filed application therefor prior to the end of such month shall be entitled to such benefit for such month if he files application therefor prior to—

(A) the end of the twelfth month immediately succeeding such month in any case where the individual (i) is filing application for a benefit under subsection (e) or (f) of this section, and satisfies paragraph (1)(B) of such subsection by reason of clause (ii) thereof, or (ii) is filing application for a benefit under subsection (b), (c), or (d) of this section on the basis of the wages and self-employment income of a person entitled to disability insurance benefits, or

(B) the end of the sixth month immediately succeeding such month in any case where subparagraph (A) does not apply.

Any benefit under this subchapter for a month prior to the month in which application is filed shall be reduced, to any extent that may be necessary, so that it will not render erroneous any benefit which, before the filing of such application, the Commissioner of Social Security has certified for payment for such prior month.

(2) An application for any monthly benefits under this section filed before the first month in which the applicant satisfies the requirements for such benefits shall be deemed a valid application (and shall be deemed to have been filed in such first month) only if the applicant satisfies the requirements for such benefits before the Commissioner of Social Security makes a final decision on the application and no request under section 405(b) of this title for notice and opportunity for a hearing thereon is made or, if such a request is made, before a decision based upon the evidence adduced at the hearing is made (regardless of whether such decision becomes the final decision of the Commissioner of Social Security).

(3) Notwithstanding the provisions of paragraph (1), an individual may, at his option, waive entitlement to any benefit referred to in paragraph (1) for any one or more consecutive months (beginning with the earliest month for which such individual would otherwise be entitled to such benefit) which occur before the month in which such individual files application for such benefit; and, in such case, such individual shall not be considered as entitled to such benefits for any such month or months before such individual filed such application. An individual shall be deemed to have waived such entitlement for any such month for which such benefit would, under the second sentence of paragraph (1), be reduced to zero.

(4)(A) Except as provided in subparagraph (B), no individual shall be entitled to a monthly benefit under subsection (a), (b), (c), (e), or (f) of this section for any month prior to the month in which he or she files an application for benefits under that subsection if the amount of the monthly benefit to which such individual would otherwise be entitled for any such month would be subject to reduction pursuant to subsection (q) of this section.

(B)(i) If the individual applying for retroactive benefits is a widow, surviving divorced wife, or widower and is under a disability (as defined in section 423(d) of this title), and such individual would, except for subparagraph (A), be entitled to retroactive benefits as a disabled widow or widower or disabled surviving divorced wife for any month before attaining the age of 60, then subparagraph (A) shall not apply with respect to such month or any subsequent month.

(ii) Subparagraph (A) does not apply to a benefit under subsection (e) or (f) of this section for the month immediately preceding the month of application, if the insured individual died in that preceding month.

(iii) As used in this subparagraph, the term "retroactive benefits" means benefits to which an individual becomes entitled for a month prior to the month in which application for such benefits is filed.

(5) In any case in which it is determined to the satisfaction of the Commissioner of Social Security that an individual failed as of any date to apply for monthly insurance benefits under this subchapter by reason of misinformation provided to such individual by any officer or employee of the

Social Security Administration relating to such individual's eligibility for benefits under this subchapter, such individual shall be deemed to have applied for such benefits on the later of—

(A) the date on which such misinformation was provided to such individual, or

(B) the date on which such individual met all requirements for entitlement to such benefits (other than application therefor).

(k) Simultaneous entitlement to benefits

(1) A child, entitled to child's insurance benefits on the basis of the wages and self-employment income of an insured individual, who would be entitled, on filing application, to child's insurance benefits on the basis of the wages and self-employment income of some other insured individual, shall be deemed entitled, subject to the provisions of paragraph (2) of this subsection, to child's insurance benefits on the basis of the wages and self-employment income of such other individual if an application for child's insurance benefits on the basis of the wages and self-employment income of such other individual has been filed by any other child who would, on filing application, be entitled to child's insurance benefits on the basis of the wages and self-employment income of both such insured individuals.

(2)(A) Any child who under the preceding provisions of this section is entitled for any month to child's insurance benefits on the wages and self-employment income of more than one insured individual shall, notwithstanding such provisions, be entitled to only one of such child's insurance benefits for such month. Such child's insurance benefits for such month shall be the benefit based on the wages and self-employment income of the insured individual who has the greatest primary insurance amount, except that such child's insurance benefits for such month shall be the largest benefit to which such child could be entitled under subsection (d) of this section (without the application of section 403(a) of this title) or subsection (m) of this section if entitlement to such benefit would not, with respect to any person, result in a benefit lower (after the application of section 403(a) of this title) than the benefit which would be applicable if such child were entitled on the wages and self-employment income of the individual with the greatest primary insurance amount. Where more than one child is entitled to child's insurance benefits pursuant to the preceding provisions of this paragraph, each such child who is entitled on the wages and self-employment income of the same insured individuals shall be entitled on the wages and self-employment income of the same such insured individual.

(B) Any individual (other than an individual to whom subsection (e)(3) or (f)(3) of this section applies) who, under the preceding provisions of this section and under the provisions of section 423 of this title, is entitled for any month to more than one monthly insurance benefit (other than an old-age or disability insurance benefit) under this subchapter shall be entitled to only one such monthly benefit for such month, such benefit to be the largest of the monthly benefits to which he (but for this subparagraph) would otherwise be entitled for such month. Any individual who is entitled for any month to more than one widow's or widower's insurance benefit to which subsection (e)(3) or (f)(3) of this section applies shall be entitled to only one such benefit for such month, such benefit to be the largest of such benefits.

(3)(A) If an individual is entitled to an old-age or disability insurance benefit for any month and to any other monthly insurance benefit for such month, such other insurance benefit for such month, after any reduction under subsection (q), subsection (e)(2) or (f)(2) of this section, and any reduction under section 403(a) of this title, shall be reduced, but not below zero, by an amount equal to such old-age or disability insurance benefit (after reduction under such subsection (q) of this section).

(B) If an individual is entitled for any month to a widow's or widower's insurance benefit to which subsection (e)(3) or (f)(3) of this section applies and to any other monthly insurance benefit under this section (other than an old-age insurance benefit), such other insurance benefit for such month, after any reduction under subparagraph (A) of this paragraph, any reduction under subsection (q) of this section, and any reduction under section 403(a) of this title, shall be reduced, but not below zero, by an amount equal to such widow's or widower's insurance benefit after any reduction or reductions under such subparagraph (A) and such section 403(a).

(4) Any individual who, under this section and section 423 of this title, is entitled for any month to both an old-age insurance benefit and a disability insurance benefit under this subchapter shall be entitled to only the larger of such benefits for such month, except that, if such individual so elects, he shall instead be entitled to only the smaller of such benefits for such month.

(5)(A) The amount of a monthly insurance benefit of any individual for each month under subsection (b), (c), (e), (f), or (g) of this section (as determined after application of the provisions of subsection (q) of this section and the preceding provisions of this subsection) shall be reduced (but not below zero) by an amount equal to two-thirds of the amount of any monthly periodic benefit payable to such individual for such month which is based upon such individual's earnings while in the service of the Federal Government or any State (or political subdivision thereof, as defined in section 418(b)(2) of this title) if, during any portion of the last 60 months of such service ending with the last day such individual was employed by such entity—

(i) such service did not constitute "employment" as defined in section 410 of this title, or

(ii) such service was being performed while in the service of the Federal Government, and constituted "employment" as so defined solely by reason of—

(I) clause (ii) or (iii) of subparagraph (G) of section 410(a)(5) of this title, where the lump-sum payment described in such clause (ii) or the cessation of coverage described in such clause (iii) (whichever is applicable) was received or occurred on or after January 1, 1988, or

(II) an election to become subject to the Federal Employees' Retirement System provided in chapter 84 of Title 5 or the Foreign Service Pension System provided in subchapter II of chapter 8 of title I of the Foreign Service Act of 1980 [22 U.S.C.A. 4071 et seq.] made pursuant to law after December 31, 1987, unless subparagraph (B) applies.

The amount of the reduction in any benefit under this subparagraph, if not a multiple of $0.10, shall be rounded to the next higher multiple of $0.10.

(B)(i) Subparagraph (A)(i) shall not apply with respect to monthly periodic benefits based wholly on service as a member of a uniformed service (as defined in section 410(m) of this title).

(ii) Subparagraph (A)(ii) shall not apply with respect to monthly periodic benefits based in whole or in part on service which constituted "employment" as defined in section 410 of this title if such service was performed for at least 60 months in the aggregate during the period beginning January 1, 1988, and ending with the close of the first calendar month as of the end of which such individual is eligible for benefits under this subsection and has made a valid application for such benefits.

(C) For purposes of this paragraph, any periodic benefit which otherwise meets the requirements of subparagraph (A), but which is paid on other than a monthly basis, shall be allocated on a basis equivalent to a monthly benefit (as determined by the Commissioner of Social Security) and such equivalent monthly benefit shall constitute a monthly periodic benefit for purposes of subparagraph (A). For purposes of this subparagraph, the term "periodic benefit" includes a benefit payable in a lump sum if it is a commutation of, or a substitute for, periodic payments.

(*l*) Entitlement to survivor benefits under railroad retirement provisions

If any person would be entitled, upon filing application therefor to an annuity under section 2 of the Railroad Retirement Act of 1974 [45 U.S.C.A. § 231a], or to a lump-sum payment under section 6(b) of such Act [45 U.S.C.A. § 231e(b)], with respect to the death of an employee (as defined in such Act) no lump-sum death payment, and no monthly benefit for the month in which such employee died or for any month thereafter, shall be paid under this section to any person on the basis of the wages and self-employment income of such employee.

(m) Repealed. Pub.L. 97–35, Title XXII, § 2201(b)(10), Aug. 13, 1981, 95 Stat. 831

(n) Termination of benefits upon removal of primary beneficiary

(1) If any individual is (after September 1, 1954) removed under section 1227(a) of Title 8 (other than under paragraph (1)(C) of such section) or under section 1182(a)(6)(A) of Title 8, then, notwithstanding any other provisions of this subchapter—

(A) no monthly benefit under this section or section 423 of this title shall be paid to such individual, on the basis of his wages and self-employment income, for any month occurring (i) after the month in which the Commissioner of Social Security is notified by the Attorney General or the Secretary of Homeland Security that such individual has been so removed, and (ii) before the month in which such individual is thereafter lawfully admitted to the United States for permanent residence,

(B) if no benefit could be paid to such individual (or if no benefit could be paid to him if he were alive) for any month by reason of subparagraph (A), no monthly benefit under this section shall be paid, on the basis of his wages and self-employment income, for such month to any other person who is not a citizen of the United States and is outside the United States for any part of such month, and

(C) no lump-sum death payment shall be made on the basis of such individual's wages and self-employment income if he dies (i) in or after the month in which such notice is received, and (ii) before the month in which he is thereafter lawfully admitted to the United States for permanent residence.

Section 403(b), (c), and (d) of this title shall not apply with respect to any such individual for any month for which no monthly benefit may be paid to him by reason of this paragraph.

(2)(A) In the case of the removal of any individual under any of the paragraphs of section 1227(a) of Title 8 (other than under paragraph (1)(C) of such section) or under section 1182(a)(6)(A) of Title 8, the revocation and setting aside of citizenship of any individual under section 1451 of Title 8 in any case in which the revocation and setting aside is based on conduct described in section 1182(a)(3)(E)(i) of Title 8 (relating to participation in Nazi persecution), or the renunciation of nationality by any individual under section 1481(a)(5) of Title 8 pursuant to a settlement agreement with the Attorney General where the individual has admitted to conduct described in section 1182(a)(3)(E)(i) of Title 8 (relating to participation in Nazi persecution) occurring after December 18, 2014, the Attorney General or the Secretary of Homeland Security shall notify the Commissioner of Social Security of such removal, revocation and setting aside, or renunciation of nationality not later than 7 days after such removal, revocation and setting aside, or renunciation of nationality (or, in the case of any such removal, revocation and setting aside, of[1] renunciation of nationality that has occurred prior to December 18, 2014, not later than 7 days after December 18, 2014).

(B)(i) Not later than 30 days after December 18, 2014, the Attorney General shall certify to the Committee on Ways and Means of the House of Representatives and the Committee on Finance of the Senate that the Commissioner of Social Security has been notified of each removal, revocation and setting aside, or renunciation of nationality described in subparagraph (A).

(ii) Not later than 30 days after each notification with respect to an individual under subparagraph (A), the Commissioner of Social Security shall certify to the Committee on Ways and Means of the House of Representatives and the Committee on Finance of the Senate that such individual's benefits were terminated under this subsection.

(3) For purposes of paragraphs (1) and (2) of this subsection—

(A) an individual against whom a final order of removal has been issued under section 1227(a)(4)(D) of Title 8 on grounds of participation in Nazi persecution shall be considered to have been removed under such section as of the date on which such order became final;

(B) an individual with respect to whom an order admitting the individual to citizenship has been revoked and set aside under section 1451 of Title 8 in any case in which the revocation and setting aside is based on conduct described in section 1182(a)(3)(E)(i) of Title 8 (relating to participation in Nazi persecution), concealment of a material fact about such conduct, or willful misrepresentation about such conduct shall be considered to have been removed as described in paragraph (1) as of the date of such revocation and setting aside; and

(C) an individual who pursuant to a settlement agreement with the Attorney General has admitted to conduct described in section 1182(a)(3)(E)(i) of Title 8 (relating to participation in Nazi persecution) and who pursuant to such settlement agreement has lost status as a national of the United States by a renunciation under section 1481(a)(5) of Title 8 shall be considered to have been removed as described in paragraph (1) as of the date of such renunciation.

(4) In the case of any individual described in paragraph (3) whose monthly benefits are terminated under paragraph (1)—

(A) no benefits otherwise available under this section based on the wages and self-employment income of any other individual shall be paid to such individual for any month after such termination; and

(B) no supplemental security income benefits under subchapter XVI shall be paid to such individual for any such month, including supplementary payments pursuant to an agreement for Federal administration under section 1382e(a) of this title and payments pursuant to an agreement entered into under section 212(b) of Public Law 93–66 [2]

(*o*) Application for benefits by survivors of members and former members of uniformed services

In the case of any individual who would be entitled to benefits under subsection (d), (e), (g), or (h) of this section upon filing proper application therefor, the filing with the Administrator of Veterans' Affairs by or on behalf of such individual of an application for such benefits, on the form described in section 5105 of Title 38, shall satisfy the requirement of such subsection (d), (e), (g), or (h) that an application for such benefits be filed.

(p) Extension of period for filing proof of support and applications for lump-sum death payment

In any case in which there is a failure—

(1) to file proof of support under subparagraph (B) of subsection (h)(1) of this section, or under clause (B) of subsection (f)(1) of this section as in effect prior to the Social Security Act Amendments of 1950, within the period prescribed by such subparagraph or clause, or

(2) to file, in the case of a death after 1946, application for a lump-sum death payment under subsection (i) of this section, or under subsection (g) of this section as in effect prior to the Social Security Act Amendments of 1950, within the period prescribed by such subsection,

any such proof or application, as the case may be, which is filed after the expiration of such period shall be deemed to have been filed within such period if it is shown to the satisfaction of the Commissioner of Social Security that there was good cause for failure to file such proof or application within such period. The determination of what constitutes good cause for purposes of this subsection shall be made in accordance with regulations of the Commissioner of Social Security.

(q) Reduction of benefit amounts for certain beneficiaries

(1) Subject to paragraph (9), if the first month for which an individual is entitled to an old-age, wife's, husband's, widow's, or widower's insurance benefit is a month before the month in which such individual attains retirement age, the amount of such benefit for such month and for any subsequent month shall, subject to the succeeding paragraphs of this subsection, be reduced by—

(A) $5/9$ of 1 percent of such amount if such benefit is an old-age insurance benefit, $25/36$ of 1 percent of such amount if such benefit is a wife's or husband's insurance benefit, or $19/40$ of 1 percent of such amount if such benefit is a widow's or widower's insurance benefit, multiplied by

(B)(i) the number of months in the reduction period for such benefit (determined under paragraph (6)), if such benefit is for a month before the month in which such individual attains retirement age, or

(ii) if less, the number of such months in the adjusted reduction period for such benefit (determined under paragraph (7)), if such benefit is (I) for the month in which such individual attains age 62, or (II) for the month in which such individual attains retirement age.

(2) If an individual is entitled to a disability insurance benefit for a month after a month for which such individual was entitled to an old-age insurance benefit, such disability insurance benefit for each month shall be reduced by the amount such old-age insurance benefit would be reduced under paragraphs (1) and (4) for such month had such individual attained retirement age (as defined in section 416(*l*) of this title) in the first month for which he most recently became entitled to a disability insurance benefit.

(3)(A) If the first month for which an individual both is entitled to a wife's, husband's, widow's, or widower's insurance benefit and has attained age 62 (in the case of a wife's or husband's insurance benefit) or age 50 (in the case of a widow's or widower's insurance benefit) is a month for which such individual is also entitled to—

(i) an old-age insurance benefit (to which such individual was first entitled for a month before he attains retirement age (as defined in section 416(*l*) of this title)), or

(ii) a disability insurance benefit,

then in lieu of any reduction under paragraph (1) (but subject to the succeeding paragraphs of this subsection) such wife's, husband's, widow's, or widower's insurance benefit for each month shall be reduced as provided in subparagraph (B), (C), or (D).

(B) For any month for which such individual is entitled to an old-age insurance benefit and is not entitled to a disability insurance benefit, such individual's wife's or husband's insurance benefit shall be reduced by the sum of—

(i) the amount by which such old-age insurance benefit is reduced under paragraph (1) for such month, and

(ii) the amount by which such wife's or husband's insurance benefit would be reduced under paragraph (1) for such month if it were equal to the excess of such wife's or husband's insurance benefit (before reduction under this subsection) over such old-age insurance benefit (before reduction under this subsection).

(C) For any month for which such individual is entitled to a disability insurance benefit, such individual's wife's, husband's, widow's, or widower's insurance benefit shall be reduced by the sum of—

(i) the amount by which such disability insurance benefit is reduced under paragraph (2) for such month (if such paragraph applied to such benefit), and

(ii) the amount by which such wife's, husband's, widow's, or widower's insurance benefit would be reduced under paragraph (1) for such month if it were equal to the excess of such wife's, husband's, widow's, or widower's insurance benefit (before reduction under this subsection) over such disability insurance benefit (before reduction under this subsection).

(D) For any month for which such individual is entitled neither to an old-age insurance benefit nor to a disability insurance benefit, such individual's wife's, husband's, widow's, or widower's insurance benefit shall be reduced by the amount by which it would be reduced under paragraph (1).

(E) Notwithstanding subparagraph (A) of this paragraph, if the first month for which an individual is entitled to a widow's or widower's insurance benefit is a month for which such individual is also entitled to an old-age insurance benefit to which such individual was first entitled for that month or for a month before she or he became entitled to a widow's or widower's benefit, the reduction in such widow's or widower's insurance benefit shall be determined under paragraph (1).

(4) If—

(A) an individual is or was entitled to a benefit subject to reduction under paragraph (1) or (3) of this subsection, and

(B) such benefit is increased by reason of an increase in the primary insurance amount of the individual on whose wages and self-employment income such benefit is based,

then the amount of the reduction of such benefit (after the application of any adjustment under paragraph (7)) for each month beginning with the month of such increase in the primary insurance amount shall be computed under paragraph (1) or (3), whichever applies, as though the increased primary insurance amount had been in effect for and after the month for which the individual first became entitled to such monthly benefit reduced under such paragraph (1) or (3).

(5)(A) No wife's or husband's insurance benefit shall be reduced under this subsection—

(i) for any month before the first month for which there is in effect a certificate filed by him or her with the Commissioner of Social Security, in accordance with regulations prescribed by the Commissioner of Social Security, in which he or she elects to receive wife's or husband's insurance benefits reduced as provided in this subsection, or

(ii) for any month in which he or she has in his or her care (individually or jointly with the person on whose wages and self-employment income the wife's or husband's insurance benefit is based) a child of such person entitled to child's insurance benefits.

(B) Any certificate described in subparagraph (A)(i) shall be effective for purposes of this subsection (and for purposes of preventing deductions under section 403(c)(2) of this title)—

(i) for the month in which it is filed and for any month thereafter, and

(ii) for months, in the period designated by the individual filing such certificate, of one or more consecutive months (not exceeding 12) immediately preceding the month in which such certificate is filed;

except that such certificate shall not be effective for any month before the month in which he or she attains age 62, nor shall it be effective for any month to which subparagraph (A)(ii) applies.

(C) If an individual does not have in his or her care a child described in subparagraph (A)(ii) in the first month for which he or she is entitled to a wife's or husband's insurance benefit, and if such first month is a month before the month in which he or she attains retirement age (as defined in section 416(*l*) of this title), he or she shall be deemed to have filed in such first month the certificate described in subparagraph (A)(i).

(D) No widow's or widower's insurance benefit for a month in which he or she has in his or her care a child of his or her deceased spouse (or deceased former spouse) entitled to child's insurance benefits shall be reduced under this subsection below the amount to which he or she would have been entitled had he or she been entitled for such month to mother's or father's insurance benefits on the basis of his or her deceased spouse's (or deceased former spouse's) wages and self-employment income.

(6) For purposes of this subsection, the "reduction period" for an individual's old-age, wife's, husband's, widow's, or widower's insurance benefit is the period—

(A) beginning—

(i) in the case of an old-age insurance benefit, with the first day of the first month for which such individual is entitled to such benefit,

(ii) in the case of a wife's or husband's insurance benefit, with the first day of the first month for which a certificate described in paragraph (5)(A)(i) is effective, or

(iii) in the case of a widow's or widower's insurance benefit, with the first day of the first month for which such individual is entitled to such benefit or the first day of the month in which such individual attains age 60, whichever is the later, and

(B) ending with the last day of the month before the month in which such individual attains retirement age.

(7) For purposes of this subsection, the "adjusted reduction period" for an individual's old-age, wife's, husband's, widow's, or widower's insurance benefit is the reduction period prescribed in paragraph (6) for such benefit, excluding—

(A) any month in which such benefit was subject to deductions under section 403(b), 403(c)(1), 403(d)(1), or 422(b) of this title,

(B) in the case of wife's or husband's insurance benefits, any month in which such individual had in his or her care (individually or jointly with the person on whose wages and self-employment income such benefit is based) a child of such person entitled to child's insurance benefits,

(C) in the case of wife's or husband's insurance benefits, any month for which such individual was not entitled to such benefits because of the occurrence of an event that terminated her or his entitlement to such benefits,

(D) in the case of widow's or widower's insurance benefits, any month in which the reduction in the amount of such benefit was determined under paragraph (5)(D),

(E) in the case of widow's or widower's insurance benefits, any month before the month in which she or he attained age 62, and also for any later month before the month in which she or he attained retirement age, for which she or he was not entitled to such benefit because of the occurrence of an event that terminated her or his entitlement to such benefits, and

(F) in the case of old-age insurance benefits, any month for which such individual was entitled to a disability insurance benefit.

(8) This subsection shall be applied after reduction under section 403(a) of this title and before application of section 415(g) of this title. If the amount of any reduction computed under paragraph (1), (2), or (3) is not a multiple of $0.10, it shall be increased to the next higher multiple of $0.10.

(9) The amount of the reduction for early retirement specified in paragraph (1)—

(A) for old-age insurance benefits, wife's insurance benefits, and husband's insurance benefits, shall be the amount specified in such paragraph for the first 36 months of the reduction period (as defined in paragraph (6)) or adjusted reduction period (as defined in paragraph (7)), and five-twelfths of 1 percent for any additional months included in such periods; and

(B) for widow's insurance benefits and widower's insurance benefits, shall be periodically revised by the Commissioner of Social Security such that—

(i) the amount of the reduction at early retirement age as defined in section 416(*l*) of this title shall be 28.5 percent of the full benefit; and

(ii) the amount of the reduction for each month in the reduction period (specified in paragraph (6)) or the adjusted reduction period (specified in paragraph (7)) shall be established by linear interpolation between 28.5 percent at the month of attainment of early retirement age and 0 percent at the month of attainment of retirement age.

(10) For purposes of applying paragraph (4), with respect to monthly benefits payable for any month after December 1977 to an individual who was entitled to a monthly benefit as reduced under paragraph (1) or (3) prior to January 1978, the amount of reduction in such benefit for the first month for which such benefit is increased by reason of an increase in the primary insurance amount of the individual on whose wages and self-employment income such benefit is based and for all subsequent months (and similarly for all subsequent increases) shall be increased by a percentage equal to the percentage increase in such primary insurance amount (such increase being made in accordance with the provisions of paragraph (8)). In the case of an individual whose reduced benefit under this section is increased as a result of the use of an adjusted reduction period (in accordance with paragraphs (1) and (3) of this subsection), then for the first month for which such increase is effective, and for all subsequent months, the amount of such reduction (after the application of the previous sentence, if applicable) shall be determined—

(A) in the case of old-age, wife's, and husband's insurance benefits, by multiplying such amount by the ratio of (i) the number of months in the adjusted reduction period to (ii) the number of months in the reduction period,

(B) in the case of widow's and widower's insurance benefits for the month in which such individual attains age 62, by multiplying such amount by the ratio of (i) the number of months in the reduction period beginning with age 62 multiplied by $^{19}/_{40}$ of 1 percent, plus the number of months in the adjusted reduction period prior to age 62 multiplied by $^{19}/_{40}$ of 1 percent to (ii) the number of months in the reduction period multiplied by $^{19}/_{40}$ of 1 percent, and

(C) in the case of widow's and widower's insurance benefits for the month in which such individual attains retirement age (as defined in section 416(*l*) of this title), by multiplying such amount by the ratio of (i) the number of months in the adjusted reduction period multiplied by $^{19}/_{40}$ of 1 percent to (ii) the number of months in the reduction period beginning with age 62 multiplied by $^{19}/_{40}$ of 1 percent, plus the number of months in the adjusted reduction period prior to age 62 multiplied by $^{19}/_{40}$ of 1 percent,

such determination being made in accordance with the provisions of paragraph (8).

(11) When an individual is entitled to more than one monthly benefit under this subchapter and one or more of such benefits are reduced under this subsection, paragraph (10) shall apply separately to each such benefit reduced under this subsection before the application of subsection (k) of this section (pertaining to the method by which monthly benefits are offset when an individual is entitled to more than one kind of benefit) and the application of this paragraph shall operate in conjunction with paragraph (3).

(r) Presumed filing of application by individuals eligible for old-age insurance benefits and for wife's or husband's insurance benefits

(1) If an individual is eligible for a wife's or husband's insurance benefit (except in the case of eligibility pursuant to clause (ii) of subsection (b)(1)(B) or subsection (c)(1)(B), as appropriate), in any month for which the individual is entitled to an old-age insurance benefit, such individual shall be deemed to have filed an application for wife's or husband's insurance benefits for such month.

(2) If an individual is eligible (but for subsection (k)(4)) for an old-age insurance benefit in any month for which the individual is entitled to a wife's or husband's insurance benefit (except in the case of entitlement pursuant to clause (ii) of subsection (b)(1)(B) or subsection (c)(1)(B), as appropriate), such individual shall be deemed to have filed an application for old-age insurance benefits—

(A) for such month, or

(B) if such individual is also entitled to a disability insurance benefit for such month, in the first subsequent month for which such individual is not entitled to a disability insurance benefit.

(3) For purposes of this subsection, an individual shall be deemed eligible for a benefit for a month if, upon filing application therefor in such month, he would be entitled to such benefit for such month.

(s) Child over specified age to be disregarded for certain benefit purposes unless disabled

(1) For the purposes of subsections (b)(1), (c)(1), (g)(1), (q)(5), and (q)(7) of this section and paragraphs (2), (3), and (4) of section 403(c) of this title, a child who is entitled to child's insurance benefits under subsection (d) of this section for any month, and who has attained the age of 16 but is not in such month under a disability (as defined in section 423(d) of this title), shall be deemed not entitled to such benefits for such month, unless he was under such a disability in the third month before such month.

(2) So much of subsections (b)(3), (c)(4), (d)(5), (g)(3), and (h)(4) of this section as precedes the semicolon, shall not apply in the case of any child unless such child, at the time of the marriage referred to therein, was under a disability (as defined in section 423(d) of this title) or had been under such a disability in the third month before the month in which such marriage occurred.

(3) The last sentence of subsection (c) of section 403 of this title, subsection (f)(1)(C) of section 403 of this title, and subsections (b)(3)(B), (c)(6)(B), (f)(3)(B), and (g)(6)(B) of section 416 of this title shall not apply in the case of any child with respect to any month referred to therein unless in such month or the third month prior thereto such child was under a disability (as defined in section 423(d) of this title).

(t) Suspension of benefits of aliens who are outside United States; residency requirements for dependents and survivors

(1) Notwithstanding any other provision of this subchapter, no monthly benefits shall be paid under this section or under section 423 of this title to any individual who is not a citizen or national of the United States for any month which is—

(A) after the sixth consecutive calendar month during all of which the Commissioner of Social Security finds, on the basis of information furnished to the Commissioner by the Attorney General or information which otherwise comes to the Commissioner's attention, that such individual is outside the United States, and

(B) prior to the first month thereafter for all of which such individual has been in the United States.

For purposes of the preceding sentence, after an individual has been outside the United States for any period of thirty consecutive days he shall be treated as remaining outside the United States until he has been in the United States for a period of thirty consecutive days.

(2) Subject to paragraph (11), paragraph (1) of this subsection shall not apply to any individual who is a citizen of a foreign country which the Commissioner of Social Security finds has in effect a social insurance or pension system which is of general application in such country and under which—

(A) periodic benefits, or the actuarial equivalent thereof, are paid on account of old age, retirement, or death, and

(B) individuals who are citizens of the United States but not citizens of such foreign country and who qualify for such benefits are permitted to receive such benefits or the actuarial equivalent thereof while outside such foreign country without regard to the duration of the absence.

(3) Paragraph (1) of this subsection shall not apply in any case where its application would be contrary to any treaty obligation of the United States in effect on August 1, 1956.

(4) Subject to paragraph (11), paragraph (1) of this subsection shall not apply to any benefit for any month if—

(A) not less than forty of the quarters elapsing before such month are quarters of coverage for the individual on whose wages and self-employment income such benefit is based, or

(B) the individual on whose wages and self-employment income such benefit is based has, before such month, resided in the United States for a period or periods aggregating ten years or more, or

(C) the individual entitled to such benefit is outside the United States while in the active military or naval service of the United States, or

(D) the individual on whose wages and self-employment income such benefit is based died, before such month, either (i) while on active duty or inactive duty training (as those terms are defined in section 410(*l*)(2) and (3) of this title) as a member of a uniformed service (as defined in section 410(m) of this title), or (ii) as the result of a disease or injury which the Secretary of Veterans Affairs determines was incurred or aggravated in line of duty while on active duty (as defined in section 410(*l*)(2) of this title), or an injury which he determines was incurred or aggravated in line of duty while on inactive duty training (as defined in section 410(*l*)(3) of this title), as a member of a uniformed service (as defined in section 410(m) of this title), if the Secretary of Veterans Affairs determines that such individual was discharged or released from the period of such active duty or inactive duty training under conditions other than dishonorable, and if the Secretary of Veterans Affairs certifies to the Commissioner of Social Security his determinations with respect to such individual under this clause, or

(E) the individual on whose employment such benefit is based had been in service covered by the Railroad Retirement Act of 1937 or 1974 [45 U.S.C.A. §§ 228a et seq., 231 et seq.] which was treated as employment covered by this chapter pursuant to the provisions of section 5(k)(1) of the Railroad Retirement Act of 1937 [45 U.S.C.A. § 228e(k)(1)] or section 18(2) of the Railroad Retirement Act of 1974 [45 U.S.C.A. § 231q(2)];

except that subparagraphs (A) and (B) of this paragraph shall not apply in the case of any individual who is a citizen of a foreign country that has in effect a social insurance or pension system which is of general application in such country and which satisfies subparagraph (A) but not subparagraph (B) of paragraph (2), or who is a citizen of a foreign country that has no social insurance or pension system of general application if at any time within five years prior to the month in which the Social Security Amendments of 1967 are enacted (or the first month thereafter for which his benefits are subject to suspension under paragraph (1)) payments to individuals residing in such country were withheld by the Treasury Department under sections 3329(a) and 3330(a) of Title 31.

(5) No person who is, or upon application would be, entitled to a monthly benefit under this section for December 1956 shall be deprived, by reason of paragraph (1) of this subsection, of such benefit or any other benefit based on the wages and self-employment income of the individual on whose wages and self-employment income such monthly benefit for December 1956 is based.

(6) If an individual is outside the United States when he dies and no benefit may, by reason of paragraph (1) or (10) of this subsection, be paid to him for the month preceding the month in which he dies, no lump-sum death payment may be made on the basis of such individual's wages and self-employment income.

(7) Subsections (b), (c), and (d) of section 403 of this title shall not apply with respect to any individual for any month for which no monthly benefit may be paid to him by reason of paragraph (1) of this subsection.

(8) The Attorney General shall certify to the Commissioner of Social Security such information regarding aliens who depart from the United States to any foreign country (other than a foreign country which is territorially contiguous to the continental United States) as may be necessary to enable the Commissioner of Social Security to carry out the purposes of this subsection and shall otherwise aid, assist, and cooperate with the Commissioner of Social Security in obtaining such other information as may be necessary to enable the Commissioner of Social Security to carry out the purposes of this subsection.

(9) No payments shall be made under part A of subchapter XVIII of this chapter with respect to items or services furnished to an individual in any month for which the prohibition in paragraph (1) against payment of benefits to him is applicable (or would be if he were entitled to any such benefits).

(10) Notwithstanding any other provision of this subchapter, no monthly benefits shall be paid under this section or under section 423 of this title, for any month beginning after June 30, 1968, to an individual who is not a citizen or national of the United States and who resides during such month in a foreign country if payments for such month to individuals residing in such country are withheld by the Treasury Department under sections 3329(a) and 3330(a) of Title 31.

(11)(A) Paragraph (2) and subparagraphs (A), (B), (C), and (E) of paragraph (4) shall apply with respect to an individual's monthly benefits under subsection (b), (c), (d), (e), (f), (g), or (h) of this section only if such individual meets the residency requirements of this paragraph with respect to those benefits.

(B) An individual entitled to benefits under subsection (b), (c), (e), (f), or (g) of this section meets the residency requirements of this paragraph with respect to those benefits only if such individual has resided in the United States, and while so residing bore a spousal relationship to the person on whose wages and self-employment income such entitlement is based, for a total period of not less than 5 years. For purposes of this subparagraph, a period of time for which an individual bears a spousal relationship to another person consists of a period throughout which the individual has been, with respect to such other person, a wife, a husband, a widow, a widower, a divorced wife, a divorced husband, a surviving divorced wife, a surviving divorced husband, a surviving divorced mother, a surviving divorced father, or (as applicable in the course of such period) any two or more of the foregoing.

(C) An individual entitled to benefits under subsection (d) of this section meets the residency requirements of this paragraph with respect to those benefits only if—

(i)(I) such individual has resided in the United States (as the child of the person on whose wages and self-employment income such entitlement is based) for a total period of not less than 5 years, or

(II) the person on whose wages and self-employment income such entitlement is based, and the individual's other parent (within the meaning of subsection (h)(3) of this section), if any, have each resided in the United States for a total period of not less than 5 years (or died while residing in the United States), and

(ii) in the case of an individual entitled to such benefits as an adopted child, such individual was adopted within the United States by the person on whose wages and self-employment income such entitlement is based, and has lived in the United States with such person and received at least one-half of his or her support from such person for a period (beginning before such individual attained age 18) consisting of—

(I) the year immediately before the month in which such person became eligible for old-age insurance benefits or disability insurance benefits or died, whichever occurred first, or

(II) if such person had a period of disability which continued until he or she became entitled to old-age insurance benefits or disability insurance benefits or died, the year immediately before the month in which such period of disability began.

(D) An individual entitled to benefits under subsection (h) of this section meets the residency requirements of this paragraph with respect to those benefits only if such individual has resided in the United States, and while so residing was a parent (within the meaning of subsection (h)(3) of this section) of the person on whose wages and self-employment income such entitlement is based, for a total period of not less than 5 years.

(E) This paragraph shall not apply with respect to any individual who is a citizen or resident of a foreign country with which the United States has an agreement in force concluded pursuant to section 433 of this title, except to the extent provided by such agreement.

(u) Conviction of subversive activities, etc.

(1) If any individual is convicted of any offense (committed after August 1, 1956) under—

(A) chapter 37 (relating to espionage and censorship), chapter 105 (relating to sabotage), or chapter 115 (relating to treason, sedition, and subversive activities) of Title 18, or

(B) section 783 of Title 50,

then the court may, in addition to all other penalties provided by law, impose a penalty that in determining whether any monthly insurance benefit under this section or section 423 of this title is payable to such individual for the month in which he is convicted or for any month thereafter, in determining the amount of any such benefit payable to such individual for any such month, and in determining whether such individual is entitled to insurance benefits under part A of subchapter XVIII of this chapter for any such month, there shall not be taken into account—

(C) any wages paid to such individual or to any other individual in the calendar year in which such conviction occurs or in any prior calendar year, and

(D) any net earnings from self-employment derived by such individual or by any other individual during a taxable year in which such conviction occurs or during any prior taxable year.

(2) As soon as practicable after an additional penalty has, pursuant to paragraph (1) of this subsection, been imposed with respect to any individual, the Attorney General shall notify the Commissioner of Social Security of such imposition.

(3) If any individual with respect to whom an additional penalty has been imposed pursuant to paragraph (1) of this subsection is granted a pardon of the offense by the President of the United States, such additional penalty shall not apply for any month beginning after the date on which such pardon is granted.

(v) Waiver of benefits

(1) Notwithstanding any other provisions of this subchapter, and subject to paragraph (3), in the case of any individual who files a waiver pursuant to section 1402(g) of the Internal Revenue Code of 1986 and is granted a tax exemption thereunder, no benefits or other payments shall be payable under this subchapter to him, no payments shall be made on his behalf under part A of subchapter XVIII of this chapter, and no benefits or other payments under this subchapter shall be payable on the basis of his wages and self-employment income to any other person, after the filing of such waiver.

(2) Notwithstanding any other provision of this subchapter, and subject to paragraph (3), in the case of any individual who files a waiver pursuant to section 3127 of the Internal Revenue Code of 1986 and is granted a tax exemption thereunder, no benefits or other payments shall be payable under this subchapter to him, no payments shall be made on his behalf under part A of subchapter XVIII of this chapter, and no benefits or other payments under this subchapter shall be payable on the basis of his wages and self-employment income to any other person, after the filing of such waiver.

(3) If, after an exemption referred to in paragraph (1) or (2) is granted to an individual, such exemption ceases to be effective, the waiver referred to in such paragraph shall cease to be applicable in the case of benefits and other payments under this subchapter and part A of subchapter XVIII of this chapter to the extent based on—

(A) his wages for and after the calendar year following the calendar year in which occurs the failure to meet the requirements of section 1402(g) or 3127 of the Internal Revenue Code of 1986 on which the cessation of such exemption is based, and

(B) his self-employment income for and after the taxable year in which occurs such failure.

(w) Increase in old-age insurance benefit amounts on account of delayed retirement

(1) The amount of an old-age insurance benefit (other than a benefit based on a primary insurance amount determined under section 415(a)(3) of this title as in effect in December 1978 or section 415(a)(1)(C)(i) of this title as in effect thereafter) which is payable without regard to this subsection to an individual shall be increased by—

(A) the applicable percentage (as determined under paragraph (6)) of such amount, multiplied by

(B) the number (if any) of the increment months for such individual.

(2) For purposes of this subsection, the number of increment months for any individual shall be a number equal to the total number of the months—

(A) which have elapsed after the month before the month in which such individual attained retirement age (as defined in section 416(*l*) of this title) or (if later) December 1970 and prior to the month in which such individual attained age 70, and

(B) with respect to which—

(i) such individual was a fully insured individual (as defined in section 414(a) of this title),

(ii) such individual either was not entitled to an old-age insurance benefit or, if so entitled, did not receive benefits pursuant to a request under subsection (z) by such individual that benefits not be paid, and

(iii) such individual was not subject to a penalty imposed under section 1320a–8a of this title.

(3) For purposes of applying the provisions of paragraph (1), a determination shall be made under paragraph (2) for each year, beginning with 1972, of the total number of an individual's increment months through the year for which the determination is made and the total so determined shall be applicable to such individual's old-age insurance benefits beginning with benefits for January of the year following the year for which such determination is made; except that the total number applicable in the case of an individual who attains age 70 after 1972 shall be determined through the month before the month in which he attains such age and shall be applicable to his old-age insurance benefit beginning with the month in which he attains such age.

(4) This subsection shall be applied after reduction under section 403(a) of this title.

(5) If an individual's primary insurance amount is determined under paragraph (3) of section 415(a) of this title as in effect in December 1978, or section 415(a)(1)(C)(i) of this title as in effect thereafter, and, as a result of this subsection, he would be entitled to a higher old-age insurance benefit if his primary insurance amount were determined under section 415(a) of this title (whether before, in, or after December 1978) without regard to such paragraph, such individual's old-age insurance benefit based upon his primary insurance amount determined under such paragraph shall be increased by an amount equal to the difference between such benefit and the benefit to which he would be entitled if his primary insurance amount were determined under such section without regard to such paragraph.

(6) For purposes of paragraph (1)(A), the "applicable percentage" is—

(A) 1/12 of 1 percent in the case of an individual who first becomes eligible for an old-age insurance benefit in any calendar year before 1979;

(B) 1/4 of 1 percent in the case of an individual who first becomes eligible for an old-age insurance benefit in any calendar year after 1978 and before 1987;

(C) in the case of an individual who first becomes eligible for an old-age insurance benefit in a calendar year after 1986 and before 2005, a percentage equal to the applicable percentage in effect under this paragraph for persons who first became eligible for an old-age insurance benefit in the preceding calendar year (as increased pursuant to this subparagraph), plus 1/24 of 1 percent if the calendar year in which that particular individual first becomes eligible for such benefit is not evenly divisible by 2; and

(D) 2/3 of 1 percent in the case of an individual who first becomes eligible for an old-age insurance benefit in a calendar year after 2004.

(x) Limitation on payments to prisoners, certain other inmates of publicly funded institutions, fugitives, probationers, and parolees

(1)(A) Notwithstanding any other provision of this subchapter, no monthly benefits shall be paid under this section or under section 423 of this title to any individual for any month ending with or during or beginning with or during a period of more than 30 days throughout all of which such individual—

(i) is confined in a jail, prison, or other penal institution or correctional facility pursuant to his conviction of a criminal offense,

(ii) is confined by court order in an institution at public expense in connection with—

(I) a verdict or finding that the individual is guilty but insane, with respect to a criminal offense,

(II) a verdict or finding that the individual is not guilty of such an offense by reason of insanity,

(III) a finding that such individual is incompetent to stand trial under an allegation of such an offense, or

(IV) a similar verdict or finding with respect to such an offense based on similar factors (such as a mental disease, a mental defect, or mental incompetence),

(iii) immediately upon completion of confinement as described in clause (i) pursuant to conviction of a criminal offense an element of which is sexual activity, is confined by court order in an institution at public expense pursuant to a finding that the individual is a sexually dangerous person or a sexual predator or a similar finding,

(iv) is fleeing to avoid prosecution, or custody or confinement after conviction, under the laws of the place from which the person flees, for a crime, or an attempt to commit a crime, which is a felony under the laws of the place from which the person flees, or, in jurisdictions that do not define crimes as felonies, is punishable by death or imprisonment for a term exceeding 1 year regardless of the actual sentence imposed, or

(v) is violating a condition of probation or parole imposed under Federal or State law.

(B)(i) For purposes of clause (i) of subparagraph (A), an individual shall not be considered confined in an institution comprising a jail, prison, or other penal institution or correctional facility during any month throughout which such individual is residing outside such institution at no expense (other than the cost of monitoring) to such institution or the penal system or to any agency to which the penal system has transferred jurisdiction over the individual.

(ii) For purposes of clauses (ii) and (iii) of subparagraph (A), an individual confined in an institution as described in such clause (ii) shall be treated as remaining so confined until—

(I) he or she is released from the care and supervision of such institution, and

(II) such institution ceases to meet the individual's basic living needs.

(iii) Notwithstanding subparagraph (A), the Commissioner shall, for good cause shown, pay the individual benefits that have been withheld or would otherwise be withheld pursuant to clause (iv) or (v) of subparagraph (A) if the Commissioner determines that—

(I) a court of competent jurisdiction has found the individual not guilty of the criminal offense, dismissed the charges relating to the criminal offense, vacated the warrant for arrest of the individual for the criminal offense, or issued any similar exonerating order (or taken similar exonerating action), or

(II) the individual was erroneously implicated in connection with the criminal offense by reason of identity fraud.

(iv) Notwithstanding subparagraph (A), the Commissioner may, for good cause shown based on mitigating circumstances, pay the individual benefits that have been withheld or would otherwise be withheld pursuant to clause (iv) or (v) of subparagraph (A) if the Commissioner determines that—

(I) the offense described in clause (iv) or underlying the imposition of the probation or parole described in clause (v) was nonviolent and not drug-related, and

(II) in the case of an individual from whom benefits have been withheld or otherwise would be withheld pursuant to subparagraph (A)(v), the action that resulted in the violation of a condition of probation or parole was nonviolent and not drug-related.

(2) Benefits which would be payable to any individual (other than a confined individual to whom benefits are not payable by reason of paragraph (1)) under this subchapter on the basis of the wages and self-employment income of such a confined individual but for the provisions of paragraph (1), shall be payable as though such confined individual were receiving such benefits under this section or section 423 of this title.

(3)(A) Notwithstanding the provisions of section 552a of Title 5 or any other provision of Federal or State law, any agency of the United States Government or of any State (or political subdivision thereof) shall make available to the Commissioner of Social Security, upon written request, the name and social security account number of any individual who is confined as described in paragraph (1) if the confinement is under the jurisdiction of such agency and the Commissioner of Social Security requires such information to carry out the provisions of this section.

(B)(i) The Commissioner shall enter into an agreement under this subparagraph with any interested State or local institution comprising a jail, prison, penal institution, or correctional facility, or comprising any other institution a purpose of which is to confine individuals as described in paragraph (1)(A)(ii). Under such agreement—

(I) the institution shall provide to the Commissioner, on a monthly basis and in a manner specified by the Commissioner, the first, middle, and last names, Social Security account numbers or taxpayer identification numbers, prison assigned inmate numbers, last known addresses, dates of birth, confinement commencement dates, dates of release or anticipated dates of release, dates of work release, and, to the extent available to the institution, such other identifying information concerning the individuals confined in the institution as the Commissioner may require for the purpose of carrying out paragraph (1) and clause (iv) of this subparagraph and other provisions of this subchapter; and

(II) the Commissioner shall pay to the institution, with respect to information described in subclause (I) concerning each individual who is confined therein as described in paragraph (1)(A), who receives a benefit under this subchapter for the month preceding the first month of such confinement, and whose benefit under this subchapter is determined by the Commissioner to be not payable by reason of confinement based on the information provided by the institution, $400 (subject to reduction under clause (ii)) if the institution furnishes the information to the Commissioner within 30 days after the date such individual's confinement in such institution begins, or $200 (subject to reduction under clause (ii)) if the institution furnishes the information after 30 days after such date but within 90 days after such date.

(ii) The dollar amounts specified in clause (i)(II) shall be reduced by 50 percent if the Commissioner is also required to make a payment to the institution with respect to the same individual under an agreement entered into under section 1382(e)(1)(I) of this title.

(iii) There are authorized to be transferred from the Federal Old-Age and Survivors Insurance Trust Fund and the Federal Disability Insurance Trust Fund, as appropriate, such sums as may be necessary to enable the Commissioner to make payments to institutions required by clause (i)(II).

(iv) The Commissioner shall maintain, and shall provide on a reimbursable basis, information obtained pursuant to agreements entered into under this paragraph to any agency administering a Federal or federally-assisted cash, food, or medical assistance program for eligibility and other administrative purposes under such program, for statistical and research activities conducted by Federal and State agencies, and to the Secretary of the Treasury for the purposes of tax administration, debt collection, and identifying, preventing, and recovering improper payments under federally funded programs.

(v)(I) The Commissioner may disclose information received pursuant to this paragraph to any officer, employee, agent, or contractor of the Department of the Treasury whose official duties require such information to assist in the identification, prevention, and recovery of improper payments or in the collection of delinquent debts owed to the United States, including payments certified by the head of an executive, judicial, or legislative paying agency, and payments made to individuals whose eligibility, or continuing eligibility, to participate in a Federal program (including those administered by a State or political subdivision thereof) is being reviewed.

(II) Notwithstanding the provisions of section 552a of Title 5, or any other provision of Federal or State law, the Secretary of the Treasury may compare information disclosed under subclause (I) with any other personally identifiable information derived from a Federal system of records or similar records maintained by a Federal contractor, a Federal grantee, or an entity administering a Federal program or activity, and may redisclose such comparison of information to any paying or administering agency and to the head of the Federal Bureau of Prisons and the head of any State agency charged with the administration of prisons with respect to inmates whom the Secretary of the Treasury has determined may have been issued, or facilitated in the issuance of, an improper payment.

(III) The comparison of information disclosed under subclause (I) shall not be considered a matching program for purposes of section 552a of Title 5.

(C) Notwithstanding the provisions of section 552a of Title 5 or any other provision of Federal or State law (other than section 6103 of the Internal Revenue Code of 1986 [Title 26, U.S.C.A.] and section 1306(c) of this title), the Commissioner shall furnish any Federal, State, or local law enforcement officer, upon the written request of the officer, with the current address, Social Security number, and photograph (if applicable) of any beneficiary under this subchapter, if the officer furnishes the Commissioner with the name of the beneficiary, and other identifying information as reasonably required by the Commissioner to establish the unique identity of the beneficiary, and notifies the Commissioner that—

(i) the beneficiary is described in clause (iv) or (v) of paragraph (1)(A); and

(ii) the location or apprehension of the beneficiary is within the officer's official duties.

(y) Limitation on payments to aliens

Notwithstanding any other provision of law, no monthly benefit under this subchapter shall be payable to any alien in the United States for any month during which such alien is not lawfully present in the United States as determined by the Attorney General.

(z) Voluntary suspension

(1)(A) Except as otherwise provided in this subsection, any individual who has attained retirement age (as defined in section 416(*l*) of this title) and is entitled to old-age insurance benefits may request that payment of such benefits be suspended—

(i) beginning with the month following the month in which such request is received by the Commissioner, and

(ii) ending with the earlier of the month following the month in which a request by the individual for a resumption of such benefits is so received or the month following the month in which the individual attains the age of 70.

(2) An individual may not suspend such benefits under this subsection, and any suspension of such benefits under this subsection shall end, effective with respect to any month in which the individual becomes subject to—

(A) mandatory suspension of such benefits under subsection (x);

(B) termination of such benefits under subsection (n);

(C) a penalty under section 1320a–8a of this title imposing nonpayment of such benefits; or

(D) any other withholding, in whole or in part, of such benefits under any other provision of law that authorizes recovery of a debt by withholding such benefits.

(3) In the case of an individual who requests that such benefits be suspended under this subsection, for any month during the period in which the suspension is in effect—

(A) no retroactive benefits (as defined in subsection (j)(4)(B)(iii)) shall be payable to such individual;

(B) no monthly benefit shall be payable to any other individual on the basis of such individual's wages and self-employment income; and

(C) no monthly benefit shall be payable to such individual on the basis of another individual's wages and self-employment income.

(Aug. 14, 1935, c. 531, Title II, § 202, 49 Stat. 623; Aug. 10, 1939, c. 666, Title II, § 201, 53 Stat. 1362; 1946 Reorg. Plan No. 2, § 4, eff. July 16, 1946, 11 F.R. 7873, 60 Stat. 1095; Aug. 10, 1946, c. 951, Title IV, §§ 402, 403(a), 404(a), 405(a), 60 Stat. 986, 987; Aug. 28, 1950, c. 809, Title I, § 101(a), 64 Stat. 482; 1953 Reorg. Plan No. 1, §§ 5, 8, eff. Apr. 11, 1953, 18 F.R. 2053, 67 Stat. 631; Aug. 14, 1953, c. 483, § 2, 67 Stat. 580; Sept. 1, 1954, c. 1206, Title I, §§ 102(i), 105(a), 107, 110, 68 Stat. 1073, 1079, 1083, 1085; Aug. 9, 1955, c. 685, § 2, 69 Stat. 621; Aug. 1, 1956, c. 836, Title I, §§ 101(a) to (c), 102(c), (d)(1) to (10), 103(c)(1) to (3), 113, 114(a), 118(a), 121(a), 70 Stat. 807, 810 to 814, 818, 831, 832, 835, 838; Aug. 1, 1956, c. 837, Title IV, §§ 403(a), 407, 70 Stat. 871, 876; Pub.L. 85–238, §§ 1, 3(a) to (g), Aug. 30, 1957, 71 Stat. 518; Pub.L. 85–798, § 1, Aug. 28, 1958, 72 Stat. 964; Pub.L. 85–840, Title I, § 101(e), Title II, § 205(b) to (i), Title III, §§ 301(a)(1), (b)(1), (c)(1), 303, 304(a)(1), 305(a), 306(a), 307(a) to (e), Aug. 28, 1958, 72 Stat. 1017, 1021 to 1024, 1026, 1027, 1029 to 1032; Pub.L. 85–857, § 13(i)(1), Sept. 2, 1958, 72 Stat. 1265; Pub.L. 85–927, § 301, Sept. 6, 1958, 72 Stat. 1783; Pub.L. 86–70, § 32(c)(1), June 25, 1959, 73 Stat. 149; Pub.L. 86–624, § 30(c)(1), July 12, 1960, 74 Stat. 420; Pub.L. 86–778, Title I, § 103(a)(1), (j)(2)(C), (D), Title II, §§ 201(a), (b), 202(a), 203(a), 205(a), (b), 208(d), 211(i) to (l), Title III, § 301(a), Title IV, § 403(d), Sept. 13, 1960, 74 Stat. 936, 937, 946, 947, 949, 952, 957 to 959, 969;

Pub.L. 87–64, Title I, §§ 102(a), (b)(1), (2)(A), (3), (e), 104(a) to (d), June 30, 1961, 75 Stat. 131, 134 to 136, 138, 139; Pub.L. 89–97, Title I, § 104(a), Title III, §§ 303(d), 304(a) to (j), 306(a), (b), (c)(1) to (9), 307(a), (b), 308(a), (b), (d)(1), (2)(A), (3) to (5), (12), (13), 319(d), 323(a), 324(a), 328(a), 333(a) to (c), 334(e), (f), 339(b), 343(a), July 30, 1965, 79 Stat. 334, 367 to 379, 392, 397, 398, 400, 403 to 405, 410, 412; Pub.L. 90–248, Title I, §§ 103(a) to (d), 104(a) to (c), 112(a), 151(a) to (d)(1), (2), 157(a), (b), 158(c)(1), (2), 162(a)(1), (b)(1), (c)(1), (2), January 2, 1968, 81 Stat. 828 to 832, 838, 860, 867, 868, 871; Pub.L. 91–172, Title X, § 1004(a) to (c), Dec. 30, 1969, 83 Stat. 741; Pub.L. 92–223, § 1, Dec. 28, 1971, 85 Stat. 802; Pub.L. 92–603, Title I, §§ 102(a), (b), (d) to (f), 103(a), (b), 107(a), 108(a) to (e), 109(a), 110(a), 111(a), 112(a), 113(b), 114(a) to (c), 116(b), (c), Oct. 30, 1972, 86 Stat. 1335, 1336, 1338 to 1340, 1343 to 1348, 1350; Pub.L. 93–66, Title II, § 240(a), July 9, 1973, 87 Stat. 161; Pub.L. 93–233, §§ 1(f), (g), 18(b), Dec. 31, 1973, 87 Stat. 947, 948, 967; Pub.L. 93–445, Title III, § 301, Oct. 16, 1974, 88 Stat. 1357; Pub.L. 95–216, Title II, §§ 203, 204(a) to (d), 205(a), (b), Title III, §§ 331(a) to (c), 332(a)(1), (2), 334(a) to (d)(4)(A), (5), (6), (e), 336(a), (b), 337(b), 353(f)(1), Dec. 20, 1977, 91 Stat. 1527 to 1529, 1541 to 1548, 1554; Pub.L. 95–600, Title VII, § 703(j)(14)(A), Nov. 6, 1978, 92 Stat. 2942; Pub.L. 96–265, Title III, §§ 303(b)(1)(B) to (D), 306(a), June 9, 1980, 94 Stat. 451, 452, 457; Pub.L. 96–473, §§ 5(b), 6(a), Oct. 19, 1980, 94 Stat. 2265; Pub.L. 96–499, Title X, § 1011(a), Dec. 5, 1980, 94 Stat. 2655; Pub.L. 97–35, Title XXII, §§ 2201(b)(10), (11), (d), (f), 2202(a)(1), 2203(a), (b)(1), (c)(1), (d)(1), (2), 2205(a)(1), 2206(b)(1), 2210(a), Aug. 13, 1981, 95 Stat. 831 to 838, 841; Pub.L. 97–123, § 2(e), Dec. 29, 1981, 95 Stat. 1660; Pub.L. 97–455, § 7(c), Jan. 12, 1983, 96 Stat. 2501; Pub.L. 98–21, Title I, §§ 111(a)(7), 113(d), 114(a) to (c)(1), 131(a)(1) to (3)(G), (b)(1) to (3)(F), (c), 132(a), 133(a), (b), 134(a), (b), Title II, § 201(b), (c)(1)(A), Title III, §§ 301(a), (b), 302, 306(a), (d) to (h), 307(a), 309(a) to (e), 334(a), 337(a), 339(a), 340(a), (b), Apr. 20, 1983, 97 Stat. 72, 79, 92, 93, 95, 97, 98, 108, 111 to 116, 130, 131, 133 to 135; Pub.L. 98–369, Div. B, Title VI, §§ 2661(b) to (f), 2662(c)(1), 2663(a)(2), July 18, 1984, 98 Stat. 1156, 1159, 1160; Pub.L. 99–272, Title XII, §§ 12104(a), 12107(a), Apr. 7, 1986, 100 Stat. 285, 286; Pub.L. 99–514, Title XVIII, § 1883(a)(1) to (3), Oct. 22, 1986, 100 Stat. 2916; Pub.L. 100–203, Title IX, §§ 9007(a) to (e), 9010(b) to (d), Dec. 22, 1987, 101 Stat. 1330–289 to 1330–293; Pub.L. 100–647, Title VIII, §§ 8004(a), (b), 8007(b), 8010(a), (b), 8014(a), Nov. 10, 1988, 102 Stat. 3780, 3782, 3788, 3790; Pub.L. 101–239, Title X, §§ 10203(a), 10301(a), (b), 10302(a)(1), Dec. 19, 1989, 103 Stat. 2473, 2481; Pub.L. 101–508, Title V, §§ 5103(c)(2)(A), (B), (d), 5116(a), Nov. 5, 1990, 104 Stat. 1388–252, 253, 274; Pub.L. 101–649, Title VI, § 603(b)(5), Nov. 29, 1990, 104 Stat. 5085; Pub.L. 102–54, § 13(q)(3)(C), June 13, 1991, 105 Stat. 279; Pub.L. 103–296, Title I, § 107(a)(4), Title III, §§ 308(a), 321(a)(2) to (5), (b)(1), (c)(2), Aug. 15, 1994, 108 Stat. 1478, 1522, 1535 to 1538; Pub.L. 103–387, § 4(a), Oct. 22, 1994, 108 Stat. 4076; Pub.L. 104–121, Title I, § 104(a)(1), (b)(1), (2), Mar. 29, 1996, 110 Stat. 851, 852; Pub.L. 104–208, Div. C, Title V, § 503(a), Sept. 30, 1996, 110 Stat. 3009–671; Pub.L. 106–169, Title II, § 207(b), Dec. 14, 1999, 113 Stat. 1838; Pub.L. 106–170, Title IV, § 402(a)(1), (b)(1), (d)(1), (2), Dec. 17, 1999, 113 Stat. 1907 to 1909; Pub.L. 106–182, § 4(b), Apr. 7, 2000, 114 Stat. 199; Pub.L. 108–203, Title II, § 203(a), Title IV, §§ 412(a), (b), 418(a) to (b)(4)(B)(vi), (5), 420A(a), Mar. 2, 2004, 118 Stat. 509, 527, 528, 531 to 533, 535; Pub.L. 113–67, Div. A, Title II, § 204(a)(1), (b)(1), Dec. 26, 2013, 127 Stat. 1179, 1180; Pub.L. 113–270, §§ 3, 4, Dec. 18, 2014, 128 Stat. 2948; Pub.L. 114–74, Title VIII, §§ 831(a)(1), (2), (b)(1), (2), Nov. 2, 2015, 129 Stat. 611, 612, 613.)

[1] So in original. Probably should be "or".

[2] So in original. Probably should be a period at the end.

Commentary

Astrue v. Capato, 132 S.Ct. 2021 (2012), holds that the Social Security Act does not grant children's benefits to children posthumously conceived by in vitro fertilization if they are not entitled to inherit from the decedent under state intestacy law. Moreover, the Act's exclusion of such children satisfies the rational basis standard of the equal protection clause. *Astrue* overrules *Gillett-Netting v. Barnhart, 317 F.3d 593 (9th Cir. 2004)*, which reached the opposite conclusion.

§ 416. Additional definitions

For the purposes of this subchapter—

(a) Spouse; surviving spouse

(1) The term "spouse" means a wife as defined in subsection (b) of this section or a husband as defined in subsection (f) of this section.

(2) The term "surviving spouse" means a widow as defined in subsection (c) of this section or a widower as defined in subsection (g) of this section.

(b) Wife

The term "wife" means the wife of an individual, but only if she (1) is the mother of his son or daughter, (2) was married to him for a period of not less than one year immediately preceding the day on which her application is filed, or (3) in the month prior to the month of her marriage to him (A) was entitled to, or on application therefor and attainment of age 62 in such prior month would have been entitled to, benefits under subsection (b), (e), or (h) of section 402 of this title, (B) had attained age eighteen and was entitled to, or on application therefor would have been entitled to, benefits under subsection (d) of such section (subject, however, to section 402(s) of this title), or (C) was entitled to, or upon application therefor and attainment of the required age (if any) would have been entitled to, a widow's, child's (after attainment of age 18), or parent's insurance annuity under section 231a of Title 45. For purposes of clause (2), a wife shall be deemed to have been married to an individual for a period of one year throughout the month in which occurs the first anniversary of her marriage to such individual. For purposes of subparagraph (C) of section 402(b)(1) of this title, a divorced wife shall be deemed not to be married throughout the month in which she becomes divorced.

(c) Widow

(1) The term "widow" (except when used in the first sentence of section 402(i) of this title) means the surviving wife of an individual, but only if (A) she is the mother of his son or daughter, (B) she legally adopted his son or daughter while she was married to him and while such son or daughter was under the age of eighteen, (C) he legally adopted her son or daughter while she was married to him and while such son or daughter was under the age of eighteen, (D) she was married to him at the time both of them legally adopted a child under the age of eighteen, (E) except as provided in paragraph (2), she was married to him for a period of not less than nine months immediately prior to the day on which he died, or (F) in the month prior to the month of her marriage to him (i) she was entitled to, or on application therefor and attainment of age 62 in such prior month would have been entitled to, benefits under subsection (b), (e), or (h) of section 402 of this title, (ii) she had attained age eighteen and was entitled to, or on application therefor would have been entitled to, benefits under subsection (d) of such section (subject, however, to section 402(s) of this title), or (iii) she was entitled to, or upon application therefor and attainment of the required age (if any) would have been entitled to, a widow's, child's (after attainment of age 18), or parent's insurance annuity under section 231a of Title 45.

(2) The requirements of paragraph (1)(E) in connection with the surviving wife of an individual shall be treated as satisfied if—

(A) the individual had been married prior to the individual's marriage to the surviving wife,

(B) the prior wife was institutionalized during the individual's marriage to the prior wife due to mental incompetence or similar incapacity,

(C) during the period of the prior wife's institutionalization, the individual would have divorced the prior wife and married the surviving wife, but the individual did not do so because such divorce would have been unlawful, by reason of the prior wife's institutionalization, under the laws of the State in which the individual was domiciled at the time (as determined based on evidence satisfactory to the Commissioner of Social Security),

(D) the prior wife continued to remain institutionalized up to the time of her death, and

(E) the individual married the surviving wife within 60 days after the prior wife's death.

(d) Divorced spouses; divorce

(1) The term "divorced wife" means a woman divorced from an individual, but only if she had been married to such individual for a period of 10 years immediately before the date the divorce became effective.

(2) The term "surviving divorced wife" means a woman divorced from an individual who has died, but only if she had been married to the individual for a period of 10 years immediately before the date the divorce became effective.

(3) The term "surviving divorced mother" means a woman divorced from an individual who has died, but only if (A) she is the mother of his son or daughter, (B) she legally adopted his son or daughter while she was married to him and while such son or daughter was under the age of 18, (C) he legally adopted her son or daughter while she was married to him and while such son or daughter was under the age of 18, or (D) she was married to him at the time both of them legally adopted a child under the age of 18.

(4) The term "divorced husband" means a man divorced from an individual, but only if he had been married to such individual for a period of 10 years immediately before the date the divorce became effective.

(5) The term "surviving divorced husband" means a man divorced from an individual who has died, but only if he had been married to the individual for a period of 10 years immediately before the divorce became effective.

(6) The term "surviving divorced father" means a man divorced from an individual who has died, but only if (A) he is the father of her son or daughter, (B) he legally adopted her son or daughter while he was married to her and while such son or daughter was under the age of 18, (C) she legally adopted his son or daughter while he was married to her and while such son or daughter was under the age of 18, or (D) he was married to her at the time both of them legally adopted a child under the age of 18.

(7) The term "surviving divorced parent" means a surviving divorced mother as defined in paragraph (3) of this subsection or a surviving divorced father as defined in paragraph (6).

(8) The terms "divorce" and "divorced" refer to a divorce a vinculo matrimonii.

(e) Child

The term "child" means (1) the child or legally adopted child of an individual, (2) a stepchild who has been such stepchild for not less than one year immediately preceding the day on which application for child's insurance benefits is filed or (if the insured individual is deceased) not less than nine months immediately preceding the day on which such individual died, and (3) a person who is the grandchild or stepgrandchild of an individual or his spouse, but only if (A) there was no natural or adoptive parent (other than such a parent who was under a disability, as defined in section 423(d) of this title) of such person living at the time (i) such individual became entitled to old-age insurance benefits or disability insurance benefits or died, or (ii) if such individual had a period of disability which continued until such individual became entitled to old-age insurance benefits or disability insurance benefits, or died, at the time such period of disability began, or (B) such person was legally adopted after the death of such individual by such individual's surviving spouse in an adoption that was decreed by a court of competent jurisdiction within the United States and such person's natural or adopting parent or stepparent was not living in such individual's household and making regular contributions toward such person's support at the time such individual died. For purposes of clause (1), a person shall be deemed, as of the date of death of an individual, to be the legally adopted child of such individual if such person was either living with or receiving at least one-half of his support from such individual at the time of such individual's death and was legally adopted by such individual's surviving spouse after such individual's death but only if (A) proceedings for the adoption of the child had been instituted by such individual before his death, or (B) such child was adopted by such individual's surviving spouse before the end of two years after (i) the day on which such individual died or (ii) August 28, 1958. For purposes of clause (2), a person who is not the stepchild of an individual shall be deemed the stepchild of such individual if such individual was not the mother or adopting mother or the father or adopting father of such person and such individual and the mother or adopting mother, or the father or adopting father, as the case may be, of such person went through a marriage ceremony resulting in a purported marriage between them which, but for a legal impediment described in the last sentence of subsection (h)(1)(B) of this section, would have been a valid marriage. For purposes of clause (2), a child shall be deemed to have been the stepchild of an individual for a period of one year throughout the month in which occurs the expiration of such one year. For purposes of clause (3), a person shall be deemed to have no natural or adoptive parent living (other than a parent who was under a disability) throughout the most recent month in which a natural or adoptive parent (not under a disability) dies.

(f) Husband

The term "husband" means the husband of an individual, but only if (1) he is the father of her son or daughter, (2) he was married to her for a period of not less than one year immediately preceding the day on which his application is filed, or (3) in the month prior to the month of his marriage to her (A) he was entitled to, or on application therefor and attainment of age 62 in such prior month would have been entitled to, benefits under subsection (c), (f) or (h) of section 402 of this title, (B) he had attained age eighteen and was entitled to, or on application therefor would have been entitled to, benefits under subsection (d) of such section (subject, however, to section 402(s) of this title), or (C) he was entitled to, or upon application therefor and attainment of the required age (if any) he would have been entitled to, a widower's, child's (after attainment of age 18), or parent's insurance annuity under section 231a of Title 45. For purposes of clause (2), a husband shall be deemed to have been married to an individual for a period of one year throughout the month in which occurs the first anniversary of his marriage to her. For purposes of subparagraph (C) of section 402(c)(1) of this title, a divorced husband shall be deemed not to be married throughout the month which he becomes divorced.

(g) Widower

(1) The term "widower" (except when used in the first sentence of section 402(i) of this title) means the surviving husband of an individual, but only if (A) he is the father of her son or daughter, (B) he legally adopted her son or daughter while he was married to her and while such son or daughter was under the age of eighteen, (C) she legally adopted his son or daughter while he was married to her and while such son or daughter was under the age of eighteen, (D) he was married to her at the time both of them legally adopted a child under the age of eighteen, (E) except as provided in paragraph (2), he was married to her for a period of not less than nine months immediately prior to the day on which she died, or (F) in the month before the month of his marriage to her (i) he was entitled to, or on application therefor and attainment of age 62 in such prior month would have been entitled to, benefits under subsection (c), (f) or (h) of section 402 of this title, (ii) he had attained age eighteen and was entitled to, or on application therefor would have been entitled to, benefits under subsection (d) of such section (subject, however, to section 402(s) of this title), or (iii) he was entitled to, or on application therefor and attainment of the required age (if any) he would have been entitled to, a widower's, child's (after attainment of age 18), or parent's insurance annuity under section 231a of Title 45.

(2) The requirements of paragraph (1)(E) in connection with the surviving husband of an individual shall be treated as satisfied if—

(A) the individual had been married prior to the individual's marriage to the surviving husband,

(B) the prior husband was institutionalized during the individual's marriage to the prior husband due to mental incompetence or similar incapacity,

(C) during the period of the prior husband's institutionalization, the individual would have divorced the prior husband and married the surviving husband, but the individual did not do so because such divorce would have been unlawful, by reason of the prior husband's institutionalization, under the laws of the State in which the individual was domiciled at the time (as determined based on evidence satisfactory to the Commissioner of Social Security),

(D) the prior husband continued to remain institutionalized up to the time of his death, and

(E) the individual married the surviving husband within 60 days after the prior husband's death.

(h) Determination of family status

(1)(A)(i) An applicant is the wife, husband, widow, or widower of a fully or currently insured individual for purposes of this subchapter if the courts of the State in which such insured individual is domiciled at the time such applicant files an application, or, if such insured individual is dead, the courts of the State in which he was domiciled at the time of death, or, if such insured individual is or was not so domiciled in any State, the courts of the District of Columbia, would find that such applicant and such insured individual were validly married at the time such applicant files such application or, if such insured individual is dead, at the time he died.

(ii) If such courts would not find that such applicant and such insured individual were validly married at such time, such applicant shall, nevertheless be deemed to be the wife, husband, widow, or widower, as the case may be, of such insured individual if such applicant would, under the laws applied by such courts in determining the devolution of intestate personal property, have the same status with respect to the taking of such property as a wife, husband, widow, or widower of such insured individual.

(B)(i) In any case where under subparagraph (A) an applicant is not (and is not deemed to be) the wife, widow, husband, or widower of a fully or currently insured individual, or where under subsection (b), (c), (d), (f), or (g) of this section such applicant is not the wife, divorced wife, widow, surviving divorced wife, husband, divorced husband, widower, or surviving divorced husband of such individual, but it is established to the satisfaction of the Commissioner of Social Security that such applicant in good faith went through a marriage ceremony with such individual resulting in a purported marriage between them which, but for a legal impediment not known to the applicant at the time of such ceremony, would have been a valid marriage, then, for purposes of subparagraph (A) and subsections (b), (c), (d), (f), and (g) of this section, such purported marriage shall be deemed to be a valid marriage. Notwithstanding the preceding sentence, in the case of any person who would be deemed under the preceding sentence a wife, widow, husband, or widower of the insured individual, such marriage shall not be deemed to be a valid marriage unless the applicant and the insured individual were living in the same household at the time of the death of the insured individual or (if the insured individual is living) at the time the applicant files the application. A marriage that is deemed to be a valid marriage by reason of the preceding sentence shall continue to be deemed a valid marriage if the insured individual and the person entitled to benefits as the wife or husband of the insured individual are no longer living in the same household at the time of the death of such insured individual.

(ii) The provisions of clause (i) shall not apply if the Commissioner of Social Security determines, on the basis of information brought to the Commissioner's attention, that such applicant entered into such purported marriage with such insured individual with knowledge that it would not be a valid marriage.

(iii) The entitlement to a monthly benefit under subsection (b) or (c) of section 402 of this title, based on the wages and self-employment income of such insured individual, of a person who would not be deemed to be a wife or husband of such insured individual but for this subparagraph, shall end with the month before the month in which such person enters into a marriage, valid without regard to this subparagraph, with a person other than such insured individual.

(iv) For purposes of this subparagraph, a legal impediment to the validity of a purported marriage includes only an impediment (I) resulting from the lack of dissolution of a previous marriage or otherwise arising out of such previous marriage or its dissolution, or (II) resulting from a defect in the procedure followed in connection with such purported marriage.

(2)(A) In determining whether an applicant is the child or parent of a fully or currently insured individual for purposes of this subchapter, the Commissioner of Social Security shall apply such law as would be applied in determining the devolution of intestate personal property by the courts of the State in which such insured individual is domiciled at the time such applicant files application, or, if such insured individual is dead, by the courts of the State in which he was domiciled at the time of his death, or, if such insured individual is or was not so domiciled in any State, by the courts of the District of Columbia. Applicants who according to such law would have the same status relative to taking intestate personal property as a child or parent shall be deemed such.

(B) If an applicant is a son or daughter of a fully or currently insured individual but is not (and is not deemed to be) the child of such insured individual under subparagraph (A), such applicant shall nevertheless be deemed to be the child of such insured individual if such insured individual and the mother or father, as the case may be, of such applicant went through a marriage ceremony resulting in a purported marriage between them which, but for a legal impediment described in the last sentence of paragraph (1)(B), would have been a valid marriage.

(3) An applicant who is the son or daughter of a fully or currently insured individual, but who is not (and is not deemed to be) the child of such insured individual under paragraph (2) of this subsection, shall nevertheless be deemed to be the child of such insured individual if:

(A) in the case of an insured individual entitled to old-age insurance benefits (who was not, in the month preceding such entitlement, entitled to disability insurance benefits)—

(i) such insured individual—

(I) has acknowledged in writing that the applicant is his or her son or daughter,

(II) has been decreed by a court to be the mother or father of the applicant, or

(III) has been ordered by a court to contribute to the support of the applicant because the applicant is his or her son or daughter,

and such acknowledgment, court decree, or court order was made not less than one year before such insured individual became entitled to old-age insurance benefits or attained retirement age (as defined in subsection (*l*) of this section), whichever is earlier; or

(ii) such insured individual is shown by evidence satisfactory to the Commissioner of Social Security to be the mother or father of the applicant and was living with or contributing to the support of the applicant at the time such applicant's application for benefits was filed;

(B) in the case of an insured individual entitled to disability insurance benefits, or who was entitled to such benefits in the month preceding the first month for which he or she was entitled to old-age insurance benefits—

(i) such insured individual—

(I) has acknowledged in writing that the applicant is his or her son or daughter,

(II) has been decreed by a court to be the mother or father of the applicant, or

(III) has been ordered by a court to contribute to the support of the applicant because the applicant is his or her son or daughter,

and such acknowledgment, court decree, or court order was made before such insured individual's most recent period of disability began; or

(ii) such insured individual is shown by evidence satisfactory to the Commissioner of Social Security to be the mother or father of the applicant and was living with or contributing to the support of that applicant at the time such applicant's application for benefits was filed;

(C) in the case of a deceased individual—

(i) such insured individual—

(I) had acknowledged in writing that the applicant is his or her son or daughter,

(II) had been decreed by a court to be the mother or father of the applicant, or

(III) had been ordered by a court to contribute to the support of the applicant because the applicant was his or her son or daughter,

and such acknowledgment, court decree, or court order was made before the death of such insured individual, or

(ii) such insured individual is shown by evidence satisfactory to the Commissioner of Social Security to have been the mother or father of the applicant, and such insured individual was living with or contributing to the support of the applicant at the time such insured individual died.

For purposes of subparagraphs (A)(i) and (B)(i), an acknowledgment, court decree, or court order shall be deemed to have occurred on the first day of the month in which it actually occurred.

(i) Disability; period of disability

(1) Except for purposes of sections 402(d), 402(e), 402(f), 423, and 425 of this title, the term "disability" means (A) inability to engage in any substantial gainful activity by reason of any medically determinable physical or mental impairment which can be expected to result in death or has lasted or can be expected to last for a continuous period of not less than 12 months, or (B) blindness; and the term "blindness" means central visual acuity of 20/200 or less in the better eye with the use of a correcting lens. An eye which is accompanied by a limitation in the fields of vision such that the widest diameter of the visual field subtends an angle no greater than 20 degrees shall be considered for purposes of this paragraph as having a central visual acuity of 20/200 or less. The provisions of paragraphs (2)(A), (2)(B), (3), (4), (5), and (6) of section 423(d) of this title shall be applied for purposes of determining whether an individual is under a disability within the meaning of the first sentence of this paragraph in the same manner as they are applied for purposes of paragraph (1) of such section. Nothing in this subchapter shall be construed as authorizing the Commissioner of Social Security or any other officer or employee of the United States to interfere in any way with the practice of medicine or with relationships between practitioners of medicine and their patients, or to exercise any supervision or control over the administration or operation of any hospital.

(2)(A) The term "period of disability" means a continuous period (beginning and ending as hereinafter provided in this subsection) during which an individual was under a disability (as defined in paragraph (1)), but only if such period is of not less than five full calendar months' duration or such individual was entitled to benefits under section 423 of this title for one or more months in such period.

(B) No period of disability shall begin as to any individual unless such individual files an application for a disability determination with respect to such period; and no such period shall begin as to any individual after such individual attains retirement age (as defined in subsection (*l*) of this section). In the case of a deceased individual, the requirement of an application under the preceding sentence may be satisfied by an application for a disability determination filed with respect to such individual within 3 months after the month in which he died.

(C) A period of disability shall begin—

(i) on the day the disability began, but only if the individual satisfies the requirements of paragraph (3) on such day; or

(ii) if such individual does not satisfy the requirements of paragraph (3) on such day, then on the first day of the first quarter thereafter in which he satisfies such requirements.

(D) A period of disability shall end with the close of whichever of the following months is the earlier: (i) the month preceding the month in which the individual attains retirement age (as defined in subsection (*l*) of this section), or (ii) the month preceding (I) the termination month (as defined in section 423(a)(1) of this title), or, if earlier (II) the first month for which no benefit is payable by reason of section 423(e) of this title, where no benefit is payable for any of the succeeding months during the 36–month period referred to in such section. The provisions set forth in section 423(f) of this title with respect to determinations of whether entitlement to benefits under this subchapter or subchapter XVIII of this chapter based on the disability of any individual is terminated (on the basis of a finding that the physical or mental impairment on the basis of which such benefits are provided has ceased, does not exist, or is not disabling) shall apply in the same manner and to the same extent with respect to determinations of whether a period of disability has ended (on the basis of a finding that the physical or mental impairment on the basis of which the finding of disability was made has ceased, does not exist, or is not disabling).

(E) Except as is otherwise provided in subparagraph (F), no application for a disability determination which is filed more than 12 months after the month prescribed by subparagraph (D) as the month in which the period of disability ends (determined without regard to subparagraph (B) and this subparagraph) shall be accepted as an application for purposes of this paragraph.

(F) An application for a disability determination which is filed more than 12 months after the month prescribed by subparagraph (D) as the month in which the period of disability ends (determined without regard to subparagraphs (B) and (E)) shall be accepted as an application for purposes of this paragraph if—

(i) in the case of an application filed by or on behalf of an individual with respect to a disability which ends after January 1968, such application is filed not more than 36 months after the month in which such disability ended, such individual is alive at the time the application is filed, and the Commissioner of Social Security finds in accordance with regulations prescribed by the Commissioner that the failure of such individual to file an application for a disability determination within the time specified in subparagraph (E) was attributable to a physical or mental condition of such individual which rendered him incapable of executing such an application, and

(ii) in the case of an application filed by or on behalf of an individual with respect to a period of disability which ends in or before January 1968—

(I) such application is filed not more than 12 months after January 1968,

(II) a previous application for a disability determination has been filed by or on behalf of such individual (1) in or before January 1968, and (2) not more than 36 months after the month in which his disability ended, and

(III) the Commissioner of Social Security finds in accordance with regulations prescribed by the Commissioner, that the failure of such individual to file an application within the then specified time period was attributable to a physical or mental condition of such individual which rendered him incapable of executing such an application.

In making a determination under this subsection, with respect to the disability or period of disability of any individual whose application for a determination thereof is accepted solely by reason of the provisions of this subparagraph (F), the provisions of this subsection (other than the provisions of this subparagraph) shall be applied as such provisions are in effect at the time such determination is made.

(G) An application for a disability determination filed before the first day on which the applicant satisfies the requirements for a period of disability under this subsection shall be deemed a valid application (and shall be deemed to have been filed on such first day) only if the applicant satisfies the requirements for a period of disability before the Commissioner of Social Security makes a final decision on the application and no request under section 405(b) of this title for notice and opportunity for a hearing thereon is made or, if such a request is made, before a decision based upon the evidence adduced at the hearing is made (regardless of whether such decision becomes the final decision of the Commissioner of Social Security).

(3) The requirements referred to in clauses (i) and (ii) of paragraph (2)(C) of this subsection are satisfied by an individual with respect to any quarter only if—

(A) he would have been a fully insured individual (as defined in section 414 of this title) had he attained age 62 and filed application for benefits under section 402(a) of this title on the first day of such quarter; and

(B)(i) he had not less than 20 quarters of coverage during the 40-quarter period which ends with such quarter, or

(ii) if such quarter ends before he attains (or would attain) age 31, not less than one-half (and not less than 6) of the quarters during the period ending with such quarter and beginning after he attained the age of 21 were quarters of coverage, or (if the number of quarters in such period is less than 12) not less than 6 of the quarters in the 12-quarter period ending with such quarter were quarters of coverage, or

(iii) in the case of an individual (not otherwise insured under clause (i)) who, by reason of clause (ii), had a prior period of disability that began during a period before the quarter in which he or she attained age 31, not less than one-half of the quarters beginning after such individual attained age 21 and ending with such quarter are quarters of coverage, or (if the number of quarters in such period is less than 12) not less than 6 of the quarters in the 12-quarter period ending with such quarter are quarters of coverage;

except that the provisions of subparagraph (B) of this paragraph shall not apply in the case of an individual who is blind (within the meaning of "blindness" as defined in paragraph (1)). For purposes of subparagraph (B) of this paragraph, when the number of quarters in any period is an odd number, such number shall be reduced by one, and a quarter shall not be counted as part of any period if any part of such quarter was included in a prior period of disability unless such quarter was a quarter of coverage.

(j) Periods of limitation ending on nonwork days

Where this subchapter, any provision of another law of the United States (other than the Internal Revenue Code of 1986) relating to or changing the effect of this subchapter, or any regulation issued by the Commissioner of Social Security pursuant thereto provides for a period within which an act is required to be done which affects eligibility for or the amount of any benefit or payment under this subchapter or is necessary to establish or protect any rights under this subchapter, and such period ends on a Saturday, Sunday, or legal holiday, or on any other day all or part of which is declared to be a nonwork day for Federal employees by statute or Executive order, then such act shall be considered as done within such period if it is done on the first day thereafter which is not a Saturday, Sunday, or legal holiday or any other day all or part of which is declared to be a nonwork day for Federal employees by statute or Executive order. For purposes of this subsection, the day on which a period ends shall include the day on which an extension of such period, as authorized by law or by the Commissioner of Social Security pursuant to law, ends. The provisions of this subsection shall not extend the period during which benefits under this subchapter may (pursuant to section 402(j)(1) or 423(b) of this title) be paid for months prior to the day application for such benefits is filed, or during which an application for benefits under this subchapter may (pursuant to section 402(j)(2) or 423(b) of this title) be accepted as such.

(k) Waiver of nine-month requirement for widow, stepchild, or widower in case of accidental death or in case of serviceman dying in line of duty, or in case of remarriage to same individual

The requirement in clause (E) of subsection (c)(1) of this section or clause (E) of subsection (g)(1) of this section that the surviving spouse of an individual have been married to such individual for a period of not less than nine months immediately prior to the day on which such individual died in order to qualify as such individual's widow or widower, and the requirement in subsection (e) of this section that the stepchild of a deceased individual have been such stepchild for not less than nine months immediately preceding the day on which such individual died in order to qualify as such individual's child, shall be deemed to be satisfied, where such individual dies within the applicable nine-month period, if—

(1) his death—

(A) is accidental, or

(B) occurs in line of duty while he is a member of a uniformed service serving on active duty (as defined in section 410(*l*)(2) of this title),

unless the Commissioner of Social Security determines that at the time of the marriage involved the individual could not have reasonably been expected to live for nine months, or

(2)(A) the widow or widower of such individual had been previously married to such individual and subsequently divorced and such requirement would have been satisfied at the time of such divorce if such previous marriage had been terminated by the death of such individual at such time instead of by divorce; or

(B) the stepchild of such individual had been the stepchild of such individual during a previous marriage of such stepchild's parent to such individual which ended in divorce and such requirement would have been satisfied at the time of such divorce if such previous marriage had been terminated by the death of such individual at such time instead of by divorce;

except that paragraph (2) of this subsection shall not apply if the Commissioner of Social Security determines that at the time of the marriage involved the individual could not have reasonably been expected to live for nine months. For purposes of paragraph (1)(A) of this subsection, the death of an individual is accidental if he receives bodily injuries solely through violent, external, and accidental means and, as a direct result of the bodily injuries and independently of all other causes, loses his life not later than three months after the day on which he receives such bodily injuries.

(*l*) Retirement age

(1) The term "retirement age" means—

(A) with respect to an individual who attains early retirement age (as defined in paragraph (2)) before January 1, 2000, 65 years of age;

(B) with respect to an individual who attains early retirement age after December 31, 1999, and before January 1, 2005, 65 years of age plus the number of months in the age increase factor (as determined under paragraph (3)) for the calendar year in which such individual attains early retirement age;

(C) with respect to an individual who attains early retirement age after December 31, 2004, and before January 1, 2017, 66 years of age;

(D) with respect to an individual who attains early retirement age after December 31, 2016, and before January 1, 2022, 66 years of age plus the number of months in the age increase factor (as determined under paragraph (3)) for the calendar year in which such individual attains early retirement age; and

(E) with respect to an individual who attains early retirement age after December 31, 2021, 67 years of age.

(2) The term "early retirement age" means age 62 in the case of an old-age, wife's, or husband's insurance benefit, and age 60 in the case of a widow's or widower's insurance benefit.

(3) The age increase factor for any individual who attains early retirement age in a calendar year within the period to which subparagraph (B) or (D) of paragraph (1) applies shall be determined as follows:

(A) With respect to an individual who attains early retirement age in the 5-year period consisting of the calendar years 2000 through 2004, the age increase factor shall be equal to two-twelfths of the number of months in the period beginning with January 2000 and ending with December of the year in which the individual attains early retirement age.

(B) With respect to an individual who attains early retirement age in the 5-year period consisting of the calendar years 2017 through 2021, the age increase factor shall be equal to two-twelfths of the number of months in the period beginning with January 2017 and ending with December of the year in which the individual attains early retirement age.

(Aug. 14, 1935, c. 531, Title II, § 216, as added Aug. 28, 1950, c. 809, Title I, § 104(a), 64 Stat. 510; amended July 18, 1952, c. 945, § 3(d), 66 Stat. 771; Sept. 1, 1954, c. 1206, Title I, § 106(d), 68 Stat. 1080; Aug. 1, 1956, c. 836, Title I, §§ 102(a), (d)(12), 103(c)(6), 70 Stat. 809, 815, 818; Pub.L. 85–109, § 1, July 17, 1957, 71 Stat. 308; Pub.L. 85–238, § 3(h), Aug. 30, 1957, 71 Stat. 519; Pub.L. 85–840, Title II, §§ 201, 203, 204(a), Title III, §§ 301(a)(2), (b)(2), (c)(2), (d), (e), 302(a), 305(b), Aug. 28, 1958, 72 Stat. 1020, 1021, 1026–1028, 1030; Pub.L. 86–778, Title II, §§ 207(a)–(c), 208(a)–(c), Title IV, §§ 402(e), 403(c), Title VII, § 703, Sept. 13, 1960, 74 Stat. 950–952, 968, 969, 994; Pub.L. 87–64, Title I, §§ 102(b)(2)(D), (c)(1), (2)(B), (3)(C), 105, June 30, 1961, 75 Stat. 134, 135, 139; Pub.L. 88–650, § 1(a) to (c), Oct. 13, 1964, 78 Stat. 1075; Pub.L. 89–97, Title III, §§ 303(a)(1), (b)(1), (2), 304(l), 306(c)(13), 308(c), (d)(2)(B), 328(b), 334(a) to (d), 339(a), 344(a), July 30, 1965, 79 Stat. 366, 367, 370, 373, 377, 378, 400, 404, 405, 409, 412; Pub.L. 90–248, Title I, §§ 104(d)(2), 105(a), 111(a), 150(a), 156(a) to (d), 158(d), 172(a), (b), Jan. 2, 1968, 81 Stat. 832, 833, 837, 860, 866, 869, 877; Pub.L. 92–603, Title I, §§ 104(g), 113(a), 115(b), 116(d), 117(a), 118(b), 145(a), Oct. 30, 1972, 86 Stat. 1341, 1347, 1349 to 1351, 1370; Pub.L. 93–445, Title III, § 304, Oct. 16, 1974, 88 Stat. 1358; Pub.L. 95–216, Title III, § 337(a), Dec. 20, 1977, 91 Stat. 1548; Pub.L. 96–265, Title III, §§ 303(b)(2)(B), 306(b), June 9, 1980, 94 Stat. 453, 457; Pub.L. 96–473, § 5(a)(2), Oct. 19, 1980, 94 Stat. 2265; Pub.L. 97–35, Title XXII, §§ 2202(a)(2), 2203(b)(2), (c)(2), (d)(3), (4), Aug. 13, 1981, 95 Stat. 835–837; Pub.L. 98–21, Title II, § 201(a), (c)(1)(D), Title III, §§ 301(c), 303, 304(c), 306(c), 309(j), (k), 332(a), 333(a), Apr. 20, 1983, 97 Stat. 107, 109, 111, 112, 114, 117, 129; Pub.L. 98–369, Div. B, Title VI, §§ 2661(l), 2662(c)(1), 2663(a)(11), July 18, 1984, 98 Stat. 1158, 1159, 1164; Pub.L. 98–460, §§ 2(b), 4(a)(2), Oct. 9, 1984, 98 Stat. 1796, 1800; Pub.L. 100–203, Title IX, § 9010(e)(1), Dec. 22, 1987, 101 Stat. 1330–294; Pub.L. 101–508, Title V, §§ 5103(b)(1), 5104(a), 5119(a), (b), Nov. 5, 1990, 104 Stat. 1388–251, 1388–254, 1388–278, 1388–279; Pub.L. 103–296, Title I, § 107(a)(4), Title III, § 321(c)(6)(H), Aug. 15, 1994, 108 Stat. 1478, 1538; Pub.L. 108–203, Title IV, § 414(a) to (c), Mar. 2, 2004, 118 Stat. 529, 530.)

Validity

The United States Supreme Court has held that certain provisions of the Social Security Act, as amended (section 339(a) of Pub.L. 89–97; 42 U.S.C.A. § 416(h)(3)), prohibiting eligibility for disability benefits for certain nonlegitimated illegitimates born after onset of disability, violates the equal protection of the law guaranteed by the due process provisions of U.S.C.A.Const. Amend. 5. Jimenez v. Weinberger, U.S.Ill. 1974, 417 U.S. 628, 94 S.Ct. 2496, 41 L.Ed.2d 363.

Commentary

The 2011 decision of the Justice Department not to enforce the Defense of Marriage Act, 1 U.S.C. § 7 (see Commentary to that section), should permit California same-sex married persons and registered domestic partners to qualify for spousal benefits under subsection (h)(1)(A)(ii).

Applying subsection (h)(2)(A), *Campbell v. Apfel, 177 F.3d 890 (9th Cir. 1999)*, holds that whether an Oregon child born out of wedlock is the child of a deceased California insured must be determined according to California intestacy law, not California's choice of law rules. Because California intestacy law would not recognize the Oregon child as an heir and the child did not otherwise qualify as decedent's child under subsection (h)(3)(C), the Oregon child was not eligible for social security child's insurance benefits.

Astrue v. Capato, 132 S.Ct. 2021 (2012), holds that the Social Security Act does not grant children's benefits to children posthumously conceived by in vitro fertilization who are not entitled to inherit from the decedent under state intestacy law. Moreover, the Act's exclusion of such children satisfies the rational basis standard of the equal protection clause. *Astrue* overrules *Gillett-Netting v. Barnhart, 317 F.3d 593 (9th Cir. 2004)*, which reached the opposite conclusion.

SUBCHAPTER IV—GRANTS TO STATES FOR AID AND SERVICES TO NEEDY FAMILIES WITH CHILDREN AND FOR CHILD-WELFARE SERVICES

PART D—CHILD SUPPORT AND ESTABLISHMENT OF PATERNITY

§ 651. Authorization of appropriations

For the purpose of enforcing the support obligations owed by noncustodial parents to their children and the spouse (or former spouse) with whom such children are living, locating noncustodial parents, establishing paternity, obtaining child and spousal support, and assuring that assistance in obtaining support will be available under this part to all children (whether or not eligible for assistance under a state program funded under part A of this subchapter) for whom such assistance is requested, there is hereby authorized to be appropriated for each fiscal year a sum sufficient to carry out the purposes of this part. *(Aug. 14, 1935, c. 531, Title IV, § 451, as added Pub.L. 93–647, § 101(a), Jan. 4, 1975, 88 Stat. 2351; amended Pub.L. 97–35, Title XXIII, § 2332(a), Aug. 13, 1981, 95 Stat. 861; Pub.L. 98–378, § 2, Aug. 16, 1984, 98 Stat. 1305; Pub.L. 104–193, Title I, § 108(c)(1),*

Title III, § 395(d)(1)(A), Aug. 22, 1996, 110 Stat. 2165, 2259.)

§ 652. Duties of Secretary

(a) Establishment of separate organizational unit; duties

The Secretary shall establish, within the Department of Health and Human Services a separate organizational unit, under the direction of a designee of the Secretary, who shall report directly to the Secretary and who shall—

(1) establish such standards for State programs for locating noncustodial parents, establishing paternity, and obtaining child support and support for the spouse (or former spouse) with whom the noncustodial parent's child is living as he determines to be necessary to assure that such programs will be effective;

(2) establish minimum organizational and staffing requirements for State units engaged in carrying out such programs under plans approved under this part;

(3) review and approve State plans for such programs;

(4)(A) review data and calculations transmitted by State agencies pursuant to section 654(15)(B) of this title on State program accomplishments with respect to performance indicators for purposes of subsection (g) of this section and section 658a of this title;

(B) review annual reports submitted pursuant to section 654(15)(A) of this title and, as appropriate, provide to the State comments, recommendations for additional or alternative corrective actions, and technical assistance; and

(C) conduct audits, in accordance with the Government auditing standards of the Comptroller General of the United States—

(i) at least once every 3 years (or more frequently, in the case of a State which fails to meet the requirements of this part concerning performance standards and reliability of program data) to assess the completeness, reliability, and security of the data and the accuracy of the reporting systems used in calculating performance indicators under subsection (g) of this section and section 658a of this title;

(ii) of the adequacy of financial management of the State program operated under the State plan approved under this part, including assessments of—

(I) whether Federal and other funds made available to carry out the State program are being appropriately expended, and are properly and fully accounted for; and

(II) whether collections and disbursements of support payments are carried out correctly and are fully accounted for; and

(iii) for such other purposes as the Secretary may find necessary;

(5) assist States in establishing adequate reporting procedures and maintain records of the operations of programs established pursuant to this part in each State, and establish procedures to be followed by States for collecting and reporting information required to be provided under this part, and establish uniform definitions (including those necessary to enable the measurement of State compliance with the requirements of this part relating to expedited processes) to be applied in following such procedures;

(6) maintain records of all amounts collected and disbursed under programs established pursuant to the provisions of this part and of the costs incurred in collecting such amounts;

(7) provide technical assistance to the States to help them establish effective systems for collecting child and spousal support and establishing paternity, and specify the minimum requirements of an affidavit to be used for the voluntary acknowledgment of paternity which shall include the social security number of each parent and, after consultation with the States, other common elements as determined by such designee;

(8) receive applications from States for permission to utilize the courts of the United States to enforce court orders for support against noncustodial parents and, upon a finding that (A) another State has not undertaken to enforce the court order of the originating State against the noncustodial parent within a reasonable time, and (B) that utilization of the Federal courts is the only reasonable method of enforcing such order, approve such applications;

(9) operate the Federal Parent Locator Service established by section 653 of this title;

(10) not later than three months after the end of each fiscal year, beginning with the year 1977, submit to the Congress a full and complete report on all activities undertaken pursuant to the provisions of this part, which report shall include, but not be limited to, the following:

(A) total program costs and collections set forth in sufficient detail to show the cost to the States and the Federal Government, the distribution of collections to families, State and local governmental units, and the Federal Government; and an identification of the financial impact of the provisions of this part, including—

(i) the total amount of child support payments collected as a result of services furnished during the fiscal year to individuals receiving services under this part;

(ii) the cost to the States and to the Federal Government of so furnishing the services; and

(iii) the number of cases involving families—

(I) who became ineligible for assistance under State programs funded under part A of this subchapter during a month in the fiscal year; and

(II) with respect to whom a child support payment was received in the month;

(B) costs and staff associated with the Office of Child Support Enforcement;

(C) the following data, separately stated for cases where the child is receiving assistance under a State program funded under part A of this subchapter (or foster care maintenance payments under part E of this subchapter), or formerly received such assistance or payments and the State is continuing to collect support assigned to it pursuant to section 608(a)(3) of this title or under section 671(a)(17) or 1396k of this title, and for all other cases under this part:

(i) the total number of cases in which a support obligation has been established in the fiscal year for which the report is submitted;

(ii) the total number of cases in which a support obligation has been established;

(iii) the number of cases in which support was collected during the fiscal year;

(iv) the total amount of support collected during such fiscal year and distributed as current support;

(v) the total amount of support collected during such fiscal year and distributed as arrearages;

(vi) the total amount of support due and unpaid for all fiscal years; and

(vii) the number of child support cases filed in each State in such fiscal year, and the amount of the collections made in each State in such fiscal year, on behalf of children residing in another State or against parents residing in another State;

(D) the status of all State plans under this part as of the end of the fiscal year last ending before the report is submitted, together with an explanation of any problems which are delaying or preventing approval of State plans under this part;

(E) data, by State, on the use of the Federal Parent Locator Service, and the number of locate requests submitted without the noncustodial parent's social security account number;

(F) the number of cases, by State, in which an applicant for or recipient of assistance under a State program funded under part A of this subchapter has refused to cooperate in identifying and locating the noncustodial parent and the number of cases in which refusal so to cooperate is based on good cause (as determined by the State);

(G) data, by State, on use of the Internal Revenue Service for collections, the number of court orders on which collections were made, the number of paternity determinations made and the number of parents located, in sufficient detail to show the cost and benefits to the States and to the Federal Government;

(H) the major problems encountered which have delayed or prevented implementation of the provisions of this part during the fiscal year last ending prior to the submission of such report; and

(I) compliance, by State, with the standards established pursuant to subsections (h) and (i) of this section; and

(11) not later than October 1, 1996, after consulting with the State directors of programs under this part, promulgate forms to be used by States in interstate cases for—

(A) collection of child support through income withholding;

(B) imposition of liens; and

(C) administrative subpoenas.

(b) Certification of child support obligations to Secretary of the Treasury for collection

The Secretary shall, upon the request of any State having in effect a State plan approved under this part, certify to the Secretary of the Treasury for collection pursuant to the provisions of section 6305 of the Internal Revenue Code of 1986 the amount of any child support obligation (including any support obligation with respect to the parent who is living with the child and receiving assistance under the State program funded under part A of this subchapter) which is assigned to such State or is undertaken to be collected by such State pursuant to section 654(4) of this title. No amount may be certified for collection under this subsection except the amount of the delinquency under a court or administrative order for support and upon a showing by the State that such State has made diligent and reasonable efforts to collect such amounts utilizing its own collection mechanisms, and upon an agreement that the State will reimburse the Secretary of the Treasury for any costs involved in making the collection. All reimbursements shall be credited to the appropriation accounts which bore all or part of the costs involved in making the collections. The Secretary after consultation with the Secretary of the Treasury may, by regulation, establish criteria for accepting amounts for collection and for making certification under this subsection including imposing such limitations on the frequency of making such certifications under this subsection.

(c) Payment of child support collections to States

The Secretary of the Treasury shall from time to time pay to each State for distribution in accordance with the provisions of section 657 of this title the amount of each collection made on behalf of such State pursuant to subsection (b) of this section.

(d) Child support management information system

(1) Except as provided in paragraph (3), the Secretary shall not approve the initial and annually updated advance automated data processing planning document, referred to in section 654(16) of this title, unless he finds that such document, when implemented, will generally carry out the objectives of the management system referred to in such subsection, and such document—

(A) provides for the conduct of, and reflects the results of, requirements analysis studies, which include consideration of the program mission, functions, organization, services, constraints, and current support, of, in, or relating to, such system,

(B) contains a description of the proposed management system referred to in section 654(16) of this title, including a description of information flows, input data, and output reports and uses,

(C) sets forth the security and interface requirements to be employed in such management system,

(D) describes the projected resource requirements for staff and other needs, and the resources available or expected to be available to meet such requirements,

(E) contains an implementation plan and backup procedures to handle possible failures,

(F) contains a summary of proposed improvement of such management system in terms of qualitative and quantitative benefits, and

(G) provides such other information as the Secretary determines under regulation is necessary.

(2)(A) The Secretary shall through the separate organizational unit established pursuant to subsection (a) of this section, on a continuing basis, review, assess, and inspect the planning, design, and operation of, management information systems referred to in section 654(16) of this title, with a view to determining whether, and to what extent, such systems meet and continue to meet requirements imposed under paragraph (1) and the conditions specified under section 654(16) of this title.

(B) If the Secretary finds with respect to any statewide management information system referred to in section 654(16) of this title that there is a failure substantially to comply with criteria, requirements, and other undertakings, prescribed by the advance automated data processing planning document theretofore approved by the Secretary with respect to such system, then the Secretary shall suspend his approval of such document until there is no longer any such failure of such system to comply with such criteria, requirements, and other undertakings so prescribed.

(3) The Secretary may waive any requirement of paragraph (1) or any condition specified under section 654(16) of this title, and shall waive the single statewide system requirement under sections 654(16) and 654a of this title, with respect to a State if—

(A) the State demonstrates to the satisfaction of the Secretary that the State has or can develop an alternative system or systems that enable the State—

(i) for purposes of section 609(a)(8) of this title, to achieve the paternity establishment percentages (as defined in subsection (g)(2) of this section) and other performance measures that may be established by the Secretary;

(ii) to submit data under section 654(15)(B) of this title that is complete and reliable;

(iii) to substantially comply with the requirements of this part; and

(iv) in the case of a request to waive the single statewide system requirement, to—

(I) meet all functional requirements of sections 654(16) and 654a of this title;

(II) ensure that calculation of distributions meets the requirements of section 657 of this title and accounts for distributions to children in different families or in different States or sub-State jurisdictions, and for distributions to other States;

(III) ensure that there is only one point of contact in the State which provides seamless case processing for all interstate case processing and coordinated, automated intrastate case management;

(IV) ensure that standardized data elements, forms, and definitions are used throughout the State;

(V) complete the alternative system in no more time than it would take to complete a single statewide system that meets such requirement; and

(VI) process child support cases as quickly, efficiently, and effectively as such cases would be processed through a single statewide system that meets such requirement;

(B)(i) the waiver meets the criteria of paragraphs (1), (2), and (3) of section 1315(c) of this title; or

(ii) the State provides assurances to the Secretary that steps will be taken to otherwise improve the State's child support enforcement program; and

(C) in the case of a request to waive the single statewide system requirement, the State has submitted to the Secretary separate estimates of the total cost of a single statewide system that meets such requirement, and of any such alternative system or systems, which shall include estimates of the cost of developing and completing the system and of operating and maintaining the system for 5 years, and the Secretary has agreed with the estimates.

(e) Technical assistance to States

The Secretary shall provide such technical assistance to States as he determines necessary to assist States to plan, design, develop, or install and provide for the security of, the management information systems referred to in section 654(16) of this title.

(f) Regulations

The Secretary shall issue regulations to require that State agencies administering the child support enforcement program under this part enforce medical support included as part of a child support order whenever health care coverage is available to the noncustodial parent at a reasonable cost. A State agency administering the program under this part may enforce medical support against a custodial parent if health care coverage is available to the custodial parent at a reasonable cost, notwithstanding any other provision of this part. Such regulation shall also provide for improved information exchange between such State agencies and the State agencies administering the State medicaid programs under subchapter XIX of this chapter with respect to the availability of health insurance coverage. For purposes of this part, the term "medical support" may include health care coverage, such as coverage under a health insurance plan (including payment of costs of premiums, co-payments, and deductibles) and payment for medical expenses incurred on behalf of a child.

(g) Performance standards for State paternity establishment programs

(1) A State's program under this part shall be found, for purposes of section 609(a)(8) of this title, not to have complied substantially with the requirements of this part unless, for any fiscal year beginning on or after October 1, 1994, its paternity establishment percentage for such fiscal year is based on reliable data and (rounded to the nearest whole percentage point) equals or exceeds—

(A) 90 percent;

(B) for a State with a paternity establishment percentage of not less than 75 percent but less than 90 percent for such fiscal year, the paternity establishment percentage of the State for the immediately preceding fiscal year plus 2 percentage points;

(C) for a State with a paternity establishment percentage of not less than 50 percent but less than 75 percent for such fiscal year, the paternity establishment percentage of the State for the immediately preceding fiscal year plus 3 percentage points;

(D) for a State with a paternity establishment percentage of not less than 45 percent but less than 50 percent for such fiscal year, the paternity establishment percentage of the State for the immediately preceding fiscal year plus 4 percentage points;

(E) for a State with a paternity establishment percentage of not less than 40 percent but less than 45 percent for such fiscal year, the paternity establishment percentage of the State for the immediately preceding fiscal year plus 5 percentage points; or

(F) for a State with a paternity establishment percentage of less than 40 percent for such fiscal year, the paternity establishment percentage of the State for the immediately preceding fiscal year plus 6 percentage points.

In determining compliance under this section, a State may use as its paternity establishment percentage either the State's IV–D paternity establishment percentage (as defined in paragraph (2)(A)) or the State's statewide paternity establishment percentage (as defined in paragraph (2)(B)).

(2) For purposes of this section—

(A) the term "IV–D paternity establishment percentage" means, with respect to a State for a fiscal year, the ratio (expressed as a percentage) that the total number of children—

(i) who have been born out of wedlock,

(ii) (I) except as provided in the last sentence of this paragraph, with respect to whom assistance is being provided under the State program funded under part A of this subchapter in the fiscal year or, at the option of the State, as of the end of such year, or (II) with respect to whom services are being provided under the State's plan approved under this part in the fiscal year or, at the option of the State, as of the end of such year pursuant to an application submitted under section 654(4)(A)(ii) of this title, and

(iii) the paternity of whom has been established or acknowledged,

bears to the total number of children born out of wedlock and (except as provided in such last sentence) with respect to whom assistance was being provided under the State program funded under part A of this subchapter as of the end of the preceding fiscal year or with respect to whom services were being provided under the State's plan approved under this part as of the end of the preceding fiscal year pursuant to an application submitted under section 654(4)(A)(ii) of this title;

(B) the term "statewide paternity establishment percentage" means, with respect to a State for a fiscal year, the ratio (expressed as a percentage) that the total number of minor children—

(i) who have been born out of wedlock, and

(ii) the paternity of whom has been established or acknowledged during the fiscal year,

bears to the total number of children born out of wedlock during the preceding fiscal year; and

(C) the term "reliable data" means the most recent data available which are found by the Secretary to be reliable for purposes of this section.

For purposes of subparagraphs (A) and (B), the total number of children shall not include any child with respect to whom assistance is being provided under the State program funded under part A of this subchapter by reason of the death of a parent unless paternity is established for such child or any child with respect to whom an applicant or recipient is found by the State to qualify for a good cause or other exception to cooperation pursuant to section 654(29) of this title.

(3)(A) The Secretary may modify the requirements of this subsection to take into account such additional variables as the Secretary identifies (including the percentage of children in a State who are born out of wedlock or for whom support has not been established) that affect the ability of a State to meet the requirements of this subsection.

(B) The Secretary shall submit an annual report to the Congress that sets forth the data upon which the paternity establishment percentages for States for a fiscal year are based, lists any additional variables the Secretary has identified under subparagraph (A), and describes State performance in establishing paternity.

(h) Prompt State response to requests for child support assistance

The standards required by subsection (a)(1) of this section shall include standards establishing time limits governing the period or periods within which a State must accept and respond to requests (from States, jurisdictions thereof, or individuals who apply for services furnished by the State agency under this part or with respect to whom an assignment pursuant to section 608(a)(3) of this title is in effect) for assistance in establishing and enforcing support orders, including requests to locate noncustodial parents, establish paternity, and initiate proceedings to establish and collect child support awards.

(i) Prompt State distribution of amounts collected as child support

The standards required by subsection (a)(1) of this section shall include standards establishing time limits governing the period or periods within which a State must distribute, in accordance with section 657 of this title, amounts collected as child support pursuant to the State's plan approved under this part.

(j) Training of Federal and State staff, research and demonstration programs, and special projects of regional or national significance

Out of any money in the Treasury of the United States not otherwise appropriated, there is hereby appropriated to the Secretary for each fiscal year an amount equal to 1 percent of the total amount paid to the Federal Government pursuant to a plan approved under this part during the immediately preceding fiscal year (as determined on the basis of the most recent reliable data available to the Secretary as of the end of the third calendar quarter following the end of such preceding fiscal year) or the amount appropriated under this paragraph [1] for fiscal year 2002, whichever is greater, which shall be available for use by the Secretary, either directly or through grants, contracts, or interagency agreements, for—

(1) information dissemination and technical assistance to States, training of State and Federal staff, staffing studies, and related activities needed to improve programs under this part (including technical assistance concerning State automated systems required by this part); and

(2) research, demonstration, and special projects of regional or national significance relating to the operation of State programs under this part.

The amount appropriated under this subsection shall remain available until expended.

(k) Denial of passports for nonpayment of child support

(1) If the Secretary receives a certification by a State agency in accordance with the requirements of section 654(31) of this title that an individual owes arrearages of child support in an amount exceeding $2,500, the Secretary shall transmit such certification to the Secretary of State for action (with respect to denial, revocation, or limitation of passports) pursuant to paragraph (2).

(2) The Secretary of State shall, upon certification by the Secretary transmitted under paragraph (1), refuse to issue a passport to such individual, and may revoke, restrict, or limit a passport issued previously to such individual.

(3) The Secretary and the Secretary of State shall not be liable to an individual for any action with respect to a certification by a State agency under this section.

(*l*) Facilitation of agreements between State agencies and financial institutions

The Secretary, through the Federal Parent Locator Service, may aid State agencies providing services under State programs operated pursuant to this part and financial institutions doing business in two or more States in reaching agreements regarding the receipt from such institutions, and the transfer to the State agencies, of information that may be provided pursuant to section 666(a)(17)(A)(i) of this title, except that any State that, as of July 16, 1998, is conducting data matches pursuant to section 666(a)(17)(A)(i) of this title shall have until January 1, 2000, to allow the Secretary to obtain such information from such institutions that are operating in the State. For purposes of section 3413(d) of Title 12, a disclosure pursuant to this subsection shall be considered a disclosure pursuant to a Federal statute.

(m) Comparisons with insurance information

(1) In general

The Secretary, through the Federal Parent Locator Service, may—

(A) compare information concerning individuals owing past-due support with information maintained by insurers (or their agents) concerning insurance claims, settlements, awards, and payments; and

(B) furnish information resulting from the data matches to the State agencies responsible for collecting child support from the individuals.

(2) Liability

An insurer (including any agent of an insurer) shall not be liable under any Federal or State law to any person for any disclosure provided for under this subsection, or for any other action taken in good faith in accordance with this subsection.

(n) The Secretary shall use the authorities otherwise provided by law to ensure the compliance of the United States with any multilateral child support convention to which the United States is a party.

(*o*) Data exchange standards for improved interoperability

(1) Designation

The Secretary shall, in consultation with an interagency work group established by the Office of Management and Budget and considering State government perspectives, by rule, designate data exchange standards to govern, under this part—

(A) necessary categories of information that State agencies operating programs under State plans approved under this part are required under applicable Federal law to electronically exchange with another State agency; and

(B) Federal reporting and data exchange required under applicable Federal law.

(2) Requirements

The data exchange standards required by paragraph (1) shall, to the extent practicable—

(A) incorporate a widely accepted, non-proprietary, searchable, computer-readable format, such as the eXtensible Markup Language;

(B) contain interoperable standards developed and maintained by intergovernmental partnerships, such as the National Information Exchange Model;

(C) incorporate interoperable standards developed and maintained by Federal entities with authority over contracting and financial assistance;

(D) be consistent with and implement applicable accounting principles;

(E) be implemented in a manner that is cost-effective and improves program efficiency and effectiveness; and

(F) be capable of being continually upgraded as necessary.

(3) Rule of construction

Nothing in this subsection shall be construed to require a change to existing data exchange standards found to be effective and efficient.

(Aug. 14, 1935, c. 531, Title IV, § 452, as added Pub.L. 93–647, § 101(a), Jan. 4, 1975, 88 Stat. 2351; amended Pub.L. 95–30, Title V, § 504(a), May 23, 1977, 91 Stat. 163; Pub.L. 96–265, Title IV, §§ 402(a), 405(c), (d), June 9, 1980, 94 Stat. 462, 464, 465; Pub.L. 96–272, Title III, § 301(b), June 17, 1980, 94 Stat. 527; Pub.L. 97–35, Title XXIII, § 2332(b), Aug. 13, 1981, 95 Stat. 861; Pub.L. 97–248, Title I, § 175(a)(1), Sept. 3, 1982, 96 Stat. 403; Pub.L. 98–369, Div. B, Title VI, § 2663(c)(12), (j)(2)(B)(viii), July 18, 1984, 98 Stat. 1166, 1170; Pub.L. 98–378, §§ 4(b), 9(a)(1), 13(a), (b), 16, Aug. 16, 1984, 98 Stat. 1312, 1316, 1319, 1321; Pub.L. 100–203, Title IX, § 9143(a), Dec. 22, 1987, 101 Stat. 1330–322; Pub.L. 100–485, Title I, §§ 111(a), 121(a), 122(a), 123(b), (d), Oct. 13, 1988, 102 Stat. 2348, 2351, 2353; Pub.L. 101–239, Title X, § 10403(a)(1)(B)(i), Dec. 19, 1989, 103 Stat. 2487; Pub.L. 103–66, Title XIII, § 13721(a), Aug. 10, 1993, 107 Stat. 658; Pub.L. 103–432, Title II, § 213, Oct. 31, 1994, 108 Stat. 4461; Pub.L. 104–35, § 1(b), Oct. 12, 1995, 109 Stat. 294; Pub.L. 104–193, Title I, § 108(c)(2) to (9), Title III, §§ 301(c)(1), (2), 316(e)(1), 324(a), 331(b), 341(c), 342(b), 343(a), 345(a), 346(a), 370(a)(1), 395(d)(1)(B), Aug. 22, 1996, 110 Stat. 2165, 2200, 2216, 2223, 2230, 2232 to 2234, 2237 to 2239, 2252, 2259; Pub.L. 104–208, Div. A, Title I, § 101(e) [Title II, § 215], Sept. 30, 1996, 110 Stat. 3009–255; Pub.L. 105–33, Title V, §§5513(a)(1), (2), 5540, 5541(a), 5556(c), Aug. 5, 1997, 111 Stat. 619, 630, 637; Pub.L. 105–200, Title I, §§ 102(a), Title II, § 201(e)(1)(A), Title IV, §§ 401(c)(2), 406(b), 407(b), July 16, 1998, 112 Stat. 647, 657, 662, 671, 672; Pub.L. 106–169, Title IV, § 401(f), Dec. 14, 1999, 113 Stat. 1858; Pub.L. 109–171, Title VII, §§ 7303(a), 7304, 7306(a), 7307(a)(2)(A)(i), (b), (c), Feb. 8, 2006, 120 Stat. 145, 146; Pub.L. 113–183, Title III, §§ 301(a)(1), 304(a), Sept. 29, 2014, 128 Stat. 1943, 1947.)

[1] So in original. Probably should be "subsection".

Commentary

Eunique v. Powell, 302 F.3d 971 (9th Cir. 2002), holds that the State Department's refusal of a passport under subsection (k) of this section does not unconstitutionally violate a support obligor's freedom to travel internationally.

§ 653. Federal Parent Locator Service

(a) Establishment; purpose

(1) The Secretary shall establish and conduct a Federal Parent Locator Service, under the direction of the designee of the Secretary referred to in section 652(a) of this title, which shall be used for the purposes specified in paragraphs (2) and (3).

(2) For the purpose of establishing parentage or establishing, setting the amount of, modifying, or enforcing child support obligations, the Federal Parent Locator Service shall obtain and transmit to any authorized person specified in subsection (c) of this section—

(A) information on, or facilitating the discovery of, the location of any individual—

(i) who is under an obligation to pay child support;

(ii) against whom such an obligation is sought;

(iii) to whom such an obligation is owed; or

(iv) who has or may have parental rights with respect to a child,

including the individual's social security number (or numbers), most recent address, and the name, address, and employer identification number of the individual's employer;

(B) information on the individual's wages (or other income) from, and benefits of, employment (including rights to or enrollment in group health care coverage); and

(C) information on the type, status, location, and amount of any assets of, or debts owed by or to, any such individual.

(3) For the purpose of enforcing any Federal or State law with respect to the unlawful taking or restraint of a child, or making or enforcing a child custody or visitation determination, as defined in section 663(d)(1) of this title, the Federal Parent Locator Service shall be used to obtain and transmit the information specified in section 663(c) of this title to the authorized persons specified in section 663(d)(2) of this title.

(b) Disclosure of information to authorized persons

(1) Upon request, filed in accordance with subsection (d) of this section, of any authorized person, as defined in subsection (c) of this section for the information described in subsection (a)(2) of this section, or of any authorized person, as defined in section 663(d)(2) of this title for the information described in section 663(c) of this title, the Secretary shall, notwithstanding any other provision of law, provide through the Federal Parent Locator Service such information to such person, if such information—

(A) is contained in any files or records maintained by the Secretary or by the Department of Health and Human Services; or

(B) is not contained in such files or records, but can be obtained by the Secretary, under the authority conferred by subsection (e) of this section, from any other department, agency, or instrumentality of the United States or of any State, and is not prohibited from disclosure under paragraph (2).

(2) No information shall be disclosed to any person if the disclosure of such information would contravene the national policy or security interests of the United States or the confidentiality of census data. The Secretary shall give priority to requests made by any authorized person described in subsection (c)(1) of this section. No information shall be disclosed to any person if the State has notified the Secretary that the State has reasonable evidence of domestic violence or child abuse and the disclosure of such information could be harmful to the custodial parent or the child of such parent, provided that—

(A) in response to a request from an authorized person (as defined in subsection (c) of this section and section 663(d)(2) of this title), the Secretary shall advise the authorized person that the Secretary has been notified that there is reasonable evidence of domestic violence or child abuse and that information can only be disclosed to a court or an agent of a court pursuant to subparagraph (B); and

(B) information may be disclosed to a court or an agent of a court described in subsection (c)(2) of this section or section 663(d)(2)(B) of this title, if—

(i) upon receipt of information from the Secretary, the court determines whether disclosure to any other person of that information could be harmful to the parent or the child; and

(ii) if the court determines that disclosure of such information to any other person could be harmful, the court and its agents shall not make any such disclosure.

(3) Information received or transmitted pursuant to this section shall be subject to the safeguard provisions contained in section 654(26) of this title.

(c) "Authorized person" defined

As used in subsection (a) of this section, the term "authorized person" means—

(1) any agent or attorney of any State or Indian tribe or tribal organization (as defined in subsections (e) and (*l*) of section 5304 of Title 25), having in effect a plan approved under this part, who has the duty or authority under such plans to seek to recover any amounts owed as child and spousal support (including, when authorized under the State plan, any official of a political subdivision);

(2) the court which has authority to issue an order or to serve as the initiating court in an action to seek an order against a noncustodial parent for the support and maintenance of a child, or any agent of such court;

(3) the resident parent, legal guardian, attorney, or agent of a child (other than a child receiving assistance under a State program funded under part A of this subchapter) (as determined by regulations prescribed by the Secretary) without regard to the existence of a court order against a noncustodial parent who has a duty to support and maintain any such child;

(4) a State agency that is administering a program operated under a State plan under subpart 1 of part B of this subchapter, or a State plan approved under subpart 2 of part B of this subchapter or under part E of this subchapter; and

(5) an entity designated as a Central Authority for child support enforcement in a foreign reciprocating country or a foreign treaty country for purposes specified in section 659a(c)(2) of this title.

(d) Form and manner of request for information

A request for information under this section shall be filed in such manner and form as the Secretary shall by regulation prescribe and shall be accompanied or supported by such documents as the Secretary may determine to be necessary.

(e) Compliance with request; search of files and records by head of any department, etc., of United States; transmittal of information to Secretary; reimbursement for cost of search; fees

(1) Whenever the Secretary receives a request submitted under subsection (b) of this section which he is reasonably satisfied meets the criteria established by subsections (a), (b), and (c) of this section, he shall promptly undertake to provide the information requested from the files and records maintained by any of the departments, agencies, or instrumentalities of the United States or of any State.

(2) Notwithstanding any other provision of law, whenever the individual who is the head of any department, agency, or instrumentality of the United States receives a request from the Secretary for information authorized to be provided by the Secretary under this section, such individual shall promptly cause a search to be made of the files and records maintained by such department, agency, or instrumentality with a view to determining whether the information requested is contained in any such files or records. If such search discloses the information requested, such individual shall immediately transmit such information to the Secretary, except that if any information is obtained the disclosure of which would contravene national policy or security interests of the United States or the confidentiality of census data, such information shall not be transmitted and such individual shall immediately notify the Secretary. If such search fails to disclose the information requested, such individual shall immediately so notify the Secretary. The costs incurred by any such department, agency, or instrumentality of the United States or of any State in providing such information to the Secretary shall be reimbursed by him in an amount which the Secretary determines to be reasonable payment for the information exchange (which amount shall not include payment for the costs of obtaining, compiling, or maintaining the information). Whenever such services are furnished to an individual specified in subsection (c)(3) of this section, a fee shall be charged such individual. The fee so charged shall be used to reimburse the Secretary or his delegate for the expense of providing such services.

(3) The Secretary of Labor shall enter into an agreement with the Secretary to provide prompt access for the Secretary (in accordance with this subsection) to the wage and unemployment compensation claims information and data maintained by or for the Department of Labor or State employment security agencies.

(f) Arrangements and cooperation with State and tribal agencies

The Secretary, in carrying out his duties and functions under this section, shall enter into arrangements with State and tribal agencies administering State and tribal plans approved under this part for such State and tribal agencies to accept from resident parents, legal guardians, or agents of a child described in subsection (c)(3) of this section and to transmit to the Secretary requests for information with regard to the whereabouts of noncustodial parents and otherwise to cooperate with the Secretary in carrying out the purposes of this section.

(g) Reimbursement for reports by State agencies

The Secretary may reimburse Federal and State agencies for the costs incurred by such entities in furnishing information requested by the Secretary under this section in an amount which the Secretary determines to be reasonable payment for the information exchange (which amount shall not include payment for the costs of obtaining, compiling, or maintaining the information).

(h) Federal Case Registry of Child Support Orders

(1) In general

Not later than October 1, 1998, in order to assist States in administering programs under State plans approved under this part and programs funded under part A of this subchapter, and for the other purposes specified in this section, the Secretary shall establish and maintain in the Federal Parent Locator Service an automated registry (which shall be known as the "Federal Case Registry of Child Support Orders"), which shall contain abstracts of support orders and other information described in paragraph (2) with respect to each case and order in each State case registry maintained pursuant to section 654a(e) of this title, as furnished (and regularly updated), pursuant to section 654a(f) of this title, by State agencies administering programs under this part.

(2) Case and order information

The information referred to in paragraph (1) with respect to a case or an order shall be such information as the Secretary may specify in regulations (including the names, social security numbers or other uniform identification numbers, and State case identification numbers) to identify the individuals who owe or are owed support (or with respect to or on behalf of whom support obligations are sought to be established), and the State or States which have the case or order. Beginning not later than October 1, 1999, the information referred to in paragraph (1) shall include the names and social security numbers of the children of such individuals.

(3) Administration of Federal tax laws

The Secretary of the Treasury shall have access to the information described in paragraph (2) for the purpose of administering those sections of the Internal Revenue Code of 1986 which grant tax benefits based on support or residence of children.

(i) National Directory of New Hires

(1) In general

In order to assist States in administering programs under State plans approved under this part and programs funded under part A of this subchapter, and for the other purposes specified in this section, the Secretary shall, not later than October 1, 1997, establish and maintain in the Federal Parent Locator Service an automated directory to be known as the National Directory of New Hires, which shall contain the information supplied pursuant to section 653a(g)(2) of this title.

(2) Data entry and deletion requirements

(A) In general

Information provided pursuant to section 653a(g)(2) of this title shall be entered into the data base maintained by the National Directory of New Hires within two business days after receipt, and shall be deleted from the data base 24 months after the date of entry.

(B) 12–month limit on access to wage and unemployment compensation information

The Secretary shall not have access for child support enforcement purposes to information in the National Directory of New Hires that is provided pursuant to section 653a(g)(2)(B) of this title, if 12 months has elapsed since the date the information is so provided and there has not been a match resulting from the use of such information in any information comparison under this subsection.

(C) Retention of data for research purposes

Notwithstanding subparagraphs (A) and (B), the Secretary may retain such samples of data entered in the National Directory of New Hires as the Secretary may find necessary to assist in carrying out subsection (j)(5) of this section.

(3) Administration of Federal tax laws

The Secretary of the Treasury shall have access to the information in the National Directory of New Hires for purposes of administering section 32 of the Internal Revenue Code of 1986, or the advance payment of the earned income tax credit under section 3507 of such Code, and verifying a claim with respect to employment in a tax return.

(4) List of multistate employers

The Secretary shall maintain within the National Directory of New Hires a list of multistate employers that report information regarding newly hired employees pursuant to section 653a(b)(1)(B) of this title, and the State which each such employer has designated to receive such information.

(j) Information comparisons and other disclosures

(1) Verification by Social Security Administration

(A) In general

The Secretary shall transmit information on individuals and employers maintained under this section to the Social Security Administration to the extent necessary for verification in accordance with subparagraph (B).

(B) Verification by SSA

The Social Security Administration shall verify the accuracy of, correct, or supply to the extent possible, and report to the Secretary, the following information supplied by the Secretary pursuant to subparagraph (A):

(i) The name, social security number, and birth date of each such individual.

(ii) The employer identification number of each such employer.

(2) Information comparisons

For the purpose of locating individuals in a paternity establishment case or a case involving the establishment, modification, or enforcement of a support order, the Secretary shall—

(A) compare information in the National Directory of New Hires against information in the support case abstracts in the Federal Case Registry of Child Support Orders not less often than every 2 business days; and

(B) within 2 business days after such a comparison reveals a match with respect to an individual, report the information to the State agency responsible for the case.

(3) Information comparisons and disclosures of information in all registries for subchapter IV program purposes

To the extent and with the frequency that the Secretary determines to be effective in assisting States to carry out their responsibilities under programs operated under this part, part B of this subchapter, or part E of this subchapter and programs funded under part A of this subchapter, the Secretary shall—

(A) compare the information in each component of the Federal Parent Locator Service maintained under this section against the information in each other such component (other than the comparison required by paragraph (2)), and report instances in which such a comparison reveals a match with respect to an individual to State agencies operating such programs; and

(B) disclose information in such components to such State agencies.

(4) Provision of new hire information to the Social Security Administration

The National Directory of New Hires shall provide the Commissioner of Social Security with all information in the National Directory.

(5) Research

The Secretary may provide access to data in each component of the Federal Parent Locator Service maintained under this section and to information reported by employers pursuant to section 653a(b) of this title for research purposes found by the Secretary to be likely to contribute to achieving the purposes of part A of this subchapter or this part, but without personal identifiers.

(6) Information comparisons and disclosure for enforcement of obligations on Higher Education Act loans and grants

(A) Furnishing of information by the Secretary of Education

The Secretary of Education shall furnish to the Secretary, on a quarterly basis or at such less frequent intervals as may be determined by the Secretary of Education, information in the custody of the Secretary of Education for comparison with information in the National Directory of New Hires, in order to obtain the information in such directory with respect to individuals who—

(i) are borrowers of loans made under Title IV of the Higher Education Act of 1965 that are in default; or

(ii) owe an obligation to refund an overpayment of a grant awarded under such title.

(B) Requirement to seek minimum information necessary

The Secretary of Education shall seek information pursuant to this section only to the extent essential to improving collection of the debt described in subparagraph (A).

(C) Duties of the Secretary

(i) Information comparison; disclosure to the Secretary of Education

The Secretary, in cooperation with the Secretary of Education, shall compare information in the National Directory of New Hires with information in the custody of the Secretary of Education, and disclose information in that Directory to the Secretary of Education, in accordance with this paragraph, for the purposes specified in this paragraph.

(ii) **Condition on disclosure**

The Secretary shall make disclosures in accordance with clause (i) only to the extent that the Secretary determines that such disclosures do not interfere with the effective operation of the program under this part. Support collection under section 666(b) of this title shall be given priority over collection of any defaulted student loan or grant overpayment against the same income.

(D) **Use of information by the Secretary of Education**

The Secretary of Education may use information resulting from a data match pursuant to this paragraph only—

(i) for the purpose of collection of the debt described in subparagraph (A) owed by an individual whose annualized wage level (determined by taking into consideration information from the National Directory of New Hires) exceeds $16,000; and

(ii) after removal of personal identifiers, to conduct analyses of student loan defaults.

(E) **Disclosure of information by the Secretary of Education**

(i) **Disclosures permitted**

The Secretary of Education may disclose information resulting from a data match pursuant to this paragraph only to—

(I) a guaranty agency holding a loan made under part B of Title IV of the Higher Education Act of 1965 on which the individual is obligated;

(II) a contractor or agent of the guaranty agency described in subclause (I);

(III) a contractor or agent of the Secretary; and

(IV) the Attorney General.

(ii) **Purpose of disclosure**

The Secretary of Education may make a disclosure under clause (i) only for the purpose of collection of the debts owed on defaulted student loans, or overpayments of grants, made under Title IV of the Higher Education Act of 1965.

(iii) **Restriction on redisclosure**

An entity to which information is disclosed under clause (i) may use or disclose such information only as needed for the purpose of collecting on defaulted student loans, or overpayments of grants, made under Title IV of the Higher Education Act of 1965.

(F) **Reimbursement of HHS costs**

The Secretary of Education shall reimburse the Secretary, in accordance with subsection (k)(3) of this section, for the additional costs incurred by the Secretary in furnishing the information requested under this subparagraph.

(7) **Information comparisons for housing assistance programs**

(A) **Furnishing of information by HUD**

Subject to subparagraph (G), the Secretary of Housing and Urban Development shall furnish to the Secretary, on such periodic basis as determined by the Secretary of Housing and Urban Development in consultation with the Secretary, information in the custody of the Secretary of Housing and Urban Development for comparison with information in the National Directory of New Hires, in order to obtain information in such Directory with respect to individuals who are participating in any program under—

(i) the United States Housing Act of 1937 (42 U.S.C. 1437 et seq.);

(ii) section 1701q of Title 12;

(iii) section 1715*l*(d)(3), 1715*l*(d)(5), or 1715z–1 of Title 12;

(iv) section 8013 of this title; or

(v) section 1701s of Title 12.

(B) **Requirement to seek minimum information**

The Secretary of Housing and Urban Development shall seek information pursuant to this section only to the extent necessary to verify the employment and income of individuals described in subparagraph (A).

(C) **Duties of the Secretary**

(i) **Information disclosure**

The Secretary, in cooperation with the Secretary of Housing and Urban Development, shall compare information in the National Directory of New Hires with information provided by the Secretary of Housing and Urban Development with respect to individuals described in subparagraph (A), and shall disclose information in such Directory regarding such individuals to the Secretary of Housing and Urban Development, in accordance with this paragraph, for the purposes specified in this paragraph.

(ii) **Condition on disclosure**

The Secretary shall make disclosures in accordance with clause (i) only to the extent that the Secretary determines that such disclosures do not interfere with the effective operation of the program under this part.

(D) Use of information by HUD

The Secretary of Housing and Urban Development may use information resulting from a data match pursuant to this paragraph only—

(i) for the purpose of verifying the employment and income of individuals described in subparagraph (A); and

(ii) after removal of personal identifiers, to conduct analyses of the employment and income reporting of individuals described in subparagraph (A).

(E) Disclosure of information by HUD

(i) Purpose of disclosure

The Secretary of Housing and Urban Development may make a disclosure under this subparagraph only for the purpose of verifying the employment and income of individuals described in subparagraph (A).

(ii) Disclosures permitted

Subject to clause (iii), the Secretary of Housing and Urban Development may disclose information resulting from a data match pursuant to this paragraph only to a public housing agency, the Inspector General of the Department of Housing and Urban Development, and the Attorney General in connection with the administration of a program described in subparagraph (A). Information obtained by the Secretary of Housing and Urban Development pursuant to this paragraph shall not be made available under section 552 of Title 5.

(iii) Conditions on disclosure

Disclosures under this paragraph shall be—

(I) made in accordance with data security and control policies established by the Secretary of Housing and Urban Development and approved by the Secretary;

(II) subject to audit in a manner satisfactory to the Secretary; and

(III) subject to the sanctions under subsection (*l*)(2) of this section.

(iv) Additional disclosures

(I) Determination by secretaries

The Secretary of Housing and Urban Development and the Secretary shall determine whether to permit disclosure of information under this paragraph to persons or entities described in subclause (II), based on an evaluation made by the Secretary of Housing and Urban Development (in consultation with and approved by the Secretary), of the costs and benefits of disclosures made under clause (ii) and the adequacy of measures used to safeguard the security and confidentiality of information so disclosed.

(II) Permitted persons or entities

If the Secretary of Housing and Urban Development and the Secretary determine pursuant to subclause (I) that disclosures to additional persons or entities shall be permitted, information under this paragraph may be disclosed by the Secretary of Housing and Urban Development to a private owner, a management agent, and a contract administrator in connection with the administration of a program described in subparagraph (A), subject to the conditions in clause (iii) and such additional conditions as agreed to by the Secretaries.

(v) Restrictions on redisclosure

A person or entity to which information is disclosed under this subparagraph may use or disclose such information only as needed for verifying the employment and income of individuals described in subparagraph (A), subject to the conditions in clause (iii) and such additional conditions as agreed to by the Secretaries.

(F) Reimbursement of HHS costs

The Secretary of Housing and Urban Development shall reimburse the Secretary, in accordance with subsection (k)(3) of this section, for the costs incurred by the Secretary in furnishing the information requested under this paragraph.

(G) Consent

The Secretary of Housing and Urban Development shall not seek, use, or disclose information under this paragraph relating to an individual without the prior written consent of such individual (or of a person legally authorized to consent on behalf of such individual).

(8) Information comparisons and disclosure to assist in administration of unemployment compensation programs

(A) In general

If, for purposes of administering an unemployment compensation program under Federal or State law, a State agency responsible for the administration of such program transmits to the Secretary the names and social security account numbers of individuals, the Secretary shall disclose to such State agency information on such individuals and their employers maintained in the National Directory of New Hires, subject to this paragraph.

(B) Condition on disclosure by the Secretary

The Secretary shall make a disclosure under subparagraph (A) only to the extent that the Secretary determines that the disclosure would not interfere with the effective operation of the program under this part.

(C) Use and disclosure of information by State agencies

(i) In general

A State agency may not use or disclose information provided under this paragraph except for purposes of administering a program referred to in subparagraph (A).

(ii) Information security

The State agency shall have in effect data security and control policies that the Secretary finds adequate to ensure the security of information obtained under this paragraph and to ensure that access to such information is restricted to authorized persons for purposes of authorized uses and disclosures.

(iii) Penalty for misuse of information

An officer or employee of the State agency who fails to comply with this subparagraph shall be subject to the sanctions under subsection *(l)* (2) of this section to the same extent as if such officer or employee was an officer or employee of the United States.

(D) Procedural requirements

State agencies requesting information under this paragraph shall adhere to uniform procedures established by the Secretary governing information requests and data matching under this paragraph.

(E) Reimbursement of costs

The State agency shall reimburse the Secretary, in accordance with subsection (k)(3) of this section, for the costs incurred by the Secretary in furnishing the information requested under this paragraph.

(9) Information comparisons and disclosure to assist in Federal debt collection

(A) Furnishing of information by the Secretary of the Treasury

The Secretary of the Treasury shall furnish to the Secretary, on such periodic basis as determined by the Secretary of the Treasury in consultation with the Secretary, information in the custody of the Secretary of the Treasury for comparison with information in the National Directory of New Hires, in order to obtain information in such Directory with respect to persons—

(i) who owe delinquent nontax debt to the United States; and

(ii) whose debt has been referred to the Secretary of the Treasury in accordance with section 3711(g) of Title 31.

(B) Requirement to seek minimum information

The Secretary of the Treasury shall seek information pursuant to this section only to the extent necessary to improve collection of the debt described in subparagraph (A).

(C) Duties of the Secretary

(i) Information disclosure

The Secretary, in cooperation with the Secretary of the Treasury, shall compare information in the National Directory of New Hires with information provided by the Secretary of the Treasury with respect to persons described in subparagraph (A) and shall disclose information in such Directory regarding such persons to the Secretary of the Treasury in accordance with this paragraph, for the purposes specified in this paragraph. Such comparison of information shall not be considered a matching program as defined in section 552a of Title 5.

(ii) Condition on disclosure

The Secretary shall make disclosures in accordance with clause (i) only to the extent that the Secretary determines that such disclosures do not interfere with the effective operation of the program under this part. Support collection under section 666(b) of this title shall be given priority over collection of any delinquent Federal nontax debt against the same income.

(D) Use of information by the Secretary of the Treasury

The Secretary of the Treasury may use information provided under this paragraph only for purposes of collecting the debt described in subparagraph (A).

(E) Disclosure of information by the Secretary of the Treasury

(i) Purpose of disclosure

The Secretary of the Treasury may make a disclosure under this subparagraph only for purposes of collecting the debt described in subparagraph (A).

(ii) Disclosures permitted

Subject to clauses (iii) and (iv), the Secretary of the Treasury may disclose information resulting from a data match pursuant to this paragraph only to the Attorney General in connection with collecting the debt described in subparagraph (A).

(iii) **Conditions on disclosure**

Disclosures under this subparagraph shall be—

(I) made in accordance with data security and control policies established by the Secretary of the Treasury and approved by the Secretary;

(II) subject to audit in a manner satisfactory to the Secretary; and

(III) subject to the sanctions under subsection (*l*)(2) of this section.

(iv) **Additional disclosures**

(I) **Determination by Secretaries**

The Secretary of the Treasury and the Secretary shall determine whether to permit disclosure of information under this paragraph to persons or entities described in subclause (II), based on an evaluation made by the Secretary of the Treasury (in consultation with and approved by the Secretary), of the costs and benefits of such disclosures and the adequacy of measures used to safeguard the security and confidentiality of information so disclosed.

(II) **Permitted persons or entities**

If the Secretary of the Treasury and the Secretary determine pursuant to subclause (I) that disclosures to additional persons or entities shall be permitted, information under this paragraph may be disclosed by the Secretary of the Treasury, in connection with collecting the debt described in subparagraph (A), to a contractor or agent of either Secretary and to the Federal agency that referred such debt to the Secretary of the Treasury for collection, subject to the conditions in clause (iii) and such additional conditions as agreed to by the Secretaries.

(v) **Restrictions on redisclosure**

A person or entity to which information is disclosed under this subparagraph may use or disclose such information only as needed for collecting the debt described in subparagraph (A), subject to the conditions in clause (iii) and such additional conditions as agreed to by the Secretaries.

(F) **Reimbursement of HHS costs**

The Secretary of the Treasury shall reimburse the Secretary, in accordance with subsection (k)(3) of this section, for the costs incurred by the Secretary in furnishing the information requested under this paragraph. Any such costs paid by the Secretary of the Treasury shall be considered costs of implementing section 3711(g) of Title 31 in accordance with section 3711(g)(6) of Title 31 and may be paid from the account established pursuant to section 3711(g)(7) of Title 31.

(10) **Information comparisons and disclosure to assist in administration of supplemental nutrition assistance program benefits**

(A) **In general**

If, for purposes of administering a supplemental nutrition assistance program under the Food and Nutrition Act of 2008 [7 U.S.C. 2011 et seq.], a State agency responsible for the administration of the program transmits to the Secretary the names and social security account numbers of individuals, the Secretary shall disclose to the State agency information on the individuals and their employers maintained in the National Directory of New Hires, subject to this paragraph.

(B) **Condition on disclosure by the Secretary**

The Secretary shall make a disclosure under subparagraph (A) only to the extent that the Secretary determines that the disclosure would not interfere with the effective operation of the program under this part.

(C) **Use and disclosure of information by State agencies**

(i) **In general**

A State agency may not use or disclose information provided under this paragraph except for purposes of administering a program referred to in subparagraph (A).

(ii) **Information security**

The State agency shall have in effect data security and control policies that the Secretary finds adequate to ensure the security of information obtained under this paragraph and to ensure that access to such information is restricted to authorized persons for purposes of authorized uses and disclosures.

(iii) **Penalty for misuse of information**

An officer or employee of the State agency who fails to comply with this subparagraph shall be subject to the sanctions under subsection (*l*)(2) of this section to the same extent as if the officer or employee were an officer or employee of the United States.

(D) **Procedural requirements**

State agencies requesting information under this paragraph shall adhere to uniform procedures established by the Secretary governing information requests and data matching under this paragraph.

(E) Reimbursement of costs

The State agency shall reimburse the Secretary, in accordance with subsection (k)(3) of this section, for the costs incurred by the Secretary in furnishing the information requested under this paragraph.

(11) Information comparisons and disclosures to assist in administration of certain veterans benefits

(A) Furnishing of information by Secretary of Veterans Affairs

Subject to the provisions of this paragraph, the Secretary of Veterans Affairs shall furnish to the Secretary, on such periodic basis as determined by the Secretary of Veterans Affairs in consultation with the Secretary, information in the custody of the Secretary of Veterans Affairs for comparison with information in the National Directory of New Hires, in order to obtain information in such Directory with respect to individuals who are applying for or receiving—

(i) needs-based pension benefits provided under chapter 15 of Title 38 or under any other law administered by the Secretary of Veterans Affairs;

(ii) parents' dependency and indemnity compensation provided under section 1315 of Title 38;

(iii) health care services furnished under subsections (a)(2)(G), (a)(3), or (b) of section 1710 of Title 38; or

(iv) compensation paid under chapter 11 of Title 38 at the 100 percent rate based solely on unemployability and without regard to the fact that the disability or disabilities are not rated as 100 percent disabling under the rating schedule.

(B) Requirement to seek minimum information

The Secretary of Veterans Affairs shall seek information pursuant to this paragraph only to the extent necessary to verify the employment and income of individuals described in subparagraph (A).

(C) Duties of the Secretary

(i) Information disclosure

The Secretary, in cooperation with the Secretary of Veterans Affairs, shall compare information in the National Directory of New Hires with information provided by the Secretary of Veterans Affairs with respect to individuals described in subparagraph (A), and shall disclose information in such Directory regarding such individuals to the Secretary of Veterans Affairs, in accordance with this paragraph, for the purposes specified in this paragraph.

(ii) Condition on disclosure

The Secretary shall make disclosures in accordance with clause (i) only to the extent that the Secretary determines that such disclosures do not interfere with the effective operation of the program under this part.

(D) Use of information by Secretary of Veterans Affairs

The Secretary of Veterans Affairs may use information resulting from a data match pursuant to this paragraph only—

(i) for the purposes specified in subparagraph (B); and

(ii) after removal of personal identifiers, to conduct analyses of the employment and income reporting of individuals described in subparagraph (A).

(E) Reimbursement of HHS costs

The Secretary of Veterans Affairs shall reimburse the Secretary, in accordance with subsection (k)(3) of this section, for the costs incurred by the Secretary in furnishing the information requested under this paragraph.

(F) Consent

The Secretary of Veterans Affairs shall not seek, use, or disclose information under this paragraph relating to an individual without the prior written consent of such individual (or of a person legally authorized to consent on behalf of such individual).

(G) Expiration of authority

The authority under this paragraph shall be in effect as follows:

(i) During the period beginning on December 26, 2007, and ending on November 18, 2011.

(ii) During the period beginning on the date of the enactment of the Department of Veterans Affairs Expiring Authorities Act of 2013 and ending 180 days after that date.

(k) Fees

(1) For SSA verification

The Secretary shall reimburse the Commissioner of Social Security, at a rate negotiated between the Secretary and the Commissioner, for the costs incurred by the Commissioner in performing the verification services described in subsection (j) of this section.

(2) For information from State directories of new hires

The Secretary shall reimburse costs incurred by State directories of new hires in furnishing information as required by section 653a(g)(2) of this title, at rates which the Secretary determines to be reasonable (which rates shall not include payment for the costs of obtaining, compiling, or maintaining such information).

(3) For information furnished to State and Federal agencies

A State or Federal agency that receives information from the Secretary pursuant to this section or section 652(m) of this title shall reimburse the Secretary for costs incurred by the Secretary in furnishing the information, at rates which the Secretary determines to be reasonable (which rates shall include payment for the costs of obtaining, verifying, maintaining, and comparing the information).

(*l*) Restriction on disclosure and use

(1) In general

Information in the Federal Parent Locator Service, and information resulting from comparisons using such information, shall not be used or disclosed except as expressly provided in this section, subject to section 6103 of the Internal Revenue Code of 1986.

(2) Penalty for misuse of information in the National Directory of New Hires

The Secretary shall require the imposition of an administrative penalty (up to and including dismissal from employment), and a fine of $1,000, for each act of unauthorized access to, disclosure of, or use of, information in the National Directory of New Hires established under subsection (i) of this section by any officer or employee of the United States or any other person who knowingly and willfully violates this paragraph.

(m) Information integrity and security

The Secretary shall establish and implement safeguards with respect to the entities established under this section designed to—

(1) ensure the accuracy and completeness of information in the Federal Parent Locator Service; and

(2) restrict access to confidential information in the Federal Parent Locator Service to authorized persons, and restrict use of such information to authorized purposes.

(n) Federal government reporting

Each department, agency, and instrumentality of the United States shall on a quarterly basis report to the Federal Parent Locator Service the name and social security number of each employee and the wages paid to the employee during the previous quarter, except that such a report shall not be filed with respect to an employee of a department, agency, or instrumentality performing intelligence or counter-intelligence functions, if the head of such department, agency, or instrumentality has determined that filing such a report could endanger the safety of the employee or compromise an ongoing investigation or intelligence mission.

(*o*) Use of set-aside funds

Out of any money in the Treasury of the United States not otherwise appropriated, there is hereby appropriated to the Secretary for each fiscal year an amount equal to 2 percent of the total amount paid to the Federal Government pursuant to a plan approved under this part during the immediately preceding fiscal year (as determined on the basis of the most recent reliable data available to the Secretary as of the end of the third calendar quarter following the end of such preceding fiscal year) or the amount appropriated under this paragraph[1] for fiscal year 2002, whichever is greater, which shall be available for use by the Secretary, either directly or through grants, contracts, or interagency agreements, for operation of the Federal Parent Locator Service under this section, to the extent such costs are not recovered through user fees. Amounts appropriated under this subsection shall remain available until expended.

(p) "Support order" defined

As used in this part, the term "support order" means a judgment, decree, or order, whether temporary, final, or subject to modification, issued by a court or an administrative agency of competent jurisdiction, for the support and maintenance of a child, including a child who has attained the age of majority under the law of the issuing State, or of the parent with whom the child is living, which provides for monetary support, health care, arrearages, or reimbursement, and which may include related costs and fees, interest and penalties, income withholding, attorneys' fees, and other relief. *(Aug. 14, 1935, c. 531, Title IV, § 453, as added Pub.L. 93–647, § 101(a), Jan. 4, 1975, 88 Stat. 2353; amended Pub.L. 97–35, Title XXIII, § 2332(c), Aug. 13, 1981, 95 Stat. 862; Pub.L. 98–369, Div. B, Title VI, § 2663(c)(13), (j)(2)(B)(ix), July 18, 1984, 98 Stat. 1166, 1170; Pub.L. 98–378, §§ 17, 19(a), Aug. 16, 1984, 98 Stat. 1321, 1322; Pub.L. 100–485, Title I, § 124(a), Oct. 13, 1988, 102 Stat. 2353; Pub.L. 104–193, Title I, § 108(c)(10), Title III, §§ 316(a) to (f), 345(b), 366, 395(d)(1)(C), (2)(A), Aug. 22, 1996, 110 Stat. 2166, 2214 to 2216, 2237, 2250, 2259, 2260; Pub.L. 104–208, Div. A, Title I, § 101(e) [Title II, § 215], Sept. 30, 1996, 110 Stat. 3009–255; Pub.L. 105–33, Title V, §§ 5534(a), 5535, 5541(b), 5543, 5553, 5556(c), Aug. 5, 1997, 111 Stat. 627, 629, 630, 631, 636, 637; Pub.L. 105–34, Title X, § 1090(a)(2), Aug. 5, 1997, 111 Stat. 961; Pub.L. 105–89, Title I, § 105, Nov. 19, 1997, 111 Stat. 2120; Pub.L. 105–200, Title IV, §§ 402(a), (b), 410(d), July 16, 1998, 112 Stat. 668, 669, 673; Pub.L. 106–113, Div. B, § 1000(a)(5) [Title III, § 303(a)], Nov. 29, 1999, 113 Stat. 1536, 1501A–304; Pub.L. 108–199, Div. G, Title II, § 217(a), Jan. 23, 2004, 118 Stat. 394; Pub.L. 108–295, § 3, Aug. 9, 2004, 118 Stat. 1091; Pub.L. 108–447, Div. H, Title VI, § 643, Dec. 8, 2004, 118 Stat. 3283; Pub.L. 109–171, Title VII, §§ 7305, 7306(b), Feb. 8, 2006, 120 Stat. 145, 146; Pub.L. 109–250, § 2, July 27, 2006, 120 Stat. 652; Pub.L. 110–157, Title III, § 301(a), Dec. 26, 2007, 121 Stat. 1833; Pub.L. 110–234, Title IV, § 4002(b)(1)(A), (B), (2)(V), May 22, 2008, 122 Stat. 1095, 1097; Pub.L. 110–246, § 4(a), Title IV, § 4002(b)(1)(A), (B), (2)(V), June 18, 2008, 122 Stat. 1664, 1857, 1858; Pub.L. 110–351, Title I, § 105, Oct. 7, 2008, 122 Stat. 3957; Pub.L. 112–37, § 17(b), Oct. 5, 2011, 125 Stat. 398; Pub.L. 113–37, § 3(a), Sept. 30, 2013, 127 Stat. 525; Pub.L. 113–79, Title IV, § 4030(p), Feb. 7, 2014, 128 Stat. 815; Pub.L. 113–183, Title III, §§ 301(a)(2), (b), 302(a), (c), Sept. 29, 2014, 128 Stat. 1943, 1945, 1946.)*

[1] So in original. Probably should be "subsection".

§ 653a. State Directory of New Hires

(a) Establishment

(1) In general

(A) Requirement for States that have no directory

Except as provided in subparagraph (B), not later than October 1, 1997, each State shall establish an automated directory (to be known as the "State Directory of New Hires") which shall contain information supplied in accordance with subsection (b) of this section by employers on each newly hired employee.

(B) States with new hire reporting law in existence

A State which has a new hire reporting law in existence on August 22, 1996, may continue to operate under the State law, but the State must meet the requirements of subsection (g)(2) of this section not later than October 1, 1997, and the requirements of this section (other than subsection (g)(2) of this section) not later than October 1, 1998.

(2) Definitions

As used in this section:

(A) Employee

The term "employee"—

(i) means an individual who is an employee within the meaning of chapter 24 of the Internal Revenue Code of 1986; and

(ii) does not include an employee of a Federal or State agency performing intelligence or counterintelligence functions, if the head of such agency has determined that reporting pursuant to paragraph (1) with respect to the employee could endanger the safety of the employee or compromise an ongoing investigation or intelligence mission.

(B) Employer

(i) In general

The term "employer" has the meaning given such term in section 3401(d) of the Internal Revenue Code of 1986 and includes any governmental entity and any labor organization.

(ii) Labor organization

The term "labor organization" shall have the meaning given such term in section 152(5) of Title 29, and includes any entity (also known as a "hiring hall") which is used by the organization and an employer to carry out requirements described in section 158(f)(3) of Title 29 of an agreement between the organization and the employer.

(C) Newly hired employee

The term "newly hired employee" means an employee who—

(i) has not previously been employed by the employer; or

(ii) was previously employed by the employer but has been separated from such prior employment for at least 60 consecutive days.

(b) Employer information

(1) Reporting requirement

(A) In general

Except as provided in subparagraphs (B) and (C), each employer shall furnish to the Directory of New Hires of the State in which a newly hired employee works, a report that contains the name, address, and social security number of the employee, the date services for remuneration were first performed by the employee, and the name and address of, and identifying number assigned under section 6109 of the Internal Revenue Code of 1986 to, the employer.

(B) Multistate employers

An employer that has employees who are employed in 2 or more States and that transmits reports magnetically or electronically may comply with subparagraph (A) by designating 1 State in which such employer has employees to which the employer will transmit the report described in subparagraph (A), and transmitting such report to such State. Any employer that transmits reports pursuant to this subparagraph shall notify the Secretary in writing as to which State such employer designates for the purpose of sending reports.

(C) Federal government employers

Any department, agency, or instrumentality of the United States shall comply with subparagraph (A) by transmitting the report described in subparagraph (A) to the National Directory of New Hires established pursuant to section 653 of this title.

(2) Timing of report

Each State may provide the time within which the report required by paragraph (1) shall be made with respect to an employee, but such report shall be made—

(A) not later than 20 days after the date the employer hires the employee; or

(B) in the case of an employer transmitting reports magnetically or electronically, by 2 monthly transmissions (if necessary) not less than 12 days nor more than 16 days apart.

(c) Reporting format and method

Each report required by subsection (b) of this section shall, to the extent practicable, be made on a W–4 form or, at the option of the employer, an equivalent form, and may be transmitted by 1st class mail, magnetically, or electronically.

(d) Civil money penalties on noncomplying employers

The State shall have the option to set a State civil money penalty which shall not exceed—

(1) $25 per failure to meet the requirements of this section with respect to a newly hired employee; or

(2) $500 if, under State law, the failure is the result of a conspiracy between the employer and the employee to not supply the required report or to supply a false or incomplete report.

(e) Entry of employer information

Information shall be entered into the data base maintained by the State Directory of New Hires within 5 business days of receipt from an employer pursuant to subsection (b) of this section.

(f) Information comparisons

(1) In general

Not later than May 1, 1998, an agency designated by the State shall, directly or by contract, conduct automated comparisons of the social security numbers reported by employers pursuant to subsection (b) of this section and the social security numbers appearing in the records of the State case registry for cases being enforced under the State plan.

(2) Notice of match

When an information comparison conducted under paragraph (1) reveals a match with respect to the social security number of an individual required to provide support under a support order, the State Directory of New Hires shall provide the agency administering the State plan approved under this part of the appropriate State with the name, address, and social security number of the employee to whom the social security number is assigned, and the name and address of, and identifying number assigned under section 6109 of the Internal Revenue Code of 1986 to, the employer.

(g) Transmission of information

(1) Transmission of wage withholding notices to employers

Within 2 business days after the date information regarding a newly hired employee is entered into the State Directory of New Hires, the State agency enforcing the employee's child support obligation shall transmit a notice to the employer of the employee directing the employer to withhold from the income of the employee an amount equal to the monthly (or other periodic) child support obligation (including any past due support obligation) of the employee, unless the employee's income is not subject to withholding pursuant to section 666(b)(3) of this title.

(2) Transmissions to the National Directory of New Hires

(A) New hire information

Within 3 business days after the date information regarding a newly hired employee is entered into the State Directory of New Hires, the State Directory of New Hires shall furnish the information to the National Directory of New Hires.

(B) Wage and unemployment compensation information

The State Directory of New Hires shall, on a quarterly basis, furnish to the National Directory of New Hires information concerning the wages and unemployment compensation paid to individuals, by such dates, in such format, and containing such information as the Secretary of Health and Human Services shall specify in regulations.

(3) Business day defined

As used in this subsection, the term "business day" means a day on which State offices are open for regular business.

(h) Other uses of new hire information

(1) Location of child support obligors

The agency administering the State plan approved under this part shall use information received pursuant to subsection (f)(2) of this section to locate individuals for purposes of establishing paternity and establishing, modifying, and enforcing child support obligations, and may disclose such information to any agent of the agency that is under contract with the agency to carry out such purposes.

(2) Verification of eligibility for certain programs

A State agency responsible for administering a program specified in section 1320b–7(b) of this title shall have access to information reported by employers pursuant to subsection (b) of this section for purposes of verifying eligibility for the program.

(3) Administration of employment security and workers' compensation

State agencies operating employment security and workers' compensation programs shall have access to information reported by employers pursuant to subsection (b) of this section for the purposes of administering such programs.

(Aug. 14, 1935, c. 531, Title IV, § 453A, as added Pub.L. 104–193, Title III, § 313(b), Aug. 22, 1996, 110 Stat. 2209; amended Pub.L. 105–33, Title V, § 5533, Aug. 5, 1997, 111 Stat. 627; Pub.L. 111–291, Title VIII, § 802(a), (b), Dec. 8, 2010, 124 Stat. 3157; Pub.L. 112–40, Title II, § 253(a), Oct. 21, 2011, 125 Stat. 422.)

§ 654. State plan for child and spousal support

A State plan for child and spousal support must—

(1) provide that it shall be in effect in all political subdivisions of the State;

(2) provide for financial participation by the State;

(3) provide for the establishment or designation of a single and separate organizational unit, which meets such staffing and organizational requirements as the Secretary may by regulation prescribe, within the State to administer the plan;

(4) provide that the State will—

(A) provide services relating to the establishment of paternity or the establishment, modification, or enforcement of child support obligations, as appropriate, under the plan with respect to—

(i) each child for whom (I) assistance is provided under the State program funded under part A of this subchapter, (II) benefits or services for foster care maintenance are provided under the State program funded under part E of this subchapter, (III) medical assistance is provided under the State plan approved under subchapter XIX of this chapter, or (IV) cooperation is required pursuant to section 2015(*l*)(1) of Title 7, unless, in accordance with paragraph (29), good cause or other exceptions exist;

(ii) any other child, if an individual applies for such services with respect to the child (except that, if the individual applying for the services resides in a foreign reciprocating country or foreign treaty country, the State may opt to require the individual to request the services through the Central Authority for child support enforcement in the foreign reciprocating country or the foreign treaty country, and if the individual resides in a foreign country that is not a foreign reciprocating country or a foreign treaty country, a State may accept or reject the application); and

(B) enforce any support obligation established with respect to—

(i) a child with respect to whom the State provides services under the plan; or

(ii) the custodial parent of such a child;

(5) provide that (A) in any case in which support payments are collected for an individual with respect to whom an assignment pursuant to section 608(a)(3) of this title is effective, such payments shall be made to the State for distribution pursuant to section 657 of this title and shall not be paid directly to the family, and the individual will be notified on a monthly basis (or on a quarterly basis for so long as the Secretary determines with respect to a State that requiring such notice on a monthly basis would impose an unreasonable administrative burden) of the amount of the support payments collected, and (B) in any case in which support payments are collected for an individual pursuant to the assignment made under section 1396k of this title, such payments shall be made to the State for distribution pursuant to section 1396k of this title, except that this clause shall not apply to such payments for any month after the month in which the individual ceases to be eligible for medical assistance;

(6) provide that—

(A) services under the plan shall be made available to residents of other States on the same terms as to residents of the State submitting the plan;

(B)(i) an application fee for furnishing such services shall be imposed on an individual, other than an individual receiving assistance under a State program funded under part A or E of this subchapter, or under a State plan approved under subchapter XIX of this chapter, or who is required by the State to cooperate with the State agency administering the program under this part pursuant to subsection (*l*) or (m) of section 2015 of Title 7, and shall be paid by the individual applying for such services, or recovered from the absent parent, or paid by the State out of its own funds (the payment of which from State funds shall not be considered as an administrative cost of the State for the operation of the plan, and shall be considered income to the program), the amount of which (I) will not exceed $25 (or such higher or lower amount (which shall be uniform for all States) as the Secretary may determine to be appropriate for any fiscal year to reflect increases or decreases in administrative costs), and (II) may vary among such individuals on the basis of ability to pay (as determined by the State); and

(ii) in the case of an individual who has never received assistance under a State program funded under part A of this subchapter and for whom the State has collected at least $500 of support, the State shall impose an annual fee of $25 for each case in which services are furnished, which shall be retained by the State from support collected on behalf of the individual (but not from the first $500 so collected), paid by the individual applying for the services, recovered from the absent parent, or paid by the State out of its own funds (the payment of which from State funds shall not be considered as an administrative cost of the State for the operation of the plan, and the fees shall be considered income to the program);

(C) a fee of not more than $25 may be imposed in any case where the State requests the Secretary of the Treasury to withhold past-due support owed to or on behalf of such individual from a tax refund pursuant to section 664(a)(2) of this title;

(D) a fee (in accordance with regulations of the Secretary) for performing genetic tests may be imposed on any individual who is not a recipient of assistance under a State program funded under part A of this subchapter; and

(E) any costs in excess of the fees so imposed may be collected—

(i) from the parent who owes the child or spousal support obligation involved; or

(ii) at the option of the State, from the individual to whom such services are made available, but only if such State has in effect a procedure whereby all persons in such State having authority to order child or spousal support are informed that such costs are to be collected from the individual to whom such services were made available;

(7) provide for entering into cooperative arrangements with appropriate courts and law enforcement officials and Indian tribes or tribal organizations (as defined in subsections (e) and (*l*) of section 5304 of Title 25) (A) to assist the agency administering the plan, including the entering into of financial arrangements with such courts and officials in order to assure optimum results under such program, and (B) with respect to any other matters of common concern to such courts or officials and the agency administering the plan;

(8) provide that, for the purpose of establishing parentage, establishing, setting the amount of, modifying, or enforcing child support obligations, or making or enforcing a child custody or visitation determination, as defined in section 663(d)(1) of this title, the agency administering the plan will establish a service to locate parents utilizing—

(A) all sources of information and available records; and

(B) the Federal Parent Locator Service established under section 653 of this title,

and shall, subject to the privacy safeguards required under paragraph (26), disclose only the information described in sections 653 and 663 of this title to the authorized persons specified in such sections for the purposes specified in such sections;

(9) provide that the State will, in accordance with standards prescribed by the Secretary, cooperate with any other State—

(A) in establishing paternity, if necessary;

(B) in locating a noncustodial parent residing in the State (whether or not permanently) against whom any action is being taken under a program established under a plan approved under this part in another State;

(C) in securing compliance by a noncustodial parent residing in such State (whether or not permanently) with an order issued by a court of competent jurisdiction against such parent for the support and maintenance of the child or children or the parent of such child or children with respect to whom aid is being provided under the plan of such other State;

(D) in carrying out other functions required under a plan approved under this part; and

(E) not later than March 1, 1997, in using the forms promulgated pursuant to section 652(a)(11) of this title for income withholding, imposition of liens, and issuance of administrative subpoenas in interstate child support cases;

(10) provide that the State will maintain a full record of collections and disbursements made under the plan and have an adequate reporting system;

(11)(A) provide that amounts collected as support shall be distributed as provided in section 657 of this title; and

(B) provide that any payment required to be made under section 656 or 657 of this title to a family shall be made to the resident parent, legal guardian, or caretaker relative having custody of or responsibility for the child or children;

(12) provide for the establishment of procedures to require the State to provide individuals who are applying for or receiving services under the State plan, or who are parties to cases in which services are being provided under the State plan—

(A) with notice of all proceedings in which support obligations might be established or modified; and

(B) with a copy of any order establishing or modifying a child support obligation, or (in the case of a petition for modification) a notice of determination that there should be no change in the amount of the child support award, within 14 days after issuance of such order or determination;

(13) provide that the State will comply with such other requirements and standards as the Secretary determines to be necessary to the establishment of an effective program for locating noncustodial parents, establishing paternity, obtaining support orders, and collecting support payments and provide that information requests by parents who are residents of other States be treated with the same priority as requests by parents who are residents of the State submitting the plan;

(14)(A) comply with such bonding requirements, for employees who receive, disburse, handle, or have access to, cash, as the Secretary shall by regulations prescribe;

(B) maintain methods of administration which are designed to assure that persons responsible for handling cash receipts shall not participate in accounting or operating functions which would permit them to conceal in the accounting records the misuse of cash receipts (except that the Secretary shall by regulations provide for exceptions to this requirement in the case of sparsely populated areas where the hiring of unreasonable additional staff would otherwise be necessary);

(15) provide for—

(A) a process for annual reviews of and reports to the Secretary on the State program operated under the State plan approved under this part, including such information as may be necessary to measure State compliance with Federal requirements for expedited procedures, using such standards and procedures as are required by the Secretary, under which the State agency will determine the extent to which the program is operated in compliance with this part; and

(B) a process of extracting from the automated data processing system required by paragraph (16) and transmitting to the Secretary data and calculations concerning the levels of accomplishment (and rates of improvement) with respect to applicable performance indicators (including paternity establishment percentages) to the extent necessary for purposes of sections 652(g) and 658a of this title;

(16) provide, for the establishment and operation by the State agency in accordance with an (initial and annually updated) advance automated data processing planning document approved under section 652(d) of this title, of a statewide automated data processing and information retrieval system meeting the requirements of section 654a of this title designed effectively and efficiently to assist management in the administration of the State plan, so as to control, account for, and monitor all the factors in the support enforcement collection and paternity determination process under such plan;

(17) provide that the State will have in effect an agreement with the Secretary entered into pursuant to section 663 of this title for the use of the Parent Locator Service established under section 653 of this title, and provide that the State will accept and transmit to the Secretary requests for information authorized under the provisions of the agreement to be furnished by such Service to authorized persons, will impose and collect (in accordance with regulations of the Secretary) a fee sufficient to cover the costs to the State and to the Secretary incurred by reason of such requests, will transmit to the Secretary from time to time (in accordance with such regulations) so much of the fees collected as are attributable to such costs to the Secretary so incurred, and during the period that such agreement is in effect will otherwise comply with such agreement and regulations of the Secretary with respect thereto;

(18) provide that the State has in effect procedures necessary to obtain payment of past-due support from overpayments made to the Secretary of the Treasury as set forth in section 664 of this title, and take all steps necessary to implement and utilize such procedures;

(19) provide that the agency administering the plan—

(A) shall determine on a periodic basis, from information supplied pursuant to section 508 of the Unemployment Compensation Amendments of 1976, whether any individuals receiving compensation under the State's unemployment compensation law (including amounts payable pursuant to any agreement under any Federal unemployment compensation law) owe child support obligations which are being enforced by such agency; and

(B) shall enforce any such child support obligations which are owed by such an individual but are not being met—

(i) through an agreement with such individual to have specified amounts withheld from compensation otherwise payable to such individual and by submitting a copy of any such agreement to the State agency administering the unemployment compensation law; or

(ii) in the absence of such an agreement, by bringing legal process (as defined in section 659(i)(5) of this title) to require the withholding of amounts from such compensation;

(20) provide, to the extent required by section 666 of this title, that the State (A) shall have in effect all of the laws to improve child support enforcement effectiveness which are referred to in that section, and (B) shall implement the procedures which are prescribed in or pursuant to such laws;

(21)(A) at the option of the State, impose a late payment fee on all overdue support (as defined in section 666(e) of this title) under any obligation being enforced under this part, in an amount equal to a uniform percentage determined by the State (not less than 3 percent nor more than 6 percent) of the overdue support, which shall be payable by the noncustodial parent owing the overdue support; and

(B) assure that the fee will be collected in addition to, and only after full payment of, the overdue support, and that the imposition of the late payment fee shall not directly or indirectly result in a decrease in the amount of the support which is paid to the child (or spouse) to whom, or on whose behalf, it is owed;

(22) in order for the State to be eligible to receive any incentive payments under section 658a of this title, provide that, if one or more political subdivisions of the State participate in the costs of carrying out activities under the State plan during any period, each such subdivision shall be entitled to receive an appropriate share (as determined by the State) of any such incentive payments made to the State for such period, taking into account the efficiency and effectiveness of the activities carried out under the State plan by such political subdivision;

(23) provide that the State will regularly and frequently publicize, through public service announcements, the availability of child support enforcement services under the plan and otherwise, including information as to any application fees for such services and a telephone number or postal address at which further information may be obtained and will publicize the availability and encourage the use of procedures for voluntary establishment of paternity and child support by means the State deems appropriate;

(24) provide that the State will have in effect an automated data processing and information retrieval system—

(A) by October 1, 1997, which meets all requirements of this part which were enacted on or before October 13, 1988; and

(B) by October 1, 2000, which meets all requirements of this part enacted on or before August 22, 1996, except that such deadline shall be extended by 1 day for each day (if any) by which the Secretary fails to meet the deadline imposed by section 344(a)(3) of the Personal Responsibility and Work Opportunity Reconciliation Act of 1996;

(25) provide that if a family with respect to which services are provided under the plan ceases to receive assistance under the State program funded under part A of this subchapter, the State shall provide appropriate notice to the family and continue to provide such services, subject to the same conditions and on the same basis as in the case of other individuals to whom services are furnished under the plan, except that an application or other request to continue services shall not be required of such a family and paragraph (6)(B) shall not apply to the family;

(26) have in effect safeguards, applicable to all confidential information handled by the State agency, that are designed to protect the privacy rights of the parties, including—

(A) safeguards against unauthorized use or disclosure of information relating to proceedings or actions to establish paternity, or to establish, modify, or enforce support, or to make or enforce a child custody determination;

(B) prohibitions against the release of information on the whereabouts of 1 party or the child to another party against whom a protective order with respect to the former party or the child has been entered;

(C) prohibitions against the release of information on the whereabouts of 1 party or the child to another person if the State has reason to believe that the release of the information to that person may result in physical or emotional harm to the party or the child;

(D) in cases in which the prohibitions under subparagraphs (B) and (C) apply, the requirement to notify the Secretary, for purposes of section 653(b)(2) of this title, that the State has reasonable evidence of domestic violence or child abuse against a party or the child and that the disclosure of such information could be harmful to the party or the child; and

(E) procedures providing that when the Secretary discloses information about a parent or child to a State court or an agent of a State court described in section 653(c)(2) or 663(d)(2)(B) of this title, and advises that court or agent that the Secretary has been notified that there is reasonable evidence of domestic violence or child abuse pursuant to section 653(b)(2) of this title, the court shall determine whether disclosure to any other person of information received from the Secretary could be harmful to the parent or child and, if the court determines that disclosure to any other person could be harmful, the court and its agents shall not make any such disclosure;

(27) provide that, on and after October 1, 1998, the State agency will—

(A) operate a State disbursement unit in accordance with section 654b of this title; and

(B) have sufficient State staff (consisting of State employees) and (at State option) contractors reporting directly to the State agency to—

(i) monitor and enforce support collections through the unit in cases being enforced by the State pursuant to paragraph 4 (including carrying out the automated data processing responsibilities described in section 654a(g) of this title); and

(ii) take the actions described in section 666(c)(1) of this title in appropriate cases;

(28) provide that, on and after October 1, 1997, the State will operate a State Directory of New Hires in accordance with section 653a of this title;

(29) provide that the State agency responsible for administering the State plan—

(A) shall make the determination (and redetermination at appropriate intervals) as to whether an individual who has applied for or is receiving assistance under the State program funded under part A of this subchapter, the State program under part E of this subchapter, the State program under subchapter XIX of this chapter, or the supplemental nutrition assistance program, as defined under section 2012(*l*) of Title 7, is cooperating in good faith with the State in establishing the paternity of, or in establishing, modifying, or enforcing a support order for, any child of the individual by providing the State agency with the name of, and such other information as the State agency may require with respect to, the noncustodial parent of the child, subject to good cause and other exceptions which—

(i) in the case of the State program funded under part A of this subchapter, the State program under part E of this subchapter, or the State program under subchapter XIX of this chapter shall, at the option of the State, be defined, taking into account the best interests of the child, and applied in each case, by the State agency administering such program; and

(ii) in the case of the supplemental nutrition assistance program, as defined under section 2012(*l*) of Title 7, shall be defined and applied in each case under that program in accordance with section 2015(*l*)(2) of Title 7;

(B) shall require the individual to supply additional necessary information and appear at interviews, hearings, and legal proceedings;

(C) shall require the individual and the child to submit to genetic tests pursuant to judicial or administrative order;

(D) may request that the individual sign a voluntary acknowledgment of paternity, after notice of the rights and consequences of such an acknowledgment, but may not require the individual to sign an acknowledgment or otherwise relinquish the right to genetic tests as a condition of cooperation and eligibility for assistance under the State program funded under part A of this subchapter, the State program under part E of this subchapter, the State program under subchapter XIX of this chapter, or the supplemental nutrition assistance program, as defined under section 2012(*l*) of Title 7; and

(E) shall promptly notify the individual and the State agency administering the State program funded under part A of this subchapter, the State agency administering the State program under part

E of this subchapter, the State agency administering the State program under subchapter XIX of this chapter, or the State agency administering the supplemental nutrition assistance program, as defined under section 2012(*l*) of Title 7, of each such determination, and if noncooperation is determined, the basis therefor;

(30) provide that the State shall use the definitions established under section 652(a)(5) of this title in collecting and reporting information as required under this part;

(31) provide that the State agency will have in effect a procedure for certifying to the Secretary, for purposes of the procedure under section 652(k) of this title, determinations that individuals owe arrearages of child support in an amount exceeding $2,500, under which procedure—

(A) each individual concerned is afforded notice of such determination and the consequences thereof, and an opportunity to contest the determination; and

(B) the certification by the State agency is furnished to the Secretary in such format, and accompanied by such supporting documentation, as the Secretary may require;

(32)(A) provide that any request for services under this part by a foreign reciprocating country, a foreign treaty country, or a foreign country with which the State has an arrangement described in section 659a(d) of this title shall be treated as a request by a State;

(B) provide, at State option, notwithstanding paragraph (4) or any other provision of this part, for services under the plan for enforcement of a spousal support order not described in paragraph (4)(B) entered by such a country (or subdivision); and

(C) provide that no applications will be required from, and no costs will be assessed for such services against, the foreign reciprocating country, foreign treaty country, or foreign individual (but costs may at State option be assessed against the obligor);

(33) provide that a State that receives funding pursuant to section 628 of this title and that has within its borders Indian country (as defined in section 1151 of Title 18) may enter into cooperative agreements with an Indian tribe or tribal organization (as defined in subsections (e) and (*l*) of section 5304 of Title 25), if the Indian tribe or tribal organization demonstrates that such tribe or organization has an established tribal court system or a Court of Indian Offenses with the authority to establish paternity, establish, modify, or enforce support orders, or to enter support orders in accordance with child support guidelines established or adopted by such tribe or organization, under which the State and tribe or organization shall provide for the cooperative delivery of child support enforcement services in Indian country and for the forwarding of all collections pursuant to the functions performed by the tribe or organization to the State agency, or conversely, by the State agency to the tribe or organization, which shall distribute such collections in accordance with such agreement; and

(34) include an election by the State to apply section 657(a)(2)(B) of this title or former section 657(a)(2)(B) of this title (as in effect for the State immediately before the date this paragraph first applies to the State) to the distribution of the amounts which are the subject of such sections and, for so long as the State elects to so apply such former section, the amendments made by subsection (b)(1) of section 7301 of the Deficit Reduction Act of 2005 shall not apply with respect to the State, notwithstanding subsection (e) of such section 7301.

The State may allow the jurisdiction which makes the collection involved to retain any application fee under paragraph (6)(B) or any late payment fee under paragraph (21). Nothing in paragraph (33) shall void any provision of any cooperative agreement entered into before August 22, 1996, nor shall such paragraph deprive any State of jurisdiction over Indian country (as so defined) that is lawfully exercised under section 1322 of Title 25. *(Aug. 14, 1935, c. 531, Title IV, § 454, as added Pub.L. 93–647, § 101(a), Jan. 4, 1975, 88 Stat. 2354; amended Pub.L. 94–88, Title II, § 208(b), (c), Aug. 9, 1975, 89 Stat. 436; Pub.L. 95–30, Title V, § 502(a), May 23, 1977, 91 Stat. 162; Pub.L. 96–265, Title IV, § 405(b), June 9, 1980, 94 Stat. 463; Pub.L. 96–611, § 9(a), Dec. 28, 1980, 94 Stat. 3571; Pub.L. 97–35, Title XXIII, §§ 2331(b), 2332(d), 2333(a), (b), 2335(a), Aug. 13, 1981, 95 Stat. 860, 862, 863; Pub.L. 97–248, Title I, §§ 171(a), (b)(1), 173(a), Sept. 3, 1982, 96 Stat. 401, 403; Pub.L. 98–369, Div. B, Title VI, § 2663(c)(14), (j)(2)(B)(x), July 18, 1984, 98 Stat. 1166, 1170; Pub.L. 98–378, §§ 3(a), (c) to (f), 5(b), 6(a), 11(b)(1), 12(a), (b), 14(a), 21(d), Aug. 16, 1984, 98 Stat. 1306, 1310, 1311, 1314, 1318, 1319, 1320, 1324; Pub.L. 100–203, Title IX, §§ 9141(a)(2), 9142(a), Dec. 22, 1987, 101 Stat. 1330–321, 1330–322; Pub.L. 100–485, Title I, §§ 104(a), 111(c), 123(a), (d), Oct. 13, 1988, 102 Stat. 2348, 2349, 2352, 2353; Pub.L. 104–35, § 1(a), Oct. 12, 1995, 109 Stat. 294; Pub.L. 104–193, Title I, § 108(c)(11), (12), Title III, §§ 301(a), (b), 302(b)(2), 303(a), 304(a), 312(a), 313(a), 316(g)(1), 324(b), 332, 333, 342(a), 343(b), 344(a)(1), (4), 370(a)(2), 371(b), 375(a), (c), 395(d)(1)(D), (2)(B), Aug. 22, 1996, 110 Stat. 2166, 2199, 2204, 2205, 2207, 2209, 2218, 2223, 2230, 2233, 2234, 2236, 2252, 2254, 2256, 2259, 2260; Pub.L. 105–33, Title V, §§ 5531(a), 5542(c), 5545, 5546(a), 5548, 5552, 5556(b), Aug. 5, 1997, 111 Stat. 625, 631, 633, 635, 637; Pub.L. 106–169, Title IV, § 401(g), (h), Dec. 14, 1999, 113 Stat. 1858; Pub.L. 109–171, Title VII, §§ 7301(b)(1)(C), 7303(b), 7310(a), Feb. 8, 2006, 120 Stat. 143, 145, 147; Pub.L. 110–234, Title IV, §§ 4002(b)(1)(A), (B), (2)(V), 4115(c)(2)(H), May 22, 2008, 122 Stat. 1095, 1097, 1110; Pub.L. 110–246, § 4(a), Title IV, §§ 4002(b)(1)(A), (B), (2)(V), 4115(c)(2)(H), June 18, 2008, 122 Stat. 1664, 1857, 1858, 1871; Pub. L. 113–79, Title IV, § 4030(v), Feb. 7, 2014, 128 Stat. 815; Pub.L. 113–183, Title III, § 301(c), Sept. 29, 2014, 128 Stat. 1943.)*

§ 654a. Automated data processing

(a) In general

In order for a State to meet the requirements of this section, the State agency administering the State program under this part shall have in operation a single statewide automated data processing and information retrieval system which has the capability to perform the tasks specified in this section with the frequency and in the manner required by or under this part.

(b) Program management

The automated system required by this section shall perform such functions as the Secretary may specify relating to management of the State program under this part, including—

(1) controlling and accounting for use of Federal, State, and local funds in carrying out the program; and

(2) maintaining the data necessary to meet Federal reporting requirements under this part on a timely basis.

(c) Calculation of performance indicators

In order to enable the Secretary to determine the incentive payments and penalty adjustments required by sections 652(g) and 658a of this title, the State agency shall—

(1) use the automated system—

(A) to maintain the requisite data on State performance with respect to paternity establishment and child support enforcement in the State; and

(B) to calculate the paternity establishment percentage for the State for each fiscal year; and

(2) have in place systems controls to ensure the completeness and reliability of, and ready access to, the data described in paragraph (1)(A), and the accuracy of the calculations described in paragraph (1)(B).

(d) Information integrity and security

The State agency shall have in effect safeguards on the integrity, accuracy, and completeness of, access to, and use of data in the automated system required by this section, which shall include the following (in addition to such other safeguards as the Secretary may specify in regulations):

(1) Policies restricting access

Written policies concerning access to data by State agency personnel, and sharing of data with other persons, which—

(A) permit access to and use of data only to the extent necessary to carry out the State program under this part; and

(B) specify the data which may be used for particular program purposes, and the personnel permitted access to such data.

(2) Systems controls

Systems controls (such as passwords or blocking of fields) to ensure strict adherence to the policies described in paragraph (1).

(3) Monitoring of access

Routine monitoring of access to and use of the automated system, through methods such as audit trails and feedback mechanisms, to guard against and promptly identify unauthorized access or use.

(4) Training and information

Procedures to ensure that all personnel (including State and local agency staff and contractors) who may have access to or be required to use confidential program data are informed of applicable requirements and penalties (including those in section 6103 of the Internal Revenue Code of 1986), and are adequately trained in security procedures.

(5) Penalties

Administrative penalties (up to and including dismissal from employment) for unauthorized access to, or disclosure or use of, confidential data.

(e) State case registry

(1) Contents

The automated system required by this section shall include a registry (which shall be known as the "State case registry") that contains records with respect to—

(A) each case in which services are being provided by the State agency under the State plan approved under this part; and

(B) each support order established or modified in the State on or after October 1, 1998.

(2) Linking of local registries

The State case registry may be established by linking local case registries of support orders through an automated information network, subject to this section.

(3) Use of standardized data elements

Such records shall use standardized data elements for both parents (such as names, social security numbers and other uniform identification numbers, dates of birth, and case identification numbers), and contain such other information (such as on case status) as the Secretary may require.

(4) Payment records

Each case record in the State case registry with respect to which services are being provided under the State plan approved under this part and with respect to which a support order has been established shall include a record of—

(A) the amount of monthly (or other periodic) support owed under the order, and other amounts (including arrearages, interest or late payment penalties, and fees) due or overdue under the order;

(B) any amount described in subparagraph (A) that has been collected;

(C) the distribution of such collected amounts;

(D) the birth date and, beginning not later than October 1, 1999, the social security number, of any child for whom the order requires the provision of support; and

(E) the amount of any lien imposed with respect to the order pursuant to section 666(a)(4) of this title.

(5) Updating and monitoring

The State agency operating the automated system required by this section shall promptly establish and update, maintain, and regularly monitor, case records in the State case registry with respect to which services are being provided under the State plan approved under this part, on the basis of—

(A) information on administrative actions and administrative and judicial proceedings and orders relating to paternity and support;

(B) information obtained from comparison with Federal, State, or local sources of information;

(C) information on support collections and distributions; and

(D) any other relevant information.

(f) Information comparisons and other disclosures of information

The State shall use the automated system required by this section to extract information from (at such times, and in such standardized format or formats, as may be required by the Secretary), to share and compare information with, and to receive information from, other data bases and information comparison services, in order to obtain (or provide) information necessary to enable the State agency (or the Secretary or other State or Federal agencies) to carry out this part, subject to section 6103 of the Internal Revenue Code of 1986. Such information comparison activities shall include the following:

(1) Federal Case Registry of Child Support Orders

Furnishing to the Federal Case Registry of Child Support Orders established under section 653(h) of this title (and update as necessary, with information including notice of expiration of orders) the minimum amount of information on child support cases recorded in the State case registry that is necessary to operate the registry (as specified by the Secretary in regulations).

(2) Federal Parent Locator Service

Exchanging information with the Federal Parent Locator Service for the purposes specified in section 653 of this title.

(3) Temporary family assistance and medicaid agencies

Exchanging information with State agencies (of the State and of other States) administering programs funded under part A of this subchapter, programs operated under a State plan approved under subchapter XIX of this chapter, and other programs designated by the Secretary, as necessary to perform State agency responsibilities under this part and under such programs.

(4) Intrastate and interstate information comparisons

Exchanging information with other agencies of the State, agencies of other States, and interstate information networks, as necessary and appropriate to carry out (or assist other States to carry out) the purposes of this part.

(5) Private industry councils receiving welfare-to-work grants

Disclosing to a private industry council (as defined in section 603(a)(5)(D)(ii) of this title) to which funds are provided under section 603(a)(5) of this title the names, addresses, telephone numbers, and identifying case number information in the State program funded under part A of this subchapter, of noncustodial parents residing in the service delivery area of the private industry council, for the purpose of identifying and contacting noncustodial parents regarding participation in the program under section 603(a)(5) of this title.

(g) Collection and distribution of support payments

(1) In general

The State shall use the automated system required by this section to assist and facilitate the collection and disbursement of support payments through the State disbursement unit operated under section 654b of this title, through the performance of functions, including, at a minimum—

(A) transmission of orders and notices to employers (and other debtors) for the withholding of income—

(i) within 2 business days after receipt of notice of, and the income source subject to, such withholding from a court, another State, an employer, the Federal Parent Locator Service, or another source recognized by the State;

(ii) using uniform formats prescribed by the Secretary; and

(iii) at the option of the employer, using the electronic transmission methods prescribed by the Secretary;

(B) ongoing monitoring to promptly identify failures to make timely payment of support; and

(C) automatic use of enforcement procedures (including procedures authorized pursuant to section 666(c) of this title) if payments are not timely made.

(2) Business day defined

As used in paragraph (1), the term "business day" means a day on which State offices are open for regular business.

(h) Expedited administrative procedures

The automated system required by this section shall be used, to the maximum extent feasible, to implement the expedited administrative procedures required by section 666(c) of this title. *(Aug. 14, 1935, c. 531, Title IV, § 454A, as added and amended Pub.L. 104–193, Title III, §§ 311, 312(c), 325(b), 344(a)(2), Aug. 22, 1996, 110 Stat. 2205, 2208, 2226, 2235; Pub.L. 105–34, Title X, § 1090(a)(1), Aug. 5,*

1997, 111 Stat. 961; Pub.L. 106–113, Div. B, §1000(a)(4) [Title VIII, § 805(a)(1)], Nov. 29, 1999, 113 Stat. 1535, 1501A–285; Pub.L. 113–183, Title III, § 306(a), Sept. 29, 2014, 128 Stat. 1949.)

§ 654b. Collection and disbursement of support payments

(a) State disbursement unit

(1) In general

In order for a State to meet the requirements of this section, the State agency must establish and operate a unit (which shall be known as the "State disbursement unit") for the collection and disbursement of payments under support orders—

(A) in all cases being enforced by the State pursuant to section 654(4) of this title; and

(B) in all cases not being enforced by the State under this part in which the support order is initially issued in the State on or after January 1, 1994, and in which the income of the noncustodial parent is subject to withholding pursuant to section 666(a)(8)(B) of this title.

(2) Operation

The State disbursement unit shall be operated—

(A) directly by the State agency (or 2 or more State agencies under a regional cooperative agreement), or (to the extent appropriate) by a contractor responsible directly to the State agency; and

(B) except in cases described in paragraph (1)(B), in coordination with the automated system established by the State pursuant to section 654a of this title.

(3) Linking of local disbursement units

The State disbursement unit may be established by linking local disbursement units through an automated information network, subject to this section, if the Secretary agrees that the system will not cost more nor take more time to establish or operate than a centralized system. In addition, employers shall be given 1 location to which income withholding is sent.

(b) Required procedures

The State disbursement unit shall use automated procedures, electronic processes, and computer-driven technology to the maximum extent feasible, efficient, and economical, for the collection and disbursement of support payments, including procedures—

(1) for receipt of payments from parents, employers, and other States, and for disbursements to custodial parents and other obligees, the State agency, and the agencies of other States;

(2) for accurate identification of payments;

(3) to ensure prompt disbursement of the custodial parent's share of any payment; and

(4) to furnish to any parent, upon request, timely information on the current status of support payments under an order requiring payments to be made by or to the parent, except that in cases described in subsection (a)(1)(B) of this section, the State disbursement unit shall not be required to convert and maintain in automated form records of payments kept pursuant to section 666(a)(8)(B)(iii) of this title before the effective date of this section.

(c) Timing of disbursements

(1) In general

Except as provided in paragraph (2), the State disbursement unit shall distribute all amounts payable under section 657(a) of this title within 2 business days after receipt from the employer or other source of periodic income, if sufficient information identifying the payee is provided. The date of collection for amounts collected and distributed under this part is the date of receipt by the State disbursement unit, except that if current support is withheld by an employer in the month when due and is received by the State disbursement unit in a month other than the month when due, the date of withholding may be deemed to be the date of collection.

(2) Permissive retention of arrearages

The State disbursement unit may delay the distribution of collections toward arrearages until the resolution of any timely appeal with respect to such arrearages.

(d) Business day defined

As used in this section, the term "business day" means a day on which State offices are open for regular business.

(Aug. 14, 1935, c. 531, Title IV, § 454B, as added Pub.L. 104–193, Title III, § 312(b), Aug. 22, 1996, 110 Stat. 2207; amended 105–33, Title V, § 5549, Aug. 5, 1997, 111 Stat. 633.)

§ 655. Payments to States

(a) Amounts payable each quarter

(1) From the sums appropriated therefor, the Secretary shall pay to each State for each quarter an amount—

(A) equal to the percent specified in paragraph (2) of the total amounts expended by such State during such quarter for the operation of the plan approved under section 654 of this title,

(B) equal to the percent specified in paragraph (3) of the sums expended during such quarter that are attributable to the planning, design, development, installation or enhancement of an automatic data processing and information retrieval system (including in such sums the full cost of the hardware components of such system); and [1]

(C) equal to 66 percent of so much of the sums expended during such quarter as are attributable to laboratory costs incurred in determining paternity, and

(D) equal to 66 percent of the sums expended by the State during the quarter for an alternative statewide system for which a waiver has been granted under section 652(d)(3) of this title, but only to the extent that the total of the sums so expended by the State on or after July 16, 1998, does not exceed the least total cost estimate submitted by the State pursuant to section 652(d)(3)(C) of this title in the request for the waiver;

except that no amount shall be paid to any State on account of amounts expended from amounts paid to the State under section 658a of this title or to carry out an agreement which it has entered into pursuant to section 663 of this title. In determining the total amounts expended by any State during a quarter, for purposes of this subsection, there shall be excluded an amount equal to the total of any fees collected or other income resulting from services provided under the plan approved under this part.

(2) The percent applicable to quarters in a fiscal year for purposes of paragraph (1)(A) is—

(A) 70 percent for fiscal years 1984, 1985, 1986 and 1987,

(B) 68 percent for fiscal years 1988 and 1989, and

(C) 66 percent for fiscal year 1990 and each fiscal year thereafter.

(3)(A) The Secretary shall pay to each State, for each quarter in fiscal years 1996 and 1997, 90 percent of so much of the State expenditures described in paragraph (1)(B) as the Secretary finds are for a system meeting the requirements specified in section 654(16) of this title (as in effect on September 30, 1995) but limited to the amount approved for States in the advance planning documents of such States submitted on or before September 30, 1995.

(B)(i) The Secretary shall pay to each State or system described in clause (iii), for each quarter in fiscal years 1996 through 2001, the percentage specified in clause (ii) of so much of the State or system expenditures described in paragraph (1)(B) as the Secretary finds are for a system meeting the requirements of sections 654(16) and 654a of this title.

(ii) The percentage specified in this clause is 80 percent.

(iii) For purposes of clause (i), a system described in this clause is a system that has been approved by the Secretary to receive enhanced funding pursuant to the Family Support Act of 1988 (Public Law 100–485; 102 Stat. 2343) for the purpose of developing a system that meets the requirements of sections 654(16) of this title (as in effect on and after September 30, 1995) and 654a of this title, including systems that have received funding for such purpose pursuant to a waiver under section 1315(a) of this title.

(4)(A)(i) If—

(I) the Secretary determines that a State plan under section 654 of this title would (in the absence of this paragraph) be disapproved for the failure of the State to comply with a particular subparagraph of section 654(24) of this title, and that the State has made and is continuing to make a good faith effort to so comply; and

(II) the State has submitted to the Secretary a corrective compliance plan that describes how, by when, and at what cost the State will achieve such compliance, which has been approved by the Secretary,

then the Secretary shall not disapprove the State plan under section 654 of this title, and the Secretary shall reduce the amount otherwise payable to the State under paragraph (1)(A) of this subsection for the fiscal year by the penalty amount.

(ii) All failures of a State during a fiscal year to comply with any of the requirements referred to in the same subparagraph of section 654(24) of this title shall be considered a single failure of the State to comply with that subparagraph during the fiscal year for purposes of this paragraph.

(B) In this paragraph:

(i) The term "penalty amount" means, with respect to a failure of a State to comply with a subparagraph of section 654(24) of this title—

(I) 4 percent of the penalty base, in the case of the first fiscal year in which such a failure by the State occurs (regardless of whether a penalty is imposed under this paragraph with respect to the failure);

(II) 8 percent of the penalty base, in the case of the second such fiscal year;

(III) 16 percent of the penalty base, in the case of the third such fiscal year;

(IV) 25 percent of the penalty base, in the case of the fourth such fiscal year; or

(V) 30 percent of the penalty base, in the case of the fifth or any subsequent such fiscal year.

(ii) The term "penalty base" means, with respect to a failure of a State to comply with a subparagraph of section 654(24) of this title during a fiscal year, the amount otherwise payable to the State under paragraph (1)(A) of this subsection for the preceding fiscal year.

(C)(i) The Secretary shall waive a penalty under this paragraph for any failure of a State to comply with section 654(24)(A) of this title during fiscal year 1998 if—

(I) on or before August 1, 1998, the State has submitted to the Secretary a request that the Secretary certify the State as having met the requirements of such section;

(II) the Secretary subsequently provides the certification as a result of a timely review conducted pursuant to the request; and

(III) the State has not failed such a review.

(ii) If a State with respect to which a reduction is made under this paragraph for a fiscal year with respect to a failure to comply with a subparagraph of section 654(24) of this title achieves compliance with such subparagraph by the beginning of the succeeding fiscal year, the Secretary shall increase the amount otherwise payable to the State under paragraph (1)(A) of this subsection for the succeeding fiscal year by an amount equal to 90 percent of the reduction for the fiscal year.

(iii) The Secretary shall reduce the amount of any reduction that, in the absence of this clause, would be required to be made under this paragraph by reason of the failure of a State to achieve compliance with section 654(24)(B) of this title during the fiscal year, by an amount equal to 20 percent of the amount of the otherwise required reduction, for each State performance measure described in section 658a(b)(4) of this title with respect to which the applicable percentage under section 658a(b)(6) of this title for the fiscal year is 100 percent, if the Secretary has made the determination described in section 658a(b)(5)(B) of this title with respect to the State for the fiscal year.

(D) The Secretary may not impose a penalty under this paragraph against a State with respect to a failure to comply with section 654(24)(B) of this title for a fiscal year if the Secretary is required to impose a penalty under this paragraph against the State with respect to a failure to comply with section 654(24)(A) of this title for the fiscal year.

(5)(A)(i) If–

(I) the Secretary determines that a State plan under section 654 of this title would (in the absence of this paragraph) be disapproved for the failure of the State to comply with subparagraphs (A) and (B)(i) of section 654(27) of this title, and that the State has made and is continuing to make a good faith effort to so comply; and

(II) the State has submitted to the Secretary, not later than April 1, 2000, a corrective compliance plan that describes how, by when, and at what cost the State will achieve such compliance, which has been approved by the Secretary,

then the Secretary shall not disapprove the State plan under section 654 of this title, and the Secretary shall reduce the amount otherwise payable to the State under paragraph (1)(A) of this subsection for the fiscal year by the penalty amount

(ii) All failures of a State during a fiscal year to comply with any of the requirements of section 654b of this title shall be considered a single failure of the State to comply with subparagraphs (A) and (B)(i) of section 654(27) of this title during the fiscal year for purposes of this paragraph.

(B) In this paragraph:

(i) The term "penalty amount" means, with respect to a failure of a State to comply with subparagraphs (A) and (B)(i) of section 654(27) of this title—

(I) 4 percent of the penalty base, in the case of the 1st fiscal year in which such a failure by the State occurs (regardless of whether a penalty is imposed in that fiscal year under this paragraph with respect to the failure), except as provided in subparagraph (C)(ii) of this paragraph;

(II) 8 percent of the penalty base, in the case of the 2nd such fiscal year;

(III) 16 percent of the penalty base, in the case of the 3rd such fiscal year;

(IV) 25 percent of the penalty base, in the case of the 4th such fiscal year; or

(V) 30 percent of the penalty base, in the case of the 5th or any subsequent such fiscal year.

(ii) The term "penalty base" means, with respect to a failure of a State to comply with subparagraphs (A) and (B)(i) of section 654(27) of this title during a fiscal year, the amount otherwise payable to the State under paragraph (1)(A) of this subsection for the preceding fiscal year.

(C)(i) The Secretary shall waive all penalties imposed against a State under this paragraph for any failure of the State to comply with subparagraphs (A) and (B)(i) of section 654(27) of this title if the Secretary determines that, before April 1, 2000, the State has achieved such compliance.

(ii) If a State with respect to which a reduction is required to be made under this paragraph with respect to a failure to comply with subparagraphs (A) and (B)(i) of section 654(27) of this title achieves such compliance on or after April 1, 2000, and on or before September 30, 2000, then the penalty amount applicable to the State shall be 1 percent of the penalty base with respect to the failure involved.

(D) The Secretary may not impose a penalty under this paragraph against a State for a fiscal year for which the amount otherwise payable to the State under paragraph (1)(A) of this subsection is reduced under paragraph (4) of this subsection for failure to comply with section 654(24)(A) of this title.

(b) Estimate of amounts payable; installment payments

(1) Prior to the beginning of each quarter, the Secretary shall estimate the amount to which a State will be entitled under subsection (a) of this section for such quarter, such estimates to be based on (A) a report filed by the State containing its estimate of the total sum to be expended in such quarter in accordance with the provisions of such subsection, and stating the amount appropriated or made available by the State and its political subdivisions for such expenditures in such quarter, and if such amount is less than the State's proportionate share of the total sum of such estimated expenditures, the source or sources from which the difference is expected to be derived, and (B) such other investigation as the Secretary may find necessary.

(2) Subject to subsection (d) of this section, the Secretary shall then pay, in such installments as he may determine, to the State the amount so estimated, reduced or increased to the extent of any overpayment or underpayment which the Secretary determines was made under this section to such State for any prior quarter and with respect to which adjustment has not already been made under this subsection.

(3) Upon the making of any estimate by the Secretary under this subsection, any appropriations available for payments under this section shall be deemed obligated.

(c) Repealed. Pub.L. 97–248, Title I, § 174(b), Sept. 3, 1982, 96 Stat. 403

(d) State reports

Notwithstanding any other provision of law, no amount shall be paid to any State under this section for any quarter, prior to the close of such quarter, unless for the period consisting of all prior quarters for which payment is authorized to be made to such State under subsection (a) of this section, there shall have been submitted by the State to the Secretary, with respect to each quarter in such period (other than the last two quarters in such period), a full and complete report (in such form and manner and containing such information as the Secretary shall prescribe or require) as to the amount of child support collected and disbursed and all expenditures with respect to which payment is authorized under subsection (a) of this section.

(e) Special project grants for interstate enforcement; appropriations

(1) In order to encourage and promote the development and use of more effective methods of enforcing support obligations under this part in cases where either the children on whose behalf the support is sought or their noncustodial parents do not reside in the State where such cases are filed, the Secretary is authorized to make grants, in such amounts and on such terms and conditions as the Secretary determines to be appropriate, to States which propose to undertake new or innovative methods of support collection in such cases and which will use the proceeds of such grants to carry out special projects designed to demonstrate and test such methods.

(2) A grant under this subsection shall be made only upon a finding by the Secretary that the project involved is likely to be of significant assistance in carrying out the purpose of this subsection; and with respect to such project the Secretary may waive any of the requirements of this part which would otherwise be applicable, to such extent and for such period as the Secretary determines is necessary or desirable in order to enable the State to carry out the project.

(3) At the time of its application for a grant under this subsection the State shall submit to the Secretary a statement describing in reasonable detail the project for which the proceeds of the grant are to be used, and the State shall from time to time thereafter submit to the Secretary such reports with respect to the project as the Secretary may specify.

(4) Amounts expended by a State in carrying out a special project assisted under this section shall be considered, for purposes of section 658(b) of this title (as amended by section 5(a) of the Child Support Enforcement Amendments of 1984), to have been expended for the operation of the State's plan approved under section 654 of this title.

(5) There is authorized to be appropriated the sum of $7,000,000 for fiscal year 1985, $12,000,000 for fiscal year 1986, and $15,000,000 for each fiscal year thereafter, to be used by the Secretary in making grants under this subsection.

(f) Direct Federal funding to Indian tribes and tribal organizations

The Secretary may make direct payments under this part to an Indian tribe or tribal organization that demonstrates to the satisfaction of the Secretary that it has the capacity to operate a child support enforcement program meeting the objectives of this part, including establishment of paternity, establishment, modification, and enforcement of support orders, and location of absent parents. The Secretary shall promulgate regulations establishing the requirements which must be met by an Indian tribe or tribal organization to be eligible for a grant under this subsection. *(Aug. 14, 1935, c. 531, Title IV, § 455, as added Pub.L. 93–647, § 101(a), Jan. 4, 1975, 88 Stat. 2355; amended Pub.L. 94–88, Title II, §§ 201(c), 205, Aug. 9, 1975, 89 Stat. 433, 435; Pub.L. 94–365, § 3, July 14, 1976, 90 Stat. 990; Pub.L. 95–59, § 4, June 30, 1977, 91 Stat. 255; Pub.L. 96–178, § 2(a), Jan. 2, 1980, 93 Stat. 1295; Pub.L. 96–265, Title IV, §§ 404(a), 405(a), 407(a), (b), June 9, 1980, 94 Stat. 463, 467; Pub.L. 96–611, §§ 9(c), 11(c), Dec. 28, 1980, 94 Stat. 3573, 3574; Pub.L. 97–35, Title XXIII, § 2333(c), Aug. 13, 1981, 95 Stat. 863, as amended Pub.L. 97–248, Title I, § 171(b)(2), Sept. 3, 1982, 96 Stat. 401; Pub.L. 97–248, Title I, § 174(a), (b), Sept. 3, 1982, 96 Stat. 403; Pub.L. 98–378, §§ 4(a), 6(b), 8, Aug. 16, 1984, 98 Stat. 1311, 1314, 1315; Pub.L. 100–485, Title I, §§ 112(a), 123(c), Oct. 13, 1988, 102 Stat. 2350, 2352; Pub.L. 104–193, Title III, §§ 344(b)(1), (c), 375(b), 395(d)(1)(E), Aug. 22, 1996, 110 Stat. 2236, 2237, 2256, 2259; Pub.L. 105–33, Title V, §§ 5546(b), (c), 5555(a), Aug. 5, 1997, 111 Stat. 631, 632, 636; Pub.L. 105–200, Title I, §§ 101(a), 102(b), Title II, § 201(f)(2)(B), July 16, 1998, 112 Stat. 645, 648, 658; Pub.L. 105–306, § 4(a)(1), Oct. 28, 1998, 112 Stat. 2926; Pub.L. 106–113, Div. B, §1000(a)(4) [Title VIII, § 807(a)], Nov. 29, 1999, 113 Stat. 1535, 1501A–286; Pub.L. 106–169, Title IV, § 401(i), Dec. 14, 1999, 113 Stat. 1858; Pub.L. 109–171, Title VII, §§ 7308(a), 7309(a), Feb. 8, 2006, 120 Stat. 147.)*

[1] So in original. The "; and" probably should be a comma.

§ 655a. Provision for reimbursement of expenses

For purposes of section 655 of this title, expenses incurred to reimburse State employment offices for furnishing information requested of such offices—

(1) pursuant to section 49b(b) of Title 29, or

(2) by a State or local agency charged with the duty of carrying a State plan for child support approved under this part,

shall be considered to constitute expenses incurred in the administration of such State plan. *(Pub.L. 94–566, Title V, § 508(b), Oct. 20, 1976, 90 Stat. 2689; Pub.L. 104–193, Title I, § 110(a), Aug. 22, 1996, 110 Stat. 2171; Pub.L. 105–220, Title III, § 302(b), Aug. 7, 1998, 112 Stat. 1081.)*

§ 656. Support obligation as obligation to State; amount; discharge in bankruptcy

(a) Collection processes

(1) The support rights assigned to the State pursuant to section 608(a)(3) of this title or secured on behalf of a child receiving foster care maintenance payments shall constitute an obligation owed to such State by the individual responsible for providing such support. Such obligation shall be deemed for collection purposes to be collectible under all applicable State and local processes.

(2) The amount of such obligation shall be—

(A) the amount specified in a court order which covers the assigned support rights, or

(B) if there is no court order, an amount determined by the State in accordance with a formula approved by the Secretary.

(3) Any amounts collected from a noncustodial parent under the plan shall reduce, dollar for dollar, the amount of his obligation under subparagraphs (A) and (B) of paragraph (2).

(b) Nondischargeability

A debt (as defined in section 101 of Title 11) owed under State law to a State (as defined in such section) or municipality (as defined in such section) that is in the nature of support and that is enforceable under this part is not released by a discharge in bankruptcy under Title 11. *(Aug. 14, 1935, c. 531, Title IV, § 456, as added Pub.L. 93–647, § 101(a), Jan. 4, 1975, 88 Stat. 2356; amended Pub.L. 95–598, Title III, § 328, Nov. 6, 1978, 92 Stat. 2679; Pub.L. 97–35, Title XXIII, § 2334(a), Aug. 13, 1981, 95 Stat. 863; Pub.L. 98–369, Div. B, Title VI, § 2663(c)(15), July 18, 1984, 98 Stat. 1167; Pub.L. 98–378, § 11(b)(2), Aug. 16, 1984, 98 Stat. 1318; Pub.L. 104–193, Title I, § 108(c)(13), Title III, §§ 374(b), 395(d)(2)(C), Aug. 22, 1996, 110 Stat. 2166, 2255, 2260; Pub.L 105–33, Title V, §§ 5513(a)(3), 5556(d), Aug. 5, 1997, 111 Stat. 619, 637.)*

§ 657. Distribution of collected support

(a) In general

Subject to subsections (d) and (e), the amounts collected on behalf of a family as support by a State pursuant to a plan approved under this part shall be distributed as follows:

(1) Families receiving assistance

In the case of a family receiving assistance from the State, the State shall—

(A) pay to the Federal Government the Federal share of the amount collected, subject to paragraph (3)(A);

(B) retain, or pay to the family, the State share of the amount collected, subject to paragraph (3)(B); and

(C) pay to the family any remaining amount.

(2) Families that formerly received assistance

In the case of a family that formerly received assistance from the State:

(A) Current support

To the extent that the amount collected does not exceed the current support amount, the State shall pay the amount to the family.

(B) Arrearages

Except as otherwise provided in an election made under section 654(34) of this title, to the extent that the amount collected exceeds the current support amount, the State—

(i) shall first pay to the family the excess amount, to the extent necessary to satisfy support arrearages not assigned pursuant to section 608(a)(3) of this title;

(ii) if the amount collected exceeds the amount required to be paid to the family under clause (i), shall—

(I) pay to the Federal Government the Federal share of the excess amount described in this clause, subject to paragraph (3)(A); and

(II) retain, or pay to the family, the State share of the excess amount described in this clause, subject to paragraph (3)(B); and

(iii) shall pay to the family any remaining amount.

(3) Limitations

(A) Federal reimbursements

The total of the amounts paid by the State to the Federal Government under paragraphs (1) and (2) of this subsection with respect to a family shall not exceed the Federal share of the amount assigned with respect to the family pursuant to section 608(a)(3) of this title.

(B) State reimbursements

The total of the amounts retained by the State under paragraphs (1) and (2) of this subsection with respect to a family shall not exceed the State share of the amount assigned with respect to the family pursuant to section 608(a)(3) of this title.

(4) Families that never received assistance

In the case of any other family, the State shall distribute to the family the portion of the amount so collected that remains after withholding any fee pursuant to section 654(6)(B)(ii) of this title.

(5) Families under certain agreements

Notwithstanding paragraphs (1) through (3), in the case of an amount collected for a family in accordance with a cooperative agreement under section 654(33) of this title, the State shall distribute the amount collected pursuant to the terms of the agreement.

(6) State option to pass through additional support with Federal financial participation

(A) Families that formerly received assistance

Notwithstanding paragraph (2), a State shall not be required to pay to the Federal Government the Federal share of an amount collected on behalf of a family that formerly received assistance from the State to the extent that the State pays the amount to the family.

(B) Families that currently receive assistance

(i) In general

Notwithstanding paragraph (1), in the case of a family that receives assistance from the State, a State shall not be required to pay to the Federal Government the Federal share of the excepted portion (as defined in clause (ii)) of any amount collected on behalf of such family during a month to the extent that—

(I) the State pays the excepted portion to the family; and

(II) the excepted portion is disregarded in determining the amount and type of assistance provided to the family under such program.

(ii) Excepted portion defined

For purposes of this subparagraph, the term "excepted portion" means that portion of the amount collected on behalf of a family during a month that does not exceed $100 per month, or in the case of a family that includes 2 or more children, that does not exceed an amount established by the State that is not more than $200 per month.

(b) Continuation of assignments

(1) State option to discontinue pre-1997 support assignments

(A) In general

Any rights to support obligations assigned to a State as a condition of receiving assistance from the State under part A of this subchapter and in effect on September 30, 1997 (or such earlier date on or after August 22, 1996, as the State may choose), may remain assigned after such date.

(B) Distribution of amounts after assignment discontinuation

If a State chooses to discontinue the assignment of a support obligation described in subparagraph (A), the State may treat amounts collected pursuant to the assignment as if the amounts had never been assigned and may distribute the amounts to the family in accordance with subsection (a)(4) of this section.

(2) State option to discontinue post-1997 assignments

(A) In general

Any rights to support obligations accruing before the date on which a family first receives assistance under part A of this subchapter that are assigned to a State under that part and in effect before the implementation date of this section may remain assigned after such date.

(B) Distribution of amounts after assignment discontinuation

If a State chooses to discontinue the assignment of a support obligation described in subparagraph (A), the State may treat amounts collected pursuant to the assignment as if the amounts had never been assigned and may distribute the amounts to the family in accordance with subsection (a)(4) of this section.

(c) Definitions

As used in subsection (a) of this section:

(1) Assistance

The term "assistance from the State" means—

(A) assistance under the State program funded under part A of this subchapter or under the State plan approved under part A of this subchapter (as in effect on the day before August 22, 1996); and

(B) foster care maintenance payments under the State plan approved under part E of this subchapter.

(2) Federal share

The term "Federal share" means that portion of the amount collected resulting from the application of the Federal medical assistance percentage in effect for the fiscal year in which the amount is distributed.

(3) Federal medical assistance percentage

The term "Federal medical assistance percentage" means—

(A) 75 percent, in the case of Puerto Rico, the Virgin Islands, Guam, and American Samoa; or

(B) the Federal medical assistance percentage (as defined in section 1396d(b) of this title, as such section was in effect on September 30, 1995) in the case of any other State.

(4) State share

The term "State share" means 100 percent minus the Federal share.

(5) Current support amount

The term "current support amount" means, with respect to amounts collected as support on behalf of a family, the amount designated as the monthly support obligation of the noncustodial parent in the order requiring the support or calculated by the State based on the order.

(d) Gap payments not subject to distribution under this section

At State option, this section shall not apply to any amount collected on behalf of a family as support by the State (and paid to the family in addition to the amount of assistance otherwise payable to the family) pursuant to a plan approved under this part if such amount would have been paid to the family by the State under section 602(a)(28) of this title, as in effect and applied on the day before August 22, 1996.

(e) Amounts collected for child for whom foster care maintenance payments are made

Notwithstanding the preceding provisions of this section, amounts collected by a State as child support for months in any period on behalf of a child for whom a public agency is making foster care maintenance payments under part E of this subchapter (42 U.S.C. 670 et seq.)—

(1) shall be retained by the State to the extent necessary to reimburse it for the foster care maintenance payments made with respect to the child during such period (with appropriate reimbursement of the Federal Government to the extent of its participation in the financing);

(2) shall be paid to the public agency responsible for supervising the placement of the child to the extent that the amounts collected exceed the foster care maintenance payments made with respect to the child during such period but not the amounts required by a court or administrative order to be paid as support on behalf of the child during such period; and the responsible agency may use the payments in the manner it determines will serve the best interests of the child, including setting such payments aside for the child's future needs or making all or a part thereof available to the person responsible for meeting the child's day-to-day needs; and

(3) shall be retained by the State, if any portion of the amounts collected remains after making the payments required under paragraphs (1) and (2), to the extent that such portion is necessary to reimburse the State (with appropriate reimbursement to the Federal Government to the extent of its participation in the financing) for any past foster care maintenance payments (or payments of assistance under the State program funded under part A of this subchapter (42 U.S.C. 601 et seq.)) which were made with respect to the child (and with respect to which past collections have not previously been retained);

and any balance shall be paid to the State agency responsible for supervising the placement of the child, for use by such agency in accordance with paragraph (2). *(Aug. 14, 1935, c. 531, Title IV, § 457, as added Pub.L. 93–647, § 101(a), Jan. 4, 1975, 88 Stat. 2356; amended Pub.L. 95–171, § 11, Nov. 12, 1977, 91 Stat. 1357; Pub.L. 97–35, Title XXIII, § 2332(e), Aug. 13, 1981, 95 Stat. 862; Pub.L. 98–369, Div. B, Title VI, § 2640(b), July 18, 1984, 98 Stat. 1145; Pub.L. 98–378, §§ 7(a), 11(a), Aug. 16, 1984, 98 Stat. 1315, 1317; Pub.L. 99–514, Title XVIII, §§ 1883(b)(6), 1899(a), Oct. 22, 1986, 100 Stat. 2917, 2957; Pub.L. 100–203, Title IX, § 9141(a)(1), Dec. 22, 1987, 101 Stat. 1330–321; Pub.L. 100–485, Title I, § 102(b), Oct. 13, 1988, 102 Stat. 2346; Pub.L. 104–193, Title III, § 302(a), Aug. 22, 1996, 110 Stat. 2200; Pub.L. 105–33, Title V, §§ 5532(a), (b)(1), (c) to (h), 5547, Aug. 5, 1997, 111 Stat. 626, 627, 632; Pub.L. 106–169, Title III, § 301(a), (b), Title IV, § 401(j), (k), Dec. 14, 1999, 113 Stat. 1857, 1858; Pub.L. 109–171, Title VII, §§ 7301(b)(1)(A), (B)(i), (iii), (2), (c), 7310(b), Feb. 8, 2006, 120 Stat. 141 to 143, 147.)*

§ 658a. Incentive payments to States.

(a) In general

In addition to any other payment under this part, the Secretary shall, subject to subsection (f) of this section, make an incentive payment to each State for each fiscal year in an amount determined under subsection (b) of this section.

(b) Amount of incentive payment

(1) In general

The incentive payment for a State for a fiscal year is equal to the incentive payment pool for the fiscal year, multiplied by the State incentive payment share for the fiscal year.

(2) Incentive payment pool

(A) In general

In paragraph (1), the term "incentive payment pool" means—

(i) $422,000,000 for fiscal year 2000;

(ii) $429,000,000 for fiscal year 2001;

(iii) $450,000,000 for fiscal year 2002;

(iv) $461,000,000 for fiscal year 2003;

(v) $454,000,000 for fiscal year 2004;

(vi) $446,000,000 for fiscal year 2005;

(vii) $458,000,000 for fiscal year 2006;

(viii) $471,000,000 for fiscal year 2007;

(ix) $483,000,000 for fiscal year 2008; and

(x) for any succeeding fiscal year, the amount of the incentive payment pool for the fiscal year that precedes such succeeding fiscal year, multiplied by the percentage (if any) by which the CPI for such preceding fiscal year exceeds the CPI for the second preceding fiscal year.

(B) CPI

For purposes of subparagraph (A), the CPI for a fiscal year is the average of the Consumer Price Index for the 12-month period ending on September 30 of the fiscal year. As used in the preceding sentence, the term "Consumer Price Index" means the last Consumer Price Index for all-urban consumers published by the Department of Labor.

(3) State incentive payment share

In paragraph (1), the term "State incentive payment share" means, with respect to a fiscal year—

(A) the incentive base amount for the State for the fiscal year; divided by

(B) the sum of the incentive base amounts for all of the States for the fiscal year.

(4) Incentive base amount

In paragraph (3), the term "incentive base amount" means, with respect to a State and a fiscal year, the sum of the applicable percentages (determined in accordance with paragraph (6)) multiplied by the corresponding maximum incentive base amounts for the State for the fiscal year, with respect to each of the following measures of State performance for the fiscal year:

(A) The paternity establishment performance level.

(B) The support order performance level.

(C) The current payment performance level.

(D) The arrearage payment performance level.

(E) The cost-effectiveness performance level.

(5) Maximum incentive base amount

(A) In general

For purposes of paragraph (4), the maximum incentive base amount for a State for a fiscal year is—

(i) with respect to the performance measures described in subparagraphs (A), (B), and (C) of paragraph (4), the State collections base for the fiscal year; and

(ii) with respect to the performance measures described in subparagraphs (D) and (E) of paragraph (4), 75 percent of the State collections base for the fiscal year.

(B) Data required to be complete and reliable

Notwithstanding subparagraph (A), the maximum incentive base amount for a State for a fiscal year with respect to a performance measure described in paragraph (4) is zero, unless the Secretary determines, on the basis of an audit performed under section 652(a)(4)(C)(i) of this title, that the data which the State submitted pursuant to section 654(15)(B) of this title for the fiscal year and which is used to determine the performance level involved is complete and reliable.

(C) State collections base

For purposes of subparagraph (A), the State collections base for a fiscal year is equal to the sum of—

(i) 2 times the sum of—

(I) the total amount of support collected during the fiscal year under the State plan approved under this part in cases in which the support obligation involved is required to be assigned to the State pursuant to part A or E of this subchapter [section 601 et seq. or 670 et seq. of this title] or subchapter XIX of this chapter [section 1396 et seq. of this title]; and

(II) the total amount of support collected during the fiscal year under the State plan approved under this part in cases in which the support obligation involved was so assigned but, at the time of collection, is not required to be so assigned; and

(ii) the total amount of support collected during the fiscal year under the State plan approved under this part in all other cases.

(6) Determination of applicable percentages based on performance levels

(A) Paternity establishment

(i) Determination of paternity establishment performance level

The paternity establishment performance level for a State for a fiscal year is, at the option of the State, the IV–D paternity establishment percentage determined under section 652(g)(2)(A) of this title or the statewide paternity establishment percentage determined under section 652(g)(2)(B) of this title.

(ii) Determination of applicable percentage

The applicable percentage with respect to a State's paternity establishment performance level is as follows:

If the paternity establishment performance level is:		The applicable
At least:	But less than:	percentage is:
80%		100
79%	80%	98
78%	79%	96
77%	78%	94
76%	77%	92
75%	76%	90
74%	75%	88
73%	74%	86
72%	73%	84
71%	72%	82
70%	71%	80
69%	70%	79
68%	69%	78
67%	68%	77
66%	67%	76
65%	66%	75
64%	65%	74
63%	64%	73
62%	63%	72
61%	62%	71
60%	61%	70
59%	60%	69
58%	59%	68
57%	58%	67
56%	57%	66
55%	56%	65
54%	55%	64
53%	54%	63
52%	53%	62
51%	52%	61
50%	51%	60
0%	50%	0.

Notwithstanding the preceding sentence, if the paternity establishment performance level of a State for a fiscal year is less than 50 percent but exceeds by at least 10 percentage points the paternity establishment performance level of the State for the immediately preceding fiscal year, then the applicable percentage with respect to the State's paternity establishment performance level is 50 percent.

(B) Establishment of child support orders

(i) Determination of support order performance level

The support order performance level for a State for a fiscal year is the percentage of the total number of cases under the State plan approved under this part in which there is a support order during the fiscal year.

(ii) **Determination of applicable percentage**

The applicable percentage with respect to a State's support order performance level is as follows:

If the support order performance level is: At least:	But less than:	The applicable percentage is:
80%		100
79%	80%	98
78%	79%	96
77%	78%	94
76%	77%	92
75%	76%	90
74%	75%	88
73%	74%	86
72%	73%	84
71%	72%	82
70%	71%	80
69%	70%	79
68%	69%	78
67%	68%	77
66%	67%	76
65%	66%	75
64%	65%	74
63%	64%	73
62%	63%	72
61%	62%	71
60%	61%	70
59%	60%	69
58%	59%	68
57%	58%	67
56%	57%	66
55%	56%	65
54%	55%	64
53%	54%	63
52%	53%	62
51%	52%	61
50%	51%	60
0%	50%	0.

Notwithstanding the preceding sentence, if the support order performance level of a State for a fiscal year is less than 50 percent but exceeds by at least 5 percentage points the support order performance level of the State for the immediately preceding fiscal year, then the applicable percentage with respect to the State's support order performance level is 50 percent.

(C) Collections on current child support due

(i) Determination of current payment performance level

The current payment performance level for a State for a fiscal year is equal to the total amount of current support collected during the fiscal year under the State plan approved under this part divided by the total amount of current support owed during the fiscal year in all cases under the State plan, expressed as a percentage.

(ii) Determination of applicable percentage

The applicable percentage with respect to a State's current payment performance level is as follows:

If the current payment performance level is: At least:	But less than:	The applicable percentage is:
80%		100
79%	80%	98
78%	79%	96
77%	78%	94
76%	77%	92
75%	76%	90
74%	75%	88
73%	74%	86
72%	73%	84
71%	72%	82
70%	71%	80
69%	70%	79
68%	69%	78
67%	68%	77
66%	67%	76
65%	66%	75
64%	65%	74
63%	64%	73
62%	63%	72
61%	62%	71
60%	61%	70
59%	60%	69
58%	59%	68
57%	58%	67
56%	57%	66
55%	56%	65
54%	55%	64
53%	54%	63
52%	53%	62
51%	52%	61
50%	51%	60
49%	50%	59
48%	49%	58
47%	48%	57
46%	47%	56
45%	46%	55
44%	45%	54
43%	44%	53
42%	43%	52
41%	42%	51
40%	41%	50
0%	40%	0.

Notwithstanding the preceding sentence, if the current payment performance level of a State for a fiscal year is less than 40 percent but exceeds by at least 5 percentage points the current payment performance level of the State for the immediately preceding fiscal year, then the applicable percentage with respect to the State's current payment performance level is 50 percent.

(D) Collections on child support arrearages

(i) Determination of arrearage payment performance level

The arrearage payment performance level for a State for a fiscal year is equal to the total number of cases under the State plan approved under this part in which payments of past-due child support were received during the fiscal year and part or all of the payments were distributed to the family to whom the past-due child support was owed (or, if all past-due child support owed to the family was, at the time of receipt, subject to an assignment to the State, part or all of the payments were retained by the State) divided by the total number of cases under the State plan in which there is past-due child support, expressed as a percentage.

(ii) Determination of applicable percentage

The applicable percentage with respect to a State's arrearage payment performance level is as follows:

If the arrearage payment performance level is: At least:	But less than:	The applicable percentage is:
80%		100
79%	80%	98
78%	79%	96
77%	78%	94
76%	77%	92
75%	76%	90
74%	75%	88
73%	74%	86
72%	73%	84
71%	72%	82
70%	71%	80
69%	70%	79
68%	69%	78
67%	68%	77
66%	67%	76
65%	66%	75
64%	65%	74
63%	64%	73
62%	63%	72
61%	62%	71
60%	61%	70
59%	60%	69
58%	59%	68
57%	58%	67
56%	57%	66
55%	56%	65
54%	55%	64
53%	54%	63
52%	53%	62
51%	52%	61
50%	51%	60
49%	50%	59
48%	49%	58
47%	48%	57
46%	47%	56
45%	46%	55
44%	45%	54
43%	44%	53
42%	43%	52
41%	42%	51
40%	41%	50
0%	40%	0.

Notwithstanding the preceding sentence, if the arrearage payment performance level of a State for a fiscal year is less than 40 percent but exceeds by at least 5 percentage points the arrearage payment performance level of the State for the immediately preceding fiscal year, then the applicable percentage with respect to the State's arrearage payment performance level is 50 percent.

(E) Cost-effectiveness

(i) Determination of cost-effectiveness performance level

The cost-effectiveness performance level for a State for a fiscal year is equal to the total amount collected during the fiscal year under the State plan approved under this part divided by the total amount expended during the fiscal year under the State plan, expressed as a ratio.

(ii) Determination of applicable percentage

The applicable percentage with respect to a State's cost-effectiveness performance level is as follows:

If the cost-effectiveness performance level is: At least:	But less than:	The applicable percentage is:
5.00		100
4.50	4.99	90
4.00	4.50	80
3.50	4.00	70
3.00	3.50	60
2.50	3.00	50
2.00	2.50	40
0.00	2.00	0.

(c) Treatment of interstate collections

In computing incentive payments under this section, support which is collected by a State at the request of another State shall be treated as having been collected in full by both States, and any amounts expended by a State in carrying out a special project assisted under section 655(e) of this title shall be excluded.

(d) Administrative provisions

The amounts of the incentive payments to be made to the States under this section for a fiscal year shall be estimated by the Secretary at/or before the beginning of the fiscal year on the basis of the best information available. The Secretary shall make the payments for the fiscal year, on a quarterly basis (with each quarterly payment being made no later than the beginning of the quarter involved), in the amounts so estimated, reduced or increased to the extent of any overpayments or underpayments which the Secretary determines were made under this section to the States involved for prior periods and with respect to which adjustment has not already been made under this subsection. Upon the making of any estimate by the Secretary under the preceding sentence, any appropriations available for payments under this section are deemed obligated.

(e) Regulations

The Secretary shall prescribe such regulations as may be necessary governing the calculation of incentive payments under this section, including directions for excluding from the calculations certain closed cases and cases over which the States do not have jurisdiction.

(f) Reinvestment

A State to which a payment is made under this section shall expend the full amount of the payment to supplement, and not supplant, other funds used by the State—

(1) to carry out the State plan approved under this part; or

(2) for any activity (including cost-effective contracts with local agencies) approved by the Secretary, whether or not the expenditures for the activity are eligible for reimbursement under this part, which may contribute to improving the effectiveness or efficiency of the State program operated under this part.

(Aug. 14, 1935, c. 531, § 458, formerly § 458A, as added Pub.L. 105–200, Title II, § 201(a), July 16, 1998, 112 Stat. 648, renumbered § 458, Pub.L. 105–200, Title II, § 201(f)(2)(A), July 16, 1998, 112 Stat. 658.)

§ 659. Consent by United States to income withholding, garnishment, and similar proceedings for enforcement of child support and alimony obligations

(a) Consent to support enforcement

Notwithstanding any other provision of law (including section 407 of this title and section 5301 of Title 38), effective January 1, 1975, moneys (the entitlement to which is based upon remuneration for employment) due from, or payable by, the United States or the District of Columbia (including any agency, subdivision, or instrumentality thereof) to any individual, including members of the Armed Forces of the United States, shall be subject, in like manner and to the same extent as if the United States or the District of Columbia were a private person, to withholding in accordance with State law enacted pursuant to subsections (a)(1) and (b) of section 666 of this title and regulations of the Secretary under such subsections, and to any other legal process brought, by a State agency administering a program under a State plan approved under this part or by an individual obligee, to enforce the legal obligation of the individual to provide child support or alimony.

(b) Consent to requirements applicable to private person

With respect to notice to withhold income pursuant to subsection (a)(1) or (b) of section 666 of this title, or any other order or process to enforce support obligations against an individual (if the order or process contains or is accompanied by sufficient data to permit prompt identification of the individual and the moneys involved), each governmental entity specified in subsection (a) of this section shall be subject to the same requirements as would apply if the entity were a private person, except as otherwise provided in this section.

(c) Designation of agent; response to notice or process

(1) Designation of agent

The head of each agency subject to this section shall—

(A) designate an agent or agents to receive orders and accept service of process in matters relating to child support or alimony; and

(B) annually publish in the Federal Register the designation of the agent or agents, identified by title or position, mailing address, and telephone number.

(2) Response to notice or process

If an agent designated pursuant to paragraph (1) of this subsection receives notice pursuant to State procedures in effect pursuant to subsection (a)(1) or (b) of section 666 of this title, or is effectively served with any order, process, or interrogatory, with respect to an individual's child support or alimony payment obligations, the agent shall—

(A) as soon as possible (but not later than 15 days) thereafter, send written notice of the notice or service (together with a copy of the notice or service) to the individual at the duty station or last-known home address of the individual;

(B) within 30 days (or such longer period as may be prescribed by applicable State law) after receipt of a notice pursuant to such State procedures, comply with all applicable provisions of section 666 of this title; and

(C) within 30 days (or such longer period as may be prescribed by applicable State law) after effective service of any other such order, process, or interrogatory, withhold available sums in response to the order or process, or answer the interrogatory.

(d) Priority of claims

If a governmental entity specified in subsection (a) of this section receives notice or is served with process, as provided in this section, concerning amounts owed by an individual to more than 1 person—

(1) support collection under section 666(b) of this title must be given priority over any other process, as provided in section 666(b)(7) of this title;

(2) allocation of moneys due or payable to an individual among claimants under section 666(b) of this title shall be governed by section 666(b) of this title and the regulations prescribed under such section; and

(3) such moneys as remain after compliance with paragraphs (1) and (2) shall be available to satisfy any other such processes on a first-come, first-served basis, with any such process being satisfied out of such moneys as remain after the satisfaction of all such processes which have been previously served.

(e) No requirement to vary pay cycles

A governmental entity that is affected by legal process served for the enforcement of an individual's child support or alimony payment obligations shall not be required to vary its normal pay and disbursement cycle in order to comply with the legal process.

(f) Relief from liability

(1) Neither the United States, nor the government of the District of Columbia, nor any disbursing officer shall be liable with respect to any payment made from moneys due or payable from the United States to any individual pursuant to legal process regular on its face, if the payment is made in accordance with this section and the regulations issued to carry out this section.

(2) No Federal employee whose duties include taking actions necessary to comply with the requirements of subsection (a) of this section with regard to any individual shall be subject under any law to any disciplinary action or civil or criminal liability or penalty for, or on account of, any disclosure of information made by the employee in connection with the carrying out of such actions.

(g) Regulations

Authority to promulgate regulations for the implementation of this section shall, insofar as this section applies to moneys due from (or payable by)—

(1) the United States (other than the legislative or judicial branches of the Federal Government) or the government of the District of Columbia, be vested in the President (or the designee of the President);

(2) the legislative branch of the Federal Government, be vested jointly in the President pro tempore of the Senate and the Speaker of the House of Representatives (or their designees),[1] and

(3) the judicial branch of the Federal Government, be vested in the Chief Justice of the United States (or the designee of the Chief Justice).

(h) Moneys subject to process

(1) In general

Subject to paragraph (2), moneys payable to an individual which are considered to be based upon remuneration for employment, for purposes of this section—

(A) consist of—

(i) compensation payable for personal services of the individual, whether the compensation is denominated as wages, salary, commission, bonus, pay, allowances, or otherwise (including severance pay, sick pay, and incentive pay);

(ii) periodic benefits (including a periodic benefit as defined in section 428(h)(3) of this title) or other payments—

(I) under the insurance system established by subchapter II of this chapter;

(II) under any other system or fund established by the United States which provides for the payment of pensions, retirement or retired pay, annuities, dependents' or survivors' benefits, or similar amounts payable on account of personal services performed by the individual or any other individual;

(III) as compensation for death under any Federal program;

(IV) under any Federal program established to provide "black lung" benefits; or

(V) by the Secretary of Veterans Affairs as compensation for a service-connected disability paid by the Secretary to a former member of the Armed Forces who is in receipt of retired or retainer pay if the former member has waived a portion of the retired or retainer pay in order to receive such compensation;

(iii) worker's compensation benefits paid or payable under Federal or State law;

(iv) benefits paid or payable under the Railroad Retirement System,[1] and

(v) special benefits for certain World War II veterans payable under subchapter VIII of this chapter [42 U.S.C.A. § 1001 et seq.]; but

(B) do not include any payment—

(i) by way of reimbursement or otherwise, to defray expenses incurred by the individual in carrying out duties associated with the employment of the individual;

(ii) as allowances for members of the uniformed services payable pursuant to chapter 7 of Title 37, as prescribed by the Secretaries concerned (defined by section 101(5) of Title 37) as necessary for the efficient performance of duty; or

(iii) of periodic benefits under title 38, United States Code, except as provided in subparagraph (A)(ii)(V).

(2) Certain amounts excluded

In determining the amount of any moneys due from, or payable by, the United States to any individual, there shall be excluded amounts which—

(A) are owed by the individual to the United States;

(B) are required by law to be, and are, deducted from the remuneration or other payment involved, including Federal employment taxes, and fines and forfeitures ordered by court-martial;

(C) are properly withheld for Federal, State, or local income tax purposes, if the withholding of the amounts is authorized or required by law and if amounts withheld are not greater than would be the case if the individual claimed all dependents to which he was entitled (the withholding of additional amounts pursuant to section 3402(i) of the Internal Revenue Code of 1986 may be permitted only when the individual presents evidence of a tax obligation which supports the additional withholding);

(D) are deducted as health insurance premiums;

(E) are deducted as normal retirement contributions (not including amounts deducted for supplementary coverage); or

(F) are deducted as normal life insurance premiums from salary or other remuneration for employment (not including amounts deducted for supplementary coverage).

(i) Definitions

For purposes of this section—

(1) United States

The term "United States" includes any department, agency, or instrumentality of the legislative, judicial, or executive branch of the Federal Government, the United States Postal Service, the Postal Regulatory Commission, any Federal corporation created by an Act of Congress that is wholly owned by the Federal Government, and the governments of the territories and possessions of the United States.

(2) Child support

The term "child support", when used in reference to the legal obligations of an individual to provide such support, means amounts required to be paid under a judgment, decree, or order, whether temporary, final, or subject to modification, issued by a court or an administrative agency of competent jurisdiction, for the support and maintenance of a child, including a child who has attained the age of majority under the law of the issuing State, or a child and the parent with whom the child is living, which provides for monetary support, health care, arrearages or reimbursement, and which may include other related costs and fees, interest and penalties, income withholding, attorney's fees, and other relief.

(3) Alimony

(A) In general

The term "alimony", when used in reference to the legal obligations of an individual to provide the same, means periodic payments of funds for the support and maintenance of the spouse (or former spouse) of the individual, and (subject to and in accordance with State law) includes separate maintenance, alimony pendente lite, maintenance, and spousal support, and includes attorney's fees, interest, and court costs when and to the extent that the same are expressly made recoverable as such pursuant to a decree, order, or judgment issued in accordance with applicable State law by a court of competent jurisdiction.

(B) Exceptions

Such term does not include—

(i) any child support; or

(ii) any payment or transfer of property or its value by an individual to the spouse or a former spouse of the individual in compliance with any community property settlement, equitable distribution of property, or other division of property between spouses or former spouses.

(4) Private person

The term "private person" means a person who does not have sovereign or other special immunity or privilege which causes the person not to be subject to legal process.

(5) Legal process

The term "legal process" means any writ, order, summons, or other similar process in the nature of garnishment—

(A) which is issued by—

(i) a court or an administrative agency of competent jurisdiction in any State, territory, or possession of the United States;

(ii) a court or an administrative agency of competent jurisdiction in any foreign country with which the United States has entered into an agreement which requires the United States to honor the process; or

(iii) an authorized official pursuant to an order of such a court or an administrative agency of competent jurisdiction or pursuant to State or local law; and

(B) which is directed to, and the purpose of which is to compel, a governmental entity which holds moneys which are otherwise payable to an individual to make a payment from the moneys to another party in order to satisfy a legal obligation of the individual to provide child support or make alimony payments.

(Aug. 14, 1935, c. 531, Title IV, § 459, as added Pub.L. 93–647, § 101(a), Jan. 4, 1975, 88 Stat. 2357; amended Pub.L. 95–30, Title V, § 501(a), (b), May 23, 1977, 91 Stat. 157; Pub.L. 98–21, Title III, § 335(b)(1), Apr. 20, 1983, 97 Stat. 130; Pub.L. 104–193, Title III, § 362(a), Aug. 22, 1996, 110 Stat. 2242; Pub.L. 105–33, Title V, §§ 5542(a), (b), Aug. 5, 1997, 111 Stat. 631; Pub.L. 106–169, Title II, § 251(b)(3), Dec. 14, 1999, 113 Stat. 1855; Pub.L. 109–435, Title VI, § 604(f), Dec. 20, 2006, 120 Stat. 3242.)

[1] So in original. Probably should be a semicolon.

§ 659a. International support enforcement

(a) Authority for declarations

(1) Declaration

The Secretary of State, with the concurrence of the Secretary of Health and Human Services, is authorized to declare any foreign country (or a political subdivision thereof) to be a foreign reciprocating country if the foreign country has established, or undertakes to establish, procedures for the establishment and enforcement of duties of support owed to obligees who are residents of the United States, and such procedures are substantially in conformity with the standards prescribed under subsection (b) of this section.

(2) Revocation

A declaration with respect to a foreign country made pursuant to paragraph (1) may be revoked if the Secretaries of State and Health and Human Services determine that—

(A) the procedures established by the foreign country regarding the establishment and enforcement of duties of support have been so changed, or the foreign country's implementation of such procedures is so unsatisfactory, that such procedures do not meet the criteria for such a declaration; or

(B) continued operation of the declaration is not consistent with the purposes of this part.

(3) Form of declaration

A declaration under paragraph (1) may be made in the form of an international agreement, in connection with an international agreement or corresponding foreign declaration, or on a unilateral basis.

(b) Standards for foreign support enforcement procedures

(1) Mandatory elements

Support enforcement procedures of a foreign country which may be the subject of a declaration pursuant to subsection (a)(1) of this section shall include the following elements:

(A) The foreign country (or political subdivision thereof) has in effect procedures, available to residents of the United States—

(i) for establishment of paternity, and for establishment of orders of support for children and custodial parents; and

(ii) for enforcement of orders to provide support to children and custodial parents, including procedures for collection and appropriate distribution of support payments under such orders.

(B) The procedures described in subparagraph (A), including legal and administrative assistance, are provided to residents of the United States at no cost.

(C) An agency of the foreign country is designated as a Central Authority responsible for—

(i) facilitating support enforcement in cases involving residents of the foreign country and residents of the United States; and

(ii) ensuring compliance with the standards established pursuant to this subsection.

(2) Additional elements

The Secretary of Health and Human Services and the Secretary of State, in consultation with the States, may establish such additional standards as may be considered necessary to further the purposes of this section.

(c) Designation of United States Central Authority

It shall be the responsibility of the Secretary of Health and Human Services to facilitate support enforcement in cases involving residents of the United States and residents of foreign reciprocating countries or foreign treaty countries, by activities including—

(1) development of uniform forms and procedures for use in such cases;

(2) notification of foreign reciprocating countries and foreign treaty countries of the State of residence of individuals sought for support enforcement purposes, on the basis of information provided by the Federal Parent Locator Service; and

(3) such other oversight, assistance, and coordination activities as the Secretary may find necessary and appropriate.

(d) Effect on other laws

States may enter into reciprocal arrangements for the establishment and enforcement of support obligations with foreign countries that are not foreign reciprocating countries or foreign treaty countries of this section, to the extent consistent with Federal law.

(e) References

In this part:

(1) Foreign reciprocating country

The term "foreign reciprocating country" means a foreign country (or political subdivision thereof) with respect to which the Secretary has made a declaration pursuant to subsection (a).

(2) Foreign treaty country

The term "foreign treaty country" means a foreign country for which the 2007 Family Maintenance Convention is in force.

(3) 2007 Family Maintenance Convention

The term "2007 Family Maintenance Convention" means the Hague Convention of 23 November 2007 on the International Recovery of Child Support and Other Forms of Family Maintenance.

(Aug. 14, 1935, c. 531, Title IV, § 459A, as added Pub.L. 104–193, Title III, § 371(a), Aug. 22, 1996, 110 Stat. 2252; amended Pub.L. 113–183, Title III, § 301(d), Sept. 29, 2014, 128 Stat. 1944.)

§ 660. Civil action to enforce child support obligations; jurisdiction of district courts

The district courts of the United States shall have jurisdiction, without regard to any amount in controversy, to hear and determine any civil action certified by the Secretary of Health and Human Services under section 652(a)(8) of this title. A civil action under this section may be brought in any judicial district in which the claim arose, the plaintiff resides, or the defendant resides. *(Aug. 14, 1935, c. 531, Title IV, § 460, as added Pub.L. 93–647, § 101(a), Jan. 4, 1975, 88 Stat. 2358; amended Pub.L. 98–369, Div. B, Title VI, § 2663(j)(2)(B)(xi), July 18, 1984, 98 Stat. 1170.)*

CHAPTER 143—INTERCOUNTRY ADOPTIONS

§ 14901. Findings and purposes

(a) Findings

Congress recognizes—

(1) the international character of the Convention on Protection of Children and Co-operation in Respect of Intercountry Adoption (done at The Hague on May 29, 1993); and

(2) the need for uniform interpretation and implementation of the Convention in the United States and abroad,

and therefore finds that enactment of a Federal law governing adoptions and prospective adoptions subject to the Convention involving United States residents is essential.

(b) Purposes

The purposes of this chapter are—

(1) to provide for implementation by the United States of the Convention;

(2) to protect the rights of, and prevent abuses against, children, birth families, and adoptive parents involved in adoptions (or prospective adoptions) subject to the Convention, and to ensure that such adoptions are in the children's best interests; and

(3) to improve the ability of the Federal Government to assist United States citizens seeking to adopt children from abroad and residents of other countries party to the Convention seeking to adopt children from the United States.

(Pub.L. 106–279, § 2, Oct. 6, 2000, 114 Stat. 825.)

§ 14902. Definitions

As used in this chapter:

(1) Accredited agency

The term "accredited agency" means an agency accredited under subchapter II of this chapter to provide adoption services in the United States in cases subject to the Convention.

(2) Accrediting entity

The term "accrediting entity" means an entity designated under section 14922(a) of this title to accredit agencies and approve persons under subchapter II of this chapter.

(3) Adoption service

The term "adoption service" means—

(A) identifying a child for adoption and arranging an adoption;

(B) securing necessary consent to termination of parental rights and to adoption;

(C) performing a background study on a child or a home study on a prospective adoptive parent, and reporting on such a study;

(D) making determinations of the best interests of a child and the appropriateness of adoptive placement for the child;

(E) post–placement monitoring of a case until final adoption; and

(F) where made necessary by disruption before final adoption, assuming custody and providing child care or any other social service pending an alternative placement.

The term "providing", with respect to an adoption service, includes facilitating the provision of the service.

(4) Agency

The term "agency" means any person other than an individual.

(5) Approved person

The term "approved person" means a person approved under subchapter II of this chapter to provide adoption services in the United States in cases subject to the Convention.

(6) Attorney General

Except as used in section 14944 of this title, the term "Attorney General" means the Attorney General, acting through the Commissioner of Immigration and Naturalization.

(7) Central authority

The term "central authority" means the entity designated as such by any Convention country under Article 6(1) of the Convention.

(8) Central authority function

The term "central authority function" means any duty required to be carried out by a central authority under the Convention.

(9) Convention

The term "Convention" means the Convention on Protection of Children and Co-operation in Respect of Intercountry Adoption, done at The Hague on May 29, 1993.

(10) Convention adoption

The term "Convention adoption" means an adoption of a child resident in a foreign country party to the Convention by a United States citizen, or an adoption of a child resident in the United States by an individual residing in another Convention country.

(11) Convention record

The term "Convention record" means any item, collection, or grouping of information contained in an electronic or physical document, an electronic collection of data, a photograph, an audio or video tape, or any other information storage medium of any type whatever that contains information about a specific past, current, or prospective Convention adoption (regardless of whether the adoption was made final) that has been preserved in accordance with section 14941(a) of this title by the Secretary of State or the Attorney General.

(12) Convention country

The term "Convention country" means a country party to the Convention.

(13) Other Convention country

The term "other Convention country" means a Convention country other than the United States.

(14) Person

The term "person" shall have the meaning provided in section 1 of Title 1 and shall not include any agency of government or tribal government entity.

(15) Person with an ownership or control interest

The term "person with an ownership or control interest" has the meaning given such term in section 1320a–3(a)(3) of this title.

(16) Secretary

The term "Secretary" means the Secretary of State.

(17) State

The term "State" means the 50 States, the District of Columbia, the Commonwealth of Puerto Rico, the Commonwealth of the Northern Mariana Islands, Guam, and the Virgin Islands.

(Pub.L. 106–279, § 3, Oct. 6, 2000, 114 Stat. 826.)

SUBCHAPTER I—UNITED STATES CENTRAL AUTHORITY

§ 14911. Designation of central authority

(a) In general

For purposes of the Convention and this chapter—

(1) the Department of State shall serve as the central authority of the United States; and

(2) the Secretary shall serve as the head of the central authority of the United States.

(b) Performance of central authority functions

(1) Except as otherwise provided in this chapter, the Secretary shall be responsible for the performance of all central authority functions for the United States under the Convention and this chapter.

(2) All personnel of the Department of State performing core central authority functions in a professional capacity in the Office of Children's Issues shall have a strong background in consular affairs, personal experience in international adoptions, or professional experience in international adoptions or child services.

(c) Authority to issue regulations

Except as otherwise provided in this chapter, the Secretary may prescribe such regulations as may be necessary to carry out central authority functions on behalf of the United States. *(Pub.L. 106–279, Title I, § 101, Oct. 6, 2000, 114 Stat. 827.)*

§ 14912. Responsibilities of the Secretary of State

(a) Liaison responsibilities

The Secretary shall have responsibility for—

(1) liaison with the central authorities of other Convention countries; and

(2) the coordination of activities under the Convention by persons subject to the jurisdiction of the United States.

(b) Information exchange

The Secretary shall be responsible for—

(1) providing the central authorities of other Convention countries with information concerning—

(A) accredited agencies and approved persons, agencies and persons whose accreditation or approval has been suspended or canceled, and agencies and persons who have been temporarily or permanently debarred from accreditation or approval;

(B) Federal and State laws relevant to implementing the Convention; and

(C) any other matters necessary and appropriate for implementation of the Convention;

(2) not later than the date of the entry into force of the Convention for the United States (pursuant to Article 46(2)(a) of the Convention) and at least once during each subsequent calendar year, providing to the central authority of all other Convention countries a notice requesting the central authority of each such country to specify any requirements of such country regarding adoption, including restrictions on the eligibility of persons to adopt, with respect to which information on the prospective adoptive parent or parents in the United States would be relevant;

(3) making responses to notices under paragraph (2) available to—

(A) accredited agencies and approved persons; and

(B) other persons or entities performing home studies under section 14921(b)(1) of this title;

(4) ensuring the provision of a background report (home study) on prospective adoptive parent or parents (pursuant to the requirements of section 14923(b)(1)(A)(ii) of this title), through the central authority of each child's country of origin, to the court having jurisdiction over the adoption (or, in the case of a child emigrating to the United States for the purpose of adoption, to the competent authority in the child's country of origin with responsibility for approving the child's emigration) in adequate time to be considered prior to the granting of such adoption or approval;

(5) providing Federal agencies, State courts, and accredited agencies and approved persons with an identification of Convention countries and persons authorized to perform functions under the Convention in each such country; and

(6) facilitating the transmittal of other appropriate information to, and among, central authorities, Federal and State agencies (including State courts), and accredited agencies and approved persons.

(c) Accreditation and approval responsibilities

The Secretary shall carry out the functions prescribed by the Convention with respect to the accreditation of agencies and the approval of persons to provide adoption services in the United States in cases subject to the Convention as provided in subchapter II of this chapter. Such functions may not be delegated to any other Federal agency.

(d) Additional responsibilities

The Secretary—

(1) shall monitor individual Convention adoption cases involving United States citizens; and

(2) may facilitate interactions between such citizens and officials of other Convention countries on matters relating to the Convention in any case in which an accredited agency or approved person is unwilling or unable to provide such facilitation.

(e) Establishment of registry

The Secretary and the Attorney General shall jointly establish a case registry of all adoptions involving immigration of children into the United States and emigration of children from the United States, regardless of whether the adoption occurs under the Convention. Such registry shall permit tracking of pending cases and retrieval of information on both pending and closed cases.

(f) Methods of performing responsibilities

The Secretary may—

(1) authorize public or private entities to perform appropriate central authority functions for which the Secretary is responsible, pursuant to regulations or under agreements published in the Federal Register; and

(2) carry out central authority functions through grants to, or contracts with, any individual or public or private entity, except as may be otherwise specifically provided in this chapter.

(Pub.L. 106–279, Title I, § 102, Oct. 6, 2000, 114 Stat. 828.)

§ 14913. Responsibilities of the Attorney General

In addition to such other responsibilities as are specifically conferred upon the Attorney General by this chapter, the central authority functions specified in Article 14 of the Convention (relating to the filing of applications by prospective adoptive parents to the central authority of their country of residence) shall be performed by the Attorney General. *(Pub.L. 106–279, Title I, § 103, Oct. 6, 2000, 114 Stat. 829.)*

§ 14914. Annual report on intercountry adoptions

(a) Reports required

Beginning 1 year after the date of the entry into force of the Convention for the United States and each year thereafter, the Secretary, in consultation with the Attorney General and other appropriate agencies, shall submit a report describing the activities of the central authority of the United States under this chapter during the preceding year to the Committee on International Relations, the Committee on Ways and Means, and the Committee on the Judiciary of the House of Representatives and the Committee on Foreign Relations, the Committee on Finance, and the Committee on the Judiciary of the Senate.

(b) Report elements

Each report under subsection (a) of this section shall set forth with respect to the year concerned, the following:

(1) The number of intercountry adoptions involving immigration to the United States, regardless of whether the adoption occurred under the Convention, including the country from which each child emigrated, the State to which each child immigrated, and the country in which the adoption was finalized.

(2) The number of intercountry adoptions involving emigration from the United States, regardless of whether the adoption occurred under the Convention, including the country to which each child immigrated and the State from which each child emigrated.

(3) The number of Convention placements for adoption in the United States that were disrupted, including the country from which the child emigrated, the age of the child, the date of the placement for adoption, the reasons for the disruption, the resolution of the disruption, the agencies that handled the placement for adoption, and the plans for the child, and in addition, any information regarding disruption or dissolution of adoptions of children from other countries received pursuant to section 622(b)(12) of this title.

(4) The average time required for completion of a Convention adoption, set forth by country from which the child emigrated.

(5) The current list of agencies accredited and persons approved under this chapter to provide adoption services.

(6) The names of the agencies and persons temporarily or permanently debarred under this chapter, and the reasons for the debarment.

(7) The range of adoption fees charged in connection with Convention adoptions involving immigration to the United States and the median of such fees set forth by the country of origin.

(8) The range of fees charged for accreditation of agencies and the approval of persons in the United States engaged in providing adoption services under the Convention.

(Pub.L. 106–279, Title I, § 104, Oct. 6, 2000, 114 Stat. 829; Pub.L. 109–288, § 6(f)(9), Sept. 28, 2006, 120 Stat. 1248.)

SUBCHAPTER II—PROVISIONS RELATING TO ACCREDITATION AND APPROVAL

§ 14921. Accreditation or approval required in order to provide adoption services in cases subject to the Convention

(a) In general

Except as otherwise provided in this subchapter, no person may offer or provide adoption services in connection with a Convention adoption in the United States unless that person—

(1) is accredited or approved in accordance with this subchapter; or

(2) is providing such services through or under the supervision and responsibility of an accredited agency or approved person.

(b) Exceptions

Subsection (a) of this section shall not apply to the following:

(1) Background studies and home studies

The performance of a background study on a child or a home study on a prospective adoptive parent, or any report on any such study by a social work professional or organization who is not providing any other adoption service in the case, if the background or home study is approved by an accredited agency.

(2) Child welfare services

The provision of a child welfare service by a person who is not providing any other adoption service in the case.

(3) Legal services

The provision of legal services by a person who is not providing any adoption service in the case.

(4) Prospective adoptive parents acting on own behalf

The conduct of a prospective adoptive parent on his or her own behalf in the case, to the extent not prohibited by the law of the State in which the prospective adoptive parent resides.

(Pub.L. 106–279, Title II, § 201, Oct. 6, 2000, 114 Stat. 830.)

§ 14922. Process for accreditation and approval; role of accrediting entities

(a) Designation of accrediting entities

(1) In general

The Secretary shall enter into agreements with one or more qualified entities under which such entities will perform the duties described in subsection (b) of this section in accordance with the Convention, this subchapter, and the regulations prescribed under section 14923 of this title, and upon entering into each such agreement shall designate the qualified entity as an accrediting entity.

(2) Qualified entities

In paragraph (1), the term "qualified entity" means—

(A) a nonprofit private entity that has expertise in developing and administering standards for entities providing child welfare services and that meets such other criteria as the Secretary may by regulation establish; or

(B) a public entity (other than a Federal entity), including an agency or instrumentality of State government having responsibility for licensing adoption agencies, that—

(i) has expertise in developing and administering standards for entities providing child welfare services;

(ii) accredits only agencies located in the State in which the public entity is located; and

(iii) meets such other criteria as the Secretary may by regulation establish.

(b) **Duties of accrediting entities**

The duties described in this subsection are the following:

(1) **Accreditation and approval**

Accreditation of agencies, and approval of persons, to provide adoption services in the United States in cases subject to the Convention.

(2) **Oversight**

Ongoing monitoring of the compliance of accredited agencies and approved persons with applicable requirements, including review of complaints against such agencies and persons in accordance with procedures established by the accrediting entity and approved by the Secretary.

(3) **Enforcement**

Taking of adverse actions (including requiring corrective action, imposing sanctions, and refusing to renew, suspending, or canceling accreditation or approval) for noncompliance with applicable requirements, and notifying the agency or person against whom adverse actions are taken of the deficiencies necessitating the adverse action.

(4) **Data, records, and reports**

Collection of data, maintenance of records, and reporting to the Secretary, the United States central authority, State courts, and other entities (including on persons and agencies granted or denied approval or accreditation), to the extent and in the manner that the Secretary requires.

(5) **Report on use of Federal funding**

Not later than 90 days after an accrediting entity receives Federal funding authorized by section 14943 of this title, the entity shall submit a report to the Committee on Foreign Relations of the Senate and the Committee on Foreign Affairs of the House of Representatives that describes—

(A) the amount of such funding the entity received; and

(B) how such funding was, or will be, used by the entity.

(c) **Remedies for adverse action by accrediting entity**

(1) **Correction of deficiency**

An agency or person who is the subject of an adverse action by an accrediting entity may re-apply for accreditation or approval (or petition for termination of the adverse action) on demonstrating to the satisfaction of the accrediting entity that the deficiencies necessitating the adverse action have been corrected.

(2) **No other administrative review**

An adverse action by an accrediting entity shall not be subject to administrative review.

(3) **Judicial review**

An agency or person who is the subject of an adverse action by an accrediting entity may petition the United States district court in the judicial district in which the agency is located or the person resides to set aside the adverse action. The court shall review the adverse action in accordance with section 706 of Title 5, and for purposes of such review the accrediting entity shall be considered an agency within the meaning of section 701 of such title.

(d) **Fees**

The amount of fees assessed by accrediting entities for the costs of accreditation shall be subject to approval by the Secretary. Such fees may not exceed the costs of accreditation. In reviewing the level of such fees, the Secretary shall consider the relative size of, the geographic location of, and the number of Convention adoption cases managed by the agencies or persons subject to accreditation or approval by the accrediting entity. *(Pub.L. 106–279, Title II, § 202, Oct. 6, 2000, 114 Stat. 831; Pub.L. 112–276, § 3(b), Jan. 14, 2013, 126 Stat. 2467.)*

§ 14923. Standards and procedures for providing accreditation or approval

(a) **In general**

(1) **Promulgation of regulations**

The Secretary, shall, by regulation, prescribe the standards and procedures to be used by accrediting entities for the accreditation of agencies and the approval of persons to provide adoption services in the United States in cases subject to the Convention.

(2) **Consideration of views**

In developing such regulations, the Secretary shall consider any standards or procedures developed or proposed by, and the views of, individuals and entities with interest and expertise in international adoptions and family social services, including public and private entities with experience in licensing and accrediting adoption agencies.

(3) **Applicability of notice and comment rules**

Subsections (b), (c), and (d) of section 553 of Title 5 shall apply in the development and issuance of regulations under this section.

(b) **Minimum requirements**

(1) **Accreditation**

The standards prescribed under subsection (a) of this section shall include the requirement that accreditation of an agency may not be provided or continued under this subchapter unless the agency meets the following requirements:

(A) **Specific requirements**

(i) The agency provides prospective adoptive parents of a child in a prospective Convention adoption a copy of the medical records of the child (which, to the fullest extent practicable, shall include an English-language translation of such records) on a date which is not later than the earlier of the date that is 2 weeks before: (I) the adoption; or (II) the date on which the prospective parents travel to a foreign country to complete all procedures in such country relating to the adoption.

(ii) The agency ensures that a thorough background report (home study) on the prospective adoptive parent or parents has been completed in accordance with the Convention and with applicable Federal and State requirements and transmitted to the Attorney General with respect to each Convention adoption. Each such report shall include a criminal background check and a full and complete statement of all facts relevant to the eligibility of the prospective adopting parent or parents to adopt a child under any requirements specified by the central authority of the child's country of origin under section 14912(b)(3) of this title, including, in the case of a child emigrating to the United States for the purpose of adoption, the requirements of the child's country of origin applicable to adoptions taking place in such country. For purposes of this clause, the term "background report (home study)" includes any supplemental statement submitted by the agency to the Attorney General for the purpose of providing information relevant to any requirements specified by the child's country of origin.

(iii) The agency provides prospective adoptive parents with a training program that includes counseling and guidance for the purpose of promoting a successful intercountry adoption before such parents travel to adopt the child or the child is placed with such parents for adoption.

(iv) The agency employs personnel providing intercountry adoption services on a fee for service basis rather than on a contingent fee basis.

(v) The agency discloses fully its policies and practices, the disruption rates of its placements for intercountry adoption, and all fees charged by such agency for intercountry adoption.

(B) Capacity to provide adoption services

The agency has, directly or through arrangements with other persons, a sufficient number of appropriately trained and qualified personnel, sufficient financial resources, appropriate organizational structure, and appropriate procedures to enable the agency to provide, in accordance with this chapter, all adoption services in cases subject to the Convention.

(C) Use of social service professionals

The agency has established procedures designed to ensure that social service functions requiring the application of clinical skills and judgment are performed only by professionals with appropriate qualifications and credentials.

(D) Records, reports, and information matters

The agency is capable of—

(i) maintaining such records and making such reports as may be required by the Secretary, the United States central authority, and the accrediting entity that accredits the agency;

(ii) cooperating with reviews, inspections, and audits;

(iii) safeguarding sensitive individual information; and

(iv) complying with other requirements concerning information management necessary to ensure compliance with the Convention, this chapter, and any other applicable law.

(E) Liability insurance

The agency agrees to have in force adequate liability insurance for professional negligence and any other insurance that the Secretary considers appropriate.

(F) Compliance with applicable rules

The agency has established adequate measures to comply (and to ensure compliance of their agents and clients) with the Convention, this chapter, and any other applicable law.

(G) Nonprofit organization with State license to provide adoption services

The agency is a private nonprofit organization licensed to provide adoption services in at least one State.

(2) Approval

The standards prescribed under subsection (a) of this section shall include the requirement that a person shall not be approved under this subchapter unless the person is a private for-profit entity that meets the requirements of subparagraphs (A) through (F) of paragraph (1) of this subsection.

(3) Renewal of accreditation or approval

The standards prescribed under subsection (a) of this section shall provide that the accreditation of an agency or approval of a person under this subchapter shall be for a period of not less than 3 years and not more than 5 years, and may be renewed on a showing that the agency or person meets the requirements applicable to original accreditation or approval under this subchapter.

(c) Temporary registration of community based agencies

(1) One-year registration period for medium community based agencies

For a 1–year period after the entry into force of the Convention and notwithstanding subsection (b) of this section, the Secretary may provide, in regulations issued pursuant to subsection (a) of this section, that an agency may register with the Secretary and be accredited to provide adoption services in the United States in cases subject to the Convention during such period if the agency has provided adoption services in fewer than 100 intercountry adoptions in the preceding calendar year and meets the criteria described in paragraph (3).

(2) Two-year registration period for small community-based agencies

For a 2–year period after the entry into force of the Convention and notwithstanding subsection (b) of this section, the Secretary may provide, in regulations issued pursuant to subsection (a) of this section, that an agency may register with the Secretary and be accredited to provide adoption services in the United States in cases subject to the Convention during such period if the agency has provided adoption services in fewer than 50 intercountry adoptions in the preceding calendar year and meets the criteria described in paragraph (3).

(3) Criteria for registration

Agencies registered under this subsection shall meet the following criteria:

(A) The agency is licensed in the State in which it is located and is a nonprofit agency.

(B) The agency has been providing adoption services in connection with intercountry adoptions for at least 3 years.

(C) The agency has demonstrated that it will be able to provide the United States Government with all information related to the elements described in section 14914(b) of this title and provides such information.

(D) The agency has initiated the process of becoming accredited under the provisions of this chapter and is actively taking steps to become an accredited agency.

(E) The agency has not been found to be involved in any improper conduct relating to intercountry adoptions.

(Pub.L. 106–279, Title II, § 203, Oct. 6, 2000, 114 Stat. 832.)

§ 14924. Secretarial oversight of accreditation and approval

(a) Oversight of accrediting entities

The Secretary shall—

(1) monitor the performance by each accrediting entity of its duties under section 14922 of this title and its compliance with the requirements of the Convention, this chapter, other applicable laws, and implementing regulations under this chapter; and

(2) suspend or cancel the designation of an accrediting entity found to be substantially out of compliance with the Convention, this chapter, other applicable laws, or implementing regulations under this chapter.

(b) Suspension or cancellation of accreditation or approval

(1) Secretary's authority

The Secretary shall suspend or cancel the accreditation or approval granted by an accrediting entity to an agency or person pursuant to section 14922 of this title when the Secretary finds that—

(A) the agency or person is substantially out of compliance with applicable requirements; and

(B) the accrediting entity has failed or refused, after consultation with the Secretary, to take appropriate enforcement action.

(2) Correction of deficiency

At any time when the Secretary is satisfied that the deficiencies on the basis of which an adverse action is taken under paragraph (1) have been corrected, the Secretary shall—

(A) notify the accrediting entity that the deficiencies have been corrected; and

(B)(i) in the case of a suspension, terminate the suspension; or

(ii) in the case of a cancellation, notify the agency or person that the agency or person may reapply to the accrediting entity for accreditation or approval.

(c) Debarment

(1) Secretary's authority

On the initiative of the Secretary, or on request of an accrediting entity, the Secretary may temporarily or permanently debar an agency from accreditation or a person from approval under this subchapter, but only if—

(A) there is substantial evidence that the agency or person is out of compliance with applicable requirements; and

(B) there has been a pattern of serious, willful, or grossly negligent failures to comply or other aggravating circumstances indicating that continued accreditation or approval would not be in the best interests of the children and families concerned.

(2) Period of debarment

The Secretary's debarment order shall state whether the debarment is temporary or permanent. If the debarment is temporary, the Secretary shall specify a date, not earlier than 3 years after the date of the order, on or after which the agency or person may apply to the Secretary for withdrawal of the debarment.

(3) Effect of debarment

An accrediting entity may take into account the circumstances of the debarment of an agency or person that has been debarred pursuant to this subsection in considering any subsequent application of the agency or person, or of any other entity in which the agency or person has an ownership or control interest, for accreditation or approval under this subchapter.

(d) Judicial review

A person (other than a prospective adoptive parent), an agency, or an accrediting entity who is the subject of a final action of suspension, cancellation, or debarment by the Secretary under this subchapter may petition the United States District Court for the District of Columbia or the United States district court in the judicial district in which the person resides or the agency or accrediting entity is located to set aside the action. The court shall review the action in accordance with section 706 of Title 5.

(e) Failure to ensure a full and complete home study

(1) In general

Willful, grossly negligent, or repeated failure to ensure the completion and transmission of a background report (home study) that fully complies with the requirements of section 14923(b)(1)(A)(ii) of this title shall constitute substantial noncompliance with applicable requirements.

(2) Regulations

Regulations promulgated under section 14923 of this title shall provide for—

(A) frequent and careful monitoring of compliance by agencies and approved persons with the requirements of section 14923(b)(A)(ii)[1] of this title; and

(B) consultation between the Secretary and the accrediting entity where an agency or person has engaged in substantial noncompliance with the requirements of section 14923(b)(A)(ii)[1] of this title, unless the accrediting entity has taken appropriate corrective action and the noncompliance has not recurred.

(3) Repeated failures to comply

Repeated serious, willful, or grossly negligent failures to comply with the requirements of section 14923(b)(1)(A)(ii) of this title by an agency or person after consultation between Secretary and the accrediting entity with respect to previous noncompliance by such agency or person shall constitute a pattern of serious, willful, or grossly negligent failures to comply under subsection (c)(1)(B) of this section.

(4) Failure to comply with certain requirements

A failure to comply with the requirements of section 14923(b)(1)(A)(ii) of this title shall constitute a serious failure to comply under subsection (c)(1)(B) of this section unless it is shown by clear and convincing evidence that such noncompliance had neither the purpose nor the effect of determining the outcome of a decision or proceeding by a court or other competent authority in the United States or the child's country of origin.

(Pub.L. 106–279, Title II, § 204, Oct. 6, 2000, 114 Stat. 835.)

[1] So in original. Probably should be section "14923(b)(1)(A)(ii)".

§ 14925. Universal accreditation requirements

(a) In general

The provisions of Title II and section 404 of the Intercountry Adoption Act of 2000 (42 U.S.C. 14901 et seq.[, 42 U.S.C. 14944]), and related implementing regulations, shall apply to any person offering or providing adoption services in connection with a child described in section 1101(b)(1)(F) of Title 8, to the same extent as they apply to the offering or provision of adoption services in connection with a Convention adoption. The Secretary of State, the Secretary of Homeland Security, the Attorney General (with respect to section 404(b) of the Intercountry Adoption Act of 2000 (42 U.S.C. 14944[(b)])), and the accrediting entities shall have the duties, responsibilities, and authorities under title II and title IV of the Intercountry Adoption Act of 2000 [42 U.S.C. 14921 et seq., 14941 et seq.] and related implementing regulations with respect to a person offering or providing such adoption services, irrespective of whether such services are offered or provided in connection with a Convention adoption.

(b) Effective date

The provisions of this section shall take effect 18 months after January 14, 2013.

(c) Transition rule

This Act shall not apply to a person offering or providing adoption services as described in subsection (a) in the case of a prospective adoption in which—

(1) an application for advance processing of an orphan petition or petition to classify an orphan as an immediate relative for a child is filed before the date that is 180 days after January 14, 2013; or

(2) the prospective adoptive parents of a child have initiated the adoption process with the filing of an appropriate application in a foreign country sufficient such that the Secretary of State is satisfied before the date that is 180 days after January 14, 2013.

(Pub.L. 112–276, § 2, Jan. 14, 2013, 126 Stat. 2466.)

SUBCHAPTER III—RECOGNITION OF CONVENTION ADOPTIONS IN THE UNITED STATES

§ 14931. Adoptions of children immigrating to the United States

(a) Legal effect of certificates issued by the Secretary of State

(1) Issuance of certificates by the Secretary of State

The Secretary of State shall, with respect to each Convention adoption, issue a certificate to the adoptive citizen parent domiciled in the United States that the adoption has been granted or, in the case of a prospective adoptive citizen parent, that legal custody of the child has been granted to the citizen parent for purposes of emigration and adoption, pursuant to the Convention and this chapter, if the Secretary of State—

(A) receives appropriate notification from the central authority of such child's country of origin; and

(B) has verified that the requirements of the Convention and this chapter have been met with respect to the adoption.

(2) Legal effect of certificates

If appended to an original adoption decree, the certificate described in paragraph (1) shall be treated by Federal and State agencies, courts, and other public and private persons and entities as conclusive evidence of the facts certified therein and shall constitute the certification required by section 1154(d)(2) of Title 8.

(b) Legal effect of Convention adoption finalized in another Convention country

A final adoption in another Convention country, certified by the Secretary of State pursuant to subsection (a) of this section or section 14932(c) of this title, shall be recognized as a final valid adoption for purposes of all Federal, State, and local laws of the United States.

(c) Condition on finalization of Convention adoption by State court

In the case of a child who has entered the United States from another Convention country for the purpose of adoption, an order declaring the adoption final shall not be entered unless the Secretary of State has issued the certificate provided for in subsection (a) of this section with respect to the adoption. *(Pub.L. 106–279, Title III, § 301, Oct. 6, 2000, 114 Stat. 837.)*

§ 14932. Adoptions of children emigrating from the United States

(a) Duties of accredited agency or approved person

In the case of a Convention adoption involving the emigration of a child residing in the United States to a foreign country, the accredited agency or approved person providing adoption services, or the prospective adoptive parent or parents acting on their own behalf (if permitted by the laws of such other Convention country in which they reside and the laws of the State in which the child resides), shall do the following:

(1) Ensure that, in accordance with the Convention—

(A) a background study on the child is completed;

(B) the accredited agency or approved person—

(i) has made reasonable efforts to actively recruit and make a diligent search for prospective adoptive parents to adopt the child in the United States; and

(ii) despite such efforts, has not been able to place the child for adoption in the United States in a timely manner; and

(C) a determination is made that placement with the prospective adoptive parent or parents is in the best interests of the child.

(2) Furnish to the State court with jurisdiction over the case—

(A) documentation of the matters described in paragraph (1);

(B) a background report (home study) on the prospective adoptive parent or parents (including a criminal background check) prepared in accordance with the laws of the receiving country; and

(C) a declaration by the central authority (or other competent authority) of such other Convention country—

(i) that the child will be permitted to enter and reside permanently, or on the same basis as the adopting parent, in the receiving country; and

(ii) that the central authority (or other competent authority) of such other Convention country consents to the adoption, if such consent is necessary under the laws of such country for the adoption to become final.

(3) Furnish to the United States central authority—

(A) official copies of State court orders certifying the final adoption or grant of custody for the purpose of adoption;

(B) the information and documents described in paragraph (2), to the extent required by the United States central authority; and

(C) any other information concerning the case required by the United States central authority to perform the functions specified in subsection (c) of this section or otherwise to carry out the duties of the United States central authority under the Convention.

(b) Conditions on State court orders

An order declaring an adoption to be final or granting custody for the purpose of adoption in a case described in subsection (a) of this section shall not be entered unless the court—

(1) has received and verified to the extent the court may find necessary—

(A) the material described in subsection (a)(2) of this section; and

(B) satisfactory evidence that the requirements of Articles 4 and 15 through 21 of the Convention have been met; and

(2) has determined that the adoptive placement is in the best interests of the child.

(c) Duties of the Secretary of State

In a case described in subsection (a) of this section, the Secretary, on receipt and verification as necessary of the material and information described in subsection (a)(3) of this section, shall issue, as applicable, an official certification that the child has been adopted or a declaration that custody for purposes of adoption has been granted, in accordance with the Convention and this chapter.

(d) Filing with registry regarding non-Convention adoptions

Accredited agencies, approved persons, and other persons, including governmental authorities, providing adoption services in an intercountry adoption not subject to the Convention that involves the emigration of a child from the United States shall file information required by regulations jointly issued by the Attorney General and the Secretary of State for purposes of implementing section 14912(e) of this title. *(Pub.L. 106–279, Title III, § 303, Oct. 6, 2000, 114 Stat. 839.)*

SUBCHAPTER IV—ADMINISTRATION AND ENFORCEMENT

§ 14941. Access to Convention records

(a) Preservation of Convention records

(1) In general

Not later than 180 days after October 6, 2000, the Secretary, in consultation with the Attorney General, shall issue regulations that establish procedures and requirements in accordance with the Convention and this section for the preservation of Convention records.

(2) Applicability of notice and comment rules

Subsections (b), (c), and (d) of section 553 of Title 5 shall apply in the development and issuance of regulations under this section.

(b) Access to Convention records

(1) Prohibition

Except as provided in paragraph (2), the Secretary or the Attorney General may disclose a Convention record, and access to such a record may be provided in whole or in part, only if such record is maintained under the authority of the Immigration and Nationality Act [8 U.S.C. 1101 et seq.] and disclosure of, or access to, such record is permitted or required by applicable Federal law.

(2) Exception for administration of the Convention

A Convention record may be disclosed, and access to such a record may be provided, in whole or in part, among the Secretary, the Attorney General, central authorities, accredited agencies, and approved persons, only to the extent necessary to administer the Convention or this chapter.

(3) Penalties for unlawful disclosure

Unlawful disclosure of all or part of a Convention record shall be punishable in accordance with applicable Federal law.

(c) Access to non-Convention records

Disclosure of, access to, and penalties for unlawful disclosure of, adoption records that are not Convention records, including records of adoption proceedings conducted in the United States, shall be governed by applicable State law. *(Pub.L. 106–279, Title IV, § 401, Oct. 6, 2000, 114 Stat. 841.)*

§ 14942. Documents of other Convention countries

Documents originating in any other Convention country and related to a Convention adoption case shall require no authentication in order to be admissible in any Federal, State, or local court in the United States, unless a specific and supported claim is made that the documents are false, have been altered, or are otherwise unreliable. *(Pub.L. 106–279, Title IV, § 402, Oct. 6, 2000, 114 Stat. 841.)*

§ 14943. Authorization of appropriations; collection of fees

(a) Authorization of appropriations

(1) In general

There are authorized to be appropriated such sums as may be necessary to agencies of the Federal Government implementing the Convention and the provisions of this chapter.

(2) Availability of funds

Amounts appropriated pursuant to paragraph (1) are authorized to remain available until expended.

(b) Assessment of fees

(1) The Secretary may charge a fee for new or enhanced services that will be undertaken by the Department of State to meet the requirements of this chapter with respect to intercountry adoptions under the Convention and comparable services with respect to other intercountry adoptions. Such fee shall be prescribed by regulation and shall not exceed the cost of such services.

(2) Fees collected under paragraph (1) shall be retained and deposited as an offsetting collection to any Department of State appropriation to recover the costs of providing such services. Such fees shall remain available for obligation until expended.

(c) Repealed. Pub.L. 112–276, § 3(a), Jan. 14, 2013, 126 Stat. 2467

(Pub.L. 106–279, Title IV, § 403, Oct. 6, 2000, 114 Stat. 841; Pub.L. 107–228, Div. A, Title II, § 211(a), Sept. 30, 2002, 116 Stat. 1365; Pub.L. 112–276, § 3(a), Jan. 14, 2013, 126 Stat. 2467.)

§ 14944. Enforcement

(a) Civil penalties

Any person who—

(1) violates section 14921 of this title;

(2) makes a false or fraudulent statement, or misrepresentation, with respect to a material fact, or offers,

gives, solicits, or accepts inducement by way of compensation, intended to influence or affect in the United States or a foreign country—

(A) a decision by an accrediting entity with respect to the accreditation of an agency or approval of a person under subchapter II of this chapter;

(B) the relinquishment of parental rights or the giving of parental consent relating to the adoption of a child in a case subject to the Convention; or

(C) a decision or action of any entity performing a central authority function; or

(3) engages another person as an agent, whether in the United States or in a foreign country, who in the course of that agency takes any of the actions described in paragraph (1) or (2),

shall be subject, in addition to any other penalty that may be prescribed by law, to a civil money penalty of not more than $50,000 for a first violation, and not more than $100,000 for each succeeding violation.

(b) Civil enforcement

(1) Authority of Attorney General

The Attorney General may bring a civil action to enforce subsection (a) of this section against any person in any United States district court.

(2) Factors to be considered in imposing penalties

In imposing penalties the court shall consider the gravity of the violation, the degree of culpability of the defendant, and any history of prior violations by the defendant.

(c) Criminal penalties

Whoever knowingly and willfully violates paragraph (1) or (2) of subsection (a) of this section shall be subject to a fine of not more than $250,000, imprisonment for not more than 5 years, or both. *(Pub.L. 106–279, Title IV, § 404, Oct. 6, 2000, 114 Stat. 842.)*

SUBCHAPTER V—GENERAL PROVISIONS

§ 14951. Recognition of Convention adoptions

Subject to Article 24 of the Convention, adoptions concluded between two other Convention countries that meet the requirements of Article 23 of the Convention and that became final before the date of entry into force of the Convention for the United States shall be recognized thereafter in the United States and given full effect. Such recognition shall include the specific effects described in Article 26 of the Convention. *(Pub.L. 106–279, Title V, § 501, Oct. 6, 2000, 114 Stat. 843.)*

§ 14952. Special rules for certain cases

(a) Authority to establish alternative procedures for adoption of children by relatives

To the extent consistent with the Convention, the Secretary may establish by regulation alternative procedures for the adoption of children by individuals related to them by blood, marriage, or adoption, in cases subject to the Convention.

(b) Waiver authority

(1) In general

Notwithstanding any other provision of this chapter, to the extent consistent with the Convention, the Secretary may, on a case-by-case basis, waive applicable requirements of this chapter or regulations issued under this chapter, in the interests of justice or to prevent grave physical harm to the child.

(2) Nondelegation

The authority provided by paragraph (1) may not be delegated.

(Pub.L. 106–279, Title V, § 502, Oct. 6, 2000, 114 Stat. 843.)

§ 14953. Relationship to other laws

(a) Preemption of inconsistent State law

The Convention and this chapter shall not be construed to preempt any provision of the law of any State or political subdivision thereof, or prevent a State or political subdivision thereof from enacting any provision of law with respect to the subject matter of the Convention or this chapter, except to the extent that such provision of State law is inconsistent with the Convention or this chapter, and then only to the extent of the inconsistency.

(b) Applicability of the Indian Child Welfare Act

The Convention and this chapter shall not be construed to affect the application of the Indian Child Welfare Act of 1978 (25 U.S.C. 1901 et seq.).

(c) Relationship to other laws

Sections 3506(c), 3507, and 3512 of Title 44 shall not apply to information collection for purposes of sections 14914, 14922(b)(4), and 14932(d) of this title or for use as a Convention record as defined in this chapter. *(Pub.L. 106–279, Title V, § 503, Oct. 6, 2000, 114 Stat. 843.)*

§ 14954. No private right of action

The Convention and this chapter shall not be construed to create a private right of action to seek administrative or judicial relief, except to the extent expressly provided in this chapter. *(Pub.L. 106–279, Title V, § 504, Oct. 6, 2000, 114 Stat. 843.)*

TITLE 45

RAILROADS

CHAPTER 9—RETIREMENT OF RAILROAD EMPLOYEES

SUBCHAPTER IV—RAILROAD RETIREMENT ACT OF 1974

§ 231m. Assignability; exemption from levy

(a) Except as provided in subsection (b) of this section and the Internal Revenue Code of 1986 [26 U.S.C.A. § 1 et seq.], notwithstanding any other law of the United States, or of any State, territory, or the District of Columbia, no annuity or supplemental annuity shall be assignable or be subject to any tax or to garnishment, attachment, or other legal process under any circumstances whatsoever, nor shall the payment thereof be anticipated [1]

(b)(1) This section shall not operate to exclude the amount of any supplemental annuity paid to an individual under section 231a(b) of this title from income taxable pursuant to the Federal income tax provisions of the Internal Revenue Code of 1986 [26 U.S.C.A. § 1 et seq.].

(2) This section shall not operate to prohibit the characterization or treatment of that portion of an annuity under this subchapter which is not computed under section 231b(a), 231c(a), or 231c(f) of this title, or any portion of a supplemental annuity under this subchapter, as community property for the purposes of, or property subject to, distribution in accordance with a court decree of divorce, annulment, or legal separation or the terms of any court-approved property settlement incident to any such court decree. The Board shall make payments of such portions in accordance with any such characterization or treatment or any such decree or settlement.

(3)(A) Payments made pursuant to paragraph (2) of this subsection shall not require that the employee be entitled to an annuity under section 231a(a)(1) of this title: Provided, however, That where an employee is not entitled to such an annuity, payments made pursuant to paragraph (2) may not begin before the month in which the following three conditions are satisfied:

(i) The employee has completed ten years of service in the railroad industry or, five years of service all of which accrues after December 31, 1995.

(ii) The spouse or former spouse attains age 62.

(iii) The employee attains age 62 (or if deceased, would have attained age 62).

(B) Payments made pursuant to paragraph (2) of this subsection shall terminate upon the death of the spouse or former spouse, unless the court document provides for termination at an earlier date. Notwithstanding the language in a court order, that portion of payments made pursuant to paragraph (2) which represents payments computed pursuant to section 231b(f)(2) of this title shall not be paid after the death of the employee.

(C) If the employee is not entitled to an annuity under section 231a(a)(1) of this title, payments made pursuant to paragraph (2) of this subsection shall be computed as though the employee were entitled to an annuity. *(Aug. 29, 1935, c. 812, § 14, as restated June 24, 1937, c. 382, pt. I, 50 Stat. 307, as restated Oct. 16, 1974, Pub.L. 93–445, Title I, § 101, 88 Stat. 1345; amended Aug. 12, 1983, Pub.L. 98–76, Title IV, § 419(a), 97 Stat. 438; Oct. 22, 1986, Pub.L. 99–514, § 2, 100 Stat. 2095; Dec. 23, 2008, Pub.L. 110–458, Title I, § 110(a)(1), 122 Stat. 5112.)*

[1] So in original. Probably should be followed by a period.

CONVENTION ON THE CIVIL ASPECTS OF INTERNATIONAL CHILD ABDUCTION

[Hague Convention]

The States signatory to the present Convention,

Firmly convinced that the interests of children are of paramount importance in matters relating to their custody.

Desiring to protect children internationally from the harmful effects of their wrongful removal or retention and to establish procedures to ensure their prompt return to the State of their habitual residence, as well as to secure protection for rights of access.

Have resolved to conclude a Convention to this effect, and have agreed upon the following provisions—

Chapter I SCOPE OF THE CONVENTION

Article I

The objects of the present Convention are—

(a) to secure the prompt return of children wrongfully removed to or retained in any Contracting State; and

(b) to ensure that rights of custody and of access under the law of one Contracting State are effectively respected in the Other Contracting States.

Article 2

Contracting States shall take all appropriate measures to secure within their territories the implementation of the objects of the Convention. For this purpose they shall use the most expeditious procedures available.

Article 3

The removal or the retention of a child is to be considered wrongful where—

(a) it is in breach of rights of custody attributed to a person, an institution, or any other body, either jointly or alone, under the law of the State in which the child was habitually resident immediately before the removal or retention; and

(b) at the time of removal or retention those rights were actually exercised, either jointly or alone, or would have been so exercised but for the removal or retention.

The rights of custody mentioned in subparagraph (a) above, may arise in particular by operation of law or by reason of a judicial or administrative decision, or by reason of an agreement having legal effect under the law of that State.

Article 4

The convention shall apply to any child who was habitually resident in a Contracting State immediately before any breach of custody or access rights. The Convention shall cease to apply when the child attains the age of 16 years.

Article 5

For the purposes of this Convention—

(a) "rights of custody" shall include rights relating to the care of the person of the child, and, in particular, the right to determine the child's place of residence;

(b) "rights of access" shall include the right to take a child for a limited period time to a place other than the child's habitual residence.

Chapter II CENTRAL AUTHORITIES

Article 6

A Contracting State shall designate a Central Authority to discharge the duties which are imposed by the Convention upon such authorities.

Federal States, States with more than one system of law or States having autonomous territorial organizations shall be free to appoint more than one Central Authority and to specify the territorial extent of their powers. When a State has appointed more than one Central Authority, it shall designate the Central Authority to which applications may be addressed for transmission to the appropriate Central Authority within that State.

Article 7

Central Authorities shall cooperate with each other and promote cooperation amongst the competent authorities in their respective States to secure the prompt return of children and to achieve the other objects of this Convention.

In particular, either directly or through any intermediary, they shall take all appropriate measures—

(a) to discover the whereabouts of a child who has been wrongfully removed or retained;

(b) to prevent further harm to the child or prejudice to interested parties by taking or causing to be taken provisional measures;

(c) to secure the voluntary return of the child or to bring about an amicable resolution of the issues;

(d) to exchange, where desirable, information relating to the social background of the child;

(e) to provide information of a general character as to the law of their State in connection with the a application of the Convention;

(f) to initiate or facilitate the institution of judicial or administrative proceedings with a view to obtaining the return of the child and, in a proper case, to make arrangements for organizing or securing the effective exercise of rights of access;

(g) where the circumstances so require, to provide or facilitate the provision of legal counsel and advisers;

(h) to provide such administrative arrangements as may be necessary and appropriate to secure the safe return of the child;

(i) to keep each other informed with respect to the operation of this Convention and, as far as possible, to eliminate any obstacles to its application.

Chapter III RETURN OF CHILDREN

Article 8

Any person, institution or other body claiming that a child has been removed or retained in breach of custody rights may apply to the Central Authority of the child's habitual residence or to the Central Authority of any other Contracting State for assistance in securing the return of the child.

The application shall contain—

(a) information concerning the identity of the applicant, of the child and of the person alleged to have removed or retained the child;

(b) where available, the date of birth of the child;

(c) the grounds on which the applicant's claim for return of the child is based;

(d) all available information relating to the whereabouts of the child and the identity of the person with whom the child is presumed to be.

The application may be accompanied or supplemented by—

(e) an authenticated copy of any relevant decision or agreement;

(f) a certificate or an affidavit emanating from a Central Authority, or other competent authority of the State of the child's habitual residence, or from a qualified person, concerning the relevant law of that State;

(g) any other relevant document.

Article 9

If the Central Authority which receives an application referred to in Article 8 has reason to believe that the child is in another contracting State, it shall directly and without delay transmit the application to the Central Authority of that Contracting State and inform the requesting Central Authority, or the applicant, as the case may be.

Article 10

The Central Authority of the State where the child is shall take or cause to be taken all appropriate measures in order to obtain the voluntary return of the child.

Article 11

The judicial or administrative authorities of Contracting States shall act expeditiously in proceedings for the return of children.

If the judicial or administrative authority concerned has not reached a decision within six weeks from the date of commencement of the proceedings, the applicant or the Central Authority of the requested State, on its own initiative or if asked by the Central Authority of the requesting State, shall have the right to request a statement of the reasons for the delay. If a reply is received by the Central Authority of the requested State, that Authority shall transmit the reply to the Central Authority of the requesting State, or to the applicant, as the case may be.

Article 12

Where a child has been wrongfully removed or retained in terms of Article 3 and, at the date of the commencement of the proceedings before the judicial or administrative authority of the Contracting State where the child is, a period of less than one year has elapsed from the date of the wrongful removal or retention, the authority concerned shall order the return of the child forthwith.

The judicial or administrative authority, even where the proceedings have been commenced after the expiration of the period of one year referred to in the preceding paragraph, shall also order the return of the child, unless it is demonstrated that the child is now settled in its new environment.

Where the judicial or administrative authority in the requested State has reason to believe that the child has been taken to another State, it may stay the proceedings or dismiss the application for the return of the child.

Article 13

Notwithstanding the provisions of the preceding Article, the judicial or administrative authority of the requested State is not bound to order the return of the child if the person, institution or other body which opposes its return establishes that—

(a) the person, institution or other body having the care of the person of the child was not actually exercising custody rights at the time of removal or retention, or had consented to or subsequently acquiesced in the removal or retention; or

(b) there is a grave risk that his or her return would expose the child to physical or psychological harm or otherwise place the child in an intolerable situation.

The judicial or administrative authority may also refuse to order the return of the child if it finds that the child objects to being returned and has attained an age and degree of maturity at which it is appropriate to take account of its views.

In considering the circumstances referred to in this Article, the judicial or administrative authorities shall take into account the information relating to the social background of the child provided by the Central Authority or other competent authority of the child's habitual residence.

Article 14

In ascertaining whether there has been a wrongful removal or retention within the meaning of Article 3, the judicial or administrative authorities of the requested State may take notice directly of the law of, and of the judicial or administrative decisions, formally recognized or not in the State of the habitual residence of the child, without recourse to the specific procedures for the proof of that law or for the recognition of foreign decisions which would otherwise be applicable.

Article 15

The judicial or administrative authorities of a Contracting State may, prior to the making of an order for the return of the child, request that the applicant obtain from the authorities of the State of habitual residence of the child a decision or other determination that the removal or retention was wrongful within the meaning of Article 3 of the Convention, where such a decision or determination may be obtained in that State. The Central Authorities of the Contracting States shall so far as practicable assist applicants to obtain such a decision or determination.

Article 16

After receiving notice of a wrongful removal or retention of a child in the sense of Article 3, the judicial or administrative authorities of the Contracting State to which the child has been removed or in which it has been retained shall not decide on the merits of rights of custody until it has been determined that the child is not to be returned under this Convention or unless an application under this Convention is not lodged within a reasonable time following receipt of the notice.

Article 17

The sole fact that a decision relating to custody has been given in or is entitled to recognition in the requested State shall not be a ground for refusing to return a child under this Convention, but the judicial or administrative authorities of the requested State may take account of the reasons for that decision in applying this Convention.

Article 18

The provisions of this Chapter do not limit the power of a the judicial or administrative authority to order the return of the child at any time.

Article 19

A decision under this Convention concerning the return of the child shall not be taken to be a determination on the merits of any custody issue.

Article 20

The return of the child under the provisions of Article 12 may be refused if this would not be permitted by the fundamental principles of the requested State relating to the protection of human rights and fundamental freedoms.

Chapter IV RIGHTS OF ACCESS

Article 21

An application to make arrangements for organizing or securing the effective exercise of rights of access may be presented to the Central Authorities of the Contracting States in the same way as an application for the return of a child.

The Central Authorities are bound by the obligations of cooperation which are set forth in Article 7 to promote the peaceful enjoyment of access rights and the fulfillment of any conditions to which the exercise of those rights may be subject. The Central Authorities shall take steps to remove, as far as possible, all obstacles to the exercise of such rights. The Central Authorities either directly or through intermediaries, may initiate or assist in the institution of proceedings with a view to organizing or protecting these rights and securing respect for the conditions to which the exercise of these rights may be subject.

Chapter V GENERAL PROVISIONS

Article 22

No security, bond or deposit, however, described, shall be required to guarantee the payment of costs and expenses in the judicial or administrative proceedings falling with the scope of this Convention.

Article 23

No legalization or similar formality may be required in the context of this Convention.

Article 24

Any application, communication or other document sent to the Central Authority of the requested State shall be in the original language, and shall be accompanied by a translation into the official language or one of the official languages of the requested State or, where that is not feasible, a translation into French or English.

However, a Contracting State may by making a reservation in accordance with Article 42, object to the use of either French or English, but not both, in any application, communication or other document sent to its Central Authority.

Article 25

Nationals of the Contracting States and persons who are habitually resident within those States shall be entitled in matters concerned with the application of this Convention to legal aid and advice in any other Contracting State on the same conditions as if they themselves were nationals of and habitually resident in that State.

Article 26

Each Central Authority shall bear its own costs in applying this Convention.

Central Authorities and other public services of Contracting States shall not impose any charges in relation to applications submitted under this Convention. In particular, they may not require any payment from the applicant towards the costs and expenses of the proceedings or, where applicable, those arising from the participation of legal counsel or advisers. However, they may require the payment of the expenses incurred or to be incurred in implementing the return of the child.

However, a Contracting State may, by making a reservation in accordance with Article 42, declare that it shall not be bound to assume any costs referred to in the preceding paragraph resulting from the participation of legal counsel or advisers or from court proceedings, except insofar as those costs may be covered by its system of legal aid and advice.

Upon ordering the return of a child or issuing an order concerning rights of access under this Convention, the judicial or administrative authorities may, where appropriate, direct the person who removed or retained the child, or who prevented the exercise of rights of access, to pay necessary expenses incurred by or on behalf of the applicant, including travel expenses, any costs incurred or payments made for locating the child, the costs of legal representation of the applicant, and those of returning the child.

Article 27

When it is manifest that the requirements of this Convention are not fulfilled or that the application is otherwise not well founded, a Central Authority is not bound to accept the application. In that case, the Central Authority shall forthwith inform the applicant or the Central Authority through which the application was submitted, as the case may be, of its reasons.

Article 28

A Central Authority may require that the application be accompanied by a written authorization empowering it to act on behalf of the applicant, or to designate a representative so to act.

Article 29

This Convention shall not preclude any person, institution or body who claims that there has been a breach of custody or access rights within the meaning of Article 3 or 21 from applying directly to the judicial or administrative authorities of a Contracting State, whether or not under the provisions of this Convention.

Article 30

Any application submitted to the Central Authorities or directly to the judicial or administrative authorities of a Contracting State in accordance with the terms of this Convention, together with documents and any other information appended thereto or provided by a Central Authority, shall be admissible in the courts or administrative authorities of the Contracting State.

Article 31

In relation to a State which in matters of custody of children has two or more systems of law applicable in different territorial units—

(a) any reference to habitual residence in that State shall be construed as referring to habitual residence in a territorial unity of that State;

(b) any reference to the law of the State of habitual residence shall be construed as referring to the law of the territorial unit in that State where the child habitually resides.

Article 32

In relation to a State which in matters of custody of children has two or more systems of law applicable to different categories of persons, any reference to the law of that State shall be construed as referring to the legal system specified by the law of that State.

Article 33

A state within which different territorial units have their own rules of law in respect of custody of children shall not be bound to apply this Convention where a State with a unified system of law would not be bound to do so.

Article 34

This Convention shall take priority in matters within its scope over the Convention of October 5, 1961 concerning the powers of authorities and the law applicable in respect of the protection of minors, as between Parties to both Conventions. Otherwise the present Convention shall not restrict the application of an international instrument in force between the State of origin and the State addressed or other law of the State addressed for the purposes of obtaining the return of a child who has been wrongfully removed or retained or of organizing access rights.

Article 35

This Convention shall apply as between Contracting States only to wrongful removals or retentions occurring after its entry into force in those States.

Where a declaration has been made under Article 39 or 40, the reference in the preceding paragraph to a Contracting State shall be taken to refer to the territorial unit or units in relation to which this Convention applies.

Article 36

Nothing in this Convention shall prevent two or more Contracting States, in order to limit the restrictions to which the return of the child may be subject, from agreeing among themselves to derogate from any provisions of this Convention which may imply such a restriction.

Chapter VI FINAL CLAUSES

Article 37

The Convention shall be open for signature by the States which were Members of the Hague Conference on Private International Law at the time of its Fourteenth Session.

It shall be ratified, accepted or approved and the instruments of ratification, acceptance or approval shall be deposited with the Ministry of Foreign Affairs of the Kingdom of the Netherlands.

Article 38

Any other State may accede to the Convention.

The instrument of accession shall be deposited with the Ministry of Foreign Affairs of the Kingdom of the Netherlands.

The Convention shall enter into force for a state acceding to it on the first day of the third calendar month after the deposit of its instrument of accession.

The accession will have effect only as regards the relations between the acceding State and such Contracting States as will have declared their acceptance of the accession. Such a declaration will also have to be made by any Member State ratifying, accepting, or approving the Convention after an accession. Such declaration shall be deposited at the Ministry of Foreign Affairs of the Kingdom of the Netherlands; this Ministry shall forward, through diplomatic channels, a certified copy to each of the Contracting States.

The Convention will enter into force as between the acceding State and the State that has declared its acceptance of the accession on the first day of the third calendar month after the deposit of the declaration of acceptance.

Article 39

Any State may at the time of signature, ratification, acceptance, approval or accession, declare that the Convention shall extend to all the territories for the international relations of which it is responsible, or to one or more of them. Such a declaration shall take effect at the time the Convention enters into force for that State.

Such declaration, as well as any subsequent extension, shall be notified to the Ministry of Foreign Affairs of the Kingdom of the Netherlands.

Article 40

In a Contracting State has two or more territorial units in which different systems of law are applicable in relations to matters dealt with in this Convention, it may at the time of signature, ratification, acceptance, approval or accession declare that this Convention shall extend to all its territorial units or only to one or more of them and may modify this declaration by submitting another declaration at any time.

Any such declaration shall be notified to the Ministry of Foreign Affairs of the Kingdom of the Netherlands and shall state expressly the territorial units to which the Convention applies.

Article 41

Where a Contracting State has a system of government under which executive, judicial and legislative powers are distributed between central or other authorities within that State, its signature or ratification, acceptance or approval of, or accession to this Convention, or its making of any declaration in terms of Article 40 shall carry no implication as to the internal distribution of powers within that State.

Article 42

Any State may, not later than the time of ratification, acceptance, approval or accession, or at the time of making a declaration in terms of Article 39 or 40, make one or both of the reservations provided for in Article 24 and Article 26, third paragraph. No other reservation shall be permitted.

Any State may at any time withdraw a reservation it has made. The withdrawal shall be notified to the Ministry of Foreign Affairs of the Kingdom of the Netherlands.

The reservation shall cease to have effect on the first day of the third calendar month after the notification referred to in the preceding paragraph.

Article 43

The Convention shall enter into force on the first day of the third calendar month after the deposit of the third instrument of ratification, acceptance , approval or accession referred to in Articles 37 and 38.

Thereafter the Convention shall enter into force—

(1) for each State ratifying, accepting, approving or acceding to it subsequently, on the first day of the third calendar month after the deposit of its instrument of ratification, acceptance, approval or accession;

(2) for any territory or territorial unit to which the Convention has been extended in conformity with Article 39 or 40, on the first day of the third calendar month after the notification referred to in that Article.

Article 44

The Convention shall remain in force for five years from the date of its entry into force in accordance with the first paragraph of Article 43 even for States which subsequently have ratified, accepted, approved it or acceded to it. If there has been no denunciation, it shall be renewed tacitly every five years.

Any denunciation shall be notified to the Ministry of Foreign Affairs of the Kingdom of the Netherlands at least six months before the expiry of the five year period. It may be limited to certain of the territories of territorial unity to which the convention applies.

The denunciation shall have effect only as regards the State which has notified it. The Convention shall remain in force for the other Contracting States.

Article 45

The Ministry of Foreign Affairs of the Kingdom of the Netherlands shall notify the States Members of the Conference, and the States which have acceded in accordance with Article 38, of the following—

(1) the signatures and ratifications, acceptances, and approvals referred to in Article 37;

(2) the accessions referred to in Article 38;

(3) the date on which the Convention enters into force in accordance with Article 43;

(4) the extensions referred to in Article 39;

(5) the declarations referred to in Articles 38 and 40;

(6) the reservations referred to in Article 24 and Article 26, third paragraph, and the withdrawals referred to in Article 42;

(7) the denunciations referred to in Article 44.

In witness whereof the undersigned, being duly authorized thereto, have signed this Convention.

Done at The Hague, on the 25th day of October 1980 in the English and French languages, both texts being equally authentic, in a single copy which shall be deposited in the archives of the Government of the Kingdom of the Netherlands, and of which a certified copy shall be sent, through diplomatic channels, to each of the States Members of the Hague Conference on Private International Law at the date of its Fourteenth Session.

On July 1, 1988 the Hague Convention entered into force in the United States. A total of 55 countries have ratified this multinational agreement. In addition, a number of nonmember nations have "acceded" to the Convention with a member nation. The Convention does not apply to abductions that took place before a nation ratified the Convention or before two nations acceded to the Convention with respect to each other.

Nations which have ratified or acceded to the Convention with respect to the United States as of January 1, 2006 are:

Albania (August 1, 2007)
Andorra (July 1, 2011)
Argentina (June 1, 1991)
Armenia (June 1, 2007)
Australia (January 1, 1987)
Austria (October 1, 1988)
Bahamas (January 1, 1994)
Belarus (April 1, 1998)
Belgium (May 1, 1999)
Belize (September 1, 1989)
Bolivia (October 1, 2016)
Bosnia & Herzegovina (March 6, 1992)
Brazil (January 1, 2000)
Bulgaria (August 1, 2003)
Burkina Faso (August 1, 1992)
Canada (December 1, 1983)
Chile (May 1, 1994)
China, People's Republic of Hong Kong Admin. Region (April 25, 1965) and Macau (February 4, 1969)
Colombia (March 1, 1996)
Costa Rica (February 1, 1999)
Croatia (December 1, 1991)
Cyprus (February 1, 1995)
Czech Republic (March 1, 1998)
Denmark (July 1, 1991)
Dominican Republic (November 1, 2004)
Ecuador (April 1, 1992)
El Salvador (May 1, 2001)
Estonia (July 1, 2001)
Fiji (June 1, 1999)
Finland (August 1, 1994)
Former Yugoslav Republic of Macedonia (December 1, 1991)
France (December 1, 1983)
Gabon (March 1, 2011)
Georgia (October 1, 1997)
Germany (December 1, 1990)
Greece (June 1, 1993)
Guatemala (May 1, 2002)
Hungary (July 1, 1986)
Guinea (February 1, 2012)
Honduras (March 1, 1994)
Iceland (November 1, 1996)
Iraq (June 1, 2014)
Ireland (October 1, 1991)
Israel (December 1, 1991)
Italy (May 1, 1995)
Jamaica (May 1, 2017)
Japan (April 1, 2014)
Kazakhstan (September 1, 2013)
Korea, Republic of (March 1, 2013)
Latvia (February 1, 2002)
Lesotho (September 1, 2012)
Lithuania (September 1, 2002)
Luxembourg (January 1, 1987)
Malta (January 1, 2000)
Mauritius (June 1, 1993)
Mexico (September 1, 1991)
Monaco (February 1, 1993)
Montenegro (June 3, 2006)
Morocco (June 1, 2010)
Netherlands (September 1, 1990)
New Zealand (August 1, 1991)
Nicaragua (March 1, 2001)
Norway (April 1, 1989)
Pakistan (March 1, 2017)
Panama (May 1, 1994)
Paraguay (August 1, 1998)
Peru (August 1, 2001)
Philippines (June 1, 2016)
Poland (November 1, 1992)
Portugal (December 1, 1983)
Republic of Moldova (July 1, 1998)
Romania (February 1, 1993)
Russian Federation (October 1, 2011)
Saint Kitts and Nevis (August 1, 1994)
San Marino (March 1, 2007)
Serbia (April 27, 1992)
Seychelles (August 1, 2008)
Singapore (March 1, 2011)
Slovakia (February 1, 2001)
Slovenia (June 1, 1994)
South Africa (October 1, 1997)
Spain (September 1, 1987)
Sri Lanka (December 1, 2001)
Sweden (June 1, 1989)
Switzerland (January 1, 1984)
Thailand (November 1, 2002)
Trinidad and Tobago (September 1, 2000)
Turkmenistan (March 1, 1998)
Tunsia (October 1, 2017)
Turkey (August 1, 2000)
Ukraine (September 1, 2006)
United Kingdom of Great Britain and Northern Ireland (August 1, 1986)
United States of America (July 1, 1988)
Uruguay (February 1, 2000)
Uzbekistan (August 1, 1999)
Venezuela (January 1, 1997)
Zambia (November 1, 2014)
Zimbabwe (July 1, 1995).

Commentary

The Fifth Circuit Court of Appeals vacated a district court order returning a child to his mother in the U.K. when the mother had earlier consented a to a Texas state court's exercise of jurisdiction with respect to the child's custody. The court reasoned that the Hague Convention could not be used to undo the earlier Texas custody order when the Hague petitioner consented to jurisdiction of the Texas court. *Larbie v. Larbie, 690 F.3d 295 (2012), cert. denied, 133 S.Ct. 1455 (2013).*

In *Chafin v. Chafin, 133 S.Ct 1017, 185 L.Ed.2d 1 (2013)*, the United States Supreme Court held that a father's appeal from a district court order directing his daughter's return to Scotland as her country of habitual residence was not rendered moot by the fact that the mother had returned to Scotland with her daughter.

On remand of *Chafin*, the Court of Appeals held that unless the district court could find that the change of habitual residence was 'unequivocally clear' as evidenced by settled intent to change the child's residence, or the court could confidently conclude that the child's attachments had changed such that returning her to the original residence would be extremely disruptive, the court must conclude that Scotland remained her country of habitual residence. *Chafin v. Chafin, 742 F.3d 934 (11th Cir. 2013)*.

Darin v. Olivero-Huffman, 746 F.3d 1 (1st Cir. 2014), reversed an order denying an Argentine father's petition for the return of his child to their habitual Argentine residence, because the evidence did not establish that the father consented to the American mother's retention of the child in the United States when, at the end of a family trip to the United States, the mother announced her intention to retain the child in the United States when the father's visa expired. The mother's unlawful retention of the child began when she announced her intention to keep the child in the United States.

Hollis v. O'Driscoll, 739 F.3d 108 (2d Cir. 2014), affirmed a judgment ordering a mother to return the child to New Zealand, which had been the child's habitual residence before the New Zealand mother and child visited and remained in New York, when the parents had no agreement to change the child's habitual residence and the child was not acclimated to New York, even though the mother and child did not have stable accommodations in New Zealand.

Taveras v. Taveraz, 477 F.3d 767 (6th Cir. 2007), held that a federal district court properly dismissed a Dominican Republic father's claim, under the Hague Convention, that the custodial mother improperly abducted their children to the United States because (1) the Hague Convention only provides remedies for *custodial* parents and the mother had, under Dominican Republic law, full guardianship and custody of the children; and (2) the court lacked jurisdiction under the Hague Convention because the United States had not yet declared its acceptance of the Dominican Republic's accession to the Hague Convention. *Taveras* additionally held that the district court lacked subject matter jurisdiction of a child abduction claim against a custodial parent under the Alien Tort Claims Act (28 U.S.C. § 1350).

Papakosmas v. Papakosmas, 483 F.3d 617 (9th Cir. 2007), held that a mother's removal of her children from Greece was not wrongful within in the meaning of the Hague Convention when the children's habitual residence remained in California.

Under the Convention, if a child has a well-established "habitual residence," the child cannot acquire a new habitual residence unless both parents intend to have the child relinquish the former habitual residence in order to acquire a new one. *Mozes v. Mozes, 239 F.3d 1067 (9th Cir. 2001)*. *Mozes* formulates a standard for acquisition of a new habitual residence. There must be (1) a settled intention to abandon the habitual residence left behind and (2) an actual change in geography combined with the passage of a period of time sufficient for the children to acclimatize to the new residence. Id. at 1075–76, 1078. In *Koch v. Koch, 450 F.3d 703 (2006)*, the Seventh Circuit Court of Appeals adopted the *Mozes* intention-of-the-parents approach to "habitual residence," and praised it for its flexibility and capacity to allow the parents to understand and control the jurisdictional consequences of selecting or changing a child's residence. *Murphy v. Sloan, 764 F.3d 1144 (9th Cir. 2014), cert. denied*, reaffirmed the Ninth Circuit's adherence to the *Mozes* standard, which looks to the parents' last shared intent to determine a child's habitual residence

Valenzuela v. Michel, 736 F.3d 1173 (9th Cir. 2013), held that substantial evidence supported the district court's determination that Mexico was not the children's habitual residence when the parties had a shared intent to abandon Mexico as the children's habitual residence. *Valenzuela* also suggests an alternative rationale for the district court's conclusion that the children were not unlawfully retained by the father under the Convention: When, by agreement of the parents, the children had alternating habitual residences in the United States and Mexico, the father's retention of the children in the United States was not unlawful because the parents had a settled intent to abandon Mexico as the children's *sole* habitual residence and the children were thus habitually resident in the United States when the father retained them in Arizona.

Having found that a child had alternating habitual residences in Pittsburgh and Berlin, and that the child had fully acclimatized to Pittsburgh when the father sought his return to Berlin, *Blackledge v. Blackledge, 866 F.3d 169 (3d Cir. 2017)*, reasoned that Pittsburgh was his habitual residence when the father sought his return to Berlin, and therefore the child's retention in Pittsburgh was not wrongful. Effectively, *Blackledge* adopted the alternative rationale of Valenzuela, supra.

Delgado v. Osuna, 837 F.3d 571 (5th Circuit 2016), affirmed a denial of a father's petition for return of his children to Venezuela, because the evidence established the parents' shared intent to abandon Venezuela as the children's habitual residence, even though the parties never shared an intent that the children remain in the United States.

Applying the "last shared intention" standard to the determination of a child's habitual residence, *Mota v. Castillo, 692 F.3d 108 (2nd Cir. 2012)*, concluded that Mexico remained the child's habitual residence when the child but not the child's mother succeeded in crossing the border illegally and joining the father in New York, because the parents did not share an intention that the child would live in the United States without her mother.

With *Mota*, compare *Sanchez-Londono v. Gonzales, 752 F.3d 533 (1st Cir. 2014)*, affirming denial of an alien mother's petition for return of her child to Colombia because the child had acclimatized to living in the United States at the time of her retention and the parents' last shared intention was that the child reside in the United States when the parties had agreed that the child's subsequent stay with the mother in Columbia would be temporary and there was no condition that the child would return to Columbia if the mother did not gain admission to the United States.

Also applying the "last shared intention" standard, *Hoffmann v. Sender, 716 F.3d 282 (2nd Cir. 2013)*, affirmed a district court order that the parties' children be returned to Canada when the mother initiated divorce proceedings against the father before he joined his family in New York and the father's consent to the children's move from Canada to New York was conditioned upon the belief that they were moving to New York as a family.

Berezowsky v. Ojeda, 765 F.3d 456 (5th Cir. 2014), cert. denied, applied the last shared intention standard in holding that the district court erred in granting a mother's petition for return to Mexico of a child born in Texas and taken by his father to Texas, when the mother failed to prove that the parents shared an intent or settled purpose regarding their child's habitual residence.

When the United States was the child's habitual residence when a foreign custody order was entered, the Hague Convention remedy of return cannot be used to enforce the foreign custody order. The Convention is an "anti-abduction" treaty, not a means for enforcement of conflicting custody orders. *Redmond v. Redmond, 724 F.3d 729 (7th Cir. 2013)*.

For discussion of Article 3 wrongful removal and the meaning of "habitually resident," see *Feder v. Evans–Feder, 63 F.3d 217, (3d Cir. 1995)* (reversing district court and holding that mother's retention of child in United States was presumptively wrongful under the Convention because habitual residence of child had been established in Australia); *Friedrich v. Friedrich, 983 F.2d 1396 (6th Cir. 1993)*; and *In re Ponath, 829 F.Supp. 363 (D.Utah 1993)* (coerced residence does not establish habitual residence).

In *Holder v. Holder, 392 F.3d 1009 (2004)*, the Ninth Circuit sustained a district court's conclusion that a family's short-term residence on an American military base in Germany did not establish Germany as the children's habitual residence under this convention.

On May 11, 2005, the California Supreme Court granted review to *Ferraris v. Alexander* in which the superseded opinion of the court of appeal, *23 Cal.Rptr.3d 592 (2005)*, held that a trial court properly denied a father's petition under this convention for the father's return of his child to Italy because the father failed to prove that Italy was the child's habitual residence.

Resolving a conflict among the Circuit Courts of Appeal, in *Abbott v. Abbott, 130 S.Ct. 1983, 176 L.Ed.2d 789 (2010)*, the United States Supreme Court held that a "ne exeat" clause requiring a parent's consent before the other parent may take their child to another country, gives a non-consenting parent a protectable "right to custody" within the meaning of Article 3.

Martinez v. Cahue, 826 F.3d 983 (7th Cir. 2016), held that the father of a child born out of wedlock, who signed a voluntary declaration of paternity and had a right to 'constant visitation and overnight visits twice a week' under a written signed contract with the child's mother, which contract had never been memorialized in a court order, had no 'custody rights' within the meaning of Article 3, because under the law of Illinois, where the child was born and resided until his mother removed him to Mexico, the mother of a child born out of wedlock has sole custody of the child absent a court order to the contrary. Thus, for purposes of the Convention, only the mother had authority to determine the legal residence of the child.

When father's occasional visits with his child constituted an exercise of his custody rights, the quality of his visits with the child, which might be an issue in a domestic custody proceeding, was improperly considered by the trial court in a Hague proceeding to return the child to his habitual residence. *Rodriguez v. Yanez, 817 F.3d 466 (5th Cir. 2016)*.

Ozaltin v. Ozaltin, 708 F.3d 355 (2d Cir. 2013), held that (1) a district court properly ordered a mother to return the parties' children to Turkey because their father retained rights of custody under Turkish law, even though mother had been awarded primary custody of the children; and (2) there is a federal right of action to enforce rights of access protected by the Hague Convention. But see *Cantor v. Cohen, 442 F.3d 196 (4th Cir. 2006)*, holding that there is no federal right of action to enforce rights of access under the Hague Convention, reasoning that Article 21 requires that application must be made to the "Central Authorities of the Contracting State."

Compare *White v. White, 718 F.3d 300 (4th Cir. 2013)*, holding that the mother's removal of the parties' child was not in breach of the father's rights of custody under the Hague Convention when Swiss law permitted the custodial parent to remove the child from Switzerland without obtaining the consent of the other parent or the court.

In re Marriage of Witherspoon, 155 Cal.App.4th 963, 66 Cal.Rptr.3d 586 (2007), held that a trial court properly found that a mother had made a prima facie case for return of her children to Germany on the ground that it was their habitual residence, but that the court erred in failing to make factual findings on whether various Hague Convention exceptions to return, which were raised by the father, were applicable.

In re B. del C.S.B., 559 F.3d 999 (9th Cir. 2009), held that a child with unlawful immigration status may nevertheless be "settled" in a new country for purposes of Article 12. Accord, *Lozano v. Alvarez, 697 F.3d 41 (2nd Cir. 2012)*.

Relying on Articles 11, 12, and 16, *Bardales v. Duarte, 181 Cal.App.4th 1262, 104 Cal.Rptr.3d 899 (2010)*, held that a state trial court has power to dismiss a Hague Convention petition for delayed prosecution.

In *Lozano v. Montoya Alvarez, 134 S.Ct. 1224 (2014)*, the United States Supreme Court held that the one-year period of Article 12, during which the court must order the return of the child to his habitual residence, is not subject to equitable tolling when the abducting parent conceals the child's whereabouts from the other parent. If the proceeding is commenced more than one year after wrongful removal of the child, the court must order the return of the child, unless the child is now settled in his new environment. *Lozano* overrules *Duarte v. Bardales, 526 F.3d 563 (9th Cir. 2008)* and *Furnes v. Reeves, 362 F.3d 702 (11th Cir. 2004)*, which applied the doctrine of equitable tolling during the child's concealment.

Alcala v. Hernandez, 826 F.3d 161 (4th Cir. 2016), affirmed a district court order denying the return of two children unlawfully removed from Mexico more than one year before the Hague petition was filed, because the children were settled in their new environment within the meaning of this Convention, even though the mother and children did not have legal immigration status, when they were unlikely to be deported in the near future.

Compare *Hernandez v. Garcia Pena, 820 F.3d 782 (5th Cir. 2016)*, which held that an otherwise adequate well-settled defense to return had not been established when the abducting mother and child were already in removal proceedings that seriously threatened their ability to remain in the United States.

With respect to immigration status, under the federal Immigration and Nationality Act, 8 USC ? 1101(27)(J), an undocumented immigrant child may be eligible for Special Immigrant Juvenile (SIJ) status. The first step in obtaining SIJ status is securing SIJ findings from a state court, including a family, probate or juvenile court. Effective July 1, 2016, California Rule of Court 5.130 governs requests for SIJ findings in child custody proceedings. Required SIJ findings parallel the Convention's grave risk of harm exception.

For treatment of the Article 13 "grave risk" exception, compare *Nunez-Escudero v. Tice–Menley, 58 F.3d 374 (8th Cir. 1995)* (trial court erred in refusing to return young child to Mexico because of grave risk of harm from separation from his mother; issue is not determination of custody but instead whether the agencies and courts of Mexico, the place of the child's habitual residence, can properly protect the child from harm) with *Ponath,* supra. Similarly, *Gaudin v. Remis, 415 F.3d 1038 (2005)*, held that the district court erred in denying a petition for the return of two abducted children under the "grave risk of . . . psychological harm" exception (Article 13) without considering alternative remedies that would allow return of the children to the home country and protect them from harm. *In re Marriage of Eaddy, 144 Cal.App.4th 1202, 51 Cal.Rptr.3d 172 (2006)*, held that the trial court erred in denying a parent's petition for the return of her daughter to Australia when Australia was the child's habitual residence and there was insufficient evidence that return would create a grave risk to the child. *Cuellar v. Joyce, 596 F.3d. 505 (9th Cir. 2010)*, also holds that a district court incorrectly applied the "grave risk" exception in denying a Panamanian mother's petition for return of a child abducted by her American father.

Although sustaining a trial court finding of 'grave risk' to the child if the child were returned to Italy without his mother, *Maurizio R. v. L.C., 201 Cal.App.4th 616, 135 Cal.Rptr.3d 93 (2011), review denied,* nevertheless concluded that the trial court erred in conditioning the child's return to Italy on the mother's willingness to accompany the child to Italy and risk Italian criminal prosecution for child abduction, a prosecution initiated by the child's Italian father but which the father was now powerless to withdraw. Instead, the trial court should have granted the father's petition for return and appointed a guardian to accompany the child back to Italy.

Ortiz v. Martinez, 789 F.3d 722 (7th Cir. 2015), affirmed the denial of a father's petition for the return of his daughter to Mexico City because the mother had established that the child would face grave risk of physical harm if she were returned to Mexico, based on clear and convincing evidence that the father had sexually abused her in the past. *Ortiz*, applying the clear error standard of review, gave great deference to the district court's determinations about the credibility of witnesses.

Souratgar v. Lee, 720 F.3d 96 (2d Cir. 2013), affirmed an order returning the parties' child to Singapore, holding that spousal domestic abuse alone, without clear and convincing evidence that it would cause a grave risk to the child, was not sufficient to decline to return the child to the habitual residence.

Gomez v. Fuenmayor, 812 F.3d 1005 (11th Cir. 2016), held that significant threats and actual murderous violence directed against a parent can constitute a grave risk of physical and psychological harm to a child even if the threats and violence are not aimed directly against the child.

The fact that, during the pendency of the children's appeal from an order of requiring their return to Mexico, the American government granted the children asylum on the ground that they had a 'well-founded fear of persecution' in Mexico, is relevant to, although not dispositive of, the issue of 'grave risk of harm,' as well as the Article 20 'protection of human rights' exception. Consequently, *Sanchez v. R.G.L., 743 F.3d 945 (5th Cir. 2014)*, vacated the district court's return order and remanded to the district court. *Sanchez* also held that the petitioning parent's excusable failure to sue the proper party did not deprive the district court of jurisdiction and that the children, although non-parties, had standing to appeal the return order as *de facto* parties. On rehearing of *Sanchez, 761 F.3d 495 (2014)*, the Fifth Circuit again vacated the district court's return order and remanded to the district court, ruling that joinder of the United States government, as the children's legal custodian, was required because relief might otherwise be ineffective, and that the discretionary grant of asylum would not supersede the enforceability of a district court order that the children be returned to their mother in Mexico.

Noergaard v. Noergaard, 244 Cal.App.4th 76, 197 Cal.Rptr.3d 546 (2015), review denied, holding that due process requires a trial court to conduct an evidentiary hearing on a parent's claim that a child would face grave risk of harm if returned to her habitual residence, reversed a trial court order granting a father's Hague Convention petition to return the child to the father's custody in Denmark without granting the mother an evidentiary hearing on her claim that the child would face a grave risk of psychological and physical harm if she were returned.

Kahn v. Fatima, 680 F.3d 781 (7th Cir. 2012), held that a district court erred in ordering a child returned to her habitual residence without making factual findings concerning the mother's claim that the child faced a great risk of harm if returned.

However, *West v. Dobrev, 735 F.3d 921 (10th Cir. 2013)*, holds that the district court may deny a parent an evidentiary hearing on the grave risk of harm exception when the parent's declarations do not allege a prima facie of case of grave risk of harm. Furthermore, West suggests that the is no requirement under the Convention, the International Child Abduction Remedies Act, or the Fifth Amendment due process clause that discovery or an evidentiary hearing be conducted as a matter of right in cases arising under the Convention.

Ermini v. Vittori, 758 F.3d 153 (2d Cir. 2014), affirmed a trial court's conclusion that an autistic child's separation from his American treatment program and from his devoted healthy older sibling would cause the child grave risk of harm. Consequently, the trial court declined to return the two children from New York to Italy, their habitual residence, where comparable autism treatment was not available. *Ermini* additionally held that the trial court erred when it denied a Hague Convention petition without prejudice to renewal if the autistic child became unable to participate in the American program or the Italian family court issued a final order requiring return of the children to Italy, reasoning that dismissal of a Hague Convention petition must always be *with prejudice* in order to achieve the goals of the Convention.

Applying the Article 13 exception for a mature child who objects to return to his country of habitual residence, *Escobar v. Flores, 183 Cal.App.4th 737, 107 Cal.Rptr.3d 596 (2010)* held that a trial court properly refused to order the return of an 8–year-old child under the Hague Convention when the child objected to return and the court found that the child had reached a level of maturity at which it was appropriate to take into account his views.

By contrast, *Garcia v. Pinelo, 808 F.3d 1158 (7th Cir. 2015)*, sustained a district court's grant of father's petition to return a child to Mexico, on the ground that the trial court did not abuse its discretion in declining to follow the wishes of a mature 13-year-old boy, who preferred to remain in the United States with his mother. Escobar and Garcia are reconcilable as appellate acknowledgement of trial court discretion.

Notwithstanding an abducting parent's wrongful behavior, *Custodio v. Samillan, 842 F.3d 1084 (8th Circ. 2016)*, affirmed a trial court's denial of return based on the mature child exception when a 15-year-old child expressed cogent reasons for remaining in the United States with his mother and siblings. *Custodio* also held that a child who had reached the age of 16 is no longer subject to the Hague Convention, regardless of the child's age when the child was abducted or wrongfully retained, or when the Convention is invoked.

When a trial court declined to return a child to Mexico, her country of habitual residence, having found that although not yet 10 years old, she was nevertheless a mature child who expressed a preference to remain in the United States, *Rodriguez v. Yanez, 817 F.3d 466 (5th Cir. 2016)*, held that expressing a preference is not equivalent to an objection to return to Mexico, and therefore remanded the case to the trial court to talk to the child and make findings on whether she objected to returning to Mexico.

Applying subsection (a) of Article 13, *Gonzalez-Caballero v. Mena, 251 F.3d 789 (9th Cir. 2001)*, holds that the federal district court properly denied a Panamanian mother's petition to return her daughter to Panama on the ground that the mother consented to the removal of the child to the United States.

See also *Wipranik v. Superior Court, 63 Cal.App.4th 315, 73 Cal.Rptr.2d 734 (1998)*, (rejecting mother's petition for rehearing on procedural grounds).

As to appeals and stay of proceedings as to judgment or order affecting custody generally, see Code of Civil Procedure § 917.7

Relying on Article 16, which requires that state custody proceedings be stayed pending resolution of a Hague Convention wrongful removal or retention claim, *Barzilay v. Barzilay, 536 F.3d 844 (8th Cir. 2008)*, held that a federal district court abused its discretion in abstaining, under the *Younger* doctrine, from hearing a Hague Convention claim while a state court custody proceeding was pending.

An American court must decline to grant comity to a foreign court's Hague Convention order when the foreign court misapplied the provisions of the Hague Convention. *Asvesta v. Petroutsas, 580 F.3d 1000 (9th Cir. 2009)*.

The Fourth Circuit Court of Appeals held that the district court properly granted comity to an earlier German decision denying, on the ground that the father had consented to the children's move to Germany, a father's Hague Convention petition for return of his children to North Carolina, and the German court's decision neither clearly misinterpreted the Hague Convention nor failed to meet a minimal standard of reasonableness. *Smedley v. Smedley, 772 F.3d 184 (4th Cir. 2014)*.

Patrick v. Rivera-Lopez, 708 F.3d 15 (1st Cir. 2013), holds that Article 22 deprives a district court of power to require a parent to post a bond.

CALIFORNIA RULES OF COURT

Title 3

CIVIL RULES

Division 11

LAW AND MOTION

Chapter 7

CIVIL PETITIONS

Rule 3.1365. Petitions under the California Environmental Quality Act

Rules for petitions for relief brought under the California Environmental Quality Act have been renumbered and moved to division 22 of these rules, beginning with rule 3.2200. *(Adopted, eff. July 1, 2014.)*

Rule 3.1370. Emancipation of minors

A petition for declaration of the emancipation of a minor must comply with rule 5.605. *(Formerly Rule 270, adopted, eff. July 1, 1994. Renumbered Rule 3.1370 and amended, eff. Jan. 1, 2007.)*

Research References

Treatises and Practice Aids

Witkin, California Summary 10th Parent and Child § 303, in General.

Witkin, California Summary 10th Parent and Child § 304, Notice Of Hearing.

Rule 3.1372. Petitions for relief from financial obligations during military service

(a) Application

This rule applies to petitions for relief from financial obligations made by a servicemember under Military and Veterans Code section 409.3.

(b) Service of petition

Service of the petition for relief and all supporting papers must be made in the manner provided by law for service of summons in civil actions.

(c) No memorandum required

Unless ordered by the court, no memorandum is required in support of or opposition to a petition for relief. *(Adopted, eff. Jan. 1, 2012.)*

Title 5

FAMILY AND JUVENILE RULES

Disposition Table

California Rules of Court Reorganization

(From former rule number to new rule number)

Title 5. Family and Juvenile Rule—Divisions 1 & 2

The following table from the Judicial Council of California shows the disposition of Divisions 1 and 2 of Title 5, "Family and Juvenile Rules", as reorganized by the Judicial Council, effective January 1, 2013. The reorganization was adopted by the Judicial Council on February 28, 2012.

Old Rule Number	New Rule Number	Title
		Title 5. Family and Juvenile Rules
5.1	5.1	Title
		Division 1. Family Rules
		Chapter 1. General Provisions
5.5	5.2(a)	Division title; application of rules and laws
5.10	5.2(b)	Definitions and use of terms
5.15	5.2(f)	Extensions of time
5.20	5.2(c)	Application of rules
5.21	5.2(d)	General law applicable
5.22	5.2(e)	Law applicable to other proceedings
5.25	5.7(a)	Use of forms
5.26	5.7(b)	Forms in nonfamily law proceedings
5.27	5.7(c)	Interstate forms
5.28	5.76	Domestic partnerships
5.35	5.430	Minimum standards for the Office of the Family Law Facilitator
5.70	5.425(f)	Nondisclosure of attorney assistance in preparation of court documents
5.71	5.425(e)	Procedures to be relieved as counsel on completion of limited scope representation
5.83	5.83	Family centered case resolution
5.92	5.92	Request for court order; response
5.93	5.427	Attorney's fees and costs
		Chapter 2. Procedural Rules
5.100	5.16(a)	Designation of parties
5.102	5.16(b)	Parties to proceeding
5.104	5.17	Other causes of action
5.106	5.18	Injunctive relief and reservation of jurisdiction
5.108	5.74	Pleadings and amended pleadings
5.110	5.50	Papers issued by the court
5.112	5.68(c)	Continuing jurisdiction
5.114	5.60(b)	Request for alternative relief
5.116	5.411	Stipulated judgments
5.118	5.111.	Declarations supporting and responding to a request for court order
5.119	5.113	Live testimony

Old Rule Number	New Rule Number	Title
5.120	5.62	Appearance by respondent or defendant
5.121	5.63	Motion to quash proceeding or responsive relief
5.122	5.401	Default
5.124	5.402	Request for default; forms
5.126	5.390(c)	Alternate date of valuation
5.128	5.260(a); 5.427(e)(2)	Financial declarations;
5.130	5.77	Summary dissolution
5.134	5.413	Notice of entry of judgment
5.136	5.415	Completion of notice of entry of judgment
5.140	5.2(g)	Implied procedures
5.146	5.405	Judgment checklists (separate report)
5.147	5.407	Review of default and uncontested judgment documents submitted on the basis of declaration under Family code section 2336 (separate report)
5.148	5.409	Default and uncontested hearings on judgments submitted on the basis of declarations under Family code section 2336 (separate report)
		Chapter 3. Joinder of Parties
5.150	5.24, subparagraph and 5.24(a)(1)	Joinder of persons claiming interest
5.152	5.24(b)	"Claimant" defined
5.154	5.24(c)	Persons who may seek joinder
5.156	5.24(d)	Form of joinder application
5.158	5.24(e)	Court order on joinder
5.160	5.24(a)(2)	Pleading rules applicable
5.162	5.29	Joinder of employee pension benefit plan
		Chapter 4. Bifurcation and Appeals
5.175	5.390(a), (b), (d)	Bifurcation of issues
5.180	5.392	Interlocutory appeals
		Chapter 5. Child Custody
5.210	5.210	Court-connected child custody mediation
5.215	5.215	Domestic violence protocol for Family Court Services
5.220	5.220	Court-ordered child custody evaluations
5.225	5.225	Appointment requirements for child custody evaluators
5.230	5.230	Domestic violence training standards for court-appointed child custody investigators and evaluators
5.235	5.235	Ex parte communication in child custody proceedings
5.240	5.240	Appointment of counsel to represent a child in family law proceedings
5.241	5.241	Compensation of counsel appointed to represent a child in a family law proceeding
5.242	5.242	Qualifications, rights, and responsibilities of counsel appointed to represent a child in family law proceedings

Old Rule Number	New Rule Number	Title
5.250	5.250	Children's participation and testimony in family court proceedings
		Chapter 6. Certification of Statewide Uniform Guideline Support Calculators
5.275	5.275	Standards for computer software to assist in determining support
		Chapter 7. Rules for Title IV–D Support Actions
5.300	5.300	Purpose, authority, and definitions
5.305	5.305	Hearing of matters by a judge under Family Code sections 4251(a) and 4252(b)(7)
5.310	5.310	Use of existing family law forms
5.311	5.311	Implementation of new and revised governmental forms by local child support agencies
5.315	5.315	Memorandum of points and authorities
5.320	5.320	Attorney of record in support actions under title IV–D of the Social Security Act
5.324	5.324	Telephone appearance in title IV–D hearings and conferences
5.325	5.325	Procedures for clerk's handling of combined summons and complaint
5.330	5.330	Procedures for child support case registry form
5.335	5.335	Procedures for hearings on interstate income withholding orders
5.340	5.340	Judicial education for child support commissioners
5.350	5.350	Procedures for hearings to set aside voluntary declarations of paternity when no previous action has been filed
5.355	5.355	Minimum standards of training for court clerk staff whose assignment includes title IV–D child support cases
5.360	5.360	Appearance by local child support agency
5.365	5.365	Procedure for consolidation of child support orders
5.370	5.370	Party designation in interstate and intrastate cases
5.375	5.375	Procedure for a support obligor to file a motion regarding mistaken identity
		Chapter 11. Domestic Violence Cases
5.380	5.380	Agreement and judgment of parentage in Domestic Violence Prevention Act cases
5.381	5.381	Modification of child custody, visitation, and support orders in Domestic Violence Prevention Act cases
		Division 2. Rules Applicable in Family and Juvenile Proceedings **Chapter 1. Contact and Coordination**
5.400	5.451	Contact after adoption agreement
5.450	5.445	Court communication protocol for domestic violence and child custody orders

Old Rule Number	New Rule Number	Title
5.410	5.460	Request for sibling contact information
5.475	5.475	Custody and visitation orders following termination of a juvenile court proceeding or probate court guardianship proceeding
		Chapter 2. Indian Child Welfare Act
5.480	5.480	Application
5.481	5.481	Inquiry and notice
5.482	5.482	Proceedings after notice
5.483	5.483	Transfer of case
5.484	5.484	Placement of an Indian child
5.485	5.485	Termination of parental rights
5.486	5.486	Petition to invalidate orders
5.487	5.487	Adoption record keeping

Derivation Table

California Rules of Court Reorganization

(From new rule number to former rule number)

Title 5. Family and Juvenile Rules–Divisions 1 & 2

The following table from the Judicial Council of California shows the derivation of Divisions 1 and 2 of Title 5, "Family and Juvenile Rules", as reorganized by the Judicial Council, effective January 1, 2013. The reorganization was adopted by the Judicial Council on February 28, 2012.

New Rule Number	Old Rule Number	Title
		Title 5. Family and Juvenile Rules
5.1	5.1	Title
		Division 1. Family Rules
		Chapter 1. General Provisions
		Article 1. General Provisions
5.2	5.5, 5.10, 5.15, 5.20, 5.21, 5.22, 5.140	Division title, application of rules and laws
5.4	New	Preemption; local rules and forms
		Article 2. Use of Forms
5.7	5.25, 5.26, 5.27	Use of forms
		Article 3. Appearance by Telephone
5.9	New	Appearance by telephone
		Article 5. Discovery
5.12	New	Discovery motions
		Article 6. Sanctions
5.14	New	Sanctions for violations of rules of court in family law cases
		Chapter 2. Parties and Joinder of Parties
		Article 1. Parties to Proceedings
5.16	5.100, 5.102	Designation of parties
5.17	5.104	Other causes of action
5.18	5.106	Injunctive relief and reservation of jurisdiction
		Article 2. Joinder of Parties
5.24	5.150, 5.152, 5.154, 5.156, 5.158, 5.160	Joinder of persons claiming interest

New Rule Number	Old Rule Number	Title
		Article 3. Joinder of Employee Pension Benefit Plan
5.29	5.162	Joinder of employee pension benefit plan
		Chapter 3. Filing Fees and Fee Waivers
		Article 1. Filing Fees and Fee Waivers
5.40	New	Filing Fees
5.41	New	Waiver of fees and costs
		Article 2. Special Procedures
5.43	New	Fee Waiver denials; voided actions; dismissal
5.45	New	Repayment of waived court fees and costs in family law support actions
5.46	New	Waiver of fees and costs —Supreme Court or Court of Appeal
		Chapter 4. Starting and Responding to a Family Law Case; Service of Papers
		Article 1. Summonses, Notices, and Declarations
5.50	5.110	Papers issued by the court
5.52	New	Declaration Under Uniform Child Custody Jurisdiction and Enforcement Act (UCCJEA)
		Article 2. Initial Pleadings
5.60	5.114 and new provisions	Petition or complaint; alternative relief
5.62	5.120	Appearance by respondent or defendant
5.63	5.121	Motion to quash proceeding or responsive relief
		Article 3. Service of Papers
5.66	New	Proof of service
		Article 4. Manner of Service
5.68	5.112 and new provisions	Manner of service of summons and petition; response; jurisdiction
5.72	New	Court order for service of summons by publication or posting when respondent's address is unknown
		Article 5. Pleadings and Amended Pleadings
5.74	5.108 (b) and (c)	Pleadings and amended pleadings
		Article 6. Specific Proceedings
5.76	5.28	Domestic partnerships
5.77	5.130	Summary dissolution
		Chapter 5. Family Centered Case Resolution Plans
5.83	5.83	Family centered case resolution
		Chapter 6. Request for Court Orders
		Article 1. General Provisions
5.90	New	Format of papers
5.91	5.110(c)	Individual restraining order
		Article 2. Filing and Service
5.92	5.92	Request for court order; response

New Rule Number	Old Rule Number	Title
5.94	New	Order shortening time; other filing requirements
5.96	New	Place and manner of filing
		Article 3. Meet-and-Confer Conferences
5.98	New	Meet-and-confer requirements; document exchange
		Article 4. Evidence at Hearing
5.111	5.118	Declarations supporting and responding to a request for court order
5.112.1	New	Declaration page limitation; exemptions
5.113	5.119	Live testimony
5.115	New	Judicial notice
		Article 5. Reporting and Preparation of Order After Hearing
5.123	New	Reporting of hearing proceedings
5.125	New	Preparation, service, and submission of order after hearing
		Chapter 7. Request for Emergency Orders (Ex Parte Orders)
		Article 1. Request for emergency orders
5.151	New	Request for emergency orders; application; required documents
		Article 2. Notice, Service, Appearance
5.165	New	Requirements for notice
5.167	New	Service of application; temporary restraining orders
5.169	New	Personal appearance at hearing for temporary emergency orders
		Article 3. Procedural matters not requiring notice (Non–Emergency Orders)
5.170	New	Matters not requiring notice to other parties
		Chapter 8. Child Custody and Visitation (Parenting Time) Proceedings
		Article 1. Child Custody Mediation
5.210	5.210	Court-connected child custody mediation
5.215	5.215	Domestic violence protocol for Family Court Services
		Article 2. Child Custody Investigations and Evaluations
5.220	5.220	Court-ordered child custody evaluations
5.225	5.225	Appointment requirements for child custody evaluators
5.230	5.230	Domestic violence training standards for court-appointed child custody investigators and evaluators
		Article 3. Ex Parte Communications
5.235	5.235	Ex parte communication in child custody proceedings
		Article 4. Counsel Appointed to Represent A Child

New Rule Number	Old Rule Number	Title
5.240	5.240	Appointment of counsel to represent a child in family law proceedings
5.241	5.241	Compensation of counsel appointed to represent a child in a family law proceeding
5.242	5.242	Qualifications, rights, and responsibilities of counsel appointed to represent a child in family law proceedings
		Article 5. Children's Participation in Family Court
5.250	5.250	Children's participation and testimony in family court proceedings
		Chapter 9. Child, Spousal, and Domestic Partner Support
		Article 1. General Provisions
5.260	5.128 and new provisions	General provisions regarding support cases
		Article 2. Certification of Statewide Uniform Guideline Support Calculators
5.275	5.275	Standards for computer software to assist in determining support
		Chapter 10. Government Child Support Cases (Title IV–D Support Cases)
5.300	5.300	Purpose, authority, and definitions
5.305	5.305	Hearing of matters by a judge under Family Code sections 4251(a) and 4252(b)(7)
5.310	5.310	Use of existing family law forms
5.311	5.311	Implementation of new and revised governmental forms by local child support agencies
5.315	5.315	Memorandum of points and authorities
5.320	5.320	Attorney of record in support actions under title IV–D of the Social Security Act
5.324	5.324	Telephone appearance in title IV–D hearings and conferences
5.325	5.325	Procedures for clerk's handling of combined summons and complaint
5.330	5.330	Procedures for child support case registry form
5.335	5.335	Procedures for hearings on interstate income withholding orders
5.340	5.340	Judicial education for child support commissioners
5.350	5.350	Procedures for hearings to set aside voluntary declarations of paternity when no previous action has been filed
5.355	5.355	Minimum standards of training for court clerk staff whose assignment includes title IV–D child support cases
5.360	5.360	Appearance by local child support agency
5.365	5.365	Procedure for consolidation of child support orders
5.370	5.370	Party designation in interstate and intrastate cases

New Rule Number	Old Rule Number	Title
5.375	5.375	Procedure for a support obligor to file a motion regarding mistaken identity
		Chapter 11. Domestic Violence Cases
		Article 1. Domestic Violence Prevention Act Cases
5.380	5.380	Agreement and judgment of parentage in Domestic Violence Prevention Act cases
5.381	5.381	Modification of child custody, visitation, and support orders in Domestic Violence Prevention Act cases
		Article 2. Tribal Court Protective Orders
5.386	5.386	Procedures for filing a tribal court protective order
		Chapter 12. Separate Trials (Bifurcation)[1] and Interlocutory Appeals
		Article 1. Separate Trials
5.390	5.126 and 5.175	Bifurcation of issues
		Article 2. Interlocutory Appeals
5.392	5.180	Interlocutory appeals
		Chapter 13. Trials and Long–Cause Hearings
5.393	New	Setting trials and long-cause hearings
5.394	New	Trial or hearing brief
		Chapter 14. Default and Judgments
5.401	5.122	Default
5.402	5.124	Request for default; forms
5.405	5.146	Judgment checklists
5.407	5.147	Review of default and uncontested judgment documents submitted on the basis of declarations under Family code section 2336
5.409	5.148	Default and uncontested hearings on judgments submitted on the basis of declarations under Family code section 2336
5.411	5.116	Stipulated judgments
5.413	5.134	Notice of entry of judgment
5.415	5.136	Completion of notice of entry of judgment
		Chapter 15. Settlement Services
5.420	New	Domestic violence procedures for court-connected settlement services providers
		Chapter 16. Limited Scope Representation; Attorney Fees and Costs
		Article 1. Limited Scope Representation
5.425	5.70, 5.71 and new provisions	Limited scope representation; application of rules
		Article 2. Attorney's Fees and Costs
5.427	5.93	Attorney's fees and costs
		Chapter 17. Family Law Facilitator
5.430	5.35	Minimum standards for the Office of the Family Law Facilitator
		Chapter 18. Court Coordination Rules
5.440	New	Related cases

New Rule Number	Old Rule Number	Title
5.445	5.450	Court communication protocol for domestic violence and child custody orders
		Division 2. Rules Applicable in Family and Juvenile Proceedings
		Chapter 1. Contact and Coordination
5.451	5.400	Contact after adoption agreement
5.460	5.410	Request for sibling contact information
5.475	5.475	Custody and visitation orders following termination of a juvenile court proceeding or probate court guardianship proceeding
		Chapter 2. Indian Child Welfare Act
5.480	5.480	Application
5.481	5.481	Inquiry and notice
5.482	5.482	Proceedings after notice
5.483	5.483	Transfer of case
5.484	5.484	Placement of an Indian child
5.485	5.485	Termination of parental rights
5.486	5.486	Petition to invalidate orders
5.487	5.487	Adoption record keeping

[1] So in copy.

Rule

5.1. Title.

Rule 5.1. Title

The rules in this title may be referred to as the Family and Juvenile Rules. *(Adopted, eff. Jan. 1, 2007.)*

Research References

Forms

West's California Code Forms, Civil Procedure § 901 Form 13, Rules on Appeal--Rule 8.124--Notice Of Election to Proceed.

West's California Code Forms, Civil Procedure § 1005 Form 35, Motions and Orders--Request for Telephone Appearance--Governmental--Official Form.

West's California Code Forms, Civil Procedure § 1005 Form 37, Motions and Orders--Order After Hearing--Governmental--Official Form.

West's California Code Forms, Civil Procedure § 1005 Form 38, Motions and Orders--Short Form Order After Hearing--Governmental--Official Form.

West's California Code Forms, Civil Procedure § 1005 Form 39, Motions and Orders--Order to Show Cause--Governmental--Official Form.

West's California Code Forms, Civil Procedure § 1005 Form 40, Motions and Orders--Request for Order and Supporting Declaration--Governmental--Official Form.

West's California Code Forms, Civil Procedure § 1005 Form 42, Motions and Orders--Stipulation and Order--Governmental--Official Form.

West's California Code Forms, Civil Procedure § 1005 Form 43, Motions and Orders--Stipulation and Order Waiving Unassigned Arrears--Official Form.

West's California Code Forms, Civil Procedure § 1005 Form 14, Motions and Orders--Order to Show Cause (Family Law, Uniform Parentage)--Official Form.

West's California Code Forms, Civil Procedure § 1005 Form 15, Motions and Orders--Temporary Orders--Attachment to Order to Show Cause--Family Law--Official Form.

West's California Code Forms, Civil Procedure § 1005 Form 18, Motions and Orders--Request for Order (Family Law)--Official Form.

West's California Code Forms, Civil Procedure § 1005 Form 29, Motion and Orders--Application for Separate Trial Attachment (Family Law)--Official Form.

Division 1

FAMILY RULES

Chapter 1

GENERAL PROVISIONS

Article 1

GENERAL PROVISIONS

Rule 5.2. Division title; definitions; application of rules and laws

(a) Division title

The rules in this division may be referred to as the Family Rules.

(b) Definitions and use of terms

As used in this division, unless the context or subject matter otherwise requires, the 19 following definitions apply:

(1) "Family Code" means that code enacted by chapter 162 of the Statutes of 1992 and any subsequent amendments to that code.

(2) "Action" is also known as a lawsuit, a case, or a demand brought in a court of law to defend or enforce a right, prevent or remedy a harm, or punish a crime. It includes all the proceedings in which a party requests orders that are available in the lawsuit.

(3) "Proceeding" is a court hearing in an action under the Family Code, including a hearing that relates to the dissolution or nullity of a marriage or domestic partnership, legal separation, custody and support of minor children, a parent and child relationship, adoptions, local child support agency actions under the Family Code, contempt proceedings relating to family law or local child support agency matters, and any action filed under the Domestic Violence Prevention Act, Uniform Parentage Act, Uniform Child Custody Jurisdiction and Enforcement Act, Indian Child Welfare Act, or Uniform Interstate Family Support Act.

(4) "Dissolution" is the legal term used for "divorce." "Divorce" commonly refers to a marriage that is legally ended.

(5) "Attorney" means a member of the State Bar of California. "Counsel" means an attorney.

(6) "Party" is a person appearing in an action. Parties include both self-represented persons and persons represented by an attorney of record. Any designation of a party encompasses the party's attorney of record, including "party," "petitioner," "plaintiff," "People of the State of California," "applicant," "defendant," "respondent," "other parent," "other parent/party," "protected person," and "restrained person."

(7) "Best interest of the child" is described in Family Code section 3011.

(8) "Parenting time," "visitation," and "visitation (parenting time)" refer to how parents share time with their children.

(9) "Property" includes assets and obligations.

(10) "Local rule" means every rule, regulation, order, policy, form, or standard of general application adopted by a court to govern practice and procedure in that court.

(c) Application of rules

The rules in this division apply to every action and proceeding to which the Family Code applies and, unless these rules elsewhere explicitly make them applicable, do not apply to any other action or proceeding that is not found in the Family Code.

(d) General law applicable

Except as otherwise provided in these rules, all provisions of law applicable to civil actions generally apply to a proceeding under the Family Code if they would otherwise apply to such proceeding without reference to this rule. To the extent that these rules conflict with provisions in other statutes or rules, these rules prevail.

(e) Law applicable to other proceedings

In any action under the Family Code that is not considered a "proceeding" as defined in (b), all provisions of law applicable to civil actions generally apply. Such an action must be commenced by filing an appropriate petition, and the respondent must file an appropriate response within 30 days after service of the summons and a copy of the petition.

(f) Extensions of time

The time within which any act is permitted or required to be done by a party under these rules may be extended by the court upon such terms as may be just.

(g) Implied procedures

In the exercise of the court's jurisdiction under the Family Code, if the course of proceeding is not specifically indicated by statute or these rules, any suitable process or mode of proceeding may be adopted by the court that is consistent with the spirit of the Family Code and these rules. *(Adopted, eff. Jan. 1, 2013.)*

Commentary

Relying on Family Code section 211 and former California Rules of Court, Rules 5.21, 5.106, and 5.118 (now Rules 5.2(d), 5.18, and 5.111), *In re Marriage of Guasch, 201 Cal.App.4th 942, 134 Cal.Rptr.3d 358 (2011)*, affirmed a judgment in favor of a wife, who was not the debtor spouse, that quashed a judgment creditor's writ of execution and enjoined further enforcement against community property, without requiring the wife to post an undertaking under Code of Civil Procedure section 529. *Guasch* declined to read the requirement of section 529 into Family Code section 2010(e), upon which the trial court relied in granting the wife relief.

Research References

Treatises and Practice Aids

Witkin, California Summary 10th Community Property § 241, Statutory Requirement Of Division.

Witkin, California Summary 10th Husband and Wife § 5, Generally Applicable Procedures.
Witkin, California Summary 10th Husband and Wife § 11, Family Law Rules.
Witkin, California Summary 10th Husband and Wife § 67, in General.
Witkin, California Summary 10th Husband and Wife § 82, in General.
Witkin, California Summary 10th Husband and Wife § 99, in General.
Witkin, California Summary 10th Husband and Wife § 144, in General.

Rule 5.4. Preemption; local rules and forms

Each local court may adopt local rules and forms regarding family law actions and proceedings that are not in conflict with or inconsistent with California law or the California Rules of Court. Effective January 1, 2013, local court rules and forms must comply with the Family Rules. *(Adopted, eff. Jan. 1, 2013.)*

Research References

Treatises and Practice Aids
Witkin, California Summary 10th Husband and Wife § 11, Family Law Rules.

Article 2

USE OF FORMS

Rule 5.7. Use of forms

(a) Status of family law and domestic violence forms

All forms adopted or approved by the Judicial Council for use in any proceeding under the Family Code, including any form in the FL, ADOPT, DV, and EJ series, are adopted as rules of court under the authority of Family Code section 211; article VI, section 6 of the California Constitution; and other applicable law.

(b) Forms in nonfamily law proceedings

The forms specified by this division may be used, at the option of the party, in any proceeding involving a financial obligation growing out of the relationship of parent and child or husband and wife or domestic partners, to the extent they are appropriate to that proceeding.

(c) Interstate forms

Notwithstanding any other provision of these rules, all Uniform Interstate Family Support Act forms approved by either the National Conference of Commissioners on Uniform State Laws or the U.S. Department of Health and Human Services are adopted for use in family law and other support actions in California. *(Adopted, eff. Jan. 1, 2013.)*

Research References

Treatises and Practice Aids
Witkin, California Summary 10th Husband and Wife § 12, Judicial Council Forms.

Article 3

APPEARANCE BY TELEPHONE

Rule 5.9. Appearance by telephone

(a) Application

This rule applies to all family law cases, except for actions for child support involving a local child support agency. Rule 5.324 governs telephone appearances in governmental child support cases.

(b) Telephone appearance

The court may permit a party to appear by telephone at a hearing, conference, or proceeding if the court determines that a telephone appearance is appropriate.

(c) Need for personal appearance

(1) At its discretion, the court may require a party to appear in person at a hearing, conference, or proceeding if the court determines that a personal appearance would materially assist in the determination of the proceedings or in the effective management or resolution of the particular case.

(2) If, at any time during a hearing, conference, or proceeding conducted by telephone, the court determines that a personal appearance is necessary, the court may continue the matter and require a personal appearance.

(d) Local rules

Courts may develop local rules to specify procedures regarding appearances by telephone. *(Adopted, eff. Jan. 1, 2013.)*

Research References

Treatises and Practice Aids
Witkin, California Summary 10th Husband and Wife § 11A, (New) Generally Applicable Procedures.
Witkin, California Summary 10th Parent and Child § 259A, (New) Military Deployment.

Article 4

DISCOVERY

Rule 5.12. Request for order regarding discovery

(a) Use of terms

In a family law proceeding, the term "request for order" has the same meaning as the terms "motion" or "notice of motion" when they are used in the Code of Civil Procedure.

(b) Applicable law

A request for order regarding discovery in family court is subject to the provisions for discovery motions under Code of Civil Procedure sections 2016.010 through 2036.050 and Family Code sections 2100 through 2113 regarding disclosure of assets and liabilities.

(c) Applicable rules

Discovery proceedings brought in a case under the Family Code must comply with applicable civil rules for motions, including:

(1) The format of supplemental and further discovery (rule 3.1000);

(2) Oral deposition by telephone, videoconference, or other remote electronic means (rule 3.1010);

(3) Separate statement requirements (rule 3.1345);

(4) Service of motion papers on nonparty deponent (rule 3.1346); and

(5) Sanctions for failure to provide discovery (rule 3.1348). *(Adopted, eff. Jan. 1, 2013. As amended, eff. July 1, 2016.)*

Research References

Treatises and Practice Aids

Witkin, California Summary 10th Husband and Wife § 11A, (New) Generally Applicable Procedures.

Article 5

SANCTIONS

Rule 5.14. Sanctions for violations of rules of court in family law cases

(a) Application

This sanctions rule applies to any action or proceeding brought under the Family Code.

(b) Definition

For purposes of the rules in this division:

(1) "Sanctions" means a monetary fine or penalty ordered by the court.

(2) "Person" means a party, a party's attorney, a law firm, a witness, or any other individual or entity whose consent is necessary for the disposition of the case.

(c) Sanctions imposed on a person

In addition to any other sanctions permitted by law, the court may order a person, after written notice and an opportunity to be heard, to pay reasonable monetary sanctions to the court or to an aggrieved person, or both, for failure without good cause to comply with the applicable rules. The sanction must not put an unreasonable financial burden on the person ordered to pay.

(d) Notice and procedure

Sanctions must not be imposed under this rule except on a request for order by the person seeking sanctions or on the court's own motion after the court has provided notice and an opportunity to be heard.

(1) A party's request for sanctions must:

(A) State the applicable rule of court that has been violated;

(B) Describe the specific conduct that is alleged to have violated the rule; and

(C) Identify the party, attorney, law firm, witness, or other person against whom sanctions are sought.

(2) The court on its own motion may issue an order to show cause that must:

(A) State the applicable rule of court that has been violated;

(B) Describe the specific conduct that appears to have violated the rule; and

(C) Direct the attorney, law firm, party, witness, or other person to show cause why sanctions should not be imposed for violation of the rule.

(e) Award of expenses

In addition to the sanctions awardable under this rule, the court may order the person who has violated an applicable rule of court to pay to the party aggrieved by the violation that party's reasonable expenses, including reasonable attorney's fees and costs, incurred in connection with the motion or request for order for sanctions.

(f) Order

A court order awarding sanctions must be in writing and must recite in detail the conduct or circumstances justifying the order. *(Adopted, eff. Jan. 1, 2013.)*

Commentary

This section, effective January 1, 2013, prospectively overrules the portion of *In re Marriage of Bianco, 221 Cal.App.4th 826, 164 Cal.Rptr.3d 785 (2013)*, that reversed an award of Rule 2.30(b) sanctions against an attorney and her co-counsel for pre-2013 violations of the Rules of Court on the ground that Rule 2.30 was not applicable in family law proceedings.

Research References

Forms

California Practice Guide: Rutter Family Law Forms Form 1:32, Glossary Of Common Family Law Terms, Phrases and Concepts (Enclosure to Form 1:31).

Treatises and Practice Aids

Witkin, California Summary 10th Husband and Wife § 11, Family Law Rules.

Chapter 2

PARTIES AND JOINDER OF PARTIES

Article 1

PARTIES TO PROCEEDINGS

Rule 5.16. Designation of parties

(a) Designation of parties

(1) In cases filed under the Family Code, the party starting the case is referred to as the "petitioner," and the other party is the "respondent."

(2) In local child support agency actions, the local child support agency starts the case and is the petitioner or plaintiff in the case. The parent sued by the child support agency is the "respondent" or "defendant," and the parent who is not the defendant is referred to as the "Other Parent." Every other proceeding must be prosecuted and defended in the names of the real parties in interest.

(b) **Parties to proceeding**

(1) The only persons permitted to be parties to a proceeding for dissolution, legal separation, or nullity of marriage are the spouses, except as provided in (3), a third party who is joined in the case under rule 5.24, or a local child support agency that intervenes in the case.

(2) The only persons permitted to be parties to a proceeding for dissolution, legal separation, or nullity of domestic partnership are the domestic partners, except as provided in (3), a third party who is joined in the case under rule 5.24, or a local child support agency that intervenes in the case.

(3) In a nullity proceeding, the case can be started by the spouses or domestic partners. The case may also be started by a parent or guardian, conservator, or other person specified in Family Code section 2211. For this type of case, the person starting the case is a party and the caption on all papers must be appropriately changed to reflect that fact.

(4) The only persons permitted to be parties to a proceeding under the Domestic Violence Prevention Act are those identified in Family Code section 6211.

(5) The only persons permitted to be parties to a family law proceeding to establish parentage are the presumed or putative parents of the minor child, the minor child, a third party who is joined in the case under rule 5.24, or a local child support agency that intervenes in the case. *(Adopted, eff. Jan. 1, 2013.)*

Research References

Treatises and Practice Aids

Witkin, California Summary 10th Husband and Wife § 76, in General.

Witkin, California Summary 10th Husband and Wife § 317, Nature Of Proceedings.

Rule 5.17. Other causes of action

A party in a family law proceeding may only ask that the court make orders against or involving the other party, or any other person, that are available to the party in these rules, Family Code sections 17400, 17402, and 17404, or other sections of the California Family Code. *(Adopted, eff. Jan. 1, 2013.)*

Research References

Forms

California Practice Guide: Rutter Family Law Forms Form 4:12, Request for Order to Strike Petition.

Treatises and Practice Aids

Witkin, California Summary 10th Husband and Wife § 82, in General.

Rule 5.18. Injunctive relief and reservation of jurisdiction

(a) **Injunctive relief**

When a party in a family law case applies for a court order under rule 5.92, the court may grant injunctive or other relief against or for the following persons to protect the rights of either or both parties:

(1) A person who has or claims an interest in the case;

(2) A person who would be a necessary party to a complete disposition of the issues in the case, but is not permitted to be a party under rule 5.16; or

(3) A person who is acting as a trustee, agent, custodian, or similar fiduciary with respect to any property subject to disposition by the court in the proceeding, or other matter subject to the jurisdiction of the court in the proceeding.

(b) **Reservation of jurisdiction**

If the court is unable to resolve the issue in the proceeding under the Family Code, the court may reserve jurisdiction over the particular issue until such time as the rights of such person and the parties to the proceeding under the Family Code have been determined in a separate action or proceeding. *(Adopted, eff. Jan. 1, 2013.)*

Commentary

Relying on Family Code section 211 and former California Rules of Court, Rules 5.21, 5.106, and 5.118 (now Rules 5.2(d), 5.18, and 5.111), *In re Marriage of Guasch, 201 Cal.App.4th 942, 134 Cal.Rptr.3d 358 (2011)*, affirmed a judgment in favor of a wife, who was not the debtor spouse, that quashed a judgment creditor's writ of execution and enjoined further enforcement against community property, without requiring the wife to post an undertaking under Code of Civil Procedure section 529. *Guasch* declined to read the requirement of section 529 into Family Code section 2010(e), upon which the trial court relied in granting the wife relief.

Article 2

JOINDER OF PARTIES

Rule 5.24. Joinder of persons claiming interest

A person who claims or controls an interest in any matter subject to disposition in the proceeding may be joined as a party to the family law case only as provided in this chapter.

(a) **Applicable rules**

(1) All provisions of law relating to joinder of parties in civil actions generally apply to the joinder of a person as a party to a family law case, except as otherwise provided in this chapter.

(2) The law applicable to civil actions generally governs all pleadings, motions, and other matters pertaining to that portion of the proceeding as to which a claimant has been joined as a party to the proceeding in the same manner as if a separate action or proceeding not subject to these rules had been filed, except as otherwise provided in this chapter or by the court in which the proceeding is pending.

(b) **"Claimant" defined**

For purposes of this rule, a "claimant" is an individual or an entity joined or sought or seeking to be joined as a party to the family law proceeding.

(c) **Persons who may seek joinder**

(1) The petitioner or the respondent may apply to the court for an order joining a person as a party to the case who has or claims custody or physical control of any of the minor children subject to the action, or visitation rights with respect to such children, or who has in his or her possession or

control or claims to own any property subject to the jurisdiction of the court in the proceeding.

(2) A person who has or claims custody or physical control of any of the minor children subject to the action, or visitation rights with respect to such children, may apply to the court for an order joining himself or herself as a party to the proceeding.

(3) A person served with an order temporarily restraining the use of property that is in his or her possession or control or that he or she claims to own, or affecting the custody of minor children subject to the action, or visitation rights with respect to such children, may apply to the court for an order joining himself or herself as a party to the proceeding.

(d) Form of joinder application

(1) All applications for joinder other than for an employee pension benefit plan must be made by serving and filing form a *Notice of Motion and Declaration for Joinder* (form FL–371). The hearing date must be less than 30 days from the date of filing the notice. The completed form must state with particularity the claimant's interest in the proceeding and the relief sought by the applicant, and it must be accompanied by an appropriate pleading setting forth the claim as if it were asserted in a separate action or proceeding.

(2) A blank copy of *Responsive Declaration to Motion for Joinder and Consent Order for Joinder* (form FL–373) must be served with the *Notice of Motion* and accompanying pleading.

(e) Court order on joinder

(1) *Mandatory joinder*

(A) The court must order that a person be joined as a party to the proceeding if ~~any person~~ the court discovers that person has physical custody or claims custody or visitation rights with respect to any minor child of the marriage, domestic partnership, or to any minor child of the relationship.

(B) Before ordering the joinder of a grandparent of a minor child in the proceeding under Family Code section 3104, the court must take the actions described in section 3104(a).

(2) *Permissive joinder*

The court may order that a person be joined as a party to the proceeding if the court finds that it would be appropriate to determine the particular issue in the proceeding and that the person to be joined as a party is either indispensable for the court to make an order about that issue or is necessary to the enforcement of any judgment rendered on that issue.

In deciding whether it is appropriate to determine the particular issue in the proceeding, the court must consider its effect upon the proceeding, including:

(A) Whether resolving that issue will unduly delay the disposition of the proceeding;

(B) Whether other parties would need to be joined to make an effective judgment between the parties;

(C) Whether resolving that issue will confuse other issues in the proceeding; and

(D) Whether the joinder of a party to determine the particular issue will complicate, delay, or otherwise interfere with the effective disposition of the proceeding.

(3) *Procedure upon joinder*

If the court orders that a person be joined as a party to the proceeding under this rule, the court must direct that a summons be issued on *Summons (Joinder)* (form FL–375) and that the claimant be served with a copy of *Notice of Motion and Declaration for Joinder* (form FL–371), the pleading attached thereto, the order of joinder, and the summons. The claimant has 30 days after service to file an appropriate response. *(Adopted, eff. Jan. 1, 2013. As amended, eff. Jan. 1, 2017.)*

Research References

Forms

California Practice Guide: Rutter Family Law Forms Form 3:20, Memorandum in Support Of Motion and Declaration for Joinder.

California Practice Guide: Rutter Family Law Forms Form 7:16, Memorandum in Support Of Motion and Declaration for Joinder (Nonparent Custody Claim).

California Practice Guide: Rutter Family Law Forms Form 7:19, Memorandum in Support Of Motion and Declaration for Joinder (Grandparent Visitation Claim).

California Transactions Forms--Family Law § 5:3, Rights Of Non-parents Generally.

California Transactions Forms--Family Law § 5:5, Rights Of Grand-parents and Close Relatives.

California Transactions Forms--Family Law § 3:13, Rights Of Third Parties.

Treatises and Practice Aids

Witkin, California Summary 10th Community Property § 239, Claims Of Third Parties.

Witkin, California Summary 10th Husband and Wife § 76, in General.

Witkin, California Summary 10th Husband and Wife § 78, Joinder Of Third Persons.

Witkin, California Summary 10th Husband and Wife § 82, in General.

Witkin, California Summary 10th Husband and Wife § 87, Methods Of Obtaining Orders.

Witkin, California Summary 10th Parent and Child § 268, Parties and Pleading.

Article 3

EMPLOYEE PENSION BENEFIT PLAN

Rule

Rule 5.29. Joinder of employee pension benefit plan

(a) Request for joinder

Every request for joinder of employee pension benefit plan and order and every pleading on joinder must be submitted on *Request for Joinder of Employee Benefit Plan and Order* (form FL–372) and *Pleading on Joinder—Employee Benefit Plan* (form FL–370).

(b) Summons

Every summons issued on the joinder of employee pension benefit plan must be on *Summons (Joinder)* (form FL–375).

(c) Notice of Appearance

Every notice of appearance of employee pension benefit plan and responsive pleading filed under Family Code section 2063(b) must be given on *Notice of Appearance and Response of Employee Benefit Plan* (form FL–374). *(Adopted, eff. Jan. 1, 2013.)*

Research References

Treatises and Practice Aids

Witkin, California Summary 10th Husband and Wife § 79, in General.

Chapter 3

FILING FEES AND FEE WAIVERS

Article 1

FILING FEES AND FEE WAIVERS

Rule 5.40. Filing Fees

(a) Filing fees

Parties must pay filing fees to the clerk of the court at the time the parties file papers with the court.

(b) Authority

The amount of money required to pay filing fees in family court is established by the Uniform Civil Fees and Standard Fee Schedule Act of 2005 under Government Code section 70670 et seq. and is subject to change. The act covers fees the court may charge parties to file the first papers in a family law proceeding, motions, or other papers requiring a hearing. It also covers filing fees that courts may charge in proceedings relating to child custody or visitation (parenting time) to cover the costs of maintaining mediation services under Family Code section 3160 et seq.

(c) Other fees

(1) The court must not charge filing fees that are inconsistent with law or with the California Rules of Court and may not impose any tax, charge, or penalty upon a proceeding, or the filing of any pleading allowed by law, as provided by Government Code section 68070.

(2) In the absence of a statute or rule authorizing or prohibiting a fee by the superior court for a particular service or product, the court may charge a reasonable fee not to exceed the costs of providing the service or product, if the Judicial Council approves the fee, as provided by Government Code section 70631. Approved fees must be clearly posted and accessible to the public. *(Adopted, eff. Jan. 1, 2013.)*

Research References

Treatises and Practice Aids

Witkin, California Summary 10th Husband and Wife § 12A, (New) in General.

Rule 5.41. Waiver of fees and costs

If unable to afford the costs to file an action in family court, a party may request that the court waive fees and costs. The procedure and forms needed to request an initial fee waiver in a family law action are the same as for all other civil actions, unless otherwise provided by a statute or the California Rules of Court.

(a) Forms

The forms required to request a fee waiver may be obtained from the clerk of the court, the public law library, or online at the California Courts website.

(b) Rules

Rules 3.50–3.56 of the California Rules of Court (title 3, division 2) govern fee waivers in family law cases. Parties may refer to the civil rules for information about:

(1) Applying for a fee waiver (rule 3.51);

(2) Forms for requesting a fee waiver (rule 3.51);

(3) How the court makes an order on a fee waiver application (rule 3.52);

(4) The time required for the court to grant a fee waiver (rule 3.53);

(5) The confidentiality of fee waiver applications and hearings (rule 3. 54);

(6) Court fees and costs included in an initial fee waiver (rule 3.55); and

(7) Additional court fees and costs that may be included in the fee waiver (rule 3.56). *(Adopted, eff. Jan. 1, 2013.)*

Research References

Treatises and Practice Aids

Witkin, California Summary 10th Husband and Wife § 12C, (New) Waiver Of Fees and Costs.

Article 2

SPECIAL PROCEDURES

Rule 5.43. Fee waiver denials; voided actions; dismissal

(a) Voided paperwork

The clerk of the court must void the papers that were filed with a petitioner's or respondent's fee waiver application if 10 days pass after notice of the fee waiver denial and petitioner or respondent has not:

(1) Paid the fees owed;

(2) Submitted a new *Request to Waive Court Fees* (form FW–001) if the fee waiver was denied because the first form was incomplete; or

(3) Requested a hearing using *Request for Hearing About Court Fee Waiver Order (Superior Court)* (form FW–006).

(b) Effect of voided petition or complaint; dismissal or continuation of case

(1) *No response or notice of appearance filed*

If a petition or complaint is voided under (a) and a response to the petition or complaint has not been filed, or respondent has not appeared in the action, the court may dismiss the case without prejudice. If the court dismisses the case, the clerk of the court must notify the parties.

(2) *Response or notice of appearance filed; case continuation or dismissal*

If a petition or complaint is voided and a response has been filed with the court, or respondent has appeared in the action, the court must:

(A) Review the response, or documents constituting respondent's appearance, to determine whether or how the case will proceed based on the relief requested;

(B) Notify the parties of the court's determination; and

(C) Refund filing fees paid by the respondent if the court dismisses the case.

(Adopted, eff. Jan. 1, 2013.)

Research References

Treatises and Practice Aids

Witkin, California Summary 10th Husband and Wife § 12C, (New) Waiver Of Fees and Costs.

Rule 5.45. Repayment of waived court fees and costs in family law support actions

(a) Determination of repayment required

When a judgment or support order is entered in a family law case, the court may order either party to pay all or part of the fees and costs that the court waived under Government Code section 68637. The court must consider and determine the repayment of waived fees as required by Government Code section 68637(d) and (e). The rule does not apply to actions initiated by a local child support agency.

(b) Required forms

(1) An order determining repayment of waived initial fees must be made on *Order to Pay Waived Court Fees and Costs (Superior Court)* (form FL–336). An order for payment of waived court fees must be accompanied by a blank *Application to Set Aside Order to Pay Waived Court Fees—Attachment* (form FL–337).

(2) An order granting or denying a request to set aside an order to pay waived court fees and costs must be made on *Order After Hearing on Motion to Set Aside Order to Pay Waived Court Fees (Superior Court)* (form FL–338). *(Adopted, eff. Jan. 1, 2013.)*

Research References

Treatises and Practice Aids

Witkin, California Summary 10th Husband and Wife § 12C, (New) Waiver Of Fees and Costs.

Witkin, California Summary 10th Parent and Child § 714, Preparing and Sending Record.

Rule 5.46. Waiver of fees and costs—Supreme Court or Court of Appeal

(a) Application

Rule 8.26 of the appellate rules specifies the procedure and forms for applying for an initial waiver of court fees and costs in the Supreme Court or Court of Appeal.

(b) Information

Parties may refer to rule 8.26 for information about:

(1) Applying for a fee waiver in appeals, writ proceedings, and petitions for review;

(2) Required forms requesting a fee waiver;

(3) The confidentiality of fee waiver applications and hearings;

(4) Time required for the court to grant a fee waiver; and

(5) Denial of a fee waiver application. *(Adopted, eff. Jan. 1, 2013.)*

Research References

Treatises and Practice Aids

Witkin, California Summary 10th Husband and Wife § 12C, (New) Waiver Of Fees and Costs.

Witkin, California Summary 10th Parent and Child § 714, Preparing and Sending Record.

Chapter 4

STARTING AND RESPONDING TO A FAMILY LAW CASE; SERVICE OF PAPERS

Article 1

SUMMONSES, NOTICES, AND DECLARATIONS

Rule

Rule 5.50. Papers issued by the court

(a) Issuing the summons; form

If a summons is required to commence a family law case, the clerk of the court must issue the summons using the same procedure for issuing a summons in civil actions, generally.

(1) The clerk of the court must:

(A) Issue a *Summons (Family Law)* (form FL–110) for divorces, legal separations, or annulment cases involving married persons or domestic partnerships;

(B) Issue a *Summons (Uniform Parentage—Petition for Custody and Support)* (form FL–210) for parentage or custody and support cases;

(C) Issue a *Summons (UIFSA)* (form FL–510) when a party seeks to establish or enforce child support orders from other states; and

(D) Process a *Summons and Complaint or Supplemental Complaint Regarding Parental Obligations* (form FL–600) as specified in rule 5.325.

(2) The clerk of the court must not give the original summons to the petitioner, but must maintain it in the court file, except for support cases initiated by a local child support agency.

(b) Automatic temporary family law restraining order in summons; handling by clerk

Under Family Code section 233, in proceedings for dissolution, legal separation, or nullity of a marriage or domestic partnership and in parentage proceedings, the clerk of the court must issue a summons that includes automatic temporary (standard) restraining orders.

(1) The summons and standard restraining orders must be issued and filed in the same manner as a summons in a civil action and must be served and enforced in the manner prescribed for any other restraining order.

(2) If service is by publication, the publication need not include the standard restraining orders.

(c) Individual restraining order

(1) On application of a party and as provided in the Family Code, a court may issue any individual restraining order that appears to be reasonable or necessary, including those automatic temporary restraining orders in (b) included in the family law summons under Family Code section 233.

(2) Individual restraining orders supersede the standard family law restraining orders in the Family Law and Uniform Parentage Act summonses. *(Adopted, eff. Jan. 1, 2013. As amended, eff. Jan. 1, 2016.)*

Research References

Treatises and Practice Aids

Witkin, California Summary 10th Husband and Wife § 6, Order in Summons.

Witkin, California Summary 10th Husband and Wife § 7, Other Ex Parte Orders.

Witkin, California Summary 10th Husband and Wife § 75, Process.

Rule 5.52. Declaration Under Uniform Child Custody Jurisdiction and Enforcement Act (UCCJEA)

(a) Filing requirements; application

(1) Petitioner and respondent must each complete, serve, and file a *Declaration Under Uniform Child Custody Jurisdiction and Enforcement Act (UCCJEA)* (form FL–105/GC–120) if there are children of their relationship under the age of 18 years.

(2) The form is a required attachment to the petition and response in actions for divorce, to establish parentage, or actions for custody and support of minor children.

(b) Duty to update information

In any action or proceeding involving custody of a minor child, a party has a continuing duty to inform the court if he or she obtains further information about a custody proceeding in a California court or any other court concerning a child who is named in the petition, complaint, or response. To comply with this duty, a party must file an updated UCCJEA form with the court and have it served on the other party. *(Adopted, eff. Jan. 1, 2013.)*

Research References

Treatises and Practice Aids

Witkin, California Summary 10th Parent and Child § 181, Information in First Pleading.

Article 2

INITIAL PLEADINGS

Rule 5.60. Petition or complaint; alternative relief

(a) Format

A party starting a family law case must file an appropriate petition or complaint using a form approved by the Judicial Council. Where the Judicial Council has not approved a specific petition or complaint form, the party must submit the petition or complaint in an appropriate format under Trial Court Rules, rules 2.100 through 2.119.

(b) Request for alternative relief

The petitioner or respondent may request alternative relief when filing a family law action. The request for alternative relief must be indicated in the petition or response. *(Adopted, eff. Jan. 1, 2013.)*

Research References

Treatises and Practice Aids

Witkin, California Summary 10th Husband and Wife § 83, Petition.

Witkin, California Summary 10th Husband and Wife § 84, Response.

Witkin, California Summary 10th Husband and Wife § 11A, (New) Generally Applicable Procedures.

Rule 5.62. Appearance by respondent

(a) Use of terms

In a family law proceeding, the term "request for order" has the same meaning as the terms "motion" or "notice of motion" when they are used in the Code of Civil Procedure.

(b) Appearance

Except as provided in Code of Civil Procedure section 418.10 and Family Code sections 2012 and 3409, a respondent is deemed to have made a general appearance in a proceeding when he or she files:

(1) A response or answer;

(2) A request for order to strike, under section 435 of the Code of Civil Procedure;

(3) A request for order to transfer the proceeding under section 395 of the Code of Civil Procedure; or

(4) A written notice of his or her appearance.

(c) Notice required after appearance

After appearance, the respondent or his or her attorney is entitled to notice of all subsequent proceedings of which notice is required to be given by these rules or in civil actions generally.

(d) No notice required

Where a respondent has not appeared, notice of subsequent proceedings need not be given to the respondent except as provided in these rules. *(Adopted, eff. Jan. 1, 2013. As amended, eff. July 1, 2016.)*

Rule 5.63. Request for order to quash proceeding or responsive relief

(a) Use of terms

In a family law proceeding, the term "request for order" has the same meaning as the terms "motion" or "notice of motion" when they are used in the Code of Civil Procedure.

(b) Respondent's application

Within the time permitted to file a response, the respondent may move to quash the proceeding, in whole or in part, for any of the following reasons:

(1) Lack of legal capacity to sue;

(2) Prior judgment or another action pending between the same parties for the same cause;

(3) Failure to meet the residence requirement of Family Code section 2320; or

(4) Statute of limitations in Family Code section 2211.

(c) Service of respondent's request for order to quash

The request for order to quash must be served in compliance with Code of Civil Procedure section 1005(b). If the respondent files a request for order to quash, no default may be entered, and the time to file a response will be extended until 15 days after service of the court's order denying the request for order to quash.

(d) Petitioner's application

Within 15 days after the filing of the response, the petitioner may move to quash, in whole or in part, any request for affirmative relief in the response for the grounds set forth in (a).

(e) Waiver

The parties are deemed to have waived the grounds set forth in (b) if they do not file a request for order to quash within the time frame set forth.

(f) Relief

When a request for order to quash is granted, the court may grant leave to amend the petition or response and set a date for filing the amended pleadings. The court may also dismiss the action without leave to amend. The action may also be dismissed if the request for order has been sustained with leave to amend and the amendment is not made within the time permitted by the court. *(Adopted, eff. Jan. 1, 2013. As amended, eff. July 1, 2016.)*

Research References

Forms

California Practice Guide: Rutter Family Law Forms Form 4:19, Request for Order to Quash Proceeding.

Article 3

SERVICE OF PAPERS

Rule 5.66. Proof of service

(a) Requirements to file proof of service

Parties must file with the court a completed form to prove that the other party received the petition or complaint or response to petition or complaint.

(b) Methods of proof of service.

(1) The proof of service of summons may be on a form approved by the Judicial Council or a document or pleading containing the same information required in *Proof of Service of Summons* (form FL–115).

(2) The proof of service of response to petition or complaint may be on a form approved by the Judicial Council or a document or pleading containing the same information required in *Proof of Service by Mail* (form FL–335) ~~or~~, *Proof of Personal Service* (form FL–330), or *Proof of Electronic Service* (form POS–050/EFS–050). *(Adopted, eff. Jan. 1, 2013. As amended, eff. Jan. 1, 2017.)*

Article 4

MANNER OF SERVICE

Rule 5.68. Manner of service of summons and petition; response; jurisdiction

(a) Service of summons and petition

The petitioner must arrange to serve the other party with a summons, petition, and other papers as required by one of the following methods:

(1) Personal service (Code Civ. Proc., § 415.10);

(2) Substituted service (Code Civ. Proc., § 415.20);

(3) Service by mail with a notice and acknowledgment of receipt (Code Civ. Proc., § 415.30);

(4) Service on person outside of the state (Code Civ. Proc., § 415.40);

(5) Service on a person residing outside of the United States, which must be done in compliance with service rules of the following:

(A) Hague Convention on the Service Abroad of Judicial and Extrajudicial Documents in Civil or Commercial Matters; or

(B) Inter–American Convention on Letters Rogatory and the Additional Protocol to the Inter–American Convention on Letters Rogatory.

(6) Service by posting or publication (Code Civ. Proc., §§ 415.50 and 413.30).

(b) Service of response to petition

A response to a family law petition may be served by the methods described in (a) but may also be served by mail without notice and acknowledgment of receipt.

(c) Continuing jurisdiction

The court has jurisdiction over the parties and control of all subsequent proceedings from the time of service of the summons and a copy of the petition. A general appearance of the respondent is equivalent to personal service within this state of the summons and a copy of the petition upon him or her. *(Adopted, eff. Jan. 1, 2013. As amended, eff. Jan. 1, 2014.)*

Rule 5.72. Court order for service by publication or posting when respondent's address is unknown

If the respondent cannot be found to be served a summons by any method described in Code of Civil Procedure sections 415.10 through 415.40, the petitioner may request an order for service of the summons by publication or posting under Code of Civil Procedure sections 415.50 and 413.30, respectively.

(a) Service of summons by publication or posting; forms

To request service of summons by publication or posting, the petitioner must complete and submit to the court *Application for Order for Publication or Posting* (form FL–980) and *Order for Publication or Posting* (form FL–982). Alternatively, petitioner may complete and submit it to the court pleadings containing the same information as forms FL–980 and FL–982. The petitioner must list all the reasonable diligent efforts that have been made to find and serve the respondent.

(b) Service of summons by posting; additional requirements

Service of summons by posting may be ordered only if the court finds that the petitioner is eligible for a waiver of court fees and costs.

(1) To request service by posting, the petitioner must have obtained an order waiving court fees and costs. If the petitioner's financial situation has improved since obtaining the approved order on court fee waiver, the petitioner must file a *Notice to Court of Improved Financial Situation or Settlement* (form FW–010). If the court finds that the petitioner no longer qualifies for a fee waiver, the court may order service by publication of the documents.

(2) *Proof of Service by Posting* (form FL–985) (or a pleading containing the same information as form FL–985) must be completed by the person who posted the documents and then filed with the court once posting is completed. *(Adopted, eff. Jan. 1, 2013. As amended, eff. Jan. 1, 2014.)*

Research References

Treatises and Practice Aids

Witkin, California Summary 10th Husband and Wife § 11A, (New) Generally Applicable Procedures.

Article 5

PLEADINGS AND AMENDED PLEADINGS

Rule 5.74. Pleadings and amended pleadings

(a) Definitions

(1) "Pleading" means a petition, complaint, application, objection, answer, response, notice, request for orders, statement of interest, report, or account filed in proceedings under the Family Code.

(2) "Amended pleading" means a pleading that completely restates and supersedes the pleading it amends for all purposes.

(3) "Amendment to a pleading" means a pleading that modifies another pleading and alleges facts or requests relief materially different from the facts alleged or the relief requested in the modified pleading. An amendment to a pleading does not restate or supersede the modified pleading but must be read together with that pleading.

(4) "Supplement to a pleading" and "supplement" mean a pleading that modifies another pleading but does not allege facts or request relief materially different from the facts alleged or the relief requested in the supplemented pleading. A supplement to a pleading may add information to or may correct omissions in the modified pleading.

(b) Forms of pleading

(1) The forms of pleading and the rules by which the sufficiency of pleadings is to be determined are solely those prescribed in these rules.

(2) Demurrers, motions for summary adjudication, and motions for summary judgment must not be used in family law actions.

(c) Amendment to pleadings

(1) Amendments to pleadings, amended pleadings, and supplemental pleadings may be served and filed in conformity with the provisions of law applicable to such matters in civil actions generally, but the petitioner is not required to file a reply if the respondent has filed a response.

(2) If both parties have filed initial pleadings (petition and response), there may be no default entered on an amended pleading of either party. *(Adopted, eff. Jan. 1, 2013. As amended, eff. Jan. 1, 2014.)*

Research References

Treatises and Practice Aids

Witkin, California Summary 10th Husband and Wife § 82, in General.

Witkin, California Summary 10th Husband and Wife § 84, Response.

Witkin, California Summary 10th Husband and Wife § 86, in General.

Article 6

SPECIFIC PROCEEDINGS

Rule 5.76. Domestic partnerships

To obtain a dissolution, a legal separation, or an annulment of a domestic partnership:

(1) Persons who qualify for a summary dissolution as described in the booklet *Summary Dissolution Information* (form FL–810) may act to dissolve their partnership through the California Secretary of State using forms found at *www.sos.ca.gov* or in the superior court following the procedures described in form FL–810.

(2) For persons who do not qualify for a summary dissolution proceeding, all forms and procedures used for the dissolution, legal separation, or annulment of a domestic partnership are the same as those used for the dissolution,

legal separation, or annulment of a marriage. *(Adopted, eff. Jan. 1, 2013. As amended, eff. Jan. 1, 2015.)*

Research References

Treatises and Practice Aids

Witkin, California Summary 10th Husband and Wife § 34, Termination Of Status.

Rule 5.77. Summary dissolution

(a) Declaration of disclosure

To comply with the preliminary disclosure requirements of chapter 9 (beginning with section 2100) of part 1 of division 6 of the Family Code in proceedings for summary dissolution, each joint petitioner must complete and give each other copies of the following documents before signing a property settlement agreement or completing a divorce:

(1) An *Income and Expense Declaration* (form FL–150).

(2) Either of the following documents listing separate and community property assets and obligations:

(A) *Declaration of Disclosure* (form FL–140) and either a *Schedule of Assets and Debts* or a *Property Declaration* (form FL–160) with all attachments; or

(B) The completed worksheet pages indicated in *Summary Dissolution Information* (form FL–810).

(3) A written statement of all investment, business, or other income-producing opportunities that came up after the date of separation based on investments made or work done during the marriage or domestic partnership and before the date of separation.

(4) All tax returns filed by the spouse or domestic partner in the two year period before exchanging the worksheets or forms described in (2).

(b) Fee for filing

The joint petitioners must pay one fee for filing a *Joint Petition for Summary Dissolution of Marriage* (form FL–800) unless both parties are eligible for a fee waiver order. The fee is the same as that charged for filing a *Petition—Marriage* (form FL–100). No additional fee may be charged for the filing of any form prescribed for use in a summary dissolution proceeding. *(Adopted, eff. Jan. 1, 2013. As amended, eff. July 1, 2013.)*

Research References

Treatises and Practice Aids

Witkin, California Summary 10th Community Property § 234, Scope Of Disclosure Requirements.

Witkin, California Summary 10th Husband and Wife § 126, Joint Petition.

Chapter 5

FAMILY CENTERED CASE RESOLUTION PLANS

Rule 5.83. Family centered case resolution

(a) Purpose

This rule establishes processes and procedures for courts to manage cases from initial filing to final disposition in an effective and timely manner. It is intended to advance the goals of Family Code section 2450(a) and Standards of Judicial Administration, standard 5.30.

(b) Definitions

(1) "Family centered case resolution process" refers to the process employed by the court to ensure that family law cases move through the court process from filing to final disposition in a timely, fair, and effective manner.

(2) "Disposition" refers to final judgment, dismissal, change of venue, or consolidation of the case into a lead case. Courts may continue a case in, or return a case to, the family centered case resolution process after disposition.

(3) "Status conference" refers to court events scheduled with the parties and attorneys for the purpose of identifying the current status of the case and determining the next steps required to reach disposition.

(4) "Family centered case resolution conference" refers to a conference scheduled with parties, attorneys, and a judicial officer to develop and implement a family centered case resolution plan under Family Code section 2451.

(c) Family centered case resolution process

(1) Beginning January 1, 2012, courts must develop a family centered case resolution process which must be fully implemented by January 1, 2013. The family centered case resolution process must identify and assist all dissolution, legal separation, nullity, and parentage cases to progress through the court process toward disposition effectively in a timely manner. The court may identify other family law case types to include in the family centered case resolution process.

(2) For cases filed on or after January 1, 2013, the court must include as part of the family centered case resolution process a review of all dissolution, legal separation, nullity, and parentage cases within at least 180 days from the date of the initial filing and at a minimum, at least every 180 days thereafter until disposition in order to determine the most appropriate next steps to help ensure an effective, fair, and timely resolution. Unless the court determines that procedural milestones are being met, the review must include at least one of the following: (1) a status conference or (2) a family centered case resolution conference. Nothing in this section prohibits courts from setting more frequent review dates.

(3) If, after 18 months from the date the petition was filed, both parties have failed to participate in the case resolution process as determined by the court, the court's obligation for further review of the case is relieved until the case qualifies for dismissal under Code of Civil Procedure section 583.210 or 583.310, or until the parties reactivate participation in the case, and the case is not counted toward the goals for disposition set out in (c)(5).

(4) In deciding whether a case is progressing in an effective and timely manner, the court should consider procedural milestones including the following:

(A) A proof of service of summons and petition should be filed within 60 days of case initiation;

(B) If no response has been filed, and the parties have not agreed on an extension of time to respond, a request to enter default should be submitted within 60 days after the date the response was due;

(C) The petitioner's preliminary declaration of disclosure should be served within 60 days of the filing of the petition;

(D) When a default has been entered, a judgment should be submitted within 60 days of the entry of default;

(E) Whether a trial date has been requested or scheduled; and

(F) When the parties have notified the court that they are actively negotiating or mediating their case, a written agreement for judgment is submitted within six months of the date the petition was filed, or a request for trial date is submitted.

(5) For dissolution, legal separation, and nullity cases initially filed on or after January 1, 2014, the goals of any family centered case resolution process should be to finalize dispositions as follows:

(A) At least 20 percent are disposed within 6 months from the date the petition was filed;

(B) At least 75 percent are disposed within 12 months from the date the petition was filed; and

(C) At least 90 percent are disposed within 18 months from the date the petition was filed.

(6) The court may select various procedural milestones at which to assist cases in moving toward disposition in an effective and timely manner. Types of assistance that can be provided include the following:

(A) Notifying the parties and attorneys by mail, telephone, e-mail, or other electronic method of communication of the current status of the case and the next procedural steps required to reach disposition;

(B) Implementing a schedule of status conferences for cases to identify the status of the case and determine the next steps required to progress toward disposition;

(C) Providing assistance to the parties at the time scheduled for hearings on requests for orders to identify the status of the case and determine the next steps required to reach disposition;

(D) Providing financial and property settlement opportunities to the parties and their attorneys with judicial officers or qualified attorney settlement officers;

(E) Scheduling a family centered case resolution conference to develop and implement a family centered case resolution plan under Family Code section 2451.

(7) In deciding that a case requires a family centered case resolution conference, the court should consider, in addition to procedural milestones, factors including the following:

(A) Difficulty in locating and serving the respondent;

(B) Complexity of issues;

(C) Nature and extent of anticipated discovery;

(D) Number and locations of percipient and expert witnesses;

(E) Estimated length of trial;

(F) Statutory priority for issues such as custody and visitation of minor children;

(G) Extent of property and support issues in controversy;

(H) Existence of issues of domestic violence, child abuse, or substance abuse;

(I) Pendency of other actions or proceedings that may affect the case; and

(J) Any other factor that would affect the time for disposition.

(d) Family centered case resolution conferences

(1) The court may hold an initial family centered case resolution conference to develop a specific case resolution plan. The conference is not intended to be an evidentiary hearing.

(2) Family centered case resolution conferences must be heard by a judicial officer. On the court's initiative or at the request of the parties, to enhance access to the court, the conference may be held in person, by telephone, by videoconferencing, or by other appropriate means of communication.

(3) At the conference, counsel for each party and each self-represented litigant must be familiar with the case and must be prepared to discuss the party's positions on the issues.

(4) With the exception of mandatory child custody mediation and mandatory settlement conferences, before alternative dispute resolution (ADR) is included in a family centered case resolution plan under Family Code section 2451(a)(2), the court must inform the parties that their participation in any court recommended ADR services is voluntary and that ADR services can be part of a plan only if both parties voluntarily opt to use these services. Additionally, the court must:

(A) Inform the parties that ADR may not be appropriate in cases involving domestic violence and provide information about separate sessions; and

(B) Ensure that all court-connected providers of ADR services that are part of a family centered case resolution plan have been trained in assessing and handling cases that may involve domestic violence.

(5) Nothing in this rule prohibits an employee of the court from reviewing the file and notifying the parties of any deficiencies in their paperwork before the parties appear in front of a judicial officer at a family centered case resolution conference. This type of assistance can occur by telephone, in person, in writing, or by other means approved by the court, on or before each scheduled family centered case resolution conference. However, this type of procedural assistance is not intended to replace family centered case resolution plan management or to create a barrier to litigants' access to a judicial officer.

(e) Family centered case resolution plan order

(1) Family centered case resolution plans as ordered by the court must comply with Family Code sections 2450(b) and 2451.

(2) The family centered case resolution plan order should set a schedule for subsequent family centered case resolution

conferences and otherwise provide for management of the case.

(f) Family centered case resolution order without appearance

If the court determines that appearances at a family centered case resolution conference are not necessary, the court may notify the parties and, if stipulated, issue a family centered case resolution order without an appearance at a conference.

(g) Family centered case resolution information

(1) Upon the filing of first papers in dissolution, legal separation, nullity, or parentage actions the court must provide the filing party with the following:

(A) Written information summarizing the process of a case through disposition;

(B) A list of local resources that offer procedural assistance, legal advice or information, settlement opportunities, and domestic violence services;

(C) Instructions for keeping the court informed of the person's current address and phone number, and e-mail address;

(D) Information for self-represented parties about the opportunity to meet with court self-help center staff or a family law facilitator; and

(E) Information for litigants on how to request a status conference, or a family centered case resolution conference earlier than or in addition to, any status conference or family centered case resolution conferences scheduled by the court.

(Adopted, eff. Jan. 1, 2012. As amended, eff. Jan. 1, 2016.)

Research References

Forms

West's California Judicial Council Forms FL-107-INFO, Legal Steps for a Divorce or Legal Separation.

Treatises and Practice Aids

Witkin, California Summary 10th Husband and Wife § 71, Case Management.

Chapter 6

REQUEST FOR COURT ORDERS

Article 1

GENERAL PROVISIONS

Rule 5.90. Format of papers

The rules regarding the format of a request for order are the same as the rules for format of motions in civil rules 3.1100 through 3.1116, except as otherwise provided in these Family Rules. *(Adopted, eff. Jan. 1, 2013.)*

Research References

Treatises and Practice Aids

Witkin, California Summary 10th Husband and Wife § 87, Methods Of Obtaining Orders.

Rule 5.91. Individual restraining order

On a party's request for order and as provided in the Family Code, a court may issue any individual restraining order that appears to be reasonable or necessary, including those automatic temporary restraining orders included in the family law summons. Individual orders supersede the standard family law restraining orders in the Family Law and Uniform Parentage Act summonses. *(Adopted, eff. Jan. 1, 2013. As amended, eff. Jan. 1, 2016.)*

Research References

Treatises and Practice Aids

Witkin, California Summary 10th Husband and Wife § 6, Order in Summons.

Article 2

FILING AND SERVICE

Rule 5.92. Request for court order; responsive declaration

(a) Application

(1) In a family law proceeding under the Family Code:

(A) The term "request for order" has the same meaning as the terms "motion" or "notice of motion" when they are used in the Code of Civil Procedure;

(B) A *Request for Order* (form FL–300) must be used to ask for court orders, unless another Judicial Council form has been adopted or approved for the specific request; and

(C) A *Responsive Declaration to Request for Order* (form FL–320) must be used to respond to the orders sought in form FL–300, unless another Judicial Council form has been adopted or approved for the specific purpose.

(2) In an action under the Domestic Violence Prevention Act, a *Request for Order* (form FL–300) must be used to request a modification or termination of all orders made after a hearing on *Restraining Order After Hearing* (form DV–130).

(3) In a local child support action under the Family Code, any party other than the local child support agency must use *Request for Order* (form FL–300) to ask for court orders.

(b) Request for order; required forms and filing procedure

(1) The *Request for Order* (form FL–300) must set forth facts sufficient to notify the other party of the moving party's contentions in support of the relief requested.

(2) When a party seeks orders for spousal or domestic partner support, attorney's fees and costs, or other orders relating to the parties' property or finances:

(A) The party must complete an *Income and Expense Declaration* (form FL–150) and file it with the *Request for Order* (form FL–300); and

(B) The *Income and Expense Declaration* (form FL–150) must be current, as described in rule 5.260 and include the documents specified in form FL–150 that demonstrate the party's income.

(3) When seeking child support orders:

(A) A party must complete an *Income and Expense Declaration* (form FL150) and file it with the *Request for Order* (form FL–300);

(B) The *Income and Expense Declaration* (form FL–150) must be current, as described in rule 5.260 and include the documents specified in the form that demonstrate the party's income; and

(C) A party may complete a current *Financial Statement (Simplified)* (form FL–155) instead of a current *Income and Expense Declaration* (form FL–150) only if the party meets the requirements listed in form FL–155.

(4) The moving party may be required to complete, file, and have additional forms or attachments served along with a *Request for Order* (form FL–300) when seeking court orders for child custody and visitation (parenting time), attorney's fees and costs, support, and other financial matters. For more information, see *Information Sheet for Request for Order* (form FL–300–INFO).

(5) The moving party must file the documents with the court clerk to obtain a court date and then have a filed copy served on all parties in the case within the timelines required by law.

(6) No memorandum of points and authorities need be filed with a *Request for Order* (form FL–300) unless required by the court on a case-by-case basis.

(c) Request for temporary emergency (ex parte) orders

If the moving party seeks temporary emergency orders pending the hearing, the moving party must:

(1) Comply with rules 5.151 through 5.169 of the California Rules of Court;

(2) Complete and include a proposed *Temporary Emergency (Ex Parte) Orders* (form FL–305) with the *Request for Order* (form FL–300); and

(3) Comply with specified local court procedures and/or local court rules about reserving the day for the temporary emergency hearing, submitting the paperwork to the court, and use of local forms.

(d) Request for order shortening time (for service or time until the hearing)

If the moving party seeks an order for a shorter time to serve documents or a shorter time until the hearing:

(1) The moving party must submit the request as a temporary emergency order on form FL–300 and comply with the requirements of rules 5.151 through 5.169 of the California Rules of Court; and

(2) The moving party's request must be supported by a declaration or a statement of facts showing good cause for the court to prescribe shorter times for the filing and service of the *Request for Order* (form FL–300) than the times specified in Code of Civil Procedure section 1005.

(3) The court may issue the order shortening time in the "Court Orders" section of the *Request for Order* (form FL–300).

(e) Issuance by court clerk

The court clerk's authority to issue a *Request for Order* (form FL–300) as a ministerial act is limited to those orders or notices:

(1) For the parties to attend orientation and confidential mediation or child custody recommending counseling; and

(2) That may be delegated by a judicial officer and do not require the use of judicial discretion.

(f) Request for order; service requirements

(1) The *Request for Order* (form FL–300) and appropriate documents or orders must be served in the manner specified for the service of a summons in Code of Civil Procedure sections 415.10 through 415.95, including personal service, if:

(A) The court granted temporary emergency orders pending the hearing;

(B) The responding party has not yet appeared in the case as described in rule 5.62; or

(C) The court ordered personal service on the other party.

(2) A *Request for Order* (form FL–300) must be served as specified in Family Code section 215 if filed after entry of a family law judgment or after a permanent order was made in any proceeding in which there was at issue the custody, visitation (parenting time), or support of a child.

(A) Requests to change a judgment or permanent order for custody, visitation (parenting time), or support of a child may be served by mail on the other party or parties only if the moving party can verify the other parties' current address.

(B) *Declaration Regarding Address Verification* (form FL–334) may be used as the address verification required by Family Code section 215. The completed form, or a declaration that includes the same information, must be filed with the proof of service of the *Request for Order*.

(3) All other requests for orders and appropriate documents may be served as specified in Code of Civil Procedure section 1010 et seq., including service by mail.

(4) The following blank forms must be served with a *Request for Order* (form FL–300):

(A) *Responsive Declaration to Request for Order* (form FL–320); and

(B) *Income and Expense Declaration* (form FL–150), when the requesting party is serving a competed FL–150 or FL–155.

(g) Responsive declaration to request for order; procedures

To respond to the issues raised in the *Request for Order* (form FL–300) and accompanying papers, the responding party must complete, file, and have a *Responsive Declaration to Request for Order* (form FL–320) served on all parties in the case.

(1) The *Responsive Declaration to Request for Order* (form FL–320) must set forth facts sufficient to notify the other party of the declarant's contentions in response to the request for order and in support of any relief requested.

(2) The responding party may request relief related to the orders requested in the moving papers. However, unrelated relief must be sought by scheduling a separate hearing using *Request for Order* (form FL–300) and following the filing and service requirements for a *Request for Order* described in this rule.

(3) A completed *Income and Expense Declaration* (form FL–150) must be filed with the *Responsive Declaration to Request for Order* (form FL–320) following the same requirements specified above in rule 5.92(b)(2) and (b)(3).

(4) The responding party may be required to complete, file, and serve additional forms or attachments along with a *Responsive Declaration to Request for Order* (form FL–320) when responding to a *Request for Order* (form FL–300) about child custody and visitation (parenting time), attorney fees and costs, support, and other financial matters. For more information, read *Information Sheet: Responsive Declaration to Request for Order* (form FL–320–INFO).

(5) No memorandum of points and authorities need be filed with a *Responsive Declaration to Request for Order* (form FL–320) unless required by the court on a case-by-case basis.

(6) A *Responsive Declaration to Request for Order* (form FL–320) may be served on the parties by mail, unless otherwise required by court order. *(Adopted, eff. July 1, 2012. As amended, eff. July 1, 2016.)*

Research References

Forms

West's California Judicial Council Forms FL-300, Request for Order.
West's California Judicial Council Forms FL-320, Responsive Declaration to Request for Order.

Treatises and Practice Aids

Witkin, California Summary 10th Husband and Wife § 5, Generally Applicable Procedures.
Witkin, California Summary 10th Husband and Wife § 87, Methods Of Obtaining Orders.
Witkin, California Summary 10th Husband and Wife § 199, Supporting Documents.
Witkin, California Summary 10th Husband and Wife § 200, Response.
Witkin, California Summary 10th Husband and Wife § 207, Modification.
Witkin, California Summary 10th Husband and Wife § 289, in General.
Witkin, California Summary 10th Husband and Wife § 384, Orders After Notice and Hearing.
Witkin, California Summary 10th Parent and Child § 265, Application and Decision.

Rule 5.94. Order shortening time; other filing requirements; request to continue hearing ~~and extend temporary emergency (ex parte) orders~~

(a) Order shortening time

The court, on its own motion or on application for an order shortening time supported by a declaration showing good cause, may prescribe shorter times for the filing and service of papers than the times specified in Code of Civil Procedure section 1005.

(b) Time for filing proof of service

Proof of service of the *Request for Order* (FL–300) and supporting papers should be filed five court days before the hearing date.

(c) Filing of late papers

No papers relating to a request for order or responsive declaration to the request may be rejected for filing on the ground that they were untimely submitted for filing. If the court, in its discretion, refuses to consider a late filed paper, the minutes or order must so indicate.

(d) Timely submission to court clerk

The papers requesting an order or responding to the request are deemed timely filed if they are submitted:

(1) Before the close of the court clerk's office to the public; and

(2) On or before the day the papers are due.

(e) Failure to timely serve request for order ~~and temporary emergency (ex parte) orders~~

The *Request for Order* (form FL–300) or other moving papers such as an order to show cause, along with any ~~and~~ temporary emergency (ex parte) orders~~(form FL–305)~~, will expire on the date and time of the scheduled hearing if the requesting party fails to:

(1) Have the other party timely served before the hearing with the *Request for Order* (form FL–300) or other moving papers, such as an order to show cause; supporting documents; and any ~~orders issued on~~ temporary emergency (ex parte) orders ~~(form FL–305)~~; or

(2) Obtain a court order to continue the hearing.

(f) Procedures to request continued hearing date ~~and extension of temporary emergency (ex parte) orders~~

~~(1) If a *Request for Order* (form FL–300) that includes temporary emergency orders is not timely served on the other party before the date of the hearing, and the party granted the temporary emergency (ex parte) orders wishes to proceed with the request, he or she must ask the court to continue the hearing date. On a showing of good cause, or on its own motion, the court may:~~

~~(A) Continue the hearing and extend the expiration date of the temporary emergency orders until the end of the continued hearing or to another date ordered by the court.~~

~~(B) Modify the temporary emergency (ex parte) orders.~~

~~(C) Terminate the temporary emergency (ex parte) orders.~~

~~(2) The party served with a *Request for Order* (form FL–300) that includes temporary emergency (ex parte) orders:~~

~~(A) Is entitled to one continuance for a reasonable period of time to respond and, thereafter, to a continuance based on a showing of good cause.~~

~~(B) Must file and serve a *Responsive Declaration to Request for Order* (form FL–320) as required by the court order.~~

~~(3) The following procedures apply to either party's request to continue the hearing:~~

~~(A) The party asking for the continuance must complete and submit an original *Request and Order to Continue Hearing and Extend Temporary Emergency (Ex Parte) Orders* (form FL–306) with two copies for the court to review, as follows:~~

~~(i) The form should be submitted to the court no later than five court days before the hearing date originally set on the *Request for Order*.~~

~~(ii) The party may present the form to the court at the hearing of the *Request for Order*.~~

~~(iii) The party who makes an oral request to the court on the date of the hearing is also required to complete and submit form FL–306 if the court grants the request.~~

~~(B) After the court signs and files form FL–306, a filed copy must be served on the other party, unless the court orders otherwise. If the continuance is granted:~~

~~(i) Before the other party is served with notice of the hearing and temporary emergency (ex parte) orders, then form FL–306 must be attached as the cover page and served along with the *Request for Order* (form FL–300), the original or modified temporary emergency (ex parte) orders, and supporting documents.~~

~~(ii) To the responding party, and the party who asked for the temporary emergency order was absent when the continuance was granted, then form FL–306 must be attached as the cover page to any documents the court orders served on that party.~~

~~(iii) Service must be in the manner required by rule 5.92 or as ordered by the court.~~

~~(C) If the *Request and Order to Continue Hearing and Extend Temporary Emergency (Ex Parte) Orders* (form FL–306), *Request for Order* (FL–300), original or modified temporary emergency order, and supporting documents are not timely served on the other party, and the requesting party wishes to proceed with the hearing, he or she must repeat the procedures in this rule.~~

(1) If a *Request for Order* (form FL–300), order to show cause, or other moving paper is not timely served on the other party before the date of the hearing, and the party requesting the order wishes to proceed with the request, he or she must ask the court to continue the hearing date.

(2) On a showing of good cause or on its own motion, the court may:

(A) Continue the hearing and set a new date; and

(B) Modify or terminate any temporary emergency (ex parte) orders initially granted with the *Request for Order,* order to show cause, or other moving paper.

(3) If the court grants a continuance and makes no change to the temporary emergency (ex parte) orders, those orders are extended until the time of the continued hearing or to another date specified by the court.

(4) The party served with a *Request for Order* (form FL–300), order to show cause, or other moving paper that includes temporary emergency (ex parte) orders:

(A) Is entitled to one continuance as a matter of course for a reasonable period of time to respond. A second or subsequent request by the responding party to continue the hearing must be supported by facts showing good cause for the continuance;

(B) May ask the court to continue the hearing by using *Request to Continue Hearing* (form FL–306); and

(C) Must file and serve a *Responsive Declaration to Request for Order* (form FL–320) before the date of the new hearing, as required by law or described in *Order on Request to Continue Hearing* (form FL–307).

(5) The following procedures apply to either party's request to continue the hearing:

(A) The party asking for the continuance must complete and submit an original *Request to Continue Hearing* (form FL–306) with two copies for the court to review, as follows:

(i) The form should be submitted to the court no later than five court days before the hearing date set on the *Request for Order*, order to show cause, or other moving papers.

(ii) The party may present the form to the court on the date of the hearing.

(iii) The party who, on the date of the hearing, makes an oral request to the court to continue the hearing, is not required to complete form FL–306, but must complete and submit an *Order on Request to Continue Hearing* (form FL–307) if the court grants the request.

(B) Along with form FL–306, the party asking for the continuance must submit to the court an *Order on Request to Continue Hearing* (form FL–307) with the caption and initial items completed as described on the form.

(C) After the court signs and files form FL–307, a filed copy must be served on the other party as follows, unless the court orders otherwise:

(i) If the continuance is granted, an *Order on Request to Continue Hearing* (form FL–307) must be attached as the cover page and served, along with the *Request for Order* (form FL–300) or other moving papers such as an order to show cause and any temporary emergency (ex parte) orders and supporting documents.

(ii) If the court grants the responding party's request for a continuance, and the party who asked for the order was absent when the continuance was granted, then an *Order on Request to Continue Hearing* (form FL–307) must be attached as the cover page to any documents the court orders served on that party.

(iii) Service must be in the manner required by rule 5.92 or as ordered by the court.

(D) If the *Order on Request to Continue Hearing* (form FL–307), *Request for Order* (FL–300) or order to show cause, original or modified temporary emergency (ex parte) order, and supporting documents are not timely served on the other party, and the requesting party wishes to proceed with the hearing, he or she must repeat the procedures in this rule unless the opposing party agrees to waive notice and proceed with the hearing.

(Adopted, eff. Jan. 1, 2013. As amended, eff. July 1, 2016; Sept. 1, 2017.)

Research References

Forms

West's California Judicial Council Forms FL-306/JV-251, Application and Order for Reissuance Of Request for Order / Temporary Emergency Orders / Other.

Rule 5.96. Place and manner of filing

(a) Papers filed in clerk's office

All papers relating to a request for order proceeding must be filed in the clerk's office, unless otherwise provided by local rule or court order.

(b) General schedule

The clerk must post a general schedule showing the days and departments for hearing the matters indicated in the *Request for Order* (form FL–300).

(c) Duty to notify court of settlement

If the matter has been settled before the scheduled court hearing date, the moving party must immediately notify the court of the settlement. *(Adopted, eff. Jan. 1, 2013.)*

Article 3

MEET–AND–CONFER CONFERENCES

Rule 5.98. Meet-and-confer requirements; document exchange

(a) Meet and confer

All parties and all attorneys are required to meet and confer in person, by telephone, or as ordered by the court, before the date of the hearing relating to a *Request for Order* (FL–300). During this time, parties must discuss and make a good faith attempt to settle all issues, even if a complete settlement is not possible and only conditional agreements are made. The requirement to meet and confer does not apply to cases involving domestic violence.

(b) Document exchange

Before or while conferring, parties must exchange all documentary evidence that is to be relied on for proof of any material fact at the hearing. At the hearing, the court may decline to consider documents that were not given to the other party before the hearing as required under this rule. The requirement to exchange documents does not relate to documents that are submitted primarily for rebuttal or impeachment purposes. *(Adopted, eff. Jan. 1, 2013.)*

Research References

Treatises and Practice Aids

Witkin, California Summary 10th Husband and Wife § 11A, (New) Generally Applicable Procedures.

Article 4

EVIDENCE AT HEARINGS

Rule 5.111. Declarations supporting and responding to a request for court order

Along with a *Request for Order* (form FL–300) or a *Responsive Declaration* (form FL–320), a party must file a supporting declaration with the court clerk and serve it on the other party. The declarations must comply with the following requirements:

(a) Length of declarations

A declaration included with a request for court order or a responsive declaration must not exceed 10 pages in length. A reply declaration must not exceed 5 pages in length, unless:

(1) The declaration is of an expert witness; or

(2) The court grants permission to extend the length of a declaration.

(b) Form, format, and content of declarations

(1) The form and format of each declaration submitted in a case filed under the Family Code must comply with the requirements set out in California Rules of Court, rule 2.100 et seq.

(2) A declaration must be based on personal knowledge and explain how the person has acquired that knowledge. The statements in the declaration must be admissible in evidence.

(c) Objections to declarations

(1) If a party thinks that a declaration does not meet the requirements of (b)(2) the party must file their objections in writing at least 2 court days before the time of the hearing, or any objection will be considered waived, and the declaration may be considered as evidence. Upon a finding of good cause, objections may be made in writing or orally at the time of the hearing.

(2) If the court does not specifically rule on the objection raised by a party, the objection is presumed overruled. If an appeal is filed, any presumed overrulings can be challenged. *(Adopted, eff. Jan. 1, 2013.)*

Commentary

In re Marriage of Shimkus, 244 Cal.App.4th 1262, 198 Cal.Rptr.3d 799 (2016), held that declarations in support of a request for a court order (RFO) are not automatically admitted into evidence, because Family Code section 217 requires live testimony absent a stipulation of the parties or a finding of good cause. Although this Rule of Court requires that declarations be filed in support of an RFO, those declarations are not automatically evidence that may be considered by the court in making its findings or order.

Relying on Family Code section 211 and former California Rules of Court, Rules 5.21, 5.106, and 5.118 (now Rules 5.2(d), 5.18, and 5.111), *In re Marriage of Guasch, 201 Cal.App.4th 942, 134 Cal.Rptr.3d 358 (2011)*, affirmed a judgment in favor of a wife, who was not the debtor spouse, that quashed a judgment creditor's writ of execution and enjoined further enforcement against community property, without requiring the wife to post an undertaking under Code of Civil Procedure section 529. *Guasch* declined to read the requirement of section 529 into Family Code section 2010(e), upon which the trial court relied in granting the wife relief.

In re Marriage of Shimkus, 244 Cal.App.4th 1262, 198 Cal.Rptr.3d 799 (2016), held that declarations in support of a request for a court order (RFO) are not automatically admitted into evidence, because Family Code section 217 requires live testimony absent a stipulation of the parties or a finding of good cause. Although this Rule of Court requires that declarations be filed in support of an RFO, those declarations are not automatically evidence that may be considered by the court in making its findings or order.

Research References

Treatises and Practice Aids

Witkin, California Summary 10th Husband and Wife § 87, Methods Of Obtaining Orders.

Witkin, California Summary 10th Husband and Wife § 11A, (New) Generally Applicable Procedures.

Witkin, California Summary 10th Husband and Wife § 199, Supporting Documents.

Witkin, California Summary 10th Husband and Wife § 200, Response.

Witkin, California Summary 10th Husband and Wife § 207, Modification.

Witkin, California Summary 10th Husband and Wife § 289, in General.

Rule 5.112.1. Declaration page limitation; exemptions

The Judicial Council form portion of a declaration does not count toward the page limitation for declarations specified in rule 5.111. In addition, the following documents may be attached to a *Request for Order* (form FL–300) or *Responsive Declaration* (form FL–320) without being counted toward the page limitation for declarations:

(1) An *Income and Expense Declaration* (form FL–150) and its required attachments;

(2) A *Financial Statement (Simplified)* (form FL–155) and its required attachments;

(3) A *Property Declaration* (form FL–160) and required attachments;

(4) Exhibits attached to declarations; and

(5) A memorandum of points and authorities. *(Adopted, eff. Jan. 1, 2013.)*

Rule 5.113. Live testimony

(a) Purpose

Under Family Code section 217, at a hearing on any request for order brought under the Family Code, absent a stipulation of the parties or a finding of good cause under (b), the court must receive any live, competent, and admissible testimony that is relevant and within the scope of the hearing.

(b) Factors

In addition to the rules of evidence, a court must consider the following factors in making a finding of good cause to refuse to receive live testimony under Family Code section 217:

(1) Whether a substantive matter is at issue—such as child custody, visitation (parenting time), parentage, child support, spousal support, requests for restraining orders, or the characterization, division, or temporary use and control of the property or debt of the parties;

(2) Whether material facts are in controversy;

(3) Whether live testimony is necessary for the court to assess the credibility of the parties or other witnesses;

(4) The right of the parties to question anyone submitting reports or other information to the court;

(5) Whether a party offering testimony from 1 a non-party has complied with Family Code section 217(c); and

(6) Any other factor that is just and equitable.

(c) Findings

If the court makes a finding of good cause to exclude live testimony, it must state its reasons on the record or in writing. The court is required to state only those factors on which the finding of good cause is based.

(d) Minor children

When receiving or excluding testimony from minor children, in addition to fulfilling the requirements of Evidence Code section 765, the court must follow the procedures in Family Code section 3042 and rule 5.250 of the California Rules of Court governing children's testimony.

(e) Witness lists

Witness lists required by Family Code section 217(c) must be served along with the request for order or responsive papers in the manner required for the service of those documents (*Witness List* (form FL–321) may be used for this purpose). If no witness list has been served, the court may require an offer of proof before allowing any nonparty witness to testify.

(f) Continuance

The court must consider whether or not a brief continuance is necessary to allow a litigant adequate opportunity to prepare for questioning any witness for the other parties. When a brief continuance is granted to allow time to prepare for questioning witnesses, the court should make appropriate temporary orders.

(g) Questioning by court

Whenever the court receives live testimony from a party or any witness it may elicit testimony by directing questions to the parties and other witnesses. *(Adopted, eff. Jan. 1, 2013.)*

Research References

Forms

California Practice Guide: Rutter Family Law Forms Form 5:9.1, Witness List.

West's California Judicial Council Forms FL-321, Witness List.

Treatises and Practice Aids

Witkin, California Summary 10th Husband and Wife § 5, Generally Applicable Procedures.

Rule 5.115. Judicial notice

A party requesting judicial notice of material under Evidence Code section 452 or 453 must provide the court and each party with a copy of the material. If the material is part of a file in the court in which the matter is being heard, the party must specify in writing the part of the court file sought to be judicially noticed and make arrangements with the clerk to have the file in the courtroom at the time of the hearing. *(Adopted, eff. Jan. 1, 2013.)*

Research References

Treatises and Practice Aids

Witkin, California Summary 10th Husband and Wife § 11A, (New) Generally Applicable Procedures.

Article 5

REPORTING AND PREPARATION OF ORDER AFTER HEARING

Rule 5.123. Reporting of hearing proceedings

A court that does not regularly provide for reporting of hearings on a request for order or motion must so state in its local rules. The rules must also provide a procedure by which a party may obtain a court reporter in order to provide the party with an official verbatim transcript. *(Adopted, eff. Jan. 1, 2013.)*

Research References

Treatises and Practice Aids

Witkin, California Summary 10th Husband and Wife § 11A, (New) Generally Applicable Procedures.

Rule 5.125. Preparation, service, and submission of order after hearing

The court may prepare the order after hearing and serve copies on the parties or their attorneys. Alternatively, the court may order one of the parties or attorneys to prepare the proposed order as provided in these rules. The court may also modify the timelines and procedures in this rule when appropriate to the case.

(a) In general

The term "party" or "parties" includes both self-represented persons and persons represented by an attorney of record. The procedures in this rule requiring a party to perform action related to the preparation, service, and submission of an order after hearing include the party's attorney of record.

(b) Submission of proposed order after hearing to the court

Within 10 calendar days of the court hearing, the party ordered to prepare the proposed order must:

(1) Serve the proposed order to the other party for approval; or

(2) If the other party did not appear at the hearing or the matter was uncontested, submit the proposed order directly to the court without the other party's approval. A copy must also be served to the other party or attorney.

(c) Other party approves or rejects proposed order after hearing

(1) Within 20 calendar days from the court hearing, the other party must review the proposed order to determine if it accurately reflects the orders made by the court and take one of the following actions:

(A) Approve the proposed order by signing and serving it on the party or attorney who drafted the proposed order; or

(B) State any objections to the proposed order and prepare an alternate proposed order. Any alternate proposed order prepared by the objecting party must list the findings and orders in the same sequence as the proposed order. After serving any objections and the alternate proposed order to the party or attorney, both parties must follow the procedure in (e).

(2) If the other party does not respond to the proposed order within 20 calendar days of the court hearing, the party ordered to prepare the proposed order must submit the proposed order to the court without approval within 25 calendar days of the hearing date. The correspondence to the court and to the other party must include:

(A) The date the proposed order was served on the other party;

(B) The other party's reasons for not approving the proposed order, if known;

(C) The date and results of any attempts to meet and confer, if relevant; and

(D) A request that the court sign the proposed order.

(d) Failure to prepare proposed order after hearing

(1) If the party ordered by the court to prepare the proposed order fails to serve the proposed order to the other party within 10 calendar days from the court hearing, the other party may prepare the proposed order and serve it to the party or attorney whom the court ordered to prepare the proposed order.

(2) Within 5 calendar days from service of the proposed order, the party who had been ordered to prepare the order must review the proposed order to determine if it accurately reflects the orders made by the court and take one of the following actions:

(A) Approve the proposed order by signing and serving it to the party or attorney who drafted the proposed order; or

(B) State any objections to the proposed order and prepare an alternate proposed order. Any alternate proposed order by the objecting party must list the findings and orders in the same sequence as the proposed order. After serving any objections and the alternate proposed order to the other party or attorney, both parties must follow the procedure in (e).

(3) If the party does not respond as described in (2), the party who prepared the proposed order must submit the proposed order to the court without approval within 5 calendar days. The cover letter to the court and to the other party or attorney must include:

(A) The facts relating to the preparation of the order, including the date the proposed order was due and the date the proposed order was served to the party whom the court ordered to draft the proposed order;

(B) The party's reasons for not preparing or approving the proposed order, if known;

(C) The date and results of any attempts to meet and confer, if relevant; and

(D) A request that the court sign the proposed order.

(e) Objections to proposed order after hearing

(1) If a party objects to the proposed order after hearing, both parties have 10 calendar days following service of the objections and the alternate proposed order after hearing to meet and confer by telephone or in person to attempt to resolve the disputed language.

(2) If the parties reach an agreement, the proposed findings and order after hearing must be submitted to the court within 10 calendar days following the meeting.

(3) If the parties fail to resolve their disagreement after meeting and conferring, each party will have 10 calendar days following the date of the meeting to submit to the court and serve on each other the following documents:

(A) A proposed *Findings and Order After Hearing* (FL–340) (and any form attachments);

(B) A copy of the minute order or official transcript of the court hearing; and

(C) A cover letter that explains the objections, describes the differences in the two proposed orders, references the relevant sections of the transcript or minute order, and includes the date and results of the meet25 and-confer conferences.

(f) Unapproved order signed by the court; requirements

Before signing a proposed order submitted to the court without the other party's approval, the court must first compare the proposed order after hearing to the minute order; official transcript, if available; or other court record.

(g) Service of order after hearing signed by the court

After the proposed order is signed by the court, the court clerk must file the order. The party who prepared the order must serve an endorsed-filed copy to the other party. *(Adopted, eff. Jan. 1, 2013.)*

Research References

Treatises and Practice Aids

Witkin, California Summary 10th Husband and Wife § 11A, (New) Generally Applicable Procedures.

Article 6

SPECIAL IMMIGRANT JUVENILE FINDINGS

Rule 5.130. Request for special immigrant juvenile findings

(a) Application

This rule applies to a request by or on behalf of a minor child who is a party or the child of a party in a proceeding under the Family Code for the judicial findings needed as a basis for filing a federal petition for classification as a Special Immigrant Juvenile (SIJ). This rule also applies to an opposition to such a request, a hearing on such a request or opposition, and judicial findings in response to such a request.

(b) Request for findings

Unless otherwise required by law or this rule, the rules in this chapter governing a request for court orders in family law proceedings also apply to a request for SIJ findings in those proceedings.

(1) *Who may file*

Any person—including the child's parent, the child if authorized by statute, the child's guardian ad litem, or an attorney appointed to represent the child—authorized by the Family Code to file a petition, response, request for order, or responsive declaration to a request for order in a proceeding to determine custody of a child may file a request for SIJ findings with respect to that child.

(2) *Form of request*

A request for SIJ findings must be made using *Confidential Request for Special Immigrant Juvenile Findings—Family Law* (form FL–356). The completed form may be filed in any proceeding under the Family Code in which a party is requesting sole physical custody of the child who is the subject of the requested findings:

(A) At the same time as, or any time after, the petition or response;

(B) At the same time as, or any time after, a *Request for Order* (form FL–300) or a *Responsive Declaration to Request for Order* (form FL–320) requesting sole physical custody of the child; or

(C) In an initial action under the Domestic Violence Prevention Act, at the same time as, or any time after, a *Request for Domestic Violence Restraining Order (Domestic Violence Prevention)* (form DV–100) or *Response to Request for Domestic Violence Restraining Order (Domestic Violence Prevention)* (form DV–120) requesting sole physical custody of the child.

(3) *Separate filing*

A request on form FL–356 filed at the same time as any of the papers in (A), (B), or (C) must be filed separately from, and not as an attachment to, that paper.

(4) *Separate form for each child*

A separate form FL–356 must be filed for each child for whom SIJ findings are requested.

(c) Notice of hearing

Notice of a hearing on a request for SIJ findings must be served with a copy of the request and all supporting papers in the appropriate manner specified in rule 5.92~~(a)(6)(A)–(C)~~(f)(1), (2) or (3), as applicable, on the following persons:

(1) All parties to the underlying family law case;

(2) All alleged, biological, and presumed parents of the child who is the subject of the request; and

(3) Any other person who has physical custody or is likely to claim a right to physical custody of the child who is the subject of the request.

(d) Response to request

Any person entitled under (c) to notice of a request for SIJ findings with respect to a child may file and serve a response to such a request using *Confidential Response to Request for Special Immigrant Juvenile Findings* (form FL–358).

(e) Hearing on request

To obtain a hearing on a request for SIJ findings, a person must file and serve a *Confidential Request for Special Immigrant Juvenile Findings—Family Law* (form FL–356) for each child who is the subject of such a request.

(1) A request for SIJ findings and a request for an order of sole physical custody of the same child may be heard and determined together.

(2) The court may consolidate into one hearing separate requests for SIJ findings for more than one sibling or half sibling named in the same family law case or in separate family law cases.

(3) If custody proceedings relating to siblings or half siblings are pending in multiple departments of a single court or in the courts of more than one California county, the departments or courts may communicate about consolidation consistent with the procedures and limits in Family Code section 3410(b)–(e).

(f) Separate findings for each child

The court must make separate SIJ findings with respect to each child for whom a request is made, and the clerk must issue a separate *Special Immigrant Juvenile Findings* (form FL–357) for each child with respect to whom the court makes SIJ findings.

(g) Confidentiality (Code Civ. Proc., § 155(c))

The forms *Confidential Request for Special Immigrant Juvenile Findings—Family Law* (form FL–356), *Confidential Response to Request for Special Immigrant Juvenile Findings* (form FL–358), and *Special Immigrant Juvenile Findings* (form FL–357) must be kept in a confidential part of the case file or, alternatively, in a separate, confidential file. Any information regarding the child's immigration status contained in a record related to a request for SIJ findings kept in the public part of the file must be redacted to prevent its inspection by any person not authorized under Code of Civil Procedure section 155(c). *(Adopted, eff. July 1, 2016. As amended, eff. Sept. 1, 2017.)*

Research References

Treatises and Practice Aids

Witkin, California Summary 10th Community Property § 234, Scope Of Disclosure Requirements.

Witkin, California Summary 10th Husband and Wife § 126, Joint Petition.

Chapter 7

REQUEST FOR EMERGENCY ORDERS (EX PARTE ORDERS)

Article 1

REQUEST FOR EMERGENCY ORDERS (EX PARTE ORDERS)

Rule 5.151. Request for temporary emergency (ex parte) orders; application; required documents

(a) Application

The rules in this chapter govern applications for emergency orders (also known as ex parte applications) in family law cases, unless otherwise provided by statute or rule. These rules may be referred to as "the emergency orders rules." Unless specifically stated, these rules do not apply to ex parte applications for domestic violence restraining orders under the Domestic Violence Prevention Act.

(b) Purpose

The purpose of a request for emergency orders is to address matters that cannot be heard on the court's regular hearing calendar. In this type of proceeding, notice to the other party is shorter than in other proceedings. Notice to the other party can also be waived under exceptional and other circumstances as provided in these rules. The process is used to request that the court:

(1) Make orders to help prevent an immediate danger or irreparable harm to a party or to the children involved in the matter;

(2) Make orders to help prevent immediate loss or damage to property subject to disposition in the case; or

(3) Make orders about procedural matters, including the following:

(A) Setting a date for a hearing on the matter that is sooner than that of a regular hearing (granting an order shortening time for hearing);

(B) Shortening or extending the time required for the moving party to serve the other party with the notice of the hearing and supporting papers (grant an order shortening time for service); and

(C) Continuing a hearing or trial.

(c) Required documents

A request for emergency orders must be in writing and must include all of the following completed documents:

(1) *Request for Order* (form FL–300) that identifies the relief requested.

(2) When relevant to the relief requested, a current *Income and Expense Declaration* (form FL–150) or *Financial Statement (Simplified)* (form FL–155) and *Property Declaration* (form FL–160).

(3) *Temporary Emergency (Ex Parte) Orders* (form FL–305) to serve as the proposed temporary order.

(4) A written declaration regarding notice of application for emergency orders based on personal knowledge. *Declaration Regarding Notice and Service of Request for Temporary Emergency (Ex Parte) Orders* (form FL–303), a local court form, or a declaration that contains the same information as form FL–303 may be used for this purpose.

(5) A memorandum of points and authorities only if required by the court.

(d) Contents of application and declaration

(1) *Identification of attorney or party*

An application for emergency orders must state the name, address, and telephone number of any attorney known to the applicant to be an attorney for any party or, if no such attorney is known, the name, address, and telephone number of the party, if known to the applicant.

(2) *Affirmative factual showing required in written declarations*

The declarations must contain facts within the personal knowledge of the declarant that demonstrate why the matter is appropriately handled as an emergency hearing, as opposed to being on the court's regular hearing calendar.

An applicant must make an affirmative factual showing of irreparable harm, immediate danger, or any other statutory basis for granting relief without notice or with shortened notice to the other party.

(3) *Disclosure of previous applications and orders*

An applicant should submit a declaration that fully discloses all previous applications made on the same issue and whether any orders were made on any of the applications, even if an application was previously made upon a different state of facts. Previous applications include an order to shorten time for service of notice or an order shortening time for hearing.

(4) *Disclosure of change in status quo*

The applicant has a duty to disclose that an emergency order will result in a change in the current situation or status quo. Absent such disclosure, attorney's fees and costs incurred to reinstate the status quo may be awarded.

(5) *Applications regarding child custody or visitation (parenting time)*

Applications for emergency orders granting or modifying child custody or visitation (parenting time) under Family Code section 3064 must:

(A) Provide a full, detailed description of the most recent incidents showing:

(i) Immediate harm to the child as defined in Family Code section 3064(b); or

(ii) Immediate risk that the child will be removed from the State of California.

(B) Specify the date of each incident described in (A);

(C) Advise the court of the existing custody and visitation (parenting time) arrangements and how they would be changed by the request for emergency orders;

(D) Include a copy of the current custody orders, if they are available. If no orders exist, explain where and with whom the child is currently living; and

(E) Include a completed *Declaration Under Uniform Child Custody Jurisdiction and Enforcement Act (UCCJEA)* (FL–105) if the form was not already filed by a party or if the information has changed since it was filed.

(e) Contents of notice and declaration regarding notice of emergency hearing

(1) *Contents of notice*

When notice of a request for emergency orders is given, the person giving notice must:

(A) State with specificity the nature of the relief to be requested;

(B) State the date, time, and place for the presentation of the application;

(C) State the date, time, and place of the hearing, if applicable; and

(D) Attempt to determine whether the opposing party will appear to oppose the application (if the court requires a hearing) or whether he or she will submit responsive pleadings before the court rules on the request for emergency orders.

(2) *Declaration regarding notice*

An application for emergency orders must be accompanied by a completed declaration regarding notice that includes one of the following statements:

(A) The notice given, including the date, time, manner, and name of the party informed, the relief sought, any response, and whether opposition is expected and that, within the applicable time under rule 5.165, the applicant informed the opposing party where and when the application would be made;

(B) That the applicant in good faith attempted to inform the opposing party but was unable to do so, specifying the efforts made to inform the opposing party; or

(C) That, for reasons specified, the applicant should not be required to inform the opposing party.

(Adopted, eff. Jan. 1, 2013. As amended, eff. July 1, 2016.)

Research References

Forms

West's California Judicial Council Forms FL-303, Declaration Regarding Notice and Service Of Request for Temporary Emergency (Ex Parte) Orders.

West's California Judicial Council Forms FL-305, Temporary Emergency Court Orders.

Article 2

NOTICE, SERVICE, APPEARANCE

Rule 5.165. Requirements for notice

(a) Method of notice

Notice of appearance at a hearing to request emergency orders may be given by telephone, in writing, or by voicemail message.

(b) Notice to parties

A party seeking emergency orders under this chapter must give notice to all parties or their attorneys so that it is received no later than 10:00 a.m. on the court day before the matter is to be considered by the court. After providing notice, each party must be served with the documents requesting emergency orders as described in rule 5.167 or as required by local rule. This rule does not apply to a party seeking emergency orders under the Domestic Violence Prevention Act.

(1) *Explanation for shorter notice*

If a party provided notice of the request for emergency orders to all parties and their attorneys later than 10:00 a.m. the court day before the appearance, the party must request in a declaration regarding notice that the court approve the shortened notice. The party must provide facts in the declaration that show exceptional circumstances that justify the shorter notice.

(2) *Explanation for waiver of notice (no notice)*

A party may ask the court to waive notice to all parties and their attorneys of the request for emergency orders. To make the request, the party must file a written declaration signed under penalty of perjury that includes facts showing good cause not to give the notice. A judicial officer may approve a waiver of notice for good cause, which may include that:

(A) Giving notice would frustrate the purpose of the order;

(B) Giving notice would result in immediate and irreparable harm to the applicant or the children who may be affected by the order sought;

(C) Giving notice would result in immediate and irreparable damage to or loss of property subject to disposition in the case;

(D) The parties agreed in advance that notice will not be necessary with respect to the matter that is the subject of the request for emergency orders; and

(E) The party made reasonable and good faith efforts to give notice to the other party, and further efforts to give notice would probably be futile or unduly burdensome.

(c) Notice to the court

The court may adopt a local rule requiring that the party provide additional notice to the court that he or she will be requesting emergency orders the next court day. The local rule must include a method by which the party may give notice to the court by telephone. *(Adopted, eff. Jan. 1, 2013.)*

Rule 5.167. Service of application; temporary restraining orders

(a) Service of documents requesting emergency orders

A party seeking emergency orders and a party providing written opposition must serve the papers on the other party or on the other party's attorney at the first reasonable opportunity before the hearing. Absent exceptional circumstances, no hearing may be conducted unless such service has been made. The court may waive this requirement in extraordinary circumstances if good cause is shown that imminent harm is likely if documents are provided to the other party before the hearing. This rule does not apply in cases filed under the Domestic Violence Prevention Act.

(b) Service of temporary emergency orders

If the judicial officer signs the applicant's proposed emergency orders, the applicant must obtain and have the conformed copy of the orders personally served on all parties. *(Adopted, eff. Jan. 1, 2013.)*

Rule 5.169. Personal appearance at hearing for temporary emergency orders

Courts may require all parties to appear at a hearing before ruling on a request for emergency orders. Courts may also make emergency orders based on the documents submitted without requiring the parties to appear at a hearing. *(Adopted, eff. Jan. 1, 2013.)*

Research References

Forms

West's California Judicial Council Forms FL-303, Declaration Regarding Notice and Service Of Request for Temporary Emergency (Ex Parte) Orders.

West's California Judicial Council Forms FL-305, Temporary Emergency Court Orders.

Article 3

PROCEDURAL MATTERS NOT REQUIRING NOTICE (NON–EMERGENCY ORDERS)

Rule 5.170. Matters not requiring notice to other parties

The courts may consider a party's request for order on the following issues without notice to the other parties or personal appearance at a hearing:

(1) Applications to restore a former name after judgment;

(2) Stipulations by the parties;

(3) An order or judgment after a default court hearing;

(4) An earnings assignment order based on an existing support order;

(5) An order for service of summons by publication or posting;

(6) An order or judgment that the other party or opposing counsel approved or agreed not to oppose; and

(7) Application for an order waiving filing fees. *(Adopted, eff. Jan. 1, 2013.)*

Research References

Treatises and Practice Aids

Witkin, California Summary 10th Husband and Wife § 20, After Judgment Of Dissolution or Nullity.

Witkin, California Summary 10th Husband and Wife § 11A, (New) Generally Applicable Procedures.

Witkin, California Summary 10th Husband and Wife § 12C, (New) Waiver Of Fees and Costs.

Witkin, California Summary 10th Husband and Wife § 251, Issuance Of Order.

Chapter 8

CHILD CUSTODY AND VISITATION (PARENTING TIME) PROCEEDINGS

Article 1

CHILD CUSTODY MEDIATION

Rule 5.210. Court-connected child custody mediation

(a) Authority

This rule of court is adopted under article VI, section 6 of the California Constitution and Family Code sections 211, 3160, and 3162(a).

(b) Purpose

This rule sets forth standards of practice and administration for court-connected child custody mediation services that are consistent with the requirements of Family Code section 3161.

(c) Definitions

(1) "Best interest of the child" is defined in Family Code section 3011.

(2) "Parenting plan" is a plan describing how parents or other appropriate parties will share and divide their decision making and caretaking responsibilities to protect the health, safety, welfare, and best interest of each child who is a subject of the proceedings.

(d) Responsibility for mediation services

(1) Each court must ensure that:

(A) Mediators are impartial, competent, and uphold the standards of practice contained in this rule of court.

(B) Mediation services and case management procedures implement state law and allow sufficient time for parties to receive orientation, participate fully in mediation, and develop a comprehensive parenting plan without unduly compromising each party's right to due process and a timely resolution of the issues.

(C) Mediation services demonstrate accountability by:

(i) Providing for acceptance of and response to complaints about a mediator's performance;

(ii) Participating in statewide data collection efforts; and

(iii) Disclosing the use of interns to provide mediation services.

(D) The mediation program uses a detailed intake process that screens for, and informs the mediator about, any restraining orders or safety-related issues affecting any party or child named in the proceedings to allow compliance with relevant law or court rules before mediation begins.

(E) Whenever possible, mediation is available from bilingual mediators or other interpreter services that meet the requirements of Evidence Code sections 754(f) and 755(a) and section 18 of the California Standards of Judicial Administration.

(F) Mediation services protect, in accordance with existing law, party confidentiality in:

(i) Storage and disposal of records and any personal information accumulated during the mediation process;

(ii) Interagency coordination or cooperation regarding a particular family or case; and

(iii) Management of child abuse reports and related documents.

(G) Mediation services provide a written description of limitations on the confidentiality of the process.

(H) Within one year of the adoption of this rule, the court adopts a local court rule regarding ex parte communications.

(2) Each court-connected mediator must:

(A) Maintain an overriding concern to integrate the child's best interest within the family context;

(B) Inform the parties and any counsel for a minor child if the mediator will make a recommendation to the court as provided under Family Code section 3184; and

(C) Use reasonable efforts and consider safety issues to:

(i) Facilitate the family's transition and reduce acrimony by helping the parties improve their communication skills, focus on the child's needs and areas of stability, identify the family's strengths, and locate counseling or other services;

(ii) Develop a comprehensive parenting agreement that addresses each child's current and future developmental needs; and

(iii) Control for potential power imbalances between the parties during mediation.

(e) Mediation process

All court-connected mediation processes must be conducted in accordance with state law and include:

(1) Review of the intake form and court file, if available, before the start of mediation;

(2) Oral or written orientation or parent education that facilitates the parties' informed and self-determined decision making about:

(A) The types of disputed issues generally discussed in mediation and the range of possible outcomes from the mediation process;

(B) The mediation process, including the mediator's role; the circumstances that may lead the mediator to make a particular recommendation to the court; limitations on the confidentiality of the process; and access to information communicated by the parties or included in the mediation file;

(C) How to make best use of information drawn from current research and professional experience to facilitate the mediation process, parties' communication, and co-parenting relationship; and

(D) How to address each child's current and future developmental needs;

(3) Interviews with children at the mediator's discretion and consistent with Family Code section 3180(a). The mediator may interview the child alone or together with other interested parties, including stepparents, siblings, new or step-siblings, or other family members significant to the child. If interviewing a child, the mediator must:

(A) Inform the child in an age-appropriate way of the mediator's obligation to disclose suspected child abuse and neglect and the local policies concerning disclosure of the child's statements to the court; and

(B) With parental consent, coordinate interview and information exchange among agency or private professionals to reduce the number of interviews a child might experience;

(4) Assistance to the parties, without undue influence or personal bias, in developing a parenting plan that protects the health, safety, welfare, and best interest of the child and that optimizes the child's relationship with each party by including, as appropriate, provisions for supervised visitation in high-risk cases; designations for legal and physical custody; a description of each party's authority to make decisions that affect the child; language that minimizes legal, mental health, or other jargon; and a detailed schedule of the time a child is to spend with each party, including vacations, holidays, and special occasions, and times when the child's contact with a party may be interrupted;

(5) Extension of time to allow the parties to gather additional information if the mediator determines that such information will help the discussion proceed in a fair and orderly manner or facilitate an agreement;

(6) Suspension or discontinuance of mediation if allegations of child abuse or neglect are made until a designated agency performs an investigation and reports a case determination to the mediator;

(7) Termination of mediation if the mediator believes that he or she is unable to achieve a balanced discussion between the parties;

(8) Conclusion of mediation with:

(A) A written parenting plan summarizing the parties' agreement or mediator's recommendation that is given to counsel or the parties before the recommendation is presented to the court; and

(B) A written or oral description of any subsequent case management or court procedures for resolving one or more outstanding custody or visitation issues, including instructions for obtaining temporary orders;

(9) Return to mediation to resolve future custody or visitation disputes.

(f) Training, continuing education, and experience requirements for mediator, mediation supervisor, and family court services director

As specified in Family Code sections 1815 and 1816:

(1) All mediators, mediation supervisors, and family court service directors must:

(A) Complete a minimum of 40 hours of custody and visitation mediation training within the first six months of initial employment as a court-connected mediator;

(B) Annually complete 8 hours of related continuing education programs, conferences, and workshops. This requirement is in addition to the annual 4–hour domestic violence update training described in rule 5.215; and

(C) Participate in performance supervision and peer review.

(2) Each mediation supervisor and family court services director must complete at least 24 hours of additional training each calendar year. This requirement may be satisfied in part by the domestic violence training required by Family Code section 1816.

(g) Education and training providers

Only education and training acquired from eligible providers meet the requirements of this rule. "Eligible providers" includes the Judicial Council and may include educational institutions, professional associations, professional continuing education groups, public or private for-profit or not-for-profit groups, and court-connected groups.

(1) Eligible providers must:

(A) Ensure that the training instructors or consultants delivering the education and training programs either meet the requirements of this rule or are experts in the subject matter;

(B) Monitor and evaluate the quality of courses, curricula, training, instructors, and consultants;

(C) Emphasize the importance of focusing child custody mediations on the health, safety, welfare, and best interest of the child;

(D) Develop a procedure to verify that participants complete the education and training program; and

(E) Distribute a certificate of completion to each person who has completed the training. The certificate must document the number of hours of training offered, the number of hours the person completed, the dates of the training, and the name of the training provider.

(2) Effective July 1, 2005, all education and training programs must be approved by Judicial Council staff in consultation with the Family and Juvenile Law Advisory Committee.

(h) Ethics

Mediation must be conducted in an atmosphere that encourages trust in the process and a perception of fairness. To that end, mediators must:

(1) Meet the practice and ethical standards of the Code of Ethics for the Court Employees of California and of related law;

(2) Maintain objectivity, provide and gather balanced information for both parties, and control for bias;

(3) Protect the confidentiality of the parties and the child in making any collateral contacts and not release information about the case to any individual except as authorized by the court or statute;

(4) Not offer any recommendations about a party unless that party has been evaluated directly or in consultation with another qualified neutral professional;

(5) Consider the health, safety, welfare, and best interest of the child in all phases of the process, including interviews with parents, extended family members, counsel for the child, and other interested parties or collateral contacts;

(6) Strive to maintain the confidential relationship between the child who is the subject of an evaluation and his or her treating psychotherapist;

(7) Operate within the limits of his or her training and experience and disclose any limitations or bias that would affect his or her ability to conduct the mediation;

(8) Not require children to state a custodial preference;

(9) Not disclose any recommendations to the parties, their attorneys, or the attorney for the child before having gathered the information necessary to support the conclusion;

(10) Disclose to the court, parties, attorneys for the parties, and attorney for the child conflicts of interest or dual relationships and not accept any appointment except by court order or the parties' stipulation;

(11) Be sensitive to the parties' socioeconomic status, gender, race, ethnicity, cultural values, religion, family structures, and developmental characteristics; and

(12) Disclose any actual or potential conflicts of interest. In the event of a conflict of interest, the mediator must suspend mediation and meet and confer in an effort to resolve the conflict of interest to the satisfaction of all parties or according to local court rules. The court may order mediation to continue with another mediator or offer the parties alternatives. The mediator cannot continue unless the parties agree in writing to continue mediation despite the disclosed conflict of interest. *(Formerly Rule 1257.1, adopted, eff. July 1, 2001. As amended, eff. Jan. 1, 2002. Renumbered Rule 5.210 and amended, eff. Jan. 1, 2003. As amended, eff. Jan. 1, 2005; Jan. 1, 2007; Jan. 1, 2016.)*

Research References

Forms

West's California Code Forms, Family § 3160, Comment Overview--Mediation Of Custody and Visitation Issues.

Treatises and Practice Aids

Witkin, California Summary 10th Parent and Child § 278, in General.

Rule 5.215. Domestic violence protocol for Family Court Services

(a) Authority

This rule of court is adopted under Family Code sections 211, 1850(a), and 3170(b).

(b) Purpose

This rule sets forth the protocol for Family Court Services' handling of domestic violence cases consistent with the requirement of Family Code section 3170(b).

(c) Definitions

(1) "Domestic violence" is used as defined in Family Code sections 6203 and 6211.

(2) "Protective order" is used as defined in Family Code section 6215, "Emergency protective order"; Family Code section 6218, "Protective order"; and Penal Code section 136.2 (orders by court). "Domestic violence restraining order" is synonymous with "protective order."

(3) "Mediation" refers to proceedings described in Family Code section 3161.

(4) "Evaluation" and "investigation" are synonymous terms.

(5) "Family Court Services" refers to court-connected child custody services and child custody mediation made available by superior courts under Family Code section 3160.

(6) "Family Court Services staff" refers to contract and employee mediators, evaluators, investigators, and counselors who provide services on behalf of Family Court Services.

(7) "Differential domestic violence assessment" is a process used to assess the nature of any domestic violence issues in the family so that Family Court Services may provide services in such a way as to protect any victim of domestic violence from intimidation, provide services for perpetrators, and correct for power imbalances created by past and prospective violence.

(d) Family Court Services: Description and duties

(1) *Local protocols*

Family Court Services must handle domestic violence cases in accordance with pertinent state laws and all applicable rules of court and must develop local protocols in accordance with this rule.

(2) *Family Court Services duties relative to domestic violence cases*

Family Court Services is a court-connected service that must:

(A) Identify cases in Family Court Services that involve domestic violence, and code Family Court Services files to identify such cases;

(B) Make reasonable efforts to ensure the safety of victims, children, and other parties when they are participating in services provided by Family Court Services;

(C) Make appropriate referrals; and

(D) Conduct a differential domestic violence assessment in domestic violence cases and offer appropriate services as available, such as child custody evaluation, parent education, parent orientation, supervised visitation, child custody mediation, relevant education programs for children, and other services as determined by each superior court.

(3) *No negotiation of violence*

Family Court Services staff must not negotiate with the parties about using violence with each other, whether either party should or should not obtain or dismiss a restraining order, or whether either party should cooperate with criminal prosecution.

(4) *Domestic violence restraining orders*

Notwithstanding the above, to the extent permitted under Family Code section 3183(c), in appropriate cases, Family Court Services staff may recommend that restraining orders be issued, pending determination of the controversy, to protect the well-being of the child involved in the controversy.

(5) *Providing information*

Family Court Services staff must provide information to families accessing their services about the effects of domestic violence on adults and children. Family Court Services programs, including but not limited to orientation programs, must provide information and materials that describe Family Court Services policy and procedures with respect to domestic violence. Whenever possible, information delivered in video or audiovisual format should be closed-captioned.

(6) *Separate sessions*

In a Family Court Services case in which there has been a history of domestic violence between the parties or in which a protective order as defined in Family Code section 6218 is in effect, at the request of the party who is alleging domestic violence in a written declaration under penalty of perjury or who is protected by the order, the Family Court Services mediator, counselor, evaluator, or investigator must meet with the parties separately and at separate times. When appropriate, arrangements for separate sessions must protect the confidentiality of each party's times of arrival, departure, and meeting with Family Court Services. Family Court Services must provide information to the parties regarding their options for separate sessions under Family Code sections 3113 and 3181. If domestic violence is discovered after mediation or evaluation has begun, the Family Court Services staff member assigned to the case must confer with the parties separately regarding safety-related issues and the option of continuing in separate sessions at separate times. Family Court Services staff, including support staff, must not respond to a party's request for separate sessions as though it were evidence of his or her lack of cooperation with the Family Court Services process.

(7) *Referrals*

Family Court Services staff, where applicable, must refer family members to appropriate services. Such services may include but are not limited to programs for perpetrators, counseling and education for children, parent education, services for victims, and legal resources, such as family law facilitators.

(8) *Community resources*

Family Court Services should maintain a liaison with community-based services offering domestic violence prevention assistance and support so that referrals can be made based on an understanding of available services and service providers.

(e) Intake

(1) *Court responsibility*

Each court must ensure that Family Court Services programs use a detailed intake process that screens for, and informs staff about, any restraining orders, dependency petitions under Welfare and Institutions Code section 300, and other safety-related issues affecting any party or child named in the proceedings.

(2) *Intake form*

Any intake form that an agency charged with providing family court services requires the parties to complete before the commencement of mediation or evaluation must state that, if a party alleging domestic violence in a written declaration under penalty of perjury or a party protected by a protective order so requests, the Family Court Services staff must meet with the parties separately and at separate times.

(3) *Review of intake form and case file*

All Family Court Services procedures must be conducted in accordance with state law and must include review of intake forms and court files, when available, by appropriate staff.

(f) Screening

(1) *Identification of domestic violence*

Screening for a history of domestic violence incidents must be done throughout the Family Court Services process. As early in the case as possible, Family Court Services staff should make every effort to identify cases in which incidents of domestic violence are present. The means by which Family Court Services elicits screening information may be determined by each program. Screening techniques may include but are not limited to questionnaires, telephone interviews, standardized screening devices, and face-to-face interviews.

(2) *Procedures for identification*

Procedures for identifying domestic violence may include, but are not limited to: (a) determination of an existing emergency protective order or domestic violence restraining order concerning the parties or minor; (b) review of court papers and declarations; (c) telephone interviews; (d) use of an intake form; (e) orientation; (f) information from attorneys, shelters, hospital reports, Child Protective Services, police reports, and criminal background checks; and (g) other collateral sources. Questions specific to incidents of domestic violence should request the following information: date of the parties' separation, frequency of domestic violence, most recent as well as past incidents of domestic violence, concerns about future domestic violence, identities of children and other individuals present at domestic violence incidents or otherwise exposed to the domestic violence, and severity of domestic violence.

(3) *Context for screening*

In domestic violence cases in which neither party has requested separate sessions at separate times, Family Court Services staff must confer with the parties separately and privately to determine whether joint or separate sessions are appropriate.

(g) Safety issues

(1) *Developing a safety plan*

When domestic violence is identified or alleged in a case, Family Court Services staff must consult with the party alleging domestic violence away from the presence of the party against whom such allegations are made and discuss the existence of or need for a safety plan. Safety planning may include but is not limited to discussion of safe housing, workplace safety, safety for other family members and children, access to financial resources, and information about local domestic violence agencies.

(2) *Safety procedures*

Each Family Court Services office should develop safety procedures for handling domestic violence cases.

(3) *Confidential addresses*

Where appropriate, Family Court Services staff must make reasonable efforts to keep residential addresses, work addresses, and contact information—including but not limited to telephone numbers and e-mail addresses—confidential in all cases and on all Family Court Services documents.

(h) Support persons

(1) *Support person*

Family Court Services staff must advise the party protected by a protective order of the right to have a support person attend any mediation orientation or mediation sessions, including separate mediation sessions, under Family Code section 6303.

(2) *Excluding support person*

A Family Court Services staff person may exclude a domestic violence support person from a mediation session if the support person participates in the mediation session or acts as an advocate or the presence of a particular support person disrupts the process of mediation. The presence of the support person does not waive the confidentiality of the process, and the support person is bound by the confidentiality of the process.

(i) Accessibility of services

To effectively address domestic violence cases, the court must make reasonable efforts to ensure the availability of safe and accessible services that include, but are not limited to:

(1) *Language accessibility*

Whenever possible, Family Court Services programs should be conducted in the languages of all participants, including those who are deaf. When the participants use only a language other than spoken English and the Family Court Services staff person does not speak their language, an interpreter—certified whenever possible—should be assigned to interpret at the session. A minor child of the parties must not be used as an interpreter. An adult family member may act as an interpreter only when appropriate interpreters are not available. When a family member is acting as an interpreter, Family Court Services staff should attempt to establish, away from the presence of the potential interpreter and the other party, whether the person alleging domestic violence is comfortable with having that family member interpret for the parties.

(2) *Facilities design*

To minimize contact between the parties and promote safety in domestic violence cases, courts must give consideration to the design of facilities. Such considerations must include but are not limited to the following: separate and secure waiting areas, separate conference rooms for parent education and mediation, signs providing directions to Family Court Services, and secure parking for users of Family Court Services.

(j) Training and education

(1) *Training, continuing education, and experience requirements for Family Court Services staff*

All Family Court Services staff must participate in programs of continuing instruction in issues related to domestic violence, including child abuse, as may be arranged for and provided to them, under Family Code section 1816(a).

(2) *Advanced domestic violence training*

Family Court Services staff must complete 16 hours of advanced domestic violence training within the first 12 months of employment and 4 hours of domestic violence update training each year thereafter. The content of the 16 hours of advanced domestic violence training and 4 hours of domestic violence update training must be the same as that required for court-appointed child custody investigators and evaluators as stated in rule 5.230. Those staff members employed by Family Court Services on January 1, 2002, who have not already fulfilled the requirements of rule 5.230 must participate in the 16–hour training within one year of the rule's effective date.

(3) *Support staff*

Family Court Services programs should, where possible, enable support staff, including but not limited to clerical staff, to participate in training on domestic violence and in handling domestic violence cases appropriately. *(Formerly Rule 1257.2, adopted, eff. Jan. 1, 2002. Renumbered Rule 5.215 and amended, eff. Jan. 1, 2003. As amended, eff. Jan. 1, 2007; Jan. 1, 2016.)*

Research References

Forms

California Practice Guide: Rutter Family Law Forms Form 1:32, Glossary Of Common Family Law Terms, Phrases and Concepts (Enclosure to Form 1:31).

Treatises and Practice Aids

Witkin, California Summary 10th Husband and Wife § 10A, (New) Ex Parte Communications With Mediator or Evaluator.

Witkin, California Summary 10th Husband and Wife § 370, in General.

Article 2

CHILD CUSTODY INVESTIGATIONS AND EVALUATIONS

Rule 5.220. Court-ordered child custody evaluations

(a) Authority

This rule of court is adopted under Family Code sections 211 and 3117.

(b) Purpose

Courts order child custody evaluations, investigations, and assessments to assist them in determining the health, safety, welfare, and best interest of children with regard to disputed custody and visitation issues. This rule governs both court-connected and private child custody evaluators appointed under Family Code section 3111, Evidence Code section 730, or Code of Civil Procedure section 2032.

(c) Definitions

For purposes of this rule:

(1) A "child custody evaluator" is a court-appointed investigator as defined in Family Code section 3110.

(2) The "best interest of the child" is as defined in Family Code section 3011.

(3) A "child custody evaluation" is an expert investigation and analysis of the health, safety, welfare, and best interest of children with regard to disputed custody and visitation issues.

(4) A "full evaluation, investigation, or assessment" is a comprehensive examination of the health, safety, welfare, and best interest of the child.

(5) A "partial evaluation, investigation, or assessment" is an examination of the health, safety, welfare, and best interest of the child that is limited by court order in either time or scope.

(6) "Evaluation," "investigation," and "assessment" are synonymous.

(d) Responsibility for evaluation services

(1) Each court must:

(A) Adopt a local rule by January 1, 2000, to:

(i) Implement this rule of court;

(ii) Determine whether a peremptory challenge to a court-appointed evaluator is allowed and when the challenge must be exercised. The rules must specify whether a family court services staff member, other county employee, a mental health professional, or all of them may be challenged;

(iii) Allow evaluators to petition the court to withdraw from a case;

(iv) Provide for acceptance of and response to complaints about an evaluator's performance; and

(v) Address ex parte communications.

(B) Give the evaluator, before the evaluation begins, a copy of the court order that specifies:

(i) The appointment of the evaluator under Evidence Code section 730, Family Code section 3110, or Code of Civil Procedure 2032; and

(ii) The purpose and scope of the evaluation.

(C) Require child custody evaluators to adhere to the requirements of this rule.

(D) Determine and allocate between the parties any fees or costs of the evaluation.

(2) The child custody evaluator must:

(A) Consider the health, safety, welfare, and best interest of the child within the scope and purpose of the evaluation as defined by the court order;

(B) Strive to minimize the potential for psychological trauma to children during the evaluation process; and

(C) Include in the initial meeting with each child an age-appropriate explanation of the evaluation process, including limitations on the confidentiality of the process.

(e) Scope of evaluations

All evaluations must include:

(1) A written explanation of the process that clearly describes the:

(A) Purpose of the evaluation;

(B) Procedures used and the time required to gather and assess information and, if psychological tests will be used, the role of the results in confirming or questioning other information or previous conclusions;

(C) Scope and distribution of the evaluation report;

(D) Limitations on the confidentiality of the process; and

(E) Cost and payment responsibility for the evaluation.

(2) Data collection and analysis that are consistent with the requirements of Family Code section 3118; that allow the evaluator to observe and consider each party in comparable ways and to substantiate (from multiple sources when possible) interpretations and conclusions regarding each child's developmental needs; the quality of attachment to each parent and that parent's social environment; and reactions to the separation, divorce, or parental conflict. This process may include:

(A) Reviewing pertinent documents related to custody, including local police records;

(B) Observing parent-child interaction (unless contraindicated to protect the best interest of the child);

(C) Interviewing parents conjointly, individually, or both conjointly and individually (unless contraindicated in cases involving domestic violence), to assess:

(i) Capacity for setting age-appropriate limits and for understanding and responding to the child's needs;

(ii) History of involvement in caring for the child;

(iii) Methods for working toward resolution of the child custody conflict;

(iv) History of child abuse, domestic violence, substance abuse, and psychiatric illness; and

(v) Psychological and social functioning;

(D) Conducting age-appropriate interviews and observation with the children, both parents, stepparents, step- and half-siblings conjointly, separately, or both conjointly and separately, unless contraindicated to protect the best interest of the child;

(E) Collecting relevant corroborating information or documents as permitted by law; and

(F) Consulting with other experts to develop information that is beyond the evaluator's scope of practice or area of expertise.

(3) A written or oral presentation of findings that is consistent with Family Code section 3111, Family Code section 3118, or Evidence Code section 730. In any presentation of findings, the evaluator must:

(A) Summarize the data-gathering procedures, information sources, and time spent, and present all relevant information, including information that does not support the conclusions reached;

(B) Describe any limitations in the evaluation that result from unobtainable information, failure of a party to cooperate, or the circumstances of particular interviews;

(C) Only make a custody or visitation recommendation for a party who has been evaluated. This requirement does not preclude the evaluator from making an interim recommendation that is in the best interest of the child; and

(D) Provide clear, detailed recommendations that are consistent with the health, safety, welfare, and best interest of the child if making any recommendations to the court regarding a parenting plan.

(f) Cooperation with professionals in another jurisdiction

When one party resides in another jurisdiction, the custody evaluator may rely on another qualified neutral professional for assistance in gathering information. In order to ensure a thorough and comparably reliable out-of-jurisdiction evaluation, the evaluator must:

(1) Make a written request that includes, as appropriate:

(A) A copy of all relevant court orders;

(B) An outline of issues to be explored;

(C) A list of the individuals who must or may be contacted;

(D) A description of the necessary structure and setting for interviews;

(E) A statement as to whether a home visit is required;

(F) A request for relevant documents such as police records, school reports, or other document review; and

(G) A request that a written report be returned only to the evaluator and that no copies of the report be distributed to parties or attorneys;

(2) Provide instructions that limit the out-of-jurisdiction report to factual matters and behavioral observations rather than recommendations regarding the overall custody plan; and

(3) Attach and discuss the report provided by the professional in another jurisdiction in the evaluator's final report.

(g) Requirements for evaluator qualifications, training, continuing education, and experience

All child custody evaluators must meet the qualifications, training, and continuing education requirements specified in Family Code sections 1815, 1816, and 3111, and rules 5.225 and 5.230.

(h) Ethics

In performing an evaluation, the child custody evaluator must:

(1) Maintain objectivity, provide and gather balanced information for both parties, and control for bias;

(2) Protect the confidentiality of the parties and children in collateral contacts and not release information about the case to any individual except as authorized by the court or statute;

(3) Not offer any recommendations about a party unless that party has been evaluated directly or in consultation with another qualified neutral professional;

(4) Consider the health, safety, welfare, and best interest of the child in all phases of the process, including interviews with parents, extended family members, counsel for the child, and other interested parties or collateral contacts;

(5) Strive to maintain the confidential relationship between the child who is the subject of an evaluation and his or her treating psychotherapist;

(6) Operate within the limits of the evaluator's training and experience and disclose any limitations or bias that would affect the evaluator's ability to conduct the evaluation;

(7) Not pressure children to state a custodial preference;

(8) Inform the parties of the evaluator's reporting requirements, including, but not limited to, suspected child abuse and neglect and threats to harm one's self or another person;

(9) Not disclose any recommendations to the parties, their attorneys, or the attorney for the child before having gathered the information necessary to support the conclusion;

(10) Disclose to the court, parties, attorney for a party, and attorney for the child conflicts of interest or dual relationships; and not accept any appointment except by court order or the parties' stipulation; and

(11) Be sensitive to the socioeconomic status, gender, race, ethnicity, cultural values, religion, family structures, and developmental characteristics of the parties.

(i) Service of the evaluation report

A *Notice Regarding Confidentiality of Child Custody Evaluation Report* (form FL–328) must be attached as the first page of the child custody evaluation report when a court-ordered child custody evaluation report is filed with the clerk of the court and served on the parties or their attorneys, and any counsel appointed for the child, to inform them of the confidential nature of the report and the potential consequences for the unwarranted disclosure of the report.

(j) Cost-effective procedures for cross-examination of evaluators

Each local court must develop procedures for expeditious and cost-effective cross-examination of evaluators, including, but not limited to, consideration of the following:

(1) Videoconferences;

(2) Telephone conferences;

(3) Audio or video examination; and

(4) Scheduling of appearances. *(Formerly Rule 1257.3, adopted, eff. Jan. 1, 1999. As amended, eff. July 1, 1999. Renumbered Rule 5.220 and amended, eff. Jan. 1, 2003. As amended, eff. July 1, 2003; Jan. 1, 2004; Jan. 1, 2007; Jan. 1, 2010.)*

Commentary

In 2015, Family Code section 3111 was amended to overrule *In re Marriage of Winternitz, 235 Cal.App.4th 644, 185 Cal.Rptr.3d 458 (2015), review denied* (affirming a trial court order denying a mother's request to strike a defective child custody evaluation report).

In re Marriage of Adams, 209 Cal.App.4th 1543, 148 Cal.Rptr.3d 83 (2012), reversed (1) an order denying a father's motion to remove a child custody evaluator who had acted outside the scope of an Evidence Code section 730 evaluation and had demonstrated bias against the father; and (2) the resultant order modifying custody.

When a child custody evaluator demonstrated bias in favor of one parent, *Leslie O. v. Superior Court, 231 Cal.App.4th 1191, 180 Cal.Rptr.3d 863 (2014)*, invoking subsection (h)(1), held that the trial court erred in denying the other parent's motion to remove the child custody evaluator and strike the evaluator's report.

Research References

Forms

California Practice Guide: Rutter Family Law Forms Form 7:5, Stipulation Appointing Child Custody Evaluator (Attorney-Drafted).

California Practice Guide: Rutter Family Law Forms Form 7:8, Notice Regarding Confidentiality Of Child Custody Evaluation Report.

California Practice Guide: Rutter Family Law Forms Form 1:32, Glossary Of Common Family Law Terms, Phrases and Concepts (Enclosure to Form 1:31).

California Transactions Forms--Family Law § 2:70, Deciding Custody.

West's California Judicial Council Forms FL-327, Order Appointing Child Custody Evaluator.

West's California Judicial Council Forms FL-328, Notice Regarding Confidentiality Of Child Custody Evaluation Report.

West's California Judicial Council Forms FL-329-INFO, Child Custody Evaluation Information Sheet.

Treatises and Practice Aids

Witkin, California Summary 10th Parent and Child § 253, Move-Away Cases.

Witkin, California Summary 10th Parent and Child § 275, in General.
Witkin, California Summary 10th Parent and Child § 276, Report.

Rule 5.225. Appointment requirements for child custody evaluators

(a) Purpose

This rule provides the licensing, education and training, and experience requirements for child custody evaluators who are appointed to conduct full or partial child custody evaluations under Family Code sections 3111 and 3118, Evidence Code section 730, or chapter 15 (commencing with section 2032.010) of title 4 of part 4 of the Code of Civil Procedure. This rule is adopted as mandated by Family Code section 3110.5.

(b) Definitions

For purposes of this rule:

(1) A "child custody evaluator" is a court-appointed investigator as defined in Family Code section 3110.

(2) A "child custody evaluation" is an investigation and analysis of the health, safety, welfare, and best interest of a child with regard to disputed custody and visitation issues conducted under Family Code sections 3111 and 3118, Evidence Code section 730, or Code of Civil Procedure section 2032.010 et seq.

(3) A "full evaluation, investigation, or assessment" is a child custody evaluation that is a comprehensive examination of the health, safety, welfare, and best interest of the child.

(4) A "partial evaluation, investigation, or assessment" is a child custody evaluation that is limited by the court in terms of its scope.

(5) The terms "evaluation," "investigation," and "assessment" are synonymous.

(6) "Best interest of the child" is described in Family Code section 3011.

(7) A "court-connected evaluator" is a superior court employee or a person under contract with a superior court who conducts child custody evaluations.

(c) Licensing requirements

A person appointed as a child custody evaluator meets the licensing criteria established by Family Code section 3110.5(c)(1)–(5), if:

(1) The person is licensed as a:

(A) Physician and is either a board certified psychiatrist or has completed a residency in psychiatry;

(B) Psychologist;

(C) Marriage and family therapist; or

(D) Clinical social worker.

(2) A person may be appointed as an evaluator even if he or she does not have a license as described in (c)(1) if:

(A) The court certifies that the person is a court-connected evaluator who meets all the qualifications specified in (j); or

(B) The court finds that all the following criteria have been met:

(i) There are no licensed or certified evaluators who are willing and available, within a reasonable period of time, to perform child custody evaluations;

(ii) The parties stipulate to the person; and

(iii) The court approves the person.

(d) Education and training requirements

Before appointment, a child custody evaluator must complete 40 hours of education and training, which must include all the following topics:

(1) The psychological and developmental needs of children, especially as those needs relate to decisions about child custody and visitation;

(2) Family dynamics, including, but not limited to, parent-child relationships, blended families, and extended family relationships;

(3) The effects of separation, divorce, domestic violence, child sexual abuse, child physical or emotional abuse or neglect, substance abuse, and interparental conflict on the psychological and developmental needs of children and adults;

(4) The assessment of child sexual abuse issues required by Family Code section 3118; local procedures for handling child sexual abuse cases; the effect that court procedures may have on the evaluation process when there are allegations of child sexual abuse; and the areas of training required by Family Code section 3110.5(b)(2)(A)–(F), as listed below:

(A) Children's patterns of hiding and disclosing sexual abuse in a family setting;

(B) The effects of sexual abuse on children;

(C) The nature and extent of sexual abuse;

(D) The social and family dynamics of child sexual abuse;

(E) Techniques for identifying and assisting families affected by child sexual abuse; and

(F) Legal rights, protections, and remedies available to victims of child sexual abuse;

(5) The significance of culture and religion in the lives of the parties;

(6) Safety issues that may arise during the evaluation process and their potential effects on all participants in the evaluation;

(7) When and how to interview or assess adults, infants, and children; gather information from collateral sources; collect and assess relevant data; and recognize the limits of data sources' reliability and validity;

(8) The importance of addressing issues such as general mental health, medication use, and learning or physical disabilities;

(9) The importance of staying current with relevant literature and research;

(10) How to apply comparable interview, assessment, and testing procedures that meet generally accepted clinical, forensic, scientific, diagnostic, or medical standards to all parties;

(11) When to consult with or involve additional experts or other appropriate persons;

(12) How to inform each adult party of the purpose, nature, and method of the evaluation;

(13) How to assess parenting capacity and construct effective parenting plans;

(14) Ethical requirements associated with the child custody evaluator's professional license and rule 5.220;

(15) The legal context within which child custody and visitation issues are decided and additional legal and ethical standards to consider when serving as a child custody evaluator;

(16) The importance of understanding relevant distinctions among the roles of evaluator, mediator, and therapist;

(17) How to write reports and recommendations, where appropriate;

(18) Mandatory reporting requirements and limitations on confidentiality;

(19) How to prepare for and give court testimony;

(20) How to maintain professional neutrality and objectivity when conducting child custody evaluations; and

(21) The importance of assessing the health, safety, welfare, and best interest of the child or children involved in the proceedings.

(e) Additional training requirements

In addition to the requirements described in this rule, before appointment, child custody evaluators must comply with the basic and advanced domestic violence training requirements described in rule 5.230.

(f) Authorized education and training

The education and training described in (d) must be completed:

(1) After January 1, 2000;

(2) Through an eligible provider under this rule; and

(3) By either:

(A) Attending and participating in an approved course; or

(B) Serving as an instructor in an approved course. Each course taught may be counted only once. Instructors may claim and receive credit for only actual classroom time.

(g) Experience requirements

To satisfy the experience requirements of this rule, persons appointed as child custody evaluators must have participated in the completion of at least four partial or full court-appointed child custody evaluations within the preceding three years, as described below. Each of the four child custody evaluations must have resulted in a written or an oral report.

(1) The child custody evaluator participates in the completion of the child custody evaluations if the evaluator:

(A) Independently conducted and completed the child custody evaluation; or

(B) Materially assisted another child custody evaluator who meets all the following criteria:

(i) Licensing or certification requirements in (c);

(ii) Education and training requirements in (d);

(iii) Basic and advanced domestic violence training in (e);

(iv) Experience requirements in (g)(1)(A) or (g)(2); and

(v) Continuing education and training requirements in (h).

(2) The court may appoint an individual to conduct the child custody evaluation who does not meet the experience requirements described in (1), if the court finds that all the following criteria have been met:

(A) There are no evaluators who meet the experience requirements of this rule who are willing and available, within a reasonable period of time, to perform child custody evaluations;

(B) The parties stipulate to the person; and

(C) The court approves the person.

(3) Those who supervise court-connected evaluators meet the requirements of this rule by conducting or materially assisting in the completion of at least four partial or full court-connected child custody evaluations in the preceding three years.

(h) Appointment eligibility

After completing the licensing requirements in (c), the initial education and training requirements described in (d) and (e), and the experience requirements in (g), a person is eligible for appointment as a child custody evaluator.

(i) Continuing education and training requirements

(1) After a child custody evaluator completes the initial education and training requirements described in (d) and (e), the evaluator must complete these continuing education and training requirements to remain eligible for appointment:

(A) Domestic violence update training described in rule 5.230; and

(B) Eight hours of update training covering the subjects described in (d).

(2) The time frame for completing continuing education and training in (1) is as follows:

(A) A newly trained court-connected or private child custody evaluator who recently completed the education and training in (d) and (e) must:

(i) Complete the continuing education and training requirements of this rule within 18 months from the date he or she completed the initial education and training; and

(ii) Specify on form FL–325 or FL–326 the date by which he or she must complete the continuing education and training requirements of this rule.

(B) All other court-connected or private child custody evaluators must complete the continuing education and training requirements in (1) as follows:

(i) Court-connected child custody evaluators must complete the continuing education and training requirements within the 12–month period immediately preceding the date he or she signs the *Declaration of Court–Connected Child Custody Evaluator Regarding Qualifications* (form FL–325), which must be submitted as provided by (*l*) of this rule.

(ii) Private child custody evaluators must complete the continuing education and training requirements within the 12–month period immediately preceding his or her appointment to a case.

(3) Compliance with the continuing education and training requirements of this rule is determined at the time of appointment to a case.

(j) Court–connected evaluators

A court-connected evaluator who does not meet the education and training requirements in (d) may conduct child custody evaluations if, before appointment, he or she:

(1) Completed at least 20 of the 40 hours of education and training required by (d);

(2) Completes the remaining hours of education and training required by (d) within 12 months of conducting his or her first evaluation as a court-connected child custody evaluator;

(3) Complied with the basic and advanced domestic violence training requirements under Family Code sections 1816 and 3110.5 and rule 5.230;

(4) Complies with the experience requirements in (g); and

(5) Is supervised by a court-connected child custody evaluator who meets the requirements of this rule.

(k) Responsibility of the courts

Each court:

(1) Must develop local court rules that:

(A) Provide for acceptance of and response to complaints about an evaluator's performance; and

(B) Establish a process for informing the public about how to find qualified evaluators in that jurisdiction;

(2) Must use an *Order Appointing Child Custody Evaluator* (form FL–327) to appoint a private child custody evaluator or a court-connected evaluation service. Form FL–327 may be supplemented with local court forms;

(3) Must provide the Judicial Council with a copy of any local court forms used to implement this rule;

(4) As feasible and appropriate, may confer with education and training providers to develop and deliver curricula of comparable quality and relevance to child custody evaluations for both court-connected and private child custody evaluators; and

(5) Must use form *Declaration of Court–Connected Child Custody Evaluator Regarding Qualifications* (form FL–325) to certify that court-connected evaluators have met all the qualifications for court-connected evaluators under this rule for a given year. Form FL–325 may be supplemented with local court rules or forms.

***(l)* Child custody evaluator**

A person appointed as a child custody evaluator must:

(1) Submit to the court a declaration indicating compliance with all applicable education, training, and experience requirements:

(A) Court-connected child custody evaluators must submit a *Declaration of Court–Connected Child Custody Evaluator Regarding Qualifications* (form FL–325) to the court executive officer or his or her designee. Court-connected child custody evaluators practicing as of January 1 of a given year must submit the form by January 30 of that year. Court-connected evaluators beginning practice after January 1 must submit the form before any work on the first child custody evaluation has begun and by January 30 of every year thereafter; and

(B) Private child custody evaluators must complete a *Declaration of Private Child Custody Evaluator Regarding Qualifications* (form FL–326) and file it with the clerk's office no later than 10 days after notification of each appointment and before any work on each child custody evaluation has begun;

(2) At the beginning of the child custody evaluation, inform each adult party of the purpose, nature, and method of the evaluation, and provide information about the evaluator's education, experience, and training;

(3) Use interview, assessment, and testing procedures that are consistent with generally accepted clinical, forensic, scientific, diagnostic, or medical standards;

(4) Have a license in good standing if licensed at the time of appointment, except as described in (c)(2) and Family Code section 3110.5(d);

(5) Be knowledgeable about relevant resources and service providers; and

(6) Before undertaking the evaluation or at the first practical moment, inform the court, counsel, and parties of possible or actual multiple roles or conflicts of interest.

(m) Use of interns

Court-connected and court-appointed child custody evaluators may use interns to assist with the child custody evaluation, if:

(1) The evaluator:

(A) Before or at the time of appointment, fully discloses to the parties and attorneys the nature and extent of the intern's participation in the evaluation;

(B) Obtains the written agreement of the parties and attorneys as to the nature and extent of the intern's participation in the evaluation after disclosure;

(C) Ensures that the extent, kind, and quality of work performed by the intern being supervised is consistent with the intern's training and experience;

(D) Is physically present when the intern interacts with the parties, children, or other collateral persons in the evaluation; and

(E) Ensures compliance with all laws and regulations governing the professional practice of the supervising evaluator and the intern.

(2) The interns:

(A) Are enrolled in a master's or doctorate program or have obtained a graduate degree qualifying for licensure or certification as a clinical social worker, marriage and family therapist, psychiatrist, or psychologist;

(B) Are currently completing or have completed the coursework necessary to qualify for their degree in the subjects of child abuse assessment and spousal or partner abuse assessment; and

(C) Comply with the applicable laws related to the practice of their profession in California when interns are:

(i) Accruing supervised professional experience as defined in the California Code of Regulations; and

(ii) Providing professional services for a child custody evaluator that fall within the lawful scope of practice as a licensed professional.

(n) Education and training providers

"Eligible providers" includes the Judicial Council and may include educational institutions, professional associations, professional continuing education groups, public or private for-profit or not-for-profit groups, and court-connected groups. Eligible providers must:

(1) Ensure that the training instructors or consultants delivering the training and education programs either meet the requirements of this rule or are experts in the subject matter;

(2) Monitor and evaluate the quality of courses, curricula, training, instructors, and consultants;

(3) Emphasize the importance of focusing child custody evaluations on the health, safety, welfare, and best interest of the child;

(4) Develop a procedure to verify that participants complete the education and training program;

(5) Distribute a certificate of completion to each person who has completed the training. The certificate must document the number of hours of training offered, the number of hours the person completed, the dates of the training, and the name of the training provider; and

(6) Meet the approval requirements described in (*o*).

(*o*) Program approval required

All education and training programs must be approved by Judicial Council staff in consultation with the Family and Juvenile Law Advisory Committee. Education and training courses that were taken between January 1, 2000, and July 1, 2003, may be applied toward the requirements of this rule if they addressed the subjects listed in (d) and either were certified or approved for continuing education credit by a professional provider group or were offered as part of a related postgraduate degree or licensing program. *(Formerly Rule 1257.4, adopted, eff. Jan. 1, 2002. Renumbered Rule 5.225 eff. Jan. 1, 2003. As amended, eff. Jan. 1, 2005; Jan. 1, 2007; Jan. 1, 2011; Jan. 1, 2015; Jan. 1, 2016.)*

Research References

Forms

West's California Code Forms, Family § 3111 Form 2, Declaration Of Court-Connected Child Custody Evaluator Regarding Qualifications.

West's California Judicial Council Forms FL-325, Declaration Of Court-Connected Child Custody Evaluator Regarding Qualifications.

West's California Judicial Council Forms FL-326, Declaration Of Private Child Custody Evaluator Regarding Qualifications.

Treatises and Practice Aids

Witkin, California Summary 10th Parent and Child § 275, in General.

Rule 5.230. Domestic violence training standards for court-appointed child custody investigators and evaluators

(a) Authority

This rule of court is adopted under Family Code sections 211 and 3111(d) and (e).

(b) Purpose

Consistent with Family Code sections 3020 and 3111, the purposes of this rule are to require domestic violence training for all court-appointed persons who evaluate or investigate child custody matters and to ensure that this training reflects current research and consensus about best practices for conducting child custody evaluations by prescribing standards that training in domestic violence must meet. Effective January 1, 1998, no person may be a court-appointed investigator under Family Code section 3111(d) or Evidence Code section 730 unless the person has completed domestic violence training described here and in Family Code section 1816.

(c) Definitions

For purposes of this rule, "court-appointed investigator" is considered to be synonymous with "court-appointed evaluator" as defined in Family Code section 3110.

(d) Mandatory training

Persons appointed as child custody investigators under Family Code section 3110 or Evidence Code section 730, and persons who are professional staff or trainees in a child custody or visitation evaluation or investigation, must complete basic training in domestic violence issues as described in Family Code section 1816 and, in addition:

(1) *Advanced training*

Sixteen hours of advanced training must be completed within a 12–month period. The training must include the following:

(A) Twelve hours of instruction, as approved by Judicial Council staff, in:

(i) The appropriate structuring of the child custody evaluation process, including, but not limited to, maximizing safety for clients, evaluators, and court personnel; maintaining objectivity; providing and gathering balanced information from both parties and controlling for bias; providing for separate sessions at separate times (as specified in Family Code section 3113); and considering the impact of the evaluation report and recommendations with particular attention to the dynamics of domestic violence;

(ii) The relevant sections of local, state, and federal law or rules;

(iii) The range, availability, and applicability of domestic violence resources available to victims, including, but not limited to, battered women's shelters, specialized counseling, drug and alcohol counseling, legal advocacy, job training, parenting classes, battered immigrant victims, and welfare exceptions for domestic violence victims;

(iv) The range, availability, and applicability of domestic violence intervention available to perpetrators, including, but not limited to, arrest, incarceration, probation, applicable Penal Code sections (including Penal Code section 1203.097, which describes certified treatment programs for batterers), drug and alcohol counseling, legal advocacy, job training, and parenting classes; and

(v) The unique issues in family and psychological assessment in domestic violence cases, including the following concepts:

a. The effects of exposure to domestic violence and psychological trauma on children; the relationship between child physical abuse, child sexual abuse, and domestic violence; the differential family dynamics related to parent-child attachments in families with domestic violence; intergenerational transmission of familial violence; and manifestations of post-traumatic stress disorders in children;

b. The nature and extent of domestic violence, and the relationship of gender, class, race, culture, and sexual orientation to domestic violence;

c. Current legal, psychosocial, public policy, and mental health research related to the dynamics of family violence, the impact of victimization, the psychology of perpetration, and the dynamics of power and control in battering relationships;

d. The assessment of family history based on the type, severity, and frequency of violence;

e. The impact on parenting abilities of being a victim or perpetrator of domestic violence;

f. The uses and limitations of psychological testing and psychiatric diagnosis in assessing parenting abilities in domestic violence cases;

g. The influence of alcohol and drug use and abuse on the incidence of domestic violence;

h. Understanding the dynamics of high-conflict relationships and abuser/victim relationships;

i. The importance of, and procedures for, obtaining collateral information from probation departments, children's protective services, police incident reports, restraining order pleadings, medical records, schools, and other relevant sources;

j. Accepted methods for structuring safe and enforceable child custody and parenting plans that assure the health, safety, welfare, and best interest of the child, and safeguards for the parties; and

k. The importance of discouraging participants in child custody matters from blaming victims of domestic violence for the violence and from minimizing allegations of domestic violence, child abuse, or abuse against any family member.

(B) Four hours of community resource networking intended to acquaint the evaluator with domestic violence resources in the geographical communities where the families being evaluated may reside.

(2) *Annual update training*

Four hours of update training are required each year after the year in which the advanced training is completed. These four hours must consist of instruction focused on, but not limited to, an update of changes or modifications in local court practices, case law, and state and federal legislation related to domestic violence, and an update of current social science research and theory, particularly in regard to the impact on children of exposure to domestic violence.

(e) Education and training providers

Only education and training acquired from eligible providers meets the requirements of this rule. "Eligible providers" includes the Judicial Council and may include educational institutions, professional associations, professional continuing education groups, public or private for-profit or not-for-profit groups, and court-connected groups.

(1) Eligible providers must:

(A) Ensure that the training instructors or consultants delivering the education and training programs either meet the requirements of this rule or are experts in the subject matter;

(B) Monitor and evaluate the quality of courses, curricula, training, instructors, and consultants;

(C) Emphasize the importance of focusing child custody evaluations on the health, safety, welfare, and best interest of the child;

(D) Develop a procedure to verify that participants complete the education and training program; and

(E) Distribute a certificate of completion to each person who has completed the training. The certificate must document the number of hours of training offered, the number of hours the person completed, the dates of the training, and the name of the training provider.

(2) Effective July 1, 2005, all education and training programs must be approved by Judicial Council staff in consultation with the Family and Juvenile Law Advisory Committee.

(f) Local court rules

Each local court may adopt rules regarding the procedures by which child custody evaluators who have completed the training in domestic violence as mandated by this rule will notify the local court. In the absence of such a local rule of court, child custody evaluators must attach copies of their certificates of completion of the initial 12 hours of advanced instruction and of the most recent annual 4–hour update training in domestic violence to each child custody evaluation report.

(g) Previous training accepted

Persons attending training programs offered after January 1, 1996, that meet all of the requirements set forth in subdivision (d)(1)(A) of this rule are deemed to have met the minimum standards set forth in subdivision (d)(1)(A) of this rule, but they must still meet the minimum standards listed in subdivisions (d)(1)(B) and (d)(2) of this rule. *(Formerly Rule 1257.7, adopted, eff. Jan. 1, 1999. As amended, eff. Jan. 1, 2002. Renumbered Rule 5.230 and amended, eff. Jan. 1, 2003. As amended, eff. Jan. 1, 2004; Jan. 1, 2005; Jan. 1, 2007; Jan. 1, 2016.)*

Research References

Forms

California Transactions Forms--Family Law § 2:70, Deciding Custody.

West's California Judicial Council Forms FL-325, Declaration Of Court-Connected Child Custody Evaluator Regarding Qualifications.

West's California Judicial Council Forms FL-326, Declaration Of Private Child Custody Evaluator Regarding Qualifications.

Treatises and Practice Aids

Witkin, California Summary 10th Husband and Wife § 370, in General.

Witkin, California Summary 10th Parent and Child § 275, in General.

Article 3

EX PARTE COMMUNICATION

Rule 5.235. Ex parte communication in child custody proceedings

(a) Purpose

Generally, ex parte communication is prohibited in legal proceedings. In child custody proceedings, Family Code section 216 recognizes specific circumstances in which ex parte communication is permitted between court-connected or court-appointed child custody mediators or evaluators and the attorney for any party, the court-appointed counsel for a child, or the court. This rule of court establishes mandatory statewide standards of practice relating to when, and between whom, ex parte communication is permitted in child custody proceedings. This rule applies to all court-ordered child custody mediations or evaluations. As in Family Code section 216, this rule of court does not restrict communications between a court-connected or court-appointed child custody mediator or evaluator and a party in a child custody proceeding who is self-represented or represented by counsel.

(b) Definitions

For purposes of this rule,

(1) "Communication" includes any verbal statement made in person, by telephone, by voicemail, or by videoconferencing; any written statement, illustration, photograph, or other tangible item, contained in a letter, document, e-mail, or fax; or other equivalent means, either directly or through third parties.

(2) "Ex parte communication" is a direct or indirect communication on the substance of a pending case without the knowledge, presence, or consent of all parties involved in the matter.

(3) A "court-connected mediator or evaluator" is a superior court employee or a person under contract with a superior court who conducts child custody evaluations or mediations.

(4) A "court-appointed mediator or evaluator" is a professional in private practice appointed by the court to conduct a child custody evaluation or mediation.

(c) Ex parte communication prohibited

In any child custody proceeding under the Family Code, ex parte communication is prohibited between court-connected or court-appointed mediators or evaluators and the attorney for any party, a court-appointed counsel for a child, or the court, except as provided by this rule.

(d) Exception for parties' stipulation

The parties may enter into a stipulation either in open court or in writing to allow ex parte communication between a court-connected or court-appointed mediator or evaluator and:

(1) The attorney for any party; or

(2) The court.

(e) Ex parte communication permitted

In any proceeding under the Family Code, ex parte communication is permitted between a court-connected or court-appointed mediator or evaluator and (1) the attorney for any party, (2) the court-appointed counsel for a child, or (3) the court, only if:

(1) The communication is necessary to schedule an appointment;

(2) The communication is necessary to investigate or disclose an actual or potential conflict of interest or dual relationship as required under rule 5.210(h)(10) and (h)(12);

(3) The court-appointed counsel for a child is interviewing a mediator as provided by Family Code section 3151(c)(5);

(4) The court expressly authorizes ex parte communication between the mediator or evaluator and court-appointed counsel for a child in circumstances other than described in (3); or

(5) The mediator or evaluator is informing the court of the belief that a restraining order is necessary to prevent an imminent risk to the physical safety of the child or party.

(f) Exception for mandated duties and responsibilities

This rule does not prohibit ex parte communication for the purpose of fulfilling the duties and responsibilities that:

(1) A mediator or evaluator may have as a mandated reporter of suspected child abuse;

(2) A mediator or evaluator may have to warn of threatened violent behavior against a reasonably identifiable victim or victims;

(3) A mediator or evaluator may have to address a case involving allegations of domestic violence under Family Code sections 3113, 3181, and 3192 and rule 5.215; and

(4) The court may have to investigate complaints. *(Adopted, eff. July 1, 2006. As amended, eff. Jan. 1, 2007.)*

Research References

Treatises and Practice Aids

Witkin, California Summary 10th Husband and Wife § 10A, (New) Ex Parte Communications With Mediator or Evaluator.

Witkin, California Summary 10th Parent and Child § 275, in General.

Witkin, California Summary 10th Parent and Child § 278, in General.

Article 4

COUNSEL APPOINTED TO REPRESENT A CHILD

Rule 5.240. Appointment of counsel to represent a child in family law proceedings

(a) Appointment considerations

In considering appointing counsel under Family Code section 3150, the court should take into account the following factors, including whether:

(1) The issues of child custody and visitation are highly contested or protracted;

(2) The child is subjected to stress as a result of the dispute that might be alleviated by the intervention of counsel representing the child;

(3) Counsel representing the child would be likely to provide the court with relevant information not otherwise readily available or likely to be presented;

(4) The dispute involves allegations of physical, emotional, or sexual abuse or neglect of the child.

(5) It appears that one or both parents are incapable of providing a stable, safe, and secure environment;

(6) Counsel is available for appointment who is knowledgeable about the issues being raised regarding the child in the proceeding;

(7) The best interest of the child appears to require independent representation; and

(8) If there are two or more children, any child would require separate counsel to avoid a conflict of interest.

(b) Request for appointment of counsel

The court may appoint counsel to represent the best interest of a child in a family law proceeding on the court's own motion or if requested to do so by:

(1) A party;

(2) The attorney for a party;

(3) The child, or any relative of the child;

(4) A mediator under Family Code section 3184;

(5) A professional person making a custody recommendation under Family Code sections 3111 and 3118, Evidence Code section 730, or Code of Civil Procedure section 2032.010 et seq.;

(6) A county counsel, district attorney, city attorney, or city prosecutor authorized to prosecute child abuse and neglect or child abduction cases under state law; or

(7) A court-appointed guardian ad litem or special advocate;

(8) Any other person who the court deems appropriate.

(c) Orders appointing counsel for a child

The court must issue written orders when appointing and terminating counsel for a child.

(1) The appointment orders must specify the:

(A) Appointed counsel's name, address, and telephone number;

(B) Name of the child for whom counsel is appointed; and

(C) Child's date of birth.

(2) The appointment orders may include the:

(A) Child's address, if appropriate;

(B) Issues to be addressed in the case;

(C) Tasks related to the case that would benefit from the services of counsel for the child;

(D) Responsibilities and rights of the child's counsel;

(E) Counsel's rate or amount of compensation;

(F) Allocation of fees payable by each party or the court;

(G) Source of funds and manner of reimbursement for counsel's fees and costs;

(H) Allocation of payment of counsel's fees to one party subject to reimbursement by the other party;

(I) Terms and amount of any progress or installment payments; and

(J) Ability of the court to reserve jurisdiction to retroactively modify the order on fees and payment.

(3) Courts may use *Order Appointing Counsel for a Child* (form FL–323) or may supplement form FL–323 with local forms developed under rule 10.613.

(d) Panel of counsel eligible for appointment

(1) Each court may create and maintain a list or panel of counsel meeting the minimum qualifications of this rule for appointment.

(2) If a list or panel of counsel is maintained, a court may appoint counsel not on the list or panel in special circumstances, taking into consideration factors including language, culture, and the special needs of a child in the following areas:

(A) Child abuse;

(B) Domestic violence;

(C) Drug abuse of a parent or the child;

(D) Mental health issues of a parent or the child;

(E) Particular medical issues of the child; and

(F) Educational issues.

(3) If the court maintains a panel of counsel eligible for appointment and the court appoints counsel who is not on the panel, the court must state the reason for not appointing a panel counsel in writing or on the record.

(4) Any lists maintained from which the court might appoint counsel should be reviewed at least annually to ensure that those on the list meet the education and training requirements. Courts should ask counsel annually to update their information and to notify the court if any changes would make them unable to be appointed.

(e) Complaint procedures

By January 1, 2010, each court must develop local court rules in accordance with rule 10.613 that provide for acceptance and response to complaints about the performance of the court-appointed counsel for a child.

(f) Termination of appointment

On entering an appearance on behalf of a child, counsel must continue to represent that child until:

(1) The conclusion of the proceeding for which counsel was appointed;

(2) Relieved by the court;

(3) Substituted by the court with other counsel;

(4) Removed on the court's own motion or request of counsel or parties for good cause shown; or

(5) The child reaches the age of majority or is emancipated. *(Adopted, eff. Jan. 1, 2008. As amended, eff. Jan. 1, 2013.)*

Commentary

Applying Family Code section 3150, *In re Marriage of Metzger, 224 Cal.App.4th 1441, 169 Cal.Rptr.3d 382 (2014), review denied,* held that judicial appointment of counsel to represent the parties' minor child in a custody dispute did not violate the father's constitutional rights. Moreover, Metzger held that the trial court did not abuse its discretion in appointing counsel, because at least four of this Rule's subsection (a) factors favored the appointment of counsel.

Research References

Forms

California Transactions Forms--Family Law § 2:72, Counsel for the Children.

West's California Judicial Council Forms FL-323, Order Appointing Counsel for a Child.

West's California Judicial Council Forms FL-321-INFO, Attorney for Child in a Family Law Case--Information Sheet.

Treatises and Practice Aids

Witkin, California Summary 10th Parent and Child § 272, in General.

Rule 5.241. Compensation of counsel appointed to represent a child in a family law proceeding

(a) Determination of counsel's compensation

The court must determine the reasonable sum for compensation and expenses for counsel appointed to represent the child in a family law proceeding, and the ability of the parties to pay all or a portion of counsel's compensation and expenses.

(1) The court must set the compensation for the child's counsel:

(A) At the time of appointment;

(B) At the time the court determines the parties' ability to pay; or

(C) Within a reasonable time after appointment.

(2) No later than 30 days after counsel is relieved as attorney of record, the court may make a redetermination of counsel's compensation:

(A) On the court's own motion;

(B) At the request of a party or a party's counsel; or

(C) At the request of counsel for the child.

(b) Determination of ability to pay

The court must determine the respective financial ability of the parties to pay all or a portion of counsel's compensation.

(1) Before determining the parties' ability to pay:

(A) The court should consider factors such as the parties' income and assets reasonably available at the time of the determination, and eligibility for or existence of a fee waiver under Government Code section 68511.3; and

(B) The parties must have on file a current *Income and Expense Declaration* (form FL–150) or *Financial Statement (Simplified)* (form FL–155).

(2) The court should determine the parties' ability to pay:

(A) At the time counsel is appointed;

(B) Within 30 days after appointment; or

(C) At the next subsequent hearing.

(3) No later than 30 days after counsel is relieved as attorney of record, the court may redetermine the parties' ability to pay:

(A) On the court's own motion; or

(B) At the request of counsel or the parties.

(c) Payment to counsel

(1) If the court determines that the parties have the ability to pay all or a portion of the fees, the court must order that the parties pay in any manner the court determines to be reasonable and compatible with the parties' financial ability, including progress or installment payments.

(2) The court may use its own funds to pay counsel for a child and seek reimbursement from the parties.

(3) The court must inform the parties that the failure to pay fees to the appointed counsel or to the court may result in the attorney or the court initiating legal action against them to collect the money.

(d) Parties' inability to pay

If the court finds that the parties are unable to pay all or a portion of the cost of the child's counsel, the court must pay the portion the parties are unable to pay. *(Adopted, eff. Jan. 1, 2008.)*

Research References

Forms

California Transactions Forms--Family Law § 2:72, Counsel for the Children.

West's California Judicial Council Forms FL-323, Order Appointing Counsel for a Child.

West's California Judicial Council Forms FL-321-INFO, Attorney for Child in a Family Law Case--Information Sheet.

Treatises and Practice Aids

Witkin, California Summary 10th Parent and Child § 272, in General.

Rule 5.242. Qualifications, rights, and responsibilities of counsel appointed to represent a child in family law proceedings

(a) Purpose

This rule governs counsel appointed to represent the best interest of the child in a custody or visitation proceeding under Family Code section 3150.

(b) General appointment requirements

To be eligible for appointment as counsel for a child, counsel must:

(1) Be an active member in good standing of the State Bar of California;

(2) Have professional liability insurance or demonstrate to the court that he or she is adequately self-insured; and

(3) Meet the education, training, and experience requirements of this rule.

(c) Education and training requirements

Effective January 1, 2009, before being appointed as counsel for a child in a family law proceeding, counsel must have completed at least 12 hours of applicable education and training which must include all the following subjects:

(1) Statutes, rules of court, and case law relating to child custody and visitation litigation;

(2) Representation of a child in custody and visitation proceedings;

(3) Special issues in representing a child, including the following:

(A) Various stages of child development;

(B) Communicating with a child at various developmental stages and presenting the child's view;

(C) Recognizing, evaluating and understanding evidence of child abuse and neglect, family violence and substance abuse, cultural and ethnic diversity, and gender-specific issues;

(D) The effects of domestic violence and child abuse and neglect on children; and

(E) How to work effectively with multidisciplinary experts.

(d) Annual education and training requirements

Effective January 1, 2010, to remain eligible for appointment as counsel for a child, counsel must complete during each calendar year a minimum of eight hours of applicable education and training in the subjects listed in (c).

(e) Applicable education and training

(1) Education and training that addresses the subjects listed in (c) may be applied toward the requirements of this rule if completed through:

(A) A professional continuing education group;

(B) An educational institution;

(C) A professional association;

(D) A court-connected group; or

(E) A public or private for-profit or not-for-profit group.

(2) A maximum of two of the hours may be by self-study under the supervision of an education provider that provides evidence of completion.

(3) Counsel may complete education and training courses that satisfy the requirements of this rule offered by the education providers in (1) by means of video presentations or other delivery means at remote locations. Such courses are not self-study within the meaning of this rule.

(4) Counsel who serve as an instructor in an education and training course that satisfies the requirements of this rule may receive 1.5 hours of course participation credit for each hour of course instruction. All other counsel may claim credit for actual time he or she attended the education and training course.

(f) Experience requirements

(1) Persons appointed as counsel for a child in a family law proceeding must have represented a party or a child in at least six proceedings involving child custody within the preceding five years as follows:

(A) At least two of the six proceedings must have involved contested child custody and visitation issues in family law; and

(B) Child custody proceedings in dependency or guardianship cases can count for no more than three of the six required for appointment.

(2) Courts may develop local rules that impose additional experience requirements for persons appointed as counsel for a child in a family law proceeding.

(g) Alternative experience requirements

Counsel who does not meet the initial experience requirements in (f) may be appointed to represent a child in a family law proceeding if he or she meets one of the following alternative experience requirements. Counsel must:

(1) Be employed by a legal services organization, a governmental agency, or a private law firm that has been approved by the presiding or supervising judge of the local family court as qualified to represent a child in family law proceedings and be directly supervised by an attorney in an organization, an agency, or a private law firm who meets the initial experience requirements in (f);

(2) Be an attorney working in consultation with an attorney approved by the presiding or supervising judge of the local family court as qualified to represent a child in family law proceedings; or

(3) Demonstrate substantial equivalent experience as determined by local court rule or procedure.

(h) Compliance with appointment requirements

A person appointed as counsel for a child must:

(1) File a declaration with the court indicating compliance with the requirements of this rule no later than 10 days after being appointed and before beginning work on the case. Counsel may complete the *Declaration of Counsel for a Child Regarding Qualifications* (form FL–322) or other local court forms for this purpose; and

(2) Notify the court within five days of any disciplinary action taken by the State Bar of California, stating the basis of the complaint, result, and notice of any reproval, probation, or suspension.

(i) Rights of counsel for a child

Counsel has rights relating to the representation of a child's best interest under Family Code sections 3111, 3151, 3151.5, 3153, and Welfare and Institutions Code section 827, which include the right to:

(1) Reasonable access to the child;

(2) Seek affirmative relief on behalf of the child;

(3) Notice to any proceeding, and all phases of that proceeding, including a request for examination affecting the child;

(4) Take any action that is available to a party to the proceeding, including filing pleadings, making evidentiary objections, and presenting evidence;

(5) Be heard in the proceeding, which may include presenting motions and orders to show cause and participating in settlement conferences and trials, seeking writs, appeals, and arbitrations;

(6) Access the child's medical, dental, mental health, and other health-care records, and school and educational records;

(7) Inspect juvenile case files subject to the provisions of Welfare and Institutions Code section 827;

(8) Interview school personnel, caretakers, health-care providers, mental health professionals, and others who have assessed the child or provided care to the child; however, the release of this information to counsel does not constitute a waiver of the confidentiality of the reports, files, and any disclosed communications;

(9) Interview mediators, subject to the provisions of Family Code sections 3177 and 3182;

(10) Receive reasonable advance notice of and the right to refuse any physical or psychological examination or evaluation, for purposes of the proceeding, that has not been ordered by the court;

(11) Assert or waive any privilege on behalf of the child;

(12) Seek independent psychological or physical examination or evaluation of the child for purposes of the proceeding on approval by the court;

(13) Receive child custody evaluation reports;

(14) Not be called as a witness in the proceedings;

(15) Request the court to authorize release of relevant reports or files, concerning the child represented by the counsel, of the relevant local child protective services agency; and

(16) Receive reasonable compensation and expenses for representing the child, the amount of which will be determined by the court.

(j) Responsibilities of counsel for a child

Counsel is charged with the representation of the child's best interest. The role of the child's counsel is to gather evidence that bears on the best interest of the child and present that admissible evidence to the court in any manner appropriate for the counsel of a party. If the child so desires, the child's counsel must present the child's wishes to the court.

(1) Counsel's duties, unless under the circumstances it is inappropriate to exercise the duties, include those under Family Code section 3151:

(A) Interviewing the child;

(B) Reviewing the court files and all accessible relevant records available to both parties; and

(C) Making any further investigations that counsel considers necessary to ascertain the facts relevant to the custody or visitation hearings.

(2) Counsel must serve notices and pleadings on all parties consistent with the requirements for parties.

(3) Counsel may introduce and examine witnesses, present arguments to the court concerning the child's welfare, and participate further in the proceeding to the degree necessary to represent the child adequately.

(4) In any case in which counsel is representing a child who is called to testify in the proceeding, counsel must:

(A) Provide information to the child in an age-appropriate manner about the limitations on confidentiality and the possibility that information provided to the court may be on the record and provided to the parties in the case;

(B) Allow but not require the child to state a preference regarding custody or visitation and, in an age-appropriate manner, provide information about the process by which the court will make a decision;

(C) Provide procedures relevant to the child's participation and, if appropriate, provide an orientation to the courtroom where the child will be testifying; and

(D) Inform the parties and then the court about the client's desire to provide input.

(k) Other considerations

Counsel is not required to assume the responsibilities of a social worker, probation officer, child custody evaluator, or mediator and is not expected to provide nonlegal services to the child. Subject to the terms of the court's order of appointment, counsel for a child may take the following actions to implement his or her statutory duties in representing a child in a family law proceeding:

(1) Interview or observe the child as appropriate to the age and circumstances of the child. In doing so, counsel should consider all possible interview or observation environments and select a location most conducive to both conducting a meaningful interview of the child and investigating the issues relevant to the case at that time.

(2) In a manner and to the extent consistent with the child's age, level of maturity, and ability to understand, and consistent with the order of appointment for the case:

(A) Explain to the child at their first meeting counsel's role and the nature of the attorney-client relationship (including confidentiality issues); and

(B) Advise the child on a continuing basis of possible courses of action and of the risks and benefits of each course of action.

(3) Actively participate in the representation of the child at any hearings that affect custody and visitation of the child and attend and participate in any other hearings relevant to the child. In doing so, counsel may, as appropriate:

(A) Take positions relevant to the child on legal issues before the court;

(B) Seek and advocate for services for the child;

(C) Prepare for any hearings or trials;

(D) Work to settle contested issues and to define trial issues;

(E) Prepare witnesses, including the child if the child is to testify;

(F) Introduce and examine witnesses on behalf of the child;

(G) Cross–examine other witnesses;

(H) Make appropriate evidentiary objections;

(I) Review court files and other pertinent records;

(J) Prepare motions to advance the child's interest, including motions to quash subpoenas for the child and other protective orders;

(K) Present arguments to advance the child's interest;

(L) Prepare trial briefs and other documents if appropriate; and

(M) Request appointment of separate appellate counsel.

(4) Conduct thorough, continuing, and independent investigations and discovery to protect the child's interest, which may include:

(A) Obtaining necessary authorizations for the release of information.

(B) Reviewing the child's social services, mental health, drug and alcohol, medical, law enforcement, education, and other records relevant to the case;

(C) Reviewing the court files of the child and his or her siblings, case-related records of the social service agency, and case-related records of other service providers;

(D) Contacting attorneys for the parties and nonlawyer guardians ad litem, Court Appointed Special Advocates (CASAs), and other service professionals, to the extent permitted by local rule, for background information;

(E) Contacting and meeting with the child's parents, legal guardians, or caretakers, with permission of their attorneys;

(F) Interviewing witnesses and individuals involved with the child, including school personnel, child welfare caseworkers, foster parents and other caretakers, neighbors, relatives, coaches, clergy, mental health professionals, physicians, law enforcement officers, and other potential witnesses;

(G) Reviewing relevant photographs, video or audio recordings, and other evidence;

(H) Documenting the results of these investigations;

(I) Monitoring compliance with court orders as appropriate, including the provision for and effectiveness of any court-ordered services;

(J) Promoting the timely progression of the case through the judicial system;

(K) Investigating the interests of the child beyond the scope of the proceeding and reporting to the court other interests of the child that may need to be protected by the institution of other administrative or judicial proceedings; however, counsel is not responsible for instituting those proceedings or representing the child in them unless expressly appointed by the court for that purpose; and

(L) After learning of other existing administrative or judicial proceedings involving the child, communicating and cooperating with others to the extent necessary and appropriate to protect the child's interest.

(5) Taking all other steps to represent the child adequately as appropriate to the case, including becoming knowledgeable in other areas affecting minors including:

(A) The Indian Child Welfare Act;

(B) Information about local experts who can provide evaluation, consultation, and testimony; and

(C) Delinquency, dependency, probate, family law, and other proceedings.

(Adopted, eff. Jan. 1, 2008. As amended, eff. Jan. 1, 2012; Jan. 1, 2016.)

Research References

Forms

California Transactions Forms--Family Law § 2:72, Counsel for the Children.

West's California Judicial Council Forms FL-322, Declaration Of Counsel for a Child Regarding Qualifications.

West's California Judicial Council Forms FL-323, Order Appointing Counsel for a Child.

West's California Judicial Council Forms FL-321-INFO, Attorney for Child in a Family Law Case--Information Sheet.

Treatises and Practice Aids

Witkin, California Summary 10th Parent and Child § 272, in General.

Witkin, California Summary 10th Parent and Child § 273, Rights and Duties.

Article 5

CHILDREN'S PARTICIPATION IN FAMILY COURT

Rule 5.250. Children's participation and testimony in family court proceedings

(a) Children's participation

This rule is intended to implement Family Code section 3042. Children's participation in family law matters must be considered on a case-by-case basis. No statutory mandate, rule, or practice requires children to participate in court or prohibits them from doing so. When a child wishes to participate, the court should find a balance between protecting the child, the statutory duty to consider the wishes of and input from the child, and the probative value of the child's input while ensuring all parties' due process rights to challenge evidence relied upon by the court in making custody decisions.

(b) Determining if the child wishes to address the court

(1) The following persons must inform the court if they have information indicating that a child in a custody or visitation (parenting time) matter wishes to address the court:

(A) A minor's counsel;

(B) An evaluator;

(C) An investigator; and

(D) A child custody recommending counselor who provides recommendations to the judge under Family Code section 3183.

(2) The following persons may inform the court if they have information indicating that a child wishes to address the court:

(A) A party; and

(B) A party's attorney.

(3) In the absence of information indicating a child wishes to address the court, the judicial officer may inquire whether the child wishes to do so.

(c) Guidelines for determining whether addressing the court is in the child's best interest

(1) When a child indicates that he or she wishes to address the court, the judicial officer must consider whether involving the child in the proceedings is in the child's best interest.

(2) If the child indicating an interest in addressing the court is 14 years old or older, the judicial officer must hear from that child unless the court makes a finding that addressing the court is not in the child's best interest and states the reasons on the record.

(3) In determining whether addressing the court is in a child's best interest, the judicial officer should consider the following:

(A) Whether the child is of sufficient age and capacity to reason to form an intelligent preference as to custody or visitation (parenting time);

(B) Whether the child is of sufficient age and capacity to understand the nature of testimony;

(C) Whether information has been presented indicating that the child may be at risk emotionally if he or she is permitted or denied the opportunity to address the court or that the child may benefit from addressing the court;

(D) Whether the subject areas about which the child is anticipated to address the court are relevant to the court's decisionmaking process; and

(E) Whether any other factors weigh in favor of or against having the child address the court, taking into consideration the child's desire to do so.

(d) Guidelines for receiving testimony and other input

(1) If the court precludes the calling of a child as a witness, alternatives for the court to obtain information or other input from the child may include, but are not limited to:

(A) The child's participation in child custody mediation under Family Code section 3180;

(B) Appointment of a child custody evaluator or investigator under Family Code section 3110 or Evidence Code section 730;

(C) Admissible evidence provided by the parents, parties, or witnesses in the proceeding;

(D) Information provided by a child custody recommending counselor authorized to provide recommendations under Family Code section 3183(a); and

(E) Information provided from a child interview center or professional so as to avoid unnecessary multiple interviews.

(2) If the court precludes the calling of a child as a witness and specifies one of the other alternatives, the court must require that the information or evidence obtained by alternative means and provided by a professional or nonparty:

(A) Be in writing and fully document the child's views on the matters on which the child wished to express an opinion;

(B) Describe the child's input in sufficient detail to assist the court in its adjudication process;

(C) Be provided to the court and to the parties by an individual who will be available for testimony and cross-examination; and

(D) Be filed in the confidential portion of the family law file.

(3) On deciding to take the testimony of a child, the judicial officer should balance the necessity of taking the child's testimony in the courtroom with parents and attorneys present with the need to create an environment in which the child can be open and honest. In each case in which a child's testimony will be taken, courts should consider:

(A) Where the testimony will be taken, including the possibility of closing the courtroom to the public or hearing from the child on the record in chambers;

(B) Who should be present when the testimony is taken, such as: both parents and their attorneys, only attorneys in the case in which both parents are represented, the child's attorney and parents, or only a court reporter with the judicial officer;

(C) How the child will be questioned, such as whether only the judicial officer will pose questions that the parties have submitted, whether attorneys or parties will be permitted to cross-examine the child, or whether a child advocate or expert in child development will ask the questions in the presence of the judicial officer and parties or a court reporter; and

(D) Whether a court reporter is available in all instances, but especially when testimony may be taken outside the presence of the parties and their attorneys and, if not, whether it will be possible to provide a listening device so that testimony taken in chambers may be heard simultaneously by the parents and their attorneys in the courtroom or to otherwise make a record of the testimony.

(4) In taking testimony from a child, the court must take special care to protect the child from harassment or embarrassment and to restrict the unnecessary repetition of questions. The court must also take special care to ensure that questions are stated in a form that is appropriate to the witness's age or cognitive level. If the child is not represented by an attorney, the court must inform the child in an age-appropriate manner about the limitations on confidentiality and that the information provided to the court will be on the record and provided to the parties in the case. In the process of listening to and inviting the child's input, the court must allow but not require the child to state a preference regarding custody or visitation and should, in an age-appropriate manner, provide information about the process by which the court will make a decision.

(5) In any case in which a child will be called to testify, the court may consider the appointment of minor's counsel for

that child. The court may consider whether such appointment will cause unnecessary delay or otherwise interfere with the child's ability to participate in the process. In addition to adhering to the requirements for minor's counsel under Family Code section 3151 and rules 5.240, 5.241, and 5.242, minor's counsel must:

(A) Provide information to the child in an age-appropriate manner about the limitations on confidentiality and indicate to the child the possibility that information provided to the court will be on the record and provided to the parties in the case;

(B) Allow but not require the child to state a preference regarding custody or visitation (parenting time) and, in an age-appropriate manner, provide information about the process by which the court will make a decision;

(C) Provide procedures relevant to the child's participation and, if appropriate, provide an orientation to the courtroom where the child will be testifying; and

(D) Inform the parties and then the court about the client's desire to provide input.

(6) No testimony of a child may be received without such testimony being heard on the record or in the presence of the parties. This requirement may not be waived by stipulation.

(e) Responsibilities of court-connected or appointed professionals

A child custody evaluator, a child custody recommending counselor, an investigator, or a mediator appointed or assigned to meet with a child in a family court proceeding must:

(1) Provide information to the child in an age-appropriate manner about the limitations on confidentiality and the possibility that information provided to the professional may be shared with the court on the record and provided to the parties in the case;

(2) Allow but not require the child to state a preference regarding custody and visitation (parenting time), and, in an age-appropriate manner, provide information about the process by which the court will make a decision; and

(3) Provide to the parents of the child participating in the court process information about local court procedures relevant to the child's participation and information about how to best support the child in an age-appropriate manner during the court process.

(f) Methods of providing information to parents and supporting children

Courts should provide information to parties and parents and support for children when children want to participate or testify or are otherwise involved in family law proceedings. Such methods may include but are not limited to:

(1) Having court-connected professionals meet jointly or separately with the parents or parties to discuss alternatives to having a child provide direct testimony;

(2) Providing an orientation for a child about the court process and the role of the judicial officer in making decisions, how the courtroom or chambers will be set up, and what participating or testifying will entail;

(3) Providing information to parents or parties before and after a child participates or testifies so that they can consider the possible effect on their child of participating or not participating in a given case;

(4) Including information in child custody mediation orientation presentations and publications about a child's participation in family law proceedings;

(5) Providing a children's waiting room; and

(6) Providing an interpreter for the child, if needed.

(g) Education and training

Education and training content for court staff and judicial officers should include information on children's participation in family court processes, methods other than direct testimony for receiving input from children, and procedures for taking children's testimony. *(Adopted, eff. Jan. 1, 2012.)*

Research References

Treatises and Practice Aids

Witkin, California Summary 10th Parent and Child § 208, Child's Preference.

Witkin, California Summary 10th Parent and Child § 225A, (New) Right Of Child to Express Preference.

Witkin, California Summary 10th Wills and Probate § 916, in General.

Chapter 9

CHILD, SPOUSAL, AND DOMESTIC PARTNER SUPPORT

Article 1

GENERAL PROVISIONS

Rule 5.260. General provisions regarding support cases

(a) Financial declarations

Except as provided below, for all hearings involving child, spousal, or domestic partner support, both parties must complete, file, and serve a current *Income and Expense Declaration* (form FL–150) on all parties.

(1) A party requesting support orders must include a current, completed *Income and Expense Declaration* (form FL–150) with the *Request for Order* (form FL–300) that is filed with the court and served on all parties.

(2) A party responding to a request for support orders must include a current, completed *Income and Expense Declaration* (form FL–150) with the *Responsive Declaration to Request for Order* (form FL–320) that is filed with the court and served on all parties.

(3) "Current" means the form has been completed within the past three months providing no facts have changed. The form must be sufficiently completed to allow the court to make an order.

(4) In child support hearings, a party may complete a current *Financial Statement (Simplified)* (form FL–155) instead of a current *Income and Expense Declaration* (form FL–150) if he or she meets the requirements allowing submission of a *Financial Statement (Simplified)* (form FL–155).

(5) *Financial Statement (Simplified)* (form FL–155) is not appropriate for use in proceedings to determine or modify spousal or domestic partner support, to determine or modify family support, or to determine attorney's fees and costs.

(b) Deviations from guideline child support in orders and judgments

(1) If a party contends that the amount of support as calculated under the statewide uniform guideline formula is inappropriate, that party must file a declaration stating the amount of support alleged to be proper and the factual and legal bases justifying a deviation from guideline support under Family Code section 4057.

(2) In its discretion, for good cause shown, the court may deviate from the amount of guideline support resulting from the computer calculation. If the court finds good cause to deviate from the statewide uniform guideline formula for child support, the court must state its findings in writing or on the record as required by Family Code sections 4056, 4057, and 4065.

(3) Stipulated agreements for child support that deviate from the statewide uniform guideline must include either a *Non–Guideline Child Support Findings Attachment* (form FL–342(A)) or language in the agreement or judgment conforming with Family Code sections 4056 and 4065.

(c) Request to change prior support orders

The supporting declaration submitted in a request to change a prior child, spousal, or domestic partner support order must include specific facts demonstrating a change of circumstances. No change of circumstances must be shown to change a previously agreed upon child support order that was below the child support guidelines.

(d) Notification to the local child support agency

The party requesting court orders must provide the local child support agency timely notice of any request to establish, change, or enforce any child, spousal, or domestic partner support order if the agency is providing support enforcement services or has intervened in the case as described in Family Code section 17400.

(e) Judgment for support

(1) If child support is an issue in a judgment:

(A) Each party should file a proposed support calculation with the proposed judgment that sets forth the party's assumptions with regard to gross income, tax filing status, time-share, add-on expenses, and any other factor relevant to the support calculation.

(B) The moving party should file the documents in (A) with the proposed judgment if the judgment is based on respondent's default or a stipulation of the parties.

(C) The court may use and must permit parties or their attorneys to use any software certified by the Judicial Council to present support calculations to the court.

(2) If spousal or domestic partner support is an issue in a judgment:

(A) Use of support calculation software is not appropriate when requesting a judgment or modification of a judgment for spousal or domestic partner support.

(B) Petitioner or the parties may use *Spousal or Partnership Support Declaration Attachment* (form FL–157) to address the issue of spousal or domestic partner support under Family Code section 4320 when relevant to the case.

(Adopted, eff. Jan. 1, 2013.)

Research References

Forms

California Practice Guide: Rutter Family Law Forms Form 1:32, Glossary Of Common Family Law Terms, Phrases and Concepts (Enclosure to Form 1:31).

Treatises and Practice Aids

Witkin, California Summary 10th Husband and Wife § 198, Order to Show Cause or Motion.

Witkin, California Summary 10th Husband and Wife § 199, Supporting Documents.

Witkin, California Summary 10th Husband and Wife § 200, Response.

Witkin, California Summary 10th Husband and Wife § 207, Modification.

Witkin, California Summary 10th Husband and Wife § 278, Necessity Of Showing.

Witkin, California Summary 10th Husband and Wife § 289, in General.

Witkin, California Summary 10th Husband and Wife § 326, Time and Notice Requirements.

Witkin, California Summary 10th Parent and Child § 411, Factors Rebutting Presumption.

Witkin, California Summary 10th Parent and Child § 414, Stipulated Support Agreements.

Witkin, California Summary 10th Parent and Child § 439, Modification or Termination Of Support Order.

Article 2

CERTIFICATION OF STATEWIDE UNIFORM GUIDELINE SUPPORT CALCULATORS

Rule 5.275. Standards for computer software to assist in determining support

(a) Authority

This rule is adopted under Family Code section 3830.

(b) Standards

The standards for computer software to assist in determining the appropriate amount of child or spousal support are:

(1) The software must accurately compute the net disposable income of each parent as follows:

(A) Permit entry of the "gross income" of each parent as defined by Family Code section 4058;

(B) Either accurately compute the state and federal income tax liability under Family Code section 4059(a) or permit the entry of a figure for this amount; this figure, in the default state of the program, must not include the tax consequences of any spousal support to be ordered;

(C) Ensure that any deduction for contributions to the Federal Insurance Contributions Act or as otherwise permitted by Family Code section 4059(b) does not exceed the allowable amount;

(D) Permit the entry of deductions authorized by Family Code sections 4059(c) through (f); and

(E) Permit the entry of deductions authorized by Family Code section 4059(g) (hardship) while ensuring that any deduction subject to the limitation in Family Code section 4071(b) does not exceed that limitation.

(2) Using examples provided by the Judicial Council, the software must calculate a child support amount, using its default settings, that is accurate to within 1 percent of the correct amount. In making this determination, the Judicial Council must calculate the correct amount of support for each example and must then calculate the amount for each example using the software program. Each person seeking certification of software must supply a copy of the software to the Judicial Council. If the software does not operate on a standard Windows 95 or later compatible or Macintosh computer, the person seeking certification of the software must make available to the Judicial Council any hardware required to use the software. The Judicial Council may delegate the responsibility for the calculation and determinations required by this rule.

(3) The software must contain, either on the screen or in written form, a glossary defining each term used on the computer screen or in printed hard copy produced by the software.

(4) The software must contain, either on the screen or in written form, instructions for the entry of each figure that is required for computation of child support using the default setting of the software. These instructions must include but not be limited to the following:

(A) The gross income of each party as provided for by Family Code section 4058;

(B) The deductions from gross income of each party as provided for by Family Code section 4059 and subdivision (b)(1) of this rule;

(C) The additional items of child support provided for in Family Code section 4062; and

(D) The following factors rebutting the presumptive guideline amount: Family Code section 4057(b)(2) (deferred sale of residence) and 4057(b)(3) (income of subsequent partner).

(5) In making an allocation of the additional items of child support under subdivision (b)(4)(C) of this rule, the software must, as its default setting, allocate the expenses one-half to each parent. The software must also provide, in an easily selected option, the alternative allocation of the expenses as provided for by Family Code section 4061(b).

(6) The software or a license to use the software must be available to persons without restriction based on profession or occupation.

(7) The sale or donation of software or a license to use the software to a court or a judicial officer must include a license, without additional charge, to the court or judicial officer to permit an additional copy of the software to be installed on a computer to be made available by the court or judicial officer to members of the public.

(c) Expiration of certification

Any certification provided by the Judicial Council under Family Code section 3830 and this rule must expire one year from the date of its issuance unless another expiration date is set forth in the certification. The Judicial Council may provide for earlier expiration of a certification if (1) the provisions involving the calculation of tax consequences change or (2) other provisions involving the calculation of support change.

(d) Statement of certified public accountant

If the software computes the state and federal income tax liability as provided in subdivision (b)(1)(B) of this rule, the application for certification, whether for original certification or for renewal, must be accompanied by a statement from a certified public accountant that[1]

(1) The accountant is familiar with the operation of the software;

(2) The accountant has carefully examined, in a variety of situations, the operation of the software in regard to the computation of tax liability;

(3) In the opinion of the accountant the software accurately calculates the estimated actual state and federal income tax liability consistent with Internal Revenue Service and Franchise Tax Board procedures;

(4) In the opinion of the accountant the software accurately calculates the deductions under the Federal Insurance Contributions Act (FICA), including the amount for social security and for Medicare, and the deductions for California State Disability Insurance and properly annualizes these amounts; and

(5) States which calendar year the statement includes and must clearly indicate any limitations on the statement. The Judicial Council may request a new statement as often as it determines necessary to ensure accuracy of the tax computation.

(e) Renewal of certification

At least three months prior to the expiration of a certification, a person may apply for renewal of the certification. The renewal must include a statement of any changes made to the software since the last application for certification. Upon request, the Judicial Council will keep the information concerning changes confidential.

(f) Modifications to the software

The certification issued by the Judicial Council under Family Code section 3830 and this rule imposes a duty upon the person applying for the certification to promptly notify the Judicial Council of all changes made to the software during the period of certification. Upon request, the Judicial Council will keep the information concerning changes confidential. The Judicial Council may, after receipt of information concerning changes, require that the software be recertified under this rule.

(g) Definitions

As used in this chapter:

(1) "Software" refers to any program or digital application used to calculate the appropriate amount of child or spousal support.

(2) "Default settings" refers to the status in which the software first starts when it is installed on a computer system. The software may permit the default settings to be changed by the user, either on a temporary or a permanent basis, if (1) the user is permitted to change the settings back to the default without reinstalling the software, (2) the computer screen prominently indicates whether the software is set to the default settings, and (3) any printout from the software prominently indicates whether the software is set to the default settings.

(3) "Contains" means, with reference to software, that the material is either displayed by the program code itself or is found in written documents supplied with the software.

(h) Explanation of discrepancies

Before the Judicial Council denies a certificate because of failure to comply with the standards in paragraph (b)(1) or (b)(2) of this rule, the Judicial Council may request the person seeking certification to explain the differences in results.

(i) Application

An application for certification must be on a form supplied by the Judicial Council and must be accompanied by an application fee of $250.

(j) Acceptability in the courts

(1) In all actions for child or family support brought by or otherwise involving the local child support agency under title IV–D of the Social Security Act, the Department of Child Support Services' California Guideline Child Support Calculator software program must be used by:

(A) Parties and attorneys to present support calculations to the court; and

(B) The court to prepare support calculations.

(2) In all non-title IV–D proceedings, the court may use and must permit parties or attorneys to use any software certified by the Judicial Council under this rule. *(Formerly Rule 1258, adopted, eff. Dec. 1, 1993. As amended, eff. Jan. 1, 2000. Renumbered Rule 5.275 and amended, eff. Jan. 1, 2003. As amended, eff. Jan. 1, 2007; Jan. 1, 2009; Jan. 1, 2016.)*

[1] So in copy.

Research References

Forms

California Practice Guide: Rutter Family Law Forms Form 5:2, Request for Order Re Child Custody, Child Support, Spousal Support, Attorney Fees, etc.

California Practice Guide: Rutter Family Law Forms Form 6:11, Request for Order Re Guideline Child Support, Temporary "Guideline" Spousal Support and Family Code S4062 "Add-On" Child Support.

Treatises and Practice Aids

Witkin, California Summary 10th Husband and Wife § 192, Use Of Guidelines.

Witkin, California Summary 10th Parent and Child § 394, . in General.

Chapter 10

GOVERNMENT CHILD SUPPORT CASES (TITLE IV–D SUPPORT CASES)

Rule 5.300. Purpose, authority, and definitions

(a) Purpose

The rules in this chapter are adopted to provide practice and procedure for support actions under title IV–D of the Social Security Act [1] and under California statutory provisions concerning these actions.

(b) Authority

These rules are adopted under Family Code sections 211, 3680(b), 4251(a), 4252(b), 10010, 17404, 17432, and 17400.

(c) Definitions

As used in these rules, unless the context requires otherwise, "title IV–D support action" refers to an action for child or family support that is brought by or otherwise involves the local child support agency under title IV–D of the Social Security Act. *(Formerly Rule 1280, adopted, eff. July 1, 1997. Renumbered Rule 5.300 and amended, eff. Jan. 1, 2003. As amended, eff. Jan. 1, 2007.)*

[1] See 42 U.S.C.A. § 651 et seq.

Research References

Treatises and Practice Aids

Witkin, California Summary 10th Husband and Wife § 316, Rules and Forms.

Rule 5.305. Hearing of matters by a judge under Family Code sections 4251(a) and 4252(b)(7)

(a) Exceptional circumstances

The exceptional circumstances under which a judge may hear a title IV–D support action include:

(1) The failure of the judge to hear the action would result in significant prejudice or delay to a party including added cost or loss of work time;

(2) Transferring the matter to a commissioner would result in undue consumption of court time;

(3) Physical impossibility or difficulty due to the commissioner being geographically separate from the judge presently hearing the matter;

(4) The absence of the commissioner from the county due to illness, disability, death, or vacation; and

(5) The absence of the commissioner from the county due to service in another county and the difficulty of travel to the county in which the matter is pending.

(b) Duty of judge hearing matter

A judge hearing a title IV–D support action under this rule and Family Code sections 4251(a) and 4252(b)(7) must make an interim order and refer the matter to the commissioner for further proceedings.

(c) Discretion of the court

Notwithstanding (a) and (b) of this rule, a judge may, in the interests of justice, transfer a case to a commissioner for hearing. *(Formerly Rule 1280.1, adopted, eff. July 1, 1997. Renumbered Rule 5.305 and amended, eff. Jan. 1, 2003. As amended, eff. Jan. 1, 2007.)*

Research References

Treatises and Practice Aids

Witkin, California Summary 10th Husband and Wife § 327, Hearing.

Rule 5.310. Use of existing family law forms

When an existing family law form is required or appropriate for use in a title IV–D support action, the form may be used notwithstanding the absence of a notation for the other parent as a party under Family Code section 17404. The caption of the form must be modified by the person filing it by adding the words "Other parent:" and the name of the other parent to the form. *(Formerly Rule 1280.2, adopted, eff. July 1, 1997. Renumbered Rule 5.310 and amended, eff. Jan. 1, 2003. As amended, eff. Jan. 1, 2007.)*

Research References

Treatises and Practice Aids

Witkin, California Summary 10th Husband and Wife § 316, Rules and Forms.

Rule 5.311. Implementation of new and revised governmental forms by local child support agencies

(a) General extended implementation

A local child support agency providing services as required by Family Code section 17400 must implement any new or revised form approved or adopted by the Judicial Council for support actions under title IV–D of the Social Security Act, [1] and under California statutory provisions concerning these actions, within six months of the effective date of the form. During that six-month period, the local child support agency may properly use and file the immediately prior version of the form.

(b) Judgment regarding parental obligations

When the local child support agency files a proposed judgment or proposed supplemental judgment in any action using *Judgment Regarding Parental Obligations (Governmental)* (form FL–630), a final judgment or supplemental judgment may be filed on:

(1) The same version of the form that was used with the initial action or that was filed as an amended proposed judgment; or

(2) The most current version of the form, unless there have been amendments to the form that result in substantial changes from the filed version. If the most current version of the form has been substantially changed from the filed version, then the filed version must be used for the final judgment. A substantial change is one that would change the relief granted in a final judgment from that noticed in a proposed or amended proposed judgment. *(Adopted, eff. Jan. 1, 2004. As amended, eff. Jan. 1, 2007.)*

[1] See 42 U.S.C.A. § 651 et seq.

Research References

Treatises and Practice Aids

Witkin, California Summary 10th Husband and Wife § 316, Rules and Forms.

Rule 5.315. Memorandum of points and authorities

Notwithstanding any other rule, including rule 313, a notice of motion in a title IV–D support action must not be required to contain points and authorities if the notice of motion uses a form adopted or approved by the Judicial Council. The absence of points and authorities under these circumstances may not be construed by the court as an admission that the motion is not meritorious and cause for its denial. *(Formerly Rule 1280.3, adopted, eff. July 1, 1997. Renumbered Rule 5.315 and amended, eff. Jan. 1, 2003. As amended, eff. Jan. 1, 2007.)*

Research References

Treatises and Practice Aids

Witkin, California Summary 10th Husband and Wife § 316, Rules and Forms.

Rule 5.320. Attorney of record in support actions under title IV–D of the Social Security Act [1]

The attorney of record on behalf of a local child support agency appearing in any action under title IV–D of the Social Security Act is the director of the local child support agency, or if the director of that agency is not an attorney, the senior attorney of that agency or an attorney designated by the director for that purpose. Notwithstanding any other rule, including but not limited to rule 2.100–2.119, the name, address, and telephone number of the county child support agency and the name of the attorney of record are sufficient for any papers filed by the child support agency. The name of the deputy or assistant district attorney or attorney of the child support agency, who is not attorney of record, and the State Bar number of the attorney of record or any of his or her assistants are not required. *(Formerly Rule 1280.4, adopted, eff. July 1, 1997. As amended, eff. Jan. 1, 2001. Renumbered Rule 5.320 and amended, eff. Jan. 1, 2003. As amended, eff. Jan. 1, 2007.)*

[1] See 42 U.S.C.A. § 651 et seq.

Research References

Treatises and Practice Aids

Witkin, California Summary 10th Husband and Wife § 318, Agency's Representation Of Public Interest.

Rule 5.324. Telephone appearance in title IV–D hearings and conferences

(a) Purpose

This rule is intended to improve the administration of the high volume of title IV–D child support hearings and conferences. Participation by both parents is needed for fair and accurate child support orders. The opportunity to appear by telephone fosters parental participation.

(b) Definition

"Telephone appearance," as used in this rule, includes any appearance by telephonic, audiovisual, videoconferencing, digital, or other electronic means.

(c) Permissibility of telephone appearances

Upon request, the court, in its discretion, may permit a telephone appearance in any hearing or conference related to an action for child support when the local child support agency is providing services under title IV–D of the Social Security Act.

(d) Exceptions

A telephone appearance is not permitted for any of the following except as permitted by Family Code section 5700.3164930:

(1) Contested trials, contempt hearings, orders of examination, and any matters in which the party or witness has been subpoenaed to appear in person; and

(2) Any hearing or conference for which the court, in its discretion on a case-by-case basis, decides that a personal appearance would materially assist in a determination of the proceeding or in resolution of the case.

(e) Request for telephone appearance

(1) A party, an attorney, a witness, a parent who has not been joined to the action, or a representative of a local child support agency or government agency may request permission of the court to appear and testify by telephone. The local child support agency may request a telephone appearance on behalf of a party, a parent, or a witness when the local child support agency is appearing in the title IV–D support action, as defined by rule 5.300(c). The court may also, on its own motion, allow a telephone appearance.

(2) A party, an attorney, a witness, a parent who has not been joined to the action, or a representative of a local child support agency or government agency who wishes to appear by telephone at a hearing must file a request with the court clerk at least 12 court days before the hearing. A local child support agency that files the request for telephone appearance on behalf of a party, a parent, or a witness must file the request with the court clerk at least 12 court days before the hearing. This request must be served on the other parties, the local child support agency, and attorneys, if any. Service must be by personal delivery, fax, express mail, or other means reasonably calculated to ensure delivery by the close of the next court day.

(3) The mandatory *Request for Telephone Appearance (Governmental)* (form FL–679) must be filed to request a telephone appearance.

(f) Opposition to telephone appearance

Any opposition to a request to appear by telephone must be made by declaration under penalty of perjury under the laws of the State of California. It must be filed with the court clerk and served at least eight court days before the court hearing. Service on the person or agency requesting the telephone appearance; all parties, including the other parent, a parent who has not been joined to the action, the local child support agency; and attorneys, if any, must be accomplished using one of the methods listed in (e)(2).

(g) Shortening time

The court may shorten the time to file, submit, serve, respond, or comply with any of the procedures specified in this rule.

(h) Notice by court

At least five court days before the hearing, the court must notify the person or agency requesting the telephone appearance, the parties, and attorneys, if any, of its decision. The court may direct the court clerk, the court-approved vendor, the local child support agency, a party, or an attorney to provide the notification. This notice may be given in person or by telephone, fax, express mail, e-mail, or other means reasonably calculated to ensure notification no later than five court days before the hearing date.

(i) Need for personal appearance

If, at any time during the hearing, the court determines that a personal appearance is necessary, the court may continue the matter and require a personal appearance.

(j) Vendors, procedure, audibility, reporting, and information

Rule 3.670(j)–(q) applies to telephone appearances under this rule.

(k) Technical equipment

Courts that lack the technical equipment to implement telephone appearances are exempt from the rule. *(Adopted, eff. July 1, 2005. As amended, eff. Jan. 1, 2007; Jan. 1, 2008; July 1, 2008; July 1, 2011; Jan. 1, 2014; Jan. 1, 2017.)*

Research References

Forms

West's California Judicial Council Forms FL-679, Request for Telephone Appearance.

Treatises and Practice Aids

Witkin, California Summary 10th Husband and Wife § 11A, (New) Generally Applicable Procedures.

Witkin, California Summary 10th Husband and Wife § 327, Hearing.

Rule 5.325. Procedures for clerk's handling of combined summons and complaint

(a) Purpose

This rule provides guidance to court clerks in processing and filing the *Summons and Complaint or Supplemental Complaint Regarding Parental Obligations (Governmental)* (form FL–600) for actions under Family Code section 17400 or 17404.

(b) Filing of complaint and issuance of summons

The clerk must accept the *Summons and Complaint or Supplemental Complaint Regarding Parental Obligations (Governmental)* (form FL–600) for filing under Code of Civil Procedure section 411.10. The clerk must issue the original summons in accordance with Code of Civil Procedure section 412.20 by filing the original form FL–600 and affixing the seal of the court. The original form FL–600 must be retained in the court's file.

(c) Issuance of copies of combined summons and complaint

Upon issuance of the original summons, the clerk must conform copies of the filed form FL–600 to reflect that the complaint has been filed and the summons has been issued. A copy of form FL–600 so conformed must be served on the defendant in accordance with Code of Civil Procedure section 415.10 et seq.

(d) Proof of service of summons

Proof of service of the *Summons and Complaint or Supplemental Complaint Regarding Parental Obligations (Governmental)* (form FL–600) must be on the form prescribed by rule 2.150 or any other proof of service form that meets the requirements of Code of Civil Procedure section 417.10.

(e) Filing of proposed judgment and amended proposed judgment

The proposed judgment must be an attachment to the *Summons and Complaint or Supplemental Complaint Regarding Parental Obligations (Governmental)* (form FL–600) and must not be file-endorsed separately. An amended proposed judgment submitted for filing must be attached to the *Declaration for Amended Proposed Judgment* (form FL–616), as required by Family Code section 17430(c), and a proof of service by mail, if appropriate. Upon filing, the *Declaration for Amended Proposed Judgment* may be file-endorsed. The amended proposed judgment must not be file-endorsed. *(Formerly Rule 1280.5, adopted, eff. July 1, 1998. Renumbered Rule 5.325 and amended, eff. Jan. 1, 2003. As amended, eff. Jan. 1, 2007.)*

Research References

Treatises and Practice Aids

Witkin, California Summary 10th Husband and Wife § 83, Petition.
Witkin, California Summary 10th Husband and Wife § 324, Pleadings.

Rule 5.330. Procedures for child support case registry form

(a) Purpose

This rule provides guidance to court clerks in processing the *Child Support Case Registry Form* (form FL–191).

(b) Application

This rule applies to any action or proceeding in which there is an order for child support or family support except for cases in which the local child support agency provides support enforcement services under Family Code section 17400. This rule does not apply to cases in which the local child support agency provides support enforcement services under Family Code section 17400.

(c) Requirement that form be filed

The court must require that a *Child Support Case Registry Form* (form FL–191), completed by one of the parties, be filed each time an initial court order for child support or family support or a modification of a court order for child support or family support is filed with the court. A party attempting to file an initial judgment or order for child support or family support or a modification of an order for child or family support without a completed *Child Support Case Registry Form* (form FL–191) must be given a blank form to complete. The form must be accepted if legibly handwritten in ink or typed. No filing fees may be charged for filing the form.

(d) Distribution of the form

Copies of the *Child Support Case Registry Form* (form FL–191) must be made available by the clerk's office and the family law facilitator's office to the parties without cost. A blank copy of the *Child Support Case Registry Form* (form FL–191) must be sent with the notice of entry of judgment to the party who did not submit the judgment or order.

(e) Items on form that must be completed

A form must be considered complete if items 1b, 1c, 2, 5, and 6 are completed. Either item 3 or item 4 must also be completed as appropriate. If the form is submitted with the judgment or order for court approval, the clerk must complete item 1a once the judgment or order has been signed by the judicial officer and filed.

(f) Clerk handling of form

The completed *Child Support Case Registry Form* (form FL–191) must not be stored in the court's file. It should be date and time stamped when received and stored in an area to which the public does not have access. At least once per month all forms received must be mailed to the California Department of Social Services.

(g) Storage of confidential information

Provided that all information is kept confidential, the court may keep either a copy of the form or the information provided on the form in an electronic format. *(Formerly Rule 1280.6, adopted, eff. July 1, 1999. Renumbered Rule 5.330 and amended, eff. Jan. 1, 2003. As amended, eff. Jan. 1, 2007.)*

Research References

Treatises and Practice Aids

Witkin, California Summary 10th Parent and Child § 384, Information Required.
Witkin, California Summary 10th Parent and Child § 427, Collection Of Information About Support Obligations.

Rule 5.335. Procedures for hearings on interstate income withholding orders

(a) Purpose

This rule provides a procedure for a hearing under Family Code section 4945 in response to an income withholding order.

(b) Filing of request for hearing

A support obligor may contest the validity or enforcement of an income withholding order by filing a completed request for hearing. A copy of the income withholding order must be attached.

(c) Filing fee

The court must not require a filing fee to file the request for hearing under this rule.

(d) Creation of court file

Upon receipt of the completed request for hearing and a copy of the income withholding order, the clerk must assign a case number and schedule a court date. The court date must be no earlier than 30 days from the date of filing and no later than 45 days from the date of filing.

(e) Notice of hearing

The support obligor must provide the clerk with envelopes addressed to the obligor, the support enforcement agency that sent the income withholding order, and the obligor's employer. The support obligor must also provide an envelope addressed to the person or agency designated to receive the support payments if that person or agency is different than the support enforcement agency that sent the income withholding order. The support obligor must provide sufficient postage to mail each envelope provided. Upon scheduling the hearing, the clerk must mail a copy of the request for hearing in each envelope provided by the support obligor.

(f) Use of court file in subsequent proceedings

Any subsequent proceedings filed in the same court that involve the same parties and are filed under the Uniform Interstate Family Support Act (UIFSA) [1] must use the file number created under this rule.

(g) Definitions

As used in this rule:

(1) An "income withholding order" is the *Order/Notice to Withhold Income for Child Support* (form FL–195) issued by a child support enforcement agency in another state; and

(2) A "request for hearing" is the *Request for Hearing Regarding Wage and Earnings Assignment (Family Law—Governmental—UIFSA)* (form FL–450). *(Formerly Rule 1280.7, adopted, eff. July 1, 1999. Renumbered Rule 5.335 and amended, eff. Jan. 1, 2003. As amended, eff. Jan. 1, 2007.)*

[1] See Family Code § 4900 et seq.

Rule 5.340. Judicial education for child support commissioners

Every commissioner whose principal judicial assignment is to hear child support matters must attend the following judicial education programs:

(1) *Basic child support law education*

Within six months of beginning an assignment as a child support commissioner, the judicial officer must attend a basic educational program on California child support law and procedure designed primarily for judicial officers. The training program must include instruction on both state and federal laws concerning child support. A judicial officer who has completed the basic educational program need not attend the basic educational program again.

(2) *Continuing education*

The judicial officer must attend an update on new developments in child support law and procedure at least once each calendar year.

(3) *Other child support education*

To the extent that judicial time and resources are available, the judicial officer is encouraged to attend additional educational programs on child support and other related family law issues.

(4) *Other judicial education*

The requirements of this rule are in addition to and not in lieu of the requirements of rule ~~10.501(e)~~10.462. *(Formerly Rule 1280.8, adopted, eff. July 1, 1999. Renumbered Rule 5.340 and amended, eff. Jan. 1, 2003. As amended, eff. Jan. 1, 2007; Jan. 1, 2017.)*

Research References

Treatises and Practice Aids

Witkin, California Summary 10th Husband and Wife § 327, Hearing.

Rule 5.350. Procedures for hearings to set aside voluntary declarations of paternity when no previous action has been filed

(a) Purpose

This rule provides a procedure for a hearing to set aside a voluntary declaration of paternity under Family Code section 7575(c).

(b) Filing of request for hearing

A person who has signed a voluntary declaration of paternity, or a local child support agency, may ask that the declaration be set aside by filing a completed *Request for Hearing and Application to Set Aside Voluntary Declaration of Paternity* (form FL–280).

(c) Creation of court file

On receipt of the completed request for hearing, the clerk must assign a case number and schedule a court date. The court date must be no earlier than 31 days after the date of filing and no later than 45 days after the date of filing.

(d) Notice of hearing

The person who is asking that the voluntary declaration of paternity be set aside must serve, either by personal service or by mail, the request for hearing and a blank *Responsive Declaration to Application to Set Aside Voluntary Declaration of Paternity* (form FL–285) on the other person who signed the voluntary declaration of paternity. If the local child support agency is providing services in the case, the person requesting the set-aside must also serve a copy of the request for hearing on the agency.

(e) Order after hearing

The decision of the court must be written on the *Order After Hearing on Motion to Set Aside Voluntary Declaration of Paternity* (form FL–290). If the voluntary declaration of paternity is set aside, the clerk must mail a copy of the order to the Department of Child Support Services in order that the voluntary declaration of paternity be purged from the records.

(f) Use of court file in subsequent proceedings

Pleadings in any subsequent proceedings, including but not limited to proceedings under the Uniform Parentage Act, that involve the parties and child named in the voluntary declaration of paternity must be filed in the court file that was initiated by the filing of the *Request for Hearing and Application to Set Aside Voluntary Declaration of Paternity* (form FL–280). *(Formerly Rule 1280.10, adopted, eff. July 1, 2000. Renumbered Rule 5.350 and amended, eff. Jan. 1, 2003. As amended, eff. Jan. 1, 2006; Jan. 1, 2007.)*

Research References

Treatises and Practice Aids

Witkin, California Summary 10th Husband and Wife § 320, in General.

Witkin, California Summary 10th Parent and Child § 34, Rescinding or Setting Aside Declaration.

Rule 5.355. Minimum standards of training for court clerk staff whose assignment includes title IV–D child support cases

Any court clerk whose assignment includes title IV–D child support cases must participate in a minimum of six hours of continuing education annually in federal and state laws concerning child support and related issues. *(Formerly Rule 1280.11, adopted, eff. July 1, 2000. Renumbered Rule 5.355 and amended, eff. Jan. 1, 2003. As amended, eff. Jan. 1, 2007.)*

Rule 5.360. Appearance by local child support agency

When a local child support agency is providing services as required by Family Code section 17400, that agency may appear in any action or proceeding that it did not initiate by giving written notice to all parties, on *Notice Regarding Payment of Support* (form FL–632), that it is providing services in that action or proceeding under title IV–D of the Social Security Act. The agency must file the original of the notice in the action or proceeding with proof of service by mail on the parties. On service and filing of the notice, the court must not require the local child support agency to file any other notice or pleading before that agency appears in the action or proceeding. *(Formerly Rule 1280.12, adopted, eff. Jan. 1, 2001. Renumbered Rule 5.360 and amended, eff. Jan. 1, 2003. As amended, eff. Jan. 1, 2007.)*

Research References

Treatises and Practice Aids

Witkin, California Summary 10th Husband and Wife § 317, Nature Of Proceedings.

Rule 5.365. Procedure for consolidation of child support orders

(a) When an order of consolidation of actions has been made under section 1048(a) of the Code of Civil Procedure in cases in which a local child support agency is appearing under section 17400 of the Family Code, or when a motion to consolidate or combine two or more child support orders has been made under section 17408 of the Family Code, the cases in which those orders were entered must be consolidated as follows:

(1) *Priority of consolidation*

The order consolidating cases that contain child support orders must designate the primary court file into which the support orders must be consolidated and must also designate the court files that are subordinate. Absent an order upon showing of good cause, the cases or child support orders must be consolidated into a single court file according to the following priority, including those cases or orders initiated or obtained by a local child support agency under division 17 of the Family Code that are consolidated under either section 1048(a) of the Code of Civil Procedure or section 17408 of the Family Code:

(A) If one of the cases or child support orders to be consolidated is in an action for nullity, dissolution, or legal separation brought under division 6 of the Family Code, all cases and orders so consolidated must be consolidated into that action, which must be the primary file.

(B) If none of the cases or child support orders to be consolidated is in an action for nullity, dissolution, or legal separation, but one of the child support orders to be consolidated has been issued in an action under the Uniform Parentage Act (Fam. Code, div. 12, pt. 3), all orders so consolidated must be consolidated into that action, which must be the primary file.

(C) If none of the cases or child support orders to be consolidated is in an action for nullity, dissolution, or legal separation or in an action under the Uniform Parentage Act, but one of the child support orders to be consolidated has been issued in an action commenced by a *Petition for Custody and Support of Minor Children* (form FL–260), all orders so consolidated must be consolidated into that action, which must be the primary file.

(D) If none of the cases or child support orders to be consolidated is in an action for nullity, dissolution, or legal separation or in an action under the Uniform Parentage Act, the case or cases with the higher number or numbers must be consolidated into the case with the lowest number, which must be the primary file. Child support orders in cases brought under the Domestic Violence Protection Act (Fam. Code, div. 10, pt. 4) or any similar law may be consolidated under this rule. However, a domestic violence case must not be designated as the primary file.

(2) *Notice of consolidation*

Upon issuance of the consolidation order, the local child support agency must prepare and file in each subordinate case a *Notice of Consolidation* (form FL–920), indicating that the support orders in those actions are consolidated into the primary file. The notice must state the date of the consolidation, the primary file number, and the case number of each of the cases so consolidated. If the local child support agency was not a participant in the proceeding in which the consolidation was ordered, the court must designate the party to prepare and file the notice.

(b) Subsequent filings in consolidated cases

Notwithstanding any other rule, including but not limited to rule 367, upon consolidation of cases with child support orders, all filings in those cases, whether dealing with child support or not, must occur in the primary court action and must be filed under that case, caption, and number only. All further orders must be issued only in the primary action, and no further orders may be issued in a subordinate court file. All enforcement and modification of support orders in consolidated cases must occur in the primary court action regardless of in which action the order was originally issued. *(Formerly Rule 1280.13, adopted, eff. Jan. 1, 2001. Renumbered Rule 5.365 and amended, eff. Jan. 1, 2003. As amended, eff. Jan. 1, 2007.)*

Research References

Treatises and Practice Aids

Witkin, California Summary 10th Husband and Wife § 325, Consolidation Of Claims.

Rule 5.370. Party designation in interstate and intrastate cases

When a support action that has been initiated in another county or another state is filed, transferred, or registered in a superior court of this state under the Uniform Interstate Family Support Act (Fam. Code, div. 9, pt. 5, ch. 6, commencing with § 4900), the intercounty support enforcement provisions of the Family Code (div. 9, pt. 5, ch. 8, art. 9, commencing with § 5600), or any similar law, the party designations in the caption of the action in the responding court must be as follows:

(1) *New actions initiated under the Uniform Interstate Family Support Act*

The party designation in the superior court of this state, responding to new actions initiated under the Uniform Interstate Family Support Act (Fam. Code, div. 9, pt. 5, ch. 6, commencing with § 4900), must be the party designation that appears on the first page of *the Uniform Support Petition* (form FL–500/OMB 0970–0085) in the action.

(2) *Registered orders under the Uniform Interstate Family Support Act or state law*

The party designation in all support actions registered for enforcement or modification must be the one that appears in the original (earliest) order being registered. *(Formerly Rule 1280.14, adopted, eff. Jan. 1, 2001. Renumbered Rule 5.370 and amended, eff. Jan. 1, 2003. As amended, eff. Jan. 1, 2007.)*

Rule 5.372. Transfer of title IV–D cases between ~~to a~~ tribal court and state court

(a) Purpose

This rule is intended to define the procedure for transfer of title IV–D child support cases ~~from~~ between a California superior court ~~to~~ and a tribal court.

(b) Definitions

(1) "Tribal court" means any tribal court of a federally recognized Indian tribe located in California that is receiving funding from the federal government to operate a child support program under title IV–D of the Social Security Act (42 U.S.C. § 654 et seq.).

(2) "Superior court" means a superior court of the state of California.

(3) "Title IV–D child support cases" include all cases where title IV–D services are being provided whether the case originates from the local child support agency's filing of a summons and complaint or later becomes a title IV–D case when the local child support agency registers a child support order or intervenes in a child support action by filing a change of payee.

(c) Disclosure of related case

A party must disclose in superior court whether there is any related action in tribal court in the first pleading, in an attached affidavit, or under oath. A party's disclosure of a related action must include the names and addresses of the parties to the action, the name and address of the tribal court where the action is filed, the case number of the action, and the name of judge assigned to the action, if known.

(d) Notice of intent to transfer case

Before filing a motion for case transfer of a child support matter from a superior court to a tribal court, the party requesting the transfer, the state title IV–D agency, or the tribal IV–D agency must provide the parties with notice of their right to object to the case transfer and the procedures to make such an objection.

(e) Determination of concurrent jurisdiction by a superior court

(1) The superior court may, on its own motion or on the motion of any party and after notice to the parties of their right to object, transfer a child support and custody provision of an action in which the state is providing services under ~~California~~ Family Code section 17400 to a tribal court, as defined in (a). This provision applies to both prejudgment and postjudgment cases.

(2) The motion for transfer to a tribal court must include the following information:

(A) Whether the child is a tribal member or eligible for tribal membership;

(B) Whether one or both of the child's parents are tribal members or eligible for tribal membership;

(C) Whether one or both of the child's parents live on tribal lands or in tribal housing, work for the tribe, or receive tribal benefits or services;

(D) Whether there are other children of the obligor subject to child support obligations;

(E) Any other factor supporting the child's or parents' connection to the tribe.

(3) When ruling on a motion to transfer, the superior court must first make a threshold determination that concurrent jurisdiction exists. Evidence to support this determination may include:

(A) Evidence contained within the motion for transfer;

(B) Evidence agreed to by stipulation of the parties; and

(C) Other evidence submitted by the parties or by the tribe.

The court may request that the tribal child support agency or the tribal court submit information concerning the tribe's jurisdiction.

(4) There is a presumption of concurrent jurisdiction if the child is a tribal member or eligible for tribal membership. If concurrent jurisdiction is found to exist, the transfer to tribal court will occur unless a party has objected ~~in a timely manner~~ within 20 days after service of notice of the right to object referenced in subdivision (e)(1) above. On the filing of a timely objection to the transfer, the superior court must conduct a hearing on the record considering all the relevant factors set forth in (f). The objecting party has the burden of proof to establish good cause not to transfer to tribal court.

(f) Evidentiary considerations

(1) In making a determination on the ~~application~~ motion for case transfer, the superior court must consider:

~~(1) The nature of the action;~~

~~(2) The interests of the parties;~~

~~(3)~~(A) The identities of the parties;

~~(4)~~(B) The convenience of the parties and witnesses;

~~(5) Whether state or tribal law will apply;~~

~~(6)~~(C) The remedy available in the superior court or tribal court; and

~~(7)~~(D) Any other factors deemed necessary by the superior court.

(2) In making a determination on the motion for case transfer, the superior court may not consider the perceived adequacy of tribal justice systems.

(3) The superior court may, after notice to all parties, attempt to resolve any procedural issues by contacting the tribal court concerning a motion to transfer. The superior court must allow the parties to participate in, and must prepare a record of, any communication made with the tribal court judge.

(g) Order on request to transfer

If ~~T~~the superior court denies the request for transfer, the court must state on the record the basis for denying the request. If the superior court grants the request for transfer, it must issue a final order on the request to transfer including a determination of whether concurrent jurisdiction exists.

(h) Proceedings after order granting transfer

Once the superior court has granted the application to transfer~~,~~ and has received confirmation that the tribal court has accepted jurisdiction, the superior court clerk must deliver a copy of the entire file, including all pleadings and orders, to the clerk of the tribal court within 20 days of confirmation that the tribal court has accepted jurisdiction. With the exception of a filing by a tribal court as described by subdivision (i) of this rule, the superior court may not accept any further r filings in the state court action in relation to the issues of child support and custody that were transferred to the tribal court.

(i) Transfer of proceedings from tribal court

(1) If a tribal court determines that it is not in the best interest of the child or the parties for the tribal court to retain jurisdiction of a child support case, the tribe may, upon noticed motion to all parties and the state child support agency, file a motion with the superior court to transfer the case to the jurisdiction of the superior court along with copies of the tribal court's order transferring jurisdiction and the entire file.

(2) The superior court must notify the tribal court upon receipt of the materials and the date scheduled for the hearing of the motion to transfer.

(3) If the superior court has concurrent jurisdiction, it must not reject the case.

(4) No filing fee may be charged for the transfer of a title IV–D child support case from a tribal court. *(Adopted, eff. Jan. 1, 2014. As amended, eff. Jan. 1, 2018.)*

Research References

Treatises and Practice Aids

Witkin, California Summary 10th Husband and Wife § 308, Background and Scope.

Rule 5.375. Procedure for a support obligor to file a motion regarding mistaken identity

(a) Purpose

This rule applies to a support obligor who claims that support enforcement actions have erroneously been taken against him or her by the local child support agency because of a mistake in the support obligor's identity. This rule sets forth the procedure for filing a motion in superior court to establish the mistaken identity under Family Code section 17530 after the support obligor has filed a claim of mistaken identity with the local child support agency and the claim has been denied.

(b) Procedure for filing motion in superior court

The support obligor's motion in superior court to establish mistaken identity must be filed on *Request for Order* (form FL–300) with appropriate attachments. The support obligor must also file as exhibits to the request for order a copy of the claim of mistaken identity that he or she filed with the local child support agency and a copy of the local child support agency's denial of the claim. *(Formerly Rule 1280.15, adopted, eff. Jan. 1, 2001. Renumbered Rule 5.375 and amended, eff. Jan. 1, 2003. As amended, eff. Jan. 1, 2007; Jan. 1, 2013.)*

Research References

Treatises and Practice Aids

Witkin, California Summary 10th Husband and Wife § 331, Relief from Order Based on Mistaken Identity.

Chapter 11

DOMESTIC VIOLENCE CASES

Article 1

DOMESTIC VIOLENCE PREVENTION ACT CASES

Rule

Rule 5.380. Agreement and judgment of parentage in Domestic Violence Prevention Act cases

(a) No requirement to open separate case; no filing fee

(1) If the court accepts the agreement of parentage and issues a judgment of parentage, the court may not require a party to open a separate parentage or other type of case in which to file the judgment. The court may open a separate type of case, but the court must not charge a fee for filing the judgment of parentage in the new case.

(2) When a judgment of parentage is filed in a Domestic Violence Prevention Act case in which a restraining order is currently in effect, no filing fee may be charged.

(b) Retention

The judgment must be retained by the court as a paternity record under Government Code section 68152.

(c) Notice of Entry of Judgment

When an *Agreement and Judgment of Parentage* (form DV–180) is filed, the court must ~~mail~~ serve a *Notice of Entry of Judgment* (form FL–190) on the parties. *(Adopted, eff. Jan. 1, 2012. As amended, eff. Jan. 1, 2017.)*

Research References

Treatises and Practice Aids

Witkin, California Summary 10th Husband and Wife § 383, Temporary Custody and Visitation.

Rule 5.381. Modification of child custody, visitation, and support orders in Domestic Violence Prevention Act cases

(a) Application of rule

This rule addresses court procedures for the modification of child custody, visitation, and support orders in accordance with Family Code section 6340(a).

(b) Filing fees

A filing fee may be charged on a request to modify a child custody, visitation, or support order only after a protective order, as defined in Family Code section 6218, is no longer in effect. The filing fee, if charged, is the same as the filing fee for a motion, application, or any other paper requiring a hearing after the first paper.

(c) Retention

The court must retain any child custody, visitation, or support order filed in a Domestic Violence Prevention Act as a Family Law order under Government Code section 68152(c)(5). *(Adopted, eff. Jan. 1, 2012.)*

Research References

Treatises and Practice Aids

Witkin, California Summary 10th Husband and Wife § 384, Orders After Notice and Hearing.

Article 2

TRIBAL COURT PROTECTIVE ORDERS

Rule 5.386. Procedures for filing a tribal court protective order

(a) Request for written procedures for filing a tribal court protective order

At the request of any tribal court located within the county, a court must adopt a written procedure or local rule to permit the fax or electronic filing of any tribal court protective order that is entitled to be registered under Family Code section 6404.

(b) Process for registration of order

The written procedure or local rule developed in consultation with the local tribal court or courts must provide a process for:

(1) The tribal court or courts to contact a representative of the superior court to inform him or her that a request for registration of a tribal court protective order will be made;

(2) Confirmation of receipt of the request for registration of the order; and

(3) Return of copies of the registered order to the tribal court or the protected person.

(c) No filing fee required

In accordance with Family Code section 6404(b), no fee may be charged for the fax or electronic filing registration of a tribal court protective order.

(d) Facsimile coversheet

The *Fax Transmission Cover Sheet for Registration of Tribal Court Protective Order* (form DV–610) or similar cover sheet established by written procedure or local rule must be used when fax filing a tribal court protective order. The cover sheet must be the first page transmitted, to be followed by any special handling instructions needed to ensure that the document will comply with local rules. Neither the cover sheet nor the special handling instructions are to be filed in the case. The court is not required to keep a copy of the cover sheet. *(Adopted, eff. July 1, 2012.)*

Research References

Forms

West's California Judicial Council Forms DV-610, Fax Transmission Cover Sheet for Registration Of Tribal Court Protective Order.

Treatises and Practice Aids

Witkin, California Summary 10th Husband and Wife § 389, Foreign Orders.

Chapter 12

SEPARATE TRIALS (BIFURCATION) AND INTERLOCUTORY APPEALS

Article 1

SEPARATE TRIALS

Rule 5.390. Bifurcation of issues

(a) Request for order to bifurcate

As part of the noticed *Request for Order* (FL–300) of a party, the stipulation of the parties, case management, or the court's own motion, the court may bifurcate one or more issues to be tried separately before other issues are tried. A party requesting a separate trial or responding to a request for a separate trial must complete *Application or Response to Application for Separate Trial* (form FL–315).

(b) When to bifurcate

The court may separately try one or more issues before trial of the other issues if resolution of the bifurcated issue is likely to simplify the determination of the other issues. Issues that may be appropriate to try separately in advance include:

(1) Validity of a postnuptial or premarital agreement;

(2) Date of separation;

(3) Date to use for valuation of assets;

(4) Whether property is separate or community;

(5) How to apportion increase in value of a business;

(6) Existence or value of business or professional goodwill;

(7) Termination of status of a marriage or domestic partnership;

(8) Child custody and visitation (parenting time);

(9) Child, spousal, or domestic partner support;

(10) Attorney's fees and costs;

(11) Division of property and debts;

(12) Reimbursement claims; or

(13) Other issues specific to a family law case.

(c) Alternate date of valuation

Requests for separate trial regarding alternate date of valuation under Family Code section 2552(b) must be accompanied by a declaration stating the following:

(1) The proposed alternate valuation date;

(2) Whether the proposed alternate valuation date applies to all or only a portion of the assets and, if the *Request for Order* (FL–300) is directed to only a portion of the assets, the declaration must separately identify each such asset; and

(3) The reasons supporting the alternate valuation date.

(d) Separate trial to terminate status of marriage or domestic partnership

(1) All pension plans that have not been divided by court order that require joinder must be joined as a party to the case before a petitioner or respondent may file a request for a separate trial to terminate marital status or the domestic partnership. Parties may refer to *Retirement Plan Joinder—Information Sheet* (form FL–318–INFO) to help determine whether their retirement benefit plans must be joined.

(2) The party not requesting termination of status may ask the court:

(A) To order that the judgment granting a dissolution include conditions that preserve his or her claims in retirement benefit plans, health insurance, and other assets; and

(B) For other orders made as conditions to terminating the parties' marital status or domestic partnership.

(3) The court must use *Bifurcation of Status of Marriage or Domestic Partnership—Attachment* (form FL–347) as an attachment to the order after hearing in these matters.

(4) In cases involving division of pension benefits acquired by the parties during the marriage or domestic partnership, the court must use *Pension Benefits—Attachment to Judgment* (form FL–348) to set out the orders upon severance of the status of marriage or domestic partnership. The form serves as a temporary qualified domestic relations order and must be attached to the status-only judgment and then served on the plan administrator. It can also be attached to a judgment to allow the parties time to prepare a qualified domestic relations order.

(e) Notice by clerk

Within 10 days after the order deciding the bifurcated issue and any statement of decision under rule 3.1591 have been filed, the clerk must ~~mail~~ serve copies to the parties and file a certificate of mailing or a certificate of electronic service. *(Adopted, eff. Jan. 1, 2013. As amended, eff. Jan. 1, 2017.)*

Research References

Forms

California Practice Guide: Rutter Family Law Forms Form 8:8, Request for Order Re Separate Trial Re Alternate Valuation Date (Community Bank Accounts).

California Practice Guide: Rutter Family Law Forms Form 1:32, Glossary Of Common Family Law Terms, Phrases and Concepts (Enclosure to Form 1:31).

Treatises and Practice Aids

Witkin, California Summary 10th Community Property § 193, in General.

Witkin, California Summary 10th Husband and Wife § 106, Court Rule.

Article 2

INTERLOCUTORY APPEALS

Rule

Rule 5.392. Interlocutory appeals

(a) Applicability

This rule does not apply to appeals from the court's termination of marital status as a separate issue, or to appeals from other orders that are separately appealable.

(b) Certificate of probable cause for appeal

(1) The order deciding the bifurcated issue may include an order certifying that there is probable cause for immediate appellate review of the issue.

(2) If it was not in the order, within 10 days after the clerk ~~mails~~ serves the order deciding the bifurcated issue, a party may notice a motion asking the court to certify that there is probable cause for immediate appellate review of the order. The motion must be heard within 30 days after the order deciding the bifurcated issue is ~~mailed~~ served.

(3) The clerk must promptly ~~mail~~ serve notice of the decision on the motion to the parties. If the motion is not determined within 40 days after ~~mailing of~~ serving the order on the bifurcated issue, it is deemed granted on the grounds stated in the motion.

(c) Content and effect of certificate

(1) A certificate of probable cause must state, in general terms, the reason immediate appellate review is desirable, such as a statement that final resolution of the issue:

(A) Is likely to lead to settlement of the entire case;

(B) Will simplify remaining issues;

(C) Will conserve the courts' resources; or

(D) Will benefit the well-being of a child of the marriage or the parties.

(2) If a certificate is granted, trial of the remaining issues may be stayed. If trial of the remaining issues is stayed, unless otherwise ordered by the trial court on noticed motion, further discovery must be stayed while the certification is pending. These stays terminate upon the expiration of time for filing a motion to appeal if none is filed, or upon the Court of Appeal denying all motions to appeal, or upon the Court of Appeal decision becoming final.

(d) Motion to appeal

(1) If the certificate is granted, a party may, within 15 days after the ~~mailing of~~ court serves the notice of the order granting it, serve and file in the Court of Appeal a motion to appeal the decision on the bifurcated issue. On ex parte application served and filed within 15 days, the Court of Appeal or the trial court may extend the time for filing the motion to appeal by not more than an additional 20 days.

(2) The motion must contain:

(A) A brief statement of the facts necessary to an understanding of the issue;

(B) A statement of the issue; and

(C) A statement of why, in the context of the case, an immediate appeal is desirable.

(3) The motion must include or have attached:

(A) A copy of the decision of the trial court on the bifurcated issue;

(B) Any statement of decision;

(C) The certification of the appeal; and

(D) A sufficient partial record to enable the Court of Appeal to determine whether to grant the motion.

(4) A summary of evidence and oral proceedings, if relevant, supported by a declaration of counsel may be used when a transcript is not available.

(5) The motion must be accompanied by the filing fee for an appeal under rule 8.100(c) and Government Code sections 68926 and 68926.1.

(6) A copy of the motion must be served on the trial court.

(e) Proceedings to determine motion

(1) Within 10 days after service of the motion, an adverse party may serve and file an opposition to it.

(2) The motion to appeal and any opposition will be submitted without oral argument, unless otherwise ordered.

(3) The motion to appeal is deemed granted unless it is denied within 30 days from the date of filing the opposition or the last document requested by the court, whichever is later.

(4) Denial of a motion to appeal is final forthwith and is not subject to rehearing. A party aggrieved by the denial of the motion may petition for review by the Supreme Court.

(f) Proceedings if motion to appeal is granted

(1) If the motion to appeal is granted, the moving party is deemed an appellant, and the rules governing other civil appeals apply except as provided in this rule.

(2) The partial record filed with the motion will be considered the record for the appeal unless, within 10 days from the date notice of the grant of the motion is ~~mailed~~ served, a party notifies the Court of Appeal of additional portions of the record that are needed for the full consideration of the appeal.

(3) If a party notifies the court of the need for an additional record, the additional material must be secured from the trial court by augmentation under rule 8.155, unless it appears to the Court of Appeal that some of the material is not needed.

(4) Briefs must be filed under a schedule set for the matter by the Court of Appeal.

(g) Review by writ or appeal

The trial court's denial of a certification motion under (b) does not preclude review of the decision on the bifurcated issue by extraordinary writ.

(h) Review by appeal

None of the following precludes review of the decision on the bifurcated issue upon appeal of the final judgment:

(1) A party's failure to move for certification under (b) for immediate appeal;

(2) The trial court's denial of a certification motion under (b) for immediate appeal;

(3) A party's failure to move to appeal under (d); and

(4) The Court of Appeals denial of a motion to appeal under (d). *(Formerly Rule 1269.5, adopted eff. July 1, 1989. As amended, eff. Jan. 1, 1994; Jan. 1, 2002. Renumbered Rule 5.180 and amended, eff. Jan. 1, 2003. As amended, eff. Jan. 1, 2007. Renumbered Rule 5.392, eff. Jan. 1, 2013. As amended, eff. Jan. 1, 2017.)*

Research References

Treatises and Practice Aids

Witkin, California Summary 10th Husband and Wife § 123, Certification Procedure for Bifurcated Issues.

Chapter 13

TRIALS AND LONG–CAUSE HEARINGS

Rule 5.393. Setting trials and long-cause hearings

(a) Definitions

For purposes of this rule:

(1) A "trial day" is defined as a period no less than two and a half hours of a single court day.

(2) A "long-cause hearing" is defined as a hearing on a request for order that extends more than a single court day.

(3) A "trial brief" or "hearing brief" is a written summary or statement submitted by a party that explains to a judge the party's position on particular issues that will be part of the trial or hearing.

(b) Conference with judge before trial or long-cause hearing

The judge may schedule a conference with the parties and their attorneys before any trial or long-cause hearing.

(1) *Time estimates*

During the conference, each party must provide an estimate of the amount of time that will be needed to complete the trial or long-cause hearing. The estimate must take into account the time needed to examine witnesses and introduce evidence at the trial.

(2) *Trial or hearing brief*

The judge must determine at the conference whether to require each party to submit a trial or hearing brief. If trial briefs will be required, they must comply with the requirements of rule 5.394. Any additional requirements to the brief must be provided to the parties in writing before the end of the conference.

(c) Sequential days

Consistent with the goal of affording family law litigants continuous trials and long-cause hearings without interruption, when trials or long-cause hearings are set, they must be scheduled on as close to sequential days as the calendar of the trial judge permits.

(d) Intervals between trial or hearing days

When trials or long-cause hearings are not completed in the number of days originally scheduled, the court must schedule the remaining trial days as soon as possible on the earliest available days with the goal of minimizing intervals between days for trials or long-cause hearings. *(Adopted, eff. Jan. 1, 2013.)*

Research References

Treatises and Practice Aids

Witkin, California Summary 10th Husband and Wife § 99, in General.

Rule 5.394. Trial or hearing brief

(a) Contents of brief

For cases in which the judge orders each party to complete a trial or hearing brief or other pleading, the contents of the brief must include at least:

(1) The statistical facts and any disputes about the statistical facts. Statistical facts that may apply to the case could include:

(A) Date of the marriage or domestic partnership;

(B) Date of separation;

(C) Length of marriage or domestic partnership in years and months; and

(D) Names and ages of the parties' minor children;

(2) A brief summary of the case;

(3) A statement of any issues that need to be resolved at trial;

(4) A brief statement summarizing the contents of any appraisal or expert report to be offered at trial;

(5) A list of the witnesses to be called at trial and a brief description of the anticipated testimony of each witness, as well as name, business address, and statement of qualifications of any expert witness;

(6) Any legal arguments on which a party intends to rely; and

(7) Any other matters determined by the judge to be necessary and provided to the parties in writing.

(b) Service of brief

The parties must serve the trial or hearing brief on all parties and file the brief with the court a minimum of 5 court days before the trial or long-cause hearing. *(Adopted, eff. Jan. 1, 2013.)*

Research References

Treatises and Practice Aids

Witkin, California Summary 10th Husband and Wife § 99, in General.

Chapter 14

DEFAULT PROCEEDINGS AND JUDGMENTS

Rule

Rule 5.401. Default

(a) Entry of default

Upon proper application of the petitioner, the clerk must enter a default if the respondent or defendant fails within the time permitted to:

(1) Make an appearance as stated in rule 5.62;

(2) File a notice of motion to quash service of summons under section 418.10 of the Code of Civil Procedure; or

(3) File a petition for writ of mandate under section 418.10 of the Code of Civil Procedure.

(b) Proof of facts

(1) The petitioner may apply to the court for the relief sought in the petition at the time default is entered. The court must require proof to be made of the facts stated in the petition and may enter its judgment based on that proof.

(2) The court may permit the use of a completed *Income and Expense Declaration* (form FL–150) or *Financial Statement (Simplified)* (form FL–155) and *Property Declaration* (form FL–160) for all or any part of the proof required or permitted to be offered on any issue to which they are relevant.

(c) Disposition of all matters required

A judgment based on a default must include disposition of all matters subject to the court's jurisdiction for which a party seeks adjudication or an explicit reservation of jurisdiction over any matter not proposed for disposition at that time. *(Adopted, eff. Jan. 1, 2013.)*

Research References

Treatises and Practice Aids

Witkin, California Summary 10th Husband and Wife § 101, Entry Of Default and Application for Relief.

Witkin, California Summary 10th Husband and Wife § 102, Requirement Of Proof.

Rule 5.402. Request for default; forms

(a) Forms

No default may be entered in any proceeding unless a request has been completed on a *Request to Enter Default* (form FL–165) and filed by the petitioner. However, an *Income and Expense Declaration* (form FL–150) or *Financial Statement (Simplified)* (form FL–155) are not required if the petition contains no request for support, costs, or attorney's fees. A *Property Declaration* (form FL–160) is not required if the petition contains no request for property.

(b) Service address required

For the purpose of completing the declaration of mailing, unless service was by publication and the address of respondent is unknown, it is not sufficient to state that the address of the party to whom notice is given is unknown or unavailable. *(Adopted, eff. Jan. 1, 2013.)*

Research References

Treatises and Practice Aids

Witkin, California Summary 10th Husband and Wife § 87, Methods Of Obtaining Orders.

Witkin, California Summary 10th Husband and Wife § 101, Entry Of Default and Application for Relief.

Rule 5.405. Judgment checklists

The *Judgment Checklist—Dissolution/Legal Separation* (form FL–182) lists the forms that courts may require to complete a judgment based on default or uncontested judgment in dissolution or legal separation cases based on a declaration under Family Code section 2336. The court may not require any additional forms or attachments. *(Formerly Rule 5.146, adopted, eff. July 1, 2012. Renumbered Rule 5.405, eff. Jan. 1, 2013.)*

Research References

Forms

West's California Judicial Council Forms FL-182, Judgment Checklist--Dissolution/Legal Separation.

Treatises and Practice Aids

Witkin, California Summary 10th Husband and Wife § 102, Requirement Of Proof.

Rule 5.407. Review of default and uncontested judgments submitted on the basis of declaration under Family Code section 2336

Once a valid proof of service of summons has been filed with the court or respondent has made a general appearance in the case:

(a) Court review

The court must conduct a procedural review of all the documents submitted for judgment based on default or uncontested judgments submitted under Family Code section 2336 and notify the attorneys or self-represented litigants who submitted them of all identified defects.

(b) Notice of errors and omissions

Basic information for correction of the defects must be included in any notification to attorneys or self-represented litigants made under (a). *(Formerly Rule 5.147, adopted, eff. July 1, 2012. Renumbered Rule 5.407 and amended, eff. Jan. 1, 2013.)*

Research References

Treatises and Practice Aids

Witkin, California Summary 10th Husband and Wife § 102, Requirement Of Proof.

Rule 5.409. Default and uncontested judgment hearings on judgments submitted on the basis of declarations under Family Code section 2336

The decision to hold a hearing in a case in which a judgment has been submitted on the basis of a declaration under Family Code section 2336 should be made on a case-by-case basis at the discretion of the court or request of a party. Courts must allow judgments in default and uncontested cases to be submitted by declaration pursuant to section 2336 and must not require that a hearing be conducted in all such cases. *(Formerly Rule 5.148, adopted, eff. July 1, 2012. Renumbered Rule 5.409, eff. Jan. 1, 2013.)*

Research References

Treatises and Practice Aids

Witkin, California Summary 10th Husband and Wife § 102, Requirement Of Proof.

Witkin, California Summary 10th Parent and Child § 714, Preparing and Sending Record.

Rule 5.411. Stipulated judgments

(a) Format

A stipulated judgment (which must be attached to form FL–180 or form FL–250) may be submitted to the court for signature as an uncontested matter or at the time of the hearing on the merits and must contain the exact terms of any judgment proposed to be entered in the case. At the end, immediately above the space reserved for the judge's signature, the stipulated judgment must contain the following:

The foregoing is agreed to by:

____

______________ ______________
(Petitioner) (Respondent)

____

Approved as conforming to the agreement of the parties:

____

______________ ______________
(Attorney for Petitioner) (Attorney for Respondent)

____

(b) Disposition of all matters required

A stipulated judgment must include disposition of all matters subject to the court's jurisdiction for which a party seeks adjudication or an explicit reservation of jurisdiction over any matter not proposed for disposition at that time. A stipulated judgment constitutes a written agreement between the parties as to all matters covered by the stipulation. *(Adopted, eff. Jan. 1, 2013.)*

Research References

Forms

California Practice Guide: Rutter Family Law Forms Form 1:32, Glossary Of Common Family Law Terms, Phrases and Concepts (Enclosure to Form 1:31).

Treatises and Practice Aids

Witkin, California Summary 10th Husband and Wife § 112, Contents Of Judgment.

Rule 5.413. Notice of entry of judgment

(a) Notice by clerk

Notwithstanding Code of Civil Procedure section 664.5, the clerk must give notice of entry of judgment, using *Notice of Entry of Judgment* (form FL–190), to the attorney for each party or to the party if self-represented, of the following:

(1) A judgment of legal separation;

(2) A judgment of dissolution;

(3) A judgment of nullity;

(4) A judgment establishing parental relationship (on form FL–190); or

(5) A judgment regarding custody or support.

(b) Notice to local child support agency form

This rule applies to local child support agency proceedings except that the notice of entry of judgment must be on *Notice of Entry of Judgment and Proof of Service by Mail* (form FL–635). *(Adopted, eff. Jan. 1, 2013.)*

Research References

Treatises and Practice Aids

Witkin, California Summary 10th Husband and Wife § 110, Entry Of Judgment.

Rule 5.415. Completion of notice of entry of judgment

(a) Required attachments

Every person who submits a judgment for signature by the court must submit:

(1) Stamped envelopes addressed to the parties (if they do not have attorneys), or to the attorneys of record (if the parties are represented) that show the address of the court clerk as the return address; and

(2) An original and at least two additional copies of the *Notice of Entry of Judgment* (form FL–190).

(b) Fully completed

Form FL–190 must be fully completed except for the designation of the date entered, the date of mailing, and signatures. It must specify in the certificate of mailing the place where notices have been given to the other party.

(c) Address of respondent or defendant

If there has been no appearance by the other party, the address stated in the affidavit of mailing in part 3 of the *Request to Enter Default* (form FL–165) must be the party's last known address and must be used for mailing form FL–190 to that party. In support proceedings initiated by the local child support agency, an envelope addressed to the child support agency need not be submitted. If service was by publication and the address of respondent or defendant is unknown, those facts must be stated in place of the required address.

(d) Consequences of failure to comply

Failure to complete the form or to submit the envelopes is cause for refusal to sign the judgment until compliance with the requirements of this rule.

(e) Application to local child support agencies

This rule applies to local child support agency proceedings filed under the Family Code except that:

(1) The local child support agency must use form *Notice of Entry of Judgment and Proof of Service by Mail* (form FL–635);

(2) The local child support agency may specify in the certificate of mailing that the address where the *Notice of Entry of Judgment* (form FL–190) was mailed is on file with the local child support agency; and

(3) An envelope addressed to the local child support agency need not be submitted. *(Adopted, eff. Jan. 1, 2013.)*

Research References

Treatises and Practice Aids

Witkin, California Summary 10th Husband and Wife § 110, Entry Of Judgment.

Chapter 15

SETTLEMENT SERVICES

Rule 5.420. Domestic violence procedures for court-connected settlement service providers

(a) Purpose

This rule sets forth the protocol for court-connected settlement service providers handling cases involving domestic violence and not involving child custody or visitation (parenting time).

(b) Definitions

(1) "Domestic violence" is used as defined in Family Code sections 6203 and 6211.

(2) "Protective order" is synonymous with "domestic violence restraining order" as well as the following:

(A) "Emergency protective order" under Family Code section 6215;

(B) "Protective order" under Family Code section 6218;

(C) "Restraining order" under Welfare and Institutions Code section 213.5; and

(D) "Orders by court" under Penal Code section 136.2.

(3) "Settlement service(s)" refers to voluntary procedures in which the parties in a family law case agree to meet with a neutral third party professional for the purpose of identifying the issues involved in the case and attempting to reach a resolution of those issues by mutual agreement.

(c) Duties of settlement service providers

Courts providing settlement services must develop procedures for handling cases involving domestic violence. In developing these procedures, courts should consider:

(1) Reviewing court files or, if available, intake forms, to inform the person providing settlement services of any existing protective orders or history of domestic violence;

(2) Making reasonable efforts to ensure the safety of parties when they are participating in services;

(3) Avoiding negotiating with the parties about using violence with each other, whether either party should or should not obtain or dismiss a restraining order, or whether either party should cooperate with criminal prosecution;

(4) Providing information and materials that describe the settlement services and procedures with respect to domestic violence;

(5) Meeting first with the parties separately to determine whether joint meetings are appropriate in a case in which there has been a history of domestic violence between the parties or in which a protective order is in effect;

(6) Conferring with the parties separately regarding safety-related issues and the option of continuing in separate sessions at separate times if domestic violence is discovered after services have begun;

(7) Protecting the confidentiality of each party's times of arrival, departure, and meeting for separate sessions when appropriate; and

(8) Providing information to parties about support persons participating in joint or separate sessions.

(d) Training and education

All settlement service providers should participate in programs of continuing instruction in issues related to domestic violence, including child abuse. *(Adopted, eff. Jan. 1, 2013.)*

Research References

Treatises and Practice Aids

Witkin, California Summary 10th Husband and Wife § 371, Civil Remedies.

Chapter 16

LIMITED SCOPE REPRESENTATION; ATTORNEY'S FEES AND COSTS

Article 1

LIMITED SCOPE REPRESENTATION

Rule 5.425. Limited scope representation; application of rules

(a) Definition

"Limited scope representation" is a relationship between an attorney and a person seeking legal services in which they have agreed that the scope of the legal services will be limited to specific tasks that the attorney will perform for the person.

(b) Application

This rule applies to limited scope representation in family law cases. Rules 3.35 through 3.37 apply to limited scope representation in civil cases.

(c) Types of limited scope representation

These rules recognize two types of limited scope representation:

(1) *Noticed representation*

This type occurs when an attorney and a party notify the court and other parties of the limited scope representation. The procedures in (d) and (e) apply only to cases involving noticed limited scope representation.

(2) *Undisclosed representation*

In this type of limited scope representation, a party contracts with an attorney to draft or assist in drafting legal documents, but the attorney does not make an appearance in the case. The procedures in (f) apply to undisclosed representation.

(d) Noticed limited scope representation

(1) A party and an attorney must provide the required notice of their agreement for limited scope representation by serving other parties and filing with the court a *Notice of Limited Scope Representation* (form FL–950).

(2) After the notice in (1) is received and until a ~~substitution of attorney~~ *Substitution of Attorney—Civil* (form MC–050), or a *Notice of Completion of Limited Scope Representation* (form FL–955) with the "Final" box checked, or an order to be relieved as attorney is filed and served:

(A) The attorney must be served only with documents that relate ~~only~~ to the issues identified in the *Notice of Limited Scope Representation* (form FL–950); and

(B) ~~The party must be served directly with~~ Documents that relate to all other issues outside the scope of the attorney's representation must be served directly on the party or the attorney representing the party on those issues.

(3) Electronic service of notices and documents described in this rule is permitted if the client previously agreed in writing to accept service of documents electronically from the attorney.

(4) Before being relieved as counsel, the limited scope attorney must file and serve the order after hearing or judgment following the hearing or trial at which he or she provided representation unless:

(A) Otherwise directed by the court; or

(B) The party agreed in the *Notice of Limited Scope Representation* (form FL–950) that completion of the order after hearing is not within the scope of the attorney's representation.

(e) Procedures to be relieved as counsel on completion of limited scope representation if client has not signed a substitution of attorney

An attorney who has completed the tasks specified in the *Notice of Limited Scope Representation* (form FL–950) may use the following procedures to request that he or she be relieved as attorney ~~in cases in which the attorney has appeared before the court as an attorney of record and~~ if the client has not signed a *Substitution of Attorney—Civil* (form MC–050):

(1) *~~Application~~ Notice of completion of limited scope representation*

~~An application to be relieved as attorney on completion of limited scope representation under Code of Civil Procedure section 284(2) must be directed to the client and made on the *Application to Be Relieved as Counsel Upon Completion of Limited Scope Representation* (form FL–955).~~ The limited scope attorney must serve the client with the following documents:

(A) A *Notice of Completion of Limited Scope Representation* (form FL–955) with the "Proposed" box marked and the deadline for the client to file the objection completed by the attorney;

(B) *Information for Client About Notice of Completion of Limited Scope Representation* (form FL–955–INFO); and

(C) A blank *Objection to Proposed Notice of Completion of Limited Scope Representation* (form FL–956).

~~(2) *Filing and service of application*~~

~~The application to be relieved as attorney must be filed with the court and served on the client and on all other parties or attorneys for parties in the case. The client must also be served with a blank *Objection to Application to Be Relieved as Counsel on Completion of Limited Scope Representation* (form FL–956).~~

~~(3)~~(2) *No objection*

~~If no objection is served and filed with the court within 15 days from the date that the *Application to Be Relieved as Counsel on Completion of Limited Scope Representation* (form FL–955) is served on the client, the attorney making the application must file an updated form FL–955 indicating the lack of objection, along with a proposed *Order on Application to Be Relieved as Counsel on Completion of Limited Scope Representation* (form FL–958). The clerk must then forward the order for judicial signature.~~ If the client does not file and serve an *Objection to Proposed Notice of Completion of Limited Scope Representation* (form FL–956) within 10 calendar days from the date that the *Notice of Completion of Limited Scope Representation* (form FL–955) was served, the limited scope attorney:

(A) Must serve the client and the other parties or, if represented, their attorneys, with a *Notice of Completion of Limited Scope Representation* (form FL–955) with the "Final" box marked;

(B) Must file the final *Notice of Completion of Limited Scope Representation* (form FL–955) with the court, and attach the proofs of service of both the "Proposed" and "Final" notices of completion;

(C) May not be charged a fee to file the final notice of completion, even if the attorney has not previously made an appearance in the case; and

(D) Is deemed to be relieved as attorney on the date that the final notice of completion is served on the client.

~~(4)~~(3) *Objection*

~~If an objection to the application is served and filed within 15 days, the clerk must set a hearing date on the *Objection to Application to Be Relieved as Counsel on Completion of Limited Scope Representation* (form FL–956). The hearing must be scheduled no later than 25 days from the date the objection is filed. The clerk must send the notice of the hearing to the parties and the attorney.~~ If the client files the *Objection to Proposed Notice of Completion of Limited Scope Representation* (form FL–956) within 10 calendar days from the date that the proposed notice of completion was served, the following procedures apply:

(A) The clerk must set a hearing date on the *Objection to Proposed Notice of Completion of Limited Scope Representation* (form FL–956) to be conducted no later than 25 court days from the date the objection is filed.

(B) The court may charge a motion fee to file the objection and schedule the hearing.

(C) The objection—including the date, time, and location of the hearing—must be served on the limited scope attorney and all other parties in the case (or on their attorneys, if they are represented). Unless the court orders a different time for service, the objection must be served by the deadline specified in *Information for Client About Notice of Completion of Limited Scope Representation* (form FL–955–INFO).

(D) If the attorney wishes, he or she may file and serve a *Response to Objection to Proposed Notice of Completion of Limited Scope Representation* (form FL–957). Unless otherwise directed by the court, any response should be filed with the court and served on the client and other parties, or their attorneys, at least nine court days before the hearing.

(E) Unless otherwise directed by the court, the attorney must prepare the *Order on Completion of Limited Scope Representation* (form FL–958) and obtain the judge's signature.

(F) The attorney is responsible for filing and serving the order on the client and other parties after the hearing, unless the court directs otherwise.

(G) If the court finds that the attorney has completed the agreed-upon work, the representation is concluded upon service of the signed *Order on Completion of Limited Scope Representation* (form FL–958).

~~(5) *Service of the order*~~

~~If no objection is served and filed and the proposed order is signed, the attorney who filed the *Application to Be Relieved as Counsel on Completion of Limited Scope Representation* (form FL–955) must serve a copy of the signed order on the client and on all parties or the attorneys for all parties who have appeared in the case. The court may delay the effective date of the order relieving the attorney until proof of service of a copy of the signed order on the client has been filed with the court.~~

(f) Nondisclosure of attorney assistance in preparation of court documents

(1) *Nondisclosure*

In a family law proceeding, an attorney who contracts with a client to draft or assist in drafting legal documents, but does not make an appearance in the case, is not required to disclose within the text of the document that he or she was involved in preparing the documents.

(2) *Attorney's fees*

If a litigant seeks a court order for attorney's fees incurred as a result of document preparation, the litigant must disclose to the court information required for a proper determination of attorney's fees, including the name of the attorney who assisted in the preparation of the documents, the time involved or other basis for billing, the tasks performed, and the amount billed.

(3) *Applicability*

This rule does not apply to an attorney who has made a general appearance or has contracted with his or her client to make an appearance on any issue that is the subject of the pleadings. *(Adopted, eff. Jan. 1, 2013. As amended, eff. Sept. 1, 2017.)*

Research References

Forms

California Practice Guide: Rutter Family Law Forms Form 1:32, Glossary Of Common Family Law Terms, Phrases and Concepts (Enclosure to Form 1:31).

West's California Judicial Council Forms FL-158, Supporting Declaration for Attorney's Fees and Costs Attachment.

West's California Judicial Council Forms FL-319, Request for Attorney's Fees and Costs Attachment.

West's California Judicial Council Forms FL-346, Attorney's Fees and Costs Order Attachment.

Treatises and Practice Aids

Witkin, California Summary 10th Husband and Wife § 74, Limited Scope Legal Representation.

Article 2

ATTORNEY'S FEES AND COSTS

Rule 5.427. Attorney's fees and costs

(a) Application

This rule applies to attorney's fees and costs based on financial need, as described in Family Code sections 2030, 2032, 3121, 3557, and 7605.

(b) Request

(1) Except as provided in Family Code section 2031(b), to request attorney's fees and costs, a party must complete, file and serve the following documents:

(A) *Request for Order (form FL–300)*;

(B) *Request for Attorney's Fees and Costs Attachment* (form FL–319) or a comparable declaration that addresses the factors covered in form FL–319;

(C) A current *Income and Expense Declaration* (form FL–150);

(D) A personal declaration in support of the request for attorney's fees and costs, either using *Supporting Declaration for Attorney's Fees and Costs Attachment* (form FL–158) or a comparable declaration that addresses the factors covered in form FL–158; and

(E) Any other papers relevant to the relief requested.

(2) The party requesting attorney's fees and costs must provide the court with sufficient information about the attorney's hourly billing rate; the nature of the litigation; the attorney's experience in the particular type of work demanded; the fees and costs incurred or anticipated; and why the requested fees and costs are just, necessary, and reasonable.

(c) Response to request

To respond to the request for attorney's fees and costs, a party must complete, file, and serve the following documents:

(1) *Responsive Declaration to Request for Order* (form FL–320);

(2) A current *Income and Expense Declaration* (form FL–150);

(3) A personal declaration responding to the request for attorney's fees and costs, either using *Supporting Declaration for Attorney's Fees and Costs Attachment* (form FL–158) or a comparable declaration that addresses the factors covered in form FL–158; and

(4) Any other papers relevant to the relief requested.

(d) Income and expense declaration

Both parties must complete, file, and serve a current *Income and Expense Declaration* (form FL–150). A *Financial Statement (Simplified)* (form FL155) is not appropriate for use in proceedings to determine or modify attorney's fees and costs.

(1) "Current" is defined as being completed within the past three months, provided that no facts have changed. The form must be sufficiently completed to allow determination of the issues.

(2) When attorney's fees are requested by either party, the section on the *Income and Expense Declaration* (form FL–150) related to the amount in savings, credit union, certificates of deposit, and money market accounts must be fully completed, as well as the section related to the amount of attorney's fees incurred, currently owed, and the source of money used to pay such fees.

(e) Court findings and order

The court may make findings and orders regarding attorney's fees and costs by using *Attorney's Fees and Costs Order Attachment* (form FL–346). This form is an attachment to *Findings and Order After Hearing* (form FL–340), *Judgment* (form FL–180), and *Judgment (Uniform Parentage—Custody and Support)* (form FL–250). *(Formerly Rule 5.93, adopted, eff. Jan. 1, 2012. As amended, eff. July 1, 2012. Renumbered Rule 5.427, eff. Jan. 1, 2013.)*

Commentary

The Judicial Council form for requesting attorney fees and costs pendente lite in a dissolution proceeding is not mandatory so long as comparable declarations are submitted. To the extent that a local court rule makes the Judicial Council form mandatory, it is unenforceable because it conflicts with California Rule of Court 5.427(b)(1)(B), which makes the form optional. *In re Marriage of Sharples, 223 Cal.App.4th 160, 166 Cal.Rptr.3d 818 (2014).*

Research References

Treatises and Practice Aids

Witkin, California Summary 10th Husband and Wife § 203A, (New) Attorneys' Fees and Costs.

Witkin, California Summary 10th Parent and Child § 19, General Provisions.

Witkin, California Summary 10th Parent and Child § 363, Applicability Of Family Code Custody Provisions.

Witkin, California Summary 10th Parent and Child § 426, Action by Child or Parent.

Chapter 17

FAMILY LAW FACILITATOR

Rule 5.430. Minimum standards for the Office of the Family Law Facilitator

(a) Authority

These standards are adopted under Family Code section 10010.

(b) Family law facilitator qualifications

The Office of the Family Law Facilitator must be headed by at least one attorney, who is an active member of the State Bar of California, known as the family law facilitator. Each family law facilitator must possess the following qualifications:

(1) A minimum of five years experience in the practice of law, which must include substantial family law practice including litigation and/or mediation;

(2) Knowledge of family law procedures;

(3) Knowledge of the child support establishment and enforcement process under Title IV–D of the federal Social Security Act (42 U.S.C. § 651 et seq.);

(4) Knowledge of child support law and the operation of the uniform state child support guideline; and

(5) Basic understanding of law and psychological issues related to domestic violence.

(c) Substituted experience

Courts may substitute additional experience, skills, or background appropriate to their community for the qualifications listed above.

(d) Desirable experience

Additional desirable experience for a family law facilitator may include experience in working with low-income, semiliterate, self–represented, or non–English–speaking litigants.

(e) Service provision

Services may be provided by other paid and volunteer members of the Office of the Family Law Facilitator under the supervision of the family law facilitator.

(f) Protocol required

Each court must develop a written protocol to provide services when a facilitator deems himself or herself disqualified or biased.

(g) Grievance procedure

Each court must develop a written protocol for a grievance procedure for processing and responding to any complaints against a family law facilitator.

(h) Training requirements

Each family law facilitator should attend at least one training per year for family law facilitators provided by the Judicial Council. *(Formerly Rule 1208, adopted, eff. Jan. 1, 2000. Renumbered Rule 5.35 and amended, eff. Jan. 1, 2003. As amended, eff. Jan. 1, 2007. Renumbered Rule 5.430, eff. Jan. 1, 2013.)*

Research References

Treatises and Practice Aids

Witkin, California Summary 10th Parent and Child § 383, in General.

Chapter 18

COURT COORDINATION RULES

Article 1

RELATED CASES

Rule 5.440. Related cases

Where resources permit, courts should identify cases related to a pending family law case to avoid issuing conflicting orders and make effective use of court resources.

(a) Definition of "related case"

For purposes of this rule, a pending family law case is related to another pending case, or to a case that was dismissed with or without prejudice, or to a case that was disposed of by judgment, if the cases:

(1) Involve the same parties or the parties' minor children;

(2) Are based on issues governed by the Family Code or by the guardianship provisions of the Probate Code; or

(3) Are likely for other reasons to require substantial duplication of judicial resources if heard by different judges.

(b) Confidential information

Other than forms providing custody and visitation (parenting time) orders to be filed in the family court, where the identification of a related case includes a disclosure of information relating to a juvenile dependency or delinquency matter involving the children of the parties in the pending family law case, the clerk must file that information in the confidential portion of the court file.

(c) Coordination of title IV–D cases

To the extent possible, courts should coordinate title IV–D (government child support) cases with other related family law matters. *(Adopted, eff. Jan. 1, 2013.)*

Research References

Treatises and Practice Aids

Witkin, California Summary 10th Husband and Wife § 68, in General.

Witkin, California Summary 10th Husband and Wife § 308, Background and Scope.

Rule 5.445. Court communication protocol for domestic violence and child custody orders

(a) Definitions

For purposes of this rule:

(1) "Criminal court protective order" means any court order issued under California Penal Code section 136.2 arising from a complaint, an information, or an indictment in which the victim or witness and the defendant have a relationship as defined in Family Code section 6211.

(2) "Court" means all departments and divisions of the superior court of a single county.

(3) "Cases involving child custody and visitation" include family, juvenile, probate, and guardianship proceedings.

(b) Purpose

(1) This rule is intended to:

(A) Encourage courts to share information about the existence and terms of criminal court protective orders and other orders regarding child custody and visitation that involve the defendant and the victim or witness named in the criminal court protective orders.

(B) Encourage courts hearing cases involving child custody and visitation to take every action practicable to ensure that they are aware of the existence of any criminal court protective orders involving the parties to the action currently before them.

(C) Encourage criminal courts to take every action practicable to ensure that they are aware of the existence of any child custody or visitation court orders involving the defendant in the action currently before them.

(D) Permit appropriate visitation between a criminal defendant and his or her children under civil court orders, but at the same time provide for the safety of the victim or witness by ensuring that a criminal court protective order is not violated.

(E) Protect the rights of all parties and enhance the ability of law enforcement to enforce orders.

(F) Encourage courts to establish regional communication systems with courts in neighboring counties regarding the existence of and terms of criminal court protective orders.

(2) This rule is not intended to change the procedures, provided in Family Code section 6380, for the electronic entry of domestic violence restraining orders into the Domestic Violence Restraining Order System.

(c) Local rule required

Every superior court must, by January 1, 2004, adopt local rules containing, at a minimum, the following elements:

(1) *Court communication*

A procedure for communication among courts issuing criminal court protective orders and courts issuing orders involving child custody and visitation, regarding the existence and terms of criminal protective orders and child custody and visitation orders, including:

(A) A procedure requiring courts issuing any orders involving child custody or visitation to make reasonable efforts to determine whether there exists a criminal court protective order that involves any party to the action; and

(B) A procedure requiring courts issuing criminal court protective orders to make reasonable efforts to determine whether there exist any child custody or visitation orders that involve any party to the action.

(2) *Modification*

A procedure by which the court that has issued a criminal court protective order may, after consultation with a court that has issued a subsequent child custody or visitation order, modify the criminal court protective order to allow or restrict contact between the person restrained by the order and his or her children.

(3) *Penal Code section 136.2*

The requirements of Penal Code section 136.2(f)(1) and (2). *(Formerly Rule 5.500, adopted, eff. Jan. 1, 2003. As amended, eff. Jan. 1, 2005. Renumbered Rule 5.450 and amended, eff. Jan. 1, 2007. Renumbered Rule 5.445, eff. Jan. 1, 2013.)*

Research References

Treatises and Practice Aids

Witkin, California Summary 10th Husband and Wife § 383, Temporary Custody and Visitation.

Witkin, California Summary 10th Parent and Child § 286, Where Domestic Violence is Alleged and Protective Order is Issued.

Division 2

RULES APPLICABLE IN FAMILY AND JUVENILE PROCEEDINGS

Chapter 1

CONTACT AND COORDINATION

Rule 5.451. Contact after adoption agreement

(a) Applicability of rule

This rule applies to any adoption of a child. The adoption petition must be filed under Family Code sections 8714 and 8714.5. If the child is a dependent of the juvenile court, the adoption petition may be filed in that juvenile court and the clerk must open a confidential adoption file for the child, and this file must be separate and apart from the dependency file, with an adoption case number different from the dependency case number. For the purposes of this rule, a "relative" is defined as follows:

(1) An adult related to the child or the child's sibling or half-sibling by blood or affinity, including a relative whose status is preceded by the word "step," "great," "great-great," or "grand"; or

(2) The spouse or domestic partner of any of the persons described in (1) even if the marriage or domestic partnership was terminated by dissolution or the death of the spouse related to the child.

(b) Contact after adoption agreement

An adoptive parent or parents~~,~~; a birth relative or relatives, including a birth parent or parents or any siblings of a child who is the subject of an adoption petition~~,~~; or an Indian tribe that the child is a member of and the child may enter into a written agreement permitting postadoption contact between the child and birth relatives, including the birth parent or parents or any siblings, or an Indian tribe. No prospective adoptive parent or birth relative may be required by court order to enter into a contact-after-adoption agreement.

(c) Court approval; time of decree

If, at the time the adoption petition is granted, the court finds that the agreement is in the best interest of the child, the court may enter the decree of adoption and grant postadoption contact as reflected in the approved agreement.

(d) Terms of agreement

The terms of the agreement are limited to the following, although they need not include all permitted terms:

(1) Provisions for visitation between the child and a birth parent or parents;

(2) Provisions for visitation between the child and other identified birth relatives, including siblings or half-siblings of the child;

(3) Provisions for contact between the child and a birth parent or parents;

(4) Provisions for contact between the child and other identified birth relatives, including siblings or half-siblings of the child;

(5) Provisions for contact between the adoptive parent or parents and a birth parent or parents;

(6) Provisions for contact between the adoptive parent or parents and other identified birth relatives, including siblings or half-siblings of the child;

(7) Provisions for the sharing of information about the child with a birth parent or parents;

(8) Provisions for the sharing of information about the child with other identified birth relatives, including siblings or half-siblings of the child; and

(9) The terms of any contact after adoption agreement entered into under a petition filed under Family Code section 8714 must be limited to the sharing of information about the child unless the child has an existing relationship with the birth relative.

(e) Child a party

The child who is the subject of the adoption petition is a party to the agreement whether or not specified as such.

(1) Written consent by a child 12 years of age or older to the terms of the agreement is required for enforcement of the agreement, unless the court finds by a preponderance of the evidence that the agreement is in the best interest of the child and waives the requirement of the child's written consent.

(2) If the child has been found by a juvenile court to be described by section 300 of the Welfare and Institutions Code, an attorney must be appointed to represent the child for purposes of participation in and consent to any contact after adoption agreement, regardless of the age of the child. If the child has been represented by an attorney in the dependency proceedings, that attorney must be appointed for the additional responsibilities of this rule. The attorney is required to represent the child only until the adoption is decreed and dependency terminated.

(f) Form and provisions of the agreement

The agreement must be prepared and submitted on *Contact After Adoption Agreement* (form ADOPT–310) with appropriate attachments.

(g) Report to the court

The department or agency participating as a party or joining in the petition for adoption must submit a report to the court. The report must include a criminal record check and descriptions of all social service referrals. If a contact after adoption agreement has been submitted, the report must include a summary of the agreement and a recommendation as to whether it is in the best interest of the child.

(h) Enforcement of the agreement

The court that grants the petition for adoption and approves the contact after adoption agreement must retain jurisdiction over the agreement.

(1) Any petition for enforcement of an agreement must be filed on *Request to: Enforce, Change, End Contact After Adoption Agreement* (form ADOPT–315). The form must not be accepted for filing unless completed in full, with documentary evidence attached of participation in, or attempts to participate in, mediation or other dispute resolution.

(2) The court may make its determination on the petition without testimony or an evidentiary hearing and may rely solely on documentary evidence or offers of proof. The court may order compliance with the agreement only if:

(A) There is sufficient evidence of good-faith attempts to resolve the issues through mediation or other dispute resolution; and

(B) The court finds enforcement is in the best interest of the child.

(3) The court must not order investigation or evaluation of the issues raised in the petition unless the court finds by clear and convincing evidence that:

(A) The best interest of the child may be protected or advanced only by such inquiry; and

(B) The inquiry will not disturb the stability of the child's home to the child's detriment.

(4) Monetary damages must not be ordered.

(i) Modification or termination of agreement

The agreement may be modified or terminated by the court. Any petition for modification or termination of an agreement must be filed on *Request to: Enforce, Change, End Contact After Adoption Agreement* (form ADOPT–315). The form must not be accepted for filing unless completed in full, with documentary evidence attached of participation in, or attempts to participate in, mediation or other appropriate dispute resolution.

(1) The agreement may be terminated or modified only if:

(A) All parties, including the child of 12 years or older, have signed the petition or have indicated on the *Answer to Request to: Enforce, Change, End Contact After Adoption Agreement* (form ADOPT–320) their consent or have executed a modified agreement filed with the petition; or

(B) The court finds all of the following:

(i) The termination or modification is necessary to serve the best interest of the child;

(ii) There has been a substantial change of circumstances since the original agreement was approved; and

(iii) The petitioner has participated in, or has attempted to participate in, mediation or appropriate dispute resolution.

(2) The court may make its determination without testimony or evidentiary hearing and may rely solely on documentary evidence or offers of proof.

(3) The court may order modification or termination without a hearing if all parties, including the child of 12 years or older, have signed the petition or have indicated on the *Answer to Request to: Enforce, Change, End Contact After Adoption Agreement* (form ADOPT–320) their consent or have executed a modified agreement filed with the petition.

(j) Costs and fees

The fee for filing a *Request to: Enforce, Change, End Contact After Adoption Agreement* (form ADOPT–315) must not exceed the fee assessed for the filing of an adoption petition. Costs and fees for mediation or other appropriate dispute resolution must be assumed by each party, with the exception of the child. All costs and fees of litigation, including any court-ordered investigation or evaluation, must be charged to the petitioner unless the court finds that a party other than the child has failed, without good cause, to comply with the approved agreement; all costs and fees must then be charged to that party.

(k) Adoption final

Once a decree of adoption has been entered, the court may not set aside the decree, rescind any relinquishment, modify or set aside any order terminating parental rights, or modify or set aside any other orders related to the granting of the adoption petition, due to the failure of any party to comply with the terms of a postadoption contact agreement or any subsequent modifications to it. *(Formerly Rule 1180, adopted, eff. July 1, 1998. As amended, eff. July 1, 2001. Renumbered Rule 5.400 and amended, eff. Jan. 1, 2003. As amended, eff. July 1, 2003; Jan. 1, 2007. Renumbered Rule 5.451 and amended, eff. Jan. 1, 2013. As amended, eff. Jan. 1, 2018.)*

Research References

Treatises and Practice Aids

Witkin, California Summary 10th Parent and Child § 104, in General.

Rule 5.460. Request for sibling contact information

(a) Applicability of rule

This rule applies to all persons wishing to exchange contact information with their adopted siblings and all adopted persons wishing to have contact with their siblings, regardless of whether the adoption occurred in juvenile or family court.

(b) Definitions

As used in this rule:

(1) "Adoptee" means any person adopted under California law.

(2) "Department" means the California Department of Social Services (CDSS).

(3) "Licensed adoption agency" means an agency licensed by the department to provide adoption services and includes a licensed county adoption agency and a licensed private adoption agency under Family Code sections 8521, 8530, and 8533.

(4) "Confidential intermediary" means either the department or a licensed adoption agency that provided adoption services for either sibling.

(5) "Alternate confidential intermediary" means a named entity or person designated by the court in place of a licensed adoption agency when the court finds that the agency would experience economic hardship by serving as confidential intermediary.

(6) "Sibling" means a biological sibling, half-sibling, or stepsibling of the adoptee.

(7) "Waiver" means *Waiver of Rights to Confidentiality for Siblings*, department form AD 904A (used for adoptees or siblings over the age of 18 years) or AD 904B (used for adoptees or siblings under the age of 18).

(8) "Consent" means the consent contained within the Department form AD 904B. It is the approval of the filing of a waiver by a person under the age of 18 years obtained from an adoptive parent, a legal parent, a legal guardian, or a dependency court when a child is currently a dependent of the court.

(9) "Petition" means Judicial Council form *Request for Appointment of Confidential Intermediary* (form ADOPT–330).

(10) "Order" means Judicial Council form *Order for Appointment of Confidential Intermediary* (form ADOPT–331).

(c) Waiver submitted by person under the age of 18 years

(1) *Adoptee or sibling waiver*

Each adoptee or sibling under the age of 18 years may submit a waiver to the department or the licensed adoption agency, provided that a consent is also completed.

(2) *Court consent*

If the sibling is currently under the jurisdiction of the juvenile court and his or her parent or legal guardian is unable or unavailable to sign the consent, the court may sign it.

(d) No waiver on file—sibling requesting contact

If, after contacting the department or licensed adoption agency, the sibling who is seeking contact learns that no waiver is on file for the other sibling, the sibling seeking contact should use the following procedure to ask the court that finalized the adoption of either sibling to designate a confidential intermediary to help locate the other sibling:

(1) *Sibling's request*

(A) A sibling requesting contact under Family Code section 9205 must file a petition and submit a blank order to the court that finalized the adoption of either sibling.

(B) If the sibling requesting contact is under the age of 18 years, the petition must be filed through the sibling's duly appointed guardian ad litem under Code of Civil Procedure section 373 or through the sibling's attorney.

(2) *Appointment of a confidential intermediary*

(A) The court must grant the petition unless the court finds that it would be detrimental to the adoptee or sibling with whom contact is sought. The court may consider any and all relevant information in making this determination, including, but not limited to, a review of the court file.

(B) The court will appoint the department or licensed adoption agency that provided adoption services for either sibling as the confidential intermediary.

(C) If the court finds that the licensed adoption agency that conducted the adoptee's adoption is unable to serve as the intermediary, owing to economic hardship, the court may then appoint any one of the following who agrees to serve as an alternate confidential intermediary:

(i) A CASA volunteer or CASA program staff member;

(ii) A court-connected mediator;

(iii) An adoption service provider as defined in Family Code section 8502(a);

(iv) An attorney; or

(v) Another California licensed adoption agency or the California Department of Social Services' Adoptions Support Bureau when no other individuals are available.

(D) When an alternate confidential intermediary is appointed, the licensed adoption agency must provide to the court all records related to the adoptee or sibling for inspection by the alternate confidential intermediary.

(3) *Role of the confidential intermediary*

(A) The confidential intermediary must:

(i) Have access to all records of the adoptee or the sibling, including the court adoption file and adoption agency or CDSS files of either sibling;

(ii) Make all reasonable efforts to locate the adoptee, the sibling, or the adoptive or birth parent;

(iii) Attempt to obtain the consent of the adoptee, the sibling, or the adoptive or birth parent; and

(iv) Notify any located adoptee, sibling, or adoptive or birth parent that consent is optional, not required by law, and does not affect the status of the adoption.

(B) The confidential intermediary must not make any further attempts to obtain consent if the individual denies the request for consent.

(C) The confidential intermediary must use information found in the records of the adoptee or the sibling for authorized purposes only and must not disclose any information obtained in this procedure unless specifically authorized.

(4) *Adopted sibling seeking contact with a sibling who is a dependent child*

An adoptee seeking contact with his or her sibling who is a dependent child must follow the procedure set forth under Welfare and Institutions Code section 388(b) to seek contact with the sibling. *(Formerly Rule 5.410, adopted, eff. Jan. 1, 2008. Renumbered Rule 5.460 and amended, eff. Jan. 1, 2013.)*

Research References

Treatises and Practice Aids

Witkin, California Summary 10th Parent and Child § 152, Contact Between Adoptees and Others.

Rule 5.475. Custody and visitation orders following termination of a juvenile court proceeding or probate court guardianship proceeding

(a) Custody and visitation order from other courts or divisions

On termination of juvenile court jurisdiction under rule 5.700 or termination of a probate guardianship under rule 7.1008, the juvenile court or probate court will direct the transmission of its custody or visitation orders to any superior court in which a related family law custody proceeding or probate guardianship proceeding is pending for filing in that proceeding.

If no such proceeding is pending, the court terminating jurisdiction will direct the transmission of its order to the superior court of, in order of preference, the county in which the parent with sole physical custody resides; if none, the county where the child's primary residence is located; or, if neither exists, a county or location where any custodial parent resides.

(1) *Procedure for filing custody or visitation orders from juvenile or probate court*

(A) Except as directed in subparagraph (B), on receiving the custody or visitation order of a juvenile court or probate court, the clerk of the receiving court must file the order in any pending nullity, dissolution, legal separation, Uniform Parentage Act, Domestic Violence Prevention Act, or other family law custody proceeding, or in any probate guardianship proceeding that affects custody or visitation of the child.

(B) If the only pending proceeding related to the child in the receiving court is filed under Family Code section 17400 et seq., the clerk must proceed as follows.

(i) If the receiving court has issued a custody or visitation order in the pending proceeding, the clerk must file the received order in that proceeding.

(ii) If the receiving court has not issued a custody or visitation order in the pending proceeding, the clerk must not file the received order in that proceeding, but must instead proceed under subparagraph (C).

(C) If no dependency, family law, or guardianship proceeding affecting custody or visitation of the child is pending, the order must be used to open a new custody proceeding in the receiving court. The clerk must immediately open a family law file without charging a filing fee, assign a case number, and file the order in the new case file.

(2) *Endorsed filed copy—clerk's certificate of mailing*

Within 15 court days of receiving the order, the clerk must send an endorsed filed copy of the order showing the case number assigned by the receiving court by first-class mail to: each of the child's parents and to the court that issued the order, with a completed clerk's certificate of mailing, for inclusion in the issuing court's file.

(b) Modification of former guardian visitation orders—custodial parent

When a parent has custody of the child following termination of a probate guardianship, a former guardian's request for modification of the probate court visitation order, including an order denying visitation, must be brought in a proceeding under the Family Code.

(c) Independent action for former guardian visitation

(1) If the court terminated a guardianship under the Probate Code and did not issue a visitation order, the former guardian may maintain an independent action for visitation if a dependency proceeding is not pending. The former guardian may bring the action without the necessity of a separate joinder action.

(2) If the child has at least one living parent and has no guardian, visitation must be determined in a proceeding under the Family Code. If the child does not have at least one living parent, visitation must be determined in a guardianship proceeding, which may be initiated for that purpose.

(3) *Declaration Under Uniform Child Custody Jurisdiction and Enforcement Act (UCCJEA)* (form FL–105/GC–120) must be filed with a petition or motion for visitation by a former guardian. *(Adopted, eff. Jan. 1, 2006. As amended, eff. Jan. 1, 2007; Jan. 1, 2008; Jan. 1, 2013; Jan. 1, 2016.)*

Research References

Forms

West's California Code Forms, Civil Procedure § 1005 Form 35, Motions and Orders--Request for Telephone Appearance--Governmental--Official Form.

West's California Code Forms, Civil Procedure § 1005 Form 37, Motions and Orders--Order After Hearing--Governmental--Official Form.

West's California Code Forms, Civil Procedure § 1005 Form 38, Motions and Orders--Short Form Order After Hearing--Governmental--Official Form.

West's California Code Forms, Civil Procedure § 1005 Form 39, Motions and Orders--Order to Show Cause--Governmental--Official Form.

West's California Code Forms, Civil Procedure § 1005 Form 40, Motions and Orders--Request for Order and Supporting Declaration--Governmental--Official Form.

West's California Code Forms, Civil Procedure § 1005 Form 42, Motions and Orders--Stipulation and Order--Governmental--Official Form.

West's California Code Forms, Civil Procedure § 1005 Form 43, Motions and Orders--Stipulation and Order Waiving Unassigned Arrears--Official Form.

West's California Code Forms, Civil Procedure § 1005 Form 14, Motions and Orders--Order to Show Cause (Family Law, Uniform Parentage)--Official Form.

West's California Code Forms, Civil Procedure § 1005 Form 15, Motions and Orders--Temporary Orders--Attachment to Order to Show Cause--Family Law--Official Form.

West's California Code Forms, Civil Procedure § 1005 Form 18, Motions and Orders--Request for Order (Family Law)--Official Form.

West's California Code Forms, Civil Procedure § 1005 Form 29, Motion and Orders--Application for Separate Trial Attachment (Family Law)--Official Form.

Treatises and Practice Aids

Witkin, California Summary 10th Parent and Child § 370, in General.

Witkin, California Summary 10th Wills and Probate § 930, Termination Of Guardianship.

Chapter 2

INDIAN CHILD WELFARE ACT

Rule 5.480. Application

This chapter addressing the Indian Child Welfare Act (25 United States Code section 1901 et seq.) as codified in various sections of the California Family, Probate, and Welfare and Institutions Codes, applies to most proceedings involving Indian children that may result in an involuntary foster care placement; guardianship or conservatorship placement; custody placement under Family Code section 3041; declaration freeing a child from the custody and control of one or both parents; termination of parental rights; or adoptive placement. This chapter applies to:

(1) Proceedings under Welfare and Institutions Code section 300 et seq.;

(2) Proceedings under Welfare and Institutions Code sections 601 and 602 et seq., whenever the child is either in foster care or at risk of entering foster care. In these proceedings, inquiry is required in accordance with rule

5.481(a). The other requirements of this chapter contained in rules 5.481 through 5.487 apply only if:

(A) The court's jurisdiction is based on conduct that would not be criminal if the child were 18 years of age or over;

(B) The court has found that placement outside the home of the parent or legal guardian is based entirely on harmful conditions within the child's home. Without a specific finding, it is presumed that placement outside the home is based at least in part on the child's criminal conduct, and this chapter shall not apply; or

(C) The court is setting a hearing to terminate parental rights of the child's parents.

(3) Proceedings under Family Code section 3041;

(4) Proceedings under the Family Code resulting in adoption or termination of parental rights; and

(5) Proceedings listed in Probate Code section 1459.5 and rule 7.1015.

This chapter does not apply to voluntary foster care and guardianship placements where the child can be returned to the parent or Indian custodian on demand. *(Adopted, eff. Jan. 1, 2008. As amended, eff. Jan. 1, 2013; July 1, 2013.)*

Research References

Forms

West's California Judicial Council Forms ICWA-030, Notice Of Child Custody Proceeding for Indian Child (Indian Child Welfare Act).

West's California Judicial Council Forms ADOPT-200, Adoption Request.

West's California Judicial Council Forms ICWA-030(A), Attachment to Notice Of Child Custody Proceeding for Indian Child (Indian Child Welfare Act).

Treatises and Practice Aids

Witkin, California Summary 10th Parent and Child § 78, Child Of Indian Ancestry.

Witkin, California Summary 10th Parent and Child § 218, Statutory Rule.

Witkin, California Summary 10th Parent and Child § 522, Nature and Scope Of Indian Child Welfare Act.

Witkin, California Summary 10th Parent and Child § 523, Definitions.

Witkin, California Summary 10th Parent and Child § 524, Jurisdiction.

Witkin, California Summary 10th Parent and Child § 526, Determination Of Indian Status.

Witkin, California Summary 10th Parent and Child § 529, Formal Requisites.

Witkin, California Summary 10th Parent and Child § 532, in General.

Witkin, California Summary 10th Parent and Child § 535, Placement Standards and Preferences.

Witkin, California Summary 10th Parent and Child § 587, Persons Entitled to be Present.

Witkin, California Summary 10th Parent and Child § 886, Conduct Of Hearing.

Witkin, California Summary 10th Parent and Child § 896, General Requirements.

Witkin, California Summary 10th Parent and Child § 288C, (New) Applicable Law.

Witkin, California Summary 10th Wills and Probate § 915A, (New) Special Provisions Applicable to Indian Children.

Rule 5.481. Inquiry and notice

(a) Inquiry

The court, court-connected investigator, and party seeking a foster-care placement, guardianship, conservatorship, custody placement under Family Code section 3041, declaration freeing a child from the custody or control of one or both parents, termination of parental rights, or adoption have an affirmative and continuing duty to inquire whether a child is or may be an Indian child in all proceedings identified in rule 5.480. The court, court-connected investigator, and party include the county welfare department, probation department, licensed adoption agency, adoption service provider, investigator, petitioner, appointed guardian or conservator of the person, and appointed fiduciary.

(1) The party seeking a foster-care placement, guardianship, conservatorship, custody placement under Family Code section 3041, declaration freeing a child from the custody or control of one or both parents, termination of parental rights, or adoption must ask the child, if the child is old enough, and the parents, Indian custodian, or legal guardians whether the child is or may be an Indian child and must complete the *Indian Child Inquiry Attachment* (form ICWA–010(A)) and attach it to the petition unless the party is filing a subsequent petition, and there is no new information.

(2) At the first appearance by a parent, Indian custodian, or guardian in any dependency case; or in juvenile wardship proceedings in which the child is at risk of entering foster care or is in foster care; or at the initiation of any guardianship, conservatorship, proceeding for custody under Family Code section 3041, proceeding to terminate parental rights proceeding to declare a child free of the custody and control of one or both parents, or adoption proceeding; the court must order the parent, Indian custodian, or guardian if available, to complete *Parental Notification of Indian Status* (form ICWA–020).

(3) If the parent, Indian custodian, or guardian does not appear at the first hearing, or is unavailable at the initiation of a proceeding, the court must order the person or entity that has the inquiry duty under this rule to use reasonable diligence to find and inform the parent, Indian custodian, or guardian that the court has ordered the parent, Indian custodian, or guardian to complete *Parental Notification of Indian Status* (form ICWA–020).

(4) If the social worker, probation officer, licensed adoption agency, adoption service provider, investigator, or petitioner knows or has reason to know that an Indian child is or may be involved, that person or entity must make further inquiry as soon as practicable by:

(A) Interviewing the parents, Indian custodian, and "extended family members" as defined in 25 United States Code sections 1901 and 1903(2), to gather the information listed in Welfare and Institutions Code section 224.2(a)(5), Family Code section 180(b)(5), or Probate Code section 1460.2(b)(5), which is required to complete the *Notice of Child Custody Proceeding for Indian Child* (form ICWA–030);

(B) Contacting the Bureau of Indian Affairs and the California Department of Social Services for assistance in identifying the names and contact information of the tribes in which the child may be a member or eligible for membership; and

(C) Contacting the tribes and any other person that reasonably can be expected to have information regarding the child's membership status or eligibility.

(5) The circumstances that may provide reason to know the child is an Indian child include the following:

(A) The child or a person having an interest in the child, including an Indian tribe, an Indian organization, an officer of the court, a public or private agency, or a member of the child's extended family, informs or otherwise provides information suggesting that the child is an Indian child to the court, the county welfare agency, the probation department, the licensed adoption agency or adoption service provider, the investigator, the petitioner, or any appointed guardian or conservator;

(B) The residence or domicile of the child, the child's parents, or an Indian custodian is or was in a predominantly Indian community; or

(C) The child or the child's family has received services or benefits from a tribe or services that are available to Indians from tribes or the federal government, such as the U.S. Department of Health and Human Services, Indian Health Service, or Tribal Temporary Assistance to Needy Families benefits.

(b) Notice

(1) If it is known or there is reason to know that an Indian child is involved in a proceeding listed in rule 5.480, except for a wardship proceeding under Welfare and Institutions Code sections 601 and 602 et seq., the social worker, petitioner, or in probate guardianship and conservatorship proceedings, if the petitioner is unrepresented, the court must send *Notice of Child Custody Proceeding for Indian Child* (form ICWA–030) to the parent or legal guardian and Indian custodian of an Indian child, and the Indian child's tribe, in the manner specified in Welfare and Institutions Code section 224.2, Family Law Code section 180, and Probate Code section 1460.2.

(2) If it is known or there is reason to know that an Indian child is involved in a wardship proceeding under Welfare and Institutions Code sections 601 and 602 et seq., the probation officer must send *Notice of Child Custody Proceeding for Indian Child* (form ICWA–030) to the parent or legal guardian, Indian custodian, if any, and the child's tribe, in accordance with Welfare and Institutions Code section 727.4(a)(2) in any case described by rule 5.480(2)(A)–(C).

(3) The circumstances that may provide reason to know the child is an Indian child include the circumstances specified in (a)(5).

(4) Notice to an Indian child's tribe must be sent to the tribal chairperson unless the tribe has designated another agent for service. *(Adopted, eff. Jan. 1, 2008. As amended, eff. Jan. 1, 2013; July 1, 2013.)*

Commentary

California provides a higher standard of protection for the rights of an Indian child's parents than does the federal Indian Child Welfare Act. Compare Family Code section 170, Welfare and Institutions Code section 224, and this rule with 25 U.S.C. § 1903. Thus a trial court, a court-connected investigator, and a petitioner have an affirmative duty to inquire whether a child is or may be an Indian child in proceedings for foster care placement, guardianship, conservatorship, custody placement with a non-parent pursuant to Family Code section 3041, a declaration freeing a child from parental custody and control, termination of parental rights, or adoption. *In re Noreen G., 181 Cal.App.4th 1359, 105 Cal.Rptr.3d 521 (2010), review denied.*

When a dependent child's parent was adopted, the agency does not have a duty to investigate the parent's adoption records to determine whether the parent had Indian ancestry. *In re C.Y., 208 Cal.App.4th 34, 144 Cal.Rptr.3d 516 (2012). C.Y.* notes that subsection (a) of this rule contemplates that initial inquiry would be made only to the child's parents.

Research References

Forms

West's California Judicial Council Forms ICWA-020, Parental Notification Of Indian Status.

Treatises and Practice Aids

Witkin, California Summary 10th Parent and Child § 522, Nature and Scope Of Indian Child Welfare Act.

Witkin, California Summary 10th Parent and Child § 526, Determination Of Indian Status.

Witkin, California Summary 10th Parent and Child § 528, in General.

Witkin, California Summary 10th Parent and Child § 529, Formal Requisites.

Witkin, California Summary 10th Parent and Child § 896, General Requirements.

Witkin, California Summary 10th Parent and Child § 288E, (New) Notice Of Proceedings.

Witkin, California Summary 10th Parent and Child § 693C, (New) Nonemergency Removal from Prospective Adoptive Parent.

Rule 5.482. Proceedings after notice

(a) Timing of proceedings

(1) If it is known or there is reason to know that a child is an Indian child, the court hearing must not proceed until at least 10 days after the parent, Indian custodian, the tribe, or the Bureau of Indian Affairs have received notice, except as stated in sections (a)(2) and (3).

(2) The detention hearing in dependency cases and in delinquency cases in which the probation officer has assessed that the child is in foster care or it is probable the child will be entering foster care described by rule 5.480(2)(A)–(C) may proceed without delay, provided that:

(A) Notice of the detention hearing must be given as soon as possible after the filing of the petition initiating the proceeding; and

(B) Proof of notice must be filed with the court within 10 days after the filing of the petition.

(3) The parent, Indian custodian, or tribe must be granted a continuance, if requested, of up to 20 days to prepare for the proceeding, except for specified hearings in the following circumstances:

(A) The detention hearing in dependency cases and in delinquency cases described by rule 5.480(2)(A)–(C);

(B) The jurisdiction hearing in a delinquency case described by rule 5.480(2)(A)–(C) in which the court finds the continuance would not conform to speedy trial considerations under Welfare and Institutions Code section 657; and

(C) The disposition hearing in a delinquency case described by rule 5.480(2)(A)–(C) in which the court finds good cause to deny the continuance under Welfare and Institutions Code section 682. A good cause reason includes when probation is recommending the release of a detained child to his or her parent or to a less restrictive placement. The court must follow the placement preferences under rule 5.484 when holding the disposition hearing.

(b) Proof of notice

Proof of notice filed with the court must include *Notice of Child Custody Proceeding for Indian Child* (form ICWA–030), return receipts, and any responses received from the Bureau of Indian Affairs and tribes.

(c) When there is no information or response from a tribe

(1) If after notice has been provided as required by federal and state law and neither the tribe nor the Bureau of Indian Affairs has provided a determinative response within 60 days after receiving that notice, then the court may determine that the Indian Child Welfare Act does not apply to the proceedings, provided that the court must reverse its determination of the inapplicability of the act and must apply it prospectively if a tribe or the Bureau of Indian Affairs subsequently confirms that the child is an Indian child.

(2) If at any time, based on the petition or other information, the court knows or has reason to know the child is an Indian child, the court must proceed as if the child were an Indian child.

(3) The court is not required to delay proceedings until a response to notice is received.

(d) Intervention

The Indian child's tribe and Indian custodian may intervene, orally or in writing, at any point in the proceedings and may, but are not required to, file with the court the *Notice of Designation of Tribal Representative and Notice of Intervention in a Court Proceeding Involving an Indian Child* (form ICWA–040) to give notice of their intent to intervene.

(e) Posthearing actions

Whenever an Indian child is removed from a guardian, conservator, other custodian, foster home, or institution for placement with a different guardian, conservator, custodian, foster home, institution, or preadoptive or adoptive home, the placement must comply with the placement preferences and standards specified in Welfare and Institutions Code section 361.31.

(f) Consultation with tribe

Any person or court involved in the placement of an Indian child in a proceeding described by rule 5.480 must use the services of the Indian child's tribe, whenever available through the tribe, in seeking to secure placement within the order of placement preference specified in rule 5.484.

(Adopted, eff. Jan. 1, 2008. As amended, eff. Jan. 1, 2013; July 1, 2013; Aug. 15, 2016.)

Validity

For validity of this rule, see In re Abbigail A. (2016) 204 Cal.Rptr.3d 760, 375 P.3d 879.

Commentary

When a child may be eligible for tribal membership but is not an *Indian child*, as defined by Indian Child Welfare Act, 25 U.S.C. § 1903(4) and California Welfare and Institutions Code § 224.1(a), former subsection (c) of this Rule requires a court to proceed as if the child were an Indian child and take steps to secure tribal membership for the child. *In re Abbigail A., 1 Cal.5th 83, 375 P.3d 879, 204 Cal.Rptr.3d 760 (2016)*, held that former subsection (c) was invalid because it conflicts with the legislative definition of *Indian child*, which is limited to a child who is either an enrolled member of a tribe or a biological child of an enrolled member of a tribe. By contrast, subsection (c)(2) of Rule 5.484 is not invalid because it applies only to a child who satisfies the statutory definition of *Indian child*.

Research References

Treatises and Practice Aids

Witkin, California Summary 10th Parent and Child § 527, Procedure Where Child May be Indian Child.

Witkin, California Summary 10th Parent and Child § 528, in General.

Witkin, California Summary 10th Parent and Child § 531, Determining Adequacy Of Notice.

Witkin, California Summary 10th Parent and Child § 532, in General.

Witkin, California Summary 10th Parent and Child § 533, Participation by Indian Tribe.

Witkin, California Summary 10th Parent and Child § 534, Out-Of-Home Placement or Guardianship.

Witkin, California Summary 10th Parent and Child § 535, Placement Standards and Preferences.

Witkin, California Summary 10th Parent and Child § 537, Proceedings After Termination or Removal.

Rule 5.483. Transfer of case

(a) Mandatory transfer of case to tribal court with exclusive jurisdiction

The court must order transfer of a case to the tribal court of the child's tribe if:

(1) The Indian child is a ward of the tribal court; or

(2) The Indian child is domiciled or resides within a reservation of an Indian tribe that has exclusive jurisdiction over Indian child custody proceedings under section 1911 or 1918 of title 25 of the United States Code.

(b) Presumptive transfer of case to tribal court with concurrent state and tribal jurisdiction

Unless the court finds good cause under subdivision (d), the court must order transfer of a case to the tribal court of the child's tribe if the parent, the Indian custodian, or the child's tribe requests.

(c) Documentation of request to transfer a case to tribal court

The parent, the Indian custodian, or the child's tribe may request transfer of the case, either orally or in writing or by filing *Notice of Petition and Petition to Transfer Case Involving an Indian Child to Tribal Jurisdiction* (form ICWA–050).

If the request is made orally, the court must document the request and make it part of the record.

(d) Cause to deny a request to transfer to tribal court with concurrent state and tribal jurisdiction

(1) One or more of the following circumstances constitutes mandatory good cause to deny a request to transfer:

(A) One or both of the child's parents objects to the transfer in open court or in an admissible writing for the record;

(B) The child's tribe does not have a "tribal court" or any other administrative body as defined in section 1903 of the Indian Child Welfare Act: "a court with jurisdiction over child custody proceedings and which is either a Court of Indian Offenses, a court established and operated under the code or custom of an Indian tribe, or any other administrative body of a tribe which is vested with authority over child custody proceedings;" or

(C) The tribal court of the child's tribe declines the transfer.

(2) One or more of the following circumstances may constitute discretionary good cause to deny a request to transfer:

(A) The evidence necessary to decide the case cannot be presented in the tribal court without undue hardship to the parties or the witnesses, and the tribal court is unable to mitigate the hardship by making arrangements to receive and consider the evidence or testimony by use of remote communication, by hearing the evidence or testimony at a location convenient to the parties or witnesses, or by use of other means permitted in the tribal court's rules of evidence or discovery;

(B) The proceeding was at an advanced stage when the request to transfer was received and the petitioner did not make the request within a reasonable time after receiving notice of the proceeding, provided the notice complied with statutory requirements. Waiting until reunification efforts have failed and reunification services have been terminated before filing a request to transfer may not, by itself, be considered an unreasonable delay;

(C) The Indian child is over 12 years of age and objects to the transfer; or

(D) The parents of a child over five years of age are not available and the child has had little or no contact with his or her tribe or members of the child's tribe.

(3) If it appears that there is good cause to deny a transfer, the court must hold an evidentiary hearing on the transfer and make its findings on the record.

(e) Evidentiary considerations

The court may not consider socioeconomic conditions and the perceived adequacy of tribal social services, tribal probation, or the tribal judicial systems in its determination that good cause exists to deny a request to transfer to tribal court with concurrent state and tribal jurisdiction.

(f) Evidentiary burdens

(1) The burden of establishing good cause to deny a request to transfer is on the party opposing the transfer.

(2) If the court believes, or any party asserts, that good cause to deny the request exists, the reasons for that belief or assertion must be stated in writing, in advance of the hearing, and made available to all parties who are requesting the transfer, and the petitioner must have the opportunity to provide information or evidence in rebuttal of the belief or assertion.

(g) Order on request to transfer

(1) The court must issue its final order on the *Order on Petition to Transfer Case Involving an Indian Child to Tribal Jurisdiction* (form ICWA–060).

(2) When a matter is being transferred from the jurisdiction of a juvenile court, the order must include:

(A) All of the findings, orders, or modifications of orders that have been made in the case;

(B) The name and address of the tribe to which jurisdiction is being transferred;

(C) Directions for the agency to release the child case file to the tribe having jurisdiction under section 827.15 of the Welfare and Institutions Code;

(D) Directions that all papers contained in the child case file must be transferred to the tribal court; and

(E) Directions that a copy of the transfer order and the findings of fact must be maintained by the transferring court.

(h) Advisement when transfer order granted

When the court grants a petition transferring a case to tribal court under Welfare and Institutions Code section 305.5, Family Code section 177(a), or Probate Code section 1459.5(b) and rule 5.483, the court must advise the parties orally and in writing that any appeal to the order for transfer to a tribal court must be made before the transfer to tribal jurisdiction is finalized and that failure to request and obtain a stay of the order for transfer will result in a loss of appellate jurisdiction.

(i) Proceeding after transfer

When, under Welfare and Institutions Code section 305.5, Family Code section 177(a), or Probate Code section 1459.5(b), the court transfers any proceeding listed in rule 5.480, the court must proceed as follows:

(1) Dismiss the proceeding or terminate jurisdiction if the court has received proof that the tribal court has accepted the transfer of jurisdiction;

(2) Make an order transferring the physical custody of the child to a designated representative of the tribal court (not necessarily the same "designated representative" identified in the *Notice of Designation of Tribal Representative and Notice of Intervention in a Court Proceeding Involving an Indian Child* (form ICWA–040)); and

(3) Include in the *Order on Petition to Transfer Case Involving an Indian Child to Tribal Jurisdiction* (form ICWA–060) all contact information for the designated tribal court representative. *(Adopted, eff. Jan. 1, 2008. As amended, eff. Jan. 1, 2013; Jan. 1, 2016.)*

Research References

Forms

West's California Judicial Council Forms ICWA-050, Notice Of Petition and Petition to Transfer Case Involving an Indian Child to Tribal Jurisdiction.

West's California Judicial Council Forms ICWA-060, Order on Petition to Transfer Case Involving an Indian Child to Tribal Jurisdiction.

Treatises and Practice Aids

Witkin, California Summary 10th Parent and Child § 524, Jurisdiction.

Rule 5.484. Placement of an Indian child

(a) Evidentiary burdens

In any child custody proceeding listed in rule 5.480, the court may not order placement of an Indian child unless it finds by clear and convincing evidence that continued custody with the parent or Indian custodian is likely to cause the Indian child serious emotional or physical damage and it considers evidence regarding prevailing social and cultural standards of the child's tribe, including that tribe's family organization and child-rearing practices.

(1) Testimony by a "qualified expert witness," as defined in Welfare and Institutions Code section 224.6, Family Code section 177(a), and Probate Code section 1459.5(b), is required before a court orders a child placed in foster care or terminates parental rights.

(2) Stipulation by the parent, Indian custodian, or tribe, or failure to object, may waive the requirement of producing evidence of the likelihood of serious damage only if the court is satisfied that the person or tribe has been fully advised of the requirements of the Indian Child Welfare Act and has knowingly, intelligently, and voluntarily waived them. Any such stipulation must be agreed to in writing.

(3) Failure to meet non–Indian family and child-rearing community standards, or the existence of other behavior or conditions that meet the removal standards of Welfare and Institutions Code section 361, will not support an order for placement absent the finding that continued custody with the parent or Indian custodian is likely to cause serious emotional or physical damage.

(b) Standards and preferences in placement of an Indian child

(1) Unless the court finds good cause to the contrary, all placements of Indian children in any proceeding listed in rule 5.480 must follow the specified placement preferences in Family Code section 177(a), Probate Code section 1459(b), and Welfare and Institutions Code section 361.31.

(2) The court may deviate from the preference order only for good cause, which may include the following considerations:

(A) The requests of the parent or Indian custodian;

(B) The requests of the Indian child, when of sufficient age;

(C) The extraordinary physical or emotional needs of the Indian child as established by a qualified expert witness; or

(D) The unavailability of suitable families based on a documented diligent effort to identify families meeting the preference criteria.

(3) The burden of establishing good cause for the court to deviate from the preference order is on the party requesting that the preference order not be followed.

(4) The tribe, by resolution, may establish a different preference order, which must be followed if it provides for the least restrictive setting.

(5) The preferences and wishes of the Indian child, when of sufficient age, and the parent must be considered, and weight given to a consenting parent's request for anonymity.

(6) When no preferred placement is available, active efforts must be made and documented to place the child with a family committed to enabling the child to have visitation with "extended family members," as defined in rule 5.481(a)(4)(A), and participation in the cultural and ceremonial events of the child's tribe.

(c) Active efforts

In addition to any other required findings to place an Indian child with someone other than a parent or Indian custodian, or to terminate parental rights, the court must find that active efforts have been made, in any proceeding listed in rule 5.480, to provide remedial services and rehabilitative programs designed to prevent the breakup of the Indian family, and must find that these efforts were unsuccessful.

(1) The court must consider whether active efforts were made in a manner consistent with the prevailing social and cultural conditions and way of life of the Indian child's tribe.

(2) Efforts to provide services must include pursuit of any steps necessary to secure tribal membership for a child if the child is eligible for membership in a given tribe, as well as attempts to use the available resources of extended family members, the tribe, tribal and other Indian social service agencies, and individual Indian caregivers. *(Adopted, eff. Jan. 1, 2008. As amended, eff. Jan. 1, 2013.)*

Commentary

When a child may be eligible for tribal membership but is not an *Indian child*, as defined by Indian Child Welfare Act, 25 U.S.C. § 1903(4), and California Welfare and Institutions Code § 224.1(a), former subsection (c) of Rule 5.842 required a court to proceed as if the child were an Indian child and take steps to secure tribal membership for the child. *In re Abbigail A., 1 Cal.5th 83, 375 P.3d 879, 204 Cal.Rptr.3d 760 (2016)*, ruled that subsection (c) was invalid because it conflicts with the legislative definition of *Indian child*, which is limited to a child who is either an enrolled member of a tribe or a biological child of an enrolled member of a tribe. By contrast, subsection (c)(2) of this Rule is not invalid because it applies only to a child who satisfies the statutory definition of *Indian child*.

Research References

Forms

West's California Judicial Council Forms JV-421, Dispositional Attachment: Removal from Custodial Parent--Placement With Nonparent (Welf. & Inst. Code, §§ 361, 361.2).

Treatises and Practice Aids

Witkin, California Summary 10th Parent and Child § 528, in General.

Witkin, California Summary 10th Parent and Child § 532, in General.

Witkin, California Summary 10th Parent and Child § 534, Out-Of-Home Placement or Guardianship.

Witkin, California Summary 10th Parent and Child § 535, Placement Standards and Preferences.

Rule 5.485. Termination of parental rights

(a) Evidentiary burdens

The court may only terminate parental rights to an Indian child or declare an Indian child free of the custody and control of one or both parents if at the hearing terminating parental rights or declaring the child free of the custody and control of one or both parents, the court:

(1) Finds by clear and convincing evidence that active efforts to provide remedial services and rehabilitative programs designed to prevent the breakup of the Indian family were made; and

(2) Makes a determination, supported by evidence beyond a reasonable doubt, including testimony of one or more "qualified expert witnesses" as defined in Welfare and Institutions Code section 224.6 and Family Code section 177(a), that the continued custody of the child by the parent is likely to result in serious emotional or physical damage to the child.

(b) When parental rights may not be terminated

The court may not terminate parental rights to an Indian child or declare a child free from the custody and control of one or both parents if the court finds a compelling reason for determining that termination of parental rights would not be in the child's best interest. Such a reason may include:

(1) Termination of parental rights would substantially interfere with the child's connection to his or her tribal community or the child's tribal membership rights; or

(2) The child's tribe has identified guardianship, long-term foster care with a fit and willing relative, or another planned permanent living arrangement for the child. *(Adopted, eff. Jan. 1, 2008. As amended, eff. Jan. 1, 2013.)*

Research References

Forms

West's California Judicial Council Forms JV-320, Orders Under Welfare and Institutions Code Sections 366.26, 727.3, 727.31.

Treatises and Practice Aids

Witkin, California Summary 10th Parent and Child § 536, Termination Of Parental Rights.

Witkin, California Summary 10th Parent and Child § 689, in General.

Rule 5.486. Petition to invalidate orders

(a) Who may petition

Any Indian child who is the subject of any action for foster-care placement, guardianship placement, or termination of parental rights; any parent or Indian custodian from whose custody such child was removed; and the Indian child's tribe may petition the court to invalidate the action on a showing that the action violated the Indian Child Welfare Act.

(b) Court of competent jurisdiction

If the Indian child is a dependent child or ward of the juvenile court or the subject of a pending petition, the juvenile court is a court of competent jurisdiction with the authority to hear the request to invalidate the foster placement or termination of parental rights.

(c) Request to return custody of the Indian child

If a final decree of adoption is vacated or set aside, or if the adoptive parents voluntarily consent to the termination of their parental rights, a biological parent or prior Indian custodian may request a return of custody of the Indian child.

(1) The court must reinstate jurisdiction.

(2) In a juvenile case, the juvenile court must hold a new disposition hearing in accordance with 25 United States Code section 1901 et seq. where the court may consider all placement options as stated in Welfare and Institutions Code sections 361.31(b), (c), (d), and (h).

(3) The court may consider placement with a biological parent or prior Indian custodian if the biological parent or prior Indian custodian can show that placement with him or her is not detrimental to the child and that the placement is in the best interests of the child.

(4) The hearing on the request to return custody of an Indian child must be conducted in accordance with statutory requirements and the relevant sections of this rule. *(Adopted, eff. Jan. 1, 2008. As amended, eff. Jan. 1, 2013.)*

Research References

Treatises and Practice Aids

Witkin, California Summary 10th Parent and Child § 537, Proceedings After Termination or Removal.

Rule 5.487. Adoption record keeping

(a) Copies of adoption decree and other information to the Secretary of the Interior

After granting a decree of adoption of an Indian child, the court must provide the Secretary of the Interior with a copy of the decree and the following information:

(1) The name and tribal affiliation of the Indian child;

(2) The names and addresses of the biological parents;

(3) The names and addresses of the adoptive parents; and

(4) The agency maintaining files and records regarding the adoptive placement.

(b) Affidavit of confidentiality to the Bureau of Indian Affairs

If a biological parent has executed an affidavit requesting that his or her identity remain confidential, the court must provide the affidavit to the Bureau of Indian Affairs, which must ensure the confidentiality of the information. *(Adopted, eff. Jan. 1, 2008. As amended, eff. Jan. 1, 2013.)*

Research References

Forms

West's California Judicial Council Forms ICWA-030, Notice Of Child Custody Proceeding for Indian Child (Indian Child Welfare Act).

West's California Judicial Council Forms ADOPT-200, Adoption Request.

West's California Judicial Council Forms ICWA-030(A), Attachment to Notice Of Child Custody Proceeding for Indian Child (Indian Child Welfare Act).

Treatises and Practice Aids

Witkin, California Summary 10th Parent and Child § 150, Confidentiality Of Information.

Chapter 3

ADOPTIONS UNDER THE HAGUE ADOPTION CONVENTION

Rule 5.490. Adoption of a child resident in the United States by a resident of a foreign country party to the Convention of 29 May 1993 on Protection of Children and Cooperation in Respect of Intercountry Adoption (Convention or Hague Adoption Convention)

(a) Purpose

The rules in this chapter are adopted to provide practice and procedure for intercountry adoptions conducted under the Hague Adoption Convention and applicable California law.

(b) Applicability of rule

This rule applies to any adoption of a child resident in the United States by an individual or individuals residing in a convention country, as defined in Family Code section 8900.5(f), if, in connection with the adoption, the child has moved or will move between the United States and the convention country.

(c) Adoption request and attachments

(1) The *Adoption Request* (form ADOPT–200) and *Verification of Compliance with Hague Adoption Convention Attachment* (ADOPT–216) must allege specific facts about the applicability of the Hague Adoption Convention and whether the petitioner is seeking a California adoption, will be petitioning for a Hague Adoption Certificate, or will be seeking a Hague Custody Declaration.

(2) The court must determine whether a child resident in the United States has been or will be moved to a convention country in connection with an adoption by an individual or individuals residing in a convention country.

(d) Evidence required to verify compliance with the Hague Adoption Convention

If the Hague Adoption Convention applies to the case, and the court is asked to issue findings and an order supporting a request for the U.S. Department of State to issue a Hague Adoption Certificate or a Hague Custody Declaration for the adoption placement, the court must receive sufficient evidence to conclude that the child is eligible for adoption and find that the placement is in the best interest of the child. The court must receive evidence of all of the following:

(1) The adoption agency or provider is accredited by the Council on Accreditation, is supervised by an accredited primary provider, or is acting as an exempted provider, as defined in Family Code section 8900.5(g), to provide intercountry adoption services for convention cases;

(2) A child background study has been completed and transmitted to a foreign authorized entity in accordance with the regulations governing convention adoptions with proof that the necessary consents have been obtained and the reason for its determination that the proposed placement is in the child's best interest, based on the home study and child background study and giving due consideration to the child's upbringing and his or her ethnic, religious, and cultural background;

(3) The child is eligible for adoption under California law;

(4) The adoption agency or provider has made reasonable efforts, as described under 22 Code of Federal Regulations section 96.54(a), to place the child in the United States, but was unable to do so, or an exception to this requirement applies to the case. Such reasonable efforts include: (1) disseminating information on the child and his or her availability for adoption through print, media, and Internet resources designed to communicate with potential prospective adoptive parents in the United States; (2) listing information about the child on a national or state adoption exchange or registry for at least 60 calendar days after the birth of the child; (3) responding to inquiries about adoption of the child; and (4) providing a copy of the child background study to potential U.S. prospective adoptive parent(s);

(5) The agency has determined that the placement is in the child's best interest;

(6) A home study on the petitioner(s) has been completed, which includes:

(A) Information on the petitioner(s), such as identity, eligibility and suitability to adopt, background, family and medical history, social environment, reasons for adoption, ability to undertake an intercountry adoption, an assessment of their ability to care for the child, and the characteristics of the child for whom they would be qualified to care;

(B) Confirmation that a competent authority has determined that the petitioner is eligible and suited to adopt and has ensured that the petitioner has been counseled as necessary; and

(C) The results of criminal background checks;

(7) The Hague Adoption Convention authority designated by the receiving country has declared that the child will be permitted to enter and reside permanently or on the same basis as the adopting parent(s) in the receiving country, and has consented to the adoption;

(8) All appropriate consents have been obtained in writing in accordance with the following standards:

(A) Counseling was provided to any biological or legal parent or legal guardian consenting to the adoption;

(B) All biological or legal parents or legal guardians were informed of the legal effect of adoption;

(C) Such consent was freely given without inducement by compensation;

(D) Such consent was not subsequently withdrawn; and

(E) Consents were taken only after the birth of the child.

(9) As appropriate in light of the child's age and maturity, the child has been counseled and informed of the effects of the adoption and the child's views have been considered. If the child's consent is required, the child has also been counseled and informed of the effects of granting consent and has freely given consent expressed or evidenced in writing in the required legal form without any inducement by compensation of any kind;

(10) The adoption agency or provider has committed to taking all steps to ensure the secure transfer of the child, including obtaining permission for the child to leave the United States;

(11) The adoption agency or provider has agreed to keep the receiving country's designated Hague Adoption Convention authority informed about the status of the case;

(12) The petitioner consents to adoption or has agreed to accept custody of the child for purposes of adoption;

(13) The adoption agency or provider demonstrates that any contact between the birth family and the adoptive family complies with applicable state law and federal regulations governing the timing of such communications; and

(14) The adoption agency or provider certifies that no one is deriving improper financial gain from the adoption and describes the financial arrangement with the prospective adoptive family.

(e) Court findings required to support the application for a Hague Adoption Certificate or Hague Custody Declaration

The court must make findings relating to the application for a Hague Adoption Certificate or Hague Custody Declaration from the Department of State. To meet the requirements for issuance of the certificate or declaration, the findings must include that:

(1) The adoption is in the child's best interest;

(2) The substantive regulatory requirements set forth in 22 Code of Federal Regulations sections 97.3(a)–(k) have been met; and

(3) The adoption services provider meets the requirements of 22 Code of Federal Regulations part 96.

(f) Court findings to verify that all Hague Adoption Convention requirements have been met

If the court is satisfied that all Hague Adoption Convention requirements have been met, the court must make findings of fact and order the following:

(1) The child is eligible for adoption;

(2) The grant of custody with respect to the proposed adoption is in the child's best interest; and

(3) The court grants custody of the child to the named family for purposes of adoption, as applicable.

(g) Petitioner's intent to finalize adoption

If the adoption is not finalized in California, a petition for a Hague Custody Declaration must state specific facts indicating that the petitioner intends to finalize the adoption in petitioner's country of residence or that petitioner will return to California after any required post-placement supervisory period to finalize the adoption in a superior court of California. *(Adopted, eff. July 1, 2013.)*

Research References

Treatises and Practice Aids

Witkin, California Summary 10th Parent and Child § 137, in General.

Rule 5.491. Adoption of a child resident in the United States by a resident of a foreign country not party to the Hague Adoption Convention

The adoption of a child resident in the United States by a resident of a foreign country not party to the Hague Adoption Convention must conform to the law governing California adoptions. *(Adopted, eff. July 1, 2013.)*

Research References

Treatises and Practice Aids

Witkin, California Summary 10th Parent and Child § 137, in General.

Rule 5.492. Adoption by a United States resident of a child resident in a foreign country that is party to the Hague Adoption Convention

A United States resident who plans to adopt, in California, a child resident in a foreign country that is party to the Hague Adoption Convention must provide to the California court the required proof, in the form of a Hague Custody Declaration, that all required Hague Adoption Convention findings have been made by the child's country of residence. *(Adopted, eff. July 1, 2013.)*

Research References

Treatises and Practice Aids

Witkin, California Summary 10th Parent and Child § 140, Petition, Hearing, and Order.

Chapter 4

PROTECTIVE ORDERS

Rule

Rule 5.495. Firearm relinquishment procedures

(a) Application of rule

This rule applies when a family or juvenile law domestic violence protective order as defined in Family Code section 6218 or Welfare and Institutions Code section 213.5 is issued or in effect.

(b) Purpose

This rule addresses situations in which information is presented to the court about firearms and provides the court with options for appropriately addressing the issue. This rule is intended to:

(1) Assist courts issuing domestic violence protective orders in determining whether a restrained person has a firearm in or subject to his or her immediate possession or control.

(2) Assist courts that have issued domestic violence protective orders in determining whether a restrained person has complied with the court's order to relinquish, store, or sell the firearm under Family Code section 6389(c).

(c) Firearm determination

When relevant information is presented to the court at any noticed hearing that a restrained person has a firearm, the court must consider that information to determine, by a preponderance of the evidence, whether the person subject to a protective order as defined in Family Code section 6218 or Welfare and Institutions Code section 213.5 has a firearm in or subject to his or her immediate possession or control in violation of Family Code section 6389.

(d) Determination procedures

(1) In making a determination under this rule, the court may consider whether the restrained person filed a firearm relinquishment, storage, or sales receipt or if an exemption from the firearm prohibition was granted under Family Code section 6389(h).

(2) The court may make the determination at any noticed hearing when a domestic violence protective order is issued, at a subsequent review hearing, or at any subsequent family or juvenile law hearing while the order remains in effect.

(3) If the court makes a determination that the restrained person has a firearm in violation of Family Code section 6389, the court must make a written record of the determination and provide a copy to any party who is present at the hearing and, upon request, to any party not present at the hearing.

(e) Subsequent review hearing

(1) When presented with information under (c), the court may set a review hearing to determine whether a violation of Family Code section 6389 has taken place.

(2) The review hearing must be held within 10 court days after the noticed hearing at which the information was presented. If the restrained person is not present when the court sets the review hearing, the protected person must provide notice of the review hearing to the restrained person at least 2 court days before the review hearing, in accordance with Code of Civil Procedure 414.10, by personal service or by mail to the restrained person's last known address.

(3) The court may for good cause extend the date of the review hearing for a reasonable period or remove it from the calendar.

(4) The court must order the restrained person to appear at the review hearing.

(5) The court may conduct the review hearing in the absence of the protected person.

(6) Nothing in this rule prohibits the court from permitting a party to appear by telephone under California Rules of Court, rule 5.9.

(f) Child custody and visitation

(1) If the court determines that the restrained person has a firearm in violation of Family Code section 6389, the court must consider that determination when deciding whether the restrained person has overcome the presumption in Family Code section 3044.

(2) An order for custody or visitation issued at any time during a family law matter must be made in a manner that ensures the health, safety, and welfare of the child and the safety of all family members, as specified in Family Code section 3020. The court must consider whether the best interest of the child, based on the circumstances of the case, requires that any visitation or custody arrangement be limited to situations in which a third person, specified by the court, is present, or that visitation or custody be suspended or denied, as specified in Family Code section 6323(d).

(3) An order for visitation issued at any time during a juvenile court matter must not jeopardize the safety of the child, as specified in Welfare and Institutions Code section 362.1.

(g) Other orders

(1) The court may consider a determination that the restrained person has a firearm in violation of Family Code section 6389 in issuing:

(A) An order to show cause for contempt under section 1209(a)(5) of the Code of Civil Procedure for failure to comply with the court's order to surrender or sell a firearm; or

(B) An order for money sanctions under section 177.5 of the Code of Civil Procedure.

(2) This rule should not be construed to limit the court's power to issue orders it is otherwise authorized or required to issue. *(Adopted, eff. July 1, 2014.)*

Advisory Committee Comment

When issuing a family or juvenile law domestic violence protective order as defined in Family Code section 6218 or Welfare and Institutions Code section 213.5, ex parte or after a noticed hearing, the court is required to order a restrained person "to relinquish any firearm in [that person's] immediate possession or control or subject to [that person's] immediate possession or control." (Fam. Code, § 6389(c)(1).) Several mandatory Judicial Council forms—*Temporary Restraining Order* (form DV–110), *Restraining Order After Hearing* (form DV–130), and *Notice of Hearing and Temporary Restraining Order—Juvenile* (form JV–250)—include mandatory orders in bold type that the restrained person must sell to or store with a licensed gun dealer or turn in to a law enforcement agency any guns or other firearms within his or her immediate possession or control within 24 hours after service of the order and must file a receipt with the court showing compliance with the order within 48 hours of receiving the order. California law requires personal service of the request for and any temporary protective order at least five days before the hearing, unless the court issues an order shortening time for service. Therefore, by the date of the hearing, the restrained person should have relinquished, stored, or sold his or r her firearms and submitted a receipt to the court.

Courts are encouraged to develop local procedures to calendar firearm relinquishment review hearings for restrained persons.

Section (f) of this rule restates existing law on the safety and welfare of children and family members and recognizes the safety issues associated with the presence of prohibited firearms.

Although this rule does not require the court to compel a restrained person to testify, the court may wish to advise a party of his or her privilege against self-incrimination under the Fifth Amendment to the United States Constitution. The court may also consider whether to grant use immunity under Family Code section 6389(d).

Division 3

JUVENILE RULES

Chapter 1

PRELIMINARY PROVISIONS—TITLE AND DEFINITIONS

Rule 5.500. Division title

The rules in this division may be referred to as the Juvenile Rules. *(Adopted, eff. Jan. 1, 2007.)*

Research References

Treatises and Practice Aids

Witkin, California Summary 10th Parent and Child § 286, Where Domestic Violence is Alleged and Protective Order is Issued.
Witkin, California Summary 10th Parent and Child § 444, Scope and Organization.
Witkin, California Summary 10th Wills and Probate § 916, in General.

Rule 5.501. Preliminary provisions

(a) Application of rules (§§ 200–945)

The rules in this division solely apply to every action and proceeding to which the juvenile court law (Welf. & Inst. Code, div. 2, pt. 1, ch. 2, § 200 et seq.) applies, unless they are explicitly made applicable in any other action or proceeding. The rules in this division do not apply to an action or proceeding heard by a traffic hearing officer, nor to a rehearing or appeal from a denial of a rehearing following an order by a traffic hearing officer.

(b) Authority for and purpose of rules (Cal. Const., art. VI, §§ 6, 265)

The Judicial Council adopted the rules in this division under its constitutional and statutory authority to adopt rules for court administration, practice, and procedure that are not inconsistent with statute. These rules implement the purposes of the juvenile court law by promoting uniformity in practice and procedure and by providing guidance to judicial officers, attorneys, social workers, probation officers, and others participating in the juvenile court.

(c) Rules of construction

Unless the context otherwise requires, these preliminary provisions and the following rules of construction govern the construction of these rules:

(1) Insofar as these rules are substantially the same as existing statutory provisions relating to the same subject matter, these rules must be construed as restatements of those statutes; and

(2) Insofar as these rules may add to existing statutory provisions relating to the same subject matter, these rules must be construed so as to implement the purposes of the juvenile court law.

(d) Severability clause

If a rule or a subdivision of a rule in this division is invalid, all valid parts that are severable from the invalid part remain in effect. If a rule or a subdivision of a rule in this division is invalid in one or more of its applications, the rule or subdivision remains in effect in all valid applications that are severable from the invalid applications. *(Formerly Rule 1400, adopted, eff. Jan. 1, 1990. Renumbered Rule 5.501 and amended, eff. Jan. 1, 2007.)*

Research References

Treatises and Practice Aids

Witkin, California Summary 10th Parent and Child § 443, Nature and Purpose.
Witkin, California Summary 10th Parent and Child § 444, Scope and Organization.

Rule 5.502. Definitions and use of terms

Definitions (§§ 202(e), 303, 319, 361, 361.5(a)(3), 450, 628.1, 636, 726, 727.3(c)(2), 727.4(d), 4512(j), 4701.6(b), 11400(v), 11400(y), 16501(f)(16); 20 U.S.C. § 1415; 25 U.S.C. § 1903(2))

As used in these rules, unless the context or subject matter otherwise requires:

(1) "Affinity" means the connection existing between one spouse or domestic partner and the blood or adoptive relatives of the other spouse or domestic partner.

(2) "At risk of entering foster care" means that conditions within a child's family may require that the child be removed from the custody of a parent or guardian and placed in foster care unless or until those conditions are resolved.

(3) "CASA" means Court Appointed Special Advocate as defined in rule 5.655.

(4) "Child Abuse Prevention and Treatment Act (CAPTA) guardian ad litem for a child subject to a juvenile dependency petition" is defined in rule 5.662.

(5) "Child" means a person under the age of 18 years.

(6) "Clerk" means the clerk of the juvenile court.

(7) "Court" means the juvenile court and includes any judicial officer of the juvenile court.

(8) "Court-ordered services" or "court-ordered treatment program" means child welfare services or services provided by an appropriate agency ordered at a dispositional hearing at which the child is declared a dependent child or ward of the court, and any hearing thereafter, for the purpose of maintaining or reunifying a child with a parent or guardian.

(9) "Date the child entered foster care" means:

(A) In dependency, the date on which the court sustained the petition filed under section 300 or 60 days after the "initial removal" of the child as defined below, whichever is earlier; or

(B) In delinquency, the date 60 days after the date on which the child was initially removed from the home, unless one of the following exceptions applies:

(i) If the child is detained pending foster care placement and remains detained for more than 60 days, then the "date the child entered foster care" means the date the court declares the child a ward and orders the child placed in foster care under the supervision of the probation officer;

(ii) If, before the child is placed in foster care, the child is committed to a ranch, camp, school, or other institution pending placement, and remains in that facility for more than 60 days, then the "date the child entered foster care" is the date the child is physically placed in foster care; or

(iii) If, at the time the wardship petition was filed, the child was a dependent of the juvenile court and in out-of-home placement, then the "date the child entered foster care" is the date defined in (A).

(10) "De facto parent" means a person who has been found by the court to have assumed, on a day-to-day basis, the role of parent, fulfilling both the child's physical and psychological needs for care and affection, and who has assumed that role for a substantial period.

(11) "Detained" means any removal of the child from the person or persons legally entitled to the child's physical custody, or any release of the child on home supervision under section 628.1 or 636. A child released or placed on home supervision is not detained for the purposes of federal foster care funding.

(12) "Domestic partner" means one of two adults who have chosen to share one another's lives in an intimate and committed relationship of mutual caring as described in Family Code section 297.

(13) "Educational rights holder" means the adult identified or appointed by the court to make educational or developmental-services decisions for a child, nonminor, or nonminor dependent. If the court limits a parent's or guardian's decisionmaking rights and appoints an educational rights holder, the appointed rights holder acts as the child's or youth's parent, spokesperson, decision maker, and "authorized representative" as described in sections 4512(j) and 4701.6(b) in regard to all matters related to educational or developmental-services needs, including those described in sections 319, 361, 726, 4512, 4646–4648, and 4700–4731; Education Code sections 56028(b)(2), 56050, and 56055; Government Code sections 7579.5 and 7579.6; chapter 33 (commencing with section 1400) of title 20 of the United States Code; and part 300 (commencing with section 300.1) of title 34 of the Code of Federal Regulations, unless the court orders otherwise. An appointed educational rights holder is entitled to access to educational and developmental-services records and information to the extent permitted by law, including by sections 4514 and 5328, and to the same extent as a parent, as that term is used in title 20 United States Code section 1232g and defined in title 34 Code of Federal Regulations part 99.3.

(14) "Foster care" means residential care provided in any of the settings described in section 11402.

(15) "Foster parent" includes a relative with whom the child is placed.

(16) "General jurisdiction" means the jurisdiction the juvenile court maintains over a nonminor under section 303(b) at the time of the dismissal of dependency jurisdiction, delinquency jurisdiction, or transition jurisdiction for the purpose of considering a request to resume its dependency jurisdiction or to assume or resume its transition jurisdiction over the person as a nonminor dependent.

(17) "Guardian" means legal guardian of the child.

(18) "Hearing" means a noticed proceeding with findings and orders that are made on a case-by-case basis, heard by either of the following:

(A) A judicial officer, in a courtroom, in which the proceedings are recorded by a court reporter; or

(B) An administrative panel, provided that the hearing meets the conditions described in section 366.3(d) and (e) for dependents and section 727.4(d)(7)(B) for delinquents.

(19) "Indian child" means any unmarried person under 18 years of age who is either (a) a member of an Indian tribe or (b) eligible for membership in an Indian tribe and is the biological child of a member of an Indian tribe. In a court proceeding defined in section 224.1(d), the term also means a youth who satisfies the conditions in either (a) or (b), above, is 18 years of age but not yet 21 years of age, and remains under the jurisdiction of the juvenile court, unless that youth, directly or through his or her attorney, chooses not to be considered an Indian child for purposes of the proceeding.

(20) "Indian child's tribe" means (a) the Indian tribe of which the Indian child is a member or is eligible for membership, or (b), if an Indian child is a member of, or eligible for membership in, more than one tribe, the Indian tribe with which the Indian child has the more significant contacts, as determined under section 224.1(e).

(21) "Initial removal" means the date on which the child, who is the subject of a petition filed under section 300 or 600, was taken into custody by the social worker or a peace officer, or was deemed to have been taken into custody under section 309(b) or 628(c), if removal results in the filing of the petition before the court.

(22) "Member of the household," for purposes of section 300 proceedings, means any person continually or frequently found in the same household as the child.

(23) "Modification of parental rights" means a modification of parental rights through a tribal customary adoption under Welfare and Institutions Code section 366.24.

(24) "90–day Transition Plan" means the personalized plan developed at the direction of a child currently in a foster care placement during the 90–day period before the child's planned exit from foster care when she or he attains 18 years of age or, if applicable, developed at the direction of a nonminor during the 90–day period prior to his or her anticipated exit from foster care. A 90–day Transition Plan must also be developed for and at the direction of a former foster child who remains eligible for Independent Living Program services during the 90–day period before he or she attains 18 years of age. The plan is as detailed as the child or nonminor chooses and includes information about a power of attorney for health care and specific options regarding housing, health insurance, education, local opportunities for mentors and continuing support services, workforce supports, and employment services. Inclusion of information in the plan relating to sexual health, services, and resources to ensure the child or nonminor is informed and prepared to make healthy decisions about his or her life is encouraged.

(25) "Nonminor" means a youth at least 18 years of age and not yet 21 years of age who remains subject to the court's dependency, delinquency, or general jurisdiction under section 303 but is not a "nonminor dependent."

(26) "Nonminor dependent" means a youth who is a dependent or ward of the court, or a nonminor under the transition jurisdiction of the court, is at least 18 years of age and not yet 21 years of age, and:

(A) Was under an order of foster care placement on his or her 18th birthday;

(B) Is currently in foster care under the placement and care authority of the county welfare department, the county probation department, or an Indian tribe that entered into an agreement under section 10553.1; and

(C) Is participating in a current Transitional Independent Living Case Plan as defined in this rule.

(27) "Notice" means a paper to be filed with the court accompanied by proof of service on each party required to be served in the manner prescribed by these rules. If a notice or other paper is required to be given to or served on a party, the notice or service must be given to or made on the party's attorney of record, if any.

(28) "Notify" means to inform, either orally or in writing.

(29) "Petitioner," in section 300 proceedings, means the county welfare department; "petitioner," in section 601 and 602 proceedings, means the probation officer or prosecuting attorney.

(30) "Preadoptive parent" means a licensed foster parent who has been approved to adopt a child by the California State Department of Social Services, when it is acting as an adoption agency, or by a licensed adoption agency, or, in the case of an Indian child for whom tribal customary adoption is the permanent plan, the individual designated by the child's identified Indian tribe as the prospective adoptive parent.

(31) "Probation officer," in section 300 proceedings, includes a social worker in the county agency responsible for the administration of child welfare.

(32) "Punishment" means the imposition of sanctions, as defined in section 202(e), on a child declared a ward of the court after a petition under section 602 is sustained. A court order to place a child in foster care must not be used as punishment.

(33) "Reasonable efforts" or "reasonable services" means those efforts made or services offered or provided by the county welfare agency or probation department to prevent or eliminate the need for removing the child, or to resolve the issues that led to the child's removal in order for the child to be returned home, or to finalize the permanent placement of the child.

(34) "Relative" means

(A) An adult who is related to the child by blood, adoption, or affinity within the fifth degree of kinship. This term includes:

(i) A parent, sibling, grandparent, aunt, uncle, nephew, niece, great-grandparent, great-aunt or -uncle (grandparents' sibling), first cousin, great-great-grandparent, great-great-aunt or -uncle (great-grandparents' sibling), first cousin once removed (parents' first cousin), and great-great-great-grandparent;

(ii) A stepparent or stepsibling; and

(iii) The spouse or domestic partner of any of the persons described in subparagraphs (A)(i) and (ii), even if the marriage or partnership was terminated by death or dissolution; or

(B) An extended family member as defined by the law or custom of an Indian child's tribe. (25 U.S.C. § 1903(2).)

(35) "Removal" means a court order that takes away the care, custody, and control of a dependent child or ward from the child's parent or guardian, and places the care, custody, and control of the child with the court, under the supervision of the agency responsible for the administration of child welfare or the county probation department.

(36) "Section" means a section of the Welfare and Institutions Code unless stated otherwise.

(37) "Sibling group" means two or more children related to each other by blood, adoption, or affinity through a common legal or biological parent.

(38) "Social study," in section 300, 601, or 602 proceedings, means any written report provided to the court and all parties and counsel by the social worker or probation officer in any matter involving the custody, status, or welfare of a child in a dependency or wardship proceeding.

(39) "Social worker," in section 300 proceedings, means an employee of the county child welfare agency and includes a probation officer performing the child welfare duties.

(40) "Subdivision" means a subdivision of the rule in which the term appears.

(41) "Transition dependent" means a ward of the court at least 17 years and five months of age but not yet 18 years of age who is subject to the court's transition jurisdiction under section 450.

(42) "Transition jurisdiction" means the juvenile court's jurisdiction over a child or nonminor described in Welfare and Institutions Code section 450.

(43) "Transitional independent living case plan" means a child's case plan submitted for the last review hearing held

before he or she turns 18 years of age or a nonminor dependent's case plan, developed with the child or nonminor dependent and individuals identified as important to him or her, signed by the child or nonminor dependent and updated every six months, that describes the goals and objectives of how the child or nonminor will make progress in the transition to living independently and assume incremental responsibility for adult decision making; the collaborative efforts between the child or nonminor dependent and the social worker, probation officer, or Indian tribe and the supportive services as described in the Transitional Independent Living Plan (TILP) to ensure the child's or nonminor dependent's active and meaningful participation in one or more of the eligibility criteria described in subdivision (b) of section 11403; the child or nonminor dependent's appropriate supervised placement setting; the child or nonminor dependent's permanent plan for transition to living independently; and the steps the social worker, probation officer, or Indian tribe is taking to ensure the child or nonminor dependent achieves permanence, including maintaining or obtaining permanent connections to caring and committed adults, as set forth in paragraph (16) of subdivision (f) of section 16501.1.

(44) "Transitional Independent Living Plan" means the written unique, individualized service delivery plan for a child or nonminor mutually agreed upon by the child or nonminor and the social worker or probation officer that identifies the child's or nonminor's current level of functioning, emancipation goals, and the specific skills needed to prepare the child or nonminor to live independently upon leaving foster care.

(45) "Tribal customary adoption" means adoption by and through the tribal custom, traditions, or law of an Indian child's tribe as defined in Welfare and Institutions Code section 366.24 and to which a juvenile court may give full faith and credit under 366.26(e)(2). Termination of parental rights is not required to effect a tribal customary adoption. *(Formerly Rule 1401, adopted, eff. Jan. 1, 1990. As amended, eff. July 1, 1992; July 1, 1997; Jan. 1, 1998; Jan. 1, 1999; Jan. 1, 2001; July 1, 2002; Jan. 1, 2003. Renumbered Rule 5.502 and amended, eff. Jan. 1, 2007. As amended, eff. Jan. 1, 2008; July 1, 2010; Jan. 1, 2011; Jan. 1, 2012; July 1, 2012; Jan. 1, 2014; Jan. 1, 2016.)*

Commentary

In re Ashley P., 62 Cal.App.4th 23, 72 Cal.Rptr.2d 383 (1998), addresses the (a)(6) definition of "de facto parent" (juvenile court should not have denied custodial grandparent's request for de facto parent status; requests for de facto parent spouse status should be liberally granted).

Applying subsection (8), *In re Jacob E., 121 Cal.App.4th 909, 18 Cal.Rptr.3d 15 (2004), review denied,* held that a juvenile court properly denied de facto parent status to a grandmother who did not adequately perform the role of a parent to a child whose mother's rights had been terminated. Interpreting Welfare and Institutions Code § 366.26(j) and Family Code § 8704, *In re Jacob E.* further held that the grandmother was not entitled to a hearing before the child was removed from her custody because the grandmother had not been identified as a prospective adoptive parent.

In re Bryan D., 199 Cal.App.4th 127, 130 Cal.Rptr.3d 821 (2011), sustained a juvenile court's finding that a dependent child's grandmother was not a presumed mother within the meaning of section 7611(d). Although the grandmother received the child into her home and performed all parental responsibilities with respect to the child, there was no evidence that she ever held the child out as her own child rather than as a grandchild. However, the juvenile court abused its discretion in denying the grandmother de facto parent status when the grandmother's conduct was the cause of the dependency proceeding but was not fundamentally inconsistent with the role of a parent.

Research References

Forms

West's California Judicial Council Forms JV-536, Local Educational Agency Response to Jv-535--Appointment Of Surrogate Parent.

Treatises and Practice Aids

Witkin, California Summary 10th Parent and Child § 4, Public Welfare Services.

Witkin, California Summary 10th Parent and Child § 523, Definitions.

Witkin, California Summary 10th Parent and Child § 582, De Facto Parents.

Witkin, California Summary 10th Parent and Child § 587, Persons Entitled to be Present.

Witkin, California Summary 10th Parent and Child § 629, Limitations on Parental Control.

Witkin, California Summary 10th Parent and Child § 763, Investigation, Release, and Conditions.

Witkin, California Summary 10th Parent and Child § 893, Limitations on Parental Control.

Witkin, California Summary 10th Parent and Child § 452A, (New) Persons Within Jurisdiction.

Witkin, California Summary 10th Parent and Child § 688A, (New) Tribal Customary Adoption.

Witkin, California Summary 10th Parent and Child § 699A, (New) in General.

Rule 5.504. Judicial Council forms

(a) Explanation of Judicial Council legal forms

Rules 1.30–1.37 and 2.131–2.134 apply to Judicial Council legal forms, including forms applicable to the juvenile court.

(b) Electronically produced forms

The forms applicable to juvenile court may be produced entirely by computer, word-processor printer, or similar process, or may be produced by the California State Department of Social Services Child Welfare Systems Case Management System.

(c) Implementation of new and revised mandatory forms

To help implement mandatory Judicial Council juvenile forms:

(1) New and revised mandatory forms produced by computer, word-processor printer, or similar process must be implemented within one year of the effective date of the form. During that one-year period the court may authorize the use of a legally accurate alternative form, including any existing local form or the immediate prior version of the Judicial Council form.

(2) Until January 1, 20179, a court may produce court orders in any form or format as long as:

(A) The document is substantively identical to the mandatory Judicial Council form it is modifying;

(B) Any electronically generated form is identical in both language and legally mandated elements, including all notices and advisements, to the mandatory Judicial Council form it is modifying;

(C) The order is an otherwise legally sufficient court order, as provided in rule 1.31(g), concerning orders not on Judicial Council mandatory forms; and

(D) The court sends written notice of its election to change the form or format of the mandatory form to the Family and Juvenile Law Advisory Committee and submits additional informational reports as requested by the committee.

(Formerly Rule 1402, adopted, eff. Jan. 1, 1991. As amended, eff. July 1, 1991; Jan. 1, 1992; July 1, 1992; Jan. 1, 1993; Jan. 1, 1994; Jan. 1, 1998; Jan. 1, 2001; Jan. 1, 2006; July 1, 2006. Renumbered Rule 5.504 and amended, eff. Jan. 1, 2007. As amended, eff. Jan. 1, 2012; Jan. 1, 2017.)

Research References

Forms

West's California Judicial Council Forms JV-100, Juvenile Dependency Petition (Version One) (Welfare and Institutions Code, S300 et seq.).
West's California Judicial Council Forms JV-110, Juvenile Dependency Petition (Version Two) (Welfare and Institutions Code, S300 et seq.).
West's California Judicial Council Forms JV-120, Serious Physical Harm (S300(a)).
West's California Judicial Council Forms JV-121, Failure to Protect (S300(B)).
West's California Judicial Council Forms JV-122, Serious Emotional Damage (S300(C)).
West's California Judicial Council Forms JV-123, Sexual Abuse (S300(D)).
West's California Judicial Council Forms JV-124, Severe Physical Abuse (S300(E)).
West's California Judicial Council Forms JV-125, Caused Another Child's Death Through Abuse or Neglect (S300(F)).
West's California Judicial Council Forms JV-126, No Provision for Support (S300(G)).
West's California Judicial Council Forms JV-127, Freed for Adoption (S300(H)).
West's California Judicial Council Forms JV-128, Cruelty (S300(i)).
West's California Judicial Council Forms JV-129, Abuse Of Sibling (S300(i)).
West's California Judicial Council Forms JV-140, Notification Of Mailing Address.
West's California Judicial Council Forms JV-150, Supplemental Petition for More Restrictive Placement (Attachment)(Welfare and Institutions Code, S387).
West's California Judicial Council Forms JV-190, Waiver Of Rights--Juvenile Dependency.
West's California Judicial Council Forms JV-280, Notice Of Review Hearing.
West's California Judicial Council Forms JV-310, Proof Of Service Under Section 366.26 Of the Welfare and Institutions Code.
West's California Judicial Council Forms JV-320, Orders Under Welfare and Institutions Code Sections 366.26, 727.3, 727.31.
West's California Judicial Council Forms JV-575, Petition to Obtain Report Of Law Enforcement Agency.
West's California Judicial Council Forms JV-590, Order to Seal Juvenile Records.
West's California Judicial Council Forms JV-600, Juvenile Wardship Petition.
West's California Judicial Council Forms JV-610, Child Habitually Disobedient S601(a).
West's California Judicial Council Forms JV-611, Child Habitually Truant S601(B).
West's California Judicial Council Forms JV-620, Violation Of Law by Child.
West's California Judicial Council Forms JV-710, Juvenile Fitness Hearing Order.
West's California Judicial Council Forms JV-735, Juvenile Notice Of Violation Of Probation.
West's California Judicial Council Forms JV-740, Petition to Modify, Change, or Set Aside Previous Orders--Change Of Circumstances.
West's California Judicial Council Forms JV-101(A), Additional Children Attachment (Juvenile Dependency Petition).

Treatises and Practice Aids

Witkin, California Summary 10th Parent and Child § 445, Judicial Council Forms.

Rule 5.505. Juvenile dependency court performance measures

(a) Purpose

The juvenile dependency court performance measures and related procedures set forth in this rule are intended to:

(1) Protect abused and neglected children by assisting courts in promoting children's placement in safe and permanent homes, enhancing their well-being and that of their families, and ensuring that all participants receive timely and fair treatment;

(2) Assist trial courts in meeting the mandated timelines for dependency hearings, securing due process for all litigants, and, in collaboration with the child welfare agency, improving safety, permanency, and well-being outcomes for children and families under the jurisdiction of the juvenile dependency court; and

(3) Assist courts in making well-informed resource allocation decisions.

(b) Performance measures

Detailed definitions of the performance measures and descriptions of the methods for producing the performance measures in accordance with (c)(2) and (3) are contained in the Judicial Council-approved *Implementation Guide to Juvenile Dependency Court Performance Measures.*

The juvenile dependency court performance measures are:

(1) *Hearing timeliness:*

(A) Percentage of children for whom the initial hearing is completed within the statutory time frame following the filing of the initial petition;

(B) Percentage of children for whom the jurisdictional hearing is completed within the statutory time frame following the initial hearing;

(C) Percentage of children for whom the disposition hearing is completed within the statutory time frame following the finding of jurisdiction;

(D) Percentage of children for whom a 3–month or other interim review hearing is held;

(E) Percentage of children for whom the 6–month review hearing is completed within 6 months of the date the child entered foster care;

(F) Percentage of children for whom the 12–month permanency hearing is completed within 12 months of the date the child entered foster care;

(G) Percentage of children for whom the 18–month review hearing is completed within 18 months of the date of original protective custody;

(H) Percentage of children for whom the first section 366.26 hearing is completed within 120 days of the termination of reunification services;

(I) Percentage of children whose postpermanency hearing is completed within 6 months of the section 366.26 hearing or the last postpermanency hearing;

(J) Percentage of children in long-term foster care whose subsequent section 366.26 hearing is completed within 12 months of the previous section 366.26 hearing;

(K) Percentage of children whose adoption is finalized within 180 days after termination of parental rights;

(L) Median time from disposition or section 366.26 hearing to order establishing guardianship;

(M) Percentage of children for whom the first and subsequent postpermanency review hearings are completed within the statutory time frame;

(N) Percentage of hearings delayed by reasons for delay and hearing type;

(O) Median time from filing of original petition to implementation of a permanent plan by permanent plan type; and

(P) Median time from filing of original petition to termination of jurisdiction by reason for termination of jurisdiction.

(2) *Court procedures and due process:*

(A) Percentage of cases in which all hearings are heard by one judicial officer;

(B) Percentage of cases in which all parties and other statutorily entitled individuals are served with a copy of the original petition;

(C) Percentage of hearings in which notice is given to all statutorily entitled parties and individuals within the statutory time frame;

(D) Percentage of hearings in which child or parents are present if statutorily entitled to be present;

(E) Percentage of hearings in which a judicial inquiry is made when a child 10 years of age or older is not present at hearing;

(F) Percentage of hearings in which other statutorily entitled individuals who are involved in the case (e.g., CASA volunteers, caregivers, de facto parents, others) are present;

(G) Percentage of cases in which legal counsel for parents, children, and the child welfare agency are present at every hearing;

(H) Point at which children and parents are assigned legal counsel;

(I) Percentage of cases in which legal counsel for children or parents changes;

(J) Percentage of cases in which no reunification services are ordered and reasons;

(K) Percentage of cases for which youth have input into their case plans; and

(L) Cases in compliance with the requirements of the Indian Child Welfare Act (ICWA).

(3) *Child safety in the child welfare system:*

(A) Percentage of children who are not victims of another substantiated maltreatment allegation within 6 and 12 months after the maltreatment incident that led to the filing of the initial petition; and

(B) For all children served in foster care during the year, percentage of children who were not victims of substantiated maltreatment by a foster parent or facility staff member.

(4) *Child permanency:*

(A) Percentage of children reunified in less than 12 months;

(B) Percentage of children who were reunified but reentered foster care within 12 months;

(C) Percentage of children who were discharged from foster care to a finalized adoption within 24 months;

(D) Percentage of children in foster care who were freed for adoption;

(E) Percentage of children in long-term foster care who were discharged to a permanent home before their 18th birthdays;

(F) Of children discharged to emancipation or aging out of foster care, percentage who were in foster care 3 years or longer;

(G) Percentage of children with multiple foster-care placements;

(5) *Child and family well-being:*

(A) Percentage of children 14 years of age or older with current transitional independent living plans;

(B) Percentage of children for whom a section 391 termination of jurisdiction hearing was held;

(C) Percentage of section 391 termination of jurisdiction hearings that did not result in termination of jurisdiction and reasons jurisdiction did not terminate;

(D) Percentage of youth present at section 391 termination of jurisdiction hearing with judicial confirmation of receipt of all services and documents mandated by section 391(b)(1–5);

(E) Percentage of children placed with all siblings who are also under court jurisdiction, as appropriate;

(F) Percentage of children placed with at least one but not all siblings who are also under court jurisdiction, as appropriate;

(G) For children who have siblings under court jurisdiction but are not placed with all of them, percentage of cases in which sibling visitation is not ordered and reasons;

(H) Percentage of cases in which visitation is not ordered for parents and reasons;

(I) Number of visitation orders for adults other than parents and siblings, (e.g., grandparents, other relatives, extended family members, others) as appropriate;

(J) Number of cases in which the court has requested relative-finding efforts from the child welfare agency;

(K) Percentage of children placed with relatives;

(L) For children 10 years of age or older and in foster care for at least 6 months, percentage for whom the court has inquired whether the social worker has identified persons important to the child; and

(M) For children 10 years of age or older in foster care for at least 6 months, percentage for whom the court has made orders to enable the child to maintain relationships with persons important to that child.

(c) Data collection

(1) California's Court Case Management System (CCMS) family and juvenile law module must be capable of collecting the data described in the *Implementation Guide to Juvenile Dependency Court Performance Measures* in order to calculate the performance measures and to produce performance measure reports.

(2) Before implementation of the CCMS family and juvenile law module, each local court must collect and submit to the Judicial Council the subset of juvenile dependency data described in (b) and further delineated in the *Implementation Guide to Juvenile Dependency Court Performance Measures* that it is reasonably capable of collecting and submitting with its existing court case management system and resources.

(3) On implementation of the CCMS family and juvenile law module in a local court, and as the necessary data elements become electronically available, the local court must collect and submit to the Judicial Council the juvenile dependency data described in (b) and further delineated in the *Implementation Guide to Juvenile Dependency Court Performance Measures*. For the purposes of this subdivision, "implementation of the CCMS family and juvenile law module" in a local court means that the CCMS family and juvenile law module has been deployed in that court, is functioning, and has the ability to capture the required data elements and that local court staff has been trained to use the system.

(d) Use of data and development of measures before CCMS implementation

Before CCMS implementation, the Judicial Council must:

(1) Establish a program to assist the local courts in collecting, preparing, analyzing, and reporting the data required by this rule;

(2) Establish a procedure to assist the local courts in submitting the required data to the Judicial Council;

(3) Use the data submitted under (c)(2) to test and refine the detailed definitions of the performance measures and descriptions of the methods for producing the performance measures described in the *Implementation Guide to Juvenile Dependency Court Performance Measures;*

(4) Consult with local courts about the accuracy of the data submitted under (c)(2). After such consultation, use data to generate aggregate data reports on performance measures, consistent with section 16543, while not disclosing identifying information about children, parents, judicial officers, and other individuals in the dependency system; and

(5) Assist the courts in using the data to achieve improved outcomes for children and families in the dependency system, make systemic improvements, and improve resource allocation decisions.

(e) Use of data after CCMS implementation

On implementation of CCMS, the Judicial Council must:

(1) Use the data submitted under (c)(3) to conduct ongoing testing, refining, and updating of the information in the *Implementation Guide to Juvenile Dependency Court Performance Measures;*

(2) Use the data submitted under (c)(3) to generate aggregate data reports on performance measures, consistent with section 16543, while not disclosing identifying information about children, parents, judicial officers, and other individuals in the dependency system;

(3) Upon the request of any local court, extract data from the system and prepare county-level reports to meet data reporting requirements; and

(4) Assist the courts in using the data to achieve improved outcomes for children and families in the dependency system, make systemic improvements, and improve resource allocation decisions. *(Adopted, eff. Jan. 1, 2009. As amended, eff. Jan. 1, 2016.)*

Research References

Treatises and Practice Aids

Witkin, California Summary 10th Parent and Child § 441, Advisory Committees and Commissions.

Witkin, California Summary 10th Parent and Child § 444, Scope and Organization.

Chapter 2

COMMENCEMENT OF JUVENILE COURT PROCEEDINGS

Rule

Rule 5.510. Proper court; determination of child's residence; exclusive jurisdiction

(a) Proper court (§§ 327, 651)

The proper court in which to commence proceedings to declare a child a dependent or ward of the court is the juvenile court in the county:

(1) In which the child resides;

(2) In which the child is found; or

(3) In which the acts take place or the circumstances exist that are alleged to bring the child within the provisions of section 300 or 601 or 602.

(b) Determination of residence—general rule (§ 17.1)

Unless otherwise provided in the juvenile court law or in these rules, the residence of a child must be determined under section 17.1.

(c) Exclusive jurisdiction (§§ 304, 316.2, 726.4)

(1) Once a petition has been filed under section 300, the juvenile court has exclusive jurisdiction of the following:

(A) All issues regarding custody and visitation of the child; and

(B) All issues and actions regarding the parentage of the child under rule 5.635 and Family Code section 7630.

(2) Once a petition has been filed under section 601 or 602, the juvenile court has exclusive jurisdiction to hear an action filed under Family Code section 7630. *(Formerly Rule 1403, adopted, eff. Jan. 1, 1991. As amended, eff. Jan. 1, 1999. Renumbered Rule 5.510 and amended, eff. Jan. 1, 2007. As amended, eff. Jan. 1, 2015.)*

Research References

Treatises and Practice Aids

Witkin, California Summary 10th Parent and Child § 369, Dependency Proceeding Pending.

Witkin, California Summary 10th Parent and Child § 444, Scope and Organization.

Witkin, California Summary 10th Parent and Child § 456, Proper Court.

Witkin, California Summary 10th Parent and Child § 520, Jurisdiction.

Witkin, California Summary 10th Parent and Child § 886, Conduct Of Hearing.

Rule 5.512. Joint assessment procedure

(a) Joint assessment requirement (§ 241.1)

Whenever a child appears to come within the description of section 300 and either section 601 or section 602, the responsible child welfare and probation departments must conduct a joint assessment to determine which status will serve the best interest of the child and the protection of society.

(1) The assessment must be completed as soon as possible after the child comes to the attention of either department.

(2) Whenever possible, the determination of status must be made before any petition concerning the child is filed.

(3) The assessment report need not be prepared before the petition is filed but must be provided to the court for the hearing as stated in (e).

(4) If a petition has been filed, on the request of the child, parent, guardian, or counsel, or on the court's own motion, the court may set a hearing for a determination under section 241.1 and order that the joint assessment report be made available as required in (f).

(b) Proceedings in same county

If the petition alleging jurisdiction is filed in a county in which the child is already a dependent or ward, the child welfare and probation departments in that county must assess the child under a jointly developed written protocol and prepare a joint assessment report to be filed in that county.

(c) Proceedings in different counties

If the petition alleging jurisdiction is filed in one county and the child is already a dependent or ward in another county, a joint assessment must be conducted by the responsible departments of each county. If the departments cannot agree on which will prepare the joint assessment report, then the department in the county where the petition is to be filed must prepare the joint assessment report.

(1) The joint assessment report must contain the recommendations and reasoning of both the child welfare and the probation departments.

(2) The report must be filed at least 5 calendar days before the hearing on the joint assessment in the county where the second petition alleging jurisdictional facts under sections 300, 601, or 602 has been filed.

(d) Joint assessment report

The joint assessment report must contain the joint recommendation of the probation and child welfare departments if they agree on the status that will serve the best interest of the child and the protection of society, or the separate recommendation of each department if they do not agree. The report must also include:

(1) A description of the nature of the referral;

(2) The age of the child;

(3) The history of any physical, sexual, or emotional abuse of the child;

(4) The prior record of the child's parents for abuse of this or any other child;

(5) The prior record of the child for out-of-control or delinquent behavior;

(6) The parents' cooperation with the child's school;

(7) The child's functioning at school;

(8) The nature of the child's home environment;

(9) The history of involvement of any agencies or professionals with the child and his or her family;

(10) Any services or community agencies that are available to assist the child and his or her family;

(11) A statement by any counsel currently representing the child; and

(12) A statement by any CASA volunteer currently appointed for the child.

(e) Hearing on joint assessment

If the child is detained, the hearing on the joint assessment report must occur as soon as possible after or concurrent with the detention hearing, but no later than 15 court days after the order of detention and before the jurisdictional hearing. If the child is not detained, the hearing on the joint assessment must occur before the jurisdictional hearing and within 30 days of the date of the petition. The juvenile court must conduct the hearing and determine which type of jurisdiction over the child best meets the child's unique circumstances.

(f) Notice and participation

At least 5 calendar days before the hearing, notice of the hearing and copies of the joint assessment report must be provided to the child, the child's parent or guardian, all attorneys of record, any CASA volunteer, and any other juvenile court having jurisdiction over the child. The notice must be directed to the judicial officer or department that will conduct the hearing.

(g) Conduct of hearing

All parties and their attorneys must have an opportunity to be heard at the hearing. The court must make a determination regarding the appropriate status of the child and state its reasons on the record or in a written order.

(h) Notice of decision after hearing

Within 5 calendar days after the hearing, the clerk of the juvenile court must transmit the court's findings and orders to any other juvenile court with current jurisdiction over the child.

(i) Local protocols

On or before January 1, 2004, the probation and child welfare departments of each county must adopt a written protocol for the preparation of joint assessment reports, including procedures for resolution of disagreements between the probation and child welfare departments, and submit a copy to the Judicial Council. *(Formerly Rule 1403.5, adopted, eff. Jan. 1, 2003. Renumbered Rule 5.512 and amended, eff. Jan. 1, 2007.)*

Validity

For validity of this rule, see In re M.V. (App. 1 Dist. 2014) 171 Cal.Rptr.3d 519, 225 Cal.App.4th 1495.

Research References

Treatises and Practice Aids

Witkin, California Summary 10th Parent and Child § 450, Dual Bases Of Jurisdiction.

Witkin, California Summary 10th Parent and Child § 959, Delinquency and Dependency Status.

Rule 5.514. Intake; guidelines

(a) Role of juvenile court

It is the duty of the presiding judge of the juvenile court to initiate meetings and cooperate with the probation department, welfare department, prosecuting attorney, law enforcement, and other persons and agencies performing an intake function. The goal of the intake meetings is to establish and maintain a fair and efficient intake program designed to promote swift and objective evaluation of the circumstances of any referral and to pursue an appropriate course of action.

(b) Purpose of intake program

The intake program must be designed to:

(1) Provide for settlement at intake of:

(A) Matters over which the juvenile court has no jurisdiction;

(B) Matters in which there is insufficient evidence to support a petition; and

(C) Matters that are suitable for referral to a nonjudicial agency or program available in the community;

(2) Provide for a program of informal supervision of the child under sections 301 and 654; and

(3) Provide for the commencement of proceedings in the juvenile court only when necessary for the welfare of the child or protection of the public.

(c) Investigation at intake (§§ 309, 652.5)

The probation officer or the social worker must conduct an investigation and determine whether:

(1) The matter should be settled at intake by:

(A) Taking no action;

(B) Counseling the child and any others involved in the matter; or

(C) Referring the child, the child's family, and any others involved to other agencies and programs in the community for the purpose of receiving services to prevent or eliminate the need for removal;

(2) A program of informal supervision should be undertaken for not more than six months under section 301 or 654; or

(3) A petition should be filed under section 300 or 601, or the prosecuting attorney should be requested to file a petition under section 602.

(d) Mandatory referrals to the prosecuting attorney (§ 653.5)

Notwithstanding (c), the probation officer must refer to the prosecuting attorney, within 48 hours, all affidavits requesting that a petition be filed under section 602 if it appears to the probation officer that:

(1) The child, regardless of age:

(A) Is alleged to have committed an offense listed in section 707(b);

(B) Has been referred for the sale or possession for sale of a controlled substance under chapter 2 of division 10 of the Health and Safety Code;

(C) Has been referred for a violation of Health and Safety Code section 11350 or 11377 at a school, or for a violation of Penal Code sections 245.5, 626.9, or 626.10;

(D) Has been referred for a violation of Penal Code section 186.22;

(E) Has previously been placed on informal supervision under section 654; or

(F) Has been referred for an alleged offense in which restitution to the victim exceeds $1,000;

(2) The child was 16 years of age or older on the date of the alleged offense and the referral is for a felony offense; or

(3) The child was under 16 years of age on the date of the alleged offense and the referral is not the first referral for a felony offense.

Except for the offenses listed in (1)(C), the provisions of this subdivision do not apply to narcotics and drug offenses listed in Penal Code section 1000.

(e) Informal supervision (§§ 301, 654)

(1) If the child is placed on a program of informal supervision for not more than six months under section 301, the social worker may file a petition at any time during the

six-month period. If the objectives of a service plan under section 301 have not been achieved within six months, the social worker may extend the period up to an additional six months, with the consent of the parent or guardian.

(2) If a child is placed on a program of informal supervision for not more than six months under section 654, the probation officer may file a petition under section 601, or request that the prosecuting attorney file a petition under section 602, at any time during the six-month period, or within 90 days thereafter. If a child on informal supervision under section 654 has not participated in the specific programs within 60 days, the probation officer must immediately file a petition under section 601, or request that the prosecuting attorney file one under section 602, unless the probation officer determines that the interests of the child and the community can be adequately protected by continuing under section 654. *(Formerly Rule 1404, adopted, eff. Jan. 1, 1991. As amended, eff. Jan. 1, 1994; Jan. 1, 1995; Jan. 1, 2001. Renumbered Rule 5.514 and amended, eff. Jan. 1, 2007.)*

Research References

Treatises and Practice Aids

Witkin, California Summary 10th Parent and Child § 560, Intake Program.

Witkin, California Summary 10th Parent and Child § 561, Investigation by Social Worker.

Witkin, California Summary 10th Parent and Child § 563, Program Of Supervision.

Witkin, California Summary 10th Parent and Child § 765, Intake Program.

Witkin, California Summary 10th Parent and Child § 766, Investigation by Probation Officer.

Witkin, California Summary 10th Parent and Child § 767, in General.

Rule 5.516. Factors to consider

(a) Settlement at intake (§ 653.5)

In determining whether a matter not described in rule 5.514(d) should be settled at intake, the social worker or probation officer must consider:

(1) Whether there is sufficient evidence of a condition or conduct to bring the child within the jurisdiction of the court;

(2) If the alleged condition or conduct is not considered serious, whether the child has previously presented significant problems in the home, school, or community;

(3) Whether the matter appears to have arisen from a temporary problem within the family that has been or can be resolved;

(4) Whether any agency or other resource in the community is available to offer services to the child and the child's family to prevent or eliminate the need to remove the child from the child's home;

(5) The attitudes of the child, the parent or guardian, and any affected persons;

(6) The age, maturity, and capabilities of the child;

(7) The dependency or delinquency history, if any, of the child;

(8) The recommendation, if any, of the referring party or agency; and

(9) Any other circumstances that indicate that settling the matter at intake would be consistent with the welfare of the child and the protection of the public.

(b) Informal supervision

In determining whether to undertake a program of informal supervision of a child not described by rule 5.514(d), the social worker or probation officer must consider:

(1) If the condition or conduct is not considered serious, whether the child has had a problem in the home, school, or community that indicates that some supervision would be desirable;

(2) Whether the child and the parent or guardian seem able to resolve the matter with the assistance of the social worker or probation officer and without formal court action;

(3) Whether further observation or evaluation by the social worker or probation officer is needed before a decision can be reached;

(4) The attitudes of the child and the parent or guardian;

(5) The age, maturity, and capabilities of the child;

(6) The dependency or delinquency history, if any, of the child;

(7) The recommendation, if any, of the referring party or agency;

(8) The attitudes of affected persons; and

(9) Any other circumstances that indicate that a program of informal supervision would be consistent with the welfare of the child and the protection of the public.

(c) Filing of petition

In determining whether to file a petition under section 300 or 601 or to request the prosecuting attorney to file a petition under section 602, the social worker or probation officer must consider:

(1) Whether any of the statutory criteria listed in rules 5.770 and 5.772 relating to the fitness of the child are present;

(2) Whether the alleged conduct would be a felony;

(3) Whether the alleged conduct involved physical harm or the threat of physical harm to person or property;

(4) If the alleged condition or conduct is not serious, whether the child has had serious problems in the home, school, or community that indicate that formal court action is desirable;

(5) If the alleged condition or conduct is not serious, whether the child is already a ward or dependent of the court;

(6) Whether the alleged condition or conduct involves a threat to the physical or emotional health of the child;

(7) Whether a chronic, serious family problem exists after other efforts to resolve the problem have been made;

(8) Whether the alleged condition or conduct is in dispute and, if proven, whether court-ordered disposition appears desirable;

(9) The attitudes of the child and the parent or guardian;

(10) The age, maturity, and capabilities of the child;

(11) Whether the child is on probation or parole;

(12) The recommendation, if any, of the referring party or agency;

(13) The attitudes of affected persons;

(14) Whether any other referrals or petitions are pending; and

(15) Any other circumstances that indicate that the filing of a petition is necessary to promote the welfare of the child or to protect the public.

(d) Certification to juvenile court

Copies of the certification, the accusatory pleading, any police reports, and the order of a superior court, certifying that the accused person was under the age of 18 on the date of the alleged offense, must immediately be delivered to the clerk of the juvenile court.

(1) On receipt of the documents, the clerk must immediately notify the probation officer, who must immediately investigate the matter to determine whether to commence proceedings in juvenile court.

(2) If the child is under the age of 18 and is in custody, the child must immediately be transported to the juvenile detention facility. *(Formerly Rule 1405, adopted, eff. Jan. 1, 1991. As amended, eff. Jan. 1, 2001. Renumbered Rule 5.516 and amended, eff. Jan. 1, 2007.)*

Research References

Treatises and Practice Aids

Witkin, California Summary 10th Parent and Child § 560, Intake Program.

Witkin, California Summary 10th Parent and Child § 563, Program Of Supervision.

Witkin, California Summary 10th Parent and Child § 564, in General.

Witkin, California Summary 10th Parent and Child § 765, Intake Program.

Witkin, California Summary 10th Parent and Child § 769, Factors in Authorizing Program.

Witkin, California Summary 10th Parent and Child § 772, Discretion Of Probation Officer and Prosecutor.

Rule 5.518. Court-connected child protection/dependency mediation

(a) Purpose (§ 350)

This rule establishes mandatory standards of practice and administration for court-connected dependency mediation services in accordance with section 350. This rule is intended to ensure fairness, accountability, and a high quality of service to children and families and to improve the safety, confidentiality, and consistency of dependency mediation programs statewide.

(b) Definitions

(1) "Dependency mediation" is a confidential process conducted by specially trained, neutral third-party mediators who have no decision-making power. Dependency mediation provides a nonadversarial setting in which a mediator assists the parties in reaching a fully informed and mutually acceptable resolution that focuses on the child's safety and best interest and the safety of all family members. Dependency mediation is concerned with any and all issues related to child protection.

(2) "Safety and best interest of the child" refers to the child's physical, psychological, and emotional well-being. Determining the safety and best interest of the child includes consideration of all of the following:

(A) The preservation and strengthening of the family and family relationships whenever appropriate and possible;

(B) The manner in which the child may be protected from the risk of future abuse or neglect;

(C) The child's need for safety, stability, and permanency;

(D) The ongoing need of the child to cope with the issues that caused his or her involvement in the juvenile dependency system;

(E) The child's need for continuity of care and the effect that removal and subsequent placements have had, or may have, on the child; and

(F) The child's education, which includes the child's participation, progress, need for assistance, cognitive development and, if applicable, early childhood education and care, the need for special education and related services, and the extent to which the child has or has had limited English proficiency (LEP).

(3) "Safety of family members" refers to the physical, psychological, and emotional well-being of all family members, with consideration of the following:

(A) The role of domestic violence in creating a perceived or actual threat for the victim; and

(B) The ongoing need of family members to feel safe from physical, emotional, and psychological abuse.

(4) "Differential domestic violence assessment" is a process used to assess the nature of any domestic violence issues in the family so that the mediator may conduct the mediation in such a way as to protect any victim of domestic violence from intimidation and to correct for power imbalances created by past violence and the fear of prospective violence.

(5) "Protocols" refer to any local set of rules, policies, and procedures developed and implemented by juvenile dependency mediation programs. All protocols must be developed in accordance with pertinent state laws, California Rules of Court, and local court rules.

(c) Responsibility for mediation services

(1) Each court that has a dependency mediation program must ensure that:

(A) Dependency mediators are impartial, are competent, and uphold the standards established by this rule;

(B) Dependency mediators maintain an appropriate focus on issues related to the child's safety and best interest and the safety of all family members;

(C) Dependency mediators provide a forum for all interested persons to develop a plan focused on the best interest of the child, emphasizing family preservation and strengthening and the child's need for permanency;

(D) Dependency mediation services and case management procedures are consistent with applicable state law without compromising each party's right to due process and a timely resolution of the issues;

(E) Dependency mediation services demonstrate accountability by:

(i) Providing for the processing of complaints about a mediator's performance; and

(ii) Participating in any statewide and national data-collection efforts;

(F) The dependency mediation program uses an intake process that screens for and informs the mediator about any restraining orders, domestic violence, or safety-related issues affecting the child or any other party named in the proceedings;

(G) Whenever possible, dependency mediation is conducted in the shared language of the participants. When the participants speak different languages, interpreters, court-certified when possible, should be assigned to translate at the mediation session; and

(H) Dependency mediation services preserve, in accordance with pertinent law, party confidentiality, whether written or oral, by the:

(i) Storage and disposal of records and any personal information accumulated by the mediation program; and

(ii) Management of any new child abuse reports and related documents.

(2) Each dependency mediator must:

(A) Attempt to assist the mediation participants in reaching a settlement of the issues consistent with preserving the safety and best interest of the child, first and foremost, and the safety of all family members and participants;

(B) Discourage participants from blaming the victim and from denying or minimizing allegations of child abuse or violence against any family member;

(C) Be conscious of the values of preserving and strengthening the family as well as the child's need for permanency;

(D) Not make any recommendations or reports of any kind to the court, except for the terms of any agreement reached by the parties;

(E) Treat all mediation participants in a manner that preserves their dignity and self–respect;

(F) Promote a safe and balanced environment for all participants to express and advocate for their positions and interests;

(G) Identify and disclose potential grounds on which a mediator's impartiality might reasonably be challenged through a procedure that allows for the selection of another mediator within a reasonable time. If a dependency mediation program has only one mediator and the parties are unable to resolve the conflict, the mediator must inform the court;

(H) Identify and immediately disclose to the participants any reasonable concern regarding the mediator's continuing capacity to be impartial, so they can decide whether the mediator should withdraw or continue;

(I) Promote the participants' understanding of the status of the case in relation to the ongoing court process, what the case plan requires of them, and the terms of any agreement reached during the mediation; and

(J) Conduct an appropriate review to evaluate the viability of any agreement reached, including the identification of any provision that depends on the action or behavior of any individual who did not participate in creating the agreement.

(d) Mediation process

The dependency mediation process must be conducted in accordance with pertinent state laws, applicable rules of court, and local protocols. All local protocols must include the following:

(1) The process by which cases are sent to mediation, including:

(A) Who may request mediation;

(B) Who decides which cases are to be sent to mediation;

(C) Whether mediation is voluntary or mandatory;

(D) How mediation appointments are scheduled; and

(E) The consequences, if any, to a party who fails to participate in the mediation process.

(2) A policy on who participates in the mediation, according to the following guidelines:

(A) When at all possible, dependency mediation should include the direct and active participation of the parties, including but not limited to the child, the parents or legal guardian, a representative of the child protective agency, and, at some stage, their respective attorneys.

(B) The child has a right to participate in the dependency mediation process accompanied by his or her attorney. If the child makes an informed choice not to participate, then the child's attorney may participate. If the child is unable to make an informed choice, then the child's attorney may participate.

(C) Any attorney who has not participated in the mediation must have an opportunity to review and agree to any proposal before it is submitted to the court for approval.

(D) As appropriate, other family members and any guardian ad litem, CASA volunteer, or other involved person or professional may participate in the mediation.

(E) A mediation participant who has been a victim of violence allegedly perpetrated by another mediation participant has the right to be accompanied by a support person. Unless otherwise invited or ordered to participate under the protocols developed by the court, a support person may not actively participate in the mediation except to be present as a source of emotional support for the alleged victim.

(3) A method by which the mediator may review relevant case information before the mediation.

(4) A protocol for providing mediation in cases in which domestic violence or violence perpetrated by any other mediation participant has, or allegedly has, occurred. This protocol must include specialized procedures designed to protect victims of domestic violence from intimidation by perpetrators. The protocol must also appropriately address all family violence issues by encouraging the incorporation of

appropriate safety and treatment interventions in any settlement. The protocol must require:

(A) A review of case-related information before commencing the mediation;

(B) The performance of a differential domestic violence assessment to determine the nature of the violence, for the purposes of:

(i) Assessing the ability of the victim to fully and safely participate and to reach a noncoerced settlement;

(ii) Clarifying the history and dynamics of the domestic violence issue in order to determine the most appropriate manner in which the mediation can proceed; and

(iii) Assisting the parties, attorneys, and other participants in formulating an agreement following a discussion of appropriate safeguards for the safety of the child and family members; and

(C) A mediation structure designed to meet the need of the victim of violence for safety and for full and noncoerced participation in the process, which structure must include:

(i) An option for the victim to attend the mediation session without the alleged perpetrator being present; and

(ii) Permission for the victim to have a support person present during the mediation process, whether he or she elects to be seen separately from or together with the alleged perpetrator.

(5) An oral or written orientation that facilitates participants' safe, productive, and informed participation and decision making by educating them about:

(A) The mediation process, the typical participants, the range of disputes that may be discussed, and the typical outcomes of mediation;

(B) The importance of keeping confidential all communications, negotiations, or settlement discussions by and between the participants in the course of mediation;

(C) The mediator's role and any limitations on the confidentiality of the process; and

(D) The right of a participant who has been a victim of violence allegedly perpetrated by another mediation participant to be accompanied by a support person and to have sessions with the mediators separate from the alleged perpetrator.

(6) Protocols related to the inclusion of children in the mediation, including a requirement that the mediator explain in an age-appropriate way the mediation process to a participating child. The following information must be explained to the child:

(A) How the child may participate in the mediation;

(B) What occurs during the mediation process;

(C) The role of the mediator;

(D) What the child may realistically expect from the mediation, and the limits on his or her ability to affect the outcome;

(E) Any limitations on the confidentiality of the process;

(F) The child's right to be accompanied, throughout the mediation, by his or her attorney and other support persons; and

(G) The child's right to leave the mediation session if his or her emotional or physical well-being is threatened.

(7) Policy and procedures for scheduling follow-up mediation sessions.

(8) A procedure for suspending or terminating the process if the mediator determines that mediation cannot be conducted in a safe or an appropriately balanced manner or if any party is unable to participate in an informed manner for any reason, including fear or intimidation.

(9) A procedure for ensuring that each participant clearly understands any agreement reached during the mediation, and a procedure for presenting the agreement to the court for its approval. This procedure must include the requirement that all parties and the attorneys who participate in the agreement review and approve it and indicate their agreement in writing before its submission to the court.

(e) Education, experience, and training requirements for dependency mediators

Dependency mediators must meet the following minimum qualifications:

(1) Possession of one or more of the following:

(A) A master's or doctoral degree in psychology, social work, marriage and family therapy, conflict resolution, or another behavioral science substantially related to family relationships, family violence, child development, or conflict resolution from an accredited college or university; or

(B) A juris doctorate or bachelor of laws degree;

(2) At least two years of experience as an attorney, a referee, a judicial officer, a mediator, or a child welfare worker in juvenile dependency court, or at least three years of experience in mediation or counseling, preferably in a setting related to juvenile dependency or domestic relations; and

(3) Completion of at least 40 hours of initial dependency mediation training before or within 12 months of beginning practice as a dependency mediator. Currently practicing dependency mediators must complete the required 40 hours of initial training by January 1, 2006. The training must cover the following subject areas as they relate to the practice of dependency mediation:

(A) Multiparty, multi-issue, multiagency, and high-conflict cases, including:

(i) The roles and participation of parents, other family members, children, attorneys, guardians ad litem, children's caregivers, the child welfare agency staff, CASA volunteers, law enforcement, mediators, the court, and other involved professionals and interested participants in the mediation process;

(ii) The impact that the mediation process can have on a child's well-being, and when and how to involve the child in the process;

(iii) The methods to help parties collaboratively resolve disputes and jointly develop plans that consider the needs and best interest of the child;

(iv) The disclosure, recantation, and denial of child abuse and neglect;

(v) Adult mental health issues; and

(vi) The rights to educational and developmental services recognized or established by state and federal law and strategies for appropriately addressing the individual needs of persons with disabilities;

(B) Physical and sexual abuse, exploitation, emotional abuse, endangerment, and neglect of children, and the impacts on children, including safety and treatment issues related to child abuse, neglect, and family violence;

(C) Family violence, its relevance to child abuse and neglect, and its effects on children and adult victims, including safety and treatment issues related to child abuse, neglect, and family violence;

(D) Substance abuse and its impact on children;

(E) Child development and its relevance to child abuse, neglect, and child custody and visitation arrangements;

(F) Juvenile dependency and child welfare systems, including dependency law;

(G) Interfamilial relationships and the psychological needs of children, including, but not limited to:

(i) The effect of removal or nonremoval of children from their homes and family members; and

(ii) The effect of terminating parental rights;

(H) The effect of poverty on parenting and familial relationships;

(I) Awareness of differing cultural values, including cross-generational cultural issues and local demographics;

(J) An overview of the special needs of dependent children, including their educational, medical, psychosocial, and mental health needs; and

(K) Available community resources and services for dealing with domestic and family violence, substance abuse, and housing, educational, medical, and mental health needs for families in the juvenile dependency system.

(f) Substitution for education or experience

The court, on a case-by-case basis, may approve substitution of experience for the education, or education for the experience, required by (e)(1) and (e)(2).

(g) Continuing education requirements for mediators

In addition to the 40 hours of training required by (e)(3), all dependency mediators, mediation supervisors, program coordinators and directors, volunteers, interns, and paraprofessionals must participate in at least 12 hours per year of continuing instruction designed to enhance dependency mediation practice, skills, and techniques, including at least 4 hours specifically related to the issue of family violence.

(h) Volunteers, interns, or paraprofessionals

Dependency mediation programs may use volunteers, interns, or paraprofessionals as mediators, but only if they are supervised by a professional mediator who is qualified to act as a professional dependency mediator as described in (e). They must meet the training and continuing education requirements in (e)(3) and (g) unless they co-mediate with another professional who meets the requirements of this rule. They are exempt from meeting the education and experience requirements in (e)(1) and (e)(2).

(i) Education and training providers

Only education and training acquired from eligible providers meet the requirements of this rule. "Eligible providers" includes the Judicial Council and may include educational institutions, professional associations, professional continuing education groups, public or private for-profit or not-for-profit groups, and court-connected groups.

(1) Eligible providers must:

(A) Ensure that the training instructors or consultants delivering the education and training programs either meet the requirements of this rule or are experts in the subject matter;

(B) Monitor and evaluate the quality of courses, curricula, training, instructors, and consultants;

(C) Emphasize the importance of focusing dependency mediations on the health, safety, welfare, and best interest of the child;

(D) Develop a procedure to verify that participants complete the education and training program; and

(E) Distribute a certificate of completion to each person who has completed the training. The certificate must document the number of hours of training offered, the number of hours the person completed, the dates of the training, and the name of the training provider.

(2) Effective July 1, 2005, all education and training programs must be approved by Judicial Council staff in consultation with the Family and Juvenile Law Advisory Committee.

(j) Ethics/standards of conduct

Mediators must:

(1) Meet the standards of the applicable code of ethics for court employees.

(2) Maintain objectivity, provide information to and gather information from all parties, and be aware of and control their own biases.

(3) Protect the confidentiality of all parties, including the child. Mediators must not release information or make any recommendations about the case to the court or to any individual except as required by statute (for example, the requirement to make mandatory child abuse reports or reports to authorities regarding threats of harm or violence). Any limitations to confidentiality must be clearly explained to all mediation participants before any substantive issues are discussed in the mediation session.

(4) Maintain the confidential relationship between any family member or the child and his or her treating counselor, including the confidentiality of any psychological evaluations.

(5) Decline to provide legal advice.

(6) Consider the health, safety, welfare, and best interest of the child and the safety of all parties and other participants in all phases of the process and encourage the formulation of settlements that preserve these values.

(7) Operate within the limits of their training and experience and disclose any limitations or bias that would affect their ability to conduct the mediation.

(8) Not require the child to state a preference for placement.

(9) Disclose to the court, to any participant, and to the participant's attorney any conflicts of interest or dual relationships, and not accept any referral except by court order or the parties' stipulation. In the event of a conflict of interest, the mediator must suspend mediation and meet and confer in an effort to resolve the conflict of interest either to the satisfaction of all parties or according to local court rules. The court may order mediation to continue with another mediator or offer the parties an alternative method of resolving the issues in dispute.

(10) Not knowingly assist the parties in reaching an agreement that would be unenforceable for a reason such as fraud, duress, illegality, overreaching, absence of bargaining ability, or unconscionability.

(11) Protect the integrity of the mediation process by terminating the mediation when a party or participant has no genuine interest in resolving the dispute and is abusing the process.

(12) Terminate any session in which an issue of coercion, inability to participate, lack of intention to resolve the issues at hand, or physical or emotional abuse during the mediation session is involved. *(Formerly Rule 1405.5, adopted, eff. Jan. 1, 2004. As amended, eff. Jan. 1, 2005. Renumbered Rule 5.518 and amended, eff. Jan. 1, 2007. As amended, eff. Jan. 1, 2008; Jan. 1, 2014; Jan. 1, 2016.)*

Research References

Treatises and Practice Aids

Witkin, California Summary 10th Parent and Child § 589, Informality and Control by Court.

Rule 5.520. Filing the petition; application for petition

(a) Discretion to file (§§ 325, 650)

Except as provided in sections 331, 364, 604, 653.5, 654, and 655, the social worker or probation officer has the sole discretion to determine whether to file a petition under section 300 and 601. The prosecuting attorney has the sole discretion to file a petition under section 602.

(b) Filing the petition (§§ 325, 650)

A proceeding in juvenile court to declare a child a dependent or a ward of the court is commenced by the filing of a petition.

(1) In proceedings under section 300, the social worker must file the petition;

(2) In proceedings under section 601, the probation officer must file the petition; and

(3) In proceedings under section 602, the prosecuting attorney must file the petition. The prosecuting attorney may refer the matter back to the probation officer for appropriate action.

(c) Application for petition (§§ 329, 331, 653, 653.5, 655)

Any person may apply to the social worker or probation officer to commence proceedings. The application must be in the form of an affidavit alleging facts showing the child is described in sections 300, 601, or 602. The social worker or probation officer must proceed under sections 329, 653, or 653.5. The applicant may seek review of a decision not to file a petition by proceeding under section 331 or 655. *(Formerly Rule 1406, adopted, eff. Jan. 1, 1991. Renumbered Rule 5.520 and amended, eff. Jan. 1, 2007.)*

Research References

Treatises and Practice Aids

Witkin, California Summary 10th Parent and Child § 561, Investigation by Social Worker.

Witkin, California Summary 10th Parent and Child § 562, Application to Social Worker.

Witkin, California Summary 10th Parent and Child § 564, in General.

Witkin, California Summary 10th Parent and Child § 766, Investigation by Probation Officer.

Witkin, California Summary 10th Parent and Child § 772, Discretion Of Probation Officer and Prosecutor.

Witkin, California Summary 10th Parent and Child § 607A, (New) Educational and Developmental Services Decisions.

Rule 5.522. Remote filing

(a) Applicability and definitions

(1) This rule applies to juvenile court proceedings in courts that permit fax or electronic filing by local rule.

(2) As used in this rule, "fax," "fax transmission," "fax machine," and "fax filing," are defined in rule 2.301. A fax machine also includes any electronic device capable of receiving a fax transmission, as defined in rule 2.301.

(3) As used in this rule, "electronic filing" is defined in rule 2.250. Rule 2.250 also defines other terms used in this rule related to electronic filing, such as "document," "electronic filer," "electronic filing service provider," "regular filing hours," and "close of business."

(b) Electronic filing

(1) A court may allow for the electronic filing of documents in juvenile dependency and delinquency proceedings as provided under, and consistent with, rule 2.252 et seq.

(2) A court may allow for the electronic filing of documents directly with the court or may provide by local rule for indirect filing through an electronic filing service provider that has in place systems to ensure the integrity and confidentiality of transmission of records and adheres to the requirements of rule 2.256(a)(1).

(3) Electronic filing must be conducted in a manner that preserves and ensures the confidentiality of records by encryption or other secure methods.

(4) This rule does not incorporate the electronic service provisions in rule 2.251.

(c) Fax filing

(1) *Juvenile court documents that may be filed by fax*

The following documents may be filed in juvenile court by the use of a fax machine: petitions filed under sections 300, 342, 387, 388, 601, 602, 777, and 778. Other documents may be filed by the use of a fax machine if permitted by local rule as specified in (a).

(2) *Persons and agencies that may file by fax*

Only the following persons and agencies may file documents by the use of a fax machine, as stated in (c)(1):

(A) Any named party to the proceeding;

(B) Any attorney of record in the proceeding;

(C) The county child welfare department;

(D) The probation department;

(E) The office of the district attorney;

(F) The office of the county counsel; and

(G) A Court Appointed Special Advocate (CASA) volunteer appointed in the case.

(3) *Procedures for fax filing*

A person described in (c)(2) may file by fax directly to any juvenile court that has provided for fax filing by local rule. The local rule or other written instruction must provide the fax telephone number or numbers for filings and the business hours during which fax filings will be accepted.

(4) *Mandatory cover sheet*

A fax filing must be accompanied by *Fax Filing Cover Sheet* (form JV–520). The cover sheet must be the first page of the transferred document. The court is not required to retain or file a copy of the cover sheet.

(5) *Signatures*

Notwithstanding any provision of law to the contrary, a signature produced by fax transmission is an original signature.

(6) *Confidentiality requirements*

To secure the confidentiality of the documents subject to filing by fax, the following procedures are required:

(A) The clerk's office designated to receive such documents must have either a separate fax machine dedicated solely to the receipt of the documents described in (c)(1) or a fax machine that is set up with a protocol to preserve the confidentiality of the documents described in (c)(1); and

(B) Any document received for fax filing must be filed or submitted to the court immediately on receipt and must not be placed or stored where anyone not entitled to access may examine it.

(Formerly Rule 1406.5, adopted, eff. Jan. 1, 1999. Renumbered Rule 5.522 and amended, eff. Jan. 1, 2007. As amended, eff. Jan. 1, 2015.)

Research References

Forms

West's California Judicial Council Forms JV-520, Fax Filing Cover Sheet.

Treatises and Practice Aids

Witkin, California Summary 10th Parent and Child § 564, in General.

Witkin, California Summary 10th Parent and Child § 657, Filing, Setting for Hearing, and Notice.

Witkin, California Summary 10th Parent and Child § 663, Form, Content, and Filing.

Witkin, California Summary 10th Parent and Child § 771, in General.

Witkin, California Summary 10th Parent and Child § 908, Notice and Setting for Hearing.

Witkin, California Summary 10th Parent and Child § 910, in General.

Rule 5.524. Form of petition; notice of hearing

(a) Form of petition—dependency (§§ 332, 333)

The petition to declare a child a dependent of the court must be verified and may be dismissed without prejudice if not verified. The petition must contain the information stated in section 332.

(b) Form of petition—delinquency (§§ 656, 656.1, 656.5, 661)

The petition to declare a child a ward of the court must be verified and may be dismissed without prejudice if not verified. The petition must contain the information stated in sections 656, 656.1, 656.5, 661, and, if applicable, the intent to aggregate other offenses under section 726.

(c) Use of forms

Dependency petitions must be filed on a Judicial Council form. The filing party must use *Juvenile Dependency Petition (Version One)* (form JV–100) with the *Additional Children Attachment (Juvenile Dependency Petition)* (form JV–101) when appropriate, or *Juvenile Dependency Petition (Version Two)* (form JV–110) as prescribed by local rule or practice. Rules 1.31 and 1.32 govern the use of mandatory and optional forms, respectively.

(d) Amending the petition (§§ 348, 678)

Chapter 8 of title 6 of part 2 of the Code of Civil Procedure, beginning at section 469, applies to variances and amendments of petitions and proceedings in the juvenile court.

(e) Notice of hearing—dependency (§§ 290.1, 290.2, 297, 338)

(1) When the petition is filed, the probation officer or social worker must serve a notice of hearing under section 290.1, with a copy of the petition attached. On filing of the petition, the clerk must issue and serve notice as prescribed in section 290.2, along with a copy of the petition. CASA volunteers are entitled to the same notice as stated in sections 290.1 and 290.2.

(2) If the county and the court choose to allow notice by electronic mail of hearings under sections 290.1–295, the court must develop a process for obtaining consent from persons entitled to notice that complies with the notice statute and ensures that notice can be effectuated according to statutory timelines.

(f) Notice of hearing—delinquency (§§ 630, 630.1, 658, 659, 660)

(1) Immediately after the filing of a petition to detain a child, the probation officer or the prosecuting attorney must issue and serve notice as prescribed in section 630.

(2) When a petition is filed, the clerk must issue and serve a notice of hearing in accordance with sections 658, 659, and 660 with a copy of the petition attached.

(3) After reasonable notification by minor's counsel or his or her parent or guardian, the clerk must provide notice to the minor's attorney as stated in section 630.1.

(g) Waiver of service (§§ 290.2, 660)

A person may waive service of notice by a voluntary appearance noted in the minutes of the court, or by a written waiver of service filed with the clerk.

(h) Oral notice (§§ 290.1, 630)

Notice required by sections 290.1 and 630 may be given orally. The social worker or probation officer must file a declaration stating that oral notice was given and to whom. *(Formerly Rule 1407, adopted, eff. Jan. 1, 1991. As amended, eff. Jan. 1, 1992; Jan. 1, 1995; Jan. 1, 2001; Jan. 1, 2006. Renumbered Rule 5.524 and amended, eff. Jan. 1, 2007. As amended, eff. July 1, 2016.)*

Research References

Forms

West's California Judicial Council Forms JV-180, Request to Change Court Order.

Treatises and Practice Aids

Witkin, California Summary 10th Parent and Child § 564, in General.
Witkin, California Summary 10th Parent and Child § 565, Form and Content.
Witkin, California Summary 10th Parent and Child § 566, Notices, Citations, Warrants, and Subpenas.
Witkin, California Summary 10th Parent and Child § 600, Petition and Notice Of Hearing.
Witkin, California Summary 10th Parent and Child § 656, Form and Content.
Witkin, California Summary 10th Parent and Child § 664, in General.
Witkin, California Summary 10th Parent and Child § 668, Subsequent Petition.
Witkin, California Summary 10th Parent and Child § 773, Form and Content.
Witkin, California Summary 10th Parent and Child § 774, Variance and Amendment.
Witkin, California Summary 10th Parent and Child § 776, Persons Entitled to Notice.
Witkin, California Summary 10th Parent and Child § 778, Service Of Notice.
Witkin, California Summary 10th Parent and Child § 820, Petition and Setting for Hearing.
Witkin, California Summary 10th Parent and Child § 908, Notice and Setting for Hearing.
Witkin, California Summary 10th Parent and Child § 911, Hearing and Determination.

Rule 5.526. Citation to appear; warrants of arrest; subpoenas

(a) Citation to appear (§§ 338, 661)

In addition to the notice required under rule 5.524, the court may issue a citation directing a parent or guardian to appear at a hearing.

(1) The citation must state that the parent or guardian may be required to participate in a counseling program, and the citation may direct the child's present caregiver to bring the child to court.

(2) The citation must be personally served at least 24 hours before the time stated for the appearance.

(b) Warrant of arrest (§§ 339, 662)

The court may order a warrant of arrest to issue against the parent, guardian, or present custodian of the child if:

(1) The citation cannot be served;

(2) The person served does not obey it; or

(3) The court finds that a citation will probably be ineffective.

(c) Protective custody or warrant of arrest for child (§§ 340, 663)

The court may order a protective custody warrant or a warrant of arrest for a child if the court finds that:

(1) The conduct and behavior of the child may endanger the health, person, welfare, or property of the child or others; or

(2) The home environment of the child may endanger the health, person, welfare, or property of the child.

(d) Subpoenas (§§ 341, 664)

On the court's own motion or at the request of the petitioner, child, parent, guardian, or present caregiver, the clerk must issue subpoenas requiring attendance and testimony of witnesses and the production of papers at a hearing. If a witness appears in response to a subpoena, the court may order the payment of witness fees as a county charge in the amount and manner prescribed by statute. *(Formerly Rule 1408, adopted, eff. Jan. 1, 1991. As amended, eff. Jan. 1, 2006. Renumbered Rule 5.526 and amended, eff. Jan. 1, 2007.)*

Research References

Treatises and Practice Aids

Witkin, California Summary 10th Parent and Child § 444, Scope and Organization.
Witkin, California Summary 10th Parent and Child § 566, Notices, Citations, Warrants, and Subpenas.
Witkin, California Summary 10th Parent and Child § 779, Citation.
Witkin, California Summary 10th Parent and Child § 780, Arrest Warrant.
Witkin, California Summary 10th Parent and Child § 781, Subpenas to Witnesses.

Chapter 3

GENERAL CONDUCT OF JUVENILE COURT PROCEEDINGS

Rule 5.530. Persons present

(a) Separate session; restriction on persons present (§§ 345, 675)

All juvenile court proceedings must be heard at a special or separate session of the court, and no other matter may be heard at that session. No person on trial, awaiting trial, or accused of a crime, other than a parent, de facto parent, guardian, or relative of the child, may be present at the hearing, except while testifying as a witness.

(b) Persons present

The following persons are entitled to be present:

(1) The child or nonminor dependent;

(2) All parents, de facto parents, Indian custodians, and guardians of the child or, if no parent or guardian resides within the state or their places of residence are not known, any adult relative residing within the county or, if none, the adult relative residing nearest the court;

(3) Counsel representing the child or the parent, de facto parent, guardian, adult relative, or Indian custodian or the tribe of an Indian child;

(4) The probation officer or social worker;

(5) The prosecuting attorney, as provided in (c) and (d);

(6) Any CASA volunteer;

(7) In a proceeding described by rule 5.480, a representative of the Indian child's tribe;

(8) The court clerk;

(9) The official court reporter, as provided in rule 5.532;

(10) At the court's discretion, a bailiff; and

(11) Any other persons entitled to notice of the hearing under sections 290.1 and 290.2.

(c) Presence of prosecuting attorney—section 601–602 proceedings (§ 681)

In proceedings brought under section 602, the prosecuting attorney must appear on behalf of the people of the State of California. In proceedings brought under section 601, the prosecuting attorney may appear to assist in ascertaining and presenting the evidence if:

(1) The child is represented by counsel; and

(2) The court consents to or requests the prosecuting attorney's presence, or the probation officer requests and the court consents to the prosecuting attorney's presence.

(d) Presence of petitioner's attorney—section 300 proceedings (§ 317)

In proceedings brought under section 300, the county counsel or district attorney must appear and represent the petitioner if the parent or guardian is represented by counsel and the juvenile court requests the attorney's presence.

(e) Others who may be admitted (§§ 346, 676, 676.5)

Except as provided below, the public must not be admitted to a juvenile court hearing. The court may admit those whom the court deems to have a direct and legitimate interest in the case or in the work of the court.

(1) If requested by a parent or guardian in a hearing under section 300, and consented to or requested by the child, the court may permit others to be present.

(2) In a hearing under section 602:

(A) If requested by the child and a parent or guardian who is present, the court may admit others.

(B) Up to two family members of a prosecuting witness may attend to support the witness, as authorized by Penal Code section 868.5.

(C) Except as provided in section 676(b), members of the public must be admitted to hearings concerning allegations of the offenses stated in section 676(a).

(D) A victim of an offense alleged to have been committed by the child who is the subject of the petition, and up to two support persons chosen by the victim, are entitled to attend any hearing regarding the offense.

(E) Any persons, including the child, may move to exclude a victim or a support person and must demonstrate a substantial probability that overriding interests will be prejudiced by the presence of the individual sought to be excluded. On such motion, the court must consider reasonable alternatives to the exclusion and must make findings as required under section 676.5.

(f) Participation of incarcerated parent in dependency proceedings (§§ 290.1–294, 316.2, 349, 361.5(e); Pen. Code § 2625)

The incarcerated parent of a child on behalf of whom a petition under section 300 has been filed may appear and participate in dependency proceedings as provided in this subdivision.

(1) Notice must be sent to an incarcerated parent of a detention hearing under section 319 as required by sections 290.1 and 290.2; a jurisdictional hearing under section 355 or a dispositional hearing under section 358 or 361 as required by section 291; a review hearing under section 366.21, 366.22, or 366.25 as required by section 293; or a permanency planning hearing under section 366.26 as required by section 294.

(A) Notice to an incarcerated parent of a jurisdictional hearing, a dispositional hearing, or a section 366.26 permanency planning hearing at which termination of parental rights is at issue must inform the incarcerated parent of his or her right to be physically present at the hearing and explain how the parent may secure his or her presence or, if he or she waives the right to be physically present, appearance and participation.

(B) Notice to an incarcerated parent of a detention hearing, a review hearing, or any other hearing in a dependency proceeding must inform the incarcerated parent of his or her options for requesting physical or telephonic appearance at and participation in the hearing.

(C) The county welfare department must use the prisoner location system developed by the Department of Corrections and Rehabilitation to facilitate timely and effective notice of hearings to incarcerated parents.

(2) The court must order an incarcerated parent's temporary removal from the institution where he or she is confined and production before the court at the time appointed for any jurisdictional hearing held under section 355 or dispositional hearing held under section 358 or 361, and any permanency planning hearing held under section 366.26 in which termination of parental rights is at issue.

(3) For any other hearing in a dependency proceeding, including but not limited to a detention hearing or a review hearing, the court may order the temporary removal of the

incarcerated parent from the institution where he or she is confined and the parent's production before the court at the time appointed for that hearing.

(4) No hearing described in (2) may be held without the physical presence of the incarcerated parent and the parent's attorney unless the court has received:

(A) A knowing waiver of the right to be physically present signed by the parent; or

(B) A declaration, signed by the person in charge of the institution in which the parent is incarcerated, or his or her designated representative, stating that the parent has, by express statement or action, indicated an intent not to be physically present at the hearing.

(5) When issuing an order under (2) or (3), the court must require that *Order for Prisoner's Appearance at Hearing Affecting Parental Rights* (form JV–450) and a copy of *Prisoner's Statement Regarding Appearance at Hearing Affecting Parental Rights* (form JV–451) be attached to the notice of hearing and served on the parent, the parent's attorney, the person in charge of the institution, and the sheriff's department of the county in which the order is issued by the person responsible for giving notice of the hearing at issue not less than 15 days before the date of the hearing.

(6) The court may, at the request of any party or on its own motion, permit an incarcerated parent, who has waived his or her right to be physically present at a hearing described in (2) or who has not been ordered to appear before the court, to appear and participate in a hearing by videoconference consistent with the requirements of rule 5.531. If video technology is not available, the court may permit the parent to appear by telephone consistent with the requirements of rule 5.531. The court must inform the parent that, if no technology complying with rule 5.531 is available, the court may proceed without his or her appearance and participation.

(7) The presiding judge of the juvenile court in each county should convene representatives of the county welfare department, the sheriff's department, parents' attorneys, and other appropriate entities to develop:

(A) Local procedures or protocols to ensure an incarcerated parent's notification of, transportation to, and physical presence at court hearings involving proceedings affecting his or her child as required or authorized by Penal Code section 2625 and this rule unless he or she has knowingly waived the right to be physically present; and

(B) Local procedures or protocols, consistent with (f)(6) and rule 5.531, to facilitate the appearance and participation by videoconference or telephone of an incarcerated parent who has knowingly waived the right to be physically present.

(Formerly Rule 1410, adopted, eff. Jan. 1, 1990. As amended, eff. Jan. 1, 1995; Jan. 1, 1997; Jan. 1, 2001; Jan. 1, 2005. Renumbered Rule 5.530 and amended, eff. Jan. 1, 2007. As amended, eff. Jan. 1, 2012; July 1, 2013.)

Commentary

For the definition of a *de facto parent*, see California Rules of Court, Rule 5.502 (10) and accompanying Commentary.

Research References

Forms

West's California Judicial Council Forms JV-450, Order for Prisoner's Appearance at Hearing Affecting Parental Rights.

West's California Judicial Council Forms JV-451, Prisoner's Statement Regarding Appearance at Hearing Affecting Parental Rights.

Treatises and Practice Aids

Witkin, California Summary 10th Parent and Child § 12, Parental or Marital Rights Of Prisoners.

Witkin, California Summary 10th Parent and Child § 444, Scope and Organization.

Witkin, California Summary 10th Parent and Child § 567, Statutory Rights.

Witkin, California Summary 10th Parent and Child § 586, Hearing is Usually Private.

Witkin, California Summary 10th Parent and Child § 587, Persons Entitled to be Present.

Witkin, California Summary 10th Parent and Child § 588, Persons Who May be Admitted.

Witkin, California Summary 10th Parent and Child § 592, Participation by District Attorney.

Witkin, California Summary 10th Parent and Child § 593, Participation by Foster Parent.

Witkin, California Summary 10th Parent and Child § 782, Statutory Rights.

Witkin, California Summary 10th Parent and Child § 808, in General.

Witkin, California Summary 10th Parent and Child § 809, Victims and Support Persons.

Witkin, California Summary 10th Parent and Child § 810, Interested Persons.

Witkin, California Summary 10th Parent and Child § 811, Members Of the Public.

Witkin, California Summary 10th Parent and Child § 815, Participation by District Attorney.

Witkin, California Summary 10th Parent and Child § 288C, (New) Applicable Law.

Rule 5.531. Appearance by telephone (§ 388; Pen. Code § 2625)

(a) Application

The standards in (b) apply to any appearance or participation in court by telephone, videoconference, or other digital or electronic means authorized by law.

(b) Standards for local procedures or protocols

Local procedures or protocols must be developed to ensure the fairness and confidentiality of any proceeding in which a party is permitted by statute, rule of court, or judicial discretion to appear by telephone. These procedures or protocols must, at a minimum:

(1) Ensure that the party appearing by telephone can participate in the hearing in real time, with no delay in aural or, if any, visual transmission or reception;

(2) Ensure that the statements of participants are audible to all other participants and court staff and that the statements made by a participant are identified as being made by that participant;

(3) Ensure that the proceedings remain confidential as required by law;

(4) Establish a deadline of no more than three court days before the proceeding for notice to the court by the party or

party's attorney (if any) of that party's intent to appear by telephone, and permit that notice to be conveyed by any method reasonably calculated to reach the court, including telephone, fax, or other electronic means;

(5) Permit the party, on a showing of good cause, to appear by telephone even if he or she did not provide timely notice of intent to appear by telephone;

(6) Permit a party to appear in person for a proceeding at the time and place for which the proceeding was noticed, even if that party had previously notified the court of an intent to appear by telephone;

(7) Ensure that any hearing at which a party appears by telephone is recorded and reported to the same extent and in the same manner as if he or she had been physically present;

(8) Ensure that the party appearing by telephone is able to communicate confidentially with his or her attorney (if any) during the proceeding and provide timely notice to all parties of the steps necessary to secure confidential communication; and

(9) Provide for the development of the technological capacity to accommodate appearances by telephone that comply with the requirements of this rule.

(c) No independent right

Nothing in this rule confers on any person an independent right to appear by telephone, videoconference, or other electronic means in any proceeding. *(Adopted, eff. Jan. 1, 2012.)*

Research References

Forms

West's California Judicial Council Forms JV-450, Order for Prisoner's Appearance at Hearing Affecting Parental Rights.

West's California Judicial Council Forms JV-451, Prisoner's Statement Regarding Appearance at Hearing Affecting Parental Rights.

Treatises and Practice Aids

Witkin, California Summary 10th Parent and Child § 12, Parental or Marital Rights Of Prisoners.

Witkin, California Summary 10th Parent and Child § 699A, (New) in General.

Rule 5.532. Court reporter; transcripts

(a) Hearing before judge (§§ 347, 677)

If the hearing is before a judge or a referee acting as a temporary judge by stipulation, an official court reporter or other authorized reporting procedure must record all proceedings.

(b) Hearing before referee (§§ 347, 677)

If the hearing is before a referee not acting as a temporary judge, the judge may direct an official court reporter or other authorized reporting procedure to record all proceedings.

(c) Preparation of transcript (§§ 347, 677)

If directed by the judge or if requested by a party or the attorney for a party, the official court reporter or other authorized transcriber must prepare a transcript of the proceedings within such reasonable time after the hearing as the judge designates and must certify that the proceedings have been correctly reported and transcribed. If directed by the judge, the official court reporter or authorized transcriber must file the transcript with the clerk of the court. *(Formerly Rule 1411, adopted, eff. Jan. 1, 1990. Renumbered Rule 5.532 and amended, eff. Jan. 1, 2007.)*

Research References

Treatises and Practice Aids

Witkin, California Summary 10th Parent and Child § 591, Reporter and Transcript.

Witkin, California Summary 10th Parent and Child § 814, Reporter and Transcript.

Rule 5.534. General provisions—all proceedings

~~**(a) Control of proceedings (§§ 350, 680)**~~

~~The court must control all proceedings with a view to quickly and effectively ascertaining the jurisdictional facts and all information relevant to the present condition and welfare of the child.~~

~~**(b) Conduct of proceedings (§§ 350, 680)**~~

~~Unless there is a contested issue of fact or law, the proceedings must be conducted in a nonadversarial atmosphere.~~

~~**(c) Testimony of child in chambers (§ 350)**~~

~~In a hearing under section 300 et seq., a child may testify in chambers and outside the presence of the child's parent or guardian if the parent or guardian is represented by counsel who is present, subject to the right of the parent or guardian to have the court reporter read back the child's testimony, and if the court determines, based on the petitioner's report or other offers of proof or other evidence, that any of the following circumstances exist:~~

~~(1) Testimony in chambers is necessary to ensure truthful testimony;~~

~~(2) The child is likely to be intimidated by a formal courtroom setting; or~~

~~(3) The child is afraid to testify in front of the parent or guardian.~~

~~**(d) Burden of proof (§§ 350, 701.1)**~~

~~Meeting the burden of proof:~~

~~(1) In any hearing under section 300 in which the county welfare agency has the burden of proof, the court may consider whether the burden of proof has been met only after completion of the agency's case and the presentation of any material evidence offered by the child. The court may then, on motion of any party or on the court's own motion, order whatever action the law requires if the court, based on all the evidence then before it, finds that the burden of proof has not been met.~~

~~(2) In any hearing under section 601 or 602, after the completion of the petitioner's case, the court may, on the motion of any party or on the court's own motion, order whatever action the law requires if the court, based on all the evidence then before it, finds that the burden of proof has not been met.~~

~~(e)~~(a) De facto parents

On a sufficient showing, the court may recognize the child's present or previous custodian as a de facto parent and grant him or her standing to participate as a party in the dispositional hearing and any hearing thereafter at which the status of the dependent child is at issue. The de facto parent may:

(1) Be present at the hearing;

(2) Be represented by retained counsel or, at the discretion of the court, by appointed counsel; and

(3) Present evidence.

~~(f)~~(b) Relatives

(1) On a sufficient showing, the court may permit a relative of the child or youth to:

(A) Be present at the hearing; and

(B) Address the court.

(2) A relative of the child has the right to submit information about the child to the court at any time. Written information about the child may be submitted to the court using *Relative Information* (form JV–285) or in a letter to the court.

(3) When a relative is located through the investigation required by rule 5.637, the social worker or probation officer must give that relative:

(A) The written notice required by section 309 or 628 and the "Important Information for Relatives" document as distributed in California Department of Social Services All County Letter No. 09–86;

(B) A copy of *Relative Information* (form JV–285), with the county and address of the court, the child's name and date of birth, and the case number already entered in the appropriate caption boxes by the social worker; and

(C) A copy of *Confidential Information* (form JV–287).

(4) When form JV–285 or a relative's letter is received by the court, the clerk must provide the social worker or probation officer, all self-represented parties, and all attorneys with a copy of the completed form or letter.

(5) When form JV–287 is received by the court, the clerk must place it in a confidential portion of the case file.

~~(g)~~(c) Right to counsel (§§ 317, 633, 634, 700)

At each hearing, the court must advise any self-represented child, parent, or guardian of the right to be represented by counsel and, if applicable, of the right to have counsel appointed, subject to a claim by the court or the county for reimbursement as provided by law.

~~(h)~~(d) Appointment of counsel (§§ 317, 353, 633, 634, 700)

(1) In cases petitioned under section 300:

(A) The court must appoint counsel for the child unless the court finds that the child would not benefit from the appointment and makes the findings required by rule 5.660(b); and

(B) The court must appoint counsel for any parent or guardian unable to afford counsel if the child is placed in out-of-home care or the recommendation of the petitioner is for out-of-home care, unless the court finds the parent or guardian has knowingly and intelligently waived the right to counsel.

(2) In cases petitioned under section 601 or 602:

(A) The court must appoint counsel for any child who appears without counsel, unless the child knowingly and intelligently waives the right to counsel. If the court determines that the parent or guardian can afford counsel but has not retained counsel for the child, the court must appoint counsel for the child and order the parent or guardian to reimburse the county;

(B) The court may appoint counsel for a parent or guardian who desires but cannot afford counsel; and

(C) If the parent has retained counsel for the child and a conflict arises, the court must take steps to ensure that the child's interests are protected.

~~(i)~~(e) Tribal representatives (25 U.S.C. §§ 1911, 1931–1934)

The tribe of an Indian child is entitled to intervene as a party at any stage of a dependency proceeding concerning the Indian child.

(1) The tribe may appear by counsel or by a representative of the tribe designated by the tribe to intervene on its behalf. When the tribe appears as a party by a representative of the tribe, the name of the representative and a statement of authorization for that individual or agency to appear as the tribe must be submitted to the court in the form of a tribal resolution or other document evidencing an official act of the tribe.

(2) If the tribe of the Indian child does not intervene as a party, the court may permit an individual affiliated with the tribe or, if requested by the tribe, a representative of a program operated by another tribe or Indian organization to:

(A) Be present at the hearing;

(B) Address the court;

(C) Receive notice of hearings;

(D) Examine all court documents relating to the dependency case;

(E) Submit written reports and recommendations to the court; and

(F) Perform other duties and responsibilities as requested or approved by the court.

~~(j)~~(f) Appointment of educational rights holder (§§ 319, 361, 366, 366.27, 726, 727.2; Gov. Code, §§ 7579.5–7579.6)

(1) If the court limits, even temporarily, the rights of a parent or guardian to make educational or developmental-services decisions for a child under rule 5.649, the court must immediately proceed under rule 5.650 to appoint a responsible adult as educational rights holder for the child.

(2) If a nonminor or nonminor dependent youth chooses not to make educational or developmental-services decisions for him- or herself or is deemed by the court to be incompetent, and the court also finds that the appointment of an educational rights holder would be in the best interests of the youth, then the court must immediately proceed under rule 5.650 to appoint or continue the appointment of a responsible adult as educational rights holder for the youth.

~~(k)~~(g) Advisement of hearing rights (§§ 301, 311, 341, 630, 702.5, 827)

(1) The court must advise the child, parent, and guardian in section 300 cases, and the child in section 601 or section 602 cases, of the following rights:

(A) ~~Any~~ The right to assert the privilege against self-incrimination;

(B) The right to confront and cross-examine the persons who prepared reports or documents submitted to the court by the petitioner and the witnesses called to testify at the hearing;

(C) The right to use the process of the court to bring in witnesses; and

(D) The right to present evidence to the court.

(2) The child, parent, guardian, and their attorneys have:

(A) The right to receive probation officer or social worker reports; and

(B) The right to inspect the documents used by the preparer of the report.

(3) Unless prohibited by court order, the child, parent, guardian, and their attorneys also have the right to receive all documents filed with the court.

~~(l)~~(h) Notice

At each hearing under section 300 et seq., the court must determine whether notice has been given as required by law and must make an appropriate finding noted in the minutes.

~~(m)~~(i) Address of parent or guardian—notice (§ 316.1)

At the first appearance by a parent or guardian in proceedings under section 300 et seq., the court must order each parent or guardian to provide a mailing address.

(1) The court must advise that the mailing address provided will be used by the court, the clerk, and the social services agency for the purposes of notice of hearings and the mailing of all documents related to the proceedings.

(2) The court must advise that until and unless the parent or guardian, or the attorney of record for the parent or guardian, submits written notification of a change of mailing address, the address provided will be used, and notice requirements will be satisfied by appropriate service at that address.

(3) *Notification of Mailing Address* (form JV–140) is the preferred method of informing the court and the social services agency of the mailing address of the parent or guardian and change of mailing address.

(A) The form must be delivered to the parent or guardian, or both, with the petition.

(B) The form must be available in the courtroom, in the office of the clerk, and in the offices of the social services agency.

(C) The form must be printed and made available in both English and Spanish.

(4) If the county and the court allow notice of hearings under sections 290.1–295 by electronic mail, persons who are entitled to notice and who want to receive notice of hearings by electronic mail must indicate their consent by filing *E-Mail Notice of Hearing: Consent, Withdrawal of Consent, Address Change (Juvenile Dependency)* (form EFS–005–JV/JV–141).

~~(n)~~(j) Caregiver notice and right to be heard (§§ 290.1–297, 366.21)

For cases filed under section 300 et seq.:

(1) For any child who has been removed from the home, the court must ensure that notice of statutory review hearings, permanency hearings, and section 366.26 hearings has been provided to the current caregiver of the child, including foster parents, preadoptive parents, relative caregivers, and nonrelative extended family members. Notice of dispositional hearings also must be provided to these individuals when the dispositional hearing is serving as a permanency hearing under section 361.5(f).

(2) The current caregiver has the right to be heard in each proceeding listed in paragraph (1), including the right to submit information about the child to the court before the hearing. Written information about the child may be submitted to the court using the Caregiver Information Form (form JV–290) or in the form of a letter to the court.

(3) At least 10 calendar days before each hearing listed in paragraph (1), the social worker must provide to the current caregiver:

(A) A summary of his or her recommendations for disposition, and any recommendations for change in custody or status;

(B) *Caregiver Information Form* (form JV–290); and

(C) *Instruction Sheet for Caregiver Information Form* (form JV–290–INFO).

(4) If the caregiver chooses to provide written information to the court using form JV–290 or by letter, the caregiver must follow the procedures set forth below. The court may waive any element of this process for good cause.

(A) If filing in person, the caregiver must bring the original document and 8 copies to the court clerk's office for filing no later than five calendar days before the hearing.

(B) If filing by mail, the caregiver must mail the original document and 8 copies to the court clerk's office for filing no later than seven calendar days before the hearing.

(5) When form JV–290 or a caregiver letter is received by mail the court clerk must immediately file it.

(6) When form JV–290 or a caregiver letter is filed, the court clerk must provide the social worker, all unrepresented parties, and all attorneys with a copy of the completed form or letter immediately upon receipt. The clerk also must complete, file, and distribute *Proof of Service—Juvenile* (form JV–510). The clerk may use any technology designed to speed the distribution process, including drop boxes in the courthouse, e-mail, fax, or other electronic transmission, as defined in rule 2.250, to distribute the JV–290 form or letter and proof of service form.

~~(o) Periodic reports (§ 365)~~

~~The court may require the petitioner or any other agency to submit reports concerning a child or youth subject to the jurisdiction of the court.~~

~~(p) Presence of child (§ 349)~~

~~(1) A child who is the subject of a juvenile court hearing is entitled to be present at the hearing. If the child is present at the hearing, the court must allow the child, if the child so desires, to address the court and participate in the hearing.~~

~~(2) If the child is 10 years of age or older and he or she is not present at the hearing, the court must determine whether~~

~~the child was properly notified of his or her right to attend the hearing and ask why the child is not present at the hearing and whether the child was given an opportunity to attend. If the court finds that the child was not properly notified or that the child wished to be present and was not given an opportunity to be present, the court must continue the hearing to allow the child to attend unless the court finds that it is in the best interest of the child not to continue the hearing. Any such continuance must be only for that period of time necessary to provide notice and secure the presence of the child. The court may issue any and all orders reasonably necessary to ensure that the child has an opportunity to attend.~~ *(Formerly Rule 1412, adopted, eff. Jan. 1, 1991. As amended, eff. Jan. 1, 1994; July 1, 1995; Jan. 1, 1997; Jan. 1, 2000; July 1, 2002; Jan. 1, 2005. Renumbered Rule 5.534 and amended, eff. Jan. 1, 2007. As amended, eff. Oct. 1, 2007; Jan. 1, 2008; Jan. 1, 2010; Jan. 1, 2011; Jan. 1, 2014; Jan. 1, 2016; July 1, 2016; Jan. 1, 2017.)*

Commentary

In re Vanessa M., 138 Cal.App.4th 1121, 41 Cal.Rptr.3d 909 (2006), holds that a juvenile court violated a father's due process rights in barring his testimony as an "evidence sanction" for his failure to appear for several court dates during a multi-day jurisdictional hearing, at the conclusion of which the court adjudged the father's daughter a dependent of the court and removed her from her father's custody.

In re Damion B., 202 Cal.App.4th 880, 135 Cal.Rptr.3d 742 (2011), review denied, held that de facto parents were not deprived of their subsection (e) right to present evidence even though they were not permitted to call witnesses at an 18-month review hearing, when they were represented by appointed counsel, the trial court had received their Caregiver Information Forms into evidence, and the de facto parents were unable to specify what testimony they wanted to present.

Research References

Forms

West's California Judicial Council Forms JV-140, Notification Of Mailing Address.
West's California Judicial Council Forms JV-285, Relative Information.
West's California Judicial Council Forms JV-287, Confidential Information.
West's California Judicial Council Forms JV-290, Caregiver Information Form.
West's California Judicial Council Forms JV-295, De Facto Parent Request.
West's California Judicial Council Forms JV-296, De Facto Parent Statement.
West's California Judicial Council Forms JV-297, De Facto Parent Order.
West's California Judicial Council Forms JV-298, Order Ending De Facto Parent Status.
West's California Judicial Council Forms ICWA-040, Notice Of Designation Of Tribal Representative and Notice Of Intervention in a Court Proceeding Involving an Indian Child.
West's California Judicial Council Forms JV-290-INFO, Instruction Sheet for Caregiver Information Form.

Treatises and Practice Aids

Witkin, California Summary 10th Parent and Child § 533, Participation by Indian Tribe.
Witkin, California Summary 10th Parent and Child § 555, Investigation, Detention, and Release.
Witkin, California Summary 10th Parent and Child § 567, Statutory Rights.
Witkin, California Summary 10th Parent and Child § 570, in General.
Witkin, California Summary 10th Parent and Child § 571, in General.
Witkin, California Summary 10th Parent and Child § 576, in General.
Witkin, California Summary 10th Parent and Child § 578, Confrontation and Cross-Examination.
Witkin, California Summary 10th Parent and Child § 579, in General.
Witkin, California Summary 10th Parent and Child § 582, De Facto Parents.
Witkin, California Summary 10th Parent and Child § 588, Persons Who May be Admitted.
Witkin, California Summary 10th Parent and Child § 589, Informality and Control by Court.
Witkin, California Summary 10th Parent and Child § 596, Disposition Where Burden Of Proof Not Met.
Witkin, California Summary 10th Parent and Child § 602, Explanation and Information.
Witkin, California Summary 10th Parent and Child § 610, Notice Of Hearing.
Witkin, California Summary 10th Parent and Child § 613, Commencement Of Hearing.
Witkin, California Summary 10th Parent and Child § 629, Limitations on Parental Control.
Witkin, California Summary 10th Parent and Child § 666, Scope Of Hearing.
Witkin, California Summary 10th Parent and Child § 670, Notice Of Hearing.
Witkin, California Summary 10th Parent and Child § 673, Child in Foster Care.
Witkin, California Summary 10th Parent and Child § 681, Notice.
Witkin, California Summary 10th Parent and Child § 763, Investigation, Release, and Conditions.
Witkin, California Summary 10th Parent and Child § 782, Statutory Rights.
Witkin, California Summary 10th Parent and Child § 787, in General.
Witkin, California Summary 10th Parent and Child § 788, Duty to Provide Counsel.
Witkin, California Summary 10th Parent and Child § 803, Right to Counsel.
Witkin, California Summary 10th Parent and Child § 810, Interested Persons.
Witkin, California Summary 10th Parent and Child § 813, Informality and Control by Court.
Witkin, California Summary 10th Parent and Child § 823, Explanation and Information.
Witkin, California Summary 10th Parent and Child § 825, in General.
Witkin, California Summary 10th Parent and Child § 826, Confrontation and Cross-Examination.
Witkin, California Summary 10th Parent and Child § 864, Commencement Of Proceeding.
Witkin, California Summary 10th Parent and Child § 878, Sufficiency Of Evidence.
Witkin, California Summary 10th Parent and Child § 893, Limitations on Parental Control.
Witkin, California Summary 10th Parent and Child § 288C, (New) Applicable Law.
Witkin, California Summary 10th Parent and Child § 607A, (New) Educational and Developmental Services Decisions.

Rule 5.536. General provisions—proceedings held before referees

(a) Referees—appointment; powers (Cal. Const., art. VI, § 22)

One or more referees may be appointed under section 247 to perform subordinate judicial duties assigned by the presiding judge of the juvenile court.

(b) Referee as temporary judge (Cal. Const., art. VI, § 21)

If the referee is an attorney admitted to practice in this state, the parties may stipulate under rule 2.816 that the referee is acting as a temporary judge with the same powers as a judge of the juvenile court. An official court reporter or other authorized reporting procedure must record all proceedings. *(Formerly Rule 1415, adopted, eff. Jan. 1, 1990. Renumbered Rule 5.536 and amended, eff. Jan. 1, 2007.)*

Research References

Treatises and Practice Aids

Witkin, California Summary 10th Parent and Child § 465, Qualifications and Appointment.

Witkin, California Summary 10th Parent and Child § 466, Referee as Temporary Judge.

Witkin, California Summary 10th Parent and Child § 814, Reporter and Transcript.

Rule 5.538. Conduct of proceedings held before a referee not acting as a temporary judge

(a) General conduct (§§ 248, 347, 677)

Proceedings heard by a referee not acting as a temporary judge must be conducted in the same manner as proceedings heard by a judge, except:

(1) An official court reporter or other authorized reporting procedure must record the proceedings if directed by the court; and

(2) The referee must inform the child and parent or guardian of the right to seek review by a juvenile court judge.

(b) Furnishing and serving findings and order; explanation of right to review (§ 248)

After each hearing before a referee, the referee must make findings and enter an order as provided elsewhere in these rules. In each case, the referee must cause all of the following to be done promptly:

(1) Furnish a copy of the findings and order to the presiding judge of the juvenile court.

(2) Furnish to the child (if the child is 14 or more years of age or, if younger, as requested) a copy of the findings and order, with a written explanation of the right to seek review of the order by a juvenile court judge.

(3) Serve the parent and guardian—and counsel for the child, parent, and guardian—a copy of the findings and order, with a written explanation of the right to seek review of the order by a juvenile court judge.

(A) Service is deemed complete at the time of personal, in-court service as provided in Welfare and Institutions Code section 248, subdivision (b)(1).

(B) If personal, in-court service as in (A) is not possible, service must be by mail to the last known address and is deemed complete at the time of mailing as provided in subdivision (b)(2) of that section.

(Formerly Rule 1416, adopted, eff. Jan. 1, 1990. Renumbered Rule 5.538 and amended, eff. Jan. 1, 2007. As amended, eff. Jan. 1, 2016.)

Research References

Treatises and Practice Aids

Witkin, California Summary 10th Parent and Child § 468, Conduct Of Proceedings.

Witkin, California Summary 10th Parent and Child § 469, Findings, Explanation, and Order.

Witkin, California Summary 10th Parent and Child § 470, When Orders Become Effective.

Witkin, California Summary 10th Parent and Child § 693, Termination Of Parental Rights.

Witkin, California Summary 10th Parent and Child § 712, Notice Of Appeal.

Rule 5.540. Orders of referees not acting as temporary judges

(a) Effective date of order (§ 250)

Except as provided in (b) and subject to the right of review provided for in rule 5.542, all orders of a referee become effective immediately and continue in effect unless vacated or modified on rehearing by order of a juvenile court judge.

(b) Orders requiring express approval of judge (§§ 249, 251)

The following orders made by a referee do not become effective unless expressly approved by a juvenile court judge within two court days:

(1) Any order removing a child from the physical custody of the person legally entitled to custody; or

(2) Any order the presiding judge of the juvenile court requires to be expressly approved.

(c) Finality date of order

An order of a referee becomes final 10 calendar days after service of a copy of the order and findings under rule 5.538, if an application for rehearing has not been made within that time or if the judge of the juvenile court has not within the 10 days ordered a rehearing on the judge's own motion under rule 5.542. *(Formerly Rule 1417, adopted, eff. Jan. 1, 1990. Renumbered Rule 5.540 and amended, eff. Jan. 1, 2007.)*

Research References

Treatises and Practice Aids

Witkin, California Summary 10th Parent and Child § 469, Findings, Explanation, and Order.

Witkin, California Summary 10th Parent and Child § 470, When Orders Become Effective.

Witkin, California Summary 10th Parent and Child § 472, Application.

Witkin, California Summary 10th Parent and Child § 693, Termination Of Parental Rights.

Witkin, California Summary 10th Parent and Child § 712, Notice Of Appeal.

Witkin, California Summary 10th Parent and Child § 720, Notice Of Intent.

Witkin, California Summary 10th Parent and Child § 725, Notice Of Intent and Record.

Rule 5.542. Rehearing of proceedings before referees

(a) Application for rehearing (§ 252)

An application for a rehearing of a proceeding before a referee not acting as a temporary judge may be made by the child, parent, or guardian at any time before the expiration of 10 calendar days after service of a copy of the order and findings. The application may be directed to all, or any specified part of, the order or findings and must contain a brief statement of the factual or legal reasons for requesting the rehearing.

(b) If no formal record (§ 252)

A rehearing must be granted if proceedings before the referee were not recorded by an official court reporter or other authorized reporting procedure.

(c) Hearing with court reporter (§ 252)

If the proceedings before the referee have been recorded by an official court reporter or other authorized reporting procedure, the judge of the juvenile court may, after reading the transcript of the proceedings, grant or deny the application for rehearing. If the application is not denied within 20 calendar days following the date of receipt of the application, or within 45 calendar days if the court for good cause extends the time, the application must be deemed granted.

(d) Rehearing on motion of judge (§ 253)

Notwithstanding (a), at any time within 20 court days after a hearing before a referee, the judge, on the judge's own motion, may order a rehearing.

(e) Hearing de novo (§ 254)

Rehearings of matters heard before a referee must be conducted de novo before a judge of the juvenile court. A rehearing of a detention hearing must be held within two court days after the rehearing is granted. A rehearing of other matters heard before a referee must be held within 10 court days after the rehearing is granted.

(f) Advisement of appeal rights—rule 5.590

If the judge of the juvenile court denies an application for rehearing directed in whole or in part to issues arising during a contested jurisdiction hearing, the judge must advise, either orally or in writing, the child and the parent or guardian of all of the following:

(1) The right of the child, parent, or guardian to appeal from the court's judgment;

(2) The necessary steps and time for taking an appeal;

(3) The right of an indigent appellant to have counsel appointed by the reviewing court; and

(4) The right of an indigent appellant to be provided a free copy of the transcript. *(Formerly Rule 1418 adopted, eff. Jan. 1, 1991. Renumbered Rule 5.542 and amended, eff. Jan. 1, 2007.)*

Research References

Treatises and Practice Aids

Witkin, California Summary 10th Parent and Child § 471, Nature Of Proceeding.
Witkin, California Summary 10th Parent and Child § 472, Application.
Witkin, California Summary 10th Parent and Child § 473, Denial.
Witkin, California Summary 10th Parent and Child § 474, Grant.
Witkin, California Summary 10th Parent and Child § 475, Rehearing on Court's Own Motion.
Witkin, California Summary 10th Parent and Child § 693, Termination Of Parental Rights.
Witkin, California Summary 10th Parent and Child § 712, Notice Of Appeal.
Witkin, California Summary 10th Parent and Child § 850, Review Of Order.

Rule 5.544. Prehearing motions (§ 700.1)

Unless otherwise ordered or specifically provided by law, prehearing motions and accompanying points and authorities must, absent a waiver, be served on the child and opposing counsel and filed with the court:

(1) At least 5 judicial days before the date the jurisdiction hearing is set to begin if the child is detained or the motion is one to suppress evidence obtained as a result of an unlawful search and seizure; or

(2) At least 10 judicial days before the date the jurisdiction hearing is set to begin if the child is not detained and the motion is other than one to suppress evidence obtained as a result of an unlawful search and seizure.

Prehearing motions must be specific, noting the grounds, and supported by points and authorities. *(Formerly Rule 1419, adopted, eff. Jan. 1, 1991. Renumbered Rule 5.544 and amended, eff. Jan. 1, 2007.)*

Rule 5.546. Prehearing discovery

(a) General purpose

This rule must be liberally construed in favor of informal disclosures, subject to the right of a party to show privilege or other good cause not to disclose specific material or information.

(b) Duty to disclose police reports

After filing the petition, petitioner must promptly deliver to or make accessible for inspection and copying by the child and the parent or guardian, or their counsel, copies of the police, arrest, and crime reports relating to the pending matter. Privileged information may be omitted if notice of the omission is given simultaneously.

(c) Affirmative duty to disclose

Petitioner must disclose any evidence or information within petitioner's possession or control favorable to the child, parent, or guardian.

(d) Material and information to be disclosed on request

Except as provided in (g) and (h), petitioner must, after timely request, disclose to the child and parent or guardian, or their counsel, the following material and information within the petitioner's possession or control:

(1) Probation reports prepared in connection with the pending matter relating to the child, parent, or guardian;

(2) Records of statements, admissions, or conversations by the child, parent, or guardian;

(3) Records of statements, admissions, or conversations by any alleged coparticipant;

(4) Names and addresses of witnesses interviewed by an investigating authority in connection with the pending matter;

(5) Records of statements or conversations of witnesses or other persons interviewed by an investigating authority in connection with the pending matter;

(6) Reports or statements of experts made regarding the pending matter, including results of physical or mental

examinations and results of scientific tests, experiments, or comparisons;

(7) Photographs or physical evidence relating to the pending matter; and

(8) Records of prior felony convictions of the witnesses each party intends to call.

(e) Disclosure in section 300 proceedings

Except as provided in (g) and (h), the parent or guardian must, after timely request, disclose to petitioner relevant material and information within the parent's or guardian's possession or control. If counsel represents the parent or guardian, a disclosure request must be made through counsel.

(f) Motion for prehearing discovery

If a party refuses to disclose information or permit inspection of materials, the requesting party or counsel may move the court for an order requiring timely disclosure of the information or materials. The motion must specifically and clearly designate the items sought, state the relevancy of the items, and state that a timely request has been made for the items and that the other party has refused to provide them. Each court may by local rule establish the manner and time within which a motion under this subdivision must be made.

(g) Limits on duty to disclose—protective orders

On a showing of privilege or other good cause, the court may make orders restricting disclosures. All material and information to which a party is entitled must be disclosed in time to permit counsel to make beneficial use of them.

(h) Limits on duty to disclose—excision

When some parts of the materials are discoverable under (d) and (e) and other parts are not discoverable, the nondiscoverable material may be excised and need not be disclosed if the requesting party or counsel has been notified that the privileged material has been excised. Material ordered excised must be sealed and preserved in the records of the court for review on appeal.

(i) Conditions of discovery

An order of the court granting discovery under this rule may specify the time, place, and manner of making the discovery and inspection and may prescribe terms and conditions. Discovery must be completed in a timely manner to avoid the delay or continuance of a scheduled hearing.

(j) Failure to comply; sanctions

If at any time during the course of the proceedings the court learns that a person has failed to comply with this rule or with an order issued under this rule, the court may order the person to permit the discovery or inspection of materials not previously disclosed, grant a continuance, prohibit a party from introducing in evidence the material not disclosed, dismiss the proceedings, or enter any other order the court deems just under the circumstances.

(k) Continuing duty to disclose

If subsequent to compliance with these rules or with court orders a party discovers additional material or information subject to disclosure, the party must promptly notify the child and parent or guardian, or their counsel, of the existence of the additional matter. *(Formerly Rule 1420, adopted, eff. Jan. 1, 1990. Renumbered Rule 5.546 and amended, eff. Jan. 1, 2007.)*

Research References

Treatises and Practice Aids

Witkin, California Summary 10th Parent and Child § 612, Discovery.
Witkin, California Summary 10th Parent and Child § 860, Nature and Purpose Of Rule.
Witkin, California Summary 10th Parent and Child § 861, Duty to Disclose.
Witkin, California Summary 10th Parent and Child § 862, Restrictions on Duty to Disclose.
Witkin, California Summary 10th Parent and Child § 863, Motion to Compel Disclosure.

Rule 5.548. Granting immunity to witnesses

(a) Privilege against self-incrimination

If a person is called as a witness and it appears to the court that the testimony or other evidence being sought may tend to incriminate the witness, the court must advise the witness of the privilege against self-incrimination and of the possible consequences of testifying. The court must also inform the witness of the right to representation by counsel and, if indigent, of the right to have counsel appointed.

(b) Authority of judge to grant immunity

If a witness refuses to answer a question or to produce evidence based on a claim of the privilege against self-incrimination, a judge may grant immunity to the witness under (c) or (d) and order the question answered or the evidence produced.

(c) Request for immunity—section 602 proceedings

In proceedings under section 602, the prosecuting attorney may make a written or oral request on the record that the court order a witness to answer a question or produce evidence. The court must then proceed under Penal Code section 1324.

(1) After complying with an order to answer a question or produce evidence and if, but for those Penal Code sections or this rule, the witness would have been privileged to withhold the answer given or the evidence produced, no testimony or other information compelled under the order or information directly or indirectly derived from the testimony or other information may be used against the witness in any criminal case, including any juvenile court proceeding under section 602.

(2) The prosecuting attorney may request an order granting the witness use or transactional immunity.

(d) Request for immunity—section 300 or 601 proceedings

In proceedings under section 300 or 601, the prosecuting attorney or petitioner may make a written or oral request on the record that the judge order a witness to answer a question or produce evidence. They may also make the request jointly.

(1) If the request is not made jointly, the other party must be given the opportunity to show why immunity is not to be granted and the judge may grant or deny the request as deemed appropriate.

(2) If jointly made, the judge must grant the request unless the judge finds that to do so would be clearly contrary to the

public interest. The terms of a grant of immunity must be stated in the record.

(3) After complying with the order and if, but for this rule, the witness would have been privileged to withhold the answer given or the evidence produced, any answer given, evidence produced, or information derived there from must not be used against the witness in a juvenile court or criminal proceeding.

(e) No immunity from perjury or contempt

Notwithstanding (c) or (d), a witness may be subject to proceedings under the juvenile court law or to criminal prosecution for perjury, false swearing, or contempt committed in answering or failing to answer or in producing or failing to produce evidence in accordance with the order. *(Formerly Rule 1421, adopted, eff. Jan. 1, 1990. As amended, eff. Jan. 1, 1998. Renumbered Rule 5.548 and amended, eff. Jan. 1, 2007.)*

Research References

Forms

Am. Jur. Pl. & Pr. Forms Witnesses § 1, Introductory Comments.

Treatises and Practice Aids

Witkin, California Summary 10th Parent and Child § 621, Immunity Of Witnesses.

Witkin, California Summary 10th Parent and Child § 879, in General.

Witkin, California Summary 10th Parent and Child § 880, Immunity in Welf.C. 601 Proceeding.

Witkin, California Summary 10th Parent and Child § 881, Immunity in Welf.C. 602 Proceeding.

Rule 5.550. Continuances

(a) Cases petitioned under section 300 (§§ 316.2, 352, 354)

(1) The court must not continue a hearing beyond the time set by statute unless the court determines the continuance is not contrary to the interest of the child. In considering the child's interest, the court must give substantial weight to a child's needs for stability and prompt resolution of custody status, and the damage of prolonged temporary placements.

(2) Continuances may be granted only on a showing of good cause, and only for the time shown to be necessary. Stipulation between counsel of parties, convenience of parties, and pending criminal or family law matters are not in and of themselves good cause.

(3) If a child has been removed from the custody of a parent or guardian, the court must not grant a continuance that would cause the disposition hearing under section 361 to be completed more than 60 days after the detention hearing unless the court finds exceptional circumstances. In no event may the disposition hearing be continued more than six months after the detention hearing.

(4) In order to obtain a continuance, written notice with supporting documents must be filed and served on all parties at least two court days before the date set for hearing, unless the court finds good cause for hearing an oral motion.

(5) The court must state in its order the facts requiring any continuance that is granted.

(b) Cases petitioned under section 601 or 602 (§ 682)

(1) A continuance may be granted only on a showing of good cause and only for the time shown to be necessary. Stipulation between counsel or parties and convenience of parties are not in and of themselves good cause.

(2) In order to obtain a continuance, written notice with supporting documents must be filed and served on all parties at least two court days before the date set for the hearing, unless the court finds good cause for failure to comply with these requirements.

(3) The court must state in its order the facts requiring any continuance that is granted.

(4) If the child is represented by counsel, failure of counsel or the child to object to an order continuing a hearing beyond the time limit is deemed a consent to the continuance.

(c) Continuances of detention hearings (§§ 319, 322, 635, 636, 638)

(1) On the motion of the child, parent, or guardian, the court must continue the detention hearing for one court day or for a reasonable period to permit the moving party to prepare any relevant evidence on the issue of detention. Unless otherwise ordered by the court, the child must remain in custody pending the continued hearing.

(2) At the initial detention hearing, if the court continues the hearing under (c)(1) or for any other reason, or sets the matter for rehearing, the court must either find that the continuance of the child in the parent's or guardian's home is contrary to the child's welfare or order the child released to the custody of the parent or guardian. The court may enter this finding on a temporary basis, without prejudice to any party, and reevaluate the finding at the time of the continued detention hearing. *(Formerly Rule 1422, adopted, eff. Jan. 1, 1991. As amended, eff. Jan. 1, 1998; Jan. 1, 1999; July 1, 2002. Renumbered Rule 5.550 and amended, eff. Jan. 1, 2007. As amended, eff. July 1, 2016.)*

Commentary

Applying subsection (c), *In re Jasmine S., 153 Cal.App.4th 835, 63 Cal.Rptr.3d 593 (2007)*, held that an attorney representing siblings in dependency proceedings may be disqualified if the children have an actual, present conflict of interest, but not if they only have a potential conflict of interest.

Research References

Forms

West's California Judicial Council Forms JV-406, Continuance--Dependency General.

Treatises and Practice Aids

Witkin, California Summary 10th Parent and Child § 594, in General.

Witkin, California Summary 10th Parent and Child § 595, Limitations on Continuances.

Witkin, California Summary 10th Parent and Child § 601, Continuance Of Hearing.

Rule 5.552. Confidentiality of records (§§ 827, 828)

(a) Definitions

For the purposes of this rule, "juvenile case file" includes:

(1) All documents filed in a juvenile court case;

(2) Reports to the court by probation officers, social workers of child welfare services programs, and CASA volunteers;

(3) Documents made available to probation officers, social workers of child welfare services programs, and CASA volunteers in preparation of reports to the court;

(4) Documents relating to a child concerning whom a petition has been filed in juvenile court that are maintained in the office files of probation officers, social workers of child welfare services programs, and CASA volunteers;

(5) Transcripts, records, or reports relating to matters prepared or released by the court, probation department, or child welfare services program; and

(6) Documents, video or audio tapes, photographs, and exhibits admitted into evidence at juvenile court hearings.

~~(c)~~(b) Petition

Juvenile case files may only be obtained or inspected in accordance with sections 827 and 828. They may not be obtained or inspected by civil or criminal subpoena. With the exception of those persons permitted to inspect juvenile ~~court records~~ case files without court authorization under sections 827 and 828, every person or agency seeking to inspect or obtain juvenile ~~court records~~ case files must petition the court for authorization using ~~*Petition*~~ *Request for Disclosure of Juvenile Case File* (form JV–570).

(1) The specific ~~records~~ files sought must be identified d based on knowledge, information, and belief that such ~~records~~ files exist and are relevant to the purpose for which they are being sought.

(2) Petitioner must describe in detail the reasons the ~~records~~ files are being sought and their relevancy to the proceeding or purpose for which petitioner wishes to inspect or obtain the ~~records~~ files.

~~(d)~~(c) Notice of petition for disclosure

(1) At least 10 days before the petition is submitted to the court, the petitioner must personally or by first-class mail serve *Request for Disclosure of Juvenile Case File* (form JV–570), *Notice of Request for Disclosure of Juvenile Case File* (form JV–571), and a blank copy of *Objection to Release of Juvenile Case File* (form JV–572) on the following:

(A) The county counsel, city attorney, or any other attorney representing the petitioning agency in a dependency action if the child's petition was filed under section 300;

(B) The district attorney if the child's petition was filed under section 601 or 602;

(C) The child if the child is 10 years of age or older;

(D) The attorney of record for the child who remains a ward or dependent of the court;

(E) The parents of the child if:

(i) The child is under 18 years of age; or

(ii) The child's petition was filed under section 300;

(F) The guardians of the child if:

(i) The child is under 18 years of age; or

(ii) The child's petition was filed under section 300;

(G) The probation department or child welfare agency, or both, if applicable;

(H) The Indian child's tribe; and

(I) The child's CASA volunteer.

(2) The petitioner must complete *Proof of Service—Request for Disclosure* (form JV–569) and file it with the court.

(3) If the petitioner does not know the identity or address of any of the parties in ~~(d)~~(c)(1) above, the clerk must:

(A) Serve personally or by first-class mail to the last known address a copy of *Request for Disclosure of Juvenile Case File* (form JV–570), *Notice of Request for Disclosure of Juvenile Case File* (form JV–571), and a blank copy of *Objection to Release of Juvenile Case File* (form JV–572); and

(B) Complete *Proof of Service—Request for Disclosure* (form JV–569) and file it with the court.

(4) For good cause, the court may, on the motion of the person seeking the order or on its own motion, shorten the time for service of the petition for disclosure.

~~(e)~~(d) Procedure

(1) The court must review the petition and, if petitioner does not show good cause, deny it summarily.

(2) If petitioner shows good cause, the court may set a hearing. The clerk must notice the hearing to the persons and entities listed in ~~(d)~~(c)(1) above.

(3) Whether or not the court holds a hearing, if the court determines that there may be information or documents in the records sought to which the petitioner may be entitled, the juvenile court judicial officer must conduct an in camera review of the juvenile case file and any objections and assume that all legal claims of privilege are asserted.

(4) In determining whether to authorize inspection or release of juvenile case files, in whole or in part, the court must balance the interests of the child and other parties to the juvenile court proceedings, the interests of the petitioner, and the interests of the public.

(5) If the court grants the petition, the court must find that the need for discovery outweighs the policy considerations favoring confidentiality of juvenile case files. The confidentiality of juvenile case files is intended to protect the privacy rights of the child.

(6) The court may permit disclosure of juvenile case files only insofar as is necessary, and only if petitioner shows by a preponderance of the evidence that the records requested are necessary and have substantial relevance to the legitimate need of the petitioner.

(7) If, after in-camera review and review of any objections, the court determines that all or a portion of the juvenile case file may be disclosed, the court must make appropriate orders, specifying the information to be disclosed and the procedure for providing access to it.

(8) The court may issue protective orders to accompany authorized disclosure, discovery, or access.

~~(f)~~(e) Reports of law enforcement agencies (§ 828)

~~Except for records sealed under section 389 or 781, or Penal Code section 1203.45, information gathered and retained by a law enforcement agency regarding the taking of a~~

~~child into custody may be disclosed without court authorization to another law enforcement agency, including a school district police or security department, or to any person or agency that has a legitimate need for the information for the purposes of official disposition of a case.~~

~~(1) If the law enforcement agency retaining the report is notified under section 1155 that the child has escaped from a secure detention facility, the agency must release the name of the child and any descriptive information on specific request by any agency or individual whose attempts to apprehend the child will be assisted by the information requested.~~

~~(2) In the absence of a specific request, the law enforcement agency retaining the report may release information about a child reported to have escaped from a secure detention facility if the agency determines that the information is necessary to assist in the apprehension of the child or the protection of members of the public from substantial physical harm.~~

~~(3)~~ Except as authorized under section 828, all others seeking to inspect or obtain ~~such reports~~ information gathered and retained by a law enforcement agency regarding the taking of a child into custody must petition the juvenile court for authorization~~,~~ using *Petition to Obtain Report of Law Enforcement Agency* (form JV–575).

~~**(g) School notification**~~

~~When a child enrolled in a public school is found to have committed one of the offenses described in section 827(b)(2), the court must provide written notice of the offense and the disposition to the superintendent of the school district within seven days. The superintendent must disseminate information to the principal of the school the child attends, and the principal may disseminate information to any teacher or administrator for the purposes of the rehabilitation of the child or the protection of other students and staff.~~

~~(h)~~(f) Other applicable statutes

Under no circumstances must this rule or any section of it be interpreted to permit access to or release of records protected under any other federal or state law, including Penal Code section 11165 et seq., except as provided in those statutes, or to limit access to or release of records permitted under any other federal or state statute~~, including Government Code section 13968~~. *(Formerly Rule 1423 adopted, eff. July 1, 1992. As amended, eff. Jan. 1, 1994; July 1, 1995; July 1, 1997; Jan. 1, 2001; Jan. 1, 2004. Renumbered Rule 5.552 and amended, eff. Jan. 1, 2007. As amended, eff. Jan. 1, 2009; Jan. 1, 2018.)*

Research References

Forms

West's California Judicial Council Forms JV-569, Proof Of Service--Request for Disclosure.

West's California Judicial Council Forms JV-570, Request for Disclosure Of Juvenile Case File.

West's California Judicial Council Forms JV-571, Notice Of Request for Disclosure Of Juvenile Case File.

West's California Judicial Council Forms JV-572, Objection to Release Of Juvenile Case File.

West's California Judicial Council Forms JV-573, Order on Request for Disclosure Of Juvenile Case File.

West's California Judicial Council Forms JV-574, Order After Judicial Review.

West's California Judicial Council Forms JV-575, Petition to Obtain Report Of Law Enforcement Agency.

Treatises and Practice Aids

Witkin, California Summary 10th Parent and Child § 492, in General.

Witkin, California Summary 10th Parent and Child § 493, Persons Entitled to Inspect Records.

Witkin, California Summary 10th Parent and Child § 498, Authorized Disclosure About Specified Crimes.

Witkin, California Summary 10th Parent and Child § 500, Disclosure on Petition.

Validity

A prior version of this court rule was declared invalid to the extent that it limits the discretion of the juvenile court to disclose juvenile court records, beyond that provided in statutes, in In re Elijah S. (App. 1 Dist. 2005) 24 Cal.Rptr.3d 16, 125 Cal.App.4th 1532.

Rule 5.553. Juvenile case file of a deceased child

When the juvenile case file of a deceased child is sought, the court must proceed as follows:

(1) Under section 827(a)(2) if the request is made by a member of the public; or

(2) Under section 16502.5 if the request is made by a county board of supervisors. *(Adopted, eff. Jan. 1, 2009.)*

Research References

Forms

West's California Judicial Council Forms JV-569, Proof Of Service--Request for Disclosure.

West's California Judicial Council Forms JV-570, Request for Disclosure Of Juvenile Case File.

West's California Judicial Council Forms JV-571, Notice Of Request for Disclosure Of Juvenile Case File.

West's California Judicial Council Forms JV-572, Objection to Release Of Juvenile Case File.

West's California Judicial Council Forms JV-573, Order on Request for Disclosure Of Juvenile Case File.

West's California Judicial Council Forms JV-574, Order After Judicial Review.

Treatises and Practice Aids

Witkin, California Summary 10th Parent and Child § 494, Records Of Dependent Children.

Rule 5.555. Hearing to consider termination of juvenile court jurisdiction over a nonminor—dependents or wards of the juvenile court in a foster care placement and nonminor dependents (§§ 224.1(b), 303, 366.31, 391, 451, 452, 607.2, 607.3, 16501.1~~(f)~~(g)(16))

(a) Applicability

(1) This rule applies to any hearing during which the termination of the juvenile court's jurisdiction over the following nonminors will be considered:

(A) A nonminor dependent as defined in section 11400(v);

(B) A ward or dependent of the juvenile court who is 18 years of age or older and subject to an order for a foster care placement; or

(C) A ward who was subject to an order for foster care placement at the time he or she attained 18 years of age, or a dependent of the juvenile court who is 18 years of age or older and is living in the home of the parent or former legal guardian.

(2) Nothing in the Welfare and Institutions Code or the California Rules of Court restricts the ability of the juvenile court to maintain dependency jurisdiction or delinquency jurisdiction over a person, 18 years of age or older, who does not meet the eligibility requirements for status as a nonminor dependent and to proceed as to that person under the relevant sections of the Welfare and Institutions Code and California Rules of Court.

(b) Setting a hearing

(1) A court hearing must be placed on the appearance calendar and ~~held~~ completed before ~~prior to terminating~~ juvenile court jurisdiction is terminated.

(2) The hearing under this rule may be held during any regularly scheduled review hearing or a hearing ~~required~~ on a petition filed under section ~~366 (g), 366.3, 366.31, 727.2, or 727.3 or rule 5.903~~ 388 or section 778.

(3) Notice of the hearing must be given as required by section 295.

(4) Notice of the hearing to the parents of a nonminor dependent as defined in section 11400(v) is not required, unless the parent~~s are~~ is receiving court-ordered family reunification services or the nonminor is living in the home of the parent or former legal guardian.

~~(4)~~(5) If juvenile court jurisdiction was resumed after having previously been terminated, a hearing under this rule must be held if the nonminor dependent wants juvenile court jurisdiction terminated again. The social worker or probation officer is not required to file the 90–day Transition Plan, and the court need not make the findings described in (d)(1)(L)(iii) or (d)(2)(E)(vi).

~~(5)~~(6) The hearing must be continued for no more than five court days for the submission of additional information as ordered by the court if the court determines that the report, the Transitional Independent Living Plan, the Transitional Independent Living Case Plan, ~~(TILCP)~~ if required, or the 90–day Transition Plan submitted by the social worker or probation officer does not provide the information required by (c) and the court is unable to make the findings and orders required by (d).

(c) Reports

(1) ~~In addition to complying with all other statutory and rule requirements applicable to the report prepared by the social worker or probation officer for any hearing during which termination of the court's jurisdiction will be considered,~~ The report prepared by the social worker or probation officer for a hearing under this rule must, in addition to any other elements required by law, include:

(A) Whether remaining under juvenile court jurisdiction is in the nonminor's best interests and the facts supporting the conclusion reached;

(B) The specific criteria in section 11403(b) met by the nonminor that make him or her eligible to remain under juvenile court jurisdiction as a nonminor dependent as defined in section 11400(v);

(C) For a nonminor to whom the Indian Child Welfare Act applies, when and how the nonminor was provided with information about the right to continue to be considered an Indian child for the purposes of the ongoing application of the Indian Child Welfare Act to him or her as a nonminor;

(D) Whether the nonminor has applied for title XVI Supplemental Security Income benefits and, if so, the status of ~~any in-progress~~ that application ~~pending for title XVI Supplemental Security Income benefits~~, and whether remaining under juvenile court jurisdiction until a final decision has been issued is in the nonminor's best interests;

(E) Whether the nonminor has applied for Special Immigrant Juvenile status or other immigration relief and, if so, the status of ~~any in-progress~~ that application, ~~pending for Special Immigrant Juvenile Status or other applicable application for legal residency~~ and whether an active juvenile court case is required for that application;

(F) When and how the nonminor was provided with information about the potential benefits of remaining under juvenile court jurisdiction as a nonminor dependent, and the social worker's or probation officer's assessment of the nonminor's understanding of those benefits;

(G) When and how the nonminor was informed that if juvenile court jurisdiction is terminated, the court maintains general jurisdiction over him or her for the purpose of resuming jurisdiction and he or she has the right to file a request to return to foster care and have the juvenile court resume jurisdiction over him or her as a nonminor dependent until he or she has attained the age of 21 years;

(H) When and how the nonminor was informed that if juvenile court dependency jurisdiction or transition jurisdiction is continued over him or her, he or she has the right to have that jurisdiction terminated;

(I) ~~For a nonminor who is not present for the hearing:~~ If the social worker or probation officer has reason to believe that the nonminor will not appear at the hearing, documentation of the basis for that belief, including:

(i) Documentation of the nonminor's statement that he or she ~~did~~ does not wish to appear in ~~court~~ person or by telephone for the ~~scheduled~~ hearing; or

(ii) Documentation of ~~the~~ reasonable efforts ~~made~~ to ~~locate~~ find the nonminor when his or her ~~current~~ location is unknown;

(J) Verification that the nonminor was provided with the information, documents, and services as required under section 391(e); and

(K) When and how a nonminor who is under delinquency jurisdiction was provided with the notices and information required under section 607.5.

(2) The social worker or probation officer must file with the report a completed *Termination of Juvenile Court Jurisdiction—Nonminor* (form JV–365).

(3) The social worker or probation officer must also file with the report the nonminor's:

(A) Transitional Independent Living Case Plan when recommending continuation of juvenile court jurisdiction;

(B) Most recent Transitional Independent Living Plan ~~(TILP)~~; and

(C) Completed 90–day Transition Plan.

(4) The social worker's or probation officer's report and all documents required by ~~(c)~~(2)–(3) must be filed with the court at least 10 calendar days before the hearing, and the social worker or probation officer must provide copies of the report and other documents to the nonminor, the nonminor's parents, and all attorneys of record. If the nonminor is under juvenile court jurisdiction as a nonminor dependent, the social worker or probation officer is not required to provide copies of the report and other documents to the nonminor dependent's parent, unless the ~~nonminor dependent's~~ parent~~s are~~ is receiving court-ordered family reunification services.

(d) Findings and orders.

~~In addition to complying with all other statutory and rule requirements applicable to the hearing,~~ The court must, in addition to any other determinations required by law, make the following ~~judicial~~ findings and orders ~~must be made~~ and include~~d~~ them in the written ~~court~~ documentation of the hearing:

(1) *Findings*

(A) Whether the nonminor had the opportunity to confer with his or her attorney about the issues currently before the court;

(B) Whether remaining under juvenile court jurisdiction is in the nonminor's best interests and the facts in support of the finding made;

(C) Whether the nonminor meets one or more of the eligibility criteria in section 11403(b) to remain in foster care as a nonminor dependent under juvenile court jurisdiction and, if so, the specific criteria in section 11403(b) met by the nonminor;

(D) For a nonminor to whom the Indian Child Welfare Act applies, whether the nonminor was provided with information about the right to continue to be considered an Indian child for the purposes of the ongoing application of the Indian Child Welfare Act to him or her;

(E) Whether the nonminor has an ~~in-progress~~ application pending for title XVI Supplemental Security Income benefits, and if ~~such an application is pending~~ so, whether it is in the nonminor's best interests to continue juvenile court jurisdiction until a final decision has been issued to ensure that the nonminor receives continued assistance with the application process;

(F) Whether the nonminor has an ~~in-progress~~ application pending for Special Immigrant Juvenile status or other ~~applicable application for legal residency~~ immigration relief, and whether an active juvenile court case is required for that application;

(G) Whether the nonminor understands the potential benefits of remaining in foster care under juvenile court jurisdiction;

(H) Whether the nonminor has been informed that if juvenile court jurisdiction is continued, he or she may have the right to have juvenile court jurisdiction terminated and that the court will maintain general jurisdiction over him or her for the purpose of resuming dependency jurisdiction or assuming or resuming transition jurisdiction over him or her as a nonminor dependent;

(I) Whether the nonminor has been informed that if juvenile court jurisdiction is terminated, he or she has the right to file a request to return to foster care and have the juvenile court resume jurisdiction over him or her as a nonminor dependent until he or she has attained the age of 21 years;

(J) Whether the nonminor was provided with the information, documents, and services as required under section 391(e) and, if not, whether juvenile court jurisdiction should be continued to ensure that all information, documents, and services are provided;

(K) Whether a nonminor who is under delinquency jurisdiction was provided with the notices and information required under section 607.5; and

(L) Whether the nonminor's:

(i) Transitional Independent Living Case Plan, if required, includes a plan for a placement the nonminor believes is consistent with his or her need to gain independence, reflects the agreements made between the nonminor and social worker or probation officer to obtain independent living skills, and sets out the benchmarks that indicate how both will know when independence can be achieved;

(ii) Transitional Independent Living Plan identifies the nonminor's level of functioning, emancipation goals, and ~~the~~ specific skills ~~he or she~~ needsed to prepare ~~to live independently~~ for independence and successful adulthood ~~up~~on leaving foster care; and

(iii) 90–day Transition Plan is a concrete individualized plan that specifically covers the following areas: housing, health insurance, education, local opportunities for mentors and continuing support services, workforce supports and employment services, and information that explains how and why to designate a power of attorney for health care.

(M) For a nonminor who ~~is not present~~ does not appear in person or by telephone for the hearing, whether ~~the reason for his or her failure to appear was~~:

(i) The nonminor~~'s~~ expressed a wish ~~to~~ not to appear ~~in court~~ for the ~~scheduled~~ hearing; or

(ii) The nonminor's ~~current~~ location remains unknown ~~although~~ and, if so, whether reasonable efforts were made to ~~locate~~ find the nonminor.

(N) For a nonminor who has attained 21 years of age the court is only required to find that:

(i) Notice was given as required by law.

(ii) The nonminor was provided with the information, documents, and services required under section 391(e), and a completed *Termination of Juvenile Court Jurisdiction—Nonminor* (form JV– 365) was filed with the court.

(iii) The 90–day Transition Plan is a concrete, individualized plan that specifically covers the following areas: housing, health insurance, education, local opportunities for mentoring and continuing support services, workforce supports and employment services, and information that explains how and why to designate a power of attorney for health care.

(iv) The nonminor has attained 21 years of age and is no longer subject to the jurisdiction of the court under section 303.

(2) *Orders*

(A) For a nonminor who meets one or more of the eligibility criteria in section 11403(b) to remain in placement under dependency jurisdiction as a nonminor dependent or under transition jurisdiction as a nonminor dependent, the court must order the continuation of juvenile court jurisdiction unless the court finds that:

(i) The nonminor does not wish to remain under juvenile court jurisdiction as a nonminor dependent;

(ii) The nonminor is not participating in a reasonable and appropriate Transitional Independent Living Case Plan; or

(iii) Reasonable efforts were made to locate the nonminor whose current location is unknown.

(B) When juvenile court jurisdiction is continued for the nonminor to remain in placement as a nonminor dependent:

(i) Order a permanent plan consistent with the nonminor's Transitional Independent Living Plan or Transitional Independent Living Case Plan;

(ii) Continue the nonminor's status as an Indian child for the purposes of the ongoing application of the Indian Child Welfare Act unless he or she has elected not to have his or her status as an Indian child continued; and

(iii) Set a status review hearing under rule 5.903 within six months of the date of his or her most recent status review hearing.

(C) For a nonminor who does not meet and does not intend to meet the eligibility requirements for nonminor dependent status but who is otherwise eligible to and will remain under juvenile court jurisdiction in a foster care placement, the court must set an appropriate statutory review hearing~~ under section on 366.21, 366.22, 366.25, 366.3, 727.2, or 727.3~~ within six months of the date of the nonminor's most recent status review hearing.

(D) For a nonminor whose current location is unknown, the court may enter an order for termination of juvenile court jurisdiction only after finding that reasonable efforts were made to locate the nonminor;

(E) For a nonminor~~ (1)~~ who does not meet one or more of the eligibility criteria of section 11403(b) and is not otherwise eligible to remain under juvenile court jurisdiction,~~ (2) who does~~ or, alternatively, who meets one or more of the eligibility criteria of section 11403(b) but either does not wish to remain under the jurisdiction of the juvenile court as a nonminor dependent,~~ or (3) who does meet one or more of the eligibility criteria of section 11403(b) but~~ or is not participating in a reasonable and appropriate Transitional Independent Living Case Plan, the court may order the termination of juvenile court jurisdiction only after entering the following findings~~ and orders~~:

(i) The nonminor was provided with the information, documents, and services as required under section 391(e);

(ii) The nonminor was informed of the options available to him or her to assist with the transition from foster care to independence;

(iii) The nonminor was informed that if juvenile court jurisdiction is terminated, he or she has the right to file a request to return to foster care and~~ to file a request to~~ have the juvenile court resume jurisdiction over him or her as a nonminor dependent until he or she has ~~attained the age of~~ reached 21 years of age;

(iv) The nonminor was provided with a copy of *How to Return to Juvenile Court Jurisdiction and Foster Care* (form JV–464–INFO), *Request to Return to Juvenile Court Jurisdiction and Foster Care* (form JV–466), *Confidential Information—Request to Return to Juvenile Court Jurisdiction and Foster Care* (form JV–468), and an endorsed filed copy of the *Termination of Juvenile Court Jurisdiction—Nonminor* (form JV–365);

(v) The nonminor had an opportunity to confer with his or her attorney regarding the issues currently before the court;

(vi) The nonminor's 90–day Transition Plan includes specific options regarding housing, health insurance, education, local opportunities for mentors and continuing support services, workforce supports and employment services, and information that explains how and why to designate a power of attorney for health care.

(F) For a nonminor who has attained 21 years of age and is no longer subject to the jurisdiction of the juvenile court under section 303, the court must enter an order that juvenile court jurisdiction is dismissed and that the attorney for the nonminor dependent is relieved 60 days from the date of the order.

(Adopted, eff. Jan. 1, 2012. As amended, eff. July 1, 2012; July 1, 2013; Jan. 1, 2014; Jan. 1, 2016; Jan. 1, 2017.)

Research References

Forms

West's California Judicial Council Forms JV-365, Termination Of Juvenile Court Jurisdiction--Nonminor.

West's California Judicial Council Forms JV-367, Findings and Orders After Hearing to Consider Termination Of Juvenile Court Jurisdiction Over a Nonminor.

Treatises and Practice Aids

Witkin, California Summary 10th Parent and Child § 444, Scope and Organization.

Witkin, California Summary 10th Parent and Child § 669, in General.

Witkin, California Summary 10th Parent and Child § 673, Child in Foster Care.

Witkin, California Summary 10th Parent and Child § 697, Status Review Hearings.

Witkin, California Summary 10th Parent and Child § 898, Court Supervision Of Child.

Witkin, California Summary 10th Parent and Child § 452C, (New) Termination Of Jurisdiction.

Witkin, California Summary 10th Parent and Child § 452F, (New) Termination Of Jurisdiction Over Nonminor.

Witkin, California Summary 10th Parent and Child § 521A, (New) Continuation or Termination Of Jurisdiction Over Nonminor or Nonminor Dependent.

Witkin, California Summary 10th Parent and Child § 669A, (New) Review Hearings Just Before and After Minor Attains Age 18.

Witkin, California Summary 10th Parent and Child § 699A, (New) in General.
Witkin, California Summary 10th Parent and Child § 699B, (New) Status Review Hearings.
Witkin, California Summary 10th Parent and Child § 899A, (New) Hearing Before Termination Of Jurisdiction.

Chapter 4

SUBSEQUENT PETITIONS AND MODIFICATIONS

Rule 5.560. General provisions

(a) General authority of the court (§ 385)

Subject to the procedural requirements prescribed by this chapter, an order made by the court may at any time be changed, modified, or set aside.

(b) Subsequent petitions (§§ 297, 342, 360(b), 364)

All procedures and hearings required for an original petition are required for a subsequent petition. Petitioner must file a subsequent petition if:

(1) A child has previously been found to be a person described by section 300 and the petitioner alleges new facts or circumstances, other than those sustained in the original petition, sufficient to again describe the child as a person under section 300 based on these new facts or circumstances;

(2) At or after the disposition hearing the court has ordered that a parent or guardian retain custody of the dependent child and the petitioner receives information providing reasonable cause to believe the child is now, or once again, described by section 300(a), (d), or (e); or

(3) The family is unwilling or unable to cooperate with services previously ordered under section 301.

(c) Supplemental petition (§§ 297, 387)

A supplemental petition must be used if petitioner concludes that a previous disposition has not been effective in the protection of a child declared a dependent under section 300 and seeks a more restrictive level of physical custody. For purposes of this chapter, a more restrictive level of custody, in ascending order, is

(1) Placement in the home of the person entitled to legal custody;

(2) Placement in the home of a noncustodial parent;

(3) Placement in the home of a relative or friend;

(4) Placement in a foster home; or

(5) Commitment to a private institution.

(d) Petition for modification hearing (§§ 297, 388, 778)

A petition for modification hearing must be used if there is a change of circumstances or new evidence that may require the court to:

(1) Change, modify, or set aside an order previously made; or

(2) Terminate the jurisdiction of the court over the child.

(e) Filing of petition (§§ 297, 388, 778)

A petition for modification hearing may be filed by:

(1) The probation officer, the parent, the guardian, the child, the attorney for the child, or any other person having an interest in a child who is a ward if the requested modification is not for a more restrictive level of custody;

(2) The social worker, regarding a child who is a dependent, if the requested modification is not for a more restrictive level of custody; or

(3) The parent, the guardian, the child, the attorney for the child, or any other person having an interest in a child who is a dependent.

(f) Clerical errors

Clerical errors in judgments, orders, or other parts of the record may be corrected by the court at any time on the court's own motion or on motion of any party and may be entered nunc pro tunc. *(Formerly Rule 1430, adopted, eff. Jan. 1, 1991. As amended, eff. Jan. 1, 2001; Jan. 1, 2006. Renumbered Rule 5.560 and amended, eff. Jan. 1, 2007. As amended, eff. July 1, 2007.)*

Research References

Treatises and Practice Aids

Witkin, California Summary 10th Parent and Child § 444, Scope and Organization.
Witkin, California Summary 10th Parent and Child § 654, Power to Modify or Correct.
Witkin, California Summary 10th Parent and Child § 655, Nature and Purpose.
Witkin, California Summary 10th Parent and Child § 662, Nature and Purpose.
Witkin, California Summary 10th Parent and Child § 668, Subsequent Petition.
Witkin, California Summary 10th Parent and Child § 905, in General.
Witkin, California Summary 10th Parent and Child § 910, in General.

Rule 5.565. Hearing on subsequent and supplemental petitions (§§ 342, 364, 386, 387)

(a) Contents of subsequent and supplemental petitions (§§ 342, 364, 387)

A subsequent petition and a supplemental petition must be verified and, to the extent known to the petitioner, contain the information required in an original petition as described in rule 5.524. A supplemental petition must also contain a concise statement of facts sufficient to support the conclusion that the previous disposition has not been effective in the protection of the child or, in the case of a dependent child placed with a relative, that the placement is not appropriate in view of the criteria in section 361.3.

(b) Setting the hearing (§§ 334, 342, 364, 386, 387)

When a subsequent or supplemental petition is filed, the clerk must immediately set it for hearing within 30 days of the filing date. The hearing must begin within the time limits prescribed for jurisdiction hearings on original petitions under rule 5.670.

(c) Notice of hearing (§§ 290.1, 290.2, 292, 297)

For petitions filed under sections 342 or 387, notice must be provided in accordance with sections 290.1, 290.2, and 291. Notice for petitions filed under section 364 must be provided as stated in section 292.

(d) Initial hearing (§ 387)

Chapter 12, article 1 of these rules applies to the case of a child who is the subject of a supplemental or subsequent petition.

(e) Requirement for bifurcated hearing

The hearing on a subsequent or supplemental petition must be conducted as follows:

(1) The procedures relating to jurisdiction hearings prescribed in chapter 12, article 2 apply to the determination of the allegations of a subsequent or supplemental petition. At the conclusion of the hearing on a subsequent petition the court must make a finding that the allegations of the petition are or are not true. At the conclusion of the hearing on a supplemental petition the court must make findings that:

(A) The factual allegations are or are not true; and

(B) The allegation that the previous disposition has not been effective is or is not true.

(2) The procedures relating to disposition hearings prescribed in chapter 12, article 3 apply to the determination of disposition on a subsequent or supplemental petition. If the court finds under a subsequent petition that the child is described by section 300(a), (d), or (e), the court must remove the child from the physical custody of the parent or guardian, if removal was not ordered under the previous disposition.

(f) Supplemental petition (§ 387)—permanency planning

If a dependent child was returned to the custody of a parent or guardian at the 12–month review or the 18–month review or at an interim review between 12 and 18 months and a 387 petition is sustained and the child removed once again, the court must set a hearing under section 366.26 unless the court finds there is a substantial probability of return within the next 6 months or, if more than 12 months had expired at the time of the prior return, within whatever time remains before the expiration of the maximum 18–month period. *(Formerly Rule 1431, adopted, eff. Jan. 1, 1990. As amended, eff. Jan. 1, 1992; July 1, 1995; Jan. 1, 1999; July 1, 1999; Jan. 1, 2001; Jan. 1, 2006. Renumbered Rule 5.565 and amended, eff. Jan. 1, 2007. As amended, eff. July 1, 2010.)*

Research References

Treatises and Practice Aids

Witkin, California Summary 10th Parent and Child § 463, Transfer-In Hearing.
Witkin, California Summary 10th Parent and Child § 655, Nature and Purpose.
Witkin, California Summary 10th Parent and Child § 656, Form and Content.
Witkin, California Summary 10th Parent and Child § 657, Filing, Setting for Hearing, and Notice.
Witkin, California Summary 10th Parent and Child § 658, Hearing.
Witkin, California Summary 10th Parent and Child § 661, Hearing After Supplemental Petition is Sustained.
Witkin, California Summary 10th Parent and Child § 668, Subsequent Petition.

Rule 5.570. Request to change court order (petition for modification)

(a) Contents of petition (§§ 388, 778)

A petition for modification must be liberally construed in favor of its sufficiency. The petition must be verified and, to the extent known to the petitioner, must contain the following:

(1) The name of the court to which the petition is addressed;

(2) The title and action number of the original proceeding;

(3) The name and age of the child, nonminor, or nonminor dependent;

(4) The address of the child, nonminor, or nonminor dependent, unless confidential under (c);

(5) The name and address of the parent or guardian of the child or nonminor;

(6) The date and general nature of the order sought to be modified;

(7) A concise statement of any change of circumstance or new evidence that requires changing the order or, for requests under section 388(c)(1)(B), a concise statement of the relevant action or inaction of the parent or guardian;

(8) A concise statement of the proposed change of the order;

(9) A statement of the petitioner's relationship or interest in the child, nonminor, or nonminor dependent, if the petition is made by a person other than the child, nonminor, or nonminor dependent; and

(10) A statement whether or not all parties agree to the proposed change.

(b) 388 petition

A petition under Welfare and Institutions Code section 388 must be made on form *Request to Change Court Order* (form JV–180).

(c) Confidentiality

The addresses and telephone numbers of the person requesting to change the court order; the child, nonminor, or nonminor dependent; and the caregiver may be kept confidential by filing *Confidential Information (Request to Change Court Order)* (form JV–182) with form JV–180. Form JV–182 must be kept in the court file under seal, and only the court, the agency, and the attorney for the child, nonminor, or nonminor dependent may have access to this information.

(d) Denial of hearing

The court may deny the petition ex parte if:

(1) The petition filed under section 388(a) or section 778(a) fails to state a change of circumstance or new evidence that may require a change of order or termination of jurisdiction or fails to show that the requested modification would promote the best interest of the child, nonminor, or nonminor dependent.

(2) The petition filed under section 388(b) fails to demonstrate that the requested modification would promote the best interest of the dependent child;

(3) The petition filed under section 388(b) or 778(b) requests visits with a nondependent child and demonstrates that sibling visitation is contrary to the safety and well-being of any of the siblings;

(4) The petition filed under section 388(b) or 778(b) requests visits with a nondependent sibling who remains in the custody of a mutual parent who is not subject to the court's jurisdiction; or

(5) The petition filed under section 388(c) fails to state facts showing that the parent has failed to visit the child or that the parent has failed to participate regularly and make substantive progress in a court-ordered treatment plan or fails to show that the requested termination of services would promote the best interest of the child.

(e) Grounds for grant of petition (§§ 388, 778)

(1) If the petition filed under section 388(a) or section 778(a) states a change of circumstance or new evidence and it appears that the best interest of the child, nonminor, or nonminor dependent may be promoted by the proposed change of order or termination of jurisdiction, the court may grant the petition after following the procedures in (f), (g), and (h), or (i).

(2) If the petition is filed under section 388(b) and it appears that the best interest of the child, nonminor, or nonminor dependent may be promoted by the proposed recognition of a sibling relationship or other requested orders, the court may grant the petition after following the procedures in (f), (g), and (h).

(3) If the petition is filed under section 388(b), the request is for visitation with a sibling who is not a dependent of the court and who is in the custody of a parent subject to the court's jurisdiction, and that sibling visitation is not contrary to the safety and well-being of any of the siblings, the court may grant the request after following the procedures in (f), (g), and (h).

(4) If the petition is filed under section 778(b), the request is for visitation with a sibling who is not a dependent of the court and who is in the custody of a parent subject to the court's jurisdiction, and that sibling visitation is not contrary to the safety and well being of the ward or any of the siblings, the court may grant the request after following the procedures in (f), (g), and (i).

(5) For a petition filed under section 388(c)(1)(A), the court may terminate reunification services during the time periods described in section 388(c)(1) only if the court finds by a preponderance of evidence that reasonable services have been offered or provided, and, by clear and convincing evidence, that the change of circumstance or new evidence described in the petition satisfies a condition in section 361.5(b) or (e). The court may grant the petition after following the procedures in (f), (g), and (h).

(6) For a petition filed under section 388(c)(1)(B), the court may terminate reunification services during the time periods described in section 388(c)(1) only if the court finds by a preponderance of evidence that reasonable services have been offered or provided, and, by clear and convincing evidence, that action or inaction by the parent or guardian creates a substantial likelihood that reunification will not occur. Such action or inaction includes, but is not limited to, failure to visit the child or failure to participate regularly and make substantive progress in a court-ordered treatment program. In determining whether the parent or guardian has failed to visit the child or to participate regularly or make progress in a court-ordered treatment plan, the court must consider factors including, but not limited to, the parent or guardian's incarceration, institutionalization, or participation in a residential substance abuse treatment program. The court may grant the petition after following the procedures in (f), (g), and (h).

(7) If the petition filed under section 388(a) is filed before an order terminating parental rights and is seeking to modify an order that reunification services need not be provided under section 361.5(b)(4), (5), or (6) or to modify any orders related to custody or visitation of the child for whom reunification services were not ordered under section 361.5(b)(4), (5), or (6), the court may modify the orders only if the court finds by clear and convincing evidence that the proposed change is in the best interests of the child. The court may grant the petition after following the procedures in (f), (g), and (h).

(f) Hearing on petition

If all parties stipulate to the requested modification, the court may order modification without a hearing. If there is no such stipulation and the petition has not been denied ex parte under section (d), the court must either:

(1) order that a hearing on the petition be held within 30 calendar days after the petition is filed; or

(2) order a hearing for the parties to argue whether an evidentiary hearing on the petition should be granted or denied. If the court then grants an evidentiary hearing on the petition, that hearing must be held within 30 calendar days after the petition is filed.

(g) Notice of petition and hearing (§§ 388, 778)

The clerk must cause notice of the hearing to be given to the persons and in the same manner prescribed by rule 5.524. The caregiver of the child, nonminor, or nonminor dependent and the tribe of an Indian child must be similarly notified. The parent or legal guardian of a nonminor dependent must not be notified unless the nonminor dependent requests that he or she receive notice or the parent or legal guardian is receiving court-ordered family reunification services.

(h) Conduct of hearing (§ 388)

(1) The petitioner requesting the modification under section 388 has the burden of proof.

(A) If the request is for the removal of the child from the child's home, the petitioner must show by clear and convincing evidence that the grounds for removal in section 361(c) exist.

(B) If the request is for termination of court-ordered reunification services, the petitioner must show by clear and convincing evidence that one of the conditions in section 388(c)(1)(A) or (B) exists and must show by a preponderance of the evidence that reasonable services have been offered or provided.

(C) If the request is to modify an order that reunification services were not ordered under section 361.5(b)(4), (5), or (6) or to modify any orders related to custody or visitation of the child for whom reunification services were not ordered under section 361.5(b)(4), (5), or (6), the petitioner must show by clear and convincing evidence that the proposed change is in the best interests of the child.

(D) All other requests require a preponderance of the evidence to show that the child's welfare requires such a modification.

(E) If the request is for visitation with a sibling who is not a dependent of the court, the court may grant the request unless the court determines that the sibling remains in the custody of a mutual parent who is not subject to the court's jurisdiction or that sibling visitation is contrary to the safety and well-being of any of the siblings.

(2) The hearing must be conducted as a dispositional hearing under rules 5.690 and 5.695 if:

(A) The request is for termination of court-ordered reunification services; or

(B) There is a due process right to confront and cross-examine witnesses.

Otherwise, proof may be by declaration and other documentary evidence, or by testimony, or both, at the discretion of the court.

(i) Conduct of hearing (§ 778)

(1) The petitioner requesting the modification under section 778(a) has the burden of proving by a preponderance of the evidence that the ward's welfare requires the modification. Proof may be by declaration and other documentary evidence, or by testimony, or both, at the discretion of the court.

(2) If the request is for sibling visitation under section 778(b), the court may grant the request unless the court determines that the sibling remains in the custody of a mutual parent who is not subject to the court's jurisdiction or that sibling visitation is contrary to the safety and well-being of any of the siblings.

(j) Petitions for juvenile court to resume jurisdiction over nonminors (§§ 388(e), 388.1)

A petition filed by or on behalf of a nonminor requesting that the court resume jurisdiction over the nonminor as a nonminor dependent is not subject to this rule. Petitions filed under section 388(e) or section 388.1 are subject to rule 5.906. *(Formerly Rule 1432, adopted, eff. Jan. 1, 1991. As amended, eff. Jan. 1, 1992; July 1, 1995; July 1, 2000; July 1, 2002; Jan. 1, 2003. Renumbered Rule 5.570 and amended, eff. Jan. 1, 2007. As amended, eff. Jan. 1, 2009; Jan. 1, 2010; Jan. 1, 2014; Jan. 1, 2016.)*

Commentary

Despite the discretion allowed the juvenile court by subsection (f), *In re Matthew P., 71 Cal.App.4th 841, 84 Cal.Rptr.2d 269 (1999),* holds that the juvenile court violated the de facto parents' due process rights by admitting the reports of social workers in a modification hearing without allowing the de facto parents to cross examine the social workers.

Research References

Forms

West's California Judicial Council Forms JV-180, Request to Change Court Order.

West's California Judicial Council Forms JV-182, Confidential Information (Request to Change Court Order).

West's California Judicial Council Forms JV-183, Court Order on Form Jv-180, Request to Change Court Order.

West's California Judicial Council Forms JV-184, Order After Hearing on Form Jv-180, Request to Change Court Order.

Treatises and Practice Aids

Witkin, California Summary 10th Parent and Child § 458, Conditions for Transfer.

Witkin, California Summary 10th Parent and Child § 463, Transfer-In Hearing.

Witkin, California Summary 10th Parent and Child § 643, Duration Of Services.

Witkin, California Summary 10th Parent and Child § 663, Form, Content, and Filing.

Witkin, California Summary 10th Parent and Child § 664, in General.

Witkin, California Summary 10th Parent and Child § 666, Scope Of Hearing.

Witkin, California Summary 10th Parent and Child § 698, Other Procedures.

Witkin, California Summary 10th Parent and Child § 910, in General.

Witkin, California Summary 10th Parent and Child § 911, Hearing and Determination.

Witkin, California Summary 10th Parent and Child § 693B, (New) Designation Of Prospective Adoptive Parent.

Rule 5.575. Joinder of agencies

(a) Basis for joinder (§§ 362, 365, 727)

The court may, at any time after a petition has been filed, following notice and a hearing, join in the proceedings any agency (as defined in section 362) that the court determines has failed to meet a legal obligation to provide services to a child or a nonminor or nonminor dependent youth for whom a petition has been filed under section 300, 601, or 602. The court may not impose duties on an agency beyond those required by law.

(b) Notice and Hearing

On application by a party, counsel, or CASA volunteer, or on the court's own motion, the court may set a hearing and require notice to the agency or provider subject to joinder.

(1) Notice of the hearing must be given to the agency on *Notice of Hearing on Joinder—Juvenile* (form JV–540). The notice must clearly describe the legal obligation at issue, the facts and circumstances alleged to constitute the agency's failure to meet that obligation, and any issues or questions the court expects the agency to address at the hearing.

(2) The hearing must be set to occur within 30 calendar days of the signing of the notice by the court. The hearing will proceed under the provisions of rule 5.570(h) or (i), as appropriate.

(3) The clerk must cause the notice to be served on the agency and all parties, attorneys of record, the CASA volunteer, any other person or entity entitled to notice under section 291 or 658, and, if the hearing might address educational or developmental-services issues, the educational

rights holder by first-class mail within 5 court days of the signing of the notice.

(4) Nothing in this rule prohibits agencies from meeting before the hearing to coordinate the delivery of services. The court may request, using section 8 of form JV–540, that agency representatives meet before the hearing and that the agency or agencies submit a written response to the court at least 5 court days before the hearing. *(Formerly Rule 1434, adopted, eff. Jan. 1, 2002. As amended, eff. Jan. 1, 2006. Renumbered Rule 5.575 and amended, eff. Jan. 1, 2007. As amended, eff. Jan. 1, 2014.)*

Research References

Treatises and Practice Aids

Witkin, California Summary 10th Parent and Child § 624, in General.

Witkin, California Summary 10th Parent and Child § 892, in General.

Rule 5.580. Hearing on violation of probation (§ 777)

(a) Notice of hearing (§§ 656, 658, 660)

Notice of a hearing to be held under section 777 must be issued and served as provided in sections 658, 660, and 777 and prepared:

(1) By the probation officer if the child has been declared a ward under section 601; or

(2) By the probation officer or the district attorney if the child is a ward or is on probation under section 602, and the alleged violation of probation is not a crime.

(b) Motion to dismiss

If the probation officer files the notice of hearing, before jeopardy attaches the prosecuting attorney may move the court to dismiss the notice and request that the matter be referred to the probation officer for appropriate action under section 777(a)(3).

(c) Detention hearing

If the child has been brought into custody, the procedures described in rules 5.524 and 5.752 through 5.764 must be followed.

(d) Report of probation officer

Before every hearing the probation officer must prepare a report on those matters relevant to a determination of whether the child has violated a condition of probation. The report must be furnished to all parties at least 48 hours, excluding noncourt days, before the beginning of the hearing unless the child is represented by counsel and waives the right to service of the report.

(e) Evidence considered

The court must consider the report prepared by the probation officer and other relevant and material evidence offered by the parties to the proceeding.

(1) The court may admit and consider reliable hearsay evidence as defined by section 777(c).

(2) The probation officer or prosecuting attorney must prove the alleged violation by a preponderance of the evidence. *(Formerly Rule 1433, adopted, eff. Jan. 1, 1990. As amended, eff. Jan. 1, 1992; Jan. 1, 2001; Jan. 1, 2006. Renumbered Rule 5.580 and amended, eff. Jan. 1, 2007.)*

Research References

Treatises and Practice Aids

Witkin, California Summary 10th Parent and Child § 444, Scope and Organization.

Witkin, California Summary 10th Parent and Child § 908, Notice and Setting for Hearing.

Witkin, California Summary 10th Parent and Child § 909, Report and Hearing.

Chapter 5

APPELLATE REVIEW

Rule 5.585. Rules governing appellate review

The rules in title 8, chapter 5 govern appellate review of judgments and orders in cases under Welfare and Institutions Code section 300, 601, or 602. *(Adopted, eff. July 1, 2010.)*

Research References

Treatises and Practice Aids

Witkin, California Summary 10th Parent and Child § 444, Scope and Organization.

Witkin, California Summary 10th Parent and Child § 692, in General.

Witkin, California Summary 10th Parent and Child § 695, Legal Guardianship.

Witkin, California Summary 10th Parent and Child § 700, Right to Appeal.

Witkin, California Summary 10th Parent and Child § 708, Counsel on Appeal.

Witkin, California Summary 10th Parent and Child § 709, in General.

Witkin, California Summary 10th Parent and Child § 712, Notice Of Appeal.

Witkin, California Summary 10th Parent and Child § 713, in General.

Witkin, California Summary 10th Parent and Child § 782, Statutory Rights.

Witkin, California Summary 10th Parent and Child § 913, Minor's Right to Appeal.

Witkin, California Summary 10th Parent and Child § 914, Notification Of Appeal Rights.

Witkin, California Summary 10th Parent and Child § 915, in General.

Witkin, California Summary 10th Parent and Child § 919, Record on Appeal.

Rule 5.590. Advisement of right to review in Welfare and Institutions Code section 300, 601, or 602 cases

(a) Advisement of right to appeal

If at a contested hearing on an issue of fact or law the court finds that the child is described by Welfare and Institutions Code section 300, 601, or 602 or sustains a supplemental or subsequent petition, the court after making its disposition order other than orders covered in (b) must advise, orally or in writing, the child, if of sufficient age, and, if present, the parent or guardian of:

(1) The right of the child, parent, and guardian to appeal from the court order if there is a right to appeal;

(2) The necessary steps and time for taking an appeal;

(3) The right of an indigent appellant to have counsel appointed by the reviewing court; and

(4) The right of an indigent appellant to be provided with a free copy of the transcript.

(b) Advisement of requirement for writ petition to preserve appellate rights when court orders hearing under section 366.26

When the court orders a hearing under Welfare and Institutions Code section 366.26, the court must advise all parties and, if present, the child's parent, guardian, or adult relative, that if the party wishes to preserve any right to review on appeal of the order setting the hearing under Welfare and Institutions Code section 366.26, the party is required to seek an extraordinary writ by filing a *Notice of Intent to File Writ Petition and Request for Record (California Rules of Court, Rule 8. 450)* (form JV–820) or other notice of intent to file a writ petition and request for record and a *Petition for Extraordinary Writ (California Rules of Court, Rules 8.452, 8.456)* (form JV–825) or other petition for extraordinary writ.

(1) The advisement must be given orally to those present when the court orders the hearing under Welfare and Institutions Code section 366.26.

(2) Within one day after the court orders the hearing under Welfare and Institutions Code section 366.26, the advisement must be sent by first-class mail by the clerk of the court to the last known address of any party who is not present when the court orders the hearing under Welfare and Institutions Code section 366.26.

(3) The advisement must include the time for filing a notice of intent to file a writ petition.

(4) Copies of *Petition for Extraordinary Writ (California Rules of Court, Rules 8.452, 8.456)* (form JV–825) and *Notice of Intent to File Writ Petition and Request for Record (California Rules of Court, Rule 8.450)* (form JV–820) must be available in the courtroom and must accompany all mailed notices informing the parties of their rights.

(c) Advisement requirements for appeal of order to transfer to tribal court

When the court grants a petition transferring a case to tribal court under Welfare and Institutions Code section 305.5, Family Code section 177(a), or Probate Code section 1459.5(b), and rule 5.483, the court must advise the parties orally and in writing, that an appeal of the order must be filed before the transfer to tribal jurisdiction is finalized, and that failure to request and obtain a stay of the order for transfer will result in a loss of appellate jurisdiction. *(Formerly Rule 1435, adopted, eff. Jan. 1, 1990. As amended, eff. Jan. 1, 1992; Jan. 1, 1993; Jan. 1, 1994; Jan. 1, 1995; July 1, 1999. Renumbered Rule 5.585 and amended, eff. Jan. 1, 2007. Renumbered Rule 5.590 and amended, eff. July 1, 2010. As amended, eff. Jan. 1, 2016.)*

Commentary

In re A.O., 242 Cal.App.4th 145, 194 Cal.Rptr.3d 826 (2015), held that a juvenile court's failure to advise a mother of her right to appeal at the conclusion of a disposition hearing, as required by this Rule, was a special circumstance that excused the mother's failure to file a timely appeal.

Research References

Forms

West's California Judicial Council Forms JV-320, Orders Under Welfare and Institutions Code Sections 366.26, 727.3, 727.31.

Treatises and Practice Aids

Witkin, California Summary 10th Parent and Child § 524, Jurisdiction.

Witkin, California Summary 10th Parent and Child § 692, in General.

Witkin, California Summary 10th Parent and Child § 695, Legal Guardianship.

Witkin, California Summary 10th Parent and Child § 700, Right to Appeal.

Witkin, California Summary 10th Parent and Child § 713, in General.

Witkin, California Summary 10th Parent and Child § 717, in General.

Witkin, California Summary 10th Parent and Child § 782, Statutory Rights.

Witkin, California Summary 10th Parent and Child § 914, Notification Of Appeal Rights.

Witkin, California Summary 10th Parent and Child § 919, Record on Appeal.

Witkin, California Summary 10th Parent and Child § 675A, (New) Setting Selection and Implementation Hearing.

Rule 5.595. Stay pending appeal

The court must not stay an order or judgment pending an appeal unless suitable provision is made for the maintenance, care, and custody of the child. *(Formerly Rule 1436, adopted, eff. Jan. 1, 1993. As amended, eff. Jan. 1, 1994; Jan. 1, 1995; Jan. 1, 2006. Renumbered Rule 5.595 and amended, eff. Jan. 1, 2007. As amended, eff. July 1, 2010.)*

Research References

Treatises and Practice Aids

Witkin, California Summary 10th Parent and Child § 444, Scope and Organization.

Witkin, California Summary 10th Parent and Child § 709, in General.

Witkin, California Summary 10th Parent and Child § 716, in General.

Witkin, California Summary 10th Parent and Child § 920, Review by Extraordinary Writ.

Chapter 6

EMANCIPATION

Rule 5.605. Emancipation of minors

(a) Petition

A petition for declaration of emancipation of a minor must be submitted on *Petition for Declaration of Emancipation of Minor, Order Prescribing Notice, Declaration of Emancipation, and Order Denying Petition* (form MC–300). Only the minor may petition the court for emancipation, and the petition may be filed in the county in which the minor can provide a verifiable residence address. The petitioner must complete and attach to the petition *Emancipation of Minor—Income and Expense Declaration* (form MC–306).

(b) Dependents and wards of the juvenile court

Petitions to emancipate a child who is a dependent or ward of the juvenile court must be filed and heard in juvenile court.

(c) Court

The petition to emancipate a minor other than a dependent or ward of the juvenile court must be filed and will be heard in juvenile court or other superior court department so designated by local rule or by order of the presiding judge.

(d) Filing fee

Unless waived, the petitioner must pay the filing fee as specified. The ability or inability to pay the filing fee is not in and of itself evidence of the financial responsibility of the minor as required for emancipation.

(e) Declaration of emancipation without hearing

If the court finds that all notice and consent requirements have been met or waived, and that emancipation is not contrary to the best interest of the petitioner, the court may grant the petition without a hearing. The presiding judge of the superior court must develop a protocol for the screening, evaluation, or investigation of petitions.

(f) Time limits

The clerk of the court in which the petition is filed must immediately provide or direct the petitioner to provide the petition to the court. Within 30 days from the filing of the petition, the court must (1) grant the petition, (2) deny the petition, or (3) set a hearing on the petition to be conducted within 30 days thereafter. The clerk must immediately provide the petitioner with an endorsed-filed copy of the court's order.

(g) Notice

If the court orders the matter set for hearing, the clerk must notify the district attorney of the time and date of the hearing, which must be within 30 days of the order prescribing notice and setting for hearing. The petitioner is responsible for notifying all other persons to whom the court requires notice. *(Formerly Rule 1437, adopted, eff. July 1, 1994. As amended, eff. Jan. 1, 1995. Renumbered Rule 5.605 and amended, eff. Jan. 1, 2007.)*

Research References

Forms

West's California Code Forms, Family § 7110, Comment Overview--Emancipation Of Minor.

Treatises and Practice Aids

Witkin, California Summary 10th Parent and Child § 303, in General.

Witkin, California Summary 10th Parent and Child § 304, Notice Of Hearing.

Witkin, California Summary 10th Parent and Child § 444, Scope and Organization.

Chapter 7

INTERCOUNTY TRANSFERS

Rule

Rule 5.610. Transfer–out hearing

(a) Determination of residence—special rule on intercounty transfers (§§ 375, 750)

(1) For purposes of rules 5.610 and 5.612, the residence of the child is the residence of the person who has the legal right to physical custody of the child according to prior court order, including:

(A) A juvenile court order under section 361.2; and

(B) An order appointing a guardian of the person of the child.

(2) If there is no order determining custody, both parents are deemed to have physical custody.

(3) The juvenile court may make a finding of paternity under rule 5.635. If there is no finding of paternity, the mother is deemed to have physical custody.

(4) For the purposes of transfer of wardship, residence of a ward may be with the person with whom the child resides with approval of the court.

(b) Verification of residence

The residence of the person entitled to physical custody may be verified ~~by that person in court or~~ by declaration of a social worker or probation officer in the transferring or receiving county.

(c) Transfer to county of child's residence (§§ 375, 750)

(1) After making its jurisdictional finding, the court may order the case transferred to the juvenile court of the child's residence if:

(A) The petition was filed in a county other than that of the child's residence; or

(B) The child's residence was changed to another county after the petition was filed.

(2) If the court decides to transfer a delinquency case, the court must order the transfer before beginning the disposition hearing without adjudging the child to be a ward.

(3) If the court decides to transfer a dependency case, the court may order the transfer before or after the disposition hearing.

(d) Transfer on subsequent change in child's residence (§§ 375, 750)

If, after the child has been placed under a program of supervision, the residence is changed to another county, the court may, on an application for modification under rule 5.570, transfer the case to the juvenile court of the other county.

(e) Conduct of hearing

(1) The request for transfer must be made on *Motion for Transfer Out* (form JV–548), which must include all required information.

(2) After the court determines the identity and residence of the child's custodian, the court must consider whether transfer of the case would be in the child's best interest. The court may not transfer the case unless it determines that the transfer will protect or further the child's best interest.

(f) Date of transfer-in hearing

(1) If the transfer-out motion is granted, the sending court must set a date certain for the transfer-in hearing in the receiving court: within 5 court days of the transfer-out order if the child is in custody, and within 10 court days of the transfer-out order if the child is out of custody. The sending court must state on the record the date, time, and location of the hearing in the receiving court.

(2) The website for every court must include up-to-date contact information for the court clerks handling dependency and delinquency matters, as well as up-to-date information on when and where transfer-in hearings are held.

~~(f)~~(g) Order of transfer (§§ 377, 752)

The order of transfer must be entered on *Juvenile Court Transfer–Out Orders* (form JV–550), which must include all required information and findings.

~~(g)~~(h) Modification of form JV–550

Juvenile Court Transfer Orders (form JV–550) may be modified as follows:

(1) Notwithstanding the mandatory use of form JV–550, the form may be modified for use by a formalized regional collaboration of courts to facilitate the efficient processing of transfer cases among those courts if the modification has been approved by the Judicial Council of California.

(2) The mandatory form must be used by a regional collaboration when transferring a case to a court outside the collaboration or when accepting a transfer from a court outside the collaboration.

~~(h)~~(i) Transport of child and transmittal of documents (§§ 377, 752)

(1) If the child is ordered transported in custody to the receiving county, the child must be delivered to the receiving county ~~within 7 court days~~ at least two business days before the transfer-in hearing, and the clerk of the court of the transferring county must prepare a certified copy of the complete case file so that it may be transported with the child to the court of the receiving county.

(2) If the child is not ordered transported in custody, the clerk of the transferring court must transmit to the clerk of the court of the receiving county within ~~10~~ five court days a certified copy of the complete case file.

(3) The file may be transferred electronically, if possible. A certified copy of the complete case file is deemed an original.

~~(i)~~(j) Appeal of transfer order (§§ 379, 754)

The order of transfer may be appealed by the transferring or receiving county and notice of appeal must be filed in the transferring county, under rule 8.400. Notwithstanding the filing of a notice of appeal, the receiving county must assume jurisdiction of the case on receipt and filing of the order of transfer. *(Formerly Rule 1425, adopted, eff. Jan. 1, 1990. As amended, eff. Jan. 1, 1992; Jan. 1, 1993; July 1, 1999; Jan. 1, 2004. Renumbered 5.610 and amended, eff. Jan. 1, 2007. As amended, eff. Jan. 1, 2015; Jan. 1, 2017.)*

Commentary

Reading this section together with Welfare and Institutions Code Section 375, *In re Christopher T., 60 Cal.App.4th 1282, 71 Cal.Rptr.2d 116 (1998), review denied April 15, 1998,* holds that a juvenile court may transfer a dependency proceeding from the county where a parent resides to the county where the dependent child has relocated with his guardians.

In re Nia A., 246 Cal.App.4th 1241, 201 Cal.Rptr.3d. 424 (2016), held that a juvenile court erred in transferring a dependency case to a different county based on a county protocol that required transfer whenever there is a potential conflict of interest, without considering the best interests of the child and finding that transfer is in the best interests of the child, as required by subsection (e) of this rule.

Research References

Forms

West's California Judicial Council Forms JV-550, Juvenile Court Transfer Orders.

Treatises and Practice Aids

Witkin, California Summary 10th Parent and Child § 444, Scope and Organization.
Witkin, California Summary 10th Parent and Child § 456, Proper Court.
Witkin, California Summary 10th Parent and Child § 457, in General.
Witkin, California Summary 10th Parent and Child § 458, Conditions for Transfer.
Witkin, California Summary 10th Parent and Child § 459, Residence Of Child.
Witkin, California Summary 10th Parent and Child § 460, Appeal from Determination Of Residence.
Witkin, California Summary 10th Parent and Child § 461, Transfer-Out Hearing and Order.
Witkin, California Summary 10th Parent and Child § 462, Appeal from Transfer Order.
Witkin, California Summary 10th Parent and Child § 463, Transfer-In Hearing.
Witkin, California Summary 10th Parent and Child § 598, in General.
Witkin, California Summary 10th Parent and Child § 819, Time Of Hearing.

Rule 5.612. Transfer–in hearing

(a) Procedure on transfer (§§ 378, 753)

~~(1)~~ On receipt and filing of a certified copy of a transfer order, the receiving court must accept jurisdiction of the case. The receiving court may not reject the case. The clerk of the receiving court must ~~immediately place the transferred case on the court calendar for a transfer-in hearing~~ confirm the transfer-in hearing date scheduled by the sending court and ensure that date is on the receiving court's calendar. The receiving court must notify the transferring court on receipt and filing of the certified copies of the transfer order and complete case file.

~~(A) Within two court days after the transfer-out order and documents are received if the child has been transported in custody and remains detained; or~~

~~(B) Within 10 court days after the transfer-out order and documents are received if the child is not detained in custody.~~

~~(2) No requests for additional time for the transfer-in hearing may be approved. The clerk must immediately cause notice to be given to the child and the parent or guardian, orally or in writing, of the time and place of the transfer-in hearing. The receiving court must notify the transferring court on receipt and filing of the certified copies of the transfer order and complete case file.~~

(b) Conduct of hearing

At the transfer-in hearing, the court must:

(1) Advise the child and the parent or guardian of the purpose and scope of the hearing;

(2) Provide for the appointment of counsel if appropriate; and

(3) If the child was transferred to the county in custody, determine whether the child must be further detained under rule 5.667.

(c) Subsequent proceedings

The proceedings in the receiving court must commence at the same phase as when the case was transferred. The court may continue the hearing for an investigation and report to a date not to exceed 10 court days if the child is in custody or 15 court days if the child is not detained in custody.

(d) Limitation on more restrictive custody (§§ 387, 777)

If a disposition order has already been made in the transferring county, a more restrictive level of physical custody may not be ordered in the receiving county, except after a hearing on a supplemental petition under rule 5.565.

(e) Setting six-month review (§ 366)

When an order of transfer is received and filed relating to a child who has been declared a dependent, the court must set a date for a six-month review within six months of the disposition or the most recent review hearing.

(f) Change of circumstances or additional facts (§§ 388, 778)

If the receiving court believes that a change of circumstances or additional facts indicate that the child does not reside in the receiving county, a transfer-out hearing must be held under rules 5.610 and 5.570. The court may direct the department of social services or the probation department to seek a modification of orders under section 388 or 778 and under rule 5.570. *(Formerly Rule 1426, adopted, eff. Jan. 1, 1990. As amended, eff. Jan. 1, 1992; July 1, 1999; Jan. 1, 2004. Renumbered Rule 5.612 and amended eff. Jan. 1, 2007. As amended, eff. Jan. 1, 2017.)*

Research References

Forms

West's California Judicial Council Forms JV-550, Juvenile Court Transfer Orders.

Treatises and Practice Aids

Witkin, California Summary 10th Parent and Child § 457, in General.

Witkin, California Summary 10th Parent and Child § 459, Residence Of Child.

Witkin, California Summary 10th Parent and Child § 461, Transfer-Out Hearing and Order.

Witkin, California Summary 10th Parent and Child § 463, Transfer-In Hearing.

Rule 5.613. Transfer of nonminor dependents

(a) Purpose

This rule applies to requests to transfer the county of jurisdiction of a nonminor dependent as allowed by Welfare and Institutions Code section 375. This rule sets forth the procedures that a court is to follow when it seeks to order a transfer of a nonminor dependent and those to be followed by the court receiving the transfer. All other intercounty transfers of juveniles are subject to rules 5.610 and 5.612.

(b) Transfer-out hearing

(1) *Determination of residence—special rule on intercounty transfers (§§ 17.1, 375)*

(A) For purposes of this rule, the residence of a nonminor dependent who is placed in a planned permanent living arrangement may be either the county in which the court that has jurisdiction over the nonminor is located or the county in which the nonminor has resided continuously for at least one year as a nonminor dependent and the nonminor dependent has expressed his or her intent to remain.

(B) If a nonminor dependent's dependency jurisdiction has been resumed, or if transition jurisdiction has been assumed or resumed by the juvenile court that retained general jurisdiction over the nonminor under section 303, the county that the nonminor dependent is residing in may be deemed the county of residence of the nonminor dependent. The court may make this determination if the nonminor has established a continuous physical presence in the county for one year as a nonminor and has expressed his or her intent to remain in that county after the court grants the petition to resume jurisdiction. The period of continuous physical presence includes any period of continuous residence immediately before filing the petition.

(2) *Verification of residence*

The residence of a nonminor may be verified by declaration of a social worker or probation officer in the transferring or receiving county.

(3) *Transfer to county of nonminor's residence (§ 375)*

If the court is resuming dependency jurisdiction or assuming or resuming transition jurisdiction of a nonminor for whom the court has retained general jurisdiction under section 303(b) as a result of a petition filed under section 388(e), after granting the petition, the court may order the transfer of the case to the juvenile court of the county in which the nonminor is living if the nonminor establishes residency in that county as provided in (b)(1) and the court finds that the transfer is in the minor's best interest.

(4) *Transfer on change in nonminor's residence (§ 375)*

If a nonminor dependent under the dependency or transition jurisdiction of the court is placed in a planned permanent living arrangement in a county other than the county with jurisdiction over the nonminor, the court may, on an application for modification under rule 5.570, transfer the case to the juvenile court of the county in which the nonminor is living if the nonminor establishes residency in that county as provided in (b)(1).

(5) *Conduct of hearing*

(A) The request for transfer must be made on *Motion for Transfer Out* (form JV–548), which must include all required information.

(B) After the court determines whether a nonminor has established residency in another county as required in (b)(1), the court must consider whether transfer of the case would be in the nonminor's best interest. The court may not transfer the case unless it determines that the nonminor supports the transfer and that the transfer will protect or further the nonminor's best interest.

(C) If the transfer-out motion is granted, the sending court must set a date certain for the transfer-in hearing in the receiving court, which must be within 10 court days of the transfer-out order. The sending court must state on the record the date, time, and location of the hearing in the receiving court.

(6) *Order of transfer (§ 377)*

The order of transfer must be entered on *Juvenile Court Transfer–Out Orders—Nonminor Dependent* (form JV–552), which must include all required information and findings.

(7) *Modification of form JV–552*

Juvenile Court Transfer–Out Orders—Nonminor Dependent (form JV–552) may be modified as follows:

(A) Notwithstanding the mandatory use of form JV–552, the form may be modified for use by a formalized regional collaboration of courts to facilitate the efficient processing of transfer cases among those courts if the modification has been approved by the Judicial Council.

(B) The mandatory form must be used by a regional collaboration when transferring a case to a court outside the collaboration or when accepting a transfer from a court outside the collaboration.

(8) *Transmittal of documents (§ 377)*

The clerk of the transferring court must transmit to the clerk of the court of the receiving county no later than five court days from the date of the transfer-out order a certified copy of the entire nonminor file and, at a minimum, all documents associated with the last status review hearing held before the nonminor reached majority, including the court report and all findings and orders. The files may be transferred electronically, if possible. A certified copy of the complete case file is deemed an original.

(9) *Appeal of transfer order (§ 379)*

The order of transfer may be appealed by the transferring or receiving county, and notice of appeal must be filed in the transferring county, under rule 8.400. Notwithstanding the filing of a notice of appeal, the receiving county must assume jurisdiction of the case on receipt and filing of the order of transfer.

(c) Transfer-in hearing

(1) *Procedure on transfer (§ 378)*

On receipt and filing of a certified copy of a transfer order, the receiving court must accept jurisdiction of the case. The receiving court may not reject the case. The receiving court must notify the transferring court on receipt and filing of the certified copies of the transfer order and complete case file. The clerk of the receiving court must confirm the transfer-in hearing date scheduled by the sending court and ensure that date is on the receiving court's calendar.

(2) *Conduct of hearing*

At the transfer-in hearing, the court must:

(A) Advise the nonminor of the purpose and scope of the hearing; and

(B) Provide for the appointment of counsel, if appropriate.

(3) *Subsequent proceedings*

The proceedings in the receiving court must commence at the same phase as when the case was transferred. The court may continue the hearing for an investigation and a report to a date not to exceed 15 court days.

(4) *Setting six-month review (§ 366.31)*

When an order of transfer is received and filed relating to a nonminor dependent, the court must set a date for a six-month review within six months of the most recent review hearing or, if the sending court transferred the case immediately after assuming or resuming jurisdiction, within six months of the date a voluntary reentry agreement was signed.

(5) *Change of circumstances or additional facts (§§ 388, 778)*

If the receiving court believes that a change of circumstances or additional facts indicate that the nonminor does not reside in the receiving county, a transfer-out hearing must be held under this rule and rule 5.570. The court may direct the department of social services or the probation department to seek a modification of orders under section 388 or section 778 and under rule 5.570. *(Adopted, eff. Jan. 1, 2017.)*

Rule 5.614. Courtesy supervision (§§ 380, 755)

The court may authorize a child placed on probation, a ward, or a dependent child to live in another county and to be placed under the supervision of the other county's county welfare agency or probation department with the consent of the agency or department. The court in the county ordering placement retains jurisdiction over the child. *(Formerly Rule 1427, adopted, eff. Jan. 1, 1990. Renumbered Rule 5.614 and amended, eff. Jan. 1, 2007.)*

Research References

Treatises and Practice Aids

Witkin, California Summary 10th Parent and Child § 464, Continuing Jurisdiction Outside County.

Rule 5.616. Interstate Compact on the Placement of Children

(a) Applicability of rule (Fam. Code, § 7900 et seq.)

This rule implements the purposes and provisions of the Interstate Compact on the Placement of Children (ICPC, or the compact). California juvenile courts must apply this rule when placing children who are dependents or wards of the juvenile court and for whom placement is indicated in any other state, the District of Columbia, or the U.S. Virgin Islands.

(1) This rule applies to expedited placements as described in (h).

(2) This rule does not apply to placements made under the Interstate Compact for Juveniles (Welf. & Inst. Code, § 1400 et seq.).

(b) Definitions (Fam. Code, § 7900 et seq.; ICPC Regulations)

(1) "Placement" is defined in article 2(d) of the compact. It includes placements with a relative, as defined in Regulation No. 3, paragraph 4, item 56; a legal guardian of the child; a placement recipient who is not related to the child; or a residential facility or group home as defined in Regulation No. 4.

(A) A court's directing or making an award of custody to a parent of the child or placing a child with his or her parent is not a placement requiring compliance with this rule.

(B) The following situations each constitute a placement, and the compact must be applied:

(i) An order causing a child to be sent or brought to a person, other than a parent, in a compact jurisdiction without a specific date of return to the sending jurisdiction;

(ii) An order causing a child to be sent or brought to a person, other than a parent, in a compact jurisdiction with a return date more than 30 days from the start of the visit or beyond the ending date of a school vacation period, under Regulation No. 9;

(iii) An out-of-state placement for the purpose of an anticipated adoption, whether independent, private, or public;

(iv) An out-of-state placement with a related or unrelated caregiver in a licensed or approved foster home;

(v) An out-of-state placement with relatives, except when a parent or relative sends or brings the child to the relative's home in the receiving state, as defined in article 8(a) of the ICPC; or

(vi) An out-of-state group home or residential placement of any child, including a child adjudicated delinquent.

(2) "Child," for the purposes of ICPC placement, includes nonminor dependents up to age 21. If a California nonminor dependent is to be placed out of state, the placing county may request supervision from the receiving state, but such services are discretionary. If the receiving state will not supervise the nonminor dependent, the sending county must make other supervision arrangements, which may include contracting with a private agency to provide the supervision.

(3) "Parent," as used in this rule, does not include de facto parents or legal guardians.

(4) ICPC Regulations Nos. 3, 4, 5, 9, 10, 11, and 12 contain additional definitions that apply to California ICPC cases, except where inconsistent with this rule or with California law.

(c) Compact requirements (Fam. Code, § 7901; ICPC Regulations)

Whenever the juvenile court makes a placement in another jurisdiction included in the compact or reviews a placement plan, the court must adhere to the provisions and regulations of the compact.

(1) Cases in which out-of-state placement is proposed in order to place a child for public adoption, in foster care, or with relatives, and where the criteria for expedited placement are not met, must meet all requirements of Regulation No. 2, except where inconsistent with California law.

(2) Expedited placement cases must meet the requirements in (h) and of Regulation No. 7, except where the requirements of Regulation No. 7 are inconsistent with California law.

(3) Cases in which out-of-state placement is proposed in order to place a child in a residential facility or group home must meet all the requirements of Regulation No. 4, except where inconsistent with California law.

(d) Notice of intention; authorization (Fam. Code, § 7901)

A sending jurisdiction must provide to the designated receiving jurisdiction written notice of intention to place the child, using Form ICPC–100A: Interstate Compact on the Placement of Children Request.

(1) The representative of the receiving jurisdiction may request and receive additional information as the representative deems necessary.

(2) The child must not be placed until the receiving jurisdiction has determined that the placement is not contrary to the interest of the child and has so notified the sending jurisdiction in writing.

(e) Placement of delinquent children in institutional care (Fam. Code, §§ 7901, art. 6, and 7908; ICPC Reg. No. 4, § 2)

(1) Before the placement, the court has held a properly noticed hearing at which the child, parent, and guardian have had an opportunity to be heard;

(2) The court has found that equivalent facilities for the child are not available in the sending jurisdiction; and

(3) Institutional care in the other jurisdiction is in the best interest of the child and will not produce undue hardship for the child or his or her family.

(f) Relocation of Family Units (ICPC Reg. No. 1)

(1) The ICPC applies to family relocation cases when the child has been placed and continues to live with a family approved by California, the family relocates to another state with the child, and supervision by California is ongoing.

(2) The ICPC does not apply when the family with whom the child is placed relocates to another state and there will be no ongoing supervision by the sending state or the relocation will be temporary (90 days or less) and will not recur.

(3) Additional procedural requirements for cases involving relocation of family units are in ICPC Regulation No. 1.

(g) Placing a Child With an Out–of–State Parent (Fam. Code, §§ 7901, art. 5(b), and 7906; ICPC Reg. No. 2, § 3)

When a child will be placed with his or her parent in another state, compliance with the requirements of the ICPC is not required. However, the court has discretion to take the steps it deems necessary to ensure the child's safety and well-being in that placement. Those steps may include:

(1) Directing the child welfare agency to request an independent, non–ICPC home study or courtesy check;

(2) Directing the child welfare agency to enter into a contract with a public or private agency in the receiving state to obtain a home study or other needed information;

(3) Directing the child welfare agency to enter into an informal agreement with a public or private agency in the receiving state, or requesting a courtesy check from such an agency, to obtain needed information; or

(4) Any other steps that the court deems necessary to ensure the child's safety and well-being.

(h) Expedited placement (ICPC Reg. No. 7)

When seeking expedited approval of an out-of-state placement of a child with a relative or guardian, a California court may designate a proposed placement as an expedited placement by using procedures described in this section.

(1) Expedited placement under Regulation No. 7 does not apply to any situation in which a California child is being placed with his or her parent in another state.

(2) Before the court orders an expedited placement, the court must make express findings that the child is a dependent child removed from and no longer residing in the home of a parent and now being considered for placement in another state with a stepparent, grandparent, adult aunt or uncle, adult sibling, or legal guardian. In addition, the court must find that the child to be placed meets at least one of the following criteria:

(A) Unexpected dependency due to the sudden or recent incarceration, incapacitation, or death of a parent or guardian. *Incapacitation* means the parent or guardian is unable to care for the child due to the parent's medical, mental, or physical condition;

(B) The child is 4 years of age or younger;

(C) The child is part of a group of siblings who will be placed together, where one or more of the siblings is 4 years of age or younger;

(D) The child to be placed, or any of the child's siblings in a sibling group to be placed, has a substantial relationship with the proposed placement resource as defined in section 5(c) of Regulation No. 7; or

(E) The child is in an emergency placement.

(3) Before the court orders an expedited placement, the child welfare agency must provide to the court, at a minimum, the documents required by section 7(a) and (b) of Regulation No. 7:

(A) A signed statement of interest from the potential placement, or a written statement from the assigned case manager affirming that the potential placement resource confirms appropriateness for the ICPC expedited placement decision process. The statement must include all items listed in Regulation No. 7, section 7(a); and

(B) A statement from the assigned case manager or other child welfare agency representative stating that he or she knows of no reason why the child could not be placed with the proposed placement and that the agency has completed and is prepared to send all required paperwork.

(4) On findings of the court under (h)(2) and (3) that the child meets the criteria for an expedited placement and that the required statements have been provided to the court, the case must proceed as follows:

(A) The court must enter an order for expedited placement, stating on the record or in the written order the factual basis for that order. If the court is also requesting provisional approval of the proposed placement, the court must so order, and must state on the record or in the written order the factual basis for that request.

(B) The court's findings and orders must be noted in a written order using *Expedited Placement Under the Interstate Compact on the Placement of Children: Findings and Orders* (form JV–567), which must include the name, address, e-mail address, telephone number, and fax number of the clerk of court or designated court administrator.

(C) The order must be transmitted by the court to the sending agency of the court's jurisdiction within 2 business days of the hearing or consideration of the request.

(D) The sending child welfare agency must be ordered to transmit to the county ICPC Liaison in the sending jurisdiction within 3 business days of receipt of the order the following:

(i) A copy of the completed *Expedited Placement Under the Interstate Compact on the Placement of Children: Findings and Orders* (form JV–567); and

(ii) A completed Interstate Compact on the Placement of Children Request (form ICPC–100A), along with form ICPC–101, the statements required under section (h)(3), above, and all required supporting documentation.

(E) Within 2 business days after receipt of the paperwork, the county ICPC Liaison of the sending jurisdiction must transmit the documents described in (D) to the compact administrator of the receiving jurisdiction with a request for an expedited placement decision, as well as any request for provisional placement.

(5) The compact administrator of the receiving jurisdiction must determine immediately, and no later than 20 business days after receipt, whether the placement is approved and must transmit the completed written report and form ICPC 100A, as required by Regulation 7, section 9, to the county ICPC Liaison in the sending jurisdiction.

(6) The transmission of any documentation, request for information, or decision may be by overnight mail, fax, e-mail, or other recognized, secure method of communication. The receiving state may also request original documents or certified copies if it considers them necessary for a legally sufficient record.

(7) When California is the sending state and there appears to be a lack of compliance with Regulation No. 7 requirements by state officials or the local child welfare agency in the receiving state regarding the expedited placement request,

the California judicial officer may communicate directly with the judicial officer in the receiving state.

(A) This communication may y be by telephone, e-mail, or any other recognized, secure communication method.

(B) The California judicial officer may do any one or more of the following:

(i) Contact the appropriate judicial officer in the receiving state to discuss the situation and possible solutions.

(ii) Provide, or direct someone else to provide, the judicial officer of the receiving state with copies of relevant documents and court orders.

(iii) Request assistance with obtaining compliance.

(iv) Use *Request for Assistance With Expedited Placement Under the Interstate Compact on the Placement of Children* (form JV–565) to communicate the request for assistance to the receiving state judicial officer. When this form is used, a copy should be provided to the county ICPC Liaison in the sending jurisdiction.

(8) All other requirements, exceptions, timelines, and instructions for expedited placement cases, along with procedures for provisional approval or denial of a placement and for removal of a child from the placement, are stated in Regulation No. 7.

(i) Authority of sending court or agency to place child; timing (ICPC Reg. No. 2, § 8(d), and Reg. No. 4, § 8)

(1) When the receiving state has approved a placement resource, the sending court has the final authority to determine whether to use the approved placement resource. The sending court may delegate that decision to the sending state child welfare agency or probation department.

(2) For proposed placements of children for adoption, in foster care, or with relatives, the receiving state's approval expires six months from the date form ICPC–100A was signed by the receiving state.

(3) For proposed placements of children in residential facilities or group homes, the receiving state's approval expires 30 calendar days from the date form ICPC–100A was signed by the receiving state. The 30–day time frame can be extended by mutual agreement between the sending and receiving states.

(j) Ongoing jurisdiction

If a child is placed in another jurisdiction under the terms of the compact, the sending court must not terminate its jurisdiction until the child is adopted, reaches majority, or is emancipated, or the dependency is terminated with the concurrence of the receiving state authority. *(Formerly Rule 1428, adopted, eff. Jan. 1, 1999. Renumbered Rule 5.616 and amended, eff. Jan. 1, 2007. As amended, eff. Jan. 1, 2013; Jan. 1, 2014.)*

Validity

The definition of "Placement" in a prior version of this rule (subd. (b)(1)) was held invalid in the decision of In re C.B. (App. 4 Dist. 2010) 116 Cal.Rptr.3d 294, 188 Cal.App.4th 1024.

Research References

Forms

California Transactions Forms--Family Law § 6:129, Documents to be Prepared.

West's California Judicial Council Forms JV-565, Request for Assistance With Expedited Placement Under the Interstate Compact on the Placement Of Children.

West's California Judicial Council Forms JV-567, Expedited Placement Under the Interstate Compact on the Placement Of Children: Findings and Orders.

Treatises and Practice Aids

Witkin, California Summary 10th Parent and Child § 80, Interstate Placement Of Children for Adoption.

Witkin, California Summary 10th Parent and Child § 444, Scope and Organization.

Chapter 8

GENERAL COURT AUTHORITY

Rule

Rule 5.620. Orders after filing under section 300

(a) Exclusive jurisdiction (§ 304)

Once a petition has been filed alleging that a child is described by section 300, and until the petition is dismissed or dependency is terminated, the juvenile court has exclusive jurisdiction to hear proceedings relating to the custody of the child and visitation with the child and establishing a guardianship for the child.

(b) Restraining orders (§ 213.5)

After a petition has been filed under section 300, and until the petition is dismissed or dependency is terminated, the court may issue restraining orders as provided in rule 5.630. A temporary restraining order must be prepared on *Notice of Hearing and Temporary Restraining Order—Juvenile* (form JV–250). An order after hearing must be prepared on *Restraining Order—Juvenile* (form JV–255).

(c) Custody and visitation (§ 361.2)

If the court sustains a petition, finds that the child is described by section on 300, and removes physical custody from a parent or guardian, it may order the child placed in the custody of a previously noncustodial parent as described in rule 5.695(a)(7)(A) or (B).

(1) This order may be entered at the dispositional hearing, at any subsequent review hearing under rule 5.708(k), or on granting a request under section 388 for custody and visitation orders.

(2) If the court orders legal and physical custody to the previously noncustodial parent and terminates dependency jurisdiction under rule 5.695(a)(7)(A), the court must proceed under rule 5.700.

(3) If the court orders custody to the noncustodial parent subject to the continuing supervision of the court, the court may order services provided to either parent or to both parents under section 361.2(b)(3). If the court orders the

provision of services, it must review its custody determination at each subsequent hearing held under section 366 and rule 5.708.

(d) Appointment of a legal guardian of the person (§§ 360, 366.26)

If the court finds that the child is described by section 300, it may appoint a legal guardian at the disposition hearing as described in rule 5.695(b), or at the hearing under section 366.26 as described in rule 5.735. The juvenile court maintains jurisdiction over the guardianship, and petitions to terminate or modify such guardianships must be heard in juvenile court under rule 5.740(c).

(e) Termination or modification of previously established guardianships (§ 728)

At any time after the filing of a petition under section 300 and until the petition is dismissed or dependency is terminated, the court may terminate or modify a guardianship of the person previously established by the juvenile court or the probate court. If the social worker recommends to the court, by filing *Juvenile Dependency Petition (Version One)* (form JV–100) and *Request to Change Court Order* (form JV–180), that an existing guardianship be modified or terminated, the court must order the appropriate county agency to file the recommended motion.

(1) The hearing on the motion may be held simultaneously with any regularly scheduled hearing regarding the child. Notice requirements under Probate Code section 1511 apply.

(2) If the court terminates or modifies a previously established probate guardianship, the court must provide notice of the order to the probate court that made the original appointment. The clerk of the probate court must file the notice in the probate file and send a copy of the notice to all parties of record identified in that file. *(Formerly Rule 1429.1, adopted, eff. Jan. 1, 2000. Renumbered Rule 5.620 and amended, eff. Jan. 1, 2007. As amended, eff. Jan. 1, 2014; Jan. 1, 2016.)*

Commentary

In re Xavier R., 201 Cal.App.4th 1398, 134 Cal.Rptr.3d 410 (2011), held that a juvenile court may terminate a Probate Code guardianship pursuant to Welfare and Institutions Code section 728 after reunification services have been offered, without first granting a petition to terminate reunification services under this section, because section 728 gives the court authority to terminate Probate Code guardianships at any point in a dependency proceeding. Moreover, subsection (e) of this Rule does not require a petition to terminate reunification services before hearing a motion to terminate a guardianship.

Research References

Forms

West's California Judicial Council Forms JV-245, Request for Restraining Order--Juvenile.

Treatises and Practice Aids

Witkin, California Summary 10th Parent and Child § 369, Dependency Proceeding Pending.

Witkin, California Summary 10th Parent and Child § 444, Scope and Organization.

Witkin, California Summary 10th Parent and Child § 453, Jurisdiction Over Adults.

Witkin, California Summary 10th Parent and Child § 520, Jurisdiction.

Witkin, California Summary 10th Parent and Child § 627, in General.

Witkin, California Summary 10th Parent and Child § 628, Legal Guardianship.

Witkin, California Summary 10th Parent and Child § 695, Legal Guardianship.

Rule 5.625. Orders after filing of petition under section 601 or 602

(a) Restraining orders (§ 213.5)

After a petition has been filed under section 601 or 602, and until the petition is dismissed or wardship is terminated, the court may issue restraining orders as provided in rule 5.630. A temporary restraining order must be prepared on *Notice of Hearing and Temporary Restraining Order—Juvenile* (form JV–250). An order after hearing must be prepared on *Restraining Order—Juvenile* (form JV–255).

(b) Appointment of a legal guardian of the person (§ 728)

At any time during wardship of a person under 18 years, the court may appoint a guardian, or may terminate or modify a previously established guardianship, in accordance with the requirements in rule 5.815. *(Formerly Rule 1429.3, adopted, eff. Jan. 1, 2000. As amended, eff. Jan. 1, 2003. Renumbered Rule 5.625 and amended, eff. Jan. 1, 2007. As amended, eff. Jan. 1, 2014.)*

Research References

Forms

West's California Judicial Council Forms JV-245, Request for Restraining Order--Juvenile.

Treatises and Practice Aids

Witkin, California Summary 10th Parent and Child § 453, Jurisdiction Over Adults.

Witkin, California Summary 10th Parent and Child § 892, in General.

Rule 5.630. Restraining orders

(a) Court's authority

After a petition has been filed under section 300, 601, or 602, and until the petition is dismissed or dependency or wardship is terminated, or the ward is no longer on probation, the court may issue restraining orders as provided in section 213.5.

(b) Application for restraining orders

(1) Application for restraining orders may be made orally at any scheduled hearing regarding the child who is the subject of a petition under section 300, 601, or 602, or may be made by written application, or may be made on the court's own motion.

(2) The written application must be submitted on *Request for Restraining Order—Juvenile* (form JV–245).

(3) A person requesting a restraining order in writing must submit to the court with the request a completed *Confidential CLETS Information Form* (form CLETS–001) under rule 1.51.

(c) Definition of abuse

The definition of abuse in Family Code section 6203 applies to restraining orders issued under Welfare and Institutions Code section 213.5.

(d) Applications—procedure

The application may be submitted without notice, and the court may grant the petition and issue a temporary order.

(1) In determining whether or not to issue the temporary restraining order without notice, the court must consider all documents submitted with the application and may review the contents of the juvenile court file regarding the child.

(2) The temporary restraining order must be prepared on *Notice of Hearing and Temporary Restraining Order—Juvenile* (form JV–250) and must state on its face the date of expiration of the order.

(e) Continuance

(1) The court may grant a continuance under Welfare and Institutions Code section 213.5.

(2) Either *Request and Order to Continue Hearing (Temporary Restraining Order—Juvenile)* (form JV–251) or a new *Notice of Hearing and Temporary Restraining Order—Juvenile* (form JV–250) must be used for this purpose.

(f) Hearing on application for restraining order

(1) Proof may be by the application and any attachments, additional declarations or documentary evidence, the contents of the juvenile court file, testimony, or any combination of these.

(2) The order after hearing must be prepared on *Restraining Order—Juvenile* (form JV–255) and must state on its face the date of expiration of the order.

(g) Service of restraining order

When service of *Notice of Hearing and Temporary Restraining Order—Juvenile* (form JV–250) or *Restraining Order—Juvenile* (form JV–255) is made, it must be served with a blank *Proof of Firearms Turned In, Sold, or Stored* (form DV–800/JV–252) and *How Do I Turn In, Sell, or Store My Firearms?* (form DV–800–INFO/JV–252–INFO). Failure to serve form JV–252 or JV–252–INFO does not make service of form JV–250 or form JV–255 invalid.

(h) Firearm relinquishment

The firearm relinquishment procedures in rule 5.495 apply to restraining orders issued under section 213.5.

(i) Expiration of restraining order

If the juvenile case is dismissed, the restraining order remains in effect until it expires or is terminated.

(j) Criminal records search (§ 213.5 and Stats.2001, ch. 572, § 7)

(1) Except as provided in (3), before any hearing on the issuance of a restraining order the court must ensure that a criminal records search is or has been conducted as described in Family Code section 6306(a). Before deciding whether to issue a restraining order, the court must consider the information obtained from the search.

(2) If the results of the search indicate that an outstanding warrant exists against the subject of the search, or that the subject of the search is currently on parole or probation, the court must proceed under section 213.5(k)(3).

(3) The requirements of (1) and (2) must be implemented in those courts identified by the Judicial Council as having resources currently available for these purposes. All other courts must implement the requirements to the extent that funds are appropriated for this purpose in the annual Budget Act.

(k) Modification of restraining order

(1) A restraining order may be modified on the court's own motion or in the manner provided for in Welfare and Institutions Code section 388 and rule 5.560.

(2) A termination or modification order must be made on *Change to Restraining Order After Hearing* (form JV–257). A new *Restraining Order—Juvenile* (form JV–255) may be prepared in addition to form JV–257. *(Formerly Rule 1429.5, adopted, eff. Jan. 1, 2000. As amended, eff. Jan. 1, 2003; Jan. 1, 2004. Renumbered Rule 5.630 and amended, eff. Jan. 1, 2007. As amended, eff. Jan. 1, 2012; Jan. 1, 2014; July 1, 2014; July 1, 2016.)*

Research References

Forms

West's California Judicial Council Forms JV-245, Request for Restraining Order--Juvenile.

West's California Judicial Council Forms JV-247, Answer to Request for Restraining Order--Juvenile.

West's California Judicial Council Forms DV-800/JV-252, Proof Of Firearms Turned In, Sold, or Stored (Domestic Violence Prevention).

Treatises and Practice Aids

Witkin, California Summary 10th Parent and Child § 444, Scope and Organization.

Witkin, California Summary 10th Parent and Child § 453, Jurisdiction Over Adults.

Witkin, California Summary 10th Parent and Child § 834, Orders.

Chapter 9

PARENTAGE

Rule 5.635. Parentage

(a) Authority to declare; duty to inquire (§ 316.2, 726.4)

The juvenile court has a duty to inquire about and to attempt to determine the parentage of each child who is the subject of a petition filed under section 300, 601, or 602. The court may establish and enter a judgment of parentage under the Uniform Parentage Act. (Fam. Code, § 7600 et seq.) Once a petition has been filed to declare a child a dependent or ward, and until the petition is dismissed or dependency or wardship is terminated, the juvenile court with jurisdiction over the action has exclusive jurisdiction to hear an action filed under Family Code section 7630.

(b) Parentage inquiry (§§ 316.2, 726.4)

At the initial hearing on a petition filed under section 300 or at the dispositional hearing on a petition filed under section 601 or 602, and at hearings thereafter until or unless parentage has been established, the court must inquire of the child's parents present at the hearing and of any other appropriate person present as to the identity and address of any and all presumed or alleged parents of the child. Questions, at the discretion of the court, may include the following and others that may provide information regarding parentage:

(1) Has there been a judgment of parentage?

(2) Was the mother married or did she have a registered domestic partner at or after the time of conception?

(3) Did the mother believe she was married or believe she had a registered domestic partner at or after the time of conception?

(4) Was the mother cohabiting with another adult at the time of conception?

(5) Has the mother received support payments or promises of support for the child or for herself during her pregnancy or after the birth of the child?

(6) Has a man formally or informally acknowledged paternity, including the execution and filing of a voluntary declaration of paternity under Family Code section 7570 et seq., and agreed to have his name placed on the child's birth certificate?

(7) Have genetic tests been administered, and, if so, what were the results?

(8) Has the child been raised jointly with another adult or in any other co-parenting arrangement?

(c) Voluntary declaration

If a voluntary declaration as described in Family Code section 7570 et seq. has been executed and filed with the California Department of Child Support Services, the declaration establishes the paternity of a child and has the same force and effect as a judgment of paternity by a court. A man is presumed to be the father of the child under Family Code section 7611 if the voluntary declaration has been properly executed and filed.

(d) Issue raised; inquiry

If, at any proceeding regarding the child, the issue of parentage is addressed by the court:

(1) The court must ask the parent or the person alleging parentage, and others present, whether any parentage finding has been made, and, if so, what court made it, or whether a voluntary declaration has been executed and filed under the Family Code;

(2) The court must direct the court clerk to prepare and transmit *Parentage Inquiry—Juvenile* (form JV–500) to the local child support agency requesting an inquiry regarding whether parentage has been established through any superior court order or judgment or through the execution and filing of a voluntary declaration under the Family Code;

(3) The office of child support enforcement must prepare and return the completed *Parentage Inquiry—Juvenile* (form JV–500) within 25 judicial days, with certified copies of any such order or judgment or proof of the filing of any voluntary declaration attached; and

(4) The juvenile court must take judicial notice of the prior determination of parentage.

(e) No prior determination

If the local child support agency states, or if the court determines through statements of the parties or other evidence, that there has been no prior determination of parentage of the child, the juvenile court must take appropriate steps to make such a determination.

(1) Any alleged father and his counsel must complete and submit *Statement Regarding Parentage (Juvenile)* (form JV–505). Form JV–505 must be made available in the courtroom.

(2) To determine parentage, the juvenile court may order the child and any alleged parents to submit to genetic tests and proceed under Family Code section 7550 et seq.

(3) The court may make its determination of parentage or nonparentage based on the testimony, declarations, or statements of the alleged parents. The court must advise any alleged parent that if parentage is determined, the parent will have responsibility for the financial support of the child, and, if the child receives welfare benefits, the parent may be subject to an action to obtain support payments.

(f) Notice to office of child support enforcement

If the court establishes parentage of the child, the court must sign *Parentage—Finding and Judgment (Juvenile)* (form JV–501) and direct the clerk to transmit the signed form to the local child support agency.

(g) Dependency and delinquency; notice to alleged parents

If, after inquiry by the court or through other information obtained by the county welfare department or probation department, one or more persons are identified as alleged parents of a child for whom a petition under section 300, 601, or 602 has been filed, the clerk must provide to each named alleged parent, at the last known address, by certified mail, return receipt requested, a copy of the petition, notice of the next scheduled hearing, and *Statement Regarding Parentage (Juvenile)* (form JV–505) unless:

(1) The petition has been dismissed;

(2) Dependency or wardship has been terminated;

(3) The alleged parent has previously filed a form JV–505 denying parentage and waiving further notice; or

(4) The alleged parent has relinquished custody of the child to the county welfare department.

(h) Dependency and delinquency; alleged parents (§§ 316.2, 726.4)

If a person appears at a hearing in dependency matter or at a hearing under section 601 or 602 and requests a judgment of parentage on form JV–505, the court must determine:

(1) Whether that person is the biological parent of the child; and

(2) Whether that person is the presumed parent of the child, if that finding is requested. *(Formerly Rule 1413, adopted, eff. July 1, 1995. As amended, eff. Jan. 1, 1999; Jan. 1, 2001; Jan. 1, 2006; July 1, 2006. Renumbered Rule 5.635 and amended, eff. Jan. 1, 2007. As amended, eff. Jan. 1, 2015.)*

Commentary

Under subsection (h), when a man alleged to be a child's biological father appears at a detention hearing and requests a parentage determination, a juvenile court *must* make a determination of the dependent child's biological paternity. *In re J.H., 198 Cal.App.4th 635, 130 Cal.Rptr.3d 389 (2011)*. *In re B.C., 205 Cal.App.4th 1306, 140 Cal.Rptr.3d 881 (2012)*, held that a trial court erred in requiring an alleged father to pay for paternity testing in dependency proceedings, because subsection (h) required the court to determine whether he was the child's father.

In re Baby Boy V., 140 Cal.App.4th 1108, 45 Cal.Rptr.3d 198 (2006), holds that a juvenile court improperly denied a request for a paternity test by a man who came forward as soon as he learned of the existence of a child of whom he believed he was the father (a *Kelsey S.* father entitled to presumed father status; see commentary to Family Code Section 7611) and terminated the man's parental rights in order to free the child for adoption. Under subsection (h) of this rule, a court juvenile court must grant permission when a man requests a finding of paternity and must, upon request, determine whether a man is a presumed father.

Research References

Forms

West's California Judicial Council Forms JV-500, Paternity Inquiry.
West's California Judicial Council Forms JV-501, Paternity--Finding and Judgment.

Treatises and Practice Aids

Witkin, California Summary 10th Parent and Child § 46, in General.
Witkin, California Summary 10th Parent and Child § 444, Scope and Organization.
Witkin, California Summary 10th Parent and Child § 583, Alleged Father.
Witkin, California Summary 10th Parent and Child § 603, Identification Of Presumed or Alleged Fathers.
Witkin, California Summary 10th Parent and Child § 882, Findings.
Witkin, California Summary 10th Parent and Child § 886, Conduct Of Hearing.

Rule 5.637. Family finding (§§ 309(e), 628(d))

(a) Within 30 days of a child's removal from the home of his or her parent or guardian, if the child is in or at risk of entering foster care, the social worker or probation officer must use due diligence in conducting an investigation to identify, locate, and notify all the child's adult relatives.

(b) The social worker or probation officer is not required to notify a relative whose personal history of family or domestic violence would make notification inappropriate. *(Adopted, eff. Jan. 1, 2011.)*

Research References

Forms

West's California Judicial Council Forms JV-285, Relative Information.

Treatises and Practice Aids

Witkin, California Summary 10th Parent and Child § 444, Scope and Organization.
Witkin, California Summary 10th Parent and Child § 555, Investigation, Detention, and Release.
Witkin, California Summary 10th Parent and Child § 625, Preparation Of Social Study.
Witkin, California Summary 10th Parent and Child § 763, Investigation, Release, and Conditions.

Chapter 10

MEDICATION, MENTAL HEALTH, AND EDUCATION

Rule 5.640. Psychotropic medications

(a) Definition (§§ 369.5(d), 739.5(d))

For the purposes of this rule, "psychotropic medication" means those medications prescribed to affect the central nervous system to treat psychiatric disorders or illnesses. They may include, but are not limited to, anxiolytic agents, antidepressants, mood stabilizers, antipsychotic medications, anti–Parkinson agents, hypnotics, medications for dementia, and psychostimulants.

(b) Authorization to administer (§§ 369.5, 739.5)

(1) Once a child is declared a dependent child of the court and is removed from the custody of the parents or guardian, only a juvenile court judicial officer is authorized to make orders regarding the administration of psychotropic medication to the child, unless, under (e), the court orders that the parent or legal guardian is authorized to approve or deny the medication.

(2) Once a child is declared a ward of the court, removed from the custody of the parents or guardian, and placed into foster care, as defined in Welfare and Institutions Code section 727.4, only a juvenile court judicial officer is authorized to make orders regarding the administration of psychotropic medication to the child, unless, under (e), the court orders that the parent or legal guardian is authorized to approve or deny the medication.

~~(3) The court must grant or deny the application using *Order on Application for Psychotropic Medication* (form JV–223).~~

(c) Procedure to obtain authorization

(1) To obtain authorization to administer psychotropic medication to a dependent child of the court who is removed from the custody of the parents or legal guardian, or to a ward of the court who is removed from the custody of the parents or legal guardian and placed into foster care, the following forms must be completed and filed with the court:

(A) *Application for Psychotropic Medication* (form JV–220); ~~and~~

(B) *Physician's Statement—Attachment* (form JV–220(A)), unless the request is to continue the same medication and maximum dosage by the same physician ~~that~~ who completed the most recent JV–220(A); then the physician may complete *Physician's Request to Continue Medication—Attachment* (form JV–220(B))~~.~~; and

(C) *Proof of Notice of Application* (form JV–221).

(2) The child, caregiver, parents or legal guardians, child's Indian tribe, and Court Appointed Special Advocate, if any, may provide input on the mediations being prescribed.

(A) Input can be by *Child's Opinion About the Medicine* (form JV–218) or *Statement About Medicine Prescribed* (form JV–219); letter; talking to the judge at a court hearing; or through the social worker, probation officer, attorney of record, or Court Appointed Special Advocate.

(B) If form JV–218 or form JV–219 is filed, it must be filed within four court days after receipt of notice of the pending application for psychotropic medication. If a hearing is set on the application, form JV–218 and form JV–219 may be filed at any time before, or at, the hearing.

(C) Input from a Court Appointed Special Advocate can also be by a court report under local rule.

(3) *Input on Application for Psychotropic Medication* (form JV–222) may be filed by a parent or guardian, his or her attorney of record, a child's attorney of record, a child's Child Abuse Prevention and Treatment Act guardian ad litem appointed under rule 5.662 of the California Rules of Court, or the Indian child's tribe. If form JV–222 is filed, it must be filed within four court days of receipt of notice of the application.

(4) Additional information may be provided to the court through the use of local forms that are consistent with this rule.

(5) Local county practice and local rules of court determine the procedures for completing and filing the forms ~~and for the provision of notice~~, except as otherwise provided in this rule. ~~The person or persons responsible for providing notice as required by local court rules or local practice protocols are encouraged to use the most expeditious manner of service possible to ensure timely notice.~~

(6) *Application for Psychotropic Medication* (form JV–220) may be completed by the prescribing physician, medical office staff, child welfare services staff, probation officer, or the child's caregiver. If the applicant is the social worker or probation officer, he or she must complete all items on form JV–220. If the applicant is the prescribing physician, medical office staff, or child's caregiver, he or she must complete and sign only page one of form JV–220.

(7) The physician prescribing the administration of psychotropic c medication for the child must complete and sign *Physician's Statement—Attachment* (form JV–220(A)) or, if it is a request to continue the same medication by the same physician ~~that~~ who completed the most recent JV–220(A), then the physician ~~may~~ must complete and sign *Physician's Statement—Attachment* (form JV–220(A)) or *Physician's Request to Continue Medication—Attachment* (form JV–220(B)).

~~(7)~~(8) The court must approve, deny, or set the matter for a hearing within seven court days of the receipt of the completed form JV–220 and form JV–220(A) or form JV–220(B).

(9) The court must grant or deny the application using *Order on Application for Psychotropic Medication* (form JV–223).

~~(8)~~(10) Notice of the application must be provided to the parents or legal guardians, their attorneys of record, the child's attorney of record, the child's Child Abuse Prevention and Treatment Act guardian ad litem, the child's current caregiver, the child's Court Appointed Special Advocate, if any, and where a child has been determined to be an Indian child, the Indian child's tribe (see also 25 U.S.C. § 1903(4)–(5); Welf. and Inst. Code, §§ 224.1(a) and (e) and 224.3).

(A) If the child is living in a group home or short-term residential therapeutic center, notice to the caregiver must be by notice to the group home administrator, or to the administrator's designee, as defined in California Code of Regulations, title 22, ~~regulation~~ section 84064.

(B) Local county practice and local rules of court determine the procedures for the provision of notice, except as otherwise provided in this rule. The person or persons responsible for providing notice as required by local court rules or local practice protocols are encouraged to use the most expeditious manner of service possible to ensure timely notice.

(C) Notice must be provided as follows:

~~(A)~~(i) Notice to the parents or legal guardians and their attorneys of record must include:

~~(i)~~a. A statement that a physician is asking to treat the child's emotional or behavioral problems by beginning or continuing the administration of psychotropic medication to the child and the name of the psychotropic medication;

~~(ii)~~b. A statement that an *Application for Psychotropic Medication* (form JV–220) and a *Physician's Statement—Attachment* (form JV–220(A)) or *Physician's Request to Continue Medication—Attachment* (form JV–220(B)) are pending before the court;

~~(iii)~~c. A copy of *Guide to Psychotropic Medication Forms* (form JV–217–INFO);

~~(iv)~~d. A blank copy of *Statement About Medicine Prescribed* (form JV–219); and

~~(v)~~e. A blank copy of *Input on Application for Psychotropic Medication* (form JV–222).

~~(B)~~(ii) Notice to the child's current caregiver and Court Appointed Special Advocate, if one has been appointed, must include only:

~~(i)~~a. A statement that a physician is asking to treat the child's emotional or behavioral problems by beginning or continuing the administration of psychotropic medication to the child and the name of the psychotropic medication;

~~(ii)~~b. A statement that an *Application for Psychotropic Medication* (form JV–220) and a *Physician's Statement—Attachment* (form JV–220(A)) or *Physician's Request to Continue Medication—Attachment* (form JV–220(B)) are pending before the court;

~~(iii)~~c. A copy of *Guide to Psychotropic Medication Forms* (form JV–217–INFO);

~~(iv)~~d. A blank copy of *Child's Opinion About the Medicine* (form JV–218); and

~~(v)~~e. A blank copy of *Statement About Medicine Prescribed* (form JV–219).

~~(C)~~(iii) Notice to the child's attorney of record and any Child Abuse Prevention and Treatment Act guardian ad litem for the child must include:

~~(i)~~a. A completed copy of *Application for Psychotropic Medication* (form JV–220);

~~(ii)~~b. A completed copy of *Physician's Statement—Attachment* (form JV–220(A)) or *Physician's Request to Continue Medication—Attachment* (form JV–220(B));

~~(iii)~~c. A copy of *Guide to Psychotropic Medication Forms* (form JV–217–INFO) or information on how to obtain a copy of the form;

~~(iv)~~d. A blank copy of *Input on Application for Psychotropic Medication* (form JV–222) or information on how to obtain a copy of the form; and

~~(v)~~e. A blank copy of *Child's Opinion About the Medicine* (form JV–218) or information on how to obtain a copy of the form.

~~(D)~~(iv) Notice to the Indian child's tribe must include:

~~(I)~~a. A statement that a physician is asking to treat the child's emotional or behavioral problems by beginning or continuing the administration of psychotropic medication to the child, and the name of the psychotropic medication;

~~(ii)~~b. A statement that an *Application for Psychotropic Medication* (form JV–220) and a *Physician's Statement—Attachment* (form JV–220(A)) or *Physician's Request to Continue Medication—Attachment* (form JV–220(B)) are pending before the court;

~~(iii)~~c. A copy of *Guide to Psychotropic Medication Forms* (form JV–217–INFO) or information on how to obtain a copy of the form;

~~(iv)~~d. A blank copy of *Input on Application for Psychotropic Medication* (form JV–222) or information on how to obtain a copy of the form; and

~~(v)~~e. A blank copy of *Child's Opinion About the Medicine* (form JV–218) or information on how to obtain a copy of the form.

~~(vi)~~f. A blank copy of *Statement About Medicine Prescribed* (form JV–219) or information on how to obtain a copy of the form.

~~(E)~~(v) Proof of notice of the application regarding psychotropic medication must be filed with the court using *Proof of Notice of Application* (form JV–221).

~~(9)~~(11) If all the required information is not included in the request for authorization, the court must order the applicant to provide the missing information and set a hearing on the application.

~~(10)~~(12) The court may grant the application without a hearing or may set the matter for hearing at the court's discretion. If the court sets the matter for a hearing, the clerk of the court must provide notice of the date, time, and location of the hearing to the parents or legal guardians, their attorneys of record, the dependent child if 12 years of age or older, a ward of the juvenile court of any age, the child's attorney of record, the child's current caregiver, the child's social worker or probation officer, the social worker's or probation officer's attorney of record, the child's Child Abuse Prevention and Treatment Act guardian ad litem, the child's Court Appointed Special Advocate, if any, and the Indian child's tribe at least two court days before the hearing. Notice must be provided to the child's probation officer and the district attorney, if the child is a ward of the juvenile court.

(d) Conduct of hearing on application

At the hearing on the application, the procedures described in rule 5.570 and section 349 must be followed. The court may deny, grant, or modify the application for authorization. If the court grants or modifies the application for authorization, the court must set a date for review of the child's progress and condition. This review must occur at every status review hearing and may occur at any other time at the court's discretion.

(e) Delegation of authority (§§ 369.5, 739.5)

~~After consideration of an application and attachments and a review of the case file,~~ If a child is removed from the custody of his or her parent or legal guardian, the court may order that the parent ~~be~~ is authorized to approve or deny the administration of psychotropic medication. The order must be based on the ~~following~~ findings in section 369.5 or section 739.5, which must be included in the order.~~: (1) the parent poses no danger to the child, and (2) the parent has the capacity to understand the request and the information provided and to authorize the administration of psychotropic medication to the child, consistent with the best interest of the child.~~ The court may use *Order Delegating Judicial Authority Over Psychotropic Medication* (form JV–216) to document the findings and order.

(f) Continued treatment

If the court grants the request or modifies and then grants the request, the order for authorization is effective until terminated or modified by court order or until 180 days from the order, whichever is earlier.

(g) Progress review

(1) After approving any application for authorization, regardless of whether the approval is made at a hearing, the court must set a progress review.

(2) A progress review must occur at every status review hearing and may occur at any other time at the court's discretion.

(3) If the progress review is held at the time of the status review hearing, notice under section 293 or 295 must include a statement that the hearing will also be a progress review on previously ordered psychotropic medication, and must include a blank copy of *Child's Opinion About the Medicine* (form JV–218) and a blank copy of *Statement About Medicine Prescribed* (form JV–219).

(4) If the progress review is not held at the time of the status review hearing, notice must be provided as required under section 293 or 295; must include a statement that the hearing will be a progress review on previously ordered psychotropic medication; and must include a blank copy of *Child's Opinion About the Medicine* (form JV–218) and a blank copy of *Statement About Medicine Prescribed* (form JV–219).

(5) Before each progress review, the social worker or probation officer must file a completed *County Report About Psychotropic Medication* (form JV–224) at least 10 calendar days before the hearing. If the progress review is set at the same time as a status review hearing, form JV–224 must be attached to and filed with the report.

(6) The child, caregiver, parents or legal guardians, and Court Appointed Special Advocate, if any, may provide input at the progress review as stated in (c)(2).

(7) At the progress review, the procedures described in section 349 must be followed.

(h) Copy of order to caregiver

(1) Upon the approval or denial of the application, the county child welfare agency, probation department, or other person or entity who submitted the request must provide the child's caregiver with a copy of the court order approving or denying the request.

(2) The copy of the order must be provided in person or mailed within two court days of when the order is signed.

(3) If the court approves the request, the copy of the order must include the last two pages of form JV–220(A) or the last two pages of form JV–220(B) and all medication information sheets (medication monographs) that were attached to form JV–220(A) or form JV–220(B).

(4) If the child resides in a group home or short-term residential therapeutic program, a copy of the order, the last two pages of form JV–220(A) or the last two pages of form JV–220(B), and all medication information sheets (medication monographs) that were attached to ~~the~~ form JV–220(A) or form JV–220(B) must be provided to the group home administrator, or to the administrator's designee, as defined in California Code of Regulations, ~~regulation~~ title 22, section 84064.

(5) If the child changes placement, the social worker or probation officer must provide the new caregiver with a copy of the order, the last two pages of form JV–220(A) or the last two pages of form JV–220(B), and the medication information sheets (medication monographs) that were attached to form JV–220(A) or form JV–220(B).

(i) Emergency treatment (§ 369(d))

(1) Psychotropic medications may be administered without court authorization in an emergency situation. An emergency situation occurs when:

(A) A physician finds that the child requires psychotropic medication to treat a psychiatric disorder or illness; and

(B) The purpose of the medication is:

(i) To protect the life of the child or others, or

(ii) To prevent serious harm to the child or others, or

(iii) To treat current or imminent substantial suffering; and

(C) It is impractical to obtain authorization from the court before administering the psychotropic medication to the child.

(2) Court authorization must be sought as soon as practical but in no case more than two court days after the emergency administration of the psychotropic medication.

(j) Section 601–602 wardships; local rules

A local rule of court may be adopted providing that authorization for the administration of such medication to a child declared a ward of the court under sections 601 or 602 and removed from the custody of the parent or guardian for placement in a facility that is not considered a foster-care placement may be similarly restricted to the juvenile court. If the local court adopts such a local rule, then the procedures under this rule apply; any reference to social worker also applies to probation officer.

(k) Public health nurses

Information may be provided to public health nurses as governed by Civil Code section 56.103. *(Formerly Rule 1432.5, adopted, eff. Jan. 1, 2001. As amended, eff. Jan. 1, 2003. Renumbered Rule 5.640 and amended, eff. Jan. 1, 2007. As amended, eff. Jan. 1, 2008; Jan. 1, 2009; Jan. 1, 2014; July 1, 2016; Jan. 1, 2018.)*

Research References

Forms

West's California Judicial Council Forms JV-218, Child's Opinion About the Medicine.

West's California Judicial Council Forms JV-219, Statement About Medicine Prescribed.

West's California Judicial Council Forms JV-220, Application and Order for Authorization to Administer Psychotropic Medication.

West's California Judicial Council Forms JV-221, Proof Of Notice: Application Regarding Psychotropic Medication.

West's California Judicial Council Forms JV-222, Opposition to Application Regarding Psychotropic Medication.

West's California Judicial Council Forms JV-223, Order Regarding Application for Psychotropic Medication.

West's California Judicial Council Forms JV-224, Order Regarding Eligibility for Special Immigrant Juvenile Status.

West's California Judicial Council Forms JV-220(A), Prescribing Physician's Statement--Attachment.

West's California Judicial Council Forms JV-220(B), Physician's Request to Continue Medication--Attachment.

West's California Judicial Council Forms JV-217-INFO, Guide to Psychotropic Medication Forms.

West's California Judicial Council Forms JV-219-INFO, Information About Psychotropic Medication Forms.

Treatises and Practice Aids

Witkin, California Summary 10th Parent and Child § 444, Scope and Organization.

Witkin, California Summary 10th Parent and Child § 629, Limitations on Parental Control.

Rule 5.645. Mental health or condition of child; court procedures

(a) Doubt concerning the mental health of a child (§§ 357, 705, 6550, 6551)

Whenever the court believes that the child who is the subject of a petition filed under section 300, 601, or 602 is mentally disabled or may be mentally ill, the court may stay the proceedings and order the child taken to a facility designated by the court and approved by the State Department of Mental Health as a facility for 72–hour treatment and evaluation. The professional in charge of the facility must submit a written evaluation of the child to the court.

(b) Findings regarding a mental disorder (§ 6551)

Article 1 of chapter 2 of part 1 of division 5 (commencing with section 5150) applies.

(1) If the professional reports that the child is not in need of intensive treatment, the child must be returned to the juvenile court on or before the expiration of the 72–hour

period, and the court must proceed with the case under section 300, 601, or 602.

(2) If the professional in charge of the facility finds that the child is in need of intensive treatment for a mental disorder, the child may be certified for not more than 14 days of involuntary intensive treatment according to the conditions of sections 5250(c) and 5260(b). The stay of the juvenile court proceedings must remain in effect during this time.

(A) During or at the end of the 14 days of involuntary intensive treatment, a certification may be sought for additional treatment under sections commencing with 5270.10 or for the initiation of proceedings to have a conservator appointed for the child under sections commencing with 5350. The juvenile court may retain jurisdiction over the child during proceedings under sections 5270.10 et seq. and 5350 et seq.

(B) For a child subject to a petition under section 602, if the child is found to be gravely disabled under sections 5300 et seq., a conservator is appointed under those sections, and the professional in charge of the child's treatment or of the treatment facility determines that proceedings under section 602 would be detrimental to the child, the juvenile court must suspend jurisdiction while the conservatorship remains in effect. The suspension of jurisdiction may end when the conservatorship is terminated, and the original 602 matter may be calendared for further proceedings.

(c) Findings regarding mental retardation (§ 6551)

Article 1 of chapter 2 of part 1 of division 5 (commencing with section 5150) applies.

(1) If the professional finds that the child is mentally retarded and recommends commitment to a state hospital, the court may direct the filing in the appropriate court of a petition for commitment of a child as a mentally retarded person to the State Department of Developmental Services for placement in a state hospital.

(2) If the professional finds that the child is not mentally retarded, the child must be returned to the juvenile court on or before the expiration of the 72–hour period, and the court must proceed with the case under section 300, 601, or 602.

(3) The jurisdiction of the juvenile court must be suspended while the child is subject to the jurisdiction of the appropriate court under a petition for commitment of a mentally retarded person, or under remand for 90 days for intensive treatment or commitment ordered by that court.

(d) Doubt as to capacity to cooperate with counsel (§§ 601, 602; Pen. Code, § 1367)

(1) If the court finds that there is substantial evidence that a child who is the subject of a petition filed under section 601 or 602 lacks sufficient present ability to consult with counsel and assist in preparing his or her defense with a reasonable degree of rational understanding, or lacks a rational as well as factual understanding of the nature of the charges or proceedings against him or her, the court must suspend the proceedings and conduct a hearing regarding the child's competence. Evidence is substantial if it raises a reasonable doubt about the child's competence to stand trial.

(A) The court must appoint an expert to examine the child to evaluate whether the child suffers from a mental disorder, developmental disability, developmental immaturity, or other condition and, if so, whether the condition or conditions impair the child's competency.

(B) To be appointed as an expert, an individual must be a:

(i) Licensed psychiatrist who has successfully completed four years of medical school and either four years of general psychiatry residency, including one year of internship and two years of child and adolescent fellowship training, or three years of general psychiatry residency, including one year of internship and one year of residency that focus on children and adolescents and one year of child and adolescent fellowship training; or

(ii) Clinical, counseling, or school psychologist who has received a doctoral degree in psychology from an educational institution accredited by an organization recognized by the Council for Higher Education Accreditation and who is licensed as a psychologist.

(C) The expert, whether a licensed psychiatrist or psychologist, must:

(i) Possess demonstrable professional experience addressing child and adolescent developmental issues, including the emotional, behavioral, and cognitive impairments of children and adolescents;

(ii) Have expertise in the cultural and social characteristics of children and adolescents;

(iii) Possess a curriculum vitae reflecting training and experience in the forensic evaluation of children;

(iv) Be familiar with juvenile competency standards and accepted criteria used in evaluating juvenile competence;

(v) Possess a comprehensive understanding of effective interventions as well as treatment, training, and programs for the attainment of competency available to children and adolescents; and

(vi) Be proficient in the language preferred by the child, or if that is not feasible, employ the services of a certified interpreter and use assessment tools that are linguistically and culturally appropriate for the child.

(2) Nothing in this rule precludes involvement of clinicians with other professional qualifications from participation as consultants or witnesses or in other capacities relevant to the case.

(3) Following the hearing on competence, the court must proceed as directed in section 709. *(Formerly Rule 1498, adopted, eff. Jan. 1, 1999. Renumbered Rule 5.645 and amended, eff. Jan. 1, 2007. As amended, eff. Jan. 1, 2009; Jan. 1, 2012.)*

Research References

Treatises and Practice Aids

Witkin, California Summary 10th Parent and Child § 567, Statutory Rights.

Witkin, California Summary 10th Parent and Child § 799, Competency to Stand Trial.

Rule 5.649. Right to make educational or developmental-services decisions

The court must identify the educational rights holder for the child on form JV–535 at each hearing in a dependency or delinquency proceeding. Unless his or her rights have been limited by the court under this rule, the parent or guardian holds the educational and developmental-services decisionmaking rights for his or her child. In addition, a nonminor or nonminor dependent youth holds the rights to make educational and developmental-services decisions for himself or herself unless rule 5.650(b) applies.

(a) Order (§§ 361, 366, 366.27, 366.3, 726, 727.2; 20 U.S.C. § 1415; 34 C.F.R. § 300.300)

At the dispositional hearing and each subsequent review or permanency hearing, the court must determine whether the rights of a parent or guardian to make educational or developmental-services decisions for the child should be limited.

If necessary to protect a child who is adjudged a dependent or ward of the court under section 300, 601, or 602, the court may limit a parent's or guardian's rights to make educational or developmental-services decisions for the child by making appropriate, specific orders on *Order Designating Educational Rights Holder* (form JV–535).

(b) Temporary order (§ 319)

At the initial hearing on a petition filed under section 325 or at any time before a child is adjudged a dependent or the petition is dismissed, the court may, on making the findings required by section 319(g)(1), use form JV–535 to temporarily limit a parent's or guardian's rights to make educational or developmental-services decisions for the child. An order made under section 319(g) expires on dismissal of the petition, but in no circumstances later than the conclusion of the hearing held under section 361.

If the court does temporarily limit the parent's or guardian's rights to make educational or developmental-services decisions, the court must, at the dispositional hearing, reconsider the need to limit those rights and must identify the authorized educational rights holder on form JV–535.

(c) No delay of initial assessment

The child's initial assessment to determine any need for special education or developmental services need not be delayed to obtain parental or guardian consent or for the appointment of an educational rights holder if one or more of the following circumstances is met:

(1) The court has limited, even temporarily, the educational or developmental-services decisionmaking rights of the parent or guardian, and consent for an initial assessment has been given by an individual appointed by the court to represent the child;

(2) The local educational agency or regional center, after reasonable efforts, cannot locate the parent or guardian; or

(3) Parental rights have been terminated or the guardianship has been set aside.

(d) Judicial Determination

If the court determines that the child is in need of any assessments, evaluations, or services—including special education, mental health, developmental, and other related services—the court must direct an appropriate person to take the necessary steps to request those assessments, evaluations, or services.

(e) Filing of order

Following the dispositional hearing and each statutory review hearing, the party that has requested a modification, limitation, or restoration of educational or developmental-services decisionmaking rights must complete form JV–535 and any required attachments to reflect the court's orders and submit the completed form within five court days for the court's review and signature. If no request is made, the child's or youth's attorney must complete and file the form. The court may direct the appropriate party to attach *Attachment to Order Designating Educational Rights Holder* (form JV–535(A)) to document the court's findings and orders. *(Adopted, eff. Jan. 1, 2014.)*

Research References

Treatises and Practice Aids

Witkin, California Summary 10th Parent and Child § 567, Statutory Rights.

Witkin, California Summary 10th Parent and Child § 629, Limitations on Parental Control.

Witkin, California Summary 10th Parent and Child § 673, Child in Foster Care.

Witkin, California Summary 10th Parent and Child § 782, Statutory Rights.

Witkin, California Summary 10th Parent and Child § 893, Limitations on Parental Control.

Witkin, California Summary 10th Parent and Child § 607A, (New) Educational and Developmental Services Decisions.

Rule 5.650. Appointed educational rights holder

(a) Order and appointment (§§ 319, 361, 366, 366.27, 366.3, 726, 727.2; Gov. Code, §§ 7579.5–7579.6; 20 U.S.C. § 1415; 34 C.F.R. § 300.519)

Whenever it limits, even temporarily, the rights of a parent or guardian to make educational or developmental-services decisions for a child, the court must use form JV–535 to appoint a responsible adult as educational rights holder or to document that one of the following circumstances exists:

(1) The child is a dependent child or ward of the court and has a court-ordered permanent plan of placement in a planned permanent living arrangement. The caregiver may, without a court order, exercise educational decisionmaking rights under Education Code section 56055 and developmental-services decisionmaking rights under section 361 or 726, and is not prohibited from exercising those rights by section 361, 726, or 4701.6(b), or by 34 Code of Federal Regulations section 300.519 or 303.422; or

(2) The court cannot identify a responsible adult to serve as the child's educational rights holder under section 319, 361, or 726 or under Education Code section 56055; and

(A) The child is a dependent child or ward of the court and is or may be eligible for special education and related services or already has a valid individualized education program, and the court:

(i) Refers the child to the local educational agency for the appointment of a surrogate parent under section 361 or 726, Government Code section 7579.5, and title 20 United States Code section 1415; and

(ii) Will, with the input of any interested person, make developmental-services decisions for the child; or

(B) The appointment of a surrogate parent is not warranted, and the court will, with the input of any interested person, make educational and developmental-services decisions for the child.

(C) If the court must temporarily make educational or developmental-services decisions for a child before disposition, it must order that every effort be made to identify a responsible adult to make future educational or developmental-services decisions for the child.

(b) Nonminor and nonminor dependent youth (§§ 361, 726, 366.3)

The court may, using form JV–535, appoint or continue the appointment of an educational rights holder to make educational or developmental-services decisions for a nonminor or nonminor dependent youth if:

(1) The youth has chosen not to make educational or developmental-services decisions for himself or herself or is deemed by the court to be incompetent; and

(2) With respect to developmental-services decisions, the court also finds that the appointment or continuance of a rights holder would be in the best interests of the youth.

(c) Limits on appointment (§§ 319, 361, 726; Ed. Code, § 56055; Gov. Code, § 7579.5(i)–(j); 34 C.F.R. §§ 300.519, 303.422)

(1) The court must determine whether a responsible adult relative, nonrelative extended family member, or other adult known to the child is available and willing to serve as the educational rights holder and, if one of those adults is available and willing to serve, should consider appointing that person before appointing or temporarily appointing a responsible adult not known to the child.

(2) The court may not appoint any individual as the educational rights holder if that person is excluded under, or would have a conflict of interest as defined by, section 361(a) or 726(c), Education Code section 56055, Government Code section 7579.5(i)–(j), 20 United States Code section 1415(b)(2), or 34 Code of Federal Regulations section 300.519 or 303.422.

(d) Referral for appointment of surrogate parent (§§ 361, 726; Gov. Code, § 7579.5; 20 U.S.C. § 1415)

(1) If the court has limited a parent's or guardian's right to make educational decisions for a child and cannot identify a responsible adult to act as the educational rights holder, and the child is or may be eligible for special education and related services or already has an individualized education program, the court must use form JV–535 to refer the child to the responsible local educational agency for prompt appointment of a surrogate parent under Government Code section 7579.5.

(2) If the court refers a child to the local educational agency for appointment of a surrogate parent, the court must order that *Local Educational Agency Response to JV–535—Appointment of Surrogate Parent* (form JV–536) be attached to form JV–535 and served by first-class mail on the local educational agency no later than five court days from the date the order is signed.

(3) The court must direct the local educational agency that when the agency receives form JV–535 requesting prompt appointment of a surrogate parent, the agency must make reasonable efforts to identify and appoint a surrogate parent within 30 calendar days of service of the referral.

(A) Whenever the local educational agency appoints a surrogate parent for a dependent or ward under Government Code section 7579.5(a)(1), it must notify the court on form JV–536 within five court days of the appointment and, at the same time, must send copies of the notice to the child's attorney and to the social worker or probation officer identified on the form.

(B) If the local educational agency does not appoint a surrogate parent within 30 days of receipt of a judicial request, it must notify the court within the next five court days on form JV–536 of the following:

(i) Its inability to identify and appoint a surrogate parent; and

(ii) Its continuing reasonable efforts to identify and appoint a surrogate parent.

(4) Whenever a surrogate parent resigns or the local educational agency terminates the appointment of a surrogate parent, replaces a surrogate parent, or appoints another surrogate parent, it must notify the court, the child's attorney, and the social worker or probation officer on form JV–536 within five court days of the resignation, termination, replacement, or appointment. The child's attorney, the social worker, or the probation officer may request a hearing for appointment of a new educational rights holder by filing *Request for Hearing Regarding Child's Access to Services* (form JV–539) and must provide notice of the hearing as provided in (g)(2). The court may, on its own motion, direct the clerk to set a hearing.

(e) Transfer of parent's or guardian's educational or developmental-services decisionmaking rights to educational rights holder

When the court appoints an educational rights holder after limiting a parent's or guardian's educational or developmental-services decisionmaking rights, those parental decisionmaking rights—including the right to notice of educational or developmental-services meetings and activities, to participation in educational or developmental-services meetings and activities, and to decisionmaking authority regarding the child's education or developmental services, including the authority under sections 4512 and 4701.6, Education Code section 56028, 20 United States Code sections 1232g and 1401(23), and 34 Code of Federal Regulations section 300.30—are transferred to the educational rights holder unless the court specifies otherwise in its order.

(1) When returning a child to a parent or guardian, the court must consider the child's educational and developmental-services needs. The parent's or guardian's educational and developmental-services decisionmaking rights are reinstated when the court returns custody to the parent or guardian unless the court finds specifically that continued limitation of parental decisionmaking rights is necessary to protect the child.

(2) If the court appoints a guardian for the child under rule 5.735 or 5.815, all of the parent's or previous guardian's educational and developmental-services decisionmaking rights transfer to the newly appointed guardian unless the

court determines that limitation of the new guardian's decisionmaking rights is necessary to protect the child.

(f) Authority and responsibilities (§§ 317, 319, 360, 361, 635, 706.5, 726, 4514, 4646–4648, 4700–4731, 5328; Ed. Code, §§ 56055, 56340, 56345; Gov. Code, §§ 7579.5, 95014–95020; 34 C.F.R. § 300.519)

(1) The educational rights holder acts as and holds the rights of the parent or guardian with respect to all decisions regarding the child's education and developmental services, and is entitled:

(A) To access records and to authorize the disclosure of information to the same extent as a parent or guardian under the Family Educational Rights and Privacy Act (FERPA), 20 United States Code section 1232g;

(B) To be given notice of and participate in all meetings or proceedings relating to school discipline;

(C) To advocate for the interests of a child or youth with exceptional needs in matters relating to:

(i) The identification and assessment of those needs;

(ii) Instructional or service planning and program development—including the development of an individualized family service plan, an individualized educational program, an individual program plan, or the provision of other services and supports, as applicable;

(iii) Placement in the least restrictive program appropriate to the child's or youth's educational or developmental needs;

(iv) The review or revision of the individualized family service plan, the individualized education program, or the individual program plan; and

(v) The provision of a free, appropriate public education.

(D) To attend and participate in the child's or youth's individualized family service plan, individualized education program, individual program plan, and other educational or service planning meetings; to consult with persons involved in the provision of the child's or youth's education or developmental services; and to sign any written consent to educational or developmental services and plans; and

(E) Notwithstanding any other provision of law, to consent to the child's or youth's individualized family service plan, individualized education program, or individual program plan, including any related nonemergency medical services, mental health treatment services, and occupational or physical therapy services provided under sections 7570–7587 of the Government Code.

(2) The educational rights holder is responsible for investigating the child's or youth's educational and developmental-services needs, determining whether those needs are being met, and acting on behalf of the child or youth in all matters relating to the provision of educational or developmental services, as applicable, to ensure:

(A) The stability of the child's or youth's school placement. At any hearing following a change of educational placement, the educational rights holder must submit a statement to the court indicating whether the proposed change of placement is in the child's or youth's best interest and whether any efforts have been made to keep the pupil in the school of origin;

(B) Placement in the least restrictive educational program appropriate to the child's or youth's individual needs;

(C) The child's or youth's access to academic resources, services, and extracurricular and enrichment activities;

(D) The child's or youth's access to any educational and developmental services and supports needed to meet state standards for academic achievement and functional performance or, with respect to developmental services, to promote community integration, an independent, productive, and normal life, and a stable and healthy environment;

(E) The prompt and appropriate resolution of school disciplinary matters;

(F) The provision of any other elements of a free, appropriate public education; and

(G) The provision of any appropriate early intervention or developmental services required by law, including the California Early Intervention Services Act or the Lanterman Developmental Disabilities Services Act.

(3) The educational rights holder is also responsible for:

(A) Meeting with the child or youth at least once and as often as necessary to make educational or developmental-services decisions that are in the best interest of the child or youth;

(B) Being culturally sensitive to the child or youth;

(C) Complying with all federal and state confidentiality laws, including, but not limited to, sections 362.5, 827, 4514, and 5328, as well as Government Code section 7579.5(f);

(D) Participating in, and making decisions regarding, all matters affecting the child's or youth's educational or developmental-services needs—including, as applicable, the individualized family service planning process, the individualized education program planning process, the individual program planning process, the fair hearing process (including mediation and any other informal dispute resolution meetings), and as otherwise specified in the court order—in a manner consistent with the child's or youth's best interest; and

(E) Maintaining knowledge and skills that ensure adequate representation of the child's or youth's needs and interests with respect to education and developmental services.

(4) Before each statutory review hearing, the educational rights holder must do one or more of the following:

(A) Provide information and recommendations concerning the child's or youth's educational or developmental-services needs to the assigned social worker or probation officer;

(B) Make written recommendations to the court concerning the child's or youth's educational or developmental-services needs;

(C) Attend the review hearing and participate in any part of the hearing that concerns the child's or youth's education or developmental services.

(5) The educational rights holder may provide the contact information for the child's or youth's attorney to the local educational agency.

(g) Term of service; resignation (§§ 319, 361, 726; Gov. Code § 7579.5)

(1) An appointed educational rights holder must make educational or developmental-services decisions for the child or youth until:

(A) The dismissal of the petition or the conclusion of the dispositional hearing, if the rights holder is appointed under section 319(g);

(B) The rights of the parent or guardian to make educational or developmental-services decisions for the child are fully restored;

(C) The dependent or ward reaches 18 years of age, unless he or she chooses not to make his or her own educational or developmental-services decisions or is deemed incompetent by the court, in which case the court may, if it also finds that continuation would be in the best interests of the youth, continue the appointment until the youth reaches 21 years of age or the court's jurisdiction is terminated;

(D) The court appoints another responsible adult as educational rights holder for the child or youth under this rule;

(E) The court appoints a successor guardian or conservator; or

(F) The court designates an identified foster parent, relative caregiver, or nonrelative extended family member to make educational or developmental-services decisions because:

(i) Reunification services have been terminated and the child is placed in a planned permanent living arrangement with the identified caregiver under section 366.21(g)(5), 366.22, 366.26, 366.3(i), 727.3(b)(5), or 727.3(b)(6); and

(ii) The foster parent, relative caregiver, or nonrelative extended family member is not otherwise excluded from making education or developmental-services decisions by the court, by section 361 or 726, or by 34 Code of Federal Regulations section 300.519 or 303.422.

(2) If an appointed educational rights holder resigns his or her appointment, he or she must give notice to the court and to the child's attorney and may use *Educational Rights Holder Statement* (form JV–537) to provide this notice. Once notice is received, the child's or youth's attorney, or the social worker or probation officer may request a hearing for appointment of a new educational rights holder by filing form JV–539.

The attorney for the party requesting the hearing must provide notice of the hearing to

(A) The parents or guardians, unless otherwise indicated on the most recent form JV–535, parental rights have been terminated, or the child has reached 18 years of age;

(B) Each attorney of record;

(C) The social worker or probation officer;

(D) The CASA volunteer; and

(E) All other persons or entities entitled to notice under section 293.

The hearing must be set within 14 days of receipt of the request for hearing. The court may, on its own motion, direct the clerk to set a hearing.

(h) Service of order

Whenever the order identifies or appoints a new or different educational rights holder or includes any other changes, the clerk will provide a copy of the completed and signed form JV–535, form JV–535(A) if attached, and any received form JV–536 or JV–537 to:

(1) The child, if 10 years of age or older, or youth;

(2) The attorney for the child or youth;

(3) The social worker or probation officer;

(4) The Indian child's tribe, if applicable, as defined in rule 5.502;

(5) The local foster youth educational liaison, as defined in Education Code section 48853.5;

(6) The county office of education foster youth services coordinator;

(7) The regional center service coordinator, if applicable; and

(8) The educational rights holder.

The completed and signed form must be provided no later than five court days from the date the order is signed. The clerk must also ensure that any immediately preceding educational rights holder, surrogate parent, or authorized representative, if any, is notified that the previous court order has been vacated and their appointment terminated.

The clerk will make copies of the form available to the parents or guardians, unless otherwise indicated on the form, parental rights have been terminated, or the child has reached 18 years of age and reunification services have been terminated; to the CASA volunteer; and, if requested, to all other persons or entities entitled to notice under section 293.

(i) Education and training of educational rights holder

If the educational rights holder, including a parent or guardian, asks for assistance in obtaining education and training in the laws incorporated in rule 5.651(a), the court must direct the clerk, social worker, or probation officer to inform the educational rights holder of all available resources, including resources available through the California Department of Education, the California Department of Developmental Services, the local educational agency, and the local regional center.

(j) Notice of and participation in hearings

(1) The educational rights holder must receive notice of all regularly scheduled juvenile court hearings and other judicial hearings that might affect the child's or youth's education and developmental services, including joint assessment hearings under rule 5.512 and joinder proceedings under rule 5.575.

(2) The educational rights holder may use form JV–537 to explain any educational or developmental-services needs to the court. The court must permit the educational rights holder to attend and participate in those portions of a court hearing, nonjudicial hearing, or mediation that concern

education or developmental services. *(Formerly Rule 1499, adopted, eff. July 1, 2002. As amended, eff. Jan. 1, 2004. Renumbered Rule 5.650 and amended, eff. Jan. 1, 2007. As amended, eff. Jan. 1, 2008; Jan. 1, 2014; Jan. 1, 2015.)*

Research References

Forms

West's California Judicial Council Forms JV-536, Local Educational Agency Response to Jv-535--Appointment Of Surrogate Parent.
West's California Judicial Council Forms JV-537, Educational Rights Holder Statement.
West's California Judicial Council Forms JV-710, Juvenile Fitness Hearing Order.

Treatises and Practice Aids

Witkin, California Summary 10th Parent and Child § 629, Limitations on Parental Control.
Witkin, California Summary 10th Parent and Child § 672, Child in Custody Of Parent or Guardian.
Witkin, California Summary 10th Parent and Child § 893, Limitations on Parental Control.
Witkin, California Summary 10th Parent and Child § 607A, (New) Educational and Developmental Services Decisions.

Rule 5.651. Educational and developmental-services decisionmaking rights

(a) Applicability (§§ 213.5, 319(g), 358, 358.1, 361(a), 362(a), 364, 366.21, 366.22, 366.23, 366.26, 366.27(b), 366.3(e), 726, 727.2(e), 4500 et seq., 11404.1; Ed. Code, §§ 48645 et seq., 48850 et seq., 49069.5, 56028, 56055, and 56155 et seq.; Gov. Code, §§ 7573–7579.6; 20 U.S.C. § 1400 et seq.; 29 U.S.C. § 794; 42 U.S.C. § 12101 et seq.)

This rule incorporates all rights with respect to education or developmental services recognized or established by state or federal law and applies:

(1) To any child, or any nonminor or nonminor dependent youth, for whom a petition has been filed under section 300, 601, or 602 until the petition is dismissed or the court has terminated dependency, delinquency, or transition jurisdiction over that person; and

(2) To every judicial hearing related to, or that might affect, the child's or youth's education or receipt of developmental services.

(b) Conduct of hearings

(1) To the extent the information is available, at the initial or detention hearing the court must consider:

(A) Who holds educational and developmental-services decisionmaking rights, and identify the rights holder or holders;

(B) Whether the child or youth is enrolled in, and is attending, the child's or youth's school of origin, as that term is defined in Education Code section 48853.5(f);

(C) If the child or youth is at risk of removal from or is no longer attending the school of origin, whether:

(i) In accordance with the child's or youth's best interest, the educational liaison, as described in Education Code section 48853.5(b), (d), and (e), in consultation with, and with the agreement of, the child or youth and the parent, guardian, or other person holding educational decisionmaking rights, recommends the waiver of the child's or youth's right to attend the school of origin;

(ii) Before making any recommendation to move a foster child or youth from his or her school of origin, the educational liaison provided the child or youth and the person holding the right to make educational decisions for the child or youth with a written explanation of the basis for the recommendation and how this recommendation serves the foster child's or youth's best interest as provided in Education Code section 48853.5(e)(7);

(iii) If the child or youth is no longer attending the school of origin, the local educational agency obtained a valid waiver of the child's or youth's right to continue in the school of origin under Education Code section 48853.5(e)(1) before moving the child or youth from that school; and

(iv) The child or youth was immediately enrolled in the new school as provided in Education Code section 48853.5(e)(8).

(D) In a dependency proceeding, whether the parent's or guardian's educational or developmental-services decisionmaking rights should be temporarily limited and an educational rights holder temporarily appointed using form JV–535; and

(E) Taking into account other statutory considerations regarding placement, whether the out-of-home placement:

(i) Is the environment best suited to meet the exceptional needs of a child or youth with disabilities and to serve the child's or youth's best interest if he or she has a disability; and

(ii) Promotes educational stability through proximity to the child's or youth's school of origin.

(2) At the dispositional hearing and at all subsequent hearings described in (a)(2), the court must:

(A) Consider and determine whether the child's or youth's educational, physical, mental health, and developmental needs, including any need for special education and related services, are being met;

(B) Identify the educational rights holder on form JV–535; and

(C) Direct the rights holder to take all appropriate steps to ensure that the child's or youth's educational and developmental needs are met.

The court's findings and orders must address the following:

(D) Whether the child's or youth's educational, physical, mental health, and developmental-services needs are being met;

(E) What services, assessments, or evaluations, including those for developmental services or for special education and related services, the child or youth may need;

(F) Who must take the necessary steps for the child or youth to receive any necessary assessments, evaluations, or services;

(G) If the child's or youth's educational placement changed during the period under review, whether:

(i) The child's or youth's educational records, including any evaluations of a child or youth with a disability, were transferred to the new educational placement within two business days of the request for the child's or youth's enrollment in the new educational placement; and

(ii) The child or youth is enrolled in and attending school.

(H) Whether the parent's or guardian's educational or developmental-services decisionmaking rights should be limited or, if previously limited, whether those rights should be restored.

(i) If the court finds that the parent's or guardian's educational or developmental-services decisionmaking rights should not be limited or should be restored, the court must explain to the parent or guardian his or her rights and responsibilities in regard to the child's education and developmental services as provided in rule 5.650(e), (f), and (j); or

(ii) If the court finds that the parent's or guardian's educational or developmental-services decisionmaking rights should be or remain limited, the court must designate the holder of those rights. The court must explain to the parent or guardian why the court is limiting his or her educational or developmental-services decisionmaking rights and must explain the rights and responsibilities of the educational rights holder as provided in rule 5.650(e), (f), and (j); and

(I) Whether, in the case of a nonminor or nonminor dependent youth who has chosen not to make educational or developmental-services decisions for himself or herself or has been deemed incompetent, it is in the best interests of the youth to appoint or to continue the appointment of an educational rights holder.

(c) Reports for hearings related to, or that may affect, education or developmental services

This subdivision applies at all hearings, including dispositional and joint assessment hearings. The court must ensure that, to the extent the information was available, the social worker or the probation officer provided the following information in the report for the hearing:

(1) The child's or youth's age, behavior, educational level, and developmental status and any discrepancies between that person's age and his or her level of achievement in education or level of cognitive, physical, and emotional development;

(2) The child's or youth's educational, physical, mental health, or developmental needs;

(3) Whether the child or youth is participating in developmentally appropriate extracurricular and social activities;

(4) Whether the child or youth is attending a comprehensive, regular, public or private school;

(5) Whether the child or youth may have physical, mental, or learning-related disabilities or other characteristics indicating a need for developmental services or special education and related services as provided by state or federal law;

(6) If the child is 0 to 3 years old, whether the child may be eligible for or is already receiving early intervention services or services under the California Early Intervention Services Act (Gov. Code, § 95000 et seq.) and, if the child is already receiving services, the specific nature of those services;

(7) If the child is between 3 and 5 years old and is or may be eligible for special education and related services, whether the child is receiving the early educational opportunities provided by Education Code section 56001 and, if so, the specific nature of those opportunities;

(8) Whether the child or youth is receiving special education and related services or any other services through a current individualized education program and, if so, the specific nature of those services;

(i) A copy of the current individualized education program should be attached to the report unless disclosure would create a risk of harm. In that case, the report should explain the risk.

(9) Whether the child or youth is receiving services under section 504 of the Rehabilitation Act of 1973 (29 U.S.C. § 701 et seq.) and, if so, the specific nature of those services;

(i) A copy of any current Section 504 plan should be attached to the report unless disclosure would create a risk of harm. In that case, the report should explain the risk.

(10) Whether the child or youth is or may be eligible for developmental services or is already receiving developmental services and, if that person is already receiving services, the specific nature of those services;

(i) A copy of any current individualized family service plan or individual program plan should be attached to the report unless disclosure would create a risk of harm. In that case, the report should explain the risk.

(11) Whether the parent's or guardian's educational or developmental-services decisionmaking rights have been or should be limited or restored;

(12) If the social worker or probation officer recommends that the court limit the parent's or guardian's rights to make educational or developmental-services decisions, the reasons those rights should be limited and the actions that the parent or guardian may take to restore those rights if they are limited;

(13) If the parent's or guardian's educational or developmental-services decisionmaking rights have been limited, the identity of the designated or appointed educational rights holder or surrogate parent;

(14) Recommendations and case plan goals to meet the child's or youth's identified educational, physical, mental health, and developmental-services needs, including all related information listed in section 16010(a) as required by section 16010(b);

(15) Whether any orders to direct an appropriate person to take the necessary steps for the child to receive assessments, evaluations, or services, including those for developmental services or for special education and related services, are requested; and

(16) In the case of a joint assessment, separate statements by the child welfare department and the probation department, each addressing whether the child or youth may have a disability and whether the child or youth needs developmental services or special education and related services or qualifies for any assessment or evaluation required by state or federal law.

(d) Continuance, stay, or suspension (§§ 357, 358, 702, 705)

If the court continues the dispositional hearing under rule 5.686 or 5.782 or stays the proceedings or suspends jurisdiction under rule 5.645, the child must continue to receive all services or accommodations required by state or federal law.

(e) Change of placement affecting the child's or youth's educational stability (§§ 16010, 16010.6; Ed. Code §§ 48850–48853.5)

This subdivision applies to all changes of placement, including the initial placement and any subsequent change of placement.

(1) At any hearing to which this rule applies that follows a decision to change the child's or youth's placement to a location that could lead to removal from the school of origin, the placement agency must demonstrate that, and the court must determine whether:

(A) The social worker or probation officer notified the court, the child's or youth's attorney, and the educational rights holder or surrogate parent, no more than one court day after making the placement decision, of the proposed placement decision.

(B) If the child or youth had a disability and an active individualized education program before removal, the social worker or probation officer, at least 10 days before the change of placement, notified in writing the local educational agency that provided a special education program for the child or youth before removal and the receiving special education local plan area, as described in Government Code section 7579.1, of the impending change of placement.

(2) After receipt of the notice in (1):

(A) The child's or youth's attorney must, as appropriate, discuss the proposed placement change and its effect on the child's or youth's right to attend the school of origin with the child or youth and the person who holds educational rights. The child's or youth's attorney may request a hearing by filing form JV–539. If requesting a hearing, the attorney must:

(i) File form JV–539 no later than two court days after receipt of the notice in (1); and

(ii) Provide notice of the hearing date, which will be no later than five court days after the form was filed, to the parents or guardians, unless otherwise indicated on form JV–535, parental rights have been terminated, or the youth has reached 18 years of age and reunification services have been terminated; the social worker or probation officer; the educational rights holder or surrogate parent; the foster youth educational liaison; the Court Appointed Special Advocate (CASA) volunteer; and all other persons or entities entitled to notice under section 293.

(B) The person who holds educational rights may request a hearing by filing form JV–539 no later than two court days after receipt of the notice in (1). After receipt of the form, the clerk must notify the persons in (e)(2)(A)(ii) of the hearing date.

(C) The court on its own motion may direct the clerk to set a hearing.

(3) If removal from the school of origin is disputed, the child or youth must be allowed to remain in the school of origin pending this hearing and pending the resolution of any disagreement between the child or youth, the parent, guardian, or educational rights holder, and the local educational agency.

(4) If the court sets a hearing, the social worker or probation officer must provide a report no later than two court days after the hearing is set that includes the information required by (b)(1)(C) as well as the following:

(A) Whether the foster child or youth has been allowed to continue his or her education in the school of origin to the extent required by Education Code section 48853.5(e)(1);

(B) Whether a dispute exists regarding the request of a foster child or youth to remain in the school of origin and whether the foster child or youth has been allowed to remain in the school of origin pending resolution of the dispute;

(C) Information addressing whether the information-sharing and other requirements in section 16501.1(c)(4) and Education Code section 49069.5 have been met;

(D) Information addressing how the proposed change serves the best interest of the child or youth;

(E) The responses of the child, if over 10 years old, or youth; the child's or youth's attorney; the parent, guardian, or other educational rights holder; the foster youth educational liaison; and the child's or youth's CASA volunteer to the proposed change of placement, specifying whether each person agrees or disagrees with the proposed change and, if any person disagrees, stating the reasons; and

(F) A statement from the social worker or probation officer confirming that the child or youth has not been segregated in a separate school, or in a separate program within a school, because the child or youth is placed in foster care.

(f) Court review of proposed change of placement affecting the right to attend the school of origin

(1) At a hearing set under (e)(2), the court must:

(A) Determine whether the placement agency and other relevant parties and advocates have fulfilled their obligations under section 16000(b), 16010(a), and 16501.1(f)(8);

(B) Determine whether the proposed school placement meets the requirements of this rule and Education Code sections 48853.5 and 49069.5, and whether the placement is in the best interest of the child or youth;

(C) Determine what actions are necessary to ensure the protection of the child's or youth's educational and developmental-services rights; and

(D) Make any findings and orders needed to enforce those rights, which may include an order to set a hearing under section 362 to join the necessary agencies regarding provision of services, including the provision of transportation services, so that the child or youth may remain in his or her school of origin.

(2) When considering whether it is in the child's or youth's best interest to remove him or her from the school of origin, the court must consider the following:

(A) Whether the parent, guardian, or other educational rights holder believes that removal from the school of origin is in the child's or youth's best interest;

(B) How the proposed change of placement will affect the stability of the child's or youth's school placement and the child's or youth's access to academic resources, services, and extracurricular and enrichment activities;

(C) Whether the proposed school placement would allow the child or youth to be placed in the least restrictive educational program; and

(D) Whether the child or youth has the educational and developmental services and supports, including those for special education and related services, necessary to meet state academic achievement standards.

(3) The court may make its findings and orders on *Findings and Orders Regarding Transfer From School of Origin* (form JV–538). *(Adopted, eff. Jan. 1, 2008. As amended, eff. Jan. 1, 2014.)*

Validity

For validity of this rule, see In re Ivan N. (App. 4 Dist. 2016) 202 Cal.Rptr.3d 338.

Research References

Forms

West's California Judicial Council Forms JV-417, Dispositional Attachment: In-Home Placement With Formal Supervision (Welf. & Inst. Code, 361).

West's California Judicial Council Forms JV-420, Dispositional Attachment: Removal from Custodial Parent--Placement With Previously Noncustodial Parent (Welf. & Inst. Code, §§ 361, 361.2).

West's California Judicial Council Forms JV-538, Findings and Orders Regarding Transfer from School Of Origin.

West's California Judicial Council Forms JV-539, Request for Hearing Regarding Child's Access to Services.

Treatises and Practice Aids

Witkin, California Summary 10th Parent and Child § 567, Statutory Rights.

Witkin, California Summary 10th Parent and Child § 602, Explanation and Information.

Witkin, California Summary 10th Parent and Child § 626, Conduct Of Hearing.

Witkin, California Summary 10th Parent and Child § 635, in General.

Witkin, California Summary 10th Parent and Child § 672, Child in Custody Of Parent or Guardian.

Witkin, California Summary 10th Parent and Child § 782, Statutory Rights.

Witkin, California Summary 10th Parent and Child § 898, Court Supervision Of Child.

Rule 5.652. Access to pupil records for truancy purposes

(a) Conditions of access (Ed. Code, § 49076)

Education Code section 49076 authorizes a school district to permit access to pupil records, including accurate copies, to any judicial officer or probation officer without consent of the pupil's parent or guardian and without a court order for the purposes of:

(1) Conducting a truancy mediation program for the pupil; or

(2) Presenting evidence in a truancy proceeding under section 681(b).

(b) Written certification

The judicial officer or probation officer may request pupil records but must certify in writing that the requested information will be used only for purposes of truancy mediation or a truancy petition. A judicial officer or probation officer must complete and file *Certified Request for Pupil Records—Truancy* (form JV–530) and serve it with *Local Educational Agency Response to JV–530* (form JV–531), by first-class mail to the local educational agency.

(c) Local educational agency response

Form JV–531 must be completed by the local educational agency and returned to the requesting judicial officer or probation officer within 15 calendar days of receipt of the request with copies of any responsive pupil records attached. After receipt the judicial officer or probation officer must file form JV–531 and the attached pupil records in the truancy proceedings.

(1) The school district must inform by telephone or other means, or provide written notification to, the child's parent or guardian within 24 hours of the release of the information.

(2) If a parent's or guardian's educational rights have been terminated, the school must notify the child's surrogate parent, relative, or other individual responsible for the child's education. *(Formerly Rule 1499.5, adopted, eff. July 1, 2002. Renumbered Rule 5.652 and amended, eff. Jan. 1, 2007.)*

Research References

Treatises and Practice Aids

Witkin, California Summary 10th Parent and Child § 444, Scope and Organization.

Witkin, California Summary 10th Parent and Child § 730, Truancy.

Chapter 11

ADVOCATES FOR PARTIES

Rule 5.655. Program requirements for Court Appointed Special Advocate programs

Text of Rule 5.655 effective until Jan. 1, 2019. See, also, Rule 5.655 effective Jan. 1, 2019.

(a) General provisions

A Court Appointed Special Advocate (CASA) program must comply with this rule to be eligible to receive Judicial Council funding. The Judicial Council may consider compliance with the guidelines delineated in the *CASA Program Policies and Procedures Manual* when determining eligibility for and amount of program funding.

(b) Definitions

(1) A CASA program is the local child advocate program that adheres to this rule; has been designated by the local presiding juvenile court judge to recruit, screen, select, train, supervise, and support lay volunteers for appointment by the court to help define the best interest of children in juvenile court dependency and wardship proceedings; and has completed one development grant year and one "start-up" year.

(2) Judicial Council staff may create a *CASA Program Policies and Procedures Manual* containing recommended program policies and procedures. If Judicial Council staff create a manual, it will be developed in collaboration with the California CASA Association and California CASA program directors. The protocols will address program and fiscal management, and the recruitment, screening, selection, training, and supervision of lay volunteers.

(3) A CASA volunteer is a person who has been recruited, screened, selected, and trained, who is being supervised and supported by a local CASA program, and who has been appointed by the juvenile court as a sworn officer of the court to help define the best interest of a child or children in juvenile court dependency and wardship proceedings.

(4) A "dependency proceeding" is a legal action brought on behalf of an allegedly abused, neglected, or abandoned child under section 300 et seq. The action is designed to protect children, preserve and reunify families, and find permanent homes for children who cannot be returned to their parents. Dependency proceedings include actions to appoint a legal guardian, terminate parental rights, and facilitate adoptions for dependent children of the juvenile court.

(5) A "wardship proceeding" is a legal action involving a child under the age of 18 years who is alleged to be:

(A) A person described under section 601 (who is beyond parental control or habitually disobedient or truant); or

(B) A person described under section 602 (who has violated any state or federal law or any city or county ordinance).

(c) Recruiting, screening, and selecting CASA volunteers

(1) A CASA program must adopt and adhere to a written plan for the recruitment of potential CASA volunteers. The program staff, in its recruitment effort, must address the demographics of the jurisdiction by making all reasonable efforts to ensure that individuals representing all racial, ethnic, linguistic, and economic sectors of the community are recruited and made available for appointment as CASA volunteers.

(2) A CASA program must adopt and adhere to the following minimum written procedures for screening potential CASA volunteers under section 102(e):

(A) A written application that generates minimum identifying data; information regarding the applicant's education, training, and experience; minimum age requirements; and current and past employment.

(B) Notice to the applicant that a formal security check will be made, including inquiries through appropriate law enforcement agencies, regarding any criminal record, driving record, or other record of conduct that would disqualify the applicant from service as a CASA volunteer. The security check must include fingerprinting. Refusal to consent to a formal security check is grounds for rejecting an applicant.

(C) A minimum of three completed references regarding the character, competence, and reliability of the applicant and his or her suitability for assuming the role of a CASA volunteer.

(D) A personal interview or interviews by a person or persons approved by the presiding juvenile court judge or designee, to probe the essential areas of concern with respect to the qualities of an effective CASA volunteer. A written, confidential record of the interview and the interviewer's assessments and observations must be made and retained in the advocate's file.

(3) If a CASA program allows its volunteers to transport children, the program must ensure that each volunteer transporting children:

(A) Possesses a valid and current driver's license;

(B) Possesses personal automobile insurance that meets the minimum state personal automobile insurance requirements;

(C) Obtains permission from the child's guardian or custodial agency; and

(D) Provides the CASA program with a Department of Motor Vehicles driving record report annually.

(4) A CASA program must adopt a written preliminary procedure for selecting CASA candidates to enter the CASA training program. The selection procedure must state that any applicant found to have been convicted of or to have current charges pending for a felony or misdemeanor involving a sex offense, child abuse, or child neglect must not be accepted as a CASA volunteer. This policy must be stated on the volunteer application form.

(5) An adult otherwise qualified to act as a CASA must not be discriminated against based on marital status, socioeconomic factors, race, national origin, ethnic group identification, religion, age, sex, sexual orientation, color, or disability or because of any other characteristic listed or defined in Government Code section 11135 or Welfare and Institutions Code section 103.

(d) Initial training of CASA volunteers (§ 102(d))

A CASA program must adopt and adhere to a written plan for the initial training of CASA volunteers.

(1) The initial training curriculum must include at least 30 hours of formal instruction. This curriculum must include mandatory training topics as listed in section 102(d). The curriculum may also include additional appropriate topics.

(2) The final selection process is contingent on the successful completion of the initial training program, as deter-

mined by the presiding judge of the juvenile court or designee.

(e) Oath

At the completion of training, and before assignment to any child's case, the CASA volunteer must take a court-administered oath describing the duties and responsibilities of the advocate under section 103(f). The CASA volunteer must also sign a written affirmation of that oath. The signed affirmation must be retained in the volunteer's file.

(f) Duties and responsibilities

CASA volunteers serve at the discretion of the court having jurisdiction over the proceeding in which the volunteer has been appointed. A CASA volunteer is an officer of the court and is bound by all court rules under section 103(e). A CASA program must develop and adopt a written description of duties and responsibilities, consistent with local court rules.

(g) Prohibited activities

A CASA program must develop and adopt a written description of activities that are prohibited for CASA volunteers. The specified prohibited activities must include:

(1) Taking a child to the CASA volunteer's home;

(2) Giving legal advice or therapeutic counseling;

(3) Giving money or expensive gifts to the child or family;

(4) Being related to any parties involved in a case or being employed in a position and/or agency that might result in a conflict of interest; and

(5) Any other activities prohibited by the local juvenile court.

(h) The appointment of CASA volunteers

The CASA program director must develop, with the approval of the presiding juvenile court judge, a written procedure for the selection of cases and the appointment of CASA volunteers for children in juvenile court proceedings.

(i) Oversight, support, and supervision of CASA volunteers

A CASA program must adopt and adhere to a written plan, approved by the presiding juvenile court judge, for the oversight, support, and supervision of CASA volunteers in the performance of their duties. The plan must:

(1) Include a grievance procedure that covers grievances by any person against a volunteer or CASA program staff and grievances by a volunteer against a CASA program or program staff. The grievance procedure must:

(A) Be incorporated into a document that contains a description of the roles and responsibilities of CASA volunteers. This document must be provided:

(i) When a copy of the court order that appointed the CASA volunteer is provided to any adult involved with the child's case, including but not limited to, teachers, foster parents, therapists, and health-care workers; and

(ii) To any person, including a volunteer, who has a grievance against a volunteer or a CASA program employee.

(B) Include a provision that documentation of any grievance filed by or against a volunteer must be retained in the volunteer's personnel file.

(2) Include a provision for the ongoing training and continuing education of CASA volunteers. Ongoing training opportunities must be provided at least monthly under section 103(a). CASA volunteers must participate in a minimum of 12 hours of continuing education in each year of service.

(j) Removal, resignation, and termination of a CASA volunteer

The CASA program must adopt a written plan for the removal, resignation, or involuntary termination of a CASA volunteer, including the following provisions:

(1) A volunteer may resign or be removed from an individual case at any time by the order of the juvenile court presiding judge or designee.

(2) A volunteer may be involuntarily terminated from the program by the program director.

(3) The volunteer has the right to appeal termination by the program director under the program's grievance procedure.

(k) CASA program administration and management

A CASA program must adopt and adhere to a written plan for program governance and evaluation that includes the following as applicable:

(1) Articles of incorporation, bylaws, and a board of directors. Any CASA program that functions under the auspices of a public agency or private entity must specify in its plan a clear administrative relationship with the parent organization and clearly delineated delegations of authority and accountability. No CASA program may function under the auspices of a probation department or department of social services. CASA programs may receive funds from probation departments, local child welfare agencies, and the California Department of Social Services if:

(A) The CASA program and the contributing agency develop a memorandum of understanding (MOU) or contract stating that the funds will be used only for general operating expenses as determined by the receiving CASA program, and the contributing agency will not oversee or monitor the funds;

(B) A procedure resolving any conflict between the CASA program and contributing agency is implemented so that conflict between the two agencies does not affect funding or the CASA program's ability to retain an independent evaluation separate from that of the contributing agency's; and

(C) Any MOU or contract between a CASA program and the contributing agency is submitted to and approved by Judicial Council staff.

(2) A clear statement of the purpose or mission of the CASA program and express goals and objectives to further that purpose. Where the CASA program is not an independent nonprofit organization, but instead functions under the auspices of a public agency or a private entity, an active advisory council must be established. The advisory council for CASA programs functioning under the auspices of a public agency or a private entity will not function as the governing body of the CASA program. The board of directors for the private entity or the public agency manage-

ment will function as the governing body for the CASA program, with guidance from the advisory council.

(3) A procedure for the recruitment, selection, hiring, and evaluation of an executive director for the CASA program.

(4) An administrative manual containing personnel policies, record-keeping practices, and data collection practices.

(5) Local juvenile court rules developed in consultation with the presiding judge of the juvenile court or a designee, as specified in section 100. One local rule must specify when CASA reports are to be submitted to the court, who is entitled to receive a copy of the report, and who will copy and distribute the report. This rule must also specify that the CASA court report must be distributed to the persons entitled to receive it at least two court days before the hearing for which the report was prepared.

(*l*) Finance, facility, and risk management

(1) A CASA program must adopt a written plan for fiscal control. The fiscal plan must include an annual audit, conducted by a qualified professional, that is consistent with generally accepted accounting principles and the audit protocols in the program's contract with the Judicial Council.

(2) The fiscal plan must include a written budget with projections that guide the management of financial resources and a strategy for obtaining necessary funding for program operations.

(3) When the program has accounting oversight, it must adhere to written operational procedures in regard to accounting control.

(4) The CASA program's board of directors must set policies for and exercise control over fundraising activities carried out by its employees and volunteers.

(5) The CASA program must have the following insurance coverage for its staff and volunteers:

(A) General liability insurance with limits of liability of not less than $1 million ($1,000,000) for each person per occurrence/aggregate for bodily injury and not less than $1 million ($1,000,000) per occurrence/aggregate for property damage;

(B) Nonowned automobile liability insurance and hired vehicle coverage with limits of liability of not less than $1 million ($1,000,000) combined single limit per occurrence and in the aggregate;

(C) Automobile liability insurance meeting the minimum state automobile liability insurance requirements, if the program owns a vehicle; and

(D) Workers' compensation insurance with a minimum limit of $500,000.

(6) The CASA program must require staff, volunteers, and members of the governing body, when applicable, to immediately notify the CASA program of any criminal charges against themselves.

(7) The nonprofit CASA program must plan for the disposition of property and confidential records in the event of its dissolution.

(m) Confidentiality

The presiding juvenile court judge and the CASA program director must adopt a written plan governing confidentiality of case information, case records, and personnel records. The written plan must include the following provisions:

(1) All information concerning children and families in the juvenile court process is confidential. Volunteers must not give case information to anyone other than the court, the parties and their attorneys, and CASA staff.

(2) CASA volunteers are required by law (Pen. Code, § 11166 et seq.) to report any reasonable suspicion that a child is a victim of child abuse or serious neglect as described by Penal Code section 273.

(3) The child's original case file must be maintained in the CASA office by a custodian of records and must remain there. Copies of documents needed by a volunteer must be restricted to those actually needed to conduct necessary business outside of the office. No one may have access to the child's original case file except on the approval of the CASA program director or presiding judge of the juvenile court. Controls must be in place to ensure that records can be located at any time. The office must establish a written procedure for the maintenance of case files.

(4) The volunteer's personnel file is confidential. No one may have access to the personnel file except the volunteer, the CASA program director or a designee, or the presiding judge of the juvenile court. *(Formerly Rule 1424, adopted, eff. July 1, 1994. As amended, eff. Jan. 1, 1995; Jan. 1, 2000; Jan. 1, 2001; Jan. 1, 2005. Renumbered Rule 5.655 and amended, eff. Jan. 1, 2007. As amended, eff. Jan. 1, 2010; Jan. 1, 2016.)*

Research References

Treatises and Practice Aids

Witkin, California Summary 10th Parent and Child § 3, in General.
Witkin, California Summary 10th Parent and Child § 444, Scope and Organization.
Witkin, California Summary 10th Parent and Child § 572, Appointment Of Guardian Ad Litem or Child Advocate.

Rule 5.655. Program requirements for Court Appointed Special Advocate programs

Text of Rule 5.655 effective Jan. 1, 2019. See, also, Rule 5.655 effective until Jan. 1, 2019.

(a) General provisions

(1) A Court Appointed Special Advocate (CASA) program is a child advocacy program that recruits, screens, selects, trains, supervises, and supports lay volunteers for appointment by the court to help define the best interest of children and nonminors under the jurisdiction of the e juvenile court, including the dependency and delinquency courts.

(2) To be authorized to serve children and nonminors in a county, the CASA program must be designated by the presiding judge of the juvenile court.

(3) A CASA program must comply with this rule to be eligible to receive Judicial Council funding. ~~The Judicial Council may consider compliance with the guidelines delineated in the *CASA Program Policies and Procedures Manual* when determining eligibility for and amount of program funding.~~

~~**(b) Definitions**~~

~~(1) A Casa program is the local child advocate program that adheres to this rule; has been designated by the local presiding juvenile court judge to recruit, screen, select, train, supervise, and support lay volunteers for appointment by the court to help define the best interest of children in juvenile court dependency and wardship proceedings; and has completed one development grant year and one "start-up" year.~~

~~(2) Judicial Council staff may create a *CASA Program Policies and Procedures Manual* containing recommended program policies and procedures. If Judicial Council staff create a manual, it will be developed in collaboration with the California CASA Association and California CASA program directors. The protocols will address program and fiscal management, and the recruitment, screening, selection, training, and supervision of lay volunteers.~~

~~(3) A CASA volunteer is a person who has been recruited, screened, selected, and trained, who is being supervised and supported by a local CASA program, and who has been appointed by the juvenile court as a sworn officer of the court to help define the best interest of a child or children in juvenile court dependency and wardship proceedings.~~

~~(4) A "dependency proceeding" is a legal action brought on behalf of an allegedly abused, neglected, or abandoned child under section 300 et seq. The action is designed to protect children, preserve and reunify families, and find permanent homes for children who cannot be returned to their parents. Dependency proceedings include actions to appoint a legal guardian, terminate parental rights, and facilitate adoptions for dependent children of the juvenile court.~~

~~(5) A "wardship proceeding" is a legal action involving a child under the age of 18 years who is alleged to be:~~

~~(A) A person described under section 601 (who is beyond parental control or habitually disobedient or truant); or~~

~~(B) A person described under section 602 (who has violated any state or federal law or any city or county ordinance).~~

(b) CASA program administration and management

(1) The court's designation of the CASA program must take the form of a memorandum of understanding (MOU) between the CASA program and the designating court.

(A) The MOU must state that the relationship between the CASA program and the designating court can be terminated for convenience by either the CASA program or the designating court.

(B) A CASA program may serve children and nonminors in more than one court if the program executes an MOU with each court.

(C) The CASA program and the designating court must be the only parties to the MOU.

(D) The MOU must indicate when and how the CASA program will have access to the juvenile case file and the nonminor dependent court file if applicable.

(2) A CASA program must function as a nonprofit organization or under the auspices of a public agency or nonprofit organization, and must adopt and adhere to a written plan for program governance and evaluation. The plan must include the following, as applicable:

(A) Articles of incorporation, a board of directors, and bylaws that specify a clear administrative relationship with the parent organization and clearly delineated delegations of authority and accountability.

(B) A clear statement of the purpose or mission of the CASA program that express goals and objectives to further that purpose. Where the CASA program is not an independent organization, but instead functions under the auspices of a public agency or a nonprofit organization, an active advisory council must be established. The role of the advisory council for CASA programs functioning under the auspices of a public agency or a nonprofit organization includes but is not limited to developing and approving policies for CASA, developing the CASA program's budget, promoting a collaborative relationship with the umbrella organization, monitoring and evaluating program operations, and developing and implementing fundraising activities to benefit the CASA program. The board of directors for the nonprofit organization or management of the public agency will function as the governing body for the CASA program, with guidance from the advisory council.

(C) A procedure for the recruitment, selection, hiring, and evaluation of an executive director for the CASA program.

(D) An administrative manual containing personnel policies, record-keeping practices, and data collection practices.

(E) Local juvenile court rules developed in consultation with the presiding judge of the juvenile court or a designee, as specified in section 100. One local rule must specify when CASA reports are to be submitted to the court, who is entitled to receive a copy of the report, and who will copy and distribute the report. This rule must also specify that the CASA court report must be distributed to the persons entitled to receive it at least two court days before the hearing for which the report was prepared.

(3) No CASA program may function under the auspices of a probation department or department of social services. CASA programs may receive funds from probation departments, local child welfare agencies, and the California Department of Social Services if:

(A) The CASA program and the contributing agency develop an MOU stating that the funds will be used only for general operating expenses as determined by the receiving CASA program, and the contributing agency will not oversee or monitor the funds;

(B) A procedure resolving any conflict between the CASA program and contributing agency is implemented so that conflict between the two agencies does not affect funding or the CASA program's ability to retain an independent evaluation separate from that of the contributing agency's; and

(C) Any MOU between a CASA program and the contributing agency is submitted to and approved by Judicial Council staff.

(4) If a CASA program serves more than one county, the CASA program is encouraged to seek representation on the board of directors and/or advisory council from each county it serves.

(c) Finance, facility, and risk management

(1) A CASA program must adopt a written plan for fiscal control. The fiscal plan must include an annual audit, conducted by a qualified professional, that is consistent with generally accepted accounting principles and the audit protocols in the program's Judicial Council contract.

(2) The fiscal plan must include a written budget with projections that guide the management of financial resources and a strategy for obtaining necessary funding for program operations.

(3) When the program has accounting oversight, it must adhere to written operational procedures in regard to accounting control.

(4) The CASA program's board of directors must set policies for and exercise control over fundraising activities carried out by its employees and volunteers.

(5) The CASA program must have the following insurance coverage for its staff and volunteers:

(A) General liability insurance with liability limits of not less than $1 million ($1,000,000) for each person per occurrence/aggregate for bodily injury, and not less than $1 million ($1,000,000) per occurrence/aggregate for property damage;

(B) Nonowned automobile liability insurance and hired vehicle coverage with liability limits of not less than $1 million ($1,000,000) combined single limit per occurrence and in the aggregate;

(C) Automobile liability insurance meeting the minimum state automobile liability insurance requirements, if the program owns a vehicle; and

(D) Workers' compensation insurance with a minimum limit of $500,000.

(6) The CASA program must require staff, volunteers, and members of the governing body, when applicable, to immediately notify the CASA program of any criminal charges against themselves.

(7) The nonprofit CASA program must plan for the disposition of property and confidential records in the event of its dissolution.

(d) Confidentiality

The presiding juvenile court judge and the CASA program director must adopt a written plan governing confidentiality of case information, case records, and personnel records. The plan must be included in the MOU or a local cal rule. The written plan must include the following provisions:

(1) All information concerning children and families, including nonminors, in the juvenile court process is confidential. Volunteers must not give case information to anyone other than the court, the parties and their attorneys, and CASA staff.

(2) CASA volunteers are required by law (Pen. Code, § 11166 et seq.) to report any reasonable suspicion that a child is a victim of child abuse or serious neglect as described by Penal Code section 273a.

(3) The child's original case file must be maintained in the CASA office by a custodian of records and must remain there. Copies of documents needed by a volunteer must be restricted to those actually needed to conduct necessary business outside of the office. No one may have access to the child's original case file except on the approval of the CASA program director or presiding judge of the juvenile court. Controls must be in place to ensure that records can be located at any time. The office must establish a written procedure for the maintenance of case files.

(4) If the nonminor provides consent for the CASA volunteer to obtain his or her nonminor dependent court file, the procedures stated in paragraph (3) related to maintenance of the case file must be followed.

(5) The volunteer's personnel file is confidential. No one may have access to the personnel file except the volunteer, the CASA program director or a designee, or the presiding judge of the juvenile court.

(e)~~(e)~~ Recruiting, screening, and selecting CASA volunteers

(1) ~~A CASA program must adopt and adhere to a written plan for the recruitment of potential CASA volunteers. The program staff, in its recruitment effort, must address the demographics of the jurisdiction by making all reasonable efforts to ensure that individuals representing all racial, ethnic, linguistic, and economic sectors of the community are recruited and made available for appointment as CASA volunteers.~~A CASA volunteer is a person who has been recruited, screened, selected, and trained; is being supervised and supported by a local CASA program; and has been appointed by the juvenile court as a sworn officer of the court to help define the best interest of children or nonminors in juvenile court dependency and wardship proceedings.

(2) A CASA program must adopt and adhere to a written n plan for the recruitment of potential CASA volunteers. The program staff, in its recruitment effort, must address the demographics of the jurisdiction by making all reasonable efforts to ensure that individuals representing all racial, ethnic, linguistic, and economic sectors of the community are recruited and made available for appointment as CASA volunteers.

(3)~~(2)~~ A CASA program must adopt and adhere to the following minimum written procedures for screening potential CASA volunteers under section 102(e):

(A) A written application that generates minimum identifying data; information regarding the applicant's education, training, and experience; minimum age requirements; and current and past employment.

(B) Notice to the applicant that a formal security check will be made, with inquiries through appropriate law enforcement agencies—including but not limited to the Department of Justice, Federal Bureau of Investigations, and the Child Abuse Index—regarding any criminal record, driving record, or other record of conduct that would disqualify the applicant from service as a CASA volunteer. The security check must include fingerprinting. Refusal to consent to a formal security check is grounds for rejecting an applicant.

(C) A minimum of three completed references regarding the character, competence, and reliability of the applicant and his or her suitability for assuming the role of a CASA volunteer.

~~(D) A personal interview or interviews by a person or persons approved by the presiding juvenile court judge or designee, to probe the essential areas of concern with respect to the qualities of an effective CASA volunteer. A written, confidential record of the interview and the interviewer's assessments and observations must be made and retained in the advocate's file.~~

(4)~~(3)~~ If a CASA program allows its volunteers to transport children, the program must ensure that each volunteer transporting children:

(A) Possesses a valid and current driver's license;

(B) Possesses personal automobile insurance that meets the minimum state personal automobile insurance requirements;

(C) Obtains permission from the child's guardian or custodial agency; and

(D) Provides the CASA program with a Department of Motor Vehicles driving record report annually.

(5)~~(4)~~ A CASA program must adopt a written preliminary procedure for selecting CASA candidates to enter the CASA training program. The selection procedure must state that any applicant found to have been convicted of or to have current charges pending for a felony or misdemeanor involving a sex offense, child abuse, or child neglect must not be accepted as a CASA volunteer. This policy must be stated on the volunteer application form.

(6)~~(5)~~ An adult otherwise qualified to act as a CASA must not be discriminated against based on marital status, socioeconomic factors, race, national origin, ethnic group identification, religion, age, sex, sexual orientation, color, or disability or because of any other characteristic listed or defined in Government Code section 11135 or Welfare and Institutions Code section 103.

(f)~~(d)~~ Initial training of CASA volunteers (§ 102(d))

A CASA program must adopt and adhere to a written plan for the initial training of CASA volunteers.

(1) The initial training curriculum must include at least 30 hours of formal instruction. This curriculum must include mandatory training topics as listed in section 102(d). The curriculum may also include additional appropriate topics, such as those stated in California Rules of Court, rule 5.664.

(2) The final selection process is contingent on the successful completion of the initial training program, as determined by the presiding judge of the juvenile court or designee.

(g)~~(e)~~ Oath

At the completion of training, and before assignment to any child~~'s~~ or nonminor's case, the CASA volunteer must take a court-administered oath describing the duties and responsibilities of the advocate under section 103(f). The CASA volunteer must also sign a written affirmation of that oath. The signed affirmation must be retained in the volunteer's file.

(h)~~(f)~~ Duties and responsibilities

CASA volunteers serve at the discretion of the court having jurisdiction over the proceeding in which the volunteer has been appointed. A CASA volunteer is an officer of the court and is bound by all court rules under section 103(e). A CASA program must develop and adopt a written description of duties and responsibilities, consistent with local court rules.

(i)~~(g)~~ Prohibited activities

A CASA program must develop and adopt a written description of activities that are prohibited for CASA volunteers. The specified prohibited activities must include:

(1) Taking a child or nonminor to the CASA volunteer's home;

(2) Giving legal advice or therapeutic counseling;

(3) Giving money or expensive gifts to the child, nonminor, or family of the child or nonminor;

(4) Being related to any parties involved in a case or being employed in a position and/or agency that might result in a conflict of interest; and

(5) Any other activities prohibited by the local juvenile court.

(j)~~(h)~~ The appointment of CASA volunteers

The CASA program director must develop, with the approval of the presiding juvenile court judge, a written procedure for the selection of cases and the appointment of CASA volunteers for children and nonminors in juvenile court proceedings.

(k)~~(i)~~ Oversight, support, and supervision of CASA volunteers

A CASA program must adopt and adhere to a written plan, approved by the presiding juvenile court judge, for the oversight, support, and supervision of CASA volunteers in the performance of their duties. The plan must:

(1) Include a grievance procedure that covers grievances by any person against a volunteer or CASA program staff and grievances by a volunteer against a CASA program or program staff. The grievance procedure must:

(A) Be incorporated into a document that contains a description of the roles and responsibilities of CASA volunteers. This document must be provided:

(i) When a copy of the court order that appointed the CASA volunteer is provided to any adult involved with the child's or nonminor's case, including but not limited to~~,~~ teachers, foster parents, therapists, and health-care workers;

(ii) To the nonminor upon appointment of the CASA; and

~~(ii)~~(iii) To any person, including a volunteer, who has a grievance against a volunteer or a CASA program employee.

(B) Include a provision that documentation of any grievance filed by or against a volunteer must be retained in the volunteer's personnel file.

(2) Include a provision for the ongoing training and continuing education of CASA volunteers. Ongoing training opportunities must be provided at least monthly under section 103(a). CASA volunteers must participate in a minimum of 12 hours of continuing education in each year of service.

~~**(l) Finance, facility, and risk management**~~

~~(1) A CASA program must adopt a written plan for fiscal control. The fiscal plan must include an annual audit, conducted by a qualified professional, that is consistent with generally accepted accounting principles and the audit protocols in the program's contract with the Judicial Council.~~

~~(2) The fiscal plan must include a written budget with projections that guide the management of financial resources and a strategy for obtaining necessary funding for program operations.~~

~~(3) When the program has accounting oversight, it must adhere to written operational procedures in regard to accounting control.~~

~~(4) The CASA program's board of directors must set policies for and exercise control over fundraising activities carried out by its employees and volunteers.~~

~~(5) The CASA program must have the following insurance coverage for its staff and volunteers:~~

~~(A) General liability insurance with limits of liability of not less than $1 million ($1,000,000) for each person per occurrence/aggregate for bodily injury and not less than $1 million ($1,000,000) per occurrence/aggregate for property damage;~~

~~(B) Nonowned automobile liability insurance and hired vehicle coverage with limits of liability of not less than $1 million ($1,000,000) combined single limit per occurrence and in the aggregate;~~

~~(C) Automobile liability insurance meeting the minimum state automobile liability insurance requirements, if the program owns a vehicle; and~~

~~(D) Workers' compensation insurance with a minimum limit of $500,000.~~

~~(6) The CASA program must require staff, volunteers, and members of the governing body, when applicable, to immediately notify the CASA program of any criminal charges against themselves.~~

~~(7) The nonprofit CASA program must plan for the disposition of property and confidential records in the event of its dissolution.~~

~~(l)~~j Removal, resignation, and termination of a CASA volunteer

The CASA program must adopt a written plan for the removal, resignation, or involuntary termination of a CASA volunteer, including the following provisions:

(1) A volunteer may resign or be removed from an individual case at any time by the order of the juvenile court presiding judge or designee.

(2) A volunteer may be involuntarily terminated from the program by the program director.

(3) The volunteer has the right to appeal termination by the program director under the program's grievance procedure.

~~**(m) Confidentiality**~~

~~The presiding juvenile court judge and the CASA program director must adopt a written plan governing confidentiality of case information, case records, and personnel records. The written plan must include the following provisions:~~

~~(1) All information concerning children and families in the juvenile court process is confidential. Volunteers must not give case information to anyone other than the court, the parties and their attorneys, and CASA staff.~~

~~(2) CASA volunteers are required by law (Pen. Code, § 11166 et seq.) to report any reasonable suspicion that a child is a victim of child abuse or serious neglect as described by Penal Code section 273.~~

~~(3) The child's original case file must be maintained in the CASA office by a custodian of records and must remain there. Copies of documents needed by a volunteer must be restricted to those actually needed to conduct necessary business outside of the office. No one may have access to the child's original case file except on the approval of the CASA program director or presiding judge of the juvenile court. Controls must be in place to ensure that records can be located at any time. The office must establish a written procedure for the maintenance of case files.~~

~~(4) The volunteer's personnel file is confidential. No one may have access to the personnel file except the volunteer, the CASA program director or a designee, or the presiding judge of the juvenile court.~~ *(Formerly Rule 1424, adopted, eff. July 1, 1994. As amended, eff. Jan. 1, 1995; Jan. 1, 2000; Jan. 1, 2001; Jan. 1, 2005. Renumbered Rule 5.655 and amended, eff. Jan. 1, 2007. As amended, eff. Jan. 1, 2010; Jan. 1, 2016; Jan. 1, 2019.)*

Research References

Treatises and Practice Aids

Witkin, California Summary 10th Parent and Child § 3, in General.
Witkin, California Summary 10th Parent and Child § 444, Scope and Organization.
Witkin, California Summary 10th Parent and Child § 572, Appointment Of Guardian Ad Litem or Child Advocate.

Rule 5.660. Attorneys for parties (§§ 317, 317.5, 317.6, 353, 366.26, 16010.6)

(a) Local rules

On or before January 1, 2002, the superior court of each county must amend its local rules regarding the representation of parties in dependency proceedings.

(1) The local rules must be amended after consultation by the court with representatives of the State Bar of California; local offices of the county counsel, district attorney, public defender, and other attorneys appointed to represent parties in these proceedings; county welfare departments; child advocates; current or recent foster youth; and others selected by the court in accordance with standard 5.40(c) of the Standards of Judicial Administration.

(2) The amended rules must address the following as needed:

(A) Representation of children in accordance with other sections of this rule;

(B) Timelines and procedures for settlements, mediation, discovery, protocols, and other issues related to contested matters;

(C) Procedures for the screening, training, and appointment of attorneys representing parties, with particular attention to the training requirements for attorneys representing children;

(D) Establishment of minimum standards of experience, training, and education of attorneys representing parties, including additional training and education in the areas of substance abuse and domestic violence as required;

(E) Establishment of procedures to determine appropriate caseloads for attorneys representing children;

(F) Procedures for reviewing and resolving complaints by parties regarding the performance of attorneys;

(G) Procedures for informing the court of interests of the dependent child requiring further investigation, intervention, or litigation; and

(H) Procedures for appointment of a Child Abuse Prevention and Treatment Act (CAPTA) guardian ad litem, who may be an attorney or a CASA volunteer, in cases in which a prosecution is initiated under the Penal Code arising from neglect or abuse of the child.

(3) Appropriate local forms may be used.

(b) Attorneys for children

The court must appoint counsel for a child who is the subject of a petition under section 300 and is unrepresented by counsel, unless the court finds that the child would not benefit from the appointment of counsel.

(1) In order to find that a child would not benefit from the appointment of counsel, the court must find all of the following:

(A) The child understands the nature of the proceedings;

(B) The child is able to communicate and advocate effectively with the court, other counsel, other parties, including social workers, and other professionals involved in the case; and

(C) Under the circumstances of the case, the child would not gain any benefit by being represented by counsel.

(2) If the court finds that the child would not benefit from representation by counsel, the court must make a finding on the record as to each of the criteria in (1) and state the reasons for each finding.

(3) If the court finds that the child would not benefit from representation by counsel, the court must appoint a CASA volunteer for the child, to serve as the CAPTA guardian ad litem, as required in section 326.5.

(c) Conflict of interest guidelines for attorneys representing siblings

(1) *Appointment*

(A) The court may appoint a single attorney to represent a group of siblings involved in the same dependency proceeding.

(B) An attorney must decline to represent one or more siblings in a dependency proceeding, and the court must appoint a separate attorney to represent the sibling or siblings, if, at the outset of the proceedings:

(i) An actual conflict of interest exists among those siblings; or

(ii) Circumstances specific to the case present a reasonable likelihood that an actual conflict of interest will arise among those siblings.

(C) The following circumstances, standing alone, do not necessarily demonstrate an actual conflict of interest or a reasonable likelihood that an actual conflict of interest will arise:

(i) The siblings are of different ages;

(ii) The siblings have different parents;

(iii) There is a purely theoretical or abstract conflict of interest among the siblings;

(iv) Some of the siblings appear more likely than others to be adoptable; or

(v) The siblings may have different permanent plans.

(2) *Withdrawal from appointment or continued representation*

(A) An attorney representing a group of siblings has an ongoing duty to evaluate the interests of each sibling and assess whether there is an actual conflict of interest.

(B) The following circumstances, standing alone, do not necessarily demonstrate an actual conflict of interest:

(i) The siblings are of different ages;

(ii) The siblings have different parents;

(iii) There is a purely theoretical or abstract conflict of interest among the siblings;

(iv) Some of the siblings are more likely to be adopted than others;

(v) The siblings have different permanent plans;

(vi) The siblings express conflicting desires or objectives, but the issues involved are not material to the case; or

(vii) The siblings give different or contradictory accounts of the events, but the issues involved are not material to the case.

(C) It is not necessary for an attorney to withdraw from representing some or all of the siblings if there is merely a reasonable likelihood that an actual conflict of interest will develop.

(D) If an attorney believes that an actual conflict of interest existed at appointment or developed during representation, the attorney must take any action necessary to ensure that the siblings' interests are not prejudiced, including:

(i) Notifying the juvenile court of the existence of an actual conflict of interest among some or all of the siblings; and

(ii) Requesting to withdraw from representation of some or all of the siblings.

(E) If the court determines that an actual conflict of interest exists, the court must relieve an attorney from representation of some or all of the siblings.

(F) After an actual conflict of interest arises, the attorney may continue to represent one or more siblings whose interests do not conflict only if:

(i) The attorney has successfully withdrawn from the representation of all siblings whose interests conflict with those of the sibling or siblings the attorney continues to represent;

(ii) The attorney has exchanged no confidential information with any sibling whose interest conflicts with those of the sibling or siblings the attorney continues to represent; and

(iii) Continued representation of one or more siblings would not otherwise prejudice the other sibling or siblings.

(d) Competent counsel

Every party in a dependency proceeding who is represented by an attorney is entitled to competent counsel.

(1) *Definition*

"Competent counsel" means an attorney who is a member in good standing of the State Bar of California, who has participated in training in the law of juvenile dependency, and who demonstrates adequate forensic skills, knowledge and comprehension of the statutory scheme, the purposes and goals of dependency proceedings, the specific statutes, rules of court, and cases relevant to such proceedings, and procedures for filing petitions for extraordinary writs.

(2) *Evidence of competency*

The court may require evidence of the competency of any attorney appointed to represent a party in a dependency proceeding.

(3) *Experience and education.*

(A) Only those attorneys who have completed a minimum of eight hours of training or education in the area of juvenile dependency, or who have sufficient recent experience in dependency proceedings in which the attorney has demonstrated competency, may be appointed to represent parties. Attorney training must include:

(i) An overview of dependency law and related statutes and cases;

(ii) Information on child development, child abuse and neglect, substance abuse, domestic violence, family reunification and preservation, and reasonable efforts; and

(iii) For any attorney appointed to represent a child, instruction on cultural competency and sensitivity relating to, and best practices for, providing adequate care to lesbian, gay, bisexual, and transgender youth in out-of-home placement.

(B) Within every three years, attorneys must complete at least eight hours of continuing education related to dependency proceedings.

(4) *Standards of representation*

Attorneys or their agents are expected to meet regularly with clients, including clients who are children, regardless of the age of the child or the child's ability to communicate verbally, to contact social workers and other professionals associated with the client's case, to work with other counsel and the court to resolve disputed aspects of a case without contested hearing, and to adhere to the mandated timelines. The attorney for the child must have sufficient contact with the child to establish and maintain an adequate and professional attorney-client relationship. The attorney for the child is not required to assume the responsibilities of a social worker and is not expected to perform services for the child that are unrelated to the child's legal representation.

(5) *Attorney contact information*

The attorney for a child for whom a dependency petition has been filed must provide his or her contact information to the child's caregiver no later than 10 days after receipt of the name, address, and telephone number of the child's caregiver. If the child is 10 years of age or older, the attorney must also provide his or her contact information to the child for whom a dependency petition has been filed no later than 10 days after receipt of the caregiver's contact information. The attorney may give contact information to a child for whom a dependency petition has been filed who is under 10 years of age. At least once a year, if the list of educational liaisons is available online from the California Department of Education, the child's attorney must provide, in any manner permitted by section 317(e)(4), his or her contact information to the educational liaison of each local educational agency serving the attorney's clients in foster care in the county of jurisdiction.

(6) *Caseloads for children's attorneys*

The attorney for a child must have a caseload that allows the attorney to perform the duties required by section 317(e) and this rule, and to otherwise adequately counsel and represent the child. To enhance the quality of representation afforded to children, attorneys appointed under this rule must not maintain a maximum full-time caseload that is greater than that which allows them to meet the requirements stated in (3), (4), and (5).

(e) Client complaints

The court must establish a process for the review and resolution of complaints or questions by a party regarding the performance of an appointed attorney. Each party must be informed of the procedure for lodging the complaint. If it is determined that an appointed attorney has acted improperly or contrary to the rules or policies of the court, the court must take appropriate action.

(f) CASA volunteer as CAPTA guardian ad litem (§ 326.5)

If the court makes the findings as outlined in (b) and does not appoint an attorney to represent the child, the court must appoint a CASA volunteer as the CAPTA guardian ad litem of the child.

(1) The required training of CASA volunteers is stated in rule 5.655.

(2) The caseload of a CASA volunteer acting as a CAPTA guardian ad litem must be limited to 10 cases. A case may include siblings, absent a conflict.

(3) CASA volunteers must not assume the responsibilities of attorneys for children.

(4) The appointment of an attorney to represent the child does not prevent the appointment of a CASA volunteer for that child, and courts are encouraged to appoint both an

attorney and a CASA volunteer for the child in as many cases as possible.

(g) Interests of the child

At any time following the filing of a petition under section 300 and until juvenile court jurisdiction is terminated, any interested person may advise the court of information regarding an interest or right of the child to be protected or pursued in other judicial or administrative forums.

(1) *Juvenile Dependency Petition (Version One)* (form JV–100) and *Request to Change Court Order* (form JV–180) may be used.

(2) If the attorney for the child, or a CASA volunteer acting as a CAPTA guardian ad litem, learns of any such interest or right, the attorney or CASA volunteer must notify the court immediately and seek instructions from the court as to any appropriate procedures to follow.

(3) If the court determines that further action on behalf of the child is required to protect or pursue any interests or rights, the court must appoint an attorney for the child, if the child is not already represented by counsel, and do one or all of the following:

(A) Refer the matter to the appropriate agency for further investigation and require a report to the court within a reasonable time;

(B) Authorize and direct the child's attorney to initiate and pursue appropriate action;

(C) Appoint a guardian ad litem for the child. The guardian may be the CASA volunteer already appointed as a CAPTA guardian ad litem or a person who will act only if required to initiate appropriate action; or

(D) Take any other action to protect or pursue the interests and rights of the child.

(Formerly Rule 1438, adopted, eff. Jan. 1, 1996. As amended, eff. July 1, 1999; July 1, 2001; Jan. 1, 2003; Jan. 1, 2005; Jan. 1, 2006. Renumbered Rule 5.660 and amended, eff. Jan. 1, 2007. As amended, eff. Jan. 1, 2014; Jan. 1, 2015.)

Research References

Treatises and Practice Aids

Witkin, California Summary 10th Parent and Child § 569, Protection Of Interests and Rights.

Witkin, California Summary 10th Parent and Child § 571, in General.

Witkin, California Summary 10th Parent and Child § 572, Appointment Of Guardian Ad Litem or Child Advocate.

Witkin, California Summary 10th Parent and Child § 573, Powers and Duties Of Counsel.

Witkin, California Summary 10th Parent and Child § 574, in General.

Witkin, California Summary 10th Parent and Child § 580, Right to Competent Counsel.

Witkin, California Summary 10th Parent and Child § 574A, (New) Guidelines for Sibling Representation.

Rule 5.661. Representation of the child on appeal

(a) Definition

For purposes of this rule, "guardian ad litem" means a person designated as the child's Child Abuse Prevention and Treatment Act (CAPTA) guardian ad litem as defined in rule 5.662.

(b) Child as appellant

A notice of appeal on behalf of the child must be filed by the child's trial counsel, guardian ad litem, or the child if the child is seeking appellate relief from the trial court's judgment or order.

(c) Recommendation from child's trial counsel or guardian ad litem

(1) In any juvenile dependency proceeding in which a party other than the child files a notice of appeal, if the child's trial counsel or guardian ad litem concludes that, for purposes of the appeal, the child's best interests cannot be protected without the appointment of separate counsel on appeal, the child's trial counsel or guardian ad litem must file a recommendation in the Court of Appeal requesting appointment of separate counsel.

(2) A child's trial counsel or guardian ad litem who recommends appointment of appellate counsel for a child who is not an appellant must follow the procedures outlined in (d)–(g).

(d) Time for trial counsel or guardian ad litem to file the recommendation with the Court of Appeal

A recommendation from the child's trial counsel or guardian ad litem may be filed at any time after a notice of appeal has been filed, but absent good cause, must be filed in the Court of Appeal no later than 20 calendar days after the filing of the last appellant's opening brief.

(e) Service of recommendation

The child's trial counsel or guardian ad litem must serve a copy of the recommendation filed in the Court of Appeal on the district appellate project and the trial court.

(f) Factors to be considered

The following are factors to be considered by a child's trial counsel or guardian ad litem in making a recommendation to the Court of Appeal:

(1) An actual or potential conflict exists between the interests of the child and the interests of any respondent;

(2) The child did not have an attorney serving as his or her guardian ad litem in the trial court;

(3) The child is of a sufficient age or development such that he or she is able to understand the nature of the proceedings and,

(A) The child expresses a desire to participate in the appeal, or

(B) The child's wishes differ from his or her trial counsel's position;

(4) The child took a legal position in the trial court adverse to that of one of his or her siblings, and an issue has been raised in an appellant's opening brief regarding the siblings' adverse positions;

(5) The appeal involves a legal issue regarding a determination of parentage, the child's inheritance rights, educational rights, privileges identified in division 8 of the Evidence Code, consent to treatment, or tribal membership;

(6) Postjudgment evidence completely undermines the legal underpinnings of the juvenile court's judgment under

review, and all parties recognize this and express a willingness to stipulate to reversal of the juvenile court's judgment;

(7) The child's trial counsel or guardian ad litem, after reviewing the appellate briefs, believes that the legal arguments contained in the respondents' briefs do not adequately represent or protect the best interests of the child; and

(8) The existence of any other factors relevant to the child's best interests.

(g) Form of recommendation

The child's trial counsel, the guardian ad litem, or the child may use *Recommendation for Appointment of Appellate Attorney for Child* (form JV–810). Any recommendation for an appellate attorney for the child must state a factual basis for the recommendation, include the information provided on form JV–810, and be signed under penalty of perjury. *(Adopted, eff. July 1, 2007. As amended, eff. Jan. 1, 2015.)*

Research References

Forms

West's California Judicial Council Forms JV-810, Recommendation for Appointment Of Appellate Attorney for Child (California Rules Of Court, Rule 5.661).

Treatises and Practice Aids

Witkin, California Summary 10th Parent and Child § 708, Counsel on Appeal.

Witkin, California Summary 10th Parent and Child § 712, Notice Of Appeal.

Rule 5.662. Child Abuse Prevention and Treatment Act (CAPTA) guardian ad litem for a child subject to a juvenile dependency petition

(a) Authority

This rule is adopted under section 326.5.

(b) Applicability

The definition of the role and responsibilities of a CAPTA guardian ad litem in this rule applies exclusively to juvenile dependency proceedings and is distinct from the definitions of guardian ad litem in all other juvenile, civil, and criminal proceedings. No limitation period for bringing an action based on an injury to the child commences running solely by reason of the appointment of a CAPTA guardian ad litem under section 326.5 and this rule.

(c) Appointment

A CAPTA guardian ad litem must be appointed for every child who is the subject of a juvenile dependency petition under section 300. An attorney appointed under rule 5.660 will serve as the child's CAPTA guardian ad litem under section 326.5. If the court finds that the child would not benefit from the appointment of counsel, the court must appoint a CASA volunteer to serve as the child's CAPTA guardian ad litem. The court must identify on the record the person appointed as the child's CAPTA guardian ad litem.

(d) General duties and responsibilities

The general duties and responsibilities of a CAPTA guardian ad litem are:

(1) To obtain firsthand a clear understanding of the situation and needs of the child; and

(2) To make recommendations to the court concerning the best interest of the child as appropriate under (e) and (f).

(e) Attorney as guardian ad litem

The specific duties and responsibilities of the child's court-appointed attorney who is appointed to serve as the child's CAPTA guardian ad litem are stated in section 317(e) and rule 5.660.

(f) CASA volunteer as CAPTA guardian ad litem

The specific duties and responsibilities of the child's CASA volunteer who is appointed to serve as the child's CAPTA guardian ad litem are stated in section 102(c) and rule 5.655. *(Formerly Rule 1448, adopted, eff. Jan. 1, 2003. Renumbered Rule 5.662 and amended, eff. Jan. 1, 2007.)*

Research References

Treatises and Practice Aids

Witkin, California Summary 10th Parent and Child § 572, Appointment Of Guardian Ad Litem or Child Advocate.

Witkin, California Summary 10th Parent and Child § 708, Counsel on Appeal.

Witkin, California Summary 10th Parent and Child § 709, in General.

Rule 5.663. Responsibilities of children's counsel in delinquency proceedings (§§ 202, 265, 633, 634, 634.6, 679, 700)

(a) Purpose

This rule is designed to ensure public safety and the protection of the child's best interest at every stage of the delinquency proceedings by clarifying the role of the child's counsel in delinquency proceedings. This rule is not intended to affect any substantive duty imposed on counsel by existing civil standards or professional discipline standards.

(b) Responsibilities of counsel

A child's counsel is charged in general with defending the child against the allegations in all petitions filed in delinquency proceedings and with advocating, within the framework of the delinquency proceedings, that the child receive care, treatment, and guidance consistent with his or her best interest.

(c) Right to representation

A child is entitled to have the child's interests represented by counsel at every stage of the proceedings, including postdispositional hearings. Counsel must continue to represent the child unless relieved by the court on the substitution of other counsel or for cause.

(d) Limits to responsibilities

A child's counsel is not required:

(1) To assume the responsibilities of a probation officer, social worker, parent, or guardian;

(2) To provide nonlegal services to the child; or

(3) To represent the child in any proceedings outside of the delinquency proceedings. *(Formerly Rule 1479, adopted, eff. July 1, 2004. Renumbered Rule 5.663 and amended, eff. Jan. 1, 2007.)*

Research References

Treatises and Practice Aids

Witkin, California Summary 10th Parent and Child § 444, Scope and Organization.

Rule 5.664. Training requirements for children's counsel in delinquency proceedings (§ 634.3)

(a) Definition

"Competent counsel" means an attorney who is a member, in good standing, of the State Bar of California, who provides representation in accordance with Welfare and Institutions Code section 634.3(a)(1)–(3), and who has participated in training in the law and practice of juvenile delinquency as defined in this rule.

(b) Education and training requirements

(1) Only those attorneys who, during each of the most recent three calendar years, have dedicated at least 50 percent of their practice to juvenile delinquency and demonstrated competence or who have completed a minimum of 12 hours of training or education during the most recent 12–month period in the area of juvenile delinquency, may be appointed to represent youth.

(2) *Attorney training must include:*

(A) An overview of delinquency law and related statutes and cases;

(B) Trial skills, including drafting and filing pretrial motions, introducing evidence at trial, preserving the record for appeal, filing writs, notices of appeal, and posttrial motions;

(C) Advocacy at the detention phase;

(D) Advocacy at the dispositional phase;

(E) Child and adolescent development, including training on interviewing and working with adolescent clients;

(F) Competence and mental health issues, including capacity to commit a crime and the effects of trauma, child abuse, and family violence, as well as crossover issues presented by youth involved in the dependency system;

(G) Police interrogation methods, suggestibility of juveniles, and false confessions;

(H) Counsel's ethical duties, including racial, ethnic, and cultural understanding and addressing bias;

(I) Cultural competency and sensitivity relating to, and best practices for, providing adequate care to lesbian, gay, bisexual, and transgender youth;

(J) Understanding of the effects of and how to work with victims of human trafficking and commercial sexual exploitation of children and youth;

(K) Immigration consequences and the requirements of Special Immigrant Juvenile Status;

(L) General and special education, including information on school discipline;

(M) Extended foster care;

(N) Substance abuse;

(O) How to secure effective rehabilitative resources, including information on available community-based resources;

(P) Direct and collateral consequences of court involvement;

(Q) ~~Fitness~~ <u>Transfer of jurisdiction to criminal court</u> hearings and advocacy in adult court;

(R) Appellate advocacy; and

(S) Advocacy in the postdispositional phase.

(c) Continuing education requirements

(1) To remain eligible for appointment to represent delinquent youth, attorneys must engage in annual continuing education in the areas listed in (b)(2), as follows:

(A) Attorneys must complete at least 8 hours per calendar year of continuing education, for a total of 24 hours, during each MCLE compliance period.

(B) An attorney who is eligible to represent delinquent youth for only a portion of the corresponding MCLE compliance period must complete training hours in proportion to the amount of time the attorney was eligible. An attorney who is eligible to represent delinquent youth for only a portion of a calendar year must complete two hours of training for every three months of eligibility.

(C) The 12 hours of initial training may be applied toward the continuing training requirements for the first compliance period.

(2) Each individual attorney is responsible for complying with the training requirements in this rule; however, offices of the public defender and other agencies that work with delinquent youth are encouraged to provide MCLE training that meets the training requirements in (b)(2).

(3) Each individual attorney is encouraged to participate in policy meetings or workgroups convened by the juvenile court and to participate in local trainings designed to address county needs.

(d) Evidence of competency

The court may require evidence of the competency of any attorney appointed to represent a youth in a delinquency proceeding, including requesting documentation of trainings attended. The court may also require attorneys who represent youth in delinquency proceedings to complete Declaration of Eligibility for Appointment to Represent Youth in Delinquency Court (JV–700). *(Adopted, eff. July 1, 2016. As amended, eff. May 22, 2017.)*

Research References

Forms

West's California Judicial Council Forms JV-419, Guardianship--Consent and Waiver Of Rights.

West's California Judicial Council Forms JV-700, Declaration Of Eligibility for Appointment to Represent Youth in Delinquency Court.

West's California Judicial Council Forms JV-419A, Guardianship--Child's Consent and Waiver Of Rights.

Treatises and Practice Aids

Witkin, California Summary 10th Parent and Child § 522, Nature and Scope Of Indian Child Welfare Act.

Witkin, California Summary 10th Parent and Child § 523, Definitions.

Witkin, California Summary 10th Parent and Child § 524, Jurisdiction.

Witkin, California Summary 10th Parent and Child § 526, Determination Of Indian Status.
Witkin, California Summary 10th Parent and Child § 527, Procedure Where Child May be Indian Child.
Witkin, California Summary 10th Parent and Child § 528, in General.
Witkin, California Summary 10th Parent and Child § 529, Formal Requisites.
Witkin, California Summary 10th Parent and Child § 531, Determining Adequacy Of Notice.
Witkin, California Summary 10th Parent and Child § 532, in General.
Witkin, California Summary 10th Parent and Child § 534, Out-Of-Home Placement or Guardianship.
Witkin, California Summary 10th Parent and Child § 535, Placement Standards and Preferences.
Witkin, California Summary 10th Parent and Child § 536, Termination Of Parental Rights.
Witkin, California Summary 10th Parent and Child § 537, Proceedings After Termination or Removal.
Witkin, California Summary 10th Parent and Child § 896, General Requirements.

Chapter 12

CASES PETITIONED UNDER SECTION 300

Article 1

INITIAL HEARING

Rule 5.667. Service and notice

(a) In court order of notice (§ 296)

The court may order the child, or any parent or guardian or Indian custodian of the child who is present in court, to appear again before the court, social worker, probation officer, or county financial officer at a specified time and place as stated in the order.

(b) Language of notice

If it appears that the parent or guardian does not read English, the social worker must provide notice in the language believed to be spoken by the parent or guardian. *(Formerly Rule 1440, adopted, eff. Jan. 1, 1998. As amended, eff. Jan. 1, 2006. Renumbered Rule 5.667 and amended, eff. Jan. 1, 2007.)*

Research References

Treatises and Practice Aids

Witkin, California Summary 10th Parent and Child § 444, Scope and Organization.
Witkin, California Summary 10th Parent and Child § 463, Transfer-In Hearing.
Witkin, California Summary 10th Parent and Child § 589, Informality and Control by Court.
Witkin, California Summary 10th Parent and Child § 598, in General.
Witkin, California Summary 10th Parent and Child § 600, Petition and Notice Of Hearing.
Witkin, California Summary 10th Parent and Child § 657, Filing, Setting for Hearing, and Notice.
Witkin, California Summary 10th Parent and Child § 668, Subsequent Petition.
Witkin, California Summary 10th Parent and Child § 706, Waiver Of Appellate Review.

Rule 5.668. Commencement of hearing—explanation of proceedings (§§ 316, 316.2)

(a) Commencement of hearing

At the beginning of the initial hearing on the petition, whether the child is detained or not detained, the court must give advisement as required by rule 5.534 and must inform each parent and guardian present, and the child, if present:

(1) Of the contents of the petition;

(2) Of the nature of, and possible consequences of, juvenile court proceedings;

(3) If the child has been taken into custody, of the reasons for the initial detention and the purpose and scope of the detention hearing; and

(4) If the petition is sustained and the child is declared a dependent of the court and removed from the custody of the parent or guardian, the court-ordered reunification services must be considered to have been offered or provided on the date the petition is sustained or 60 days after the child's initial removal, whichever is earlier. The time for services must not exceed 12 months for a child three years of age or older ~~aged three or over~~ at the time of the initial removal and must not exceed 6 months for a child who was under ~~the age of~~ three years of age or who is in a sibling group in which one sibling was under three years of age at the time of the initial removal if the parent or guardian fails to participate regularly and make substantive progress in any court-ordered treatment program.

(b) Parentage inquiry

The court must also inquire of the child's mother and of any other appropriate person present as to the identity and address of any and all presumed or alleged parents of the child as set forth in section 316.2. ~~Questions, at the discretion of the court, may include:~~

~~(1) Has there been a judgment of parentage?~~

~~(2) Was the mother married, or did she believe she was married, at or any time after the time of conception?~~

~~(3) Was the mother cohabiting at the time of conception?~~

~~(4) Has the mother received support payments or promises of support for the child or for the mother during her pregnancy?~~

~~(5) Has anyone formally or informally acknowledged parentage, including through the execution of a voluntary declaration under Family Code section 7571?~~

~~(6) Have tests to determine biological parentage been administered and, if so, what were the results?~~

(c) Health and education information (§ 16010)

The court must order each parent and guardian present either to complete *Your Child's Health and Education* (form JV–225) or to provide the information necessary for the social worker or probation officer, court staff, or representative of the local child welfare agency to complete the form. The social worker or probation officer assigned to the dependency matter must provide the child's attorney with a copy of the completed form. Before each periodic status review hearing, the social worker or probation officer must obtain and include in the reports prepared for the hearing all information necessary to maintain the accuracy of form JV–225. *(Formerly Rule 1441, adopted, eff. Jan. 1, 1998. As amended, eff. Jan. 1, 1999; Jan. 1, 2001; Jan. 1, 2002. Renumbered Rule 5.668 and amended, eff. Jan. 1, 2007. As amended, eff. Jan. 1, 2008; Jan. 1, 2015; Jan. 1, 2017.)*

Research References

Treatises and Practice Aids

Witkin, California Summary 10th Parent and Child § 567, Statutory Rights.

Witkin, California Summary 10th Parent and Child § 602, Explanation and Information.

Witkin, California Summary 10th Parent and Child § 603, Identification Of Presumed or Alleged Fathers.

Rule 5.670. Initial hearing; detention hearings; time limit on custody; setting jurisdiction hearing; visitation (§§ 309, 311, 313, 315, 362.1)

(a) Child not detained; filing petition, setting hearing

If the social worker does not take the child into custody but determines that a petition concerning the child should be filed, the social worker must file a petition with the clerk of the juvenile court as soon as possible. The clerk must set an initial hearing on the petition within 15 court days.

~~**(b) Time limit on custody, filing petition, setting hearing (§§ 311, 313)**~~

~~If the social worker takes the child into custody, the social worker must immediately file a petition with the clerk of the juvenile court, and the clerk must immediately set the matter for hearing on the detention hearing calendar. A child who is detained must be released within 48 hours, excluding noncourt days, unless a petition has been filed.~~

~~**(d) Detention hearing—time of (§ 315)**~~

~~Unless the child has been released sooner, the matter concerning a child who is taken into custody must be brought before the juvenile court for a detention hearing as soon as possible, but in any event before the end of the next court day after a petition has been filed. At the detention hearing, the court must determine whether the child is to continue to be detained in custody. If the detention hearing is not commenced within that time, the child must be immediately released from custody.~~

~~(e)~~(b) Detention hearing—warrant cases, transfers in, changes in placement.

Notwithstanding ~~(c)~~ section 309(b), and unless the child has been released sooner, a detention hearing must be held as soon as possible, but no later than 48 hours, excluding noncourt days, after the child arrives at a facility within the county if:

(1) The child was taken into custody in another county and transported in custody to the requesting county under a protective custody warrant issued by the juvenile court;

(2) The child was taken into custody in the county in which a protective custody warrant was issued by the juvenile court; or

(3) The matter was transferred from the juvenile court of another county under rule 5.610 and the child was ordered transported in custody.

At the hearing the court must determine whether the child is to continue to be detained in custody. If the hearing is not commenced within that time, the child must be immediately released from custody.

~~**(f) Setting jurisdiction hearing (§ 334)**~~

~~If the child is not detained, the court must set a jurisdiction hearing to be held within 30 days of the date the petition is filed. If the court orders the child to be detained, the court must set a jurisdiction hearing within 15 court days of the order of detention.~~

~~(g)~~(c) Visitation

(1) The court must consider the issue of visitation between the child and other persons, determine if contact pending the jurisdiction hearing would be beneficial or detrimental to the child, and make appropriate orders.

(2) The court must consider the issue of visitation between the child and any sibling who was not placed with the child, and who was taken into custody with the child or is otherwise under the court's jurisdiction, and enter an order for sibling visitation pending the jurisdiction hearing, unless the court finds by clear and convincing evidence that sibling interaction between the child and the sibling is contrary to the safety or well-being of either child. *(Formerly Rule 1442, adopted, eff. Jan. 1, 1998. Renumbered Rule 5.670 and amended, eff. Jan. 1, 2007. As amended, eff. July 1, 2011; Jan. 1, 2017.)*

Research References

Forms

West's California Judicial Council Forms JV-400, Visitation Attachment: Parents, Legal Guardian, Indian Custodian, Other Important Person.

West's California Judicial Council Forms JV-401, Visitation Attachment: Sibling.

West's California Judicial Council Forms JV-402, Visitation Attachment: Grandparent.

Treatises and Practice Aids

Witkin, California Summary 10th Parent and Child § 598, in General.

Witkin, California Summary 10th Parent and Child § 600, Petition and Notice Of Hearing.

Witkin, California Summary 10th Parent and Child § 607, Findings and Orders.

Witkin, California Summary 10th Parent and Child § 609, Time for Hearing.

Rule 5.672. Continuances

(a) Detention hearing; right to one-day continuance; custody pending continued hearing (§§ 319, 322)

On motion of the child, parent, or guardian, the court must continue the detention hearing for one court day. Unless otherwise ordered by the court, the child must remain detained pending completion of the detention hearing or a rehearing. The court must either find that continuance in the home of the parent or guardian is contrary to the child's welfare or order the child released to the custody of the parent or guardian. The court may enter this finding on a temporary basis, without prejudice to any party, and reevaluate the finding at the time of the continued detention hearing.

(b) Initial hearing; child not detained

If the child is not detained, motions for continuances of the initial hearing must be made and ruled on under rule 5.550. *(Formerly Rule 1443, adopted, eff. Jan. 1, 1998. As amended, eff. July 1, 2002. Renumbered Rule 5.672 and amended, eff. Jan. 1, 2007.)*

Research References

Forms

West's California Judicial Council Forms JV-405, Continuance--Dependency Detention Hearing.

West's California Judicial Council Forms JV-406, Continuance--Dependency General.

Treatises and Practice Aids

Witkin, California Summary 10th Parent and Child § 598, in General.

Witkin, California Summary 10th Parent and Child § 601, Continuance Of Hearing.

Rule 5.674. Conduct of hearing; admission, no contest, submission

(a) Admission, no contest, submission

(1) At the initial hearing, whether or not the child is detained, the parent or guardian may admit the allegations of the petition, plead no contest, or submit the jurisdictional determination to the court based on the information provided to the court and waive further jurisdictional hearing.

(2) If the court accepts an admission, a plea of no contest, or a submission from each parent and guardian with standing to participate as a party, the court must then proceed according to rules 5.682 and 5.686.

(b) Detention hearing; general conduct (§ 319; 42 U.S.C. § 600 et seq.)

(1) The court must read, consider, and reference any reports submitted by the social worker and any relevant evidence submitted by any party or counsel. All detention findings and orders must appear in the written orders of the court.

(2) The findings and orders that must be made on the record are:

(A) Continuance in the home is contrary to the child's welfare;

(B) Temporary placement and care are vested with the social services agency;

(C) Reasonable efforts have been made to prevent removal; and

(D) The findings and orders required to be made on the record under section 319.

~~**(c) Detention hearing; examination by court (§ 319)**~~

~~Subject to (d), the court must examine the child's parent, guardian, or other person having knowledge relevant to the issue of detention and must receive any relevant evidence that the petitioner, the child, a parent, a guardian, or counsel for a party wishes to present.~~

~~(d)~~(c) Detention hearing; rights of child, parent, or guardian (§§ 311, 319)

At the detention hearing, the child, the parent, and the guardian have the right to assert the privilege against self-incrimination and the right to confront and cross-examine:

(1) The preparer of a police report, probation or social worker report, or other document submitted to the court; and

(2) Any person examined by the court under ~~(c)~~ section 319. If the child, parent, or guardian asserts the right to cross-examine preparers of documents submitted for court consideration, the court may not consider any such report or document unless the preparer is made available for cross-examination.

(d) No parent or guardian present and not noticed (§ 321)

If the court orders the child detained at the detention hearing and no parent or guardian is present and no parent or guardian has received actual notice of the detention hearing, a parent or guardian may file an affidavit alleging the failure of notice and requesting a detention rehearing. The clerk must set the rehearing for a time within 24 hours of the filing of the affidavit, excluding noncourt days. At the rehearing the court must proceed under rules 5.670–5.678.

(e) Hearing for further evidence; prima facie case (§ 321)

If the court orders the child detained, and the child, a parent, a guardian, or counsel requests that evidence of the prima facie case be presented, the court must set a prima facie hearing for a time within 3 court days to consider evidence of the prima facie case or set the matter for jurisdiction hearing within 10 court days. If at the hearing the petitioner fails to establish the prima facie case, the child must be released from custody. *(Formerly Rule 1444, adopted, eff. Jan. 1, 1998. As amended, eff. July 1, 2002. Renumbered Rule 5.674 and amended, eff. Jan. 1, 2007. As amended, eff. Jan. 1, 2016; Jan. 1, 2017.)*

Research References

Treatises and Practice Aids

Witkin, California Summary 10th Parent and Child § 567, Statutory Rights.

Witkin, California Summary 10th Parent and Child § 576, in General.

Witkin, California Summary 10th Parent and Child § 578, Confrontation and Cross-Examination.

Witkin, California Summary 10th Parent and Child § 604, in General.
Witkin, California Summary 10th Parent and Child § 605, Rights Of Child, Parent, and Guardian.
Witkin, California Summary 10th Parent and Child § 607, Findings and Orders.

Rule 5.676. Requirements for detention

(a) Requirements for detention (§ 319)

No child may be ordered detained by the court unless the court finds that:

(1) A prima facie showing has been made that the child is described by section 300;

(2) Continuance in the home of the parent or guardian is contrary to the child's welfare; and

(3) One or more of the grounds for detention in rule 5.678 is found.

(b) Evidence required at detention hearing

In making the findings required to support an order of detention, the court may rely solely on written police reports, probation or social worker reports, or other documents. The reports relied on must include:

(1) A statement of the reasons the child was removed from the parent's custody;

(2) A description of the services that have been provided, including those under section 306, and of any available services or safety plans that would prevent or eliminate the need for the child to remain in custody;

(3) If a parent is enrolled in a certified substance abuse treatment facility that allows a dependent child to reside with his or her parent, information and a recommendation regarding whether the child can be returned to the custody of that parent;

(4) Identification of the need, if any, for the child to remain in custody; and

(5) If continued detention is recommended, information about any parent or guardian of the child with whom the child was not residing at the time the child was taken into custody and about any relative or nonrelative extended family member as defined under section 362.7 with whom the child may be detained. *(Formerly Rule 1445, adopted, eff. Jan. 1, 1998. As amended, eff. July 1, 2002. Renumbered Rule 5.676 and amended, eff. Jan. 1, 2007. As amended, eff. Jan. 1, 2016.)*

Research References

Treatises and Practice Aids

Witkin, California Summary 10th Parent and Child § 604, in General.

Rule 5.678. Findings in support of detention; factors to consider; reasonable efforts; detention alternatives

(a) Findings in support of detention (§ 319; 42 U.S.C., § 600 et seq.)

The court must order the child released from custody unless the court finds that:

(1) A prima facie showing has been made that the child is described by section 300;

(2) Continuance in the home of the parent or guardian is contrary to the child's welfare; and

(3) Any of the following grounds exist:

(A) There is a substantial danger to the physical health of the child or the child is suffering severe emotional damage, and there are no reasonable means to protect the child's physical or emotional health without removing the child from the parent's or guardian's physical custody;

(B) The child is a dependent of the juvenile court who has left a placement;

(C) The parent, guardian, or responsible relative is likely to flee the jurisdiction of the court with the child; or

(D) The child is unwilling to return home and the petitioner alleges that a person residing in the home has physically or sexually abused the child.

(b) Factors to consider

In determining whether to release or detain the child under (a), the court must consider the following:

(1) Whether the child can be returned home if the court orders services to be provided, including services under section 306; and

(2) Whether the child can be returned to the custody of his or her parent who is enrolled in a certified substance abuse treatment facility that allows a dependent child to reside with his or her parent.

(c) Findings of the court—reasonable efforts (§ 319; 42 U.S.C., § 600 et seq.)

(1) Whether the child is released or detained at the hearing, the court must determine whether reasonable efforts have been made to prevent or eliminate the need for removal and must make one of the following findings:

(A) Reasonable efforts have been made; or

(B) Reasonable efforts have not been made.

(2) The court must not order the child detained unless the court, after inquiry regarding available services, finds that there are no reasonable services that would prevent or eliminate the need to detain the child or that would permit the child to return home.

(3) If the court orders the child detained, the court must:

(A) Determine if there are services that would permit the child to return home pending the next hearing and state the factual bases for the decision to detain the child;

(B) Specify why the initial removal was necessary; and

(C) If appropriate, order services to be provided as soon as possible to reunify the child and the child's family.

(d) Order of the court (§ 319, 42 U.S.C., § 600 et seq.)

If the court orders the child detained, the court must order that temporary care and custody of the child be vested with the county welfare department pending disposition or further order of the court.

(e) Detention alternatives (§ 319)

The court may order the child detained in the approved home of a relative, an emergency shelter, another suitable licensed home or facility, a place exempt from licensure if specifically designated by the court, or the approved home of a nonrelative extended family member as defined in section 362.7.

(1) In determining the suitability of detention with a relative or a nonrelative extended family member, the court must consider the recommendations of the social worker based on the approval of the home of the relative or nonrelative extended family member, including the results of checks of criminal records and any prior reports of alleged child abuse.

(2) The court must order any parent and guardian present to disclose the names, residences (if known), and any identifying information of any maternal or paternal relatives of the child. *(Formerly Rule 1446, adopted, eff. Jan. 1, 1998. As amended, eff. Jan. 1, 1999; July 1, 2002. Renumbered Rule 5.678 and amended, eff. Jan. 1, 2007. As amended, eff. Jan. 1, 2016.)*

Commentary

In re Ashly F., 225 Cal.App.4th 803, 170 Cal.Rptr.3d 523 (2014), reversed a dispositional order removing children from the parental home, finding that the evidence did not support the juvenile court's finding that reasonable efforts had been made to prevent the minors' removal and there were no reasonable means to protect the minors other than removing them from their home, as required by subsections (c)(1) and (d) of Welfare and Institutions Code section 361. For further discussion of reasonable efforts and means, see subsection (c) of this Rule and subsection (a)(1)(B)(i) of Rule 5.690.

Research References

Forms

West's California Judicial Council Forms JV-410, Findings and Orders After Detention Hearing (Welf. & Inst. Code, S319.

Treatises and Practice Aids

Witkin, California Summary 10th Parent and Child § 599, Grounds for Detention.

Witkin, California Summary 10th Parent and Child § 607, Findings and Orders.

Article 2

JURISDICTION

Rule

Rule 5.682. Commencement of jurisdiction hearing—advisement of trial rights; admission, no contest, submission

~~(a) Petition read and explained (§ 353)~~

~~At the beginning of the jurisdiction hearing, the petition must be read to those present. On request of the child or the parent, guardian, or adult relative, the court must explain the meaning and contents of the petition and the nature of the hearing, its procedures, and the possible consequences.~~

~~(b)~~(a) Rights explained (§§ 341, 353, 361.1)

After giving the advisement required by rule 5.534, the court must advise the parent or guardian of the following rights:

(1) The right to a hearing by the court on the issues raised by the petition; and

~~(2) The right to assert any privilege against self-incrimination1;~~

~~(3) The right to confront and to cross-examine all witnesses called to testify;~~

~~(4) The right to use the process of the court to compel attendance of witnesses on behalf of the parent or guardian; and~~

~~(5)~~(2) The right, if the child has been removed, to have the child returned to the parent or guardian within two working days after a finding by the court that the child does not come within the jurisdiction of the juvenile court under section 300, unless the parent or guardian and the child welfare agency agree that the child will be released on a later date.

~~(c)~~(b) Admission of allegations; prerequisites to acceptance

The court must then inquire whether the parent or guardian intends to admit or deny the allegations of the petition. If the parent or guardian neither admits nor denies the allegations, the court must state on the record that the parent or guardian does not admit the allegations. If the parent or guardian wishes to admit the allegations, the court must first find and state on the record that it is satisfied that the parent or guardian understands the nature of the allegations and the direct consequences of the admission, and understands and waives the rights in ~~(b)~~ (a) and (e)(3).

~~(d)~~(c) Parent or guardian must admit

An admission by the parent or guardian must be made personally by the parent or guardian.

~~(e)~~(d) Admission, no contest, submission

The parent or guardian may elect to admit the allegations of the petition~~,~~ or plead no contest~~, or submit the jurisdictional determination to the court based on the information provided to the court~~ and waive further jurisdictional hearing. The parent or guardian may elect to submit the jurisdictional determination to the court based on the information provided to the court and choose whether to waive further jurisdictional hearing. If the parent or guardian submits to the jurisdictional determination in writing, *Waiver of Rights—Juvenile Dependency* (form JV–190) ~~may~~ must be completed by the parent or guardian and counsel and submitted to the court.

~~(f)~~(e) Findings of court (§ 356)

After admission, plea of no contest, or submission, the court must make the following findings noted in the order of the court:

(1) Notice has been given as required by law;

(2) The birthdate and county of residence of the child;

(3) The parent or guardian has knowingly and intelligently waived the right to a trial on the issues by the court, the right to assert the privilege against self-incrimination, and the right to confront and to cross-examine adverse witnesses and to use the process of the court to compel the attendance of witnesses on the parent or guardian's behalf;

(4) The parent or guardian understands the nature of the conduct alleged in the petition and the possible consequences of an admission, plea of no contest, or submission;

(5) The admission, plea of no contest, or submission by the parent or guardian is freely and voluntarily made;

(6) There is a factual basis for the parent or guardian's admission;

(7) Those allegations of the petition as admitted are true as alleged; or ~~and~~

(8) Whether the allegations of the petition as submitted are true as alleged; and

~~(8)~~(9) The child is described ~~under~~ by one or more specific subdivisions of section 300.

~~(g)~~(f) Disposition

After accepting an admission, plea of no contest, or submission, the court must proceed to a disposition hearing under rule~~s 5.686 and~~ 5.690. *(Formerly Rule 1449, adopted, eff. Jan. 1, 1991. As amended, eff. Jan. 1, 2005. Renumbered Rule 5.682 and amended, eff. Jan. 1, 2007. As amended, eff. Jan. 1, 2017.)*

Research References

Forms

West's California Judicial Council Forms JV-412, Findings and Orders After Jurisdictional Hearing (Welf. & Inst. Code, S356).

Treatises and Practice Aids

Witkin, California Summary 10th Parent and Child § 444, Scope and Organization.
Witkin, California Summary 10th Parent and Child § 567, Statutory Rights.
Witkin, California Summary 10th Parent and Child § 576, in General.
Witkin, California Summary 10th Parent and Child § 578, Confrontation and Cross-Examination.
Witkin, California Summary 10th Parent and Child § 604, in General.
Witkin, California Summary 10th Parent and Child § 613, Commencement Of Hearing.
Witkin, California Summary 10th Parent and Child § 614, Determination by Admission, No Contest, or Submission.

Rule 5.684. Contested hearing on petition

(a) Contested jurisdiction hearing (§ 355)

If the parent or guardian denies the allegations of the petition, the court must hold a contested hearing and determine whether the allegations in the petition are true.

(b) Admissibility of evidence—general (§§ 355, 355.1)

Except as provided in sections 355(c) and 355.1 and (c)~~,~~ ~~(d),~~ and ~~(e)~~ (d) of this rule, the admission and exclusion of evidence must be in accordance with the Evidence Code as it applies to civil cases.

(c) Reports

(1) A social study, with hearsay evidence contained in it, is admissible ~~and is sufficient to support a finding that the child is described by section 300.~~ as provided in section 355.

~~(1)~~(2) The social study must be provided to all parties and their counsel by the county welfare department within a reasonable time before the hearing.

~~(2) The preparer of the report must be made available for cross-examination on the request of any party. The preparer may be on telephone standby if the preparer can be present in court within a reasonable time.~~

~~**(d) Hearsay in the report (§ 355)**~~

~~If a party makes an objection with reasonable specificity to particular hearsay in the report and provides petitioner a reasonable period to meet the objection, that evidence must not be sufficient in and of itself to support a jurisdictional finding, unless:~~

~~(1) The hearsay is admissible under any statutory or judicial hearsay exception;~~

~~(2) The hearsay declarant is a child under 12 years of age who is the subject of the petition, unless the objecting party establishes that the statement was produced by fraud, deceit, or undue influence and is therefore unreliable;~~

~~The hearsay declarant is a peace officer, a health practitioner, a social worker, or a teacher and the statement would be admissible if the declarant were testifying in court; or~~

~~The hearsay declarant is available for cross-examination.~~

~~(e)~~(d) Inapplicable privileges (Evid. Code, §§ 972, 986)

The privilege not to testify or to be called as a witness against a spouse or domestic partner, and the confidential marital communication privilege, does not apply to dependency proceedings.

~~(f)~~(e) Findings of court—allegations true (§ 356)

If the court determines by a preponderance of the evidence that the allegations of the petition are true, the court must make findings on each of the following, noted in the minutes:

(1) Notice has been given as required by law;

(2) The birthdate and county of residence of the child;

(3) The allegations of the petition are true; and

(4) The child is described ~~under~~ by one or more ~~specific~~ subdivisions of section 300.

~~(g)~~(f) Disposition and continuance pending disposition hearing (§§ 356, 358)

After making the findings in ~~(f)~~(e), the court must proceed to a disposition hearing under rule~~s 5.686 and~~ 5.690. The court may continue the disposition hearing as provided in section 358.

~~(h)~~(g) Findings of court—allegations not proved (§§ 356, 361.1)

If the court determines that the allegations of the petition have not been proved by a preponderance of the evidence, the court must dismiss the petition and terminate any detention orders relating to the petition. The court must order that the child be returned to the physical custody of the parent or guardian immediately but, in any event, not more than two working days following the date of that finding, unless the parent or guardian and the agency with custody of the child agree to a later date for the child's release. The court must make the following findings, noted in the order of the court:

(1) Notice has been given as required by law;

(2) The birthdate and county of residence of the child; and

(3) The allegations of the petition are not proved. *(Formerly Rule 1450, adopted, eff. Jan. 1, 1991. As amended, eff. July 1, 1997; Jan. 1, 2005. Renumbered Rule 5.684 and amended, eff. Jan. 1, 2007. As amended, eff. Jan. 1, 2017.)*

Research References

Forms

West's California Judicial Council Forms JV-412, Findings and Orders After Jurisdictional Hearing (Welf. & Inst. Code, S356).

Treatises and Practice Aids

Witkin, California Summary 10th Parent and Child § 615, in General.

Witkin, California Summary 10th Parent and Child § 617, in General.

Witkin, California Summary 10th Parent and Child § 618, Admissibility and Weight Of Social Study.

Witkin, California Summary 10th Parent and Child § 620, Privileges.

Witkin, California Summary 10th Parent and Child § 622, Findings and Order.

Article 3

DISPOSITION

Rule

Rule 5.690. General conduct of disposition hearing

(a) Social study (§§ 280, 358, 358.1, 360, 361.5, 16002(b))

The petitioner must prepare a social study of the child. The social study must include a discussion of all matters relevant to disposition and a recommendation for disposition.

(1) The petitioner must comply with the following when preparing the social study:

(A) If petitioner recommends that the court appoint a legal guardian, petitioner must prepare an assessment under section 360(a), to be included in the social study report prepared for disposition or in a separate document.

(B) If petitioner recommends removal of the child from the home, the social study must include:

(i) A discussion of the reasonable efforts made to prevent or eliminate removal and a recommended plan for reuniting the child with the family, including a plan for visitation;

(ii) A plan for achieving legal permanence for the child if efforts to reunify fail; and

(iii) A statement that each parent has been advised of the option to participate in adoption planning and to voluntarily relinquish the child if an adoption agency is willing to accept the relinquishment, and the parent's response.

(C) The social study ~~should~~ must include a discussion of the social worker's efforts to comply with rule 5.637, including but not limited to:

(i) The number of relatives identified and the relationship of each to the child;

(ii) The number and relationship of those relatives described by item (i) who were located and notified;

(iii) The number and relationship of those relatives described by item (ii) who are interested in ongoing contact with the child; and

(iv) The number and relationship of those relatives described by item (ii) who are interested in providing placement for the child.

(D) If siblings are not placed together, the social study must include an explanation of why they have not been placed together in the same home, what efforts are being made to place the siblings together, or why making those efforts would be contrary to the safety and well-being of any of the siblings.

~~(D)~~(E) If petitioner alleges that section 361.5(b) applies, the social study must state why reunification services should not be provided.

~~(E)~~(F) All other relevant requirements of sections 358 and 358.1.

(2) The petitioner must submit the social study and copies of it to the clerk at least 48 hours before the disposition hearing is set to begin, and the clerk must make the copies available to the parties and attorneys. A continuance within statutory time limits must be granted on the request of a party who has not been furnished a copy of the social study in accordance with this rule.

(b) Evidence considered (§§ 358, 360)

The court must receive in evidence and consider the social study, a guardianship assessment, the report of any CASA volunteer, the case plan, and any relevant evidence offered by petitioner, the child, or the parent or guardian. The court may require production of other relevant evidence on its own motion. In the order of disposition, the court must state that the social study and the study or evaluation by the CASA volunteer, if any, have been read and considered by the court.

(c) Case plan (§ 16501.1)

Whenever child welfare services are provided, the social worker must prepare a case plan.

(1) A written case plan must be completed and filed with the court by the date of disposition or within 60 calendar days of initial removal or of the in-person response required under section 16501(f) if the child has not been removed from his or her home, whichever occurs first.

(2) The court must consider the case plan and must find as follows:

(A) The social worker solicited and integrated into the case plan the input of the child, the child's family, the child's identified Indian tribe, including consultation with the child's tribe on whether tribal customary adoption as defined in section 366.24 is an appropriate permanent plan for the child if reunification is unsuccessful; and other interested parties, or

(B) The social worker did not solicit and integrate into the case plan the input of the child, the child's family, the child's identified Indian tribe, and other interested parties. If the court finds that the social worker did not solicit and integrate into the case plan the input of the child, the child's family, the child's identified Indian tribe, and other interested parties, the court must order that the social worker solicit and integrate into the case plan the input of the child, the child's family, the child's identified Indian tribe, and other interested parties, unless the court finds that each of these participants was unable, unavailable, or unwilling to participate.

(3) For a child 12 years of age or older and in a permanent placement, the court must consider the case plan and must find as follows:

(A) The child was given the opportunity to review the case plan, sign it, and receive a copy; or

(B) The child was not given the opportunity to review the case plan, sign it, and receive a copy. If the court makes such a finding, the court must order the agency to give the child the opportunity to review the case plan, sign it, and receive a copy.

(C) Whether the case plan was developed in compliance with and meets the requirements of section 16501.1(g). If the court finds that the development of the case plan does not comply with section 16501.1(g) the court must order the agency to comply with the requirements of section 16501.1(g).

(Formerly Rule 1455, adopted, eff. Jan. 1, 1991. As amended, eff. July 1, 1995; Jan. 1, 2000. Renumbered Rule 5.690 and amended, eff. Jan. 1, 2007. As amended, eff. Jan. 1, 2009; July 1, 2010; Jan. 1, 2011; Jan. 1, 2017.)

Commentary

In re Ashly F., 225 Cal.App.4th 803, 170 Cal.Rptr.3d 523 (2014), reversed a dispositional order removing children from the parental home, finding that the evidence did not support the juvenile court's finding that reasonable efforts had been made to prevent the minors' removal and there were no reasonable means to protect the minors other than removing them from their home, as required by subsections (c)(1) and (d) of Welfare and Institutions Code section 361. For further discussion of reasonable efforts and means, see Rules of Court, Rule 5.678(c) and subsection (a)(1)(B)(i) of this Rule.

Research References

Treatises and Practice Aids

Witkin, California Summary 10th Parent and Child § 4, Public Welfare Services.

Witkin, California Summary 10th Parent and Child § 10, Rights Of Foster Children.

Witkin, California Summary 10th Parent and Child § 334, Offer Of Less Detrimental Alternatives.

Witkin, California Summary 10th Parent and Child § 444, Scope and Organization.

Witkin, California Summary 10th Parent and Child § 614, Determination by Admission, No Contest, or Submission.

Witkin, California Summary 10th Parent and Child § 622, Findings and Order.

Witkin, California Summary 10th Parent and Child § 624, in General.

Witkin, California Summary 10th Parent and Child § 625, Preparation Of Social Study.

Witkin, California Summary 10th Parent and Child § 626, Conduct Of Hearing.

Witkin, California Summary 10th Parent and Child § 664, in General.

Rule 5.695. Findings and orders of the court—disposition

(a) Orders of the court (§§ 245.5, 358, 360, 361, 361.2, 390)

At the disposition hearing, the court may:

(1) Dismiss the petition with specific reasons stated in the minutes;

(2) Place the child under a program of supervision ~~as provided in~~ for a time period consistent with section 301 and order that services be provided;

(3) Appoint a legal guardian for the child without declaring dependency and order the clerk to issue letters of guardianship, which are not subject to the confidential protections of juvenile court documents as described in section 827;

(4) Declare dependency and appoint a legal guardian for the child if the requirements of section 360 are met and order the clerk to issue letters of guardianship, which are not subject to the confidential protections of juvenile court documents as described in section 827;

(5) Declare dependency, permit the child to remain at home, and order that services be provided;

(6) Declare dependency, permit the child to remain at home, limit the control to be exercised by the parent or guardian, and order that services be provided; or

(7) Declare dependency, remove physical custody from the parent or guardian, and:

(A) After stating on the record or in writing the factual basis for the order, order custody to a noncustodial parent, terminate jurisdiction, and direct that *Custody Order—Juvenile—Final Judgment* (form JV–200) be prepared and filed under rule 5.700;

(B) After stating on the record or in writing the factual basis for the order, order custody to a noncustodial parent with services to one or both parents; or

(C) Make a placement order and consider granting specific visitation rights to the child's grandparents.

~~**(b) Appointment of a legal guardian (§ 360)**~~

~~(1) At the disposition hearing, the court may appoint a legal guardian for the child if:~~

~~(A) The parent has advised the court that the parent does not wish to receive family maintenance services or family reunification services;~~

~~(B) The parent has executed and submitted *Waiver of Reunification Services (Juvenile Dependency)* (form JV–195);~~

~~(C) The court finds that the parent, and the child if of sufficient age and comprehension, knowingly and voluntarily waive their rights to reunification services and agree to the appointment of the legal guardian; and~~

~~(D) The court finds that the appointment of the legal guardian is in the best interest of the child.~~

~~(2) If the court appoints a legal guardian, it must:~~

~~(A) State on the record or in the minutes that it has read and considered the assessment;~~

~~(B) State on the record or in the minutes its findings and the factual bases for them;~~

~~(C) Advise the parent that no reunification services will be offered or provided;~~

~~(D) Make any appropriate orders regarding visitation between the child and the parent or other relative, including any sibling; and~~

~~(E) Order the clerk to issue letters of guardianship, which are not subject to the confidential protections of juvenile court documents as described in section 827.~~

~~(3) The court may appoint a legal guardian without declaring the child a dependent of the court. If dependency is declared, a six-month review hearing must be set.~~

~~(c)~~(b) Limitations on parental control (§§ 245.5, 361, 362; Gov. Code, § 7579.5)

(1) If a child is declared a dependent, the court may clearly and specifically limit the control over the child by a parent or guardian.

(2) If the court orders that a parent or guardian retain physical custody of the child subject to court-ordered supervision, the parent or guardian must be ordered to participate in child welfare services or services provided by an appropriate agency designated by the court.

(3) The court must consider whether it is necessary to limit the rights of the parent or guardian to make educational or developmental-services decisions for the child or youth. If the court limits those rights, it must follow the procedures in rules 5.649–5.651.

~~(d)~~(c) Removal of custody—required findings (§ 361)

The court may not order a dependent removed from the physical custody of a parent or guardian with whom the child resided at the time the petition was filed, unless the court ~~finds~~makes one or more of the findings in subdivision (c) of section 361 by clear and convincing evidence.~~ any of the following:~~

~~(1) There is a substantial danger to the physical health, safety, protection, or physical or emotional well-being of the child, or will be if the child is returned home, and there is no reasonable alternative means to protect that child;~~

~~(2) The parent or guardian is unwilling to have physical custody of the child and has been notified that if the child remains out of the parent's or guardian's physical custody for the period specified in section 366.26, the child may be declared permanently free of his or her custody and control;~~

~~(3) The child is suffering severe emotional damage, as indicated by extreme anxiety, depression, withdrawal, or untoward aggressive behavior toward self or others, and no reasonable alternative means to protect the child's emotional health exists;~~

~~(4) The child has been sexually abused by a parent or guardian or member of the household or other person known to his or her parent and there is no reasonable alternative means to protect the child or the child does not wish to return to the parent or guardian; or~~

~~(5) The child has been left without any provisions for his or her support and there is no parent or guardian available to maintain or provide for the care, custody, and control of the child.~~

~~(e)~~(d) Reasonable efforts finding

The court must consider whether reasonable efforts to prevent or eliminate the need for removal have been made and make one of the following findings:

(1) Reasonable efforts have been made to prevent removal; or

(2) Reasonable efforts have not been made to prevent removal.

~~(f)~~(e) Family-finding determination (§ 309)

(1) If the child is removed, the court must consider and determine whether the social worker has exercised due diligence in conducting the required investigation to identify, locate, and notify the child's relatives. The court may consider the activities listed in ~~(g)~~(f) as examples of due diligence. The court must document its determination by making a finding on the record.

If the dispositional hearing is continued, the court may set a hearing to be held 30 days from the date of removal or as soon as possible thereafter to consider and determine whether the social worker has exercised due diligence in conducting the required investigation to identify, locate, and notify the child's relatives.

(2) If the court finds that the social worker has not exercised due diligence, the court may order the social worker to exercise due diligence in conducting an investigation to identify, locate, and notify the child's relatives—except for any individual the social worker identifies as inappropriate to notify under rule 5.637(b)—and may require a written or oral report to the court.

~~(g)~~(f) Due diligence (§ 309)

When making the determination required in ~~(f)~~(e), the court may consider, among other examples of due diligence, whether the social worker has done any of the following:

(1) Asked the child, in an age-appropriate manner and consistent with the child's best interest, about his or her relatives;

(2) Obtained information regarding the location of the child's relatives;

(3) Reviewed the child's case file for any information regarding relatives;

(4) Telephoned, e-mailed, or visited all identified relatives;

(5) Asked located relatives for the names and locations of other relatives;

(6) Used Internet search tools to locate relatives identified as supports; or

(7) Developed tools, including a genogram, family tree, family map, or other diagram of family relationships, to help the child or parents to identify relatives.

~~(h)~~(g) Provision of reunification services (§ 361.5)

(1) Unless the court makes a finding that reunification services need not be provided under subdivision (b) of section 361.5~~ Except as provided in (6),~~ if a child is removed from the custody of a parent or legal guardian, the court must order the county welfare department to provide reunification services to the child and the child's mother and statutorily presumed parent, or the child's legal guardian, to facilitate reunification of the family as required in section 361.5.~~ For a child who was three years of age or older on the date of initial~~

~~removal, services must be provided during the time period beginning with the dispositional hearing and ending 12 months after the date the child entered foster care, as defined by section 361.49. For a child who was under three years of age on the date of initial removal, services must be provided for a period of 6 months from the dispositional hearing, but no longer than 12 months from the date the child entered foster care, as defined by section 361.49. The time period for the provision of family reunification services must be calculated consistent with section 361.5(a). The court must inform the parent or legal guardian of a child who was under three when initially removed that failure to participate regularly and make substantive progress in court-ordered treatment programs may result in the termination of reunification efforts after 6 months from the date of the dispositional hearing.~~

~~(2) If a child is a member of a sibling group removed from parental custody at the same time, and one member of the sibling group was under three at the time of the initial removal, reunification services for some or all members of the sibling group may be limited to 6 months from the dispositional hearing, and no later than 12 months from the date the children entered foster care. The court must inform the parent or legal guardian of a child who is a member of such a sibling group that failure to participate regularly and make substantive progress in court-ordered treatment programs may result in termination of reunification efforts after 6 months for one or more members of the sibling group.~~

~~(3)~~(2) On a finding and declaration of paternity by the juvenile court or proof of a prior declaration of paternity by any court of competent jurisdiction, the juvenile court may order services for the child and the biological father, if the court determines that such services will benefit the child.

~~(4) Any motion to terminate reunification services before the permanency hearing set under section 366.21(f) for a child age three or older, or before the 6-month review hearing set under section 366.21(e) for a child under age three, must follow the requirements in section 388(c) and rule 5.570. A motion to terminate reunification services at the 6-month review hearing is not required if the court finds by clear and convincing evidence that one or more of the circumstances described in section 361.5(a)(2) and rule 5.710(c)(1)(A) is true.~~

~~(5)~~(3) If a child is removed from the custody of a parent or guardian, and reunification services are ordered, the court must order visitation between the child and the parent or guardian for whom services are ordered. Visits are to be as frequent as possible, consistent with the well-being of the child.

~~(6)~~(4) Reunification services must not be provided when the parent has voluntarily relinquished the child and the relinquishment has been filed with the State Department of Social Services, or if the court has appointed a guardian under section 360. ~~Reunification services need not be provided to a parent or guardian if the court finds, by clear and convincing evidence, any of the following:~~

~~(A) The whereabouts of the parent or guardian are unknown. This finding must be supported by a declaration or by proof that a reasonably diligent search has failed to locate the parent. Posting or publishing notice is not required.~~

~~(B) The parent or guardian is suffering from a mental disability described in chapter 2 (commencing with section 7820) of part 4 of division 12 of the Family Code that renders the parent incapable of using those services.~~

~~(C) The child had been previously declared a dependent under any subdivision of section 300 as a result of physical or sexual abuse; following that adjudication the child had been removed from the custody of the parent or guardian under section 361; the child has been returned to the custody of the parent or guardian from whom the child had been taken originally; and the child is being removed under section 361 because of additional physical or sexual abuse.~~

~~(D) The parent or guardian of the child has caused the death of another child through abuse or neglect.~~

~~(E) The child was brought within the jurisdiction of the court under (e) of section 300 because of the conduct of that parent or guardian.~~

~~(F) The child is a dependent as a result of the determination that the child, a sibling, or a half-sibling suffered severe sexual abuse, as defined in section 361.5(b)(6), by the parent or guardian or that the parent or guardian inflicted severe physical harm, as defined in section 361.5(b)(6), on the child, a sibling, or a half-sibling, and the court finds that attempts to reunify would not benefit the child. The court must specify on the record the basis for the finding that the child suffered severe sexual abuse or the infliction of severe physical harm.~~

~~(G) The parent or guardian is not receiving reunification services for a sibling or half-sibling of the child, for reasons under (C), (E), or (F).~~

~~(H) The child was conceived as a result of the parent having committed an offense listed in Penal Code section 288 or 288.5, or by an act described by either section but committed outside California.~~

~~(I) The court has found that the child is described by (g) of section 300, that the child was willfully abandoned by the parent or guardian, and that the abandonment constituted serious danger to the child as defined in section 361.5(b)(9).~~

~~(J) The court has terminated reunification services for a sibling or half-sibling of the child because the parent failed to reunify with the sibling or half-sibling, and the parent or guardian has not made a reasonable effort to treat the problems that led to the removal of the sibling or half-sibling from that parent or guardian.~~

~~(K) The parental rights of a parent over any sibling or half-sibling of the child have been terminated, and the parent has not subsequently made a reasonable effort to treat the problem that led to the removal of the sibling or half-sibling.~~

~~(L) The parent or guardian has been convicted of a violent felony as defined in Penal Code section 667.5(c).~~

~~(M) The parent or guardian has a history of extensive, abusive, and chronic use of alcohol or other drugs and has not sought or participated in treatment during the three years immediately prior to the filing of the petition under~~

~~section 300, or has failed, on at least two prior occasions, to comply with an available and accessible treatment program described in the case plan required by section 358.1, and the removal of the child is based in whole or in part on the risk to the child presented by the use of alcohol or other drugs.~~

~~(N) The parent or guardian, who must be represented by counsel, has advised the court through the execution and submission of *Waiver of Reunification Services (Juvenile Dependency)* (form JV–195) that that parent or guardian does not wish to receive family maintenance or reunification services and does not wish the child returned or placed in the custody of that parent or guardian. The court may accept the waiver only on a finding on the record that the parent or guardian has knowingly and intelligently waived the right to services.~~

~~(O) On at least one occasion, the parent or guardian has abducted the child or a sibling or half-sibling from placement and has refused to disclose the abducted child's whereabouts or has refused to return custody of the abducted child to the placement or to the social worker.~~

~~(7) In deciding whether to order reunification in any case in which petitioner alleges that section 361.5(b) applies, the court must consider the report prepared by petitioner, which must discuss the factors contained in section 361.5(c).~~

~~(8) If the petitioner alleges that section 361.5(c) applies, the report prepared for disposition must address the issue of reunification services. At the disposition hearing, the court must consider the factors stated in section 361.5.~~

~~(9) If the court finds under (6)(A) that the whereabouts of the parent or guardian are unknown and that a diligent search has failed to locate the parent or guardian, the court may not order reunification services and must set the matter for a 6-month review hearing. If the parent or guardian is located prior to the 6-month review and requests reunification services, the welfare department must seek a modification of the disposition orders. The time limits for reunification services must be calculated from the date of the initial removal, and not from the date the parent is located or services are ordered.~~

~~(10) If the court finds that allegations under (6)(B) are proved, the court must nevertheless order reunification services unless evidence by mental health professionals establishes by clear and convincing evidence that the parent is unlikely to be able to care for the chIld within the n♪xt 12 months.~~

~~(11) If the court finds that the allegations under (6)(C), (D), (F), (G), (H), (I), (J), (K), (L), (M), (N), or (O) have been proved, the court may not order reunification services unless the party seeking the order for services proves by clear and convincing evidence that reunification is in the best interest of the child. If (6)(F) is found to apply, the court must consider the factors in section 361.5(h) in determining whether the child will benefit from services and must specify on the record the factual findings on which it based its determination that the child will not benefit.~~

~~(12) If the court finds that the allegations under (6)(E) have been proved, the court may not order reunification services unless it finds, based on consideration of factors in section 361.5(b) and (c), that services are likely to prevent reabuse or continued neglect or that failure to attempt reunification will be detrimental to the child.~~

~~(13) If the parent or guardian is institutionalized, incarcerated, or detained by the United States Department of Homeland Security, or has been deported to his or her country of origin, the court must order reunification services unless it finds by clear and convincing evidence that the services would be detrimental to the child, with consideration of the factors in section 361.5(e). The court may order reunification services with an institutionalized, incarcerated, detained, or deported biological father whose paternity has been declared by the juvenile court or another court of competent jurisdiction, if the court determines that such services would benefit the child, with consideration of the factors in section 361.5(e).~~

~~(14)~~(5) ~~If, with the exception of (6)(A)~~Except when the order is made under paragraph (1) of subdivision (b) of section 361.5, if the court orders no reunification services for every parent otherwise eligible for such services ~~under (1) and (2)~~, the court must conduct a hearing under section on 366.26 within 120 days and:

(A) Order that the social worker provide a copy of the child's birth certificate to the caregiver consistent with sections 16010.4(e)(5) and 16010.5(b)–(c); and

(B) Order that the social worker provide a child or youth 16 years of age or older with a certified copy of his or her birth certificate unless the court finds that provision of the birth certificate would be inappropriate.

~~(15)~~(6) A judgment, order, or decree setting a hearing under section 366.26 is not an immediately appealable order. Review may be sought only by filing a *Notice of Intent to File Writ Petition and Request for Record (California Rules of Court, Rule 8.450)* (form JV–820) or other notice of intent to file a writ petition and request for record, and a *Petition for Extraordinary Writ (California Rules of Court, Rules 8.452, 8.456)* (form JV–825) or other petition for extraordinary writ. If a party wishes to preserve any right to review on appeal of the findings and orders made under this rule, the party must seek an extraordinary writ under rules 8.450 and 8.452.

~~(16)~~(7) A judgment, order, or decree setting a hearing under section 366.26 may be reviewed on appeal following the order of the 366.26 hearing only if the following have occurred:

(A) An extraordinary writ was sought by the timely filing of a *Notice of Intent to File Writ Petition and Request for Record (California Rules of Court, Rule 8.450)* (form JV–820) or other notice of intent to file a writ petition and request for record, and a *Petition for Extraordinary Writ (California Rules of Court, Rules 8.452, 8.456)* (form JV–825) or other petition for extraordinary writ; and

(B) The petition for extraordinary writ was summarily denied or otherwise not decided on the merits.

~~(17)~~(8) Review on appeal of the order setting a hearing under section 366.26 is limited to issues raised in a previous petition for extraordinary writ that were supported by an adequate record.

~~(18)~~(9) Failure to file a notice of intent to file a writ petition and request for record and a petition for extraordinary writ review within the period specified by rules 8.450 and

8.452 to substantively address the issues challenged, or to support the challenge by an adequate record, precludes subsequent review on appeal of the findings and orders made under this rule.

~~(19)~~(10) When the court orders a hearing under section 366.26, the court must advise orally all parties present, and by first-class mail for parties not present, that if the party wishes to preserve any right to review on appeal of the order setting the hearing under section 366.26, the party must seek an extraordinary writ by filing a *Notice of Intent to File Writ Petition and Request for Record (California Rules of Court, Rule 8.450)* (form JV–820) or other notice of intent to file a writ petition and request for record and a *Petition for Extraordinary Writ (California Rules of Court, Rules 8.452, 8.456)* (form JV–825) or other petition for extraordinary writ.

(A) Within 24 hours of the hearing, notice by first-class mail must be provided by the clerk of the court to the last known address of any party who is not present when the court orders the hearing under section 366.26.

(B) Copies of *Petition for Extraordinary Writ (California Rules of Court, Rules 8.452, 8.456)* (form JV–825) and *Notice of Intent to File Writ Petition and Request for Record (California Rules of Court, Rule 8.450)* (form JV–820) must be available in the courtroom and must accompany all mailed notices informing the parties of their rights.

~~(i)~~(h) Information regarding termination of parent-child relationship (§§ 361, 361.5)

If a child is removed from the physical custody of the parent or guardian under either section 361 or 361.5, the court must:

(1) State the facts on which the decision is based; and

(2) Notify the parents that their parental rights may be terminated if custody is not returned within 6 months of the dispositional hearing or within 12 months of the date the child is determined to have entered foster care, whichever time limit is applicable.

~~**(j) Setting 6–month review (§§ 361.5, 366).** Review of the status of every dependent child must be performed within 6 months after the date of the original disposition order, and no later than 6 months after the date the child is determined to have entered foster care; the review must be scheduled on the appearance calendar. The court must advise the dependent child of the child's right to petition for modifications of court orders as required in section 353.1.~~

~~**(k) Fifteen-day reviews (§ 367).** If a child is detained pending the execution of the disposition order, the court must review the case at least every 15 calendar days to determine whether the delay is reasonable. During each review the court must inquire about the action taken by the probation or welfare department to carry out the court's order, the reasons for the delay, and the effect of the delay on the child.~~

~~(l)~~(i) Setting a hearing under section 366.26

At the disposition hearing, the court may not set a hearing under section 366.26 to consider termination of the rights of only one parent unless that parent is the only surviving parent, or the rights of the other parent have been terminated by a California court of competent jurisdiction or by a court of competent jurisdiction of another state under the statutes of that state, or the other parent has relinquished custody of the child to the county welfare department. *(Formerly Rule 1456, adopted, eff. Jan. 1, 1991. As amended, eff. Jan. 1, 1993; July 1, 1993; Jan. 1, 1994; Jan. 1, 1995; July 1, 1995; Jan. 1, 1996; July 1, 1997; Jan. 1, 1999; July 1, 1999; Jan. 1, 2001; July 1, 2001; July 1, 2002; Jan. 1, 2004; Jan. 1, 2006. Renumbered Rule 5.695 and amended, eff. Jan. 1, 2007. As amended, eff. Jan. 1, 2008; Jan. 1, 2010; Jan. 1, 2011; Jan. 1, 2014; Jan. 1, 2015; Jan. 1, 2017.)*

Commentary

A juvenile court may not award child custody to a noncustodial parent without first removing the child from the custodial parent. *In re Miguel C., 198 Cal.App.4th 965, 129 Cal.Rptr.3d 684 (2011).*

Research References

Forms

West's California Judicial Council Forms JV-415, Findings and Orders After Dispositional Hearing (Welf. & Inst. Code, S361 et seq.).

West's California Judicial Council Forms JV-416, Dispositional Attachment: Dismissal Of Petition With or Without Informal Supervision (Welf. & Inst. Code, S360(B)).

West's California Judicial Council Forms JV-417, Dispositional Attachment: In-Home Placement With Formal Supervision (Welf. & Inst. Code, 361).

West's California Judicial Council Forms JV-418, Dispositional Attachment: Appointment Of Guardian (Welf. & Inst. Code, 360(a)).

West's California Judicial Council Forms JV-419, Guardianship--Consent and Waiver Of Rights.

West's California Judicial Council Forms JV-420, Dispositional Attachment: Removal from Custodial Parent--Placement With Previously Noncustodial Parent (Welf. & Inst. Code, §§ 361, 361.2).

West's California Judicial Council Forms JV-421, Dispositional Attachment: Removal from Custodial Parent--Placement With Nonparent (Welf. & Inst. Code, §§ 361, 361.2).

West's California Judicial Council Forms JV-419A, Guardianship--Child's Consent and Waiver Of Rights.

Treatises and Practice Aids

Witkin, California Summary 10th Parent and Child § 334, Offer Of Less Detrimental Alternatives.

Witkin, California Summary 10th Parent and Child § 555, Investigation, Detention, and Release.

Witkin, California Summary 10th Parent and Child § 627, in General.

Witkin, California Summary 10th Parent and Child § 628, Legal Guardianship.

Witkin, California Summary 10th Parent and Child § 629, Limitations on Parental Control.

Witkin, California Summary 10th Parent and Child § 630, Bases for Removal.

Witkin, California Summary 10th Parent and Child § 631, Procedure.

Witkin, California Summary 10th Parent and Child § 633, in General.

Witkin, California Summary 10th Parent and Child § 637, Priority Right Of Noncustodial Parent.

Witkin, California Summary 10th Parent and Child § 641, Visitation Rights.

Witkin, California Summary 10th Parent and Child § 642, in General.

Witkin, California Summary 10th Parent and Child § 643, Duration Of Services.

Witkin, California Summary 10th Parent and Child § 644, Persons Entitled to Services.

Witkin, California Summary 10th Parent and Child § 646, Incarcerated or Institutionalized Parent or Guardian.
Witkin, California Summary 10th Parent and Child § 647, in General.
Witkin, California Summary 10th Parent and Child § 648, Parent or Guardian Absent, Unwilling, or Incapable.
Witkin, California Summary 10th Parent and Child § 649, Previous Occurrences.
Witkin, California Summary 10th Parent and Child § 650, Abuse, Neglect, or Abduction Of Child.
Witkin, California Summary 10th Parent and Child § 651, Criminal or Addictive Behavior.
Witkin, California Summary 10th Parent and Child § 652, Determination Whether to Order Services.
Witkin, California Summary 10th Parent and Child § 664, in General.
Witkin, California Summary 10th Parent and Child § 673, Child in Foster Care.
Witkin, California Summary 10th Parent and Child § 695, Legal Guardianship.
Witkin, California Summary 10th Parent and Child § 717, in General.

Rule 5.700. Termination of jurisdiction—custody and visitation orders (§§ 302, 304, 361.2, 362.4, 726.5)

When the juvenile court terminates its jurisdiction over a dependent or ward of the court and places the child in the home of a parent, it may issue an order determining the rights to custody of and visitation with the child. The court may also issue protective orders as provided in section 213.5 or as described in Family Code section 6218.

(a) Effect of order

Any order issued under this rule continues in effect until modified or terminated by a later order of a superior court with jurisdiction to make determinations about the custody of the child. The order may be modified or terminated only if the superior court finds both that:

(1) There has been a significant change of circumstances since the juvenile court issued the order; and

(2) Modification or termination of the order is in the best interest of the child.

(b) Preparation and transmission of order

The order must be prepared on *Custody Order—Juvenile—Final Judgment* (form JV–200). The court must direct either the parent, parent's attorney, county counsel, or clerk to:

(1) Prepare the order for the court's signature; and

(2) Transmit the order within 10 calendar days after the order is signed to any superior court where a proceeding described in (c)(1) is pending or, if no such proceeding exists, to the superior court of, in order of preference:

(A) The county in which the parent who has been given sole physical custody resides;

(B) The county in which the children's primary residence is located if no parent has been given sole physical custody; or

(C) A county or other location where any parent resides.

(c) Procedures for filing order—receiving court

On receiving a juvenile court custody order transmitted under (b)(2), the clerk of the receiving court must immediately file the juvenile court order as follows.

(1) Except as provided in paragraph (2), the juvenile court order must be filed in any pending nullity, dissolution, legal separation, guardianship, Uniform Parentage Act, Domestic Violence Prevention Act, or other family law custody proceeding and, when filed, becomes a part of that proceeding.

(2) If the only pending proceeding related to the child in the receiving court is filed under Family Code section 17400 et seq., the clerk must proceed as follows.

(A) If the receiving court has issued a custody or visitation order in the pending proceeding, the clerk must file the received order in that proceeding.

(B) If the receiving court has not issued a custody or visitation order in the pending proceeding, the clerk must not file the received order in that proceeding, but must instead proceed under paragraph (3).

(3) If no dependency, family law, or guardianship proceeding affecting custody or visitation of the child is pending, the order must be used to open a new custody proceeding in the receiving court. The clerk must immediately open a family law file without charging a filing fee, assign a case number, and file the order in the new case file.

(d) Endorsed filed copy—clerk's certificate of mailing

Within 15 court days of receiving the order, the clerk of the receiving court must send an endorsed filed copy of the order showing the case number assigned by the receiving court by first-class mail to the child's parents and the originating juvenile court, with a completed clerk's certificate of mailing, for inclusion in the child's file. *(Formerly Rule 1457, adopted, eff. Jan. 1, 1990. As amended, eff. Jan. 1, 1994; Jan. 1, 2001. Renumbered Rule 5.700 and amended, eff. Jan. 1, 2007. As amended, eff. Jan. 1, 2016.)*

Research References

Forms

West's California Judicial Council Forms JV-200, Custody Order - Juvenile - Final Judgment.
West's California Judicial Council Forms JV-205, Visitation Order--Juvenile.
West's California Judicial Council Forms JV-206, Reasons for No or Supervised Visitation--Juvenile.

Treatises and Practice Aids

Witkin, California Summary 10th Parent and Child § 370, in General.
Witkin, California Summary 10th Parent and Child § 627, in General.
Witkin, California Summary 10th Parent and Child § 637, Priority Right Of Noncustodial Parent.
Witkin, California Summary 10th Parent and Child § 653, Ex Parte Orders Pending Nullity or Dissolution Proceedings.
Witkin, California Summary 10th Parent and Child § 669, in General.
Witkin, California Summary 10th Parent and Child § 676, in General.
Witkin, California Summary 10th Parent and Child § 678, Twelve-Month Review.
Witkin, California Summary 10th Parent and Child § 679, Eighteen-Month Review.

Witkin, California Summary 10th Parent and Child § 892, in General.

Rule 5.705. Setting a hearing under section 366.26

At a disposition hearing, a review hearing, or at any other hearing regarding a dependent child, the court must not set a hearing under section 366.26 to consider termination of the rights of only one parent unless that parent is the only surviving parent, or the rights of the other parent have been terminated by a California court of competent jurisdiction or by a court of competent jurisdiction of another state under the statutes of that state, or the other parent has relinquished custody of the child to the county welfare department. *(Formerly Rule 1459, adopted, eff. July 1, 1990. As amended, eff. Jan. 1, 1994; July 1, 1997. Renumbered Rule 5.705 and amended, eff. Jan. 1, 2007.)*

Research References

Treatises and Practice Aids

Witkin, California Summary 10th Parent and Child § 689, in General.

Article 4

REVIEWS, PERMANENT PLANNING

Rule

Rule 5.706. Family maintenance review hearings (§ 364)

~~(a) Setting of hearing (§ 364)~~

~~If the child remains in the custody of the parent or legal guardian, a review hearing must be held within six months after the date of the original dispositional hearing and no less frequently than once every six months thereafter as long as the child remains a dependent.~~

~~(b)~~(a) Notice (§ 292)

The petitioner or the court clerk must give notice of review hearings on *Notice of Review Hearing* (form JV–280), in the manner provided in section 292, to all persons required to receive notice under section 292 and to any CASA volunteer that has been appointed on the case.

~~(c) Reports (§ 364)~~

~~At least 10 calendar days before the hearing, the petitioner must file a supplemental report with the court describing the services offered to the family, the progress made by the family in eliminating the conditions or factors requiring court supervision, and the petitioner's recommendation regarding the necessity of continued supervision. A copy of the report must be provided to all parties at least 10 calendar days before the hearing.~~

~~(d)~~(b) Court considerations and findings

(1) The court must consider the report prepared by the petitioner, the report of any CASA volunteer, and the case plan submitted for this hearing.

(2) In considering the case plan submitted for the hearing, the court must find as follows:

(A) The child was actively involved in the development of his or her own case plan as age and developmentally appropriate; or

(B) The child was not actively involved in the development of his or her own case plan. If the court makes such a finding, the court must order the agency to actively involve the child in the development of his or her own case plan, unless the court finds that the child is unable, unavailable, or unwilling to participate; and

(C) Each parent was actively involved in the development of the case plan; or

(D) Each parent was not actively involved in the development of the case plan. If the court makes such a finding, the court must order the agency to actively involve each parent in the development of the case plan, unless the court finds that each parent is unable, unavailable, or unwilling to participate.

~~(e)~~(c) Conduct of hearing (§ 364)

~~(1) *The court must determine whether continued supervision is necessary.* The court must terminate its dependency jurisdiction unless the court finds that the petitioner has established by a preponderance of the evidence that existing conditions would justify initial assumption of jurisdiction under section 300 or that such conditions are likely to exist if supervision is withdrawn. Failure of the parent or legal guardian to participate regularly in any court-ordered treatment program constitutes prima facie evidence that the conditions that justified initial assumption of jurisdiction still exist and that continued supervision is necessary.~~

~~(2)~~ If the court retains jurisdiction, the court must order continued services and set a review hearing within six months. ~~under this rule.~~ The court must determine whether continued supervision is necessary under section 364(c).

~~(f)~~(d) Reasonable cause (§ 364)

In any case in which the court has ordered that a parent or legal guardian retain physical custody of a child subject to supervision by a social worker, and the social worker subsequently receives a report of acts or circumstances that indicate there is reasonable cause to believe that the child is a person described under section 300(a), (d), or (e), the social worker must file a subsequent petition under section 342 or a supplemental petition under section 387. If, as a result of the proceedings under the section 342 or 387 petition, the court finds that the child is a person described in section 300(a), (d), or (e), the court must remove the child from the care, custody, and control of the child's parent or legal guardian and must commit the child to the care, custody, and control of the social worker under section 361.

~~(g)~~ (e) Child's education (§§ 361, 366, 366.1)

The court must consider the child's education, including whether it is necessary to limit the right of the parent or legal guardian to make educational or developmental-services decisions for the child, following the requirements and procedures in rules 5.649, 5.650, and 5.651 and in section 361(a). *(Adopted, eff. Jan. 1, 2010. As amended, eff. Jan. 1, 2017.)*

Research References

Forms

West's California Judicial Council Forms JV-425, Findings and Orders After In-Home Status Review Hearing (Welf. & Inst. Code, S364).

West's California Judicial Council Forms JV-426, Findings and Orders After In-Home Status Review Hearing--Child Placed With Previously Noncustodial Parent (Welf. & Inst. Code, §§ 364, 366.21).

Treatises and Practice Aids

Witkin, California Summary 10th Parent and Child § 669, in General.

Witkin, California Summary 10th Parent and Child § 670, Notice Of Hearing.

Witkin, California Summary 10th Parent and Child § 671, Supplemental Report.

Witkin, California Summary 10th Parent and Child § 672, Child in Custody Of Parent or Guardian.

Rule 5.707. Review or dispositional hearing requirements for child approaching majority (§§ 224.1, 366(a)(1)(F), 366.3, 366.31, 16501.1(f)(16))

(a) Reports

At the last review hearing before the child attains 18 years of age held under section 366.21, 366.22, 366.25, or 366.3, or at the dispositional hearing held under section 360 if no review hearing will be set before the child attains 18 years of age, in addition to complying with all other statutory and rule requirements applicable to the report prepared by the social worker for the hearing, the report must include a description of:

(1) The child's plans to remain under juvenile court jurisdiction as a nonminor dependent including the criteria in section 11403(b) that he or she plans to meet;

(2) The efforts made by the social worker to help the child meet one or more of the criteria in section 11403(b);

(3) For an Indian child to whom the Indian Child Welfare Act applies, his or her plans to continue to be considered an Indian child for the purposes of the ongoing application of the Indian Child Welfare Act to him or her as a nonminor dependent;

(4) Whether the child has applied for and, if so, the status of any in-progress application pending for title XVI Supplemental Security Income benefits and, if such an application is pending, whether it will be in the child's best interest to continue juvenile court jurisdiction until a final decision is issued to ensure that the child receives continued assistance with the application process;

(5) Whether the child has an in-progress application pending for Special Immigrant Juvenile Status or other applicable application for legal residency and whether an active dependency case is required for that application;

(6) The efforts made by the social worker toward providing the child with the written information, documents, and services described in section 391, and to the extent that the child has not yet been provided with them, the barriers to providing the information, documents, or services and the steps that will be taken to overcome those barriers by the date the child attains 18 years of age;

(7) When and how the child was informed of his or her right to have juvenile court jurisdiction terminated when he or she attains 18 years of age;

(8) When and how the child was provided with information about the potential benefits of remaining under juvenile court jurisdiction as a nonminor dependent and the social worker's assessment of the child's understanding of those benefits; and

(9) When and how the child was informed that if juvenile court jurisdiction is terminated after he or she attains 18 years of age, he or she has the right to file a request to return to foster care and have the juvenile court resume jurisdiction over him or her as a nonminor dependent.

(b) Transitional Independent Living Case Plan

At the last review hearing before the child attains 18 years of age held under section 366.21, 366.22, 366.25, or 366.3, or at the dispositional hearing held under section 360 if no review hearing will be set before the child attains 18 years of age, the child's Transitional Independent Living Case Plan:

(1) Must be submitted with the social worker's report prepared for the hearing at least 10 calendar days before the hearing; and

(2) Must include:

(A) The individualized plan for the child to satisfy one or more of the criteria in section 11403(b) and the child's anticipated placement as specified in section 11402; and

(B) The child's alternate plan for his or her transition to independence, including housing, education, employment, and a support system in the event the child does not remain under juvenile court jurisdiction after attaining 18 years of age.

(c) Findings

(1) At the last review hearing before the child attains 18 years of age held under section 366.21, 366.22, 366.25, or 366.3, or at the dispositional hearing held under section 360 if no review hearing will be set before the child attains 18 years of age, in addition to complying with all other statutory and rule requirements applicable to the hearing, the court must make the following findings in the written court documentation of the hearing:

(A) Whether the child's Transitional Independent Living Case Plan includes a plan for the child to satisfy one or more of the criteria in section 11403(b) and the specific criteria it is anticipated the child will satisfy;

(B) Whether there is included in the child's Transitional Independent Living Case Plan an alternative plan for the child's transition to independence, including housing, education, employment, and a support system in the event the child does not remain under juvenile court jurisdiction after attaining 18 years of age;

(C) For an Indian child to whom the Indian Child Welfare Act applies, whether he or she intends to continue to be considered an Indian child for the purposes of the ongoing application of the Indian Child Welfare Act to him or her as a nonminor dependent;

(D) Whether the child has an in-progress application pending for title XVI Supplemental Security Income benefits and, if such an application is pending, whether it is in the child's best interest to continue juvenile court jurisdiction until a final decision has been issued to ensure that the child receives continued assistance with the application process;

(E) Whether the child has an in-progress application pending for Special Immigrant Juvenile Status or other applicable application for legal residency and whether an active dependency case is required for that application;

(F) Whether all the information, documents, and services in sections 391(e) were provided to the child, and whether the barriers to providing any missing information, documents, or services can be overcome by the date the child attains 18 years of age;

(G) Whether the child has been informed of his or her right to have juvenile court jurisdiction terminated when he or she attains 18 years of age;

(H) Whether the child understands the potential benefits of remaining under juvenile court jurisdiction as a nonminor dependent; and

(I) Whether the child has been informed that if juvenile court jurisdiction is terminated after he or she attains 18 years of age, he or she has the right to file a request to return to foster care and have the juvenile court resume jurisdiction over him or her as a nonminor dependent.

(2) The hearing must be continued for no more than five court days for the submission of additional information as ordered by the court if the court finds that the report and Transitional Independent Living Case Plan submitted by the social worker do not provide the information required by (a) and (b) and the court is unable to make all the findings required by (c)(1).

(d) Orders

(1) For a child who intends to remain under juvenile court jurisdiction as a nonminor dependent, as defined in section 11400(v), after attaining 18 years of age, the court must set a nonminor dependent status review hearing under rule 5.903 within six months from the date of the current hearing.

(2) For a child who does not intend to remain under juvenile court as a nonminor dependent, as defined in section 11400(v), after attaining 18 years of age, the court must:

(A) Set a hearing under rule 5.555 for a date within one month after the child's 18th birthday, for the child who requests that the juvenile court terminate its jurisdiction after he or she attains 18 years of age; or

(B) Set a hearing under section 366.21, 366.22, 366.25, or 366.3 no more than six months from the date of the current hearing, for a child who will remain under juvenile court jurisdiction in a foster care placement.

(Adopted, eff. Jan. 1, 2012. As amended, eff. July 1, 2012; Jan. 1, 2014; Jan. 1, 2016.)

Research References

Forms

West's California Judicial Council Forms JV-460, Attachment: Additional Findings and Orders for Child Approaching Majority--Dependency.

Treatises and Practice Aids

Witkin, California Summary 10th Parent and Child § 625, Preparation Of Social Study.
Witkin, California Summary 10th Parent and Child § 626, Conduct Of Hearing.
Witkin, California Summary 10th Parent and Child § 671, Supplemental Report.
Witkin, California Summary 10th Parent and Child § 673, Child in Foster Care.
Witkin, California Summary 10th Parent and Child § 697, Status Review Hearings.
Witkin, California Summary 10th Parent and Child § 669A, (New) Review Hearings Just Before and After Minor Attains Age 18.

Rule 5.708. General review hearing requirements

~~**(a) Setting of review hearings (§ 366)**~~

~~The status of every dependent child who has been removed from the custody of the parent or legal guardian must be reviewed periodically but no less frequently than once every 6 months until the section 366.26 hearing is completed. Review hearings must be set as described in rule 5.710 (for 6 month review hearings), rule 5.715 (for 12 month permanency hearings), rule 5.720 (for 18 month permanency review hearings), or rule 5.722 (for 24 month subsequent permanency review hearings).~~

~~(b)~~(a) Notice of hearing (§ 293)

The petitioner or the clerk must serve written notice of review hearings on *Notice of Review Hearing* (form JV–280), in the manner provided in sections 224.2 or 293 as appropriate, to all persons or entities entitled to notice under sections 224.2 and 293 and to any CASA volunteer, educational rights holder, or surrogate parent appointed to the case.

~~(c)~~(b) Reports (§§ 366.05, 366.1, 366.21, 366.22, 366.25, 16002)

Before the hearing, the social worker must investigate and file a report describing the services offered to the family, progress made, and, if relevant, the prognosis for return of the child to the parent or legal guardian.

(1) The report must include:

(A) Recommendations for court orders and the reasons for those recommendations;

(B) A description of the efforts made to achieve legal permanence for the child if reunification efforts fail;

(C) A factual discussion of each item listed in sections 366.1 and 366.21(c); and

(D) A factual discussion of the information required by section 16002(b).

(2) At least 10 calendar days before the hearing, the social worker must file the report and provide copies to the parent or legal guardian and his or her counsel, to counsel for the child, to any CASA volunteer, and, in the case of an Indian child, to the child's identified Indian tribe. The social worker must provide a summary of the recommendations to any foster parents, relative caregivers, or certified foster parents who have been approved for adoption.

(3) The court must read and consider, and state on the record that it has read and considered, the report of the social worker, the report of any CASA volunteer, the case plan submitted for the hearing, any report submitted by the child's caregiver under section 366.21(d), and any other evidence.

~~**(d) Return of child—detriment finding g (§§ 366.21, 366.22, 366.25).**~~

~~(1) If the child was removed from the custody of the parent or legal guardian, the court must order the child returned unless the court finds by a preponderance of the evidence that return of the child to the parent or legal guardian would create a substantial risk of detriment to the safety, protection, or physical or emotional well-being of the child. The social worker has the burden of establishing that detriment.~~

~~(2) The court must consider whether the child can be returned to the custody of his or her parent who is enrolled in a certified substance abuse treatment facility that allows a dependent child to reside with his or her parent.~~

~~(3) Failure of the parent or legal guardian to regularly participate and make substantive progress in any court-ordered treatment program is prima facie evidence that continued supervision is necessary or that return would be detrimental.~~

~~(4) In making its determination about whether returning the child would be detrimental, the court must consider the following:~~

~~(A) The social worker's report and recommendations and the report and recommendations of any CASA volunteer who has been appointed on the case;~~

~~(B) The efforts or progress demonstrated by the parent or legal guardian; and~~

~~(C) The extent to which the parent or legal guardian availed himself or herself of the services provided, taking into account the particular barriers to an incarcerated or institutionalized parent or legal guardian's access to court-mandated services and the ability to maintain contact with his or her child.~~

~~(5) If the parent or legal guardian agreed to submit fingerprints to obtain criminal history information as part of the case plan, the court must consider the criminal history of the parent or legal guardian after the child's removal to the extent that the criminal record is substantially related to the welfare of the child or the parent's or legal guardian's ability to exercise custody and control regarding his or her child.~~

~~(6) Regardless of whether the child is returned home, the court must specify the factual basis for its conclusion that the return would or would not be detrimental.~~

~~**(e)**~~**(c) Reasonable services (§§ 366, 366.21, 366.22, 366.25, 366.3)**

(1) If the child is not returned to the custody of the parent or legal guardian, the court must consider whether reasonable services have been offered or provided. The court must find that~~:~~

~~(A) R~~reasonable services have been offered or provided~~;~~ or

~~(B) Reasonable services~~ have not been offered or provided.

~~(2) The following factors are not sufficient, in and of themselves, to support a finding that reasonable services have not been offered or provided:~~

~~(A) The child has been placed in a preadoptive home or with a family that is eligible to adopt the child;~~

~~(B) The case plan includes services to achieve legal permanence for the child if reunification cannot be accomplished; or~~

~~(C) Services to achieve legal permanence for the child if reunification efforts fail are being provided concurrently with reunification services.~~

(2) If the child is not returned to the custody of the parent or legal guardian, the court must consider the safety of the child and make the findings listed in sections 366(a) and 16002.

~~**(f)**~~**(d) Educational and developmental-services needs (§§ 361, 366, 366.1, 366.3)**

The court must consider the educational and developmental-services needs of each child and nonminor or nonminor dependent, including whether it is necessary to limit the rights of the parent or legal guardian to make educational or developmental-services decisions for the child. If the court limits those rights or, in the case of a nonminor or nonminor dependent who has chosen not to make educational or developmental-services decisions for him- or herself or has been deemed incompetent, finds that appointment would be in the best interests of the nonminor or nonminor dependent, the court must appoint a responsible adult as the educational rights holder as defined in rule 5.502. Any limitation on the rights of a parent or guardian to make educational or developmental-services decisions for the child must be specified in the court order. The court must follow the procedures in rules 5.649–5.651.

~~**(g)**~~**(e) Case plan (§§ 16001.9, 16501.1).**

The court must consider the case plan submitted for the hearing and must determine:

(1) Whether the child was actively involved, as age- and developmentally appropriate, in the development of ~~his or her own~~ the case plan and plan for permanent placement. If the court finds ~~that~~ the child ~~or youth~~ was not appropriately involved, the court must order the agency to actively involve the child in the development of ~~his or her own~~ the case plan and plan for permanent placement, unless the court finds ~~that~~ the child is unable, unavailable, or unwilling to participate.

(2) Whether each parent or legal guardian was actively involved in the development of the case plan and plan for permanent placement. If the court finds that any parent or legal guardian was not actively involved, the court must order the agency to actively involve that parent or legal guardian in the development of the case plan and plan for permanent

placement, unless the court finds that the parent is unable, unavailable, or unwilling to participate.

(3) In the case of an Indian child, whether the agency consulted with the Indian child's tribe, as defined in rule 5.502, and the tribe was actively involved in the development of the case plan and plan for permanent placement, including consideration of tribal customary adoption as an appropriate permanent plan for the child if reunification is unsuccessful.

If the court finds that the agency did not consult the Indian child's tribe, the court must order the agency to do so, unless the court finds that the tribe is unable, unavailable, or unwilling to participate.

(4) For a child 12 years of age or older in a permanent placement, whether the child was given the opportunity to review the case plan, sign it, and receive a copy. If the court finds that the child was not given this opportunity, the court must order the agency to give the child the opportunity to review the case plan, sign it, and receive a copy.

(5) Whether the case plan was developed in compliance with and meets the requirements of section 16501.1(g). If the court finds that the development of the case plan does not comply with section 16501.1(g), the court must order the agency to comply with the requirements of section 16501.1(g).

~~**(h) Out-of-state placement (§§ 361.21, 366)**~~

~~If the child has been placed out of the state, the court must consider whether the placement continues to be the most appropriate placement for the child and in the child's best interest. If the child is in an out-of-state group home, the court must follow the requirements in section 361.21.~~

~~**(i) Title IV–E findings (§ 366)**~~

~~Regardless of whether or not the child is returned home, the court must consider the safety of the child and must determine all of the following:~~

~~(1) The continuing necessity for and appropriateness of the placement;~~

~~(2) The extent of the agency's compliance with the case plan in making reasonable efforts or, in the case of an Indian child, active efforts as described in section 361.7, to return the child to a safe home and to complete any steps necessary to finalize the permanent placement of the child. These steps include efforts to maintain relationships between a child who is 10 years or older who has been in an out-of-home placement for 6 months or longer and individuals other than the child's siblings who are important to the child, consistent with the child's best interest;~~

~~(3) The extent of progress that has been made by the parents or legal guardians toward alleviating or mitigating the causes necessitating placement in foster care; and~~

~~(4) The likely date by which the child may be returned to and safely maintained in the home or placed for adoption, legal guardianship, or in another planned permanent living arrangement.~~

~~(j)~~(f) Sibling findings; additional findings (§§ 366, 16002)

(1) The court must determine whether the child has other siblings under the court's jurisdiction. If so, the court must make the additional determinations required by section 366(a)(1)(D); and

(2) The court must enter any additional findings as required by section 366 and section 16002.

~~(k)~~(g) Placement with noncustodial parent (§ 361.2)

If at any review hearing the court places the child with a noncustodial parent, or if the court has previously made such a placement, the court may, after stating on the record or in writing the factual basis for the order:

(1) Continue supervision and reunification services;

(2) Order custody to the noncustodial parent, continue supervision, and order family maintenance services; or

(3) Order custody to the noncustodial parent, terminate jurisdiction, and direct that *Custody Order—Juvenile—Final Judgment* (form JV–200) be prepared and filed under rule 5.700.

~~(*l*)~~(h) Setting a hearing under section 366.26 for one parent

The court may not set a hearing under section 366.26 to consider termination of the rights of only one parent unless:

(1) That parent is the only surviving parent;

(2) The rights of the other parent have been terminated by a California court of competent jurisdiction or by a court of competent jurisdiction of another state under the statutes of that state; or

(3) The other parent has relinquished custody of the child to the county welfare department.

~~**(m) Setting a hearing under section 366.26; reasonable services requirement (§§ 366.21, 366.22)**~~

~~At any 6-month, 12-month, or 18-month hearing, the court may not set a hearing under section 366.26 unless the court finds by clear and convincing evidence that reasonable services have been provided or offered to the parent or legal guardian.~~

~~(n)~~(i) Requirements on setting a section 366.26 hearing (§§ 366.21, 366.22, 366.25)

The court must make the following orders and determinations when setting a hearing under section 366.26:

~~(1) The court must terminate reunification services to the parent or legal guardian and:~~

~~(A) Order that the social worker provide a copy of the child's birth certificate to the caregiver as consistent with sections 16010.4(e)(5) and 16010.5(b)–(c); and~~

~~(B) Order that the social worker provide a child 16 years of age or older with a copy of his or her birth certificate unless the court finds that provision of the birth certificate would be inappropriate.~~

~~(2) The court must continue to permit the parent or legal guardian to visit the child, unless it finds that visitation would be detrimental to the child;~~

~~(3) If the child is 10 years of age or older and is placed in an out-of-home placement for 6 months or longer, the court must enter any other appropriate orders to enable the child to maintain relationships with other individuals who are important to the child, consistent with the child's best interest. Specifically, the court:~~

~~(A) Must determine whether the agency has identified individuals, in addition to the child's siblings, who are important to the child and will maintain caring, permanent relationships with the child, consistent with the child's best interest;~~

~~(B) Must determine whether the agency has made reasonable efforts to nurture and maintain the child's relationships with those individuals, consistent with the child's best interest; and~~

~~(C) May make any appropriate order to ensure that those relationships are maintained.~~

~~(4) The court must direct the county child welfare agency and the appropriate county or state adoption agency to prepare an assessment under section 366.21(i), 366.22(c), or 366.25(b);~~

~~(5)~~(1) The court must ensure that notice is provided as required by section 294.

~~(6)~~(2) The court must follow all procedures in rule 5.590 regarding writ petition rights, advisements, and forms.

~~(o)~~(j) Appeal of order setting section 366.26 hearing

An appeal of any order setting a hearing under section 366.26 must follow the procedures in rules 8.400–8.416. *(Adopted, eff. Jan. 1, 2010. As amended, eff. July 1, 2010; Jan. 1, 2014; Jan. 1, 2015; Jan. 1, 2016; July 1, 2016; Jan. 1, 2017.)*

Research References

Forms

West's California Judicial Council Forms JV-403, Sibling Attachment: Contact and Placement.
West's California Judicial Council Forms JV-426, Findings and Orders After In-Home Status Review Hearing--Child Placed With Previously Noncustodial Parent (Welf. & Inst. Code, §§ 364, 366.21).
West's California Judicial Council Forms JV-430, Findings and Orders After Six-Month Prepermanency Hearing (Welf. & Inst. Code, S361.21(E)).
West's California Judicial Council Forms JV-431, Six-Month Prepermanency Attachment: Child Reunified (Welf. & Inst. Code, S361.21(E)).
West's California Judicial Council Forms JV-432, Six-Month Prepermanency Attachment: Reunification Services Continued (Welf. & Inst. Code, S366.21(E)).
West's California Judicial Council Forms JV-433, Six-Month Prepermanency Attachment: Reunification Services Terminated (Welf. & Inst. Code, S366.21(E)).
West's California Judicial Council Forms JV-435, Findings and Orders After 12-Month Permanency Hearing (Welf. & Inst. Code, S366.21(F)).
West's California Judicial Council Forms JV-436, Twelve-Month Permanency Attachment: Child Reunified (Welf. & Inst. Code, S366.21(F)).
West's California Judicial Council Forms JV-437, Twelve-Month Permanency Attachment: Reunification Services Continued (Welf. & Inst. Code, S366.21(F)).
West's California Judicial Council Forms JV-438, Twelve-Month Permanency Attachment: Reunification Services Terminated (Welf. & Inst. Code, S366.21(F)).
West's California Judicial Council Forms JV-440, Findings and Orders After 18-Month Permanency Hearing (Welf. & Inst. Code, S366.22).
West's California Judicial Council Forms JV-441, Eighteen-Month Permanency Attachment: Child Reunified (Welf. & Inst. Code, S366.22).
West's California Judicial Council Forms JV-442, Eighteen-Month Permanency Attachment: Reunification Services Terminated (Welf. & Inst. Code, S366.22).
West's California Judicial Council Forms JV-443, Eighteen-Month Permanency Attachment: Reunification Services Continued (Welf. & Inst. Code, S366.22).
West's California Judicial Council Forms JV-455, Findings and Orders After 24-Month Permanency Hearing (Welf. & Inst. Code, S366.25).
West's California Judicial Council Forms JV-456, Twenty-Four-Month Permanency Attachment: Child Reunified (Welf. & Inst. Code, S366.25).
West's California Judicial Council Forms JV-457, Twenty-Four-Month Permanency Attachment: Reunification Services Terminated (Welf. & Inst. Code, S366.25).

Treatises and Practice Aids

Witkin, California Summary 10th Parent and Child § 444, Scope and Organization.
Witkin, California Summary 10th Parent and Child § 627, in General.
Witkin, California Summary 10th Parent and Child § 669, in General.
Witkin, California Summary 10th Parent and Child § 670, Notice Of Hearing.
Witkin, California Summary 10th Parent and Child § 671, Supplemental Report.
Witkin, California Summary 10th Parent and Child § 673, Child in Foster Care.
Witkin, California Summary 10th Parent and Child § 674, Return Of Child.
Witkin, California Summary 10th Parent and Child § 675, Reunification Services.
Witkin, California Summary 10th Parent and Child § 676, in General.
Witkin, California Summary 10th Parent and Child § 677, Scheduling Selection and Implementation Hearing.
Witkin, California Summary 10th Parent and Child § 678, Twelve-Month Review.
Witkin, California Summary 10th Parent and Child § 679, Eighteen-Month Review.
Witkin, California Summary 10th Parent and Child § 681, Notice.
Witkin, California Summary 10th Parent and Child § 682, Preliminary Assessment.
Witkin, California Summary 10th Parent and Child § 675A, (New) Setting Selection and Implementation Hearing.
Witkin, California Summary 10th Parent and Child § 679A, (New) Twenty-Four Month Review.

Rule 5.710. Six-month review hearing

(a) Determinations and conduct of hearing (§§ 364, 366, 366.1, 366.21)

At the hearing, the court and all parties must comply with all relevant requirements and procedures in rule 5.708, General review hearing requirements. The court must make all appropriate findings and orders specified in rule 5.708 and proceed under section 366.21(e) and (g), and as follows:

(1) *Order return of the child or find that return would be detrimental*

If the child is returned, the court may order the termination of dependency jurisdiction or order continued dependency services and set a review hearing within 6 months.

(2) *Place with noncustodial parent*

If the court has previously placed or at this hearing places the child with a noncustodial parent, the court must follow the procedures in rule 5.708(g) and section 361.2.

(3) *Set a section 366.26 hearing*

If the court does not return custody of the child to the parent or legal guardian, the court may set a hearing under section 366.26 within 120 days, as provided in (b).

(4) *Continue the case for a 12–month permanency hearing*

If the child is not returned and the court does not set a section 366.26 hearing, the court must order that any reunification services previously ordered will continue to be offered to the parent or legal guardian, if appropriate. The court may modify those services as appropriate or order additional services reasonably believed to facilitate the return of the child to the parent or legal guardian. The court must set a date for the next hearing no later than 12 months from the date the child entered foster care as defined in section 361.49.

(b) Setting a section 366.26 hearing (§§ 366.21, 366.215)

(1) The court may set a hearing under section 366.26 within 120 days if any of the conditions in section 366.21(e) are met; or the parent is deceased.

(2) At the hearing, the court and all parties must comply with all relevant requirements and procedures related to section 366.26 hearings in rule 5.708, General review hearing requirements. The court must make all appropriate findings and orders specified in rule 5.708. *(Formerly Rule 1460, adopted, eff. Jan. 1, 1990. As amended, eff. Jan. 1, 1992; Jan. 1, 1993; Jan. 1, 1995; July 1, 1995; July 1, 1997; Jan. 1, 1999; July 1, 1999; Jan. 1, 2000; Jan. 1, 2001; July 1, 2002; Jan. 1, 2004; Jan. 1, 2005; Jan. 1, 2006. Renumbered Rule 5.710 and amended, eff. Jan. 1, 2007. As amended, eff. Jan. 1, 2010; Jan. 1, 2011; Jan. 1, 2014; Jan. 1, 2015; Jan. 1, 2017; Jan. 1, 2018.)*

Validity

A prior version of this rule was held invalid in the decision of M.V. v. Superior Court (App. 4 Dist. 2008) 83 Cal.Rptr.3d 864, 167 Cal.App.4th 166.

Research References

Forms

West's California Judicial Council Forms JV-430, Findings and Orders After Six-Month Prepermanency Hearing (Welf. & Inst. Code, S361.21(E)).

West's California Judicial Council Forms JV-431, Six-Month Prepermanency Attachment: Child Reunified (Welf. & Inst. Code, S361.21(E)).

West's California Judicial Council Forms JV-432, Six-Month Prepermanency Attachment: Reunification Services Continued (Welf. & Inst. Code, S366.21(E)).

West's California Judicial Council Forms JV-433, Six-Month Prepermanency Attachment: Reunification Services Terminated (Welf. & Inst. Code, S366.21(E)).

Treatises and Practice Aids

Witkin, California Summary 10th Parent and Child § 444, Scope and Organization.

Witkin, California Summary 10th Parent and Child § 643, Duration Of Services.

Witkin, California Summary 10th Parent and Child § 669, in General.

Witkin, California Summary 10th Parent and Child § 670, Notice Of Hearing.

Witkin, California Summary 10th Parent and Child § 671, Supplemental Report.

Witkin, California Summary 10th Parent and Child § 672, Child in Custody Of Parent or Guardian.

Witkin, California Summary 10th Parent and Child § 673, Child in Foster Care.

Witkin, California Summary 10th Parent and Child § 674, Return Of Child.

Witkin, California Summary 10th Parent and Child § 675, Reunification Services.

Witkin, California Summary 10th Parent and Child § 676, in General.

Witkin, California Summary 10th Parent and Child § 677, Scheduling Selection and Implementation Hearing.

Witkin, California Summary 10th Parent and Child § 681, Notice.

Witkin, California Summary 10th Parent and Child § 682, Preliminary Assessment.

Witkin, California Summary 10th Parent and Child § 701, in General.

Rule 5.715. Twelve-month permanency hearing

(a) Requirement for 12–month review; setting of hearing (§§ 293, 366.21).

The case of any dependent child whom the court has removed from the custody of the parent or legal guardian must be set for a permanency hearing within 12 months of the date the child entered foster care, as defined in section 361.49, and no later than 18 months from the date of the initial removal.

(b) Determinations and conduct of hearing (§§ 309(e), 361.5, 366, 366.1, 366.21)

At the hearing, the court and all parties must comply with all relevant requirements and procedures in rule 5.708, General review hearing requirements. The court must make all appropriate findings and orders specified in rule 5.708 and proceed under section 366.21(f) and (g), and as follows:

(1) The requirements in rule 5.708(c) must be followed in entering a reasonable services finding.

(2) If the court has previously placed or at this hearing places the child with a noncustodial parent, the court must follow the procedures in rule 5.708(g) and section 361.2.

(3) The court may order that the name and address of the foster home remain confidential.

(4) In the case of an Indian child, if the child is not returned to his or her parent or legal guardian, the court must determine whether:

(A) The agency has consulted the child's tribe about tribal customary adoption;

(B) The child's tribe concurs with tribal customary adoption; and

(C) Tribal customary adoption is an appropriate permanent plan for the child.

(5) If the child is not returned to his or her parent or legal guardian and the court terminates reunification services, the court must find as follows:

(A) The agency has made diligent efforts to locate an appropriate relative; or

(B) The agency has not made diligent efforts to locate an appropriate relative. If the court makes such a finding, the court or administrative review panel must order the agency to make diligent efforts to locate an appropriate relative; and

(C) Each relative whose name has been submitted to the agency as a possible caregiver has been evaluated as an appropriate placement resource; or

(D) Each relative whose name has been submitted to the agency as a possible caregiver has not been evaluated as an appropriate placement resource. If the court makes such a finding, the court must order the agency to evaluate as an appropriate placement resource each relative whose name has been submitted to the agency as a possible caregiver.

(Formerly Rule 1461, adopted, eff. Jan. 1, 1990. As amended, eff. Jan. 1, 1992; Jan. 1, 1993; Jan. 1, 1994; Jan. 1, 1995; July 1, 1995; July 1, 1996; July 1, 1997; Jan. 1, 1999; July 1, 1999; Jan. 1, 2000; Jan. 1, 2001; Jan. 1, 2004; Jan. 1, 2005; Jan. 1, 2006. Renumbered Rule 5.715 and amended, eff. Jan. 1, 2007. As amended, eff. Jan. 1, 2010; July 1, 2010; Jan. 1, 2014; Jan. 1, 2017; Jan. 1, 2018.)

Research References

Forms

West's California Judicial Council Forms JV-435, Findings and Orders After 12-Month Permanency Hearing (Welf. & Inst. Code, S366.21(F)).

West's California Judicial Council Forms JV-436, Twelve-Month Permanency Attachment: Child Reunified (Welf. & Inst. Code, S366.21(F)).

West's California Judicial Council Forms JV-437, Twelve-Month Permanency Attachment: Reunification Services Continued (Welf. & Inst. Code, S366.21(F)).

West's California Judicial Council Forms JV-438, Twelve-Month Permanency Attachment: Reunification Services Terminated (Welf. & Inst. Code, S366.21(F)).

Treatises and Practice Aids

Witkin, California Summary 10th Parent and Child § 669, in General.

Witkin, California Summary 10th Parent and Child § 673, Child in Foster Care.

Witkin, California Summary 10th Parent and Child § 674, Return Of Child.

Witkin, California Summary 10th Parent and Child § 675, Reunification Services.

Witkin, California Summary 10th Parent and Child § 678, Twelve-Month Review.

Witkin, California Summary 10th Parent and Child § 681, Notice.

Witkin, California Summary 10th Parent and Child § 682, Preliminary Assessment.

Witkin, California Summary 10th Parent and Child § 701, in General.

Rule 5.720. Eighteen-month permanency review hearing

~~(a) Requirement for 18-month permanency review hearing; setting of hearing; notice (§§ 293, 366.22)~~

~~For any dependent child whom the court has removed from the custody of the parent or legal guardian, and who was not returned at the 6- or 12-month review hearing, a permanency review hearing must be held no later than 18 months from the date of the initial removal. Notice of the hearing must be given as provided in section 293 and rule 5.708(b).~~

~~(b)~~(a) Determinations and conduct of hearing (§§ 309(e), 361.5, 366.22)

At the hearing the court and all parties must comply with all relevant requirements and procedures in rule 5.708, General review hearing requirements. The court must make all appropriate findings and orders specified in rule 5.708, and proceed under section 366.22 and as follows:

~~(1) The court must order the child returned to the custody of the parent or legal guardian unless the court finds the petitioner has established, by a preponderance of the evidence, that return would create a substantial risk of detriment to the safety, protection, or physical or emotional well-being of the child. Failure of the parent or legal guardian to regularly participate and make substantive progress in a court-ordered treatment program is prima facie evidence that continued supervision is necessary or that return would be detrimental. The requirements in rule 5.708(d) must be followed in establishing detriment. The requirements in rule 5.708(e) must be followed in entering a reasonable services finding.~~

~~(2)~~(1) If the court has previously placed or at this hearing places the child with a noncustodial parent, the court must follow the procedures in rule 5.708~~(k)~~(g) and section 361.2.

~~(3)~~(2) ~~If the court does not order return of the child to the custody of the parent or legal guardian, the court must specify the factual basis for its finding of risk of detriment and do one of the following:~~The court may order that the name and address of the foster home remain confidential.

~~(A) Continue the case for a subsequent permanency review hearing not later than 24 months from the date of the initial removal if the court finds that there is a substantial probability that the child will be returned within that time or that reasonable services have not been offered or provided. To extend services to the 24-month point, the court must also find by clear and convincing evidence that additional reunification services are in the best interest of the child and that the parent or legal guardian is making significant and consistent progress in a substance abuse treatment program, or a parent or legal guardian has recently been discharged from incarceration, institutionalization, or the custody of the United States Department of Homeland Security and is making significant and consistent progress in establishing a safe home for the child's return. The court must also inform the parent or legal guardian that, if the child cannot be returned home by the subsequent permanency review hearing, a hearing under section 366.26 may be instituted.~~

~~In order to find a substantial probability that the child will be returned within the 24-month period, the court must find all of the following:~~

~~(i) The parent or legal guardian has consistently and regularly contacted and visited the child;~~

~~(ii) The parent or legal guardian has made significant and consistent progress in the prior 18 months in resolving the problems that led to the removal of the child; and~~

~~(iii) The parent or legal guardian has demonstrated the capacity and ability both to complete the objectives of his or her substance abuse treatment plan as evidenced by reports from a substance abuse provider, as applicable, or to complete a treatment plan postdischarge from incarceration, institutionalization, or detention or following deportation to his or her country of origin or his or her return to the United States, and to provide for the child's safety, protection, physical and emotional health, and special needs.~~

~~(B) Terminate reunification services and order that the child remain in a planned permanent living arrangement, if it finds by clear and convincing evidence already presented, including a recommendation by the appropriate state or county adoption agency, that there is a compelling reason for determining that a section 366.26 hearing is not in the best interest of the child because the child is not a proper subject for adoption and has no one willing to accept legal guardianship.~~

~~(i) If the court orders that the child remain in a planned permanent living arrangement, it must identify the foster care setting by name and identify a specific permanency goal for the child.~~

~~(ii)~~

~~(iii) The court must continue to permit the parent or legal guardian to visit the child, unless it finds that visitation would be detrimental to the child;~~

~~(iv) If the child is 10 years of age or older and is placed in out-of-home placement for six months or longer, the court must enter any other appropriate orders to enable the child to maintain relationships with other individuals who are important to the child, consistent with the child's best interest. Specifically, the court:~~

~~a. Must determine whether the agency has identified individuals, in addition to the child's siblings, who are important to the child and will maintain caring, permanent relationships with the child, consistent with the child's best interest;~~

~~b. Must determine whether the agency has made reasonable efforts to nurture and maintain the child's relationships with those individuals, consistent with the child's best interest; and~~

~~c. May make any appropriate order to ensure that those relationships are maintained.~~

~~(C) If (1), (3)(A), or (3)(B) do not apply, the court must terminate reunification services and order a hearing under section 366.26 within 120 days. The court and all parties must comply with all relevant requirements, procedures, and findings and orders related to section 366.26 hearings in rule 5.708.~~

~~(4)~~(3) In the case of an Indian child, I~~i~~f the child is not returned to his or her parent or legal guardian, the court must ~~consider and state, for the record, in-state and out-of-state options for permanent placement, including, in the case of an Indian child,~~ determine whether:

(A) The agency has consulted the child's tribe about tribal customary adoption;

(B) The child's tribe concurs with tribal customary adoption; and

(C) Tribal customary adoption is an appropriate permanent plan for the child.

(4) If the child is not returned to his or her parent or legal guardian and the court terminates reunification services, the court must find as follows:

(A) The agency has made diligent efforts to locate an appropriate relative; or

(B) The agency has not made diligent efforts to locate an appropriate relative. If the court makes such a finding, the court must order the agency to make diligent efforts to locate an appropriate relative; and

(C) Each relative whose name has been submitted to the agency as a possible caregiver has been evaluated as an appropriate placement resource; or

(D) Each relative whose name has been submitted to the agency as a possible caregiver has not been evaluated as an appropriate placement resource. If the court makes such a finding, the court must order the agency to evaluate as an appropriate placement resource each relative whose name has been submitted to the agency as a possible caregiver.

(Formerly Rule 1462, adopted, eff. Jan. 1, 1990. As amended, eff. July 1, 1991; Jan. 1, 1992; Jan. 1, 1993; Jan. 1, 1994; Jan. 1, 1995; July 1, 1995; July 1, 1997; Jan. 1, 1999; July 1, 1999; Jan. 1, 2001; Jan. 1, 2005; Jan. 1, 2006; July 1, 2006. Renumbered Rule 5.720 and amended, eff. Jan. 1, 2007. As amended, eff. July 1, 2007; Jan. 1, 2010; July 1, 2010; Jan. 1, 2014; Jan. 1, 2015; Jan. 1, 2017.)

Commentary

In re Marilyn A., 148 Cal.App.4th 285, 55 Cal.Rptr.3d 647 (2007), held that a juvenile court may return a dependent child to a parent's home at an 18-month dependency hearing, but also continue services and court supervision to ensure the child's safety. *Marilyn A.* relies on the broad discretion conferred on the court by subsection (a) of Welfare and Institutions Code section 366.22 and the explicit authorization, by Cal. Rules of Ct., Rule 5.710(e)(2), of continued services and court supervision at six-month reviews.

Research References

Forms

West's California Judicial Council Forms JV-440, Findings and Orders After 18-Month Permanency Hearing (Welf. & Inst. Code, S366.22).

West's California Judicial Council Forms JV-441, Eighteen-Month Permanency Attachment: Child Reunified (Welf. & Inst. Code, S366.22).

West's California Judicial Council Forms JV-442, Eighteen-Month Permanency Attachment: Reunification Services Terminated (Welf. & Inst. Code, S366.22).

West's California Judicial Council Forms JV-443, Eighteen-Month Permanency Attachment: Reunification Services Continued (Welf. & Inst. Code, S366.22).

Treatises and Practice Aids

Witkin, California Summary 10th Parent and Child § 669, in General.

Witkin, California Summary 10th Parent and Child § 673, Child in Foster Care.

Witkin, California Summary 10th Parent and Child § 674, Return Of Child.

Witkin, California Summary 10th Parent and Child § 675, Reunification Services.

Witkin, California Summary 10th Parent and Child § 679, Eighteen-Month Review.
Witkin, California Summary 10th Parent and Child § 681, Notice.
Witkin, California Summary 10th Parent and Child § 682, Preliminary Assessment.
Witkin, California Summary 10th Parent and Child § 701, in General.

Rule 5.722. Twenty-four-month subsequent permanency review hearing

~~**(a) Requirement for 24-month subsequent permanency review hearing; setting of hearing; notice (§ 366.25)**~~

~~For any dependent child whom the court has removed from the custody of the parent or legal guardian, and whose case has been continued under section 366.22(b), the subsequent permanency review hearing must be held no later than 24 months from the date of initial removal. Notice must be provided as described in rule 5.708.~~

~~(b)~~(a) Determinations and conduct of hearing (§§ 309(e), 366, 366.1, 366.25).

At the hearing, the court and all parties must comply with all relevant requirements and procedures in rule 5.708, General review hearing requirements. The court must make all appropriate findings and orders specified in rule 5.708, and proceed under section 366.25 and as follows:

(1) ~~The court must order the child returned to the custody of the parent or legal guardian unless the court finds that petitioner has established by a preponderance of the evidence that return would create a substantial risk of detriment to the safety, protection, or physical or emotional well-being of the child. Failure of the parent or legal guardian to regularly participate and make substantive progress in a court-ordered treatment program is prima facie evidence that return would be detrimental. The requirements in rule 5.708(d) must be followed in establishing detriment.~~The requirements in rule 5.708~~(e)~~(c) must be followed in entering a reasonable services finding.

(2) If the court does not order the return of the child to the custody of the parent or legal guardian, the court must specify the factual basis for its finding of risk of detriment~~and do one of the following:~~.

~~(A) If the court finds by clear and convincing evidence, including a recommendation by the appropriate state or county adoption agency, that there is a compelling reason for determining that a section 366.26 hearing is not in the best interest of the child because the child is not a proper subject for adoption and has no one willing to accept legal guardianship, the court must terminate reunification services and order that the child remain in a planned permanent living arrangement.~~

~~(i) If the court orders that the child remain in a planned permanent living arrangement, it must identify the foster care setting by name and identify a specific permanency goal for the child.~~

~~(ii)~~(3) The court may order that the name and address of the foster home remain confidential. The court and all parties must comply with all relevant requirements, procedures, findings, and orders related to section 366.26 hearings in rule 5.708 (h)–(j).

~~(iii) The court must continue to permit the parent or legal guardian to visit the child, unless it finds that visitation would be detrimental to the child.~~

~~(iv) If the child is 10 years of age or older and is placed in out-of-home placement for six months or longer, the court must enter any other appropriate orders to enable the child to maintain relationships with other individuals who are important to the child, consistent with the child's best interest. Specifically, the court:~~

~~a. Must determine whether the agency has identified individuals, in addition to the child's siblings, who are important to the child and will maintain caring, permanent relationships with the child, consistent with the child's best interest;~~

~~b. Must determine whether the agency has made reasonable efforts to nurture and maintain the child's relationships with those individuals, consistent with the child's best interest; and~~

~~c. May make any appropriate order to ensure that those relationships are maintained.~~

~~(B) If (1) or (2)(A) do not apply, the court must terminate reunification services and order that a hearing be held under section 366.26 within 120 days. *(l)–(o).*~~

~~(3)~~(4) In the case of an Indian child, ~~I~~if the child is not returned to his or her parent or legal guardian, the court must ~~consider and state, for the record, in-state and out-of-state options for permanent placement, including, in the case of an Indian child,~~ determine whether:

(A) The agency has consulted the child's tribe about tribal customary adoption;

(B) The child's tribe concurs with tribal customary adoption; and

(C) Tribal customary adoption is an appropriate permanent plan for the child.

(5) If the child is not returned to his or her parent or legal guardian and the court terminates reunification services, the court must find as follows:

(A) The agency has made diligent efforts to locate an appropriate relative; or

(B) The agency has not made diligent efforts to locate an appropriate relative. If the court makes such a finding, the court must order the agency to make diligent efforts to locate an appropriate relative; and

(C) Each relative whose name has been submitted to the agency as a possible caregiver has been evaluated as an appropriate placement resource; or

(D) Each relative whose name has been submitted to the agency as a possible caregiver has not been evaluated as an appropriate placement resource. If the court makes such a finding, the court must order the agency to evaluate as an appropriate placement resource each relative whose name has been submitted to the agency as a possible caregiver.

(Adopted, eff. Jan. 1, 2010. As amended, eff. July 1, 2010; Jan. 1, 2017.)

Research References

Forms

West's California Judicial Council Forms JV-455, Findings and Orders After 24-Month Permanency Hearing (Welf. & Inst. Code, S366.25).

West's California Judicial Council Forms JV-456, Twenty-Four-Month Permanency Attachment: Child Reunified (Welf. & Inst. Code, S366.25).

West's California Judicial Council Forms JV-457, Twenty-Four-Month Permanency Attachment: Reunification Services Terminated (Welf. & Inst. Code, S366.25).

Treatises and Practice Aids

Witkin, California Summary 10th Parent and Child § 673, Child in Foster Care.

Witkin, California Summary 10th Parent and Child § 674, Return Of Child.

Witkin, California Summary 10th Parent and Child § 675, Reunification Services.

Witkin, California Summary 10th Parent and Child § 679A, (New) Twenty-Four Month Review.

Rule 5.725. Selection of permanent plan (§§ 366.24, 366.26, 727.31)

(a) Application of rule

This rule applies to children who have been declared dependents or wards of the juvenile court.

~~(1) Only section 366.26 and division 12, part 3, chapter 5 (commencing with section 7660) of the Family Code or Family Code sections 8604, 8605, 8606, and 8700 apply for the termination of parental rights. Part 4 (commencing with section 7800) of division 12 of the Family Code does not apply.~~

~~(2)~~(1) The court may not terminate the rights of only one parent under section 366.26 unless that parent is the only surviving parent; or unless the rights of the other parent have been terminated ~~under division 12, part 3, chapter 5 (commencing with section 7660), or division 12, part 4 (commencing with section 7800) of the Family Code, or Family Code sections 8604, 8605, or 8606~~ by a California court of competent jurisdiction or by a court of competent jurisdiction of another state under the statutes of that state; or unless the other parent has relinquished custody of the child to the welfare department.

~~(3)~~(2) Only sections 366.26 and 727.31 apply ~~applies~~ for establishing legal guardianship.

~~(4)~~(3) For termination of the parental rights of an Indian child, the procedures in this rule and in rule 5.485 must be followed.

(b) Notice of hearing (§ 294)

In addition to the requirements stated in section 294, notice must be given to any CASA volunteer, ~~the child's present caregiver~~ Indian custodian, and ~~any~~ de facto parent on *Notice of Hearing on Selection of a Permanent Plan* (form JV-300).

(c) Report

Before the hearing, petitioner must prepare an assessment under section 366.21(i). At least 10 calendar days before the hearing, the petitioner must file the assessment, provide copies to each parent or guardian and all counsel of record, and provide a summary of the recommendations to the present custodians of the child, to any CASA volunteer, and to the tribe of an Indian child.

(d) Conduct of hearing

At the hearing, the court must state on the record that the court has read and considered the report of petitioner, the report of any CASA volunteer, the case plan submitted for this hearing, any report submitted by the child's caregiver under section 366.21(d), and any other evidence, and must proceed under section 366.26 and as follows:

(1) In the case of an Indian child, after the agency has consulted with the tribe, when the court has determined with the concurrence of the tribe that tribal customary adoption is the appropriate permanent plan for the child, order a tribal customary adoption in accordance with section 366.24.~~; or~~

~~(2) Order parental rights terminated and the child placed for adoption if the court determines, by clear and convincing evidence, that it is likely the child will be adopted, unless:~~

~~(A) At each and every hearing at which the court was required to consider reasonable efforts or services, the court has found that reasonable efforts were not made or that reasonable services were not offered or provided; or~~

~~(B) The child is living with a relative who is unable or unwilling to adopt the child because of circumstances that do not include an unwillingness to accept legal or financial responsibility for the child, but who is willing and capable of providing the child with a stable and permanent environment through legal guardianship, and removal from the home of the relative would be detrimental to the emotional well-being of the child. For an Indian child, "relative" includes an "extended family member," as defined in the federal Indian Child Welfare Act (25 U.S.C. § 1903(2)); or~~

~~(C) The court finds a compelling reason to determine that termination would be detrimental to the child because of the existence of one of the following circumstances:~~

~~(i) The parents or guardians have maintained regular visitation and contact with the child and the child would benefit from continuing the relationship;~~

~~(ii) A child 12 years of age or older objects to termination of parental rights;~~

~~(iii) The child is placed in a residential treatment facility and adoption is unlikely or undesirable while the child remains in that placement, and continuation of parental rights will not prevent the finding of an adoptive home if the parents cannot resume custody when residential care is no longer needed;~~

~~(iv) The child is living with a foster parent or Indian custodian who is unable or unwilling to adopt the child because of exceptional circumstances, but who is willing and capable of providing the child with a stable and permanent home, and removal from the home of the foster parent or Indian custodian would be detrimental to the emotional well-being of the child. This exception does not apply to (1) a child under 6 or (2) a child who has a sibling under 6 who is also a dependent and with whom the child should be placed permanently; or~~

~~(v) There would be a substantial interference with the child's relationship with a sibling, taking into consider-~~

~~ation the nature and extent of the relationship. To make this determination, the court may consider whether the child was raised in the same home as the sibling, whether the child and the sibling shared common experiences or have close and strong bonds, and whether ongoing contact with the sibling is in the child's best interest. For purposes of this subdivision, determination of the child's best interest may include a comparison of the child's long-term emotional interest with the benefit of legal permanence in an adoptive home.~~

~~(vi) The child is an Indian child and termination of parental rights would substantially interfere with the child's connection to his or her tribal community or the child's tribal membership rights, or the child's tribe has identified guardianship, long-term foster care with a fit and willing relative, tribal customary adoption, or another planned permanent living arrangement as the appropriate permanent plan for the child.~~

~~(3) The court must not fail to find that the child is likely to be adopted based on the fact that the child is not yet placed in a preadoptive home or with a relative or foster family willing to adopt the child.~~

~~(4)~~(2) The party claiming that termination of parental rights would be detrimental to the child has the burden of proving the detriment.

~~(5) If the court finds termination of parental rights to be detrimental to the child for reasons stated in (2)(B), the court must state the reasons in writing or on the record.~~

~~(6) If termination of parental rights would not be detrimental to the child, but the child is difficult to place for adoption because the child (1) is a member of a sibling group that should stay together; (2) has a diagnosed medical, physical, or mental handicap; or (3) is 7 years of age or older and no prospective adoptive parent is identified or available, the court may, without terminating parental rights, identify adoption as a permanent placement goal and order the public agency responsible for seeking adoptive parents to make efforts to locate an appropriate adoptive family for a period not to exceed 180 days. During the 180-day period, in order to identify potential adoptive parents, the agency responsible for seeking adoptive parents for each child must, to the extent possible, ask each child who is 10 years of age or older and who is placed in out-of-home placement for six months or longer to identify any individuals who are important to the child. The agency may ask any other child to provide that information, as appropriate. After that period the court must hold another hearing and proceed according to (1), (2), or (7).~~

~~(7)~~(3) If the court finds that ~~(2)(A) or (2)(B)~~ section 366.26(c)(1)(A) or section 366.26(c)(2)(A) applies, the court must appoint the present custodian or other appropriate person to become the child's legal guardian or must order the child to remain in foster care.

(A) ~~If the court orders that the child remain in foster care, it must identify the foster care setting by name and identify a specific permanency goal for the child.~~If the court orders that the child remain in foster care, ~~The court~~ it may order that the name and address of the foster home remain confidential.

~~(B) Legal guardianship must be given preference over foster care when it is in the interest of the child and a suitable guardian can be found.~~

~~(C) A child who is 10 years of age or older who is placed in a out-of-home placement for six months or longer must be asked to identify any adults who are important to him or her in order for the agency to investigate and the court to determine whether any of those adults would be appropriate to serve as legal guardians. Other children may be asked for this information, as age and developmentally appropriate.~~

~~(D)~~(B) If the court finds that removal of the child from the home of a foster parent or relative who is not willing to become a legal guardian for the child would be seriously detrimental to the emotional well-being of the child, then the child must not be removed. The foster parent or relative must be willing to provide, and capable of providing, a stable and permanent home for the child and must have substantial psychological ties with the child.

~~(E) The court must make an order for visitation with each parent or guardian unless the court finds by a preponderance of the evidence that the visitation would be detrimental to the child.~~

~~(8)~~(4) The court must consider the case plan submitted for this hearing and must ~~find as follows:~~ make the required findings and determinations in rule 5.708(e).

~~(A) The child was actively involved in the development of his or her own case plan and plan for permanent placement as age and developmentally appropriate, including being asked for a statement regarding his or her permanent placement plan, and the case plan contains the social worker's assessment of those stated wishes; or~~

~~(B) The child was not actively involved in the development of his or her own case plan and plan for permanent placement, including being asked for a statement regarding his or her permanent placement plan and the case plan does not contain the social worker's assessment of those stated wishes. If the court makes such a finding, the court must order the agency to actively involve the child in the development of his or her own case plan and plan for permanent placement, including asking the child for a statement regarding his or her permanent plan, unless the court finds that the child is unable, unavailable, or unwilling to participate. If the court finds that the case plan does not contain the social worker's assessment of the child's stated wishes, the court must order the agency to submit the assessment to the court; and~~

~~(C) In the case of an Indian child, the agency consulted with the child's tribe and the tribe was actively involved in the development of the case plan and plan for permanent placement, including consideration of whether tribal customary adoption is an appropriate permanent plan for the child if reunification is unsuccessful; or~~

~~(D) In the case of an Indian child, the agency did not consult with the child's tribe. If the court makes such a finding, the court must order the agency to consult with the tribe, unless the court finds that the tribe is unable, unavailable, or unwilling to participate.~~

~~(9) For a child 12 years of age or older and in a permanent placement, the court must consider the case plan and must find as follows:~~

~~(A) The child was given the opportunity to review the case plan, sign it, and receive a copy; or~~

~~(B) The child was not given the opportunity to review the case plan, sign it, and receive a copy. If the court makes such a finding, the court must order the agency to give the child the opportunity to review the case plan, sign it, and receive a copy.~~

~~(10) If no adult is available to become legal guardian, and no suitable foster home is available, the court may order the care, custody, and control of the child transferred to a licensed foster family agency, subject to further orders of the court.~~

(e) Procedures—adoption

(1) The court must follow the procedures in section 366.24 or 366.26, as appropriate.

~~(1) The court may not terminate parental rights or order adoption if a review of the prior findings and orders reveals that at each and every prior hearing at which the court was required to consider reasonable efforts or services the court found that reasonable efforts had not been made or that reasonable services had not been offered or provided. If at any prior hearing the court found that reasonable efforts had been made or that reasonable services had been offered or provided, the court may terminate parental rights.~~

(2) An order of the court terminating parental rights, ordering adoption under section 366.26 or, in the case of an Indian child, ordering tribal customary adoption under section 366.24, is conclusive and binding on the child, the parent, and all other persons who have been served under the provisions of section 294. The order may not be set aside or modified by the court, except as provided in section 366.26(i)(3) and rules 5.538, 5.540, and 5.542 with regard to orders by a referee.

~~(3) If the court declares the child free from custody and control of the parents, the court must at the same time order the child referred to a licensed county adoption agency for adoptive placement. A petition for adoption of the child may be filed and heard in the juvenile court but may not be granted until the appellate rights of all parents have been exhausted.~~

~~(4) In the case of an Indian child for whom tribal customary adoption has been ordered in accordance with section 366.24, the court may continue the hearing for up to 120 days to permit the tribe to complete the process for tribal customary adoption. In its discretion, the court may grant a further continuance not exceeding 60 days.~~

~~(A) No less than 20 days before the date set for the continued hearing, the tribe must file the completed tribal customary adoption order with the court.~~

~~(B) The social worker must file an addendum report with the court at least 7 days before the hearing.~~

~~(C) If the tribe does not file the tribal customary adoption order within the designated time period, the court must make new findings and orders under section 366.26(b) and select a new permanent plan for the child.~~

(f) Procedures—legal guardianship

The proceedings for appointment of a legal guardian for a dependent child of the juvenile court must be in the juvenile court as provided in rule 5.735.

(g) Purpose of termination of parental rights

The purpose of termination of parental rights is to free the child for adoption. Therefore, the court must not terminate the rights of only one parent unless that parent is the only surviving parent, or the rights of the other parent have been terminated by a California court of competent jurisdiction or by a court of competent jurisdiction of another state under the statutes of that state, or the other parent has relinquished custody of the child to the county welfare department. The rights of all parents—whether natural, presumed, biological, alleged, or unknown—must be terminated in order to free the child for adoption.

(h) Advisement of appeal rights

The court must advise all parties of their appeal rights as provided in rule 5.585 and section 366.26(*1*). *(Formerly Rule 1463, adopted, eff. Jan. 1, 1991. As amended, eff. Jan. 1, 1992; July 1, 1992; Jan. 1, 1994; July 1, 1994; Jan. 1, 1995; July 1, 1995; July 1, 1997; Jan. 1, 1999; July 1, 1999; July 1, 2002; Jan. 1, 2005; Jan. 1, 2006. Renumbered Rule 5.725 and amended, eff. Jan. 1, 2007. As amended, eff. Jan. 1, 2009; Jan. 1, 2010; July 1, 2010; Jan. 1, 2015; Jan. 1, 2017.)*

Commentary

Interpreting subsection (b), *In re Caitlin B., 78 Cal.App.4th 1190, 93 Cal.Rptr.2d 480 (2000), review denied May 24, 2000*, holds that the mother of two dependent children lacks standing to challenge an order terminating parental rights on the ground that the children's alleged fathers were not given notice of the proceeding, because her interest was in the continuation of her parental rights, not those of other persons with whom she had no continuing relationship.

Research References

Forms

West's California Judicial Council Forms JV-300, Notice Of Hearing on Selection Of a Permanent Plan.

West's California Judicial Council Forms JV-310, Proof Of Service Under Section 366.26 Of the Welfare and Institutions Code.

West's California Judicial Council Forms JV-320, Orders Under Welfare and Institutions Code Sections 366.26, 727.3, 727.31.

Treatises and Practice Aids

Witkin, California Summary 10th Parent and Child § 680, Statutory Procedure is Exclusive.

Witkin, California Summary 10th Parent and Child § 681, Notice.

Witkin, California Summary 10th Parent and Child § 682, Preliminary Assessment.

Witkin, California Summary 10th Parent and Child § 685, Hearing.

Witkin, California Summary 10th Parent and Child § 686, Alternative Dispositions.

Witkin, California Summary 10th Parent and Child § 687, Termination Of Parental Rights to Free Child for Adoption.

Witkin, California Summary 10th Parent and Child § 688, Other Alternatives.

Witkin, California Summary 10th Parent and Child § 689, in General.

Witkin, California Summary 10th Parent and Child § 690, Benefit to Child.

Witkin, California Summary 10th Parent and Child § 692, in General.

Witkin, California Summary 10th Parent and Child § 693, Termination Of Parental Rights.
Witkin, California Summary 10th Parent and Child § 695, Legal Guardianship.
Witkin, California Summary 10th Parent and Child § 899, Termination Of Parental Rights.

Rule 5.726. Prospective adoptive parent designation (§§ 366.26(n), 16010.6)

(a) Request procedure

A dependent child's caregiver may be designated as a prospective adoptive parent. The court may make the designation on its own motion or on a request by a caregiver, the child, a social worker, the child's identified Indian tribe, or the attorney for any of these parties.

(1) A request for designation as a prospective adoptive parent may be made at a hearing where parental rights are terminated or a plan of tribal customary adoption is ordered or thereafter, whether or not the child's removal from the home of the prospective adoptive parent is at issue.

(2) A request may be made orally.

(3) If a request for prospective adoptive parent designation is made in writing, it must be made on *Request for Prospective Adoptive Parent Designation* (form JV–321).

(4) The address and telephone number of the caregiver and the child may be kept confidential by filing *Confidential Information—Prospective Adoptive Parent (form JV–322),* with form JV–321. Form JV–322 must be kept in the court file under seal, and only the court, the child's attorney, the agency, and the child's CASA volunteer may have access to this information.

(b) ~~Criteria for designation as prospective adoptive parent~~ Facilitation steps. ~~A caregiver must meet the following criteria to be designated as a prospective adoptive parent:~~

~~(1) The child has lived with the caregiver for at least six months;~~

~~(2) The caregiver currently expresses a commitment to adopt the child; and~~

~~(3) The caregiver has taken at least one step to facilitate the adoption process.~~ Steps to facilitate the adoption process include:~~—~~ those listed in section 366.26(n)(2) and, in the case of an Indian child when tribal customary adoption has been identified as the child's permanent plan, the child's identified Indian tribe has designated the caregiver as the prospective adoptive parent.

~~(A) Applying for an adoption home study;~~

~~(B) Cooperating with an adoption home study;~~

~~(C) Being designated by the court or the licensed adoption agency as the adoptive family;~~

~~(D) In~~ ;

~~(E) Requesting de facto parent status;~~

~~(F) Signing an adoptive placement agreement;~~

~~(G) Discussing a postadoption contact agreement with the social worker, child's attorney, child's CASA volunteer, adoption agency, or court;~~

~~(H) Working to overcome any impediments that have been identified by the California Department of Social Services and the licensed adoption agency; and~~

~~(I) Attending any of the classes required of prospective adoptive parents.~~

(c) Hearing on request for prospective adoptive parent designation

(1) The court must ~~evaluate~~ determine whether the caregiver meets the criteria in ~~(b)~~ section 366.26(n)(1).

~~(1) The petitioner must show on the request that the caregiver meets the criteria in (b).~~

(2) If the court finds ~~that the petitioner does not show~~ that the caregiver does not meet~~s~~ the criteria in ~~(b),~~ section 366.26(n)(1), the court may deny the request without a hearing.

(3) If the court finds ~~that the petitioner has shown~~ that the ~~current~~ caregiver meets the criteria in ~~(b),~~ section 366.26(n)(1), the court must set a hearing as set forth in (4) below.

(4) If it appears to the court that the request for designation as a prospective adoptive parent will be contested, or if the court wants to receive further evidence on the request, the court must set a hearing.

(A) If the request for designation is made at the same time ~~as an objection~~ a petition is filed to object to removal of the child from the caregiver's home, the court must set a hearing as follows:

(i) The hearing must be set as soon as possible and not later than five court days after the ~~objection~~ petition objecting to removal is filed with the court.

(ii) If the court for good cause ~~is unable to~~ cannot set the matter for hearing five court days after the petition objecting to removal is filed, the court must set the matter for hearing as soon as possible.

(iii) The matter may be set for hearing more than five court days after the ~~objection~~ petition objecting to removal is filed if this delay is necessary to allow participation by the child's identified Indian tribe or the child's Indian custodian.

(B) If the request for designation is made before ~~a request for removal is filed~~ the agency serves notice of a proposed removal or before an emergency removal has occurred, the court must ~~order that the~~ set a hearing ~~be set at a time~~ within 30 calendar days after the ~~filing of the~~ request for designation is made.

(5) If all parties stipulate to the ~~request for~~ designation of the caregiver as a prospective adoptive parent, the court may order the designation without a hearing.

(d) Notice of designation hearing

After the court has ordered a hearing on a request for prospective adoptive parent designation, notice of the hearing must be as described below.

(1) The following participants must be noticed:

(A) The adoption agency;

(B) The current caregiver,

(C) The child's attorney;

(D) The child, if the child is 10 years of age or older;

(E) The child's identified Indian tribe if any;

(F) The child's Indian custodian if any; and

(G) The child's CASA program if any.

(2) If the request for designation ~~was~~ is made at the same time as a request for hearing on a proposed or emergency removal, notice of the designation hearing must be provided with notice of the hearing on proposed removal~~hearing~~, as stated in rule 5.727(f).

(3) If the request for designation ~~was~~ is made before ~~a request for removal was filed~~ the agency serves notice of a proposed removal or before an emergency removal occurred, notice must be as follows:

(A) Service of the notice must be either by first-class mail sent at least 15 calendar days before the hearing date to the last known address of the person to be noticed, or by personal service on the person at least 10 calendar days before the hearing.

(B) *Prospective Adoptive Parent Designation Order* (form JV–327) must be used to provide notice of a hearing on the request for prospective adoptive parent designation.

(C) The clerk must provide notice of the hearing to the participants listed in (1) above, if the court, caregiver, or child requested the hearing.

(D) The child's attorney must provide notice of the hearing to the participants listed in (1) above, if the child's attorney requested the hearing.

(E) *Proof of Notice* (form JV–326) must be filed with the court before the hearing on the request for prospective adoptive parent designation.

(e) Termination of designation

If the prospective adoptive parent no longer meets the criteria in ~~rule 5.726(b),~~ section 366.26(n)(1), a request to vacate the order designating the caregiver as a prospective adoptive parent may be filed under section 388 and rule 5.570.

(f) Confidentiality

If the telephone or address of the caregiver or the child is confidential, all forms must be kept in the court file under seal. Only the court, the child's attorney, the agency, and the child's CASA volunteer may have access to this information.

(Formerly Rule 1463.1, adopted, eff. July 1, 2006. Renumbered Rule 5.726 and amended, eff. Jan. 1, 2007. As amended, eff. Jan. 1, 2008; July 1, 2010; Jan. 1, 2017.)

Research References

Forms

West's California Judicial Council Forms JV-321, Request for Prospective Adoptive Parent Designation.

West's California Judicial Council Forms JV-322, Confidential Information--Prospective Adoptive Parent.

West's California Judicial Council Forms JV-323, Notice Of Intent to Remove Child and Proof Of Notice, Objection to Removal, and Order After Hearing.

West's California Judicial Council Forms JV-326, Proof Of Notice.

West's California Judicial Council Forms JV-327, Prospective Adoptive Parent Designation Order.

West's California Judicial Council Forms JV-328, Prospective Adoptive Parent Order After Hearing.

Treatises and Practice Aids

Witkin, California Summary 10th Parent and Child § 693A, (New) in General.

Witkin, California Summary 10th Parent and Child § 693B, (New) Designation Of Prospective Adoptive Parent.

Rule 5.727. Proposed removal (§ 366.26(n))

(a) Application of rule

This rule applies, after termination of parental rights or, in the case of tribal customary adoption, modification of parental rights, to the removal by the Department of Social Services (DSS) or a licensed adoption agency of a dependent child from a prospective adoptive parent ~~under rule 5.726(b)~~ or from a caregiver who may meet the criteria for designation as a prospective adoptive parent ~~under rule 5.726(b)~~ in section 366.26(n)(1). This rule does not apply if the caregiver requests the child's removal.

(b) Participants to be served with notice

Before removing a child from the home of a prospective adoptive parent ~~under rule 5.726(b)~~ as defined in section 366.26(n)(1) or from the home of a caregiver who may meet the criteria of a prospective adoptive parent ~~under rule 5.726(b)~~ in section 366.26(n)(1), and as soon as possible after a decision is made to remove the child, the agency must notify the following participants of the proposed removal:

(1) The court;

(2) The current caregiver, if that caregiver either is a designated prospective adoptive parent or, on the date of service of the notice, meets the criteria in ~~rule 5.726(b)~~ section 366.26(n)(1);

(3) The child's attorney;

(4) The child, if the child is 10 years of age or older;

(5) The child's identified Indian tribe if any;

(6) The child's Indian custodian if any; and

(7) The child's CASA program if any.

(c) Form of notice

DSS or the agency must provide notice on *Notice of Intent to Remove Child* (form JV–323). A blank copy of *Objection to Removal* (form JV–325) and *Request for Prospective Adoptive Parent Designation* (form JV–321) must also be provided to all participants listed in (b) except the court.

(d) Service of notice

DSS or the agency must serve notice of its intent to remove a child as follows:

(1) DSS or the agency must serve notice either by first-class mail, sent to the last known address of the person to be noticed, or by personal service.

(2) If service is by first-class mail, service is completed and time to respond is extended by five calendar days.

(3) Notice to the child's identified Indian tribe and Indian custodian must ~~be given under rule 5.481~~ comply with the requirements of section 224.2.

(4) ~~Proof of service of the notice on~~ *Proof of Notice* (form JV–326) must be filed with the court before the hearing on the proposed removal.

(e) Objection to proposed removal

Each participant who receives notice under (b) may object to the proposed removal of the child and may request a hearing.

(1) A request for hearing on the proposed removal must be made on *Objection to Removal* (form JV–325).

(2) A request for hearing on the proposed removal must be made within five court or seven calendar days from the date of notification, whichever is longer. If service of the notification is by mail, time to ~~respond~~ request a hearing is extended by five calendar days.

(3) The court must ~~order~~ set a hearing as follows:

(A) The hearing must be set as soon as possible and not later than five court days after the objection is filed with the court.

(B) If the court for good cause is unable to set the matter for hearing five court days after the petition is filed, the court must set the matter for hearing as soon as possible.

(C) The matter may be set for hearing more than five court days after the objection is filed if this delay is necessary to allow participation by the child's identified Indian tribe or the child's Indian custodian.

(f) Notice of hearing on proposed removal

After the court has ordered a hearing on a proposed removal, notice of the hearing must be as follows:

(1) The clerk must provide notice of the hearing to the agency and the participants listed in (b) above, if the court, caregiver, or child requested the hearing.

(2) The child's attorney must provide notice of the hearing to the agency and the participants listed in (b) above, if the child's attorney requested the hearing.

(3) Notice must be ~~either~~ by personal service or by telephone. Notice by personal service must include a copy of the completed forms *Notice of Intent to Remove Child* (form JV–323) and *Objection to Removal* (form JV–325). Telephone notice must include the reasons for and against the removal, as indicated on forms JV–323 and JV–325.

(4) ~~Proof of notice on~~ *Proof of Notice* (form JV–326) must be filed with the court before the hearing on the proposed removal.

(g) Burden of proof

At a hearing on an intent to remove the child, the agency intending to remove the child must prove by a preponderance of the evidence that the proposed removal is in the best interest of the child.

(h) Confidentiality

If the telephone or address of the caregiver or the child is confidential, all forms must be kept in the court file under seal. Only the court, the child's attorney, the agency, and the child's CASA volunteer may have access to this information.

(i) Appeal

If the court order made after a hearing on an intent to remove a child is appealed, the appeal must be ~~made~~ brought as a petition for writ review under rules 8.454 and 8.456.

(Formerly Rule 1463.3, adopted, eff. July 1, 2006. Renumbered Rule 5.727 and amended, eff. Jan. 1, 2007. As amended, eff. Jan. 1, 2008; July 1, 2010; Jan. 1, 2011; Jan. 1, 2017.)

Research References

Forms

West's California Judicial Council Forms JV-322, Confidential Information--Prospective Adoptive Parent.

West's California Judicial Council Forms JV-323, Notice Of Intent to Remove Child and Proof Of Notice, Objection to Removal, and Order After Hearing.

West's California Judicial Council Forms JV-325, Objection to Removal.

West's California Judicial Council Forms JV-326, Proof Of Notice.

West's California Judicial Council Forms JV-328, Prospective Adoptive Parent Order After Hearing.

Treatises and Practice Aids

Witkin, California Summary 10th Parent and Child § 693A, (New) in General.

Witkin, California Summary 10th Parent and Child § 693C, (New) Nonemergency Removal from Prospective Adoptive Parent.

Rule 5.728. Emergency removal (§ 366.26(n))

(a) Application of rule

This rule applies, after termination of parental rights or, in the case of tribal customary adoption, modification of parental rights, to the removal by the Department of Social Services (DSS) or a licensed adoption agency of a dependent child from the home of a prospective adoptive parent ~~under rule 5.726(b)~~ or ~~from~~ a caregiver who may meet the criteria for designation as a prospective adoptive parent ~~under rule 5.726(b)~~ in section 366.26(n)(1) when the DSS or the licensed adoption agency has determined a removal must occur immediately due to a risk of physical or emotional harm. This rule does not apply if the child~~'s removal is carried out~~ is removed at the request of the caregiver.

(b) Participants to be noticed

After removing a child from the home of a prospective adoptive parent ~~under rule 5.726(b)~~, or from the home of a caregiver who may meet the criteria of a prospective adoptive parent ~~under rule 5.726(b)~~ in section 366.26(n)(1), because of ~~immediate~~ risk of physical or emotional harm, the agency must notify the following participants of the emergency removal:

(1) The court;

(2) The ~~current~~ caregiver, ~~if that caregiver either~~ who is a ~~designated~~ prospective adoptive parent or who, on the date of service of the notice, ~~meets~~ may meet the criteria in ~~rule 5.726(b)~~ section 366.26(n)(1);

(3) The child's attorney;

(4) The child if the child is 10 years of age or older;

(5) The child's identified Indian tribe if any;

(6) The child's Indian custodian if any; and

(7) The child's CASA program if any.

(c) Form and service of notice

Notice of Emergency Removal (form JV–324) must be used to provide notice of an emergency removal, as described below.

(1) The agency must provide notice of the emergency removal as soon as possible but no later than two court days after the removal.

(2) Notice must be either by telephone or by personal service of the form.

(3) Telephone notice must include the reasons for removal as indicated on the form, and notice of the right to object to the removal.

(4) Whenever possible, the agency, at the time of the removal, must give a blank copy of ~~the form~~ *Request for Prospective Adoptive Parent Designation* (form JV–321) and a blank copy of *Objection to Removal* (form JV–325) to the caregiver and, if the child is 10 years of age or older, to the child.

(5) Notice to the court must be served by filing ~~of the form~~ *Notice of Emergency Removal* (form JV–324) and *Proof of Notice* (form JV–326) with the court. ~~The proof of notice included on the form must be completed when the form is filed with the court.~~

(6) *Proof of Notice* (form JV–326) must be filed with the court before the hearing on the proposed removal.

(d) Objection to emergency removal

Each participant who receives notice under (b) may object to the removal of the child and may request a hearing.

(1) A request for hearing on the emergency removal must be made on *Objection to Removal* (form JV–325).

(2) The court must ~~order~~ set a hearing as follows:

(A) The hearing must be set as soon as possible and not later than five court days after the ~~objection~~ petition objecting to removal is filed with the court.

(B) If the court for good cause ~~is unable to~~ cannot set the matter for hearing within five court days after the petition objecting to removal is filed, the court must set the matter for hearing as soon as possible.

(C) The matter may be set for hearing more than five court days after the ~~objection~~ petition objecting to removal is filed if this delay is necessary to allow participation by the child's identified Indian tribe or the child's Indian custodian.

(e) Notice of ~~emergency removal~~ hearing on emergency removal

After the court has ordered a hearing on an emergency removal, notice of the hearing must be as follows:

~~(1) Notice must be either by personal service or by telephone. Notice by personal service must include a copy of *Notice of Emergency Removal* (form JV–324). Telephone notice must include the reasons for and against the removal, as indicated on forms JV–324 and JV–325.~~

~~(2)~~(1) The clerk must provide notice of the hearing to the agency and the participants listed in (b) above, if the court, ~~the~~ caregiver, or ~~the~~ child requested the hearing.

~~(3)~~(2) The child's attorney must provide notice of the hearing to the agency and the participants listed in (b) above, if the child's attorney requested the hearing.

(3) Notice must be by personal service or by telephone. Notice by personal service must include a copy of the completed *Notice of Emergency Removal* (form JV–324). Telephone notice must include the reasons for and against the removal, as indicated on forms JV–324 and JV–325.

(4) ~~Proof of notice on~~ *Proof of Notice* (form JV–326) must be filed with the court before the hearing on the emergency removal.

(f) Burden of proof

At a hearing on an emergency removal, the agency that removed the child must prove by a preponderance of the evidence that the removal is in the best interest of the child.

(g) Confidentiality

If the telephone or address of the caregiver or the child is confidential, all forms must be kept in the court file under seal. Only the court, the child's attorney, the agency, and the child's CASA volunteer and program may have access to this information. *(Formerly Rule 1463.5, adopted, eff. July 1, 2006. Renumbered Rule 5.728 and amended, eff. Jan. 1, 2007. As amended, eff. Jan. 1, 2008; July 1, 2010; Jan. 1, 2017.)*

Research References

Forms

West's California Judicial Council Forms JV-322, Confidential Information--Prospective Adoptive Parent.

West's California Judicial Council Forms JV-324, Notice Of Emergency Removal, Objection to Removal, and Order After Hearing.

West's California Judicial Council Forms JV-325, Objection to Removal.

West's California Judicial Council Forms JV-326, Proof Of Notice.

Treatises and Practice Aids

Witkin, California Summary 10th Parent and Child § 693A, (New) in General.

Witkin, California Summary 10th Parent and Child § 693D, (New) Emergency Removal from Prospective Adoptive Parent.

Rule 5.730. Adoption (§§ 366.24, 366.26(e), Fam. Code, § 8600 et seq.)

(a) Procedures—adoption

(1) The petition for the adoption of a dependent child who has been freed for adoption may be filed in the juvenile court with jurisdiction over the dependency.

(2) All adoption petitions must be completed on *Adoption Request* (form ADOPT–200) and must be verified. In addition, the petitioner must complete *Adoption Agreement* (form ADOPT–210) and *Adoption Order* (form ADOPT–215).

(3) A petitioner seeking to adopt an Indian child must also complete *Adoption of Indian Child* (form ADOPT–220). If applicable, *Parent of Indian Child Agrees to End Parental Rights* (form ADOPT–225) may be filed.

(4) The clerk must open a confidential adoption file for each child and this file must be separate and apart from the dependency file, with an adoption case number different from the dependency case number.

(b) Notice

The clerk of the court must give notice of the adoption hearing to:

(1) Any attorney of record for the child;

(2) Any CASA volunteer;

(3) The child welfare agency;

(4) The tribe of an Indian child; and

(5) The California Department of Social Services. The notice to the California Department of Social Services must include a copy of the completed *Adoption Request* (form ADOPT–200) and a copy of any adoptive placement agreement or agency joinder filed in the case.

(c) Hearing

If the petition for adoption is filed in the juvenile court, the proceeding for adoption must be heard in juvenile court once appellate rights have been exhausted. Each petitioner and the child must be present at the hearing. The hearing may be heard by a referee if the referee is acting as a temporary judge.

(d) Record

The record must reflect that the court has read and considered the assessment prepared for the hearing held under section 366.26 and as required by section 366.22(b), the report of any CASA volunteer, and any other reports or documents admitted into evidence.

(e) Assessment

The preparer of the assessment may be called and examined by any party to the adoption proceeding.

(f) Consent

(1) At the hearing, each adoptive parent must execute *Adoption Agreement* (form ADOPT–210) in the presence of and with the acknowledgment of the court.

(2) If the child to be adopted is 12 years of age or older, he or she must also execute *Adoption Agreement* (form ADOPT–210), except in the case of a tribal customary adoption.

(g) Dismissal of jurisdiction

If the petition for adoption is granted, the juvenile court must dismiss the dependency, terminate jurisdiction over the child, and vacate any previously set review hearing dates. A completed *Termination of Dependency (Juvenile)* (form JV–364) must be filed in the child's juvenile dependency file. *(Formerly Rule 1464, adopted, eff. July 1, 1995. As amended, eff. Jan. 1, 1996; Jan. 1, 1999; Jan. 1, 2004. Renumbered Rule 5.730 and amended, eff. Jan. 1, 2007. As amended, eff. July 1, 2010; Jan. 1, 2017.)*

Research References

Forms

California Transactions Forms--Family Law § 6:98, Form Drafting Considerations.

California Transactions Forms--Family Law § 6:152, Client Interview and Form Drafting Considerations in Handling ICWA Issues.

California Transactions Forms--Family Law § 6:153, Matters to Consider in Handling Adoption With ICWA Issues.

West's California Judicial Council Forms JV-364, Termination Of Dependency.

West's California Judicial Council Forms ADOPT-200, Adoption Request.

West's California Judicial Council Forms ADOPT-210, Adoption Agreement.

West's California Judicial Council Forms ADOPT-215, Adoption Order.

Treatises and Practice Aids

Witkin, California Summary 10th Parent and Child § 118, Petition.

Witkin, California Summary 10th Parent and Child § 694, Adoption Proceeding.

Rule 5.735. Legal guardianship

(a) Proceedings in juvenile court (§ 366.26(d))

The proceedings for the appointment of a legal guardian for a dependent child must be in the juvenile court. The request for appointment of a guardian must be included in the social study report prepared by the county welfare department or in the assessment prepared for the hearing under section 366.26. Neither a separate petition nor a separate hearing is required.

(b) Notice; hearing

Notice for the guardianship hearing must be given under section 294, and the hearing must proceed under section 366.26.

~~**(c) Conduct of hearing**~~

~~(1) Before appointing a guardian, the court must read and consider the social study report specified in section 366.26 and note its consideration in the minutes of the court.~~

~~(2) The preparer of the social study report may be called in and examined by any party to the proceedings.~~

~~(d)~~(c) Findings and orders

(1) If the court finds that legal guardianship is the appropriate permanent plan, the court must appoint the guardian and order the clerk to issue letters of guardianship, which will not be subject to the confidentiality protections ~~of juvenile court documents as~~ described in section 827.

(2) The court ~~may~~ must issue orders regarding visitation of the child by a parent or ~~other relative~~ former guardian, unless the court finds that visitation would be detrimental to the physical or emotional well-being of the child.

(3) The court may issue orders regarding visitation of the child by a relative.

~~(3)~~(4) On appointment of a guardian under section 366.26, the court may terminate dependency.

~~(e)~~(d) Notification of appeal rights

The court must advise all parties of their appeal rights as provided in rule ~~5.585~~ 5.590. *(Formerly Rule 1464, adopted, eff. Jan. 1, 1991. Renumbered Rule 1465 and amended, eff. July 1, 1995. As amended, eff. July 1, 1997; July 1, 1999; Jan. 1, 2006. Renumbered Rule 5.735 and amended, eff. Jan. 1, 2007. As amended, eff. Jan. 1, 2017.)*

Research References

Treatises and Practice Aids

Witkin, California Summary 10th Parent and Child § 695, Legal Guardianship.

Rule 5.740. Hearings subsequent to a permanent plan (§§ 366.26, 366.3, 16501.1)

(a) Review hearings—adoption and guardianship

Following an order for termination of parental rights or, in the case of tribal customary adoption, modification of parental rights, or a plan for the establishment of a guardianship under section 366.26, the court must retain jurisdiction and conduct review hearings at least every 6 months to ensure the expeditious completion of the adoption or guardianship.

(1) At the review hearing, the court must consider the report of the petitioner required by section 366.3(g), the report of any CASA volunteer, the case plan submitted for this hearing, and any report submitted by the child's caregiver under section 366.21(d); inquire about the progress being made to provide a permanent home for the child; consider the safety of the child; and enter findings as required by section 366.3(e).

(2) The court or administrative review panel must consider the case plan and make the findings and determinations concerning the child in rule 5.708(e).

~~(2)~~(3) When adoption is granted, the court must terminate its jurisdiction.

~~(3)~~(4) When legal guardianship is granted, the court may continue dependency jurisdiction if it is in the best interest of the child, or the court may terminate dependency jurisdiction and retain jurisdiction over the child as a ward of the guardianship.

~~(4)~~(5) Notice of the hearing must be given as provided in section 295.

(6) If the child is not placed for adoption, the court or administrative review panel must find as follows:

(A) Whether the agency has made diligent efforts to locate an appropriate relative. If the court or administrative review panel finds the agency has not made diligent efforts to locate an appropriate relative, the court or administrative review panel must order the agency to do so.

(B) Whether each relative whose name has been submitted to the agency as a possible caregiver has been evaluated as an appropriate placement resource. If the court or administrative review panel finds the agency has not evaluated each relative whose name has been submitted as a possible caregiver, the court or administrative review panel must order the agency to do so.

(b) Review hearings—relative care or foster care

Following the establishment of a plan other than those provided for in (a), review hearings must be conducted at least every 6 months by the court or by a local administrative review panel.

(1) At the review hearing, the court or administrative review panel must consider the report of the petitioner, the report of any CASA volunteer, the case plan submitted for this hearing, and any report submitted by the child's caregiver under section 366.21(d); inquire about the progress being made to provide a permanent home for the child; consider the safety of the child; and enter findings ~~regarding each item listed in~~ as required by section 366.3(e).

(2) The court or administrative review panel must consider the case plan submitted for this hearing and ~~must find as follows:~~ make the findings and determinations concerning the child in rule 5.708(e).

~~(A) The child was actively involved in the development of his or her own case plan and plan for permanent placement as age and developmentally appropriate; or~~

~~(B) The child was not actively involved in the development of his or her own case plan and plan for permanent placement as age and developmentally appropriate. If the court or administrative review panel makes such a finding, the court must order the agency to actively involve the child in the development of his or her own case plan and plan for permanent placement, unless the court finds that the child is unable, unavailable, or unwilling to participate.~~

~~(3) For a child 12 years of age or older and in a permanent placement, the court must consider the case plan and must find as follows:~~

~~(A) The child was given the opportunity to review the case plan, sign it, and receive a copy; or~~

~~(B) The child was not given the opportunity to review the case plan, sign it, and receive a copy. If the court makes such a finding, the court must order the agency to give the child the opportunity to review the case plan, sign it, and receive a copy.~~

(3) If the child is not placed for adoption, the court or administrative review panel must find as follows:

(A) Whether the agency has made diligent efforts to locate an appropriate relative. If the court or administrative review panel finds the agency has not made diligent efforts to locate an appropriate relative, the court or administrative review panel must order the agency to do so.

(B) Whether each relative whose name has been submitted to the agency as a possible caregiver has been evaluated as an appropriate placement resource. If the court or administrative review panel finds the agency has not evaluated each relative whose name has been submitted as a possible caregiver, the court or administrative review panel must order the agency to do so.

(4) No less frequently than once every 12 months, the court must conduct a review of the previously ordered permanent plan to consider whether the plan continues to be appropriate for the child. The review of the permanent plan may be combined with the 6–month review.

(5) If circumstances have changed since the permanent plan was ordered, the court may order a new permanent plan under section 366.26 at any subsequent hearing, or any party may seek a new permanent plan by a motion filed under section 388 and rule 5.570.

(6) Notice of the hearing must be given as provided in section 295.

(7) The court must continue the child in foster care unless the parents prove, by a preponderance of the evidence, that further efforts at reunification are the best alternative for the child. In those cases, the court may order reunification services for a period not to exceed 6 months.

~~(8) At a review held 12 months after an original or subsequent order for the child to remain in foster care, the court must consider all permanency planning options, including whether the child should be returned to a parent or guardian, placed for adoption, or appointed a legal guardian. If the court orders that the child remain in foster care, it must identify the foster care setting by name and identify a specific permanency goal for the child. The court may order that the name and address of the foster home remain confidential.~~

~~(9) At a review held 12 months after an original or subsequent order for the child to remain in foster care, the court must order a hearing under section 366.26 unless the court finds by clear and convincing evidence that there is a~~

~~compelling reason for determining that a section 366.26 hearing is not in the child's best interest because the child is being returned to the home of the parent, the child is not a proper subject for adoption, or there is no one available to assume guardianship.~~

~~(10) If the court makes the findings in (9), the court may order that the child remain in foster care.~~

(c) Hearing on petition to terminate guardianship or modify guardianship orders

A petition to terminate a guardianship established by the juvenile court, to appoint a successor guardian, or to modify or supplement orders concerning ~~the~~ a guardianship must be filed in the juvenile court. The procedures described in rule 5.570 must be followed, and *Request to Change Court Order* (form JV–180) must be used.

(1) Proceedings on a petition to terminate a guardianship established under section 366.26 must be heard in the juvenile court. If dependency was terminated at the time of or subsequent to the appointment of the guardian, and dependency is later declared in another county, proceedings to terminate the guardianship may be held in the juvenile court with current dependency jurisdiction.

(2) Not less than 15 court days before the hearing date, the ~~petitioner must serve~~ clerk must cause notice of the hearing ~~on~~ to be given to the department of social services; the guardian; the child, if 10 years or older; parents whose parental rights have not been terminated; the court that established the guardianship, if in another county; and counsel of record for those entitled to notice.

(3) At the hearing on the petition to terminate the guardianship, the court may do one of the following:

(A) Deny the petition to terminate guardianship;

(B) Deny the petition and request the county welfare department to provide services to the guardian and the ward for the purpose of maintaining the guardianship, consistent with section 301; or

(C) Grant the petition to terminate the guardianship.

(4) If the petition is granted and the court continues or resumes dependency, the court must order that a new plan be developed to provide stability and permanency to the child. Unless the court has already scheduled a hearing to review the child's status, the court must conduct a hearing within 60 days. Parents whose parental rights have not been terminated must be notified of the hearing on the new plan. The court may consider further efforts at reunification only if the parent proves, by a preponderance of the evidence, that the efforts would be the best alternative for the child.

(5) If the court terminates a guardianship established in another county, the clerk of the county of current dependency jurisdiction must transmit a certified copy of the order terminating guardianship within 15 days to the court that established the original guardianship. *(Formerly Rule 1465, adopted, eff. Jan. 1, 1991. As amended, eff. Jan. 1, 1992; Jan. 1, 1993; Jan. 1, 1994; July 1, 1994. Renumbered Rule 1466 and amended, eff. July 1, 1995. As amended, eff. Jan. 1, 1998; Jan. 1, 1999; July 1, 1999; July 1, 2002; Jan. 1, 2005; Jan. 1, 2006. Renumbered Rule 5.740 and amended, eff. Jan. 1, 2007. As amended, eff. July 1, 2010; Jan. 1, 2012; Jan. 1, 2015; Jan. 1, 2017.)*

Research References

Forms

West's California Judicial Council Forms JV-403, Sibling Attachment: Contact and Placement.

West's California Judicial Council Forms JV-445, Findings and Orders After Postpermanency Hearing--Parental Rights Terminated; Permanent Plan Of Adoption (Welf. & Inst. Code, S366.3).

West's California Judicial Council Forms JV-446, Findings and Orders After Postpermanency Hearing--Permanent Plan Other Than Adoption (Welf. & Inst. Code, S366.3).

Treatises and Practice Aids

Witkin, California Summary 10th Parent and Child § 444, Scope and Organization.

Witkin, California Summary 10th Parent and Child § 521, Termination Of Jurisdiction.

Witkin, California Summary 10th Parent and Child § 628, Legal Guardianship.

Witkin, California Summary 10th Parent and Child § 695, Legal Guardianship.

Witkin, California Summary 10th Parent and Child § 696, Continuing Jurisdiction.

Witkin, California Summary 10th Parent and Child § 697, Status Review Hearings.

Witkin, California Summary 10th Parent and Child § 698, Other Procedures.

Witkin, California Summary 10th Parent and Child § 699, Notice.

Chapter 13

CASES PETITIONED UNDER SECTIONS 601 AND 602

Article 1

INITIAL APPEARANCE

Rule 5.752. Initial hearing; detention hearings; time limit on custody; setting jurisdiction hearing

(a) Child not detained; filing petition, setting hearing

If the child is not taken into custody and the authorized petitioner (district attorney or probation officer) determines that a petition or notice of probation violation concerning the child should be filed, the petition or notice must be filed with the clerk of the juvenile court as soon as possible. The clerk must set an initial hearing on the petition within 15 court days.

(b) Time limit on custody; filing petition (§§ 604, 631, 631.1)

A child must be released from custody within 48 hours, excluding noncourt days, after first being taken into custody unless a petition or notice of probation violation has been filed either within that time or before the time the child was first taken into custody.

(c) Time limit on custody—willful misrepresentation of age (§ 631.1)

If the child willfully misrepresents the child's age to be 18 years or older, and this misrepresentation causes an unavoidable delay in investigation that prevents the filing of a petition or of a criminal complaint within 48 hours, excluding noncourt days, after the child has been taken into custody, the child must be released unless a petition or complaint has been filed within 48 hours, excluding noncourt days, from the time the true age is determined.

(d) Time limit on custody—certification of child detained in custody (§ 604)

A child must be released from custody within 48 hours, excluding noncourt days, after certification to juvenile court under rules 4.116 and 5.516(d) unless a petition has been filed.

(e) Time limit for detention hearing—warrant or nonward charged with nonviolent misdemeanor (§ 632)

A detention hearing must be set and commenced as soon as possible, but no later than 48 hours, excluding noncourt days, after the child has been taken into custody, if:

(1) The child has been taken into custody on a warrant or by the authority of the probation officer; or

(2) The child is not on probation or parole and is alleged to have committed a misdemeanor not involving violence, the threat of violence, or the possession or use of a weapon.

(f) Time limit for detention hearing—felony, violent misdemeanor, or ward (§ 632)

A detention hearing must be set and commenced as soon as possible, but no later than the expiration of the next court day after the petition or notice of probation violation has been filed, if:

(1) The child is alleged to have committed a felony;

(2) The child is alleged to have committed a misdemeanor involving violence, the threat of violence, or the possession or use of a weapon; or

(3) The child is a ward currently on probation or parole.

(g) Time limit for hearing—arrival at detention facility (§ 632)

A detention hearing must be set and commenced as soon as possible, but no later than 48 hours, excluding noncourt days, after the child arrives at a detention facility within the county if:

(1) The child was taken into custody in another county and transported in custody to the requesting county;

(2) The child was ordered transported in custody when transferred by the juvenile court of another county under rule 5.610; or

(3) The child is a ward temporarily placed in a secure facility pending a change of placement.

(h) Time limit for hearing—violation of home supervision (§§ 628.1, 636)

A child taken into custody for a violation of a written condition of home supervision, which the child has promised in writing to obey under section 628.1 or 636, must be brought before the court for a detention hearing as soon as possible, but no later than 48 hours, excluding noncourt days, after the child was taken into custody.

(i) Time limits—remedy for not observing (§§ 632, 641)

If the detention hearing is not commenced within the time limits, the child must be released immediately, or, if the child is a ward under section 602 awaiting a change of placement, the child must be placed in a suitable, nonsecure facility. *(Formerly Rule 1471, adopted, eff. Jan. 1, 1998. Renumbered Rule 5.752 and amended, eff. Jan. 1, 2007.)*

Research References

Treatises and Practice Aids

Witkin, California Summary 10th Parent and Child § 444, Scope and Organization.

Witkin, California Summary 10th Parent and Child § 764, Retention Of Custody.

Witkin, California Summary 10th Parent and Child § 819, Time Of Hearing.

Witkin, California Summary 10th Parent and Child § 820, Petition and Setting for Hearing.

Witkin, California Summary 10th Parent and Child § 908, Notice and Setting for Hearing.

Rule 5.754. Commencement of initial hearing—explanation, advisement, admission

(a) Explanation of proceedings (§ 633)

At the beginning of the initial hearing, whether the child is detained or not detained, the court must give the advisement required by rule 5.534 and must inform the child and each parent and each guardian present of the following:

(1) The contents of the petition;

(2) The nature and possible consequences of juvenile court proceedings; and

(3) If the child has been taken into custody, the reasons for the initial detention and the purpose and scope of the initial hearing.

(b) Admission of allegations; no contest plea

If the child wishes to admit the allegations of the petition or enter a no contest plea at the initial hearing, the court may accept the admission or plea of no contest and must proceed according to rule 5.778. *(Formerly Rule 1472, adopted, eff. Jan. 1, 1998. Renumbered Rule 5.754 and amended, eff. Jan. 1, 2007.)*

Research References

Forms

West's California Judicial Council Forms JV-642, Initial Appearance Hearing--Juvenile Delinquency.

Treatises and Practice Aids

Witkin, California Summary 10th Parent and Child § 782, Statutory Rights.

Witkin, California Summary 10th Parent and Child § 823, Explanation and Information.

Witkin, California Summary 10th Parent and Child § 824, Admission Of Allegations.

Witkin, California Summary 10th Parent and Child § 826, Confrontation and Cross-Examination.

Rule 5.756. Conduct of detention hearing

(a) Right to inspect (§ 827)

The child, the parent, the guardian, and counsel are permitted to inspect and receive copies of police reports, probation reports, and any other documents filed with the court or made available to the probation officer in preparing the probation recommendations.

(b) Examination by court (§ 635)

Subject to the child's privilege against self-incrimination, the court may examine the child, the parent, the guardian, and any other person present who has knowledge or information relevant to the issue of detention and must consider any relevant evidence that the child, the parent, the guardian, or counsel presents.

(c) Evidence required

The court may base its findings and orders solely on written police reports, probation reports, or other documents. *(Formerly Rule 1473, adopted, eff. Jan. 1, 1998. Renumbered Rule 5.756 and amended, eff. Jan. 1, 2007.)*

Research References

Treatises and Practice Aids

Witkin, California Summary 10th Parent and Child § 782, Statutory Rights.

Witkin, California Summary 10th Parent and Child § 825, in General.

Witkin, California Summary 10th Parent and Child § 826, Confrontation and Cross-Examination.

Rule 5.758. Requirements for detention; prima facie case

(a) Requirements for detention (§§ 635, 636)

The court must release the child unless the court finds that:

(1) A prima facie showing has been made that the child is described by section 601 or 602;

(2) Continuance in the home is contrary to the child's welfare; and

(3) One or more of the grounds for detention stated in rule 5.760 exist. However, except as provided in sections 636.2 and 207, no child taken into custody solely on the basis of being a person described in section 601 may be detained in juvenile hall or any other secure facility.

(b) Detention in adult facility

A child must not be detained in a jail or lockup used for the confinement of adults, except as provided in section 207.1. *(Formerly Rule 1474, adopted, eff. Jan. 1, 1998. As amended, eff. July 1, 2002. Renumbered Rule 5.758 and amended, eff. Jan. 1, 2007.)*

Research References

Forms

West's California Judicial Council Forms JV-642, Initial Appearance Hearing--Juvenile Delinquency.

Treatises and Practice Aids

Witkin, California Summary 10th Parent and Child § 751, in General.

Witkin, California Summary 10th Parent and Child § 755, Secure Detention Of Status Offender.

Witkin, California Summary 10th Parent and Child § 827, in General.

Rule 5.760. Detention hearing; report; grounds; determinations; findings; orders; factors to consider for detention; restraining orders

(a) Conduct of detention hearing (§§ 635, 636)

The court must consider the written report of the probation officer and any other evidence and may examine the child, any parent or guardian, or any other person with relevant knowledge of the child.

(b) Written detention report (§§ 635, 636)

If the probation officer has reason to believe that the child is at risk of entering foster care placement, the probation officer must submit a written report to the court that includes the following:

(1) The reasons the child has been removed;

(2) Any prior referral for abuse or neglect of the child and any prior filing of a petition regarding the child under section 300;

(3) The need, if any, for continued detention;

(4) Available services to facilitate the return of the child;

(5) Whether there are any relatives able and willing to provide effective care and control over the child;

(6) Documentation that continuance in the home is contrary to the child's welfare; and

(7) Documentation that reasonable efforts were made to prevent or eliminate the need for removal of the child from the home and documentation of the nature and results of the services provided.

(c) Grounds for detention (§§ 625.3, 635, 636)

(1) The child must be released unless the court finds that continuance in the home of the parent or legal guardian is contrary to the child's welfare, and one or more of the following grounds for detention exist:

(A) The child has violated an order of the court;

(B) The child has escaped from a commitment of the court;

(C) The child is likely to flee the jurisdiction of the court;

(D) It is a matter of immediate and urgent necessity for the protection of the child; or

(E) It is reasonably necessary for the protection of the person or property of another.

(2) If the child is a dependent of the court under section 300, the court's decision to detain must not be based on the child's status as a dependent of the court or the child welfare services department's inability to provide a placement for the child.

(3) The court may order the child placed on home supervision under the conditions stated in sections 628.1 and 636, or detained in juvenile hall or in a suitable place designated by the court.

(4) If the court orders the release of a child who is a dependent of the court under section 300, the court must

order the child welfare services department either to ensure that the child's current caregiver takes physical custody of the child or to take physical custody of the child and place the child in a licensed or approved placement.

(d) Required determinations before detention

Before detaining the child, the court must determine whether continuance in the home of the parent or legal guardian is contrary to the child's welfare and whether there are available services that would prevent the need for further detention. The court must make these determinations on a case-by-case basis and must state the evidence relied on in reaching its decision.

(1) If the court determines that the child can be returned to the home of the parent or legal guardian through the provision of services, the court must release the child to the parent or guardian and order that the probation department provide the required services.

(2) If the child cannot be returned to the home of the parent or legal guardian, the court must state the facts on which the detention is based.

(e) Required findings to support detention (§ 636)

If the court orders the child detained, the court must make the following findings on the record and in the written order. The court must reference the probation officer's report or other evidence relied on to make its determinations:

(1) Continuance in the home of the parent or guardian is contrary to the child's welfare;

(2) Temporary placement and care is the responsibility of the probation officer pending disposition or further order of the court; and

(3) Reasonable efforts have been made to prevent or eliminate the need for removal of the child, or reasonable efforts were not made.

(f) Required orders to support detention (§ 636)

If the court orders the child detained, the court must make the following additional orders:

(1) As soon as possible, the probation officer must provide services that will enable the child's parent or legal guardian to obtain such assistance as may be needed to effectively provide the care and control necessary for the child to return home; and

(2) The child's placement and care must be the responsibility of the probation department pending disposition or further order of the court.

(g) Factors—violation of court order

Regarding ground for detention (c)(1), the court must consider:

(1) The specificity of the court order alleged to have been violated;

(2) The nature and circumstances of the alleged violation;

(3) The severity and gravity of the alleged violation;

(4) Whether the alleged violation endangered the child or others;

(5) The prior history of the child as it relates to any failure to obey orders or directives of the court or probation officer;

(6) Whether there are means to ensure the child's presence at any scheduled court hearing without detaining the child;

(7) The underlying conduct or offense that brought the child before the juvenile court; and

(8) The likelihood that if the petition is sustained, the child will be ordered removed from the custody of the parent or guardian at disposition.

(h) Factors—escape from commitment

Regarding ground for detention (c)(2), the court must consider whether or not the child:

(1) Was committed to the California Department of Corrections and Rehabilitation, Division of Juvenile Justice; or a county juvenile home, ranch, camp, forestry camp, or juvenile hall; and

(2) Escaped from the facility or the lawful custody of any officer or person in which the child was placed during commitment.

(i) Factors—likely to flee

Regarding ground for detention (c)(3), the court must consider whether or not:

(1) The child has previously fled the jurisdiction of the court or failed to appear in court as ordered;

(2) There are means to ensure the child's presence at any scheduled court hearing without detaining the child;

(3) The child promises to appear at any scheduled court hearing;

(4) The child has a prior history of failure to obey orders or directions of the court or the probation officer;

(5) The child is a resident of the county;

(6) The nature and circumstances of the alleged conduct or offense make it appear likely that the child would flee to avoid the jurisdiction of the court;

(7) The child's home situation is so unstable as to make it appear likely that the child would flee to avoid the jurisdiction of the court; and

(8) Absent a danger to the child, the child would be released on modest bail or own recognizance were the child appearing as an adult in adult court.

(j) Factors—protection of child

Regarding ground for detention (c)(4), the court must consider whether or not:

(1) There are means to ensure the care and protection of the child until the next scheduled court appearance;

(2) The child is addicted to or is in imminent danger from the use of a controlled substance or alcohol; and

(3) There exist other compelling circumstances that make detention reasonably necessary.

(k) Factors—protection of person or property of another

Regarding ground for detention (c)(5), the court must consider whether or not:

(1) The alleged offense involved physical harm to the person or property of another;

(2) The prior history of the child reveals that the child has caused physical harm to the person or property of another or has posed a substantial threat to the person or property of another; and

(3) There exist other compelling circumstances that make detention reasonably necessary.

(*l*) Restraining orders

As a condition of release or home supervision, the court may issue restraining orders as stated in rule 5.630 or orders restraining the child from any or all of the following:

(1) Molesting, attacking, striking, sexually assaulting, or battering, or from any contact whatsoever with an alleged victim or victim's family;

(2) Presence near or in a particular area or building; or

(3) Associating with or contacting in writing, by phone, or in person any adult or child alleged to have been a companion in the alleged offense. *(Formerly Rule 1475, adopted, eff. Jan. 1, 1998. As amended, eff. Jan. 1, 2001; July 1, 2002; Jan. 1, 2006. Renumbered Rule 5.760 and amended, eff. Jan. 1, 2007. As amended, eff. Jan. 1, 2016.)*

Research References

Forms

West's California Judicial Council Forms JV-642, Initial Appearance Hearing--Juvenile Delinquency.

Treatises and Practice Aids

Witkin, California Summary 10th Parent and Child § 820, Petition and Setting for Hearing.
Witkin, California Summary 10th Parent and Child § 821, Probation Officer's Report and Recommendation.
Witkin, California Summary 10th Parent and Child § 825, in General.
Witkin, California Summary 10th Parent and Child § 827, in General.
Witkin, California Summary 10th Parent and Child § 828, Statutory Grounds.
Witkin, California Summary 10th Parent and Child § 829, Violation Of Order.
Witkin, California Summary 10th Parent and Child § 830, Escape from Confinement.
Witkin, California Summary 10th Parent and Child § 831, Minor Likely to Flee.
Witkin, California Summary 10th Parent and Child § 832, Protection Of Minor.
Witkin, California Summary 10th Parent and Child § 833, Protection Of Another.
Witkin, California Summary 10th Parent and Child § 834, Orders.

Rule 5.762. Detention rehearings

(a) No parent or guardian present and not noticed

If the court orders the child detained at the detention hearing and no parent or guardian is present and no parent or guardian has received actual notice of the detention hearing, a parent or guardian may file an affidavit alleging the failure of notice and requesting a detention rehearing. The clerk must set the rehearing within 24 hours of the filing of the affidavit, excluding noncourt days. At the rehearing, the court must proceed under rules 5.752–5.760.

(b) Parent or guardian noticed; parent or guardian not present (§ 637)

If the court determines that the parent or guardian has received adequate notice of the detention hearing, and the parent or guardian fails to appear at the hearing, a request from the parent or guardian for a detention rehearing must be denied, absent a finding that the failure was due to good cause.

(c) Parent or guardian noticed; preparers available (§ 637)

If a parent or guardian received notice of the detention hearing, and the preparers of any reports or other documents relied on by the court in its order detaining the child are present at court or otherwise available for cross-examination, there is no right to a detention rehearing. *(Formerly Rule 1476, adopted, eff. Jan. 1, 1998. Renumbered Rule 5.762 and amended, eff. Jan. 1, 2007.)*

Research References

Treatises and Practice Aids

Witkin, California Summary 10th Parent and Child § 826, Confrontation and Cross-Examination.

Rule 5.764. Prima facie hearings

(a) Hearing for further evidence; prima facie case (§ 637)

If the court orders the child detained, and the child or the child's attorney requests that evidence of the prima facie case be presented, the court must set a prima facie hearing for a time within three court days to consider evidence of the prima facie case.

(b) Continuance (§ 637)

If the court determines that a prima facie hearing cannot be held within three court days because of the unavailability of a witness, a reasonable continuance not to exceed five court days may be granted. If at the hearing petitioner fails to establish the prima facie case, the child must be released from custody. *(Adopted, eff. Jan. 1, 2007.)*

Research References

Forms

West's California Judicial Council Forms JV-688, Continuance--Juvenile Delinquency.

Treatises and Practice Aids

Witkin, California Summary 10th Parent and Child § 444, Scope and Organization.
Witkin, California Summary 10th Parent and Child § 826, Confrontation and Cross-Examination.
Witkin, California Summary 10th Parent and Child § 908, Notice and Setting for Hearing.

Article 2

FITNESS HEARINGS

Rule

Rule 5.766. General provisions

(a) ~~Fitness hearing~~ Hearing on transfer of jurisdiction to criminal court (§ 707)

A child who is the subject of a petition under section 602~~(a)~~ and who was 14 years or older at the time of the alleged felony offense may be considered for prosecution under the general law in a court of criminal jurisdiction. The ~~prosecuting attorney~~ district attorney or other appropriate prosecuting officer may ~~request a hearing to determine whether the child is a fit and proper subject to be dealt with under the juvenile court law~~ make a motion to transfer the child from juvenile court to a court of criminal jurisdiction, in one of the following circumstances:

~~(3)~~(1) ~~Under section 707(c),~~ The child was 14 years or older at the time of the alleged offense listed in section 707(b).

~~(1)~~(2) ~~Under section 707(a)(1),~~ The child was 16 years or older at the time of the alleged felony offense~~if the offense is not listed in section 707(b)~~.

~~(2) Under section 707(a)(2), the child was 16 years or older at the time of the alleged felony offense not listed in section 707(b) and has been declared a ward of the court under section 602 on at least one prior occasion and:~~

~~(A) The child has previously been found to have committed two or more felony offenses; and~~

~~(B) The felony offenses in the previously sustained petitions were committed when the child was 14 years or older.~~

(b) Notice (§ 707)

Notice of the ~~fitness~~ transfer hearing must be given at least five judicial days before the ~~fitness~~ hearing. In no case may notice be given following the attachment of jeopardy.

(c) Prima facie showing

On the child's motion, the court must determine whether a prima facie showing has been made that the offense alleged is an offense that makes the child subject to transfer as set forth in subdivision (a).

~~(c)~~(d) Time of ~~fitness~~ transfer hearing—rules 5.774, 5.776

The ~~fitness~~ transfer of jurisdiction hearing must be held and the court must rule on the ~~issue of fitness~~ the [1] request to transfer jurisdiction before the jurisdiction hearing begins. Absent a continuance under rule 5.776 or the child's waiver of the statutory time period to commence the jurisdiction hearing, the jurisdiction hearing must begin within the time limits under rule 5.774. *(Formerly Rule 1480, adopted, eff. Jan. 1, 1991. As amended, eff. Jan. 1, 1996; Jan. 1, 2001. Renumbered Rule 5.766 and amended, eff. Jan. 1, 2007. As amended, eff. May 22, 2017.)*

[1] So in original.

Research References

Treatises and Practice Aids

Witkin, California Summary 10th Parent and Child § 444, Scope and Organization.

Witkin, California Summary 10th Parent and Child § 840, in General.

Rule 5.768. Report of probation officer

(a) Contents of report (§ 707)

The probation officer must ~~investigate the issue of fitness~~ prepare and submit to the court a report on the behavioral patterns and social history of the child being considered. The report must include information relevant to the determination of whether ~~or not~~ the child ~~would be amenable to the care, treatment, and training program available through the facilities of the juvenile court, including information regarding all of the criteria listed in rules 5.770 and 5.772~~ should be retained under the jurisdiction of the juvenile court or transferred to the jurisdiction of the criminal court, including information regarding all of the criteria in section 707(a)(2). The report must also include any written or oral statement offered by the victim pursuant to section 656.2. ~~The report may also include information concerning:~~

~~(1) The social, family, and legal history of the child;~~

~~(2) Any statement the child chooses to make regarding the alleged offense;~~

~~(3) Any statement by a parent or guardian;~~

~~(4) If the child is or has been under the jurisdiction of the court, a statement by the social worker, probation officer, or Youth Authority parole agent who has supervised the child regarding the relative success or failure of any program of rehabilitation; and~~

~~(5) Any other information relevant to the determination of fitness.~~

(b) Recommendation of probation officer (§§ 281, 707)

If the court, under section 281, orders the probation officer to include a recommendation, ~~T~~the probation officer must make a recommendation to the court as to whether the child ~~is a fit and proper subject to be dealt with under the juvenile court law~~ should be retained under the jurisdiction of the juvenile court or transferred to the jurisdiction of the criminal court.

(c) Copies furnished

The probation officer's report on the behavioral patterns and social history of the child must be furnished to the child, the parent or guardian, and all counsel at least ~~24 hours~~ two court days before commencement of the ~~fitness~~ hearing on the motion. A continuance of at least 24 hours must be granted on the request of any party who has not been furnished the probation officer's report in accordance with this rule. *(Formerly Rule 1481, adopted, eff. Jan. 1, 1991. Renumbered Rule 5.768 and amended, eff. Jan. 1, 2007. As amended, eff. May 22, 2017.)*

Research References

Treatises and Practice Aids

Witkin, California Summary 10th Parent and Child § 841, Probation Officer's Investigation and Report.

Rule 5.770. Conduct of ~~fitness~~ transfer of jurisdiction hearing under section 707~~(a)(1)~~

(a) Burden of proof (§ 707~~(a)(1)~~)

In a ~~fitness~~ transfer of jurisdiction hearing under section 707~~(a)(1)~~, the burden of proving that ~~the child is unfit~~ there should be a transfer of jurisdiction to criminal court jurisdiction is on the petitioner, by a preponderance of the evidence.

(b) Criteria to consider (§ 707~~(a)(1)~~)

Following receipt of the probation officer's report and any other relevant evidence, the court may ~~find that~~ order that the child ~~is not a fit and proper subject to be dealt with under juvenile court law~~ be transferred to the jurisdiction of the criminal court if the court finds:

(1) The child was 16 years or older at the time of ~~the~~ any alleged felony offense, ~~and~~ or the child was 14 or 15 years at the time of an alleged felony offense listed in section 707(b); and

(2) The child ~~would not be amenable to the care, treatment, and training program available through facilities of the juvenile court,~~ should be transferred to the jurisdiction of the criminal court based on an evaluation of all of the ~~following~~ criteria in section 707(a)(2) as provided in that section.~~:~~

~~(A) The degree of criminal sophistication exhibited by the child;~~

~~(B) Whether the child can be rehabilitated before the expiration of jurisdiction;~~

~~(C) The child's previous delinquent history;~~

~~(D) The results of previous attempts by the court to rehabilitate the child; and~~

~~(E) The circumstances and gravity of the alleged offense.~~

(c) ~~Findings under section 707(a)(1)~~ Basis for order of transfer

~~The findings must be stated in the order.~~

~~(1) *Finding of fitness*~~

~~The court may find the child to be fit and state that finding.~~

~~(2) *Finding of unfitness*~~

~~If the court determines the child is unfit, the court must find that:~~

~~(A) The child was 16 years or older at the time of the alleged offense; and~~

~~(B) The child would not be amenable to the care, treatment, and training program available through the juvenile court because of one or a combination of more than one of the criteria listed in (b)(2).~~

If the court orders a transfer of jurisdiction to the criminal court, the court must recite the basis for its decision in an order entered on the minutes.

~~**(d) Maintenance of juvenile court jurisdiction**~~

~~If the court determines that one or more of the criteria listed in (b)(2) apply to the child, the court may nevertheless find that the child is amenable to the care, treatment, and training program available through the juvenile court and may find the child to be a fit and proper subject to be dealt with under juvenile court law.~~

~~**(e) Extenuating circumstances**~~

~~The court may consider extenuating or mitigating circumstances in the evaluation of each relevant criterion.~~

~~(f)~~(d) Procedure following findings

(1) If the court finds the child ~~to be fit~~ should be retained within the jurisdiction of the juvenile court, the court must proceed to jurisdiction hearing under rule 5.774.

(2) If the court finds the child ~~to be unfit~~ should be transferred to the jurisdiction of the criminal court, the court must make orders under section 707.1 relating to bail and to the appropriate facility for the custody of the child, or release on own recognizance pending prosecution. The court must set a date for the child to appear in criminal court and dismiss the petition without prejudice upon the date of that appearance.

(3) When the court rules on the request to transfer the child to the jurisdiction of the criminal court, the court must advise all parties present that appellate review of the order must be by petition for extraordinary writ. The advisement may be given orally or in writing when the court makes the ruling. The advisement must include the time for filing the petition for extraordinary writ as set forth in subdivision (g) of this rule.

~~(g)~~(e) Continuance to seek review

If the prosecuting attorney informs the court orally or in writing that a review ~~of a finding of fitness~~ of the court's decision not to transfer jurisdiction to the criminal court will be sought and requests a continuance of the jurisdiction hearing, the court must grant a continuance for not less than two judicial days to allow time within which to obtain a stay of further proceedings from the reviewing judge or appellate court.

~~(h)~~(f) Subsequent role of judicial officer

Unless the child objects, the judicial officer who has conducted a ~~fitness~~ hearing on a motion to transfer jurisdiction may participate in any subsequent contested jurisdiction hearing relating to the same offense.

~~(i)~~(g) Review of ~~fitness~~ determination on a motion to transfer jurisdiction to criminal court

An order ~~that a child is or is not a fit and proper subject to be dealt with under the juvenile court law~~ granting or denying a motion to transfer jurisdiction of a child to the criminal court is not an appealable order. Appellate review of the order is by petition for extraordinary writ. Any petition for review of a judge's order ~~determining the child unfit~~ to transfer jurisdiction of the child to the criminal court, or denying an application for rehearing of the referee's determination ~~of unfitness~~ to transfer jurisdiction of the child to the criminal court, must be filed no later than 20 days after the child's first arraignment on an accusatory pleading based on the allegations that led to the ~~unfitness determination~~ transfer of jurisdiction order.

(h) Postponement of plea prior to transfer hearing

If a hearing for transfer of jurisdiction has been noticed under section 707, the court must postpone the taking of a plea to the petition until the conclusion of the transfer hearing, and no pleas that may have been entered already may be considered as evidence at the hearing. *(Formerly Rule 1482, adopted, eff. Jan. 1, 1991. As amended, eff. Jan. 1, 1996; Jan. 1, 2001; July 1, 2002. Renumbered Rule 5.770 and amended, eff. Jan. 1, 2007. As amended, eff. May 22, 2017.)*

Research References

Treatises and Practice Aids

Witkin, California Summary 10th Parent and Child § 772, Discretion Of Probation Officer and Prosecutor.
Witkin, California Summary 10th Parent and Child § 836, Criteria to Determine Fitness.
Witkin, California Summary 10th Parent and Child § 841, Probation Officer's Investigation and Report.
Witkin, California Summary 10th Parent and Child § 842, Conduct Of Hearing.
Witkin, California Summary 10th Parent and Child § 844, in General.
Witkin, California Summary 10th Parent and Child § 849, Finding Of Fitness.
Witkin, California Summary 10th Parent and Child § 850, Review Of Order.
Witkin, California Summary 10th Parent and Child § 851, Criminal Charge and Proceeding.

Article 3

JURISDICTION

Rule 5.774. Setting petition for hearing—detained and nondetained cases; waiver of hearing

(a) Nondetention cases (§ 657)

If the child is not detained, the jurisdiction hearing on the petition must begin within 30 calendar days from the date the petition is filed.

(b) Detention cases (§ 657)

If the child is detained, the jurisdiction hearing on the petition must begin within 15 judicial days from the date of the order of the court directing detention. If the child is released from detention before the jurisdiction hearing, the court may reset the jurisdiction hearing within the time limit in (a).

(c) Tolling of time period

Any period of delay caused by the child's unavailability or failure to appear must not be included in computing the time limits of (a) and (b).

(d) Dismissal

Absent a continuance under rule 5.776, when a jurisdiction hearing is not begun within the time limits of (a) and (b), the court must order the petition dismissed. This does not bar the filing of another petition based on the same allegations as in the original petition, but the child must not be detained.

(e) Waiver of hearing (§ 657)

At the detention hearing, or at any time thereafter, a child may admit the allegations of the petition or plead no contest and waive further jurisdiction hearing. The court may accept the admission or no contest plea and proceed according to rules 5.778 and 5.782. *(Formerly Rule 1485, adopted, eff. Jan. 1, 1991. Renumbered Rule 5.774 and amended, eff. Jan. 1, 2007.)*

Research References

Treatises and Practice Aids

Witkin, California Summary 10th Parent and Child § 444, Scope and Organization.
Witkin, California Summary 10th Parent and Child § 775, Setting Petition for Hearing.
Witkin, California Summary 10th Parent and Child § 824, Admission Of Allegations.
Witkin, California Summary 10th Parent and Child § 840, in General.
Witkin, California Summary 10th Parent and Child § 842, Conduct Of Hearing.
Witkin, California Summary 10th Parent and Child § 856, in General.
Witkin, California Summary 10th Parent and Child § 857, Dismissal for Delay in Commencement.
Witkin, California Summary 10th Parent and Child § 858, Refiling After Dismissal.
Witkin, California Summary 10th Parent and Child § 859, Continuance.
Witkin, California Summary 10th Parent and Child § 889, Dismissal in Interests Of Justice.

Rule 5.776. Grounds for continuance of jurisdiction hearing

(a) Request for continuance; consent (§ 682)

A continuance may be granted only on a showing of good cause and only for the time shown to be necessary. Stipulation between counsel or parties and convenience of parties are not in and of themselves good cause.

(1) In order to obtain a continuance, written notice with supporting documents must be filed and served on all parties at least two court days before the date set for the hearing, unless the court finds good cause for failure to comply with these requirements. Absent a waiver of time, a child may not be detained beyond the statutory time limits.

(2) The court must state in its order the facts requiring any continuance that is granted.

(3) If the child is represented by counsel and no objection is made to an order setting or continuing the jurisdiction hearing beyond the time limits of rule 5.774, consent must be implied.

(b) Grounds for continuance—mandatory (§ 700)

The court must continue the jurisdiction hearing for:

(1) A reasonable period to permit the child and the parent, guardian, or adult relative to prepare for the hearing; and

(2) No more than seven calendar days:

(A) For appointment of counsel;

(B) To enable counsel to become acquainted with the case; or

(C) To determine whether the parent, guardian, or adult relative can afford counsel.

(c) Grounds for continuance—discretionary (§§ 700.5, 701)

The court may continue the jurisdiction hearing for no more than seven calendar days to enable the petitioner to subpoena witnesses if the child has made an extrajudicial admission and denies it, or has previously indicated to the court or petitioner an intention to admit the allegations of the petition, and at the time set for jurisdiction hearing denies the allegations.

(d) Grounds for continuance—section 654.2 (§§ 654.2, 654.3, 654.4)

In a case petitioned under section 602, the court may, with the consent of the child and the parent or guardian, continue the jurisdiction hearing for six months. If the court grants the continuance, the court must order the child and the parent or guardian to participate in a program of supervision under section 654, and must order the parent or guardian to participate with the child in a program of counseling or education under section 654. *(Formerly Rule 1486, adopted, eff. Jan. 1, 1991. Renumbered Rule 5.776 and amended, eff. Jan. 1, 2007.)*

Research References

Forms

West's California Judicial Council Forms JV-688, Continuance--Juvenile Delinquency.

Treatises and Practice Aids

Witkin, California Summary 10th Parent and Child § 787, in General.

Witkin, California Summary 10th Parent and Child § 817, Discretionary Continuance.

Witkin, California Summary 10th Parent and Child § 857, Dismissal for Delay in Commencement.

Witkin, California Summary 10th Parent and Child § 859, Continuance.

Rule 5.778. Commencement of hearing on section 601 or section 602 petition; right to counsel; advisement of trial rights; admission, no contest

(a) Petition read and explained (§ 700)

At the beginning of the jurisdiction hearing, the petition must be read to those present. On request of the child, or the parent, guardian, or adult relative, the court must explain the meaning and contents of the petition, the nature of the hearing, the procedures of the hearing, and possible consequences.

(b) Rights explained (§ 702.5)

After giving the advisement required by rule 5.534, the court must advise those present of each of the following rights of the child:

(1) The right to a hearing by the court on the issues raised by the petition;

(2) The right to assert the privilege against self-incrimination;

(3) The right to confront and to cross-examine any witness called to testify against the child; and

(4) The right to use the process of the court to compel the attendance of witnesses on the child's behalf.

(c) Admission of allegations; prerequisites to acceptance

The court must then inquire whether the child intends to admit or deny the allegations of the petition. If the child neither admits nor denies the allegations, the court must state on the record that the child does not admit the allegations. If the child wishes to admit the allegations, the court must first find and state on the record that it is satisfied that the child understands the nature of the allegations and the direct consequences of the admission, and understands and waives the rights in (b).

(d) Consent of counsel—child must admit

Counsel for the child must consent to the admission, which must be made by the child personally.

(e) No contest

The child may enter a plea of no contest to the allegations, subject to the approval of the court.

(f) Findings of the court (§ 702)

On an admission or plea of no contest, the court must make the following findings noted in the minutes of the court:

(1) Notice has been given as required by law;

(2) The birthdate and county of residence of the child;

(3) The child has knowingly and intelligently waived the right to a hearing on the issues by the court, the right to confront and cross-examine adverse witnesses and to use the process of the court to compel the attendance of witnesses on the child's behalf, and the right to assert the privilege against self-incrimination;

(4) The child understands the nature of the conduct alleged in the petition and the possible consequences of an admission or plea of no contest;

(5) The admission or plea of no contest is freely and voluntarily made;

(6) There is a factual basis for the admission or plea of no contest;

(7) Those allegations of the petition as admitted are true as alleged;

(8) The child is described by section 601 or 602; and

(9) In a section 602 matter, the degree of the offense and whether it would be a misdemeanor or felony had the offense been committed by an adult. If any offense may be found to be either a felony or misdemeanor, the court must consider which description applies and expressly declare on the record that it has made such consideration and must state its determination as to whether the offense is a misdemeanor or a felony. These determinations may be deferred until the disposition hearing.

(g) Disposition

After accepting an admission or plea of no contest, the court must proceed to disposition hearing under rules 5.782 and 5.785. *(Formerly Rule 1487, adopted, eff. Jan. 1, 1991. As amended, eff. Jan. 1, 1998. Renumbered Rule 5.778 and amended, eff. Jan. 1, 2007.)*

Research References

Forms

West's California Judicial Council Forms JV-618, Waiver Of Rights--Juvenile Delinquency.

West's California Judicial Council Forms JV-642, Initial Appearance Hearing--Juvenile Delinquency.
West's California Judicial Council Forms JV-644, Jurisdiction Hearing--Juvenile Delinquency.

Treatises and Practice Aids

Witkin, California Summary 10th Parent and Child § 782, Statutory Rights.
Witkin, California Summary 10th Parent and Child § 824, Admission Of Allegations.
Witkin, California Summary 10th Parent and Child § 855, in General.
Witkin, California Summary 10th Parent and Child § 864, Commencement Of Proceeding.
Witkin, California Summary 10th Parent and Child § 865, Personal Admission.
Witkin, California Summary 10th Parent and Child § 866, Conditions for Acceptance.
Witkin, California Summary 10th Parent and Child § 867, Findings.
Witkin, California Summary 10th Parent and Child § 869, No Contest in Lieu Of Admission.

Rule 5.780. Contested hearing on section 601 or section 602 petition

(a) Contested jurisdiction hearing (§ 701)

If the child denies the allegations of the petition, the court must hold a contested hearing to determine whether the allegations in the petition are true.

(b) Admissibility of evidence—general (§ 701)

In a section 601 matter, the admission and exclusion of evidence must be in accordance with the Evidence Code as it applies in civil cases. In a section 602 matter, the admission and exclusion of evidence must be in accordance with the Evidence Code as it applies in criminal cases.

(c) Probation reports

Except as otherwise provided by law, the court must not read or consider any portion of a probation report relating to the contested petition before or during a contested jurisdiction hearing.

(d) Unrepresented children (§ 701)

If the child is not represented by counsel, objections that could have been made to the evidence must be deemed made.

(e) Findings of court—allegations true (§ 702)

If the court determines by a preponderance of the evidence in a section 601 matter, or by proof beyond a reasonable doubt in a section 602 matter, that the allegations of the petition are true, the court must make findings on each of the following, noted in the order:

(1) Notice has been given as required by law;

(2) The birthdate and county of residence of the child;

(3) The allegations of the petition are true;

(4) The child is described by section 601 or 602; and

(5) In a section 602 matter, the degree of the offense and whether it would be a misdemeanor or a felony had the offense been committed by an adult. If any offense may be found to be either a felony or a misdemeanor, the court must consider which description applies and expressly declare on the record that it has made such consideration, and must state its determination as to whether the offense is a misdemeanor or a felony. These determinations may be deferred until the disposition hearing.

(f) Disposition

After making the findings in (e), the court must then proceed to disposition hearing under rules 5.782 and 5.785.

(g) Findings of court—allegations not proved (§ 702)

If the court determines that the allegations of the petition have not been proved by a preponderance of the evidence in a 601 matter, or beyond a reasonable doubt in a 602 matter, the court must make findings on each of the following, noted in the order:

(1) Notice has been given as required by law;

(2) The birthdate and county of residence of the child; and

(3) The allegations of the petition have not been proved.

The court must dismiss the petition and terminate detention orders related to this petition. *(Formerly Rule 1488, adopted, eff. Jan. 1, 1991. As amended, eff. Jan. 1, 1998. Renumbered Rule 5.780 and amended, eff. Jan. 1, 2007.)*

Research References

Forms

West's California Judicial Council Forms JV-644, Jurisdiction Hearing--Juvenile Delinquency.

Treatises and Practice Aids

Witkin, California Summary 10th Parent and Child § 870, in General.
Witkin, California Summary 10th Parent and Child § 871, Time for Consideration Of Probation Report and Social Study.
Witkin, California Summary 10th Parent and Child § 872, in General.
Witkin, California Summary 10th Parent and Child § 878, Sufficiency Of Evidence.
Witkin, California Summary 10th Parent and Child § 882, Findings.
Witkin, California Summary 10th Parent and Child § 894, Degree Of Offense.
Witkin, California Summary 10th Parent and Child § 895, Alternative Felony Misdemeanor.

Rule 5.782. Continuance pending disposition hearing

(a) Continuance pending disposition hearing (§ 702)

If the court finds that the child is described by section 601 or 602, it must proceed to a disposition hearing. The court may continue the disposition hearing up to 10 judicial days if the child is detained. If the child is not detained, the court may continue the disposition hearing up to 30 calendar days from the date of the filing of the petition and up to an additional 15 calendar days for good cause shown.

(b) Detention pending hearing (§ 702)

The court may release or detain the child during the period of the continuance.

(c) Observation and diagnosis (§ 704)

If the child is eligible for commitment to the Youth Authority, the court may continue the disposition hearing up to 90 calendar days and order the child to be placed temporarily at a Youth Authority diagnostic and treatment center for observation and diagnosis. The court must order the Youth Authority to submit a diagnosis and recommendation within 90 days, and the probation officer or any other peace officer designated by the court must place the child in the diagnostic and treatment center and return the child to the court. After return from the diagnostic and treatment center, the child must be brought to court within 2 judicial days. A disposition hearing must be held within 10 judicial days thereafter. *(Formerly Rule 1489, adopted, eff. Jan. 1, 1991. Renumbered Rule 5.782 and amended, eff. Jan. 1, 2007.)*

Research References

Forms

West's California Judicial Council Forms JV-688, Continuance--Juvenile Delinquency.

Treatises and Practice Aids

Witkin, California Summary 10th Parent and Child § 444, Scope and Organization.

Witkin, California Summary 10th Parent and Child § 824, Admission Of Allegations.

Witkin, California Summary 10th Parent and Child § 883, Continuance Pending Disposition Hearing.

Article 4

DISPOSITION

Rule 5.785. General conduct of hearing

(a) Social study (§§ 280, 702, 706.5)

The probation officer must prepare a social study of the child, which must contain all matters relevant to disposition, including any parole status information, and a recommendation for disposition.

(1) In any case in which the probation officer is recommending placement in foster care or in which the child is already in foster care placement or pending placement under an earlier order, the social study must include a case plan as described in (c).

(2) The probation officer must submit the social study and copies of it to the clerk at least 48 hours before the disposition hearing is set to begin, and the clerk must make the copies available to the parties and attorneys. A continuance of up to 48 hours must be granted on the request of a party who has not been furnished a copy of the social study in accordance with this rule.

(b) Evidence considered (§ 706)

The court must receive in evidence and consider the social study and any relevant evidence offered by the petitioner, the child, or the parent or guardian. The court may require production of other relevant evidence on its own motion. In the order of disposition the court must state that the social study has been read and considered by the court.

(c) Case plan

When a child is detained and is at risk of entering foster care placement, the probation officer must prepare a case plan.

(1) The plan must be completed and filed with the court by the date of disposition or within 60 calendar days of initial removal, whichever occurs first.

(2) The court must consider the case plan and must find as follows:

(A) The probation officer solicited and integrated into the case plan the input of the child, the child's family, in a case described by rule 5.480(2)(A)–(C) the child's identified Indian tribe, and other interested parties; or

(B) The probation officer did not solicit and integrate into the case plan the input of the child, the child's family, in a case described by rule 5.480(2)(A)–(C) the child's identified Indian tribe, and other interested parties. If the court finds that the probation officer did not solicit and integrate into the case plan the input of the child, the child's family, the child's identified Indian tribe, and other interested parties, the court must order that the probation officer solicit and integrate into the case plan the input of the child, the child's family, in a case described by rule 5.480(2)(A)–(C) the child's identified Indian tribe, and other interested parties, unless the court finds that each of these participants was unable, unavailable, or unwilling to participate.

(3) For a child 12 years of age or older and in a permanent placement, the court must consider the case plan and must find as follows:

(A) The child was given the opportunity to review the case plan, sign it, and receive a copy; or

(B) The child was not give the opportunity to review the case plan, sign it, and receive a copy. If the court makes such a finding, the court must order the probation officer to give the child the opportunity to review the case plan, sign it, and receive a copy, unless the court finds that the child was unable, unavailable, or unwilling to participate.

(4) If the probation officer believes that the child will be able to return home through reasonable efforts by the child, the parents or guardian, and the probation officer, the case plan must include the elements described in section 636.1(b).

(5) If the probation officer believes that foster care placement is the most appropriate disposition for the child, the case plan must include all of the information required by section 706.6. *(Formerly Rule 1492, adopted, eff. Jan. 1, 1991. As amended, eff. July 1, 2002. Renumbered Rule 5.785 and amended, eff. Jan. 1, 2007. As amended, eff. July 1, 2013.)*

Research References

Forms

West's California Judicial Council Forms JV-665, Disposition--Juvenile Delinquency.

West's California Judicial Council Forms JV-667, Custodial and Out Of Home Placement Disposition Attachment.

Treatises and Practice Aids

Witkin, California Summary 10th Parent and Child § 444, Scope and Organization.

Witkin, California Summary 10th Parent and Child § 884, Social Study.

Witkin, California Summary 10th Parent and Child § 885, Case Plan.
Witkin, California Summary 10th Parent and Child § 886, Conduct Of Hearing.
Witkin, California Summary 10th Parent and Child § 887, in General.

Rule 5.790. Orders of the court

(a) Findings and orders of the court (§§ 654, 654.1, 654.2, 654.3, 654.4, 725, 725.5, 782)

At the disposition hearing:

(1) If the court has not previously considered whether any offense is a misdemeanor or felony, the court must do so at this time and state its finding on the record. If the offense may be found to be either a felony or a misdemeanor, the court must consider which description applies and must expressly declare on the record that it has made such consideration and must state its finding as to whether the offense is a misdemeanor or a felony.

(2) The court may then:

(A) Dismiss the petition in the interests of justice and the welfare of the child or, if the child does not need treatment or rehabilitation, with the specific reasons stated in the minutes;

(B) Place the child on probation for no more than six months, without declaring the child a ward; or

(C) Declare the child a ward of the court.

(b) Conditions of probation (§§ 725, 726, 727, 729.2, 729.9, 729.10)

If the child is placed on probation, with or without wardship, the court must set reasonable terms and conditions of probation. Unless the court finds and states its reasons on the record that any of the following conditions is inappropriate, the court must:

(1) Require the child to attend school;

(2) Require the parent to participate with the child in a counseling or education program; and

(3) Require the child to be at the child's residence between 10:00 p.m. and 6:00 a.m. unless accompanied by a parent or a guardian or an adult custodian.

(c) Custody and visitation (§ 726.5)

(1) At any time when a child is a ward of the juvenile court, the court may issue an order determining the custody of or visitation with the child. An order issued under this subdivision continues in effect until modified or terminated by a later order of the juvenile court.

(2) At the time wardship is terminated, the court may issue an order determining custody of or visitation with the child, as described in rule 5.700.

(d) Removal of custody—required findings (§ 726)

The court must not order a ward removed from the physical custody of a parent or guardian unless the court finds:

(1) The parent or guardian has failed or neglected to provide, or is incapable of providing, proper maintenance, training, and education for the child;

(2) The child has been on probation in the custody of the parent or guardian and during that time has failed to reform; or

(3) The welfare of the child requires that physical custody be removed from the parent or guardian.

(e) Removal of custody—orders regarding reunification services (§ 727.2)

(1) Whenever the court orders the care, custody, and control of the child to be under the supervision of the probation officer for placement, the court must order the probation department to ensure the provision of reunification services to facilitate the safe return of the child to his or her home or the permanent placement of the child and to address the needs of the child while in foster care.

(2) Reunification services need not be provided to the parent or guardian if the court finds, by clear and convincing evidence, that one or more of the exceptions listed in section 727.2(b) is true.

(f) Family-finding determination (§ 628(d))

(1) If the child is detained or at risk of entering foster care, the court must consider and determine whether the probation officer has exercised due diligence in conducting the required investigation to identify, locate, and notify the child's relatives. The court may consider the activities listed in (g) as examples of due diligence. The court must document its determination by making a finding on the record.

If the dispositional hearing is continued, the court may set a hearing to be held 30 days from the date of detention or as soon as possible thereafter to consider and determine whether the probation officer has exercised due diligence in conducting the required investigation to identify, locate, and notify the child's relatives.

(2) If the court finds that the probation officer has not exercised due diligence, the court may order the probation officer to exercise due diligence in conducting an investigation to identify, locate, and notify the child's relatives—except for any individual the probation officer identifies who is inappropriate to notify under rule 5.637(b)—and may require a written or oral report to the court.

(g) Due Diligence

When making the determination required in (f), the court may consider, among other examples of due diligence, whether the probation officer has done any of the following:

(1) Asked the child, in an age-appropriate manner and consistent with the child's best interest, about his or her relatives;

(2) Obtained information regarding the location of the child's relatives;

(3) Reviewed the child's case file for any information regarding relatives;

(4) Telephoned, e-mailed, or visited all identified relatives;

(5) Asked located relatives for the names and locations of other relatives;

(6) Used Internet search tools to locate relatives identified as supports; or

(7) Developed tools, including a genogram, family tree, family map, or other diagram of family relationships, to help the child or parents to identify relatives.

(h) Wardship orders (§§ 726, 727, 727.1, 730, 731)

The court may make any reasonable order for the care, supervision, custody, conduct, maintenance, support, and medical treatment of a child adjudged a ward of the court.

(1) Subject to the provisions of section 727, the court may order the ward to be on probation without the supervision of the probation officer and may impose on the ward reasonable conditions of behavior.

(2) The court may order the care, custody, control, and conduct of the ward to be under the supervision of the probation officer in the home of a parent or guardian.

(3) If the court orders removal of custody under (d), it must authorize the probation officer to place the ward with a person or organization described in section 727. The decision regarding choice of placement must take into account the following factors:

(A) That the setting is safe;

(B) That the setting is the least restrictive or most family-like environment that is appropriate for the child and available;

(C) That the setting is in close proximity to the parent's home; and

(D) That the setting is the environment best suited to meet the child's special needs and best interest.

The selection must consider, in order of priority, placement with relatives, tribal members, and foster family, group care, and residential treatment under Family Code section 7950.

(4) If the child was declared a ward under section 602, the court may order treatment or commitment of the child under section 730 or 731.

(5) The court may limit the control exercised over the ward by a parent or guardian. Orders must clearly specify all limitations. In particular, the court must consider whether it is necessary to limit the rights of the parent or guardian to make educational or developmental-services decisions for the child. If the court limits those rights, it must follow the procedures in rules 5.649–5.651.

(i) California Department of Corrections and Rehabilitation, Division of Juvenile Justice

If, at the time of the disposition hearing, the child is a ward of the California Department of Corrections and Rehabilitation, Division of Juvenile Justice (DJJ) under a prior commitment, the court may either recommit or return the child to the DJJ. If the child is returned to the DJJ, the court may:

(1) Recommend that the ward's parole status be revoked;

(2) Recommend that the ward's parole status not be revoked; or

(3) Make no recommendation regarding revocation of parole.

(j) Fifteen-day reviews (§ 737)

If the child or nonminor is detained pending the implementation of a dispositional order, the court must review the case at least every 15 days as long as the child is detained. The review must meet all the requirements in section 737. *(Formerly Rule 1493, adopted, eff. Jan. 1, 1991. As amended, eff. Jan. 1, 1998; July 1, 2002; Jan. 1, 2004; Jan. 1, 2006. Renumbered Rule 5.790 and amended, eff. Jan. 1, 2007. As amended, eff. Jan. 1, 2008; Jan. 1, 2014; Jan. 1, 2015; Jan. 1, 2016.)*

Research References

Forms

West's California Judicial Council Forms JV-624, Terms and Conditions.
West's California Judicial Council Forms JV-665, Disposition--Juvenile Delinquency.
West's California Judicial Council Forms JV-667, Custodial and Out Of Home Placement Disposition Attachment.
West's California Judicial Council Forms JV-732, Commitment to the California Department Of Corrections and Rehabilitation, Division Of Juvenile Facilities.

Treatises and Practice Aids

Witkin, California Summary 10th Parent and Child § 763, Investigation, Release, and Conditions.
Witkin, California Summary 10th Parent and Child § 886, Conduct Of Hearing.
Witkin, California Summary 10th Parent and Child § 889, Dismissal in Interests Of Justice.
Witkin, California Summary 10th Parent and Child § 890, Probation Without Wardship.
Witkin, California Summary 10th Parent and Child § 892, in General.
Witkin, California Summary 10th Parent and Child § 893, Limitations on Parental Control.
Witkin, California Summary 10th Parent and Child § 897, Reunification Services.
Witkin, California Summary 10th Parent and Child § 904, Temporary Detention.
Witkin, California Summary 10th Parent and Child § 942, Types Of Sanctions.
Witkin, California Summary 10th Parent and Child § 955, Judge Must be Satisfied Of Benefit.

Rule 5.795. Required determinations

(a) Felony or misdemeanor (§ 702)

Unless determined previously, the court must find and note in the minutes the degree of the offense committed by the youth, and whether it would be a felony or a misdemeanor had it been committed by an adult. If any offense may be found to be either a felony or a misdemeanor, the court must consider which description applies and expressly declare on the record that it has made such consideration and must state its determination as to whether the offense is a misdemeanor or a felony.

(b) Physical confinement (§ 726)

If the youth is declared a ward under section 602 and ordered removed from the physical custody of a parent or guardian, the court must specify and note in the minutes the maximum period of confinement under section 726. *(Formerly Rule 1494, adopted, eff. Jan. 1, 1991. As amended, eff. Jan. 1, 2001; Jan. 1, 2003. Renumbered Rule 5.795 and amended, eff. Jan. 1, 2007.)*

Research References

Forms

West's California Judicial Council Forms JV-665, Disposition--Juvenile Delinquency.

West's California Judicial Council Forms JV-667, Custodial and Out Of Home Placement Disposition Attachment.

West's California Judicial Council Forms JV-732, Commitment to the California Department Of Corrections and Rehabilitation, Division Of Juvenile Facilities.

Treatises and Practice Aids

Witkin, California Summary 10th Parent and Child § 944, in General.

Rule 5.800. Deferred entry of judgment

(a) Eligibility (§ 790)

A child who is the subject of a petition under section 602 alleging violation of at least one felony offense may be considered for a deferred entry of judgment if all of the following apply:

(1) The child is 14 years or older at the time of the hearing on the application for deferred entry of judgment;

(2) The offense alleged is not listed in section 707(b);

(3) The child has not been previously declared a ward of the court based on the commission of a felony offense;

(4) The child has not been previously committed to the California Department of Corrections and Rehabilitation, Division of Juvenile Justice;

(5) If the child is presently or was previously a ward of the court, probation has not been revoked before completion; and

(6) The child meets the eligibility standards stated in Penal Code section 1203.06.

(b) Procedures for consideration (§ 790)

(1) Before filing a petition alleging a felony offense, or as soon as possible after filing, the prosecuting attorney must review the child's file to determine if the requirements of (a) are met. If the prosecuting attorney's review reveals that the requirements of (a) have been met, the prosecuting attorney must file *Determination of Eligibility—Deferred Entry of Judgment—Juvenile* (form JV–750) with the petition.

(2) If the court determines that the child is eligible and suitable for a deferred entry of judgment, and would derive benefit from education, treatment, and rehabilitation efforts, the court may grant deferred entry of judgment.

(c) Citation (§ 792)

The court must issue *Citation and Written Notification for Deferred Entry of Judgment—Juvenile* (form JV–751) to the child's custodial parent, guardian, or foster parent. The form must be personally served on the custodial adult at least 24 hours before the time set for the appearance hearing.

(d) Determination without a hearing; supplemental information (§ 791)

(1) The court may grant a deferred entry of judgment as stated in (2) or (3).

(2) If the child admits each allegation contained in the petition as charged and waives the right to a speedy disposition hearing, the court may summarily grant the deferred entry of judgment.

(3) When appropriate, the court may order the probation department to prepare a report with recommendations on the suitability of the child for deferred entry of judgment or set a hearing on the matter, with or without the order to the probation department for a report.

(A) The probation report must address the following:

(i) The child's age, maturity, educational background, family relationships, motivation, any treatment history, and any other relevant factors regarding the benefit the child would derive from education, treatment, and rehabilitation efforts; and

(ii) The programs best suited to assist the child and the child's family.

(B) The probation report must be submitted to the court, the child, the prosecuting attorney, and the child's attorney at least 48 hours, excluding noncourt days, before the hearing.

(e) Written notification of ineligibility (§ 790)

If it is determined that the child is ineligible for deferred entry of judgment, the prosecuting attorney must complete and provide to the court, the child, and the child's attorney *Determination of Eligibility—Deferred Entry of Judgment—Juvenile* (form JV–750).

(f) Conduct of hearing (§§ 791, 794)

At the hearing, the court must consider the declaration of the prosecuting attorney, any report and recommendations from the probation department, and any other relevant material provided by the child or other interested parties.

(1) If the child consents to the deferred entry of judgment, the child must enter an admission as stated in rule 5.778(c) and (d). A no-contest plea must not be accepted.

(2) The child must waive the right to a speedy disposition hearing.

(3) After acceptance of the child's admission, the court must set a date for review of the child's progress and a date by which the probation department must submit to the court, the child, the child's parent or guardian, the child's attorney, and the prosecuting attorney a report on the child's adherence to the conditions set by the court. Although the date set may be any time within the following 36 months, consideration of dismissal of the petition may not occur until at least 12 months have passed since the court granted the deferred entry of judgment.

(4) If the court grants the deferred entry of judgment, the court must order search-and-seizure probation conditions and may order probation conditions regarding the following:

(A) Education;

(B) Treatment;

(C) Testing for alcohol and other drugs, if appropriate;

(D) Curfew and school attendance requirements;

(E) Restitution; and

(F) Any other conditions consistent with the identified needs of the child and the factors that led to the conduct of the child.

(g) Compliance with conditions; progress review

Twelve months after the court granted the deferred entry of judgment and on receipt of the progress report ordered at the hearing on the deferred entry of judgment, the court may:

(1) Find that the child has complied satisfactorily with the conditions imposed, dismiss the petition, seal the court records in compliance with section 793(c), and vacate the date set for review hearing; or

(2) Confirm the review hearing. At the hearing the court must:

(A) Find that the child has complied satisfactorily with the conditions imposed, dismiss the petition, and seal the court records in compliance with section 793(c); or

(B) Find that the child has not complied satisfactorily with the conditions imposed, lift the deferred entry of judgment, and set a disposition hearing.

(h) Failure to comply with conditions (§ 793)

(1) Before the date of the progress hearing, if the child is found to have committed a misdemeanor offense or more than one misdemeanor offense on a single occasion, the court may schedule a hearing within 15 court days.

(A) At the hearing, the court must follow the procedure stated in rule 5.580 (d) and (e) to determine if the deferred entry of judgment should be lifted, with a disposition hearing to be conducted thereafter.

(B) The disposition hearing must be conducted as stated in rules 5.785 through 5.795.

(C) The child's admission of the charges under a deferred entry of judgment must not constitute a finding that a petition has been sustained unless a judgment is entered under section 793(b).

(2) Before the date of the progress hearing, on the court's own motion, or if the court receives a declaration from the probation department or the prosecuting attorney alleging that the child has not complied with the conditions imposed or that the conditions are not benefiting the child, or if the child is found to have committed a felony offense or two or more misdemeanor offenses on separate occasions, the court must schedule a hearing within 10 court days.

(A) At the hearing, the court must follow the procedure stated in rule 5.580 (d) and (e) to determine if the deferred entry of judgment should be lifted, with a disposition hearing to be conducted thereafter.

(B) The disposition hearing must be conducted as stated in rules 5.785 through 5.795.

(C) The child's admission of the charges under a deferred entry of judgment must not constitute a finding that a petition has been sustained unless a judgment is entered under section 793(b).

(3) If the child is found to have committed a felony offense or two or more misdemeanor offenses on separate occasions, the court must schedule a disposition hearing within 10 court days. The disposition hearing must be conducted as stated in rules 5.785 through 5.795.

(4) If the judgment previously deferred is imposed and a disposition hearing is scheduled under section 793(a), the juvenile court must report the complete criminal history of the child to the Department of Justice under section 602.5. *(Formerly Rule 1495, adopted, eff. Jan. 1, 2001. As amended, eff. Jan. 1, 2006. Renumbered Rule 5.800 and amended, eff. Jan. 1, 2007. As amended, eff. July 1, 2010.)*

Research References

Forms

West's California Judicial Council Forms JV-760, Deferred Entry Of Judgment Order.

Treatises and Practice Aids

Witkin, California Summary 10th Parent and Child § 891, Deferred Entry Of Judgment.

Rule 5.805. California Department of Corrections and Rehabilitation, Division of Juvenile Justice, commitments

If the court orders the youth committed to the California Department of Corrections and Rehabilitation, Division of Juvenile Justice (DJJ):

(1) The court must complete *Commitment to the California Department of Corrections and Rehabilitation, Division of Juvenile Justice* (form JV–732).

(2) The court must specify whether the offense is one listed in section 707(b) or subdivision (c) of Penal Code section 290.008.

(3) The court must order the probation department to forward to the DJJ all required medical information, including previously executed medical releases.

(4) If the youth is taking a prescribed psychotropic medication, the DJJ may continue to administer the medication for up to 60 days, provided that a physician examines the youth on arrival at the facility, and the physician recommends that the medication continue.

(5) The court must provide to the DJJ information regarding the youth's educational needs, including the youth's current individualized education program if one exists. To facilitate this process, the court must ensure that the probation officer communicates with appropriate educational staff. *(Formerly Rule 1494.5, adopted, eff. Jan. 1, 2003. As amended, eff. Jan. 1, 2006. Renumbered Rule 5.805 and amended, eff. Jan. 1, 2007. As amended, eff. Jan. 1, 2014.)*

Research References

Forms

West's California Judicial Council Forms JV-732, Commitment to the California Department Of Corrections and Rehabilitation, Division Of Juvenile Facilities.

Treatises and Practice Aids

Witkin, California Summary 10th Parent and Child § 444, Scope and Organization.

Witkin, California Summary 10th Parent and Child § 942, Types Of Sanctions.

Witkin, California Summary 10th Parent and Child § 951, in General.

Witkin, California Summary 10th Parent and Child § 952, Duties Of Court on Commitment.

Article 5

REVIEWS AND SEALING

Rule 5.810. Reviews, hearings, and permanency planning

(a) Six–month status review hearings (§§ 727.2, 11404.1)

For any ward removed from the custody of his or her parent or guardian under section 726 and placed in a home under section 727, the court must conduct a status review hearing no less frequently than once every six months from the date the ward entered foster care. The court may consider the hearing at which the initial order for placement is made as the first status review hearing.

(1) *Consideration of reports (§ 727.2(d))*

The court must review and consider the social study report and updated case plan submitted by the probation officer and the report submitted by any CASA volunteer, and any other reports filed with the court under section 727.2(d).

(2) *Return of child if not detrimental (§ 727.2(f))*

At any status review hearing before the first permanency hearing, the court must order the return of the ward to the parent or guardian unless it finds the probation department has established by a preponderance of evidence that return would create a substantial risk of detriment to the safety, protection, or physical or emotional well-being of the ward. The probation department has the burden of establishing that detriment. In making its determination, the court must review and consider all reports submitted to the court and must consider the efforts and progress demonstrated by the child and the family and the extent to which the child availed himself or herself of the services provided.

(3) *Findings and orders (§ 727.2(e))*

The court must consider the safety of the ward and make findings and orders that determine the following:

(A) The continuing necessity for and appropriateness of the placement;

(B) The extent of the probation department's compliance with the case plan in making reasonable efforts to safely return the child to the child's home and to complete whatever steps are necessary to finalize the permanent placement of the child;

(C) Whether it is necessary to limit the rights of the parent or guardian to make educational or developmental-services decisions for the child. If the court limits those rights or, if the ward is 18 years of age or older and has chosen not to make educational or developmental-services decisions for him- or herself or has been deemed incompetent, finds that it is in the best interests of the ward, the court must appoint a responsible adult as the educational rights holder as defined in rule 5.502. Any limitation on the rights of a parent or guardian to make educational or developmental-services decisions for a ward must be specified in the court order. The court must follow the procedures in rules 5.649–5.651;

(D) The extent of progress that has been made by the child and parent or guardian toward alleviating or mitigating the causes necessitating placement in foster care;

(E) The likely date by which the child may return to and be safely maintained in the home or placed for adoption, legal guardianship, or another permanent plan;

(F) In the case of a child who is 16 years of age or older, the services needed to assist the child in making the transition from foster care to independent living;

(G) Whether the child was actively involved, as age- and developmentally appropriate, in the development of his or her own case plan and plan for permanent placement. If the court finds that the child was not appropriately involved, the court must order the probation department to actively involve the child in the development of his or her own case plan and plan for permanent placement, unless the court finds that the child is unable, unavailable, or unwilling to participate;

(H) Whether each parent was actively involved in the development of the case plan and plan for permanent placement. If the court finds that any parent was not actively involved, the court must order the probation department to actively involve that parent in the development of the case plan and plan for permanent placement, unless the court finds that the parent is unable, unavailable, or unwilling to participate; and

(I) If sibling interaction has been suspended and will continue to be suspended, that sibling interaction is contrary to the safety or well-being of either child.

(4) *Basis for Findings and Orders (§ 727.2(e))*

The determinations required by (a)(3) must be made on a case-by-case basis, and the court must reference, in its written findings, the probation officer's report and any other evidence relied on in reaching its decision.

(b) Permanency planning hearings (§§ 727.2, 727.3, 11404.1)

A permanency planning hearing for any ward who has been removed from the custody of a parent or guardian and not returned at a previous review hearing must be held within 12 months of the date the ward entered foster care as defined in section 727.4(d)(4). However, when no reunification services are offered to the parents or guardians under section 727.2(b), the first permanency planning hearing must occur within 30 days of disposition.

(1) *Consideration of reports (§ 727.3)*

The court must review and consider the social study report and updated case plan submitted by the probation officer and the report submitted by any CASA volunteer, and any other reports filed with the court under section 727.3(a)(2).

(2) *Findings and orders (§§ 727.2(e), 727.3(a))*

At each permanency planning hearing, the court must consider the safety of the ward and make findings and orders regarding the following:

(A) The continuing necessity for and appropriateness of the placement;

(B) The extent of the probation department's compliance with the case plan in making reasonable efforts to safely return the child to the child's home and to complete whatever steps are necessary to finalize the permanent placement of the child;

(C) The extent of progress that has been made by the child and parent or guardian toward alleviating or mitigating the causes necessitating placement in foster care;

(D) The permanent plan for the child, as described in (3);

(E) Whether the child was actively involved, as age- and developmentally appropriate, in the development of his or her own case plan and plan for permanent placement. If the court finds that the child was not appropriately involved, the court must order the probation officer to actively involve the child in the development of his or her own case plan and plan for permanent placement, unless the court finds that the child is unable, unavailable, or unwilling to participate; and

(F) Whether each parent was actively involved in the development of the case plan and plan for permanent placement. If the court finds that any parent was not actively involved, the court must order the probation department to actively involve that parent in the development of the case plan and plan for permanent placement, unless the court finds that the parent is unable, unavailable, or unwilling to participate; and

(G) If sibling interaction has been suspended and will continue to be suspended, that sibling interaction is contrary to the safety or well-being of either child.

(3) *Selection of a permanent plan (§ 727.3(b))*

At the first permanency planning hearing, the court must select a permanent plan. At subsequent permanency planning hearings that must be held under section 727.2(g) and rule 5.810(c), the court must either make a finding that the current permanent plan is appropriate or select a different permanent plan, including returning the child home, if appropriate. The court must choose from one of the ~~following~~ permanent plans~~,~~ listed in section 727.3(b) ~~which are, in order of priority:~~.

~~(A) A permanent plan that immediately returns the child to the physical custody of the parent or guardian. This plan must be the permanent plan unless no reunification services were offered under section 727.2(b), or unless the court finds that the probation department has established by a preponderance of evidence that return would create a substantial risk of detriment to the safety, protection, or physical or emotional well being of the ward. The probation department has the burden of establishing that detriment. In making its determination, the court must review and consider all reports submitted to the court and must consider the efforts or progress, or both, demonstrated by the child and family and the extent to which the child availed himself or herself of the services provided.~~

~~(B) A permanent plan of return of the child to the physical custody of the parent or guardian, after 6 additional months of reunification services. The court may not order this plan unless the court finds that there is a substantial probability that the child will be able to return home within 18 months of the date of initial removal or that reasonable services have not been provided to the parent or guardian.~~

~~(C) A permanent plan of adoption. When this plan is identified, the court must order that a hearing under section 727.31 be held within 120 days.~~

~~(D) A permanent plan of legal guardianship. When this plan is ordered, the court must set a hearing under the procedures described in section 728 and rule 5.815.~~

~~(E) A permanent plan of placement with a fit and willing relative. When this plan is ordered, the court must specify that the child will be placed with the appropriate relative on a permanent basis.~~

~~(F) A permanent plan of placement in a planned permanent living arrangement. The court may order this permanent plan only after considering, and ruling out, each of the other permanent plan options listed above. If, after doing so, the court concludes that a planned permanent living arrangement is the most appropriate permanent plan for the child, it must also enter a finding, by clear and convincing evidence, that there is a compelling reason, as defined in section 727.3(c), for determining that a plan of termination of parental rights and adoption is not in the best interest of the child. When a planned permanent living arrangement is ordered, the court must specify the type of placement. The court must also specify the goal of the placement, which may include, but is not limited to, a goal of the child returning home, emancipation, guardianship, or permanent placement with a relative.~~

(4) *Involvement of parents or guardians*

If the child has a continuing involvement with his or her parents or legal guardians, they must be involved in the planning for permanent placement. The permanent plan order must include an order regarding the nature and frequency of visitation with the parents or guardians.

(c) Postpermanency status review hearings (§ 727.2)

A postpermanency status review hearing must be conducted for wards in placement no less frequently than once every six months.

(1) *Consideration of reports (§ 727.2(d))*

The court must review and consider the social study report and updated case plan submitted for this hearing by the probation officer and the report submitted by any CASA volunteer, and any other reports filed with the court under section 727.2(d).

(2) *Findings and orders (§ 727.2(g))*

At each postpermanency status review hearing, the court must consider the safety of the ward and make findings and orders regarding the following:

(A) Whether the current permanent plan continues to be appropriate. If not, the court must select a different permanent plan, including returning the child home, if appropriate. If the plan is another planned permanent living arrangement, the court must meet the requirements set forth in Welfare and Institutions Code section 727.3(a)(5);

(B) The continuing necessity for and appropriateness of the placement;

(C) The extent of the probation department's compliance with the case plan in making reasonable efforts to complete whatever steps are necessary to finalize the permanent plan for the child;

(D) Whether the child was actively involved, as age and developmentally appropriate, in the development of his or her own case plan and plan for permanent placement. If the court finds that the child was not appropriately involved, the court must order the probation department to actively involve the child in the development of his or her own case plan and plan for permanent placement, unless the court finds that the child is unable, unavailable, or unwilling to participate; and

(E) If sibling interaction has been suspended and will continue to be suspended, sibling interaction is contrary to the safety or well-being of either child.

(d) Notice of hearings; service; contents (§ 727.4)

No earlier than 30 nor later than 15 calendar days before each hearing date, the probation officer must serve written notice on all persons entitled to notice under section 727.4, as well as the current caregiver, any CASA volunteer or educational rights holder, and all counsel of record. A *Notice of Hearing—Juvenile Delinquency Proceeding* (form JV–625) must be used.

(e) Report (§§ 706.5, 706.6, 727.2(c), 727.3(a)(1), 727.4(b), 16002)

Before each hearing described above, the probation officer must investigate and prepare a social study report that must include an updated case plan and all of the information required in sections 706.5, 706.6, 727.2, 727.3, and 16002.

(1) The report must contain recommendations for court findings and orders and must document the evidentiary basis for those recommendations.

(2) At least 10 calendar days before each hearing, the probation officer must file the report and provide copies of the report to the ward, the parent or guardian, all attorneys of record, and any CASA volunteer. *(Formerly Rule 1496, adopted, eff. Jan. 1, 1991. As amended, eff. Jan. 1, 1998; Jan. 1, 2001; Jan. 1, 2003; Jan. 1, 2004; Jan. 1, 2006. Renumbered Rule 5.810 and amended, eff. Jan. 1, 2007. As amended, eff. Jan. 1, 2014; Jan. 1, 2016; Jan. 1, 2018.)*

Research References

Forms

West's California Judicial Council Forms JV-320, Orders Under Welfare and Institutions Code Sections 366.26, 727.3, 727.31.

West's California Judicial Council Forms JV-672, Findings and Orders After Six-Month Prepermanency Hearing--Delinquency.

West's California Judicial Council Forms JV-674, Findings and Orders After Permanency Hearing--Delinquency.

West's California Judicial Council Forms JV-678, Findings and Orders After Postpermanency Hearing--Delinquency.

Treatises and Practice Aids

Witkin, California Summary 10th Parent and Child § 444, Scope and Organization.

Witkin, California Summary 10th Parent and Child § 896, General Requirements.

Witkin, California Summary 10th Parent and Child § 898, Court Supervision Of Child.

Rule 5.812. Additional requirements for any hearing to terminate jurisdiction over child in foster care and for status review or dispositional hearing for child approaching majority (§§ 450, 451, 727.2(i)–(j), 778)

(a) Hearings subject to this rule

The following hearings are subject to this rule:

(1) The last review hearing under section 727.2 or 727.3 before the child turns 18 years of age and a dispositional hearing under section 702 for a child under an order of foster care placement who will attain 18 years of age before a subsequent review hearing will be held. If the hearing is the last review hearing under section 727.2 or 727.3, the hearing must be set at least 90 days before the child attains his or her 18th birthday and within six months of the previous hearing held under section 727.2 or 727.3.

(2) Any review hearing held under section 727.2 or 727.3 for a child less than 18 years of age during which a recommendation to terminate juvenile court jurisdiction will be considered;

(3) Any hearing to terminate juvenile court jurisdiction over a child less than 18 years of age who is subject to an order for foster care placement; and

(4) Any hearing to terminate juvenile court jurisdiction over a child less than 18 years of age who is not currently subject to an order for foster care placement but was previously removed from the custody of his or her parents or legal guardian as a dependent of the juvenile court and an order for a foster care placement as a dependent of the juvenile court was in effect at the time the juvenile court adjudged the child to be a ward of the juvenile court under section 725.

(b) Conduct of the hearing

(1) The hearing must be held before a judicial officer and recorded by a court reporter.

(2) The hearing must be continued for no more than five court days for the submission of additional information as ordered by the court if the court finds that the report and, if required, the Transitional Independent Living Case Plan and Transitional Independent Living Plan submitted by the probation officer do not provide the information required by (c) and the court is unable to make all the findings required by (d).

(c) Reports

(1) In addition to complying with all other statutory and rule requirements applicable to the report prepared by the probation officer for a hearing described in (a)(1)–(4), the report must state whether the child was provided with the notices and information required under section 607.5 and include a description of:

(A) The child's progress toward meeting the case plan goals that will enable him or her to be a law-abiding and productive member of his or her family and the community.

(B) If reunification services have not been previously terminated, the progress of each parent or legal guardian toward participating in case plan service activities and meeting the case plan goals developed to resolve his or her issues that were identified and contributed to the child's removal from his or her custody.

(C) The current ability of each parent or legal guardian to provide the care, custody, supervision, and support the child requires in a safe and healthy environment.

(D) For a child previously determined to be a dual status child for whom juvenile court jurisdiction as a dependent was suspended under section 241.1(e)(5)(A), a joint assessment by the probation department and the child welfare services agency under section 366.5 regarding the detriment, if any, to the child of a return to the home of his or her parents or legal guardian and a recommendation on the resumption of dependency jurisdiction. The facts in support of the opinions expressed and the recommendations made must be included in the joint assessment section of the report. If the probation department and the child welfare services agency do not agree, the child welfare services agency must file a separate report with facts in support of its opinions and recommendations.

(E) For a child previously determined to be a dual status child for whom the probation department was designated the lead agency under section 241.1(e)(5)(B), the detriment, if any, to the child of a return to the home of his or her parents or legal guardian and the probation officer's recommendation regarding the modification of the court's jurisdiction over the child from that of a dual status child to that of a dependent under section 300 and the facts in support of the opinion expressed and the recommendation made.

(F) For a child other than a dual status child, the probation officer's recommendation regarding the modification of the juvenile court's jurisdiction over the child from that of a ward under section 601 or 602 to that of a dependent under section 300 or to that of a transition dependent under section 450 and the facts in support of his or her recommendation.

(2) For the review hearing held on behalf of a child approaching majority described in (a)(1) and any hearing described in (a)(2) or (a)(3) held on behalf of a child more than 17 years, 5 months old and less than 18 years of age, in addition to complying with all other report requirements set forth in (c)(1), the report prepared by the probation officer must include:

(A) The child's plans to remain under juvenile court jurisdiction as a nonminor dependent including the criteria in section 11403(b) that he or she plans to meet;

(B) The efforts made by the probation officer to help the child meet one or more of the criteria in section 11403(b);

(C) For an Indian child, his or her plans to continue to be considered an Indian child for the purposes of the ongoing application of the Indian Child Welfare Act to him or her as a nonminor dependent;

(D) Whether the child has applied for and, if so, the status of any in-progress application pending for title XVI Supplemental Security Income benefits and, if such an application is pending, whether it is in the child's best interest to continue juvenile court jurisdiction until a final decision has been issued to ensure that the child receives continued assistance with the application process;

(E) Whether the child has an in-progress application pending for Special Immigrant Juvenile Status or other applicable application for legal residency and whether an active juvenile court case is required for that application;

(F) The efforts made by the probation officer toward providing the child with the written information, documents, and services described in section 391 and, to the extent that the child has not yet been provided with them, the barriers to providing the information, documents or services and the steps that will be taken to overcome those barriers by the date the child attains 18 years of age;

(G) When and how the child was informed that upon reaching 18 years of age he or she may request the dismissal of juvenile court jurisdiction over him or her under section 778;

(H) When and how the child was provided with information regarding the potential benefits of remaining under juvenile court jurisdiction as a nonminor dependent and the probation officer's assessment of the child's understanding of those benefits;

(I) When and how the child was informed that if juvenile court jurisdiction is terminated after he or she attains 18 years of age, he or she has the right to file a request to return to foster care and have the juvenile court assume or resume transition jurisdiction over him or her as a nonminor dependent; and

(J) The child's Transitional Independent Living Case Plan and Transitional Independent Living Plan, which must include:

(i) The individualized plan for the child to satisfy one or more of the criteria in section 11403(b) and the child's anticipated placement as specified in section 11402; and

(ii) The child's alternate plan for his or her transition to independence, including housing, education, employment, and a support system in the event the child does not remain under juvenile court jurisdiction after attaining 18 years of age.

(d) Findings

(1) At the hearing described in (a)(1)–(4), in addition to complying with all other statutory and rule requirements applicable to the hearing, the court must make the following findings in the written documentation of the hearing:

(A) Whether the rehabilitative goals for this child have been met and juvenile court jurisdiction over the child as a ward is no longer required. The facts supporting the finding must be stated on the record.

(B) For a dual status child for whom dependency jurisdiction was suspended under section 241.1(e)(5)(A), whether the return to the home of the parents or legal guardian would be detrimental to the minor. The facts supporting the finding must be stated on the record.

(C) For a child previously determined to be a dual status child for whom the probation department was designated the lead agency under section 241.1(e)(5)(B), whether the return to the home of the parents or legal guardian would be detrimental to the minor. The facts supporting the finding must be stated on the record.

(D) For a child other than a dual status child:

(i) Who was not subject to the court's dependency jurisdiction at the time he or she was adjudged a ward and is currently subject to an order for a foster care placement, whether the child appears to come within the description of section 300 and cannot be returned home safely. The facts supporting the finding must be stated on the record;

(ii) Who was subject to an order for a foster care placement as a dependent of the court at the time he or she was adjudged a ward, whether the child remains within the description of a dependent child under section 300 and whether the return to the home of the parents or legal guardian would create a substantial risk of detriment to the child's safety, protection, or physical or emotional well-being. The facts supporting the findings must be stated on the record;

(iii) Whether reunification services have been terminated;

(iv) Whether the matter has been set for a hearing to terminate parental rights or establish a guardianship; and

(v) Whether the minor intends to sign a mutual agreement for a placement in a supervised setting as a nonminor dependent.

(2) At the review hearing held on behalf of a child approaching majority described in (a)(1) and any hearing under (a)(2) or (a)(3) held on behalf of a child more than 17 years, 5 months old and less than 18 years of age, in addition to complying with all other statutory and rule requirements applicable to the hearing, the court must make the following findings in the written documentation of the hearing:

(A) Whether the child's Transitional Independent Living Case Plan, if required, or Transitional Independent Living Plan includes:

(i) A plan specific to the child for him or her to satisfy one or more of the criteria in section 11403(b) and the specific criteria in section 11403(b) it is anticipated the child will satisfy; and

(ii) The child's alternate plan for his or her transition to independence, including housing, education, employment, and a support system in the event the child does not remain under juvenile court jurisdiction after attaining 18 years of age.

(B) For an Indian child to whom the Indian Child Welfare Act applies, whether he or she intends to continue to be considered an Indian child for the purposes of the ongoing application of the Indian Child Welfare Act to him or her as a nonminor dependent;

(C) Whether the child has an in-progress application pending for title XVI Supplemental Security Income benefits and, if such an application is pending, whether it is in the child's best interest to continue juvenile court jurisdiction until a final decision has been issued to ensure that the child receives continued assistance with the application process;

(D) Whether the child has an in-progress application pending for Special Immigrant Juvenile Status or other applicable application for legal residency and whether an active juvenile court case is required for that application;

(E) Whether the child has been informed that he or she may decline to become a nonminor dependent;

(F) Whether the child has been informed that upon reaching 18 years of age he or she may request the dismissal of juvenile court jurisdiction over him or her under section 778;

(G) Whether the child understands the potential benefits of remaining under juvenile court jurisdiction as a nonminor dependent;

(H) Whether the child has been informed that if after reaching 18 years of age juvenile court jurisdiction is terminated, he or she has the right to file a request to return to foster care and have the juvenile court assume or resume transition jurisdiction over him or her as a nonminor dependent;

(I) Whether all the information, documents, and services in sections 391(e) were provided to the child, and whether the barriers to providing any missing information, documents, or services can be overcome by the date the child attains 18 years of age; and

(J) Whether the notices and information required under section 607.5 were provided to a child who is or was subject to an order for foster care placement.

(e) Orders

(1) For a child previously determined to be a dual status child for whom dependency jurisdiction was suspended under section 241.1(e)(5)(A), dependency jurisdiction must be resumed if the court finds that the child's rehabilitative goals have been achieved and a return to the home of the parents or legal guardian would be detrimental to the child.

(2) For a child previously determined to be a dual status child for whom the probation department was designated the lead agency under section 241.1(e)(5)(B), the court must terminate dual status, dismiss delinquency jurisdiction, and continue dependency jurisdiction with the child welfare services department responsible for the child's placement if the court finds that the child's rehabilitative goals have been achieved and a return to the home of the parents or legal guardian would be detrimental to the child.

(3) For a child who comes within the description of section 450(a), other than a child described in (e)(1) or (e)(2), the court must enter an order modifying its jurisdiction over him or her from delinquency jurisdiction to transition jurisdiction and set a nonminor dependent status review hearing under rule 5.903 within six months of the last hearing held under section 727.2.

(4) For a child who was not subject to the court's dependency jurisdiction at the time he or she was adjudged a ward and is currently subject to an order for a foster care placement, the court must:

(A) Order the probation department or the child's attorney to submit an application under section 329 to the county child welfare services department to commence a proceeding to declare the child a dependent of the court by filing a petition under section 300 if the court finds:

(i) The child does not come within the description of section 450(a);

(ii) The rehabilitative goals for the child included in his or her case plan have been met and delinquency jurisdiction is no longer required; and

(iii) The child appears to come within the description of section 300 and a return to the home of the parents or legal guardian may be detrimental to his or her safety, protection, or physical or emotional well-being.

(B) Set a hearing to review the county child welfare services department's decision within 20 court days of the date the order to file an application under section 329 was entered and at that hearing:

(i) Affirm the county child welfare services department's decision not to file a petition under section 300; or

(ii) Order the county child welfare services department to file a petition under section 300.

(C) If the court affirms the decision not to file a petition under section 300 or a petition filed under section 300 is not sustained, the court may:

(i) Return the child to the home of the parents or legal guardian and set a progress report hearing within the next six months;

(ii) Return the child to the home of the parents or legal guardian and terminate juvenile court jurisdiction over the child; or

(iii) Continue the child's foster care placement and set a hearing under section 727.2 no more than six months from the date of the most recent hearing held under 727.2.

(5) For a child who was subject to an order for foster care placement as a dependent of the court at the time he or she was adjudged a ward, the court must modify its delinquency jurisdiction over the child by vacating the order terminating jurisdiction over the child as a dependent of the court and resuming dependency jurisdiction over him or her if the court finds that:

(A) The child does not come within the description of section 450(a);

(B) The rehabilitative goals for the child included in his or her case plan have been met and delinquency jurisdiction may not be required; and

(C) The child remains within the description of a dependent child under section 300 and a return to the home of a parents or legal guardian would create a substantial risk of detriment to his or her safety, protection, or physical or emotional well-being.

(6) At a hearing described in (a)(1) for a child approaching majority or at any hearing described in (a)(2) or (a)(3) held on behalf of a child more than 17 years, 5 months old and less than 18 years old that did not result in modification of jurisdiction over the child from delinquency jurisdiction to dependency jurisdiction or transition jurisdiction, the court must:

(A) Return the child to the home of the parents or legal guardian and set a progress report hearing within the next six months; or

(B) Return the child to the home of the parents or legal guardian and terminate juvenile court jurisdiction over the child; or

(C) Continue the child's foster care placement and:

(i) For the child who intends to meet the eligibility requirements for status as a nonminor dependent after attaining 18 years of age, set a nonminor dependent status review hearing under rule 5.903 no more than six months from the most recent hearing held under section 727.2; or

(ii) For the child who does not intend to meet the eligibility requirements for nonminor dependent status after attaining 18 years of age:

a. Set a hearing to terminate delinquency jurisdiction under section 607.2(b)(4) and section 607.3 for a date within one month after the child's 18th birthday; or

b. Set a hearing under section 727.2 no more than six months from the date of the most recent hearing held under section 727.2 for the child who will remain under delinquency jurisdiction in a foster care placement.

(7) At any hearing under (a)(2) or (a)(3) held on behalf of a child 17 years, 5 months old or younger that did not result in modification of jurisdiction over the child from delinquency jurisdiction to dependency jurisdiction, the court must:

(A) Return the child to the home of the parents or legal guardian and set a progress report hearing within the next six months;

(B) Return the child to the home of the parents or legal guardian and terminate juvenile court jurisdiction over the child; or

(C) Continue the child's out-of-home placement and set a hearing under section 727.2 to occur within six months of the most recent hearing under section 727.2.

(8) At any hearing under (a)(4) on behalf of a child less than 18 years of age that did not result in modification of jurisdiction over the child from delinquency jurisdiction to dependency jurisdiction, the court must:

(A) Return the child to the home of the parents or legal guardian and set a progress report hearing within the next six months;

(B) Return the child to the home of the parents or legal guardian and terminate juvenile court jurisdiction over the child; or

(C) Continue the child's out-of-home placement and set a progress report hearing within the next six months.

(f) Modification of jurisdiction—conditions

Whenever the court modifies its jurisdiction over a dependent or ward under section 241.1, 607.2, or 727.2, the court must ensure that all of the following conditions are met:

(1) The petition under which jurisdiction was taken at the time the dependent or ward was originally removed from his

or her parents or legal guardian and placed in foster care is not dismissed until after the new petition is sustained; and

(2) The order modifying the court's jurisdiction contains all of the following provisions:

(A) A reference to the original removal findings, the date those findings were made, and a statement that the finding "continuation in the home is contrary to the child's welfare" and the finding "reasonable efforts were made to prevent removal" made at that hearing remain in effect;

(B) A statement that the child continues to be removed from the parents or legal guardian from whom the child was removed under the original petition; and

(C) Identification of the agency that is responsible for placement and care of the child based upon the modification of jurisdiction.

(Adopted, eff. Jan. 1, 2012. As amended, eff. July 1, 2012; Jan. 1, 2014; Jan. 1, 2016.)

Research References

Forms

West's California Judicial Council Forms JV-680, Findings and Orders for Child Approaching Majority--Delinquency.

West's California Judicial Council Forms JV-681, Attachment: Hearing for Dismissal--Additional Findings and Orders--Foster Care Placement--Delinquency.

Treatises and Practice Aids

Witkin, California Summary 10th Parent and Child § 898, Court Supervision Of Child.

Witkin, California Summary 10th Parent and Child § 452D, (New) Modification Of Jurisdiction.

Witkin, California Summary 10th Parent and Child § 452E, (New) Termination Of Jurisdiction Over Minor.

Rule 5.813. Modification to transition jurisdiction for a ward older than 18 years and younger than 21 years of age (§§ 450, 451)

(a) Purpose

This rule provides the procedures that must be followed when it appears to a probation officer that a ward who is at least 18 years of age and younger than 21 years of age has met his or her rehabilitative goals and wants to remain in extended foster care under the jurisdiction of the court.

(b) Setting and conduct of hearing

(1) The probation officer must request a hearing for the court to consider modifying delinquency jurisdiction to transition jurisdiction.

(2) The hearing must be held before a judicial officer and recorded by a court reporter.

(3) The hearing must be continued for no more than five court days for the submission of additional evidence as ordered by the court if the court finds that the report and, if required, the Transitional Independent Living Case Plan submitted by the probation officer do not provide the information required by (d) and the court is unable to make all the findings required by (e).

(c) Notice of hearing

(1) The probation officer must serve written notice of the hearing in the manner provided in section 295.

(2) Proof of service of notice must be filed by the probation officer at least five court days before the hearing.

(d) Reports

At least 10 calendar days before the hearing, the probation officer must submit a report to the court that includes information regarding:

(1) Whether the ward is a nonminor who was subject to an order for foster care placement on the day of the ward's 18th birthday and is within the age eligibility requirements for extended foster care;

(2) Whether the ward was removed from the physical custody of his or her parents, adjudged to be a ward of the juvenile court under section 725, and ordered into foster care placement as a ward; or whether the ward was removed from the custody of his or her parents as a dependent of the court with an order for foster care placement in effect at the time the court adjudged him or her to be a ward of the juvenile court under section 725 and was ordered into a foster care placement as a ward, including the date of the initial removal findings—"continuance in the home is contrary to the child's welfare" and "reasonable efforts were made to prevent removal"—as well as whether the ward continues to be removed from the parents or legal guardian from whom the child was removed under the original petition;

(3) Whether the ward's rehabilitative goals as stated in the case plan have been met and whether juvenile court jurisdiction over the ward is no longer required;

(4) Whether the probation officer recommends the modification of juvenile court jurisdiction over the ward from that of a ward under section 601 or 602 to that of a nonminor dependent under section 450 and the facts in support of that recommendation;

(5) Whether the ward signed a mutual agreement with the probation department or social services agency for placement in a supervised setting as a nonminor dependent and, if so, a recommendation as to which agency should be responsible for placement and care of the nonminor dependent;

(6) Whether the ward plans to meet at least one of the conditions in section 11403(b) and what efforts the probation officer has made to help the ward meet any of the conditions;

(7) When and how the ward was informed of the benefits of remaining under juvenile court jurisdiction as a nonminor dependent and the probation officer's assessment of the ward's understanding of those benefits;

(8) When and how the ward was informed that he or she may decline to become a nonminor dependent and have the juvenile court terminate jurisdiction at a hearing under section 391 and rule 5.555; and

(9) When and how the ward was informed that if juvenile court jurisdiction is terminated, he or she can file a request to return to foster care and have the court resume jurisdiction over him or her as a nonminor.

(e) Findings

At the hearing described in (a), the court must make the following findings:

(1) Whether notice has been given as required by law;

(2) Whether the nonminor comes within the description of section 450;

(3) Whether the ward has been informed that he or she may decline to become a nonminor dependent and have juvenile court jurisdiction terminated at a hearing set under rule 5.555;

(4) Whether the ward was informed that if juvenile court jurisdiction is terminated, the ward can file a request to return to foster care and may have the court resume jurisdiction over the ward as a nonminor;

(5) Whether the benefits of remaining under juvenile court jurisdiction as a nonminor dependent were explained and whether the ward understands them;

(6) Whether the ward has signed a mutual agreement with the probation department for placement in a supervised setting as a nonminor dependent;

(7) Whether the ward's Transitional Independent Living Case Plan includes a plan for the ward to satisfy at least one of the conditions in section 11403(b); and

(8) Whether the ward has had an opportunity to confer with his or her attorney.

(f) Orders

For a child who comes within the description of section 450(a), the court must enter the following orders:

(1) An order modifying the court's jurisdiction over the child from delinquency to transition jurisdiction and setting a nonminor dependent status review hearing under section 366.31 and rule 5.903 within six months of the last hearing held under section 727.2 or 366.31. The order modifying the court's jurisdiction must contain all of the following provisions:

(A) A reference to the initial removal findings, the date those findings were made, and a statement that the findings—"continuance in the home is contrary to the child's welfare" and "reasonable efforts were made to prevent removal"—made at that hearing remain in effect;

(B) A statement that the nonminor dependent continues to be removed from the parents or legal guardian from whom the nonminor dependent was removed under the original petition; and

(C) Identification of the agency that is responsible for placement and care of the nonminor dependent based on the modification of jurisdiction.

(2) An order continuing the appointment of the attorney of record or appointing a new attorney as the attorney of record for the nonminor dependent. *(Adopted, eff. Jan. 1, 2014.)*

Research References

Forms

West's California Judicial Council Forms JV-683, Findings and Orders After Hearing to Modify Delinquency Jurisdiction to Transition Jurisdiction for Ward Older Than 18 Years Of Age.

Treatises and Practice Aids

Witkin, California Summary 10th Parent and Child § 452D, (New) Modification Of Jurisdiction.

Rule 5.814. Modification to transition jurisdiction for a ward older than 17 years, 5 months of age and younger than 18 years of age (§§ 450, 451)

(a) Purpose

This rule provides the procedures that must be followed to modify delinquency jurisdiction to transition jurisdiction for a ward who is older than 17 years, 5 months of age, younger than 18 years of age, and:

(1) Has met his or her rehabilitative goals;

(2) Is under a foster care placement order;

(3) Wants to remain in extended foster care under the transition jurisdiction of the juvenile court;

(4) Is not receiving reunification services; and

(5) Does not have a hearing set for termination of parental rights or establishment of guardianship.

(b) Setting and conduct of hearing

(1) The probation officer must request a hearing for the court to consider modifying delinquency jurisdiction to transition jurisdiction.

(2) The hearing must be held before a judicial officer and recorded by a court reporter.

(3) The hearing must be continued for no more than five court days for the submission of additional evidence as ordered by the court if the court finds that the report and, if required, the Transitional Independent Living Case Plan submitted by the probation officer, do not provide the information required by (d) and the court is unable to make all the findings required by (e).

(c) Notice of hearing

(1) The probation officer must serve written notice of the hearing in the manner provided in section 295.

(2) Proof of service of notice must be filed by the probation officer at least five court days before the hearing.

(d) Reports

At least 10 calendar days before the hearing, the probation officer must submit a report to the court that includes information regarding:

(1) Whether the ward is subject to an order for foster care placement and is older than 17 years, 5 months of age and younger than 18 years of age;

(2) Whether the ward was removed from the physical custody of his or her parents, adjudged to be a ward of the juvenile court under section 725, and ordered into foster care placement as a ward; or whether the ward was removed from the custody of his or her parents as a dependent of the court with an order for foster care placement in effect at the time the court adjudged him or her to be a ward of the juvenile court under section 725 and was ordered into a foster care placement as a ward, including the date of the initial removal findings—"continuance in the home is contrary to the child's welfare" and "reasonable efforts were made to prevent removal"—as well as whether the ward continues to be

removed from the parents or legal guardian from whom the child was removed under the original petition;

(3) Whether the ward's rehabilitative goals as stated in the case plan have been met and whether juvenile court jurisdiction over the ward is no longer required;

(4) Whether each parent or legal guardian is currently able to provide the care, custody, supervision, and support the child requires in a safe and healthy environment;

(5) Whether the probation officer recommends the modification of the juvenile court's jurisdiction over the ward from that of a ward under section 601 or 602 to that of a transition dependent under section 450;

(6) Whether the ward signed a mutual agreement with the probation department or social services agency for placement in a supervised setting as a transition dependent and, if so, a recommendation as to which agency should be responsible for placement and care of the transition dependent;

(7) Whether the ward plans to meet at least one of the conditions in section 11403(b) and what efforts the probation officer has made to help the ward meet any of these conditions;

(8) When and how the ward was informed of the benefits of remaining under juvenile court jurisdiction as a transition dependent and the probation officer's assessment of the ward's understanding of those benefits;

(9) When and how the ward was informed that he or she may decline to become a transition dependent and have the juvenile court terminate jurisdiction at a hearing under section 391 and rule 5.555; and

(10) When and how the ward was informed that if juvenile court jurisdiction is terminated, he or she can file a request to return to foster care and have the court resume jurisdiction over him or her as a nonminor.

(e) Findings

At the hearing, the court must make the following findings:

(1) Whether notice has been given as required by law;

(2) Whether the ward comes within the description of section 450;

(3) Whether the ward has been informed that he or she may decline to become a transition dependent and have juvenile court jurisdiction terminated at a hearing set under rule 5.555;

(4) Whether the ward's return to the home of his or her parent or legal guardian would create a substantial risk of detriment to the ward's safety, protection, or physical or emotional well-being. The facts supporting this finding must be stated on the record;

(5) Whether reunification services have been terminated;

(6) Whether the ward's case has been set for a hearing to terminate parental rights or establish a guardianship;

(7) Whether the ward intends to sign a mutual agreement with the probation department or social services agency for placement in a supervised setting as a nonminor dependent;

(8) Whether the ward was informed that if juvenile court jurisdiction is terminated, the ward can file a request to return to foster care and may have the court resume jurisdiction over the ward as a nonminor dependent;

(9) Whether the benefits of remaining under juvenile court jurisdiction as a nonminor dependent were explained and whether the ward understands them;

(10) Whether the ward's Transitional Independent Living Case Plan includes a plan for the ward to satisfy at least one of the conditions in section 11403(b); and

(11) Whether the ward has had an opportunity to confer with his or her attorney.

(f) Orders

For a child who comes within the description of section 450(a), the court must enter the following orders:

(1) An order modifying the court's jurisdiction over the child from delinquency to transition jurisdiction and adjudging the ward a transition dependent pending his or her 18th birthday and status as a nonminor dependent under the transition jurisdiction of the court. The order modifying the court's jurisdiction must contain all of the following provisions:

(A) A reference to the initial removal findings, the date those findings were made, and a statement that the findings—"continuance in the home is contrary to the child's welfare" and "reasonable efforts were made to prevent removal"—made at that hearing remain in effect;

(B) A statement that the child continues to be removed from the parents or legal guardian from whom the child was removed under the original petition; and

(C) Identification of the agency that is responsible for placement and care of the child based on the modification of jurisdiction.

(2) An order continuing the appointment of the attorney of record, or appointing a new attorney, as the attorney of record for the nonminor dependent.

(3) An order setting a nonminor dependent status review hearing under section 366.31 and rule 5.903 within six months of the last hearing held under section 727.2 or 727.3. *(Adopted, eff. Jan. 1, 2014.)*

Research References

Treatises and Practice Aids

Witkin, California Summary 10th Parent and Child § 452D, (New) Modification Of Jurisdiction.

Rule 5.815. Appointment of legal guardians for wards of the juvenile court; modification or termination of guardianship

(a) Proceedings in juvenile court (§ 728)

Proceedings for the appointment of a legal guardian for a child who is a ward of the juvenile court under section 725(b) may be held in the juvenile court.

(b) Recommendation for guardianship (§ 728(c))

On the recommendation of the probation officer supervising the child, the motion of the attorney representing the child, or the court's own motion and order that a legal guardian should be appointed for the child, the court must set a hearing to consider the establishment of a legal guardianship and must order the probation officer to prepare an assessment that includes:

(1) A review of the existing relationship between the child and the proposed guardian;

(2) A summary of the child's medical, developmental, educational, mental, and emotional status;

(3) A social history of the proposed guardian, including a screening for criminal records and any prior referrals for child abuse or neglect;

(4) An assessment of the ability of the proposed guardian to meet the child's needs and the proposed guardian's understanding of the legal and financial rights and responsibilities of guardianship; and

(5) A statement confirming that the proposed guardian has been provided with a copy of *Guardianship Pamphlet* (form JV–350) or *Guardianship Pamphlet (Spanish)* (form JV–350S).

(c) Forms

The probation officer or child's attorney may use *Juvenile Wardship Petition* (form JV–600) and *Petition to Modify Previous Orders—Change of Circumstances* (form JV–740) to request that a guardianship hearing be set.

(d) Notice (§ 728(c))

The clerk must provide notice of the hearing to the child, the child's parents, and other individuals as required by section 294.

(e) Conduct of hearing

The court must read and consider the assessment prepared by the probation officer and any other evidence. The preparer of the assessment must be available for examination by the court or any party to the proceedings.

(f) Findings and orders

If the court finds that establishment of a legal guardianship is necessary or convenient and consistent with the rehabilitation and protection of the child and with public safety, the court must appoint a legal guardian and order the clerk to issue letters of guardianship (*Letters of Guardianship (Juvenile)* (form JV–330)).

(1) The court may issue orders regarding visitation and contact between the child and a parent or other relative.

(2) After the appointment of a legal guardian, the court may continue juvenile court wardship and supervision or may terminate wardship.

(g) Modification or termination of the guardianship, or appointment of a co-guardian or successor guardian

A petition to terminate a guardianship established by the juvenile court, to appoint a co-guardian or successor guardian, or to modify or supplement orders regarding the guardianship must be filed and heard in juvenile court. The procedures described in rule 5.570 must be followed, and *Juvenile Wardship Petition* (form JV–600) and *Petition to Modify Previous Orders—Change of Circumstances* (form JV–740) must be used. The hearing on the motion may be held simultaneously with any regularly scheduled hearing regarding the child. *(Formerly Rule 1496.2, adopted, eff. Jan. 1, 2003. As amended, eff. July 1, 2006. Renumbered Rule 5.815 and amended, eff. Jan. 1, 2007. As amended, eff. July 1, 2016.)*

Research References

Treatises and Practice Aids

Witkin, California Summary 10th Parent and Child § 892, in General.

Rule 5.820. Termination of parental rights for child in foster care for 15 of the last 22 months

(a) Requirement (§§ 727.32(a), 16508.1)

Whenever a child has been declared a ward and has been in any foster care placement for 15 of the most recent 22 months, the probation department must follow the procedures described in section 727.31 to terminate the parental rights of the child's parents. The probation department is not required to follow these procedures if it has documented a compelling reason in the probation file, as defined in section 727.3(c), for determining that termination of parental rights would not be in the child's best interest, or if it has not provided the family with reasonable efforts necessary to achieve reunification.

(1) If the probation department sets a hearing under section 727.31, it must also make efforts to identify an approved family for adoption.

(2) If the probation department has determined that a compelling reason exists, it must document that reason in the case file. The documentation may be a separate document or may be included in another court document, such as the social study prepared for a permanency planning hearing.

(b) Calculating time in foster care (§ 727.32(d))

The following guidelines must be used to determine if the child has been in foster care for 15 of the most recent 22 months:

(1) Determine the date the child entered foster care, as defined in rule 5.502(a)(9). In some cases, this will be the date the child entered foster care as a dependent.

(2) Calculate the total number of months since the date in (1) that the child has spent in foster care. Do not start over if a new petition is filed or for any other reason.

(3) If the child is in foster care for a portion of a month, calculate the total number of days in foster care during that month. Add one month to the total number of months for every 30 days the child is in foster care.

(4) Exclude time during which the child was detained in the home of a parent or guardian; the child was living at home on formal or informal probation, at home on a trial home visit, or at home with no probationary status; the child was a runaway or "absent without leave" (AWOL); or the child was out of home in a non–foster care setting, including juvenile hall; California Department of Corrections and Rehabilitation, Division of Juvenile Justice; a ranch; a camp; a school; or any other locked facility.

(5) Once the total number of months in foster care has been calculated, determine how many of those months occurred within the most recent 22 months. If that number is 15 or more, the requirement in (a) applies.

(6) If the requirement in (a) has been satisfied once, there is no need to take additional action or provide additional documentation after any subsequent 22–month period. *(Formerly Rule 1496.3, adopted, eff. Jan. 1, 2003. As amended, eff.*

Jan. 1, 2006. Renumbered Rule 5.820 and amended, eff. Jan. 1, 2007.)

Research References

Treatises and Practice Aids

Witkin, California Summary 10th Parent and Child § 899, Termination Of Parental Rights.

Rule 5.825. Freeing wards for adoption

(a) Applicable law (§§ 294, 366.26, 727.2, 727.3, 727.31)

Except as provided in section 727.31, the procedures for termination of parental rights to free children described in that section for adoption are stated in sections 294 and 366.26. Rules 5.725 and 5.730 are applicable to these proceedings.

(b) Joint county protocol

In each county, the county probation department and the county child welfare department must jointly develop a protocol for freeing wards for adoption. The protocol should address questions such as:

(1) When and how will wards be referred to the licensed county adoption agency, or State Department of Social Services when it is acting as the adoption agency, for a determination of whether the ward is adoptable, as described by section 727.3(i)(2)?

(2) Once a finding has been made that the permanent plan for the ward must be adoption and the case is set for a section 727.31 hearing, how will the referral be made to the licensed county adoption agency, or to the State Department of Social Services when it is acting as the adoption agency, to prepare an adoption assessment, as required by section 727.3(j)?

(3) Will the probation department continue to have ongoing case management and supervision of the case, pending the termination of parental rights hearing?

(4) Will the probation department or the child welfare department prepare the notices and other legal documents required before a termination of parental rights hearing?

(5) In counties in which different judicial officers hear delinquency and dependency matters, what procedure will be used to ensure that the dependency judge will hear each 727.31 hearing?

(6) Will the probation department or the child welfare department prepare the petition for adoption and other forms needed after the 727.31 hearing to complete the adoption process? *(Formerly Rule 1496.5, adopted, eff. Jan. 1, 2001. As amended, eff. Jan. 1, 2006. Renumbered Rule 5.825 and amended, eff. Jan. 1, 2007.)*

Research References

Treatises and Practice Aids

Witkin, California Summary 10th Parent and Child § 899, Termination Of Parental Rights.

Rule 5.830. Sealing records (§ 781)

(a) Sealing records—former wards

(1) A former ward of the court may apply to petition the court to order juvenile records sealed. Determinations under section 781 may be made by the court in any county in which wardship was terminated. A court may seal the records of another court when it determines that it is appropriate to do so, and must make a determination on sealing those records if the case has been transferred to its jurisdiction under rules 5.610 and 5.612.

(2) At the time jurisdiction is terminated or the case is dismissed, the court must provide or instruct the probation department to provide form JV–595–INFO, *How to Ask the Court to Seal Your Records,* and form JV–595, *Request to Seal Juvenile Records*, to the ward if the court does not seal the ward's records under section 786. If the court does seal the ward's records under section 786, the court must provide or instruct the probation department to provide form JV–596–INFO, *Sealing of Records for Satisfactory Completion of Probation,* and a copy of the sealing order as provided in rule 5.840.

(3) *Application—submission*

(A) The application for a petition to seal records must be submitted to the probation department in the county in which wardship was terminated.

(B) The application for a petition to seal juvenile records may be submitted on form JV–595, *Request to Seal Juvenile Records,* or on another form that includes all required information.

(4) *Investigation*

If the applicant is at least 18 years of age, or if it has been at least five years since the applicant's probation was last terminated or since the applicant was cited to appear before a probation officer or was taken before a probation officer under section 626 or before any officer of a law enforcement agency, the probation officer must do all of the following:

(A) Prepare the petition;

(B) Conduct an investigation under section 781 and compile a list of cases and contact addresses of every agency or person that the probation department knows has a record of the ward's case—including the date of each offense, case number(s), and date when the case was closed—to be attached to the sealing petition;

(C) Prepare a report to the court with a recommendation supporting or opposing the requested sealing; and

(D) Within 90 days from receipt of the application if only the records of the investigating county are to be reviewed, or within 180 days from receipt of the application if records of other counties are to be reviewed:

(i) File the petition;

(ii) Set the matter for a hearing, which may be nonappearance; and

(iii) Notify the prosecuting attorney of the hearing.

(5) The court must review the petition and the report of the probation officer, and the court must grant or deny the petition.

(6) If the petition is granted, the court must order the sealing of all records described in section 781 using form JV–590, *Order to Seal Juvenile Records—Welfare and Institutions Code Section 781*, or a similar form. The order must apply in the county of the court hearing the petition and in all other counties in which there are juvenile records concerning the petitioner. If the court determines that sealing the records of another court for a petition that has not been transferred is

inappropriate, it must inform the petitioner that a petition to seal those records can be filed in the county where the other court is located.

(b) Sealing—nonwards

(1) For all other persons described in section 781, application may be submitted to the probation department in any county in which there is a juvenile record concerning the petitioner, and the procedures of (a) must be followed.

(2) When jurisdiction is terminated or the case is closed, the probation department must provide the following forms to individuals described under section 781(h)(1)(A) and (B):

(A) If the individual's records have not been sealed under section 786, form JV–595–INFO, *How to Ask the Court to Seal Your Records,* and form JV–595, *Request to Seal Juvenile Records;* or

(B) If the individual's records have been sealed under section 786, form JV–596–INFO, *Sealing of Records for Satisfactory Completion of Probation,* and a copy of the sealing order.

(c) Destruction of records

All records sealed must be destroyed according to section 781(d).

(d) Distribution of order

The clerk of the issuing court must:

(1) Send a copy of the order to each agency and official listed in the order; and

(2) Send a certified copy of the order to the clerk in each county in which a record is ordered sealed.

(e) Deadline for sealing

Each agency and official notified must immediately seal all records as ordered. *(Formerly Rule 1499, adopted, eff. Jan. 1, 1991. Renumbered Rule 1497, eff. Jan. 1, 1999. Renumbered Rule 5.830 and amended, eff. Jan. 1, 2007. As amended, eff. July 1, 2016.)*

Research References

Forms

West's California Judicial Council Forms JV-590, Order to Seal Juvenile Records.

West's California Judicial Council Forms JV-591, Acknowledgment Of Juvenile Record Sealed.

West's California Judicial Council Forms JV-595, Request to Seal Juvenile Records.

West's California Judicial Council Forms JV-595-INFO, How to Ask the Court to Seal Your Records.

Treatises and Practice Aids

Witkin, California Summary 10th Parent and Child § 444, Scope and Organization.

Witkin, California Summary 10th Parent and Child § 503, Petition and Order.

Rule 5.840. Dismissal of petition and sealing of records (§ 786)

(a) Applicability

This rule states the procedures to dismiss and seal the records of minors who are subject to section 786.

(b) Dismissal of petition

If the court finds that a minor subject to this rule has satisfactorily completed his or her informal or formal probation supervision, the court must order the petition dismissed. The court must not dismiss a petition if it was sustained based on the commission of an offense listed in subdivision (b) of section 707 when the minor was 14 or older unless the finding on that offense has been dismissed or was reduced to an offense not listed in subdivision (b) of section 707. The court may also dismiss prior petitions filed or sustained against the minor if they appear to the satisfaction of the court to meet the sealing and dismissal criteria in section 786. An unfulfilled order, condition, or restitution or an unpaid restitution fee must not be deemed to constitute unsatisfactory completion of probation supervision. The court may not extend the period of supervision or probation solely for the purpose of deferring or delaying eligibility for dismissal and sealing under section 786.

(c) Sealing of records

For any petition dismissed by the court under section 786, the court must also order sealed all records in the custody of the court, law enforcement agencies, the probation department, and the Department of Justice pertaining to those dismissed petition(s) using form JV–596, *Dismissal and Sealing of Records—Welfare and Institutions Code Section 786,* or a similar form. The court may also seal records pertaining to these cases in the custody of other public agencies upon a request by an individual who is eligible to have records sealed under section 786, if the court determines that sealing the additional record(s) will promote the successful reentry and rehabilitation of the individual. The prosecuting attorney, probation officer, and court must have access to these records as specifically provided in section 786. Access to the records for research purposes must be provided as required in section 787.

(d) Destruction of records

The court must specify in its order the date by which all sealed records must be destroyed. For court records this date may be no earlier than the date the subject of the order attains age 21 and no later than the end of the time frame set forth in section 781(d). For all other records, the date may be no earlier than the date the subject of the order attains age 18, and no later than the time frame set forth in section 781(d) unless that time frame expires prior to the date the subject attains 18 years of age.

(e) Distribution of order

The clerk of the issuing court must send a copy of the order to each agency and official listed in the order and provide a copy of the order to the individual whose records have been sealed and his or her attorney. The court shall also provide or instruct the probation department to provide the individual with form JV–596–INFO, *Sealing of Records for Satisfactory Completion of Probation*.

(f) Deadline for sealing

Each agency, individual, and official notified must immediately seal all records as ordered and advise the court that its sealing order has been completed using form JV–591, *Acknowledgment of Juvenile Record Sealed,* or another means. *(Adopted, eff. July 1, 2016.)*

Research References

Forms

West's California Judicial Council Forms JV-591, Acknowledgment Of Juvenile Record Sealed.

West's California Judicial Council Forms JV-595-INFO, How to Ask the Court to Seal Your Records.

West's California Judicial Council Forms JV-596-INFO, Sealing Of Records for Satisfactory Completion Of Probation.

Chapter 14

NONMINOR DEPENDENT

Rule 5.900. Nonminor dependent—preliminary provisions (§§ 224.1(b), 295, 303, 366, 366.3, 388, 391, 607(a))

(a) Applicability

(1) The provisions of this chapter apply to nonminor dependents as defined in section 11400(v).

(2) Nothing in the Welfare and Institutions Code or in the California Rules of Court restricts the ability of the juvenile court to maintain dependency jurisdiction or delinquency jurisdiction over a person, 18 years of age and older, who does not meet the eligibility requirements for status as a nonminor dependent and to proceed as to that person under the relevant sections of the Welfare and Institutions Code and California Rules of Court.

(b) Purpose

(1) Maintaining juvenile court jurisdiction under sections 300 or 450 over a person as a nonminor dependent is the result of a consensual agreement between the person and child welfare services agency or the probation department for a voluntary placement in a supervised setting and includes the agreement between the social worker or probation officer and the person to work together to implement the mutually developed supervised placement agreement or reentry agreement.

(2) Maintaining juvenile court jurisdiction and supervision by the child welfare services agency or probation department under sections 300, 450, 601, or 602 over a person as a nonminor dependent is for the purpose of implementing the mutually developed Transitional Independent Living Case Plan and providing support, guidance, and foster care services to the person as a nonminor dependent so he or she is able to successfully achieve independence, including relationships with caring and committed adults who can serve as lifelong connections.

(c) Legal status

(1) Nothing in the Welfare and Institutions Code, including sections 340, 366.2, and 369.5, or in the California Rules of Court provides legal custody of a nonminor dependent to the child welfare services agency or the probation department or abrogates any right the nonminor dependent, as a person who has attained 18 years of age, may have as an adult under California law.

(2) A nonminor dependent retains all his or her legal decisionmaking authority as an adult. The decisionmaking authority of a nonminor dependent under delinquency jurisdiction may be limited by and subject to the care, supervision, custody, conduct, and maintenance orders in section 727.

(d) Conduct of hearings

(1) All hearings involving a person who is a nonminor dependent must be conducted in a manner that respects the person's legal status as an adult.

(2) Unless there is a contested issue of fact or law, the hearings must be informal and nonadversarial and all parties must work collaboratively with the nonminor dependent as he or she moves toward the achievement of his or her Transitional Independent Living Case Plan goals.

(3) The nonminor dependent may designate his or her attorney to appear on his or her behalf at a hearing under this chapter.

(e) Telephone appearance

(1) The person who is the subject of the hearing may appear, at his or her request, by telephone at a hearing to terminate juvenile court jurisdiction held under rule 5.555, a status review hearing under rule 5.903, or a hearing on a request to have juvenile court jurisdiction resumed held under rule 5.906. Rule 5.531 applies to telephone appearances under this paragraph.

(2) The court may require the nonminor dependent or the person requesting to return to juvenile court jurisdiction and foster care to appear personally on a showing of good cause and a showing that the personal appearance will not create an undue hardship for him or her.

(3) The telephone appearance must be permitted at no cost to the nonminor dependent or the person requesting to return juvenile court jurisdiction and foster care.

(f) Separate court file

The clerk of the superior court must open a separate court file for nonminor dependents under the dependency, delinquency, or transition jurisdiction of the court that ensures the confidentiality of the nonminor dependent and allows access only to those listed in section 362.5. *(Adopted, eff. Jan. 1, 2012. As amended, eff. Jan. 1, 2014.)*

Research References

Treatises and Practice Aids

Witkin, California Summary 10th Parent and Child § 444, Scope and Organization.

Witkin, California Summary 10th Parent and Child § 699A, (New) in General.

Witkin, California Summary 10th Parent and Child § 699B, (New) Status Review Hearings.

Rule 5.903. Nonminor dependent status review hearing (§§ 224.1(b), 295, 366.1, 366.3, 366.31)

(a) Purpose

The primary purpose of the nonminor dependent status review hearing is to focus on the goals and services described in the nonminor dependent's Transitional Independent Living Case Plan and the efforts and progress made toward achieving independence and establishing lifelong connections with caring and committed adults.

(b) Setting and conduct of a nonminor dependent status review hearing

(1) A status review hearing for a nonminor dependent conducted by the court or by a local administrative review panel must occur no less frequently than once every 6 months.

(2) The hearing must be placed on the appearance calendar, held before a judicial officer, and recorded by a court reporter under any of the following circumstances:

(A) The hearing is the first hearing following the nonminor dependent's 18th birthday;

(B) The hearing is the first hearing following the resumption of juvenile court jurisdiction over a person as a nonminor dependent under rule 5.906;

(C) The nonminor dependent or the nonminor dependent's attorney requests that the hearing be conducted by the court; or

(D) It has been 12 months since the hearing was conducted by the court.

(3) The hearing may be attended, as appropriate, by participants invited by the nonminor dependent in addition to those entitled to notice under (c).

(4) The nonminor dependent may appear by telephone as provided in rule 5.900 at a hearing conducted by the court.

(5) The hearing must be continued for no more than five court days for the social worker, probation officer, or nonminor dependent to submit additional information as ordered by the court if the court determines that the report and Transitional Independent Living Case Plan submitted by the social worker or probation officer do not provide the information required by (d)(1) and the court is unable to make all the findings and orders required by (e).

(c) Notice of hearing (§ 295)

(1) The social worker or probation officer must serve written notice of the hearing in the manner provided in section 295, and to all persons required to receive notice under section 295, except notice to the parents of the nonminor dependent is not required.

(2) The written notice served on the nonminor dependent must include:

(A) A statement that he or she may appear for the hearing by telephone; and

(B) Instructions about the local court procedures for arranging to appear and appearing at the hearing by telephone.

(3) Proof of service of notice must be filed by the social worker or probation officer at least five court days before the hearing.

(d) Reports

(1) The social worker or probation officer must submit a report to the court that includes information regarding:

(A) The continuing necessity for the nonminor dependent's placement and the facts supporting the conclusion reached;

(B) The appropriateness of the nonminor dependent's current foster care placement;

(C) The nonminor dependent's plans to remain under juvenile court jurisdiction including the criteria in section 11403(b) that he or she meets;

(D) The efforts made by the social worker or probation officer to help the nonminor dependent meet the criteria in section 11403(b);

(E) Verification that the nonminor dependent was provided with the information, documents, and services as required under section 391(e);

(F) How and when the Transitional Independent Living Case Plan was developed, including the nature and the extent of the nonminor dependent's participation in its development, and for the nonminor dependent who has elected to have the Indian Child Welfare Act continue to apply, the extent of consultation with the tribal representative;

(G) The efforts made by the social worker or probation officer to comply with the nonminor dependent's Transitional Independent Living Case Plan, including efforts to finalize the permanent plan and prepare him or her for independence;

(H) Progress made toward meeting the Transitional Independent Living Case Plan goals and the need for any modifications to assist the nonminor dependent in attaining the goals;

(I) The efforts made by the social worker or probation officer to maintain relationships between the nonminor dependent and individuals who are important to him or her, including the efforts made to establish and maintain relationships with caring and committed adults who can serve as a lifelong connection;

(J) The efforts made by the social worker or probation officer to establish or maintain the nonminor dependent's relationship with his or her siblings who are under the juvenile court's jurisdiction as required in section 366(a)(1)(D);

(K) For a nonminor dependent whose case plan is continued court-ordered family reunification services, the information required in section 366.31(d); and

(L) For a nonminor who has returned to the home of the parent or former legal guardian, whether continued juvenile court jurisdiction is necessary and the facts in support of that conclusion.

(2) The social worker or probation officer must submit with his or her report the Transitional Independent Living Case Plan.

(3) The social worker or probation officer must file with the court the report prepared for the hearing and the Transitional Independent Living Case Plan at least 10 calendar days before the hearing, and provide copies of the report and other documents to the nonminor dependent, all attorneys of record, and for the nonminor dependent who has elected to have the Indian Child Welfare Act continue to apply, the tribal representative.

(e) Findings and orders

The court must consider the safety of the nonminor dependent, and the following judicial findings and orders must be made and included in the written court documentation of the hearing:

(1) *Findings*

(A) Whether notice was given as required by law;

(B) Whether the nonminor dependent's continuing placement is necessary;

(C) Whether the nonminor dependent's current placement is appropriate;

(D) Whether the Transitional Independent Living Case Plan includes a plan for the nonminor dependent to satisfy one or more of the criteria in section 11403(b);

(E) The specific criteria in section 11403(b) the nonminor dependent satisfied since the last hearing held under this rule;

(F) The specific criteria in section 11403(b) it is anticipated the nonminor dependent will satisfy during the next six months;

(G) Whether reasonable efforts were made and assistance provided by the social worker or probation officer to help the nonminor dependent establish and maintain compliance with section 11403(b);

(H) Whether the nonminor dependent was provided with the information, documents, and services as required under section 391(e);

(I) Whether the Transitional Independent Living Case Plan was developed jointly by the nonminor dependent and the social worker or probation officer, reflects the living situation and services that are consistent in the nonminor dependent's opinion with what he or she needs to gain independence, and sets out the benchmarks that indicate how both will know when independence can be achieved;

(J) For the nonminor dependent who has elected to have the Indian Child Welfare Act continue to apply, whether the representative from his or her tribe was consulted during the development of the Transitional Independent Living Case Plan;

(K) Whether reasonable efforts were made by the social worker or probation officer to comply with the Transitional Independent Living Case Plan, including efforts to finalize the nonminor dependent's permanent plan and prepare him or her for independence;

(L) Whether the Transitional Independent Living Case Plan includes appropriate and meaningful independent living skill services that will assist him or her with the transition from foster care to independent living;

(M) Whether the nonminor dependent signed and received a copy of his or her Transitional Independent Living Case Plan;

(N) The extent of progress made by the nonminor dependent toward meeting the Transitional Independent Living Case Plan goals and any modifications needed to assist in attaining the goals;

(O) Whether reasonable efforts were made by the social worker or probation officer to maintain relationships between the nonminor dependent and individuals who are important to him or her, including the efforts made to establish and maintain relationships with caring and committed adults who can serve as lifelong connections;

(P) Whether reasonable efforts were made by the social worker or probation officer to establish or maintain the nonminor dependent's relationship with his or her siblings who are under the juvenile court's jurisdiction as required in section 366(a)(1)(D);

(Q) For a nonminor dependent whose case plan is continued court-ordered family reunification services, the findings required in section 366.31(d); and

(R) For a nonminor who has returned to the home of the parent or former legal guardian, whether continued juvenile court jurisdiction is necessary.

(2) *Orders*

(A) Order the continuation of juvenile court jurisdiction and set a nonminor dependent review hearing under this rule within six months, and:

(i) Order a permanent plan consistent with the nonminor dependent's Transitional Independent Living Case Plan, and

(ii) Specify the likely date by which independence is anticipated to be achieved; and

(iii) For a nonminor dependent whose parents are receiving court-ordered family reunification services:

a. Order the continuation of reunification services;

b. Order the termination of reunification services; or

c. Order that the nonminor may reside in the home of the parent or former legal guardian and that juvenile court jurisdiction is terminated or that juvenile court jurisdiction is continued under section 303(a) and a status review hearing is set for within six months.

(B) Order the continuation of juvenile court jurisdiction and set a hearing to consider termination of juvenile court jurisdiction over a nonminor under rule 5.555 within 30 days; or

(C) Order termination of juvenile court jurisdiction pursuant to rule 5.555 if this nonminor dependent status review hearing was heard at the same time as a hearing under rule 5.555.

(Adopted, eff. Jan. 1, 2012. As amended, eff. Jan. 1, 2014.)

Research References

Forms

West's California Judicial Council Forms JV-281, Notice Of Hearing--Nonminor Dependent Review Hearing / Other.

Treatises and Practice Aids

Witkin, California Summary 10th Parent and Child § 673, Child in Foster Care.

Witkin, California Summary 10th Parent and Child § 697, Status Review Hearings.

Witkin, California Summary 10th Parent and Child § 452E, (New) Termination Of Jurisdiction Over Minor.

Witkin, California Summary 10th Parent and Child § 452F, (New) Termination Of Jurisdiction Over Nonminor.

Witkin, California Summary 10th Parent and Child § 669A, (New) Review Hearings Just Before and After Minor Attains Age 18.

Witkin, California Summary 10th Parent and Child § 699A, (New) in General.

Witkin, California Summary 10th Parent and Child § 699B, (New) Status Review Hearings.

Witkin, California Summary 10th Parent and Child § 699C, (New) Request for Resumption Of Jurisdiction.

Rule 5.906. Request by nonminor for the juvenile court to resume jurisdiction (§§ 224.1(b), 303, 388(e), 388.1)

(a) Purpose

This rule provides the procedures that must be followed when a nonminor wants to have juvenile court jurisdiction assumed or resumed over him or her as a nonminor dependent as defined in subdivisions (v) or (aa) of section 11400.

(b) Contents of the request

(1) The request to have the juvenile court assume or resume jurisdiction must be made on the *Request to Return to Juvenile Court Jurisdiction and Foster Care* (form JV–466).

(2) The request must be liberally construed in favor of its sufficiency. It must be verified by the nonminor or if the nonminor is unable to provide verification due to a medical condition, the nonminor's representative, and to the extent known to the nonminor or the nonminor's representative, must include the following information:

(A) The nonminor's name and date of birth;

(B) The nonminor's address and contact information, unless the nonminor requests that this information be kept confidential from those persons entitled to access to the juvenile court file, including his or her parents, by filing *Confidential Information—Request to Return to Juvenile Court Jurisdiction and Foster Care* (form JV–468). Form JV–468 must be kept in the court file under seal, and only the court, the child welfare services agency, the probation department, or the Indian tribe with an agreement under section 10553.1 to provide child welfare services to Indian children (Indian tribal agency), the attorney for the child welfare services agency, the probation department, or the Indian tribe, and the nonminor's attorney may have access to this information;

(C) The name and action number or court file number of the nonminor's case and the name of the juvenile court that terminated its dependency jurisdiction, delinquency jurisdiction, or transition jurisdiction;

(D) The date the juvenile court entered the order terminating its dependency jurisdiction, delinquency jurisdiction, or transition jurisdiction;

(E) If the nonminor wants his or her parents or former legal guardians to receive notice of the filing of the request and the hearing, the name and residence addresses of the nonminor's parents or former guardians;

(F) The name and telephone number of the court-appointed attorney who represented the nonminor at the time the juvenile court terminated its dependency jurisdiction, delinquency jurisdiction, or transition jurisdiction if the nonminor wants that attorney to be appointed to represent him or her for the purposes of the hearing on the request;

(G) If the nonminor is an Indian child within the meaning of the Indian Child Welfare Act and chooses to have the Indian Child Welfare Act apply to him or her, the name of the tribe and the name, address, and telephone number of his or her tribal representative;

(H) If the nonminor had a Court Appointed Special Advocate (CASA) when he or she was a dependent or ward of the court and wants the CASA to receive notice of the filing of the request and the hearing, the CASA's name;

(I) The condition or conditions under section 11403(b) that the nonminor intends to satisfy; and

(J) Whether the nonminor requires assistance to maintain or secure an appropriate, supervised placement, or is in need of immediate placement and will agree to a supervised placement under a voluntary reentry agreement.

(3) The court may dismiss without prejudice a request filed under this rule that is not verified.

(c) Filing the request

(1) The form JV–466 must be completed and verified by the nonminor or the nonminor's representative if the nonminor is unable to provide verification due to a medical condition, and may be filed by the nonminor or the county child welfare services, probation department, or Indian tribe (placing agency) on behalf of the nonminor.

(2) For the convenience of the nonminor, the form JV–466 and, if the nonminor wishes to keep his or her contact information confidential, the *Confidential Information—Request to Return to Juvenile Court Jurisdiction and Foster Care* (form JV–468) may be:

(A) Filed with the juvenile court that maintained general jurisdiction or for cases petitioned under section 388.1, in the court that established the guardianship or had jurisdiction when the adoption was finalized; or

(B) Submitted to the juvenile court in the county in which the nonminor currently resides, after which:

(i) The court clerk must record the date and time received on the face of the originals submitted and provide a copy of the originals marked as received to the nonminor at no cost to him or her.

(ii) To ensure receipt of the original form JV–466 and, if submitted, the form JV–468 by the court of general jurisdiction within five court days as required in section 388(e), the court clerk must forward those originals to the clerk of the court of general jurisdiction within two court days of submission of the originals by the nonminor.

(iii) The court in the county in which the nonminor resides is responsible for all costs of processing, copying, and forwarding the form JV–466 and form JV–468 to the clerk of the court of general jurisdiction.

(iv) The court clerk in the county in which the nonminor resides must retain a copy of the documents submitted.

(v) The form JV–466 and, if submitted, the form JV–468 must be filed immediately upon receipt by the clerk of the juvenile court of general jurisdiction.

(C) For a nonminor living outside the state of California, the form JV–466 and, if the nonminor wishes to keep his or her contact information confidential, the form JV–468 must be filed with the juvenile court of general jurisdiction.

(3) If form JV–466 is filed by the nonminor, within two court days of its filing with the clerk of the court in the county

of general jurisdiction, the clerk of that court must notify the placing agency that was supervising the nonminor when juvenile court jurisdiction was terminated that the nonminor has filed form JV–466 and provide the placing agency with the nonminor's contact information. The notification must be by telephone, fax, e-mail, or other method approved by the presiding juvenile court judge that will ensure prompt notification and inform the placing agency that a copy of form JV–466 will be served on the agency and that one is currently available in the office of the juvenile court clerk.

(4) If form JV–466 has not been filed at the time the nonminor completes the voluntary reentry agreement described in section 11400(z), the placing agency must file form JV–466 on the nonminor's behalf within 15 court days of the date the voluntary reentry agreement was signed, unless the nonminor files form JV–466 prior to the expiration of the 15 court days.

(5) No filing fees are required for the filing of form JV–466 and, if filed, form JV–468. An endorsed, filed copy of each form filed must be provided at no cost to the nonminor or the placing agency that filed the request on the nonminor's behalf.

(d) Determination of prima facie showing

(1) Within three court days of the filing of form JV–466 with the clerk of the juvenile court of general jurisdiction, a juvenile court judicial officer must review the form JV–466 and determine whether a prima facie showing has been made that the nonminor meets all of the criteria set forth below in (d)(1)(A)–(D) and enter an order as set forth in (d)(2) or (d)(3).

(A) The nonminor was previously under juvenile court jurisdiction subject to an order for foster care placement on the date he or she attained 18 years of age, or the nonminor is eligible to seek assumption on of dependency jurisdiction pursuant to the provisions of subdivision (c) of section 388.1;

(B) The nonminor has not attained 21 years of age;

(C) The nonminor wants assistance to maintain or secure an appropriate, supervised placement or is in need of immediate placement and agrees to a supervised placement under a voluntary reentry agreement; and

(D) The nonminor intends to satisfy at least one of the eligibility criteria in section 11403(b).

(2) If the court determines that a prima facie showing has not been made, the court must enter a written order denying the request, listing the issues that resulted in the denial and informing the nonminor that a new form JV–466 may be filed when those issues are resolved.

(A) The court clerk must serve on the nonminor:

(i) A copy of the written order;

(ii) A blank copy of *Request to Return to Juvenile Court Jurisdiction and Foster Care* (form JV–466) and *Confidential Information—Request to Return to Juvenile Court Jurisdiction and Foster Care* (form JV–468);

(iii) A copy of *How to Ask to Return to Juvenile Court Jurisdiction and Foster Care* (form JV–464–INFO); and

(iv) The names and contact information for those attorneys approved by the court to represent children in juvenile court proceedings who have agreed to provide a consultation to any nonminor whose request was denied due to the failure to make a prima facie showing.

(B) The court clerk must serve on the placing agency a copy of the written order.

(C) Service must be by personal service or first-class mail within two court days of the issuance of the order.

(D) A proof of service must be filed.

(3) If the judicial officer determines that a prima facie showing has been made, the judicial officer must issue a written order:

(A) Directing the court clerk to set the matter for a hearing, and

(B) Appointing an attorney to represent the nonminor solely for the hearing on the request.

(e) Appointment of attorney

(1) If the nonminor included on the form JV–466 a request for the appointment of the court-appointed attorney who represented the nonminor during the period of time he or she was a ward or dependent or nonminor dependent, the judicial officer must appoint that attorney solely for the hearing on the request, if the attorney is available to accept such an appointment.

(2) If the nonminor did not request the appointment of his or her former court-appointed attorney, the judicial officer must appoint an attorney to represent the nonminor solely for the hearing on the request. The attorney must be selected from the panel or organization of attorneys approved by the court to represent children in juvenile court proceedings.

(3) In addition to complying with the requirements in (g)(1) for service of notice of the hearing, the juvenile court clerk must notify the attorney of his or her appointment as soon as possible, but no later than one court day from the date the order for his or her appointment was issued under (d)(3). This notification must be made by telephone, fax, e-mail, or other method approved by the presiding juvenile court judge that will ensure prompt notification. The notice must also include the nonminor's contact information and inform the attorney that a copy of the form JV–466 will be served on him or her and that one is currently available in the office of the juvenile court clerk.

(4) If the request is granted, the court must continue the attorney's appointment to represent the nonminor regarding matters related to his or her status as a nonminor dependent until the jurisdiction of the juvenile court is terminated, unless the court finds that the nonminor would not benefit from the appointment of an attorney.

(A) In order to find that a nonminor would not benefit from the appointment of an attorney, the court must find all of the following:

(i) The nonminor understands the nature of the proceedings;

(ii) The nonminor is able to communicate and advocate effectively with the court, other attorneys, and other parties, including social workers, probation officers, and other professionals involved in the case; and

(iii) Under the circumstances of the case, the nonminor would not gain any benefit from representation by an attorney.

(B) If the court finds that the nonminor would not benefit from representation by an attorney, the court must make a finding on the record as to each of the criteria in (e)(4)(A) and state the reasons for each finding.

(5) Representation of the nonminor by the court-appointed attorney for the hearing on the request to return to juvenile court jurisdiction and for matters related to his or her status as a nonminor dependent must be at no cost to the nonminor.

(6) If the nonminor chooses to be represented by an attorney other than a court-appointed attorney, the fees for an attorney retained by the nonminor are the nonminor's responsibility.

(f) Setting the hearing

(1) Within two court days of the issuance of the order directing the court clerk to do so, the court clerk must set a hearing on the juvenile court's calendar within 15 court days from the date the form JV–466 was filed with the court of general jurisdiction.

(2) The hearing must be placed on the appearance calendar, heard before a juvenile court judicial officer, and recorded by a court reporter.

(g) Notice of hearing

(1) The juvenile court clerk must serve notice as soon as possible, but no later than five court days before the date the hearing is set, as follows:

(A) The notice of the date, time, place, and purpose of the hearing and a copy of the form JV–466 must be served on the nonminor, the nonminor's attorney, the child welfare services agency, the probation department, or the Indian tribal agency that was supervising the nonminor when the juvenile court terminated its delinquency, dependency, or transition jurisdiction over the nonminor, and the attorney for the child welfare services agency, the probation department, or the Indian tribe.

(B) The notice of the date, time, place, and purpose of the hearing must be served on the nonminor's parents only if the nonminor included in the form JV–466 a request that notice be provided to his or her parents.

(C) The notice of the date, time, place, and purpose of the hearing must be served on the nonminor's tribal representative if the nonminor is an Indian child and indicated on the form JV–466 his or her choice to have the Indian Child Welfare Act apply to him or her as a nonminor dependent.

(D) The notice of the date, time, place, and purpose of the hearing must be served on the local CASA office if the nonminor had a CASA and included on the form JV–466 a request that notice be provided to his or her former CASA.

(2) The written notice served on the nonminor dependent must include:

(A) A statement that the nonminor may appear for the hearing by telephone; and

(B) Instructions regarding the local juvenile court procedures for arranging to appear and appearing at the hearing by telephone.

(3) Service of the notice must be by personal service or by first-class mail.

(4) Proof of service of notice must be filed by the juvenile court clerk at least two court days prior to the hearing.

(h) Reports

(1) The social worker, probation officer, or Indian tribal agency case worker (tribal case worker) must submit a report to the court that includes:

(A) Confirmation that the nonminor was previously under juvenile court jurisdiction subject to an order for foster care placement when he or she attained 18 years of age and that he or she has not attained 21 years of age, or is eligible to petition the court to assume jurisdiction over the nonminor pursuant to section 388.1;

(B) The condition or conditions under section 11403(b) that the nonminor intends to satisfy;

(C) The social worker, probation officer, or tribal case worker's opinion as to whether continuing in a foster care placement is in the nonminor's best interests and recommendation about the assumption or resumption of juvenile court jurisdiction over the nonminor as a nonminor dependent;

(D) Whether the nonminor and the placing agency have entered into a reentry agreement for placement in a supervised setting under the placement and care responsibility of the placing agency;

(E) The type of placement recommended if the request to return to juvenile court jurisdiction and foster care is granted;

(F) If the type of placement recommended is a placement in a setting where minor dependents also reside, the results of the background check of the nonminor under section 16504.5.

(i) The background check under section 16504.5 is required only if a minor dependent resides in the placement under consideration for the nonminor.

(ii) A criminal conviction is not a bar to a return to foster care and the resumption of juvenile court jurisdiction over the nonminor as a nonminor dependent.

(2) At least two court days before the hearing, the social worker, probation officer, or tribal case worker must file the report and any supporting documentation with the court and provide a copy to the nonminor and to his or her attorney of record; and

(3) If the court determines that the report and other documentation submitted by the social worker, probation officer, or tribal case worker does not provide the information required by (h)(1) and the court is unable to make the findings and orders required by (i), the hearing must be continued for no more than five court days for the social worker, probation officer, tribal case worker, or nonminor to submit additional information as ordered by the court.

(i) Findings and orders

The court must read and consider, and state on the record that it has read and considered, the report; the supporting documentation submitted by the social worker, probation officer, or tribal case worker; the evidence submitted by the nonminor; and any other evidence. The following judicial findings and orders must be made and included in the written court documentation of the hearing:

(1) *Findings*

(A) Whether notice was given as required by law;

(B) Whether the nonminor was previously under juvenile court jurisdiction subject to an order for foster care placement when he or she attained 18 years of age, or meets the requirements of subparagraph (5) of subdivision (c) of section 388.1;

(C) Whether the nonminor has attained 21 years of age;

(D) Whether the nonminor intends to satisfy a condition or conditions under section 11403(b);

(E) The condition or conditions under section 11403(b) that the nonminor intends to satisfy;

(F) Whether continuing or reentering and remaining in a foster care placement is in the nonminor's best interests;

(G) Whether the nonminor and the placing agency have entered into a reentry agreement for placement in a supervised setting under the placement and care responsibility of the placing agency; and

(H) Whether a nonminor who is an Indian child chooses to have the Indian Child Welfare Act apply to him or her as a nonminor dependent.

(2) *Orders*

(A) If the court finds that the nonminor has not attained 21 years of age, that the nonminor intends to satisfy at least one condition under section 11403(b), and that the nonminor and placing agency have entered into a reentry agreement, the court must:

(i) Grant the request and enter an order assuming or resuming juvenile court jurisdiction over the nonminor as a nonminor dependent and vesting responsibility for the nonminor's placement and care with the placing agency;

(ii) Order the social worker, probation officer, or tribal case worker to develop with the nonminor and file with the court within 60 days a new Transitional Independent Living Case Plan;

(iii) Order the social worker or probation officer to consult with the tribal representative regarding a new Transitional Independent Living Case Plan for the nonminor who chooses to have the Indian Child Welfare Act apply to him or her as a nonminor dependent and who is not under the supervision of a tribal case worker;

(iv) Set a nonminor dependent status review hearing under rule 5.903 within the next six months; and

(v) Make the findings and enter the appropriate orders under (e)(4) regarding appointment of an attorney for the nonminor.

(B) If the court finds that the nonminor has not attained 21 years of age, but the nonminor does not intend to satisfy at least one of the conditions under section 11403(b) and/or the nonminor and placing agency have not entered into a reentry agreement, the court must:

(i) Enter an order denying the request, listing the reasons for the denial, and informing the nonminor that a new form JV–466 may be filed when those circumstances change;

(ii) Enter an order terminating the appointment of the attorney appointed by the court to represent the nonminor, effective seven calendar days after the hearing; and

(iii) In addition to the service of a copy of the written order as required in (i)(3), the juvenile court clerk must cause to be served on the nonminor a blank copy of the *Request to Return to Juvenile Court Jurisdiction and Foster Care* (form JV–466) and *Confidential Information—Request to Return to Juvenile Court Jurisdiction and Foster Care* (form JV–468), and a copy of *How to Ask to Return to Juvenile Court Jurisdiction and Foster Care* (form JV–464–INFO).

(C) If the court finds that the nonminor is over 21 years of age, the court must:

(i) Enter an order denying the request to have juvenile court jurisdiction resumed; and

(ii) Enter an order terminating the appointment of the attorney appointed by the court to represent the nonminor, effective seven calendar days after the hearing.

(3) *Findings and orders: service*

(A) The written findings and order must be served by the juvenile court clerk on all persons provided with notice of the hearing under (g)(1).

(B) Service must be by personal service or first-class mail within three court days of the issuance of the order.

(C) A proof of service must be filed.

(Adopted, eff. Jan. 1, 2012. As amended, eff. July 1, 2012; Jan. 1, 2014; Jan. 1, 2016.)

Research References

Forms

West's California Judicial Council Forms JV-466, Request to Return to Juvenile Court Jurisdiction and Foster Care.

West's California Judicial Council Forms JV-468, Confidential Information--Request to Return to Juvenile Court Jurisdiction and Foster Care.

West's California Judicial Council Forms JV-470, Findings and Orders Regarding Prima Facie Showing on Nonminor's Request to Reenter Foster Care.

West's California Judicial Council Forms JV-472, Findings and Orders After Hearing to Consider Nonminor's Request to Reenter Foster Care.

West's California Judicial Council Forms JV-464-INFO, How to Ask to Return to Juvenile Court Jurisdiction and Foster Care.

Treatises and Practice Aids

Witkin, California Summary 10th Parent and Child § 444, Scope and Organization.

Witkin, California Summary 10th Parent and Child § 699A, (New) in General.

Witkin, California Summary 10th Parent and Child § 699B, (New) Status Review Hearings.

Witkin, California Summary 10th Parent and Child § 699C, (New) Request for Resumption Of Jurisdiction.

Title 7

PROBATE RULES

Chapter 7

SPOUSAL OR DOMESTIC PARTNER PROPERTY PETITIONS

Rule 7.301. Spousal or domestic partner property petition filed with petition for probate

A petition for spousal or domestic partner property determination or confirmation must be filed separately from a petition for probate of will or for letters of administration, even if both petitions are filed at the same time. The two petitions must be filed under the same case number. *(Adopted, eff. Jan. 1, 2000. As amended, eff. Jan. 1, 2002; Jan. 1, 2007.)*

Research References

Forms

West's California Code Forms, Probate § 13651 Form 1, Spousal or Domestic Partner Property Petition-- Judicial Council Form DE-221.

Treatises and Practice Aids

Witkin, California Summary 10th Wills and Probate § 4, Probate Rules.

Witkin, California Summary 10th Wills and Probate § 829, Nature Of Proceeding.

Title 8

APPELLATE RULES

Division 1

RULES RELATING TO THE SUPREME COURT AND COURTS OF APPEAL

Chapter 5

JUVENILE APPEALS AND WRITS

Article 1

GENERAL PROVISIONS

Rule 8.400. Application

The rules in this chapter govern:

(1) Appeals from judgments or appealable orders in:

(A) Cases under Welfare and Institutions Code sections 300, 601, and 602; and

(B) Actions to free a child from parental custody and control under Family Code section 7800 et seq. and Probate Code section 1516.5; ~~and~~

(2) Appeals of orders requiring or dispensing with an alleged father's consent for the adoption of a child under Family Code section 7662 et seq.; and

~~(2)~~(3) Writ petitions under Welfare and Institutions Code sections 366.26 and 366.28. *(Formerly Rule 37, adopted, eff. Jan. 1, 2005. As amended, eff. Jan. 1, 2006. Renumbered Rule 8.400 and amended, eff. Jan. 1, 2007. As amended, eff. Jan. 1, 2008; July 1, 2010; Jan. 1, 2017.)*

Research References

Forms

West's California Judicial Council Forms JV-800, Notice Of Appeal--Juvenile.

Treatises and Practice Aids

Witkin, California Summary 10th Parent and Child § 355, Review on Appeal.

Witkin, California Summary 10th Parent and Child § 444, Scope and Organization.

Witkin, California Summary 10th Parent and Child § 460, Appeal from Determination Of Residence.

Witkin, California Summary 10th Parent and Child § 709, in General.

Witkin, California Summary 10th Parent and Child § 712, Notice Of Appeal.

Witkin, California Summary 10th Parent and Child § 716, in General.

Witkin, California Summary 10th Parent and Child § 895, Alternative Felony Misdemeanor.

Witkin, California Summary 10th Parent and Child § 918, in General.

Witkin, California Summary 10th Parent and Child § 675A, (New) Setting Selection and Implementation Hearing.

Rule 8.401. Confidentiality

(a) References to juveniles or relatives in documents

To protect the anonymity of juveniles involved in juvenile court proceedings:

(1) In all documents filed by the parties in proceedings under this chapter, a juvenile must be referred to by first name and last initial; but if the first name is unusual or other circumstances would defeat the objective of anonymity, the initials of the juvenile may be used.

(2) In opinions that are not certified for publication and in court orders, a juvenile may be referred to either by first name and last initial or by his or her initials. In opinions that are certified for publication in proceedings under this chapter, a juvenile must be referred to by first name and last initial; but if the first name is unusual or other circumstances would defeat the objective of anonymity, the initials of the juvenile may be used.

(3) In all documents filed by the parties and in all court orders and opinions in proceedings under this chapter, if use of the full name of a juvenile's relative would defeat the objective of anonymity for the juvenile, the relative must be referred to by first name and last initial; but if the first name is unusual or other circumstances would defeat the objective of anonymity for the juvenile, the initials of the relative may be used.

(b) Access to filed documents

(1) Except as provided in (2)–(3), the record on appeal and documents filed by the parties in proceedings under this chapter may be inspected only by the reviewing court and appellate project personnel, the parties or their attorneys, and other persons the court may designate.

(2) Filed documents that protect anonymity as required by (a) may be inspected by any person or entity that is considering filing an amicus curiae brief.

(3) Access to records that are sealed or confidential under authority other than Welfare and Institutions Code section 827 is governed by rules 8.45–8.47 and the applicable statute, rule, sealing order, or other authority.

(c) Access to oral argument

The court may limit or prohibit public admittance to oral argument. *(Adopted, eff. July 1, 2010. As amended, eff. Jan. 1, 2012; Jan. 1, 2014.)*

Research References

Forms

West's California Judicial Council Forms JV-800, Notice Of Appeal--Juvenile.

Treatises and Practice Aids

Witkin, California Summary 10th Parent and Child § 444, Scope and Organization.

Witkin, California Summary 10th Parent and Child § 709, in General.

Article 2

APPEALS

Rule 8.403. Right to appointment of appellate counsel and prerequisites for appeal

(a) Welfare and Institutions Code section 601 or 602 proceedings

In appeals of proceedings under Welfare and Institutions Code section 601 or 602, the child is entitled to court-appointed counsel.

(b) Welfare and Institutions Code section 300 proceedings

(1) Any judgment, order, or decree setting a hearing under Welfare and Institutions Code section 366.26 may be reviewed on appeal following the order at the Welfare and Institutions Code section 366.26 hearing only if:

(A) The procedures in rules 8.450 and 8.452 regarding writ petitions in these cases have been followed; and

(B) The petition for an extraordinary writ was summarily denied or otherwise not decided on the merits.

(2) The reviewing court may appoint counsel to represent an indigent child, parent, or guardian.

(3) Rule 5.661 governs the responsibilities of trial counsel in Welfare and Institutions Code section 300 proceedings with regard to appellate representation of the child. *(Adopted, eff. July 1, 2010. As amended, eff. Jan. 1, 2013.)*

Research References

Treatises and Practice Aids

Witkin, California Summary 10th Parent and Child § 444, Scope and Organization.

Witkin, California Summary 10th Parent and Child § 701, in General.

Witkin, California Summary 10th Parent and Child § 708, Counsel on Appeal.

Witkin, California Summary 10th Parent and Child § 913, Minor's Right to Appeal.

Rule 8.404. Stay pending appeal

The court must not stay an order or judgment pending an appeal unless suitable provision is made for the maintenance, care, and custody of the child. *(Adopted, eff. July 1, 2010.)*

Research References

Treatises and Practice Aids

Witkin, California Summary 10th Parent and Child § 709, in General.

Witkin, California Summary 10th Parent and Child § 713, in General.

Witkin, California Summary 10th Parent and Child § 919, Record on Appeal.

Rule 8.405. Filing the appeal

(a) Notice of appeal

(1) To appeal from a judgment or appealable order under these rules, the appellant must file a notice of appeal in the superior court. Any notice of appeal on behalf of the child in a Welfare and Institutions Code section 300 proceeding must be authorized by the child or the child's CAPTA guardian ad litem.

(2) The appellant or the appellant's attorney must sign the notice of appeal.

(3) The notice of appeal must be liberally construed, and is sufficient if it identifies the particular judgment or order being appealed. The notice need not specify the court to which the appeal is taken; the appeal will be treated as taken to the Court of Appeal for the district in which the superior court is located.

(b) Superior court clerk's duties

(1) When a notice of appeal is filed, the superior court clerk must immediately:

(A) Send a notification of the filing to:

(i) Each party other than the appellant, including the child if the child is 10 years of age or older;

(ii) The attorney of record for each party;

(iii) Any person currently awarded by the juvenile court the status of the child's de facto parent;

(iv) Any Court Appointed Special Advocate (CASA) volunteer;

(v) If the court knows or has reason to know that an Indian child is involved, the Indian custodian, if any, and tribe of the child or the Bureau of Indian Affairs, as required under Welfare and Institutions Code section 224.2; and

(vi) The reviewing court clerk; and

(B) Notify the reporter by telephone and in writing to prepare a reporter's transcript and deliver it to the clerk within 20 days after the notice of appeal is filed.

(2) The notification must show the name of the appellant, the date it was sent, the number and title of the case, and the date the notice of appeal was filed. If the information is available, the notification must also include:

(A) The name, address, telephone number, e-mail address, and California State Bar number of each attorney of record in the case;

(B) The name of the party that each attorney represented in the superior court; and

(C) The name, address, telephone number and e-mail address of any unrepresented party.

(3) The notification to the reviewing court clerk must also include a copy of the notice of appeal and any sequential list of reporters made under rule 2.950.

(4) A copy of the notice of appeal is sufficient notification if the required information is on the copy or is added by the superior court clerk.

(5) The sending of a notification is a sufficient performance of the clerk's duty despite the discharge, disqualification, suspension, disbarment, or death of the attorney.

(6) Failure to comply with any provision of this subdivision does not affect the validity of the notice of appeal. *(Adopted, eff. July 1, 2010. As amended, eff. Jan. 1, 2016.)*

Research References

Forms

West's California Judicial Council Forms JV-800, Notice Of Appeal--Juvenile.

Treatises and Practice Aids

Witkin, California Summary 10th Parent and Child § 712, Notice Of Appeal.

Rule 8.406. Time to appeal

(a) Normal time

(1) Except as provided in (2) and (3), a notice of appeal must be filed within 60 days after the rendition of the judgment or the making of the order being appealed.

(2) In matters heard by a referee not acting as a temporary judge, a notice of appeal must be filed within 60 days after the referee's order becomes final under rule 5.540(c).

(3) When an application for rehearing of an order of a referee not acting as a temporary judge is denied under rule 5.542, a notice of appeal from the referee's order must be filed within 60 days after that order is served under rule 5.538(b)(3) or 30 days after entry of the order denying rehearing, whichever is later.

(b) Cross-appeal

If an appellant timely appeals from a judgment or appealable order, the time for any other party to appeal from the same judgment or order is either the time specified in (a) or 20 days after the superior court clerk sends notification of the first appeal, whichever is later.

(c) No extension of time; late notice of appeal

Except as provided in rule 8.66, no court may extend the time to file a notice of appeal. The superior court clerk must mark a late notice of appeal "Received [date] but not filed," notify the party that the notice was not filed because it was late, and send a copy of the marked notice of appeal to the district appellate project.

(d) Premature notice of appeal

A notice of appeal is premature if filed before the judgment is rendered or the order is made, but the reviewing court may treat the notice as filed immediately after the rendition of judgment or the making of the order. *(Adopted, eff. July 1, 2010. As amended, eff. July 1, 2010; Jan. 1, 2016.)*

Research References

Forms

West's California Judicial Council Forms JV-800, Notice Of Appeal--Juvenile.

Treatises and Practice Aids

Witkin, California Summary 10th Parent and Child § 357, Effect Of Late Appeal.

Witkin, California Summary 10th Parent and Child § 712, Notice Of Appeal.

Rule 8.407. Record on appeal

(a) Normal record: clerk's transcript

The clerk's transcript must contain:

(1) The petition;

(2) Any notice of hearing;

(3) All court minutes;

(4) Any report or other document submitted to the court;

(5) The jurisdictional and dispositional findings and orders;

(6) The judgment or order appealed from;

(7) Any application for rehearing;

(8) The notice of appeal and any order pursuant to the notice;

(9) Any transcript of a sound or sound-and-video recording tendered to the court under rule 2.1040;

(10) Any application for additional record and any order on the application;

(11) Any opinion or dispositive order of a reviewing court in the same case; and~~;~~

(12) Any written motion or notice of motion by any party, with supporting and opposing memoranda and attachments, and any written opinion of the court.

(b) Normal record: reporter's transcript

The reporter's transcript must contain any oral opinion of the court and:

~~(1) Except as provided in (2), the oral proceedings at any hearing that resulted in the order or judgment being appealed;~~

~~(2)~~(1) In appeals from dispositional orders, the oral proceedings at hearings on:

(A) Jurisdiction;~~ and~~

(B) Disposition;~~ and~~

~~(B)~~(C) Any motion by the appellant that was denied in whole or in part; and

(D) In cases under Welfare and Institutions Code section 300 et seq., hearings:

(i) On detention; and

(ii) At which a parent of the child made his or her initial appearance.

(2) In appeals from an order terminating parental rights under Welfare and Institutions Code section 300 et seq., the oral proceedings at all section 366.26 hearings.

(3) ~~Any oral opinion of the court~~ In all other appeals, the oral proceedings at any hearing that resulted in the order or judgment being appealed.

(c) Application in superior court for addition to normal record

(1) Any party or Indian tribe that has intervened in the proceedings may apply to the superior court for inclusion of any oral proceedings in the reporter's transcript.

(2) An application for additional record must describe the material to be included and explain how it may be useful in the appeal.

(3) The application must be filed in the superior court with the notice of appeal or as soon thereafter as possible, and will be treated as denied if it is filed after the record is sent to the reviewing court.

(4) The clerk must immediately present the application to the trial judge.

(5) Within five days after the application if filed, the judge must order that the record include as much of the additional material as the judge finds proper to fully present the points raised by the applicant. Denial of the application does not preclude a motion in the reviewing court for augmentation under rule 8.155.

(6) If the judge does not rule on the application within the time prescribed by (5), the requested material-other than exhibits-must be included in the clerk's transcript or the reporter's transcript without a court order.

(7) The clerk must immediately notify the reporter if additions to the reporter's transcript are required under (5) or (6).

(d) Agreed or settled statement

To proceed by agreed or settled statement, the parties must comply with rule 8.344 or 8.346, as applicable.

(e) Transmitting exhibits

Exhibits that were admitted in evidence, refused, or lodged may be transmitted to the reviewing court as provided in rule 8.224. *(Formerly Rule 37.1, adopted, eff. Jan. 1, 2005. Renumbered Rule 8.404 and amended, eff. Jan. 1, 2007. Renumbered Rule 8.407 and amended, eff. July 1, 2010. As amended, eff. Jan. 1, 2014; Jan. 1, 2017.)*

Research References

Treatises and Practice Aids

Witkin, California Summary 10th Parent and Child § 713, in General.

Witkin, California Summary 10th Parent and Child § 721, Record.

Witkin, California Summary 10th Parent and Child § 725, Notice Of Intent and Record.

Witkin, California Summary 10th Parent and Child § 919, Record on Appeal.

Rule 8.408. Record in multiple appeals in the same case

If more than one appeal is taken from the same judgment or related order, only one appellate record need be prepared, which must be filed within the time allowed for filing the record in the latest appeal. *(Formerly Rule 8.406, adopted, eff. Jan. 1, 2007. Renumbered Rule 8.408, eff. July 1, 2010.)*

Research References

Treatises and Practice Aids

Witkin, California Summary 10th Parent and Child § 713, in General.

Witkin, California Summary 10th Parent and Child § 714, Preparing and Sending Record.

Witkin, California Summary 10th Parent and Child § 919, Record on Appeal.

Rule 8.409. Preparing and sending the record

(a) Application

This rule applies to appeals in juvenile cases except cases governed by rule 8.416.

(b) Form of record

The clerk's and reporter's transcripts must comply with rules 8.45–8.47, relating to sealed and confidential records, and with rule 8.144.

(c) Preparing and certifying the transcripts

Within 20 days after the notice of appeal is filed:

(1) The clerk must prepare and certify as correct an original of the clerk's transcript and one copy each for the appellant, the respondent, the child's Indian tribe if the tribe has intervened, and the child if the child is represented by counsel on appeal or if a recommendation has been made to the Court of Appeal for appointment of counsel for the child under rule 8.403(b)(2) and that recommendation is either pending with or has been approved by the Court of Appeal but counsel has not yet been appointed; and

(2) The reporter must prepare, certify as correct, and deliver to the clerk an original of the reporter's transcript and the same number of copies as (1) requires of the clerk's transcript. On request, and unless the trial court orders otherwise, the reporter must provide the Court of Appeal and any party with a copy of the reporter's transcript in computer-readable format. Each computer-readable copy must comply with the ~~format, labeling, content, and numbering requirements of Code of Civil Procedure section 271(b)~~ requirements of rule 8.144(a)(4).

(d) Extension of time

(1) The superior court may not extend the time to prepare the record.

(2) The reviewing court may order one or more extensions of time for preparing the record, including a reporter's transcript, not exceeding a total of 60 days, on receipt of:

(A) A declaration showing good cause; and

(B) In the case of a reporter's transcript, certification by the superior court presiding judge, or a court administrator designated by the presiding judge, that an extension is reasonable and necessary in light of the workload of all reporters in the court.

(e) Sending the record

(1) When the transcripts are certified as correct, the court clerk must immediately send:

(A) The original transcripts to the reviewing court, noting the sending date on each original; and

(B) One copy of each transcript to the appellate counsel for the following, if they have appellate counsel:

(i) The appellant;

(ii) The respondent;

(iii) The child's Indian tribe if the tribe has intervened; and

(iv) The child.

(2) If appellate counsel has not yet been retained or appointed for the appellant or the respondent, or if a recommendation has been made to the Court of Appeal for appointment of counsel for the child under rule 8.403(b)(2) and that recommendation is either pending with or has been approved by the Court of Appeal but counsel has not yet been appointed, when the transcripts are certified as correct, the clerk must send that counsel's copy of the transcripts to the district appellate project. If a tribe that has intervened is not represented by counsel when the transcripts are certified as correct, the clerk must send that counsel's copy of the transcripts to the tribe.

(3) The clerk must not send a copy of the transcripts to the Attorney General or the district attorney unless that office represents a party. *(Formerly Rule 37.2, adopted, eff. Jan. 1, 2005. Renumbered Rule 8.408 and amended, eff. Jan. 1, 2007. Renumbered Rule 8.409 and amended, eff. July 1, 2010. As amended, eff. Jan. 1, 2013; Jan. 1, 2014; Jan. 1, 2015; Jan. 1, 2017.)*

Research References

Treatises and Practice Aids

Witkin, California Summary 10th Parent and Child § 713, in General.

Witkin, California Summary 10th Parent and Child § 714, Preparing and Sending Record.

Witkin, California Summary 10th Parent and Child § 919, Record on Appeal.

Rule 8.410. Augmenting and correcting the record in the reviewing court

(a) Omissions

If, after the record is certified, the superior court clerk or the reporter learns that the record omits a document or transcript that any rule or order requires to be included, without the need for a motion or court order, the clerk must promptly copy and certify the document or the reporter must promptly prepare and certify the transcript and the clerk must promptly send the document or transcript—as an augmentation of the record—to all those who are listed under 8.409(e).

(b) Augmentation or correction by the reviewing court

(1) On motion of a party or on its own motion, the reviewing court may order the record augmented or corrected as provided in rule 8.155(a) and (c).

(2) If, after the record is certified, the trial court amends or recalls the judgment or makes any other order in the case, the trial court clerk must notify each entity and person to whom the record is sent under rule 8.409(e). *(Adopted, eff. July 1, 2010. As amended, eff. Jan. 1, 2015.)*

Research References

Treatises and Practice Aids

Witkin, California Summary 10th Parent and Child § 713, in General.

Witkin, California Summary 10th Parent and Child § 721, Record.

Witkin, California Summary 10th Parent and Child § 725, Notice Of Intent and Record.

Witkin, California Summary 10th Parent and Child § 919, Record on Appeal.

Rule 8.411. Abandoning the appeal

(a) How to abandon

An appellant may abandon the appeal at any time by filing an abandonment of the appeal.. The abandonment must be authorized by the appellant and signed by either the appellant or the appellant's attorney of record. In a Welfare and Institutions Code section 300 proceeding in which the child is the appellant, the abandonment must be authorized by the child or, if the child is not capable of giving authorization, by the child's CAPTA guardian ad litem.

(b) Where to file; effect of filing

(1) If the record has not been filed in the reviewing court, the appellant must file the abandonment in the superior court. The filing effects a dismissal of the appeal and restores the superior court's jurisdiction.

(2) If the record has been filed in the reviewing court, the appellant must file the abandonment in that court. The reviewing court may dismiss the appeal and direct immediate issuance of the remittitur.

(c) Clerk's duties

(1) If the abandonment is filed in the superior court, the clerk must immediately send a notification of the abandonment to:

(A) Every other party;

(B) The reviewing court; and

(C) The reporter if the appeal is abandoned before the reporter has filed the transcript.

(2) If the abandonment is filed in the reviewing court and the reviewing court orders the appeal dismissed, the clerk must immediately send a notification of the order of dismissal to every party. *(Adopted, eff. July 1, 2010. As amended, eff. Jan. 1, 2016.)*

Research References

Treatises and Practice Aids

Witkin, California Summary 10th Parent and Child § 715A, (New) Abandoning Appeal.

Witkin, California Summary 10th Parent and Child § 919A, (New) Abandoning Appeal.

Rule 8.412. Briefs by parties and amici curiae

(a) Contents, form, and length

(1) Rule 8.200 governs the briefs that may be filed by parties and amici curiae.

(2) Except as provided in (3), rule 8.204 governs the form and contents of briefs. Rule 8.216 also applies in appeals in which a party is both appellant and respondent.

(3) Rule 8.360(b) governs the length of briefs.

(b) Time to file

(1) Except in appeals governed by rule 8.416, the appellant must serve and file the appellant's opening brief within 40 days after the record is filed in the reviewing court.

(2) The respondent must serve and file the respondent's brief within 30 days after the appellant's opening brief is filed.

(3) The appellant must serve and file any reply brief within 20 days after the respondent's brief is filed.

(4) In dependency cases in which the child is not an appellant but has appellate counsel, the child must serve and file any brief within 10 days after the respondent's brief is filed.

(5) Rule 8.220 applies if a party fails to timely file an appellant's opening brief or a respondent's brief, but the period specified in the notice required by that rule must be 30 days.

(c) Extensions of time

The superior court may not order any extensions of time to file briefs. Except in appeals governed by rule 8.416, the reviewing court may order extensions of time for good cause.

(d) Failure to file a brief

(1) Except in appeals governed by rule 8.416, if a party fails to timely file an appellant's opening brief or a respondent's brief, the reviewing court clerk must promptly notify the party's counsel or the party, if not represented, in writing that the brief must be filed within 30 days after the notice is sent and that failure to comply may result in one of the following sanctions:

(A) If the brief is an appellant's opening brief:

(i) If the appellant is the county, the court will dismiss the appeal;

(ii) If the appellant is other than the county and is represented by appointed counsel on appeal, the court will relieve that appointed counsel and appoint new counsel;

(iii) If the appellant is other than the county and is not represented by appointed counsel, the court will dismiss the appeal.

(B) If the brief is a respondent's brief, the court will decide the appeal on the record, the opening brief, and any oral argument by the appellant.

(2) If a party fails to comply with a notice under (1), the court may impose the sanction specified in the notice.

(3) Within the period specified in the notice under (1), a party may apply to the presiding justice for an extension of that period for good cause. If an extension is granted beyond the 30–day period and the brief is not filed within the extended period, the court may impose the sanction under (2) without further notice.

(e) Additional service requirements

(1) A copy of each brief must be served on the superior court clerk for delivery to the superior court judge.

(2) A copy of each brief must be served on the child's trial counsel, or, if the child is not represented by trial counsel, on the child's guardian ad litem appointed under rule 5.662.

(3) If the Court of Appeal has appointed counsel for any party:

(A) The county child welfare department and the People must serve two copies of their briefs on that counsel; and

(B) Each party must serve a copy of its brief on the district appellate project.

(4) In delinquency cases the parties must serve copies of their briefs on the Attorney General and the district attorney. In all other cases the parties must not serve copies of their briefs on the Attorney General or the district attorney unless that office represents a party.

(5) The parties must not serve copies of their briefs on the Supreme Court under rule 8.44(b)(1). *(Formerly Rule 37.3, adopted, eff. Jan. 1, 2005. Renumbered Rule 8.412 and amended, eff. Jan. 1, 2007. As amended, eff. July 1, 2007; July 1, 2010; Jan. 1, 2016.)*

Research References

Forms

West's California Judicial Council Forms JV-816, Application for Extension Of Time to File Brief (Juvenile Delinquency Case).
West's California Judicial Council Forms JV-817, Application for Extension Of Time to File Brief (Juvenile Dependency Case).
West's California Judicial Council Forms APP-012, Stipulation for Extension Of Time to File Brief (Civil Case).

Treatises and Practice Aids

Witkin, California Summary 10th Parent and Child § 711, Expedited Appeal.
Witkin, California Summary 10th Parent and Child § 715, Briefs.

Rule 8.416. Appeals from all terminations of parental rights; dependency appeals in Orange, Imperial, and San Diego Counties and in other counties by local rule

(a) Application

(1) This rule governs:

(A) Appeals from judgments or appealable orders of all superior courts terminating parental rights under Welfare and Institutions Code section 366.26 or freeing a child from parental custody and control under Family Code section 7800 et seq.; and

(B) Appeals from judgments or appealable orders in all juvenile dependency cases of:

(i) The Superior Courts of Orange, Imperial, and San Diego Counties; and

(ii) Other superior courts when the superior court and the District Court of Appeal with jurisdiction to hear appeals from that superior court have agreed and have adopted local rules providing that this rule will govern appeals from that superior court.

(2) In all respects not provided for in this rule, rules 8.403–8.412 apply.

(b) Form of record

(1) The clerk's and reporter's transcripts must comply with rules 8.45–8.467, relating to sealed and confidential records, and, except as provided in (2) and (3), with rule 8.144.

(2) In appeals under (a)(1)(A), the cover of the record must prominently display the title "Appeal From [Judgment or Order] Terminating Parental Rights Under [Welfare and Institutions Code Section 366.26 or Family Code Section 7800 et seq.]," whichever is appropriate.

(3) In appeals under (a)(1)(B), the cover of the record must prominently display the title "Appeal From [Judgment or Order] Under [Welfare and Institutions Code Section 300 et seq. or Family Code Section 7800 et seq.]," whichever is appropriate.

(c) Preparing, certifying, and sending the record

(1) Within 20 days after the notice of appeal is filed:

(A) The clerk must prepare and certify as correct an original of the clerk's transcript and one copy each for the appellant, the respondent, the district appellate project, the child's Indian tribe if the tribe has intervened, and the child if the child is represented by counsel on appeal or if a recommendation has been made to the Court of Appeal for appointment of counsel for the child under rule 8.403(b)(2) and that recommendation is either pending with or has been approved by the Court of Appeal but counsel has not yet been appointed; and

(B) The reporter must prepare, certify as correct, and deliver to the clerk an original of the reporter's transcript and the same number of copies as (A) requires of the clerk's transcript. On request, and unless the trial court orders otherwise, the reporter must provide the Court of Appeal and any party with a copy of the reporter's transcript in computer-readable format. Each computer-readable copy must comply with the ~~format, labeling, content, and numbering requirements of Code of Civil Procedure section 271(b)~~ requirements of rule 8.144(a)(4).

(2) When the clerk's and reporter's transcripts are certified as correct, the clerk must immediately send:

(A) The original transcripts to the reviewing court by the most expeditious method, noting the sending date on each original; and

(B) One copy of each transcript to the district appellate project and to the appellate counsel for the following, if they have appellate counsel, by any method as fast as United States Postal Service express mail:

(i) The appellant;

(ii) The respondent;

(iii) The child's Indian tribe if the tribe has intervened; and

(iv) The child.

(3) If appellate counsel has not yet been retained or appointed for the appellant or the respondent or if a recommendation has been made to the Court of Appeal for appointment of counsel for the child under rule 8.403(b)(2) and that recommendation is either pending with or has been approved by the Court of Appeal but counsel has not yet been appointed, when the transcripts are certified as correct, the clerk must send that counsel's copies of the transcripts to the district appellate project. If a tribe that has intervened is not represented by counsel when the transcripts are certified as correct, the clerk must send that counsel's copy of the transcripts to the tribe.

(d) Augmenting or correcting the record

(1) Except as provided in (2) and (3), rule 8.410 governs any augmentation or correction of the record.

(2) An appellant must serve and file any motion for augmentation or correction within 15 days after receiving the record. A respondent must serve and file any such motion within 15 days after the appellant's opening brief is filed.

(3) The clerk and the reporter must prepare any supplemental transcripts within 20 days, giving them the highest priority.

(4) The clerk must certify and send any supplemental transcripts as required by (c).

(e) Time to file briefs

(1) To permit determination of the appeal within 250 days after the notice of appeal is filed, the appellant must serve and file the appellant's opening brief within 30 days after the record is filed in the reviewing court.

(2) Rule 8.412(b) governs the time for filing other briefs.

(f) Extensions of time

The superior court may not order any extensions of time to prepare the record or to file briefs; the reviewing court may order extensions of time, but must require an exceptional showing of good cause.

(g) Failure to file a brief

Rule 8.412(d) applies if a party fails to timely file an appellant's opening brief or a respondent's brief, but the period specified in the notice required by that rule must be 15 days.

(h) Oral argument and submission of the cause

(1) Unless the reviewing court orders otherwise, counsel must serve and file any request for oral argument no later than 15 days after the appellant's reply brief is filed or due to be filed. Failure to file a timely request will be deemed a waiver.

(2) The court must hear oral argument within 60 days after the appellant's last reply brief is filed or due to be filed, unless the court extends the time for good cause or counsel waive argument.

(3) If counsel waive argument, the cause is deemed submitted no later than 60 days after the appellant's reply brief is filed or due to be filed. *(Formerly Rule 37.4, adopted, eff. Jan. 1, 2005. Renumbered Rule 8.416 and amended, eff. Jan. 1, 2007. As amended, eff. July 1, 2010; Jan. 1, 2015; Jan. 1, 2017.)*

Research References

Forms

West's California Judicial Council Forms JV-817, Application for Extension Of Time to File Brief (Juvenile Dependency Case).

Treatises and Practice Aids

Witkin, California Summary 10th Parent and Child § 444, Scope and Organization.

Witkin, California Summary 10th Parent and Child § 531, Determining Adequacy Of Notice.

Witkin, California Summary 10th Parent and Child § 711, Expedited Appeal.

Witkin, California Summary 10th Parent and Child § 713, in General.
Witkin, California Summary 10th Parent and Child § 714, Preparing and Sending Record.
Witkin, California Summary 10th Parent and Child § 715, Briefs.
Witkin, California Summary 10th Parent and Child § 675A, (New) Setting Selection and Implementation Hearing.

Article 3

WRITS

Rule 8.450. Notice of intent to file writ petition to review order setting hearing under Welfare and Institutions Code section 366.26

(a) Application

Rules 8.450–8.452 and 8.490 govern writ petitions to review orders setting a hearing under Welfare and Institutions Code section 366.26.

(b) Purpose

Rules 8.450–8.452 are intended to encourage and assist the reviewing courts to determine on their merits all writ petitions filed under these rules within the 120–day period for holding a hearing under Welfare and Institutions Code section 366.26.

(c) Who may file

The petitioner's trial counsel, or in the absence of trial counsel, the party, is responsible for filing any notice of intent and writ petition under rules 8.450–8.452. Trial counsel is encouraged to seek assistance from or consult with attorneys experienced in writ procedure.

(d) Extensions of time

The superior court may not extend any time period prescribed by rules 8.450–8.452. The reviewing court may extend any time period but must require an exceptional showing of good cause.

(e) Notice of intent

(1) A party seeking writ review under rules 8.450–8.452 must file in the superior court a notice of intent to file a writ petition and a request for the record.

(2) The notice must include all known dates of the hearing that resulted in the order under review.

(3) The notice must be authorized by the party intending to file the petition and must be signed by that party or by the attorney of record for that party.

(4) The date of the order setting the hearing is the date on which the court states the order on the record orally, or issues an order in writing, whichever occurs first. The notice of intent must be filed according to the following timeline requirements:

(A) If the party was present at the hearing when the court ordered a hearing under Welfare and Institutions Code section 366.26, the notice of intent must be filed within 7 days after the date of the order setting the hearing.

(B) If the party was notified of the order setting the hearing only by mail, the notice of intent must be filed within 12 days after the date the clerk mailed the notification.

(C) If the party was notified of the order setting the hearing by mail, and the notice was mailed to an address outside California but within the United States, the notice of intent must be filed within 17 days after the date the clerk mailed the notification.

(D) If the party was notified of the order setting the hearing by mail, and the notice was mailed to an address outside the United States, the notice of intent must be filed within 27 days after the date the clerk mailed the notification.

(E) If the order was made by a referee not acting as a temporary judge, the party has an additional 10 days to file the notice of intent as provided in rule 5.540(c).

(f) Premature or late notice of intent to file writ petition

(1) A notice of intent to file a writ petition under Welfare and Institutions Code section 366.26 is premature if filed before an order setting a hearing under Welfare and Institutions Code section 366.26 has been made.

(2) If a notice of intent is premature or late, the superior court clerk must promptly:

(A) Mark the notice of intent "Received [date] but not filed;"

(B) Return the marked notice of intent to the party with a notice stating that:

(i) The notice of intent was not filed either because it is premature, as no order setting a hearing under Welfare and Institutions Code section 366.26 has been made, or because it is late; and

(ii) The party should contact his or her attorney as soon as possible to discuss this notice, because the time available to take appropriate steps to protect the party's interests may be short; and

(C) Send a copy of the marked notice of intent and clerk's notice to the party's counsel of record, if applicable.

(g) Sending the notice of intent

(1) When the notice of intent is filed, the superior court clerk must immediately ~~mail~~ send a copy of the notice to:

(A) The attorney of record for each party;

(B) Each party, including the child if the child is 10 years of age or older;

(C) Any known sibling of the child who is the subject of the hearing if that sibling either is the subject of a dependency proceeding or has been adjudged to be a dependent child of the juvenile court as follows:

(i) If the sibling is under 10 years of age, on the sibling's attorney;

(ii) If the sibling is 10 years of age or over, on the sibling and the sibling's attorney.

(D) The mother, the father, and any presumed and alleged parents;

(E) The child's legal guardian, if any;

(F) Any person currently awarded by the juvenile court the status of the child's de facto parent;

(G) The probation officer or social worker;

(H) Any Court Appointed Special Advocate (CASA) volunteer;

(I) The grandparents of the child, if their address is known and if the parents' whereabouts are unknown; and

(J) If the court knows or has reason to know that an Indian child is involved, the Indian custodian, if any, and tribe of the child or the Bureau of Indian Affairs as required under Welfare and Institutions Code section 224.2.

(2) The clerk must promptly send by first-class mail, e-mail, or fax a copy of the notice of intent and a list of those to whom the notice of intent was sent to:

(A) The reviewing court; and

(B) The petitioner if the clerk ~~mailed~~ sent the notice of intent to the Indian custodian, tribe of the child, or the Bureau of Indian Affairs.

(3) If the party was notified of the order setting the hearing only by mail, the clerk must include the date that the notification was mailed.

(h) Preparing the record

When the notice of intent is filed, the superior court clerk must:

(1) Immediately notify each court reporter by telephone and in writing to prepare a reporter's transcript of the oral proceedings at each session of the hearing that resulted in the order under review and deliver the transcript to the clerk within 12 calendar days after the notice of intent is filed; and

(2) Within 20 days after the notice of intent is filed, prepare a clerk's transcript that includes the notice of intent, proof of service, and all items listed in rule 8.407(a).

(i) Sending the record

When the transcripts are certified as correct, the superior court clerk must immediately send:

(1) The original transcripts to the reviewing court by the most expeditious method, noting the sending date on each original, and

(2) One copy of each transcript to each counsel of record and any unrepresented party by any means as fast as United States Postal Service express mail.

(j) Reviewing court clerk's duties

(1) The reviewing court clerk must immediately lodge the notice of intent. When the notice is lodged, the reviewing court has jurisdiction of the writ proceedings.

(2) When the record is filed in the reviewing court, that court's clerk must immediately notify the parties, stating the date on which the 10–day period for filing the writ petition under rule 8.452(c)(1) will expire. *(Formerly Rule 38, adopted, eff. Jan. 1, 2005. As amended, eff. Jan. 1, 2006; July 1, 2006. Renumbered Rule 8.450 and amended, eff. Jan. 1, 2007. As amended, eff. Jan. 1, 2008; Jan. 1, 2009; July 1, 2010; Jan. 1, 2013; Jan. 1, 2017.)*

Commentary

Maribel M. v Superior Court, 61 Cal.App.4th 1469, 72 Cal.Rptr.2d 536 (1998), holds that the amendment to Rule 39.1B, effective January 1, 1998, is unconstitutional to the extent it would bar summary denial on the merits of Rule 39.1B petitions, because the amendment is inconsistent with controlling law, Welfare and Institutions Code 366.26(1), which allows summary denial.

Glen C. v. Superior Court, 78 Cal.App.4th 570, 93 Cal.Rptr.2d 103 (2000), announces that future petitions for writ review of juvenile court orders denying reunification services or setting implementation hearings will be summarily denied if they fail to comply with the procedural requirements of this section and Welfare and Institutions Code § 366.26. *Glen C.* also threatens to report attorneys who file procedurally inadequate petitions to the State Bar or to initiate sanction proceedings against them.

Applying Welfare and Institutions Code Section 366.26 (*l*) and subsection (d) of this Rule, *In re Charmice G., 66 Cal.App.4th 659, 78 Cal.Rptr.2d 212 (1998),* ruled that an order setting a Section 366.26 hearing is not an appealable order. Thus an order setting a hearing may be challenged only by special writ as provided in Section 366.26 (*l*), or by appeal from the subsequent order entered after the permanency planning hearing. *In re Anthony B., 72 Cal.App.4th 1017, 85 Cal.Rptr.2d 594 (1999),* holds that a party cannot appeal a collateral order (denying the mother supervised visitation) made at a hearing at which an order setting a Section 366.26 hearing is scheduled, unless the party first seeks writ review of the order under subsection (*l*).

Interpreting this rule and Welfare and Institutions Code section 366.26(*l*)(3), *In re A.H., 218 Cal.App.4th 337, 159 Cal.Rptr.3d 891 (2013), review denied,* held that parents who became upset and walked out of the 18-month review hearing before the judge could orally advise them of the writ requirement for challenging an order setting a section 366.26 hearing and who also failed to notify the court of a change in their permanent mailing address did not show good cause for noncompliance with the writ requirement. Thus the trial court properly denied a motion to vacate or modify, under section 388, a default judgment that placed the two dependent children with relatives.

In a dependency proceeding, the "waiver rule" ordinarily bars an appellate court from examining objections to prior appealable orders in an appeal from a subsequent appealable order. The waiver rule may, however, be relaxed when the defect complained of fundamentally undermined the statutory scheme and prevented the parent from securing the protections of the statutory scheme as a whole. *In re Janee J., 74 Cal.App.4th 198, 87 Cal.Rptr.2d 634 (1999), review denied November 17, 1999.*

Research References

Forms

West's California Judicial Council Forms JV-820, Notice Of Intent to File Writ Petition and Request for Record to Review Order Setting a Hearing Under Welfare and Institutions Code Section 366.26.

Treatises and Practice Aids

Witkin, California Summary 10th Parent and Child § 444, Scope and Organization.

Witkin, California Summary 10th Parent and Child § 701, in General.

Witkin, California Summary 10th Parent and Child § 705, in General.

Witkin, California Summary 10th Parent and Child § 716, in General.
Witkin, California Summary 10th Parent and Child § 717, in General.
Witkin, California Summary 10th Parent and Child § 720, Notice Of Intent.
Witkin, California Summary 10th Parent and Child § 721, Record.
Witkin, California Summary 10th Parent and Child § 722, Writ Petition and Response.
Witkin, California Summary 10th Parent and Child § 725, Notice Of Intent and Record.
Witkin, California Summary 10th Parent and Child § 920, Review by Extraordinary Writ.

Rule 8.452. Writ petition to review order setting hearing under Welfare and Institutions Code section 366.26

(a) Petition

(1) The petition must be liberally construed and must include:

(A) The identities of the parties;

(B) The date on which the superior court made the order setting the hearing;

(C) The date on which the hearing is scheduled to be held;

(D) A summary of the grounds of the petition; and

(E) The relief requested.

(2) The petition must be accompanied by a memorandum.

(b) Contents of the memorandum

(1) The memorandum must provide a summary of the significant facts, limited to matters in the record.

(2) The memorandum must state each point under a separate heading or subheading summarizing the point and support each point by argument and citation of authority.

(3) The memorandum must support any reference to a matter in the record by a citation to the record. The memorandum should explain the significance of any cited portion of the record and note any disputed aspects of the record.

(c) Serving and filing the petition and response

(1) The petition must be served and filed within 10 days after the record is filed in the reviewing court. The petitioner must serve a copy of the petition on:

(A) Each attorney of record;

(B) Any unrepresented party, including the child if the child is 10 years of age or older;

(C) Any known sibling of the child who is the subject of the hearing if that sibling either is the subject of a dependency proceeding or has been adjudged to be a dependent child of the juvenile court as follows:

(i) If the sibling is under 10 years of age, on the sibling's attorney;

(ii) If the sibling is 10 years of age or over, on the sibling and the sibling's attorney.

(D) The child's Court Appointed Special Advocate (CASA) volunteer;

(E) Any person currently awarded by the juvenile court the status of the child's de facto parent; and

(F) If the court sent the notice of intent to file the writ petition to an Indian custodian, tribe, or Bureau of Indian Affairs, then to that Indian custodian, tribe of the child, or the Bureau of Indian Affairs as required under Welfare and Institutions Code section 224.2.

(2) Any response must be served on each of the people and entities listed above and filed:

(A) Within 10 days—or, if the petition was served by mail, within 15 days—after the petition is filed; or

(B) Within 10 days after a respondent receives a request from the reviewing court for a response, unless the court specifies a shorter time.

(d) Order to show cause or alternative writ

If the court intends to determine the petition on the merits, it must issue an order to show cause or alternative writ.

(e) Augmenting or correcting the record in the reviewing court

(1) Except as provided in (2) and (3), rule 8.410 governs any augmentation or correction of the record.

(2) The petitioner must serve and file any request for augmentation or correction within 5 days—or, if the record exceeds 300 pages, within 7 days; or, if the record exceeds 600 pages, within 10 days—after receiving the record. A respondent must serve and file any such request within 5 days after the petition is filed or an order to show cause has issued, whichever is later.

(3) A party must attach to its motion a copy, if available, of any document or transcript that the party wants added to the record. The pages of the attachment must be consecutively numbered, beginning with the number one. If the reviewing court grants the motion, it may augment the record with the copy.

(4) If the party cannot attach a copy of the matter to be added, the party must identify it as required under rules 8.122 and 8.130.

(5) An order augmenting or correcting the record may grant no more than 15 days for compliance. The clerk and the reporter must give the order the highest priority.

(6) The clerk must certify and send any supplemental transcripts as required by rule 8.450(h). If the augmentation or correction is ordered, the time to file any petition or response is extended by the number of additional days granted to augment or correct the record.

(f) Stay

The reviewing court may stay the hearing set under Welfare and Institutions Code section 366.26, but must require an exceptional showing of good cause.

(g) Oral argument

(1) The reviewing court must hear oral argument within 30 days after the response is filed or due to be filed, unless the court extends the time for good cause or counsel waive argument.

(2) If argument is waived, the cause is deemed submitted not later than 30 days after the response is filed or due to be filed.

(h) Decision

(1) Absent exceptional circumstances, the reviewing court must decide the petition on the merits by written opinion.

(2) The reviewing court clerk must promptly notify the parties of any decision and must promptly send a certified copy of any writ or order to the court named as respondent.

(3) If the writ or order stays or prohibits proceedings set to occur within 7 days or requires action within 7 days—or in any other urgent situation—the reviewing court clerk must make a reasonable effort to notify the clerk of the respondent court by telephone or e-mail. The clerk of the respondent court must then notify the judge or officer most directly concerned.

(4) The reviewing court clerk need not give telephonic or e-mail notice of the summary denial of a writ, unless a stay previously issued will be dissolved.

(i) Filing, modification, finality of decision, and remittitur

Rule 8.490 governs the filing, modification, finality of decisions, and remittitur in writ proceedings under this rule. *(Formerly Rule 38.1, adopted, eff. Jan. 1, 2005. As amended, eff. Jan. 1, 2006. Renumbered Rule 8.452 and amended, eff. Jan. 1, 2007. As amended, eff. July 1, 2010; Jan. 1, 2017.)*

Commentary

See Rule 8.450.

Research References

Forms

West's California Judicial Council Forms JV-825, Petition for Extraordinary Writ (Cal. Rules Of Court, Rules 8.452, 8.456).

West's California Judicial Council Forms JV-826, Denial Of Petition (California Rules Of Court, Rules 8.452, 8.456).

Treatises and Practice Aids

Witkin, California Summary 10th Parent and Child § 701, in General.

Witkin, California Summary 10th Parent and Child § 705, in General.

Witkin, California Summary 10th Parent and Child § 716, in General.

Witkin, California Summary 10th Parent and Child § 717, in General.

Witkin, California Summary 10th Parent and Child § 720, Notice Of Intent.

Witkin, California Summary 10th Parent and Child § 721, Record.

Witkin, California Summary 10th Parent and Child § 722, Writ Petition and Response.

Witkin, California Summary 10th Parent and Child § 723, Hearing and Decision.

Witkin, California Summary 10th Parent and Child § 727, Hearing and Decision.

Witkin, California Summary 10th Parent and Child § 920, Review by Extraordinary Writ.

Rule 8.454. Notice of intent to file writ petition under Welfare and Institutions Code section 366.28 to review order designating specific placement of a dependent child after termination of parental rights

(a) Application

Rules 8.454–8.456 and 8.490 govern writ petitions to review placement orders following termination of parental rights entered on or after January 1, 2005. "Posttermination placement order" as used in this rule and rule 8.456 refers to orders following termination of parental rights.

(b) Purpose

The purpose of this rule is to facilitate and implement Welfare and Institutions Code section 366.28. Delays caused by appeals from court orders designating the specific placement of a dependent child after parental rights have been terminated may cause a substantial detriment to the child.

(c) Who may file

The petitioner's trial counsel, or, in the absence of trial counsel, the party, is responsible for filing any notice of intent and writ petition under rules 8.454–8.456. Trial counsel is encouraged to seek assistance from, or consult with, attorneys experienced in writ procedure.

(d) Extensions of time

The superior court may not extend any time period prescribed by rules 8.454–8.456. The reviewing court may extend any time period, but must require an exceptional showing of good cause.

(e) Notice of intent

(1) A party seeking writ review under rules 8.454–8.456 must file in the superior court a notice of intent to file a writ petition and a request for the record.

(2) The notice must include all known dates of the hearing that resulted in the order under review.

(3) The notice must be authorized by the party intending to file the petition and signed by the party or by the attorney of record for that party.

(4) The notice must be served and filed within 7 days after the date of the posttermination placement order or, if the order was made by a referee not acting as a temporary judge, within 7 days after the referee's order becomes final under rule 5.540(c). The date of the posttermination placement order is the date on which the court states the order on the record orally or in writing, whichever first occurs.

(5) If the party was notified of the posttermination placement order only by mail, the notice of intent must be filed within 12 days after the date that the clerk mailed the notification.

(f) Premature or late notice of intent to file writ petition

(1) A notice of intent to file a writ petition under Welfare and Institutions Code section 366.28 is premature if filed before a date for a posttermination placement order has been made. The reviewing court may treat the notice as filed immediately after the posttermination order has been made.

(2) The superior court clerk must mark a late notice of intent to file a writ petition under section 366.28 "Received [date] but not filed," notify the party that the notice was not filed because it was late, and send a copy of the marked notice to the party's counsel of record, if applicable.

(g) Sending the notice of intent

(1) When the notice of intent is filed, the superior court clerk must immediately ~~mail~~ send a copy of the notice to:

(A) The attorney of record for each party;

(B) Each party, including the child if the child is 10 years of age or older;

(C) Any known sibling of the child who is the subject of the hearing if that sibling either is the subject of a dependency proceeding or has been adjudged to be a dependent child of the juvenile court as follows:

(i) If the sibling is under 10 years of age, on the sibling's attorney;

(ii) If the sibling is 10 years of age or over, on the sibling and the sibling's attorney;

(D) Any prospective adoptive parent;

(E) The child's legal guardian if any;

(F) Any person currently awarded by the juvenile court the status of the child's de facto parent;

(G) The probation officer or social worker;

(H) The child's Court Appointed Special Advocate (CASA) volunteer, if any; and

(I) If the court knows or has reason to know that an Indian child is involved, the Indian custodian, if any, and tribe of the child or the Bureau of Indian Affairs as required under Welfare and Institutions Code section 224.2.

(2) The clerk must promptly send by first-class mail, e-mail, or fax a copy of the notice of intent and a list of those to whom the notice of intent was sent to:

(A) The reviewing court; and

(B) The petitioner if the clerk ~~mailed~~ sent a copy of the notice of intent to the Indian custodian, tribe of the child, or the Bureau of Indian Affairs.

(3) If the party was notified of the post placement order only by mail, the clerk must include the date that the notification was mailed.

(h) Preparing the record

When the notice of intent is filed, the superior court clerk must:

(1) Immediately notify each court reporter by telephone and in writing to prepare a reporter's transcript of the oral proceedings at each session of the hearing that resulted in the order under review and to deliver the transcript to the clerk within 12 calendar days after the notice of intent is filed; and

(2) Within 20 days after the notice of intent is filed, prepare a clerk's transcript that includes the notice of intent, proof of service, and all items listed in rule 8.407(a).

(i) Sending the record

When the transcripts are certified as correct, the superior court clerk must immediately send:

(1) The original transcripts to the reviewing court by the most expeditious method, noting the sending date on each original; and

(2) One copy of each transcript to each counsel of record and any unrepresented party and unrepresented custodian of the dependent child by any means as fast as United States Postal Service express mail.

(j) Reviewing court clerk's duties

(1) The reviewing court clerk must promptly lodge the notice of intent. When the notice is lodged, the reviewing court has jurisdiction over the writ proceedings.

(2) When the record is filed in the reviewing court, that court's clerk must immediately notify the parties, stating the date on which the 10–day period for filing the writ petition under rule 8.456(c)(1) will expire. *(Formerly Rule 38.2, adopted, eff. Jan. 1, 2005. As amended, eff. Jan. 1, 2006; July 1, 2006. Renumbered Rule 8.454 and amended, eff. Jan. 1, 2007. As amended, eff. Jan. 1, 2008; Jan. 1, 2009; July 1, 2010; July 1, 2013; Jan. 1, 2017.)*

Research References

Forms

West's California Judicial Council Forms JV-822. Notice Of Intent to File Writ Petition and Request for Record to Review Order Designating or Denying Specific Placement Of a Dependent Child After Termination Of Parental Rights...

Treatises and Practice Aids

Witkin, California Summary 10th Parent and Child § 704, Miscellaneous Orders.

Witkin, California Summary 10th Parent and Child § 716, in General.

Witkin, California Summary 10th Parent and Child § 724, in General.

Witkin, California Summary 10th Parent and Child § 725, Notice Of Intent and Record.

Witkin, California Summary 10th Parent and Child § 920, Review by Extraordinary Writ.

Witkin, California Summary 10th Parent and Child § 693C, (New) Nonemergency Removal from Prospective Adoptive Parent.

Rule 8.456. Writ petition under Welfare and Institutions Code section 366.28 to review order designating or denying specific placement of a dependent child after termination of parental rights

(a) Petition

(1) The petition must be liberally construed and must include:

(A) The identities of the parties;

(B) The date on which the superior court made the posttermination placement order;

(C) A summary of the grounds of the petition; and

(D) The relief requested.

(2) The petition must be accompanied by a memorandum.

(b) Contents of memorandum

(1) The memorandum must provide a summary of the significant facts, limited to matters in the record.

(2) The memorandum must state each point under a separate heading or subheading summarizing the point and support each point by argument and citation of authority.

(3) The memorandum must support any reference to a matter in the record by a citation to the record. The memorandum should explain the significance of any cited portion of the record and note any disputed aspects of the record.

(c) Serving and filing the petition and response

(1) The petition must be served and filed within 10 days after the record is filed in the reviewing court. The petitioner must serve the petition on:

(A) Each attorney of record;

(B) Any unrepresented party, including the child if the child is 10 years of age or older;

(C) Any known sibling of the child who is the subject of the hearing if that sibling either is the subject of a dependency proceeding or has been adjudged to be a dependent child of the juvenile court as follows:

(i) If the sibling is under 10 years of age, on the sibling's attorney;

(ii) If the sibling is 10 years of age or over, on the sibling and the sibling's attorney;

(D) Any prospective adoptive parent;

(E) The child's Court Appointed Special Advocate (CASA) volunteer;

(F) Any person currently awarded by the juvenile court the status of the child's de facto parent; and

(G) If the court sent the notice of intent to file the writ petition to an Indian custodian, tribe, or Bureau of Indian Affairs, then to that Indian custodian, tribe, or the Bureau of Indian Affairs as required under Welfare and Institutions Code section 224.2.

(2) Any response must be served on each of the people and entities listed in (1) and filed:

(A) Within 10 days—or, if the petition was served by mail, within 15 days—after the petition is filed; or

(B) Within 10 days after a respondent receives a request from the reviewing court for a response, unless the court specifies a shorter time.

(d) Order to show cause or alternative writ

If the court intends to determine the petition on the merits, it must issue an order to show cause or alternative writ.

(e) Augmenting or correcting the record in the reviewing court

(1) Except as provided in (2) and (3), rule 8.410 governs augmentation or correction of the record.

(2) The petitioner must serve and file any request for augmentation or correction within 5 days—or, if the record exceeds 300 pages, within 7 days; or, if the record exceeds 600 pages, within 10 days—after receiving the record. A respondent must serve and file any such request within 5 days after the petition is filed or an order to show cause has issued, whichever is later.

(3) A party must attach to its motion a copy, if available, of any document or transcript that it wants added to the record. The pages of the attachment must be consecutively numbered, beginning with the number one. If the reviewing court grants the motion, it may augment the record with the copy.

(4) If the party cannot attach a copy of the matter to be added, the party must identify it as required under rules 8.122 and 8.130.

(5) An order augmenting or correcting the record may grant no more than 15 days for compliance. The clerk and the reporter must give the order the highest priority.

(6) The clerk must certify and send any supplemental transcripts as required by rule 8.454(i). If the augmentation or correction is ordered, the time to file any petition or response is extended by the number of additional days granted to augment or correct the record.

(f) Stay

A request by petitioner for a stay of the posttermination placement order will not be granted unless the writ petition shows that implementation of the superior court's placement order pending the reviewing court's decision is likely to cause detriment to the child if the order is ultimately reversed.

(g) Oral argument

(1) The reviewing court must hear oral argument within 30 days after the response is filed or due to be filed, unless the court extends the time for good cause or counsel waive argument.

(2) If argument is waived, the cause is deemed submitted not later than 30 days after the response is filed or due to be filed.

(h) Decision

(1) Absent exceptional circumstances, the reviewing court must review the petition and decide it on the merits by written opinion.

(2) The reviewing court clerk must promptly notify the parties of any decision and must promptly send a certified copy of any writ or order to the court named as respondent.

(3) If the writ or order stays or requires action within 7 days—or in any other urgent situation—the reviewing court clerk must make a reasonable effort to notify the clerk of the respondent court by telephone or e-mail. The clerk of the respondent court must then notify the judge or officer most directly concerned.

(4) The reviewing court clerk need not give telephonic or e-mail notice of the summary denial of a writ, unless a stay previously issued and will be dissolved.

(5) Rule 8.490 governs the filing, modification, finality of decisions, and remittitur in writ proceedings under this rule.

(i) Right to appeal other orders

This section does not affect the right of a parent, a legal guardian, or the child to appeal any order that is otherwise appealable and that is issued at a hearing held under Welfare and Institutions Code section 366.26. *(Formerly Rule 38.3, adopted, eff. Jan. 1, 2005. As amended, eff. Jan. 1, 2006; Feb. 24, 2006. Renumbered Rule 8.456 and amended, eff. Jan. 1, 2007. As amended, eff. July 1, 2010; Jan. 1, 2017.)*

Research References

Forms

West's California Judicial Council Forms JV-825, Petition for Extraordinary Writ (Cal. Rules Of Court, Rules 8.452, 8.456).

West's California Judicial Council Forms JV-826, Denial Of Petition (California Rules Of Court, Rules 8.452, 8.456).

Treatises and Practice Aids

Witkin, California Summary 10th Parent and Child § 444, Scope and Organization.

Witkin, California Summary 10th Parent and Child § 704, Miscellaneous Orders.

Witkin, California Summary 10th Parent and Child § 716, in General.

Witkin, California Summary 10th Parent and Child § 717, in General.

Witkin, California Summary 10th Parent and Child § 722, Writ Petition and Response.

Witkin, California Summary 10th Parent and Child § 723, Hearing and Decision.

Witkin, California Summary 10th Parent and Child § 724, in General.
Witkin, California Summary 10th Parent and Child § 725, Notice Of Intent and Record.
Witkin, California Summary 10th Parent and Child § 726, Writ Petition.
Witkin, California Summary 10th Parent and Child § 727, Hearing and Decision.
Witkin, California Summary 10th Parent and Child § 920, Review by Extraordinary Writ.

Article 4

HEARING AND DECISION

Rule 8.470. Hearing and decision in the Court of Appeal

Except as provided in rules 8.400–8.456, rules 8.252–8.272 govern hearing and decision in the Court of Appeal in juvenile cases. *(Formerly Rule 38.4, adopted, eff. Jan. 1, 2005. As amended, eff. July 1, 2005. Renumbered Rule 8.470 and amended, eff. Jan. 1, 2007.)*

Research References

Treatises and Practice Aids

Witkin, California Summary 10th Parent and Child § 444, Scope and Organization.

Rule 8.472. Hearing and decision in the Supreme Court

Rules 8.500–8.552 govern hearing and decision in the Supreme Court in juvenile cases. *(Formerly Rule 38.5, adopted, eff. Jan. 1, 2005. As amended, eff. July 1, 2005. Renumbered Rule 8.472 and amended, eff. Jan. 1, 2007.)*

Rule 8.474. Procedures and data

(a) Procedures

The judges and clerks of the superior courts and the reviewing courts must adopt procedures to identify the records and expedite the processing of all appeals and writs in juvenile cases.

(b) Data

The clerks of the superior courts and the reviewing courts must provide the data required to assist the Judicial Council in evaluating the effectiveness of the rules governing appeals and writs in juvenile cases. *(Formerly Rule 38.6, adopted, eff. Jan. 1, 2005. Renumbered Rule 8.474, eff. Jan. 1, 2007. As amended, eff. Jan. 1, 2016.)*

Research References

Treatises and Practice Aids

Witkin, California Summary 10th Parent and Child § 355, Review on Appeal.
Witkin, California Summary 10th Parent and Child § 444, Scope and Organization.
Witkin, California Summary 10th Parent and Child § 709, in General.
Witkin, California Summary 10th Parent and Child § 716, in General.

Title 9

RULES ON LAW PRACTICE, ATTORNEYS, AND JUDGES

Division 2

ATTORNEY ADMISSION AND DISCIPLINARY PROCEEDINGS AND REVIEW OF STATE BAR PROCEEDINGS

Chapter 2

ATTORNEY DISCIPLINARY PROCEEDINGS

Rule 9.22. Suspension of members of the State Bar for failure to comply with judgment or order for child or family support

(a) Annual State Bar recommendation for suspension of delinquent members

Under Family Code section 17520, the State Bar is authorized to transmit to the Supreme Court on an annual basis the names of those members listed by the State Department of Social Services as delinquent in their payments of court-ordered child or family support with a recommendation for their suspension from the practice of law.

(b) Condition for reinstatement of suspended members

A member suspended under this rule may be reinstated only after receipt by the Supreme Court of notification from the State Bar that the member's name has been removed from the State Department of Social Services list.

(c) Additional recommendation for suspension by the State Bar

Under Family Code section 17520(*l*), the State Bar is further authorized to promptly transmit to the Supreme Court with a recommendation for their suspension from the practice of law the names of those members previously listed by the State Department of Social Services as delinquent in their payments of court-ordered child or family support, who obtained releases under Family Code section 17520(h), and who have subsequently been identified by the Department of Social Services as again being delinquent.

(d) Authorization for the Board of Governors of the State Bar to adopt rules and regulations

The Board of Governors of the State Bar is authorized to adopt such rules and regulations as it deems necessary and appropriate in order to comply with this rule. The rules and regulations of the State Bar must contain procedures governing the notification, suspension, and reinstatement of members of the State Bar in a manner not inconsistent with Family Code section 17520. *(Formerly Rule 962, adopted, eff. Jan. 31, 1993. As amended, eff. April 1, 1996. Renumbered Rule 9.22 and amended, eff. Jan. 1, 2007.)*

Research References

Treatises and Practice Aids

Witkin, California Summary 10th Husband and Wife § 338, Nonissuance, Nonrenewal, or Suspension Of License.

STANDARDS OF JUDICIAL ADMINISTRATION

Title 5

STANDARDS FOR CASES INVOLVING CHILDREN AND FAMILIES

Standard 5.20. Uniform standards of practice for providers of supervised visitation

(a) Scope of service

This standard defines the standards of practice, including duties and obligations, for providers of supervised visitation under Family Code sections 3200 and 3200.5. Unless specified otherwise, the standards of practice are designed to apply to all providers of supervised visitation, whether the provider is a friend, relative, paid independent contractor, employee, intern, or volunteer operating independently or through a supervised visitation center or agency. The goal of these standards of practice is to assure the safety and welfare of the child, adults, and providers of supervised visitation. Once safety is assured, the best interest of the child is the paramount consideration at all stages and particularly in deciding the manner in which supervision is provided. Each court is encouraged to adopt local court rules necessary to implement these standards of practice.

(b) Definition

Family Code section 3200 defines the term "provider" as including any individual or supervised visitation center that monitors visitation. Supervised visitation is contact between a noncustodial party and one or more children in the presence of a neutral third person.

(c) Type of provider

Who provides the supervision and the manner in which supervision is provided depends on different factors, including local resources, the financial situation of the parties, and the degree of risk in each case. While the court makes the final decision as to the manner in which supervision is provided and any terms or conditions, the court may consider recommendations by the attorney for the child, the parties and their attorneys, Family Court Services staff, evaluators, and therapists. As specified in Family Code section 3200.5, in any case in which the court has determined that there is domestic violence or child abuse or neglect, as defined in section 11165.6 of the Penal Code, and the court determines supervision is necessary, the court must consider whether to use a professional or nonprofessional provider based on the child's best interest.

(d) Qualifications of nonprofessional providers

(1) A "nonprofessional provider" is any person who is not paid for providing supervised visitation services. Unless otherwise ordered by the court or stipulated by the parties, the nonprofessional provider must:

(A) Have no record of a conviction for child molestation, child abuse, or other crimes against a person;

(B) Have proof of automobile insurance if transporting the child;

(C) Have no current or past court order in which the provider is the person being supervised; and

(D) Agree to adhere to and enforce the court order regarding supervised visitation.

(2) Unless otherwise ordered by the court or stipulated by the parties, the nonprofessional provider should:

(A) Be 21 years of age or older;

(B) Have no record of conviction for driving under the influence (DUI) within the last 5 years;

(C) Not have been on probation or parole for the last 10 years;

(D) Have no civil, criminal, or juvenile restraining orders within the last 10 years; and

(E) Not be financially dependent on the person being supervised.

(e) Qualifications of professional providers

A "professional provider" is any person paid for providing supervised visitation services, or an independent contractor, employee, intern, or volunteer operating independently or through a supervised visitation center or agency. The professional provider must:

(1) Be 21 years of age or older;

(2) Have no record of conviction for driving under the influence (DUI) within the last 5 years;

(3) Not have been on probation or parole for the last 10 years;

(4) Have no record of a conviction for child molestation, child abuse, or other crimes against a person;

(5) Have proof of automobile insurance if transporting the child;

(6) Have no civil, criminal, or juvenile restraining orders within the last 10 years;

(7) Have no current or past court order in which the provider is the person being supervised;

(8) Be able to speak the language of the party being supervised and of the child, or the provider must provide a neutral interpreter over the age of 18 who is able to do so;

(9) Agree to adhere to and enforce the court order regarding supervised visitation;

(10) Meet the training requirements stated in (f); and

(11) Sign a declaration or *Declaration of Supervised Visitation Provider* (form FL–324) stating that all requirements to be a professional provider have been met.

(f) Training for providers

(1) Each court is encouraged to make available to all providers informational materials about the role of a provider, the terms and conditions of supervised visitation, and the legal responsibilities and obligations of a provider under this standard.

(2) In addition, professional providers must receive 24 hours of training that includes the following subjects:

(A) The role of a professional provider;

(B) Child abuse reporting laws;

(C) Record–keeping procedures;

(D) Screening, monitoring, and termination of visitation;

(E) Developmental needs of children;

(F) Legal responsibilities and obligations of a provider;

(G) Cultural sensitivity;

(H) Conflicts of interest;

(I) Confidentiality;

(J) Issues relating to substance abuse, child abuse, sexual abuse, and domestic violence; and

(K) Basic knowledge of family and juvenile law.

(g) Safety and security procedures

All providers must make every reasonable effort to assure the safety and welfare of the child and adults during the visitation. Professional providers should establish a written protocol, with the assistance of the local law enforcement agency, that describes the emergency assistance and responses that can be expected from the local law enforcement agency. In addition, the professional provider should:

(1) Establish and state in writing minimum security procedures and inform the parties of these procedures before the commencement of supervised visitation;

(2) Conduct comprehensive intake and screening to understand the nature and degree of risk for each case. The procedures for intake should include separate interviews with the parties before the first visit. During the interview, the provider should obtain identifying information and explain the reasons for temporary suspension or termination of a visit under this standard. If the child is of sufficient age and capacity, the provider should include the child in part of the intake or orientation process. Any discussion should be presented to the child in a manner appropriate to the child's developmental stage;

(3) Obtain during the intake process:

(A) Copies of any protective order;

(B) Current court orders;

(C) Any Judicial Council form relating to supervised visitation orders;

(D) A report of any written records of allegations of domestic violence or abuse; and

(E) An account of the child's health needs if the child has a chronic health condition; and

(4) Establish written procedures that must be followed in the event a child is abducted during supervised visitation.

(h) Ratio of children to provider

The ratio of children to a professional provider must be contingent on:

(1) The degree of risk factors present in each case;

(2) The nature of supervision required in each case;

(3) The number and ages of the children to be supervised during a visit;

(4) The number of people, as provided in the court order, visiting the child during the visit;

(5) The duration and location of the visit; and

(6) The experience of the provider.

(i) Conflict of interest

All providers should maintain neutrality by refusing to discuss the merits of the case or agree with or support one party over another. Any discussion between a provider and the parties should be for the purposes of arranging visitation and providing for the safety of the children. In order to avoid a conflict of interest, the professional provider should not:

(1) Be financially dependent on the person being supervised;

(2) Be an employee of the person being supervised;

(3) Be an employee of or affiliated with any superior court in the county in which the supervision is ordered unless specified in the employment contract; or

(4) Be in an intimate relationship with the person being supervised.

(j) Maintenance and disclosure of records for professional providers

(1) Professional providers must keep a record for each case, including the following:

(A) A written record of each contact and visit;

(B) Who attended the visit;

(C) Any failure to comply with the terms and conditions of the visitation; and

(D) Any incidence of abuse as required by law.

(2) Case recordings should be limited to facts, observations, and direct statements made by the parties, not personal conclusions, suggestions, or opinions of the provider. All contacts by the provider in person, in writing, or by telephone with either party, the children, the court, attorneys, mental health professionals, and referring agencies should be documented in the case file. All entries should be dated and signed by the person recording the entry.

(3) If ordered by the court or requested by either party or the attorney for either party or the attorney for the child, a report about the supervised visit must be produced. These reports should include facts, observations, and direct statements and not opinions or recommendations regarding future visitation. The original report must be sent to the court if so ordered, or to the requesting party or attorney, and copies should be sent to all parties, their attorneys, and the attorney for the child.

(4) Any identifying information about the parties and the child, including addresses, telephone numbers, places of employment, and schools, is confidential, should not be disclosed, and should be deleted from documents before

releasing them to any court, attorney, attorney for the child, party, mediator, evaluator, mental health professional, social worker, or referring agency, except as required in reporting suspected child abuse.

(k) Confidentiality

Communications between parties and providers of supervised visitation are not protected by any privilege of confidentiality. Professional providers should, whenever possible, maintain confidentiality regarding the case except when:

(1) Ordered by the court;

(2) Subpoenaed to produce records or testify in court;

(3) Requested to provide information about the case by a mediator or evaluator in conjunction with a court-ordered mediation, investigation, or evaluation;

(4) Required to provide information about the case by Child Protective Services; or

(5) Requested to provide information about the case by law enforcement.

(*l*) Delineation of terms and conditions

The provider bears the sole responsibility for enforcement of all the terms and conditions of any supervised visitation. Unless otherwise ordered by the court, the provider should implement the following terms and conditions:

(1) Monitor conditions to assure the safety and welfare of the child;

(2) Enforce the frequency and duration of the visits as ordered by the court;

(3) Avoid any attempt to take sides with either party;

(4) Ensure that all contact between the child and the noncustodial party is within the provider's hearing and sight at all times, and that discussions are audible to the provider;

(5) Speak in a language spoken by the child and the noncustodial party;

(6) Allow no derogatory comments about the other parent, his or her family, caretaker, child, or child's siblings;

(7) Allow no discussion of the court case or possible future outcomes;

(8) Allow neither the provider nor the child to be used to gather information about the other party or caretaker or to transmit documents, information, or personal possessions;

(9) Allow no spanking, hitting, or threatening the child;

(10) Allow no visits to occur while the visiting party appears to be under the influence of alcohol or illegal drugs;

(11) Allow no emotional, verbal, physical, or sexual abuse;

(12) Allow no contact between the custodial and noncustodial parents unless ordered by the court; and

(13) Ensure that the parties follow any additional rules stated by the provider or the court.

(m) Safety considerations for sexual abuse cases

In cases where there are allegations of sexual abuse, in addition to the requirements of (*l*), the provider should comply with the following terms and conditions, unless otherwise ordered by the court:

(1) Allow no exchanges of gifts, money, or cards;

(2) Allow no photographing, audiotaping, or videotaping of the child;

(3) Allow no physical contact with the child such as lap sitting, hair combing, stroking, hand holding, hugging, wrestling, tickling, horseplaying, changing diapers, or accompanying the child to the bathroom;

(4) Allow no whispering, passing notes, hand signals, or body signals; and

(5) Allow no supervised visitation in the location where the alleged sexual abuse occurred.

(n) Legal responsibilities and obligations of a provider

All nonprofessional providers of supervised visitation should, and all professional providers must:

(1) Advise the parties before commencement of supervised visitation that no confidential privilege exists;

(2) Report suspected child abuse to the appropriate agency, as provided by law, and inform the parties of the provider's obligation to make such reports; and

(3) Suspend or terminate visitation under (p).

(*o*) Additional legal responsibilities of professional providers

In addition to the legal responsibilities and obligations required in (n), professional providers must:

(1) Prepare a written contract to be signed by the parties before commencement of the supervised visitation. The contract should inform each party of the terms and conditions of supervised visitation; and

(2) Review custody and visitation orders relevant to the supervised visitation.

(p) Temporary suspension or termination of supervised visitation

(1) All providers must make every reasonable effort to provide a safe visit for the child and the noncustodial party.

(2) However, if a provider determines that the rules of the visit have been violated, the child has become acutely distressed, or the safety of the child or the provider is at risk, the visit may be temporarily interrupted, rescheduled at a later date, or terminated.

(3) All interruptions or terminations of visits must be recorded in the case file.

(4) All providers must advise both parties of the reasons for interruption of a visit or termination.

(q) Additional requirements for professional providers

Professional providers must state the reasons for temporary suspension or termination of supervised visitation in writing and provide the written statement to both parties, their attorneys, the attorney for the child, and the court.

(Formerly § 26.2, adopted, eff. Jan. 1, 1998. Renumbered Standard 5.20 and amended, eff. Jan. 1, 2007. As amended, eff. Jan. 1, 2015.)

Standard 5.30. Family court matters

(a) Judicial assignments to family court

In a court with a separate family court, the presiding judge of the superior court should assign judges to the family court to serve for a minimum of three years. In selecting judges for family court assignments, the presiding judge should consider, in addition to rule 10.603(c)(1)(A) of the California Rules of Court, the judge's prior experience in family law litigation and mediation, as well as whether the judge prefers to serve in a family law department.

(b) Case assignment to same department

To the extent possible, family law actions related to the same family should be assigned to the same judicial officer for all purposes, so that all decisions that are made in a case through final judgment are issued by the same judicial officer.

(c) Importance of family court

The supervising judge in the family court, in consultation with the presiding judge of the superior court, should:

(1) Motivate and educate other judges regarding the significance of family court; and

(2) Work to ensure that sufficient judicial officers, court staff, family law facilitators, child custody mediators and evaluators, interpreters, financial resources, and adequate facilities are assigned to the family court to allow adequate time to hear and decide the matters before it.

(d) Compensation for court-appointed attorneys

The supervising judge of the family court should ensure that court-appointed attorneys in the family court are compensated at a level equivalent to attorneys appointed by the court in comparable types of cases.

(e) Training and education

Family court law is a specialized area of the law that requires dedication and study. The supervising judge of the family court has a responsibility to maintain high-quality services in family court. The quality of services provided by judicial officers and court staff depends, in significant part, on appropriate training and education, from the beginning of the family court assignment and on a continuing basis thereafter.

(1) Family court judicial officers, family law facilitators, child custody mediators and evaluators, interpreters, other court staff, and court-appointed attorneys should have sufficient training to perform their jobs competently.

(2) The supervising judge of the family court should promote access to printed, electronic, Internet, and other family law resources.

(f) Unique role of a family court

Under the direction of the presiding judge of the superior court, the family court, to the extent that it does not interfere with the adjudication process or violate any ethical constraints, is encouraged to:

(1) Provide active leadership within the community in determining the needs of, and obtaining and developing resources and services for children and families who participate in the family law court system;

(2) Investigate and determine the availability of specific prevention, intervention, and treatment services in the community for families who come before the family courts;

(3) Take an active role in helping the court develop rules and procedures that will result in the ordering of appropriate treatment and services for children and families;

(4) Exercise a leadership role in the development and maintenance of services for self-represented and financially disadvantaged litigants;

(5) Take an active part in the formation of a community-wide network to promote and coordinate private- and public-sector efforts to focus attention and resources on the needs of family law litigants;

(6) Educate the community and its institutions, including the media, concerning the role of the family court in meeting the complex needs of families;

(7) Encourage the development of community services and resources to assist families and children in the family court system, including self-help information; supervised visitation; substance abuse and drug prevention, intervention, and treatment; services for families with domestic violence issues; counseling; parenting education; vocational training; mediation; alternative dispute resolution options; and other resources to support families;

(8) Manage cases more efficiently and effectively to avoid conflicting orders;

(9) Take an active role in promoting completion of cases in a timely manner;

(10) Appoint counsel for children in appropriate family law custody cases; and

(11) Ensure that the best interest of children is served throughout the family court process.

(g) Appointment of attorneys and other persons

A court should follow the guidelines of standard 10.21 of the California Standards of Judicial Administration when appointing attorneys, arbitrators, mediators, referees, masters, receivers, and other persons. *(Adopted, eff. Jan. 1, 2007.)*

Standard 5.40. Juvenile court matters

(a) Assignments to juvenile court

The presiding judge of the superior court should assign judges to the juvenile court to serve for a minimum of three years. Priority should be given to judges who have expressed an interest in the assignment.

(b) Importance of juvenile court

The presiding judge of the juvenile court, in consultation with the presiding judge of the superior court, should:

(1) Motivate and educate other judges regarding the significance of juvenile court.

(2) Work to ensure that sufficient judges and staff, facilities, and financial resources are assigned to the juvenile court to allow adequate time to hear and decide the matters before it.

(c) Standards of representation and compensation

The presiding judge of the juvenile court should:

(1) Encourage attorneys who practice in juvenile court, including all court-appointed and contract attorneys, to continue their practice in juvenile court for substantial periods of time. A substantial period of time is at least two years and preferably from three to five years.

(2) Confer with the county public defender, county district attorney, county counsel, and other public law office leaders and encourage them to raise the status of attorneys working in the juvenile courts as follows: hire attorneys who are interested in serving in the juvenile court for a substantial part of their careers; permit and encourage attorneys, based on interest and ability, to remain in juvenile court assignments for significant periods of time; and work to ensure that attorneys who have chosen to serve in the juvenile court have the same promotional and salary opportunities as attorneys practicing in other assignments within a law office.

(3) Establish minimum standards of practice to which all court-appointed and public office attorneys will be expected to conform. These standards should delineate the responsibilities of attorneys relative to investigation and evaluation of the case, preparation for and conduct of hearings, and advocacy for their respective clients.

(4) In conjunction with other leaders in the legal community, ensure that attorneys appointed in the juvenile court are compensated in a manner equivalent to attorneys appointed by the court in other types of cases.

(d) Training and orientation

The presiding judge of the juvenile court should:

(1) Establish relevant prerequisites for court-appointed attorneys and advocates in the juvenile court.

(2) Develop orientation and in-service training programs for judicial officers, attorneys, volunteers, law enforcement personnel, court personnel, and child advocates to ensure that all are adequately trained concerning all issues relating to special education rights and responsibilities, including the right of each child with exceptional needs to receive a free, appropriate public education and the right of each child with educational disabilities to receive accommodations.

(3) Promote the establishment of a library or other resource center in which information about juvenile court practice (including books, periodicals, videotapes, and other training materials) can be collected and made available to all participants in the juvenile system.

(4) Ensure that attorneys who appear in juvenile court have sufficient training to perform their jobs competently, as follows: require that all court-appointed attorneys meet minimum training and continuing legal education standards as a condition of their appointment to juvenile court matters; and encourage the leaders of public law offices that have responsibilities in juvenile court to require their attorneys who appear in juvenile court to have at least the same training and continuing legal education required of court-appointed attorneys.

(e) Unique role of a juvenile court judge

Judges of the juvenile court, in consultation with the presiding judge of the juvenile court and the presiding judge of the superior court, to the extent that it does not interfere with the adjudication process, are encouraged to:

(1) Provide active leadership within the community in determining the needs of and obtaining and developing resources and services for at-risk children and families. At-risk children include delinquents, dependents, and status offenders.

(2) Investigate and determine the availability of specific prevention, intervention, and treatment services in the community for at-risk children and their families.

(3) Exercise their authority by statute or rule to review, order, and enforce the delivery of specific services and treatment for at-risk children and their families.

(4) Exercise a leadership role in the development and maintenance of permanent programs of interagency cooperation and coordination among the court and the various public agencies that serve at-risk children and their families.

(5) Take an active part in the formation of a community-wide network to promote and unify private and public sector efforts to focus attention and resources for at-risk children and their families.

(6) Maintain close liaison with school authorities and encourage coordination of policies and programs.

(7) Educate the community and its institutions through every available means, including the media, concerning the role of the juvenile court in meeting the complex needs of at-risk children and their families.

(8) Evaluate the criteria established by child protection agencies for initial removal and reunification decisions and communicate the court's expectations of what constitutes "reasonable efforts" to prevent removal or hasten return of the child.

(9) Encourage the development of community services and resources to assist homeless, truant, runaway, and incorrigible children.

(10) Be familiar with all detention facilities, placements, and institutions used by the court.

(11) Act in all instances consistent with the public safety and welfare.

(f) Appointment of attorneys and other persons

For the appointment of attorneys, arbitrators, mediators, referees, masters, receivers, and other persons, each court should follow rule 10.611 and the guidelines of standard 10.21.

(g) Educational rights of children in the juvenile court

The juvenile court should be guided by certain general principles:

(1) A significant number of children in the juvenile court process have exceptional needs that, if properly identified and assessed, would qualify such children to receive special education and related services under federal and state education law (a free, appropriate public education) (see Ed. Code, § 56000 et seq. and 20 U.S.C. § 1400 et seq.);

(2) Many children in the juvenile court process have disabilities that, if properly identified and assessed, would qualify such children to receive educational accommodations (see § 504 of the Rehabilitation Act of 1973 [29 U.S.C. § 794; 34 C.F.R. § 104.1 et seq.]);

(3) Unidentified and unremediated exceptional needs and unaccommodated disabilities have been found to correlate strongly with juvenile delinquency, substance abuse, mental health issues, teenage pregnancy, school failure and dropout, and adult unemployment and crime; and

(4) The cost of incarcerating children is substantially greater than the cost of providing special education and related services to exceptional needs children and providing educational accommodations to children with disabilities.

(h) Role of the juvenile court

The juvenile court should:

(1) Take responsibility, with the other juvenile court participants at every stage of the child's case, to ensure that the child's educational needs are met, regardless of whether the child is in the custody of a parent or is suitably placed in the custody of the child welfare agency or probation department and regardless of where the child is placed in school. Each child under the jurisdiction of the juvenile court with exceptional needs has the right to receive a free, appropriate public education, specially designed, at no cost to the parents, to meet the child's unique special education needs. (See Ed. Code, § 56031 and 20 U.S.C. § 1401(8).) Each child with disabilities under the jurisdiction of the juvenile court has the right to receive accommodations. (See § 504 of the Rehabilitation Act of 1973 [29 U.S.C. § 794; 34 C.F.R. § 104.1 et seq. (1980)].) The court should also ensure that each parent or guardian receives information and assistance concerning his or her child's educational entitlements as provided by law.

(2) Provide oversight of the social service and probation agencies to ensure that a child's educational rights are investigated, reported, and monitored. The court should work within the statutory framework to accommodate the sharing of information between agencies. A child who comes before the court and is suspected of having exceptional needs or other educational disabilities should be referred in writing for an assessment to the child's school principal or to the school district's special education office. (See Ed. Code, §§ 56320–56329.) The child's parent, teacher, or other service provider may make the required written referral for assessment. (See Ed. Code, § 56029.)

(3) Require that court reports, case plans, assessments, and permanency plans considered by the court address a child's educational entitlements and how those entitlements are being satisfied, and contain information to assist the court in deciding whether the right of the parent or guardian to make educational decisions for the child should be limited by the court under Welfare and Institutions Code section 361(a) or 726(b). Information concerning whether the school district has met its obligation to provide educational services to the child, including special educational services if the child has exceptional needs under Education Code section 56000 et seq., and to provide accommodations if the child has disabilities as defined in section 504 of the Rehabilitation Act of 1973 (29 U.S.C. § 794; 34 C.F.R. § 104.1 et seq. (1980)) should also be included, along with a recommendation for disposition.

(4) Facilitate coordination of services by joining the local educational agency as a party when it appears that an educational agency has failed to fulfill its legal obligations to provide special education and related services or accommodations to a child in the juvenile court who has been identified as having exceptional needs or educational disabilities. (See Welf. & Inst. Code, §§ 362(a), 727(a).)

(5) Make appropriate orders limiting the educational rights of a parent or guardian who cannot be located or identified, or who is unwilling or unable to be an active participant in ensuring that the child's educational needs are met, and appoint a responsible adult as educational representative for such a child or, if a representative cannot be identified and the child may be eligible for special education and related services or already has an individualized education program, use form JV–535 to refer the child to the local educational agency for special education and related services and prompt appointment of a surrogate parent. (Welf. & Inst. Code, §§ 361, 726; Ed. Code, § 56156.)

(6) Ensure that special education, related services, and accommodations to which the child is entitled are provided whenever the child's school placement changes. (See Ed. Code, § 56325.) *(Formerly § 24, adopted, eff. July 1, 1989. As amended, eff. July 1, 1992; Jan. 1, 1999; Jan. 1, 2001; Jan. 1, 2004. Renumbered Standard 5.40 and amended, eff. Jan. 1, 2007.)*

Standard 5.45. Resource guidelines for child abuse and neglect cases

(a) Guidelines

To improve the fair and efficient administration of child abuse and neglect cases in the California juvenile dependency system, judges and judicial officers assigned to the juvenile court, in consultation with the presiding judge of the juvenile court and the presiding judge of the superior or consolidated court, are encouraged to follow the resource guidelines of the National Council of Juvenile and Family Court Judges, titled "Resource Guidelines: Improving Court Practice in Child Abuse & Neglect Cases." The guidelines are meant to be goals to help courts achieve, among other objectives, the following:

(1) Adherence to statutory timelines;

(2) Effective calendar management;

(3) Effective representation by counsel;

(4) Child–friendly court facilities;

(5) Timely and thorough reports and services to ensure informed judicial decisions, including reasonable efforts findings; and

(6) Minimum time allocations for specified hearings.

(b) Distribution of guidelines

Judicial Council staff will distribute a copy of the resource guidelines to each juvenile court and will provide individual copies to judicial officers and court administrators on written request. *(Formerly § 24.5, adopted, eff. July 1, 1997. Renumbered Standard 5.45 and amended, eff. Jan. 1, 2007. As amended, eff. Jan. 1, 2016.)*

JUDICIAL COUNCIL FORMS

Reproducible copies of the forms appear in *West's California Judicial Council Forms*. Copies of the forms are available in electronic format from West and on the Internet at http://www.courtinfo.ca.gov.

To order *California Judicial Council Forms*—call West at 1–800–762–5272 or order online at west.thomson.com.

FAMILY LAW

Dissolution, Legal Separation and Annulment

The forms listed below are pertinent to the statutes and rules appearing in the preceding divisions of this publication:

FL–100 * Petition—Marriage/Domestic Partnership

FL–105/GC–120 * Declaration Under Uniform Child Custody Jurisdiction and Enforcement Act (UCCJEA)

FL–105(A)/GC–120(A) * Attachment to Declaration Under Uniform Child Custody Jurisdiction and Enforcement Act (UCCJEA)

FL–107–INFO Legal Steps for a Divorce or Legal Separation

FL–110 * Summons (Family Law)

FL–120 * Response—Marriage/Domestic Partnership

FL–140 * Declaration of Disclosure (Family Law)

FL–141 * Declaration Regarding Service of Declaration of Disclosure and Income and Expense Declaration (Family Law)

FL–144 Stipulation and Waiver of Final Declaration of Disclosure

FL–150 * Income and Expense Declaration

FL–155 Financial Statement (Simplified)

FL–157 Spousal or Partner Support Declaration Attachment

FL–158 Supporting Declaration for Attorney's Fees and Costs Attachment

FL–160 * Property Declaration (Family Law)

FL–161 * Continuation of Property Declaration (Family Law)

FL–165 * Request to Enter Default (Family Law—Uniform Parentage)

FL–170 * Declaration for Default or Uncontested Dissolution or Legal Separation

FL–174 Family Centered Case Resolution Order

FL–180 * Judgment

FL–190 * Notice of Entry of Judgment (Family Law—Uniform Parentage—Custody and Support)

FL–191 * Child Support Case Registry Form

FL–192 Notice of Rights Responsibilities (Health–Care Costs and Reimbursement Procedures)

Parentage Actions

FL–200 Petition to Establish Parental Relationship (Uniform Parentage)

FL–210 * Summons (Uniform Parentage—Petition for Custody and Support)

FL–220 Response to Petition to Establish Parental Relationship (Uniform Parentage)

FL–230 * Declaration for Default or Uncontested Judgment (Uniform Parentage—Custody and Support)

FL–235 Advisement and Waiver of Rights Re: Establishment of Parental Relationship (Uniform Parentage)

FL–240 * Stipulation for Entry of Judgment Re: Establishment of Parental Relationship (Uniform Parentage)

FL–250 * Judgment (Uniform Parentage—Custody and Support)

FL–260 Petition for Custody and Support of Minor Children

FL–270 Response to Petition for Custody and Support of Minor Children

FL–272 * Notice of Motion to Set Aside Judgment of Paternity (Family Law—Government)

FL–274 Information Sheet for Completing Notice of Motion to Set Aside Judgment of Paternity (Family Law—Governmental)

FL–276 * Response to Notice of Motion to Set Aside Judgment of Paternity (Family Law—Governmental)

FL–278 * Order After Hearing on Motion to Set Aside Judgment of Paternity (Family Law—Governmental)

FL–280 * Request for Hearing and Application to Set Aside Voluntary Declaration of Paternity (Family Law—Governmental)

FL–281 Information Sheet for Completing Request for Hearing and Application to Set Aside Voluntary Declaration of Paternity (Family Law—Governmental)

FL–285 * Responsive Declaration to Application to Set Aside Voluntary Declaration of Paternity (Family Law—Governmental)

FL–290 * Order After Hearing on Motion to Set Aside Voluntary Declaration of Paternity (Family Law—Governmental)

Motions and Attachments

FL–300 * Request for Order

FL–303 Declaration Regarding Notice and Service of Request for Temporary Emergency (Ex Parte) Orders

FL–305 * Temporary Emergency (Ex Parte) Orders

FL–306 Request to Continue Hearing

FL—310 * Application for Order and Supporting Declaration

FL–311 Child Custody and Visitation (Parenting Time) Application Attachment

FL–312 * Request for Child Abduction Prevention Orders

FL–315 * Request or Response to Request for Separate Trial (Family Law)

FL–316 Request for Orders Regarding Noncompliance With Disclosure Requirements

FL–318–INFO Retirement Plan Joinder—Information Sheet (Family Law)

FL–319 Request for Attorney's Fees and Costs Attachment

FL–320 * Responsive Declaration to Request for Order

FL–321 Witness List

FL–321–INFO Attorney for Child in a Family Law Case—Information Sheet

FL–321–INFO C Attorney for Child in a Family Law Case—Information Sheet

FL–321–INFO K Attorney for Child in a Family Law Case—Information Sheet

FL–321–INFO S Attorney for Child in a Family Law Case—Information Sheet

FL–321–INFO V Attorney for Child in a Family Law Case—Information Sheet

FL–322 Declaration of Counsel for a Child Regarding Qualifications

FL–323 Order Appointing Counsel for a Child

FL–324 Declaration of Supervised Visitation Provider

FL–325 * Declaration of Court–Connected Child Custody Evaluator Regarding Qualifications

FL–326 * Declaration of Private Child Custody Evaluator Regarding Qualifications

FL–327 * Order Appointing Child Custody Evaluator

FL–328 * Notice Regarding Confidentiality of Child Custody Evaluation Report

FL–329–INFO Child Custody Evaluation Information Sheet

FL–334 Declaration Regarding Address Verification—Postjudgment Request to Modify a Child Custody, Visitation, or Child Support Order

FL–335 Proof of Service by Mail

FL–341 Child Custody and Visitation (Parenting Time) Order Attachment

FL–341(A) * Supervised Visitation Order?

FL–341(B) * Child Abduction Prevention Order Attachment

FL–341(C) Children's Holiday Schedule Attachment

FL–341(D) Additional Provisions—Physical Custody Attachment

FL–341(E) Joint Legal Custody Attachment

FL–342 * Child Support Information and Order Attachment

FL–342(A) * Non–Guideline Child Support Findings Attachment

FL–343 Spousal, Partner, or Family Support Order Attachment

FL–344 * Property Order Attachment to Findings and Order After Hearing

FL–345 Property Order Attachment to Judgment

FL–347 * Bifurcation of Status of Marriage or Domestic Partnership—Attachment (Family Law)

FL–350 * Stipulation to Establish or Modify Child Support and Order

FL–348 Pension Benefits—Attachment to Judgment (Attach to Form FL–180)

FL–360 * Request for Hearing and Application to Set Aside Support Order Under Family Code Section 3691

FL–365 * Responsive Declaration to Application to Set Aside Support Order

FL–367 * Order After Hearing on Motion to Set Aside Support Order

FL–370 * Pleading on Joinder—Employee Benefit Plan

FL–371 * Notice of Motion and Declaration for Joinder

FL–372 * Request for Joinder of Employee Benefit Plan Order

FL–374 * Notice of Appearance and Response of Employee Benefit Plan

FL–380 * Application for Expedited Child Support Order

FL–381 * Response to Application for Expedited Child Support Order and Notice of Hearing

FL–382 * Expedited Child Support Order

FL–390 * Notice of Motion and Motion for Simplified Modification of Order for Child, Spousal, or Family Support

FL–391 Information Sheet—Simplified Way to Change Child, Spousal, or Family Support

FL–392 * Responsive Declaration to Motion for Simplified Modification of Order for Child, Spousal, or Family Support

FL–393 Information Sheet—How to Oppose a Request to Change Child, Spousal, or Family Support

FL–395 * Ex Parte Application for Restoration of Former Name After Entry of Judgment and Order (Family Law)

FL–396 * Request for Production of an Income and Expense Declaration After Judgment

FL–397 * Request for Income and Benefit Information From Employer

FL–398 * Notice of Activation of Military Service and Deployment and Request to Modify a Support Order

Enforcement

FL–400 * Order for Child Support Security Deposit and Evidence of Deposit

FL–401 * Application for Disbursement and Order for Disbursement from Child Support Security Deposit

FL–410 * Order to Show Cause and Affidavit for Contempt

FL–411 * Affidavit of Facts Constituting Contempt (Financial and Injunctive Orders)

FL–412 * Affidavit of Facts Constituting Contempt (Domestic Violence/Custody and Visitation)

FL–415 Findings and Orders Regarding Contempt (Family Law—Domestic Violence Prevention—Uniform Parentage—Governmental)

FL–420 * Declaration of Payment History (Family Law—Governmental—Uniform Parentage Act)

FL–421 Payment History Attachment (Family Law—Governmental—Uniform Parentage Act)

FL–430 * Ex Parte Application to Issue, Modify, or Terminate an Earnings Assignment Order

FL–435 * Earnings Assignment Order for Spousal or Partner Support (Family Law)

FL–440 Statement for Registration of California Support Order

FL–450 * Request for Hearing Regarding Earnings Assignment (Family Law—Governmental—UIFSA)

FL–455 * Stay of Service of Earnings Assignment and Order

FL–460 Qualified Domestic Relations Order for Support (Earnings Assignment Order for Support)

FL–461 Attachment to Qualified Domestic Relations Order for Support (Earnings Assignment Order for Support)

FL–470 * Application and Order for Health Insurance Coverage

FL–475 * Employer's Health Insurance Return

FL–478 * Request and Notice of Hearing Regarding Health Insurance Assignment

FL–478–INFO Information Sheet and Instructions for Request and Notice of Hearing Regarding Health Insurance Assignment

FL–480 * Abstract of Support Judgment

FL–485 * Notice of Delinquency

FL–490 * Application to Determine Arrearages

Interstate Actions

FL–510 * Summons (UIFSA)

FL–520 * Response to Uniform Support Petition (UIFSA)

FL–530 * Judgment Regarding Parental Obligations (UIFSA)

FL–560 * Ex Parte Application for Transfer and Order (UIFSA)

FL–570 Notice of Registration of Out-of-State Support Order

FL–575 * Request for Hearing Regarding Registration of Support Order

FL–580 Registration of Out–of–State Custody Order

FL–585 Request for Hearing Regarding Registration of Out-of-State Custody Decree

FL–590A * UIFSA Child Support Order Jurisdictional Attachment

FL–592 * Notice of Registration of an International Hague Convention Support Order

FL–594 * Request for Hearing Regarding Registration of an International Hague Convention Support Order

Governmental Child Support

FL–600 * Summons and Complaint or Supplemental Complaint Regarding Parental Obligations

FL–605 * Notice and Acknowledgment of Receipt

FL–610 * Answer to Complaint or Supplemental Complaint Regarding Parental Obligations (Governmental)

FL–615 * Stipulation for Judgment or Supplemental Judgment Regarding Parental Obligations and Judgment (Governmental)

FL–615 S * Stipulation for Judgment or Supplemental Judgment Regarding Parental Obligations and Judgment (Governmental)

FL–616 * Declaration for Amended Proposed Judgment (Governmental)

FL–620 * Request to Enter Default Judgment (Governmental)

FL–625 * Stipulation and Order

FL–625 S * Stipulation and Order (Governmental)

FL–626 Stipulation and Order Waiving Unassigned Arrears (Governmental)

FL–626 C Stipulation and Order Waiving Unassigned Arrears (Governmental)

FL–626 K Stipulation and Order Waiving Unassigned Arrears (Governmental)

FL–626 S Stipulation and Order Waiving Unassigned Arrears (Governmental)

FL–626 T Stipulation and Order Waiving Unassigned Arrears (Governmental)

FL–627 * Order for Genetic (Parentage) Testing

FL–630 * Judgment Regarding Parental Obligations

FL–632 * Notice Regarding Payment of Support (Governmental)

FL–634 * Notice of Change of Responsibility for Managing Child Support Case (Governmental)

FL–634 S * Notice of Change of Responsibility for Managing Child Support Case (Governmental)

FL–635 * Notice of Entry of Judgment and Proof of Service by Mail (Governmental)

FL–640 * Notice and Motion to Cancel (Set Aside) Support Order Based on Presumed Income (Governmental)

FL–643 Declaration of Obligor's Income During Judgment Period—Presumed Income Set–Aside Request

FL–645 * Notice to Local Child Support Agency of Intent to Take Independent Action to Enforce Support Order (Governmental)

FL–646 * Response of Local Child Support Agency to Notice of Intent to Take Independent Action to Enforce Support Order (Governmental)

FL–650 * Statement for Registration of California Support Order (Governmental)

FL–651 * Notice of Registration of California Support Order (Governmental)

FL–660 * Ex Parte Motion by Local Child Support Agency and Declaration for Joinder of Other Parent (Governmental)

FL–661 Notice of Motion and Declaration for Joinder of Other Parent in Governmental Action (Governmental)

FL–662 * Responsive Declaration to Motion for Joinder of Other Parent—Consent Order of Joinder (Governmental)

FL–662 INFO Information Sheet for Responsive Declaration to Motion for Joinder of Other Parent—Consent Order of Joinder

FL–663 * Stipulation and Order for Joinder of Other Parent (Governmental)

FL–663 C * Stipulation and Order for Joinder of Other Parent (Governmental)

FL–663 K * Stipulation and Order for Joinder of Other Parent (Governmental)

FL–663 S * Stipulation and Order for Joinder of Other Parent (Governmental)

FL–663 T * Stipulation and Order for Joinder of Other Parent (Governmental)

FL–663 V * Stipulation and Order for Joinder of Other Parent (Governmental)

FL–665 * Findings and Recommendation of Commissioner

FL–666 * Notice of Objection (Governmental)

FL–667 * Review of Commissioner's Findings of Fact and Recommendation (Governmental)

FL–670 * Notice of Motion for Judicial Review of License Denial (Governmental)

FL–676 * Request for Judicial Determination of Support Arrearages or Adjustment of Arrearages Due to Incarceration or Involuntary Institutionalization

FL–679 * Request for Telephone Appearance (Governmental)

FL–683 * Order to Show Cause (Governmental)

FL–684 * Request for Order and Supporting Declaration (Governmental)

FL–685 * Response to Governmental Notice of Motion or Order to Show Cause (Governmental)

FL–687 * Order After Hearing

FL–688 * Short Form Order After Hearing

FL–692 * Minutes and Order or Judgment

FL–693 Guideline Findings Attachment (Governmental)

Summary Dissolutions

FL–800 * Joint Petition for Summary Dissolution

FL–810 * Summary Dissolution Information

FL–820 * Request for Judgment, Judgment of Dissolution of Marriage, and Notice of Entry of Judgment (Family Law—Summary Dissolution)

FL–830 * Notice of Revocation of Joint Petition for Summary Dissolution (Family Law—Summary Dissolution)

Miscellaneous

FL–910 Request of Minor to Marry or Establish a Domestic Partnership

FL–915 Order on Request of Minor to Marry or Establish a Domestic Partnership

FL–920 Notice of Consolidation

FL–935 Application and Order for Appointment of Guardian Ad Litem of Mino —Family Law

FL–940 Office of the Family Law Facilitator Disclosure

FL–940 C Office of the Family Law Facilitator Disclosure

FL–940 V Office of the Family Law Facilitator Disclosure

FL–945 Family Law Information Center Disclosure

FL–950* Notice of Limited Scope Representation

FL–955* Notice of Completion of Limited Scope Representation

FL–956* Objection to Application to be Relieved as Counsel Upon Completion of Limited Scope Representation

FL–957* Response to Objection to Propsed Notice of Completion of Limited Scope Representation

FL–958* Order on Completion of Limited Scope Representation

FL–970 * Request and Declaration for Final Judgment of Dissolution of Marriage (Family Law)

Chinese, Korean, Spanish. Tagalog and Vietnamese language versions of particular forms have been approved by the Judicial Council.

JUVENILE

The forms listed below are pertinent to the statutes and rules appearing in the preceding divisions of this publication:

JV–100 * Juvenile Dependency Petition (Version One)

JV–100(S) * Juvenile Dependency Petition (Version One)

JV–101(A) * Additional Children Attachment—Juvenile Dependency Petition

JV–101(A)S * Additional Children Attachment—Juvenile Dependency Petition

JV–110 * Juvenile Dependency Petition (Version Two)

JV–110S * Juvenile Dependency Petition (Version Two)

JV–120 Serious Physical Harm (§ 300(a))

JV–120S Serious Physical Harm (§ 300(a))

JV–121 Failure to Protect (§ 300(b))

JV–121S Failure to Protect (§ 300(b))

JV–122 Serious Emotional Damage (§ 300(c))

JV–122S Serious Emotional Damage (§ 300(c))

JV–123 * Sexual Abuse (§ 300(d))

JV–123S * Sexual Abuse (§ 300(d))

JV–124 Severe Physical Abuse (§ 300(e))

JV–124S Severe Physical Abuse (§ 300(e))

JV–125 Caused Another Child's Death Through Abuse or Neglect (§ 300(f))

JV–125S Caused Another Child's Death Through Abuse or Neglect (§ 300(f))

JV–126 No Provision for Support (§ 300(g))

JV–126S No Provision for Support (§ 300(g))

JV–127 Freed for Adoption (§ 300(h))

JV–127S Freed for Adoption (§ 300(h))

JV–128 Cruelty (§ 300(i))

JV–128S Cruelty (§ 300(i))

JV–129 Abuse of Sibling (§ 300(i))

JV–129S Abuse of Sibling (§ 300(i))

JV–140 * Notification of Mailing Address

JV–140S * Notification of Mailing Address

JV–150 * Supplemental Petition for More Restrictive Placement (Attachment) (Welfare and Institutions Code, § 387)

JV–150S * Supplemental Petition for More Restrictive Placement (Attachment) (Welfare and Institutions Code, § 387)
JV–180 * Request to Change Court Order
JV–180S * Request to Change Court Order
JV–182 * Confidential Information (Request to Change Court Order)
JV–183 * Court Order on Form JV–180, Request to Change Court Order
JV–184 * Order After Hearing on Form JV–180, Request to Change Court Order
JV–185 Child's Information Sheet—Request to Change Court Order
JV–190 * Waiver of Rights—Juvenile Dependency
JV–190S * Waiver of Rights—Juvenile Dependency
JV–195 * Waiver of Reunification Services
JV–195S * Waiver of Reunification Services
JV–200 * Custody Order—Juvenile—Final Judgment
JV–200S * Custody Order—Juvenile—Final Judgment
JV–205 * Visitation Order—Juvenile
JV–206 Reasons for No or Supervised Visitation—Juvenile
JV–210 Application to Commence Proceedings by Affidavit and Decision by Social Worker (Welf. & Inst. Code, § 329)
JV–215 Application to Review Decision by Social Worker Not to Commence Proceedings (Welf. & Inst. Code, § 331)
JV–215S Application to Review Decision by Social Worker Not to Commence Proceedings (Welf. & Inst. Code, § 331)
JV–216 Order Delegating Judicial Authority Over Psychotropic Medication
JV–217–INFO Guide to Psychotropic Medication Forms
JV–218 Child's Opinion About the Medicine
JV–219 Statement About Medicine Prescribed
JV–219–INFO S * Information about Psychotropic Medication Forms
JV–220 * Application for Psychotropic Medication
JV–220S * Application Regarding Psychotropic Medication
JV–220(A) * Physician's Statement—Attachment
JV–220(A)S * Prescribing Physician's Statement—Attachment
JV–220(B) * Physician's Request to Continue Medication—Attachment
JV–221 * Proof of Notice of Application
JV–221S * Proof of Notice: Application Regarding Psychotropic Medication
JV–222 * Input on Application for Psychotropic Medication
JV–222S * Opposition to Application Regarding Psychotropic Medication
JV–223 * Order on Application for Psychotropic Medication
JV–223S * Order Regarding Application for Psychotropic Medication
JV–224 * County Report on Psychotropic Medication
JV–245 * Request for Restraining Order—Juvenile
JV–247 * Answer to Request For Restraining Order—Juvenile
JV–250 * Notice of Hearing and Temporary Restraining Order—Juvenile
JV–251 Request and Order to Continue Hearing
JV–252/DV–800 Proof of Firearms Turned In or Sold (Domestic Violence Prevention)
JV–252C/DV–800 Proof of Firearms Turned In or Sold (Domestic Violence Prevention)
JV–252K/DV–800 Proof of Firearms Turned In or Sold (Domestic Violence Prevention)
JV–252S/DV–800 Proof of Firearms Turned In or Sold (Domestic Violence Prevention)
JV–252V/DV–800 Proof of Firearms Turned In or Sold (Domestic Violence Prevention)
JV–255 * Restraining Order–Juvenile
JV–280 * Notice of Review Hearing
JV–280S * Notice of Review Hearing
JV–281 Notice Of Hearing—Nonminor
JV–285 Relative Information
JV–285S Relative Information
JV–287 Confidential Information
JV–287S Confidential Information
JV–290 Caregiver Information Form
JV–290C Caregiver Information Form
JV–290K Caregiver Information Form
JV–290S Caregiver Information Form
JV–290V Caregiver Information Form
JV–290–INFO Instructions to Complete the Caregiver Information Form
JV–290–INFO C Instructions to Complete the Caregiver Information Form
JV–290–INFO K Instructions to Complete the Caregiver Information Form
JV–290–INFO S Instructions to Complete the Caregiver Information Form
JV–290–INFO V Instructions to Complete the Caregiver Information Form
JV–295 * De Facto Parent Request
JV–295S * De Facto Parent Request
JV–296 * De Facto Parent Statement
JV–296S * De Facto Parent Statement
JV–297 * De Facto Parent Order
JV–297S * De Facto Parent Order
JV–298 * Order Ending De Facto Parent Status
JV–298S * Order Ending De Facto Parent Status
JV–299 De Facto Parent Pamphlet
JV–299C De Facto Parent Pamphlet
JV–299K De Facto Parent Pamphlet

JV–299S De Facto Parent Pamphlet

JV–299V De Facto Parent Pamphlet

JV–300 * Notice of Hearing on Selection of a Permanent Plan

JV–300S * Notice of Hearing on Selection of a Permanent Plan

JV–305 * Citation for Publication Under Welfare and Institutions Code Section 294

JV–305S * Citation for Publication Under Welfare and Institutions Code Section 294

JV–310 * Proof of Service Under Section 366.26 of the Welfare and Institutions Code

JV–310S * Proof of Service Under Section 366.26 of the Welfare and Institutions Code

JV–320 * Orders Under Welfare and Institutions Code Sections 366.24, 366.26, 727.3, 727.31

JV–321 * Request for Prospective Adoptive Parent Designation

JV–322 * Confidential Information—Prospective Adoptive Parent

JV–323 * Notice of Intent to Remove Child

JV–324 * Notice of Emergency Removal

JV–325 * Objection to Removal

JV–326 * Proof of Notice

JV–327 * Prospective Adoptive Parent Designation Order

JV–328 * Prospective Adoptive Parent Order After Hearing

JV–330 * Letters of Guardianship (Juvenile)

JV–330S * Letters of Guardianship (Juvenile)

JV–364 * Termination of Dependency

JV–364S * Termination of Dependency

JV–365 * Termination of Juvenile Court Jurisdiction—Nonminor

JV–367 * Findings And Orders After Hearing To Consider Termination of Juvenile Court Jurisdiction Over A Nonminor

JV–400 Visitation Attachment: Parental, Legal Guardian, Indian Custodian, Other Important Person

JV–401 Visitation Attachment: Sibling

JV–402 Visitation Attachment: Grandparent

JV–403 Sibling Attachment Contact and Placement

JV–405 Continuance—Dependency Detention Hearing

JV–406 Continuance—General

JV–410 Findings and Orders After Detention Hearing (Welfare and Institutions Code, § 319)

JV–412 Findings and Orders After Jurisdictional Hearing (Welfare and Institutions Code, § 356)

JV–415 Findings and Orders After Dispositional Hearing

JV–416 Dispositional Attachment: Dismissal of Petition With or Without Informal Supervision (Welfare and Institutions Code, § 360(b))

JV–417 Dispositional Attachment: In-Home Placement With Formal Supervision (Welfare and Institutions Code, § 361)

JV–418 Dispositional Attachment: Appointment of Guardian (Welfare and Institutions Code, § 360(a))

JV–419 Guardianship—Consent and Waiver of Rights

JV–419A Guardianship—Child's Consent and Waiver of Rights

JV–420 Dispositional Attachment: Removal From Custodial Parent—Placement With Previously Noncustodial Parent (Welfare and Institutions Code, §§ 361, 361.2)

JV–421 Dispositional Attachment: Removal From Custodial Parent—Placement With Nonparent

JV–425 Findings and Orders After In-Home Status Review Hearing (Welfare and Institutions Code, § 364)

JV–426 Findings and Orders After In-Home Status Review Hearing—Child Placed With Previously Noncustodial Parent (Welfare and Institutions Code, §§ 364, 366.21)

JV–430 Findings and Orders After Six-Month Status Review Hearing

JV–431 Six-Month Prepermanency Attachment: Child Reunified (Welfare and Institutions Code, § 366.21(e))

JV–432 Six-Month Prepermanency Attachment: Reunification Services Continued

JV–433 Six-Month Prepermanency Attachment: Reunification Services Terminated

JV–435 Findings and Orders After 12–Month Permanency Hearing

JV–436 Twelve-Month Permanency Attachment: Child Reunified (Welfare and Institutions Code, § 366.21(f))

JV–437 Twelve-Month Permanency Attachment: Reunification Services Continued (Welfare and Institutions Code, § 366.21(f))

JV–438 Twelve-Month Permanency Attachment: Reunification Services Terminated

JV–440 Findings and Orders After 18–Month Permanency Hearing

JV–441 Eighteen-Month Permanency Attachment: Child Reunified (Welfare and Institutions Code, § 366.22)

JV–442 Eighteen-Month Permanency Attachment: Reunification Services Terminated

JV–443 Eighteen-Month Permanency Attachment: Reunification Services Continued

JV–445 Findings and Orders After Postpermanency Hearing—Parental Rights Terminated; Permanent Plan of Adoption

JV–446 Findings and Orders After Postpermanency Hearing—Permanent Plan Other Than Adoption

JV–448 Order Granting Authority to Consent to Medical, Surgical, and Dental Care (Welfare and Institutions Code, § 366.27)

JV–450 * Order for Prisoner's Appearance at Hearing Affecting Parental Rights

JV–455 Findings and Orders After 24–Month Permanency Hearing

JV–456 Twenty-four–Month Permanency Attachment: Child Reunified (Welfare & Institutions Code § 366.25)

JV–457 Twenty-four–Month Permanency Attachment: Reunification Services Terminated

JV–460 Attachment: Additional Findings and Orders for Child Approaching Majority—Dependency

JV–464–INFO * How to Ask to Return to Juvenile Court Jurisdiction and Foster Care

JV–474 Nominor Dependent—Consent to Copy and Inspect Nonminor Dependent Court File

JV–475 Agreement of Adoption of Nonminor Dependent

JV–477 Consent of Spouse or Registered Partner to Adoption of Nonminor Dependent

JV–479 Order of Adoption of Nonminor Dependent

JV–500 * Parentage Inquiry

JV–500S * Parentage Inquiry

JV–501 * Parentage—Finding and Judgment (Juvenile)

JV–501S * Parentage—Finding and Judgment (Juvenile)

JV–505 * Statement Regarding Parentage (Juvenile)

JV–505S * Statement Regarding Parentage (Juvenile)

JV–535 * Findings and Orders Limiting Right to Make Educational Decisions for the Child, Appointing Educational Representative, and Determining Child's Educational Needs

JV–535S * Findings and Orders Limiting Right to Make Educational Decisions for the Child, Appointing Educational Representative, and Determining Child's Educational Needs

JV–536 * Local Educational Agency Response to JV–535—Appointment of Surrogate Parent

JV–537 Educational Representative or Surrogate Parent Information

JV–537S Educational Representative or Surrogate Parent Information

JV–538 Findings and Orders Regarding Transfer from School of Origin

JV–539 Request for Hearing Regarding Child's Access to Services

JV–540 * Notice of Hearing on Joinder—Juvenile

JV–540S * Notice of Hearing on Joinder—Juvenile

JV–548 * Motion for Transfer Out

JV–550 * Juvenile Court Transfer-Out Orders

JV–550S * Juvenile Court Transfer Orders

JV–552 * Juvenile Court Transfer-Out Orders—Nominor Dependent

JV–565 * Request for Assistance With Expedited Placement Under the Interstate Compact on the Placement of Children

JV–565S * Findings and Request for Assistance Under Interstate Compact on the Placement of Children (ICPC)

JV–567 * Expedited Placement Under the Interstate Compact on the Placement of Children; Findings and Orders

JV–569 * Proof of Service—Request for Disclosure

JV–570 * Request for Disclosure of Juvenile Case File

JV–571 * Notice of Request for Disclosure of Juvenile Case File

JV–572 * Objection to Release of Juvenile Case File

JV–573 * Order on Request for Disclosure of Juvenile Case File

JV–574 * Order After Judicial Review

JV–575 * Petition to Obtain Report of Law Enforcement Agency

JV–575S * Petition to Obtain Report of Law Enforcement Agency

JV–590 * Order to Seal Juvenile Records

JV–590S * Order to Seal Juvenile Records

JV–591 Acknowledgment of Juvenile Record Sealed

JV–595 Request to Seal Juvenile Records

JV–595–INFO* How to Ask the Court to Seal your Records

JV–600 Juvenile Wardship Petition

JV–610 Child Habitually Disobedient § 601(a)

JV–610S Child Habitually Disobedient § 601(a)

JV–611 Child Habitually Truant § 601(b)

JV–611S Child Habitually Truant § 601(b)

JV–618 Waiver of Rights—Juvenile Delinquency

JV–618C Waiver of Rights—Juvenile Delinquency

JV–618K Waiver of Rights—Juvenile Delinquency

JV–618S Waiver of Rights—Juvenile Delinquency

JV–618V Waiver of Rights—Juvenile Delinquency

JV–620 * Violation of Law by Child

JV–620S * Violation of Law by Child

JV–624 Terms and Conditions

JV–642 Initial Appearance Hearing—Juvenile Delinquency

JV–644 Jurisdiction Hearing—Juvenile Delinquency

JV–665 Disposition—Juvenile Delinquency

JV–667 Custodial and Out-of-Home Placement Disposition Attachment

JV–674 Findings and Orders After Permanency Hearing—Delinquency

JV–678 Findings and Orders After Postpermanency Hearing—Delinquency

JV–680 Attachment: Additional Findings and Orders for Minor Approaching Majority—Delinquency

JV–683 Findings and Orders After Hearing to Modify Delinquency Jurisdiction to Transition Jurisdiction for Ward Older Than 18 Years of Age

JV–688 Continuance—Juvenile Delinquency

JV–710 Juvenile Fitness Hearing Order

JV–732 * Commitment to the California Department of Corrections and Rehabilitation, Division of Juvenile Facilities

JV–735 Juvenile Notice of Violation of Probation

JV–740 Petition to Modify, Change, or Set Aside Previous Orders—Change of Circumstances

JV–760 Deferred Entry of Judgment Order

JV–800 Notice of Appeal—Juvenile

JV–810 Recommendation for Appointment of Appellate Attorney for Child

JV–816 Application for Extension of Time to File Brief (Juvenile Delinquency Case)

JV–817 Application for Extension of Time to File Brief (Juvenile Dependency Case)

JV–820 Notice of Intent to File Writ Petition and Request for Record to Review Order Setting a Hearing under Welfare and Institutions Code Section 366.26 (California Rules of Court, Rule 8.450)

JV–822 Notice of Intent to File Writ Petition and Request for Record to Review Order Designating or Denying Specific Placement of a Dependent Child after Termination of Parental Rights

JV–825 Petition for Extraordinary Writ

JV–826 Denial of Petition (California Rules of Court, Rules 8.452, 8.456)

JV–826S Denial of Petition (California Rules of Court, Rules 8.452, 8.456)

JV–828 Notice of Action (California Rules of Court, Rule 8.452)

Chinese, Korean, Spanish and Vietnamese language versions of particular forms have been approved by the Judicial Council.

ADOPTION

The forms listed below are pertinent to the statutes and rules appearing in the preceding divisions of this publication:

ADOPT–200 * Adoption Request

ADOPT–210 * Adoption Agreement

ADOPT–215 * Adoption Order

ADOPT–216 * Verification of Compliance with Hague Adoption Convention Attachment

ADOPT–230 * Adoption Expenses

ADOPT–310 * Contact After Adoption Agreement

ADOPT–315 * Request to: Enforce, Change, End Contact After Adoption Agreement

ADOPT–320 * Answer to Request to: Enforce, Change, End Contact After Adoption Agreement

ADOPT–325 * Judge's Order to: Enforce, Change, End Contact After Adoption Agreement

ADOPT–330 * Request for Appointment of Confidential Intermediary

ADOPT–331 * Order for Appointment of Confidential Intermediary

ALTERNATIVE DISPUTE RESOLUTION

The forms listed below are pertinent to the statutes and rules appearing in the preceding divisions of this publication:

ADR–103 Petition to Confirm, Correct, or Vacate Attorney-Client Fee Arbitration Award (Alternative Dispute Resolution)

ADR–105 Information Regarding Rights After Attorney-Client Fee Arbitration (Alternative Dispute Resolution)

ADR–110 Order Appointing Referee

ADR–111 Report of Referee (Alternative Dispute Resolution)

CIVIL

The forms listed below are pertinent to the statutes and rules appearing in the preceding divisions of this publication:

CIV–025 Application and Order for Reissuance of Order to Show Cause and Temporary Restraining Order

CIVIL HARASSMENT PREVENTION

The forms listed below are pertinent to the statutes and rules appearing in the preceding divisions of this publication:

CH–100 * Request for Civil Harassment Restraining Orders

CH–110 * Temporary Restraining Order (CLETS–TCH) (Civil Harassment)

CH–115 * Request to Continue Court Hearing

CH–115–INFO How to Ask for a New Hearing Date

CH–120 * Response to Request for Civil Harassment Restraining Orders

CH–130 * Civil Harassement Restraining Order After Hearing (CLETS–CHO)

CH–200 Proof of Personal Service (Civil Harassment)

CH–250 Proof of Service of Response by Mail (Civil harshening)

CH–600 * Request to Modify/Terminate Civil Harassment Restraining Order

CH–610 * Notice of Hearing or Request to Modify/Terminate Civil Harassment Restraining Order

CH–620 * Response to Request to Modify/Terminate Civil Harassment Restraining Order

CH–630 * Order on Request to Modify/Terminate Civil Harassment Restraining Order

CH–800 Proof of Firearms Turned In, Sold, or Stored (Civil Harassment)

CLAIM AND DELIVERY

The forms listed below are pertinent to the statutes and rules appearing in the preceding divisions of this publication:

CD–200 * Temporary Restraining Order (Claim and Delivery)

CRIMINAL LAW

The forms listed below are pertinent to the statutes and rules appearing in the preceding divisions of this publication:

CR-160 * Criminal Protective Order—Domestic Violence (CLETS–CPO)

CR-165 * Notice of Termination of Protective Order in Criminal Proceeding (CLETS-CANCEL)

DISABILITY ACCESS LITIGATION

The forms listed below are pertinent to the statutes and rules appearing in the preceding divisions of this publication:

DAL–012 Proof of Service—Disability Access Litigation

DOMESTIC VIOLENCE PREVENTION:

The forms listed below are pertinent to the statutes and rules appearing in the preceding divisions of this publication:

DV–100 * Request for Domestic Violence Restraining Order

DV–101 Description of Abuse

DV–101C Description of Abuse (Chinese)
DV–101K Description of Abuse (Korean)
DV–101S Description of Abuse (Spanish)
DV–101V Description of Abuse (Vietnamese)
DV–105 * Request for Child Custody and Visitation Orders
DV–108 * Request for Order: No Travel with Children (Domestic Violence Prevention)
DV–109 * Notice of Court Hearing (Domestic Violence)
DV–109C * Notice of Court Hearing (Domestic Violence) (Chinese)
DV–109K * Notice of Court Hearing (Domestic Violence) (Korean)
DV–109S * Notice of Court Hearing (Domestic Violence) (Spanish)
DV–109V * Notice of Court Hearing (Domestic Violence) (Vietnamese)
DV–110 * Temporary Restraining Order (CLETS—TRO)
DV–110C * Temporary Restraining Order (CLETS—TRO) (Domestic Violence) (Chinese)
DV–110K * Temporary Restraining Order (CLETS—TRO) (Domestic Violence) (Korean)
DV–110S * Temporary Restraining Order (CLETS—TRO) (Domestic Violence) (Spanish)
DV–110V * Temporary Restraining Order (CLETS—TRO) (Domestic Violence) (Vietnamese)
DV–112 Waiver of Hearing on Denied Request for Temporary Restraining Order
DV–112C Waiver of Hearing on Denied Request for Temporary Restraining Order (Chinese)
DV–112K Waiver of Hearing on Denied Request for Temporary Restraining Order (Korean)
DV–112S Waiver of Hearing on Denied Request for Temporary Restraining Order (Spanish)
DV–112V Waiver of Hearing on Denied Request for Temporary Restraining Order (Vietnamese)
DV–115 * Request to Continue Court Hearing and Reissue Temporary Restraining Order (Domestic Violence Prevention)
DV–115C * Request to Continue Court Hearing and Reissue Temporary Restraining Order (Domestic Violence Prevention)
DV–115K * Request to Continue Court Hearing and Reissue Temporary Restraining Order (Domestic Violence Prevention)
DV–115S * Request to Continue Court Hearing and Reissue Temporary Restraining Order (Domestic Violence Prevention)
DV–115V * Request to Continue Court Hearing and Reissue Temporary Restraining Order (Domestic Violence Prevention)
DV–116 * Notice of New Hearing and Order on Reissuance
DV–116C * Notice of New Hearing and Order on Reissuance
DV–116K * Notice of New Hearing and Order on Reissuance
DV–116S * Notice of New Hearing and Order on Reissuance
DV–116V * Notice of New Hearing and Order on Reissuance
DV–120 * Response to Request for Domestic Violence Restraining Order
DV–130 * Restraining Order After Hearing (CLETS–OAH) (Order of Protection)
DV–130C * Restraining Order After Hearing (CLETS–OAH) (Order of Protection) (Chinese)
DV–130K * Restraining Order After Hearing (CLETS–OAH) (Order of Protection) (Korean)
DV–130S * Restraining Order After Hearing (CLETS–OAH) (Order of Protection) (Spanish)
DV–130V * Restraining Order After Hearing (CLETS–OAH) (Order of Protection) (Vietnamese)
DV–140 * Child Custody and Visitation Order (Domestic Violence)
DV–145 * Order: No Travel with Children (Domestic Violence Prevention)
DV–150 * Supervised Visitation and Exchange Order
DV–180* Agreement and Judgment of Parentage
DV–200 Proof of Personal Service (CLETS)
DV–200C Proof of Personal Service (CLETS) (Chinese)
DV–200K Proof of Personal Service (CLETS) (Korean)
DV–200S Proof of Personal Service (CLETS) (Spanish)
DV–200V Proof of Personal Service (CLETS) (Vietnamese)
DV–250 Proof of Service by Mail (CLETS) (Domestic Violence Prevention)
DV–250C Proof of Service by Mail (CLETS) (Domestic Violence Prevention) (Chinese)
DV–250K Proof of Service by Mail (CLETS) (Domestic Violence Prevention) (Korean)
DV–250S Proof of Service by Mail (CLETS) (Domestic Violence Prevention) (Spanish)
DV–250V Proof of Service by Mail (CLETS) (Domestic Violence Prevention) (Vietnamese)
DV–400 * Findings and Order to Terminate Restraining Order After Hearing (CLETS- CANCEL)
DV–600* Order to Register Out-of-State or Tribal Court Protective/Restraining Order
DV–610 Fax Transmission Cover Sheet for Registration of Tribal Court Protective Order
DV–700 * Request to Renew Restraining Order (Domestic Violence Prevention)
DV–710 * Notice of Hearing to Renew Restraining Order
DV–800/JV-252 Proof of Firearms Turned In, Sold, or Stored (Domestic Violence Prevention)
DV–805 * Proof of Enrollment for Batterer Intervention Program
DV–815 Batterer Intervention Program Progress Report
DV–900 * Order Transferring Wireless Phone Account

DV–901 * Attachment to Order Transferring Wireless Phone Account

Chinese, Korean, Spanish and Vietnamese language versions of particular forms have been approved by the Judicial Council.

ELDER OR DEPENDENT ADULT ABUSE PREVENTION

The forms listed below are pertinent to the statutes and rules appearing in the preceding divisions of this publication:

EA–100 * Request for Elder or Dependent Adult Abuse Restraining Orders

EA–800 Proof of Firearms Turned In, Sold, or Stored

ELECTRONIC FILING AND SERVICE

The forms listed below are pertinent to the statutes and rules appearing in the preceding divisions of this publication:

EFS–005–JV/JV–141 E-Mail Notice of Hearing: Consent, Withdrawal of Consent, Address Change

EMERGENCY PROTECTIVE ORDER

The forms listed below are pertinent to the statutes and rules appearing in the preceding divisions of this publication:

EPO–001 * Emergency Protective Order (CLETS–EPO) (Domestic Violence, Child Abuse, Elder or Dependent Adult Abuse, or Stalking)

ENFORCEMENT OF JUDGMENT

The forms listed below are pertinent to the statutes and rules appearing in the preceding divisions of this publication:

EJ–190 Application for and Renewal of Judgment

EJ–195 * Notice of Renewal of Judgment

INDIAN CHILD WELFARE ACT

The forms listed below are pertinent to the statutes and rules appearing in the preceding divisions of this publication:

ICWA–020 * Parental Notification of Indian Status

ICWA–020S * Parental Notification of Indian Status

ICWA–030 * Notice of Child Custody Proceeding for Indian Child

ICWA–030S * Notice of Child Custody Proceeding for Indian Child

ICWA–030(A) Attachment to Notice of Child Custody Proceeding for Indian Child (Indian Child Welfare Act)

ICWA–030(A)S Attachment to Notice of Child Custody Proceeding for Indian Child (Indian Child Welfare Act)

ICWA–040 Notice of Designation of Tribal Representative and Notice of Intervention in a Court Proceeding Involving an Indian Child

ICWA–050 Notice of Petition and Petition to Transfer Case Involving an Indian Child to Tribal Jurisdiction

ICWA–060 * Order on Petition to Transfer Case Involving an Indian Child to Tribal Jurisdiction

NAME CHANGES

The forms listed below are pertinent to the statutes and rules appearing in the preceding divisions of this publication:

NC–100 * Petition for Change of Name (Change of Name)

NC–110 * Attachment to Petition for Change of Name

NC–110G * Supplemental Attachment to Petition for Change of Name (Declaration of Guardian)

NC–120 * Order to Show Cause for Change of Name (Change of Name)

NC–121 * Proof of Service of Order to Show Cause

NC–130 * Decree Changing Name (Change of Name)

NC–130G * Decree Changing Name (Change of Name of Minor by Guardian)

NC–200 * Petition for Change of Name and Gender

NC–220 * Order to Show Cause for Change of Name

NC–230 * Decree Changing Name and Gender

NC–400 * Confidential Cover Sheet—Name Change Proceeding Under Address Confidentiality Program (Safe at Home) (Change of Name)

NC–400–INFO Information Sheet for Name Change Proceedings Under Address Confidentiality Program (Safe at Home)

NC–410 * Application to File Documents Under Seal in Name Change Proceeding Under Address Confidentiality Program (Safe at Home)

NC–420 * Declaration in Support of Application to File Documents Under Seal in Name Change Proceeding Under Address Confidentiality Program (Safe at Home)

NC–425 Order on Application to File Documents Under Seal in Name Change Proceeding Under Address Confidentiality Program (Safe at Home)

PROBATE:

Decedents' Estates

The forms listed below are pertinent to the statutes and rules appearing in the preceding divisions of this publication:

DE–111 * Petition for Probate

DE–140 * Order for Probate

DE–147 * Duties and Liabilities of Personal Representative

DE–150 * Letters

DE–221 * Spousal or Domestic Partner Property Petition (Probate—Decedents' Estates)

DE–226 * Spousal of Domestic Partner Property Order (Probate—Decedents' Estates)

DE–295/GC–395 * Ex Parte Petition for Final Discharge and Order (Probate—Decedents' Estates and Conservatorships and Guardianships)

Guardianships and Conservatorships

The forms listed below are pertinent to the statutes and rules appearing in the preceding divisions of this publication:

GC–010 * Certification of Attorney Concerning Qualifications for Court Appointment in Conservatorships or Guardianships

GC–011 * Annual Certification of Court-Appointed Attorney (Probate—Guardianships and Conservatorships)

GC–020 * Notice of Hearing—Guardianship or Conservatorship (Probate—Guardianships and Conservatorships)

GC–020(C) * Clerk's Certificate of Posting Notice of Hearing—Guardianship or Conservatorship (Probate—Guardianship or Conservatorships)

GC–020(P) Proof of Personal Service of Notice of Hearing—Guardianship or Conservatorship (Probate—Guardianships and Conservatorships)

GC–021 * Order Dispensing with Notice

GC–120/FL–105 * Declaration Under Uniform Child Custody Jurisdiction and Enforcement Act (UCCJEA)

GC–120/FL–105 S * Declaration Under Uniform Child Custody Jurisdiction and Enforcement Act (UCCJEA)

GC–120(A)/FL–105(A) * Attachment to Declaration Under Uniform Child Custody Jurisdiction and Enforcement Act (UCCJEA)

GC–210(CA) * Guardianship Petition—Child Information Attachment (Probate—Guardianships and Conservatorships)

GC–210(PE) Petition to Extend Guardianship of the Person

GC–211 * Consent of Proposed Guardian, Nomination of Guardian, and Consent to Appointment of Guardian and Waiver of Notice

GC–212 * Confidential Guardian Screening Form

GC–251 * Confidential Guardianship Status Report

GC–255 * Petition for Termination of Guardianship (Probate—Guardianships and Conservatorships)

GC–260 * Order Terminating Guardianship (Probate—Guardianships and Conservatorships)

GC–330 Order Appointing Court Investigator (Probate—Guardianships and Conservatorships)

GC–331 Order Appointing Court Investigator (Review and Successor Conservator Investigations) (Probate—Guardianships and Conservatorships)

GC–332 Order Setting Biennial Review Investigation and Directing Status Report Before Review (Probate—Guardianships and Conservatorships)

GC–505 Forms You Need to Ask the Court to Appoint a Guardian of the Person (Probate—Guardianships and Conservatorships)

GC–505S Forms You Need to Ask the Court to Appoint a Guardian of the Person (Probate—Guardianships and Conservatorships)

GC–510 What Is "Proof of Service" in a Guardianship? (Probate—Guardianships and Conservatorships)

GC–510S What Is "Proof of Service" in a Guardianship? (Probate—Guardianships and Conservatorships)

PROOF OF SERVICE

The forms listed below are pertinent to the statutes and rules appearing in the preceding divisions of this publication:

POS–030 Proof of Service by First–Class Mail—Civil (Proof of Service) Information Sheet for Proof of Service By First–Class Mail—Civil

POS–040 Proof of Service—Civil

RECEIVERSHIPS

The forms listed below are pertinent to the statutes and rules appearing in the preceding divisions of this publication:

RC–200 Ex Parte Order Appointing Receiver and Order to Show Cause and Temporary Restraining Order—Rents, Issues, and Profits

RC–210 Order Confirming Appointment of Receiver and Preliminary Injunction—Rents, Issues, and Profits

RC–300 Order to Show Cause and Temporary Restraining Order—Rents, Issues, and Profits

RC–310 Order Appointing Receiver after Hearing and Preliminary Injunction—Rents, Issues, and Profits

SCHOOL VIOLENCE PREVENTION

The forms listed below are pertinent to the statutes and rules appearing in the preceding divisions of this publication:

SV–100 * Petition for Private Postsecondary School Violence Restraining Orders

SV–110 * Temporary Restraining Order (CLETS-TSV)

SV–115 * Request to Continue Court Hearing and to Reissue Temporary Restraining Order

SV–115–INFO How to Ask for a New Hearing Date

SV–120 * Response to Petition for Private Postsecondary School Violence Restraining Orders

SV–120–INFO How Can I Respond to a Petition for Private Postsecondary School Violence Restraining Orders? (Private Postsecondary School Violence Prevention)

SV–130 * Private Postsecondary School Violence Restraining Order After Hearing (CLETS-SVO)

SV–600 * Request to Modify/Terminate Private Postsecondary School Violence Restraining Order

SV–610 * Notice of Hearing on Request to Modify/Terminate Private Postsecondary School Violence Restraining Order

SV–620 * Response to Request to Modify/Terminate Private Postsecondary School Violence Restraining Order

SV–630 * Order on Request to Modify/Terminate Private Postsecondary School Violence Restraining Order

SV–800 Proof of Firearms Turned In, Sold, or Stored (Private Postsecondary School Violence Prevention

SMALL CLAIMS

The forms listed below are pertinent to the statutes and rules appearing in the preceding divisions of this publication:

SC–114 Request to Amend Claim Before Hearing (Small Claims)

SC–132 * Attorney-Client Fee Dispute (Attachment to Notice of Entry of Judgment)

SC–202A * Decision on Attorney-Client Fee Dispute (Small Claims)

UNLAWFUL DETAINER (LANDLORD/TENANT)

The forms listed below are pertinent to the statutes and rules appearing in the preceding divisions of this publication:

UD–105 Answer—Unlawful Detainer

WAGE GARNISHMENT

The forms listed below are pertinent to the statutes and rules appearing in the preceding divisions of this publication:

WG–002 * Earnings Withholding Order

WG–004 * Earnings Withholding Order for Support (Wage Garnishment)

WG–026 * Claim of Exemption and Financial Declaration (State Tax Liability)

WG–030 * Earnings Withholding Order for Elder and Dependent Adult Abuse

WORKPLACE VIOLENCE PREVENTION

The forms listed below are pertinent to the statutes and rules appearing in the preceding divisions of this publication:

WV–100 * Petition for Workplace Violence Restraining Orders

WV–100–INFO How Do I Get an Order to Prohibit Workplace Violence? (Workplace Violence Prevention)

WV–109 * Notice of Court Hearing (Workplace Violence Prevention)

WV–110 * Temporary Restraining Order (CLETS-TWH)

WV–115–INFO How to Ask for a New Hearing Date

WV–116 * Notice of New Hearing Date and Order on Reissuance

WV–120 * Response to Petition for Workplace Violence Restraining Orders

WV–120–INFO How Can I Respond to a Petition for Workplace Violence Restraining Orders?

WV–130 * Workplace Violence Restraining Order After Hearing (CLETS-WHO)

WV–200 Proof of Personal Service (Workplace Violence Prevention)

WV–250 Proof of Service of Response by Mail (Workplace Violence Prevention)

WV–600 * Request to Modify/Terminate Workplace Violence Restraining Order

WV–610 * Notice of Hearing on Request to Modify/Terminate Workplace Violence Restraining Order

WV–620 * Response to Request to Modify/Terminate Workplace Violence Restraining Order

WV–630 * Order on Request to Modify/Terminate Workplace Violence Restraining Order

WV–800 Proof of Firearms Turned In, Sold, or Stored (Workplace Violence Prevention)

MISCELLANEOUS

The forms listed below are pertinent to the statutes and rules appearing in the preceding divisions of this publication:

MC–012 * Memorandum of Costs After Judgment, Acknowledgment of Credit, and Declaration of Accrued Interest

MC–275 Petition for Writ of Habeas Corpus

MC–300 * Petition for Declaration of Emancipation of Minor, Order Prescribing Notice, Declaration of Emancipation, and Order Denying Petition

MC–305 Notice of Hearing—Emancipation of Minor

MC–306 * Emancipation of Minor—Income and Expense Declaration

MC–310 Declaration of Emancipation of Minor After Hearing

MC–315 Emancipated Minor's Application to California Department of Motor Vehicles

MC–350(A–13b(5)) Medical Service Provider Attachment to Petition to Approve Compromise of Claim or Action or Disposition of Proceeds of Judgment (Miscellaneous)

MC–350 * Petition to Approve Compromise of Disputed Claim or Pending Action or Disposition of Proceeds of Judgment for Minor or Person with a Disability (Miscellaneous)

MC–350EX * Expedited Petition to Approve Compromise of Disputed Claim or Pending Action or Disposition of Proceeds of Judgment for Minor or Person With A Disability (Miscellaneous)

MC–351 * Order Approving Compromise of Disputed Claim or Pending Action or Disposition of Proceeds of Judgment for Minor or Person with a Disability (Miscellaneous)

MC–355 * Order to Deposit Money into Blocked Account

MC–356 * Receipt and Acknowledgment of Order for the Deposit of Money into Blocked Account

MC–1000 Request for Review of Denial of Request to Remove Name From Gan Database

* Adopted for mandatory use by all courts.

CALIFORNIA JURY INSTRUCTIONS

This table indicates where sections of the California Codes appearing in this pamphlet are referenced in the California Jury Instructions—Civil, 8th (BAJI), the Judicial Council of California Civil Jury Instructions (CACI) and California Jury Instructions–Criminal, 6th Edition (CALJIC)

FAMILY CODE

6910 .... CACI 531
6211 .... CALJIC 2.50.02
7540 .... CALJIC 16.153
7556 .... CALJIC 16.153
7613 .... CALJIC 16.153

CIVIL CODE

38 .... BAJI 10.55
39 .... BAJI 10.55
43.6 .... CACI 513
44 .... BAJI 7.00; CACI 1700
45 .... BAJI 7.00; CACI 1700, 1702, 1704, 1706, 1707
45a .... BAJI 7.09, 7.11; CACI 1701, 1703, 1704
46 ....BAJI 7.00. 7.09, 7.11; CACI 1700, 1702, 1704, 1706, 1707
47 ....BAJI 7.05, 7.05.1, 7.36, 7.86, 7.86.1; CACI 1501, 1520, 1605, 1723, 1731, 2711
49 .... BAJI 7.97
50 .... BAJI 7.55; CACI 1304
51 .... BAJI 7.92, 7.92.1; CACI 3060, 3067
52.4 .... BAJI 7.92.3
52.45 .... BAJI 7.92.4
1569 .... CACI 333; CALJIC 9.62
1570 .... CACI 333
1572 .... CALJIC 9.60, 9.62
1575 .... CACI 3117
1620 .... BAJI 10.56; CACI 305, 2401, 2402, 2403
1621 .... BAJI 10.56
1708.5.5 .... BAJI 7.57
1708.6 .... BAJI 7.96
1708.9 .... BAJI 7.95.3
1714 .... CACI 433, 1620, 1622, 1623
2295 .... CACI 3724, 3725
2342 .... BAJI 10.97.2
2343 .... BAJI 10.97.3
3294 .... BAJI 2.62, 7.10.1; 7.12, 7.12.1, 10.43, 12.25, 14.61, 14.71, 14.72.1, 14.72.2, 14.73, 14.73.1, 14.75, 16.81; CACI 1623, 2433, 3940, 3941, 3942, 3943, 3944, 3945, 3946, 3947, 3948, 3949
3318 .... CACI 10.97.4
3439.01 .... CACI 4204, 4205
3439.02 .... CACI 4205, 4206
3439.03 .... CACI 4202, 4203, 4207
3439.04 .... CACI 4200, 4201, 4202, 4203
3439.05 .... CACI 4202, 4203
3439.07 .... CACI 4200
3439.08 .... CACI 4207

CODE OF CIVIL PROCEDURE

340 .... BAJI 12.70
340.5 .... BAJI 6.20; CACI 500, 3103
340.6 .... CACI 610, 611
352 .... CACI 610, 611
376 .... BAJI 14.30, 15.00
377.60 .... CACI 3921
527.6 .... BAJI 7.20, 7.58
685.010 .... BAJI 16.90
1161.3 .... CACI 4328

EVIDENCE CODE

1010 .... BAJI 6.00.1.1, 6.00.2

GOVERNMENT CODE

12945.2 .... CACI 2601

PENAL CODE

270 .... CALJIC 16.151, 16.152, 16.153, 16.155, 16.156
270e .... CALJIC 16.153
272 .... CALJIC 16.160, 16.160.1
273 .... CALJIC 4.80, 9.36
273a .... CALJIC 9.36.5, 9.37, 9.38, 16.170, 16.172
273ab .... CALJIC 9.36.5, 9.36.6
273d .... CALJIC 2.50.04, 9.36
273.5 .... CALJIC 9.35, 9.35.01
277 .... CALJIC 9.70.5, 9.71, 9.72
278 .... CALJIC 9.70
278.5 .... CALJIC 9.60, 9.71, 9.71.5, 16.135
279 .... CALJIC 9.72
13700 .... CALJIC 2.50.02, 9.35

PROBATE CODE

1400, et seq. .... CACI 4013

WELFARE AND INSTITUTIONS CODE

300 .... CALJIC 16.161
601 .... CALJIC 16.162

TABLE OF CASES

References are to division of publication and provision in which the case is referenced

Abbreviations

Fam C = Family Code
Related Cal Stats = Related California Statutes
Bus & Prof C = Business and Professions Code
Civ C = Civil Code
CCP = Code of Civil Procedure
Corp C = Corporations Code
Educ C = Education Code
Evid C = Evidence Code
Gov C = Government Code
Pen C = Penal Code
Prob C = Probate Code
W & I C = Welfare and Institutions Code
Related Fed Stats = Related Federal Statutes
USCA = United States Code Annotated
Hague Convention = Hague Convention on International Child Abduction
Cal R Ct = California Rules of Court

A

A.A., In re, 114 Cal.App.4th 771, 7 Cal.Rptr.3d 755 (2003), review denied—Fam C §§ 7611, 7612
A.A, In re, 164 Cal.Rptr.3d (2013)—Related Cal Stats: W & I C §§ 300, 355.1
A.A. v. Superior Court, 209 Cal.App.4th 237, 146 Cal.Rptr.3d 805 (2012)—Related Cal Stats: W & I C § 361.5
A.B., Adoption of, 2 Cal.App.5th 912, 206 Cal.Rptr.3d 531 (2016)—Fam C § 7822
Abandonato v. Coldren, 41 Cal.App.4th 264, 48 Cal.Rptr.2d 429 (1996)—Related Cal Stats: CCP §§ 128.5, 128.7
Abargil, In re Marriage of, 106 Cal.App.4th 1294, 131 Cal.Rptr.2d 429 (2003)—Fam C § 7501
Abbett Electric Corp. v. Storek, 22 Cal.App.4th 1460, 27 Cal. Rptr.2d 845 (1994), review denied 6/23/94—Fam C § 2581
Abbigail A., In re, 173 Cal.Rptr.3d 191 (2014)—Selected Fed Stats: 25 USCA § 1903; Cal R Ct 5.482, 5.484
Abbigail A., In re, 1 Cal.5th 83, 375 P.3d 879, 204 Cal.Rptr.3d 760 (2016)—Cal R Ct 5.482, 5.484
Abbott v. Abbott, 130 S.Ct. 1983, 176 L.Ed.2d 789 (2010)—Hague Convention
Abdi (Mahamud) v. Commissioner, T.C. Memo 2015-41—Related Fed Stats: 26 USCA §§ 32, 152
Ablamis v. Roper, 937 F.2d 1450 (9th Cir. 1991)—Fam C § 2610
Abram L., In re, 219 Cal.App.4th 452, 161 Cal.Rptr.3d 837 (2013)—Related Cal Stats: W & I C § 361.2
Abrams, In re Marriage of, 105 Cal.App.4th 979, 130 Cal.Rptr.2d 16 (2003), review denied 5/14/03—Fam C § 7501
A.C., In re, 13 Cal.App.5th 661, 220 Cal.Rptr.3d 725 (2017)—Fam C § 3421
A.C., In re, 130 Cal.App.4th 854, 30 Cal.Rptr.3d 431 (2005)—Fam C §§ 3402, 3403, 3421, 3424
A.C., In re, 155 Cal.App.4th 282, 65 Cal.Rptr.3d 767 (2007), review denied—Related Cal Stats: W & I C § 306.6
A.C., In re, 166 Cal.App.4th 146, 82 Cal.Rptr.3d 542 (2008), review denied—Related Cal Stats: CCP § 372
A.C., In re, 169 Cal.App.4th 636, 88 Cal.Rptr.3d 1 (2008)—Related Cal Stats: W & I C §§ 361.2, 361.5
A.C., In re, 186 Cal.App.4th 976, 112 Cal.Rptr.3d 593 (2010)—Related Cal Stats: W & I C §§ 387, 388
Adam D., In re, 183 Cal.App.4th 1250, 108 Cal.Rptr.3d 611 (2010)—Related Cal Stats: W & I C § 360
Adam N., In re, 101 Cal.Rptr.2d 181 (2000)—Related Fed Stats: 25 USCA §§ 1903, 1912
Adams, In re Marriage of, 209 Cal.App.4th 1543, 148 Cal.Rptr.3d 83 (2012)—Cal R Ct 5.220
Adams, In re Marriage of, 52 Cal.App.4th 911, 60 Cal.Rptr.2d 811 (1997), review denied 5/14/97—Related Cal Stats: CCP § 128.5
Addison v. Addison, 62 Cal.2d 558, 43 Cal.Rptr. 97, 399 P.2d 897 (1965)—Fam C §§ 125, 912
Adoption of (see name of party)
Adoptive Couple v. Baby Girl, 133 S.Ct. 2552 (2013)—Related Fed Stats: 25 USCA § 1912
Adrianna P., In re, 166 Cal.App.4th 44, 81 Cal.Rptr.3d 918 (2008)—Related Cal Stats: W & I C §§ 361.2, 361.5
A.E., In re, 228 Cal.App.4th 820, 175 Cal.Rptr.3d 629 (2014)—Related Cal Stats: W & I C § 361
A.G., In re, 12 Cal.App.5th 994, 219 Cal.Rptr.3d 239 (2017)—Related Cal Stats: W & I C § 361.5
A.G. v. C.S., 246 Cal.App.4th 1269, 201 Cal.Rptr.3d 552 (2016)—Related Cal Stats: CCP § 632
Agricultural Prorate Commission v. Superior Court, 30 Cal. App. 2d 154, 85 P.2d 898 (1938)—Fam C § 242
A.H., In re, 218 Cal.App.4th 337, 159 Cal.Rptr.3d 891 (2013), review denied—Related Cal Stats: W & I C § 366.26; Cal R Ct 8.450
A.K., In re, 12 Cal.App.5th 492, 218 Cal.Rptr.3d 845 (2017), review denied—Related Cal Stats: W & I C § 361.3
A.L., In re, 188 Cal.App.4th 138, 115 Cal.Rptr.3d 560 (2010)—Related Cal Stats: W & I C §§ 362, 366.26, 388
Alameda, County of v. Johnson, 28 Cal.App.4th 259, 33 Cal.Rptr.2d 483 (1994)—Fam C § 17402
Alanna A, In re, 135 Cal.App.4th 555, 37 Cal.Rptr.3d 579 (2005)—Related Cal Stats: W & I C § 366.21
Alayah J., In re, 9 Cal.App.5th 469, 215 Cal.Rptr.3d 140 (2017)—Related Cal Stats: W & I C § 388
Albert T., In re, 144 Cal.App.4th 207, 50 Cal.Rptr.3d 227 (2006)—Related Cal Stats: W & I C § 361.5
Alcala v. Hernandez, 826 F.3d 161 (4th Cir. 2016)—Hague Convention
Alderson v. Alderson, 180 Cal.App.3d 450, 225 Cal.Rptr. 610 (1986), review denied 7/16/86—Fam C § 290
Alex R. v. Superior Court of Los Angeles County, 248 Cal.App.4th 1, 203 Cal.Rptr.3d 251 (2016)—Fam C § 7635
Alexander, In re Marriage of, 212 Cal.App.3d 677, 261 Cal.Rptr. 9 (1989)—Fam C § 1100
Alexander B., In re, 121 Cal.Rptr.2d 512 (2002)—Related Cal Stats: Pen C § 2625; W & I C § 366.26
Alexander M., Adoption of, 94 Cal.App.4th 430, 114 Cal.Rptr.2d 218 (2001)—Fam C §§ 7611, 7664, 8604
Alexandria M., In re, 156 Cal.App.4th 1088, 68 Cal.Rptr.3d 10 (2007)—Related Cal Stats: W & I C § 364
Alexandria P., In re, 228 Cal.App.4th 1322, 176 Cal.Rptr.3d 468 (2014)—Selected Fed Stats:25 USCA §§ 1915, 1915
Alexander P., In re, 4 Cal.App.5th 475, 209 Cal.Rptr.3d 130 (2016), review denied—Related Cal Stats: W & I C § 316.2

B

Barthold, In re Marriage of, 158 Cal.App.4th 1301, 70 Cal.Rptr.3d 691 (2008)—Related Cal Stats: CCP § 1008

Barzilay v. Barzilay, 536 F.3d 844 (8th Cir. 2008)—Related Fed Stats: 42 USCA § 11601; Hague Convention

Baumann (Stanley K. and Tomi L.) v. Commissioner, T.C. Memo 2005–31, 89 T.C.M. (CCH) 790 (U.S. Tax Ct. 2005)—Related Fed Stats: 26 USCA § 6015

Baxter (Linda J.) v. Commissioner, T.C. Memo. 1999-190, 77 T.C.M. (CCH) 2137 (U.S. Tax Ct. 1999)—Related Fed Stats: 26 USCA §§ 71, 215

B.C., In re, 205 Cal.App.4th 1306, 140 Cal.Rptr.3d 881 (2012)—Cal R Ct 5.635

B.C., In re Adoption of, 195 Cal.App.4th 913, 125 Cal.Rptr.3d 727 (2011)—Fam C § 9102

B. del C.S.B., In re, 559 F.3d 999 (9th Cir. 2009)—Hague Convention

Beach, People v., 194 Cal.App.3d 955, 240 Cal.Rptr. 50 (1987), review denied 12/2/87—Fam C §§ 3060, 3061, 3062, 3063, 3064

Beal Bank, SSB v. Arter and Hadden, LLP, 42 Cal.4th 503, 66 Cal.Rptr.3d 52, 167 P.3d 666 (2007)—Related Cal Stats: CCP § 340.6

Beam v. Bank of America, 6 Cal.3d 12, 98 Cal.Rptr. 137 (1971)—Fam C § 2640

Beatrice M., In re, 29 Cal.App.4th 1411, 35 Cal.Rptr.2d 162 (1994), review denied 1/19/95—Related Cal Stats: W & I C § 366.26

Becherer (Timothy R.) v. Commissioner, T.C. Memo 2004–282, 88 T.C.M. (CCH) 617 (U.S. Tax Ct. 2004)—Related Fed Stats: 26 USCA § 6015

Beck, In re Marriage of, 57 Cal.App.4th 341, 67 Cal.Rptr.2d 79 (1997)—Fam C § 4336

Becker v. Williams, 777 F.3d 1035 (9th Cir. 2015)—Fam C § 2610

Begic (Belma) v. Commissioner, T.C. Memo 2007–74, 93 T.C.M. (CCH) 1242 (U.S. Tax Ct. 2007)—Related Fed Stats: 26 USCA § 6015

Begier v. Strom, 46 Cal.App.4th 877, 54 Cal.Rptr.2d 158 (1996)—Fam C § 3027; Related Cal Stats: Civ C § 47

Bell, In re Marriage of, 49 Cal.App.4th 300, 56 Cal.Rptr.2d 623 (1996), review denied 12/11/96—Fam C § 2602

Bellio, In re Marriage of, 105 Cal.App.4th 630, 129 Cal.Rptr.2d 556 (2003)—Fam C § 1612

Belot v. Commissioner, T.C. Memo 2016-113 (U.S. Tax Ct.)—Related Fed Stats: 26 U.S.C.A. § 1041

Beltran, In re Marriage of, 183 Cal.App.3d 292, 227 Cal.Rptr. 924 (1986)—Fam C § 2602

Ben C., In re Conservatorship of, 40 Cal.4th 529, 53 Cal.Rptr.3d 856, 150 P.3d 738 (2007)—Fam C § 7822; Related Cal Stats: W & I C § 366.26

Bendetti, In re Marriage of, 214 Cal.App.4th 863, 154 Cal.Rptr.3d 329 (2013)—Fam C § 2030

Benham (Thomas B.) v. Commissioner, T.C. Memo. 2000–165, 79 T.C.M. (CCH) 2054 (U.S. Tax Ct. 2000)—Related Fed Stats: 26 USCA §§ 71, 215

Benjamins, In re Marriage of, 26 Cal.App.4th 423, 31 Cal.Rptr.2d 313 (1994)—Fam C §§ 271, 4330, 4337

Bennett v. McCall, 19 Cal.App.4th 122, 23 Cal.Rptr.2d 268 (1993), review denied 12/30/93—Related Cal Stats: CCP § 340.6

Benson, In re Marriage of, 171 Cal.App.3d 907, 217 Cal.Rptr. 589 (1985)—Fam C § 4335

Benson, In re Marriage of, 36 Cal.4th 1096, 116 P.3d 1152, 32 Cal.Rptr.3d 471 (2005)—Fam C §§ 852, 1611

Benson v. City of Los Angeles, 60 Cal.2d 355, 33 Cal.Rptr. 257 (1963)—Fam C § 2610

Ben–Yehosua, In re Marriage of, 91 Cal.App.3d 259, 154 Cal.Rptr. 80 (1979)—Fam C § 125

Bereznak & Heminger, In re Marriage of, 110 Cal.App.4th 1062, 2 Cal.Rptr.3d (2003)—Fam C § 4065

Berezowsky v. Ojeda, 765 F.3d 456 (5th Cir. 2014), cert. denied—Related Fed Stats: Hague Convention

Berg v. Traylor, 148 Cal.App.4th 809, 56 Cal.Rptr.3d 140 (2007)—Fam C §§ 1612, 6710

Bergen v. Wood, 14 Cal.App.4th 854, 18 Cal.Rptr.2d 75 (1993), review denied 7/15/93—Fam C § 2251

Berger, In re Marriage of, 170 Cal.App.4th 1070, 88 Cal.Rptr.3d 766 (2009)—Fam C §§ 4057, 4058

Berger, United States v., 574 F.3d 1202 (9th Cir. 2009)—Fam C § 910

Bergeron v. Boyd, 223 Cal.App.4th 877, 167 Cal.Rptr 3d 426 (2014), review denied—Related Cal Stats: Civ C § 47

Bergman, In re Marriage of, 168 Cal.App.3d 742, 214 Cal.Rptr. 661 (1985)—Fam C § 2550

Bernal (Kathryn) v. Commissioner, 20 T.C. 102 (U.S. Tax Court 2003)—Related Fed Stats: 26 USCA § 66

Berry (Michael K.) v. Commissioner, T.C. Memo 2005–91, 89 T.C.M. (CCH) 1090 (U.S. Tax Ct. 2005)—Fam C § 4337; Related Fed Stats: 26 USCA §§ 71, 215

Berry (Thomas D.) v. Commissioner, T.C. Memo. 2000–373, 80 T.C.M. (CCH) 825 (U.S. Tax Ct. 2000)—Related Fed Stats: 26 USCA § 71

Bertrand, In re Marriage of, 33 Cal.App.4th 437, 39 Cal.Rptr.2d 151 (1995)—Fam C § 4504

Beust, In re Marriage of, 23 Cal.App.4th 24, 28 Cal.Rptr.2d 201 (1994), review denied 6/23/94—Fam C §§ 3591, 4320

Beverly, In re, 374 B.R. 221 (U.S. Bankr. App. Pan., 9th Cir. 2007)—Fam C §§ 721, 850, 851, 852, 916; Related Cal Stats: Civ C § 3493.04

B.G., In re, 11 Cal.3d 679, 114 Cal.Rptr. 444 (1974)—Fam C §§ 3040, 3041

B.H., In re, 243 Cal.App.4th 729, 196 Cal.Rptr.3d 718 (2016)—Related Cal Stats: W & I C § 361.5

B.H., In re, 241 Cal.App.4th 603, 194 Cal.Rptr.3d 226 (2015)—Related Fed Stats: 25 U.S.C.A. § 1912

Biallas, In re Marriage of, 65 Cal.App.4th 755, 76 Cal.Rptr.2d 717 (1998)—Fam C § 7501

Bianco, In re Marriage of, 221 Cal.App.4th 826, 164 Cal.Rptr.3d 785 (2013)—Cal R Ct 5.14

Bibb, Estate of, 87 Cal.App.4th 461, 104 Cal.Rptr.2d 415 (2001), review denied 5/16/01—Fam C § 852

Bidna v. Rosen, 19 Cal.App.4th 27, 23 Cal.Rptr.2d 251 (1993), review denied 12/30/93—Fam C § 271

Biggums–Slayton, In re Marriage of, 86 Cal.App.4th 653, 103 Cal. Rptr.2d 545 (2001), review denied 5/16/01—Fam C § 3064

Billings (David Bruce) v. Commissioner, 127 T.C. No.2 (2006)—Related Fed Stats: 26 USCA § 6015

Birnbaum, In re Marriage of, 211 Cal.App.3rd 1508, 260 Cal. Rptr.2d 210 (1989)—Fam C §§ 3022, 3087

Bir's Estate, In re, 83 Cal.App.2d 256, 188 P.2d 499 (1948)—Fam C § 308

B.L., In re, 204 Cal.App.4th 1111, 139 Cal.Rptr.3d 525 (2012)—Related Cal Stats: W & I C § 361.5

Blackledge v. Blackledge, 866 F.3d 169 (3d Cir. 2017)—Hague Convention

Blair, Estate of, 199 Cal.App.3d 161, 244 Cal.Rptr. 627 (1988)—Fam C §§ 2040, 2581

Blatt v. Commissioner, 102 T.C. 77, Tax Ct. Rep. (CCH) 49,641 (1994)—Related Fed Stats: 26 USCA § 1041

Blazer, In re Marriage of, 176 Cal.App.4th 1438, 99 Cal.Rptr.3d 42 (2009)—Fam C § 4320

Block (Evelyn B.) v. Commissioner, 120 T.C. 62 (U.S. Tax Ct. 2003)—Related Fed Stats: 26 USCA § 6015

Blumenthal v. Superior Court, 137 Cal.App.4th 672, 40 Cal.Rptr.3d 509 (2006)—Fam C § 2330.3

Boblitt, In re Marriage of, 223 Cal.App.4th 1004, 167 Cal.Rptr.3d 777 (2014)—Fam C § 218

Boblitt v. Boblitt, 190 Cal.App.4th 603, 118 Cal.Rptr.3d 788 (2010)—Fam C § 4320

TABLE OF CASES

Bock (Debra) v. Commissioner, T.C. Memo 2007–41, 93 T.C.M. (CCH) 927 (U.S. Tax Ct. 2007)—Related Fed Stats: 26 USCA § 6015

Bodo, In re Marriage of, 198 Cal.App.4th 373, 129 Cal.Rptr.3d 298 (2011)—Fam C § 4065

Boeseke v. Boeseke, 10 Cal.3d 844, 112 Cal.Rptr. 401 (1974)—Fam C § 1100

Boggs v. Boggs, 117 S.Ct. 1754, 138 L.Ed.2d 45 (1997)—Fam C § 2610

Boltinghouse (Michael K.) v. Commissioner, T.C. Memo. 2003–134, 85 T.C.M. (CCH) 1277 (U.S. Tax Court 2003)—Related Fed Stats: 26 USCA § 152

Bonanno, Estate of, 165 Cal.App.4th 7, 80 Cal.Rptr.3d 560 (2008)—Related Cal Stats: Prob C § 13500

Bonds, In re Marriage of, 5 P.3d 815, 99 Cal.Rptr.2d 252 (2000)—Fam C § 1615

Bonnie P. v. Superior Court, 134 Cal.App.4th 1249, 37 Cal.Rptr.3d 77 (2005)—Fam C § 7120

Bono v. Clark, 103 Cal.App.4th 1409, 128 Cal.Rptr.2d 31 (2002), review denied 3/5/03—Fam C §§ 2552, 2640

Bonvino, In re Marriage of, 241 Cal.App.4th 1411, 194 Cal.Rptr.3d 754 (2015)—Fam C § 2640

Boozer v. Wilder, 381 F.3d 931 (9th Cir. 2004)—Related Fed Stats: 26 USCA § 1911

Borelli v. Brusseau, 12 Cal.App.4th 647, 16 Cal.Rptr.2d 16 (1993), review denied 4/1/93—Fam C §§ 720, 1620, 4300

Borges, Marriage of, 83 Cal.App.3d 771, 148 Cal.Rptr. 118 (1978)—Fam C § 2650

Borson, In re Marriage of, 37 Cal.App.3d 632, 112 Cal.Rptr. 432 (1974)—Fam C § 2030

Bouley v. Long Beach Memorial Medical Center, 127 Cal.App.4th 601, 25 Cal.Rptr.3d 813 (2005)—Related Cal Stats: CCP § 377.60

Boutte v. Nears, 50 Cal.App.4th 162, 57 Cal.Rptr.2d 655 (1996)—Fam C § 4062

Bower, In re Marriage of, 96 Cal.App.4th 893, 117 Cal.Rptr.2d 520 (2002)—Fam C § 4323

B.R., In re, 176 Cal.App.4th 773, 97 Cal.Rptr.3d 890 (2009)—Related Fed Stats: 25 USCA § 1903

Brace, In re, 566 B.R. 13 (B.A.P. 9th Cir. 2017)—Fam C §§ 760, 850, 851, 852, 2581

Branco, In re Marriage of, 47 Cal.App.4th 1621, 55 Cal.Rptr.2d 493 (1996)—Fam C § 2640

Branco v. UFCW–Northern California Employers Joint Pension Plan, 279 F.3d 1154 (9th Cir.2002)—Fam C § 2610

Brandes, In re Marriage of, 239 Cal.App.4th 1461, 192 Cal.Rptr.3d 1 (2015), review denied—Fam C § 2640

Brandes, Marriage of, 239 Cal.App.4th 1461, 192 Cal.Rptr.3d 1 (2015)—Related Cal Stats: Prob C § 5305

Brandon C., In re, 71 Cal.App.4th 1530, 84 Cal.Rptr.2d 505 (1999)—Related Cal Stats: W & I C § 366.26

Brandon M., In re, 54 Cal.App.4th 1387, 63 Cal.Rptr.2d 671 (1997), review denied 8/20/97—Related Fed Stats: 25 USCA § 1903

Brandon T., In re, 164 Cal.App.4th 1400, 80 Cal.Rptr.3d 287 (2008), review denied—Related Cal Stats: W & I C § 366.26

Braud, In re Marriage of, 45 Cal.App.4th 797, 53 Cal.Rptr.2d 179 (1996)—Fam C §§ 770, 2550, 2640, 3800, 3802, 3808, 4057

Bray, Estate of, 230 Cal.App.2d 136, 40 Cal.Rptr. 750 (1964)—Fam C § 770

Brekke v. Wills, 125 Cal.App.4th 1400, 23 Cal.Rptr.3d 609 (2004), review denied—Related Cal Stats: CCP § 527.6

Breanna S., In re, 8 Cal.App.5th 636, 214 Cal.Rptr.3d 98 (2017)—Related Cal Stats: W & I C § 224.2; Related Fed Stats: 25 USCA § 1912

Brequia Y., In re, 57 Cal.App.4th 1060, 67 Cal.Rptr.2d 389 (1997)—Related Cal Stats: W & I C § 366.22

Brewer, In re Marriage of, 93 Cal.App.4th 1334, 113 Cal.Rptr.2d 849 (2001) Fam C §§ 2102, 2120, 2121, 2122, 2125

Brewer v. Carter, 218 Cal.App.4th 1312, 160 Cal.Rptr.3d 853 (2013)—Fam C § 3427

Brian C. v. Ginger K., 77 Cal.App.4th 1198, 92 Cal.Rptr.2d 294 (2000)—Fam C §§ 7540, 7611

Brian P., In re, 99 Cal.App.4th 616, 1333F, 121 Cal.Rptr.2d 326 (2002)—Related Cal Stats: W & I C § 366.26

Brianna M., In re, 163 Cal.Rptr.3d 665 (2013)—Fam C §§ 7575, 7611; Related Cal Stats: W & I C § 361.5

Briana V., In re, 236 Cal.App.4th 297, 186 Cal.Rptr.3d 397 (2015)—Related Cal Stats: W & I C § 300

Bridget R., In re, 41 Cal.App.4th 1483, 49 Cal.Rptr.2d 507 (1996), review denied 5/15/96, cert. denied by Cindy R. v. James R., 519 U.S. 1060 (1997), cert. denied by Dry Creek Rancheria v. Bridget and Lucy R., 520 U.S. 1181 (1997)—Related Fed Stats: 25 USCA §§ 1913, 1914

Brigden, In re Marriage of, 80 Cal.App.3d 380, 145 Cal.Rptr. 716 (1978)—Fam C § 2601

Brinkman, In re Marriage of, 111 Cal.App.4th 1281, 4 Cal.Rptr.3d 722 (2003)—Fam C § 3651

Britel, Estate of, 236 Cal.App.4th 127, 186 Cal.Rptr 3d 321 (2015), review denied—Related Cal Stats: Prob C § 6453

Brittany C., In re, 76 Cal.App.4th 847, 90 Cal.Rptr.2d 737 (1999), review denied 2/16/00—Related Cal Stats: W & I C § 366.26

Brody v. Kroll, 53 Cal.Rptr.2d 280 (1996), review denied 9/4/96—Fam C § 7501

Brooke C., In re, 127 Cal.App.4th 377, 25 Cal.Rptr.3d 590 (2005)—Related Fed Stats: 25 USCA § 1912

Brooks & Robinson, In re Marriage of, 169 Cal.App.4th 176, 86 Cal.Rptr.3d 624 (2008)—Fam C §§850, 852, 1100; Related Cal Stats: Evid C § 662

Brossoit v. Brossoit, 31 Cal.App.4th 361, 36 Cal.Rptr.2d 919 (1995)—Fam C § 3421

Brothers v. Kern, 154 Cal.App.4th 126, 64 Cal.Rptr.3d 239 (2007)—Fam C §§ 4057, 4058

Brown, In re Marriage of, 35 Cal.App.4th 785, 41 Cal.Rptr.2d 506 (1995)—Fam C § 3591

Brown and Yana, Marriage of, 37 Cal.4th 947, 38 Cal.Rptr.3d 610, 127 P.3d 28 (2006)—Fam C § 7501

Bruce (Jason Alan) v. Commissioner, T.C. Summary Opinion 2014-46 (U.S. Tax Court 2014)—Selected Fed Stats: 26 USCA § 152

Brunson v. Brunson, 168 Cal.App.3d 786, 214 Cal.Rptr. 378 (1985)—Fam C § 2556

Bryan D., In re, 199 Cal.App.4th 127, 130 Cal.Rptr.3d 821 (2011)—Fam C § 7611; Cal R Ct 5.502

Bryant, In re Marriage of, 91 Cal.App.4th 789, 110 Cal.Rptr.2d 791 (2001)—Fam C § 7501

Bryce C., In re, 12 Cal.4th 226, 906 P.2d 1275, 48 Cal.Rptr.2d 120 (1995)—Fam C §§ 7822, 7860, 7863, 7895

B.T., In re, 193 Cal.App.4th 685, 122 Cal.Rptr.3d 651 (2011)—Related Cal Stats: W & I C § 300

Buckely, In re, 10 Cal.3d 237, 514 P.2d 1201, 110 Cal.Rptr. 121 (1973)—Related Cal Stats: CCP § 1222

Buckley, In re Marriage of, 133 Cal.App.3d 927, 184 Cal.Rptr. 290 (1982)—Fam C § 2210

Buford, In re Marriage of, 155 Cal.App.3d 74, 202 Cal.Rptr. 20 (1984)—Fam C § 2550

Bukaty, In re Marriage of, 180 Cal.App.3d 143, 225 Cal.Rptr.2d 492 (1986)—Fam C § 4336

Buol, In re Marriage of, 39 Cal.3d 751, 705 P.2d 354, 218 Cal.Rptr. 31 (1985)—Fam C §§ 291, 2580, 2581, 2640

Burchard v. Garay, 42 Cal.3d 531, 229 Cal.Rptr. 800, 724 P.2d 486 (1986)—Fam C § 3022

Burch v. George, 7 Cal.4th 246, 27 Cal.Rptr.2d 165 (1994)—Related Cal Stats: Prob C §§ 100, 21310, 21311, 21313

Burden, Estate of, 146 Cal.App.4th 1021, 53 Cal.Rptr.3d 390 (2007), review denied 5/9/07—Related Cal Stats: Prob C § 6453

Burgess, In re Marriage of, 13 Cal.4th 25, 913 P.2d 473, 51 Cal.Rptr.2d 444 (1996)—Fam C § 7501

Bukaty, In re Marriage of, 180 Cal.App.3d 143, 225 Cal.Rptr.2d 492 (1986)—Fam C § 4320

Burkes v. Commissioner, T.C. Memo. 1998–61, 75 T.C.M. (CCH) 1772 (1998)—Related Fed Stats: 26 USCA §§ 71, 215

Burkhart v. Burkhart, 180 Cal.App.3d 198, 204, 225 Cal.Rptr. 390 (1986)—Fam C § 4338

Burkle, In re Marriage of, 139 Cal.App.4th 712, 43 Cal.Rptr.3d 181 (2006)—Fam C §§ 721, 1100

Burkle v. Burkle, 144 Cal.App.4th 387, 50 Cal.Rptr.3d 436 (2006), review denied 2/21/07—Fam C §§ 271, 2550; Related Cal Stats: CCP § 128.7

Burkle v. Burkle, 135 Cal.App.4th 1045, 37 Cal.Rptr.3d 805 (2006), review denied—Fam C § 2024.6

Burlini, In re Marriage of, 143 Cal.App.3d 65, 191 Cal.Rptr. 541 (1993)—Fam C § 4320

Burnham v. California Public Employees' Retirement System, 208 Cal.App.4th 1576, 146 Cal.Rptr.3d 607 (2012)—Fam C § 2251

Burquet v. Brumbaugh, 223 Cal.App.4th 1140, 167 Cal.Rptr.3d 664 (2014), review denied—Fam C § 6320

Buser, In re Marriage of, 190 Cal.App.3d 639, 235 Cal.Rptr. 785 (1987), review denied 7/2/87—Fam C § 3082

Bush v. Rogers, 42 Cal.App.2d 477, 109 P.2d 379 (1941)—Fam C § 1102

Butler & Gill, In re Marriage of, 53 Cal.App.4th 462, 61 Cal.Rptr.2d 781 (1997)—Fam C § 4057

Buzzanca, In re Marriage of, 61 Cal.App.4th 1410, 72 Cal.Rptr.2d 280 (1998), review denied 6/10/98—Fam C §§ 7610, 7613

Byers v. Cathcart, 57 Cal.App.4th 805, 67 Cal.Rptr.2d 398 (1997)—Related Cal Stats: CCP § 527.6

Byrd v. Blanton, 149 Cal.App.3d 987, 197 Cal.Rptr. 190 (1983)—Fam C § 1102

Byrne v. Laura, 52 Cal.App.4th 1054, 60 Cal.Rptr.2d 908 (1997), review denied 5/28/97—Fam C §§ 300, 2251;—Related Cal Stats: Civ C § 683; Prob C § 21700

C

C., In re Marriage of, 57 Cal.App.4th 1100, 67 Cal.Rptr.2d 508 (1997)—Fam C § 4057

Caballero v. Caballero, 27 Cal.App.4th 1139, 33 Cal.Rptr.2d 46 (1994)—Related Cal Stats: CCP § 372

Cabral v. Martins, 177 Cal.App.4th 471, 99 Cal.Rptr.3d 394 (2009), review denied—Related Cal Stats: CC § 1714.4, 1714.41; CCP §§ 425.16, 425.17, 425.18

Cadwell-Faso & Faso, In re Marriage of, 191 Cal.App.4th 945, 119 Cal.Rptr.3d 818 (2011), review denied—Fam C § 1615

Cairo, In re Marriage of, 204 Cal.App.3d 1255, 251 Cal.Rptr. 731 (1988)—Fam C §§ 2581, 2625, 2640

Caitlin B., In re, 78 Cal.App.4th 1190, 93 Cal.Rptr.2d 480 (2000), review denied 5/24/00—Related Cal Stats: W & I C § 366.26; Cal R Ct 5.725

Campbell, In re Marriage of, 74 Cal.App.4th 1058, 88 Cal.Rptr.2d 580 (1999), review denied 11/17/99—Fam C § 852

Campbell, In re Marriage of, 136 Cal.App.4th 502, 38 Cal.Rptr.3d 908 (2006) review denied—Fam C § 4337

Campbell v. Apfel, 177 F.3d 890 (9th Cir. 1999)—Related Fed Stats: 42 USCA § 416

Campbell (Phyllis E.) v. Commissioner, T.C. Memo. 2006–24, 91 T.C.M. (CCH) 735 (U.S. Tax Ct. 2006)—Related Fed Stats: 26 USCA § 6015

Campi, In re Marriage of, 212 Cal.App.4th 1565, 152 Cal.Rptr.3d 179 (2013)—Fam C § 2552

Campos, In re Marriage of, 108 Cal.App.4th 839, 134 Cal.Rptr.2d 300 (2003)—Fam C § 7501

Cantarella, In re Marriage of, 191 Cal.App.4th 916, 119 Cal.Rptr.3d 829 (2011)—Fam C §§ 306, 425

Cantor v. Cohen, 442 F.3d 196 (4th Cir. 2006)—Related Fed Stats: 42 USCA § 11603; Hague Convention

Carbaugh, In re, 278 B.R. 512 (10th Cir. BAP 2002)—Related Fed Stats: 11 USCA §§ 362, 541

Cardew v. Cardew, 192 Cal.App.2d 502, 13 Cal.Rptr. 620 (1961)—Fam C § 803

Carissa G., In re, 76 Cal.App.4th 731, 90 Cal.Rptr.2d 561 (1999), review denied 2/16/00—Related Cal Stats: W & I C § 350

Carlebach (Leah M.) v. Commissioner, 139 T.C., No. 1 (2012)—Related Fed Stats: 26 USCA § 152

Carlos E., In re, 129 Cal.App.4th 1408, 29 Cal.Rptr.3d 317 (2005), review denied—Related Cal Stats: W & I C § 361.5

Carlos G., In re, 88 Cal.Rptr.2d 623 (1999) denied review and depublished 12/1/1999—Related Fed Stats: 25 USCA § 1912

Carlsen, In re Marriage of, 50 Cal.App.4th 212, 57 Cal.Rptr.2d 630 (1996)—Fam C §§ 4057.5, 4059, 4072

Carlson v. Eassa, 54 Cal.App.4th 684, 62 Cal.Rptr.2d 884 (1997)—Fam C § 17406

Carlton & D'Allessandro, In re Marriage of, 91 Cal.App.4th 1213, 111 Cal.Rptr.2d 329 (2001)—Fam C §§ 4057, 4057.5, 4058, 4059

Carmen M., In re, 141 Cal.App.4th 478, 46 Cal.Rptr.3d 117 (2006)—Related Cal Stats: W & I C §§ 202, 359, 362

Carmona v. Carmona, 544 F.3d 988 (9th Cir. 2008)—Fam C § 2610; Related Fed Stats: 5 USCA §§ 8339, 8341; 29 USCA §§ 1055, 1056

Carnall, In re Marriage of, 216 Cal.App.3d 1010, 265 Cal.Rptr. 271 (1989)—Fam C § 2610

Carney, In re Marriage of, 24 Cal.3d 725, 598 P.2d 36, 157 Cal.Rptr. 383 (1979)—Fam C §§ 3022, 3049

Carrillo, People v., 162 Cal.App.3d 585, 208 Cal.Rptr. 684 (1984)—Fam C § 3010

Carroll v. Superior Court, 101 Cal.App.4th 1423, 124 Cal.Rptr.2d 891 (2002)—Related Cal Stats: W & I C § 366.26

Carter, In re Marriage of, 26 Cal.App.4th 1024, 33 Cal.Rptr.2d 1 (1994)—Fam C § 4057

Case, Guardianship of, 57 Cal. App. 2d 844, 135 P.2d 681 (1943)—Fam C § 3010

Casey D., In re, 70 Cal.App.4th 38, 82 Cal.Rptr.2d 426 (1999)—Related Cal Stats: W & I C § 366.26

Casimir, Estate of, 19 Cal.App.3d 773, 97 Cal.Rptr. 623 (1971)—Fam C § 2346

Cassady v. Signorelli, 49 Cal.App.4th 55, 56 Cal.Rptr.2d 545 (1996), review denied 11/20/96—Fam C § 7501

Cassandra B., In re, 125 Cal.App.4th 199, 22 Cal.Rptr.3d 686 (2004), review denied—Related Cal Stats: W & I C § 213.5

Castiglioni, Estate of, 40 Cal.App.4th 367, 47 Cal.Rptr.2d 288 (1995), review denied 2/15/96—Fam C § 2640; Related Cal Stats: Prob C § 251

Castle (Susan L.) v. Commissioner, T.C. Memo 2002–142, 83 T.C.M. (CCH) 1788 (U.S. Tax Ct. 2002)—Related Fed Stats: 26 USCA § 6015

Cauley, In re Marriage of, 138 Cal.App.4th 1100, 41 Cal.Rptr.3d 902 (2006) review denied—Fam C §§ 3591, 4325

C.B., In re, 190 Cal.App.4th 102, 117 Cal.Rptr.3d 846 (2010)—Fam C §§ 7901, 7907; Related Cal Stats: W & I C § 366.26

C.C., In re, 111 Cal.App.4th 76, 3 Cal.Rptr.3d 354 (2003), review denied—Related Cal Stats: W & I C § 361.5

C.C., In re, 172 Cal.App.4th 1481, 92 Cal.Rptr.3d 168 (2009)—Related Cal Stats: W & I C § 362.1

Cecilia and David W., In re Marriage of, 241 Cal.App.4th 1277, 194 Cal.Rptr.3d 559 (2015)—Fam C § 3910

Ceja v. Rudolph & Sletten, 56 Cal.4th 1113, 302 P.3d 211, 158 Cal.Rptr.3d 211 (2013)—Fam C § 2251

Ceja v. Rudolph & Sletten, 125 Cal.Rtpr.3d 98 (2011)—Fam C § 2251

Celia S. v. Hugo H., 3 Cal.App.5th 655, 207 Cal.Rptr.3d 756 (2016)—Fam C § 3044

Celine R., In re, 31 Cal.4th 45, 1 Cal.Rptr.3d 432, 71 P.3d 787 (2003)—Related Cal Stats: W & I C § 366.26

Centinela Hospital Medical Center v. Superior Court, 215 Cal. App.3d 971, 263 Cal.Rptr. 672 (1989), review denied—Fam C § 2251

Cervantes, In re, 219 F.3d 955 (9th Cir. 2000)—Related Fed Stats: 11 USCA § 523

Cesar V. v. Superior Court, 91 Cal.App.4th 1023, 111 Cal.Rptr.2d 243 (2001)—Related Cal Stats: W & I C § 361.3

Cesnalis, In re Marriage of, 106 Cal.App.4th 1267, 131 Cal.Rptr.2d 436 (2003), review denied 6/18/03—Fam C § 4337

Chabak v. Monroy, 154 Cal.App.4th 1502, 65 Cal.Rptr.3d 641 (2007)—Related Cal Stats: Civ C § 47

Chafin v. Chafin, 133 S.Ct 1017, 185 L.Ed.2d 1 (2013)—Hague Convention

Chafin v. Chafin, 742 F.3d 934 (11th Cir. 2013)—Hague Convention

Chakko, In re Marriage of, 115 Cal.App.4th 104, 8 Cal.Rptr.3d 699 (2004)—Fam C § 2107

Chalmers v. Hirschkop, 213 Cal.App.4th 289, 152 Cal.Rptr.3d 361 (2013)—Fam C § 3101

Chambers (Horace M.) v. Commissioner, T.C. Memo. 2000–218, 80 T.C.M. (CCH) 73 (U.S. Tax Ct. 2000)—Related Fed Stats: 26 USCA §§ 61, 215

Chandler, In re Marriage of, 60 Cal.App.4th 124, 70 Cal.Rptr.2d 109 (1997)—Fam C §§ 4057, 4062

Chanel S., In re, 45 Cal.App.4th 1250, 53 Cal.Rptr.2d 253 (1996)—Fam C §§ 7822, 7851, 7860, 7863, 7895

Chang, In re, 163 F.3d 1138 (9th Cir. 1998), cert. denied sub. nom. Chang v. Beaupied, 119 S.Ct. 2029, 143 L.Ed.2d 1039 (1999)—Related Fed Stats: 11 USCA § 523

Chantal, In re, 13 Cal.4th 196, 913 P.2d 1075, 51 Cal.Rptr.2d 866 (1996)—Fam C § 3190;—Related Cal Stats: W & I C § 362.4

Chapman, In re Marriage of, 191 Cal.App.3d 1308, 237 Cal.Rptr. 84 (1987)—Fam C §§ 4320, 4336

Charisma R. v. Kristina S., 175 Cal.App.4th 361, 96 Cal.Rptr.3d 26 (2009)—Fam C §§ 7610, 7611, 7650, 8814

Charisma R. v. Kristina S., 140 Cal.App.4th 301, 44 Cal.Rptr.3d 332 (2006)—Fam C §§ 7610, 7611, 7650, 8814

Charles Schwab & Co. v. Debickero, 593 F.3d 916 (9th Cir. 2010)—Related Fed Stats: 26 USCA § 408; 29 USCA § 1055

Charlotte D., In re, 45 Cal.4th 1140, 90 Cal.Rptr.3d 724, 202 P.3d 1109 (2009)—Related Cal Stats: Prob C § 1516.5

Charlotte V., In re, 6 Cal.App.5th 51, 210 Cal.Rptr.3d 650 (2016)—Related Cal Stats: W & I C § 224.2

Charlton (Fredie Lynn) v. Commissioner, 114 T.C. No. 22 (U.S. Tax Ct. 2000)—Related Fed Stats: 26 USCA § 6015

Charmice G., In re, 66 Cal.App.4th 659, 78 Cal.Rptr.2d 212 (1998)—Related Cal Stats: W & I C § 366.26; Cal R Ct 8.450

Chen (Paul) v. Commissioner, T.C. Memo 2006–160, 92 T.C.M. (CCH) 95 (U.S. Tax Ct. 2006)—Related Fed Stats: 26 USCA § 6015

Cheriton, In re Marriage of, 92 Cal.App.4th 269, 111 Cal.Rptr.2d 755 (2001), review denied 12/19/01—Fam C § 4058

Cheryl P. v. Superior Court, 139 Cal.App.4th 87, 42 Cal.Rptr.3d 504 (2006)—Related Cal Stats: W & I C § 361.5

Cheshire (Kathryn) v. Commissioner, 115 T.C. No. 15 (U.S. Tax Ct. 2000)—Related Fed Stats: 26 USCA § 6015

Chester, In re Marriage of, 37 Cal.App.4th 1624, 44 Cal.Rptr.2d 717 (1995)—Fam C § 4820; Related Fed Stats: 28 USCA § 1738B

Cheyanna M. v. A.C. Nielson Co., 66 Cal.App.4th 855, 78 Cal. Rptr.2d 335 (1998)—Fam C § 7630; Related Cal Stats: Civ C § 43.1; CCP § 377.60; Prob C § 6453

Cheyenne B., In re, 203 Cal.App.4th 1361, 138 Cal.Rptr.3d 267 (2012), review denied—Fam C §§ 7573, 7611, 7612

Chiosie (Keith) v. Commissioner, T.C. Memo. 2000–117, 79 T.C.M. (CCH) 1812 (U.S. Tax Ct. 2000)—Related Fed Stats: 26 USCA § 7703

Chodos v. Cole, 210 Cal.App.4th 692, 148 Cal.Rptr.3d 451 (2012), review denied—Related Cal Stats: CCP § 425.16

Christian G., In re Guardianship of, 195 Cal.App.4th 581, 124 Cal.Rptr.3d 642 (2011)—Related Cal Stats: Prob C § 1513

Cristian I., In re, 224 Cal.App.4th 1088, 169 Cal.Rptr.3d 265 (2014)—Fam C § 3424

Christina A., In re, 91 Cal.App.4th 1153, 111 Cal.Rptr.2d 310 (2001)—Related Cal Stats: W & I C §§ 361.5, 366, 366.21

Christina L. v. Chauncey B., 229 Cal.App.4th 731, 177 Cal.Rptr.3d 178 (2014)—Fam C §§ 3011, 3022, 3044

Christina M., In re, 36 Cal.App.4th 1249, 43 Cal.Rptr.2d 52 (1995)—Fam C §§ 7901, 7907

Christine M. v. Superior Court, 69 Cal.App.4th 1233, 82 Cal.Rptr.2d 220 (1999)—Related Cal Stats: W & I C § 366.26

Christopher M., In re, 113 Cal.App.4th 155, 6 Cal.Rptr.3d 197 (2003)—Fam C §§ 7575, 7630

Christopher M., In re, 228 Cal.App.4th 1310, 175 Cal.Rptr.3d 837 (2014)—Related Cal Stats: W & I C § 300

Christopher T., In re, 60 Cal.App.4th 1282, 71 Cal.Rptr.2d 116 (1998), review denied 4/15/98—Related Cal Stats: W & I C § 375; Cal R Ct 5.605

Christy, In re Marriage of, 26 Cal.App.4th 256 (1994), rehearing granted 7/11/94—Fam C § 271

Cicely L., In re, 28 Cal.App.4th 1697, 34 Cal.Rptr.2d 345 (1994)—Related Cal Stats: W & I C §§ 366.21, 366.26

City and County of (see name of city)

Claralyn S., In re Guardianship of, 148 Cal.App.3d 81, 195 Cal.Rptr. 646 (1983), hearing denied 12/15/83—Fam C § 7630

Clarissa H., Adoption of, 105 Cal.App.4th 120, 129 Cal.Rptr.2d 223 (2003)—Fam C § 7894

Clark, Estate of, 94 Cal.App. 453, 271 P. 542 (1928)—Fam C § 770

Clark v. Superior Court, 62 Cal.App.4th 576, 73 Cal.Rptr.2d 53 (1998)—Fam C §§ 17400, 17402, 17404

Claudia S., In re, 131 Cal.App.4th 236, 31 Cal.Rptr.3d 697 (2005)—Related Cal Stats: W & I C § 290.2

Clay W., In re, 88 Cal.Rptr.2d 629 (1999), review denied and depublished 11/23/1999—Related Cal Stats: W & I C § 300

Clements, In re Marriage of, 134 Cal.App.3d 737, 184 Cal.Rptr. 756 (1982)—Fam C § 916

Clevenger v. Clevenger, 189 Cal.App.2d 658, 11 Cal.Rptr.707 (1961)—Fam C §§ 3900, 7611

Clifford S. v. Superior Court, 38 Cal.App.4th 747, 45 Cal.Rptr.2d 333 (1995)—Related Cal Stats: W & I C § 361.5

C.M. v. M.C., 7 Cal.App.5th 1188, 213 Cal.Rptr.3d 351 (2017), review denied—Fam C § 7962

CMRE Financial Services, Inc. v. Parton, 184 Cal.App.4th 263, 109 Cal.Rptr.3d 139 (2010), review denied—Fam C §§ 914, 916

Cochran, In re Marriage of, 89 Cal.App.4th 1144, 103 Cal.Rptr.2d 901 (2001)—Fam C § 2640

Cochran v. Cochran, 56 Cal.App.4th 1115, 66 Cal.Rptr.2d 337 (1997)—Fam C § 2251

Cochran v. Cochran, 89 Cal.App.4th 283, 106 Cal.Rptr.2d 899 (2001)—Fam C §§ 300, 2251

Codoni v. Codoni, 103 Cal.App.4th 18, 126 Cal.Rptr.2d 423 (2002)—Fam C §§ 4950, 5700.601, 5700.602, 5700.603, 17400

Cody B., In re, 153 Cal.App.4th 1004, 63 Cal.Rptr.3d 652 (2007)—Fam C § 7611

Cody C., In re, 121 Cal.App.4th 1297, 17 Cal.Rptr.3d 928 (2004), review denied—Related Cal Stats: W & I C § 366.26

Cody S., In re, 56 Cal.App.4th 230, 65 Cal.Rptr.2d 22 (1997)—Related Cal Stats: W & I C § 366.21

Coefield, In re Marriage of, 92 Cal.App.3d 959, 155 Cal.Rptr. 335 (1979)—Fam C § 2346

Cohen, In re Marriage of, 6 Cal.App.5th 1014, 207 Cal.Rptr.3d 846 (2016), review denied—Fam C § 4065

Cohn, In re Marriage of, 65 Cal.App.4th 923, 76 Cal.Rptr.2d 866 (1998)—Fam C § 4058

Colburn v. Northern Trust Company, 151 Cal.App.4th 439, 59 Cal.Rptr.3d 828 (2007), review denied 8/8/07—Related Cal Stats: Prob C § 21320

Cole Y., In re, 233 Cal.App.4th 1444, 183 Cal.Rptr.3d 308 (2015)—Related Cal Stats: W & I C § 302

D

Dandona & Araluce, In re Marriage of, 91 Cal.App.4th 1120, 111 Cal.Rptr.2d 390 (2001)—Fam C § 3653

Daniel B., In re, 231 Cal.App.4th 663, 180 Cal.Rptr.3d 26 (2014)—Related Cal Stats: W & I C § 362

Daniel C. H., In re, 220 Cal.App.3d 814, 269 Cal.Rptr. 624 (1990), review denied 8/1/90—Fam C § 3025

Daniel H., In re, 99 Cal.App.4th 804, 121 Cal.Rptr.2d 475 (2002), review denied—Related Cal Stats: W & I C § 366.26

Daniel M., In re, 110 Cal.App.4th 703, 1 Cal.Rptr.3d 897 (2003)—Related Fed Stats: 25 USCA § 1903

Daniele G., Adoption of, 87 Cal.App.4th 1392, 105 Cal.Rptr.2d 341 (2001)—Fam C §§ 3041, 7505, 8804, 8814.5

Daniels, In re Marriage of, 19 Cal.App.4th 1102, 23 Cal.Rptr.2d 865 (1993)—Fam C § 271

D'Anthony D., In re, 230 Cal.App.4th 292, 178 Cal.Rptr.3d 574 (2014)—Related Cal Stats: W & I C § 361.2

Dargan, In re Marriage of, 118 Cal.App.4th 1167, 13 Cal.Rptr.3d 522 (2004), review denied—Fam C §§ 1620, 2310

Dargie v. Patterson, 176 Cal. 714, 169 P. 360 (1917)—Fam C §§ 1100, 2601

Daria D. v. Superior Court, 61 Cal.App.4th 606, 71 Cal.Rptr.2d 668 (1998)—Related Cal Stats: W & I C §§ 361.5, 366.21

Darin v. Olivero-Huffman, 746 F.3d 1 (1st Cir. 2014)—Hague Convention

Darlice C., In re, 105 Cal.App.4th 459, 129 Cal.Rptr.2d 472 (2003)—Related Cal Stats: W & I C § 366.26

DaSilva v. DaSilva, 119 Cal.App.4th 1030, 15 Cal.Rptr.3d 59 (2004)—Fam C § 4055

Dato-Nodurft (Antoinette J.) v. Commissioner, T.C. Memo. 2004-119, 87 T.C.M. (CCH) 1338 (U.S. Tax Ct. 2004)—Related Fed Stats: 26 USCA § 71

Daugherty, In re Marriage of, 232 Cal.App.4th 463, 181 Cal.Rptr.3d 427 (2014)—Fam C §§ 4058, 4504

Davenport, People v., 219 Cal.App.3d 885, 268 Cal.Rptr. 501 (1990), review denied 7/18/90—Fam C § 753

David B. v. Superior Court, 140 Cal.App.4th 772, 44 Cal.Rptr.3d 799 (2006)—Related Cal Stats: W & I C § 366.22

David and Martha M., In re Marriage of, 140 Cal.App.4th 96, 44 Cal.Rptr.3d 388 (2006)—Related Cal Stats: W & I C §§ 302, 362.4

David B., In re, 12 Cal.App.5th 633, 219 Cal.Rptr.3d 108 (2017)—Related Cal Stats: W & I C § 303

David R., In re, 151 Cal.Rptr.3d 253 (2012)—Related Cal Stats: W & I C §§ 300, 355.1

Davis, In re Marriage of, 120 Cal.App.4th 1007, 16 Cal.Rptr.3d 220 (2004)—Fam C § 2610

Davis, In re Marriage of, 61 Cal.4th 846, 352 P.3d 401, 189 Cal.Rptr.3d 835 (2015)—Fam C §§ 70, 771

Davis (Patrick A.) v. Commissioner, T.C. Memo 2014-147 (U.S. Tax Court 2014)—Selected Fed Stats: 26 USCA § 151

Dawn D. v. Superior Court, 17 Cal.4th 932, 952 P.2d 1139, 72 Cal.Rptr.2d 871 (1998)—Fam C § 7630

D.B., In re, 239 Cal.App.4th 1073, 191 Cal.Rptr.3d 641 (2015)—Related Cal Stats: W & I C § 364

D.C., In re, 195 Cal.App.4th 1010, 124 Cal.Rptr.3d 795 (2011), review denied—Related Cal Stats: W & I C § 300

Deborah M. v. Superior Court, 128 Cal.App.4th 1181, 27 Cal. Rptr.3d 757 (2005)—Fam C § 3041.5

Deffner, In re Marriage of, 49 Cal.Rptr.3d 424 (2006), review denied and depublished 1/24/07—Fam C § 2122

de Guigne, In re Marriage of, 97 Cal.App.4th 1353, 119 Cal.Rptr.2d 430 (2002)—Fam C §§ 4057, 4057.5, 4058, 4062, 4320

Dekker, In re Marriage of, 17 Cal.App.4th 842, 21 Cal.Rptr.2d 642 (1993), review denied—Fam C § 2640

Delaney, In re Marriage of, 111 Cal.App.4th 991, 4 Cal.Rptr.3d 378 (2003)—Fam C § 721; Related Cal Stats: Evid C § 662

Delarosarauda, People v. 227 Cal.App.4th 205, 173 Cal.Rptr.3d 512 (2014), review denied—Related Cal Stats: Pen C § 273.5

Delgado v. Osuna, 837 F.3d 571 (5th Circuit 2016)—Hague Convention

D'Elia v. D'Elia, 58 Cal.App.4th 415, 68 Cal.Rptr.2d 324 (1997)—Fam C §§ 721, 2100, 2102, 2105

Della Zoppa v. Della Zoppa, 86 Cal.App.4th 1144, 103 Cal.Rptr.2d 901 (2001)—Fam C §§ 300, 2251

Dellaria, In re Marriage of, 172 Cal.App.4th 196, 90 Cal.Rptr.3d 802 (2009), review denied—Fam C § 2550

DeLong (Brendon) v. Commissioner, T.C. Memo. 2013-70—Related Fed Stats: 26 USCA §§ 71, 215

DeLoreto, Estate of, 118 Cal.App.4th 1048, 13 Cal.Rptr.3d 513 (2004)—Related Cal Stats: Prob C § 21115

Dennis H., In re, 88 Cal.App.4th 94, 105 Cal.Rptr.2d 705 (2001), review denied 7/18/01—Related Cal Stats: W & I C § 350

Department of Social Services v. Superior Court, 58 Cal.App.4th 721, 68 Cal.Rptr.2d 239 (1997), review denied 1/21/98—Fam C § 8704; Related Cal Stats: W & I C §§ 366.26, 366.3

DePasse, Estate of, 97 Cal.App.4th 92, 118 Cal.Rptr.2d 143 (2002), review denied 6/26/02—Fam C §§ 306, 425, 2251

De Prieto, In re Marriage of, 104 Cal.App.4th 748, 128 Cal.Rptr.2d 380 (2002)—Fam C §§ 4722, 4726

Derek W., In re, 73 Cal.App.4th 823, 86 Cal.Rptr.2d 739 (1999)—Related Cal Stats: W & I C § 366.26

Derrick S., In re, 156 Cal.App.4th 436, 67 Cal.Rptr.3d 367 (2007)—Related Cal Stats: W & I C §§ 361.5, 366.21

Desiree F., In re, 83 Cal.App.4th 460, 99 Cal.Rptr.2d 688 (2000)—Related Fed Stats: 25 USCA § 1912

Destein, In re Marriage of, 91 Cal.App.4th 1385, 111 Cal.Rptr.2d 487 (2001)—Fam C § 4058

Devin M., In re, 58 Cal.App.4th 1538, 68 Cal.Rptr.2d 666 (1997), review denied 12/23/97—Related Cal Stats: W & I C § 366.26

Devlin, In re Marriage of, 138 Cal.App.3d 804, 189 Cal.Rptr. 1 (1982)—Fam C §§ 780, 2603

D.H., In re, 14 Cal.App.5th 719, 222 Cal.Rptr.3d 305 (2017)—Related Cal Stats: W & I C § 366.26

Diana B., Guardianship of, 30 Cal.App.4th 1766, 36 Cal.Rptr.2d 447 (1994)—Fam C §§ 3040, 3041

Dick, In re Marriage of, 15 Cal.App.4th 144, 18 Cal.Rptr.2d 743 (1993), review denied 8/26/93—Fam C §§ 2320, 3600

Dieden v. Schmidt, 104 Cal.App.4th 645, 128 Cal.Rptr.2d 365 (2002), review denied 3/19/03—Related Cal Stats: Civ C § 683

Dietz, In re Marriage of, 176 Cal.App.4th 387, 97 Cal.Rptr.3d 616 (2009)—Fam C § 3591

Diosdado v. Diosdado, 97 Cal.App.4th 470, 118 Cal.Rptr.2d 494 (2002)—Fam C §§ 1620, 2310

D.M., In re, 210 Cal.App.4th 541, 148 Cal.Rptr.3d 349 (2012), review denied—Fam C §§ 7611, 7612; Related Cal Stats: W & I C § 361.5

D.M., In re, 242 Cal.App.4th 634, 195 Cal.Rptr.3d 402 (2015)—Related Cal Stats: W & I C § 300

D.M. v. Superior Court, 173 Cal.App.4th 1117, 93 Cal.Rptr.3d 418 (2009), review denied—Related Cal Stats: W & I C § 300

D.M., In re, 205 Cal.App.4th 283, 140 Cal.Rptr.3d 311 (2012)—Related Cal Stats: W & I C § 366.26

D.N., In re, 218 Cal.App.4th 1246, 161 Cal.Rptr.3d 151 (2013)—Related Cal Stats: W & I C § 224.3

D.O., In re, 247 Cal.App.4th 166, 201 Cal.Rptr.3d 642 (2016)—Related Cal Stats: W & I C § 366.26

Dobles v. San Diego Dept. of Social Services, 114 S.Ct. 1221 (1994)—Related Cal Stats: W & I C § 366.26

Doe v. Mann, 415 F.3d 1038 (9th Cir., 2005)—Related Fed Stats: 25 USCA §§ 1911, 1918

Dollaga, In re, 260 B.R. 493 (9th Cir. BAP, 2001)—Related Fed Stats: 11 USCA § 523

Donaldson, In re Guardianship of, 178 Cal.App.3d 477, 223 Cal. Rptr. 707 (1986)—Fam C § 3010

Donnovan J., In re, 58 Cal.App.4th 1474, 68 Cal.Rptr.2d 714 (1997)—Fam C § 3190; Related Cal Stats: W & I C § 362.4

E

F

G

Gill, United States v., 264 F.3d 929 (9th Cir. 2001)—Related Fed Stats: 18 USCA § 228
Gillmore, In re Marriage of, 29 Cal.3d 418, 629 P.2d 1, 174 Cal.Rptr. 493 (1981)—Fam C § 2610
Gilmore v. Gilmore, 45 Cal.2d 142, 287 P.2d 769 (1955)—Fam C § 2640
Giorgianni v. Crowley, 197 Cal.App.4th 1462, 129 Cal.Rptr.3d 546 (2011)—Related Cal Stats: Bus & Prof C § 6204
G.L., In re, 222 Cal.App.4th 1153, 166 Cal.Rptr.3d 579 (2014)—Related Cal Stats: W & I C § 361.5
Gladys L., In re, 141 Cal.App.4th 845, 46 Cal.Rptr.3d 434 (2006)—Related Cal Stats: W & I C § 366.26
Glen C. v. Superior Court, 78 Cal.App.4th 570, 93 Cal.Rptr.2d 103 (2000)—Related Cal Stats: W & I C § 366.26; Cal R Ct 8.450
Glickman v. Collins, 13 Cal.3d 852, 120 Cal.Rptr. 76 (1975)—Fam C § 721
Gloria A., In re, 213 Cal.App.4th 476, 152 Cal.Rptr.3d 550 (2013)—Fam C § 3402
G.M., In re, 181 Cal.App.4th 552, 105 Cal.Rptr.3d 32 (2010)—Related Cal Stats: W & I C § 366.26
Goetz and Lewis, In re Marriage of, 203 Cal.App.3d 514, 250 Cal.Rptr. 30 (1988)—Fam C §§ 2010, 3040, 3101
Goldberg, In re Marriage of, 22 Cal.App.4th 265, 27 Cal.Rptr.2d 298 (1994), review denied 5/19/94—Fam C § 2211
Gomez v. Fuenmayor, 812 F.3d 1005 (11th Cir. 2016)—Hague Convention
Gonzales (Marie A.) v. Commissioner, T.C. Memo. 1999–332, 78 T.C.M. (CCH) 527 (U.S. Tax Ct. 1999)—Related Fed Stats: 26 USCA §§ 71, 215
Gonzalez, In re Marriage of, 168 Cal.App.3d 1021, 214 Cal.Rptr. 634 (1985)—Fam C § 4360
Gonzalez v. Gutierrez, 311 F.3d 942 (9th Cir. 2002)—Related Fed Stats: 42 USCA § 11603; Hague Convention
Gonzalez v. Munoz, 156 Cal.App.4th 413, 67 Cal.Rptr.3d 317 (2007)—Fam C §§ 6323, 6340
Gonzalez–Caballero v. Mena, 251 F.3d 789 (9th Cir. 2001)—Related Fed Stats: 42 USCA § 11603; Hague Convention
Goodarzirad, Marriage of, 185 Cal.App.3d 1020, 230 Cal.Rptr. 203 (1986)—Fam C §§ 58, 3587, 3910
Goodman & Gruen, In re Marriage of, 191 Cal.App.4th 627, 120 Cal.Rptr.3d 184 (2011)—Fam C § 3603
Goold v. Superior Court, 145 Cal.App.4th 1, 51 Cal.Rptr.3d 455 (2006)—Fam C § 2040; CCP § 1218
Goosmann, In re Marriage of, 26 Cal.App.4th 838, 31 Cal.Rptr.2d 613 (1994)—Fam C § 4009
Gootee v. Lightner, 224 Cal.App.3d 587, 274 Cal.Rptr. 697 (1990)—Related Cal Stats: Civ C § 47
Gowan, In re Marriage of, 54 Cal.App.4th 80, 62 Cal.Rptr.2d 453 (1997)—Fam C § 2610
Gowdy, In re Marriage of, 178 Cal.App.3d 1228, 224 Cal.Rptr. 400 (1986)—Fam C § 2640
Grace C., In re, 190 Cal.App.4th 1470, 119 Cal.Rptr.3d 474 (2010)—Related Cal Stats: W & I C § 362.4
Grace P., In re, 8 Cal.App.5th 605, 213 Cal.Rptr.3d 714 (2017)—Related Cal Stats: W & I C § 366.26
Graham, In re Marriage of, 109 Cal.App.4th 1321, 135 Cal.Rptr.2d 685 (2003)—Fam C § 2641
Grahm v. Superior Court, 132 Cal.App.4th 1193, 34 Cal.Rptr.3d 270 (2005)—Fam C § 3422
Gram, In re Marriage of, 25 Cal.App.4th 859, 30 Cal.Rptr.2d 792 (1994)—Fam C § 2610
Green, In re Marriage of, 56 Cal.4th 1130, 302 P.3d 562, 158 Cal.Rptr.3d 247 (2013)—Fam C. § 2610
Green, In re Marriage of, 140 Cal.Rptr.3d 915 (2012)—Fam C § 2610
Green, In re Marriage of, 143 Cal.App.4th 1312, 49 Cal.Rptr.3d 908 (2006)—Fam C § 272
Green, In re Marriage of, 213 Cal.App.3d 14, 261 Cal.Rptr. 294 (1989)—Fam C § 2552
Green v. Uccelli, 207 Cal.App.3d 1112, 255 Cal.Rptr. 315 (1989)—Fam C §§ 214, 271
Greenberg, In re Marriage of, 194 Cal.App.4th 1095, 125 Cal. Rptr.3d 238 (2011)—Fam C § 271
Greene v. Williams, 9 Cal.App.3d 559, 88 Cal.Rptr. 261 (1970)—Fam C § 2211
Greenway, In re Marriage of, 217 Cal.App.4th 628, 158 Cal.Rptr.3d 364 (2013), review denied—Related Cal Stats: Prob C §§ 810, 811, 1900
Griffis, In re Marriage of, 187 Cal.App.3d 156, 231 Cal.Rptr. 510 (1986)—Fam C §§ 2581, 2640
Grolemund v. Cafferata, 17 Cal.2d 679, 111 P.2d 641 (1941), cert. denied 314 U.S. 612 (1941)—Fam C § 2625
Grossman v. Commissioner, 182 F.3d 275 (4th Cir. 1999)—Related Fed Stats: 26 USCA § 6015
Gruntz, In re, 202 F.3d 1074 (9th Cir. en banc 2000)—Related Cal Stats: Pen C § 270;—Related Fed Stats: 11 USCA § 362
G.S.R., In re, 159 Cal.App.4th 1202, 72 Cal.Rptr.3d 398 (2008)—Related Cal Stats: W & I C § 366.26
Guardianship of (see name of party)
Guasch, In re Marriage of, 201 Cal.App.4th 942, 134 Cal.Rptr.3d 358 (2011)—Fam C §§ 211, 2010; Related Cal Stats: CCP § 529; Cal R Ct 5.2, 5.18, 5.21, 5.106, 5.111
Guess v. Bernhardson, 242 Cal.App.4th 821, 195 Cal.Rptr.3d 349 (2015), review denied—Related Cal Stats: CCP § 697.320
Guidotti, Estate of, 90 Cal.App.4th 1403, 109 Cal.Rptr.2d 674 (2001)—Related Cal Stats: Civ C § 710
Guilardi, In re Marriage of, 200 Cal.App.4th 770, 132 Cal.Rptr.3d 798 (2011), review denied—Fam C § 2030
Guo & Sun, In re Marriage of, 186 Cal.App.4th 1491, 112 Cal. Rptr.3d 906 (2010)—Fam C § 2251
Guo v. Xiao, 228 Cal.App.4th 812, 175 Cal.Rptr.3d 635 (2014)—Fam C §§ 6203, 6320
G.W., In re, 173 Cal.App.4th 1428, 94 Cal.Rptr.3d 53 (2009), review denied—Related Cal Stats: W & I C §§ 361.4, 387

H

Hafner, Estate of, 184 Cal.App.3d 1371, 229 Cal.Rptr. 676 (1986), review denied 11/20/86—Fam C §§ 306, 2251
Haggard v. Haggard, 38 Cal.App.4th 1566, 45 Cal.Rptr.2d 638 (1995)—Fam C §§ 4057, 4059, 4071
Haines, In re, 210 B.R. 586 (1997)—Related Fed Stats: 11 USCA § 523
Haines, In re Marriage of, 33 Cal.App.4th 277, 39 Cal.Rptr.2d 673 (1995)—Fam C §§ 721, 852, 1100;—Related Cal Stats: Evid C § 662
Hale Exemption Trust v. Commissioner, T.C. Memo. 2001-89, 81 T.C.M. (CCH) 1507 (U.S. Tax Ct. 2001)—Related Fed Stats: 26 USCA § 6015
Haley A., Adoption of, sub. nom. Petition of Mark A., 930 P.2d 401, 60 Cal.Rptr.2d 608 (1997)—Fam C § 8804
Hall, In re Marriage of, 81 Cal.App.4th 313, 96 Cal.Rptr.2d 772 (2000)—Fam C § 4056
Hall and Frencher, In re Marriage of, 247 Cal.App.4th 23, 201 Cal.Rptr.3d 769 (2016)—Fam C § 4504
Hall v. Hall, 222 Cal.App.3d 578, 271 Cal.Rptr. 773 (1990), review denied Fam C § 1611
Hamer, In re Marriage of, 81 Cal.App.4th 712, 97 Cal.Rptr.2d 195 (2000)—Fam C §§ 3556, 3651, 4502; Related Cal Stats: CCP §§ 695.211, 695.221
Hamilton v. Washington State Plumbing and Pipefitting Industry Pension Plan, 433 F.3d 1091 (9th Cir. 2006)—Fam C § 2610;—Related Fed Stats: 29 USCA §§ 1055, 1056
Hannah S., In re Adoption of, 142 Cal.App.4th 998, 48 Cal.Rptr.3d 605 (2006)—Related Fed Stats: 25 USCA § 1913
Hardin, In re Marriage of, 38 Cal.App.4th 448, 45 Cal.Rptr.2d 308 (1995)—Fam C § 771

I

J

K

L

M

N

O

Obergefell v. Hodges, 135 S.Ct. 2584 (2015)—Related Fed Stats: 26 USCA § 6013; 28 USCA § 1738C

Obos v. Scripps Psychological Associates, 59 Cal.App.4th 103, 69 Cal.Rptr.2d 30 (1997)—Related Cal Stats: Civ C § 47

O.C., In re, 5 Cal.App.5th 1173, 210 Cal.Rptr.3d 467 (2016)—Related Cal Stats: W & I C § 224.2

Ocegueda v. Perreira, 232 Cal.App.4th 1079, 181 Cal.Rptr.3d 845 (2015), review denied—Fam C §§ 3402, 3421

O'Connell, In re Marriage of, 8 Cal.App.4th 565, 10 Cal.Rptr.2d 334 (1992)—Fam C § 4360

O'Connor, In re Marriage of, 59 Cal.App.4th 877, 69 Cal.Rptr.2d 480 (1998), review denied 2/18/98—Fam C §§ 2030, 2032

Oddino, In re Marriage of, 16 Cal.4th 67, 939 P.2d 1266, 65 Cal.Rptr.2d 566 (1997)—Fam C § 2610;—Related Fed Stats: 29 USCA § 1056

Ohio v. Barron, 52 Cal.App.4th 62, 60 Cal.Rptr.2d 342 (1997)—Fam C § 17402

O.K., In re, 106 Cal.App.4th 152, 130 Cal.Rptr.2d 276 (2003), review denied 5/14/03—Related Fed Stats: 25 USCA §§ 1903, 1912

O'Kane v. Irvine, 47 Cal.App.4th 207, 54 Cal.Rptr.2d 549 (1996)—Fam C § 6209

Okerson (John R.) v. Commissioner, 123 T.C. Memo 258 (U.S. Tax Ct. 2004)—Fam C § 4337; Related Fed Stats: 26 USCA §§ 71, 215

Oliverez, In re Marriage of, 238 Cal.App.4th 1242, 190 Cal.Rptr.3d 436 (2015)—Related Cal Stats CCP § 1008

Olivia J., Guardianship of, 84 Cal.App.4th 1146, 101 Cal.Rptr.2d 364 (2000)—Fam C § 3041; Related Cal Stats: Prob C § 1514

Olmstead v. Arthur J. Gallagher & Co., 32 Cal.4th 804, 11 Cal. Rptr.3d 298, 86 P.3d 354 (2004)—Related Cal Stats: CCP §§ 128.5, 128.7

Olsen, In re Marriage of, 24 Cal.App.4th 1702, 30 Cal.Rptr.2d 306 (1994), review denied 9/7/94—Fam C § 2556

Olson, In re Marriage of, 14 Cal.App.4th 1, 17 Cal.Rptr.2d 480 (1993)—Fam C §§ 3600, 4320

Olson, In re Marriage of, 238 Cal.App.4th 1458, 190 Cal.Rptr.3d 715 (2015)—Fam C §§ 3022, 3087

O'Neill v. Tichy, 19 Cal.App.4th 114, 25 Cal.Rptr.2d 162 (1993), review denied 1/13/94—Related Cal Stats: CCP § 340.6

Orange. County of v. Carl D., 76 Cal.App.4th 429, 90 Cal.Rptr.2d 440 (1999)—Fam C § 3556

Orange, County of v. Dabbs, 29 Cal.App.4th 999, 35 Cal.Rptr.2d 79 (1994)—Fam C § 17402

Orange, County of v. Ivansco, 67 Cal.App.4th 328, 78 Cal.Rptr.2d 886 (1998)—Fam C § 4059

Orange, County of v. Leslie B., 14 Cal.App.4th 976, 17 Cal.Rptr.2d 797 (1993)—Fam C § 7540

Orange, County of v. Quinn, 97 Cal.App.4th 956, 118 Cal.Rptr.2d 833 (2002)—Fam C §§ 3600, 3601; Related Cal Stats: CCP § 583.161

Orange, County of v. Rosales, 99 Cal.App.4th 1214, 121 Cal.Rptr.2d 788 (2002)—Fam C §§ 3600, 3601; Related Cal Stats: CCP § 583.161

Orange, County of v. Smith, 132 Cal.App.4th 1434, 34 Cal.Rptr.3d 383 (2005), review denied—Fam C §§ 4057, 4058

Orange, County of v. Superior Court, 155 Cal.App.4th 1253, 66 Cal.Rptr.3d 689 (2007)—Fam C §§ 7575, 7646

Ordlock (Lois E.) v. Commissioner, 533 F.3d 1136 (9th Cir. 2008)—Related Fed Stats: 26 USCA § 6015

Oregon, State of v. Vargas, 70 Cal.App.4th 1123, 83 Cal.Rptr.2d 229 (1999)—Fam C § 4058

Oriola v. Thaler, 84 Cal.App.4th 397, 100 Cal.Rptr.2d 822 (2000)—Fam C § 6210

Oropallo, In re Marriage of, 68 Cal.App.4th 997, 80 Cal.Rptr.2d 669 (1998)—Related Cal Stats: CCP § 580d

Ortiz v. Martinez, 789 F.3d 722 (7th Cir. 2015)—Related Fed Stats: Hague Convention

O.S., In re, 102 Cal.App.4th 1402, 126 Cal.Rptr.2d 571 (2002)—Related Cal Stats: W & I C § 366.26

Osgood v. Landon, 127 Cal.App.4th 425, 25 Cal.Rptr.3d 379 (2005)—Fam C § 7501

Ostler and Smith, In re Marriage of, 223 Cal.App.3d 33, 272 Cal.Rptr. 560 (1990)—Fam C § 4320

Ostrander, In re Marriage of, 53 Cal.App.4th 63, 61 Cal.Rptr.2d 348 (1997), review denied 4/23/97—Fam C § 4336

Ousterman, In re Marriage of, 46 Cal.App.4th 1090, 54 Cal.Rptr.2d 403 (1996)—Fam C § 3591

Oyakawa v. Gillett, 8 Cal.App.4th 628, 10 Cal.Rptr.2d 469 (1992)—Fam C § 1000

Ozaltin v. Ozaltin, 708 F.3d 355 (2d Cir. 2013)—Related Fed Stats: 42 USCA § 11603; Hague Convention

P

P.A., In re, 198 Cal.App.4th 974, 130 Cal.Rptr.3d 556 (2011)—Fam C §§ 7573, 7611, 7612

P.A., In re, 155 Cal.App.4th 1197, 66 Cal.Rptr.3d 783 (2007)—Related Cal Stats: W & I C § 300

Pablo S. v. Superior Court, 98 Cal.App.4th 292, 119 Cal.Rptr.2d 523 (2002)—Related Cal Stats: W & I C § 361.5

Padilla, In re Marriage of, 932 P.2d 756, 61 Cal.Rptr.2d 809 (1997)—Fam C § 3556

Padilla, In re Marriage of, 38 Cal.App.4th 1212, 45 Cal.Rptr.2d 555 (1995)—Fam C § 4058

Pangilinan v. Palisoc, 227 Cal.App.4th 765, 174 Cal.Rptr.3d 114 (2014)—Fam C § 7630

Papakosmas v. Papakosmas, 483 F.3d 617 (9th Cir. 2007)—Hague Convention

Papenthien v. Papenthien, 120 F.3d 1025 (9th Cir. 1997)—Related Cal Stats: CCP § 340.15

Parker v. Harbert, 212 Cal.App.4th 1172, 151 Cal.Rptr.3d 642 (2013)—Fam C § 271

Parson v. Parson, 49 Cal.App.4th 537, 56 Cal.Rptr.2d 686 (1996), review denied 12/18/96—Related Cal Stats: Prob C § 6540

Patience v. Snyder, 93 Cal.Rptr.2d 265 (2000)—Related Cal Stats: Civ C § 683.2

Patrick v. Alacer Corp, 167 Cal.App.4th 995, 84 Cal.Rptr.3d 642 (2008), review denied—Fam C §§ 751, 2640

Patrick v. Rivera-Lopez, 708 F.3d 15 (1st Cir. 2013)—Hague Convention

Patrick S. III, In re, 218 Cal.App.4th 1254, 160 Cal.Rptr.3d 832 (2013)—Related Cal Stats: W & I C § 361.2

Patton v. Denver Post Corp., 326 F.3d 1148 (10th Cir. 2003)—Related Fed Stats: 29 USCA § 1056

Paul, In re Marriage of, 173 Cal.App.3rd 913, 219 Cal.Rptr. 318 (1985)—Fam C § 4320

Paul E., In re, 39 Cal.App.4th 996, 46 Cal.Rptr.2d 289 (1995)—Related Cal Stats: W & I C § 361

Paulin, In re Marriage of, 46 Cal.App.4th 1378, 54 Cal.Rptr.2d 314 (1996)—Fam C §§ 4059, 4071

P.C., In re, 165 Cal.App.4th 98, 80 Cal.Rptr.3d 595 (2008)—Related Cal Stats: W & I C § 366.26

Pearlstein, In re Marriage of, 137 Cal.App.4th 1361, 40 Cal.Rptr.3d 910 (2006)—Fam C §§ 4057, 4058

Pedregon, In re Marriage of, 107 Cal.App.4th 1284, 132 Cal.Rptr.2d 861 (2003)—Fam C §§ 3900, 7611

Pedro N., In re, 35 Cal.App.4th 183, 41 Cal.Rptr.2d 819 (1995)—Related Cal Stats: W & I C §§ 366.21, 366.26; Related Fed Stats: 25 USCA §§ 1911, 1912

Pedro Z., In re, 190 Cal.App.4th 12, 117 Cal.Rptr.3d 605 (2010)—Related Cal Stats: W & I C §§ 361.2, 361.5

Pendleton & Fireman, In re Marriage of, 24 Cal.4th 39, 99 Cal. Rptr.2d 278, 5 P.3d 839 (2000)—Fam C § 1612

Q

R

S

Stewart v. Gomez, 47 Cal.App.4th 1748, 55 Cal.Rptr.2d 531 (1996)—Fam C §§ 4058, 4059
Stewart v. Thorpe Holding Co. Profit Sharing Plan, 207 F.3d 1143 (9th Cir. 2000)—Related Fed Stats: 29 USCA § 1056
Stierlen v. Stierlen, 6 Cal.App. 420, 92 P. 329 (1907)—Fam C § 309
Stimel, In re Marriage of, 49 Cal.App.4th 991, 57 Cal.Rptr.2d 18 (1996)—Fam C § 4360
Stitt, In re Marriage of, 147 Cal.App.3d 579, 195 Cal.Rptr. 172 (1983)—Fam C §§ 1000, 2602, 2625
Stoll, In re Marriage of, 63 Cal.App.4th 837, 74 Cal.Rptr.2d 506 (1998)—Fam C § 2640
Stone v. Davis, 148 Cal.App.4th 596, 55 Cal.Rptr.3d 833 (2007)—Fam C § 5700.205
Stoner, In re Marriage of, 147 Cal.App.3d 858, 195 Cal.Rptr. 351 (1983)—Fam C § 2640
Stover v. Bruntz, 12 Cal.App.5th 19, 218 Cal.Rptr.3d 551 (2017)—Fam C § 3653
Strauss v. Horton, 46 Cal.4th 364, 93 Cal.Rptr.3d 591, 207 P.3d 48 (2009)—Fam C §§ 300, 308.5
Strong v. State Board of Equalization, 155 Cal.App.4th 1182, 66 Cal.Rptr.3d 657 (2007), review denied—Fam C §§ 297, 297.5
Stuard v. Stuard, 244 Cal.App.4th 768, 199 Cal.Rptr.3d 821 (2016)—Fam C § 3104
Stupp & Schilders, In re Marriage of, 11 Cal.App.5th 907, 217 Cal.Rptr.3d 825 (2017)—Fam C § 4331
Suarez, In re, 400 Bankr. 732 (U.S. Bankr. App. Pan., 9th Cir. 2009)—Related Cal Stats: W & I C § 523
Suleman v. Superior Court, 180 Cal.App.4th 1287, 103 Cal.Rptr.3d 651 (2010)—Related Cal Stats: Prob C § 1510
Sullivan, In re Marriage of, 37 Cal.3d 762, 691 P.2d 1020, 209 Cal.Rptr. 354 (1984)—Fam C § 2641
Summer H., In re, 139 Cal.App.4th 1315, 43 Cal.Rptr.3d 682 (2006)—Related Cal Stats: W & I C §§ 360, 361.4
Summers, In re, 332 F.3d 1240 (9th Cir. 2003)—Fam C §§ 850, 852;—Related Cal Stats: Evid C § 662
Susan H. v. Jack S., 30 Cal.App.4th 1435, 37 Cal.Rptr.2d 120 (1994)—Fam C §§ 7540, 7541
S.W., In re, 131 Cal.App.4th 838, 32 Cal.Rptr.3d 192 (2005)—Related Cal Stats: W & I C § 361.4
S.W., In re, 148 Cal.App.4th 1501, 56 Cal.Rptr.3d 665 (2007) review denied 6/13/07—Fam C §§ 3402, 3421
Sweeney, In re Marriage of, 76 Cal.App.4th 343, 90 Cal.Rptr.2d 298 (1999)—Fam C §§ 291, 4502
Suzanna L., In re, 104 Cal.App.4th 223, 127 Cal.Rptr.2d 860 (2002)—Fam C §§ 175, 7800, 7802, 7810, 7880
S.Y. v. S.B., 201 Cal.App.4th 1023, 134 Cal.Rptr.3d 1 (2011), review denied—Fam C §§ 7610, 7611, 7650, 8814
Sylvia R., In re, 55 Cal.App.4th 559, 64 Cal.Rptr.2d 93 (1997)—Related Cal Stats: W & I C § 388

T

Tallman, In re Marriage of, 22 Cal.App.4th 1697, 28 Cal.Rptr.2d 323 (1994)—Fam C § 2640
Tameka M., In re, 33 Cal.App.4th 1747, 40 Cal.Rptr.2d 64 (1995)—Related Cal Stats: W & I C § 366.21
Tamika C., In re, 131 Cal.App.4th 1153, 32 Cal.Rptr.3d 597 (2005)—Related Cal Stats: W & I C § 391
Tamika T., In re, 97 Cal.App.4th 1114, 118 Cal.Rptr.2d 873 (2002), review denied 7/10/02—Related Cal Stats: W & I C § 366.26
Tamraz, In re Marriage of, 24 Cal.App.4th 1740, 30 Cal.Rptr.2d 233 (1994), review denied 7/27/94—Fam C § 2346
Tanis H., In re, 59 Cal.App.4th 1218, 69 Cal.Rptr.2d 380 (1997)—Fam C § 7611
Tanyann W., In re, 97 Cal.App.4th 675, 118 Cal.Rptr.2d 596 (2002)—Related Cal Stats: W & I C § 361.5
Taschen, In re Marriage of, 134 Cal.App.4th 681, 36 Cal.Rptr.3d 286 (2005), review denied Related Cal Stats: Civ C § 51
Tassi v. Tassi, 160 Cal.App.2d 680, 325 P.2d 872 (1958)—Fam C § 2640
Tate v. Wilburn, 184 Cal.App.4th 150, 109 Cal.Rptr.3d 18 (2010), review denied—Related Cal Stats: CCP § 1008
Tavares, In re Marriage of, 151 Cal.App.4th 620, 60 Cal.Rptr.3d 39 (2007), rehearing denied 8/8/07—Fam C § 3651
Taveras v. Taveraz, 477 F.3d 767 (6th Cir. 2007)—Hague Convention
Taylor v. George, 34 Cal.2d 552, 212 P.2d 505 (1949)—Fam C § 3952
Taylor v. Superior Court, 218 Cal.App.3d 1185, 267 Cal.Rptr. 519 (1990)—Fam C § 4012
Taylor v. Taylor, 192 Cal. 71, 218 P. 756 (1923)—Fam C § 2660
Taylor, In re, 737 F.3d 670 (10th Cir. 2013)—Related Fed Stats: 11 USCA § 523
Taylor J., In re, 223 Cal.App.4th 1446, 168 Cal.Rptr.3d 149 (2014)—Related Cal Stats: W & I C § 361.5
Teichman, In re, 774 F.2d 1395 (9th Cir. 1985)—Fam C § 1100;—Related Fed Stats: 11 USCA § 523
Tejeda, In re Marriage of, 179 Cal.App.4th 973, 102 Cal.Rptr.3d 361 (2009)—Fam C § 2251
Teneka W., In re, 37 Cal.App.4th 721, 43 Cal.Rptr.2d 666 (1995), review denied 11/2/95—Related Cal Stats: W & I C § 366.26
Teresa J. v. Superior Court, 102 Cal.App.4th 366, 125 Cal.Rptr.2d 506 (2002)—Fam C § 8700; Related Cal Stats: W & I C § 361
Terrance B., In re, 144 Cal.App.4th 965, 50 Cal.Rptr.3d 815 (2006), review denied 2/7/07—Related Cal Stats: W & I C § 388
Terry, In re Marriage of, 80 Cal.App.4th 921, 95 Cal.Rptr.2d 760 (2000), review denied 7/26/00—Fam C § 4322
T.G., In re, 215 Cal.App.4th1, 155 Cal.Rptr.3d 1 (2013)—Related Cal Stats: W & I C § 366.26
T.G., In re, 242 Cal.App.4th 976, 195 Cal.Rptr.3d 649 (2015)—Related Cal Stats: W & I C § 361.5
T.H., In re, 190 Cal.App.4th 1119, 119 Cal.Rptr.3d 1 (2010)—Related Cal Stats: W & I C § 362.4
Tharp, In re Marriage of, 188 Cal.App.4th 1295, 116 Cal.Rptr.3d 375 (2010), review denied—Fam C §§ 271, 2030, 2032, 2107
Therman, People v., 236 Cal.App.4th 1276, 187 Cal.Rptr.3d 492 (2015)—Related Cal Stats: Pen C § 13700
Thomas R., In re, 145 Cal.App.4th 726, 51 Cal.Rptr.3d 864 (2006)—Related Cal Stats: W & I C § 366.26
Thorne & Raccina, In re Marriage of, 203 Cal.App.4th 492, 136 Cal.Rptr.3d 887 (2012)—Fam C §§ 2122, 2556
Thornton, In re Marriage of, 95 Cal.App.4th 251, 115 Cal.Rptr.2d 380 (2002)—Fam C § 4337
Thornton, Estate of, 1 Cal.2d 1, 33 P.2d 1 (1934)—Fam C § 125
Thornton, In re Marriage of, 135 Cal.App.3d 500, 185 Cal.Rptr. 388 (1982)—Fam C § 2320
Thweatt, In re Marriage of, 96 Cal.App.3d 530, 157 Cal.Rptr. 826 (1979)—Fam C § 4323
Tietge v. Western Province of Servites, 55 Cal.App.4th 382, 64 Cal.Rptr.2d 53 (1997), review denied 8/13/97—Related Cal Stats: CCP § 340.1
Tintocalis v. Tintocalis, 20 Cal.App.4th 1590, 25 Cal.Rptr.2d 655 (1993)—Fam C § 4360
T.K., Adoption of, 240 Cal.App.4th 1392, 194 Cal.Rptr.3d 606 (2015)—Fam C §§ 7611, 8604
Tolces v. Trask, 76 Cal.App.4th 285, 90 Cal.Rptr.2d 294 (1999)—Fam C § 17520
Tomaier v. Tomaier, 23 Cal. 2d 754, 146 P.2d 905 (1944)—Fam C § 2660
Tong & Samson, In re Marriage of, 197 Cal.App.4th 23, 127 Cal.Rptr.3d 857 (2011)—Fam C § 4320
Tonya M. v. Superior Court, 42 Cal.4th 836, 69 Cal.Rptr.3d 96, 172 P.3d 402 (2007)—Related Cal Stats: W & I C §§ 361.5, 366.21
Torres, In re Marriage of, 62 Cal.App.4th 1357, 73 Cal.Rptr.2d 344 (1998)—Fam C §§ 3408, 3421; Related Fed Stats: 28 USCA § 1738A

U

V

W

X

Y

Z

INDEX

Abbreviations

1 § _	United States Code Annotated
5 § _	United States Code Annotated
10 § _	United States Code Annotated
11 § _	United States Code Annotated
18 § _	United States Code Annotated
22 § _	United States Code Annotated
25 § _	United States Code Annotated
26 § _	United States Code Annotated
28 § _	United States Code Annotated
29 § _	United States Code Annotated
42 § _	United States Code Annotated
45 § _	United States Code Annotated
Const	Constitution of California
Bus & P	Business and Professions Code
CC	Civil Code
CCP	Code of Civil Procedure
Corp	Corporations Code
Educ	Education Code
Evid	Evidence Code
Fam	Family Code
Gov	Government Code
Ins	Insurance Code
Pen	Penal Code
Prob	Probate Code
Veh	Vehicle Code
Welf & I	Welfare and Institutions Code
CFR	Code of Federal Regulations